THE CATHOLIC STUDENT BIBLE

AF797059

CONTRIBUTORS

Cele Breen, S.C.L. Jeanette Lucinio, S.P.

Graziano Marcheschi Biagio Mazza

SCHOLARLY ADVISORY BOARD

Donald Senior, C.P. Mary Ann Getty

John J. Collins

EDUCATORS ADVISORY BOARD

Maureen Gallager Judy Connolly, S.S.N.D.

James A. DiGiacomo, S.J.

THE CATHOLIC STUDENT BIBLE

Jean Marie Hiesberger
General Editor

NEW AMERICAN BIBLE

Including the Revised Psalms and
the Revised New Testament

Translated from the Original Languages
with Critical Use of All the Ancient Sources

WILLIAM H. SADLIER, INC. New York

OXFORD UNIVERSITY PRESS
New York Oxford

OXFORD UNIVERSITY PRESS
Oxford New York
Athens Auckland Bangkok Bombay Calcutta
Cape Town Dar es Salaam Delhi Florence
Hong Kong Istanbul Karachi Kuala Lumpur Madrid
Madras Melbourne Mexico City Nairobi Paris
Singapore Tokyo Taipei Toronto
and associated companies in
Berlin Ibadan

Copyright © 1995 by Oxford University Press, Inc.

Published by Oxford University Press, Inc.
198 Madison Avenue, New York, NY 10016

Oxford is a registered trademark of Oxford University Press

Oxford Reading Guides, Articles, copyright © 1990, 1995 by Oxford University Press, Inc.
All rights reserved. No part of this publication may be reproduced, stored in a retrieval system, or transmitted, in any form or by any means, electronic, mechanical, photocopying, recording, or otherwise, without the prior permission of Oxford University Press.

Nihil Obstat
Reverend John G. Lodge, S.T.L., S.S.L., S.T.D., Censor Deputatus
February 24, 1995
Imprimatur
Reverend David M. Hynous, O.P., Vice-Chancellor/Delegate of the Local Ordinary
February 24, 1995

Scripture texts used in this work are taken from the New American Bible.
The Old Testament of the New American Bible copyright © 1970 by the Confraternity of Christian Doctrine (CCD), Washington, D.C. (Books 1 Samuel and 2 Maccabees copyright © 1969);
Revised New Testament of the New American Bible copyright © 1986 CCD;
Revised Psalms of the New American Bible copyright © 1991 CCD.
All rights reserved. No part of the New American Bible may be reproduced, or transmitted in any form or by any means, including electronic, or mechanical, or photocopying, or by any information and retrieval system without permission in writing from the copyright owner.

Nihil Obstat
Stephen J. Hartdegen, O.F.M., S.S.L., and Christian P. Ceroke, O. Carm.., S.T.D.
Imprimatur
†Patrick Cardinal O'Boyle, D.D., Archbishop of Washington
July 27 1970

THE REVISED NEW TESTAMENT

Nihil Obstat
Stephen J. Hartdegen, O.F.M., S.S.L., Censor Deputatus
Imprimatur
†James A. Hickey, S.T.D., J.C.D., Archbishop of Washington
August 27, 1986

THE REVISED PSALMS

Imprimatur
Most Reverend Daniel E. Pilarczyk, President, National Conference of Catholic Bishops
October 10, 1991

1 3 5 7 9 8 6 4 2
Printed in the United States of America

Contents

NEW TESTAMENT READING GUIDES

The Gospels and Acts, RG 302

Paul and His Writings, RG 396

The Pastoral Letters, RG 445

The Catholic Letters and the Book of Revelation, RG 463

THE NEW AMERICAN BIBLE / THE OLD TESTAMENT

THE NEW AMERICAN BIBLE / THE NEW TESTAMENT

Special Study Aids in the Reading Guides
A Selected List

Definitions and Discussions

Charts and Diagrams

Maps

Abbreviations of Books of the Bible

Acts	Acts of the Apostles
Am	Amos
Bar	Baruch
1 Chr	1 Chronicles
2 Chr	2 Chronicles
Col	Colossians
1 Cor	1 Corinthians
2 Cor	2 Corinthians
Dn	Daniel
Dt	Deuteronomy
Eccl	Ecclesiastes
Eph	Ephesians
Est	Esther
Ex	Exodus
Ez	Ezekial
Ezr	Ezra
Gal	Galatians
Gn	Genesis
Hb	Habakkuk
Heb	Hebrews
Hg	Haggai
Hos	Hosea
Is	Isaiah
Jas	James
Jb	Job
Jdt	Judith
Jer	Jeremiah
Jgs	Judges
Jl	Joel
Jn	John
1 Jn	1 John
2 Jn	2 John
3 Jn	3 John
Jon	Jonah
Jos	Joshua
Jude	Jude
1 Kgs	1 Kings
2 Kgs	2 Kings
Lam	Lamentations
Lk	Luke
Lv	Leviticus
Mal	Malachi
1 Mc	1 Maccabees
2 Mc	2 Maccabees
Mi	Micah
Mk	Mark
Mt	Matthew
Na	Nahum
Neh	Nehemiah
Nm	Numbers
Ob	Obadiah
Phil	Philippians
Phlm	Philemon
Prv	Proverbs
Ps(s)	Psalms
1 Pt	1 Peter
2 Pt	2 Peter
Rom	Romans
Ru	Ruth
Rv	Revelation
Sir	Sirach
1 Sm	1 Samuel
2 Sm	2 Samuel
Song(Sg)	Song of Songs
Tb	Tobit
1 Thes	1 Thessalonians
2 Thes	2 Thessalonians
Ti	Titus
1 Tm	1 Timothy
2 Tm	2 Timothy
Wis	Wisdom
Zec	Zechariah
Zep	Zephaniah

Note For greater clarity and convenience, the footnotes and cross-references are printed at the bottom of each page and cross-indexed in the text itself. An *asterisk* (*) in the text indicates that there is a footnote to the text in question. Each footnote is in turn clearly marked with the number of the chapter and the verse to which it pertains. Similarly a *superior letter* ([a]) in the text indicates that there is a cross-reference to a particular verse. The reference itself is also clearly marked with the same letter. Hence, the reader is always aware of a footnote or a cross-reference simply *by reading the text.*

[ ] Indicates a gloss. / = Divides verse // = Parallel

Simple Key to References

Gn 1,1 refers to the Book of Genesis, chapter 1, verse 1.

Gn 1,1a refers to the Book of Genesis, chapter 1, the first part of verse 1.

Gn 1,1f refers to the Book of Genesis, chapter 1, verse 1 and the following verse (2).

Gn 1,1–10 refers to the Book of Genesis, chapter 1, verses 1 to 10 inclusive.

Gn 1,1–10.14 refers to the Book of Genesis, chapter 1, verses 1 to 10 inclusive and verse 14.

Gn 1,1–2,3 refers to the Book of Genesis, chapter 1, verse 1 to chapter 2, verse 3 inclusive.

Gn 1,1; 2,3 refers to the Book of Genesis, chapter 1, verse 1 and chapter 2, verse 3.

THE CATHOLIC STUDENT BIBLE

General Introduction

The book you hold in your hand contains one of humanity's greatest treasures. No one can deny that the Bible has had a profound impact on world civilization. Its epic stories, its powerful language and images have left their imprint on human history, especially in cultures touched by Judaism and Christianity.

For the Christian, the Bible has an importance far more profound than its impact on culture. The Christian believes that through the turbulent and wonderful chapters of biblical history, God speaks to us. Although expressed in genuinely human terms and through very human authors, the Bible is, at the same time, the Word of God for us. Therefore, as Christians we reverence and love the Scriptures and seek to understand them as much as we can.

INTRODUCING THE BIBLE

The Bible is not a single, unified book, even though it is bound under one cover and bears a single title. It is, in fact, a collection of some 73 different works by different authors, using very different styles and perspectives, composed over a span of several centuries, and in three different languages (Hebrew, Aramaic, Greek). Most of the Old Testament (46 books) was written in Hebrew, but parts of the books of Daniel (2,4–7,28), Ezra (4,6–6,18; 7,12–26), and one verse from Jeremiah (10,11) were originally composed in Aramaic, a Middle Eastern language related to but different from Hebrew. All 27 of the New Testament books were composed in Greek.

The rich diversity of the Bible is one of its glories because it allows the story of God's people to be told from various perspectives. It also presents a challenge to the reader, who should be aware of the different cultural, historical, and literary contexts of each biblical book. But there is a deeper unity to the Bible that binds together these individual pieces of literature. Through the many biblical books flows the continuing saga of God's love for Israel and for the community of Christians. Each of the biblical authors, no matter how much separated in time, culture, and literary style, shares a conviction that God's presence is felt in human history and that God invites the human family to respond with faith and integrity.

Forming a "Bible" from Diverse Books: The Story of the Canon

The gathering of these diverse writings into a single collection or "book" (the literal meaning of the word "bible") was itself a long-term and difficult process. The Jewish or Hebrew canon ultimately recognizes 39 books, divided into three major categories:

1. The Law (sometimes referred to as the Pentateuch, or first five books of the Bible): Genesis, Exodus, Leviticus, Numbers, Deuteronomy.

2. The Prophets: Subdivided into the "Former Prophets": Joshua, Judges, 1 and 2 Samuel, 1 and 2 Kings; and the "Latter Prophets": Isaiah, Jeremiah, Ezekiel, and the "Twelve" (Hosea, Joel, Amos, Obadiah, Jonah, Micah, Nahum, Habakkuk, Zephaniah, Haggai, Zechariah, Malachi).
3. The Writings: Psalms, Proverbs, Job, Song of Songs, Ruth, Lamentations, Ecclesiastes, Esther, Daniel, Ezra-Nehemiah, 1 and 2 Chronicles.

There are seven other books that Roman Catholics (and Orthodox Christians) consider part of their Scriptures. Judaism reverences these books and considers them sacred, but they are not part of their "canon" or official list. These books are: Tobit, Judith, 1 and 2 Maccabees, Wisdom, Ecclesiasticus (or Sirach), and Baruch. There are also some additional passages in the books of Daniel and Esther.

All Christians agree on the 27 books to be included in the New Testament. But there is a dispute about some of the books in the Old Testament. As noted above, Roman Catholics and Orthodox Christians agree on the 46 books that make up the Old Testament (the Orthodox include additional books in their canon: 1 and 2 Esdras; the Prayer of Manasseh; Psalm 151; 3 Maccabees). Judaism and Protestant Christians hold to the shorter list of 39 books sketched above.

The reason for this divergence is that earliest Christianity used an ancient Greek translation of the Old Testament (called the Septuagint) as its Bible. This Greek version of the Bible included 46 books. Since most of the early Christians were Greek-speaking, this is the Bible they preferred. But when Judaism officially set out to determine *its* canon at the end of the first century, it drew up a shorter list of 39 books: those written in Hebrew. In the Reformation period, Protestants went back to this shorter, Hebrew canon, considering it more authentic.

Reading, Studying, and Praying the Scriptures

From the beginning of its existence, the Bible has been the object of intense study, prayerful reading, and even heated debate. The Bible is not meant to be a coffee-table book.

In many ways the Bible took shape in prayer and reflection. The various biblical authors reflected on significant events in the life of Israel, of Jesus, and of the early church. Their discovery of God's presence working within history gives the Bible its force. For all Christians the Bible has unique authority as writings inspired by God's Spirit working within the communities of Israel and the church, and impelling the biblical writers to give expression in human words to their faith perspective.

Judaism has always maintained a rich tradition of reflection on its Scriptures. The rabbis lovingly studied every detail of the biblical text and saw an infinite possibility of applications to everyday life. The Scriptures were reverenced as God's Word and took a central place within the prayer life of the synagogue. Christian tradition has had the same character. Until the late Middle Ages, almost all of the church's theology and teaching was little more than an elaboration of the biblical text.

For most Christians, reading the Bible has a more modest, yet still important goal. They turn to the Scriptures for inspiration in living out their life of faith. Such inspiration can be gained in many different ways.

For some, the Scriptures are an important stimulant for prayer. The words of the Psalms, the challenge of the prophets, the compassionate mission of Jesus, the soaring words of Paul—

all of these give form and expression to the longing of our own hearts as we seek the face of God. Very often the biblical words are able to express the feelings and fears and hopes we could not put into words ourselves. And in reaching out to the Bible we unite ourselves with the faith of countless generations of Christians who found the same solace and strength in the Scriptures.

For others, probing the Scriptures either in private or with a group of fellow Christians helps guide and illumine their daily life. Study of the biblical text and discussion of its meaning with other thoughtful Christians can help us understand our own experience of faith and expand our perspective on what it means to be a believer in the modern world. This approach works best when the participant is not afraid to reflect on his or her own experience, and then relate that reflection to the ideas and images of the Bible. Very often the Bible opens its treasures when we bring to it questions and hopes that spring from our life of faith. Then, in turn, the biblical message can give new insight and nourishment to our faith experience.

MEETING THE BIBLICAL TEST

As you begin to read the Bible, you will encounter passages of great beauty and profound meaning along with sections that may seem very distant from your life and concerns. The Reading Guides and other materials are intended to help you in your first encounter with these readings, and the notes and introductions attached to the *New American Bible* translation are meant to provide guidance at the moment of reading the text.

But there is another ingredient present when you read the Bible—you! You as a human person; you as a Christian; you as a Catholic. How does this have an impact on your encounter with the Bible?

First, you must remember that the Bible is a book about human beings, people with concerns like yours. The characters in the text of the Bible lived long ago and in a faraway place, but they shared many of your worries and hopes. They had families—parents, children, brothers and sisters, aunts and uncles—and all the joys and problems that families bring. They wondered about the world and their place in it, and tried to understand things as best they could. They wanted people, rich and poor, to obey the law and act fairly—and they wondered how to set up their society so that people would act according to the best parts of their nature. They had governments of which they could be proud, and other governments that they didn't like. They worried about events in foreign countries, and how those events might affect their lives.

As you meet these people and read the writings they have left behind, try first of all to see the people behind the words. Try to understand their concerns and their ideals. The Guides and the other materials will help you with this. Above all, try to keep in mind the whole story, and remember that each individual is only one part of a long, long history that stretches from the earliest beginnings of the Hebrews in ancient times up through the beginnings of the Christian church in the time of the apostles. Each life story becomes a part of this larger story and brings the larger story that much further along.

Second, try to see these people as part of a larger society. They existed in a community, whether it was the community of the people of Israel or the people of the early church. And their membership in a community did not mean that they all agreed with each other completely. You will encounter plenty of disagreement in the pages of the Bible: prophets disagreeing with kings, priests disagreeing with prophets, apostles disagreeing with one another. But there are two things to remember about these disagreements. First, they took place within the society of Israel or the early Christian church, that is, among people who would continue to talk to one another and have dealings with one another despite disagreements. The second thing to remember is that these were disagreements among people who shared a great purpose: They were arguments about how Israel might be most faithful to God or how the early Christians could best carry out the will of the Lord Jesus.

As a member of a Christian community, you too are a part of a society. You too have relationships with others in that community, even with those people who might disagree with you about one thing or another. And you too are part of a group that is trying to carry out a larger mission in our country and in the world.

Finally, as you read the Bible you may wonder how you encounter God in these words. Sometimes the answer is easy. When you read in Isaiah 53,5 words like these:

> "But he was pierced for our offenses,
> crushed for our sins,
> Upon him was the chastisement that makes us whole,
> by his stripes we were healed."

or in the Gospels words like these from Matthew 5,7:

> "Blessed are the merciful,
> for they will be shown mercy."

it is not hard to think that God is speaking directly through the text. But there are other places where things may not seem so clear. At those places it is important to remember that God can use all of life and all of experience to speak to us, but not always in the same way. Sometimes the message is a negative one.

That is why a Catholic understanding of the Bible can be helpful. Like the sacraments in the Catholic Church, the Bible uses human materials and human experience to convey God's presence. God speaks to us from within our human lives, not only from the outside. And sometimes our human lives, and the experiences that form a part of them, are less than we might hope they would be. The same is true of the people of the Bible. There are no characters in the Hebrew Scriptures, for instance, who receive more honor than Moses or King David. Yet the Bible tells us the bad, as well as the good, about them: Moses killed a man in anger (Ex 2,11–14) and King David committed adultery (2 Sm, Chapters 11 and 12). Likewise, the New Testament shows us Paul losing his temper (Gal 3,1–3) and the disciples running away when Jesus is arrested in the garden (Mt 26,56).

The lesson we can draw from such passages, and other difficult and painful episodes, is that *all* of life is involved in our understanding of God. The Bible does not try to gloss things over or pretend that they are better than they are. God uses it all, even the bad parts, to carry on the story.

Following are some guidelines for you in using this study Bible to come to a better knowledge of the Scriptures. It is the hope of the contributors that you will browse through the entire book before beginning to read or study a part. Doing so will help you become familiar and comfortable with the many parts of this treasure so that you can use all it has to offer from the text itself to the general introductions to the maps, essays, glossary, or charts.

FEATURES

In striving to help bring these pages alive, the contributors have chosen to forego long, explanatory essays and use instead a variety of features such as the following:

Most of the Reading Guides present information and background to situate what you are going to read before you start. These opening passages will enhance your understanding and equip you to get more out of what you read. Within the Guides themselves you will find brief themes developed on significant and interesting topics, such as "Did it Really Happen?" or "What are the Parables?" or "Was Solomon the Author of Proverbs?" A chart within the Reading Guides, called *At a Glance,* is often provided to show the overview of the book you are beginning, in order to contextualize its contents. You will also find boxes, scattered throughout the study materials, that provide pertinent definitions or explanations of words appearing in an essay. (Other definitions are given parenthetically in the essay, and still others are contained in the glossary.) Other boxed information includes material that is related to the essay, such as social habits of biblical times. *Questions for Discussion or Reflection* is the last feature in each book, and helps make application of the text to life whether you use this book alone or with others.

POPULAR EDITIONS FOR SPECIAL READERS

The contributors to this volume were keenly aware, as the Pontifical Biblical Commission reminded us recently in "The Interpretation of the Bible in the Church" (*Origins*, CNS documentary service, Jan. 6, 1994, vol. 23: no 29), "The Scriptures, as given to the Church, are the communal treasure of the entire body of believers. . ." (page 516). "There is another form of publication, more short-term in nature, which renders a very great service by its ability to adapt itself to a variety of readers, from the well educated to children of catechism age, reaching biblical groups, apostolic movements, and religious congregations. Exegetes who have a gift for popularization provide an extremely useful and fruitful work, one that is indispensable if the fruit of exegetical studies is to be dispersed as widely as need demands. In this area, the need to make the biblical message something real for today is ever more obvious. This requires that exegetes take into consideration the reasonable demands of educated and cultural persons of our time, clearly distinguishing for their benefit what is to be regarded as the true historical and inspired meaning" (page 518).

APPLICATION TO LIFE

In preparing the study text for this volume, the contributors also remembered that "the biblical texts have been composed with respect to circumstances of the past and in language conditioned by a variety of times and seasons. To reveal their significance for men and women of today, it is necessary to apply their message to contemporary circumstances and to express it in language adapted to the present time" (*Origins*, page 520). Thus the questions for reflection or discussion are geared to real life. You will undoubtedly think of other ways to integrate the message of this book into your daily living. That, of course, is the challenge and the grace of the book we call the Bible.

HOW TO USE THIS VOLUME

Catholics today are highly interested in the Bible, whether they're studying it in parochial school settings, informal study groups, structured classes, or alone. Some ways to make good use of this resource are:

1. Page through an entire book and its study guide before beginning.
2. Read the questions before starting, so they are in your mind as you read the text.
3. Use the questions as a model, but adapt them to yourself and your group. Think about what is important for this particular group at this time—that we have a challenge? that we keep up hope? that we grow in faith?—and create the questions appropriate to your need.
4. Remember to allow time for reflection before beginning a discussion.
5. As you read, put yourself into the text by asking: What was the message for the people at the time of its writing? What is the message for today?
6. Challenge yourself to put the primary message or insight into language for your peers.
7. Explore the heart of a passage or book by deciding how you would preach on it in your parish if this were Sunday's reading.
8. In preparing for a class, jot down phrases you want to come back to. Reflect on why those were important. What feeling was evoked, what memory recalled, what idea sparked? Such insights shared (and only when you feel comfortable doing so) can be part of breaking the word open for others.

CONCLUSION

The Bible is your family album, the story of your heritage. It is the book of a faith-seeking community. You, as a member of that community, share in its present and future. Understanding and connecting with the past through study, prayer, and reflection will help you be a part of creating its future by living an informed faith-filled life. It is our hope that this story will truly become your story in your heart, your mind, and your actions.

The Reverend Donald Senior, C.P.
Jean Marie Hiesberger
and the Editors of Oxford University Press

The Importance of Story

When you want to get someone's attention, tell a story. Human beings have loved stories for as long as they've been able to tell them. In fact, much of what we know about the past has been preserved because of stories. Even before there were historians, people shaped what they knew about important events and situations into stories that could be easily remembered and repeated. Stories have always been popular because they help us organize and understand life.

THE BIBLE AS STORY

Throughout this study guide you'll be reminded that before it is anything else, sacred scripture is a story. That's not to say that what we read in the Bible is made up, that there is no historical basis to the characters and events we encounter in the pages of scripture. Far from it. But whether reading the Old Testament or the New, in scripture you'll find the features of good storytelling—plot, characters, and settings that help you get caught up in the emotion and dynamic energy of the events being recounted.

God Teaches through the Events of Our Lives

This emphasis on story points to a great biblical truth: People learn about God through the events of their lives. We might have a notion that scripture relates a succession of "mountain-top" events where God dictates laws and teachings to religious giants like Moses. But, except for the giving of the Ten Commandments, scripture narrates no such events. The usual way that the people of Israel discovered who God is and how God deals with people was through their life experience. Even when prophets raised their voices to deliver God's messages to the people, they were usually commenting on how the people were (or were not) living their lives. Look at the mess you're in, a prophet might say to the nation. God is speaking to you through the tragic events you're experiencing!

The Jewish people's understanding of a "covenant" provides a fine example. It was first considered to be an eternal and unconditional pledge made by God to the people (I am your God and you will always be my people whom I will protect), but over the course of many years it came to be understood instead that it was conditional on the people's behavior toward God and one another. *If* you are faithful to your part of the bargain—that is, love me and each other—*then* I will be faithful to mine. It took a lot of life experience to get to that realization, a lot of paying the price for unfaithfulness, before the people realized that God would not be their divine warrior fighting on the side of Israel no matter what.

There's a lesson here for the modern reader as well as for the ancient believer: God has made all of life holy, and it is in and through the events of our God-given lives that we will encounter and know our God. We must therefore pay close attention to the details of life, since it is there, on a daily basis, that God is revealed.

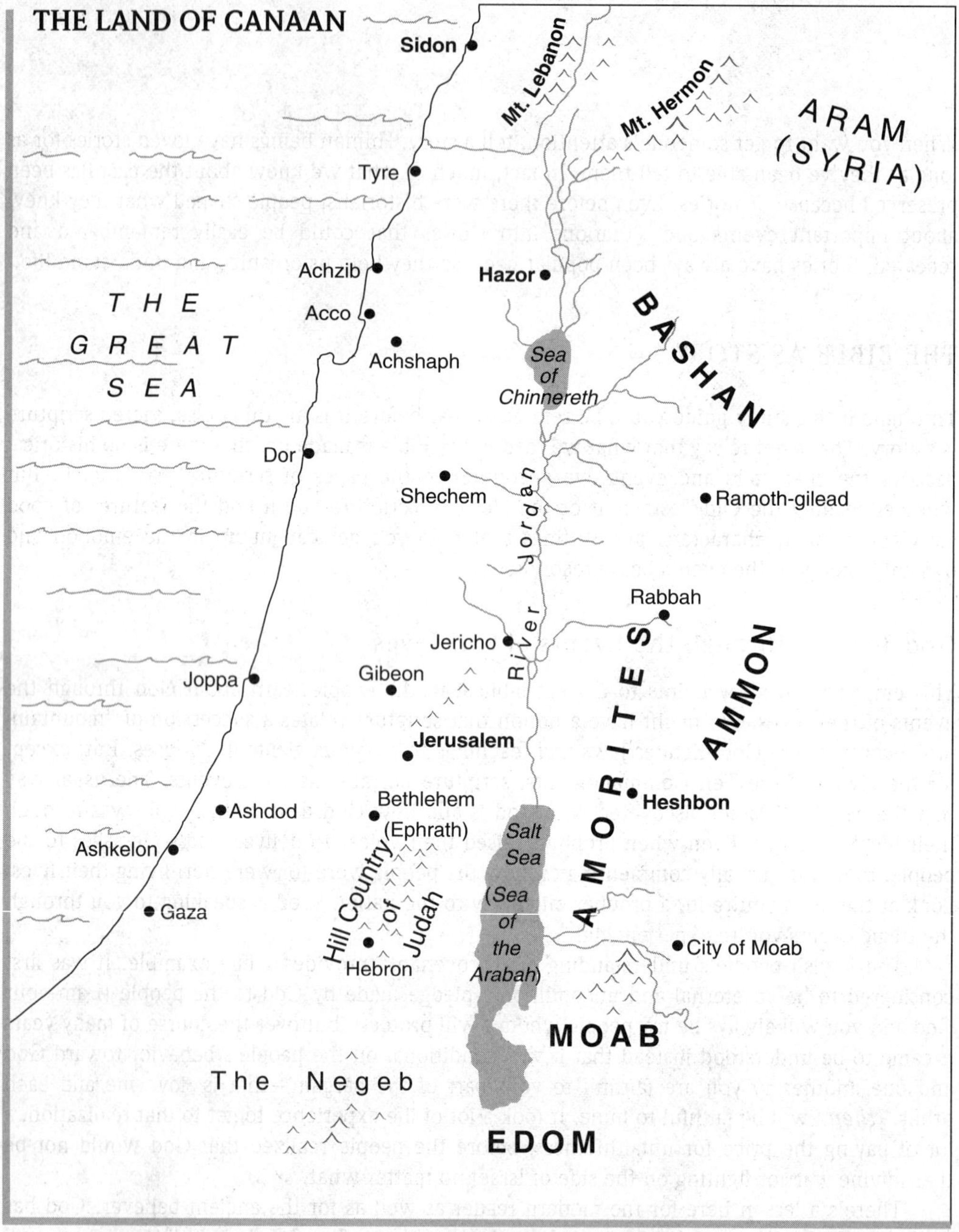
THE LAND OF CANAAN
Sidon
Mt. Lebanon
Mt. Hermon
ARAM (SYRIA)
Tyre
Achzib
Hazor
THE GREAT SEA
Acco
Achshaph
Sea of Chinnereth
BASHAN
Dor
Shechem
River Jordan
Ramoth-gilead
Rabbah
Jericho
AMMON
Joppa
Gibeon
Jerusalem
AMORITES
Heshbon
Ashdod
Bethlehem (Ephrath)
Salt Sea (Sea of the Arabah)
Ashkelon
Hill Country of Judah
Gaza
Hebron
City of Moab
MOAB
The Negeb
EDOM

The Old Testament Is All One Story

Because the scriptures were written by many different authors over the course of many centuries; because, at times, the same story is told by several authors; because the storytelling is often interrupted by lists of laws, genealogies, and prayers; and because the "story" is spread out over more than one thousand pages, it is difficult to get a sense of the whole, of how characters and events relate to one another. To get a better sense of who came first and of how events flow together, it may be a good idea to "tell the story" of God's people all at once.

What follows is an attempt to do just that. The telling will be very informal, it will hit only "highlights" in the history of the Hebrew people, and it will take considerable artistic license with the presentation of the colorful characters in the story. The intent is to provide a sense of flow, to grasp the continuity of people and events we may know only in isolated or fragmentary form. Elsewhere in the Reading Guides questions of historical accuracy occur. That is not our concern here.

THE STORY OF THE OLD TESTAMENT

Prehistory: Creation and Sin

The story begins "in the beginning" when everything was a "formless wasteland" and "darkness covered" it (Gn 1,1). It was by God's act that it was raised into light, order, and life; and when it came to be, it was wondrous, it was holy, and it was "good"! God made woman and man to resemble the divine goodness, but God also made them free, and freedom meant that things would not always be as God would want them. And soon enough they weren't. The man and woman God created decided to do things their own way. This original rebellion against God's will didn't take long to grow. Soon one brother (Cain) killed another (Abel), and evil spread throughout the earth.

THE FLOOD AND THE TOWER OF BABEL

God grieved and regretted having created human beings, so God decided to destroy them and start again. From all the people of the earth God saved one family: Noah's. For forty days his ark floated above the flood waters as Noah's family and two of every animal waited safely inside. When the ark finally rested on the top of Mt. Ararat, God made a covenant with Noah promising never again to destroy the earth by flood. And while the waters of the earth never again grew so high as to drown all life, human sin did grow—right up to the skies.

Human pride swelled up into a tower of arrogance. In the city of Babel the people built a tall tower that would "make a name" for them. They refused to spread out over the earth as God desired, so God confused the people by making them babble, unable to understand one another, and people have had a hard time understanding each other ever since.

Folk History: The Patriarchs and Matriarchs

ABRAHAM AND SARAH

Because in the Garden God's original plan got spoiled, God conceived a new plan. God decided to choose a people who could live out this plan for righting the imbalance that happened at the beginning. God wanted a new people, a nation that had not been before, and to begin God chose one man and one woman. The man was Abram, and his wife, Sarai, was the woman. Though Sarai was barren, God promised Abram that he would one day have a son and through him become the father of a whole nation that would possess the land of Canaan. Fearing her barrenness would prevent God's promise from being fulfilled, Sarai encouraged Abram to father a child through her young maidservant, Hagar. Abram slept with Hagar and she conceived. But soon her pregnancy caused her to look down on her mistress, Sarai. In retaliation, Sarai began mistreating Hagar, who then ran away into the desert. God's angel told Hagar to return to her mistress Sarai and submit to her. She did and bore a son whom Abram named Ishmael.

But God had chosen Abram and *Sarai* as channels of the promise. Abram's heir would be his wife's son. So time passed, and when Abram and Sarai were long past their prime, they finally had a son. This boy, through whom God's promises would be fulfilled, was named Isaac.

ISAAC AND REBEKAH AND JACOB

Isaac married a beautiful woman named Rebekah and though she, too, had seemed to be sterile, eventually she bore two sons, twins, named Esau and Jacob. The boys wrestled even in the womb. Esau was born first with Jacob holding onto his heel. Much of their life together was lived the same way: struggling for superiority, fighting to be first.

Esau was Isaac's favorite, but Rebekah favored Jacob. When Isaac was near death he planned to give the first-born Esau his special blessing. But Rebekah wanted Jacob to receive it, so she helped him trick Isaac, who was nearly blind, into thinking that Jacob was really Esau. Jacob dressed in his brother's clothes so he would smell like him and put animal skins on his arms and neck so he would be hairy like his brother. Isaac realized Jacob didn't sound like Esau, but he did feel and smell like him, so Isaac spoke the words of blessing over the younger boy.

When Esau came to Isaac to receive his promised blessing Isaac asked, "Who are you?"

"I am Esau, your first-born."

Trembling, Isaac asked, "Who was it, then, that I just blessed?" It's a tragic, heart-rending scene when Isaac and Esau realize how they've been betrayed by their son and brother. But the word of blessing was spoken, and the spoken word is powerful and cannot be "unspoken" or reversed.

Esau became so angry at being deceived that he planned to kill his brother, but Rebekah got wind of the plan and sent Jacob away to find safety and a wife among the daughters of her brother, Laban.

JOSEPH

Jacob married two sisters: Rachel, whom he loved, and Leah, who was forced upon him by her scheming father. Jacob (also referred to as Israel [see explanation and genealogical chart on page RG 45 at the end of Genesis notes]) had contracted that he would be permitted to marry Rachel after working for her father Laban for seven years. But on the wedding day, Laban substituted the older Leah for her younger sister Rachel. Since she was heavily veiled, Jacob didn't know he was being deceived until it was too late. He had to agree to work for Laban an extra seven years in order to marry Rachel, the woman he really loved.

Eventually tension arose between Jacob and Laban, so the Lord instructed Jacob to return to Canaan, the land of his relatives. During his return trip, Jacob had a remarkable experience. During the night he wrestled with a man whom he came to realize was a messenger of God in human form. Jacob demanded a blessing from this stranger before agreeing to release him. The divine messenger responded by changing Jacob's name to Israel, which means "he struggles with God."

Soon after this encounter, Jacob met his brother Esau. Jacob feared his brother still harbored anger and resentment, but Esau overwhelmed him with forgiving love. Esau threw his arms around Jacob's neck and kissed him. The long-separated brothers stood together and wept.

Custom permitted Jacob to have children not only by his two wives, but by each wife's maid as well. Of his twelve sons, Jacob's favorite was Joseph, the first of Rachel's two boys. Jacob's other sons resented and envied Joseph's favored status, so they got rid of him by selling him to slave merchants who took him to Egypt.

But in Egypt, Joseph rose to great prominence through his ability to interpret dreams. By correctly interpreting one of Pharaoh's dreams, he helped Egypt prepare for a famine. When the famine came seven years later, Joseph's brothers traveled to Egypt where, because of Joseph, food had been stored in abundance. Kneeling before Joseph, whom they did not recognize, the brothers asked for grain to bring back to their family. Joseph decided to find out whether his brothers had changed or whether they were still the jealous and selfish men who had sold him into slavery. By pretending to believe that they were spies, Joseph was able to force his brothers to return home so they could bring back to Egypt his only full brother Benjamin, the other son of Joseph's mother Rachel.

Reluctantly, Jacob consented to let his new favorite son go to Egypt. Joseph now concocted a scheme to make Benjamin look like a thief. Announcing that only Benjamin would be punished for the theft, he gave the others permission to return home. But, knowing that the loss of Benjamin would kill their father, one of the boys volunteered to remain in Egypt in place of Benjamin. Joseph now saw that his brothers truly had changed. He revealed his true identity and told them to go bring their father and families from Canaan to Egypt where they would live off the fat of the land.

SAFETY IN EGYPT

God had set out to create a new people. Through Abraham and Sarah that people was conceived. But, just like a human embryo that needs a womb of nurturance and safety to grow, this infant nation needed a womb where it could be nourished and protected until it was strong enough to stand on its own. That womb was Egypt. Alone in the land of Canaan, this little clan's survival would have been risky at best. But in Egypt the Pharaoh laid the nation's best resources in the lap of this small tribe.

At some point, babies must be born. If it were up to them, they might not choose to leave the security and comfort of life in the womb. And so labor sets in to thrust them, willingly or not, into a world of growth and challenge.

SLAVERY

In Egypt the descendants of Jacob and Joseph were fruitful. The embryonic nation of Israel had grown numerous and powerful. They were rich and comfortable. God's promises to Abraham, Isaac, and Jacob — the promises of land and nationhood — were a distant memory. So, as in human birth, it took labor pains to move Israel out of its womb of comfort. Israel's labor pains were just that, the pain of forced labor — slavery.

The Egyptians feared the great numbers and the power of the growing Hebrew population. So first they turned the Israelites into slaves, but eventually they ordered the cruel killing of all their newborn male children. The Hebrew midwives, however, refused to cooperate with this ruthless scheme, so a new order was given that every newborn boy would be thrown in the river.

MOSES

Now Moses enters the story. His mother had set the infant Moses adrift on the river in the hope of saving him from Pharaoh's death decree. Found and adopted by Pharaoh's daughter, he grew up in Pharaoh's lavish court, but he eventually discovered his Hebrew roots and encountered God in a dramatic and life-transforming way at the burning bush. Here God chose Moses as midwife for his people, making him the one who would deliver them—sometimes against their will—into the land of promise.

EXODUS

The story of Moses' interaction with Pharaoh could be amusing if it weren't so tragic. Repeatedly Moses returned to Pharaoh to warn him that he must let the Israelite people go or suffer dire consequences. Each time Pharaoh agreed, only to renege at the last moment. Ten plagues afflicted Egypt before Pharaoh finally allowed the Hebrew people to leave. And even though the last was the most terrible plague, the death of the first-born of every Egyptian home, Pharaoh once again tried to prevent God's people from following Moses to their destiny. He pursued them to the edge of the Red Sea and there, helplessly, watched his troops perish as the Hebrews escaped in safety "with the water like a wall to their right and to their left" (Ex 14,22). Despite Yahweh's amazing display of strength and loyalty in delivering Israel from the hands of the Egyptians, the people quickly began to question God's protection and the wisdom of following Moses. Because of this lack of faith, the Israelites' journey through the desert became a protracted ordeal lasting forty years.

THE PROMISED LAND

Finally, however, the people arrived at the land of promise. Moses, because of his own momentary lapse during the desert wanderings, was allowed to see but not to enter this land flowing with milk and honey. Led by Joshua, Moses' successor, the Israelites began to conquer and settle in Canaan. After Joshua's death, a pattern began to emerge in the life of the nation. The people fell into sin (usually idolatry); calamity struck (always perceived as God's punishment); Israel repented; God relented and forgave.

JUDGES

The calamities that struck Israel during their times of unfaithfulness most often took the form of some external danger—an enemy nation threatening attack—and Israel's response was usually to fall to its knees and beg forgiveness. God reacted by raising up a military leader whose charismatic qualities ensured victory against the threatening enemy. These leaders were called judges. Once the danger passed, their work was done and they returned to peaceful anonymity. Many times Israel replayed this four-fold pattern of unfaithfulness, punishment, repentance, and deliverance through a charismatic leader before they finally began to clamor for a king.

DEMANDS FOR A KING

The people grew tired of having to hope (and pray!) God would grant them a leader each time they got themselves into a jam. "Why don't we have a king like other nations?" they asked. "Someone we can rely on who will always be there to save us." Samuel, the prophet, realized they were asking for a human leader to usurp God's rightful role among the people. "God is your safety," he asserted. "He alone is your king!" But the people demanded and eventually got what they wanted.

SAUL

Saul, anointed Israel's first king, began well but ended badly. He disobeyed God's instructions, became extremely jealous of David, and eventually even resorted to consulting mediums and witches. During a fierce battle, he received word of his sons' deaths and he despaired. He knew God had repented of having chosen him king, so he asked his armor-bearer to slay him, but the man refused. Rather than relying on and embracing God's forgiving mercy, Saul threw himself upon his own sword and embraced death instead.

DAVID

Who would be Israel's new king? God had already decided. Samuel had been sent to the house of Jesse to anoint one of his sons as Saul's successor. As each of seven sturdy young brothers was paraded before him Samuel heard God's judgment: "No, not this one." Samuel was surprised, but God told him: "God does not see as you see. You judge by appearance, but the Lord looks into the heart."

"Aren't there any other brothers?" asked Samuel. "Well, yes, there's the youngest, the runt you might say, tending sheep on the hillside. His name is David." They sent for him. He was ruddy, handsome, and splendid. And when he was anointed, the spirit of the Lord rushed upon him.

As soon as David came to the throne he got to work uniting the kingdom and made Jerusalem his seat of power. This lowly shepherd boy, this teller of tales, this poet and musician, had also become a great warrior and would now be Israel's greatest king. Among the giants of Israel's history David stands tall. But despite being venerated for his political, military, and religious leadership, David is also remembered as a murderer.

Though he could have had any woman in the kingdom, David's eyes one day settled on Bathsheba, a woman married to Uriah, one of his generals. David had her brought to him and he had intercourse with her. Soon she discovered she was pregnant. To cover up his wrongdoing, David recalled Bathsheba's husband from battle in the hope that he would have sexual relations with his wife and then believe the child she carried was his own. But Uriah remained faithful to the practice of refraining from sexual relations while still involved in a military campaign. So David resorted to treachery. He ordered Uriah back to the front lines, and instructed his generals to withdraw, leaving Uriah unprotected and doomed to die.

The prophet Nathan came to David under the ruse of seeking judgment in a case. A man in your kingdom, he told him, has large flocks of sheep. His neighbor is a poor man who owns but a single lamb. Yet, when the rich man wished to entertain a guest, he did not take a lamb from his own flock. Instead he stole and slew the neighbor's only lamb and served it to his guest. "Tell me who the man is," insisted David, "for he deserves to die!" Poignantly and pointedly, Nathan answered, "You are the man" (2 Sm 12,7). Here we see the difference between David and his predecessor Saul. Confronted with his failure and sin, David did not despair. Instead of falling on his sword like Saul, he fell upon his knees and asked forgiveness.

SOLOMON

David was succeeded by his son Solomon. Renowned for his proverbial wisdom and for his magnificent building projects, Solomon nonetheless ended tragically. The opulence and pageantry of his court and his many foreign wives eventually turned his heart away from the Lord, his God. Seeing that his heart was elsewhere, the Lord said to Solomon, "Since you have not kept my covenant . . . I will deprive you of the kingdom and give it to your servant."

TWO KINGDOMS

One of his sons, Rehoboam, took the throne after Solomon's death to become the last king to reign over a united kingdom. The Northern ten tribes soon broke away, leaving David's line to rule over two small tribes in the South. The one kingdom had become two rival nations, Israel in the North and Judah in the South.

PROPHETS

Governments that endure are usually characterized by some kind of system of checks and balances. In the United States the Congress and the judiciary balance each other's power and that of the presidency. In Israel it was the prophets who helped achieve balance, though not through the exercise of power but through political and religious influence. Throughout the history of both kingdoms, the voices of the prophets rang out, reminding the people of God's promises, calling the kings to fidelity, comforting those who were troubled, and troubling those who were comfortable.

FALL OF THE NORTHERN AND SOUTHERN KINGDOMS

Each kingdom experienced periods of stability and prosperity, but often the prosperity came at the expense of the poor, who were exploited by the rich citizens. The prophets' voices were crucial at these times, pointing out that such injustice was in direct violation of God's will. The Northern kingdom eventually fell into the clutches of Assyria which, in 721 B.C., conquered Israel and deported many of its citizens.

One hundred thirty-five years later, the same fate befell the Southern kingdom, only for them it was at the hands of the Babylonians. The great Temple was destroyed, the prominent citizens of Judah were taken into exile, and the nation was no more.

EXILE AND RETURN

While in exile the prophet Ezekiel spoke words of future restoration and renewal. Announcing a new covenant to be written on hearts instead of stone, he raised the people's hopes that God would eventually restore the nation and its Temple. When Babylonia fell to the Persian conqueror, Cyrus, the people's expectations were fulfilled. Eventually the Temple was restored, but never again would Israel be a world power. Though Israel again experienced brief periods of autonomy, it became more like a coin tossed among world powers. After the Persian conquerors came the Greeks, then finally the Romans, who stuffed Israel into their pocket for good.

Questions for Discussion or Reflection

1. What is your favorite Old Testament story? What does it tell you about your image of God? What does it tell you about yourself?
2. In what ways is it helpful to read the Old Testament as one continuous story? What insights do you gain? What questions does it raise for you?
3. How do your life stories reveal God's presence and activity in your life?

The Pentateuch

WHAT IS THE PENTATEUCH?

In the United States, the Constitution, the Declaration of Independence, and the Bill of Rights stand as the foundational documents on which the democratic system of government is based. No matter what new laws are written or policies are made, every piece of legislation, every judicial decision is ultimately judged in light of those original documents.

The foundation documents for the people of Israel are the books we now commonly refer to as the Pentateuch, the first five books of the Bible. These books do more than introduce the rest of the Bible: they are the very foundation on which the rest of the scriptures stand. The Pentateuch serves as the blueprint or constitution by which all other scripture is interpreted. By understanding the special nature and special role of these first five books of the Old Testament, we will have a better understanding of the entire Bible.

The name "Pentateuch" means a five-part writing. So, rather than five distinct books, what we're really dealing with is one book in five volumes. Even in biblical times the Pentateuch was considered a single work. Jewish tradition calls it "Torah," which is often translated as "law" but really means "teaching" or "instruction." In the Torah we find the basic teachings of the Jewish faith. The chart below gives an overview of the Pentateuch.

The Pentateuch

Genesis	Origins: Creation and stories of primeval times. Abraham, Isaac, Jacob, Joseph: The great ancestors of the Jewish people.
Exodus	God chooses Moses to deliver Israelites from slavery in Egypt. The giving of the Law at Mt. Sinai. Many laws regarding daily life and religious practice.
Leviticus	Laws for the people of God relating to sacrifice, priesthood, and religious feasts. Recurring call to be "holy" as God is holy.
Numbers	More laws. Desert wanderings and military exploits on the way to Promised Land. Repeated acts of unfaithfulness to God and Moses extend the wandering to forty years.
Deuteronomy	A "second law" that sums up the significance of the Exodus. Moses' farewell speech delivered at the borders of the Promised Land in which Moses warns people they must obey the covenant or risk losing the land.

Oddly, the Table of Contents of the *New American Bible* lists eight books under the heading "Pentateuch" and groups the books of the Old Testament into four categories: The Pentateuch, The Historical Books, The Wisdom Books, and the Prophetic Books. Jewish Bibles group the biblical books differently, under three headings:

The Law (Torah)

Genesis; Exodus; Leviticus; Numbers; Deuteronomy

The Prophets

Former Prophets: Joshua; Judges; 1 Samuel, 2 Samuel (regarded as one book); 1 Kings, 2 Kings (regarded as one book).

Latter Prophets: Isaiah; Jeremiah; Ezekiel; The Book of the Twelve (minor prophets).

The Writings

Psalms; Job; Proverbs; Ruth; Song of Songs; Ecclesiastes; Lamentations; Esther; Daniel; Ezra-Nehemiah; 1 Chronicles, 2 Chronicles (regarded as one book).

This arrangement helps us see that the Pentateuch is the source from which all the other books of the Old Testament flow. It may be surprising to find books of history together with those of prophetic writing in the "Prophets" column. But there's an important message in that fact: The teaching of the prophets and Israel's life-experience both call the people back to fidelity to the teachings of the Pentateuch. In our own lives, we often have to face unpleasant consequences of our own actions. Often, these experiences remind us of the differences between right and wrong that we learned when we were younger. In the same way, Israel had both the words of the prophets and their own history to help them determine how well or how poorly they had lived out the message of the Pentateuch in their life as a nation. Even when they were deaf to the prophets' words, the messes they frequently found themselves in were sufficient to remind them that they had indeed been unfaithful to God and the law.

The Writings are a group of books that also flow out of the Pentateuch. Primarily they contain reflections and explanations intended to help us live the message of the Torah. In short, all the other books of the Old Testament are the result of Israel's reflection on the Torah.

TaNaK Modern Hebrew uses the acronym TNK (pronounced "Tenak") to refer to the Bible. The acronym consists of the first letters of the Hebrew words for the Law (Torah), the Prophets (Nebi'im), and the Writings (Ketubim).

The Pentateuch and the Canon of Scripture

None of the books in the Bible got there by accident. Every decision about whether to include a certain book was carefully thought out, discussed, and probably hotly debated. The final decisions make a difference. When we read the books of the Bible we read them as part of a collection of books, and how we interpret the message of a book is determined, at least in part, by where that book stands in relation to other books. So as we begin to study the Old Testament we will want to determine why Genesis, Exodus, Leviticus, Numbers, and Deuteronomy appear in that order.

How do we do that? By asking questions about the books themselves, about the times during which they were written, and about their meaning for us today. For example:

1. Literary Shape: What kind of literature is this? Is it poetry, story, history, prophecy, myth, or some other form of writing?
2. Historical Development: How did separate pieces of writing composed by different authors come to be put together to make the present book?
3. Actual History: What was happening in Israel during the period this book describes?
4. Religious Significance: What is the religious message of the book for a modern reader?

Canon Canon is the term used to refer to the list of officially approved books contained in the Bible. It comes from a Greek word meaning "regulation" or "rule" and from a Hebrew word meaning "reed." A canon, then, is a measuring stick or ruler used to decide what does and does not fit in.

Story and Law

We said above that one of the first questions we put to a scripture text is "What kind of literature is it?" It's easy to see from just looking at the pages of the *New American Bible* that the bulk of the Pentateuch is prose rather than poetry. If you examine the five books carefully, you'll soon find two kinds of prose dominate: laws and stories (narratives). Generally, each book contains large sections of each. Sections of stories regularly alternate with sections of laws, but within every story segment you'll find scattered laws and commands, and in every listing of laws you'll find a healthy episode or two of story. The breakdown of laws and narratives is illustrated in the table here.

	Stories	Laws
Genesis	All Stories (Gn 1–50)	
Exodus	Half Stories (Ex 1–19; 24; 31–34)	Half Laws (Ex 20–23; 25–30; 35–40)
Leviticus		All Laws (Lv 1–27)
Numbers	Half Stories (Nm 1–19; 20–26; 31–33)	Half Laws (Nm 1–10; 18–19; 27–30; 34–36)
Deuteronomy		All Laws (Dt 1–34)

The stories of the Pentateuch are part of a larger story that continues into the books listed under the Former Prophets (Joshua, Judges, Samuel, Kings). The Pentateuch wraps its many laws in a package of stories that trace the "history" of the world from the moment of creation down to the time of the total collapse of the nation of Israel, just before the Babylonian exile.

THE LARGER PICTURE

The Pentateuch ends with the chosen people standing on the borders of the Promised Land. But the story continues. The books of Joshua and Judges tell the story of the people's entry into the land: stories of conquest and the gradual settling of the land and stories of great military leaders called judges. 1 and 2 Samuel recount how the people abandoned tribal rule and accepted kingship. 1 and 2 Kings present stories of the life of Israel under the kings up to the time of the exile.

The rich blending of laws and story in the Pentateuch is intentional. Its purpose is to help readers see the many laws as part of their unfolding story. They were not merely regulations tacked on to their life here and there; they were the very stuff of which their life as a nation was made. Without the Law, Israel would have had no story to tell.

A modern reader might be puzzled to find lists of the laws the Congress passed in a given period as part of a history of the United States. But in order to understand the history and culture of the country, we would have to know about the laws. Likewise, in biblical times awareness of the Law brought with it an awareness of how the lives of the ancestors were guided by the same laws. It made the Israelites aware of their continuity with those who went before them. They might think, "Our ancestors obeyed these laws, and we obey these laws, and as a result we are one!"

This sense of continuity helped the Hebrews see the Law as a gift from God. It not only taught them *how* to live, but, more importantly, it helped assure that they *would* live because by being faithful to the Law the people were maintaining their end of their relationship with God: "If you keep my commandments, I will be your God and you will be my people." Fidelity meant protection, and protection meant existence!

	Stories	Laws
Genesis	From Creation to the days of the Patriarchs	
Exodus Leviticus Numbers	Leaving slavery in Egypt. Meeting God at Mt. Sinai. Desert wanderings and reaching the borders of the Promised Land.	Laws delivered to Moses on Mt. Sinai that are to become the basis of the covenant between God and Israel, and many more laws Moses "receives" from God that govern every aspect of daily life.
Deuteronomy		Moses sums up the law and applies it to life in the land.

The Structure of the Pentateuch

Try thinking about the structure of the Pentateuch in this way. Basically it looks like a plan-within-a-plan. The plan begins in Genesis with God creating a good world so humanity can come to know and share in God's goodness. When humanity fails to live up to God's hopes (Gn 1–11), God chooses a family, Abraham's, that will be God's special means of revealing the divine goodness to all nations (Gn 12–50). This people will discover God's goodness through hardship (slavery) and deliverance (Exodus) and learn to be an obedient and holy people (Leviticus and Nm 1–10). Then God will lead them to a promised land (Nm 10–36) which they will keep only if they remain obedient and loyal (Deuteronomy). The diagram on the next page illustrates this plan-within-a-plan structure.

God's Plan: Create Humanity to Praise and Share God's Goodness

First Plan		New Plan: Choose family-nation to teach all nations to praise and share God's goodness.	
Creation. Adam and Eve and all creation are created good.	Gn 1–2	Promise to Patriarchs: Abraham, Isaac, Jacob, Joseph.	Gn 12–50
Sin. Human sin and alienation grow.	Gn 3–11	Escape from Egypt to Mt. Sinai.	Ex 1–15
		Laws given to teach Israel to be a holy people.	Ex 19–40 Lv 1–27 Nm 1–10
		Journey to the Promised Land.	Nm 10–36
		Summary of law. Ready to enter Land.	Dt 1–34

HISTORY IN THE BIBLE

Anywhere something of importance happens today newspaper and television reporters, photographers, and video cameras record every moment. We live in a world of instant replays where you don't have to wonder what someone said or did; you can even play it back in slow motion. In the ancient world, such technology, of course, was not available.

In a culture like ours, so dominated by science, we value exact observation and documentation for its own sake. We expect historians to prove the claims they make in their books with clear documentation. And we expect them to be unbiased reporters, not propaganda peddlers. That's a lot to ask in any age since even trained historians are never totally free of bias and have their own point of view that colors what they write. If modern historians are never entirely objective even when that is what's expected of them, then we certainly cannot hope for that kind of objectivity from ancient writers who never made it their goal.

Even if they had wanted that kind of accuracy, ancient writers had no way to get much of the historical information. The reason that little or no information was preserved for its own sake was that history was seen not as a record of "what happened," but as a lesson people were to learn from. History was written to teach that one kind of behavior or attitude was more appropriate than another. It was written more like what we would call editorials, which take sides and argue for their favorite causes.

The bottom line is that ancient "history" was more interested in explaining *why* something happened than in *what* happened. It was more concerned with the meaning of events than in an accurate record of those events.

History or Theology?

While the Pentateuch is a complete story, it is in no way a complete history. It picks and chooses the events and themes it wants to talk about. And it only talks about those things that will teach a religious lesson. What we have here is a handbook or rule book for right living, a theology book much more than any real history of the people. That's why laws are so generously sprinkled in among the stories. They were part of the lesson the stories were meant to teach.

Clearly, many of the stories in the Pentateuch are not at all about ordinary time in history. Genesis 1–11, for example, does not fit the category of history telling because it treats the creation of the world and the first events of human existence without any historical concreteness. By trying to answer universal questions—questions like Why did God make humans this way? Why do we sin? Why do we die? Why is it hard to obey God? Why are men and women different?—the stories of Genesis 1–11 fall into the literary genre of myth. Even the stories of the patriarchs and matriarchs in Genesis 12–50 are not like modern history. Though based on real history, they resemble folktale hero stories, and it is hard to pin them down to exact locations and events.

Myth "Myth" has many different meanings. Often it is used to refer to something that is false or unreliable: "The story of George Washington chopping down the cherry tree is a myth." But that familiar use of the word is misleading. Narrowly defined, the term refers to traditional stories about heroes, gods, or demi-gods. Defined very broadly, myth is any idea put into story form that people live by and from which they see meaning in their lives. Thus, for instance, Americans have a national ideal of people from various parts of the world coming to this country and being able to participate in "the American dream" of a better life for themselves and their children. The "truth" of this ideal is almost irrelevant; it is nevertheless a powerful motivation in our country.

Scholars generally understand myths as attempts by ancient peoples to explain how certain things came into existence through the action of divine beings. Myths narrate a "sacred history" and are therefore special, sacred stories. But rather than providing answers, myths offer insights. They get at the core meaning of life and reality. For ancient peoples "myth" meant a "true story," and, indeed, what distinguishes myths is that they are stories that *can* be believed. One of the early church fathers defined myth as "What is believed always, everywhere, and by everybody." J.R.R. Tolkien has said, "Just as speech is invention about objects and ideas, myth is invention about truth." But instead of facts, myths offer the metaphorical truths that lie beyond facts. As a form of poetry, myth neither competes with nor contradicts scientific knowledge; it exists alongside of it. A.K. Coomaraswamy has observed, "Myth embodies the nearest approach to absolute truth that can be stated in words."

Keep these insights in mind when you run into problems of logic in one of the books. For example, in Genesis 4 Cain and Abel are the only two children of Adam and Eve. Yet, after killing Abel, Cain is banished and, we are told, has "relations with his wife." If this were a real history, we would have to ask how Cain could have a wife when Adam and Eve were the only other living human beings at the time.

The author's intent obviously centers not on literal facts, but on a religious lesson, here concerning how the world came to be populated. Whether or not that lesson is consistent with what has previously been said doesn't concern the author.

But while it is important not to make the mistake of thinking that the Pentateuch is a record of history, it is also important not to think of it as just a clever story pulled from someone's imagination. It is a masterwork, a work of genius that makes God known to us. In beautiful language and powerful imagery it speaks of humanity's tendency toward sin, about the failure of most of the world to know God, and of God's choice of Israel to demonstrate to the world God's loving concern for humanity. The marvelous storytelling of the Pentateuch reveals God by focusing on a number of central events: the choice of the patriarchs, the giving of the Law, the making of a covenant, and the guidance through the wilderness to a promised land.

Good storytelling can give us pleasure, teach us about history, and give us philosophical and theological insights. As a great work of storytelling the Pentateuch is multilayered. It tells history, but it does not allow us to question it too closely about exact descriptions. It presents religious and theological lessons, but warns us not to treat it like a catechism filled with lists of truths. Most of all it tells a story. The story teaches us by letting us compare our experience with that of the Hebrew people. As we read we begin to discover that their story and our story are intertwined, that the God who was at work in the lives of the Hebrew people works in similar ways in our own lives.

Patriarchs The forefathers of the Israelites, i.e., Abraham, Isaac, and Jacob. Because he figures so prominently in the Genesis patriarchal stories, Joseph is often designated a patriarch as well. The New Testament also refers to David and the twelve sons of Jacob as patriarchs. The term overlooks the significance of the wives of these men without whom God's plan would not have moved forward. These matriarchs, Sarah, Rebekah, Rachel, and Leah, can be included by the use of expressions like "forebears," "ancestors," or "patriarchs and matriarchs."

Historical Dating of Pentateuch Traditions

Despite many difficulties, we are not completely in the dark when it comes to dating some of the events of the Pentateuch. Archaeological digs in ancient sites have produced tablets and other records that offer a good idea of what each different period in the second millenium B.C. was like, so we can date the major events of the Pentateuch with a fair degree of confidence.

The patriarchal narratives fall somewhere between 2000 and 1500 B.C., the Exodus event between 1450 and 1250 B.C., and the invasion of the land of Palestine around 1250 to 1200 B.C. Nonbiblical historical information makes some dates more likely than others: Since Egypt was governed by foreign rulers between 1750 B.C. and 1550 B.C., the story of how Joseph, a foreigner, rises to power best fits this time period. Exodus 1,11 says the enslaved Israelites built the cities of Pithom and Raamses, pointing to the reign of Sethi I as the period of enslavement and the reign of Ramesses II as the time of the Exodus.

HOW SCHOLARS STUDY THE PENTATEUCH: THE ART OF INTERPRETATION

Studying the Bible is not easy. Because it was written over many centuries by people living in cultures very different from our own, we cannot simply expect to pick up a Bible and be able

Did Moses Write the Pentateuch?

For more than two thousand years Moses was considered the author of the Pentateuch even though no book of the Bible specifically names him as the author. The Pentateuch was often called "the Book of Moses," and throughout the Bible there are frequent references to the "law of Moses." Jesus, like most of his contemporaries, took for granted that Moses authored the Pentateuch.

But even in the ancient world some questioned whether Moses could really have written the entire Pentateuch. How, for example could Moses have written about his own death as in Deuteronomy 34,5–12? Many of the laws supposedly written by Moses deal with situations that occurred much later than the time when Moses led the people through the desert. Other evidence in the Bible leads scholars to believe the Pentateuch did not exist in its present state until approximately 450 B.C.—nearly 800 years after Moses' death.

No one can say for certain who did write the Pentateuch, but there is no question that Moses played a unique and important role in the events recorded in these books. Modern scholars don't try to prove that Moses directly authored the written books of the Pentateuch. As Catholics, our belief that the Bible is divinely inspired makes the identity of its human author an issue of limited importance. Whatever else we may say, Moses may be regarded as the founder of the Israelite faith.

to grasp its meaning in its entirety. On the other hand, we must not be intimidated by the amount of scholarly knowledge it takes to understand the Bible properly so that we start to feel it belongs only to some special caste. The reality lies somewhere in the middle. With some scholarly help, like that provided by this study guide and the excellent footnotes of the *New American Bible*, a layperson should be able to read the Bible intelligently and find in it religious meaning for his or her life.

Despite those who would argue for one over the other, it is clear that the Bible must be read on two levels at once. The first is the level of Scripture, that is, the word of God, God's authoritative and inspired communication to humanity which we read by the light of faith. For the second level, reading the Bible as the literature of a particular culture, we must draw on the insights of archaeology, history, ancient languages, and the many other fields that can open up the ancient world that produced these texts. Unless we're reading on both these levels, we will miss part of the Bible's message.

It is also important to remember that we can't read on either level all by ourselves. We need the biblical scholar to interpret the text by means of scientific, linguistic, and cultural tools. And we need the theologian and religious leader to interpret the Bible according to the tradition of our church.

When we read the Bible we're looking for two things: what the text meant to its original author and audience, and what it means now to us, its modern readers. We must be careful, however, not to let one meaning cancel out the other. When we seek the original meaning of a text, we don't rule out the possibility that over the centuries a particular text may have taken on more meaning than even the author intended. So what it meant then and what it means now are not necessarily the same thing.

Some modern churchgoers have rejected scholarly theories and methods of study because they feel these have robbed the Bible of its status as God's inspired word and have turned it into an ordinary literary document. Why so negative a reaction? Maybe because some scholars approach the Bible with the assumption that they may not use God as the explanation for anything. While they would not deny the possibility of miracles, they believe that what is called the critical method requires them to propose natural explanations whenever such explanations are plausible. Even discussions of inspiration are considered off-limits by some scholars. If you read the Bible only on this level, you might think it would tell you little of religious value.

But here's the heart of the matter: The critical method helps us to unlock and clarify what is going on in a text. How? First, by connecting the text to historical events that we may have learned about through nonbiblical sources; second, by helping us understand unusual cultural customs; and third, by helping us understand special literary styles of expression that are no longer in use today.

Without scientific study we would not comprehend those things that are not part of our culture. When archaeologists dig up clay tablets that contain long-lost information, biblical scholars become the bridge that connects that information with the Bible. They study how language works, how people hand down traditions, and how they record events and tell folk tales. All this helps us understand how biblical stories and laws were put together.

Exegesis The critical or scholarly explanation of a Bible passage. (The term means "to bring out" and refers to the process of explaining meaning.)

Hermeneutics is a term often used interchangeably with exegesis. While exegesis tries to discover what a passage meant in its original context (time and place of composition), hermeneutics uses exegesis to ask what the text means for us now. (The term comes from Hermes, the Greek messenger god, and means "interpretation.")

All writing is interpretation. The ancient authors interpreted what they thought God was communicating; the churches and synagogues interpret what these words of revelation mean for their congregations. Modern scholars and believing readers must also interpret and decide what relevance these long-ago stories and events have for their lives. Everyone who reads the Bible asks "What does it mean?" But we can find a full answer only if our reading is illuminated by the twin lights of faith and scientific knowledge of the past. And nowhere in the Bible is this more crucial than in reading the Pentateuch.

The study of the Pentateuch has a long history that can be traced back even to the time of Jesus as illustrated in the chart on the next page.

New Testament Times

In New Testament times, Jesus and the authors of various New Testament books referred to texts from the Bible, which at that time was simply the Hebrew Scriptures, what Christians now call the Old Testament. Usually they were referring to stories that were cited as proofs for something Jesus or one of the apostles was teaching. Some stories from the Pentateuch were treated as what has been called a *type*, in which an Old Testament figure is seen as a foreshad-

How the Bible Has Been Read in History	
New Testament Times (Jesus and writers of New Testament books)	Scripture viewed as prophecy of Jesus, and used to show connection between Jesus and what went before him.
Early Church (The time after the Apostles to the 6th century)	Scripture read allegorically. Literal meaning rejected because Bible contains deeper meanings put there (inspired) by God. Therefore Bible always says more than the author intended to say.
Medieval Period (From the 7th century through the Renaissance and Reformation)	Allegorical reading still predominates. Growing respect for literal meaning of text. But much of Old Testament still viewed as prediction of Jesus.
Modern Study (From the 17th century to the 20th century)	Critical study of texts. Four sources theory and *source criticism* developed. Development of *form criticism*, the search for literary genres and the earliest and smallest literary units of tradition, and *transmission history,* the account of how the current texts came to be.

owing of a later character, like Abraham who is seen as a forerunner of the Christian believer, or Isaac who is seen as a foreshadowing of Jesus. The New Testament treats many passages from the Pentateuch, the prophets, and psalms as a type of prophecy that predicts Jesus and helps explain his suffering, death, and resurrection. It would be fair to say that the New Testament uses the Bible primarily to show the deep connection between Jesus and what went before him.

Early Church

The early church (the community of believers during the four centuries after the death of the Apostles) saw the Bible operating on three levels of meaning. First, there was the *literal* or *historical* meaning of the text. Then there was the *spiritual* or *allegorical* sense: a deep, often hidden, layer that went beyond the literal. The third level expressed the *moral* lesson the text meant to teach.

Level two, the spiritual level, was considered most important. Since scripture is inspired writing, pious believers thought it therefore must contain layers of meaning that even the author was not aware of. God, after all, was using the ancient author to point the way to Jesus. The meaning of a passage, then, could not be limited to what the author intended to say. The full meaning was much deeper, more spiritual, and not immediately obvious.

This attitude led to an almost total disregard for the literal meaning of the text. All the focus was on the so-called spiritual meaning intended by God. Because of the conviction that every word of scripture contained a prophecy about Jesus, and thus always said more than it seemed to say, the allegorical method flourished in the early church.

The Medieval Period

The medieval world was largely a period in love with the allegorical approach, and students of the Bible relied heavily on the opinions of the early church writers regarding each passage of scripture. But the rise of scholasticism in the 12th and 13th centuries shifted the focus to a clear and literal interpretation of Bible texts. Medieval thinkers, however, lacked a knowledge of Hebrew and Greek with which to study the original words, and they still viewed the Bible as prophecy rather than as a history of a people's experience of God working in their lives. So they, too, read the Bible more as a book about Christ and the church than about Israel.

Modern Study

Truly modern study of the Bible began with a French priest named Richard Simon (1678) who detected different literary styles within the Book of Genesis. He concluded that Moses didn't write the Pentateuch from scratch, but probably was quoting sources (more than one) that existed before him. This insight earned him church condemnation, but it also opened the door for further critical study.

In the next century scholars began investigating the biblical passages that regularly call God by the proper name "Yahweh" (the *New American Bible* renders it as "LORD"), and those that call God by the more generic term, "Elohim" (which the *NAB* renders as "God"). Even though the passages that use the two names are intermixed, they run through the entire Pentateuch (up to the Book of Numbers) as two complete, parallel stories.

New questions arose. Were these two separate written works that told the same history of Israel, or was one original story embellished and eventually turned into two different versions? The debate was intense. Then scholars began to notice that the so called "Elohist" passages really contained two separate accounts themselves. The one that was more narrative and interested in God's great interventions in history was called the Elohist strand, while the other, which was more concerned with priestly and ritual actions, was called the Priestly strand.

By the mid-1800s scholars generally agreed that there were in fact three independent versions of the Pentateuch's basic story, which could be labeled with the initials J (for German "Jahvist"), E (for Elohist), and P for (Priestly). The Book of Deuteronomy was considered a fourth and totally separate source of its own, and received the label D.

Eventually a German scholar, Julius Wellhausen, proposed dates for the writing of each version and speculated on the historical situation that created the need for each different telling of the history. All this came to be known as the "four sources theory," and the method is called *source criticism*." We say "sources" because we don't know exactly who is responsible for each of these four traditions. Was it a single author-editor or, more likely, a group of author-editors? What is clear is that each strand responds to a particular situation or need in the life of the nation and incorporates the particular worldview of its author-editor. This theory is outlined in the table on the next page.

J and E existed side by side while the two kingdoms lasted from 930 to 722 B.C. (See the guide to the historical books.) When the Northern kingdom fell, its E story was carried down to Judah by refugees, and there it was eventually combined (around 700 B.C.) with J into a single account. Still later, when Judah itself fell in 587 B.C. and during its exile, D and P were combined with JE to make our final JEPD. Editors from the Priestly circles applied the final touches. Each of the sources has a distinctive style and emphasis, as described in the table on page RG 28.

Four Sources Theory

Source and Characteristics	Why Written
"J" Yahwist Written in 10th or 9th century B.C. Literary artist. Loves stories. Focus on the heart. Earthy, frank language. Emphasis on God's closeness with humanity. Uses name Yahweh for God (traditionally spelled Jehovah, hence the "J"). Favors strong leaders like David. Southern tradition.	Written in Jerusalem to show that promises to Abraham were fulfilled in the empire of David.
"E" Elohist Written after 900 B.C. Uses Elohim for God's name. Stresses role of the prophet. Contains strong tone of challenge and stress on morality. Emphasizes role of Jacob and the significance of Northern kingdom ideas and places. Northern tradition reflecting anti-Jerusalem view. Like D it stresses covenant with Moses is more important than kingship.	After the division of the kingdom, this version written to provide the North's official account of the tradition.
"P" Priestly Much of the material dates to 8th and 7th centuries B.C., but some materials probably written in 6th century B.C. Very strong interest in ritual and priesthood. Less focus on story and more on religious symbols. Style is more formal. God is more distant, less intimately involved with human beings. Stresses obedience to law and permanence of God's blessing. The dominant tradition in Pentateuch. Reflects Southern point of view. The P editors arranged the four sources into our present Pentateuch around 500 B.C.	Some of the P material reflects and responds to the needs of the exiles in the 6th century B.C.
"D" Deuteronomist Written in 8th and 7th centuries B.C. Emphasizes role of family (parents) for instruction and fidelity to covenant. Moralistic: Stresses preaching and exhortation. Style is eloquent; many often-repeated verbal formulas. Emphasizes Jerusalem as sole place of worship. Northern tradition which stresses covenant over kingship.	It reassesses the J and E traditions in light of pagan inroads and unfaithful kings.

The Four Sources and the Four "*P*s"

Who	What	How
Yahwist	Emphasizes role of *P*oet	Storytelling
Elohist	Emphasizes role of *P*rophet	Challenging
Priestly	Emphasizes role of *P*riest	Legislating
Deuteronomist	Emphasizes role of *P*arents	Exhorting

All this speculation on sources led to even more research into the original units that made up each source. Where did the individual incidents, poems, stories, and laws come from? This search for the earliest and smallest units of the tradition gave birth to a new way of studying the Bible called *form criticism.* By identifying the special form of a poem or hymn or law or narrative, scholars thought they could probably determine the cultural-historical situation from which it came.

Some scholars have focused on the *transmission history* of a text, looking at how traditions get passed on and grow or change. Before reaching the final form they have today, original statements, stories, and laws went through a process of being combined with other units, and then combined again in still larger works. Study of how collections grew and how stories were sometimes arranged into a new order helps us understand how they were used and the meaning they were given by different generations. For example, the story of Exodus was the story of escaping from an oppressive situation. However, later on, in the context of the law and the land, the story of Exodus became a story about the celebration of a feast year after year: the Passover. The bread, the lamb, and the bitter herbs all became parts of the yearly ritual Passover celebration.

REFLECTING ON THE MESSAGE OF THE PENTATEUCH

Like navigating a vast ocean, finding our way through the vast array of materials in the Pentateuch can be challenging. A lighthouse now and then can make the going easier. The Pentateuch provides these in the form of themes and topics that recur over and over again. The demand for obedience to God's will, which is seen as a sign of faith, and God's giving of the covenant, which is seen as a sign of God's love, are examples of such lighthouses. Whether it's Adam and Eve's failure to obey, or Moses' own failure when striking the rock for water in Numbers 20, it is clear that obedience is a major issue. Many other examples could be given. In fact, it is difficult trying to limit the themes to a specific number. Every time we read, new themes may capture our imagination or move our hearts.

We will have an easier time understanding the major theological themes of the Pentateuch if we remember that more than being a book *of* or *by* God, the Bible is a book *about* God. Through its many themes and stories, the Pentateuch reveals a God Israel has come to know as the one God, who acts in human history, and who has chosen Israel in a special way. All the themes of the Pentateuch reveal God's intimate relationship with people, emphasizing the need for humanity to respond to God's initiative.

Ten Central Themes

GOD CREATED A GOOD WORLD

When Genesis tells us God spoke the world into being, it means that creation was no accident, but part of a divine plan causing all things to work together in harmony. God judged all creation as "very good" (Gn 1,31). Thus, no matter how bad things get, we must remember that the original blessing is never fully lost and that, ultimately, goodness will prevail.

GOD HAS BLESSED HUMAN LIFE

Twice Genesis tells us that God blessed the human race (Gn 1,28; 9,1). If the world is good, so is all life within it.

HUMANITY HAS A TENDENCY TO SIN

Much of the biblical story presents human beings as disobedient and sinful, ignoring God's will. Many of the laws, therefore, center on atonement (particularly in Leviticus) and on the need to repent and turn back to God (Deuteronomy particularly).

GOD IS A GOD OF MERCY

If humanity tends toward rebellion, God tends toward forgiveness and mercy. God spares Adam and Eve, Cain and Noah, and others in order to give the human race a new start each time after it sins. In the Exodus event, God is revealed above all else as a liberating God.

GOD KEEPS PROMISES

God promised Noah, Abraham, Isaac, Jacob, and Moses that they would become a great people, and repeatedly the Pentateuch stresses the fulfillment of that promise. Israel's God is a God of the future, not one patterned on the recurring cycles of nature. God inspires hope. Believers can expect that God can act in new and decisive ways.

THE COVENANT BINDS GOD TO ISRAEL

All people believe their god relates to them somehow, but only in Israel do we find a relationship based on love, permanent loyalty, and respect for the human partner. The covenant is the heart of biblical faith because it expresses a unique bond between God and people.

THE LAW EXPRESSES ISRAEL'S BOND TO GOD

The covenant establishes a relationship, but the laws of the Pentateuch show how that relationship can be lived out by the people. Laws are not restrictive rules; they're a joyful way of life that expresses faith in actions as well as words.

WORSHIP IS PRAISE IS THANKSGIVING

An odd way to express a simple but important idea: To pray is to praise, and to praise is to thank God. The Pentateuch constantly reminds Israel of what God has done for them, and the laws express the need to rejoice and give thanks to God in everything.

RELIGIOUS LIFE IS LIFE IN COMMUNITY

God chose a people, not a lot of all-star individuals. Single hearts and voices can't know and praise God properly. Only human minds and voices joined together can do that. God's many faces can be seen only if we share our memories and relate to one another in love.

GOD DIRECTS ALL OF HISTORY

The central conviction of Israel—that there is one, and only one, God—leads to recognition of God's lordship over all peoples and all events. God blesses and punishes, sets obstacles and shows the way through them. All things are in God's hands, so the only thing that makes sense is to walk in the ways of the Lord.

Ten Themes of Biblical Spirituality for Today

The theological themes of the Pentateuch offer rich implications for our own spiritual life as disciples of the one God we find there. Following are some of the important personal demands the message of the Pentateuch places on our lives.

ALL THINGS IN OUR LIFE MUST FLOW FROM FAITH

The stories of the Pentateuch reveal that no part of life is outside of God's plan. We must live believing that God's will can be known and followed in all of life's situations.

OUR PRAYER AND OUR DAILY LIFE MUST BE ONE

We must not, like Solomon Grundy, pray on Sunday and go to hell for what we do on Monday. Nothing is so secular that God cannot be a part of it. Our worship and prayer should relate to the real problems and decisions we face in daily life. The Bible speaks of wars and politics more than of anything else, and yet there is not a single area of life where God is not present.

WE MUST RESPECT GOD'S HOLINESS

The Bible often speaks of God with beautiful human imagery, but it never allows us to forget that God is also the all-powerful creator of the universe who cannot be represented by idols or treated like just another human being. The Pentateuch balances notions of God's closeness to the world with the clear recognition that our job is to do God's will—not try to make God do our will.

WE MUST IMITATE GOD'S HOLINESS

Since we are made in God's image and likeness, we have a responsibility to act like God. God cares for the poor, the widow, the alien, and the orphan—and so must we. (See how Leviticus 19 outlines our duties to our neighbor.)

HOLINESS MUST BE TRANSLATED INTO COMPASSION

Forgiveness is the hallmark of God's holiness. God claims to be a God who bestows "mercy down to the thousandth generation, on the children of those who love me" (Ex 20,6) and who forgives "wickedness and crime and sin" (Ex 34,7). Holiness is best expressed not in private prayer, but in our forgiving and merciful behavior toward each other.

LIFE IS A JOURNEY

Among the oldest of metaphors for human existence, this image is deeply rooted in the Pentateuch itself. Abraham is called to a new land; Jacob must find God far from home. Joseph must go to Egypt, and Israel must cross the desert to find a Promised Land. The journey motif not only stresses the future to which we go, even more, it emphasizes the value of the journey itself, for the God toward whom we move is already with us on the road.

LIFE'S JOURNEY REQUIRES TRUST IN GOD

What's needed on a risk-filled journey with God? Trust! The Pentateuch asserts that God's guidance never fails even when the people turn from God's way. Keeping God's commandments builds our courage and confidence; we learn to trust in God's promises and find peace.

WE ARE PEOPLE OF THE LAND

The Promised Land dominates the stories of the Pentateuch. Israel was in love with her land and never lost her infatuation with it even when it was taken from her. Israel never wanted to be divorced from the concrete realities of everyday life and never embraced asceticism as an ideal. Its spirituality was hardheaded and included wrestling with the proper use of the land and its resources, working for justice in social settings, and molding politics and economics to the demands of God's law. Genesis says that we are from the earth and to the earth we shall return (Gn 3,19). Then we must take the earth seriously!

FAITH IS A FAMILY AFFAIR

Much of Israel's religious practice was centered in the home: sabbath observance, Passover, prayer, teaching children the law. The home-centered religious practices narrated in the Pentateuch can teach us much about how our own families can celebrate together, teach one another about God, and give concrete witness to what we believe.

PRAYER MUST FILL OUR LIVES

The Pentateuch provides numerous examples both of public prayer and of the private prayers of great individuals responding to every experience of God's presence in their lives. Israel's need and ability to pray in all situations eventually gave birth to the Psalms, a collection of prayers and hymns that express the whole range of human feelings before God. Their boldness and yet humility provide modern believers with an example of how we can live our lives as prayer.

Questions for Discussion or Reflection

1. How does the biblical writer's sense of history differ from a modern understanding of history?
2. Which level dominates your reading of Scripture: the literal/historical, spiritual/allegorical, or moral?
3. What kinds of questions surface in your mind when you consider the possibility that Moses did not author the Pentateuch?
4. Which is your favorite story from the books of the Pentateuch? What does it tell you about your image of God? What does it tell you about yourself?
5. Were you surprised to learn that Protestants, Catholics, and Jews each have a different order and emphasis in their collections of Old Testament books in their Bibles? What kinds of questions does that raise for you?

6. What is the Hebrew understanding of law? What role did it play in their lives? Is your understanding of law anything like that of the Israelites?

7. What do you understand "myth" to mean? Is it an appropriate term to use in reference to some of the stories of Genesis? Why or why not?

GENESIS READING GUIDE

At a Glance

Who are the main players?	Adam and Eve, Cain and Abel, Noah, Abraham, Sarah, Isaac, Rebekah, Jacob, Rachel, Joseph
What should I look for?	Creation of the world; Human rebellion and sin; The beginning of the nation of Israel; God's Promises: Covenants with Noah and Abraham
When did this take place?	Prehistory and c. 1800 B.C. to 1300 B.C.
Where did these events occur?	The area now called the Middle East: i.e., Egypt, Jordan, Lebanon, Israel, Syria, Turkey, Iraq, Saudi Arabia
Why was this book written?	To make the point that God created all things and created them good; that human beings broke faith with God and are responsible for evil in the world; that God never stops loving humanity and, through Abraham, formed a people to whom and through whom God has been revealed.
What's the story?	God creates a good world. Man and woman sin. Noah and family survive the flood. Abraham receives God's promises and trusts God even to the point of being willing to sacrifice his own son. Through Isaac and Jacob, Abraham's clan begins to grow. In Egypt, Joseph provides safe-haven for the fledgling nation and it begins to prosper and multiply.

Genesis is not the first book of the Bible by accident. Everything it contains was intentionally chosen to set the stage for all that follows. While the fascinating stories of Genesis make great reading all on their own, to fully understand the book's purpose we must also pay attention to its religious message and the key themes it develops. A quick reading of all fifty chapters to get the drift of the "plot" might be the best way to start. Then, after getting a sense of the style of the book, a second more careful reading will reveal much more.

STRUCTURE OF GENESIS

Most often scholars divide Genesis into two parts: Chapters 1–11 and 12–50. While the parts seem to constitute a single, continuous story, there are actually significant differences between them in both subject matter and in the kind of literature they contain. The first eleven chapters, often referred to as the "primeval history," discuss the creation of the world and the first human beings—the ancestors of all humanity. The second part, on the other hand, describes

Differences Between the Two Major Divisions of Genesis

Topic	Genesis 1–11	Genesis 12–50
Time	Set in time before human history	Set in historical times well known to ancient records
Place	Locations vague: somewhere to the East	Locations exact: Palestine and Egypt and northern Mesopotamia
Persons	Characters seem like symbols, little is known of their lives	Characters have names and behave like typical people of the second millennium B.C.
Stories	Many stories can be classified as myths; they resemble those known from Mesopotamia	Sagalike stories and epic history narratives similar to oral lore of tribal groups
Events	Most events seem to have supernatural quality	Major events resemble normal human experience
Purpose	Describes the origins of humanity long before Israel's time	Traces the direct tribal ancestors of Israel itself

the very specific ancestors of Israel itself. Genesis 1–11 falls into the literary category of "myth" (see box, RG 21) in which every story seems to model the proper relationship between God and humans. The stories of the latter part of Genesis, however, relate specific events in the life of what came to be a particular nation, Israel.

The characters and worlds of the two sections are very different. The world of the primeval history bears little resemblance to the world we live in. In that world people lived incredibly long lives and spoke directly with God. In contrast, Abraham, Isaac, Jacob, and the other people described in Chapters 12–50, seem to live out their joys and struggles in a world like ours, making decisions that affect the whole history of the nation.

The chart above illustrates some of the significant differences between the two parts.

Subdivisions of Genesis 1–50

By breaking down the two-part division of the Book of Genesis into smaller units, we can get a clearer picture of the relationship between the two parts.

Note how the four major sections of the primeval history match the four sections of the folk history of Israel's founders. Each column reveals growth, for better or worse: In the primeval history, sin grows; in the folk history, Israel. The editors' effort to show that there are stages in the history of humanity, and of Israel in particular, clearly succeeds. Each period of history has major impact on those that follow; therefore, as we read Genesis, we should keep our eyes open for signs of growth and development.

Genesis 1–11 Primeval History	Genesis 12–50 Folk History
Genesis 1–3 The story of God's creation and the first human sin.	Genesis 12–25 Abraham is chosen to receive God's special blessing.
Genesis 4–5 The evil sin grows and spreads through the world.	Genesis 21–27 The son, Isaac, inherits the promise and passes it on.
Genesis 6–10 Evil overwhelms the world; God must begin again with a new blessing.	Genesis 27–36; 48–50 Jacob in turn receives the promise; he is blessed with the twelve sons who will become Israel.
Genesis 10–11 People again multiply across the earth but sin persists.	Genesis 37–50 Joseph brings the promise to Egypt and remains completely faithful to God.

Another way to organize Genesis is to break it down into four blocs of material that focus on major characters. When we do this, as the chart below illustrates, we see that the "plot" of Genesis centers on major decisions made by key individuals.

We may be surprised to find that Genesis ends with Abraham's descendants living in Egypt instead of in the land of promise. But the book's ending reminds us that the story will continue: God's promise is not forgotten and Israel's future lies elsewhere.

Division of Genesis into Four Blocs of Material

A	The Prologue: primeval history of humankind's original blessing and failure through sin	Gn 1–11
B	The story of Abraham: his call and response; his blessing and promise	Gn 12–25
C	The stories of Abraham's son Isaac and grandson Jacob and how they carry on the blessing	Gn 26–36
D	The story of Joseph in Egypt: preparation for God's great self-revelation in the Exodus	Gn 37–50

Division by the Special *Toledoth* Lists

The *New American Bible* points out that Genesis contains internal markers that help divide and organize the material. These markers are the genealogical lists, *toledoth,* that always begin "these are the descendants of . . ." (Note: the *NAB* sometimes varies the translation of that phrase but in Hebrew it is always the same). These lists help make the point that while generations come and go, God's plan moves ahead no matter what. Sometimes appearing at the beginning and sometimes at the end of a section, the lists group together all the members of a

The *Toledoth* Lists	
Gn 2,4a	Begins the second story of creation
Gn 5,1	Introduces the long break between the first family and the days of Noah
Gn 6,9	Introduces the story of the flood
Gn 10,1	Marks the great expansion of people all over the world
Gn 11,10	Marks the addition of a new list of the nations of the world by the P source
Gn 11,27	Begins the story of Abraham
Gn 25,12	Closes off the life of Abraham's "other" family through Hagar and Ishmael
Gn 25,19	Opens the story of Jacob's birth and destiny
Gn 36,1	Ends the role of Jacob's twin, Esau, and directs us to Jacob's children, especially Joseph
Gn 36,9	A repetition within the Esau list that marks its conclusion
Gn 37,2	Marks the opening of the story of Joseph and his brothers that continues to the end of Genesis

family line or tribe to signal a break with the events that have just been recounted. The chart above illustrates where these lists appear and the purpose they serve.

In architecture, form follows function; that is, the shape of a building is determined by the purpose it will serve. That is true in writing as well. The way a writer organizes material, and the choices made regarding the overall shape of the writing, reveal much about the purpose of the writing. Our purpose in identifying the major outline of Genesis and of naming its various subdivisions is to show that what we have here is a continuous story that runs not only from the beginning to the end of Genesis, but through the entire Pentateuch as well. Once we grasp the overall outline, we can begin to see how individual incidents fit into it.

THE PRIMEVAL HISTORY OF GENESIS 1–11

Thus far we have looked primarily at the structure of the Book of Genesis. As we look more closely now at the first eleven chapters, we should keep four points in mind.

1. According to form criticism they are chiefly a combination of myths and genealogical tables.
2. Source critics find here a combination of the Yahwist (J) and Priestly (P) sources.
3. Similar, and older, versions of many of the Genesis stories have been found in the literature of the ancient Near East.
4. The final masterpiece is unique: It is neither like the J or P accounts taken by themselves, nor, in its purpose and beauty, like any other people's version. (See essay, page RG 37.)

The interweaving of the J and P sources in these chapters accounts for the fact that some stories seem to be told twice, with different details. For example, both J and P authors have a list of ancestors between Adam and Noah, a flood story (the two are now hopelessly intermixed into a single account), and a table of nations (Gn 10–11) that also is interwoven into a single list.

The Theology of the Yahwist Source

The incidents chosen by the J author to tell the story of creation focus on the tension between God's goodness and human beings' disobedience. Adam and Eve, Cain and Abel, the wicked generation of the flood, the sons of Noah, and the builders of the tower of Babel all received plenty of evidence of God's love. Yet each generation chose to disobey by embracing one of the deadly vices: greed, envy, lust, pride.

Look at the pattern the Yahwist author uses to structure each story:

God	People
1. acts lovingly toward humanity,	
	2. disobey God and sin,
3. announces punishment,	
	4. are punished,
5. shows mercy and gives a new blessing.	

This repeated pattern itself conveys a message: Because humanity repeatedly failed to respond to God's offering of intimate love, sin spread and contaminated all people. Now God must find a new way to demonstrate control over the earth and all of history, and to show love for humanity. As with Adam and Eve and Noah and his family, God begins this new round by again choosing a single family, Abraham's, and giving them a special revelation of divine goodness to share with the world.

The Theology of the Priestly Source

If later Israelites had only the version of their history given in the J Source—sin, punishment, mercy, and the promise of being formed into a chosen people—they might have misunderstood it as promising absolute control over the land and great power for Abraham's descendants. But by the time the Priestly writers were gathering their own accounts, Israel had already experienced military defeats and the loss of ten of the twelve tribes. Israel was wondering if God really was in control and would stand by them in hard times.

The Priestly writers apparently wanted to make sure the promises spoken in the creation stories would suggest two things: first, that God's control over world events was greater than any human power; and second, that it would be shown in ways besides Israel's political fortunes. In other words, Israel's misfortunes did not mean that God had lost control. P clearly states that humans are made in the image of God (Gn 1,27 and 9,6) to govern the earth and fill it, but P's stress is not on humanity's independent power; rather, an important element of being made in the image of God is humanity's responsibility to act as God would act.

The genealogies of Chapters 5 and 10–11 are also part of P's insistence that God has a plan that can't be derailed by human whims, nor even upset by human sin. God is always in charge—even when we are experiencing just punishment. God's blessing *can* be relied on: We must learn trust! By stressing the goodness of creation and God's blessing of humanity, P's larger vision brought hope to Israel at a time when circumstances could have led it to despair.

ESSAY

Are Some Genesis Stories Just Rewrites of Ancient Myths?

Sometimes readers point to the similarities between the biblical creation stories and myths of ancient Near Eastern people as a way of discrediting the Bible texts. Since they are derived from pagan myths, they argue, the Bible stories have no more than literary value. But the fact that a biblical writer may have borrowed legends from neighboring cultures in no way diminishes the theological value of the writing.

It is the biblical author's final product, not the original myth, that we believe is inspired, and that we have canonized into the body of Scripture. And this final form differs significantly in purpose and theology from the myths the inspired writer not only may have borrowed, but perhaps was also trying to debunk.

To take just two examples: The story of the creation of humanity and the story of the flood both have parallels among ancient Mesopotamian myths. Many of the similarities are even quite striking. But their overall messages are clearly different, especially in their presentation and understanding of God.

The Babylonian creation story called *Enuma Elish* presumes the existence of many gods who haphazardly created the world while fighting among themselves. Their creation is therefore partly good and partly evil, and human beings are nothing more than their slaves. Against this view of creation the biblical writer presents a theology that asserts one, and only one, God who creates consciously and out of love. God's creation is all good and human beings are not slaves, but are made in God's own image and are given dominion over the earth.

The Noah flood story has a close parallel in the *Epic of Gilgamesh,* possibly the oldest of recorded human stories. In the tale, Gilgamesh sets out to find an ancestor who has achieved immortality. The ancestor tells of having survived a great flood and of how he helped save humanity. In details, this flood account is surprisingly similar to the Genesis story. But the two versions present very different images of God.

The Babylonians believed there was an ongoing struggle between gods and humans. Their unpredictable gods found humans annoying and often erupted in hostility toward them. Human beings could never be sure of how to please their gods, nor of what would anger them. Genesis, on the other hand, presents a God who never changes God is eternally just, yet loving and faithful. Israel's God punishes only when human beings have committed real wrong. And their God is always eager to forgive.

It is important to remember that being related to and derived from similar stories of the ancient Near East in no way compromises the religious truth or value of the stories we find in Genesis.

The Overall Message of Genesis 1–11

The combining of J and P reveals the full range of Hebrew thought regarding the origins of humanity:

> God is good and all God created is good.
> Human beings are morally obligated to obey God's plan.
> God alone is worthy of worship.

By the way they used and reshaped Canaanite myths and subtly attacked pagan religious practices, the J and P authors and editors made the point that Canaanite worship and beliefs pervert God's plan. The Israelites did use elements from beliefs of other Near Eastern peoples—for example, creation being a fight between God and Chaos. However, they always modified these in a way that made clear their belief in God's sovereignty over creation. In the same way they took over planting and harvesting celebrations but distanced themselves from the fertility cults they were rejecting.

Notes on Individual Passages

Gn 1,1–2,4a

The Priestly creation story contains patterns that structure the individual days and the entire week.

Pattern One: Each day contains a five-point framework:

> *Opening:* "And God said . . ."
> *Command:* "Let there be . . ."
> *Fulfillment:* "And so it was . . ."
> *Judgment:* "And God saw that it was good . . ."
> *Naming:* "Evening came, and morning followed—the first day . . ."

Pattern Two: The six days of creation are divided into two matched panels of three days each as shown in the chart here. During the first three days of creation we see God building a

Prologue: Introductory statement asserting God's control of chaos			
Three Days of Separation		Three Days of Integration	
Day 1	God creates heavens and separates light from darkness	Day 4	Sun, moon, and stars join the sky
Day 2	God separates waters above (rain) from waters below (oceans)	Day 5	Birds and fish are added to sky and waters
Day 3	God separates land from waters and adds vegetation to land	Day 6	Animals populate the land and, finally, humans
Day 7 Epilogue: God rests, fully in control of all creation			

vast stage of heavens, water, and land by separating one from the other. During the second three days God populates the stage with its primary actors, and the creation becomes one integrated whole. The goodness of the creation is celebrated on the climactic seventh day. This day becomes the model of rest and celebration of God's goodness that humans are to follow each week.

Gn 2,4b–3,24

This is the Yahwist account of creation, a much older story than the Priestly version of Chapter 1. Although we can detect here some story themes borrowed from Mesopotamia, the biblical account is unique as a whole and more sophisticated in its vision than anything else found in the ancient world. This account of creation and sin presents some key biblical insights: Man is created first, at the beginning of creation, and all other creatures are made for him. Woman alone, among God's other creatures, is equal to the man and is a suitable partner for him. Intimacy is the chief characteristic of the relationship between God and human beings. Sin is a pervasive reality, but it is the result of human choice, not God's.

Gn 4,1–16

In the story of Cain and Abel we see that the evil of sin grows and leads even to fratricide. Sin results in alienation, first from God and self, and then from one another. The message is becoming clearer that humanity's downhill slide away from God can be stopped only by God's love and mercy.

Gn 4,17–22; 5,1–32

The genealogies of Genesis 4–5 with the enormous ages of the patriarchs are not intended to be taken literally. A Sumerian list of kings who lived before the flood ascribes even more astounding ages to its monarchs. The lists bridge the time gap between the creation accounts and the story of the flood, and they show that human beings have indeed multiplied as God ordered in Gn 1,28. Lists like these were a device used by ancient people to speculate on how long the world has existed.

Gn 6,1–9,27

Two observations should be remembered during your study of the flood account. First, it must have been very important to the biblical writers, because both the Yahwist and Priestly traditions had their own version of the flood and they considered each important enough to save. Second, the biblical story bears strong resemblance to other ancient flood stories told in Babylon and Syria (see essay, RG 37). What makes the biblical account unique and religiously important is what it teaches us about God. In the pagan versions God's motives for destroying humanity are either left out or trivialized (human noisiness kept the gods awake). But the Genesis story insists that God acted out of justice and in response to people's moral evil. The relationship between God and people is not characterized by the constant tension of the pagan versions, but by intimate love that continues despite the flood. The story's final image is the rainbow, promising hope and blessing.

Gn 9,28–10,32

By being placed after the flood story, this second set of genealogies links the prehistoric flood with the call of Abraham in the very real towns of Ur and Haran in Mesopotamia. Like the genealogy of Genesis 4,17–5,32 it connects major moments in the history of God's interventions in human life and tells how, after the flood, people spread out to fill the far corners of the earth. The genealogy is a composite of two separate lists, one from the P school and the other from J. Look at the text and see how easy it is to pick out the more colorful J list with its bits of stories (10,8–30) from the much drier P list which gives names and nothing more (9,29–10,7 and 10,21–24).

Gn 11,1–9

The J writer has crafted an ironic and even humorous story. Having ignored God's earlier command to "fill the earth" (Gn 1,29; 9,1), people are united and speak one language. In addition, they want to "make a name for themselves," that is, without any help from God. God attacks this arrogance and forces the people both to disperse and to populate the earth by confusing their language. Note that the great temple they were building to glorify themselves is so small by divine standards that God has to "come down" to see it. Several wordplays add to the humor and irony of this story that makes the point that the growth of sin even turns nation against nation.

Gn 11,10–32

In this genealogy the ages of the patriarchs are greatly reduced (compare with Gn 5,1–32). These, of course, are not meant to be taken literally, but as a device showing that growing sin has brought the "golden age" to an end. More sin means less life. Besides illustrating the disintegrating effects of sin, the genealogies show continuity in human history from the dawn of time to Abraham. The periods recorded in the genealogies were times of blessing sandwiched in between times of sin and punishment, as illustrated in the chart on page RG 41.

THE GREAT ANCESTOR NARRATIVES OF GENESIS 12–50

Since humanity as a whole proves stubbornly unresponsive to God's love, God shifts gears and chooses a single people who will respond to God's self-revelation and will testify about God's goodness to all nations. This second major part of Genesis tells the story of God's new plan by focusing on the lives of four patriarchal figures: Abraham, Isaac, Jacob, and Joseph. Through each character, God's plan moves a step forward toward fulfillment. The blueprint for this new plan is contained in the story of Abraham's call at the beginning of Chapter 12. The first three verses not only describe his call but also present the other major themes that will dominate Genesis and much of Israel's history:

verse 1	the promise of a land for his family;
verse 2	the promise of blessing through empire and fame, and probably children ("a great nation");
verse 3	the promise to rule other nations and to mediate God's blessing to them.

The promises of a son to carry on the name and a land of their own echo especially loudly in the stories that follow. But Israel did not read these promises as guarantees that life would be rosy. These stories record Israel's failures as well as successes, disobedience as well as obedi-

Key Moments of Sin and Punishment (and Giving the Blessing)	Genealogy Lists (Living the Blessing)
Genesis 1,2–4,16 The story of creation. The blessings and sins of the first generations.	
	Genesis 4,17–5,32 The long age of blessing of the ten great patriarchs before Noah's time.
Genesis 6,1–9,27 Sin. Flood as punishment. Blessing on Noah, followed by further sin by his sons.	
	Genesis 9,28–10,32 The lists of all the nations known to ancient Israel. Shows the blessing of fertility and having dominion over the earth.
Genesis 11,1-9 After blessing, sin again rises up out of human pride.	
	Genesis 11,10–32 God's blessing continues, now focusing on one family, that of Terah and Abraham.
Genesis 12,1ff The story of Abraham and the new direction of God's blessing.	

ence, lessons of deep faith and of sinful lack of trust. Because the Bible is the product of a faith-seeking community, Israel consistently found in its history evidence of God working even through their mistakes, guiding this puny people through all their troubles, helping them overcome obstacles, and bringing them blessing even in the land of their enemy, Egypt.

The Literary Issues of Genesis 12–50

We can better appreciate what a masterpiece of storytelling Genesis is when we realize that whoever edited the book pulled together three different sources into one continuous story. Scholars have been able to identify many passages that came from J, and others that came from P. A third source, the Elohist, which is close to J in spirit but does not yet use the name Yahweh for God, has also been detected in these chapters. The three sources can be easily

J, E, P Sources in the Abraham and Sarah Story			
What Happened	J version	E version	P version
Abraham receives promise of land and/or a son.	Gn 12,1–3	Gn 15,1–6	Gn 12,4–9
God makes a covenant with Abraham.	Gn 15,7–12	Gn 15,13–16	Gn 17,1–14
A son is born and the line of the promise is secured.	Gn 16,1–16; 18,1–19	Gn 21,1–21	Gn 17,15–27
Abraham's life ends.	Gn 25,1–6	Gn 22,1–13	Gn 23,1–20
Places stress on Abraham's	Faith	Obedience	Fidelity

identified when they each tell their own version of the same story. The chart above shows how the three sources intertwine to tell the Abraham and Sarah story. In telling the story, each source stresses a different aspect of Abraham's personality. J extols his trust in the promise of land and a son, while E marvels at his obedience even to sacrificing his son. P stresses his fidelity to religious regulations, especially circumcision.

The stories of the great patriarchs and matriarchs existed in oral form long before J, E, or P ever wrote a word. The three literary sources did more than simply write down the stories, however. They carefully composed them in a way that revealed their religious value and more clearly pointed to the lessons in the stories. As you read, be aware that the writing contains two kinds of information: the original description of what happened, and Israel's later reflection on what happened. As a people of faith, Israel saw many events as clear experiences of God's hand guiding them through history.

The Historical Setting of the Patriarchal Stories

Scholars generally agree that the customs and events described in Genesis 12–50 best fit the period from 1900 to 1500 B.C. From what we know of the ancient world through nonbiblical sources we can say that items like the names of the patriarchs, customs like the adoption of an heir (Gn 15,1–3) and marrying a sister (12,10–20), and Abraham's and Isaac's seminomadic lifestyle and their negotiations for grazing and water rights reflect this period of history. The story of Joseph rising to the position of prime minister in Egypt is also most plausible in this period when Egypt was ruled by foreign invaders, the Hyksos, who may have been more likely to allow a fellow foreigner to assume power than the strong Egyptian leaders who took control around 1500 B.C.

These examples make the dating of the Genesis stories likely, but not certain. Archaeological finds, however, continue to present a picture of this part of the world that matches well with the descriptions found in Genesis.

Abraham and Sarah, Genesis 12–25

There are several ways to get more out of the Abraham narrative. One way is to read it as the story of a man who is a homeless alien in Chapter 12 and has become a wealthy landowner by the time he and Sarah are buried on their own land in Chapters 23 and 25. Another way is to follow the series of promises made to Abraham and Sarah as they are slowly but surely fulfilled. Two sets of promises run parallel throughout these chapters:

	Promise of a Son		Promise of Land
Gn 12,2	I make you a great nation	Gn 12,1	"go to a land I indicate"
Gn 15,5	at the night covenant	Gn 12,7	at the terebinth of Moreh
Gn 17,4	the P covenant	Gn 13,14	at the departure of Lot
Gn 17,16	the promise of Isaac	Gn 15,18	at the night covenant
Gn 18,10	the three angels	Gn 17,8	the P covenant
Gn 18,18	recap of 12,2f	Gn 24,7	the messenger for Isaac
Gn 21,12	a promise to Isaac	Gn 26,4	repeated promise to Isaac
Gn 22,17	at the sacrifice of Isaac		
Gn 26,4	promise repeated to Isaac		

A third and perhaps the most religiously fruitful way of reading Genesis 12–25 is to see it as a story of Abraham and Sarah's struggle to continue believing in and trusting God. They struggle because, like most believers, Abraham and Sarah create almost as many obstacles to God's plan as they do faith-filled responses (see below). Remember, the Bible presents its lead characters honestly, warts and all.

	Trusting Responses		Obstacles
Gn 12,1–9	Abraham leaves home	Gn 12,10–20	Abraham pretends Sarah is his sister
Gn 14,1–24	War and blessing of Melchizedek	Gn 13,1–8	Lot allowed to choose the land
Gn 15,1–21	The covenant with God	Gn 16,1–14	Abraham has a son by his slave wife
Gn 17,1–27	Abraham's covenant renewed	Gn 18,1–15	Sarah doubts the promise of a son
Gn 18,16–33	Abraham intercedes for Sodom	Gn 20,1–18	Abraham nearly repeats his denial of Sarah
Gn 21,1–20	The birth of Isaac		
Gn 21,21–33	Abraham establishes rights to water		
Gn 22,1–14	Abraham passes test of sacrificing Isaac		
Gn 23,1–20	Abraham buys land		

The story of Abraham and Sarah climaxes in the great moment of the test in Chapter 22. After Abraham proves himself fully obedient to God's will at that awful moment when he nearly sacrifices his son, the story comes to a rapid conclusion. The promise of a son is secured, Abraham's purchase of a tomb and a small piece of land foreshadows the eventual possession of the entire land God had promised, and so Abraham's role now passes on to Isaac.

Isaac and Rebekah, Genesis 24–27

We may be surprised to find so little space given to the life of Isaac, one of the three great patriarchs of Israel. Though he plays an important role in the life of Abraham as the promised son, his role is primarily passive, even in the great scene where he is nearly sacrificed. In Isaac, continuity with Abraham is clearly established, for God appears twice to Isaac repeating to him the promises made to Abraham. But Isaac himself seems to do little to advance God's plan.

It would be easy to think of Isaac simply as a transitional character between Abraham and Jacob except for the presence in his life of his remarkable wife, Rebekah. The story of the messenger persuading Rebekah and her brother Laban to permit her to marry Isaac is a masterpiece of ancient writing (Gn 24). A total of 67 verses is given to describing this one event. Rebekah will become the key player in the next step of God's plan, the selection of her son Jacob over his older brother, Esau.

Jacob, Genesis 27–36

The theme of promise that dominates the patriarchal stories continues here, but to it is added the theme of rivalry between brothers. When we see how that rivalry is played out, and the other forms of trickery and dishonesty that color Jacob's career, we might be surprised, even horrified. We'll better appreciate the value and religious message of this part of the patriarchal history if we keep a few points in mind.

1. The overall purpose of Genesis 12–50 is to show God's promise being carried out *despite all obstacles.* We shouldn't be surprised then that Jacob, like Abraham, is himself one of those obstacles.
2. These chapters consist of many hero-type folktales that had been told for generations. When these were gathered into written form and their religious meaning highlighted, even the less edifying details were kept and cherished.
3. We're dealing here with a world very different from our own, which didn't share our refined sense of ethics. Craftiness and the ability to outfox an opponent were not incompatible with ancient people's standards of honesty and fair play. And we don't have to agree with or like all of what we find in these stories.
4. Israel is recounting its own history here, not the pious biography of a saint.

Israel saw God working in the events of these stories. In them it recognized a God who had chosen to work through a people that was as imperfect as its leaders. And this very fact built their faith, for it proved that everything works for the good in God's plan. Israel realized God writes straight with crooked lines—including the choice of a younger son (Jacob) over the rightful leader, the older son (Esau), and following the advice of a mother rather than the good judgment of a father of the promise, Isaac himself. These stories are reminders that despite their faults, the patriarchs never completely turned away from God, and that despite its faults, neither did Israel.

Jacob stands as a model for Israel in addition to being its founding father. Three times God appears to him. God passes on to Jacob the promise made to Abraham and Isaac, wrestles with him and changes his name, and assures him he will father a great nation. In turn, Jacob acknowledges God as the only god of Israel. But those encounters changed more than wily Jacob's name, for he emerged from them as a principled and decent human being. Israel found in Jacob's life a mirror of its own struggle to live out the covenant with God.

Joseph, Genesis 37–50

Like those that precede it, Joseph's story can be read in two ways: to find the traditions and themes that reach far back into Israel's history, and to learn the theological purpose of the story as part of the overall religious message of Genesis. Scholars see the Yahwist and Elohist sources woven together to form this one unified story. The slight differences and inconsistencies found in the text are sure give-aways that two sources were blended into one. An obvious example occurs in Chapter 37 where, in alternating sets of verses, J names Joseph's father *Israel,* states that his *long coat* caused his brothers' jealousy, that his brother *Judah* interceded for him, and that *Ishmaelite* merchants bought him; while the E writer names the father *Jacob,* blames Joseph's *dreams* for causing the jealousy, credits *Reuben* with interceding for Joseph, and says *Midianite* merchants carried him off to Egypt.

Scholars also agree that the Joseph story contains many elements of the Wisdom tradition

The Tribes of Israel

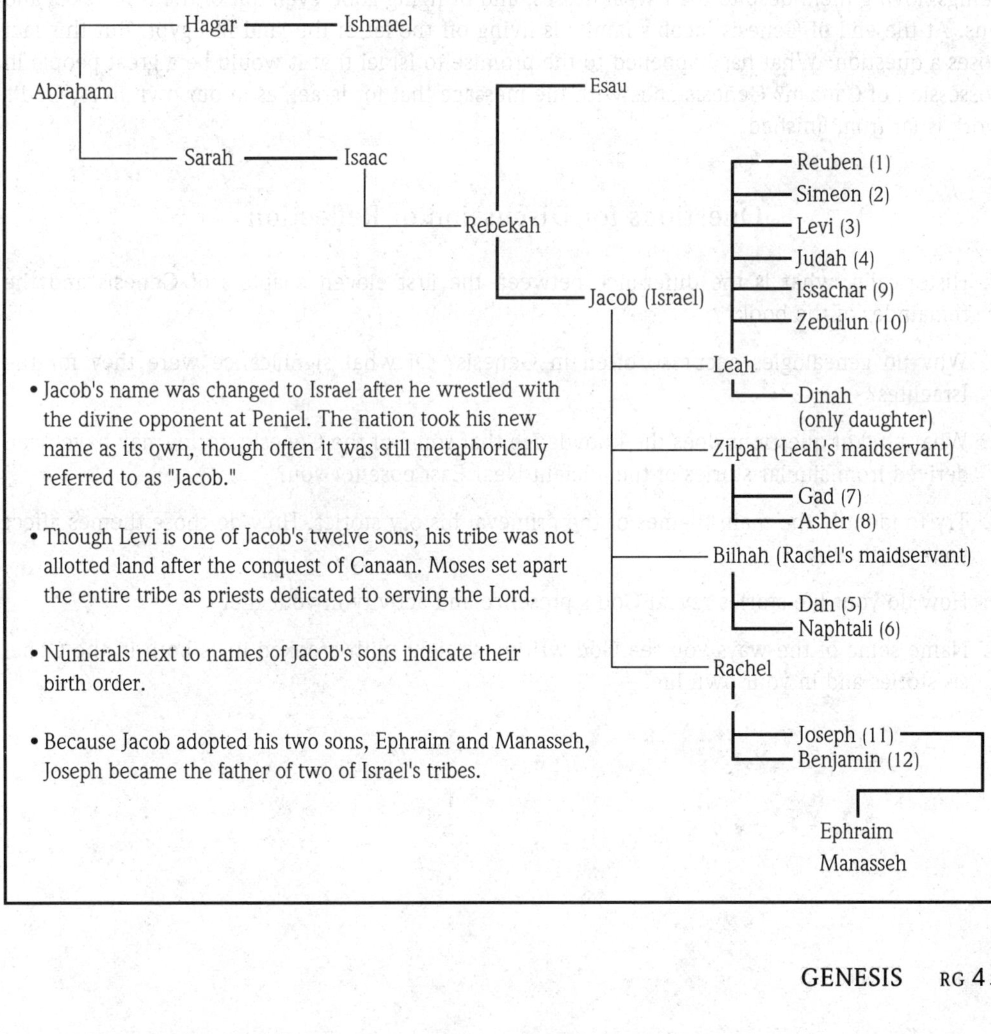

- Jacob's name was changed to Israel after he wrestled with the divine opponent at Peniel. The nation took his new name as its own, though often it was still metaphorically referred to as "Jacob."
- Though Levi is one of Jacob's twelve sons, his tribe was not allotted land after the conquest of Canaan. Moses set apart the entire tribe as priests dedicated to serving the Lord.
- Numerals next to names of Jacob's sons indicate their birth order.
- Because Jacob adopted his two sons, Ephraim and Manasseh, Joseph became the father of two of Israel's tribes.

of Israel. Joseph fits the image of the ideal man offered by the Book of Proverbs: He says only what is appropriate, keeps his own counsel, accepts misunderstandings, is hard-working and disciplined, is a fine administrator, interprets dreams, plays political games well, and avoids getting involved with foreign women. Most of all, Joseph is a devout, God-fearing man who knows God's ways are different from ours.

The Joseph story is more like a short novel than the string of saga-like stories that make up the previous chapters. There is a wonderful dramatic unity to the narrative: From start to finish, each part of the story fits into the whole like the pieces of a puzzle. If any piece were missing, the story simply wouldn't work. Some genius took all the old themes and separate traditions and created a literary work of art, the earliest such masterpiece that we know anywhere.

Again God has written straight with crooked lines. Joseph, one of the youngest of Jacob's twelve sons, is the instrument God uses to fulfill the promise to the patriarchs. The older and supposedly more deserving brothers are bypassed. What Joseph does is done entirely through divine guidance. Though his vanity caused him initial troubles, God's grace overcomes it and brings this lowly Palestinian shepherd to a position of power in Egypt second only to Pharaoh.

In the story of Joseph, as in all of Genesis, we see God working through flawed human beings, loving them despite their weaknesses, and bringing good even out of their mistakes and sins. At the end of Genesis Jacob's family is living off the fat of the land in Egypt. But this fact poses a question: What has happened to the promise to Israel that it would be a great people in possession of Canaan? Genesis ends with the message that for Israel, as in our own lives, God's work is far from finished.

Questions for Discussion or Reflection

1. Historically, what is the difference between the first eleven chapters of Genesis and the remainder of the book?
2. Why do genealogies occur so often in Genesis? Of what significance were they for the Israelites?
3. What kind of questions does the knowledge that some of the Genesis stories may have been derived from similar stories of the ancient Near East pose for you?
4. Try to identify the main themes of the primeval history stories. How do those themes affect your spirituality?
5. How do your life stories reveal God's presence and activity in your life?
6. Name some of the ways you see God writing straight with crooked lines both in the Genesis stories and in your own life.

EXODUS READING GUIDE

At a Glance

Who are the main players?	Moses, Miriam, Aaron Zipporah, Jethro Pharaoh, Pharaoh's daughter Joshua Bezalel and Oholiab
What should I look for?	Slavery Deliverance: The Passover God's Guidance The Ten Commandments The Covenant at Sinai Importance of laws and public worship
When did this take place?	Probably around 1270 B.C. Another possible date is 1440 B.C.
Where did these events occur?	Egypt Midian (Modern Saudi Arabia) The Sinai Peninsula: The Sinai Desert and Mt. Sinai (also called Mt. Horeb)
Why was this book written?	To make sure Israel never forgot God's saving act of delivering them from slavery in Egypt; that it was God who made Israel a nation and swore, at Sinai, to be their God forever; that the law is a sign of God's love and presence among them.
What's the story?	Joseph's family settles and prospers in Egypt, but after his death the Israelites become so numerous that the Egyptians fear them and force them into slavery. God chooses Moses to lead the people from slavery to freedom in the Promised Land. It takes ten plagues to convince Pharaoh to let the Israelites go. Finally, they escape across the Red Sea. After long wanderings in the desert, the Israelites make a covenant with God at Mt. Sinai and receive the law to guide their life as a nation.

STRUCTURE OF EXODUS

The story that started in Genesis continues in Exodus and does not end until the last of the five books of the Pentateuch. Because it is part of this "five-part writing," Exodus was never meant to be treated as a separate book. "Exodus" is the Latin form of the Greek name for the book, *Exodos,* and the word itself means "a going out" or "departure." Exodus tells of how the Israelites lost their position of comfort and security in Egypt; how they were enslaved, delivered from slavery, and eventually led through a barren desert to a meeting with God at Mount Sinai. But this journey takes you only halfway through the book, to the end of Chapter 18. The other twenty-two chapters focus on two significant events that take place at the mountain: first, the making of a covenant between God and the people that included acceptance of God's law; and second, the giving of the chief elements of public worship, which were building a sanctuary tent and ark to serve as God's throne and establishing priestly ministers. So Exodus is an intentional mixture of stories and laws. Why? Because the Hebrews believed that the mercy God demonstrated in delivering them from slavery was the same mercy that motivated God to give them laws and institutions for public worship. The people believed those laws and institutions were signs of God's promise to remain with them forever.

Exodus is essential reading for anyone who would understand the Old Testament, for a great deal that is of significance in the rest of the Hebrew Scriptures flows out of the first half of this book. We should not be surprised, therefore, that, like Genesis, this important book was artistically and intentionally put together. It begins with a surprise. Instead of being the privileged guests of the Egyptian empire as in the time of Joseph, the Hebrews are now slaves. What has happened to God's promise of land and nationhood?

Just as it would in an exciting, action-packed novel, the answer begins to unfold: through the birth of Moses, God is already setting a plan in motion for fulfilling the promise. But the unfolding is really a series of starts and stops that keeps the final outcome in question, creating tension and suspense through much of the book. Just when a situation seems on the verge of being resolved, the same issue rises up again in a new form: Will the people follow Moses? Will they remain faithful in the desert? Will Moses continue to trust God despite the many obstacles? These questions are never quite resolved, so the tension mounts right up to the moment Moses and the people arrive at the Mountain of God.

The second half of the book has its tense moments as well: Note, for example, the people's idolatry in Chapter 32. But, by describing God's giving of the Law and the people's oath to keep the covenant, the latter part of the book also establishes an orderly balance and a sense of security. The detailed and well-planned description of the sanctuary, together with interlocking passages of legal and liturgical descriptions, also contribute to the sense of balance in the second half of the book. When we reach the final chapter, God's glory descends into the sanctuary and the people are united in harmony with God as they were at the beginning of the book, though now under far different circumstances. The diagram on the next page illustrates how the book is like an interlocking puzzle in which each stage prepares for the next.

The three geographical regions in which God meets Israel, and which track the people's journey from slavery to freedom, provide another way of dividing the book, as illustrated here.

Egypt	Exodus 1–12	In Egypt God works wonders to free the people from slavery.
Wilderness	Exodus 13–18	God guides the people safely through the wilderness to personal encounter with God.
Mount Sinai	Exodus 19–40	At Mt. Sinai God establishes a community based on covenant, law, and worship.

Throughout the book, we see God clearly in control of events. Moses is the leading character, but this is a story of God's power and authority exercised over every land and king. The book's novel-like structure surfaces in the many sudden and unexpected plot twists. Hopeless situations and near-defeats are suddenly transformed into hope and triumph. The book's structure follows that of the lament psalms: A time of desperate need spurs the people to cry for help; God responds with mercy, and the people sing their thanks and praise (compare Pss 7, 10, and 53).

NOTES ON INDIVIDUAL PASSAGES

Because the final editor combined into one story the individual retelling of these events by each of the three major sources who recorded them (J, E, and P), you may notice some inconsistencies and duplications in the book. But since this work was done so carefully and smoothly, you are not likely to notice it without careful examination. Where necessary, historical information that sheds light on particular passages will be provided.

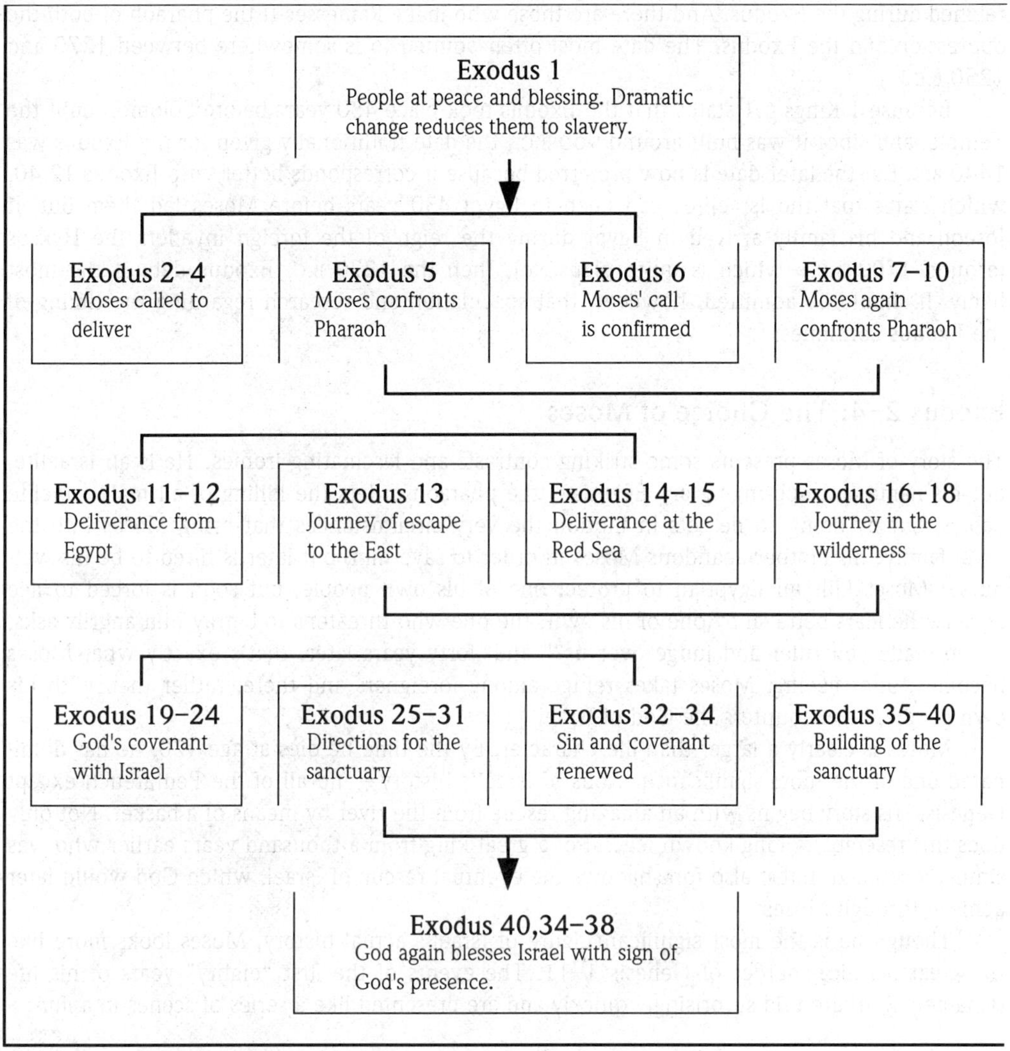

Exodus 1: The Story Continues: —The Egyptian Setting

At the start of the book, a poignant line announces the Hebrew people's dramatic change of fortune: "Then a new king, who knew nothing of Joseph, came to power in Egypt." But who was this new pharaoh and when did he begin oppressing the Hebrews? Exact dating of the Exodus, of course, is nearly impossible, but most discussions center on the reign of Pharaoh Ramesses II of the 19th Dynasty. Some scholars claim the pharaoh of the oppression was his predecessor, Seti I, making Ramesses II the pharaoh of the Exodus event. Others believe Ramesses II was himself the pharaoh of the oppression and that his successor, Merneptah, reigned during the Exodus. And there are those who make Ramesses II the pharaoh of both the oppression and the Exodus. The date most often pointed to is somewhere between 1270 and 1250 B.C.

Because 1 Kings 6,1 states that the Exodus took place 480 years before Solomon built the Temple, and since it was built around 960 B.C., the date traditionally given for the Exodus was 1440 B.C. But the later date is now preferred because it corresponds better with Exodus 12,40, which states that the Israelites had been in Egypt 430 years before Moses led them out. If Joseph and his family arrived in Egypt during the reign of the foreign invaders the Hyksos (around 1700 B.C.—which is quite plausible), then the 1270 B.C. Exodus date is the most likely. It should be admitted, however, that speculation and research regarding the timing of the Exodus continues.

Exodus 2–4: The Choice of Moses

The story of Moses presents some striking contrasts and fascinating ironies: He is an Israelite, but his name and upbringing are Egyptian; the pharaoh orders the killing of all male Israelite babies, but by doing so he sets in motion the very circumstances that bring Moses into the royal family; his mother abandons Moses in order to save him, but later is hired to be his wet-nurse; Moses kills an Egyptian to protect one of his own people, but soon is forced to flee because he fears betrayal by one of his own; the one who threatens to betray him angrily asks, "Who made you ruler and judge over us?" and, forty years later, that's exactly what Moses becomes; after fleeing, Moses takes refuge among foreigners and there, rather than with his own people, he encounters the God of Israel.

Moses is clearly a larger-than-life character. By the time he dies at age 120, he has dominated one of the most significant periods of Israel's history—and all of the Pentateuch except Genesis. His story begins with an amazing rescue from the river by means of a basket. Not only does this resemble a long-known legend of a great king from a thousand years earlier who was similarly rescued, but it also foreshadows the eventual rescue of Israel, which God would later achieve through Moses.

Though he is the most significant figure of Israel's actual history, Moses looks more like the great mythical heroes of Genesis 1–11. The events of the first "eighty" years of his life (Chapters 2–4) are told surprisingly quickly and are presented like a series of scenes in a film:

1. The near miraculous circumstances surrounding Moses' birth and rescue hint at his special mission.
2. The situation worsens—Moses is not respected by his own people and is forced to flee.
3. While Moses is living among foreigners, God asks him to do the near-impossible; very reluctantly, Moses accepts (Ex 3,1–12).
4. God communicates more intimately with Moses than with anyone else and even reveals to him the divine name, "I am who am" (Ex 3,12–22).
5. God reassures the insecure Moses and, grudgingly, assigns his brother, Aaron, as his spokesperson (Ex 4,1–22).
6. Persuaded by the miraculous signs he performed, the people believe Moses and accept his mission.

The call of Moses is the first instance of an oft-repeated biblical call-pattern that shows up in the call of other great prophets and leaders. This pattern is illustrated in the table below. Note the elements as they occur in the Moses story and see how they parallel the sequence of events in the other stories.

Biblical Call-Patterns

Apparition	God appears and speaks to Moses.	Ex 3,1–4
Motive	God gives reason for coming.	Ex 3,4–9
Commission	God commissions Moses for his task.	Ex 3,10
Objection	Moses protests he is unworthy and unqualified.	Ex 3,11
Reassurance	God reassures Moses and insists he serve.	Ex 3,12
Sign	God gives a sign or prediction.	Ex 3,12; 4,1–5

Listed below are places you can find the elements of this same pattern in the call of other prophets and leaders.

	Gideon	Isaiah	Jeremiah	Ezekiel
Apparition	Jgs 6,11f	Is 6,1f	Jer 1,4	Ez 1,1–28a
Motive	Jgs 6,12f	Is 6,3–7	Jer 1,5	Ez 1,28b–2,2
Commission	Jgs 6,14	Is 6,8–10	Jer 1,5	Ez 2,3–5
Objection	Jgs 6,15	Is 6,11	Jer 1,6	Ez 2,6–8
Reassurance	Jgs 6,16	Is 6,11f	Jer 1,7f	Ez 2,6f
Sign	Jgs 6,17	—	Jer 1,9f	Ez 2,8 – 3,11

The revelation of the divine name is an especially important moment in the story. God prepares Moses by first announcing, "I am the God of Abraham, the God of Isaac, and the God of Jacob," and by insisting that love and compassion are God's motives for coming to Moses and intervening in the lives of the Israelites. God then responds to Moses' question: If they ask me your name, what shall I say? God's answer is both surprising and mysterious, for God's is no ordinary name. Several versions of the divine name occur in the text: "I am who am," "I AM," and "He who is" (or better, "He who causes to be"). Names, especially in the Bible, are handles one can use to control another (note that in C.B. radio jargon a person's broadcast nickname is called his or her "handle"). God's response makes it clear the Israelites will be given no handle on God. God's true identity is beyond their understanding, for God is pure power and being. But the name also suggests that God's existence has a purpose; here it is closely connected with the survival of Israel. By claiming to be the God of Abraham, Isaac, and Jacob, God is assuring Israel that "I am with you totally."

YHWH In Hebrew only the consonants of words are written down; vowels are suggested by "points" added to the word. Hence the divine name is sometimes referred to as the *Tetragrammaton* (Greek for "four letters"). Much debate surrounds the meaning of the name, but most agree it is a form of the verb "to be."

As a sign of reverence, Jews from the time of the exile onward have refrained from speaking the name aloud (some of the Dead Sea Scrolls substitute four dots for the letters, refraining even from *writing* the name). In the Hebrew text, the letters *YHWH* were surrounded by vowel points for the word *'Adonai* ("my Lord"), to indicate that when the text was read aloud, the reader should substitute *'Adonai* for *Yahweh.* Misunderstanding of the significance of the vowel points used with the consonants for the divine name resulted, in the 16th century, in the word *Yehowah,* "Jehovah." Today, pious Jews will frequently substitute the term *ha-shem, has-sem* "the Name." The divine name occurs 6,823 times in the Old Testament. Everywhere else the divine name appears in the third-person form, *Yahweh.* Only in Exodus 3,14 do we find the unique first-person form "I am who am."

Following the Jewish custom, Christians do not normally speak the name in prayer, but replace it with the title "LORD." Whenever you see the word in the *New American Bible,* printed with large and small capitals, it is replacing the Hebrew word *Yahweh.*

Exodus 5–12: Confrontation with the Pharaoh

The biblical plagues dominate these chapters and contribute to the dramatic, even cinematic feel of this part of the story. There is no shortage of excitement and suspense. First Moses pleads with Pharaoh to allow the Israelites to go and worship the Lord (5,1–13). Pharaoh not only refuses, he increases the work of the slave laborers, prompting the Israelite foremen to grumble that Moses is making matters worse for them (5,14–21). An apparent repeat of the call of Moses opens Chapter 6 in what is probably a retelling of the story by the P source. But instead of feeling redundant, the retelling serves to emphasize that Moses can rely on God to do exactly what God promised.

The fight for freedom shifts into high gear when God starts sending plagues upon Egypt. The chart on the next page gives details regarding the plagues that should help us keep in mind two important points:

1. Each of the first nine plagues can be seen as an intensification of naturally occurring phenomena (e.g., small organisms still turn the Nile red during flood times; ancient Egyptian documents describe the calamity of being overrun by frogs; flies and gnats are a chronic nuisance in that area even today; sandstorms and desert dust are known to block out the sun's light [see *NAB* footnote at Ex 7,14]).
2. The Israelites saw the hand of God in the timing of these events and in the obvious control God exerted over them. In other words, the miracle was found not in the fact that the plagues happened (they could happen any time), but in *when* they happened. Such timing could only be explained as God's intervention.

The pharaoh is in a battle of wills with the Lord, and we might wonder if God's power can overcome Pharaoh's hardheartedness. The unfolding action is a little like the story of the

The Ten Plagues

Plague What Happened	Duplicated by Egyptians	Naturally occurring phenomenon	Pharaoh starts to relent
Blood River Nile metaphorically "turned to blood" making most of Egypt's water undrinkable.*†	Yes	Yes	No
Frogs Frogs came up out of the Nile and "covered the land."*	No	Yes	Yes
Gnats The "dust of Egypt" turned into huge swarms of gnats.*†	No	Yes	No
Flies Swarms of flies invaded every home in Egypt.*	No	Yes	Yes
Disease Fatal disease afflicted all Egyptian livestock but none of the Israelites' animals.†	No	Yes	No
Boils Festering boils broke out on all Egyptian people and animals.*†	No	Yes	No
Hail Worst hail storm ever destroyed livestock and crops.*†‡	No	Yes	Yes
Locusts Countless locusts devoured what few crops were left.*‡	No	Yes	Yes
Darkness Total darkness covered Egypt for three days.*	No	Yes	Yes
Death of Firstborn Firstborn son of every Egyptian family died also firstborn among livestock.*†	No	No	Yes

*Plague affected humans †Plague affected livestock ‡Plague affected crops

Greek hero Sisyphus, who must push a boulder up a mountain only to have it roll back down every time he reaches the summit. Each time Pharaoh reaches the point of relenting, he reneges at the last moment, and the hard work of pushing events in God's direction starts all over again.

The tenth and last plague, however, is decisive. Terrifying and chilling in our eyes, it was for Israel a clear sign of God's favor and protection. The firstborn males of the Egyptians perish while those of the Israelites are spared. In Israel's eyes this event marked God's clear choice of Israel as his favored nation, the firstborn of all the peoples of the earth. The Passover feast was developed as a celebration of the miracle of the "passing over" of the angel of death and the liberation of Israel from slavery.

So important was this ritual in the life of Israel that it is written into the account of the actual event. Instead of describing a fear-filled meal eaten in haste—as it probably occurred—the text describes the full liturgical ritual as it was *later* celebrated in memory of the original events. The theology of the Book of Exodus (and Christian theology as well) stresses the oneness of later rituals and original events. The Hebrew concept of remembrance *(zakir)* emphasizes that remembering makes the past present again. What our ancestors experienced in Egypt and the desert, we relive and celebrate again in our feasts. The Catholic Mass is a perfect example of the notion that ritual remembering makes past events present now, for we believe that when we remember what Jesus did, he becomes uniquely present among the assembly.

Exodus 13–15: Escape through the Sea

In addition to two tellings of the escape through the sea, these chapters list two additional practices the Israelites are to observe to remember how God delivered them from death and slavery: refraining from any food containing yeast, and consecration to God of all first-born males (13,1–16). These practices, in fact, may have existed among the Israelites and their pagan neighbors for generations before the time of the Exodus. But Israel's history persuaded them to give these practices a whole new meaning: They became reminders that Israel's life as a nation depended on the love and mercy of the God who delivered them from death.

The first telling of the flight through the sea (13,17–14,31) is a dramatic and detailed prose description. The second (15,1–21) is a poetic rendition, which probably derived from a feast-day hymn. It is also considered by many to be the oldest written text in the Bible, probably written during the 200-year period when Israel was ruled by judges, before the establishment of the monarchy. It presents God as a fierce warrior fighting on behalf of the people.

The first and older half of the song (verses 1–12) recounts the actual battle God wages against Egypt, while the second half tells how God led Israel through the desert to the promised land. Verses 13–18 in the second half refer to events that have not yet happened at this point in the story (the eventual conquest and settlement of Canaan), leading scholars to conclude that the second half was probably composed later than the first part of the song.

Exodus 16–18: Hardships in the Desert of Sinai

Scholars have more questions than answers regarding the route of the Exodus and especially the leg of the journey that brought the Israelites from the sea to the foot of Mt. Sinai. The itinerary of that two-month trek is listed for us, but unfortunately few of the places can be identified with any certainty: Even the place where the Israelites crossed the "Red Sea" and

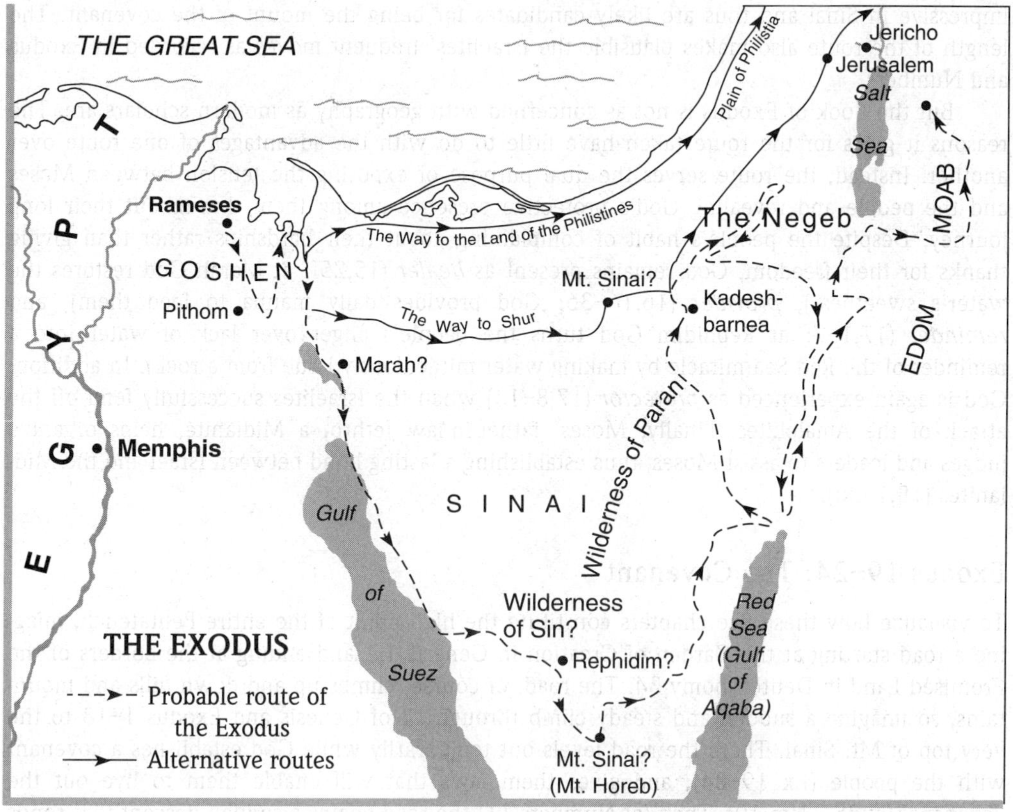

the location of Mt. Sinai are debated. The Hebrew name for "Red Sea" has two other meanings: "reed sea" or the "sea of chaos." If the correct meaning is "reed sea," then any of a number of marshy lakes might be the actual crossing site (though it is possible today's Red Sea was once called the "Sea of Reeds"). If "sea of chaos" is the correct reading, then anyone's guess might do since the name is symbolic, representing the place where God would destroy pharaoh's army—the servants of chaotic evil.

While no definitive answer can be given about the route of the Exodus, scholars offer three possible options, which are shown on the map above. Least likely is the northern and shortest route that would have led them through the so-called "Way to the Land of the Philistines" (13,17 notes God's decision to avoid the Philistines for fear that the possibility of conflict with them would turn the Israelites back toward Egypt). The second route would have traversed the Sinai peninsula, also in the northern area moving eastward. This was a major caravan route that passes near Kadesh-barnea, where according to Deuteronomy 2,14 Israel camped for thirty-eight years, and it went through territory known to be hospitable to nomadic groups. The map lists it as "The Way to Shur." Most favored and most probable, however, is the circular route along and around the southern part of the Sinai. What recommends this longest route is the fact that because Egyptians mined gems here, it is quite possible that Moses could have known it. Also, several of the mountain peaks found here are among the most impressive in Sinai and thus are likely candidates for being the mount of the covenant. The length of the route also makes plausible the Israelites' frequent moves as recorded in Exodus and Numbers.

But the Book of Exodus is not as concerned with geography as modern scholars are. The reasons it gives for the route taken have little to do with the advantages of one route over another. Instead, the route serves the dual purpose of exposing the tension between Moses and the people and revealing God's protective presence among them throughout their long journey. Despite the people's habit of complaining about their hardships rather than giving thanks for their freedom, God remains present as *healer* (15,25f: at Marah God restores the water's sweetness), *provider* (16,16–36: God provides daily manna to feed them), and *reminder* (17,1–7: at Rephidim God turns the people's anger over lack of water into a reminder of the Red Sea miracle by making water miraculously issue from a rock). In addition, God is again experienced as *protector* (17,8–13) when the Israelites successfully fend off the attack of the Amalekites. Finally, Moses' father-in-law Jethro, a Midianite, helps organize judges and leaders to assist Moses, thus establishing a lasting bond between Israel and the Midianites (18,1–26).

Exodus 19–24: The Covenant

To visualize how these five chapters constitute the high point of the entire Pentateuch, imagine a road starting at the Garden of Creation in Genesis 1,1 and ending at the borders of the Promised Land in Deuteronomy 34. The road, of course, climbs up and down hills and mountains, so imagine a sudden and steady climb through all of Genesis and Exodus 1–18 to the very top of Mt. Sinai. There the road levels out temporarily while God establishes a covenant with the people (Ex 19–24), and gives them laws that will enable them to live out the covenant (Ex 25 — Nm 10). Then (at Numbers 11) the road begins a sudden descent that sends it to the edge of the Jordan River (at the end of Deuteronomy). When the Israelites looked back at human history, that's the God-directed route they saw history following, with Israel playing a central role in the history.

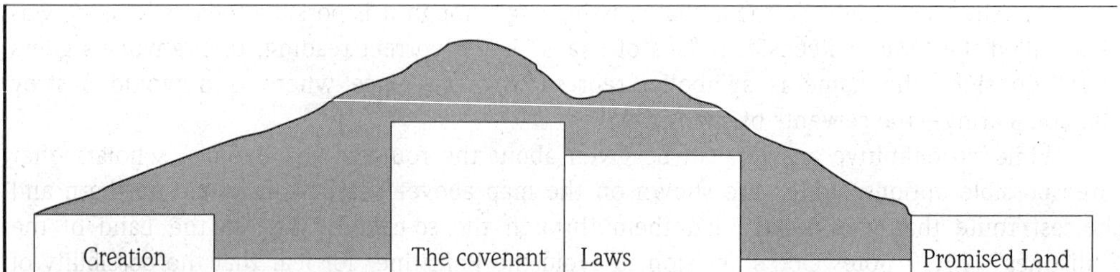

Chapters 19 to 24 are unified by their common focus on the law. The events recounted here are divided into four stages:

1. Israel prepares to meet God and receive the law (Ex 19,1–25).
2. God gives general laws (the Ten Commandments) (Ex 20,1–21).

Slavery in the Bible

It may be shocking to find in the Bible a reference to human beings as "property" (21,21). Remembering that all biblical literature arose out of the culture in which it was written may soften the blow a bit, but it may still be jarring to see apparent approval of slavery in the pages of scripture. Recalling that God's ways are gradually revealed to Israel throughout its history (e.g., the concept of life after death is a late development in their theology) may help put things in perspective. Christians believe that only in Jesus was God's self-revelation complete, yet even the New Testament made accommodation for slavery. God's people were still on the path of discovering God's ways and will.

It should be mentioned that the laws listed in Exodus represented an enlightened view of slavery. Other nations treated slaves as objects rather than as persons, according them no formal rights. Israel, aware of its own enslavement in Egypt, made laws to ensure humane treatment of slaves, provided for their rights, limited the time of enslavement (for Israelite slaves), and allowed slaves to assume positions of responsibility and prestige.

3. God gives specific laws (Ex 21,22–23,33).
4. Israel accepts God's laws and seals the covenant with God (Ex 24,1–18).

Note the difference between the commandments and the more specific laws that follow. The commandments present the basic demands of a healthy relationship with God—loving God and neighbor. Limited to ten (for easy memorizing and counting on the fingers), they state simple demands but don't say what will happen if one disobeys them, while the laws of Chapters 21–23 list the consequences of breaking each specific law. These laws are called "The Covenant Code" because, by looking at practical situations and stipulating the proper way to settle each case, they teach Israel how to live the covenant justly.

The giving of the Law is surrounded by solemn moments of impressive ritual. In Chapter 19 Moses, alone, several times ascends the mountain to God, creating a sense of holiness and reverence. His solitary climb resembles the once-a-year, solitary entrance of the high priest into the Holy of Holies of the Temple. When the people embrace the covenant in Chapter 24, they seal the pact with two rituals: a sprinkling with blood (24,3–8), and a meal in which Moses, Aaron, and the seventy elders feast with God. Lawgiving and ritual thus combine in a setting of divine holiness and human sanctification to impress on the reader that the Law is the God-given means to becoming holy as God is holy.

God's Self-Description Chapter 34,6–7—the most quoted and alluded to passage in the Old Testament—provides a sublime understanding of who God is: "The LORD, the LORD, a merciful and gracious God, slow to anger and rich in kindness and fidelity, continuing his kindness for a thousand generations, and forgiving wickedness and crime and sin; yet not declaring the guilty guiltless."

Exodus 25–40: Establishing God's Home in Israel

It may well be that there is more material describing the Tabernacle than there is about any other single topic in the Bible. This material helps emphasize one of the themes of Exodus: God is not only a transcendent and mighty warrior God, but also a gracious God who has chosen to live in the midst of the people.

Chapter 25–31 and 35–40 essentially repeat each other by giving directions for building and furnishing the tabernacle and by describing in detail how the directions were carried out. In between, however, are stories of Israel's first failure to keep the covenant—the worship of the golden calf. This placement is probably no accident. Here, as in the previous section, structure reveals the writer's purpose: In the preceding section two ritual events were wrapped around the giving of the Law to make a statement about the intimate connection between law and holiness. Now, by inserting the story of Israel's infidelity between the two halves of the sanctuary narratives, the writer is saying that worship and fidelity to the covenant are inseparably interlocked; the covenant cannot be followed faithfully if the people are not rooted in worship of God.

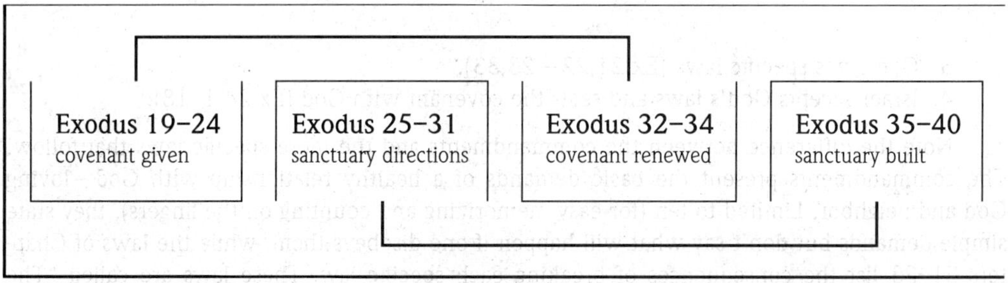

THE THEOLOGY OF THE COVENANT

Because the giving of the covenant is the central moment of the entire Pentateuch, reflection on the meaning of the term "covenant" (the Hebrew word is *berit*) will yield a better understanding of Israel's faith. But first, some general points:

1. A covenant, like a contract, is a solemn agreement, legally binding on both parties, but made with a religious ritual.
2. Covenants can be made between individuals, between nations, or between a god and people.
3. Several types of royal covenants or treaties are known from the ancient Near East. A *royal grant* was an unconditional covenant between a king and a loyal servant. A *parity treaty* was made by equals who agreed to respect each other's rights and interests and accepted mutual responsibility. A *Suzerain-vassal treaty* was a covenant between a great king and the lesser kings of nations conquered or threatened by him. Vassal treaties were not an equal proposition; the vassal agreed to faithfully execute a long list

of demands, while the king promised nothing more specific than kindnesss and protection.

4. Once solemnly made, these treaties were considered binding for all time.
5. The most common form of vassal treaty known from ancient times contains six parts which, in a general way, can also be found in the Sinai covenant (Ex 19–24).

The similarities as outlined in the chart below are of interest, but they must not be pushed too far. Later in the tradition legal treaty language became commonplace, such as in the covenant summary statement often found in the prophets, "You shall be my people and I will be your God" (Jer 7,23; 11,4; 24,7; Ex 11,20; 14,11; Hos 2,25, etc.). But Exodus is first of all a record of Israel's momentous encounter with God, and of her promise to worship the Lord who was the savior and loving benefactor of this small and insignificant group of refugees.

The notion of covenant confirmed in Israel's mind the special and unique relationship they enjoyed with God. God had shown Israel special favor by revealing the divine name to them, saving them from slavery, choosing to live among them in the tabernacle, and giving them laws to govern their life and ensure a just society among them. Initially the covenant was celebrated in worship with a sense of unalterable national destiny, a kind of "We can't lose because God is on our side" attitude. The later prophets like Jeremiah and Ezekiel, however, emphasized that while even disasters did not mean God had abandoned them, the people's faithlessness could bring punishment upon the nation.

Ancient Treaties and the Sinai Covenant

Typical 13th-century B.C. Hittite vassal-type treaty	Elements of typical vassal-type treaty found in the Sinai covenant
A preamble stating names of the parties	Ex 20,2: "I am the LORD your God who brought you out of Egypt, out of the land of slavery."
Historical listing of the good things the king has done	Ex 20,2 (19,4): "You yourselves have seen what I did in Egypt, and how I carried you on eagles' wings and brought you to myself."
Duties the vassal must perform	Ex 20,3–17; 20,23 – 23,17: The commandments and the laws governing daily life
An order to save the document and read it publicly	Ex 24,3–8; 24,12: Blood-sprinkling ceremony and giving of the tablets of the Law to be kept among the people.
List of gods who witness the treaty	There are *no* divine witnesses because there is no other god who can testify to what the Lord does.
Lists of curses the gods will inflict on those who break the treaty and blessings for those who keep it	Ex 20,5f; 23,25: "I the LORD your God am a jealous God, inflicting punishment for their fathers' wickedness on the children of those who hate me . . . but bestowing mercy to the thousandth generation, on the children of those who love me and keep my commandments."

Questions for Discussion or Reflection

1. Why do you think God chose Israel? Did it have to do with who they were and what they did? What insights does the following verse offer regarding this question: "I who show favors to whom I will, I who grant mercy to whom I will" (Ex 33,19)? What does this say about God's willingness to put up with us despite our many and repeated failings?

2. In Exodus we see close connections between worship and law and between law and holiness. Can you state what the connections are? Why is law enshrined in worship? How does observance of the law lead to holiness?

3. Some say the heart of the Old Testament is found in God's command to Moses when Pharaoh pursues the fleeing Israelites: "Go forward," God says. God tells them to move and pursue freedom; to yield to the call to greatness; to stop complaining, take action, and follow their dream. Has God ever given you that same command? When? Why? Can one be afraid of freedom? Why is slavery or dependence sometimes more attractive than freedom?

4. With which of the characters of Exodus can you most easily identify? Is it because of their strengths or their weaknesses? How does it feel to know you have some of the same strengths and weaknesses as these great characters of Exodus?

5. How important is the concept of remembering in your life? What kinds of memories do you live with most? Does your remembering "make the past present again"?

ESSAY

Did It Really Happen?

Often people reading scripture will ask, "But did it really happen?" The "it" might be the parting of the Red Sea, any one of the ten plagues, Jesus' walking on the water, or even his rising from the dead. Today some teachers, theologians, and scripture scholars might answer, "It doesn't really matter. You miss the point when you ask such a question. The 'truth' of the event is contained not in the literal, historical *fact* of the event, but in the meaning the event had for those who recorded it." Many Bible readers will not accept that answer at all; and even those who do may often go away thinking that, in fact, it really *does* matter.

First let's admit what's right about the above answer. Yes, the "truth" of the event lies in the meaning the event had for those who recorded it. But then one has to ask another question: Would the event have held the meaning it did, would it have been cherished and preserved by our ancestors in faith, if it did not embody a kernel, at least, of historical truth?

Let's take the Exodus. What seems clear is that, in this event, the Israelites experienced God acting decisively in their history. God's activity was so marvelous, in fact, that it impressed their imaginations forever. From that moment on Israel could rely on God no matter what the circumstance because they knew without question that God was *able,* and not only able but also *willing,* to intervene in the events of human history. The memory of the Exodus became something the Israelites could stake their lives on.

The resurrection of Jesus was, for the first disciples, such a sustaining memory. No matter what else we can say about the resurrection, we must acknowlege that whatever took place so impressed the disciples that it completely changed their lives. They left the upper room and risked their very lives because they had seen God work so decisively in the life of Jesus. Now they *knew* that death was not the final answer: They could believe that all the little deaths they would experience in their lives could lead to new life, resurrection if you will, because God had demonstrated that possibility in the life of Jesus.

When we talk of paschal-mystery spirituality as the realization that the daily "deaths" we experience also lead to new life, we are not just making metaphors about a metaphor. Certainly one could study the cycle of life as demonstrated in nature's cycle of seasons and make some statements about how death and life are just flip sides of the same coin. For example, one could talk about being *like* a caterpillar who must "die" in order to experience "new life." Caterpillars make for rich metaphors because they spin cocoons and turn into butterflies, but they don't really "die" and come to life again. They do something *like* dying and rising, so they point to the possibility of that reality. Metaphoric images about the possibility of "rising" from the "little deaths" of daily experience are available without Jesus. If Jesus' death and rising said nothing more about human life than that, then Christianity would offer no new information for human experience. If watching a caterpillar turn into a butterfly teaches the same message as the resurrection, if the cycles of human life itself could have taught the first disciples that death is not the final word, why did they make the resurrection moment the centerpiece of their teaching about Jesus? Could it be because Jesus' resurrection convinced them they were not kidding themselves when they believed death is not the final word? Could it be that now they believed they could say with certainty that the "death" of losing a job, of a divorce, or of a crippling illness can lead to new life because in a concrete, historical moment—the life of Jesus—God had decisively demonstrated that death *can* be overcome? Could it be that they experienced God's sovereignty over death in a way they had never experienced it before and decided that if God could do that, then even in their lives anything is possible?

A friend belongs to a community that cherishes a memory of its early days before she became a member. The group is an alternative parish that exists side-by-side with a traditional parish in a large archdiocese. When the priest the group hired to be its full-time presider was called on the carpet by the parish pastor, some of the community folks insisted on going with him to answer for the community's behavior. After these folks explained what they were doing and why to the pastor and members of the parish council, instead of being chastised they were asked to help the official parish implement some of the strategies the alternative community had developed. The incident is fondly referred to as "the night the Christians ate the lions." That meeting has become a sustaining memory for that community; so much so, in fact, that someone like my friend, who was not a member when it happened, cherishes it as much as those who were.

Then, say in a hundred years, suppose someone demonstrates that the meeting never really took place, or at least did not occur in the way it has been enshrined in the story. Maybe the parish council members never really asked for help from the alternative folks, and the best that could be said was that a resigned and grudging tolerance of the alternative community resulted. It would be hard to imagine that the memory could continue to nourish and sustain that community. (Are any school children still taught the story of George Washington and the cherry tree now that we know that incident is apocryphal?)

ESSAY (Continued)

The stories in the Bible cover a wide range, from those that are accounts of historical incidents to those that are meant only to make a point. For instance, the events of the first conquest of Jerusalem in 597 B.C., told in 2 Kings 24,10–17, are also related in ancient Babylonian records. The parables of Jesus, on the other hand, are not records of events that really took place. When Jesus told the story of the Good Samaritan (Luke 10,29–37), his audience knew that it was not an actual happening, even though it talks about things (robberies, travelers and so on) that are realistic. The parables are stories told to illustrate a particular teaching. (See the essay on Parables in the Reading Guides to the Gospels.)

With any given incident, each reader will have to decide which is more central: the history or the meaning. Except where reason and scholarship tell us a story is clearly non-historical (Jonah's being swallowed by the whale, for example), we may find it helpful to approach scripture—even its more miraculous stories—from this viewpoint: These are the sustaining memories the tradition has chosen to cherish; what the historical kernel is we cannot say with certainty, but with the assent of faith we believe it must have been something clear, concrete, and decisive enough to stake your life on.

LEVITICUS READING GUIDE

At a Glance

Who are the main players?	Moses, Aaron Aaron's sons: Abihu, Nadab, Eleazar, Ithamar
What should I look for?	Holiness of God and nation; relationship of law and people's holiness; Significance of physical perfection Religious ritual and worship; sacrificial offerings Levites and priesthood
When did this take place?	It is presented as perhaps two years after the Exodus from Egypt, during the Israelites' year-long stay camped at Mt. Sinai. (Possible date: around 1272 B.C or 1442 B.C.) The laws were actually completed over a long period of time, perhaps 1000 B.C. to 600 B.C.
Where did these events occur?	In the Sinai peninsula, at the foot of Mt. Sinai (also called Mt. Horeb)
Why was this book written?	To answer the question: How can a sinful people serve a perfect and holy God? To teach the ways of holiness: observance of law and religious ritual. To serve as a guidebook: teaching priests and people how to worship the Lord and live holy lives.
What's the story?	Leviticus contains few characters and almost no story line. The book is a very detailed compilation of rules and regulations governing worship and daily life.

If you were working your way through the Bible one book at a time, your reading might come to a grinding halt at Leviticus. All the elements you might normally expect are missing here: plot, poetry, stories of suspense or deep emotion—even the characters are few. Yet the book holds a venerated place in Jewish tradition. That is because the book is rich with laws that define Jewish life and practice. Of the 613 binding commandments found in the Pentateuch, 247 are right here in Leviticus. Despite the fact that a major portion of the laws, those pertaining to temple sacrifice, became impossible to observe when the Jerusalem Temple was destroyed in 70 B.C., Leviticus remains the most important statement of Torah for Judaism. Its laws are much studied and debated because Judaism has always found in their rich diversity the "teaching" or "way" it needed to follow to be faithful and beloved sons and daughters of God.

In Judaism *Torah* carries a positive and joyful connotation, not the narrow and restrictive meaning "Law" often conjures among modern people. Because it means "teaching" or "guide," Torah is celebrated in Judaism as a gift from God that leads to God's favor and salvation. The best expression of this attitude can be found in Psalm 119, the longest Psalm in the psalter, which, for 176 verses, exults in praise and gratitude for the Law.

Christians come to Leviticus with a very different attitude. Whether horrified by the details of animal sacrifice, or disgusted by the discussions of bodily emissions, or turned off by the many restrictive rules governing what can and cannot be eaten, Christians find little to celebrate here, preferring to emphasize instead the concept of "freedom from the law" that St. Paul stresses in his letters. What Christians who approach the book with these biases miss are the profound insights into the mystery of God that are woven into the fabric of Leviticus. Like golden thread, the insights into the holiness, majesty, power, and love of God shine through regularly and reveal the enduring value of the book. By keeping our eyes on the "big picture" rather than on individual laws, we can focus on the most important question the book raises: How would following these laws make Israel different from other nations?

To tap its fullest meaning, we must approach the book from two angles: First, we can ask what religious insights and meaning the ancient Israelites found in its various laws and practices. Second, we can explore how its major themes reveal the enduring character and purpose of God. Israel relied on these themes for their understanding of God, and Christianity has made them central in its own teaching. Take, for example, the concept of sacrifice. Without knowing the importance of sacrifice in Leviticus as a means of relating to God, Christians would find the meaning of Jesus' death and an understanding of Eucharist difficult to articulate.

STRUCTURE OF LEVITICUS

Leviticus exhibits the style of the Priestly (P) source whose work is found throughout the Pentateuch—and who is always concerned with classifying and listing things in their proper place (see the P creation story in Genesis 1 and the list of nations in Genesis 11,10–32). Another major concern of the P writer is defining the difference between the world of the sacred and that of everyday life. Like wise parents teaching a child how to relate to fire, the P source knows God is not to be dealt with lightly. One must respect fire and understand its power if one is to deal with it and live. P deals directly with the life-and-death question of what is appropriate and inappropriate when relating with God.

Leviticus has two major divisions that are quite different in spirit. Chapters 1–16 live up to the name of the book, which basically means "That which pertains to the levitical priests."

(The Hebrew title is the opening word of the text, *wayyigra,* meaning "And he [the LORD] called"). Chapters 17–27, however, deal with larger areas of community behavior and public worship that express the unique identity of Israel and the call to holiness inherent in the covenant. A simple outline of the book is shown here.

Outline of Leviticus

Part I

- A. Laws governing the five types of sacrifice (Lv 1–7)
- B. The ceremony of ordination of Aaron and his sons (Lv 8–10)
- C. Laws governing legal purity regarding animals, childbirth, leprosy, and sexuality (Lv 11–15)
- D. The observance of the Day of Atonement (Lv 16)

Part II

- A. Moral and ethical laws of holiness (Lv 17–20)
- B. Ritual (liturgical) requirements for holiness (Lv 21–25)
- C. Blessings and curses for following and breaking the covenant (Lv 26) [Serves as a conclusion to Chapters 17–25 and to entire book]
- D. Regulations for redeeming offerings vowed to God (Lv 27) [Added later to the book as an appendix]

In Part I of the outline we find a twice-repeated pattern of *laws* followed by *actions.* After the many regulations on sacrifice in Chapters 1–7, there follows a narrative explanation of the role of priests and a description of Aaron's first major sacrifice. Chapter 11 begins a new set of regulations, this time relating to proper use of food and respect for bodily functions. What follows in Chapter 16 is an elaborate description of the annual Day of Atonement, the ritual that cleansed the people of guilt from all their sins. The message in this pattern of laws-followed-by-actions is simple: Worship and daily life are closely connected—what we celebrate in worship flows out of how we live our lives.

Like Part I, Part II of Leviticus, often referred to as "The Law of Holiness," is also dominated by the theme of holiness. This section of laws has a moralistic and preachy tone that sets it apart from the first sixteen chapters, which merely list laws one after another. These later laws are of two types: Chapter 1–20 focus on moral laws that govern the way we relate as social beings living in community, while Chapters 21–25 deal with regulations for priests and liturgical worship. Chapter 26 is an impressive chapter that caps the collection of laws and serves as a conclusion of the whole book.

All commentators agree that the viewpoint that dominates and unites Leviticus is Priestly. Those editors gathered here all the laws that governed the various activities that the priests were expected to monitor—everything from public worship to private matters like food and clothing, skin diseases, and sexual activity, as well as truly ethical questions about just and loving relationships among the people.

The laws of Leviticus were not written all at once. Groups of laws written at different times were joined by the Priestly editors into an ever-growing collection. Though three different sets of sacrifice laws, detected by their unique stylistic features, have been identified in Chapters 1–7, and though the style of the first sixteen chapters differs noticeably from that of

Holiness and Purity

The twin emphases on holiness and ritual purity found in Leviticus reflect attitudes that on the surface might seem contradictory but, in actuality, are complementary.

The stress on holiness expressed the Israelites' belief that God lived among them. Holiness, in fact, might be defined as awareness of and respect for the divine presence that surrounds people everywhere. For Israel the implications were obvious: If a just and merciful God had chosen to "tabernacle" (make a home) among them, then they must be a just and merciful people. Over and over again in Leviticus we hear the refrain: "Be holy because I, the LORD your God, am holy." The expectation was that by living among them, God would rub off on the people.

A doubly opposite expectation is reflected in the stress on ritual purity: The people must not rub off on God. Yes, God was willing to live among them, but God's ways were still light-years away from human ways. People were not to approach God carelessly or take God for granted. Instead, the people were to foster an attitude of carefulness toward God, approaching God as worthily as possible. Keep in mind that ritual uncleanness in itself was not considered harmful or even sinful. Daily life, after all, made uncleanness impossible to avoid. God is the holy one; human beings of necessity fall short of God's holiness. The point, then, was not that one always had to be ritually clean, but that one could not approach God unless he or she was clean. Coming into the presence of God in an unclean state was truly dangerous, for God's holiness could not abide it. While Exodus taught the people how to make holy objects, Leviticus teaches them how to be holy people.

So all the laws regarding holiness and ritual purity point to the same reality: a holy, just, and loving God dwells among us calling us to be a holy, compassionate people; because our God is everywhere, even in ordinary day-to-day life, we must take care to keep our lives pure so that in every aspect of our lives we can stand worthily before the Lord whose greatness so transcends our ordinary, puny existence.

the rest of the book, the editors, nevertheless, have blended these elements into a book that, after Deuteronomy, is the most unified of the five in the Pentateuch.

Because so much of the material in Leviticus is not a part of modern Christian religious practice, a look at each section of the above outline should increase our understanding.

Leviticus 1–7: The Topic of Sacrifice

The five types of sacrifice that are named in these chapters are described in the table on the next page. When more than one was presented, the sequence of offerings was as follows: first, the guilt or sin offering, which gave people a way of dealing with their sinfulness. The burnt offering followed, demonstrating the people's total dedication to God. Finally came the peace or fellowship offering, which established communion with God and others in the community. This sequence of expiation to dedication to fellowship reveals the importance and theology of Israel's system of sacrifice: To achieve communion with God one first had to be forgiven and totally committed to the Lord.

Sacrifices of the Old Testament

Type of sacrifice What (elements)	Why (function)	Where (citation)
Holocaust or whole burnt offering		
Male and unblemished cattle, sheep and goats, birds (pigeons for the poor)	Because wholly consumed, it acknowledges God as Lord of life: atones for sins; joyful worship	Lv 1,1–17; 6,8–13; 8,18–21; 22,17
The grain (or cereal) offering		
Grain, flour, frankincense, oil, bread. Only symbolic portion burned, rest eaten by priests	Substitute for expensive animal offering; thanksgiving for good crops; joyful worship	Lv 2,1–16; 6,14–23
The peace offering		
Any unblemished animal—male or female (cattle or sheep and goats, but not birds since too small for group to eat)	A "well-being sacrifice"; not burned up, but eaten by offerers and families. Only fat parts (considered choicest) were burned to God	Lv 3,1–17; 7,11–34
Sin offering or "purgation offering"		
If offender were whole people or a priest: Bull; ordinary person: goat; poor: bird or some fine flour.	To atone for usually unintentional sin (violating something sacred)	Lv 4,1–5,13; 6,24–30
Blood sprinkled on altar in outer courtyard if lay offender; in holy interior if priest or whole people offended	Atone for loss of holiness Cleansing from impurity	
The guilt or reparation offering		
A ram sheep (its blood sprinkled on altar) The original wrong must be undone, then additional compensation must be offered to God.	While sin offering cleansed the defiled object or person, guilt offering is a "pay-back" to God for something we should have given or done—atonement to remove guilt	Lv 5,14–26; 7,1–6

Theology of Sacrifice
Expiation + dedication = fellowship OR Being forgiven + being committed = communion with God

Leviticus 8–10: The Anointing and Service of Aaron and His Sons

Chapters 25–31 of Exodus gave instructions about religious ritual that are finally put into practice in these chapters of Leviticus. (The instructions for the building of the Tent and Ark had already been followed by the end of Exodus, but those regarding sacrifice and the consecration of priests are not implemented until now.) Chapter 8 details the installation of Aaron and his descendants as priests of Israel. Chapter 9 narrates the first sacrifice, and Chapter 10 deals with infractions of the sacrificial rules.

All three chapters reinforce the message that sacrifices must be approached with deadly seriousness. Close attention to the details of ritual is absolutely necessary, for ritual improperly done will not bring the glory of the Lord into their midst. So serious is this requirement that two of Aaron's sons are struck dead for failing to follow ceremonial rules and approaching God's presence carelessly.

Priests are reminded always to distinguish between the sacred and profane, the clean and unclean. Among other ways, they are to do this by refraining from customs that show disrespect for God's holiness such as improper dress, stepping outside the Tent of Meeting, and drinking alcoholic beverages. Even excess zeal that violates sacrificial regulations is dangerous. Aaron's sons Eleazar and Ithamar, for example, had refused to eat the portion of the sacrifice to which they, as priests, had been entitled. They allowed it, instead, to be burnt as an offering to God. They were permitted to get away with this transgression only because they had given up to God what was rightfully theirs. Had it been the other way around, however, they might well have been struck dead.

These chapters reinforce the belief that idolatry is very alluring and the holiness of God easily transgressed. The role of the priests, then, becomes extremely important, for by their careful observance of religious ritual they help preserve the people's relationship with God.

Leviticus 11–15: The Laws of Purity

While the discussion of holiness and purity on page RG 65 deals with this topic, some additional comments may aid our understanding of this area that is so foreign to modern Christian experience.

These chapters deal with four types of uncleanness:

1. Animals	Lv 11,1–47
2. Childbirth	Lv 12,1–8
3. Contagious disease	Lv 13,1 – 14,57
4. Genital discharges	Lv 15,1–33

The many regulations that fill these chapters govern (1) which animals are and are not fit for eating, (2) when quarantine is necessary to deal with contagious diseases or infected homes,

Clean and Unclean

Various reasons are proposed for certain animals being designated clean and others unclean:

1. Medical: reducing exposure to infectious diseases and animals known to carry disease and parasites.
2. Religious: some animals are "defective" and fail to reflect God's original plan of creation.
3. Arbitrary: simply a means of setting Israel apart from its neighbors.

Note that Chapter 10 of Acts of the Apostles indicates there is nothing inherently wrong with the animals Leviticus labels unclean.

and (3) how purification is achieved by both men and women following sexual emissions. Though other purity regulations controlled the nation's life (see Ex 12–13 and Dt 20), those listed here deal with matters that come under the direct supervision of the priests.

The basis for all these laws is the belief that many areas of human life touch and express the mystery of God. Birth and death and sexuality are such holy areas because they are at the very heart of the divine mystery that controls our lives. As such, those areas cannot be defiled by anything impure or unworthy. Humans penetrate the set-apart world of the sacred not only on holy days, or when they enter a holy place or participate in rituals performed by a consecrated (and thus "holy") person, but also through common everyday moments that involve life and death—like the awesome experience of sexual activity and the sometimes dangerous loss of blood or other bodily fluids.

Reading through all the rules, you might begin to wonder why one animal is deemed clean and edible while another is not. Scholars vary in their opinions. Some say there is sound primitive science underlying the regulations reflected in such rules as the mandatory quarantine of persons with infectious diseases or the ban on pork—long recognized as a carrier of parasites. Others argue that the reason is religious. Some in this group insist certain animals are forbidden because they seem imperfect—freaks of nature perhaps, but certainly not what was intended in the creation. Fish that swim, birds that fly, and animals that graze are fully in God's plan, but flightless birds like ostriches, sea creatures that walk like animals, and animals that crawl close to the ground like insects seem to be aberrations, and must be shunned. Some scholars who hold for a religious basis for the division between clean and unclean think the divisions are mostly arbitrary—simply a way of making the Israelites different from other people. Canaanites used pigs in their worship, so for the Israelites they were forbidden. Sharing a meal was a very important part of Middle Eastern hospitality, but their strict dietary laws prevented the Israelites from being able to mix socially with their pagan neighbors. The best guess, perhaps, is that a blend of all these motivations influenced those who drew up the lists of clean and unclean foods.

Leviticus 16: The Day of Atonement

The feast of the Day of Atonement described in Chapter 16 was seen as a way of making up for all the instances of impurity that had defiled the land throughout the year. The description of this important ritual is the climax to all the preceding material from Chapter 1 onward regarding sacrifice, priestly service, and purity. At one level or other, all those issues deal with the need for atonement. Note how atonement was at the center of most religious practice: The sacrifices always included some atoning function; ritual mistakes requiring atonement were a constant danger in priestly service; and, of course, daily life presented innumerable opportunities for intentional and especially unintentional impurity that required atoning. With this constant need for atonement, it was certainly reassuring that once a year the wickedness and rebellion of all the people could be laid onto a goat that would carry the sins off into the wilderness.

The actual rite probably did not originate in Israel: Other ancient cultures observed the practice of laying the sins of the people onto an animal and then slaughtering it. The desert was the traditional place of evil and demons, so by banishing the goat into the desert the people, in effect, were telling it to "Go to hell!"

The instructions regarding the ritual end with the command to do this forever. In the ritual of Yom Kippur, celebrated annually by Jews each September–October, that command is still obeyed.

Scapegoat The term scapegoat is derived from the word Azazel (Lv 16,8), which possibly may have been a name of Satan that is used nowhere but in this book and chapter. Ancient editions translated the word as "the escaping goat," which eventually became the English word "scapegoat." Today it means anyone who is blamed for wrongs committed by others.

Leviticus 17–25: The Holiness Code

Chapter 1–16 dealt with ritual purity—all the behaviors and regulations that help overcome the natural barrier between God and humanity. Chapters 17–25 have a different focus: Rather than emphasizing what must be avoided in order to remain holy, they stress those positive things that must be done in order to grow in holiness.

While the long lists of laws in Chapters 1–16 dealt mainly with liturgical requirements, the sermon-like verses of Chapters 17–25 deal with the moral obligations of living in community. From how to worship a holy God, the focus has shifted to how to live a holy life. Because the Holiness Code of Chapters 17–25 resembles the homiletic style of the Book of Deuteronomy and the fiery oratory of the prophet Ezekiel, scholars think it may have been composed at the same time as these other writings, possibly around the time of the Babylonian Exile of 587 B.C.

The Code itself can be divided into two parts: Chapters 17–20 cover laws for living a just and holy life binding on all members of the community, and Chapters 21–25 deal mostly with priestly matters of public worship.

Though these lists might seem endless as you read them, remember that these (and the laws listed in Exodus, Numbers, and Deuteronomy) are the nation's entire collection of laws. Compared to modern lawbooks, these are remarkably short and easy to understand. Read the laws and you'll note they are not grouped in any systematic way—an inspiring law like the command to love your neighbor as yourself (Lv 19,18) stands beside one that tells you not to plant your field with two kinds of seed (Lv 19,19). A law forbidding turning your daughter into a prostitute is followed by one ordering observance of the Sabbath, which is followed by one about consulting mediums, and by another that says you should stand when an elderly person enters the room (Lv 19,30–32).

These laws comprise an *ideal* code, and it is likely that some of the laws were never really put into practice. For example, the Jubilee Year—which mandated that every fifty years debts were forgiven, Israelite slaves were set free, and all property leased or bought reverted to its original owners—may never actually have been practiced. But it does point to some remarkable characteristics of Israelite law.

Their laws established Israel as a nation apart, different from all their neighbors. Israel protected the rights of the weak and the poor. Punishment was not allowed to be excessive, but had to be proportionate to the crime ("An eye for an eye"). Sexuality was to be treated as sacred and not allowed to degenerate into immorality. What went on inside a person was as important as what went on outside—that is, your heart had to be pure as well as your actions. The poor could get justice just as readily as the rich, and even foreigners were assured fair treatment. And property rights never took precedence over human rights. Encoded in this system of laws was the belief that the followers of a compassionate God who "led them out of Egypt" must be known, in turn, for their own compassion and justice.

Leviticus 26: The Conclusion of the Holiness Code

This chapter ends both the Holiness Code and the entire book. The regulations regarding how to worship God and how to live as God's holy people have been spelled out. Blessings are promised for those who will obey the covenant, curses for those who will defy it.

The chapter reflects the postexilic attitude of the Priestly editors and shows signs of having been written with the benefits of hindsight: It predicts blessings but also the eventual curse of exile for disobedience. It also adds a promise of renewed blessing and assurance that God will not forget the covenant completely (Lv 26,45). The reference to "uncircumcised hearts" (Lv 26,41) also anticipates the spirit of the exilic prophets Jeremiah (see Jer 9,26) and Ezekiel, who announced that God was about to establish a new covenant that would be written on people's hearts. This covenant would be obeyed not out of fear of the law, but out of love of the Lord.

The upbeat and hopeful final verses of Chapter 26 were the original ending of Leviticus. Chapter 27 was added later to deal with the question of how to handle vows, sometimes rashly made, of dedicating certain people, animals, or objects to the Lord. When it was inappropriate to actually offer the vowed item, like a family member or an animal that was unclean, monetary value could be assigned to the item and the money, rather than the person or object itself, could be given over to the Lord.

Circumcision In Israel, the medical ritual practice of circumcision initiated a male into the covenant and nation and allowed him to participate in public worship. By speaking of "uncircumcised hearts," Leviticus is pointing out that more than a surgical procedure is needed to be a true follower of God. One's inner attitude is also critical. Moses (Dt 10,16) also calls the people to circumcise "the foreskin of their hearts" by loving the Lord and ending their disobedience. In essence, following the law is a call to a deeper relationship with God.

Questions for Discussion or Reflection

1. What is your attitude toward law? Do you see it as gift, burden, restriction, source of freedom? How does contemporary culture view law?
2. Where in your own life do you see signs of the pattern: forgiveness + dedication = communion with God. Do you think this is a necessary pattern? What forces in your life work against this equation?
3. Has your attitude toward Leviticus changed at all as a result of your reading? In what ways? What value, if any, do you find in reading through such long lists of laws?
4. From your reading of the scholarly opinions regarding the reason for the purity laws (health, religious, setting people apart), which reasons do you find most convincing and why? Can you find any practices in Catholic tradition that may have sprung from similar motivations?
5. How do you feel about the Hebrew attitude toward God's holiness, especially the extreme concern about not violating it? Is there anything of value here to guide contemporary Catholic liturgical practice? Is the call in Leviticus to be holy as God is holy realistic? Do you see it as a guiding principle in your life, the life of the Church? What changes woul you have to make in order to live this principle? What changes would church leaders need to make?

NUMBERS READING GUIDE

At a Glance

Who are the main players?	Moses Aaron and Miriam Joshua and Caleb Balaam Korah, Eleazar
What should I look for?	Grumbling and rebellion of the people Characterizations of God's wrath God's faithfulness despite people's sin Importance of priests and Levites in developing fidelity through proper ritual and holiness God's use of foreign prophet/magician Balaam
When did this take place?	During the 38 years of Israel's wanderings in the desert following the sealing of the covenant at Sinai
Where did these events occur?	Three main sites: 1. Mt. Sinai—preparing to set out for Promised Land 2. Kadesh—rebellion causes long delay, followed by eventual journey to Moab 3. The plains of Moab—readying to enter and conquer the Promised Land
Why was this book written?	To show the consequences of Israel's murmuring and rebellion against the Lord; that God's wrath is to be taken seriously, but God's grace and mercy always prevail, and God will be faithful to the promises made to the Patriarchs; that God's plan for Israel and all peoples will not be thwarted; that the call to holiness and purity cannot be ignored, especially by soldiers fighting a "holy war"; and that trust in God is not an option for God's people.

What's the story?

No sooner is the covenant at Sinai sealed, than the people start grumbling against the Lord. God punishes some, but Moses' prayers persuade God to spare the nation. Spies sent into the land of Canaan return with reports of giants and argue against invasion. Joshua and Caleb disagree, but the people refuse to move. Because of their lack of trust, God decides none of the generation that left Egypt will be allowed to enter the Promised Land. The "wandering" period begins and lasts till all adults who left Egypt have died in the desert (except Joshua and Caleb). God uses the pagan prophet Balaam to speak blessings on Israel as they prepare to enter the beautiful land of God's promise.

OVERVIEW OF NUMBERS

We will look first at some characteristics that give us a basic orientation to the Book of Numbers (while the English name refers to the census lists recorded in Chapters 1 and 26, the Hebrew name [*bemidbar,* "in the desert"] tells more about the content of the book).

The Book Recounts a Journey

The focus of all the stories and legal lists in Numbers is either on *preparation* for the journey, *problems faced* during the journey, or *attitudes* that *threaten* the journey from Mt. Sinai to the Promised Land. This journey is no ordinary trip. It is a journey of conquest, a military campaign that won't be completed until the end of the Book of Joshua. Most of the laws and the elaborate preparations for leaving Sinai deal with proper military behavior: Soldiers fighting a war for God had to meet special standards of holiness and single-mindedness.

Numbers Flows from Leviticus

Leviticus stressed the importance of holiness in the ordinary areas of life, such as food, clothing, sickness, morality, and worship. Numbers intensifies those expectations for holiness. It insists that Israel will succeed as a nation and live prosperously in the land only if the people are totally committed to God.

Numbers Combines Narratives and Laws

Exodus contained stories and laws; Leviticus mostly laws. Numbers again combines laws and stories. Significantly, each collection of laws relates to the lessons learned from the experiences narrated in the stories.

Finally, the Book Concentrates on the Promise of the Land

Genesis saw the promise of a son fulfilled. Now the land dominates Israel's thinking. As a great and fearsome force, the people advance against the enemy in the hope of finding prosperity and an end to the deprivation and suffering they experienced in the desert.

A CLOSE LOOK AT THE CHAPTERS OF NUMBERS

The structure of the Book of Numbers is dominated by Israel's movement toward the land that God first promised them in Genesis (12,1–3). The book is most commonly divided, in fact, into three large blocs that correspond to the major stages of that journey: (1) preparation, (2) journey through the desert, and (3) arrival at the borders of Promised Land. We will use these major divisions of the book to group the chapters and provide a summary of their contents.

Numbers 1,1 – 10,10: The Camp Prepares for a Holy War

Chapter 1: A census is taken of all males able to go to war; but Levites, who serve in the sanctuary, are exempted.

Chapter 2: The newly commissioned soldiers are organized into a military camp that can defend itself and move quickly in time of danger.

Chapter 3: The tribe of Levi is given the special role of dwelling around and caring for the tabernacle (and ark) at the center of camp. By being set apart in this way, the Levites substitute for the nation's firstborn males who were supposed to be set apart for the Lord. The entire fighting force, then, becomes a consecrated army linked to the holy service of God through the levitical substitutes.

Chapter 4: A list of the duties of the Levites for moving the holy objects of the sanctuary when marching.

Chapter 5: A list of laws regarding uncleanness, theft, adultery, and other sins that would defile the army's holy status as God's soldiers.

Chapter 6: A list of rules for the Nazirites – men who take strict vows of total dedication to the Lord (Samson, John the Baptist, and St. Paul are biblical characters who took the Nazirite vow). The preparation of the camp is completed and Chapter 6 ends with Aaron blessing the camp.

How Many Were There?

According to biblical numbers, some two million Israelites (including women and children) journeyed from Egypt to Canaan. But scholars have long debated the reliability of that figure. How could so huge a group live for 40 years in a desolate desert area? Could the Sinai peninsula feed such numbers – even with miraculous supplies of quail and manna? Would Egypt have dared to stand in the way of a fighting force of 600,000 men? Some scholars argue that the numbers are not to be understood literally. They claim there are various ways of interpreting the word "thousands" that do not yield the high mathematical totals that a literal reading demands. It is also quite possible that in telling the story, later generations cited numbers that proudly reflected the later and more stable situation of the time of King David. But, while the actual numbers may have been considerably lower than stated, the book's message that God miraculously led a large band of people through many trials and dangers to the safety of the Promised Land is not changed.

Chapter 7: These next four chapters deal with liturgical regulations for the sanctuary, including, in this chapter, sacrifices and gift-giving.

Chapter 8: Regulations regarding purification of Levites for their service and limits to their length of service.

Chapter 9: The Israelites celebrate the first anniversary of the Passover event and are told that the camp will be guided on the journey by the divine pillars of cloud and fire.

Chapter 10: This first major section concludes as the silver trumpets summon the people to leave Sinai with the ark leading the army of Israel.

Numbers 10,11–20,13: The Journey from Sinai to Canaan

Chapter 11: Numbers duplicates some of the grumblings already recorded in Exodus 13–18. The first incident of grumbling is punished by fire. But Moses intercedes and saves the people. Immediately the people complain again about lack of meat. An exasperated Moses asks for help in leading the people, and God instructs him to share his authority with seventy elders.

Chapter 12: Even his brother and sister challenge Moses' authority and so are punished with leprosy. But again, Moses intercedes and they are healed.

Chapter 13: The Israelites reach the southern borders of the Promised Land and advance straight into it. Scouts bring back reports of how rich the land is, but terrify the people with exaggerated claims about the fierceness of the inhabitants.

Chapter 14: Joshua and Caleb are willing to attack Canaan, but the people, full of fear from the scouts' report, first cower and then openly rebel against Moses. God threatens punishment, but relents at Moses' intercession. However, God decrees that no one of this generation shall enter the Promised Land except for Joshua and Caleb.

Chapter 15: Laws regarding sacrificial offerings and respect for the Sabbath that will guide the people once they possess the land are inserted here.

Chapter 16: Some Levites, possibly wanting more people to be permitted to function as priests, rebel against Moses and are punished by death.

Chapter 17: Through the miraculous budding of Aaron's staff, God's choice of Aaron as priest is confirmed.

Chapter 18: Following the discussion of Aaron's role of reconciling the people to God, laws are listed regulating the proper payment of priests and Levites for their service in the sanctuary.

Chapter 19: The theme of uncleanness has run through the preceding chapters, especially regarding those who approach the sanctuary. This chapter describes a ritual for preparing holy water to be used for purifying anyone who has become unclean.

Chapter 20: Recounts another grumbling incident—regarding lack of water—and this time even Moses and Aaron fail to trust God; as a consequence they are forbidden to enter the Promised Land.

Chapters 10 to 20 have emphasized several points:

1. The people's loyalty to God is very fragile.
2. In order to possess the land, the Israelites must remain pure in their actions and totally faithful to God.

3. The role of the priests is critical for maintaining Israel's purity and fidelity through proper ritual.

Numbers 20,14–36,13: Arrival at the Jordan River, and Preparation for Assault on the Promised Land

Chapter 21: Grumbling resumes and God punishes the people by means of poisonous snakes. Those bitten are healed by looking at a bronze serpent. The conquest of Canaan begins with Israel's defeat of the Amorites.

Chapter 22: Fearing the Israelites, the king of Moab hires the prophet, Balaam, to forecast evil for Israel.

Chapters 23–24: Balaam attempts to curse Israel, but God permits only blessings to come from his mouth. He foresees the greatness of Israel in the coming centuries and the destruction of Moab and Edom by King David.

Chapter 25: At Balaam's suggestion, Moabite women invite Israelite men to their orgiastic religious services where the men even offer sacrifice to the pagan gods. All who participated at Baal-peor in this violation of the first commandment are put to death.

Chapter 26: Repentant, the nation renews its dedication to the Lord, symbolized by a second census that calls forth fighting men for the war ahead.

Chapters 27–30: Before the fighting, however, another set of laws is set forth that will regulate Israel's future agricultural and urban life styles. These laws deal with duties of one family to another, inheritance laws for widows and daughters, and rules for religious celebrations in the new land.

Chapter 31: The fighting resumes with a major victory over Midian seen as revenge for the role Midian played in leading Israel into idolatry.

Chapter 32: Three of the tribes conquer land on the eastern side of the Jordan. Reluctantly, Moses allows them to keep it but demands a promise that they will help conquer Palestine when the time comes.

Chapters 33–34: The final chapters provide a summary. Chapter 33 lists all the stopping places along the forty-year journey from Egypt to Canaan. God solemnly warns Israel to take the land, to drive out its inhabitants and destroy all religious sites, and to divide the land among the tribes. Moses defines the land's generous boundaries (Nm 34,1–15).

Chapters 35–36: At the end of the book there is a series of laws that once again illustrate the nature of the stories that preceded them. They deal with tricky boundary issues; special cities for the Levites, towns set aside to provide asylum for accused persons; murders in territory between tribes; and property rights for women and the defenseless.

Conclusion

Throughout the book, stories are used to teach lessons. Clear connections are also made between present laws and the lessons of the past that made the laws necessary. Israel believed God was setting them apart as a nation unique among the nations of the earth. How could they retain this unique identity and resist the temptation to become like their neighbors? The answer was clear: by remembering their life in the desert and applying the lessons they had learned.

MAJOR RELIGIOUS TOPICS OF NUMBERS

While keeping the journey narrative moving forward, the Priestly editors of Numbers emphasize certain themes over others. Ritual and worship matters are very important, as are questions regarding the duties of priests and Levites. Laws governing conflicts over land also receive attention. But the themes that dominate are theological; that is, issues that center on God's power to fulfill the promise made to Abraham and the other patriarchs. Of these topics four require more detailed attention:

1. the authority of Moses, Aaron, and the elders
2. the people's murmuring and lack of trust
3. God's use of the prophet Balaam
4. the use of war to advance God's plan for Israel.

Moses and Aaron and Priests and Levites

The primacy of Moses in the Pentateuch can hardly be questioned. And yet that is exactly what the people did often during their journeys. Even his sister and brother questioned his right to sole authority. Moses says little in his own defense. He leaves that to God, and God does not disappoint. More than 150 times in Numbers we are told God spoke to Moses directly, and through him to Israel. Those who questioned Moses' role were reminded that God's relationship with Moses was unique.

Yet God does allow Moses to share the burden of leadership with Aaron and some elders of the community. Even a giant like Moses could not bear the weight of leading this fickle and complaining people all alone. Moses and Aaron were from the tribe of Levi, a tribe that got bad press in Genesis, where they were considered violent renegades. Exodus, however, points out that the Levites were the only tribe that did not worship the golden calf, and Deuteronomy adds that the Levites alone were faithful at Massah and Meribah where Moses struck water from the rock.

While the majority of Bible references speak of the Levites as temple assistants distinct from priests (who had to be descendants of Aaron), a few passages do refer to them as priests. It is possible that originally the Levites did perform some priestly functions, but then lost that role to a branch of Aaron's family.

Numbers renders the Levites high praise and presents four sets of regulations for their service:

1. Only they can carry the Ark of the Covenant (Nm 1,49–53) and other sacred objects. This was a high and holy privilege.
2. They are consecrated to God as substitutes for each firstborn male in the nation (who by law was to be set aside for God's service). Because of this honor, they cannot serve in the military nor own land.
3. In open rebellion, some Levites demand the right to be priests (Nm 16–17). But God punishes them severely, and the incident serves as a reminder that Levites are not to do priestly ministry.
4. Moses sets aside certain cities as refuge centers for people suspected of crimes (Nm 35,2–8). The Levites (in contradiction of other texts that say they never owned land) are given these towns. Here they probably served as administrators of justice and as priests for these small communities far removed from Jerusalem.

Instances of Grumbling and Rebellion

Nm 11,1	At Taberah, the people grumble against Moses; God sends consuming fire, but the people are spared through Moses' prayer.
Nm 11,4	At Kibroth-hattaavah, people grumble over lack of meat; first God sends a plague, but then miraculous quail for food.
Nm 12,1–16	Miriam and Aaron rebel against Moses' sole authority; Miriam is punished with leprosy, but later is healed by God.
Nm 14,1–38	At the very edge of the Promised Land, the people cringe in fear, refusing to attack and take possession of the land; they accuse Moses of leading them to their deaths. God decides none of them will ever enter the Promised Land.
Nm 16,1–36	Korah, Dathan, and Abiram lead 250 council members in open rebellion against Moses; they are destroyed by fire from heaven.
Nm 17,6–15	Again the people grumble against Moses and Aaron; God's threatened punishment is averted by Aaron's ritual action.
Nm 17,27–28	The Israelites express panic and despair.
Nm 20,2–13	People grumble about lack of water; Moses strikes the rock and God sends water, but Moses won't be allowed to enter the Promised Land.
Nm 21,4–9	More grumbling about food, so God sends poisonous snakes; all who are bitten are saved by looking at a bronze serpent made by Moses.

The Murmuring Tradition

In the desert, the people repeatedly grumble and rebel against God. The table above lists these incidents, some of which are also found in Exodus 14–18. The stories that most resemble each other are those in Nm 11,4 and Ex 16,3 and in Nm 20,1–13 and Ex 17,2, which might be borrowed from the J or E sources. But all the other instances of grumbling reflect the Priestly interest in showing how God punished the people and then allowed the leaders, Moses or Aaron, to intercede and save them.

Through all these grumbling incidents, the Priestly editors emphasize that the community must atone for sin and seek purification through *liturgy.* Even the bronze serpent episode is an example of healing through ritual action.

No Admittance! God's decision to bar the entire generation that left Egypt from entry to the Promised Land may seem harsh. But remember: God dramatically saved the Israelites from slavery, and yet many seemed actually to prefer that state of life. All those with the heart of a slave were then doomed to die in the desert. Only those who could appropriate the radical freedom God was offering could enter the land of promise.

The Balaam Oracles

A character who is as mysterious as he is fascinating takes the stage in Chapters 22 through 24. Balaam is no typical biblical prophet. He is more a magician-for-hire, a foreigner belonging to a nomadic clan who is well-known to and well-regarded by even the kings of his day. One king, Balak, tries to hire him to prophesy *against* Israel, but Balaam is able to utter only words of blessing for God's people: "How can I curse whom God has not cursed? . . . It is a blessing I have been given to pronounce" (Nm 23,8–20) and curses on their enemies.

Because the stories in Numbers seem to be a compilation of material from the J and E sources as well as the Priestly, we get two rather contradictory views of Balaam. Chapters 22–24 present him favorably as willing to do what the Lord asks of him, though even here there is a vague indication that Balaam was willing to be led more by greed than God's will (see footnote at Nm 22,22). Yet, after being rebuked by his own donkey (the only talking animal in the Bible), he does deliver four moving oracles about the destiny of Israel. God could use even this foreign prophet of questionable character to do the divine will.

In Chapter 31, however, we learn Balaam was slaughtered by the Israelites because he had led the people into sexual immorality and the worship of false gods. Even New Testament books seem to pick up on a tradition that Balaam was a false teacher motivated by greed. In all, nine biblical books refer to Balaam, a sign of the importance given him and the events he dominates. His prophecies confirm Israel's eventual victory in its battle for the Promised Land.

The Conquest by the Tribes

Numerous differences in the lists of tribes suggest that there is not a clear tradition about which tribes actually made up the original people of Israel. Compare the lists on the next page, noting the numeral beside each name which indicates the order in which the name appears on the actual list.

While most lists begin with Reuben, Jacob's firstborn son, others start with Judah, the chief tribe in the Priestly view. Most of the tribal lists that appear after the Book of Exodus omit the name of Joseph and include instead the names of his two sons, Ephraim and Manasseh, the grandsons Jacob had adopted as his own sons. In effect, then, there were *thirteen* tribes of Israel. But the lists never exceed twelve, because usually either Simeon or (more often) Levi is left off. Levi does not appear on most lists because, since it was not allotted territory in the Promised Land, it lost its status as a tribe, though it survived in Israel's history as a class of priestly assistants.

There are several clues in Numbers that indicate that relationships among the tribes were not always smooth: Joshua and Caleb quarrelled with the other scouts in Chapters 13–14, and Chapter 32 records how two and a half tribes wanted to remain on the east side of the Jordan River rather than enter Canaan. Their reluctance to fight may indicate that few actually joined the invasion with Joshua. The constant substitution of Ephraim and Manasseh for Joseph, on the other hand, may mean that it was these two tribes that were Joshua's best fighters and allies.

The Theology of the Priestly Writers

The end of the Book of Exodus already presented the P school's primary theology: God's presence in Israel will be found in the sanctuary (a tent during the desert years, a temple later).

Tribal Lists in the Books of Genesis, Numbers, and Deuteronomy

Gn 49,1–27	Nm 1,5–15	Nm 1,20–43	Nm 2,3–29; 7,12–83	Nm 13,4–15	Nm 26,5–50	Nm 34,19–28	Dt 33,1–29
Reuben 1	Reuben 1	Reuben 1	Reuben 4	Reuben 1	Reuben 1	—	Reuben 1
Simeon 2	Simeon 2	Simeon 2	Simeon 5	Simeon 2	Simeon 2	Simeon 2	*Levi* 3
Judah 4	Judah 3	Judah 4	Judah 1	Judah 3	Judah 4	Judah 1	Judah 2
Issachar 6	Issachar 4	Issachar 5	Issachar 2	Issachar 4	Issachar 5	Issachar 8	Issachar 8
Zebulun 5	Zebulun 5	Zebulun 6	Zebulun 3	Zebulun 7	Zebulun 6	Zebulun 7	Zebulun 7
Joseph 11	Ephraim 6	Ephraim 7	Ephraim 7	Ephraim 5	Ephraim 8	Ephraim 6	Ephraim 5
Levi 3	Manasseh 7	Manasseh 8	Manasseh 8	Manasseh 8	Manasseh 7	Manasseh 5	Manasseh 6
Benjamin 12	Benjamin 8	Benjamin 9	Benjamin 9	Benjamin 6	Benjamin 9	Benjamin 3	Benjamin 4
Dan 7	Dan 9	Dan 10	Dan 10	Dan 9	Dan 10	Dan 4	Dan 10
Asher 9	Asher 10	Asher 11	Asher 11	Asher 10	Asher 11	Asher 9	Asher 12
Gad 8	Gad 11	Gad 3	Gad 6	Gad 12	Gad 3	—	Gad 9
Naphtali 10	Naphtali 12	Naphtali 12	Naphtali 12	Naphtali 11	Naphtali 12	Naphtali 10	Naphtali 11

Israel's proper response to God's presence among them is observance of the laws of holiness and sacrifice. In Numbers, however, the P authors add important specifications about how this holiness is to be lived out: (1) through national institutions and (2) through relations among the tribes.

Moreover, Israel must never neglect its system of religious worship no matter what the circumstances. God will surely punish disobedience, but the intercession of priests and leaders can deter God's wrath and bring blessing. Most important, nothing can prevent God's will from being fulfilled and no one leader, not even Moses, is indispensable.

The end of Numbers finds the people still without a home, but equipped with all the tools of worship and obedience to enable them to hold on until God's promises are fulfilled. Now Moses can depart and the conquest begin. But, for editorial reasons, Moses' death is delayed till the end of Deuteronomy.

ESSAY

Holy War

For many modern readers that title may seem an oxymoron—a striking contradiction in terms. One might ask, "Can war ever be *holy?*" Numbers 31 says that God told Moses to take vengeance on the Midianites. Our ears may hear that order differently than did the writers and ancient readers of the Bible. What they heard was an expression of the life and death struggle between the Lord and the Canaanite gods. They were reminded that *in their founding days* God was a warrior who fought for them against their enemies. We might hear in that order a random decision to punish innocent people for the sake of God's "chosen people," Israel. But the Israelites heard something different. In their view, the Canaanites were a wicked and sinful people who deserved the punishment God was doling out to them through Israel. In Deuteronomy Moses bluntly tells the Israelites that "it is not because of your merits or the integrity of your heart that you are going in to take possession of their land; but the LORD, your God, is driving these nations out before you on account of their wickedness" (Dt 9,5). In the thrusting aside of the native people of Canaan, Israel also saw God fulfilling the promise of land made to the patriarchs.

But God did not victimize some innocent, unsuspecting nation. When, in Numbers 31, God ordered the destruction of all the Midianites, including the women, it was because they had been the ones who followed Balaam's advice and seduced the Israelites into fornication and idolatry at Baal-peor. We have already mentioned that one of the primary purposes of Israel's dietary and purity regulations was ensuring that the nation would be different from all its neighbors. To be different Israel had to be pure, and to be pure Israel had to avoid the infection of sexual excess and idolatry; and the best way to prevent contamination was to remove all possible sources of infection. Those are fierce standards. But Israel saw God inflicting equally brutal punishment on itself for its own unfaithfulness.

We must also recognize that the authors of these texts were trying to justify their conquests. It was therefore in their interest to emphasize that the war had God's command behind it, and that the inhabitants who were driven out deserved their fate. Some of the descriptions must be read bearing in mind that they were written by the winning side.

Deuteronomy 20 specifies restrictions for holy war that make it less than total massacre. Numbers, too, embodies some elements of this later attitude. Now, purity and obedience are to be the hallmarks of God's army, not vengeance. It seems as if the editors of Numbers were trying to soften the old stories of total war and call instead for a total commitment of life to God. The stories of old were plenty exciting, but they were not to be models for present behavior! Over the centuries Israel's theology of war developed, as reflected in the teachings of several prophets who said that war was not the way to do God's will (see Is 7,1–14; Hos 10,13f; Jer 21,3–10; Jer 34,1–5). In Numbers we find the earlier and later viewpoints on war mixed together.

Questions for Discussion or Reflection

1. As you ponder the forty-year journey of the Israelites through the desert, what insights do you get about your own journey: the ebb and flow of your relationship with God, the ups and downs in your own commitment?
2. How has your reading of Numbers affected your way of viewing the role of priests and the function of liturgy in the contemporary church?
3. What do you make of God's use of Balaam? The overall biblical judgment of Balaam is negative. Does this seem justified to you? What do you think caused Balaam to go from being an apparent convert to being the slaughtered victim of the Israelites?
4. Why do you think Israel kept alive the "murmuring tradition"? What lessons did they learn from that part of their history? What do those events teach you?
5. Could you use the words *holy* and *war* in the same sentence? How did Israel grow in their understanding of God's use of war? What insights does Christianity bring to that conversation?

DEUTERONOMY READING GUIDE

At a Glance

Who are the main players?	Moses Joshua
What should I look for?	Treaty/covenant structure of the book Review of Israel's history and God's saving activity Warm, personal tone of the writing Stress on God's love for the people Emphasis on laws and teaching of laws to children
When did this take place?	At the end of the forty years of wandering, as Israel prepares to enter the Promised Land
Where did these events occur?	The river Jordan's east bank, in the territory of Moab where the Jordan meets the Dead Sea
Why was this book written?	To remind the Israelites of God's great love for them, of the mighty saving deeds God had performed for them, and that they must choose fidelity to the covenant in order to reap its benefits
What's the story?	Poised to enter the land of promise, the Israelites hear three major speeches from Moses, who takes a final opportunity to admonish and instruct the people before his death. The book is a lengthy sermon in which Moses, like an elderly parent, tells his children what really matters and encourages them to choose carefully and well. Having done so, he blesses the tribes and goes off to die.

READING THE BOOK OF DEUTERONOMY

We can start our examination of the last book of the Pentateuch by naming some of its special characteristics. First, the book is structured like one of the suzerain-vassal treaties typical of the ancient Near East. Second, the theology of Deuteronomy also runs through the historical books of Joshua, Judges, Samuel, and Kings, making Deuteronomy a kind of preface to these books. Third, Deuteronomy has a distinctive style that sets it apart from all the other writing in the Pentateuch: It reads like a sermon, spoken entirely by Moses, full of urgent pleas for obedience and thundering warnings about what will happen if the people don't obey the law. Fourth, scholars believe Deuteronomy was written about the 7th century B.C., long after the time of Moses, so it is really looking backward at Israel's history even though it is written as if it were looking ahead to Israel's movement into the land.

We will examine these and other features shortly, but first let us look at the basic outline of the book. Some commentators divide the book very simply into three major addresses of Moses:

1. First Address: Review of Israel's History (1,1 – 4,43)
2. Second Address: God's Covenant and Elaboration of the Law (4,44 – 26,19)
3. Third Address: Moses' Summary and Farewell (27,1 – 33,29)
   Death and Burial of Moses (34,1–10)

This simple outline makes clear that the core of the book is in fact a new presentation of the law that restates many of the laws presented earlier in Exodus through Numbers (*Deuteronomos* is Greek for "second law" or "repetition of the law").

The Covenant Structure of the Book

Another way of viewing the shape of the book is provided by its vassal-treaty format. There were six typical parts to a covenant treaty between kings and vassals which, in a vague way, also can be found in the structure of the first thirty chapters of Deuteronomy. The six parts are listed here with indications of where the same pattern can be found in Deuteronomy. As you can see, the treaty-document structure of the book is incomplete because there is no mention of other gods witnessing the sealing of the treaty, but since there *are* no other gods besides the Lord, that role could not be filled.

1. A preamble that identified the great king giving the treaty	Dt 1,1
2. A historical prologue listing his gracious deeds to the lesser king/vassal	Dt 1, 2 – 4, 43
3. The legal stipulations binding on the lesser king/vassal	Dt 4,44 – 26,19
a. Introduction and warnings	Dt 4,44 – 11,32
b. The laws in detail	Dt 12,1 – 26,19
4. The provisions for public reading of the document	Dt 27,8
5. The list of gods who witnessed the treaty	none
6. The curses and blessings that will come to those who break or keep the treaty	Dt 27,1 – 28,68

The book bears a resemblance to two other types of ancient writing: the farewell speech of a great leader, and an aging father's wisdom passed on to his son. Most likely, Deuteronomy is a combination of these two kinds of literature, which accounts for the very personal, tender, and parental tone of the writing.

The Unique Style of the Book

From beginning to end, Deuteronomy has the feel of an extemporaneous first-person speech. Unlike the other books of the Pentateuch which show evidence of being patchwork quilts of material drawn together from the J, E, and P sources, Deuteronomy stands alone as an independent source. Even its vocabulary differs from that of the other books. Certain phrases that are repeated often throughout the book help establish Deuteronomy's special character. Note the following examples:

1. These are the ordinances, statutes, and decrees which the Lord, your God, has enjoined on you (cf. 4,45; 5,1; 6,20; etc.); take care to observe them (4,5; 5,1; 6,3; 7,12; 8,1; etc.)
2. You must learn them, or teach them in the land (5,1; 5,31; 11,19; etc.) and teach them to your children (4,9; 4,10; 11,19; etc.)
3. In the land you are about to enter to possess (5,31; 6,1; 6,10; 6,18; 9,5; etc.)
4. So that you might live long and prosper (4,40; 5,33; 6,2f; 6,24; 11,9; etc.)
5. You will love the Lord your God with all your heart and soul (6,5; 10,12; 11,13; etc.)
6. Do not turn aside after other gods to serve them (6,14; 7,4; 8,19; 11,16; etc.)
7. Do not forget the Lord (8,11; 6,12; etc.)
8. I set before you today a blessing and a curse (11,26; cf. 30,19)
9. The land which the LORD swore to our fathers (6,10; 6,18; 6,23; 7,13; 10,11; etc.); a land flowing with milk and honey (6,3; 11,9; etc.)
10. Do what is right and good (6,18; cf. 12,28; 13,19; etc.)

The repeated use of these phrases and the overall repetitive style of Deuteronomy contributes to the extemporaneous feel of the writing. It sounds like a preacher working hard to get a message across. This is persuasive oratory whose goal is to make its audience choose and change. By referring constantly to the land as "flowing with milk and honey . . . a good land . . . a land that God swore to your ancestors," and by constantly recalling God's good deeds toward Israel, especially God's help against foreign opposition, Deuteronomy's intense and repetitive language helps make the book's main point: The people must be obedient when they take possession of the land.

The Historical Perspective of the Book

Some people may assume that Israel was always run like a theocracy where knowledge and observance of the law could be taken for granted. They may also assume that the Bible, as we know it today, was always available to guide the people of ancient Israel. The reality, of course, was much different. As this reading guide has often pointed out, the books we now call the Pentateuch did not exist as we now know them until late in Israel's history; probably the J and E sources were not pulled together to form Genesis, Exodus, Leviticus, and Numbers until the reign of King Hezekiah (715–687 B.C.). What existed before the books were formalized and finalized were stories, traditions, laws, and legends which were mostly passed on orally and, if they were written at all, were available to very few.

Most scholars agree that Deuteronomy is not as old as the sources that were pulled together to make up the rest of the Pentateuch. Instead, it was first written centuries after Moses in an attempt to inspire Israel to remember and renew its commitment to the covenant Moses had negotiated between the people and God. But despite its claim to be God's chosen people, Israel often failed in its covenant commitments; sometimes, in fact, it seemed to forget it ever had made commitments to God.

ESSAY

Obedience = Reward: Is It That Simple?

Deuteronomy seems to offer a very simple formula for life: obey and you'll be rewarded; disobey and you'll be punished. The national history of Israel as presented by the biblical writers, though often with the benefit of hindsight, would indicate that the formula basically worked. It is hard to say whether or not Israel would have received constant blessing if they had remained consistently faithful, because theirs is a story of forgetfulness and infidelity more than of loyal obedience. But what is clear is that Israel saw moments and enjoyed periods of great blessing only to watch them dissolve into times of tragic misfortune (a pattern that especially dominates the Book of Judges).

Moses clearly states that God had established a special relationship with Israel and that Israel's part of the bargain was to live by the covenant made at Sinai. But God's self-disclosure to Israel and all believers develops throughout the Old Testament. In fact, even the understanding in Deuteronomy that God will act on behalf of Israel only if the people keep their part of the treaty, is a development of earlier theologies that saw God as a warrior who would fight for Israel no matter what. In their infancy as God's people, Israel perhaps needed a mighty, warrior God who would destroy their enemies, solve their problems, and reward their every good deed. But they learned to view God differently.

It would be naive for Christians today to think they could live by Deuteronomy's simple formula of "do good and be blessed." Christians believe that Jesus continued God's self-revelation. From Jesus we learn that while peace is promised—a peace the world does not understand—it is also a peace that we can, indeed must, find even in the midst of trial, suffering, and possibly persecution. Jesus warned his followers to expect poverty and rejection, and to expect it most when they are most faithful! One of the great truths of the Christian tradition, which some Christians seem eager to ignore, is that pain and suffering are an inevitable part of the journey to union with God. Much as we would like it to be otherwise, these are necessary ingredients for the growth and maturity of any Christian. Without them our life is usually out of balance; we are tempted to think we don't need God anymore. Pain often provides a corrective to indifference and self-indulgence. Despite our fear of it, it may be said that we need to suffer. We could not have the courage to say this if the God we worship had not been crucified. But from Jesus we learned that death leads to life. And so we can risk following him knowing there are no guarantees except his love, support, and final peace.

Such a time was the reign of the idolatrous King Manasseh, who ruled Judah longer than any other king (687–642 B.C.). The king who followed him after a brief period, Josiah (640–609 B.C.), initiated a reform. He rejected the idolatry of his predecessor and called for renewed obedience of the law. It was during his reign that the Book of Deuteronomy first appeared. The story goes that during the rebuilding of the Temple a "Book of the Law" was found that greatly moved the young king: Upon hearing it read aloud, he tore his garments and wept. Immediately he consulted a well-known prophetess, Huldah, who declared the book's message authentic. Convinced more than ever, the king fully embraced the book's program of reform and called the nation to repentance.

Was Deuteronomy this "Book of the Law" found in the Temple? Most scholars think so. One reason for their assumption is that the reform program Josiah undertook (as described in 2 Kings 23) contains all the same elements laid down in the law code of Deuteronomy (Chapters 12–26). If Deuteronomy did serve as Josiah's blueprint for reform, then at least the core of the present book was known by 622 B.C.

But the detective work is not yet complete. Closer examination of Deuteronomy reveals that it strongly resembles ideas and books that were brought to Judah from the northern kingdom of Israel (the kingdom was split in two after Solomon's reign, with the northern ten tribes becoming Israel, and the two southern tribes becoming Judah). Almost 100 years earlier, in 722 B.C., Israel was destroyed by the Assyrians and many leaders, including those who had attempted reform in the North, fled to the southern kingdom. With them they brought ideas that can be found in Deuteronomy: the love of God, the covenant as relationship, the imagery of a father leading a son. In addition, Deuteronomy expresses doubt about the king's faithfulness, which is more typical of a northern viewpoint than of the South where the beloved King David had ruled. Other factors also point to the possibility that the deuteronomic tradition may have taken its earliest shape in the North.

Interestingly enough, a reform similar to Josiah's had been started in Judah nearly 100 years earlier by King Hezekiah, around 715 B.C. But did Hezekiah know about the teachings of Deuteronomy back then? It is just possible that the refugees who had fled the destruction of the North only seven years earlier brought with them the fundamental deuteronomic teachings, traditions, and laws, and that these influenced Hezekiah's reform.

But one hundred years passed between the reigns of Hezekiah and Josiah. What happened to Deuteronomy during that time? Since the unfaithful king Manasseh reigned during the bulk of those years, and since he violently opposed reform, the book may have been lost, or, most likely, it may be that the reformers hid the already written book, or just kept it to themselves until a more receptive king took the throne.

The Development of the Religious Perspective of the Book

This understanding of the possible historical development of Deuteronomy leads us to a discussion of how its religious outlook may have developed. After the North and South went their separate ways following the death of Solomon (about 930 B.C.), the northern kingdom, Israel, soon fell into the worst forms of idolatry. Of course there were voices of protest against the infidelity, most likely coming from the followers of the prophets Elijah and Elisha, who violently opposed the pagan cults, and from the levitical priests whose job it was to teach and maintain the covenant. These groups put together a restatement of the law that clearly warned the people that if they did not keep the covenant, they would lose the land.

Assyria proved the reformers right when it destroyed the North in 722 B.C. Left homeless, many fled to Judah where Hezekiah would soon become king. Though their stories of disobedience-leading-to-disaster impressed Hezekiah and his priests, a strange irony prevented the reform ideas from taking hold. In 701 B.C. Assyria attempted to invade even Judah, but the small nation was miraculously spared. The people's conclusion: God is so much on our side that we have nothing to fear; God promised never to abandon David's dynasty nor his city, Jerusalem, so no matter what we do, God will protect us. They couldn't have been more wrong.

The *Shema* Perhaps the most important, and certainly the most quoted, statement of belief for Israel was what is called the *Shema,* verses 4–9 of Chapter 6 of Deuteronomy: "Hear, O Israel! The LORD is our God, the LORD alone! Therefore, you shall love the LORD, your God, with all your heart, and with all your soul, and with all your strength. Take to heart these words which I enjoin on you today. Drill them into your children." It was this commitment that the northern kings neglected and forgot and which brought about the destruction of the North and, later, the South.

By the time of Josiah, the Assyrian empire was falling apart, so Judah began to retake the old northern kingdom of Israel. After the discovery of the book in the Temple, Josiah decided to use Deuteronomy's reform program to try to draw the half-believing northerners into a unified nation. It was at this point that the book was enlarged to its present size, except for its opening and closing chapters.

Concerns peculiar to the South were now added to those that were more characteristic of the North. So in addition to its harsh criticism of pagan gods, its warlike strategy against Canaanite religion, and its strong endorsement of Moses as a charismatic leader, Deuteronomy now took on two more emphases: (1) the necessity of a single place of worship where God's name would dwell (Dt 12,1–14), and (2) the frequent use of the verb *choose,* particularly in reference to God's special choice of the house of David and of the Temple of Jerusalem as the divine dwelling place.

During or shortly after the reign of Josiah, the followers of Deuteronomy used the deuteronomic standards of obedience-in-the-land as a lens through which to look at the entire history and at each ruler of Israel from Joshua down to their own time. They wrote a history of Israel in which all their leaders and past events were judged according to the principles set down in Deuteronomy. The reforming power of the book was now evident not only in its own pages, but also in the pages of Joshua, Judges, 1 and 2 Samuel, and 1 and 2 Kings.

IMPORTANT THEMES OF DEUTERONOMY

The Importance of the Covenant

While Deuteronomy has the shape of a vassal treaty, it is also written like a speech of Moses, which reminds the people of God's miraculous care for them in the desert. It also casts God in the role of loving father caring for his son, and as a mother giving life to her child. The father-son language is typical of covenant treaties of the times, which used love as the motivation for loyalty between the parties. In Deuteronomy, love and fidelity are everything!

Strong Words The influence of Deuteronomy is seen even in the life of Jesus. His responses to Satan's three temptations all come from Deuteronomy (6,13; 6,16; 8,3). In the desert preparing for his mission, Jesus draws on the lessons Israel learned during its own desert experience to set the course of his journey.

Jesus also quoted Deuteronomy when asked what was the greatest commandment (the *Shema*). In all, twenty-one New Testament books quote Deuteronomy almost 100 times, a testimony to its great influence. But that influence is found more in the basic themes of the New Testament than in any specific quotes. Jesus' whole ministry is an embodiment of the deuteronomic attitude of total dedication to God, as well as Deuteronomy's other core teachings: God's love and fatherhood, doing more than the minimum the law requires, and letting faith guide us to choose obedience over disobedience. The New Testament authors learned from Deuteronomy to value singlemindedness and to see all of life as an integrated whole.

The Law Is Not Simply Laws, but Total Commitment

In contrast with Exodus, Deuteronomy talks frequently about *why* laws need to be obeyed. And the reason is love. Before Deuteronomy, the Pentateuch seldom mentions that word as a motive for following the covenant, but this book repeatedly speaks of God's love for the people and their need to respond in kind. In Exodus obedience was a duty, in Deuteronomy it is an act of love. God gave the law for the people's good, much the way a father would lay out rules for a child out of concern for his or her welfare. The emphasis on knowing, teaching, reading, and writing the law is not a sign of legalism, but a reflection of the deeper and more permanent commitment to the Lord that lies beneath.

The Land and God's Blessing Are Conditional

On page RG 84 is an essay that describes how Israel learned that God's promise of blessing depended on whether or not they kept the covenant: Blessing and curse follow obedience and disobedience. The people of Israel learned that lesson from the events of their lives. Another lesson they had to learn was that even God's gift of the land could be taken away if they misused it or failed to create a just and honest society. By writing Deuteronomy as a farewell speech given by Moses in the desert, the authors make his warnings come from a period *before* the people took possession of Canaan. The writers are saying: Remember what it was like to have no land? Well, that could be the case again if you don't heed Moses' warnings. The book may have been most influential once the exile began (about 587 B.C.), since then readers could see that this tragedy resulted from their failure to obey the Lord as Moses had warned. It spoke to their misery and to their repentant hearts!

There Is To Be One Sanctuary

One of the objectives of Deuteronomy is to focus the people's attention on Jerusalem as the central place of worship so that they would not be distracted by local shrines and cult centers that often had pagan connections. But since, at the time that Moses is supposedly speaking, the choice of Jerusalem as the nation's capital by King David is still hundreds of years off, the city is never mentioned by name, only alluded to with such references as "the place which the LORD, your God, chooses as the dwelling place for his name" (12,11) and "the place which the LORD chooses from among your tribes" (12,14).

Deuteronomy Updates the Covenant Law

We've already mentioned that many of the laws listed in Deuteronomy are a restatement of the laws found in Israel's earliest law code, the "Covenant Code" found in Exodus 20,22–23,33. But there is also a difference. In Deuteronomy the laws are stated in a way that addresses the town and city life that had developed in Israel during the centuries since the Exodus. These laws have been fine-tuned to meet the needs of people living under conditions very different from those of the times when the laws were originally written. They accent the obligations of people to each other and especially to the weak and dispossessed, a need that became more visible and pressing once city life developed.

Conclusion

By the time Deuteronomy was written, Israel was no longer a loose-knit alliance of desert tribes. It had become a kingdom. In this new life situation, Israel needed a reinterpretation and summary of the meaning of the events told in the other books of the Pentateuch. Deuteronomy provides this summary in the form of a "repetition of the law." But Deuteronomy does more than look back at its history, it also anticipates its future in the land, which will be narrated in the historical books that follow. Thus Deuteronomy links those books written by historians from its own school of thought with the earlier Pentateuch traditions. The diagram below illustrates this relationship.

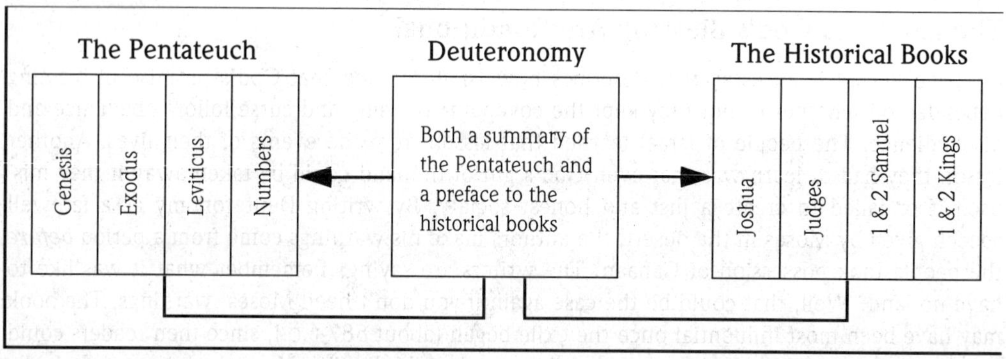

Questions for Discussion or Reflection

1. Scholars claim that Deuteronomy was written near the end of Israel's life as an independent kingdom, hundreds of years after Moses. Why then is it written as if it were composed by Moses himself? Does this feel dishonest to you? Does it change your understanding and/or appreciation of the book?

2. Moses reminds the people that God chose them not because of their merit, but out of pure love (see 7,7; 9,5; and 9,24). Do you ever feel chosen simply out of love, or do you feel your have to try to earn God's favor through goodness and fidelity?

3. The kingdom of Judah had begun to think that God would never abandon David's dynasty nor the city of Jerusalem. What aspects of the contemporary church do you feel God would never abandon? Have there been seemingly eternal aspects of church life that God let go of in the past?

4. Deuteronomy presents the motivation that underlies the similar laws found in Exodus calling for obedience out of *love* rather than *duty.* Which motivation do you think is at the core of your own observance of the law?

5. Deuteronomy contains some strong messages about the importance of justice for the health of society. Concern for the poor and weak is incorporated into the laws of the land. What contemporary laws embody this same concern? Is it appropriate for civil laws to demand concern for the needy?

The Historical Books

The story of the Israelite people is told in three major units of the Bible: the Pentateuch, the deuteronomistic history, and the chronicler's history. You won't find these designations used in the Bible itself, however, because they are divisions identified by scholars who see a unity among certain groups of books. By studying the writing style, subject matter, and major themes of each book, scholars are able to conclude that a major collection was put together by one person or a small group working together.

The ancient authors of the Bible usually began by collecting and organizing stories and oral traditions that already existed. Since each major section of the Bible covers centuries of history, it is not possible for any section to be a single person's eyewitness account. The ancient writers turned the preexisting materials with which they started into the final form that became the Bible. Sometimes they did this by simply taking over the old stories with little or no change; other times they rewrote the original story. Scholars often can tell the difference between the older material the writer started with and the final form given to the writing. Both are important. The *older* material tells us what had been valued by the ancient tradition. The *final form* tells us what the author thought was important and worth emphasizing at the time the collection was being shaped.

The reading guides up to this point have dealt with the Bible's first five books, the Pentateuch. The next section of the reading guide will deal with seven books (Joshua, Judges, 1 and 2 Samuel, and 1 and 2 Kings [Ruth is a later addition]) which are called the *deuteronomistic history* because the Book of Deuteronomy serves as a kind of preface to the whole collection. The last group of historical books (1 and 2 Chronicles, Ezra, and Nehemiah) begins with the Books of Chronicles and therefore is called the *chronicler's history.* By telling the same story from different perspectives, the Bible gives us a clue that we have much to learn not just from the story itself, but also from its unique point of view.

THE DEUTERONOMISTIC HISTORY

Joshua, Judges, 1 and 2 Samuel, and 1 and 2 Kings

The books we commonly refer to by these titles and treat as independent works are actually part of a continous story that starts in Genesis and ends in 2 Kings. However, these historical books existed as an independent unit, with the Book of Deuteronomy as its preface, long before the Genesis-to-Kings collection was pulled together into its present form. But even before they became a unit, the individual works of this deuteronomistic history also existed independently as stories and traditions (also referred to as "sources") which sometimes were written and sometimes were known only in oral form.

It is clear that the deuteronomistic writers who wrote the history of Israel used such sources. They even mention some of their sources (none of which have survived) in the history itself: "The Book of Jashar" (Jos 10,13), "The Book of the Chronicles of Solomon" (1 Kgs

11,41), "The Book of the Chronicles of the Kings of Judah" (1 Kgs 14,29), and "The Book of the Chronicles of the Kings of Israel" (1 Kgs 14,19).

The deuteronomistic writers did not force their original sources to blend into one completely consistent story. They did not even try to blot out the contradictions, inconsistencies, or duplications that resulted from combining several sources. While they did impress an overall unity or perspective on the material they brought together, they also respected their sources and allowed them to speak for themselves, even if that meant letting them disagree with each other.

Deuteronomic Vision of the Pattern of Israel's History

1. God's offer of love
2. Israel's faithlessness and sin
3. God's just punishment
4. Israel's repentance and cry for help
5. God's forgiveness and mercy
6. Israel's renewed sinfulness

DATE AND PURPOSE OF THE DEUTERONOMISTIC HISTORY

The final edition of the deuteronomic books was most likely put together during and after the exile that followed the destruction of Jerusalem in 586 B.C. Much of it, however, may already have been written down during the reign of Josiah, the reformer King of Judah (d. 609 B.C.). This dating helps us to understand, in part, the overall purpose of the history, which was to explain why the nation collapsed and why the people were led into exile. God did not abandon the covenant, says this history; the people did. Israel deserved destruction because of its sin. By refusing to heed God's constant warnings and shows of mercy, Israel sealed its fate. God was not obligated to stand by one particular country or king. Without the people's voluntary fidelity to the covenant, all bets were off.

The history, however, is not essentially a pessimistic work. Signs of hope can be detected in the repeated calls for repentance and in the high value the authors place on God's promise to David of an everlasting dynasty. The recurring pattern in Israel's history of sin, punishment, cry for help, and deliverance told the people that despite their sin and God's punishment, deliverance was possible again, *if* they returned to the Lord and asked for help.

THE LITERARY CHARACTER OF THE DEUTERONOMISTIC HISTORY

The cliches and repetitions used by the deuteronomistic writers make their style easy to recognize, though it is more noticeable in the original than in any translation.

The deuteronomistic writers pulled together the sometimes detailed and well-written and sometimes sketchy stories of Israel's kings; then they added long speeches that would help readers understand the theological significance of each of the stages of Israel's history. The speeches (Jos 1,11–15; Jos 23; 1 Sm 12; 2 Sm 7; 1 Kgs 8,14–61), which usually are put into the mouths of main characters at critical moments of Israel's past, impose a religious interpretation on the events of Israel's history. They express the vision that God's initial offer of love was followed by Israel's sin, which was followed by God's mercy, only to be followed by more sin.

Typical Deuteronomistic Phrases

"to follow other gods"
"to serve other gods"
"the city that the LORD has chosen"
"to sacrifice and burn incense at high places"
"you will know that the LORD alone is God"
"to walk in the ways of the LORD"
"to keep all the commandments"
"to provoke the LORD to anger"

Besides "looking back" and explaining why things happened as they did, these speeches also "look forward" to Israel's future and urge the people to live differently. Past and future are viewed through the same glasses: If Israel obeys the law all goes well; if it does not, it is punished.

THEOLOGICAL CONCERNS OF THE DEUTERONOMISTIC HISTORY

While it would be difficult to reduce the theology of the deuteronomistic writers to one simple statement, certain key elements do stand out. The Book of Deuteronomy, which sets the tone for this whole history, asked the people to choose between life and death, between blessing and curse, with clear consequences resulting from each option. The deuteronomistic writers saw all the events of Israel's history either as *blessings* that flowed from their obedience or as *curses* that resulted from disobedience of the law, the foremost of which was the first commandment: "I, the LORD, am your God . . . you shall not have other gods besides me" (Dt 5,6–7). The reign of each king of Israel, in fact, was evaluated according to how faithful he and the nation had been to this single law.

By constantly interpreting Israel's history as the fulfillment of God's promises to bless or curse in response to the people's level of fidelity, these books take on a prophetic quality. Indeed, the prophets play a very prominent role in this history, for it is they who make sure God's warnings and promises are never forgotten in Israel and who draw the connections between the people's behavior and the consequences they suffered. For this reason, Jewish tradition refers to these books as "Former Prophets" rather than as "Historical Books."

By recognizing the theological agenda of the deuteronomistic writers, we can better understand that what we have here is not a complete history of Israel, but a theological history told from the particular viewpoint of the deuteronomistic writers: Obedience brings prosperity, disobedience brings destruction.

One Law

Despite repeated references to keeping the laws, commandments, and statutes, for the deuteronomistic writers all laws are reducible to one: Worship the LORD and the LORD alone. Even the writers' interest in centralized worship in the Jerusalem Temple is a reflection of their concern for obedience of this one law.

ESSAY

Needed: Bible "Quadrafocals" to Correct 21st-Century Vision

People who have to wear glasses or contacts easily understand the concept of corrected vision. Even those with so-called perfect or 20/20 vision may have used a magnifying glass or binoculars to see something clearly that was beyond the normal range of our eyes.

We also need "lenses" that correct our way of seeing things to read the Bible with greater understanding. Unfortunately we can't take the prescription to the optical shop to buy such lenses, but we can use the prescription to form lenses of awareness for ourselves.

When we approach a biblical text, we need at least "quadrafocals" or four corrections for our modern day vision:

1. Sometimes the reader thinks that the words of the Bible were written down just as an event was happening and have been passed on always as a written text. So the first correction makes us aware that most of the material was originally spoken, whether we're dealing with a prophet's oracle or a gospel story.
2. The next correction reminds us that this spoken message was passed on by word of mouth many times and over long periods of time. This process of handing on the message means that it was adapted to the situation of those who passed it on.
3. Eventually, the message was written down. Once again the prescription calls for an awareness of the situation of the writer's community. The present-day reader needs to recall when and where was this written, and what was going on that caused this particular passage or book to be saved in writing.
4. Many texts require yet another correction because they have been collected and edited at a much later date and under different circumstances than the original writing. This is true of many parts of the Bible, for example, the Pentateuch, the Prophets, the Psalms, and the New Testament. Editing raises more questions. Why are the texts arranged this way? Were new parts written and added at the time of the editing? Did the editor strengthen or soften a phrase to fit the community's theology?

There seems to be no end to this process of correcting our vision. It is like the systems theory which says that when you change one thing, everything in the system changes. (For example, when one piece of furniture is moved in a living room, often the whole room gets rearranged.) Once "quadrafocals" have been worn, the faithful reader often experiences the need for a fifth or sixth lens.

One might say that following this prescription is too hard or too complicated. There is help. Corrective lenses are provided by commentaries and study guides. It is true that studying ancient texts from a culture and in a language very different from our own is hard work, but centuries of believers attest to the value of struggling with the word of God.

HOW TO READ THE DEUTERONOMISTIC HISTORY

In referring to this work as a history we must be clear about what we mean by that designation (see also RG 20). All history writing is a process of selection, organization, and interpretation. No history simply tells what happened. Every history tells some of the things that happened, while leaving out other things. That very selection process imposes an interpretation on the events. History is never objective in a strict sense because the facts it presents can't exist in isolation from the way a historian uses them.

The deuteronomistic writers have taken many stories and combined them to form one story that communicates a fairly simple message to its audience: Learn from the past. Therefore, the focus of our study will not be on what actually happened, but on what the writers were trying to teach through the events they recounted.

JOSHUA READING GUIDE

At a Glance

Who are the main players?	Joshua Rahab the prostitute Achan Caleb Eleazar, son of Aaron Phineas the high priest
What should I look for?	The superiority of faith over military might Punishment of evil; reward of good Joshua's leadership Israel's God-given success The people's fidelity and careful observance of the law The book's pervasive sense of hope
When did this take place?	During the period following the wandering in the desert, beginning c. 1250 B.C. or 1406 B.C.
Where did these events occur?	In the land of Canaan—the land promised to Abraham—which is today's Israel
Why was this book written?	To record Israel's conquest of Canaan and the fulfillment of God's promise to give Israel the Promised Land
What's the story?	Still camped east of the Jordan River, the Israelites spy on Jericho, then prepare to march across the river. Joshua leads many successful campaigns of conquest in northern, southern, and central Canaan. Finally conquered, the land is allotted to the tribes. Joshua makes a farewell speech during which the covenant is renewed. Joshua dies and is buried.

FORMATION OF THE BOOK OF JOSHUA

The editing work of the deuteronomistic writers is apparent in the distinctive vocabulary and theological perspective that crop up throughout the book (see Jos 1,1–18; 8,30–35; 12; 21,43–22,6; 23,1–6). We cannot reconstruct the whole history of its development as a book, but when we eliminate the passages associated with the deuteronomistic writers, we find that Chapters 1–12 consist of stories that originally told of isolated military successes and defeats. Eventually, some of these stories were combined either before they reached the hands of the deuteronomistic editors or by those editors themselves. Chapters 13–21 are built largely on preexisting geographical lists (town or boundary lists) that show, without the benefit of narrative, the extent of Israel's conquest of the Promised Land.

Sagas and Lists

Chapters 1–12: In telling the story of Israel's conquest of Canaan, the authors of Joshua drew upon old stories called sagas. A *saga* is a story, in historical form but with many elements (drama, foreshadowing, striking events) that resemble fiction. It is almost always concerned with heroic characters and the formative events of a people's history. It is different from *legend* in that it dwells less on the marvelous or supernatural; it differs from *chronicle* in that it emphasizes narrative interest over lists of characters and events, that is, stories that contain a kernel of historical truth, but whose main concern is the poetic or theological truth that is expressed by the story. Sagas tell the events of the *past* in a way that sheds light on the *present* experience of the reader. Thus, the story of the conquest was not just a record of Israel's past, it was a source that could continuously reveal to Israel the state of its present relationship with God.

Many of the sagas found in the first half of Joshua are etiological stories. Such stories are told to offer an explanation, usually about the origin or cause of something, like how a city got its name, how a particular custom originated, or why animals or humans behave in a certain way.

Chapters 13–21: This part of the book is concerned with how the land was distributed among the tribes. These chapters were probably put together from actual lists, that is, very ancient government documents that had been used for taxation purposes or to settle boundary disputes.

The Book of Joshua in Context

We can think of the Book of Joshua as being part of a puzzle-within-a-puzzle. The first puzzle of which it is a piece is what we have called the deuteronomistic history (the Books of Deuteronomy, Joshua, Judges, 1 and 2 Samuel, and 1 and 2 Kings). Deuteronomy serves as a preface to this history and sets down the conditions for a successful conquest and occupation of Canaan: If Israel obeys God's law it will conquer the land and settle it in peaceful prosperity. The first step, conquest and distribution of the land, is successfully completed in Joshua. But the succeeding books reveal that the second step, peaceful settlement of the land, is ultimately unsuccessful because of Israel's infidelity to God's law.

The larger puzzle of which the deuteronomistic history is a part is the ongoing story of Israel as God's chosen people, a story that began in Genesis with God's promise to Abraham of land and descendants (Gen 12,1–3). By the end of Deuteronomy the promise of countless descendants has been fulfilled, though the land is not yet given. But in Joshua, as Israel takes full possession of Canaan, we see the complete fulfillment of God's promise.

Because Joshua is not a complex book, it can be easily divided into two parts: (1) the conquest of the land of Canaan (Chapters 1–12), and (2) the distribution of the land (Chapters 13–21). But the book's authors have inserted speeches given by Joshua both at the beginning (Chapter 1) and end of the book (Chapters 23–24) to serve as preface and epilogue and to firmly place the meaning of the recorded events in a theological context.

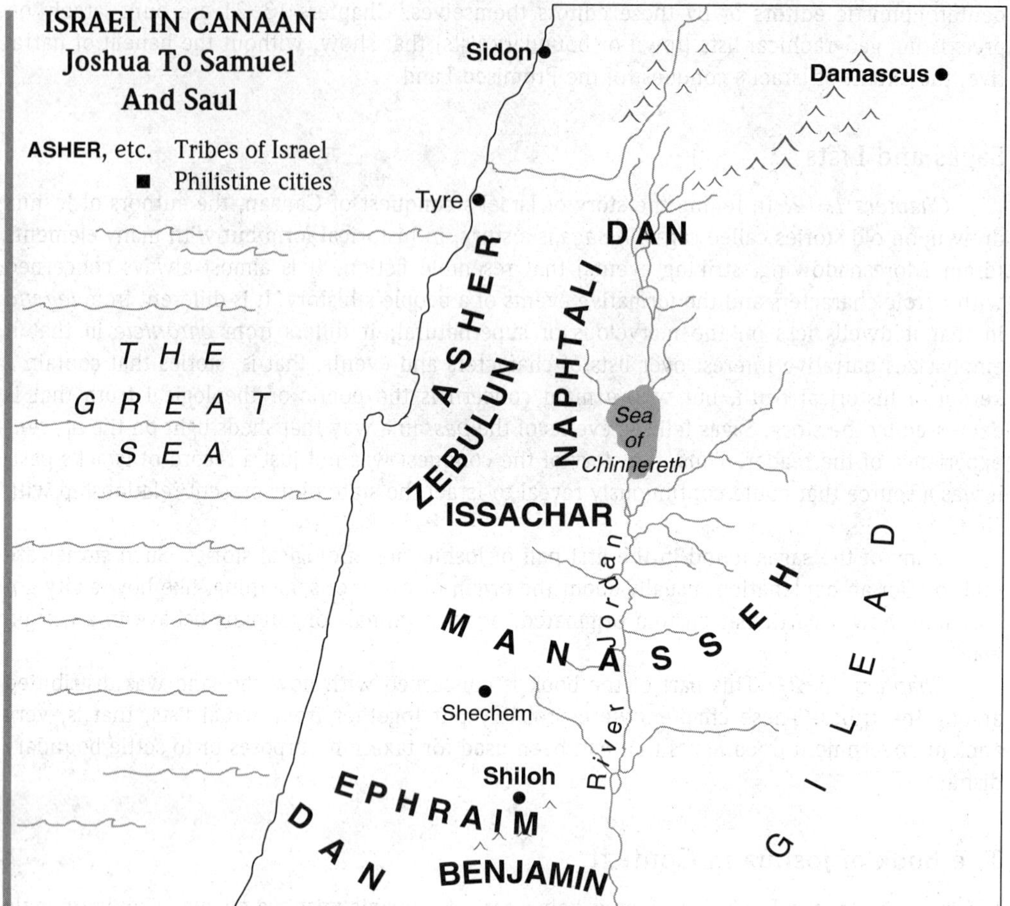
ISRAEL IN CANAAN
Joshua To Samuel
And Saul
ASHER, etc. Tribes of Israel
Philistine cities
Sidon
Damascus
Tyre
DAN
ASHER
NAPHTALI
ZEBULUN
THE GREAT SEA
Sea of Chinnereth
ISSACHAR
MANASSEH
River Jordan
GILEAD
Shechem
Shiloh
EPHRAIM
DAN
BENJAMIN
Jerusalem
Ekron
Ashdod
Ashkelon
Gaza
Gath?
REUBEN
Sea of Arabah (The Salt Sea)
JUDAH
SIMEON
The Negeb

READING THE BOOK OF JOSHUA

Outline of the Book of Joshua

Jos 1,1 – 5,15	Introduction: Joshua's authority and entry into the land
Jos 6,1 – 12,24	The conquest of the land
Jos 13,1 – 21,45	Distribution of the land
Jos 22,1 – 24,33	Epilogue: Joshua's farewell, departure of Transjordan tribes, and renewal of covenant

Introduction (Jos 1,1–18)

Several significant theological themes are set forth in the introduction and color the writing of the rest of the chapters. First is the question of fidelity and obedience: Though the conquest of Canaan is ultimately God's doing, the people aid or hinder its progress depending on how obedient they are to God's law. The second and third concepts, central to Israel's theology, center on the notion of the Lord as a warrior God who leads Israel in battle, and the land as God's gift to Israel.

No matter how offensive modern readers might find it, there is no easy way to dismiss the biblical notion of a warrior God. That concept is central to Israel's foundational experience of God in the Exodus and in the Books of Joshua, Judges, and 1 and 2 Samuel. Yet one must not conclude from this that God gives war unqualified approval.

It is important to remember that the ancient Near Eastern world in which Israel lived experienced war as a common, recurring reality. A discussion of holy war is found on page RG 80. The belief that God acts within war, giving victory or punishing through defeat, was shared by Israel's neighbors. It is also important to realize that the treatment of war in Joshua and Judges represents the deuteronomistic writers' attempt to make the events of Israel's experience conform with deuteronomic law (Dt 20,16f). They are painting an idealized picture of the conquest as God's holy war in which all things that oppose God's will (the pagan nations) are utterly destroyed. In reality, the land was not fully conquered till much later, but the theological point is that God was giving the land to Israel and removing all obstacles in its path.

> ***Herem*** The practice of sacrificing all the spoils of war to God, sometimes referred to as "the ban." If carried out literally, this meant destroying all human and animal life, and keeping none of war's booty for oneself. If it was ever carried out in practice, it would have been only in times of greatest danger.

A central belief of the deuteronomistic writers becomes apparent: God governs every aspect of Israel's life; even war, then, is a sign of God's care for Israel. Fighting on their behalf testifies to God's love and concern for the people. While a modern reader might prefer to hear "rejoice not when your enemy falls" (Prv 24,17), the ancient reader found in the warrior God image, and in the Old Testament God's call to take up arms, a clear theological statement that God can use anything to achieve the divine will, even the human tragedy of war.

The biblical perspective on the land of Canaan is that it belongs to God. God makes a gift of the land to Israel in fulfillment of the promise made to Abraham. By winning the land in battle for Israel, the Lord provides this homeless people with a place to live. This rich land, "flowing with milk and honey," gives God's people a new identity, as well as a sense of belonging and security.

Besides referring to the actual territory that Israel comes to possess, the land also represents the sacred trust that exists between God and the people. Though it is a great blessing from God, the land is also a source of temptation for Israel. The Canaanite inhabitants of the land had been worshipers of fertility gods; now Israel finds itself frequently tempted to worship those Canaanite idols. Possession of the land in peace is assured only as long as Israel remains faithful: Infidelity will just as surely result in loss of the land. The Books of Judges, 1 and 2 Samuel, and 1 and 2 Kings record Israel's tragic failure to obey God's law and their subsequent loss of their treasured, God-given land.

Joshua Sends Spies; Crossing the Jordan (Jos 2,1–5,1)

The tale of the spies explains the survival of Rahab's family despite the order to destroy all life in Jericho. The crossing of the Jordan obviously and closely parallels the crossing of the Red Sea and, like the former event, it (1) demonstrates the power of God, (2) affirms the role of God's chosen leader (here Joshua), and (3) demonstrates the people's commitment to obey God and the leaders God has selected. This mighty action of the Lord strikes fear in the nations who soon are to be driven out of the land: Before even a single battle is fought, the nations tremble before the Lord.

The clear parallels between Moses and Joshua help establish the leadership of Moses' successor. Besides the obvious parallel of the river crossing itself, in which Joshua exercises a role like that of Moses in the Red Sea crossing, two other features confirm Joshua's role as leader: (1) like Moses, Joshua is obedient to God's commands, and (2) God exalts Joshua and assures him he will receive divine support, just as Moses did.

Caleb and Rahab

Minor characters often play major roles. Caleb and Joshua were among the twelve spies who first entered Canaan. While the others returned with fear and advised retreat, only Caleb and Joshua trusted in God and believed they could conquer the land. Because of their faith, they became the only two of the entire generation that left Egypt to actually enter the Promised Land.

Rahab, though a prostitute, recognized the hand of God working through the Israelites, so she helped them. Subsequently, not only was she spared, she also became an ancestor of King David and, ultimately, even of Jesus. The New Testament holds her up as an example of faith (Jas 2,25 and Heb 11,31).

The Conquest of Jericho (Jos 6,1–27)

This story, which may have had a long prehistory before being written in its present form, clearly expresses Israel's belief that God was fighting its battle. God's role and presence in the battle is represented by the Ark that is carried before the army. The victory, achieved by a miracle, is the obvious work of God. The deuteronomic theology, which says victory comes only if Joshua and the people obey God's commands, finds expression in the call for obedience found in Chapter 6,17–19, and in the acknowledgement that the people did obey the laws of *herem* (holy war).

The Sin of Achan and the Conquest of Ai (Jos 7,1 – 8,35)

Defeat so close on the heels of victory! Even Joshua fell on his face and trembled. The deuteronomists' point is clear: Disobedience brings defeat as surely as obedience brings victory. While the battle of Jericho demonstrates the steps that lead to success, the battle of Ai is a recipe for how *not* to fight a battle. The ban (*herem*) was violated when Achan greedily took war booty from Jericho for himself; in addition, Israel adopted a battle plan against Ai, suggested by overconfident spies, without first consulting with the Lord. Thus the sin of self-reliance combined with disobedience, and tragedy resulted: The army lost the battle and Achan lost his life. The deuteronomic recipe for success is simple: obedience and trust in God.

The Conquest of the Entire Land (Jos 9,1 – 12,24)

The remainder of the story of the conquest clearly illustrates the absolute necessity of relying on the Lord for military success. When, for a second time, the Israelites fail to consult with God about a serious decision, the Gibeonites trick them into making a covenant that violates the Israelites' own law (Jos 9,1–27). But the rest of this section depicts an Israel that has learned its lesson. The people become totally obedient to the laws of holy war, exterminating all conquered opponents. With God fighting for them, Israel completes its conquest of Canaan, and Joshua, the successor of Moses, is depicted as an exemplary leader, totally obedient to the Lord.

For many reasons, the historicity of the events surrounding the conquest are called into question. Chapters 13–21 of Joshua indicate that much of the land still remains under the control of the Canaanites, not Israel. The Book of Judges presents the conquest as a more gradual takeover. In addition, there is little archaeological evidence to support what is found in Joshua. Some evidence even seems to contradict the claims of the book.

Archaeological evidence clearly demonstrates that some of the cities of Canaan *were* conquered by military activity, leading some scholars to assert the authenticity of the military conquest, but the *identity* of the conquerors cannot be determined conclusively. Some scholars believe that internal peasant uprisings were mostly responsible for the overthrow of the governments in Canaan. Other scholars think that the Israelites gradually infiltrated the land, settled in, and eventually achieved dominance. Does each of these views represent part of the truth? Probably. What is certain, however, is that the actual conquest of Canaan was a much more complicated process than what is presented in the Book of Joshua.

All or Some? Compare Jos 13,1 with 11,23. After being told Joshua "captured the whole country," we suddenly learn that "a very large part of the land still remains to be conquered." Apparently historical reality does not square with the theological presupposition, not fully realized till the time of King David, that God's promise to Abraham would be fulfilled. By offering a "total conquest" view, the authors of Joshua anticipate (by several hundred years) what they know eventually came to pass.

DISTRIBUTION OF THE LAND (JOS 13,1–21,45)

The second part of the Book of Joshua begins like the first, with a command from the Lord. Now Joshua is told to distribute the conquered land, and the chapters that follow describe the apportionment.

Special Cities (Jos 20,1–21,45)

Cities of Refuge. In the Israelite tribal society that prevailed before centralized government was established, those who committed murder were punished by the family of the victim. In order to protect those who had caused an accidental death, special cities were set up where the family of the deceased could not hunt down the perpetrator. These cities of refuge, however, did not protect those who killed intentionally.

Levitical Cities. Because of their special calling to serve the Lord, the tribe of Levi was allotted no land. Instead, they were given cities within the boundaries of the other tribes' lands. By moving into these towns, four in each tribe's territory, the Levites were scattered among all the people, which enabled them to teach God's law and lead worship in all parts of the land. The towns also provided some measure of financial security for the Levites, who could not rely on inheritance of land as a source of economic stability.

Through This Lens Chapter 21 verse 45 states the theological perspective of the entire Book of Joshua: "Not a single promise that the LORD made to the house of Israel was broken; every one was fulfilled."

CONCLUSION

Dismissal of the Transjordan Tribes (Jos 22,1–34)

The tribes that had chosen to settle on the east side of the Jordan had been asked to help conquer the West and had been promised that they could return to the land Moses had granted them once the job was done.

When they are dismissed, with blessings and fraternal good wishes, the eastern tribes build an altar that causes a grave misunderstanding. The western tribes take it as an act of apostasy, an attempt to set up a rival and illegitimate worship site. Civil war is averted when the eastern tribes explain that they built the altar only as a sign of unity between the tribes, not as a place of sacrifice to compete with the Lord's tabernacle.

Joshua's Farewell Speech (Jos 23,1–16)

Joshua is old; the conquest is complete; a new era is dawning. So, like Moses, Joshua gives a farewell speech. Using language and theology typical of deuteronomistic writing, Joshua exhorts the people to remain faithful to the Lord. Despite the full conquest of the land, some other nations still remain in Israel. Only faithful obedience to the Lord will ensure the blessing that these nations eventually will be driven out. But if the Israelites worship other gods, they will be cursed and *they* will be driven off the land.

The Shechem Assembly (Jos 24,1–28)

Here we find what seems to be a second "farewell speech," one that follows the pattern of the "suzerainty treaties" discussed on page RG 59: The people renew their covenant with the Lord and agree to accept the blessings and curses that flow from keeping or breaking their promise of fidelity. Faithful to the end, Joshua dies and is buried "in the land of his inheritance" (Jos 24,30).

Your Choice One of Scripture's beloved and famous lines is spoken by Joshua: Decide today whom you will serve. . . . As for me and my household, we will serve the LORD (Jos 24,15).

The Continuing Significance of the Book of Joshua

The Book of Joshua affirms God's faithfulness and God's direct involvement in human history. In war, it was God who fought. In peace, God was responsible. All that happens to Israel reveals the hand of God. Yet personal responsibility is not ignored. Joshua 24,31 asserts: "Israel served the LORD during the entire lifetime of Joshua." From their obedience to the Lord flowed the blessings of peace and prosperity. But rarely in their history could such a statement be made again, and rarely, therefore, would they be so blessed.

Quesions for Discussion or Reflection

1. All God's promises to Israel were eventually fulfilled, but often the timing was not at all what Israel expected. What implications does this have for our own prayer lives and our relationships with God?

2. "As for me and my household," says Joshua, "we will serve the LORD." Have you ever faced a situation where you had to choose whether to do things God's way or not? Did you ever have to stand up publicly to announce or defend your choice? Could you if the need arose?

3. The Levites were to lead worship of the Lord on behalf of the people, so the cities they were given were scattered throughout the land. Though many Israelites lived far from Jerusalem, none was more than a day's journey from a levitical city. What does that tell you about Israel's attitude toward worship? How does that compare or contrast with our contemporary attitudes toward worship?

4. Joshua is presented as a very successful leader because he *obeyed* God's law. Is the concept of obedience an important part of your spirituality? Why or why not? Is it old-fashioned to talk of obedience, or is it the purest form of worship? Why?

JUDGES READING GUIDE

At a Glance

Who are the main players?	Othniel Ehud Deborah and Jael Gideon and his son Abimelech Jephthah and his daughter Samson and Delilah
What should I look for?	The issue of God's lordship over Israel Israel's repeated apostasy The fourfold pattern of disobedience/oppression/cries for help/deliverance God's faithfulness despite the people's infidelity God's use of charismatic leaders to rescue Israel The imperfection of God's chosen leaders and lack of real heroes Sad, tragic, often ugly stories that seem out of place in the Bible
When did this take place?	During the period after the conquest of Canaan and before the establishment of the monarchy: probably the years between 1220 and 1000 B.C.
Where did these events occur?	In the land of Canaan
Why was this book written?	To document Israel's moral downfall and its inevitable consequences; to reiterate the deuteronomic theme that fidelity leads to blessing, but infidelity to certain and tragic punishment (including possible loss of the land); and to help explain why God permitted Israel to change its system of government to monarchy
What's the story?	The Israelites continue their conquest of the Promised Land. But the Canaanite natives who had not been driven out by the Israelites regroup and counterattack. In addition, the Israelites begin to adopt the customs and idolatrous worship of their pagan neighbors. A series of twelve leaders, each in a time of grave national crisis, arises to rouse the people and lead them against the threatening enemy. And every time, in response to the people's repentance, the Lord has mercy and rescues Israel.

FORMATION AND STRUCTURE OF THE BOOK OF JUDGES

Like the Book of Joshua, the Book of Judges went through several stages of development. It began as a group of independent and unrelated stories, told orally, that related the activities of some local hero or "judge." Many of these sagas, though they often contain exaggerations and embellishments, are clearly based on some historical facts. The stories were eventually pulled together and placed into a common context: holy war. In this context, the focus of the stories is on God, who fights for Israel and uses the local hero as an instrument to achieve victory.

Judges The judges of the Bible were not people who wore black robes and presided over a court. Instead, they were Spirit-led, charismatic leaders who rose up in times of crisis to lead the nation in battle against a threatening enemy. A better term might be "warlords" or "military heroes." The personalities of these guerilla freedom fighters were often seriously flawed. The term is also applied to local elders who settled disputes among the tribes.

Though some of the stories contain etiological elements that seek to explain why certain places got their names or how certain customs originated, what binds the stories together is the theological frame the deuteronomic writers weave around the entire collection. As used by these writers, the stories reveal Israel's failure to live out the central demand of the covenant, which is stated in the first commandment: "I am the LORD your God, you shall have no other gods before me" (Ex 20,2).

The people's infidelity is played out in a four-act drama that is often repeated and always follows the same pattern:

1. Israel sins by turning to other gods;
2. The Lord punishes Israel by allowing an enemy to conquer it;
3. The people repent and beg God for help;
4. The Lord sends a deliverer (a judge) who rescues Israel from their foe.

This "sin–punishment–cry for help–deliverance" pattern is the theological frame that surrounds the entire book. The pattern is repeated in the story of each judge, so while the book moves forward in time, it also has a cyclic character.

Whatever the original meaning or purpose of the stories, the theological message they now convey is clear: Sin brings punishment; repentance brings deliverance. That is also the basic message of deuteronomistic theology, and it runs through the whole of the Book of Judges.

Key Verse In whole or in part, this verse is repeated four times in the later chapters of Judges. It states the main problem of the age of judges and serves as an indictment of the people's disobedience: "In those days Israel had no king; everyone did what he thought best" (17,6; 18,1; 19,1; 21,25).

The Book of Judges in Context

The death of Joshua left a leadership vacuum that would not be filled consistently until the beginning of the monarchy some 200 years later. The Book of Judges fills in the gap between eras by describing the transitional stage between conquest and monarchy—the age of judges. By demonstrating Israel's need for strong and faithful leadership, the Book of Judges provides a compelling argument for the eventual establishment of the monarchy.

READING THE BOOK OF JUDGES

The Book of Judges can be easily divided into three sections, as outlined in the table here.

I. Introduction 1,1—3,6	1. Israel's failure to fully conquer the land 2. Israel's disobedience as cause of their failure	
	Major Judges	Minor Judges
II. Exploits of the judges 3,7—16,31	1 Othniel (3,7–11)	
	2 Ehud (3,12–30)	
	3	Shamgar (3,31)
	4 Deborah (4,1—5,31)	
	5 Gideon (6,1—8,35)	
	Abimelech, the illegitimate judge (9,1–57)	
	6	Tola (10,1–2)
	7	Jair (10,3–5)
	8 Jephthah (10,6—12,7)	
	9	Ibzon (12,8–10)
	10	Elon (12,11–12)
	11	Abdon (12,13–15)
	12 Samson (13,1—16,31)	
III. Appendices 17,1—21,25	1. Idol worship in the tribe of Dan 2. Outrage against a concubine and Israel's first civil war	

Introduction (Jgs 1,1—3,6)

The beginning of the Book of Judges presents an alternate view or tradition regarding the conquest. This introduction combines ancient fragments to make the point that, despite the impression given by the Book of Joshua, the conquest is far from complete.

A simple explanation for why Israel has been unable to conquer the land is given in Jgs 2,1–5 by the angel of the Lord who appears at Bochim: Israel has disobeyed the Lord. As a result, God will not drive out the inhabitants of the land, and the lure of idolatry will be a constant temptation for Israel. This theological interpretation of Israel's history runs throughout

Judges. In fact, the book's overriding theme is that idolatry will always lead to punishment, but if the people repent God will be merciful.

How Did the Israelites Enter the Land?

If the land was not conquered in a quick series of decisive battles, then how did the Israelites occupy Canaan? A possible three-step explanation:

1. Assimilation: Coming out of the desert, tribal groups settled in sparsely populated areas on the outskirts of the desert and in land between the various city-states.
2. Alliances and conversions: The new religion of the Israelites may have been attractive, especially to the natives who were oppressed by rulers of the city-states. Some natives may have accepted the covenant and allied with Israelites.
3. Military battles: Some city-states were conquered through military campaigns waged by Joshua and his army. Others were conquered in later generations.

Exploits of the Judges (Jgs 3,7 – 16,31)

The individual stories of the judges are used by the deuteronomistic writers to make the theological point that though the Lord punishes Israel for its sins, nevertheless the Lord will not abandon the people, but hears their cries and sends someone to deliver them from oppression. While the judges were local leaders, the writers present them as leaders of all of Israel to underscore their concern for the unity of the tribes.

OTHNIEL (JGS 3,7-11)

The story of this first judge does little more than name the four-act drama of sin, punishment, repentance, and deliverance that will recur throughout the book. Here we find the Bible's first reference to the Spirit of the Lord coming upon someone. The Spirit transforms the soon-to-be judges, giving them the gift of leadership and making them God's instruments of deliverance.

EHUD (JGS 3,12-30)

Originally a secular narrative, the story of Ehud is given a theological significance by the deuteronomistic writers. This is a striking and graphic folktale that incorporates elements of humor that may strike us as crude: The king of Moab is so fat that Ehud's sword disappears when he strikes the king in the belly; the servants assume the king is lingering in the bathroom ("he is only relieving himself in the closet of the cool chamber [3,24]") when in fact he is dead.

DEBORAH AND BARAK (JGS 4,1 – 5,31)

Two versions of the same story—one prose, one poetry—tell of a battle won by Israel against the superior forces of the Canaanites. No explanation or apology is offered for the fact that a woman is serving as judge and prophetess. Deborah calls the tribes to battle under the leadership of Barak. But the general won't go to war without Deborah at his side. Another woman, Jael, becomes the hero of the battle, just as Deborah had predicted: Through treachery, and in flagrant violation of the laws of hospitality, Jael kills the Canaanite general Sisera.

The Song of Deborah in Chapter 5, probably one of the oldest pieces of writing in the Bible, is typical of the songs women sang to welcome soldiers returning from war. The poem recounts a theophany (a manifestation of God) and makes the point that the battle victory was the Lord's, for God was fighting a holy war on behalf of the people.

GIDEON (JGS 6,1 – 8,35)

The story begins with the deuteronomistic perspective that because the people "did evil in the eyes of the LORD (6,1)" they were delivered into the hands of the Midianites. An angel appears to Gideon to inform him he has been chosen to deliver Israel from its enemies. Gideon is terrified both by the task he's given and by the fact that he has seen God (in the form of the angel): Like others of his day, Gideon believed that anyone who saw God face-to-face would die. The angel reassures him and the Spirit of the Lord comes upon Gideon.

Gideon becomes a charismatic and effective general, leading into battle a company of 300 men, reduced by the Lord from an army of 32,000. The Lord intentionally shrinks Gideon's forces to make it clear that the victory achieved is God's doing, not the result of Israel's strength. Employing clever scare tactics and the advantage of surprise, Israel wins the battle.

The tribal leaders ask Gideon to become their king. Normally a judge led only as long as there was need; once the enemy was defeated, judges returned to their original occupation. But now the tribes want a permanent leader to protect them from their enemies. Gideon refuses the title but willingly enjoys many of the privileges of kingship. At one point he concedes to the making of an idol (8,22–27). For the deuteronomistic writers this sinful lapse of faith will lead eventually to the destruction of Gideon's family.

ABIMELECH (JGS 9,1-57)

The sin–punishment–repentance–deliverance pattern is interrupted with the story of Abimelech. Among the kingly privileges Gideon allowed himself was the right to many wives in many towns. Through them he fathered many sons, which in turn allowed him to assert his authority over the towns. One of these sons is Abimelech. In contrast to the judges, who were selected and mandated by the Lord to lead Israel, Abimelech usurps power after slaying seventy of his own brothers. The deuteronomistic writers see this story through a theological lens: Because his leadership is unauthorized and illegitimate, the Lord instigates a rebellion against Abimelech. In addition to Abimelech's use of treachery to win power, the Shechemites who

Ambivalence to Monarchy

The Bible contains much evidence that Israel was always divided about the institution of the monarchy: Some saw it as a practical, logical and necessary development in the nation's history; others saw it as evidence of apostasy—an abandonment of the Lord, the one true king of Israel. The story of Abimelech clearly preserves some of the negative attitude toward kingship. But the observation that everyone "did as he thought best" indicates that strong leadership became increasingly necessary.

accepted his kingship over them had not first consulted the Lord; they acted only according to their own will.

One of the Bible's few fables appears at Jgs 9,8–15. Composed by Jotham, a son of Gideon who escaped Abimelech's massacre, this wonderful fable satirizes kingship. Kings, it suggests, like the bramble bush (*NAB* "buckthorn") have nothing to offer but trouble and pain. In battle, Abimelech is fatally wounded by a woman who throws a millstone from a besieged tower; but rather than endure the disgrace of dying at the hands of a woman, Abimelech asks his armor-bearer to kill him with his sword.

JEPHTHAH (JGS 10,6 – 12,7)

Again the people sin against the Lord; again they are punished; and again the Lord chooses an unlikely hero to save them. Jephthah, a harlot's son and the leader of a band of outlaws, is the people's and the Lord's choice for a leader. After the Lord's Spirit comes upon him, Jephthah makes a superfluous and foolish vow to sacrifice "who (*or* what) ever comes out of the doors of my house" upon his return from a successful battle. Scholars are not agreed on whether the Hebrew text assumes that the intended victim was to be human or not. But whether or not he planned on a human sacrifice, that indeed is what Jephthah offers—and not just any human, but his own daughter. Human sacrifice was practiced by the Israelites, though rarely, despite the fact that their law forbade it and the prophets fiercely condemned it.

The point of the story seems to be focused on Jephthah's vow which, like any vow, once made had to be kept. It also indicts Jephthah for lack of faith. The coming of the Spirit of the Lord upon him should have been guarantee enough that he would win in battle. Relying on vows and pagan practices betrays a lack of trust in the Lord's willingness to defend Israel.

Since no greater disgrace could befall a Hebrew woman than to die childless, Jephthah's daughter requests time to mourn her virginity. While we might be horrified by the events of this story, we must not forget they are taking place in a culture where such practices were acceptable. We also must realize that the inspired author simply related the events without indicating approval of them.

SAMSON (JGS 13,1 – 16,31)

Samson, probably the best known of the judges, seems an odd choice for a biblical hero. His life is marked by striking contrasts. The positives: He is the only judge whose birth was announced by an angel, a sign of divine favor and great destiny; that the spirit of the Lord came upon him is said more often of Samson than of any other judge; he is dedicated from birth as a Nazirite, a religious group that took special vows to consecrate themselves to the Lord. But Samson is also a man of excesses. The negatives: He is repeatedly and tragically controlled by his sexual passions; he breaks all the Nazirite vows; endowed with great strength, he uses his power only to carry out personal vendettas, not to liberate the people from Philistine domination.

Ironically, in his strengths and weaknesses Samson embodies the entire nation. On the plus side: His birth is the result of divine intervention; he is dedicated to God; and he stands out as chosen and uniquely gifted among the people. But Israel's tragedy is also mirrored in his life: Israel often prostituted herself to pagan gods bringing judgment and destruction on herself, and Samson, slave to his passions, runs after foreign women, even prostitutes, thus bringing about his own destruction.

Despite Samson's many weaknesses, the Lord chose to use him. That God is active in all that Samson does is a clear teaching of this book. Though his motives were often narrow and self-centered, Samson's exploits do diminish the power of the Philistines and help keep Israel in one piece. His sexual escapades are never condemned outright, but neither are they approved by the authors. Certainly we are clearly shown that his downfall is a direct result of his inability to say no to a woman. Another theological statement focuses on the seriousness of breaking vows: Samson has broken his and suffers for his disobedience. Ultimately, however, we are left with the impression that Samson's tragedy serves the Lord's purposes, for out of Samson's defeat the Lord brings victory over the Philistines.

Nazirite Vows

Nazirites, who could be male or female, took their three vows either for a designated period of time or for life:

1. Abstain from wine and strong drink.
2. Avoid contact with any dead body.
3. Refrain from cutting the hair.

Though he was best at vow number three, Samson breaks all the vows, for by revealing his secret he becomes indirectly responsible for having his hair cut by Delilah.

Two Appendices (Jgs 17,1 – 21,25)

The final chapters of the Book of Judges contain two episodes that illustrate the disintegration of Israelite society that resulted from the lack of leadership. Thus they make a case for the transition to monarchy that we will see in 1 Samuel.

THE SANCTUARY AT DAN (JGS 17,1 – 18,31)

The first episode deals with the deterioration of Israelite worship. Micah sets up a local worship center at Dan (in violation of the Lord's command to have only *one* worship center in Israel) and then compounds his error by even setting up images of idols. All this he does with the aid of a Levite who claims to be descended from Moses and who seems to be willing to work for the highest bidder, for later he leaves Micah to join the service of the Danites.

OUTRAGE AT GIBEAH AND CIVIL WAR (JGS 19,1 – 21,25)

This jarring and horrific story presents many difficulties. A Levite who has gone to bring back his concubine finds himself confronted with the possibility of homosexual rape. To save himself, he offers the men of Gibeah his own concubine, whom they take and ravish repeatedly until she dies. The tragedy of the story lies not only in the depravity of Gibeah's citizens, but also in the callous and self-serving behavior of a man who allows a defenseless woman to be so brutalized. When the Levite finds her dead at his doorstep, he shows no concern for her. Instead, he sets out to muster Israel's tribes to avenge her death.

Gibeah was a town of the tribe of Benjamin, so what the Levite is calling for is civil war against a brother tribe. After intense fighting, all but 600 Benjaminite men are slaughtered; all the Benjaminite towns, with all their inhabitants, are destroyed. Soon the Israelites begin to grieve over their actions—they've nearly wiped out one of Israel's tribes. They had taken an oath not to give any of their daughters in marriage to the surviving Benjaminites; but since they wanted to keep the tribe from totally disappearing, the men of Israel decide to find wives elsewhere for the survivors. They slaughter most of the population of Jabesh-gilead and take 400 of their young women to the Benjaminites. Since these are not enough, they encourage the rest of the Benjaminites to seize wives for themselves from among the girls of Shiloh in order to rebuild their tribe.

Certainly these are shocking events. But we must not project our own concerns and morals into the story. In this culture women were considered little more than possessions, so the Levites' behavior would not have appeared as awful then as it does now to us. In the ancient view, the real criminals were the men of Gibeah who violated the laws of hospitality and who sought to inflict perverse violence on the Levite. Though the tribes carry their vengeance to almost unimaginable extremes, their determination to right the injustice done to the concubine is a positive value in the story.

These stories reveal that in many ways Israel has become its own worst enemy. Edited by authors writing at the time of King David, the stories serve to reveal the corruption that results when there is "no king and everyone (does) what he (thinks) best" (21,25). No better argument could be made for Israel's need for a king.

CONTINUING SIGNIFICANCE OF THE BOOK OF JUDGES

Despite some of the distasteful and difficult aspects of the Book of Judges, three theological concepts that we should remember are embedded in the stories: First, God is depicted as acting decisively on behalf of those who are politically oppressed. Second, we are shown that any action that does not conform with God's will ultimately fail. Third, negative experiences are made lessons for the future: Defeat helps the people recognize their guilt and brings them to repentance and greater fidelity to the covenant.

We might not completely agree with the simplistic deuteronomistic theology presented in Judges: Sin always brings punishment; trust in God always brings deliverance. Seldom is human life so neat. But the primary emphasis of the deuteronomistic history is on God's patience and willingness to forgive if people repent. Only lack of repentance makes punishment necesssary. In addition, the deuteronomists' simple equation between sin and punishment is challenged and complemented in other books of the Bible, especially the Book of Job.

Questions for Discussion or Reflection

1. Have you seen the typical pattern of the Book of Judges—sin, punishment, crying out to the Lord, deliverance—played out in your own life?
2. Why does the Book of Judges view the characterization "everyone did as he saw fit" so negatively? To what sin or weakness does the expression point?

3. Did the Israelites' problems stem from outside factors or from internal problems and weaknesses? In your own life, which is the greater source of trouble, circumstances or weaknesses?
4. With all its gritty and gruesome tales, its less than heroic heroes, and its overt and ugly violence, does the Book of Judges still hold a message that is worth hearing?
5. Can you make sense of the holy war concept as depicted in the Book of Judges? Does God fight wars? Can war ever be holy?

RUTH READING GUIDE

At a Glance

Who are the main players?	Naomi Ruth, her daughter-in-law Boaz
What should I look for?	The loyalty of Ruth The felt but unseen presence of God The notion of redemption that runs throughout God's use of a non-Israelite to advance the divine plan
When did this take place?	During the days of the judges, before the establishment of the monarchy (c. 1200–1000 B.C.). The book, however, was probably written sometime during the period of the monarchy.
Where did these events occur?	In the land of Moab, east of the Dead Sea; and in Bethlehem
Why was this book written?	To show that fidelity and integrity are possible even when faithlessness abounds; to illustrate God's faithfulness and protection; to demonstrate that kindness, piety, and loyalty bear good fruit
What's the story?	Because of famine Naomi's family migrates to Moab where her sons marry Moabite women. Later, Naomi's husband and sons die, so she prepares to return home. One daughter-in-law, Ruth, insists on going back to Canaan with her. There she meets and marries Boaz, a kinsman. They bear a child, Obed, who will become the grandfather of King David.

Ruth and Rest of the Bible

- The Book of Ruth is one of only three books in the Bible that bears the name of a woman (the others are Esther and Judith).
- Ruth and the harlot Tamar are two of the four women mentioned in Matthew's genealogy of Jesus.
- In the Hebrew text, the introduction that presents the problem (1,1–5) and the conclusion that states the solution to Naomi and Ruth's troubles (4,13–17) both contain exactly 71 words.

RUTH AS STORY

The Book of Ruth is a well-crafted Hebrew short story. It uses great artistry to tell a simple tale of ordinary people and everyday events. Compact, dramatic, focused, and full of warmth and beauty, the story both entertains and instructs. Its characters are people we can like and identify with: We feel their pain and rejoice when their problems are resolved.

We have no way of verifying the historicity of the events of the story, but there are good reasons to believe King David's ancestors were Moabite, as the story indicates. In any case, the story is a work of art which illustrates that even in difficult times people of integrity can live the covenant faithfully. Ruth, Naomi, and Boaz are models of goodness, loyalty, and kindness. They put into heroic practice the covenant "theory" that so many others had come to ignore. Because God never directly speaks or acts in the story, the book teaches its readers to be attentive to the subtle and invisible presence of God in all of life.

Scholarly opinion regarding the date of composition of the Book of Ruth has shifted. The consensus used to favor a later date for the writing of the book (during or after the exile—as late as 400 B.C.—when its purpose might have been to counteract the nationalistic exclusivism of Ezra, who had forbidden intermarriage with foreign women). But today scholars prefer an earlier date—sometime during the period of the monarchy (8th to 10th centuries B.C.). The style and theology of the book both argue for the earlier dating.

Theology in the Book of Ruth

Because it narrates events that occur during the time of the judges, the Greek and Latin Bibles placed the Book of Ruth between Judges and 1 Samuel. But Ruth does not reflect the theological thought or style of the writers who compiled the deuteronomistic history, the story of Israel from the conquest to the exile as found in the Books of Joshua, Judges, 1 and 2 Samuel, and 1 and 2 Kings. Ruth, therefore, really is not part of the deuteronomistic history.

The Book of Ruth presents God as present in the ordinary events of everyday life. Though God is clearly in control, God's will is accomplished by human decisions and human actions. Such a subtle presence contrasts sharply with the God of Moses who parted waters and sent thunder from the sky. This subtlety requires that we pay extra attention to the characters Ruth, Naomi, and Boaz, for it is in their actions, their love for one another, that God's love is revealed in the story.

READING THE BOOK OF RUTH

Outline of the Book of Ruth

Ru 1,1–5	Stating the problem: Naomi's emptiness
Ru 1,6–22	Ruth's loyalty to Naomi: the return to Bethlehem
Ru 2,1–23	Ruth gleans in the field of Boaz
Ru 3,1–18	Naomi's plan: Ruth and Boaz on the threshing floor
Ru 4,1–12	Boaz pursues his claim and announces marriage to Ruth
Ru 4,13–17	Ruth bears a son: The problem is resolved; Naomi's emptiness is filled
Ru 4,18–22	Genealogical appendix

The Scene Is Set (Ru 1,1–5)

The introduction tells us two significant things about the conditions that prevailed at the time of the story: It was the age of the judges, a time of moral decay and political disunity; and it was a time of famine. Unstated, but implied in Naomi's dialogue, is the patriarchal structure of the society which presumed that a woman would be cared for by her father, husband, or sons. Lacking all three, Naomi, or any widow in the same circumstances, faced a life of certain poverty and destitution.

The situation in the land closely mirrors Naomi's personal dilemma: Both are empty. The land lacks food and Naomi lacks husband and sons. Her "emptiness," says Naomi, cannot be cured. She can have no more sons to give in marriage to replace the husbands her daughters-in-law have lost. So she tells the young women to return to their family homes. But the story demonstrates the power and mercy of God, who is capable of reversing Naomi's situation. By the end, Naomi has a descendant through Ruth. She who was empty is made full.

Naomi Returns to Bethlehem (Ru 1,6–22)

In contrast to the first scene, which covered a span of years with few words, this scene uses many words to relate a brief episode. The length of the scene reveals the importance the author gives it. Naomi sees her situation as hopeless: She is too old to remarry and bear more children. She will be destitute and alone, she thinks. Her widowed daughters-in-law, expected to stand by their mother-in-law, thus share Naomi's desperate situation. But Naomi refuses to let them suffer with her. She insists that they return to their own Moabite families where they can remarry.

While Orpah agrees to return to her family, Ruth will not abandon Naomi. The contrast between the women makes Ruth's virtue stand out: Orpah did nothing wrong, but Ruth certainly did better. By being willing to share Naomi's problem, Ruth becomes the route to a solution. Throughout the book, in fact, human beings are the clear mediators of God's love and protection. God is behind all the good that happens, but it happens because of people like Ruth and Boaz who are willing to live good and faithful lives, not because of direct divine intervention.

Ruth Gleans in the Field of Boaz (Ru 2,1–23)

Though it seems that chance is at work here, the inspired authors want us to see God's hand guiding Ruth to enter the fields of Boaz, a prominent relative of Naomi. Because he has heard of Ruth's kindness to her mother-in-law, Boaz gives strict orders that the men do her no harm (an unmarried woman alone in the fields would have been easy prey), and he allows her to

Gleaning Israel's law required that widows and orphans and the poor be cared for. One way this was done was to allow the poor to "glean" the fields, that is, to gather the grain left behind by the reapers. Landowners were not allowed to pick up what the laborers had dropped or missed. It was to be left for the poor.

gather a large quantity of barley. Boaz is presented as an honorable and selfless man. His interest in Ruth is motivated by her kindness and loyalty to Naomi. He is as good to her as she has been to her mother-in-law.

Boaz and Ruth on the Threshing Floor (Ru 3,1–18)

In a scene that has clear sexual overtones, Naomi sends Ruth to the threshing floor where Boaz is sleeping. Naomi tells Ruth to bathe and dress in her finest clothes and then lie at Boaz's "feet," a Hebrew euphemism for male genitals. Ruth does lay beside him, and when Boaz awakens she asks him to spread his cloak over her, a symbolic gesture that would represent his willingness to take her for his wife. But despite the seemingly compromising situation Ruth enters, her relationship with Boaz remains honorable throughout. Never does he take advantage of her; he strives, instead, to protect her good reputation.

Boaz Pursues His Claim (Ru 4,1–12)

We have only limited knowledge of the customs that governed the circumstances involved here. We know that deuteronomic law dictated that a man had to marry his brother's widow if she had not borne children before her husband's death. In this way the living brother would produce heirs for his decreased brother. But Boaz is not Ruth's brother-in-law. Was the law extended to more distant relatives in unusual circumstances like these? Did various regions develop their own variations on the law? Both are possible explanations.

Levirate Marriage Israelite law (Dt 25,5–25) required that the brother of a man who died without a male heir had to marry the widow and that their first male child would "carry on the name of the dead brother so that his name may not be blotted out from Israel." The Sadducees who question Jesus in Mark 12,18–27 are referring to this same law.

Another explanation centers on a different issue: land redemption. Relatives were expected to redeem family land that had been lost because of debt. Perhaps Naomi's husband had sold his land when they moved to Moab, and now she wants to redeem it but lacks the funds to do so. Boaz somehow connects redemption of the land with marriage to Ruth. While the unnamed kinsman is willing to redeem the land, he does not want to marry Ruth (since the first male child they would have would be considered the heir of Ruth's dead husband, the property he would redeem would go to this son, rather than to the kinsman's own heirs). Wanting to avoid such entanglements, the kinsman waives his right to redeem the land and clears the way for Boaz to marry Ruth.

The Birth of a Son (Ru 4,13–17)

Both the introduction and the conclusion of the story focus on Naomi. It is Ruth who bears a child, but the boy is seen as a blessing for Naomi: His birth balances the tragedy of death that entered her life at the beginning of the story. For the blessing she brings into Naomi's life, Ruth is credited with being better than "seven (the perfect number of) sons." The announcement that David would descend from the child, Obed, climaxes the entire story.

Continuing Significance of the Story of Ruth

The story of Ruth reaffirms that God can work through the worst of tragedies and in the worst of times. Darkness can be turned to light, sadness into joy, if we allow God's love to flow through us. God's will is accomplished in and achieved through us when we become bearers of God's love to one another. Most often this happens in subtle and ordinary ways rather than through striking miracles. The story of Ruth confirms the value of our acts of kindness and faithfulness in God's plan of salvation. Through the fact that Ruth was a foreigner, it also reasserts the belief that God's love and salvation are available to all the world.

Questions for Discussion or Reflection

1. Why is it significant that Ruth, the great-grandmother of King David, was a foreigner?
2. The Book of Ruth never shows God directly intervening in the lives of the main characters. Though we know God is influencing events, it happens in unspectacular, everyday kinds of ways. How does that relate to the ways you experience God in your life? How does this contrast with the ways we see God acting in other books of the Bible?
3. In ancient Palestine, a woman without a man in her life was destined for hardship. How does this consideration shed even more favorable light on the character of Ruth? Besides loyalty, what other admirable qualities do you see in Ruth? In Naomi?
4. After the death of her husband and sons Naomi says, "Call me Mara, because the Almighty has made it (my life) very bitter for me" (Ru 1,20). How do you feel about expressing bitterness or even anger to God? In the end, Naomi's bitterness is turned to blessing. Can you think of situations in your life when good came out of seemingly hopeless circumstances?

1 AND 2 SAMUEL READING GUIDE

At a Glance

Who are the main players?	Eli Hannah Samuel Saul Jonathan David Goliath Bathsheba Joab, David's general Absalom, David's son
What should I look for?	The transition in Israel from theocracy to monarchy The system of checks and balances: king's power is checked by God's law and the voice of the prophet How Saul's and David's sins have both personal and national consequences The theme of obedience to God: "Obedience is better than sacrifice" (1 Sm 15,22)
When did this take place?	From the end of the age of the judges through the monarchy of David: approximately 1083 B.C. to 1000 B.C.
Where did these events occur?	The land of Israel; especially Ramah, birthplace of Samuel; Shiloh, Israel's center of worship; the desert where David fled; Gath, where David moved his family; Ziklag, the city from which David conducted numerous raids; Mount Gilboa, site of Saul's final battle and death
Why was this book written?	To depict Israel's transition from theocracy to democracy by narrating the life of Samuel and the reigns of Israel's first two kings, Saul and David
What's the story?	Samuel, the last judge, anoints Saul as first king of Israel. Saul begins well but ends badly, becoming obsessed with jealousy and hatred of David. Saul turns to occult practices and eventually commits suicide. David succeeds him on the throne and unites Israel into a powerful kingdom. Though he never abandons the Lord, David's own sins bring strife to his family and nation.

The Books of Samuel were not written from start to finish by a single author or even a group of authors. Individual stories and blocks of material about the fascinating characters in these books had existed long before anyone pulled them together and gave them their present form. Although it is not as evident here as in the Book of Judges, the same deuteronomistic editors who shaped that book shaped these.

As Israel changed, so did its literature. During the tribal era, it produced heroic *sagas* filled with astounding events. But when Israel became a state, *historical* writing developed. The Books of Samuel combine sagas, like the story of David and Goliath, with historical writing, like the report in 2 Samuel 8 of David's conquest of the Moabites and Edomites.

All history has a subjective side, something we can call a "point of view." Even the most "objective" historians must select and then organize facts, and as they do it they are guided by their own ideas of what is important and valuable. Their lenses may be rose or grey or blue, but every historian looks at history through some kind of glasses. The deuteronomistic writers looked at Israel's history through "worship"-colored glasses; that is, their chief preoccupation was the question: Was Israel faithful or not to its commitment to worship God at Jerusalem? All the good and evil that happened to Israel, according to them, resulted directly from how the nation's history answered that question.

The Books of Samuel offer a theological interpretation of how the monarchy was established in Israel. Their basic theological presupposition is this: David, who conquered Jerusalem and made it Israel's religious center, must have been God's chosen leader.

READING THE BOOKS OF SAMUEL

The theological perspective of the deuteronomist editors colors their presentation of the lives of Samuel, Saul, and David. Their viewpoint is this: Total obedience to God's law brings success; disobedience brings failure. Since the deuteronomists see David succeed despite his sins, they conclude that basically he must have been loyal to the Lord. Saul, on the other hand, fails, so they concluded he must have been disloyal.

Outline of 1 and 2 Samuel

1 Sm 1,1 – 3,21	Birth and youth of Samuel
1 Sm 4,1 – 7,	Loss and return of the Ark of the Covenant
1 Sm 7,2–17	Samuel as judge
1 Sm 8,1 – 12,25	Establishment of the monarchy
1 Sm 13,1 – 15,35	Reign and rejection of Saul
1 Sm 16,1 – 2 Sm 5,5	David becomes king of Judah and Israel
2 Sm 5,6 – 24,25	Reign of King David
2 Sm 21,1 – 24,25	Appendices

Samuel's Birth and Youth (1 Sm 1,1 – 3,21)

In Scripture, the circumstances of a child's birth often provide hints about the child's destiny. Samuel's destiny as one chosen by God for special service is foreshadowed by his mother Hannah's barrenness. Harassed by her husband's other wife who has borne numerous children, Hannah prays that God remove her misery by granting her a son. When her prayer is answered, she fulfills her promise to dedicate the boy to God and raise him as a Nazirite (1,22). Samuel is clearly a gift from God, special and destined for greatness.

After consecrating Samuel to God, Hannah prays a beautifully poetic prayer. Mary's Magnificat (Lk 1,46–55) resembles Hannah's prayer. Hannah praises God for reversing fortunes by bringing down the mighty and raising up the lowly, for making the barren fertile, and for defending the weak and lowly.

Hannah leaves Samuel in the care of Eli the priest at the shrine in Shiloh. While Samuel grew in stature and favor before God and people, the sons of Eli committed grave sins of greed and desecration, making them clearly unworthy for their service as priests of the Lord.

Samuel's special role in God's plan is highlighted by the story of his call (3,1–21). He is God's chosen servant: Reared as a priest, he is later given a prophetic ministry as well. He will also function as a military leader or judge, Israel's last and finest. Thus, the major institutions of

Barren Women Besides Hannah, there are four other seemingly barren Old Testament women who were divinely blessed with a son: Sarah (Gn 11,30); Rebekah (Gn 25,21); Rachel (Gn 29,31); and Samson's mother (Jgs 13,3). In the New Testament, there is Mary's cousin Elizabeth (Lk 1,7).

ancient Israel—priest, prophet, and judge—are all manifested in this one man who also anointed Israel's first two kings.

Loss and Return of the Ark (1 Sm 4,1—7,1)

In this story the Ark's primary significance is military. Its capture by the Philistines is a devastating blow. In Israel the Ark's presence in the battlefield signified God's presence fighting for the people. Is God's presence now lost? Ancient people believed that capturing an enemy's god and setting it up in your own temple indicated your gods were much more powerful than your enemy's. But this story shows that Israel's God works differently. Despite the Ark's capture, Yahweh is still very much in control. This is pointedly (even humorously) demonstrated by the idol of the god Dagon twice falling down in worship before the Ark. Wherever it is held captive, the Ark causes disease and devastation. Every town to which it is sent experiences turmoil.

The Philistines soon learn whose god is most powerful and quickly resolve to return the Ark to Israel. But more than lampooning the god Dagon, the deuteronomistic writers use this story to illustrate that the prophecy God spoke through Samuel (that Eli's family would be punished for their wrongdoing [2,27–36]) is beginning to be fulfilled.

The Ark of the Covenant

The most sacred of Israel's possessions, the Ark was a box of acacia wood measuring approximately 4′ × 2 ½′ × 2 ½′. Kept in the Holy of Holies of the tent and later the Temple, it contained the Tablets of the Law (and possibly also a jar of desert manna and Aaron's rod). It was considered God's throne and signified God's presence among people (at times it was virtually identified with God). Anyone who desecrated it was instantly struck down.

Samuel as Judge (1 Sm 7,2–17)

When Samuel reappears in Chapter 7, he is a military leader or judge leading the fight against the Philistines. The degree of his success is overstated (7,13), for the Philistines are not completely subjugated till the reign of David. But by stressing Samuel's military victories, the deuteronomistic writers make a theological point regarding kingship: Israel does not really need a king to lead its battles, for God can use anyone at any time to bring the chosen people victory.

Establishment of the Monarchy (1 Sm 8,1—12,25)

Throughout most of its history, Israel remained ambivalent about monarchy. One of the distinguishing characteristics of its literature is the fact that it preserves both strands of thinking: promonarchy and anti-monarchy. Which attitude came first is hard to say. But by mingling negative with positive overtones, the deuteronomistic writers prepare the reader for the negative assessment of the whole institution of the monarchy presented in the Books of Kings, and for the more immediate downfall of Israel's first king, Saul.

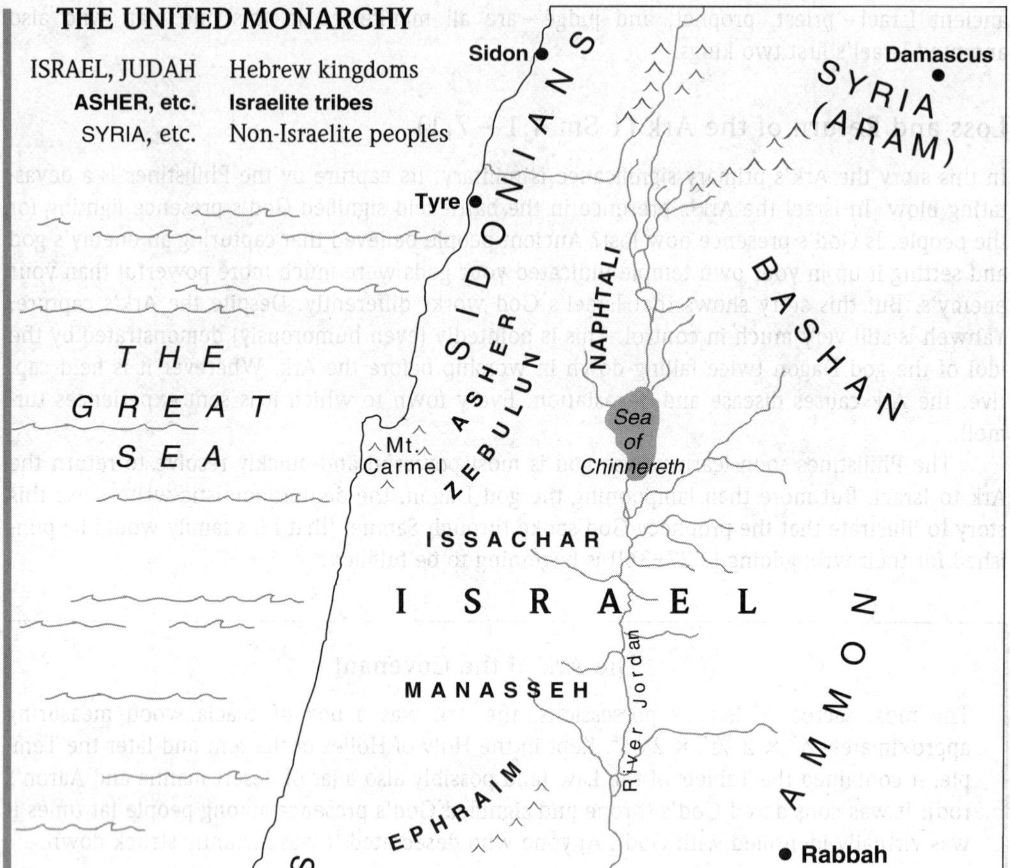
THE UNITED MONARCHY
ISRAEL, JUDAH Hebrew kingdoms
ASHER, etc. Israelite tribes
SYRIA, etc. Non-Israelite peoples
Sidon
Damascus
SYRIA (ARAM)
SIDONIANS
Tyre
NAPHTALI
ASHER
BASHAN
ZEBULUN
THE GREAT SEA
Sea of Chinnereth
Mt. Carmel
ISSACHAR
ISRAEL
MANASSEH
River Jordan
AMMON
EPHRAIM
Rabbah
BENJAMIN
Jerusalem
PHILISTINES
Salt Sea (Sea of the Arabah)
JUDAH
Gaza
MOAB
The Negeb
Kir-hareseth
AMALEK
EDOM

REQUEST FOR A KING AND SAMUEL'S OPPOSITION (1 SM 8,1–22)

Since the Philistine military threat would not go away, Israel was in constant need of strong leadership. Other nations relied on kings who would be succeeded by their sons when the king got old. Israel had no such assurance of continuity when a leader like Samuel died. So they asked for a king because they wanted to be "like all other nations" (8,20). But Israel was not supposed to be like other nations. Samuel resisted—perhaps because he was unhappy that his own sons were being rejected as potential future leaders. God instructed Samuel to warn the people that a king would bring higher taxes, forced labor, and a military draft.

Israel's king was the Lord; therefore the request for a human king was theologically repugnant. But in the end God relented. Since theological theory and historical practice seem to conflict, the text, accordingly, reflects ambivalence about God's decision. Perhaps God opposed the people's motive for wanting a king—"to be like other nations"—more than the idea of monarchy itself. The editors, unable to dispute the historical reality that monarchy existed for centuries in Israel, assume the theological position that therefore God must have accepted it.

SAUL ANOINTED KING BY SAMUEL (1 SM 9,1–11,15)

The story presents Saul in a positive light: His good looks and stature are signs of God's favor. Before his anointing, Saul had never heard of Samuel nor ever dreamed of kingship. Many folk stories depict their hero as someone on a mission to find something that is lost who instead finds something unexpected and better. Saul has been looking for asses but ends up with a crown. Three signs will confirm his selection by God: The asses will be found (10,2); he will be offered bread intended for sacrifice (10,4); and most importantly, the Spirit of the Lord will come upon him as it had upon the judges (10,6).

The ambivalence toward monarchy demonstrated in Chapter 8 continues here: While the Lord accepts kingship and designates Saul the first king, nevertheless, by wanting a king the people have proven their lack of faith.

Saul seems to have returned to private life at the start of Chapter 11. Led by the Spirit and acting more like a warrior judge than a king, he leads a victorious battle against the Ammonites.

Saul and David—First Impressions

We meet Saul chasing after donkeys—animals as stubborn as he turns out to be and possibly symbols of those who demanded a king despite God's displeasure. They were also a sign of his family's wealth. David, on the other hand, is introduced as a simple shepherd tending to his father's flock. Later he will shepherd Israel.

SAMUEL'S ADDRESS AND ACCEPTANCE OF THE KINGSHIP (1 SM 12,1–25)

Chapter 12 confirms the Lord's acceptance of kingship. After publicly asserting his own honesty, Samuel sets out to demonstrate the irrationality of Israel's request for a king by narrating how God always saved Israel in her times of need. The people have done evil in asking for a king, yet God permits it. But the Lord is still the ultimate authority in Israel and failure to follow God's law will bring just punishment.

The deuteronomistic writers present Samuel as the bridge between the eras of judges and kings. This address brings the era of judges to an end and sets the stage for prophets to take on greater importance. The people will not have to depend solely on the king, for the prophet (whose power is here demonstrated by the thunderstorm [11,18]) will act on their behalf in four ways: (1) interceding and praying for them; (2) teaching them what is right; (3) exhorting them to worship the Lord alone; and (4) warning them of punishment when they disobey. The prophet checks and balances the king's power and mediates the Lord's judgment.

The Reign and Rejection of Saul (1 Sm 13,1 – 15,35)

In this section, the deuteronomistic writers' main interest is in demonstrating why Saul failed as Israel's king.

SAUL IS REBUKED FOR DISOBEYING SAMUEL (1 SM 13,1–22)

The crime seems trivial, but the consequences are serious. While waiting to attack the Philistines, Saul's soldiers begin to desert because Samuel does not arrive at the expected time. Overanxious, Saul disregards Samuel's order to wait for him and offers the sacrifice himself. Disobedience to the Lord's prophet is disobedience to the Lord; consequently Saul's kingdom will not endure.

Because of the Philistine monopoly on iron, the Israelites have no metal weapons, we are told, but the Philistines are armed with swords and spears. In light of this disparity of weapons, an Israelite victory can only be the Lord's doing.

JONATHAN AND THE DEFEAT OF THE PHILISTINES AT MICHMASH (1 SM 13,23–14,46)

Demonstrating amazing bravado, Jonathan, aided only by his armor-bearer, takes on and kills some twenty Philistines. Saul, too, leads a successful battle, but a rashly made decision threatens the safety of the army and demonstrates Saul's unfitness to reign as king. Saul had impulsively ordered his army to fast until nightfall on the day of battle, putting them at an unnecessary disadvantage. Knowing nothing of his father's order, Jonathan unwittingly breaks the fast. Later, Saul is willing to kill his son for the inadvertent violation despite the fact that Jonathan had made the greatest contribution to the day's victory. Saul's behavior appears clearly egocentric and ill-conceived. Increasingly he seems ill-suited to lead God's people. Some commentators believe the story is also meant to indicate that Jonathan, too, is unacceptable as Saul's successor because, despite being uninformed, Jonathan did violate the oath and thus stands guilty. Though Jonathan's life is spared (an animal is sacrificed in his place), a sense of doom remains.

WAR WITH THE AMALEKITES AND REJECTION OF SAUL (1 SM 14,47–15,35)

This story focuses on Saul's failure to obey a command God gave through the prophet Samuel. In violation of God's direct order, Saul refuses to enforce the *ban* against Israel's old enemies the Amalekites. (See the definition of *herem* in Joshua RG 97.) He spares their king and won't slaughter the best of the herds of sheep and oxen, destroying only what was worthless. Because of his disobedience and greed, Saul guarantees eventual forfeit of the throne. He is still king for now, but the end is near.

David Becomes King of Judah and Israel (1 Sm 16,1–2 Sm 5,5)

The stories of David that make up this section may have been drawn from an ancient document called the History of the Rise of David (1 Sm 16,1–2 Sm 5,10), though some scholars question whether the document actually existed. What is clear is that the deuteronomistic writers have adapted the material, from whatever source, to advance their theological agenda.

SAMUEL ANOINTS DAVID AND DAVID SERVES SAUL (1 SM 16,1-23)

David is God's chosen one. All he does is viewed and judged from that perspective. The Lord is on his side, so all he does succeeds. Saul is another story. The Lord regrets making him king, so all his efforts fail. Saul has become moody and depressed, tormented by "an evil spirit" (16,14). A great irony occurs: Seeking relief from his foul moods, Saul takes David, his future rival and successor, as his servant. David's skillful harp playing soothes the king's troubled spirit. Who would suspect this youthful poet would one day replace the warrior king?

DAVID AND GOLIATH (1 SM 17,1-55)

Here is a storytelling masterpiece. Note that David's connection with Saul established in the previous chapter is not acknowledged here. Apparently this story originally stood alone, not connected to the preceding events. Here David does not yet know Saul, nor has he entered his service as harp player.

Throughout the Books of Samuel the contrast between Saul and David is repeatedly drawn. This story adds details to the sketch. David, the inexperienced underdog, readily challenges the veteran Goliath. But he relies on more than his youthful agility to combat the giant's armor and experience. Most of all he relies on the Lord. Saul, on the other hand, had repeatedly proven his lack of faith, his inadequate trust, his unwillingness to obey. David's faith is unshakable. His courage is born of his total trust in God. The qualities that make him superior to Saul as a candidate for kingship are all demonstrated here: courage, military skill, and, most importantly, faith in the Lord.

DAVID AND JONATHAN (1 SM 18,1-5)

David and Jonathan's deep and lasting friendship is established in their first encounter. Jonathan's gesture of giving David his mantle, military dress, and weapons can be seen as a symbolic act of turning over to David the right of succession.

SAUL'S JEALOUSY OF DAVID (1 SM 18,6-30)

It would seem David cannot fail. Everything he touches turns into a golden opportunity. David's success is not lost on Saul, who grows more jealous with each of David's achievements. His jealousy becomes a cancer driving him even to an attempt on David's life. Yet Saul's every move, even those calculated to bring David down, contribute instead to David's growing success.

Saul's Jealousy Already declining, Saul gets a push on his downward spiral of jealousy and resentment when the women of Israel come out to greet him singing this song: "Saul has slain his thousands and David his *ten thousands*."

Saul loved and hated David. He promises to make his daughter, Merob, David's wife, then marries her to another man. He offers another daughter, Michal, but only on the condition that first David do the impossible: deliver to Saul the foreskins of a hundred Philistines. David not only meets the demand, he doubles it and wins a great military victory in the process. Instead of getting killed trying, David marries Michal, and Saul watches another plot to undermine his rival blow up in his own face. Recognizing that the Lord's hand is upon David, Saul hates and fears him all the more.

SAUL'S PURSUIT OF DAVID AND DAVID'S ESCAPES (1 SM 19,1–28,2)

Saul is obsessed with David. He fears him and suspects disloyalty. These nine chapters chronicle Saul's efforts to capture David and David's numerous escapes. Saul wants to kill David, but he allows his son Jonathan to persuade him to let David return to court. But soon his anger boils over again, and now it is Saul's daughter Michal who helps David escape. Even Samuel conspires to obstruct Saul's efforts against David. Throughout, David's innocence and loyalty are reaffirmed. David flees not because of any real crime, but because of Saul's obsessive attempts to destroy him.

David flees with his men and comes to the town of Nob where the tabernacle had been relocated after Shiloh's destruction. He lies to the priests in order to get food for himself and his men, an action that receives no comment from the narrator. The priests seek out God's will for David (22,10,15) and allow him to take the sword of Goliath, indicating their approval of David as future king. By acting like a madman, David narrowly escapes capture by the king of Gath, then delivers his parents to the safety of the land of Moab (the home of his great-grandmother Ruth) to protect them from Saul's vengeance.

No negative judgment is made on any of David's actions (not even his lies to the priests). But Saul is depicted as becoming increasingly irrational. Though he had been unwilling to enforce the *ban* against his enemies, Saul now carries it out against his own people. He butchers the residents of Nob, including the priests David had tricked into helping him, and even the "children and infants." This tragic massacre fulfills the prophecy that Eli's family would be cut off from Israel's priesthood (2,31–36). Though one priest survives and gives his support to David, he, too, is later removed from the priesthood when Solomon sends him into exile, thus leaving no descendant of Eli serving as priest.

Saul keeps David on the run, but David does nothing without first consulting the Lord. God grants David much success in battle and in evading Saul. Even his fleeing reveals David's noble character: Twice he has an opportunity to secretly kill Saul but, despite the encouragement of his men, he refuses to harm the Lord's anointed. Chapters 24–26 emphasize David's innocence—even Saul recognizes it—and his selection as Israel's next king (24,21f).

In Chapter 27 David makes a desperate and startling decision: Driven by Saul's incessant harassment, he joins forces with Israel's hated enemies, the Philistines. While working as a

The Philistines The fighting between Israel and her archenemies was constant. The Books of 1 and 2 Samuel record at least thirteen military encounters between Israel and the Philistines. Israel's success always depended on the degree of her faith in the Lord. Of the thirteen battles, Israel was victorious eleven times and one battle was a draw.

paid mercenary for the Philistines, David takes care never to attack Israel itself, but only her enemies, though he convinces the Philistines that he *is* attacking his own people.

THE FINAL DAYS OF SAUL'S REIGN (1 SM 28,3 – 2 SM 1,27)

Saul's last days are desperate and sad. When he receives no answers from God to his questions of how to handle a Philistine invasion, he panics and seeks out a sorceress to help him consult the ghost of Samuel. The dead prophet offers no comfort, but instead reminds Saul that God has rejected him as king and that he and his sons will lose both the upcoming battle and their lives.

When David reappears, we find him in a serious predicament: He has sworn loyalty to the Philistine king, Achish, yet now that king wants to send David into battle against his own people. What will David do? As usual, his behavior is beyond reproach. Because of circumstances, David betrays neither side: The Philistine generals don't trust him, and they force him to leave. So David battles another of Israel's chief enemies, the Amalekites, and distinguishes himself in every way.

While David is enjoying every success, Saul has become a total failure. Rather than die at the hands of the Philistines like his two sons, Saul takes his own life. The once great and beloved leader is dead. As testimony to his former greatness, his soldiers march all night to retrieve and bury Saul's body. Interestingly, the start of the second Book of Samuel presents a different version of Saul's death: An Amalekite youth, probably lying to win favor with David, claims that he killed Saul at the king's own request. The boy wins nothing from David but a death sentence.

One might expect David to rejoice, but instead Saul's death brings him great grief. David expresses his sorrow in a mournful poem he chants for Saul and Jonathan (2 Sm 1,17–27).

DAVID BECOMES KING OF JUDAH AND ISRAEL (2 SM 2,1 – 5,5)

After consulting the Lord, David travels to Hebron, where he is anointed king of Judah. But the northern territory is under the rule of Saul's son Ishbaal who has been placed on the throne by Saul's general, Abner, the real power in Israel. A fight between representative warriors of each side—Joab's warriors representing David and Abner's representing Ishbaal—soon escalates into an all-out civil war between Israel and Judah. A series of murders and assassinations follows that results in the deaths of Abner and Ishbaal. The deuteronomistic writers make it very clear that David is innocent of the killings; he even punishes those who assassinated his rival, Ishbaal. But the result is that David benefits and becomes Israel's king (2 Sm 5,1–15).

The Reign of King David (2 Sm 5,6 – 24,25)

In this section the deuteronomistic writers advance their basic theological theme: because he is God's chosen, David will find success in all his efforts, but he will also suffer the consequences of all his sins. Interwoven with this dominant theme are concerns about who will rule after David dies, and Solomon's choice as David's successor.

The Lord is with David. Everything points to this fact: his choice as king of Israel, his military victories, the continued blessing of children in his life. David's first achievement as king of Judah and Israel was to take the city of Jerusalem, an act of the greatest political and theological significance. The city not only becomes the political capital of the empire, but, in the view of the deuteronomistic writers, the only legitimate place to worship the Lord.

DAVID DEFEATS THE PHILISTINES AND BRINGS THE ARK TO JERUSALEM (2 SM 5,17–6,23)

When they hear David has become king of both Israel and Judah, the Philistines immediately attack. But the Lord gives David the victory. This triumph, coupled with the previous conquest of Jerusalem, makes it possible for David to bring the Ark from the house of Abinadab, where it was taken after the Philistines returned it, to the capital city, Jerusalem. A man named Uzzah tries to keep the Ark from falling during transport and is struck dead—harsh punishment for apparently well-intentioned behavior. But since the Ark represented God's very presence, it could be touched only by those who were consecrated. Uzzah's death emphasized the Ark's unparalleled holiness.

David dances naked before the Ark, and his wife, Michal (Saul's daughter), rebukes him for such undignified behavior. But David won't let her rain on his parade, insisting he'll be even more enthusiastic (and undignified) in honoring the Lord who chose him over Saul as Israel's king.

The Promise to David

"Your house and your kingdom shall endure forever before me; your throne shall stand firm forever." Like the covenants with Noah (Gn 9) and Abraham (Gn 15), the promise to David is unconditional, whereas the covenant with Moses at Sinai (Ex 19–24) contained a major condition ("*If* you obey my laws . . .").

GOD'S PROMISE TO DAVID (2 SM 7,1-29)

2 Samuel 7 is an enormously significant text. God's promise to David of an eternal dynasty becomes the basis for Israel's expectation of a messiah after the Davidic dynasty abruptly comes to an end with the destruction of Jerusalem in 586 B.C. The New Testament sees the prophecy fulfilled in Jesus, the Son of David and eternal king. This text climaxes the story of David's rise to power and prepares the way for the future that will be shaped largely by David's dynasty.

Ancient Near Eastern literature sees a connection between building a temple and establishing a dynasty. Nathan's prophecy contains an interesting play on words that may be inferring this connection. The Hebrew word for "house" can also mean both temple and dynasty. David wants to build God a house (temple); but the Lord insists on building a house (dynasty) for David. The promise of an *eternal* dynasty manifests the Lord's approval of kingship; the ambivalence present when the monarchy was first established is nowhere in evidence here.

DAVID'S EXPLOITS (2 SM 8,1–9,13)

These episodes reveal David's noble character. He wins battles (8,1–18) and rules justly over all; he is the ideal king who shows mercy even to the family of his enemies. In ancient times new kings routinely killed all the relatives of the former king to eliminate any potential rival for the throne. But, because his love of Saul's family never wanes, David keeps his promise to Jonathan not to harm his relatives.

DAVID AND BATHSHEBA (2 SM 10,1 – 12,25)

One day David sees Bathsheba bathing and immediately decides he must have her. David is king, so what he wants he gets. We are told nothing of Bathsheba's feelings, but we know she is the wife of one of David's generals who is away battling the Ammonites. After his lust conceives a child, David conceives a cover-up. He calls Uriah home from battle in the hope that he will have sexual relations with his wife and then think the child she carries is his. But Uriah spoils the plan: In keeping with the rules of holy war, he refuses to sleep with Bathsheba. David's plot turns drastic and cold-blooded. Uriah's murder, carried out by Joab, costs the lives of other men as well. Now David can marry Bathsheba and hide his double sin from all—but not from the Lord.

Enter Nathan with a heartrending story of abusive power. David does not hesitate in pronouncing judgment on the antagonist of Nathan's tale: "The man merits death!" But Nathan shocks him with the words, "You are the man!" David's uniqueness and true greatness is revealed in his sincere and humble repentance. God forgives him, but his sin will have consequences. The child born of his lust will die and he will live out his life in the shadow of a sword. The stories that follow (the murder of Amnon and the rebellions of Absalom and Sheba) embody the violence that now will never leave David's house. The second child of David and Bathsheba, however, will be a bright light that comes from their union. He will be Israel's next king, favored by the Lord.

THE RAPE OF TAMAR AND ABSALOM'S REVENGE (2 SM 13,1 – 14,33)

Prior to David's sin with Bathsheba we heard nothing of problems in his reign. Now, as if set in motion by David's offense, problems multiply.

Like father, like son. Amnon lusts for his half-sister Tamar and will not rest till he has her. Though the customs of the times would have permitted a marriage between a half-brother and -sister, Amnon yields to lust rather than custom and rapes his sister. At times David's dealings with his sons were overindulgent, but taking no action against Amnon reveals a serious weakness, even blindness in David.

It falls to Absalom to avenge Tamar. He waits two years, but eventually he slays his brother and in the process becomes next in line for the throne. Absalom goes into exile and David mourns the loss of both sons until Joab persuades him to bring Absalom back.

REBELLIONS OF ABSALOM AND SHEBA (2 SM 15,1 – 20,26)

Absalom now consolidates his rebellious efforts, suggesting David is a poor enforcer of justice and claiming that if he were king, justice would reign. When he hears of Absalom's rebellion, David flees Jerusalem, barefoot and weeping, in a procession that resembles a penitential rite.

Absalom marches out in pursuit of his father and David stands ready to meet him. But the soldiers won't let the king risk his life, so David asks them to deal gently with Absalom. The king's forces quickly rout the rebels and Joab, in direct disobedience of David's orders, kills Absalom. David's reaction to his son's death (19,1) is one of Scripture's most moving passages. But the troops are shaken by David's bitter mourning. Joab warns the king he must set the example for the troops and let them rejoice in their victory. David listens and soon regains the support of his forces.

With the rebellion crushed, David returns triumphant to Jerusalem. But tension exists between the peoples of Judah and Israel, a fact that sets the stage for the next rebellion led by Sheba of the tribe of Benjamin. Joab pursues Sheba and quickly brings his rebellion to an end.

Appendices (2 Sm 21,1 – 24,25)

Except that they all speak about David's reign, these final chapters seem to have no common thread.

THE GIBEONITES ARE AVENGED; BATTLES WITH THE PHILISTINES (2 SM 21,1–22)

Behind this story are ancient religious beliefs that national disasters are the result of sin. The famine here resulted from Saul's illegal slaughter of the Gibeonites, and such sins must be atoned in order to restore balance to nature. Seven sons and grandsons of Saul are executed to make atonement for his sin. Saul's concubine, Rizpah, protects their decaying bodies, moving David to provide belated proper burial for Saul and Jonathan.

What can we make of the claim in verse 19 that it was the warrior Elhanan who slew Goliath? Possible explanations include the following: perhaps the name Goliath became mistakenly associated with David's victim who was actually a different Philistine; a later period may have romanticized Goliath's slaying as David's own doing; 1 Chronicles 20,5 credits Elhanan with the killing of Goliath's brother, which would mean David and Elhanan are both giant-killers.

DAVID'S SONG AND LAST WORDS (2 SM 22–23)

David's hymn (which, with some variations, reappears as Psalm 18) gives thanks to the Lord for military victories. The song reasserts God's faithfulness, the need for obedience, and God's promise to David of an everlasting dynasty.

David's last words review his career and acknowledge him as God's favorite, the recipient of an eternal covenant.

DAVID TAKES A CENSUS (2 SM 24,1–25)

Ancient writers sometimes confused primary and secondary causes. They believed that since God is all-powerful, God ultimately causes everything, no matter what the immediate causes might seem to be. Eventually they came to see that their all-loving God might permit but never "cause" evil. While this passage claims that God incited David to take the census, the same story retold in 1 Chronicles 21 blames it all on "Satan." The census is viewed as evil because it reflects arrogant pride, a willingness on David's part to put his trust in the size of his army rather than in the protection of the Lord. Even Joab feared angering the Lord by counting Israel's fighting forces.

CONTINUING SIGNIFICANCE OF THE BOOKS OF SAMUEL

The deuteronomistic writers teach us a valuable lesson through their conviction that human history and God's purposes are inextricably bound together. The Books of Samuel remind us that God is ever present in our lives both as individuals and as a nation. That God is acting in our own lives today may be less obvious, but is no less certain, than in the times of Saul and David. These books take on greater meaning for us when we read them as stories of people who, despite distance of time and place, are little different from ourselves: The truth of our lives can be found in theirs.

Questions for Discussion or Reflection

1. Given the seriousness of some of David's sins, can it still be said that he was "a man after God's own heart"? Why? In some ways, Saul's sins were less grievous than David's. Why then did God repent of choosing Saul yet never repent of choosing David?
2. God promised David an eternal monarchy, yet in 586 B.C. Jerusalem fell. No king reigns over Israel today. Has God's promise been kept? How?
3. What does David's sinfulness say to you about your own imperfections? Can you serve God and still be a sinner? Judging from the careers of Saul and David, what sins can most distance you from God?
4. When Israel moved from theocracy to monarchy, God set in place a system of checks and balances, with the prophet's voice serving to counter the king's power. Would the church today benefit from such a system of checks and balances? Can you point to any checks and balances already in place in the church?

1 AND 2 KINGS READING GUIDE

At a Glance

Who are the main players?	David Solomon Bathsheba Adonijah, half-brother of Solomon Rehoboam, son of Solomon and first king of Judah after split Jeroboam, first king of Israel after split Elijah the prophet Elisha, his assistant and successor Ahab, a king of Israel Jezebel, his wife Shunammite woman Naaman, general cured of leprosy Jehu, a king of Israel Hezekiah, a king of Judah Sennacherib, Assyrian king Isaiah, prophet in Judah Manasseh, worst king of Judah Josiah, reformer king of Judah Jehoiakim, a king of Judah Zedekiah, last king of Judah Nebuchadnezzar, king of Babylon
What should I look for?	How all kings are judged according to their fidelity to the covenant, not by political, social, or economic standards How the authors pay most attention to the very faithful and very unfaithful kings or those who most interacted with one of God's prophets How the behavior of the king powerfully impacts the life of the nation, especially as regards idolatry The importance of the Temple in the nation's life How David's reign is used as a standard to measure the reigns of all later kings The importance given to the role of prophets The frequency with which events are seen as the fulfillment of prophecy

When did this take place?	During a period of 400 years from approximately 961 B.C. to 561 B.C., that is, from the end of the reign of David to the Babylonian exile
Where did these events occur?	In the land of Israel which becomes divided into two parts: Israel in the North and Judah in the South
Why was this book written?	To help explain the exile; to tell the people that their infidelity to the covenant brought about the collapse of the nation, and to narrate the complete history of the monarchy
What's the story?	David's reign comes to an end and he is succeeded by his son Solomon whose reign is described in great detail. After Solomon's reign the kingdom is divided in two: Israel in the North, with its own centers of worship to rival Jerusalem, and Judah in the South. Twenty kings, all judged unfaithful, rule the northern kingdom over a period of approximately 200 years until the North collapses in 722–721 B.C. and its population is led into exile. In the South David's descendants (20 in all, though one was a usurper) rule for a period of about 360 years, until the time of the Babylonian exile in 586 B.C. Several of the southern kings attempt reform but ultimately their efforts are too little, too late.

In order to understand the process of editing and reediting that the Books of Kings went through, it is necessary to review the major events of Israel's history.

Israel was a united nation only during the reigns of Saul, David, and Solomon. Immediately after Solomon's death the ten northern tribes rejected the leadership of David's family and, under the leadership of Jeroboam, set up their own kingdom, Israel, with its own centers of worship at Dan and Bethel. The deuteronomistic writers judge this as a sinful act of idolatry that leads to the eventual downfall of the north in 721 B.C. at the hands of the Assyrians. All the northern kings who maintained this sinful system are therefore condemned. The two southern tribes continued on their own as the tiny kingdom of Judah with its capital at Jerusalem.

Two of Judah's kings, Hezekiah and Josiah, attempted to reform the nation's worship. During the reform of good king Josiah, a law code resembling the law code in the Book of Deuteronomy was found in the Temple and immediately implemented. Worship was centralized in Jerusalem, but after Josiah is killed in battle against Egypt the reform unravels. Less than 25 years after his death, Jerusalem is destroyed and all its people led into exile.

FORMATION OF THE BOOKS OF KINGS

Like most of the other books of the Old Testament, these books are compiled from various sources. The most obvious sources are these three:

1. *Official court documents* or *annals* that contained the dates and record of each king's reign. Highly selective in their choice of details, the deuteronomistic writers' chief concern is the loyalty or disloyalty of each king to proper worship of the Lord in Jerusalem.
2. *Temple writings* drawn either from court annals or temple archives that demonstrate the importance of the temple in the life of the nation.

3. *Prophetic narratives* that highlight the life of each prophet and focus on how their prophetic words were later fulfilled. These stories enhance the character and power of the prophet by accenting miraculous events in his ministry.

An early draft of the Books of Kings was probably written sometime between the start of Josiah's reform (621 B.C.) and his death in 609 B.C. Though Judah prospered, the northern kingdom had already been destroyed. This version explains that the cause of the North's collapse was Israel's willingness to abandon Jerusalem and establish rival worship sites in the North. According to the deuteronomists, the South does well under Josiah because he, like David, is wholly faithful to the Lord.

But then a second tragedy occurs. The South also collapses, so a new version is needed to explain this new disaster. Josiah's predecessor, Manasseh, gets the blame. His wickedness had been so great that Josiah's goodness was able only to postpone God's just and inevitable punishment.

Having recounted the last days of Moses (Deuteronomy), the conquest and settlement of Canaan (Judges), and the establishment of the monarchy under David (1 and 2 Samuel), the deuteronomistic history now continues in the Books of Kings with the story of the next 400 years of the monarchy and of the destruction of Israel and Judah.

One Book Becomes Two

Originally one book, 1 and 2 Kings was split only because when it was translated from Hebrew into Greek and Latin it did not fit on one scroll. Hebrew uses no vowels, only consonants, and is therefore very compact. But when the book was translated into languages that use vowels, more space was required, so it was divided in two.

READING THE BOOKS OF KINGS

Outline of 1 and 2 Kings

1 Kgs 1,1 – 11,43	The rise and reign of Solomon: Solomon's wisdom, his extravagant wealth, and even the deuteronomistic writers' negative judgment of his rule take a back seat to details of the building, furnishing, and dedication of the Temple.
1 Kgs 12,2 – 2 Kgs 17,41	The two kingdoms, Israel and Judah: The writers ignore or gloss over many historical events in favor of focusing on the religious practices of each king (of special interest is whether or not the king worshiped in the Jerusalem Temple). Much attention is also given to the prophets through whom God speaks and directs the flow of events in the life of Israel and Judah.
2 Kgs 18,1 – 25,30	The Kingdom of Judah: Judah survives on its own for about 120 years after the fall of Israel. The deuteronomistic writers intentionally focus on the reigns of the two reformer kings, Hezekiah and Josiah.

Chronological Tables of Rulers

The United Monarchy

The length of Saul's reign is not known; David and Solomon are each said to have ruled for forty years, which is often used as a general and somewhat indefinite number. Their reigns must have fallen between about 1020 and 922 (931) B.C., perhaps as follows:

Saul	1020–1000 B.C.
David	1000–961 (or 1000–965) B.C.
Solomon	961–922 (or 965–931) B.C.

The Divided Monarchy, Judah and Israel

Problems of chronology of the kings of Israel and Judah permit no easy solution. The following tables are based upon two widely accepted systems of chronology, one developed by W. F. Albright, and the other by E. R. Thiele. The dates of Thiele's system (3rd ed.), which are enclosed within parentheses, are presented in simplified form apart from coregencies and simultaneous claims to the throne. The two columns show the chronological relationships of the kings of the two kingdoms.

JUDAH	ISRAEL
Rehoboam—922 (931)	922 (931)—Jeroboam I
Abijam—915 (913)	
Asa—913 (911)	
	901 (910)—Nadab
	900 (909)—Baasha
	877 (886)—Elah
	876 (885)—Zimri
	876 (885)—Omri, Tibni
	(880)—Omri
Jehoshaphat—873 (870)	
	869 (874)—Ahab
	850 (853)—Ahaziah
Jehoram—849 (848)	849 (852)—Jehoram (Joram)
Ahaziah—842 (841)	842 (841)—Jehu

Athaliah – 842 (841)	
Joash (Jehoash) – 837 (835)	
	815 (814) – Jehoahaz
	801 (798) – Jehoash (Joash)
Amaziah – 800 (796)	
	786 (782) – Jeroboam II
Azariah (Uzziah) – 783 (767)	
	746 (753) – Zechariah
	745 (752) – Shallum
	745 (752) – Menahem
Jotham – 742 (740)	
	738 (742) – Pekahiah
	737 (740) – Pekah
Ahaz – 735 (732)	
	732 (732) – Hoshea
	721 (723/22) – Fall of Samaria
Hezekiah – 715 (716)	
Manasseh – 687 (687)	
Amon – 642 (643)	
Josiah – 640 (641)	
Jehoahaz – 609 (609)	
Jehoiakim – 609 (609)	
Jehoiachin – 598 (598)	
Zedekiah – 597 (597)	
Fall of Jerusalem – 587 (586)	

The Rise and Reign of Solomon (1 Kgs 1,1 – 11,43)

Besides showing great interest in the Temple, the deuteronomistic writers present their basic theological stance: The success of Israel and her kings depends entirely on their obedience of the Mosaic law.

SOLOMON BECOMES KING (1 KGS 1,1 – 2,46)

David is old and unable to rule. His son Adonijah, next in the line of succession, claims the throne. David's general Joab and his priest, Abiathar, both support Adonijah. But the prophet Nathan and Solomon's mother Bathsheba have different plans. They persuade David to name Solomon king instead.

David's final instructions to Solomon reiterate the promise to David of eternal dynasty, but, significantly, here the deuteronomistic writers present the promise in conditional terms: *If* his sons remain faithful to the Lord, *then* David's throne will stand secure.

Once Solomon is made king, Adonijah asks to marry David's concubine, Abishag. Solomon sees this as a masked attempt by Adonijah to regain his lost throne, for in the ancient world a person would marry the former king's wife or concubine in order to assert his claim to kingship. Solomon has Adonijah executed and soon thereafter, the general Joab and the old man Shimei as well. The deuteronomistic writers don't even comment on this ruthless behavior. They are more concerned with whether or not the king faithfully worships the Lord and the Lord alone. Because early in his career Solomon did so, and because he built the Temple, all his other behavior is seen as secondary.

THE WISDOM OF SOLOMON (1 KGS 3,1 – 5,14)

Solomon marries an Egyptian princess, probably a politically important move, but possibly also a hint that Solomon was relying on military alliances with powerful neighbors rather than on God to safeguard his nation.

Solomon is said to worship at "high places," a practice that is normally condemned by the deuteronomistic writers since usually these are associated with pagan Canaanite worship. At this time, however, they were probably used as places of authentic worship of the Lord and, since the Temple was not yet built, they are not seen as competing with Israel's central and only legitimate place of worship.

Solomon's confirmation as king contrasts sharply with that of Saul and David. Samuel anointed Saul and David and immediately the Spirit of the Lord descended on them. There is

He Told Them So

Samuel warned the people that a king could make life more difficult rather than more pleasant. Solomon proved him right. To support his building projects and lavish lifestyle, he introduced a national taxation system and forced labor; then he turned to idolatry as a result of marrying so many foreign wives and brought judgment on the nation. Samuel told them so!

no report of Solomon's anointing nor of the Spirit of God being with him. In the Books of Kings the Spirit of the Lord is associated with prophets, not kings. This makes the prophet's role all the more important. Kings may wield power, but it is the prophets who now represent God's will and speak God's word.

Solomon prays for practical wisdom that will enable him to govern well. In later tradition his wisdom will be equated with vast theoretical knowledge and with the ability to answer all questions, but here it is immediately put to practical use. The phrase used to describe Solomon's wisdom, "an understanding (literally, listening) heart," implies not just intelligence but insight. In one of Scripture's best known stories, Solomon cleverly distinguishes the true mother from the false, thus proving his prayer was answered.

BUILDING OF THE TEMPLE (1 KGS 5,15–7,51)

Much detail is given regarding the building of the Temple and its furnishings, but the meaning of many of the architectural terms is lost and the purpose of some of the furnishings is not known. Rectangular in shape and similar to pagan temples, the building had three sections: a vestibule, the temple proper, and the Holy of Holies which housed the Ark of the Covenant. The forced labor and taxes that enabled Solomon to build the Temple may also have contributed to the break-up of the kingdom after his death.

THE DEDICATION OF THE TEMPLE (1 KGS 8,1–9,9)

After the Ark of the Covenant is brought in, a dark cloud fills the Temple, signifying both the presence of the Lord and the Lord's acceptance of the Temple. Solomon's prayer presents two different theologies of the Temple, which reflect the nation's pre- and postexilic experience. Before the exile, the nation expected that the Temple would stand for all time. Hence, in verse 13, the Temple is called the place where God will dwell forever. But then the Temple was destroyed. So to deal with that reality, and to counter the possibility that the people will think God can be contained in a building of stone and mortar and lose a sense of God's transcendence, the deuteronomists speak of the Temple as the place where God's *name* dwells (verse 20, "honor" in *NAB,* "name" in Hebrew). Loss of the Temple, then, is not loss of the Lord, only of the place where God is honored.

The Temple is also the place where God hears the people's prayers, especially prayers for forgiveness, and where the people know for sure that God is accessible. Notice that when Solomon recalls the promise to David he phrases it conditionally: "Someone from your line (shall always) sit on the throne of Israel, provided only that your descendants look to their conduct . . ." (8,25). This conditional promise, repeated in 1 Kgs 9,6–9 where the Lord appears again to warn Solomon, prepares the way for Solomon's eventual rejection by the Lord.

JUDGMENT AGAINST SOLOMON (1 KGS 9,10–11,43)

Solomon's reign surpassed all others in riches and his wisdom astonished all. Even the Queen of Sheba was overwhelmed by the splendor of his court and his great wisdom. But the very excesses that brought him fame also brought judgment upon Solomon. His program of taxation and forced labor (needed to maintain his lavish living) added strain to the already shaky relationship between the North (Israel) and South (Judah) and contributed to the division of the kingdom.

But the deuteronomistic writers see Solomon's failure to worship the Lord and the Lord

Solomon's Temple

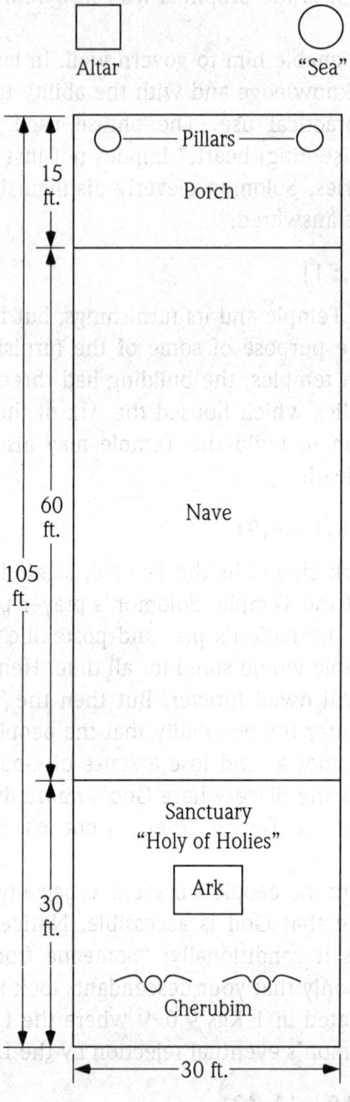

Note: There is little reliable information about the arrangement. This diagram shows the main elements.

alone as his greatest fault and the chief reason why the kingdom split. Though he lapsed into idolatry only in old age (a factor that somewhat lessens his guilt) he nonetheless allowed his many wives, whom he married in violation of God's law about intermarriage with foreigners, to persuade him to build altars to their gods. This idolatry must be punished. God will not forget the promise to David, so the Davidic dynasty will continue to reign, but they will reign only over the single tribe of Judah.

The Two Kingdoms, Israel and Judah (1 Kgs 12,1–2 Kgs 17,41)

The deuteronomistic writers are interested only in a religious or covenantal assessment of the reigns of each of the kings of the northern kingdom, Israel. Social, economic, and political factors are disregarded in favor of the overriding deuteronomic concern: the failure of the northern kings to worship the Lord in Jerusalem and their persistence in following the example of Jeroboam by worshiping in Dan and Bethel. Politically significant kings like Omri and Jeroboam II, who conquered enemies and ruled during times of great political and economic power, are dismissed in a few verses because they "did evil in the eyes of the LORD" by not worshiping in Jerusalem.

The deuteronomic writers weave stories of the prophets Elijah (1 Kgs 17,1–2 Kgs 1,16) and Elisha (2 Kgs 2–13) into their treatment of the reigns of the kings of Israel. The writers' understanding of the roles of kings and prophets, detailed below, color their perception of Israel's history.

Kingship In the ancient Near East a king was viewed either as an "adopted" son of god (as in Mesopotamia) or as a god himself (as in Egypt). With absolute authority, kings maintained order, defended the nation from enemies, and dispensed justice. Kings also had important religious roles, so much so that kingship and priesthood were essentially flip sides of the same coin.

In many ways, Israel's kings resembled those of their neighbors: They led the military, upheld justice, maintained order, functioned as priests by offering sacrifice, and were considered the Lord's "adopted" sons. But in the area of absolute authority there was significant difference: Israel's kings were *not* absolute, for they too were under the law. In fact, the deuteronomistic writers define kingship as fearing the Lord and keeping the commandments. Israel's was more like a constitutional monarchy where the Law of Moses was the constitution that made demands even on the king.

Prophecy According to the Book of Deuteronomy (18,9–22) prophets speak on God's behalf to both king and people. Primarily prophets *indict* and *warn*: they indict the king, and by extension the people, for not obeying God's commandments and they warn the king and people of impending punishment in the hope of getting them to repent.

The surest test of a true prophet, of course, is seeing whether or not the prophecy comes true (Dt 18,20–22). Consequently, the Books of Kings repeatedly point out the fulfillment of specific prophecies. But while prophets may do miracles, their most important task is to motivate the people to worship only the one, true Lord (Dt 13).

DIVISION OF THE KINGDOM (1 KGS 12,1–24)

Rehoboam ascends the throne and continues the forced-labor policy of his father Solomon, which all the more angers and alienates the northern tribes. But, for the deuteronomistic writers, Rehoboam's stubbornness and stupidity are merely serving the purposes of the Lord to dismantle the nation and give the lion's share to Jeroboam (1 Kgs 11,30–38).

THE REIGN OF JEROBOAM, KING OF ISRAEL: 922–901 B.C. (1 KGS 12,25 – 14,20)

The Lord promised Jeroboam a lasting dynasty in Israel if he would keep God's commandments. All such hope is quickly dashed because Jeroboam violates God's laws by establishing worship sites to rival Jerusalem at Dan and Bethel. He also sets up golden calves as objects of worship, thereby condemning himself and dooming the northern kingdom to destruction. The stories of the man of God who is sent to speak an oracle against the altar at Bethel and of Jeroboam's disguised wife seeking a favorable oracle for her sick son both serve to reiterate God's irreversible judgment against Jeroboam for his sin. Jeroboam apparently forgot that God had said, "I will build you an enduring house, if you listen to all I command you" (11,38).

Because many of the kings of Israel and Judah are dealt with so briefly, they are listed here chronologically with a brief notation of the deuteronomic judgment on their career.

KINGS OF ISRAEL AND JUDAH

Rehoboam, King of Judah   922–915 B.C.   1 Kgs 14,21–31

Uniquely, here the people are judged instead of the king. They worship as the pagans and so are punished with a foreign invasion and the looting of the Temple.

Jeroboam, King of Israel   922–901 B.C.   1 Kgs 12,25 – 14,20

He establishes worship in the North, away from Jerusalem, and is condemned.

Abijam, King of Judah   915–913 B.C.   1 Kgs 15,1–8

He is condemned because his heart was not true to the Lord.

Asa, King of Judah   913–873 B.C.   1 Kgs 15,9–24

Judged more positively than his father Abijam. He banished male temple prostitutes, destroyed pagan images, and even deposed his own queen mother for idolatry, but he did not remove the pagan "high places."

Nadab, King of Israel   901–900 B.C.   1 Kgs 15,25–32

Sinned like his father Jeroboam. His murder by Baasha ends Israel's first dynasty.

Baasha King of Israel   900–877 B.C.   1 Kgs 15,33 – 16,7

Continues evils of Jeroboam. Condemned by prophet Jehu.

Elah, King of Israel   877–876 B.C.   1 Kgs 16,8–14

Israel's second dynasty ends with his death during a coup—staged while he was getting drunk—thus fulfilling Jehu's prophecy.

Zimri, King of Israel   876 B.C.   1 Kgs 16,15–20

His seven-day reign ends in suicide. He's condemned as other kings: for doing evil in God's sight.

Omri, King of Israel   876–869 B.C.   1 Kgs 16,21–28

He gets high marks from secular historians as powerful ruler. His dynasty lasted four generations; he established Samaria as capital of Israel, accumulated wealth, and expanded boundaries. But he receives little notice here because he "did evil . . . beyond any of his predecessors."

Ahab, King of Israel   869–850 B.C.   1 Kgs 16,29–34

Israel's religiously worst king. His reign overlaps much of the ministry of Elijah the prophet. Like Solomon, he is condemned because he allows his foreign wife to lead him into pagan worship. (More below on Ahab's reign.)

THE PROPHET ELIJAH: THE DROUGHT (1 KGS 17,1-24)

Elijah gets no introduction, possibly because the beginning of the story of this man who is one of the Old Testament's most important figures has been lost. The stories about Elijah are filled with miraculous happenings because the deuteronomic writers use miracle stories to illustrate God's power flowing through the prophets.

Elijah first announces that henceforth rain will fall only at his command. During the ensuing drought he is cared for first by ravens, then by a widow who shares her last meal with him and is rewarded with an unending supply of food. Heroes being fed by animals and finding an unfailing food supply are common themes of folklore. When the generous widow's son suddenly dies, Elijah, in a dramatic scene, lies upon the boy and cries to the Lord. God hears Elijah's lament and restores the boy's life.

ELIJAH AND THE PROPHETS OF BAAL (1 KGS 18,1-46)

High drama and comic satire can both be found in the exciting confrontation between Elijah and the prophets of Baal on Mt. Carmel. At issue is a simple question: Who's in charge, Baal or the Lord? The answer will be found by seeing who can end the drought and bring life back to the land.

After entering Canaan, the Israelites had become very attracted to the fertility god, Baal, who was believed to control the fertility of the land. So the people had added worship of Baal to their worship of the Lord. But such syncretism was strongly opposed by the deuteronomistic writers. The God of Israel was a jealous God who did not tolerate divided loyalties. On Mt. Carmel the Lord's control of the rain demonstrates conclusively that no other god answers prayer, and no other god controls the land's fertility. Jezebel's vindictive efforts to humiliate Elijah fail miserably. Instead, her prophets are ridiculed (Elijah comments in 1 Kgs 18,27 that the prophets should "call louder . . . [because Baal] may have *retired,*" a euphemism for *relieving himself*) and killed for claiming to be what they are not (Dt 18,20).

Syncretism The blending together of beliefs and practices from different faith traditions or religions is called syncretism.

ELIJAH ON MT. HOREB (1 KGS 19,1-21)

The importance of Elijah's pilgrimage to Mt. Horeb (also called Mt. Sinai) is underscored by how clearly it parallels the story of Moses and the Exodus:

Moses	**Elijah**
Climbs Mt. Sinai	Climbs Mt. Horeb (same mountain)
Journeys forty years	Journeys forty days and nights
Fed by God with quail and manna	Fed by God through an angel
Learns God's will	Learns God's will
Hides in cleft of rock	Hides in cleft of rock

On the same mountain where Moses met God, Elijah encounters the Lord in the still, small voice (*NAB* "whispering sound"), rather than in the more dramatic (and more usual) ways God might be expected to be experienced: wind, earthquake, and fire. God's presence is an assurance that Israel has not been abandoned by the Lord. Mercifully, God will bring together those who refused to worship Baal as a remnant of hope.

By tossing his mantle onto Elisha (19,19–21), Elijah "anoints" him to be his successor and transfers his power to him.

Remnant A theologically important concept that refers to those who will survive the judgment that God will send upon the nation. The remnant becomes the basis for hope in the future when God will use these survivors to reestablish the nation/kingdom.

CONDEMNATIONS OF AHAB (1 KGS 20–21)

The true power in Israel is the Lord; therefore no king is absolute and no king is above the law. Two episodes illustrate this unique aspect of Israel's understanding of kingship.

First, an unnamed prophet brings Ahab God's promise of victory in battle against the Arameans, but also the expectation that Ahab will sacrifice the king of Aram in accordance with the practice of holy war or *herem* (the sacrifice of all the spoils of war to God). Because Ahab, like Saul before him, refuses to carry out *herem,* he is condemned.

Second, Ahab later wants to purchase a privately owned vineyard, but the owner, Naboth, refuses to sell because the law prohibits ancestral property from being sold (Lv 25). Supported by Ahab, Jezebel shows her contempt for Israel's law. She has Naboth killed and his property confiscated. This unwillingness to submit to the law of the Lord brings condemnation on Ahab and Jezebel. But because Ahab repents, God delays the destruction of his dynasty until the next generation.

KINGS OF ISRAEL AND JUDAH

Jehoshaphat, King of Judah 873–849 B.C. 1 Kgs 22,41–45

In all of 1 Kings he and his father Asa are the only kings praised for doing what "pleased the LORD." He brought peace and prosperity to Judah.

Ahaziah, King of Israel 850–849 B.C. 1 Kgs 22,52–2 Kgs 1,28

Baal worshiper, weak and spiteful. Condemned by Elijah for consulting pagan god. Tries to arrest Elijah to nullify his negative prophecy, but as always, every attempt to avoid or undo God's prophetic word is hopeless.

Joram, King of Israel 849–842 B.C. 2 Kgs 3,1–3

Though better than his parents, Ahab and Jezebel, still he persisted in the "sin of Jeroboam." As prophesied (1 Kgs 21,29), his murder ends the dynasty of Omri and Ahab.

ELIJAH TRANSFERS AUTHORITY TO ELISHA (2 KGS 2,1–25)

Elijah's power and greatness are once more demonstrated through a spectacular event: Elijah is taken up to heaven in a fiery chariot. Before he goes, however, Elisha asks that he inherit a double portion of Elijah's spirit. Soon it is clear that Elisha has done so, for he begins performing great miracles like dividing the Jordan's waters, purifying spring water at Jericho (2,21), and even calling down fatal curses (2,24). Beyond doubt, he is Elijah's rightful successor.

Worthy Persons In the Bible, only two persons were deemed worthy to be taken up by God without dying: Enoch (Gn 5,24) and Elijah (2 Kgs 2,11).

ELISHA NARRATIVES (2 KGS 3,4–4,44)

First we learn that the prophet sometimes used music to help him be open and receptive to the Spirit (3,15). Then we have two stories that reveal the character and power of the prophet Elisha and closely parallel events in the life of the prophet Elijah.

In one story Elisha multiplies oil for the widow of a fellow prophet just as Elijah had multiplied flour and oil for the widow of Zarephath (1 Kgs 17,7–17). Then he brings back to life the son of the Shunammite woman in the same way that Elijah had restored the widow's son in 1 Kgs 17, only here the story is richer and the woman's character better drawn. But the point is the same: Life and blessing are God's alone to give.

Two more episodes, neutralizing a poisoned stew (4,38–41) and multiplying loaves of bread (4,42–44), demonstrate the prophet's power and the goodness of the Lord.

ELISHA CURES NAAMAN'S LEPROSY (2 KGS 5,1–27)

What is remarkable here is that a pagan confesses Israel's God as the only God of all the earth. Having heard of Elisha from an Israelite serving girl, Naaman travels to Israel seeking a cure for his leprosy. After his healing, he takes home two mule-loads of earth from Israel to set up an altar to Yahweh in his homeland (since a god could not be worshiped apart from his own land).

Elisha's servant Gehazi secretly tries to profit from Naaman's cure but instead receives Naaman's disease as just punishment for his greed.

ELISHA AND THE ARAMEAN SIEGE (2 KGS 6,8–7,20)

This is a strange story that alternates with humor and horror. As the story opens, Elisha gets divine help to trick the forces of the king of Aram. At this point, there is humor and much confidence in the air. But shortly the king of Aram besieges the city and such a desperate famine results that the citizens begin to eat their own children. The king of Israel blames Elisha, but the prophet insists that God's deliverance will soon be manifested. Humor follows this tragic scene when the entire Aramean army is routed by imaginary sounds of chariots and horses. Fearing a great army is attacking, the enemy flees before what was actually four lepers looking for food. Once more God's word and God's true prophet are vindicated.

KINGS OF ISRAEL AND JUDAH

Jehoram, King of Judah 849–842 B.C. 2 Kgs 8,16–24

Judah fares well for 60 years under Asa and Jehoshaphat, but under Jehoram it relapses into idolatry. Married to the daughter of Ahab and Jezebel, Jehoram adopts worship of Baal and thus receives harsh condemnation from the deuteronomistic writers.

Ahaziah, King of Judah 842 B.C. 2 Kgs 8,25–29

Son of Jehoram, he is dominated by his mother Athaliah, Ahab's daughter. Murdered by Jehu, he is condemned like his father.

KINGS OF ISRAEL AND JUDAH (Continued)

Jehu, King of Israel 842–815 B.C. 2 Kgs 9,1 – 10,36

Overthrows Joram, son of Ahab, and sets out to rid Israel of Ahab's influence. Kills all the priests of Baal, plus Jezebel and 70 princes. Though he rids Israel of the cult of Baal, this brutally violent man receives negative evaluation from deuteronomistic writers.

Athaliah, Queen of Judah 842–837 B.C. 2 Kgs 11,1–20

After her son Ahaziah's death, she kills her grandchildren to eliminate any rivals to the throne. But one child, Joash, survives. Hidden for seven years, he reemerges and overthrows Athaliah with the help of the military and the priest Jehoiada.

Joash, King of Judah 837–800 B.C. 2 Kgs 12,1–22

Religious fervor returned to Judah during this period. Temple of Baal was destroyed after Athaliah's death. Joash, her grandson, repairs the Lord's Temple in Jerusalem under guidance of priest Jehoiada, but other priests are unresponsive to his initiative. After Jehoiada's death, Joash succumbs to idolatry, and even has prophet Zechariah, son of Jehoiada, stoned. He's finally killed by his own servants.

Jehoahaz, King of Israel 815–801 B.C. 2 Kgs 13,1–9

The pattern found in Book of Judges of sin, punishment, repentance, and deliverance is found again here: After his father Jehu had eliminated Baal worship, Jehoahaz reinstated it. As a consequence the nation was subjugated by the Aramites. Jehoahaz repents and a military leader frees Israel. But despite this deliverance the people persist in their sins of idolatry.

Joash, King of Israel 801–786 B.C. 2 Kgs 13,10–25

(This is *not* the same king as Joash of Judah.) Joash has good relationship with the prophet Elisha. Through Elisha he receives power to defeat his enemies and thus recovers much lost territory. In a unique occurrence, a dead person is brought to life through contact with the corpse of a holy person, Elisha. Nowhere else does such a thing occur in the Old Testament.

Amaziah, King of Judah 800–783 B.C 2 Kgs 14,1–22

The deuteronomistic writers say he "pleased the LORD, yet not like his forefather David." He kills those who killed his father Joash and engages in military exploits, including an ill-advised campaign against Israel that resulted in the plundering of the Jerusalem Temple by Israel's king.

Jeroboam II, King of Israel 786–746 B.C. 2 Kgs 14,23–29

He reigns over a period of peace and prosperity in Israel and regains much lost territory. But like his predecessors he perpetuates the sin of Jeroboam. Yet God seeks to save, not destroy the people.

Azariah, King of Judah 783–742 B.C. 2 Kgs 15,1–7

Also called Uzziah, he reigns longest among Judah's kings. He strengthens the kingdom but is afflicted with leprosy, probably as punishment for not destroying "the high places."

Zechariah, King of Israel 746–745 B.C. 2 Kgs 15,8–12

His six-month reign brings to an end the dynasty of Jehu as prophesied in 10,30.

KINGS OF ISRAEL AND JUDAH (Continued)

Shallum, King of Israel 745 B.C. 2 Kgs 15,13–16

His one-month reign ends with his assassination, reflecting the nation's instability.

Menahem, King of Israel 745–738 B.C. 2 Kgs 15,17–22

He begins his reign with a brutal attack on a town that resisted him, and there he "ripped open all the pregnant women." Assyria begins its attacks on Israel during his pro-Assyrian reign.

Pekahiah, King of Israel 744–732 B.C. 2 Kgs 15,23–26

Continues his father's pro-Assyrian policy. Israel is slipping into anarchy prior to his assassination.

Pekah, King of Israel 738–732 B.C. 2 Kgs 15,27–31

Attempts to unseat king of Judah, but Judah gets help from Assyria, which invades Israel and carries off part of the population. He, too, is assassinated.

Jotham, King of Judah 742–732 B.C. 2 Kgs 15,32–38

He did what pleased the Lord, but did not remove "the high places." He built one of the Temple gates and was attacked by King Pekah of Israel.

Ahaz, King of Judah 732–715 B.C. 2 Kgs 16,1–20

Attacked by the king of Aram and King Pekah of Israel, Ahaz uses Temple funds to hire the king of Assyria to help him fight off the aggressors. He builds a new altar for the Temple copied from an altar he had seen in Damascus when he had gone to show gratitude and loyalty to his victorious Assyrian overlord. But for this corruption of Temple worship (and other idolatry including sacrificing his own son) Ahaz is condemned by the deuteronomistic writers.

Hoshea, King of Israel 732–722 B.C. 2 Kgs 17,1–6

Israel's last king. Inexplicably judged more positively than other kings: "He did evil in the sight of the LORD, yet not to the extent of the kings of Israel before him" (17,2). He offends Assyria by refusing to pay tribute and by making an alliance with Egypt, thus provoking an Assyrian attack that results in collapse of the nation and permanent exile.

CONDEMNATION OF ISRAEL AND WARNING TO JUDAH (2 KGS 17,7–41)

Why did the northern kingdom fall? For the deuteronomists this question is far more important theologically than politically. Their answer is to be expected: because Israel lapsed into pagan worship and did not repent despite the prophets' repeated warnings. While the sin of Jeroboam (setting up rival worship sites at Bethel and Dan) is the reason given throughout the Books of Kings, the bulk of the reasons listed in verses 7–20 apply more to Judah than to Israel. There is a purpose here. The deuteronomists are packing a warning to Judah inside their condemnation of Israel: Do as the Israelites did, and you'll be punished as they were.

The Kingdom of Judah (2 Kgs 18,1–25,30)

The careers of the kings of Judah who reigned after the fall of Israel (722–721 B.C.) are covered in this final section. Hezekiah and Josiah implement reforms that, tragically, are short-lived.

Consequently Judah will fall like Israel. Though most of the story is negative, it ends on a positive note: the release from prison of Jehoiachin, Judah's last legitimate king.

KINGS OF JUDAH

Hezekiah, King of Judah   715–686 B.C.   2 Kgs 18,1 – 20,21

Hezekiah revolted against Assyria, whose vassal he had been. Assyria's king, Sennacherib, attacks Judah and lays siege to Jerusalem. The biblical account claims that, in keeping with the prophecy of Isaiah (19,21–31), Jerusalem was miraculously saved and Sennacherib was routed. But Assyrian records claim that a victorious Sennacherib captured 46 of Judah's cities.

Hezekiah's reforms in worship clear the way for God's deliverance of Judah. Despite Sennacherib's warnings that no god can keep Jerusalem from his grasp (18,29–35 and 19,10–13) the Lord does rescue the city and people. Hezekiah, however, remains Sennacherib's vassal – a fact the deuteronomistic writers simply ignore.

Isaiah the prophet ministered during Hezekiah's reign. He heals the king of a fatal illness and announces God will add 15 years to his life. But Isaiah also announces that Judah's ultimate doom will come at the hands of the Babylonians.

Manasseh, King of Judah   686–642 B.C.   2 Kgs 21,1–18

By far the worst of Judah's rulers, Manasseh undoes most of Hezekiah's reforms. Deuteronomistic writers see punishment as result of sin, and when they look for a cause of Judah's destruction they find it in Manasseh's sinful reign. Even the reforms of Josiah, who follows him, can't cancel the punishment that Manasseh's backward slide into idolatry (to please his Assyrian overlords) has merited.

Amon, King of Judah   642–640 B.C.   2 Kgs 21,19–26

Amon continues his father's sinful policies and is assassinated by his own servants.

Josiah, King of Judah   640–609 B.C.   2 Kgs 22,1 – 23,30

Coming to the throne at age eight, Josiah reigns at a time when Assyria's strength is declining. The deuteronomists rate him Judah's best king for the depth of his sincerity and piety. His reforms, which eliminate all traces of pagan worship, are so thorough that they even extend into regions of the North. A scroll of the Law of Moses is discovered when the Temple is being repaired, causing much excitement. Josiah immediately authenticates it (through the prophetess Huldah) and puts it into practice. Tragically, he undertakes an ill-advised campaign against Egypt and is killed in battle.

Jehoahaz, King of Judah   609 B.C.   2 Kgs 23,31–34

His three-month reign is terminated by Pharaoh Necho of Egypt who replaces him with a puppet king.

Jehoiakim, King of Judah   609–598 B.C.   2 Kgs 23,36 – 24,7

Babylon is gaining power during his reign, so Jehoiakim switches allegiance to Nebuchadnezzar, Babylon's king. But he also seeks help from Egypt when he decides to rebel against Babylon. For this Babylon attacks Jerusalem, but the deuteronomists see the attack as a direct result of the sins of Manasseh and as well-deserved punishment for Judah.

KINGS OF JUDAH (Continued)

Jehoiachin, King of Judah 598 B.C. 2 Kgs 24,8–17

Nebuchadnezzar of Babylon besieges Jerusalem in 597 B.C. Jehoiachin surrenders and is carried off into exile together with Jerusalem's prominent and powerful citizens and thousands of artisans and soldiers.

Zedekiah, King of Judah 597–586 B.C. 2 Kgs 24,18–25,7

Uncle of Jehoiachin, he is put on the throne by Nebuchadnezzar. When he rebels against Babylon, the city is besieged for nearly two years, resulting in acute starvation. Finally, the city is sacked, the Temple destroyed, officials executed, and the king and citizens are carried off to Babylonian exile.

JUDAH AFTER THE BABYLONIAN CONQUEST (2 KGS 25,8-30)

The devastation of Jerusalem is a clear sign that no hope remains in Judah. Hope has gone into exile in Babylon, and only there will God begin anew.

The Book of Jeremiah (Chapters 40–41) adds details to the scant information provided here. The Babylonians appoint Gedaliah as governor, but he rules over the remnant in Judah only a short time before he is assassinated by relatives of Judah's royal family.

The book ends with a report on King Jehoiachin. After 37 years he is released from prison and treated with great respect in Babylon. It may be the deuteronomistic writers want to say that despite their negative assessment of Jehoiachin, the line of David has not been snuffed out.

The Reasons The deuteronomists leave no doubt about why they believe Israel and Judah fell. Here's where you can find their reasons clearly presented.

Why Israel fell: 2 Kgs 17,7–21.

Why Judah fell: 2 Kgs 21,10–16.

CONTINUING SIGNIFICANCE OF THE BOOKS OF KINGS

The histories related in 1 and 2 Kings teach Israel what pleases the Lord and what it takes to build a new community: obedience and absolute loyalty to the Lord. With God, destruction, punishment, and death are never the final word. God's chastisement is always a means to an end. If punishment is necessary to open a people's eyes, then punishment must be seen as an act of God's love. While the Books of Kings justify God's actions against sinful Israel and Judah, they also do much more, for they teach that God is merciful and ever willing to offer new opportunities and new beginnings.

Questions for Discussion or Reflection

1. Why do you think that Solomon, who had received everything he could possibly want at the hands of the Lord, could still slip into false worship of other gods? What were the personal (internal) and cultural (external) reasons for his sin? Are people in positions of power more susceptible to temptation than others?

2. What do you make of Israel's and Judah's fascination with idols? Why were they so easily led astray? What was the attraction of the pagan religions for God's chosen people? In today's society, do you see signs of idolatry? Are cults, New Age philosophies, and interest in astrology, witchcraft, and mediums similar to the practices condemned in the Books of Kings? What are the "idols" in your life—money, fame, power, other people?

3. How important is the miraculous in your own faith life and in your appreciation of Scripture? What do amazing events like those reported in the ministries of Elijah and Elisha signify for you? What would happen to your faith if the Bible reported no such events? Can the miraculous be found in contemporary life? Why or why not?

4. Israel and Judah were both conquered by nations that the deuteronomistic writers would undoubtedly have considered even more wicked than they were. Why then were Israel and Judah destroyed? Were the Lord's expectations of the chosen people higher than the expectations of other nations? Are God's expectations of you different from those of others in your life? Why or why not?

The Chronicler's History and the Later Histories

1 AND 2 CHRONICLES READING GUIDE

The First Book of Chronicles is part of a larger work that includes the Second Book of Chronicles, Ezra, and Nehemiah. This chronicler's history begins with Adam (1 Chr 1,1) and concludes with the writer's own day, the fifth century following the restoration of the Jerusalem Temple after the Babylonian Exile (587 to 539 B.C.).

Like Genesis 1, the chronicler's history begins with Adam but repeats none of the stories found in the Priestly history. Chapters 1–9 are little more than genealogical lists taken from Bible texts and other sources available to the author. The narrative material begins with the story of Saul's death and burial (10,1–14). This, perhaps, is the chronicler's way of stating that Israel's story really begins with David, Saul's successor as king.

Like the deuteronomic history of Israel (Joshua, Judges, Samuel, and Kings, with Deuteronomy as its preface), the chronicler's history tells the story of the Israelite kingdoms and their fall. The deuteronomic history tries to explain why they fell. Even though the chronicler tells the story of Israel's past, the author's real purpose is to sketch out the prospects for Israel's future.

Cult The ritual and religious practices at a temple or other place of worship.

For the chronicler, what really counts are the validity of Judah's cultic institutions and continuity with the past. The author wanted to defend the legitimacy of the Davidic dynasty and the Temple of Jerusalem. By presenting the Judah of the chronicler's day as a worshiping community that was a direct extension of the community that God had established centuries before, the author aimed to show that Israel could secure its future by continuing to worship God according to the pattern set by David. Israel's hope then, resided not in the revelation that a messiah could guarantee its future but in the belief that careful observance of the cultic institutions, handed down by Judah's priests, would be its security. These cultic institutions were kept alive by the remnant that survived the exile and returned to Jerusalem. For the chronicler, the exile was just an unfortunate interruption in the otherwise unbroken history of the worshiping community of Judah.

The Septuagint (the ancient Greek translation of the Hebrew Bible) entitled the Books of Chronicles "Paraleipomenon" ("that which was left out"). This was also the name used in the Douay-Rheims version and some other Roman Catholic versions. Those responsible for the Septuagint considered Chronicles a sort of supplement to the Books of Samuel and Kings. The placement of these books differs in Bibles used by Jews. In Christian Bibles, the Old Testament ends with the prophets. The final text is Malachi's prophecy of the return of Elijah who will announce the "day of the LORD" (Mal 3,23f). The church reads a messianic meaning in this

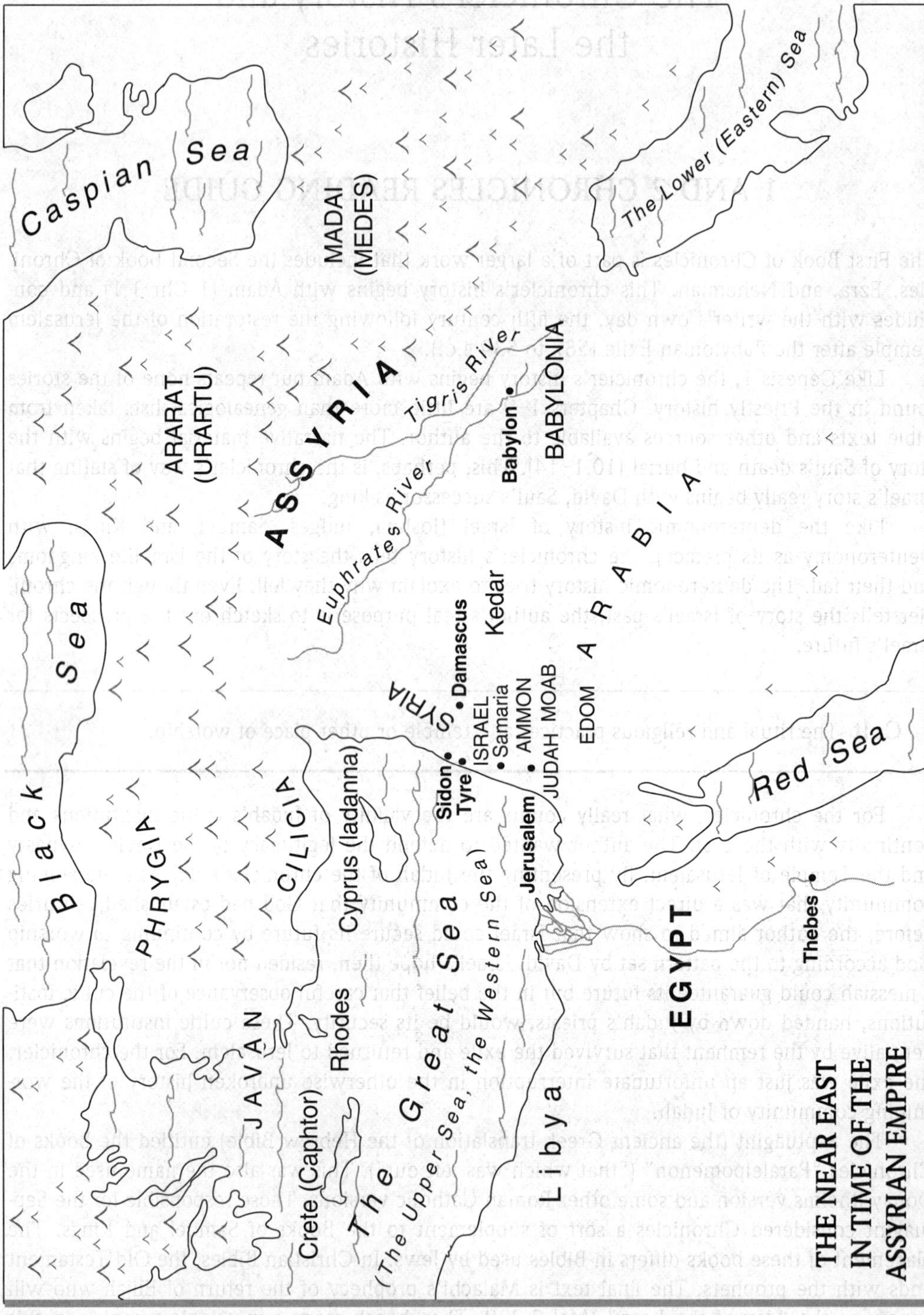

THE NEAR EAST IN TIME OF THE ASSYRIAN EMPIRE

text and identifies John the Baptist, the precursor of Jesus, as the returning Elijah (Mt 11–14; 17,11–13). But in the Hebrew Bible arranged by the rabbis, the prophetic books follow the books of Moses (the Torah or the Pentateuch) since the early rabbis viewed the prophets as explainers of the Torah. The Hebrew Bible has a third part called the "Writings," a collection of books that belong to neither the Torah nor the Prophets. The last books of this collection are 1 and 2 Chronicles. Thus the Hebrew Bible ends with the decree of Cyrus (2 Chr 36,23) that calls for the people of Judah to return to Jerusalem and rebuild the Temple there.

READING THE FIRST BOOK OF CHRONICLES

The First Book of Chronicles has a very simple arrangement: Chapters 1 – 9,34 are extensive genealogical lists; Chapters 9,35 – 29,30 tell the story of David.

The Genealogies

The genealogies of Chronicles extend from Adam to the return from the Babylonian Exile. The author uses the genealogies from the Book of Genesis in his own tables that begin with the descent from Adam to Abraham. From there the focus is on the twelve sons of Jacob. The chronicler arrives at the centerpiece of his presentation once the genealogy reaches Judah, one of Jacob's twelve sons. From here the author traces Judah's descendants down to David and his relatives. Chapter 3 lists David's descendants, all the kings of the Davidic dynasty and their descendants into the period after the Babylonian Exile. The genealogies of the other tribes follow but are not as extensive as the one for Judah except for the tribe of Levi. The chronicler had a special interest in the priestly tribe of Levi and the cult which they ministered. Finally, the genealogies of Saul's descendants frame a list of those who returned from the Babylonian Exile. From this reading one is left with the impression that the true beginning of Israel was not at Sinai with the giving of the Torah, as the Priestly history would have it, but with the rise of David.

The History of David's Reign

This section begins with a report on Saul's death and burial (10,1–12), along with a short editorial comment on the dangers Saul's reign posed for Israel because Saul was not faithful to God. Saul is little more than a figure of contrast for David, whose portrait the chronicler painted with strokes of piety and fidelity.

The chronicler wanted to make David's rise to power more impressive than the version found in the deuteronomic history (2 Sm 1–20), one of the sources he used. For example, 2 Samuel states that "the men of Judah" anointed David as king of their tribe following Saul's death. David ruled over Judah seven years before the elders of Israel chose him as king over the rest of the tribes (2 Sm 5,1–5). The chronicler, however, states that "all Israel" made David king immediately following Saul's death (1 Chr 11,1–3). And while the deuteronomic historian paints David's decision to bring the Ark into Jerusalem as a decision made by David alone, the chronicler portrays the same event as an act approved by all the people. The Ark's entrance into Jerusalem highlights the role of the Levites as David appoints them to carry it into the city. And since the king also commissions them to be singers in the Temple, they sing a psalm. The deuteronomic history does not contain these details. The rest of David's story is devoted to the

Shalom The Hebrew word for peace. It is reflected in the name *Solomon,* in Hebrew, *Shelomo.* A contrast is drawn between Solomon, the peaceful man, and David, who waged great wars. David was prevented from building the Temple not only because all his time was taken up in battle but also because he shed much blood, which made him ritually unfit for the task.

plans for the building of the Temple which Solomon, David's son, would eventually carry out. This makes Solomon a central figure in the chronicler's story.

The negative features of the story of David and Solomon that are recorded by the deuteronomic historian are omitted in the chronicler's version. Nothing is said about how Solomon succeeded David as king (2 Sm 12,1–12; 1 Kgs 1–2). Nothing is said about David's adultery with Bathsheba and the prophet Nathan's condemnation of David (2 Sm 12, 1–12). Nor does the chronicler make mention of the two revolts against David (2 Sm 15–18; 20,1–22).

Solomon's role is to complete the work David began. This seems to be a deliberate effort by the chronicler to imitate the transition from Moses to Joshua (Dt 21 and Jos 1). The author considered Solomon's succession to David as important as Joshua's succession to Moses.

The Establishment and Importance of the Temple

Worship is one of the chronicler's principle concerns. The author tries to show that Judah's future is dependent upon its fidelity to the proper forms of worship that God revealed to David. God blesses Judah and Judah worships God.

For the chronicler, the Temple and its liturgy symbolized God's continuous presence among the people of Judah. As long as the priests offered the correct sacrifices at the appropriate times in the presence of a grateful people, the Lord would dwell with Judah. Even though there were temples and sanctuaries elsewhere, for the chronicler, the Temple in Jerusalem was the only true place of worship. David built this Temple under the same kind of divine guidance that led Moses to build the tabernacle in the wilderness. The chronicler considered sacrifice at any other place to be illegitimate.

Chapters 23–27 are important for the chronicler's general purpose; proper worship and proper personnel to conduct the liturgy are described in detail. The division of duties among the priests, the Levites, and the Temple slaves is shown here.

The Priests
(chief religious officials)
Duties: blow the trumpets, minister in inner sanctuary, offer sacrifice on the altar, burn incense

The Levites
("lower clergy")
Duties: carry the Ark, singers, gatekeepers, judges, prophets, fund raisers

Temple Slaves
Duty: to help the Levites

Our Worship Heritage

The sacrament of orders in the Roman Catholic Church is largely a part of our heritage from ancient Israel. The rituals of ordination recognize this. The division of orders mirrors, to some extent, the chronicler's division of temple personnel:

episcopacy (bishops)	priests
presbyterate (priests)	Levites
diaconate (deacons)	Temple slaves

Even though status, role, and interrelationships in the church are different from the Old Testament's cultic personnel, there is a concern in the church for a hierarchy among those concerned with worship. However, there is not a single instance in the New Testament of anyone called "priest" presiding at Christian worship. The people experienced the presence of God in worship. The value the church places on worship and priesthood finds a strong support in the chronicler's history.

READING THE SECOND BOOK OF CHRONICLES

The Second Book continues the story of Israel with Solomon's ascent to the throne of David. As the *NAB* Introduction to 2 Chronicles says: The portrait of Solomon is an idealized one; he appears second only to David. This is in keeping with the author's purpose: stressing the supreme importance of the Temple and its worship. Judah's kings are judged by their attitude toward the Temple and its cult: one people united in worship of the one true God in one temple in one place, Jerusalem.

After Solomon's death, the Davidic-Solomonic empire broke up into two national states of Israel in the north and Judah in the south. The chronicler, though, all but ignores the northern kingdom and focuses all the attention on the southern kingdom, Judah. Why did he bother to retell the story of the monarchy in the South when there already existed the deuteronomic history of the Davidic dynasty? The author reinterpreted the material in order to give his readers a new understanding of the Davidic dynasty.

Politics, too, may have been at work here. This depends, however, upon the question of dating the books to the end of the 5th century B.C. At this time there was great strain between the people of the North and of the South. This caused the animosity that grew over the years and continued even into the New Testament period. Samaritan sources record that the division began when Eli left Shechem and established a high-priestly line at Shiloh (11th century B.C.). According to biblical tradition, (2 Kgs 17) the separation took place in the 8th century B.C. when the people of the former northern kingdom intermarried with foreign peoples whom the Assyrians introduced into their territory. Although it is not possible to treat either account as straight history, they do point to important concerns. The chronicler claimed that the Samaritans did not have true priesthood, and therefore their cult was worthless.

This attitude toward outsiders offers a striking example of the unwillingness to accept too great a diversity among those who considered themselves to be worshipers of the Lord. The complex reasons were in part political and economic. Samaria, apparently, wanted to control Jerusalem while the leadership of the Jerusalem community wanted to remain independent of such control. There were also religious and liturgical reasons. The people of the North wished to help with the rebuilding of the Jerusalem temple (Ezr 4,2) but the people of Judah refused their help. Perhaps they doubted the Samaritans' sincerity. There were also historical reasons for the rift. The tribes in the North and the South developed somewhat independently of one another and cherished their independence fiercely. Their union under David and Solomon was an exceptional intermission. Whatever the reasons for the strain, the Samaritan community, though small, has been in existence continuously even to the present day.

The Second Book of Chronicles is divided as follows:

2 Chr 1,1–9,31	The reign of Solomon
2 Chr 10,1–27,9	The monarchy before Hezekiah
2 Chr 28,1–36,1	Reforms of Hezekiah and Josiah
2 Chr 36,2–23	End of the kingdom

ESSAY

Relationship among Christian Churches

Until Vatican Council II the attitude of Catholics was similar to the lack of tolerance that the chronicler showed toward religious diversity. Restoration of Christian unity was one of the principal concerns of the Council's *Decree on Ecumenism.* Like the chronicler who in part was responsible for the rift between Jew and Samaritan, the Catholic Church, says the Council, shares in responsibility for the divisions among Christian churches. Of the two main kinds of division within Christianity, that which separates East from West most resembles the separation between Jew and Samaritan that developed during the last four centuries before Christ. Tensions that had existed for a long time came to a head in 1054 A.D. with the excommunication of the Patriarch of Constantinople by the papal legate and the patriarch's excommunication of the pope's delegate. Four centuries later, other divisions arose as the result of the Protestant Reformation. The differences between Christian churches are not simply theological but also historical, political, sociological, cultural, and even psychological. The Council suggested that dialogue among Christian churches focus first on what the churches share: the Scriptures, belief in Christ, baptism, and the Eucharist. We will recognize, then, that customs and doctrine will not necessarily be obstacles to unity. We will recognize that diversity and helpful adaptations to differences of culture contribute to the church's beauty.

Questions for Discussion or Reflection

1. The Second Vatican Council emphasized that the church is the entire people of God. For centuries the term *church* tended to mean the higher clergy. In one chapter of Vatican II's *Constitution on the Church,* the council spoke of "the universal call to holiness." How does this reverse the age-old idea that only "the ordained" have a special vocation to holiness?

2. What impact has the reemergence of lay ministry had upon the life of the church?
3. Describe how ministry and Holy Orders are related.
4. The term *catholic* means *universal.* How do you understand this?
5. How willing are you to live with religious diversity?
6. What contributions do various cultures, customs, and religious understandings make to the church's perception of God, of Christ, and of herself?

EZRA AND NEHEMIAH READING GUIDE

The Books of Ezra and Nehemiah are the only narrative accounts of the period after the Babylonian Exile (587–539 B.C.) that have survived in the Hebrew Bible.

Originally Ezra and Nehemiah were a single work. In fact, Nehemiah doesn't even have its own title in Jewish Bibles.

The Books of Ezra and Nehemiah do not give a reliable chronology of the restoration of Judah. They are more interested in presenting the religious dimension of the renewed life of Judah.

There are important political reasons why the Persian rulers were concerned about conditions in Judah. The beginning of both Nehemiah's and Ezra's missions coincided with Egyptian revolts against Persia's imperialism. It was important to have a sympathetic Judah at their back as they moved against rebellious Egypt. The following list of the Kings of Persia will be useful for dating the events mentioned in Ezra-Nehemiah.

The Kings of Persia

Cyrus	538–529 B.C.	Darius II	423–404 B.C.
Cambyses	529–521 B.C.	Artaxerxes II	404–358 B.C.
Darius I	521–485 B.C.	Artaxerxes III	358–337 B.C.
Xerxes	485–464 B.C.	End of the Persian Empire	331 B.C.
Artaxerxes I	464–423 B.C.	(Defeat of Darius III)	336–330 B.C.

READING THE BOOK OF EZRA

Outline of the Book of Ezra

Ezr 1,1 – 6,22 The Return from Exile
Ezr 7,1 – 10,44 The Deeds of Ezra

Timeline: Postexilic Literature

OT Sources	Events in Jerusalem	Persian Rulers
	586 B.C. to 500 B.C.	
	586: Fall of Jerusalem to Babylon; second and final deportation; diaspora Jews in Babylon	550–530: Cyrus II (the Great) 539: Fall of Babylonian Empire to Cyrus the Great
Ezra 1–6	538: First wave of the return to Jerusalem begins (groups continue to drift back over the next century). Zerubbabel begins rebuilding the temple in Jerusalem. Samaritans thwart their efforts; rebuilding project halts.	538: Cyrus the Great issues Edict of Toleration, allowing Jews to return home 530–522: Cambyses II 522–486: Darius I
Haggai and Zechariah 1–8	520: The prophets Haggai and Zechariah call for the rebuilding of the temple to continue; work begins. 515: In March, the second temple is finished.	
	500 B.C. to 400 B.C.	
[Esther?] Nehemiah's Memoirs: Neh 1–7 and Neh 11–13 [Jonah and Ruth?] Malachi	444–432: Nehemiah hears of the plight of Jerusalem while in Persia. He is appointed governor of Judah; the walls around Jerusalem are rebuilt.	486–465: Xerxes I ("Ahasuerus" in the Book of Esther) 465–423: Artaxerxes I [Age of Pericles in Athens] 423: Xerxes II 423–404: Darius II 404–358: Artaxerxes II
	400 B.C. to 331 B.C.	
The "I" narrative—Ezr 7,11–9,15 The "he" narrative—Ezr 10 and Neh 8–10 The king's letter—Ezr 7,12–26 The lists—Ezr 8,1–14; Ezr 10,18–44; Neh 10,1–27	398(?): Ezra, priest and scribe, institutes reforms of worship. End of OT history, c. 400	331: Alexander the Great conquers the Persian Empire (defeat of Darius III); Age of Socrates, Plato, Aristotle, rise of Hellenism

The Return from Exile and Rebuilding of the Temple

The most striking feature of this section is not apparent to those who read it in translation. While the rest of the Book of Ezra is in Hebrew, 4,7–6,18 are in Aramaic. This is due to the author's citing of a few official Persian documents relating to the restoration of Judah.

Chapters 1–3 cover the return from exile. Cyrus, the king of Persia, proclaimed that every exile from Judah who was ready to return to Jerusalem to rebuild its Temple should do so. The following verses describe the return itself. Chapter 2 gives a list of names of the returnees. At the top of the list is Zerubbabel, a member of the Davidic family and Jeshua, a member of a prominent priestly family. These two play an important role in Chapter 3 in the revival of worship in Jerusalem.

There were problems with the rebuilding. Opposition came from "the enemies of Judah and Benjamin" and from "the people of the land." Both tried to convince the Persians that restoration of Jerusalem was an act of political disloyalty. In the end all opposition failed and the people of Judah completed their project with full support of Persian imperial authorities.

The Four Stages of Return from Exile

1. Return under Cyrus (538 B.C.) led by Sheshbazzar who began rebuilding the temple but left it unfinished because of local opposition.
2. Return under Darius I (521–485 B.C.) led by Zerubbabel and Jeshua who completed the temple.
3. A group led by Ezra in either 458 or 398 B.C. who brought a copy of the Mosaic law.
4. Another group in 445 B.C. under Artaxerxes I (464–423 B.C.) led by Nehemiah to build the walls of Jerusalem and attempt to establish purity of community and worship. Nehemiah came as governor with his own retinue. He did not, strictly speaking, lead a group of returning exiles.

Ezra's Mission

The genealogy in 7,1–5 shows that Ezra was a Zadokite priest. (The Zadokite priests were those associated with the Jerusalem Temple before the Babylonian Exile. Zadok was a priest who served David and Solomon.) Ezra was an expert in the Torah which the priests who were in exile developed while in Babylon. An imperial commission given to Ezra from Artaxerxes includes information about contributions to the Temple in Jerusalem and the order to reestablish Judahite society based on the "law of God." By acceptance or rejection of the Torah, Judahites define themselves as belonging to or rejecting membership in the Jewish community. This means that in the view of the Persian government, the Priestly version of ancient Israel's ancestral faith was the "official" religion of Judah. The author's account of Ezra's journey seems to have been modeled on the Exodus from Egypt, the crossing of the Jordan, and the occupation of the land.

Aramaic was a common language of a diverse peoples that made up the empire and was the official language of the administration. The use of Hebrew and Aramaic shows that the people were bilingual. Originally Aramaic was the language of the Arameans. It is a Semitic language that is related to Hebrew. Because Arameans were active in commercial affairs in the Near East, the language became widely known. By the sixth century B.C., it became the most commonly used Semitic language and was generally used in Palestine until Greek became the official language after the conquest of Alexander the Great in the fourth century B.C.. Aramaic remained the language of the common people until the seventh century A.D., when Arabic replaced it. Aramaic was the language of Jesus, although he may have known Greek as well.

The Problem of Mixed Marriages

The remaining two chapters deal with Jews who have married outside their religious community. Ezra finds their behavior unacceptable and recites a long penitential prayer on their behalf. The people ask Ezra for help to set matters straight. The Hebrew text is unclear about the action taken in this matter, but some Jewish men probably divorced their non-Jewish wives in response to Ezra's urging.

Exclusivism in Ezra

In denouncing mixed marriages, Ezra speaks of the Jews as a "holy race." He accuses the people of desecrating themselves with "the people of the land" (Canaanites, Hittites, Perizzites, Jebusites, Ammonites, Moabites, Egyptians, and Amorites). The Jewish community faced the same threats to its existence as did the Israelite tribes centuries before the establishment of the Israelite national state (13th to 11th centuries, B.C.). At that time Israel faced hostile neighbors and was unable to defend herself adequately. There was little unity or even cooperation among the tribes in the 11th century. The prophet Samuel responded to these problems by establishing the monarchy. The king provided order and stability to the foundering Israelite tribes. The Davidic dynasty lasted from the 11th to the 5th centuries B.C., and furnished a sense of continuity. But in the 5th century B.C, Persian imperialism made the reestablishment of Judah's native dynasty impossible. Ezra provided the community with another source of stability and continuity—the Torah, which the Jews came to see as encompassing an eternal order given to Moses by God. This notion made the Jewish community exclusive and led to the idea of a "holy race" which was to remain unsullied by contact with the nations. To counteract the danger of Jews being absorbed by the non-Jewish culture that surrounded them, Ezra taught that there was a very specific criterion for membership in the Jewish community—heredity. Mixed marriages were no longer permissible and, under Ezra, the community was not open to outsiders.

Elevating heredity to the position of defining the people of God is understandable, yet it separated Israel from other nations. The Samaritans whom Ezra's decrees excluded from the people of God considered him their archenemy. In contrast, the Talmud considers Ezra to be a second Moses because he restored observance of the Torah when the people had forgotten about it. Early Christianity also had to deal with Ezra's legacy as it faced the consequences of its highly successful mission to the Gentiles (Acts 10,1 – 15,35). The early church abandoned the views of Ezra on membership in the people of God.

We need to see Ezra's notion of a "holy race" against the backdrop of the cultural assumptions of ancient Near Eastern people. The key word here is *holy.* According to Ezra, part of observance of the Torah revolved around separation from all that was not *ritually* pure. *Holy* is a cultic term, not a moral one implying that the Jews were ethically superior to other nations. Books such as Jonah and Ruth reminded their readers among the Jews that Gentiles, too, could please God.

Here and Now: The Call to Inclusion

The Book of Ezra speaks to a beleaguered religious community on the brink of extinction. The circumstances faced by Ezra's community are not those faced by the human community today. In our time, the threat to human existence comes from ignorance, prejudice, and hatred that keeps the peoples of the world apart. The Second Vatican Council recognized this when it decided to issue a separate document dealing with non-Christian religions. The Council declared that all peoples comprise a single community with a single final goal: God. All the religions of the world have come about from the universal attempt to probe the mystery of the divine. Catholics are encouraged to speak and work with followers of other religions. They are to acknowledge, preserve, and promote the spiritual and moral values found in these non-Christian religions. Judaism and Islam (the other two monotheistic faiths) are singled out by the Council for special attention. Any form of persecution and hatred that existed between Christians and Jews at any time is condemned. The Church has rejected any type of discrimination directed at people because of their religion and calls upon all Catholics to maintain "good fellowship" with all peoples by living with them in peace.

READING THE BOOK OF NEHEMIAH

It is important to see the work of both Nehemiah and Ezra against the deplorable conditions that the prophet Malachi describes (see Mal 1–2). Without the strong communal structures that Ezra and Nehemiah provided for Judah, the people would have found it impossible to live according to the high ideals of their ancestral religion since they lacked a healthy social and religious life. Nehemiah was a man of good practical sense, combined with deep faith in God. He was a layman, and his generous dedication of talents to the service of God and God's people remains an example for lay people today.

Outline of the Book of Nehemiah

Neh 1,1 – 7,22 The deeds of Nehemiah
Neh 8,1 – 13,31 Promulgation of the Law

The Rebuilding of Jerusalem

Because of bad reports that came to the Persian imperial court from Jerusalem, the emperor Artaxerxes I agreed to send Nehemiah, his cupbearer, to rebuild the city. There was great opposition from the governors of neighboring provinces who even proposed military action against Jerusalem. When their criticism and threats failed to dissuade Nehemiah, they began to plot against his life. Some within the Judahite community associated themselves with these plots against Nehemiah. This internal opposition came from the upper classes who had stake in maintaining the status quo. But despite all this opposition, Nehemiah completed the project of rebuilding the walls of the city in just fifty-two days.

From the time of David, Jerusalem was the central city of ancient Israel—at least for those devoted to the Davidic monarchy. David and Solomon wanted their Temple to solidify their capital's importance in the hearts of their people. But in spite of its great splendor, the Babylonians leveled the Temple and the city around it in 587 B.C. Although the Temple was rebuilt and Nehemiah refortified the city, the second Temple was never as elaborate as the one built by Solomon. Jerusalem was no longer a symbol of unity of North and South. It was, now, the center for preserving the particular worship of the Jewish community.

The Promulgation of the Torah

At this point the Nehemiah memoirs break off and Chapters 8–10 describe a ritual that Ezra conducts. This ceremony brings closure to the rebuilding of the city and the restoration of its religious life. The community heard the words of the Torah and responded by celebrating the Feast of Booths according to its prescriptions. Two weeks later they began a fast, and then Ezra made a great confession of sin in the name of the people.

The Confession

Nehemiah 9,6–37 is one of the important creedal statements in the Old Testament. It recounts Israel's experience of God from the time of Abraham to the period of restoration. This remarkable act of faith acknowledges God's goodness and fidelity despite Israel's failure to keep the commandments. The similar prayer of confession in Ezra 9,7–15 suggests that these two confessions were originally parts of the same prayer.

The Agreement of the People

Chapter 10 contains a written pledge made by those listed in verses 1b–29 to observe the Torah of Moses. Among the specific points made in this pledge are the prohibition of marriage with Gentiles and the observance of the sabbath. Those who made the pledge promised to provide firewood for the altar, first fruits for sacrifice, and tithes for the support of the Levites. Chapter 11 begins with a lottery used to resettle Jerusalem. Nehemiah 12 begins with lists of priests and Levites, followed by a description of the dedication of the walls. The book concludes with a list of the various reform measures that the people pledged themselves to observe.

ESSAY

The Torah

An important theme in both Ezra and Nehemiah is the Torah as a written official guide for the life of the Jewish community. In Nehemiah 8–10, Ezra reads the law, the people confess their failure to observe it, and then they agree to live according to its precepts. Unfortunately, too many Christians have very distorted notions of the Torah. These may have arisen because of the tense atmosphere in the Gospels which recount Jesus' debates with the Pharisees regarding the interpretation of the Torah and the bitter exchanges between Paul and some early Christians who thought that the Torah should be observed by everyone. But both Jesus and Paul often gave praise to the Torah: "Do you think that I have come to abolish the law or the prophets. . . . Whoever breaks one of the least of these commandments and teaches others to do so will be called the least in the kingdom of heaven. . . ." (Mt 5,17–19) and "So then the law is holy, and the commandment is holy and righteous and good" (Rom 7,12). Still the word "law" has a negative ring to it in the ears of most Christians.

The key to understanding and appreciating the Torah is to discover where it came from. Like most important words in the Hebrew Bible, *Torah* is used in several different ways. *Torah* could have come from the Hebrew word *yarah* which means to cast lots, to point the way, or to instruct. *Torah* may have derived from the instructions priests gave to the people.

In the Bible, *Torah* usually refers to God's instructions to Moses at Sinai that he handed on to ancient Israel. In the Book of Deuteronomy, *Torah* takes on a more extensive sense and becomes that which determines Israel's cultural, religious, and national identity. The prophets use *Torah* in several ways: cultic regulations, God's moral commands and ethical norms, and even the divine teachings given through the prophets. The Psalms praise both the Torah and those who live by it.

The early rabbis believed that they were responsible for transmitting not only the written Torah but also an oral Torah which contained the teachings of revered sages who furthered the obligations of the law beyond the words of the written Torah and made violations of the written Torah much more difficult. Around 200 A.D., Rabbi Judah the Prince committed this oral law to writing in a work called the Mishnah. This was the beginning of the Talmud (the code of rabbinical teaching on the manner of observing the law). In Judaism today, *Torah* refers not only to the Books of Moses but to the Talmud and the entire Jewish ethical tradition.

The Bible often speaks of Israel as God's children. Some people understood the Torah as the teaching given by the loving parent, God, to the child, Israel. In this light, the giving of Torah is an act of highest love. Jews of ancient Israel or modern times do not experience Torah as a burden, but as a way to life and as a source of joy. This devotion to ethical principles—the attitude of self-examination and self-correction that comes from loving observance and the preservation of identity through a specific moral code—are values that Christians could learn from Judaism, ancient and modern.

Ritual Purity

At first glance, the Books of Ezra and Nehemiah may seem to be concerned with racial or ethnic discrimination. Though this could have been at work here, it is important to note that the emphasis on purity primarily involves cult and ritual. Mixing two peoples in marriage or in worship offends the Near Eastern notion of order. Exclusion of Gentiles from worship did not come from a belief in ethnic superiority but was associated with the rebuilding of the Temple and the restoration program led by both Ezra and Nehemiah.

According to the Gospel of John in the New Testament, Christians worship in "Spirit and in truth" (Jn 4,23), transcending these ethnic patterns. Paul makes it clear that in Jesus there is "no Jew or Greek" (Gal 3,28). And Matthew writes that Jesus' final command was to "make disciples of all nations" (Mt 28,19). This did not occur to the first Christians automatically. The Acts of the Apostles shows that the inclusion of the Gentiles into the Christian community was a matter of spirited debate among Jewish Christians (Acts 15,1–35).

The synagogue also struggled with the question of inclusion or exclusion of the Gentiles. Some rabbis favored the more exclusive strain as found in Deuteronomy, Ezra, and Nehemiah. Others endorsed the more inclusive tendencies in texts such as Isaiah 56, which states that the Temple was to be "a house of prayer for *all* peoples."

Questions for Reflection or Discussion

1. Christians cannot make use of the specific way Ezra responded to the problems of his day. They can, however, imitate his passionate commitment to the survival of his people. What calls Christians today to this kind of passionate commitment?
2. What kinds of exclusion do you see in the world in which you live?
3. The teachings of the Torah are not considered a burden but as principles or a moral code given by a loving parent to the children. What teachings do you view in this manner?

The Apocrypha The Catholic Bible includes seven Old Testament books that are not part of Jewish and Protestant Bibles. These books are sometimes referred to as The Apocrypha (meaning "hidden" or "concealed" works) but more often as the Deuterocanonical books (meaning "second" canon).

The books in question were all originally written in Greek rather than Hebrew. For that reason they were not incorporated into the Jewish Bible when the official list of inspired books was finalized by a group of rabbis meeting at the Council of Jamnia in 90 A.D. The books are: Tobit, Judith, Wisdom, Sirach, Baruch, and 1 and 2 Maccabees.

St. Jerome had expressed doubt about the value of these books and considered them less important than the other canonical books. During the Reformation Protestant leaders chose to remove these books from the Old Testament in an effort to be rid of excess baggage and to get back to their scriptural roots. Another factor may have been that some passages in these books were believed to support certain "Catholic" beliefs like the value of prayer for the dead and the existence of purgatory.

TOBIT READING GUIDE

The Book of Tobit is a complex literary work with a very simple moral. The book tells the tragedies and triumphs in the lives of three people: Tobit, Sarah, and Tobiah. The author, by weaving the stories together in three different but related plots, has a theological purpose: to show that God can manage the circumstances of people's lives to bring God's plans to fulfillment. The primary message is simple: God rewards those who are faithful.

APPROACHING THE BOOK: THE LITERARY FORM OF TOBIT

This book is a kind of religious novel. The historical and geographical details are there simply to provide a setting for the story. The author confuses the kings of Assyria, shows ignorance of the topography of Mesopotamia, and dates Tobit's exile earlier than it could have been. There is little to suggest that the author meant this work to be historical.

The book is the work of a single author and not the product of tradition. What is especially important to notice is how the author tells the stories of Tobit and his relative Sarah. Both suffer undeservedly. This cleverly told story is short enough to read in a single sitting. One key to understanding the purpose of the story is the unfolding of how God answers the prayers of the innocent Tobit and Sarah in a way they hardly expected. The story assumes God's determination to reward the just. When they suffer, there is a limit to that suffering. Once the limit occurs, God will intervene, sometimes miraculously.

THE JUDAISM OF THE BOOK

The Book of Tobit was probably written in the second century B.C.; it is not known where. It reveals a form of Judaism that accepts magic and sees angels and demons as having important roles to play in the drama between God and human beings. This differs sharply from the books such as Judith and Esther where human beings are in control of their own destiny without any intervention from angels or demons. The author of Tobit considers angels to be more than God's messengers: They mediate prayers in God's throne room; they oppose demons; and they authorize the writing of books. While angels make their negotiations for good people, demons are malicious powers.

The Book of Tobit reflects the importance that the Book of Deuteronomy came to have in early Judaism. This is especially clear in Tobit 14,4–7 which claims that the exile happened because of Israel's infidelity. But it maintains that the exile is not God's final judgment on Israel; rather there is hope for mercy, and the Temple in Jerusalem is the only legitimate place for worship. Fidelity to God is measured in terms of fulfillment of the Torah, just as Deuteronomy preaches.

Finally, Tobit seems to reflect the circumstances of Jews in the diaspora (Jewish settlements outside Palestine). The book depicts Gentiles as unsympathetic to Tobit's activities and as responsible for persecuting him. The book presents marriage within Judaism as a duty. It teaches that God is supreme over all people and is present to those in exile in the midst of their suffering. It emphasizes the need to preserve Jewish identity in the diaspora achieved through the family. This emphasis on the family is the reason that Tobit remained popular in the church even though the book did not become part of the Jewish canon of the Old Testament.

READING THE BOOK OF TOBIT

The only way to savor the book's literary artistry and to appreciate its religious perspectives is to follow the way the author unfolds the events of Tobit's, Sarah's, and their families' lives. Notice how the stories of Tobit and Sarah parallel one another:

Tobit's piety (2,1–7)	Sarah's innocence (3,14)
Tobit's blindness (2,9–10)	Sarah's demon (3,8)
Tobit's reproach (2,14)	Sarah's reproach (3,7–10)
Tobit's prayer (3,1–6)	Sarah's prayer (3,10–15)

God hears these prayers but responds to them in a totally unexpected manner. Though Tobit and Sarah felt abandoned by God, God was, nonetheless, with them in the midst of their suffering. The reader should notice the movement in the book from despair to thanksgiving and praise.

About Angels and Demons

The Book of Tobit reflects the belief of early Judaism in angels and demons as supernatural beings. The first form of this belief seems to be "the messenger of the Lord" which belongs to the earliest narratives in the Hebrew Bible. In some of these stories the messenger is not different from the Lord (see Gn 16,13; 21,18; 31,13). Since God confronts people directly in many early stories, the appearance of angels is somewhat rare. As people begin to think of God as far beyond the human sphere, angels appear more regularly in the stories. Ideas develop about good angels and bad angels (demons), a hierarchy of angels, and the various duties of angels. It is possible to see popular imagination at work in the description of angels. They wear white garments and have wings. Around the turn of the era, there appear in a few Jewish texts what seems to be the belief that it was permissible to portray figures from Israel's past, especially Adam and Jacob, as angels. Some Jews must have held that it was possible for a select few to transcend humanity and become angels. However, not all Jews believed in angels. The Acts of the Apostles asserts that the Pharisees, who represented more liberal, popular belief, acknowledged the existence of angels while the Sadducees rejected the existence of angels as well as belief in spirits and the resurrection from the dead.

Questions for Discussion or Reflection

1. All the biblical short stories are told from the third person point of view, that is, the narrator tells us about the characters by describing their actions through dialogue and speech. How would the story of the Book of Tobit be affected if it were told by the characters themselves? Choose a character who interests you and pick a particular scene or episode from the story. Allow that person to tell the story from his or her own point of view. Give lots of details, emotional reactions, and insights *based on* the story.
2. The purpose of the book is to move its readers from despair to prayer. The most important message in this story is that God is with Tobit even when Tobit does not experience the divine presence. Reflect upon God's fidelity to you in time of suffering and pray Tobit's Song of Praise (13,1–18).
3. Have you had an experience similar to Tobit's in your own life?

JUDITH READING GUIDE

THE BOOK'S LITERARY FORM

There have been several attempts to classify the Book of Judith according to its literary type. Clearly it is not history. It is useless to try to read it against the backdrop of Jewish history or that of other nations in the ancient world. There are just too many historical errors. Is it then a historical novel, *midrash,* or a fictional drama? None of these is completely satisfactory. The book is the result of a conscious, faith-filled meditation on God's providential care for Israel. The story shows how the invisible hand of God rescues Israel through the hand of Judith.

> **Midrash** is the expansion, probing and exposition of biblical texts to bring out their full new meaning for changed circumstances.

Over the centuries this story has attracted remarkable attention from writers, artists, and composers. Mozart and Beethoven chose Judith as the subject of their musical compositions. Painters have represented her story on canvas, and sculptors even carved her story in stone on the great cathedral of Chartres in France. The reason for all this attention is that Judith's story is such a good one. It is a heroic tale in which an unlikely character overcomes the cowardice of her own people in the face of the enemy.

The Book of Judith is a piece of literature for difficult times. It was hoped that the reader would take to heart the lesson that God was still the master of history who could save Israel from her enemies. There is a parallel with the time of the Exodus: As God had delivered the people by the hand of Moses, so God could deliver them by the hand of the pious widow Judith.

The heroine's name is probably not a proper name. It simply means "Jewish woman." Judith is more than an individual: She is a composite of all the women who have saved Israel in the past by their piety, wisdom, and action. These heroines saved the people of ancient Israel when the more usual channels of leadership (the king, priests, and other notables) were not able to meet the challenges of faith.

The first people to hear the story of Judith lived in a traditional society in which roles assigned to men and women were clearly distinct. Change, if it took place at all, occurred very slowly. This story offers a surprising contradiction to what the culture assumed the role and status of women should be. In this story the men proved to be utter failures in the face of the threats of the king Nebuchadnezzar and Holofernes, the commander of his armies. The impact that this story made on a traditional society such as early Judaism is difficult for us to appreciate since we live in a society where change occurs much more quickly.

But on the other hand, the Book of Judith is quite conservative in its outlook. By rescuing her people from destruction at the hands of Gentiles, Judith is a model for the Jewish woman as the preserver of tradition. Judith is a paradigm for the Jewish woman who protects her family from intrusions from the outside that threaten to dilute their loyalty to their ancestral religion. The heroine of the book carries out the role assigned her by her culture, but also surpasses that role.

The Image of Women in the Church

A type of tension similar to that in Judith is visible in the U.S. Bishops' Pastoral Response to Women's Concerns for Church and Society, *Partners in the Mystery of Redemption* (1988). The first draft attempted to integrate the responses the bishops received from Catholic women through conversations that were part of this first draft. Reading these responses makes it clear that there is great diversity among Catholic women. "The typical Catholic woman" doesn't exist. Like Judith, Catholic women see themselves as preservers of what is best in the tradition, though some are ready to cross what they perceive as artificial barriers set up by that tradition. The Book of Judith offers a model for the process of contemporary theological reflection on the role and status of women in the church. The book itself is a product of early Judaism's reflection on the role of women in its social and religious system. At the very least, the book sees women as, at times, better fit to be instruments of salvation than men—a conclusion that was most unexpected in the cultural milieu in which it rose.

THE IRONY OF THE BOOK

The story of Judith is full of unexpected turns. The most obvious, especially to those who first hear or read the story, is that a woman—not a man—saved Judah in time of severe distress. Judith is more faithful and resourceful than any of the men of Bethulia. She is more eloquent than the king and more courageous than the leading citizens of the city. Yet Judith is a very unlikely heroine. As a childless widow, she occupied a very low place in the social hierarchy. While the king, priests, and leaders show themselves incapable of dealing with the crisis, Judith stands up to the threat posed by Holofernes and takes decisive action to end that threat.

The means she uses to accomplish her end may offend some. She uses her beauty to gain access to the enemy camp and to beguile Holofernes. Judith, though, is using the one weapon she has available to her. This leads to the second irony. Judith destroys the enemy not with military might but with her charm and disarming beauty.

Finally, Judith is a childless widow, yet the book portrays her as the mother of faith. That is why the high priests praise her so highly. The Latin hymn, *Tota pulchra es,* applies these words in praise of Mary. The story of Judith provides the liturgy with an appropriate image for the Virgin Mary as the Mother of the Church.

THE JUDAISM OF THE BOOK

The Book of Judith affirms that the deliverance of the Jews of Bethulia depends not on power and might but on fidelity to the law. The author portrays Judith as living according to the law as Jews interpreted it at the time. As a widow, she lives in a state of mourning marked by fasting. She prays daily at the hour of the incense offering in the Temple. She observes Jewish dietary laws. She purifies herself by bathing in running water at the appropriate time. Judith criticizes the people for violating the law of first fruits and tithes. But while the book presents Judith's obedience to the Torah as the key to Israel's deliverance, it shows a type of flexibility that is able to respond to a person such as Achior the Ammonite, who wishes to join the Israelites in the service of God. According to Deuteronomy, Israel was never to admit an Ammonite into their community. The issue of inclusion and exclusion was a perplexing one for Judaism, as it was also for the first Christians (see Acts 10,1–49; 11,1–8, 15,1–12).

Questions for Discussion or Reflection

1. What are the role expectations out of which you live your life?
2. To what degree have these been decided by society's role expectations for you as a man or a woman?
3. What would you restructure, if you could? Can you imagine ways of organizing your life differently?
4. What are some experiences of women's faith that have nourished your life?
5. What are the ways that women's faith continues to sustain the church?
6. What insights do women gain from their experience that men in society and in the church need to hear?
7. Scripture uses both masculine and feminine images as revelatory of God. How does thinking and speaking of God through both masculine and feminine images make a difference in our sense of the divine?
8. In what ways have you made an effort to use inclusive language in prayer?
9. Has there been any effort in your parish to deal with questions of inclusive language? If not, what action could you take to bring attention to this issue?

Some of the above questions have been taken from the *New Leaven Booklet Series:* "In God's Image" and "Women, Faithful for the Future." Kansas City: Leaven Press 1985.

ESTHER READING GUIDE

The central concern of the Book of Esther is the survival of the Jewish minority in the midst of a world that is growing more hostile to it. This book tells the story of Mordecai, a Jewish courtier in the service of the Persian emperors, and his beautiful and courageous niece, Esther, and how they averted one threat to Jewish survival. The book was intended to console Israel and remind them that God's providence continually cares for them, never abandoning them when they serve God faithfully or turn to God, asking for forgiveness. God does not intervene directly to resolve the problem, but even though the divine action may be hidden, it is nonetheless real.

STRUCTURE OF THE BOOK

A confusing aspect to the arrangement of this book in the *New American Bible* is the order and numbering of its chapters and verses. Besides the familiar numbering common to the rest of the Bible, there are six chapters that have letter identification scattered in the midst of chapters that have the usual number identification. This is the result of the way the Book of Esther has come down to us.

This book has survived in two forms: a shorter Hebrew text and a longer version preserved in the Septuagint (the ancient Greek version of the Hebrew Bible). The Greek has about 107 verses more than the Hebrew. When St. Jerome revised the Old Latin translation and compared these two ancient versions, he concluded that the extra verses in Greek were not inspired. Jerome took these verses out of their proper context and put them in an appendix at the end of the book. The Greek additions also did not become part of the Jewish canon, and their place in the canon of the Roman Catholic Church wasn't settled until the Council of Trent in the 16th century. Protestant churches do not accept the additions to Esther as canonical. The arrangement in this *New American Bible* attempts to follow the order of the Greek version without losing the arrangement of numbering of chapters and verses that is universally followed. The table on the next page compares the two versions.

The purpose of the Greek additions to the Hebrew version of Esther is clear. They introduce a religious element into a secular story. The Hebrew version is a tale about how the Jews were able to outsmart their enemies and does not make a single reference to God. The additions also lend an air of authenticity by introducing "documents" (B,107;E,1–24) that make the book read as if it were a historical work. This is important to encourage the celebration of the Feast of Purim with which the story became associated.

Purim The holiday named for the pur (lot) Haman cast to determine when the Jews would be destroyed. Purim is the feast celebrated on the 14th and 15th of Adar (around the first of March) commemorating the deliverance of the Jews from Haman's pogrom (an officially organized massacre).

Hebrew Bible	Greek Septuagint
1,1 – 3,13	A. Mordecai's dream; the conspiracy against the king
3,14 – 4,17	B. The royal edict of Haman
	C. The prayers of Mordecai and Esther
5,1–2 (omitted in Septuagint)	D. Expansion of the account of Esther's audience with the king
5,3 – 8,12	E. The royal edict of Mordecai
8,13 – 10,3	F. Explanation of Mordecai's dream, conclusion, and post-script

Source: Carol A. Newsom and Sharon H. Ringe, (ed.), *Women's Bible Commentary* (London: John Knox Press, 1992) 126.

THE STORY AND ITS PERSONALITIES

The story takes place in the diaspora (the Jewish settlements outside of the land of Israel) and makes no reference to the homeland of the Jews. Two royal officials, Mordecai the Jew and Haman the Agagite, vie for power and position in the court of the Persian emperor. The rivalry between them soon sweeps up the entire Jewish community because of their particular customs and patterns of behavior. When Esther joins her relative, Mordecai, in a plan to frustrate Haman's murderous plots, the tension is resolved. What was to have been an officially organized massacre of the Jews becomes a celebration of the Jews because Haman and his conspiracy fail.

The Name Esther The name Esther was a Mesopotamian name. Her Jewish name was Hadassah, which means "myrtle."

The story begins with the dethronement of Vashti, the queen of Persia. Vashti refused to obey the command of her drunken husband, Ahasuerus, king of Persia, when during a banquet he ordered her to "display her beauty" before his male courtiers. Because she refused to submit to this indignity, the king's officials advised him to remove her as queen. They feared that their own wives might imitate and refuse to obey their orders. The king issued a decree deposing Vashti and declaring that "every man should be lord of his own home."

Unlike Judith, Esther is hardly a model for feminists. She participates in the process to replace Vashti, who is the real heroine according to a feminist reading of this text. Vashti lost her crown but preserved her dignity. Esther betrayed the queen by seeking to replace her. While this story shows that the author was familiar with the royal court and the administrative system of Persia, the story of Esther is fictional and was not intended to report an actual event. It is an early Jewish novella on the theme of the persecuted righteous and their deliverance.

Novella A novella is a fictional piece of writing in prose not designed as historical. It is written by a single author and meant to be read, not recited. The plot moves from tension to complication to resolution, concentrating on the development of characters and situa-

THE BOOK OF ESTHER AND THE FEAST OF PURIM

According to F, 10, God wished the Jews to celebrate the feast on the 14th and 15th of Adar to celebrate their deliverance. The Bible mentions this feast nowhere else except a possible allusion in 2 Mc 15,36 that mentions Mordecai's day. Did the feast come first and the story of Esther later or did the feast come from the book? It may be that the Jews in the Persian diaspora adopted a local spring festival and attached a story of deliverance to it. Passover, the principal Jewish spring festival, shows a similar origin. Passover was a festival celebrated by nomads as they changed grazing areas for their flocks in spring. The Israelites attached the story of the deliverance from Egypt to this celebration. Since the Torah did not mandate the observance of Purim, the story of Esther serves to promote a religious celebration commemorating the story of a frustrated massacre and the secular triumph of the Jews over their enemies. They are to observe this feast by mourning and fasting, by giving of gifts—especially to the poor—and by remembering the story of Esther. These prescriptions give a religious dimension to what was a purely secular story. The Jews are to understand their survival not just in nationalistic terms but as a religious obligation.

The story of Esther describes intrigues and plots, power plays and schemes for murder. The Bible text does not approve the action of either Esther or Mordecai but only the results. What God intended was the survival of the Jewish community. God did not dictate the means for that survival: The human personalities in the story controlled these. Perhaps the Hebrew version's refusal to speak about God directly in the story was an attempt to emphasize the importance of the Jews taking the matter of their survival into their own hands. The additions to the Hebrew version, however, show that some people saw this reticence as something that needed correction. The list below summarizes these additions.

Additions to the Book of Esther

Additions A and F	Mordecai's dream makes it clear that God controls the destiny of Israel.
Addition B	The decree of the Persian king against the Jews emphasizes the peculiarity of Jewish customs and alleges that they are not loyal to him.
Addition C	The deliverance of the Jews is in response to the prayers of Mordecai and Esther.

Addition D	The king's change of opinion regarding the Jews resulted from God's answer to Esther's prayer.
Addition E	God condemns the enemy of Israel. The Jews are innocent. The king acclaims the God of the Jews sovereign over all.

Questions for Discussion or Reflection

How do Christians read a book so highly saturated with Jewish nationalism? The message of the Book of Esther has an important role for the Christian canon. It offers an opportunity to check the tendency to spiritualize the people of ancient Israel and their descendants today. Where Vatican Council II declared that there is a spiritual bond between Jews and Christians, the Book of Esther asserts that the preservation of the Jewish people is a *religious obligation.* The presence of the Book of Esther in the Christian canon is a statement of the religious importance of the Jewish people as an ethnic group. It makes the sin of anti-Semitism even more shameful than the irrational injustice that most Christians understand it to be today.

1. Where do you see anti-Semitism in the contemporary world?
2. Give examples of the Christian response to such situations.

Stories about living outside one's land and community of faith contribute to a special feeling of vulnerability. People cut off from their roots can feel lost and menaced. Today there are more and more people who can identify with the Jewish characters from the tales of the diaspora. Immigrants, migrants, refugees and the undocumented all feel the dislocation that comes with being on the move.

3. What does it mean to be an alien? What does it mean to be alienated? Aliens are often alienated. Why?
4. Why do people reject and condemn others' religious beliefs? How is it possible to do this in a pluralistic world?

A Prayer for Those Who Wander

O God of a Pilgrim People, journey with us
as we seek the proper path of our becoming.
From our mother's womb until the tomb
You mark the passing moments until we rest in You.
May we not wander aimlessly in search of ultimate meaning,
but lead us gently and firmly
to the oasis deep within You,
and show us how to pitch our tents
in the valley of your love.*

*Miriam Therese Winter, *Woman Wisdom* (New York: Crossroad, 1991) 86.

1 MACCABEES READING GUIDE

By 326 B.C., Alexander the Great had conquered the lands surrounding the eastern end of the Mediterranean. At his sudden death in 323 B.C., however, his empire fell apart into three separate sections. One, which included Egypt and parts of present-day Israel, Jordan, and Lebanon, was ruled by Ptolemy, one of Alexander's generals. Another general, Seleucus, ruled a territory including what is now Syria, Iran, and Iraq, and extending eastward at one point as far as India. The portion of the empire centered on Greece was ruled (and fought over) by various members of Alexander's family and court.

The word "Maccabee" derives from the Hebrew word for hammer and was the nickname for Judas, a leader in the Jewish revolt against the Seleucid ruler Antiochus Epiphanes (165–161 B.C.). The nickname later became a designation for other members of Judas's family who succeeded him in the revolt. Judas and his brothers became known as "the Maccabees" and "Maccabean" came to designate the period of Jewish history that witnessed the successful revolt against the Seleucid Empire.

After the revolt, the descendants of the Maccabees took over religious and later political leadership of the Jewish community in Palestine. They ruled an independent Judah from about 164 B.C. (beginning with Judas Maccabee) until Pompey conquered Palestine for Rome in 63 B.C. This dynasty was called the "Hasmonean" dynasty. That name comes from the ancestor Asamonaeus whom Josephus (a 1st century A.D. Jewish historian) identifies as the father of Mattathias, who was the father of Judas and his brothers. It was Mattathias who started the revolt against Antiochus.

WHAT IS THE MACCABEAN LITERATURE?

There are four books of the Maccabees that have survived from early Judaism. None are in the Hebrew Bible and so are not included in Jewish or Protestant Bibles. An overview of the contents of these books follows.

First Book of Maccabees Historical narrative of events in life of Jewish community in and around Jerusalem from 175 B.C. to 104 B.C. (Included by Jerome in Vulgate; became part of the Catholic canon.)

Second Book of Maccabees Abridgement of a five-volume history of the Maccabees that no longer exists. Covers period in Palestine from 180 B.C. to 161 B.C. (Became part of Catholic canon.)

Third Book of Maccabees A misnamed work that has nothing to do with the exploits of the Maccabees. It is a first-century B.C work that describes the persecution of the Jews in Egypt under Ptolemy IV (221–203 B.C.). (Included in the canon of Eastern Christianity.)

Fourth Book of Maccabees A first-century A.D. tract on religious reason as exemplified by Jewish martyrs during the Maccabean revolt. (No Christian tradition accepts this book as divinely inspired though some Eastern churches include it as an appendix to the Bible and it has had some influence in their spirituality.)

HISTORY AND THEOLOGY IN FIRST MACCABEES

Unlike the Books of Tobit, Judith, and Esther, which use historical events and persons as a backdrop for what are fictional tales, the First Book of Maccabees is a historical narrative. The author tries to show the significance of the events in the middle of second-century B.C. Palestine. But the book is more than a catalogue of events. Its purpose was to affirm the legitimacy of the Hasmonean high-priestly dynasty, whose right to rule derived from the achievements of their ancestors:

1. The Maccabees saved the Jews from persecution.
2. They restored observance of the Torah.
3. They set up an era of peace and prosperity.

The author believed that it was God's will that the Hasmoneans assume leadership over the Jews of Palestine. The members of this dynasty were not without their opponents. After all, they ruled as kings when many Jews believed that the only legitimate political leaders ought to be descendants of David. As a priestly family the Hasmoneans were not of David's tribe (Judah), let alone his family. In addition, the Hasmoneans functioned as high priests even though they were not descendants of Aaron, as required by tradition. The chief opponents of the Hasmoneans were the Hasidim, who were the spiritual ancestors of the Essenes and the Pharisees.

Hasidim were the "pious ones" who saw themselves as the careful observers of the Law. They were sometimes not very prudent in their self-styled devotion to the Torah (see 1 Mc 7,8–18).

The First Book of Maccabees reflects a type of pragmatism that was incompatible with the religious zeal of the Hasidim. 1 Maccabees 8 is lavish in its praise of the Romans. This shows that the Hasmoneans were willing to compromise with foreigners when circumstances made it necessary. Later the Pharisees adopted the same position, and so did the early church (see Rom 13,1–7 and 1 Pt 2,13–17).

First Maccabees also shows that both Spartans and Romans, the major political powers of the day, recognized the Hasmoneans as the political leaders of the Jewish people.

READING THE BOOK

The story told in this book is part of a much larger story: the Hellenization in the eastern Mediterranean. It was the dream of Alexander the Great, who conquered this area in the fourth century B.C. to take the culture of Greece and wed it to the cultures of the ancient Near East so that people could benefit from the best of each. But his premature death in 323 B.C prevented him from fulfilling that dream. Alexander's generals divided his empire among themselves. The area of the former Israelite kingdoms came under the control of Ptolemy, who ruled from Egypt. Ptolemy permitted the Jews to practice their religion without much interference. The process of Hellenization grew in the other areas of Jewish cultural, political, and economic life. Some Jews resisted Hellenization while others eagerly accepted the new wave that was sweeping the world.

Hellenization was the shift of western Greek culture to the oriental eastern Mediterranean region.

The region of the ancient Mesopotamian Empire fell to another of Alexander's generals: Seleucus. He thought that the territory of the old Judahite and Israelite kingdoms rightfully belonged to him. The Ptolemies and Seleucids fought over this region until it passed into the hands of the Seleucids in 200 B.C. At first the Jews were permitted to practice their religion. But circumstances changed in 168 B.C. when the Seleucid king Antiochus IV Epiphanes seized upon the opportunity provided by divisions within the Jewish community. He favored the Jewish Hellenizers for reasons that were partly economic but also in some part cultural. To ensure the victory of the Jewish Hellenizers, Antiochus forbade the practice of the Jewish religion. Without anyone to resist his policies, the future of Judaism looked bleak.

Seleucid was the name of the Greek dynasty that ruled in Syria following the death of Alexander the Great. The name derived from Seleucus, one of Alexander's generals.

Mattathias (1 Mc 1,1 – 2,70)

The first chapter sets the scene for the bloody confrontation between the Jews and the Seleucids. It describes the Hellenization of Jerusalem, the military attacks on the city by two Seleucid armies, and the prohibition of Jewish religious practices. The king's efforts at destroying the Jewish religion culminated in the setting up of an altar to Zeus Olympus upon the altar of holocausts, the holy place in the Temple where burnt offerings were made. Tradition remembers this transformation of the Temple into a shrine for Zeus as the "horrible abomination" (Dn 11,31; 12,11).

The second chapter importantly describes the specific type of opposition that the Maccabees and their followers mounted against the Hellenization of Antiochus and his Jewish collaborators. Not all Jews who opposed Antiochus responded in the same way. While some reacted with a type of passive resistance, the Maccabees, in the person of Mattathias, opposed these policies militantly. A key text is 2,23–46, which describes Mattathias's fury at the prospect of Jewish apostasy. By comparing Mattathias's response with that of Phineas (see Nm 25,6–14), the author implies that Mattathias's action prevented God's anger from consuming the Jews because of their apostasy. This merited the high-priestly office for the Hasmoneans. Mattathias became the leader of a large guerilla force whose aim was to end the Seleucid military domination of the Jews and the banning of their religion.

The Militancy of First Maccabees

The United States Bishops' Pastoral, *The Challenge of Peace,* asserts that "the sacred scriptures provide the foundation for confronting war and peace today" (27). In trying to formulate a Christian response to these issues, one has to face the armed resistance of 1 Maccabees to the Seleucid persecution. Theologically, they were responding from the religious traditions of ancient Israel.

It is important to remember that the response of the Maccabees was not the only response among religious Jews in Palestine. Though there was an agreement that they ought to oppose Antiochus, there was a variety of viewpoints on how they ought to resist. While the Maccabees insisted on violent resistance, there were others who opted for martyrdom, nonviolent resistance, and even pacificism in the face of the threat of anti-Jewish laws.

While 2 Maccabees shares the militancy of 1 Maccabees, it expands the meaning of the revolution by adding martyrdom as another way the faithful may contribute to the final victory over their enemies. The blood of martyrs who died rather than violate the Torah cries to God for vengeance and thereby seals the victory for the Jews.

The Book of Daniel also reflects the traditions of holy war, but it presents the belief that the real conflict takes place not on earth but in heaven where God will be victorious over the powers of evil. Resistance is necessary but nonviolent and expresses itself in willingness to suffer and even die for the sake of the Torah. Daniel can offer nonviolent resistance because of confidence in the resurrection of the faithful (Dn 12,2f). The Book of Daniel gives credit for the victory over Antiochus not to the Maccabees but to God's initiative.

In their pastoral letter, the bishops recognize that the scriptures reflect many historical situations (28). They could also have noted as well that the scriptures reflect varied responses to the same historical circumstances. While we can understand the militancy of the Maccabees, such a response makes little sense in a nuclear age. There is no comparison between warfare of the second century B.C. and warfare today.

Mattathias's Farewell

Chapter 2 ends with Mattathias's statement in which he turns over his military authority to his sons, commending to them the example of Israelite heroes of the past to support his militant ideology.

Judas (1 Mc 3,1–9,22)

About forty percent of the story centers on the exploits of Judas, who succeeded his father as leader of the Jewish guerilla forces. Though the text acclaims his exploits and praises his bravery, the author is careful to imply that Judas's victories came because of divine help. Judas prays before every battle. He reminds his army of how God helped their ancestors in the face of overwhelming odds. Judas dismissed those Deuteronomy exempts from war (3,56, see Dt 20,5–8). That, and the way he dealt with the defeated enemy and the spoils of war, exemplify a man who was certain that he was fighting in accord with a divine command. Finally, Judas praises God when he celebrates his victories.

Hanukkah or the Feast of Dedication A Jewish feast celebrating the purification and rededication of the Second Temple during the Maccabean revolt. Judas Maccabee mandated the observance of this festival. Three years to the day after Antiochus's "horrible abomination" of the Temple, the Maccabees gained control of the area, purified the Temple, and rebuilt the altar. Josephus calls this festival "the feast of lights": The rededication involved rekindling the Temple's menorah (a lamp stand with seven branches). Jews observe this festival at home by lighting one candle on a special Hanukkah menorah each night. The family is reminded of how one day's supply of oil lasted for the full eight days of the original festival until the priests could obtain more oil for the menorah in the Temple. This festival is a glorification of the deeds of those who refused to give up their faith.

Jonathan (1 Mc 9,23 – 12,54)

Judas dies in battle and his brother Jonathan succeeds him. While the text hails Jonathan's military exploits, of particular importance is his acceptance of the appointment as high priest from the Seleucid king Alexander who succeeded Antiochus.

Simon (1 Mc 13,1 – 16,24)

When Jonathan is assassinated by the followers of Tryphon, the pretender to the Syrian throne, the succession passes to his brother Simon. The First Book of Maccabees reaches its climax with the succession of Simon as leader and high priest. Remember, the purpose of the book is the establishment of the Hasmonean house as the legitimate political and religious dynasty for the Jews in Palestine.

A poem in 14,4–15 is a combination of biblical themes suggesting that with Simon has come to the Jews a state of peace and prosperity not seen since the days of David and Solomon. A beleaguered minority stood up to a powerful empire for the sake of their religion. The author of 1 Maccabees believed that God was working through the Hasmonean family.

However, the book closes on a tragic note. Simon is murdered by a political rival who is captured and executed by John, Simon's son. The succession is safe and another Hasmonean, John Hyrcanus, continues the line of those "men to whom it was granted to achieve Israel's salvation" (5,62).

FIRST MACCABEES IN CATHOLIC TRADITION

This book is not part of the Hebrew Bible. There is no evidence that it formed part of the Qumran library, and Josephus did not include it on the list of his sacred books. Reverence for the book by the early church's theologians was perhaps the reason that the Councils of Florence and Trent affirmed it canonically. But it has never had a real impact on Christian theology, and its use in the liturgy is minimal.

The Story of the Maccabees in Music

George Frederick Handel's oratorio *Judas Maccabeus* tells the story of the Maccabean revolt. It includes the famous chorus "Hallelujah, Amen."

2 MACCABEES READING GUIDE

THE RELATIONSHIP BETWEEN 1 AND 2 MACCABEES

The Second Book of Maccabees does not continue the history of the Jewish revolt against the Seleucid Empire but is an abridgement of a five-volume work on the Maccabees by one Jason of Cyrene (2 Mc 2,23). This longer work has not come down to us. The unknown editor who is responsible for the present form of 2 Maccabees wished to simplify Jason's work so that readers could remember its most important features (2 Mc 2,25). The book is not simply a digest of a much longer work. There are portions of the book that do not come from Jason but were written by the person who made the abridgement.

Second Maccabees begins its story of the Jews in Palestine with the reign of the Syrian king Seleucus IV when Onias III was the high priest and ends with the defeat of the Syrian army by Judas Maccabee. The period extends from approximately 180 to 160 B.C. The story overlaps with that in 1 Mc 1,10–7,5, with great similarity between 2 Mc 8–15 and 1 Mc 3–7.

Second Maccabees is less defensive of the Hasmonean dynasty and gives more emphasis to God's justice in rewarding the faithful and punishing both Jews and Greeks who disregard the divine will. The book focuses on those Jews who accepted death rather than be guilty of an act of disobedience.

READING THE BOOK

The book begins with two letters directed to the Jewish community in Egypt, calling them to celebrate a festival in honor of the rededication of the Temple following the victory of the Maccabees over the Seleucids. Since the Torah could not mandate the celebration of the feast of Hanukkah, the leadership of the Jewish community had to take this special step to encourage its observance.

The Jewish community in Egypt built its own temple under the direction of Onias IV, the last legitimate high priest. Perhaps these letters were directed to the Jews in Egypt to keep them from forgetting their ties with Palestine. But it could be that the person responsible for the present form of 2 Maccabees added these letters to the story of the Maccabees in order to make the book into a festal scroll for Hanukkah as the Book of Esther is for the Feast of Purim.

ESSAY

Hellenization is a term that describes Greek culture, ideals, and institutions that reached their peak in fifth-century B.C. Athens and came to have momentous influence throughout the eastern Mediterranean. Until the time of Alexander the Great, the region was oriented culturally to the East. The Israelite kingdoms could not help falling under the political, economic, and cultural sway of the eastern empires: Assyria, Babylon, and Persia. Alexander effected a genuine cultural reorientation that lasted until the Moslem conquest in the seventh century A.D.

The city or "polis" with its marketplace *(agora),* colonnaded streets, temples, theaters, and gymnasium was the instrument of economic prosperity, and of the spread of Hellenism as well. Throughout Palestine the Greeks remade ancient cities. Even Jerusalem was made over (1 Mc 1,11–14).

It is not surprising that there was resistance among some Jews to Hellenization. After all, the Jews had a very traditional culture in which change occurred only gradually. There were people—especially among the upper class of Jewish society—who embraced the new cultural wave. At first the Hellenism the Jews faced was a mild type. The Ptolemies who ruled Judah from the time of Alexander's death in 332 B.C. until 200 B.C were the least culturally aggressive of the Hellenistic dynasties. Matters changed dramatically under the Seleucid king Antiochus IV, who imposed Hellenism upon the Jews. His policies sparked the Maccabean revolt.

Like 1 Maccabees, 2 Maccabees is also opposed to the forced Hellenization program of Antiochus. It is intensely devoted to the Torah. Death, even suicide (2 Mc 14,37–46) is preferable to violating the Torah. The reward for such loyalty for the individual is resurrection and for the community is the possession of Jerusalem.

Despite this opposition to Hellenism, it plays into the hands of the author, when 2 Maccabees appeals to the emotions of its readers. The work doesn't hesitate to describe the death of Jewish martyrs in vivid detail. This approach is typical of Hellenistic history writing. It is impossible to escape the influence of Hellenistic culture. The miraculous episodes in 2 Maccabees are also comparable to episodes in Greek histories.

As opposed to the Greeks as 2 Maccabees is, it is not simplistic in the way it deals with Jews and Greeks. It presents some Greeks as sympathetic to the Jews. Antiochus even converts on his deathbed. The Jews do not object to the rule of the Greeks as such. The Jews can be good citizens. What they do object to are the abuses that came with Antiochus.

There comes a point when the pious must choose. With Hellenism there came a whole collection of gods and goddesses. There were even deified kings. But more subtle were the novelties in philosophy and ethics. For the pious Jew, Hellenism represented a religious ideology and practice that was completely foreign. But there was no escaping the influence of Greek culture at this time and on into the future. For example, almost 700 years later during the Byzantine period (4th to 6th centuries A.D.) there were a few synagogues in Palestine that had decorative motifs that included a zodiac complete with the god Helios in the center of the mosaic floor.

Second Maccabees represents an earlier view that rejected any compromise with Hellenism. There are absolute values that do not allow any compromise. Even in the face of death, the righteous will choose fidelity to the Torah and be confident that such a choice is not in vain because of their belief in the resurrection.

The Story of the Maccabees (2 Mc 3,1 – 15,36)

The author has a theological purpose in the way the story of the Maccabees is presented. The events of Jewish history from the time of Onias the high priest to the time of Judas Maccabee show a God who cares for the Jewish people by rewarding the faithful and punishing evildoers. The author uses a scheme first devised by the authors of the deuteronomic history of Israel, who told how Israel came to own the land under Joshua and then how Israel lost the land under its kings. Infidelity transformed a blessing into a curse.

Blessing – Sin – Punishment

1. Period of *blessing* (3,1–40): during the time of Onias III when people observe the Torah.
2. Period of *sin* (4,1 – 5,10): during the time of the high priests Jason and Menelaus when the people and the leaders violate the Torah and follow the customs of the Greeks.
3. Period of *punishment* (5,11 – 6,17): Antiochus is the agent of God's judgment.

Turning Point – Blessing

1. The prayers of the people and the heroic death of the Jewish martyrs bring a change in circumstances. Although the book is aware of the victories of Judas Maccabee that ended the domination of Antiochus, it assumes that the death of the martyrs turned God's anger to mercy and made the victories possible.
2. The cycle is complete: *blessing* has returned to the Jewish community.

Another story runs parallel to this story of salvation: retribution. The enemies of the Jews come to a terrible end:

- Antiochus dies in agony (9,8).
- The Greek who murdered Onias is himself killed (4,38).
- The general who commanded the siege against Jerusalem is dead and his head hangs from the citadel of the city (15,35).
- The wicked among the Jews suffer under divine judgment.
- The high priests Jason and Menelaus both come to miserable ends (5,1–10 and 13,7f).

THE BOOK'S INFLUENCE IN CHRISTIAN THEOLOGY

This section of the book has influenced the development of the notion in Christian theology that suffering can have a positive value. Suffering can be a form of divine education. God did not send suffering to destroy the Jewish people but to discipline them. God's people are never abandoned. The suffering of the innocent leads the author to affirm his belief in the resurrection of the dead (7,9; 7,11; 7,14; 7,23; 14,46). This enables the Jewish martyrs to accept their suffering, for God will deliver the faithful despite their death at the hands of the wicked.

One of the most important texts in this book for Roman Catholic theology is 12,42–46. The author tries to show that Judas Maccabee believed in the resurrection of the dead since he ordered prayers and sacrifices for those who had fallen in battle. Such prayers would be useless unless Judas believed that they would rise again (12,44). This text is sometimes used as support for the Roman Catholic belief in purgatory and the power of prayers for the living and the dead. Another important text for Roman Catholics is 2 Mc 15,12–16. Here Judas Maccabee sees the prophet Jeremiah in a dream praying for the Jews and Jerusalem. Catholic tradition accepts this text as one support for the belief in the power of the intercession of the saints.

The Epilogue (2 Mc 15,37–39)

The author ends his work rather abruptly with a hope that readers will find his work pleasant reading.

Question for Discussion or Reflection

1. Use your imagination and picture yourself viewing the earth from outer space, much as the astronauts have done. Imagine you have two hours to ponder the sight. What would your thoughts be? What hopes would you have for peoples of the world? Read the prayer of Jesus during the last discourse (Jn 17,1–26) and let it become your prayer for world peace.

The Wisdom Books

At a Glance

Job	A dramatic poem that treats the problem of suffering of the innocent, and of retribution.
Psalms	A collection of religious songs under the major headings of hymns, laments, and songs of thanksgiving.
Proverbs	An anthology of mostly short sayings in poetical form whose purpose is to teach wisdom for successful living.
Ecclesiastes	A treatise on the vanity, or emptiness, of all things. The book is concerned with the purpose and value of human life.
The Song of Songs	A collection of love poems full of sensuous imagery. It could be seen as a portrayal of ideal human love.
Wisdom	Oratory from the Jewish community of Alexandria about one hundred years before the coming of Christ, the author explaining traditions and themes familiar to Judaism but reinterpreting them from the experience of living in a Hellenistic culture.
Sirach	A collection of proverbs dealing with moral instruction, written to show that real wisdom was to be found in the traditions of Israel and not in the godless philosophy of the day.

Some of the literature that originated in the period of the Davidic-Solomonic monarchy (10th century B.C.) suggests that at that time every aspect of human life took on a new aspect. Israel claimed that it encountered God *through* human experience, not *in addition* to it. A new question was being asked: What kind of role does God play in everyday life? The answers to that question in no way contributed to what we have come to know as "salvation history." Instead, they form a "guide for successful living." Since every person in every culture must struggle with the questions of life, this literature has universal appeal. This might explain why, even today, people of other religious cultures can more easily identify with the teaching of the wisdom books than with the other books found in the Bible.

Wisdom is the ability to perceive the order of the universe and to live in accord with it.

The Israelites believed that their God was the great Creator-God, the one responsible for the world and everything in it. By observing the regularity in creation, they concluded that there was some kind of order inherent in nature itself. If they could understand how this order operated and then attune their lives with it, they would be successful and at peace.

The writers of wisdom literature used various teaching techniques such as storytelling, exhortation, warning, and questioning. They also used proverbs, riddles, parables, and metaphors to instruct, advise, and persuade. Usually there were very definite lessons they wanted to teach, so it should not surprise us to come across what appears to be "the moral of the story."

The sages were humanists; that is, they were concerned with the study of human beings and attentive to human welfare, values, and dignity. They taught that whatever benefited humanity was a good to be pursued; and whatever was harmful should be avoided. The gauge for judging the value of any undertaking was the degree of success or happiness that it brought. Success was a concrete sign of the wisdom of the person who succeeded.

Although the wise woman or man believed that there was a right way of behaving, there was no insistence on a rigid standard that would fit everybody. The wise person was the one who had a store of wisdom gained from experience and who knew which way of behaving was appropriate for each situation. Conformity to the inherent governing principles of the world would result in a life filled with success and prosperity. Adversity or misfortune was the result of some failure to conform to these governing principles. The idea that the good shall be rewarded and the evil shall be punished undergirds most of the wisdom literature.

Israel's wisdom tradition did not develop in a vacuum. It was part of a much broader movement within the Near Eastern world. There is a remarkable similarity between the biblical wisdom material and some Egyptian, Mesopotamian, and Canaanite texts. The non-Israelite texts are significantly older than the comparable biblical material. More likely than not, Israel borrowed from its neighbors and adapted and reinterpreted when necessary. But despite the similarities, Israel's wisdom tradition is clearly in accord with its Yahwistic faith. It may not focus on specifics of religion, but it is highly ethical, fundamentally monotheistic, and, at times, equates wisdom with fidelity to the law of Israel.

JOB READING GUIDE

At a Glance

Prologue (1,1–2,13)	Job, an oriental chieftain, suffers sudden and complete reversal of fortune.
First Cycle of Speeches (3,1–14,22)	Job's friends visit him. He protests his innocence, not knowing why he is afflicted.
Second Cycle of Speeches (15,1–21,34)	Job's visitors insist his plight is a punishment for personal wrongdoing and an invitation from God to repentance.
Third Cycle of Speeches (22,1–28,28)	Job's visitors insist his misfortune is a punishment for evil. Job insists on his innocence.
Job's Final Summary of His Cause (29,1–31,37)	Job rejects his friends' inadequate explanation and calls for a response from God.
Elihu's Speeches (32,1–37,24)	Elihu offers counsel but still insists on Job's affliction as a sign of error.
The Lord's Speech (38,1–42,6)	God answers not by justifying God's actions before humankind but by referring to God's omniscience and almighty power. Job is content with this.
Epilogue (42,7–17)	Job, vindicated, is compensated by double payment.

ABOUT THE BOOK OF JOB

There is no agreement about the book's date, its place of origin, or the source of some of its parts. There is not even total agreement as to its principal theme. The richness of the book and its universal appeal prevent us from easily categorizing it.

Evidence from the book itself is often given in support of a date before the Babylonian exile (7th century B.C.). Job's complaints are reminiscent of the lamentations of Jeremiah and some consider the book an outcry of impending destruction of Jerusalem and deportation into exile. However, similarities with the theology and style of Deutero-Isaiah (the portion of Isaiah beginning with Chapter 40) seem to tip the scale in favor of a postexilic dating (6th to 5th century B.C). It certainly appeared before the 3rd century B.C. when "Satan" appears as a proper name (1 Chr 21,1) instead of the designated role of an adversary in a court of justice, as is found in the Book of Job.

Job's struggle with suffering is a universal problem. There are older Near Eastern accounts of innocent sufferers that may have influenced the author of Job. The names and places of origin of Job's three visitors suggest foreign influence and even borrowing. Still, whatever in the book that may have originated elsewhere has been used here with Israelite theology in mind.

Like most pieces of ancient literature, Job is a composite rather than the work of a single author. It appears to be a prose folktale (1,1 – 2,13; 42,7–17) within which extensive poetic speeches (3,1 – 42,6) have been inserted. Even within the speeches, we can detect units believed to have originated from someone other than the principal author. But regardless of when or from whom these different sections originated, they all belong to the final form, and it is this final form that has been handed down to us as sacred Scripture. Therefore we should read it as a unified literary work.

Why Do the Good Suffer?

The universal appeal of the Book of Job stems from the nature of the questions by this innocent man. Who has not struggled with the dilemma of bewildering suffering? Who has not cried out to God, "Why?"

As the drama unfolds, each section of the Book of Job has its own dynamic. The prose prologue plays an important role in the theological message of the book. Job's innocence is established beyond any doubt and we see who is responsible for Job's misfortune. It is God who permits the righteous man to suffer in order to test the quality of his integrity. Job never knows this, nor do his visitors. It is important that the reader know what took place in heaven as we listen to the theological debate that follows. By the many arguments of the poetic speeches adding layer upon layer of accusation and rebuttal, the author brings us into the very midst of the impasse of this pointless debate. Only God can resolve this.

Job demands a hearing and God does confront him, but in a manner surpassing Job's imagining. God answers Job from the midst of creative power. The epilogue and its last verses of prose complete the reworked folktale. Job's question "Why?" is never answered. All he knows is that the innocent can indeed suffer for no apparent reason and with no guarantee that the reason will ever be disclosed.

THE LITERARY STYLE

The simple understanding of the story about the innocent man stricken and rewarded in the end for his faithfulness does not accurately represent the story of Job. It is merely the plot of the folktale that frames the poetic dialogues that compose the principal part of the book. The more we understand how the form of the book works, the more we will discover the message within it.

In the following ways, the literary style of the author contributes to the development of the book's message.

1. *The dialogues:* Speeches in Hebrew poetic form. Each time Job cries out about his sorry state, either Eliphaz, Bildad, or Zophar offer counsel or attempt to convince him of his error. The cycles of speech proceed in orderly fashion.
2. *The use of nature as means of instruction:* This is characteristic of the wisdom tradition. While it occurs throughout the entire book, nowhere else does it have the effect it does in God's speeches. By not directly addressing Job's question, God does not ignore Job's concerns. This is the way the author uses nature as a teaching tool.
3. *Poetry:* The kind found within the book is unlike classical or contemporary poetry. There is no rhyme and the rhythm follows tonal patterns that are lost when the original Hebrew is translated.
4. *Lawsuit:* Again and again Job demands that God meet him in court where his case will be tried and he will be found innocent (23,2–4).
5. *Lament:* Job cries out to God in complaint and laments the day of his birth (3,1–10) and life itself (10,1–7), and he pleads for help (13,20–27).

Parallelism is a feature often found in the poetry of the Bible, especially in the wisdom books. It is the correspondence of thought in successive half lines. The thought in the first line is repeated in the second:

Does God pervert judgment,
and does the Almighty distort justice? (Jb 8,3)

or contrasted (there is no clear example in Job):

Hatred stirs up disputes,
but love covers all offenses. (Prv 10,12)

or advanced:

Pity me, pity me, O my friends,
for the hand of God has struck me! (Jb 19,21)

Parallelism is used effectively in Job as an aid in furthering the arguments of the various speakers.

Onomasticon An ancient Near Eastern pattern meaning "naming" (Greek). A constructed listing of names of things that had similar characteristics, probably a prescientific attempt at classifying natural phenomena. See God's questions to Job about the wonders of the universe.

THE MESSAGE

While the Book of Job is a poetic narrative, it is also a theological statement made up of several themes intricately interwoven. The way we understand this theology will influence the way we perceive the arguments in this book. The themes here are not in any order of importance but as they appear in the book.

Reward and Punishment

The belief that goodness should be rewarded and evil punished undergirds most of the wisdom literature. This theory probably arose out of life experience itself. When in the natural course of events it does not happen, someone in authority steps in to see that justice is done. This we need in order to live with a certain degree of security.

Job's real agony, however, seems to lie in the incomprehensibility of his situation. Because he is suffering, he must have sinned. Because his suffering is so intense, his sin must be great. Job's visitors argue this point and try to persuade him to repent because they assume he is guilty. This same kind of thinking prompted the apostles to ask Jesus whether it was the sin of the blind man or of his parents that resulted in the man's blindness (see Jn 9,2).

Job holds to this theory as well, but he makes his claim from a different point of view. Since he has done nothing wrong to deserve such misfortune, he blames God who he believes is the architect of the order of the universe. It is God who usually decides who will be rewarded and who will be punished and accomplishes this through the laws set at creation. When these laws fail, the tradition of Israel claims that God intervenes to enforce justice. So from Job's point of view, God has failed to do this in his case.

Since the speeches argue in defense of or in opposition to Job's innocence, one would think that when God finally does thunder from the whirlwind, everything would become clear. But the question of justice is not addressed. Instead, the issue is the creative wisdom and power of God. This is not an avoidance of the question. Remember that God is cast in the role of a wisdom teacher who asks rhetorical questions and makes reference to the natural world in order to make a point. God leads Job to see that just as there is much in nature he cannot understand, so there is much in human experience that is beyond him. In this way God reveals the inadequacy of the theory of retribution. Happiness and success are not rewards for righteous living, nor are grief and failure punishment for unfaithfulness. Suffering is not a sure sign of alienation from God.

Once we are convinced that certain suffering is undeserved, we are faced with a very troubling question: Why does God seem to allow injustice to occur? If Job didn't believe God is a moral God, the question of evil would take a totally different turn. If God is not righteous then Job's suffering might be just as difficult to bear but would not be the puzzle it is. He would know that he could not depend on God. Such a view was foreign to Israel's faith. Job's counselors never question God's integrity, and Job does so only reluctantly and at the risk of falsely accusing God.

Another view: God could be moral but not able to control evil completely. This is the theory held by some thinkers concerning the Holocaust when they cannot explain why God allowed so many millions of innocent people to be exterminated during World War II. A contemporary book by Harold S. Kushner, *Why Do Bad Things Happen to Good People?* maintains this argument. This thinking is not found in the Bible. Israel believed its God was the undisputed creator (see Is 45,7; Am 3,6).

Theodicy Theodicy, from the Greek for "justifying God," is the name given to our attempt to explain the problem of evil, while at the same time maintaining the belief that God is a moral creator who is in control and who loves those who suffer.

Perhaps God is both moral and omnipotent but unconcerned about simple people. Surely the Almighty has more important things to do than worry about the fortunes or misfortunes of one person. The traditions of Israel contradict this notion as well. From the stories of their ancestors we see God portrayed as attentive to the most personal needs of the individual (see Genesis). This memory causes Job to lament his present situation. How could God, who cared for him in earlier years, turn against him now?

While theodicy is not an issue for Job or for his visitors, it is of major importance for the author of this book, who depicts God as all-powerful and provident and a God of unchallenged goodness. At the end, the question of suffering may be left unanswered but the integrity of God is no longer questioned.

Disinterested Piety

In a very real sense, the drama of the book stems from Satan's challenge found in 1,9: "Is it for nothing that Job is God-fearing?" It's easy to be loyal to God when things are going right and he is happy with life. Take away these good things and Job will not only give up his way of integrity, he will actually curse God. God takes the dare.

Twice Job is assaulted and he neither curses God nor veers from his attachment to God. His confidence has not been shaken and he actually praises God. It is probable that he did expect to be blessed for being faithful. So the question remains: Was Job faithful for the sake of reward or was his piety really disinterested?

Job's laments and pleading show that he does not look for reward; he wants vindication. He is not concerned about possessions; he insists that his integrity be acknowledged. When he finally understands the lesson God set out to teach him, he is silent and seems content with his new insights. Now we know that the depth of Job's piety is based on his relationship with God, not on some promise of reward.

We must remember that at that time Israelites did not have a clear idea of reward or punishment in an afterlife, as Christian theology teaches. If justice was not meted out in this life, they had no hope at all for retribution. This serves to challenge the quality of our own fidelity.

Suffering

Although the customary way of understanding suffering was a punishment for sin, the Book of Job does provide other explanations for it. The prologue itself tells us that God allowed Job's misfortunes to befall him so that Job's integrity might be tested (1,11; 2,3–5). In the Book of Genesis "God put Abraham to the test" (Gn 22,1) and told him to sacrifice his son Isaac. The difference, however, is that in the end Abraham was told that he had been tested while Job never knows about God's dealings with Satan.

Suffering is sometimes seen as a source of moral discipline, a warning against sin and a defense against pride and self-satisfaction.

Other interpretations include suffering endured for others (the Suffering Servant: Is 52,13—53,12); undergoing purification (Ps 66,10); a necessary way of accomplishing the will of God (Joseph in Egypt: Gn 50,20). Only the first two explanations are found in the Book of Job.

The ancient Near East offered another explanation referred to as the "curse of the evil deed." It claimed that those who engage in evil infect themselves in the process: "He who digs a pit falls into it" (Prv 26,27). God does not intervene to punish.

Biblical writers appear to be more interested in the reason and purpose of suffering than in its origin. They offer temporary explanations to strengthen people in their struggle. Circumstances change and the advice might cease to be appropriate, which is precisely the case in Job. No one seems able to offer him an adequate explanation for his suffering.

ESSAY

Experience and Tradition

A fundamental principle underlies wisdom thinking and plays an important role in the Book of Job. It is the relationship between experience and tradition in the formation of new theological understanding. We have all been taught the importance of conforming our lives to the teachings of our religious tradition. A new and sometimes conflicting attitude is developing today: that it is the tradition that must conform to contemporary life. In fact, a more complete understanding shows that there should be a dynamic relationship between the two where each is influenced and refashioned by the other.

In the Book of Job we see that neither Job nor the men who came to visit him took note of this dynamic. From where Job stands there is something seriously wrong with the order of things. Not willing to question his own integrity and not ready to challenge the tradition, Job finds fault with God.

The others also evaluate Job's life according to the traditional way of interpreting suffering. God is justified in afflicting Job, and the tradition is adequate in explaining the situation.

Job's experience of innocent suffering calls for a new and more critical look at the tradition. It is strange that neither he nor his counselors challenge this unbending interpretation of theology because it is precisely the ability to be faithful yet flexible in new situations that constitutes wisdom. Perhaps the author of the book wanted to demonstrate what can happen when theology is rigidly applied.

The Catholic Bishops of the United States have consciously included reflection on contemporary experience in the process of writing their most recent pastoral letters. They are keenly aware of the need to be faithful to official teaching while at the same time realistic about the changes in the world. They have frequently held open hearings in order to gain insights from the experience of other people before writing their documents. This practice can both endorse new wisdom and contest the old. For that reason it has been applauded by some and criticized by others.

The God of Mystery

Up to this point the themes have focused our attention on Job. Now we turn our gaze toward God. In his complaints, Job characterizes God as powerful and oppressive when near and unconcerned when at a distance. Job's companions describe God as a prosecuting judge. But the image unveiled in the speeches of the Lord is quite different.

God is indeed powerful, but it is a wondrous awe-inspiring power. It is true that God is transcendent, but this does not prevent God from being attentive to the mountain goat about to kid (see 39,1). Finally, God does not assume the role of divine judge to find Job guilty. Instead, God as the divine teacher leads Job to new horizons of understanding. Now Job understands that he has been treading on mystery—"things too wonderful for me" (42,3). This provident yet mysterious God of creation is the same God who works in the life of each of us yet remains a mystery.

Questions for Discussion or Reflection

1. The theory of retribution continues in our thinking today. When we fail or come upon hard times we frequently ask: What have I done to deserve this? Why is God punishing me? Perhaps like Job we have to learn that not everything can be explained according to the theory. Life is too complicated to be forced into one pattern.

2. Job's faithfulness can also be an encouragement to us. Here is a man who is not willing to accept unquestioningly what he considers a grave injustice. He rejects the instruction and counsel of those regarded as teachers of the religious tradition. Job is not blindly docile in his suffering. Nor is he afraid to complain to God in his frustration. But we must understand Job's anger correctly. He does not really argue with God because he is suffering but because he sees a conflict between his undeserved suffering and the justice of God. The Job who curses God is no less pious than the Job who acknowledged, "The LORD gave and the LORD has taken away" (1,21). Devout people certainly do have their differences with God. We are reminded of the great Teresa of Avila, who in frustration complained to God, "No wonder you have so few friends."

3. It is because of the theme of undeserved suffering that Job has enjoyed a favored place in the literature of the world and in the hearts of countless people. No one is protected from undeserved personal misfortunes such as the sudden and tragic death of loved ones, human exploitation or betrayal, the unexpected collapse of a business or career, or from natural disasters. The horrors of war, of ethnic, racial, sexual, or other social discrimination, and of the brutality that victimizes untold children, women, and men defy all standards of justice. Over the centuries, Job has stood as a proof that suffering is not a sure sign of infidelity. He continues to be a source of consolation for many today who suffer innocently.

PSALMS READING GUIDE

The Book of Psalms, also known as the Psalter, is really a collection of books, each of which ends with a short doxology or hymn of praise. The editors of the *New American Bible* have indicated this arrangement of the Psalms by adding subdivisions within the text.

The First Book
Psalms 1–41 ends with doxology in 41,14

The Second Book
Psalms 42–72 ends with 72,18f

The Third Book
Psalms 73–89 ends with 89,53

The Fourth Book
Psalms 90–106, ends with 106,48

The Fifth Book
Psalms 107–150 ends with an entire Psalm of praise (Ps 150)

There is evidence within the Book of Psalms itself that our present anthology was composed of even earlier collections. Several psalms, found principally in the first book, are attributed to David. (This may account for the popular but probably not historically accurate tradition that David himself wrote most of the psalms.) Several psalms in the second and third books are ascribed to Korah and Asaph, the two great guilds of temple singers during the period of the Second Temple (see 1 Chr 6,33f; 25,1f). These groupings may have been the original collections around which other psalms clustered. Finally, the fifth book is made up of a number of Songs of Ascent and psalms of praise known as the Hallel ("praise") or Hallelujah collection.

Elohist Psalter *Elohim* (translated God) is preferred in the second and third books.

Yahwist Psalter *Yahweh* (translated LORD) is generally used in the first, the fourth, and the fifth collections.

Most scholars believe that Elohim is a substitution made by a postexilic editor who wished to show reverence due the divine name (Yahweh) by avoiding its use. (You can actually see this process at work if you compare Psalm 14 with Psalm 53. LORD in Psalm 14, representing the word "Yahweh," is changed to God in Psalm 53.)

All of these collections overlap, so it is difficult to identify precisely the original groupings. It is enough to know that the compilers had an array of psalms from which to choose. There is other psalmody in the Bible, for example, the Song of Moses in Exodus 15 and the Song of Deborah in Judges 5. This indicates that there were many more psalms than have been preserved here.

TYPES OF PSALMS

Hymns

The hymn is a song praising God. While many hymns appear to be prayers of individuals, they seem to have been composed for use in the liturgies of Israel's major festivals.

THE STRUCTURE OF A HYMN (PSS 8, 19, 29, 33, 100, 103–104, 111, 113, 114, 117, 135, 136, 145–150)

It begins with a call to praise, suggesting that this type of psalm originated within a community setting with a liturgical leader calling others to prayer. This introduction is followed by an account of the wondrous acts of God that cause us to stand in awe. Having proclaimed God's glorious deeds, the psalm ends with a repetition of the initial call to praise, some expression of exaltation of God, and a plea for God's blessing.

HYMNS OF THE LORD'S KINGSHIP (PSS 47, 93, 96–99)

These are a distinct group among the psalms. Their focus is the Lord, the universal king. Some scholars claim that they were composed for an annual celebration: the feast of the Enthronement of the Lord. But no account of such a festival can be found in the Bible itself. For that reason, and because they fit the general hymnic pattern, they are included in this category.

THE SONGS OF ZION (PSS 46, 48, 76, 84, 87, 122)

These psalms extol Zion as God's holy mountain and Jerusalem as the city God chose to inhabit. We are not certain about the cultic setting at which the songs of Zion were sung. We may be heirs of Israel's songs, but we do not know more than a few general facts about its cultic calendar, and we cannot reconstruct its system of worship.

Laments

The type of psalm that occurs most frequently in the Psalter is the lament. Nearly a third of the psalms belong to this category. Depending on who the speaker is supposed to be, they are further classified as community laments or laments of the individual.

Community Laments

(Pss 12, 14, 44, 53, 58, 60, 74, 79, 80, 83, 85, 90, 94, 106, 123, 126, 137)

- Associated with official cultic worship of Israel
- Used when people were gathered to fast and pray because of national humiliation or distress
- Israel's rivals were viewed as opposed to the Lord
- A recital of the former deeds that God accomplished in the history of the nation
- Purpose: to remind God of past favors and encourage God to grant new ones
- Used to remind people of God's earlier blessings and to instill confidence in their hearts

Laments of the Individual

(Pss 3–7, 13, 17, 22, 25–28, 31, 35, 36, 38–40, 42–43, 51, 52, 54–57, 59, 61, 63, 64, 67–71, 77, 86, 88, 102, 109, 120, 130, 140–143)

- Prayerful responses to personal misfortunes such as illness or persecution
- An integral part of personal liturgical devotion
- Frequently suffering people went to the Temple or a shrine to request deliverance. Laments with trust in God were prayed for the community gathered around the one suffering

The structure of the lament is not exactly the same in every case. Still, laments usually consist of an invocation similar to the introduction in hymns; a plea for deliverance from misfortune; some kind of praise of God, often an expression of confidence that God will come to the rescue of the community or the individual; and a vow to perform an act of worship in gratitude for God's intervention. Some laments include an acknowledgment of guilt or an assertion of innocence. Finally, there usually is a curse hurled at those responsible for the situation that brought about the lament. This last feature has caused considerable difficulty for those who wish to use the psalms in their own prayer.

Thanksgiving

It is difficult to classify these psalms because expressions of confidence and gratitude are often found within the laments. There are some psalms that might be considered explicit psalms of confidence:

- Communal Psalms (Pss 115, 125, 129)
- Individual Psalms (Pss 11, 16, 23, 62, 91, 121, 131)
- Psalms of Thanksgiving (Pss 9–10, 30, 32, 41, 116, 138)

It is the subject matter rather than the form that characterizes this type of psalm. Thanksgiving psalms are similar to hymns in that they praise the marvelous works of God. Like the laments, they were probably part of the communal or personal liturgical life of the people and were used when thanksgiving was in order.

Royal Psalms

Various occasions in the king's life form the setting for these psalms, coronation hymns (Pss 2, 72, 101, 110), an anniversary hymn (Ps 132), a royal wedding song (Ps 45), petitions in behalf of the warrior-king (Pss 20, 144), and prayers of thanksgiving for his success (Pss 18, 21). These psalms are often referred to as "messianic psalms," since "messiah" means "anointed one" and that is what a king was. They take on new meaning in the Christian tradition when they are applied to Jesus, the supremely "anointed one" of God.

God's Special Envoy

Israel was a nation that perceived its king as the representative of the whole people before God, and as God's special envoy for the people. This assured the king the special place he enjoyed.

Wisdom Poems

These poems (Pss 1, 37, 49, 73, 112, 119, 127, 128) are clearly different in content and style from those psalms which probably originated in and were used during liturgical celebrations. The wisdom tradition in general is concerned with the problem of evil, the suffering of the righteous, and the justice of God. These same themes, along with the language and imagery of the wisdom tradition, are found in these psalms. The purpose of these psalms is to call people to listen and learn, not to pray.

The sages of ancient Israel used several techniques that helped people learn. Some of these appear in the wisdom psalms. One of the most popular was the acrostic arrangement. In this form the letters of the alphabet in order determine the beginning letter of the first word of each successive line (Ps 37 along with hymns 111; 119). Because they follow this pattern, some commentators include them as wisdom poems rather than hymns (Ps 145), laments (Ps 125), or thanksgiving psalms (Pss 9–10, 34).

It is difficult to know how and why this type of psalm originated and was included in various collections. And why does the Psalter begin with a wisdom poem (Ps 1)? Most likely a compiler after the exile placed this psalm first when there was neither Temple nor temple worship and those responsible for the religious life of the community wanted to keep the psalms alive in the Israelite tradition. The psalms might have been seen as a treasury for the much-needed instruction and prayer of the people. Placing the psalms into five books might have been patterned after the Torah of five books of Moses, wherein the major teachings of the faith were found.

Various Psalms

These are other psalms, like Songs of Ascent (going up to the Temple) used during pilgrimage (Pss 120–134) or those for processions around Jerusalem (Pss 15, 24, 95). Since people frequently came to the Temple or to a shrine in search of some word from the Lord, some psalms trace their origin to a style of prophetic speech. And then a few psalms don't fit into any of the categories we have mentioned. They are either stories about the feats of the Lord (Pss 78, 105), combinations of other psalm forms (Pss 108, 133, 139), or general liturgical songs (Ps 134).

THE PIETY OF THE PSALMIST

The psalms generally speak *to* God rather than *about* God. If we look carefully at the sentiments of these songs, we will be able to detect the piety of ancient Israel, a piety to which we are heirs. It will be helpful to return to the classifications (Types of Psalms: hymns, laments, thanksgiving, etc.) as we explore the piety of Israel contained in the psalms.

Praise

Praise is that sentiment that wells up in us when we are overwhelmed by the wonders around us or by God's gracious care of us in the events of life. This is not something we are taught but something we experience. Who has not been swept away by the extravagance of a sunset, by the delicacy of spring's awakening, by the refreshment of a gentle breeze, by the magnitude of the ocean's horizon, or by the night sky's depths? The psalmist does not seem to be able to find words adequate to describe the grandeur of creation (Pss 8, 29, 104, 148) and calls upon all the forces of nature to join the psalmist in praising God.

Other hymns applaud God for marvelous deeds performed on behalf of Israel. Since the greatest experience of deliverance was liberation from the oppression of Egypt, the Exodus became the symbol of all liberation. God is the tireless savior, and the psalmist's praise acknowledges the nation's total dependence on God for its continued survival. The biblical hymns are not flights of fancy of people protected from the hard realities of life. They are songs of praise of people who, despite misfortune, persist in their reliance on an all-powerful and attentive God. The Lord who is acclaimed as the sole and eternal king over the nations arises from the concept of God as victor over the cosmic conflict at the time of creation, bringing order out of chaos (see the creation narrative in Genesis 1).

The Songs of Zion

These songs contain some of the same imagery as do the psalms in honor of the Lord King. Ancient Canaanite mythology, from which much of the Israelite imagery originated, tells of the cosmic battle mentioned above. After the forces of evil have been conquered, a palace is built for the victor on the summit of the highest mountain. From this summit the hero holds sway over the entire universe.

Israel revered Zion as this sacred mountain and revered the Temple as the palace of the victorious creator God. We can observe the drama of the cosmic scene of primordial creation shifting from Zion and the Jerusalem Temple to the political and cultural world of Israel. God's creative power is now associated with the nation and, because of the close connection between Zion and David, specifically with the monarchy.

In these psalms God is praised as totally committed to the welfare of Israel. This creator-God is not distant from the people but lives in their midst, allowing them to approach the divine presence mysteriously dwelling in the Temple. Other nations were also allowed to worship the Lord in this holy place.

Grief, Fear, Repentance, and Confidence

We all have a certain sense about how life is supposed to unfold. Everyone agrees that basic to our human nature is the desire to be happy. When we have not attained what we believe is our right, or we lose it, we cry out in protest.

This natural human instinct, coupled with the conviction of God's special love and care, led Israel to expect security in a hostile world, success in undertakings, and a life of serenity and prosperity for the nation and for each individual within this nation. This state of affairs is what the Bible refers to as *shalom,* or peace. Psalms of lament grew out of the absence of such peace.

Communal laments apply to some national disaster that has already taken place. Depending on the date of the particular psalm, this calamity could have been:

- the fall of the northern kingdom of Israel (about 722 B.C.)
- the Babylonian exile (about 586 B.C.)
- the Maccabean conflict (about 167 B.C.)

Allusions to the vulnerability of the nation would fit any one of these emergencies, as it would the description of the destruction of the Temple (515 B.C.; see the Reading Guide to Ezra and Nehemiah).

The fact that the psalmist cries out to God indicates that Israel's belief in God's saving power is based on former saving events in the history of the people (Pss 44,2–4; 74,2; 83,10). Even as the people cried out in complaint, they were proclaiming God's all-encompassing power and declaring God's continued concern for them based on covenantal promises.

At times Israel felt it was the innocent victim of the aggression of another nation. But there were also instances when it admitted that the straits in which it found itself were directly related to its own sinfulness. Suffering at the hand of another was seen as a punishment from God for violation of the covenant. Many of the sentiments found in the communal laments are found in the individual complaints as well. In distress they turn to God for release. On occasion, they question why God has allowed them to be besieged in the first place. But their confidence in God rests in remembering past blessings and reliance on God's own faithfulness to covenant promises.

Gratitude

Gratitude is obvious in the psalms. The structure and content of thanksgiving psalms resemble those of the hymn. There can be no thanksgiving until God has first been praised for the goodness that he has accomplished.

National Loyalty

National loyalty flows from the royal psalms out of Israel's pride in her nation. Since the king was perceived as the representative of the whole people before God and as God's special envoy, loyalty to the king and to the nation was considered an act of devotion to God. These psalms originated from such events as coronations, royal weddings, or danger to the king during warfare, and would be considered today as a type of patriotism.

An Understanding Heart

This is a trait of religious sentiment that implicitly reveals expressions of Israelite piety. The wisdom poems generally do not address God but are usually directed toward the community. The piety of the psalmist is not as clearly demonstrated here as in the prayers we have already examined. But if we look carefully, we will see the way the poet treats prominent themes.

The problem of evil, the suffering of the innocent, and the justice of God are all facets of the same issue: the right order of the universe. Evil that is clearly not a punishment for wrongdoing can challenge the sovereignty of God over creation. God either cannot repress evil or is unwilling to do so. While Job and Ecclesiastes live with the unanswered question of innocent suffering, the wisdom psalms do not challenge the prevailing situation. They presume that the suffering of the righteous is due to some legitimate purpose which God will reveal at the appropriate time (see 1 Kgs 3,9–12).

Enthusiasm, Humility, and Faithfulness

These traits characterize the processional psalms that invite the observant Israelite to participate with heart and soul in various liturgical celebrations. Passover or Unleavened Bread, Pentecost or Feast of Weeks, and Sukkoth or the Feast of Tabernacles were all commemorated with pilgrimages to Jerusalem. Psalms were sung as people approached the city. There were shouts of profound joy as well as humble acknowledgments of the need for pure hearts when approaching the holy city and the Temple of the Lord.

THE THEOLOGY IN THE PSALMS

The expressions of piety found within the Book of Psalms give us insight into the theology of ancient Israel. It will be helpful to look at it in a systematic fashion.

The God of Israel

The portrait of God sketched in the Psalms draws together all of the divine traits found in the rest of the Israelite tradition. This God is

- the creator of the universe (Ps 8,4)
- the source of all life (Ps 36,10)
- enthroned in heaven (Ps 47,6)
- yet dwelling in Jerusalem (Ps 76,3)
- Israel's exclusive liberator (Ps 66,6)
- yet gradually seen as concerned for all people (Ps 117)

This majestic God inspires both fear (Ps 89,8) and confidence (Ps 23) and is demanding (Ps 75,83) as well as forgiving (Ps 85,3). Above everything God is "merciful and gracious . . . slow to anger and abounding in kindness" (Ps 103,8; see Ps 86,5). The Lord is the "covenant partner." Everything that is important to Israel flows from this perception of God.

The Image of God

The human person is held in high regard in the psalms. Honored as the culmination of creation, humanity is given responsibility for the other living creatures of the earth (Ps 8; see Gn 1). The psalmist marvels at this singular work of divine artistry.

Why should God be personally committed to such an insignificant being (Pss 8,5; 144,3f)? As extraordinary as they are, humans live a fleeting life (Ps 39,5f) and then perish like flowers in the field (Ps 103,15f). Realization of the impermanence of life becomes even starker when we remember that the psalmist did not have any clear notion of life after death. Human dignity was related to life in this world. In the mind of the psalmist

- human beings are thoroughly understood by and totally dependent on God (Ps 139);
- God provides for their basic needs (Ps 65,10–14) and protects them from harm (Ps 121);
- God is the guardian of the poor and the afflicted (Ps 40,18), of defenseless widows and orphans (Ps 68,6) and the *anawim* or lowly (Ps 147,6).

Male Imagery

It's important to note that the psalms come from a society where the male person was the norm for what is human. The language and imagery that issued from this fact have caused great distress to some feminists. Without perpetuating this male-preferred situation and by making appropriate substitutions while reading or meditating, we can still value the psalms for their religious insight and sentiment.

Natural Creation

The psalms reveal a special regard for creation as the handiwork of God (Ps 104). This may have originated from a polytheistic belief that the mysterious powers in nature are really manifestations of various deities. As Israel's understanding developed, these came to be seen as expressions of the Lord. God is revealed in the thunderstorm (Ps 29) and in the design of the natural world (Ps 65,7), where creation is no longer seen as a rival for the homage of the people but as a partner in the praise of God (Ps 148).

The Future

Ancient Israel was interested in both the future of the nation and the fate of the individual. The positive view it takes on this issue of *eschatology* stems from its faith in the goodness of God. Despite the struggles of attempting to live in a quarrelsome world, Israel believed that the final victory would be the Lord's. Individuals, too, clung to the conviction that God would right all wrongs and that they would enjoy the happiness that was their due.

The psalms that praise the kingship of the Lord describe God's defeat of the forces of evil and the restoration of the nation (Ps 14,7). The gods of other nations will be recognized as the empty idols that they are (Ps 95,5), and all peoples will join in praising the Lord (Ps 96,7–10). According to some royal psalms, this final turning point in history will be brought about by the agency of a "messiah" (Ps 2,7–9).

An earlier theology taught that reward and punishment would be worked out in the community or down through the generations. But this theory was challenged in the face of the prosperity of the wicked. In response, the psalmist claimed that such prosperity would not last and the upright should not envy sinners (Ps 37,2). Still, the apparently peaceful death of the prosperous wicked and the suffering of the righteous remained an unresolved problem.

Sheol The psalms say very little about life beyond the grave, but they frequently mention a shadowy existence known as *Sheol* (Ps 49,15). This was a place of neither reward nor punishment, but merely of darkness and dust, the abode of the dead. While Israel did not have a clear idea of a life after death, it entertained the possibility that the dead did not cease to exist.

The Psalms and the New Testament

It is clear that the early Christian community did not tend to distinguish between explicit theological statements on one hand and prayer on the other. For them, the psalms were not only vehicles of prayer but also contained important statements of faith, statements that found their fulfillment in the person and mission of Jesus (see Lk 24,44). The New Testament cites various psalms. Five seem to be referred to more than the rest:

- The messianic psalms 2 and 110: cited in discussions of Jesus' Messianic preeminence (Acts 13,33 and Heb 1,5)
- The individual laments 22 and 69: used in descriptions of Jesus' passion and death, suggesting that the psalmist was foretelling Jesus' suffering
- The communal psalm of thanksgiving: Psalm 118 speaks of the rejected stone that becomes the cornerstone (v.22; see Mt 21,42) and the blessedness of the one who comes in the name of the Lord (v.26; see Mk 11,9)

The early Christian theologians developed the theology of the psalms in ways that would enhance their understanding of Jesus the Christ.

ESSAY

The Psalms Today

Most people become acquainted with the psalms because they are incorporated into the regular prayer life of the church. Others may be more familiar through personal prayer and private devotion. Anyone interested in psalms will want to know more about how they function as a means of prayer and how they shape our minds and hearts. We cannot arrive at this insight by limiting our examination of the psalms to their historical or literary analysis. While they are religious literature, they are also a means to spiritual transformation.

The psalms are some of the most beautiful poetry that the human spirit has created. One need not be familiar with the historical situations from which the psalms originated in order to appreciate them. Like all classic poetry they speak to every culture and every age.

Reflective, even contemplative reading can plunge us into the religious dispositions of the psalmist and serve as a vehicle carrying us back into them. We may not come to the psalms with hearts filled with praise, thanksgiving, or grief, but the world mirrored there resonates with our own. We know that world, or at least we sense that we should know it, and we cry out with praise, thanksgiving, or grief. This poetic imagery can become a starting point of meditation on the psalms.

For Jews and Christians the psalms are the voice of their respective faith. The psalms have served as a prism that spreads before us the many facets of our relationship with God. Gilead, Manasseh, and Ephraim (see Ps 60,9) may be unfamiliar names to many, but they were beneficiaries of God's promise of protection of which we are heirs.

Liturgy is not merely a celebration of some past event. It is an enactment in which and through which promises and claims that were made in the past become present realities. Exodus was a concrete historical event. But whenever Israel reenacted this event, the reality of the Exodus became present with all its power and possibility. When we enter the world sketched by the laments, *we* are plunged into fear and distress and *we* cry out to the Lord. Now these are *our* sentiments; this is *our* prayer.

Making the Psalms Real Today

Ideas for Communal and Individual Prayer

1. As we praise God for the splendor of creation and acknowledge that the universe belongs to this divine architect and not to us, we should be moved to profound respect for the world of which we are a part. Allow the hymns of praise to instill in us the dispositions necessary to become responsible stewards of the treasures of creation.
2. The hymns extolling the Lord for having delivered Israel from the threats of extinction depict God as the ever-present savior. In praising God as faithful liberator, Israel acknowledged God's enduring commitment to justice. As we pray these hymns, we too should find ourselves committed to justice and respect for the autonomy of all nations.
3. The Lord is acclaimed as champion in the cosmic struggle with the threatening forces of chaos. Acknowledging that these forces were never completely destroyed, these psalms claim that the Lord is nevertheless in charge and deserving of our undivided devotion. If we praise the Lord in this fashion, we can hardly allow anything—wealth, power, national loyalty—to rival the allegiance we have pledged to God.
4. The songs of Zion honor this mountain as the dwelling place of God to which all nations are invited. The Lord is not in some distant, remote place, inaccessible to people, but in the midst of people, approachable, even inviting. But a warning here. Whenever a nation confused being *elect* with being *elite,* it faced prophetic condemnation (see Jer 7,26). We are not above this same temptation.
5. Laments are the largest category of psalms in the Bible. Some people think that prayer should be primarily praise, petition, or thanksgiving. We have become so accustomed to seeing ourselves as "Alleluia People" that we relegate any mention of suffering and pain to prayers of petition. But it is natural to complain, even to complain to God. The laments are not only protests of our grief or anger but also testimonies to our belief that the compassionate God of the past will surely be faithful to us and deliver us once again.
6. Solidarity with those who suffer is another way to enter into the world of the laments. As we share their suffering, their prayer becomes our own. Laments can strengthen us in our commitments to justice and peace.
7. Laments are often admissions of guilt, pleas for forgiveness, and promises of amendment. When we pray the laments in this spirit, we confess that God is a just yet forgiving judge, and we pledge ourselves to lives of faithfulness to our own covenanted responsibilities.
8. Psalms of thanksgiving help us remember that whatever we enjoy has come to us from the hand of a gracious God. We cannot claim any gifts by right, and so we would do well to be as generous with these gifts toward others as God has been toward us.
9. One of the characteristics of the wisdom poetry is its lavish use of nature imagery. The balance and regularity of the natural world are held up as examples after which society and human relationships should be patterned. But we cannot allow reflection on the harmony in nature to hinder us from addressing the more challenging issues of the wisdom psalms:

the problem of evil, the suffering of the righteous, and the justice of God. As these hymns become our own, their interests will become our commitments.

10. The processional psalms remind us that, while God is indeed in our midst and accessible to us, God is still God—holy and transcendent. In rejecting an earlier conviction that we are unworthy to approach God, we have emphasized a kind of familiarity with God. In a society so focused on human progress and human accomplishment, together with technological advances and the secularization of our society, it is not surprising that there is an apparent loss of people's appreciation of the transcendent.

PROVERBS READING GUIDE

At a Glance

First Section: Instruction (1,1–7 and 1,8f.18)	The student is addressed as "my son" and exhorted to listen to the teaching that is advanced.
Second Section: The proverbs of Solomon (10,1–22,16)	Each verse is a saying in its own right. Meaning does not depend on what precedes or follows it. Sometimes called *sentence literature.* These use contrasting ideas to make their points.
Third Section: The sayings of the wise (22,17–24,22)	Patterned after a collection of an Egyptian scribe, Amen-em-Ope (an example of Israel's literary borrowing).
Fourth and Fifth Sections: Also sayings of the wise and proverbs of Solomon (24,23–34)	Collections linked with court of Hezekiah, Judean king (7th century B.C.) who inaugurated religious reform and literary activity.
Sixth and Seventh Sections: The words of Agur and numerical proverbs (30,1–33)	30,1–6 very short section followed by collection distinguished by the use of numbers, which have much in common with the riddle.
Eighth Section: The words of Lemuel (31,1–9) and the ideal wife (31,10–31)	The advice given to Lemuel, king of Massa, by his mother followed by a poem describing the ideal wife.

THE PROVERB

There is no word in English that adequately translates the Hebrew *mashal.* It embraces a broad category of literary forms: oracle (Nm 23,7); discourse (Jb 29,1); parable (Ps 78,2); taunt-song (Is 14,4). In each case there is a lesson to be learned, and for this reason the *mashal* might be best understood as "an example from life" intended to instruct. This is the word that identifies two major collections as The Proverbs of Solomon (10,1; 25,1), and from which the book receives its name.

The root meaning of *mashal* is "likeness" or "comparison," as in "like mother like daughter," or in the contrast, "better safe than sorry." As a comparison, it usually consists of two parts in the same kind of poetic construction. The sentence (which is the purest form of the proverb) is distinct from the instruction (which is much longer—sometimes an essay). Both sentence and instruction are expressed in poetic form, the two parts being either compared or contrasted in parallel balance of "thought rhyme." This parallelism (see Reading Guide to Job, Literary Style) is an easily recognizable feature of Hebrew poetry.

Three Major Types of Parallelism

1. *Synonymous parallelism:* The second half of the line repeats the thought with a slight variation:

   On the way of wisdom I direct you
   I lead you on straightforward paths (4,11).

2. *Antithetic parallelism:* These contrasting ideas are not precise opposites and ultimately they communicate the same idea:

   The memory of the just will be blessed,
   but the name of the wicked will rot (10,7).

3. *Synthetic parallelism:* The second part of this saying neither repeats nor contrasts the initial idea but advances it and moves it toward a new thought:

   Gray hair is a crown of glory;
   it is gained by virtuous living (16,31).

Because synonymous parallelism does not demand exact equivalence, antithetic parallelism does not require precise contrast, and synthetic parallelism extends the scope of the proverb, the second half of these poetic lines can be drawn from a wide variety of possibilities. The result is a collection of sayings that are remarkable for their accuracy and adaptability of expression.

It is important to appreciate the prominence of poetry in the Bible. Israel did not casually choose to express itself in poetic form. Its very perception of reality was poetic. The modern world of science and technology does not always grasp, much less appreciate, the aesthetic perspective of the ancient world. Because we tend to perceive reality scientifically, we insist on the language of exact science. When ancient Israel encountered reality, it expressed itself in artistic thought patterns and literary forms. This in no way minimizes the validity and truthfulness of its perception, or of ours for that matter. They are two very different ways of looking at reality and talking about it. They have one very important thing in common, however: Both the proverbial view and the scientific view are based on noticing *patterns* or *recurrences* in life and calling attention to them.

Wisdom is not a collection of quaint catchy phrases which suggest that life will unfold according to plan if we just follow the directions. Proverbs are artistically honed images of specific facets of life, and from these we can learn something about our own living. They direct our attention to the commonplace and offer us the opportunity to gain insight into the complexities of life. Different proverbs do this in different ways. The wise person is the one who understands life from more than one proverbial point of view and can discern the appropriate way of responding to it.

Our comprehension of proverbs depends upon our ability to recognize what very different things might have in common:

> The way of an eagle in the air,
> the way of a serpent upon a rock,
> The way of a ship on the high seas,
> and the way of a man with a maiden (30,19).

None of these "ways" is a distinctly defined route. This kind of analogy works the way riddles do when people challenge each other's wit.

Proverbs do not command; they persuade. They do not dictate what must be done; they describe how things work. Their purpose is not to indoctrinate, but to educate. They are not precepts that call for obedience, but sayings that invite prudent response. The Book of Proverbs clearly insists on the importance of living an ethical life. The ethics it promotes, however, issued from reflection on life rather than from conformity to law.

Was Solomon the Author of Proverbs?

The first verse of the Book of Proverbs states that Solomon is the author of the proverbs. There was a tradition that this king had not only human insight but vast knowledge as well (see 1 Kgs 3,4–14; 16–28). Ancient people believed that wisdom belonged by right to their gods, and since the king was the human representative of the god, it was the special possession of the king. Since Solomon ruled during a time of splendor and enlightenment, he became known in popular devotion as the wise man par excellence. His reputation gave credibility to wisdom, and as more wisdom writing was attributed to him, his reputation grew. Attributing the authorship of Proverbs to Solomon gives the book the status of official teaching and credits the king with comprehensive wisdom.

There is a possibility that the *real* royai authority behind the Proverbs is King Hezekiah. Collections of proverbs could well have been compiled during the time of his religious reform, and he could have ascribed them to Solomon. We do not have enough information to accurately reconstruct this historical period. The Book of Proverbs itself, however, attests to both Hezekiah's influence (25,1) and Solomon's reputation (1,1; 10,1; 25,1).

THE TEACHER AND THE STUDENT

All scholars agree that the primary education of ancient Israelite youth took place in the home and was the responsibility of the father, and as Proverbs 1,8 tells us, the mother. Some commentators do not believe that women played a role in the education of sons. The inclusion of "mother," they contend, is merely for the sake of poetic parallelism (see above). While this may be the case in this instance, such poetic construction could not have been imagined without some grounding in experience. Important information and operating principles or hereditary occupations, such as the monarchy, the priesthood, and the scribal class, were handed down within the family and perhaps the extended family. Education in these professions might have been added to ordinary family training.

The texts in the Bible show that Israelite kings modeled their courts after other ancient Near Eastern nations. They appointed men to advise them, to administer royal policies, and to keep official records. These men, of course, had to be trained. But we should not automatically conclude that these centers were exclusive places for the teaching of wisdom. If wisdom is the way a culture addresses the fundamental questions of life, then all members of that society are trained in it. While intelligence is an innate quality, wisdom is acquired by learning from others and from life experience. Such wisdom is not unchanging, nor does it belong only to certain people. It grows up within a society and belongs to everybody.

My Son . . . Some insist that the relationship between teacher and student was like father and son. In patriarchal societies, women seldom benefit from education. While this is true, the inclusion of "your mother's teaching" (1,8) argues for a family setting of wisdom teaching.

THE WAY OF WISDOM

Wisdom came to be understood in several ways. "The way of wisdom," a phrase that scholars use, refers to a way of operating that is proper in human society, in the world of nature, or on the cosmic plane.

Practical or Folk Wisdom

Such guidance in ordinary life is properly concerned with the way people interact with one another. Since peace and harmony can only exist where social order is preserved, whatever guaranteed such order was followed. Whatever threatened it was avoided. The theory that the wise will enjoy peace and prosperity and the fool suffer the consequences of foolishness came from this reasoning:

> The virtue of the upright saves them,
> but the faithless are caught in their own intrigue (11,6).

Proverbs declares that there are only two ways open to men and women: the way of the wise (those who learn from experience) or the way of the foolish (those who do not). Since successful living demands an ongoing search for meaning, one can never settle for solutions of the past. New situations constantly present themselves; new choices must be made. The wise follow "the way of wisdom" by drawing from the accumulated wisdom of the past and, in an imaginative way, understand how it corresponds to new situations.

The Need to Survive and Prosper in the Natural World

By reflectively observing nature and its movements, people have been led to recognize a certain amount of regularity in its operations and similarity in its display. As this regularity was charted and similarities noted, a kind of nature wisdom developed that was the precursor of the physical sciences. People learned how to live in harmony with nature, and through comparison and contrast, they drew lessons from nature for their daily lives.

Like snow in summer, or rain in harvest,
honor for a fool is out of place (26,1).

Some have questioned the religious value of folk wisdom, because there is no mention of God. The proverbs appear to be human-centered rather than God-centered. We must be careful not to compare the humanistic point of view of the ancient Near East with a kind of modern humanism, which is faithless. Israel never questioned that the divine power was working to hold the world in proper balance. The wisdom tradition was built on the conviction that God expected people to use their human abilities to their fullest. Whether God is mentioned explicitly or not, Israelite wisdom was religious teaching. The ethical quality of the proverbs, the way they help in telling right from wrong, should be seen as evidence of their religious character.

Primordial Divine Wisdom

The ancient Near Eastern world believed that there was a kind of wisdom that was beyond their comprehension. They believed that there was some kind of reliable yet mysterious cosmic order within which they lived that revealed the wisdom of the creator-god. This cosmic order not only predated the natural world but was actually responsible for its existence. Of all kinds of wisdom, it alone contains the secrets of the universe and the answers to all questions. The sages knew that this was the only wisdom that would satisfy the human search for meaning.

From of old I was poured forth,
at the first, before the earth (8,23).

Israel believed that God was the creator of all things, so it spoke of a theological dimension to each of these three manifestations of wisdom. Although theological expression is more explicit in later biblical writings, it was never absent from Israel's worldview.

Who Were the Wisdom Teachers?

Scholars hold various opinions regarding the identity of the wisdom teachers and what they taught. Some believe that there was a professional class of teachers attached to the court and appointed to train young men in the arts of diplomacy. They claim that much of the wisdom we find in Proverbs is specialized knowledge taught in designated schools. Other scholars maintain that elders of the family were the ones who handed down the tradition to the next generation. Still others believe that wisdom was part of the common cultural heritage of the people and that all members of the society were formed in its teaching.

THE TEACHINGS OF THE WISE

The emphasis of wisdom is on the human person in general rather than on a nation as a collective group. Its scope is universal, not exclusively Israelite. The counsel offered addresses issues from everyday life rather than from cultic experience. It is concerned with pragmatic ends, not transcendent values. If we expect this teaching to address topics not found within this range, not only will we find it wanting, but we might miss the riches that are to be found there.

Fear of the Lord

"The fear of the LORD is the beginning of wisdom." Several variations of this saying appear in the Book of Proverbs. Israel did not view this reverential fear as merely an attitude of mind. It was the foundation of its moral conduct, which included respect, loyalty, obedience, and covenant love.

In Proverbs, "fear of the LORD" is linked with wisdom, which is practical knowledge that comes from reflecting on experience. There are two quite distinct ideas that, when brought together, significantly reinterpret the meaning of wisdom. This can be seen by comparing:

The beginning of wisdom is: get wisdom (4,7)

with

The beginning of wisdom is the fear of the LORD (9,10).

In the first proverb, ordinary life is the source of wisdom. In the second, wisdom flows from religious faith. This change of perspective may be the result of the sages trying to bridge the gap between the wisdom teaching they held in common with other Near Eastern nations and that which was distinctly Israelite.

Israel also believed that behind the breathtaking order of the universe was an all-wise and all-powerful God. They believed that the more they knew about their world, the more they would discover about God. And the more they knew God and were committed to the Lord, the more they were in harmony with the order placed in the world by this divine wisdom.

Fear of the Lord This is best characterized as awe and reverence rather than terror and dread. Awe is awakened when one realizes the transcendence of a God who is protective, not threatening.

Yahweh The Hebrew word we translate as LORD is the name of Israel's God. "Fear of the LORD" became the summation of Israelite piety—the best expression of the religion of Judaism.

Training in Virtue

In the wisdom tradition, the emphasis on the individual person rather than on the nation should not be understood as a kind of privatized individualism as we know it today. It was precisely as a member of the covenant community that an Israelite searched for meaning in the events of life.

The connection between wisdom and personal virtue is clear and frequently used:

- The way of wisdom is the way of virtue. It is also the only way to happiness (Prv 10–13).
- Many proverbs praise self-control, especially restraint in speech (21,23).
- When one does speak, it should be with words that are pleasing (16,14), not foolish (14,23).
- One should be disciplined in other areas of life as well: "With closest custody, guard your heart" (4,23). Honesty (13,5), diligence (6,6–11), docility (13,10), and humility (22,14) are virtues recommended to the young.
- If they live their lives according to this counsel, they are promised a good reputation (22,1) and long life (10,27).
- They are not to be overconfident of their own ability but to put their trust in the Lord (3,5).

Warnings Against Seduction

There are numerous warnings against the seduction of adulterous women. In a strict patriarchal society, the virtue of men would be of primary concern; women were treated as property and confined in restrictive seclusion in order to guarantee their fidelity and thus assure the legitimacy of the male's offspring. Only women of questionable virtue move freely in such societies, and these are precisely the women about whom the young men are cautioned (see 2,16–19; 6,20–6,35).

A significant amount of instruction is social in its focus. It is bent on developing relationships necessary for social tranquility. The proverbs give us hints about the settings within which they might have been effective. The family plays a prominent role as the primary setting for education:

- Young people are to heed the teaching of their parents (1,8; 6,20).
- Much counsel is given about the training and chastisement of the young (22,6; 13,1; 24; 19,18).

Even though the influence of Yahwism may not be easily detected in some of the proverbs' instruction, the covenant's call to justice is clear. Despite the fact that riches were viewed as fitting reward for righteous living, dangers of possessing wealth were still acknowledged (28,3–8; 11,2; 21,13). The poor were to be respected, for they too came from the hand of God (14,31; 22,2) and sometimes were more virtuous than the rich (28,6).

Advice was given to the ruled and the ruler:

- Subjects esteem the king because he exercises power over them (16,14f).
- Kings are bound to be fair and upright (16,10–12).

Israelite influence can be seen here. In other nations of the ancient world, the king had the last word, and that word could not be questioned. In Israel, the king may have been revered as the legitimate representative of God, but he, too, was a member of the covenant community and was obliged to obey the Mosaic law.

This kind of moral teaching presupposes an almost mechanical view of retribution. The universal order is neat and reliable. Rewards and punishments are the result of particular styles of living. The Book of Proverbs does not question the status quo. The theory of retribution is not challenged here as it is in Job and Ecclesiastes.

The Role of Wisdom

The Bible explicitly states that God alone is the creator. However, wisdom claims to have had some part in creation (8,30). One way to reconcile this to traditional faith is to understand the

Wisdom—Who Is She?

In the very first chapter (1,20–33), Wisdom is depicted as a woman who goes through the city looking for disciples. Some scholars claim that this mysterious figure was originally a Canaanite deity. Others say she was early Israelite. They have long believed that Israel moved from believing in many gods (polytheism), to believing that other nations may have their gods but Israel worships only one (monolatry), to believing there *is* only one God (monotheism). It is possible that the ancestors of Israel believed in a goddess of wisdom from whom this figure originated. Many of the traits that characterize her are found throughout the book in proverbs that describe either the wise teacher or wisdom itself. This woman is frequently contrasted with a second woman, Folly (9,13), who attempts to seduce the simple into her ways.

It is not unusual to find personification in Hebrew poetry. The prophets used it:

> Break out together in song, O ruins of Jerusalem! (Is 52,9)

as did the psalmists:

> Let the rivers clap their hands, the mountains shout with them for joy (Ps 98,8).

What is unusual is that wisdom is characterized as a woman. Several explanations for this have been offered:

1. This could be a remnant of ancient Near Eastern (even Israelite) worship of a goddess of wisdom.
2. Or it may be merely a development based upon the feminine form of the word *hokmah,* wisdom.
3. But the most likely explanation can be found in the society itself. Wisdom is regarded as the most desirable possession. In this patriarchal male-preferred society, it is understandable that it was personified as a woman. The same is true for folly. Women are no more inherently seductive than are men. However, they are a better representation of what men find enticing.

figure of wisdom as the personification of a divine attribute. This view, then, is merely a stylistic feature of the author and is not foreign to the Bible. The kindness, truth, and justice of God have also been personified (see Ps 85,10–14).

This explanation, though, does not take into account that wisdom is identified as an entity separate from the creator (8,22). This is more than personification; it is closer to hypostasization (taking what is normally a personal trait and transforming it into a person with its own existence). Once wisdom is created, she has a life of her own. She existed before the rest of creation, and she appears to be active beyond space and time. According to some commentators, this suggests a mythological origin. This would certainly not be against biblical religion. Other sections of the Bible contain mythological elements, for example, the garden with the talking serpent (Gn 2–3) and the sea dragon (Is 27,1).

Whatever the origin of this puzzling figure, she is no longer perceived as a goddess. She probably represents that inaccessible dimension of wisdom that we all desire but that resides with God alone, that kind of wisdom that is within creation but beyond us. This mysterious figure reminds us that the fullness of wisdom cannot be gained through human experience. It belongs to God.

THE ROLE OF WISDOM TODAY

Proverbs may not be popular reading today because it seems to describe a world that does not exist—a world that has a proper order and in which events follow a cause-and-effect sequence. We know that life is very unpredictable and the events of life cannot be foreseen.

The world of Proverbs seems to be the world of the comfortable, not the world of those who struggle. Even directions about justice are given from the point of view of those who are in charge. Since persons supported by the status quo seldom challenge it, Proverbs might well be seen as a guide to "Win Friends, Influence People, and Get Ahead in the World, As We Have It." Advocates of justice and peace usually turn to the prophets for inspiration, not to the Proverbs.

Such evaluation of the wisdom tradition misses a few very important points:

- Proverbs does not claim to describe everything, but each proverb does depict a snippet of life. Together they offer a collage, not a blueprint.
- The process that produces proverbs may be more important than the content of the proverbs themselves. It teaches us the importance of serious reflection on experience and the need to adjust our behavior as circumstances change.

The Wisdom Method of Reflection

With human experience as their starting point, contemporary theologians have developed their insights. The Base Communities of Latin America and Bible discussion groups in North America have realized that they encounter God *through* human experience, not *despite* it.

1. Reflecting upon your ordinary experiences of this past week, think of an event that could be the basis for a contemporary proverb. Jot it down.

2. If you are with others, test out the wisdom of your proverb with the group. Does it resonate with others' experience?
3. Remember a wise person you have encountered in your lifetime (a grandparent, parent, teacher, etc.). Do you remember some bit of wisdom they often offered their hearers?
4. Many people struggle with parenting today. Look through the Book of Proverbs. Which ones offer valuable guidance for the training of children and youth in our contemporary world? If you are a parent, how might you apply them today? If you are a young person, how would you want them applied to you?

ECCLESIASTES READING GUIDE

You may not be as familiar with the Book of Ecclesiastes as you are with other writings from the wisdom tradition. But you are probably not unfamiliar with some of its expressions: "There's nothing new under the sun!" and "You can't take it with you!" This shows that the thinking of Ecclesiastes is not foreign to our contemporary worldview.

ABOUT THE BOOK

Ecclesiastes demonstrates some of the literary characteristics of a Royal Testament, a common type of literature in the ancient Near East intended for the instruction of the king's successor. It

Who Was Qoheleth?

The very first verse identifies the speaker as "David's son, Qoheleth, king of Jerusalem." There is no biblical mention of a Davidic son by this name, so some other meaning must be intended. The exact meaning of Qoheleth is debated. It probably comes from the Hebrew word *qahal,* assembly, and refers to someone who calls forth or presides over a meeting, perhaps for the purpose of teaching. The form of the word *Qoheleth* suggests that it is not a name, but rather a participle that designates someone who does something. The Greek word used to translate *qahal* is *ekklesia,* a citizens' assembly in Greece. The one who presides over this particular assembly is called Ecclesiastes or Preacher.

The man is further designated as king of Israel. This is an obvious reference to Solomon, the one revered in popular devotion as the wise king. The author claims that Solomon is the speaker, and therefore his teaching has the authority of Solomon's wisdom. From the outset it has authority even though it may prove to be unorthodox. Because the author uses instruction, proverbial quotations, contrasting proverbs, rhetorical questions, parables, the words of the wise, and their riddles, the characterization of Qoheleth is of a respected teacher of wisdom.

was written in the third person and claimed to be advice gleaned from the experience of life. Although the book begins with a kind of third-person descriptive prologue (1,1–11) and ends with an epilogue also in the third person (12,9–14), everything else suggests but one speaker and, despite some conflicting statements, one point of view.

The language of the book resembles the kind of Hebrew that appeared during a very late biblical period and was used almost exclusively for literary purposes. The inclusion of several Aramaic words has led scholars to date the book around the 3rd century B.C. The place of origin is more difficult to determine. Some say Phoenicia, others suggest Egypt. Because the wisdom tradition was common to the ancient Near East, precise identification of origin is difficult.

Ecclesiastes is one of the five books that make up the *Megilloth.* It was read during the harvest celebration of Sukkoth, also known as Tabernacles or Booths. This major pilgrim feast was so called because the harvesters lived in booths as they gathered their crops. It is not clear how this practice began or why Ecclesiastes was chosen. Perhaps the somber tone of the book fit the dreariness of autumn. Although reading the book was not always a consistent synagogue practice, Ecclesiastes continues to be considered part of the *Megilloth.*

Megilloth or "Scrolls" This is a special collection in the Hebrew Bible that also includes Song of Songs, Ruth, Lamentations, and Esther. These books were read during various liturgical festivals and were gathered together for the sake of convenience.

A Note About the Ending

The book clearly begins with the distinctive, "Vanity of vanities, says Qoheleth, vanity of vanities! All things are vanity!" (1,2) and ends on the same tone: "Vanity of vanities, says Qoheleth, all things are vanity!" (12,8). What some consider a kind of prologue (1,1–11) might well come from the original author. The epilogue (12,9–14) is different: At least one, possibly two people besides the main author have added something. Whoever added verses 9–11 plainly agreed with Qoheleth's conclusions despite their critical and sometimes singular viewpoint. The tone changes with verse 12, which begins with the same Hebrew word as verse 9. This might be a second epilogue. The student, identified only here in the manner found frequently in Proverbs, is warned about too much speculation and is advised to trust in the punishing justice of God, a theme that Qoheleth, in contrast, consistently challenged.

It appears that the author created a literary character, Qoheleth, and attributed Solomonic authority to him to give his own instruction credibility. A later editor further authenticated this teaching by explicitly assuring the reader of Qoheleth's wisdom. However, with two short verses, a second editor tried to temper Qoheleth's statements. There are two possible explanations for this inconsistent ending:

1. The book was already well enough accepted so that it could not be dismissed by the critics. Still, someone appended a caution to what might be considered questionable teaching.

2. If only one editor agreed with Qoheleth's teaching, that person realized that without some kind of tempering it would not be preserved. The last verses restate the traditional view of punishment and seem to return the entire teaching to the circle of orthodoxy.

A CRITICAL POINT OF VIEW

There is a wide range of scholarly opinion regarding the meaning of the book. Qoheleth has been described as a skeptic, a cynic, or more positively, a pragmatist. His view of life has been called everything from pessimistic and fatalistic to realistic. Some judge his religious outlook as pleasure-seeking, while others think it is faithful to Israelite values. It is clear that he is disillusioned with certain parts of his society, yet he lacks the enthusiasm of a reformer or the vision of a mystic. Because of this some critics label him a frustrated man who is resigned to the injustice and meaninglessness of life and has decided to make the most of fleeting pleasures. Careful reading of Qoheleth will show that he does not really despair of life but of unrealistic expectations regarding it. His real struggle is with the meaning of life, especially from the perspective of the theory of retribution (see Introduction to Wisdom Books).

Retribution This theory claims that there is a direct relationship between the uprightness of one's behavior and the good fortune that one enjoys.

A Chase after the Wind

Qoheleth sets out to discover everything within human experience (1,13). Since he is a king, he has both wealth and the leisure to embark on this quest. As one with extraordinary wisdom (1,16), he of all people is equipped to experience life to the full. But what he really sought was always beyond his grasp, "a chase after the wind" (1,17). It is clear that in his search for wisdom, he was looking for something else as well. Qoheleth next turned to the search of self-gratification. In many ways he was successful, but still he was not satisfied (2,1–11). He accomplished everything he set his mind to in his search to answer the fundamental question:

What profit has man from all the labor
which he toils at under the sun? (1,3)

He constantly arrived at the same conclusion: There is no lasting gain, no tangible dividend, . . . "with nothing gained under the sun" (2,11).

According to the theory of retribution, Qoheleth's wisdom and wealth would be perceived as a concrete proof of his goodness and the guarantee of his future prosperity. But Qoheleth really does not enjoy his good fortune, so he questions its value. Since death comes to everyone, he wonders, "Why then should I be wise? Where is the profit for me?" (2,15). It is not life, nor the search for fulfillment in life, that frustrates him. What he loathes is the profitlessness of human striving. It is not fulfilling. He is asking more of life than success and prosperity.

Since death comes to all, any advantage one might have because of righteousness, wisdom, or wealth, is only temporary, and therefore questionable. Maybe the fool who disregards the rules of society may actually have an edge over the one who conforms to them at the cost of enjoyment. So he wonders if perhaps life itself is "a chase after the wind."

Nothing Is New under the Sun

We have already seen how the wisdom teachers appealed to the obvious order within the natural world as they urged people to live in obedience to the acceptable social custom (see Proverbs: The Way of Wisdom, page RG 198). The author of Job used the same technique with a slightly different twist. There Job was overwhelmed by the wonders of nature and led to acknowledge the incomprehensible dimension of life (see Job: Reward and Punishment, page RG 181). The author of Ecclesiastes also directs our attention to the regularity in nature (1,2–11), but does so in order to highlight its monotony. The sun rises and sets day after day. Although the wind appears to be irregular, upon observation its paths can be predicted. Though the sea is constantly fed, it is never full. The regularity of the earth appears to be lacking any progress. There is nothing new under the sun.

What advantage does the earth have in being so constant? The sage urges us to learn another lesson from nature. Human striving for gain is nothing but wearisome labor that must be repeated and repeated with no promise of conclusion and no assurance of satisfaction. Human life is basically the same regardless of the society or the generation into which one is born. Life itself follows the same cycles, and experiences are quite similar. Momentous events seldom interfere with the fundamental rhythms of existence. As nature repeats itself, so does human history. Nothing seems to have lasting significance.

An Appointed Time

"There is an appointed time for everything . . . under the heavens." In what may be the most familiar section of the entire book, Qoheleth declares that each event of human life has its own appointed time. Each event is linked in poetic construction with its opposite. There are two ways of understanding the pattern:

1. Juxtaposing opposites is a way of expressing totality. It encompasses both poles and everything in between. For examples, "knowledge of good and evil" (Gn 2,9–17) means comprehensive knowledge; "bone and flesh" (Gn 2,23) refers to the entire body.
2. A second poetic form is an expression of relativity. The circumstances of life determine what is fitting and what is not. What is appropriate at one time can be out of place when circumstances change. This may be the author's way of insisting that there are no absolutes; everything is relative to everything else. There is a time to die as well as a time to be born. Neither seems to have an advantage over the other. Still, we do not know the rules that govern these appointed times, so we are helpless and may feel that we are at their mercy.

The task of living is not easy. Qoheleth explains why in 3,11. This verse may be the most difficult one in the book because of the questions surrounding the translation and interpretation of the Hebrew *olam.* Although some versions translate the word as "world," or "future," or even "ignorance," the *New American Bible* renders it as "the timeless." God has put *olam* in the human heart, and we want to know and understand, even to control everything in the world. It seems that while human beings are finite, their desires transcend the limits of time. Though Qoheleth described the world as fixed and closed, there is an urgency in the human heart that seeks to burst the confines of restrictive determinism in order to delight in the wonders of freedom and mystery.

> You have made us for yourself, O Lord,
> and our hearts are restless
> until they rest in you. (St. Augustine)

All Is Vanity

This is the expression that has come to characterize the entire book. The Hebrew word *hebel,* which is here translated as vanity, can also be rendered as vapor or thin air. It means pointlessness or futility and refers to something that may be real but that has little or no lasting substance.

Qoheleth accomplished all his goals and yet he declares, "All is vanity!" All the energy he put into his projects was pointless. We might expect him to advise others against ever trying to be happy but he does not. On the contrary, he urges people to enjoy what they have. Then what is it about life that he regards as vanity?

Qoheleth observed in the lives of others what Job experienced in his own. That is, the inadequacy of the theory of retribution. The righteous do not always enjoy the good things of life, nor are the wicked always deprived of them (4,1; 8,10f). While Qoheleth shares this insight with Job, his dissatisfaction in the face of his own prosperity and success has led him a step further in challenging the theory. It is not only that a righteous person sometimes does not prosper; it is also that, even when one does realize some desired goal, there is no guarantee of fulfillment. To suppose that the attainment of goals, even noble ones, can fulfill human longings is, to Qoheleth, vanity.

THE WISDOM OF THE SAGE

The wisdom of Qoheleth consists not only in a critical examination of everything that is supposed to bring happiness, but also in positive advice. Although he finds fault with some aspects of human striving, he encourages something that is often overlooked in busy lives. The key to true fulfillment may well be to relish the simple pleasures of life that are at hand (2,24; 3,13–22; 5,19; 8,15; 9,9). These pleasures can be experienced in the very act of living: in eating, in drinking, in the work itself rather than in the wealth that one may hope to produce by it. The pleasure, like everything, has come from the hand of God and should be enjoyed.

Life is not a business transaction with a strict *quid pro quo* (this for that) return. Such a rigid interpretation of retribution will only end in disappointment. To wait in anticipation of something more than the natural satisfaction that accompanies human activity is foolish, because the future is uncertain.

Qoheleth objects to making human accomplishment the primary goal in life. He calls upon all to find pleasure in what they are doing and, if they are fortunate enough to become successful in the process, to see this as a gift from God as well.

Questions for Discussion or Reflection

1. Ecclesiastes is not an account of Qoheleth's journey in faith but more like jottings on his experiments in living. He seems to have gone right to the core of things. What are some of the fundamental goals of people?

2. The complexity of modern society and the instability of the world's economy make it more difficult to amass wealth today than in the past. For this reason, the strain and conflict that accompanies "upward mobility" have been heightened. This is true for nations as well as for individuals. Where does much of the injustice in present society stem from? Do people really believe that having more will make them happy? Give examples.

3. Qoheleth criticized those who judged the worth of human endeavor by the amount of output rather than the quality of input. Today he would most likely criticize any attitude or system that placed more value on the product than on the person producing it. Think of examples in present business practices that would come under his scrutiny in this regard.

4. Many people spend a lifetime climbing the ladder of prominence and power. What do you think about ambition? How would Qoheleth challenge the struggle for "upward mobility"?

5. A strict interpretation of retribution frequently includes the notion that God is bound to respond to our actions with proper reward or punishment. Looking at the scripture itself, find passages where Qoheleth reminds us that God is not bound by our interpretive theories.

6. Qoheleth insists that the primary goal of life is living. Every other end is secondary or "a chase after the wind." This is a profoundly religious teaching, for he believes that it was the creator who placed the desire for happiness within the human heart, made living an exciting adventure, and willed that every person be given the chance to find pleasure in it. The creed of materialism denies this basic conviction. How are we seduced into believing that material possessions can satisfy the human heart?

THE SONG OF SONGS READING GUIDE

No book in the Old Testament is more difficult to interpret than the Song of Songs. It is clearly a collection of love poems full of sensuous imagery. No apparent theological or moral values are held up and the Song never even mentions God. It is no wonder that its acceptance into the canon of inspired writings has been seriously questioned. The very character of the book has led to many distinct interpretations.

ABOUT THE BOOK

Scholars agree that the book did not originate as a single composition. They recognize that it is a collection of poems of various length, but they suggest different ways of gathering these poems into sections. Some scholars see a pattern of separation, longing, and union. Others maintain that while these elements are present, they do not follow a particular pattern. Others see unity in verbal echoes, for instance the repetitions in 2,6–7; 3,5; 8,3–4. Since there is no narrative plot and the speakers are neither identified nor introduced, one can only speculate about the original intention of the compiler.

Language and Authorship

This short book has an unusually large number of uncommon words. Its 117 verses contain 49 words that appear nowhere else in the Old Testament. This adds to the difficulty of understanding it, for we are prevented from comparing the meaning of a word in one context with its meaning in another. This unfamiliar vocabulary opens the poem to many interpretations, but it also allows for rich diversity.

Like Proverbs and Ecclesiastes, the Song is associated with Solomon. Attribution to the famous king is only found in the editorial introduction (1,1) and is preceded by a preposition that can be translated in various ways: "by" Solomon; "to" Solomon; "for" Solomon; "of" Solomon; "concerning" Solomon. This does not mean Solomon was the author. Connecting the king's name to the Song probably gave credibility to the Song and linked it to the other wisdom traditions. Since the book includes other references to Solomon (3,7–11; 8,11f) some interpreters identify Solomon as the amorous shepherd. But because the king never speaks in these passages, the references could be merely figurative allusions to fabulous wealth.

The geographic references are wide-reaching. Northern locations are mentioned (2,1; 3,9; 4,8; 6,4; 7,5–6), as are places in Transjordan (4,1) and Judah (1,14; 3,5). This variety may reflect the early northern Israelite source of some of the original poems and a later southern (perhaps Jerusalem) setting for the final edition. The appearance of the Persian word for orchard or park (4,13) suggests a date after the exile in Babylon (after 539 B.C).

The Song of Songs is also found in the *Megilloth,* or festal scroll (see page RG 205). It is read on the last day of the celebration of Passover. Perhaps the announcement of the end of winter (2,11) made the poem suitable for a spring festival. Reference to horses and chariots of Pharaoh (1,9) is an allusion to Exodus, the event commemorated at Passover.

Several different voices are heard in the Song of Songs, as outlined in the following table:

Voices in the Song of Songs

Daughters of Jerusalem	A chorus of voices
Bride	Meaning is not clear. Hebrew text refers to a young woman betrothed but not yet married to a man. While the text alludes to the sexual union of the lovers, it never describes a marriage. The male partner is not necessarily a "groom."
Lover	There seem to be two distinct lovers, one a royal figure from Jerusalem (1,12–17; 3,6–11) and the other a rustic youth from the north (1,7f; 2,8–17). Nowhere is there a combination of the two.

Who are these mysterious lovers? The way one understands the meaning and function of the book will influence the way one identifies the characters within it. If these are ancient wedding songs, then the lovers are bride and groom. If it is love poetry like the poems of ancient Egypt, then the "bride" is understood in a figurative sense; her partner the man with whom she is intimately involved. He is called "lover," not "husband."

FORM AND MEANING

For more than two thousand years, the Song of Songs has been not only a source of fascination but also something of a riddle. Its very uniqueness has made understanding it a challenge. There are four ways of interpreting it: allegorical, cultic, dramatic, and literal. Each of these approaches reveals different possibilities for our religious enrichment. All of them have gained acceptance within Roman Catholic tradition. It is interesting to note that while the first and preferred method of interpreting the Bible has been the literal approach, the opposite has been true with this book. It seems that much of the sexual imagery has been so explicit or suggestive as to offend the sensitivities of many of the faithful. Therefore commentators have presumed that the poems were not intended to be literally understood but must have some concealed religious meaning.

Interpretation When we talk about interpretation, it is important to distinguish between what the book *meant* in the past and what it *means* for the present. Those interpreters who use a strict historical-critical approach insist that the original sense must be the focus of our explanation. Discovering the earliest form and meaning of the book is crucial. It is this original meaning, they would argue, that continues to be revelatory for us today. Other commentators do not categorize methods as "right" or "wrong" but as "helpful" or "not helpful." They would be more open to various interpretations of the Song of Songs.

What Is Allegory?

An allegory is a comparison between two areas of human experience, usually a concrete or everyday area and an abstract one more removed from ordinary experience. For example, justice in our courts is often represented as a beautiful woman wearing a blindfold and holding balancing scales. The woman's beauty symbolizes the attractions of justice: Just as we are drawn to beauty, so we should be drawn to justice. Her blindfold symbolizes the impartiality of justice. No matter how important or unimportant the person who appears before her, she is concerned only with the merits of the case each presents. The balancing scales symbolize the idea that decisions are made according to public standards and anyone can observe how they are made. By using everyday images, the allegorical figure helps us understand our ideals of justice.

Allegorical Interpretations

An allegorical method presumes that the surface meaning of a figure of speech signifies some deeper spiritual truth. This approach was quite popular in ancient Jewish circles (Philo, 20 B.C.–54 A.D.) as well as among early Christian writers (Origen, A.D. 185–254). Jewish commentators who allegorize the Song interpret it as symbolizing God's relationship with Israel, tracing it from the time of the Exodus to the coming of the messiah. They believe it celebrates God's steadfast love bestowed on Israel and describes the fickleness that characterized Israel's attitude toward its divine lover.

As Christians began to read the Hebrew traditions in light of their faith in Christ, this allegorical method produced new meanings. They identified the lovers as Christ and the church. Some read it as a description of the mystical union of God and the individual soul. Some of the most profound theology in the Christian mystical tradition is grounded in this kind of allegorical interpretation of the Song. The works of St. Bernard of Clairvaux and St. John of the Cross are chief examples of this kind of writing.

The bride has even been explained as the Virgin Mary. Though not easily accommodated to the poem, this interpretation has been quite prominent within the Roman Catholic tradition. One reason for this is the belief that Mary is the exemplar of the individual soul in union with God. A stronger reason for this interpretation is the fact that sections of the Song are read during the liturgy on several Marian feasts. Thus by association this interpretation has come into popular devotion to Mary.

Cultic Interpretation

A second way of understanding the Song of Songs assumes that it was originally a liturgical reenactment of a drama that takes place in nature each spring. In a well-known fertility myth of the ancient Near Eastern world, the great god (the Canaanite Baal or the Babylonian Tammuz) dies after the harvest and is mourned by the fertility goddess (Anath or Ishtar respectively). She frantically searches for him during the barrenness of winter. Her efforts are successful and they are finally united. Nature is revived with the coming of spring and the cycle of life continues. The fact that this book was read during the festival of Passover seems to support the theory that Israel was influenced by the agricultural celebrations of the time.

There is ample evidence in the Bible of Israel's use and reinterpretation of Canaanite cultic practices. A nomadic festival took on historical meaning when it was used to commemorate God's deliverance of the people from Egyptian bondage. It was associated with the Feast of Unleavened Bread after the people had settled in Canaan and had moved from a nomadic to an agricultural form of life. These two festivals merged into one celebration, and elements of both became details of the standard story of the first Passover celebration.

Passover is probably a combination of two festivals: an early nomadic celebration intended to ensure the fertility of the flock, and an agricultural one, the Feast of Unleavened Bread, intended to ensure the growth of the crop.

The Song of Songs includes several features that are characteristic of fertility liturgies. Women always play a prominent role in these cultic reenactments. There is frequently a chorus of women and a goddess who is separated from her lover. The speakers are seldom named, and there are more monologues than dialogues. The goddess is sometimes a bride, sometimes a sister, sometimes a mother; the beloved is depicted as a king, but more frequently as a shepherd. While it is quite possible that this ritual drama was never incorporated into the official liturgy of Israel, it could have enjoyed widespread acceptance in isolated rural communities (see Ez 8,14).

The commentators who reject this theory do so because there is no explicit evidence that Israel included the rite of the dying/rising god in its ritual. They do not deny the popular acceptance, but any association with fertility religion would have worked against the book's inclusion in the canon.

Dramatic Interpretation

This third approach has had a long history in the church's tradition. As early as the second century of the Christian era, Origen claimed that the Song was a wedding poem written in dramatic form by Solomon himself. Some interpreters today divide the book into a drama of five movements:

1. The anticipation and meeting of the lovers (1,1 – 2,17)
2. The separation (3,1–11)
3. Reunion (4,1 – 5,1)
4. A second separation (5,2 – 6,3)
5. Final union (6,4 – 8,14)

The commentators assign the speeches to the characters, as indicated in the *New American Bible,* and identify the various scenes by means of subtitles within the text.

The two major characters are the royal shepherd and the Shulammite maiden. A two-character interpretation has serious deficiencies. There is no dramatic development, and the book lacks ethical purpose. A three-character approach was developed to address these weaknesses. It distinguishes two male individuals, the king and the shepherd. The king tries to win the love of the maiden, but she remains faithful to her shepherd lover. In the first interpretation the royal shepherd is worthy of the faithful love of the Shulammite. This personage might well represent Solomon. In the second interpretation, the king is a villain who tries to seduce the maiden with the promise of luxury and comfort. One wonders how this disapproving portrait of Solomon could survive as part of the wisdom tradition, which ascribed wisdom to the very king who is depicted in this manner.

The weaknesses of this approach are obvious. Since the biblical text does not supply names for the speeches, the decisions about their identification are influenced by the biases of the interpreter. Stage directions are imposed from without rather than discovered within the poems themselves. Finally, there is neither story line nor character development, essential traits of good drama.

Literal Interpretation

It may be that the original meaning of the Song is found in its literal interpretation. The Song of Songs is most likely a collection of love poems that neither symbolize divine love nor were developed from fertility rites. It teaches no lesson; it tells no story. It simply celebrates the passion of human love. While some believe that the poems are secular, others doubt that purely secular love songs would ever be admitted to the canon. These latter commentators believe that the poems are examples of Judean wedding songs. They also discover traces of a poetic form called *wasf,* an Arabic word meaning description. These are poems that use images from nature to describe parts of the male or female body. This may explain some of the strange imagery found in the Song (see 4,1–5; 7,2–6).

If this is really the meaning of the Song of Songs, why was the book considered inspired and thus included in the Bible? One can only offer a hypothetical answer. Israel may have followed some of the same wedding customs as did its Syrian neighbor, celebrating the event for seven days. During the festivities, the bride was characterized as "maiden" and the groom as "king." On the eve of the wedding the girl would dance for her lover and recite *wasfs* for his enjoyment. Representing the man as "king" and the extravagance of the celebration could blend quite easily with the tradition about Solomon's erotic adventures (see 1 Kgs 11,1). Some believe that one of the poems was actually composed on the occasion of one of his marriages (3,6–11). What was initially a collection of wedding songs was now regarded as a description of the king's sexual adventures and was joined with two other writings that claim divine inspiration and Solomonic authorship (Proverbs and Ecclesiastes).

Each of the three books attributed to Solomon addresses some of the central issues of life that are basic to the wisdom thinking of the ancient Near East, Israel included.

- Proverbs provides directions on how to achieve peace and prosperity by coming to an understanding of order and stability in the world.
- In Ecclesiastes, Qoheleth addresses the search for meaning in life.
- The Song of Songs celebrates a fundamental human emotion—erotic love.

None of these books fits into the category of "salvation history," but each one is an example of the "way of wisdom."

Once the writings were associated with Solomon and the wisdom attributed to him, it was not long before they possessed their own authoritative significance. This seems to have been enough to ensure inclusion in the canon. Although the three books are quite distinct, they have come to represent different moments in the life of the same man.

- The Song of Songs reveals a young, passionate, unguarded Solomon.
- Proverbs shows a moderate but optimistic man who has learned from his experience of life.
- The musings of Qoheleth in Ecclesiastes come from someone who comes to the end of life challenging the enduring value of human accomplishment.

The quality of these human, but nonetheless theological, concerns is evidence of their religious value. Ascribing them to Solomon provided them with canonical status.

An Independent Woman in a Patriarchal Society

The portrait of the maiden is exceptional for literature from a patriarchal and male-dominated society. This is not the image of a sexually naive and passive woman, dependent upon a man for protection and sustenance. It is the woman who takes the initiative in this romantic pursuit. She utters almost twice as much of the erotic poetry as does the man. Her language is quite explicit, and she shatters any stereotypes that suggest that women may be romantic but not sexually inclined. The Song of Songs does not portray male dominance and female subordination. The maiden is an independent person. She has her own vineyard (1,6) and is encouraged to pasture her flocks (1,8), occupations normally assigned to men. This wisdom book teaches that human passion is both noble and ennobling. Its attraction and vitality are natural to both men and women.

WISDOM TEACHING

From each of the interpretive approaches described above, what does the Song of Songs teach us? What is its theological value? We have considered four different methods of interpretation, so there are four distinct answers to these questions.

1. *The Allegorical Approach*
   A symbolic approach provides us with a figurative way of understanding the nature of our relationship with God, which is dynamic, energizing, and mutually loving. Contrary to an image of God as an impassive creator or avenging judge, the Song of Songs offers us a portrait of a passionate lover, one who desires union with us. Some may find this notion scandalous, but the wisdom tradition (especially Job and Ecclesiastes) repeatedly teaches something about God or human nature that has been unconventional.
2. *The Cultic Interpretation*
   At the heart of the dying/rising ritual is the conviction that death does not have the final victory. The love of the grieving goddess is strong enough to bring her lover back to her and revitalize the lifeless earth.

3. *The Dramatic Interpretation*
   Understanding the poem as a dialogue or interaction among various characters provides an example of faithful love. The fidelity of the bride is held up for all to admire and imitate. This image of a faithful woman conforms to the one found in other places in the wisdom tradition (see Prv 31,10–31).
4. *The Literal Interpretation*
   Seeing the work as lyrical poetry makes no apology for its erotic interpretation. It affirms that sexuality is one of the gifts that God gave for our enjoyment (see Prv 5,15–21; Eccl 9,9). The sexual pleasure is not sought promiscuously but pursued only within the context of a faithful and exclusive commitment.

Questions for Discussion or Reflection

1. If the most basic way of experiencing God's love and saving presence is through human friendship, what does this tell us about who God is?
2. How do we know that God is personal? When applied to God, what does this mean?
3. What is our culture's attitude toward the human body? What are some of the ways we are allured into this prevalent attitude without our recognizing it? How does the Song of Songs proclaim a different message?
4. How has the sense of dualism of body/spirit shaped your spirituality? How has this dualism affected Catholic perception of good and evil? Of sexuality? Of sin?
5. In our culture, permanent commitments are no longer cherished nor are they the customary pattern. If love is death to self, what are the ways people choose safer, more practical activities than loving?
6. What will it take to begin recognizing the mystery of God in all of human life as well as in committed human love and sexuality?

THE BOOK OF WISDOM READING GUIDE

At a Glance

The reward of justice, 1,1 – 6,21	At first glance it might seem a restatement of the doctrine of retribution. A closer look will reveal that traditional views are challenged and radically new ideas are introduced.
Praise of wisdom by Solomon, 6,22 – 11,1	The book receives its name from this section. Wisdom is personified. The author may have felt that Solomonic authority would be necessary in order to gain acceptance of this reinterpretation.
Special providence of God during the Exodus, 11,2 – 19,22	The *midrash* extols the ancestral God of Israel. This *midrash* provides "historical" basis for continued trust in the God of Israel.

BACKGROUND FOR UNDERSTANDING THE BOOK OF WISDOM

The last half of the 4th century saw rapid and sweeping changes in the ancient world. Alexander the Great had brought the entire eastern world under the influence of Greek culture, thereby unifying a diverse, disorganized world. This, however, threatened the integrity of other cultures and religious perspectives. With his death in 323 B.C., the empire was divided among his followers and three independent, hostile kingdoms were formed. Two of these kingdoms played an important role in the affairs of the Jewish nation. Ptolemy gained control of Egypt and established himself in Alexandria; Seleucus triumphed over Babylon and made Antioch his center. Each kingdom contributed to the shaping of the biblical tradition.

Hellenization was forced upon the Jewish community by the Seleucid ruler Antiochus Epiphanes (See Reading Guides for 1 and 2 Maccabees and the Book of Daniel). However, the influence of the Ptolemies is more relevant to the understanding of the wisdom literature. It preceded the influence of the Seleucids and seems to have been well received. A large colony of Jews lived in Alexandria and adapted itself to Greek language and culture. This was the group that translated its religious traditions from Hebrew into Greek, producing what has come to be known as the Septuagint.

Septuagint The Latin for seventy, frequently designated LXX, Septuagint is the name for the main ancient Greek translation of the Hebrew Bible with additions. Tradition claimed that 70 scribes, working independently of each other, labored over the translation of the Bible for 70 days in 70 different locations and produced identical versions. This was seen as evidence of the inspired nature of the translation. Most likely it took decades, but this did not detract from the reverence accorded the Septuagint over the years.

This Greek version was probably the one in popular use during the first century of the Christian era. During the same era, the Jewish community adopted the older Palestinian or Hebrew version of the Bible as its official text. The Christian practice of adding their own writings to the collection may have contributed to this decision.

Christians continued to revere the Alexandrian tradition of the Septuagint. Scholars comparing Old Testament citations used by New Testament writers conclude that a good number, if not all of them, came from the Alexandrian rather than from the earlier Palestinian version. At the time of the Reformation, the official version of the Old Testament became a point of disagreement among Christian denominations. Protestant churches retained the shorter, more ancient Hebrew canon, while the Roman Church accepted the wider Greek canon, preserving an early church tradition. This explains why some Bibles include such books as Wisdom and Sirach,while others do not.

Deuterocanonical ("second listing"). Those books accepted as Scripture by Catholics but not found in the Hebrew canon.

Apocryphal (originally meaning "hidden"). Understood as inspirational but not canonical by Protestants.

ABOUT THE BOOK

Over the centuries this book has been called "The Book of Wisdom" (from the Latin translations), "the Wisdom of Solomon" (from the Septuagint), or variations of either title. Although the author does not explicitly identify himself as Solomon, speaking in the first person, he does describe himself as such (7,5; 8,21; 9,7f; see 1 Kgs 3,5–15). The author may have presumed that the unconventional character of the book's ideas might need the authority of Solomon to be accepted as orthodox teaching. (For explanation of Solomonic authorship see the Reading Guide for Proverbs; Ecclesiastes; Song of Songs.)

The book suggests an origin from within the Jewish community of Alexandria. It is clear that the author was steeped in the history of the Exodus (11,2–16; 12,23–27; 16,2 – 19,22), was acquainted with the religious practices of Egypt (15,14 – 16,1), and was well versed in Hellenistic philosophy and science (6,22 – 11,1). The author reinterpreted his own heritage and critiqued the traditions, practices, and insights of the other two cultures. He did this to support those Jews who were questioning the relevance of their ancient faith in the face of radical cultural changes they were undergoing.

Date of the Book

Most scholars date it somewhere during the first century B.C. The primary threat at this time did not arise from the Hellenizing Greeks but from the Hellenized Jews themselves. The outside oppression at the time of the Maccabean Revolt had given way to a subtle undermining of traditional teaching and values. Even religious leaders were not immune to this kind of worldliness. The author appears to have been concerned that

a. the pious not be led astray,
b. those enthralled by Greek culture be convinced of the work of their own religious heritage,
c. those already carried away by the currents of change be rescued.

Literary Features of the Book

It originated in Greek. The form is natural and free-flowing, not awkward as might be the case if this were a translation from Hebrew.

a. The vocabulary reveals an author who possessed an extensive comprehension of Hellenistic learning.
b. References to earlier religious tradition correspond to the style of the Alexandrian rather than the Palestinian version.
c. The thought is similar to what is found in Jewish-Alexandrian works of this period.
d. The author frequently employed a form of expression that resembles the *diatribe* – a method of argument developed by the Cynic and Stoic philosophers of Greece that creates imaginary opponents who raise questions that the philosopher refutes.

Despite these Greek characteristics, this is basically a Jewish work. It is not difficult to detect the influence of Hebrew parallelism in the poetry. (See the Reading Guide for Job for an explanation of parallelism). The description of God's care during the Exodus is a kind of homiletic *midrash.* The Greeks, especially Philo, developed allegory as a principal method of interpreting traditions. It is significant that the author of Wisdom employed *midrash* rather than allegory. This further verifies the Jewish, rather than Greek, origin of the book.

> **Midrash** Midrash is a kind of interpretation that the Jewish community devised in order to apply the Bible to new situations. Thus a law *(halakah)* was restated or a narrative *(haggadah)* retold in such a way as to give new direction to a new generation.

WISDOM TEACHING

The unifying theme of this biblical book is "the praise of wisdom." Each of the three major sections addresses this theme from its own distinctive point of view. Each section will highlight the significant theological elements found there.

The Reward of Justice (1,1 – 6,21)

The first section is often called "The Book of Eschatology." In it we find the destinies of the righteous and of the wicked described in vivid contrast. The righteous, regardless of their obvious suffering, "are in the hand of God" (3,1), while the wicked "shall receive a punishment to match their thoughts" (3,10). This entire section serves as a summons to fidelity to the religious traditions of Israel, a fidelity that will guarantee the rewards of wisdom.

> **Eschatology** This traditionally refers to the last or final things: the end of the age, death, judgment, reward, and punishment.

This is not a restatement of the doctrine of retribution but a radical departure from the traditional understanding.

1. The author insisted that childlessness, a condition that brought reproach in ancient society (see Gn 16,4; 1 Sm 1,7) is not a mark of divine displeasure (3,13f; 4,1). Moral, not physical fruitfulness is emphasized.
2. The author denied that suffering itself presupposes sin. In fact, an untimely death may be a righteous person's rescue from the wickedness of life (4,14). We are reminded of the popular saying: "The good die young." The author agreed with Job and Qoheleth that virtue is not always rewarded in this life, nor is evil punished. Whoever thinks that death of the righteous is an affliction or destruction is foolish (3,2f). It is rather a trial they must endure to be with God.
3. The author brought two earlier creation narratives together and reinterpreted them. The statement about being made in God's image (2,23), an allusion to Genesis 1,16.28, is followed by the claim that the devil's envy brought death into the world (2,24), a reinterpretation of Genesis. Some think that the latter refers to Cain's envy which resulted in the death of Abel (Gn 4,1–6). Another writer of this time says that Satan led Eve astray (Enoch 69,6). The author of Wisdom was the first biblical writer to identify the serpent of the Genesis account with the devil.

What about Life after Death?

In the Book of Wisdom, the reader is introduced for the first time to the Greek concept of *psyche* (soul, 1,11: 3,1). Although in some passages the word is used with the same meaning as the Hebrew *nephesh* (*being* or *life,* 12,6; 14,5; 16,9), in other places it clearly marks the adoption of the body-spirit dualism that is part of the Greek understanding of human nature. The Greeks held that human nature was a combination of a perishable material body and an eternal spiritual soul. This combination was dissolved at death. We must be careful, however, not to take this Greek thought further than the author did. Nowhere does this book speak of an immortal soul.

Life after death is quite different from the earlier perception of *Sheol,* the abode of the dead (see RG 192; see also RG 234). There is just enough ambiguity in the words "immortality" (3,4; 4,1; 8,13.17; 15,3) and "incorruptibility" (2,23; 6,18f) to prevent us from making definite statements about the author's view. One thing seems clear. Immortality is not an inherent quality of human nature; it is the result of union with wisdom (8,13.17; 15,3). Although 2,23 claims that God made humans to be imperishable, 6,18 suggests that incorruptibility is possible only when one is faithful to wisdom.

We are not sure if the author was speaking of physical death, of physical death followed by spiritual death, or of spiritual death alone. The thought does seem to be directed to spiritual death. St. Paul will have to face the same question when dealing with the unexpected deaths of Christians (1 Thes 4,13–18). Unlike the author of Wisdom, his answer is quite specific.

Praise of Wisdom by Solomon (6,22–11,1)

The second major section of the book is an address acclaiming the glories of wisdom. It is from this section that the book receives its name, and it is from here that we find a representation of personified Wisdom (see Proverbs Reading Guide: "Wisdom—Who Is She?"). This representation of Wisdom is quite different from that found in earlier tradition. The author may have realized that he needed to claim the authority of Solomon to gain acceptance for this reinterpretation. This section begins with an account of his humble origin, his own prayer for wisdom, and God's immeasurable gift in answering his plea (7,1–7; also see 9,1–18). This is an allusion to the prayer of Solomon (1 Kgs 3,5–15), and it characterizes the author as the wise king.

The description of Wisdom is composed of elements from:

- Israelite tradition (7,22a; see Prv 8,30);
- the cult of the Egyptian deity Isis (goddess of wisdom and patron of culture whose praises were extolled in the form of listings similar to those found in 7,22–8,1);
- Hellenistic philosophy and science (see 8,7 for mention of the cardinal virtues of Plato). This may be the way the author argues for the superiority of the religion of Israel. The author confers on the figure of Wisdom the characteristics of Isis already found in the Israelite tradition and draws upon Hellenistic religious and scientific concepts to praise her as he argues that *real* wisdom is a gift from God bestowed on the faithful.

Christianity and the Book of Wisdom

In this book wisdom is referred to as "the spirit of the Lord" (1,7). The theology of this verse functions significantly in the liturgy of Pentecost. Although spirit played a major role in Stoic philosophy, it was clearly a theme in Jewish tradition as well. The author ascribed to Wisdom what earlier writers attributed to the spirit of the Lord:

- the creative power of the world (7,22,a; see Jdt 16,14);
- the source of Joseph's honor in Egypt (10,13; see Gn 41,38);
- the inspiration that prepared Moses for the Exodus and led the people through the wilderness (10,16f; see Is 63,11.14).

What is the influence of the figure of Wisdom on New Testament writings? Some scholars believe that the influence is direct. Others hold that there was a treasury of thought, imagery, and language that served as a common source. Whichever the case may be, the figure of Wisdom was reinterpreted by early Christian theologians as they struggled to understand Jesus the Christ.

Paul explicitly referred to Christ as the wisdom of God (1 Cor 1,24.30). The most obvious example of this is found in the Gospel according to John. There we find Jesus described in ways that Wisdom had been depicted earlier: as being with God in the beginning before the world existed (Jn 1,1; 17,5; see Wis 2,22); as sent from heaven to accomplish the will of God (Jn 6,38; see Wis 9,10). Current scholarship is only beginning to seek the implications of this imagery for Christology.

Earlier traditions spoke of "a spirit of wisdom" (Is 11,2), but here Wisdom itself is called a spirit (1,6; 7,22). The author has brought two different concepts together by joining intelligence with energy of power. By doing this, he could speak of wisdom-spirit as "an aura of the might of God" (7,25).

This section ends with a summary of the way Wisdom guided the ancestors of Israel by bringing them out of Egypt, through the agency of Moses (see Hos 12,14); and by enabling them to prosper (10,1–11,1). It is clear that Wisdom, once thought to be the possession of the king, was now to be understood as the constant companion of true Israelites, those faithful ones of the past as well as committed Jews of the present.

Special Providence of God during the Exodus (11,2–19,22)

At this point there is an observable shift in focus. The poem in praise of Wisdom gives way to *midrash* that praises the God of Israel. This version of the experience of the Exodus and the time in the wilderness illustrates two points:

1. The sufferings that befell the Egyptians were the direct result of their sinfulness (11,16).
2. The very elements that afflicted the Egyptians benefited the Israelites (11,5).

This reading of the past is done through creative selection of biblical data as well as addition of material not found anywhere else.

The author did not set out to recount historical facts but seemed intent on addressing the challenge raised by Hellenism. His goal was to remind the Alexandrian Jews that once before they had suffered at the hands of the Egyptians and, in the face of impossible odds, had been rescued. This *midrash* provides a "historical" basis for continued trust in the God of Israel.

There are two digressions within this third division of the book. Both of them are found in the second example of God's providence:

1. A testimony to God's mercy (11,17 – 12,22). Although it breaks the *midrashic* line of thought, it may have been prompted by the mention of punishment in the preceding line (11,16).
2. A condemnation of idolatry (13,1 – 15,17). It follows the claim that the Egyptians "saw and recognized the true God whom before they had refused to know" (12,27), but continued in their idolatry. The language used in the condemnation of nature worship (13,1–9) may be the best example of the author's broad grasp of scientific knowledge.

THEOLOGY IN A NEW CONTEXT

The author of Wisdom did not set out in search of new theological insights. Since he was committed to proving the enduring value of the religion of Israel, he explained traditions and themes that were familiar to the Jews of his day. What made his contribution unique was the method that he employed as he went about his task.

Throughout its history, Israel had been forced by circumstances to deal with religious and cultural tensions of other societies. The Bible itself shows that these encounters were sometimes peaceful and at other times violent and destructive. Whatever the situation may have been, elements from those cultures found their way into the traditions of Israel. It was the religion of Israel that reinterpreted features of other cultures and then assimilated these new ideas into their own perspective. Israel seldom took seriously the religious worldview of the other culture.

This attitude changed with the Hellenization of the world. It was precisely the attraction of Greek civilization that threatened Jewish faith. The community wrestled with an agonizing dilemma: Could one accept the prevailing culture and remain faithful to the traditions of the ancestors? The author of Wisdom undertook the task of answering this question in the affirmative. He did not try to reconcile Judaism with Hellenism but used the ideas, the language, and the literary style of Greek culture to demonstrate the excellence of the Jewish faith.

In taking Greek culture seriously, this theologian did what theologians after him would have to do whenever cultural lines were crossed. The challenge of interpretation facing him was not so different from the one facing us: that is, to adapt and transfer a religious heritage that originated in one cultural context into another His purpose was a defense of the ancestral faith. Ours is the proclamation of the word of God. We have much to learn from this wisdom teacher and his method of theological reinterpretation.

Questions for Discussion or Reflection

Many good, intelligent Catholics worry when it seems that the Church's teachings are changing: more favorable attitude toward non-Catholics, a greater role for the laity in Church matters, a relaxation of the laws of fast and abstinence, changes in the liturgy, and different explanations of traditional beliefs.

Spend a few moments in silence and compare the contemporary Catholic experience with the situation being addressed to the Jewish community by the author of the Book of Wisdom.

1. How do you see the Book of Wisdom as a source of understanding the changing appearance of Catholic practice and theological reinterpretation?
2. Theologians tell us the only good way of judging changes to be good or bad is the common sense way of looking at the history of the Church's teaching or practice. How would your common sense judge a change such as the Sacrament of Reconciliation from once in a lifetime to the current practice; or the celebration of the Eucharist from Latin to the vernacular language? How can you discover more about the Church's history of such practices?
3. Do you perceive what is handed down to us as the Christian tradition as a way of life rather than just words?

SIRACH (ECCLESIASTICUS) READING GUIDE

The book appears to be a collection of proverbs organized in such a way as to resemble short essays. While there is no explicit arrangement in the book itself, one can divide the material into themes and according to literary form.

At a Glance

Chapters 1–43	Moral instruction, similar to that in the rest of the wisdom literature
1,1–29; 24,1–31	Two poems praising wisdom
42,15–43,35	A poem extolling God's activity in nature
Chapters 44,1–49,16; 50,1–24	Poems acclaiming time-honored heroes of Israel and the high priest Simon
Epilogue: 50,25–29	A denunciation of some of the traditional enemies of Israel and a subscription identifying the author
Two appendices	A psalm of thanksgiving for deliverance from danger (51,1–12) and a personal testimony in the form of an acrostic poem (see Psalms: Wisdom Poems)

ABOUT THE BOOK

Over the years the Book of Sirach has been known by different names: "The Wisdom of Jesus Ben Sira" (of which Sirach is the Greek form); "The Book of Sirach" (a shortened title); "Ecclesiasticus" (from the Latin for Book of the Church, a designation that probably stems from its frequent use as a catechetical aid in the early centuries of the Western Church).

Sirach is the only biblical book that:

- Identifies its author (50,27)
- Refers to its translator (a grandson of Ben Sira)

- Dates its translation ("the 38th year of the reign of King Euergetes," sometime after 132 B.C. (see the Foreword preceding Chapter 1)

Although the prophetic books claim to originate from the prophets and do locate their ministry during the reign of specific kings (for example, Hos 1,1; Is 1,1; Jer 1,2f; etc.), the references there are to the activity of the prophets, not to the books that bear the prophets' names. Here we have a clear reference to when the book was written.

The Foreword also provides us with some interesting information about the composition of the biblical canon (the official list of inspired books). Three times the grandson of Ben Sira speaks of "the law, the prophets, and the later authors" (or "the rest of the books"). This tells us that by the second century B.C. the Jewish community already had what came to be known as a tripartite (three-part) Bible. Scholars believe that the first two parts (the Law and the Prophets) most likely include the books as we have them today. The third part (the Writings) was probably quite fluid well into the Christian era.

Like the Book of Wisdom, Sirach belongs to the collection called Deuterocanonical by Roman Catholics or Apocryphal by Protestants (see RG 217). The Foreword, which is considered historical introduction and not inspired instruction, recounts the translator's arrival in Egypt, where he discovered that the Jews' "valuable teaching" had been rendered from Hebrew into Greek, the language of the day. This inspired him to undertake the translation of his grandfather's teachings. The Hebrew version from which he worked seems to have dropped out of sight until copies of it were found in 1896.

It is not clear why the Jews did not accept Sirach as canonical. Some commentators offer these reasons:

1. Ben Sira was interested in the Temple and cult (concerns of a first century A.D. group called Sadducees).
2. He did not seem to believe in the resurrection of the body held by a rival religious group of the first century called the Pharisees.

Therefore the Pharisaic rabbis who decided on the canon rejected Sirach. Whatever the case may be, its absence from the Jewish list explains why it is missing from the Protestant canon.

The way the high priest Simon is described (50,1–21) leads one to conclude he had recently died. This would locate the writing of the original Hebrew version of Sirach sometime during the first quarter of the second century (200–175) B.C. The description of Simon's priestly performance suggests that the author was quite familiar with the Jerusalem ritual and perhaps was even a resident of the city and wrote there.

THE REASON FOR WRITING

The Hellenization of the Near East had already taken hold among the educated upper classes by the time Ben Sira put his teachings into writing (see the essay on Hellenization on RG 174). Many Jews must have wondered whether their ancient traditions could match the breadth and depth of Greek thought. Being a well-traveled man (34,11) and an observant Jew, Ben Sira would have witnessed the decline in fervor that overtook his fellow Jews, and it would have troubled him. His object in writing was to show the Jews of his day that real wisdom was to be found in the traditions of Israel and not in the godless philosophy of the day. He intended his work to be a guide to every circumstance of life:

- Ben Sira exhorted his readers to study the ancient traditions to find direction needed to cope with their new, challenging situation (2,10).
- He warned against trying to live according to the standards of both Judaism and Hellenism (2,12).
- He condemned those who chose Hellenism over Judaism (2,13f).
- He identified the wise ("those who fear the LORD") as those who were faithful to the religion of Israel (2,15–17).

Although most of Ben Sira's wisdom teaching is quite conventional, the way he blended it with Israel's history and its legal and cultic traditions is distinctive. Earlier wisdom writing showed little interest in Israelite matters. Ben Sira's way of arguing in favor of fidelity to Judaism was:

- To claim that true wisdom resided in Israel (24,1–21)
- To use history to support this claim (44,1 – 49,16)
- To identify Wisdom with the Law of Moses (24,22), giving this a place of honor above the traditions of other cultures
- To demonstrate a profound concern for the cult and role of the priesthood (46,6–20; 47,12f; 50,1–21)

If we are correct in determining the date of the translation, then it is probable that the final form of this book appeared after the Maccabean Revolt but before the writing of the Wisdom of Solomon. This helps us to see how Israel's response to Hellenism varied with time. Ben Sira did not adapt to the process of Hellenization to the extent the author of Wisdom did. If "traditionalist" means holding unchanged the answers of the past because they alone can meet the problems of the present, then Ben Sira can be called traditionalist in his response to Hellenism.

WISDOM TEACHING

Like the Book of Proverbs, the primary focus of Ben Sira's teaching is moral guidance. The book is like an instructional manual containing maxims, many of which are grouped according to topic. A series of short essays addresses topics such as duties toward God, toward one's parents, and toward rulers. There are instructions on how to train children, how to choose friends, and how to guard one's speech. There are warnings against excess, laziness, and foolishness. Whatever one needs to succeed in life, while at the same time remaining faithful to the traditions of the elders, is addressed in the instruction.

Like Proverbs, Sirach celebrates the glories of personified Wisdom (Chapters 1 and 24). But it takes the characterization a step further than the earlier work. Here we see Wisdom searching for a place to dwell and finally pitching her tent in Jerusalem. Traces of this poetic characterization can be found in the Gospel of John where the Word, present with God from the beginning and involved in the creation of all things, "pitched his tent among us" (Jn 1,1–14).

Ben Sira's poems describing the role of divine wisdom in creation (16,22 – 17,18; 39,12–35; 42,15 – 43,35) are really commentaries on the opening chapters of Genesis. The rather technical way he develops his thought shows us the extent to which Ben Sira was influenced by the scientific knowledge of his day.

The book contains some of the harshest statements about women found in the Bible. Proverbs may have warned the naive youth to beware of wily and seductive women, but this

The Influence of Sirach on Jewish and Christian Communities

The New Testament writers primarily used the ancient Greek version of the Hebrew Bible called the Septuagint, which contained additional works such as Sirach. It is not surprising that the influence of Sirach can be detected in some of their writings. The Letter of James is a clear example of this. Both books address questions of pride (Sir 10,7; Jas 4,6) and humility (Sir 3,18; Jas 1,9), of rich and poor (Sir 10,19–24; Jas 2,1–6), and of true wisdom (Sir 19,17–21; Jas 3,13–17), to name but a few.

There are also parallels between directives found in Sirach and those in the Gospels. This includes teaching on magnanimity (Sir 29,12; Mt 6,19) and forgiveness (Sir 28,2; Mk 11,25) and against placing false hope in possessions (Sir 11,18f; Lk 12,16–21).

Although the canonical status of Sirach was and remains a question for debate, from the time of its appearance it has been very influential in both the Jewish and Christian communities. Over the years it has served as a kind of handbook of practical ethics, and its teachings can be found in the liturgical texts of both groups. The discovery at Qumran of a scroll of Sirach is evidence that the book was venerated as Scripture by this Jewish sectarian group. It also appears in copies of liturgical scrolls that were read in synagogues around the 10th century A.D. Finally, the book is quoted as Scripture at least once in the Talmud.

The early church theologians Cyprian (3rd century A.D.) and Jerome (4th century A.D.) attest to Christian use of the book. Clement of Alexandria (2nd century A.D.) quotes it so often that his citations have come to be considered an authoritative version of the text. This book continues to exercise its influence even today. Passages from Sirach are used as lectionary readings. For most Catholics, the liturgical celebration is their primary exposure to the Bible. The teachings of Ben Sira continue to exhort hearers to fidelity to the tradition and upright moral living.

author seems to speak disparagingly against women in general. Ben Sira is the one who blames woman for sin and death (25,23). He expected wives to be subservient to their husbands, for he seems to be in favor of punishment, even including divorce, if they refuse to obey (25,24f). Perhaps the worst example of this misogyny is found in the description of the unwed daughter (42,9–14). The author considers her a liability, and his concern is exclusively with the reputation of the father. As with biblical passages about slavery and other practices of ancient society, we need to use care in present-day interpretation. Nothing in these writings can or should be used to deny the proper rights and responsibilities of women today.

The author holds a traditional view of retribution (4,11–19; 7,1–3; 16,1–21; 21,1–10). Reward or punishment after death does not seem to be the concern of this wisdom teacher (14,15–19). He counsels mourning at the death of another but cautions his reader to moderation in the acceptable expression of grief. The reason the display should be temperate is that the dead are dead and nothing can be changed by uncontrolled sorrow (38,1–23).

While this view of death may be similar to earlier notions of retribution, it was not universally held in Israel at this time. Hope of reward after death for fidelity during persecution is found in other writings of this period (for example Dn 12,1–3; 2 Mc 7,9–29). Although Ben

Sira probably lived before the Maccabean Revolt (events surrounding this period are recorded in other books mentioned above), his grandson-translator certainly lived after the rebellion, and he upheld his ancestor's traditional view.

Many interpreters regard Ben Sira as a Proto-Sadducee because of his adherence to the traditional notion of retribution and rejection of any life after death, as well as his support of the priesthood and his interest in the cult. Although the Sadducees probably did not exist until after the Maccabean Revolt, many of the theological views found in this book were adopted by this aristocratic priestly party.

RELEVANCE TO MODERN LIFE

In response to the Vatican document *Decree on the Training of Priests* (16), moral theologians are reexamining the moral instructions found in Scripture. They are not looking for ageless answers to contemporary questions, but searching in an attempt to discover how moral decisions were made in the past. Biblical specialists provide them with insight into the manner in which writers, especially the teachers of wisdom, brought the time-honored religious tradition to bear upon new situations.

The Book of Sirach, with its essay-like instruction, remains a source of information in this area. It opens a window into a community struggling with its identity as it finds itself at the crossroads of traditional religion and contemporary culture. While we may not be able to follow their specific advice, we can learn from their example how to reinterpret the tradition creatively, yet remain loyal to its revelatory message.

Prayer

Divine Wisdom,
you led men and women to put
into the Bible words that
would bring us closer to you.
Help us search the holy Scriptures
better each day. Enlighten us in
these changing times to acquire the
wisdom and grace to understand
your call, reinterpreting it for
our contemporary lives while
remaining loyal to its eternal
message.
Let your word, like good seed,
take root in our hearts
and bear fruit in our lives.
We ask this through Christ our Lord. Amen.

Questions for Discussion or Reflection

1. Choose several maxims from Sirach that especially appeal to you. Why do you think they are appropriate for life today?
2. Give examples that are inappropriate for the way we live today.
3. If you were Ben Sira, what ten teachings would you leave for your children and their children?
4. Where do most people today find the principles by which they live?

The Prophets

PROPHETIC THEMES

Before getting into the individual characteristics and message of each of the prophetic books, it will be important to talk a little about prophets and prophecies. When you think of prophecy, what immediately comes to mind? For most people, the common understanding is that a prophet is a person who predicts the future. This is not, however, all that the Bible means.

A biblical prophet is a person deeply concerned with the present-day events that affect the moral and spiritual lives of people. Having experienced God's presence and love in a profound way, the prophet becomes attuned to the perspective of God in individual lives and in the life of the community. Taking on the perspective of God awakens the prophet to concerns of justice—especially concern for the poor, the afflicted, the alienated, and the marginalized. It's as if the prophet, having become a very intimate friend of God, consults with God on various matters, and then feels compelled to share those insights and discussions with the rest of the community. Thus, the prophet uses all possible imaginative techniques to communicate with the people: symbols, stories, word plays, and forms and patterns of speech common to that day.

The prophet, through that personal relationship with God, takes on God's very mind and heart. This leads the prophet to assess people and events not on the basis of wealth, status, or possessions, but rather on the basis of the value and dignity of every single person created in the image and likeness of God. This viewpoint is so much the prophet's own that the prophet dares to speak for God, often using the phrase, "Thus says the LORD. . . ." This conviction comes to the surface most clearly when the prophet perceives the lack of justice, fidelity, or compassion in individual lives and especially in the life and actions of the community. These experiences of injustice call the prophet forth to speak, no matter what the cost. The prophet's challenge is hard to listen to because the prophet speaks of matters that go counter to the accepted actions within the community, whether in religion, culture, or politics. Usually, the prophet's message concerns a movement away from being preoccupied with our own selfish concerns, to a movement toward being concerned for others—especially those who have no power: the poor, the widows, the afflicted, the outcasts, the alienated, the marginalized, the stranger.

As an integral part of this community, the prophet's own challenge is to renounce self-righteousness and to speak as one, like all the rest, in continual need of healing and conversion. Self-righteousness is not the true stance of the prophet, although that danger is ever present. Rather, the prophet speaks as a member of this sinful community. Despite this stance, the messenger is often clearly unpopular, because the message is painful. Think about it for yourself: Would you want to live with someone who constantly pointed out your injustices or social evils, as if God were constantly watching you?

In speaking from the perspective of God, the prophet always laments over the injustices and points out and accuses the wrongdoers, hoping for repentance and reform. Usually, a warning is included, in which the prophet, in a general manner, tells of possible dire consequences if matters are not corrected, or if attitudes are not changed. The prophet's message always demands a change of heart, mind, and attitudes—aligning them to the very mind, heart, and attitudes of God. Only in this manner can justice once again prevail and God be intimately present to the community.

The prophet's message is not always one of doom and gloom. Rather, the prophet continually reminds the people of God's faithful love and concern for them. In this context, the prophet offers the opportunity and the guidance for the community to realign itself with God's love, reconciliation, and peace. But the challenge is that this reality will only occur if the people continue to do the Lord's work, the work of justice. Just as God is faithful, the prophet spurs the people on to be faithful also. God's love and peace will be manifest if the people attend to the concerns of the poor and to the works of justice. Reform of self in order to be of service to others is the key message of all the prophets. In order for the reform to take place, the prophet continually reminds the people of God's loving arms and faithful watch on the people's behalf. If the people continue to remember God's love and fidelity toward them, then justice will indeed flourish in the land.

THE DEVELOPMENT OF THE PROPHETIC COLLECTIONS

Many of the books of the Bible were written much later than the time period and the event they recount. This is true for the collection of the prophetic books. The development of the prophetic material follows a pattern somewhat like this. First the prophet experiences life within a believing faith community. This community nourishes and sustains the prophet's relationship with God and enables the prophet to grow in intimacy with God and others. Sometime during the prophet's life, God is experienced more intimately and more profoundly, to such an extent that the prophet feels called to delve into the whole mystery of God as it relates to the community. The prophet develops an acute sensitivity to violations of justice, especially toward the poor and rejected. The prophet has an inherent need to call these incidents to the attention of the community. Often, warnings of dire consequences accompany the prophet's words, challenging the community to action on behalf of those who are experiencing injustice.

There are those in the community who reject the prophet's message and try to outshout, silence, imprison, exile, or kill the prophet. Others see the wisdom in the prophet's words and begin to live and act accordingly. This segment of the community preserves the message and memory of the prophet by acting on the challenge and by passing the words and story on to anyone who will listen. In this process of handing on the stories, the words of the prophet are shaped and reshaped, often refashioned and reinterpreted so that they speak not only to the prophet's original audience but also to the present reality and life of the community. Sooner or later the words and stories are preserved in written form. Finally, some individual or group of disciples collects, combines, and edits the written material into a single work, though in part its form might resemble an anthology of oracles.

There is, nevertheless, a viewpoint for these prophetic collections. This viewpoint, the theology of the book, reflects the human relationship with God and tries to be faithful to the living memory of the original prophet. At the same time, it continues the living and active tradition in its relevance to changing historical times and experiences of the believing community.

Thus, the words of the prophet still challenge our own generation and times in the same way that they challenged the prophet's own generation and times.

ISAIAH READING GUIDE

THREE IN ONE: THE BOOK OF ISAIAH

Since the Bible presents us with a single work, under one title, it is natural to assume that the entire Book of Isaiah was written by one person called Isaiah. Scholarly research, however, has shown that one person could not have written the entire book. Close analysis reveals that the people, places, and events mentioned span several centuries. This is important to realize as you attempt to read this well-known and beloved book of the Bible. It is a book that has had a significant influence both on Old and New Testaments, with Isaiah being one of the books most often quoted in the New Testament.

At least three different authors or communities, at three different times in Israel's history, contributed materials that were actually compiled and edited into the one book we now know as Isaiah. Conventionally, biblical scholars have assigned names to each of the three collections of materials in the Book of Isaiah: First Isaiah, or Isaiah of Jerusalem, Chapters 1–39; Second or Deutero-Isaiah, Chapters 40–55; and Third or Trito-Isaiah, Chapters 56–66.

Isaiah of Jerusalem

First Isaiah, or Isaiah of Jerusalem (Chapters 1–39) is usually dated to a very turbulent period in the history of Israel, 740–687 B.C. First Isaiah witnessed the events that led Assyria, at the invitation of Ahaz, the king of Judah, to annihilate and exile the Northern Kingdom of Israel, in 721, as well as to place Judah itself under the control of the Assyrians, forcing it to pay high tribute to Assyria. Isaiah of Jerusalem was still ministering in 701 when Hezekiah, king of Judah and the son of Ahaz, grew tired of being subject to Assyria and asked Egypt for help in rebelling against Assyria. In response to this rebellious league against him, Sennacherib, the king of Assyria, came back and captured all the key Judean towns, ultimately surrounding Jerusalem. In the biblical version of the story, a plague sent by God broke out, and Sennacherib retreated with the spoils and booty from the other cities. The Assyrian version of the story, found recorded in a recent archeological discovery known as Taylor's prism, is that Hezekiah knew he was defeated, so he called a truce and agreed to pay a very large sum of money if Sennacherib would leave and not destroy the city. Sennacherib agreed, and the battle ended.

Isaiah in Babylonia

Second or Deutero (from the Greek word meaning second) Isaiah, Chapters 40–55, covers the years 540–537 B.C., in Babylonia. Babylonia, roughly modern-day Iraq, had defeated the previous superpower, Assyria, in 612, when Babylonia captured Assyria's capital city, Nineveh. Nebuchadnezzar, the king of Babylonia, went on a campaign to capture as much territory as he could handle. In 587, he captured the Southern Kingdom of Judah, destroyed Jerusalem and its temple, and exiled or deported the people of Judah to Babylonia. From 587–538, the people of Judah were in Babylonia, without land, temple, or roots. In 538, Cyrus, the king of the Persians, defeated the Babylonian empire and restored the people to their homeland. It was during the last few years of the Babylonian exile, and the beginning of the return under Cyrus, that Second Isaiah spoke to the people in Babylonia.

Isaiah of the Return from Exile

Third Isaiah, also known as Trito (the Greek word meaning third) Isaiah, Chapters 56–66, is dated to the period after the return of the people from Babylon, 537–500 B.C. There was great joy in returning, but soon worry, depression, and defeat set in because of the vast amount of work that needed to be done to rebuild the land, the city walls and structures, and the Temple. These preoccupations were further complicated by the attitude of some of those who returned to the land. Even though they had come to see their exile as a consequence of their faithlessness, and their liberation as God's new mighty act that renewed the covenant relationship, people still sinned, acted from motives of avarice and greed, and showed injustice toward the poor and oppressed. These chapters presume the Temple had been rebuilt, dating them after 515 B.C. Judah had become a province of Persia, and the people were caught up in the frustrating process of rebuilding the land and their Jewish identities. It is in this context that Third Isaiah speaks to the people. These three blocks of material, each with its unique message, were pulled together by editors, who gave them final shape.

The description above helps us set a context for reading and understanding Isaiah. Unless we are familiar with the historical background, the prophet's words will not be clear, because we won't understand the specific references. God speaks and acts in and through the human events and through people. To know what God is saying, therefore, we must read the signs of the times. Only those who see matters from God's perspective will be true guides in reading the signs of the times.

Process of Transforming Life Experience into a Text and Beyond

1. An experience—immediate or of long duration
2. Reflection on that experience—a duration of time
3. Verbal articulation of that experience—storytelling and reshaping of story over a period of time
4. Written texts—collections of stories, sayings, rituals, insights, wisdom, proverbs, poetry, narration
5. Editing of the written material into a coherent whole with an overarching point of view or theology

This entire process is perpetually repeated every time an individual or a community reads or hears and experiences the text as speaking directly to them. The application of the text to their own personal lived experience initiates this process over and over. In this context, the text becomes a living document able to speak to those willing to listen and take it to heart.

At some point, certain texts were made definitive or accepted as canonical, and no more changes could be made to the text. But up to that point, the text was still in a process of shaping and reshaping. At the time of canonization, these texts, along with the entire shaping process, were considered inspired by God, and therefore metaphorically called the Word of God.

FIRST ISAIAH

Overview of Chapters 1–39

First Isaiah, or Isaiah of Jerusalem, speaks from the very turbulent events of 742–700 B.C. In its final form, the work begins with a particular message to Jerusalem in Chapters 1–12. It then addresses the nations as a whole in Chapters 13–23, and finally speaks about the fate of the whole world in Chapters 24–27, which probably do not go back to Isaiah of Jerusalem. Chapters 28–39 will be discussed later.

The account of the prophet's call usually provides significant clues to the prophet's perspective. (See the explanation below.) Chapter 6 of Isaiah recounts First Isaiah's call.

Biblical Vocation Call Pattern

1. God significantly enters a human life.
2. God gives a mandate or a mission.
3. The person being called usually objects.
4. God makes creative use of this objection.
5. God reassures.

Some Biblical Texts Indicative of this Pattern:

- Exodus 3,1–12
- Jeremiah 1,4–10
- Isaiah 6,1–8
- Isaiah 40,1–9
- Luke 1,28–38

Isaiah experiences the Lord as king and glorious majesty during temple worship and prayer. This majestic, overwhelming, holy presence is suffused in and through "all the earth." The prophet's experience of this presence leads to his perception of himself as a person, like everyone else, full of imperfections, infidelities, and weaknesses. Yet, when the Lord touches and cleanses the mouth of the prophet with a fiery ember, the prophet is empowered to speak in spite of his weak and sinful human condition. The prophet sees the need for someone to speak to the people, feels called to respond to this need, and volunteers as the spokesperson for the Lord. Isaiah will speak the Lord's message but the people will not listen or understand. When Isaiah asks how long this will continue, he receives the answer: until all is destroyed, laid waste, and made desolate.

Thus, the message that Isaiah brings, the people will not listen to, and therefore destruction will come upon both the people and the land. Yet, throughout there is the ultimate hope for peace, harmony, and messianic salvation. No matter how stubborn the people are in their refusal to listen and repent, God will still work peace and future salvation in and through that very stubbornness and refusal. Suffering and punishment will prove to be a purifying, refining fire that will bring the community closer to God and that will make them more concerned with each other, especially the poor, the oppressed, and the alienated.

Now that we have completed this overview of Isaiah of Jerusalem's main themes, we can turn to an explanation of specific passages. Remember, however, that the original prophetic material has been shaped and reshaped as it has been handed down and further modified by the final editors into a message that will be pertinent to their own particular community. The editors will even add material that will stress a particular aspect of the original message. Therefore, while Isaiah's call is located in Chapter 6, the editors have provided a summary chapter, Chapter 1, showing what Isaiah's message was to be, and how the people would respond, along with how God would eventually work out the loving plan of salvation.

Isaiah, Chapters 1–6

Chapter 1 of Isaiah boldly states that unless the community repents its injustices and cares for the poor and defenseless in their midst, God will bring severe punishment upon the people. God punishes them (for instance, by the Assyrian conquest) not to destroy them, but rather to purify them, so that they will become a more just and loving community. (See the essay on God and suffering).

Isaiah 2,1–5 speaks of a vision of future peace in a passage that is one of the most quoted and best-known passages of all Scripture. It speaks of that ideal time when instruments of war are turned into tools of peace—tools that can be used for meeting the hungers of the human family. This is the ideal to which God has called Israel and the entire community, the vision that is integral to Isaiah's message as prophet. Yet Chapter 2,6 to Chapter 5 continue what must have been Isaiah's enduring, poorly received, and unheard message. In this section the prophet calls to mind the selfishness of the people, their lack of justice, their lack of concern for others, and their utter disregard for the loving relationship into which God called Israel. Chap-

Life After Death

Did you know that Isaiah is one of the first Old Testament authors to have proposed that death is not the end of life? We might find it hard to believe, but the entire Old Testament, with a few minor exceptions, seems to accept the notion that there is no life after death. After death, one exists in a world of shadows, characterized by unreality, forgetfulness, and inactivity. The most common name for this place, at times personified as a being, was Sheol, often translated as Hades, or the Nether World. The belief was that, after death, one lived most vitally in the children and family who would remember you and carry on your name, in the spotless reputation that you would be known for, and in having been part of a nation that God would continually care for and sustain. Isaiah seems to suggest that this is not enough. Unjust or overwhelming suffering, along with God's continual fidelity and love for each person, almost demands that death not be the end. Rather Isaiah envisions a continuance of life after death in which all wrongs will be righted. Peace and joy will be the characteristics of this continually deeper and ever-growing love relationship with God and with all people.

ESSAY

God and Suffering

A theological perspective that Isaiah seems to espouse focuses on God as an impatient parent who is fed up with the sinful actions of the children. Punishment is seen by the parent as a means of redirecting or redefining the focus and perspective of the child. Isaiah seems to be saying that God punishes in order to purify the sinful actions and inclinations of the people. Other nations are used by God as instruments to accomplish this punishing and purifying process.

A question that needs to be asked is whether this is an image of God that makes sense to us today? Does this image of God speak to our experience and consciousness of what we have come to understand as God? Just as corporal punishment of children is no longer really tolerated or in any way considered an appropriate form of punishment for wrong acts, so this image of God as child-punisher has to be also reevaluated. We have come to realize that suffering is not something that God causes to happen in order to help us learn a lesson. Rather, suffering is part and parcel of what it means to be human, what it means to live a limited human existence.

God is experienced as one who is always life-giving, life-enhancing, life-producing. God uses all the experiences of our lives as means by which we can enter into a greater personal and loving relationship with him. Suffering and pain are key moments in our experience that get us in touch with our limited existence and force us to realize that we are not the center of the universe. It is at these particular moments that God invites us to an ever deeper relationship, challenging us to believe very firmly that new life will come out of this seemingly life-denying experience. God is always on the side of life, on our side, in the sense of a loved one who is faithful no matter what the sorrow or pain. It is this fidelity of God toward the people that is truly Isaiah's message.

God brings about redemption in and through those very experiences of pain and sorrow that bring us to our knees. God doesn't cause the pain and suffering, but rather, God uses it to bring new life out of death. This is what we mean when we speak of the Christian life as one deeply imbedded in the Paschal Mystery. God doesn't cause the pain, nor does God free us from this very human experience. Rather, God transforms our very pain and sorrow into an occasion of greater understanding of self as human, of deeper sympathy with others in pain, and of greater depth in our personal, loving relationship with God and all of creation.

ter 6 relates Isaiah's vocation call experience, a willingness to devote himself to the work of the Lord despite the frustration, futility, and hardships that the work and message will bring.

The Book of Immanuel

Chapters 7–12, usually referred to as the "Book of Immanuel" because it contains the famous verses of the Immanuel prophecy (Is 7,12), deal with salvation that comes only with reliance on God, and not on one's own strength or alliances for security. Isaiah 7,9 clearly expresses the intent of this whole section, as well as all of the Book of Isaiah, when it states that "unless your faith is firm, you shall not be firm." Faith in God is the root that will maintain us no matter what comes along. Yet even if we are overwhelmed by what comes along, God will continue to be with us (Immanuel), bringing new life, birth, and creation out of death, destruction, and pain. Although the material in these chapters comes from different times in Isaiah's ministry, it has been carefully arranged to stress the themes of reliance on God and God's fidelity to the promises made to the people.

Oracles Against the Nations

Chapters 13–23 make up a collection of oracles against the nations. The prophet uses these to show that God will not allow Israel to be unjust indefinitely. Just because the Israelites have an established relationship with God does not mean that they can do whatever they want. God will draw the line at some point, and Isaiah's message is exactly that: You can't go on being unjust and expect to get away with it.

Usually, God's plan for punishment of the people was understood by the prophets to be the key reason that other nations were successful in defeating Israel. God uses other nations to accomplish his purifying purposes upon the community of Israel. However, God does not allow the other nations to overstep their bounds either. God makes sure that other nations merely accomplish the purifying punishment desired, and no more. The key to these oracles in Isaiah is that the final editors have inserted another revolutionary concept, that of universal salvation. They saw God's saving hand operative even in these foreign nations. Like Israel, they will not be completely destroyed. Rather, there is hope that they too, after experiencing their own purification through suffering, will ultimately place their reliance on God, and God alone. They too, like Israel, will be saved. (See the essay on God and universal salvation).

The Apocalypse of Isaiah

Chapters 24–27 are referred to as the "Apocalypse of Isaiah." *Apocalypse,* a style of writing, is a term meaning to reveal or to draw aside the veil of the mysteries of life, and discern God's plan at work in and through the events of the day, especially those experiences that are the most puzzling or opaque to such insights, like pain and suffering. Often such writings were intended primarily to offer encouragement and support to those suffering and oppressed. Highly symbolic language was used to reveal how God would ultimately accomplish the plan of salvation, especially how salvation would be brought out of the pain, suffering, and evil in the midst of the community.

These chapters of Isaiah provide a future vision, a peek into the end times, when all the ruin, destruction, and suffering will be put into perspective, and new life will come out of it. Those who have remained faithful, those who have continually trusted in the Lord, will be fully rewarded and recompensed with new life, and the defeat of death (25,7f,19). Full intimacy with God, explored here in the image of an eternal divine banquet on God's holy mountain (25,6ff.), will be reestablished.

The defeat of death and the universal salvation of all nations are two of the most revolutionary concepts found in the Book of Isaiah, if not in the entire Old Testament. Up to this time, future survival was seen exclusively in terms of the memory of an individual living on in the family, in the children, and in the survival of the nation of Israel.

ESSAY

God and Universal Salvation

The Book of Isaiah proposes a theological perspective concerning God's relationship to other nations that is truly radical and was probably very shocking to the people of that time. The book states that God is a God of all nations, and that just as God has dealt with Israel, so God deals with all the other nations. God has chosen other nations to enter into relationship with, as well as to work out their salvation. While Israel has a special place in God's heart, this does not mean that God rejects or shuns the other nations. God blesses those nations just as God has blessed Israel (Is 19,16–25).

The vision that Isaiah presents is one in which all nations will come together to worship the Lord on God's holy mountain. Along with this vision comes the radical proposal that God's house is a house of prayer for all peoples (Is 56,7), and not just for Israel. As a matter of fact, the Book of Isaiah looks forward to the day when people from other nations will serve the Lord and be ministers in God's house, the Temple (Is 56,1–8).

These are radical insights and theological perspectives that should cause us to evaluate our own present-day understanding of who God is, and how God operates with regard to other nations, other beliefs, and other religions. Is God the God of all peoples and all creation? Do we really believe this? If so, what are the implications of this belief, when we speak of the religious beliefs, practices, and traditions of other nations, and other religions that differ from Christianity? Does God speak to those people the way we believe God has spoken to us Christians in the person of Christ? No one faith expression captures completely the reality of God. No one faith experience has all the answers to life's questions. We should be open to other faith expressions, searching for ways that all could benefit from the insights and emphases that others have explored and developed.

This is exactly the challenge that Vatican II presented to us. It emphasized the fact that God's Spirit blows where it wills. This should force us to be attuned to the signs of our time and age, so as to be able to discern how the Spirit is speaking to us today. Isaiah's vision of all nations worshiping the Lord on God's holy mountain is a vision and an ideal that still challenges us today. How open are we to the challenge? Or are we scandalized and shocked by this challenge just as the people of Isaiah's time probably were? God is the God of all nations and all peoples. How catholic, meaning universal, are we in our vision of God and God's relationship to all peoples and all religions?

Later Addition to First Isaiah

Chapters 28–33 and 34–35 are later additions made by a second editor or group who were inspired by the words and tradition of Isaiah of Jerusalem. It is important to remember that inspiration applies to the entire process that resulted in the biblical text, not just to one author but also to those who collected and edited the material, as well as those who reflected upon and reshaped the original words or message of Isaiah. In other words, the final book that we know as Isaiah is the result of a whole tradition, begun by Isaiah and ending when the final editing touches were placed on the entire book. Chapters 28–33 and 34–35, though they are the work of a different group of editors, are consistent with the previous 27 chapters.

They stress once again the need to put away all injustice and to trust in God. Since the people will refuse to listen, God will punish the people, yet this punishment will lead to a greater experience of the need to place faith and trust completely in God. The vision of 35,5–6 focuses on the lame, deaf, and blind placing their trust in God, and establishing their home in the new Jerusalem that God has prepared for those who have placed their complete trust and faith in the Lord. After the pain and anguish caused by the purifying punishment, God will gather all the scattered and bring them back home to a new Jerusalem which will be faithful to the loving relationship God has initiated.

Historical Appendix to First Isaiah

Chapters 36–39 are a historical appendix provided by the editors and based primarily on 2 Kings 18,13 – 20,19, giving a quick summary of the historical events surrounding the oracles of First Isaiah of Jerusalem. This quick summary is intended to provide a link back to the message of Isaiah and the actual historical events surrounding Hezekiah and Sennacharib (see page RG 231). Also, this summary provides a link forward to the Babylonian attack and the destruction of Jerusalem, as well as the exile of the people to Babylonia. The time that has elapsed between Chapter 39 and Chapter 40 is approximately 150 years. Second Isaiah, Chapters 40–55, picks up the themes of First Isaiah, especially God's plan for universal salvation, and expands them significantly.

SECOND ISAIAH

Second Isaiah speaks to a community that has indeed experienced the terrifying, purifying punishment of God, and still continues to do so. The Babylonians have defeated Assyria, and in 583 B.C. they captured and destroyed Jerusalem and exiled all its people. Second Isaiah speaks in the very midst of this exile, observing how it is about to end, with Cyrus, king of the Persians, referred to as God's anointed, coming to defeat the Babylonians and setting God's people free. The tone of Second Isaiah is one of comfort, hope, restoration, and of God's loving arms reaching out to comfort and console the people.

Overture to Second Isaiah's Symphony

Like an overture to a good piece of music, Chapter 40 summarizes, in beautiful poetry, all the key themes of Chapters 40–55. At the time when Israel is most discouraged and ready to despair, Isaiah speaks God's word of comfort and love to the people. The setting for Second Isaiah's message is the entire world, for God's saving action on behalf of the people will be so evident that all will see and experience God's saving plan, love, and power. Greed, corruption, and reliance on false gods are again condemned, making their elimination the key condition upon which God's loving, saving activity will become realized.

The Suffering Servant

Chapters 41–48 take up several themes which are beautifully and poetically developed by Second Isaiah. The "servant" theme is one that has great meaning, both in its application to Israel as the suffering servant of God, and to Jesus, the ultimate model of the suffering servant of God. There are at least four servant passages in all of Second Isaiah: 42,1–4; 49,1–7; 50,4–11; 52,13–53,12.

Another rich theme that Second Isaiah explores concerns the comparison that is made between God's saving action on behalf of the people now in Babylonia, and God's foundational saving action on behalf of the people in their Exodus from Egypt. Second Isaiah exhorts the people to be faithful to God, for God is about to unleash a new salvation experience for the people, just like the one their ancestors experienced in the desert. Second Isaiah uses the image of God as the master engineer who will design and build a superhighway right through the desert so that Israel will be able to take a direct route back to its home. What God did for the people in the beginning of their relationship he will do again, to show his great love and fidelity toward the people. Second Isaiah emphasizes the fact that God is still faithful now, as God was in the infancy stages of Israel's growth. God continues to work in their midst those great and mighty deeds that were worked in the midst of their ancestors. Faith and reliance on God are the only key requirements for God's mighty deeds to take place.

Salvation Involves Suffering

Chapters 49–55 have a less exalted, less hopeful tone, with more of a tragic sense of what is needed to bring about God's plan. One aspect of this deeper view is the prophet's identification of himself as the suffering servant. Another is in the recognition of the importance of suffering.

Salvation will come about, but often through the mediation of one who suffers with and for the people, as an ultimate example and model of what suffering is all about. It is in this context that these passages about the suffering servant were not only identified with Second Isaiah and with the whole people of God, but also most especially with Jesus, as the ultimate model of what it means to live a fully human existence, with all its limitations. In Chapters 49–55 the hopeful message of joy and comfort is still there, but it is deepened through the realization that the very messenger of the good news must endure pain and suffering for the good news to take root in the minds and hearts of the community.

THIRD ISAIAH

Isaiah of the Return

With these ideas in mind, we now move to Third Isaiah, whose melancholy tone is much more pronounced than that in Second Isaiah. Third Isaiah presumes a time when the people have returned from exile and have rebuilt the Temple. From a variety of sources, the date can be set any time after 515 B.C. The people are home, changed and purified by their experience of suffering, yet authentic worship and a concern for justice are not central to the lives of the restored people of God.

The author of Third Isaiah, whether one person or a community of persons, experiences this lack in the community and is moved to use the vision of the Isaiah tradition to address the current situation. The author reinterprets the message of Isaiah of Jerusalem and Isaiah of the Exile to address the needs of the community of that time, resulting in the Isaiah of the Return.

Chapters 56–59 pick up themes of the previous chapters, especially themes of salvation in and through suffering. Suffering has the potential of making the worshiping community more sensitive to the needs of others who suffer in their midst, especially the foreigner, the outcast, and the marginalized. These people are welcomed into the house of God—a radical proposal—because of the key insight developed in 56,7 that the house of God is a house of prayer for all peoples. Yet worship can also result in self-righteousness and complacency. We have done our part in worship, God. When are you going to do yours?

Ritual and Life Are Related

Third Isaiah challenges this complacency by connecting worship with actions that flow from worship. If worship does not lead to a greater concern for those who are in need, if it does not lead to justice for the oppressed and outcasts, then worship is indeed meaningless. Chapter 57,1–2 continues a theme central to the whole of Isaiah (see Chapters 24–27, especially 25,7f,19), that of death not overcoming the just ones, but rather a belief in the continuation of life after death, especially for the just, for those who have tried to rely on God, and who are concerned for the poor, the needy, and the alienated.

Suffering as Purifying Fire

Chapters 60–62 form the heart of Third Isaiah's message. By using a variety of images reminiscent of Second Isaiah, Third Isaiah speaks of the salvation that has come upon the community once the purifying punishment has ended. Because of the fidelity of the community to God during this time of testing and trial, God will more than reward the people. Not only will God restore the people to their former glory, but God will make them a light to all nations. All the nations will see what God has done for the people, and they will stream toward Israel, and bask in the light and warmth of the people in intimate relationship with their God.

Third Isaiah emphasizes that the clear sign of this salvation will be that of the Jubilee experience. The Jubilee (every 50 years) celebration, like the sabbatical experience (every 7 years) was a time of celebration and joy that spilled out into every facet of the community's life. During this time, the community is to remind itself forcibly that everything belongs to God. Thus, the land is to lie fallow, and what grows on it belongs to all people. Debts are to be wiped out, offenses are to be forgiven, the needy are to be taken care of, and all are to be at peace. Salvation is to spill into every facet of life and make itself visible to all people and nations. Jesus himself understood his mission and ministry in terms of the insights communicated here by Third Isaiah, even quoting them, and applying them to his own vocation as God's salvation to the people.

Reliance on God Brings Eternal Rewards

Chapters 63–66 are parallel to the key themes in Chapters 56–59. Sorrow is expressed over the sins of the community and the need of the community to be punished because of its sinfulness and injustice. The punishment of the people by God for their injustice is seen as the only way that God could curb the excesses, greed, and selfishness of this sinful people. Yet, once the punishment is accomplished, God reaches out with double the effort to restore the people and make them even better and greater than before. A universality is evident in the salvation theme, where Jew and Gentile will live as one and worship God together. Those who refuse to rely on God will be severely punished, but those who trust in God will be abundantly rewarded.

CONCLUSION

Thus ends the Book of Isaiah, a book that spans about 200 years. Throughout that period of turmoil, tension, and suffering, Isaiah focuses on one key theme: reliance, trust, faith, and confidence in God. This trust in God will lead to the recognition that God and others are the center of the universe, and not you. Faith in God enables us to risk reaching out to others in their need and pain, even when this might lead to conflict, frustration, and rejection by others. The book can probably be summed up by a phrase Paul uses in his letter to the Romans: "All things work unto God for those who love the Lord," and another Pauline text which states that "eye has not seen, ear has not heard, what God has ready for those who love him."

Questions for Discussion or Reflection

1. First Isaiah's message is very hard on people's ears. They don't like the sound of it. How receptive are you to words that challenge your established notions about your life, community, society, or culture? How would you respond to the bearer of that message? What would you do with the content of the message?
2. Fidelity and trust amid trial and tribulation will result in eternal reward and loving intimacy with God at the divine banquet on God's holy mountain. What impact do you think such a message has on those who are undergoing trials and suffering? How much of this do you really believe? How does it affect the way you live your life, especially as you experience suffering and pain?
3. Recall an experience in which someone offered hope, comfort, and consolation to you while you were very much taken up with your pain and suffering. How did this make you feel? How did you respond to the person? What words or gestures did you use to show your feelings?
4. How do you understand the role of the suffering servant as portrayed by Second Isaiah? How was this image applied to Jesus? What role does it play in the life of a Christian? In your life?
5. Third Isaiah emphasizes the fact that suffering has the potential of making individuals or communities sensitive to the needs and suffering of others. Why is this so? Recall an experience in which you came to such a realization. What insights would you want to share from your experience concerning the redemptive qualities of suffering?
6. In the Book of Isaiah, God's constant and tender love reaches out continually toward those who suffer. How true is this to your experience of life? What message would you wish to convey to those who are suffering? What role would God play in your message?

JEREMIAH READING GUIDE

JEREMIAH: THE PERSON, THE MESSAGE

In Jeremiah's case, the prophet's life speaks as loudly as the message. Both need to be examined if the book is to have its full impact.

Jeremiah's name, in Hebrew, means "The Lord raises up." In the very life and words of Jeremiah, it is the Lord who rises up to meet Jeremiah. In Jeremiah's struggle to determine what God wanted and how God wanted it, we also see our own struggle in trying to live in a loving, faithful relationship to God. With Jeremiah, we realize that this is not easy. God's word comes to us not in clearly defined terms and directions, but rather in the messiness of life, with all its ambiguities and fuzziness.

Like Jeremiah, our struggle in relating to God is to be on the journey of life, continually asking where God is in all of this. Where is God in the good times? Where is God in the bad times? Where is God at those times when I am in need? Why doesn't God leave me alone? It's not that Jeremiah wants to live without God. Jeremiah can't live without God. Jeremiah can't ignore God, either in his life or in the life of the community.

Jeremiah's life and message is continually intermixed with all these questions and concerns. While desiring to be faithful and obedient to God's message at work in his life, Jeremiah is continually overwhelmed by it. This feeling causes him to question God, to get angry at God, to entertain doubt, to feel abandoned by God. However, Jeremiah doesn't allow himself the luxury of getting stuck in this mode of living. His love of God is like "a fire burning in my heart, imprisoned in my bones" (Jer 20,9).

All these aspects of Jeremiah's reactions to God are most clearly expressed in passages scattered throughout his book, known as the Confessions of Jeremiah (12,1–5; 15,10–21; 17,12–18; 18,18–23; 20,7–18). In these passages Jeremiah vents his anger and frustration, yet he continually works through the anger by placing his reliance on God, who, no matter what the situation, is always faithful. Through the venting, Jeremiah arrives at a sense of peace and renewed commitment to that loving relationship with God, along with all that the relationship demands.

If Jeremiah the person is the message as much as his words are, then we need to look at the very human gyrations that Jeremiah endures in order to work out God's purpose in his life and in the life of the community. This is as much our own journey with God as it is Jeremiah's. This is one of the reasons that Jeremiah's journey with God has often been compared with Jesus' journey with God. Jesus, like Jeremiah, had to struggle with faith, doubt, and feelings of abandonment to determine what the will of God was for him, as he worked out that relationship with God in his own life and community. This is the struggle of every person who tries to live in relationship with God and attempts to be continually faithful to God, no matter what the results.

JEREMIAH, THE BOOK

Jeremiah lived during very disturbing and unsettled times in the history of God's people. The full range of these changes was reflected in the gamut of emotional and spiritual reactions which they elicited from the person of Jeremiah. The table below gives the historical background to Jeremiah. However, the development of the book as a story, and as a collection of the words and actions of Jeremiah, follows a different format. This can be sketched out in the table of literary background shown on the next page.

The Book of Jeremiah is clearly a tradition, begun by the prophet and continued by disciples who composed a major part of what is entitled in 1,1 "the words of Jeremiah." "Words" mean actions as well as statements, disciples' response as well as the master's leadership.

Historical Background

Chapters 1–6	Reign of King Josiah (640–609 B.C. Collapse of the Assyrian Empire Independence of many vassal states like Babylonia and Judah Deuteronomic reform at Jerusalem (2 Chr 34f) Reunification of all Israel (2 Kgs 23) Violent death of Josiah while attempting to block the Egyptian army at the pass of Megiddo (2 Chr 35,20–25) Josiah's son, Jehoahaz, taken captive to Egypt; another son, Jehoiakim, installed as king (2 Chr 36,1–8)
Chapters 7–20	Reign of Jehoiakim (609–597 B.C.), a ruthless tyrant despised by Jeremiah Nebuchadnezzar defeats Egypt at Carchemesh in Syria (605 B.C.), takes Jerusalem in 603 B.C. for the Babylonians and confirms Jehoiakim in office 601 B.C. Jehoiakim revolts. Babylonians return to Jerusalem in 597 B.C. Jehoiakim is dead; his son Jehoiachin is taken captive to Babylon and Zedekiah is installed as king (2 Chr 36, 9f)
Chapters 21–33	Reign of Zedekiah (597–587 B.C.) Chapters 30–33 come from an earlier period.
Chapters 34–45	Fall and last days of Jerusalem (587–583 B.C.) City and temple destroyed, August, 587 B.C. Most of the people deported Gedaliah governor; Jeremiah remains at Jerusalem Gedaliah assassinated; people flee to Egypt, dragging Jeremiah with them, 583 B.C. Third Babylonian deportation, 582 B.C. Jeremiah dies in Egypt
Chapters 46–51	Oracles against the Nations
Chapter 52	Historical appendix

Literary Background

Chapter 1	The prologue, or Jeremiah's prophetic call from God.
Chapters 2–25	The preaching of the prophet. The ordering of the material in this section remains close to the chronology of Jeremiah's life.
Chapters 26–45	A disciple's justification of the prophet, with a message of hope from Jeremiah in Chapters 30–33. Chapters 30–33 probably represent Jeremiah's earliest preaching. By placing it in the middle of the book, Jeremiah's followers showed that they never gave up on the hopeful message of the prophet, despite the tragic events of Chapters 2–29.
Chapters 46–51	The Oracles against the Nations. These balance well with Jeremiah's call to be "a prophet to the nations" at the beginning (1,4f).
Chapter 52	A fulfillment of Jeremiah's threats, concluding hopefully with the release from prison of King Jehoiachin.

Sources of the Book of Jeremiah

The organization of the book indicates a long, complex development. The sources of this development are the sermons of the prophet himself, usually in poetry. Jeremiah is usually associated with traditions that developed in the northern kingdom, especially the focus on the Exodus and the covenant. While working out of these traditions, Jeremiah is not a slave to them, but rather stamps his words with his own uniqueness and individuality. Chapters 2–25 and 30–33 are uniquely Jeremiah: very personal, agonizing, continually interacting with the community and God.

The ultimate example of Jeremiah's struggle with his vocation and mission from God is located in sections of the book called the "Confessions" of Jeremiah. In these Confessions Jeremiah argues with God and anguishes over his vocation and the message God has given him to proclaim to the community: 12,1–5; 15,10–21; 17,12–18; 18,18–23; 20,7–18. These Confessions might have originally been a diary of Jeremiah which was possibly split up and inserted into the text by an editor. The insertion of these Confessions at particular places in the text is confirmed by the fact that wherever they appear, the sequence of the verses is disturbed.

There are two long prose sections about Jeremiah (Chapters 26–29; 34–45) which are generally considered to have been collected and edited by Jeremiah's secretary, Baruch. Even though they tell of Jeremiah, the key purpose of these sections is theological and not necessarily biographical.

The Book of Jeremiah also contains sermons based on phrases from a number of discourses from the Book of Deuteronomy. These sermons are evident in 7,1 – 8,3; 11,1–17; 16,1–13; 21,1–10. It is possible that these sermons were originally discourses preached by disciples of Jeremiah, reflecting upon the prophet's words or actions.

The Editing of Jeremiah's Preaching

The development of the text of the Book of Jeremiah has an extensive and complex history. Scholars have arrived at several conclusions regarding this complex history of the text:

1. The prophet's words were originally preserved in separate booklets.
2. Several editions of the book were made during the prophet's lifetime; several more editions were made after his death.
3. The book contains not only the words of Jeremiah based on the preaching of the prophet, but also extended accounts about him, as well as sermons based on his words.
4. Jeremiah might not have intended all of his words, most especially his confessions, to become public property.

We should not focus simply on Jeremiah as being inspired by God. Rather, we need to focus on an inspired Jeremiah tradition, in which inspiration was shared among prophet, disciples, editors, and community.

Introduction and Call to Prophecy (Chapter 1)

This chapter represents more than God's call to the prophet. Either Jeremiah or one of his disciples fashioned the call into the accepted form of describing a prophetic vocation. (See other examples of this form in Ex 3; Is 6 and 40; Lk 1,5–38.) In doing this, the editors affirmed in the very beginning of the book what God wanted for the prophet and for the community. Two separate visions (verses 11–16) anticipate the fulfillment of Jeremiah's prophecy about the destruction of Jerusalem. The final words of encouragement (verses 17–19) are present in other places throughout the book, especially in the Confessions.

Oracles from the Reign of Josiah (Chapters 2–6)

Jeremiah's basic attitude centered on the tender love of God as manifested in the covenant during the days of Moses (2,2f). Sin brings its own punishment, but this punishment can be purifying and transforming (2,19.30; 4,14). Chapter 3,12 into Chapter 4 repeats one of Jeremiah's key themes: Return to the Lord. In these chapters Jeremiah makes several very radical observations. In 3,14–18 a whole new series of religious and civic leaders is called for, along with the removal of the necessity of the Ark of the Covenant, and the call to welcome foreigners to the new Temple.

Oracles from the Reign of Jehoiakim (Chapters 7–20)

In this section we meet the first of the famous sermons in the style and theological content of the Book of Deuteronomy. These sermons were probably composed by disciples of Jeremiah reflecting on earlier texts of Jeremiah. Chapter 7 is the most important of these sermons. When Jeremiah threatened the destruction of the Temple, the people shouted, "Blasphemy." Yet Jeremiah reminded them of such an occurrence at an earlier time, at Shiloh, done by an act of God. The preservation of the Temple did not depend blindly upon divine promises, nor upon more and better ceremonies. Rather, it depended on the following: "If you thoroughly reform your ways . . . if each of you deals justly with his neighbor; if you no longer oppress the resident alien, the orphan, and the widow, . . . will I remain with you" (7,5–7).

The first of Jeremiah's Confessions occurs at 12,1–5. Jeremiah's complaint against God is courageous, tender, impatient, and obedient. God never answers Jeremiah's initial question but addresses his faith, basically encouraging him to continue his task even though things are going to get worse.

Many symbols and parables are used to communicate the message: Jeremiah's celibacy (Chapter 17), the potter (Chapters 18–20), and the purchase of a field (Chapter 32). Visions and symbolic actions were key vehicles used by prophets to get people's attention and to communicate their message in a way that would make an impression and be remembered by the community.

Oracles from the Last Years of Jerusalem (Chapters 21–25)

Most of Chapter 21, like Chapter 7, is a sermon along the lines of the Book of Deuteronomy, developed by Jeremiah's disciples as they reflected on his words to the community. In Chapter 22, Jeremiah explodes in anger against the greedy, cruel, and devious King Jehoiakim, wishing for him "the burial of an ass" (verses 13–19). Along with this outburst, there is an elegy to Jehoiakim's successor, King Jehoiachin, a young man lost to the Babylonian exile.

In Chapter 23 Jeremiah reaffirms his loyalty to the Davidic dynasty, but only on the condition that the entire family tree be cut to the roots. From these roots, God will raise a new shoot to shepherd the people rightly. This chapter also severely denounces false prophets, individuals who claim insights into God's ways but only end up fostering their own greed and immorality. They condone sin in others to excuse their own sin.

Chapter 25 announces the "70 years" of exile (verse 11). "Seventy years" is used several times in Jeremiah and in other parts of the Old Testament. This number, like seven, should be taken as a symbolic number indicating completion and fulfillment. In other words, it announces that the exile will run its full course, but it will also be completed and come to an end.

Biographical Accounts about Jeremiah (Chapters 26–29 and 34–45)

Baruch, Jeremiah's secretary, shows how true the prophecies of Jeremiah were, especially about the destruction of Jerusalem and its Temple. By showing us the eventual reality of the exile and its destruction, Baruch contrasts the truth of Jeremiah's message from God with the falsity of those prophets who chose to believe themselves and not God. In this fashion, Jeremiah is shown to be the prophet faithful to God, involved in the agony of the community, and yet already preparing for the restoration of the people, the land, and the coming of the messianic age.

The Book of Consolation (Chapters 30–33)

The editor gathered this material from various moments in the life of Jeremiah, most especially from his earliest preaching. That editor placed it here between Chapter 29, a letter of encouragement to those in exile since 597 B.C., and Chapters 34–45, detailing in a gruesome fashion the end of Jerusalem and the second deportation to Babylonia in 587 B.C. As a result of this editing, words intended for a different context were reinterpreted to apply to this particular context. This process occurs often in Scripture, especially when a new context shows a new way of looking at the text and of applying that text to this new situation.

Oracles against the Nations (Chapters 46–51; Appendix, Chapter 52)

These oracles are intended to show that God is in control and that God will overcome all hostile powers. By doing this, God will insure that the covenant and the divine plans will be fulfilled. Israel's exile into foreign lands does not mean the end of Israel. The appendix, Chapter 52, ends with a ray of hope for all exiles: King Jehoiachin is released from prison. It is significant that a prophet of doom like Jeremiah ends on a hopeful note.

JEREMIAH, THE PROPHET

Jeremiah hails from the town of Anathoth, 3.6 miles northeast of Jerusalem. His father, Hilkiah, may have been the one by that name who found the book of the Law of Moses (the Book of Deuteronomy) during the repair of the Temple by King Josiah in 622 B.C. (2 Kgs 22,8). This fact partially explains the influence of Deuteronomy on Jeremiah.

Politics helped to form the message of Jeremiah. The words and actions of Jeremiah were intimately caught up with the political happenings of the day, particularly the demise of the Assyrian Empire and the rise of Babylonia as the world power. This was the context in which Jeremiah spoke God's word to the people of Israel.

Jeremiah's ministry began in 627 B.C. With the collapse of the Assyrian Empire, he joyfully announced the return of the northern tribes. This is the context for Chapters 30–31 of Jeremiah. Jeremiah also condemned idolatry at Jerusalem but was strangely silent during the deuteronomic reform under King Josiah. In 609 B.C. Josiah was killed in battle against the Egyptians. His son Jehoiakim succeeded him and revolted against the new world power, the Babylonians. They responded by capturing Jerusalem in 597 B.C., sacking the city and deporting many of its leading citizens.

King Zedekiah was warned by Jeremiah not to join with the Egyptians in another rebellion against the Babylonians. Zedekiah gave in to the rebellion temptation and the Babylonians once again stormed the city in July, 587 B.C. They burned Jerusalem and the Temple to the ground. The king and the people were all deported to Babylonia. Jeremiah was left behind, choosing to remain in the land as a sign of hope for the future (Jer 40,1–6). When the remaining few in Jerusalem rejected his advice to stay on the land and fled to Egypt, they dragged Jeremiah with them (Jer 42,1—43,7). There Jeremiah died, leaving behind a tradition and a book.

The character of Jeremiah shines brightly from any page of the book. Jeremiah manifests

- Joyful optimism (Chapter 31)
- Honest, painful struggling with God (12,1–5; 15,10–21; 20,7–18)
- Courage in confronting kings (Chapter 37)
- Agony over the tragic fate of Jerusalem (8,18—9,10)
- Perseverance amid continuous rejection (20,9)
- Irritability and, at times, a desire for revenge, showing itself especially in his Confessions, prayer diary jottings never intended for the public eye (12,1–5; 15,10–21; 17,12–18; 18,18–23; 20,7–18)
- Sensitivity to the beauties and wonder of nature (1,11; 2,13; 4,25)
- Celibacy, by choice, a hard choice from which he suffered much (16,1–4); yet at the same time it kept him in tune with the suffering of the people and their need to trust and have faith in God, leading to peace.

Jeremiah gave a solid focus to the piety of Israel. This focus centered on the laments against pain and evil, as well as the bold questioning of God and God's motives. Examples of laments and questioning existed before Jeremiah, but not to the extent or degree exemplified by him. Jeremiah's Confessions were such deep questionings of God that they became seared in the community's consciousness, never to be forgotten. They have the same effect on modern readers.

The Message of Jeremiah

Central to Jeremiah's message is the attitude of compassion and prayer. This is intimately linked to fidelity to a covenant inscribed upon the heart. Four crucial themes central to Jeremiah are the new covenant, sin and atonement, faith and prayer, and true and false prophecy. Each will be briefly addressed.

The New Covenant

The key passage for this theme of the new covenant is Jeremiah 30–33, the Book of Consolation. These passages of hope were reinterpreted to apply to the context of restoration after exile. There are frequent references to "the days are coming" or "the coming days." Before Jeremiah, the Israelites thought mostly in terms of a future fulfillment of God's promises in a single great day of the Lord. Under Jeremiah's influence this future "day" began to appear in stages: first suffering; then "the coming days" or the in-between period; and finally, the definite completion of all the hopes and promises.

Jeremiah's "new" covenant written on the heart is closely tied with the Mosaic covenant of Mount Sinai. This covenant of Exodus 34,6f had already bonded Israel with a compassionate, forgiving God. Jeremiah's covenant was "new" in that it reminded people of the covenant terms they had forgotten or neglected. This idea of the new covenant, one which was taken into the personality or character of each person, greatly influenced Jesus and the early church, and continues to influence our current understanding of what it means to be a member of the people of God.

Sin and Atonement

Jeremiah realistically declares that sin brings its own sorrow. People are transformed, for good or bad, into those very things that they seek or desire. Yet the punishment resulting from sin can be a source of purification of our desires, and a strengthening of our resolve to change our lives. All this is linked to God's compassion, leading us to hope in being forgiven and restored. This sequence of sin—suffering—repentance—forgiveness—new life undergirds the theology of the deuteronomic books of Joshua, Judges, 1 and 2 Samuel, and 1 and 2 Kings. By recovering this existing tradition and applying it to the present reality of the community, Jeremiah makes this tradition new again, bringing it to life with new meaning and vigor.

Faith and Prayer

Jeremiah continually bares his heart and soul as he struggles in his relationship to God and to the community. This wrestling with God is most evident in his Confessions (12,1–5; 15,10–21; 17,12–18; 18,18–23; 20,7–18). In these prayer experiences, Jeremiah confronts God with defiant and bold questions. Yet, throughout the questioning and the doubts, Jeremiah never wavers from his reliance on God's fidelity and concern for him and for the community. God never resolves Jeremiah's questions or concerns, yet this venting out to God seems to help Jeremiah in coming to grips with his own pain, anguish, and struggle.

Jeremiah arrives at the conviction that his relationship with God is the only one he can depend upon, and once again he finds peace and reassurance in that reality. The recounting of this human experience of Jeremiah proved to be very powerful and very attractive to the community, for it modeled for them a realistic relationship to God and to one another.

True and False Prophecy

Throughout his ministry Jeremiah had to struggle with the charge of being a false prophet because the message that he proclaimed was neither acceptable nor popular. The criteria for determining a true prophet just did not fit the personality, mission, prayer life, or credentials that Jeremiah exhibited. Jeremiah is the classic example of the rejected prophet. Despite continuous rejection and persecution, Jeremiah eventually became one of the most popular and accepted prophets. His genuine expressions of piety made an impact on the community for generations to come. His spontaneous and continuous interaction with God, openly and honestly, authenticated the genuineness of his mission and message.

True prophecy is usually judged by the lasting impact that the prophet and the message have on the community. This long-term community acceptance of the prophet also determined which prophet's words and works were to be preserved in the collection of books that came to be known as the Bible. Jeremiah has proven to be a true prophet indeed.

Questions for Discussion or Reflection

1. The Confessions of Jeremiah reveal him as a person of deep prayer and spirituality, especially in times of great doubt, uncertainty, and questioning. How do you respond to God when confronted with similar situations in life? Where is God for you at these times? How do anger, frustration, anxiety, doubts, and questions enhance your relationship to God? What do faith, fidelity, hope, and trust mean at such times in life?

2. Fidelity to God and God's message brought rejection, unpopularity, and persecution to the life of Jeremiah. Have there been times when you have been rejected because of your fidelity to God? How did you feel about this? What role did your friends play at this time of rejection by others? How did you maintain your integrity and your fidelity to God?

3. For Jeremiah, the message and vision of God as lived out in his life influenced the political and social realities of his day. What role does your relationship to God play as you interact with others at home, at work, and in the political arena? How does your relationship to God influence the political and social realities of your community? How do you respond to those who decry the mixing of religion and politics? What are the dangers when religion and politics become too friendly? What kind of distance should be maintained between religion and politics?

4. Despite many setbacks and disappointments, Jeremiah maintained a hopeful stance in life. What are the things in life that give you hope? How do they do this? What role does your relationship to God play in the things that give you hope in life?

LAMENTATIONS READING GUIDE

THE HUMAN REALITY

Imagine what feelings would surface if you experienced the loss of someone who had been of great significance in your life. It could be the death of a loved one, of a mentor or guide, of a person who was instrumental in being supportive and kind when you needed it the most. Now imagine that, at the same time that this special loss occurs, your home, your means of income, all your personal possessions, as well as all that was of material value to you, were also gone or destroyed. Add to this the fact that your former supports, your church, your priests, your community, were no longer there to lend a helping hand in this time of sorrow.

Imagine the feelings that would stir in you. Imagine the anger, frustration, despair, and hopelessness that would overwhelm you. Imagine the questions that you would be hurling at God. Imagine also the feelings of guilt you would experience. Was there something that you should have done, that you could have done to prevent or minimize any or all of this pain, suffering, or destruction? If you can relate to this overwhelming human experience of pain, suffering, and privation, then you can begin to understand the human context out of which the Book of Lamentations was written.

THE STRUCTURE OF LAMENTATIONS

The Book of Lamentations, traditionally associated with Jeremiah the prophet, is a series of five poems written in the traditional stock language of lament. The poems are used as a means to vent grief and anguish over the great pain, suffering, and calamity that the community has experienced.

What is the calamity? The Babylonian exile of 587 B.C. In that year Babylonia, the dominant power of the Middle East, arrived in Israel to prevent an insurrection by Judah. In the process, the army destroyed Jerusalem and its Temple and exiled to Babylonia all the leaders of Judah, as well as the wealthy and the powerful. Only the poor, the uneducated, the farmers and sheep herders were left in the land. It is believed that these people gathered periodically at the remains of the Jerusalem Temple to pray and to ritualize their pain of loss and destruction. It is from the prayer experiences at these ritualizing events and times that these laments have their possible origin.

The Book of Lamentations consists of five chapters or poems which, with the exception of the last chapter or poem, are structured in an acrostic or alphabetical arrangement. The acrostic style, a common poetic device, structured poems by making the first letter of each stanza begin with each successive letter of the Hebrew alphabet. Since there are twenty-two letters in the Hebrew alphabet, there are twenty-two stanzas in each poem. Chapter (or poem) 3 has twenty-two stanzas, but the three lines of each stanza all begin with the same letter of the alphabet. Thus Chapter 3 contains sixty-six verses because each letter of the alphabet is repeated three times in a particular stanza before moving on to the next stanza. The final poem, Chapter 5, even though it contains twenty-two verses, does not follow this traditional acrostic format.

The Five Lamentations

The five chapters are not intended to solve the problem of suffering. Rather, they let us remain sorrowing in God's presence.

Praying with the Book

Lamentation	Structure
First	Begins with the sorrow of the author at the sight of the ruined city (verses 1–11) Jerusalem herself comes alive and confesses her sins, her hopes, and her anger against the enemy (verses 12–22)
Second	This lament lays the devastated city before God, in all its pain and horror (verses 1–10) Verses 11–12 find the poet revealing the sorrow present in his own heart Verses 13–22 are the poet's address, from the very depths of his compassion, to the city of Jerusalem
Third	An individual cry of sorrow during which the poet speaks in his own name Verses 25–47 are the voices of others who are also greatly baffled by the tragedy The most complex of all the laments
Fourth	Similar in tone to the first two laments Verses 1–10 relate the end of the nobles and the children, followed in verses 11–12 by a meditation on Jerusalem Verses 13–20 place the main responsibility for the horror on the religious leaders The poem ends with a curse on the enemy (verses 21–22)
Fifth	Traditionally entitled the "Prayer of Jeremiah," this lament deals entirely with the topic of rejection and tragedy In its beauty and serenity, it asks very little of God, only that the Lord remember

Authorship and Place in the Bible

While there are quite a few signs pointing to someone other than Jeremiah, tradition, nevertheless, has designated Jeremiah the prophet as the author of Lamentations. 2 Chr 35,25 attests to this tradition very clearly. Christian tradition points to a hillside cave north of the walled city of Jerusalem as the place where Jeremiah wept over the city and composed these laments. Lamentations is placed after the Book of Jeremiah as a direct result of this connection with Jeremiah. Lamentations thus becomes a part of the tradition of Jeremiah in reflecting upon suffering as a way of doing penance for sin.

The themes of Lamentations link with the second and third parts of Isaiah (Is 40–55 and 56–66). Each deals with the horrendous problem of the destruction of Jerusalem, the Babylonian exile, and the return to a miserable postexilic Jerusalem. Prayer bonded the disciples of Isaiah in exile with those of Jeremiah among the ruins of Jerusalem. Lamentations also links well with the traditions found in Deuteronomy and Hosea. These books, with their stress on sensitivity, compassion, and fidelity, enabled the authors of Lamentations to remain faithful to God when God seemed totally absent.

Even though the five poems of Lamentations have much in common, it is difficult to decide upon a single author. They are better explained by traditions of prayer amid Israelites struggling to survive in the rubble of Jerusalem.

Laments

The church used readings from the Book of Lamentations to lament the death of Jesus during its Holy Week services. During the special service known as "Tenebrae" or Darkness Service before daybreak, readings from the Book of Lamentations were sung, hauntingly set to the rhythms of Gregorian Chant. In the very midst of its anguish, the church community still placed its faith in God, sustained in its sorrow by prayer and lament. Jewish people also sang these laments on the ninth day of Ab (July–August), sorrowfully remembering the two destructions of Jerusalem, by the Babylonians in 587 B.C., and by the Romans in 70 A.D.

Orderly Disorder

Why was this particular format used in the composition of the poetry in the Book of Lamentations? Many reasons are given. Some scholars suggest that this technique was primarily a memory device. In other words, it would be easier to remember the next stanza of a poem if you knew what letter of the alphabet it began with. Others suggest that this technique was related to the belief that the letters of the alphabet, created by God to communicate with the people, held magical powers. When used artistically and completely, this alphabetical focus would reveal the mysteries of whatever topic one was exploring. Still others relate this technique primarily to the manner in which the scribes and rabbis taught their lessons. A creative and forceful suggestion is that this technique gives an individual or a community the feeling that they have covered the topic exhaustively, from A to Z.

This last suggestion seems very applicable in the context of laments, expressions surfacing from the venting of pain and grief. Venting pain and grief, if unchecked, can easily go overboard and get out of control. This acrostic form and structure enables one to cover the topic exhaustively, while at the same time knowing that there is a structural ending to the lament. Psychologically, it provides for the release and expression of grief and pain, within a prescribed structure and time, something beneficial to all parties concerned. The poetic structure implies that God is still in control; all is not lost. Good order must return and Israel's theology must absorb and teach the lessons of Jerusalem's destruction and exile. Lamentations, however, asks that this process not be hurried. Israel needs space for mourning, time for disorder.

Prayer Beyond Theology

This book is a triumph of faith over theology. When theology is inadequate to the task of making sense of the events the community has experienced and endured, then the only other response is blind faith sustained by prayer. At such times, prayer does what nothing else can do: It sustains us in God's presence with our agony and anger. Israelites prayed to God in the place that God had abandoned. They gathered in the Temple ruins, a dead place that paradoxically comes alive to speak to the community (Lam 1,12). Israel seemed to survive less by theological tradition, more as a community at prayer before a compassionate God.

Questions for Discussion or Reflection

1. Recall an experience of deep pain and sorrow. How did you respond to the experience? What supports were there to sustain you? What challenges did you need to address or confront?
2. How do you respond when your experience of life does not fit the explanations you have been given? When life becomes very confusing and overwhelming, where do you turn for help? Where is God for you in all this searching and wandering?
3. Recall a time when an artistic creation, such as music, poetry, art, nature, etc., helped you to arrive at some peace in the midst of chaos and confusion. How did this happen? Why did it bring you to some sense of peace and order?
4. What is the role of the community toward the individual who is undergoing pain and suffering? What if the whole community is suffering greatly? What are some appropriate ways for the community to respond to the crisis?

BARUCH READING GUIDE

A SPIRITUALITY FOR DISPLACED PEOPLE

With only a few exceptions, the entire Old Testament centers on God's action with the chosen people Israel in the Promised Land. Only a few books admit the possibility of an Israelite living permanently outside the Promised Land: Tobit, Baruch, Wisdom, and possibly Esther. The first three never became part of the Hebrew canon, the list of books considered inspired by God, and therefore part of the Bible. They are not part of either the Jewish or Protestant versions of the Bible. "Apocryphal" is the Protestant name for these books, a name derived from the Greek word meaning "hidden." Catholics refer to them as "Deuterocanonical", also from the Greek meaning "second canon." This word distinguishes these books, along with some other books, as separate from the first canon, the books universally accepted as inspired and part of the Bible. As part of the Apocrypha or Deuterocanonical books, Baruch manifests its homelessness or foreign existence. While the holy city, Jerusalem, remains the source of unity and tradition, Baruch declares that God is also found in foreign territory.

In our homelessness, Baruch seems to impart a sense of	
Prayer	No matter what the situation, we can always turn to God.
Biblical traditions	Reliance on the traditions articulated in the Scriptures, like Isaiah 40–66 and Job 28, will offer guidance when the way is lost or confused.
Hope	No matter what, the odds are in our favor, and we shall not be overwhelmed.
Strength	We must not give in to the pressure of a foreign culture, especially when it goes against our core beliefs and values.
Realism	We need to come to practical terms with life where we are.
Humility	By fasting and repentance, we admit mistakes made, and we remove guilt without blaming ourselves, others, or fate.

Baruch, like Tobit and Wisdom, is a guide for people who are separated or lost, physically or emotionally, from their normal environment. Baruch helps people, displaced physically or mentally, to get established and focused on the way of peace with God and neighbor. The book can be a guide for today's displaced people, even though the context and situation are obviously different. In the context of homelessness, Baruch seeks to impart a clear sense of direction or focus, as outlined in the table above.

READING THE BOOK OF BARUCH

Baruch is an honorary title, inspired by the person with this name who wrote down and preserved the preaching of Jeremiah (Jer 36,5–32). Early Christians considered this book a strong supporter of the Jeremiah tradition. Two other books, which were not included in the Bible, were also attributed to Jeremiah's secretary. It seems that this tradition was rather popular, or caught the imagination of the people who composed them.

Outline of the Book of Baruch

1,1–14	Introduction recalling the Feast of Tabernacles and the renewal of the covenant
1,15 – 3,8	Offers to God a humble confession of sin
3,9 – 4,4	A reflection in the style of wisdom literature, acting as a bridge to conversion and renewed loyalty to God's law
4,5 – 5,9	A response of consolation, forgiveness, and renewed hope to the humble confession of sin in 1,15 – 3,8
6,1–72	In a letter format, idolatry is ridiculed with irony and sarcasm. There is a question concerning this chapter: Was it part of the original editing of the book, or was it added later on by another editor?

Introduction (1,1–14)

The purpose of this section is not to provide details but to set a mood of exile and separation. Many details exist in this section, but they are out of place both in time and situation. The dating is imprecise, i.e., "the fifth year" of what? Outside of this passage nothing is known of the high priest Jehoiakim or of the return of the silver vessels to the Temple. The Babylonian emperor Nebuchadnezzar never had a son called Belshazzar, a difficulty also existing in Daniel 5,2. Despite these difficulties with the details, the entire setting of the introduction concerns itself with exile from home and family, along with all that exile entails. The exile provides a framework for those who are displaced or estranged, either physically or emotionally, to understand their situation. Displaced people need solidarity, religious assemblies, outreach in helping others, and a point of contact for unity. This section sets these needs in context and offers them as guides for dealing with homelessness.

A Penitential Prayer (1,15–3,8)

This is a style of prayer common in the Bible: Ezra 9,6–15; Nehemiah 1,5–11; 9,5–37; Daniel 9,4–19. These prayers were probably derived from a common collection of prayers for exiles. The prayer does not encourage violence to regain freedom but rather counsels acceptance of the government in control. Yet moral ideals and practices are not to be abandoned, even in such conditions. The prayer recalls God's fidelity to the people during their miseries in Egypt, and how God was compassionate and faithful during their sufferings and their desert journey.

In a manner typical of the biblical literature after the exile, the Bible quotes the Bible. In Baruch 2,21–23 several prophecies of Jeremiah are blended together: Jer 7,34; 27,12; and possibly 29,5–7. These quotes are not taken word for word but rather are adapted to the new situation. The reference to an eternal covenant in 2,34f brings to mind the covenant announcement in Jeremiah 31,31–34; 32,40. God's eternal promises and plans are operative today, here and now, in our own experience of exile.

In Praise of Divine Wisdom (3,9–4,4)

This section is parallel to Job 28 and Sirach 24, both books within the wisdom tradition of the Jewish people. Because of these parallels, and Baruch's influence on later works in Judaism, Baruch provides a key link between the earlier and the later development of the wisdom tradition in Judaism.

The section stresses that God's wisdom lies hidden in creation (3,15–31) and that this wisdom is revealed in bits and pieces in God's law given to Moses (3,32–4,4). The many references to the land of Canaan, and its ancestors and traditions, revive a new sense of appreciation and respect for the land, especially for those in exile who might tend to forget. Even though God's wisdom lies hidden in creation, uncovering it can be very elusive, even for the greatest thinkers and holy ones. Therefore, obedience to the law is essential. It is this obedience to the law that keeps the people attuned to God's way and keeps their moral perspective focused. Only in this fashion can the people draw close to the mysteries of love and fidelity to God, self, family, and community.

Lament and Song of Consolation (4,5 – 5,9)

During this lament, voices that provide needed hope for a desolate people surface slowly and repetitively. Meditating on the promises expressed in Isaiah 40–55 and 56–66, the people renew their hopes and are reminded once again of God's love and fidelity. In 4,5–9a, the prophet talks encouragingly to the people Israel. In 4,9b–16, Jerusalem addresses a lament about her lost children to her neighbors. In 4,17–29, Jerusalem turns and speaks to her people in exile. In 4,30 – 5,9, the prophet addresses Jerusalem in words of hope and consolation based on Isaiah. God will manifest power and glory in and through Jerusalem, and she shall rejoice greatly as God rescues the people once again and returns them to their land and their holy city.

Letter of Jeremiah (6,1–72)

The author of this section is different from the author of the rest of the book. Often, this chapter is not included as part of the Book of Baruch, but rather as a separate book altogether, referred to as the Letter of Jeremiah. However, for our purposes, this chapter is treated as an integral part of the final editing of the Book of Baruch.

Drawing upon a tradition about Jeremiah as a letter writer (Jer 29) and a depositor of divine secrets (2 Mc 2,2), the author, most probably a synagogue preacher, attacks idolatry with great irony and sarcasm. This attack seems to be modeled on earlier prophets (Jer 10,1–16 and Is 44,9–20). The gist of the attack focuses on the inability of these carved idols to do anything for themselves or for their human creators. Why fear or be threatened by such silliness? The sermon gathers momentum with its frequent refrain, which the gathered community would quickly learn and repeat: verses 14, 22, 28, 39, 44, 50, 56, 64, and the grand finale, 71f. Here, idolatry seems more foolish than threatening.

Religious Teaching of Baruch

The author of Baruch drew heavily upon Jeremiah and Second Isaiah (Is 40–55), and also upon postexilic writers like Job, Third Isaiah (Is 56–66), and even one as late as Sirach (around 190 B.C.) to produce something different from any one of these. The Bible, in quoting or alluding to the Bible, is no literalist. Rather, the Bible finds the living word of God at home among the people of each age.

Because of the dangers of living in exile, several key themes are meant to reinforce the peoples' identity, as well as their core beliefs, values, and traditions. These themes are summarized in the table that follows.

Who was Baruch? We are not sure. If the author was a single individual, at least for Chapters 1–5, then this person was able to pick and choose through a variety of sacred traditions: at times siding with Jeremiah, at times going in a different direction; learning from Isaiah 40–66, Job, and even Sirach. The Sirach reference places the author after 190 B.C. Although writing from outside Jerusalem, the author was still in enough contact to write originally in Hebrew and to believe in the Holy City as a bond of unity.

A significant source for the book seems to lead in the direction of a tradition of prayer and preaching in the synagogue. An editor from somewhere in exile gathered the material into a single book, at the earliest about 180 B.C., or possibly around 150 B.C., the end of the Maccabean revolt.

Key Themes in Baruch's Religious Teaching

Monotheism	This is beyond dispute. All other gods are to be scorned (Chapter 6). Israel's God created all of creation (3,32–35) and is enthroned in the highest heaven (3,3). God is the supreme source of wisdom (3,12–32), justice (1,15; 2,6–10), and mercy (2,27; 3,1; 5,9).
Sin	Sin is an act of rebellion (1,22; 4,7) which disrupts and repudiates God's wisdom for the universe (2,12). Sinis seen in terms of communal sin and national apostasy (1, 16–20; 2,1–6). Sin always brings suffering in its wake (1, 13–15; 2,1–5).
Repentance	This is the principal reason for putting together the Book of Baruch. Israel needs to be honest in confessing her faults (2,14; 3,2). She needs to return to the sole fount of goodness (2,8; 4,28).
Hope	Hope is the dominant attitude in this book. Life is limited to this earth and to the future generations (2,17), and it concludes no traditions about the messiah. Yet, eternity is a key focus. God abides eternally (3,3) and establishes an eternal covenant with Israel (2,35). Salvation is from an eternal God (4,8). Eternity pervades God's consolation to Israel (4,10.21–24.35 5,5,2) as well as announcements of eternal joy (4,23–29; 5,1–4).

Questions for Discussion or Reflection

1. Recount an experience in which you realized how different you really were from most of the people and things around you: e.g., travel in a foreign country, not knowing the language, customs, traditions, beliefs of a group you were with, etc. How did this situation make you feel? Name some of the things you did to relieve these feelings. What did this experience teach you about yourself and others?

2. If all your familiar, recognizable roots and supports were removed from you, what would be some of the things that you would continue to rely on for anchoring your identity, your human dignity, your religious beliefs?

3. What sorts of situations in our world are similar to the Israelites' experience of exile? How do people in our day maintain their balance when hope seems to be very distant, and restoration to normal living does not seem to be at all realistic?

4. How do you relate to God in all of this disorientation? How do you relate to self and others? What would you say to God? to yourself? to others?

EZEKIEL READING GUIDE

EZEKIEL, THE PERSON

The book opens in 593/2 B.C. with Ezekiel already in exile at a village called Tel Abib (1,1; 3,15). The village was on the banks of the river Chebar, in the capital city of Babylon. It is not clear when Ezekiel made the 900-mile journey northward from Israel, eastward across Syria, then southward down the Euphrates River into modern-day Iraq. The Babylonians may have deported him in 597 B.C., the year of their first attack on Jerusalem. Or he may have gone freely to join the exiles sometime before 593/2 B.C. The latest date in the book is 571 B.C. (29,17). He was born of a priestly family (1,3), and was married (24,16–18).

Although the written text is the starting point, writing seems to have been of secondary importance to Ezekiel. The focus throughout the book is on symbolic actions, gestures, public demonstrations of faith, confrontations with others, and a total focus on God. Ezekiel is continually being ordered to prophesy and say, hear the word (6,2–3; 13,2; 34,2); speak and say (14,4; 20,3); propose a riddle and speak this proverb (17,2); raise a lament and say (19,1–3; 27,2f). This focus on action and speaking make Ezekiel truly a public person in the community. This may explain how he could be objective and distant, and yet intensely present with his audience.

Ezekiel continually speaks in the first person singular, yet it is not he who speaks but the Lord speaking through him. Ezekiel remains obedient to God, like clay in the hands of the potter, never questioning God's complete control over all things. Ezekiel's prophetic career was very colorful, even puzzling, with all kinds of strange symbolic actions. Gifted as well with visions and mystical insights, Ezekiel is an interesting and intriguing character.

No matter how we regard the prophet's unusual behavior and miraculous gifts, Ezekiel remained a strong, influential person in his community. Elders gathered round him (8,1; 14,1; 20,1); the messenger from Jerusalem came first to Ezekiel (32,21f), as did other people (33,30–33). Also, Ezekiel had an extraordinary influence on later prophecy and the history of Judaism.

Theological Background

Ezekiel combined and spoke out of various theological traditions. Like Hosea, Jeremiah, and other prophets usually associated with the northern part of Israel, Ezekiel merges the Exodus tradition into his prophecy (Chapters 16 and 20). Jeremiah and Ezekiel both speak of a new covenant written within the person (Jer 31,31–34; Ez 30,26f), leading to a more personal responsibility for the covenant (Jer 31,27–30; Ez 18). As Isaiah, Micah, and traditions associated with the South and Jerusalem did, Ezekiel emphasizes the importance of the holy city and its Temple.

The rituals and the traditions of the Temple greatly affected Ezekiel. This may explain his tendency to include many details in his account of events. It also may explain why he frequently expresses himself in symbolic actions and stories. Storytelling to communicate God's message finds its way into Ezekiel's preaching. Priesthood and prophecy blended well within the person of Ezekiel, and it shows throughout this book.

EZEKIEL, THE MESSAGE

Ezekiel's message can be summarized under five topics:

1. The centrality of the Temple and the Lord's presence
2. The awesome wonder of God
3. Individual responsibility
4. Prophecy and beyond
5. The influence of Ezekiel on the New Testament

The Centrality of the Temple and the Lord's Presence

Ezekiel's book of prophecy opens with a vision of the Lord enthroned as in the Temple. The book closes with the sacred stream flowing from the Temple altar (47,1–12) and with the proclamation of Jerusalem's new name, *yahweh shamah,* "the LORD is here" (48,35). In Ezekiel, God is portrayed either in the Temple, or in a style that is associated with the Temple.

The vision that begins the book also dominates the whole book and is associated with the presence of the Lord with the prophet and the people: God anointing Ezekiel as prophet (Chapter 1); God departing from the Temple and the city, setting it up for destruction (Chapter 10); God preparing for the resurrection of the people (37,1); and God reconsecrating the new messianic Temple and city (43,1–9). These events are told in priestly language involving priestly details and symbols. But Ezekiel the priest is also Ezekiel the prophet. Thus prophecy is evident throughout these priestly descriptions.

Ezekiel, the prophet, insists that the Temple is not holy of itself, but only because the Lord is present there. The Lord's presence requires that the people practice justice. The Lord can therefore choose to depart from the Temple, and reappear in foreign lands, areas that priests considered unclean. The announcement in Chapter 34 of the destruction of Jerusalem and its Temple led to the second major period in Ezekiel's preaching, which focused on the new purified Israel. The images used here are also those of one at home with priestly language and Temple worship.

The Awesome Wonder of God

Ezekiel's God is overpowering and awesome, reaching beyond human relationships (24,15–24) and human explanations (20,25f). God is not someone to be argued with, as in Jeremiah; nor someone agonizing over the fate of the people, as in Hosea. Unlike the second and third parts of Isaiah, as well as Hosea and Jeremiah, Ezekiel does not portray the Lord as parent or kinsperson. For Ezekiel, God is close, yet also very distant.

A phrase constantly used by Ezekiel to portray God's majestic and overpowering presence is "the glory of the LORD" (1,28; 3,12–23; 8,4; 10,4). This phrase usually accompanies the vision of the cherubim or the four living creatures. Still another word is "holiness." The name of the Lord is usually qualified as holy. These two words, *glory* and *holy,* are usually associated with events that take us beyond normal human existence. Although the Lord is continually communicating through the prophet, the character of the prophet is lost within the overpowering message of the Lord.

Individual Responsibility

Ezekiel is generally referred to in any discussions on this topic. With Jeremiah he quotes a well-known proverb, only to prove how wrong it really is: "Fathers have eaten sour grapes, thus their children's teeth are on edge" (Ez 18,2; Jer 31,29). Both prophets insist that this proverb is a denial of the actual reality of a situation, along with a refusal to take responsibility for one's actions. Ultimately, this proverb blames others for one's present condition. In a long chapter Ezekiel insists that "only the one who sins shall die" (18,4).

For Ezekiel, the entire nation is God's chosen people. Thus each individual Israelite is personally responsible for the living out of the covenant. Each person lives or dies according to his or her virtuous or wicked way of life. Ezekiel focuses not only on exterior behavior, but also on interior change of heart (11,19; 18,31; 36,26f). Here, as well as with Ezekiel 18,2, we see important points of comparison with Jeremiah (see Jer 31,31–34). Both prophets speak of a new heart.

Prophecy and Beyond

While remaining within the prophetic tradition of Israel that he inherited, Ezekiel also went beyond it. He changed the tradition in many ways; prophecy after him would never be the same as before. After the return from exile, prophets like Haggai, Zechariah, Joel, and Malachi seem as much priest as prophet. Their words and preaching seem to be more concerned with liturgical action in the Temple, or about the Temple itself, than with social justice and compassion.

Ezekiel had turned the style of prophecy in the direction of the apocalyptic movement. Apocalyptic prophets are called "seers" rather than prophets because of the awesome mysteries they foresee about Israel's future. To communicate these mysteries, they resort to symbols rather than plain speech. At times, these symbols are so beyond human comprehension and discernment that angels are needed to interpret the vision or the symbol. Apocalyptic prophets actually speak of present realities and situations in the context of the ultimate end of all things, using visions, dreams, and all sorts of symbols.

Apocalyptic means "drawing aside the veil" so as to perceive mysteries hidden in God.

Influence on the New Testament

Ezekiel's influence on the New Testament shows up in the Gospels whenever Jesus refers to himself as the "Son of Man—ben-Adam." This title reflects someone absorbed within humanity (Adam) and overwhelmed before God's mighty presence (Ez 2,2f). Ezekiel's notion of the "son of man" seems to have been more influential on Jesus than the more exalted "son of man" in Daniel (Daniel 7,13f). Ezekiel's image of the shepherd, in Chapter 34, influenced Jesus' use of the image of the good shepherd (Jn 10).

It is in the Book of Revelation that the influence of Ezekiel shows up consistently: the four living creatures (Ez 1; Rv 4,6–9); a voice like the sound of many waters (Ez 1,24; Rv 1,15); God from the land of Magog (Ez 38–39; Rv 20,8); the seer being carried to a high mountain (Ez 40,2; Rv 21,10). The Book of Revelation tends to change or simplify the stranger features of Ezekiel's prophecy.

EZEKIEL, THE BOOK

The overall plan of the book can be clearly seen from the way it is structured. There are two major sections to the book: one condemning Jerusalem to total destruction (Chapters 1–24) and the other announcing the resurrection of a new people and a new Jerusalem (Chapters 25–48). A second organizing structure, overlapping the first, can also be seen as dividing the book into two major sections: Ezekiel the prophet (Chapters 1–39) and Ezekiel the priest (Chapters 40–48). If we follow this latter breakdown, we notice various subdivisions to each major section:

- Chapters 1–39, Ezekiel the Prophet

Chapters 1–3	The call to prophesy
Chapters 4–24	The condemnation of Jerusalem
Chapters 25–32	The oracles against the nations
Chapters 33–37	Israel's revival and transformation
Chapters 38–39	The final defeat of world forces

- Chapters 40–48, Ezekiel the Priest

Chapters 40–43	The new Temple
Chapters 44–46	The new way of life
Chapters 47–48	The new promised land

Major Historical Developments

The format of the book follows national and world events as these affected Israel:

Chapters 4–24	The nations are God's instruments for punishing a sinful people. After the exile, the prophet prepares for the rebirth of his people through:
Chapters 25–32	Oracles that proclaim the destruction of those foreign nations responsible for Israel's suffering and exile, especially Egypt and Tyre.
Chapters 33–37	Speeches and visions that announce Israel's religious renewal beyond anyone's expectations.
Chapters 38–39	Because the restoration of the people was not completely final, Ezekiel foresees another victory for the Lord, against the most powerful of the world's forces.
Chapters 40–48	Description of the Lord finally achieving the total peace of Jerusalem and the transformation of the Promised Land into paradise.

Literary Unity

In its final form, Ezekiel contains several key themes and repetitions that run throughout, giving it a sense of unity. Identical words and phrases appear at different places throughout the book, as illustrated by these examples:

- "the hand of the LORD came upon me" 1,3; 3,14–22; 8,1; 33,22; 37,1; 40,1.
- "know that I the LORD" 6,7.10.13.14; 7,4.9.27; 11,10.12; 32,15; 33,29; 38,23.
- "I, the LORD, have spoken" 5,13.15.17; 12,25; 17,24; 21,22; 22,14; 34,24; 36,36.
- "glory of the LORD," "glory of the God of Israel" 1,28; 3,12.23; 8,4; 9,3; 10,4–18.19; 11,22.23; 43,2.4.5; 44,4.
- "rebellious house" 2,5.6.7.8; 3,9.26.27; 12.2.3.9.15; 17,12; 24,3; 44,6
- "abominations" 5,9.11; 6,9.11; 7,3.4.8.9; 8,6.9.13.15.17; 9,4; 11,18.21; 12,16; 14,6; 16,2.22.43.47.51.58; 20,4; 33,26,29; 43,8; 44,6.7.13.

Visions

The book is bonded together by a series of visions, especially that of the four living creatures in Chapter 1. Visions introduce key sections of Ezekiel's prophecy:

- The four living creatures (1,4—3,15) Vision of the witnesses to Ezekiel's call to be a prophet
- Idolatry in the Temple (Chapters 8–11) Vision of the activity that seals the ultimate destruction of Jerusalem
- The dry bones (Chapter 37) Vision that prepares for the resurrection of exiled Israel to new life
- New Jerusalem (Chapters 40 and 43) Vision that prepares for the resurrection of Jerusalem and the Temple to new splendor and glory
- Stream of water flowing from the altar (47,1–12) Vision of new life restored once more at the very heart of Israel, and also the vision that brings Ezekiel's prophecy to a close

MAJOR SECTIONS OF THE BOOK OF EZEKIEL

The Four Living Creatures (Chapters 1–3)

This opening vision sets the tone and scene for the entire book. The editors have united the entire prophecy of Ezekiel around the cherubim, the four living creatures who once upheld the throne of the Lord in the Holy of Holies of the Jerusalem Temple (Ex 25,17–22). In Chapter 3, other elements are added to the vision (the prophet as watchman 24,25–27; as stricken dumb, Chapter 33, etc.), elements that will be picked up later in the book and further elaborated. The four living creatures appear first in 1,4–28. They reappear in 8,1–4; 10; 11,22f, providing the setting for the eventual destruction of the Temple. In Chapter 37, Ezekiel can speak words he could not speak while on the plain in Chapter 3. Ezekiel 43,1–9 echoes many of the phrases from the beginning vision, as well as undoing the curse placed upon Jerusalem with the departure of the glory of the Lord in 10,18–23. New life and new beginnings are in store for Israel.

Symbolic Actions (Chapters 4–12)

Not only the visions, but many symbolic actions surround Ezekiel. Each symbolic action follows a precise pattern:

1. A command from the Lord
2. The carrying out of that command by Ezekiel, with all the care and attention required in response to God's command
3. The meaning that this action has for Israel

Because of this pattern, Ezekiel sometimes seems to be almost like a robot, acting blindly on divine orders. This strong preference for patterns may be Ezekiel's answer to the chaos that resulted from Israel's lack of faithfulness.

The first set of four symbolic actions occurs in 4,1–5,17. In these verses, the fiery destruction of Jerusalem and its long journey into exile are symbolically acted out by Ezekiel. This sequence of events is shown in the table here. Symbols, words, and actions all combine to tell the community the reality of their fate, because of their infidelity and idolatry.

Symbolic Actions of the Destruction and Exile of Israel

4,1-3	Siege of Jerusalem is acted out in picture form of a ramp, battering rams, and other actions of siege.
4,4-8	The long siege is symbolized by the prophet lying for 360 days on his left side, and 40 days on his right side, while bound with cords.
4,9-17	The hunger and thirst of the siege are acted out by the prophet in eating and drinking very little while lying on his side.
5,1-17	The shaving of the hair from the head and beard (a very demeaning action for an Israelite male—2 Sm 10,4), and the burning of some of the hair, as well as the striking with the sword and the scattering of the hair, are all symbolic of the burning of Jerusalem and the dispersal of the survivors.

Editors reinterpreted Ezekiel's symbolic actions and visions. Additions are inserted at different places. One example is in 5,3f, where a small amount of hair is preserved in the hem of the garment, to show that not all will be lost in the destruction and the exile. This symbolic action with the hair is given four related but separate interpretations: 5,7–10.11–13.14f.16f.

There are other symbolic actions in the book that portray further the destruction of the city and the exile. Further symbols of exile are:

12,1–16	Packing one's baggage and crawling through a hole in the city wall
12,17–20	Eating and drinking with trembling and horror
21,11f	Groaning bitterly
21,19–22	Clapping hands and waving a sword
24,15–17	Ezekiel not mourning the death of his wife, just as the people are not to mourn the death of Jerusalem

Symbolic actions also extend to hopeful prophecies for the future as in 37,15–28. Here the symbolic tying of two sticks together shows that the people from both the northern and southern kingdoms who survive the destruction will be united peacefully under a Davidic prince around the sanctuary.

Other Literary Forms (Chapters 13–24)

Ezekiel the book displays many literary forms as it tries in creative ways to get the message of destruction and exile across to the community. The table below shows some examples of the various literary forms used.

Variety of Literary Forms in Chapters 13–24

13,1-23	Two *prophecies of woe* against false prophets, both male and female
14,1-23	A *legal case* against idol-worshipers
15,1-8	A scornful *disputation* with the inhabitants of Jerusalem
16,1-63	An *allegory* about Jerusalem
17,1-24	A *fable,* featuring an eagle, a cedar, and a vine
18,1-32	A long *disputation* on personal responsibility
19,1-14	A funeral *dirge,* ridiculing Jerusalem, speaking to her as if already dead
20,1-44	A *prophetic speech,* about God's interventions to save Israel, with a litany of the people's infidelities
21,1-37	Three *prophecies of doom* linked by the image of a sword
22,1-37	*Prophecy and allegory* decreeting the punishment of Jerusalem, a city of blood and guilt
23,1-49	A long *allegory* about two immoral sisters
24,1-14	An *allegory*
24,15-27	A *symbolic action*

This ends the first major part of Ezekiel's prophecy, which emphasized the fact that God is determined to destroy Jerusalem, too wicked to be purified any further. Ezekiel will now await the news of the city's destruction in Chapter 33 and then begin to reconstruct a new people. First, however, the editor records the oracles against the nations, Chapters 25–32.

Oracles Against the Nations (Chapters 25–32)

Making prophetic speeches condemning foreign nations, and singing mocking laments over their death are consistent biblical patterns: Amos 1,2 – 2,16; Isaiah 13–23; Jeremiah 46–51. This pattern probably has its source in Temple prayers for victory, as well as in ritual curses against the enemy.

Ezekiel concentrates his speeches against the nations of Egypt and Tyre, both of which represent forces that caused harm and division within Israel. There are seven oracles against the nations. Seven is a symbolic number representing perfection. Thus seven oracles represent the complete defeat of the enemy forces, as well as the seven nations of Palestine that Joshua was told to defeat so that Israel could gain the land (Dt 7,1–4).

In many prophetical books, the oracles against the nations are placed between the section condemning Israel and that announcing her revival. This pattern shows a belief of the editors that God overcomes every obstacle, first in Israel's sins (Is 1–12; Ez 1–24; Zep 1,2 – 2,3), and then in the nations' opposition (Is 13–23; Ez 25–32; Zep 2,4–15), before resurrecting Israel to new life (Is 24–26; 34–35; Ez 33–48; Zep 3,1–20).

Message of Consolation (Chapters 33–37)

Chapter 33 recalls earlier passages and moves into a new age for Israel. The prophet as watchman (verses 1–9) links with 3,16–21 and Ezekiel's initial call. The passage on individual responsibility for one's actions (verses 10–20) links with Chapter 18, a key passage in understanding Ezekiel's notion of sin, guilt, and punishment. The arrival of the fugitive from Jerusalem and the end of Ezekiel's muteness (verses 21f) links well with 3,22–27 and 24,25–27. The final verses 23–33 insist that salvation is reserved for those exiles who have been internally transformed, anticipating 36,16–38.

Chapter 34 comes from a long tradition of referring to kings as shepherds: 2 Sm 5,2; Mi 5,4; Jer 2,8; 3,15; 23,1–6. Ezekiel's passage in turn influenced Zechariah 11,4–17, and together they helped to form New Testament readings like Mark 6,34 and John 10.

Chapter 36,16–38 makes an interesting study with Jeremiah 31,31–37. Both speak of an internal renewal, with Ezekiel introducing many external details or rituals to accompany the internal transformation.

Chapter 37,1–14 uses two different images to tell of Israel's revival. In verses 1–11, the dry bones in the valley come together to form enfleshed people. In verses 12–14, the bones rise out of a grave. Ezekiel's prophecy over the dead bones enables him to summon the spirit that brings them back to life.

The Lord's World Victory (Chapters 38–39)

After the purifying renewal of Israel during the exile and the return to the Promised Land, why did Israel not experience the final glorious fulfillment of God's promises? The crisis behind Chapters 38–39 may be the long, dreary, frustrating stretch of existence after the return from exile. This is the in-between period of time, between the initial renewal of Israel and the definitive, everlasting victory of peace that was still to come.

One way of looking at this final victory was through the origins of an apocalyptic literary form. The key to this literary form is that the forces of good are always at war with the forces of evil. God's mighty intervention on behalf of the forces of good is the only way that the forces of evil will ever be finally defeated. During severe crises, preachers and writers turn to the final day of the Lord as a means of offering hope and consolation to those enduring pain or suffering. Some excellent examples from scripture are Daniel 7–12 and the Book of Revelation.

For Ezekiel, the forces of Gog from Magog represent the forces of evil that have to be defeated before final and lasting peace can be experienced by Israel. The final verses of this section (39,21–29) may once have concluded the Book of Ezekiel. These verses summarize well the goals of Ezekiel's preaching.

Vision of the New Temple, Land, and Community (Chapters 40–48)

Visions surround this final section (40,1—44,4; 47,1–12). Between these visions and after 47,12, Ezekiel provides rules or instructions for the community and its leadership. These instructions are developed still further by Ezekiel's disciples or editors of his material. Some of the outstanding passages are summarized in the table below. The Book of Ezekiel ends fittingly with the new name for Jerusalem, "The LORD is here" (48,35).

Important Passages from Chapters 40–48

43,1–9	The glory of the Lord reverses the journey of Chapter 10 and returns to its place above the Ark of the Covenant, between the wings of the cherubim. This return promises the Temple a place in the final age.
44,4–31	Ezekiel takes a strong stand against the more open positions of Deuteronomy and Third Isaiah (56–66). In verses 5–9 Ezekiel forbids all foreigners from entering the Temple. Also, Ezekiel favors the priestly family of the Zadokites, over all the other Levite families. The Zadokites are "the only Levites who may come near to minister to the LORD" (40,46; 43,19).
45,18–23	This section includes a calendar of feasts.
46,2	This verse drops the title of king and reduces the heir of the Davidic royalty to the rank of a "prince." Royal privileges and power are being transferred to the high priest. The eternal promises made to David are no longer applied to his heirs but are understood as promises for the future Messiah.
47,1–12	This passage offers a vision of fresh water, flowing from the altar, down the Kidron Valley, into the Dead Sea. This is part of the biblical tradition that declares symbolically that all life flows from God, enthroned at the Temple. The Temple becomes a symbol of the messianic era and mirrors God's true and everlasting home in heaven.

Questions for Discussion or Reflection

1. God appears in unexpected places. Ezekiel sees God in the alien, defiled land of Babylonia. It is here that God speaks to Ezekiel. How do we place expectations on God? Where are the places in our lives where we would never expect God to be?

2. Complete obedience and blind faith are Ezekiel's response to God's word and command. What is your response to God's word and command in your life? What demands does God place on you? How do you respond? What kind of relationship to God is required for us to begin to respond to God in the same manner that Ezekiel did?

3. Ezekiel insists that internal conversion must be manifested in external actions and rituals. How do you react to this stance that Ezekiel advances? How does this stance take shape in your daily living? What are the benefits of such a stance? What are the dangers in focusing on rituals and external actions as indicators of internal disposition?

4. God's presence in the midst of the people is the essential component of Ezekiel's God. How is God present in your life? In your community? What are some clear indicators of God's presence? When is God's presence not so clear? How do we focus on God at such times? What are some symbols that help us to focus on God's presence in our midst?

DANIEL READING GUIDE

At a Glance

When	Mainly during the 2nd century B.C.
Where	Judah
Main Focus	Hope: God is reliable

THE AUTHORSHIP AND DATE OF DANIEL

The Book of Daniel was written by an unknown author probably in the middle of the second century B.C., but it presents itself as the composition of a wise Israelite, Daniel, during the fifth century B.C. This false attribution of authorship was a common practice in the ancient world, when a composition needed the extra authority of a prominent author or the extra authority of having been written a long time before.

Daniel therefore predicts the future that is already known to the author. This means that, in reading the book, we must concentrate on the lessons that the author thought were important for contemporary readers. If we do not pay attention to this, we will be misled into concentrating on Daniel as a predictor of the future.

Outline of the Book of Daniel

Dn 1–6	Stories of Daniel and his companions. These may have once been independent stories.
Dn 7–12	Revelations as told by Daniel and composed during the persecution of the Jews by Antiochus IV Epiphanes of Syria (168–64 B.C.).
Dn 13–14	These "additions" were added sometime later, probably before the Christian era.

THE TALES (CHAPTERS 1–6)

These stories are similar to historical novels: They mention historical names and places but they are fictional. They are not concerned with historical accuracy but, instead, carry a religious message, like the parables of Jesus. Daniel, like Noah and Job, may never have existed, but that does not take away from the religious value of the stories.

The stories paint an ideal picture of the life of Jewish exiles in Babylon. The situation is idealized in order to express hope and define acceptable behavior. The message of these tales is relevant today. The modern situation of religious people living in the secular world is not so far removed from ancient Jews living in the pagan world of Babylon. The message has two facets: It affirms the possibility of living in a Gentile environment, and it insists on the importance of fidelity to the essentials of the Jewish tradition.

Affirmation of the Gentile Environment

This affirmation is demonstrated in the story in Chapter 1 when Daniel and his companions are trained and even excel in "the language and literature of the Chaldeans." They express no reservations about this training. In Chapter 2, Daniel, with God's assistance, is able to interpret the king's dream when the Babylonian wise men fail. There are more instances of Daniel's ability to interpret mysteries in Chapters 4 and 5.

Several instances in these chapters reveal Daniel's attitude toward Gentile kingship. One dream foretells that all Gentile kingdoms will eventually be destroyed, but there is no urgency about this prophecy. God has willed a long Gentile rule and Jews can find fulfillment in the service of a pagan king. The stories about King Nebuchadnezzar and King Belshazzar make it clear that Gentile kings must be subject to God and not become too proud or arrogant. They must act with restraint. If they do this, Daniel has no objection to their rule. Only when the kings exceed their limits do they incur the judgment of God.

The Importance of Fidelity

This second facet of the message is presented in the actions of Daniel and his companions. They remain faithful to their Jewish religion even as they enjoy their success at the pagan court. They refuse to eat the king's food, because it is not *kosher* (Chapter 1). The three youths refuse to worship the king's statue, at the risk of death (Chapter 3). Daniel refuses to depart from his custom of daily prayer even at the cost of being thrown into the lions' den. Each time the Jews ultimately win the respect of their rulers and become more successful.

The stories of the fiery furnace and the lions' den, like all miracle stories, are meant to arouse a sense of wonder. They are not realistic stories. The essential point in Daniel's stories is that God has the power to save, or to do what is for the best. Daniel and his companions trust in God, and this liberates them to do whatever they ought to do regardless of the immediate circumstances. This attitude is expressed in the words of the three youths: "If our God, whom we serve, can save us from the white-hot furnace and from your hands, O king, may he save us! But even if he will not, know, O king that we will not serve your god or worship the golden statue which you set up." Their fidelity is not conditional.

Daniel 1–6 conveys a sense that God is in control and that all will work out for the best. The will of God can be exercised through the rule of pagan kings. True religion does not require any particular political system.

Apocalyptic Literature

Daniel's visions (Chapters 7–12) belong to a kind of literature called apocalyptic (see Glossary, *apocalypse*). This word is from the Greek for "revelation" and has come to be associated with a particular kind of revelation, with certain recurring characteristics. The table below lists some of those characteristics, some examples from Daniel, and a few of the ways the characteristics function.

Characteristics	Function
1. Heavy Use of Symbolism *Example:* Beasts = kingdoms; sea = chaos	Veils the meaning. Lack of specificity adds sense of mystery. Allows long-term interpretation.
2. Angels and Demons *Example:* Interpreting angel; Michael the archangel	Angels emphasize supernatural, add to sense of mystery and dramatize divine control.
3. Pseudonymity *Example:* Second-century author writes as if living during the Exile	Antiquity adds to prestige of writings. Allows accurate "predictions" which foster hope and inspire right conduct.
4. Determinism *Example:* History has fixed duration—70 weeks of years	Divine control. Course of history is set with fate of righteous and wicked. Human decisions not predetermined.
5. Predictions of the End *Example:* End persecution (Dan) and/or end of the world	During persecution, easier to keep going if the specific day of relief is known.

These characteristics create numerous difficulties for the modern reader and call for some caution in interpreting books like Daniel.

1. *Heavy Use of Symbolism.* Apocalyptic authors do not speak directly but use symbols or images instead. For example, all scholars agree that King Antiochus is a major figure in Daniel, but his name is never mentioned. He appears as the eleventh horn on a beast. Sometimes this veiled language might be used to save the community from persecution from the king. It also strengthens the impression of supernatural origin and allows later generations to make their own interpretations. This characteristic can easily lead to misinterpretation and misapplications. Two hundred years later the eleventh horn might have been interpreted as the Roman emperor instead of Antiochus. In our own time the beasts rising out of the sea might be interpreted as meaning the outbreak of the Second World War. It is important to remember that the author of Daniel was speaking of persecution in the 2nd century B.C., and not predicting any later event. The Book of Daniel can help us understand our modern situation because it describes patterns that recur throughout history, but it cannot be used to predict specific events or persons in our world. The same can be said for the New Testament Book of Revelation.
2. *Angels and Demons.* The first thing to remember when trying to interpret the meaning of the heavenly beings in Daniel is that, like other apocalypses, this is a work of imagination. The author is trying to build up hope in the people by saying that earthly war is not entirely under earthly control. To understand an apocalypse, we should ask, not, "Do these angels exist?" but, "What do they stand for?"
3. *Pseudonymity.* Many readers today consider the practice of claiming ancient authorship and, therefore, accurate predictions as deceptive and unethical. This was, however, widely accepted in the ancient world and helped the people believe in the real predictions of what was to come. The question is not whether Daniel really predicted all these things in advance, but whether his stance in the face of religious persecutions is a valid one.
4. *Determinism.* In dealing with the notion of fixed periods of history, the modern reader needs to remember that human decisions are not predetermined. On the contrary, the Book of Daniel is basically a call for decision in a time of crisis. The fact that God has control over history strengthens the people's hope and their ability to make decisions.
5. *Predictions of the End.* Whether the end predicted was of persecution or of the world, the point of the specific predictions was, again, to encourage people to stand firm in their faith in the midst of suffering.

The problems of interpreting apocalyptic literature can be minimized if the believer reads for inspiration or exhortation rather than information. It can have ethical value and relevance for modern times if the focus is placed on the attitudes and actions it was designed to support.

A SYMBOLIC VISION (CHAPTER 7)

This vision of four human kingdoms that will be followed by a kingdom set up by God is one of the most famous and influential of all apocalyptic visions. In biblical poetry the sea is often a symbol of chaos, of all that is opposed to God; that is the point Daniel makes when he represents the pagan kingdoms as beasts from the sea. This is much more negative than the view of pagan kingdoms in Daniel 1–6. The experience of persecution colored the author's perception of all Gentile kingdoms.

After the vision of the four beasts, Daniel sees a judgment scene in which the "Ancient One" sits on a throne, the fourth beast is condemned to the fire, and "one like a son of man" appears on the clouds of heaven. There have been a variety of interpretations of this "son of man" figure. Early Christian tradition, beginning with the Gospels, identified this figure with Jesus Christ, but that could not have been the case in the 2nd century B.C. Jewish tradition identified the "son of man" as the Messiah. Modern scholarship is divided between two interpretations: a symbol for Israel, or Michael the archangel. Either interpretation, however, can be understood as representing the triumph of the Jewish people over their persecutors under their heavenly patron.

The message of the vision is one of hope. Even when the opposing forces seem overwhelming, the power of God will eventually defeat them. The symbolism of the vision (beasts, fire, figure riding on the cloud) expresses the message with exceptional power and vividness. The image has been used over and over again in new situations. It provides language to express the power of evil that erupts from time to time in human affairs (for example, the Holocaust), and it can also express a hope that does not depend on human power. A similar symbolic vision is found in Chapter 8 and, again, the message is one of hope.

PROPHECY REINTERPRETED (CHAPTER 9)

A prophecy of Jeremiah provides the basis for a different kind of revelation in this chapter. Jeremiah prophesied in the 8th century that the land would be subject to Babylon for 70 years. The Second Book of Chronicles credits Cyrus of Persia with fulfilling the prophecy (after 50 years had passed). Zechariah related it to the rebuilding of the Temple (after 66 years). The author of Daniel obviously does not think the prophecy has been fulfilled, but rather than discard it as a failure, he reinterprets it. Seventy years, he says, really means 70 weeks of years or 490 years. Like the dreams and visions of earlier chapters, Jeremiah's number is treated as a symbol. It is not meant to stand for an exact number of years. Rather, it reminds the readers that they can depend on God's promises even when the time of fulfillment is completely unknown.

Daniel's prayer in Chapter 9 contains another important reminder: We should not expect our prayers to alter the course of events. Daniel receives a revelation in response to his prayer, but his prayer does not result in a shortening of the time of trial.

DANIEL'S APOCALYPTIC VIEW OF HISTORY (CHAPTERS 10–12)

This long vision explains to Daniel that the ongoing war between Judah and her enemies is not the whole picture. The earthly battle is only a reflection of the more important heavenly battle between the archangels Michael and Gabriel opposing the angelic princes of Persia and Greece. The vision shows that Michael will eventually be victorious (12,1) and the resurrection will follow. It is important to notice some key points about history in the vision.

1. The vision presumes that the outcome of warfare between human kingdoms depends on God's power, not human power (illustrated by the battle between the angelic powers).
2. The vision gives the impression that what happens in history is fixed in advance. It is written as if Daniel is writing during the exile, some 400 years before the actual events of persecution under Antiochus Epiphanes. This is done not to deceive, but to build up confidence in the prediction about the death of the king (11,40–55) and the resurrection (12,1–3).
3. The vision clearly affirms the resurrection of individuals (the only book of the Hebrew Bible to do so). Other books use the language of resurrection to refer to the restoration of the Jewish nation but not of individuals. This new emphasis was probably influenced by the experience of martyrdom in the time of persecution (see 2 Maccabees 7).

Belief in the resurrection made an enormous difference to Judaism and was essential to the beginnings of Christianity. Before this, Jewish religion taught that the reward for a just life was to see one's children's children to the fourth generation and the welfare of the nation as a whole. Now, however, pious Jews were being put to death for obeying the Law and were being cut off from the traditional reward. Just as the 70-year prediction of Jeremiah was reinterpreted in a new situation, so too, the reward of a just life had to be reinterpreted. Belief in life beyond the grave put martyrdom in a new perspective.

For Daniel, the Jews who remained faithful in the time of persecution were the wise persons (11,33–35). These put their trust in Michael and the heavenly world and apparently did not join in the fighting. The faithful stance of these wise teachers illustrates the ethical stance of the Book of Daniel, which is the most enduring message of the book.

The apocalyptic message of Chapters 10–12 has some basic beliefs in common with the older stories found in Chapters 1–6, although the stories are more optimistic. Both affirm the belief that God rules all kingdoms and has the power to save, and that the individual must act with integrity even at the cost of life itself. This last is helped by the belief in the resurrection.

It is important to remember when reading Daniel that apocalyptic writing comes out of difficult, troubled times and, therefore, the writer's position may be presented as the only right way of seeing things. Daniel presents one possible way in which a faithful person might respond to a situation of oppression and persecution. It would be a mistake to think that it is the only appropriate response. The Bible presents many different responses in a variety of situations.

THE ADDITIONS OR APPENDIX (CHAPTERS 13–14)

These are independent stories added here probably because Daniel happens to be one of the characters.

Susanna

This story may be described as a parable because it reverses our expectations. Daniel appears as a young but wise judge, as suggested by his name (Dan comes from the Hebrew verb "to judge"). Usually elders who have been appointed judges are the righteous ones, and the word of a young woman would carry little weight against theirs. However, it is characteristic of biblical narrative that the underdog prevails or is justified.

The story of Susanna is similar to the rest of Daniel in her response when she is trapped: "Yet it is better for me to fall into your power without guilt than to sin before the LORD" (13,14).

Bel and the Dragon

Daniel 14 contains two stories that make fun of pagan idolatry and are not meant to be taken as accurate descriptions of Babylonian religion. The Babylonians are portrayed as excessively stupid, and the stories are more fantastic than Daniel 6. Although the fantastic elements give the tale a lighthearted quality, the background here is more tense than Daniel 1–6. Bel and the Dragon allows for no ecumenical relations with pagan religion and reflects a more serious situation than indicated in Daniel 1–6. The present-day reader must remember that biblical stories are shaped by historical circumstances, and this effects how we read them.

Questions for Discussion or Reflection

1. What are the situations that might condition your fidelity to God (e.g., standard of living, government policies, job requirements, etc.)?
2. In what ways do faithful companions help us to be faithful?
3. What are the convictions that strengthen your hope or enable you to make ethical decisions?
4. Are there any symbols that remind you of these convictions?
5. Think about your patterns of prayer. Do you usually pray to change God, to change events or conditions, to change yourself, or to strengthen your fidelity?
6. How does your prayer reflect the circumstances of your life? Give some examples.
7. Can you identify any apocalyptic characteristics in the ways you express your faith?

The Twelve Minor Prophets

The authors of this collection (referred to as the Book of the Twelve) are called *minor* prophets because their writings are short compared to the four *major* prophets, Isaiah, Jeremiah, Ezekiel, and Daniel. Like the others, however, they were "here and now" kinds of people dealing with specific situations; so it is important to know as much as possible about the time and place of their activity (see the timeline on RG 152):

1. This collection covers a period of about 300 years of prophetic activity.
2. Amos, Hosea, and Micah were active in the 8th century B.C. at the same time Isaiah was beginning his career. Recall that there were two kingdoms at this time. Hosea was in the north and Micah in the south. Amos was from the southern kingdom but prophesied in the north.
3. Zephaniah, Nahum, and Habakkuk were active toward the end of the 7th century B.C. during the Babylonian period.
4. Haggai and Zechariah (Chapters 1–8) were involved in the rebuilding of the Temple in Jerusalem in 520 B.C.
5. Joel, Jonah, Obadiah, and Malachi are from the time after the *exile* (called the postexilic period) but are more difficult to date. (See "Exile and Return" on RG 14.)

Most of these books are made up of short poetic *oracles* or messages from God delivered through the prophets. The Book of Jonah, which is a short story, is an exception.

We can discover a pattern in the content of these books: sin followed by judgment followed by salvation or the promise of restoration. Not all of the prophets get to the end of the pattern (Amos), while others focus primarily on restoration (Haggai and Zechariah). Within this overall pattern there is diversity, as well as some dominant themes:

1. Most of these prophets focus on the sins of their own people. There are a few exceptions, but generally you could say that these prophets are critical of those around them.
2. They concentrate on two kinds of sin. *Social sin,* the mistreatment of the poor, the weak and the unprotected, is clearly denounced in Amos and Micah but is found throughout the collection. *Cultic sin,* the worship of false gods and abuses within their own religious rituals, is also condemned. We'd expect the prophets to be hard on the people of Israel when they worship gods other than the Lord. They are even stronger when it comes to the worship of the Lord that is only empty ritual. Amos and Micah draw social and cultic sin together. They condemn the cult of their people because it makes them too comfortable and distracts them from the injustices of their society.
3. These prophets take the common biblical belief that God acts in history and then they add to it. They teach that whatever actually happens is the work of God. They understood the destruction of the northern kingdom in 721 B.C. and the southern kingdom of Judah in 587/6 B.C. as acts of divine judgment.
4. Salvation and restoration become more prominent after the exile but they are also evident in earlier prophets, most notably Hosea. It is appropriate to talk of restoration after a time of destruction. Very often the prophets imagine a situation that is very dif-

ferent from the present. This is the case especially with the postexilic prophets when they are trying to encourage the people in the rebuilding of the Temple. The phrase "on that day" often introduces prophecies of transformation. The reader needs to be aware that some of these messages of hope may have been added at a later date by the editors of the prophetic books.

Taken as a whole, the Book of the Twelve is both a reflection on the past and a lesson for the future. The editors of the prophetic books were heavily influenced by the theology of Deuteronomy which, briefly stated is: Sin does not go unpunished, but God is ultimately merciful and wants only the repentance and restoration of Israel. This call to repentance can be heard throughout this collection.

HOSEA READING GUIDE

At a Glance

When	8th century B.C.
Where	Northern kingdom of Israel
Main Focus	Fidelity to the God of the covenant

Hosea's work appears first in the collection of minor prophets, sometimes called The Book of the Twelve. Although not chronologically first, Hosea provides a good introduction to these prophets. He is unrivaled for the beauty of his poetry and the emotional power of his oracles.

Hosea lived at a time of great difficulty and instability for the northern kingdom of Israel, caused by the westward expansion of the mighty Assyrian empire. During Hosea's time Assyria moved from merely being a threat to actually bringing about the end of the northern kingdom in 722 B.C. Even before this tragic date, there was unrest in the kingdom. In the 14 years between the death of Jeroboam II and 722, five kings ruled.

We get an insight into the personal life of Hosea from his use of the metaphor of marriage. Like some of the other prophets, he uses metaphor not just as a matter of spoken or written words; his life itself conveys his message. This speaks clearly of his total involvement in his prophecy. Even his children are given symbolic names, "not pitied" (Lo-ruhama, 1,6) and "not my people" (Lo-ammi, 1,8). The prophet and his family are living signs of God's concern for the welfare of his people.

Outline of the Book of Hosea

Hosea is usually divided into two parts:

Hos 1–3	The metaphor of marriage		
Hos 4–14	Oracles of Israel's destruction		
	Two exceptions:	Prophecy of restoration	11,8–11
		Invitation to repentance	14,2–9

ESSAY

MSL: Metaphor as a Second Language

The study of any type of literature would be enhanced by a good course on metaphor. This is especially true for the study of the Bible. This need for the language of metaphor, image, or symbol comes from the Bible itself. In order to respond to the thinking of the biblical writers, to get to their message, one must be able to use this language because it was their language. The need also arises from our modern pragmatic, conceptual approach. As one participant in an adult Bible study class said, "Can't you skip the flowery stuff and cut to the bottom line? Tell us what it means."

Metaphor is especially appropriate to convey meaning in the Bible because it reminds us that we are dealing with the divine, with a reality that can never be fully understood. This is one way of describing *mystery.* A mystery is not something that our reason cannot grasp; it does not put an end to our efforts to comprehend it. Rather, it is a never-ending process of coming to new understanding. The love of God for us is a mystery, not because we cannot understand what love is, but because we cannot comprehend the fullness of God's love, no matter how hard we try. When Israel tried to put into words how God had entered into relationship with them or how God acted in their history, they were at a loss for words. The language of metaphor at least allowed them to point to the reality that was beyond what was tangible or measurable.

The Bible is full of metaphors. In Hosea we have a prime example of the beauty of metaphorical language and its power to convey meaning that is almost beyond our power to communicate. Perhaps his most famous is the "lived metaphor" of his marriage to Gomer, which portrays Israel as the unfaithful spouse. In other places he compares Israel to a "cake unturned" (7,8), a "wild ass" (8,9), or a "luxuriant vine" (10,1). These examples have an emotional effect that evokes a response in the reader because of the many associations they carry.

Another striking example is in Chapter 11 of Hosea which begins, "When Israel was a child I loved him." The reference is to the Exodus event, but the effect is very different from our response to the Pentateuch. By portraying Israel as a child, Hosea paints a vivid picture of God as the loving parent, teaching the infant to walk and lifting it up. The comparison strongly implies that Israel should have the same kind of bond with the Lord that a toddler has with its parents.

The metaphorical language of the Bible points the reader to something beyond our ability to completely understand, to the mystery of God.

THE METAPHOR OF HOSEA'S MARRIAGE (CHAPTERS 1–3)

The Lord's first recorded words to Hosea capture the power of this metaphor, "Go take a harlot wife . . .". It may be that Gomer was not a harlot at the time of her marriage to Hosea. However, many scholars see the choice of a harlot wife as a deliberate symbolic act on the part of the prophet. And if, as some think, Gomer was not only a prostitute but a cult prostitute serving the pagan god Baal (see below), then Hosea's action is even more dramatic. In any case, the prophet's message is clear: Israel's behavior toward God is like that of an unfaithful spouse. This metaphor illustrates several significant insights:

1. *Covenant*

   Hosea believes that God and Israel are bound together by the covenant given to Moses, symbolized here by the marriage covenant, an agreement that forms the basis of a relationship. Hosea's words, "you are my people" and "My God" (2,25), recall not only the standard marriage formula but the covenant language of Exodus as well.

2. *Idolatry and Infidelity*

   A major problem addressed by Hosea was idolatry, specifically the cult of the Canaanite god Baal. Baal was a real temptation for the people because he was a fertility god who was supposed to guarantee the productivity of the land, animals, and people. Think about how much farmers and ranchers depend on good weather for their livelihood and you get a feel for the strength of this temptation.

   The worship of Baal may have included sexual acts with prostitutes. If Gomer was such a prostitute, then Hosea's comparison was all the more pronounced: Israel's covenant with the Lord, understood as marriage, contrasted with the worship of Baal, understood as prostitution. Gomer exemplified the behavior of Israel, by straying from the marital relationship.

   Hosea was not concerned just with Israel's participation in the Baal fertility rites. Her infidelity was more pervasive, as he says in 4,1–3:

   > There is no fidelity, no mercy,
   > no knowledge of God in the land.
   > False swearing, lying, murder, stealing and adultery!
   > in their lawlessness, bloodshed follows bloodshed.
   > Therefore, the land mourns . . .

   According to Hosea, one cannot pick and choose when it comes to the Lord. As we say of some things today, "It's a package deal." When the Israelites acknowledge the Lord as lord, they have to accept the covenant code of ethics as well.

3. *Understanding of God*

   Hosea understands God as the best in human nature, only more so. And, for him, a faithful marriage is the culmination of love between a man and a woman. Therefore, the love between the Lord and Israel is best understood as a faithful marriage.

LAND AND DESERT

While Hosea is developing the marriage metaphor, he weaves in the familiar Exodus images of the promised land and the desert with all their rich associations. This allows him to accomplish several things in a short space:

1. He recalls the foundational experience of Exodus/Covenant that gave Israel its identity as a people. This reminds the people of what is really important, their covenant with God.

ESSAY

Concentric Circle Thinking and Writing

Sometimes reading the Bible can be confusing. For example, you might be reading along focusing on one idea and a new image is introduced, and even another. Or, you are reading a text and you think, "Haven't I read this before?" What at first seems confusing can really be helpful to understanding the biblical message.

This could be called concentric circle thinking or writing. It is a way of organizing information that many of the biblical writers felt at home with, though it may seem strange to us. The way we've been taught to think or reason is more linear; you go through certain steps in a particular order and you come to a conclusion, at least most of the time. The people who produced the Bible generally thought in a more circular fashion. It doesn't mean that they weren't logical; it's a different kind of logic.

Picture someone throwing a rock into a pond or lake. When the rock hits the water there is a splash—that's the main point of the writer. Then a circle appears and begins to expand—the development of the main point. Another circle appears and moves out—a related idea is added and developed. Soon there are several concentric circles all visible and moving at the same time.

The book of the prophet Hosea is a good example of this; his images sometimes seem to be tumbling over one another. In Chapter 2, Hosea is in the process of developing the marriage metaphor, comparing Israel to his own unfaithful wife. Then he brings in the image of the desert, then back to his harlot wife. Several lines later he is talking about laying waste her vines and fig trees, building a wall against her, then leading her into the desert to allure her. Later on there's talk of the covenant and more marriage talk and several more images in between. Finally the chapter ends with two quotes, "You are my people," and the response, "My God!"

By going around and around and bringing in all kinds of familiar words and images, Hosea is pleading with his people to once again be faithful to the Lord who is faithful to them. He has already said that God is like a faithful spouse; he brings up the desert to remind them of God's saving action on their behalf and of the covenant relationship. He warns them about how destructive unfaithfulness can be to a relationship. Even though he knows that they won't really listen and will suffer the consequences, he sows the seeds of hope.

When you are reading this circular kind of structuring, it is important to remember not to get caught in trying to figure out what is first, second, or third. Let the images circle around. Through the use of a commentary, try to find out what the people of Hosea's time would have heard when these words were spoken or read to them. Let the message just sink in.

2. The prophet focuses on the gift of the land "flowing with milk and honey," the primary symbol of salvation from ancient times. This is where the prophet delivers the threat with full force: The land will be reduced to a desert. Since there is no belief in an afterlife at this time, to lose the land is to undo the Exodus. The expression, "to have the rug pulled out from under you," is apt. For Israel it was that and more.
3. Hosea transforms the desert image; it is not only a place of wandering and death but a place where a man might court a young woman in privacy. He is suggesting that away from the cult of Baal and other abuses, after being stripped down by the Assyrians, something new is possible, a new Exodus.

So, hope is introduced. It may not be full-fledged, flag-waving hope, but it is there. After all, Hosea is a realist. Second Isaiah (Is 40–55) will develop this new Exodus theme after the Exile, and it reappears in the Dead Sea Scrolls and in the New Testament.

Questions for Discussion or Reflection

1. An important lesson we learn from Hosea has to do with theological method, that is, that the way to knowledge of God is through the observation of human experience.
   a. How is God like a faithful spouse, a loving parent, a friend seeking an enduring relationship?
   b. What does infidelity do to human relationships? Would the same things apply to our relationship to God?

2. Words Worth Pondering and Remembering from Hosea, 11,1–4:

"When Israel was a child, I loved him,
  out of Egypt I called my son.
The more I called them,
  the farther they went from me,
Sacrificing to the Baals
  and burning incense to idols.
Yet it was I who taught Ephraim to walk,
  who took them in my arms;
I drew them with human cords,
  with bands of love;
I fostered them like one
  who raises an infant to his cheeks;
Yet, though I stooped to feed my child,
  they did not know that I was their healer."

Memorize this passage as a reminder to yourself that the God of the Old Testament cannot be characterized only as a harsh God, as sometimes happens.

JOEL READING GUIDE

At a Glance

When	Around 400 B.C.
Where	Judah
Main Focus	Universal judgment

The Book of Joel gives no references to known historical events to indicate when it was written. There are indications, however, that point to a time of deprivation and exploitation, probably after the Babylonian exile, around 400 B.C. The reference in 4,6 to Jews sold into slavery suggests a time when Judah was weak and a time when contacts between Greeks and the Near East were increasing. Also, the apocalyptic imagery of the Day of the Lord and judgment of the nations is characteristic of the period after the exile. These circumstances are significant for understanding why the prophet predicts cosmic upheaval and radical change.

Outline of the Book of Joel

The book moves from specific concern with the plague of locusts to a more general prophecy of universal judgment:

Jl 1,1 – 2,17	The plague of locusts and prayer for deliverance
Jl 2,18–27	Reply and reassurance from God
Jl 3	Future time when God will intercede
Jl 4	Final judgment of the nations and salvation for the elect

THE DAY OF THE LORD

The theme of the Day of the Lord runs through the book as a unifying thread. This theme with its two related aspects, the vision of plenty and the desire for vengeance, is important for understanding Joel's message.

In Amos (8th century B.C.), the meaning of the Day of the Lord shifts from the original festive day to one of a day of darkness, not light. By the time the Book of Joel was written, any great disaster might be called a "Day of the Lord."

In developing this theme, Joel starts with something specific, the plague of locusts. He takes something that was surely terrible and uses it to teach the people what the real disaster, the Day of the Lord, will be like. The locust plague is a rehearsal, an image of the end of the world, the day of judgment of the nations.

The locusts transform the land from being like the "garden of Eden" to a "desert waste" (2,3). Joel also describes them as an invading army, with the Lord at their head (2,11), affirming the conviction that whatever happens is the work of God. The people respond to the plague in a way typical of the ancient world, by bringing offerings and libations. Joel also responds typically, like other Hebrew prophets, by turning the crisis into an occasion for reform and repentance. In 2,13 we find a classic expression of the prophetic view of proper ritual: "Rend your hearts, not your garments."

In our day we do not usually regard natural disasters as visitations from God, or seek relief primarily through rituals. But in Joel's time, the situation was beyond human control. The ritual was the only thing they could do. It was a way of expressing their desperation and their hope that God would give them relief. And the prophet, by urging reform, was trying to bring some good out of a bad situation. This is a good example of the "here and now" attitude of the prophets. For them, salvation is primarily concerned with the welfare of the people on earth.

In Chapter 3, the Day of the Lord takes on a different meaning. It now refers to the Day of Judgment and the passage suggests the end of the world: "The sun will be turned to darkness, and the moon to blood, . . ." (3,4). We are dealing here with the language of metaphor. The darkening of the sun and moon is a way of expressing a time of tumult and confusion; the world as we have known it will be turned upside down. Unlike later apocalyptic writers, who took the image of the end of the world literally, Joel looks for a transformation of this world rather than a new creation.

Vision of Plenty

Joel's hope for the transformation of the earth is captured in his prediction of a time of plenty. It is a natural reaction to the locust plague and also appeals to the universal hope for freedom from hunger. In a time of scarcity, Joel comforts his people with the promise that they will eat and be filled (2,26). This is very common in the prophets and serves two functions: It gives hope to the poor and it gives a goal for people to work toward.

Vengeance on the Nations

The occasional desire for vengeance in the Hebrew scriptures can be distasteful to Christians, though not unknown to their experience. Joel's presentation of Judah's desire for vengeance recalls the "eye for an eye" attitude. It is not enough that Judah flow with wine and milk; the hated neighbor Edom must be a desert waste (4,19). If their enemy sold Jews into slavery, then the enemy's children must be sold. Some prophets called for peace, calling the people to beat their swords into plowshares (Is 2,4; Mi 4,3); Joel calls for a showdown.

Vengeance is not noble, but it is understandable in some situations. We must not overlook the fact that the prophet's call for vengeance is a call for justice. In Joel it is a protest of the powerless who had seen their children sold into slavery.

Perhaps we could apply that characteristic insight of the prophets, discerning the good within a bad situation, to vengeance. If poor, oppressed people in our day express a desire for vengeance, wanting to see the tables turned on their more powerful neighbors, maybe our reaction might be tempered by our reading of the prophets. Is their situation, their desperation due to injustice?

Questions for Discussion or Reflection

1. Try this as an examination of conscience about vengeance. For one week be aware of all the people who might feel like "turning the tables" on you. Some might be very personal; others might be directed toward you as a member of a group. For example:
    - people of a different cultural or religious group;
    - people of third world countries;

- people who come to the soup kitchen;
- someone who works for the competition;
- checkers/cashiers at the grocery store;
- waiters and waitresses;
- secretaries;
- ushers at ball games/movies.

2. Words Worth Pondering and Remembering from Joel 2,13:

   "Rend your hearts, not your garments,
   and return to the LORD, your God."

   What attitudes of my heart need to be changed in order to return to the Lord? Remember, for those who heard Joel, "heart" meant the very center of a person, where decisions are made.

AMOS READING GUIDE

At a Glance

When	8th century B.C.
Where	Northern kingdom of Israel
Main Focus	Social justice: All equal before God

AMOS, THE PROPHET

Only one episode of Amos's career is recounted in this book. Although he came from the southern kingdom of Judah, Amos proclaimed his oracles in the northern kingdom, especially around the temple of Bethel. (After the northern tribes split off from Judah to form their own kingdom, King Jeroboam set up two official sanctuaries at Dan and Bethel to discourage people from worshiping at the Jerusalem Temple.) Amaziah, the priest at Bethel, was worried because Amos was prophesying against the king in the temple precincts. The priest could not afford to offend the king, so he told Amos to go back to Judah. The reply of Amos (7,14) about not being a prophet, nor belonging to a company of prophets, until the Lord called him, points to his independence. He did not have to rely for support on the priest or the king. He could take care of himself working as a shepherd or a dresser of sycamores (a kind of fig tree).

This independence, added to his obvious personal conviction, gave rise to a style that is blunt and sometimes offensive. He calls the women of Samaria "cows of Bashan" (4,1) and tells the priest that his wife will be a harlot in the city (7,17). He had nothing to gain by soft-pedaling his message. He was not a trusted adviser to the king, as the prophet Nathan was to David; and as an outsider, he had no hope of influencing the upper classes. He simply proclaims the doom that is coming.

AMOS AND THE COVENANT

Amos consistently treats Israel the same as the other nations in the sight of God. Did the prophet consider Israel as a chosen nation and, therefore, special in any sense? Certainly Amos considered the Exodus as fundamental to Israel's identity, but this did not give the Israelites any guarantees nor put them into a position of privilege. Rather, it gave them more responsibility.

Two passages make this very clear. Chapter 3, verse 2 says, "You alone have I favored; more than all the families of the earth." The modern-day reader is probably surprised to read the verse that follows: "Therefore I will punish you for all your crimes." Amos's audience was no doubt shocked and maybe even angered. This was not what they wanted to hear. Similarly and even more bluntly, we read in 9,7: "Did I not bring the Israelites from the land of Egypt as I brought the Philistines from Caphtor and the Arameans from Kir?" Israel is special but so is every other nation.

ORGANIZATION OF THE BOOK

Outline of the Book of Amos

Am 1–2	Oracles against the nations ending with a denunciation of Israel
Am 3,1 – 5,9	"Words" – three long oracles (strings of short utterances). Note that verses 7–9 are out of order.
Am 5,7 – 6,14	Three "woes" against Israel and Judah
Am 7,1 – 9,8b	Visions of destruction
Am 9,8c–15	An epilogue, probably added later

Oracles Against the Nations (Chapters 1–2)

The book begins with oracles of judgment against Israel's immediate neighbors (present-day Lebanon, Syria, Jordan, and part of the occupied territory of Palestine). It is not unusual for a prophet to denounce other nations, but what is unusual is that Amos goes on to pronounce a similar judgment on Israel. He insists that Israel is no different from other nations in the eyes of God. According to Amos, any nation that sins against humanity deserves punishment. Moab is condemned for burning to lime the bones of the King of Edom (2,1); Israel is condemned for selling the just man for silver and the poor man for a pair of sandals (2,6).

The oracle in 2,6–16 is in the form of a speech in which a "lawsuit" is brought against Israel for failing to keep the Sinai covenant. This style of writing follows a pattern: recalling God's action on behalf of Israel in the Exodus; pointing out Israel's unfaithfulness in not keeping the commandments; usually issuing a threat. Many scholars think that this recollection of the Exodus may have been added by an editor of the prophetic books who wanted to put the prophetic preaching in the context of the theology of Deuteronomy as found in the Books of Joshua, Judges, Samuel, and Kings. This opinion seems reasonable because Amos's own focus was broader. He believed that people of any nation are bound by the requirements of justice, whether or not they know the law of Moses. In other words, Amos affirms the natural law as it was understood in the ancient Near East. Paul makes the same point in the first chapter of

Romans when he says that pagan idolaters have no excuse, "for what can be known about God is evident to them."

> **Editor at Work**
>
> An example of one way scholars discover the hand of an editor at work is found in the lawsuit speech (2,6–16). Here, one could say, the clue is theological. Throughout the oracles, Amos denounces Israel and the neighboring nations for behavior that is anti-human or against nature. The prophet's messages were not limited to those bound by the law of Moses. So, when the oracle is presented in a covenant pattern typical of the theology of Deuteronomy, a flag goes up for the interpreter with the question, "Is this Amos or a later editor fitting Amos into a specific theological view?"
>
> Other clues that might attract attention have to do with vocabulary, writing style, and historical references. One who is thoroughly familiar with a particular biblical text in the original language will notice words, phrases, or ways of expression that are not typical of the work as a whole and will ask the question. Similarly, if something that seems more at home in the 5th century shows up in an 8th-century document, it is likely some editorial work has been done.

Words and Woes (3,1 – 6,14)

The three "words" of Amos are really a string of shorter oracles, mainly concerned with Israel's sins. There is a short section in 3,3–8, however, that is important because it focuses for the reader part of what Amos believes about God. This kind of insight helps the reader in understanding the rest of the prophet's work.

For Amos, everything that happens is God's doing. The order in nature is God's design. Nothing happens by chance. The acts of God in history are not confined to special events but take in everything, good as well as bad. (There was no devil in Israel's religion at this time to blame for the evil in the world.) This basic conviction about God accounts for Amos's interpretation of political events. For example, if Assyria is more powerful than Israel, this is not by chance; it is God's will. All this is another way of saying that Amos is a radical monotheist; he not only ignores other gods, but he attributes everything that happens to the God of Israel.

In both the "words and the woes," Amos criticizes the cult of Israel, its religious rituals and practices. In 4,4, he uses a pun, a play on words, to make his point. The words for "sin-offering" and "sin" in Hebrew are so similar that the people would, no doubt, understand Amos's implication, that they come to the sanctuary at Bethel to sin, rather than to make an offering for sin.

The prophet's sharpest critique of the cult is the "woe" against those who yearn for the Day of the Lord (5,18–25). This yearning was expressed in a major harvest festival in the fall, an occasion celebrating the victory of the God of Israel and the defeat of God's enemies. Amos turns a celebration into its opposite, a day of judgment. He was the first prophet to speak of the Day of the Lord as a day of judgment on Israel.

Amos goes on to issue a broadside against all the festivals of Israel. His point is not that all ritual is necessarily bad, but that ritual is not the essence of religion. The essence of religion is social justice. If ritual furthers justice, well and good, but too often it does not. Amos thought that ritual made the upper classes complacent, so much so that they thought that God would protect them no matter what and that they need not be concerned about the plight of the poor. They could leave the festival and go back to cheating in the marketplace (8,5). Amos labels all this as self-delusion.

In the final "woe" in Chapter 6, Amos predicts that the upper classes of both kingdoms, "the complacent in Zion [and] the overconfident on the mount of Samaria," would be the first to go into exile. They had sold the poor into slavery while they lived in luxury. Amos knew what he was talking about; he knew that the practice of the Assyrians was to take the upper classes into exile so there would be no one left to organize a revolt. In his view, it was a fate they richly deserved.

Visions of Destruction (7,1 – 9,8b)

Amos is so moved by the enormity of the destruction he envisions that, at first, he intercedes and God relents. Once again, using a play on words, he makes the point that the time for forgiveness has run out. The vision is of a basket of ripe fruit. The Hebrew for "ripe fruit" is similar to the word for "end," so, "the time is ripe" (8,2) can be translated "the end has come."

This was the first time that the idea of the "end" was proclaimed in ancient Israel. For Amos, the end was the end of Israel as an independent nation that had existed for 200 years. It was primarily the Israel of the upper classes that would end. The peasants would continue to suffer under Assyria but, for them, it probably didn't make much difference whether they paid taxes to a foreign power or to oppressive Israelite landlords. For Amos and for the peasants, what mattered was not political identity but the living conditions of the poor within society.

Epilogue (9,8c–15)

Another example of the work of an editor is found in the epilogue. The force of Amos's prophecy was in its finality, as we read in the last line before the epilogue (9,8a and b), "The eyes of the Lord God are on this sinful kingdom: I will destroy it from off the face of the earth." In the very next line, a later editor adds, "But I will not destroy the house of Jacob completely, says the Lord."

The editor puts the prophecy of Amos in a broader historical perspective, that of the whole of Israel. The message of the prophets of Israel, in general, was not of destruction but of hope. Death and destruction have their place and time, but hope remains. Ultimate optimism is an essential ingredient of biblical faith.

Questions for Discussion or Reflection

1. In the ancient world it was the role of the prophet to be the conscience of the nation and to speak up for the powerless.
   a. Who are the powerless of our day?
   b. Who speaks for them? Religious leaders? Social workers?
   c. Do you ever feel responsible to speak for the powerless? Discuss/journal your answer.

2. Words Worth Pondering and Remembering from Amos, 5,23–24:

"Away with your noisy songs!
I will not listen to the melodies of your harps.
But if you would offer me holocausts,
then let justice surge like water,
and goodness like an unfailing stream."

How would you answer someone who said that justice issues have no place in worship?

OBADIAH READING GUIDE

At a Glance

When	6th or early 5th century B.C.
Where	Judah
Main Focus	Vengeance

The Book of Obadiah gives no information about the prophet, but the oracles against Edom indicate that the prophecy comes at the time when the Jews were returning to Judah from exile in Babylon.

Edom (later called Idumaea) was a small state to the south of Judah. The Edomites took advantage of Judah after the Babylonian invasion and pillaged their land. The hatred between Judah and Edom was still strong after the exile, as seen in these oracles. Long after Edom ceased to be a threat to the Jews, the rabbis used the name Edom as a code word for Rome, the hated enemy of their day.

Outline of the Book of Obadiah

Obadiah is the shortest of the prophetic books with only 21 verses:

Verses 1–14	Short oracles against Edom
Verses 15–16	An oracle against all the nations
Verses 17–21	Prediction of restoration for Judah

ORACLES AGAINST EDOM AND THE NATIONS (1–16)

Oracles of vengeance against Edom were common in the time after the Exile (compare Jer 49,7–22; Joel 4,19). Obadiah then extends this vengeance to all the nations. The basic message of these oracles is stated clearly in verse 15, "As you have done, so it shall be done to you."

Once more the reader is challenged to deal with the notion of vengeance. The prophet says that if you do violence to your neighbors and gloat over their distress, you deserve the same treatment. When the prophet extends the attack beyond Edom to all the nations, he uses the familiar motif of the Day of the Lord. Here it refers to the day of judgment, not the end of the world. The judgment is based on the law of retribution: As you have done, so it will be done to you.

THE RESTORATION OF JUDAH (17–21)

Modest hope is expressed at the end of Obadiah. Judah will rule over its neighbors and this kingdom will be the Lord's. There is a slight notion of vengeance in this image of the kingdom, but the hope for the survival of the people is far more significant.

Questions for Discussion or Reflection

Words Worth Pondering and Remembering from Obadiah, verse 15b:

> "As you have done, so shall it be done to you,
> your deed shall come back upon your own head."

Compare this expression of vengeance to the so-called golden rule: "Do to others whatever you would have them do to you." Have you ever thought of the golden rule as an expression of vengeance or retribution?

JONAH READING GUIDE

At a Glance

When	Set in 8th century B.C., written in 5th century B.C.
Where	Judah
Main Focus	God's mercy

Jonah is unique among the prophetic books. It is a story rather than a series of oracles. Jonah is himself a sort of anti-prophet: His actions are the opposite of what we expect of prophets. The story is more a fable, because of the role of the fish (like the animals in Aesop's fables). It's also a parable, a short story that goes against the expected. (See the discussion of Parables in the New Testament Reading Guides, pp. RG 311–314). It is clearly meant to be humorous. It was written sometime in the postexilic period, but has a different outlook from other writings of that period.

The chapter headings reveal the outline of the book. The long psalm in Chapter 2 was probably added by a later editor, who focused on the miracle of Jonah's survival.

To appreciate Jonah we need to consider that:

1. the book is deliberately humorous;
2. it is about the proper attitude to foreign nations, not about Jonah's miraculous escape from drowning;
3. the story is mildly critical of the religious zeal usually connected with prophecy.

THE STORY'S HUMOR

The humor is apparent from verse one: A prophet shamelessly disobeys a divine command; pagan sailors fear the Lord of Israel; wicked Assyrians and even animals repent; a fish swallows a man and then spits him up on the shore.

The author is not interested in historical plausibility; he uses this fantastic tale to teach a theological lesson. Ironically, in this "prophetic book", the prophet is not given the dignity usually associated with the office, nor are his convictions taken seriously. The reader is asked to reconsider the stereotype of both pagan and prophet.

THE ATTITUDE TO FOREIGN NATIONS

The wickedness of Assyria is the premise of this story, and Jonah is upset at being sent to preach to those who seem not to deserve God's mercy. Incredibly, the Assyrians repent and Jonah questions whether they deserve divine forgiveness. One might react thus if the leaders of some dictatorial regime made a show of repentance for their crimes and were pardoned. It is not that Jonah is exceptionally narrow-minded, but rather that his God is exceptionally tolerant. To God the Creator, Assyrians are as important as Israelites (or, in our terms, no racial or ethnic group is beyond redemption).

The last verse of the book recognizes that ordinary Assyrians are no more guilty of the crimes of their nation than are the cattle. In any case, guilt or innocence is not the point; the astonishing magnanimity of God is the message. The Book of Jonah sees God in the same terms as the much later Book of Wisdom 11,24: "For you love all things that are and loathe nothing that you have made, for what you hated, you would not have fashioned." The penitent Assyrian is as great a contradiction as the "good Samaritan" of the Gospel, and as hard to accept, given the situation of the Jews of the postexilic period in which the book was written.

THE PERSPECTIVE ON PROPHETIC ZEAL

Jonah reacts to God's mercy by sulking and praying for death (4,8). He is a prophet in the same mold as Elijah who, with great zeal for destroying sinners, had done the same in 1 Kgs 19,4f. But the Book of Jonah sees the limitations of prophetic zeal. Jonah is well-intentioned and acts out of a long tradition, but God rebukes him mildly. Earlier, Hosea had broadened the tradition by recognizing that it is more fitting for God to have mercy than to punish. This book goes further and extends that mercy to foreign nations. Even prophets must learn that reconciliation is a higher value than strict retribution. Not all the prophetic books reflect this insight, but it is the view affirmed for Christianity in the Gospels.

The Sign of Jonah

The episode in the belly of the fish, a minor humorous motif in the story, acquires greater meaning in later tradition. It is taken to prefigure (Mt 12,39f) Jesus' time in the tomb. Jonah is a frequent symbol of the Resurrection in early Christian art. In Chapter 2 the belly of the fish is equated with the netherworld, and Jonah's regret about being there is that he is separated from God's presence. Jonah asks to be restored to that presence, which is the fullness of life for most Old Testament writers.

The Relevance of Jonah

Jonah's message is as urgent in today's world as it was in his time. It teaches us not only tolerance and understanding for those who are different from us, but also forgiveness for those who have truly behaved wickedly, if they are willing to accept it.

The sign of Jonah is a sign of hope that we can afford to forgive the injustices of life. The wicked deeds of the oppressor are not as final as they seem. Belief in resurrection is often associated with a hope for the damnation of the wicked. The Book of Jonah, read in the light of the New Testament and Christian tradition, suggests that resurrection can also give a larger perspective on life, one which has room for tolerance and forgiveness.

Questions for Discussion or Reflection

1. Jonah's message of tolerance and forgiveness is a hard word and should not be sentimentalized. Perhaps it could prompt us to pray often for the grace to be tolerant and to forgive. It might focus our prayer and strengthen our petition if we brought to our prayer those individuals and groups that we think deserve to be punished. Describe a difficult situation that was solved or at least relieved by using humor. What exactly does humor contribute to a tense situation?
2. How do you respond when something good happens to someone you consider a rival or a competitor (it could be a neighbor, a co-worker or a sibling)? What does the message of Jonah say about your response?

MICAH READING GUIDE

At a Glance

When	8th century B.C.
Where	Southern kingdom of Judah
Main Focus	Social justice and honesty

Micah, in his role as prophet, resembles Jeremiah. He spoke out against prophets who wanted to be popular. They said what people wanted to hear and were more concerned about their own well-being than that of the nation. Micah saw the role of the true prophet "to declare to Jacob his crimes and to Israel his sins" (3,8). Because of this position, Micah stands as a lonely figure. Like Jeremiah, he was not successful in reaching the people, but trusted that God would vindicate him (7,7–10).

Outline of the Book of Micah

Mi 1–3	Impending judgment
Mi 4–5	(Added later) Restoration
Mi 6	Indictment of Israel
Mi 7	The prophet's reflection

THE IMPENDING JUDGMENT (CHAPTERS 1–3)

Micah begins with a description of an apparition of God. In Israel's tradition, such appearances of God were associated with God's saving action, for example, as on Sinai. But in Micah, God is not coming to save but to judge. Eighth-century Israel experiences God's presence in the invasion of the Assyrian army rather than in Sinai's fire and earthquake. According to Micah, the destruction would center on Jerusalem and Samaria, home to the royalty and ruling classes.

In Chapter 2, the prophet gives the reason for the coming destruction: The rich force the small property owners into debt and eventually seize their property. It is only right, says Micah, that the Assyrians will seize the land from the rich.

In Chapter 3, Micah attacks the complacency and illusion of some religious teaching and practice. It is not enough to say that no evil can come upon Israel because the Lord is in its midst. Such faith is not virtue for Micah. Virtue is in the practice of justice and in facing reality honestly. Faith cannot be based on any religious institution, no matter how sacred. Micah's prophecy that Zion would be plowed like a field was not what people wanted to hear. The prophecy was not fulfilled in Micah's time, but his words were justified later.

THE PROPHECIES OF RESTORATION (CHAPTERS 4–5)

As indicated above, these prophecies of restoration were probably added to Micah after the Babylonian exile. Two of them in particular show us the work of the postexilic editor. The prophecy of the restoration of the house of the Lord in Micah 4,1–3 is also found in Isaiah 2,24. The idea of nations streaming to Jerusalem is not new, but it speaks of the time after the exile when Jews who lived in other lands came to Jerusalem on pilgrimage. The placement of this prophecy immediately after the prediction that Zion would become a plowed field is typical of the editors of the prophetic books. They often spoke of hope after destruction or judgment. In the same way, the Temple and its rituals had taken on too much importance in the 8th century; now, after the exile, the Temple has a potential for uniting the people and strengthening faith.

The prophecy about Bethlehem in Micah 5,1–4 is familiar to Christians for obvious reasons. The postexilic editor had at least two reasons for inserting it here. First, to build up hope, suggesting that David's kingly line would be restored. But, second, by mentioning Bethlehem rather than Jerusalem, the editor is pointing to a humbler, more simple monarchy free of big-city corruption.

THE INDICTMENT OF ISRAEL (CHAPTER 6)

Micah recalls the covenant, God's faithfulness, and Israel's failure in a speech that sounds like a courtroom scene (compare Amos 2). The prophet returns to the themes of justice and honesty in his indictment of Israel's false religion, which included performing rituals to further their own interests.

Micah's solutions sound simple on the surface. True religion is not based on certain rituals or beliefs, only this, "to do the right and to love goodness, and to walk humbly with your God" (6,8). Notice the emphasis on action.

Questions for Discussion or Reflection

1. Notice the power of Micah's image, that Zion will be like a plowed field. In the context of the approaching Assyrian invasion it feels like total destruction. On the other hand, a description of a freshly plowed field can have a positive sense of growth, harvest, and prosperity. Don't pass over the biblical images too quickly.
   a. How is it possible that one event can be both destructive and life-giving?
   b. What might we learn from such an event?
2. Words Worth Pondering and Remembering from Micah, 6,8:

   "You have been told, O man, what is good,
   and what the LORD requires of you:
   Only to do the right and to love goodness,
   and to walk humbly with your God."

   Micah would probably not be happy that these words have been put to music and are used in many churches unless the song moves people to acts of justice.

NAHUM READING GUIDE

At a Glance

When	612 B.C.
Where	Judah
Main Focus	Fall of Nineveh

Outline of the Book of Nahum

Na 1,2 – 2,1.3 The Lord's coming in judgment
Na 2,2 – 3,19 The fall of Nineveh

NAHUM'S MESSAGE

Nahum's sole concern is the fall of the Assyrian capital city of Nineveh. The prophet is euphoric:

> "See, upon the mountains there advances
> the bearer of good news, announcing peace!
> Celebrate. . . . For nevermore shall you be
> invaded by the scoundrel . . . (2,1)."

It is characteristic of biblical prophecy that the fall of one Gentile nation at the hands of another is assumed to be the work of the Lord.

A JEALOUS GOD

The opening verse of Nahum's prophecy is somewhat shocking to modern ears: "A jealous and avenging God is the Lord" (1,2). However, this image of God is neither new nor incompatible with a God of mercy and love. In the Book of Exodus, the Lord is called a "warrior" (15,3) and described as jealous on Sinai (20,50). Even Nahum, in the very next verse after "jealous and avenging," says that "The LORD is slow to anger . . ." (1,3).

The modern reader could, no doubt, benefit by taking on the ancient Hebrew's ability to deal with ambiguity when it comes to God. This means letting diverse or seemingly contradictory statements about God stand side by side. It is an acknowledgment that God is beyond our ability to completely explain. It also allows God's wrath to be seen as an expression of justice.

A SHORT-SIGHTED PROPHECY

Judah's freedom, proclaimed by Nahum, was short-lived. It was only 15 years before another oppressor would lay siege to Jerusalem. Nahum's short prophecy is a lesson in realistic hope; no power lasts forever, but neither is complete freedom attained in this life.

Nahum's influence can be seen in the Book of Revelation. John uses the image of the harlot from Nahum (3,4) in anticipating the fall of Rome.

Questions for Discussion or Reflection

Words Worth Pondering and Remembering from Nahum, 1, 2a.3a.7:

> "A jealous and avenging God is the LORD,
> an avenger is the LORD, and angry; . . .
> The LORD is slow to anger, yet great in power,
> and the LORD never leaves the guilty unpunished. . . .
> The LORD is good, a refuge on the day of distress;
> He takes care of those who have recourse to him, . . ."

Try the both/and approach when thinking about God. See how many times you can fill in the blanks:

God is both ______________ and ______________.

HABAKKUK READING GUIDE

At a Glance

When	605–597 B.C.
Where	Judah
Main Focus	Faith in God's justice

Outline of the Book of Habakkuk

Hb 1–2	A dialogue between the prophet and the Lord
Hb 3	A hymn of faith

THE DIALOGUE (CHAPTERS 1–2)

Habakkuk's prophecy comes shortly after that of Nahum (see timeline for Nahum), when the Babylonian threat was even more obvious, but Habakkuk is more reflective than Nahum. He reacts to the immediate danger but he also seeks to understand the problem. He asks the age-old questions: Why do the wicked prevail over the just? How can God allow such a situation to exist? Is God just? These types of questions, called theodicy or the effort to explain the existence of evil, are more typical of wisdom literature (particularly Job) and apocalyptic (see Apocalypse) literature than of prophecy.

Habakkuk was concerned first of all with the injustice within Jewish society. He applies the woes in Chapter 2 to the arrogant and wealthy. This section is similar to Chapter 22 of Jeremiah, written at about the same time (609–598 B.C.), accusing King Jehoiakim of oppression and exploitation. Habakkuk's woes could be directed to the king as well.

Habakkuk's answer to the questions of God's justice is not an explanation but a promise that the situation will be set aright in the future. At first the solution seems worse than the problem: God will raise up the Babylonians (1,6–11). Just as Isaiah (Chapter 10) had spoken of Assyria as the rod of the Lord's anger, Babylon will bring about the downfall of King Jehoiakim. The comparison to Isaiah continues in the implied hope of Habakkuk; like the rod which would eventually be destroyed, so too will Babylon. It is unclear in the prophecy whether Habakkuk is referring to Babylon or the wicked in Judah because their behavior is similar (the wicked devouring the just). The lesson, however, is clear. Even though justice is not apparent in the world, one should trust in the Lord and be patient.

RIGHTEOUSNESS AND FAITH (CHAPTER 3)

Faith according to Habakkuk might be closer to the traditional Christian understanding of hope. For the prophet, faith is simply the trust in God that enables one to wait for the future. The person who only looks at the present and sees no justice in the world and, therefore, judges that God is not in control lacks faith. The righteous or faithful one takes a longer view, trusts that justice will prevail, and is content to wait for it.

This hope in the future is expressed poetically in the hymn in Chapter 3. God, coming in triumph as a warrior, stands in a long tradition of such hymns (see Dt 33, Jgs 5, Mi 1). The early hymns of this kind referred to God's past activity on behalf of Israel. Habakkuk expects this in the future. It will be directed against "the people who attack us" (3,16), presumably the Babylonians but maybe the Jewish oppressors as well. The prophet envisages a decisive intervention of God to wipe out all wickedness and oppression. This whole description of the future is close to what we find later in the apocalyptic literature and explains why Habakkuk was popular in apocalyptic circles, for example, the Dead Sea Scrolls include a commentary on Habakkuk.

Questions for Discussion or Reflection

Words Worth Pondering and Remembering from Habakkuk, 2,3:

"For the vision still has its time,
presses on to fulfillment, and will not disappoint;
If it delays, wait for it,
it will surely come, it will not be late."

The faith of Habakkuk is a faith against appearances. It is a faith that encourages us to trust in God's activity in our midst. It is a faith that also encourages us to work against oppression and exploitation, especially when the task seems impossible. How is this a timely faith for us today?

ZEPHANIAH READING GUIDE

At a Glance

When	Reign of Josiah, 640–609 B.C.
Where	Judah
Main Focus	Day of the Lord

Zephaniah prophesied a little earlier than Nahum and Habakkuk and at the same time that Jeremiah was getting started, during the reign of Josiah who instituted the deuteronomic reform (2 Kgs 22–23). Idolatry is one of Zephaniah's themes, since purifying Temple worship was the focus of the reform, but almost everything is expressed in terms of the Day of the Lord.

A DAY OF JUDGMENT FOR JUDAH (CHAPTER 1)

The first oracle on the Day of the Lord is directed against Judah for idolatry and lack of faith in the Lord (1,12). Zephaniah emphasizes not the sins of Judah but the destructiveness of the Day of the Lord. It is portrayed in cosmic terms: God will make an end of all who live on earth. The day of judgment is a vindication of the majesty of God against the unworthiness of the people.

A DAY OF JUDGMENT ON THE NATIONS (CHAPTER 2)

Judah is not the only object of the Lord's wrath. Chapter 2 lists the surrounding nations, and seems to build up to Assyria, the most arrogant of all. The prophet quotes Nineveh's boast: "There is no other than I" (2,15), echoing that of Babylon a century earlier (Is 47,10). The most fundamental human sin is self-divinization, and it is seen again and again throughout the Bible. Zephaniah's prophecies of the Day of the Lord dramatize the gulf between God and humanity and are basically a put-down of human pride.

REPROACH AND PROMISE FOR JERUSALEM (CHAPTER 3)

Chapter 3 does not use the phrase "Day of the Lord" but deals with related themes. The phrase "on that day" (3,11) refers to the Day of the Lord and is often used to introduce additions to the prophetic books in this period after the exile.

Jerusalem is denounced as the tyrannical city that accepts no correction (3,1–8), which may refer to the failure of the reform or the rejection of the prophet. Finally, the last oracle (3,11–20) promises restoration for Jerusalem, when God "will leave as a remnant in your midst a people humble and lowly." This reference to the remnant, familiar from the preaching of Isaiah, could be a sign of Isaiah's influence on Zephaniah, but it is more likely that it is another example of an optimistic oracle added on by an editor.

Whether or not these last words come from Zephaniah, they have their own validity. Just as the judgments on Assyria and Babylon were not God's last words to Israel, hope is still possible even after the destructive Day of the Lord.

Questions for Discussion or Reflection

World and local events often contribute to a certain despair or at least a skeptical attitude toward life. What are your sources of hope? How do you contribute to the hope of your community?

HAGGAI READING GUIDE

At a Glance

When	Around 520 B.C.
Where	Judah
Main Focus	Rebuilding the Temple

There are two main focuses of Haggai's prophetic work, and they both have to do with the Temple and the difficult situation of the returned exiles (the "remnant of the people"). Along with Zechariah, Haggai encourages the people to complete the Temple (Ezr 5,1), and then he must help them deal with their disappointment after its completion.

EXHORTATION TO REBUILD (CHAPTER 1)

The reasons for delaying the completion of the Temple all make sense, whether in ancient or modern times. The returned exiles were poverty-stricken; in addition, they were suffering under drought and crop failure. It was obvious that they needed houses for shelter and God did not. Haggai's interpretation of this situation was that their difficulties were due to the fact that they had not rebuilt the Temple but had concentrated instead on rebuilding their own homes.

There is wisdom in the prophet's exhortation to rebuild the Temple. The morale of the community would also be built by working on a common project, especially one that would focus the people's attention on God. Recall the experience of the poor European immigrant communities in the United States in the late 19th and early 20th centuries. They built impressive churches and schools at great sacrifice to themselves. Their value to these communities was enormous, not just economically but as a sign of their faith in God and what they could accomplish by working together.

THE REACTION TO THE FINISHED TEMPLE (CHAPTER 2)

The completion of the Temple was a disappointment. Those who could remember Solomon's Temple lamented because this new Temple was so puny by comparison (2,3). Not only that, the completion did not bring about the reversal of fortunes that Haggai had predicted. His reaction is typical of prophets whose predictions don't come to pass. He says it is delayed and the reason for the delay is that the people are not observing the purity laws and their offerings are unclean. He ends by reaffirming that God will shake the heavens and the earth when conditions are right.

This situation points out the problem with prophecies that make specific predictions. The hopes raised are good for the morale of the community, but only for a time. When they are not fulfilled, it leads to disillusionment. The same problem will tend to discredit apocalyptic and messianic expectations of later times.

THE LESSONS OF HAGGAI

There are two lessons to be learned from Haggai. One is that hope should not be focused on specific predictions, and the other is the value of religious symbols and ritual for bringing people together. The Temple may not have satisfied immediate expectations, but it contributed to Jewish life for the next 500 years and far outweighed the initial disappointments.

Questions for Discussion or Reflection

1. Words Worth Pondering and Remembering from Haggai, 2,4c–5:

   "For I am with you says the LORD of Hosts.
   This is the pact I made with you
   when you came out of Egypt,
   And my spirit continues in your midst;
   do not fear!"

   Spend some time reflecting on those expressions of your faith that sustain you through the specific disappointments and difficulties of life. Try writing them down.

2. What are some of the specific things you bargain for with God? (If I get this job, then I will . . .?) What happens to your hope when things don't work out?

ZECHARIAH READING GUIDE

At a Glance

When	Around 520 B.C., chapters 1–8; Much later, chapters 9–14
Where	Judah
Main Focus	Encouragement of returned exiles, chapters 1–8; Apocalyptic visions, chapters 9–14

The Book of Zechariah contains the work of more than one prophet. It is named for the prophet who, along with Haggai, encouraged the people to complete the Temple after their return from the exile. His work is found in Chapters 1–8. The prophet of Chapters 9–14 comes from a much later time. Some scholars point to a third prophet as the author of Chapters 12–14.

THE ORIGINAL ZECHARIAH (CHAPTERS 1–8)

These oracles are a series of visions that are explained to the prophet by an angel. This is the first time that the interpreting angel appears in biblical literature; it becomes common in later apocalyptic writings. The visions show the prophet's view of what is really going on in these times after the exile, revealing something that is hidden from the ordinary person. It is God's activity that is hidden. The prophet wants to assure the returned exiles that God is active among them. For example, the first vision shows four horsemen sent by God to patrol the earth to indicate that God is in control, although not visible. Similarly, in Chapter 2, four heavenly blacksmiths come to beat down the nations and an angelic "man" makes preparations for the restoration of Jerusalem. All this is aimed at building up the confidence of the struggling community.

High Priest and Governor

When Zechariah prophesied to the returned exiles, the monarchy had been destroyed and there was no king. The Persians ruled the area. Zerubbabel, a descendant of David, was governor and Joshua was the High Priest. In the absence of a king, the High Priest had additional power and authority.

Up until the time of the Babylonian exile, the prophets had been sharply critical of the king and usually the priests as well. Prophets like Amos condemned the monarchy and its religious practices for making the people complacent and, therefore, unfaithful. In this new situation, Zechariah takes a different stance and comes to the defense of the leaders, in opposition to their critics.

In the vision in Chapter 3, the High Priest, Joshua, stands before the angel of the Lord and is accused by Satan. This is one of the earliest appearances of Satan in the Old Testament (see Job 1–2 and 1 Chr 21,1). Satan is not yet portrayed as the Devil; rather, he is an angel in the service of God, serving as a prosecuting attorney. In Zechariah's vision, Satan represents the people in the community who are criticizing Joshua and receives a stinging rebuke from the angel of the Lord. Zechariah's point is not that Joshua is without fault, but that criticism is not appropriate when the community is struggling.

The prophet is equally positive about Zerubbabel, the governor. In Chapter 4, the two leaders are pictured as olive trees, because both priest and king were anointed with oil. This is the source of the title "messiah" or "anointed one". In Chapter 6, the prophet goes further and says that he has been commanded to make a crown for Zerubbabel. To make a king of a Davidic prince would have been extremely dangerous because the Persian rulers would, no doubt, have seen this as an act of rebellion. We don't know whether Zechariah ever carried it out, but we do know that the understanding of the monarchy became more and more idealized in the minds of the people in this period after the exile. The people hoped for a future messiah-king, the anointed one who would make Jerusalem again a holy city (8,3). Zechariah's visions helped keep alive this dream of justice and freedom.

The Appreciation of Ritual

A positive view of ritual is another contrast to earlier prophets that we see in Zechariah. He shows that ritual is powerful in expressing human desires because it engages the emotions and motivations of the people performing it. In 5,5–11, he relates a vision of wickedness, pictured as a woman, placed in a bushel container and shipped off to Babylon (similar to the Scapegoat ritual in Lv 16). The ritual action of getting rid of wickedness is meant to strengthen the people's resolve to rid society of evil and to move them to action.

Zechariah also appreciates the limits of ritual. After the experience of the exile and the destruction of the Temple, Zechariah knew the importance of sacrifice but still leaned more toward the position of Hosea; "It is love that I desire, not sacrifice" (Hos 6,6).

MESSIANIC ORACLE AND ALLEGORY OF THE SHEPHERDS CHAPTERS 9–11

The messianic oracle in Chapter 9 is famous because of its association with the Palm Sunday passages in Matthew 21,5 and John 12,15. The ass was not as humble an animal in the ancient world as in modern times and was used by the nobility in Genesis and Judges. Here, however, the image is used to recall an earlier, simpler time to express the hope for a ruler to restore Solomon's empire without the arrogance of the monarchy, symbolized by the horses and chariots. Although the messianic age is usually described as a time of universal disarmament, the messianic oracle in Chapter 9 sounds very war-like. The point here, similar to what is found in later apocalyptic writing, is that the Lord will fight for Judah. The human role is to maintain purity and be obedient to the law. This role of the Lord as warrior is in accord with much of Israelite tradition (see Ex 15,3).

The allegory of the shepherds in Chapter 11 must be read against the background of two passages in Ezekiel, because Zechariah 11 reverses this earlier prophet's predictions of salvation. Chapter 34 is against the shepherds of Israel who exploited their flock. The mood changes, however, from judgment to salvation as the Lord takes over as shepherd. In Chapter 37, Ezekiel takes two sticks, representing the two kingdoms of Israel and Judah, and joins them together, signifying that they would be one nation under David their king. In Zechariah 11 there are also exploitive shepherds but no movement to salvation, only slaughter. Also in Zechariah there are two staffs symbolizing two covenants, one with the nations and one between Judah and Israel. Both are broken in the course of the prophecy.

It is not clear when this prophecy was written or what context it addressed, but it is clearly an expression of extreme dissatisfaction and disillusionment with the situation after the exile. There is not a hint of the support for the institutional leaders found in Chapters 1–8 or of the dream of justice and freedom. This anonymous prophet (sometimes called Deutero-Zechariah or "Second" Zechariah) can only proclaim judgment and try to make the people see reality for what it is.

CHAPTERS 12–14

The last three chapters of Zechariah are even more confusing than Chapters 9–11. There is persistent criticism of the rulers, especially in Chapter 13: a "song of the sword" against the shepherd with a prediction that only a third of the people will be spared; and a surprising prediction of the end of prophecy. A motif of a final battle in Jerusalem runs through these chapters, especially 12 and 14, with the prophet expressing hope for reconciliation (between the leaders in Jerusalem and the people they oppressed) and a remarkable universalism (wanting to include the Egyptians in the worship of the true God).

After Haggai and Zechariah, prophets seemed to have lost status. This was partly due to the failure of predictions, the conflict between prophets themselves, and the willingness of some to mislead the people for their own gain. Although some of this could be said of some earlier times, these late postexilic prophets do not command the same respect as their predecessors; their real names are not even used (e.g., Deutero-Zechariah).

Questions for Discussion or Reflection

1. Zechariah's attitude toward the institutions and their leadership differed from the earlier prophets. He was more supportive because the community was struggling. Pick an institution to which you belong, your local church or local government, and list some ways in which you can be both supportive and yet constructively critical.
2. What values govern whether or not you give support to designated leaders?

MALACHI READING GUIDE

At a Glance

When	5th century B.C.
Where	Judah
Main Focus	Critical of Judah, mainly priesthood

We do not know who wrote these last three chapters that make up the last prophetic book. "Malachi" is not a proper name but means "my messenger." The word is taken from 3,1, "Lo, I am sending my messenger," to designate the one through whom this word of the Lord is given. The book is made up of six oracles; all, except the first, are critical of Judah, the priesthood, and the breaches of faith by the people.

THE PRIESTHOOD (1,6 – 2,9)

Malachi, like many prophets before him, is critical of the priesthood. However, the prophet is not opposed to the priesthood as a whole; in fact, he has the greatest respect for the ideal of the priesthood. His problem with the priests is that they have been offering cheap sacrifices, sick and lame animals. His point is that an offering represents the person bringing it. No one would offer a sick animal to the governor, so why would the priests offer one to God?

A familiar and somewhat surprising line is found in 1,11, "from the rising of the sun, even to its setting, my name is great among the nations." It is not certain what the prophet had in mind, because the Gentiles did not worship the Lord explicitly. It could refer to those Jews who were spread out among all the nations (the diaspora) or to the Persian kings who were generous in supporting the Temple. A third possibility would point to a decidedly broad-minded and liberal attitude. Since the Lord is called the God of Heaven (Ezr 6,10), then the High God of the Persians and other deities could also be acknowledged as "the God of

Heaven." This would mean that the Gentiles worshiped the same God as the Jews! This is quite broad-minded.

BREACHES OF FAITH (2,10–17)

Another surprising phrase is found in the third oracle (2,10–16). The prophet begins with the question: "Have we not all the one Father?" Then he denounces two breaches of faith: Judah "has married an idolatrous woman" (2,11) and the divorce of "the wife of your youth" (2,14).

The usual explanation for this passage is that Jewish men were divorcing the Jewish wives of their youth and marrying Gentile women, possibly for social reasons. This led to their involvement in the cult of pagan deities. So, the question, "Have we not all one Father?" is addressed only to Jews and does not reflect as universal an attitude as it seems.

Another interpretation is based on the fact that there is no other evidence that Jews in the postexilic period divorced their Jewish wives. Once a marriage had been entered into, it was sacred. The Jewish men should have seen to it that their offspring were "godly" (2,15). Conversion of the spouses, rather than divorce, was the solution. The "one Father," then, is the creator of all, Jews and Gentiles. Ethnic distinctions do not matter if one is willing to recognize the one God.

If this interpretation is correct, Malachi exhibits some of the spirit of St. Paul in his openness to the Gentiles. It also points to the diversity of opinion in Judaism at this time. Ezekiel (44,7) insisted that no "foreigners, uncircumcised in heart and flesh" be admitted to the Temple.

THE DAY OF THE LORD (CHAPTER 3)

The final chapter of the book is dominated by the expectation that God will come in judgment, an adaptation of the traditional Day of the Lord. It is from this chapter that Handel borrowed the image of the refiner's fire for his *Messiah.* Malachi is also the source of the motif of the messenger who prepares the way and is first identified as Elijah the prophet. In the New Testament, John the Baptist is cast in this role (Mt 11,14; 17,12f). It is likely that the prophet we call Malachi saw himself in this role.

The final oracle of Malachi is also the conclusion of all the prophetic books. The editors refer to Moses as a way of reinforcing the laws of the Pentateuch. They also underline the theme of the coming judgment. The prophetic books not only remind us of the past but motivate us in the present by making us look into the future.

Questions for Discussion or Reflection

1. One interpretation of Malachi's teaching is that ethnic distinctions do not matter if one is willing to recognize the one God. Test that out in your life.
2. How do you ensure that all ethnic groups feel welcome in your church, at your place of work or study, in your home?

The Gospels and Acts

THE SYNOPTIC GOSPELS

Because of their striking similarities, the three Gospels of Matthew, Mark and Luke have traditionally been called the "synoptic" Gospels, from the Greek meaning to "view together." The observer of these three Gospels would, in fact, notice many parallels among these stories of Jesus if they were laid side by side. (See the "Harmony of the Gospels" that follows.)

At the same time, the synoptic Gospels are different from John's Gospel. For example, in each of the synoptic Gospels, Jesus begins his public ministry of teaching and healing in Galilee, travels with his disciples on a single purposeful journey to Jerusalem, and there experiences final rejection, death and, ultimately, resurrection. Jesus' sayings in these Gospels are generally either succinct and pointed or in the story form of the parable; his actions are characterized by marvelous healings and exorcisms; a major theme of his preaching is the advent of the "Rule of God." In John, on the other hand, Jesus moves back and forth between Galilee and Judea and his teaching is often expressed in long, meditative discourses. There are no parables in John, no exorcisms, and fewer healing stories; the Rule of God motif plays a very minor role.

But the three synoptic Gospels develop their own distinct view of Jesus and his mission. Mark, for instance, begins his story of Jesus with his baptism at the Jordan, whereas Matthew, by means of the Infancy Narrative at the beginning of the Gospel, traces Jesus' origin back into the history of Israel. Luke, too, begins with an infancy narrative, but gives much more positive emphasis to Jerusalem than either Mark or Matthew. In Luke's Gospel the young Jesus goes to Jerusalem to listen to the teachers in the Temple courtyard, and the disciples of Jesus will gather to pray after his resurrection in the Jerusalem Temple. Luke also adds a second volume to his Gospel; the Acts of the Apostles picks up the story of Jesus and his apostles where the Gospel left off, and shows its continuing force as the community of the Risen Christ moves out into the world.

Both the similarities and the differences among the synoptic Gospels have led to ongoing debate about their interrelationship. Analyses of the style and content of Mark led scholars to conclude that Mark was the first Gospel written, with Matthew and Luke directly dependent on Mark. The presence of other material in Matthew and Luke that was not found in Mark, such as the sayings of Jesus in the Sermon on the Mount, led to the hypothesis of an additional source for Matthew and Luke. This hypothetical source of material—which scholars call "Q" (from the German word *Quelle* or "source")—was probably a collection of sayings and parables of Jesus that circulated in the earliest Christian community. Independently of each other, if this hypothesis is correct, Matthew and Luke blended this source with their new renditions of Mark and perhaps with some other materials or traditions specific to their own communities.

Scholars assume, therefore, that Mark was the first Gospel to be written and that Mark, in fact, set the basic format for the story of Jesus, a format that both Matthew and Luke used as the starting point for their own narratives. This relationship accounts for the similarities among the Gospels. Each Gospel writer's particular interpretation of Mark, the use of other sources, and the unique pastoral and theological perspectives of the writers and their local churches lead to the distinctiveness of each of the synoptics.

The issue of the relationship of John's Gospel to the synoptics is more problematic. Until the midpoint of this century most modern biblical scholars assumed that John knew of the synoptic Gospels and that his own Gospel was a very distinctive variation on the synoptic tradition. But more recently, a significant number of scholars speculate that John may represent an independent stream of tradition that had little, if any, contact with the synoptic Gospels.

THE FOUR GOSPELS AT A GLANCE

Matthew	Mark	Luke	John
DATE OF WRITING			
70–90 A.D.	65–70 A.D.	70–90 A.D.	90–100 A.D.
PLACE OF WRITING			
Antioch in Syria	Rome	Greece	Syria or Palestine
TARGET AUDIENCE			
Jewish Christians	Gentiles	Greeks	All Christians
PURPOSE FOR WRITING			
To assert that Jesus is the long-awaited Messiah who fulfills Israel's hopes and the words of the prophets	To present the person of Jesus through his actions and miracles	To give an orderly account of the ministry of Jesus so readers will rely on the gospel to build their faith	To lead to faith in Jesus as God's son so those who believe will gain eternal life
PORTRAIT OF JESUS			
Promised Messiah	Suffering servant, hidden Messiah	Son of Man	Son of God/Word of God
CHARACTER OF THE AUTHOR			
Teacher/Catechist	Storyteller	Historian	Theologian
MAJOR EMPHASIS			
Jesus' teachings	Jesus' actions	Jesus' humanity	Jesus' teachings
THEMES			
Jesus fulfilled Old Testament prophecy	The identity of Jesus	Salvation is a joyous surprise	The role of "signs" in building faith
Jesus identifies with the lowly	The importance of the cross	Salvation is offered to everyone	Dualistic struggle between forces of light and darkness
Jesus is the world's savior, not just Israel's	Discipleship	Jesus identifies with the lowly and respects and defends the dignity of all	Faith in Jesus necessary for eternal life
		Mary is the first disciple	Jesus is the divine Son of God

HARMONY OF THE GOSPELS

	Matthew	Mark	Luke	John
The Divinity of Jesus				1,1–5
Announcement of the Birth of John the Baptist			1,5–25	
The Betrothal of the Virgin Mary	1,18		1,27	
The Announcement of the Birth of Jesus			1,26–38	
Mary Visits Elizabeth			1,39–56	
Joseph's Dream	1,20–25			
The Birth of John the Baptist			1,57–80	
The Birth of Jesus			2,1–7	
The Visit by the Shepherds			2,8–20	
The Circumcision and Naming of Jesus			2,21	
The Presentation in the Temple			2,22–29	
The Genealogy of Jesus	1,1–17		3,23–38	
The Visit of the Magi	2,1–12			
The Flight to Egypt	2,13–15			
The Massacre of the Infants	2,16–18			
The Return from Egypt	2,19–23		2,39	
The Boy Jesus in the Temple			2,41	
With the Teachers in the Temple			2,46–50	
Youth of Jesus			2,51	
The Preaching of John the Baptist	3,1–4	1,1–8	3,1–18	1,6–15
Baptism by John	3,6	1,5	3,21	
The First Testimony of the Baptist to Christ	3,11–12	1,7–8		1,29–34
The Baptism of Jesus	3,13–17	1,9–11	3,21–22	
The Temptation of Jesus	4,1–11	1,12–13	4,1–13	
John the Baptist's Testimony to Himself				1,19–35
The Call of the First Disciples	4,18–22	1,16–20	5,1–11	1,37–51
First Miracle at Cana				2,1–11
Visit to Capernaum				2,12
Cleansing of the Temple	21,12–13	11,15–17	19,45–46	2,13–23
Nicodemus				3,1–21
The Final Witness of the Baptist				3,22–36
The Samaritan Woman				4,1–42

	Matthew	Mark	Luke	John
The Return to Galilee				4,43–45
The Second Sign at Cana				4,46–54
The Cure on a Sabbath				5,1–47
Imprisonment of John the Baptist	4,12; 14, 3	1,14–15		3,24
The Beginning of the Galilean Ministry	4,12–17	1,14–15	4,14–15	
The Rejection at Nazareth	13,54–58	6,1–4	4,16–27	
Jesus Preaches at Capernaum	4,13–17			
The Cure of a Demoniac		1,23–27	4,33–36	
The Cure of Peter's Mother-in-law	8,14–15	1,29–31	4,38–39	
Other Healings	8,16–17	1,32–34	4,40–41	
Circuit through Galilee		1,38–39	4,42–44	
The Cleansing of a Leper	8,1–4	1,40–45	5,12–18	
Retirement for Solitary Prayer		1,45	5,16	
The Healing of a Paralytic	9,1–8	2,1–12	5,18–25	
Call of Matthew	9,9–17	2,13–22	5,27–39	
Ministering to a Great Multitude	4,23–25		6,17–19	
Picking Grain on the Sabbath	12,1–8	2,23–28	6,1–5	
The Man with the Withered Hand	12,9–14	3,1–6	6,6–11	
Retirement for Solitary Prayer			6,12	
The Mission of the Twelve	10,1–4	3,13–19 6,7–13	6,13–16 9,1–6	
The Sermon on the Mount	5,1–12		6,20–26	
The Healing of the Centurion's Servant	8,5–13		7,1–10	
The Raising of the Widow's Son			7,11–17	
The Messengers from John the Baptist	11,2–19		7,18–35	
The Pardon of the Sinful Woman			7,36–50	
The Beatitudes	5,2–12		6,20–26	
Galilean Women Follow Jesus			8,1–3	
Jesus and Beelzebul	12,22–28	3,23–30	11,14–23	
Blasphemy against the Holy Spirit	12,31–32			
The Return of the Unclean Spirit	12,43–45		11,24–26	
The True Family of Jesus	12,46–50	3,31–35	8,19–21	
The Parable of the Sower	13,1–9	4,1–9 4,14–20	8,6–8 8,11–15	
The Parable of the Weeds among the Wheat	13,24–30			

	Matthew	Mark	Luke	John
The Parable of the Mustard Seed	13,31–32	4,30–32	13,18–19	
The Parable of the Yeast	13,33		13,20–21	
The Parable of the Lamp	5,15	4,21	8,16; 11,33	
The Parable of the Buried Treasure	13,44			
The Parable of the Fine Pearl	13,45–46			
The Parable of the Thrown Net	13,47–48			
The Calming of the Storm at Sea	8,24–27	4,37–41	8,23–25	
The Healing of the Gergesene Demoniacs	8,28–34	5,1–20	8,26–39	
The Parable of the Bridegroom	9,15			
The Parable of the New Cloth	9,16	2,21	5,36	
The Parable of the New Wine in Old Bottles	9,17	2,22	5,37–38	
Miracles: Jairus' Daughter and the Woman with a Hemorrhage	9,18–26	5,22–43	8,41–56	
The Healing of Two Blind Men	9,27–31			
The Healing of a Mute Person	9,32–34			
The Mission of the Twelve	10,1–4	6,7–12	9,1–6	
Herod's Opinion of Jesus	14,1–12	6,14–29	9,7–9	
The Return of the Twelve and the Feeding of the Five Thousand	14,13–21	6,31–44	9,10–17	6,1–14
The Walking on the Water	14,22–33	6,47–52		6,16–21
The Bread of Life Discourse				6,22–65
Retirement for Solitary Prayer	14,23	6,46		
The Tradition of the Elders	15,1–20	7,1–23		
The Canaanite Woman's Faith	15,24–29	7,24–30		
The Healing of Many People	15,29–31			
The Feeding of the Four Thousand	15,32–39	8,1–9		
The Demand for a Sign: Weather	16,1–4	8,11–13	12,54–56	
The Leaven of the Pharisees and Sadducees	16,5–12	8,14–21		
Peter's Confession of Christ	16,13–20	8,27–30	9,18–20	
The First Prediction of the Passion	16,21–23	8,31–38	9,22–27	
The Transfiguration of Jesus	17,1–8	9,2–8	9,28–36	
The Healing of a Boy with a Demon	17,14–21	9,14–25	9,37–43	
The Second Prediction of the Passion	17,22–23	9,30–32	9,43–45	
Payment of the Temple Tax	17,24–27			
The Greatest in the Kingdom	18,1–5	9,33–37	9,46–48	

	Matthew	Mark	Luke	John
The Parable of the Lost Sheep	18,10–14		15,1–7	
A Brother Who Sins	18,15–20		17,3–4	
A Lesson on Self-denial	18,18			
The Parable of the Unforgiving Servant	18,23–35			
The Departure for Jerusalem			9,51–52	
The Jealousy of the Samaritans			9,53	
The Anger of James and John			9,54–56	
The Feast of Tabernacles				7,1–10
The First Dialogue				7,14–31
Officers Sent to Arrest Jesus				7,32–36
The Woman Caught in Adultery				8,1–11
The Light of the World				8,12–20
Jesus Threatened with Stoning				8,59
The Man Born Blind				9,1–41
The Good Shepherd				10,1–21
The Mission of the Seventy-two			10,1–12	
The Return of the Seventy-two			10,17–20	
The Parable of the Good Samaritan			10,29–37	
The Visit to Martha and Mary			10,38–42	
The Lord's Prayer	6,9–13		11,1–4	
Jesus and Beelzebul	12,22–45	3, 23–30	11,14–23	
The Demand for a Sign: Jonah	12,38–42		11,29–32	
God's Providence to Birds and Flowers	10,29–31		12,6–7; 12,24; 12,27–28	
The Parable of the Rich Fool			12,16–20	
A Call to Repentance			13,1–5	
The Parable of the Barren Fig Tree			13,6–9	
The Cure of the Crippled Woman on the Sabbath			13,10–17	
The Feast of Dedication				10,22–42
The Attempt to Stone Jesus				10,31
Jesus Retires across the Jordan				10,40
Salvation and Rejection	7,13–14; 7,21–23		13,22–30	
Herod's Desire to Kill Jesus			13,31–33	

	Matthew	Mark	Luke	John
The Healing of the Man with Dropsy on the Sabbath			14,1–6	
The Parable of the Great Feast	22,1–14		14,15–24	
The Parable of the Lost Sheep	18,10–14		15,1–7	
The Parable of the Lost Coin			15,8–10	
The Parable of the Prodigal Son			15,11–32	
The Parable of the Dishonest Steward			16,1–8	
The Parable of the Rich Man and Lazarus			16,19–31	
The Raising of Lazarus				11,38–44
The Return of Jesus from Peraea to Bethany				11,11–16
The Resurrection of Lazarus				11,38–44
The Session of the Sanhedrin				11,45–54
The Last Passover				11,55
The Last Journey in Jerusalem	19,1	10,1	17,11	
The Cleansing of the Ten Lepers			17,11–19	
The Parable of the Persistent Widow			18,1–8	
The Parable of the Pharisee and the Tax Collector			18,9–14	
Marriage and Divorce	19,1–12	10,1–12		
Blessing of the Children	19,13–15	10,13–16	18,15–17	
The Rich Young Man	19,16–30	10,17–22	18,18–23	
The Workers in the Vineyard	20,1–16			
The Third Prediction of the Passion	20,17–19	10,32–34	18,31–34	
The Request of James and John	20,20–28	10,35–45		
The Healing of Two Blind Men	20,29–34	10,46–52	18,35–43	
Zacchaeus the Tax Collector			19,1–10	
The Parable of the Talents	25,14–30		10,11–27	
The Supper in Simon's House	26,6–13	14,3–9		12,1–9
Mary Anoints Jesus	26,7–13	14,3–9	12,3–8	
The Entry into Jerusalem	21,1–11	11,1–10	19,29–44	12,12–19
The Survey of the Temple		11,11		
The Cursing of the Fig Tree	21,18–19	11,12–14		
The Cleansing of the Temple	21,12–17	11,15–18		
The Lesson of the Fig Tree	21,20–22	11,20–25		
The Authority of Jesus Questioned	21,23–27	11,27–33	20,1–8	

	Matthew	Mark	Luke	John
The Parable of the Two Sons	21,28–32			
The Parable of the Tenants	21,33–46	12,1–12	20,9–19	
The Wedding Feast	22,1–14		14,15–24	
Paying Taxes to the Emperor	22,15–22	12,13–17	20,20–26	
The Question about the Resurrection	22,23–33	12,18–27	20,27–39	
The Greatest Commandment	22,34–40	12,28–34	11,25–28	
The Question about David's Son	22,41–46	12,35–37	20,41–44	
Denunciation of the Scribes and Pharisees	23,1–33	12,38–40	11,37–54	
The Poor Widow's Contribution		12,41–44	21,1–4	
The Coming of Jesus' Hour				12,20–23
The Destruction of the Temple Foretold	24,1–2	13,1–3		
The Parable of the Ten Virgins	25,1–13		19,11–27	
The Judgment of Nations	25,31–46			
The Conspiracy Against Jesus	26,3–5	14,1–2	22,1–2	
The Betrayal by Judas	26,14–16	14,10–11	22,3–6	18,2–5
Preparation of the Passover	26,17–19	14,12–16	22,7–13	
The Washing of the Disciples' Feet				13,1–17
The Lord's Supper	26,26	14,22	22,14	
The Betrayal Foretold	26,21	14,18	22,21	13,21
The Giving of the Morsel				13,26–27
The Departure of Judas				13,30
Peter's Denial Predicted	26,31–35	14,27–31	22,21–23	13,36
Blessing the Cup	26,27–28	14,23–24	22,17	
Last Supper Discourses				14,1–14
The Prayer of Jesus				17,1
The Hymn	26,30	14,26		
The Agony in the Garden	26,36; 26,44	14,32–42	22,39–46	18,1
Jesus is Comforted by the Angel			22,43–44	
The Sleep of the Apostles	26,40–45	14,37–41	22,45–46	
The Betrayal and Arrest of Jesus	26,47–50	14,43–45	22,47	18,1–14
Peter Smites Malchus	26,51	14,47	22,50	18,10
Jesus Heals the Ear of Malchus			22,51	
Jesus Forsaken by His Disciples	26,56	14,50		

	Matthew	Mark	Luke	John
Jesus Led to Annas				18,12–13
Jesus Before the Sanhedrin	26,57	14,53	22,66	
Peter Follows Jesus	26,58	14,54	22,55	18,15
The High Priest's Adjuration	26,63	14,61	22,66	
Jesus Condemned	26,66–67	14,64–65	22,70–71	
Peter's Denial of Jesus	26,69–75	14,66–72	22,54–62	18,17–27
Jesus before Pilate	27,1	15,1	23,1	18,28
The Death of Judas	27,3			
Pilate Comes out to the People				18,29
Pilate Speaks to Jesus Privately				18,33
Mockery by the Soldiers	27,27	15,15	22,63–65	19,1
Jesus Crowned with Thorns	27,29	15,17		19,2
Jesus Exhibited by Pilate				19,5
Jesus Questioned by Pilate	27,11	15,2	23,2	
Jesus Sent by Pilate to Herod			23,6–11	
The Sentence of Death	27,15	15,6	23,17	19,12–16
Pilate Receives a Message from his Wife	27,19			
Pilate Washes his Hands	27,24			
Pilate Releases Barnabas	27,26	15,15	23,25	
Pilate Delivers Jesus to Be Crucified	27,26	15,15	23,25	19,16
The Way of the Cross	27,32	15,21	23,26	
The Crucifixion	27,33–44	15,22–32	23,33–43	19,17–30
The Death of Jesus	27,45–56	5,33–41	23,44–49	
The Burial of Jesus	27,57–61	15,42–47	23,50–56	19,38–42
The Guard at the Tomb	27,62–66			
The Resurrection of Jesus	28,1–10	16,1–8	24,1–12	20,1–10
The Report of the Guards	28,11–15			
The Appearance to Mary Magdalene		16,9		20,14
The Appearance to the Women Returning Home	28,9			
The Appearance to Two Disciples Going to Emmaus		16,12	24,13	
The Appearance to Peter			24,34	
The Appearance to the Disciples in Jerusalem			24,36	20,19

	Matthew	Mark	Luke	John
The Appearance to the Eleven Apostles		16,14		
The Appearance to Thomas				20,27
The Appearance to the Seven Disciples				21,1–22
Jesus and Peter				21,15–19
The Commissioning of the Disciples	28,16–20	16,14		
The Ascension of Jesus		16,19–20	24,50–43	

PARABLES

The word *parable* comes from a Greek word that means "to throw alongside" or "compare." A parable is a story about a situation, usually one that would be very familiar to the hearers. The story is told in order to make a point about another reality, moral or spiritual, that is not as easy to speak of in down-to-earth terms.

Jesus' parables are *similes* (statements comparing one thing with another by using *like* or *as,* such as, "The kingdom of heaven is like a mustard seed . . ." in Mt 13,31) or *metaphors* (statements identifying one thing with another, for instance, "Beware of false prophets, who come to you in sheep's clothing, but underneath are ravenous wolves" in Mt 7,15). Sometimes these comparisons grow into stories. They make their points by using everyday objects and characters drawn from real-life situations in families, farms, the marketplace, and the courts of kings. Jesus used parables as a main part of his teaching, and their primary purpose was to reveal some dimension of God's Kingdom.

As you read through the parables keep in mind this combination of day-to-day reality and great spiritual insight. The parables are famous, rightly so, for their ability to take the most ordinary situations—cleaning house, growing grapes, the rivalry between two brothers, the preparations for a wedding, the story of a mugging in a bad part of town—and find in them an endless source of spiritual meaning.

The parables can be grouped into three categories according to their length and complexity.

1. Similes and metaphors that have minimal elaboration and are basically "one-liners." Some examples are the lamp under the basket (Mt 5,14–16); the mustard seed (Mt 13,31–32); and the two debtors (Lk 7,41–43).
2. Comparisons that are more extended; these are more elaborate than the simple metaphors above, but are not yet full-blown stories like those in category 3. Some examples are the two sons (Mt 21,28–32); the growing seed (Mk 4,26–29); the rich fool (Lk 12,16–21); and the unprofitable servants (Lk 17,7–10).
3. Stories that contain characters, dialogue, plot, and setting; these stories have a clear beginning, middle, and end. Some examples are the good Samaritan (Lk 10,30–37); the prodigal son (Lk 15,11–32); the wicked vinedressers (Mt 21,33–41); and the wise and foolish virgins (Mt 25,1–13).

Parables were used by Jesus to reveal the Kingdom he came to initiate through his life and ministry. But, ironically, Jesus also used them to obscure his teaching (Mk 4,11–12). Knowledge of the Kingdom is available to all who sincerely seek it, but it requires some effort. Parables make their point indirectly so people will only discover their truth if their ears and eyes are open and if they have the heart of a seeker. Even the disciples of Jesus did not always understand the significance of his parables. However, because they were committed to Jesus, they sought, and the doors of understanding were opened to them. Those who stand on the "outside" at a safe distance from Jesus, unwilling to make a commitment, are locked into misunderstanding. They are unable to "hear" the truth expressed in the parables because they are unwilling to open their ears and eyes and hearts.

For many centuries parables were viewed primarily as allegories in which every element carried some kind of symbolic significance or hidden meaning. For example, St. Augustine allegorized the parable of the prodigal son. He saw the victim as Adam, the robbers as Satan and his angels, the priest and Levite who walked by as representative of the Torah and the prophets, the Samaritan as Jesus, and the inn as the church, etc. But scholars would say Augustine went way beyond what Jesus intended. The point the parable was meant to make (that God's love is extravagant and unconditional) almost gets lost in the elaborate analogy. Modern scholarship has therefore turned away from that kind of interpretation, insisting that parables make only a single point. The details of the story have just one point of contact with the spiritual teaching the story is trying to convey.

Although modern readers have moved away from an overly allegorical reading of parables, avoiding allegorical interpretations entirely is not an absolute rule. Some parables, in fact, do have more than one point of contact with the teaching they convey. The parable of the sower is one of them. One must be careful, of course, to make sure that the points of contact they discover are coming *from* the text, not being read *into* the text. Besides the parable of the sower (Mk 4,14–20), see the parable of the wheat among the weeds (Mt 13,37–40) as another example of a parable that does have more than one point of contact with the teaching it presents. However, the general approach is that interpretation is derived from the story as a whole, rather than from its individual details.

The parables are designed to make us see differently. They don't just present moral teaching; they offer a whole new way of perceiving how God rules over and is present in our lives. They also help us understand how we are converted by this presence, and thus how we enter God's Kingdom. Certain truths just cannot be explained directly. So we resort to imagination. Because they appeal to the imagination, parables can touch us in ways that an abstract explanation cannot. They supply jolts to the imagination ("The kingdom of heaven is like yeast that a woman took and mixed with three measures of wheat flour until the whole batch was leavened." Mt 13,33). They penetrate deeper and plant their truth inside us.

But they do much more than provide folksy examples that make a point. They shake us up, make us ask questions. They challenge our categories and make us think our way through to a conclusion. Often they do this by reversing our expectations: A host who is stood up by the guests invites the poor, the lame, and the blind to his banquet (Lk 14,21); the owner of a vineyard pays those hired *last* the same amount as those hired *first* (Mt 20,8); a man acquires a treasure not because of his hard work, but out of dumb luck (Mt 13,44).

Most of us approach life with certain expectations or a particular worldview: The good are rewarded and the bad are punished; those who work harder and longer get paid more than those who work fewer hours, etc. Then we read a parable and it shakes us up, it turns our world upside down: The *prodigal* got the party, not the good older brother; the workers hired last were paid as much as those hired first! We become disoriented by such a perspective. But if we do the work the parable calls for, we will be rewarded; if we seek, we will discover the profound truth the parable wants to teach us. For example, the parable of the good Samaritan is not a pious story about being compassionate, but a radical challenge to consider as "neighbor" those we had previously viewed as "enemy." Out of this seeking and struggle a sense of reorientation emerges.

The parables invite us into a process of questioning. Within that process, we become an essential part of their meaning. They are incomplete in themselves. They invite and await a response. Our response completes the process that they initiate. Their truth does not stand alone. It combines with our efforts and springs to life in our hearts as a revelation of God's mysterious Kingdom.

PARABLES IN THE SYNOPTIC GOSPELS

Parable	Matthew	Mark	Luke
The Weeds among the Wheat	13,24–30		
The Buried Treasure	13,44		
The Fine Pearl	13,45–46		
The Thrown Net	13,47–48		
The Unforgiving Servant	18,21		
The Workers in the Vineyard	20,1 – 16		
The Two Sons	21,28 – 30		
The Wedding Feast	22,2 – 14		
The Talents	25,14 – 30		
The Judgment of Nations	25,31 – 46		
Seed Grows of Itself		4,26 – 29	
Need for Watchfulness		13,32 – 37	
The Two Debtors			7,41–42
The Good Samaritan			10,30–35
The Importunate Friend			11,5–8
The Rich Fool			12,16–20
The Vigilant and Faithful Servants			12,35–40
The Faithful and Prudent Steward			12,42–48
The Barren Fig Tree			13,6–9
The Great Feast			14,15–24
The Tower			14,28–30
The King Marching into Battle			14,31–33
The Lost Coin			15,8–10
The Prodigal Son			15,11–32
The Dishonest Steward			16,1–8

(Continued)

Parable	Matthew	Mark	Luke
The Rich Man and Lazarus			16,19–31
Attitude of a Servant			17,7–10
The Persistent Widow			18,2–5
The Pharisee and the Tax Collector			18,9–14
The Ten Gold Coins			19,11–27
The Two Foundations	7,24–29		6,46–49
The Yeast	13,33		13,20–21
The Lost Sheep	18,10–14		15,1–7
The Lamp	5,15	4,21	8,16 11,33
The New Cloth	9,16	2,21	5,36
The New Wine in Old Wineskins	9,17	2,22	5,37–38
The Sower	13,1–9	4,1–9	8,4–8
The Mustard Seed	13,31–32	4,30–34	13,18–19
The Tenants	21,33–46	12,1–12	20,9–19
The Lesson of the Fig Tree	24,32–35	13,28–31	21,29

MATTHEW STUDY GUIDE

At a Glance

Who wrote the Gospel, and for whom was it written?	Traditionally attributed to the Apostle Matthew (identified in Mark's Gospel as the tax collector Levi). But most scholars today do not accept this judgment. Recent scholarship concludes Matthew was a Greek-speaking Jewish convert to Christianity probably living at the end of the first century in Antioch of Syria and writing for a Jewish audience.
Who are the main players?	John the Baptist Mary Joseph Herod Jesus the disciples Mary Magdalene the religious leaders Caiphas the high priest Pilate
When was the Gospel written?	Probable date somewhere between 70–90 A.D.
Healings in Matthew	Cleansing a leper 8,2–4 (Mk, Lk) The centurion's servant 8,5–13 (Lk) Peter's mother-in-law 8,14–15 (Mk, Lk) Evening time healing of the sick 8,16–17 (Mk, Lk) The paralytic 9,2–8 (Mk, Lk) The woman with a hemorrhage 9,20–22 (Mk, Lk) Two blind men 9,27–31 The mute demoniac 9,32–34 The man with a withered hand 12,10–13 (Mk, Lk) The blind and mute demoniac 12,22–32 (Lk) The Canaanite woman's daughter 15,21–28 (Mk) The boy with a demon 17,14–20 (Mk, Lk) Two blind men 20,30–34 (Mk, Lk) (Mk and Lk indicate the healing miracle is recounted in Mark and Luke as well.)

Other miracles found in Matthew	Calming the storm at sea 8,23–27 (Mk, Lk) The Gadarene demoniacs cured 8,28–34 (Mk, Lk) Raising the official's daughter 9,18. 23–26 (Mk, Lk) Feeding the five thousand 14,13–21 (Mk, Lk, Jn) Walking on the water 14,22–33 (Mk,Jn) Feeding the four thousand 15,32–38 (Mk) Finding tax payment in fish's mouth 17,24–27 Cursing the fig tree 21,18 (Mk) (Mk, Lk and Jn indicate the miracle story also occurs in Mark, Luke or John)
Parables found only in Matthew	Weeds and wheat 13,24–30 The hidden treasure 13,44 The pearl of great price 13,45–46 The dragnet 13,47–50 The lost sheep 18,12–14 The unforgiving servant 18,23–35 The workers in the vineyard 20,1–16 The two sons 21,28–32 The wedding feast 22,2–14 The wise and foolish virgins 25,1–13
Stories told only in Matthew	Joseph's dream 1,20–24 The visit of the Magi 2,1–12 The flight to Egypt 2,13–15 The massacre of the infants 2,16–18 The death of Judas 27,3–10 The dream of Pilate's wife 27,19 The dead rise after Jesus' resurrection 27,52 Guards are posted at Jesus' tomb 27,62–66 The resurrection earthquake 28,2–4
When Jesus prays in Matthew	The Lord's Prayer 6,9–15 Praising the Father 11,25 Blessing the children 19,13 When multiplying loaves and fishes 14,9; 15,36 At the Last Supper 26,26–27 In the garden of Gethsemane 26,36–44 On the cross 27,46
Matthew's portrait of Jesus	Paints Jesus as a lawgiver and Messiah, the great teacher of Israel
Matthew's unique perspective	A convert to Christianity, Matthew traces Jesus' origins back into the history of Israel. He has great interest in showing that Jesus is the promised Messiah who fulfills Old Testament prophecy ("Son of David" and other messianic language is utilized throughout). His Jesus is a kind of catechist, teaching the law and preaching the kingdom of God.

While all share common elements, each of the Gospels is unique. Matthew has traditionally held a place of honor among the four Gospels because it had long been considered the first written. Though that thinking has changed, it still contains elements that set it apart: Matthew contains more of Jesus' sayings than any of the other Gospels; more forcefully than the other Gospels, it connects the story of Jesus with the story of the people of Israel; and it does all this in the form of a powerful story.

Why Matthew Isn't Matthew Anymore

Scholars no longer believe Matthew the apostle is Matthew the evangelist (Gospel writer). Why? 1. Because he uses 90 percent of Mark's Gospel: Why, ask the scholars, would one of the Twelve who was an eyewitness to the life of Jesus depend so heavily on the account of a non-eyewitness? 2. His theological perspective, his command of the Greek language, and his apparent rabbinic training all indicate Matthew the evangelist was probably a *second generation* Jewish Christian.

A Story

Matthew's Gospel contains an unfolding plot, fascinating characters, and various settings. In other words, it has all the elements of a good story. The plot traces Jesus' life from his birth, through his ministry of some success and much rejection, to his death and the final triumph of his resurrection. The characters are sometimes flat and one-dimensional (the Pharisees), and sometimes well developed (Jesus, Peter). And the settings, even though briefly described, help establish the drama and reality of the various scenes. These are characteristics of all good stories.

Of course, in calling the Gospel a story we don't imply that it is "made up" or void of any history. What we mean is that, like a good novel or fine film, it has the ability to catch us up and carry us along by involving us in the intensity and drama of the events being related.

A Fund of Teaching

Matthew's Gospel is so rich with the sayings of Jesus (many of which also appear in Luke's Gospel) that past commentators have often considered it a kind of "catechism" or teacher's manual. But Matthew is not offering actual "transcripts" of Jesus' talks. He organizes Jesus' sayings into discourses or speeches that are like patchwork quilts, containing little logical progression. The sayings, like the similar colored patches of a quilt, are grouped together around a common motif. Through these discourses, Matthew puts the reader in touch with the transforming power of Jesus' teaching.

The Jewish Heritage of Jesus and the Early Church

No one reading Matthew's Gospel can fail to notice the Jewishness of Jesus and the continuity with Israel's history that Jesus represents. The genealogy of Jesus that opens the Gospel and that reaches back to the very origins of Israel is a prime example of Matthew's determination to connect Jesus with Jewish history. Other evidence of Matthew's intense interest in Jesus' Jewish heritage can also be listed: fifty-three direct quotations from and seventy-six other references to the Old Testament fill the Gospel; much concern for Jewish law and customs of ritual purity and prayer is evident throughout; a no-punches-pulled approach characterizes his critique of the Jewish leaders who rejected Jesus and failed to live holy lives.

Matthew's Anti-Semitism

Matthew hits the Jewish leaders hard. His Jesus repeatedly blasts them for hypocrisy and lack of faith. The reader is told not to imitate these insincere show-offs. Matthew's harsh critique may reflect the wall of bitterness and hostility that rose up between Judaism and Jewish Christianity in the early decades of the church. Confronted with a shocking and baffling reversal of expectations (the very Jews to whom Jesus had come rejected him while many Gentiles eagerly embraced his teaching), Matthew registers his disappointment through his characterization of the Jewish leaders. It should be remembered, however, that it is the leaders he criticizes, not the Jewish people as a whole. Sadly, Matthew's negative characterization has often been used as justification for anti-semitism (itself an odious violation of gospel teaching).

But Matthew's Gospel would be welcome reading for a Gentile as well as a Jew interested in Jesus. While stressing that Jesus fulfilled God's promises to Israel, he also asserts that Jesus extends those promises of salvation to all the world. The church's universal mission stands out as another major theme of this Gospel.

READING THROUGH MATTHEW'S GOSPEL

The *NAB* introduction and the footnotes contained in the Gospel text are helpful resources for an informed reading of Matthew. The following commentary supplements those resources by looking at themes and characteristics of each section of Matthew's Gospel.

I. The Origin of Jesus (1,1 – 2,23). The birth and infancy of Jesus
II. Preparation for the Ministry of Jesus (3,1 – 4,17). The temptation in the desert and the ministry of John the Baptist help prepare for Jesus' mission
III. The Galilean Ministry of Jesus (4,17 – 16,12). Jesus' ministry from entrance into Galilee to his announcement of the passion and his plan to go to Jerusalem. Major subdivisions include:
   A. Sermon on the Mount (4,17 – 7,29)
   B. Jesus the healer (8,1 – 9,35)
   C. The mission discourse (9,36 – 11,1)
   D. Mounting hostility to Jesus (11,2 – 12,50)
   E. The parable discourse (13,1-53)
   F. The Kingdom and the disciples (13,54 – 16,12)
IV. The Way to Jerusalem (16,13 – 20,34). Jesus' journey to Jerusalem. Jesus predicts his passion and resurrection three times (16,21; 17,22f; 20,17-19) and instructs disciples on cost of discipleship (18,1-35).
V. Final Teaching in Jerusalem (21,1 – 25,46). Jesus' final exchanges with his opponents in Jerusalem – condemnation of scribes and Pharisees (21,12 – 23,39) and discourse on end times and judgment (24,1 – 25,46).
VI. Jesus' Death and Resurrection (26,1 – 28,20). Passion narrative and burial of Jesus (26,1 – 27,66). The empty tomb (28,1-15) and Jesus' final appearance and ascension (28,16-20)

THE ORIGIN OF JESUS (1,1 – 2,23)

Right from the start Matthew underlines Jesus' Jewish heritage. He is "son of David, son of Abraham" (1,1). From this beginning to the end of the Gospel, Matthew announces repeatedly and loudly that Jesus is the promised Messiah through whom God's longed-for salvation would be realized.

Old Testament Allusions Some of Matthew's quotations of the Old Testament come early. See 1,23; 2,6; 2,15; 2,18; 2,23. Examples of his allusions to Old Testament people and events are the hostility of Herod which recalls Pharaoh's hard-heartedness toward Israel; and the Bethlehem star which recalls Balaam's prophecy of a coming savior (Nm 24,17).

A Messiah Close to His People

Surprisingly, the promised Messiah is not met with applause and fanfare. Instead he is threatened with death. Innocents are killed because of him. He and his family imitate Israel's painful history by being forced into exile and then returning from Egypt in a kind of new exodus. But even then they are fugitives unable to return home to Bethlehem, forced instead to live as displaced persons in Nazareth (2,22f). From all this emerges another of Matthew's themes, namely Jesus' identification with the "least" – the outcast poor of society.

But Jesus is also identified with Israel's struggle for freedom. Throughout that struggle God was with Israel, never abandoning the people. Matthew's Gospel names Jesus "Emmanuel," which means "God is with us." And in this Gospel Jesus demonstrates his commitment to being "with us" through his extraordinary compassion for the suffering (see the healings in Chapters 8–9), by identifying himself with the "least" (Mt 25,31–46), and by promising to be with the church as it does his work in the world (28,20; 18,20).

Jesus as Messiah of Israel and Savior of the World

No sooner has the story begun than we are given signals that Jesus' mission is intended not just for Israel, but for the whole world. The Magi, foreign wise men, come seeking Jesus to pay him homage (2,1–12). Even his family tree contains hints that Jesus' influence will reach the nations. His genealogy surprisingly contains the names of four women, all foreigners (one, Tamar, seduced her own father-in-law, another, Rahab, was a prostitute, and a third, Bathsheba, committed adultery, making Ruth the only model ancestor). Yet all four of these "outsiders" were part of Jesus' history and their presence in his genealogy suggests that Jesus, in turn, will become part of the history of the world.

That Jesus, too, is an outsider is a major theme of Matthew's Gospel. Matthew stresses Jesus' rejection by his own people while pointing out how various Gentiles respond to Jesus with exemplary faith. Though Matthew notes that Jesus' historical ministry was directed at Israel ("I have been sent to the lost sheep of the house of Israel" 15,24), he also announces that the good news of salvation would extend to all nations (28,19).

Gentile Believers Among the non-Jews who demonstrated faith in Jesus were the centurion whose servant was healed (8,15–13); the Gadarene demoniacs (8,28–34); the Canaanite woman (15,21–28); and the centurion at the crucifixion (27,54).

By being the only evangelist to stress the significance of Jesus' name ("God saves" see note at 1,21), Matthew hints at Jesus' saving ministry. And throughout he is portrayed as a savior who liberates people from their awful burdens of oppression, sickness, and sin. Jesus heals, forgives sin (9,1–8), longs for the justice or righteousness of God (3,15), and urges his disciples to willingly suffer for the sake of justice (5,10).

Lacking the chorus of angels and folksy shepherds, and offering only a fleeting glimpse of the tender mother and child, Matthew's nativity story creates a very different mood from Luke's. Here we find danger and death instead of angel voices and bleating lambs. But here, too, is the promise that God is with us despite and in the midst of danger, sin, and death.

The innocence of childhood might prefer Luke's story, but sober adulthood will look to Matthew's Christmas story for the hope it offers in the face of contemporary violence and persecution.

PREPARATION FOR THE MINISTRY OF JESUS (3,1 – 4,17)

This brief section serves as a transition between the infancy narrative and the beginning of Jesus' ministry in Galilee. John the Baptist's preaching in the desert opens the section and Jesus' entry into Galilee ends it. In between we find two of Matthew's major themes.

The Dawn of the New Age

Israel had long awaited the return of the prophet Elijah whose coming would signal the end of the world and the appearance of the kingdom of God. Matthew sees the promise of Elijah's return fulfilled in the person of John the Baptist. John declares the nearness of God's kingdom and prepares the way for Jesus who, being greater than John, is the one who ushers in the kingdom. Matthew's awareness that the coming of Jesus represents the culmination of God's plan for salvation runs throughout the Gospel. Jesus, the "beloved son" (3,17) of God has come to dispel darkness and offer hope to all people who stumble in the dark of sin and death.

Repentance and Good Deeds

In Matthew's Gospel repentance means a change in one's way of thinking and acting. Real change is evident in the good deeds that flow from it. When John and Jesus call for repentance they are challenging their listeners not to rely on their status as children of Abraham (3,15), but to respond concretely to God's love offered in Jesus.

Jesus' temptations in the desert illustrate this same point. As he did in the details of his birth, Jesus here relives the experience of Israel in the desert. Only his story ends differently. Similarly tempted, Jesus does *not* yield to temptation and sin as Israel did in the desert. Jesus practices what he preaches. He demands fidelity to God and teaches how by being fiercely faithful himself.

THE GALILEAN MINISTRY OF JESUS (4,17 – 16,12)

This section constitutes a major portion of Matthew's Gospel. It begins with Jesus' entry into Galilee and covers the bulk of his ministry.

The Sermon on the Mount (4,17 – 7,29)

The best known part of this Gospel is the Sermon on the Mount, the first of Jesus' five great discourses in Matthew. Jesus announces the kingdom and the repentance it requires, attracting not only the first of his disciples, but also great throngs of broken, needy people who are hungry for his message of divine mercy and love. Jesus speaks with power, Matthew suggests, for his words change people's lives as surely as his healing hands.

The Sermon on the Mount consists of groups of Jesus' sayings that are clustered around four themes. Like different spools of yarn thrown into the same basket, we'll need to unravel them one at a time.

Matthew's Five Discourses

I. The Sermon on the Mount 4,17 – 7,29
II. The Mission Discourse 9,36 – 11,1
III. The Parable Discourse 13,1–53
IV. The Discourse on Community 18,1–35
V. The Discourse on the Final Age and Judgment 24,1 – 25,46

A NEW TEACHING FOR A NEW AGE

Jesus, Messiah and authoritative teacher, offers new insights into God's will to those living in the final era of salvation that dawned at his birth. That's the conviction that runs all through Matthew. For Matthew's Jesus, God's will does not negate the revelation that came through the Old Testament Law of Moses, it merely brings it to fullness and completion (5,17; and read the footnotes on that text).

In the Beatitudes we hear the beams that supported the world's way of doing things starting to creak and crumble. God is doing something new, and at the end of the world God's grace will fully triumph. God will finally satisfy those who seek peace and "hunger and thirst for righteousness." In the new age that is now dawning, old wisdom becomes inadequate. Thus Jewish law regarding anger, adultery, divorce, taking oaths, retaliation, and attitudes toward enemies gets a radical new interpretation from Jesus (5,21–28).

LOVE CALLS FOR COMMITTED ACTION

Jesus says, "Not everyone who says to me, 'Lord, Lord,' will enter the kingdom of heaven, but only the one wh does the will of my Father in heaven." These are hard, uncompromising words that call for sentiment to be put into action. As stated earlier, Matthew puts a high value on good deeds, but he does not call for frantic action done for its own sake. All good must be motivated by the kind of unconditional love God has for humanity. The sun nourishes weeds as well as wheat, and God's love falls on both good and bad. So a disciple of Jesus loves enemies as well as friends. This "hard" saying captures the spirit of all of Jesus' teaching on human relationships. The implications that flow from the command to love as lavishly and indiscriminately as God does are obvious: One must be truthful (5,33–37), avoid retaliation (5,38–39), and refuse to exploit another through lust or manipulation (5,27–30). These are not recommendations, they are *demands* of the law of love.

IMAGE OF GOD

The God of Jesus is a close, devoted, and loving God who expects simplicity and honesty from us and wants us to pray with trust and total confidence. God does not love us because we deserve it, for God loves even the unjust and the enemy (5,45–48). Before such a God we have no choice but to be ourselves, not putting on airs, but relating as we would to a loving parent who knows us completely (6,9–15).

LIVING THE SERMON ON THE MOUNT

Some hear the words of the sermon as impossible ideals livable only by perfect people. Others claim they were intended only for Jesus' listeners who expected the imminent end of the world and thus could respond with heroic virtue. But in the sermon Jesus offered neither clear-cut laws to guide all human behavior, nor abstract, near-impossible ideals. As the core of Jesus' teaching, the sermon offers practical guidance on how, with God's grace, we can live and be faithful to the Gospel. The sermon asserts the possibility of living differently, and of being transformed in the process.

Jesus the Healer (8,1 – 9,35)

In this powerful section, Matthew presents Jesus the healer. Though he draws most of his material here from Mark's Gospel, Matthew significantly edits the material he borrows. He wants to concentrate on Jesus' most essential actions and words, so he shortens Mark's stories and eliminates some of Mark's most colorful details.

Matthew arranges the stories of this section into three groups, each with its own dominant motif:

Group 1	8,1–17	Emphasizes Jesus' healing power. (The leper, centurion's servant, Peter's mother-in-law)
Group 2	8,18 – 9,17	Emphasizes the demands of discipleship. (Calming the storm, healing the demoniacs, the paralytic)
Group 3	9,18–34	Emphasizes the indispensable role of faith in the healing stories. (The official's daughter, the woman with a hemorrhage, two blind men, the mute demoniac)

We will now look more closely at each of these three dominant themes.

CHRISTOLOGY

The first three healing stories reveal Jesus to be a Messiah of both power and compassion. On the one hand he fulfills the prophetic promise of Isaiah 53,4 ("He took away our infirmities and bore our diseases"), but at the same time he demonstrates his willingness to stand compassionately with all those who suffer sickness and fear death.

CONDITIONS OF DISCIPLESHIP

The second group of stories reveal the demands of discipleship: total commitment to the Kingdom of God (8,18–23), readiness to deal with fearful, life-threatening experiences (the storm 8,24–27), and mystifying encounters with evil (the demoniacs 8,28–34). Unlike the hard-hearted Pharisees, the true disciple sees that Jesus is driven only by mercy and compassion.

FAITH

Real faith is nothing more than simple trust in Jesus' ability to heal and transform us. All the characters in these four stories demonstrate that expectant faith in very active ways. All those who are healed take some initiative: The leper disregards the law in approaching

Jesus; the woman dares to touch him; the Gentile official begs help of a Jewish nobody; the friends of the paralytic find a way to reach Jesus. Their active trust leads them to expect a response and they get it. Is there a lesson there for us who also seek transformation in our lives?

The Mission Discourse (9,36 – 11,1)

We now move into the second of the five great discourses in Matthew. Like Jesus himself who confined his mission to the land of Israel, the apostles are sent only to Israelite towns, not to the Gentiles. They are to proclaim the Kingdom of God and to heal, and they are to be motivated by the same compassion that drove Jesus to reach out to the crowds who were "troubled and abandoned, like sheep without a shepherd" (9,36–38).

Though the twelve disciples are commissioned to preach and heal, they are not yet commissioned to teach. That will come only after the resurrection when they will better understand Jesus' mission. Besides sharing in Jesus' ministry of healing and proclaiming the Kingdom, another theme typical of Matthew surfaces here: Disciples must know that following Jesus means walking a bumpy road where hostility, rejection, or indifference may be waiting around every corner.

The Twelve Apostles

Peter, formerly Simon	Matthew, tax collector
Andrew, Peter's brother	James, son of Alphaeus
James, son of Zebedee	Thaddaeus (or Jude son of James)
John, James's brother	Simon the Cananean (zealot)
Philip, a fisherman	Judas Iscariot, Jesus' betrayer
Bartholomew (or Nathanael)	Matthias later succeeds Judas to restore the number to twelve (Acts 1,15–26)
Thomas (name means "Twin")	

But despite those harsh realities, disciples are to be unafraid and confident, relying on the power of the gospel. The God who watches sparrows and clothes the flowers of the field has also numbered each hair on their heads.

Though here the mission of Jesus and the twelve is limited to Israel, later, after the resurrection, it will explode into the entire world.

Mounting Hostility to Jesus and His Mission (11,2 – 12,50)

Jesus warned that his message would be opposed. Now opposition hits him (and the Baptist) square in the face.

John is in prison awaiting death. He sends his disciples to Jesus with the poignant question: "Are you the one who is to come, or should we look for another?" We can hear 2000 years of longing in that question. Jesus uses the inquiry to summarize his great deeds and to comment on John's ministry and his own. No one else in all the Gospels receives praise like Jesus gives John here.

One of the Gospel's most beautiful passages, which sheds light on the nature of the relationship between Jesus and his Father ("No one knows the Father except the son . . . " 11,25–27), is juxtaposed against scenes of opposition from enemies who are unable to recognize Jesus for who he is and who attack him for violating the Sabbath.

Another of Matthew's themes now emerges: judgment. Opposition to Jesus will not go unnoticed. Those who reject him (like the unrepentant towns of 11,20–24) will bear responsibility. Matthew makes it very clear that good intentions alone are never enough. To avoid judgment, a tree must bear good fruit (12,33). And blood kinship alone does not make one family with Jesus, but doing God's will does (12,50).

The Parable Discourse (13,1–53)

Parables are meant to turn things upside down. Their method and their purpose is ironic, that is, saying one thing but meaning another. These cunning stories can at the same time reveal and veil the mystery of the Kingdom. They can open eyes to truth, but only if one is willing to look beneath the surface where the fuller meaning lies.

The major themes of Matthew's Gospel reemerge in the parables of this section:

Theme	Parables
The certain triumph of the Kingdom	The sower (13,1–9), the mustard seed (13,31f), and the yeast (13,33f)
Discipleship: True disciples surrender everything for the sake of the beauty of God's reign	The buried treasure, the pearl of great price, and the dragnet (13,44–46)

Many of the parables also convey clear moral messages. For example, the parable of the weeds among wheat (13,24–30) teaches that the church is a mixed bag of good and evil, just like the rest of the world. But in the end all will be judged and justice will triumph.

The conclusion of the parable discourse restates Matthew's unique perspective on Jesus. Matthew firmly believed Jesus had not come to do away with the traditions of Judaism, but to give them new meaning. He is the householder who can bring from the storehouse "both the new and the old" (13,52). Jesus does not abolish the Law, he brings it to life for each new generation.

The Kingdom and the Disciples (13,54 – 16,12)

In this section Jesus continues to teach and heal while his opponents — mainly the Pharisees — continue their resistance. Though the section eludes a single classification, it is dominated by the haunting story of Jesus walking on the water. In the dark of gloom of the sea of Galilee, a light of understanding begins to dawn on the disciples, who start to comprehend the awesome identity of the astonishing Messiah.

Three motifs run through these chapters:

THE INCLUSIVE MISSION OF JESUS

In Matthew's Gospel, as in Mark's, Jesus' ministry tears down walls and breaks boundaries. Many of Jesus' actions force people's eyes and minds to open. But when he ventures into the

Gentile region of Tyre and Sidon, it is his own vision that is seemingly expanded by a Canaanite woman who won't take no for an answer (15,21–28). The woman asks help for her daughter, but Jesus clings to his commitment to minister only to the Israelites. She persists, and her active, expectant faith wins him over. If Matthew's church was making the mistake of thinking only Jews could become Christians, this story would challenge them to broaden their understanding of their mission and realize that God wants all people within the boundaries of the Kingdom.

The only miracle recorded by all four evangelists is found in this section (14,15–21). Together with the second miraculous feeding story it reinforces the theme of God's liberality. Once more the disciples see in Jesus the embodiment of God's big-hearted compassion.

Miracles Of the four Gospels, Mark's records the most miracles. The only miracle recorded in all four Gospels is the feeding of the five thousand. Matthew, Mark, and Luke share ten miracles: Peter's mother-in-law; storm calmed; demoniacs cured; leper cured; daughter of Jairus raised; woman with hemorrhage; paralytic; man with withered hand; boy with a demon; two blind men. The only miracle common to Matthew, Mark, and John is Jesus walking on water.

OPPOSITION AND REJECTION

Jesus encountered opposition every step of the way. But perhaps the most bitter was that in his own hometown (13,54–58) where his neighbors' mockery and lack of faith kept him from working "many mighty deeds" (13,58).

Through the controversy over the washing of hands before meals (15,1–20) Matthew offers an explanation for the stubbornness of Jesus' opponents: They have forgotten that the Law was given as a sign and source of God's love. Now some religious leaders have allowed their own human traditions to "nullify the word of God" (15,6). By placing good but secondary values ahead of those that are truly essential, they have turned the Law into a millstone hung around people's necks. Here, too, Matthew makes the point that Jesus came not to nullify the Law, but to insist that true fidelity is motivated first of all by love.

THE DISCIPLES

Of the three evangelists who record the miracle of Jesus walking on the water, only Matthew adds the detail that Peter walked on water too. Stories of Peter are important in this Gospel, as is the term "little faith" (14,31) that Matthew uses to explain why Peter sank in the waves. The disciples admit their faith is not as strong as it should be, but they do not reject Jesus. Instead, they acclaim him as "the Son of God" (14,33) and—though hesitantly—understand his teaching (16,12).

THE WAY TO JERUSALEM (16,13–20,34)

In this section Jesus asks his disciples the chief question of the entire Gospel: "Who do you say that I am?" (16,15). After Peter's confession that Jesus is "the Messiah, the Son of the living God" (16,16), Jesus begins to speak openly about his impending death. He then announces his

JERUSALEM IN NEW TESTAMENT TIMES

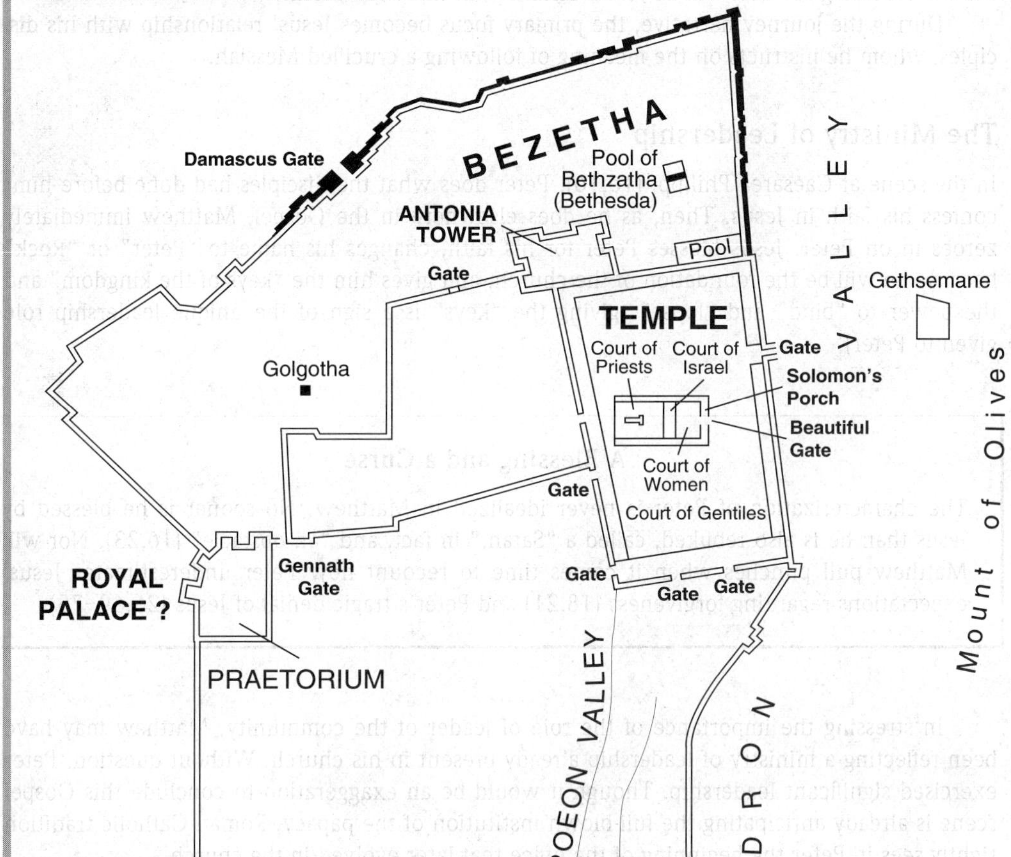

intent to go to Jerusalem, thus introducing a "journey" motif into the story. Two more predictions of his own death (17,22f; 20,17–19) will keep the reader focused on Jerusalem and the fate that awaits Jesus there. But first, in the transfiguration event (17,1–8), where Jesus encounters Moses and Elijah—representatives of Old Testament Law and prophets, whose presence confirms Jesus' role as the fulfillment of both—the disciples are given a glimpse of the resurrected glory that will be Jesus' once he has faced his destiny.

During the journey narrative, the primary focus becomes Jesus' relationship with his disciples, whom he instructs on the meaning of following a crucified Messiah.

The Ministry of Leadership

In the scene at Caesarea Philippi (16,16), Peter does what the disciples had done before him: confess his faith in Jesus. Then, as he does elsewhere in the Gospel, Matthew immediately zeroes in on Peter. Jesus blesses Peter for his faith, changes his name to "Peter" or "Rock" because he will be the foundation of the church, and gives him the "keys of the kingdom" and the power to "bind" and "loose" (giving the "keys" is a sign of the unique leadership role given to Peter).

A Blessing and a Curse

The characterization of Peter is never idealized in Matthew. No sooner is he blessed by Jesus than he is also rebuked, called a "Satan," in fact, and "an obstacle" (16,23). Nor will Matthew pull punches when it comes time to recount how Peter underestimates Jesus' expectations regarding forgiveness (18,21) and Peter's tragic denial of Jesus (26,69–75).

In stressing the importance of the role of leader of the community, Matthew may have been reflecting a ministry of leadership already present in his church. Without question, Peter exercised significant leadership. Though it would be an exaggeration to conclude this Gospel scene is already anticipating the full-blown institution of the papacy, Roman Catholic tradition rightly sees in Peter the beginning of the office that later evolved in the church.

The Church Matthew's concern for the Christian church is reflected in the fact that the word for church (*ekklesia* in Greek) is used only in his Gospel. It occurs when Jesus says of Peter " . . . on this rock I will build my church" (16,18).

Life in the Community

The Discourse on Community, the fourth of Matthew's major discourses, occurs here. It is built around two parables, the Lost Sheep (18,10–14) and the Unforgiving Servant (18,21–35), that communicate the two major themes of this discourse.

The Lost Sheep parable reveals God's great interest in the weak or alienated members of the community. Community members are to be humble and should never "scandalize" or shun those who are weak or living on the margins of the church (18,6–10).

The parable of the Unforgiving Servant stresses the need for reconciliation: To be forgiven, we must be willing to forgive. Suggestions are offered for settling disputes, but the dominant message is that we must love even our enemies in imitation of a God who loves us lavishly and unconditionally.

The message for the church cannot be missed: Institutional concerns and money matters, important as they are, must always take a back seat to our care for one another.

FINAL TEACHING IN JERUSALEM (21,1–25,46)

Jesus, always the unlikely Messiah, now enters Jerusalem in triumph, but he does so riding a donkey's colt—which Matthew interprets as a sign of humility. Still pursuing his divinely given mission to call Israel to repentance, Jesus fearlessly drives the money changers from the Temple. Next he takes up teaching in the Temple area but encounters renewed resistance from the Pharisees, who have now acquired powerful allies in the "chief priests and elders of the people"—all of whom are members of the Sanhedrin.

Sanhedrin A council of 70 members that functioned as the chief political and religious authority for Jews of Jesus' day.

This section contains two clusters of sayings and parables. In the first, 23,1–39, Jesus blasts the Scribes and Pharisees for their hypocrisy and infidelity. The second cluster of sayings and parables forms the so-called "Eschatological Discourse" or the discourse on the end of the world. This last of Matthew's five discourses (24,36–25,46) contemplates the ultimate fate both of the Temple and all of human history.

The Authority of Jesus

Like a fine conductor, Matthew orchestrates the elements of this section to trumpet a grand Messiah chorus. Jesus' triumphant entry into Jerusalem shakes the entire city (21,10). Strength and authority accompany him wherever he goes. On his own authority this "Lord of the sabbath" (12,8) drives the money-changers from the Temple and reasserts the Temple's proper role as a house of prayer (21,12–27). And he backs down from none of the religious authorities who challenge him—not the scribes or the chief priests, not the elders of the people, nor the Sadducees. Matthew leaves no room for doubt about Jesus' status as Messiah and true Teacher of Israel.

And what is the source of Jesus' authority? He is the Son of God. For Matthew the evidence is clear and irresistible. Even the parable of the tenants affirms it (21,33–46). In that allegory Jesus describes himself as the vineyard owner's son and "heir." And later he asserts his preeminence even over King David who called the future Messiah his "Lord" (22,41–46).

When Jesus is questioned about the Law, his reaction is typical of Matthew's Gospel: He reinterprets, never rejects, the Law. Though surrounded by hostile opponents, Jesus fields their questions with the poise and ease of a master teacher, reminding them that the "whole law and the prophets" (22,40) depend on the command to love God and neighbor.

Jesus and His Opponents

Suddenly the tone changes. The poised Jesus shifts into an offensive mode, hammering the scribes and Pharisees for their hypocrisy and infidelity. Jesus points to them as negative role models, the opposite of what disciples should be. Through the series of seven "woes" (i.e., "Woe to" — a phrase used by the prophets to express horror over sin and the punishment it will bring), Matthew reveals the values that really matter to Jesus:

- Practicing what you preach (23,3)
- Showing compassion rather than burdening others (23,4)
- Not using religion for self-glorification (23,5f)
- Letting mercy and justice guide interpretation of the law (23,23–38)
- Expecting religious leaders to show respect rather than arrogance toward the community (23,8–12)

These harsh and sobering condemnations are directed not only at the Jewish leaders, but at Matthew's own Christian readers to encourage them to truly live the Gospel, not pay it hollow lip-service. The Church cautions us never to let these blunt condemnations of the religious leaders influence our attitude toward Jews today.

Judgment

In the eschatological discourse we find a theme we've seen before in Matthew: The true disciple is a doer of good deeds. Look at the many examples that state and restate that point:

- The "faithful and prudent servant" is the one caring for the house and doing good for the needy (24,45–51)
- The "wise virgins" are those who have their oil ready (25,1–13)
- The servant who is rewarded when the master returns is the one who used his or her talents (25,14–30)
- Those who inherit the Kingdom are those who live the law of love by feeding, clothing, visiting, and welcoming the needy (25,31–46)

There is no better lesson on the value of good deeds than the climactic parable of the sheep and goats. The "sheep" are blessed because in life they showed compassion even though they did not realize it was the risen Lord who was present in the needy they served. The good do good. Hypocrites just talk about it. Matthew's Jesus has little tolerance for that.

JESUS' DEATH AND RESURRECTION (26,1 – 28,20)

Matthew's version of the Passion is cast in light and shadow: Jesus' lordship is acknowledged, but only after he dies and only by a Gentile soldier who declares, "Clearly this was the Son of

God!" (27,54). Positive examples of discipleship contrast sharply with the cowardice and betrayal from Jesus' closest friends. From the cross Jesus speaks no words of forgiveness as in Luke, but expresses abandonment instead: "My God, my God, why have you forsaken me?" (27, 46). Matthew's Passion is not only sadder than Luke's and John's, it also contains a garden scene that embodies more sorrow than is found anywhere else in the Gospels. Yet throughout, Jesus retains his majesty as the Messiah of Israel and, in the end, he is gloriously vindicated in his resurrection.

The Majesty of Jesus

Though gloomy clouds surround him, signs of Jesus' majesty penetrate the darkness, giving evidence of the obscured but glorious "sun" that waits to be revealed. The majestic Son of God has foreknowledge of what lies ahead:

- He knows the leaders plot against him (26,1f)
- He knows he soon will die (26,12.18)
- He knows that Judas will betray him (26,25) and that Peter will deny him (26,34)
- He is even in control of when he will be arrested: not until he's confronted his betrayer (26,50)
- In response to the high priest's demand that he identify himself, Jesus states with calm, majestic certitude that he will be revealed as the Son of Man coming in glory and exalted at God's right hand (26,64).

Matthew's passion story makes one overwhelming claim: God's son will not be destroyed by death, for he is lord over death as well as life. Climactic testimony to this fact is given when, at the moment of Jesus' death, the earth convulses violently and tombs give up their dead.

The Dawn of the New Age

The death of Jesus changes everything. For Matthew, Jesus' death was an ultimate act of love that summarized his entire mission. But because his death (and resurrection) fulfilled God's promise of salvation to Israel, it was also the center point of all history. What came before it was one age; everything after it would be a whole new era.

Human history turned a corner, and in this final age of human experience people would have to respond to God's grace in a new way. Matthew provides startling evidence that history is transformed: Nature reacts to Jesus' death with dramatic signs. The dead walk out of their tombs—just as in Ezekiel's vision of the dry bones being restored to life (Ez 37). In Jesus, death is conquered at last; now resurrection reigns.

Another piece of Matthew's theology of history centers on the fact that the Jewish people and their leaders rejected Jesus. Ironically, it is because the effort with the Jews had failed that the Gospel can now be preached to the Gentiles. Though he seems to present hope that Israel may someday embrace Jesus' message (see 23,39), Matthew, like Paul in Romans 9–11, believes that Israel's failure becomes a graced opportunity for the Gentiles. That, of course, must not be construed as God's rejection of Israel. Vatican II reaffirmed what Paul had clearly said: Israel remains God's special possession; God will never abandon the promises made to the chosen people. Christians can rightly pray for others to accept the truth of Jesus, but they must never impose their faith.

Examples and Counterexamples

Using examples, both positive and negative, of people reacting to crisis, Matthew allows the Passion to teach his readers about discipleship.

The negative examples are plentiful: The religious leaders never stop opposing Jesus; the disciples fall asleep three times while Jesus prays in the Garden, then they all desert him; Judas betrays him then kills himself rather than seek forgiveness; and, with oaths and curses, Peter denies him three times.

But there are also bright spots: At Bethany, despite protests from the disciples, a woman anoints Jesus in a final gesture of kindness (26,6–13); Pilate's wife intervenes on behalf of "that holy man" (27,19); the centurion and his men confess Jesus as "the Son of God" (27,54); the wealthy Joseph of Arimathea, disregarding public opinion, buries Jesus in his own tomb. And then, of course, there's Jesus. What better example could there be of faithful discipleship than Jesus enduring rejection, abandonment, and unbearable pain all for the sake of his Father's will?

The Resurrection (28,1–20)

Though none of the evangelists tries to describe the actual moment of the resurrection, Matthew comes closest in mentioning an "earthquake" and "an angel of the Lord" rolling away the stone from the tomb.

The original ending of Mark's Gospel dealt only briefly with the resurrection: The tomb is found empty and the angel announces Jesus' victory over death. But Matthew, in borrowing from Mark, adds important details to his source about both Jesus' disciples and his opponents. *Disciples:* Jesus appears first to the women as they leave the tomb (28,9f) and then to the disciples in Galilee (28,16–20). *Opponents:* As we've seen throughout the Gospel, the leaders of the people never let down their guard: Even after hearing the amazing report of what happened at the tomb, they refuse to believe in Christ's triumph and instead bribe the guards to invent a story about the disciples snatching Jesus' body.

The great commission scene (28,16–20) accomplishes much for Matthew. First it reasserts the triumphant, majestic image of Jesus that Matthew has consistently presented. Then we hear a reprise of several of Matthew's other themes: (1) concern for the church; (2) the church's universal mission—the risen Jesus commissions the disciples to go "make disciples of all nations," initiating the Gentiles into the community of the church and teaching them

Mountaintop Experiences

Throughout the Gospel, as throughout the Old Testament, special revelations occur on mountaintops. Ancient peoples considered mountains the homes of gods and the likely place for a divine encounter (Moses and Elijah both meet God on mountaintops).

In Matthew, the temptation of Jesus, the Sermon on the Mount, the transfiguration, the healing of the crowds (15,29–31), and the commission (28,16–20) all occur on mountaintops.

all Jesus had commanded; (3) Jesus as teacher; and (4) realistic portrayal of the disciples—the disciples (now numbering only "eleven" as Judas' tragic fate is not ignored) get no cosmetic make-over. Matthew presents them as realistically as ever, for he tells us that even when they encountered the risen Jesus they "doubted" (28,17)!

The conclusion of the Gospel recalls its beginning: The one who was named "Emmanuel," "God is with us," (1,23) now makes a final promise: "I am with you always, until the end of the age" (28,20). The church will never be without a firm foundation: Jesus the Lord.

Questions for Discussion or Reflection

1. What can we learn about Jesus from the genealogy/infancy narrative? What is the significance of the women in the genealogy? In what ways do the details of his birth confirm the truth of Jesus' name "Emmanuel"?

2. What values of society do the Beatitudes challenge? After reading the Sermon on the Mount what changes do you think would be in order for the nation—and for yourself?

3. Throughout the Gospel (and especially in Chapters 14–17) Jesus harshly criticizes the religious leaders. What is the basis for his criticism? Given that some scholars think Jesus may have been a Pharisee himself, why is he especially critical of them?

4. In Chapter 18 Matthew presents parables and teachings on humility and forgiveness. What does it mean to "become like children?" Does it have more to do with innocence or with recognition of one's dependence? What is the role of forgiveness and reconciliation in the life of a Christian?

5. Paul alludes to the paradox that because the Jews rejected Jesus, the Gospel can be proclaimed to the Gentiles. Can this be viewed as the unfolding of God's plan? What is the nature of the continuing relationship between God and the Jewish people? Can Christians ever use religious reasons to justify anti-Semitism?

MARK READING GUIDE

At a Glance

Who wrote the Gospel, and for whom was it written?	Most likely a Gentile disciple of Peter writing for other Gentiles. It was the unanimous opinion of the early church, and remains the opinion of many today, that he was John Mark, the companion of Paul first mentioned in Acts 12,12.
Who are the main players?	John the Baptist Jesus The twelve disciples, especially Peter, James, and John Pilate The religious opponents
When was the Gospel written?	Scholars believe it was the first Gospel written. Probable date of composition between 65 and 70 A.D., possibly in Rome.

Healings in Mark	A leper 1,40 (Mt, Lk) Peter's mother-in-law 1,30 (Mt, Lk) Evening healings of the sick 1,32 (Mt, Lk) A paralytic 2,3 (Mt, Lk) A man with a withered hand 3,1 (Mt, Lk) The woman with a hemorrhage 5,25 (Mt, Lk) The Syrophoenician woman's daughter 7,24 (Mt) A deaf-mute man 7,31 (only in Mk) A blind paralytic at Bethsaida 8,22 (only in Mk) The epileptic boy 9,17 (Mt, Lk) The blind Bartimaeus 10,46 (Mt, Lk) (Mt and Lk indicate the healing miracle is recounted in Matthew and Luke as well.)
Other miracles found in Mark	Cure of a demoniac in synagogue 1,23 (Lk) Calming the storm 4,35 (Mt, Lk) Curing the Gerasene demoniacs 5,1 (Mt, Lk) Raising Jairus's daughter 5,22 (Mt, Lk) Feeding the five thousand 6,30 (Mt, Lk, Jn) Walking on the water 6,48 (Mt, Lk, Jn) Feeding the four thousand 8,1 (Mt) Withering the fig tree 11,12 (Mt) (Mt, Lk, and Jn indicate the miracle story also occurs in Matthew, Luke or John)
Miracles and parables found only in Mark	Though all but 31 of Mark's verses are quoted by either Luke or Matthew, two parables and two miracles are found only in Mark: *Parables:* The growing seed 4,26–29 The traveling householder 13,34–37 *Healings:* A deaf man 7,31–37 The blind man at Bethsaida 8,22–26 (Mark has fewer parables than the other synoptics: Matthew = 20, Luke = 28, Mark = 9)
When Jesus prays in Mark	In a deserted place 1,35 In the garden at Gethsemane 14,32–40 On the cross 15,34
Mark's portrait of Jesus	Paints Jesus as the unrecognized (hidden), suffering Messiah
Mark's unique perspective	Though the shortest Gospel, Mark often contains more vivid detail than Matthew or Luke. Mark stresses Jesus' suffering: Jesus is the prophesied Messiah who came not as a king, but as a *servant.* Mark is a storyteller who focuses more on what Jesus *did* than on what he *said;* he thus reveals Jesus as a man of power and decisive action. Because he was rejected by the Jews to whom he went first, Jesus expanded his mission to Gentiles. Through his many miracles, Jesus manifests his divine status as God's only son.

Mark's Details

Though his is the shortest Gospel, Mark often includes colorful details the other synoptics leave out. These details give the impression of an authentic eye-witness account which some believe Mark got from Peter. Here are some examples of Mark's vivid style:

- 1,35 Jesus awakened "very early *before dawn.*"
- 4,38 During a terrible storm, Jesus rests in the stern of the boat *"sleeping on a cushion."*
- 5,1–5 Mark says of the Gerasene demoniac: *"no one could restrain him . . . even with a chain."*
- 5,42 Jesus raises from the dead a girl who was *"a child of twelve."*
- 9,3 When transfigured, Jesus' clothes became dazzlingly white—*"such as no fuller (bleach) on earth could bleach them."*

Mark may not only have written the first of the four New Testament Gospels, he may even have invented the literary form. He took the Christian message, the proclamation of the good news of the Kingdom of God, and shaped it into a powerful, dynamic story that not only preserved the church's memory of Jesus but also turned that memory into a force that would radically change people's lives.

Mark wrote at a time of crisis for the early church. In Rome, Nero had launched a bitter persecution against the Christian community. Some members remained heroically faithful and even accepted martyrdom. But others abandoned their faith rather than face death. Addressed to these Roman Christians, Mark's account of the crucified Jesus and his disciples provided encouragement and instruction for a troubled church.

CHARACTERISTICS OF MARK'S GOSPEL

As you read, there are several themes of Mark's Gospel that you should be on the lookout for.

A Theology in Narrative

Mark gave his announcement of the good news of salvation (the literal meaning of the word *gospel*) the form of a story. He avoided abstractions and dove right into a breathless account of Jesus' ministry using a blunt style that some may find a bit jarring (in 3,21 his family comes to bring him home because they think "he is out of his mind;" and in 7,27 he compares ministering to Gentiles to throwing food to dogs).

The urgency in his tone combines with his strong language to propel this shortest of the four Gospels toward its climax—the crucifixion, the central event of Mark's narrative and the event for which Jesus was born. Mark has no time for an infancy narrative, for elegant prose, or for lengthy discourses like those in Matthew. His purpose is clearly to assert that Jesus is the Son of God, and this is what he does.

Mark's urgency helps communicate his theological message: There is no time to waste in responding to the message and mission of Jesus. Mark's story is packed with conflicts between Jesus and his religious opponents and between Jesus and demonic forces. Mark wants to let his readers know that following Jesus demands radical life-changes that inevitably will put them, too, in conflict with the forces of this world.

Christology

Jesus himself poses the central question of Mark's Gospel: "Who do you say that I am?" (8,29). Yet, ironically, in this Gospel Jesus works very hard to keep his identity as the Messiah a secret. But the secret keeps "leaking" out through everything Jesus says and does: He heals, expels demons, argues with opponents, teaches his disciples, shares parables, and, most importantly, he dies and rises from the dead. All this proclaims Jesus' unmistakable identity as the Son of God and the Messiah.

Jesus' healings and exorcisms were evidence that God was breaking into human history offering liberation and salvation. But for Mark the most convincing sign of that fact was the cross. Real faith in Jesus means embracing his cross. The liberation and salvation Jesus came to bring were only made possible by his death. Yes, he was "Messiah," healer, "Son of Man," but those titles can only be understood in the context of Jesus' redemptive death.

Mark in the Liturgy

Until Vatican II revised the lectionary, Mark was rarely heard in Roman Catholic liturgy. Mark had been largely ignored because the Gospel was considered a poor condensation of Matthew's Gospel. His literary style is unsophisticated and at times embarrassingly blunt. Today, Mark's Gospel is used for an entire year (Year B) in the 3-year cycle of the Sunday lectionary.

Discipleship

Another irony is found when we look at the disciples of Jesus and the role they play in Mark's story. Mark is very intent on teaching what it means to be a disciple of Jesus. And yet the disciples, Jesus' inner circle, do no better than anyone else at understanding who Jesus is and what he came to do. First they openly misunderstand Jesus, and then they totally abandon him.

In Mark the disciples are both historical figures and object lessons. Mark wanted his readers to see themselves in the disciples, who failed Jesus but received his love and forgiveness nonetheless. The Gospel ends with hope and promise of renewal: The "young man" at the tomb asks the women to tell the disciples to go to Galilee where they will see Jesus again. The same hope is offered to the reader who, like the disciples, may have been slow to understand Jesus, and may even have failed him, but who now can hope for the same forgiveness and renewal Jesus offered the disciples.

The Messianic Secret

It may seem curious that throughout Mark's Gospel (seven times in all) Jesus tries to keep his true identity a secret: He instructs those he heals, his disciples, and even demons not to talk about his miracles or reveal who he is. And he has good reasons. Jesus knows the kind of Messiah the people want and expect. He is not prepared to be that kind of Messiah—a military leader overthrowing Roman rule, or an easy Messiah who fills empty stomachs and relieves every burden. Jesus has come to be a suffering Messiah, not a king of glory and triumph. Jesus' consistent effort in Mark's Gospel to conceal his identity as Messiah is called the messianic secret.

READING THROUGH MARK'S GOSPEL

Try reading all of Mark at one sitting; the compact story makes for compelling reading. Then you can begin to focus on individual passages.

A look at the map on page RG 336 will help you understand how Mark uses geography to organize his story of Jesus into four main parts:

1. The *Judean desert,* where Jesus is baptized by John;
2. *Galilee,* the locus of most of Jesus' ministry;

3. The *journey to Jerusalem,* as Jesus prepares to embrace his fate; and
4. *Jerusalem* itself, where the story climaxes in death and resurrection.

Thus, the basic outline of Mark's Gospel can be sketched simply in four parts:

I. Overture in the Desert (1,1–13). In the Judean desert John preaches a baptism of repentance. Jesus accepts John's baptism and, at that very moment, his identity as God's son is revealed. Jesus then goes off alone and is tempted by Satan.

II. The Galilean Ministry of Jesus (1,14–8,21). In Galilee, the northern region of Israel, Jesus embarks on his public ministry. The central events are:
   A. Announcing the Kingdom of God (1,14–15)
   B. Calling his first disciples (1,16–45)
   C. Tangling with the religious leaders (2,1–3,6)
   D. Experiencing continued opposition and misundertanding (3,7–4,34)
   E. Expanding his mission to include Gentile territory (4,35–8,21)

III. The Journey from Galilee to Jerusalem (8,22–10,52). Starting in Caesarea Philippi, where Peter acknowledges Jesus as the Christ, Jesus and the disciples travel down to Jerusalem for Jesus' upcoming passion. Much teaching on discipleship is found in this section.

IV. Death and Resurrection in Jerusalem (11,1–16,8). The story climaxes in Jerusalem where Jesus:
   A. Enters triumphantly into the city and then drives the money-changers from the Temple (11,1–12,44)
   B. Predicts the destruction of the Temple (13,1–37)
   C. Is arrested, tried, flogged, and crucified (14,1–15,47)
   D. Achieves victory over death and the grave (16,1–8)

The Gospel of Mark originally ended at Chapter 16,8. Writers other than the evangelist appended additional endings they felt made for a smoother, more suitable conclusion.

The following comments are meant to complement the *NAB* introduction and the detailed notes found within the biblical text. We will examine each of the four major sections for its themes and characteristics.

OVERTURE (1,1–13)

A desert can be many things: a *place of new beginnings*—Israel, after all, was led into the desert and there forged into a people covenanted to God. But it can also be a *place of testing*—it was in the desert that the Israelites first rebelled against the Lord and discovered their true character. The desert setting of Mark's Gospel provides opportunities for Jesus to replay Israel's history. Jesus comes to the desert to inaugurate his mission, and in the desert he is put to the test by Satan.

Just like the overture of an orchestral piece, Mark's brief introduction announces the major themes that will surface again throughout the Gospel:

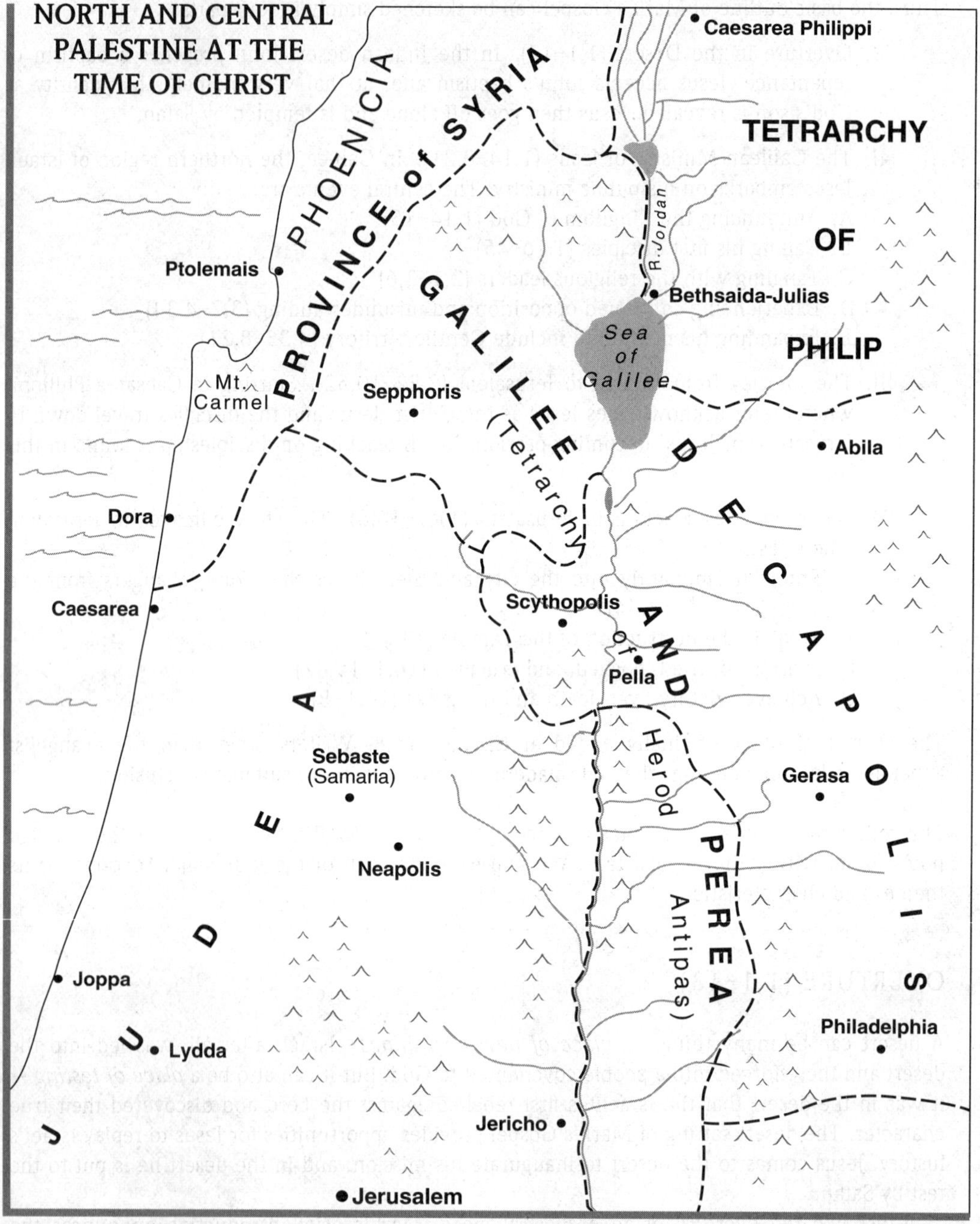
NORTH AND CENTRAL PALESTINE AT THE TIME OF CHRIST
Caesarea Philippi
PROVINCE of SYRIA
PHOENICIA
TETRARCHY OF PHILIP
R. Jordan
Ptolemais
Bethsaida-Julias
Sea of Galilee
GALILEE (Tetrarchy)
Mt. Carmel
Sepphoris
Abila
DECAPOLIS
Dora
Caesarea
Scythopolis
of
Pella
Herod
Gerasa
Sebaste (Samaria)
Neapolis
PEREA
Antipas)
JUDEA
Joppa
Philadelphia
Lydda
Jericho
Jerusalem

1. *A new age is beginning.* John, dressed like the long-awaited Elijah who was to return at the end of the world, comes as the herald of a new age. By casting John in this light, Mark indicates that God is doing something new. People must reform their lives to be ready for God's new dawn.
2. *Jesus is the Son of God.* At his baptism, God's voice announces Jesus' true identity; then God's Spirit descends on Jesus to fill him with power for his messianic mission. Christology (understanding the nature of Jesus) will remain a major concern of the Gospel.
3. *Jesus' ministry will be marked by conflict with the forces of darkness.* What Jesus experienced in the desert is but a preview of what is to come: In carrying out his mission, Jesus will often confront opponents and cast out demons. Struggle is a constant in any effort for true liberation.

THE GALILEAN MINISTRY OF JESUS (1,14–8,21)

This major section, which constitutes half the Gospel, can be divided into five distinctive segments.

The Keynote of Jesus' Mission (1,14–15)

A single verse, 1,15, announces three major themes of Mark's Gospel:

"This is the time of fulfillment." What Israel had longed for is finally here: the new and final age of salvation. And Jesus is the one who ushers it in. In this new age, old ways will have to yield to new responses, just like new wine must be poured into new wineskins (2,18–22).

"The Kingdom of God is at hand." The "Kingdom of God" is a biblical symbol that expresses Israel's hope for a time when God would rule the earth with justice and peace. Jesus not only announces the rule of God, he actually inaugurates it by healing, working for justice, and freely giving his life for others.

"Repent and believe in the gospel." The gospel of Jesus demands a response, a turning around: repentance. Jesus asks his disciples to see, hear, and think differently; to view reality with eyes of faith and to change their lives accordingly.

The Call of the Disciples and Jesus' First Day of Ministry (1,16–45)

In Mark's account, Jesus gets busy immediately. Set in the small fishing village of Capernaum where Mark situates most of Jesus' ministry, this section is typical of Mark's portrayal of Jesus: As soon as he's chosen his disciples, Jesus tackles sickness and pain and casts out demons wherever he meets them.

THE CALL OF THE DISCIPLES (1,16–20)

The importance of discipleship is reinforced by the fact that Jesus' first act is the calling of his disciples to join him in his ministry. A theology of discipleship is compressed into this brief episode:

- Discipleship is a gift: Jesus calls them, the disciples don't volunteer.
- Disciples follow Jesus: that's the essence of the call; nothing is more important.
- Discipleship is a privilege, and it is defined here as "fishing" for people.

EXORCISM AND HEALING (1,20–45)

Again the beginning is typical of the rest of Jesus' ministry. Jesus enters a synagogue and liberates a man tormented by an "unclean spirit" (called "unclean" because they separated their victim from the worship of God). The demons, unlike most of the humans in Mark's story, recognize Jesus and even announce his identity. That Jesus can expel the demon with words alone causes the crowd to marvel at his "authority." The exorcisms, which occur frequently in Mark, are an important part of his overall design. They demonstrate in the most dramatic terms the ultimate purpose of Jesus' mission: to free humanity from the power of death in all its forms.

"Immediately" Mark's succinct and simple style makes frequent use of a Greek word that can be translated as "at once," "quickly," "just then," and "immediately." The word is used over 40 times in the short 16 chapters of the Gospel, adding to the urgency and immediacy of Mark's account and giving the impression that Jesus was constantly active.

Conflict (2,1 – 3,6)

The more Jesus continues to heal, the greater the opposition that builds against him. Five stories of conflict between Jesus and the scribes and Pharisees crowd this section. They culminate in the leaders' plot to kill Jesus. Though it is still far off, Mark has already set our sights on the passion.

Note that Jesus and the leaders disagree on precisely the issues that are at the heart of Jesus' mission: healing and forgiveness of sins. The very things that make Jesus distinctive are what anger the Pharisees: Jesus associates with sinners and outcasts and refuses to allow the law to override compassion. For Jesus, healing on the Sabbath is simply putting the spirit ahead of the letter of the Law, but for the Pharisees, it is the final straw.

In the discussion on fasting (2,18–22), Mark reiterates his message that Jesus has ushered in a new age that will operate by new standards. The images here are of newness and change. The arrival of the "bridegroom" calls for new ways of seeing and responding. When he describes faith in this new age, Mark uses images of perception — "hearing," "seeing," "understanding" — and stresses the need to perceive differently.

The call of Levi reminds us that the call to discipleship is a gift that God can give to anyone — the sinner as well as the just. This point is lost on the Pharisees who criticize Jesus for eating with "tax collectors and sinners." But Jesus responds that it was precisely for sinners (the "sick") that he came (2,17).

Like Jesus, those who take the Gospel seriously had best be prepared for opposition and conflict, for those who live by the ways of the world will bitterly resent the Gospel's insistence on justice and compassion. And even the church needs the reminder of Jesus' example so that it does not neglect to care for the sick, disabled, and society's outcasts.

The Company They Keep

If it is true that a person can be known by the company he or she keeps, then here are some hints regarding the kind of person Jesus was. In Mark, he spent time with, healed and/or touched the following:

- A paralyzed man 2,1–12
- A demon-possessed man 5,1–15
- A leader of the synagogue 5,22
- A woman with a chronic bleeding problem 5,22
- A young girl 5,41
- A Gentile mother of a possessed child 7,25–30
- A boy with an evil spirit 9,17–27
- A group of little children 10,13–16
- A rich young man 10,17–23
- A blind beggar 10,46
- The Jewish religious authorities 12,13–37

The Mystery of the Kingdom (3,7 – 4,34)

Several elements — the portrayal of Jesus' family, the portrayal of the disciples, and the series of parables — all work together in this section to amplify Mark's message that the Kingdom is a mysterious reality that is beyond human control. God grants it to those who are called to be Jesus' disciples.

The disciples present a great irony: Though they are the privileged few called to be followers of Jesus, they are always out of step, unable to understand what Jesus is really all about (4,13).

One might expect that Jesus' family would be the first to express faith in him, yet two scenes here demonstrate the opposite. In 3,21 his "relatives" want to take Jesus home because they think "he is out of his mind." In a later scene of the same incident, Jesus' "mother and his brothers" also come to take him back home (3,31–35). Jesus responds by shunning his uncomprehending family and, pointing to the disciples gathered around him, announces that "whoever does the will of God" is his brother and sister and mother (3,35).

The reason for all this misunderstanding is provided by the parable discourse (4,1–34). Jesus, like his parables, is a mysterious revelation of God's Kingdom. Understanding does not come easily. It is a gift given by God, not taken; nor is it earned solely through our own effort. While Mark respects human freedom, his point is that God is always in control — even a person's rejection of Jesus is somehow part of God's overall will and plan.

The seed parables teach another important point. All three — the sower casting seed onto fertile and infertile ground (4,3–9), the tiny mustard seed (4,30–32), and the seed growing while the farmer sleeps (4,26–29) — all make the point that the Kingdom has a life of its own. It grows unnoticed, even into our own lives. Because of this hidden but sure growth, the Kingdom's ultimate triumph is assured. No opposition can prevent the final harvest from being lavishly abundant, "thirty, sixty, and a hundredfold."

The Universal Mission of Jesus (4,35 – 8,21)

In this section, that begins to bring to an end the Galilean ministry of Jesus, the Sea of Galilee takes on prominence as a symbolic boundary between Jew and Gentile (the western shore was mostly Jewish, while the eastern shore was mainly Gentile).

Crossing the Sea several times, Jesus and the disciples make excursions into Gentile territory. Among the Gerasenes (5,1) Jesus frees a man from a horrifying demon. Later, on another missionary journey that takes him through the Decapolis (on the eastern side of the Sea of Galilee), Jesus encounters the Syrophoenician woman whose daughter he heals (7,24–30).

Decapolis A loosely-knit confederation of Gentile cities north of the Dead Sea and east of the Sea of Galilee. Though the word is Greek for "ten cities," the actual number was greater and varied over time.

Several blocks of material give a missionary flavor to this section: Jesus sends the twelve disciples out to preach and expel unclean spirits, giving them full participation in his own ministry (6,7–13). Herod's murder of John the Baptist and Jesus' continuing disputes with his enemies are stark reminders that discipleship comes at a high cost (6,14–29). And the two miraculous feedings of the huge and hungry crowds, one on the *Jewish* side and one on the *Gentile* side of the lake, give insight into the universal nature of Jesus' mission.

Following are some of this section's major themes:

The Universality of the Gospel. Human tendencies toward exclusion are strong. We today are no different from the early church in our need to combat attitudes of division and racism. Mark's Gospel gives evidence of both the need to overcome these tendencies and the courage it takes to do so.

Jesus heals the Gerasene demoniac (5,1–20), the Greek woman's daughter (7,24–30), and the deaf-mute from the Decapolis (7,31–37), but to do so he and the disciples must endure the terror of the storm in order to get to the Gentile side of the lake. Crossing religious and cultural boundaries can indeed be terrifying, but to follow Jesus we must be willing to venture even into the storms of racial and cultural division.

Nourishing God's People. The two feeding stories reveal the nature of Jesus' mission. He must feed God's hungry people (a lesson the disciples who want to send the crowd away hungry—and we today as well—apparently need to learn). The feeding stories both recall the miraculous feeding of Israel with manna during the Exodus, and anticipate the Eucharistic meal (notice how Jesus takes, blesses, breaks, and gives the bread exactly as he does at the last supper, 14,22).

The Struggle of the Disciples. Jesus' ministry in Galilee draws to a close. The disciples have seen many wonders (calming the storm, 4,38–41; walking on water, 6,45–51) and have heard Jesus' parables and words of instruction. Yet they are still stumbling in the dark of misunderstanding about who Jesus is. After so much evidence, Jesus' question echoes with judgment and pathos: "Do you still not understand?" (8,21).

Mark's Gentile Audience

One indication that Mark's Gospel is addressed to a Gentile audience is the fact that he often defines Aramaic words and explains Jewish customs to his readers. For examples, look up the following: *"Talitha koum"* 5,41; handwashing regulations 7,3; *"qorban"* 7,11; and *"Eloi, Eloi, lema sabachtani?"* 15,35.

THE JOURNEY FROM GALILEE TO JERUSALEM (8,22–10,52)

Now the Galilean ministry is set aside. Significantly, Mark begins and ends this section with a healing of a blind man, symbols of the disciples' inability to see Jesus for who he is. From the northernmost section of Galilee, Caesarea Philippi, Jesus and the disciples journey to Jerusalem. But first Jesus asks the central question of the Gospel: "Who do you say that I am?" (8,29). Of course, the answer has been consistently given by the eloquent words and powerful healings that have accompanied Jesus' ministry. But those signs are not enough for either Jesus' opponents or his disciples to fully comprehend that Jesus is the Messiah.

Now Jesus begins to speak openly (8,31; 9,31; 10,33–34) about his impending death and resurrection. Understanding the cross becomes the key to understanding who Jesus is and what discipleship means. The journey toward Jerusalem becomes part of the instruction on the meaning of the cross. Jesus' trip to the holy city is very deliberate: He knows what awaits him there and he willingly accepts the Father's call to this act of selfless love for others. All who would follow Jesus, Mark suggests, must be willing to travel the same road he walks. Because Jerusalem with its great Temple is the place where Jesus will be rejected and die, the Jerusalem Temple will be replaced by a new temple, Jesus himself.

The disciples become incredibly thick-headed. To each of Jesus' passion predictions, they make patently inappropriate responses: Peter by scolding Jesus (8,32); the disciples by arguing over who is the greatest (9,33f); and James and John by requesting places of special honor in the Kingdom (10,35–37). In addition, they misjudge Jesus' willingness to spend time with little children (10,13) and can't even perform an exorcism on a sick boy (9,18)—despite having been given the power to do so (see 6,7).

Jesus intensifies his instruction on discipleship after each of the passion predictions:

- Disciples must be as humble as their master, putting aside self-interest and becoming the "servant of all" (10,35f).
- The cross is an indispensable part of the formula for discipleship. It in no way represents failure. It is instead the clearest expression of Jesus' mission.
- Rather than being concerned with self-aggrandizement or preoccupied with fears, disciples must be as willing as Jesus to give up their lives for others.

But the only way the disciples will overcome their stubborn, deep-seated spiritual blindness will be to imitate the physically blind Bartimaeus who begs Jesus to make him see (10,51). Unless they ask Jesus for the light of faith, they will remain in a darkness far more disabling then Bartimaeus' lack of sight.

DEATH AND RESURRECTION IN JERUSALEM (11,1 – 16,8)

The final phase of Jesus' story can be subdivided into four sections. The first two focus on the Temple, the latter two on the passion and the empty tomb.

Jesus and the Temple (11,1 – 12,44)

For a glowing moment Jesus' true identity shines out clearly. But the exultant crowd that greets him will soon turn a corner and become the menacing mob that calls for his execution. The peculiar story of the fig tree (11,12–14.20f) introduces a somber note into this section. With good purpose, Mark wraps the fig tree story around the story of the cleansing of the Temple. Just like the tree that failed to produce fruit, the Temple has failed to produce just and contrite hearts and authentic worship of the Lord. Jesus not only cleanses the Temple, he declares it invalid. It will be replaced by a temple "not made by hands" (14,58) that will be Jesus himself and his future community of disciples. In that new temple, love of God and neighbor will replace burnt offerings and sacrifice as forms of worship. The hypocritical leaders who delight in the trappings of religion while "devouring the houses of widows" will have no place there; but the humble, like the poor widow who gives all she has to God, will be assured a place (12,38–44).

Towards the Endtime (13,1–37)

Set in the context of Jesus' prediction that the great Temple of Herod would be leveled (and it was in 70 A.D.), this final discourse of Jesus is one of the Gospel's most puzzling, but important, passages. It focuses on the future of the Christian community and how it will carry out its mission in history after Jesus' death and resurrection. From the sayings of Jesus and Old Testament quotations that Mark has woven together in this discourse, three main themes can be identified:

Warnings of persecutions and divisions as the community carries out its mission. The world cannot end until the gospel has been proclaimed throughout the world (13,10). But that evangelization effort will be met with opposition, persecution (13,9–11), and internal divisions (13,12f).

The Christian must "stay awake." Without becoming doomsayers endlessly speculating about the end of the world, Christians must be sober and alert, aware of God's presence breaking into human history. False prophets will say, "I am he," and, "There he is" (13,6.21), but true disciples will faithfully proclaim the Gospel while anticipating God's soon-to-be-revealed presence in history.

God's triumph in history. Without denial or sugar-coating, Mark acknowledges that the Christian community will suffer and face crises, but ultimately grace will triumph and human history will be full of hope.

The Passion (14,1 – 15,47)

In keeping with the important role the passion plays in Mark's understanding of Jesus, these chapters constitute the longest single narrative of the Gospel; yet the story moves quickly to its climax at the cross.

The opening scenes (14,1–11) set contrasting moods: While Judas and the leaders plot, a faithful woman anoints Jesus' body for death. The next section is dominated by the last supper, where the broken bread and shared cup become action signs of Jesus' impending death for others. Gethsemane is a scene of profound pain and sorrow (14,32–52). As darkness closes in around Jesus, the disciples take a nap—disappointing Jesus' hope that they would keep watch with him (13,36). Then Jesus is arrested by an armed band led by one of his own disciples. The rest of the disciples flee, leaving Jesus alone to face his trials before the Sanhedrin (14,53–72) and Pilate (15,1–20), and deserting him at his crucifixion and death.

Two motifs dominate the passion story: the crisis of discipleship and the revelation of Jesus as the son of God.

The Crisis of Discipleship. Throughout the Gospel the disciples have come off rather badly, and now their behavior is outright scandalous. They professed loyalty at the last supper (14,31), but in the midst of crisis they run like frightened rabbits. Peter, the leader of the lot, denies even knowing the man he so recently confessed as the Messiah. While suffering and persecution make a hero of Jesus, it makes cowards of his friends.

The only people who come off looking good are those one would least expect: a woman who anoints Jesus despite the objections of his disciples (14,3–9); a Roman centurion who proclaims his faith in Jesus (15,39); and Joseph of Arimathea who courageously recovers and buries the body of Jesus (15,42–47). These are such unexpected disciples: a woman, a Gentile soldier, a member of the Sanhedrin. Clearly there is a lesson here for the church of Mark's day—and our own.

The Revelation of Jesus Christ, the Son of God. In the passion story we learn the answer to this Gospel's chief question: Who is Jesus? Jesus himself makes the bold announcement before the Sanhedrin: he *is* the Christ, the Son of God (14,61f). But again, the unexpected is the norm. This Messiah stands as a prisoner soon to be condemned to death. He came to liberate Israel, but he has no army or weapons. He liberates not with power and might, but by freely surrendering his life. Jesus is the son of a God who is revealed in the "weakness" of selfless giving. For Mark, it is in the shadow of the cross that Jesus is seen most clearly.

The Empty Tomb (16,1–8)

This brief but important passage is probably the original ending of Mark's Gospel. Someone writing later than Mark added the longer ending (see text notes to 16,1–8).

Jesus' Victory Over Death. The crucified Jesus has conquered death: The empty tomb proclaims the fact, and so does the mysterious "young man" who greets the women there. It is the truth of the young man's announcement that "Jesus of Nazareth, the crucified, has been raised," that makes Mark's story "gospel"—good news.

Reconciliation with the Disciples. Jesus does not wait for the disciples to come seeking him. The women are told to "go tell his disciples and Peter, 'He is going before you to Galilee; there you will see him.'" As he had promised at the last supper (14,24), Jesus will be reunited with his disciples despite their scandalous desertion of their teacher. Significantly, the messenger at the tomb instructs the women to tell the disciples *and Peter.* Peter, who had not only abandoned but denied Jesus, is singled out signifying, perhaps, not only his preeminence in the group, but the anticipation of his full rehabilitation. The hopes and dreams of the disciples that died when Jesus died will now be resurrected with him.

Back to Galilee: The Mission Begins. In Galilee, where Jesus began his ministry and first called the disciples to share it with him, is where the reunion of master and disciples will occur. But it is not clear what kind of reunion Mark has in mind. It may be a resurrection appearance, a final end-of-the-world meeting with the disciples, or perhaps a reunion in spirit—Jesus promising to be with the disciples as they go forth to spread the Gospel. Mark doesn't say, and maybe he means all of the above.

Death is conquered and the world is changed forever. The silence of the women suggests an awe-filled response to Jesus' victory over death. Some think their silence is just one more instance of failed discipleship provoked by paralyzing fear. But more likely the silence expresses wondrous reverence for the marvel of the resurrection.

Mark's Abrupt Ending

Why does Mark's Gospel end so suddenly? Some speculate that he may have been prevented from finishing the Gospel. More likely, the original ending has been lost, or perhaps Mark thought that after the empty tomb nothing more need be said. The vocabulary, literary style, and theological content of the longer ending differ enough from Mark to convince scholars it came from another's pen.

The Longer Ending (16,9–20)

Perhaps to blunt the effect of the abrupt original ending, a later writer appended the longer ending that recounts Jesus' appearance to Mary Magdalene. She breaks the silence of the other women and brings the message of Jesus' resurrection to the disciples. The brief mention of an appearance to two disciples walking to the country (16,12–13) evokes the Emmaus story of Luke's Gospel, although here, unlike in Luke, the two are not believed when they report their encounter with the risen Jesus. The report of Jesus' appearance to the eleven begins with rebukes for their lack of faith in his resurrection and concludes with a commissioning of the disciples and with promises that signs and wonders will accompany their ministry. Finally, without mention of a mountaintop, Jesus is taken up into heaven. The disciples go forth to preach and the risen Lord is with them.

Questions for Discussion or Reflection

1. Mark's Gospel is rarely named as someone's "favorite" Gospel. It has been said that while Luke appeals to children, Mark is a more adult Gospel. Do you agree? What appeals to you about this Gospel? What don't you like about Mark's presentation?
2. What motivates Mark's Jesus to keep his true identity hidden? What kind of Messiah were the people of Jesus' day expecting? How did that differ from the Messiah Jesus turned out to be? Does our world prefer the Messiah Jesus' contemporaries wanted or the one they got? Which do you prefer?

3. The central question of Mark's Gospel is "Who do you say I am?" (8,29). After reading the Gospel, how would you answer that question? In what way is Mark's portrait of Jesus different from the portraits of the other Gospels?

4. Mark's disciples stumble in the darkness of lack of understanding to the very end. Do you think this is a realistic portrayal of Jesus' closest companions? Why did they so regularly miss the point? What about those who did express their faith in Jesus—the beggars, the lame, even some Gentiles. How did they differ from the disciples? What made them able to recognize Jesus for who he truly was? Do you ever suffer from the same lack of insight?

5. The cross looms large in Mark's Gospel. Why is it so central to his understanding of who Jesus was? Paul said the cross was a scandal and a stumbling block. Yet Christianity has clung to the cross as a mark of faith and a sign of hope. What is the message of the cross? What meaning does it hold for you and your faith?

LUKE READING GUIDE

At a Glance

Who wrote the Gospel, and for whom was it written?	The unanimous tradition of the church has upheld that Luke, the "beloved physician" of Colossians (4,14) is the author of the Gospel. Probably a well-educated member of a wealthy urban family, Luke was writing for a Hellenistic (Greek) audience. Very likely from Antioch of Syria—the only Gentile among the four evangelists—he was a companion of Paul (Acts 16,10–40) who accompanied him on some of his travels.
Who are the main players?	Elizabeth An angel of the Lord Zechariah John the Baptist Mary Joseph The disciples Zacchaeus Herod the Great Pilate Mary Magdalene
When was the Gospel written?	Proposed dates vary between 63 and 90 A.D. Some evidence suggests a date between 80–85 A.D.
Healings in Luke	A leper 5,12 (Mk, Mt) The centurion's servant 7,1 (Mt) Peter's mother-in-law 4,38 (Mk, Mt) Evening healings of the sick 4,40 (Mk, Mt) A paralytic 5,18 (Mk, Mt) A man with a withered hand 6,6 (Mk, Mt) The woman with a hemorrhage 8,42 (Mk, Mt) A mute demoniac 11,14 (Mt) An epileptic boy 9,38 (Mk, Mt) Two blind men 18,35 (Mk, Mt) The crippled woman 13,11 The man with dropsy 14,1 The ten lepers 17,11 Restoring the ear of the servant Malchus 22,50 (Mt and Mk indicate the healing miracle is reported in Matthew and Mark as well.)
Other miracles reported in Luke	Casting out an unclean spirit 4,33 (Mk) Calming the storm at sea 8,22 (Mk, Mt) Curing the Gerasene demoniacs 8,26 (Mk, Mt) Raising of Jairus's daughter 8,40 (Mk, Mt) Feeding the five thousand 9,10 (Mk, Mt) Escape from hostile Nazareth crowd 4,30 The catch of fish 5,1 Raising of son of the widow of Nain 7,11–17 *Luke's is the only Gospel that does not report the miracle of walking on the sea.* (Mk, Mt, and Jn indicate the miracle story also occurs in Mark, Matthew, or John.)

Parables found only in Luke	The two debtors 7,41–43 The good Samaritan 10,30–37 A friend at midnight 11,5–13 The rich fool 12,16–21 Faithful servants 12,35–40 The vigilant steward 12,42–48 The barren fig tree 13,6–9 The great feast 14,16–24 Constructing a tower and a king preparing for war 14,25–35 The lost coin 15,8–10 The lost (prodigal) son 15,11–32 The dishonest steward 16,1–13 The rich man and Lazarus 16,19–31 The master and servants 17,7–10 The persistent widow 18,1–8 The Pharisee and the tax collector 18,9–14 The ten gold coins 19,11–27
When Jesus prays in Luke	At the Jordan River 3,21 In desert places 5,16 On a mountain 6,12 In solitude 9,18 On the Mountain of Transfiguration 9,28 In a "certain place" and teaching the "Our Father" 11,1–4 The upper room 22,32 In the garden 22,39–46 From the cross 23,34.46 With the Emmaus disciples 24,30 At the ascension 24,50 (Luke records more instances of Jesus at prayer than any other evangelist.)
Luke's portrait of Jesus	Luke's Jesus is a man of mercy and compassion with a particular concern for the poor and outcast. His Jesus prays often, especially before important events. Though he is the son of God, Luke's Jesus is also fully human and his concern for all people makes him the universal Messiah.
Luke's unique perspective	Luke aims at a clear, orderly and faith-affirming presentation of the words and deeds of Jesus. Wanting his readers to know the truth and reliability of the gospel, he pays attention to historical detail. He stresses Christian prayer and the value of renunciation. He sees the fulfillment of prophecy in Jesus and thus stresses the fidelity of the God of Jesus. His Jesus shows a special interest in sinners, women, and family life. His Gospel expresses joy at the announcement of the "good news," makes frequent use of the title "Son of Man," and reveals the active participation of the Spirit in the ministry of Jesus.

Some Accounts Found Only in Luke

- Announcements of the birth of John (1,5–25) and Jesus (1,26–38)
- Canticles of Mary (1,46–55) and Zechariah (1,67–79)
- Birth in Bethlehem, visit of the shepherds and presentation in the Temple (2,1–40)
- Twelve-year-old Jesus in the Temple (2,41–52)
- Imprisonment of John (3,19.20)
- Jesus is rejected at Nazareth (4,16–30)
- A sinful woman washes Jesus' feet (7,36–50)
- Galilean women follow Jesus (8,1–3)
- The meeting with Zacchaeus (19,1–10)
- The trial before Herod (23,6–12)

As the only Gentile among the four evangelists, Luke helped initiate a process that continues even today: He took the story of Jesus that originated in a culture different from his own and introduced it to his own culture without violating the integrity of either culture. Part of Luke's message is that the good news of Jesus is meant for all people.

Though he admits he was not an eyewitness, Luke is well qualified to present the Jesus story for, as he claims, he has investigated "everything accurately anew to write it down in an orderly sequence" (1,3). Among his sources are (1) Mark's Gospel; (2) a resource he shared with Matthew, called "Q" by scholars, that consists of sayings of Jesus; and (3) a source unique to him which scholars designate "L." His language and style reveal him to be a wealthy and well-educated city dweller (see "At a Glance").

Luke is sometimes referred to as a "historian" because he refers to events and personalities of the Roman Empire. But by no means is he a historian in the modern sense of the word. In fact, most of his so-called historical references don't seem to be accurate even by the standards of the ancient world. By his own word, Luke is writing a *diegesis,* a "narrative account," not a history, whose purpose is to provide *asphaleia,* "assurance," regarding the ministry of Jesus. Luke wants to show that everything the church preaches is firmly rooted in that ministry and in the preaching of the apostles.

Luke's "History"

Luke is sometimes characterized as the "historian" among the evangelists. While he does make historical references to Roman emperors and Jewish kings (2,1–3; 3,1–2), his details are vague and not always accurate. He also shows faulty knowledge of Palestine—its climate for instance, and the way homes were built. Clearly he is not a historian by modern standards. His chief interest is theological.

Luke's intent in presenting an "orderly" narrative is to show God working to move human history through the various periods of salvation. God has guided the process from Old Testament times and has fulfilled it in the ministry of Jesus and the Christian movement, the early church (which he records in his second volume, Acts). To create his orderly account, Luke has not only borrowed from other sources, he has made significant additions to the preexisting material. Three of his additions to Mark's Gospel are fairly evident:

1. While Mark began with the sudden appearance of John the Baptist, Luke (like Matthew) begins with a birth and infancy narrative (1,5–2,40). He also recounts a story about the adolescent Jesus in the Temple and then inserts Jesus' genealogy.
2. In Mark's Gospel the account of Jesus' trip from Galilee to Jerusalem consists of a small amount of instruction to the disciples. In Luke, however, the report of this same trip constitutes a major section of instruction. That is why most of the parables that occur in Luke are found here, while only four of the many miracles Luke records are in this section.
3. Finally, Luke and Mark differ significantly in their passion and resurrection accounts. While Mark ends his story with the women running silent from the tomb, Luke includes appearances of the risen Jesus—some of which contain instructions to the disciples. Luke's and Mark's passion accounts also differ: Among other things, Luke skips the trial before the Sanhedrin and adds an appearance before Herod.

The three sections of added material illustrate the way God's plan of salvation is being fulfilled through the events of Jesus' life:

1. The infancy narratives recall (and in symbolic ways relive) the history and hopes of Israel.
2. The journey to Jerusalem prepares for Jesus' eventual death and for the disciples' future role as missionaries.
3. The passion-resurrection account emphasizes that it was God's plan announced by the prophets that the Messiah would suffer and die.

The Tragedy of Israel

While Luke clearly suggests that there is a divine plan at work in the events of Jesus' life, he is not saying that all the things that happened were "supposed" to happen. To think that would be to miss the sense of tragedy he has about Israel's fate because, in fact, some of what was "supposed" to happen doesn't. The long-awaited Messiah was to bring God's peace and salvation to Israel. The infancy stories awaken the hope that the moment of blessing for Jews (and Gentiles) has come.

Yet three times in this Gospel Jesus laments the fact that Israel will not see that promise fulfilled. Her rejection of both Jesus and the mission of the disciples will exclude her from the day of salvation that Jesus initiated. The prophetic laments of Jesus (13,31–34; 19,41–44; 23,27–31) convey tragic sadness over the fate of the city, Jerusalem: Though it was meant to be a jewel in the heavenly crown, it was turned, instead, to rubble and dust.

While some of the Jews of his day rejected Jesus as Messiah, Christians cannot reject and persecute Jews. The church's teaching is clear on this. We share ancestors in faith with the Jewish people. Jesus' own relatives were faithful Jews who trusted in God's salvation. Luke's Jesus does not condemn but forgives those who cause his death, and he weeps as he foresees that his beloved city, Jerusalem, will not find the peace that God so yearns to give.

READING THROUGH LUKE'S GOSPEL

As with each of the Gospels, it is a good idea to read all of Luke before starting a careful study. When you do, you'll find Luke is a fine storyteller who brings stories to life with lively dialogue. As you read, be on the lookout for the following themes that run throughout the Gospel.

THEME 1: SALVATION IS A JOYOUS SURPRISE

Mary's Magnificat (1,46–55) sets the tone: Celebration, rejoicing, praising, and thanking God for the gift of salvation fill this Gospel. Salvation is more than a gift, it is a surprise, for it comes to those who least expect it—the humble, poor, oppressed, and sinners. Jesus is the embodiment of God's healing and forgiving mercy which extends even to the rich, like the tax-collector Zacchaeus, who are willing to receive it.

Christians must show the same kind of active mercy that God offers (6,36). Jesus presents a proactive God who is always seeking the lost, not waiting passively for sinners to come crawling back. His images of mercy—the shepherd and the lost sheep, the woman and the lost coin, the prodigal son's father—all show how much God is out to "get us." But some, like the prodigal's older brother, find it hard to accept such unconditional love when they have worked so hard to *earn* it.

THEME II: SALVATION INCLUDES EVERYONE

In Luke, Jesus consistently reaches out to many kinds of people. We've mentioned Zacchaeus, a rich and sinful tax collector. Samaritans, too—longtime enemies of the Jews—become exemplary disciples, so much so that today being a "Good Samaritan" (10,37) describes anyone who demonstrates unmerited mercy. Significantly, it is also a *Samaritan* leper (17,12–19) who is the only one of ten to return and give thanks to Jesus for his healing.

Luke's Gospel is also distinguished by the significant role women—another group the ancient world often excluded and oppressed—play in Jesus' ministry. Jesus praises the sinful woman who washes his feet for being more loving and hospitable than his Pharisee host (7,31–50). Mary, the sister of Martha, is welcomed to listen as a disciple at the feet of Jesus, and a group of women traveled with Jesus and financially supported him and the disciples (8,1–3).

THEME III: SPECIAL CONCERN FOR THOSE IN NEED

In Luke, salvation is not only a spiritual experience. Jesus gives it concrete shape when he heals the sick and brings their suffering to an end. But the Gospel also shows that the concrete experience of salvation is not limited to divine miracles. Christians, like the Good Samaritan, through their concrete, loving actions for each other can also bring about salvation.

Luke often contrasts rich and poor in his Gospel. Because they are fixated on money and pleasure, the rich exclude themselves from salvation (see 12,13–21; 16,19–30). Even well-meaning people like the Rich Official (or Rich Young Man, 18,18–24) are left out because they won't let go of their possessions long enough to accept what Jesus has to offer them. But that does not mean that the rich are automatically excluded from God's Kingdom. Anyone with a generous heart who shares with those in need is assured a place with Jesus. Luke presents the sayings of Jesus that call for renunciation of material goods (6,35; 9,3; 12,33; 16,13) as a way of demonstrating that Jesus is concerned only with promoting the Kingdom, not enriching himself. But Luke doesn't forget that such radical discipleship is only possible when basic human needs are met through the generosity of others. As mentioned above, for Jesus and his disciples that support came, in part, from the group of women who traveled with them (8,1–3).

THEME IV: MARY IS THE FIRST DISCIPLE

Luke's Gospel provides the basis for the special devotion Catholic Christians show to Mary. Her simple "yes" sets in motion God's work of salvation. But Catholics don't honor Mary simply because, as a virgin, she gave miraculous birth to Jesus. Luke provides the real reasons. For him Mary is the model of the faith-filled Israelite who confidently expects God's salvation, and the ideal disciple of Jesus who hears and does the word of God (8,21). It is in her faithful living that Mary finds her true source of blessing. Not only does she accept God's will in the annunciation scene, she holds dearly in her heart what she hears about Jesus from Simeon and Anna (2,25–38); and she remains a faithful disciple of Jesus, accompanying him to Calvary and gathering with the disciples in Jerusalem after the resurrection.

An Outline of Luke

Luke's Gospel begins and ends in the Jerusalem Temple. In between, the biggest block of material details Jesus' journey from Galilee to Jerusalem. Throughout, therefore, the holy city and its Temple retain central significance. The key moments of transition in the story form its outline:

- Prologue (1,1–4)
- The Infancy Narrative (1,5–2,52)
- Preparation for the Public Ministry (3,1–4,13)
- The Ministry in Galilee (4,14–9,50)
- The Journey to Jerusalem (9,51–19,27)
- The Teaching Ministry in Jerusalem (19,28–21,38)
- The Passion Narrative (22,1–23,56a)
- The Resurrection Narrative (23,56b–24,53)

In the individual sections, we will be looking for Luke's portrait of Jesus and for how Luke uses the teachings of Jesus to develop the themes of salvation and discipleship.

Discipleship Luke's formula for discipleship is clear: Don't just hear the word of God, live it. Luke uses parables, more than the other evangelists, to teach about discipleship. Look at the following parables for what they teach about the way a disciple should behave:

- The good Samaritan (10,30–37)
- The rich fool (12,16–21)
- The lost sheep; lost coin; lost (prodigal) son (15,1–32)
- Dishonest steward (16,1–13)
- Rich man and Lazarus (16,19–31)
- Pharisee and publican (18,9–14)

PROLOGUE (1,1–4)

This one-sentence prologue makes Luke's Gospel resemble other Hellenistic (Greek-influenced) literature. The last word, *asphaleia* (assurance), reveals his hope that the orderly account of Jesus' ministry he provides will confirm the trustworthiness of the Christian message proclaimed by the early church.

THE INFANCY NARRATIVE (1,5–2,52)

Structure of the Lucan Infancy Narrative

The birth announcements and actual births of Jesus and John the Baptist bear strikingly similar details, as outlined on the next page.

The birth/circumcision/naming episodes (John in 1,57–80; Jesus in 2,1–40) both speak of the joy that surrounded each child's birth. Luke leaves no doubt that God has brought these children into being: God overcomes the barrenness of aged Elizabeth—recalling other Old Testament figures like Sarah, Rachel, and Hannah—and, even more marvelously, God is able to bring Jesus into being in the womb of a young virgin from Nazareth.

Parallels in the Birth Announcements of Jesus and John

a. Neither parent expects a child at that time in life.
b. An angel appears; the parent becomes troubled and is told not to fear.
c. The child's birth is announced and his future greatness foretold.
d. The parent questions how this can happen.
e. The angel asserts that it will happen and announces a sign.
f. Zechariah is unable to speak; Mary spontaneously accepts God's will.

Jesus and John are brought together (The Visitation 1,39–56) in an episode in which John responds to the presence of Jesus by moving in his mother's womb, an indication that Jesus is the greater figure for whom John is the forerunner.

Songs of Salvation: The Canticles

The canticles contained in this section (which receive their names from the first words of their Latin translations) have become much-revered elements of Christian worship: Mary's Magnificat (1,46–55); Zechariah's Benedictus (1,68–79); the song of the angels (12,13f); and Simeon's Nunc Dimittis (2,29–32). All but the angels' song consist of phrases taken from the Greek Old Testament. Scholars believe Luke may have adapted the Magnificat and Benedictus (and possibly the Nunc Dimittis) from Jewish Christian hymns.

Mary's Magnificat, which closely resembles the Song of Hannah (1 Sm 2,1–10), celebrates God's past deeds of salvation and God's generosity toward the lowly.

Anawim The *anawim* are the "poor ones," the faithful remnant who are lowly and downtrodden. These meek and humble, but righteous, Israelites know they must depend on God for everything, including salvation.

The Benedictus picks up on the promise made to David (2 Sm 7,12f) of a king-to-come who would save the people and free them to worship without fear. Jesus will fulfill that promise.

In the Nunc Dimittis, which derives from Isaiah 40,5 and 49,6, Simeon acknowledges that in Jesus he has seen the salvation promised in Isaiah. But his prophetic vision allows Simeon to see not only the glory that the child will bring to Israel and all the world, but also the pain and division that will result from the opposition and rejection he will encounter (see 4,29; 13,33–35; 19,44–47f; 20,14.17).

Virgin Birth and Christology in the Infancy Narrative

While the canticles sing of Jesus' coming as the fulfillment of God's promises to Israel, it is in the angel Gabriel's birth announcement (1,28–37) that we find the most striking claims about who Jesus is. The announcement is made in two parts. First is the announcement that Jesus is the long-awaited Messiah of David's house who will rule forever as "Son of the Most High."

The second part of the announcement explains in what sense Jesus is the Son of God: He is actually begotten through God's intervention. Though fully human, Luke's Jesus is no ordinary human being; from the moment of his conception he is also the son of God.

Mary's virginity plays a key role in establishing the uniqueness of Jesus. And even the similarity in the circumstances of Jesus' and John's births show that God did a mightier deed in Jesus than in John. The wonder of a supposedly barren womb unexpectedly becoming fruitful does not compare with the wonder of a virgin conceiving a child. No human explanation can account for it. Radical modern scholars who contend that Mary conceived Jesus through normal human intercourse would find no friend in Luke. That Mary was a virgin is essential to his claim that Jesus is God's only son. Yet Mary's prominence results not from her physical virginity, but from her willingness to participate in God's plan of salvation.

Luke prefaces the actual birth of Jesus with a reference to Caesar Augustus and a census that was taken during his reign. No substantiation that this census ever took place has been found outside Luke's Gospel. While evidence of other universal registrations of Roman citizens does exist, those dates cannot be made to correspond with the governorship of Quirinius and the reign of King Herod, all of which would have to correspond in order for Luke's and Matthew's accounts not to be contradictory. (A provincial census of Judea was taken under Quirinius, but it did not require travel back to one's ancestral home.)

But the reference to Caesar Augustus serves a more symbolic than historical purpose. Augustus was known for bringing a lasting peace to the empire, and he was called "savior" for doing so. Luke insinuates that the true savior and bringer of peace is the child who reigns first from a manger and then from a cross.

PREPARATION FOR THE PUBLIC MINISTRY (3,1 – 4,13)

The infancy narrative has already set the tone for much of the Gospel.

1. It has introduced some of the major Christological titles: Son of David, Messiah, Savior, Lord, and Son of God.
2. It has introduced the Spirit who overshadowed Mary at Jesus' conception and who will remain with Jesus throughout his ministry.
3. Mary's Magnificat has announced that God's salvation comes in the form of "reversal," the raising up of the lowly and the bringing down of the mighty.
4. Thanksgiving, rejoicing, and prayer already have been given prominence.
5. The suggestion that Jesus will not be received with open arms has been clearly made.

Now Luke presents three more blocks of material before moving into the specifics of Jesus' ministry: (a) the role of John in preparing for Jesus' mission; (b) a genealogy, and (c) the temptation story.

The Baptist's Ministry (3,1 – 4,13)

For Luke, John belongs to the age of prophets. Jesus, on the other hand, will introduce a new, messianic age. As forerunner of God's Messiah, John anticipates on two counts the teaching of Jesus: (a) repentance and forgiveness – which in Luke are two of the components of salvation, and (b) proper handling of material possessions – sharing, avoiding greed, and acting fairly.

John's insistence on bearing good fruit and his reference to God's being able to raise up children to Abraham from the stones reinforces Luke's theme that God's word must be acted upon, not just heard. Jesus is baptized by John, but in no way does Luke suggest that Jesus was dependent on the Baptist; instead, the baptism account affirms Jesus' divine sonship and reports the descent of the Spirit on Jesus.

Genealogy of Jesus (3,23–38)

Unlike Matthew's genealogy that traces Jesus' ancestry back to Abraham, Luke's universalism takes him further—to Adam, and even to God. This Jesus is not the son of Joseph as some might mistakenly think; he is God's own son.

Temptation of Jesus (4,1–13)

Led by the Spirit, Jesus enters the desert. Satan will challenge Jesus' very identity as "Son of God," not by tempting him to some evil act, but by presenting a crisis—like God's order to Abraham that he sacrifice Isaac—that will reveal whether Jesus' faith in God can be destroyed. Though Satan "strikes out," we are given an ominous reminder that he will return. Jesus emerges as the obedient Son of God, ready to carry out God's plan of salvation no matter the cost.

THE MINISTRY IN GALILEE (4,14 – 9,50)

The introduction sets the tone: Jesus ministers "under the power of the Spirit" and wins much praise.

In Nazareth and Capernaum (4,16–44)

Despite the praise, rejection of Jesus is soon to follow. In Nazareth, Jesus quotes Isaiah and thus states the agenda of his ministry. But his skeptical neighbors cannot accept that this son of Joseph (3,23; 4,22) is the Lord's anointed. Jesus' reference to Elijah and Elisha hint at the

The Evangelists Symbolized

Since ancient times, artists have used the four living creatures of the Book of Revelation (Rv 4,7) to symbolize the four evangelists.

Mark is linked with the desert lion because his Gospel opens with John, the voice of one "crying out in the desert."

Luke is linked with the ox, a sacrificial animal, because his Gospel opens with Zechariah offering sacrifice in the Temple.

Matthew is associated with the human figure because his Gospel begins with a record of Jesus' human ancestors.

John is linked with the eagle because his Gospel starts with a hymn of praise to Jesus who uniquely can look on the face of God just as the eagle uniquely looks upon the sun.

future. Just as these prophets were sent to minister to non-Israelites, Jesus' mission will extend to the Gentiles. The reaction of his listeners is violently hostile (4,25–30), contrasting with the acclaim he receives in Capernaum where he is mobbed by eager crowds reacting to his miracles.

Jesus Gathers Disciples (5,1–39)

There will be plenty of time for fasting once Jesus, the bridegroom, is gone (5,35). Meantime, one can't mix the old with the new without risking the loss of both the container and its contents (5,39).

Next, Jesus defends the right of the disciples to feed themselves on the Sabbath on the grounds that caring for human needs and doing good take precedence over Sabbath regulations. Then, after an entire night of prayer, Jesus selects twelve followers who will be his apostles, witnesses to all he will say and do.

Sermon on the Plain (6,17–49)

Though much shorter, Luke's Sermon on the Plain parallels Matthew's Sermon on the Mount. Addressed to the disciples, it repeats the now familiar theme of reversal that characterized the Magnificat: The Kingdom is good news for the poor and oppressed, but it brings judgment against the wealthy and mighty. While commanding disciples to love enemies as well as neighbors and to be known by the "good fruit" they bear (6,27–45), he also warns them to expect persecution and opposition (6,27–30)—concrete opportunities to put their love of enemies to the test.

The Beatitudes In contrast with Matthew, Mark lists only four beatitudes or "blessed" statements which he contrasts with four "woes." Blessed refers to those who receive God's favor. The woes threaten God's wrath against those who value material wealth over the things of the Kingdom. Note that the future will see the hungry and weeping satisfied and laughing while those who are filled and laughing will hunger and weep. It is especially noteworthy that while Matthew spiritualizes the beatitudes—blessed are the poor *in spirit* (Mt 5,5), those who hunger and thirst *for righteousness* (Mt 5,6)—Luke refers to humanity's very real economic and social circumstances.

Jesus is the Promised Savior (7,1 – 9,18)

Luke uses the miracle stories in this section to announce the identity of Jesus: Jesus is savior for Jew and Gentile alike (healing the centurion's slave, 7,9); he is a great prophet in the tradition of Elijah and Elisha (raising the widow's son, 7,16); and he is indeed the "one who is to come" that the Baptist's disciples asked about (various miracles, 18,23). Luke also uses his stories to draw a sharp distinction between those who accept and those who reject the plan of God revealed in Jesus. The lawyers and Pharisees are too righteous to see the truth of Jesus, but sinners, like Levi (5,27–32) and the woman who anoints Jesus' feet (7,36–50), find in Jesus forgiveness and salvation.

Sidon
ITURAEA
ABILENE
Damascus
PROVINCE OF SYRIA
Tyre
GAULANITIS
TRACHONITIS
BATANAEA
Chorazin
Bethsaida-Julias
Capernaum
Gennesaret
Sea of Galilee
Hippos
GALILEE
Sepphoris
AURANITIS
The Great Plain
DECAPOLIS
River Jordan
MARE INTERNUM
(Mediterranean Sea)
Caesarea
Sebaste
(Samaria)
SAMARIA
KINGDOM OF HEROD
Philadelphia
Jericho
Emmaus
Jerusalem
JUDEA
Lake Asphaltitis
IDUMEA
(Dead Sea)
Masada
PALESTINE UNDER THE HERODS
Divisions, A.D. 6–37

A section on discipleship follows, dominated by the parable of the sower (8,4–15). The interpretation of the parable gives reasons why discipleship is no easy task: (a) Some will reject the initial preaching; (b) others won't have the patience or endurance to await the maturing of the harvest, and (c) some will give in to temptation, worries, riches, and worldly pleasures. The parable is framed by the mention of women who are examples of model discipleship: the women who follow and help support Jesus (8,1–3), and his mother who heard the word of God and acted on it (8,19–21).

The next section of miracles presents Jesus as savior: He saves the disciples from the storm (8,22–25), and the Gerasene from the bondage of demons (8,26–37), telling him (and all believers) to go and announce what God has done (8,38f). Then Jesus tells the twelve disciples to go and do what he does: preach and heal. As shaped by Luke, the story of feeding the five thousand that concludes the section represents Jesus' concern for the needy (see 6,21), but it also answers Satan's challenge to turn stones into bread (4,3f).

The Messiah Who Must Suffer (9,18–50)

That Jesus is a Messiah who must suffer is a truth that the disciples largely resist. In Luke Jesus calls disciples to take up their cross "daily" (9,23). That willingness is a requirement for normal Christian living, not just the attitude of those who face actual suffering and death for the sake of Jesus, as in Mark's Gospel. The transfiguration provides glimpses both of Jesus' coming glorification and his passion. But the disciples don't grasp the message of Jesus. They argue over status and exhibit jealousy, thus demonstrating their unreadiness to follow Jesus on the road of suffering.

THE JOURNEY TO JERUSALEM (9,51 – 19,27)

The journey to Jerusalem becomes a time of preparation for the disciples. Parables and miracles dominate this section. Below are some of the key themes found here.

Criticism of the Pharisee Opponents of Jesus

As he does regularly in Luke, Jesus attacks the hypocrisy of the Pharisees while sitting at a meal with them (7,37–50). Luke intends the injunctions against hypocrisy and self-aggrandizement that Jesus directs at the Pharisees to be taken to heart by the Christian reader as well. Anyone who condemns in one situation behavior they tolerate in another is no less hypocritical than the Pharisees. When Christians denounce discrimination and injustice in the world and then tolerate those same evils within the church they commit the sin of the Pharisees; and if they devote their lives to the pursuit of wealth, status, and power, they cannot claim to be living the gospel of Jesus.

Warnings About Judgment

Luke does not expect the immediate return of the risen Jesus. Christians, therefore, must remain ready for his return no matter how far off it may be. The warnings to be on guard, then, apply as much to the Christian reader as to Jesus' opponents. The warnings are severe, and the recipients are unrepentant towns (10,13–15), those who demand signs and thus show less faith than the Gentiles of Jonah's day (11,29–32), and hypocritical Pharisees (12,1–3). Irresponsible behavior cannot be justified by the presumption (or hope) that Jesus' return is far off. Like the faithful and unfaithful servants (12,35–48), the Christian, too, can be caught off guard. When tragedies happen to others, we must not assume that we are better than those who suffer, nor that God is more pleased with us (13,1–5). Otherwise, like the barren fig tree (13,6–9), we might discover that we are being given one last chance—with our time of judgment just around the corner. Though the Kingdom is present among us now (17,21), the fullness of the Kingdom is a future event. But before that fullness, when he returns in judgment, the Son of Man must suffer greatly and be rejected by his own generation (17,25).

Discipleship: Renunciation, Devotion, and Suffering

Early in the journey section Luke lays out the requirements of discipleship. Disciples must:

- Be completely devoted to the Kingdom, even to the point of renouncing normal human ties to family (9,57–62)
- Heal and preach the coming of the Kingdom (10,9)
- Face dangers, like demonic forces (10,17–20), with confidence in the power of Jesus
- Avoid anxiety and trust in the generosity of others to provide for physical needs (12,22–34)
- Subordinate all the cares of this world, even the obligations of hospitality, to the one thing necessary for salvation: hearing and keeping the word of God (11,27–38)
- Expect divisions, even within families (12,49–53)
- Endure to the end with patience and a willingness to suffer (14,25–33).

Discipleship and Material Possessions

Important teachings on discipleship and material possessions are also included in this section:

- Possessions pose a special problem for disciples. If they are not careful, riches can start possessing them. The rich official (18,18–23) demonstrates how big an obstacle wealth poses to becoming and remaining a disciple.
- Wealth is transitory: The rich farmer dies before he can build his barns (12,13–21), and the rich man who neglects the beggar Lazarus learns he can't take his riches with him to hell (16,19–31).
- Disciples must learn to share their material wealth with the unfortunate, as does the Good Samaritan (10,30–36). No matter what rationalizations one finds, it is not possible to serve both God and mammon (16,13).

Mammon Mammon is the Greek transliteration of an Aramaic word for any kind of wealth: land, cattle, money. It can also refer to that thing in which one puts one's trust. In Luke 16,13 Jesus personifies it, speaking of mammon as if it were a god.

Prayer in the Life of Disciples

Jesus provides the example and disciples are called to be prayerful like their master. Jesus is shown at prayer numerous times in this Gospel. The disciples are twice instructed about prayer: first when they ask to be taught to pray (11,1), and later when Jesus teaches them about the efficacy of prayer through the parable of the persistent widow (18,1–6). Disciples should trust in the power of prayer because if a wicked, uncaring judge can be hounded into giving the widow what she wants, how much more will our loving, compassionate God hear the prayers of faith-filled disciples? After all, ours is a God on the look-out for lost sinners, like Zacchaeus (19,1–10).

THE TEACHING MINISTRY IN JERUSALEM (19,28 – 21,38)

With Jesus' entry into the holy city, the story returns to its starting point.

The Messiah Comes to City and Temple (19,28–48)

Jesus "proceeds on his journey" not only to Jerusalem, but also to the destiny that awaits him there. The Pharisees, fearing that the jubilant cries of the crowds will bring Roman vengeance upon them, demand that Jesus silence his disciples. But Jesus rejoins that the stones would pick up the shout if the disciples stopped praising God for what they had seen (19,40). Note that here, unlike the angelic announcement of peace on earth at Jesus' birth, peace comes not on earth but to the heavens instead (19,38). In fact, Jesus weeps because Jerusalem will not receive the peace he longed to give her (19,41–44). Then he proceeds to the Temple, which he violently cleanses to restore it to its true purpose of prayer (19,45–48).

Jesus Teaches in the Temple (20,1 – 21,4)

A new section of Luke's Gospel begins with Jesus' return to the holy city: Jesus' ministry in Jerusalem. In the Temple, "his father's house" (2,49), Jesus teaches daily.

The Authority for Jesus' Actions. Jesus beats those who question his authority at their own game. Knowing his counterquestion will indict them either way, they refuse to answer. So Jesus returns the compliment (20,8).

The Tenant Farmers. The priests and scribes realize Jesus has aimed this parable at them (12,9–19): Because they have rejected the owner's son, they will soon lose the vineyard. The tone of judgment is strong. Jesus' opponents sense it and seek his life, but they hold back for fear of the people.

Tribute Due to God and Caesar. Jesus won't be trapped. He answers the religious leaders' malicious question with a counterquestion. The question is not asking whether taxation is just, but whether a religious state like Israel should be paying taxes to a pagan conqueror like Rome. Jesus' words here do not endorse dividing the world into separate spheres for church and state. Though Caesar must be paid his due, God is sovereign Lord over all. God's law supersedes the law of the state.

Resurrection of the Dead. The Sadducees pose a ridiculous question in order to debunk belief in the resurrection. Jesus first repudiates their simplistic interpretation of resurrection

Levirate Marriage This is the custom of marrying a dead brother's wife, if the brother dies without a son, so that he will not be without heirs (see Dt 2,5; Gn 38,8).

and then cites Moses to argue for belief in the resurrection of the dead: God is God of the living; since Moses calls the Lord the God of Abraham, Isaac, and Jacob, then the patriarchs must be living.

Jesus Challenges the Opposition. Now Jesus turns the tables and asks a hard question himself: How can the Messiah be David's son if David calls him Lord? The leaders' inability to answer reveals the bankrupt state of their religious authority. The Lucan contrast between rich and poor occurs twice here—in the denunciation of the scribes (20,45–47), and in Jesus' comments on the widow's offering (21,1–4). The rich give of their surplus, but the widow gave all—making her the more pious by far.

Fate of the Temple and the Coming end-time (21,5–38)

Luke's apocalyptic section resembles Mark's, but by separating the destruction of the Temple from the signs that herald the final judgment, Luke tells his readers that the end-time will not come immediately. Even false messiahs and rebellions do not mean disciples should start watching the skies. Persecution will come, but God will care for Christians who will face hostility and even death (21,12–19). The fall of Jerusalem will not bring the end of the age but the beginning of a new stage of salvation history. Christians must be vigilant and prayerful, knowing that Jesus' words will never pass away (21,29–33).

Apocalyptic The term refers to the revelation of mysterious truth that was previously hidden regarding future events that deal with the end of human history and final judgment. Both "revelation" (from Latin *revelatio*) and "apocalypse" (from Greek *apokalypsis*) mean "take away the veil."

THE PASSION NARRATIVE (22,1–23,56a)

Luke's passion narrative is not meant to be a historical report. It is a faith statement that Jesus is the suffering Messiah and God's obedient son who was raised from the dead. Luke builds a strong case for Jesus' innocence. Pilate doesn't believe the charges and three times declares him innocent. But, yielding to pressure, he hands Jesus over to die.

The Conspiracy to Kill Jesus (22,1–6)

Judas conspires with the religious leaders who have determined to put Jesus to death. Luke blames only Jewish leaders for the murderous plot, perhaps in order to exonerate the Romans and thereby avert persecution by the Roman authorities.

The Last Supper (22,7–38)

Fully aware of what lies ahead, Jesus reinterprets the cups and bread of the Passover meal. They are now the elements of a new covenant made in his own blood, not that of sacrificial animals. The Passover meal was Israel's way of remembering the Exodus; now it will become the way of remembering the new covenant initiated in Jesus' death and resurrection.

Jesus' farewell speech follows. It consists of four units: (a) prediction of betrayal (22,21–23); (b) the role of the disciples (22,24–30); (c) prophecy of Peter's denial and later rehabilitation (22,31–34); and (d) instructions for the coming crisis (22,35–38).

Though Judas' betrayal of Jesus will be the greatest sin committed by any of the disciples, they will also experience division, jealousy, and backsliding. Jesus provides the example, through his role as "one who serves," that the disciples must not imitate the culture in worrying about status and honors. At his own farewell banquet, Jesus appears as slave rather than master, reinforcing the theme, typical in Luke, that the Kingdom is a place of reversals.

Though Jesus will die after being betrayed by Judas and denied by Peter, all is not dark. Future fulfillment will see the twelve disciples occupying the thrones of the tribes of Israel and feasting in glory with Jesus. For now, Satan is at work in Judas (22,3) and in Peter's testing. So the old guidelines for missionaries (see 10,1–12) are canceled, and now missionaries must provide themselves with purse, knapsack, sandals, and even a sword, for they must be ready to face a world hostile to their preaching.

Arrest of Jesus (22,39–53)

Jesus emerges from the garden, a familiar place of prayer, as God's obedient son; he has won the inner struggle and goes forth in peace. The disciples come off better here than in Mark, for Luke excuses their failure to support Jesus in prayer by referring to their being exhausted from "grief." But Jesus urges them to pray that they not be put to the test. The mob comes for him as for a criminal, but even in these circumstances Jesus plays the healer, restoring the severed ear of the servant Malchus. Jesus accepts his arrest as part of the hour of darkness permitted by God's plan.

The Trial of Jesus (22,54—23,25)

Seeing Jesus' prediction of betrayal and denial fulfilled reinforces the perception that the events of the passion are controlled not by human decisions but by God's sovereign will. Peter's denial proves Jesus a true prophet. The scene is poignant: Jesus' look at Peter smites Peter with guilt and calls forth his tears. The appearance before the Sanhedrin is not a formal trial. The religious authorities have already decided on Jesus' fate and have sealed it with false charges. In Jesus' words they find the "evidence" they need and charge him with claiming to be the "Son of God" (22,66–71). Pilate protests Jesus' innocence each time Jesus appears before him. It is the Jewish authorities, in this Gospel as in John's, who force the hand of Pilate. Pilate even sends Jesus to Herod in order to avoid a decision, and Herod, too, can find no fault (23,6–12). Herod was looking for entertainment in Jesus, but he is disappointed by the silent prisoner and resorts to mean-spirited ridicule. Jesus proves the peacemaker, however, for the incident somehow ends the animosity between Pilate and Herod. Pointing out that even Herod could not accuse him, Pilate argues for Jesus' release. He even offers to first teach him a lesson by flogging him. But the crowd demands crucifixion. Ironically, by demanding the release of a murderer and rebel, they become guilty of the very crime of which they accused Jesus: inciting rebellion.

Crucifixion and Burial of Jesus (23,26–56a)

Luke's theme of discipleship resurfaces. Earlier Jesus had said disciples should be ready to take up their cross and follow him; here Simon and a large crowd do exactly that. Jesus is led to his death, but even in this hour of greatest need we see Jesus ministering to others. He prophesies the destruction of Jerusalem to the women who weep for him (23,26–32), revealing the grief and compassion he feels. On the cross, in an incident recorded only by Luke, Jesus offers salvation to the repentant sinner who hangs beside him (23,39–43). Jesus even forgives all those who cause his death. Luke's grammar in the original Greek indicates Jesus may have repeated his "Father, forgive them" many times.

In Luke, the crowd simply watches; only the leaders and soldiers do the mocking. They challenge Jesus to save himself from his fate, the fate that becomes the source of salvation for all who put their trust in him. Note that here Jesus addresses his last words to humans not to his mother or his followers, but to the criminal who shares the final indignity of crucifixion. An apocalyptic sign (the eclipse of the sun) and the tearing of the Temple veil mark the time of Jesus' death. A centurion asserts his innocence and the sympathetic crowd departs "beating their breasts" (23,49).

Jesus was born in a borrowed manger; now, through the generosity of Joseph, a member of the Council, he is laid to rest in a borrowed tomb. The women act quickly because of the approaching Sabbath, but they bury Jesus with dignity and honor. That they take note of the place of burial is significant. Luke is saying that there is no chance that the women went to the wrong tomb when they returned on the third day to anoint the body.

THE RESURRECTION NARRATIVE (23,56b–24,53)

The ascension of Jesus takes place in Jerusalem on Sunday (the sequence of events from the appearance on the road to Emmaus to the departure of Jesus all occur on the same "third day," though in Acts Luke mentions a period of forty days between the resurrection and ascension). Luke creates three scenes—the empty tomb, the appearance on the road, and the appearance to the disciples—that clearly spell out his faith in the resurrection.

Scene 1: The Women at the Tomb (23,56b–24,12)

The first scene finds the women at the tomb puzzling over the rolled-away stone and the missing body. Angels not only scold them for looking for the living among the dead (compare 20,38), but also remind the women that Jesus had predicted his passion and resurrection. Luke names the women who announce the resurrection to the apostles, who consider the news nonsense (24,11).

Scene 2: Jesus Appears to the Disciples (24,13–43)

Jesus appears on the road to Emmaus (24,13–35). This scene employs a motif common in folktales: a disguised god in need of hospitality. Jesus enters the disciples' discussion, explaining

Women in Luke

Luke was especially sensitive to outcasts and outsiders. Women in his day could claim few of the rights men enjoyed. But Jesus often crossed social, religious, and political barriers; he treated all people with compassion and respect. Luke reflects this by introducing thirteen women who are mentioned in no other Gospel. He also includes five incidents involving women that are not reported by any of the other evangelists:

- Raising the widow's son (7,11–17)
- Pardon of a sinful woman (7,36–50)
- Galilean women follow Jesus (8,1–11)
- Visit to Martha and Mary (10,38–42)
- Cure of a crippled woman (13,10–17)

that Moses and the prophets reveal that the suffering of the Messiah was necessary—a part of God's plan. This emphasizes that the fulfillment of Scripture is an important theme in Luke. The heart of the scene is the disciples' recognition of Jesus "in the breaking of the bread." After Jesus disappears, they realize their hearts had been burning within them all the while they were on the road in the presence of the disguised Lord.

Jesus appears to the disciples in Jerusalem (24,36–43). Luke refers to Jesus' appearance to Peter (24,34), but he fully describes only the appearance to the entire group of apostles gathered for a meal (24,36–49). This third appearance, through its use of physical details and the mention of Jesus eating, is meant to convince the reader that the apostles saw the true risen Lord, not some counterfeit ghost.

Jesus' Resurrection

Christian belief in the resurrection of Jesus cannot be supported by near-death experiences—well-intentioned as such efforts might be. Christians do not believe Jesus was *resuscitated* in the sense that his dead body came back to life in the same way as a near-death survivor's. Nor was his resurrection merely a spiritual phenomenon, i.e., he rose in the minds and hearts of his followers who experienced his presence through his teachings and his "spirit" among them. Both attitudes miss the mark. Christian belief says God transformed Jesus, body and spirit. Lazarus was resuscitated or revivified, meaning he returned to the same state of life he had enjoyed previous to his death. But Jesus was truly and fully transformed. He experienced a bodily resurrection, which meant his body was now different from anything we know or understand. His body was freed from the limitations of time and space. Disciples who had known him in life now could not recognize him. Luke shows him needing to convince the apostles that he is Jesus and to prove he is no ghost by eating fish. The transformation of Jesus gives hope to all Christians that the ultimate fate of all creation is a like transformation in the fullness of the Kingdom.

Scene 3: Jesus Commissions the Disciples (24,44–49)

Luke provides another reminder that the suffering and death of the Messiah were necessary to fulfill Scripture (24,44–46). The commissioning of the disciples is the core message of all the post-resurrection accounts. Luke is preparing for the story he will tell in Acts of how the apostles went forth to preach repentance and baptism and to establish Christian communities. Their work will both continue the ministry of Jesus and initiate a new age of salvation history.

After reviewing his ministry, Jesus assures the disciples he will send "the promise of my Father (the Spirit)" (24,49). Jesus is taken from them, and the Gospel ends where it began—in the Temple where the disciples offer constant praise to God.

WHAT WE HAVE LEARNED FROM LUKE

JESUS IS SAVIOR FOR ALL PEOPLE

No one is excluded from Jesus' ministry nor from the Kingdom he brings. The weak, outcast, and poor; women as well as men; Gentiles as much as Israelites; the mighty and the lowly—all are welcome at the banquet table of the Lord. The God of Jesus is a God of reversals, so Jesus comes as a suffering servant Messiah, not a conquering king. He takes his place with outcasts, not power-brokers or lords of finance.

DISCIPLES PARTICIPATE IN THE MISSION OF JESUS

Disciples become participants in Jesus' ministry. They embody the reversals and the counter-cultural values of the Kingdom. They abandon wealth or put it at the disposal of the needy. Disciples give without expecting in return. They don't seek security in the things of this world, but store up treasure in heaven. They seek greatness by being servants of all.

PRAYER AND WORSHIP ARE THE CENTER OF CHRISTIAN LIFE

Even a life of seeking after justice would not bring a would-be disciple into oneness with God if conscious prayer were absent from the person's life. Action and contemplation are inseparable. The Christian path consists of an inner journey of spiritual discipline and growth as well as the outer journey of ministry to God's people. Consistently in Luke's Gospel, Jesus sets the example. His life is grounded in prayer. In the garden he warns the disciples that they, too, must pray to avoid being tested. In the Lord's Prayer that reminder is shared with all of us as well.

Questions for Discussion or Reflection

1. Luke's beatitudes (Lk 6,20–26) differ in style as well as content from Matthew's (Mt 5,3–12). What significance do you find in Matthew's spiritualized beatitudes versus Luke's more economically oriented beatitudes? Which do you find more comforting? Which more challenging? What is the impact of Luke's four "woes"? What challenge do they present for your life?

2. Women play a more prominent role in Luke's Gospel than in any other. What did you find surprising or especially noteworthy about the role women play in this Gospel? Why do you think Luke includes this emphasis? In what ways has the church neglected the consciousness that this Gospel embodies regarding women?

3. Jesus is clearly a man of prayer in this Gospel. Why did Jesus need to pray? What is the proper role of prayer in the life of the Christian? Can one be a good Christian without praying? Why is "doing good" not enough to build a relationship with God?
4. The parables of Jesus often reverse people's expectations; they turn people's worlds upside down—the exemplary son never gets a party in his honor, but the profligate son does. Which parables reverse your expectations? Which are most comforting and which most disturbing?

JOHN READING GUIDE

At a Glance

Who wrote the Gospel, and for whom was it written?	The author may have been a disciple of the Apostle John, but almost certainly was not the Apostle himself, though that had been the belief from the mid-2nd century on. The Gospel itself refers to a mysterious "Beloved Disciple" (21,20–24) who scholars believe is a different person from the Apostle John, the son of Zebedee. Several things are clear: The Gospel shows the hand of more than one writer (several sources may have been combined into the one Gospel); the Gospel contains many accurate details that argue for its being based on eyewitness testimony; the Beloved Disciple may be the source of that testimony, but his story was likely told and retold within his community before being written down. So the question of *single* authorship may not be very relevant. The Gospel is addressed to all Christians of the world.
Who are the main players?	Jesus John the Baptist the twelve disciples the Beloved Disciple Lazarus Mary Martha Mary the mother of Jesus Pilate Mary Magdalene Peter
When was the Gospel written?	Most likely between 90–100 A.D. Though the place of composition traditionally was considered to be Ephesus, some scholars today propose a location in Syria or Palestine.
Healings in John	The royal official's son 4,46–54 The infirm man at the pool of Bethesda 5,1–9 The man born blind 9,1–7 *These three healings, as well as three of the miracles below, are reported only in John.* (John records no exorcisms among the healings of Jesus.)
Other miracles reported in John	Changing water into wine 2,1–11 Feeding the five thousand 6,1–13 (Mt, Mk, Lk) Walking on the water 6,19–21 (Mt, Mk) Raising of Lazarus 11,1–44 Second miraculous catch of fish 21,1–9 *The first four miracles above constitute the "seven signs" of John's Gospel that point to the true identity of Jesus. The miraculous catch is a post-resurrection miracle.* (Mt, Mk, Lk, indicate the miracle is reported in Matthew, Mark, or Luke as well.)
Parables in John	There are no parables reported by John. (Some might consider the images of the good shepherd (10,1–18) and the vine and branches (15,1–10) as parables.)
When Jesus prays in John	On the mountain, alone 6,15 Before raising Lazarus 11,41 While teaching in Jerusalem 12,27–28 The upper room Chapter 17 On the cross 19,30
John's portrait of Jesus	John's Jesus is not the suffering servant seen in the synoptics. He is a noble and divine figure who is the Son of God and the Word of God. Even in the passion, John's Jesus is not a beaten, tormented victim. Instead he has stately bearing. He is peaceful, yet powerful, and fully in charge of his destiny.

John's unique perspective	In John the eternal life that Jesus brings begins here in the present. Jesus is the unique son of God who is himself fully God. As such, he has existed forever, even before the world began. In John, Jesus' glory and power are revealed long before the resurrection. The miracles Jesus performs serve to inspire faith in him, for they reveal Jesus as a man of authority and love. For John, belief in Jesus is necessary for salvation.

Despite the various reasons proposed for the composition of this Gospel—to appeal to Greek thinkers, to oppose some heresy, to complement (or possibly correct) the synoptic Gospels—its goal is clearly stated within its own pages: to inspire faith so that, believing, one can find eternal life.

Differences between John's Gospel and the Synoptics

Synoptics	John
Jesus' teaching focuses on the Kingdom of God.	The Kingdom is not a focus of John's Gospel. He stresses instead Jesus' relationship with the Father.
Writing style makes use of proverbs, maxims and parables. Sayings of Jesus are probably closer to their original form in these Gospels. Numerous ethical teachings are given.	Retells no parables and avoids use of proverbs. He freely shapes and phrases the teachings of Jesus in his own style and imagery. The only ethical teaching here is the command to love one another.
Focuses on Jesus' human origins by recounting his conception, birth and childhood.	Focuses on Jesus as the preexistent, divine Word who was with God from the beginning.
Jesus' ministry centers on Galilee and scant time is spent in Judea. He makes only one trip to Jerusalem where he cleanses the Temple at the end of his ministry.	Jesus' ministry spans several years and includes three trips to Jerusalem in Judea. The Temple cleansing occurs at the beginning of his ministry.
The Last Supper is a Passover meal which would take place on a Friday night.	Last Supper takes place the day before Passover, which would be a Thursday evening.
The disciples only gradually realize the meaning of messiahship.	The disciples profess Jesus as Messiah from the start.
Miracles are recounted in rapid succession and tend to speak for themselves.	Miracles are related within extended narratives followed by discourses that explain their meaning and provide insight into the identity of Jesus.
Jesus starts his ministry just as John the Baptist comes to the end of his. No mention of Jesus baptizing.	John's and Jesus' ministries overlap. Jesus has a baptizing ministry at the same time as John.

Composition of the Fourth Gospel

The apparent double ending of the Gospel (20,30f and 21,24f), as well as some awkward transitions between sections, seem to reveal the work of several editors. For example, in John 14,31 Jesus ends his long discourse by saying, "Get up, let us go." Yet the discourse continues into the next three chapters with no explanation. It is possible that material like these additional chapters may have been added by disciples of the original author.

The Fourth Gospel is very literary and symbolic. Jesus often applies Old Testament symbols like light, life, water, bread, shepherd, and vine to himself. The synoptics do not speak of Jesus in such highly symbolic ways. This symbolic style of speaking about Jesus may have developed within a particular Christian community that included disciples of the author of this Gospel, who is also the author of the Johannine letters. He and his community of followers are called Johannine Christians. Because the basic Jesus story was told and retold by members of this group, the Gospel, in terms of authorship, is sometimes considered to have arisen from the community rather than from a single author.

The Fourth Gospel and the Other Gospels

The chart on the previous page illustrates some of the significant ways John differs from the synoptics. Many scholars believe that although John may have had some knowledge of synoptic tradition, he did draw on sources different from those used by Matthew, Mark and Luke.

The Fourth Gospel and the Jews

It is important when reading through John to be aware of how he uses the term "the Jews." The expression refers to certain characters in his story, not the Jewish people as a whole. In referring to the troubles in northern Ireland one might refer to the Catholics and the Protestants doing this or that against the other. But one would not mean *all* Catholics, nor *all* Protestants. The reference would be to those of either faith who participated in a certain activity, those who played a certain *role*. John's use is the same. After all, Jesus and his followers, and the evangelist himself, are all Jews. But they are not part of the group of Jewish *opponents* who resisted and rejected Jesus. The synoptics use more specific terms that name the various groups and sects of Jesus' day—Sadducees, Herodians, scribes, Pharisees. But when John wants to refer to the "bad guys" in his story he simply says "the Jews."

Herodians The Herodians were a Jewish political group who were strong supporters of the Idumean dynasty to which Herod belonged.

Catholic Church teaching is very explicit in condemning anti-Semitism as an egregious form of racism. When reading the Gospel aloud, especially with children who can't always distinguish between "the Jews" as characters in a story and their own Jewish neighbors and classmates, it may be pastorally advisable to substitute terms that honor John's intent but don't seem to implicate the entire Jewish people, e.g., "Jesus' enemies," or "the religious authorities."

READING THROUGH JOHN'S GOSPEL

Symbols, Irony, and Misunderstanding

Among John's chief devices for stating that Jesus is the Son of God are these literary tools. A symbol is something that stands for something else: for instance, an image ("the vine") that stands for a concept (the union between Jesus and the disciples). Irony is saying one thing and meaning another, sometimes even meaning the opposite of what one says. The effect of irony comes when the reader or hearer sees the double meaning. The symbols provide glimpses of Jesus' true identity. Jesus cannot be known by taking his words literally. Those who do walk in the darkness of misunderstanding. Characters in the story are at different levels of understanding about Jesus' identity. His disciples recognize him as Messiah immediately, but only gradually realize he is the divine Son of God. The crowd is often split in its opinion of him, some being very wrong while the others are partly correct (12,27–29). Throughout, the fact that the reader understands more than the characters in the story provides a consistent sense of irony.

Signs and Faith in John's Gospel

John uses miracles as a way of pointing to faith, not demanding it. Only when they are seen as "signs" that point to who Jesus is do they have value for the would-be believer. Taking miracles literally will not automatically lead to faith. After all, some of Jesus' opponents believed Jesus did miracles, but through the power of Satan! (Mk 3,22). John follows the miracles with discourses that interpret what they mean for the believer.

The Gospels present miracles as an important part of Jesus' ministry. Besides demonstrating who he was, they were signs of God's love and mercy. Should people today "believe in miracles?" Scripture certainly seems to encourage it, but for the right reasons, not to make us believe. Jesus' miracles simply point to his identity. Though miracles are signs of God's presence, they are not to be an opportunity to bargain with God: "You do this for me God, and I'll do that for you." God will act in miraculous ways at times, and we do well to seek healing through prayer. But miracles are but a small sign of God's true greatness.

Miracles Miracles are sometimes seen as events that transcend the ordinary laws of nature or even *all* the laws of nature. The Bible, while presenting the marvelous or wonderful elements of miracles, does so for a reason. God is active throughout our lives and history, but a miracle is an event in which God's participation is made manifest to all.

Some modern scholars have dismissed the Gospel miracles as later embellishments to the original Gospel preaching. Their premise is that miracles just don't happen in the real world, so the miracles of Jesus must be made up. This position ignores Jesus as the unique manifestation of God. Though using miracles as a way of proving Jesus' identity misses the main point of the Gospel miracle stories, those stories must, nonetheless, be seen as authentic memories of the extraordinary presence of God in the ministry of Jesus.

Dualism in John's Gospel

John's Gospel tends to draw sharp distinctions. One is either a believer or a nonbeliever. There is no middle ground (12,44–50). Believers are united with God, nonbelievers are not. This dualism is expressed in terms like these: light/darkness, life/death, from above (heavenly)/ from below (earthly), not judged/condemned. Although these passages may seem harsh or judgmental to us, they serve to emphasize John's presentation of the crucial nature of our choices.

Belief and Eternal Life

John introduces a perspective on salvation that may be surprising. Most Christians think of salvation as what happens at the end of life (14,2f; 17,24) or at the end of the world when Jesus returns in glory as judge (5,27–29). While John does not cancel that kind of thinking, he adds another dimension. By becoming united to Jesus through belief in him, a believer immediately, in the present moment, passes from death to new life (5,24–26; 3,16–21). Conversely, rejecting Jesus means condemnation now. In other words, we are judged at the moment we decide to accept or reject Jesus.

Jesus as God in John's Gospel

The Gospel identifies Jesus with the divine Word that is always present to God and through which God created the world (1,1–5). It also offers reasons for believing Jesus is equal to God: Jesus reveals God to the world, and Jesus does what God does—he gives life and he judges.

John also highlights Jesus' special relationship with the Father. Because of that relationship Jesus deserves the same honor given to God. The "Jews" who oppose him and seek his death are, ironically, trying to kill the very source of life.

An Outline of John

The book clearly divides into two parts: Jesus' confrontation with the world, known as the "book of signs" (Chapters 1–12); and Jesus' return to the Father, known as the "book of glory" (Chapters 13–20). The plot of the book uses a pattern of descent and ascent: Jesus comes (descends) into the world to seek "his own." Jesus meets opposition that leads to the "hour" of his crucifixion, which John views as a time of exaltation. Jesus then returns (ascends) to the Father to enjoy the glory he had from the beginning.

I. Prologue (1,1–18). A glorious hymn of praise to the preexistent Word who has come into the world.

II. The Book of Signs (1,19—12,50). Jesus confronts the world and brings God's judgment against unbelief. It consists of two parts:
   A. Gathering Witnesses to Jesus (1,19—4,54). Jesus reveals his glory to disciples and other believers before confronting the unbelief of the world.
   B. Confrontation with the World (5,1—12,50). The light of Jesus condemns the darkness of the world. Jesus confronts nonbelievers with testimony of his divine origin.

III. The Book of Glory (13,1—20,31). Jesus moves toward the time of glorification and return to the Father. This section also has two parts:
   A. The Supper Discourses (13,1—17,26). At the Last Supper Jesus announces his return to the Father and what that glorification will mean for his disciples.

B. Jesus' Arrest, Crucifixion and Resurrection (18,1 – 20,31). For John the crucifixion is no tragedy, but the moment of Jesus' exaltation and return to the Father.

IV. Epilogue: Resurrection Appearances in Galilee (21,1–25). This second conclusion reports more appearances of Jesus.

As you read through the Gospel, aware of its symbols and noting the sharp contrasts between characters in the story, remember that John wrote the Gospel to inspire faith. You might ask yourself why some characters embrace Jesus and find eternal life, while others respond with disbelief and hostility.

THE PROLOGUE (1,1-18)

If you had any doubts about the distinctiveness of this Gospel, the prologue should remove them. In it you can hear echoes of Genesis 1, where God speaks the world into existence. John offers a powerful new insight into the divine Word. It is not speech or some abstract power God uses to create. The Word is a divine *person* who has become known to us as Jesus. We call this mysterious reality of God becoming human the Incarnation. It is the unique and special revelation of Christianity.

Right from the start, John makes it clear that God can be known both as Creator, the source of all life (that is, the Father), and as the Word through whom God created everything (that is, the Son). Later the Gospel will tell us that the Spirit of God comes to all who believe. The prologue speaks of what "we" have experienced as a result of the Word becoming flesh (1,1214b.16). "We" refers to Christians who believe in Jesus and who, through Jesus, have received power to become children of God (1,12). Scholars believe the poetic lines of the prologue were adapted by John from an early hymn. The *New American Bible* indents these lines so you can distinguish them from the prose comments inserted by the author to form the introduction.

Salvation, A Gift from the Word

The gift of salvation will be given only to those who accept Jesus as the Word made flesh. Though the world and everything in it were created through the Word, still the world did not accept the Word when it came to them. Even those who were "his own . . . did not accept him" (1,11). The ultimate fate of the Word incarnate is suggested at the very start. The prologue even hints at the conflict that Jesus will experience with the Jewish leaders when it contrasts the "law" that came from Moses with the "grace and truth" that come through Jesus (1,17).

THE BOOK OF SIGNS (1,19 – 12,50)

The significance of John's reference to the miracles of Jesus as "signs" is that they serve as symbols that point to Jesus' true identity. Jesus will be known for who he is only by those who understand the symbolic meaning of his actions. The Jews who view his words and actions too literally will not understand the truth Jesus brings.

Gathering Witnesses to Jesus (1,19—4,54)

Though storm clouds can be seen in the distance, the first four chapters are basically optimistic. Jesus is gathering people who will believe in him and his mission.

JOHN TESTIFIES TO JESUS (1,19-34)

The Baptist makes it clear that he is not the Messiah, but one sent to prepare the way for him (1,19-28). Instead of an actual baptism scene as found in the synoptics, this Gospel offers a witness statement given by the Baptist. John says he has seen the Spirit descend like a dove and remain on Jesus. This is the sign God told him to look for. Now he knows that Jesus is the son of God who will baptize not with water but with the Spirit.

JESUS GATHERS DISCIPLES (1,35-51)

In almost every instance the disciples are sent to Jesus by someone else. The Baptist sends the first three and they, in turn, recruit the rest. Though they come to Jesus through the testimony of others, once they meet Jesus, they become true and willing disciples. This chapter gathers all the titles used by the early church to speak of Jesus: Lamb of God (1,36); Messiah (1,41); the one predicted by Moses and the prophets (1,45); Son of God (1,49); King of Israel (1,49); and Son of Man (1,51).

Titles of Jesus

Besides the titles used in this section, Jesus gives himself other names in this Gospel that reveal his identity and mission:

Bread of life 6,35
Light of the world 8,12
Gate for the sheep 10,7
Good shepherd 10,11
The vine 15,1

He also calls himself "the resurrection and life" (11,25) and "the way and the truth and the life" (14,6).

CANA MIRACLE MANIFESTS HIS GLORY (2,1-12)

Though the full manifestation of Jesus' glory will only be accomplished in the crucifixion, the miracle at Cana reveals his divine glory to his newly gathered disciples. Jesus first resists his mother's request (Mary is never named in this Gospel) because his "hour," i.e., his death and resurrection that will reveal his glory, has not yet come. In John Jesus makes Jewish forms of worship obsolete. In fact, Jesus is shown replacing most of the important Jewish feasts. In this story he replaces Jewish ceremonial washings (2,6).

CLEANSING OF THE TEMPLE (2,13-25)

On the first of his three visits to Jerusalem Jesus drives the merchants and money-changers from the Temple. John is announcing to his readers that Jesus will even replace the Temple itself, because Jesus *is* the Temple. But no one in the story, not even the disciples, understands

Jesus' reference to raising up the Temple in three days (2,19). It took the resurrection to open the disciples' eyes. Jesus will not trust himself to those who believe in him only because of his miracles; he is only too familiar with the inconstancy of human nature.

DIALOGUE WITH NICODEMUS (3,1-21)

When Jesus speaks with Nicodemus, and later with the Samaritan woman, he finds himself taken too literally and therefore misunderstood. Yet Jesus keeps upping the ante in the conversations, always responding with an even-more-difficult statement than the one that caused the original misunderstanding. This technique of misunderstanding is effective because the reader, who does understand, can sympathize with or marvel at the character who doesn't. Here Nicodemus never seems to get the point, though he returns later in the Gospel as a sympathetic figure (7,50–52). Jesus speaks of being born "from above," using a word that can also mean "again." Nicodemus thinks he means the latter. For John's Christian readers the reference is to rebirth through baptism.

John 3,16 is one of the best known and loved verses in this Gospel and in all of Scripture. In other contexts "world" represents the forces that are hostile to the Word. But here the world refers to all humanity, to whom God sent "his only son" as a sign of love and as a source of eternal life. Tragically some people will prefer darkness to light, and John offers an explanation: They would rather hide their evil in the dark than "live the truth," a semitic expression for doing God's will. There is a lesson here for all whose sincere offers of help to others have been rebuffed. Bringing light to those in darkness will not always be welcomed or easy.

> **John 3,16** "For God so loved the world that he gave his only Son, so that everyone who believes in him might not perish but might have eternal life."

JESUS AND JOHN THE BAPTIST (3,22–4,3)

Once more the Baptist testifies that Jesus is the one to come. He speaks of himself as the "best man" who rejoices at the arrival of the "bridegroom" (3,29), and he poignantly comments that now his task is to "decrease" while Jesus must increase (3,30). The Father has given Jesus "all things" (3,35), and out of what he has received, Jesus must give the Spirit—i.e., eternal life—to all who believe (3,33f. 36). But not all will accept the Son, and those who don't will merit judgment (3,36b).

THE SAMARITAN WOMAN (4,4-42)

Jesus is presented as a new and greater Jacob—the patriarch who met his wife at a well. (According to legend, Jacob's well contained water that bubbled to the top.) Jesus is greater than all the hopes of either Israel or Samaria, both of which expected great champions who would vindicate them and bring them glory.

Jesus speaks of living (i.e., flowing) water, but what he means is the gift of the Spirit. The woman, however, can't get past the literal until Jesus' comment about her husbands (4,18) convinces her he is a prophet. When Jesus says that henceforth believers will worship in "spirit and truth," he is referring to himself as the replacement of the Temple (see 2,13–22). After the woman accepts Jesus as Messiah and becomes a disciple, she goes out, like the apostles in Chapter 1, and recruits more.

Jesus speaks to the disciples about mission and harvest (4,31–38) and suggests that, like the woman, they too must go and preach to others. We learn that because of the woman's testimony many Samaritans became disciples. That information, coupled with the earlier reference that Jesus was baptizing more disciples than John, indicates that Jesus was winning many followers.

Samaritans The animosity between Jews and Samaritans was long-standing. The Books of Kings pass a consistently negative judgment on the northern kingdom of Israel for its infidelity to the Jerusalem Temple and the true worship of the Lord. Those who lived in the territory of the northern kingdom after the fall of the North at the hands of Assyria were non-Israelites settled there by the Assyrian overlords. These foreigners intermarried with the few Jews not carried into exile and adopted Jewish religion, but mixed it with their own polytheism. Even after the Hebrew nation was restored under Ezra and Nehemiah, the Samaritans were considered outsiders and never assimilated. The mutual hatred was so great that when Jews traveled, they would take routes that bypassed Samaria even though that meant many extra miles of travel.

HEALING THE ROYAL OFFICIAL'S SON (4,43–54)

The Samaritan woman's story concluded with the joyous announcement that Jesus is "savior of the world" (4,42). Returning to Cana, Jesus performs a miracle (from a distance, he heals a boy without ever seeing him) that further establishes his reputation and his identity as God's son. Now the stage is set for the confrontation between Jesus and those who refuse to believe.

Confrontation with the World (5,1 – 12,50)

Jesus encounters much opposition and unbelief in this section. But because it leads to Jesus' exaltation through his death and resurrection, the unbelief in no way represents failure. Despite the many obstacles, Jesus does succeed in winning many followers who are made children of God for believing Jesus is sent by the Father.

HEALING THE LAME MAN: JESUS GIVES LIFE AND JUDGES (5,1-47)

Jesus provokes the hostility of the Jewish leaders by healing a lame man on the Sabbath. But the real cause of tension is the claim to equality with God that Jesus makes through what he says and does (5,6–18). Jesus lays claim to the power of giving life and forgiving sin (5,21–22), which in the Old Testament are things only God can do. He defends his right to do these things because of his special relationship with the Father. Jesus is the son who does only what the Father has given him to do (5,30). Remember, in John, just to encounter Jesus is an experience of judgment, for one must decide whether to believe in him (and be saved) or reject him (and be lost). Jesus points out to the leaders all those things they choose to ignore that witness to him: the Baptist (5,31–35), Jesus' actions (5,36), and even Scripture (5,37–39). The leaders are so preoccupied with winning earthly glory for themselves, says Jesus, that they miss the glory of God revealed in him. For this they will be judged, not by Jesus, but by the one they have tried to use against Jesus, Moses himself.

JESUS IS THE BREAD FROM HEAVEN (6,1–71)

This section contains material also found in the synoptics, but John has molded it into a new shape by including a long discourse about Jesus being the bread of life (6,22–59). The multiplication of the loaves is the fourth of the seven signs in John that point to the identity of Jesus. These signs are primarily symbolic, and anyone who does not recognize the symbolism here will not receive Jesus as the bread of life. Earlier, Jesus promised to give the Samaritan woman living water that would give eternal life. Now he promises bread that will do the same for believers.

The bread-of-life discourse is a difficult one for Jesus' hearers to understand. Jesus identifies himself with the bread of life that comes down from heaven, sent by God. The first level of meaning in the symbol of bread is that of *faith:* in God and in Jesus. Christian tradition associates the manna and "bread of life" with the Eucharist (6,51–59). Jesus is the very source of life for Christians. Through him one develops a whole new relationship with God. And it is that new relationship, not merely believing that Jesus is God's son, that brings eternal life to the believer. The special role of the Eucharist is that it helps us sustain that relationship with God. To miss the symbolic nature of Jesus' insistence that one must eat his flesh and drink his blood would result in a ludicrous misunderstanding that would seem to endorse human sacrifice. And some of his listeners make that very mistake. But even those who understood the symbolism might have been scandalized by the way Jesus associated himself so closely with God.

Jesus' words are indeed "hard" (6,60). Many disciples abandon him because of them. Peter, however, speaks for the twelve disciples when he says in answer to Jesus' question about whether they, too, will leave him: "To whom shall we go?" (6,68). Only Jesus has the words of eternal life.

CONFLICT AND DIVISION AT THE FEAST OF TABERNACLES (7,1 – 8,59)

The Feast of Tabernacles is the backdrop for the events in this section. Jesus appropriates two of the elements of the Tabernacles ritual, light and water, to express his own identity (7,37–39; 8,12). The religious officials are seeking to put Jesus to death for various alleged crimes including leading the people astray and being demon possessed. But because it is not yet his "hour," their efforts to arrest him, and even to stone him, fail.

Through his words and actions Jesus addresses some of the objections the religious leaders level at him. For one, he asks them to explain why he can't *heal* on the Sabbath when the law permits performing *circumcision* on the Sabbath (7,19–24). And in response to the leaders' claim that Jesus' origins as son of Joseph (6,42) and the fact that they know where he comes from—when the true Messiah comes, they believe, no one will know where he comes from (7,27)—make it impossible for him to be the Messiah, Jesus says that they really don't know where he comes from for his *true* origins are "from heaven" (7,25–31.40–44). Jesus even appropriates the divine name I AM (8,28). He demands that the crowd acknowledge him, a human being, as the revealer of the God of Abraham and Moses. Because of this many turn away. But others, including the guards sent to arrest Jesus, are persuaded by his words, saying, "Never before has anyone spoken like this" (7,46).

The powerful story of the woman caught in adultery is in this section, though many scholars believe it was a later addition to this Gospel. More typical of Luke in style and subject, it reveals Jesus' power and compassion.

THE BLIND MAN BELIEVES IN JESUS (9,1–41)

Physical vision comes to the blind man instantly. But spiritual insight comes more gradually. During the process of being interrogated by the Pharisees, the blind man begins to realize that Jesus could not be the sinner the authorities accuse him of being. He acknowledges Jesus as a prophet (9,17) and claims that he must have come from God (9,33). His parents offer him no support, for they fear being thrown out of the synagogue by the "Jews." This fear probably reflects the experience of John's community that actually had been forced out of the synagogues by Jewish authorities in the period after the destruction of the Temple (after about 70 A.D.). At the end of the story the man meets Jesus again and is able to confess his faith in him while Jesus condemns the spiritual blindness of the Jewish leaders (9,39–41).

God's Mercy Revealed In this story Jesus discredits the commonly held belief that physical suffering was the result of sin. Neither the man nor his parents sinned, Jesus says. His blindness was an opportunity for God's power and mercy to be revealed.

THE TRUE SHEPHERD GIVES HIS LIFE (10,1–42)

The parable of the Good Shepherd asserts that Jesus, despite the accusations of his detractors that he leads people astray, is a true and caring leader. Jesus is willing to lay down his life for the sheep. None of the "hired hands" who claim to be leaders of the people would be so generous. (This imagery was part of Israel's traditions: see Ezekiel, Chapter 34). Again Jesus asserts his divine sonship (10,30–39), and again the people try to stone him (10,33) for his supposed blasphemy.

Shepherds In first-century Palestine shepherds tended their flocks without dogs. The sheep knew the voice of the shepherd and responded only to that voice. Sheep were often herded together into a common pen with other flocks, but when a shepherd called his flock, only those sheep that belonged to him would come out.

RAISING LAZARUS: GIFT OF LIFE MEANS DEATH (11,1–57)

This episode is built on ironies. First, the Jewish leaders try to end the life of Jesus, who is the very source of life (11,24–26). In addition, Jesus gains his largest following from this, his greatest sign. Yet, ironically, it is this success that leads the Jewish Council to decide to seek his death (11,45–47). Even the high priest speaks ironic words when he says it is better for one man to die for the sake of the people: For those who have faith, Jesus' death benefits all the world. Jesus displays genuine grief and deep concern for Lazarus and his sisters. But Christians are reminded through this episode that anyone who believes that Jesus is the resurrection should not mourn physical death in the same way the world does.

THE LIGHT IS DEPARTING (12,1–50)

In addition to the anointing at Bethany, a similar story of Jesus' anointing also occurs in the synoptics (Mk 14,3–9; Mt 26,6–13). John sets it in the home of Lazarus. Judas, the traitor,

Burying the Dead Debated among the rabbis was the question of which was the greater act of charity: burying the dead or giving alms to the poor. Those who argued for burying the dead believed it was a necessary condition for being able to rise from the dead.

protests the waste of such costly ointment that could have been sold for the benefit of the poor (12,1–8). But Jesus defends Mary, seeing in her action a preparation for his burial. Jesus enters Jerusalem triumphantly, with "the whole world (going) after him" (12,19). This comment and the arrival of Greek Gentiles who want to meet Jesus hint at the future spread of Christianity. Jesus prophesies that when he is lifted up on the cross, he will draw all people to himself (12,20–32). But for now, he bitterly laments the depth of unbelief he has encountered. On this tragic note John ends the "book of signs."

THE BOOK OF GLORY (13,1 – 20,31)

In the "book of glory" we will see some of the ways this Gospel differs from the synoptics, particularly in the Last Supper scene and in the depiction of Jesus in the passion account. The truth of who Jesus is and why he came among us is revealed most fully in his death and resurrection.

The Supper Discourses (13,1 – 17,26)

The Footwashing. Jesus models for the disciples the attitude of service that should characterize their relationships with each other and the world (13,1–20). At the place in the story where the synoptics put the institution of the Eucharist, John inserts the footwashing, suggesting the importance he places on the episode.

Judas and the Beloved Disciple. Judas, one of the twelve, is the betrayer who, despite being in Satan's grip, helps further God's plan (6,70f; 12,4–6; 13,2.11.21–30; 17,12). The Beloved Disciple is somewhat of a puzzle. While some identify him with John, the brother of James, most scholars believe he is a different personality. Closer to Jesus than any other disciple, he shares special insights into the passion and resurrection. The Johannine community from which this Gospel comes considered the Beloved Disciple the source of its tradition.

The Discourses. The fact that there is similar content in some of the discourses of this section suggests that originally they may have been composed as independent units and later woven together: e.g., Chapters 13,36 – 14,31 and Chapter 16,4–33 both deal with the disciples' grief, Jesus' departure and return, and the coming of the Advocate.

Unity. In 15,1 – 16,4a Jesus speaks of unity and the threats to unity the disciples will encounter. The hatred and persecution of the world will test their ability to love each other and to cling to Jesus, the true vine.

Jesus' Prayer. Chapter 17 contains an extended prayer of Jesus for the disciples that reveals Jesus' intimate love of the Father and his profound love for the disciples. Jesus will leave them in the world, but they do not belong to the world any more than he does (17,13–19).

Sent Forth. As Jesus was sent by the Father, so he sends the disciples into the world to be expressions of the love that exists between the Father and the Son (17,20–26).

Love Command. The only explicit command Jesus gives in this Gospel is the command to love one another. The love God demonstrated in sending Jesus and the love Jesus will demonstrate on the cross model the love disciples are called to give each other and the world.

The Advocate. The disciples don't yet understand all Jesus has told them, but the Advocate will come to complete their understanding and to help the disciples to face the trials of hatred and persecution that will inevitably come.

The Trial of Jesus

There are differences in the four evangelists' descriptions of Jesus' trial.

- Only John records a hearing before Annas (18,13–23).
- All four mention the hearing before Caiaphas (Mt 26; Mk 14; Lk 22; Jn 18).
- Only the synoptics record the hearing before the Sanhedrin (Mt 27; Mk 15; Lk 22).
- All recount the trial before Pilate (Mt 27; Mk 15; Lk 23; Jn 23).

Only in Luke is the Pilate trial interrupted by an appearance before Herod (Lk 23), after which the Pilate trial resumes.

Jesus' Arrest, Crucifixion, and Resurrection (18,1 – 20,31)

Jesus in Control. Note the dramatically different tone of this garden scene as compared with those in the synoptics. Here there is no agony, no prayer to let this cup pass. Jesus is in control of his destiny. When he dies it is because he surrenders his life, not because it is taken from him. In the garden, when Jesus identifies himself once more with the divine I AM, all his opponents fall to the ground.

Before Pilate. Jesus is first brought before the former high priest, Annas, and then sent to Caiaphas, the current high priest. During these interrogations Peter denies Jesus. Then, though they have no formal charge, the Jewish authorities hand Jesus over to Pilate. John spends more time on this trial than the synoptics. In the tug-of-war between Pilate and the Jewish authorities, Pilate comes off looking better. The exchange about Barabbas seems to be an effort on Pilate's part to resolve the problem quickly. It does not work. Pilate knows Jesus is innocent, but he has him brutally flogged in an effort to appease the chief priests. This effort also fails and Pilate finally yields to the priests' pressure rather than risk being denounced to Caesar. But Pilate wins the final round by insisting the charge against Jesus read "King of the Jews." The priests reveal how far they have drifted from the Law of God by announcing that they have no king but Caesar (19,12–22).

The Crucifixion. None of the evangelists describes the crucifixion. John generally does not include any incident mentioned in the synoptic Gospels that would imply that Jesus is not fully in control of his destiny. Hence, there is no Simon; we are told Jesus carried the cross by himself (19,17). And there are no mourning women or insults hurled at the crucified Jesus. As Jesus hangs on the cross, scripture is fulfilled (dividing of his garments, 19,24; Jesus saying, "I thirst," 19,28), showing that all these events are under God's control. Finally, Jesus entrusts his mother into the care of the beloved disciple (19,25–27) and then hands over his spirit. This is the climax of John's Gospel, the most glorious moment of Jesus' "hour of glory."

His Bones Were Not Broken

The leg bones of crucified men were broken in order to speed up their death: Since they could no longer support their weight with their legs, they slumped and suffocated. The urgency reported here was due to the need to remove the bodies before sundown and the start of the Passover feast. Since Jesus was already dead, his bones did not need to be broken, though his side was pierced—fulfilling Scripture (Ex 12,46; Zech 12,10).

The Resurrection. The flow of blood and water was biological evidence of Jesus' death. (It was later seen as a powerful theological symbol of the sacraments, baptism and Eucharist.) His proper burial in a known tomb confirms his death (19,38–42). But the tomb, remember, is in a garden—a garden, as it turns out, of new creation. Mary reacts to the empty tomb (20,1f) by fearing that the body has been stolen (possibly by the hostile religious leaders). The beloved disciple believes when he sees the empty tomb, but all he and Peter discover there are empty wrappings.

Magdalene. Reversing the order of the synoptics, John introduces angels in the tomb after Peter and the Beloved Disciple have departed. Here, too, Mary is given a message for the disciples, but in John it comes directly from Jesus, whom Mary sees but cannot at first recognize. Once she knows it is the Lord, however, she runs to announce the good news to the disciples.

Appearances of Jesus. In the Gospel of John the resurrection, Jesus' ascent to the Father, and the bestowing of the Spirit all occur on Sunday. Jesus appears to the disciples and shows his hands and feet as evidence of who he is. He then commissions them to go to the world, and he imparts the Spirit.

The appearance that includes Thomas, who needs physical evidence to believe, makes the point that those who have not seen but have believed, like John's readers, are those who are truly blessed (20,28f).

Post-Resurrection Appearances

In all, the Gospels record eight appearances of Jesus after the resurrection. John records three; the last two are unique to this Gospel.

- The disciples without Thomas (20,19–25)
- The disciples with Thomas (20,26–31)
- To seven disciples fishing (21,1–14)

EPILOGUE (21,1–25)

As the *New American Bible* introduction points out, this chapter seems to have been a later addition to the Gospel. Two characters stand out: Peter and the Beloved Disciple. The lake shore scene between Peter and the risen Jesus is moving and theologically significant: Peter both is reconciled to his Lord and inherits Jesus' role as shepherd. Peter followed Jesus in a martyr's death. The Beloved Disciple lived long but also died. It is on that disciple's reliable testimony that the Gospel is based (21,24).

WHAT WE HAVE LEARNED FROM JOHN

JESUS IS THE SON OF GOD

John's unique contribution takes the form of a story that avoids parables that speak of the Kingdom of God but focuses, instead, on the special relationship between Jesus and the Father. Jesus is like no other religious figure. He is unique in all of history because God was revealed in him in a way God never was in any other human being before or since.

SALVATION COMES THROUGH BELIEF IN THE SON

Belief in Jesus as the Son of God is necessary for salvation, i.e., eternal life. Salvation means we have an entirely new relationship with God that is made possible by Jesus. This new relationship is available to anyone who has received the grace to believe in Jesus.

JESUS' DEATH EXPRESSES GOD'S LOVE FOR HUMANITY

Though he was killed by evil people, Jesus was not the *victim* of human injustice. Jesus freely chose to die as an offering. His death on the cross revealed God's love. It also reveals that God identifies with the lowly and the suffering, not just by feeling sorry for them, but by becoming one of them. Jesus' followers must also identify with the poor and suffering. The lowly cannot be left to the powers of the world, or they may forever be victims of injustice as Jesus was.

MUTUAL LOVE AND UNITY IN THE CHURCH EXPRESSES THE LOVE OF GOD

Lack of unity among Christians is a grave scandal. For Christians to love one another is not simply a way of living a moral virtue. It is a way of revealing the love of Jesus and the mutual love of the Father and the Son to the world. Jesus reveals God's love to us and enables us to love one another.

Questions for Discussion or Reflection

1. What does discipleship mean in John's Gospel? In what ways does it resemble or differ from the picture of discipleship presented by the synoptic writers?
2. What do you think is the significance of this substitution? Instead of recounting Jesus' words over the bread and wine (the institution of the Eucharist), John focuses on Jesus' service to the disciples (the washing of feet).
3. Why does John see the crucifixion as the hour of "glory" for Jesus? In what way does it climax his ministry? What is revealed to us through Jesus' death on the cross?
4. Throughout the Gospel, various characters misunderstand Jesus, often by taking his words too literally. Yet some come to understanding and faith while others do not. Why does this happen? Is it all their doing, or does God's will also play a role? What misunderstanding of Jesus has reading this Gospel cleared up for you?

5. The miraculous signs of the Gospel are presented as evidence that Jesus really is the Messiah. They lead to faith by pointing to who Jesus is. After feeding the five thousand Jesus again meets the crowd and scolds them because they have come looking for him only because their stomachs had been filled, "not because (they) saw signs" (6,26). What is the difference Jesus is pointing to? Why is he disappointed? In your prayer life do you seek more for "signs" or for the fulfillment of your needs?

ACTS READING GUIDE

At a Glance

Who wrote the book, and for whom was it written?

From the late second century onward church tradition has held that Luke, the sometime companion of Paul and the author of the Gospel, is also the author of the Book of Acts. He was a well-educated Syrian from Antioch who was himself a Gentile convert to Christianity.

Luke addresses the Book of Acts to Theophilus, the same individual to whom he addressed the Gospel and whose name means "one who loves God." But the book is also intended for *all* who love and fear God.

When was the book written?

Sometime after the destruction of Jerusalem and the Temple, probably between 80–90 A.D.

What should I look for?

- How the Spirit-led church spreads from Jerusalem to Rome, the center of the empire
- How the church thrived even during times of opposition, demonstrating its divine guidance
- The apology for (defense of) Christianity that runs through the book
- The historical perspective on the founding of the church
- The internal struggles present in and survived in the early church
- The continuing presence of Lukan themes first seen in his Gospel: the work of the Spirit; the importance of prayer; the pervasive presence of joy; the significance of women, including Mary, the mother of Jesus

Where did these events occur?

In Jerusalem and various cities of what we now call the Middle East: Joppa, Antioch, Derbe, Lystra, Ephesus, Iconium, the island of Cyprus, Philippi, Thessalonica, Berea, Corinth, Athens, the island of Malta, Rome

Why was this book written?

- To continue Luke's record of biblical, or salvation, history and to provide a historical account of the founding of the church
- To explain that the salvation brought by Jesus has been extended to Gentiles
- To demonstrate the working of the Holy Spirit in the life of the early church
- To assert that the spread of the gospel was accomplished through the apostles who were chosen by God and commissioned by Jesus

Who are the main players?

Peter Stephen Philip Paul Cornelius James
Timothy Barnabus Lydia Titus Apollos Felix
Festus King Agrippa and Luke

What's the story? The book centers on the preaching and ministry of Peter and Paul. After the ascension, Peter begins to preach boldly and to work many miracles. Though initially he resists preaching the gospel to Gentiles, he eventually realizes that God wants all people to come to know Jesus.

Paul, a devout and zealous Jew, at first persecutes the followers of Jesus until a miraculous encounter with the risen Jesus changes his life. He becomes a missionary preaching about Jesus throughout much of the Roman empire.

After the church is established in Jerusalem, conflicts arise with Jewish authorities that climax in the martyrdom of Stephen and the imprisonment of Peter. The gospel spreads throughout the Gentile world largely due to the efforts of Paul, Barnabas, and others. Internal conflicts arise but are resolved. The book ends with Paul imprisoned in Rome where he has witnessed to the gospel in the very heart of the empire.

The story isn't finished yet. The light that dawned at Jesus' birth must now spread across the sky and illumine the whole earth (Lk 24,47; Acts 1,8). The Book of Acts begins the story of how that light spread from the relatively insignificant outpost of Jerusalem, through most of the Roman empire, and then to its very heart in Rome. But the story of that outward movement is not written in the style of what we would consider history in today's world. Luke left out significant historical events that a good historian, if that's what he was trying to be, would not have ignored—for example, riots in Rome over the name of "Chrestus" that prompted the emperor to expel the Christians. Luke's intention was broader. He wanted to record not human history, but salvation history. He wanted to tell the story of the way God worked out the plan for our salvation through special people and events.

Understanding Salvation History

One thing that salvation history has in common with world history is that it can only be put together with hindsight. Most Christians would agree that it is much easier to know where God has led you than to know where God is taking you. It was no different for the disciples. What did God want of them? They had some guideposts, of course, to help them answer that question, guideposts such as (1) their experience of Jesus and their memories of what he taught them; (2) Jesus' assurance that God would use them to initiate a new stage in the plan of salvation; (3) sections of the Old Testament Scriptures that helped them understand how Jesus' life and death fit into God's overall plan. But these resources alone would not have helped the disciples figure out where they were headed if the Holy Spirit had not intervened directly at key moments in the story; for example, the vision that helped Peter realize salvation was God's gift for all people, not just Jews (Acts 10,9–16), and the vision Paul had in Asia Minor that caused him to change his plans and travel to Greece instead (Acts 16,6–10).

The direct intervention of the Holy Spirit does not mean, however, that God turned the disciples into puppets. Paul fell to the ground, was blinded, and had a conversation with the risen Jesus. But he was never given a map of what he should say and do in order to spread the gospel. God provided signposts that pointed in the right direction, but when they reached a fork in the road the disciples had to think and pray hard about how to continue. Prayer was a great resource for them. Another was their ability to learn from past events about how God was working with them in the present.

Preaching In Acts

A large part of Acts, about one-fourth of the book, consists of sermons, eighteen in all. These are Luke's reconstructions of sermons given by Peter, Paul, and other leaders of the early church. They are not verbatim reports, but they do communicate a good sense of the flavor and the content of the teachings of the early church.

The Plan of Salvation History in Acts

The story of salvation, as Luke unfolds it in Acts, follows a two-fold pattern—one geographical, the other sociological.

As mentioned above, the spread of the gospel begins outward from Jerusalem, where Jesus ended his ministry, and follows a westward course along the Mediterranean until it reaches Rome, the capital city of the empire and the symbolic center of the known world. In a relatively short amount of time Christianity has grown from a small and frightened band of believers in Jerusalem to a world-wide movement. As a result of Paul's visits to the major cities along the roads and sea routes of his day, Christian churches dot the empire.

The second pattern of growth was foreshadowed in Jesus' own ministry. Brought first to the Jews, but rejected, the message of Jesus is now shared with Gentiles. There were some Jewish converts, of course. Apollos preached successfully in the synagogues (Acts 18,26–28), and Luke speaks of converts from both Jews and "Greeks" (a term he uses as a synonym for Gentiles). But often the door for Gentile converts to hear the gospel was opened because Jews in a particular place had shut the door on the message of Jesus (see Acts 13,44–52). Salvation history has turned a corner. Israel had held a primary place in God's plan of salvation. Even after rejecting the Messiah in the person of Jesus, Israel received another chance through the ministry of the apostles (see 3,11–26). But continued rejection by the Jews makes it clear that the story of salvation has become bigger than the story of God's involvement with Israel, it is now the story of God's dealings with all peoples.

This pattern of Jews first, then Gentiles is not a sign of God's rejection of Israel. Instead, it is a reminder that we Christians owe much to our Jewish ancestors in faith. We are forever linked as a result of God's plan of salvation. Therefore Christians shun all forms of anti-Semitism and seek greater understanding of how Jewish traditions contribute to our own faith in God.

READING THROUGH ACTS

A Good Read

Before trying to study Acts, sit down and read it through all at once. You'll notice that Acts works both as religious literature and as entertainment. Like the novels of his day, Luke packs his account with stories of persecutions, hardships, imprisonment and trials, and perilous journeys. As you read, you will not be bored.

Journey Motif

Second, you will notice that certain kinds of events tend to recur in the story: The apostles make speeches before courts and officials; they are jailed and sometimes miraculously rescued from jail or other dangers; they preach sermons; they draw much attention by working miracles; they challenge the beliefs and superstitions of the Gentiles. Significantly, all these dramatic events are organized into a pattern of journeys. The journey motif picks up on the ministry of Jesus which itself was seen as a journey, and it tells the Christian that his or her life will have to take on this character also. Christians move through life as through a journey, experiencing highs and lows, smooth roads and road-blocks, but always intent on witnessing to the good news of Jesus.

Community Life

Luke paints a fairly rosy picture of what life was like within the early Christian communities. Paul's letters, on the other hand, tell us that dissent and conflicts did arise within the churches. Luke is not trying to cover up. In fact, he, too, mentions some of the problems (e.g., Ananias and Sapphira, 5,1–11 and disagreements (e.g., Paul and Barnabas, 15,39. But his greater concern is with showing how things *ought* to be within the churches. He is even teaching Christians how to work out their problems and reminding them to always and everywhere thank God for the gift of salvation they have received.

AN OUTLINE OF ACTS

The Book of Acts splits nicely in two, with each half dominated by one of the two great figures of the early church: Peter and Paul. Peter's ministry runs through the first twelve chapters, which focus on the beginnings of the church in Palestine; Chapters 13 to 28 recount the ministry of Paul and the expansion of the church beyond Palestine to Rome. Smaller units can also be identified, as the following outline shows:

I. Peter and the Mission in Palestine
- A. Preparation for the Christian Mission (1,1–2,13). Includes the events between Easter and Peter's first missionary sermon on Pentecost.
  1. Waiting in Jerusalem (1,1–14)
  2. Replacing Judas (1,15–26)
  3. Pentecost, the coming of the Spirit (2,1–13)
- B. The Mission in Jerusalem (2,14–8,3)
  1. Two sermons by Peter (2,14–3,26)
  2. Peter and John before the Sanhedrin (4,1–31)
  3. Sharing possessions in the community (4,32–5,16)
  4. Trial before the Sanhedrin (5,17–42)
  5. Deacons for the Greek-speaking Christians (6,1–7)
  6. Trial and death of Stephen (6,8–8,3)
- C. Mission in Judea and Samaria (8,4–9,43). The gospel begins to spread into areas around Jerusalem.
  1. Philip preaches outside Jerusalem (8,4–40)

2. Conversion of Paul (9,1–30)
3. The church continues to grow (9,31–43)

II. Paul and the Mission to the Gentiles

A. Inauguration of the Gentile Mission (10,1 – 15,35). Sets the stage for Paul's mission by showing that the Gentile mission began from Jerusalem itself.
1. Conversion of Cornelius (10,1 – 11,26)
2. Paul's first missionary journey (11,27 – 14,28)
3. Gentile mission confirmed in Jerusalem (15,1–35)

B. Paul's Mission to the Ends of the Earth (15,36 – 28,31). Paul fulfills his mission by carrying the gospel from Jerusalem to Rome.
1. Second missionary journey (15,36 – 18,23)
2. Third missionary journey (18,24 – 21,14)
3. Paul's arrest and imprisonment at Jerusalem (21,15 – 26,32)
4. Paul's journey to Rome (27,1 – 28,31)

Now we will study each section of Acts in detail, looking for Luke's description of the growth of the early church. Though sometimes stumbling in the dark, the disciples never stop following the Spirit; though confronted with opposition and even deaths, they never cease sharing the good news of Jesus.

The Preparation for the Christian Mission (1,1 – 2,13)

WAITING IN JERUSALEM (1,1-14)

The risen Jesus makes a number of appearances to the disciples. Luke says the appearances lasted over a period of forty days, and he attests that the risen Jesus who appears is the same person who had died on the cross (1,3a). Jesus tells the disciples to wait in Jerusalem for the coming of the Holy Spirit, who will empower them as it had empowered Jesus at the start of his ministry (see Lk 3,22). The disciples betray their lack of insight by asking if Jesus will restore the Kingdom of Israel. Jesus tells them that salvation history will not follow the course of reestablishing Israel. Instead, they will be sent as his witnesses to announce the good news to *all* peoples, even to the ends of the earth.

The first community consists of Jesus' apostles and other followers including Jesus' mother, Mary, and some other women. Prayer and the celebration of the meal together are a

Biblical Numbers In the Bible certain numbers take on special significance. Seven, for example, is the number of perfection, while six represents imperfection – hence one must forgive seven times seven, while the Beast of Revelation is symbolized by "666." Twelve is an important number because it signifies the twelve tribes of Israel. The number forty has many associations that give it significance: Israel's wanderings in the desert lasted forty years. Various Old Testament figures spent periods of forty days or years in preparation for their missions (Moses was in exile from Egypt forty years before returning to confront Pharaoh). Because he viewed the time that the risen Jesus spent with the disciples as especially significant, Luke identifies it with the sacred number forty.

primary source of sustenance for the church. And their charity to one another is the mark by which they are known.

REPLACING JUDAS (1,15-26)

To preserve the sacred number of twelve, someone must be chosen to replace Judas among the apostles. These twelve represent the tribes of Israel and through them God will create a new Israel, the church (see text note to 1,26). An Old Testament method for discerning God's will, casting lots, is used to choose the replacement. Because the apostles are those who can "witness" to the validity of the gospel, the one chosen must be someone who followed Jesus from the start to the end of his ministry. The death of Judas is mentioned, though the details differ from Matthew 27,5, which says Judas hanged himself. Judas had died to the community and no longer shared its life or values. Despite his treachery, Judas has not derailed God's plan. It moves forward though he is left behind, justly punished for his blasphemy.

> **Casting Lots** This is the last time casting of lots is mentioned in the Bible. From Pentecost on, the disciples seek the guidance of the Holy Spirit for important decisions.

PENTECOST, THE COMING OF THE SPIRIT (2,1-13)

Strong winds and fire are often biblical signs for the presence of God. Isaiah 66,15.18 says of God's coming: "Lo, the LORD shall come in fire . . . to gather nations of every language." The day of Pentecost presents a powerful image of God doing just that—gathering all nations into one church. The Holy Spirit's presence is so powerful that not only are the humble apostles emboldened to speak with eloquent power, but the visitors from many nations are enabled to understand all they say. Pentecost undoes Babel (Gn 11,1–9) and anticipates the success of the church's missionary efforts.

The Mission in Jerusalem (2,14—8,3)

TWO SERMONS BY PETER (2,14—3,26)

Peter's first sermon is his most famous (2,14–36). Preaching on the day of Pentecost, Peter informs his listeners that the expectations of the prophets were fulfilled by the pouring out of the Spirit upon the disciples. He quotes the Old Testament to demonstrate that the crucified Jesus, now risen and reigning as Lord and Christ in heaven, is the Messiah God had promised.

Members of the crowd are "cut to the heart" (2,37) by his impassioned oratory and nearly three thousand of them accept baptism. These converts, coming as they do from the far corners of the earth, represent the universality of the gospel.

Luke presents an idealized picture of the early communities who live together in unity, drawn together by the teaching of the apostles, by fellowship, prayer, and the breaking of bread.

The healing of a man who was disabled (3,1–10) becomes the occasion for Peter to preach again (3,11–26). And again he reviews salvation history and points to Jesus as the fulfillment of the promises made to Abraham and the prophets.

PETER AND JOHN BEFORE THE SANHEDRIN (4,1–31)

A Pattern. This is the first of several "trial" scenes in Acts, all of which follow the same pattern:

1. A disciple performs a miracle that attracts attention.
2. The apostles use the opportunity to teach the people attracted by the miracle.
3. Jealous Jewish officials arrest the miracle-working missionary.
4. The missionary is put on trial.
5. The imprisoned missionary miraculously escapes.

At first the trials are orderly and peaceful. But opposition to the Christian missionary effort grows until it culminates in the murder of Stephen.

Only Jesus. The apostles never claim to have the power to work a miracle themselves, they perform miracles only in the name of Jesus and through his power (4,10). Each miracle is somehow related to the mandate of spreading the gospel. The urgency the apostles feel about preaching the gospel is explained by Peter to the Sanhedrin: "There is no salvation through anyone else, nor is there any other name . . . by which we are to be saved" (4,12).

God is in Charge. At all times, the apostles see God as very much in control. Imprisonment, and even the martyrs' deaths that will soon follow, are no more signs of defeat than was Jesus' crucifixion. God can use such events to further the plan of salvation. When the apostles are released from prison, the community responds with prayer. Suddenly, as if it were a second Pentecost, the Holy Spirit descends on all those gathered (4,23–31).

SHARING POSSESSIONS IN THE COMMUNITY (4,32–5,16)

Luke mentions again how the community members supported one another by selling their property or houses and giving the money to the apostles to use for the good of all. This way, no one was left wanting. Ananias and Sapphira, however, provide a counter-example. There was no rule that required selling goods in order to belong to the community. But this couple wants to appear as generous as the most heroic of the community, though, secretly, they withhold some of their wealth. For this they are struck dead. As with Judas, this could be Luke's way of saying that they no longer shared in the life of the community. The reason is not that they were not generous enough, but that they lied to the Holy Spirit and accepted honor they didn't deserve. Their behavior was blasphemous; they tried to "cheat" God. But God won't be cheated, or lied to.

TRIAL BEFORE THE SANHEDRIN (5,17–42)

More miracles lead to more jealousy and another imprisonment. An angel frees the disciples during the night and they return to the Temple to teach. When they are brought before the Sanhedrin, Gamaliel, a wise and respected member of the Council, argues for their release, pointing out that if they are frauds they will soon disappear; but if they are not, the Council does not want to find itself opposing God (5,39).

DEACONS FOR THE HELLENISTS (6,1–7)

Greek-speaking Jewish converts complain that their needs are not being attended to as well as those of the Jewish Christians. The apostles appoint seven deacons to take care of the daily distribution of food so that the apostles can be freed from that labor in order to pray and preach.

These seven deacons received their ministry through prayer and the laying on of hands (6,6). Although they were ordained to take care of the material needs of the poor, the two most famous of the seven deacons, Philip and Stephen, are characterized as preachers of the Word, just like the apostles they were supposed to free. This demonstrates that the church was eager to care for both the spiritual and the material needs of the community.

TRIAL AND DEATH OF STEPHEN (6,8 – 8,3)

This is the longest of the trial scenes. Luke uses it to explain, by a dramatic incident, some of the possible reasons for Christianity's movement away from its Jewish roots. Stephen's speech prepares for the future missionary work among the Gentiles. Luke ties Stephen in with the main actor in that missionary drama, Paul, by telling us Paul was present—as an approving witness—at Stephen's death (8,1). Luke also makes a connection between Stephen and Jesus: Both are falsely accused of attacking the Temple and the Law. The same charge will later be leveled at Paul. But Luke wants it known that neither Jesus, nor Stephen, nor Paul is guilty of attacking the Law or Temple. The Jerusalem community, he insists, regularly met in the Temple to pray!

Many scholars believe Luke is answering the suspicions of outsiders through these trial scenes. Christianity was a new religious movement and therefore automatically suspect. Luke is alerting his readers that whether they are Jews or pagans they have nothing to fear from Christianity because, as the rightful heir of the ancient Jewish tradition, it is both new and very old.

Stephen's speech (7,2–53) accuses Israel of failure to obey God's commands and of persecuting the prophets God sent (7,51–53). But this reminder of past infidelities causes the anger of the crowd to sweep over Stephen and the entire Christian community. Persecutions are started and Stephen is killed, the first Christian martyr. Just before his death, he has a vision of the risen Christ that recalls an image from Mark's Gospel where Jesus speaks of the "Son of Man seated at the right hand of the Power coming on the clouds of heaven" (Mk 14,62). The mob stops their ears to block his words, and falls upon him. But Stephen's vision is also a promise of vindication because it carries inherent overtones of divine judgment. Stephen dies as Jesus did, peacefully and speaking of forgiveness. But there is a difference. Whereas Jesus prayed to God, the Father, Stephen prays to Jesus, who stands at God's right hand.

Mission in Judea and Samaria (8,4 – 9,43)

PHILIP PREACHES OUTSIDE JERUSALEM (8,4–40)

A gradual shift is taking place. The gospel is beginning to spread to those who have contact with Judaism but are not, strictly speaking, Jews. The gospel is heard by the Samaritans, who had their own version of the Law of Moses, and an Ethiopian who was probably a "God-fearer," that is, one who worshiped the God of Israel but did not feel bound by Jewish law, like circumcision. Several themes surface in this section:

The missionary effort beyond Jerusalem is simply an extension of the outreach to Jews in Jerusalem. Baptism incorporates anyone into the community of believers. In Luke, baptism and the conferring of the Spirit are usually one and the same event. Here we find an exception. The Samaritans are baptized, but the Spirit is not imparted until Peter and John come from Jerusalem and lay on hands. Luke is using this episode where water baptism and receiving the Spirit are separated to indicate that the new missionary effort to non-Jews is happening with the approval and cooperation of the Jerusalem elders.

Christianity is superior to all forms of pagan superstition and religion. In the ancient world magicians could perform wonders that looked like miracles. A genuine miracle might easily be considered the work of magic. Luke is asserting two truths here: (1) The apostles work such miracles that even magicians want to tap their power to be able to do what they do, and they are willing to pay for it; and (2) the miracles of the apostles are not for sale. Simon is condemned for even suggesting it. Christians are not motivated by a desire for wealth. They give it away.

Jesus is the fulfillment of what is written in the prophets. The Ethiopian is impressed by what he hears about Jesus fulfilling the words of Isaiah. Unlike the Jews, he does not stop up his ears; instead he asks for baptism on the spot. In Luke prominent people like the Ethiopian tend to be supportive of the gospel: They listen willingly to Christian preaching; sometimes they accept baptism, other times they provide assistance to the missionaries. The gospel is attractive to rich and poor alike.

THE CONVERSION OF PAUL (9,1–30)

If Saul can be converted then surely God can use anything to advance the divine plan. Paul, formerly named Saul, had been so diligent and unrelenting in his attack on Jesus' followers that his transformation from being an enemy and persecutor of the gospel to being one of its most successful advocates is truly remarkable. Acts presents three renditions of the conversion story (9,1–30; 22,3–21; 26,9–23). In Galatians 1,11–24, Paul gives his own version. Each time the stories serve to demonstrate Paul's legitimate role as teacher of the gospel. They teach that he in fact has the authority to endorse such things as preaching to the Gentiles and excusing non-Jewish Christians from observance of the Jewish Law.

While there are a few differences in Luke's three accounts of the conversion, they have much more in common: in all three Paul is on his way to Damascus carrying letters from the high priest authorizing him to arrest Christians. He sees a bright light, falls to the ground, and hears a voice asking, "Saul, Saul, why are you persecuting me?" Paul asks who is speaking and is told it is "Jesus whom you are persecuting."

In the first two versions, when Paul rises he is blind. His temporary blindness symbolizes the spiritual blindness that temporarily had afflicted him. Paul's commission to preach to the Gentiles comes from the Lord (9,16). It is not Paul's idea to send the gospel to the far reaches of the empire. The risen Christ himself commissions him to do it. And that missionary work is the subject of the next section of the book.

THE CHURCH CONTINUES TO GROW (9,31–43)

Before Paul takes center stage, Peter has a few more scenes to play. Here he heals a man and raises a dead girl to life. Having endured the persecution that followed Stephen's martyrdom, the Christian community is at peace.

Inauguration of the Gentile Mission (10,1 – 15,35)

CONVERSION OF CORNELIUS (10,1 – 11,26)

Paul cannot become the apostle to the Gentiles until the leaders in Jerusalem officially accept Gentiles into the Christian fellowship. The eucharistic meal was the chief sign of unity among the Christian believers. Yet Paul claims that some Jewish Christians would not eat with Gentile

Christians from Antioch, probably because to do so would have violated the kosher eating laws that set Jews apart from other peoples. Peter had no such reservations, that is until stricter Jewish Christians arrived and persuaded him he should not eat with Gentiles (see Gal 2,11–14). As leader of the church, Peter may have been playing the peacemaker by avoiding offending Jewish Christians who could not begin to consider changing the kosher habits of a lifetime. Peter will need a direct vision to shake him out of his way of seeing and thinking on this subject of clean and unclean food.

After his vision Peter answers the summons to go to Cornelius' house and takes others with him to witness what has happened. It is almost as if his eyes are opening wider even as he speaks, and he is seeing more and more clearly that God is truly impartial, offering salvation through Jesus to anyone who acts justly and honors God (10,35). When Cornelius' entire household receives the Holy Spirit even before being baptized, Peter knows there can be no doubt that God has opened the door to salvation to Gentiles, too (11,18).

Christians The followers of Jesus were not always known as Christians. The name originated in Antioch (Acts 11,26) where Jews and Gentiles worshiped together in a single Christian fellowship for the first time. Before that believers were known variously as "the Way" (9,2); "the sect of the Nazoreans" (24,5) and other improvised names. The name "Christians" was probably given by outsiders and may have carried a derogatory connotation (see 26,28).

PAUL'S FIRST MISSIONARY JOURNEY (11,27 – 14,28)

Jewish Rejection. Imbedded in the story of Paul and Barnabas' missionary efforts is a principle that runs throughout Luke: Jewish rejection of the gospel opens the door for Gentiles to receive God's word with joy.

Persecution. Renewed persecution in Jerusalem brings about the death of James, the son of Zebedee, and the imprisonment of Peter—who also would have been killed if God's angel had not rescued him (12,1–19).

Death of Herod. Herod Agrippa, the Jewish king who ordered James's death and Peter's imprisonment, allows himself to be treated like a god and dies an agonizing death as punishment for his evil life and blasphemy. The Jewish historian Josephus corroborates most of Luke's details regarding Herod's death.

Preaching Pattern. Paul follows a pattern during his first missionary journey of preaching first in the Jewish synagogues and then to the Gentiles. In Pisidian Antioch, he actually states this policy (13,44–47).

Superiority of Christian Faith. Luke consistently tries to show that Christianity is superior to pagan superstition and that prominent people are drawn to the faith. He makes both points in the episode where Paul confronts a Jewish magician who had impressed the Roman proconsul on Cyprus (13,4–12). The magician is temporarily blinded (as Paul himself had been) when Paul rebukes him. The proconsul, impressed with Paul's authority, accepts the faith. At Lystra the crowd is so impressed with Paul and Barnabas that they try to worship them as gods (14,8–18). Repeatedly during the journey, the apostles are rejected and threatened by the Jews but accepted with warmth and joy by the Gentiles.

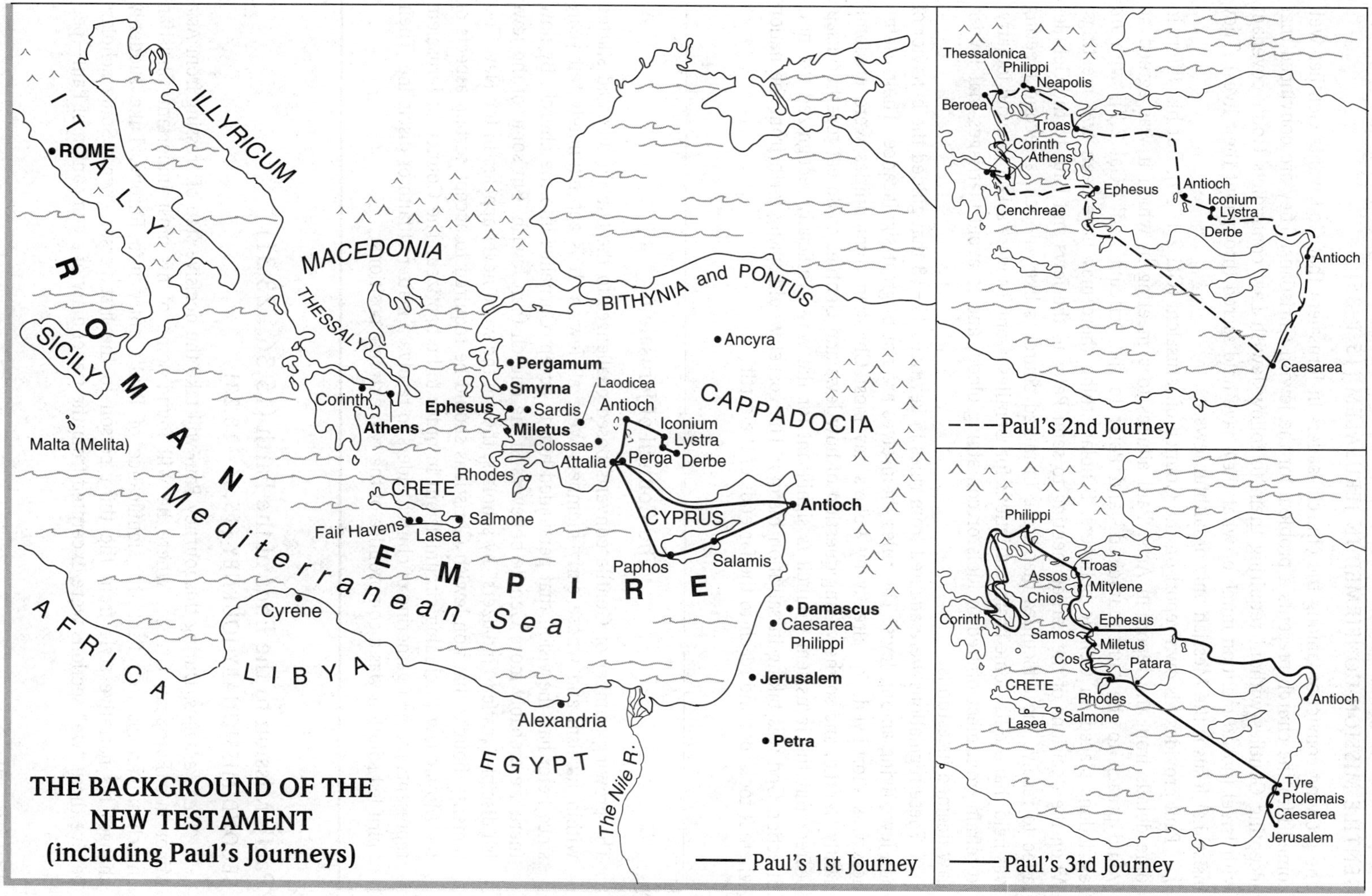

THE BACKGROUND OF THE NEW TESTAMENT (including Paul's Journeys)

GENTILE MISSION CONFIRMED IN JERUSALEM (15,1–35)

The growing conviction among the church leaders in Jerusalem that God wants Gentiles welcomed into the church presents a problem for the Jewish Christians. They are convinced that accepting Gentiles without requiring them to follow Jewish Law contradicts God's covenant with Israel (not to mention much of what they have held sacred throughout their lives). They insist that Jesus is the Messiah only of faithful Jews.

Paul provides his own report on the Council of Jerusalem (Gal 2,1–10). But his differs in some details from the report in Acts. Paul alludes to a meeting in which it was agreed he would preach to the "uncircumcised" and Peter to the "circumcised" (Gal 2,7), with *no* restrictions placed on Gentile believers. Scholars think there may have been two meetings. When the decisions of the earlier meeting to send Peter to the Jews and Paul to the Gentiles failed to resolve the difficulties that arose in mixed churches like Antioch, a second meeting was held that *did* list some basic restrictions for Gentiles. Gentiles were asked to avoid idolatry, to refrain from meat offered to idols or containing blood, and to avoid marriages that Jewish Law deemed incestuous.

These regulations were adapted from rules in Leviticus 17–18 that guided the behavior of non-Jews living among Jews. The rules themselves are not of great significance. Their usefulness was short-lived, for already by Luke's day most Christian communities were predominantly Gentile, and so the vexing question of how Jews and Gentiles could eat together disappeared. But the Jerusalem Council *is* significant for the way it officially recognized the new direction God was taking in salvation history: The gospel would spring forth from the nation where it took root and reach to the far ends of the earth.

The Council of Jerusalem

The growing number of Gentile converts posed challenges to the church that had started within Judaism and whose early members were all Jewish. It is approximately ten years since Peter had the vision that persuaded him to accept Cornelius into the church. By now there are probably more Gentile believers in the church than Jewish. But some of the Jewish disciples (called "Judaizers" by scholars, though the word never appears in the New Testament) thought that non-Jewish Christians should be required to accept certain aspects of the Mosaic law (including circumcision) in order to be baptized. The Council of Jerusalem represents the first gathering of church elders to resolve a matter of faith or discipline. Their Spirit-led solution was a compromise of the two extreme positions.

Paul's Mission to the Ends of the Earth (15,36–28,31)

SECOND MISSIONARY JOURNEY (15,36–18,23)

"We" Passages. During this journey Paul will take the decisive step of crossing from Asia Minor into European Greece, where he will found some of his most important Christian churches. Perhaps to reflect the significance of Paul's entry into Europe, Luke suddenly changes his narrative style from the third person to the first person "we." Some scholars believe these "we" sections were excerpted from the travel diary of a companion of Paul—per-

haps Luke himself. But others think that the use of "we" is a literary device meant to include the reader and draw him or her into the action, rather than a clue that suggests that the narrator traveled with Paul.

Philippi. It was not Paul's own wisdom that drew him to Europe. It was the Holy Spirit working through a dream vision (16,6–16). The ancient world often considered visions sources of divine guidance. Paul begins at Philippi, an important Roman colony. As his own letter to the Philippians reveals, Paul developed a close relationship with the believers at Philippi. The Philippians provided Paul with financial assistance for his work, and they sent dedicated men and women to participate in the missionary work of the gospel.

Familiar Themes. In Philippi (16,16–40), and later in Thessalonica (17,1–9) and Berea (17,10–15), familiar themes surface: (a) Christian belief is well received by wealthy, respectable citizens (e.g., Lydia, the cloth merchant, 16,12–15); (b) but jealousy and the loss of profits motivate some of the locals to falsely accuse the apostles of disturbing the peace and inciting rebellion. By now, Luke's readers know that the apostles are innocent of such charges and that no amount of hostility will keep them from spreading the gospel.

Athens. Paul's speech in Athens cites three areas of common ground Christianity shares with pagan philosophy:

1. God the creator of the universe has no need for an earthly temple or any form of human service (17,24f).
2. God, the creator and sustainer of all things, has granted certain areas of the earth for the nations and peoples. Humans should show gratitude for God's generosity.
3. True worship of God leaves no room for superstition or the worship of idols made with human hands.

Paul then stops listing areas of agreement and appeals for the conversion of his listeners (17,30f). God will overlook past times of ignorance, Paul says, but now God demands repentance and conversion to Jesus, whose resurrection proves that God has set him up as judge over all (17,31). But Paul is met with derision or, at best, a vague willingness to hear more later. The lack of faith does not permit a church to be founded here.

Tentmaker. In the description of Paul's stay in Corinth we not only learn that he worked to support himself while preaching there, as he did in all his churches, but also that the work he did was that of a "tentmaker" (18,3). Aquila and Priscilla, a local couple who had emigrated from Rome, befriend Paul and become his close associates. In Corinth, as elsewhere, prominent people are the first to accept the gospel, but this initial success arouses hostility from the Jews that eventually forces the apostles to turn their efforts toward the Gentiles.

Ideal Behavior. Paul is brought before the proconsul, Gallio, who refuses to meddle in what he believes are internal Jewish religious affairs. Luke considers this the ideal response from civil authorities. He knows Roman officials are not always so indifferent; after all, Aquila and Priscilla were exiled from Rome because of their religion. But Gallio does remain aloof, even to the point of allowing the ruler of the synagogue to be beaten right in front of him.

THIRD MISSIONARY JOURNEY (18,24–21,14)

Ephesus. The fourth largest city of the empire and the home of the governor of the province, Ephesus is also the location of a magnificent temple to the goddess Artemis whose devotees riot against Paul and his teaching. Here Paul meets Apollos, the silver-tongued orator who, though he had received only the baptism of John, has already become a successful missionary. There is no report of his being rebaptized, but Priscilla and Aquila help to correct his understanding of Christian faith.

Never Heard of the Holy Spirit. Paul encounters a group of disciples in Ephesus. When he asks if they have received the Holy Spirit, they say they never knew that there was a Holy Spirit. Paul lays hands on them and the Spirit comes upon them. This episode serves two functions for Luke: (a) It demonstrates that Paul is able to win converts to Christianity, and (b) it shows that, like the Samaritans in 8,15–16, these believers receive the Spirit only after they come in contact with someone who is an extension of the Jerusalem community. Both points are important for validating Paul's expanding missionary effort. He not only can win converts, but he is a legitimate representative of the leadership in Jerusalem through whom the gift of the Spirit is imparted to the church.

Near Riot. Paul's mission is very successful. His preaching and miracles attract much attention. Those who had been mired in superstition and magical practices abandon them in favor of the gospel (19,8–20). But Paul is too successful for his own good. The silversmiths whose livelihood depend on pagan worship of Artemis, fearing economic loss because so many have listened to Paul and renounced the worship of idols, rise up against the Christian missionaries. Only the intervention of the city clerk saves them.

Paul Leaves Ephesus. Paul visits several other cities and performs many miracles. He leaves Ephesus and avoids returning there to save time so that he can reach Jerusalem by Pentecost (20,16). Some scholars, however, find evidence both here and in Paul's letters (1 Cor 15,32a) to suggest Paul may have been forced out of Ephesus. Given in Miletus, Paul's farewell follows the pattern of the farewell speech genre common in Hellenistic Jewish writing. Such addresses contain standard elements: exhortation to follow the law; warnings about future disobedience (in most cases); presentation of one's own life as an example. Luke incorporates these elements into this speech. Paul is aware that he faces imprisonment in Jerusalem. He presents his life as a model of devotion to the gospel even under the worst of circumstances. He never sought to make money from his work. In fact, he always worked at a trade, and they should do the same because working wards off suspicion of greed and makes money available for helping the needy (20,33–35).

More Blessed to Give . . .

The famous saying of Jesus, "It is more blessed to give than to receive," quoted everywhere from greeting cards to Hollywood movies, is never mentioned in any of the four Gospels. Only Paul quotes it (Acts 20,35) to encourage hard work for the sake of the weak and needy.

Be Vigilant. Paul is aware that he will never again see these believers to whom he preached the gospel. He speaks with the love and concern of a dying patriarch who worries about the future struggles his children will face. So he warns them of the dangers of the future: "Savage wolves" (20,29) will fall upon them, coming even from among their own ranks to pervert the truth of the gospel. Luke's story has made us aware that the age of apostles is coming to a close. Now local leaders, called "elders" or "overseers" (20,28) will guide the community. They are not substitute apostles, of course. But they are persons who, through the imposition of hands, have been appointed *successors* to the apostles. In all circumstances, they must continue to rely on the guidance of the Spirit who directed the church through the apostolic era.

No Turning Back. Disciples in Tyre warn Paul that danger awaits him in Jerusalem. Even the Christian prophet Agabus (21,10) prophesies the specific troubles he will face. But Paul does not heed their warnings to stay away from Jerusalem. His dedication is total. He will proceed.

PAUL'S ARREST AND IMPRISONMENT AT JERUSALEM (21,15–26,32)

Throughout this section, the innocence of Paul becomes apparent to all the authorities who question him. Only his Jewish opponents persist in calling for (and secretly plotting) his death.

In Jerusalem. Paul's arrival immediately stirs controversy. James informs Paul that sincere Jewish Christians believe he has been encouraging Jewish converts to Christianity to abandon the Law of Moses. He encourages Paul to demonstrate his respect for the law by undergoing a week of ritual purification in the Temple and by paying the expenses of four men who must fulfill the requirements of a Nazirite vow they had taken. Ironically, it is this very act of piety that draws attention to Paul and gets him arrested. His arrest and imprisonment provide opportunities for Paul to make several speeches in his own defense. The first is to the Jerusalem crowd (22,1–21). He recalls his strict upbringing and his fierce devotion to the law. He admits having persecuted Christians. His new direction, he suggests, could only have resulted from God's direct intervention.

James

The James often referred to in the Book of Acts is not James, the brother of John, the son of Zebedee. He is, instead, James, "the brother of the Lord" (Mt 13,55; Mk 6,3; Acts 12,17), that is, one of four half-brothers or cousins of Jesus mentioned in the Gospels. James became the first leader or bishop of the Jerusalem community. He was killed at the instigation of the high priest and the Sanhedrin soon after the death of the Roman procurator, Festus.

Imprisonment. The Roman cohort commander orders Paul to be interrogated under torture. But Paul reveals he is a Roman citizen and therefore cannot be subjected to such treatment. The commander releases him to the Sanhedrin for trial. Paul manages to entangle the Sadducees and Pharisees in a resurrection dispute that surges to such intensity that the Roman commander must intervene to rescue Paul. Sent for safe keeping and under heavy guard to Caesarea (23,12), Paul receives a hearing from Felix, the Roman governor. Though he finds no fault in Paul, he is himself convicted by Paul's preaching about "righteousness and self-restraint" (24,25), for he is living in an adulterous marriage with Drusilla. Paul remains imprisoned for two years, but when a change in Roman administration prompts the Jews to renew their efforts to try Paul in Jerusalem, Paul plays his final card. He appeals to Caesar; i.e, he demands to be tried in an imperial court in Rome.

Divine Commission. The visit of the Jewish king, Agrippa, provides the opportunity for Paul to review his career once more. This rendition of Paul's conversion stresses the commission he received directly from Jesus to be a missionary to the Gentiles (26,16–18). Another irony surfaces. Festus and Agrippa are so convinced of Paul's innocence that they would gladly free him, but he has appealed to Caesar, and so he must go to Rome. The very tactic that was meant to save him draws Paul nearer to his death.

PAUL'S JOURNEY TO ROME (27,1 – 28,31)

These final episodes of Acts contain some of Luke's most exciting and suspenseful scenes. Besides all the other things it offers, there is no question that Acts is also interesting to read. Luke cares passionately about his subject and so, throughout the book, he uses his storytelling gifts to create suspense, fear, joy, and even tears.

Shipwreck. This is a tale of high drama. Despite a pounding storm, Paul is a calming force for his superstitious fellow travelers. His assurance comes from his trust in God and from prophetic knowledge that they will be saved. He not only reassures the crew, he even influences decisions that save the lives of everyone on board. At one point he blesses bread, breaks it, and begins to eat: Luke's words are clearly an allusion to the Eucharist (27,35). When they are shipwrecked, but safe, on the island of Malta, more wonders occur. Paul is unaffected by the bite of a poisonous snake, so the native peoples think he must be a god (28,3–6). Then Paul heals some of the local inhabitants, who respond by providing Paul and the crew with provisions for the rest of their journey (28,7–10). That Paul survives shipwreck and snakebite is just further evidence that God will provide whatever the apostle needs to fulfill his mission. Paul trusts fully in the Lord, and God never abandons him. Acts ends with Paul in Rome, meeting with inquirers and believers and explaining and teaching the faith freely (28,16–31).

WHAT WE HAVE LEARNED FROM ACTS

Luke has taught us much about the unfolding of God's plan of salvation during the apostolic age.

CHRISTIANITY'S ROOTS ARE IN JUDAISM

God led the Christian movement that began within Judaism to turn toward the Gentiles. But God's plan of salvation will forever remain rooted in the experience of Israel. Though keeping all of the Mosaic Law is no longer necessary for salvation, this Jewish ancestry and heritage are not forgotten. This shows us the importance of our history and traditions.

GOD WANTS ALL PEOPLE TO BE SAVED

The apostles overcame great difficulty to bring the good news of Jesus to cultures that were not their own. All of them accepted as God's will this movement toward becoming a truly universal church. The job is not finished. There are still many lands and cultures who await the fulfillment of the mission Jesus entrusted to the church: to bear witness to the gospel until the end of time and to the ends of the earth.

THE CHURCH IS A SPIRIT-GUIDED INSTITUTION

Popular notions sometimes suggest that the Holy Spirit works only through charismatic individuals who are often counter-cultural and antiestablishment. But the Book of Acts shows that the Spirit also works through the official leaders and structures of the community. The difficult challenge of incorporating Gentiles into the church provides an example of how the Spirit can use the leaders of the community to discern and express the will of God. Paul makes sure that he leaves behind no leadership vacuum. He establishes "elders" and "overseers" in his churches. The Book of Acts says that such institutionalization is not an impediment to the working of the Spirit.

CHRISTIANS MUST BE WILLING TO SUFFER FOR THE GOSPEL

The resistance the apostles encounter is relentless and fierce. Neither suffering nor the threat of death deters the apostles from the mission entrusted to them. It is important for Christians to observe that there is no situation in which preaching the gospel does not arouse some form of resistance.

THE CHRISTIAN COMMUNITY WILL BE KNOWN BY ITS ACTIONS

Luke's portrait of the early church provides an understanding of what features should characterize the church of any generation: gathering for prayer, the preaching of the apostles, community meals, and genuine concern for the weak and needy.

THE CHURCH CALLS PEOPLE TO RELIGIOUS CONVERSION

Just as Jesus did, and the apostles after him, the church calls people to conversion, that is, to radically change their lives. Like Jesus and the apostles, the church will come into conflict with pseudoreligion and superstition. But Christians must be careful not to be taken in by magical practices or cults or those who use religion for their own profit or aggrandizement. Religion and the church are to serve the gospel. When they do not, they are working against it. Christian life should be characterized by the sense of joy and trust in God that characterized the lives of the apostles.

Questions for Discussion or Reflection

1. Do you agree that there is no instance in which the preaching of the gospel does not awaken some form of resistance? If you agree, why is it true?
2. Were you surprised to learn there were struggles and disagreements even in the very early church? What insights can you draw from knowledge of that experience?
3. Why was the incorporation of Gentiles into the Christian community such a controversial issue? What problems did it cause? What issues did it raise for Jewish believers? What do you think of the solution that was offered by the Jerusalem leadership?
4. Often Christians will pine for the "good old days" of the early church. They point to the ideal life the community enjoyed, the simplicity and lack of institutional structure. Do you think life was really that ideal and that simple? In what way might longing for the simplicity of the "good old days" represent a negation of the work of the Spirit in the evolution of the institutional church?

Paul and His Writings

Paul was born in Tarsus, a city on the eastern end of the Mediterranean Sea, in what is now Turkey, around A.D. 10. He was a Roman citizen from birth, a status which carried certain privileges. He was, as is evident from his writings, well educated in the Greek language. He also had a good education as a Pharisee, that is, a Jew of strict observance. Luke has him say that he studied with Gamaliel, a renowned rabbi (Acts 22,3), but none of Paul's letters make this claim. Nevertheless, Paul was so zealous for the Jewish Law before his conversion that he persecuted those who, he believed, had strayed from the Law by believing that Jesus was the Christ.

After experiencing a revelation from God, however, Paul (then named Saul) himself became a Christian in about A.D. 34. To mark what he considered his totally new understanding, he changed his name to Paul. He firmly believed that his conversion included a call to preach the Christian message of salvation to all people, including the Gentiles. Paul spent the rest of his life, about thirty years, in pursuit of this mission. After spending some time in retreat and study, he undertook three missionary journeys (see RG 389). During the last of these journeys, he met with increasing opposition from some Jewish leaders and the Roman government, and was arrested and brought to Rome around A.D. 60. Between A.D. 48 and his death around A.D. 62, Paul wrote letters to communities with which he had worked, answering their questions and preaching the gospel.

There are thirteen letters or epistles ascribed to Paul. But most commentators recognize only seven of these as definitely written by the apostle; the others are attributed to disciples of Paul. The seven letters certainly written by Paul himself are Romans, First and Second Corinthians, Galatians, Philippians, First Thessalonians and Philemon. The remaining six letters (that is, Ephesians, Colossians, Second Thessalonians, First and Second Timothy, and Titus) are called "deutero-Pauline." For various reasons commentators believe that these six letters were not actually written by Paul but instead were written by later Christians familiar with his teachings. Disciples could have claimed to be writing in Paul's name in order to gain authority for their own adaptations of his teaching, an accepted practice among the ancients. In the New Testament, the Pauline writings are arranged in two groups: first, letters to communities; second, letters to individuals. Within each group they run roughly from the longest to the shortest. The letters are not arranged in the order in which they were written.

ROMANS READING GUIDE

At a Glance

Who is the main player?	Paul
What should I look for?	▪ Paul's reasoned and logical argumentation ▪ The contrast between spirit and law ▪ The inclusion of all people in God's saving action in Christ ▪ The hope for those who do not yet believe ▪ The duties of a follower of Christ

When did this take place?	Between 56–58 A.D.
Where did these events occur?	Written from Greece, most likely Corinth
Why was this letter written?	▪ To stress salvation and justification through faith in Christ ▪ To recount how God's hatred for sin is only matched by the abundant love he displayed in giving us Christ, who saves us from sin ▪ To show concern and hope for those who do not yet believe in Jesus, especially fellow Jews, and that one day all Israel will believe in Jesus as Lord and Savior ▪ To explain how belief in Jesus as the Christ demands corresponding action in every aspect of one's life
What's the story?	Paul was about to leave Greece for Jerusalem with the collection of money contributed by the Gentiles for the suffering church of Jerusalem. After that he hopes to visit Rome and personally greet the Romans. In the meantime, he is writing this letter to tell them of the good news of Jesus Christ and how all are justified through faith in Jesus as Savior and Lord.

Romans is placed at the beginning of Paul's letters. Not only is it the longest of Paul's letters, but it is one of Paul's most important works. Paul's focus in Romans is on the doctrine of "justification by faith." The meaning and understanding of this doctrine is of crucial importance to Catholics and Protestants alike.

Paul and the Roman Christians

There are a number of characteristics unique to Romans that set it apart from Paul's other letters. In Romans, Paul addresses a church he has not founded. He writes the letter seeking the Romans' acceptance and help. But first, Paul needs to deliver the collection of money from the Gentile churches to "the poor saints of Jerusalem" (15,26), who are in need. Then he will set his sights on Rome and even further west into Spain.

Paul's concerns in Romans center on the relationship among the Jewish and Gentile churches. What bonds these two groups together? How are they united despite their differences? Although Paul does not know the Roman church personally, he is bonded with them through the common faith they both share. Paul's concern in Romans for the unity in faith of all believers, and for reconciliation in the midst of differences, makes this letter significant for any age or culture.

Romans lacks the personal tone (excepting Chapter 16) that is very common to Paul's other letters. Romans comes close to being considered a circular letter, one meant to circulate to a number of readers, developing some of Paul's most basic theological ideas. In this letter, Paul develops his ideas on universal salvation, on justification by faith, and on the relationship between Israel and the church as transformed by Christ. These are some of Paul's recurring themes throughout his work, thus making the letter to the Romans a good introduction to the thought of Paul.

Romans as Diatribe

Romans serves as a summary of Paul's theology and preaching, enabling him to introduce himself to a community he does not know personally. In this manner, Romans can be considered a philosophical "diatribe." An element of the diatribe style of writing is the insertion of traces of dialogue in order to answer questions expected of the opponents. Paul will use this approach throughout Romans (3,1; 3,9; 4,1). While Paul's other letters reflect the give and take of actual dialogue, Romans is structured more along the lines of a philosophical treatise or diatribe.

> **Diatribe** A diatribe is a written exposé that tries to anticipate real or supposed objections or rebuttals. This style is very common in Paul's letter to the Romans.

READING THROUGH ROMANS

Outline of Romans

I. Address (1,1–15)

II. Body of the letter (1,16 – 15,13)
- A. Paul describes his view of the Christian life (1,16 – 11,36)
  1. Paul develops the teaching on justification by faith as already given in Christ (1,16 – 8,39)
     - a. Abraham, model of faith (4,1–25)
     - b. Effect of the two Adams (5,1 – 8,39)
  2. Paul struggles with the issue of Israel's disbelief (9,1 – 11,36)
- B. Paul arrives at some moral implications from his teachings (12,1 – 15,13)
  1. Consideration of the church and world (12,1 – 13,14)
  2. Call for reconciliation and unity (14,1 – 15,13)

III. Conclusion (15,14 – 16,27)

THE ADDRESS (1,1-15)

Paul uses the standard form of address, identifying himself and those to whom he is writing, offering both greetings and thanksgiving. Paul writes of his desire to be accepted by the Romans, especially in light of their common faith. The faith and teaching that the Romans have received and accepted from other Christian teachers is the very same faith and gospel that he, Paul, teaches. This is their bond and their source of strength and support of each other.

While Paul does not refer to the Roman community as "church", he does refer to their call to holiness. In doing this, Paul borrows terminology from the Hebrew Scriptures and traditions, that which he knew best. Thus, Paul, in attempting to create a Christian language for the Greco-Roman world, borrows many concepts and ideas from his Jewish traditions. Whenever we read Paul, we are reminded of our close relationship to our Jewish roots, and our indebtedness to Judaism in general. Like the Gentiles of Paul's day, Christians today owe a debt to Israel whose spiritual heritage we share (15,27).

Typical Structure of a Greco-Roman Letter

Structure	As It Applies to Romans	Chapters and Verses
Address	Contains the greeting and thanksgiving	1,1–15
Body	Contains the essential message	1,16 – 15,13
Conclusion	Contains Paul's journey plans, his personal greetings, and final blessing	15,14 – 16,27

BODY OF THE LETTER (1,16 – 15,13)

Paul's View of the Christian Life (1,16 – 11,36)

Paul's message in Romans is essentially a theological reflection on the meaning of "justification by faith" and the implication of this teaching for the daily life of the Christian community. The doctrine itself is developed in 1,18 – 8,39. Paul adds a separate consideration on how this doctrine affects Israel in Chapters 9–11. The ethical reflection on the effects of justification in the lives of Christians appears in 12,1 – 15,13.

Paul connects the justice of God with God's power and will to justify all people. In the Hebrew Scriptures, God's justice is revealed and cannot be completely attained through human effort or study. Yet, at the same time, Scripture continually challenges us to be just, in imitation of God who is entirely just. Thus justice is not completely foreign to us. In the Old Testament, pious persons acted in ways acceptable to God and in accord with God's covenant.

Paul's Fundamental Doctrine: Justification by Faith

Universal Sinfulness	Universal Salvation
Sinfulness of all is manifested in ▪ both Jews and Gentiles (1,18 – 3,31) ▪ Sin of all since sin of Adam (5,12–21) ▪ The human dilemma – knowing what is right (the Law) does not enable us to do what is right (7,13–25)	We are already justified by faith ▪ Exemplified by Abraham (4,1–25) ▪ Fulfilled in Christ (5,1–11; 6,1–23; 8,1–39)

In Romans, these two poles are in constant dynamic tension.

The Jewish Torah (Instruction or Law), revealed to Moses on Mt. Sinai and handed down throughout the history of the Jewish people, became the focus around which people acted justly. For the Jews, a Torah-guided individual was a "just" or "righteous" person, as Joseph is described in Matthew's infancy narrative (Mt 1,19). Thus, for the Old Testament, as for Paul, the related terms of "justice," "just," and "justified" all originate in God, who reveals how we are to act and judges us accordingly. By faithfully following the Law in all things, all people may learn the way of justice.

Paul's concerns about justification through the Law need to be explored to determine exactly what Paul understood by it. Galatians 3 also tackles this same issue. Romans deals with this matter, explaining Paul's position on it. Along with this issue, Romans deals with how the Gentiles, and all those who do not have the Law, are justified. For Paul, justification through the Law is a false hope. Paul's experience of the risen Christ, and his mission to preach justification to all, convinces Paul that justification is an act of God, given freely to all who believe. Justification based on the law can lead to blindness, ignorance, pride, and self-righteousness—blinding us to other ways in which the grace of God is operative in our midst.

Justification through the Law is insufficient for Paul because it excludes the Gentiles, who are in the same sinful predicament as the Jews (1,18—3,31). But Abraham and Christ show that all are now justified through faith. God's action in Jesus overturns the Law's verdict on Jesus' life, thus overcoming the Law by the death and resurrection of Jesus. Jesus is justified by God in contrast to the Law, with the consequence that, now, all people are potentially included among the justified, and not just those who have the Law. Thus, by accepting Jesus' gift of justification, and by living in accord with God's will, Jews and Gentiles both are saved. Following rules and regulations is not a requirement for being justified, but rather a result of already being justified. This is why Paul, after he develops his doctrine of justification, draws out the moral practical implications for everyday Christian living (12,1—15,3). The justification of all gained through the death and resurrection of Jesus has ripple effects on all humanity.

Paul's argument has very strong implications for our own day and time. If individuals think that they can be saved by obedience to the Law, then two possible attitudes or behaviors might develop. One is an attitude of pride, thinking that I can be saved by my own efforts, and don't really need or require God. The other attitude results in a state of constant and endless worry. Since I am ultimately and totally responsible for my salvation, I can never be sure that I have done all that I could in following the Law. Such constant worry can leave one close to paralysis. Paul overcomes both of these attitudes by proclaiming the new message of salvation. Salvation is accomplished not through obedience to the Law, but by means of the justifying power of the death and resurrection of Christ.

This new message of salvation, for Paul, is centered on God's justice being shared with human beings through God's action of justifying. The death of Jesus under the Law means that God went beyond the Law. Now justification is open to all who have faith that Jesus is the Messiah.

Paul is not merely replacing one human action—obedience to the Law—with another human action—faith in Jesus Christ. Rather, for Paul, faith is trust: the belief that it is God's power, not our own, and our reliance on God, not on our own abilities, that saves us. Faith is our acknowledgment that it is God's power that saves us, not our own efforts. Paul starts with the affirmation of faith in the God who justifies, most clearly seen in God's action through Jesus. The primary stress for Paul is on the goodness and power of God to save, and only then does Paul move on to show how we are all in need of such salvation. Unlike the divisions caused by the Law between Jews and Gentiles, faith in Jesus overcomes those divisions. As a result, all now have equal access to God's revelation of justice expressed in Christ. Through faith we are reconciled to God and to one another. We are redeemed by the blood of Christ, and our sins are forgiven.

JUSTIFICATION BY FAITH (1,18 – 8,39)

The focus of this entire section is the doctrine of justification by faith, as is outlined here.

Justification by Faith – The Focus of 1,18 – 8,39

Universal Sin 1,18 – 4,25)	Universal Faith (5,1 – 8,39)
Focus is on the theme of universal sin and access by all to faith and justification.	Focus is on justification through faith in Christ. Contrasts Adam and Christ; contrasts Law and faith, and contrasts what was "in the past" to "what is now."

In Chapters 1,8 – 3,31, Paul delineates how both Jews and Gentiles have sinned and continue to be slaves to sin. Chapter 1,18 – 31 lists the various sinfulness of the Gentiles, while Chapters 2,1 – 3,31 is a similar list for the Jews. Chapter 3,23 summarizes the fact that all have sinned and are deprived of the glory of God. For Paul, all of humanity has a universal need for salvation.

ABRAHAM, MODEL OF FAITH (4,1-25)

For Paul, Abraham follows the pattern of Christ, for Abraham was justified by God before any Law was given and before his own circumcision. Therefore Abraham is the ancestor of both Jews and Gentiles. Abraham's example of faith shows that all have access now to salvation through faith.

Circumcision Circumcision is the ritual removal of the foreskin of the penis of infant boys. This action continues to be symbolic of the individual's membership in the people of God. It also indicates the individual's acceptance of God's Law and teaching.

EFFECTS OF THE TWO ADAMS (5,1 – 8,39)

In Chapters 5–8, Paul contrasts Christ's saving action with the horrible consequences of the sin of the first Adam. If Adam's sin impacted all of humanity, how much more so did God's saving actions in Christ encompass all of humanity. The gospel becomes, for Paul, God's power to save all. Paul uses many words to describe this salvation: reconciliation, redemption, justification, sanctification. All these words are caught up in God's saving action through the death and resurrection of Jesus. All of Paul's thinking about Jesus is really focused on the doctrine of how Christ saves all.

JUSTIFICATION ALREADY GIVEN IN CHRIST (5,1-21)

Romans 5,1–11 serves as a transition passage between the developments of 1,18–4,25 and 5,12–8,39. In 5,1–11, Paul emphasizes the aspect of salvation that is already present in the justification and reconciliation achieved by Christ's death and resurrection. In 5,12-21, Paul adopts the image of Adam from Genesis. Adam represents all people under sin, with its curse of death. But Adam's predicament also draws God's promise of redemption. According to Genesis, there will always be a deadly struggle between evil and all humanity. Eventually, humanity will overcome evil, symbolized by the crushing of the serpent's head. Christians have always seen in this promise of ultimate victory a symbol for the work of Christ. Paul argues that if Adam's sin had such a widespread effect upon all humanity that we are still under its influence, how much more effective and powerful is the gift of salvation won through Jesus Christ. That gift is called grace, which brings eternal life (5,21).

Paul's "Justification by Faith" Argument in 5,1 – 8,39

5,1-21	Justification already given in Christ
6,1 – 7,25	Baptism has freed us from sin and the Law now plays a different role
8,1-39	The effects of the Spirit's work in us, giving us hope

FREEDOM FROM SIN AND THE ROLE OF THE LAW (6,1 – 7,25)

In this section, Paul describes what life is like when it is freed from slavery to sin. Paul's view of humankind is very evident in this section. Paul considers all people to be under some strong, controlling influence, living either for God under grace or living for sin. Living for God under grace brings with it life and freedom. Living for sin brings with it death and slavery. This new life of freedom has been won by Christ and is obtained by the believer through baptism. Through baptism, believers enter into a solidarity with Christ. Paul speaks of this solidarity with Christ using a number of images. Through baptism, we have died with Christ, and are buried with him; therefore we will be raised with him and now live with him. Entering into the death and resurrection of Christ through baptism has implications for how we should live our lives. Paul addresses these implications of our new life in Christ in Chapters 12–15. For most of Chapter 7, Paul spends time posing and answering supposed objections that he feels others may have concerning his views on the Law and its relationship to the freedom won by Christ.

THE GIFT OF THE SPIRIT (8,1–39)

Romans 8 celebrates the message of salvation. "There is no condemnation for those who are in Christ Jesus" (8,1). "Nothing can separate us from the love of God in Christ Jesus our Lord" (8,38f). Nowhere is Paul's understanding of the role of the Spirit more eloquently expressed than in Romans 8.

Paul begins Romans 8 with a consideration of the opposition between the flesh and the spirit. Adopting the Greek notion of flesh, Paul speaks of the "flesh" as the moral equivalent of "sin." In this view, flesh is mortal and must be controlled by the "spirit" (that is, the mind and will), which in Greek thought is immortal. Drawing on this same Greek tradition, Paul uses the term "spirit" to refer to the new life available to all through Christ. The Holy Spirit, Christ's very presence and life within us, is our helper and defender, coming to our aid and strengthening us. Through the Spirit, we are freed from slavery to sin and empowered to pray as children of God, saying "Abba" (8,15), "daddy." God is the loving father, helping us in our needs and continually loving us. At the end of Chapter 8, Paul exclaims that nothing can separate us from the love of God. This sets up his reflections in Chapters 9–11, in which he tackles the Jewish rejection of the Christian message, trying to make sense of what it all means.

ISRAEL AND THE JUSTICE OF GOD (9,1 – 11,36)

In this section, Paul senses the necessity of taking up the personally painful question concerning God's fidelity to the Jews. Israel's rejection of Christ was clearly a problem not only for Paul but for the early church.

Paul begins his argument by showing that the element of divine choice was operating throughout Jewish history, illustrating that God is free to show mercy as he wishes. Not all are children of Abraham simply because they descended from him. Paul cites a number of examples from the Old Testament to support God's freedom to choose as he wills. For Paul, God's mercy is God's justice. With this in mind, Paul carefully builds his arguments to show how God is now including the Gentiles among the new "Israel of God" (Gal 6,16).

Paul goes on to say that Christ, as "end of the Law" (Rom 10,4), brings justification for all who believe. Thus, the Law, which justified the Jew when contrasted to the Gentile, is rendered useless by Christ, thus eliminating the difference between Jew and Gentile. There is only one Lord who is over all and accessible to all who call upon him. That Lord is Christ.

But God has not abandoned his "disobedient" people. God's fidelity, proven in the past and present (Chapters 9 and 10) will ultimately be for the salvation of "all Israel" in the future (Chapter 11). Paul cautions all, especially the Gentiles, to remember that it is only by grace that we are saved.

Moral Implications of Paul's Teachings (12,1 – 15,13)

CONSIDERATION OF THE CHURCH AND WORLD (12,1 – 13,14)

Paul uses the image of the body to illustrate the interdependence that should exist among the members of the Christian community. Pope Pius XII used and developed further this image of the Christian community in the encyclical entitled "The Mystical Body" (*Mystici Corporis*). This papal letter stressed the various ways members of the Christian community, both now and in past ages, are related to one another. For Paul, Christians are to view themselves as one body, having many parts, each dependent on the other. Therefore, Christians "ought not to think of themselves more highly than others" (12,3).

Romans 13,1–7 takes up the question of the Christian community in relation to civil government. Paul is speaking to a community that was primarily a minority within an alien state. People of the Roman Empire were expected to practice the religion of the state. The Christian community had to live within this tension. Paul's advice to the community is to show good citizenship while not being conformed to this age or to the standards of the world around them.

Paul now speaks of the obligation believers owe to one another, asserting that love is the fulfillment of the Law. The commandments are there as a guide, and Paul lists them to remind the people of their importance. But Paul reiterates the fact that love is the ultimate fulfillment of the Law, a love modeled on Jesus.

CALL FOR RECONCILIATION AND UNITY (14,1 – 15,13)

It is evident from this section that the Christian community in Rome is experiencing division over various ethical issues such as dietary matters and the observance of certain feast days. Paul's emphasis throughout these divisions is focused on the "body" image of the community, stressing the common attitudes that are to be cultivated among the believers. He always calls them back to the faith of the community, and the responsibility they have to be united as one body. Paul continually exhorts the Christians to a fundamental harmony that is expressed in mutual respect and concern for one another. Hope, joy, and peace are linked to belief. While faith is a confession about the meaning of Jesus' death and resurrection, it is also, according to 15,7–13, acceptance of other members of the Christian community.

CONCLUSION (15,14 – 16,27)

Paul reminds the Romans about their common faith and his confidence in them. He is traveling to Jerusalem, bringing with him the money he has collected from the various churches for the needs of the Christians there. After this journey, he plans to travel to Spain, and on his way there he will stop at Rome. Paul asks for prayers for his journey and for hospitality when he visits Rome. He has spoken boldly in this letter simply because he is the Lord's minister and wishes to share that good news with them.

Paul sees the collection for Jerusalem as a symbol of the bond between Jews and Gentiles. Also important is the obligation of the wealthier members of the community to care for those less fortunate. This collection is seen by Paul as a "debt" that the Gentiles owe to the Jews, whose spiritual heritage is now shared by the Gentiles. Thus, the common faith that is shared by both Jews and Gentiles bonds them as family and links both in mutual responsibility.

It is possible that Chapter 16 was a later addition to the preceding fifteen chapters. This chapter seems almost like an afterthought. Paul commends Phoebe to the Romans, then greets numerous people as if he is well known to them, and as if he and the Romans have a number of mutual acquaintances. If Paul knows as many Romans as this chapter indicates, the uncharacteristically general and impersonal tone of Chapters 1–15 of the letter is strange.

The placement and originality of the final blessing is debated. But its appropriateness at the end of this letter is truly fitting. The blessing, or doxology, echoes several themes developed in the course of this epistle. Paul reflects the Jewish custom of celebrating the wonders of God in our midst with praise. This praise and blessing is most fitting in that God has acted on

ESSAY

Reading Only One Side of Correspondence

When reading the letters of the New Testament, it is important to remember that we are reading only one side of a two-way (at least) correspondence.

Imagine a situation like this. You go to visit your sister and she shows you a recent letter from her son who's away at college. Because you know your nephew, you understand most of the letter and can even "read between the lines." However, there's one line in the letter thanking the mother for sending "grandpa's tux" that you can't figure out. You ask and your sister explains something about a black and white sweater that had belonged to the boy's grandfather and that there had always been a joke between the two of them about it being the grandfather's tuxedo. He had written previously and asked that it be sent to him.

When we are close, geographically and in terms of time, it is easy to get an explanation of parts of letters that we don't understand because we only see one side of the correspondence. When we read ancient letters, like the letters of Paul, we always have to be aware of our disadvantage in reading only one side.

Sometimes it helps to ask ourselves some questions. For example, when we read something that sounds quite different from the surrounding material, we might wonder, "Could Paul be quoting something from the letter he received?" Or, we might say to ourselves, "Is it possible that this community was having a problem with something (e.g., people not doing their fair share of work)?" It also helps to keep in mind that Paul, and those who wrote in his name, knew the communities that he wrote to very well and therefore didn't have to include all the details that we might find helpful.

our behalf, making salvation universally available through the triumph of Jesus Christ over evil and sin.

CONCLUDING REMARKS

Throughout this introduction to Romans, a number of Paul's key themes and doctrines have been developed: justification by faith; the emphasis on the present reality of justification contrasted with the former life of sin; the inclusion of all, Jews and Gentiles, in a new Israel of God, the church. The ethical sections of Romans may be seen as a description of the church living in but not of the world. It would be hard to overestimate the influence of Romans in the development of Christian doctrine and morality throughout history. We can still benefit today from recalling the fundamentals of the Christian message put forth in Romans.

Questions for Discussion or Reflection

1. Paul's doctrine of "justification by faith" is central to his whole relationship to Jesus. What does "justification by faith" mean in your life? How does this help you to focus in on your relationship with Jesus, and with others? What role does concern and care for others play in relationship to the concept of "justification by faith"?

2. The bond and the corresponding responsibility established between Jews and Gentiles who believe in Jesus is very real and essential for Paul. How do you see your present relationship with Jews who do not regard Jesus as the Messiah? What does Paul mean when he says that Gentiles owe a debt to Jews because of the spiritual heritage that they now share? How is this fact still true today? What difference does it make in the way Christians relate and interact with Jews today?
3. Spend some time reading and reflecting on Romans 8. What does this chapter say to you about the role of the Spirit in the your life? In the life of the Christian community?
4. The power of the Spirit enables us to work toward unity and a loving relationship with one another in the person of Jesus, with God as loving father. How does this reality affect the way you relate to the Christian community? To people of other faiths, especially the Jews? To all the people of the world?

1 CORINTHIANS READING GUIDE

At a Glance

Who are the main players?	Paul, the Corinthians, Chloe, Apollos, Sosthenes
What should I look for?	▪ The mind and character of Paul ▪ Paul's understanding of community living ▪ Contrast between Christian freedom and love ▪ Paul's description of the Eucharist ▪ Paul's pastoral advice and counsel ▪ How belief in Jesus impacts everyday living
When did this take place?	Around 56 A.D.
Where did these events occur?	Written from Ephesus in Asia Minor
Why was this letter written?	▪ To answer practical questions posed to Paul by the Corinthians ▪ To address a church which struggled with living in the very midst of a pagan society ▪ To demonstrate that the model of Christ is totally adequate for addressing the concerns of community living ▪ To show the relationship between Christian freedom and Christian love ▪ To determine the place of spiritual gifts in the Christian life ▪ To specify what Christian community gatherings and rituals should look like
What's the story?	Paul is in Ephesus during his third missionary journey and he receives letters from Corinth concerning questions that the Christian community is struggling with. Paul pastorally and sensitively answers their concerns, while at the same time instructing them on how to make Jesus truly present in their midst. Love and concern for one another should be the marks of any Christian community modeling itself on Christ.

Paul wrote 1 Corinthians sometime around 56 A.D. in response to problems in the Christian community at Corinth. Paul had spent eighteen months living and working in Corinth, and he knew the community well. The problems Paul addresses are real and show the truly pastoral side of Paul. Paul's response to these problems is applicable to the present situations that the church faces.

1 Corinthians raises the issues of divisions and diversity in the church based on different ways of thinking and different worldviews. It also deals with the role of women in liturgical celebrations, along with the significance of the sacraments, especially baptism and Eucharist. Crucial to Paul's response is the meaning and importance of the resurrection. These issues are as relevant today as they were for Paul and the Corinthians. Along with the Corinthians, we need to recognize that how we act is a key indicator of what we believe. Paul's pastoral response to the Corinthians focuses on how to relate Christian faith to daily life. Today, this is still the main challenge of any Christian community.

The diversity and divisions among the Corinthians were a result of different communities of faith living side by side. They began to develop different approaches to worship and to living out their faith. Often, these approaches were at odds with one another, leading to competition among the communities as to which was the best. Paul's response to the Corinthians on the importance of unity, charity, and mutual respect based on a common faith provides us with a model for approaching our own problems. 1 Corinthians says a great deal about Paul, the pastoral leader, who encourages the Corinthians to imitate him as he imitates Christ (11,1).

READING THROUGH FIRST CORINTHIANS

1 Corinthians employs the usual letter format: an address in 1,1–9, the body of the letter in 1,10 – 15,58, and a conclusion in 16,1–24. This letter differs from the objective formal structure of the letter to the Romans. Yet a pattern is evident in this letter that may help in shedding some light on the emphasis and meaning of Paul's message. Paul's general approach to issues follows an A–B–A′ pattern. Paul introduces and begins to develop a topic (A), breaks his thought by bringing up a second issue (B), and then returns to the original topic (A′). Often, Paul uses this pattern to emphasize the middle or B statement. One example is Paul's discussion of abuses in the liturgical celebration of the Eucharist, as shown here.

11,17–22	(A)	Paul describes the abuses
11,23–25	(B)	Paul's account of Jesus' last supper
11,26–34	(A′)	Paul returns to a description of the abuses

By using this pattern, Paul tries to bring the abuses he describes into perspective. Paul reminds the Corinthians that when they gather for Eucharist, they are to act "in memory of" Jesus, recalling what he did for them, and for all Christians. There are other examples of this pattern throughout the letter. The key point to remember is that the pattern has the effect of emphasizing the middle or B section as the focus for correcting the situations described in A and A′.

Outline of 1 Corinthians

I. Address (1,1–9)
II. Body of the letter (1,10 – 15,58)
  A. Reported divisions and abuses (1,10 – 6,20)
    1. The factions (1,10 – 4,21)
    2. Moral disorders (5,1 – 6,20)
  B. Answers to the Corinthians' questions (7,1 – 11,1)
    1. Marriage and virginity (7,1–40)
    2. Offerings to idols (8,1 – 11,1)
      a. Knowledge versus charity (8,1–13; 10,1 – 11,1)
      b. The example of Paul (9,1–27)
  C. Problems in liturgical assemblies (11,2 – 14,40)
    1. Dress and appropriate actions at liturgies (11,2–16)
    2. Celebration of the Eucharist (11,17–34)
    3. The spiritual gifts (12,1 – 14,40)
  D. The resurrection (15,1–58)
III. Conclusion (16,1–24)

THE ADDRESS (1,1–9)

The address contains a greeting (1,1–3) and a thanksgiving (1,4–9). In the greeting, Paul refers to himself as an "apostle of Jesus Christ" and identifies a "brother," Sosthenes, as co-author of the letter. Paul addresses the community as a "church" which has been "sanctified in Jesus Christ" and "called to be holy." Paul thus reminds the Corinthians that, in Christ, they have a common vocation and a new identity that distinguishes them from the world around them.

Paul's thanksgiving focuses on the blessings received by the Corinthians. The thanksgiving also announces themes that Paul will develop in the letter. The Corinthians lack no spiritual gifts (1,7). Rather, the factions among them seem to stem from their envy of and competition for extraordinary gifts. Paul is concerned that these factions will destroy the unity and love they should have for one another as Christians, and he is writing to tell them about his concern.

THE BODY OF THE LETTER (1,10 – 15,58)

The whole of 1 Corinthians addresses specific issues that caused divisions and strained the very unity and life of the Corinthian community. Paul discusses the divisions he has heard about among the Corinthians in 1,10 – 6,20. He then turns to address matters that the Corinthians had themselves directed to him in 7,1 – 11,1. Finally, Paul discusses other issues that he feels are essential to the life of the community, appropriate ways of celebrating the liturgy (11,2 – 14,40), and the meaning of the resurrection (15,1–58).

Reported Factions and Abuses (1,10 – 6,20)

Reports from Corinth from Chloe (1,11) identified problems arising from two areas:

1. Competing allegiance to different leaders (1,10 – 4,21)
2. Moral disorders (5,1 – 6,20)

THE FACTIONS IN CORINTH (1,10 – 4,21)

Like many Christian groups even today, the Corinthians disagreed among themselves about which leaders were the most important and which group of Christians had more prestige and importance. Various members of the community turned to different leaders, and groups began to compete with one another for superiority and recognition. Rivalry existed even among the leaders themselves. Peter and James disagreed with Paul as to what was required of Gentile Christians with respect to the Jewish Law. Apollos was a better speaker than Paul, therefore his preaching seemed to carry more weight. These disagreements among the leaders caused many in the community to side with one leader against another.

Paul scolded the Corinthians for judging by human standards, not by God's as revealed in the cross of Jesus Christ. Paul reminded them that neither he nor Peter nor Apollos were crucified for them. The Corinthians were baptized in Christ's name and belonged to Christ. Therefore, competition within the Christian community is absurd. Only in the Lord can they boast that they are saved. Only in the riches and blessings granted by the Spirit of God can they glory.

Paul pointed out very clearly the gospel message that God's wisdom is greater than human wisdom, and that the power of the cross is greater than any human power. The Corinthians, while thinking themselves wise and sophisticated, are actually acting childish and immature. They judge by standards that are human and changing, not by standards that are divine and eternal. The riches and wisdom of God surpass all understanding and may be perceived only through wisdom that is revealed by the Spirit.

These words of Paul are words both of challenge and of encouragement for Christians today. Like the Corinthians, we too have been baptized. We celebrate the Eucharist and we strive for spiritual gifts. But our divisions and factions still tell us that we don't fully understand what it means to be the "Body of Christ." Like the Corinthians, we are challenged today to reflect on and apply the real meaning of the gospel message in our lives: not to rely on our own status and judgments but to rely on the status and insight given us by God in Christ.

MORAL DISORDERS (5,1 – 6,20)

In Chapters 5 and 6 Paul basically points to behavior that is inconsistent with belonging to the Christian community. Paul specifically mentions incest, bringing lawsuits against other members of the community, and sexual promiscuity as actions which of necessity demand the community's judgment and action.

The Corinthians had allowed a known sinner into their community without judging. Paul is concerned about this because of the impact of the sinner on the community along with the possible spreading of this sinful attitude throughout the rest of the community. Throughout this letter, Paul consistently emphasizes a key pillar of Christian living: As Christians we cannot act alone and think that it will not affect others in the community. Rather, our actions affect others, for good or evil.

Christian conversion is a turning of our minds and hearts towards God, as modeled by Jesus. For Paul, conversion requires the readiness to change not only our hearts but also our actions so that we may live in accordance with our baptism. The social dimensions of the gospel, especially when it flows from the liturgical life of the community, is at the heart of what it means to be Christian. Paul will delve further into this teaching in the next section of his letter.

Answers to the Corinthians' Questions (7,1 – 11,1)

The Corinthians themselves identified certain issues within their community that were disturbing their unity. These concerns fell into two categories:

1. Questions about marriage and virginity (7,1–40)
2. Questions about eating meat offered to idols and participation at pagan meals (8,1 – 11,1)

MARRIAGE AND VIRGINITY (7,1–40)

In Chapter 7 Paul discusses three life choices that many Christians believed were affected by baptism: marriage (7,1–15f), fidelity to Judaism signified by circumcision (7,18–20), and slavery (7,21–24). Some members of the community thought that, because of the near return of Jesus at the second coming, married people should give up the bonds and responsibilities of marriage in order to devote themselves to preparation for that coming. Paul's general advice is to "remain in the state in which you were called" (7,17. 20. 24). Why? For Paul, the particular status of the believers did not interfere with or lessen the effect of their new identity in Christ. Paul advocates no change in social status since it is unimportant in the Christian context.

Paul acknowledges his own preference for the single life, leaving one "free of anxieties" (7,32), but he does not impose this on others. Note that Paul's criticism of marriage is that it encourages our materialism, not that it encourages our sexuality. Ultimately, sexuality, circumcision, even slavery are of no significance in the new age that has dawned in Jesus. It is this very reason, the hope for a new society of equals, that made Christianity attractive to many oppressed and minority groups such as slaves, women, and people who had no status in society.

Throughout this section, and in the letter as a whole, Paul demonstrates a keen pastoral sense, allowing him to be sensitive to the needs of the Christian community in their particular context in Corinth. At the same time, Paul displays a loose interpretation and application of the tradition that he inherited from Jesus and the apostles. On various points such as mixed marriages between believers and unbelievers, on the support of the apostles by the community (9,12–27), even on central doctrines such as the Eucharist (11,23–25) and the resurrection (15,3–8), Paul demonstrates both creativity and flexibility. The Christian community today continues to use Paul's pastoral approach to guide and to respond to the needs of its members.

OFFERINGS TO IDOLS (8,1 – 11,1)

Paul responded in 8,1 – 11,1 to the Corinthians' questions about the eating of meats offered to idols and participation at public cultic meals. These issues are placed by Paul under the umbrella of love, and the demands that love for one another place on the entire community. Paul offers examples from Israel's history as well as from his own experience to demonstrate his point that love should be the guiding force in any doubtful situation.

The Corinthian community is a mix of primarily Gentile Christians, culturally Greek, with some Jewish converts. This mix is important in understanding the conflicts that arise in the community. Greek culture valued highly both intellectual and spiritual gifts, often at the expense of the human dignity of those who did not possess such gifts. Thus, such desired knowledge and gifts became a source of class distinction and pride, leading to a violation of love that every Christian community should cherish and practice.

In today's church the same central role of love should be the main drive in reconciling tensions and divisions that continue to arise. Paul indicates a direction for solving problems that continues to be appropriate for today's church. In commenting on 1 Corinthians 8,1–11,1, one is struck by the role the apostle's own life plays in presenting an example for believers to imitate. This is at the heart of Paul's message to the Corinthians.

KNOWLEDGE VERSUS CHARITY (8,1-7; 10,23–11,1)

The Corinthians apparently assumed that knowledge made some of them superior to others. Paul proposes charity as a remedy for the rivalry of the various kinds of "knowledge" that inflate the ego. This emphasis on knowledge encouraged an individualism that ran contrary to the needs of community living. Unlike knowledge, love unites, enabling the Corinthians' many gifts to supply various needs in the community. Love enables one to focus on using the gifts to build up the community, not to destroy or divide it.

In discussing the factions between the "weak and the strong," Paul speaks of "conscience." In 1 Corinthians 8 and 10, Paul gives a communal dimension to conscience and places it in a new Christian context. In this context, the individual conscience of both the "weak" and the "strong" are subordinate to the obligations of mutual charity. The weak must not judge the strong and the strong must not give a bad example to the weak. For Paul, conscience is subject to charity and concern for everyone "for whom Christ has died" (8,11).

In 10,23–11,1, Paul refers to the same principle when he responds to concerns regarding a Christian's participation in pagan meals and customs. While everything in this regard is lawful (10,23), Paul warns that everything may not be beneficial to the community, especially its weaker members. For Paul, the rightness of a decision depends upon its impact on the conscience of others in the community. Paul's focus is to win others over to Christ rather than to alienate them. In this, Paul asks the Corinthians to imitate him as he imitates Christ.

THE EXAMPLE OF PAUL (9,1-27)

This chapter represents B in the A-B-A′ of Chapters 8-10, a pattern discussed above. The B section usually creates the focus for the entire part of the letter under discussion. This is true for these particular chapters.

The Corinthians value freedom. But Paul insists that living within a community places limits on freedom. He then goes on to show that in his service of Christ and for the sake of those he ministered to, he freely gave up some privileges and freedoms so that no obstacles would be placed on his priority of preaching the gospel. Instead of demanding support from the community for his ministry, Paul freely chose to work at his own tentmaking trade to support himself so that he would not be a burden on the community. This forfeiting of privilege makes Paul more free to serve.

Paul also sees his manual support of himself as a form of discipline that keeps him focused on the essentials of his ministry: to serve and not be served, in imitation of Jesus. Discipline is essential in ministry if we are to serve others and not ourselves. Paul asks the Corinthians to imitate him in this, just as he is imitating Christ who "emptied himself and gave his life for all" (Phil 2,7).

Today, the same challenge exists for anyone involved in Christian community living. The community's actions on behalf of justice and love should be the focus of an individual's energies, while at the same time correctly forming the individual's conscience. This focus demands continual exercising of a discipline that places the needs of others on the same level as our own.

Problems in Liturgical Assemblies (11,2 – 14,40)

Paul now turns to a number of issues affecting the ways in which the Corinthians are worshipping together. These issues fall into three categories:

1. Dress and behavior at liturgies (11,2–16)
2. The celebration of the Lord's Supper (11,17–34)
3. The unity and variety of spiritual gifts (12,1–14,40)

DRESS AND BEHAVIOR AT LITURGIES (11,2–16)

The subordinate role of women in society, as well as their proper dress in the midst of public gatherings, seem to be the issues creating tensions in the Corinthian community. By their baptism, women were on equal footing with men. The freedoms allowed as a result of this equality were causing conflicts within the community. Paul addresses women's attire at liturgy simply because it is a cause of concern in the Corinthian community. Paul's response is consistent with the principles he has laid down above.

Even though they did not have to veil themselves at public gatherings as a result of their baptismal equality, Paul encourages women to do so for the sake of the community. Paul does not want their essential roles of prophecy and ministry to the community sidetracked for the superficial reason of dress. Thus, for the sake of the conscience of others, and their continual progress in Christian living, women should give up this particular freedom so that the greater community good can be served. For Paul, individual freedoms are subordinate to that fundamental, common goal of communal growth in love and peace.

THE CELEBRATION OF THE EUCHARIST (11,17–34)

There were divisions among the Corinthians on social and economic grounds. Wealthy Christians apparently hosted great meals at which the poor were either not welcomed or were treated badly. Some became drunk while others went away hungry (11,20–22.33f). Paul says that this is not the Lord's Supper and that the Corinthians are eating and drinking their own condemnation (11,27–29). Within the context of the discussion of abuses in the community's liturgical celebrations, Paul inserts his account of the institution of the Last Supper.

Paul's is the earliest written account of the institution of the Lord's Supper in the New Testament. By emphasizing that Jesus' body was given "for you," Paul reminds the Corinthians of Jesus' total gift of self in which they participate by receiving the bread and the cup. They are then warned that an "unworthy" reception would not bring salvation but rather condemnation. The command to "do this in memory" of Jesus challenges the community to be aware of what they are about when they gather, and to imitate Jesus in his care, concern, and giving of self completely for others. The insertion of "new" before "covenant" reminds the Corinthians that the Old Testament prophecy of a "new covenant" is fulfilled in Jesus (see Jer 31,31; 2 Cor 3,3.6). This is an inclusive covenant, one that is extended to all. This inclusive covenant provides the basis for a new society and a new relationship with God.

Paul's remarks about the Eucharist are as significant today as they were in the Corinthian community. The Eucharist is the greatest sacrament of unity, and it challenges us to be reconciled with all members of the whole church. We cannot celebrate the Eucharist worthily unless we are reconciled to one another (Mt 5,23–25). This is the intent of Paul's instructions to the Corinthian community. It is also the same intent that we should strive for in our community gatherings.

THE SPIRITUAL GIFTS (12,1 – 14,40)

The divisions among the Corinthians based on competition for the higher gifts continues to occupy Paul. Paul advises the Corinthians that in true conversion to Jesus Christ there is unity with others who also worship the same God. The hymn of love in 1 Corinthians 13, the B of the A–B–A′ pattern in Chapters 12–14, serves to illustrate the unity that should characterize the Corinthian community. Love is the highest spiritual gift, one which all believers must strive to acquire.

In today's church, love remains more important than all the other gifts, even more than faith and hope. This is not to minimize the importance of other gifts, but rather to set all the gifts in their proper perspective. This love is an expression of God's own love, enabling us to act mercifully and kindly toward one another. For love in action, at the service of others, is the essential message of the gospel. It is this message that Paul strove to communicate and put into action in his own life.

The Resurrection (15,1–58)

For Paul, the death, burial, and resurrection of Christ are fundamental to all Christian teaching and action. This doctrine was an integral part of the tradition that he passed on to the Corinthians. Paul implies that if the Corinthians really grasped and accepted the resurrection and its implications, many of the problems he has addressed in this letter would have been resolved.

In the first part of this chapter (15,1–11), Paul states the fundamental teaching on the resurrection. The second section (15,12–28) states emphatically that "if Christ is not risen, our faith is in vain." The resurrection forms the basis of faith and causes believers to reassess all of life and death. Christ is our hope, our assurance that we will experience the resurrection. Without the resurrection, perseverance in faith, including the sacrifices involved in suffering persecution, is pointless.

In a third section (15,29–34), Paul is trying to shame the Corinthians by showing them how absurd some of their Christian practices and beliefs are without faith in the resurrection. A fourth section (15,34–50) points to the foolishness of trying to explain what we will be like after the resurrection. Paul states that it will be totally different from what we can imagine or conceive. We will no longer be like Adam, but like Christ.

The last section (15,51–58) is a hymn celebrating God's victory, through Christ, over sin and death. Conquered by Christ, sin and death have lost their power. By the resurrection God has shown that sin and death are not the last word, but only lead to life. Therefore Paul sings God's praises for the hope the resurrection gives.

CONCLUSION (16,1–24)

Paul speaks of the collection and how it is to be taken to relieve the suffering of the saints (16,1–4). Paul then repeats his travel plans, sends greetings to his friends, and concludes with a blessing. These friends of Paul are an interesting mix of the Corinthian community, including men and women, rich and poor, powerful and ordinary people. Paul greets representatives of all categories, personally showing the acceptance and unity he has been preaching throughout the letter.

CONCLUDING REMARKS

The Corinthians were a church like ours, real people with real problems. They struggled for charity in the midst of disagreements, and for the respect of others. Paul continually stressed the role of ministers as servants of God and Jesus Christ. Paul tried to help remedy their problems by advising them to seek spiritual gifts, especially charity. Paul recognized roles for both women and men in the liturgy. He also gave many concrete examples of practical implications of living the gospel message as a community of equals. An implication that Paul continually stressed here and elsewhere was the Christian's necessity of aiding the less fortunate. The first epistle to the Corinthians is an interpretation of the gospel message that continues to challenge us with its many implications.

Questions for Discussion or Reflection

1. Paul stresses the need for the Christian community to be focused on Jesus as the ultimate model of how a Christian leader should lead. When you serve in some leadership capacity for your community, how conscious are you of modeling your leadership style on that of Jesus? When opposing points of view arise, how are they handled by those who have designated leadership positions in the community? What could show that a leader was consciously taking Jesus as a model when serving in any leadership position?
2. The individual actions of one member of the Christian community can be either helpful or hurtful to the unity and peace of the community. How does your community call others to accountability, either to praise their efforts or to censure their actions? Why is such a role essential to the on-going life and health of the community? What are the results when we do not hold each other accountable in the Christian community?
3. Liturgical gatherings and celebrations are the life blood of a Christian community. How do your celebrations and gatherings reflect the beliefs that you hold dear as a Christian community? What happens when community rituals become empty celebrations, lacking any real substance, and rarely calling us to deeper involvement with others in the world? What are some essential ingredients that make for meaningful, spirit-filled liturgical gatherings?
4. All gifts are given for the purpose of building up the body of Christ, which is the community gathered in his name. How do you use the many gifts you have been given to build up the community? How do you avoid making gifts your own personal possessions? What can we do to insure that our talents and gifts are placed at the service of others, not at our own service?

ESSAY

The Influence of Apocalyptic Thinking on Paul

Apocalyptic literature came out of hard times. It was intended to encourage the people to remain faithful during times of suffering, oppression, and disappointment. It tried to deal with the always upsetting situation of a world that was not as it should be and circumstances that were beyond individual control.

The list below shows some of the ways that apocalyptic thinking influenced Paul. It is based on four elements of Jewish apocalyptic thought that had significant impact on Paul and other New Testament writers. (For more about apocalyptic literature, see the Reading Guides to Daniel, page RG 271, and Revelation, page RG 491.)

Four Elements of Jewish Apocalyptic Thought Found in Paul

1. Salvation is for All (Universal). For the Jews all of history, good and bad, was tied to the divine plan for Israel's salvation. For Paul, this narrow view is no longer valid because with Christ, salvation is for all.
   - God shows no partiality (Rom 1,16; 3,22 and 29; 10,12; Eph 2,14)
   - "neither Jew nor Greek . . . all one in Christ" (Gal 3,28)
   - The new Israel of God is inclusive of the Gentiles (Rom 9,6; Gal 6,15)
   - Christ eliminated the barrier between Jew and Gentile, establishing peace (Col 1,20; Eph 2,15–16)
2. Salvation of the Faithful and Punishment of the Wicked. This pattern is typical of apocalyptic writers. The basis for the judgment for Paul is acceptance or rejection of the gospel.
   - The "saved" and the perishing (1 Cor 1,18; 2 Thes 2,10)
   - Judgment according to "good and evil" (2 Cor 5,10)
   - The faithful delivered from the wrath (1 Thes 1,10) but not the "enemies of the cross" (Phil 3,18; 1 Thes 2,16)
3. Dualism—Two Powers (conflict between good and evil). This is a way of explaining the tension and even hostility between how things are now and the time of fulfillment to come. In apocalyptic writings, good will eventually triumph.
   - Christ is in the process of returning all things to God (1 Cor 15,28)
   - Dangers threaten the Christian community: factions (1 Cor 1,10–25; Gal 5,13–15; Phil 2,1–4); idleness (1 Thes 4,11f; 5,14; 2 Thes 3,6–15); persecution from outside (Phil 1,28–30)
   - All creation is involved in the conflict (Rom 8,20–25; Phil 3,21)
4. The End Will Be Soon. Apocalyptic writers used this as a way of encouraging people to "hold on."
   - This influenced Paul's views on marital and social status (1 Cor 7); prayerful vigilance (1 Thes 5,1–11); enduring suffering or oppression while striving to build up the community (Phil 2,12–18)

Paul adapts these elements, avoiding the extremes of some apocalyptic thinkers. His adaptations are due to his experience as an apostle to the Gentiles and his conviction that the end-times have already begun in Christ.

2 CORINTHIANS READING GUIDE

At a Glance

Who are the main players?	Paul Titus Timothy
What should I look for?	▪ revelations into Paul's character ▪ Paul's honesty and openness ▪ most autobiographical of Paul's letters ▪ the highly emotional tone of the letter ▪ the disorganization of the letter itself ▪ the reality of the Cross in ministry ▪ Paul's defense of his ministry ▪ Paul's collection for the poor
When did this take place?	Around 57 A.D.
Where did these events occur?	Written from Macedonia during Paul's third missionary journey
Why was this letter written?	▪ To testify to Paul's authenticity as an apostle, as well as to defend his ministry ▪ To reaffirm Paul's love and concern for the Corinthians ▪ To emphasize the generosity of the Corinthians toward other Christian communities in need, especially the church in Jerusalem ▪ To boast of the suffering and cross that Paul has endured in fidelity to his ministry ▪ To acknowledge the fact that any minister will, at times, be misunderstood and badly treated, just like Christ
What's the story?	Paul, still on his third missionary journey, hears of dissensions and mistrust among the Christians at Corinth. Some are questioning his authenticity as an apostle. Paul is very offended by this charge and responds strongly and emotionally. Along the way he receives another letter from Corinth assuring him that all is well, and of their desire to see Paul once again. Paul is overjoyed at the news, and ends with praise and love of them, while, at the same time, reiterating the role of suffering involved in ministry.

Second Corinthians seems to lack an orderly sequence. Paul's tone is very emotional and rather defensive. The flow of his thought is choppy. There are indications that this "letter" is actually put together from several pieces of communication that Paul sent to the Corinthians. Of all the communities Paul deals with, his most difficult yet consistent relationship is with the Corinthians. 2 Corinthians reveals traces of an ongoing conversation between Paul and the Corinthians. Yet, all we have is this letter in its final form, so it is important to work through the letter in its final form, even though it is most likely a compilation of separate letters or letter fragments.

This letter was preserved by the early church and read at liturgical gatherings in spite of its criticisms of the Corinthians and the many challenges it raised for the community at

Corinth. The Corinthians respected Paul's authority, even though he criticized them severely. Despite these criticisms, they circulated, reflected on, and preserved his words. This is a good lesson for today's Christian community to learn. We are not the only community in history to experience mistrust between authority and ordinary people. The Corinthians experienced it long before us, and we can learn from their community.

READING THROUGH 2 CORINTHIANS

Some initial observations will help in better understanding Paul's second letter to the Corinthians. 2 Corinthians follows a rather disruptive and choppy sequence. For example, some fragments, e.g., 6,14–7,1, appear completely out of context. Also, Chapters 8 and 9 seem to have been originally two separate letters, each dealing with the collection for the poor in Jerusalem. Yet neither chapter seems to be aware of the other, and neither chapter has any relationship to the whole context of the letter in Chapters 1–7 and 10–13. Finally, Chapters 10–13 could stand alone as an explanation in defense of Paul's own spiritual experience, his vocation, and apostolic credentials.

Following the usual structure of letters at this period of time, 2 Corinthians has three main parts:

1. The address (1,1–11)
2. The body (1,12–13,10)
3. The conclusion (13,11–13)

Outline of 2 Corinthians

- I. Address (1,1–11)
- II. Body of the letter (1,12–13,10)
  - A. Crisis between Paul and the Corinthians (1,12–7,16)
    1. Past relationships (1,12–2,13)
    2. Paul's ministry (2,14–7,4)
    3. Resolution of the crisis (7,5–16)
  - B. The collection for Jerusalem (8,1–9,15)
  - C. Paul's defense of his ministry (10,1–13,10)
- III. Conclusion (13,11–13)

THE ADDRESS (1,1–11)

In the address of the letter Paul names Timothy as co-author. Timothy and Titus (2,13; 7,6; 8,16.23) were apparently more trusted by the Corinthians than Paul himself. The greeting includes a prayer glorifying and praising God whose "encouragement" is strength in affliction (1,3–4). The theme of this prayer gives us a hint as to the overall mood of this letter. Paul and the Corinthians experience much suffering, but also great consolation. The assurance of God's presence with them helps in overcoming the pain of their conflicts. Paul communicates to them his confidence that God is at work in their lives no matter what the pain or suffering.

THE BODY OF THE LETTER (1,12–13,10)

The message of 2 Corinthians is developed in three main parts:

1. In 1,12–7,16, Paul reviews his past relationship with the Corinthians.
2. In Chapters 7–8, Paul develops a theology of giving, speaking of the collection among the Gentiles. The generosity of the Corinthians in this collection is, for Paul, a sign of the readiness of the Gentiles in responding to others in and through their acceptance of Jesus. The acceptance of this help by the Jewish Christians is a sign also, for Paul, of the Jews' acceptance of the Gentiles as fellow believers in Jesus.
3. In 10,1–13,10, Paul returns to the theme of his credentials as an apostle, focusing on his own weakness and on God's call even in the midst of weakness. Paul develops a theology of suffering and uses his own experience of God's grace in his life to give concrete reality to his reflections on suffering. Many have taken great comfort in his experience of God as one who continually reassures us with the phrase: "My grace is sufficient for you, for power is made perfect in weakness" (12,9).

The Crisis between Paul and the Corinthians (1,12–7,16)

The whole relationship between Paul and the Corinthians seems to have been marked by crisis. This is clear from both letters to the Corinthians. In this section, Paul first reviews his past relationship with the Corinthians. He then moves on to talk of his particular ministry with them. In doing so, Paul mentions instances of mistrust and tension between himself and the Corinthians.

PAUL'S REVIEW OF HIS PAST RELATIONSHIP WITH THE CORINTHIANS (1,12–2,13)

In his review of his relationship with the Corinthians, Paul seems to be frustrated at their apparent lack of communication, sympathy, and confidence. Those in the community who do not like Paul interpret a change in Paul's promise to visit them as a sign that Paul is unreliable.

Paul's response to them is that his word is sincere and his care and concern is always for them. He changed his plans to visit them because of his need to write this letter to them expressing his disappointment with them (2,4). He delayed his visit to them in order to give each side time for healing (2,1–4). This delay would give the Corinthians the time to reflect on Paul's love for them and would give time for Paul to get over his disappointment in them.

In 2,5–11, there is the discussion of the community's forgiveness of someone who had offended Paul. Paul thought that decisions in these situations belonged to the community. The Corinthians did well in forgiving the person and reinstating the person into the community. Paul accepts their decision and praises them for their action of reconciliation. This is a good sign of their overcoming evil with good, as Jesus did, and of their rejection of the forces of evil in their midst. In 5,11–16, Paul speaks of the community as being entrusted with the "ministry of reconciliation." The forgiveness of one who has offended Paul is a specific example of that ministry in practice.

In 2,12–13, Paul expresses anxiety about not receiving any news from Titus concerning the Corinthians. This anxiety, Paul points out, is another sign of his love for them. It seems that this whole first section of the letter, 1,12–2,13, was written before Paul received the happy news from Titus described in 7,5–16.

PAUL'S MINISTRY (2,14–7,4)

In this section, Paul describes his own ministry and reflects on its meaning for him and for those with whom he has come into contact. The description of his ministry develops several important themes:

1. The old and the new covenant (3,1–18)
2. The paradox of the ministry (4,7–18)
3. The ministry of reconciliation (5,11–21)

Each of these themes will be discussed briefly.

THE OLD AND THE NEW COVENANT (3,1-18)

Paul reasons here from Old Testament passages, and from contrasts he makes between the spirit and the flesh. Jeremiah (31,31–34) promised the giving of a "new covenant." Ezekiel's prophesy is used to supplement this promise. Ezekiel expressed God's promise to replace human hearts of stone with hearts of flesh and to give a covenant in the Spirit (Ez 36,26–36). Exodus 34 described the relationship between God and Moses as so glorious that Moses had to come down from Mount Sinai with a veil covering his head lest the Israelites die at the sight of his glowing face.

These passages from the prophets and the Law provide the scriptural basis for Paul's description of his ministry as superior to Moses'. Paul argues that if Moses' covenant was so spectacular yet was still written on stone and in hearts of flesh, how much greater is Christ's covenant which is the fulfillment of the prophetic promise of the Spirit.

Paul contrasted the Mosaic covenant written "in ink" or "on stone" with the "new covenant" written by the "spirit" on "hearts of flesh." In this description, Paul used the phrase "old covenant" (2 Cor 3,14). This is the only time that this phrase is used in the New Testament. According to Paul, this "old" Mosaic covenant was not permanent. The "new covenant" in Christ, out of which Paul ministers, is the only one that lasts forever. Paul and the Corinthians are ministers of the new covenant, which brings life and the Spirit. Paul concludes that the covenant represented by Moses and symbolized by the flesh is inferior and did not lead to life.

This kind of logic, which is evident in other places in the New Testament, can lead to a superior, self-righteous position in relationship to the Jews and to all of the Old Testament. It has led many Christians to view the Old Testament as something that has no value. For them, the fullness of revelation is in the New Testament. Yet, many forget that Paul and even Jesus himself were Jews brought up on and trained in a relationship to God based on the Old Testament covenant and understanding of God.

Jewish and Gentile believers in Jesus as Messiah used and adapted the images and language of the Old Testament to fit their situation and needs. At times, this led to an apparent justification of one tradition at the expense of the other. Yet Christians share the same heritage and spiritual journey of the Jews. This heritage is to be continually cherished and mutually explored by Jews and Christians, so that understanding and respect for one another's traditions will emerge. The Old Testament continues to provide a rich tradition for mutual reflection and understanding among Christians and Jews.

THE PARADOX OF THE MINISTRY (4,7-18)

Paul continually marvels at God's mysterious ways in dealing with us. God has given us such great treasures in Christ and has granted us a privileged place in being able to minister to one another. Yet, what is more awesome for Paul is that "we hold this treasure in earthen vessels" (4,7). In other words, there are many forces, both spiritual (the evil powers) and political (the Romans), which could easily overwhelm us, and consistently try to do so. Yet, somehow we continue to live and minister to each other in Christ's name. For Paul, this is abundant reason for seeing God as the font and source of all our hope, confidence, and power. For hostile forces afflict only the "outer self" while the "inner self" grows strong. The apparent superiority of the powers opposing Christianity is only temporary. The unseen power of God operative among Christians lasts forever.

THE MINISTRY OF RECONCILIATION (5,11–21)

Throughout 2 Corinthians 2,14—7,4 Paul searches for meaning and value in the suffering that occurs for the sake of the Christian message. This is developed along several lines:

1. The negative is never overwhelming: There is always some experience of rescue or salvation.
2. The experience of suffering seems to be an occasion of growth and unity for the community.
3. Conversion and salvation demands a great deal of pain and change, yet they radically change believers from the old sinful reality to a whole new life and reality in Christ.
4. The challenge that all believers experience in making the reality of Christ present and active in a world that is not quite receptive to the message is a struggle for all believers: We are all called to be involved in the ministry of reconciliation of the whole world to God.

For Paul, Christ's work is not finished once and for all. Through Christ we have been given the work of reconciling the world to God (5,17–20). In order to accomplish this task, Paul sees the mission of every Christian as being involved in a spiritual battle against every "spirit" opposing God (10,3–6). In this struggle, believers are equipped by the Spirit of God with spiritual weapons that are far superior to any of the forces arrayed against them. In this context, even weakness and sin are reduced to insignificance and overcome by the power of God. This power is bestowed on all believers who together struggle to restore all things to God in Christ.

RESOLUTION OF THE CRISIS (7,5–16)

Paul returns to the concrete situation in Corinth. Titus has furnished good news about the Corinthians' warm reception of Paul's message. The conflict between Paul and the Corinthians has been resolved. Paul is happy and joyful, and there seems to be no more reason for concern about the Corinthians.

Throughout this first part of the letter Paul is concerned about the Corinthians, and they are concerned about him. Because of their unity in Christ, neither could be indifferent to or abandon the other. This realization can place all problems, misunderstandings, and worries into their proper perspective. In Christ, all can be reconciled and brought to a peaceful resolution. This is a powerful message that the Corinthians needed to hear from Paul, and a message that every Christian community needs to take to heart every time conflicts arise. This is especially true when the conflicts involve community members and their leaders. We have all been called to the ministry of reconciliation of one another, and the world, to God in Christ.

The Collection for Jerusalem (8,1 – 9,15)

Chapters 8 and 9 appear to have been two independent fragments on the importance and need of a generous and substantial offering to the church suffering a famine in Jerusalem. The importance of the collection according to Paul is that it represents the full participation of the Gentile Christians in the community of the new Israel, the church. Also, the Gentiles were "indebted" to the Jerusalem church and the other Jewish-Christian churches whose spiritual heritage they shared. Paul encourages the Corinthians to give generously as a "test of the genuineness of your love by your concern for others" (8,8). Paul also will see the acceptance of the Gentiles' offering as evidence of the Jewish-Christian's willingness to accept Gentile members. Mutual suspicion was a main cause of conflicts and problems in the early church (see Rom 15,22–33), and Paul was eager to overcome it.

Paul begins Chapter 9 as if he has not written Chapter 8. There are many ideas repeated in Chapter 9 that were raised in Chapter 8. This repetition and the apparent independence of these chapters not only from each other but from the context of the rest of the letter prompt many scholars to consider them as originally separate letters or letter fragments. Yet, they are still considered as an integral part of this letter and fit in well with Paul's message and role as apostle to the Corinthians.

Paul's Defense of his Ministry (10,1 – 13,10)

In this section Paul continues a defense of his ministry by tackling some of the concerns or charges that some members of the Corinthian community have expressed about him. They charged that he is weak (10,1–2); that he is not a good speaker (10,10); and that he is not supported by the community (11,7–10). Paul reminded the Corinthians at the beginning (10,2.11) and end (12,20 – 13,2.10) of this letter that he intended to visit them soon and deal with such issues directly in person. In the midst of his responses to charges, Paul developed a famous and memorable passage (11,1 – 12,18), his own lived theology of the cross.

PAUL'S RESPONSE TO CHARGES (10,1-18; 12,19 – 13,10)

Paul expresses an impatience in Chapters 10–13 over accusations by some of the Corinthians, charges that Paul feels should have been corrected a long time before this writing. However, Paul feels the need to address them again concerning these charges.

Some of the Corinthians appear to be snobbish and particular in how they understood themselves and in the kinds of people they would respond to or be attracted by. They considered themselves superior in knowledge and would be attracted to those who possessed similar superior knowledge and gifts. The charismatic leader or speaker with striking presence and gifted tongue was the person to whom they would truly pay attention. They were attracted to Apollos rather than Paul because of these very characteristics that they saw in Apollos and not in Paul.

The Corinthians also saw Paul's refusal to be supported by the community as a sign that Paul himself did not believe that he was on the same level as the other apostles, like Peter. Because he refused the community's support, the Corinthians believed Paul to be less of an apostle than Peter and the others, who did accept the support.

The complaint of the Corinthians was that Paul was weak. Paul hides behind the written word, and when he does show up in person, his presence is disappointing. They appear to have accused Paul of failing to visit them because his appearance was so unimpressive.

In response to all of this, Paul speaks of the gentleness and mercy of Christ (10,1–2), empowering Paul to act boldly. Paul's approach is to use everything at his disposal in order to make all things subject to Christ (10,2–6). Paul warns the Corinthians against false pride, conceits, and jealousies. He promises to visit them soon, and he will not be lenient with them if they are still caught up in these vices (13,1–10). The Corinthians should examine themselves to see if Christ is in them. For his part, Paul is confident that Christ is with him.

PAUL BOASTS OF HIS LABORS AND HIS WEAKNESS (11,1 – 12,18)

Since the Corinthians are attracted by knowledge, Paul proposes to speak of "foolishness," and asks their indulgence. In 1 Corinthians 1 – 3, Paul had described how God confuses and challenges the wise with the wisdom of the cross. In this section of 2 Corinthians, Paul talks about the role of the cross in his own life.

It seems that there are people whom Paul sarcastically calls the "superapostles" (11,5), who are leading the Corinthians astray. Paul fears that the Corinthians are like Eve (11,3), deceived by the lies of the serpent. This comparison would be insulting to the lofty Corinthians, a strategy Paul uses to bring them back to humility.

Paul continues by describing the wisdom he has learned through suffering. The experiences that the Corinthians look upon as signs of "failures" – beatings, humiliations, imprisonments, dangers – are viewed by Paul as his most important apostolic credentials. He has experienced visions, revelations, and ecstasies, which could easily have led to pride on his part. Paul suggests that the Corinthians would easily and certainly be tempted to pride by these experiences. But Paul also experienced a "thorn in the flesh . . . an angel of Satan, to beat me" (12,7). The wisdom that Paul learned from this suffering is that God's power is made perfect in weakness. In the end we can understand why Paul says, "I boast most gladly of my weaknesses, in order that the power of Christ may dwell with me" (12,9).

CONCLUDING REMARKS

Today, we are not quite sure what the particular problems were that Paul was trying to address in that Corinthian community long ago. What we do know is that Paul's correspondence with the Corinthians concerns all the suffering and anxiety it takes to create a Christian community among limited human beings. There are loud tones of frustration, pain, and suffering in Paul's words. Yet Paul does not wallow in these feelings. Paul knows that this endeavor to build community is not merely a human endeavor, but is directed and supported by the Spirit. Thus Paul's hope and confidence rest in our fidelity to that power at work among us. It is the power of the Spirit that will eventually bring fruit to all our labors, if we are only faithful and attentive to the path modeled for us by Christ. The path of the cross is the way God has chosen to bring new life out of pain, suffering, anxiety, and death. Thus, reading 2 Corinthians brings us to a whole new realization and appreciation of the role of the cross in our Christian growth in holiness, both for ourselves and for the communities with which we are involved.

Questions for Discussion or Reflection

1. Paul's second letter to the Corinthians is full of the pain, frustration, anxiety, and sorrow that is involved when limited human beings gather to create community. What has been your experience and involvement in community gathering and community building? What were the sources of hope and joy? What were the sources of pain, frustration, anxiety, and sorrow? How are all these feelings and reactions kept in balance? What role does the Spirit play in all this?
2. The ministry of reconciliation is a crucial component of Christian living. How do you put this ministry into practice? Within yourself? Within your family? Within your work place? Within your church community? Within your country?
3. Chapters 8 and 9 of 2 Corinthians emphasize the financial responsibility of a Christian community for another community that is suffering or in need. What is the basis for this responsibility of one community for another? What Gospel passages reinforce this responsibility? What are you doing to show your concern for others in need? What is your community doing? How broad or extensive is this Christian responsibility? What are the boundaries of such responsibility?
4. For Paul, to experience the cross of Christ is the true beginning of the wisdom necessary if effective ministry is to be carried out. Name times and situations when you have experienced the cross of Christ in your life. What wisdom have these experiences taught you? How has this wisdom been beneficial in your relating to and understanding the situation of others? What would you recommend to others who would wish to learn the wisdom that comes from the cross of Christ?

GALATIANS READING GUIDE

At a Glance

Who is the main player?	Paul
What should I look for?	▪ Justification by grace through faith alone ▪ Role and preaching of Judaizers ▪ Paul's conflict with Peter and James ▪ Paul's argument from Scripture ▪ Scriptures fulfilled in Christ ▪ Faith implications for Christian living
When did this take place?	Either 48–50 A.D. or 54–55 A.D.
Where did these events occur?	Uncertain but written either from Ephesus or Macedonia

Why was this letter written?	▪ to counteract false teachers ▪ to authenticate Paul's mission, teaching and ministry among the Galatians ▪ to defend his apostolic authority and his correct teaching of the gospel ▪ to manifest the total sufficiency of Christ as the only requirement for life ▪ to exhort the Galatians to put their faith into action in their everyday lives
What's the story?	Paul hears that his beloved Galatians are being misled by false teachers or Judaizers who insist that to be a follower of Christ one must first be subject to Jewish Law and practices. These teachers accuse Paul of dishonesty concerning the true requirements of faith in Christ. Paul defends his gospel and his ministry by contrasting himself with Peter and James. Arguing from Scripture, Paul demonstrates that faith and not the Law is the only requirement for salvation. In Christ we have been freed from the Law. Paul ends by exhorting the Galatians to continue to put their faith into practice by love and concern for one another.

Paul's tone in Galatians is defensive and emotional. Other Christian missionaries, referred to by Paul as Judaizers (Gal 2,14), were insisting that Gentiles must follow some aspects of the Mosaic Law, including circumcision, in order to be fully Christian. Paul saw these people as a real threat not only to his own reputation and mission, but to the gospel itself. By preaching such a message, the Judaizers were undermining Paul's authority. They were also undermining the heart of Paul's preaching, which insisted that faith in Christ was all that was required to be fully Christian.

Paul's letter to the Galatians addresses many issues that are still realities in any Christian community. Issues centering on freedom, divisions in the community even among leaders, the relationship of Christianity to Judaism, and the emphasis on faith as contrasted to good works, are as important today as they were in Paul's day. To understand these issues as addressed in Galatians, we need to understand the historical situation and context out of which Paul was writing.

Jews and Gentiles in the Pauline Churches

The focus of Galatians centers on the relationship between Judaism and the infant church that struggled to unite the non-Jews or Gentiles into the new "Israel of God" (Gal 6,16). The question of who shall belong and how is still relevant today, especially in our dialogue with other Christian churches. For Jews, membership involved circumcision and obedience to the Mosaic Law. Did these requirements for belonging also apply to Gentiles?

Since Jesus was a Jew, many of the early Christians saw the message of Jesus largely within the context of Judaism. Christianity might have remained a sect within Judaism had it revolved only around the belief that Jesus was the Messiah. Yet early Christianity was almost immediately open to the conversion of the Gentiles. Paul himself was a strict, observant Jew, who, after Jesus appeared to him and called Paul to follow him, abandoned his concern for the Law, and concentrated on the mission to the Gentiles.

In light of his God-given vocation to preach the message of Christ to non-Jews, Paul sees Christ as superior to the Law. The Law excluded Gentiles, while, in Christ, they are fully included. Thus, Paul identified himself as an apostle to the Gentiles, as committed to their conversion to Jesus as he had been committed to his observance of the Jewish Law.

Other people, such as Stephen and Peter, had preached to the Gentiles as well, and before Paul. But very few of them felt the same degree of freedom from the Jewish Law that Paul felt. A number of them insisted that some observance of the Jewish Law was necessary for full membership in Christ. This was true of Peter and James, both recognized leaders of the early church, Peter in Antioch and James in Jerusalem. Representatives of James, from the Jerusalem church, were preaching at least a minimal observance of Jewish Law, and they were gaining a significant following among the Gentile converts (see Acts 11,1–26; Gal 2,1–10).

All this was confusing for several reasons. Christianity was a child of Judaism, accepting fully its belief in one God and its high moral ideals and standards. Gentiles were pagans who did not live by such beliefs and standards. Thus, the Judaizers reasoned that the Gentiles should fulfill some basic requirement of the Jewish Law to show that they had actually converted from pagan ways.

But from the beginning of the Christian preaching, faith in Jesus, and especially the resurrection, had been the only requirement for baptism. Even Peter testified that the Gentiles, like the Jews, were saved through faith, and that "God shows no partiality" (Acts 15,9; Gal 2,6). Paul strongly opposed any additional requirement for the Gentiles. He believed that such a requirement actually went against the belief that salvation is the work of God accomplished through grace which becomes real when one expresses faith in Jesus as the Christ.

READING THROUGH GALATIANS

Galatians represents Paul's effort to correct some misrepresentations about the message he preaches. Galatians exhibits the three main parts of a letter:

1. The address (1,1–5)
2. The body (1,6 – 6,10), containing teaching (1,6 – 4,31) and applications to daily living (5,1 – 6,10)
3. The conclusion (6,11–18)

Outline of Galatians

I. Address (1,1–5)
II. Body of the letter (1,6 – 6,10)
  A. Paul's teaching (1,6 – 4,31)
    1. Defense of Paul's gospel and authority (1,6 – 2,21)
      a. Paul's vocation (1,6–24)
      b. Only one gospel (2,1–10)
      c. Paul's conflict with Peter and James (2,11–21)
    2. Faith, freedom, and the Scriptures (3,1 – 4,31)
      a. The experience of the Galatians (3,1–5; 4,1–20)
      b. The Scriptures are fulfilled in Christ (3,6–29; 4,21–31)
  B. Applications to Christian daily life (5,1 – 6,10)
III. Conclusion (6,11–18)

THE ADDRESS (1,1–5)

The address is cut short in that it does not contain the typical thanksgiving usual in this section. Galatians is the only Pauline letter without a thanksgiving. Paul seems eager to get at the issues right away. He expresses amazement that the Galatians have so quickly deserted the one who called them (1,6). Their abandonment of the gospel is the opposite of Paul's own fidelity to it (1,1). Paul insists that he himself stands faithfully rooted in Jesus Christ. Paul is an apostle not by the will of human beings, but because of a call from God.

THE BODY OF THE LETTER (1,6 – 6,10)

There are two major parts to the body of the letter: the first is focused on a summary of Paul's teaching (1,6—4,31); the second part contains applications of this teaching for the life of the community (5,1—6,10).

Paul's Teaching (1,6 – 4,31)

This section focuses on two important related themes: a defense of Paul's gospel and authority (1,6—2,21), and faith, freedom, and the Scriptures (3,1—4,31).

DEFENSE OF PAUL'S TEACHING AND AUTHORITY (1,6 – 2,21)

In Galatians we see Paul on the defensive, strongly insisting on his loyalty to the gospel. It seems that some were accusing him of shaping the gospel to please others and make himself popular. Paul insisted that his authority came from God, and he stressed several themes in his defense of the message he preached: his vocation, the oneness of the Christian message, and a review of his conflict with Peter and James.

PAUL'S VOCATION (1,6–24)

Paul speaks of his experience of turning to Christ not as a conversion but as a vocation. For Paul, this call involved a mission specifically to the Gentiles. This call came directly from God and no human beings played any role in it. Paul insists on this direct mission from God because he seems to differ from many others, including key church leaders, on the essentials of the Gentile mission. Paul received a revelation from God, and he did not consult any of the leaders of the Jerusalem church about it until three years after his call. Paul used language from the great prophets to describe his call, and he insists that he did not consult or compromise with "flesh and blood," i.e., any church leader, only with God.

THERE IS ONLY ONE GOSPEL (2,1–10)

Apparently there were those who accused Paul of lying, and of not fully explaining the gospel to his converts. They claimed that Paul neglected to inform the Gentiles that their baptism involved following certain parts of the Jewish Law. Paul claimed that it was his opponents, rather than he, who were distorting the gospel. There cannot be two versions of the same gospel message. Paul understood the challenge to his authority as also a threat to the message he preached. According to the authentic gospel preaching which Paul received directly from God, faith in Jesus as the Christ is sufficient for salvation, without any other obligations to the Jewish Law.

Paul's meeting with all the leaders of the church in Jerusalem around 50 A.D. confirmed the fact that there was only one single gospel message. The only condition that the leaders placed on Paul and the Gentiles was that they be mindful and supportive of the poor. Paul was eager to do this not because it was a Jewish Law, but because it was a concrete application of the gospel to everyday life. Paul insists that there was neither discussion nor agreement about the Gentiles following any aspect of the Jewish Law.

PAUL'S CONFLICT WITH PETER AND JAMES (2,11–21)

Paul asserts that only after the Jerusalem conference did "representatives from James" insist on some minimal observance by the Gentiles of the Jewish Law, including circumcision. Paul even confronted Peter in Antioch for caving in to the pressure of the "Judaizing" delegation from James in Jerusalem, calling Peter a coward and a liar. The picture Paul paints is of a change of mind on the part of James and Peter after the Jerusalem agreement, due to pressure from the Jerusalem church. This attitude undermined Paul's teaching and authority in Galatia and elsewhere. Paul's gospel message is that in Christ, we are all children of God, free from the Law, united as one in Christ.

This historical conflict provides the context for Paul's important concept of "justification by faith." Paul reminds Peter as a fellow Jew that "we who are Jews . . . know that a person is not justified by works of the law but through faith in Jesus Christ" (2,15f). It is Jesus rather than the Jewish Law that justifies all.

Once this historical context was forgotten by later generations of Christians, some mistakenly interpreted Paul's message as somehow considering faith as opposed to works. The reformers at the time of the Protestant Reformation were reacting to a distortion of Catholic teaching in its genuine form, which says that works are a *response* to faith, not a substitute for it. For their part, Catholics have sometimes exaggerated the role of good deeds, arguing as if they caused God's response of grace through some merit of their own. Both Protestants and Catholics have based their arguments in this debate on Paul, especially as he presents it in Galatians and Romans. As a result, some Christians read into Paul's message a split between faith and works that is not faithful to Paul's original meaning and intention.

Paul teaches that faith is expressed in living a good life. Good works are a response to faith. Paul's understanding of Christianity includes a highly developed Christian life style. Paul would see no opposition between faith and freedom on one side, and good works and obedience on the other. This is exactly what he develops in the following section of Galatians.

FAITH, FREEDOM, AND THE SCRIPTURES (3,1 – 4,31)

In this second section of Paul's teaching, he appeals to the experience of the Galatians and to the Scriptures to reinforce his teaching that faith in Christ is sufficient for the Christian.

THE EXPERIENCE OF THE GALATIANS (3,1–5; 4,1–20)

Paul insists that the Galatians have heard the true and complete gospel message from him, and that, as a result of their conversion to Christ, they have received the Spirit of God. Paul contrasts this new life in the Spirit to their old life in the flesh. Here, Paul is using the Greek understanding of flesh and spirit, which are not our current understanding of those terms. For the Greeks, there existed a tension between the flesh and the spirit, stressing the superiority of the spirit over the flesh. For them, spirit represented the immortal, life-giving aspect of human experience, whereas the body or flesh represented the weaker, sensual, mortal aspect that had to be subjugated to the spirit in order to find true happiness.

Paul asserts that the Spirit of God came upon the Galatians by faith, and not by "works of the flesh" such as circumcision. Thus faith transferred all the believers from the world of the flesh to that of the spirit. The Spirit of God empowers us to share fully in the inheritance of the promise made to Abraham and fulfilled now in Christ. Paul now takes an example from Scripture to make his point.

THE SCRIPTURES ARE FULFILLED IN CHRIST (3,6–29; 4,21–31)

Paul gives several examples from the Old Testament to show that faith in Christ is sufficient for salvation. The story of Abraham and his two sons by two different women is linked by Paul to the experience of the Galatians.

"Abraham 'believed God' and it was credited to him as righteousness" (3,6). God gave a promise to Abraham because of his faith. This promise included the "nations" or Gentiles who are blessed through Abraham. Now, Paul says the Gentiles have received the blessing of Abraham. The promise has been fulfilled in Christ.

Next Paul moves to the story of Abraham's two sons: Ishmael, born of the slave woman, Hagar; and Isaac, child of the promise and born of the freewoman, Sarah. Paul understands Ishmael and Hagar to represent slavery to the covenant on Mt. Sinai. Isaac and Sarah represent the promise fulfilled in freedom of faith without the restrictions of the Law. Paul says of the Galatians: "Now you, like Isaac, are children of the promise," that is, the promise of grace, and with it, freedom from the Law. Thus Paul's reading of the Scriptures reinforces his insistence that the Galatians are justified without the Law and freed from the Law. Therefore, to return to the Law's restrictions would be great foolishness (see 3,1).

Applications to Christian Daily Life (5,1 – 6,10)

In this section, Paul draws out the implications of his teaching for daily Christian living. Faith has consequences in the Christian's daily life. In Chapters 5 and 6 Paul calls believers to exercise their faith in their relationships with one another. A Christian's responsibility is to share in the building up of the community. Paul's emphasis is on social responsibility, something which the Catholic community has consistently emphasized. Paul specifies the relationships that should characterize the Christian community that is living the blessings of the Spirit of God (see 5,21–23).

The term *freedom* is mentioned again (5,1.13). For Paul freedom is not a license to do what you want; rather it is the choice to live freely for God (Rom 6,4) and to serve one another in love (Gal 5,13). The choice between slavery and freedom is the choice between the works of the Law and the works of the Spirit. For Paul, all humans are under some power—either of "sin" and the "flesh" or the Spirit of God and faith.

In 5,2–12, Paul refers to the specific problem of the Judaizers who are trying to convince the Galatians to be circumcised and follow some of the elements of the Jewish Law. Paul reminds the Galatians of a principle certainly upheld by Jews: Circumcision is a sign of commitment to follow the whole Law (5,3). Paul merely challenges the forcing of circumcision and Jewish Law on the Gentiles. Galatians 5,11 implies that Paul, even as a Christian, did "preach circumcision" for Jews. Paul does not argue against the role of the Law in Jewish life. Paul is innocent of the charge of undermining the Law for Jews (see Rom 9,1–5; 1 Cor 9,20; Acts 21,20–26).

In Galatians 6,1–10, Paul continues to reflect on community life, encouraging the virtues of charity, service, and humility. Christians are obliged to "bear one another's burdens." Although they are also called to "do good to all," even those outside the church, special priority is given to those in the family of faith (6,10).

CONCLUSION (6,11–18)

Paul adds a final note in his own handwriting for emphasis and concludes with a short prayer. The letter was probably dictated by Paul to a scribe. Paul again attacks the Judaizers for being insincere, since they themselves do not follow the Law. Paul speculates that they are merely trying to escape persecution from the Romans if they are caught and found to be Christian. Paul contrasts their cowardice and insincerity with his own boldness and consistency, referring to the "marks of Jesus" on his body. All that matters, Paul says, is that we are created anew in Christ (6,15). He concludes with a prayer for peace and mercy, calling down a blessing on his brothers and sisters in Christ.

CONCLUDING REMARKS

Paul's message in this letter is still very appropriate for today's Christian community, even though the historical context in which the letter was written may be different. Despite painful differences with other leaders, Paul focuses on a single gospel message communicated by all authentic Christian teachers. This message emphasizes the role of faith and the importance of community. Paul's use of Scripture illustrates that this is the same message that has been repeated and refined throughout the Old Testament. Faith is the expression of the bond between us and God, a bond lived out in relationship with others. Paul's message to Christians is to "be free" and therefore responsible for one another. There is no conflict between faith and good works, according to Paul. Faith is necessarily expressed in the everyday life of believers. Yet Paul stresses that works of faith are the result of the gift of the Spirit and a response to it. Good works are not, and never will be, a requirement for receiving the Spirit or for gaining salvation.

Questions for Discussion or Reflection

1. Freedom to do the will of God is crucial to Paul's understanding of what it means to be a follower of Christ. How free are you in the living out of your faith life? What restrictions are placed on you by others? What restrictions do you place on yourself? How valid are these restrictions? When are restrictions sources of slavery? When are restrictions sources of freedom?

2. For Paul, faith in Christ is all that is necessary for salvation. How do you react to this statement? How secure are you in placing your salvation solely on your faith stance? How does this faith stance relate to the good works that you do for others, both in private and in the community?

3. There is one authentic gospel message and all who preach are subject to proclaim that one reality. What is at the heart of your gospel message? How would you preach that message to your community? What criteria should others use to check whether your message is authentic?

4. The Judaizers were so attached to their approach and understanding of what was involved in being a follower of Christ that they lost sight of the authentic gospel message. How attached are you to your understanding of what it means to be a follower of Christ? How open are you to new ways of following Christ? What signs would you look for to check out if these new ways are truly authentic? Name the virtues and graces required if one is to be ever faithful to the gospel itself, and not just to one's own unique interpretation of the gospel.

EPHESIANS READING GUIDE

At a Glance

A "captivity" letter written from prison	As in Phil, Col, and Phlm, the author refers to his imprisonment.
Disputed authorship	Some of the language is the same as Paul's but the theology is more developed.
Time and place of writing uncertain	Probably written after Paul's death around 60 A.D. The reference to prison could be to connect it to Paul.
Major focus	▪ The mystery of the church: unity and world mission. ▪ The resolution of the tensions between Jews and Gentiles called for an adaptation of Paul's theology to new times and circumstances.

Ephesians is a letter written to a church suffering oppression from the outside and confusion and dissension from within. Some interpreters think that it was directed to a wider audience than just the community at Ephesus and was meant to be circulated to several communities.

There is a well-developed theology of Christ (*christology*) and of the church (*ecclesiology*) in both Ephesians and Colossians. This leads interpreters to suggest that both of these letters were written after Paul's death. The thinking in these areas seems to go beyond what would have been the concerns of the local churches in the very early years of Christianity, when Paul was writing and preaching. If that is the case, the disciple who wrote these letters was familiar with Paul's theology and style and adapted his message to new times and circumstances.

In the liturgy we introduce a passage from Ephesians or Colossians with the words, "A reading from the letter of Paul to the_______________." For similar reasons of convenience, we will call the author of these letters "Paul."

READING THROUGH EPHESIANS

Outline of Ephesians

Ephesians follows the pattern of a Pauline letter:

I. The Address (1,1–14)
II. The Body of the Letter (1,15–6,20)
    A. The Teaching on the Church (1,15–4,24)

1. Unity of the Church (1,15–2,22)
2. World Mission of the Church (3,1–4,24)

B. Ethical Applications (4,25–6,20)

III. Conclusion (6,21–24)

THE ADDRESS (1,1–14)

The address identifies the sender as "Paul, an apostle of Christ Jesus by the will of God," but there is nothing specific about the community at Ephesus. This would be unusual for Paul because he knew the community at Ephesus very well. It is noticing details like this that leads interpreters to their conclusions. In this case, such interpreters have concluded that Paul is not the author and that the letter was intended for a broader audience.

A blessing of God (1,3–6) replaces the personal thanksgiving usually found in Paul's letters. But, like the usual thanksgiving, it points to the major teaching section of the letter. The author proclaims the blessedness of God "who has blessed us in Christ" (1,3). The blessing is in Christ, in whom the divine plan for the salvation of all people will be achieved. It is in this context of blessing that the author will describe the mystery of the church.

THE BODY OF THE LETTER (1,15–6,20)

The Teaching on the Church (1,15–4,24)

UNITY OF THE CHURCH (1,15–2,22)

The view of the church in Ephesians is closely tied to Christ and Christ's saving work. The emphasis on the unity of the church has its roots in Paul's earlier teaching on the church as the Body of Christ, which expresses the unity of Christians and the saving work of Christ's death and resurrection.

Paul had urged the Christians in Corinth (1 Cor 12,12–27) and Rome (Rom 12,4–8) to express their unity in mutual love as members of the same body, Christ. The development of this image comes in Ephesians and Colossians when Christ is referred to as the "head of the body, the church" (Eph 1,22f; Col 1,18). Christ as head stresses his authority. Christ is portrayed as above every principality, authority, power and dominion (Eph 1,21f). These were probably the names of various classes of angels or heavenly beings (see Col 1,16 for a similar list: "thrones . . . dominions . . . principalities . . . powers"). Paul is concerned to combat the influence of angel-worshiping groups within the church.

This builds on what we find in Paul's earlier letters. He used one of the oldest christological expressions, "Jesus is Lord" (see Rom 10,9), to sum up the meaning of the early church's belief about Jesus. By his resurrection, Paul asserted, Jesus became "Lord" of all, Jews and Gentiles and every creature including angels, because in Christ's resurrection God conquered sin and death.

In this letter, images of the church as the body of Christ and Christ as head of the church illustrate the unity of the church made up of Jews and Gentiles, that is, of all people in Christ. In Ephesians, the Gentiles are described as those who were once "far off . . . strangers to the covenant of promise." Now they have "become near by the blood of Christ" (2,13). This is clearly an improvement over the situation described in Galatians and Romans in the early

50's A.D. One of the major problems facing the church at that time was the reconciliation of Jews and Gentiles under one God and one Lord. Paul himself had to struggle to resolve the tension between Israel and the Gentiles (see, for example, Rom 9–11). The teaching about the church in Ephesians reflects a resolution of these tensions.

WORLD MISSION OF THE CHURCH (3,1 – 4,24)

In Ephesians, the church, the body of Christ and the family of God, is entrusted with the work of salvation, which is to be filled "with all the fullness of God" (3,19). This means to complete the universal recognition of Jesus' lordship and bring all creation under God's reign.

Paul understands that his work is essential to God's plan. Yet, here he is in prison and that does not seem to disturb him, nor does the fact that many fail to accept the message of Christ. Salvation as well as creation is in God's hands, and God's plan is being fulfilled in mysterious ways.

The language of this letter is similar to that used by Paul in earlier letters. But the idea of the divine plan of salvation is more developed here. The church, moved by the Spirit, is bringing all to the "one God and Father of all, who is over all and through all and in all" (4,6). Notice how the writer stresses the universal or world mission by the repetition of the word "all."

Ethical Applications (4,25 – 6,20)

After describing the mystery of the church, the author goes on to instruct the Christians to express their common call to holiness and unity in their daily lives. Ephesians 5,1f says, "So be imitators of God, as beloved children, and live in love." He draws out some of the implications for living in love.

Paul acknowledges that there are already certain ways of relating to one another established by the Greco-Roman society in which the Christians live. He doesn't radically question that structure. Yet, for Paul, relationships among Christians must reflect a new perspective. Christians are motivated to a new way of thinking, determined by their common baptism. Christians share the conviction that all are in Christ and saved by Christ.

In ordinary Greco-Roman society the lines of authority and of subservience are clear. Husbands, parents, and masters all have great power over wives, children, and slaves. But the Ephesians are urged to "live in a manner worthy of the call you have received . . . bearing with one another through love" (4,1f). They are instructed to "be subordinate to one another" (5,21), to "nourish and cherish" one another, because they are members of one body (5,29f).

Paul finally urges the Ephesians to "pray at every opportunity in the Spirit" (6,18). He again asks for prayers for himself, that he may speak "the mystery of the gospel" with boldness and courage even though he is in chains (6,19f).

CONCLUSION (6,21-24)

This letter does not include the usual personal tone and greetings of Paul's authentic letters. In the conclusion, he indicates that he sends the letter with Tychicus (6,21), the name of the messenger of Colossians as well (Col 4,7). The final prayers are for peace, love, and grace.

Questions for Discussion or Reflection

The implications of being imitators of God and living in love are as much a challenge for us today as they were in the first century.

1. Who are the people, according to society's norms, that are supposed to be subservient to you (children, employees, students, people in service jobs, etc.)?
2. What are some ways in which you could relate to these people that would reflect the message of Ephesians:
   - "bear with one another in love"?
   - "be subordinate to one another"?
   - "nourish and cherish" one another?
   - "live in a manner worthy of your call"?

PHILIPPIANS READING GUIDE

At a Glance

A "captivity" letter written from prison	The author refers to his imprisonment (1,7.13.14.17), as he does in Eph, Col and Phlm.
Authentic authorship	No one denies that Paul wrote Philippians.
Time and place of writing	About 55 A.D., maybe from Ephesus. The frequent communications suggest a place closer than Rome. It appears that Paul was imprisoned in Ephesus about 55 A.D.
Major themes	▪ All themes are related to the mission of the community to proclaim the gospel. ▪ Partnership for the gospel ▪ Confident joy in spite of suffering ▪ Concern for external pressures (Judaizers) and internal divisions

READING THROUGH PHILIPPIANS

This is one of the most popular and beautiful of Paul's letters, due in part to the close relationship that Paul had with this community. The letter indicates rather free and frequent visits and letters between Paul and the Philippians through which they gave mutual encouragement to each other.

The choppy nature of this letter points to the possibility that Philippians was originally three letters combined and adapted by a later editor. According to this theory, there is a basic letter into which fragments of other letters are placed.

Outline of Philippians

The Basic Letter

I. Address (1,1–11)
II. Body of the Letter (1,12–2,18)
  A. Progress of the Gospel (1,12–26)
  B. Instructions for the Community (1,27–2,18)
III. Conclusion (2,19–3,1; 4,21–23)

Other Communications
Warnings and Instructions (3,2–21; 4,2–9)
A Thank-You Note (4,10–20)

THE ADDRESS (1,1–11)

This section, composed of the actual address, a thanksgiving, and a prayer, already hints at the special relationship Paul had with the Philippians. Notice that he does not have to defend his right to be called an apostle, as he does at the beginning of other letters. It is significant that Paul addresses the leaders of the community, specifically "bishops and deacons" ("overseers and ministers" in the *NAB* translation) at this early date, since these offices still exist today. However, the role of bishops and deacons in 58 A.D. was very loosely defined compared to today. The fact that Paul mentions them here shows the importance of leadership as well as its role in handing on the tradition he is teaching.

The thanksgiving (1,3–8) introduces the themes of confident joy and community that recur throughout the letter. These themes are even more striking when we consider the intense suffering of Paul and the Philippians expressed here. Although separated because of Paul's imprisonment, and threatened on all sides, Paul and the Philippians are "partners" in the spread of the gospel. He prays (1,9–11) that they will be strengthened and that even in hardship their love will grow.

THE BODY OF THE LETTER (1,12 – 2,18)

Progress of the Gospel (1,12–26)

Paul's main concern, his priority, is the spread of the gospel. He seems to see everything in that perspective. He refers to his own suffering and imprisonment in terms of their effects on this task. Even if some preach the gospel for the wrong reasons, it does not matter, as long as it is proclaimed.

Paul's joy, confidence, and hope, even under threat of death in prison, are amazing and understandable if two things are kept in mind. First, Paul was a committed and passionate apostle who apparently was able to pass on that enthusiasm to the Philippians, his "partners" in this mission. He draws strength from this community, knowing they will continue the preaching even if he dies in prison. Second, Paul's belief and teaching about the cross shapes how he lives. For him, the wisdom of the cross is a paradox: God's power is made perfect, finds its full expression, in weakness (1 Corinthians 1 and 2); that is why he considers death to be "gain" and knows that what he used to think of as gain is "rubbish" (3,7f).

Instructions for the Community (1,27 – 2,18)

Paul is concerned that the faith of the Philippians will be weakened both by opposition from the outside and by division from within the community. He appeals to them to "have a common mind and heart" and to be encouraged by his own suffering and the example of Christ.

Paul sums up this example of Christ, who "emptied himself," by quoting a hymn to Christ (2,6–11) that was already familiar to the Philippians. The hymn reminds them that Christ is their example of selfless, mutual service in the church. In Christ, who through his death became Lord, the Philippians recognize that they are brothers and sisters, members with one another of one believing community.

Following the hymn, Paul gives some specific instructions about how the community is to live out this example of Christ and once again returns to the theme of joy.

CONCLUSION (2,19 – 3,1)

Travel plans (2,19–30) are often part of the conclusion of Paul's letters. His news about Timothy and Epaphroditus serves the dual purpose of giving information and underlining his sense of being in partnership for the sake of the gospel, not only with Timothy but through Epaphroditus with the Philippians. The three also provide the community with an example of mutual trust and service.

Warnings and Instructions (3,2–21; 4,1–9)

There is an abrupt change of tone between verses one and two of Chapter 3; this is one of the signs that indicates that these were once separate letters. The problem Paul addresses here is with the Judaizers. These were a group made up of some of the Jewish-Christian missionaries who were undermining Paul's work with the Gentiles. The Judaizers believed that the only true Christians were those who observed the basics of the Jewish Law, including circumcision. (See the letter to the Galatians for Paul's most vehement arguments against this position.) In very strong language Paul denounces those who put their confidence in the "flesh" instead of the wisdom of the cross. He calls them "dogs" and circumcision, in these circumstances, he calls "mutilation." This argument is especially powerful because Paul himself had been an observant Jew.

Paul is not only concerned with outside influences but also with those that come from within that are harmful to the community. He begins Chapter 4 by once again urging the Philippians to live in harmony. Here he specifically refers to a conflict between some leading women of the community, Euodia and Syntyche. He calls upon some of the other leaders to aid in the reconciliation of these women, for the betterment of the community.

A Thank-You Note (4,10–20)

Paul's thanks for the help received from the Philippians and sent through Epaphroditus once again underlines the partnership he had with this community. His gratitude is not so much that he was personally aided as that the Philippians' generosity is "profit that accrues to your account" (4,17). His use of legal language strengthens the mutuality of their partnership in the common cause of spreading the gospel. Paul also speaks of this aid in liturgical terms, "a fragrant aroma, . . . a sacrifice, pleasing to God" (4,18). He uses the ancient language of liturgical offering and sacrifice to indicate that an offering of mutual love and aid by Christians to one another is a liturgy (see 2 Cor 2,14–16; Rom 12,1f and 15,17–20).

Questions for Discussion or Reflection

1. Philippians is a powerful reflection on the meaning of fidelity in the midst of trial and suffering. Think of a person you know who has remained faithful in spite of suffering.

a. What enabled the person to do this?
b. Did the people around the person have any effect on the situation?
c. Was the person's faith in God a factor?

2. Imagine that Paul has spent a few months in your parish and after leaving writes back about his concerns for the community.
a. What kinds of external pressures on people would he name?
b. What internal divisions would Paul want the community to reconcile?
c. What advice would Paul give your parish?

ESSAY

Determining the Full Meaning of a Text

We owe a tremendous debt to scholars of the Bible. Without their research, their study of ancient languages, their careful explanations of the customs and beliefs of people in the past, we would be puzzled by much that we read in the text of Scripture. Building on centuries of scholarship, modern-day scholars are able to bring a vast amount of knowledge and perception to the study of these ancient texts.

We cannot all be biblical scholars. But that does not free us from the responsibility of working hard to understand an author's meaning and how it might apply to us today. We can learn from the methods of scholarship even though we do not have the time or the inclination to be scholars ourselves. What are these methods and how can we apply them to our own reading of the texts?

First, modern scholars try not to look at writings in isolation. They compare one part of a Scripture text to another part. They look at other writings by the same author, if there are any, to see if they can find characteristics of that writer's thought that can be helpful to understanding. They try to find out as much as possible about the place and time of writing, the audience the writer had in mind, and other similar matters.

For us, this means that we should be very careful about taking a tiny piece of any writing and trying to determine what it means on its own. We need to look at "the big picture"—the writer's time and place, the audience, the context of the writing, and so on.

Second, modern scholars are very much aware of the long process that has gone on in order to bring the text to us. It was written, copied, recopied, perhaps added to or mixed together with other writings, or perhaps miscopied in some way. It is sometimes an open question whether a particular passage is an original part of the writing, and if a passage is questionable—if for instance it does not appear in early manuscripts of the writing—it is then necessary to try to find out how, when, and why it was added.

For us, this does not mean that we can simply skip over a passage that we don't agree with. It is a part of our Bible and we must accept it. But we can learn to read with a greater awareness: to try to determine when a biblical writer is making an effort to discern God's will and when the writer is "editorializing" on his or her own. And this can also help us to avoid our own tendency to "editorialize": to try to find our own viewpoint and our own opinions in the pages of the Bible, instead of listening to the biblical text and responding.

Third, scholars try very hard not to come to the text they are studying with preconceptions about what it might mean, or with ideas they might have about current issues. They try, for instance, not to assume that a biblical writer would have meant exactly what we

ESSAY (Continued)

might mean when using a particular word or phrase. This is particularly important when some phrases, like "the Word of God," have many centuries of discussion and teaching attached to them.

For us, this means that we must read carefully, without putting ideas into the biblical writer's head. The Gospel of Luke tells the story of Jesus' birth, and we read this story every Christmas—but Luke would be very surprised if he were to see a Christmas tree! It's easy to avoid mistakes like that, but some of our beliefs, ones that have grown up over the years, are more difficult to keep out of our reading of the Bible.

In our reading we depend on the labors of countless scholars, translators, commentators, and teachers who have given us a place to begin. But we can never be completely certain about the meaning or relevance of every passage in the Bible. That is why, after we have made our best efforts to gather information about the biblical writings, and after we have tried to hear what the authors are truly saying and not merely what we expect them to say, we must bring in two other ingredients. We must rely on our own spiritual growth and perceptiveness to gradually make things clearer to us. We must also remain aware of our sense of our own limitations, and approach the text in humility and openness. As we make efforts to discern the deeper meanings of the text, and as we learn to live within the meaning we can see and wait for the larger meanings we might not yet be able to grasp, we will find our understanding enriched and our lives enlarged even when we know we don't have all the answers.

COLOSSIANS READING GUIDE

At a Glance

A "captivity" letter written from prison	As in Phil, Eph, and Phlm, the author refers to his imprisonment.
Disputed authorship	Lively style and personal greetings are typical of Paul but other expressions are not.
Time and place of writing uncertain	Paul, himself, was imprisoned several times; if written by a disciple, the time could be around 60–62 A.D.
Major focus	Primacy of Christ, reconciliation of all in him; ethical implications. This focus grows out of false teaching at Colossae and is a response to a request of the founder, Epaphras.

Paul did not establish the church at Colossae, nor had he ever visited there (2,1). It was founded by one of his disciples, Epaphras (1,6–7). It is likely that Paul was not the author of Colossians, but that it was written in his name to give emphasis to the encouragement it contains—to hold onto what the Colossians have learned and believed about Christ in the face of false teaching about Christ. (For the sake of convenience, we refer to the author as "Paul" even though there is doubt about authorship.)

READING THROUGH COLOSSIANS

Outline of Colossians

This letter follows the basic style of Paul: The address and conclusion enclose the body of the letter where he lays out his teaching and its ethical implications.

- I. The Address (1,1–14)
- II. The Body of the Letter (1,15 – 4,6)
  - A. The Pauline Teaching (1,15 – 2,23)
    - 1. Hymn about Christ and Implications (1,15–23)
    - 2. Paul's Ministry and Example (1,24 – 2,3)
    - 3. Warnings against False Teachings (2,4–23)
  - B. Ethics Characterizing the True Christian (3,1 – 4,6)
- III. The Conclusion (4,7–18)

THE ADDRESS (1,1-14)

The address includes the usual greeting, a thanksgiving, and a prayer for the continued progress of the Colossians. Paul expresses his confidence in the preaching of Epaphras and the solid foundation it provided the community. He sets the stage for his message when he says that it is in Christ that "we have redemption, the forgiveness of sins" (1,14). This passage from the realm of sin and error into that of grace and truth takes place in baptism and must be lived out in the daily lives of Christians.

THE BODY OF THE LETTER (1,15 – 4,6)

Teachings of Paul (1,15–2,23)

THE HYMN ABOUT CHRIST (1,15-23)

The false preachers at Colossae are apparently saying that Christ's death and resurrection is not sufficient for salvation. It is incomplete and the Christians must add other practices drawn from Jewish and non-Jewish sources. In response to this false teaching, Paul quotes a hymn about Christ (1,15–20, see also Phil 2,6–11), which probably came from their liturgy. In the hymn, they profess and celebrate the authority and primacy of Christ in whom all "fullness was pleased to dwell, and through him to reconcile all things for him" (1,19–20). Paul stresses the redemption and peace won for us through Christ.

Quoting this hymn serves more than one purpose. By starting with something the Colossians already know and share in common, Paul affirms their faith and can build on the unity of their belief. He does not scold the Colossians for their errors but emphasizes Christ's role of reconciling the world to God as the basis of their common faith.

PAUL'S MINISTRY AND EXAMPLE (1,24 – 2,3)

Throughout Paul's writings there is a repeated pattern. He sets out the example of Christ and the example of his own ministry as a model to be followed. His confidence is somewhat surprising, but it makes sense when one examines the foundation of this practice. Paul is firmly rooted in God and his confidence is not self-reliance but, rather, hope in God. This is so clear to him that he believes that others can know the power of God and be converted by studying his own life. Paul's confidence is very realistic; he glories in his call and fidelity but also emphasizes his suffering in the service of the gospel.

In describing his own ministry, Paul adapts categories important to the Colossians and to the false teachers who are disturbing them. Because they were emphasizing "wisdom" and "perfection," Paul speaks about the "knowledge of the mystery of God, Christ, in whom are hidden all the treasures of wisdom and knowledge" (2,2f). Paul identifies the goal of his mission to "present everyone perfect in Christ" (1,28).

WARNINGS AGAINST FALSE TEACHERS (2,4-23)

Before his warnings about the false teachings, Paul once again encourages the Colossians in their faith. The false teachers presumed that something was lacking in Christ and that salvation required something more. These additional requirements were a combination of Jewish and pagan philosophies, ideals, and practices. Paul labels these as fads, "things destined to perish," and reasserts the primacy of Christ in whom dwells the fullness of God. All are members of Christ, who is the head of the body, the church. The church's task is the reconciliation of the world to God under Christ. According to Paul, these teachings are sufficient and false teaching must be avoided.

Ethics Characterizing the True Christian (3,1 – 4,6)

Paul does not present a new, uniquely Christian ethical system. Rather, he adapts elements from sources known to people of his time to form his ethical principles. What is unique for Paul is the source of the motivation and energy to fulfill these ethical principles: the commandment of love. For him, the church as the body of Christ distinguishes itself from the outside world in that the love command operates to create a new way for Christians to relate to one another.

CONCLUSION (4,7-18)

Tychicus is the messenger entrusted with the letter to the Colossians. Many think that he was accompanied by Onesimus, the former runaway slave who returned to Colossae with the letter from Paul to Philemon (see Reading Guide to Philemon).

Questions for Discussion or Reflection

1. Many people today are pulled in various directions and are searching for spiritual guidance and nourishment. Based on Paul's message in this letter, what advice would you give someone who is searching for spiritual answers?
2. Think of a person or a group with whom you disagree on some point of church practice or belief. Following Paul's example of beginning with something that the Colossians shared in common (the hymn to Christ), what are some important beliefs that you share in common with this person or group?

1 THESSALONIANS READING GUIDE

At a Glance

One of Paul's earliest letters	The communities at Philippi and Thessalonica were among Paul's first converts.
Authentic authorship	No one denies that Paul wrote 1 Thessalonians.
Time and place of writing	Around 51 A.D., probably from Corinth. Timothy was sent from Athens to Thessalonica and caught up with Paul later to report on his visit.
Major themes	Thanksgiving; relationship between faith and charity; expectation of the second coming of Christ Timothy's report is a testimony to the faith of the Thessalonians, but they are not without problems and questions.

The Christian community at Thessalonica was one of the very first that Paul established. Although his tone is affectionate, Paul experienced a great deal of persecution from both Jews and Gentiles because of his preaching. Four times in this letter he expresses gratitude for the faith of the Thessalonians, while still addressing real problems of the community.

READING THROUGH 1 THESSALONIANS

Outline of 1 Thessalonians

First Thessalonians follows the usual letter format.

- I. The Address (1,1–10)
- II. The Body of the Letter (2,1 – 5,22)
  - A. Paul's Teaching (2,1 – 3,13)
    - 1. Thanksgiving (2,13–16; 3,9–13; 5,23f; 1,2–10)
    - 2. Defense of Paul's Ministry (2,1–12; 2,17 – 3,8)
  - B. Specific Instructions (4,1 – 5,22)
    - 1. Sexual Conduct (4,2–8)
    - 2. Death and the Need for Vigilance (4,13 – 5,11)
    - 3. Church Order (5,12–22)
- III. Final Greeting (5,23–28)

THE ADDRESS (1,1-10)

The address contains a short greeting (1,1) and an extended thanksgiving (1,2–10). A distinctive feature of Paul's letters is that the thanksgiving focuses on what God has done for the community that Paul is addressing. In letters written in the first century, the thanksgiving usually centered on the health and benefits enjoyed by the sender.

The address shows Paul's concept of being part of a team of missionaries; he writes not only in his own name but with Silvanus and Timothy. Paul's trademark greeting, in its simplest form, is seen here: "Grace and peace to you, the church of ______________ in (or from) God the Father and the Lord Jesus."

THE BODY OF THE LETTER (2,1 – 5,22)

Paul's Teaching (2,1 – 3,13)

Paul's "teaching" or message to the Thessalonians is a summary of his previous relations with them. Paul expresses his gratitude for the success of this community and yet has to defend his ministry among them.

THANKSGIVING (1,2-10; 2,13-16; 3,9-13; 5,23f)

Often in Paul's letters the thanksgiving in the address hints at the themes of the letter. In this case, however, thanksgiving itself is a major theme. Four different times Paul expresses gratitude. In all four places, he speaks of the relationship between faith and charity and of the expectation of the second coming of Jesus Christ (or *Parousia*).

Although thanksgiving is a persistent thread that runs through this letter, Paul is no naive optimist. He is aware that this community is experiencing problems. There are some false teachers stirring up things in Paul's absence, and obviously some members of the community are questioning Paul's authority. Although these are threatening and painful problems, Paul returns again to his theme of thanksgiving as if to say that he is confident in the Thessalonians' perseverance.

DEFENSE OF PAUL'S MINISTRY (2,1-12; 2,17 – 3,8)

The difficulty of travel and communications in the ancient world had both positive and negative influences on the spread of Christianity. Often philosophers or religious teachers joined others who traveled for business or personal reasons. News was gathered and spread by these traveling groups, and often new converts were made along the way. These travelers were also, at times, a source of false teaching and created a difficult and persistent problem for the early church.

There seems to be such a problem at Thessalonica and Paul is unable to get back to clear it up. He warns them about ministers who are greedy or who flatter (2,5) or who rely on the community for support (2,9).

Paul not only reminds the community of the sacrifices and dedication they saw in him and his companions, but he also makes an issue about work. He repeatedly says that he is self-supporting and warns against idleness and idlers. Some Thessalonians apparently needed this reminder because they thought that, since the end of the world was near, they could quit work. Paul links working and self-support with charity. All must contribute to the upbuilding of the community. Believers are not simply to sit back and wait for the second coming of Christ, but to be actively engaged in the world.

Specific Instructions (4,1 – 5,22)

Paul always makes some practical application of his message. His concern is that faith be obvious in daily life, especially as expressed in charity.

SEXUAL CONDUCT (4,2 – 8)

His first application has to do with the relationship between chastity and charity (4,3-8). Sexual conduct was an issue that concerned the early church, which was trying to integrate Gentile as well as Jewish converts. The Greek culture had achieved a high degree of moral development; certainly the "pagans" as a group could not be considered promiscuous; and the Jews considered the obligations of marriage and the family to be linked to the covenant relationship with God.

It was this covenant link that Paul wished to preserve. Therefore, he stresses the obligation of believers to develop relationships worthy of them, showing respect for one another and for their call to holiness.

DEATH AND THE NEED FOR VIGILANCE (4,13 – 5,11)

Paul and other early Christians believed that the return of Jesus (the *Parousia*) was very near. Apparently, some in the church at Thessalonica were worried about what would happen to those Christians who died before the second coming. How would they participate in that triumphant day of Christ's return?

Paul feared that the death of fellow Christians would so shake the Thessalonians' faith that their grief would give way to doubt, discouragement, and even apostasy. He encourages them to persevere in faith and repeats the admonition: "Console one another with these words" (4,18; 5,11), that is, that the dead will rise and join the living when Christ comes.

Paul also warns them about the continued need for preparedness and vigilance, especially through the images of the pregnant woman and the thief in the night (5,2–3; see also Mt 24,43; Lk 21,23).

Paul's view of the second coming reveals his apocalyptic perspective. God is perceived as "above," beyond the clouds. There are trumpets, an archangel, and a call to judgment.

CHURCH ORDER (5,12-22)

Paul asks for respect for those who minister among the faithful and reminds Christians that there must be mutual care and concern for one another.

CONCLUSION (5,23-28)

The concluding prayer (5,23–25) and greetings (5,26–28) suggest that this letter was intended for reading in a liturgical setting. Paul says that the Thessalonians will be kept holy and spotless as they wait for the Lord's return. He requests their prayers and urges that they greet one another with a "holy kiss."

Questions for Discussion or Reflection

1. Like the Thessalonians, we may find that the death of loved ones poses painful questions. Any death leaves a hole in the fabric of a community.
   a. How can the community work together to respond helpfully when someone dies? How does your (our) faith respond? With a consoling image or a more frightening one?
   b. Does God seem closer or more remote when someone close to us has died? If closer, how can we build on this experience? If more remote, how can we be helped to close the gap?
2. Carefully re-read 5,14–22.
   a. Who are the idle, the fainthearted, the weak in my experience? Would those words ever describe me? How do I admonish, cheer, and support those around me?
   b. What could "quench the Spirit" mean in today's church?

2 THESSALONIANS READING GUIDE

At a Glance

Author unknown	This letter was probably written by a second-generation Pauline Christian.
Time and place of writing	Unknown. The speedy return of Christ (1 Thes) had already been proven wrong. The letter may have been written as late as 70 A.D. (around the time of Mark).
Major themes	Thanksgiving; apocalyptic message of consolation and hope. This is not a frightening message trying to arouse fear; rather, it is a message of encouragement to Christians suffering persecution and confusion.

This letter is a response to the situation at Thessalonica, some years after Paul's death. One problem has to do with a message that was supposedly sent to the Thessalonians by Paul, saying that the day of the Lord (the second coming of Christ) is at hand (2,2). (See "The Influence of Apocalyptic Thinking on Paul," RG 415.)

READING THROUGH 2 THESSALONIANS

Outline of 2 Thessalonians

Second Thessalonians follows the usual structure of a Pauline letter:

- I. The Address (1,1–12)
- II. The Body of the Letter (2,1 – 3, 16)
  - A. Paul's Teaching (2,1–17)
    - 1. Warning about the Second Coming (2,1–12)
    - 2. Thanksgiving and Prayer (2,13–17; see also 1,3–12; 3,16)
  - B. Ethical Instructions (3,1–16)
- III. Final Greeting (3,17f)

THE ADDRESS (1,1–12)

The address includes a greeting, a thanksgiving, and a prayer. The writer's imitation of Paul's greeting in 1 Thessalonians is quite clear. Also, similar to 1 Thessalonians, the thanksgiving is not only a part of the formal address but also a central theme in the development of the teaching part of the letter (see 1 Thessalonians).

THE BODY OF THE LETTER (2,1 – 3,16)

Paul's Teaching (2,1–17)

WARNING AGAINST MISINFORMATION ABOUT THE SECOND COMING (2,1–12)

In the earlier letters actually written by Paul, he often expressed his fear that the faith of the young church would be threatened by false teachers coming from the outside and from division within the community. The message of Christ's early return was a powerful incentive for the Christians to "hold on" and remain faithful. By the time 2 Thessalonians was written, there were still these same problems, but the added confusion and questions about the delay of the second coming of Christ made matters worse. (This situation, the delay of Christ's coming, is one of the main reasons interpreters believe that this letter was written by a later Pauline Christian.)

This problem of the delay is heightened by the claim of some agitators that they have a message from Paul that Christ would return soon. The writer's response to this situation is "do not be alarmed," and he gives a reminder that before the end some events must still take place. It is not clear exactly what these events are, but the writer carefully avoids guesswork about the times and circumstances of the *Parousia* (second coming). The standard apocalyptic images portraying the conflict between good and evil, and the ultimate victory of God over evil, are meant to focus the reader's attention on hope and vigilance against deception and alarm.

THANKSGIVING AND PRAYER (2,13–17; 1,3–12; 3,16)

Just as in 1 Thessalonians, there is a significant section of the main message of this letter devoted to thanksgiving. This author continues to make the connection between faith and love that was evident in the first letter. The difference here is the emphasis placed on the extended time of their faithfulness. He gives thanks that the community has remained strong in faith, but warns that faith must be expressed in love over time and that the time of waiting may be longer than expected. In his gratitude and prayer for the Thessalonians, the author focuses on the need to express faith in building up the community, especially in times of trouble.

Ethical Instructions (3,1–5)

Writing as if in Paul's name, the author requests prayers for himself and for the success of his mission. He instructs the Thessalonians to work, to avoid idleness, and even to avoid those who do not obey this message. He warns that idlers disrupt the peace of the community and in this way connects idleness with a lack of love or charity. Once again the apostle is presented as a model to be imitated, one who toils night and day (3,8), so as not to be a burden.

FINAL GREETING (3,17–18)

The author adds a greeting, "in my own hand," apparently as a way to ensure that this letter will be seen as coming from Paul. Yet this very way of ending, plus the absence of Paul's style of personal greetings, is one of the factors that points to a writer other than Paul.

Questions for Discussion or Reflection

Both the Christians at the time 2 Thessalonians was written and the present-day readers of the letter could benefit from the saying attributed to Augustine: "Pray (or believe) as if everything depended on God and work as if everything depended on you."

1. What are the problem areas in your life, your city, or the world that require the balance of both intense prayer and energetic work?
2. Have you have given up on praying or working for solutions for any of these problems?

The Pastoral Letters

The two letters to Timothy and the single letter to Titus have been called the "Pastoral Letters" since they deal with issues about the ongoing care of the Pauline communities. The Pastorals might be read as reflections on Christian ministry. They were probably written by disciples of Paul for leaders of communities at least a generation after the apostle's death.

Timothy and Titus are mentioned as companions and trusted and reliable partners of Paul in the authentic Pauline letters, and Timothy is also mentioned in Acts. It is likely that the names of Timothy and Titus are used in an encouraging way to stand for trusted pastors who lead local communities and are trying to guard the tradition of the Pauline churches.

These letters are written to reinforce the faith of these pastors and to encourage them, reminding them of their own Christian vocation.

1 TIMOTHY READING GUIDE

At a Glance

A "pastoral" letter	Along with 2 Tm and Titus, these are called "pastoral" because they deal with the ongoing care of the Pauline communities.
Author unknown	Probably written by a disciple of Paul
Time of writing	Possibly around the beginning of the 2nd century. Most interpreters agree that these letters were written at least a generation after Paul's death.
Major themes	Advice and warnings against false teaching and on Christian ministry Addresses the situation of the developing Christian communities: the ever-present threat of false teaching and practical reflections on ministry.

This letter is addressed to Timothy, who administered the church at Ephesus. It speaks to the ongoing problem of false teaching that always threatened the church and the practical challenges of the developing communities and their ministries.

As with other letters written in Paul's name, the author is referred to as "Paul" in this guide.

READING THROUGH 1 TIMOTHY

Organization of the Letter

This letter does not fall into the familiar structure of Paul's authentic letters or the earlier letters written in Paul's name. In that structure, the body of the letter contained a section devoted to Paul's teaching, usually based on problems or questions in the community, followed by practical application of the teaching in daily life. Unlike the reading guides for the other letters, the following comments do not follow the text of the letter, except for the three main sections. Instead, the body of this letter will be treated according to some of the themes repeated throughout the letter:

I. The address (1,1–2.12–17)
II. The body of the letter (1,3–11; 1,18 – 6,19)
   A. Advice or warnings about false teaching
   B. Advice concerning ministers
   C. Advice concerning women
III. Final recommendation and warning (6,20–21)

THE ADDRESS (1,1–2.12–17)

The address consists of a greeting (1,1–2) with the thanksgiving delayed until 1,12–17. A warning against false doctrines (1,3–11) appears between these two parts of the address. This insertion demonstrates the gravity of the author's concern with false teaching.

THE BODY OF THE LETTER (1,3–11; 1,18 – 6,19)

One way to approach the diverse material in 1 Timothy is to see it as a collection of the suggestions offered to leaders or pastors of Christian communities near the beginning of the 2nd century. (See The Pastoral Letters, page RG 445.) The advice given is not so much theological but practical, and all of it has a common theme: Members of the Christian community should distinguish themselves by their love and service to others.

Advice or Warnings about False Teaching

The threat of false teaching is a problem that afflicted the church from the beginning. In 1 Timothy the main focus is against a form of knowledge that is false; other concerns include certain spiritual practices and attitudes toward wealth.

We do not find a clear description of the content of the false teaching attacked in this letter. According to 1,4, this knowledge is concerned "with myths . . . genealogies which promote speculation rather than the plan of God . . . to be received by faith." This threat to faith is a kind of knowledge that is without any ethical or practical application for living. So the letter not only warns against this "so-called knowledge" (6,20) but also against those who would

Gnosis is the Greek word for knowledge and is the root for the word *Gnosticism* (see the Glossary). Gnosticism was a kind of religion that claimed secret knowledge for its members. It developed during the 2nd, 3rd, and 4th centuries.

It is possible that the "so-called" knowledge attacked in 1 Timothy is a sign of the beginnings of gnostic influences during New Testament times. (See the note on 1 Tm 6,20f, in the *New American Bible* text.)

reduce Christianity to a mere doctrine or to an intellectual exercise at the neglect of ethical implications.

First Timothy stresses the practical to such an extent that there is almost no reference to the content of truly Christian teaching. The letter presumes a common fund of knowledge and emphasizes that authentic Christianity should work itself out in everyday life.

The author also warns against false teachers who advocate spiritual practices, especially those suggesting renunciation of marriage or restrictions on certain foods (4,1–3) and reminds the reader: "For everything created by God is good and nothing is to be rejected when received with thanksgiving" (4,4).

Apparently there were some false teachings concerning the accumulation of wealth. The advice here puts material wealth in a right perspective: "Tell the rich . . . not to rely on so uncertain a thing as wealth but rather on God . . ." (6,17).

Advice Concerning Ministers

There is a good deal of advice directed to Timothy (the pastor of the community) himself and to other leaders. The writer impresses on Timothy the importance of his role as an example for the church and the great responsibility entrusted to him by God (1,3.18–20; 4,6–16; 6,11–17).

The experience of Paul is reviewed as a prime example to be followed; here it demonstrates God's mercy acting in the minister's life. The reference to Paul's sinful past (1,12–17) serves to illustrate the graciousness of God's mercy.

The advice to Timothy in this letter is in line with the overall practical approach. He is admonished to draw strength from the "prophetic words once spoken about you" (1,18) and to "attend to yourself and to your teaching" (4,16). Timothy should concentrate on "righteousness, devotion, faith, love, patience, and gentleness" (6,11). He should ignore the seduction of "profane babbling and the absurdities of so-called knowledge" (6,20). Constancy and perseverance in the faith is urged to demonstrate to all his reliance on God.

The concrete advice about bishops, deacons, and other ministers to the community (Chapters 5 and 6) also stresses the power of example made earlier to Timothy. This whole letter could be read as a list of rules for people in various offices and positions within the community with an emphasis on love and service to others. Even the dress and decorum of men and women at the liturgy, for example, should contribute to the building up of the community (2,8–10).

Many interpreters assume that the offices mentioned suggest that this letter must have been written late. They argue that it would have taken some years for the church to develop such a variety of roles and recognize ministers. But this is not necessarily so. These ministries arose as the church struggled to respond to its mission in the world. The office of bishop or overseer developed out of the custom of holding all things in common so that the surplus of the rich would supply the needs of the poor (see 2 Cor 8 and 9). The ministry of deacons reflected the priority of preaching the word while not neglecting the physical and material needs of the church's members (Acts 6,1–6).

Advice Concerning Women

The particular advice to women in this letter presents difficulty for many modern interpreters. Like other biblical passages that present difficulties, this one needs to be seen in its historical and cultural context. The writer of 1 Timothy betrays the bias of a male-dominated culture. The prevailing male wisdom taught that women were gullible and subject to error, as symbolized by the story of Eve who was tempted by the serpent.

To his credit, and contrary to the false teachers, the author supports marriage and sees the family as conducive to holiness. He therefore advocates the "submission" (an unfortunate word choice to modern ears) of women, which can be understood as the participation of women in marriage and family. This is not a life style unworthy of Christian women but a way in which women may, like Timothy, "persevere in faith and love and holiness" (2,15; see also 6,11).

Similarly, the author describes the vital role of widows as teachers and role models in the encouragement of younger women as wives and mothers.

FINAL RECOMMENDATION AND WARNING (6,20–21)

First Timothy ends by restating the main message of the letter: "Guard the trust" (see 1,3–10; 4,7; 6,3–5). Timothy is urged to hold firm to what he knows and to live it quietly. The simple concluding formula suggests that the letter was meant for "all" Timothy's associates.

Questions for Discussion or Reflection

First Timothy stresses the responsibility of leaders to interpret the essentials of the Christian message and to ensure that charity is distinctive of the Christian community. As a way of connecting this message to our lives today, we might ask ourselves:

1. What is the most recent issue that I have been upset about concerning the church?
2. How is this issue related to how we as members and ministers of the church are involved in the spread of the gospel or the building up of the community?

2 TIMOTHY READING GUIDE

At a Glance

A "pastoral" letter	Along with 1 Tm and Titus, these are called "pastoral" because they deal with the ongoing care of the Pauline communities.
Author unknown	Probably written by a disciple of Paul
Time of writing	Possibly around the beginning of the 2nd century. Most interpreters agree that these letters were written at least a generation after Paul's death.
Major themes	Encouragement of Timothy's ministry and warnings against false teaching. Like 1 Tm, there is still the concern with false teaching and ministry. Here, the tone of the reflections on ministry are more personal and focus on Timothy.

This letter deals with the same themes as 1 Timothy, but it has a more personal tone. The author, in Paul's name, seems to be giving the younger pastor the benefit of his experience. The elder apostle speaks of his own life, his loneliness, his lack of confidence in other human beings. Yet he is not discouraged because God is the source of his strength, as he is for Timothy.

As with the other letters written in Paul's name, the author is referred to as "Paul" in this guide.

READING THROUGH 2 TIMOTHY

Organization of the Letter

Paul's authentic letters and the earlier letters written in his name generally follow a basic pattern of first presenting his fundamental doctrine or teaching and then drawing ethical conclusions from his teaching. Second Timothy does not follow this pattern, primarily because it is more of a personal letter that combines reminders about doctrine with advice in an informal way. In general, the basic outline found in the *New American Bible* introduction will be followed:

I. The address (1,1–5)
II. The body of the letter (1,6 – 4,8)
  A. Exhortations to Timothy (1,6 – 2,13)
  B. Instructions concerning false teaching (2,14 – 4,8)
III. Personal requests and final greetings (4,9–22)

THE ADDRESS (1,1–5)

The address consists of a greeting (1,1–2) and a thanksgiving (1,3–5), following the authentic Pauline style.

THE BODY OF THE LETTER (1,6 – 4,8)

The informal structure of this letter focuses on two main themes which are developed here: the minister's experience of God and warnings against false teaching.

Exhortations to Timothy (1,6 – 2,13)

Paul is represented in 2 Timothy as giving a kind of farewell address near the end of his life, "the time of my departure is at hand" (4,6b). (Moses and Jesus were also portrayed this way.) In this typical biblical pattern, the person speaking warns his followers about coming dangers and threats to fidelity. Usually they are commissioned with authority and reminded about the source of their confidence. They are promised that God will remain with them and they will endure.

Following this pattern, the author reminds Timothy that his ministry was confirmed in the church through ordination by Paul. He further reminds Timothy that those who follow Christ will suffer persecution. This is similar to Jesus' warning to his disciples (Mt 24,9–14; Mk 13,9–13; Lk 21,12–19; Jn 15,11–27).

As in previous letters, the example of Paul is used as a model. His life and impending death are described as a liturgical sacrifice: He is being poured out like a libation, an offering of wine (4,6). He has run and finished the course (4,7). He awaits with longing the reward of God (4,6–8). This display of confidence is rooted in God and is meant to serve as encouragement to Timothy who still runs the course. Paul urges Timothy to be faithful in waiting for the appearance of Jesus Christ.

Warnings Against False Teaching (2,14–4,8)

In all three pastoral letters, the author attacks false teaching and assumes that since his readers hold the right beliefs, it is not necessary to review correct teaching or doctrine. The false teaching, for the most part, remains vague. One false teaching, however, is identified: that baptized Christians are already risen with Christ and that there is no future bodily resurrection (see the note on 2,14–19 in the *New American Bible* text). The author stresses the appropriate ethical applications that follow from true gospel teaching.

Paul urges Timothy not to become embroiled in debates: "Charge [people] . . . to stop disputing about words . . . avoid profane [and] idle talk" (2,14.16).

PERSONAL REQUESTS AND FINAL GREETINGS (4,9–22)

The personal tone and greetings of 2 Timothy mark this as the Pastoral Letter closest to Paul's own style. Like Paul, Timothy often experienced problems in his relationships with others. Also like Paul, 2 Timothy suggests that such difficulties are the occasion to add more converts to the gospel message. The letter ends with a prayer for God's Spirit to be with Timothy (singular). The plural in the last line may indicate the letter's being read and reflected upon in the liturgy.

Questions for Discussion or Reflection

The warning in this letter against engaging in useless disputes, "stop disputing about words" (2,14), must strike a chord with members of some parish committees or readers of the "Letters to the Editor" in some diocesan newspapers.

1. Can you think of some issues where disputing over words really is important to living the gospel?
2. Give some examples of situations where arguing over words was possibly a way of dodging the real issues.

TITUS READING GUIDE

At a Glance

A "pastoral" letter	Along with 1 and 2 Tm, these letters are called "pastoral" because they deal with the ongoing care of the Pauline communities.
Author unknown	Probably written by a disciple of Paul

Time of writing	Possibly around the beginning of the 2nd century. Most interpreters agree that these letters were written at least a generation after Paul's death.
Major themes	Appointment of reliable ministers to protect against false teachers Similar to 1 Tm, concerned with false teaching, the appointment and conduct of ministers, and living faithfully in society

This third "pastoral letter" is addressed to Titus, who is the administrator of the church on the large Mediterranean island of Crete. The letter is very similar to 1 Timothy and shows the same concerns for those entrusted with the care of the local communities. They are to be careful in appointing ministers who will present sound church teaching, therefore protecting the local church from the many dangers of false teaching.

As with the other letters written in Paul's name, the author of this letter will be referred to as "Paul" in this guide.

READING THROUGH TITUS

Organization of the Letter

This letter has the typical structure of an address, the body of the letter, and a short conclusion. The entire letter may be seen as an exhortation of encouragement from one pastor to another.

I. The address (1,1–4)
II. The body of the letter (1,5–3,11)
  A. Pastoral responsibilities
  B. Teaching the Christian life
III. Conclusion

THE ADDRESS (1,1-14)

The address follows the usual Pauline pattern, consisting of a greeting and a thanksgiving. The greeting is more elaborate than Paul's usual greeting, but includes many features of Paul's thinking. As with the other pastorals, the author emphasizes the apostle's role in the spread of the worldwide mission of Christ. This mission is now entrusted to Paul's "child," Titus, a fellow worker.

THE BODY OF THE LETTER (1,5–3,11)

This message is concerned with pastoral responsibilities, especially that of working with others in the preaching of the Christian message. It is also a message of encouragement from one pastor to another.

Pastoral Responsibilities (1,5–16)

Although Paul was himself a preacher who moved from one place to another in order to spread the gospel, he is presented here as seeing the need for stabilized leadership, especially to protect the church against heretical or false teaching and to be an example for others. (Compare 1,5–9 with the instructions of 1 Tm 3,1–7.) The instructions given to Titus about the administration of the church at Crete are, therefore, primarily concerned with appointing trustworthy and reliable pastors for the various duties required for the growth and development of the church there.

One of the important offices was that of *presbyter* (elder), a title that is quite close in meaning to *episcopos* (bishop, literally "overseer") in this letter (1,5f). The main function of the bishop was the overseeing of the financial or material matters in the church. Therefore his own life ought to be exemplary. He must not only avoid excess but represent a model Christian life in his own family.

This instruction about how the leaders of the community ought to live as models for others is not only valid as it stands, it also gives the author another way of warning against false teachings, and especially against the false teachers themselves. By their good conduct, the elders and bishops will show, by contrast, that the false teachers are those who preach for personal gain and personal recognition. Paul himself exemplified this: during his ministry, he always tried to be self-supporting so that his motive of spreading the gospel would be clear.

Primary among the false teachers are the Judaizers who continue to plague the Gentile Christians by advocating a return to some aspects of the Jewish Law. (See Galatians and Romans.) The writer also warns against the national tendencies of the Cretans themselves, tendencies that lead them to deceit, dishonesty, and laziness, making them easy targets for false teachers.

Teaching the Christian Life (2,1–3,11)

This section deals with the situation of the Christians developing their own life style within the civic society. Titus is encouraged to hold on to sound teaching while resisting pressures from all sides. Christians must not act in accordance with the world around them. Paul's instructions focus on how to survive while offering an alternative life style and developing integrity as Christians.

Paul lists some of the groups Titus must work with; for example, older men, younger men and women, slaves, and those in authority. It is possible that there was a problem concerning some people's interpretation of the freedoms given in baptism. Women, slaves, and citizens are all urged to strive for fidelity within the constraints of their situation, whether that be marriage, slavery, or the state.

CONCLUSION

Paul summarizes his advice to Titus by reminding him to teach others to avoid false knowledge and useless arguments. The false teachers disturb the community and its ministers. The faithful are called to vigilance and constancy.

Questions for Discussion or Reflection

The advice given in this letter, to avoid controversy and to be faithful within your "state in life," sounds a lot like the saying, "Don't rock the boat."

1. Think about the Christian church only 70 or 80 years after the death and resurrection of Jesus. Can you think of any reasons why this advice is appropriate in that situation?
2. If the writer of Titus were alive today and understood the situation of our church, what would you ask him about applying this advice today?

PHILEMON READING GUIDE

At a Glance

A "captivity" letter written from prison	Like Phil, Eph, and Col, Paul refers to his imprisonment (1.10.13.23).
Authentic authorship	No one denies that Paul wrote Philemon.
Time and place of writing	Early 60s? maybe from Rome. Indications that this was written later: reference to being an old man (9) and a development in thought on slavery.
Major theme	New ways of relating to others, based on baptism in Christ The return of the baptized slave, Onesimus, to Philemon is the occasion for this description of a new society, based on baptism.

The situation behind this letter seems, at first, to be a very personal one, involving three individuals, Paul, Onesimus, and Philemon. Because the letter is so short, it might seem to be simple. Living out its message, however, is neither simple nor limited to the purely personal.

According to the biblical text and the introduction and notes of the *New American Bible,* Onesimus, a slave, had run away from his master and had been with Paul in prison. While there with Paul, Onesimus became a Christian. Paul then sent him back to Philemon carrying this letter.

The use of phrases like "partnership in the faith . . . pay . . . owe," call to mind the letter to the Philippians. Paul seems to feel a similar closeness to Philemon and "the church at your house." This letter provides another glimpse into the structure and operation of the early church.

ORGANIZATION OF THE LETTER

Philemon follows the usual structure of a Pauline letter with an address, body, and conclusion. The informal conversational tone distinguishes this letter from others, but the content clearly puts it in a community context so typical of Paul.

Another distinguishing mark of the structure is the weaving together of the message and the ethical implications that flow from the message. It is impossible to separate them. Philemon follows a simple outline:

I. The address (1–6)
II. The body of the letter (7–22)
III. Conclusion (23–25)

THE ADDRESS (1–6)

The community context is clear in the address. Philemon is addressed, as are his wife Apphia, other members of his household, and the whole "church [that meets] at your house" (1–2). As in other letters, Paul uses the thanksgiving (4–6) to hint at his theme, the new relationship or society that is based on our baptismal relationship. He calls attention to the faith and love that Philemon has always shown the "holy ones," his fellow Christians, and calls him a "partner" in faith.

THE BODY OF THE LETTER (7–22)

Paul comes across in this letter as a master of understatement. Perhaps it is due to his mellowing, since he calls himself an old man now (9). He also calls himself the father of the slave, Onesimus; it is possible to discern the image of a parent of a child newly entering adulthood in the way he deals with Philemon and the young church at his house. He doesn't tell them what to do, though he says he has the right to order them (8). It's like the parents saying, "You know what we stand for and what we've taught you and now it's up to you." Some might say that Paul lays it on thick when he says, "With trust in your compliance, . . . knowing you will do even more than I say" (21).

Paul relies heavily on his relationship with Philemon as the model for the new relationship between Onesimus and Philemon. Paul describes himself as Philemon's brother (7), a guest of Philemon (22), and one to whom Philemon is indebted. He calls Philemon "beloved" and a "co-worker" (1).

These descriptions illustrate the various ways that Christians express their interdependence and ultimately their equality in Christ. Their common baptism provides a basis for Philemon and Onesimus (as well as the whole church) to create an entirely new way of relating to one another and to resolve the tensions between them. This letter recalls the baptismal formula quoted in Galatians 3,28: "There is neither Jew nor Greek, there is neither slave nor free person, there is not male and female; for you are all one in Christ Jesus."

Compared to Paul's comments on slavery in 1 Cor 7, Philemon shows a certain development in the apostle's thought. Although there is no definite appeal for the release of Onesimus from slavery, it is clear that Paul expects Philemon to treat Onesimus as a fellow Christian and not retaliate against him as against a runaway slave. Paul goes even further when he says, "Welcome him as you would me" (17).

CONCLUSION (23–35)

These greetings underscore the communal context in which this letter was written.

Questions for Discussion or Reflection

Today the church as a whole and local churches are faced with perplexing social problems. Like the church that met at Philemon's house, we too have pastoral letters from our bishops that challenge us to find Christian ways of solving these problems.

1. What are the most pressing social problems facing your local church? Which ones are facing the American church?

2. What are some of the recent pastoral letters from your bishops that address these issues?

3. How do the relationships created by baptism cause you to look at social problems in a different way?

HEBREWS READING GUIDE

At a Glance

The Prologue (1,1–4)	God's revelation in Jesus is superior to the covenant. Through his death and resurrection, Christians will enter into his inheritance.
The Son is higher than the angels (1,5–2,18)	Jesus was "lower than the angels" only temporarily so he could "taste death for everyone." Because he is human, Jesus can save humanity.
Jesus, faithful and compassionate high priest (3,1–5,10)	Obedient faith is the response demanded of the people of God on pilgrimage.
Jesus' eternal priesthood and sacrifice (5,11–10,39)	God's promise based on Jesus' resurrection is utterly reliable. God is bound by oath to Jesus' priesthood, by which the Christian hope is made secure.
Examples, discipline, disobedience (11,1–12,29)	Heroes and heroines of the past are examples for the readers to imitate. We have a "cloud of witnesses" to support us on the pilgrimage toward "the city of the living God."
Final exhortation, blessing, greetings (13,1–25)	Christians live in the world but are not defined by it or its values. They are never entirely at ease in the world or even in the church but are pilgrims struggling toward the "God of peace."

Since Hebrews is not a real letter but a sermon, it is best approached by being read out loud from beginning to end. Subtle points of Greek rhetoric—such as the alliteration in the opening verses—will escape the contemporary reader. But reading it aloud helps us catch the sermonic rhythms of Hebrews, its use of *we* and *you* (so natural to the sermon), and its alternating pattern of exposition and exhortation:

> For to which of the angels did God ever say: "You are my son; this day I have begotten you"? (1,5).
>
> Therefore, we must attend all the more to what we have heard, so that we may not be carried away (2,1).

Reading from beginning to end also pulls us into the powerful argument that is the outstanding characteristic of this early Christian writing.

More than reading aloud is required for the book's riches to be grasped, for this writing does not yield its treasures easily. The reflection on Melchizedek in Chapter 7 has influenced Catholic liturgy. Nowhere else in the New Testament do we find the same interpretation of Jesus as priest. Hebrews contributed significantly to the doctrinal development concerning Jesus' identity as God's son. But Hebrews resists easy absorption for two reasons: Hebrews is a sustained argument from beginning to end, and its symbols are hard to understand. We can clear the way to more intelligent reading by confronting each difficulty directly.

THE ARGUMENT

Some parts of the New Testament, like the Gospel parables, can be lifted from their context and still make sense. But in Hebrews, each part of the sermon plays a role in a complicated back-and-forth argument and explanation concerning Jesus and the Christian life. You cannot separate one section and understand it by itself. Hebrews uses a form of argument found both in Greek philosophy and rabbinic Judaism called "from the lesser to the greater." It says, "If something is true in a smaller matter, it is even more true in a parallel greater matter." In the past God's revelation came through angels, law, and priesthood. But now the perfect revelation has come through God's son, Jesus. The contrast is between "lesser" salvation and the present "greater" salvation.

Essential to the argument in Hebrews is its practical application. There is also a contrast between the response to God's Word by people of the past and the response demanded of the people today. Greater blessing and hope require a greater degree of obedience and loyalty. There is also a greater penalty for disobedience. The stakes are higher all around.

THE SYMBOLS

Hebrews demands of its readers a far more sophisticated grasp of Scripture than that possessed by most Christians today. Much of the argument is based on the complex modes of scriptural interpretation that were common in the first century. To us they may appear very strange because the New Testament world was not just like ours. This study edition gives us some help in providing complete scriptural references. Citations in the text of Hebrews are flagged with small letters; passages are identified at the bottom of each page. To fully appreciate the artistry of this book, we must study the citations in their original context as well as examine how these citations are turned to fit the argument of Hebrews. Here is an example:

> "Sacrifice and offering you did not desire,
> but a body you prepared for me;
> holocausts and sin offerings you took no delight in.
> Then I said, 'As is written of me in the scroll,
> Behold, I come to do your will, O God'" (10,5–7).

The note at the bottom of the page reads:

> A passage from Psalm 40, 7–9a is placed in the mouth of the Son at his incarnation. As usual, the author follows the Septuagint text. There is a notable difference in v 5 (= Ps 40,7b), where the Masoretic text reads "ears you have dug for me" ("ears open to obedience you gave me," *NAB*), but most Septuagint manuscripts have "a body you prepared for me," a reading obviously more suited to the interpretation of Heb.

Hebrews works within a philosophical tradition called Platonism, which saw a great gulf between the spiritual realm and the material world. This view is strikingly different from the world of present-day Christians. Hebrews understood spiritual things as eternal, unchanging; material things as transitory. Because of this, spiritual things are more real and better than the material. For platonic Jews and Christians, the "spiritual" and "material" realms were understood in terms of "heaven" and "earth."

This is how we are to understand the superiority of Jesus' priesthood. By his resurrection, Jesus entered heaven, where he is a "priest forever" (5,6), in contrast with the Jewish priesthood which was temporary. In the same way the "heavenly sanctuary" is superior to the physical tent of worship described in Chapters 8 and 9. The symbolism becomes dense and requires patience to disentangle. The basic point is that the human Messiah Jesus now shares God's life in heaven. His priesthood is therefore the ultimate and eternal "source of salvation" to others (5,9).

THE READERS

The ancient audience who heard this sermon had experienced the loss of property and friends (10,32–34). They could easily lose hope and seek an easier way of life than that offered by a crucified Messiah. This sermon addresses their longing for stability by offering them the hope for "a better homeland, a heavenly one" (11,16). This ancient community's experience can be translated into that of every age: All of us experience loss, desperation, alienation, and despair. The book's message to us is as sharp as it was to them: "Oh, that today you would hear his voice: 'Harden not your hearts'" (4,7). We, too, are called to pilgrimage through our troubles, looking to Jesus, who is still the "leader and perfecter of faith" (12,2).

THE PROLOGUE (1,1–4)

The opening sentence is elegantly constructed and introduces the central themes of Hebrews:

1. There is a contrast between God's partial revelation in the past and the perfect revelation through God's son. Jesus is superior to the covenant.
2. Jesus' divine status is clearly if symbolically expressed as his being the "very imprint" of God. This exalted identity given to the son is similar to that found in John and Paul (see Jn 1,1–4 and 1 Cor 8,6). The understanding of Jesus' sonship in Hebrews had a real influence on later doctrinal development.
3. The way God "spoke" in Jesus was through his death for others (the purification of sins), and through his resurrection.

Notice the image of enthronement: Jesus "takes his seat at the right hand." This alludes to Psalm 110,1, the favorite resurrection psalm of early Christians: "The LORD says to you, my lord: 'Take your throne at my right hand, while I make your enemies your footstool'" (see also 1,13). Hebrews cites this psalm again in Chapter 7. Enthronement runs throughout this sermon. Jesus is both priest and king; in fact, he is one by being the other. Finally, Jesus "inherits" a name better than that of the angels. Jesus goes ahead. If Christians follow him, they will enter into an inheritance (1,14; 6,12). The mention of angels introduces the next piece of the argument.

THE SON IS HIGHER THAN THE ANGELS (1,5–2,18)

A series of scriptural citations proves that the son is superior to angels. We might ask why angels require a ranking anyway? Today's view of the world has little room for angels. But in the world of the New Testament, especially in the writings of Judaism, angels were regarded as the most powerful intermediaries between God and humans. Their high place is witnessed in Galatians 4,8f and Colossians 2,18. What is the concern here? Jesus in his humanity did not appear so impressive as these "spiritual" beings. He was not only human, he suffered and died. Hebrews must overcome the scandal of a "lowly" Messiah.

As in other New Testament writings (for example, Gal 3,1–5), Hebrews argues "the greater" right out of the readers' own experience. The work of God's Spirit among them is itself powerful "witness" to the salvation accomplished through Jesus (2,3–4). Hebrews now drives home the exhortation. This "greater salvation" demands of the readers a greater response of vigilance (2,1–2).

From the perspective of the risen Lord, Hebrews now takes up the issue of Jesus' "lowliness." On the basis of Psalm 8, the author asserts that Jesus was "lower than the angels" only temporarily. And the reason for this was so that he could "taste death for everyone," that is, act as a priest. On the basis of a messianic reading of Isaiah 8,18–19, Hebrews next affirms God's (and the Messiah's) solidarity with humanity. Then Hebrews turns the tables. Because Jesus is one with those he represents before God—those who are "tested" and who "fear death"—he can be a compassionate and merciful priest. Hebrews defines priesthood in terms of identity rather than in terms of religious ceremony. Later doctrine would say that "what is not assumed [by God] cannot be saved." Precisely *because* Jesus is human, he can save humanity.

JESUS, FAITHFUL AND COMPASSIONATE HIGH PRIEST (3,1–5,10)

The next contrast is between Moses, "the servant of the house," and Jesus, "a son placed over his house" (3,4–6). The real contrast is between the people led by Moses and the Christian community hearing this sermon, a contrast between disobedience and obedient faith (3,7–13). Hebrews agrees with Paul's argument in 1 Corinthians 10,1–13, that what happened to Israel in the desert is a warning for the present.

Much is made of specific words such as *rest* and *today,* without regard to their original contexts. The reason for this is that Scripture speaks to every age in each of its words, and that every part of Scripture interprets every other part.

Hebrews says that the "rest" to which Moses led the people (the land) was not the "rest of God" (God's own life). Also, the people of old failed to enter *that* earthly rest because of their disobedience. Now Christians have hope for the real rest won by Jesus' resurrection. The point? They are to obey the call of God and not fall away (4,6). The message is not a trivial one. The readers are not engaged in a conquest of territory; they are called to share God's life, an awesome prospect (4,12–13). The comparison to the wandering Israelites also establishes a basic image of the church as a people on pilgrimage. Hebrews points the reader again to the leader of the pilgrimage, the "apostle and high priest of our confession" (3,1). In the description of Jesus as priest (4,14–5,9), Hebrews combines what has come to be called "high" and "low" christologies. It is his human existence that defines the path "all the children" are to follow. As priest, he is the example. Jesus is not only "faithful" (3,1–2) as all are called to be, he "learned obedience from what he suffered" (5,8). The implications of this statement become clear only later (see 12,1–11). We already

Pilgrimage of the Church

Vatican Council II, using this image of pilgrimage, suggested that the church is not simply an institution like other institutions. It is never fully "at home" in the world. The church is steadily moving toward the "heavenly city" like a pilgrim, although on this side of death the goal is never reached.

"High" and "Low" Christologies

High—Jesus is "from above," God's son in the fullest sense.
Low—Jesus is also fully human, "from below."

understand that Jesus' suffering deepened his faith, and his obedience was itself a form of suffering. Jesus *became* little by little, in his humanity, the perfect son of God and therefore the "leader" of all who follow him.

JESUS' ETERNAL PRIESTHOOD AND SACRIFICE (5,11–10,39)

The long middle section of the sermon argues for the superiority of Jesus' priesthood. An extended exhortation is found in 5,11–6,20, and Chapters 7–10 focus on the priestly identity and activity of Jesus.

Hebrews presupposes the readers' grasp of the "basic teaching about Christ" (6,1), but, in a rebuke as much as an exhortation, urges them beyond the milk fit for babes to the meat meant for the mature (compare Paul's use of this imagery in 1 Cor 3,1–3). This "mature teaching" is not a matter of abandoning Jesus. Hebrews calls such apostasy from Christ "recrucifying the son of God" (6,6). God's promise based on Jesus' resurrection is utterly reliable; Jesus is the "anchor of the soul" (6,19), to whose priesthood God is bound by oath (6,13). But how are we to understand Jesus' priesthood? This requires explanation. By it Christians are enabled to become "imitators of those who, through faith and patience, are inheriting the promises" (6,12).

The consideration of Jesus as priest is the climax of the "lesser to greater" argument. But because the Jewish symbols are foreign to us today, this section makes for some of the hardest reading in the New Testament. It is important to remember from the start that the book's premise is the Christian experience of the Spirit and the conviction that Jesus is the risen Lord, who has entered into the life of God (2,3–4). Only this makes Hebrews' reinterpretation of Scripture reasonable. The major turning points are noted on the next page.

Jesus and Melchizedek (7,1–28)

Both appearances in Scripture point toward Christ:

Gn 14,17–20: Melchizedek named a priest of God (although he was a Gentile), whom even Abraham acknowledged. A priest descended from Melchizedek would be superior to one descended from Abraham.

Psalm 110,4: Melchizedek's being without beginning or end (Scripture records neither his birth nor his death) is an anticipation of the Son of God whose priesthood is eternally valid.

In his resurrection, Jesus became priest, "by the power of a life that cannot be destroyed" (7,16). He remains "forever" (7,24). His sacrifice is "once for all" (7,27). "He lives forever to make intercession" (7,25). The Jewish priesthood descended from Abraham cannot compete.

The Old and New Covenants (8,1–13)

God's revelation in Jesus does not merely continue the former story, it raises it to a new plane. Jesus' death and resurrection mark an absolute beginning. Platonism is evident in 8,1–6: Moses' desert sanctuary is "the copy and shadow of the heavenly sanctuary" (8,5). Heaven is greater than earth. Hebrews turns this Platonism into an interpretation of history: The old covenant is a "shadow" of the new, pointing to but replaced by the work of Jesus. Hebrews exploits Jeremiah's promise of a new covenant "in the heart" to affirm that the old order has in fact passed.

The Priestly Act of Jesus (9,1 – 10,18)

The contrast is between the ancient cult and Jesus' death and resurrection. The complicated imagery is daunting. It would be helpful to read through Exodus 25–27 (the Dwelling in the Wilderness) and Leviticus 16 (ritual for the Day of Atonement). Hebrews hammers two points: First, Jewish sacrifices had to be repeated, so they were not effective; Jesus entered "real" life, so his sacrifice is eternally valid. Second, the old cult sacrifices animals. Jesus gave his own life in obedience to God. Now all can enter the sanctuary.

Exhortation to Fidelity (10,19–39)

In the light of this "greater salvation," Hebrews warns again of the consequences of apostasy (10,26–31). Despite their losses and trials, Christians are called to a still deeper loyalty (10,32–39). By mentioning endurance and faith as requisites for receiving the promise (10,36–38), Hebrews prepares for its final stirring exhortation.

EXAMPLES, DISCIPLINE, DISOBEDIENCE (11,1 – 12,29)

The sermon's long argument reaches its climax in this exhortation to faith, understood as loyalty, endurance, and hope. The long list of heroes and heroines of the past are examples for the readers to imitate. Just as the readers lost their property and were persecuted, so also had the believers who came before them. Yet they persevered in the search for a better homeland (11,14). Repeating the phrase "by faith" over and over, Hebrews summons the readers to join ranks with those on pilgrimage to God's presence. Unlike the desert generation that fell by the way through disobedience, these exemplars continued faithful, even though they themselves did not receive the full promise. It was left to Jesus, the "leader and perfecter of faith," to provide complete access to God through his death and resurrection. There is solid reason for Christians to hope while still on the journey.

The "cloud of witnesses" who support the commitment of the readers eventually became an article of the Christian creed, "the communion of saints." Those struggling for God on earth are not alone but are joined by those who have died and who now support them with their prayers. People of faith are joined in a solidarity of hope.

The suffering of the ancients is not trivialized. Before Jesus could sit on the throne of God he had to "endure the cross, despising its shame." The way Jesus humanly responded to God is the perfect example for Christian faith. Faith is always "evidence of things not seen," which means it is always a risk taken in the face of pain, more felt in the present than the promise of the future.

There is a connection between sonship and suffering. The remarks about fathers disciplining their children at first might seem superficial. But when we remember that Jesus, "although a son, learned obedience from what he suffered," we come to appreciate the profound correspondence between christology and Christian existence. What we suffer in our lives, if we accept it in faith, enables God to shape Jesus' own "sonship" in us. Following Jesus on pilgrimage means being purified painfully, for the goal is the holy God.

Ancient Greeks had the maxim *mathein pathein*, "to learn it is necessary to suffer." Hebrews reminds its readers that this is not a pleasant stroll but a terrible path toward "the city of the living God" (12,22), a pilgrimage whose completion means life eternal, but whose abandonment means "not seeing the Lord" (12,14). Nowhere in the New Testament is there a sterner reminder of life's tragic depths and terrifying heights than in this simple conclusion, "for our God is a consuming fire" (12,29).

FINAL EXHORTATION, BLESSING, GREETINGS (13,1-25)

Although the final chapter is made up mainly of practical instructions, it is closely joined to the theological argument of Chapters 1–12. Notice, for example, the plea to "imitate the faith" of leaders, the motivation of that faith being the eternal priesthood of Jesus who is "the same yesterday, today, and forever" (13,7–8).

The mix of advice about hospitality, marriage, and possessions, with the command to "go to Jesus outside the camp . . . for we have here no lasting city but seek the one that is to come" is typical of this sermon and of early Christianity's understanding of existence generally:

- Christians live in the world like other people and participate in its structures. But they are not defined by this world or its values, even its religious values (13,9–11).

- No institutional cult or sacrificial priesthood is made lawful by this severe writing; everything necessary has been accomplished already by Jesus.
- Christians are defined not by their liturgy but by their following the one who suffered "outside the gate, to consecrate the people by his own blood" (13,12).
- Christians are never entirely at ease in this world or even in the church. They are pilgrims, struggling toward the "God of peace" into whose care the final blessing (13,20–21) entrusts the readers of this profound and powerful sermon.

Questions for Discussion or Reflection

1. Hebrews uses the image of pilgrimage for the church. Pilgrims need the sort of attentiveness, patience, obedience, and endurance demanded by this sermon. Above all they need hope (see 6,9f). They can move lightly through the world only if convinced that their destination is truly "greater" than their present home.
   a. What is the difference between "being in the world but not of the world" and "enduring this life with an eye on heaven"?
   b. The Vatican II Document, *The Church in the Modern World,* endorses Christian life in the world. Is this in contradiction with the message of Hebrews? Explain.
   c. How does the message of Hebrews challenge the values and attitudes shaped by the media in modern culture?
2. The image of pilgrimage has been used by the mystics to describe the personal journey of the soul toward union with God in prayer. Both individual and collective applications of this image are appropriate for people who consider their true homeland to be elsewhere.
   a. If Jesus "learned obedience from what he suffered," how does suffering in faith open us to God's action of shaping Jesus' own sonship in us?
   b. How does this understanding of "obedience" differ from the popular notion of "doing what one is told"?
   c. In that "cloud of witnesses" spoken of in Hebrews, there are important people who pray for you and support you on your pilgrimage to the "city of the living God." Name some of them.
3. The pilgrimage to God in prayer has an essential component, the "dark night" of the soul which is the experience of the absence of God.
   a. What could possibly be the purpose of this purifying process? Do only saints experience this?
   b. Can such an experience be misinterpreted as a punishment for some wrongdoing? How would you encourage someone who is journeying through the dark night? What passages from Hebrews might you pray with that person?
   c. Hebrews reminds us that "our God is a consuming fire" (12,29). What do you think this means?
   d. Why is Hebrews read in the liturgy of Holy Week and throughout the Easter season? What connections can be made with our baptismal vows?

The Catholic Letters and the Book of Revelation

JAMES READING GUIDE

At a Glance

The two measures (1,1–27)	The values of the world are based on the perception of a system where God has no part. Human competition reigns. One person's gain is another person's loss.
Discrimination and the law of love (2,1–13)	"Faith in our . . . Lord Jesus Christ" (2,1) is incompatible with any form of discrimination within the Christian community.
Active faith (2,14–26)	Faith without works is dead.
The power of the tongue (3,1–12)	As action should follow conviction, so should speech conform to faith.
Friendship with God or the world (3,13–4,10)	Friendship with the world and friendship with God are opposing ways of life. The double-minded are called to conversion.
Against arrogance (4,11–5,6)	Three forms of arrogance according to the measure of the world.
Patience, plain speech, prayer (5,7–20)	The proper uses of speech in the church. The anointing for a sick member of the community.

JAMES AS MORAL EXHORTATION

Greek moral exhortation (*paraenesis*) was concerned with traditional values rather than with theory. It could take the form of short maxims or essays. *Paraenesis* also attaches its moral maxims to the imitation of models. In James, the figures of Abraham, Rahab, Job, and Elijah provide examples from Scripture of the practical virtues James encourages. But James is more than a moral treatise. It is a religious writing using symbols of Scripture. In form, James resembles most the Wisdom literature (3,13–18); the prophetic tradition is seen when he censures rich oppressors in 5,1–6; and James also appropriates the Law aspect of the Scripture. The Ten Commandments and the Law of Love alike are binding for the Christian. They are to be understood in light of the teachings of Jesus to which James alludes throughout the letter (for example 1,12; 2,5; 3,12; 5,12).

James advocates living faith and practical love. His concern is behavior. Like other moralists of his age, he is impatient with fine words that have no action. Above all, faith without practice in love is a charade.

James's first target is the Christian who is "double-minded." This person wants to live by two standards at once: that of God and that of the world. James demands a choice, not only in speech but also in the use of possessions and the practice of fairness within the community.

Readers may be surprised to find Jesus mentioned only twice (1,1; 2,1), with no reference at all to the messianic message of salvation through Jesus' death and resurrection. James's theology centers attention on God rather than on Christ.

THE TWO MEASURES (1,1–27)

The literary arrangement most resembles the Book of Proverbs. There is little connection between verses, but there is a strong correspondence between each verse and life experience. On the other hand, this is not just a collection of wise sayings. There are connections throughout the letter.

- Chapter 1 provides an index to Chapters 2 and 5.
- Theme of enduring trials (1,2–4.12–15) developed in 5,7–11.
- Opposition between rich and poor (1,9–11) recurs in 4,13—5,6.
- Control of the tongue (1,19–21) is expanded in 3,1–12.
- Carrying out words in speech (1,22–26) is enlarged by 2,14–26.
- The theme of true wisdom (1,5–8.16–18) is argued by 3,13—4,10.
- The prayer of faith (1,6–7) is amplified by 5,12–18.

The short sayings introduce the basic structural pattern throughout James: the contrast between the measure of the world and the measure of God. The measure of the world is expressed by envy: "Desire conceives and brings forth sin, and when sin reaches maturity it gives birth to death" (1,15). The values of the world are self-deceptive (1,16.27), are expressed in wrathful manner (1,19) and every sort of excess (1,2), especially the pursuit of illusory wealth (1,11). These values are based on a closed system in which God has no part. Therefore all human beings are in competition: One person's gain is another's loss.

The measure of faith is the opposite. All creation—life itself—is a gift: "All good giving and every perfect gift is from above, coming down from the Father of lights" (1,17). Because God implanted his word in the human heart, people are able to live in the way God does, "generously and ungrudgingly" (1,5). In Greek, these terms suggest the opposite of envy, which always grasps for more.

The greeting "to the twelve tribes in the dispersion" can be understood as referring to the condition of Christians "in the world but not of the world." Christians are not hostile to the world but neither are they defined by it. James's whole effort is to persuade those "of two minds" (1,8) to live by God's measure, which is the perfect "wisdom from above" (see 3,15).

DISCRIMINATION AND THE LAW OF LOVE (2,1–13)

The first essay reveals a voice like that of Paul in Galatians. James uses the same oral, dialogical style known as the *diatribe.* Vivid and lively, it is filled with rhetorical questions, exclamations, and abrupt transitions. The effect is a direct challenge to the reader—today as well as then. The challenge is heard even more clearly when the text is read aloud.

"Faith in our . . . Lord Jesus Christ" (2,1) is incompatible with any form of discrimination within the community. James sketches a lively scene that probably reflects a general situation rather than a local incident. In the background is the injunction of Leviticus 19,15, forbidding partiality in judgment.

The "Law of Love" was already stated by Jesus as the summation of Scripture. James calls the standard regulating relations in the community the "royal" law. James spells out this commandment by alluding to the Ten Commandments (2,11) and also to the specific commandments found in the original context of Leviticus 19 that accompany the original exhortation, "love your neighbor as yourself." James says that breaking any commandment means breaking the whole law, because sin is not against a law but a lawgiver. Faith in the one God excludes picking and choosing between commandments, just as it excludes picking and choosing between fellow Christians.

ACTIVE FAITH (2,14–26)

This section is often misunderstood because when James speaks of "faith" and "works," it is sometimes suggested that he is responding to Paul's teaching. In fact, James's perspective is entirely different. James isn't speaking of the commandments of the law but of active faith. He is a moralist and is concerned about the way speech is converted into action. He points to the examples of Abraham and Rahab whose faith expressed itself in action. Abraham was willing to sacrifice his son. Rahab showed hospitality to God's scouts. Pious talk does not feed the hungry nor clothe the needy. Such faith is as "dead" as a corpse; such religion is fraudulent.

We discover that James's exhortation is not based on what is specifically *Christian* but on faith in the one God. "Faith in Christ" and the teachings of Jesus do not oppose but refine the Torah. For that reason, James's teaching contains the possibility of genuine social ethics that can be extended to the world. If there is no partiality in the community based on the laws of God, then forms of discrimination in the wider world can be combatted on the same basis. James warns us that this can cut both ways. If the Christian community does not live up to its own calling, and is unjust, then it bears no witness to the world and is itself subject to condemnation (2,5–7).

THE POWER OF THE TONGUE (3,1–12)

James's concern now is for proper use of speech (1,19.26). Preoccupation with speech is typical of ancient moralists. That reservation in speech was a sign of wisdom was proverbial (see for example, Prv 10,19; 11,12). It was well known that "control of the tongue" is extremely difficult to achieve. James considers control of speech to be a mark of perfection (3,2).

Using the conventional imagery of Greek philosophy, James illustrates the disproportionate power of the tongue. Such a small organ is able to produce great harm. By comparing the tongue to a horse's bit or a ship's rudder, James shows how something so small can direct a large body. Such a little organ needs to be controlled by someone with a sense of direction. Uncontrolled speech is like a flame "setting the entire course of our lives on fire" (3,6).

"No human being can tame the tongue. It is a restless evil, full of deadly poison" (3,8). Sadly, the story of human discourse from the Garden of Eden to the latest garden party only confirms James's harsh judgment. No wonder the ancients valued guarded speech: better no speech than destructive speech.

The Value of Silence The dangers inherent in speech have helped to secure the value given to silence in the monastic/contemplative tradition both of the East and the West. Silence is the necessary precondition to "welcome the word that . . . is able to save your souls" (1,21).

The theological implications of speech are central in James's exhortation:

- James contrasts the speech that "blesses God" with that which curses human beings who are made in God's image (3,9–12).
- He combats the "two-minded" person who thinks that it is possible to have a relationship with God that disregards human obligations.
- James insists that religious language and practical human care must go together. No more than the same source can yield two kinds of water should a Christian speak with two tongues. Actions must follow convictions and speech conform to faith.

The warning is directed most of all at those who desire to be teachers in the faith community (3,1). If care is required for all speech, it is even more necessary for those who shape the minds of others according to the measure of God and not of the world.

FRIENDSHIP WITH GOD OR THE WORLD (3,13–4,10)

The verses from Chapter 3,13 to 4,10 form a single essay that contains the central framework for understanding James as a whole. It is a call to conversion in which James exhorts his readers to repentance. There is a contrast between what comes "from above" (true wisdom, God's gift), and that which originates "from below" (false wisdom, human arrogance). Readers are told to "humble" themselves so that God can "exalt" them (4,10). That "from below" James calls "the world." It treats life as though God has no claim; human success is measured by human accomplishment and acquisition. God's measure says that everything is a gift from "the Father of lights" (1,17), and that arrogance is empty pretense. As always, James has as his target the "two-minded" person who wants to live by both measures at once.

Envy Envy, says James, is the measure of the world. Notice how often the word *jealousy* occurs. God's spirit has nothing to do with envy. Envy comes from the "wisdom from below" and is associated with all the vices commonly attributed to it in Greek moral discourse, especially social unrest, murder, and war.

Envy is singled out because its underlying assumption is that your gain is my loss. That is the opposite of the spirit of community, where all gain by anyone's growth and all rejoice in anyone's good fortune. Envy causes me sorrow when another has something that I lack. And when life is measured simply in terms of what I possess—"I am what I have"—then for another to have and for me to lack is intolerable. The step is short between coveting and conflict, war and murder—not only between individuals but between nations.

At the climax of the indictment (4,4), James accuses his readers of being "adulterers," because they have broken covenant with God and with their fellow humans. The covenant is about loyalty and love. Using the language of Greek philosophy, James contrasts "friendship with the world" and "friendship with God" as opposing ways of life. Far from condemning the world as the place of human activity and God's creation, James characterizes "the world" as a place that leaves God's claim aside.

To this closed system, James now opposes the measure of faith: "God is the source of every good and perfect gift" (1,17). God "gives more grace to the humble" even as God resists the arrogant. God is not envious of humans but gives to all generously and without grudging. Humans who submit to God are lifted up by God. Their tears will rapidly turn to joy because when humans draw near to God, God also draws near to them (4,8).

AGAINST ARROGANCE (4,11 – 5,6)

James now turns to three forms of arrogance that exemplify life according to the measure of the world:

1. The practice of slander against one's neighbor (4,11–12)	Such critical speech involves a condemnation of the other and an implied assertion of one's superiority: "I am in a position to judge." Such judgment breaks the law of God. The lawgiver is also a judge. God alone is capable of saving and destroying life.
2. The practice of making big business plans without considering the fragile nature of their own existence (4,13–17)	Their speech gives them away; they assume control over the present and the future. "You are boasting in your arrogance," says James. "All such boasting is evil" (4,16). "If the Lord wills" is more than pious talk by those who refer all of life and life's projects to the one who gives and can alone sustain life.
3. The practice of the rich who withhold wages from their laborers (5,4–5)	They sin because they "know the right thing to do but do not do it" (4,17). They know because the scriptural context for the law of love in Leviticus 19,18 states plainly, "You shall not withhold overnight the wages of your day laborer" (Lv 19,13).

PATIENCE, PLAIN SPEECH, PRAYER (5,7–20)

Speech is again the underlying theme, but this time with reference to the proper use of speech in the church. The attack on oppressors (5,1–6) leads naturally to the condition of those who suffer persecution from outsiders. James recommends patience and extends the example of Job (5,11). Patience is possible for them as it is for a farmer, because the fruitful outcome of their loyalty is certain: "The coming of the Lord is at hand." In the meantime, nothing would be more natural than for the afflicted to turn on each other in resentment and hurt. James tells them, "Do not complain about one another that you may not be judged" (see Lv 19,17–18).

James repeats the commandment of Jesus (see Mt 5,33–37) that speech should be simple and straightforward, without need of oaths. And in his last exhortation, James encourages the sort of mutual correction that can build up the identity of the church (5,20).

Because the church is constituted by the word of truth (1,18), it should above all express the truth in its communal life of prayer. James specifies the sorts of prayer that are appropriate to the community's various circumstances (5,13–14) and then elaborates the prayer with anointing of a sick member. James's last example from the Torah is the prophet Elijah, whose prayer demonstrates the power of faith for those who live by God's measure (5,17–18; cf. 1,6–8). These final, down-to-earth exhortations summarize beautifully the character of James, who from beginning to end finds wisdom in practical faith and active love.

Anointing This ritual is the basis for the sacrament of anointing for the sick and has its roots in the ministry of Jesus (see 5,15).

Questions for Discussion or Reflection

1. This letter of James is addressed to Christians who are double-minded. Could this letter be addressed to modern-day Catholics? What would James point out to us as a double standard?
2. The Western world is built on the ethic of competition and economic advancement. One person or nation's gain is another's loss. Give examples from this past week's TV news that show how important being Number One is for us.
3. James assigns the cause of war to envy (4,1–3). It is remarkable that this passage which alone in the New Testament analyzes the causes of human conflict should play so small a role in moral discussions of war and peace. Why is envy such a driving force for conflict among nations, family members, ethnic groups, etc?
4. "Faith in our . . . Lord Jesus Christ" is incompatible with any form of discrimination within the community, says James. Who are the members of our community we judge should be kept on the fringes? Does this letter of James or even the teachings of Jesus warrant this exclusion?
5. Just as faith excludes our being able to pick and choose between commandments, it also forbids our picking and choosing between fellow Christians. In what way is this a profound challenge for the church today?
6. Read James's passage on control of the tongue (3,1–12). Recall experiences in your life or the life of others you know that confirm this strong message.
7. What is silence? Name different kinds of silence. Do you value it or find it oppressive? Why is silence a precondition to welcome the word of God?
8. James uses the word *adulterers* for those who have broken covenant with God and their fellow human beings. Is this word too strong to describe such persons? Explain the reason for your answer.
9. If you are alone or with a group, allow a wordless prayer to rise from the center of your being. Try to still your tongue and your thoughts, and remain simply in the presence of God for a few minutes. Then let the first word uttered by your tongue be the name of Jesus.

1 PETER READING GUIDE

At a Glance

The greeting (1,1–2)	Identifies the author and the addressees.
The gift and call of God (1,3–21)	Peter asserts the reality of God's gift and sketches the demands it places on those who receive it.
A gospel people (1,22 – 2,10)	For Christians, the basis of their new existence is the message of a crucified Messiah who was raised to new life. By patterning their behavior on his, they are being built into a glorious people.
Life within the world's structures (2,11 – 3,7)	Keeping their distance from the values of this world, Christians must live within the structures of the world.
Witness in a hostile world (3,8 – 4,6)	Christians suffered because they no longer followed the ways of their neighbors. They are to remain in the world's structures and engage outsiders in dialogue.
Community attitudes (4,7 – 5,14)	Be sober . . . be watchful. The time for serious decision is *now.* Those who suffer will share in Christ's glory.

A LETTER TO GENTILE CHRISTIANS

First Peter bears all the marks of a real letter. It was written to Christians scattered throughout the provinces of Asia Minor. Although 1 Peter may be one of the New Testament's most lively, joy-filled books, it is given far less attention than it deserves. This is partly due to the opinion of many contemporary scholars that this letter was not written by Peter but was the product of the second generation rather than the earliest Christians. There are, however, excellent reasons for considering Peter the disciple to have been the author of 1 Peter. And we know that the authority of New Testament writings does not derive from their authorship but from their inclusion in the canon. It is better to pay attention to the situation of Peter's first readers and how the message given to them retains enduring value for any age.

THE SITUATION OF THE READERS

Since the letter is addressed to Christians scattered over a wide geographical area, we do not expect detailed treatment of local problems. If we read between the lines, we will be able to learn something about Peter's readers and the characteristics they shared.

Who Were They?

1. They seem to have been recently converted. Peter reminds them of their former life but also of their initiation into the messianic community through baptism.
2. Their conversion appears to have been directly from paganism rather than from Judaism.

3. As Gentiles, they continued to live among the pagan symbols and social structures of the empire and felt pulled between allegiance to their new calling and to the culture of their world.
4. They were converts who were experiencing suffering. Some have thought this was a state-sponsored persecution of the Christian community, but Peter's positive view of the state (2,12–17) does not fit that explanation. It is more likely that Peter's readers were experiencing a sort of verbal abuse and social ostracism that Christians experienced from the beginning. This suffering was no less serious. Martyrdom is painful but swift. Corrosion of confidence is slower but terribly effective.

WHAT IS CHRISTIAN APOLOGETIC?

First Peter can best be understood as a form of apologetic literature. This is a form of writing that originated among the diaspora Jews and was taken over by the Christians. Outwardly it explains one's distinctive beliefs to the wider world in terms that outsiders can understand. Indirectly it supports community identity. First Peter is positive and open to the dominant culture. Christians are not to flee from the world but to be good citizens within the social structures. They are to be ready to demonstrate by their behavior and their speech that they pose no threat to others.

At the same time Peter works to build up the identity of the community.

1. He reminds his readers that they are called to holiness which demands a standard of behavior higher than that of their neighbors.
2. He reminds them of the fundamental transformation they have undergone in their baptism.
3. He assures them that although they are "strangers" in the world, they are part of the "household of God."

Peter brings to these new Gentile believers all the scriptural titles and symbols used of Israel to give them a sense of continuity with God's people, even though once they were "no people." In this letter we observe a thoroughly Gentile Christianity regarding itself as the "New Israel," taking up a place in the diaspora not against the world but as a witness to the world.

THE GREETING (1,1–2)

The greeting of this letter being sent to the various communities establishes more than simple identification of author and addressees. There is no need to elaborate on "Peter, Apostle of Jesus Christ," since Peter's authority is unquestioned. But the "diaspora" of Asia Minor has religious as well as geographical connotations. There is a theme also found in James and Hebrews and in Christian literature of the second century: Christians are in exile from their true homeland in heaven so long as they are on earth. They are "sojourners" precisely because they have been chosen by God and have an identity distinct from their neighbors. The greeting reminds the readers of the complexity of their experience of God: The Father has chosen them; the Son saved them by his obedient sacrifice; and the Spirit has sanctified them.

THE GIFT AND CALL OF GOD IN BAPTISM (1,3–2,10)

The opening prayer (1,3–9) is based on the blessing formula of Jewish worship: God is blessed for God's gifts to humans. Peter gives thanks for the new life of salvation given them through the resurrection of Jesus. Of course they must wait for their inheritance which is being kept for them in heaven. In the meantime they must experience the trials and sufferings of this life of faith (1,6–7). Peter places his readers between the "already" of God's grace and the "not yet" of salvation fully achieved (1,9), so typical of New Testament writings.

Despite the fact that his readers have converted from paganism, Peter inserts them into the story of Israel. "Inheritance in heaven" is contrasted with the "inheritance of the land" which was the hope of Israel. The prophets, Peter says, did not speak of their own times but spoke of the "sufferings destined for Christ and the glories to follow them" (1,11). This striking statement contains three aspects that deserve notice:

1. The superiority of the Christians' present experience; as in Hebrews, the claims of the earlier covenant are made secondary. What Christians have received in the gospel transcends even what the angels can know.
2. The Scripture is taken over completely as messianic prophecy. Everything points to Jesus.
3. As in Luke, John, and Acts, the pattern of the Messiah is spelled out in terms of "suffering, then glory." Peter's readers must follow after this same pattern.

Peter now sketches the demands this gift places on those who receive it. Their lives are to be directed by a radical obedience to the giver of this gift. They must not act as they formerly did, but are to become "different." They are to shape themselves after the one who called them with the gift of the "precious blood of Christ" (1,19). Peter again calls his readers "sojourners" (1,17). As the Jews of the diaspora were different from the pagans, so these Christians must be "different" (holy) from the world as they wait for the fulfillment of their salvation (see 1,9).

To strengthen their special identity, Peter reminds his readers of the basis of their new life in "the living and abiding word of God" (1,23), by which he means the gospel (1,25). By obedient acceptance of the message of a crucified Messiah who was raised to new life, they were given "new birth" (1,23). But immediately Peter tells them that the "spiritual milk" they now enjoy is appropriate for new converts who have just "tasted and seen that the Lord is good" (see 1 Cor 3,1–3; Heb 6,13). But now they are to mature in Christ by patterning their lives according to a new standard of moral behavior.

Peter is concerned with more than the transformation of individuals; he reminds them of their communal identity as God's house and people. The scriptural cross references to 1 Peter 1–2 (see *NAB* notes) provide an illustration of Peter's interweaving of scriptural passages and allusions in an effort to strengthen the community's identity. You will notice that the choice of passages is strikingly similar to that in Romans 9,25–33. It is less likely that Peter used Romans than that Peter and Paul shared common traditions of scriptural interpretation developed from the first days of the church.

What a paradox! The stone that God intended to be the basis for God's people Israel was rejected by them; yet the rejected one has become the basis for a new people, "a spiritual house" made up of living persons (2,4). It is clear that this refers to the crucified Jesus who was a scandal (a stone of stumbling) to his fellow Jews, who expected a glorious Messiah (see 1 Cor 1,18–23).

What About the Historical Jewish People?

First Peter does not have them in mind. He assigns the symbols of Torah for the use of Gentile-Christian addressees. Readers today cannot expect to find an answer in this text concerning the relations between Christians and Jews, for 1 Peter does not address this.

As Peter strings together the most precious memories of Israel as God's people in Torah (the teaching of the first five books of the Bible: Genesis, Exodus, Leviticus, Numbers, and Deuteronomy), he now applies them to these Gentiles, "once no people but now God's people." In the messianic community, these aliens have a home (see Eph 2,19–22).

THE CHRISTIAN IN A HOSTILE WORLD (2,11–4,11)

Christians are to keep their distance from the values of this world as "aliens and sojourners" (2,11). At the same time they have to live within the social structures of this world. Peter is convinced that if they are good citizens, they will turn away slander and persecution. The best witness they give is the practice of "good works" (2,12).

Greek philosophy had elaborated the mutual duties of those who live in a stratified society. Peter uses the traditional form of "household ethics" to sketch the Christians' social obligations. Over the empire as a whole, the emperor was considered the head of the household. In families, husbands ruled wives, parents ruled children, masters ruled slaves. This was simply the way it was. Similarly, Paul (see Col 3,18–4,1) thought that the Christian message did not require dismantling society's structures.

What is Peter Getting At?

The exhortation to wives (3,1–6) is much more extensive than that to husbands (3,7). Traditional Jewish and Greek themes, which stress the value of internal virtue over external ornamentation, are used to support the command to be submissive. Women are to be subordinate, we notice, not to all men, but to their husbands (3,5). In return, men are to regard women as fully equal in their relationship before the Lord. They are "joint heirs of the gift of life" (3,7).

In these instructions, we do not find an inspired blueprint given by God for the ideal social order or Christian family structure. What we find is the best available moral teaching applied to the real world of that age. Just as social structures of the past cannot be transferred to the present, neither can the relationships appropriate to those ancient structures be directly imitated today. But for families, then and now, good order, mutual respect, obedience, and authority are very much required. The style of those structures today is left to our human creativity.

If Christians were being harassed by the state at this time, Peter would not have portrayed the empire and its agents in such positive terms. Yet, even here, relationship with God is primary. If social obligations conflict with this primary relationship, they must give way to it: "Be free, yet without using freedom as a pretext for evil, but as slaves of God" (2,16). Obedience to God comes before all; and before God, all are slaves.

In the next section we would expect Peter to instruct both masters and slaves. Perhaps the absence of masters says something about the Christians' social status. Peter thinks of all Christians as slaves. He reminds the Christian community of the example Jesus gave as a pattern for all those who suffer unjustly. Not only did Jesus win salvation for others by his death on the cross, but in his very manner of suffering he provided the model for how Christians were to act.

Even though the Christians of Asia Minor were not subjected to persecution, torture, and death, their suffering was no less significant. Being ostracized in society works a slow poison into a community's sense of identity. They were being "insulted" (3,9), maligned and defamed (3,16), and slandered (4,4) because they no longer followed the ways of their neighbors. Becoming different (holy) causes resentment.

Peter advises Christians not to withdraw from the world but to remain there to engage outsiders in dialogue. "Give an explanation to anyone who asks you for a reason for your hope" (3,15). Christians are to follow the command of Jesus to return a blessing for a curse (see Mt 5,44).

In order to act this way with outsiders, they must treat members of the Christian community with the same qualities of sympathy and love. They are to "sanctify Christ as Lord" (3,15), which will free them from fear of outsiders (3,14). How will they do this?

1. They are to remember how Jesus "suffered for sins once" but was also raised from the dead in power.
2. Using the traditions of apocalyptic literature, Peter symbolically expresses the conviction that the resurrection was an event that not only concerned the person of Jesus but had cosmic extension.
3. "In the spirit" Jesus went to the spirits in prison to preach the good news (3,19–22). This dramatic statement is the basis for the article of the creed that says Jesus "descended into hell." God's power to save reaches everywhere, even the farthest reaches of human sin and alienation.

ADVICE TO THE PERSECUTED (4,12 – 5,11)

The time to make a decision is *now!* "The end of all things is at hand" (4,7). The time of judgment is soon (4,17). Therefore Christian life demands "resisting the devil" who through suffering such as Peter's readers are experiencing, seeks to "devour" them (5,8f). This calls for a "serious, sober" attitude and one that is always "vigilant" (4,7; 5,8). Those who experience affliction are to regard their sufferings as a share in Christ's own (4,13–14), knowing that they will also share in his glory (4,13; 5,10).

When exhorting community leaders (presbyters or elders), Peter forbids lording it over the flock (5,3). Leaders are to provide a positive example like Jesus the "shepherd and guardian of your souls" (2,25). Peter promises that when the chief Shepherd is revealed, these shepherds will receive the unfading crown of glory (5,4).

CONCLUSION (5,12–14)

First Peter ends as it began, with a description of the purpose of the letter: Hold fast to God's grace and "remain firm in it." The author says that the letter was written by "Silvanus whom I consider a faithful brother" (5,12). Silvanus could have been Peter's secretary. Such secretaries often helped the author express their thoughts in writing. Or Silvanus could have been the messenger who delivered the letter. Peter writes from "Babylon," the code name among early Christians for Rome. He sends greetings from this church at the heart of the Roman world to the small Christian communities at the edge of the empire. They are to "greet one another with a loving kiss" (5,14). This was an accepted greeting of friendship in the Greek culture but for the baptized, this joyous salutation further ritualized their identity in Christ.

The New Testament contains no writing more positive in its evaluation of the world yet more compelling in its call to holiness than 1 Peter. Martin Luther correctly noted that it is one of the New Testament writings which truly "show thee Christ."

Questions for Discussion or Reflection

1. Peter reminds the Christian community that they are God's chosen people. Baptism has brought about a fundamental transformation in them. They are not to bask in their specialness but to be sent into mission. What does this mean for Catholics today? What does "sent" mean? How are we "sent"?

2. Peter wrote this letter to urge Christians to *live* their faith. If he were writing today, what would he be asking Catholics to do?

3. In this letter, Peter encourages civil obligations. Today, as in his day, families and society at large require good order. Read 1 Peter 2,13. Cite examples of breakdown in modern society where this is lacking. What are some creative ways of rebuilding the human spirit that will effect the quality of life for families, civil institutions, and international relationships?

4. As in the Gospel of Luke and the Acts of the Apostles, the message is "suffering, then glory." This rubs against the grain of modern culture. Discuss the challenge Peter holds out to us in 3,9; 3,14; 3,18–22; 4,4; and 4,12–19.

5. Sometimes it is easier to love "outsiders" than those within the "household of the faith." What are ways we Catholics take one another for granted or fail to show appreciation? What one concrete action can you take this week to show your care, concern, and gratitude toward someone who shares your faith in Christ?

6. Newborns (the newly baptized) need "spiritual milk." But now you are mature in Christ. Read 1 Pt 2,1–3; 1 Cor 3,1–3; and Heb 6,13. Why is it easier to hold on to the spiritual sweetness of childhood faith than to accept the "solid food" mature baptismal commitment requires? Describe how your image of God, of Christ, of the church and of Scripture has changed since your childhood. Discuss the difficulty of letting go of secure religious images. Why do you think we are called to do this?

2 PETER READING GUIDE

At a Glance

Chapter 1	Establishes the authority of the writer and of the Scripture which will be used as a source of proof.
Chapter 2	Attacks the opponents' "destructive teachings" on the basis of Scripture.
Chapter 3	Presents the proper understanding of the tradition concerning God's judgment.

The *New American Bible* introduction to 2 Peter notes, "Among modern scholars there is a wide agreement that 2 Peter is a pseudonymous work. It gives the impression of being more remote in time from the apostolic period than 1 Peter. Many think it is the latest work in the New Testament and assign it to the first or even second quarter of the second century."

Pseudonymous A *pseudonymous* work is one written by a later author who attributed it to an important person according to the literary convention popular at the time.

An appreciative understanding of 2 Peter demands more than normal effort. Hard work is necessary to uncover the situation addressed by the letter. At first reading, 2 Peter seems to be a loose collection of observations within which talk about Jesus' second coming (the *parousia*) seems to play a particularly significant part. Some scholars thought that the "delay of the *parousia*" was the crisis that stimulated composition of this letter. But if we look closer, we will notice that a deeper and more persistent problem is being debated by "Peter" and his opponents: the reality of God and God's relationship to the world. The debate is between living faith and practical atheism. Because this debate is still in progress today, 2 Peter is worth hearing.

THE COMMON TRADITION (1,1–21)

The first section of the letter establishes the authority of the writer and of the shared tradition (1,1) which he represents. Extraordinary emphasis is put on the person of Peter and on the fact that he will soon die (1,13–14). These touches recall the literary style popular in early Christianity called the "farewell discourse," in which before his death a figure from the past is depicted as predicting catastrophes to come and urges his followers to be faithful. We notice in this case a strong emphasis on *memory* (1,9.12.13.15). The opponents "forget the proper knowledge" and Peter seeks to "remind" his readers of it. This emphasis on memory makes this letter resemble the form of moral exhortation called *paraenesis.*

The connection to *paraenesis* is obvious in 2 Peter 1,5–8. Here the author lists the sort of qualities that should follow upon the readers' faith. It isn't enough simply to know about the faith; a whole way of life is demanded. Those who forget this lead lives that are "idle and

Paraenesis Paraenesis spelled out moral obligations in the form of maxims or traditional sayings.

unfruitful" (1,8f). In Chapter 2, the author will show that the opponents' "destructive heresies" lead to destructive behavior, which brings down God's judgment.

In a passage that clearly corresponds to the synoptic Gospels' story of Jesus' transfiguration (see Mt 17,1–8), he affirms the Christian experience of God. The tradition out of which Peter writes is not based on speculation ("cleverly devised myths"), but on a power experienced personally by him and others; "we" saw and heard on the mountain (1,16–18)! The point is simply that the community's tradition is based not in fancy but in *fact.* This experience was of "the power and coming" of the Lord Jesus Christ. As we will learn, the promise concerning Jesus' return is the issue of contention in Chapter 3. Peter claims that the expectation of his return is based on the *reality* of his already having come.

The disciples' experience of Jesus also grounds the "prophetic message" about Jesus' return for judgment. Peter places this prophecy of Jesus (see Mt 24,29–31) among the prophecies of Scripture. Scriptural prophecies are not to be interpreted individually, but by a decision of the community, guided by the same Spirit who gave utterance in the first place.

CONDEMNATION OF FALSE TEACHERS (2,1–22)

Chapter 2 begins with Peter's attack on "false teachers" as those in line with "false prophets." These opponents are denying God's power to judge, which brings judgment on themselves. But their teaching has proven successful, convincing many (2,2); Peter's response must be vigorous and pointed.

As we have already seen, Peter was concerned with the *moral* consequences of faith. The ancient world knew something that we often ignore today, that people act on their ideas, and bad ideas lead to bad behavior. Peter pays particular attention to the *way of life* generated by the doctrines taught by these "false prophets." He attacks the "licentious ways" of the opponents (2,2), their "greed" and "lies" (2,3). They are people of "depraved desires" (2,10); they are "irrational" (2,12) and "adulterous" (2,14). Now the catalogue of vices takes a sharp turn: "They promise freedom, though they themselves are slaves of corruption, for a person is slave of whatever overcomes him" (2,19).

What sort of "freedom" did the opponents promise? Apparently, it was freedom from the fear of punishment. If God does not intervene in human affairs to punish the wicked and reward the good, then (they said) it makes sense to live immorally, looking out only for oneself, indulging in hateful behavior.

Peter answers this claim by reminding them that they are slaves to whatever appetite dominates them and controls their behavior. These Christians who once knew righteousness have turned back to a novel version of an old atheism: "The fool says in his heart, 'There is no God'" (Ps 14,1).

The second part of Peter's rebuttal is based on the conviction that the Bible stories relate the facts of history. When Scripture says that God *did* punish and reward, that is proof of God's ability to do so still. Peter's recitation of stories from Scripture asserts the fact that God does act in human history.

THE COMING OF THE LORD (3,1–18)

The specific nature of the debate emerges for the first time in this final section. A matter of principle is at stake. Jesus clearly had not yet returned to judge the world as Christians had been expecting. Scoffers challenged the very *promise* of his coming (3,4).

Those whose experience is different are not likely to be convinced. Peter appeals not to

ESSAY

Where Is Your God?

What opposition were the early Christians facing? Their neighbors in society ridiculed them for their faith in God's care for the world. The position held by the ancient skeptics such as the Epicureans and (among the Jews) Sadducees was a denial of divine providence. If there was a god, they said, he did not meddle with the world, which was a closed system of natural forces and human desires. God was not a factor to be considered, never had been, never would be. The failure of Jesus to return was only one more piece of evidence that all such prophecies were empty.

Though this debate can obviously never be resolved—it has continued down to the present day—the side of those who believe in God is still strongly represented. Ultimately, believers can point to their own experience—the experience of prayer, of worship, of service—and identify that as one basis of their faith. Another basis is community—the sense of a fellowship of believers. A third basis is tradition—really a way of being in community with those who precede us. The debate will continue, but believers will also continue to have reason to maintain their position.

In this argument, both sides base their position on a claim of *experience,* which then interprets reality as a whole:

The Skeptics	Peter
Experience shows no evidence for God's activity: "Nothing has changed."	Scripture proves that God *does* intervene (see all of Chapter 2). Peter and his companions experienced such an intervention in the transfiguration of Jesus! This is the significance of 1,16–19. Their tradition is based on the prophets, on the Lord Jesus, and on the apostles.
How can you believe that God intervenes if he is so apparently absent?	God's time cannot be measured by human time: There is an infinite distance between God and humans (3,7). The apparent delay is to bring people to repentance (3,8–9).

the opponents but to those attracted to the Christian position. He reaffirms that Jesus *will* come "like a thief in the night" (see Mt 24,43; 1 Thes 5,2; Rv 3,3), and that his coming will inaugurate "new heavens and a new earth in which righteousness dwells" (2 Pt 3,13; see Rv 21,1). Throughout his letter, Peter has been most keenly concerned with the behavior of his readers. He reasserts "what sort of persons they are to be" during the time of waiting (3,11). When all the debates are over, it is the truth of human existence that gives doctrine its authenticity. Second Peter concludes with a reference to Paul's letters that are being distorted by the opponents (3,15f). That the author refers to "all" of Paul's letters, that he makes them equivalent to Scripture, and that there is already a history of interpreting (or misinterpreting) them, are strong indications that this Peter is a writer of the second generation who defends a tradition common to the historical Peter and Paul against the threat of doctrinal and behavioral deviance.

Questions for Discussion or Reflection

1. This letter addresses the debate between living faith and practical atheism, a very contemporary subject. What is meant by "living faith" and "practical atheism"? Give examples of "practical atheism" at work in our day. Why is it so easy to be swayed by its allure?
2. Peter tells his readers that to be a Christian demands more than knowing *about* the faith; it requires a whole way of life. Why isn't mastery of religious knowledge and going to Mass on Sundays sufficient?
3. What is meant by "a whole way of life"?
4. Read 2 Pt 1,20–21. Why does the author of this letter warn about private interpretation of Scripture? Today as the church encourages its members to study the Scriptures, does this admonition still hold?
5. Read 2 Pt 2,19. Give examples of the truth of this statement in contemporary life. What does "freedom" mean to you?
6. In some Christian circles today, great emphasis is placed on "the Lord's second coming." What is the Catholic understanding of the *parousia?* How does this affect your understanding of divine providence?

1 JOHN READING GUIDE

Three letters are attributed to John in the New Testament canon. It is not easy to determine how these letters are connected to the Gospel According to John and the Book of Revelation. Scholars agree that all these came from a community of "Johannine Christianity" in the late first century, but neither their precise authorship nor their sequence has been established. We are not even sure of the location of this "Johannine Christianity," although Asia Minor seems most likely. With such uncertainty, hypotheses are abundant.

Apart from the connection to John, there are common characteristics that marked this version of belief in Jesus as the Messiah.

1. The figure of Jesus played a central role in the identity of the community.
2. These churches had experienced tragic division:
   a. In the Gospel According to John and Revelation, there is conflict between these messianists and the Jews.
   b. In the Letters and Revelation, there is also evidence of divisions within the churches.
3. This experience of division sharpened the community's symbols into a stark dualism: light and darkness, life and death, truth and falsehood, flesh and spirit.

THE THREE LETTERS

In the three letters, the conflict is within the churches and involves the proper understanding of Jesus. These letters provide a window on this serious early Christian conflict with its multiple dimensions. It is impossible to say at this distance how the letters relate to one another or to the situation. Second and Third John are real letters and claim to come from "the Elder." First John is anonymous and no letter at all, but is more like a theological treatise.

Some have thought that the three letters show three stages of the community's conflict. It might be more true that the three documents were written at the same time by the same author and sent to a single church affiliated with "the Elder." Each letter fulfills a specific function:

- 3 John recommends the bearer, Demetrius, to the church leader, Gaius.
- 2 John is a cover letter to be read to the church.
- 1 John is the centerpiece, an exhortation to a community divided by conflict.

We will consider each of the three letters separately.

THE CHARACTERISTICS OF 1 JOHN

Because it is not so closely tied to a particular situation, 1 John lends itself to every time and place. For a document that was written because of a bitter conflict, it is amazingly positive and loving in tone. For Christians through the ages it has transcended its hard beginnings and has been one of the great spiritual witnesses of the New Testament.

The structure of this letter is not obvious. Certainly it is not a genuine letter. Even as a sermon, it tends to wander a bit, repeating the same points. First John at times appears to be an argument but contains none of the substance of a debate. Readers are sometimes shocked at the lack of consistency. It seems to state something positively only to deny it a short time later. (For instance, see the statements about sinning at 2,1–2; 3,4–10; and 5,16–17.) The reason for this alternation between the ideal and the real lies in the circumstances being addressed.

These Christians saw their lives defined by a basic choice to follow Jesus. Truth, life, and light characterized them; while falsehood, darkness, and death characterized those who did not follow Jesus. They were the community of true prophesy. But now the community was divided into two hostile camps. The cause of this division is what should have been the centerpiece of unity: the proper understanding of the nature and role of Jesus.

First John's inconsistency reflects the chastened perspective caused by the trauma of division. Their symbols need reshaping. The author urges his readers away from a smug sense of their own perfection, to an awareness of their need to repent. Not only "those who went out from us" (see 2,19) have sinned. All have sinned and need the salvation offered by Jesus.

OUTLINE OF 1 JOHN

I. Opening Exhortation (1,1 – 2,17)
II. The Divided Community (2,18 – 3,24)
III. The Remnant Community (4,1 – 5,21)

OPENING EXHORTATION (1,1 – 2,17)

First John opens with a poetic prologue (1,1–4) which resembles the prologue to the fourth Gospel (Jn 1,1–18): the deliberate allusion to Genesis 1,1, "in the beginning"; the centrality of the "Word of life." In the epistle's prologue, however, the stress is placed on the community's experience of the Word in Jesus. The writer testifies to what he has "seen and heard and touched" (compare Jn 19,35). And furthermore, the experience is one shared by the readers. The language of fellowship dominates 1,3–4. Believers have fellowship with God the Father through Jesus. But they also have fellowship among themselves: "We are writing this so that our joy may be complete" (1,4). We are not sure whether the Greek text should read "your" joy or "our" joy. But both meanings harmonize with one another because of the power of Christian fellowship.

The section closes with another deliberately rhetorical statement of purpose: "I am writing to you because . . ." (2,12–14). Different groups of the community are addressed, but the message is basically one message and is more clearly spelled out by 2,15–17: The church is to live by the "will of God" and not by the standards of the "world." John's talk about "love of the world" here is very close to that in James about "a lover of the world" (Jas 4,4) and means much the same thing. The writer does not forbid love of humanity; he denounces the "worldliness" that denies God's claim on God's creation and bases existence on "sensual lust, enticement for the eyes, and a pretentious life" (2,16).

Within the framework provided by the prologue and the opening statement of purpose, the rest of this section of the sermon serves to remind the readers of the need to live by the "message we have heard from him and proclaim to you" (1,5).

The community has already heard that "God is light and there is no darkness in God at all" (1,5). But now, because of the division in this community, a new sense of reality is required. Behavior must match their ideals. They can no longer simply assume that "we are in the light" when their behavior shows that they "walk in darkness" (1,6). That is a lie. Sin does occur among them, and they need to repent of it. Likewise, it is also a lie to claim to "know God" while not keeping God's commandments (2,4).

With different vocabulary than James, but with a similar concern, John seeks to make his readers' actions match their conviction. And the great commandment of God that is to govern the life of the community is also—as in James—the law of love for neighbor, the test whether one is "in the light" or "in the darkness."

First John places special emphasis on the role of Jesus as expiation for sin (1,7; 2,2) and advocate for believers (2,1). The community's division into hostile parties makes the need for intercession clear. They cannot do it alone. It is also clear that "love" is not simply a state of mind, but something to be performed. Where there is hurt and separation, such performance is difficult.

THE DIVIDED COMMUNITY (2,18–3,24)

The severity of the community's crisis is indicated by the fact that the writer thinks that the end of all things is at hand. The author calls those who have left the community "antichrists," and in the apocalyptic scenario, the presence of the antichrist is a sign of the final tribulation (see Mt 24,24). The theme of Jesus' return occurs again in 1 Jn 2,28 and in 3,2. Typical of apocalyptic messages is the exhortation to stand fast ("remain in him," 2,24.27.28;3,6) and to avoid being deceived (2,26). (See the explanations of apocalyptic writing in the Reading Guides to Daniel and Revelation.)

The threat to the community is all the greater because it is caused by former members: "They went out from us" (2,19). It is impossible for the writer to acknowledge fully that they had ever been of one spirit with the community: "They were not really of our number." He proves this by saying, "If they had been, they would have remained" (2,19). This desperate logic indicates the shock given to a church devoted to unity and opposition to a world "out there" when it experiences division from within. The very identity of the community is called into question.

We cannot be sure what the bone of contention was between those who left and those who stayed, only that it involved the proper understanding of Jesus. The author uses language of "denial" and "confession." It seems clear that a formal doctrinal issue is at stake. Some former members refused to acknowledge Jesus as the Christ (2,22) and denied that he was a true man (4,2). The specific heresy described in this letter cannot be identified exactly, but it is a form of *docetism* or *gnosticism*. These heresies qualify those who hold them as "antichrists" in the narrow sense, but it is hard to imagine how such people could have been part of the messianic community. Such a denial of claims about Jesus would be more appropriate coming

Docetism From a Greek word meaning "to seem," docetism is a heresy that claims Christ only *seemed* to be a human being, but was actually purely God.

Gnosticism From a Greek word meaning "to know," gnosticism is a heresy that claims *knowledge,* particularly secret knowledge, is the key to salvation, and that actions are of little or no importance.

from Jews arguing against Christian preaching. The author adds other features in 3,23; 4,2f; 5,1.10. In short, John is convinced his party has the full understanding of Jesus and his opponents do not. More than that, we really do not know.

Characteristic of this writing is the ability to combine a claim to possession of "the truth" (2,21) with a demand at the same time for transformation. The community is not yet perfect. They are indeed "children of God" (see Jn 1,12), but they still need to mature. Only when he appears will they become "like him, for we shall see him as he is" (3,2). Having the truth means living the truth. In 3,4–18 John develops the strongest possible contrast between the way of the world, governed by the devil (4,8; 5,19), and the way revealed by God through Jesus. The way of the world is ruled by envy which leads to murder (the example of Cain, 3,12; compare Jas 4,1–5). The way revealed by Jesus is exactly the opposite. Life is not taken away but given, and in the giving of life, love is revealed: "The way we came to know love was that he laid down his life for us; so we ought to lay down our lives for our brothers" (1 Jn 3,16). The New Testament contains no more direct connection between the work of the Messiah and the pattern of Christian living. And lest anyone think that the giving of life is simply an attitude of mind, John spells it out clearly in terms of sharing of material possessions with the needy. He concludes in the manner of a Greek moralist, "Let us love not in word or speech but in deed and truth."

Finally, the claim to be in possession of the truth must be held with deep humility (3,19–21). It is because these Christians are in the hands of "one who is greater than our hearts and knows everything" that they know they belong to the truth. It is not their accomplishment but God's gift. Their adequate response is to act as Christ did, in love (3,23f).

THE REMNANT COMMUNITY (4,1 – 5,21)

Because the community is divided, those symbols they once shared are now being re-interpreted by opposing parties. John reminds his readers of the need to "test the spirits to see whether they belong to God" (4,1). Earlier he had spoken of the opponents as "antichrists"; now he calls them "false prophets," another favorite label in apocalyptic writing (see Mt 24,11). In this case, the proper confession of Jesus is the gauge for true and false prophecy, certifying whether the speaker belongs to God or to "the world" (4,2–4.13–16).

The last section of this sermon is filled with a mixture of confidence and caution. The community living by God's love is sure of "victory over the world" (5,4–5) even though "the whole world is under the power of the evil one" (5,19). This is because the community is not isolated but supported by the Father, Son, and Spirit, each working in and through the church (5,6–9). Even though the community is confident of its gift of "eternal life" (2,25; 5,11.13), the victory over sin and death is not complete:

- Idolatry is a temptation that needs to be avoided (5,21).
- Perfect love has not yet driven out fear (4,18).
- Mutual correction is required (5,16–17).

For this divided community, nothing can be taken for granted any longer. Their experience of division has given new urgency to discernment (5,20).

Discernment

Within this remnant community itself, discernment was also required. How could the church be sure it was living by the Spirit of God? Discernment, or "testing the spirits," has had a long tradition within Christianity. This is the process by which an individual or a community examines, in the light of the whole value structure of faith, what leads to God and a more perfect service of God and others and what detracts from this goal. Sometimes this is very difficult to distinguish.

That the Johannine community had the right confession of Jesus was taken for granted by its members. But John added the ethical dimension: Keeping the commandment of God showed their love for God (5,2f). What is that commandment? That they love one another. John joined love for God and love for neighbor in a way that they could not be separated; doing one was doing the other. "If anyone says, 'I love God,' but hates his brother, he is a liar" (4,20).

There is a certain parallel to the beginning of Genesis in the Gospel of John when Christ breathes on the apostles and gives them the Holy Spirit (Jn 20,22). It is the Spirit that secures the unity of the body (1 Cor 12,13; Eph 2,16.18; 4,4). The Good Spirit holds the body together. Divisions, factions, hurt, and separation are always suspect. However, even these can masquerade as truth. The only way a community can judge itself as being "in the truth" is to measure its members' love for one another. Since human beings do not have direct access to God, (4,12; see Jn 1,18), their relationship to God is always mediated by their relationship with each other (4,12.20–21).

Questions for Discussion or Reflection

1. For many Catholics, scrutiny of conscience has been measured by a list of faults, which contributes to forgetting that only God can reveal sin in our lives.
   a. What is the difference between awareness of sinfulness and simply making a "grocery list" of faults?
   b. How can a parish community discern whether it is "walking in the light"?
2. The Catholic Church claims to be the bearer of truth.
   a. Think of a person from another faith who seems to live his or her belief in an authentic way. What can Catholics learn from this person?
   b. What is the measuring rod for authenticity of truth according to the First Letter of John?
3. The Christian Churches of the East have a tradition of praying the "Jesus Prayer" as a kind of mantra. It is said quietly over and over again while leaving one's heart open to the action of the Holy Spirit.

Lord, Jesus Christ,
Son of the Living God,
have mercy on me, a sinner.

2 JOHN READING GUIDE

A COVER LETTER TO THE CHURCH

Unless 2 and 3 John are connected to the same moment of crisis that generated 1 John, it is hard to explain their preservation by a local church, their exchange between churches, and their eventual inclusion in the New Testament canon. In the Reading Guide for 1 John, the suggestion is made that all three letters were sent as a single packet by the "mailman" Demetrius to the local leader Gaius (see 3 John) who was still loyal to "the elder" in the dispute dividing Johannine Christianity into hostile factions.

Whereas 1 John lacks all characteristics of a letter and appears to be a sermon to be delivered aloud to an assembly (or a number of assemblies), 2 John bears all the marks of a genuine letter: the formal elements of a greeting (1–3), body of the letter (4–12), and farewell (13). It mentions the desire of the writer to visit the addressees (12).

Unlike 3 John, which is addressed to an individual, 2 John is written to the "chosen Lady" and her children (1). The designation "chosen Lady" is almost certainly an honorary title for the church itself. That it refers to a specific woman leader is doubtful if the rest of the reconstruction here being suggested makes sense. The "children," of course, are the ones really being addressed; second person verbs are predominantly in the plural. Surely such a cluster of distinctive themes makes best sense when read together with 1 John.

What distinguishes 2 John is its function. In 3 John 9, the elder says that he "is writing" (or "wrote") something to the church. This likely refers to 1 John, the exhortation to the remnant community. Second John is undoubtedly a letter of introduction to the community as such, to be read before the sermon is delivered, to identify the author, to emphasize its main teaching, and to suggest some practical actions to be taken by the community. These may or may not be fully in accord with the spirit of 1 John, but they are certainly recognizable as a response to the crisis signaled by 3 John.

STRATEGIES FOR SURVIVAL

Again we meet a split between those who "walk in the truth" and "many deceivers who have gone out into the world" (7). As in 1 John, the deceivers are labeled antichrists because they "do not acknowledge Jesus Christ as coming in the flesh." In the Reading Guide to 1 John, we

The Symbols of Johannine Christianity Evident in 2 John

Emphasis on:

- "the truth" (1.2.3)
- "walking in the truth" (4)
- "keeping the commandments" (5)
- creation of mutual joy as a mark of fellowship (12)

suggest how difficult it is to determine precisely what this denial implies. For the elder, the opponents appear as "progressives" who have gone too far in the interpretation and no longer "remain in the teaching of the Christ" (or "about" the Christ). The elder's community is portrayed as defending the traditional understanding of Jesus. The importance of right doctrine is underscored by the equation:

having Christ = having God (see 1 Jn 4,3)

For Johannine Christianity, the unique mediation of salvation by Jesus is undisputed truth. He alone is the "way, the truth, and the life" (Jn 14,6). The lesson is clear: Misconstruing the mediator means missing the good news entirely. If the elder's readers don't hold to the proper understanding, they will "lose what they worked for."

The crisis in the community is so severe that the elder calls for the extraordinary practice of excommunication. They are not to offer heretics hospitality, and they must not even greet them as brothers (10). Notice the connection, everywhere assumed in the New Testament, between message and messenger. Physical fellowship implies spiritual agreement. Thus "whoever greets him, shares in his evil works" (11). Only those who deliver the proper doctrine are to be welcomed. Here the elder recommends the same practice of shunning and exclusion of which he accuses Diotrephes in 3 John. The battle is a bitter one.

CONCLUSION

It is difficult to know what positive instruction one should draw from these ancient fragments of hostile conflicts. Perhaps it is important for the church to remember in every age that it has never been easy to establish or to secure its identity; deviance and dispute are part of community life. However, it is important for the church to reflect on whether proper doctrine is more important than the fellowship of love. Even in an age of ecumenism that issue remains unresolved.

Questions for Discussion or Reflection

1. What do you see in the Church today that keeps it from being an effective sign of Christ for the world?
2. What must we do to help correct this situation?
3. What is the course of action that the members of your parish community should take when disagreements arise?
4. How should today's Catholic Church reach out to people of other faiths?

3 JOHN READING GUIDE

A LETTER OF RECOMMENDATION

The New Testament contains two letters written explicitly to individuals, Paul's letter to Philemon, and the elder's letter to Gaius, the letter known as 3 John. Both letters take up matters of community concern, and both have the same specific function, that of recommending the bearer of the letter to the addressee. In the case of Philemon, Paul seeks to return a slave who had run away and to assure his welcome. In the case of 3 John, the elder recommends to the local church leader his courier, Demetrius. He has a good reputation from all, and "we give our testimonial as well, and you know our testimony is true" (12).

The ancient world had protocol for letters such as these. They were widely used in early Christianity, as we learn elsewhere in Paul's correspondence (see 2 Cor 3,1; Rom 16). It was natural for a missionary movement to certify its apostles with such letters, in order to ensure them a safe reception and the hospitality due such "co-workers in the truth" (3 Jn 8). Receiving such messengers, as we see also in 2 John, meant accepting their message as well. This understanding, which was widespread in Judaism, was reflected in the sayings of Jesus: "Whoever listens to you listens to me. Whoever rejects you rejects me. And whoever rejects me rejects the one who sent me" (Lk 10,16). This axiom became problematic when the Christian movement itself divided into hostile parties. Paul complained of the Corinthians' preference for apostles other than himself (2 Cor 10,12; 11,4). Third John points us directly to such a situation.

Probably neither 2 John nor 3 John would have been preserved or made part of the New Testament canon if they had not been associated with the religious message in 1 John. The Reading Guide for 1 John has proposed that the three letters of John were all part of the same packet delivered to Gaius from the elder through Demetrius, and that the two smaller letters owe their preservation to the theological weightiness of 1 John.

But if its survival was accidental and its theology minimal, 3 John is all the more precious to readers today. It provides the key to the historical circumstances presupposed by 2 and 1 John. And without 3 John, an appreciation for the sufferings of the early church would be greatly diminished.

THE POLITICS OF ECCLESIASTICAL POWER

Third John reveals that the struggle for the soul of Johannine Christianity involved structure as much as symbol, power as much as piety. The two levels of conflict were intimately connected. On one side we see the elder writing to his loyal colleague, Gaius. On the other side is Diotrephes, who "loves to dominate." Diotrephes not only asserts authority over Gaius at the local level, he refuses to acknowledge the authority of the elder over the regional church. The author says that when he comes, he will draw attention to what Diotrephes is doing (10), but this is a small threat to a rebellious chieftain. The position of the elder is a defensive one. He needs the personal loyalty of Gaius and his financial assistance as well.

Here we are brought to the political maneuvering at the heart of this battle. Diotrephes is not content to "spread evil nonsense" about the elder. He takes action to suppress the elder's authority. He refuses to receive the elder's delegates, and even more, Diotrephes expels from the church those who want to receive them (10). We can understand why the elder appreciates Gaius's reception of Demetrius, and we can grasp the significance of verses 5–8. The elder needs to find an alternative source of hospitality, since Diotrephes has taken up a position among those who "went out from us" (1 Jn 2,19) and no longer supports the elder's teaching.

Gaius is being asked to receive Demetrius (and his companions) as well as to equip them for their next stage of travel. Perhaps the elder's future messengers are also included in this request. Since the missionaries accept nothing from the "pagans" ("the world"), the need for a network of hospitality and financial support is obvious (7). As in 2 John, financial sharing is equivalent to spiritual fellowship. Helping such missionaries is being "co-workers in the truth" (8). It is clear that both parties in the dispute are using the same tactics. Here Diotrephes is shunning and excommunicating. But in 2 John we find the elder advocating the same actions among his followers.

CONCLUSION

These struggles of early Christianity are not terribly edifying, but they are instructive. Christians who long for a golden age of harmony should be reminded that there never was one. Among history's benefits is liberation from illusion. Edifying or not, these letters testify to another truth. The struggle for identity is never simply a matter of ideas or even doctrinal symbols. It involves inevitably the messy realities of money and political power.

Questions for Discussion or Reflection

1. What has been your experience of diversity in the Catholic Church?
2. St. Augustine said that Christians should manifest unity in essentials, diversity in all other things, and charity in everything. How is it possible for the Church to experience diversity and still profess unity?
3. What examples of Christian witness have inspired you? What has been a scandal to you or others?
4. How does St. Augustine's teaching in question 2 relate to the witness Christianity gives to the world?

JUDE READING GUIDE

Although Jude is among the shortest writings in the New Testament, it bristles with difficulties. Some of these have to do with placing the composition in the historical development of early Christianity. Others involve grasping its obscure references. The two sorts of problems are related. Since we do not know the author or his circumstances, we do not have a secure context for intelligent reading of the letter. And because Jude was obviously responding to some kind of specific crisis, we must attempt to construct a context if we are to understand the letter at all.

Literary puzzles are provided by Jude's literary references. He cites examples of sinners being punished. Some are readily apparent from the Bible, although a few (like Balaam) show signs of traditional Jewish biblical interpretation. Jude's reference to the "words spoken by the apostles" (17) are no more clear, since the statement is more a combination of early Christian statements on the end-time (see for example Mk 13,22; 1 Tm 4,1–3) than specific quotations.

That the author could assume that his readers were familiar with these sources presupposes either a Jewish-Christian readership, or a Gentile one familiar with Jewish apocrypha. We do not know what the ancient readers presumably understood, and the lack of literary context continues to make this letter obscure to present-day readers.

HISTORICAL SETTING

Writings like 2 Peter and Jude remind us how little we know about early Christianity apart from what is provided by Acts and Paul's letters. We cannot fit them into any development we know about, so we must rely on guesswork. Every theory is based solely on the text itself. Accuracy concerning what the text does and does not say is obviously critical to the value of any reconstruction.

Jude is obviously an argument against opponents and an exhortation to its readers to remain steadfast. However, the text contains no clear indication that Jude was opposing "false teachers" or that they were purveying any "heresy." Their "scorning of lordship" (4.8) had to do with practice rather than doctrine. Jude attacks immoral behavior rather than false teaching. He accuses his opponents of disrupting the community's love feasts. The term is usually taken to mean eucharistic meals. They are also accused of carousing and of looking after only themselves (literally "shepherding themselves"; 12). He also calls their behavior "divisive" (19). Otherwise, Jude uses all the standardized charges common to controversies of the ancient world: They are sexually immoral (7), greedy (11.16), slanderous (15), and living for their own desires (16). In short, they "live on the natural plane, devoid of the Spirit" (19). They "pervert the grace of our God into licentiousness" (4).

LIVING BY GOD'S GRACE

Letters of Paul such as 1 Corinthians attest to how difficult it was for the early Christians to translate the gift of God (grace) into consistent patterns of moral behavior. Legitimate disagreement could exist on matters of diet, work, use of possessions, and the like. It was not immediately obvious in all cases what "life in the Spirit" meant behaviorally. In the case of Jude, it appears that disagreement has overstepped the boundary of true moral deviance; hence the outrage of the author. The opponents are "perverting the gift."

Jude's first line of defense is an attack on the immoral people. He tries to demonstrate from Scripture how there have always been such troublemakers and they have always been punished; so will these. Unlike 2 Peter 2 where the emphasis is on the power of God to judge the righteous and unrighteous, the stress in Jude is on the punishment of the rebellious.

The argument is not random but carefully argued, with rhetorical effect. Notice the repetition of *these people* and similar phrases:

(8) *these dreamers* . . . also defile the flesh, scorn lordship . . .
(10) But *these people* revile what they do not understand . . .
(12) *They* are blemishes on your love feasts . . .
(16) *These people* are complainers . . . who live by their desires;
(19) *They* are the ones who cause divisions . . .

This repetition brings the examples of old to bear on present circumstances. Jude also plays on the Greek words for *keep* in verses 1,6,13,21, and 24. His opponents fail to "*keep* their place," but Jude's readers are to "*keep* themselves in the love of God," who is in turn able to "*keep* them from stumbling."

Jude's second line of defense is to edify (build up) his readers in their "most holy faith" (20). He reminds them that God dealt with troubles like these from of old, and in fact the apostles of Jesus had foretold the emergence of such rebellious "scoffers" (17–18). He reassures them that they are being "kept safe for Jesus Christ" despite these turmoils (1). Jude does not suggest that it is the believers' role to punish the scoundrel. Rather, he exhorts them to avoid such immoral behavior (23) and to build up their own faith. If the opponents are "devoid of Spirit," the believers are to "pray in the Spirit" (20). Their love for God is to be demonstrated in an attitude of mercy and care for those who waver and even for those who appear to be lost (22–23).

The use of moral outrage is not limited to the circumstances of the first century. We all have a tendency to take our relationship with God for granted and engage in unscrupulous behavior. Combining just anger at immorality with mercy for the immoral ones is a delicate and difficult art. Few writings have carried it off as well as Jude.

Questions for Discussion or Reflection

1. Jude reminds his readers that "shepherding oneself" is a blemish on the eucharistic meal of the community (12). Discuss the meaning of this statement.
2. If such individualism weakens the bond of Christian unity, what gives rootedness to believers?
3. How is the Eucharist the sign and source of unity?
4. Read verses 20–23. How are these words of Jude heard by present-day Christians?

Pray the Doxology:

To the one who is able to keep you from stumbling and to present you unblemished and exultant, in the presence of his glory, to the only God, our savior, through Jesus Christ our Lord be glory, majesty, power, and authority from ages past, now, and for ages to come.

Amen (24–25)

REVELATION READING GUIDE

OUTLINE

I. Prologue (1,1–3)
II. Letters to the churches of Asia (1,4 – 3,22)
III. God and the Lamb in heaven (4,1 – 5,14)
IV. The seven seals, trumpets, and plagues, with interludes (6,1 – 16,21)
V. The punishment of Babylon and the destruction of pagan nations (17,1 – 20,15)
VI. The new creation (21,1 – 22,5)
VII. Epilogue (22,6–21)

A BOOK OF CHRISTIAN PROPHECY

The Book of Revelation makes for difficult reading, and in fact has a long history of misinterpretation. Many people had made a fundamental mistake: taking it as a literal set of predictions delivered in the past concerning current events. Reading Revelation in that way has been popular for a long time. For many people nowadays, it has become an obsession. The "end-time" has been awaited many times without occurring. Such readings have caused distortion of lives; many individuals and groups have left livelihood and loved ones to meet the New Jerusalem, only to have their dreams destroyed. Such readings have also missed the real religious message of Revelation. They reduce its value to that of an astrological chart.

The Book of Revelation requires an *openness of faith* and an *ability to hear.* Because it engages the hearing and the seeing, images must be elicited through the imagination. A contemplative attitude is essential, along with the need not to try to pin poetic language to specific events.

Although the text calls out for such an interpretation, with its promise to reveal "what will happen soon" (22,18–19), it is critical to recognize that just such statements are standard features of a specific literary form of the ancient world, called *apocalyptic.* Two tenets should guide the faithful study of Revelation:

1. The Word of God was addressed to the people of the age when it was written.
2. A text's "fuller" meaning for successive ages is secondary and never to be divorced from its first historical meaning.

Newspapers and poetry do not communicate their "truths" in exactly the same way. Knowing the usage of a literary form is necessary for intelligent reading.

REVELATION AS PROPHECY

In other ways, Revelation transcends apocalyptic. The author is not a fictional sage from the past but a leader well known to his readers. He calls himself John (1,1.4.9; 22,8), who because of his Christian faith has been exiled to the rocky island of Patmos, a Roman penal colony.

The voice of prophecy is directed explicitly (not in coded fashion) to the seven churches of Asia Minor in Chapters 2–3. The turn of the ages had already begun. The victory of God

ESSAY

What Is Apocalyptic?

Beginning at least with the Book of Daniel in the Old Testament, the apocalyptic style became prevalent in Judaism during the New Testament period (200 B.C. to 200 A.D.). Persecutions from without and the threat of unfaithfulness from within generated this "literature of the oppressed," which quickly gained certain standard features:

1. Revelations about the future are experienced in dreams or visions.
2. The insights from these visions are communicated through a complex symbolism involving numbers, animals, and cosmic phenomena.
3. The element of prediction is usually a fiction.
4. The seer interprets events of his own age, using a figure of the past (such as Enoch) or an angelic being as a spokesperson.

The literary features express an interpretation of history. Apocalyptic defends God's justice. The "present age" appears to be under the control of evil people or even satanic powers, since those devoted to God are being persecuted. The apocalyptic transposes God's blessing to a future time, "the age to come." Just when things become humanly impossible, God will intervene (as through a messiah) to save God's own, and he will inaugurate the "Kingdom of God." Apocalyptic brings the conviction that God controls history even though experience seems to suggest that God does not.

The religious message of apocalyptic is simple. To the faithful, it says, "hold on"; to the wavering, it declares, "stand fast." It offers hope of victory to those now oppressed but remaining loyal to the one God.

Revelation fits the apocalyptic genre well. It has visions, animals, numbers, cosmic catastrophes. It has a two-page interpretation of history and its basic religious message is a call for the "endurance of the holy ones" (13,10; 14,12).

over evil has been accomplished through the death and resurrection of Jesus; even more, the faithful who have been killed already share that victory in heaven.

The self-understanding of the church in this writing is prophetic. Those who follow Jesus are "servants and prophets and saints" (11,18). Their witness is the "spirit of prophecy" (19,10). Jesus is the first and "faithful witness" (1,5) whose mission they continue. And what is their prophecy? To witness to the reality of God in the world in the face of corruption or apostasy (unfaithfulness). In the visions, it is expressed as loyalty to God in face of the idolatrous claims of the state (Rome) and even possible death.

HISTORICAL DATES TO ASSIST OUR UNDERSTANDING OF THE BOOK OF REVELATION

1. The death and resurrection of Jesus: the beginning of the 30s.
2. The martyrdom of Peter and Paul and Nero's persecution of the Christians: the 60s.
3. The capture of Jerusalem and the destruction of the Temple: 70–73.

4. After the destruction of the Temple, conflicts between Jews and Christians increased, resulting in a complete break around the year 90.
5. The emperor Domitian (81–90) imposed the practice of emperor worship. Christians were often suspect and objects of persecution because of their refusal to participate in this ritual.

THE OPENING VISION (1,1–20)

The prologue (1,1–3) and the epilogue (22,6–21) provide an explicit prophetic framework for the entire work. The understanding of prophecy as *witness,* which becomes the major theme of the book, is sounded at once (1,2). This means that the prophet is seen primarily as one who tells the truth that people need to hear, rather than primarily as one who predicts the future.

The popularity of letter writing in early Christianity is shown by the fact that this apocalyptic writing contains letters to the seven churches of Asia Minor (Chapters 2–3), and even has an epistolary greeting to introduce the work (1,4–8). The author identifies himself as one known to his readers, and he recounts the vision that provides the basis for the rest of the book. The phrasing of 1,9 suggests that John is on the Greek island of Patmos as a punishment for his witness to Jesus. The vision that now comforts him becomes an exhortation to all who are likewise oppressed.

The risen Jesus is encountered as the Son of Man (the central figure in much apocalyptic), described in the most transcendent terms available. The reader is now in the realm of visions, which means the realm of symbols. These symbolic terms are not meant literally. The terms used here and elsewhere were not invented by the writer of Revelation but are part of biblical symbolism. Of all apocalyptic writings, Revelation most artfully weaves together the themes of classical prophecy, especially of the prophet Ezekiel. You will be greatly helped in your understanding if you take notice of the footnotes and cross-references in the *New American Bible.* You will quickly realize that Revelation is a complex literary construction written by someone very much aware of the previous scriptural tradition.

The Son of Man appears with stars in his hands and standing amid the seven lampstands. Revelation makes two things clear from the start:

1. It is the risen and powerful Lord, in control of the whole universe, who is revealing all these matters.
2. This risen Lord is the one who is present to the churches (1,20), and their concerns are treated in the letters that follow.

LETTERS TO THE SEVEN CHURCHES (2,1 – 3,22)

In what are literally "spirit letters" (see 2,7) from the risen Jesus, seven churches of well-known cities in Asia Minor are issued individualized prophecies. We see at once what Revelation understands "prophecy" to be: These letters are exhortations to remain faithful to the integrity of their calling. The trials and lapses of the Johannine Christians are here put on remarkable display. We also hear fragments of sayings (such as in 2,3) that occur elsewhere in the New Testament literature (see 1 Thes 5,2 and Mk 13,33).

The letters follow the same format. There is greeting, followed by an elaborate designation of Jesus. The risen Lord analyzes each community's spiritual condition and concludes with words of warning or promise. The description of the church's struggles show how they faced opposition from without (as from the Jews), but even more, division within (as from the Nicolaitans—see note on 2,6 in the *New American Bible*). And corruption appears as a vivid possibility. Typical for Johannine literature, the opposition is pictured in terms of false prophecy (2,20). Endurance is the focus of the praise and persuasion in these letters.

The imagery of the letters is lush. Who can resist the almost fairy-tale quality of the statement: "I shall also give a white amulet upon which is inscribed a new name, which no one knows except the one who receives it" (2,17)? Beneath the poetry, however, lies grim reality. The difficulty in these letters of maintaining loyalty in the face of social exclusion and human laxity is raised to the level of a cosmic conflict between the Lord and the forces of evil in the visions that follow.

What is the Spirit Saying to the Churches?

Read the Letters aloud and fill the spaces:

	Addressed to whom	Christ described as...	Judgment?	Conversion?	What is promised?
Ephesus 2,1–7					
Smyrna 2,8–11					
Pergamum 2,12–17					
Thyatira 2,18–29					
Sardis 3,1–6					
Philadelphia 3,7–13					
Laodicea 3,14–22					

(This activity is based on a chart in Jean-Pierre Prévost's book, *How to Read the Apocalypse* [New York: Crossroad, 1993], p. 70.)

GOD AND THE LAMB IN HEAVEN (4,1–5,14)

John is "caught up in spirit" (4,2), and the rest of Revelation consists of the visions he experiences in his ecstatic state. The vision is an essential element of apocalyptic. It is found with equal frequency in early Jewish mysticism, called *Merkabah,* or "throne-chariot" mysticism. In prayer the mystic ascended through the heavens to the throne of God's presence. Much of the celestial furniture in Revelation resembles that of the *Merkabah:* the jewel-encrusted throne room (4,3–4), the sea of glass (4,6), the angelic creatures (4,6–9), and the numerous hymns sung in praise of God (5,9–13).

A dramatic departure from standard symbolism is the appearance of "a Lamb that seemed to have been slain" (5,6). Jesus is also called "Lamb of God" in John's Gospel (1,29; see also Jn 19,36, a reference to the Passover lamb). What a bold stroke to picture Jesus in animal terms, especially one so paradoxical. The obvious aspect of the lamb is its sacrificial function: Jesus was slain. But the lamb is also "the lion of the tribe of Judah" who has triumphed over death (Rv 5,5). In a powerful proclamation of Jesus' status after his resurrection, the lamb sits at "the right hand of the one who sat on the throne" (5,7; see Ps 110,1). Both figures receive the praise of the heavenly creatures (5,9–11) and indeed of all creation (5,13–14).

The special character of the visions of Revelation is shown by the problem of "the scroll" (5,1). It contains the secrets to be revealed, and because of its use in Ezekiel it is immediately recognizable as a symbol for prophecy (10,8–11; Ez 2,9–3,4). Because of his resurrection, Jesus is empowered to open the scroll (Rv 5,5). What follows is both a revelation *of* and *from* Jesus Christ (see 1,1). The visions will show "what must happen afterwards" (4,1), but the reader is not frightened, knowing from this first vision that the fundamental victory has already been accomplished.

Absorbing Understanding through Imagery

It is useless to try to tease such poetry into a train schedule. The vision here is not one of history unfolding like clockwork: It is a religious vision of God's ultimate conquest despite current appearances. Once the reader lets go of the obsessive "need to know" that twists beauty into time charts, it is possible to wonder at the powerful and religious imagination at work in these glorious images.

Take time to read carefully and even pray the beautiful acclamations of Christ in the Book of Revelation: 1,4–7; 5,1; 7,10; 19,6–7; 5,9–10; 5,13; and 11,15.

VISIONS OF COSMIC CONFLICT (6,1 – 16,21)

The next section of Revelation is the most difficult to make sense of and the most worked over for signs of the end. Candidates to fit the beast with the number 666 (13,18) have ranged from Nero to Hitler.

The visions are so structured as to give the illusion of taking place in time, linked together by the phrase "and then I saw." It is always tempting to translate a series of visions into a sequence of historical events. So readers have tried to figure out the overlapping series of sevens: Seals (6,1–17; 8,1), trumpets (8,1 – 9,21; 11,15), plagues (15,1–8), bowls (16,1–20). But neither the events of the daily newspaper nor elaborate literary analysis have ever satisfactorily unlocked this dense poetry. It is in fact more likely that all the visions repeat the same basic message: The saints on earth are locked in conflict with hostile forces. Their earthly combat finds a cosmic counterpart in the struggle between God and Satan.

This Christian community reflecting upon its experience shows two people who both "witness and testify" (the terms are interchangeable). They are killed in imitation of Jesus

The Cosmic Conflict

On one side we see all the "beasts" who oppose the faithful: the dragon (12,1–8), the first beast (13,1–10), and the second beast (13,11–17). These are not separate enemies, but masks worn by the one force of evil. As in modern horror films, the destruction of one evil force gives rise to another more horrifying still. Beneath the different masks, one visible enemy is most prevalent: the idolatrous state that persecutes the saints, enslaves them, and seeks to kill them (13,7–18).

On the other side are those loyal to God, the "servants, prophets, and saints" (11,18; 19,9f). They continue Jesus' own faithful witness to God by witnessing to Jesus. By so doing, they reject the idolatrous claims of the state for worship of the emperor. They suffer the consequences, some by shedding their blood. Revelation establishes the connection between "witness" and "martyr" by the disciples' imitation of Jesus' death.

(11,7). They are also called into heaven (11,12). This picture describes the conviction of Revelation that those who share Jesus' death also share his triumph in heaven. Scenes of suffering on earth below are alternated with serene descriptions of the saints in heaven celebrating the anticipated and certain victory of the Lamb (5,9f; 6,9–11; 7,4–7; 14,1–5; 15,2–4). Apocalyptic demands that history move in a downward curve to ever more dismal circumstances, until God finally intervenes. In Revelation, however, the final outcome is not in doubt. Not just Jesus, but also those "defeated" with him by evil *already* share in the resurrection triumph.

PUNISHMENT OF BABYLON (17,1 – 20,15)

The masks fall away, revealing as the real enemy of God's people the Roman Empire, "the great harlot who lives near the many waters" (17,1). Rome is called Babylon (17,5) because in the biblical tradition it was Babylon above all that symbolized the desecration of the Temple and the exile of the people. In typical apocalyptic fashion, the sequence of events is laid out: God has given temporary rule to the evil empire, to accomplish God's ends. It does battle against the Lamb and the people.

The persecution and suffering were undoubtedly real. These Christians were faced with the choices of all who suffer oppression. What were they to do? To resist violently and seek to overthrow Rome would be futile as well as contrary to their beliefs. But to cooperate would be to lose their identity. They chose the path of passive resistance. They did not fight the beast, but neither would they do its bidding. The path of martyrdom, however slow or fast, is not easy. For those who survive, the psychic toll is considerable. Anger at the enemy can easily turn inward; patient endurance is hard labor.

They were convinced that "the Lamb will conquer" (17,14), but in their earthly condition they had not seen it happen. The description of Rome's fall is deliciously detailed. The pent-up fury of the oppressed is released in glee over the disgrace of the oppressor. Much of this is obviously and literally wish fulfillment, the stuff of fantasy. The anger of a downtrodden people is deflected to a punishing God.

The stages of the end-time reveal how "the words of God are accomplished" (17,17). These final stages lack poetry, but this deficiency is overcome by the final vision.

THE NEW CREATION (21,1–22,21)

The conclusion to Revelation is a fitting conclusion to the Bible as a whole. The vision of a new creation (21,1) is central to the New Testament (see 2 Cor 5,17). The Christian experience of Christ was one of an absolute new beginning, rooted in the ever-new life of God. God can say, "Behold, I make all things new" (21,5), because God is "the Alpha and the Omega, the beginning and the end" of all things (21,6; 22,13). As Genesis began with the creation by a word, so the vision of the end-time recaps that beginning: Creation is renewed.

The hope expressed in Revelation is not simply that souls will be saved after death, or that evil will be conquered, or even that the saints will reign for a thousand years over a burnt-out terrain. The hope is that creation itself will be transformed. So the sight of a "New Jerusalem coming down out of heaven from God" is a vision of a civilized order, one that is intrinsically *holy* in the proper sense. Human society is based on the recognition of God's power and presence (21,3.7f).

In this city there is not even need for "religion" as a separate compartment of life. The temple of the city is "the Lord God almighty and the Lamb" (21,22). And all the city's people will be priests of [the Lord] God (21,6), showing at last that the fundamental human vocation is praise of God (22,9). There is no division between peoples; nothing is accursed (22,3). The nations will walk by the light of the Lamb (21,24), and the trees of the city "serve as medicine for the nations" (22,2). And what medicine! There will be "no more death or mourning, wailing or pain, [for] the old order has passed away" (21,4).

Great harm has come to those who have tried by force to make this vision a reality, to establish a thousand-year reign of the saints on earth. Great despair has come to those who have tried on the basis of good will to construct a society like the New Jerusalem. The vision has value precisely as challenge, as an ever-present call to all humanity for constant renewal. This does not come about by human effort but by God's gift. The transformation is not technical but organic.

But so compelling is the vision that no one who hears it can help joining in the plaintive cry of the epilogue, "Amen! Come, Lord Jesus!" The epilogue also reminds us that we are still in the in-between time when the world is not yet recreated. There is still need for the witness of prophecy and for endurance of the saints, "for let the wicked still act wickedly, and the filthy still be filthy. The righteous must still do right, and the holy still be holy" (22,11). Here is the call to the saints.

Questions For Discussion or Reflection

1. Throughout the Book of Revelation Christ is given many titles. List as many as you can find. Examples: Jesus, Christ, the firstborn from the dead, who walks among the seven golden lampstands, who has the key of David, etc.
2. Pray the Seven Beatitudes of the Book of Revelation: 1,3; 14,13; 16,15; 19,9; 20,6; 22,7; and 22,14.

3. Ancient peoples gave symbolism to special numbers. With the meaning of the numbers listed, turn to the Book of Revelation and reread the passage. You may come to a better understanding of the poetic imagery.

Number	Meaning	References
One or first	Primacy, excellence	1,17; 2,8; 22,13
Three or third	Limited	8,1; 12,14; 11,9; 4,7; 6,5; 8,7–12
Four	Whole, universality	4,6–8; 5,6–8.14; 6,1.6; 7,11; 14,3; 15,7; 19,4
Six	Imperfection	13,18
Seven	Fullness, perfection	1,4; 1,12; 1,16; 4,5; 5,1
Twelve	Continuity with the chosen people	12,1; 21,12. 14. 20. 21
Thousand	Superlative, very many	Chapters 7; 14; 20

4. Looking at the Gospels, how does Revelation's vision of God's empire compare to the announcement by Jesus of God's reign?
5. If we are still in the in-between time, what is meant by "The kingdom of God is at hand" (Mk 1,15) and "Yes, I am coming soon" (Rv 22,20)?

THE OLD TESTAMENT

THE PENTATEUCH

The Pentateuch, which consists of the first five books of the Bible (Genesis, Exodus, Leviticus, Numbers, Deuteronomy), enjoys particular prestige among the Jews as the "Law," or "Torah," the concrete expression of God's will in their regard. It is more than a body of legal doctrine, even though such material occupies many chapters, for it contains the story of the formation of the People of God: Abraham and the patriarchs, Moses and the oppressed Hebrews in Egypt, the birth of Israel in the Sinai covenant, the journey to the threshold of the Promised Land, and the "discourses" of Moses.

The grandeur of this historic sweep is the result of a careful and complex joining of several historical traditions, or sources. These are primarily four: the so-called Yahwist, Elohist, Priestly and Deuteronomic strands that run through the Pentateuch. (They are conveniently abbreviated as J, E, P and D.) Each brings to the Torah its own characteristics, its own theological viewpoint—a rich variety of interpretation that the sensitive reader will take pains to appreciate. A superficial difference between two of these sources is responsible for their names: the Yahwist prefers the name *Yahweh* (represented in translation as *Lord*) by which God revealed himself to Israel; the Elohist prefers the generic name for God, *Elohim*. The Yahwist is concrete, imaginative, using many anthropomorphisms in its theological approach, as seen, e.g., in the narrative of creation in Gn 2, compared with the Priestly version in Gn 1. The Elohist is more sober, moralistic. The Priestly strand, which emphasizes genealogies, is more severely theological in tone. The Deuteronomic approach is characterized by the intense hortatory style of Dt 5—11, and by certain principles from which it works, such as the centralization of worship in the Jerusalem temple.

However, even this analysis of the Pentateuch is an over-simplification, for it is not always possible to distinguish with certainty among the various sources. The fact is that each of these individual traditions incorporates much older material. The Yahwist was himself a collector and adapter. His narrative is made up of many disparate stories that have been reoriented, and given a meaning within the context in which they now stand; e.g., the story of Abraham and Isaac in Gn 22. Within the J and P traditions one has to reckon with many individual units; these had their own history and life-setting before they were brought together into the present more or less connected narrative.

This is not to deny the role of Moses in the development of the Pentateuch. It is true we do not conceive of him as the author of the books in the modern sense. But there is no reason to doubt that, in the events described in these traditions, he had a uniquely important role, especially as lawgiver. Even the later laws which have been added in P and D are presented as a Mosaic heritage. Moses is the lawgiver *par excellence,* and all later legislation is conceived in his spirit, and therefore attributed to him. Hence, the reader is not held to undeviating literalness in interpreting the words, "the Lord said to Moses." One must keep in mind that the Pentateuch is the crystallization of Israel's age-old relationship with God.

In presenting the story of the birth of the People of God, the Pentateuch looks back to the promises made to the patriarchs, and forward to the continuing fulfillment of these promises in later books of the Bible. The promises find their classic expression in Gn 12, 1ff. The "God of the Fathers" challenges Abraham to believe: the patriarch is to receive a people, a land, and through him the nations will somehow be blessed.

The Massoretic text of 1 and 2 Samuel has in numerous instances been corrected by the more ancient manuscripts Samuel a, b, and c from Cave 4 of Qumran, with the aid of important evidence from the Septuagint in both its oldest from and its Lucianic recension. Fragments of the lost Book of Tobit in Aramaic and in Hebrew, recovered from Cave 4 of Qumran, are in substantial agreement with the Sinaiticus Greek recension used for the translation of this book. The lost original Hebrew text of 1 Maccabees is replaced by its oldest extant form in Greek. Judith, 2 Maccabees, and parts of Esther are also translated from the Greek.

The basic text for the Psalms is not the Massoretic but one which the editors considered closer to the original inspired form, namely the Hebrew text underlying the new Latin Psalter of the Church, the *Liber Psalmorum* (1944[1], 1945[2]). Nevertheless they retained full liberty to establish the reading of the original text on sound critical principles.

The translation of Sirach, based on the original Hebrew as far as it is preserved and corrected from the ancient versions, is often interpreted in the light of the traditional Greek text. In the Book of Baruch the basic text is the Greek of the Septuagint, with some readings derived from an underlying Hebrew form no longer extant. In the deuterocanonical sections of Daniel (3, 24–90; 13, 1—14, 42), the basic text is the Greek text of Theodotion, occasionally revised according to the Greek text of the Septuagint.

In some instances in the Book of Job, in Proverbs, Sirach, Isaiah, Jeremiah, Ezekiel, Hosea, Amos, Micah, Nahum, Habakkuk, and Zechariah there is good reason to believe that the original order of lines was accidentally disturbed in the transmission of the text. The verse numbers given in such cases are always those of the current Hebrew text, though the arrangement differs. In these instances the textual notes advise the reader of the difficulty. Cases of exceptional dislocation are called to the reader's attention by footnotes.

The Books of *Genesis to Ruth* were first published in 1952; the Wisdom Books, *Job to Sirach,* in 1955; the Prophetic Books, *Isaiah to Malachi,* in 1961; and the Historical Books, *Samuel to Maccabees,* in 1969. In the present edition of *Genesis to Ruth* there are certain new features: a general introduction to the Pentateuch, a retranslation of the text of Genesis with an introduction, cross-references, and revised textual notes, besides new and expanded exegetical notes which take into consideration the various sources or literary traditions.

The revision of *Job to Sirach* includes changes in strophe division in Job and Proverbs and in titles of principal parts and sections of Wisdom and Ecclesiastes. Corrections in the text of Sirach are made in 39, 27—44, 17 on the basis of the Masada text, and in 51, 13–30 on the basis of the occurrence of this canticle in the Psalms scroll from Qumran Cave 11. In this typical edition, new corrections are reflected in the textual notes of Job, Proverbs, Wisdom, and Sirach. In the Psalms, the enumeration found in the Hebrew text is followed instead of the double enumeration, according to both the Hebrew and the Latin Vulgate texts, contained in the previous edition of this book.

In the Prophetic Books *Isaiah to Malachi,* only minor revisions have been made in the structure and wording of the texts, and in the textual notes.

The spelling of proper names in *The New American Bible* follows the customary forms found in most English Bibles since the Authorized Version.

The work of translating the Bible has been characterized as "the sacred and apostolic work of interpreting the word of God and of presenting it to the laity in translations as clear as the difficulty of the matter and the limitations of human knowledge permit" (A. G. Cicognani, Apostolic Delegate, in *The Catholic Biblical Quarterly,* 6, [1944], 389–90). In the appraisal of the present work, it is hoped that the words of the encyclical *Divino afflante Spiritu* will serve as a guide: "Let all the sons of the church bear in mind that the efforts of these resolute laborers in the vineyard of the Lord should be judged not only with equity and justice but also with the greatest charity; all moreover should abhor that intemperate zeal which imagines that whatever is new should for that very reason be opposed or suspected."

Conscious of their personal limitations for the task thus defined, those who have prepared this text cannot expect that it will be considered perfect; but they can hope that it may deepen in its readers "the right understanding of the divinely given Scriptures," and awaken in them "that piety by which it behooves us to be grateful to the God of all providence, who from the throne of his majesty has sent these books as so many personal letters to his own children" (*Divino afflante Spiritu*).

PREFACE TO THE NEW AMERICAN BIBLE

THE OLD TESTAMENT

On September 30, 1943, His Holiness Pope Pius XII issued his now famous encyclical on scripture studies, *Divino afflante Spiritu.* He wrote: "We ought to explain the original text which was written by the inspired author himself and has more authority and greater weight than any, even the very best, translation whether ancient or modern. This can be done all the more easily and fruitfully if to the knowledge of languages be joined a real skill in literary criticism of the same text."

Early in 1944, in conformity with the spirit of the encyclical, and with the encouragement of Archbishop Cicognani, Apostolic Delegate to the United States, the Bishops' Committee of the Confraternity of Christian Doctrine requested members of The Catholic Biblical Association of America to translate the sacred scriptures from the original languages or from the oldest extant form of the text, and to present the sense of the biblical text in as correct a form as possible.

The first English Catholic version of the Bible, the Douay-Rheims (1582–1609/10), and its revision by Bishop Challoner (1750) were based on the Latin Vulgate. In view of the relative certainties more recently attained by textual and higher criticism, it has become increasingly desirable that contemporary translations of the sacred books into English be prepared in which due reverence for the text and strict observance of the rules of criticism would be combined.

The New American Bible has accomplished this in response to the need of the church in America today. It is the achievement of some fifty biblical scholars, the greater number of whom, though not all, are Catholics. In particular, the editors-in-chief have devoted twenty-five years to this work. The collaboration of scholars who are not Catholic fulfills the directive of the Second Vatican Council, not only that "correct translations be made into different languages especially from the original texts of the sacred books," but that, "with the approval of the church authority, these translations be produced in cooperation with separated brothers" so that "all Christians may be able to use them."

The text of the books contained in *The New American Bible* is a completely new translation throughout. From the original and the oldest available texts of the sacred books, it aims to convey as directly as possible the thought and individual style of the inspired writers. The better understanding of Hebrew and Greek, and the steady development of the science of textual criticism, the fruit of patient study since the time of St. Jerome, have allowed the translators and editors in their use of all available materials to approach more closely than ever before the sense of what the sacred authors actually wrote.

Where the translation supposes the received text—Hebrew, Aramaic, or Greek, as the case may be—ordinarily contained in the best-known editions, as the original or the oldest extant form, no additional remarks are necessary. But for those who are happily able to study the original text of the scriptures at firsthand, a supplementary series of textual notes pertaining to the Old Testament was added originally in an appendix to the typical edition. (It is now obtainable in a separate booklet from The Catholic Biblical Association of America, The Catholic University of America, Washington, DC 20064.) These notes furnish a guide in those cases in which the editorial board judges that the manuscripts in the original languages, or the evidence of the ancient versions, or some similar source, furnish the correct reading of a passage, or at least a reading more true to the original than that customarily printed in the available editions.

The mysterious and tortuous way in which this people is brought into being is described: Despite Sarah's sterility, Isaac is finally born—to be offered in sacrifice! The promises are renewed to him eventually, and also to the devious Jacob, as if to show that the divine design will be effected, with or without human cunning. The magnificent story of Joseph is highlighted by the theme of Providence; the promise of a people is taking shape.

Israel is not formed in a vacuum, but amid the age-old civilization of Mesopotamia and the Nile. Oppression in Egypt provokes a striking intervention of God.

Yahweh reveals himself to Moses as a savior, and the epic story of deliverance is told in Exodus. This book also tells of the Sinai covenant, which is rightfully regarded as the key to the Old Testament. Through the covenant Israel becomes Yahweh's people, and Yahweh becomes Israel's God. This act of grace marks the fulfillment of the first promise; that Abraham will be the father of a great nation, God's special possession. The laws in Exodus and Leviticus (P tradition) are both early and late. They spell out the proper relationship of the federation of the Twelve tribes with the LORD. He is a jealous God, demanding exclusive allegiance; he cannot be imaged; he takes vengeance upon the wicked, and shows mercy to the good. Slowly the LORD reveals himself to his people; with remarkable honesty, Israel records the unsteady response—the murmurings and rebellions and infidelities through the desert wanderings up to the plain of Moab.

This sacred history was formed within the bosom of early Israel, guided by the spirit of God. It was sung beside the desert campfires; it was commemorated in the liturgical feasts, such as Passover; it was transmitted by word of mouth from generation to generation—until all was brought together in writing, about the sixth century B.C., when the literary formation of the Pentateuch came to an end.

The Book of Deuteronomy has a history quite peculiar to itself. Its old traditions and law code (12—26) are put forth in the form of "discourses" of Moses before his death. The extraordinarily intense and hortatory tone fits the mood of a discourse. The book contains possibly the preaching of the Levites in the northern kingdom of Israel before its fall in 721 B.C. If this book is situated in its proper historical perspective, its true impact is more vividly appreciated. It is the blueprint of the great "Deuteronomic" reform under King Josiah (640–609 B.C.). This was an attempt to galvanize the people into a wholehearted commitment to the covenant ideals, into an obedience motivated by the great commandment of love (Dt 6, 4ff). Israel has yet another chance, if it obeys. The people are poised between life and death; and they are exhorted to choose life—today (26, 16-19; 30, 15-20).

THE BOOK OF GENESIS

Genesis, the first book of the Bible, opens with the Hebrew word bereshit, which means "in the beginning." The title "Genesis" was given to the Septuagint (Greek) translation of the book, because of its concern with the origin of the world (Gn 1, 1; 2, 4), of the human race, and, in particular, of the Hebrew people.

Eleven structural units (toledoth), of unequal length and importance, present the unity and purpose of the book in terms of God's universal sovereignty, his dealings with men, and his choice and formation of a special people to be the instrument of his plan of salvation.

The tracing of the direct descendance from Adam to Jacob constitutes the major part of the book, while the genealogical tables of lateral branches are not so developed nor of such interest as those that pertain to the story of the Israelite people. In fact, these lateral branches gradually disappear from the narrative. And with the introduction of Abraham and his covenant with God, the history of humanity as such becomes contracted to the story of the descendants of Abraham through Isaac and Jacob—the chosen people.

Despite its unity of plan and purpose, the book is a complex work, not to be attributed to a single original author. Several sources, or literary traditions, that the final redactor used in his composition are discernible. These are the Yahwist (J), Elohist (E) and Priestly (P) sources, which in turn reflect older oral traditions (see Introduction to the Pentateuch).

In Genesis, the Yahwist source is the most important by reason of its teaching, its antiquity, and the continuity it gives the book. It constitutes a sacred history, continually drawing attention to the working out of God's design through his interventions in the affairs of men. The Elohist source, less well preserved, is found in fragmentary form only, depicting God's manifestations through visions and dreams rather than theophanies. Angels are God's intermediaries with men. Moreover, there is a solicitude for the divine transcendence and greater sensitivity toward the moral order. The Priestly source contains those elements—chronological data, lists, genealogies—that construct the framework of Genesis and bind its contents together. To the J and E sources it adds such legal institutions as the sabbath rest, circumcision and the alliances between God and Noah and God and Abraham.

The interpreter of Genesis will recognize at once the distinct object that sets chapters 1—11 apart: the recounting of the origin of the world and of man (primeval history). To make the truths contained in these chapters intelligible to the Israelite people destined to preserve them, they needed to be expressed through elements prevailing among that people at that time. For this reason, the truths themselves must therefore be clearly distinguished from their literary garb.

With the story of the patriarchs Abraham, Isaac and Jacob (Gn 11, 27—50, 26), the character of the narrative changes. While we do not view the account of the patriarchs as history in the strict sense, nevertheless certain of the matters recounted from the time of Abraham onward can be placed in the actual historical and social framework of the Near East in the early part of the second millennium B.C. (2000–1500), and documented by non-biblical sources.

Genesis contains many religious teachings of basic importance: the preexistence and transcendence of God, his wisdom and goodness, his power through which all things are made and on which they all depend; the special creation of man in God's image and likeness, and of woman from the substance of man; the institution of marriage as the union of one man with one woman; man's original state of innocence; man's sin of pride and disobedience, its consequences for the protoparents and their posterity. Despite the severity of their punishment, hope of reconciliation is offered by God through the first as well as the subsequent promises of salvation and blessing. Abraham is blessed for his faith and obedience, and he is to be a blessing for all nations through his offspring, Isaac, Jacob, and Jacob's sons (Gn 12, 3; 18, 18; 22, 18), of whom the Messiah, mankind's greatest blessing, will eventually be born (Gal 3, 8).

Frequent references to Genesis are found in the New Testament. Christ becomes the antithesis of Adam: sin and death come to mankind through Adam, justification and life through Jesus Christ (Rom 5, 12. 17ff). Noah's ark becomes the symbol of the church, by which men are saved from destruction through the waters of baptism (1 Pt 3, 20ff); Abraham's faith is the model for all believers; the sacrifice of his son Isaac typifies the sacrifice of Christ, Son of the Father. The liturgy, too, relates the persons of Abel, Abraham and Melchizedek to Christ in his act of sacrifice.

The Book of Genesis is divided as follows:

I. The Primeval History (1, 1—11, 26).
II. The Patriarch Abraham (11, 27—25, 18).
III. The Patriarchs Isaac and Jacob (25, 19—36, 43).
IV. Joseph and His Brothers (37, 1—50, 26).

I: The Primeval History

CHAPTER 1

First Story of Creation* 1In the beginning,
when God created the heavens and the earth,[a]
2the earth was a formless wasteland, and dark-
ness covered the abyss,* while a mighty wind
swept over the waters.[b]
3Then God said, "Let there be light," and
there was light.[c] 4God saw how good the light
was. God then separated the light from the
darkness. 5God called the light "day," and the
darkness he called "night." Thus evening came,
and morning followed—the first day.*
6Then God said, "Let there be a dome in the
middle of the waters, to separate one body of
water from the other." And so it happened:
7God made the dome, and it separated the water
above the dome from the water below it.[d] 8God
called the dome "the sky." Evening came, and
morning followed—the second day.
9Then God said, "Let the water under the sky
be gathered into a single basin, so that the dry
land may appear." And so it happened: the
water under the sky was gathered into its basin,
and the dry land appeared.[e] 10God called the dry
land "the earth," and the basin of the water he
called "the sea." God saw how good it was.
11[f]Then God said, "Let the earth bring forth
vegetation: every kind of plant that bears seed
and every kind of fruit tree on earth that bears
fruit with its seed in it." And so it happened:
12the earth brought forth every kind of plant that
bears seed and every kind of fruit tree on earth
that bears fruit with its seed in it. God saw how
good it was. 13Evening came, and morning
followed—the third day.
14Then God said: "Let there be lights in the
dome of the sky, to separate day from night. Let
them mark the fixed times, the days and the
years,[g] 15and serve as luminaries in the dome of
the sky, to shed light upon the earth." And so it
happened: 16God made the two great lights, the
greater one to govern the day, and the lesser one
to govern the night; and he made the stars.[h]
17God set them in the dome of the sky, to shed
light upon the earth, 18to govern the day and the
night, and to separate the light from the dark-

1, 1—2, 4a: This section introduces the whole Pentateuch. It shows how God brought an orderly universe out of primordial chaos.

1, 2: The abyss: the primordial ocean according to the ancient Semitic cosmogony. After God's creative activity, part of this vast body forms the salt-water seas (vv 9f); part of it is the fresh water under the earth (Ps 33, 7; Ez 31, 4), which wells forth on the earth as springs and fountains (Gn 7, 11; 8, 2; Prv 3, 20). Part of it, "the upper water" (Ps 148, 4; Dn 3, 60), is held up by the dome of the sky (Gn 1, 6f) from which rain descends on the earth (Gn 7, 11; 2 Kgs 7, 2. 19; Ps 104, 13). A mighty wind: Literally, "a wind of God," or "a spirit of God"; cf Gn 8 1.

1, 5: In ancient Israel a day was considered to begin at sunset. According to the highly artificial literary structure of Gn 1, 1—2, 4a, God's creative activity is divided into six days to teach the sacredness of the sabbath rest on the seventh day in the Israelite religion (Gn 2, 2f).

a Gn 2, 1.4: Pss 8, 4; 38—39; 90, 2; Wis 11, 17; Sir 16, 24; Jer 10, 12; 2 Mc 7, 28; Acts 14, 15; Col 1, 16f; Heb 1, 2f; 3, 4; 11, 3; Rv 4, 11. b Jer 4, 23. c 2 Cor 4, 6. d Prv 8, 27f; 2 Pt 3, 5. e Jb 38, 8; Ps 33, 7; Jer 5, 22. f Ps 104, 14. g Jb 26, 10; Ps 19, 1f; Bar 3, 33. h Dt 4, 19; Ps 136, 7ff; Wis 13, 2ff; Jer 31, 35.

ness. God saw how good it was. [19]Evening
came, and morning followed—the fourth day.
[20] [i]Then God said, "Let the water teem with
an abundance of living creatures, and on the
earth let birds fly beneath the dome of the sky."
And so it happened: [21]God created the great sea
monsters and all kinds of swimming creatures
with which the water teems, and all kinds of
winged birds. God saw how good it was, [22]and
God blessed them, saying, "Be fertile, multiply,
and fill the water of the seas; and let the birds
multiply on the earth." [j] [23]Evening came, and
morning followed—the fifth day.
[24] [k]Then God said, "Let the earth bring forth
all kinds of living creatures: cattle, creeping
things, and wild animals of all kinds." And so it
happened: [25]God made all kinds of wild animals,
all kinds of cattle, and all kinds of creeping
things of the earth. God saw how good it was.
[26] [l]Then God said: "Let us make man in our
image, after our likeness. Let them have domin-
ion over the fish of the sea, the birds of the air,
and the cattle, and over all the wild animals and
all the creatures that crawl on the ground."*

[27]God created man in his image;
in the divine image he created him;
male and female he created them.

[28]God blessed them, saying: "Be fertile and
multiply; fill the earth and subdue it. Have
dominion over the fish of the sea, the birds of the
air, and all the living things that move on the
earth." [m] [29] [n]God also said: "See, I give you every
seed-bearing plant all over the earth and every
tree that has seed-bearing fruit on it to be your
food; [30]and to all the animals of the land, all the
birds of the air, and all the living creatures that
crawl on the ground, I give all the green plants
for food." And so it happened. [31]God looked at
everything he had made, and he found it very
good. Evening came, and morning followed—
the sixth day. [o]

CHAPTER 2

[1]Thus the heavens and the earth and all their
array were completed. [p] [2]Since on the seventh
day God was finished with the work he had
been doing, he rested on the seventh day from
all the work he had undertaken. [q] [3]So God
blessed the seventh day and made it holy,
because on it he rested from all the work he had
done in creation. [r]

[4]Such is the story of the heavens and the earth
at their creation.

Second Story of Creation* At the time when
the LORD God made the earth and the
heavens— [5]while as yet there was no field shrub
on earth and no grass of the field had sprouted,
for the LORD God had sent no rain upon the
earth and there was no man to till the soil, [6]but a
stream was welling up out of the earth and was
watering all the surface of the ground— [7]the
LORD God formed man out of the clay of the
ground* and blew into his nostrils the breath of
life, and so man became a living being. [s]

[8]Then the LORD God planted a garden in
Eden,* in the east, and he placed there the man
whom he had formed. [t] [9]Out of the ground the
LORD God made various trees grow that were
delightful to look at and good for food, with the
tree of life in the middle of the garden and the
tree of the knowledge of good and bad. [u]

[10]A river rises* in Eden to water the garden;

1, 26: Man is here presented as the climax of God's creative activity; he resembles God primarily because of the dominion God gives him over the rest of creation.

2, 4b-25: This section is chiefly concerned with the creation of man. It is much older than the narrative of Gn 1, 1—2, 4a. Here God is depicted as creating man before the rest of his creatures, which are made for man's sake.

2, 7: God is portrayed as a potter molding man's body out of clay. There is a play on words in Hebrew between adam ("man") and adama ("ground"). Being: literally, "soul."

2, 8: Eden: used here as the name of a region in southern Mesopotamia; the term is derived from the Sumerian word eden, "fertile plain." A similar-sounding Hebrew word means "delight"; the garden in Eden could therefore be understood as the "garden of delight," so that, through the Greek version, it is now known also as "paradise," literally, a "pleasure park."

2, 10-14: Rises: in flood to overflow its banks. Beyond there: as one travels upstream. Branches: literally, "heads," i.e., upper courses. Eden is near the head of the Persian Gulf, where the

i Jb 12, 7-10. j Gn 8, 17. k Sir 16, 27f; Bar 3, 32. l 26f: Gn 5, 1. 3; 9, 6; Ps 8, 5f; Wis 2, 23; 10, 2; Sir 17, 1. 3f; Jas 3, 7; 1 Cor 11, 7; Eph 4, 24; Col 3, 10; 2Mt 19, 4; Mk 10, 6. m Gn 8, 17; 9, 1; Pss 8, 6-9; 115, 16; Wis 9, 2. n 29f: Gn 9, 3; Ps 104, 14f. o 1 Tm 4, 4. p Is 45, 12; Jn 1, 3. q Ex 20, 9ff; 31, 17; Heb 4, 4. 10. r Ex 20, 11; Dt 5, 14; Neh 9, 14. s Gn 3, 19; 18, 27; Tb 8, 6; Jb 34, 15; Pss 103, 14; 104, 29; Eccl 3, 20; 12, 7; Wis 7, 1; Sir 33, 10; 1 Cor 15, 245. t Is 51, 3; Ez 31, 9. u Gn 3, 22; Prv 3, 18; Rv 2, 7; 22, 2. 14.

beyond there it divides and becomes four
branches. 11 The name of the first is the Pishon;
it is the one that winds through the whole land
of Havilah, where there is gold. 12 The gold of
that land is excellent; bdellium and lapis lazuli
are also there. 13 The name of the second river is
the Gihon; it is the one that winds all through
the land of Cush.[v] 14 The name of the third river
is the Tigris; it is the one that flows east of
Asshur. The fourth river is the Euphrates.
15 The LORD God then took the man and
settled him in the garden of Eden, to cultivate
and care for it.[w] 16 The LORD God gave man this
order: "You are free to eat from any of the trees
of the garden[x] 17 except the tree of knowledge of
good and bad. From that tree you shall not eat;
the moment you eat from it you are surely
doomed to die."[y]
18 The LORD God said: "It is not good for the
man to be alone. I will make a suitable partner
for him."[z] 19 So the LORD God formed out of the
ground various wild animals and various birds of
the air, and he brought them to the man to see
what he would call them; whatever the man
called each of them would be its name. 20 The
man gave names to all the cattle, all the birds of
the air, and all the wild animals; but none
proved to be the suitable partner for the man.
21 So the LORD God cast a deep sleep on the
man, and while he was asleep, he took out one
of his ribs and closed up its place with flesh.[a]
22 The LORD God then built up into a woman the
rib that he had taken from the man. When he
brought her to the man, 23 the man said:

"This one, at last, is bone of my bones
and flesh of my flesh;
This one shall be called 'woman,'
for out of 'her man' this one has been
taken."*

24 [b]That is why a man leaves his father and
mother and clings to his wife, and the two of
them become one body.*
25 The man and his wife were both naked, yet
they felt no shame.

CHAPTER 3

The Fall of Man 1 Now the serpent was the
most cunning of all the animals that the LORD
God had made. The serpent asked the woman,
"Did God really tell you not to eat from any of
the trees in the garden?" 2 The woman answered
the serpent: "We may eat of the fruit of the trees
in the garden; 3 [c]it is only about the fruit of the
tree in the middle of the garden that God said,
'You shall not eat it or even touch it, lest you
die.' " 4 But the serpent said to the woman: "You
certainly will not die![d] 5 No, God knows well
that the moment you eat of it your eyes will be
opened and you will be like gods who know*
what is good and what is bad." 6 The woman saw
that the tree was good for food, pleasing to the
eyes, and desirable for gaining wisdom. So she
took some of its fruit and ate it; and she also
gave some to her husband, who was with her,
and he ate it.[e] 7 Then the eyes of both of them
were opened, and they realized that they were
naked; so they sewed fig leaves together and
made loincloths for themselves.
8 When they heard the sound of the LORD God
moving about in the garden at the breezy time of
the day,* the man and his wife hid themselves
from the LORD God among the trees of the
garden.[f] 9 The LORD God then called to the man
and asked him, "Where are you?" 10 He an-
swered, "I heard you in the garden; but I was
afraid, because I was naked, so I hid myself."
11 Then he asked, "Who told you that you were
naked? You have eaten, then, from the tree of

Tigris and the Euphrates join with two other streams to form a single river. The land of Cush here and in Gn 10, 8, is not Ethiopia (Nubia) as elsewhere, but the region of the Kassites east of Mesopotamia.

2, 23: There is a play on the similar-sounding Hebrew words ishsha ("woman") and ishah ("her man, her husband").

2, 24: One body: literally "one flesh"; classical Hebrew has no specific word for "body." The sacred writer stresses the fact that conjugal union is willed by God.

3, 5: Like gods who know: or "like God who knows."

3, 8: The breezy time of the day: literally "the wind of the day." On most days in Palestine a cooling breeze blows from the sea shortly before sunset.

v Sir 24, 25. w Sir 7, 15. x Ps 104, 14. y Gn 3, 2f; Rom 6, 23. z Tb 8, 6; Sir 36, 24; 1 Cor 11, 9; 1 Tm 2, 13. a Sir 17, 1; 1 Cor 11, 8f; 1 Tm 2, 13. b Mt 19, 5; Mk 10, 7; 1 Cor 7, 10f; Eph 5, 31. c Gn 2, 17; Rom 6, 23. d 4f: Wis 2, 24; Sir 25, 14; Is 14, 14; Jn 8, 44; 2 Cor 11, 3. e Gn 3, 22; 1 Tm 2, 14. f Jer 23, 24.

which I had forbidden you to eat!" 12The man
replied, "The woman whom you put here with
me—she gave me fruit from the tree, and so I
ate it." 13The LORD God then asked the woman,
"Why did you do such a thing?" The woman
answered, "The serpent tricked me into it, so I
ate it."[g]
14Then the LORD God said to the serpent:

"Because you have done this, you shall be
banned
from all the animals
and from all the wild creatures;
On your belly shall you crawl,
and dirt shall you eat
all the days of your life.[h]
15 I will put enmity between you and the
woman,
and between your offspring and hers;
He will strike at your head,
while you strike at his heel."*[i]
16To the woman he said:
"I will intensify the pangs of your
childbearing;
in pain shall you bring forth children.
Yet your urge shall be for your husband,
and he shall be your master."[j]

17To the man he said: "Because you listened
to your wife and ate from the tree of which I had
forbidden you to eat,

"Cursed be the ground because of you!
In toil shall you eat its yield
all the days of your life.[k]
18 Thorns and thistles shall it bring forth to you,
as you eat of the plants of the field.
19 By the sweat of your face
shall you get bread to eat,
Until you return to the ground,
from which you were taken;
For you are dirt,
and to dirt you shall return."[l]

20The man called his wife Eve, because she
became the mother of all the living.*
21For the man and his wife the LORD God
made leather garments, with which he clothed
them. 22Then the LORD God said: "See! The
man has become like one of us, knowing what is
good and what is bad! Therefore, he must not be
allowed to put out his hand to take fruit from the
tree of life also, and thus eat of it and live
forever."[m] 23The LORD God therefore banished
him from the garden of Eden, to till the ground
from which he had been taken. 24When he
expelled the man, he settled him east of the
garden of Eden; and he stationed the cherubim
and the fiery revolving sword, to guard the way
to the tree of life.*

CHAPTER 4

Cain and Abel 1The man had relations with
his wife Eve, and she conceived and bore Cain,
saying, "I have produced a man with the help of
the LORD."* 2Next she bore his brother Abel.
Abel became a keeper of flocks, and Cain a tiller
of the soil. 3In the course of time Cain brought
an offering to the LORD from the fruit of the soil,
4while Abel, for his part, brought one of the best
firstlings of his flock.[n] The LORD looked with
favor on Abel and his offering, 5but on Cain and
his offering he did not. Cain greatly resented this
and was crestfallen. 6So the LORD said to Cain:
"Why are you so resentful and crestfallen? 7If

3, 15: He will strike . . . at his heel: since the antecedent for he and his is the collective noun offspring, i.e., all the descendants of the woman, a more exact rendering of the sacred writer's words would be, "They will strike . . . at their heels." However, later theology saw in this passage more than unending hostility between snakes and men. The serpent was regarded as the devil (Wis 2, 24; Jn 8, 44; Rv 12, 9; 20, 2), whose eventual defeat seems implied in the contrast between head and heel. Because "the Son of God appeared that he might destroy the works of the devil" (1 Jn 3, 8), the passage can be understood as the first promise of a Redeemer for fallen mankind. The woman's offspring then is primarily Jesus Christ.

3, 20: This verse seems to be out of place; it would fit better after v 24. The Hebrew name hawwa ("Eve") is related to the Hebrew word hay ("living").

3, 24: The above rendering is based on the ancient Greek version; that of the current Hebrew is, When he expelled the man, he settled east of the garden of Eden, the cherubim.

4, 1: The Hebrew name qayin ("Cain") and the term qaniti ("I have produced") present another play on words.

g 2 Cor 11, 3. h Is 65, 25; Mi 7, 17; Rv 12, 9. i Is 7, 14; 9, 5; Rom 16, 20; 1 Jn 3, 8; Rv 12, 17. j 1 Cor 11, 3; Eph 5, 22f; 1 Tm 2, 12. k Gn 5, 29; Rom 5, 12; 8, 20; Heb 6, 8. l Gn 2, 7; Jb 10, 9; 34, 15; Pss 90, 3; 103, 14; Eccl 3, 20; 12, 7; Wis 15, 8; Sir 10, 9; 17, 2; Rom 5, 12; 1 Cor 15, 21; Heb 9, 27. m Gn 2, 9; Rv 22, 2. 14. n Ex 34, 19; Heb 11, 4.

you do well, you can hold up your head; but if
not, sin is a demon lurking* at the door: his urge
is toward you, yet you can be his master."[o]
8 Cain said to his brother Abel, "Let us go out
in the field." When they were in the field, Cain
attacked his brother Abel and killed him.[p] 9 Then
the LORD asked Cain, "Where is your brother
Abel?" He answered, "I do not know. Am I my
brother's keeper?" 10 The LORD then said: "What
have you done! Listen: Your brother's blood
cries out to me from the soil! 11 Therefore you
shall be banned from the soil that opened its
mouth to receive your brother's blood from your
hand.[q] 12 If you till the soil, it shall no longer give
you its produce. You shall become a restless
wanderer on the earth." 13 Cain said to the
LORD: "My punishment is too great to bear.
14 Since you have now banished me from the
soil, and I must avoid your presence and become
a restless wanderer on the earth, anyone may kill
me at sight." 15 "Not so!" the LORD said to him.
"If anyone kills Cain, Cain shall be avenged
sevenfold." So the LORD put a mark* on Cain,
lest anyone should kill him at sight. 16 Cain then
left the LORD's presence and settled in the land
of Nod,* east of Eden.

Descendants of Cain and Seth 17 *Cain had
relations with his wife, and she conceived and
bore Enoch. Cain also became the founder of a
city, which he named after his son Enoch. 18 To
Enoch was born Irad, and Irad became the father
of Mehujael; Mehujael became the father of
Methusael, and Methusael became the father of
Lamech. 19 Lamech took two wives; the name of
the first was Adah, and the name of the second
Zillah. 20 Adah gave birth to Jabal, the ancestor of
all who dwell in tents and keep cattle. 21 His
brother's name was Jubal; he was the ancestor of
all who play the lyre and the pipe. 22 Zillah, on
her part, gave birth to Tubalcain, the ancestor of
all who forge instruments of bronze and iron.
The sister of Tubalcain was Naamah. 23 Lamech
said to his wives:

"Adah and Zillah, hear my voice;
wives of Lamech, listen to my utterance:
I have killed a man for wounding me,
a boy for bruising me.
24 If Cain is avenged sevenfold,
then Lamech seventy-sevenfold."

25 Adam again had relations with his wife, and
she gave birth to a son whom she called Seth.
"God has granted* me more offspring in place of
Abel," she said, "because Cain slew him." 26 To
Seth, in turn, a son was born, and he named him
Enosh.

At that time men began to invoke the LORD by
name.[r]

CHAPTER 5

Generations: Adam to Noah* 1 [s]This is the
record of the descendants of Adam. When God
created man, he made him in the likeness of
God; 2 he created them male and female. When
they were created, he blessed them and named
them "man."
3 [t]Adam was one hundred and thirty years old
when he begot a son in his likeness, after his

4, 7: Demon lurking: in Hebrew, robes, literally "croucher," is used here, like the similar Akkadian term rabisu, to designate a certain kind of evil spirit.

4, 15: A mark: probably a tattoo. The use of tattooing for tribal marks has always been common among the nomads of the Near Eastern deserts.

4, 16: The land of Nod: not a definite geographic region. The term merely means "the land of nomads."

4, 17–22: In vv 12–16 Cain was presented as the archetype of nomadic peoples. The sacred author in this section follows another ancient tradition that makes Cain the prototype of sedentary peoples with higher material culture.

4, 25f: Has granted: Hebrew shat, a wordplay on the name shet ("Seth"). Enosh: in Hebrew, a synonym of adam ("man"). At the time . . . name: men began to call God by his personal name, Yahweh, rendered as "the Lord" in this version of the Bible. The ancient, so-called Yahwist source used here employs the name Yahweh long before the time of Moses. Another ancient source, the Elohist (from its use of the term Elohim, "God," instead of Yahweh, "Lord," for the pre-Mosaic period), makes Moses the first to use Yahweh as the proper name of Israel's God, previously known by other names as well; cf Ex 3, 13ff.

5, 1–32: Although this chapter, with its highly schematic form, belongs to the relatively late "Priestly document," it is based on very ancient traditions. Together with Gn 11, 10–26, its primary purpose is to bridge the genealogical gap between Adam and Abraham. Adam's line is traced through Seth, but several names in the series are the same as, or similar to, certain names in Cain's line (Gn 4, 17ff). The long lifespans attributed to these ten antediluvian patriarchs have a symbolic rather than a historical value. Babylonian tradition also recorded ten kings with fantastically high ages who reigned successively before the flood.

o Sir 7, 1; Jude 11. p Wis 10, 3; Mt 23, 35; Lk 11, 51; 1 Jn 3, 12; Jude 11. q Dt 27, 24. r 1 Chr 1, 1; Lk 3, 38. s Gn 1, 27; Wis 2, 23; Sir 17, 1; 1 Cor 11, 7; Jas 3, 9. t Gn 4, 25.

image; and he named him Seth.[u] 4 Adam lived
eight hundred years after the birth of Seth, and
he had other sons and daughters. 5 The whole
lifetime of Adam was nine hundred and thirty
years; then he died.
6 When Seth was one hundred and five years
old, he became the father of Enosh. 7 Seth lived
eight hundred and seven years after the birth of
Enosh, and he had other sons and daughters.
8 The whole lifetime of Seth was nine hundred
and twelve years; then he died.
9 When Enosh was ninety years old, he be-
came the father of Kenan. 10 Enosh lived eight
hundred and fifteen years after the birth of
Kenan, and he had other sons and daughters.
11 The whole lifetime of Enosh was nine hundred
and five years; then he died.
12 When Kenan was seventy years old, he
became the father of Mahalalel. 13 Kenan lived
eight hundred and forty years after the birth of
Mahalalel, and he had other sons and daughters.
14 The whole lifetime of Kenan was nine hun-
dred and ten years; then he died.
15 When Mahalalel was sixty-five years old, he
became the father of Jared. 16 Mahalalel lived
eight hundred and thirty years after the birth of
Jared, and he had other sons and daughters.
17 The whole lifetime of Mahalalel was eight
hundred and ninety-five years; then he died.
18 When Jared was one hundred and sixty-two
years old, he became the father of Enoch. 19 Jared
lived eight hundred years after the birth of
Enoch, and he had other sons and daughters.
20 The whole lifetime of Jared was nine hundred
and sixty-two years; then he died.
21 When Enoch was sixty-five years old, he
became the father of Methuselah. 22 Enoch lived
three hundred years after the birth of Methuse-
lah, and he had other sons and daughters. 23 The
whole lifetime of Enoch was three hundred and
sixty-five years. 24 Then Enoch walked with
God,* and he was no longer here, for God took
him.[v]
25 When Methuselah was one hundred and
eighty-seven years old, he became the father of
Lamech. 26 Methuselah lived seven hundred and
eighty-two years after the birth of Lamech, and
he had other sons and daughters. 27 The whole
lifetime of Methuselah was nine hundred and
sixty-nine years; then he died.
28 When Lamech was one hundred and eighty-
two years old, he begot a son 29 [w]and named him
Noah, saying, "Out of the very ground that the
LORD has put under a curse, this one shall bring
us relief from our work and the toil of our
hands."* 30 Lamech lived five hundred and
ninety-five years after the birth of Noah, and he
had other sons and daughters. 31 The whole
lifetime of Lamech was seven hundred and
seventy-seven years; then he died.
32 When Noah was five hundred years old, he
became the father of Shem, Ham and Japheth.[x]

CHAPTER 6

Origin of the Nephilim* 1 When men began
to multiply on earth and daughters were born to
them, 2 the sons of heaven* saw how beautiful
the daughters of man were, and so they took for
their wives as many of them as they chose.[y]
3 Then the LORD said: "My spirit* shall not
remain in man forever, since he is but flesh. His
days shall comprise one hundred and twenty
years."
4 At that time the Nephilim appeared on earth
(as well as later*), after the sons of heaven had

5, 24: In place of the usual formula, Then he died, the change to Enoch walked with God clearly implies that he did not die, but like Elijah (2 Kgs 2, 11f) was taken alive to God's abode.

5, 29: There is a similarity in sound between the Hebrew word noah, "Noah," and the verbal phrase yenahamenu, "he will bring us relief"; this latter refers both to the curse put on the soil because of the fall of man (Gn 3, 17ff) and to Noah's success in agriculture, especially in raising grapes for wine (Gn 9, 20f).

6, 1–4: This is apparently a fragment of an old legend that had borrowed much from ancient mythology. The sacred author incorporates it here, not only in order to account for the prehistoric giants of Palestine, whom the Israelites called the Nephilim, but also to introduce the story of the flood with a moral orientation—the constantly increasing wickedness of mankind.

6, 2: The sons of heaven: literally "the sons of the gods" or "the sons of God," i.e., the celestial beings of mythology.

6, 3: My spirit: the breath of life referred to in Gn 2, 7. His days . . . years: probably the time God would still let men live on earth before destroying them with the flood, rather than the maximum span of life God would allot to individual men in the future.

6, 4: As well as later: According to Nm 13, 33, when the

u 3–32: 1 Chr 1, 1–4; Lk 3, 36ff. v Wis 4, 10f; Sir 44, 16; 49, 14; Heb 11, 5. w Gn 3, 17ff. x Gn 6, 10; 10, 1. y Mt 24, 38; Lk 17, 26f.

intercourse with the daughters of man, who
bore them sons. They were the heroes of old, the
men of renown.[z]

Warning of the Flood 5*When the LORD saw
how great was man's wickedness on earth, and
how no desire that his heart conceived was ever
anything but evil,[a] 6he regretted that he had
made man on the earth, and his heart was
grieved.

7So the LORD said: "I will wipe out from the
earth the men whom I have created, and not
only the men, but also the beasts and the
creeping things and the birds of the air, for I am
sorry that I made them." 8But Noah found favor
with the LORD.

9These are the descendants of Noah. Noah, a
good man and blameless in that age,[b] 10for he
walked with God, begot three sons: Shem, Ham
and Japheth.

11In the eyes of God the earth was corrupt
and full of lawlessness.[c] 12When God saw how
corrupt the earth had become, since all mortals
led depraved lives on earth,[d] 13he said to Noah:
"I have decided to put an end to all mortals on
earth; the earth is full of lawlessness because of
them. So I will destroy them and all life on
earth.[e]

Preparation for the Flood 14"Make yourself
an ark of gopherwood,* put various compart-
ments in it, and cover it inside and out with
pitch. 15This is how you shall build it: the length
of the ark shall be three hundred cubits, its
width fifty cubits, and its height thirty cubits.*
16Make an opening for daylight* in the ark, and
finish the ark a cubit above it. Put an entrance in
the side of the ark, which you shall make with
bottom, second and third decks. 17I, on my part,
am about to bring the flood [waters] on the earth,
to destroy everywhere all creatures in which
there is the breath of life; everything on earth
shall perish.[f] 18But with you I will establish my
covenant; you and your sons, your wife and your
sons' wives, shall go into the ark.[g] 19Of all other
living creatures you shall bring two into the ark,
one male and one female, that you may keep
them alive with you. 20Of all kinds of birds, of all
kinds of beasts, and of all kinds of creeping
things, two of each shall come into the ark with
you, to stay alive. 21Moreover, you are to
provide yourself with all the food that is to be
eaten, and store it away, that it may serve as
provisions for you and for them." 22This Noah
did; he carried out all the commands that God
gave him.

CHAPTER 7

1Then the LORD said to Noah: "Go into the
ark, you and all your household, for you alone in
this age have I found to be truly just.[h] 2Of every
clean animal, take with you seven pairs, a male
and its mate; and of the unclean animals, one
pair, a male and its mate; 3likewise, of every
clean bird of the air, seven pairs, a male and a
female, and of all the unclean birds, one pair, a
male and a female. Thus you will keep their
issue alive over all the earth. 4Seven days from

Israelites invaded Palestine and found there the tall aboriginal Anakim, they likened them to the Nephilim; cf Dt 2, 10f. Perhaps the huge megalithic structures in Palestine were thought to have been built by a race of giants, whose superhuman strength was attributed to semi-divine origin. The heroes of old: the legendary worthies of ancient mythology.

6, 5—8, 22: The story of the great flood here recorded is a composite narrative based on two separate sources interwoven into an intricate patchwork. To the Yahwist source, with some later editorial additions, are usually assigned 6, 5–8; 7, 1–5. 7–10. 12. 16b. 17b. 22–23; 8, 2b-3a. 6–12. 13b. 20–22. The other sections come from the "Priestly document." The combination of the two sources produced certain duplications (e.g., 6, 13–22 of the Yahwist source, beside 7, 1–5 of the Priestly source); also certain inconsistencies, such as the number of the various animals taken into the ark (6, 19f; 7, 14f of the Priestly source, beside 7, 2f of the Yahwist source), and the timetable of the flood (8, 3–5. 13f of the Priestly source, beside 7, 4. 10. 12. 17b; 8, 6. 10. 12 of the Yahwist source). Both biblical sources go back ultimately to an ancient Mesopotamian story of a great flood, preserved in the eleventh tablet of the Gilgamesh Epic. The latter account, in some respects remarkably similar to the biblical account, is in others very different from it.

6, 14: Gopherwood: an unidentified wood not mentioned elsewhere; gopher is merely the Hebrew word for it.

6, 15: The dimensions of Noah's ark were approximately 440 × 73 × 44 feet, a foot and a half to the cubit. The ark of the Babylonian flood story was an exact cube, 120 cubits in length, width, and height.

6, 16: Opening for daylight: a conjectural rendering of the Hebrew word sohar, occurring only here. The reference is probably to an open space on all sides near the top of the ark to admit light and air. The ark also had a window or hatch, which could be opened and closed (Gn 8, 6).

z Wis 14, 6; Bar 3, 26. a Ps 14, 2f. b Wis 10, 4; Sir 44, 17. c Jb 22, 15ff. d Ps 14, 2. e Sir 40, 9f; 44, 17; Mt 24, 37ff. f Gn 7, 4. 21; 2 Pt 2, 5. g Gn 9, 9; Wis 14, 6; Heb 11, 7; 1 Pt 3, 20. h Wis 10, 4; Sir 44, 17; 2 Pt 2, 5.

now I will bring rain down on the earth for forty
days and forty nights, and so I will wipe out from
the surface of the earth every moving creature
that I have made."[i] [5]Noah did just as the LORD
had commanded him.

The Great Flood [6]Noah was six hundred years
old when the flood waters came upon the earth.
[7]Together with his sons, his wife, and his sons'
wives, Noah went into the ark because of the
waters of the flood.[j] [8]Of the clean animals and
the unclean, of the birds, and of everything that
creeps on the ground, [9][two by two] male and
female entered the ark with Noah, just as the
LORD had commanded him.[k] [10]As soon as the
seven days were over, the waters of the flood
came upon the earth.

[11]In the six hundredth year of Noah's life, in
the second month, on the seventeenth day of the
month: it was on that day that

All the fountains of the great abyss* burst
forth,
and the floodgates of the sky were opened.

[12]For forty days and forty nights heavy rain
poured down on the earth.

[13]On the precise day named, Noah and his
sons Shem, Ham and Japheth, and Noah's wife,
and the three wives of Noah's sons had entered
the ark, [14]together with every kind of wild
beast, every kind of domestic animal, every kind
of creeping thing of the earth, and every kind of
bird. [15]Pairs of all creatures in which there was
the breath of life entered the ark with Noah.
[16]Those that entered were male and female, and
of all species they came, as God had commanded
Noah. Then the LORD shut him in.

[17]The flood continued upon the earth for forty
days. As the waters increased, they lifted the ark,
so that it rose above the earth. [18]The swelling
waters increased greatly, but the ark floated on
the surface of the waters. [19]Higher and higher
above the earth rose the waters, until all the
highest mountains everywhere were submerged,
[20]the crest rising fifteen cubits higher than the
submerged mountains. [21]All creatures that
stirred on earth perished: birds, cattle, wild
animals, and all that swarmed on the earth, as
well as all mankind.[l] [22]Everything on dry land
with the faintest breath of life in its nostrils died
out. [23]The LORD wiped out every living thing on
earth: man and cattle, the creeping things and
the birds of the air; all were wiped out from the
earth. Only Noah and those with him in the ark
were left.

CHAPTER 8

[24]*The waters maintained their crest over the
earth for one hundred and fifty days, [1]and then
God remembered Noah and all the animals, wild
and tame, that were with him in the ark. So God
made a wind sweep over the earth, and the
waters began to subside. [2]The fountains of the
abyss and the floodgates of the sky were closed,
and the downpour from the sky was held back.
[3]Gradually the waters receded from the earth.
At the end of one hundred and fifty days, the
waters had so diminished [4]that, in the seventh
month, on the seventeenth day of the month,
the ark came to rest on the mountains of
Ararat.* [5]The waters continued to diminish
until the tenth month, and on the first day of the
tenth month the tops of the mountains ap-
peared.

[6]At the end of forty days Noah opened the
hatch he had made in the ark,* [7]and he sent out
a raven, to see if the waters had lessened on the
earth. It flew back and forth until the waters
dried off from the earth. [8]Then he sent out a
dove, to see if the waters had lessened on the
earth. [9]But the dove could find no place to alight
and perch, and it returned to him in the ark, for
there was water all over the earth. Putting out
his hand, he caught the dove and drew it back to
him inside the ark. [10]He waited seven days more

7, 11: Abyss: the subterranean ocean; see note on Gn 1, 2.

7, 24: This verse belongs to chapter 7 but its contents properly introduce chapter 8.

8, 4: Ararat: ancient Urartu, north of the Mesopotamian plain, part of modern Armenia.

8, 6: In the original Yahwist source, from which this verse is taken, the forty days refer to the full period of the flood itself (cf Gn 7, 4. 17); in the present context, however, they seem to refer to a period following the date just given in v 5 from the Priestly source.

i Gn 6, 17; 2 Pt 2, 5. j Wis 14, 6; 1 Pt 3, 20; 2 Pt 2, 5. k Gn 6, 19. l 21ff; Jb 22, 16; Mt 24, 39; Lk 17, 27; 2 Pt 3, 6.

and again sent the dove out from the ark. 11In
the evening the dove came back to him, and
there in its bill was a plucked-off olive leaf! So
Noah knew that the waters had lessened on the
earth. 12He waited still another seven days and
then released the dove once more; and this time
it did not come back.

13In the six hundred and first year of Noah's
life, in the first month, on the first day of the
month, the water began to dry up on the earth.
Noah then removed the covering of the ark and
saw that the surface of the ground was drying
up. 14In the second month, on the twenty-
seventh day of the month, the earth was dry.

15Then God said to Noah: 16"Go out of the
ark, together with your wife and your sons and
your sons' wives. 17Bring out with you every
living thing that is with you—all bodily crea-
tures, be they birds or animals or creeping things
of the earth—and let them abound on the earth,
breeding and multiplying on it."[m] 18So Noah
came out, together with his wife and his sons
and his sons' wives; 19and all the animals, wild
and tame, all the birds, and all the creeping
creatures of the earth left the ark, one kind after
another.

20Then Noah built an altar to the LORD, and
choosing from every clean animal and every
clean bird, he offered holocausts on the altar.
21When the LORD smelled the sweet odor, he
said to himself: "Never again will I doom the
earth because of man, since the desires of man's
heart are evil from the start;* nor will I ever
again strike down all living beings, as I have
done.[n]

22As long as the earth lasts,
seedtime and harvest,
cold and heat,
Summer and winter,
and day and night
shall not cease."[o]

CHAPTER 9

Covenant with Noah 1God blessed Noah and
his sons and said to them: "Be fertile and
multiply and fill the earth.[p] 2Dread fear of you
shall come upon all the animals of the earth and
all the birds of the air, upon all the creatures that
move about on the ground and all the fishes of
the sea; into your power they are delivered.
3[q]Every creature that is alive shall be yours to
eat; I give them all to you as I did the green
plants.* 4[r]Only flesh with its lifeblood still in it
you shall not eat.* 5For your own lifeblood, too,
I will demand an accounting: from every animal
I will demand it, and from man in regard to his
fellow man I will demand an accounting for
human life.[s]

6If anyone sheds the blood of man,
by man shall his blood be shed;
For in the image of God
has man been made.[t]

7Be fertile, then, and multiply; abound on earth
and subdue it."[u]

8God said to Noah and to his sons with him:
9"See, I am now establishing my covenant with
you and your descendants after you[v] 10and with
every living creature that was with you: all the
birds, and the various tame and wild animals
that were with you and came out of the ark. 11I
will establish my covenant with you, that never
again shall all bodily creatures be destroyed by
the waters of a flood; there shall not be another
flood to devastate the earth."[w] 12God added:
"This is the sign that I am giving for all ages to
come, of the covenant between me and you and
every living creature with you: 13[x]I set my bow
in the clouds to serve as a sign of the covenant

8, 21: From the start: literally "from his youth." It is uncertain whether this means from the beginning of the human race or from the early years of the individual.

9, 3: Antediluvian creatures, including man, are depicted as vegetarians (Gn 1, 29f), becoming carnivorous only after the flood.

9, 4: Because a living being dies when it loses most of its blood, the ancients regarded blood as the seat of life, and therefore as sacred. Although in itself the prohibition against eating meat with blood in it is comparable to the ritual laws of the Mosaic code, the Jews considered it binding on all men, because it was given by God to Noah, the new ancestor of all mankind; therefore the early Christian Church retained it for a time (Acts 15, 20. 29).

m Gn 1, 22. 28. n Sir 44, 18; Is 54, 9; Rom 7, 18. o Jer 33, 20. 25. p Gn 1, 22, 28; 8, 17; Jas 3, 7. q Gn 1, 29f; Dt 12, 15. r Lv 7, 26f; 17, 4; Dt 12, 16. 23; 1 Sm 14, 33; Acts 15, 20. s Gn 4, 10f; Ex 21, 12. t Gn 1, 26f; Lv 24, 17; Nm 35, 33; Jas 3, 9. u Gn 1, 28; 8, 17; 9, 2. v Gn 6, 18. w Sir 44, 18; Is 54, 9. x Sir 43, 12.

between me and the earth. 14 When I bring
clouds over the earth, and the bow appears in
the clouds, 15 I will recall the covenant I have
made between me and you and all living beings,
so that the waters shall never again become a
flood to destroy all mortal beings.[y] 16 As the bow
appears in the clouds, I will see it and recall the
everlasting covenant that I have established
between God and all living beings—all mortal
creatures that are on earth." 17 God told Noah:
"This is the sign of the covenant I have estab-
lished between me and all mortal creatures that
are on earth."

Noah and His Sons 18 *The sons of Noah who
came out of the ark were Shem, Ham and
Japheth. (Ham was the father of Canaan.)[z]
19 These three were the sons of Noah, and from
them the whole earth was peopled.

20 Now Noah, a man of the soil, was the first to
plant a vineyard. 21 When he drank some of the
wine, he became drunk and lay naked inside his
tent.[a] 22 Ham, the father of Canaan, saw his
father's nakedness, and he told his two brothers
outside about it. 23 Shem and Japheth, however,
took a robe, and holding it on their backs, they
walked backward and covered their father's
nakedness; since their faces were turned the
other way, they did not see their father's naked-
ness. 24 When Noah woke up from his drunken-
ness and learned what his youngest son had
done to him, 25 he said:

"Cursed be Canaan!
The lowest of slaves
shall he be to his brothers."[b]

26 He also said:

"Blessed be the LORD, the God of Shem!*
Let Canaan be his slave.
27 May God expand Japheth,*
so that he dwells among the tents of Shem;
and let Canaan be his slave."

28 Noah lived three hundred and fifty years
after the flood. 29 The whole lifetime of Noah
was nine hundred and fifty years; then he died.

CHAPTER 10

Table of the Nations* 1 These are the descen-
dants of Noah's sons, Shem, Ham and Japheth,
to whom sons were born after the flood.

2 [c]The descendants of Japheth:
Gomer,* Magog, Madai, Javan, Tubal,
Meshech and Tiras.[d]
3 The descendants of Gomer:
Ashkenaz,* Riphath and Togarmah.
4 The descendants of Javan:
Elishah,* Tarshish, the Kittim and the
Rodanim.

5 These are the descendants of Japheth, and
from them sprang the maritime nations, in their
respective lands—each with its own language—
by their clans within their nations.

6 The descendants of Ham:
Cush,* Mizraim, Put and Canaan.

9, 18–27: This story seems to be a composite of two earlier accounts; in the one, Ham was guilty, whereas in the other, it was Canaan. One purpose of the story is to justify the Israelites' enslavement of the Canaanites because of certain indecent sexual practices in the Canaanite religion. Obviously the story offers no justification for enslaving African Negroes, even though Canaan is presented as a "son" of Ham because the land of Canaan belonged to Hamitic Egypt at the time of the Israelite invasion.

9, 26: Blessed . . . Shem: perhaps the text read originally, "Blessed of the Lord be Shem," which would be expected in the context.

9, 27: In the Hebrew text there is a play on the words yapt ("expand") and yepet ("Japheth").

10, 1–32: This chapter presents a remarkably good classification of the various peoples known to the ancient Israelites; it is theologically important as stressing the basic family unity of all men on earth. The relationship between the various peoples is based partly on linguistic, partly on geographic, and partly on political grounds according to their . . . languages, . . . lands and nations: (v 31). In general, the descendants of Japheth (vv 2–5) are the peoples of the Indo-European languages to the north and west of Mesopotamia and Syria; the descendants of Ham (vv 6–20) are the Hamitic-speaking peoples of northern Africa; and the descendants of Shem (vv 21–31) are the Semitic-speaking peoples of Mesopotamia, Syria and Arabia. But there are many exceptions to this rule; the Semitic-speaking peoples of Canaan, for instance, are considered descendants of Ham, because at the time they were subject to Hamitic Egypt (vv 6. 15–19). This chapter is a composite from the Yahwist source (vv 8–19. 21. 24–30) of about the ninth century B.C., and the Priestly source (vv 1–7. 20. 22f. 31f) of a few centuries later. That is why certain tribes of Arabia are listed under both Ham (v 7) and Shem (vv 26ff).

10, 2: Gomer: the Cimmerians; Madai: the Medes; Javan: the Greeks.

10, 3: Ashkenaz: the Scythians.

10, 4: Elishah: Cyprus; the Kittim: certain inhabitants of Cyprus; the Rodanim: the inhabitants of Rhodes.

10, 6: Cush: Biblical Ethiopia, modern Nubia. Mizraim: Egypt; Put: either Punt in East Africa or Libya.

y Is 54, 9. z Gn 5, 32; 10, 1. a Lam 4, 21; Heb 2, 15. b Dt 27, 16; Wis 12, 11. c 2–8: 1 Chr 1, 5–10. d Ez 38, 2.

7 The descendants of Cush:
Seba, Havilah, Sabtah, Raamah and Sabteca.
The descendants of Raamah:
Sheba and Dedan.

8 Cush* became the father of Nimrod, who
was the first potentate on earth. 9 He was a
mighty hunter by the grace of the LORD; hence
the saying, "Like Nimrod, a mighty hunter by
the grace of the LORD." 10 The chief cities of his
kingdom were Babylon, Erech and Accad, all of
them in the land of Shinar.* 11 From that land he
went forth to Asshur,* where he built Nineveh,
Rehoboth-Ir and Calah, 12 as well as Resen,
between Nineveh and Calah,* the latter being
the principal city.

13 e Mizraim became the father of the Ludim,
the Anamim, the Lehabim, the Naphtuhim,
14 the Pathrusim,* the Casluhim, and the Caphto-
rim from whom the Philistines sprang.

15 Canaan became the father of Sidon, his first-
born, and of Heth;* 16 also of the Jebusites, the
Amorites, the Girgashites, 17 the Hivites, the
Arkites, the Sinites, 18 the Arvadites, the Zema-
rites and the Hamathites. Afterward, the clans of
the Canaanites spread out, 19 so that the Canaan-
ite borders extended from Sidon all the way to
Gerar, near Gaza, and all the way to Sodom,
Gomorrah, Admah and Zeboiim, near Lasha.*

20 These are the descendants of Ham, accord-
ing to their clans and languages, by their lands
and nations.

21 To Shem also, Japheth's oldest brother and
the ancestor of all the children of Eber, sons
were born.

22 f The descendants of Shem:
Elam, Asshur, Arpachshad, Lud and Aram.
23 The descendants of Aram:
Uz, Hul, Gether and Mash.

24 Arpachshad became the father of Shelah,
and Shelah became the father of Eber. 25 To Eber
two sons were born: the name of the first was
Peleg, for in his time the world was divided;*
and the name of his brother was Joktan.

26 Joktan became the father of Almodad, She-
leph, Hazarmaveth, Jerah, 27 Hadoram, Uzal,
Diklah, 28 Obal, Abimael, Sheba 29 Ophir, Havilah
and Jobab. All these were descendants of Joktan.
30 Their settlements extended all the way to
Sephar, the eastern hill country.

31 These are the descendants of Shem, accord-
ing to their clans and languages, by their lands
and nations.

32 These are the groupings of Noah's sons,
according to their origins and by their nations.
From these the other nations of the earth
branched out after the flood.

CHAPTER 11

The Tower of Babel* 1 The whole world
spoke the same language, using the same words.
2 While men were migrating in the east, they
came upon a valley in the land of Shinar* and
settled there. 3 They said to one another, "Come,
let us mold bricks and harden them with fire."
They used bricks for stone, and bitumen for
mortar. 4 Then they said, "Come, let us build
ourselves a city and a tower with its top in the
sky,* and so make a name for ourselves; other-
wise we shall be scattered all over the earth."

10, 8: Cush: here, the Kassites; see note on Gn 2, 10–14. Nimrod: probably Tukulti-Ninurta I (thirteenth century B.C.), the first Assyrian conqueror of Babylonia and a famous city-builder at home.

10, 10: Shinar: ancient Sumer in southern Mesopotamia, mentioned also in Gn 11, 2; 14, 1.

10, 11: Asshur: Assyria. Rehoboth-Ir: literally "wide-streets city," was probably not the name of another city, but an epithet of Nineveh; cf Jon 3, 3.

10, 12: Calah: Assyrian Kalhu, the capital of Assyria in the ninth century B.C.

10, 14: The Pathrusim: the people of upper (southern) Egypt; cf Is 11, 11; Jer 44, 1; Ez 29, 14; 30, 14. Caphtorim: Crete; for Caphtor as the place of origin of the Philistines, cf Dt 2, 23; Am 9, 7; Jer 47, 4.

10, 15: Heth: the biblical Hittites; see note on Gn 23, 3.

10, 19: Lasha: the reading of this name is uncertain; perhaps it should be "Bela"; cf Gn 14, 2.

10, 25: In the Hebrew text there is a play on the name Peleg and the word niplega, "was divided."

11, 1–9: This story, based on traditions about the temple towers or ziggurats of Babylonia, is used by the sacred writer primarily to illustrate man's increasing wickedness, shown here in his presumptuous effort to create an urban culture apart from God. The secondary motive in the story is to present an imaginative origin of the diversity of the languages among the various peoples inhabiting the earth, as well as an artificial explanation of the name "Babylon."

11, 2: Shinar: see note on Gn 10, 10.

11, 4: Tower with its top in the sky: a direct reference to the chief ziggurat of Babylon, the E-sag-ila, signifying "the house that raises high its head." Babylonian ziggurats were the earliest skyscrapers.

e 13–18: 1 Chr 1, 11–16. f 22–29: 1 Chr 1, 17–23.

5The LORD came down to see the city and the tower that the men had built. 6Then the LORD said: "If now, while they are one people, all speaking the same language, they have started to do this, nothing will later stop them from doing whatever they presume to do. 7Let us then go down and there confuse their language, so that one will not understand what another says." 8Thus the LORD scattered them from there all over the earth, and they stopped building the city. 9That is why it was called Babel,* because there the LORD confused the speech of all the world. It was from that place that he scattered them all over the earth.

The Line from Shem to Abraham* 10 [g]This is the record of the descendants of Shem. When Shem was one hundred years old, he became the father of Arpachshad, two years after the flood. 11Shem lived five hundred years after the birth of Arpachshad, and he had other sons and daughters.

12When Arpachshad was thirty-five years old, he became the father of Shelah.* 13Arpachshad lived four hundred and three years after the birth of Shelah, and he had other sons and daughters.

14When Shelah was thirty years old, he became the father of Eber. 15Shelah lived four hundred and three years after the birth of Eber, and he had other sons and daughters.

16When Eber* was thirty-four years old, he became the father of Peleg. 17Eber lived four hundred and thirty years after the birth of Peleg, and he had other sons and daughters.

18When Peleg was thirty years old, he became the father of Reu. 19Peleg lived two hundred and nine years after the birth of Reu, and he had other sons and daughters.

20When Reu was thirty-two years old, he became the father of Serug. 21Reu lived two hundred and seven years after the birth of Serug, and he had other sons and daughters.

22When Serug was thirty years old, he became the father of Nahor. 23Serug lived two hundred years after the birth of Nahor, and he had other sons and daughters.

24When Nahor was twenty-nine years old, he became the father of Terah. 25Nahor lived one hundred and nineteen years after the birth of Terah, and he had other sons and daughters.

26When Terah was seventy years old, he became the father of Abram, Nahor and Haran. [h]

II: The Patriarch Abraham

Terah 27This is the record of the descendants of Terah. Terah became the father of Abram, Nahor and Haran, and Haran became the father of Lot. 28Haran died before his father Terah, in his native land, in Ur of the Chaldeans.* 29Abram and Nahor took wives; the name of Abram's wife was Sarai, and the name of Nahor's wife was Milcah, daughter of Haran, the father of Milcah and Iscah. [i] 30Sarai was barren; she had no child.

31Terah took his son Abram, his grandson Lot, son of Haran, and his daughter-in-law Sarai, the wife of his son Abram, and brought them out of Ur of the Chaldeans, to go to the land of Canaan.* But when they reached Haran, they settled there. [j] 32The lifetime of Terah was two

11, 9: Babel: the Hebrew form of the name "Babylon"; the native name, Bab-ili, means "gate of the gods." The Hebrew word balil, "he confused," has a similar sound. Apparently the name referred originally only to a certain part of the city, the district near the gate that led to the temple area.

11, 10–26: This section is a continuation of the genealogical record given in Gn 5, 1–32; see note there. Although the ages of the patriarchs in this list are much lower than those of the antediluvian patriarchs, they are still artificial and devoid of historical value. The ages given here are from the current Hebrew text; the Samaritan and Greek texts have divergent sets of numbers in most cases.

11, 12: The Greek text has a certain Kenan (cf Gn 5, 9f) between Arpachshad and Shelah. The text is followed in Lk 3, 36.

11, 16: Eber: the eponymous ancestor of the Hebrews, "descendants of Eber" (Gn 10, 21. 24–30); see note on Gn 14, 13.

11, 28: Ur of the Chaldeans: Ur was an extremely ancient city of the Sumerians (later, of the Babylonians) in southern Mesopotamia. The Greek text has "the land of the Chaldeans." In either case, the term Chaldeans is an anachronism, because the Chaldeans were not known to history until approximately a thousand years after Abraham's time.

11, 31: The Samaritan and Greek texts include Nahor and his wife in Terah's migration to Haran. Although this is probably due to scribal harmonization, Nahor's family actually did migrate to Haran; cf Gn 24, 10; 27, 43.

g 10–26: 1 Chr 1, 24–27; Lk 3, 34ff. h Jos 24, 2; 1 Chr 1, 27. i Gn 17, 15; 20, 12. j Jos 24, 3; Neh 9, 7; Jdt 5, 6–9; Acts 7, 4.

hundred and five years; then Terah died in
Haran.*

CHAPTER 12

Abram's Call and Migration 1 The LORD said
to Abram: "Go forth from the land of your
kinsfolk and from your father's house to a land
that I will show you.[k]

2 "I will make of you a great nation,
and I will bless you;
I will make your name great,
so that you will be a blessing.[l]
3 [m]I will bless those who bless you
and curse those who curse you.
All the communities of the earth
shall find blessing in you."*

4 [n]Abram went as the LORD directed him, and
Lot went with him. Abram was seventy-five
years old when he left Haran. 5 Abram took his
wife Sarai, his brother's son Lot, all the posses-
sions that they had accumulated, and the per-
sons* they had acquired in Haran, and they set
out for the land of Canaan. When they came to
the land of Canaan, 6 Abram passed through the
land as far as the sacred place at Shechem, by the
terebinth of Moreh. (The Canaanites were then
in the land.)
7 The LORD appeared to Abram and said, "To
your descendants I will give this land." So
Abram built an altar there to the LORD who had
appeared to him.[o] 8 From there he moved on to
the hill country east of Bethel, pitching his tent
with Bethel to the west and Ai to the east. He
built an altar there to the LORD and invoked the
LORD by name. 9 Then Abram journeyed on by
stages to the Negeb.*

Abram and Sarai in Egypt 10 There was fam-
ine in the land; so Abram went down to Egypt to
sojourn there, since the famine in the land was
severe.[p] 11 When he was about to enter Egypt,
he said to his wife Sarai: "I know well how
beautiful a woman you are. 12 When the Egyp-
tians see you, they will say, 'She is his wife';
then they will kill me, but let you live. 13 Please
say, therefore, that you are my sister,* so that it
may go well with me on your account and my
life may be spared for your sake."[q] 14 When
Abram came to Egypt, the Egyptians saw how
beautiful the woman was; 15 and when Pha-
raoh's courtiers saw her, they praised her to
Pharaoh. So she was taken into Pharaoh's pal-
ace. 16 On her account it went very well with
Abram, and he received flocks and herds, male
and female slaves, male and female asses, and
camels.*
17 But the LORD struck Pharaoh and his house-
hold with severe plagues because of Abram's
wife Sarai.[r] 18 Then Pharaoh summoned Abram
and said to him: "How could you do this to me!
Why didn't you tell me she was your wife?
19 Why did you say, 'She is my sister,' so that I
took her for my wife? Here, then, is your wife.
Take her and be gone!"
20 Then Pharaoh gave men orders concerning
him, and they sent him on his way, with his wife
and all that belonged to him.

11, 32: Since Terah was seventy years old when his son Abraham was born (v 26), and Abraham was seventy-five when he left Haran (Gn 12, 4), Terah lived in Haran for sixty years after Abraham's departure. According to the tradition in the Samaritan text, Terah died when he was one hundred and forty-five years old, therefore, in the same year in which Abraham left Haran. This is the tradition followed in St. Stephen's speech: Abraham left Haran "after his father's death" (Acts 7, 4).

12, 3: Shall find blessing in you: the sense of the Hebrew expression is probably reflexive, "shall bless themselves through you" (i.e., in giving a blessing they shall say, "May you be as blessed as Abraham"), rather than passive, "shall be blessed in you." Since the term is understood in a passive sense in the New Testament (Acts 3, 25; Gal 3, 8), it is rendered here by a neutral expression that admits of both meanings. So also in the blessings given by God to Isaac (Gn 26, 4) and Jacob (Gn 28, 14).

12, 5: Persons: slaves and retainers that formed the social aggregate under the leadership of Abraham; cf Gn 14, 14.

12, 9: The Negeb: the semidesert land of southern Palestine.

12, 13: You are my sister: although Abraham's deceit may not be fully defensible, his statement was at least a half-truth; Sarah was indeed his relative, called "a sister" in Hebrew; cf Gn 20, 12. Moreover, the ancient traditions on which this story and the parallel ones in Gn 20, 1–18 and 26, 6–11 are based, probably come from the Hurrian custom of wife-sister marriage. Among the Hurrians, with whom Abraham's clan lived in close contact at Haran, a man could adopt his wife as his sister and thus give her higher status.

12, 16: Camels: domesticated camels probably did not come into common use in the ancient Near East until the end of the 2nd millennium B.C. Thus the mention of camels at the time of the patriarchs (Gn 24, 11–64; 30, 43; 31, 17. 34; 32, 8. 16; 37, 25) is seemingly an anachronism.

k Acts 7, 3; Heb 11, 8. l Gn 17, 6; Sir 44, 20; Rom 4, 17–22. m Gn 18, 18; 22, 18; Acts 3, 25; Gal 3, 8. n 4f: Gn 11, 31; Jos 24, 3; Acts 7, 4. o Ex 33, 1; Dt 34, 4; Acts 7, 5. p Gn 26, 1. q Gn 20, 12f; 26, 7. r Ps 105, 14.

CHAPTER 13

Abram and Lot Part 1 From Egypt Abram went
up to the Negeb with his wife and all that
belonged to him, and Lot accompanied him.[s]
2 Now Abram was very rich in livestock, silver
and gold.[t] 3 From the Negeb he traveled by
stages toward Bethel, to the place between
Bethel and Ai where his tent had formerly stood,
4 the site where he had first built the altar; and
there he invoked the LORD by name.[u]

5 Lot, who went with Abram, also had flocks
and herds and tents, 6 so that the land could not
support them if they stayed together; their
possessions were so great that they could not
dwell together. 7 There were quarrels between
the herdsmen of Abram's livestock and those of
Lot's. (At this time the Canaanites and the
Perizzites were occupying the land.)

8 So Abram said to Lot: "Let there be no strife
between you and me, or between your herds-
men and mine, for we are kinsmen. 9 Is not the
whole land at your disposal? Please separate
from me. If you prefer the left, I will go to the
right; if you prefer the right, I will go to the left."
10 Lot looked about and saw how well watered
the whole Jordan Plain was as far as Zoar, like
the LORD's own garden, or like Egypt. (This was
before the LORD had destroyed Sodom and
Gomorrah.) 11 Lot, therefore, chose for himself
the whole Jordan Plain and set out eastward.
Thus they separated from each other; 12 Abram
stayed in the land of Canaan, while Lot settled
among the cities of the Plain, pitching his tents
near Sodom. 13 Now the inhabitants of Sodom
were very wicked in the sins they committed
against the LORD.[v]

14 After Lot had left, the LORD said to Abram:
"Look about you, and from where you are, gaze
to the north and south, east and west;[w] 15 all the
land that you see I will give to you and your
descendants forever.[x] 16 I will make your descen-
dants like the dust of the earth; if anyone could
count the dust of the earth, your descendants
too might be counted.[y] 17 Set forth and walk
about in the land, through its length and
breadth, for to you I will give it." 18 Abram
moved his tents and went on to settle near the
terebinth of Mamre, which is at Hebron. There
he built an altar to the LORD.[z]

CHAPTER 14

The Four Kings 1 In the days of . . . ,* Amra-
phel king of Shinar, Arioch king of Ellasar,
Chedorlaomer king of Elam, and Tidal king of
Goiim 2 made war on Bera king of Sodom, Birsha
king of Gomorrah, Shinab king of Admah,
Shemeber king of Zeboiim, and the king of Bela
(that is, Zoar). 3 All the latter kings joined forces
in the Valley of Siddim (that is, the Salt Sea*).
4 For twelve years they had been subject to
Chedorlaomer, but in the thirteenth year they
rebelled. 5 *In the fourteenth year Chedorlaomer
and the kings allied with him came and defeated
the Rephaim in Ashteroth-karnaim, the Zuzim in
Ham, the Emim in Shaveh-kiriathaim, 6 and the
Horites in the hill country of Seir, as far as El-
paran, close by the wilderness.[a] 7 They then
turned back and came to Enmishpat (that is,
Kadesh), and they subdued the whole country
both of the Amalekites and of the Amorites who
dwelt in Hazazon-tamar. 8 Thereupon the king of
Sodom, the king of Gomorrah, the king of
Admah, the king of Zeboiim, and the king of
Bela (that is, Zoar) marched out, and in the
Valley of Siddim they went into battle against
them: 9 against Chedorlaomer king of Elam,
Tidal king of Goiim, Amraphel king of Shinar,
and Arioch king of Ellasar—four kings against
five. 10 Now the Valley of Siddim was full of
bitumen pits; and as the kings of Sodom and
Gomorrah fled, they fell into these, while the
rest fled to the mountains. 11 The victors seized
all the possessions and food supplies of Sodom
and Gomorrah and then went their way, 12 tak-
ing with them Abram's nephew Lot, who had

14, 1: In the days of . . . : the personal name by which the event is dated has not been preserved.

14, 3: The Salt Sea: now known as the Dead Sea.

14, 5f: The five kings came from north to south through the land east of the Jordan.

s Gn 12, 9. t Ps 112, 1ff; Prv 10, 22. u Gn 12, 8. v Gn 18, 20; Ez 16, 49; 2 Pt 2, 6ff; Jude 1, 7. w Gn 28, 14. x Gn 12, 7; Mt 5, 4; Lk 1, 55; Acts 7, 5; Gal 3, 16. y Gn 22, 17; Nm 23, 10. z Gn 14, 13. a Dt 2, 12.

been living in Sodom, as well as his posses-
sions.[b]
13A fugitive came and brought the news to
Abram the Hebrew,* who was camping at the
terebinth of Mamre the Amorite, a kinsman of
Eshcol and Aner; these were in league with
Abram. 14When Abram heard that his nephew
had been captured, he mustered three hundred
and eighteen of his retainers, born in his house,
and went in pursuit as far as Dan. 15He and his
party deployed against them at night, defeated
them, and pursued them as far as Hobah, which
is north of Damascus. 16He recovered all the
possessions, besides bringing back his kinsman
Lot and his possessions, along with the women
and the other captives.
17When Abram returned from his victory over
Chedorlaomer and the kings who were allied
with him, the king of Sodom went out to greet
him in the Valley of Shaveh (that is, the King's
Valley).
18Melchizedek, king of Salem,* brought out
bread and wine, and being a priest of God Most
High,* he blessed Abram with these words:[c]

19"Blessed be Abram by God Most High,*
the creator of heaven and earth;
20And blessed be God Most High,
who delivered your foes into your hand."

Then Abram gave him* a tenth of everything.
21The king of Sodom said to Abram, "Give me
the people; the goods you may keep." 22But
Abram replied to the king of Sodom: "I have
sworn to the LORD, God Most High,* the creator
of heaven and earth, 23that I would not take so
much as a thread or a sandal strap from anything
that is yours, lest you should say, 'I made Abram
rich.' 24Nothing for me except what my servants
have used up and the share that is due to the
men who joined me—Aner, Eshcol and Mamre;
let them take their share."

CHAPTER 15

The Covenant with Abram 1Some time after
these events, this word of the LORD came to
Abram in a vision:

"Fear not, Abram!
I am your shield;
I will make your reward very great."

2But Abram said, "O Lord GOD, what good will
your gifts be, if I keep on being childless and
have as my heir the steward of my house,
Eliezer?" 3Abram continued, "See, you have
given me no offspring, and so one of my servants
will be my heir." 4Then the word of the LORD
came to him: "No, that one shall not be your
heir; your own issue shall be your heir."[d] 5He
took him outside and said, "Look up at the sky
and count the stars, if you can. Just so," he
added, "shall your descendants be."[e] 6[f]Abram
put his faith in the LORD, who credited it to him
as an act of righteousness.*
7He then said to him, "I am the LORD who
brought you from Ur of the Chaldeans to give
you this land as a possession."[g] 8"O Lord GOD,"
he asked, "how am I to know that I shall possess
it?" 9He answered him, "Bring me a three-year-
old heifer, a three-year-old she-goat, a three-year-

14, 13: Abram the Hebrew: elsewhere in the Old Testament, until the last pre-Christian centuries, the term "Hebrew" is used only by non-Israelites, or by Israelites in speaking to foreigners, since it evidently had a disparaging connotation—something like "immigrant." The account in this chapter may, therefore, have been taken originally from a non-Israelite source, in which Abraham, a warlike sheik of Palestine, appears as a truly historical figure of profane history.

14, 18: Salem: traditionally identified with Jerusalem (Ps 76, 3), but the Hebrew text is not certain; instead of the present melek shalem ("king of Salem") the original may have been melek shelomo ("a king allied to him"). In Heb 7, 2, "king of Salem" is interpreted as "king of peace" (shalom).

14, 19: God most High: in Hebrew, el-elyon. In Canaanite texts, each element may occur separately as the name of a specific deity, or they may be applied together to a single deity, as is done here by the Canaanite priest Melchizedek. For the Israelites, el became a poetic synonym for elohim ("God"); elyon ("Most High") became one of the titles of their God Yahweh.

14, 20: Abram gave him: literally "he gave him"; but Abram is to be understood as the subject of the sentence, for the tithes were the tenth part assigned to priests; cf Heb 7, 4–10.

14, 22: Abraham uses the name of the Canaanite god el-elyon ("God, the Most High") in apposition to the name of his God, yahweh ("the Lord").

15, 6: Abraham's faith in God's promises was regarded as an act of righteousness, i.e., as expressing the "right" attitude of man toward God. In turn, God credited this to Abraham, i.e., gave him title to the fulfillment of God's promises. St. Paul (Rom 4, 1–25; Gal 3, 6–9) makes Abraham's faith a model for that of Christians.

b Gn 13, 10ff. c Ps 110, 4; Heb 5, 6. 10; 7, 1. d Gn 17, 16. e Gn 22, 17; 28, 14; Ex 32, 13; Dt 1, 10; Sir 44, 21; Rom 4, 18; Heb 11, 12. f 1 Mc 2, 52; Rom 4, 3. 9. 22; Gal 3, 6f; Jas 2, 23. g Gn 11, 31; 12, 1; Ex 32, 13; Neh 9, 7f; Acts 7, 2f.

old* ram, a turtledove, and a young pigeon."[h]
10 He brought him all these, split them in two,
and placed each half opposite the other; but the
birds he did not cut up. 11 Birds of prey swooped
down on the carcasses, but Abram stayed with
them. 12 As the sun was about to set, a trance fell
upon Abram, and a deep, terrifying darkness
enveloped him.

13 Then the LORD said to Abram: "Know for
certain that your descendants shall be aliens in a
land not their own, where they shall be enslaved
and oppressed for four hundred years.[i] 14 But I
will bring judgment on the nation they must
serve, and in the end they will depart with great
wealth.[j] 15 You, however, shall join your forefa-
thers in peace; you shall be buried at a contented
old age. 16 In the fourth time-span* the others
shall come back here; the wickedness of the
Amorites will not have reached its full measure
until then."[k]

17 When the sun had set and it was dark, there
appeared a smoking brazier* and a flaming
torch, which passed between those pieces. 18 It
was on that occasion that the LORD made a
covenant* with Abram, saying: "To your descen-
dants I give this land, from the Wadi of Egypt to
the Great River [the Euphrates],[l] 19 [m]the land of
the Kenites, the Kenizzites, the Kadmonites,
20 the Hittites, the Perizzites, the Rephaim, 21 the
Amorites, the Canaanites, the Girgashites, and
the Jebusites."

CHAPTER 16

Birth of Ishmael 1 *Abram's wife Sarai had
borne him no children. She had, however, an
Egyptian maidservant named Hagar.[n] 2 Sarai said
to Abram: "The LORD has kept me from bearing
children. Have intercourse, then, with my maid;
perhaps I shall have sons through her." Abram
heeded Sarai's request.[o] 3 Thus, after Abram had
lived ten years in the land of Canaan, his wife
Sarai took her maid, Hagar the Egyptian, and
gave her to her husband Abram to be his
concubine. 4 He had intercourse with her, and
she became pregnant. When she became aware
of her pregnancy, she looked on her mistress
with disdain.[p] 5 [q]So Sarai said to Abram: "You
are responsible for this outrage against me. I
myself gave my maid to your embrace; but ever
since she became aware of her pregnancy, she
has been looking on me with disdain. May the
LORD decide between you and me!" 6 Abram told
Sarai: "Your maid is in your power. Do to her
whatever you please." Sarai then abused her so
much that Hagar ran away from her.

7 The LORD's messenger* found her by a
spring in the wilderness, the spring on the road
to Shur,[r] 8 and he asked, "Hagar, maid of Sarai,
where have you come from and where are you
going?" She answered, "I am running away from
my mistress, Sarai." 9 But the LORD's messenger
told her: "Go back to your mistress and submit
to her abusive treatment. 10 I will make your
descendants so numerous," added the LORD's
messenger, "that they will be too many to
count.[s] 11 Besides," the LORD's messenger said
to her:

"You are now pregnant and shall bear a son;
  you shall name him Ishmael,*
For the LORD has heard you,
  God has answered you.

12 He shall be a wild ass of a man,
  his hand against everyone,
  and everyone's hand against him;
In opposition to all his kin
  shall he encamp."[t]

15, 9: Three-year-old: ritually mature.
15, 16: Time-span: the Hebrew term dor is commonly rendered as "generation," but it may signify a period of varying length. Neither this passage nor the statement about the four hundred years has any value for determining how long the Israelites were in Egypt.
15, 17: Brazier: literally "oven"; a portable one is meant here. The smoke and fire represent God's presence. Although the text does not mention it, Abraham no doubt also walked between the split carcasses. For the meaning of this strange ceremony, see note on Jer 34, 18ff.
15, 18: Made a covenant: literally "cut a covenant"; the expression derives from the ceremony of cutting the animals in two.
16, 1–6: Sarah's actions are all in keeping with the laws of the time, as known from ancient extra-biblical sources.
16, 7: The Lord's messenger: a manifestation of God in human form; therefore in v 13 the messenger is identified with the Lord himself.
16, 11: Ishmael: in Hebrew the name means "God has heard."

h Lv 1, 14. i Ex 12, 40; Nm 20, 15; Jdt 5, 9f; Is 52, 4; Acts 13, 20; Gal 3, 17. j Ex 3, 8. 21f. k 1 Kgs 21, 26. l Ex 32, 13; Neh 9, 8; Ps 105, 11; Sir 44, 21. m 19f: Dt 7, 1. n Gn 11, 30. o Gn 21, 8f; Gal 4, 22. p 1 Sm 1, 6; Prv 30, 23. q 5–16: Gn 21, 10–19. r Ex 15, 22. s Gn 17, 20; 21, 13. 18; 25, 12–18. t Gn 21, 20; 25, 18.

13 To the LORD who spoke to her she gave a name, saying, "You are the God of Vision";* she meant, "Have I really seen God and remained alive after my vision?"[u] 14 That is why the well is called Beer-lahai-roi.* It is between Kadesh and Bered.

15 Hagar bore Abram a son, and Abram named the son whom Hagar bore him Ishmael.[v] 16 Abram was eighty-six years old when Hagar bore him Ishmael.

CHAPTER 17

Covenant of Circumcision 1 When Abram was ninety-nine years old, the LORD appeared to him and said: "I am God the Almighty.* Walk in my presence and be blameless.[w] 2 Between you and me I will establish my covenant, and I will multiply you exceedingly."[x]

3 When Abram prostrated himself, God continued to speak to him: 4 "My covenant with you is this: you are to become the father of a host of nations.[y] 5 No longer shall you be called Abram; your name shall be Abraham,* for I am making you the father of a host of nations.[z] 6 I will render you exceedingly fertile; I will make nations of you; kings shall stem from you. 7 I will maintain my covenant with you and your descendants after you throughout the ages as an everlasting pact, to be your God and the God of your descendants after you.[a] 8 I will give to you and to your descendants after you the land in which you are now staying, the whole land of Canaan, as a permanent possession; and I will be their God."[b]

9 God also said to Abraham: "On your part, you and your descendants after you must keep my covenant throughout the ages. 10 This is my covenant with you and your descendants after you that you must keep: every male among you shall be circumcised.[c] 11 Circumcise the flesh of your foreskin, and that shall be the mark of the covenant between you and me.[d] 12 Throughout the ages, every male among you, when he is eight days old, shall be circumcised, including houseborn slaves and those acquired with money from any foreigner who is not of your blood.[e] 13 Yes, both the houseborn slaves and those acquired with money must be circumcised. Thus my covenant shall be in your flesh as an everlasting pact. 14 If a male is uncircumcised, that is, if the flesh of his foreskin has not been cut away, such a one shall be cut off from his people; he has broken my covenant."

15 God further said to Abraham: "As for your wife Sarai, do not call her Sarai; her name shall be Sarah.* 16 I will bless her, and I will give you a son by her. Him also will I bless; he shall give rise to nations, and rulers of peoples shall issue from him."[f] 17 Abraham prostrated himself and laughed* as he said to himself, "Can a child be born to a man who is a hundred years old? Or can Sarah give birth at ninety?"[g] 18 Then Abraham said to God, "Let but Ishmael live on by your favor!" 19 God replied: "Nevertheless, your wife Sarah is to bear you a son, and you shall call him Isaac. I will maintain my covenant with him as an everlasting pact, to be his God and the God of his descendants after him.[h] 20 As for Ishmael, I am heeding you: I hereby bless him. I will make him fertile and will multiply him exceedingly. He shall become the father of twelve chieftains, and I will make of him a great nation.[i] 21 But my covenant I will maintain with Isaac, whom Sarah shall bear to you by this time next year."[j]

16, 13: The God of Vision: in Hebrew, el-roi; hence the name of the spring. Remained alive: for the ancient notion that a person died on seeing God, cf Gn 32, 31; Ex 20, 19; Dt 4, 33; Jgs 13, 22.

16, 14: Beer-lahai-roi: probably "the well of living sight," i.e., the well where one can see (God) and yet live.

17, 1: The Almighty: traditional but incorrect rendering of the divine title shaddai, of uncertain meaning.

17, 5: Abram and Abraham are merely two forms of the same name, both meaning, "the father is exalted"; another variant form is Abiram (Nm 16, 1; 1 Kgs 16, 34). The additional -ha- in the form Abraham is explained by folk etymology as coming from abhamon goyim, "father of a host of nations."

17, 15: Sarai and Sarah are variant forms of the same name, both meaning "princess."

17, 17: Laughed: yishaq, which is the Hebrew form of the name "Isaac"; other similar explanations of the name are given in Gn 18, 12 and 21, 6.

u Gn 24, 62. v Gn 16, 2; Gal 4, 22. w Gn 35, 11; Ex 6, 3. x Gn 12, 2: 13, 16; Ex 32, 13. y Sir 44, 21; Rom 4, 17. z Neh 9, 7. a Ps 105, 42; Lk 1, 72f; Gal 3, 16. b Ex 32, 13; Dt 1, 8; 14, 2; Lk 1, 55; Acts 7, 5. c Jn 7, 22; Acts 7, 8; Rom 4, 11. d Sir 44, 21. e Lv 12, 3; Lk 1, 59; 2, 21. f Gn 18, 10; Gal 4, 23. g Rom 4, 19; Heb 11, 11f. h Gn 11, 30; 21, 2; Ex 32, 13; Sir 44, 22. i Gn 16, 10; 21, 13. 18; 25, 12–16. j Gn 18, 14; 21, 2; 26, 2–5; Rom 9, 7.

[22]When he had finished speaking with him, God departed from Abraham.

[23]Then Abraham took his son Ishmael and all his slaves, whether born in his house or acquired with his money—every male among the members of Abraham's household—and he circumcised the flesh of their foreskins on that same day, as God had told him to do. [24]Abraham was ninety-nine years old when the flesh of his foreskin was circumcised,[k] [25]and his son Ishmael was thirteen years old when the flesh of his foreskin was circumcised. [26]Thus, on that same day Abraham and his son Ishmael were circumcised; [27]and all the male members of his household, including the slaves born in his house or acquired with his money from foreigners, were circumcised with him.

CHAPTER 18

Abraham's Visitors [1]The LORD appeared to Abraham by the terebinth of Mamre, as he sat in the entrance of his tent, while the day was growing hot. [2]Looking up, he saw three men standing nearby. When he saw them, he ran from the entrance of the tent to greet them; and bowing to the ground,[l] [3]he said: "Sir,* if I may ask you this favor, please do not go on past your servant. [4]Let some water be brought, that you may bathe your feet, and then rest yourselves under the tree. [5]Now that you have come this close to your servant, let me bring you a little food, that you may refresh yourselves; and afterward you may go on your way." "Very well," they replied, "do as you have said."

[6]Abraham hastened into the tent and told Sarah, "Quick, three seahs* of fine flour! Knead it and make rolls." [7]He ran to the herd, picked out a tender, choice steer, and gave it to a servant, who quickly prepared it. [8]Then he got some curds* and milk, as well as the steer that had been prepared, and set these before them; and he waited on them under the tree while they ate.

[9]"Where is your wife Sarah?" they asked him. "There in the tent," he replied. [10]One of them* said, "I will surely return to you about this time next year, and Sarah will then have a son." Sarah was listening at the entrance of the tent, just behind him.[m] [11]Now Abraham and Sarah were old, advanced in years, and Sarah had stopped having her womanly periods.[n] [12]So Sarah laughed* to herself and said, "Now that I am so withered and my husband is so old, am I still to have sexual pleasure?" [13]But the LORD said to Abraham: "Why did Sarah laugh and say, 'Shall I really bear a child, old as I am?' [14]Is anything too marvelous for the LORD to do? At the appointed time, about this time next year, I will return to you, and Sarah will have a son."[o] [15]Because she was afraid, Sarah dissembled, saying, "I didn't laugh." But he said, "Yes you did."

Abraham Intercedes for Sodom [16]The men set out from there and looked down toward Sodom; Abraham was walking with them, to see them on their way. [17]The LORD reflected: "Shall I hide from Abraham what I am about to do, [18]now that he is to become a great and populous nation, and all the nations of the earth are to find blessing in him?[p] [19]Indeed, I have singled him out that he may direct his sons and his posterity to keep the way of the LORD by doing what is right and just, so that the LORD may carry into effect for Abraham the promises he made about him." [20][q]Then the LORD said: "The outcry against Sodom and Gomorrah is so great, and their sin so grave,* [21]that I must go down and

18, 3: Abraham addresses the leader of the group, whom he does not yet recognize as Yahweh; in the next two verses he speaks to all three men. The other two are later (Gn 19, 1) identified as messengers.

18, 6: Three seahs: one ephah, about half a bushel.

18, 8: Curds: a type of soft cheese or yoghurt.

18, 10: One of them: i.e., the Lord. Abraham now realizes this for the first time when he hears the prediction of a miraculous birth. About this time next year: literally "when the time becomes alive," i.e., at the time when birth is due after the period of gestation; the conception is understood as taking place soon after the prediction.

18, 12: Sarah laughed: see note on Gn 17, 17.

18, 20: Israelite tradition was unanimous in ascribing the destruction of Sodom and Gomorrah to the wickedness of these cities, but tradition varied in regard to the nature of this wickedness. According to the present account of the Yahwist, the sin of Sodom was homosexuality (Gn 19, 4f), which is therefore also known as sodomy; but according to Isaiah (1, 9f; 3, 9), it was a lack of social justice; Ezekiel (16, 46–51) described it as a disre-

k Gn 17, 10; Rom 4, 11. l Heb 13, 1f. m Gn 17, 19; 21, 1; 2 Kgs 4, 16; Rom 9, 9. n Gn 17, 17; Rom 4, 19; Heb 11, 11f. o Mt 19, 26; Mk 10, 27; Lk 1, 37; 18, 27; Rom 4, 21. p Lk 1, 55. q Gn 19, 13; Is 3, 9; Lk 17, 28; Jude 1, 7.

see whether or not their actions fully correspond to the cry against them that comes to me. I mean to find out."

22 While the two men walked on farther toward Sodom, the LORD remained standing before Abraham. 23 Then Abraham drew nearer to him and said: "Will you sweep away the innocent with the guilty? 24 Suppose there were fifty innocent people in the city; would you wipe out the place, rather than spare it for the sake of the fifty innocent people within it? 25 Far be it from you to do such a thing, to make the innocent die with the guilty, so that the innocent and the guilty would be treated alike! Should not the judge of all the world act with justice?"[r] 26 The LORD replied, "If I find fifty innocent people in the city of Sodom, I will spare the whole place for their sake." 27 Abraham spoke up again: "See how I am presuming to speak to my Lord, though I am but dust and ashes![s] 28 What if there are five less than fifty innocent people? Will you destroy the whole city because of those five?" "I will not destroy it," he answered, "if I find forty-five there." 29 But Abraham persisted, saying, "What if only forty are found there?" He replied, "I will forbear doing it for the sake of the forty." 30 Then he said, "Let not my Lord grow impatient if I go on. What if only thirty are found there?" He replied, "I will forbear doing it if I can find but thirty there." 31 Still he went on, "Since I have thus dared to speak to my Lord, what if there are no more than twenty?" "I will not destroy it," he answered, "for the sake of the twenty." 32 But he still persisted, "Please, let not my Lord grow angry if I speak up this last time. What if there are at least ten there?" "For the sake of those ten," he replied, "I will not destroy it."[t]

33 The LORD departed as soon as he had finished speaking with Abraham, and Abraham returned home.

CHAPTER 19

Destruction of Sodom and Gomorrah 1 The two angels reached Sodom in the evening, as Lot was sitting at the gate of Sodom. When Lot saw them, he got up to greet them; and bowing down with his face to the ground, 2 he said, "Please, gentlemen,* come aside into your servant's house for the night, and bathe your feet; you can get up early to continue your journey." But they replied, "No, we shall pass the night in the town square."[u] 3 He urged them so strongly, however, that they turned aside to his place and entered his house. He prepared a meal for them, baking cakes without leaven, and they dined.

4 [v]Before they went to bed, all the townsmen of Sodom, both young and old—all the people to the last man—closed in on the house. 5 They called to Lot and said to him, "Where are the men who came to your house tonight? Bring them out to us that we may have intimacies with them." 6 Lot went out to meet them at the entrance. When he had shut the door behind him, 7 he said, "I beg you, my brothers, not to do this wicked thing. 8 I have two daughters who have never had intercourse with men. Let me bring them out to you, and you may do to them as you please. But don't do anything to these men, for you know they have come under the shelter of my roof." 9 They replied, "Stand back! This fellow," they sneered, "came here as an immigrant, and now he dares to give orders! We'll treat you worse than them!" With that, they pressed hard against Lot, moving in closer to break down the door.[w] 10 But his guests put out their hands, pulled Lot inside with them, and closed the door; 11 at the same time they struck the men at the entrance of the house, one and all, with such a blinding light* that they were utterly unable to reach the doorway.

12 Then the angels said to Lot: "Who else belongs to you here? Your sons [sons-in-law]*

gard for the poor, whereas Jeremiah (23, 14) saw it as general immorality.

19, 2: Gentlemen: Lot does not yet know that the distinguished-looking men are God's messengers; cf Gn 18, 3.

19, 11: Blinding light: a preternatural flash that temporarily dazed the wicked men and revealed to Lot the true nature of his guests.

19, 12: Since Lot apparently had no sons, a glossator interpreted the term to mean sons-in-law.

r Dt 32, 4; Jb 8, 3. 20; Wis 12, 15. s Sir 10, 9; 17, 27. t Jer 5, 1; Ez 22, 30. u Wis 10, 6; Sir 16, 8; Ez 16, 50; Heb 13, 1f. v 4–9; Jgs 19, 22–25; Jude 1, 7. w Gn 13, 12; 2 Pt 2, 7f.

and your daughters and all who belong to you in
the city—take them away from it![x] 13We are
about to destroy this place, for the outcry
reaching the LORD against those in the city is so
great that he has sent us to destroy it."[y] 14So Lot
went out and spoke to his sons-in-law, who had
contracted marriage with his daughters.* "Get
up and leave this place," he told them; "the
LORD is about to destroy the city." But his sons-
in-law thought he was joking.
15As dawn was breaking, the angels urged Lot
on, saying, "On your way! Take with you your
wife and your two daughters who are here, or
you will be swept away in the punishment of the
city." 16When he hesitated, the men, by the
LORD's mercy, seized his hand and the hands of
his wife and his two daughters and led them to
safety outside the city. 17As soon as they had
been brought outside, he was told: "Flee for
your life! Don't look back or stop anywhere on
the Plain. Get off to the hills at once, or you will
be swept away."[z] 18"Oh, no, my lord!" replied
Lot. 19"You have already thought enough of your
servant to do me the great kindness of interven-
ing to save my life. But I cannot flee to the hills
to keep the disaster from overtaking me, and so I
shall die. 20Look, this town ahead is near
enough to escape to. It's only a small place.* Let
me flee there—it's a small place, isn't it?—that
my life may be saved." 21"Well, then," he
replied, "I will also grant you the favor you now
ask. I will not overthrow the town you speak of.
22Hurry, escape there! I cannot do anything until
you arrive there." That is why the town is called
Zoar.[a]
23The sun was just rising over the earth as Lot
arrived in Zoar;[b] 24at the same time the LORD
rained down sulphurous fire upon Sodom and
Gomorrah [from the LORD out of heaven].[c] 25He
overthrew* those cities and the whole Plain,
together with the inhabitants of the cities and
the produce of the soil.[d] 26But Lot's wife looked
back, and she was turned into a pillar of salt.[e]
27Early the next morning Abraham went to
the place where he had stood in the LORD's
presence. 28As he looked down toward Sodom
and Gomorrah and the whole region of the
Plain,* he saw dense smoke over the land rising
like fumes from a furnace.[f]
29Thus it came to pass: when God destroyed
the Cities of the Plain, he was mindful of
Abraham by sending Lot away from the up-
heaval by which God overthrew the cities where
Lot had been living.

Moabites and Ammonites* 30Since Lot was
afraid to stay in Zoar, he and his two daughters
went up from Zoar and settled in the hill
country, where he lived with his two daughters
in a cave. 31The older one said to the younger:
"Our father is getting old, and there is not a man
on earth to unite with us as was the custom
everywhere. 32Come, let us ply our father with
wine and then lie with him, that we may have
offspring by our father." 33So that night they
plied their father with wine, and the older one
went in and lay with her father; but he was not
aware of her lying down or her getting up.
34Next day the older one said to the younger:
"Last night it was I who lay with my father. Let
us ply him with wine again tonight, and then
you go in and lie with him, that we may both
have offspring by our father." 35So that night,
too, they plied their father with wine, and then
the younger one went in and lay with him; but

19, 14: It is uncertain whether Lot's sons-in-law were fully married to his daughters or only "engaged" to them (Israelite "engagement" was the first part of the marriage ceremony), or even whether the daughters involved were the same as, or different from, the two daughters who were still in their father's house.

19, 20: A small place: the Hebrew word misar, literally "a little thing," has the same root consonants as the name of the town Zoar in v 22.

19, 25: Overthrew: the consistent use of this term, literally "turned upside down," to describe the destruction of the Cities of the Plain seems to imply that their upheaval (v 29) was caused primarily by an earthquake; this would naturally be accompanied by a disastrous fire, especially in a region containing bitumen (Gn 14, 10) and its accompanying gases.

19, 28f: From the height east of Hebron, Abraham could easily see the region at the southern end of the Dead Sea, where the Cities of the Plain were probably located.

19, 30–38: This Israelite tale about the origin of Israel's neighbors east of the Jordan and the Dead Sea was told partly to ridicule these racially related but rival nations and partly to give folk etymologies for their names.

x 2 Pt 7, 9. y Is 1, 7. 9; Zep 2, 9; Lk 17, 29. z Wis 10, 6. a Wis 10, 6. b Pss 9, 6; 11, 6; 107, 34. c Wis 10, 7; Is 1, 9; 13, 19; Lam 4, 6; 17, 29; 2 Pt 2, 6. d Dt 29, 22; Jer 50, 40; Am 4, 11. e Wis 10, 7; Lk 17, 32. f Rv 9, 2; 14, 10f.

again he was not aware of her lying down or her getting up.

[36]Thus both of Lot's daughters became pregnant by their father. [37]The older one gave birth to a son whom she named Moab, saying, "From my father."* He is the ancestor of the Moabites of today.[g] [38]The younger one, too, gave birth to a son, and she named him Ammon, saying, "The son of my kin."* He is the ancestor of the Ammonites of today.[h]

CHAPTER 20

Abraham at Gerar* [1]Abraham journeyed on to the region of the Negeb, where he settled between Kadesh and Shur. While he stayed in Gerar, [2]he said of his wife Sarah, "She is my sister." So Abimelech, king of Gerar, sent and took Sarah. [3]But God came to Abimelech in a dream one night and said to him, "You are about to die because of the woman you have taken, for she has a husband." [4]Abimelech, who had not approached her, said: "O Lord, would you slay a man even though he is innocent? [5]He himself told me, 'She is my sister,' and she herself also stated, 'He is my brother.' I did it in good faith and with clean hands." [6]God answered him in the dream: "Yes, I know you did it in good faith. In fact, it was I who kept you from sinning against me; that is why I did not let you touch her. [7]Therefore, return the man's wife—as a spokesman* he will intercede for you—that your life may be saved. If you do not return her, you can be sure that you and all who are yours will certainly die."

[8]Early the next morning Abimelech called all his court officials and informed them of everything that had happened, and the men were horrified. [9]Then Abimelech summoned Abraham and said to him: "How could you do this to us! What wrong did I do to you that you should have brought such monstrous guilt on me and my kingdom? You have treated me in an intolerable way. [10]What were you afraid of," he asked him, "that you should have done such a thing?" [11]"I was afraid," answered Abraham, "because I thought there would surely be no fear of God in this place, and so they would kill me on account of my wife. [12]Besides, she is in truth my sister, but only my father's daughter, not my mother's; and so she became my wife.[i] [13]When God sent me wandering from my father's house, I asked her: 'Would you do me this favor? In whatever place we come to, say that I am your brother.' "

[14]Then Abimelech took flocks and herds and male and female slaves and gave them to Abraham; and after he restored his wife Sarah to him, [15]he said, "Here, my land lies at your disposal; settle wherever you please." [16]To Sarah he said: "See, I have given your brother a thousand shekels of silver.* Let that serve you as a vindication before all who are with you; your honor has been preserved with everyone." [17]Abraham then interceded with God, and God restored health to Abimelech, that is, to his wife and his maidservants, so that they could bear children; [18]for God had tightly closed every womb in Abimelech's household on account of Abraham's wife Sarah.

CHAPTER 21

Birth of Isaac [1]The LORD took note of Sarah as he had said he would; he did for her as he had promised.[j] [2]Sarah became pregnant and bore Abraham a son in his old age, at the set time that God had stated.[k] [3]Abraham gave the name Isaac to this son of his whom Sarah bore him.[l] [4]When his son Isaac was eight days old, Abraham circumcised him, as God had commanded.[m] [5]Abraham was a hundred years old when his son Isaac was born to him. [6]Sarah then said, "God has given me cause to laugh, and all who hear of it will laugh with me.[n] [7]Who would have told

19, 37: From my father: in Hebrew, meabi, similar in sound to the name "Moab."

19, 38: The son of my kin: in Hebrew, ben-ammi, similar in sound to the name "Ammonites."

20, 1–18: This story from the Elohist source (see note on Gn 4, 25) combines elements found in the two very similar but distinct stories of the Yahwist source in Gn 12, 10–20 and 26, 6–11.

20, 7: Spokesman: the Hebrew term nabi used here is regularly translated as "prophet," but it simply means "one who speaks on behalf of another," whether the latter is God, as in almost all cases, or another man, as in Ex 4, 16.

20, 16: A thousand shekels of silver: not a gift distinct from that of the animals and the slaves (v 14), but the monetary value of these.

g Dt 2, 9. h Dt 2, 19. i Gn 12, 13. j Gn 17, 19; 18, 10. k Gal 4, 23; Heb 11, 11. l Mt 1, 2; Lk 3, 34. m Gn 17, 10ff; Acts 7, 8. n Gn 17, 17.

Abraham," she added, "that Sarah would nurse children! Yet I have borne him a son in his old age." 8Isaac grew, and on the day of the child's weaning Abraham held a great feast.

9*Sarah noticed the son whom Hagar the Egyptian had borne to Abraham playing with her son Isaac; 10so she demanded of Abraham: "Drive out that slave and her son! No son of that slave is going to share the inheritance with my son Isaac!"[o] 11Abraham was greatly distressed, especially on account of his son Ishmael. 12But God said to Abraham: "Do not be distressed about the boy or about your slave woman. Heed the demands of Sarah, no matter what she is asking of you; for it is through Isaac that descendants shall bear your name.[p] 13As for the son of the slave woman, I will make a great nation of him also, since he too is your offspring."

14Early the next morning Abraham got some bread and a skin of water and gave them to Hagar. Then, placing the child on her back,* he sent her away. As she roamed aimlessly in the wilderness of Beer-sheba, 15the water in the skin was used up. So she put the child down under a shrub, 16and then went and sat down opposite him, about a bowshot away; for she said to herself, "Let me not watch to see the child die." As she sat opposite him, he began to cry. 17God heard the boy's cry, and God's messenger called to Hagar from heaven: "What is the matter, Hagar? Don't be afraid; God has heard the boy's cry in this plight of his.[q] 18Arise, lift up the boy and hold him by the hand; for I will make of him a great nation." 19Then God opened her eyes, and she saw a well of water. She went and filled the skin with water, and then let the boy drink.

20God was with the boy as he grew up. He lived in the wilderness and became an expert bowman, 21with his home in the wilderness of Paran. His mother got a wife for him from the land of Egypt.

The Pact at Beer-sheba 22About that time Abimelech, accompanied by Phicol, the commander of his army,* said to Abraham: "God is with you in everything you do. 23Therefore, swear to me by God at this place* that you will not deal falsely with me or with my progeny and posterity, but will act as loyally toward me and the land in which you stay as I have acted toward you." 24To this Abraham replied, "I so swear."

25Abraham, however, reproached Abimelech about a well that Abimelech's men had seized by force. 26"I have no idea who did that," Abimelech replied. "In fact, you never told me about it, nor did I ever hear of it until now."

27Then Abraham took sheep and cattle and gave them to Abimelech and the two made a pact. 28Abraham also set apart seven ewe lambs of the flock, 29and Abimelech asked him, "What is the purpose of these seven ewe lambs that you have set apart?" 30Abraham answered, "The seven ewe lambs you shall accept from me that thus I may have your acknowledgment that the well was dug by me." 31This is why the place is called Beer-sheba;* the two of them took an oath there. 32When they had thus made the pact in Beer-sheba, Abimelech, along with Phicol, the commander of his army, left and returned to the land of the Philistines.

33Abraham planted a tamarisk at Beer-sheba, and there he invoked by name the LORD, God the Eternal.* 34Abraham resided in the land of the Philistines for many years.

21, 9–19: This story of Hagar's expulsion, in the Elohist source, is in general a duplicate of the one from the Yahwist source in Gn 16, 5–14; but the two stories differ greatly in detail.

21, 14: Placing the child on her back: the phrase is translated from an emended form of the Hebrew text. In the current faulty Hebrew text, Abraham put the bread and the waterskin on Hagar's back, while her son apparently walked beside her. This reading seems to be a scribal attempt at harmonizing the present passage with the data of the Priestly source, in which Ishmael would have been at least fourteen years old when Isaac was born; compare Gn 16, 16 with 21, 5; cf 17, 25. But in the present Elohist story Ishmael is obviously a little boy, not much older than Isaac; cf vv 15, 18.

21, 22: Here and in v 32 the Greek text has ". . . Abimelech, accompanied by Ahuzzath, his councilor, and Phicol . . ."; but this is probably a secondary harmonization with Gn 26, 26. Abimelech took Phicol with him in order to intimidate Abraham by a show of strength.

21, 23: This place: Beer-sheba (v 31). Abimelech had come from Gerar (Gn 20, 2), about thirty miles west of Beer-sheba.

21, 31: Beer-sheba: the Hebrew name really means "the well of the seven," i.e., the place where there are seven wells, alluded to in the episode of the seven ewe lambs, vv 28ff; but it can also be interpreted to mean "the well of the oath."

21, 33: God the Eternal: in Hebrew, el olam, perhaps the name of the deity of the pre-Israelite sanctuary at Beer-sheba, but used by Abraham merely as a title of Yahweh; cf Is 40, 28.

o Jgs 11, 2; Gal 4, 30. p Rom 9, 7; Heb 11, 18. q Gn 16, 7.

CHAPTER 22

The Testing of Abraham 1Some time after these events, God put Abraham to the test.* He called to him, "Abraham!" "Ready!" he replied.[r] 2Then God said: "Take your son Isaac, your only one,* whom you love, and go to the land of Moriah. There you shall offer him up as a holocaust on a height that I will point out to you."[s] 3Early the next morning Abraham saddled his donkey, took with him his son Isaac, and two of his servants as well, and with the wood that he had cut for the holocaust, set out for the place of which God had told him.

4On the third day Abraham got sight of the place from afar. 5Then he said to his servants: "Both of you stay here with the donkey, while the boy and I go on over yonder. We will worship and then come back to you." 6Thereupon Abraham took the wood for the holocaust and laid it on his son Isaac's shoulders, while he himself carried the fire and the knife. 7As the two walked on together, Isaac spoke to his father Abraham: "Father!" he said. "Yes, son," he replied. Isaac continued, "Here are the fire and the wood, but where is the sheep for the holocaust?" 8"Son," Abraham answered, "God himself will provide the sheep for the holocaust." Then the two continued going forward.

9When they came to the place of which God had told him, Abraham built an altar there and arranged the wood on it. Next he tied up his son Isaac, and put him on top of the wood on the altar.[t] 10Then he reached out and took the knife to slaughter his son.[u] 11But the LORD's messenger called to him from heaven, "Abraham, Abraham!" "Yes, Lord," he answered. 12"Do not lay your hand on the boy," said the messenger. "Do not do the least thing to him. I know now how devoted you are to God, since you did not withhold from me your own beloved son."[v] 13As Abraham looked about, he spied a ram caught by its horns in the thicket. So he went and took the ram and offered it up as a holocaust in place of his son. 14Abraham named the site Yahweh-yireh;* hence people now say, "On the mountain the LORD will see."

15Again the LORD's messenger called to Abraham from heaven 16[w]and said: "I swear by myself, declares the LORD, that because you acted as you did in not withholding from me your beloved son, 17I will bless you abundantly and make your descendants as countless as the stars of the sky and the sands of the seashore; your descendants shall take possession of the gates of their enemies,[x] 18and in your descendants all the nations of the earth shall find blessing—all this because you obeyed my command."[y]

19Abraham then returned to his servants, and they set out together for Beer-sheba, where Abraham made his home.

Nahor's Descendants* 20Some time afterward, the news came to Abraham: "Milcah too has borne sons, to your brother Nahor: 21Uz, his first-born, his brother Buz, Kemuel (the father of Aram), 22Chesed, Hazo, Pildash, Jidlaph and Bethuel." 23Bethuel became the father of Rebekah. These eight Milcah bore to Abraham's brother Nahor. 24His concubine, whose name was Reumah, also bore children: Tebah, Gaham, Tahash and Maacah.

CHAPTER 23

Purchase of a Burial Place 1The span of Sarah's life was one hundred and twenty-seven years. 2She died in Kiriath-arba (that is, Hebron) in the land of Canaan, and Abraham performed the customary mourning rites for her. 3Then he left the side of his dead one and addressed the Hittites:* 4"Although I am a resident alien*

22, 1: God put Abraham to the test: to prove the firmness of Abraham's faith in God's promise that through Isaac all the nations of the earth would find blessing; cf Gn 18, 10. 18; 21, 12.

22, 2: Only one: uniquely precious, especially loved; therefore the same term is rendered in vv 12. 17 as "beloved."

22, 14: Yahweh-yireh: a Hebrew expression meaning "the Lord will see"; the reference is to the words in v 8, "God himself will see to it."

22, 20–24: A list of Aramean tribes who lived to the east and northeast of Israel, twelve in number, like the twelve tribes of Israel (Gn 35, 23) and the twelve tribes of Ishmael (Gn 25, 12–16).

23, 3: The Hittites: a non-Semitic people in Canaan; their relationship to the well-known Hittites of Asia Minor is uncertain.

r Sir 44, 20. s 2 Chr 3, 1; 1 Mc 2, 52; Heb 11, 17. t Jas 2, 21. u Wis 10, 5. v Rom 8, 32; 1 Jn 4, 9. w 16f: Gn 15, 5; Ex 32, 13; Lk 1, 73; Rom 4, 13; Heb 6, 13f; 11, 12. x Gn 24, 60. y Gn 12, 3; 18, 18; 26, 4; Sir 44, 21; Acts 3, 25; Gal 3, 16.

among you, sell me from your holdings a piece of property for a burial ground, that I may bury my dead wife."[z] 5The Hittites answered Abraham: "Please, sir, 6listen to us! You are an elect of God among us. Bury your dead in the choicest of our burial sites. None of us would deny you his burial ground for the burial of your dead." 7Abraham, however, began to bow low before the local citizens, the Hittites, 8while he appealed to them: "If you will allow me room for burial of my dead, listen to me! Intercede for me with Ephron, son of Zohar, asking him 9to sell me the cave of Machpelah that he owns; it is at the edge of his field. Let him sell it to me in your presence, at its full price, for a burial place."

10Now Ephron was present with the Hittites. So Ephron the Hittite replied to Abraham in the hearing of the Hittites who sat on his town council:* 11"Please, sir, listen to me! I give you both the field and the cave in it; in the presence of my kinsmen I make this gift. Bury your dead!" 12But Abraham, after bowing low before the local citizens, addressed Ephron in the hearing of these men: 13"Ah, if only you would please listen to me! I will pay you the price of the field. Accept it from me, that I may bury my dead there." 14Ephron replied to Abraham, "Please, 15sir, listen to me! A piece of land worth four hundred shekels* of silver—what is that between you and me, as long as you can bury your dead?" 16 [a]Abraham accepted Ephron's terms; he weighed out to him the silver that Ephron had stipulated in the hearing of the Hittites, four hundred shekels of silver at the current market value.*

17 [b]Thus Ephron's field in Machpelah, facing Mamre, together with its cave and all the trees anywhere within its limits, was conveyed 18to Abraham by purchase in the presence of all the Hittites who sat on Ephron's town council. 19After this transaction, Abraham buried his wife Sarah in the cave of the field of Machpelah, facing Mamre (that is, Hebron) in the land of Canaan. 20Thus the field with its cave was transferred from the Hittites to Abraham as a burial place.

CHAPTER 24

Isaac and Rebekah 1Abraham had now reached a ripe old age, and the LORD had blessed him in every way. 2 [c]Abraham said to the senior servant of his household, who had charge of all his possessions: "Put your hand under my thigh,* 3and I will make you swear by the LORD, the God of heaven and the God of earth, that you will not procure a wife for my son from the daughters of the Canaanites among whom I live,[d] 4but that you will go to my own land and to my kindred to get a wife for my son Isaac." 5The servant asked him: "What if the woman is unwilling to follow me to this land? Should I then take your son back to the land from which you migrated?" 6"Never take my son back there for any reason," Abraham told him. 7"The LORD, the God of heaven, who took me from my father's house and the land of my kin, and who confirmed by oath the promise he then made to me, 'I will give this land to your descendants,'—he will send his messenger before you, and you will obtain a wife for my son there.[e] 8If the woman is unwilling to follow you, you will be released from this oath. But never take my son

23, 4: A resident alien: literally "a sojourner and a settler," i.e., a long-term resident alien. Such a one would normally not have the right to own property. The importance of Abraham's purchase of the field in Machpelah, which is worded in technical legal terms, lies in the fact that it gave his descendants their first, though small, land rights in the country that God had promised the patriarch they would one day inherit as their own. Abraham therefore insists on purchasing the field and not receiving it as a gift.

23, 10: Who sat on his town council: probable meaning of the literal translation, "who came in at the gate of his city"; so also in v 18.

23, 15: Four hundred shekels: probably an exorbitant sum; Jeremiah (32, 9) paid only seventeen shekels for his field in Anathoth, though the Babylonian invasion no doubt helped to reduce the price.

23, 16: The current market value: the standard weight called a shekel varied according to time and place.

24, 2: Put your hand under my thigh: the symbolism of this act was apparently connected with the Hebrew concept of children issuing from their father's "thigh" (Gn 46, 26; Ex 1, 5). Perhaps the man who took such an oath was thought to bring the curse of sterility on himself if he did not fulfill his sworn promise. Jacob made Joseph swear in the same way (Gn 47, 29). In both these instances, the oath was taken to carry out the last request of a man upon his death.

z Gn 33, 19; Acts 7, 16; Heb 11, 9. a Acts 7, 16. b 17f: Gn 49, 29f. c 2f: Gn 47, 29. d Gn 24, 37; 28, 1f; Jgs 14, 3; Tb 4, 12. e Gn 12, 7; Ex 6, 8; Tb 5, 17; Gal 3, 16.

back there!" 9 So the servant put his hand under the thigh of his master Abraham and swore to him in this undertaking.

10 The servant then took ten of his master's camels, and bearing all kinds of gifts from his master, he made his way to the city of Nahor* in Aram Naharaim. 11 Near evening, at the time when women go out to draw water, he made the camels kneel by the well outside the city. 12 Then he prayed: "LORD, God of my master Abraham, let it turn out favorably for me* today and thus deal graciously with my master Abraham. 13 While I stand here at the spring and the daughters of the townsmen are coming out to draw water, 14 if I say to a girl, 'Please lower your jug, that I may drink,' and she answers, 'Take a drink, and let me give water to your camels, too,' let her be the one whom you have decided upon for your servant Isaac. In this way I shall know that you have dealt graciously with my master."

15 [f] He had scarcely finished these words when Rebekah (who was born to Bethuel, son of Milcah, the wife of Abraham's brother Nahor) came out with a jug on her shoulder. 16 The girl was very beautiful, a virgin, untouched by man. She went down to the spring and filled her jug. As she came up, 17 the servant ran toward her and said, "Please give me a sip of water from your jug." 18 "Take a drink, sir," she replied, and quickly lowering the jug onto her hand, she gave him a drink. 19 When she had let him drink his fill, she said, "I will draw water for your camels, too, until they have drunk their fill." 20 With that, she quickly emptied her jug into the drinking trough and ran back to the well to draw more water, until she had drawn enough for all the camels. 21 The man watched her the whole time, silently waiting to learn whether or not the LORD had made his errand successful. 22 When the camels had finished drinking, the man took out a gold ring weighing half a shekel, which he fastened on her nose, and two gold bracelets weighing ten shekels, which he put on her wrists. 23 Then he asked her: "Whose daughter are you? Tell me, please. And is there room in your father's house for us to spend the night?" 24 She answered: "I am the daughter of Bethuel the son of Milcah, whom she bore to Nahor. 25 There is plenty of straw and fodder at our place," she added, "and room to spend the night." 26 The man then bowed down in worship to the LORD, 27 saying: "Blessed be the LORD, the God of my master Abraham, who has not let his constant kindness toward my master fail. As for myself also, the LORD has led me straight to the house of my master's brother."

28 Then the girl ran off and told her mother's household about it. 29 [g] Now Rebekah had a brother named Laban. 30 As soon as he saw the ring and the bracelets on his sister Rebekah and heard her words about what the man had said to her, Laban rushed outside to the man at the spring. When he reached him, he was still standing by the camels at the spring. 31 So he said to him: "Come, blessed of the LORD! Why are you staying outside when I have made the house ready for you, as well as a place for the camels?" 32 The man then went inside; and while the camels were being unloaded and provided with straw and fodder, water was brought to bathe his feet and the feet of the men who were with him. 33 But when the table was set for him, he said, "I will not eat until I have told my tale." "Do so," they replied.

34 "I am Abraham's servant," he began. 35 "The LORD has blessed my master so abundantly that he has become a wealthy man; he has given him flocks and herds, silver and gold, male and female slaves, and camels and asses. 36 My master's wife Sarah bore a son to my master in her old age, and he has given him everything he owns. 37 My master put me under oath, saying: 'You shall not procure a wife for my son among the daughters of the Canaanites in whose land I live; 38 instead, you shall go to my

24, 10: Nahor: it is uncertain whether this is to be understood as the name of Abraham's brother (Gn 11, 27), Rebekah's grandfather (Gn 24, 15), or the city of the same name (as known from the Mari documents); Aram Naharaim, situated near Haran (Gn 11, 31) in northern Mesopotamia.

24, 12: Let it turn out favorably for me: let me have a favorable omen; cf end of v 14.

f Gn 22, 23. g Gn 27, 43.

father's house, to my own relatives, to get a wife
for my son.' 39 When I asked my master, 'What if
the woman will not follow me?' 40 he replied:
'The LORD, in whose presence I have always
walked, will send his messenger with you and
make your errand successful, and so you will get
a wife for my son from my own kindred of my
father's house.[h] 41 Then you shall be released
from my ban. If you visit my kindred and they
refuse you, then, too, you shall be released from
my ban.'

42 "When I came to the spring today, I prayed:
'LORD, God of my master Abraham, may it be
your will to make successful the errand I am
engaged on! 43 While I stand here at the spring, if
I say to a young woman who comes out to draw
water, Please give me a little water from your
jug, 44 and she answers, Not only may you have a
drink, but I will give water to your camels, too—
let her be the woman whom the LORD has
decided upon for my master's son.'

45 "I had scarcely finished saying this prayer to
myself when Rebekah came out with a jug on
her shoulder. After she went down to the spring
and drew water, I said to her, 'Please let me have
a drink.' 46 She quickly lowered the jug she was
carrying and said, 'Take a drink, and let me bring
water for your camels, too.' So I drank, and she
watered the camels also. 47 When I asked her,
'Whose daughter are you?' she answered, 'The
daughter of Bethuel, son of Nahor, born to
Nahor by Milcah.' So I put the ring on her nose
and the bracelets on her wrists. 48 Then I bowed
down in worship to the LORD, blessing the LORD,
the God of my master Abraham, who had led me
on the right road to obtain the daughter of my
master's kinsman for his son. 49 If, therefore, you
have in mind to show true loyalty to my master,
let me know; but if not, let me know that, too. I
can then proceed accordingly."

50 [i]Laban and his household said in reply:
"This thing comes from the LORD; we can say
nothing to you either for or against it. 51 Here is
Rebekah, ready for you; take her with you, that
she may become the wife of your master's son,
as the LORD has said." 52 When Abraham's ser-
vant heard their answer, he bowed to the
ground before the LORD. 53 Then he brought out
objects of silver and gold and articles of clothing
and presented them to Rebekah; he also gave
costly presents to her brother and mother. 54 Af-
ter he and the men with him had eaten and
drunk, they spent the night there.

When they were up the next morning, he
said, "Give me leave to return to my master."[j]
55 Her brother and mother replied, "Let the girl
stay with us a short while, say ten days; after
that she may go." 56 But he said to them, "Do not
detain me, now that the LORD has made my
errand successful; let me go back to my master."
57 They answered, "Let us call the girl and see
what she herself has to say about it." 58 So they
called Rebekah and asked her, "Do you wish to
go with this man?" She answered, "I do." 59 At
this they allowed their sister Rebekah and her
nurse to take leave, along with Abraham's ser-
vant and his men. 60 Invoking a blessing on
Rebekah, they said:

"Sister, may you grow
 into thousands of myriads;
And may your descendants gain possession
 of the gates of their enemies!"[k]

61 Then Rebekah and her maids started out; they
mounted their camels and followed the man. So
the servant took Rebekah and went on his way.

62 Meanwhile Isaac had gone from Beer-lahai-
roi and was living in the region of the Negeb.[l]
63 One day toward evening he went out . . . * in
the field, and as he looked around, he noticed
that camels were approaching. 64 Rebekah, too,
was looking about, and when she saw him, she
alighted from her camel 65 and asked the servant,
"Who is the man out there, walking through the
fields toward us?" "That is my master," replied
the servant. Then she covered herself with her
veil.

66 The servant recounted to Isaac all the things
he had done. 67 Then Isaac took Rebekah into his

24, 63: He went out: the meaning of the Hebrew term that follows this is obscure.

h Tb 5, 17; 10, 13. i 50f; Tb 7, 12. j Tb 7, 14; 8, 20. k Gn 22, 17. l Gn 16, 13f; 25, 11.

tent; he married her, and thus she became his
wife. In his love for her Isaac found solace after
the death of his mother Sarah.

CHAPTER 25

Abraham's Sons by Keturah 1 [m]*Abraham
married another wife, whose name was Keturah.
2 She bore him Zimran, Jokshan, Medan, Midian,
Ishbak and Shuah. 3 Jokshan became the father of
Sheba and Dedan. The descendants of Dedan
were the Asshurim, the Letushim, and the
Leummim. [n] 4 The descendants of Midian were
Ephah, Epher, Hanoch, Abida and Eldaah. All of
these were descendants of Keturah.

5 Abraham deeded everything that he owned
to his son Isaac. 6 To his sons by concubinage,
however, he made grants while he was still
living, as he sent them away eastward, to the
land of Kedem,* away from his son Isaac.

Death of Abraham 7 The whole span of Abra-
ham's life was one hundred and seventy-five
years. 8 Then he breathed his last, dying at a ripe
old age, grown old after a full life; and he was
taken to his kinsmen. 9 [o]His sons Isaac and
Ishmael buried him in the cave of Machpelah, in
the field of Ephron, son of Zohar the Hittite,
which faces Mamre, 10 the field that Abraham
had bought from the Hittites; there he was
buried next to his wife Sarah. 11 After the death
of Abraham, God blessed his son Isaac, who
made his home near Beer-lahai-roi.

Descendants of Ishmael 12 These are the de-
scendants of Abraham's son Ishmael, whom
Hagar the Egyptian, Sarah's slave, bore to Abra-
ham. 13 [p]These are the names of Ismael's sons,
listed in the order of their birth: Nebaioth
(Ishmael's first-born), Kedar, Adbeel, Mibsam, [q]
14 Mishma, Dumah, Massa, 15 Hadad, Tema, Je-
tur, Naphish and Kedemah, 16 These are the sons
of Ishmael, their names by their villages and
encampments; twelve chieftains of as many
tribal groups. [r]

17 The span of Ishmael's life was one hundred
and thirty-seven years. After he had breathed his
last and died, he was taken to his kinsmen.
18 The Ishmaelites ranged from Havilah-by-Shur,
which is on the border of Egypt, all the way to
Asshur; and each of them pitched camp* in
opposition to his various kinsmen. [s]

III: The Patriarchs Isaac and Jacob

Birth of Esau and Jacob 19 This is the family
history of Isaac, son of Abraham; Abraham had
begotten Isaac. 20 Isaac was forty years old when
he married Rebekah, the daughter of Bethuel the
Aramean of Paddan-aram and the sister of Laban
the Aramean. [t] 21 Isaac entreated the LORD on
behalf of his wife, since she was sterile. The
LORD heard his entreaty, and Rebekah became
pregnant. 22 But the children in her womb jostled
each other so much that she exclaimed, "If this
is to be so, what good will it do me!" She went
to consult the LORD, 23 and he answered her:

"Two nations are in your womb,
two peoples are quarreling while still within
you;
But one shall surpass the other,
and the older shall serve the younger. [u]

24 When the time of her delivery came, there
were twins in her womb. [v] 25 The first to emerge
was reddish,* and his whole body was like a
hairy mantle; so they named him Esau. 26 His
brother came out next, gripping Esau's heel;* so

25, 1–11: Though mentioned here, Abraham's marriage to a "concubine," or wife of secondary rank, and his death are not to be understood as happening chronologically after the events narrated in the preceding chapter.

25, 6: The land of Kedem: or "the country of the East," the region inhabited by the Kedemites or Easterners (Gn 29, 1; Jgs 6, 3. 33; Jb 1, 3; Is 11, 14). The names mentioned in vv 2ff, as far as they can be identified, are those of tribes in the Arabian desert.

25, 18: Pitched camp: literally "fell"; the same Hebrew verb is used in Jgs 7, 12 in regard to the hostile encampment of Bedouin tribes. The present passage shows the fulfillment of the prediction contained in Gn 16, 12.

25, 25: Reddish: in Hebrew, admoni, a reference to Edom, another name for Esau (v 30; 36, 1). Edom, however, was really the name of the country south of Moab where the descendants of Esau lived. It was called the "red" country because of its reddish sandstone. Hairy: in Hebrew, sear, a reference to Seir, another name for Edom (Gn 36, 8). One might expect the text to say, "So they named him Seir"; but Esau (esaw) also means "hairy."

25, 26: Esau's heel: the Hebrew is baaqeb esaw, a reference to the name Jacob; cf Gn 27, 36. Probably, however, the name Jacob has no true etymological connection with the Hebrew word for "heel" (aqeb), but is instead a shortened form of some such name as yaaqob-el ("may God protect").

m 1–4; 1 Chr 1, 32f. n Is 21, 13. o 9f: Gn 23, 3–20. p 13–16: 1 Chr 1, 29ff. q Is 60, 7. r Gn 17, 20. s Gn 16, 12. t Gn 24, 66. u Gn 27, 29; Nm 24, 18; Mal 1, 2–5; Rom 9, 11f. v Hos 12, 3.

they named him Jacob. Isaac was sixty years old when they were born.[w]

[27]As the boys grew up, Esau became a skillful hunter, a man who lived in the open; whereas Jacob was a simple man, who kept to his tents.[x] [28]Isaac preferred Esau, because he was fond of game; but Rebekah preferred Jacob. [29]Once, when Jacob was cooking a stew, Esau came in from the open, famished. [30]He said to Jacob, "Let me gulp down some of that red stuff;* I'm starving." (That is why he was called Edom.) [31]But Jacob replied, "First give me your birthright* in exchange for it."[y] [32]"Look," said Esau, "I'm on the point of dying. What good will any birthright do me?" [33]But Jacob insisted, "Swear to me first!" So he sold Jacob his birthright under oath.[z] [34]Jacob then gave him some bread and the lentil stew; and Esau ate, drank, got up, and went his way. Esau cared little for his birthright.

CHAPTER 26

Isaac and Abimelech [1] [a]There was a famine in the land (distinct from the earlier one that had occurred in the days of Abraham), and Isaac went down to Abimelech, king of the Philistines in Gerar.[b] [2]The LORD appeared to him and said: "Do not go down to Egypt, but continue to camp wherever in this land I tell you. [3]Stay in this land, and I will be with you and bless you; for to you and your descendants I will give all these lands, in fulfillment of the oath that I swore to your father Abraham.[c] [4]I will make your descendants as numerous as the stars in the sky and give them all these lands, and in your descendants all the nations of the earth shall find blessing—[d] [5]this because Abraham obeyed me, keeping my mandate (my commandments, my ordinances and my instructions)."

[6]*So Isaac settled in Gerar. [7]When the men of the place asked questions about his wife, he answered, "She is my sister." He was afraid, if he called her his wife, the men of the place would kill him on account of Rebekah, since she was very beautiful. [8]But when he had been there for a long time, Abimelech, king of the Philistines, happened to look out of a window and was surprised to see Isaac fondling his wife Rebekah. [9]He called for Isaac and said: "She must certainly be your wife! How could you have said, 'She is my sister'?" Isaac replied, "I thought I might lose my life on her account." [10]"How could you do this to us!" exclaimed Abimelech. "It would have taken very little for one of the men to lie with your wife, and you would have thus brought guilt upon us!" [11]Abimelech therefore gave this warning to all his men: "Anyone who molests this man or his wife shall forthwith be put to death."

[12]*Isaac sowed a crop in that region and reaped a hundredfold the same year. Since the LORD blessed him, [13] [e]he became richer and richer all the time, until he was very wealthy indeed. [14]He acquired such flocks and herds, and so many work animals, that the Philistines became envious of him. ([15] [f]The Philistines had stopped up and filled with dirt all the wells that his father's servants had dug back in the days of his father Abraham.) [16]So Abimelech said to Isaac, "Go away from us; you have become far too numerous for us." [17]Isaac left there and made the Wadi Gerar his regular campsite. ([18]Isaac reopened the wells which his father's servants had dug back in the days of his father Abraham and which the Philistines had stopped up after Abraham's death; he gave them the same names that his father had given them.) [19]But when Isaac's servants dug in the wadi and reached spring water in their well, [20]the shepherds of Gerar quarreled with Isaac's servants, saying, "The water belongs to us!" So the well

25, 30: Red stuff: in Hebrew, adom; another play on the word Edom, the "red" land.

25, 31: Birthright: the privilege that entitled the first-born son to a position of honor in the family and to a double share in the possessions inherited from the father.

26, 6–11: The Yahwist's version of the wife-sister episode at Gerar; the Elohist's version (Gn 20, 1–18) is connected with Abraham and Sarah.

26, 12–33: The Yahwist's version of the story about the wells at Beer-sheba; again, the Elohist's version (Gn 21, 22f) is connected with Abraham. A redactor joined the two accounts by means of the parenthetical verses 15 and 18.

w Mt 1, 2 x Gn 27, 6f. y Dt 21, 17. z Heb 12, 16. a 1–14: Gn 12, 10–20. b Gn 12, 1. c Gn 12, 7; 15, 18; Ex 32, 13; Ps 105, 9; Sir 44, 22; Heb 11, 9. d Gn 12, 3; 22, 17f; 28, 14; Ex 32, 13. e 13f: Jb 1, 3. f 15–24: Gn 21, 25–31.

was called Esek,* because they had challenged him there. [21]Then they dug another well, and they quarreled over that one too; so it was called Sitnah.* [22]When he had moved on from there, he dug still another well; but over this one they did not quarrel. It was called Rehoboth, because he said, "The LORD has now given us ample room, and we shall flourish in the land."

[23]From there Isaac went up to Beer-sheba. [24]The same night the LORD appeared to him and said: "I am the God of your father Abraham. You have no need to fear, since I am with you. I will bless you and multiply your descendants for the sake of my servant Abraham."[g] [25]So he built an altar there and invoked the LORD by name. After he had pitched his tent there, his servants began to dig a well nearby.

[26] [h]Abimelech had meanwhile come to him from Gerar, accompanied by Ahuzzath, his councilor, and Phicol, the general of his army. [27]Isaac asked them, "Why have you come to me, seeing that you hate me and have driven me away from you?" [28]They answered: "We are convinced that the LORD is with you, so we propose that there be a sworn agreement between our two sides—between you and us. Let us make a pact with you: [29]you shall not act unkindly toward us, just as we have not molested you, but have always acted kindly toward you and have let you depart in peace. Henceforth, 'The LORD's blessing be upon you!' " [30]Isaac then made a feast for them, and they ate and drank. [31]Early the next morning they exchanged oaths. Then Isaac bade them farewell, and they departed from him in peace.

[32]That same day Isaac's servants came and brought him news about the well they had been digging; they told him, "We have reached water!" [33]He called it Shibah;* hence the name of the city, Beer-sheba, to this day.

[34]*When Esau was forty years old, he married Judith, daughter of Beeri the Hittite, and Basemath, daughter of Elon the Hivite.[i] [35]But they became a source of embitterment to Isaac and Rebekah.

CHAPTER 27

Jacob's Deception* [1]When Isaac was so old that his eyesight had failed him, he called his older son Esau and said to him, "Son!" "Yes, father!" he replied. [2]Isaac then said, "As you can see, I am so old that I may now die at any time. [3]Take your gear, therefore—your quiver and bow—and go out into the country to hunt some game for me. [4]With your catch prepare an appetizing dish for me, such as I like, and bring it to me to eat, so that I may give you my special blessing* before I die."

[5]Rebekah had been listening while Isaac was speaking to his son Esau. So when Esau went out into the country to hunt some game for his father,[j] [6]Rebekah said to her son Jacob, "Listen! I overheard your father tell your brother Esau, [7]'Bring me some game and with it prepare an appetizing dish for me to eat, that I may give you my blessing with the LORD's approval before I die.' [8]Now, son, listen carefully to what I tell you. [9]Go to the flock and get me two choice kids. With these I will prepare an appetizing dish for your father, such as he likes. [10]Then bring it to your father to eat, that he may bless you before he dies." [11]"But my brother Esau is a hairy man," said Jacob to his mother Rebekah,

26, 20: Esek: "challenge."

26, 21: Sitnah: "opposition"; one might expect the text to be continued by some such words as "because they were in opposition there."

26, 33: Shibah: "seven," for the sake of a closer assonance with Beer-sheba; but the present version of the story says nothing about there being seven wells there as implied in Gn 21, 28–31. The Greek version understood the Hebrew text more logically as shebua, "oath," in keeping with the present story.

26, 34f: These verses from the Priestly source, which have no logical connection with the preceding stories, serve as an introduction to the following section on Esau's loss of his birthright by suggesting a motivation for this in Isaac's and Rebekah's dislike for Esau's Canaanite wives.

27, 1–45: What Jacob did in deceiving his father and thereby cheating Esau out of Isaac's deathbed blessing is condemned as blameworthy, not only by Hosea (12, 4) and Jeremiah (9, 3), but also, indirectly, by the Yahwist narrator of the present story, who makes the reader sympathize with Esau as the innocent victim of a cruel plot, and shows that Jacob and his mother, the instigator of the plot, paid for it by a lifelong separation from each other. The story was told because it was part of the mystery of God's ways in salvation history—his use of weak, sinful men to achieve his own ultimate purpose.

27, 4: My special blessing: "the blessing of my soul." The same expression is used also in vv 19. 25. 31. In the context it must mean something like a solemn deathbed blessing, believed to be especially efficacious.

g Gn 46, 3. h 26–33: Gn 21, 22–31; Prv 16, 7. i 34f: Gn 27, 46. j Gn 25, 28.

"and I am smooth-skinned![k] 12 Suppose my fa-
ther feels me? He will think I am making sport of
him, and I shall bring on myself a curse instead
of a blessing." 13 His mother, however, replied:
"Let any curse against you, son, fall on me! Just
do as I say. Go and get me the kids."
14 So Jacob went and got them and brought
them to his mother; and with them she prepared
an appetizing dish, such as his father liked.
15 Rebekah then took the best clothes of her
older son Esau that she had in the house, and
gave them to her younger son Jacob to wear;
16 and with the skins of the kids she covered up
his hands and the hairless parts of his neck.
17 Then she handed her son Jacob the appetizing
dish and the bread she had prepared.
18 Bringing them to his father, Jacob said,
"Father!" "Yes?" replied Isaac. "Which of my
sons are you?" 19 Jacob answered his father: "I
am Esau, your first-born. I did as you told me.
Please sit up and eat some of my game, so that
you may give me your special blessing." 20 But
Isaac asked, "How did you succeed so quickly,
son?" He answered, "The LORD, your God, let
things turn out well with me." 21 Isaac then said
to Jacob, "Come closer, son, that I may feel you,
to learn whether you really are my son Esau or
not." 22 So Jacob moved up closer to his father.
When Isaac felt him, he said, "Although the
voice is Jacob's, the hands are Esau's." 23 (He
failed to identify him because his hands were
hairy, like those of his brother Esau; so in the
end he gave him his blessing.) 24 Again he asked
him, "Are you really my son Esau?" "Certainly,"
he replied. 25 Then Isaac said, "Serve me your
game, son, that I may eat of it and then give you
my blessing." Jacob served it to him, and Isaac
ate; he brought him wine, and he drank. 26 Fi-
nally his father Isaac said to him, "Come closer,
son, and kiss me." 27 As Jacob went up and
kissed him, Isaac smelled the fragrance of his
clothes. With that, he blessed him, saying,

"Ah, the fragrance of my son
is like the fragrance of a field
that the LORD has blessed![l]

28 "May God give to you
of the dew of the heavens
And of the fertility of the earth
abundance of grain and wine.

29 [m]"Let peoples serve you,
and nations pay you homage;
Be master of your brothers,
and may your mother's sons bow down to
you.

Cursed be those who curse you,
and blessed be those who bless you."

30 Jacob had scarcely left his father, just after
Isaac had finished blessing him, when his
brother Esau came back from his hunt. 31 Then
he too prepared an appetizing dish with his
game, and bringing it to his father, he said,
"Please, father, eat some of your son's game, that
you may then give me your special blessing."
32 "Who are you?" his father Isaac asked him. "I
am Esau," he replied, "your first-born son."
33 With that, Isaac was seized with a fit of
uncontrollable trembling. "Who was it, then,"
he asked, "that hunted game and brought it to
me? I finished eating it just before you came, and
I blessed him. Now he must remain blessed!"
34 On hearing his father's words, Esau burst into
loud, bitter sobbing. "Father, bless me too!" he
begged. 35 When Isaac explained, "Your brother
came here by a ruse and carried off your
blessing," 36 Esau exclaimed, "He has been well
named Jacob! He has now supplanted me*
twice! First he took away my birthright, and
now he has taken away my blessing." Then he
pleaded, "Haven't you saved a blessing for
me?"[n] 37 Isaac replied: "I have already appointed
him your master, and I have assigned to him all
his kinsmen as his slaves; besides, I have en-
riched him with grain and wine. What then can I
do for you, son?" 38 But Esau urged his father,
"Have you only that one blessing, father? Bless

27, 36: He has now supplanted me: in Hebrew, wayyaqebeni, a wordplay on the name Jacob, yaaqob; see Jer 9, 3 and note, as well as Gn 25, 26. There is also a play between the Hebrew words bekora ("birthright") and beraka ("blessing").

k Gn 25, 25. l Gn 22, 17f; Heb 11, 20. m Gn 25, 23; 49, 8; Nm 24, 9. n Gn 25, 17, 26. 29–34; Hos 12, 4.

me too!" Isaac, however, made no reply; and
Esau wept aloud.[o] 39 Finally Isaac spoke again
and said to him:

"Ah, far from the fertile earth
shall be your dwelling;
far from the dew of the heavens above![p]
40 "By your sword you shall live,
and your brother you shall serve;
But when you become restive,
you shall throw off his yoke from your
neck."[q]

41 Esau bore Jacob a grudge because of the
blessing his father had given him. He said to
himself, "When the time of mourning for my
father comes, I will kill my brother Jacob."[r]
42 When Rebekah got news of what her older son
Esau had in mind, she called her younger son
Jacob and said to him: "Listen! Your brother
Esau intends to settle accounts with you by
killing you. 43 Therefore, son, do what I tell you:
flee at once to my brother Laban in Haran, 44 and
stay with him a while until your brother's fury
subsides 45 [until your brother's anger against you
subsides] and he forgets what you did to him.
Then I will send for you and bring you back.
Must I lose both of you in a single day?"

Jacob Sent to Laban 46 *Rebekah said to Isaac:
"I am disgusted with life because of the Hittite
women. If Jacob also should marry a Hittite
woman, a native of the land, like these women,
what good would life be to me?"[s]

CHAPTER 28

1 Isaac therefore called Jacob, greeted him
with a blessing, and charged him: "You shall not
marry a Canaanite woman![t] 2 Go now to
Paddan-aram, to the home of your mother's
father Bethuel, and there choose a wife for
yourself from among the daughters of your uncle
Laban.[u] 3 May God Almighty bless you and make
you fertile, multiply you that you may become
an assembly of peoples. 4 May he extend to you
and your descendants the blessing he gave to
Abraham, so that you may gain possession of the
land where you are staying, which he assigned
to Abraham."[v] 5 Then Isaac sent Jacob on his
way; he went to Paddan-aram, to Laban, son of
Bethuel, the Aramean, and brother of Rebekah,
the mother of Jacob and Esau.[w]

6 Esau noted that Isaac had blessed Jacob
when he sent him to Paddan-aram to get himself
a wife there, charging him, as he gave him his
blessing, not to marry a Canaanite woman, 7 and
that Jacob had obeyed his father and mother and
gone to Paddan-aram. 8 Esau realized how dis-
pleasing the Canaanite women were to his father
Isaac, 9 so he went to Ishmael, and in addition to
the wives he had, married Mahalath, the daugh-
ter of Abraham's son Ishmael and sister of
Nebaioth.[x]

Jacob's Dream at Bethel 10 Jacob departed
from Beer-sheba and proceeded toward Haran.
11 When he came upon a certain shrine,* as the
sun had already set, he stopped there for the
night. Taking one of the stones at the shrine, he
put it under his head and lay down to sleep at
that spot. 12 Then he had a dream: a stairway*
rested on the ground, with its top reaching to
the heavens; and God's messengers were going
up and down on it.[y] 13 And there was the LORD
standing beside him and saying: "I, the LORD,
am the God of your forefather Abraham and the
God of Isaac; the land on which you are lying I
will give to you and your descendants.[z] 14 These
shall be as plentiful as the dust of the earth, and
through them you shall spread out east and
west, north and south. In you and your descen-

27, 46—28, 9: This section, which is from the Priestly source and a direct sequel of Gn 26, 34f, presents a different, though not contradictory, reason for Jacob's going to Paddan-aram: namely, to preserve racial purity among the chosen people. The account of Esau's marriages is given for the purpose of explaining the racial mixture of the Edomites, who were descended in part from tribes related to Israel, in part from older peoples in Edom called Hittites, Horites or Hivites, and in part from the Ishmaelite (Arabian) tribes who later invaded the region.

28, 11: Shrine: literally "place," often used specifically of a sacred site. Here the place was Bethel (v 19), a sacred site as early as the time of Abraham (Gn 12, 8).

28, 12: Stairway: in Hebrew, sullam, traditionally but inaccurately, translated as "ladder." The corresponding verb, salal, means "to heap up" something, such as dirt for a highway or ramp. The imagery in Jacob's dream is derived from the Babylonian ziggurat or temple tower, "with its top in the sky" (Gn 11, 4), and with brick steps leading up to a small temple at the top.

o Heb 12, 17. p Heb 11, 20. q 2 Kgs 8, 20. 22; 2 Chr 21, 8. r Wis 10, 10; Ob 1, 10. s Gn 26, 34f. t Gn 24, 3f; 26, 35. u Gn 22, 22; 17, 1f. 4f. v Ex 32, 13. w Jdt 8, 26. x Gn 36, 2f. y Jn 1, 51. z Dt 1, 8; Mi 7, 28.

dants all the nations of the earth shall find blessing.[a] 15Know that I am with you; I will protect you wherever you go, and bring you back to this land. I will never leave you until I have done what I promised you."[b]

16When Jacob awoke from his sleep, he exclaimed, "Truly, the LORD is in this spot, although I did not know it!" 17In solemn wonder he cried out: "How awesome is this shrine! This* is nothing else but an abode of God, and that is the gateway to heaven!" 18Early the next morning Jacob took the stone that he had put under his head, set it up as a memorial stone,* and poured oil on top if it.[c] 19He called that site Bethel,* whereas the former name of the town had been Luz.[d]

20Jacob then made this vow: "If God remains with me, to protect me on this journey I am making and to give me enough bread to eat and clothing to wear, 21and I come back safe to my father's house, the LORD shall be my God. 22This stone that I have set up as a memorial stone shall be God's abode. Of everything you give me, I will faithfully return a tenth part to you."

CHAPTER 29

Arrival in Haran 1[e]After Jacob resumed his journey, he came to the land of the Easterners.* 2Looking about, he saw a well in the open country, with three droves of sheep huddled near it, for droves were watered from that well. A large stone covered the mouth of the well.[f] 3Only when all the shepherds were assembled there could they roll the stone away from the mouth of the well and water the flocks. Then they would put the stone back again over the mouth of the well.

4Jacob said to them, "Friends, where are you from?" "We are from Haran," they replied. 5Then he asked them, "Do you know Laban, son of Nahor?" "We do," they answered.[g] 6He inquired further, "Is he well?" "He is," they answered; "and here comes his daughter Rachel with his flock." 7Then he said: "There is still much daylight left; it is hardly the time to bring the animals home. Why don't you water the flocks now, and then continue pasturing them?" 8"We cannot," they replied, "until all the shepherds are here to roll the stone away from the mouth of the well; only then can we water the flocks."

9While he was still talking with them, Rachel arrived with her father's sheep; she was the one who tended them. 10As soon as Jacob saw Rachel, the daughter of his uncle Laban, with the sheep of his uncle Laban, he went up, rolled the stone away from the mouth of the well, and watered his uncle's sheep. 11Then Jacob kissed Rachel and burst into tears.* 12He told her that he was her father's relative, Rebekah's son, and she ran to tell her father. 13When Laban heard the news about his sister's son Jacob, he hurried out to meet him. After embracing and kissing him, he brought him to his house. Jacob then recounted to Laban all that had happened, 14and Laban said to him, "You are indeed my flesh and blood."*

Marriage to Leah and Rachel After Jacob had stayed with him a full month, 15Laban said to him: "Should you serve me for nothing just because you are a relative of mine? Tell me what your wages should be." 16Now Laban had two daughters; the older was called Leah, the younger Rachel. 17Leah had lovely eyes,* but Rachel was well formed and beautiful. 18Since Jacob had fallen in love with Rachel, he answered Laban, "I will serve you seven years for your younger daughter Rachel."* 19Laban replied, "I

28, 17: This: the stone Jacob used as a headrest; cf v 22. That: the stairway Jacob saw in his dream.

28, 18: Memorial stone: in Hebrew, masseba, a stone which might vary in shape and size, set upright and usually intended for some religious purpose. Since the custom of erecting such "sacred pillars" in Palestine went back to its pre-Israelite period, their pagan associations were often retained; therefore, later Israelite religion forbade their erection (Lv 26, 1; Dt 16, 22) and ordered the destruction of those that were associated with paganism (Ex 34, 31; Dt 12, 3).

28, 19: Bethel: i.e., "house of God"; the reference is to the abode of God in v 17.

29, 1: Easterners: see note on Gn 25, 6.

29, 11: Burst into tears: literally "raised his voice and wept," i.e., for joy.

29, 14: Flesh and blood: literally "bone and flesh," i.e., a close relative; on the Hebrew idiom, see Gn 2, 23.

29, 17: Lovely eyes: The adjective modifying eyes is often translated as "weak," but "lovely" is the more probable word.

29, 18: Jacob offers to render service (Jos 15, 16f; 1 Sm 17, 25; 18, 17) in lieu of the customary bridal price (Ex 22, 16f; Dt 22, 29).

a Gn 12, 3; 13, 14f; 15, 5f; 18, 18; 22, 17f; 26, 4; Dt 19, 8; Sir 44, 21. b Gn 31, 3. c Gn 31, 13; 35, 14f. d Gn 35, 6; 48, 3; Jos 18, 13; Jgs 1, 23; Hos 12, 4. e Wis 10, 10. f Gn 24, 11f. g Tb 7, 4.

prefer to give her to you rather than to an outsider. Stay with me." 20So Jacob served seven years for Rachel, yet they seemed to him but a few days because of his love for her.[h]

21Then Jacob said to Laban, "Give me my wife, that I may consummate my marriage with her, for my term is now completed." 22So Laban invited all the local inhabitants and gave a feast. 23At the nightfall he took his daughter Leah and brought her to Jacob, and Jacob consummated the marriage with her. 24(Laban assigned his slave girl Zilpah to his daughter Leah as her maidservant.) 25In the morning Jacob was amazed:* it was Leah! So he cried out to Laban: "How could you do this to me! Was it not for Rachel that I served you? Why did you dupe me?" 26"It is not the custom in our country," Laban replied, "to marry off a younger daughter before an older one. 27Finish the bridal week* for this one, and then I will give you the other too, in return for another seven years of service with me."[i]

28Jacob agreed. He finished the bridal week for Leah, and then Laban gave him his daughter Rachel in marriage. 29(Laban assigned his slave girl Bilhah to his daughter Rachel as her maidservant.) 30Jacob then consummated his marriage with Rachel also, and he loved her more than Leah. Thus he remained in Laban's service another seven years.[j]

Jacob's Children 31When the LORD saw that Leah was unloved, he made her fruitful, while Rachel remained barren. 32Leah conceived and bore a son, and she named him Reuben;* for she said, "It means, 'The LORD saw my misery; now my husband will love me.' "[k] 33She conceived again and bore a son, and said, "It means, 'The LORD heard that I was unloved,' and therefore he has given me this one also"; so she named him Simeon.* 34Again she conceived and bore a son, and she said, "Now at last my husband will become attached to me, since I have now borne him three sons"; that is why she named him Levi.* 35Once more she conceived and bore a son, and she said, "This time I will give grateful praise to the LORD"; therefore she named him Judah.* Then she stopped bearing children.[l]

CHAPTER 30

1When Rachel saw that she failed to bear children to Jacob, she became envious of her sister. She said to Jacob, "Give me children or I shall die!"[m] 2In anger Jacob retorted, "Can I take the place of God, who has denied you the fruit of the womb?"[n] 3She replied, "Here is my maidservant Bilhah. Have intercourse with her, and let her give birth on my knees,* so that I too may have offspring, at least through her."[o] 4So she gave him her maidservant Bilhah as a consort,* and Jacob had intercourse with her. 5When Bilhah conceived and bore a son, 6Rachel said, "God has vindicated me; indeed he has heeded my plea and given me a son." Therefore she named him Dan.* 7Rachel's maidservant Bilhah conceived again and bore a second son, 8and Rachel said, "I engaged in a fateful struggle with my sister, and I prevailed." So she named him Naphtali.*

29, 25: Jacob was amazed: he had not recognized Leah because a bride was veiled when she was brought to her bridegroom; cf Gn 24, 65.

29, 27: The bridal week: an ancient wedding lasted for seven days of festivities; cf Jgs 14, 12.

29, 32: Reuben: The literal meaning of the Hebrew name is "look, a son!" But in this case, as also with the names of all the other sons of Jacob, a symbolic rather than an etymological interpretation of the name is given, because the name and the persons were regarded as closely interrelated. The symbolic interpretation of Reuben's name, according to the Yahwist source, is based on the similar-sounding, raa beonyi, "he saw my misery." In the Elohist source, the name is explained by the similar-sounding yeehabani, "he will love me."

29, 33: Simeon: in popular etymology, related to shama, "he heard."

29, 34: Levi: related to yillaweh, "he will become attached."

29, 35: Judah: related to odeh, "I will give grateful praise."

30, 3: On my knees: in the ancient Near East, a father would take a newborn child in his lap to signify that he acknowledged it as his own; Rachel uses this ceremony in order to adopt the child and establish her legal rights to it.

30, 4: Consort: the Hebrew word normally means "wife," but here it refers to a wife of secondary rank, who did not have the full legal rights of an ordinary wife.

30, 6: Dan: explained by the term dannanni, "he has vindicated me."

30, 8: Naphtali: explained by the phrase "naptule elohim niptalti, literally, "in a divine wrestling match I have wrestled," perhaps implying the concept of an ordeal; hence the above rendering, I engaged in a fateful struggle.

h Hos 12, 13. i Hos 12, 13. j Dt 21, 15ff. k Gn 49, 3. l Mt 1, 2; Lk 3, 33. m Prv 30, 16. n 2 Kgs 5, 7. o Gn 16, 2ff.

9When Leah saw that she had ceased to bear children, she gave her maidservant Zilpah to Jacob as a consort. 10So Jacob had intercourse with Zilpah, and she conceived and bore a son. 11Leah then said, "What good luck!" So she named him Gad.* 12Then Leah's maidservant Zilpah bore a second son to Jacob; 13and Leah said, "What good fortune!"—meaning, "Women call me fortunate." So she named him Asher.*

14One day, during the wheat harvest, when Reuben was out in the field, he came upon some mandrakes* which he brought home to his mother Leah. Rachel asked Leah, "Please let me have some of your son's mandrakes." 15Leah replied, "Was it not enough for you to take away my husband, that you must now take my son's mandrakes too?" "Very well, then!" Rachel answered. "In exchange for your son's mandrakes, Jacob may lie with you tonight." 16That evening, when Jacob came home from the fields, Leah went out to meet him. "You are now to come in with me," she told him, "because I have paid for you with my son's mandrakes." So that night he slept with her, 17and God heard her prayer; she conceived and bore a fifth son to Jacob. 18Leah then said, "God has given me my reward for having let my husband have my maidservant"; so she named him Issachar.* 19Leah conceived again and bore a sixth son to Jacob; 20and she said, "God has brought me a precious gift. This time my husband will offer me presents, now that I have borne him six sons"; so she named him Zebulun.* 21Finally, she gave birth to a daughter, and she named her Dinah.

22Then God remembered Rachel; he heard her prayer and made her fruitful. 23She conceived and bore a son, and she said, "God has removed my disgrace."[p] 24So she named him Joseph,* meaning, "May the LORD add another son to this one for me!"

Jacob Outwits Laban 25After Rachel gave birth to Joseph, Jacob said to Laban: "Give me leave to go to my homeland. 26Let me have my wives, for whom I served you, and my children, too, that I may depart. You know very well the service that I have rendered you." 27Laban answered him: "If you will please. . . .

"I have learned through divination that it is because of you that God has blessed me. 28So," he continued, "state what wages you want from me, and I will pay them." 29Jacob replied: "You know what work I did for you and how well your livestock fared under my care; 30the little you had before I came has grown into very much, since the LORD's blessings came upon you in my company. Therefore I should now do something for my own household as well." 31"What should I pay you?" Laban asked. Jacob answered: "You do not have to pay me anything outright. I will again pasture and tend your flock, if you do this one thing for me: 32go through your whole flock today and remove from it every dark animal among the sheep and every spotted or speckled one among the goats.* Only such animals shall be my wages. 33In the future, whenever you check on these wages of mine, let my honesty testify against me: any animal in my possession that is not a speckled or spotted goat, or a dark sheep, got there by theft!" 34"Very well," agreed Laban. "Let it be as you say."

35That same day Laban removed the streaked and spotted he-goats and all the speckled and spotted she-goats, all those with some white on them, as well as the fully dark-colored sheep; these he left . . . in charge of his sons.* 36Then

30, 11: Gad: explained by the Hebrew term begad, literally "in luck," i.e., what good luck!

30, 13: Asher: explained by the term beoshri, literally "in my good fortune," i.e., what good fortune, and by the term ishsheruni, "they call me fortunate."

30, 14: Mandrakes: an herb whose root was anciently thought to promote conception. The Hebrew word for mandrakes, dudaim, has erotic connotations, since it sounds like the words daddayim ("breasts") and dodim ("sexual pleasure").

30, 18: Issachar: explained by the terms, sekari, "my reward," and in v 16, sakor sekartika, literally "I have hired you," i.e., I have paid for you.

30, 20: Zebulun: related to the Akkadian word zubullum, "bridegroom's gift," is explained by the terms, zebadani . . . zebed tob, "he has brought me a precious gift," and yizbeleni, "he will offer me presents."

30, 24: Joseph: explained by the words yosep, "may he add," and in v 23, asap, "he has removed."

30, 32: Dark . . . sheep . . . spotted or speckled goats: In the Near East the normal color of sheep is light gray, whereas that of goats is uniform dark brown or black. Ordinarily, therefore, Jacob would have received but few animals.

30, 35: By giving the abnormally colored animals to his sons, Laban not only deprived Jacob of his first small wages, but he also

p Lk 1, 25.

he put a three days' journey between himself and Jacob, while Jacob continued to pasture the rest of Laban's flock.

[37]Jacob, however, got some fresh shoots of poplar, almond and plane trees, and he made white stripes in them by peeling off the bark down to the white core of the shoots. [38]The rods that he had thus peeled he then set upright in the watering troughs, so that they would be in front of the animals that drank from the troughs. When the animals were in heat as they came to drink, [39]*the goats mated by the rods, and so they brought forth streaked, speckled and spotted kids. [40]The sheep, on the other hand, Jacob kept apart, and he set these animals to face the streaked or fully dark-colored animals of Laban. Thus he produced special flocks of his own, which he did not put with Laban's flock. [41]Moreover, whenever the hardier animals were in heat, Jacob would set the rods in the troughs in full view of these animals, so that they mated by the rods; [42]but with the weaker animals he would not put the rods there. So the feeble animals would go to Laban, but the sturdy ones to Jacob. [43]Thus the man grew increasingly prosperous, and he came to own not only large flocks but also male and female servants and camels and asses.

CHAPTER 31

Flight from Laban [1]Jacob learned that Laban's sons were saying, "Jacob has taken everything that belonged to our father, and he has accumulated all this wealth of his by using our father's property." [2]Jacob perceived, too, that Laban's attitude toward him was not what it had previously been. [3]Then the LORD said to Jacob, "Return to the land of your fathers, where you were born, and I will be with you." [q]

[4]So Jacob sent for Rachel and Leah to meet him where he was in the field with his flock. [5]There he said to them: "I have noticed that your father's attitude toward me is not as it was in the past; but the God of my father has been with me. [6]You well know what effort I put into serving your father; [7]yet your father cheated me and changed my wages time after time. God, however, did not let him do me any harm. [r] [8]*Whenever your father said, 'The speckled animals shall be your wages,' the entire flock would bear speckled young; whenever he said, 'The streaked animals shall be your wages,' the entire flock would bear streaked young. [9]Thus God reclaimed your father's livestock and gave it to me. [10]Once, in the breeding season, I had a dream in which I saw mating he-goats that were streaked, speckled and mottled. [11]In the dream God's messenger called to me, 'Jacob!' 'Here!' I replied. [12]Then he said, 'Note well. All the he-goats in the flock, as they mate, are streaked, speckled and mottled, for I have seen all the things that Laban has been doing to you. [13]I am the God who appeared to you in Bethel, where you anointed a memorial stone and made a vow to me. Up, then! Leave this land and return to the land of your birth.' " [s]

[14]Rachel and Leah answered him: "Have we still an heir's portion in our father's house? [15]Are we not regarded by him as outsiders?* He not only sold us; he has even used up the money that he got for us! [16]All the wealth that God reclaimed from our father really belongs to us and our children. Therefore, do just as God has told you." [t] [17]Jacob proceeded to put his children and wives on camels, [18]and he drove off with all his livestock and all the property he had acquired in Paddan-aram, to go to his father Isaac in the land of Canaan.

---

designed to prevent in this way the future breeding of such animals in the part of his flock entrusted to Jacob.

30, 39–42: Jacob's stratagem was based on the widespread notion among simple people that visual stimuli can have prenatal effects on the offspring of breeding animals. Thus, the rods on which Jacob had whittled stripes or bands or chevron marks were thought to cause the female goats that looked at them to bear kids with lighter-colored marks on their dark hair, while the gray ewes were thought to bear lambs with dark marks on them simply by visual cross-breeding with the dark goats.

31, 8–12: This Elohist account of the miraculous increase in Jacob's flock differs somewhat from the Yahwist account given in Gn 30, 32–42.

31, 15: Outsiders: literally "foreign women"; they lacked the favored legal status of native women. Used up: literally "eaten, consumed"; the bridal price that a man received for giving his daughter in marriage was legally reserved as her inalienable dowry.

q Gn 26, 3; 28, 15; 32, 10. r Jdt 8, 26. s Gn 28, 18. t Wis 10, 10f.

19 Now Laban had gone away to shear his sheep, and Rachel had meanwhile appropriated her father's household idols.[u] * 20 Jacob had hoodwinked* Laban the Aramean by not telling him of his intended flight. 21 Thus he made his escape with all that he had. Once he was across the Euphrates, he headed for the highlands of Gilead.

22 On the third day, word came to Laban that Jacob had fled. 23 Taking his kinsmen with him, he pursued him for seven days* until he caught up with him in the hill country of Gilead. 24 But that night God appeared to Laban the Aramean in a dream and warned him, "Take care not to threaten Jacob with any harm."[v]

Jacob and Laban in Gilead 25 When Laban overtook Jacob, Jacob's tents were pitched in the highlands; Laban also pitched his tents there, on Mount Gilead. 26 "What do you mean," Laban demanded of Jacob, "by hoodwinking me and carrying off my daughters like war captives?* 27 Why did you dupe me by stealing away secretly? You should have told me, and I would have sent you off with merry singing to the sound of tambourines and harps. 28 You did not even allow me a parting kiss to my daughters and grandchildren! What you have now done is a senseless thing. 29 I have it in my power to harm all of you; but last night the God of your father said to me, 'Take care not to threaten Jacob with any harm!' 30 Granted that you had to leave because you were desperately homesick for your father's house, why did you steal my gods?" 31 "I was frightened," Jacob replied to Laban, "at the thought that you might take your daughters away from me by force. 32 But as for your gods, the one you find them with shall not remain alive! If, with my kinsmen looking on, you identify anything here as belonging to you, take it." Jacob, of course, had no idea that Rachel had stolen the idols.

33 Laban then went in and searched Jacob's tent and Leah's tent, as well as the tents of the two maidservants; but he did not find the idols. Leaving Leah's tent, he went into Rachel's. 34 Now Rachel had taken the idols, put them inside a camel cushion, and seated herself upon them. When Laban had rummaged through the rest of her tent without finding them,[w] 35 Rachel said to her father, "Let not my lord feel offended that I cannot rise in your presence; a woman's period is upon me." So, despite his search, he did not find his idols.

36 Jacob, now enraged, upbraided Laban. "What crime or offense have I committed," he demanded, "that you should hound me so fiercely? 37 Now that you have ransacked all my things, have you found a single object taken from your belongings? If so, produce it here before your kinsmen and mine, and let them decide between us two.

38 "In the twenty years that I was under you, no ewe or she-goat of yours ever miscarried, and I have never feasted on a ram of your flock. 39 [x]I never brought you an animal torn by wild beasts; I made good the loss myself. You held me responsible for anything stolen by day or night.* 40 How often the scorching heat ravaged me by day, and the frost by night, while sleep fled from my eyes! 41 Of the twenty years that I have now spent in your household, I slaved fourteen years for your two daughters and six years for your flock, while you changed my wages time after time. 42 If my ancestral God, the God of Abraham and the Awesome One of Isaac, had not been on my side, you would now have sent me away empty-handed. But God saw my plight and the

31, 19: Household idols: in Hebrew, teraphim, figurines used in divination (Ez 21, 26; Zec 10, 2). Laban calls them his "gods" (v 30).

31, 20: Hoodwinked: literally "stolen the heart of," i.e., lulled the mind of. Aramean: The earliest extra-biblical references to the Arameans date from several centuries after the time of Jacob; to call Laban an Aramean and to have him speak Aramaic (v 47) would seem to be an anachronism.

31, 23: For seven days: literally "a way of seven days," a general term to designate a long distance; it would have taken a camel caravan many more days to travel from Haran to Gilead, the region east of the northern half of the Jordan.

31, 26: War captives: literally "women captured by the sword"; the women of a conquered people were treated as part of the victor's booty; cf 1 Sm 30, 2; 2 Kgs 5, 2.

31, 39: Laban's actions were contrary to the customs of the ancient Near East, as recorded in the Code of Hammurabi: "If in a sheepfold an act of god has occurred, or a lion has made a kill, the shepherd shall clear himself before the deity, and the owner of the fold must accept the loss" (par. 266); cf Ex 22, 12.

u Gn 19, 34; 1 Sm 19, 13. v Wis 10, 12. w Gn 31, 19. x Ex 22, 12.

fruits of my toil, and last night he gave judgment."[y]

[43]*Laban replied to Jacob: "The women are mine, their children are mine, and the flocks are mine; everything you see belongs to me. But since these women are my daughters, I will now do something for them and for the children they have borne. [44]Come, then, we will make a pact, you and I; the LORD shall be a witness between us."

[45]Then Jacob took a stone and set it up as a memorial stone.[z] [46]Jacob said to his kinsmen, "Gather some stones." So they got some stones and made a mound; and they had a meal there at the mound. [47]Laban called it Jegar-sahadutha,* but Jacob named it Galeed. [48]"This mound," said Laban, "shall be a witness from now on between you and me." That is why it was named Galeed— [49]and also Mizpah,* for he said: "May the LORD keep watch between you and me when we are out of each other's sight. [50]If you mistreat my daughters, or take other wives besides my daughters, remember that even though no one else is about, God will be witness between you and me."

[51]Laban said further to Jacob: "Here is this mound, and here is the memorial stone that I have set up between you and me. [52]This mound shall be witness, and this memorial stone shall be witness, that, with hostile intent, neither may I pass beyond this mound into your territory nor may you pass beyond it into mine. [53]May the God of Abraham and the god of Nahor [their ancestral deities] maintain justice between us!" Jacob took the oath by the Awesome One of Isaac. [54]He then offered a sacrifice on the mountain and invited his kinsmen to share in the meal. When they had eaten, they passed the night on the mountain.

CHAPTER 32

[1]Early the next morning, Laban kissed his grandchildren and his daughters goodbye; then he set out on his journey back home, [2]while Jacob continued on his own way. Then God's messengers encountered Jacob. [3]When he saw them he said, "This is God's encampment." So he named that place Mahanaim.*

Embassy to Esau [4]Jacob sent messengers ahead to his brother Esau in the land of Seir, the country of Edom,[a] [5]with this message: "Thus shall you say to my lord Esau: 'Your servant Jacob speaks as follows: I have been staying with Laban and have been detained there until now. [6]I own cattle, asses and sheep, as well as male and female servants. I am sending my lord this information in the hope of gaining your favor.' " [7]When the messengers returned to Jacob, they said, "We reached your brother Esau. He is now coming to meet you, accompanied by four hundred men."

[8]Jacob was very much frightened. In his anxiety, he divided the people who were with him, as well as his flocks, herds, and camels, into two camps. [9]"If Esau should attack and overwhelm one camp," he reasoned, "the remaining camp may still survive." [10]Then he prayed, "O God of my father Abraham and God of my father Isaac! You told me, O LORD, 'Go back to the land of your birth, and I will be good to you.'[b] [11]I am unworthy of all the acts of kindness that you have loyally performed for your servant: although I crossed the Jordan here with nothing but my staff, I have now grown into two companies. [12]Save me, I pray, from the hand of my brother Esau! Otherwise I fear that when he comes he will strike me down and slay the mothers and children.[c] [13]You yourself said, 'I will be very good to you, and I will make your descendants like the sands of the sea, which are too numerous to count.' "

31, 43–54: In this account of the treaty between Laban and Jacob, the Yahwist and Elohist sources are closely interwoven. The mound or cairn of stones comes from the Yahwist source, the memorial stone or stele comes from the Elohist one.

31, 47: Jegar-sahadutha: an Aramaic term meaning "mound of witness." Galeed: in Hebrew, galed, with the same meaning; also offers an explanation of the regional name Gilead.

31, 49: Mizpah: a town in Gilead; cf Jgs 10, 17; 11, 11. 34; Hos 5, 1. The Hebrew name mispa ("lookout") is allied to yisep yhwh ("may the Lord keep watch"), and also echoes the word masseba ("memorial pillar").

32, 3: Mahanaim: a town in Gilead (Jos 13, 26. 30; 21, 38; 2 Sm 2, 8; etc.). The Hebrew name means "two camps." There are other allusions to the name in vv 8. 11.

y Gn 19, 24. 29. z Gn 28, 18; 35, 14. a Gn 36, 6. b Gn 31, 3. c Gn 28, 14; 48, 16; Ex 32, 13; Heb 11, 12.

14 After passing the night there, Jacob selected
from what he had with him the following
presents for his brother Esau: 15 two hundred
she-goats and twenty he-goats; two hundred
ewes and twenty rams; 16 thirty milch camels
and their young; forty cows and ten bulls;
twenty she-asses and ten he-asses. 17 He put
these animals in charge of his servants, in
separate droves, and he told the servants, "Go
on ahead of me, but keep a space between one
drove and the next." 18 To the servant in the lead
he gave this instruction: "When my brother
Esau meets you, he may ask you, 'Whose man
are you? Where are you going? To whom do
these animals ahead of you belong?' 19 Then you
shall answer, 'They belong to your brother Jacob,
but they have been sent as a gift to my lord Esau;
and Jacob himself is right behind us.' " 20 He
gave similar instructions to the second servant
and the third and to all the others who followed
behind the droves, namely: "Thus and thus shall
you say to Esau, when you reach him; 21 and be
sure to add, 'Your servant Jacob is right behind
us.' " For Jacob reasoned, "If I first appease him
with gifts that precede me, then later, when I
face him, perhaps he will forgive me." 22 So the
gifts went on ahead of him, while he stayed that
night in the camp.

Struggle with the Angel 23 In the course of
that night, however, Jacob arose, took his two
wives, with the two maidservants and his eleven
children, and crossed the ford of the Jabbok.
24 After he had taken them across the stream and
had brought over all his possessions, 25 Jacob was
left there alone. Then some man* wrestled with
him until the break of dawn. 26 When the man
saw that he could not prevail over him, he struck
Jacob's hip at its socket, so that the hip socket
was wrenched as they wrestled.[d] 27 The man
then said, "Let me go, for it is daybreak." But
Jacob said, "I will not let you go until you bless
me." 28 "What is your name?" the man asked.
He answered, "Jacob."[e] 29 Then the man said,
"You shall no longer be spoken of as Jacob, but as
Israel,* because you have contended with divine
and human beings and have prevailed." 30 Jacob
then asked him, "Do tell me your name, please."
He answered, "Why should you want to know
my name?" With that, he bade him farewell.
31 Jacob named the place Peniel,* "Because I
have seen God face to face," he said, "yet my life
has been spared."[f]

32 At sunrise, as he left Penuel, Jacob limped
along because of his hip. 33 That is why, to this
day, the Israelites do not eat the sciatic muscle
that is on the hip socket, inasmuch as Jacob's hip
socket was struck at the sciatic muscle.

CHAPTER 33

Jacob and Esau Meet 1 Jacob looked up and
saw Esau coming, accompanied by four hundred
men. So he divided his children among Leah,
Rachel and the two maidservants, 2 putting the
maids and their children first, Leah and her
children next, and Rachel and Joseph last. 3 He
himself went on ahead of them, bowing to the
ground seven times, until he reached his
brother. 4 Esau ran to meet him, embraced him,
and flinging himself on his neck, kissed him as
he wept.

5 When Esau looked about, he saw the
women and children. "Who are these with
you?" he asked. Jacob answered, "They are the
children whom God has graciously bestowed on
your servant." 6 Then the maidservants and their
children came forward and bowed low; 7 next,
Leah and her children came forward and bowed
low; lastly, Rachel and her children came for-
ward and bowed low. 8 Then Esau asked, "What
did you intend with all those droves that I
encountered?" Jacob answered, "It was to gain
my lord's favor." 9 "I have plenty," replied Esau;

32, 25: Some man: a messenger of the Lord in human form, as is clear from vv 29ff.

32, 29: Israel: the first part of the Hebrew name Yisrael is given a popular explanation in the word sarita, "you contended"; the second part is the first syllable of elohim, "divine beings." The present incident, with a similar allusion to the name Israel, is referred to in Hos 12, 5, where the mysterious wrestler is explicitly called an angel.

32, 31: Peniel: a variant of the word Penuel (v 32), the name of a town on the north bank of the Jabbok in Gilead (Jgs 8, 8f. 17; 1 Kgs 12, 25). The name is explained as meaning "the face of God," peni-el. Yet my life has been spared: see note on Gn 16, 13.

d Hos 12, 4. e Gn 35, 10; 1 Kgs 18, 31; 2 Kgs 17, 34. f Jgs 13, 22.

“you should keep what is yours, brother.” 10“No, I beg you!” said Jacob. “If you will do me the favor, please accept this gift from me, since to come into your presence is for me like coming into the presence of God, now that you have received me so kindly. 11Do accept the present I have brought you; God has been generous toward me, and I have an abundance.” Since he so urged him, Esau accepted.

12Then Esau said, “Let us break camp and be on our way; I will travel alongside you.” 13But Jacob replied: “As my lord can see, the children are frail. Besides, I am encumbered with the flocks and herds, which now have sucklings; if overdriven for a single day, the whole flock will die. 14Let my lord, then, go on ahead of me, while I proceed more slowly at the pace of the livestock before me and at the pace of my children, until I join my lord in Seir.” 15Esau replied, “Let me at least put at your disposal some of the men who are with me.” But Jacob said, “For what reason? Please indulge me in this, my lord.” 16So on the same day that Esau began his journey back to Seir, 17Jacob journeyed to Succoth. There he built a home for himself and made booths for his livestock. That is why the place was called Succoth.*

18Having thus come from Paddan-aram, Jacob arrived safely at the city of Shechem, which is in the land of Canaan, and he encamped in sight of the city.[g] 19The plot of ground on which he had pitched his tent he bought for a hundred pieces of bullion* from the descendants of Hamor, the founder of Shechem.[h] 20He set up a memorial stone there and invoked “El, the God of Israel.”[i]

CHAPTER 34

The Rape of Dinah 1*Dinah, the daughter whom Leah had borne to Jacob, went out to visit some of the women of the land. 2When Shechem, son of Hamor the Hivite,* who was chief of the region, saw her, he seized her and lay with her by force. 3Since he was strongly attracted to Dinah, daughter of Jacob, indeed was really in love with the girl, he endeavored to win her affection. 4Shechem also asked his father Hamor, “Get me this girl for a wife.”

5Meanwhile, Jacob heard that Shechem had defiled his daughter Dinah; but since his sons were out in the fields with his livestock, he held his peace until they came home. 6Now Hamor, the father of Shechem, went out to discuss the matter with Jacob, 7just as Jacob's sons were coming in from the fields. When they heard the news, the men were shocked and seethed with indignation. What Shechem had done was an outrage in Israel; such a thing could not be tolerated.[j]

8Hamor appealed to them, saying, “My son Shechem has his heart set on your daughter. Please give her to him in marriage. 9Intermarry with us; give your daughters to us, and take our daughters for yourselves. 10Thus you can live among us. The land is open before you; you can settle and move about freely in it, and acquire landed property here.” 11Then Shechem, too, appealed to Dinah's father and brothers: “Do me this favor, and I will pay whatever you demand of me. 12No matter how high you set the bridal price, I will pay you whatever you ask; only give me the maiden in marriage.”

Revenge of Jacob's Sons 13Jacob's sons replied to Shechem and his father Hamor with guile, speaking as they did because their sister Dinah had been defiled. 14“We could not do such a thing,” they said, “as to give our sister to an uncircumcised man; that would be a disgrace for us. 15We will agree with you only on this condition, that you become like us by having

33, 17: Succoth: an important town near the confluence of the Jabbok and the Jordan (Jos 13, 27; Jgs 8, 5–16; 1 Kgs 7, 46). Booths: in Hebrew, sukkot, of the same sound as the name of the town.

33, 19: Pieces of bullion: in Hebrew, kesita, a monetary unit of which the value is now unknown. Descendants of Hamor: Hamorites, “the men of Hamor”; cf Jgs 9, 28. Hamor was regarded as the eponymous ancestor of the pre-Israelite inhabitants of Shechem.

34, 1–31: Behind the story of the rape of Dinah and the revenge of Jacob's sons on the men of the city of Shechem there probably lies a dimly recollected historical event connected with an armed conflict between the earliest Israelite tribes invading central Canaan and the Hurrian inhabitants of the Shechem region.

34, 2: Hivite: The Greek text has “Horite”; the terms were apparently used indiscriminately to designate the Hurrian or other non-Semitic elements in Palestine.

g Gn 12, 6; Jn 4, 6. h Jos 24, 32; Jn 4. 5; Acts 7, 16. i Jgs 6, 24. j 2 Sm 13, 12.

every male among you circumcised. 16Then we will give you our daughters and take yours in marriage; we will settle among you and become one kindred people with you. 17But if you do not comply with our terms regarding circumcision, we will take our daughter and go away."

18Their proposal seemed fair to Hamor and his son Shechem. 19The young man lost no time in acting in the matter, since he was deeply in love with Jacob's daughter. Moreover, he was more highly respected than anyone else in his clan. 20So Hamor and his son Shechem went to their town council and thus presented the matter to their fellow townsmen: 21"These men are friendly toward us. Let them settle in the land and move about in it freely; there is ample room in the country for them. We can marry their daughters and give our daughters to them in marriage. 22But the men will agree to live with us and form one kindred people with us only on this condition, that every male among us be circumcised as they themselves are. 23Would not the livestock they have acquired—all their animals—then be ours? Let us, therefore, give in to them, so that they may settle among us."

24All the able-bodied men of the town* agreed with Hamor and his son Shechem, and all the males, including every able-bodied man in the community, were circumcised. 25On the third day, while they were still in pain, Dinah's full brothers Simeon and Levi, two of Jacob's sons, took their swords, advanced against the city without any trouble, and massacred all the males.[k] 26After they had put Hamor and his son Shechem to the sword, they took Dinah from Shechem's house and left.[l] 27Then the other sons of Jacob followed up the slaughter and sacked the city in reprisal for their sister Dinah's defilement. 28They seized their flocks, herds and asses, whatever was in the city and in the country around. 29They carried off all their wealth, their women, and their children, and took for loot whatever was in the houses.[m]

30Jacob said to Simeon and Levi: "You have brought trouble upon me by making me loathsome to the inhabitants of the land, the Canaanites and the Perizzites. I have so few men that, if these people unite against me and attack me, I and my family will be wiped out." 31But they retorted, "Should our sister have been treated like a harlot?"

CHAPTER 35

Bethel Revisited 1God said to Jacob: "Go up now to Bethel. Settle there and build an altar there to the God who appeared to you while you were fleeing from your brother Esau."[n] 2So Jacob told his family and all the others who were with him: "Get rid of the foreign gods* that you have among you; then purify yourselves and put on fresh clothes. 3We are now to go up to Bethel, and I will build an altar there to the God who answered me in my hour of distress and who has been with me wherever I have gone." 4They therefore handed over to Jacob all the foreign gods in their possession and also the rings* they had in their ears. 5Then, as they set out, a terror from God fell upon the towns round about, so that no one pursued the sons of Jacob.

6Thus Jacob and all the people who were with him arrived in Luz [that is, Bethel] in the land of Canaan.[o] 7There he built an altar and named the place Bethel, for it was there that God had revealed himself to him when he was fleeing from his brother.[p]

8Death came to Rebekah's nurse Deborah; she was buried under the oak below Bethel, and so it was called Allon-bacuth.*

9On Jacob's arrival from Paddan-aram, God

34, 24: Every able-bodied man in the community: literally "all those who go out at the gate of the city," apparently meaning the men who go out to war. By temporarily crippling them through circumcision, Jacob's sons deprived the city of its defenders.

35, 2: Foreign gods: pagan images, including household idols (see note on Gn 31, 19), that Jacob's people brought with them from Paddan-aram.

35, 4: Rings: Earrings were often worn as amulets connected with pagan magic.

35, 8: This verse may have stood originally in some other context. Rebekah's nurse is spoken of without a name, in Gn 24, 59. Allon-bacuth: the Hebrew name means "oak of weeping."

k Gn 49, 6. l Jdt 9, 2. m Jdt 9, 3f. n Gn 28, 12f. o Gn 28, 19; Jos 18, 13; Jgs 1, 22f. p Gn 28, 12f.

appeared to him again and blessed him. 10God
said to him:

"You whose name is Jacob
shall no longer be called Jacob,
but Israel shall be your name." [q]

Thus he was named Israel. 11God also said to
him:

"I am God Almighty;
be fruitful and multiply.
A nation, indeed an assembly of nations,
shall stem from you,
and kings shall issue from your loins.
12The land I once gave
to Abraham and Isaac
I now give to you;
And to your descendants after you
will I give this land." [r]

13Then God departed from him. 14On the site
where God had spoken with him, Jacob set up a
memorial stone, and upon it he made a libation
and poured out oil. [s] 15Jacob named the site
Bethel, because God had spoken with him there.
Jacob's Family 16Then they departed from
Bethel: but while they still had some distance to
go on the way to Ephrath, Rachel began to be in
labor and to suffer great distress. 17When her
pangs were most severe, her midwife said to her,
"Have no fear! This time, too, you have a son."
18With her last breath—for she was at the point
of death—she called him Ben-oni;* his father,
however, named him Benjamin. 19 [t]Thus Rachel
died; and she was buried on the road to Ephrath
[that is, Bethlehem].* 20Jacob set up a memorial
stone on her grave, and the same monument
marks Rachel's grave to this day.
21Israel moved on and pitched his tent beyond
Migdal-eder. 22While Israel was encamped in
that region, Reuben went and lay with Bilhah,
his father's concubine. When Israel heard of it,
he was greatly offended. [u]
The sons of Jacob were now twelve. 23The
sons of Leah: Reuben, Jacob's first-born, Simeon,
Levi, Judah, Issachar, and Zebulun; 24*the sons
of Rachel: Joseph and Benjamin; 25the sons of
Rachel's maid Bilhah: Dan and Naphtali; 26the
sons of Leah's maid Zilpah: Gad and Asher.
These are the sons of Jacob who were born to
him in Paddan-aram.
27Jacob went home to his father Isaac at
Mamre, in Kiriath-arba [that is, Hebron], where
Abraham and Isaac had stayed. 28The lifetime of
Isaac was one hundred and eighty years; 29then
he breathed his last. After a full life, he died as
an old man and was taken to his kinsmen. His
sons Esau and Jacob buried him.

CHAPTER 36

Edomite Lists 1These are the descendants of
Esau [that is, Edom]. 2*Esau took his wives from
among the Canaanite women: Adah, daughter
of Elon the Hittite; Oholibamah, granddaughter
through Anah of Zibeon the Hivite; [v] 3and Base-
math, daughter of Ishmael and sister of Neba-
ioth. 4Adah bore Eliphaz to Esau; Basemath bore
Reuel; [w] 5and Oholibamah bore Jeush, Jalam and
Korah. These are the sons of Esau who were
born to him in the land of Cannan. [x]
6Esau took his wives, his sons, his daughters,
and all the members of his household, as well as
his livestock comprising various animals and all
the property he had acquired in the land of
Canaan, and went to the land of Seir, out of the
way of his brother Jacob. [y] 7Their possessions
had become too great for them to dwell to-

35, 18: Ben-oni: means either "son of my vigor" or, more likely in the context, "son of affliction." Benjamin: "son of the right hand." This may be interpreted to signify a son who is his father's help and support, but more likely its original meaning was "southerner." In the Hebrew idiom, the south lies to one's right hand, and Benjamin was the southernmost of the Rachel tribes.

35, 19: Bethlehem: the gloss comes from a later tradition that identified the site with Bethlehem, also called Ephrath or Ephratha (Jos 15, 59; Ru 4, 11; Mi 5, 1). But Rachel's grave was actually near Ramah (Jer 31, 15), a few miles north of Jerusalem, in the territory of Benjamin (1 Sm 10, 2).

35, 24ff: Benjamin is here said to have been born in Paddan-aram, either because all twelve sons of Jacob are considered as a unit, or because the Priestly source, from which vv 23–29 are taken, follows a tradition different from that of the Elohistic source found in vv 16–20.

36, 2–14: The names of Esau's wives and of their fathers given here differ considerably from their names cited from other old sources in Gn 26, 34 and 28, 9. Zibeon the Hivite: In v 20 he is called a "Horite"; see note on Gn 34, 2.

q 1 Kgs 18, 31; 2 Kgs 17, 34. r Ex 32, 13; Heb 11, 9. s Gn 28, 18; 31, 45. t Gn 48, 7; 1 Sm 10, 2; Mi 5, 2. u Gn 49, 4; 1 Chr 5, 1. v Gn 26, 34. w 1 Chr 1, 35. x 1 Chr 1, 35. y Gn 32, 4.

gether, and the land in which they were staying
could not support them because of their live-
stock. 8So Esau settled in the highlands of Seir.
[Esau is Edom.][z] 9These are the descendants of
Esau, ancestor of the Edomites, in the highlands
of Seir.

10These are the names of Esau's sons: Eliphaz,
son of Esau's wife Adah; and Reuel, son of
Esau's wife Basemath. 11 [a]The sons of Eliphaz
were Teman, Omar, Zepho, Gatam and Kenaz.
12(Esau's son Eliphaz had a concubine Timna,
and she bore Amalek to Eliphaz.) These are the
descendants of Esau's wife Adah. 13The sons of
Reuel were Nahath, Zerah, Shammah and Miz-
zah. These are the descendants of Esau's wife
Basemath.[b] 14The descendants of Esau's wife
Oholibamah—granddaughter through Anah of
Zibeon—whom she bore to Esau were Jeush,
Jalam and Korah.[c]

15The following are the clans of Esau's descen-
dants. The descendants of Eliphaz, Esau's first-
born: the clans of Teman, Omar, Zepho, Kenaz,
16Korah, Gatam and Amalek. These are the clans
of Eliphaz in the land of Edom; they are de-
scended from Adah. 17The descendants of Esau's
son Reuel: the clans of Nahath, Zerah, Shammah
and Mizzah. These are the clans of Reuel in the
land of Edom; they are descended from Esau's
wife Basemath. 18The descendants of Esau's
wife Oholibamah: the clans of Jeush, Jalam and
Korah. These are the clans of Esau's wife Oholi-
bamah, daughter of Anah. 19Such are the descen-
dants of Esau [that is, Edom] according to their
clans.

20The following are the descendants of Seir
the Horite,* the original settlers in the land:
Lotan, Shobal, Zibeon, Anah,[d] 21Dishon, Ezer
and Dishan; they are the Horite clans descended
from Seir, in the land of Edom. 22 [e]Lotan's
descendants were Hori and Hemam, and Lotan's
sister was Timna. 23Shobal's descendants were
Alvan, Mahanath, Ebal, Shepho and Onam.
24Zibeon's descendants were Aiah and Anah.
(He is the Anah who found water in the desert
while he was pasturing the asses of his father
Zibeon.) 25The descendants of Anah were Di-
shon and Oholibamah, daughter of Anah. 26The
descendants of Dishon were Hemdan, Eshban,
Ithran and Cheran. 27The descendants of Ezer
were Bilhan, Zaavan and Akan. 28The descen-
dants of Dishan were Uz and Aran. 29These are
the Horite clans: the clans of Lotan, Shobal,
Zibeon, Anah, 30Dishon, Ezer and Dishan; they
were the clans of the Horites, clan by clan, in the
land of Seir.

31 [f]The following are the kings who reigned in
the land of Edom before any king reigned over
the Israelites.* 32Bela, son of Beor, became king
in Edom; the name of his city was Dinhabah.
33When Bela died, Jobab, son of Zerah, from
Bozrah, succeeded him as king. 34When Jobab
died, Husham, from the land of the Temanites,
succeeded him as king. He defeated the Midian-
ites in the country of Moab; the name of his city
was Avith. 35When Husham died, Hadad, son of
Bedad, succeeded him as king. 36When Hadad
died, Samlah, from Masrekah, succeeded him as
king. 37When Samlah died, Shaul, from
Rehoboth-on-the-River, succeeded him as king.
38When Shaul died, Baal-hanan, son of Achbor,
succeeded him as king. 39When Baal-hanan
died, Hadar succeeded him as king; the name of
his city was Pau. (His wife's name was Meheta-
bel; she was the daughter of Matred, son of
Mezahab.)

40The following are the names of the clans of
Esau individually according to their subdivisions
and localities: the clans of Timna, Alvah, Je-
theth, 41Oholibamah, Elah, Pinon, 42Kenaz, Te-
man, Mibzar, 43Magdiel and Iram. These are the
clans of the Edomites, according to their settle-
ments in their territorial holdings. [Esau was the
father of the Edomites.]

36, 20: Seir the Horite: According to Dt 2, 12, the highlands of Seir were inhabited by Horites before they were occupied by the Edomites.

36, 31: Before any king reigned over the Israelites: obviously this statement was written after the time of Saul, Israel's first king.

z Dt 2, 4f; Jos 24, 4. a 11f: 1 Chr 1, 36. b 1 Chr 1, 37. c 1 Chr 1, 35. d 20f: 1 Chr 1, 38. e 22–28: 1 Chr 1, 39–42. f 31–43: 1 Chr 1, 45–54.

IV: Joseph and His Brothers

CHAPTER 37

Joseph Sold into Egypt 1 Jacob settled in the land where his father had stayed, the land of Canaan. 2 This is his family history. When Joseph was seventeen years old, he was tending the flocks with his brothers; he was an assistant to the sons of his father's wives Bilhah and Zilpah, and he brought his father bad reports about them.

3 Israel loved Joseph best of all his sons, for he was the child of his old age; and he had made him a long tunic. 4 When his brothers saw that their father loved him best of all his sons, they hated him so much that they would not even greet him.

5 Once Joseph had a dream, which he told to his brothers:[g] 6 "Listen to this dream I had. 7 There we were, binding sheaves in the field, when suddenly my sheaf rose to an upright position, and your sheaves formed a ring around my sheaf and bowed down to it." 8 "Are you really going to make yourself king over us?" his brothers asked him. "Or impose your rule on us?" So they hated him all the more because of his talk about his dreams.[h]

9 Then he had another dream, and this one, too, he told to his brothers. "I had another dream," he said; "this time, the sun and the moon and eleven stars were bowing down to me." 10 When he also told it to his father, his father reproved him. "What is the meaning of this dream of yours?" he asked, "Can it be that I and your mother and your brothers are to come and bow to the ground before you?" 11 So his brothers were wrought up against him but his father pondered the matter.

12 One day, when his brothers had gone to pasture their father's flocks at Shechem, 13 Israel said to Joseph, "Your brothers, you know, are tending our flocks at Shechem. Get ready; I will send you to them." "I am ready," Joseph answered. 14 "Go then," he replied; "see if all is well with your brothers and the flocks, and bring back word." So he sent him off from the valley of Hebron. When Joseph reached Shechem, 15 a man met him as he was wandering about in the fields. "What are you looking for?" the man asked him. 16 "I am looking for my brothers," he answered. "Could you please tell me where they are tending the flocks?" 17 The man told him, "They have moved on from here; in fact, I heard them say, 'Let us go on to Dothan.' " So Joseph went after his brothers and caught up with them in Dothan. 18 They noticed him from a distance, and before he came up to them, they plotted to kill him. 19 They said to one another: "Here comes that master dreamer! 20 Come on, let us kill him and throw him into one of the cisterns here; we could say that a wild beast devoured him. We shall then see what comes of his dreams."[i]

21 *When Reuben heard this, he tried to save him from their hands, saying, "We must not take his life. 22 Instead of shedding blood," he continued, "just throw him into that cistern there in the desert; but don't kill him outright." His purpose was to rescue him from their hands and restore him to his father.[j] 23 So when Joseph came up to them, they stripped him of the long tunic he had on; 24 then they took him and threw him into the cistern, which was empty and dry.

25 They then sat down to their meal. Looking up, they saw a caravan of Ishmaelites coming from Gilead, their camels laden with gum, balm and resin to be taken down to Egypt.[k] 26 Judah said to his brothers: "What is to be gained by killing our brother and concealing his blood?[l] 27 Rather, let us sell him to these Ishmaelites, instead of doing away with him ourselves. After all, he is our brother, our own flesh." His

37, 21-36: The chapter thus far is from the Yahwist source, as are also vv 25-28a. But vv 21-24 and 28b-36 are from the Elohist source. In the latter, Reuben tries to rescue Joseph, who is taken in Reuben's absence by certain Midianites; in the Yahwist source, it is Judah who saves Joseph's life by having him sold to certain Ishmaelites. Although the two variant forms in which the story was handed down in early oral tradition differ in these minor points, they agree on the essential fact that Joseph was brought as a slave into Egypt because of the jealousy of his brothers.

g Gn 42, 9. h Gn 50, 17. i Gn 44, 28. j Gn 42, 22. k Gn 43, 11. l Jb 16, 18.

brothers agreed. 28 They sold Joseph to the Ishmaelites for twenty pieces of silver.*

Some Midianite traders passed by, and they pulled Joseph up out of the cistern and took him to Egypt.[m] 29 When Reuben went back to the cistern and saw that Joseph was not in it, he tore his clothes, 30 and returning to his brothers, he exclaimed: "The boy is gone! And I—where can I turn?" 31 They took Joseph's tunic, and after slaughtering a goat, dipped the tunic in its blood. 32 They then sent someone to bring the long tunic to their father, with the message: "We found this. See whether it is your son's tunic or not." 33 He recognized it and exclaimed: "My son's tunic! A wild beast has devoured him! Joseph has been torn to pieces!"[n] 34 Then Jacob rent his clothes, put sackcloth on his loins, and mourned his son many days. 35 Though his sons and daughters tried to console him, he refused all consolation, saying, "No, I will go down mourning to my son in the nether world." Thus did his father lament him.[o]

36 The Midianites, meanwhile, sold Joseph in Egypt to Potiphar, a courtier of Pharaoh and his chief steward.[p]

CHAPTER 38*

Judah and Tamar 1 About that time Judah parted from his brothers and pitched his tent near a certain Adullamite named Hirah. 2 There he met the daughter of a Canaanite named Shua, married her, and had relations with her.[q] 3 She conceived and bore a son, whom she named Er. 4 Again she conceived and bore a son, whom she named Onan. 5 Then she bore still another son, whom she named Shelah. They were in Chezib* when he was born.[r]

6 Judah got a wife named Tamar for his first-born, Er. 7 But Er, Judah's first-born, greatly offended the LORD; so the LORD took his life.[s] 8 [t]Then Judah said to Onan, "Unite with your brother's widow, in fulfillment of your duty as brother-in-law, and thus preserve your brother's line."* 9 Onan, however, knew that the descendants would not be counted as his; so whenever he had relations with his brother's widow, he wasted his seed on the ground, to avoid contributing offspring for his brother. 10 What he did greatly offended the LORD, and the LORD took his life too. 11 Thereupon Judah said to his daughter-in-law Tamar, "Stay as a widow in your father's house until my son Shelah grows up"—for he feared that Shelah also might die like his brothers. So Tamar went to live in her father's house.

12 Years passed, and Judah's wife, the daughter of Shua, died. After Judah completed the period of mourning, he went up to Timnah for the shearing of his sheep, in company with his friend Hirah the Adullamite. 13 When Tamar was told that her father-in-law was on his way up to Timnah to shear his sheep, 14 she took off her widow's garb, veiled her face by covering herself with a shawl, and sat down at the entrance to Enaim, which is on the way to Timnah; for she was aware that, although Shelah was now grown up, she had not been given to him in marriage.[u] 15 When Judah saw her, he mistook her for a harlot, since she had covered her face. 16 So he went over to her at the roadside, and not realizing that she was his daughter-in-law, he said, "Come, let me have intercourse with you." She replied, "What will you pay me for letting you have intercourse with me?" 17 He answered, "I will send you a kid from the flock." "Very well," she said, "provided you leave a pledge until you send it." 18 Judah asked, "What pledge am I to give you?" She answered, "Your seal and

37, 28: They sold Joseph . . . silver: in the Hebrew text, these words occur between out of the cistern and (they) took him to Egypt at the end of the verse.

38, 1–30: This chapter, from the Yahwist source, has nothing to do with the Joseph story in which Judah is still living with his father and brothers. The sacred author inserted this independent account from the life of Judah at this place to mark the long lapse of time during which Joseph's family knew nothing of his life in Egypt. This is apparently a personalized history of the early days of the tribe of Judah, which interbred with several Canaanite clans, though some of these soon became extinct.

38, 5: Chezib: a variant form of Achzib (Jos 15, 44; Mi 1, 14), a town in the Judean Shephelah.

38, 8: Preserve your brother's line: literally, "raise up seed for your brother." The ancient Israelites regarded as very important their law of levirate, or "brother-in-law" marriage; see notes on Dt 25, 5; Ru 2, 20. In the present story, it is primarily Onan's violation of this law, rather than the means he used to circumvent it, that brought on him God's displeasure (vv 9f).

m Ps 105, 17; Wis 10, 13; Acts 7, 9. n Gn 44, 28. o Gn 42, 38. p Ps 105, 17. q 1 Chr 2, 3. r 1 Chr 4, 21. s 1 Chr 2, 3. t Dt 25, 5; Mt 22, 24; Mk 12, 19; Lk 20, 28. u Prv 7, 10.

cord,* and the staff you carry." So he gave them to her and had intercourse with her, and she conceived by him. [19]When she went away, she took off her shawl and put on her widow's garb again.

[20]Judah sent the kid by his friend the Adullamite to recover the pledge from the woman; but he could not find her. [21]So he asked the men of the place, "Where is the temple prostitute,* the one by the roadside in Enaim?" But they answered, "There has never been a temple prostitute here." [22]He went back to Judah and told him, "I could not find her; and besides, the men of the place said there was no temple prostitute there." [23]"Let her keep the things," Judah replied; "otherwise we shall become a laughingstock. After all, I did send her the kid, even though you were unable to find her."

[24]About three months later, Judah was told that his daughter-in-law Tamar had played the harlot and was then with child from her harlotry. "Bring her out," cried Judah; "she shall be burned." [25]But as they were bringing her out, she sent word to her father-in-law, "It is by the man to whom these things belong that I am with child. Please verify," she added, "whose seal and cord and whose staff these are." [26]Judah recognized them and said, "She is more in the right than I am, since I did not give her to my son Shelah." But he had no further relations with her.

[27]When the time of her delivery came, she was found to have twins in her womb.[v] [28]While she was giving birth, one infant put out his hand; and the midwife, taking a crimson thread, tied it on his hand, to note that this one came out first. [29] [w]But as he withdrew his hand, his brother came out; and she said, "What a breach you have made for yourself!" So he was called Perez.* [30]Afterward his brother came out; he was called Zerah.[x] *

CHAPTER 39

Joseph's Temptation [1]When Joseph was taken down to Egypt, a certain Egyptian (Potiphar, a courtier of Pharoah and his chief steward*) bought him from the Ishmaelites who had brought him there. [2] [y]But since the LORD was with him, Joseph got on very well and was assigned to the household of his Egyptian master. [3]When his master saw that the LORD was with him and brought him success in whatever he did, [4]he took a liking to Joseph and made him his personal attendant; he put him in charge of his household and entrusted to him all his possessions.[z] [5]From the moment that he put him in charge of his household and all his possessions, the LORD blessed the Egyptian's house for Joseph's sake; in fact, the LORD's blessing was on everything he owned, both inside the house and out. [6]Having left everything he owned in Joseph's charge, he gave no thought, with Joseph there, to anything but the food he ate.

Now Joseph was strikingly handsome in countenance and body. [7]After a time, his master's wife began to look fondly at him and said, "Lie with me." [8]But he refused. "As long as I am here," he told her, "my master does not concern himself with anything in the house, but has entrusted to me all he owns. [9]He wields no more authority in this house than I do, and he has withheld from me nothing but yourself, since you are his wife. How, then, could I

38, 18: Seal and cord: the cylinder seal, through which a hole was bored lengthwise so that it could be worn from the neck by a cord, was a distinctive means of identification. Apparently a man's staff was also marked with his name (Nm 17, 16f) or other sign of identification.

38, 21: Temple prostitute: the Hebrew term qedesha, literally "consecrated woman," designates a woman who had ritual intercourse with men in pagan fertility rites; cf Dt 23, 18; Hos 4, 14, where the same Hebrew word is used. Hirah the Adullamite uses a word that refers to a higher social class than that designated by the term zona, common "harlot," used in vv 15. 24.

38, 29: He was called Perez: the Hebrew word means "breach."

38, 30: He was called Zerah: a name connected here by popular etymology with a Hebrew verb for the red light of dawn, alluding apparently to the crimson thread.

39, 1: (Potiphar . . . chief steward): These words in the text serve to harmonize ch 39 from the Yahwist source, with Gn 37, 36 and 40, 1–23, from the Elohist. In the former, the Ishmaelites who bought Joseph from his brothers (Gn 37, 28) sold him to the unnamed "Egyptian master" of ch 39. In the latter, the Midianites who kidnaped Joseph (Gn 37, 28; 40, 15) sold him to Potiphar, Pharaoh's chief steward (Gn 37, 36), whose house was used as a royal prison (Gn 40, 2f).

v 1 Chr 2, 4. w Rv 4, 12; Mt 1, 3; Lk 3, 33. x Nm 26, 20; 1 Chr 2, 4; Mt 1, 3. y 1 Sm 3, 19; 10, 7; 18, 14; 2 Sm 5, 10; 2 Kgs 18, 7; Acts 7, 9. z Dn 1, 9.

commit so great a wrong and thus stand con-
demned before God?" 10 Although she tried to
entice him day after day, he would not agree to
lie beside her, or even stay near her. [a]
11 One such day, when Joseph came into the
house to do his work, and none of the household
servants were then in the house, 12 she laid hold
of him by his cloak, saying, "Lie with me!" But
leaving the cloak in her hand, he got away from
her and ran outside. 13 When she saw that he
had left his cloak in her hand as he fled outside,
14 she screamed for her household servants and
told them, "Look! my husband has brought in a
Hebrew slave to make sport of us! He came in
here to lie with me, but I cried out as loud as I
could. 15 When he heard me scream for help, he
left his cloak beside me and ran away outside."
16 She kept the cloak with her until his master
came home. 17 Then she told him the same
story: "The Hebrew slave whom you brought
here broke in on me, to make sport of me. 18 But
when I screamed for help, he left his cloak
beside me and fled outside." 19 As soon as the
master heard his wife's story about how his slave
had treated her, he became enraged. 20 He seized
Joseph and threw him into the jail where the
royal prisoners were confined. [b]
But even while he was in prison, 21 the LORD
remained with Joseph; he showed him kindness
by making the chief jailer well-disposed toward
him. [c] 22 The chief jailer put Joseph in charge of
all the prisoners in the jail, and everything that
had to be done there was done under his
management. 23 The chief jailer did not concern
himself with anything at all that was in Joseph's
charge, since the LORD was with him and
brought success to all he did.

CHAPTER 40

The Dreams Interpreted 1 Some time after-
ward, the royal cupbearer and baker gave of-
fense to their lord, the king of Egypt. 2 Pharaoh
was angry with his two courtiers, the chief
cupbearer and the chief baker, 3 and he put them
in custody in the house of the chief steward (the
same jail where Joseph was confined). 4 The chief
steward assigned Joseph to them, and he became
their attendant.
After they had been in custody for some time,
5 the cupbearer and the baker of the king of
Egypt who were confined in the jail both had
dreams on the same night, each dream with its
own meaning. 6 When Joseph came to them in
the morning, he noticed that they looked dis-
turbed. 7 So he asked Pharaoh's courtiers who
were with him in custody in his master's house,
"Why do you look so sad today?" 8 They an-
swered him, "We have had dreams, but there is
no one to interpret them for us." Joseph said to
them, "Surely, interpretations come from God.
Please tell the dreams to me." [d]
9 Then the chief cupbearer told Joseph his
dream. "In my dream," he said, "I saw a vine in
front of me, 10 and on the vine were three
branches. It had barely budded when its blos-
soms came out, and its clusters ripened into
grapes. 11 Pharaoh's cup was in my hand; so I
took the grapes, pressed them out into his cup,
and put it in Pharaoh's hand." 12 Joseph said to
him: "This is what it means. The three branches
are three days; 13 within three days Pharaoh will
lift up your head* and restore you to your post.
You will be handing Pharaoh his cup as you
formerly used to do when you were his cup-
bearer. 14 So if you will still remember, when all
is well with you, that I was here with you, please
do me the favor of mentioning me to Pharaoh, to
get me out of this place. 15 The truth is that I was
kidnaped from the land of the Hebrews, and
here I have not done anything for which I should
have been put into a dungeon."
16 When the chief baker saw that Joseph had
given this favorable interpretation, he said to
him: "I too had a dream. In it I had three wicker
baskets on my head; 17 in the top one were all
kinds of bakery products for Pharaoh, but the
birds were pecking at them out of the basket on
my head." 18 Joseph said to him in reply: "This is

40, 13: Lift up your head: signifying "pardon you." In v 19 "to lift up the head" means "to behead"; and finally, in v 20, the same expression means "to review the case (of someone)." Joseph couches his interpretation of the dreams in equivocal terms.

a 1 Mc 2, 53. b Ps 105, 18. c Acts 7, 9f. d Gn 41, 16.

what it means. The three baskets are three days; 19within three days Pharaoh will lift up your head and have you impaled on a stake, and the birds will be pecking the flesh from your body."

20And in fact, on the third day, which was Pharaoh's birthday, when he gave a banquet to all his staff, with his courtiers around him, he lifted up the heads of the chief cupbearer and chief baker. 21He restored the chief cupbearer to his office, so that he again handed the cup to Pharaoh; 22but the chief baker he impaled—just as Joseph had told them in his interpretation. 23Yet the chief cupbearer gave no thought to Joseph; he had forgotten him.

CHAPTER 41

Pharaoh's Dream 1After a lapse of two years, Pharaoh had a dream. He saw himself standing by the Nile, 2when up out of the Nile came seven cows, handsome and fat; they grazed in the reed grass. 3Behind them seven other cows, ugly and gaunt, came up out of the Nile; and standing on the bank of the Nile beside the others, 4the ugly, gaunt cows ate up the seven handsome, fat cows. Then Pharaoh woke up.

5He fell asleep again and had another dream. He saw seven ears of grain, fat and healthy, growing on a single stalk. 6Behind them sprouted seven ears of grain, thin and blasted by the east wind; 7and the seven thin ears swallowed up the seven fat, healthy ears. Then Pharaoh woke up, to find it was only a dream.

8Next morning his spirit was agitated. So he summoned all the magicians and sages of Egypt and recounted his dreams to them; but no one could interpret his dreams for him. 9Then the chief cupbearer spoke up and said to Pharaoh: "On this occasion I am reminded of my negligence. 10Once, when Pharaoh was angry, he put me and the chief baker in custody in the house of the chief steward. 11Later, we both had dreams on the same night, and each of our dreams had its own meaning. 12There with us was a Hebrew youth, a slave of the chief steward; and when we told him our dreams, he interpreted them for us and explained for each of us the meaning of his dream.[e] 13And it turned out just as he had told us: I was restored to my post, but the other man was impaled."

14Pharaoh therefore had Joseph summoned, and they hurriedly brought him from the dungeon. After he shaved and changed his clothes, he came into Pharaoh's presence.[f] 15Pharaoh then said to him: "I had certain dreams that no one can interpret. But I hear it said of you that the moment you are told a dream you can interpret it." 16"It is not I," Joseph replied to Pharaoh, "but God who will give Pharaoh the right answer."[g]

17Then Pharaoh said to Joseph: "In my dream, I was standing on the bank of the Nile, 18when up from the Nile came seven cows, fat and well-formed; they grazed in the reed grass. 19Behind them came seven other cows, scrawny, most ill-formed and gaunt. Never have I seen such ugly specimens as these in all the land of Egypt! 20The gaunt, ugly cows ate up the first seven fat cows. 21But when they had consumed them, no one could tell that they had done so, because they looked as ugly as before. Then I woke up. 22In another dream, I saw seven ears of grain, fat and healthy, growing on a single stalk. 23Behind them sprouted seven ears of grain, shriveled and thin and blasted by the east wind; 24and the seven thin ears swallowed up the seven healthy ears. I have spoken to the magicians, but none of them can give me an explanation."

25Joseph said to Pharaoh: "Both of Pharaoh's dreams have the same meaning. God has thus foretold to Pharaoh what he is about to do. 26The seven healthy cows are seven years, and the seven healthy ears are seven years—the same in each dream. 27So also, the seven thin, ugly cows that came up after them are seven years, as are the seven thin, wind-blasted ears; they are seven years of famine. 28It is just as I told Pharaoh: God has revealed to Pharaoh what he is about to do. 29Seven years of great abundance are now coming throughout the land of Egypt; 30but these will be followed by seven years of famine, when all the abundance in the land of Egypt will be forgotten. When the famine

e Dn 1, 17. f Ps 105, 20. g Gn 40, 8.

has ravaged the land, [31]no trace of the abundance will be found in the land because of the famine that follows it—so utterly severe will that famine be. [32]That Pharaoh had the same dream twice means that the matter has been reaffirmed by God and that God will soon bring it about.

[33]"Therefore, let Pharaoh seek out a wise and discerning man and put him in charge of the land of Egypt. [34]Pharaoh should also take action to appoint overseers, so as to regiment the land during the seven years of abundance. [35]They should husband all the food of the coming good years, collecting the grain under Pharaoh's authority, to be stored in the towns for food. [36]This food will serve as a reserve for the country against the seven years of famine that are to follow in the land of Egypt, so that the land may not perish in the famine."

[37]This advice pleased Pharaoh and all his officials.[h] [38]"Could we find another like him," Pharaoh asked his officials, "a man so endowed with the spirit of God?" [39]So Pharaoh said to Joseph: "Since God has made all this known to you, no one can be as wise and discerning as you are. [40]You shall be in charge of my palace, and all my people shall dart at your command. Only in respect to the throne shall I outrank you.[i] [41]Herewith," Pharaoh told Joseph, "I place you in charge of the whole land of Egypt." [42]With that, Pharaoh took off his signet ring* and put it on Joseph's finger. He had him dressed in robes of fine linen and put a gold chain about his neck. [43]He then had him ride in the chariot of his vizier, and they shouted "Abrek!"* before him.

Thus was Joseph installed over the whole land of Egypt. [44]"I, Pharaoh, proclaim," he told Joseph, "that without your approval no one shall move hand or foot in all the land of Egypt." [45]Pharaoh also bestowed the name of Zaphenath-paneah* on Joseph, and he gave him in marriage Asenath, the daughter of Potiphera, priest of Heliopolis. [46]Joseph was thirty years old when he entered the service of Pharaoh, king of Egypt.

After Joseph left Pharaoh's presence, he traveled throughout the land of Egypt. [47]During the seven years of plenty, when the land produced abundant crops, [48]he husbanded all the food of these years of plenty that the land of Egypt was enjoying and stored it in the towns, placing in each town the crops of the fields around it. [49]Joseph garnered grain in quantities like the sands of the sea, so vast that at last he stopped measuring it, for it was beyond measure.

[50]Before the famine years set in, Joseph became the father of two sons, born to him by Asenath, daughter of Potiphera, priest of Heliopolis.[j] [51]He named his first-born Manasseh,* meaning, "God has made me forget entirely the sufferings I endured at the hands of my family"; [52]and the second he named Ephraim,* meaning, "God has made me fruitful in the land of my affliction."

[53]When the seven years of abundance enjoyed by the land of Egypt came to an end, [54]the seven years of famine set in, just as Joseph had predicted. Although there was famine in all the other countries, food was available throughout the land of Egypt.[k] [55]When hunger came to be felt throughout the land of Egypt and the people cried to Pharaoh for bread, Pharaoh directed all the Egyptians to go to Joseph and do whatever he told them. [56]When the famine had spread throughout the land, Joseph opened all the cities that had grain and rationed it to the Egyptians, since the famine had gripped the land of Egypt. [57]In fact, all the world came to Joseph to obtain

41, 42: Signet ring: a finger ring in which was set a stamp seal, different from the cylinder seal such as Judah wore; see note on Gn 38, 18. This is an authentic detail. By receiving Pharaoh's signet ring, Joseph was made vizier of Egypt (v 43); the vizier was known as "seal-bearer of the king of Lower Egypt." Another authentic detail is the gold chain, a symbol of high office in ancient Egypt.

41, 43: Abrek: apparently a cry of homage, though the word's derivation and actual meaning are uncertain.

41, 45: Zaphenath-paneah: a Hebrew transcription of an Egyptian name meaning "the god speaks and he (the newborn child) lives." Asenath: means "belonging to (the Egyptian goddess) Neith." Potiphera: means "he whom Ra (the Egyptian god) gave"; a shorter form of the same name was borne by Joseph's master (Gn 37, 36). Heliopolis: in Hebrew, On, a city seven miles northeast of modern Cairo, site of the chief temple of the sun god; it is mentioned also in v 50; Gn 46, 20; Ez 30, 17.

41, 51: Manasseh: allusion to this name is in the Hebrew expression, nishshani, "he made me forget."

41, 52: Ephraim: related to the Hebrew expression hiphrani, "(God) has made me fruitful."

h Acts 7, 10. i Ps 105, 21; Wis 10, 14; 1 Mc 2, 53; Acts 7, 10. j Gn 46, 20; 48, 5. k Ps 105, 16; Acts 7, 11.

rations of grain, for famine had gripped the whole world.

CHAPTER 42

The Brothers' First Journey to Egypt [1]When Jacob learned that grain rations were available in Egypt, he said to his sons: "Why do you keep gaping at one another? [2]I hear," he went on, "that rations of grain are available in Egypt. Go down there and buy some for us, that we may stay alive rather than die of hunger."[l] [3]So ten of Joseph's brothers went down to buy an emergency supply of grain from Egypt. [4]It was only Joseph's full brother Benjamin that Jacob did not send with the rest, for he thought some disaster might befall him. [5]Thus, since there was famine in the land of Canaan also, the sons of Israel were among those who came to procure rations.[m]

[6]It was Joseph, as governor of the country, who dispensed the rations to all the people. When Joseph's brothers came and knelt down before him with their faces to the ground,[n] [7]he recognized them as soon as he saw them. But he concealed his own identity from them and spoke sternly to them. "Where do you come from?" he asked them. They answered, "From the land of Canaan, to procure food."

[8]When Joseph recognized his brothers, although they did not recognize him, [9]he was reminded of the dreams he had about them. He said to them: "You are spies.[o] You have come to see the nakedness of the land."* [10]"No, my lord," they replied. "On the contrary, your servants have come to procure food. [11]All of us are sons of the same man. We are honest men; your servants have never been spies." [12]But he answered them: "Not so! You have come to see the nakedness of the land." [13]"We your servants," they said, "were twelve brothers, sons of a certain man in Canaan; but the youngest one is at present with our father, and the other one is gone."[p] [14]"It is just as I said," Joseph persisted; "you are spies. [15]This is how you shall be tested: unless your youngest brother comes here, I swear by the life of Pharaoh that you shall not leave here. [16]So send one of your number to get your brother, while the rest of you stay here under arrest. Thus shall your words be tested for their truth; if they are untrue, as Pharaoh lives, you are spies!" [17]With that, he locked them up in the guardhouse for three days.

[18]On the third day Joseph said to them: "Do this, and you shall live; for I am a God-fearing man. [19]If you have been honest, only one of your brothers need be confined in this prison, while the rest of you may go and take home provisions for your starving families. [20]But you must come back to me with your youngest brother. Your words will thus be verified, and you will not die." To this they agreed.[q] [21]To one another, however, they said: "Alas, we are being punished because of our brother. We saw the anguish of his heart when he pleaded with us, yet we paid no heed; that is why this anguish has now come upon us."[r] [22]"Didn't I tell you," broke in Reuben, "not to do wrong to the boy? But you wouldn't listen! Now comes the reckoning for his blood."[s] [23]They did not know, of course, that Joseph understood what they said, since he spoke with them through an interpreter. [24]But turning away from them, he wept. When he was able to speak to them again, he had Simeon taken from them and bound before their eyes. [25]Then Joseph gave orders to have their containers filled with grain, their money replaced in each one's sack, and provisions given them for their journey. After this had been done for them, [26]they loaded their donkeys with the rations and departed.

[27]*At the night encampment, when one of them opened his bag to give his donkey some fodder, he was surprised to see his money in the mouth of his bag. [28]"My money has been returned!" he cried out to his brothers. "Here it is in my bag!" At that their hearts sank. Trem-

42, 9. 12: The nakedness of the land: the military weakness of the land, like human nakedness, should not be seen by strangers.

42, 27–28: These two verses are from the Yahwist source, whereas the rest of the chapter is from the Elohist source, in which the men find the money in their sacks (not "bags"—a different Hebrew word) only when they arrive home (v 35); cf Gn 43, 21.

l Acts 7, 12. m Jdt 5, 10; Acts 7, 11. n Ps 105, 21. o Gn 37, 5. p Gn 44, 20. q Gn 43, 5. r Gn 37, 18–27. s Gn 37, 22.

bling, they asked one another, "What is this that God has done to us?"

29When they got back to their father Jacob in the land of Canaan, they told him all that had happened to them. 30"The man who is lord of the country," they said, "spoke to us sternly and put us in custody as if we were spying on the land. 31But we said to him: 'We are honest men; we have never been spies. 32There were twelve of us brothers, sons of the same father; but one is gone, and the youngest one is at present with our father in the land of Canaan.' 33Then the man who is lord of the country said to us: 'This is how I shall know if you are honest men: leave one of your brothers with me, while the rest of you go home with rations for your starving families. 34When you come back to me with your youngest brother, and I know that you are honest men and not spies, I will restore your brother to you, and you may move about freely in the land.' "

35When they were emptying their sacks, there in each one's sack was his moneybag! At the sight of their moneybags, they and their father were dismayed. 36Their father Jacob said to them: "Must you make me childless? Joseph is gone, and Simeon is gone, and now you would take away Benjamin! Why must such things always happen to me!" 37Then Reuben told his father: "Put him in my care, and I will bring him back to you. You may kill my own two sons if I do not return him to you." 38But Jacob replied: "My son shall not go down with you. Now that his full brother is dead, he is the only one left. If some disaster should befall him on the journey you must make, you would send my white head down to the nether world in grief." [t]

CHAPTER 43*

The Second Journey to Egypt 1Now the famine in the land grew more severe. 2So when they had used up all the rations they had brought from Egypt, their father said to them, "Go back and procure us a little more food." 3But Judah replied: "The man strictly warned us, 'You shall not appear in my presence unless your brother is with you.' [u] 4If you are willing to let our brother go with us, we will go down to procure food for you. 5But if you are not willing, we will not go down, because the man told us, 'You shall not appear in my presence unless your brother is with you.' " [v] 6Israel demanded, "Why did you bring this trouble on me by telling the man that you had another brother?" 7They answered: "The man kept asking about ourselves and our family: 'Is your father still living? Do you have another brother?' We had to answer his questions. How could we know that he would say, 'Bring your brother down here'?"

8Then Judah urged his father Israel: "Let the boy go with me, that we may be off and on our way if you and we and our children are to keep from starving to death. [w] 9I myself will stand surety for him. You can hold me responsible for him. If I fail to bring him back, to set him in your presence, you can hold it against me forever. [x] 10Had we not dilly-dallied, we could have been there and back twice by now!"

11Their father Israel then told them: "If it must be so, then do this: Put some of the land's best products in your baggage and take them down to the man as gifts: some balm and honey, gum and resin, and pistachios and almonds. [y] 12Also take extra money along, for you must return the amount that was put back in the mouths of your bags; it may have been a mistake. 13Take your brother, too, and be off on your way back to the man. 14May God Almighty dispose the man to be merciful toward you, so that he may let your other brother go, as well as Benjamin. As for me, if I am to suffer bereavement, I shall suffer it."

15So the men got the gifts, took double the amount of money with them, and, accompanied by Benjamin, were off on their way down to Egypt to present themselves to Joseph. 16When Joseph saw Benjamin with them, he told his head steward, "Take these men into the house, and have an animal slaughtered and prepared,

43, 1–34: This chapter and the following one are from the Yahwist source, in which Judah, not Reuben as in the Elohist source, volunteers to go surety for Benjamin.

t Gn 37, 35. u Gn 44, 23. v Gn 42, 20. w Gn 42, 37. x Gn 44, 32. y Gn 45, 23.

for they are to dine with me at noon." [17]Doing as Joseph had ordered, the steward conducted the men to Joseph's house. [18]But on being led to his house, they became apprehensive. "It must be," they thought, "on account of the money put back in our bags the first time, that we are taken inside; they want to use it as a pretext to attack us and take our donkeys and seize us as slaves." [19]So they went up to Joseph's head steward and talked to him at the entrance of the house. [20]"If you please, sir," they said, "we came down here once before to procure food.[z] [21]But when we arrived at a night's encampment and opened our bags, there was each man's money in the mouth of his bag—our money in the full amount! We have now brought it back.[a] [22]We have brought other money to procure food with. We do not know who put the first money in our bags." [23]"Be at ease," he replied; "you have no need to fear. Your God and the God of your father must have put treasures in your bags for you. As for your money, I received it." With that, he led Simeon out to them.

[24]The steward then brought the men inside Joseph's house. He gave them water to bathe their feet, and got fodder for their donkeys. [25]Then they set out their gifts to await Joseph's arrival at noon, for they had heard that they were to dine there. [26]When Joseph came home, they presented him with the gifts they had brought inside, while they bowed down before him to the ground. [27]After inquiring how they were, he asked them, "And how is your aged father, of whom you spoke? Is he still in good health?"[b] [28]"Your servant our father is thriving and still in good health," they said, as they bowed respectfully. [29]When Joseph's eye fell on his full brother Benjamin, he asked, "Is this your youngest brother, of whom you told me?" Then he said to him, "May God be gracious to you, my boy!"[c] [30]With that, Joseph had to hurry out, for he was so overcome with affection for his brother that he was on the verge of tears. He went into a private room and wept there.

[31]After washing his face, he reappeared and, now in control of himself, gave the order, "Serve the meal." [32]It was served separately to him,* to the brothers, and to the Egyptians who partook of his board. (Egyptians may not eat with Hebrews; that is abhorrent to them.) [33]When they were seated by his directions according to their age, from the oldest to the youngest, they looked at one another in amazement; [34]and as portions were brought to them from Joseph's table, Benjamin's portion was five times as large as* anyone else's. So they drank freely and made merry with him.

CHAPTER 44

Final Test [1]*Then Joseph gave his head steward these instructions: "Fill the men's bags with as much food as they can carry, and put each man's money in the mouth of his bag. [2]In the mouth of the youngest one's bag put also my silver goblet, together with the money for his rations." The steward carried out Joseph's instructions. [3]At daybreak the men and their donkeys were sent off. [4]They had not gone far out of the city when Joseph said to his head steward: "Go at once after the men! When you overtake them, say to them, 'Why did you repay good with evil? Why did you steal the silver goblet from me? [5]It is the very one from which my master drinks and which he uses for divination.* What you have done is wrong.' "

[6]When the steward overtook them and repeated these words to them, [7]they remonstrated with him: "How can my lord say such things? Far be it from your servants to do such a thing! [8]We even brought back to you from the land of Canaan the money that we found in the mouths of our bags. Why, then, would we steal silver or

43, 32: Separately to him: that Joseph did not eat with the other Egyptians was apparently a matter of rank.

43, 34: Five times as large as: probably an idiomatic expression for "much larger than."

44, 1f: Replacement of the money in the men's bags is probably a redactional addition here, taken from the Yahwist account of the first visit. It is only the goblet in Benjamin's bag, not any replaced money, that plays a part in the rest of the chapter.

44, 5: Divination: seeking omens through liquids poured into a cup or bowl was a common practice in the ancient Near East; cf v 15. Even though divination was frowned on in later Israel (Lv 19, 31), it is in this place an authentic touch which the sacred author does not hesitate to ascribe to Joseph, the wisest man in Egypt.

z Gn 42, 3. a Gn 42, 27f. b Tb 7, 4. c Gn 42, 13.

gold from your master's house? [9]If any of your
servants is found to have the goblet, he shall die,
and as for the rest of us, we shall become my
lord's slaves." [10]But he replied, "Even though it
ought to be as you propose, only the one who is
found to have it shall become my slave, and the
rest of you shall be exonerated." [11]Then each of
them eagerly lowered his bag to the ground and
opened it; [12]and when a search was made,
starting with the oldest and ending with the
youngest, the goblet turned up in Benjamin's
bag. [13]At this, they tore their clothes. Then,
when each man had reloaded his donkey, they
returned to the city.

[14]As Judah and his brothers reentered Jo-
seph's house, he was still there; so they flung
themselves on the ground before him. [15]"How
could you do such a thing?" Joseph asked them.
"You should have known that such a man as I
could discover by divination what happened."
[16]Judah replied: "What can we say to my lord?
How can we plead or how try to prove our
innocence? God has uncovered your servant's
guilt.* Here we are, then, the slaves of my
lord—the rest of us no less than the one in
whose possession the goblet was found." [17]"Far
be it from me to act thus!" said Joseph. "Only
the one in whose possession the goblet was
found shall become my slave; the rest of you
may go back safe and sound to your father."

[18]Judah then stepped up to him and said: "I
beg you, my lord, let your servant speak ear-
nestly to my lord, and do not become angry with
your servant, for you are the equal of Pharaoh.
[19]*My lord asked your servants, 'Have you a
father, or another brother?' [20]So we said to my
lord, 'We have an aged father, and a young
brother, the child of his old age. This one's full
brother is dead, and since he is the only one by
that mother who is left, his father dotes on
him.'[d] [21]Then you told your servants, 'Bring him
down to me that my eyes may look on him.'
[22]We replied to my lord, 'The boy cannot leave
his father; his father would die if he were to
leave him.' [23]But you told your servants, 'Unless
your youngest brother comes back with you, you
shall not come into my presence again.'[e]
[24]When we returned to your servant our father,
we reported to him the words of my lord.

[25]"Later, our father told us to come back and
buy some food for the family. [26]So we reminded
him, 'We cannot go down there; only if our
youngest brother is with us can we go, for we
may not see the man if our youngest brother is
not with us.' [27]Then your servant our father said
to us, 'As you know, my wife bore me two sons.
[28]One of them, however, disappeared, and I had
to conclude that he must have been torn to
pieces by wild beasts; I have not seen him
since.[f] [29]If you now take this one away from
me, too, and some disaster befalls him, you will
send my white head down to the nether world
in grief.'

[30]"If then the boy is not with us when I go
back to your servant my father, whose very life is
bound up with his, he will die as soon as he sees
that the boy is missing; [31]and your servants will
thus send the white head of our father down to
the nether world in grief. [32]Besides, I, your
servant, got the boy from his father by going
surety for him, saying, 'If I fail to bring him back
to you, father, you can hold it against me
forever.'[g] [33]Let me, your servant, therefore,
remain in place of the boy as the slave of my
lord, and let the boy go back with his brothers.
[34]How could I go back to my father if the boy
were not with me? I could not bear to see the
anguish that would overcome my father."

CHAPTER 45

The Truth Revealed [1]Joseph could no longer
control himself in the presence of all his atten-
dants, so he cried out, "Have everyone with-
draw from me!" Thus no one else was about
when he made himself known to his brothers.
[2]But his sobs were so loud that the Egyptians

44, 16: Guilt: in trying to do away with Joseph when he was young.

44, 19: My lord . . . your servants: such frequently repeated expressions in Judah's speech show the formal court style used by a subject in speaking to a high official.

d Gn 42, 13. e Gn 43, 3. f Gn 37, 20. 33. g Gn 43, 9.

heard him, and so the news reached Pharaoh's
palace. 3 [h]"I am Joseph," he said to his brothers.
"Is my father still in good health?" But his
brothers could give him no answer, so dumb-
founded were they at him.

4"Come closer to me," he told his brothers.
When they had done so, he said: "I am your
brother Joseph, whom you once sold into Egypt.
5But now do not be distressed, and do not
reproach yourselves for having sold me here. It
was really for the sake of saving lives that God
sent me here ahead of you.[i] 6For two years now
the famine has been in the land, and for five
more years tillage will yield no harvest. 7God,
therefore, sent me on ahead of you to ensure for
you a remnant on earth and to save your lives in
an extraordinary deliverance. 8So it was not
really you but God who had me come here; and
he has made of me a father to Pharaoh,* lord of
all his household, and ruler over the whole land
of Egypt.

9*"Hurry back, then, to my father and tell
him: 'Thus says your son Joseph: God has made
me lord of all Egypt; come to me without delay.[j]
10You will settle in the region of Goshen,*
where you will be near me—you and your
children and grandchildren, your flocks and
herds, and everything that you own. 11Since five
years of famine still lie ahead, I will provide for
you there, so that you and your family and all
that are yours may not suffer want.' 12Surely,
you can see for yourselves, and Benjamin can see
for himself, that it is I, Joseph, who am speaking
to you. 13Tell my father all about my high
position in Egypt and what you have seen. But
hurry and bring my father down here." 14There-
upon he flung himself on the neck of his brother
Benjamin and wept, and Benjamin wept in his
arms. 15Joseph then kissed all his brothers,
crying over each of them; and only then were
his brothers able to talk with him.

16When the news reached Pharaoh's palace
that Joseph's brothers had come, Pharaoh and
his courtiers were pleased. 17So Pharaoh told
Joseph: "Say to your brothers: 'This is what you
shall do: Load up your animals and go without
delay to the land of Canaan. 18There get your
father and your families, and then come back
here to me; I will assign you the best land in
Egypt, where you will live off the fat of the
land.'[k] 19Instruct them further: 'Do this. Take
wagons from the land of Egypt for your children
and your wives and to transport your father on
your way back here. 20Do not be concerned
about your belongings, for the best in the whole
land of Egypt shall be yours.' "

21The sons of Israel acted accordingly. Joseph
gave them the wagons, as Pharaoh had ordered,
and he supplied them with provisions for the
journey. 22He also gave to each of them fresh
clothing, but to Benjamin he gave three hundred
shekels of silver and five sets of garments.
23Moreover, what he sent to his father was ten
jackasses loaded with the finest products of
Egypt and ten jennies loaded with grain and
bread and other provisions for his journey. 24As
he sent his brothers on their way, he told them,
"Let there be no recriminations on the way."

25So they left Egypt and made their way to
their father Jacob in the land of Canaan. 26When
they told him, "Joseph is still alive—in fact, it is
he who is ruler of all the land of Egypt," he was
dumbfounded; he could not believe them. 27But
when they recounted to him all that Joseph had
told them, and when he saw the wagons that
Joseph had sent for his transport, the spirit of
their father Jacob revived. 28"It is enough," said
Israel. "My son Joseph is still alive! I must go and
see him before I die."

CHAPTER 46

Migration to Egypt 1Israel set out with all that
was his. When he arrived at Beer-sheba, he
offered sacrifices to the God of his father Isaac.

45, 8: Father to Pharaoh: a term applied to a vizier in ancient Egypt.

45, 9–15: In these verses, as in Gn 46, 31–47, 5a, all from the Yahwist source, Joseph in his own name invites his father and brothers to come to Egypt. Only after their arrival is Pharaoh informed of the fact. On the other hand, in 45, 16–20 from the Elohist source, it is Pharaoh himself who invites Joseph's kinsmen to migrate to his domain.

45, 10: The region of Goshen: modern Wadi Tumilat in the eastern part of the Nile Delta.

h 3f: Acts 7, 13. i Gn 50, 20; Sir 49, 15. j Acts 7, 14. k Acts 7, 14.

2 There God, speaking to Israel in a vision by night, called, "Jacob! Jacob!" "Here I am," he answered. 3 Then he said: "I am God,* the God of your father. Do not be afraid to go down to Egypt, for there I will make you a great nation. 4 Not only will I go down to Egypt with you; I will also bring you back here, after Joseph has closed your eyes."

5 So Jacob departed from Beer-sheba, and the sons of Israel put their father and their wives and children on the wagons that Pharaoh had sent for his transport. 6 They took with them their livestock and the possessions they had acquired in the land of Canaan. Thus Jacob and all his descendants migrated to Egypt.[l] 7 His sons and his grandsons, his daughters and his granddaughters—all his descendants—he took with him to Egypt.

8 These are the names of the Israelites, Jacob and his descendants, who migrated to Egypt.

*Reuben, Jacob's first-born,[m] 9 and the sons of Reuben: Hanoch, Pallu, Hezron and Carmi.[n] 10 The sons of Simeon: Nemuel, Jamin, Ohad, Jachin, Zohar, and Shaul, son of a Canaanite woman.[o] 11 The sons of Levi: Gershon, Kohath and Merari.[p] 12 The sons of Judah: Er, Onan, Shelah, Perez and Zerah—but Er and Onan had died in the land of Canaan; and the sons of Perez were Hezron and Hamul.[q] 13 The sons of Issachar: Tola, Puah, Jashub and Shimron.[r] 14 The sons of Zebulun: Sered, Elon and Jahleel.[s] 15 These were the sons whom Leah bore to Jacob in Paddan-aram, along with his daughter Dinah—thirty-three persons in all, male and female.

16 The sons of Gad: Zephon, Haggi, Shuni, Ezbon, Eri, Arod and Areli.[t] 17 The sons of Asher: Imnah, Ishvah, Ishvi and Beriah, with their sister Serah; and the sons of Beriah: Heber and Malchiel.[u] 18 These were the descendants of Zilpah, whom Laban had given to his daughter Leah; these she bore to Jacob—sixteen persons in all.

19 The sons of Jacob's wife Rachel: Joseph and Benjamin. 20 In the land of Egypt Joseph became the father of Manasseh and Ephraim, whom Asenath, daughter of Potiphera, priest of Heliopolis, bore to him.[v] 21 The sons of Benjamin: Bela, Becher, Ashbel, Gera, Naaman, Ahiram, Shupham, Hupham and Ard.[w] 22 These were the sons whom Rachel bore to Jacob—fourteen persons in all.

23 The sons of Dan: Hushim.[x] 24 The sons of Naphtali: Jahzeel, Guni, Jezer and Shillem.[y] 25 These were the sons of Bilhah, whom Laban had given to his daughter Rachel; these she bore to Jacob—seven persons in all.

26 Jacob's people who migrated to Egypt—his direct descendants, not counting the wives of Jacob's sons—numbered sixty-six persons in all.[z] 27 Together with Joseph's sons who were born to him in Egypt—two persons—all the people comprising Jacob's family who had come to Egypt amounted to seventy persons* in all.[a]

28 Israel had sent Judah ahead to Joseph, so that he might meet him in Goshen. On his arrival in the region of Goshen, 29 Joseph hitched the horses to his chariot and rode to meet his father Israel in Goshen. As soon as he saw him, he flung himself on his neck and wept a long time in his arms. 30 And Israel said to Joseph, "At last I can die, now that I have seen for myself that Joseph is still alive."

31 Joseph then said to his brothers and his father's household: "I will go and inform Pharaoh, telling him: 'My brothers and my father's household, whose home is in the land of Canaan, have come to me. 32 The men are shep-

46, 3: I am God: more precisely according to the Hebrew text, "I am El." "El" is here a divine name, not the common noun "god."

46, 9–27: This genealogical list has here been inserted by a redactor who based it on the clan lists (Nm 26, 5–50) at the time of Moses. Therefore it includes some of Jacob's grandchildren, who would hardly have been born when Joseph was still a relatively young man. The number fourteen (v 22) is based on a garbled version of the genealogical list.

46, 27: Seventy persons: either to be understood as a round number, or arrived at by including Jacob and Joseph with the preceding persons, who add up to sixty-eight.

l Ex 1, 1; Jos 24, 4; Jdt 5, 10; Acts 7, 15. m Ex 1, 2. n Ex 6, 14; Nm 26, 5; 1 Chr 5, 3. o Ex 6, 15; Nm 26, 12; 1 Chr 4, 24. p Ex 6, 16; Nm 3, 17; 26, 57; 1 Chr 6, 1. q Gn 38, 3–10. 29f; Nm 26, 19; Rv 4, 18–22; 1 Chr 2, 5. r Nm 26, 23f; 1 Chr 7, 1. s Nm 26, 26. t Nm 26, 15f. u Nm 26, 44; 1 Chr 7, 30f. v Gn 41, 50; Nm 26, 28. 35. w Nm 26, 38; 1 Chr 7, 6; 8, 1–4. x Nm 26, 42. y Nm 26, 48f; 1 Chr 7, 13. z Ex 1, 5. a Ex 1, 5; Dt 10, 22; Acts 7, 14.

herds, having long been keepers of livestock; and they have brought with them their flocks and herds, as well as everything else they own.' [33]So when Pharaoh summons you and asks what your occupation is, [34]you must answer. 'We your servants, like our ancestors, have been keepers of livestock from the beginning until now,' in order that you may stay in the region of Goshen, since all shepherds are abhorrent to the Egyptians."

CHAPTER 47

Settlement in Goshen [1]Joseph went and told Pharaoh, "My father and my brothers have come from the land of Canaan, with their flocks and herds and everything else they own; and they are now in the region of Goshen." [2]He then presented to Pharaoh five of his brothers whom he had selected from their full number. [3]When Pharaoh asked them what their occupation was, they answered, "We, your servants, like our ancestors, are shepherds. [4]We have come," they continued, "in order to stay in this country, for there is no pasture for your servants' flocks in the land of Canaan, so severe has the famine been there. Please, therefore, let your servants settle in the region of Goshen."[b] [5]Pharaoh said to Joseph, "They may settle in the region of Goshen; and if you know any of them to be qualified, you may put them in charge of my own livestock."

Thus, when Jacob and his sons came to Joseph in Egypt, and Pharaoh, king of Egypt, heard about it, Pharaoh said to Joseph, "Now that your father and brothers have come to you, [6]the land of Egypt is at your disposal; settle your father and brothers in the pick of the land." [7]Then Joseph brought his father Jacob and presented him to Pharaoh. After Jacob had paid his respects to Pharaoh, [8]Pharaoh asked him, "How many years have you lived?" [9]Jacob replied: "The years I have lived as a wayfarer amount to a hundred and thirty. Few and hard have been these years of my life, and they do not compare with the years that my ancestors lived as wayfarers."* [10]Then Jacob bade Pharaoh farewell and withdrew from his presence.

[11]As Pharaoh had ordered, Joseph settled his father and brothers and gave them holdings in Egypt on the pick of the land, in the region of Rameses.* [12]And Joseph sustained his father and brothers and his father's whole household, down to the youngest, with food.

Joseph's Land Policy [13]Since there was no food in any country because of the extreme severity of the famine, and the lands of Egypt and Canaan were languishing from hunger, [14]Joseph gathered in, as payment for the rations that were being dispensed, all the money that was to be found in Egypt and Canaan, and he put it in Pharaoh's palace. [15]When all the money in Egypt and Canaan was spent, all the Egyptians came to Joseph, pleading, "Give us food or we shall perish under your eyes; for our money is gone." [16]"Since your money is gone," replied Joseph, "give me your livestock, and I will sell you bread in return for your livestock." [17]So they brought their livestock to Joseph, and he sold them food in return for their horses, their flocks of sheep and herds of cattle, and their donkeys. Thus he got them through that year with bread in exchange for all their livestock. [18]When that year ended, they came to him in the following one and said: "We cannot hide from my lord that, with our money spent and our livestock made over to my lord, there is nothing left to put at my lord's disposal except our bodies and our farm land. [19]Why should we and our land perish before your very eyes? Take us and our land in exchange for food, and we will become Pharaoh's slaves and our land his property; only give us seed, that we may survive and not perish, and that our land may not turn into a waste."

[20]Thus Joseph acquired all the farm land of Egypt for Pharaoh, since with the famine too much for them to bear, every Egyptian sold his

47, 9: Wayfarer . . . wayfarers: man is merely a sojourner on earth; cf Ps 39, 13.

47, 11: The region of Rameses: same as the region of Goshen; see note on Gn 45, 10. The name Rameses, however, is an anachronism, since this royal name did not come into use before the end of the fourteenth century B.C., long after the time of Joseph.

b Ex 23, 9; Dt 23, 8.

field; so the land passed over to Pharaoh, [21]and
the people were reduced to slavery, from one
end of Egypt's territory to the other. [22]Only the
priests' lands Joseph did not take over. Since the
priests had a fixed allowance from Pharaoh and
lived off the allowance Pharaoh had granted
them, they did not have to sell their land.

[23]Joseph told the people: "Now that I have
acquired you and your land for Pharaoh, here is
your seed for sowing the land. [24]But when the
harvest is in, you must give a fifth of it to
Pharaoh, while you keep four-fifths as seed for
your fields, and as food for yourselves and your
families [and as food for your children]." [25]"You
have saved our lives!" they answered. "We are
grateful to my lord that we can be Pharaoh's
slaves." [26]Thus Joseph made it a law for the land
in Egypt, which is still in force, that a fifth of its
produce should go to Pharaoh. Only the land of
the priests did not pass over to Pharaoh.

Jacob Blesses Ephraim and Manasseh

[27]Thus Israel settled in the land of Egypt, in the
region of Goshen. There they acquired property,
were fertile, and increased greatly.[c] [28]Jacob lived
in the land of Egypt for seventeen years; the
span of his life came to a hundred and forty-
seven years. [29]When the time approached for
Israel to die, he called his son Joseph and said to
him: "If you really wish to please me, put your
hand under my thigh as a sign of your constant
loyalty to me; do not let me be buried in Egypt.
[30]When I lie down with my ancestors, have me
taken out of Egypt and buried in their burial
place."[d] [31]"I will do as you say," he replied. But
his father demanded, "Swear it to me!" So
Joseph swore to him. Then Israel bowed at the
head of the bed.*

CHAPTER 48

[1]Some time afterward, Joseph was informed,
"Your father is failing." So he took along with
him his two sons, Manasseh and Ephraim.
[2]When Jacob was told, "Your son Joseph has
come to you," he rallied his strength and sat up
in bed.

[3][e]Jacob then said to Joseph: "God Almighty
appeared to me at Luz* in the land of Canaan,
and blessing me, [4]he said, 'I will make you fertile
and numerous and raise you into an assembly of
tribes, and I will give this land to your descen-
dants after you as a permanent possession.'
[5]Your two sons, therefore, who were born to
you in the land of Egypt before I joined you here,
shall be mine; Ephraim and Manasseh shall be
mine as much as Reuben and Simeon are mine.
[6]Progeny born to you after them shall remain
yours; but their heritage shall be recorded in the
names of their two brothers. [7][f]I do this because,
when I was returning from Paddan, your mother
Rachel died, to my sorrow, during the journey in
Canaan, while we were still a short distance
from Ephrath; and I buried her there on the way
to Ephrath [that is, Bethlehem]."*

[8]When Israel saw Joseph's sons, he asked,
"Who are these?" [9]"They are my sons," Joseph
answered his father, "whom God has given me
here." "Bring them to me," said his father, "that
I may bless them." [10](Now Israel's eyes were
dim from age, and he could not see well.) When
Joseph brought his sons close to him, he kissed
and embraced them. [11]Then Israel said to Jo-
seph, "I never expected to see your face again,
and now God has allowed me to see your
descendants as well!"

[12]Joseph removed them from his father's
knees and bowed down before him with his face
to the ground. [13]Then Joseph took the two,
Ephraim with his right hand, to Israel's left, and
Manasseh with his left hand, to Israel's right,
and led them to him. [14]But Israel, crossing his
hands, put out his right hand and laid it on the
head of Ephraim, although he was the younger,
and his left hand on the head of Manasseh,

47, 31: Israel bowed at the head of the bed: meaning perhaps that he gave a nod of assent and appreciation as he lay on his bed. By reading with different vowels the Hebrew word for "bed," the Greek version translated it as "staff," and understood the phrase to mean that he bowed in worship, leaning on the top of his staff; it is thus quoted in Heb 11, 21.

48, 3: Luz: an older name of Bethel (Gn 28, 19).

48, 7: Since her early death prevented Rachel from bearing more than two sons, Jacob feels justified in treating her two grandsons as if they were her own offspring.

c Ex 1, 7. d Gn 50, 5. e 3f: Gn 28, 12–15; 35, 6. f Gn 35, 19.

although he was the first-born. 15 Then he
blessed them with these words:

"May the God in whose ways
my fathers Abraham and Isaac walked,
The God who has been my shepherd
from my birth to this day,[g]
16 The Angel who has delivered me from all
harm,
bless these boys
That in them my name be recalled,
and the names of my fathers, Abraham and
Isaac,
And they may become teeming multitudes
upon the earth!"

17 When Joseph saw that his father had laid his
right hand on Ephraim's head, this seemed
wrong to him; so he took hold of his father's
hand, to remove it from Ephraim's head to
Manasseh's, 18 saying, "That is not right, father;
the other one is the first-born; lay your right
hand on his head!" 19 But his father resisted. "I
know it, son," he said, "I know. That one too
shall become a tribe, and he too shall be great.
Nevertheless, his younger brother shall surpass
him, and his descendants shall become a multi-
tude of nations." 20 So when he blessed them
that day and said, "By you shall the people of
Israel pronounce blessings; may they say, 'God
make you like Ephraim and Manasseh,' " he
placed Ephraim before Manasseh.[h]

21 Then Israel said to Joseph: "I am about to
die. But God will be with you and will restore
you to the land of your fathers. 22 [i]As for me, I
give to you, as to the one above his brothers,
Shechem, which I captured from the Amorites
with my sword and bow."*

CHAPTER 49

Jacob's Testament 1 Jacob called his sons and
said: "Gather around, that I may tell you what is
to happen to you in days to come.

2 "Assemble and listen, sons of Jacob,
listen to Israel, your father.

3 "You, Reuben, my first-born,
my strength and the first fruit of my
manhood,
excelling in rank and excelling in power!
4 Unruly as water, you shall no longer excel,
for you climbed into your father's bed
and defiled my couch to my sorrow.[j]

5 "Simeon and Levi, brothers indeed,
weapons of violence are their knives.*
6 Let not my soul enter their council,
or my spirit be joined with their company;
For in their fury they slew men,
in their willfulness they maimed oxen.[k]
7 Cursed be their fury so fierce,
and their rage so cruel!
I will scatter them in Jacob,
disperse them throughout Israel.

8 "You, Judah, shall your brothers praise
—your hand on the neck of your enemies;
the sons of your father shall bow down to
you.
9 Judah, like a lion's whelp,
you have grown up on prey, my son.
He crouches like a lion recumbent,
the king of beasts—who would dare rouse
him?[l]
10 The scepter shall never depart from Judah,
or the mace from between his legs,
While tribute is brought to him,*
and he receives the people's homage.
11 He tethers his donkey to the vine,

48, 22: Both the meaning of the Hebrew and the historical reference in this verse are obscure. By taking the Hebrew word for Shechem as a common noun meaning shoulder or mountain slope, some translators render the verse, "I give you one portion more than your brothers, which I captured . . ." The reference may be to the capture of Shechem by the sons of Jacob (Gn 34, 24–29). Shechem lay near the border separating the tribal territory of Manasseh from that of Ephraim (Jos 16, 4–9; 17, 1f. 7).

49, 5: Knives: if this is the meaning of the obscure Hebrew word here, the reference may be to the knives used in circumcising the men of Shechem (Gn 34, 24; cf Jos 5, 2).

49, 10: While tribute is brought to him: this translation is based on a slight change in the Hebrew text, which, as it stands, would seem to mean, "until he comes to Shiloh." A somewhat different reading of the Hebrew text would be, "until he comes to whom it belongs." This last has been traditionally understood in a Messianic sense. In any case, the passage foretells the supremacy of the tribe of Judah, which found its fulfillment in the Davidic dynasty and ultimately in the Messianic Son of David, Jesus Christ.

g Heb 11, 21. h Heb 11, 21. i Jos 17, 14. 17f; Jn 4. 5. j Gn 35, 22; 1 Chr 5, 1f. k Gn 34, 25. l 1 Chr 5, 2.

his purebred ass to the choicest stem.
In wine he washes his garments,
his robe in the blood of grapes.*
12 His eyes are darker than wine,
and his teeth are whiter than milk.
13 "Zebulun shall dwell by the seashore
[This means a shore for ships],
and his flank shall be based on Sidon.

14 "Issachar is a rawboned ass,
crouching between the saddlebags.
15 When he saw how good a settled life was,
and how pleasant the country,
He bent his shoulder to the burden
and became a toiling serf.

16 "Dan shall achieve justice* for his kindred
like any other tribe of Israel.
17 Let Dan be a serpent by the roadside,
a horned viper by the path,
That bites the horse's heel,
so that the rider tumbles backward.

18 "[I long for your deliverance, O LORD!]

19 "Gad shall be raided by raiders,
but he shall raid at their heels.*

20 "Asher's produce is rich,
and he shall furnish dainties for kings.

21 "Naphtali is a hind let loose,
which brings forth lovely fawns.

22 "Joseph is a wild colt,
a wild colt by a spring,
a wild ass on a hillside.
23 Harrying and attacking,
the archers opposed him;
4 But each one's bow remained stiff,
as their arms were unsteady,
By the power of the Mighty One of Jacob,
because of the Shepherd, the Rock of Israel,
25 The God of your father, who helps you,*
God Almighty, who blesses you,
With the blessings of the heavens above,
the blessings of the abyss that crouches
below,
The blessings of breasts and womb,
26 the blessings of fresh grain and blossoms,
The blessings of the everlasting mountains,
the delights of the eternal hills.
May they rest on the head of Joseph,
on the brow of the prince among his
brothers.

27 "Benjamin is a ravenous wolf;
mornings he devours the prey,
and evenings he distributes the spoils."

Farewell and Death 28 All these are the twelve
tribes of Israel, and this is what their father said
about them, as he bade them farewell and gave
to each of them an appropriate message. 29 Then
he gave them this charge: "Since I am about to
be taken to my kindred, bury me with my
fathers in the cave that lies in the field of Ephron
the Hittite, 30 the cave in the field of Machpelah,
facing on Mamre, in the land of Canaan, the
field that Abraham bought from Ephron the
Hittite for a burial ground.[m] 31 There Abraham
and his wife Sarah are buried, and so are Isaac
and his wife Rebekah, and there, too, I buried
Leah— 32 the field and the cave in it that had
been purchased from the Hittites."
33 When Jacob had finished giving these in-
structions to his sons, he drew his feet into the
bed, breathed his last, and was taken to his
kindred.

CHAPTER 50

Jacob's Funeral 1 Joseph threw himself on his
father's face and wept over him as he kissed
him. 2 Then he ordered the physicians in his
service to embalm his father. When they em-
balmed Israel, 3 they spent forty days at it, for
that is the full period of embalming; and the
Egyptians mourned him for seventy days. 4 When
that period of mourning was over, Joseph spoke
to Pharaoh's courtiers. "Please do me this favor,"

49, 11: In wine . . . the blood of grapes: Judah's clothes are poetically pictured as soaked with grape juice from trampling in the wine press, the rich vintage of his land; cf Is 63, 2.

49, 16: In Hebrew the verb for achieve justice is from the same root as the name Dan.

49, 19: In Hebrew there is a certain assonance between the name Gad and the words for "raided," "raiders" and "raid."

49, 25f: A very similar description of the agricultural riches of the tribal land of Joseph is given in Dt 33, 13–16.

m Gn 23, 17.

he said, "and convey to Pharaoh this request of mine. 5Since my father, at the point of death, made me promise on oath to bury him in the tomb that he had prepared for himself in the land of Canaan, may I go up there to bury my father and then come back?"[n] 6Pharaoh replied, "Go and bury your father, as he made you promise on oath."

7So Joseph left to bury his father; and with him went all of Pharaoh's officials who were senior members of his court and all the other dignitaries of Egypt, 8as well as Joseph's whole household, his brothers, and his father's household; only their children and their flocks and herds were left in the region of Goshen. 9Chariots, too, and charioteers went up with him; it was a very large retinue.

10When they arrived at Goren-ha-atad,* which is beyond the Jordan, they held there a very great and solemn memorial service; and Joseph observed seven days of mourning for his father. 11When the Canaanites who inhabited the land saw the mourning at Goren-ha-atad, they said, "This is a solemn funeral the Egyptians are having." That is why the place was named Abel-mizraim. It is beyond the Jordan.

12Thus Jacob's sons did for him as he had instructed them. 13They carried him to the land of Canaan and buried him in the cave in the field of Machpelah, facing on Mamre, the field that Abraham had bought for a burial ground from Ephron the Hittite.[o]

14After Joseph had buried his father he returned to Egypt, together with his brothers and all who had gone up with him for the burial of his father.

Plea for Forgiveness 15Now that their father was dead, Joseph's brothers became fearful and thought, "Suppose Joseph has been nursing a grudge against us and now plans to pay us back in full for all the wrong we did him!" 16So they approached Joseph and said: "Before your father died, he gave us these instructions: 17'You shall say to Joseph, Jacob begs you to forgive the criminal wrongdoing of your brothers, who treated you so cruelly.' Please, therefore, forgive the crime that we, the servants of your father's God, committed." When they spoke these words to him, Joseph broke into tears. 18Then his brothers proceeded to fling themselves down before him and said, "Let us be your slaves!" 19But Joseph replied to them: "Have no fear. Can I take the place of God? 20Even though you meant harm to me, God meant it for good, to achieve his present end, the survival of many people.[p] 21Therefore have no fear. I will provide for you and for your children." By thus speaking kindly to them, he reassured them.[q]

22Joseph remained in Egypt, together with his father's family. He lived a hundred and ten years. 23He saw Ephraim's children to the third generation, and the children of Manasseh's son Machir were also born on Joseph's knees.[r]

Death of Joseph 24Joseph said to his brothers: "I am about to die. God will surely take care of you and lead you out of this land to the land that he promised on oath to Abraham, Isaac and Jacob."[s] 25Then, putting the sons of Israel under oath, he continued, "When God thus takes care of you, you must bring my bones up with you from this place."[t] 26Joseph died at the age of a hundred and ten. He was embalmed and laid to rest in a coffin in Egypt.[u]

50, 10f: Goren-ha-atad: "Threshing Floor of the Brambles." Abel-mizraim: although the name really means "watercourse of the Egyptians," it is understood here, by a play on the first part of the term, to mean "mourning of the Egyptians." The site has not been identified through either reading of the name. But it is difficult to see why the mourning rites should have been held in the land beyond the Jordan when the burial was at Hebron. Perhaps an earlier form of the story placed the mourning rites beyond the Wadi of Egypt, the traditional boundary between Canaan

n Gn 47, 30. o Gn 23, 16; Acts 7, 16. p Gn 45, 5; Sir 49, 15. q Gn 47, 12. r Nm 32, 39; Jos 17, 1. s Ex 3, 8; Jos 24, 32; Heb 11, 22. t Ex 13, 19; Heb 11, 22. u Sir 49, 15.

THE BOOK OF EXODUS

The second book of the Pentateuch is called Exodus from the Greek word for "departure," because the central event narrated in it is the departure of the Israelites from Egypt. It continues the history of the chosen people from the point where the Book of Genesis leaves off. It recounts the oppression by the Egyptians of the ever-increasing descendants of Jacob and their miraculous deliverance by God through Moses, who led them across the Red Sea to Mount Sinai where they entered into a special covenant with the Lord.

These events were of prime importance to the chosen people, for they became thereby an independent nation and enjoyed a unique relationship with God. Through Moses God gave to the Israelites at Mount Sinai the "law": the moral, civil and ritual legislation by which they were to become a holy people, in whom the promise of a Savior for all mankind would be fulfilled.

The principal divisions of Exodus are:

I. The Israelites in Egypt (Ex 1, 1—12, 36).
II. The Exodus from Egypt and the Journey to Sinai (Ex 12, 37—18, 27).
III. The Covenant at Mount Sinai (Ex 19, 1—24, 18).
IV. The Dwelling and Its Furnishings (Ex 25, 1—40, 38).

I: The Israelites In Egypt

CHAPTER 1

Jacob's Descendants in Egypt 1These are the
names of the sons of Israel* who, accompanied
by their households, migrated with Jacob into
Egypt: 2*Reuben, Simeon, Levi and Judah; 3Issa-
char, Zebulun and Benjamin; 4Dan and Naph-
tali; Gad and Asher. 5The total number of the
direct descendants* of Jacob was seventy.[a] Jo-
seph was already in Egypt.
6Now Joseph and all his brothers and that
whole generation died.[b] 7But the Israelites were
fruitful and prolific. They became so numerous
and strong that the land was filled with them.
The Oppression 8Then a new king, who
knew nothing of Joseph,* came to power in
Egypt.[c] 9He said to his subjects, "Look how
numerous and powerful the Israelite people are
growing, more so than we ourselves! 10Come,
let us deal shrewdly with them to stop their
increase; otherwise, in time of war they too may
join our enemies to fight against us, and so leave
our country."
11Accordingly, taskmasters were set over the
Israelites to oppress them with forced labor.[d]
Thus they had to build for Pharaoh* the supply
cities of Pithom and Raamses. 12Yet the more
they were oppressed, the more they multiplied
and spread. The Egyptians, then, dreaded the
Israelites 13and reduced them to cruel slavery,
14making life bitter for them with hard work in
mortar* and brick and all kinds of field work—
the whole cruel fate of slaves.
Command to the Midwives 15The king of
Egypt told the Hebrew midwives, one of whom
was called Shiphrah and the other Puah,
16"When you act as midwives for the Hebrew
women and see them giving birth,* if it is a boy,
kill him; but if it is a girl, she may live." 17The

1, 1: Sons of Israel: here literally the first-generation sons of Jacob. Cf v 5. However, beginning with Ex 1, 7 the same Hebrew phrase refers to the more remote descendants of Jacob; hence, from there on, it is ordinarily rendered as "the Israelites." Households: the family in its fullest sense, including wives, children and servants.

1, 2: The sons of Jacob are listed here according to the respective mothers. Cf Gn 29, 31; 30, 20; 35, 16–26.

1, 5: Direct descendants: literally, persons coming from the loins of Jacob; hence, wives and servants are here excluded. Cf Gn 46, 26.

1, 8: Who knew nothing of Joseph: this king ignored the services that Joseph had rendered to Egypt.

1, 11: Pharaoh: not a personal name, but a title common to all the kings of Egypt.

1, 14: Mortar: either the wet clay with which the bricks were made, as in Na 3, 14, or the cement used between the bricks in building, as in Gn 11, 3.

1, 16: And see them giving birth: the Hebrew text is uncertain.

a Gn 46, 27; Dt 10, 22; Acts 7, 14. b Gn 50, 26. c 8ff: Acts 7, 18. d Dt 26, 6.

midwives, however, feared God; they did not do
as the king of Egypt had ordered them, but let
the boys live. 18So the king summoned the
midwives and asked them, "Why have you acted
thus, allowing the boys to live?" 19The midwives
answered Pharaoh, "The Hebrew women are
not like the Egyptian women. They are robust
and give birth before the midwife arrives."
20Therefore God dealt well with the midwives.
The people, too, increased and grew strong.
21And because the midwives feared God, he
built up families for them. 22Pharaoh then com-
manded all his subjects, "Throw into the river*
every boy that is born to the Hebrews,[e] but you
may let all the girls live."

CHAPTER 2

Birth and Adoption of Moses 1Now a certain
man of the house of Levi married a Levite
woman,[f] 2who conceived and bore a son. See-
ing that he was a goodly child, she hid him for
three months.[g] 3When she could hide him no
longer, she took a papyrus basket,* daubed it
with bitumen and pitch, and putting the child in
it, placed it among the reeds on the river bank.
4His sister stationed herself at a distance to find
out what would happen to him.

5Pharaoh's daughter came down to the river
to bathe, while her maids walked along the river
bank. Noticing the basket among the reeds, she
sent her handmaid to fetch it. 6On opening it,
she looked, and lo, there was a baby boy, crying!
She was moved with pity for him and said, "It is
one of the Hebrews' children." 7Then his sister
asked Pharaoh's daughter, "Shall I go and call
one of the Hebrew women to nurse the child for
you?" 8"Yes, do so," she answered. So the
maiden went and called the child's own mother.
9Pharaoh's daughter said to her, "Take this child
and nurse it for me, and I will repay you." The
woman therefore took the child and nursed it.
10When the child grew,* she brought him to
Pharaoh's daughter, who adopted him as her
son[h] and called him Moses; for she said, "I drew
him out of the water."

Moses' Flight to Midian 11On one occasion,
after Moses had grown up,* when he visited his
kinsmen[i] and witnessed their forced labor, he
saw an Egyptian striking a Hebrew, one of his
own kinsmen. 12Looking about and seeing no
one, he slew the Egyptian and hid him in the
sand. 13The next day he went out again, and
now two Hebrews were fighting! So he asked
the culprit, "Why are you striking your fellow
Hebrew?" 14But he replied, "Who has appointed
you ruler and judge over us? Are you thinking of
killing me as you killed the Egyptian?" Then
Moses became afraid and thought, "The affair
must certainly be known."

15Pharaoh, too, heard of the affair and sought
to put him to death. But Moses fled from him
and stayed in the land of Midian.[j] As he was
seated there by a well, 16seven daughters of a
priest of Midian came to draw water and fill the
troughs to water their father's flock. 17But some
shepherds came and drove them away. Then
Moses got up and defended them and watered
their flock. 18When they returned to their father
Reuel,* he said to them, "How is it you have
returned so soon today?" 19They answered, "An
Egyptian* saved us from the interference of the
shepherds. He even drew water for us and
watered the flock!" 20"Where is the man?" he
asked his daughters. "Why did you leave him
there? Invite him to have something to eat."
21Moses agreed to live with him, and the man
gave him his daughter Zipporah in marriage.
22She bore him a son, whom he named Ger-

1, 22: The river: the Nile, which was "the" river for the Egyptians.

2, 3: Basket: literally, "chest" or "ark"; the same Hebrew word is used in Gn 6, 14 for Noah's ark. Here, however, the chest was made of papyrus stalks.

2, 10: When the child grew: probably when he was weaned or a little later. Moses: in Hebrew, Mosheh; the Hebrew word for "draw out" is mashah. This explanation of the name is not intended as a scientific etymology but as a play on words. The name is probably derived from an Egyptian word for "has been born," referring the birth to a god thought to be its sponsor.

2, 11: After Moses had grown up: Acts 7, 23 indicates that this was after an interval of nearly forty years. Cf Ex 7, 7. Striking: probably in the sense of "flogging"; according to some, "slaying."

2, 18: Reuel: he was also called Jethro. Cf Ex 3, 1; 4, 18; 18, 1.

2, 19: An Egyptian: Moses was probably wearing Egyptian dress, or spoke Egyptian to Reuel's daughters.

2, 22: Gershom: the name is explained as if it came from the Hebrew word ger, "stranger," joined to the Hebrew word sham,

e Acts 7, 19. f Ex 6, 20; Nm 26, 59. g Acts 7, 20; Heb 11, 23. h Acts 7, 21; Heb 11, 24. i 11–14: Acts 7, 23–28. j Acts 7, 29; Heb 11, 27.

shom;* for he said, "I am a stranger in a foreign land."[k]

The Burning Bush 23 A long time passed, during which the king of Egypt died. Still the Israelites groaned and cried out because of their slavery. As their cry for release went up to God,[l] 24 he heard their groaning and was mindful of his covenant[m] with Abraham, Isaac and Jacob. 25 He saw the Israelites and knew. . . .

CHAPTER 3

1 Meanwhile Moses was tending the flock of his father-in-law Jethro, the priest of Midian. Leading the flock across the desert, he came to Horeb, the mountain of God.* 2 There an angel of the LORD* appeared to him in fire flaming out of a bush.[n] As he looked on, he was surprised to see that the bush, though on fire, was not consumed. 3 So Moses decided, "I must go over to look at this remarkable sight, and see why the bush is not burned."

The Call of Moses 4 When the LORD saw him coming over to look at it more closely, God called out to him from the bush, "Moses! Moses!" He answered, "Here I am." 5 God said, "Come no nearer![o] Remove the sandals from your feet, for the place where you stand is holy ground. 6 [p]I am the God of your father," he continued, "the God of Abraham, the God of Isaac, the God of Jacob."* Moses hid his face, for he was afraid to look at God. 7 But the LORD said, "I have witnessed the affliction of my people in Egypt and have heard their cry of complaint against their slave drivers, so I know well what they are suffering. 8 Therefore I have come down* to rescue them from the hands of the Egyptians and lead them out of that land into a good and spacious land, a land flowing with milk and honey, the country of the Canaanites, Hittites, Amorites, Perizzites, Hivites and Jebusites.[q] 9 So indeed the cry of the Israelites has reached me, and I have truly noted that the Egyptians are oppressing them. 10 Come, now! I will send you to Pharaoh to lead my people, the Israelites, out of Egypt."

11 But Moses said to God, "Who am I* that I should go to Pharaoh and lead the Israelites out of Egypt?" 12 He answered, "I will be with you; and this shall be your proof that it is I who have sent you: when you bring my people out of Egypt, you will worship God on this very mountain." 13 "But," said Moses to God, "when I go to the Israelites and say to them, 'The God of your fathers has sent me to you,' if they ask me, 'What is his name?' what am I to tell them?" 14 God replied, "I am who am."* Then he added, "This is what you shall tell the Israelites: I AM sent me to you."

15 God spoke further to Moses, "Thus shall you say to the Israelites: The LORD, the God of your fathers, the God of Abraham, the God of Isaac, the God of Jacob, has sent me to you.

"This is my name forever;[r]
this is my title for all generations.

16 "Go and assemble the elders* of the Israel-

"there." Some Greek and Latin manuscripts add here a passage taken from Ex 18, 4.

3, 1: The mountain of God: probably given this designation because of the divine apparitions which took place there, such as on this occasion and when the Israelites were there after the departure from Egypt.

3, 2: An angel of the Lord: the visual form under which God appeared and spoke to men is referred to indifferently in some Old Testament texts either as God's angel or as God himself. Cf Gn 16, 7. 13; Ex 14, 19. 24f; Nm 22, 22–35; Jgs 6, 11–18.

3, 6: The appearance of God caused fear of death, since it was believed that no one could see God and live; cf Gn 32, 30. The God of Abraham . . . Jacob: cited by Christ in proof of the resurrection since the patriarchs, long dead, live on in God who is the God of the living. Cf Mt 22, 32; Mk 12, 26; Lk 20, 37.

3, 8: I have come down: a figure of speech signifying an extraordinary divine intervention in human affairs. Cf Gn 11, 5. 7. Flowing with milk and honey: an expression denoting agricultural prosperity, which seems to have been proverbial in its application to Palestine. Cf Ex 13, 5; Nm 13, 27; Jos 5, 6; Jer 11, 5; 32, 22; Ez 20, 6. 15.

3, 11: Who am I: besides naturally shrinking from such a tremendous undertaking, Moses realized that, as a fugitive from Pharaoh, he could hardly hope to carry out a mission to him. Perhaps he also recalled that on one occasion even his own kinsmen questioned his authority. Cf Ex 2, 14.

3, 14: I am who am: apparently this utterance is the source of the word Yahweh, the proper personal name of the God of Israel. It is commonly explained in reference to God as the absolute and necessary Being. It may be understood of God as the Source of all created beings. Out of reverence for this name, the term Adonai, "my Lord," was later used as a substitute. The word Lord in the present version represents this traditional usage. The word "Jehovah" arose from a false reading of this name as it is written in the current Hebrew text.

3, 16: Elders: the Israelite leaders, who were usually older men. They were representatives of the people.

k Ex 18, 3. l Ex 3, 7. 9; Dt 26. 7. m Ex 6, 5; Pss 105, 8f; 106, 44f. n 2–10; Acts 7, 30–35. o Jos 5, 15. p Ex 4, 5; Mt 22, 32; Mk 12, 36; Lk 20, 37. q 8f: Gn 15, 19ff. r Ps 135, 13.

ites, and tell them: The LORD, the God of your fathers, the God of Abraham, Isaac and Jacob, has appeared to me and said: I am concerned about you and about the way you are being treated in Egypt; [17]so I have decided to lead you up out of the misery of Egypt into the land of the Canaanites, Hittites, Amorites, Perizzites, Hivites and Jebusites, a land flowing with milk and honey.

[18]"Thus they will heed your message. Then you and the elders of Israel shall go to the king of Egypt and say to him: [s] The LORD, the God of the Hebrews, has sent us word. Permit us, then, to go a three-days' journey in the desert, that we may offer sacrifice to the LORD, our God.

[19]"Yet I know that the king of Egypt will not allow you to go unless he is forced. [20]I will stretch out my hand, therefore, and smite Egypt by doing all kinds of wondrous deeds there. After that he will send you away. [21]I will even make the Egyptians so well-disposed toward this people that, when you leave, you will not go empty-handed. [22] [t]Every woman shall ask her neighbor and her house guest for silver and gold articles* and for clothing to put on your sons and daughters. Thus you will despoil the Egyptians."

CHAPTER 4

Confirmation of Moses' Mission [1]"But," objected Moses, "suppose they will not believe me, nor listen to my plea? For they may say, 'The LORD did not appear to you.'" [2]The LORD therefore asked him, "What is that in your hand?" "A staff," he answered. [3]The LORD then said, "Throw it on the ground." When he threw it on the ground it was changed into a serpent, [u] and Moses shied away from it. [4]"Now, put out your hand," the LORD said to him, "and take hold of its tail." So he put out his hand and laid hold of it, and it became a staff in his hand. [5]"This will take place so that they may believe," he continued, "that the LORD, the God of their fathers, the God of Abraham, the God of Isaac, the God of Jacob, did appear to you."

[6]Again the LORD said to him, "Put your hand in your bosom." He put it in his bosom, and when he withdrew it, to his surprise his hand was leprous, like snow. [7]The LORD then said, "Now, put your hand back in your bosom." Moses put his hand back in his bosom, and when he withdrew it, to his surprise it was again like the rest of his body. [8]"If they will not believe you, nor heed the message of the first sign, they should believe the message of the second. [9]And if they will not believe even these two signs, nor heed your plea, take some water from the river and pour it on the dry land. The water you take from the river will become blood on the dry land." [v]

Aaron's Office as Assistant [10]Moses, however, said to the LORD, "If you please, Lord, I have never been eloquent, neither in the past, nor recently, nor now that you have spoken to your servant; but I am slow of speech and tongue." [w] [11]The LORD said to him, "Who gives one man speech and makes another deaf and dumb? Or who gives sight to one and makes another blind? Is it not I, the LORD? [12]Go, then! It is I who will assist you in speaking and will teach you what you are to say." [13]Yet he insisted, "If you please, Lord, send someone else!"* [14]Then the LORD became angry with Moses and said, "Have you not your brother, Aaron the Levite? I know that he is an eloquent speaker. Besides, he is now on his way to meet you. [15]When he sees you, his heart will be glad. You are to speak to him, then, and put the words in his mouth. I will assist both you and him in speaking and will teach the two of you what you are to do. [16]He shall speak to the people for you: he shall be your spokesman,* and you shall be as God to him. [x] [17]Take this staff* in your hand; with it you are to perform the signs."

3, 22: Articles: probably jewelry. Despoil: this was permissible, that the Israelites might compensate themselves for their many years of servitude; besides, the Egyptians would give these things willingly. Cf Ex 12, 33–36.

4, 13: Send someone else: literally, "Send by means of him whom you will send," that is, "Send whom you will."

4, 16: Spokesman: literally, "mouth"; Aaron was to serve as a mouthpiece for Moses, as a prophet does for God; hence the relation between Moses and Aaron is compared to that between God and his prophet. Cf Ex 7, 1.

4, 17: This staff: probably the same as that of vv 2ff; but some understand it here of a new staff now given by God to Moses.

s Ex 5, 3. t 21f: Ex 11, 2f; 12, 35f. u Ex 7, 10. v Ex 7, 17. 19f. w Ex 6, 12. x 15f: Ex 7, 1.

Moses' Return to Egypt 18After this Moses
returned to his father-in-law Jethro and said to
him, "Let me go back, please, to my kinsmen in
Egypt, to see whether they are still living."
Jethro replied, "Go in peace."* 19In Midian[y] the
LORD said to Moses, "Go back to Egypt, for all
the men who sought your life are dead." 20So
Moses took his wife and his sons, and started
back to the land of Egypt, with them riding the
ass. The staff of God he carried with him. 21The
LORD said to him, "On your return to Egypt, see
that you perform before Pharaoh all the wonders
I have put in your power. I will make him
obstinate,* however, so that he will not let the
people go. 22 [z]So you shall say to Pharaoh: Thus
says the LORD: Israel is my son, my first-born.
23Hence I tell you: Let my son go, that he may
serve me. If you refuse to let him go, I warn you,
I will kill your son, your first-born." [a]

24*On the journey, at a place where they
spent the night, the Lord came upon Moses and
would have killed him. 25 [b]But Zipporah took a
piece of flint and cut off her son's foreskin and,
touching his person, she said, "You are a spouse
of blood to me." 26Then God let Moses go. At
that time she said, "A spouse of blood," in regard
to the circumcision.

27The LORD said to Aaron, "Go into the desert
to meet Moses." So he went, and when they
met at the mountain of God, Aaron kissed him.
28Moses informed him of all the LORD had said
in sending him, and of the various signs he had
enjoined upon him. 29Then Moses and Aaron
went and assembled all the elders of the Israel-
ites. 30Aaron told them everything the LORD had
said to Moses, and he performed the signs before
the people. 31The people believed, and when
they heard that the LORD was concerned about
them and had seen their affliction, they bowed
down in worship.

CHAPTER 5

Pharaoh's Obduracy 1After that, Moses and
Aaron went to Pharaoh and said, "Thus says the
LORD, the God of Israel: Let my people go, that
they may celebrate a feast to me in the desert."
2Pharaoh answered, "Who is the LORD, that I
should heed his plea to let Israel go? I do not
know the LORD; even if I did, I would not let
Israel go." 3They replied, "The God of the
Hebrews has sent us word. Let us go a three
days' journey in the desert, that we may offer
sacrifice to the LORD, our God;[c] otherwise he
will punish us with pestilence or the sword."

4The king of Egypt answered them, "What do
you mean, Moses and Aaron, by taking the
people away from their work? Off to your labor!
5Look how numerous the people of the land are
already," continued Pharaoh, "and yet you
would give them rest from their labor!"

6That very day Pharaoh gave the taskmasters
and foremen* of the people this order: 7"You
shall no longer supply the people with straw for
their brickmaking* as you have previously done.
Let them go and gather straw themselves! 8Yet
you shall levy upon them the same quota of
bricks as they have previously made. Do not
reduce it. They are lazy; that is why they are
crying, 'Let us go to offer sacrifice to our God.'
9Increase the work for the men, so that they
keep their mind on it and pay no attention to
lying words."

10So the taskmasters and foremen of the
people went out and told them, "Thus says
Pharaoh: I will not provide you with straw. 11Go
and gather the straw yourselves, wherever you
can find it. Yet there must not be the slightest
reduction in your work." 12The people, then,
scattered throughout the land of Egypt to gather
stubble for straw, 13while the taskmasters kept
driving them on, saying, "Finish your work, the

4, 18: Moses did not tell his father-in-law his main reason for returning to Egypt, but this secondary motive which he offered was also true.

4, 21: Make him obstinate: literally, "harden his heart." God permitted Pharaoh to be stubborn in his opposition to the departure of the Israelites. Cf Rom 9, 17f.

4, 24ff: Apparently God was angry with Moses for having failed to keep the divine command given to Abraham in Gn 17, 10ff. Moses' life is spared when his wife circumcises their son.

5, 6: The taskmasters and foremen: the former were higher officials and probably Egyptians; the latter were lower officials, chosen from the Israelites themselves. Cf v 14.

5, 7: Straw was mixed with the clay to give the sun-dried bricks greater consistency.

y Ex 2, 15, 23. z Sir 36, 11. a Ex 11, 5; 12, 29. b Is 6, 2; 7, 20. c Ex 3, 18.

same daily amount as when your straw was supplied."

Complaint of the Foremen [14]The foremen of the Israelites, whom the taskmasters of Pharaoh had placed over them, were beaten, and were asked, "Why have you not completed your prescribed amount of bricks yesterday and today, as before?"

[15]Then the Israelite foremen came and made this appeal to Pharaoh: "Why do you treat your servants in this manner? [16]No straw is supplied to your servants, and still we are told to make bricks. Look how your servants are beaten! It is you who are at fault." [17]Pharaoh answered, "It is just because you are lazy that you keep saying, 'Let us go and offer sacrifice to the LORD.' [18]Off to work, then! Straw shall not be provided for you, but you must still deliver your quota of bricks."

[19]The Israelite foremen knew they were in a sorry plight, having been told not to reduce the daily amount of bricks. [20]When, therefore, they left Pharaoh and came upon Moses and Aaron, who were waiting to meet them, [21]they said to them, "The LORD look upon you and judge! You have brought us into bad odor with Pharaoh and his servants and have put a sword in their hands to slay us."

Renewal of God's Promise [22]Moses again had recourse to the LORD and said, "Lord, why do you treat this people so badly? And why did you send me on such a mission? [23]Ever since I went to Pharaoh to speak in your name, he has maltreated this people of yours, and you have done nothing to rescue them."

CHAPTER 6

[1]Then the LORD answered Moses, "Now you shall see what I will do to Pharaoh. Forced by my mighty hand, he will send them away; compelled by my outstretched arm, he will drive them from his land."

[2]God also said to Moses, "I am the LORD. [3]As God the Almighty I appeared[d] to Abraham, Isaac and Jacob, but my name, LORD, I did not make known to them. [4]I also established my covenant with them, to give them the land of Canaan, the land in which they were living as aliens.[e] [5]And now that I have heard the groaning of the Israelites, whom the Egyptians are treating as slaves, I am mindful of my covenant.[f] [6]Therefore, say to the Israelites: I am the LORD. I will free you from the forced labor of the Egyptians and will deliver you from their slavery. I will rescue you by my outstretched arm and with mighty acts of judgment. [7]I will take you as my own people, and you shall have me as your God.[g] You will know that I, the LORD, am your God when I free you from the labor of the Egyptians [8]and bring you into the land which I swore to give to Abraham, Isaac and Jacob. I will give it to you as your own possession—I, the LORD!" [9]But when Moses told this to the Israelites, they would not listen to him because of their dejection and hard slavery.

[10]Then the LORD said to Moses, [11]"Go and tell Pharaoh, king of Egypt, to let the Israelites leave his land." [12]But Moses protested to the LORD, "If the Israelites would not listen to me, how can it be that Pharaoh will listen to me, poor speaker[h] that I am!" [13]Still, the LORD, to bring the Israelites out of Egypt, spoke to Moses and Aaron and gave them his orders regarding both the Israelites and Pharaoh, king of Egypt.

Genealogy of Moses and Aaron [14]These are the heads of the ancestral houses.* The sons of Reuben,[i] the first-born of Israel, were Hanoch, Pallu, Hezron and Carmi; these are the clans of Reuben. [15]The sons of Simeon[j] were Jemuel, Jamin, Ohad, Jachin, Zohar and Shaul, who was the son of a Canaanite woman; these are the clans of Simeon. [16]The names of the sons of Levi,[k] in their genealogical order, are Gershon, Kohath and Merari. Levi lived one hundred and thirty-seven years.

[17]The sons of Gershon,[l] as heads of clans, were Libni and Shimei. [18]The sons of Kohath[m] were Amram, Izhar, Hebron and Uzziel. Kohath

6, 14: The purpose of the genealogy here is to give the line from which Moses and Aaron sprang. Reuben and Simeon are first mentioned because, as older brothers of Levi, their names occur before his in the genealogy.

d Gn 17, 1; 35, 11. e Gn 15, 18; 17, 4–8. f Ex 2, 24. g Lv 26, 12. h Ex 6, 30. i Nm 26. 5f; 1 Chr 5, 3 j Nm 26, 12; 1 Chr 4, 24. k Nm 3, 17; 1 Chr 6, 1. 16; 23, 6. l Nm 3, 21; 1 Chr 6, 17; 23, 7. m Nm 3, 27; 1 Chr 6, 2. 18.

lived one hundred and thirty-three years. 19The sons of Merari[n] were Mahli and Mushi. These are the clans of Levi in their genealogical order.

20Amram married his aunt* Jochebed,[o] who bore him Aaron, Moses and Miriam. Amram lived one hundred and thirty-seven years. 21The sons of Izhar were Korah, Nepheg and Zichri. 22The sons of Uzziel were Mishael, Elzaphan and Sithri. 23Aaron married Amminadab's[p] daughter, Elisheba, the sister of Nahshon; she bore him Nadab, Abihu, Eleazar and Ithamar. 24The sons of Korah were Assir, Elkanah and Abiasaph. These are the clans of the Korahites. 25Aaron's son, Eleazar, married one of Putiel's daughters, who bore him Phinehas. These are the heads of the ancestral clans of the Levites. 26This is the Aaron and this the Moses to whom the LORD said, "Lead the Israelites from the land of Egypt, company by company." 27These are the ones who spoke to Pharaoh, king of Egypt, to bring the Israelites out of Egypt—the same Moses and Aaron.

Moses and Aaron before Pharaoh 28On the day the LORD spoke to Moses in Egypt 29he said, "I am the LORD. Repeat to Pharaoh, king of Egypt, all that I tell you." 30But Moses protested to the LORD, "Since I am a poor speaker,[q] how can it be that Pharaoh will listen to me?"

CHAPTER 7

1The LORD answered him, "See! I have made you as God to Pharaoh,[r] and Aaron your brother shall act as your prophet.* 2You shall tell him all that I command you. In turn, your brother Aaron shall tell Pharaoh to let the Israelites leave his land. 3Yet I will make Pharaoh so obstinate that, despite the many signs and wonders that I will work in the land of Egypt, 4he will not listen to you. Therefore I will lay my hand on Egypt and by great acts of judgment I will bring the hosts of my people, the Israelites, out of the land of Egypt, 5so that the Egyptians may learn that I am the LORD, as I stretch out my hand against Egypt and lead the Israelites out of their midst."

6Moses and Aaron did as the LORD had commanded them. 7Moses was eighty years old and Aaron eighty-three when they spoke to Pharaoh.

The Staff Turned into a Snake 8The LORD told Moses and Aaron, 9"If Pharaoh demands that you work a sign or wonder, you shall say to Aaron: Take your staff and throw it down before Pharaoh, and it will be changed into a snake."[s] 10Then Moses and Aaron went to Pharaoh and did as the LORD had commanded. Aaron threw his staff down before Pharaoh and his servants, and it was changed into a snake. 11Pharaoh, in turn, summoned wise men and sorcerers, and they also, the magicians[t] of Egypt, did likewise by their magic arts. 12Each one threw down his staff, and it was changed into a snake. But Aaron's staff swallowed their staffs. 13Pharaoh, however, was obstinate and would not listen to them, just as the LORD had foretold.

First Plague: Water Turned into Blood 14*Then the LORD said to Moses, "Pharaoh is obdurate in refusing to let the people go. 15Tomorrow morning, when he sets out for the water, go and present yourself by the river bank, holding in your hand the staff that turned into a serpent. 16Say to him: The LORD, the God of the Hebrews, sent me to you with the message: Let my people go to worship me in the desert. But as yet you have not listened. 17The LORD now says: This is how you shall know that I am the LORD. I will strike the water of the river with the staff I hold, and it shall be changed into blood.[u] 18The fish in the river shall die, and the river itself shall become so polluted that the Egyptians will be unable to drink its water."

19The LORD then said to Moses, "Say to Aaron: Take your staff and stretch out your hand over the waters of Egypt—their streams and canals and pools, all their supplies of water—

6, 20: His aunt: more exactly, "his father's sister." Later on such a marriage was forbidden. Cf Lv 18, 12. Hence, the Greek and Latin versions render here, "his cousin."

7, 1: Just as God had his prophets to speak to men in his name, so Moses had Aaron as his "prophet" to speak to Pharaoh. Cf Ex 4, 16.

7, 14: Most of the ten plagues of Egypt seem to be similar to certain natural phenomena of that country; but they are represented as supernatural at least in their greater intensity and in their occurring exactly according to Moses' commands.

n Nm 3, 20; 1 Chr 6, 19; 23, 21. o Nm 26, 59. p Ru 4, 19f; 1 Chr 2, 10. q Ex 6, 12. r Ex 4, 15f. s Ex 4, 3. t 2 Tm 3, 8. u 17–21: Ex 4, 9; Pss 78, 44; 105, 29; Wis 11, 5–7.

that they may become blood. Throughout the land of Egypt there shall be blood, even in the wooden pails and stone jars."

20 Moses and Aaron did as the LORD had commanded. Aaron raised his staff and struck the waters of the river in full view of Pharaoh and his servants, and all the water of the river was changed into blood. 21 The fish in the river died, and the river itself became so polluted that the Egyptians could not drink its water. There was blood throughout the land of Egypt. 22 But the Egyptian magicians did the same by their magic arts. So Pharaoh remained obstinate and would not listen to Moses and Aaron, just as the LORD had foretold. 23 He turned away and went into his house, with no concern even for this. 24 All the Egyptians had to dig in the neighborhood of the river for drinking water, since they could not drink the river water.

Second Plague: the Frogs 25 Seven days passed after the LORD had struck the river. 26 *Then the LORD said to Moses, "Go to Pharaoh and tell him:[v] Thus says the LORD: Let my people go to worship me. 27 If you refuse to let them go, I warn you, I will send a plague of frogs over all your territory. 28 The river will teem with frogs. They will come up into your palace and into your bedroom and onto your bed, into the houses of your servants, too, and your subjects, even into your ovens and your kneading bowls. 29 The frogs will swarm all over you and your subjects and your servants."

CHAPTER 8

1 The LORD then told Moses, "Say to Aaron: Stretch out your hand and your staff over the streams and canals and pools, to make frogs overrun the land of Egypt." 2 Aaron stretched out his hand over the waters of Egypt, and the frogs came up and covered the land of Egypt. 3 But the magicians did the same by their magic arts. They, too, made frogs overrun the land of Egypt.

4 Then Pharaoh summoned Moses and Aaron and said, "Pray the LORD to remove the frogs from me and my subjects, and I will let the people go to offer sacrifice to the LORD." 5 Moses answered Pharaoh, "Do me the favor of appointing the time when I am to pray for you and your servants and your subjects, that the frogs may be taken away from you and your houses and be left only in the river." 6 "Tomorrow," said Pharaoh. Then Moses replied, "It shall be as you have said, so that you may learn that there is none like the LORD, our God. 7 The frogs shall leave you and your houses, your servants and your subjects; only in the river shall they be left."

8 After Moses and Aaron left Pharaoh's presence, Moses implored the LORD to fulfill the promise he had made to Pharaoh about the frogs; 9 and the LORD did as Moses had asked. The frogs in the houses and courtyards* and fields died off. 10 Heaps and heaps of them were gathered up, and there was a stench in the land. 11 But when Pharaoh saw that there was a respite, he became obdurate and would not listen to them, just as the LORD had foretold.

Third Plague: the Gnats 12 Thereupon the LORD said to Moses, "Tell Aaron to stretch out his staff and strike the dust of the earth, that it may be turned into gnats[w] throughout the land of Egypt."* 13 They did so. Aaron stretched out his hand, and with his staff he struck the dust of the earth, and gnats came upon man and beast. The dust of the earth was turned into gnats throughout the land of Egypt. 14 Though the magicians tried to bring forth gnats by their magic arts, they could not do so.[x] As the gnats infested man and beast, 15 the magicians said to Pharaoh, "This is the finger of God."* Yet Pharaoh remained obstinate and would not listen to them, just as the LORD had foretold.

Fourth Plague: the Flies 16 Again the LORD told Moses, "Early tomorrow morning present yourself to Pharaoh when he goes forth to the water, and say to him: Thus says the LORD: Let my people go to worship me. 17 If you will not let

7, 26—8, 28: This is Ex 8, 1–32 in the verse enumeration of the Vulgate.

8, 9: Courtyards: some render "farmhouses."

8, 12. 17: Gnats, flies: it is uncertain what species of troublesome insects are here meant.

8, 15: The finger of God: understood by the magicians as the staff mentioned in Ex 8, 13. Cf Lk 11, 20.

v 26–29: Pss 78, 45; 105, 30. w 12f: Ps 105, 31. x Wis 17, 7.

my people go, I warn you, I will loose swarms of flies upon you and your servants and your subjects and your houses. The houses of the Egyptians and the very ground on which they stand shall be filled with swarms of flies. [18]But on that day I will make an exception of the land of Goshen: there shall be no flies where my people dwell, that you may know that I am the LORD in the midst of the earth. [19]I will make this distinction between my people and your people. This sign shall take place tomorrow." [20]This the LORD did. Thick swarms of flies entered the house of Pharaoh and houses of his servants; throughout Egypt the land was infested with flies.[y]

[21]Then Pharaoh summoned Moses and Aaron and said to them, "Go and offer sacrifice to your God in this land." [22]But Moses replied, "It is not right to do so, for the sacrifices we offer to the LORD, our God, are an abomination to the Egyptians.* If before their very eyes we offer sacrifices which are an abomination to them, will not the Egyptians stone us? [23]We must go a three days' journey in the desert to offer sacrifice to the LORD, our God, as he commands us." [24]"Well, then," said Pharaoh, "I will let you go to offer sacrifice to the LORD, your God, in the desert, provided that you do not go too far away and that you pray for me." [25]Moses answered, "As soon as I leave your presence I will pray to the LORD that the flies may depart tomorrow from Pharaoh and his servants and his subjects. Pharaoh, however, must not play false again by refusing to let the people go to offer sacrifice to the LORD." [26]When Moses left Pharaoh's presence, he prayed to the LORD; [27]and the LORD did as Moses had asked. He removed the flies from Pharaoh and his servants and subjects. Not one remained. [28]But once more Pharaoh became obdurate and would not let the people go.

CHAPTER 9

Fifth Plague: the Pestilence [1]Then the LORD said to Moses, "Go to Pharaoh and tell him: Thus says the LORD, the God of the Hebrews: Let my people go to worship me. [2]If you refuse to let them go and persist in holding them, [3]I warn you, the LORD will afflict all your livestock in the field—your horses, asses, camels, herds and flocks—with a very severe pestilence. [4]But the LORD will distinguish between the livestock of Israel and that of Egypt, so that none belonging to the Israelites will die." [5]And setting a definite time, the LORD added, "Tomorrow the LORD shall do this in the land." [6]And on the next day the LORD did so. All the livestock of the Egyptians died,[z] but not one beast belonging to the Israelites. [7]But though Pharaoh's messengers informed him that not even one beast belonging to the Israelites had died, he still remained obdurate and would not let the people go.

Sixth Plague: the Boils [8]Then the LORD said to Moses and Aaron, "Take a double handful of soot from a furnace, and in the presence of Pharaoh let Moses scatter it toward the sky. [9]It will then turn into fine dust over the whole land of Egypt and cause festering boils on man and beast throughout the land."

[10]So they took soot from a furnace and stood in the presence of Pharaoh. Moses scattered it toward the sky, and it caused festering boils on man and beast. [11]The magicians could not stand in Moses' presence, for there were boils on the magicians no less than on the rest of the Egyptians. [12]But the LORD made Pharaoh obstinate, and he would not listen to them, just as the LORD had foretold to Moses.

Seventh Plague: the Hail [13]Then the LORD told Moses, "Early tomorrow morning present yourself to Pharaoh and say to him: Thus says the LORD, the God of the Hebrews: Let my people go to worship me, [14]or this time I will hurl all my blows upon you and your servants and your subjects, that you may know that there is none like me anywhere on earth. [15]For by now I would have stretched out my hand and struck you and your subjects with such pestilence as would wipe you from the earth. [16]But

8, 22: The Egyptians would fiercely resent the sacrifice of any animal they considered sacred. Certain animals were worshiped in Egypt, at least as the symbols of various deities.

y Pss 78, 45; 105, 31; Wis 16, 9. z Ps 78, 48.

this is why I have spared you: to show you* my power and to make my name resound throughout the earth! [a] 17Will you still block the way for my people by refusing to let them go? 18I warn you, then, tomorrow at this hour I will rain down such fierce hail as there has never been in Egypt from the day the nation was founded up to the present. 19Therefore, order all your livestock and whatever else you have in the open fields to be brought to a place of safety. Whatever man or beast remains in the fields and is not brought to shelter shall die when the hail comes upon them." 20Some of Pharaoh's servants feared the warning of the LORD and hurried their servants and livestock off to shelter. 21Others, however, did not take the warning of the LORD to heart and left their servants and livestock in the fields.

22The LORD then said to Moses, "Stretch out your hand toward the sky, that hail may fall upon the entire land of Egypt, on man and beast and every growing thing in the land of Egypt." 23When Moses stretched out his staff toward the sky, the LORD sent forth hail [b] and peals of thunder. Lightning flashed toward the earth, and the LORD rained down hail upon the land of Egypt; 24and lightning constantly flashed through the hail, such fierce hail as had never been seen in the land since Egypt became a nation. 25It struck down every man and beast that was in the open throughout the land of Egypt; it beat down every growing thing and splintered every tree in the fields. 26Only in the land of Goshen, where the Israelites dwelt, was there no hail.

27Then Pharaoh summoned Moses and Aaron and said to them, "I have sinned again! The LORD is just; it is I and my subjects who are at fault. 28Pray to the LORD, for we have had enough of God's thunder and hail. Then I will let you go; you need stay no longer." 29Moses replied, "As soon as I leave the city I will extend my hands to the LORD; the thunder will cease, and there will be no more hail. Thus you shall learn that the earth is the LORD's. 30But you and your servants, I know, do not yet fear the LORD God."

31Now the flax and the barley were ruined, because the barley was in ear and the flax in bud. 32But the wheat and the spelt were not ruined, for they grow later.

33When Moses had left Pharaoh's presence and had gone out of the city, he extended his hands to the LORD. Then the thunder and the hail ceased, and the rain no longer poured down upon the earth. 34But Pharaoh, seeing that the rain and hail and thunder had ceased, sinned again: he with his servants became obdurate, 35and in his obstinacy he would not let the Israelites go, as the LORD had foretold through Moses.

CHAPTER 10

Eighth Plague: the Locusts 1Then the LORD said to Moses, "Go to Pharaoh, for I have made him and his servants obdurate in order that I may perform these signs of mine among them 2and that you may recount to your son and grandson how ruthlessly I dealt with the Egyptians and what signs I wrought among them, so that you may know that I am the LORD." [c]

3So Moses and Aaron went to Pharaoh and told him, "Thus says the LORD, the God of the Hebrews: How long will you refuse to submit to me? Let my people go to worship me. 4If you refuse to let my people go, I warn you, tomorrow I will bring locusts into your country. 5They shall cover the ground, so that the ground itself will not be visible. They shall eat up the remnant you saved unhurt from the hail, as well as all the foliage that has since sprouted in your fields. 6They shall fill your houses and the houses of your servants and of all the Egyptians; such a sight your fathers or grandfathers have not seen from the day they first settled on this soil up to the present day." With that he turned and left Pharaoh.

7But Pharaoh's servants said to him, "How long must he be a menace to us? Let the men go to worship the LORD, their God. Do you not yet realize that Egypt is being destroyed?" 8So Moses and Aaron were brought back to Pharaoh, who said to them, "You may go and worship the

9, 16: To show you: some ancient versions read, "to show through you." Cf Rom 9, 17.

a Rom 9, 17. b 23f: Pss 78, 47; 105, 32f. c Dt 6, 20ff.

LORD, your God. But how many of you will go?"
9"Young and old must go with us," Moses
answered, "our sons and daughters as well as
our flocks and herds must accompany us. That is
what a feast of the LORD means to us." 10"The
LORD help you,"* Pharaoh replied, "if I ever let
your little ones go with you! Clearly, you have
some evil in mind. 11No, no! Just you men can
go and worship the LORD.* After all, that is what
you want." With that they were driven from
Pharaoh's presence.

12The LORD then said to Moses, "Stretch out
your hand over the land of Egypt, that locusts[d]
may swarm over it and eat up all the vegetation
and whatever the hail has left." 13So Moses
stretched out his staff over the land of Egypt, and
the LORD sent an east wind* blowing over the
land all that day and all that night. At dawn the
east wind brought the locusts. 14They swarmed
over the whole land of Egypt and settled down
on every part of it. Never before had there been
such a fierce swarm of locusts, nor will there
ever be. 15They covered the surface of the whole
land, till it was black with them. They ate up all
the vegetation in the land and the fruit of
whatever trees the hail had spared. Nothing
green was left on any tree or plant throughout
the land of Egypt.

16Hastily Pharaoh summoned Moses and Aar-
on and said, "I have sinned against the LORD,
your God, and against you. 17But now, do
forgive me my sin once more, and pray the
LORD, your God, to take at least this deadly pest
from me." 18When Moses left the presence of
Pharaoh, he prayed to the LORD, 19and the LORD
changed the wind to a very strong west wind,
which took up the locusts and hurled them into
the Red Sea.* But though not a single locust
remained within the confines of Egypt, 20the
LORD made Pharaoh obstinate, and he would not
let the Israelites go.

Ninth Plague: the Darkness 21Then the
LORD said to Moses, "Stretch out your hand
toward the sky, that over the land of Egypt there
may be such intense darkness* that one can feel
it." 22So Moses stretched out his hand toward
the sky, and there was dense darkness[e] through-
out the land of Egypt for three days. 23Men
could not see one another, nor could they move
from where they were, for three days. But all the
Israelites had light where they dwelt.

24Pharaoh then summoned Moses and Aaron
and said, "Go and worship the LORD. Your little
ones, too, may go with you. But your flocks and
herds must remain." 25Moses replied, "You must
also grant us sacrifices and holocausts to offer up
to the LORD, our God. 26Hence, our livestock
also must go with us. Not an animal must be left
behind. Some of them we must sacrifice to the
LORD, our God, but we ourselves shall not know
which ones we must sacrifice to him until we
arrive at the place itself." 27But the LORD made
Pharaoh obstinate, and he would not let them
go. 28"Leave my presence," Pharaoh said to him,
"and see to it that you do not appear before me
again! The day you appear before me you shall
die!" 29Moses replied, "Well said! I will never
appear before you again."

CHAPTER 11

Tenth Plague: the Death of the First-born
1Then the LORD told Moses, "One more plague
will I bring upon Pharaoh and upon Egypt. After
that he will let you depart. In fact, he will not
merely let you go; he will drive you away.
2Instruct your people that every man is to ask his
neighbor, and every woman her neighbor, for
silver and gold articles and for clothing."[f] 3The

10, 10: The Lord help you . . . : literally, "May the LORD be with you in the same way as I let you . . ."; a sarcastic blessing intended as a curse.

10, 11: Pharaoh realized that if the men alone went they would have to return to their families. He suspected that the Hebrews had no intention of returning.

10, 13: East wind: coming across the desert from Arabia, the strong east wind brings Egypt the burning sirocco and, at times, locusts. Cf Ex 14, 21.

10, 19: The Red Sea: according to the traditional translation, but the Hebrew is literally, "the Reed Sea"; hence the Red Sea of Exodus was probably a body of shallow water somewhat to the north of the present deep Red Sea.

10, 21: Darkness: at times a storm from the south, called the khamsin, blackens the sky of Egypt with sand from the Sahara; the dust in the air is then so thick that the darkness can, in a sense, "be felt."

d 12ff: Pss 78, 46; 105, 34f. e Ps 105, 28. f 2f: Ex 3, 21f; 12, 35f.

LORD indeed made the Egyptians well-disposed toward the people; Moses himself was very highly regarded by Pharaoh's servants and the people in the land of Egypt.

4Moses then said, "Thus says the LORD: At midnight I will go forth through Egypt.[g] 5Every first-born in this land shall die,[h] from the first-born of Pharaoh on the throne to the first-born of the slave-girl at the handmill, as well as all the first-born of the animals. 6Then there shall be loud wailing throughout the land of Egypt, such as has never been, nor will ever be again. 7But among the Israelites and their animals not even a dog shall growl, so that you may know how the LORD distinguishes between the Egyptians and the Israelites. 8 [i]All these servants of yours shall then come down to me, and prostrate before me, they shall beg me, 'Leave us, you and all your followers!' Only then will I depart." With that he left Pharaoh's presence in hot anger.

9The LORD said to Moses, "Pharaoh refuses to listen to you that my wonders may be multiplied in the land of Egypt." 10Thus, although Moses and Aaron performed these various wonders in Pharaoh's presence, the LORD made Pharaoh obstinate, and he would not let the Israelites leave his land.

CHAPTER 12

The Passover Ritual Prescribed 1The LORD said to Moses and Aaron in the land of Egypt, 2"This month* shall stand at the head of your calendar; you shall reckon it the first month of the year.[j] 3Tell the whole community of Israel: On the tenth of this month every one of your families must procure for itself a lamb, one apiece for each household. 4If a family is too small for a whole lamb, it shall join the nearest household in procuring one and shall share in the lamb* in proportion to the number of persons who partake of it. 5The lamb must be a year-old male and without blemish. You may take it from either the sheep or the goats. 6You shall keep it until the fourteenth day of this month, and then, with the whole assembly of Israel present, it shall be slaughtered during the evening twilight. 7They shall take some of its blood and apply it to the two doorposts and the lintel of every house in which they partake of the lamb. 8That same night they shall eat its roasted flesh with unleavened bread and bitter herbs. 9It shall not be eaten raw or boiled, but roasted whole, with its head and shanks and inner organs. 10None of it must be kept beyond the next morning; whatever is left over in the morning shall be burned up.

11"This is how you are to eat it: with your loins girt, sandals on your feet and your staff in hand, you shall eat like those who are in flight. It is the Passover* of the LORD. 12For on this same night I will go through Egypt, striking down every first-born of the land, both man and beast, and executing judgment on all the gods of Egypt—I, the LORD! 13But the blood will mark the houses where you are. Seeing the blood, I will pass over you; thus, when I strike the land of Egypt, no destructive blow will come upon you.[k]

14"This day shall be a memorial feast for you, which all your generations shall celebrate with pilgrimage to the LORD, as a perpetual institution. 15For seven days you must eat unleavened bread. From the very first day you shall have your houses clear of all leaven. Whoever eats leavened bread from the first day to the seventh shall be cut off from Israel. 16On the first day you shall hold a sacred assembly, and likewise on the seventh. On these days you shall not do any sort of work, except to prepare the food that everyone needs.

17"Keep, then, this custom of the unleavened bread.[l] Since it was on this very day that I brought your ranks out of the land of Egypt, you

12, 2: This month: Abib, the month of "ripe grain." Cf Ex 13, 4; 23, 15; 34, 18; Dt 16, 1. It occurred near the vernal equinox, March-April. Later it was known by the Babylonian name of Nisan. Cf Neh 2, 1; Est 3, 7.

12, 4: Share in the lamb: probably, in the expenses of its purchase. Some explain, "reckon for the lamb the number of persons required to eat it." Cf Ex 12, 10.

12, 11: Passover: in Hebrew, pesach, in Aramaic, pascha. In the following verses the same root is used in the verb "to pass over." The word may be originally Egyptian, pesach, "the blow," i.e., the final plague which destroyed the Egyptian first-born.

g Ex 12, 12. h 5f: Ex 12, 29f. i Ex 12, 31ff. j 2–20: Lv 23, 5–8; Nm 9, 2–5; 28, 16ff; Dt 16, 1–8. k Heb 11, 28. l Ex 13, 3.

must celebrate this day throughout your genera-
tions as a perpetual institution. [18]From the
evening of the fourteenth day of the first month
until the evening of the twenty-first day of this
month you shall eat unleavened bread. [19]For
seven days no leaven may be found in your
houses. Anyone, be he a resident alien or a
native, who eats leavened food shall be cut off
from the community of Israel. [20]Nothing leav-
ened may you eat; wherever you dwell you may
eat only unleavened bread."

Promulgation of the Passover [21]Moses called
all the elders of Israel and said to them, "Go and
procure lambs for your families, and slaughter
them as Passover victims. [22]Then take a bunch
of hyssop,* and dipping it in the blood that is in
the basin, sprinkle the lintel and the two
doorposts with this blood.[m] But none of you
shall go outdoors until morning. [23]For the LORD
will go by, striking down the Egyptians. Seeing
the blood on the lintel and the two doorposts,
the LORD will pass over that door and not let the
destroyer come into your houses to strike you
down.

[24]"You shall observe this as a perpetual ordi-
nance for yourselves and your descendants.
[25]Thus, you must also observe this rite when
you have entered the land which the LORD will
give you as he promised. [26]When your children
ask you, 'What does this rite of yours mean?'[n]
[27]you shall reply, 'This is the Passover sacrifice of
the LORD, who passed over the houses of the
Israelites in Egypt; when he struck down the
Egyptians, he spared our houses.' "

Then the people bowed down in worship,
[28]and the Israelites went and did as the LORD
had commanded Moses and Aaron.

Death of the First-born [29]At midnight the
LORD slew every first-born in the land of Egypt,[o]
from the first-born of Pharaoh on the throne to
the first-born of the prisoner in the dungeon, as
well as all the first-born of the animals. [30]Pha-
raoh arose in the night, he and all his servants
and all the Egyptians; and there was loud
wailing throughout Egypt, for there was not a
house without its dead.

Permission To Depart [31]During the night Pha-
raoh summoned Moses and Aaron and said,
"Leave my people at once, you and the Israelites
with you! Go and worship the LORD as you said.
[32]Take your flocks, too, and your herds, as you
demanded, and begone; and you will be doing
me a favor."

[33]The Egyptians likewise urged the people on,
to hasten their departure from the land; they
thought that otherwise they would all die. [34]The
people, therefore, took their dough before it was
leavened, in their kneading bowls wrapped in
their cloaks on their shoulders. [35]The Israelites
did as Moses had commanded: they asked the
Egyptians for articles of silver and gold and for
clothing.[p] [36]The LORD indeed had made the
Egyptians so well-disposed toward the people
that they let them have whatever they asked for.
Thus did they despoil the Egyptians.

II: The Exodus From Egypt and the Journey to Sinai

Departure from Egypt [37]The Israelites set out
from Rameses[q] for Succoth, about six hundred
thousand men on foot, not counting the chil-
dren. [38]A crowd of mixed ancestry* also went
up with them, besides their livestock, very
numerous flocks and herds. [39]Since the dough
they had brought out of Egypt was not leavened,
they baked it into unleavened loaves. They had
been rushed out of Egypt and had no opportu-
nity even to prepare food for the journey.

[40]The time the Israelites had stayed in Egypt*
was four hundred and thirty years.[r] [41]At the end
of four hundred and thirty years, all the hosts of
the LORD left the land of Egypt on this very date.
[42]This was a night of vigil for the LORD, as he led

12, 22: Hyssop: a plant with many woody branchlets that made a convenient sprinkler.

12, 38: Mixed ancestry: half-Hebrew and half-Egyptian. Cf Nm 11, 4; Lv 24, 10f.

12, 40: In Egypt: according to some ancient sources, "in Canaan and Egypt," thus reckoning from the time of Abraham. Cf Gal 3, 17.

m 22f: Ex 12, 7. 13. n 26f: Ex 13, 8. 14; Dt 6, 20f. o 29f: Ex 11, 4ff; Pss 78, 51; 105, 36; 136, 10; Wis 18, 10–16. p 35f: Ex 3, 21f; 11, 2f; Ps 105, 37f. q Nm 33, 3ff. r Gn 15, 13; Acts 7, 6; Gal 3, 17.

them out of the land of Egypt; so on this same night all the Israelites must keep a vigil for the LORD throughout their generations.

Passover Regulations 43 The LORD said to Moses and Aaron, "These are the regulations for the Passover. No foreigner may partake of it. 44 However, any slave who has been bought for money may partake of it, provided you have first circumcised him. 45 But no transient alien or hired servant may partake of it. 46 It must be eaten in one and the same house; you may not take any of its flesh outside the house.[s] You shall not break any of its bones.* 47 The whole community of Israel must keep this feast. 48 If any aliens[t] living among you wish to celebrate the Passover of the LORD, all the males among them must first be circumcised, and then they may join in its observance just like the natives. But no man who is uncircumcised may partake of it. 49 The law shall be the same for the resident alien as for the native."

50 All the Israelites did just as the LORD had commanded Moses and Aaron. 51 On that same day the LORD brought the Israelites out of Egypt company by company.

CHAPTER 13

Consecration of First-born 1 The LORD spoke to Moses and said, 2 "Consecrate to me every first-born that opens the womb among the Israelites,[u] both of man and beast, for it belongs to me."

3 Moses said to the people, "Remember this day on which you came out of Egypt, that place of slavery.[v] It was with a strong hand that the LORD brought you away. Nothing made with leaven must be eaten. 4 This day of your departure is in the month of Abib. 5 Therefore, it is in this month that you must celebrate this rite, after the LORD, your God, has brought you into the land of the Canaanites, Hittites, Amorites, Hivites and Jebusites, which he swore to your fathers he would give you, a land flowing with milk and honey. 6 For seven days you shall eat unleavened bread, and the seventh day shall also be a festival to the LORD. 7 Only unleavened bread may be eaten during the seven days; no leaven and nothing leavened may be found in all your territory. 8 On this day you shall explain to your son, 'This is because of what the LORD did for me when I came out of Egypt.' 9 It shall be as a sign on your hand and as a reminder on your forehead;[w] thus the law of the LORD will ever be on your lips, because with a strong hand the LORD brought you out of Egypt. 10 Therefore, you shall keep this prescribed rite at its appointed time from year to year.

11 "When the LORD, your God, has brought you into the land of the Canaanites, which he swore to you and your fathers he would give you, 12 you shall dedicate to the LORD every son that opens the womb;[x] and all the male firstlings of your animals shall belong to the LORD. 13 Every first-born of an ass you shall redeem with a sheep. If you do not redeem it, you shall break its neck. Every first-born son you must redeem. 14 If your son should ask you later on, 'What does this mean?' you shall tell him, 'With a strong hand the LORD brought us out of Egypt, that place of slavery. 15 When Pharaoh stubbornly refused to let us go, the LORD killed every first-born in the land of Egypt, every first-born of man and of beast. That is why I sacrifice to the LORD everything of the male sex that opens the womb, and why I redeem every first-born of my sons.' 16 Let this, then, be as a sign on your hand and as a pendant on your forehead: with a strong hand the LORD brought us out of Egypt."[y]

Toward the Red Sea 17 Now, when Pharaoh let the people go, God did not lead them by way of the Philistines' land,* though this was the nearest; for he thought, should the people see that they would have to fight, they might change their minds and return to Egypt. 18 Instead, he rerouted them toward the Red Sea by way of the

12, 46: You shall not break any of its bones: the application of these words to our Lord on the cross shows that the Paschal lamb was a prophetic type of Christ, immolated to free men from the bondage of sin. Cf also 1 Cor 5, 7; 1 Pt 1, 19.

13, 17: By way of the Philistines' land: the most direct route from Egypt to Palestine, along the shore of the Mediterranean.

s Nm 9, 12; Jn 19, 36. t 47f: Nm 9, 14. u Ex 13, 12–15. v 3–10: Ex 12, 2–20. w Ex 13, 16; Dt 6, 8; 11, 18. x 12–15; Ex 13, 2; 22, 29f; 34, 19f: Nm 3, 12f; 8, 16; 18, 15; Dt 15, 19. y Ex 13, 9.

desert road. In battle array the Israelites marched out of Egypt. 19Moses also took Joseph's bones[z] along, for Joseph had made the Israelites swear solemnly that, when God should come to them, they would carry his bones away with them.

20Setting out from Succoth, they camped at Etham[a] near the edge of the desert.

21The LORD preceded them, in the daytime by means of a column of cloud to show them the way, and at night by means of a column of fire* to give them light.[b] Thus they could travel both day and night. 22Neither the column of cloud by day nor the column of fire by night ever left its place in front of the people.

CHAPTER 14

1Then the LORD said to Moses, 2*"Tell the Israelites to turn about and camp before Pi-hahiroth, between Migdol and the sea.[c] You shall camp in front of Baal-zephon, just opposite, by the sea. 3Pharaoh will then say, 'The Israelites are wandering about aimlessly in the land. The desert has closed in on them.' 4Thus will I make Pharaoh so obstinate that he will pursue them. Then I will receive glory through Pharaoh and all his army, and the Egyptians will know that I am the LORD."

This the Israelites did. 5When it was reported to the king of Egypt that the people had fled, Pharaoh and his servants changed their minds about them. "What have we done!" they exclaimed. "Why, we have released Israel from our service!" 6So Pharaoh made his chariots ready and mustered his soldiers— 7six hundred first-class chariots and all the other chariots of Egypt, with warriors on them all. 8So obstinate had the LORD made Pharaoh that he pursued[d] the Israelites even while they were marching away in triumph. 9The Egyptians, then, pursued them; Pharaoh's whole army, his horses, chariots and charioteers, caught up with them as they lay encamped by the sea, at Pi-hahiroth, in front of Baal-zephon.

Crossing of the Red Sea 10Pharaoh was already near when the Israelites looked up and saw that the Egyptians were on the march in pursuit of them. In great fright they cried out to the LORD. 11And they complained to Moses, "Were there no burial places in Egypt that you had to bring us out here to die in the desert? Why did you do this to us? Why did you bring us out of Egypt? 12Did we not tell you this in Egypt, when we said, 'Leave us alone. Let us serve the Egyptians'? Far better for us to be the slaves of the Egyptians than to die in the desert." 13But Moses answered the people, "Fear not! Stand your ground, and you will see the victory the LORD will win for you today. These Egyptians whom you see today you will never see again. 14The LORD himself will fight for you; you have only to keep still."

15Then the LORD said to Moses, "Why are you crying out to me? Tell the Israelites to go forward. 16And you, lift up your staff and, with hand outstretched over the sea, split the sea in two, that the Israelites may pass through it on dry land. 17But I will make the Egyptians so obstinate that they will go in after them. Then I will receive glory through Pharaoh and all his army, his chariots and charioteers. 18The Egyptians shall know that I am the LORD, when I receive glory through Pharaoh and his chariots and charioteers."

19The angel of God, who had been leading Israel's camp, now moved and went around behind them. The column of cloud also, leaving the front, took up its place behind them, 20so that it came between the camp of the Egyptians and that of Israel. But the cloud now became dark,* and thus the night passed without the rival camps coming any closer together all night

13, 21: A column of cloud . . . a column of fire: probably one and the same preternatural phenomenon, a central nucleus of fire surrounded by smoke; only at night was its luminous nature visible. Cf Ex 40, 38.

14, 2: These places have not been definitively identified. Even the relative position of Pi-hahiroth and Baal-zephon is not clear; perhaps the former was on the west shore of the sea, where the Israelites were, and the latter on the opposite shore.

14, 20: The cloud now became dark: the light which it ordinarily cast at night would now have been a help to the Egyptians; its present obscurity serves as a shield for the Israelites. However, the reading of the original text here is not quite certain.

z Gn 50, 25; Jos 24, 32. a Nm 33, 6. b 21f: Ex 40, 38; Nm 9, 15–22; Dt 1, 33; Neh 9, 19; Pss 78, 14; 105, 39; Wis 10, 17. c Nm 33, 7f. d 5–8: Wis 19, 3; 1 Mc 4, 9.

long. 21 Then Moses stretched out his hand over
the sea, and the LORD swept the sea with a
strong east wind throughout the night and so
turned it into dry land.[e] When the water was
thus divided, 22 the Israelites marched into the
midst of the sea on dry land, with the water like
a wall to their right and to their left.

Destruction of the Egyptians 23 The Egyp-
tians followed in pursuit; all Pharaoh's horses
and chariots and charioteers went after them
right into the midst of the sea. 24 In the night
watch just before dawn the LORD cast through
the column of the fiery cloud upon the Egyp-
tian force a glance that threw it into a panic;
25 and he so clogged their chariot wheels that
they could hardly drive. With that the Egyp-
tians sounded the retreat before Israel, because
the LORD was fighting for them against the
Egyptians.

26 Then the LORD told Moses, "Stretch out
your hand over the sea, that the water may flow
back upon the Egyptians, upon their chariots and
their charioteers." 27 So Moses stretched out his
hand over the sea, and at dawn the sea flowed
back to its normal depth. The Egyptians were
fleeing head on toward the sea, when the LORD
hurled them into its midst. 28 As the water
flowed back, it covered the chariots and the
charioteers of Pharaoh's whole army[f] which had
followed the Israelites into the sea. Not a single
one of them escaped. 29 But the Israelites had
marched on dry land through the midst of the
sea, with the water like a wall to their right and
to their left. 30 Thus the LORD saved Israel on that
day from the power of the Egyptians. When
Israel saw the Egyptians lying dead on the
seashore 31 and beheld the great power that the
LORD had shown against the Egyptians, they
feared the LORD and believed in him[g] and in his
servant Moses.

CHAPTER 15

1 Then Moses and the Israelites sang[h] this
song to the LORD:*

I will sing to the LORD, for he is gloriously
triumphant;
horse and chariot he has cast into the sea.

2 My strength and my courage is the LORD,
and he has been my savior.
He is my God, I praise him;
the God of my father, I extol him.[i]

3 The LORD is a warrior,
LORD is his name!

4 Pharaoh's chariots and army he hurled into
the sea;
the elite of his officers were submerged in
the Red Sea.

5 The flood waters covered them,
they sank into the depths like a stone.[j]

6 Your right hand, O LORD, magnificent in
power,
your right hand, O LORD, has shattered the
enemy.

7 In your great majesty you overthrew your
adversaries;
you loosed your wrath to consume them
like stubble.

8 At a breath of your anger the waters piled up,
the flowing waters stood like a mound,
the flood waters congealed in the midst of
the sea.

9 The enemy boasted, "I will pursue and over-
take them;
I will divide the spoils and have my fill of
them;
I will draw my sword; my hand shall
despoil them!"

10 When your wind blew, the sea covered them;
like lead they sank in the mighty waters.

11 Who is like to you among the gods, O LORD?
Who is like to you, magnificent in holiness?
O terrible in renown, worker of wonders,
12 when you stretched out your right hand,
the earth swallowed them!

13 In your mercy you led the people you
redeemed;

15, 1–21: This canticle (used in Christian liturgy) celebrates God's saving power, miraculously delivering his people from their enemies, and leading them to the victorious conquest of the Promised Land.

e 21f: Ex 15, 19; Pss 66, 6; 78, 13; 136, 13f; Wis 10, 18; 19, 7f; Is 63, 12f; Heb 11, 29. f 28f: Dt 11, 4; Ps 106, 11. g 31f: Ps 106, 12; Wis 10, 20. h Ex 15, 21. i Ps 118, 14; Is 12, 2. j Neh 9, 11.

in your strength you guided them to your
holy dwelling.
14 The nations heard and quaked:
anguish gripped the dwellers in Philistia.
15 Then were the princes of Edom dismayed;
trembling seized the chieftains of Moab;
All the dwellers in Canaan melted away;
16 terror and dread fell upon them.[k]
By the might of your arm they were frozen like
stone,
while your people, O LORD, passed over,
while the people you had made your own
passed over.

17 And you brought them in and planted them on
the mountain of your inheritance—
the place where you made your seat,
O LORD,
the sanctuary, O LORD, which your hands
established.
18 The LORD shall reign forever and ever.

19 They sang thus because Pharaoh's horses
and chariots and charioteers had gone into the
sea, and the LORD made the waters of the sea
flow back upon them, though the Israelites had
marched on dry land through the midst of the
sea.[l] 20 The prophetess Miriam, Aaron's sister,
took a tambourine in her hand, while all the
women went out after her with tambourines,
dancing; 21 and she led them* in the refrain:

Sing to the LORD, for he is gloriously
triumphant;
horse and chariot he has cast into the sea.[m]

At Marah and Elim 22 [n]Then Moses led Israel
forward from the Red Sea, and they marched out
to the desert of Shur. After traveling for three
days through the desert without finding water,
23 they arrived at Marah, where they could not
drink the water, because it was too bitter. Hence
this place was called Marah. 24 As the people
grumbled against Moses, saying, "What are we
to drink?" 25 he appealed to the LORD, who
pointed out to him a certain piece of wood.
When he threw this into the water, the water
became fresh.[o]

It was here that the LORD, in making rules and
regulations for them, put them to the test. 26 "If
you really listen to the voice of the LORD, your
God," he told them, "and do what is right in his
eyes: if you heed his commandments and keep
all his precepts, I will not afflict you with any of
the diseases with which I afflicted the Egyp-
tians;[p] for I, the LORD, am your healer."

27 Then they came to Elim, where there were
twelve springs of water and seventy palm trees,
and they camped there near the water.[q]

CHAPTER 16

The Desert of Sin 1 Having set out from Elim,
the whole Israelite community came into the
desert of Sin, which is between Elim and Sinai,
on the fifteenth day of the second month* after
their departure from the land of Egypt. 2 Here in
the desert the whole Israelite community grum-
bled against Moses and Aaron. 3 The Israelites
said to them, "Would that we had died at the
LORD's hand in the land of Egypt, as we sat by
our fleshpots and ate our fill of bread! But you
had to lead us into this desert to make the whole
community die of famine!"
The Quail and Manna 4 Then the LORD said to
Moses,[r] "I will now rain down bread from
heaven* for you. Each day the people are to go
out and gather their daily portion; thus will I test
them, to see whether they follow my instruc-
tions or not. 5 On the sixth day, however, when
they prepare what they bring in, let it be twice as
much as they gather on the other days." 6 So
Moses and Aaron told all the Israelites, "At

15, 21: She led them: Miriam's refrain re-echoes the first verse of this song and was probably sung as an antiphon after each verse.

16, 1: On the fifteenth day of the second month: just one full month after their departure from Egypt. Cf Ex 12, 2. 51; Nm 33, 3f. They encamped in the desert of Sin on a Friday; the murmuring (vv 2f) occurred on the sabbath, the arrival of the quail (v 13) the evening before Sunday, followed by six mornings (vv 14–27) of collecting manna before the next sabbath.

16, 4: Bread from heaven: as a gift from God, the manna is said to come down from the sky. Cf Ps 78, 25; Wis 16, 20. Perhaps it was similar to a natural substance that is still found in small quantities on the Sinai peninsula, but here it is, at least in part, clearly miraculous. Our Lord referred to the manna as a type of the Blessed Eucharist. Cf Jn 6, 32. 49–52.

k 16f: Ps 78, 53ff. l Ex 14, 21–29. m Ex 15, 1. n 22f: Nm 33, 8. o Sir 38, 5. p Dt 7, 15. q Nm 33, 9. r Pss 78, 24f; 105, 40; Jn 6, 31f; 1 Cor 10, 3.

evening you will know that it was the LORD who brought you out of the land of Egypt; 7 and in the morning you will see the glory of the LORD, as he heeds your grumbling against him.[s] But what are we that you should grumble against us? 8 When the LORD gives you flesh to eat in the evening," continued Moses, "and in the morning your fill of bread, as he heeds the grumbling you utter against him, what then are we? Your grumbling is not against us, but against the LORD."

9 Then Moses said to Aaron, "Tell the whole Israelite community: Present yourselves before the LORD, for he has heard your grumbling." 10 When Aaron announced this to the whole Israelite community, they turned toward the desert, and lo, the glory of the LORD appeared in the cloud! 11 The LORD spoke to Moses and said, 12 "I have heard the grumbling of the Israelites. Tell them: In the evening twilight you shall eat flesh, and in the morning you shall have your fill of bread, so that you may know that I, the LORD, am your God."

13 In the evening quail[t] came up and covered the camp. In the morning a dew lay all about the camp, 14 and when the dew evaporated, there on the surface of the desert were fine flakes like hoarfrost on the ground. 15 On seeing it, the Israelites asked one another, "What is this?"* for they did not know what it was. But Moses told them, "This is the bread which the LORD has given you to eat.[u]

Regulations Regarding the Manna 16 "Now, this is what the LORD has commanded. So gather it that everyone has enough to eat, an omer for each person, as many of you as there are, each man providing for those of his own tent." 17 The Israelites did so. Some gathered a large and some a small amount. 18 *But when they measured it out by the omer, he who had gathered a large amount did not have too much, and he who had gathered a small amount did not have too little.[v] They so gathered that everyone had enough to eat. 19 Moses also told them, "Let no one keep any of it over until tomorrow morning." 20 But they would not listen to him. When some kept a part of it over until the following morning, it became wormy and rotten. Therefore Moses was displeased with them.

21 Morning after morning they gathered it, till each had enough to eat; but when the sun grew hot, the manna melted away. 22 On the sixth day they gathered twice as much food, two omers for each person. When all the leaders of the community came and reported this to Moses, 23 he told them, "That is what the LORD prescribed. Tomorrow is a day of complete rest, the sabbath, sacred to the LORD. You may either bake or boil the manna, as you please; but whatever is left put away and keep for the morrow." 24 When they put it away for the morrow, as Moses commanded, it did not become rotten or wormy. 25 Moses then said, "Eat it today, for today is the sabbath of the LORD. On this day you will not find any of it on the ground. 26 On the other six days you can gather it, but on the seventh day, the sabbath, none of it will be there." 27 Still, on the seventh day some of the people went out to gather it, although they did not find any. 28 Then the LORD said to Moses, "How long will you refuse to keep my commandments and laws? 29 Take note! The LORD has given you the sabbath. That is why on the sixth day he gives you food for two days. On the seventh day everyone is to stay home and no one is to go out." 30 After that the people rested on the seventh day.

31 The Israelites called this food manna.[w] It was like coriander seed,* but white, and it tasted like wafers made with honey.

32 Moses said, "This is what the LORD has commanded. Keep an omerful of manna for your descendants, that they may see what food I gave you to eat in the desert when I brought you out

16, 15: What is this: the original man hu is thus rendered by the ancient versions, which understood the phrase as a popular etymology of the Hebrew word man, "manna"; some render, "This is manna."

16, 18: St. Paul cites this passage as an example of equitable sharing. Cf 2 Cor 8, 15.

16, 31: Coriander seed: small, round, aromatic seeds of bright brown color; the comparison, therefore, refers merely to the size and shape, not to the taste or color of the manna.

s 6f: Ex 16, 12. t Nm 11, 31; Ps 78, 27f. u Dt 8, 3. v 2 Cor 8, 15. w Nm 11, 7.

of the land of Egypt." [33]Moses then told Aaron, "Take an urn* and put an omer of manna in it. Then place it before the LORD in safekeeping for your descendants."[x] [34]So Aaron placed it in front of the commandments* for safekeeping, as the LORD had commanded Moses.

[35]The Israelites ate this manna for forty years, until they came to settled land;[y] they ate manna until they reached the borders of Canaan. [36][An omer is one tenth of an ephah.]

CHAPTER 17

Water from the Rock [1]From the desert of Sin the whole Israelite community journeyed by stages, as the LORD directed, and encamped at Rephidim.[z]

Here there was no water for the people to drink. [2]They quarreled, therefore, with Moses and said, "Give us water to drink."[a] Moses replied, "Why do you quarrel with me? Why do you put the LORD to a test?" [3]Here, then, in their thirst for water, the people grumbled against Moses, saying, "Why did you ever make us leave Egypt? Was it just to have us die here of thirst with our children and our livestock?" [4]So Moses cried out to the LORD, "What shall I do with this people? A little more and they will stone me!" [5]The LORD answered Moses, "Go over there in front of the people, along with some of the elders of Israel, holding in your hand, as you go, the staff with which you struck the river. [6]I will be standing there in front of you on the rock in Horeb. Strike the rock, and the water will flow from it for the people to drink."[b] This Moses did, in the presence of the elders of Israel. [7]The place was called Massah and Meribah,* because the Israelites quarreled there and tested the LORD, saying, "Is the LORD in our midst or not?"[c]

Battle with Amalek [8]At Rephidim, Amalek* came and waged war against Israel.[d] [9]Moses, therefore, said to Joshua, "Pick out certain men, and tomorrow go out and engage Amalek in battle. I will be standing on top of the hill with the staff of God in my hand." [10]So Joshua did as Moses told him: he engaged Amalek in battle after Moses had climbed to the top of the hill with Aaron and Hur. [11]As long as Moses kept his hands raised up, Israel had the better of the fight, but when he let his hands rest, Amalek had the better of the fight. [12]Moses' hands, however, grew tired; so they put a rock in place for him to sit on. Meanwhile Aaron and Hur supported his hands, one on one side and one on the other, so that his hands remained steady till sunset. [13]And Joshua mowed down Amalek and his people with the edge of the sword.

[14]Then the LORD said to Moses, "Write this down in a document as something to be remembered, and recite it in the ears of Joshua.[e] I will completely blot out the memory of Amalek from under the heavens." [15]Moses also built an altar there, which he called Yahweh-nissi;* [16]for he said, "The LORD takes in hand his banner; the LORD will war against Amalek through the centuries."

CHAPTER 18

Meeting with Jethro [1]Now Moses' father-in-law Jethro, the priest of Midian, heard of all that God had done for Moses and for his people Israel: how the LORD had brought Israel out of Egypt. [2]So his father-in-law Jethro took along Zipporah, Moses' wife, whom Moses had sent back to him, [3]and her two sons. One of these was called Gershom;[f] for he said, "I am a stranger in a foreign land." [4]The other was called Eliezer; for he said, "My father's God is my helper; he has rescued me from Pharaoh's sword." [5]Together with Moses' wife and sons, then, his father-in-law Jethro came to him in the desert where he was encamped near the mountain of God, [6]and he sent word to Moses, "I,

16, 33: Urn: according to the Greek translation, which is followed in Heb 9, 4, this was a golden vessel.

16, 34: The commandments: the two tablets of the ten commandments, which were kept in the ark. Cf Ex 25, 16. 21f.

17, 7: Massah . . . Meribah: Hebrew words meaning respectively, "the (place of the) test," and "the (place of the) quarreling."

17, 8: Amalek: the Amalekites were an aboriginal people of southern Palestine and the Sinai peninsula. Cf Nm 24, 20.

17, 15: Yahweh-nissi: meaning, "the LORD is my banner."

x Heb 9, 4. y Jos 5, 12. z Nm 33, 12ff. a 2–7: Nm 20, 2–13. b 5f: Dt 8, 15; Pss 78, 15f; 105, 41; Wis 11, 4; Is 43, 20; 48, 21. c Ps 95, 8f. d Dt 25, 17; 1 Sm 15, 2. e Nm 24, 20; 1 Sm 15, 3. 20. f Ex 2, 22.

Jethro, your father-in-law, am coming to you,
along with your wife and her two sons."
7 Moses went out to meet his father-in-law,
bowed down before him, and kissed him. Hav-
ing greeted each other, they went into the tent.
8 Moses then told his father-in-law of all that the
LORD had done to Pharaoh and the Egyptians for
the sake of Israel, and of all the hardships they
had had to endure on their journey, and how the
LORD had come to their rescue. 9 Jethro rejoiced
over all the goodness that the LORD had shown
Israel in rescuing them from the hands of the
Egyptians. 10 "Blessed be the LORD," he said,
"who has rescued his people from the hands of
Pharaoh and the Egyptians. 11 Now I know that
the LORD is a deity great beyond any other; for
he took occasion of their being dealt with
insolently to deliver the people from the power
of the Egyptians." 12 Then Jethro, the father-in-
law of Moses, brought a holocaust and other
sacrifices to God, and Aaron came with all the
elders of Israel to participate with Moses' father-
in-law in the meal before God.
Appointment of Minor Judges 13 The next
day Moses sat in judgment for the people, who
waited about him from morning until evening.
14 When his father-in-law saw all that he was
doing for the people, he inquired, "What sort of
thing is this that you are doing for the people?
Why do you sit alone while all the people have
to stand about you from morning till evening?"
15 Moses answered his father-in-law, "The people
come to me to consult God. 16 Whenever they
have a disagreement, they come to me to have
me settle the matter between them and make
known to them God's decisions and regula-
tions."
17 "You are not acting wisely," his father-in-
law replied. 18 "You will surely wear yourself out,
and not only yourself but also these people with
you. The task is too heavy for you;[g] you cannot
do it alone. 19 Now, listen to me, and I will give
you some advice, that God may be with you. Act
as the people's representative before God, bring-
ing to him whatever they have to say. 20 En-
lighten them in regard to the decisions and
regulations, showing them how they are to live
and what they are to do. 21 But you should also
look among all the people for able and God-
fearing men, trustworthy men who hate dishon-
est gain, and set them as officers over groups of
thousands, of hundreds, of fifties, and of tens.[h]
22 Let these men render decisions for the people
in all ordinary cases. More important cases they
should refer to you, but all the lesser cases they
can settle themselves. Thus, your burden will be
lightened, since they will bear it with you. 23 If
you do this, when God gives you orders you will
be able to stand the strain, and all these people
will go home satisfied."
24 Moses followed the advice of his father-in-
law and did all that he had suggested. 25 He
picked out able men from all Israel and put them
in charge of the people as officers over groups of
thousands, of hundreds, of fifties, and of tens.
26 They rendered decisions for the people in all
ordinary cases. The more difficult cases they
referred to Moses, but all the lesser cases they
settled themselves. 27 Then Moses bade farewell
to his father-in-law, who went off to his own
country.

III: The Covenant at Mount Sinai

CHAPTER 19

Arrival at Sinai 1 [i]In the third month after their
departure from the land of Egypt, on its first day,
the Israelites came to the desert of Sinai. 2 After
the journey from Rephidim to the desert of Sinai,
they pitched camp.
While Israel was encamped here in front of
the mountain, 3 Moses went up the mountain to
God. Then the LORD called to him and said,
"Thus shall you say to the house of Jacob; 4 tell
the Israelites: You have seen for yourselves how
I treated the Egyptians and how I bore you up on
eagle wings and brought you here to myself.[j]
5 Therefore, if you hearken to my voice and keep
my covenant, you shall be my special possession,
dearer to me than all other people,[k] though all

g Nm 11, 14. h 21. 25: Dt 1, 15; 16, 18. i 1f: Nm 33, 15. j Dt 32, 11. k Dt 7, 6; 14, 2; 26, 18f; 32, 8f.

the earth is mine. [6]You shall be to me a kingdom of priests,* a holy nation.[l] That is what you must tell the Israelites." [7]So Moses went and summoned the elders of the people. When he set before them all that the LORD had ordered him to tell them, [8]the people all answered together, "Everything the LORD has said, we will do." Then Moses brought back to the LORD the response of the people.

[9]The LORD also told him, "I am coming to you in a dense cloud,[m] so that when the people hear me speaking with you, they may always have faith in you also." When Moses, then, had reported to the LORD the response of the people, [10]the LORD added, "Go to the people and have them sanctify themselves today and tomorrow. Make them wash their garments [11]and be ready for the third day; for on the third day the LORD will come down on Mount Sinai before the eyes of all the people. [12]Set limits for the people all around the mountain,[n] and tell them: Take care not to go up the mountain, or even to touch its base. If anyone touches the mountain he must be put to death. [13]No hand shall touch him; he must be stoned to death or killed with arrows. Such a one, man or beast, must not be allowed to live. Only when the ram's horn resounds may they go up to the mountain." [14]Then Moses came down from the mountain to the people and had them sanctify themselves and wash their garments. [15]He warned them, "Be ready for the third day. Have no intercourse with any woman."

The Great Theophany [16]On the morning of the third day there were peals of thunder and lightning, and a heavy cloud over the mountain, and a very loud trumpet blast, so that all the people in the camp trembled. [17]But Moses led the people out of the camp to meet God, and they stationed themselves at the foot of the mountain.[o] [18]Mount Sinai was all wrapped in smoke, for the LORD came down upon it in fire. The smoke rose from it as though from a furnace, and the whole mountain trembled violently. [19]The trumpet blast grew louder and louder, while Moses was speaking and God answering him with thunder.

[20]When the LORD came down to the top of Mount Sinai, he summoned Moses to the top of the mountain, and Moses went up to him. [21]Then the LORD told Moses, "Go down and warn the people not to break through toward the LORD in order to see him; otherwise many of them will be struck down. [22]The priests, too, who approach the LORD must sanctify themselves; else he will vent his anger upon them." [23]Moses said to the LORD, "The people cannot go up to Mount Sinai, for you yourself warned us to set limits around the mountain to make it sacred." [24]The LORD repeated, "Go down now! Then come up again along with Aaron. But the priests and the people must not break through to come up to the LORD; else he will vent his anger upon them." [25]So Moses went down to the people and told them this.

CHAPTER 20

The Ten Commandments [1]Then God delivered all these commandments:*

[2][p]"I, the LORD, am your God, who brought you out of the land of Egypt,[q] that place of slavery. [3]You shall not have other gods besides me. [4]You shall not carve idols[r] for yourselves in the shape of anything in the sky above or on the earth below or in the waters beneath the earth; [5]you shall not bow down before them or worship them.[s] For I, the LORD, your God, am a jealous* God, inflicting punishment for their fathers' wickedness on the children of those who hate me, down to the third and fourth genera-

19, 6: Kingdom of priests: inasmuch as the whole Israelite nation was consecrated to God in a special way, it formed a race of royal priests who participated in the liturgical sacrifices, even though the actual offering of the sacrifices was the exclusive prerogative of the Aaronic priesthood. The same condition exists in the New Dispensation as regards the whole Christian people and the Christian priesthood in the strict sense. Cf Is 61, 6; 1 Pt 2, 5. 9.

20, 1–17: The precise division of these precepts into "ten commandments" is somewhat uncertain. Traditionally among Catholics vv 1–6 are considered as only one commandment, and v 17 as two. Cf Dt 5, 6–21.

20, 5: Jealous: demanding exclusive allegiance, such as a wife must have for her husband.

l 1 Pt 2, 9. m Ex 20, 21; 24, 15–18. n 12f: Ex 34, 3; Heb 12, 18f. o 16ff: Dt 4, 10ff. p 2–17; Dt 5, 6–21. q Lv 26, 13; Ps 81, 10; Hos 13, 4. r Ex 34, 17; Lv 26, 1; Dt 4, 15–19; 27, 15. s Ex 34, 7. 14; Nm 14, 18; Dt 4, 24; 6, 15.

tion; 6 but bestowing mercy down to the thou-
sandth generation, on the children of those who
love me and keep my commandments.
7 "You shall not take the name of the LORD,
your God, in vain.[t] For the LORD will not leave
unpunished him who takes his name in vain.
8 "Remember to keep holy the sabbath day.
9 Six days you may labor and do all your work,
10 but the seventh day is the sabbath of the LORD,
your God.[u] No work may be done then either by
you, or your son or daughter, or your male or
female slave, or your beast, or by the alien who
lives with you. 11 In six days the LORD made the
heavens and the earth, the sea and all that is in
them; but on the seventh day he rested.[v] That is
why the LORD has blessed the sabbath day and
made it holy.
12 [w]"Honor your father and your mother, that
you may have a long life in the land which the
Lord, your God, is giving you.[x]
13 "You shall not kill.[y]
14 "You shall not commit adultery.[z]
15 "You shall not steal.[a]
16 "You shall not bear false witness against
your neighbor.[b]
17 "You shall not covet your neighbor's house.
You shall not covet your neighbor's wife, nor his
male or female slave, nor his ox or ass, nor
anything else that belongs to him."[c]

The Fear of God 18 When the people wit-
nessed the thunder and lightning, the trumpet
blast and the mountain smoking, they all feared
and trembled.[d] So they took up a position much
farther away 19 and said to Moses, "You speak to
us, and we will listen; but let not God speak to
us, or we shall die." 20 Moses answered the
people, "Do not be afraid, for God has come to
you only to test you and put his fear upon you,
lest you should sin." 21 Still the people remained
at a distance, while Moses approached the cloud
where God was.
22 The LORD told Moses, "Thus shall you speak
to the Israelites: You have seen for yourselves
that I have spoken to you from heaven. 23 Do not
make anything to rank with me; neither gods of
silver nor gods of gold shall you make for
yourselves.[e]
24 "An altar of earth you shall make for me,
and upon it you shall sacrifice your holocausts
and peace offerings, your sheep and your oxen.[f]
In whatever place I choose for the remembrance
of my name* I will come to you and bless you.
25 If you make an altar of stone for me,[g] do not
build it of cut stone, for by putting a tool to it you
desecrate it. 26 You shall not go up by steps to my
altar, on which you must not be indecently
uncovered.

CHAPTER 21

Laws Regarding Slaves 1 "These are the
rules* you shall lay before them. 2 [h]When you
purchase a Hebrew slave, he is to serve you for
six years, but in the seventh year he shall be
given his freedom without cost. 3 If he comes
into service alone, he shall leave alone; if he
comes with a wife, his wife shall leave with him.
4 But if his master gives him a wife and she bears
him sons or daughters, the woman and her
children shall remain the master's property and
the man shall leave alone. 5 If, however, the slave
declares, 'I am devoted to my master and my
wife and children; I will not go free,' 6 his master
shall bring him to God* and there, at the door or
doorpost, he shall pierce his ear with an awl,
thus keeping him as his slave forever.
7 "When a man sells his daughter as a slave,
she shall not go free as male slaves do. 8 But if her
master, who had destined her* for himself,

20, 24: I choose for the remembrance of my name: literally, "where I make my name to be remembered": at the sacred site where God wishes to be worshiped and his name revered.

21, 1: Rules: judicial precedents to be used in settling questions of law and custom. This introductory phrase serves as the title of the following collection of civil and religious laws (chapters 21–23) which is called in Ex 24, 7, the book of the covenant.

21, 6: To God: to the sanctuary; or perhaps the phrase is to be rendered, "to the gods," in the sense of "to the judges." Cf Ps 82, 1. Since the expression "to have an open ear" meant to "obey," a pierced ear lobe was an ancient symbol of obedience. Cf Ps 40, 7.

21, 8: Destined her: intended her as a wife of second rank.

t Lv 19, 12; 24, 16. u 8ff: Ex 23, 12; 31, 13–16; 34, 21; 35, 2; Lv 23, 3. v Ex 31, 17; Gn 2, 2f. w 12–16: Mt 19, 18f; Mk 10, 19; Lk 18, 20; Rom 13, 9. x Mt 15, 4; Mk 7, 10; Eph 6, 2f. y Mt 5, 21. z Lv 18, 20; 20, 10; Dt 22, 22; Mt 5, 27. a Lv 19, 11. b Ex 23, 1; Dt 19, 16ff; Prv 19, 5. 9; 24, 28. c Rom 7, 7. d 18–21: Dt 4, 11; 5, 22–27; 18, 16; Heb 12, 18f. e Ex 20, 3f. f Dt 12, 5. 11; 14, 23; 16, 6. g Dt 27, 5; Jos 8, 31. h 2–6: Lv 25, 39ff; Dt 15, 12–18; Jer 34, 14.

dislikes her, he shall let her be redeemed. He has no right to sell her to a foreigner, since he has broken faith with her. [9]If he destines her for his son, he shall treat her like a daughter. [10]If he takes another wife, he shall not withhold her food, her clothing, or her conjugal rights. [11]If he does not grant her these three things, she shall be given her freedom absolutely, without cost to her.

Personal Injury [12]"Whoever strikes a man a mortal blow must be put to death.[i] [13]He, however, who did not hunt a man down, but caused his death by an act of God, may flee to a place which I will set apart for this purpose. [14]But when a man kills another after maliciously scheming to do so, you must take him even from my altar and put him to death. [15]Whoever strikes his father or mother shall be put to death.

[16]"A kidnaper, whether he sells his victim or still has him when caught, shall be put to death.[j]

[17]"Whoever curses his father or mother shall be put to death.[k]

[18]"When men quarrel and one strikes the other with a stone or with his fist, not mortally, but enough to put him in bed, [19]the one who struck the blow shall be acquitted, provided the other can get up and walk around with the help of his staff. Still, he must compensate him for his enforced idleness and provide for his complete cure.

[20]"When a man strikes his male or female slave with a rod so hard that the slave dies under his hand, he shall be punished. [21]If, however, the slave survives for a day or two, he is not to be punished, since the slave is his own property.

[22]"When men have a fight and hurt a pregnant woman, so that she suffers a miscarriage, but no further injury, the guilty one shall be fined as much as the woman's husband demands of him, and he shall pay in the presence of the judges.[l] [23]*But if injury ensues, you shall give life for life, [24]eye for eye, tooth for tooth, hand for hand, foot for foot, [25]burn for burn, wound for wound, stripe for stripe.

[26]"When a man strikes his male or female slave in the eye and destroys the use of the eye, he shall let the slave go free in compensation for the eye. [27]If he knocks out a tooth of his male or female slave, he shall let the slave go free in compensation for the tooth.

[28]"When an ox gores a man or a woman to death, the ox must be stoned; its flesh may not be eaten. The owner of the ox, however, shall go unpunished. [29]But if an ox was previously in the habit of goring people and its owner, though warned, would not keep it in; should it then kill a man or a woman, not only must the ox be stoned, but its owner also must be put to death. [30]If, however, a fine is imposed on him, he must pay in ransom for his life whatever amount is imposed on him. [31]This law applies if it is a boy or a girl that the ox gores. [32]But if it is a male or a female slave that it gores, he must pay the owner of the slave thirty shekels of silver, and the ox must be stoned.

Property Damage [33]"When a man uncovers or digs a cistern and does not cover it over again, should an ox or an ass fall into it, [34]the owner of the cistern must make good by restoring the value of the animal to its owner; the dead animal, however, he may keep.

[35]"When one man's ox hurts another's ox so badly that it dies, they shall sell the live ox and divide this money as well as the dead animal equally between them. [36]But if it was known that the ox was previously in the habit of goring and its owner would not keep it in, he must make full restitution, an ox for an ox; but the dead animal he may keep.

[37]*"When a man steals an ox or a sheep and slaughters or sells it, he shall restore five oxen for the one ox, and four sheep for the one sheep.[m]

21, 23ff: This section is known as the lex talionis, the law of tit for tat. The purpose of this law was not merely the enforcement of rigorous justice, but also the prevention of greater penalties than would be just. Christ refers to this passage when he exhorts Christians to cede their lawful rights for the sake of charity. Cf Mt 5, 38ff.

21, 37—22, 30: In the Vulgate, 22, 1–31.

i 12ff: Lv 24, 17; Nm 35, 15–29; Dt 4, 41f; 19, 2–5. j Dt 24, 7. k Lv 20, 9; Prv 20, 20; Mt 15, 4; Mk 7, 10. l 22–25: Lv 24, 18–21; Dt 19, 21; Mt 5, 38. m 2 Sm 12, 6.

CHAPTER 22

1 "[If a thief is caught* in the act of housebreak-
ing and beaten to death, there is no bloodguilt
involved. 2 But if after sunrise he is thus beaten,
there is bloodguilt.] He must make full restitu-
tion. If he has nothing, he shall be sold to pay for
his theft. 3 If what he stole is found alive in his
possession, be it an ox, an ass or a sheep, he shall
restore two animals for each one stolen.

4 *"When a man is burning over a field or a
vineyard, if he lets the fire spread so that it burns
in another's field, he must make restitution with
the best produce of his own field or vineyard. 5 If
the fire spreads further, and catches on to thorn
bushes, so that shocked grain or standing grain
or the field itself is burned up, the one who
started the fire must make full restitution.

Trusts and Loans 6 "When a man gives money
or any article to another for safekeeping and it is
stolen from the latter's house, the thief, if
caught, must make twofold restitution. 7 If the
thief is not caught, the owner of the house shall
be brought to God,* to swear that he himself did
not lay hands on his neighbor's property. 8 In
every question of dishonest appropriation,
whether it be about an ox, or an ass, or a sheep,
or a garment, or anything else that has disap-
peared, where another claims that the thing is
his, both parties shall present their case before
God; the one whom God convicts must make
two-fold restitution to the other.

9 "When a man gives an ass, or an ox, or a
sheep, or any other animal to another for safe-
keeping, if it dies, or is maimed or snatched
away, without anyone witnessing the fact, 10 the
custodian shall swear by the LORD that he did
not lay hands on his neighbor's property; the
owner must accept the oath, and no restitution
is to be made. 11 But if the custodian is really
guilty of theft, he must make restitution to the
owner. 12 If it has been killed by a wild beast, let
him bring it as evidence, and he need not make
restitution for the mangled animal.[n]

13 "When a man borrows an animal from his
neighbor, if it is maimed or dies while the owner
is not present, the man must make restitution.
14 But if the owner is present, he need not make
restitution. If it was hired, this was covered by
the price of its hire.

Social Laws 15 "When a man seduces a virgin
who is not betrothed, and lies with her, he shall
pay her marriage price and marry her.[o] 16 If her
father refuses to give her to him, he must still
pay him the customary marriage price for vir-
gins.*

17 "You shall not let a sorceress live.[p]

18 "Anyone who lies with an animal shall be
put to death.[q]

19 "Whoever sacrifices to any god, except to
the LORD alone, shall be doomed.[r]

20 "You shall not molest or oppress an alien,
for you were once aliens yourselves in the land
of Egypt.[s] 21 You shall not wrong any widow or
orphan. 22 If ever you wrong them and they cry
out to me, I will surely hear their cry. 23 My
wrath will flare up, and I will kill you with the
sword; then your own wives will be widows,
and your children orphans.

24 [t]"If you lend money to one of your poor
neighbors among my people, you shall not act
like an extortioner toward him by demanding
interest from him. 25 If you take your neighbor's
cloak as a pledge, you shall return it to him
before sunset; 26 for this cloak of his is the only
covering he has for his body. What else has he to
sleep in? If he cries out to me, I will hear him;
for I am compassionate.

22, 1f: If a thief is caught: this seems to be a fragment of what was once a longer law on housebreaking, which has been inserted here into the middle of a law on stealing animals. At night the householder would be justified in killing a burglar outright, but not so in the daytime, when the burglar could more easily be caught alive. He must make full restitution: this stood originally immediately after 21, 37.

22, 4: The Greek and Latin versions understood this verse as a prohibition against allowing one's cattle to graze in the field of another.

22, 7: Brought to God: see note on Ex 21, 6. Cf also Ex 22, 10.

22, 16: The customary marriage price for virgins: fifty shekels according to Dt 22, 29.

n Gn 31, 39. o 15f: Dt 22, 28f. p Lv 19, 26. 31; 20. 6. 27; Dt 18, 10f. q Lv 18, 23; Dt 27, 21. r Dt 13; 17, 2–7. s 20–23: Ex 23, 9; Lv 19, 33f; Dt 10, 18f; 24, 17f; 27, 19; Zec 7, 10. t 24–26: Lv 25, 35–38; Dt 23, 19f; 24, 10–13; Ez 18, 7f. 17f.

27“You shall not revile God,* nor curse a prince of your people.[u]

28“You shall not delay the offering of your harvest and your press. You shall give me the first-born of your sons. 29You must do the same with your oxen and your sheep; for seven days the firstling may stay with its mother, but on the eighth day you must give it to me.[v]

30“You shall be men sacred to me. Flesh torn to pieces in the field you shall not eat; throw it to the dogs.[w]

CHAPTER 23

1“You shall not repeat a false report. Do not join the wicked in putting your hand, as an unjust witness, upon anyone.[x] 2Neither shall you allege the example of the many as an excuse for doing wrong, nor shall you, when testifying in a lawsuit, side with the many in perverting justice. 3You shall not favor a poor man in his lawsuit.[y]

4“When you come upon your enemy’s ox or ass going astray, see to it that it is returned to him.[z] 5When you notice the ass of one who hates you lying prostrate under its burden, by no means desert him; help him, rather, to raise it up.

6“You shall not deny one of your needy fellow men his rights in his lawsuit. 7You shall keep away from anything dishonest. The innocent and the just you shall not put to death, nor shall you acquit the guilty. 8Never take a bribe, for a bribe blinds even the most clear-sighted and twists the words even of the just.[a] 9You shall not oppress an alien; you well know how it feels to be an alien, since you were once aliens yourselves in the land of Egypt.[b]

Religious Laws 10[c]“For six years you may sow your land and gather in its produce. 11But the seventh year you shall let the land lie untilled and unharvested, that the poor among you may eat of it and the beasts of the field may eat what the poor leave. So also shall you do in regard to your vineyard and your olive grove.

12“For six days you may do your work, but on the seventh day you must rest,[d] that your ox and your ass may also have rest, and that the son of your maidservant and the alien may be refreshed. 13Give heed to all that I have told you.

“Never mention the name of any other god; it shall not be heard from your lips.

14[e]“Three times a year you shall celebrate a pilgrim feast to me.* 15You shall keep the feast of Unleavened Bread. As I have commanded you, you must eat unleavened bread for seven days at the prescribed time in the month of Abib, for it was then that you came out of Egypt. No one shall appear before me* empty-handed. 16You shall also keep the feast of the grain harvest with the first of the crop that you have sown in the field; and finally, the feast at the fruit harvest at the end of the year, when you gather in the produce from the fields. 17Thrice a year shall all your men appear before the LORD God.

18“You shall not offer the blood of my sacrifice with leavened bread;[f] nor shall the fat of my feast be kept overnight till the next day. 19The choicest first fruits of your soil you shall bring to the house of the LORD, your God.

“You shall not boil a kid in its mother’s milk.*

Reward of Fidelity 20“See, I am sending an angel[g] before you, to guard you on the way and bring you to the place I have prepared. 21Be attentive to him and heed his voice. Do not rebel against him, for he will not forgive your sin. My authority resides in him.* 22If you heed his voice and carry out all I tell you, I will be an enemy to your enemies and a foe to your foes.

23“My angel will go before you and bring you to the Amorites, Hittites, Perizzites, Canaanites, Hivites and Jebusites; and I will wipe them out.

22, 27: God: or perhaps “the gods,” in the sense of “the judges,” as the parallel with a prince of your people suggests.

23, 14: These three feasts are elsewhere called the Passover, Pentecost and Booths. Cf Ex 34, 18–26; Lv 23; Dt 16.

23, 15: Appear before me: the original expression was “see my face”; so also in several other places, as Ex 23, 17; 34, 23f; Dt 16, 16; 31, 11.

23, 19: Boil a kid in its mother’s milk: this was part of a Canaanite ritual; hence it is forbidden here as a pagan ceremony.

23, 21: My authority resides in him: literally, “My name is within him.”

u Acts 23, 5. v Ex 13, 2; 34, 19; Lv 22, 27; Dt 15, 19. w Lv 7, 24; 17, 15; 22, 8. x 1f: Dt 19, 16ff. y Lv 19, 15. z Dt 22, 1ff. a Dt 16, 19; 27, 25; Sir 20, 28. b Ex 22, 21. c 10f: Lv 25, 3–7. d Ex 20, 8. e 14–17: Ex 34, 18. 22ff; Lv 23; Dt 16, 1–17. f 18f: Ex 34, 25f. g Ex 14, 19; 32, 34; 33, 2.

24 Therefore, you shall not bow down in worship before their gods, nor shall you make anything like them;* rather, you must demolish them and smash their sacred pillars.[h] 25 The LORD, your God, you shall worship; then I will bless your food and drink, and I will remove all sickness from your midst; 26 no woman in your land will be barren or miscarry; and I will give you a full span of life.

27 "I will have the fear of me precede you, so that I will throw into panic every nation you reach.[i] I will make all your enemies turn from you in flight, 28 and ahead of you I will send hornets* to drive the Hivites, Canaanites and Hittites out of your way. 29 But not in one year will I drive them all out before you; else the land will become so desolate that the wild beasts will multiply against you. 30 Instead, I will drive them out little by little before you, until you have grown numerous enough to take possession of the land. 31 [j]I will set your boundaries from the Red Sea to the sea of the Philistines,* and from the desert to the River; all who dwell in this land I will hand over to you to be driven out of your way. 32 You shall not make a covenant with them or their gods. 33 They must not abide in your land, lest they make you sin against me by ensnaring you into worshiping their gods."[k]

CHAPTER 24

Ratification of the Covenant 1 Moses himself was told, "Come up to the LORD, you and Aaron, with Nadab, Abihu, and seventy of the elders of Israel. You shall all worship at some distance, 2 but Moses alone is to come close to the LORD; the others shall not come too near, and the people shall not come up at all with Moses."

3 When Moses came to the people and related all the words and ordinances of the LORD, they all answered with one voice, "We will do everything that the LORD has told us."[l] 4 Moses then wrote down all the words of the LORD and, rising early the next day, he erected at the foot of the mountain an altar and twelve pillars* for the twelve tribes of Israel. 5 Then, having sent certain young men of the Israelites to offer holocausts and sacrifice young bulls as peace offerings to the LORD, 6 Moses took half of the blood and put it in large bowls; the other half he splashed on the altar. 7 Taking the book of the covenant, he read it aloud to the people, who answered, "All that the LORD has said, we will heed and do." 8 Then he took the blood and sprinkled it on the people, saying, "This is the blood of the covenant which the LORD has made with you in accordance with all these words of his."[m]

9 Moses then went up with Aaron, Nadab, Abihu, and seventy elders of Israel, 10 and they beheld the God of Israel. Under his feet there appeared to be sapphire tilework, as clear as the sky itself. 11 Yet he did not smite these chosen Israelites. After gazing on God,* they could still eat and drink.

Moses on the Mountain 12 The LORD said to Moses, "Come up to me on the mountain and, while you are there, I will give you the stone tablets[n] on which I have written the commandments intended for their instruction." 13 So Moses set out with Joshua, his aide, and went up to the mountain of God. 14 The elders, however, had been told by him, "Wait here for us until we return to you. Aaron and Hur are staying with you. If anyone has a complaint, let him refer the matter to them." 15 After Moses had gone up, a cloud covered the mountain. 16 The glory of the LORD settled upon Mount Sinai. The cloud covered it for six days, and on the seventh day he called to Moses from the midst of the cloud.[o]

23, 24: Make anything like them: some render, "act according to their conduct." Sacred pillars: objects of religious veneration at Canaanite sanctuaries.

23, 28: Hornets: some understand this figuratively of various troublesome afflictions; others translate the Hebrew word as "leprosy." Cf Dt 7, 20; Jos 24, 12; Wis 12, 8.

23, 31: The sea of the Philistines: the Mediterranean. The River: the Euphrates. Only in the time of David and Solomon did the territory of Israel come near to reaching such distant borders.

24, 4: Pillars: stone shafts or slabs, erected as symbols of the fact that each of the twelve tribes had entered into this covenant with God; not idolatrous as in Ex 23, 24, although the same Hebrew word is used in both passages. See note on Gn 28, 18.

24, 11: After gazing on God: the ancients thought that the sight of God would bring instantaneous death. Cf Ex 33, 20; Gn 16, 13; 32, 31; Jgs 6, 22f; 13, 22. Eat and drink: partake of the sacrificial meal.

h 23f: Ex 34, 10–16; Nm 33, 51f; Dt 7, 24ff. i 27ff: Dt 2, 25; 7, 20ff. j Gn 15, 18; Dt 11, 24; Jos 1, 4. k 32f: Ex 34, 12–16; Dt 7, 2ff. l Ex 19, 8. m 5–8: Heb 9, 18ff. n Ex 31, 18; 32, 15f; Dt 5, 22. o Sir 45, 4.

17 To the Israelites the glory of the LORD was seen as a consuming fire on the mountaintop.[p] 18 But Moses passed into the midst of the cloud as he went up on the mountain; and there he stayed for forty days and forty nights.[q]

IV: The Dwelling and Its Furnishings

CHAPTER 25

Collection of Materials 1 This is what the LORD then said to Moses:[r] 2 "Tell the Israelites to take up a collection for me. From every man you shall accept the contribution that his heart prompts him to give me. 3 These are the contributions you shall accept from them: gold, silver and bronze;[s] 4 violet, purple and scarlet yarn; fine linen and goat hair; 5 rams' skins dyed red, and tahash* skins; acacia wood; 6 oil for the light; spices for the anointing oil and for the fragrant incense; 7 onyx stones and other gems for mounting on the ephod and the breastpiece.

8 "They shall make a sanctuary for me, that I may dwell in their midst.[t] 9 This Dwelling and all its furnishings you shall make exactly according to the pattern that I will now show you.[u]

Plan of the Ark 10 "You shall make an ark of acacia wood,[v] two and a half cubits long, one and a half cubits wide, and one and a half cubits high. 11 Plate it inside and outside with pure gold, and put a molding of gold around the top of it. 12 Cast four gold rings and fasten them on the four supports of the ark, two rings on one side and two on the opposite side. 13 Then make poles of acacia wood and plate them with gold. 14 These poles you are to put through the rings on the sides of the ark, for carrying it; 15 they must remain in the rings of the ark and never be withdrawn. 16 In the ark you are to put the commandments which I will give you.

17 "You shall then make a propitiatory* of pure gold, two cubits and a half long, and one and a half cubits wide. 18 Make two cherubim* of beaten gold for the two ends of the propitiatory, 19 fastening them so that one cherub springs direct from each end. 20 The cherubim shall have their wings spread out above, covering the propitiatory with them; they shall be turned toward each other, but with their faces looking toward the propitiatory. 21 This propitiatory you shall then place on top of the ark. In the ark itself you are to put the commandments which I will give you. 22 There I will meet you and there, from above the propitiatory, between the two cherubim on the ark of the commandments, I will tell you all the commands that I wish you to give the Israelites.

The Table 23 "You shall also make a table of acacia[w] wood, two cubits long, a cubit wide, and a cubit and a half high. 24 Plate it with pure gold and make a molding of gold around it. 25 Surround it with a frame,* a handbreadth high, with a molding of gold around the frame. 26 You shall also make four rings of gold for it and fasten them at the four corners, one at each leg, 27 on two opposite sides of the frame as holders for the poles to carry the table. 28 These poles for carrying the table you shall make of acacia wood and plate with gold. 29 Of pure gold you shall make its plates* and cups, as well as its pitchers and bowls for pouring libations. 30 On the table you shall always keep showbread set before me.[x]

The Lampstand 31 "You shall make a lampstand of pure beaten gold[y] —its shaft and branches—with its cups and knobs and petals

25, 5: Tahash: perhaps the name of a marine animal, such as the dugong or the porpoise. The Greek and Latin versions took it for the color hyacinth.

25, 17: Propitiatory: this traditional rendering of the Hebrew term, which may mean merely "cover," is derived from its connection with the ceremony of the Day of Atonement whereby God was rendered "propitious." Cf Lv 16, 14ff.

25, 18ff: Cherubim: probably in the form of human-headed winged lions. The cherubim over the ark formed the throne for the invisible Lord. Cf Ps 80, 2. For a more detailed description of the somewhat different cherubim in the temple of Solomon, see 1 Kgs 6, 23–28; 2 Chr 3, 10–13.

25, 25: A frame: probably placed near the bottom of the legs to keep them steady. The golden table of Herod's temple is pictured thus on the Arch of Titus.

25, 29f: The plates held the showbread, that is, the holy bread which was placed upon the table every sabbath as an offering to God, and was later eaten by the priests. The cups held the incense which was strewn upon the bread. Cf Lv 24, 5–9. The libation wine was poured from the pitchers into the bowls. All these vessels were kept on the golden table.

p Ex 19, 18; Heb 12, 18. q Ex 34, 28; Dt 9, 9. r 1–7: Ex 35, 4–9. 20–29. s Ex 35, 4–9. t 8f: Ex 26, 1–30; 36, 8–38. u Acts 7, 44. v 10–22: Ex 37, 1–9; Heb 9, 1–5. w 23–30: Ex 37, 10–16. x Lv 24, 5ff. y 31–40: Ex 37, 17–24.

springing directly from it. 32Six branches are to
extend from the sides of the lampstand, three
branches on one side, and three on the other.
33*On one branch there are to be three cups,
shaped like almond blossoms, each with its knob
and petals; on the opposite branch there are to
be three cups, shaped like almond blossoms,
each with its knob and petals; and so for the six
branches that extend from the lampstand. 34On
the shaft there are to be four cups,* shaped like
almond blossoms, with their knobs and petals,
35including a knob below each of the three pairs
of branches that extend from the lampstand.
36Their knobs and branches shall so spring from
it that the whole will form but a single piece of
pure beaten gold. 37*You shall then make seven
lamps[z] for it and so set up the lamps that they
shed their light on the space in front of the
lampstand. 38These, as well as the trimming
shears and trays,* must be of pure gold. 39Use a
talent of pure gold for the lampstand and all its
appurtenances. 40See that you make them ac-
cording to the pattern shown you on the moun-
tain.[a]

CHAPTER 26

The Tent Cloth 1"The Dwelling itself you shall
make out of sheets* woven of fine linen twined
and of violet, purple and scarlet yarn, with
cherubim embroidered on them.[b] 2The length of
each shall be twenty-eight cubits, and the width
four cubits; all the sheets shall be of the same
size. 3Five of the sheets are to be sewed to-
gether, edge to edge; and the same for the other
five. 4Make loops of violet yarn along the edge of
the end sheet in one set, and the same along the
edge of the end sheet in the other set. 5There are
to be fifty loops along the edge of the end sheet
in the first set, and fifty loops along the edge of
the corresponding sheet in the second set, and
so placed that the loops are directly opposite
each other. 6Then make fifty clasps of gold, with
which to join the two sets of sheets, so that the
Dwelling forms one whole.

7"Also make sheets woven of goat hair, to be
used as a tent covering* over the Dwelling.
8Eleven such sheets are to be made; the length
of each shall be thirty cubits, and the width four
cubits: all eleven sheets shall be of the same size.
9Sew five of the sheets, edge to edge, into one
set, and the other six sheets into another set.
Use the sixth sheet double at the front of the
tent.* 10Make fifty loops along the edge of the
end sheet in one set, and fifty loops along the
edge of the end sheet in the second set. 11Also
make fifty bronze clasps and put them into the
loops, to join the tent into one whole. 12There
will be an extra half sheet of tent covering,
which shall be allowed to hang down over the
rear of the Dwelling. 13Likewise, the sheets of
the tent will have an extra cubit's length to be
left hanging down on either side of the Dwelling
to protect it. 14Over the tent itself you shall
make a covering of rams' skins dyed red, and
above that, a covering of tahash skins.

The Wooden Walls 15[c]"You shall make boards
of acacia wood as walls for the Dwelling. 16The
length of each board is to be ten cubits, and its
width one and a half cubits. 17Each board shall
have two arms* that shall serve to fasten the
boards in line. In this way all the boards of the
Dwelling are to be made. 18Set up the boards of
the Dwelling as follows: twenty boards on the
south side, 19with forty silver pedestals under
the twenty boards, so that there are two pedes-

25, 33: In keeping with the arrangement of the ornaments on the shaft, the three sets of ornaments on each branch were probably so placed that one was at the top and the other two equally spaced along the length of the branch. Knob: the cup-shaped seed capsule at the base of a flower.

25, 34f: Of the four ornaments on the shaft, one was at the top and one was below each of the three sets of side branches.

25, 37: The lamps were probably shaped like small boats, with the wick at one end; the end with the wick was turned toward the front of the lampstand.

25, 38: Trays: small receptacles for the burnt-out wicks.

26, 1: Sheets: strips of tapestry, woven of white linen, the colored threads being used for the cherubim which were embroidered on them. These sheets were stretched across the top of the Dwelling to form a roof, their free ends hanging down inside the boards which formed walls.

26, 7: Tent covering: the cloth made of sheets of goat hair to cover the Dwelling.

26, 9: Half the width of the end strip was folded back at the front of the Dwelling, thus leaving another half-strip to hang down at the rear. Cf v 12.

26, 17: Arms: literally, "hands." According to some, they served as "tongue and groove" to mortise the boards together; according to others, they were pegs at the bottom of the boards and fitted into sockets in the pedestals.

z Lv 24, 2ff; Nm 8, 2. a Heb 8, 5. b 1–14: Ex 36, 8–19. c 15–30: Ex 36, 20–34.

tals under each board, at its two arms; 20 twenty boards on the other side of the Dwelling, the north side, 21 with their forty silver pedestals, two under each board; 22 six boards for the rear of the Dwelling, to the west; 23 and two boards for the corners at the rear of the Dwelling. 24 These two shall be double at the bottom, and likewise double at the top, to the first ring. That is how both boards in the corners are to be made. 25 Thus, there shall be in the rear eight boards, with their sixteen silver pedestals, two pedestals under each board. 26 Also make bars of acacia wood: five for the boards on one side of the Dwelling, 27 five for those on the other side, and five for those at the rear, toward the west. 28 The center bar, at the middle of the boards, shall reach across from end to end. 29 Plate the boards with gold, and make gold rings on them as holders for the bars, which are also to be plated with gold. 30 You shall erect the Dwelling according to the pattern shown you on the mountain.

The Veils 31 "You shall have a veil woven of violet, purple and scarlet yarn,[d] and of fine linen twined, with cherubim embroidered on it.[e] 32 It is to be hung on four gold-plated columns of acacia wood, which shall have hooks* of gold and shall rest on four silver pedestals. 33 Hang the veil from clasps. The ark of the commandments you shall bring inside, behind this veil which divides the holy place from the holy of holies. 34 Set the propitiatory on the ark of the commandments in the holy of holies.

35 "Outside the veil you shall place the table and the lampstand, the latter on the south side of the Dwelling, opposite the table, which is to be put on the north side. 36 For the entrance of the tent make a variegated* curtain of violet, purple and scarlet yarn and of fine linen twined. 37 Make five columns of acacia wood for this curtain; have them plated with gold, with their hooks of gold; and cast five bronze pedestals for them.

CHAPTER 27

The Altar of Holocausts 1 "You shall make an altar[f] of acacia wood, on a square, five cubits long and five cubits wide; it shall be three cubits high. 2 At the four corners there are to be horns, so made that they spring directly from the altar. You shall then plate it with bronze. 3 Make pots for removing the ashes, as well as shovels, basins, forks and fire pans, all of which shall be of bronze. 4 Make a grating* of bronze network for it; this to have four bronze rings, one at each of its four corners. 5 Put it down around the altar, on the ground. This network is to be half as high as the altar. 6 You shall also make poles of acacia wood for the altar, and plate them with bronze. 7 These poles are to be put through the rings, so that they are on either side of the altar when it is carried. 8 Make the altar itself in the form of a hollow* box, just as it was shown you on the mountain.

Court of the Dwelling 9 [g]"You shall also make a court for the Dwelling. On the south side the court shall have hangings a hundred cubits long, woven of fine linen twined, 10 with twenty columns and twenty pedestals of bronze; the hooks and bands on the columns shall be of silver. 11 On the north side there shall be similar hangings, a hundred cubits long, with twenty columns and twenty pedestals of bronze; the hooks and bands on the columns shall be of silver. 12 On the west side, across the width of the court, there shall be hangings, fifty cubits long, with ten columns and ten pedestals. 13 The width of the court on the east side shall be fifty cubits. 14 On one side there shall be hangings to the extent of fifteen cubits, with three columns and three pedestals; 15 on the other side there

26, 32: Hooks: probably placed near the tops of the columns, to hold the rope from which the veils and curtains hung.

26, 36: Variegated: without definite designs such as the cherubim on the inner veil.

27, 4: Grating: it is not clear whether this was flush with the altar or at some small distance from it; in the latter case the space between the altar and the grating would be filled with stones and serve as a platform around the altar, which would otherwise be too high for the priest to reach conveniently.

27, 8: Hollow: probably filled with earth or stones when in use. Cf Ex 20, 24f.

d 2 Chr 3, 14. e 31–37: Ex 36, 35–38. f 1–8: Ex 38, 1–7. g 9–19: Ex 38, 9–20.

shall be hangings to the extent of fifteen cubits, with three columns and three pedestals.

16“At the entrance of the court there shall be a variegated curtain, twenty cubits long, woven of violet, purple and scarlet yarn and of fine linen twined. It shall have four columns and four pedestals.

17“All the columns around the court shall have bands and hooks of silver, and pedestals of bronze. 18The enclosure of the court is to be one hundred cubits long, fifty cubits wide, and five cubits high. Fine linen twined must be used, and the pedestals must be of bronze. 19All the fittings of the Dwelling, whatever be their use, as well as all its tent pegs and all the tent pegs of the court, must be of bronze.

Oil for the Lamps 20“You shall order the Israelites to bring you clear oil of crushed olives, to be used for the light, so that you may keep lamps burning regularly.[h] 21From evening to morning Aaron and his sons shall maintain them before the LORD in the meeting tent, outside the veil which hangs in front of the commandments. This shall be a perpetual ordinance for the Israelites throughout their generations.

CHAPTER 28

The Priestly Vestments 1[i]“From among the Israelites have your brother Aaron, together with his sons Nadab, Abihu, Eleazar and Ithamar, brought to you, that they may be my priests. 2For the glorious adornment of your brother Aaron you shall have sacred vestments made. 3Therefore, to the various expert workmen whom I have endowed with skill, you shall give instructions to make such vestments for Aaron as will set him apart for his sacred service as my priest. 4These are the vestments they shall make: a breastpiece, an ephod, a robe, a brocaded tunic, a miter and a sash. In making these sacred vestments which your brother Aaron and his sons are to wear in serving as my priests, 5they shall use gold, violet, purple and scarlet yarn and fine linen.

The Ephod and Breastpiece 6“The ephod* they shall make of gold thread and of violet, purple and scarlet yarn, embroidered on cloth of fine linen twined.[j] 7It shall have a pair of shoulder straps joined to its two upper ends. 8The embroidered belt on the ephod shall extend out from it and, like it, be made of gold thread, of violet, purple and scarlet yarn, and of fine linen twined.

9“Get two onyx stones and engrave on them the names of the sons of Israel: 10six of their names on one stone, and the other six on the other stone, in the order of their birth. 11As a gem-cutter engraves a seal, so shall you have the two stones engraved with the names of the sons of Israel and then mounted in gold filigree work. 12Set these two stones on the shoulder straps of the ephod as memorial stones of the sons of Israel. Thus Aaron shall bear their names on his shoulders as a reminder before the LORD. 13Make filigree rosettes of gold,[k] 14as well as two chains of pure gold, twisted like cords, and fasten the cordlike chains to the filigree rosettes.

15[l]“The breastpiece* of decision you shall also have made, embroidered like the ephod with gold thread and violet, purple and scarlet yarn on cloth of fine linen twined. 16It is to be square when folded double, a span high and a span wide. 17*On it you shall mount four rows of precious stones: in the first row, a carnelian, a topaz and an emerald; 18in the second row, a garnet, a sapphire and a beryl; 19in the third row, a jacinth, an agate and an amethyst; 20in the fourth row, a chrysolite, an onyx and a jasper. These stones are to be mounted in gold filigree work, 21twelve of them to match the names of the sons of Israel, each stone engraved

28, 6: Ephod: this Hebrew word is retained in the translation because it is the technical term for a peculiar piece of the priestly vestments, the exact nature of which is uncertain. It seems to have been a sort of apron that hung from the shoulders of the priest by shoulder straps (v 7) and was tied around his waist by the loose ends of the attached belt (v 8).

28, 15–30: Breastpiece: in shape like a modern altar burse, it was a pocketlike receptacle for holding the Urim and Thummim (v 30), and formed an integral part of the ephod, to which it was attached by an elaborate system of rings and chains. Both the ephod and its breastpiece were made of brocaded linen.

28, 17–20: The translation of the Hebrew names of some of these gems is quite conjectural.

h 20f: Lv 24, 1–4. i 1–5: Ex 39, 1; Sir 45, 7. j 6–12: Ex 39, 2–7; Sir 45, 8–14. k 13f: Ex 28, 22. 25; 39, 15. 18. l 15–21: Ex 39, 15–21.

like a seal with the name of one of the twelve tribes.

22 "When the chains of pure gold, twisted like cords, have been made for the breastpiece, 23 you shall then make two rings of gold for it and fasten them to the two upper ends of the breastpiece. 24 The gold cords are then to be fastened to the two rings at the upper ends of the breastpiece, 25 the other two ends of the cords being fastened in front to the two filigree rosettes which are attached to the shoulder straps of the ephod. 26 Make two other rings of gold and put them on the two lower ends of the breastpiece, on its edge that faces the ephod. 27 Then make two more rings of gold and fasten them to the bottom of the shoulder straps next to where they join the ephod in front, just above its embroidered belt. 28 Violet ribbons shall bind the rings of the breastpiece to the rings of the ephod, so that the breastpiece will stay right above the embroidered belt of the ephod and not swing loose from it.

29 "Whenever Aaron enters the sanctuary, he will thus bear the names of the sons of Israel on the breastpiece of decision over his heart as a constant reminder before the LORD. 30 In this breastpiece of decision[m] you shall put the Urim and Thummim,* that they may be over Aaron's heart whenever he enters the presence of the LORD. Thus he shall always bear the decisions for the Israelites over his heart in the LORD's presence.

Other Vestments 31 "The robe of the ephod[n] you shall make entirely of violet material. 32 It shall have an opening for the head in the center, and around this opening there shall be a selvage, woven as at the opening of a shirt, to keep it from being torn. 33 All around the hem at the bottom you shall make pomegranates, woven of violet, purple and scarlet yarn and fine linen twined, with gold bells between them; 34 first a gold bell, then a pomegranate, and thus alternating all around the hem of the robe. 35 Aaron shall wear it when ministering, that its tinkling may be heard as he enters and leaves the LORD's presence in the sanctuary; else he will die.

36 "You shall also make a plate of pure gold and engrave on it, as on a seal engraving, "Sacred to the LORD." 37 This plate is to be tied over the miter with a violet ribbon in such a way that it rests on the front of the miter,[o] 38 over Aaron's forehead. Since Aaron bears whatever guilt the Israelites may incur in consecrating any of their sacred gifts, this plate must always be over his forehead, so that they may find favor with the LORD.

39 [p]"The tunic of fine linen shall be brocaded. The miter shall be made of fine linen. The sash shall be of variegated work.

40 "Likewise, for the glorious adornment of Aaron's sons you shall have tunics and sashes and turbans made. 41 With these you shall clothe your brother Aaron and his sons. Anoint and ordain them,* consecrating them as my priests. 42 You must also make linen drawers for them, to cover their naked flesh from their loins to their thighs.[q] 43 Aaron and his sons shall wear them whenever they go into the meeting tent or approach the altar to minister in the sanctuary, lest they incur guilt and die. This shall be a perpetual ordinance for him and for his descendants.

CHAPTER 29

Consecration of the Priests 1 "This is the rite you shall perform in consecrating them as my priests.[r] Procure a young bull and two unblemished rams. 2 With fine wheat flour make unleavened cakes mixed with oil, and unleavened wafers spread with oil, 3 and put them in a basket. Take the basket of them along with the bullock and the two rams. 4 Aaron and his sons

28, 30: Urim and Thummim: both the meaning of these Hebrew words and the exact nature of the objects so designated are uncertain. They were apparently lots of some kind which were drawn or cast by the priest to ascertain God's decision in doubtful matters. Hence, the burse in which they were kept was called "the breastpiece of decision."

28, 41: Ordain them: literally, "fill their hands," a technical expression used solely for the installation of priests. The phrase probably originated in the custom of placing in the priests' hands the instruments or other symbols of the sacerdotal office.

m Lv 8, 8; Sir 45, 11. n 31–35: Ex 39, 20ff; Lv 8, 9; Sir 45, 10. o Ex 39, 31; Lv 8, 9. p 39–43: Ex 39, 27ff. q Ez 44, 18. r 1–8: Lv 8, 1–9.

you shall also bring to the entrance of the meeting tent, and there wash them with water. 5 Take the vestments and clothe Aaron with the tunic, the robe of the ephod, the ephod itself, and the breastpiece, fastening the embroidered belt of the ephod around him. 6 Put the miter on his head, the sacred diadem on the miter. 7 Then take the anointing oil and anoint him with it, pouring it on his head. 8 Bring forward his sons also and clothe them with the tunics, 9 gird them with the sashes, and tie the turbans on them.[s] Thus shall the priesthood be theirs by perpetual law, and thus shall you ordain Aaron and his sons.

Ordination Sacrifices 10 [t]"Now bring forward the bullock in front of the meeting tent. There Aaron and his sons shall lay their hands on its head. 11 Then slaughter the bullock before the LORD, at the entrance of the meeting tent. 12 Take some of its blood and with your finger put it on the horns of the altar. All the rest of the blood you shall pour out at the base of the altar. 13 All the fat that covers its inner organs, as well as the lobe of its liver and its two kidneys, together with the fat that is on them, you shall take and burn on the altar. 14 But the flesh and hide and offal of the bullock you must burn up outside the camp, since this is a sin offering.[u]

15 "Then take one of the rams, and after Aaron and his sons have laid their hands on its head, 16 slaughter it. The blood you shall take and splash on all the sides of the altar. 17 Cut the ram into pieces; its inner organs and shanks you shall first wash, and then put them with the pieces and with the head. 18 The entire ram shall then be burned on the altar, since it is a holocaust, a sweet-smelling oblation to the LORD.

19 "After this take the other ram, and when Aaron and his sons have laid their hands on its head, 20 slaughter it. Some of its blood you shall take and put on the tip of Aaron's right ear and on the tips of his sons' right ears and on the thumbs of their right hands and the great toes of their right feet. Splash the rest of the blood on all the sides of the altar. 21 Then take some of the blood that is on the altar, together with some of the anointing oil, and sprinkle this on Aaron and his vestments, as well as on his sons and their vestments, that his sons and their vestments may be sacred.

22 "Now, from this ram you shall take its fat: its fatty tail,* the fat that covers its inner organs, the lobe of its liver, its two kidneys with the fat that is on them, and its right thigh, since this is the ordination ram; 23 then, out of the basket of unleavened food that you have set before the LORD, you shall take one of the loaves of bread, one of the cakes made with oil, and one of the wafers. 24 All these things you shall put into the hands of Aaron and his sons, so that they may wave them as a wave offering* before the LORD. 25 After you have received them back from their hands, you shall burn them on top of the holocaust on the altar as a sweet-smelling oblation to the LORD. 26 Finally, take the breast of Aaron's ordination ram and wave it as a wave offering before the LORD; this is to be your own portion.

27 *"Thus shall you set aside the breast of whatever wave offering is waved,[v] as well as the thigh of whatever raised offering is raised up, whether this be the ordination ram or anything else belonging to Aaron or to his sons. 28 Such things are due to Aaron and his sons from the Israelites by a perpetual ordinance as a contribution. From their peace offerings, too, the Israelites shall make a contribution, their contribution to the LORD.

29 "The sacred vestments[w] of Aaron shall be passed down to his descendants, that in them they may be anointed and ordained. 30 The descendant who succeeds him as priest and who is to enter the meeting tent to minister in the

29, 22: Fatty tail: the thick layer of fat surrounding the tails of sheep and rams bred in Palestine even today. It is regarded as a choice food. Cf Lv 3, 9.

29, 24–26: Wave offering: the portions of a peace offering, breast and right thigh, which the officiating priest moved to and fro (waved) in the presence of the Lord. They were reserved for Aaron and his sons.

29, 27–30: These verses are a parenthetical interruption of the ordination ritual; v 31 belongs logically immediately after v 26.

s Lv 8, 13. t 10–26: Lv 8, 14–30. u Heb 13, 11. v 27f: Lv 7, 31–34; 10, 14f; Nm 18, 18f; Dt 18, 3. w Nm 20, 26. 28.

sanctuary shall be clothed with them for seven days.

31 [x]"You shall take the flesh of the ordination ram and boil it in a holy place. 32 At the entrance of the meeting tent Aaron and his sons shall eat the flesh of the ram and the bread that is in the basket. 33 They themselves are to eat of these things by which atonement was made at their ordination and consecration; but no layman may eat of them, since they are sacred. 34 If some of the flesh of the ordination sacrifice or some of the bread remains over on the next day, this remnant must be burned up; it is not to be eaten, since it is sacred. 35 Carry out all these orders in regard to Aaron and his sons just as I have given them to you.[y]

"Seven days you shall spend in ordaining them, 36 [z]sacrificing a bullock each day as a sin offering, to make atonement. Thus also shall you purge the altar* in making atonement for it; you shall anoint it in order to consecrate it. 37 Seven days you shall spend in making atonement for the altar and in consecrating it. Then the altar will be most sacred, and whatever touches it will become sacred.

38 *"Now, this is what you shall offer on the altar: two yearling lambs[a] as the sacrifice established for each day; 39 one lamb in the morning and the other lamb at the evening twilight. 40 With the first lamb there shall be a tenth of an ephah of fine flour mixed with a fourth of a hin of oil of crushed olives and, as its libation, a fourth of a hin of wine. 41 The other lamb you shall offer at the evening twilight, with the same cereal offering and libation as in the morning. You shall offer this as a sweet-smelling oblation to the LORD. 42 Throughout your generations this established holocaust shall be offered before the LORD at the entrance of the meeting tent, where I will meet you and speak to you.

43 "There, at the altar, I will meet the Israelites; hence, it will be made sacred by my glory.[b] 44 Thus I will consecrate the meeting tent and the altar, just as I also consecrate Aaron and his sons to be my priests. 45 I will dwell in the midst of the Israelites and will be their God. 46 They shall know that I, the LORD, am their God who brought them out of the land of Egypt, so that I, the LORD, their God, might dwell among them.

CHAPTER 30

Altar of Incense 1 "For burning incense you shall make an altar of acacia wood,[c] 2 with a square surface, a cubit long, a cubit wide, and two cubits high, with horns that spring directly from it. 3 Its grate on top, its walls on all four sides, and its horns you shall plate with pure gold. Put a gold molding around it. 4 Underneath the molding you shall put gold rings, two on one side and two on the opposite side, as holders for the poles used in carrying it. 5 Make the poles, too, of acacia wood and plate them with gold. 6 This altar you are to place in front of the veil that hangs before the ark of the commandments where I will meet you.[d]

7 "On it Aaron shall burn fragrant incense. Morning after morning, when he prepares the lamps, 8 and again in the evening twilight, when he lights the lamps, he shall burn incense. Throughout your generations this shall be the established incense offering before the LORD. 9 On this altar you shall not offer up any profane incense, or any holocaust or cereal offering; nor shall you pour out a libation upon it. 10 Once a year Aaron shall perform the atonement rite on its horns.[e] Throughout your generations this atonement is to be made once a year with the blood of the atoning sin offering. This altar is most sacred to the LORD."

Census Tax 11 The LORD also said to Moses, 12 "When you take a census[f] of the Israelites who are to be registered, each one, as he is enrolled, shall give the LORD a forfeit for his life, so that no plague may come upon them for being registered. 13 Everyone who enters the registered group must pay a half-shekel, according to the

29, 36f: Purge the altar: the construction of an altar by profane hands rendered it impure. The anointing and consecration of the altar purified it and made it sacred.

29, 38–42: A parenthesis inserted into the rubrics for consecrating the altar; v 43 belongs directly after v 37.

x 31–34: Lv 8, 31f. y Lv 8, 36. z 36f: Lv 8, 33ff. a 38–42: Nm 28, 3–8. b Ex 25, 22. c 1–5; Ex 37, 25–28. d Ex 40, 26. e Lv 16, 18. f Nm 1, 2f; 26, 2.

standard of the sanctuary shekel, twenty gerahs to the shekel. This payment of a half-shekel is a contribution to the LORD.[g] 14 Everyone of twenty years or more who enters the registered group must give this contribution to the LORD. 15 The rich need not give more, nor shall the poor give less, than a half-shekel in this contribution to the LORD to pay the forfeit for their lives. 16 [h]When you receive this forfeit money from the Israelites, you shall donate it to the service of the meeting tent, that there it may be the Israelites' reminder, before the LORD, of the forfeit paid for their lives."

The Laver 17 The LORD said to Moses, 18 "For ablutions you shall make a bronze laver with a bronze base. Place it between the meeting tent and the altar, and put water in it.[i] 19 Aaron and his sons shall use it in washing their hands and feet.[j] 20 When they are about to enter the meeting tent, they must wash with water, lest they die. Likewise when they approach the altar in their ministry, to offer an oblation to the LORD, 21 they must wash their hands and feet, lest they die. This shall be a perpetual ordinance for him and his descendants throughout their generations."

The Anointing Oil 22 The LORD said to Moses, 23 "Take the finest spices: five hundred shekels of free-flowing myrrh; half that amount, that is, two hundred and fifty shekels, of fragrant cinnamon; two hundred and fifty shekels of fragrant cane; 24 five hundred shekels of cassia—all according to the standard of the sanctuary shekel; together with a hin of olive oil; 25 and blend them into sacred anointing oil,[k] perfumed ointment expertly prepared. 26 [l]With this sacred anointing oil you shall anoint the meeting tent and the ark of the commandments, 27 the table and all its appurtenances, the lampstand and its appurtenances, the altar of incense 28 and the altar of holocausts with all its appurtenances, and the laver with its base. 29 When you have consecrated them, they shall be most sacred; whatever touches them shall be sacred. 30 Aaron and his sons you shall also anoint and consecrate as my priests.[m] 31 To the Israelites you shall say: As sacred anointing oil this shall belong to me throughout your generations. 32 It may not be used in any ordinary anointing of the body, nor may you make any other oil of a like mixture. It is sacred, and shall be treated as sacred by you. 33 Whoever prepares a perfume like this, or whoever puts any of this on a layman, shall be cut off from his kinsmen."

The Incense 34 [n]The LORD told Moses, "Take these aromatic substances: storax and onycha and galbanum, these and pure frankincense in equal parts; 35 and blend them into incense. This fragrant powder, expertly prepared, is to be salted and so kept pure and sacred. 36 Grind some of it into fine dust and put this before the commandments in the meeting tent where I will meet you. This incense shall be treated as most sacred by you. 37 You may not make incense of a like mixture for yourselves; you must treat it as sacred to the LORD. 38 Whoever makes an incense like this for his own enjoyment of its fragrance, shall be cut off from his kinsmen."

CHAPTER 31

Choice of Artisans 1 [o]The LORD said to Moses, 2 "See, I have chosen Bezalel, son of Uri, son of Hur, of the tribe of Judah, 3 and I have filled him with a divine spirit of skill and understanding and knowledge in every craft: 4 in the production of embroidery, in making things of gold, silver or bronze, 5 in cutting and mounting precious stones, in carving wood, and in every other craft. 6 As his assistant I have appointed Oholiab, son of Ahisamach, of the tribe of Dan. I have also endowed all the experts with the necessary skill to make all the things I have ordered you to make: 7 [p]the meeting tent, the ark of the commandments with the propitiatory on top of it, all the furnishings of the tent, 8 the table with its appurtenances, the pure gold lampstand with all its appurtenances, the altar of incense, 9 the altar of holocausts with all its appurtenances, the

g Mt 17, 24–27. h Ex 38, 25. i Ex 38, 8; 40, 7. 30. j 19ff: Ex 40, 31f. k Ex 37, 29. l 26–29: Ex 40, 9ff; Lv 8, 10; Nm 7, 1. m Ex 29, 7; Lv 8, 12. n 34ff: Ex 25, 6; 37, 29. o 1–6: Ex 35, 30–35. p 7–11: Ex 35, 10–19.

laver with its base, 10the service cloths,* the sacred vestments for Aaron the priest, the vestments for his sons in their ministry, 11the anointing oil, and the fragrant incense for the sanctuary. All these things they shall make just as I have commanded you."

Sabbath Laws 12[q]The LORD said to Moses, 13"You must also tell the Israelites: Take care to keep my sabbaths, for that is to be the token between you and me throughout the generations, to show that it is I, the LORD, who make you holy. 14Therefore, you must keep the sabbath as something sacred. Whoever desecrates it shall be put to death. If anyone does work on that day, he must be rooted out of his people. 15Six days there are for doing work, but the seventh day is the sabbath of complete rest, sacred to the LORD. Anyone who does work on the sabbath day shall be put to death. 16So shall the Israelites observe the sabbath, keeping it throughout their generations as a perpetual covenant. 17Between me and the Israelites it is to be an everlasting token; for in six days the LORD made the heavens and the earth, but on the seventh day he rested at his ease."

18When the LORD had finished speaking to Moses on Mount Sinai, he gave him the two tablets of the commandments, the stone tablets inscribed by God's own finger.[r]

CHAPTER 32

The Golden Calf 1When the people became aware of Moses' delay in coming down from the mountain, they gathered around Aaron and said to him, "Come, make us a god who will be our leader; as for the man Moses who brought us out of the land of Egypt, we do not know what has happened to him."[s] 2Aaron replied, "Have your wives and sons and daughters take off the golden earrings they are wearing, and bring them to me." 3So all the people took off their earrings and brought them to Aaron, 4who accepted their offering, and fashioning this gold with a graving tool, made a molten calf. Then they cried out, "This is your God, O Israel, who brought you out of the land of Egypt."[t] 5On seeing this, Aaron built an altar before the calf and proclaimed, "Tomorrow is a feast of the LORD."* 6Early the next day the people offered holocausts and brought peace offerings. Then they sat down to eat and drink, and rose up to revel.[u]

7With that, the LORD said to Moses, "Go down at once to your people, whom you brought out of the land of Egypt, for they have become depraved. 8[v]They have soon turned aside from the way I pointed out to them, making for themselves a molten calf and worshiping it, sacrificing to it and crying out, 'This is your God, O Israel, who brought you out of the land of Egypt!' 9I see how stiff-necked this people is,"[w] continued the LORD to Moses. 10"Let me alone, then, that my wrath may blaze up against them to consume them. Then I will make of you a great nation."

11But Moses implored the LORD, his God, saying,[x] "Why, O LORD, should your wrath blaze up against your own people, whom you brought out of the land of Egypt with such great power and with so strong a hand? 12Why should the Egyptians say, 'With evil intent he brought them out, that he might kill them in the mountains and exterminate them from the face of the earth'? Let your blazing wrath die down; relent in punishing your people. 13Remember your servants Abraham, Isaac and Israel, and how you swore to them by your own self, saying,[y] 'I will make your descendants as numerous as the stars in the sky; and all this land that I promised, I will give your descendants as their perpetual heritage.' " 14So the LORD relented in the punishment he had threatened to inflict on his people.

15Moses then turned and came down the mountain with the two tablets of the command-

31, 10: The service cloths: so the Greek. They were perhaps the colored cloths mentioned in Nm 4, 4–15.

32, 5: The calf . . . a feast of the Lord: from this it is clear that the golden calf was intended as an image, not of a false god, but of the Lord himself, his strength being symbolized by the strength of a young bull. The Israelites, however, had been forbidden to represent the Lord under any visible form. Cf Ex 20, 4.

q 12–17: Ex 20, 8–11; 35, 1–3. r Ex 24, 12; 32, 15f; Dt 5, 22. s Ex 32, 23; Acts 7, 40. t Ex 32, 8; 1 Kgs 12, 28. u 1 Cor 10, 7. v 7f: Dt 9, 12. 16. w 9f: Dt 9, 13; Ps 106, 23. x 11f: Nm 14, 13ff; Dt 9, 28. y Gn 22, 16f.

ments in his hands,[z] tablets that were written on
both sides, front and back; [16]tablets that were
made by God, having inscriptions on them that
were engraved by God himself.[a] [17]Now, when
Joshua heard the noise of the people shouting,
he said to Moses, "That sounds like a battle in
the camp." [18]But Moses answered, "It does not
sound like cries of victory, nor does it sound like
cries of defeat; the sounds that I hear are cries of
revelry." [19]As he drew near the camp, he saw
the calf and the dancing. With that, Moses'
wrath flared up, so that he threw the tablets
down and broke them on the base of the
mountain.[b] [20]Taking the calf they had made, he
fused it in the fire and then ground it down to
powder, which he scattered on the water* and
made the Israelites drink.[c]

[21]Moses asked Aaron, "What did this people
ever do to you that you should lead them into so
grave a sin?" Aaron replied, "Let not my lord be
angry. [22]You know well enough how prone the
people are to evil. [23]They said to me, 'Make us a
god to be our leader; as for the man Moses who
brought us out of the land of Egypt, we do not
know what has happened to him.' [24]So I told
them, 'Let anyone who has gold jewelry take it
off.' They gave it to me, and I threw it into the
fire, and this calf came out."

[25]When Moses realized that, to the scornful
joy of their foes, Aaron had let the people run
wild, [26]he stood at the gate of the camp and
cried, "Whoever is for the LORD, let him come to
me!" All the Levites[d] then rallied to him, [27]and
he told them, "Thus says the LORD, the God of
Israel: Put your sword on your hip, every one of
you! Now go up and down the camp, from gate
to gate, and slay your own kinsmen,* your
friends and neighbors!" [28]The Levites carried
out the command of Moses, and that day there
fell about three thousand of the people. [29]Then
Moses said, "Today you have been dedicated to
the LORD,* for you were against your own sons
and kinsmen, to bring a blessing upon yourselves
this day."

The Atonement [30]On the next day Moses said
to the people,[e] "You have committed a grave
sin. I will go up to the LORD, then; perhaps I may
be able to make atonement for your sin." [31]So
Moses went back to the LORD and said, "Ah, this
people has indeed committed a grave sin in
making a god of gold for themselves! [32]If you
would only forgive their sin! If you will not, then
strike me out of the book that you have writ-
ten."* [33]The LORD answered, "Him only who
has sinned against me will I strike out of my
book. [34]Now, go and lead the people whither I
have told you. My angel will go before you.
When it is time for me to punish, I will punish
them for their sin."

[35]Thus the LORD smote the people for having
had Aaron make the calf for them.

CHAPTER 33

[1]The LORD told Moses, "You and the people
whom you have brought up from the land of
Egypt, are to go up from here to the land which I
swore to Abraham, Isaac and Jacob I would give
to their descendants.[f] [2]Driving out the Canaan-
ites, Amorites, Hittites, Perizzites, Hivites and
Jebusites, I will send an angel before you[g] [3]to
the land flowing with milk and honey. But I
myself will not go up in your company, because
you are a stiff-necked people; otherwise I might
exterminate you on the way." [4]When the people
heard this bad news, they went into mourning,
and no one wore his ornaments.

[5]The LORD said to Moses, "Tell the Israelites:
You are a stiff-necked people. Were I to go up in
your company even for a moment, I would
exterminate you. Take off your ornaments, there-
fore; I will then see what I am to do with you."

32, 20: The water: the stream that flowed down Mount Sinai. Cf Dt 9, 21.

32, 27: Slay your own kinsmen: those who were especially guilty of the idolatry.

32, 29: Dedicated to the Lord: because of their zeal for the true worship of the Lord, the Levites were chosen to be special ministers of the ritual service. However, the meaning of the Hebrew here is somewhat disputed.

32, 32: The book that you have written: the list of God's intimate friends. In a similar sense St. Paul wished to be anathema from Christ for the sake of his brethren. Cf Rom 9, 3.

z Dt 9, 15. a Ex 31, 18. b Dt 9, 16f. c Dt 9, 21. d 26–29: Dt 33, 8f. e 30–34: Dt 9, 18ff. f Gn 12, 7. g Ex 23, 23.

6So, from Mount Horeb onward, the Israelites laid aside their ornaments.

Moses' Intimacy with God 7The tent,[h] which was called the meeting tent,* Moses used to pitch at some distance away, outside the camp. Anyone who wished to consult the LORD would go to this meeting tent outside the camp. 8Whenever Moses went out to the tent, the people would all rise and stand at the entrance of their own tents, watching Moses until he entered the tent. 9As Moses entered the tent, the column of cloud would come down and stand at its entrance while the LORD spoke with Moses. 10On seeing the column of cloud stand at the entrance of the tent, all the people would rise and worship at the entrance of their own tents. 11The LORD used to speak to Moses face to face,[i] as one man speaks to another. Moses would then return to the camp, but his young assistant, Joshua, son of Nun, would not move out of the tent.

12Moses said to the LORD, "You, indeed, are telling me to lead this people on;[j] but you have not let me know whom you will send with me. Yet you have said, 'You are my intimate friend,' and also, 'You have found favor with me.' 13Now, if I have found favor with you, do let me know your ways so that, in knowing you, I may continue to find favor with you. Then, too, this nation is, after all, your own people." 14"I myself,"* the LORD answered, "will go along, to give you rest." 15Moses replied, "If you are not going yourself, do not make us go up from here. 16For how can it be known that we, your people and I, have found favor with you, except by your going with us? Then we, your people and I, will be singled out from every other people on the earth." 17The LORD said to Moses, "This request, too, which you have just made, I will carry out, because you have found favor with me and you are my intimate friend."

18Then Moses said, "Do let me see your glory!" 19He answered, "I will make all my beauty pass before you, and in your presence I will pronounce my name, 'LORD'; I who show favors to whom I will, I who grant mercy to whom I will.[k] 20But my face you cannot see,[l] for no man sees me and still lives. 21Here," continued the LORD, "is a place near me where you shall station yourself on the rock. 22When my glory passes I will set you in the hollow of the rock and will cover you with my hand until I have passed by. 23Then I will remove my hand, so that you may see my back;* but my face is not to be seen."

CHAPTER 34

Renewal of the Tablets 1The LORD said to Moses, "Cut two stone tablets like the former,[m] that I may write on them the commandments which were on the former tablets that you broke. 2Get ready for tomorrow morning, when you are to go up Mount Sinai and there present yourself to me on the top of the mountain. 3No one shall come up with you, and no one is even to be seen on any part of the mountain;[n] even the flocks and the herds are not to go grazing toward this mountain." 4Moses then cut two stone tablets like the former, and early the next morning he went up Mount Sinai as the LORD had commanded him, taking along the two stone tablets.

5Having come down in a cloud, the LORD stood with him there and proclaimed his name, "LORD." 6Thus the LORD passed before him and cried out, "The LORD, the LORD, a merciful and gracious God, slow to anger and rich in kindness and fidelity, 7continuing his kindness for a thousand generations, and forgiving wickedness and crime and sin; yet not declaring the guilty guiltless, but punishing children and grandchildren to the third and fourth generation for their

33, 7–11: The meeting tent is mentioned here by anticipation; its actual construction is described in the following chapters.

33, 14: I myself: literally, "my face," that is, "my presence." To give you rest: in the Promised Land; some understand, "to put your mind at rest"; others, by a slight emendation in the text, render, "to lead you."

33, 23: You may see my back: man can see God's glory as reflected in creation, but his "face," that is, God as he is in himself, mortal man cannot behold. Cf 1 Cor 13, 12.

h Ex 29, 42f. i Nm 12, 8; Dt 34, 10; Sir 45, 4–6. j Ex 32, 34. k Rom 9, 15. l Jn 1, 18; 1 Tm 6, 16. m Dt 10, 1f. n Ex 19, 12f. 21.

fathers' wickedness!"[o] 8 Moses at once bowed down to the ground in worship. 9 Then he said, "If I find favor with you, O LORD, do come along in our company. This is indeed a stiff-necked people; yet pardon our wickedness and sins, and receive us as your own."

Religious Laws 10 "Here, then," said the LORD, "is the covenant I will make. Before the eyes of all your people I will work such marvels as have never been wrought in any nation anywhere on earth, so that this people among whom you live may see how awe-inspiring are the deeds which I, the LORD, will do at your side. 11 But you, on your part, must keep the commandments I am giving you today.[p]

"I will drive out before you the Amorites, Canaanites, Hittites, Perizzites, Hivites, and Jebusites. 12 [q]Take care, therefore, not to make a covenant with these inhabitants of the land that you are to enter; else they will become a snare among you. 13 Tear down their altars; smash their sacred pillars, and cut down their sacred poles.* 14 You shall not worship any other god, for the LORD is 'the Jealous One';* a jealous God is he. 15 Do not make a covenant with the inhabitants of that land; else, when they render their wanton worship to their gods and sacrifice to them, one of them may invite you and you may partake of his sacrifice. 16 Neither shall you take their daughters as wives for your sons; otherwise, when their daughters render their wanton worship to their gods, they will make your sons do the same.

17 "You shall not make for yourselves molten gods.[r]

18 "You shall keep the feast of Unleavened Bread.[s] For seven days at the prescribed time in the month of Abib you are to eat unleavened bread, as I commanded you; for in the month of Abib you came out of Egypt.

19 "To me belongs every first-born male that opens the womb among all your livestock, whether in the herd or in the flock.[t] 20 The firstling of an ass you shall redeem with one of the flock; if you do not redeem it, you must break its neck. The first-born among your sons you shall redeem.

"No one shall appear before me empty-handed.

21 "For six days you may work,[u] but on the seventh day you shall rest; on that day you must rest even during the seasons of plowing and harvesting.

22 [v]"You shall keep the feast of Weeks* with the first of the wheat harvest; likewise, the feast at the fruit harvest at the close of the year. 23 Three times a year all your men shall appear before the Lord, the LORD God of Israel. 24 Since I will drive out the nations before you to give you a large territory, there will be no one to covet your land when you go up three times a year to appear before the LORD, your God.

25 "You shall not offer me the blood of sacrifice with leavened bread, nor shall the sacrifice of the Passover feast be kept overnight for the next day.

26 "The choicest first fruits of your soil you shall bring to the house of the LORD, your God.

"You shall not boil a kid in its mother's milk."[w]

Radiance of Moses' Face 27 Then the LORD said to Moses, "Write down these words, for in accordance with them I have made a covenant with you and with Israel." 28 So Moses stayed there with the LORD for forty days and forty nights,[x] without eating any food or drinking any water, and he wrote on the tablets the words of the covenant, the ten commandments.

29 As Moses came down from Mount Sinai with the two tablets of the commandments in his hands, he did not know that the skin of his face had become radiant while he conversed

34, 13: Sacred poles: "Ashera" was the name of a Canaanite goddess. In her honor wooden poles (asherot) were erected, just as stone pillars (massebot) were erected in honor of the god Baal. Both were placed near the altar in a Canaanite shrine.

34, 14: The Lord is "the Jealous One": see note on Ex 20, 5. Some, by a slight emendation, render, "The LORD is jealous for his name." Cf Ez 39, 25.

34, 22: Feast of Weeks: the festival of thanksgiving for the harvest, celebrated seven weeks or fifty days after the beginning of the harvest. It was also called Pentecost (fiftieth) and coincided with the giving of the law on Mount Sinai, fifty days after the offering of the first fruits; cf Lv 23 10f; Dt 16, 9.

o 6f: Ex 20, 5f; Nm 14, 18; Dt 5, 9f; Jer 32, 18. p Ex 13, 5; 33, 2. q 12–16: Ex 23, 32f; Dt 7, 1–5; 12, 2f. r Lv 19, 4; 5, 8f. s Ex 12, 15ff; 13, 3f. t 19f: Ex 13, 2. 12f; 23, 15. u Ex 20, 9f. v 22f: Ex 23, 16f; Dt 16, 10. 13. 16. w 25f: Ex 23, 18f. x Ex 24, 18; Dt 9, 9. 18; 10, 2. 4.

with the LORD. 30 When Aaron, then, and the other Israelites saw Moses and noticed how radiant the skin of his face had become, they were afraid to come near him. 31 Only after Moses called to them did Aaron and all the rulers of the community come back to him. Moses then spoke to them. 32 Later on, all the Israelites came up to him, and he enjoined on them all that the LORD had told him on Mount Sinai. 33 When he finished speaking with them, he put a veil over his face.* 34 Whenever Moses entered the presence of the LORD to converse with him, he removed the veil until he came out again.[y] On coming out, he would tell the Israelites all that had been commanded. 35 Then the Israelites would see that the skin of Moses' face was radiant; so he would again put the veil over his face until he went in to converse with the LORD.

CHAPTER 35

Sabbath Regulations 1 Moses assembled the whole Israelite community and said to them,[z] "This is what the LORD has commanded to be done. 2 On six days work may be done, but the seventh day shall be sacred to you as the sabbath of complete rest to the LORD. Anyone who does work on that day shall be put to death. 3 You shall not even light a fire in any of your dwellings on the sabbath day."

Collection of Materials 4 Moses told the whole Israelite community, "This is what the LORD has commanded: 5 [a]Take up among you a collection for the LORD. Everyone, as his heart prompts him, shall bring, as a contribution to the LORD, gold, silver and bronze; 6 violet, purple and scarlet yarn; fine linen and goat hair; 7 rams' skins dyed red, and tahash skins; acacia wood; 8 oil for the light; spices for the anointing oil and for the fragrant incense; 9 onyx stones and other gems for mounting on the ephod and on the breastpiece.

Call for Artisans 10 [b]"Let every expert among you come and make all that the LORD has commanded: 11 the Dwelling, with its tent, its covering, its clasps, its boards, its bars, its columns and its pedestals; 12 the ark, with its poles, the propitiatory, and the curtain veil; 13 the table, with its poles and all its appurtenances, and the showbread; 14 the lampstand, with its appurtenances, the lamps, and the oil for the light; 15 the altar of incense, with its poles; the anointing oil, and the fragrant incense; the entrance curtain for the entrance of the Dwelling; 16 the altar of holocausts, with its bronze grating, its poles, and all its appurtenances; the laver, with its base; 17 the hangings of the court, with their columns and pedestals; the curtain for the entrance of the court; 18 the tent pegs for the Dwelling and for the court, with their ropes; 19 the service cloths for use in the sanctuary; the sacred vestments for Aaron, the priest, and the vestments worn by his sons in their ministry."

The Contribution 20 When the whole Israelite community left Moses' presence, 21 everyone, as his heart suggested and his spirit prompted, brought a contribution to the LORD for the construction of the meeting tent, for all its services, and for the sacred vestments. 22 Both the men and the women, all as their hearts prompted them, brought brooches, earrings, rings, necklaces and various other gold articles.[c] Everyone who could presented an offering of gold to the LORD. 23 Everyone who happened to have violet, purple or scarlet yarn, fine linen or goat hair, rams' skins dyed red or tahash skins, brought them. 24 Whoever could make a contribution of silver or bronze offered it to the LORD; and everyone who happened to have acacia wood for any part of the work, brought it. 25 All the women who were expert spinners brought hand-spun violet, purple and scarlet yarn and fine linen thread. 26 All the women who possessed the skill, spun goat hair. 27 The princes brought onyx stones and other gems for mounting on the ephod and on the breastpiece; 28 as well as spices, and oil for the light, anointing oil,

34, 33: He put a veil over his face: St. Paul sees in this a symbol of the failure of the Jews to recognize Jesus as the promised Messiah. The true spiritual meaning of the writings of Moses and the prophets is still veiled from the unbelieving Jews. Cf 2 Cor 3, 7–18.

y 33f: 2 Cor 3, 13. 16. z 1–3: Ex 31, 13–17. a 5–9: Ex 25, 2–7. b 10–19: Ex 31, 6–11. c 22–28: Ex 25, 3–7.

and fragrant incense. 29 Every Israelite man and woman brought to the LORD such voluntary offerings as they thought best, for the various kinds of work which the LORD had commanded Moses to have done.

The Artisans 30 Moses said to the Israelites,[d] "See, the LORD has chosen Bezalel, son of Uri, son of Hur, of the tribe of Judah, 31 and has filled him with a divine spirit of skill and understanding and knowledge in every craft: 32 in the production of embroidery, in making things of gold, silver or bronze, 33 in cutting and mounting precious stones, in carving wood, and in every other craft. 34 He has also given both him and Oholiab, son of Ahisamach, of the tribe of Dan, the ability to teach others. 35 He has endowed them with skill to execute all types of work: engraving, embroidering, the making of variegated cloth of violet, purple and scarlet yarn and fine linen thread, weaving, and all other arts and crafts.

CHAPTER 36

1 "Bezalel, therefore, will set to work with Oholiab and with all the experts whom the LORD has endowed with skill and understanding in knowing how to execute all the work for the service of the sanctuary, just as the LORD has commanded."[e]

2 Moses then called Bezalel and Oholiab and all the other experts whom the LORD had endowed with skill, men whose hearts moved them to come and take part in the work. 3 They received from Moses all the contributions which the Israelites had brought for establishing the service of the sanctuary. Still, morning after morning the people continued to bring their voluntary offerings to Moses. 4 Thereupon the experts who were executing the various kinds of work for the sanctuary, all left the work they were doing, 5 and told Moses, "The people are bringing much more than is needed to carry out the work which the LORD has commanded us to do." 6 Moses, therefore, ordered a proclamation to be made throughout the camp: "Let neither man nor woman make any more contributions for the sanctuary." So the people stopped bringing their offerings; 7 there was already enough at hand, in fact, more than enough, to complete the work to be done.

The Tent Cloth and Coverings 8 [f]The various experts who were executing the work, made the Dwelling with its ten sheets woven of fine linen twined, having cherubim embroidered on them with violet, purple and scarlet yarn. 9 The length of each sheet was twenty-eight cubits, and the width four cubits; all the sheets were of the same size. 10 Five of the sheets were sewed together, edge to edge; and the same for the other five. 11 Loops of violet yarn were made along the edge of the end sheet in the first set, and the same along the edge of the end sheet in the second set. 12 Fifty loops were thus put on one inner sheet, and fifty loops on the inner sheet in the other set, with the loops directly opposite each other. 13 Then fifty clasps of gold were made, with which the sheets were joined so that the Dwelling formed one whole.

14 Sheets of goat hair were also woven as a tent over the Dwelling. Eleven such sheets were made. 15 The length of each sheet was thirty cubits and the width four cubits; all eleven sheets were of the same size. 16 Five of these sheets were sewed edge to edge into one set; and the other six sheets into another set. 17 Fifty loops were made along the edge of the end sheet in one set, and fifty loops along the edge of the corresponding sheet in the other set. 18 Fifty bronze clasps were made with which the tent was joined so that it formed one whole. 19 A covering for the tent was made of rams' skins dyed red, and above that, a covering of tahash skins.

The Boards 20 [g]Boards of acacia wood were made as walls for the Dwelling. 21 The length of each board was ten cubits, and the width one and a half cubits. 22 Each board had two arms, fastening them in line. In this way all the boards of the Dwelling were made. 23 They were set up as follows: twenty boards on the south side, 24 with forty silver pedestals under the twenty boards, so that there were two pedestals under

d 30–35; Ex 31, 1–6. e 1f: Ex 31, 1. 6. f 8–19: Ex 26, 1–14. g 20–34: Ex 26, 15–29.

each board, at its two arms; 25 twenty boards on the other side of the Dwelling, the north side, 26 with their forty silver pedestals, two under each board; 27 six boards at the rear of the Dwelling, to the west; 28 and two boards at the corners in the rear of the Dwelling. 29 These were double at the bottom, and likewise double at the top, to the first ring. That is how both boards in the corners were made. 30 Thus, there were in the rear eight boards, with their sixteen silver pedestals, two pedestals under each board. 31 Bars of acacia wood were also made, five for the boards on one side of the Dwelling, 32 five for those on the other side, and five for those at the rear, to the west. 33 The center bar, at the middle of the boards, was made to reach across from end to end. 34 The boards were plated with gold, and gold rings were made on them as holders for the bars, which were also plated with gold.

The Veil 35 [h]The veil was woven of violet, purple and scarlet yarn, and of fine linen twined, with cherubim embroidered on it. 36 Four gold-plated columns of acacia wood, with gold hooks, were made for it, and four silver pedestals were cast for them.

37 The curtain for the entrance of the tent was made of violet, purple and scarlet yarn, and of fine linen twined, woven in a variegated manner. 38 Its five columns, with their hooks as well as their capitals and bands, were plated with gold; their five pedestals were of bronze.

CHAPTER 37

The Ark 1 Bezalel made the ark of acacia wood, two and a half cubits long, one and a half cubits wide, and one and a half cubits high. 2 The inside and outside were plated with gold, and a molding of gold was put around it. 3 Four gold rings were cast and put on its four supports, two rings for one side and two for the opposite side. 4 Poles of acacia wood were made and plated with gold; 5 these were put through the rings on the sides of the ark, for carrying it.

6 The propitiatory was made of pure gold, two and a half cubits long and one and a half cubits wide. 7 Two cherubim of beaten gold were made for the two ends of the propitiatory, 8 one cherub fastened at one end, the other at the other end, springing directly from the propitiatory at its two ends. 9 The cherubim had their wings spread out above, covering the propitiatory with them. They were turned toward each other, but with their faces looking toward the propitiatory.[i]

The Table 10 [j]The table was made of acacia wood, two cubits long, one cubit wide, and one and a half cubits high. 11 It was plated with pure gold, and a molding of gold was put around it. 12 A frame a handbreadth high was also put around it, with a molding of gold around the frame. 13 Four rings of gold were cast for it and fastened, one at each of the four corners. 14 The rings were alongside the frame as holders for the poles to carry the table. 15 These poles were made of acacia wood and plated with gold. 16 The vessels that were set on the table, its plates and cups, as well as its pitchers and bowls for pouring libations, were of pure gold.

The Lampstand 17 [k]The lampstand was made of pure beaten gold—its shaft and branches as well as its cups and knobs and petals springing directly from it. 18 Six branches extended from its sides, three branches on one side and three on the other. 19 On one branch there were three cups, shaped like almond blossoms, each with its knob and petals; on the opposite branch there were three cups, shaped like almond blossoms, each with its knob and petals; and so for the six branches that extended from the lampstand. 20 On the shaft there were four cups, shaped like almond blossoms, with their knobs and petals, 21 including a knob below each of the three pairs of branches that extended from the lampstand. 22 The knobs and branches sprang so directly from it that the whole formed but a single piece of pure beaten gold. 23 Its seven lamps, as well as its trimming shears and trays, were made of pure gold. 24 A talent of pure gold was used for the lampstand and its various appurtenances.

The Altar of Incense 25 [l]The altar of incense was made of acacia wood, on a square, a cubit long, a cubit wide, and two cubits high, having horns that sprang directly from it. 26 Its grate on

h 35–38: Ex 26, 31–37. i 1–9: Ex 25, 10–22. j 10–16: Ex 25, 23–30. k 17–24: Ex 25, 31–39. l 25–28: Ex 30, 1–5.

top, its walls on all four sides, and its horns were plated with pure gold; and a molding of gold was put around it. 27Underneath the molding gold rings were placed, two on one side and two on the opposite side, as holders for the poles to carry it. 28The poles, too, were made of acacia wood and plated with gold.

29The sacred anointing oil and the fragrant incense were prepared in their pure form by a perfumer.[m]

CHAPTER 38

The Altar of Holocausts 1The altar of holocausts[n] was made of acacia wood, on a square, five cubits long and five cubits wide; its height was three cubits. 2At the four corners horns were made that sprang directly from the altar. The whole was plated with bronze. 3All the utensils of the altar, the pots, shovels, basins, forks and fire pans, were likewise made of bronze. 4A grating of bronze network was made for the altar and placed round it, on the ground, half as high as the altar itself. 5Four rings were cast for the four corners of the bronze grating, as holders for the poles, 6which were made of acacia wood and plated with bronze. 7The poles were put through the rings on the sides of the altar for carrying it. The altar was made in the form of a hollow box.

8The bronze laver,[o] with its bronze base, was made from the mirrors of the women who served* at the entrance of the meeting tent.

The Court 9[p]The court was made as follows. On the south side of the court there were hangings, woven of fine linen twined, a hundred cubits long, 10with twenty columns and twenty pedestals of bronze, the hooks and bands of the columns being of silver. 11On the north side there were similar hangings, one hundred cubits long, with twenty columns and twenty pedestals of bronze, the hooks and bands of the columns being of silver. 12On the west side there were hangings, fifty cubits long, with ten columns and ten pedestals, the hooks and bands of the columns being of silver. 13On the east side the court was fifty cubits long. 14Toward one side there were hangings to the extent of fifteen cubits, with three columns and three pedestals; 15toward the other side, beyond the entrance of the court, there were likewise hangings to the extent of fifteen cubits, with three columns and three pedestals. 16The hangings on all sides of the court were woven of fine linen twined. 17The pedestals of the columns were of bronze, while the hooks and bands of the columns were of silver; the capitals were silver-plated, and all the columns of the court were banded with silver.

18At the entrance of the court there was a variegated curtain, woven of violet, purple and scarlet yarn and of fine linen twined, twenty cubits long and five cubits wide, in keeping with the hangings of the court. 19There were four columns and four pedestals of bronze for it, while their hooks were of silver. 20All the tent pegs for the Dwelling and for the court around it were of bronze.

Amount of Metal Used 21The following is an account of the various amounts used on the Dwelling, the Dwelling of the commandments, drawn up at the command of Moses by the Levites under the direction of Ithamar, son of Aaron the priest. 22However, it was Bezalel, son of Uri,[q] son of Hur, of the tribe of Judah, who made all that the Lord commanded Moses, 23and he was assisted by Oholiab, son of Ahisamach, of the tribe of Dan, who was an engraver, an embroiderer, and a weaver of variegated cloth of violet, purple and scarlet yarn and of fine linen.

24All the gold used in the entire construction of the sanctuary, having previously been given as an offering, amounted to twenty-nine talents and seven hundred and thirty shekels, according to the standard of the sanctuary shekel. 25The amount of the silver received from the community was one hundred talents and one thousand seven hundred and seventy-five shekels, according to the standard of the sanctuary shekel;

38, 8: The reflecting surface of ancient mirrors was usually of polished bronze. The women who served: cf 1 Sm 2, 22.

m Ex 30, 23ff. 34ff. n 1–7: Ex 27, 1–8; 2 Chr 1, 5. o Ex 30, 18–21. p 9–20: Ex 27, 9–19. q 22f: Ex 31, 2. 6; 35, 30. 34; 36, 1.

26one bekah apiece, that is, a half-shekel apiece,
according to the standard of the sanctuary shek-
el, was received from every man of twenty years
or more who entered the registered group; the
number of these was six hundred and three
thousand five hundred and fifty men.[r] 27One
hundred talents of silver were used for casting
the pedestals of the sanctuary and the pedestals
of the veil, one talent for each pedestal, or one
hundred talents for the one hundred pedestals.
28The remaining one thousand seven hundred
and seventy-five shekels were used for making
the hooks on the columns, for plating the
capitals, and for banding them with silver. 29The
bronze, given as an offering, amounted to sev-
enty talents and two thousand four hundred
shekels. 30With this were made the pedestals at
the entrance of the meeting tent, the bronze
altar with its bronze gratings and all the appurte-
nances of the altar, 31the pedestals around the
court, the pedestals at the entrance of the court,
and all the tent pegs for the Dwelling and for the
court around it.

CHAPTER 39

The Vestments 1With violet, purple and scar-
let yarn were woven the service cloths for use in
the sanctuary, as well as the sacred vestments[s]
for Aaron, as the LORD had commanded Moses.
2 [t]The ephod was woven of gold thread and of
violet, purple and scarlet yarn and of fine linen
twined. 3Gold was first hammered into gold leaf
and then cut up into threads, which were woven
with the violet, purple and scarlet yarn into an
embroidered pattern on the fine linen. 4Shoulder
straps were made for it and joined to its two
upper ends. 5The embroidered belt on the ephod
extended out from it, and like it, was made of
gold thread, of violet, purple and scarlet yarn,
and of fine linen twined, as the LORD had
commanded Moses. 6The onyx stones were
prepared and mounted in gold filigree work;
they were engraved like seal engravings with the
names of the sons of Israel. 7These stones were
set on the shoulder straps of the ephod as
memorial stones of the sons of Israel, just as the
LORD had commanded Moses.
8 [u]The breastpiece was embroidered like the
ephod, with gold thread and violet, purple and
scarlet yarn on cloth of fine linen twined. 9It was
square and folded double, a span high and a span
wide in its folded form. 10Four rows of precious
stones were mounted on it: in the first row a
carnelian, a topaz and an emerald; 11in the
second row, a garnet, a sapphire and a beryl;
12in the third row a jacinth, an agate and an
amethyst; 13in the fourth row a chrysolite, an
onyx and a jasper. They were mounted in gold
filigree work. 14These stones were twelve, to
match the names of the sons of Israel, and each
stone was engraved like a seal with the name of
one of the twelve tribes.
15 [v]Chains of pure gold, twisted like cords,
were made for the breastpiece, 16together with
two gold filigree rosettes and two gold rings. The
two rings were fastened to the two upper ends of
the breastpiece. 17The two gold chains were
then fastened to the two rings at the ends of the
breastpiece. 18The other two ends of the two
chains were fastened in front to the two filigree
rosettes, which were attached to the shoulder
straps of the ephod. 19Two other gold rings were
made and put on the two lower ends of the
breastpiece, on the edge facing the ephod. 20Two
more gold rings were made and fastened to the
bottom of the two shoulder straps next to where
they joined the ephod in front, just above its
embroidered belt. 21Violet ribbons bound the
rings of the breastpiece to the rings of the ephod,
so that the breastpiece stayed right above the
embroidered belt of the ephod and did not swing
loose from it. All this was just as the LORD had
commanded Moses.
The Other Vestments 22The robe of the
ephod was woven entirely of violet yarn, 23with
an opening in its center like the opening of a
shirt, with selvage around the opening to keep it
from being torn. 24At the hem of the robe
pomegranates were made of violet, purple and
scarlet yarn and of fine linen twined; 25bells of

r Nm 1, 46. s Ex 31, 10. t 2–10: Ex 28, 6–12. u 8–14: Ex 28, 15–21. v 15–21: Ex 28, 31–35.

pure gold were also made and put between the pomegranates all around the hem of the robe: 26 first a bell, then a pomegranate, and thus alternating all around the hem of the robe which was to be worn in performing the ministry—all this, just as the LORD had commanded Moses.

27 For Aaron and his sons there were also woven tunics of fine linen;[w] 28 the miter of fine linen; the ornate turbans of fine linen; drawers of linen [of fine linen twined]; 29 and sashes of variegated work made of fine linen twined and of violet, purple and scarlet yarn, as the LORD had commanded Moses. 30 The plate of the sacred diadem was made of pure gold[x] and inscribed, as on a seal engraving: "Sacred to the LORD." 31 It was tied over the miter with a violet ribbon, as the LORD had commanded Moses.

Presentation of the Work to Moses 32 Thus the entire work of the Dwelling of the meeting tent was completed. The Israelites did the work just as the LORD had commanded Moses. 33 They then brought to Moses the Dwelling, the tent with all its appurtenances, the clasps, the boards, the bars, the columns, the pedestals, 34 the covering of rams' skins dyed red, the covering of tahash skins, the curtain veil; 35 the ark of the commandments with its poles, the propitiatory, 36 the table with all its appurtenances and the showbread, 37 the pure gold lampstand with its lamps set up on it and with all its appurtenances, the oil for the light, 38 the golden altar, the anointing oil, the fragrant incense; the curtain for the entrance of the tent, 39 the altar of bronze with its bronze grating, its poles and all its appurtenances, the laver with its base, 40 the hangings of the court with their columns and pedestals, the curtain for the entrance of the court with its ropes and tent pegs, all the equipment for the service of the Dwelling of the meeting tent; 41 the service cloths for use in the sanctuary, the sacred vestments for Aaron the priest, and the vestments to be worn by his sons in their ministry. 42 The Israelites had carried out all the work just as the LORD had commanded Moses. 43 So when Moses saw that all the work was done just as the LORD had commanded, he blessed them.

CHAPTER 40

Erection of the Dwelling 1 Then the LORD said to Moses, 2 [y]"On the first day of the first month* you shall erect the Dwelling of the meeting tent.[z] 3 Put the ark of the commandments in it, and screen off the ark with the veil.[a] 4 Bring in the table and set it. Then bring in the lampstand and set up the lamps on it. 5 Put the golden altar of incense in front of the ark of the commandments, and hang the curtain at the entrance of the Dwelling. 6 Put the altar of holocausts in front of the entrance of the Dwelling of the meeting tent. 7 Place the laver between the meeting tent and the altar, and put water in it. 8 Set up the court round about, and put the curtain at the entrance of the court.

9 [b]"Take the anointing oil and anoint the Dwelling and everything in it, consecrating it and all its furnishings, so that it will be sacred. 10 Anoint the altar of holocausts and all its appurtenances, consecrating it, so that it will be most sacred. 11 Likewise, anoint the laver with its base, and thus consecrate it.

12 [c]"Then bring Aaron and his sons to the entrance of the meeting tent, and there wash them with water. 13 Clothe Aaron with the sacred vestments and anoint him, thus consecrating him as my priest. 14 Bring forward his sons also, and clothe them with the tunics. 15 As you have anointed their father, anoint them also as my priests. Thus, by being anointed, they shall receive a perpetual priesthood throughout all future generations."

16 Moses did exactly as the LORD had commanded him. 17 On the first day of the first month of the second year the Dwelling was erected. 18 It was Moses who erected the Dwelling. He placed its pedestals, set up its boards, put in its bars, and set up its columns. 19 He spread the tent over the Dwelling and put the covering

40, 2: On the first day of the first month: almost a year after the departure of the Israelites from Egypt. Cf v 17.

w 27ff: Ex 28, 39–42. x 30f: Ex 28, 36f. y 2–8: Ex 40, 16–33. z Ex 26, 30. a 3ff: Ex 26, 33ff. b 9ff: Ex 30, 26–29. c 12–15: Ex 28, 41; 29, 4–9; Lv 8, 1–13.

on top of the tent, as the LORD had commanded him. [20] [d]He took the commandments and put them in the ark; he placed poles alongside the ark and set the propitiatory upon it. [21]He brought the ark into the Dwelling and hung the curtain veil, thus screening off the ark of the commandments, as the LORD had commanded him. [22]He put the table in the meeting tent, on the north side of the Dwelling, outside the veil, [23]and arranged the bread on it before the LORD, as the LORD had commanded him.[e] [24]He placed the lampstand in the meeting tent, opposite the table, on the south side of the Dwelling, [25]and he set up the lamps before the LORD, as the LORD had commanded him. [26]He placed the golden altar in the meeting tent, in front of the veil, [27]and on it he burned fragrant incense, as the LORD had commanded him. [28]He hung the curtain at the entrance of the Dwelling. [29]He put the altar of holocausts in front of the entrance of the Dwelling of the meeting tent, and offered holocausts and cereal offerings on it, as the LORD had commanded him. [30][f]He placed the laver between the meeting tent and the altar, and put water in it for washing. [31]Moses and Aaron and his sons used to wash their hands and feet there, [32]for they washed themselves whenever they went into the meeting tent or approached the altar, as the LORD commanded Moses. [33]Finally, he set up the court around the Dwelling and the altar and hung the curtain at the entrance of the court. Thus Moses finished all the work.

God's Presence in the Dwelling [34] [g]Then the cloud covered the meeting tent, and the glory of the LORD filled the Dwelling. [35]Moses could not enter the meeting tent, because the cloud settled down upon it and the glory of the LORD filled the Dwelling. [36]Whenever the cloud rose from the Dwelling, the Israelites would set out on their journey. [37]But if the cloud did not lift, they would not go forward; only when it lifted did they go forward. [38]In the daytime the cloud of the LORD was seen over the Dwelling; whereas at night, fire was seen in the cloud by the whole house of Israel in all the stages of their journey.

d 20ff: Ex 25, 16, 21; 26, 33ff. e Ex 25, 30. f 30ff: Ex 30, 18ff. g 34–38; Nm 9, 15–22.

THE BOOK OF LEVITICUS

The name "Leviticus" was bestowed on the third book of the Pentateuch by the ancient Greek translators because a good part of this book consists of sacrificial and other ritual laws prescribed for the priests of the tribe of Levi.

Continuing the legislation given by God to Moses at Mount Sinai, Leviticus is almost entirely legislative in character; the rare narrative portions are subordinate to the main legislative theme. Generally speaking, the laws contained in this book serve to teach the Israelites that they should always keep themselves in a state of legal purity, or external sanctity, as a sign of their intimate union with the Lord. Accordingly, the central idea of Leviticus is contained in its oft-repeated injunction: "You shall be holy, because I, the LORD, am holy."

The main divisions of Leviticus are:

I. Ritual of Sacrifices (Lv 1—7).
II. Ceremony of Ordination (Lv 8—10).
III. Laws regarding Legal Purity (Lv 11—16).
IV. Code of Legal Holiness (Lv 17—26).
V. Redemption of Offerings (Lv 27).

I: Ritual of Sacrifices

CHAPTER 1

Holocausts 1The LORD called Moses, and from
the meeting tent gave him this message:
2 [a]"Speak to the Israelites and tell them: When
any one of you wishes to bring an animal
offering to the LORD, such an offering must be
from the herd or from the flock.*
3"If his holocaust* offering is from the herd, it
must be a male without blemish.[b] To find favor
with the LORD, he shall bring it to the entrance
of the meeting tent 4and there lay his hand on
the head of the holocaust, so that it may be
acceptable to make atonement for him.[c] 5He
shall then slaughter the bull before the LORD, but
Aaron's sons, the priests, shall offer up its blood
by splashing it on the sides of the altar which is
at the entrance of the meeting tent.[d] 6Then he
shall skin the holocaust and cut it up into pieces.
7After Aaron's sons, the priests, have put some
burning embers on the altar and laid some wood
on them, 8they shall lay the pieces of meat,
together with the head and the suet, on top of
the wood and embers on the altar. 9The inner
organs and the shanks, however, the offerer shall
first wash with water. The priest shall then burn
the whole offering on the altar as a holocaust, a
sweet-smelling oblation to the LORD.[e]
10"If his holocaust offering is from the flock,
that is, a sheep or a goat, he must bring a male
without blemish. 11This he shall slaughter before
the LORD at the north side of the altar. Then
Aaron's sons, the priests, shall splash its blood on
the sides of the altar. 12When the offerer has cut
it up into pieces, the priest shall lay these,
together with the head and suet, on top of the
wood and the fire on the altar. 13The inner
organs and the shanks, however, the offerer shall
first wash with water. The priest shall offer them
up and then burn the whole offering on the altar
as a holocaust, a sweet-smelling oblation to the
LORD.
14"If he offers a bird as a holocaust to the
LORD, he shall choose a turtledove or a pigeon as
his offering.[f] 15Having brought it to the altar
where it is to be burned, the priest shall snap its
head loose and squeeze out its blood against the
side of the altar.[g] 16Its crop and feathers shall be
removed and thrown on the ash heap at the east
side of the altar. 17Then, having split the bird
down the middle without separating the halves,
the priest shall burn it on the altar, over the
wood on the fire, as a holocaust, a sweet-
smelling oblation to the LORD.

CHAPTER 2

Cereal Offerings 1"When anyone wishes to
bring a cereal offering to the LORD, his offering
must consist of fine flour. He shall pour oil on it
and put frankincense over it.[h] 2When he has
brought it to Aaron's sons, the priests, one of
them shall take a handful of this fine flour and
oil, together with all the frankincense, and this
he shall burn on the altar as a token offering,* a
sweet-smelling oblation to the LORD.[i] 3The rest
of the cereal offering belongs to Aaron and his
sons. It is a most sacred oblation to the LORD.[j]
4"When the cereal offering you present is
baked in an oven, it must be in the form of
unleavened cakes made of fine flour mixed with
oil, or of unleavened wafers spread with oil. 5If
you present a cereal offering that is fried on a
griddle, it must be of fine flour mixed with oil
and unleavened.[k] 6Such a cereal offering must
be broken into pieces, and oil must be poured
over it. 7If you present a cereal offering that is
prepared in a pot, it must be of fine flour, deep-
fried in oil. 8A cereal offering that is made in any
of these ways you shall bring to the LORD,

1, 2: From the herd or from the flock: the only animals which could be used as sacrificial victims were either of the bovine class (bulls, cows and calves) or the ovine class (sheep and lambs, goats and kids). Excluded, therefore, were not only all wild animals, but also such "unclean" domestic animals as the camel and the ass. See note on Lv 11, 1ff.

1, 3: Holocaust: from the Greek word meaning "wholly burned," this is the technical term for the special type of sacrifice in which an entire animal except its hide was consumed in the fire on the altar. The primary purpose of this complete gift was to render glory and praise to God.

2, 2: Token offering: literally, "reminder." Instead of burning the whole cereal offering, they burned only this part of it on the altar; it thus corresponded to the fat of the peace offering. See note on Lv 3, 1.

a Lv 22, 18. 19. b Ex 12, 5. c Lv 3, 2. 8. 13; 4, 15; 8, 14. 22; 16, 21; Ex 29, 10. 15. d Lv 3, 8. e Lv 3, 5. 16; Ex 29, 18. f Lv 5, 7; 12, 8; Lk 2, 24. g Lv 5, 8. h Nm 15, 4. i Lv 6, 15. j Lv 7, 9f; Sir 7, 31; 1 Cor 9, 13. k 1 Chr 23, 29.

offering it to the priest, who shall take it to the altar. 9Its token offering the priest shall then lift from the cereal offering and burn on the altar as a sweet-smelling oblation to the LORD. 10The rest of the cereal offering belongs to Aaron and his sons. It is a most sacred oblation to the LORD.

11"Every cereal offering that you present to the LORD shall be unleavened, for you shall not burn any leaven or honey as an oblation to the LORD.[l] 12Such you may indeed present to the LORD in the offering of first fruits, but they are not to be placed on the altar for a pleasing odor. 13However, every cereal offering that you present to the LORD shall be seasoned with salt.[m] Do not let the salt of the covenant of your God* be lacking from your cereal offering. On every offering you shall offer salt.

14"If you present a cereal offering of first fruits to the LORD, you shall offer it in the form of fresh grits of new ears of grain, roasted by fire. 15On this cereal offering you shall put oil and frankincense. 16For its token offering the priest shall then burn some of the grits and oil, together with all the frankincense, as an oblation to the LORD.

CHAPTER 3

Peace Offerings 1"If someone in presenting a peace offering* makes his offering from the herd, he may offer before the LORD either a male or a female animal, but it must be without blemish.[n] 2He shall lay his hand on the head of his offering,[o] and then slaughter it at the entrance of the meeting tent; but Aaron's sons, the priests, shall splash its blood on the sides of the altar. 3From the peace offering he shall offer as an oblation to the LORD the fatty membrane over the inner organs, and all the fat that adheres to them,[p] 4as well as the two kidneys, with the fat on them near the loins, and the lobe of the liver,* which he shall sever above the kidneys. 5All this Aaron's sons shall then burn on the altar with the holocaust,[q] on the wood over the fire, as a sweet-smelling oblation to the LORD.

6"If the peace offering he presents to the LORD is from the flock, he may offer either a male or a female animal, but it must be without blemish. 7If he presents a lamb as his offering, he shall bring it before the LORD, 8and after laying his hand on the head of his offering, he shall slaughter it before the meeting tent; but Aaron's sons shall splash its blood on the sides of the altar. 9As an oblation to the LORD he shall present the fat of the peace offering: the whole fatty tail,* which he must sever close to the spine, the fatty membrane over the inner organs, and all the fat that adheres to them,[r] 10as well as the two kidneys, with the fat on them near the loins, and the lobe of the liver, which he must sever above the kidneys. 11All this the priest shall burn on the altar as the food of the LORD's oblation.

12"If he presents a goat, he shall bring it before the LORD, 13and after laying his hand on its head, he shall slaughter it before the meeting tent; but Aaron's sons shall splash its blood on the sides of the altar. 14From it he shall offer as an oblation to the LORD the fatty membrane over the inner organs, and all the fat that adheres to them, 15as well as the two kidneys, with the fat on them near the loins, and the lobe of the liver, which he must sever above the kidneys. 16All this the priest shall burn on the altar as the food of the sweet-smelling oblation. All the fat belongs to the LORD. 17This shall be a perpetual ordinance for your descendants wherever they may dwell. You shall not partake of any fat* or any blood."[s]

2, 13: The salt of the covenant of your God: the partaking in common of salt by those seated together at table was an ancient symbol of friendship and alliance. Cf Mk 9, 49 and Col 4, 6; and see note on Nm 18, 19.

3, 1: Peace offering: thus the ancient versions have rendered the Hebrew word, which perhaps means more exactly, "fulfillment sacrifice," offered up in fulfillment of a vow. Cf Prv 7, 14. Its characteristic feature was the sacred banquet at which the offerer and his guests partook of the meat of the sacrificed animal. Cf Lv 7, 11–21.

3, 4: The lobe of the liver: some render, "the fatty covering of the liver."

3, 9: The whole fatty tail: see note on Ex 29, 22.

3, 17: Any fat: only the fat mentioned in vv 9f. 14f is meant; other fat could be eaten by the Israelites.

l Lv 6, 16f; Mt 16, 12; Mk 8, 15; Lk 12, 1; 1 Cor 5, 7; Gal 5, 9. m Ez 43, 24. n Lv 22, 21. o Lv 1, 4. p Ex 29, 13. 22. q Lv 6, 12. r Lv 9, 19. s Lv 17, 10–14; Gn 9, 4; Dt 12, 16. 23; 15, 23.

CHAPTER 4

Sin Offerings: For Priests [1]The LORD said to Moses, [2]"Tell the Israelites: When a person inadvertently commits a sin* against some command of the LORD by doing one of the forbidden things,[t] [3]if it is the anointed priest* who thus sins and thereby makes the people also become guilty, he shall present to the LORD a young, unblemished bull as a sin offering for the sin he committed.[u] [4]Bringing the bullock to the entrance of the meeting tent, before the LORD, he shall lay his hand on its head and slaughter it before the LORD.[v] [5]The anointed priest shall then take some of the bullock's blood and bring it into the meeting tent, [6]where, dipping his finger in the blood, he shall sprinkle it seven times before the LORD, toward the veil of the sanctuary.[w] [7]The priest shall also put some of the blood on the horns of the altar[x] of fragrant incense which is before the LORD in the meeting tent. The rest of the bullock's blood he shall pour out at the base of the altar of holocausts which is at the entrance of the meeting tent. [8]From the sin-offering bullock he shall remove all the fat: the fatty membrane over the inner organs, and all the fat that adheres to them, [9]as well as the two kidneys, with the fat on them near the loins, and the lobe of the liver, which he must sever above the kidneys. [10]This is the same as is removed from the ox of the peace offering; and the priest shall burn it on the altar of holocausts. [11]The hide of the bullock and all its flesh, with its head, legs, inner organs and offal,[y] [12]in short, the whole bullock, shall be brought outside the camp to a clean place where the ashes are deposited and there be burned up in a wood fire. At the place of the ash heap, there it must be burned.

For the Community [13]"If the whole community of Israel inadvertently and without even being aware of it does something that the LORD has forbidden and thus makes itself guilty,[z] [14]should it later on become known that the sin was committed, the community shall present a young bull as a sin offering. They shall bring it before the meeting tent, [15]and here, before the LORD, the elders of the community shall lay their hands on the bullock's head.[a] When the bullock has been slaughtered before the LORD, [16]the anointed priest shall bring some of its blood into the meeting tent, [17]and dipping his finger in the blood, he shall sprinkle it seven times before the LORD, toward the veil. [18]He shall also put some of the blood on the horns of the altar of fragrant incense which is before the LORD in the meeting tent. The rest of the blood he shall pour out at the base of the altar of holocausts which is at the entrance of the meeting tent. [19]All of its fat he shall take from it and burn on the altar, [20]doing with this bullock just as he did with the other sin-offering bullock. Thus the priest shall make atonement for them, and they will be forgiven. [21]This bullock must also be brought outside the camp and burned, just as has been prescribed for the other one. This is the sin offering for the community.

For the Princes [22]"Should a prince commit a sin inadvertently by doing one of the things which are forbidden by some commandment of the LORD, his God, and thus become guilty, [23]if later on he learns of the sin he committed, he shall bring as his offering an unblemished male goat. [24]Having laid his hands on its head, he shall slaughter the goat as a sin offering before the LORD, in the place where the holocausts are slaughtered. [25]The priest shall then take some of the blood of the sin offering on his finger and put it on the horns of the altar of holocausts. The rest of the blood he shall pour out at the base of this altar. [26]All of the fat he shall burn on the altar like the fat of the peace offering.[b] Thus the priest shall make atonement for the prince's sin, and it will be forgiven.

4, 2: A sin: not necessarily a moral fault; included are all the cases of ritual uncleanness which people necessarily incurred in certain unavoidable circumstances.

4, 3: The anointed priest: his violation of the ceremonial law brought a sort of collective guilt on all the people whom he represented before God. Sin offering: more exactly, "sacrifice for remitting sin"; sin is here understood as explained above.

t Lv 5, 15. 17; Nm 15, 22–29. u Heb 7, 27. v Lv 1, 3f. w Lv 8, 11. x Lv 8, 15; 9, 9; 16, 18; Ex 29, 12. y Lv 8, 17; 9, 11; Ex 29, 14; Nm 19, 5. z Lv 5, 2–4; Nm 15, 24–26. a Lv 1, 4. b Lv 3, 3–5.

For Private Persons 27 “If a private person
commits a sin inadvertently[c] by doing one of the
things which are forbidden by the command-
ments of the LORD, and thus becomes guilty,
28 should he later on learn of the sin he commit-
ted, he shall bring an unblemished she-goat as
the offering for his sin. 29 Having laid his hand on
the head of the sin offering,[d] he shall slaughter it
at the place of the holocausts. 30 The priest shall
then take some of its blood on his finger and put
it on the horns of the altar of holocausts. The rest
of the blood he shall pour out at the base of the
altar. 31 All the fat shall be removed, just as the
fat is removed from the peace offering, and the
priest shall burn it on the altar for an odor
pleasing to the LORD.[e] Thus the priest shall
make atonement for him, and he will be for-
given.

32 “If, however, for his sin offering he presents
a lamb, he shall bring an unblemished female.
33 Having laid his hand on its head, he shall
slaughter this sin offering in the place where the
holocausts are slaughtered. 34 The priest shall
then take some of the blood of the sin offering on
his finger and put it on the horns of the altar of
holocausts. The rest of the blood he shall pour
out at the base of the altar. 35 All the fat shall be
removed, just as the fat is removed from the
peace-offering lamb,[f] and the priest shall burn it
on the altar with the other oblations of the LORD.
Thus the priest shall make atonement for the
man's sin, and it will be forgiven.

CHAPTER 5

For Special Cases 1 “If any person refuses to
give the information which, as a witness of
something he has seen or learned, he has been
adjured to give, and thus commits a sin and has
guilt to bear;[g] 2 or if someone, without being
aware of it, touches any unclean thing, as the
carcass of an unclean wild animal,[h] or that of an
unclean domestic animal, or that of an unclean
swarming creature, and thus becomes unclean
and guilty; 3 or if someone, without being aware
of it, touches some human uncleanness, what-
ever kind of uncleanness this may be, and then
recognizes his guilt; 4 or if someone, without
being aware of it, rashly utters an oath[i] to do
good or evil, such as men are accustomed to
utter rashly, and then recognizes that he is guilty
of such an oath; 5 then whoever is guilty in any
of these cases shall confess the sin he has
incurred,[j] 6 and as his sin offering for the sin he
has committed he shall bring to the LORD a
female animal from the flock, a ewe lamb or a
she-goat. The priest shall then make atonement
for his sin.

7 “If, however, he cannot afford an animal of
the flock, he shall bring to the LORD as the sin
offering for his sin two turtledoves or two
pigeons, one for a sin offering and the other for a
holocaust.[k] 8 He shall bring them to the priest,
who shall offer the one for the sin offering first.
Snapping its head loose at the neck, yet without
breaking it off completely,[l] 9 he shall sprinkle
some of the blood of the sin offering against the
side of the altar.[m] The rest of the blood shall be
squeezed out against the base of the altar. Such
is the offering for sin. 10 The other bird shall be
offered as a holocaust in the usual way. Thus the
priest shall make atonement for the sin the man
committed, and it will be forgiven.

11 “If he is unable to afford even two turtle-
doves or two pigeons, he shall present as a sin
offering for his sin one tenth of an ephah of fine
flour. He shall not put oil or frankincense on it,
because it is a sin offering. 12 When he has
brought it to the priest, the latter shall take a
handful of this flour as a token offering, and this
he shall burn as a sin offering on the altar with
the other oblations of the LORD. 13 Thus the
priest shall make atonement for the sin that the
man committed in any of the above cases, and it
will be forgiven.[n] The rest of the flour, like the
cereal offerings, shall belong to the priest.”

Guilt Offerings 14 The LORD said to Moses,
15 “If someone commits a sin by inadvertently

c Nm 15, 27. d Lv 1, 4. e Lv 1, 9; 3, 3–5. f Lv 3, 3. 9. g Prv 29, 24. h Lv 11, 24. 31. 39; 12; 13; 15. i Jgs 11, 30f; 1 Sm 14, 24; Mk 6, 23; Acts 23, 12. j Lv 26, 40; Nm 5, 7. k Lv 12, 8; Lk 2, 24. l Lv 1, 15. 17. m Lv 1, 15. n Lv 4, 26. 35.

cheating* in the LORD's sacred dues, he shall bring to the LORD as his guilt offering an unblemished ram from the flock, valued at two silver shekels according to the standard of the sanctuary shekel. 16He shall also restore what he has sinfully withheld from the sanctuary, adding to it a fifth of its value.[o] This is to be given to the priest, who shall then make atonement for him with the guilt-offering ram, and he will be forgiven.

17 [p]"If someone, without being aware of it,* commits such a sin by doing one of the things which are forbidden by some commandment of the LORD, that he incurs guilt for which he must answer, 18he shall bring as a guilt offering to the priest an unblemished ram of the flock of the established value. The priest shall then make atonement for the fault which was unwittingly committed, and it will be forgiven. 19Such is the offering for guilt; the penalty of the guilt must be paid to the LORD."

20The LORD said to Moses, 21"If someone commits a sin of dishonesty against the LORD by denying his neighbor a deposit or a pledge for a stolen article, or by otherwise retaining his neighbor's goods unjustly, 22or if, having found a lost article, he denies the fact and swears falsely about it with any of the sinful oaths that men make in such cases, 23he shall therefore, since he has incurred guilt by his sin, restore the thing that was stolen or unjustly retained by him or the deposit left with him or the lost article he found 24or whatever else he swore falsely about; on the day of his guilt offering he shall make full restitution of the thing itself, and in addition, give the owner one fifth of its value. 25As his guilt offering he shall bring to the LORD an unblemished ram of the flock of the established value. When he has presented this as his guilt offering to the priest, 26the latter shall make atonement for him before the LORD, and he will be forgiven whatever guilt he may have incurred."

CHAPTER 6

The Daily Holocaust 1The LORD said to Moses, 2"Give Aaron and his sons the following command: This is the ritual* for holocausts. The holocaust is to remain on the hearth of the altar all night until the next morning, and the fire is to be kept burning on the altar. 3The priest, clothed in his linen robe and wearing linen drawers on his body, shall take away the ashes to which the fire has reduced the holocaust on the altar, and lay them at the side of the altar. 4Then, having taken off these garments and put on other garments, he shall carry the ashes to a clean place outside the camp. 5The fire on the altar is to be kept burning; it must not go out. Every morning the priest shall put firewood on it. On this he shall lay out the holocaust and burn the fat of the peace offerings. 6The fire is to be kept burning continuously on the altar; it must not go out.

Daily Cereal Offering 7"This is the ritual of the cereal offering. One of Aaron's sons shall first present it before the LORD, in front of the altar. 8Then he shall take from it a handful of its fine flour and oil, together with all the frankincense that is on it, and this he shall burn on the altar as its token offering, a sweet-smelling oblation to the LORD. 9The rest of it Aaron and his sons may eat; but it must be eaten in the form of unleavened cakes and in a sacred place: in the court of the meeting tent they shall eat it. 10It shall not be baked with leaven. I have given it to them as their portion from the oblations of the LORD; it is most sacred, like the sin offering and the guilt offering. 11All the male descendants of Aaron may partake of it as their rightful share in the oblations of the LORD perpetually throughout

5, 15: Cheating: not offering the full amount in tithes, first fruits, etc. Guilt offering: its characteristic was a certain additional penalty imposed as reparation for the injustice involved in the fault which was atoned for by this sacrifice. However, in certain passages, e.g., Lv 14, 12f; Nm 6, 12; Ezr 10, 19, the term "guilt offering" is used for more important cases of "sin offerings" where no apparent injustice is involved.

5, 17: Without being aware of it: the case naturally presupposes that later on the offender learns of his mistake. Cf Lv 4, 13f.

6, 2: Ritual: literally, "law, instruction." Here, and in the following paragraphs, are given additional prescriptions for various kinds of sacrifices which were, in part, treated of in the preceding chapters.

o Lv 22, 14. p Lv 4, 2.

your generations. Whatever touches the oblations becomes sacred."

12*The LORD said to Moses, 13"This is the offering that Aaron and his sons shall present to the LORD [on the day he is anointed]: one tenth of an ephah of fine flour for the established cereal offering, half in the morning and half in the evening. 14It shall be well kneaded and fried in oil on a griddle when you bring it in. Having broken the offering into pieces, you shall present it as a sweet-smelling oblation to the LORD. 15Aaron's descendant who succeeds him as the anointed priest shall do likewise. This is a perpetual ordinance: for the Lord the whole offering shall be burned. 16Every cereal offering of a priest shall be a whole burnt offering; it may not be eaten."

Sin Offerings 17The LORD said to Moses, 18"Tell Aaron and his sons: This is the ritual for sin offerings. At the place where holocausts are slaughtered, there also, before the LORD, shall the sin offering be slaughtered.[q] It is most sacred. 19The priest who presents the sin offering may partake of it; but it must be eaten in a sacred place,[r] in the court of the meeting tent. 20Whatever touches its flesh shall become sacred. If any of its blood is spilled on a garment, the stained part must be washed in a sacred place. 21A clay vessel in which it has been cooked shall thereafter be broken;[s] if it is cooked in a bronze vessel, this shall be scoured afterward and rinsed with water. 22All the males of the priestly line may partake of the sin offering, since it is most sacred.[t] 23But no one may partake of any sin offering of which some blood has been brought into the meeting tent[u] to make atonement in the sanctuary; such an offering must be burned up in the fire.

CHAPTER 7

Guilt Offerings 1"This is the ritual for guilt offerings, which are most sacred. 2At the place where the holocausts are slaughtered, there also shall the guilt offering be slaughtered.[v] Its blood shall be splashed on the sides of the altar. 3[w]All of its fat shall be taken from it and offered up: the fatty tail, the fatty membrane over the inner organs, 4as well as the two kidneys with the fat on them near the loins, and the lobe of the liver, which must be severed above the kidneys. 5All this the priest shall burn on the altar as an oblation to the LORD. This is the guilt offering. 6All the males of the priestly line may partake of it; but it must be eaten in a sacred place, since it is most sacred.[x]

7"Because the sin offering and the guilt offering are alike, both having the same ritual, the guilt offering likewise belongs to the priest who makes atonement with it. 8Similarly, the priest who offers a holocaust for someone may keep for himself the hide of the holocaust that he has offered. 9[y]Also, every cereal offering that is baked in an oven or deep-fried in a pot or fried on a griddle shall belong to the priest who offers it, 10whereas all cereal offerings[z] that are offered up dry or mixed with oil shall belong to all of Aaron's sons without distinction.

Peace Offerings 11"This is the ritual for the peace offerings that are presented to the LORD. 12When anyone makes a peace offering in thanksgiving, together with his thanksgiving sacrifice he shall offer unleavened cakes mixed with oil, unleavened wafers spread with oil, and cakes made of fine flour mixed with oil and well kneaded. 13His offering shall also include loaves of leavened bread* along with the victim of his peace offering for thanksgiving. 14From each of his offerings he shall present one portion as a contribution to the LORD; this shall belong to the priest who splashes the blood of the peace offering.

15[a]"The flesh of the thanksgiving sacrifice shall be eaten on the day it is offered; none of it

6, 12–16: This is another law about the daily or "established" cereal offering. It differs in some respects from the preceding law (vv 7–11) and also from the law in Ex 29, 38–42. Hence, the words on the day he is anointed were probably added by some later scribe in order to avoid the difficulty of harmonizing this law with the other two laws on the same matter.

7, 13: Leavened bread: these loaves were not burned on the altar (cf Lv 2, 11), but were eaten at the "communion" meal which followed the sacrifice. See note on Lv 3, 1.

q Lv 7, 2. r Lv 10, 17. s Lv 11, 33; 15, 12. t Lv 7, 6; Nm 18, 10. u Lv 4, 5; Heb 13, 11. v Lv 6, 18. w 3–5: Lv 3, 4. 9f. 14–16; 4, 8f. x Lv 6, 22. y Lv 2, 3–10; Nm 18, 9; Ez 44, 29. z Lv 2, 14f. a 15–18: Lv 19, 6f.

may be kept till the next day. 16However, if the sacrifice is a votive or a free-will offering, it should indeed be eaten on the day the sacrifice is offered, but what is left over may be eaten on the next day. 17Should any flesh from the sacrifice be left over on the third day, it must be burned up in the fire. 18If, therefore, any of the flesh of the peace offering is eaten on the third day, it shall not win favor for him nor shall it be reckoned to his credit; rather, it shall be considered as refuse, and anyone who eats of it shall have his guilt to bear. 19Should the flesh touch anything unclean, it may not be eaten, but shall be burned up in the fire.

"All who are clean may partake of this flesh. 20If, however, someone while in a state of uncleanness eats any of the flesh of a peace offering belonging to the LORD, that person shall be cut off from his people. 21Likewise, if someone touches anything unclean, whether the uncleanness be of human or of animal origin or from some loathsome crawling creature, and then eats of a peace offering belonging to the LORD, that person, too, shall be cut off from his people."

Prohibition against Blood and Fat 22The LORD said to Moses, 23"Tell the Israelites: You shall not eat the fat* of any ox or sheep or goat.[b] 24Although the fat of an animal that has died a natural death or has been killed by wild beasts may be put to any other use, you may not eat it.[c] 25If anyone eats the fat of an animal from which an oblation is made to the LORD, such a one shall be cut off from his people. 26Wherever you dwell, you shall not partake of any blood, be it of bird or of animal. 27Every person who partakes of any blood shall be cut off from his people."[d]

The Portions for Priests 28The LORD said to Moses, 29"Tell the Israelites: He who presents a peace offering to the LORD shall bring a part of it as his special offering to him, 30carrying in with his own hands the oblations to the LORD. The fat is to be brought in, together with the breast, which is to be waved as a wave offering* before the LORD. 31The priest shall burn the fat on the altar,[e] but the breast belongs to Aaron and his sons. 32Moreover, from your peace offering you shall give to the priest the right leg as a raised offering. 33The descendant of Aaron who offers up the blood and fat of the peace offering shall have the right leg as his portion, 34for from the peace offerings of the Israelites I have taken the breast that is waved and the leg that is raised up, and I have given them to Aaron, the priest, and to his sons by a perpetual ordinance as a contribution from the Israelites."[f]

35This is the priestly share* from the oblations of the LORD, allotted to Aaron and his sons on the day he called them to be the priests of the LORD; 36on the day he anointed them the LORD ordered the Israelites to give them this share by a perpetual ordinance throughout their generations.

37This is the ritual for holocausts, cereal offerings, sin offerings, guilt offerings, [ordination offerings] and peace offerings, 38which the LORD enjoined on Moses at Mount Sinai at the time when he commanded the Israelites in the wilderness of Sinai to bring their offerings to the LORD.

II: Ceremony of Ordination

CHAPTER 8

Ordination of Aaron and His Sons 1The LORD[g] said to Moses,* 2"Take Aaron and his sons, together with the vestments,* the anointing oil, the bullock for a sin offering, the two rams, and the basket of unleavened food. 3Then assemble the whole community at the entrance of the meeting tent." 4And Moses did as the LORD had commanded. When the community had assembled at the entrance of the meeting tent, 5Moses told them what the LORD had ordered to be done. 6Bringing forward Aaron

7, 23: The fat: only the particular portions specified in Lv 3, 9f. 14f are meant. Ox or sheep or goat: such animals as could be sacrificed; the fat of other clean animals could be eaten.

7, 30–34: A wave offering . . . a raised offering: these ceremonies are described in Ex 29, 24–28. The Hebrew word for "raised offering" is also rendered, in certain contexts, as "contribution."

7, 35: The priestly share: literally, "the anointed part."

8, 1—9, 21: Though presented in the form of a narrative, this description of Aaron's ordination was intended to serve as a guide for all future ordinations.

8, 2: The vestments, etc.: already described in Ex 28–29.

b Lv 3, 17. c Lv 22, 8. d Lv 17, 10. e Lv 3, 11, 16. f Ex 29, 27f. g 1–36: cf Ex 29.

and his sons, he first washed them with water.[h]
7 Then he put the tunic on Aaron,[i] girded him
with the sash, clothed him with the robe, placed
the ephod on him, and girded him with the
embroidered belt of the ephod, fastening it
around him. 8 [j]He then set the breastpiece on
him, with the Urim and Thummim* in it, 9 [k]and
put the miter on his head, attaching the gold
plate, the sacred diadem, over the front of the
miter, at his forehead, as the LORD had commanded him to do.

10 Taking the anointing oil, Moses anointed
and consecrated the Dwelling, with all that was
in it.[l] 11 Then he sprinkled some of this oil seven
times on the altar, and anointed the altar, with
all its appurtenances, and the laver, with its base,
thus consecrating them. 12 He also poured some
of the anointing oil on Aaron's head, thus
consecrating him.[m] 13 Moses likewise brought
forward Aaron's sons, clothed them with tunics,
girded them with sashes, and put turbans on
them, as the LORD had commanded him to do.

Ordination Sacrifices 14 When he had brought
forward the bullock for a sin offering, Aaron and
his sons laid their hands on its head. 15 Then
Moses slaughtered it, and taking some of its
blood, with his finger he put it on the horns
around the altar, thus purifying the altar. He also
made atonement for the altar by pouring out the
blood at its base when he consecrated it.[n]
16 Taking all the fat that was over the inner
organs, as well as the lobe of the liver and the
two kidneys with their fat,[o] Moses burned them
on the altar. 17 The bullock, however, with its
hide and flesh and offal he burned in the fire
outside the camp, as the LORD had commanded
him to do.

18 He next brought forward the holocaust ram,
and Aaron and his sons laid their hands on its
head. 19 When he had slaughtered it, Moses
splashed its blood on all sides of the altar. 20 After
cutting up the ram into pieces, he burned the
head, the cut-up pieces and the suet; 21 then,
having washed the inner organs and the shanks
with water, he also burned these remaining parts
of the ram on the altar as a holocaust, a sweet-smelling oblation to the LORD, as the LORD had
commanded him to do.

22 Then he brought forward the second ram,
the ordination ram, and Aaron and his sons laid
their hands on its head. 23 When he had slaughtered it, Moses took some of its blood and put it
on the tip of Aaron's right ear, on the thumb of
his right hand, and on the big toe of his right
foot.[p] 24 Moses had the sons of Aaron also come
forward, and he put some of the blood on the
tips of their right ears, on the thumbs of their
right hands, and on the big toes of their right
feet. The rest of the blood he splashed on the
sides of the altar. 25 He then took the fat: the
fatty tail and all the fat over the inner organs, the
lobe of the liver and the two kidneys with their
fat, and likewise the right leg; 26 from the basket
of unleavened food that was set before the LORD
he took one unleavened cake, one loaf of bread
made with oil, and one wafer; these he placed
on top of the portions of fat and the right leg.
27 He then put all these things into the hands of
Aaron and his sons, whom he had wave them as
a wave offering before the LORD. 28 When he had
received them back, Moses burned them with
the holocaust on the altar as the ordination
offering, a sweet-smelling oblation to the LORD.
29 He then took the breast and waved it as a
wave offering before the LORD; this was Moses'
own portion of the ordination ram. All this was
in keeping with the LORD's command to Moses.
30 Taking some of the anointing oil and some of
the blood that was on the altar, Moses sprinkled
with it Aaron and his vestments, as well as his
sons and their vestments, thus consecrating both
Aaron and his vestments and his sons and their
vestments.

31 Finally, Moses said to Aaron and his sons,
"Boil the flesh at the entrance of the meeting
tent, and there eat it with the bread that is in the
basket of the ordination offering, in keeping with
the command I have received: 'Aaron and his

8, 8: The Urim and Thummim: see note on Ex 28, 30.

h 6f: Ex 40, 12f. i 7ff: Sir 45, 8–13. j Ex 28, 30. k Ex 28, 36. l Ex 30, 26. m Sir 45, 15. n Lv 4, 7; Heb 9, 22. o 16f: Lv 3, 4; 4, 8–11. p Lv 14, 14.

sons shall eat of it.' [32]What is left over of the flesh and the bread you shall burn up in the fire. [33]Moreover, you are not to depart from the entrance of the meeting tent for seven days, until the days of your ordination are completed; for your ordination is to last for seven days. [34]*The LORD has commanded that what has been done today be done to make atonement for you. [35]Hence you must remain at the entrance of the meeting tent day and night for seven days, carrying out the prescriptions of the LORD; otherwise you shall die; for this is the command I have received." [36]So Aaron and his sons did all that the LORD had commanded through Moses.

CHAPTER 9

Octave of the Ordination [1]On the eighth day Moses summoned Aaron and his sons, together with the elders of Israel, [2]and said to Aaron, "Take a calf for a sin offering and a ram for a holocaust, both without blemish, and offer them before the LORD. [3]Tell the elders of Israel, too: Take a he-goat for a sin offering, a calf and a lamb, both unblemished yearlings, for a holocaust, [4]and an ox and a ram for a peace offering, to sacrifice them before the LORD, along with a cereal offering mixed with oil; for today the LORD will reveal himself to you." [5]So they brought what Moses had ordered. When the whole community had come forward and stood before the LORD, [6]Moses said, "This is what the LORD orders you to do, that the glory of the LORD may be revealed to you. [7]Come up to the altar," Moses then told Aaron, "and offer your sin offering and your holocaust in atonement for yourself and for your family; then present the offering of the people in atonement for them, as the LORD has commanded."

[8]Going up to the altar, Aaron first slaughtered the calf that was his own sin offering. [9]When his sons presented the blood to him, he dipped his finger in the blood and put it on the horns of the altar. The rest of the blood he poured out at the base of the altar. [10]He then burned on the altar the fat, the kidneys and the lobe of the liver that were taken from the sin offering, as the LORD had commanded Moses; [11]but the flesh and the hide he burned up in the fire outside the camp. [12]Then Aaron slaughtered his holocaust. When his sons brought him the blood, he splashed it on all sides of the altar. [13]They then brought him the pieces and the head of the holocaust, and he burned them on the altar. [14]Having washed the inner organs and the shanks, he burned these also with the holocaust on the altar.

[15]Thereupon he had the people's offering brought up. Taking the goat that was for the people's sin offering, he slaughtered it and offered it up for sin as before. [16]Then he brought forward the holocaust, other than the morning holocaust, and offered it in the usual manner. [17]He then presented the cereal offering; taking a handful of it, he burned it on the altar. [18]Finally he slaughtered the ox and the ram, the peace offering of the people. When his sons brought him the blood, Aaron splashed it on all sides of the altar. [19]The portions of fat from the ox and from the ram, the fatty tail, the fatty membrane over the inner organs, the two kidneys, with the fat that is on them, and the lobe of the liver,[q] [20]he placed on top of the breasts and burned them on the altar, [21] [r]having first waved the breasts and the right legs as a wave offering before the LORD, in keeping with the LORD's command to Moses.

Revelation of the Lord's Glory [22]Aaron then raised his hands over the people and blessed them. When he came down from offering the sin offering and holocaust and peace offering, [23]Moses and Aaron went into the meeting tent.[s] On coming out they again blessed the people. Then the glory of the LORD was revealed to all the people. [24]Fire came forth from the LORD's presence[t] and consumed the holocaust and the remnants of the fat on the altar. Seeing this, all the people cried out and fell prostrate.

8, 34: The sense is not quite clear. Either the verse gives merely the reason why God ordered this ceremony, or it contains God's command that the same ceremony be used in all future ordinations, or it decrees a repetition of the entire ceremony on each of the seven days. At least a sin offering for atonement was made on each of these days. Cf Ex 29, 29–36.

q 19f: Lv 3, 3ff. r Lv 7, 31f. s Nm 6, 23–26. t 1 Kgs 18, 38; 2 Chr 7, 1.

CHAPTER 10

Nadab and Abihu 1During this time Aaron's
sons Nadab and Abihu* took their censers and,
strewing incense on the fire they had put in
them,[u] they offered up before the LORD profane
fire, such as he had not authorized. 2Fire*
therefore came forth from the LORD's presence
and consumed them,[v] so that they died in his
presence. 3Moses then said to Aaron, "This is as
the LORD said:

> Through those who approach me I will
> manifest my sacredness;*
> In the sight of all the people I will reveal my
> glory."[w]

But Aaron said nothing. 4Then Moses sum-
moned Mishael and Elzaphan, the sons of Aar-
on's uncle Uzziel, with the order, "Come, re-
move your kinsmen from the sanctuary and
carry them to a place outside the camp." 5So
they went in and took them, in their tunics,*
outside the camp, as Moses had commanded.

Conduct of the Priests 6Moses said to Aaron
and his sons Eleazar and Ithamar, "Do not bare
your heads* or tear your garments,[x] lest you
bring not only death on yourselves but God's
wrath also on the whole community. Your kins-
men, the rest of the house of Israel, shall mourn
for those whom the LORD's fire has smitten; 7but
do not you go beyond the entry of the meeting
tent, else you shall die; for the anointing oil of
the LORD is upon you." So they did as Moses told
them.

8The LORD said to Aaron, 9"When you are to
go to the meeting tent, you and your sons are
forbidden under pain of death, by a perpetual
ordinance throughout your generations, to drink
any wine or strong drink.[y] 10You must be able to
distinguish between what is sacred and what is
profane, between what is clean and what is
unclean;[z] 11you must teach the Israelites all the
laws that the LORD has given them through
Moses."[a]

The Eating of the Priestly Portions 12Moses
said to Aaron and his surviving sons, Eleazar and
Ithamar, "Take the cereal offering left over from
the oblations of the LORD, and eat it beside the
altar in the form of unleavened cakes.[b] Since it is
most sacred, 13you must eat it in a sacred place.
This is your due from the oblations of the LORD,
and that of your sons; such is the command I
have received. 14 [c]With your sons and daughters
you shall also eat the breast of the wave offering
and the leg of the raised offering, in a clean
place; for these have been assigned to you and
your children as your due from the peace
offerings of the Israelites. 15The leg of the raised
offering and the breast of the wave offering shall
first be brought in with the oblations, the fatty
portions, that are to be waved as a wave offering
before the LORD. Then they shall belong to you
and your children by a perpetual ordinance, as
the LORD has commanded."

16*When Moses inquired about the goat of
the sin offering, he discovered that it had all
been burned. So he was angry with the surviving
sons of Aaron, Eleazar and Ithamar, and said,
17 [d]"Why did you not eat the sin offering in the
sacred place, since it is most sacred? It has been
given to you that you might bear the guilt of the
community and make atonement for them be-
fore the LORD. 18If its blood was not brought into
the inmost part of the sanctuary, you should
certainly have eaten the offering in the sanctu-

10, 1: Nadab and Abihu: the older sons of Aaron. Cf Ex 6, 23f.

10, 2: Fire: perhaps after the manner of lightning.

10, 3: I will manifest my sacredness: the presence of God is so sacred that it strikes dead those who approach him without the proper holiness. Cf Nm 20, 13; Ez 28, 22.

10, 5: In their tunics: they were buried just as they were, with no shroud or funeral solemnities.

10, 6: Bare your heads: go without the customary head covering, as a sign of mourning. Some interpreters, however, understand it as the cutting off of one's hair, which ordinarily all the Israelites, men as well as women, let grow long. Cf Is 15, 2; Jer 7, 29. Still others understand the verb to mean "to let one's hair hang loose and wild." Cf Lv 13, 45; 21, 10, where the same phrase is used.

10, 16–19: Eleazar and Ithamar burned the entire goat of the sin offering (Lv 9, 15) instead of eating it in a sacred place (Lv 6, 19) to bear the guilt of the community. Aaron defends this action of his sons against Moses' displeasure by implying that they did not have sufficient sanctity to eat the flesh of the victim and thus perform the expiation of the people. They themselves still labored under the blow of the divine anger which struck their brothers Nadab and Abihu.

u Lv 16, 1; Nm 3, 4; 26, 61; 1 Chr 24, 2. v Nm 16, 35. w Lv 21, 17. 21. x Lv 21, 10. y Ez 44, 21. z Lv 11, 47; 20, 25; Ez 22, 26; 44, 23. a Sir 45, 16. b Lv 6, 16. c 14f: Lv 7, 34. d Lv 6, 18f.

ary, in keeping with the command I had received." [19]Aaron answered Moses, "Even though they presented their sin offering and holocaust before the LORD today, yet this misfortune has befallen me. Had I then eaten of the sin offering today, would it have been pleasing to the LORD?" [20]On hearing this, Moses was satisfied.

III: Laws Regarding Legal Purity

CHAPTER 11

Clean and Unclean Food [1]The LORD said to Moses and Aaron,* [2]"Speak to the Israelites and tell them: Of all land animals these are the ones you may eat: [3]any animal that has hoofs you may eat, provided it is cloven-footed and chews the cud. [4]But you shall not eat any of the following that only chew the cud or only have hoofs: the camel, which indeed chews the cud, but does not have hoofs and is therefore unclean for you; [5]the rock badger,* which indeed chews the cud, but does not have hoofs and is therefore unclean for you; [6]the hare, which indeed chews the cud, but does not have hoofs and is therefore unclean for you; and the pig, [7]which does indeed have hoofs and is cloven-footed, but does not chew the cud and is therefore unclean for you. [8]Their flesh you shall not eat, and their dead bodies you shall not touch; they are unclean for you.

[9]"Of the various creatures that live in the water, you may eat the following: whatever in the seas or in river waters has both fins and scales you may eat. [10]But of the various creatures that crawl or swim in the water, whether in the sea or in the rivers, all those that lack either fins or scales are loathsome for you, [11]and you shall treat them as loathsome. Their flesh you shall not eat, and their dead bodies you shall loathe. [12]Every water creature that lacks fins or scales is loathsome for you.

[13]"Of the birds, these you shall loathe and, as loathsome, they shall not be eaten:* the eagle, the vulture, the osprey, [14]the kite, the various species of falcons, [15]the various species of crows, [16]the ostrich, the nightjar, the gull, the various species of hawks, [17]the owl, the cormorant, the screech owl, [18]the barn owl, the desert owl, the buzzard, [19]the stork, the various species of herons, the hoopoe, and the bat.*

[20]"The various winged insects that walk on all fours are loathsome for you. [21]But of the various winged insects that walk on all fours you may eat those that have jointed legs for leaping on the ground; [22]hence of these you may eat the following: the various kinds of locusts,* the various kinds of grasshoppers, the various kinds of katydids, and the various kinds of crickets. [23]All other winged insects that have four legs are loathsome for you.

[24]*"Such is the uncleanness that you contract, that everyone who touches their dead bodies shall be unclean until evening, [25]and everyone who picks up any part of their dead bodies shall wash his garments and be unclean until evening. [26]All hoofed animals that are not cloven-footed* or do not chew the cud are unclean for you; everyone who touches them becomes unclean. [27]Of the various quadrupeds, all those that walk on paws* are unclean for you; everyone who touches their dead bodies shall be unclean until evening, [28]and everyone who picks up their dead bodies shall wash his garments and be unclean until evening. Such is their uncleanness for you.

[29]"Of the creatures that swarm on the ground, the following are unclean for you: the

11, 1ff: These distinctions between edible and inedible meats were probably based on traditional ideas of hygiene, but they are here given a moral, religious basis: the inedible varieties are classified as "unclean" to remind the Israelites that they are to be a pure and holy people, dedicated to the Lord.

11, 5f: According to modern zoology, the rock badger (hyrax Syriacus) is classified as an ungulate, and the hare as a rodent; neither is a ruminant. They appear to chew their food as the true ruminants do, and it is upon this appearance that the classification in the text is based.

11, 13–19. 30: The identification of the various Hebrew names for these birds and reptiles is in many cases uncertain.

11, 19: The bat: actually a mammal, but listed here with the birds because of its wings.

11, 22: The Hebrew distinguishes four classes of edible locust-like insects, but the difference between them is quite uncertain. Cf Mt 3, 4.

11, 24–28: This paragraph sharpens the prohibition against unclean animals: not only is their meat unfit for food, but contact with their dead bodies makes a person ritually unclean.

11, 26: All hoofed animals that are not cloven-footed: such as the horse and the ass.

11, 27: All those that walk on paws: such as dogs and cats.

rat, the mouse, the various kinds of lizards, 30 the
gecko, the chameleon, the agama, the skink, and
the mole. 31 Among the various swarming crea-
tures, these are unclean for you. Everyone who
touches them when they are dead shall be
unclean until evening. 32 Everything on which
one of them falls when dead becomes unclean.
Any such article that men use, whether it be an
article of wood, cloth, leather or goat hair, must
be put in water and remain unclean until eve-
ning, when it again becomes clean. 33 Should any
of these creatures fall into a clay vessel, every-
thing in it becomes unclean, and the vessel itself
you must break. 34 Any solid food that was in
contact with water, and any liquid that men
drink, in any such vessel become unclean. 35 Any
object on which one of their dead bodies falls,
becomes unclean; if it is an oven or a jar-stand,
this must be broken to pieces; they are unclean
and shall be treated as unclean by you. 36 How-
ever, a spring or a cistern for collecting water
remains clean; but whoever touches the dead
body* becomes unclean. 37 Any sort of cultivated
grain remains clean even though one of their
dead bodies falls on it; 38 but if the grain has
become moistened, it becomes unclean when
one of these falls on it.

39 "When one of the animals that you could
otherwise eat, dies of itself, anyone who touches
its dead body shall be unclean until evening;
40 and anyone who eats of its dead body shall
wash his garments and be unclean until eve-
ning;[e] so also, anyone who removes its dead
body shall wash his garments and be unclean
until evening.

41 "All the creatures that swarm on the ground
are loathsome and shall not be eaten. 42 Whether
it crawls on its belly, goes on all fours, or has
many legs, you shall eat no swarming creature:
they are loathsome. 43 Do not make yourselves
loathsome or unclean with any swarming crea-
ture through being contaminated by them.[f]
44 For I, the LORD, am your God; and you shall
make and keep yourselves holy, because I am
holy.[g] You shall not make yourselves unclean,
then, by any swarming creature that crawls on
the ground. 45 Since I, the LORD, brought you up
from the land of Egypt that I might be your God,
you shall be holy, because I am holy.

46 "This is the law for animals and birds and
for all the creatures that move about in the water
or swarm on the ground, 47 that you may distin-
guish between the clean and the unclean, be-
tween creatures that may be eaten and those
that may not be eaten."[h]

CHAPTER 12

Uncleanness of Childbirth 1 The LORD said to
Moses, 2 "Tell the Israelites: When a woman has
conceived and gives birth to a boy, she shall be
unclean* for seven days, with the same unclean-
ness as at her menstrual period.[i] 3 On the eighth
day, the flesh of the boy's foreskin shall be
circumcised,[j] 4 and then she shall spend thirty-
three days more in becoming purified of her
blood; she shall not touch anything sacred nor
enter the sanctuary till the days of her purifica-
tion are fulfilled. 5 If she gives birth to a girl, for
fourteen days she shall be as unclean as at her
menstruation, after which she shall spend sixty-
six days in becoming purified of her blood.

6 "When the days of her purification for a son
or for a daughter are fulfilled,[k] she shall bring to
the priest at the entrance of the meeting tent a
yearling lamb for a holocaust and a pigeon or a
turtledove for a sin offering. 7 The priest shall
offer them up before the LORD to make atone-
ment for her, and thus she will be clean again
after her flow of blood. Such is the law for the
woman who gives birth to a boy or a girl child.
8 *If, however, she cannot afford a lamb, she may
take two turtledoves or two pigeons,[l] the one

11, 36: Whoever touches the dead body: to remove the dead insect from the water supply.

12, 2f: The uncleanness of the woman was more serious during the first period, the seven days after the birth of a boy or the fourteen days after the birth of a girl; only during this period would the rules given in Lv 15, 19–24 apply.

12, 8: Forty days after the birth of Jesus, his Virgin Mother made this offering of the poor (Lk 2, 22. 24); since the holocaust was offered in thanksgiving for the birth of the child, this was most fittingly offered by Mary. However, because of her miraculous delivery, she was not really obliged to make the sin offering of purification.

e Lv 17, 15; 22, 8. f 43f: Lv 20, 25f. g Lv 19, 2; 20, 7. 26; Mt 5, 48; 1 Pt 1, 16. h Lv 10, 10. i Lv 15, 19. j Gn 17, 12; Jn 7, 22. k Lk 2, 22. l Lv 1, 14; Lk 2, 24.

for a holocaust and the other for a sin offering. The priest shall make atonement for her, and thus she will again be clean."

CHAPTER 13

Leprosy [1]The LORD said to Moses and Aaron, [2] [m]"If someone has on his skin* a scab or pustule or blotch which appears to be the sore of leprosy, he shall be brought to Aaron, the priest, or to one of the priests among his descendants, [3]who shall examine the sore on his skin. If the hair on the sore has turned white and the sore itself shows that it has penetrated below the skin, it is indeed the sore of leprosy; the priest, on seeing this, shall declare the man unclean. [4]If, however, the blotch on the skin is white, but does not seem to have penetrated below the skin, nor has the hair turned white, the priest shall quarantine the stricken man for seven days. [5]On the seventh day the priest shall again examine him. If he judges that the sore has remained unchanged and has not spread on the skin, the priest shall quarantine him for another seven days, [6]and once more examine him on the seventh day. If the sore is now dying out and has not spread on the skin, the priest shall declare the man clean; it was merely eczema. The man shall wash his garments and so become clean. [7]But if, after he has shown himself to the priest to be declared clean, the eczema spreads at all on his skin, he shall once more show himself to the priest. [8]Should the priest, on examining it, find that the eczema has indeed spread on the skin, he shall declare the man unclean; it is leprosy.

[9]"When someone is stricken with leprosy, he shall be brought to the priest. [10]Should the priest, on examining him, find that there is a white scab on the skin which has turned the hair white and that there is raw flesh in it, [11]it is skin leprosy that has long developed. The priest shall declare the man unclean without first quarantining him, since he is certainly unclean. [12]If leprosy breaks out on the skin* and, as far as the priest can see, covers all the skin of the stricken man from head to foot, [13]should the priest then, on examining him, find that the leprosy does cover his whole body, he shall declare the stricken man clean; since it has all turned white, the man is clean. [14]But as soon as raw flesh appears on him, he is unclean; [15]on observing the raw flesh, the priest shall declare him unclean, because raw flesh is unclean; it is leprosy. [16]If, however, the raw flesh again turns white, he shall return to the priest; [17]should the latter, on examining him, find that the sore has indeed turned white, he shall declare the stricken man clean, and thus he will be clean.

[18]"If a man who had a boil on his skin which later healed, [19]should now in the place of the boil have a white scab or a pink blotch, he shall show himself to the priest. [20]If the latter, on examination, sees that it is deeper than the skin and that the hair has turned white, he shall declare the man unclean: it is the sore of leprosy that has broken out in the boil. [21]But if the priest, on examining him, finds that there is no white hair in it and that it is not deeper than the skin and is already dying out, the priest shall quarantine him for seven days. [22]If it has then spread on the skin, the priest shall declare him unclean; the man is stricken. [23]But if the blotch remains in its place without spreading, it is merely the scar of the boil; the priest shall therefore declare him clean.

[24]"If a man had a burn on his skin, and the proud flesh of the burn now becomes a pink or a white blotch, [25]the priest shall examine it. If the hair has turned white on the blotch and this seems to have penetrated below the skin, it is leprosy that has broken out in the burn; the priest shall therefore declare him unclean and stricken with leprosy. [26]But if the priest, on examining it, finds that there is no white hair on the blotch and that this is not deeper than the skin and is already dying out, the priest shall quarantine him for seven days. [27]Should the

13, 2ff: Various kinds of skin blemishes are treated here which were not contagious but simply disqualified their subjects from association with others, especially in public worship, until they were declared ritually clean. The Hebrew term used does not refer to Hansen's disease, currently called leprosy.

13, 12ff: If leprosy breaks out on the skin: the symptoms described here point to a form of skin disease which is merely on the surface and therefore easily cured.

m Dt 24, 8.

priest, when examining it on the seventh day,
find that it has spread at all on the skin, he shall
declare the man unclean and stricken with
leprosy. 28 But if the blotch remains in its place
without spreading on the skin and is already
dying out, it is merely the scab of the burn; the
priest shall therefore declare the man clean,
since it is only the scar of the burn.

29 "When a man or a woman has a sore on the
head or cheek, 30 should the priest, on examin-
ing it, find that the sore has penetrated below
the skin and that there is fine yellow hair on it,
the priest shall declare the person unclean, for
this is scall,* a leprous disease of the head or
cheek. 31 But if the priest, on examining the scall
sore, finds that it has not penetrated below the
skin, though the hair on it may not be black, the
priest shall quarantine the person with scall sore
for seven days, 32 and on the seventh day again
examine the sore. If the scall has not spread and
has no yellow hair on it and does not seem to
have penetrated below the skin, 33 the man shall
shave himself, but not on the diseased spot.
Then the priest shall quarantine him for another
seven days. 34 If the priest, when examining the
scall on the seventh day, finds that it has not
spread on the skin and that it has not penetrated
below the skin, he shall declare the man clean;
the latter shall wash his garments, and thus he
will be clean. 35 But if the scall spreads at all on
his skin after he has been declared clean, 36 the
priest shall again examine it. If the scall has
indeed spread on the skin, he need not look for
yellow hair; the man is surely unclean. 37 If,
however, he judges that the scall has remained
in its place and that black hair has grown on it,
the disease has been healed; the man is clean,
and the priest shall declare him clean.

38 "When the skin of a man or a woman is
spotted with white blotches, 39 the priest shall
make an examination. If the blotches on the skin
are white and already dying out, it is only tetter*
that has broken out on the skin, and the person
therefore is clean.

40 "When a man loses the hair of his head, he
is not unclean merely because of his bald crown.
41 So too, if he loses the hair on the front of his
head, he is not unclean merely because of his
bald forehead. 42 But when there is a pink sore
on his bald crown or bald forehead, it is leprosy
that is breaking out there. 43 The priest shall
examine him; and if the scab on the sore of the
bald spot has the same pink appearance as that of
skin leprosy of the fleshy part of the body, 44 the
man is leprous and unclean, and the priest shall
declare him unclean by reason of the sore on his
head.

45 "The one who bears the sore of leprosy shall
keep his garments rent and his head bare, and
shall muffle his beard; he shall cry out, 'Unclean,
unclean!' 46 As long as the sore is on him he shall
declare himself unclean, since he is in fact
unclean.[n] He shall dwell apart, making his
abode outside the camp.

Leprosy of Clothes 47 "When a leprous infec-
tion* is on a garment of wool or of linen, 48 or on
woven or knitted material of linen or wool, or on
a hide or anything made of leather, 49 if the
infection on the garment or hide, or on the
woven or knitted material, or on any leather
article is greenish or reddish, the thing is indeed
infected with leprosy and must be shown to the
priest. 50 Having examined the infection, the
priest shall quarantine the infected article for
seven days.

51 "On the seventh day the priest shall again
examine the infection. If it has spread on the
garment, or on the woven or knitted material, or
on the leather, whatever be its use, the infection
is malignant leprosy, and the article is unclean.
52 He shall therefore burn up the garment, or the
woven or knitted material of wool or linen, or
the leather article, whatever it may be, which is
infected; since it has malignant leprosy, it must
be destroyed by fire. 53 But if the priest, on
examining the infection, finds that it has not
spread on the garment, or on the woven or
knitted material, or on the leather article, 54 he

13, 30: Scall: a scabby or scaly eruption of the scalp. According to some, "ringworm."

13, 39: Tetter: vitiligo, a harmless form of skin disease.

13, 47: A leprous infection: some mold or fungus growth resembling human leprosy.

n Nm 5, 2; 12, 14f; 2 Kgs 15, 5; Lk 17, 12.

shall give orders to have the infected article washed and then quarantined for another seven days.

[55]"Then the priest shall again examine the infected article after it has been washed. If the infection has not changed its appearance, even though it may not have spread, the article is unclean and shall be destroyed by fire. [56]But if the priest, on examining the infection, finds that it is dying out after the washing, he shall tear the infected part out of the garment, or the leather, or the woven or knitted material. [57]If, however, the infection again appears on the garment, or on the woven or knitted material, or on the leather article, it is still virulent and the thing infected shall be destroyed by fire. [58]But if, after the washing, the infection has left the garment, or the woven or knitted material, or the leather article, the thing shall be washed a second time, and thus it will be clean. [59]This is the law for leprous infection[o] on a garment of wool or linen, or on woven or knitted material, or on any leather article, to determine whether it is clean or unclean."

CHAPTER 14

Purification after Leprosy [1]The LORD said to Moses, [2] [p]"This is the law for the victim of leprosy at the time of his purification. He shall be brought to the priest, [3]who is to go outside the camp to examine him. If the priest finds that the sore of leprosy has healed in the leper, [4]he shall order the man who is to be purified, to get two live, clean birds, as well as some cedar wood, scarlet yarn,* and hyssop. [5]The priest shall then order him to slay one of the birds over an earthen vessel with spring water* in it. [6]Taking the living bird with the cedar wood, the scarlet yarn and the hyssop, the priest shall dip them all in the blood of the bird that was slain over the spring water, [7]and then sprinkle seven times the man to be purified from his leprosy. When he has thus purified him, he shall let the living bird fly away over the countryside. [8]The man being purified shall then wash his garments and shave off all his hair and bathe in water; only when he is thus made clean may he come inside the camp; but he shall still remain outside his tent for seven days. [9]On the seventh day he shall again shave off all the hair of his head, his beard, his eyebrows, and any other hair he may have, and also wash his garments and bathe his body in water; and so he will be clean.

Purification Sacrifices [10]"On the eighth day he shall take two unblemished male lambs, one unblemished yearling ewe lamb, three tenths of an ephah of fine flour mixed with oil for a cereal offering, and one log of oil. [11]The priest who performs the purification ceremony shall place the man who is being purified, as well as all these offerings, before the LORD at the entrance of the meeting tent. [12]Taking one of the male lambs, the priest shall present it as a guilt offering, along with the log of oil, waving them as a wave offering before the LORD. [13](This lamb he shall slaughter in the sacred place where the sin offering and the holocaust are slaughtered; because, like the sin offering, the guilt offering belongs to the priest and is most sacred.) [14]Then the priest shall take some of the blood of the guilt offering and put it on the tip of the man's right ear, the thumb of his right hand, and the big toe of his right foot.[q] [15]The priest shall also take the log of oil and pour some of it into the palm of his own left hand; [16]then, dipping his right forefinger in it, he shall sprinkle it seven times before the LORD. [17]Of the oil left in his hand the priest shall put some on the tip of the man's right ear, the thumb of his right hand, and the big toe of his right foot, over the blood of the guilt offering. [18]The rest of the oil in his hand the priest shall put on the head of the man being purified. Thus shall the priest make atonement for him before the LORD. [19]Only after he has offered the sin offering in atonement for the man's uncleanness shall the priest slaughter the holocaust [20]and offer it, together with the cereal offering, on the altar before the LORD. When the

14, 4: Scarlet yarn: probably used for tying the hyssop sprig to the cedar branchlet.

14, 5: Spring water: literally, "living water," taken from some source of running water, not from a cistern.

o Lv 14, 54. p Mt 8, 4; Mk 1, 44; Lk 5, 14. q Lv 8, 23f.

priest has thus made atonement for him, the
man will be clean.
Poor Leper's Sacrifice 21“If a man is poor and
cannot afford so much, he shall take one male
lamb for a guilt offering, to be used as a wave
offering in atonement for himself, one tenth of
an ephah of fine flour mixed with oil for a cereal
offering, a log of oil, 22and two turtledoves* or
pigeons, which he can more easily afford, the
one as a sin offering and the other as a holocaust.
23On the eighth day of his purification he shall
bring them to the priest, at the entrance of the
meeting tent before the LORD. 24Taking the guilt-
offering lamb, along with the log of oil, the priest
shall wave them as a wave offering before the
LORD. 25When he has slaughtered the guilt-
offering lamb, he shall take some of its blood,
and put it on the tip of the right ear of the man
being purified, on the thumb of his right hand,
and on the big toe of his right foot. 26The priest
shall then pour some of the oil into the palm of
his own left hand 27and with his right forefinger
sprinkle it seven times before the LORD. 28Some
of the oil in his hand the priest shall also put on
the tip of the man's right ear, the thumb of his
right hand, and the big toe of his right foot, over
the blood of the guilt offering. 29The rest of the
oil in his hand the priest shall put on the man's
head. Thus shall he make atonement for him
before the LORD. 30Then, of the turtledoves or
pigeons, such as the man can afford, 31the priest
shall offer up one as a sin offering and the other
as a holocaust, along with the cereal offering.
Thus shall the priest make atonement before the
LORD for the man who is to be purified. 32This is
the law for one afflicted with leprosy who has
insufficient means for his purification.”
Leprosy of Houses 33The LORD said to Moses
and Aaron, 34“When you come into the land of
Canaan, which I am giving you to possess, if I
put a leprous infection on any house of the land
you occupy, 35the owner of the house shall come
and report to the priest, ‘It looks to me as if my
house were infected.’ 36The priest shall then
order the house to be cleared out before he goes
in to examine the infection, lest everything in
the house become unclean. Only after this is he
to go in to examine the house. 37If the priest, on
examining it, finds that the infection on the
walls of the house consists of greenish or reddish
depressions which seem to go deeper than the
surface of the wall, 38he shall close the door of
the house behind him and quarantine the house
for seven days. 39On the seventh day the priest
shall return to examine the house again. If he
finds that the infection has spread on the walls,
40he shall order the infected stones to be pulled
out and cast in an unclean place outside the city.
41The whole inside of the house shall then be
scraped, and the mortar that has been scraped
off shall be dumped in an unclean place outside
the city. 42Then new stones shall be brought and
put in the place of the old stones, and new
mortar shall be made and plastered on the
house.

43“If the infection breaks out once more after
the stones have been pulled out and the house
has been scraped and replastered, 44the priest
shall come again; and if he finds that the
infection has spread in the house, it is corrosive
leprosy, and the house is unclean. 45It shall be
pulled down, and all its stones, beams and
mortar shall be hauled away to an unclean place
outside the city. 46Whoever enters a house while
it is quarantined shall be unclean until evening.
47Whoever sleeps or eats in such a house shall
also wash his garments. 48If the priest finds,
when he comes to examine the house, that the
infection has in fact not spread after the plaster-
ing, he shall declare the house clean, since the
infection has been healed. 49To purify the house,
he shall take two birds, as well as cedar wood,
scarlet yarn, and hyssop. 50One of the birds he
shall slay over an earthen vessel with spring
water in it. 51Then, taking the cedar wood, the
hyssop and the scarlet yarn, together with the
living bird, he shall dip them all in the blood of
the slain bird and the spring water, and sprinkle
the house seven times. 52Thus shall he purify the
house with the bird's blood and the spring

14, 22: Two turtledoves: substitutes for the two additional lambs, similar to the offering of a poor woman after childbirth. Cf Lv 12, 8.

water, along with the living bird, the cedar wood, the hyssop, and the scarlet yarn. [53]He shall then let the living bird fly away over the countryside outside the city. When he has thus made atonement for it, the house will be clean.

[54]"This is the law for every kind of human leprosy and scall, [55] [r]for leprosy of garments and houses, [56]as well as for scabs, pustules and blotches, [57]so that it may be manifest when there is a state of uncleanness and when a state of cleanness. This is the law for leprosy."

CHAPTER 15

Personal Uncleanness [1]The LORD said to Moses and Aaron, [2]"Speak to the Israelites and tell them: Every man who is afflicted with a chronic flow from his private parts is thereby unclean.[s] [3]Such is his uncleanness from this flow that it makes no difference whether the flow drains off or is blocked up; his uncleanness remains. [4]Any bed on which the man afflicted with the flow lies, is unclean, and any piece of furniture on which he sits, is unclean. [5]Anyone who touches his bed shall wash his garments, bathe in water, and be unclean until evening. [6]Whoever sits on a piece of furniture on which the afflicted man was sitting, shall wash his garments, bathe in water, and be unclean until evening. [7]Whoever touches the body of the afflicted man shall wash his garments, bathe in water, and be unclean until evening. [8]If the afflicted man spits on a clean man, the latter shall wash his garments, bathe in water, and be unclean until evening. [9]Any saddle on which the afflicted man rides, is unclean. [10]Whoever touches anything that was under him shall be unclean until evening; whoever lifts up any such thing shall wash his garments, bathe in water, and be unclean until evening. [11]Anyone whom the afflicted man touches with unrinsed hands shall wash his garments, bathe in water, and be unclean until evening. [12]Earthenware touched by the afflicted man shall be broken; and every wooden article shall be rinsed with water.

[13]"When a man who has been afflicted with a flow becomes free of his affliction, he shall wait seven days for his purification. Then he shall wash his garments and bathe his body in fresh water, and so he will be clean. [14]On the eighth day he shall take two turtledoves or two pigeons, and going before the LORD, to the entrance of the meeting tent, he shall give them to the priest, [15]who shall offer them up, the one as a sin offering and the other as a holocaust. Thus shall the priest make atonement before the LORD for the man's flow.

[16]"When a man has an emission of seed, he shall bathe his whole body in water and be unclean until evening. [17]Any piece of cloth or leather with seed on it shall be washed with water and be unclean until evening.

[18]"If a man lies carnally with a woman, they shall both bathe in water and be unclean until evening.

[19]"When a woman has her menstrual flow, she shall be in a state of impurity for seven days.[t] Anyone who touches her shall be unclean until evening. [20]Anything on which she lies or sits during her impurity shall be unclean. [21]Anyone who touches her bed shall wash his garments, bathe in water, and be unclean until evening. [22]Whoever touches any article of furniture on which she was sitting, shall wash his garments, bathe in water, and be unclean until evening. [23]*But if she is on the bed or on the seat when he touches it, he shall be unclean until evening. [24]If a man dares to lie with her, he contracts her impurity and shall be unclean for seven days;[u] every bed on which he then lies also becomes unclean.

[25]"When a woman is afflicted with a flow of blood for several days outside her menstrual period, or when her flow continues beyond the ordinary period,[v] as long as she suffers this unclean flow she shall be unclean, just as during her menstrual period. [26]Any bed on which she lies during such a flow becomes unclean, as it would during her menstruation, and any article of furniture on which she sits becomes unclean just as during her menstruation. [27]Anyone who touches them becomes unclean; he shall wash

15, 23: What is added to the legislation by this verse is uncertain in both the Hebrew and the Greek.

r Lv 13, 47–58. s Nm 5, 2. t Lv 12, 2. 5. u Lv 18, 19. v Mt 9, 20; Mk 5, 25; Lk 8, 43.

his garments, bathe in water, and be unclean
until evening.
28 "If she becomes freed from her affliction,
she shall wait seven days, and only then is she to
be purified. 29 On the eighth day she shall take
two turtledoves or two pigeons and bring them
to the priest at the entrance of the meeting tent.
30 The priest shall offer up one of them as a sin
offering and the other as a holocaust. Thus shall
the priest make atonement before the LORD for
her unclean flow.
31 "You shall warn the Israelites of their un-
cleanness, lest by defiling my Dwelling, which is
in their midst, their uncleanness be the cause of
their death.
32 "This is the law for the man who is afflicted
with a chronic flow, or who has an emission of
seed, and thereby becomes unclean; 33 as well as
for the woman who has her menstrual period, or
who is afflicted with a chronic flow; the law for
male and female; and also for the man who lies
with an unclean woman."

CHAPTER 16

The Day of Atonement 1 After the death of
Aaron's two sons, who died when they ap-
proached the LORD's presence, the LORD spoke
to Moses 2 and said to him,[w] "Tell your brother
Aaron that he is not to come whenever he
pleases into the sanctuary, inside the veil,* in
front of the propitiatory on the ark; otherwise,
when I reveal myself in a cloud above the
propitiatory, he will die. 3 Only in this way may
Aaron enter the sanctuary. He shall bring a
young bullock for a sin offering and a ram for a
holocaust. 4 He shall wear the sacred linen tunic,
with the linen drawers next his flesh, gird
himself with the linen sash and put on the linen
miter. But since these vestments are sacred, he
shall not put them on until he has first bathed his
body in water. 5 From the Israelite community he
shall receive two male goats for a sin offering
and one ram for a holocaust.[x]
6 "Aaron shall bring in the bullock, his sin
offering to atone for himself and for his house-
hold. 7 Taking the two male goats, and setting
them before the LORD at the entrance of the
meeting tent, 8 he shall cast lots to determine
which one is for the LORD and which for
Azazel.* 9 The goat that is determined by lot for
the LORD, Aaron shall bring in and offer up as a
sin offering. 10 But the goat determined by lot for
Azazel he shall set alive before the LORD, so that
with it he may make atonement by sending it off
to Azazel in the desert.
11 "Thus shall Aaron offer up the bullock, his
sin offering, to atone for himself and for his
family. When he has slaughtered it, 12 he shall
take a censer full of glowing embers from the
altar before the LORD, as well as a double
handful of finely ground fragrant incense, and
bringing them inside the veil, 13 there before the
LORD he shall put incense on the fire, so that a
cloud of incense may cover the propitiatory over
the commandments; else he will die.* 14 Taking
some of the bullock's blood, he shall sprinkle it
with his finger on the fore part of the propitiatory
and likewise sprinkle some of the blood with his
finger seven times in front of the propitiatory.[y]
15 "Then he shall slaughter the people's sin-
offering goat, and bringing its blood inside the
veil, he shall do with it as he did with the
bullock's blood, sprinkling it on the propitiatory
and before it.[z] 16 Thus he shall make atonement
for the sanctuary because of all the sinful defile-
ments and faults of the Israelites. He shall do the
same for the meeting tent, which is set up
among them in the midst of their uncleanness.
17 No one else may be in the meeting tent from
the time he enters the sanctuary to make atone-
ment until he departs. When he has made
atonement for himself and his household, as well

16, 2: The sanctuary, inside the veil: the innermost part of the sanctuary, known also as "the holy of holies." Cf Ex 26, 33f. Here the high priest was allowed to enter only once a year, on Yom Kippur, the Day of Atonement. In Heb 9, 3–12 this ceremony is applied to Christ's single act of Redemption, whereby he won for us an everlasting atonement. Propitiatory: see note on Ex 25, 17.

16, 8: Azazel: perhaps a name of Satan, used only in this chapter. The ancient versions translated this word as "the escaping goat," whence the English word "scapegoat."

16, 13: Else he will die: the smoke is to conceal the resplendent majesty of God, the sight of which would strike any man dead.

w Heb 9, 6–12. x Nm 29, 11. y Heb 9, 13. 25. z Heb 5, 1; 6, 19.

as for the whole Israelite community, 18he shall
come out to the altar before the LORD and make
atonement for it also. Taking some of the bull-
ock's and the goat's blood, he shall put it on the
horns around the altar,[a] 19and with his finger
sprinkle some of the blood on it seven times.
Thus he shall render it clean and holy, purged of
the defilements of the Israelites.

The Scapegoat 20"When he has completed the
atonement rite for the sanctuary, the meeting
tent and the altar, Aaron shall bring forward the
live goat. 21Laying both hands on its head, he
shall confess over it all the sinful faults and
transgressions of the Israelites, and so put them
on the goat's head.[b] He shall then have it led
into the desert by an attendant. 22Since the goat
is to carry off their iniquities to an isolated
region, it must be sent away into the desert.[c]

23*"After Aaron has again gone into the
meeting tent, he shall strip off and leave in the
sanctuary the linen vestments he had put on
when he entered there. 24After bathing his body
with water in a sacred place, he shall put on his
vestments, and then come out and offer his own
and the people's holocaust, in atonement for
himself and for the people, 25and also burn the
fat of the sin offering on the altar.

26"The man who has led away the goat for
Azazel shall wash his garments and bathe his
body in water; only then may he enter the camp.
27The sin-offering bullock and goat whose blood
was brought into the sanctuary to make atone-
ment, shall be taken outside the camp,[d] where
their hides and flesh and offal shall be burned up
in the fire. 28The one who burns them shall
wash his garments and bathe his body in water;
only then may he enter the camp.

The Fast 29[e]"This shall be an everlasting ordi-
nance for you: on the tenth day of the seventh
month every one of you, whether a native or a
resident alien, shall mortify himself* and shall do
no work. 30Since on this day atonement is made
for you to make you clean, so that you may be
cleansed of all your sins before the LORD, 31by
everlasting ordinance it shall be a most solemn
sabbath for you, on which you must mortify
yourselves.

32"This atonement is to be made by the priest
who has been anointed and ordained to the
priesthood in succession to his father. He shall
wear the linen garments, the sacred vestments,
33and make atonement for the sacred sanctuary,
the meeting tent and the altar, as well as for the
priests and all the people of the community.
34This, then, shall be an everlasting ordinance
for you: once a year atonement shall be made for
all the sins of the Israelites."[f]

Thus was it done, as the LORD had com-
manded Moses.

IV: Code of Legal Holiness

CHAPTER 17

Sacredness of Blood 1The LORD said to Mo-
ses, 2"Speak to Aaron and his sons, as well as to
all the Israelites, and tell them: This is what the
LORD has commanded. 3*Any Israelite who
slaughters an ox or a sheep or a goat, whether in
the camp or outside of it, 4without first bringing
it to the entrance of the meeting tent to present
it as an offering to the LORD in front of his
Dwelling, shall be judged guilty of bloodshed;
and for this, such a man shall be cut off from
among his people. 5Therefore, such sacrifices as
they used to offer up in the open field the
Israelites shall henceforth offer to the LORD,
bringing them to the priest at the entrance of the
meeting tent and sacrificing them there as peace
offerings to the LORD. 6The priest shall splash the
blood on the altar of the LORD at the entrance of
the meeting tent and there burn the fat for an

16, 23: This verse is best read after v 25. According to later Jewish practice the high priest again went into the holy of holies to remove the censer.

16, 29: Mortify himself: literally, "afflict his soul"; traditionally understood by the Jews as signifying abstinence from all food. This is the only fast day prescribed in the Mosaic law.

17, 3ff: The ancients considered blood the seat and sign of life, and therefore something sacred, even in animals. Cf Gn 9, 4f. Hence, even the ordinary butchering of an animal for meat was looked upon as having a sacrificial character, so that it should be performed at the sanctuary. This law, however, could not be carried out without great difficulty when the Israelites were scattered throughout Palestine, and so was modified in Dt 12, 20ff.

a Ex 30, 12. b Is 53, 6; 2 Cor 5, 21. c Is 53, 11. 12; Jn 1, 29; 1 Pt 2, 24. d Heb 13, 11. e Lv 23, 27. 32; Nm 29, 7. f Heb 9, 7. 25.

odor pleasing to the LORD. 7 No longer shall they offer their sacrifices to the satyrs to whom they used to render their wanton worship.[g] This shall be an everlasting ordinance for them and their descendants.

8 "Tell them, therefore: Anyone, whether of the house of Israel or of the aliens residing among them, who offers a holocaust or sacrifice 9 without bringing it to the entrance of the meeting tent to offer it to the LORD, shall be cut off from his kinsmen. 10 And if anyone, whether of the house of Israel or of the aliens residing among them, partakes of any blood, I will set myself against that one who partakes of blood and will cut him off from among his people.[h] 11 [i]Since the life of a living body is in its blood, I have made you put it on the altar, so that atonement may thereby be made for your own lives,* because it is the blood, as the seat of life, that makes atonement. 12 That is why I have told the Israelites: No one among you, not even a resident alien, may partake of blood.

13 "Anyone hunting, whether of the Israelites or of the aliens residing among them, who catches an animal or a bird that may be eaten, shall pour out its blood and cover it with earth. 14 Since the life of every living body is its blood, I have told the Israelites: You shall not partake of the blood of any meat.[j] Since the life of every living body is its blood, anyone who partakes of it shall be cut off.

15 [k]Everyone, whether a native or an alien, who eats of an animal that died of itself or was killed by a wild beast, shall wash his garments, bathe in water, and be unclean until evening, and then he will be clean. 16 If he does not wash or does not bathe his body, he shall have the guilt to bear."

CHAPTER 18

The Sanctity of Sex 1 The LORD said to Moses, 2 "Speak to the Israelites and tell them: I, the LORD, am your God. 3 You shall not do as they do in the land of Egypt, where you once lived, nor shall you do as they do in the land of Canaan, where I am bringing you; do not conform to their customs. 4 My decrees you shall carry out, and my statutes you shall take care to follow. I, the LORD, am your God. 5 Keep, then, my statutes and decrees, for the man who carries them out will find life through them. I am the LORD.[l]

6* "None of you shall approach a close relative to have sexual intercourse with her. I am the LORD. 7 [m]You shall not disgrace your father by having intercourse with your mother. Besides, since she is your own mother, you shall not have intercourse with her. 8 You shall not have intercourse with your father's wife,[n] for that would be a disgrace to your father. 9 You shall not have intercourse with your sister, your father's daughter or your mother's daughter, whether she was born in your own household or born elsewhere. 10 You shall not have intercourse with your son's daughter or with your daughter's daughter, for that would be a disgrace to your own family. 11 You shall not have intercourse with the daughter whom your father's wife bore to him, since she, too, is your sister. 12 [o]You shall not have intercourse with your father's sister, since she is your father's relative. 13 You shall not have intercourse with your mother's sister, since she is your mother's relative. 14 You shall not disgrace your father's brother by being intimate with his wife,[p] since she, too, is your aunt. 15 You shall not have intercourse with your daughter-in-law; she is your son's wife, and therefore you shall not disgrace her. 16 You shall not have intercourse with your brother's wife,* for that would

17, 11: That atonement may thereby be made for your own lives: hence, the sacrifice of an animal was a symbolic act which substituted the victim's life for the life of the offerer, who thus acknowledged that he deserved God's punishments for his sins. This idea of sacrifice is applied in Heb 9–10 to the death of Christ, inasmuch as "without the shedding of blood there is no forgiveness" (Heb 9, 22).

18, 6–18: These laws are formulated as directed to the male Israelites only, but naturally the same norms of consanguinity and affinity would apply to the women as well. Marriage, as well as casual intercourse, is here forbidden between men and women of the specified degrees of relationship.

18, 16: With your brother's wife: it was the violation of this law which aroused the wrath of John the Baptist against Herod Antipas. Cf Mk 6, 18. An exception to this law is made in Dt 25, 5.

g Ex 34, 15; Dt 32, 17; 2 Chr 11, 15; 1 Cor 10, 20. h Lv 3, 17. i Gn 9, 4. j Lv 7, 26f. k Lv 11, 39f; 22, 8. l Gal 3, 12. m 7–16: Lv 20, 11–21. n Dt 23, 1; 27, 20; 1 Cor 5, 1. o 12f: Lv 20, 19. p Lv 20, 20.

be a disgrace to your brother.[q] 17You shall not have intercourse with a woman and also with her daughter, nor shall you marry and have intercourse with her son's daughter or her daughter's daughter; this would be shameful, because they are related to her. 18While your wife is still living you shall not marry her sister as her rival; for thus you would disgrace your first wife.

19"You shall not approach a woman to have intercourse with her while she is unclean from menstruation. 20You shall not have carnal relations with your neighbor's wife, defiling yourself with her. 21[r]You shall not offer any of your offspring to be immolated to Molech,* thus profaning the name of your God. I am the LORD. 22You shall not lie with a male as with a woman; such a thing is an abomination.[s] 23You shall not have carnal relations with an animal, defiling yourself with it; nor shall a woman set herself in front of an animal to mate with it; such things are abhorrent.[t]

24"Do not defile yourselves by any of these things by which the nations whom I am driving out of your way have defiled themselves. 25Because their land has become defiled, I am punishing it for its wickedness, by making it vomit out its inhabitants. 26You, however, whether natives or resident aliens, must keep my statutes and decrees forbidding all such abominations 27by which the previous inhabitants defiled the land; 28otherwise the land will vomit you out also for having defiled it, just as it vomited out the nations before you. 29Everyone who does any of these abominations shall be cut off from among his people. 30Heed my charge, then, not to defile yourselves by observing the abominable customs that have been observed before you.[u] I, the LORD, am your God."

CHAPTER 19

Various Rules of Conduct 1The LORD said to Moses, 2"Speak to the whole Israelite community and tell them: Be holy, for I, the LORD, your God, am holy.[v] 3Revere your mother and father,[w] and keep my sabbaths. I, the LORD, am your God.

4"Do not turn aside to idols, nor make molten gods for yourselves.[x] I, the LORD, am your God.

5"When you sacrifice your peace offering to the LORD, if you wish it to be acceptable, 6it must be eaten on the very day of your sacrifice or on the following day. Whatever is left over until the third day shall be burned up in the fire. 7If any of it is eaten on the third day, the sacrifice will be unacceptable as refuse;[y] 8whoever eats of it then shall pay the penalty for having profaned what is sacred to the LORD. Such a one shall be cut off from his people.

9"When you reap the harvest of your land, you shall not be so thorough that you reap the field to its very edge, nor shall you glean the stray ears of grain.[z] 10Likewise, you shall not pick your vineyard bare, nor gather up the grapes that have fallen. These things you shall leave for the poor and the alien. I, the LORD, am your God.

11"You shall not steal. You shall not lie or speak falsely to one another.[a] 12You shall not swear falsely by my name, thus profaning the name of your God.[b] I am the LORD.

13"You shall not defraud or rob your neighbor. You shall not withhold overnight the wages of your day laborer.[c] 14You shall not curse the deaf, or put a stumbling block in front of the blind, but you shall fear your God. I am the LORD.

15"You shall not act dishonestly in rendering judgment. Show neither partiality to the weak nor deference to the mighty, but judge your fellow men justly.[d] 16You shall not go about spreading slander among your kinsmen; nor shall you stand by idly when your neighbor's life is at stake. I am the LORD.

17"You shall not bear hatred for your brother in your heart.[e] Though you may have to reprove

18, 21: Immolated to Molech: the reference is to the Canaanite custom of sacrificing children to the god Molech. The little victims were first slain and then cremated. Cf Ez 16, 20ff; 20, 26. 31; 23, 37.

q Lv 20, 21; Mt 14, 3f; Mk 6, 18. r Lv 20, 2–5; Dt 18, 10; 2 Kgs 16, 3; 21, 6. s Lv 20, 13; Rom 1, 27; 1 Cor 6, 9f. t Lv 20, 15f; Ex 22, 18. u Lv 20, 23; Dt 18, 9. v Lv 11, 44; Mt 5, 48; 1 Pt 1, 16. w Ex 20, 12. x Lv 26, 1; Ex 20, 3–5; 34, 17; Dt 27, 15. y Lv 7, 18. z Lv 23, 22; Dt 24, 19ff. a Ex 20, 15f. b Ex 20, 7; Mt 5, 33. c Dt 24, 14f. d Ex 23, 2f; Dt 1, 17; 16, 19; Ps 82, 2; Prv 24, 23. e Mt 18, 15; Lk 17, 3; Gal 6, 1; 1 Jn 3, 14.

your fellow man, do not incur sin because of him. 18 Take no revenge and cherish no grudge against your fellow countrymen. You shall love your neighbor as yourself.* I am the LORD.[f]

19 "Keep my statutes: do not breed any of your domestic animals with others of a different species; do not sow a field of yours with two different kinds of seed; and do not put on a garment woven with two different kinds of thread.

20* "If a man has carnal relations with a female slave who has already been living with another man but has not yet been redeemed or given her freedom, they shall be punished but not put to death, because she is not free. 21 The man, moreover, shall bring to the entrance of the meeting tent a ram as his guilt offering to the LORD. 22 With this ram the priest shall make atonement before the LORD for the sin he has committed, and it will be forgiven him.

23 "When you come into the land and plant any fruit tree there, first look upon its fruit as if it were uncircumcised. For three years, while its fruit remains uncircumcised,* it may not be eaten. 24 In the fourth year, however, all of its fruit shall be sacred to the LORD as a thanksgiving feast to him. 25 Not until the fifth year may you eat its fruit. Thus it will continue its yield for you. I, the LORD, am your God.

26 "Do not eat meat with the blood still in it.[g] Do not practice divination or soothsaying. 27* Do not clip your hair at the temples, nor trim the edges of your beard.[h] 28 Do not lacerate your bodies for the dead, and do not tattoo yourselves. I am the LORD.

29 "You shall not degrade your daughter by making a prostitute of her; else the land will become corrupt and full of lewdness. 30 Keep my sabbaths, and reverence my sanctuary.[i] I am the LORD.

31 "Do not go to mediums or consult fortune-tellers, for you will be defiled by them.[j] I, the LORD, am your God.

32 "Stand up in the presence of the aged, and show respect for the old: thus shall you fear your God. I am the LORD.

33 "When an alien resides with you in your land, do not molest him.[k] 34 You shall treat the alien who resides with you no differently than the natives born among you; have the same love for him as for yourself; for you too were once aliens in the land of Egypt.[l] I, the LORD, am your God.

35 "Do not act dishonestly in using measures of length or weight or capacity. 36 You shall have a true scale and true weights, an honest ephah and an honest hin.[m] I, the LORD, am your God, who brought you out of the land of Egypt. 37 Be careful, then, to observe all my statutes and decrees. I am the LORD."

CHAPTER 20

Penalties for Various Sins 1 The LORD said to Moses, 2 "Tell the Israelites: Anyone, whether an Israelite or an alien residing in Israel, who gives any of his offspring to Molech shall be put to death.[n] Let his fellow citizens stone him. 3 [o] I myself will turn against such a man and cut him off from the body of his people; for in giving his offspring to Molech, he has defiled my sanctuary and profaned my holy name. 4 Even if his fellow citizens connive at such a man's crime of giving his offspring to Molech, and fail to put him to death, 5 I myself will set my face against that man and his family and will cut off from their people both him and all who join him in his wanton

19, 18: You shall love your neighbor as yourself: cited by our Lord as the second of the two most important commandments of God. Cf Mt 22, 39; Mk 12, 31. Although in the present context the word "neighbor" is restricted to "fellow countrymen," in Lk 10, 29–37 Christ extends its meaning to embrace all men, even enemies. Cf also Mt 5. 43ff.

19, 20ff: This law seems out of its proper context here; perhaps it stood originally after Lv 20, 12. Female slave . . . given her freedom: reference is to the case treated of in Ex 21, 7–11.

19, 23ff: Uncircumcised: by analogy with a newborn boy, the newly planted tree was considered impure until "circumcised" by offering to the Lord all the fruit it bore in the fourth year.

19, 27: See note on Lv 21, 5.

f Mt 5, 43; 19, 19; 22, 39; Mk 12, 31; Rom 13, 9; Gal 5, 14; Jas 2, 8. g Lv 3, 17; Dt 18, 10; 2 Kgs 17, 17; 21, 6; 2 Chr 33, 6. h Lv 21, 5. i Lv 26, 2; Ex 20, 8. j Lv 20, 6. 27; Dt 18, 11; Is 8, 19. k Ex 22, 20; 23, 9; Jer 22, 3; Mal 3, 5. l Dt 10, 19. m Dt 25, 13. 15; Prv 11, 1; 16, 11; 20, 10; Ez 45, 10. n Lv 18, 21. o Ez 23, 39.

worship of Molech. 6 Should anyone turn to mediums and fortune-tellers and follow their wanton ways,[p] I will turn against such a one and cut him off from his people. 7 Sanctify yourselves, then, and be holy; for I, the LORD, your God, am holy.[q] 8 Be careful, therefore, to observe what I, the LORD, who make you holy, have prescribed.

9 "Anyone who curses his father or mother shall be put to death;[r] since he has cursed his father or mother, he has forfeited his life. 10 If a man commits adultery with his neighbor's wife, both the adulterer and the adulteress shall be put to death.[s] 11 If a man disgraces his father[t] by lying with his father's wife, both the man and his stepmother shall be put to death; they have forfeited their lives. 12 If a man lies with his daughter-in-law,[u] both of them shall be put to death; since they have committed an abhorrent deed, they have forfeited their lives. 13 If a man lies with a male as with a woman,[v] both of them shall be put to death for their abominable deed; they have forfeited their lives. 14 If a man marries a woman and her mother also,[w] the man and the two women as well shall be burned to death for their shameful conduct, so that such shamefulness may not be found among you. 15 If a man has carnal relations with an animal, the man shall be put to death,[x] and the animal shall be slain. 16 If a woman goes up to any animal to mate with it,[y] the woman and the animal shall be slain; let them both be put to death; their lives are forfeit. 17 If a man consummates marriage with his sister or his half-sister,[z] they shall be publicly cut off from their people for this shameful deed; the man shall pay the penalty of having had intercourse with his own sister. 18 If a man lies in sexual intercourse with a woman during her menstrual period,[a] both of them shall be cut off from their people, because they have laid bare the flowing fountain of her blood. 19 You shall not have intercourse with your mother's sister or your father's sister;[b] whoever does so shall pay the penalty of incest. 20 If a man disgraces his uncle by having intercourse with his uncle's wife, the man and his aunt shall pay the penalty by dying childless. 21 If a man marries his brother's wife and thus disgraces his brother, they shall be childless because of this incest.

22 "Be careful to observe all my statutes and all my decrees; otherwise the land where I am bringing you to dwell will vomit you out. 23 Do not conform, therefore, to the customs of the nations[c] whom I am driving out of your way, because all these things that they have done have filled me with disgust for them. 24 But to you I have said:[d] Their land shall be your possession, a land flowing with milk and honey. I am giving it to you as your own, I, the LORD, your God, who have set you apart from the other nations. 25 [e]You, too, must set apart, then, the clean animals from the unclean, and the clean birds from the unclean, so that you may not be contaminated with the uncleanness of any beast or bird or of any swarming creature in the land that I have set apart for you. 26 To me, therefore, you shall be sacred; for I, the LORD, am sacred,[f] I, who have set you apart from the other nations to be my own.

27 * "A man or a woman who acts as a medium or fortune-teller[g] shall be put to death by stoning; they have no one but themselves to blame for their death."

CHAPTER 21

Sanctity of the Priesthood 1 The LORD said to Moses, "Speak to Aaron's sons, the priests, and tell them: None of you shall make himself unclean for any dead person* among his people,[h] 2 except for his nearest relatives, his mother or father, his son or daughter, his brother 3 or his maiden sister, who is of his own family while she remains unmarried; for these he may make himself unclean. 4 But for a sister who has

20, 27: This verse is best read immediately after v 6.

21, 1: Unclean for any dead person: by preparing the corpse for burial. Cf Nm 6, 6; 19, 11–19.

p Lv 19, 31. q Lv 11, 44; 19, 2; 1 Pt 1, 16. r Ex 21, 17; Prv 20, 20; Mt 15, 4; Mk 7, 10. s Lv 18, 20; Dt 22, 22; Jn 8, 5. t Lv 18, 7f. u Lv 18, 15. v Lv 18, 22. w Lv 18, 17; Dt 27, 23. x Ex 22, 18; Dt 27, 21. y Lv 18, 23. z Lv 18, 9; Dt 27, 22. a Lv 18, 19. b Lv 18, 12f. c Lv 18, 30. d Ex 3, 8. 17; 6, 8. e Lv 11, 2–47; Dt 14, 4–20. f Lv 11, 44; Ex 19, 6; 1 Pt 1, 16. g Lv 19, 31; Ex 22, 17; Dt 18, 11. h Ez 44, 25.

married out of his family he shall not make himself unclean; this would be a profanation.

5*"The priests shall not make bare the crown of the head, nor shave the edges of the beard,[i] nor lacerate the body. 6 To their God they shall be sacred,* and not profane his name; since they offer up the oblations of the LORD, the food of their God, they must be holy.

7 "A priest shall not marry a woman who has been a prostitute or has lost her honor, nor a woman who has been divorced by her husband; for the priest is sacred to his God.[j] 8 Honor him as sacred who offers up the food of your God; treat him as sacred, because I, the LORD, who have consecrated him, am sacred.

9 "A priest's daughter who loses her honor by committing fornication and thereby dishonors her father also, shall be burned to death.

10 "The most exalted of the priests, upon whose head the anointing oil has been poured and who has been ordained to wear the special vestments, shall not bare his head* or rend his garments, 11 nor shall he go near any dead person. Not even for his father or mother may he thus become unclean 12 or leave the sanctuary;[k] otherwise he will profane the sanctuary of his God, for with the anointing oil upon him, he is dedicated to his God, to me, the LORD.

13 "The priest shall marry a virgin. 14 Not a widow or a woman who has been divorced or a woman who has lost her honor as a prostitute, but a virgin, taken from his own people, shall he marry;[l] 15 otherwise he will have base offspring among his people. I, the LORD, have made him sacred."

Irregularities 16 The LORD said to Moses, 17 "Speak to Aaron and tell him: None of your descendants, of whatever generation, who has any defect shall come forward to offer up the food of his God. 18 Therefore, he who has any of the following defects may not come forward: he who is blind, or lame, or who has any disfigurement or malformation, 19 or a crippled foot or hand, 20 or who is humpbacked or weakly or walleyed, or who is afflicted with eczema, ringworm or hernia. 21 No descendant of Aaron the priest who has any such defect may draw near to offer up the oblations of the LORD; on account of his defect he may not draw near to offer up the food of his God. 22 He may, however, partake of the food of his God: of what is most sacred as well as of what is sacred. 23 Only, he may not approach the veil nor go up to the altar on account of his defect; he shall not profane these things that are sacred to me, for it is I, the LORD, who make them sacred."

24 Moses, therefore, told this to Aaron and his sons and to all the Israelites.

CHAPTER 22

Sacrificial Banquets 1 The LORD said to Moses, 2 "Tell Aaron and his sons to respect the sacred offerings which the Israelites consecrate to me; else they will profane my holy name. I am the LORD.

3 "Tell them: If any one of you, or of your descendants in any future generation, dares, while he is in a state of uncleanness, to draw near the sacred offerings which the Israelites consecrate to the LORD, such a one shall be cut off from my presence. I am the LORD.

4 "No descendant of Aaron who is stricken with leprosy, or who suffers from a flow, may eat of these sacred offerings, unless he again becomes clean.[m] Moreover, if anyone touches a person who has become unclean by contact with a corpse, or if anyone has had an emission of seed, 5 or if anyone touches[n] any swarming creature or any man whose uncleanness, of whatever kind it may be, is contagious, 6 the one who touches such as these shall be unclean until evening and may not eat of the sacred portions until he has first bathed his body in water;[o] 7 then, when the sun sets, he again becomes

21, 5: Such mourning customs of the Canaanites were forbidden to all the Israelites, but especially to the priests. Cf Lv 19, 27f.

21, 6: Sacred: the same Hebrew word has both the active meaning of "holy," that is, keeping oneself free from profane impurities, and the passive meaning of "sacred," that is, set apart from what is profane and therefore treated with religious reverence.

21, 10: Bare his head: see note on Lv 10, 6.

i Ez 44, 20. j Ez 44, 22. k Lv 10, 7. l Ez 44, 22. m Lv 7, 20; 15, 16. n Lv 11, 24. 43. o Heb 10, 22.

clean. Only then may he eat of the sacred offerings, which are his food. 8He shall not make himself unclean by eating of any animal that has died of itself or has been killed by wild beasts.[p] I am the LORD.

9"They shall keep my charge and not do wrong in this matter; else they will die for their profanation. I am the LORD who have consecrated them.

10"Neither a lay person nor a priest's tenant or hired servant may eat of any sacred offering.[q] 11But a slave whom a priest acquires by purchase or who is born in his house may eat of his food. 12A priest's daughter who is married to a layman may not eat of the sacred contributions. 13But if a priest's daughter is widowed or divorced and, having no children, returns to her father's house, she may then eat of her father's food as in her youth. No layman, however, may eat of it. 14 [r]If such a one eats of a sacred offering through inadvertence, he shall make restitution to the priest for the sacred offering, with an increment of one fifth of the amount. 15The sacred offerings which the Israelites contribute to the LORD the priests shall not allow to be profaned[s] 16nor in the eating of the sacred offering shall they bring down guilt that must be punished; it is I, the LORD, who make them sacred."

Unacceptable Victims 17The LORD said to Moses, 18"Speak to Aaron and his sons and to all the Israelites, and tell them: When anyone of the house of Israel, or any alien residing in Israel, who wishes to offer a sacrifice, brings a holocaust as a votive offering or as a free-will offering to the LORD, 19if it is to be acceptable, the ox or sheep or goat that he offers must be an unblemished male.[t] 20You shall not offer one that has any defect, for such a one would not be acceptable for you.[u] 21When anyone presents a peace offering[v] to the LORD from the herd or the flock in fulfillment of a vow, or as a free-will offering, if it is to find acceptance, it must be unblemished; it shall not have any defect. 22One that is blind or crippled or maimed, or one that has a running sore or mange or ringworm, you shall not offer to the LORD; do not put such an animal on the altar as an oblation to the LORD. 23An ox or a sheep that is in any way ill-proportioned or stunted you may indeed present as a free-will offering, but it will not be acceptable as a votive offering. 24One that has its testicles bruised or crushed or torn out or cut off you shall not offer to the LORD. You shall neither do this in your own land 25nor receive from a foreigner any such animals to offer up as the food of your God; since they are deformed or defective,[w] they will not be acceptable for you."

26The LORD said to Moses, 27"When an ox or a lamb or a goat is born, it shall remain with its mother for seven days; only from the eighth day onward will it be acceptable, to be offered as an oblation to the LORD.[x] 28You shall not slaughter an ox or a sheep on one and the same day with its young. 29Whenever you offer a thanksgiving sacrifice to the LORD, so offer it that it may be acceptable for you; 30it must, therefore, be eaten on the same day; none of it shall be left over until the next day.[y] I am the LORD.

31"Be careful to observe the commandments which I, the LORD, give you, 32and do not profane my holy name; in the midst of the Israelites I, the LORD, must be held as sacred. It is I who made you sacred 33and led you out of the land of Egypt, that I, the LORD, might be your God."

CHAPTER 23

Holy Days 1The LORD said to Moses, 2"Speak to the Israelites and tell them: The following are the festivals of the LORD, my feast days, which you shall celebrate with a sacred assembly.

3"For six days work may be done; but the seventh day is the sabbath rest, a day for sacred assembly, on which you shall do no work. The sabbath shall belong to the LORD wherever you dwell.[z]

p Lv 17, 15; Dt 14, 21; Ez 44, 31. q 1 Sm 21, 6; Mt 12, 4. r Lv 5, 16; 27, 13. 15. 19. s Lv 19, 8; Nm 18, 32. t Lv 1, 3. 10. u Dt 15, 21; 17, 1; Mal 1, 8. 14. v Lv 3, 1. 6. w Mal 1, 14. x Ex 22, 29. y Lv 7, 15. z Ex 20, 8–11; 23, 12; 31, 14f; 34, 21; Dt 5, 12–15; Lk 13, 14.

Passover 4“These, then, are the festivals of the LORD which you shall celebrate at their proper time with a sacred assembly.[a] 5The Passover of the LORD falls on the fourteenth day of the first month, at the evening twilight.[b] 6The fifteenth day of this month is the LORD's feast of Unleavened Bread. For seven days you shall eat unleavened bread.[c] 7On the first of these days you shall hold a sacred assembly and do no sort of work.[d] 8On each of the seven days you shall offer an oblation to the LORD. Then on the seventh day you shall again hold a sacred assembly and do no sort of work.”

9The LORD said to Moses, 10“Speak to the Israelites and tell them: When you come into the land which I am giving you, and reap your harvest, you shall bring a sheaf of the first fruits of your harvest to the priest, 11who shall wave the sheaf before the LORD that it may be acceptable for you. On the day after the sabbath* the priest shall do this. 12On this day, when your sheaf is waved, you shall offer to the LORD for a holocaust an unblemished yearling lamb. 13Its cereal offering shall be two tenths of an ephah of fine flour mixed with oil, as a sweet-smelling oblation to the LORD; and its libation shall be a fourth of a hin of wine. 14Until this day, when you bring your God this offering, you shall not eat any bread* or roasted grain or fresh kernels. This shall be a perpetual statute for you and your descendants wherever you dwell.

Pentecost 15“Beginning with the day after the sabbath, the day on which you bring the wave-offering sheaf, you shall count seven full weeks,[e] 16and then on the day after the seventh week, the fiftieth* day,[f] you shall present the new cereal offering to the LORD. 17For the wave offering of your first fruits to the LORD, you shall bring with you from wherever you live two loaves of bread made of two tenths of an ephah of fine flour and baked with leaven. 18Besides the bread, you shall offer to the LORD a holocaust of seven unblemished yearling lambs, one young bull, and two rams, along with their cereal offering and libations, as a sweet-smelling oblation to the LORD. 19One male goat shall be sacrificed as a sin offering, and two yearling lambs as a peace offering.[g] 20The priest shall wave the bread of the first fruits and the two lambs as a wave offering before the LORD; these shall be sacred to the LORD and belong to the priest. 21On this same day you shall by proclamation have a sacred assembly, and no sort of work may be done. This shall be a perpetual statute for you and your descendants wherever you dwell.

22“When you reap the harvest of your land, you shall not be so thorough that you reap the field to its very edge, nor shall you glean the stray ears of your grain. These things you shall leave for the poor and the alien. I, the LORD, am your God.”

New Year's Day 23The LORD said to Moses, 24“Tell the Israelites: On the first day of the seventh month you shall keep a sabbath rest, with a sacred assembly and with the trumpet blasts as a reminder; 25you shall then do no sort of work, and you shall offer an oblation to the LORD.”

The Day of Atonement 26[h]The LORD said to Moses, 27“The tenth of this seventh month is the Day of Atonement,[i] when you shall hold a sacred assembly and mortify yourselves and offer an oblation to the LORD. 28On this day you shall not do any work, because it is the Day of Atonement, when atonement is made for you before the LORD, your God. 29Anyone who does not mortify himself on this day shall be cut off from his people; 30and if anyone does any work on this day, I will remove him from the midst of his people. 31This is a perpetual statute for you

23, 11: The sabbath: according to the Jewish tradition this was the feast day itself, the fifteenth of Nisan, which was a special day of rest. Cf v 7. However, some understand here the Saturday of the Passover week, or even the Saturday following it; cf Jn 19, 31.

23, 14: Any bread: made from the new grain. The harvest had first to be sanctified for man's use by this offering to God.

23, 16: The fiftieth: from the Greek word for this we have the name “Pentecost.” Cf 2 Mc 12, 31; Acts 2, 1. It was also called “the feast of the Seven Weeks,” or simply “the feast of Weeks” (Nm 28, 26; Dt 16, 10; Tb 2, 1). The new cereal offering: of flour made from the new grain. Pentecost was the thanksgiving feast at the end of the grain harvest, which began after Passover. Later tradition made it a commemoration of the giving of the law at Sinai.

a Ex 23, 14–19. b Nm 9, 2f; 28, 16. c Ex 12, 18; 13, 3. 10; 23, 15; 34, 18. d Ex 12, 15; Nm 28, 18. 25. e Ex 34, 22; Nm 28, 26; Dt 16, 9. f Acts 2, 1. g Nm 28, 30. h Lv 25, 9. i Lv 16, 29f; Nm 29, 7.

and your descendants wherever you dwell: you shall do no work, 32but shall keep a sabbath of complete rest and mortify yourselves. Beginning on the evening of the ninth of the month, you shall keep this sabbath of yours from evening to evening."

The Feast of Booths 33The LORD said to Moses, 34"Tell the Israelites: The fifteenth day of this seventh month[j] is the LORD's feast of Booths,* which shall continue for seven days. 35On the first day there shall be a sacred assembly, and you shall do no sort of work. 36For seven days you shall offer an oblation to the LORD, and on the eighth day you shall again hold a sacred assembly and offer an oblation to the LORD. On that solemn closing you shall do no sort of work.

37"These, therefore, are the festivals of the LORD on which you shall proclaim a sacred assembly, and offer as an oblation to the LORD holocausts and cereal offerings, sacrifices and libations, as prescribed for each day, 38in addition to those of the LORD's sabbaths, your donations, your various votive offerings and the free-will offerings that you present to the LORD.

39"On the fifteenth day, then, of the seventh month, when you have gathered in the produce of the land,[k] you shall celebrate a pilgrim feast of the LORD for a whole week. The first and the eighth day shall be days of complete rest. 40On the first day you shall gather foliage* from majestic trees, branches of palms and boughs of myrtles and of valley poplars, and then for a week you shall make merry before the LORD, your God. 41By perpetual statute for you and your descendants you shall keep this pilgrim feast of the LORD for one whole week[l] in the seventh month of the year. 42During this week every native Israelite among you shall dwell in booths, 43that your descendants[m] may realize that, when I led the Israelites out of the land of Egypt, I made them dwell in booths. I, the LORD, am your God."

44Thus did Moses announce to the Israelites the festivals of the LORD.

CHAPTER 24

The Sanctuary Light 1The LORD said to Moses, 2"Order the Israelites to bring you clear oil of crushed olives for the light, so that you may keep lamps burning regularly.[n] 3In the meeting tent, outside the veil that hangs in front of the commandments, Aaron shall set up the lamps to burn before the LORD regularly, from evening till morning. Thus, by a perpetual statute for you and your descendants, 4the lamps shall be set up on the pure gold lampstand,[o] to burn regularly before the LORD.

The Showbread 5"You shall take fine flour and bake it[p] into twelve cakes, using two tenths of an ephah of flour for each cake. 6These you shall place in two piles, six in each pile, on the pure gold table before the LORD. 7On each pile put some pure frankincense, which shall serve as an oblation to the LORD, a token offering for the bread. 8Regularly on each sabbath day this bread shall be set out afresh[q] before the LORD, offered on the part of the Israelites by an everlasting agreement. 9It shall belong to Aaron and his sons, who must eat it in a sacred place, since, as something most sacred among the various oblations to the LORD, it is his by perpetual right."

Punishment of Blasphemy 10Among the Israelites there was a man born of an Israelite mother (Shelomith, daughter of Dibri, of the tribe of Dan) and an Egyptian father. 11This man quarreled publicly with another Israelite and cursed and blasphemed the LORD's name. So the people brought him to Moses, 12who kept him in custody till a decision from the LORD should settle the case for them. 13The LORD then said to Moses, 14"Take the blasphemer outside the

23, 34: Feast of Booths: the joyful observance of the vintage and fruit harvest. Cf Dt 16, 13. During the seven days of the feast the Israelites camped in booths of branches erected on the roofs of their houses or in the streets in commemoration of their wanderings in the desert, where they dwelt in booths.

23, 40: Foliage: literally, "fruit," but here probably used in the general sense of "produce, growth." These branches were used for constructing the "booths" or huts in which the people lived during the feast. Cf Neh 8, 15. However, from about the time of Christ on, the Jews have understood this of "fruit" in the strict sense; hence, branches of lemons and oranges were carried with the other branches in joyous procession.

j Nm 29, 12; Dt 16, 13; 2 Mc 1, 9. 18; Jn 7, 2. k Ex 23, 16; Dt 16, 13. l Nm 29, 12–38. m Dt 31, 10–13. n Ex 27. 20f. o Ex 25, 31. p Ex 25, 30; 1 Kgs 7, 48; 2 Chr 4, 19; 13, 11; Heb 9, 2. q 1 Chr 9, 32.

camp, and when all who heard him have laid
their hands on his head, let the whole commu-
nity stone him. 15 Tell the Israelites: Anyone who
curses his God shall bear the penalty of his sin;
16 whoever blasphemes the name of the LORD
shall be put to death.[r] The whole community
shall stone him; alien and native alike must be
put to death for blaspheming the LORD's name.
17 "Whoever takes the life of any human being
shall be put to death;[s] 18 whoever takes the life
of an animal shall make restitution of another
animal. A life for a life![t] 19 Anyone who inflicts
an injury on his neighbor shall receive the same
in return. 20 Limb for limb, eye for eye, tooth for
tooth! The same injury that a man gives another
shall be inflicted on him in return.[u] 21 Whoever
slays an animal shall make restitution, but who-
ever slays a man shall be put to death. 22 You
shall have but one rule, for alien and native
alike.[v] I, the LORD, am your God."
23 When Moses told this to the Israelites, they
took the blasphemer outside the camp and
stoned him;[w] they carried out the command
that the LORD had given Moses.

CHAPTER 25

The Sabbatical Year 1 The LORD said to Moses
on Mount Sinai, 2 "Speak to the Israelites and tell
them: When you enter the land that I am giving
you, let the land, too, keep a sabbath for the
LORD. 3 For six years you may sow your field, and
for six years prune your vineyard, gathering in
their produce.[x] 4 But during the seventh year the
land shall have a complete rest, a sabbath for the
LORD,[y] when you may neither sow your field
nor prune your vineyard. 5 *The aftergrowth of
your harvest you shall not reap, nor shall you
pick the grapes of your untrimmed vines in this
year of sabbath rest for the land. 6 While the land
has its sabbath, all its produce will be food
equally for you yourself and for your male and
female slaves, for your hired help and the
tenants who live with you, 7 and likewise for
your livestock and for the wild animals on your
land.

The Jubilee Year 8 "Seven weeks of years shall
you count—seven times seven years—so that
the seven cycles amount to forty-nine years.
9 Then, on the tenth day of the seventh month
let the trumpet resound; on this, the Day of
Atonement, the trumpet blast shall re-echo
throughout your land. 10 This fiftieth year* you
shall make sacred by proclaiming liberty in the
land for all its inhabitants.[z] It shall be a jubilee
for you, when every one of you shall return to
his own property, every one to his own family
estate. 11 In this fiftieth year, your year of jubilee,
you shall not sow, nor shall you reap the
aftergrowth or pick the grapes from the un-
trimmed vines. 12 Since this is the jubilee, which
shall be sacred for you, you may not eat of its
produce, except as taken directly from the field.
13 "In this year of jubilee, then, every one of
you shall return to his own property. 14 There-
fore, when you sell any land to your neighbor or
buy any from him, do not deal unfairly. 15 On the
basis of the number of years since the last jubilee
shall you purchase the land from him;[a] and so
also, on the basis of the number of years for
crops, shall he sell it to you. 16 When the years
are many, the price shall be so much the more;
when the years are few, the price shall be so
much the less. For it is really the number of
crops that he sells you. 17 Do not deal unfairly,
then; but stand in fear of your god. I, the LORD,
am your God.
18 "Observe my precepts and be careful to
keep my regulations, for then you will dwell
securely in the land. 19 The land will yield its fruit
and you will have food in abundance, so that

25, 5ff: As long as the produce of the sabbatical year remains on the field, it remains available to everyone; cf v 12. In Ex 23, 10f the poor and the wild beasts that have no other source of nourishment are alone mentioned.

25, 10: Fiftieth year: to arrive at this number, the preceding year of jubilee is included in the count, and therefore this is more exactly the forty-ninth year, the seventh sabbatical year. Liberty: Israelite slaves were set free (v 50) and landed property was returned to its original owner (v 13): two important laws for preserving the social and economic equilibrium. Jubilee: derived from the Hebrew word yobel, "ram's horn," which was blown on this occasion.

r 1 Kgs 21, 10. 13; Mt 26, 65f; Jn 10, 33. s Gn 9, 5f; Ex 21, 12; Nm 35, 31; Dt 19, 11f. t Ex 21, 33f. u Dt 19, 21; Mt 5, 38. v Lv 19, 34; Ex 12, 49; Nm 15, 16. w Acts 7, 57f. x Ex 23, 10f. y 1 Mc 6, 49. 53. z Nm 36, 4; Is 61, 2; Ez 46, 17; Lk 4, 19. a Lv 27, 18. 23.

you may live there without worry.[b] 20Therefore,
do not say, 'What shall we eat in the seventh
year, if we do not then sow or reap our crop?'[c]
21I will bestow such blessings on you in the sixth
year that there will then be crop enough for
three years. 22When you sow in the eighth year,
you will continue to eat from the old crop; and
even into the ninth year, when the crop comes
in, you will still have the old to eat from.[d]
Redemption of Property 23[e]"The land shall
not be sold in perpetuity; for the land is mine,
and you are but aliens who have become my
tenants. 24Therefore, in every part of the country
that you occupy, you must permit the land to be
redeemed. 25When one of your countrymen is
reduced to poverty and has to sell some of his
property, his closest relative, who has the right
to redeem it, may go and buy back what his
kinsman has sold.[f] 26If, however, the man has
no relative to redeem his land, but later on
acquires sufficient means to buy it back in his
own name, 27he shall make a deduction from
the price in proportion to the number of years
since the sale, and then pay back the balance to
the one to whom he sold it, so that he may thus
regain his own property. 28But if he does not
acquire sufficient means to buy back his land,
what he has sold shall remain in the possession
of the purchaser until the jubilee, when it must
be released and returned to its original owner.[g]

29"When someone sells a dwelling in a walled
town, he has the right to buy it back during the
time of one full year from its sale. 30But if such a
house in a walled town has not been redeemed
at the end of a full year, it shall belong in
perpetuity to the purchaser and his descendants;
nor shall it be released in the jubilee. 31However,
houses in villages that are not encircled by walls
shall be considered as belonging to the surround-
ing farm land; they may be redeemed at any
time, and in the jubilee they must be released.

32"In levitical cities the Levites shall always
have the right to redeem the town houses that
are their property. 33Any town house of the
Levites in their cities that had been sold and not
redeemed, shall be released in the jubilee; for
the town houses of the Levites are their heredi-
tary property in the midst of the Israelites.
34Moreover, the pasture land belonging to their
cities shall not be sold at all;[h] it must always
remain their hereditary property.

35"When one of your fellow countrymen is
reduced to poverty and is unable to hold out
beside you, extend to him the privileges of an
alien or a tenant, so that he may continue to live
with you.[i] 36Do not exact interest from your
countryman either in money or in kind, but out
of fear of God let him live with you. 37[j]You are
to lend him neither money at interest nor food at
a profit. 38I, the LORD, am your God, who
brought you out of the land of Egypt to give you
the land of Canaan and to be your God.

39"When, then, your countryman becomes so
impoverished beside you that he sells you his
services, do not make him work as a slave.[k]
40Rather, let him be like a hired servant or like
your tenant, working with you until the jubilee
year, 41when he, together with his children,
shall be released from your service and return to
his kindred and to the property of his ancestors.
42Since those whom I brought out of the land of
Egypt are servants of mine, they shall not be sold
as slaves to any man. 43Do not lord it over them
harshly, but stand in fear of your God.

44"Slaves, male and female, you may indeed
possess, provided you buy them from among the
neighboring nations. 45You may also buy them
from among the aliens who reside with you and
from their children who are born and reared in
your land. Such slaves you may own as chattels,
46and leave to your sons as their hereditary
property, making them perpetual slaves. But you
shall not lord it harshly over any of the Israelites,
your kinsmen.[l]

47"When one of your countrymen is reduced
to such poverty that he sells himself to a wealthy
alien who has a permanent or a temporary
residence among you, or to one of the descen-
dants of an immigrant family, 48even after he has
thus sold his services he still has the right of

b Lv 26, 5. c Mt 6, 25. 31; Lk 12, 22. 29. d Lv 26, 10. e 1 Pt 2, 11. f Ru 2, 20; 4, 4. 6; Jer 32, 7f. g Lv 27, 24. h Nm 35, 3. i Dt 15, 7. 8. j Dt 23, 19. k 1 Kgs 9, 22. l Is 14, 1f.

redemption; he may be redeemed by one of his
own brothers, 49or by his uncle or cousin, or by
some other relative or fellow clansman; or, if he
acquires the means, he may redeem himself.
50With his purchaser he shall compute the years
from the sale to the jubilee, distributing the sale
price over these years as though he had been
hired as a day laborer. 51The more such years
there are, the more of the sale price he shall pay
back as ransom; 52the fewer years there are left
before the jubilee year, the more he has to his
credit; in proportion to his years of service shall
he pay his ransom. 53The alien shall treat him as
a servant hired on an annual basis, and he shall
not lord it over him harshly under your very
eyes. 54If he is not thus redeemed, he shall
nevertheless be released, together with his chil-
dren, in the jubilee year.[m] 55For to me the
Israelites belong as servants; they are servants of
mine, because I brought them out of the land of
Egypt, I, the LORD, your God.

CHAPTER 26

The Reward of Obedience 1"Do not make
false gods for yourselves. You shall not erect an
idol or a sacred pillar for yourselves, nor shall
you set up a stone figure for worship in your
land;[n] for I, the LORD, am your God. 2Keep my
sabbaths,[o] and reverence my sanctuary. I am the
LORD.

3*"If you live in accordance with my precepts
and are careful to observe my commandments,
4I will give you rain in due season, so that the
land will bear its crops, and the trees their fruit;[p]
5your threshing will last till vintage time, and
your vintage till the time for sowing, and you
will have food to eat in abundance, so that you
may dwell securely in your land. 6I will establish
peace in the land, that you may lie down to rest
without anxiety. I will rid the country of raven-
ous beasts, and keep the sword of war from
sweeping across your land. 7You will rout your
enemies and lay them low with your sword.
8Five of you will put a hundred of your foes to
flight, and a hundred of you will chase ten
thousand of them, till they are cut down by your
sword. 9I will look with favor upon you, and
make you fruitful and numerous, as I carry out
my covenant with you. 10So much of the old
crops will you have stored up for food that you
will have to discard them to make room for the
new.[q] 11 [r]I will set my Dwelling among you, and
will not disdain you. 12Ever present in your
midst, I will be your God, and you will be my
people; 13for it is I, the LORD, your God, who
brought you out of the land of the Egyptians and
freed you from their slavery, breaking the yoke
they had laid upon you and letting you walk
erect.

Punishment of Disobedience 14"But if you
do not heed me and do not keep all these
commandments, 15if you reject my precepts and
spurn my decrees, refusing to obey all my
commandments and breaking my covenant,
16then I, in turn, will give you your deserts. I
will punish you with terrible woes—with wast-
ing and fever to dim the eyes and sap the life.
You will sow your seed in vain, for your enemies
will consume the crop. 17I will turn against you,
till you are beaten down before your enemies
and lorded over by your foes. You will take to
flight though no one pursues you.[s]

18"If even after this you do not obey me, I will
increase the chastisement for your sins
sevenfold, 19to break your haughty confidence. I
will make the sky above you as hard as iron, and
your soil as hard as bronze, 20so that your
strength will be spent in vain; your land will
bear no crops, and its trees no fruit.

21"If then you become defiant in your unwill-
ingness to obey me, I will multiply my blows
another sevenfold, as your sins deserve. 22I will
unleash the wild beasts against you, to rob you
of your children and wipe out your livestock, till
your population dwindles away and your roads
become deserted.

23"If, with all this, you still refuse to be

26, 3–45: Since God's covenant was with the Israelite nation as a whole, these promises and threats are made primarily to the entire community. The rewards and punishments are of a temporal nature because the community as such exists only here on earth, not in the hereafter.

m Ex 21, 2f. n Lv 19, 4; Ex 20, 4; Nm 33, 52; Dt 5, 8. o Ex 20, 8. p Ps 85, 13. q Lv 25, 22. r 11f: Ex 29, 45; Ez 39, 26ff; 2 Cor 6, 16. s Dt 28, 25.

chastened by me and continue to defy me, 24I,
too, will defy you and will smite you for your
sins seven times harder than before.[t] 25I will
make the sword, the avenger of my covenant,
sweep over you. Though you then huddle to-
gether in your walled cities, I will send in
pestilence among you, till you are forced to
surrender to the enemy. 26And as I cut off your
supply of bread, ten women will need but one
oven for baking all the bread they dole out to
you in rations[u] —not enough food to still your
hunger.
27"If, despite all this, you still persist in
disobeying and defying me, 28I, also, will meet
you with fiery defiance and will chastise you
with sevenfold fiercer punishment for your sins,
29 [v]till you begin to eat the flesh of your own sons
and daughters.* 30I will demolish your high
places,[w] overthrow your incense stands, and
cast your corpses on those of your idols. In my
abhorrence of you, 31I will lay waste your cities
and devastate your sanctuaries, refusing to ac-
cept your sweet-smelling offerings. 32So devas-
tated will I leave the land that your very enemies
who come to live there will stand aghast at the
sight of it.[x] 33You yourselves I will scatter among
the nations[y] at the point of my drawn sword,
leaving your countryside desolate and your cities
deserted. 34Then shall the land retrieve its lost
sabbaths during all the time it lies waste, while
you are in the land of your enemies; then shall
the land have rest and make up for its sabbaths[z]
35during all the time that it lies desolate, enjoy-
ing the rest that you would not let it have on the
sabbaths when you lived there.
36"Those of you who survive in the lands of
their enemies I will make so fainthearted that, if
leaves rustle behind them, they will flee head-
long, as if from the sword, though no one
pursues them; 37stumbling over one another as
if to escape a weapon, while no one is after
them—so helpless will you be to take a stand
against your foes! 38You will be lost among the
Gentiles, swallowed up in your enemies' coun-
try. 39Those of you who survive in the lands of
their enemies will waste away for their own and
their fathers' guilt.[a]
40"Thus they will have to confess that they
and their fathers were guilty of having rebelled
against me and of having defied me, 41so that I,
too, had to defy them and bring them into their
enemies' land. Then, when their uncircumcised
hearts are humbled and they make amends for
their guilt, 42I will remember my covenant with
Jacob, my covenant with Isaac, and my covenant
with Abraham;[b] and of the land, too, I will be
mindful. 43But the land must first be rid of them,
that in its desolation it may make up its lost
sabbaths, and that they, too, may make good the
debt of their guilt for having spurned my pre-
cepts and abhorred my statutes. 44Yet even so,
even while they are in their enemies' land, I will
not reject or spurn them, lest, by wiping them
out, I make void my covenant with them; for I,
the LORD, am their God. 45I will remember them
because of the covenant I made with their
forefathers, whom I brought out of the land of
Egypt under the very eyes of the Gentiles,[c] that
I, the LORD, might be their God."
46*These are the precepts, decrees and laws
which the LORD had Moses promulgate on
Mount Sinai in the pact between himself and the
Israelites.

V: Redemption of Offerings

CHAPTER 27

Redemption of Votive Offerings 1The LORD
said to Moses, 2"Speak to the Israelites and tell
them: When anyone fulfills a vow of offering one
or more persons to the LORD, who are to be
ransomed at a fixed sum of money, 3for persons
between the ages of twenty and sixty, the fixed
sum, in sanctuary shekels, shall be fifty silver

26, 29: Eat the flesh of your own sons and daughters: extreme famine in cities under siege often forced their inhabitants to such dire means of subsistence. Cf Dt 28, 53; Jer 19, 9; Ez 5, 10; 2 Kgs 6, 28f.

26, 46: The Book of Leviticus seems originally to have ended here; the following chapter is an appendix.

t 24f; Jer 2, 30; Ez 5, 17; 14, 17. u Is 9, 19; Ez 4, 16; 5, 16; 14, 13; Mi 6, 14. v Is 9, 18. w 2 Chr 14, 5; 34, 3. 4. 7; Ez 6, 3–6. x 1 Kgs 9, 8; Jer 9, 11; 18, 16; 19, 8; 25, 18; Ez 5, 15. y Jer 9, 16; Zec 7, 14. z Lv 25, 2; 2 Chr 36, 21. a Ez 4, 17; 24, 23; 33, 10. b Ex 6, 5; 2 Kgs 13, 23; Ps 106, 45; Ez 16, 60. c Ex 12, 51.

shekels for a man, 4and thirty shekels for a woman; 5for persons between the ages of five and twenty, the fixed sum shall be twenty shekels for a youth, and ten for a maiden; 6for persons between the ages of one month and five years, the fixed sum shall be five silver shekels for a boy, and three for a girl; 7for persons of sixty or more, the fixed sum shall be fifteen shekels for a man, and ten for a woman. 8However, if the one who took the vow is too poor to meet the fixed sum, the person must be set before the priest, who shall determine the sum for his ransom in keeping with the means of the one who made the vow.

9"If the offering vowed to the LORD is an animal that may be sacrificed, every such animal, when vowed to the LORD, becomes sacred. 10The offerer shall not present a substitute for it by exchanging either a better for a worse one or a worse for a better one. If he attempts to offer one animal in place of another, both the original and its substitute shall be treated as sacred. 11If the animal vowed to the LORD is unclean and therefore unfit for sacrifice, it must be set before the priest, 12who shall determine its value* in keeping with its good or bad qualities, and the value set by the priest shall stand. 13If the offerer wishes to redeem the animal, he shall pay one fifth more than this valuation.[d]

14"When someone dedicates his house as sacred to the LORD, the priest shall determine its value in keeping with its good or bad points, and the value set by the priest shall stand. 15If the one who dedicated his house wishes to redeem it, he shall pay one fifth more than the price thus established, and then it will again be his.

16"If the object which someone dedicates to the LORD is a piece of his hereditary land, its valuation shall be made according to the amount of seed required to sow it, the acreage sown with a homer of barley seed being valued at fifty silver shekels. 17If the dedication of a field is made at the beginning of a jubilee period, the full valuation shall hold; 18but if it is some time after this, the priest shall estimate its money value according to the number of years left until the next jubilee year, with a corresponding rebate on the valuation.[e] 19If the one who dedicated his field wishes to redeem it, he shall pay one fifth more than the price thus established, and so reclaim it. 20If, instead of redeeming such a field, he sells it to someone else, it may no longer be redeemed; 21but at the jubilee it shall be released as sacred to the LORD; like a field that is doomed, it shall become priestly property.

22"If the field that some man dedicates to the LORD is one he had purchased and not a part of his hereditary property, 23the priest shall compute its value in proportion to the number of years until the next jubilee, and on the same day the price thus established shall be given as sacred to the LORD; 24at the jubilee,[f] however, the field shall revert to the hereditary owner of this land from whom it had been purchased.

25"Every valuation shall be made according to the standard of the sanctuary shekel. There are twenty gerahs to the shekel.

Offerings Not To Be Redeemed 26"Note that a first-born animal,[g] which as such already belongs to the LORD, may not be dedicated by vow to him. If it is an ox or a sheep, it shall be ceded to the LORD; 27but if it is an unclean animal,* it may be redeemed by paying one fifth more than its fixed value. If it is not redeemed, it shall be sold at its fixed value.

28"Note, also, that any one of his possessions which a man vows as doomed to the LORD, whether it is a human being or an animal or a hereditary field, shall be neither sold nor ransomed; everything that is thus doomed becomes most sacred to the LORD.[h] 29All human beings

27, 12: Determine its value: fix the price at which the animal may be sold to someone else. Only the original owner must pay the twenty percent tax, as a penalty for buying back what he had vowed to God. So also for houses and fields that are vowed to the Lord, as treated of in the following verses. The money from the sale or from the redemption of such vowed property naturally goes to the sanctuary.

27, 27: An unclean animal: such as the first-born of an ass, which was unfit for sacrifice. According to Ex 13, 13; 34, 20, a first-born ass was to be redeemed by offering a sheep in its stead, or was to have its neck broken. The present law is probably a later modification of the earlier one.

d Lv 22, 14. e Lv 25, 15f. f Lv 25, 10. 28. 41. g Ex 13, 2. h 1 Sm 15, 21.

that are doomed* lose the right to be redeemed; they must be put to death.
30"All tithes of the land, whether in grain from the fields or in fruit from the trees, belong to the LORD, as sacred to him.[i] 31If someone wishes to buy back any of his tithes, he shall pay one fifth more than their value. 32The tithes of the herd and the flock shall be determined by ceding to the LORD as sacred every tenth animal as they are counted by the herdsman's rod. 33It shall not matter whether good ones or bad ones are thus chosen, and no exchange may be made. If any exchange is attempted, both the original animal and its substitute shall be treated as sacred, without the right of being bought back."
34These are the commandments which the LORD gave Moses on Mount Sinai for the Israelites.

27, 29: All human beings that are doomed: according to some interpreters, this signifies the idolatrous Canaanites, who were doomed to destruction by divine authority; according to others, this drastic law was enacted for the purpose of discouraging private persons from rashly vowing their slaves or other dependents as offerings to God. Cf Ex 22, 19; Dt 13, 13–19.

i Nm 18, 21. 24; 2 Chr 31, 5f. 12; Mal 3, 8. 10.

THE BOOK OF NUMBERS

The Book of Numbers derives its name from the account of the two censuses of the Hebrew people taken, one near the beginning and the other toward the end of the journey in the desert (chapters 1 and 26). It continues the story of that journey, begun in Exodus, and describes briefly the experiences of the Israelites for a period of thirty-eight years, from the end of their encampment at Sinai to their arrival at the border of the Promised Land. Numerous legal ordinances are interspersed in the account, making the book a combination of law and history.

The various events described clearly indicate the action of God, who punishes the murmuring of the people by prolonging their stay in the desert, at the same time preparing them by this discipline to be his witnesses among the nations.

In the New Testament Christ and the Apostles derive useful lessons from such events in the Book of Numbers as the brazen serpent (Jn 3, 14f), the sedition of Korah and its consequences (1 Cor 10, 10), the prophecies of Balaam (2 Pt 2, 15f), and the water gushing from the rock (1 Cor 10, 4).

The chief divisions of the Book of Numbers are as follows:

I. Preparation for the Departure from Sinai (Nm 1, 1—10, 10).
II. From Sinai to the Plains of Moab (Nm 10, 11—22, 1).
III. On the Plains of Moab (Nm 22, 2—36, 13).

I: Preparation for the Departure from Sinai

CHAPTER 1

The Census 1In the year following that of the Israelites' departure from the land of Egypt, on the first day of the second month, the LORD said to Moses in the meeting tent in the desert of Sinai: 2*"Take a census of the whole community of the Israelites,[a] by clans and ancestral houses, registering each male individually. 3You and Aaron shall enroll in companies all the men in Israel of twenty years or more who are fit for military service.

Moses' Assistants 4"To assist you there shall be a man from each tribe, the head of his

1, 2: All Israel was divided into tribes, each tribe into clans, and each clan into ancestral houses.

a 2f: Nm 14, 29; 26, 2–51.

ancestral house. 5 [b]These are the names of those
who are to assist you:

from Reuben: Elizur, son of Shedeur;
6 from Simeon: Shelumiel, son of Zurishaddai;
7 from Judah: Nahshon, son of Amminadab;
8 from Issachar: Nethanel, son of Zuar;
9 from Zebulun: Eliab, son of Helon;
10 from Ephraim: Elishama, son of Ammihud,
and from Manasseh: Gamaliel, son of Pedah-
zur, for the descendants of Joseph;
11 from Benjamin: Abidan, son of Gideoni;
12 from Dan: Ahiezer, son of Ammishaddai;
13 from Asher: Pagiel, son of Ochran;
14 from Gad: Eliasaph, son of Reuel;
15 from Naphtali: Ahira, son of Enan."

16 [c]These were councilors of the community,
princes of their ancestral tribes, chiefs of the
troops* of Israel. 17 So Moses and Aaron took
these men who had been designated, 18 and
assembled the whole community on the first day
of the second month. Every man of twenty years
or more then declared his name and lineage
according to clan and ancestral house, 19 as the
LORD had commanded Moses.
Count of the Twelve Tribes This is their
census as taken in the desert of Sinai. 20 Of the
descendants of Reuben, the first-born of Israel,
registered by lineage in clans and ancestral
houses: when all the males of twenty years or
more who were fit for military service were
polled, 21 forty-six thousand five hundred were
enrolled in the tribe of Reuben.

22 Of the descendants of Simeon, registered by
lineage in clans and ancestral houses: when all
the males of twenty years or more who were fit
for military service were polled, 23 fifty-nine thou-
sand three hundred were enrolled in the tribe of
Simeon.

24 Of the descendants of Gad, registered by
lineage in clans and ancestral houses: when all
the males of twenty years or more who were fit
for military service were polled, 25 forty-five thou-
sand six hundred and fifty were enrolled in the
tribe of Gad.

26 Of the descendants of Judah, registered by
lineage in clans and ancestral houses: when all
the males of twenty years or more who were fit
for military service were polled, 27 seventy-four
thousand six hundred were enrolled in the tribe
of Judah.

28 Of the descendants of Issachar, registered by
lineage in clans and ancestral houses: when all
the males of twenty years or more who were fit
for military service were polled, 29 fifty-four thou-
sand four hundred were enrolled in the tribe of
Issachar.

30 Of the descendants of Zebulun, registered
by lineage in clans and ancestral houses: when
all the males of twenty years or more who were
fit for military service were polled, 31 fifty-seven
thousand four hundred were enrolled in the
tribe of Zebulun.

32 Of the descendants of Joseph—

Of the descendants of Ephraim, registered by
lineage in clans and ancestral houses: when all
the males of twenty years or more who were fit
for military service were polled, 33 forty thousand
five hundred were enrolled in the tribe of
Ephraim.

34 Of the descendants of Manasseh, registered
by lineage in clans and ancestral houses: when
all the males of twenty years or more who were
fit for military service were polled, 35 thirty-two
thousand two hundred were enrolled in the tribe
of Manasseh.

36 Of the descendants of Benjamin, registered
by lineage in clans and ancestral houses: when
all the males of twenty years or more who were
fit for military service were polled, 37 thirty-five
thousand four hundred were enrolled in the
tribe of Benjamin.

38 Of the descendants of Dan, registered by
lineage in clans and ancestral houses: when all
the males of twenty years or more who were fit
for military service were polled, 39 sixty-two

1, 16: Troops: literally "thousands"; this division of the Israelites, with its subdivisions of "hundreds, fifties and tens," was primarily for military and judicial purposes. Cf Ex 18, 21; 2 Sm 18, 1.

b 5–15: Nm 10, 14–27. c Ex 18, 21. 25.

thousand seven hundred were enrolled in the tribe of Dan.

40Of the descendants of Asher, registered by lineage in clans and ancestral houses: when all the males of twenty years or more who were fit for military service were polled, 41forty-one thousand five hundred were enrolled in the tribe of Asher.

42Of the descendants of Naphtali, registered by lineage in clans and ancestral houses: when all the males of twenty years or more who were fit for military service were polled, 43fifty-three thousand four hundred were enrolled in the tribe of Naphtali.

44It was these who were registered, each according to his ancestral house, in the census taken by Moses and Aaron and the twelve princes of Israel. 45The total number of the Israelites of twenty years or more who were fit for military service, registered by ancestral houses, 46was six hundred and three thousand five hundred and fifty.

Levites Omitted in the Census 47The Levites, however, were not registered[d] by ancestral tribe with the others.* 48For the LORD had told Moses, 49"The tribe of Levi alone you shall not enroll nor include in the census along with the other Israelites. 50You are to give the Levites charge of the Dwelling of the commandments with all its equipment and all that belongs to it. It is they who shall carry the Dwelling with all its equipment and who shall be its ministers.[e] They shall therefore camp around the Dwelling. 51When the Dwelling is to move on, the Levites shall take it down; when the Dwelling is to be pitched, it is the Levites who shall set it up.[f] Any layman who comes near it shall be put to death. 52While the other Israelites shall camp by companies, each in his own division of the camp,[g] 53the Levites shall camp around the Dwelling of the commandments.[h] Otherwise God's wrath will strike the Israelite community. The Levites, then, shall have charge of the Dwelling of the commandments." 54All this the Israelites fulfilled as the LORD had commanded Moses.

CHAPTER 2

Arrangement of the Tribes 1The LORD said to Moses and Aaron: 2"The Israelites shall camp, each in his own division, under the ensigns of their ancestral houses.[i] They shall camp around the meeting tent, but at some distance from it.

3*"Encamped on the east side, toward the sunrise, shall be the divisional camp of Judah, arranged in companies. [The prince of the Judahites was Nahshon, son of Amminadab, 4and his soldiers amounted in the census to seventy-four thousand six hundred.] 5With Judah shall camp the tribe of Issachar [their prince was Nethanel, son of Zuar, 6and his soldiers amounted in the census to fifty-four thousand four hundred] 7and the tribe of Zebulun. [Their prince was Eliab, son of Helon, 8and his soldiers amounted in the census to fifty-seven thousand four hundred. 9The total number of those registered by companies in the camp of Judah was one hundred and eighty-six thousand four hundred.] These shall be first on the march.

10"On the south side shall be the divisional camp of Reuben, arranged in companies. [Their prince was Elizur, son of Shedeur, 11and his soldiers amounted in the census to forty-six thousand five hundred.] 12Beside them shall camp the tribe of Simeon [their prince was Shelumiel, son of Zurishaddai, 13and his soldiers amounted in the census to fifty-nine thousand three hundred] 14and next the tribe of Gad. [Their prince was Eliasaph, son of Reuel, 15and his soldiers amounted in the census to forty-five thousand six hundred and fifty. 16The total number of those registered by companies in the camp of Reuben was one hundred and fifty-one thousand four hundred and fifty.] These shall be second on the march.

17"Then the meeting tent and the camp of the Levites shall set out in the middle of the line. As

1, 47: The Levites were not enrolled in this census, which was principally for military purposes, but a separate census was made of them. Cf Nm 3, 15f. 39.

2, 3–31: A similar arrangement of the tribes around the central sanctuary in the ideal Israelite state is given in Ez 48.

d Nm 2, 33; 3, 14–39; 26, 57–62. e Nm 3, 7f; 4, 2–49; 1 Chr 6, 48. f Nm 3, 10. 38; 18, 7; 2 Sm 6, 6f; 1 Chr 13, 10. g Nm 2, 2. 34. h Nm 3, 7f. 38; 8, 19; 18, 4f. i Nm 1. 52.

in camp, so also on the march, every man shall be in his proper place, with his own division.

[18]“On the west side shall be the divisional camp of Ephraim, arranged in companies. [Their prince was Elishama, son of Ammihud, [19]and his soldiers amounted in the census to forty thousand five hundred.] [20]Beside them shall camp the tribe of Manasseh [their prince was Gamaliel, son of Pedahzur, [21]and his soldiers amounted in the census to thirty-two thousand two hundred] [22]and the tribe of Benjamin. [Their prince was Abidan, son of Gideoni, [23]and his soldiers amounted in the census to thirty-five thousand four hundred. [24]The total number of those registered by companies in the camp of Ephraim was one hundred and eight thousand one hundred.] These shall be third on the march.

[25]“On the north side shall be the divisional camp of Dan, arranged in companies. [Their prince was Ahiezer, son of Ammishaddai, [26]and his soldiers amounted in the census to sixty-two thousand seven hundred.] [27]Beside them shall camp the tribe of Asher [their prince was Pagiel, son of Ochran, [28]and his soldiers amounted in the census to forty-one thousand five hundred] [29]and next the tribe of Naphtali. [Their prince was Ahira, son of Enan, [30]and his soldiers amounted in the census to fifty-three thousand four hundred. [31]The total number of those registered by companies in the camp of Dan was one hundred and fifty-seven thousand six hundred.] These shall be the last of the divisions on the march.”

[32][j]This was the census of the Israelites taken by ancestral houses. The total number of those registered by companies in the camps was six hundred and three thousand five hundred and fifty. [33]The Levites, however, were not registered with the other Israelites, for so the LORD had commanded Moses. [34]The Israelites did just as the LORD had commanded Moses; both in camp and on the march they were in their own divisions, every man according to his clan and his ancestral house.

CHAPTER 3

The Sons of Aaron [1]The following were the descendants of Aaron and Moses at the time that the LORD spoke to Moses on Mount Sinai. [2]The sons of Aaron were Nadab his first-born, Abihu, Eleazar, and Ithamar.[k] [3]These are the names of the sons of Aaron, the anointed priests who were ordained to exercise the priesthood. [4]But when Nadab and Abihu offered profane fire before the LORD in the desert of Sinai, they met death[l] in the presence of the LORD, and left no sons. Thereafter only Eleazar and Ithamar performed the priestly functions under the direction of their father Aaron.

Levites in Place of the First-born [5]Now the LORD said to Moses: [6]“Summon the tribe of Levi and present them to Aaron the priest, as his assistants.[m] [7]They shall discharge his obligations and those of the whole community before the meeting tent[n] by serving at the Dwelling. [8]They shall have custody of all the furnishings of the meeting tent and discharge the duties of the Israelites in the service of the Dwelling. [9]You shall give the Levites to Aaron and his sons;[o] they have been set aside from among the Israelites as dedicated to me. [10]But only Aaron and his descendants shall you appoint to have charge of the priestly functions.[p] Any layman who comes near shall be put to death.”

[11]The LORD said to Moses, [12]“It is I who have chosen the Levites from the Israelites in place of every first-born that opens the womb among the Israelites.[q] The Levites, therefore, are mine, [13]because every first-born is mine. When I slew all the first-born in the land of Egypt, I made all the first-born in Israel sacred to me, both of man and of beast. They belong to me; I am the LORD.”

Census of the Levites [14]The LORD said to Moses in the desert of Sinai, [15]“Take a census of the Levites by ancestral houses and clans, registering every male of a month or more.”[r] [16]Moses, therefore, took their census in accordance with the command the LORD had given him.

j 32–33: Nm 1, 46–49. k Ex 6, 23. l Nm 26, 61; Lv 10, 1f; 1 Chr 24, 2. m Nm 18, 2. n Nm 8, 24. o Nm 8, 19. p Nm 1, 51; 18, 7. q 12f: Nm 3, 41; 8, 16f; Ex 13, 2. 12. 15. r Nm 3, 39; 26, 62.

[17][s]The sons of Levi were named Gershon, Kohath and Merari. [18]The descendants of Gershon, by clans, were named Libni and Shimei. [19]The descendants of Kohath, by clans, were Amram, Izhar, Hebron and Uzziel. [20]The descendants of Merari, by clans, were Mahli and Mushi. These were the clans of the Levites by ancestral houses.

Duties of the Levitical Clans [21]To Gershon belonged the clan of the Libnites and the clan of the Shimeites; these were the clans of the Gershonites. [22]When all their males of a month or more were registered, they numbered seven thousand five hundred. [23]The clans of the Gershonites camped behind the Dwelling, to the west. [24]The prince of their ancestral house was Eliasaph, son of Lael. [25][t]At the meeting tent they had charge of whatever pertained to the Dwelling,* the tent and its covering, the curtain at the entrance of the meeting tent, [26]the hangings of the court, the curtain at the entrance of the court enclosing both the Dwelling and the altar, and the ropes.

[27]To Kohath belonged the clans of the Amramites, the Izharites, the Hebronites, and the Uzzielites; these were the clans of the Kohathites. [28]When all their males of a month or more were registered, they numbered eight thousand three hundred. They had charge of the sanctuary. [29]The clans of the Kohathites camped at the south side of the Dwelling. [30]The prince of their ancestral house was Elizaphan, son of Uzziel. [31]They had charge of whatever pertained to the ark, the table, the lampstand, the altars, the utensils with which the ministry of the sanctuary was exercised, and the veil.* [32]The chief prince of the Levites, however, was Eleazar, son of Aaron the priest; he was supervisor over those who had charge of the sanctuary.

[33]To Merari belonged the clans of the Mahlites and the Mushites; these were the clans of Merari. [34]When all their males of a month or more were registered, they numbered six thousand two hundred. [35]The prince of the ancestral house of the clans of Merari was Zuriel, son of Abihail. They camped at the north side of the Dwelling. [36]*The Merarites were charged with the care of whatever pertained to the boards of the Dwelling, its bars, columns, pedestals, and all its fittings, [37]as well as the columns of the surrounding court with their pedestals, pegs and ropes.

[38]East of the Dwelling, that is, in front of the meeting tent, toward the sunrise, were camped Moses and Aaron and the latter's sons. They discharged the obligations of the sanctuary for the Israelites. Any layman who came near was to be put to death.

[39]The total number of male Levites a month old or more whom Moses had registered by clans in keeping with the LORD's command, was twenty-two thousand.

Census and Ransom of First-born [40]The LORD then said to Moses, "Take a census of all the first-born males of the Israelites a month old or more, and compute their total number. [41]Then assign the Levites to me, the LORD, in place of all the first-born of the Israelites, as well as their cattle in place of all the first-born among the cattle of the Israelites." [42]So Moses took a census of all the first-born of the Israelites, as the LORD had commanded him. [43]When all the first-born males of a month or more were registered, they numbered twenty-two thousand two hundred and seventy-three.

[44]The LORD said to Moses: [45]"Take the Levites in place of all the first-born of the Israelites, and the Levites' cattle in place of their cattle, that the Levites may belong to me. I am the LORD. [46]As ransom for the two hundred and seventy-three first-born of the Israelites who

3, 25f: The Gershonites had two wagons for transporting these things; cf Nm 7, 7. For a description of the Dwelling, see Ex 26, 1–6; the tent, Ex 26, 7–13; its covering, Ex 26, 14; the curtain at the entrance, Ex 26, 36; the hangings of the court, Ex 27, 9–15; the curtain at the entrance of the court, Ex 27, 16; the ropes of the Dwelling, Ex 35, 18.

3, 31: The Kohathites had to carry these sacred objects on their shoulders; cf Nm 7, 9. For a description of the ark, see Ex 25, 10–22; the table, Ex 25, 23–30; the lampstand, Ex 25, 31–40; the altars, Ex 27, 1–8; 30, 1–10.

3, 36f: The Merarites had four wagons for transporting this heavy material; cf Nm 7, 8. For a description of the boards, bars, etc., of the Dwelling, see Ex 26, 15–30; the columns, pedestals, etc., of the court, Ex 27, 9–19.

s 17–20: Nm 26, 57; Gn 46, 11; Ex 6, 16–19; 1 Chr 6, 1f. 16–19. t 25–26: Ex 26, 7. 14. 36; 36, 14.

outnumber the Levites, 47you shall take five shekels for each individual, according to the standard of the sanctuary shekel, twenty gerahs to the shekel.[u] 48Give this silver to Aaron and his sons as ransom for the extra number." 49So Moses took the silver as ransom from those who were left when the rest had been redeemed by the Levites. 50From the first-born of the Israelites he received in silver one thousand three hundred and sixty-five shekels according to the sanctuary standard. 51He then gave this ransom silver to Aaron and his sons, as the LORD had commanded him.

CHAPTER 4

Duties Further Defined 1The LORD said to Moses and Aaron: 2"Among the Levites take a total of the Kohathites, by clans and ancestral houses, all the men of the Kohathites 3between thirty* and fifty years of age; these are to undertake obligatory tasks in the meeting tent.[v]

4"The service of the Kohathites in the meeting tent concerns the most sacred objects. 5In breaking camp, Aaron and his sons shall go in and take down the screening curtain* and cover the ark of the commandments with it. 6Over these they shall put a cover of tahash skin, and on top of this spread an all-violet cloth. They shall then put the poles in place. 7On the table of the Presence they shall spread a violet cloth and put on it the plates and cups, as well as the bowls and pitchers for libations; the established bread offering shall remain on the table. 8Over these they shall spread a scarlet cloth and cover all this with tahash skin. They shall then put the poles in place. 9They shall use a violet cloth to cover the lampstand with its lamps, trimming shears, and trays, as well as the various containers of oil from which it is supplied. 10The lampstand with all its utensils they shall then enclose in a covering of tahash skin, and place on a litter. 11Over the golden altar* they shall spread a violet cloth, and cover this also with a covering of tahash skin. They shall then put the poles in place. 12Taking the utensils of the sanctuary service, they shall wrap them all in violet cloth and cover them with tahash skin. They shall then place them on a litter. 13After cleansing the altar* of its ashes, they shall spread a purple cloth over it. 14On this they shall put all the utensils with which it is served: the fire pans, forks,* shovels, basins, and all the utensils of the altar. They shall then spread a covering of tahash skin over this, and put the poles in place.

15"Only after Aaron and his sons have finished covering the sacred objects and all their utensils on breaking camp, shall the Kohathites enter to carry them. But they shall not touch the sacred objects; if they do they will die.[w] These, then, are the objects in the meeting tent that the Kohathites shall carry.

16"Eleazar, son of Aaron the priest, shall be in charge of the oil for the light, the fragrant incense, the established cereal offering, and the anointing oil. He shall be in charge of the whole Dwelling with all the sacred objects and utensils that are in it."

17The LORD said to Moses and Aaron: 18"Do not let the group of Kohathite clans perish from the body of the Levites. 19That they may live and not die when they approach the most sacred objects, this is what you shall do for them: Aaron and his sons shall go in and assign to each of them his task and what he must carry; 20but the Kohathites shall not go in to look upon the sacred objects, even for an instant; if they do, they will die."[x]

21The LORD said to Moses, 22"Take a total among the Gershonites also, by ancestral houses and clans, 23of all the men between thirty and fifty years of age; these are to undertake obligatory tasks in the meeting tent. 24This is the task of the clans of the Gershonites, what they must do and what they must carry: 25they shall carry

4, 3: Thirty: at a later period the Levites began to serve when they were twenty-five (Nm 8, 24) or even only twenty years old (1 Chr 23, 24. 27; 2 Chr 31, 17; Ezr 3, 8; but cf 1 Chr 23, 3).

4, 5: The screening curtain: the veil between the inner and the outer rooms of the sanctuary. Cf Ex 26, 31–33.

4, 11: The golden altar: the altar of incense. Cf Ex 30, 1–6.

4, 13: The altar: the bronze altar of holocausts. Cf Ex 27, 1–8.

4, 14: Forks: used in turning over the sacrificed animal on the fire of the altar. Basins: to receive the sacrificial blood; cf Zec 9, 15.

u Nm 18, 16; Ex 30, 13; Lv 27, 25; Ez 45, 12. v Nm 8, 24; 1 Chr 23, 24–27. w 2 Sm 6, 6f; 1 Chr 13, 9f. x 1 Sm 6, 19.

the sheets of the Dwelling, the meeting tent with its covering and the outer wrapping of tahash skin, the curtain at the entrance of the meeting tent, [26]the hangings of the court, the curtain at the entrance of the court that encloses both the Dwelling and the altar, together with their ropes and all other objects necessary in their use. Whatever is to be done with these things shall be their task. [27]The service of the Gershonites shall be entirely under the direction of Aaron and his sons, with regard to what they must do and what they must carry; you shall make each man of them responsible for what he is to carry. [28]This, then, is the task of the Gershonites in the meeting tent; and they shall be under the supervision of Ithamar, son of Aaron the priest.

[29]"Among the Merarites, too, you shall enroll by clans and ancestral houses [30]all their men between thirty and fifty years of age; these are to undertake obligatory tasks in the meeting tent. [31] [y]This is what they shall be responsible for carrying, all the years of their service in the meeting tent: the boards of the Dwelling with its bars, columns and pedestals, [32]and the columns of the surrounding court with their pedestals, pegs and ropes. You shall designate for each man of them all the objects connected with his service, which he shall be responsible for carrying. [33]This, then, is the task of the clans of the Merarites during all their service in the meeting tent under the supervision of Ithamar, son of Aaron the priest."

Number of Adult Levites [34]So Moses and Aaron and the princes of the community made a registration among the Kohathites, by clans and ancestral houses, [35]of all the men between thirty and fifty years of age. These were to undertake obligatory tasks in the meeting tent; [36]as registered by clans, they numbered two thousand seven hundred and fifty. [37]Such was the census of all the men of the Kohathite clans who were to serve in the meeting tent, which Moses took, together with Aaron, as the LORD bade him.

[38]The registration was then made among the Gershonites, by clans and ancestral houses, [39]of all the men between thirty and fifty years of age. These were to undertake obligatory tasks in the meeting tent; [40]as registered by clans and ancestral houses, they numbered two thousand six hundred and thirty. [41]Such was the census of all the men of the Gershonite clans who were to serve in the meeting tent, which Moses took, together with Aaron, at the LORD's bidding.

[42]Then the registration was made among the Merarites, by clans and ancestral houses, [43]of all the men from thirty up to fifty years of age. These were to undertake obligatory tasks in the meeting tent; [44]as registered by clans, they numbered three thousand two hundred. [45]Such was the census of the men of the Merarite clans which Moses took, together with Aaron, as the LORD bade him.

[46]Therefore, when Moses and Aaron and the Israelite princes had completed the registration among the Levites, by clans and ancestral houses, [47]of all the men between thirty and fifty years of age who were to undertake tasks of service or transport of the meeting tent, [48]the total number registered was eight thousand five hundred and eighty. [49]According to the LORD's bidding to Moses, they gave them their individual assignments for service and for transport; so the LORD had commanded Moses.

CHAPTER 5

The Unclean Expelled [1]The LORD said to Moses: [2]"Order the Israelites to expel from camp every leper, and everyone suffering from a discharge, and everyone who has become unclean by contact with a corpse.* [z] [3]Male and female alike, you shall compel them to go out of the camp; they are not to defile the camp in which I dwell." [a] [4]The Israelites obeyed the command that the LORD had given Moses; they expelled them from the camp.

Unjust Possession [5]*The LORD said to Moses,

5, 2: For the laws regarding victims of leprosy, see Lv 13–14; those suffering from a discharge, Lv 15; the unclean by contact with a corpse, Nm 19, 11–22; Lv 21, 1–4.

5, 5–10: The basic law on unjust possession is given in Lv 5,

y Nm 3, 36f. z Nm 19, 11. 13; Lv 13, 46; 21, 1; 22, 4. a Nm 35, 34.

6 [b]"Tell the Israelites: If a man (or woman) commits a fault against his fellow man and wrongs him, thus breaking faith with the LORD, 7he shall confess the wrong he has done, restore his ill-gotten goods in full, and in addition give one fifth of their value to the one he has wronged. 8However, if the latter has no next of kin* to whom restoration of the ill-gotten goods can be made, the goods to be restored shall be the LORD's and shall fall to the priest; this is apart from the atonement ram with which the priest makes amends for the guilty man. 9Likewise, every sacred contribution that the Israelites are bound to make shall fall to the priest. [c] 10Each Israelite man may dispose of his own sacred contributions; they become the property of the priest to whom he gives them." [d]

Ordeal for a Suspected Adulteress 11The LORD said to Moses, 12"Speak to the Israelites and tell them: If a man's wife goes astray and becomes unfaithful to him 13by having intercourse with another man, [e] though her husband has not sufficient evidence of the fact, so that her impurity remains unproved for lack of a witness who might have caught her in the act; 14or if a man is overcome by a feeling of jealousy that makes him suspect his wife, whether she was actually impure or not: 15he shall bring his wife to the priest and shall take along as an offering for her a tenth of an ephah of barley meal. However, he shall not pour oil on it nor put frankincense over it, since it is a cereal offering of jealousy, a cereal offering for an appeal in a question of guilt.

16"The priest shall first have the woman come forward and stand before the LORD. 17In an earthen vessel he shall meanwhile put some holy water,* as well as some dust that he has taken from the floor of the Dwelling. [f] 18Then, as the woman stands before the LORD, the priest shall uncover her head and place in her hands the cereal offering of her appeal,* that is, the cereal offering of jealousy, while he himself shall hold the bitter water that brings a curse. 19Then he shall adjure the woman, saying to her, 'If no other man has had intercourse with you, and you have not gone astray by impurity while under the authority of your husband, be immune to the curse brought by this bitter water. 20But if you have gone astray while under the authority of your husband and have acted impurely by letting a man other than your husband have intercourse with you'— 21so shall the priest adjure the woman with this oath of imprecation—'may the LORD make you an example of malediction and imprecation* among your people by causing your thighs to waste away and your belly to swell! 22May this water, then, that brings a curse, enter your body to make your belly swell and your thighs waste away!' [g] And the woman shall say, 'Amen, amen!'* 23The priest shall put these imprecations in writing and shall then wash them off into the bitter water, 24which he is to have the woman drink, so that it may go into her with all its bitter curse. 25But first he shall take the cereal offering of jealousy from the woman's hand, and having waved this offering before the LORD, shall put it near the altar, 26where he shall take a handful of the cereal offering as its token offering and burn it on the altar. [h] Only then shall he have the woman drink the water. 27Once she has done so, if she has been impure and unfaithful to her husband, this bitter water that brings a curse will go into her, and her belly will swell and her thighs will waste away, so that she will become an example

14–26. The new item here concerns the case where the injured party has died and left no heirs, in which case the restitution must be made to the priest.

5, 8: Next of kin: literally, "redeemer," a technical term denoting the nearest relative, upon whom devolved the obligation of "redeeming" the family property, in order to keep it within the family. Cf Lv 25, 25; Ru 4, 1–6.

5, 17: Holy water: water from the laver that stood in the court of the Dwelling.

5, 18: Appeal: by which she invokes the Lord and refers her case to his decision.

5, 21: An example of malediction and imprecation: the woman's name would be used in curses and oaths to invoke a similar misfortune on another person or on oneself. Cf Is 65, 15; Jer 29, 22.

5, 22: Amen: a Hebrew word meaning, "certainly, truly," used to give assent to a statement, a curse, a blessing, a prayer, or the like; in this sense of "so be it," the Christian liturgy also uses it after prayers and blessings.

b 6ff: Lv 5, 21–25. c Dt 18, 3f; Ex 44, 29f. d Lv 10, 12–15. e Lv 18, 20; Jn 8, 4. f Nm 19, 17. g Ps 109, 18. h Lv 5, 12.

of imprecation among her people. [28]If, however, the woman has not defiled herself, but is still pure, she will be immune and will still be able to bear children.

[29]"This, then, is the law for jealousy: When a woman goes astray while under the authority of her husband and acts impurely, [30]or when such a feeling of jealousy comes over a man that he becomes suspicious of his wife, he shall have her stand before the LORD, and the priest shall apply this law in full to her. [31]The man shall be free from guilt,* but the woman shall bear such guilt as she may have."

CHAPTER 6

Laws Concerning Nazirites [1]The LORD said to Moses: [2]"Speak to the Israelites and tell them: When a man (or a woman) solemnly takes the nazirite* vow to dedicate himself to the LORD, [3]he shall abstain from wine and strong drink;[i] he may neither drink wine vinegar, other vinegar, or any kind of grape juice, nor eat either fresh or dried grapes. [4]As long as he is a nazirite he shall not eat anything of the produce of the vine; not even unripe grapes or grapeskins. [5]While he is under the nazirite vow, no razor shall touch his hair.[j] Until the period of his dedication to the LORD is over, he shall be sacred, and shall let the hair of his head grow freely. [6]As long as he is dedicated to the LORD, he shall not enter where a dead person is.[k] [7]Not even for his father or mother, his sister or brother, should they die, may he become unclean, since his head bears his dedication to God. [8]As long as he is a nazirite he is sacred to the LORD.

[9]"If someone dies very suddenly in his presence, so that his dedicated head becomes unclean, he shall shave his head on the day of his purification, that is, on the seventh day. [10]On the eighth day he shall bring two turtledoves or two pigeons to the priest at the entrance of the meeting tent. [11]The priest shall offer up the one as a sin offering and the other as a holocaust, thus making atonement for him for the sin he has committed by reason of the dead person. On the same day he shall reconsecrate his head [12]and begin anew the period of his dedication to the LORD as a nazirite, bringing a yearling lamb as a guilt offering. The previous period is not valid, because his dedicated head became unclean.

[13]"This is the ritual for the nazirite:[l] On the day he completes the period of his dedication he shall go to the entrance of the meeting tent, [14]bringing as his offering to the LORD one unblemished yearling lamb for a holocaust, one unblemished yearling ewe lamb for a sin offering, one unblemished ram as a peace offering, along with their cereal offerings and libations, [15]and a basket of unleavened cakes of fine flour mixed with oil and of unleavened wafers spread with oil. [16]The priest shall present them before the LORD, and shall offer up the sin offering and the holocaust for him. [17]He shall then offer up the ram as a peace offering to the LORD, with its cereal offering and libation, and the basket of unleavened cakes. [18]Then at the entrance of the meeting tent the nazirite shall shave his dedicated head,[m] collect the hair, and put it in the fire that is under the peace offering. [19]After the nazirite has shaved off his dedicated hair, the priest shall take a boiled shoulder of the ram, as well as one unleavened cake and one unleavened wafer from the basket, and shall place them in the hands of the nazirite. [20]The priest shall then wave them as a wave offering before the LORD. They become sacred and shall belong to the priest, along with the breast of the wave offering and the leg of the raised offering. Only after this may the nazirite drink wine.

[21]"This, then, is the law for the nazirite; this

5, 31: Free from guilt: by fulfilling his obligation of obtaining a decision in the matter.

6, 1ff: Nazirite: from the Hebrew word nazir, meaning "set apart as sacred, dedicated, vowed." The nazirite vow could be either for a limited period or for life. Those bound by this vow had to abstain from all the products of the grapevine, from cutting or shaving their hair, and from contact with a corpse. They were regarded as men of God like the prophets; cf Am 2, 11f. Examples of lifelong nazirites were Samson (Jgs 13, 4f. 7; 16, 17), Samuel (1 Sm 1, 11), and John the Baptizer (Lk 1, 15). At the time of Christ the practice of taking the nazirite vow for a limited period seems to have been quite common, even among the early Christians; cf Acts 18, 18; 21, 23f. 26.

i 3f: Jgs 13, 7. 14. j Jgs 13, 5; 16, 17; 1 Sm 1, 11. k Nm 19, 11. 16; Lv 21, 11. l Acts 21, 24, 26. m Acts 18, 18; 21, 24.

is the offering to the LORD which is included in his vow of dedication apart from anything else which his means may allow. Thus shall he carry out the law of his dedication in keeping with the vow he has taken."

The Priestly Blessing 22The LORD said to Moses: 23"Speak to Aaron and his sons and tell them: This is how you shall bless the Israelites. Say to them:

24The LORD bless you and keep you!
25The LORD let his face shine* upon you, and be
gracious to you!
26The LORD look upon you kindly and give you
peace!*

27So shall they invoke my name upon the Israelites, and I will bless them."

CHAPTER 7

Offerings of Princes 1Now, when Moses had completed the erection of the Dwelling and had anointed and consecrated it with all its equipment[n] (as well as the altar with all its equipment), 2an offering was made by the princes of Israel, who were heads of ancestral houses; the same princes of the tribes who supervised the census. 3The offering they brought before the LORD consisted of six baggage wagons and twelve oxen, that is, a wagon for every two princes, and an ox for every prince. These they presented as their offering before the Dwelling.

4The LORD then said to Moses, 5"Accept their offering, that these things may be put to use in the service of the meeting tent. Assign them to the Levites, to each group in proportion to its duties." 6So Moses accepted the wagons and oxen, and assigned them to the Levites. 7He gave two wagons and four oxen to the Gershonites[o] in proportion to their duties, 8and four wagons and eight oxen to the Merarites in proportion to their duties, under the supervision of Ithamar, son of Aaron the priest. 9He gave none to the Kohathites, because they had to carry on their shoulders the sacred objects which were their charge.[p]

10For the dedication of the altar also, the princes brought offerings before the altar on the day it was anointed.[q] 11But the LORD said to Moses, "Let one prince a day present his offering for the dedication of the altar."

12*The one who presented his offering on the first day was Nahshon, son of Amminadab, prince of the tribe of Judah. 13His offering consisted of one silver plate weighing a hundred and thirty shekels according to the sanctuary standard and one silver basin weighing seventy shekels, both filled with fine flour mixed with oil for a cereal offering; 14one gold cup of ten shekels' weight filled with incense; 15one young bull, one ram, and one yearling lamb for a holocaust; 16one goat for a sin offering; 17and two oxen, five rams, five goats, and five yearling lambs for a peace offering. This was the offering of Nahshon, son of Amminadab.

18On the second day Nethanel, son of Zuar, prince of Issachar, made his offering. 19He presented as his offering one silver plate weighing a hundred and thirty shekels according to the sanctuary standard and one silver basin weighing seventy shekels, both filled with fine flour mixed with oil for a cereal offering; 20one gold cup of ten shekels' weight filled with incense; 21one young bull, one ram, and one yearling lamb for a holocaust; 22one goat for a sin offering; 23and two oxen, five rams, five goats, and five yearling lambs for a peace offering. This was the offering of Nethanel, son of Zuar.

24On the third day it was the turn of Eliab, son of Helon, prince of the Zebulunites. 25His offering consisted of one silver plate weighing a hundred and thirty shekels according to the sanctuary standard and one silver basin weighing seventy shekels, both filled with fine flour mixed with oil for a cereal offering; 26one gold cup of ten shekels' weight filled with incense; 27one

6, 25: Let his face shine: a Hebrew idiom for "smile."
6, 26: Peace: the Hebrew word includes the idea of "prosperity, happiness."
7, 12–88: The repetitious account of the same offerings brought by each of the twelve tribal princes and the summary of them are characteristic of an official registration.

n Ex 40, 17. o 7f: Nm 4, 24–33. p Nm 3, 31; 4, 4–15. q Nm 7, 84.

young bull, one ram, and one yearling lamb for a
holocaust; 28 one goat for a sin offering; 29 and
two oxen, five rams, five goats, and five yearling
lambs for a peace offering. This was the offering
of Eliab, son of Helon.

30 On the fourth day it was the turn of Elizur,
son of Shedeur, prince of the Reubenites. 31 His
offering consisted of one silver plate weighing a
hundred and thirty shekels according to the
sanctuary standard and one silver basin weighing
seventy shekels, both filled with fine flour mixed
with oil for a cereal offering; 32 one gold cup of
ten shekels' weight filled with incense; 33 one
young bull, one ram, and one yearling lamb for a
holocaust; 34 one goat for a sin offering; 35 and
two oxen, five rams, five goats, and five yearling
lambs for a peace offering. This was the offering
of Elizur, son of Shedeur.

36 On the fifth day it was the turn of Shelu-
miel, son of Zurishaddai, prince of the Sim-
eonites. 37 His offering consisted of one silver
plate weighing a hundred and thirty shekels
according to the sanctuary standard and one
silver basin weighing seventy shekels, both filled
with fine flour mixed with oil for a cereal
offering; 38 one gold cup of ten shekels' weight
filled with incense; 39 one young bull, one ram,
and one yearling lamb for a holocaust; 40 one
goat for a sin offering; 41 and two oxen, five
rams, five goats, and five yearling lambs for a
peace offering. This was the offering of Shelu-
miel, son of Zurishaddai.

42 On the sixth day it was the turn of Eliasaph,
son of Reuel, prince of the Gadites. 43 His offer-
ing consisted of one silver plate weighing a
hundred and thirty shekels according to the
sanctuary standard and one silver basin weighing
seventy shekels, both filled with fine flour mixed
with oil for a cereal offering; 44 one gold cup of
ten shekels' weight filled with incense; 45 one
young bull, one ram, and one yearling lamb for a
holocaust; 46 one goat for a sin offering; 47 and
two oxen, five rams, five goats, and five yearling
lambs for a peace offering. This was the offering
of Eliasaph, son of Reuel.

48 On the seventh day it was the turn of
Elishama, son of Ammihud, prince of the Ephra-
imites. 49 His offering consisted of one silver plate
weighing a hundred and thirty shekels according
to the sanctuary standard and one silver basin
weighing seventy shekels, both filled with fine
flour mixed with oil for a cereal offering; 50 one
gold cup of ten shekels' weight filled with
incense; 51 one young bull, one ram, and one
yearling lamb for a holocaust; 52 one goat for a
sin offering; 53 and two oxen, five rams, five
goats, and five yearling lambs for a peace offer-
ing. This was the offering of Elishama, son of
Ammihud.

54 On the eighth day it was the turn of
Gamaliel, son of Pedahzur, prince of the Manas-
sehites. 55 His offering consisted of one silver
plate weighing a hundred and thirty shekels
according to the sanctuary standard and one
silver basin weighing seventy shekels, both filled
with fine flour mixed with oil for a cereal
offering; 56 one gold cup of ten shekels' weight
filled with incense; 57 one young bull, one ram,
and one yearling lamb for a holocaust; 58 one
goat for a sin offering; 59 and two oxen, five
rams, five goats, and five yearling lambs for a
peace offering. This was the offering of Gamaliel,
son of Pedahzur.

60 On the ninth day it was the turn of Abidan,
son of Gideoni, prince of the Benjaminites. 61 His
offering consisted of one silver plate weighing a
hundred and thirty shekels according to the
sanctuary standard and one silver basin weighing
seventy shekels, both filled with fine flour mixed
with oil for a cereal offering; 62 one gold cup of
ten shekels' weight filled with incense; 63 one
young bull, one ram, and one yearling lamb for a
holocaust; 64 one goat for a sin offering; 65 and
two oxen, five rams, five goats, and five yearling
lambs for a peace offering. This was the offering
of Abidan, son of Gideoni.

66 On the tenth day it was the turn of Ahiezer,
son of Ammishaddai, prince of the Danites. 67 His
offering consisted of one silver plate weighing a
hundred and thirty shekels according to the
sanctuary standard and one silver basin weighing
seventy shekels, both filled with fine flour mixed
with oil for a cereal offering; 68 one gold cup of
ten shekels' weight filled with incense; 69 one

young bull, one ram, and one yearling lamb for a holocaust; 70 one goat for a sin offering; 71 and two oxen, five rams, five goats, and five yearling lambs for a peace offering. This was the offering of Ahiezer, son of Ammishaddai.

72 On the eleventh day it was the turn of Pagiel, son of Ochran, prince of the Asherites. 73 His offering consisted of one silver plate weighing a hundred and thirty shekels according to the sanctuary standard and one silver basin weighing seventy shekels, both filled with fine flour mixed with oil for a cereal offering; 74 one gold cup of ten shekels' weight filled with incense; 75 one young bull, one ram, and one yearling lamb for a holocaust; 76 one goat for a sin offering; 77 and two oxen, five rams, five goats, and five yearling lambs for a peace offering. This was the offering of Pagiel, son of Ochran.

78 On the twelfth day it was the turn of Ahira, son of Enan, prince of the Naphtalites. 79 His offering consisted of one silver plate weighing a hundred and thirty shekels according to the sanctuary standard and one silver basin weighing seventy shekels, both filled with fine flour mixed with oil for a cereal offering; 80 one gold cup of ten shekels' weight filled with incense; 81 one young bull, one ram, and one yearling lamb for a holocaust; 82 one goat for a sin offering; 83 and two oxen, five rams, five goats, and five yearling lambs for a peace offering. This was the offering of Ahira, son of Enan.

84 These were the offerings for the dedication of the altar, given by the princes of Israel on the occasion of its anointing: twelve silver plates, twelve silver basins, and twelve gold cups. 85 Each silver plate weighed a hundred and thirty shekels, and each silver basin seventy, so that all the silver of these vessels amounted to two thousand four hundred shekels, according to the sanctuary standard. 86 The twelve gold cups that were filled with incense weighed ten shekels apiece, according to the sanctuary standard, so that all the gold of the cups amounted to one hundred and twenty shekels. 87 The animals for the holocausts were, in all, twelve young bulls, twelve rams, and twelve yearling lambs, with their cereal offerings; those for the sin offerings were twelve goats. 88 The animals for the peace offerings were, in all, twenty-four oxen, sixty rams, sixty goats, and sixty yearling lambs. These, then, were the offerings for the dedication of the altar after it was anointed.

The Voice 89 When Moses entered the meeting tent to speak with him, he heard the voice addressing him from above the propitiatory[r] on the ark of the commandments, from between the two cherubim; and it spoke to him. . . .

CHAPTER 8

The Lamps Set Up 1 The LORD spoke to Moses, and said, 2 "Give Aaron this command: When you set up the seven lamps,[s] have them throw their light toward the front of the lampstand." 3 Aaron did so, setting up the lamps to face toward the front of the lampstand, just as the LORD had commanded Moses. 4 The lampstand was made of beaten gold[t] in both its shaft and its branches, according to the pattern which the LORD had shown Moses.

Purification of the Levites 5 The LORD said to Moses: 6 "Take the Levites from among the Israelites and purify them.* 7 This is what you shall do to them to purify them. Sprinkle them with the water of remission;* then have them shave their whole bodies and wash their clothes, and so purify themselves. 8 They shall take a young bull, along with its cereal offering of fine flour mixed with oil; you shall take another young bull for a sin offering. 9 Then have the Levites come forward in front of the meeting tent, where you shall assemble also the whole community of the Israelites. 10 While the Levites are present before the LORD, the Israelites shall lay their hands upon them. 11 Let Aaron then offer the Levites before the LORD as a wave offering from the Israelites, thus devoting them

8, 6: Purify them: in the language of the Pentateuch only the priests were "consecrated," that is, made sacred or set aside for the Lord, in an elaborate ceremony described in Ex 29; Lv 8. The Levites were merely "purified," that is, made ritually clean for their special work.

8, 7: Water of remission: literally, "water of sin," that is, for the remission of sin.

r Ex 25, 22. s Ex 25, 37. t Ex 25, 31. 40.

to the service of the LORD. 12The Levites in turn shall lay their hands on the heads of the bullocks, which shall then be immolated, the one as a sin offering and the other as a holocaust to the LORD, in atonement for the Levites. 13Thus, then, shall you have the Levites stand before Aaron and his sons, to be offered as a wave offering to the LORD; 14and thus shall you set aside the Levites from the rest of the Israelites, that they may be mine. [u]

15"Only then shall the Levites enter upon their service in the meeting tent. You shall purify them and offer them as a wave offering; 16because they, among the Israelites, are strictly dedicated to me; I have taken them for myself in place of every first-born that opens the womb among the Israelites. [v] 17Indeed, all the first-born among the Israelites, both of man and of beast, belong to me; I consecrated them to myself on the day I slew all the first-born in the land of Egypt. [w] 18But in place of all the first-born Israelites I have taken the Levites; 19and I have given these dedicated Israelites to Aaron and his sons[x] to discharge the duties of the Israelites in the meeting tent and to make atonement for them, so that no plague may strike among the Israelites should they come near the sanctuary."

20Thus, then, did Moses and Aaron and the whole community of the Israelites deal with the Levites, carrying out exactly the command which the LORD had given Moses concerning them. 21When the Levites had cleansed themselves of sin* and washed their clothes, Aaron offered them as a wave offering before the LORD, and made atonement for them to purify them. 22Only then did they enter upon their service in the meeting tent under the supervision of Aaron and his sons. The command which the LORD had given Moses concerning the Levites was carried out.

Age Limits for Levitical Service 23The LORD said to Moses: 24"This is the rule for the Levites. Each from his twenty-fifth year onward shall perform the required service in the meeting tent.[y] 25When he is fifty years old, he shall retire from the required service and work no longer. 26His service with his fellow Levites shall consist in sharing their responsibilities in the meeting tent, but he shall not do the work. This, then, is how you are to regulate the duties of the Levites."

CHAPTER 9

Second Passover 1In the first month of the year following their departure from the land of Egypt, the LORD said to Moses in the desert of Sinai, 2"Tell the Israelites to celebrate the Passover at the prescribed time. 3The evening twilight of the fourteenth day of this month[z] is the prescribed time when you shall celebrate it, observing all its rules and regulations." 4Moses, therefore, told the Israelites to celebrate the Passover. 5And they did so, celebrating the Passover in the desert of Sinai during the evening twilight of the fourteenth day of the first month, just as the LORD had commanded Moses.

6There were some, however, who were unclean because of a human corpse and so could not keep the Passover that day. These men came up to Moses and Aaron that same day 7and said, "Although we are unclean because of a corpse, why should we be deprived of presenting the LORD's offering at its proper time along with the other Israelites?" 8Moses answered them, "Wait until I learn what the LORD will command in your regard."

9The LORD then said to Moses: 10"Speak to the Israelites and say: If any one of you or of your descendants is unclean because of a corpse, or if he is absent on a journey, he may still keep the LORD's Passover. 11But he shall keep it in the second month,[a] during the evening twilight of the fourteenth day of that month, eating it with unleavened bread and bitter herbs, 12and not leaving any of it over till morning, nor breaking any of its bones,[b] but observing all the rules of the Passover. 13However, anyone who is clean and not away on a journey, who yet fails to keep

8, 21: Cleansed themselves of sin: by having the "water of remission" sprinkled on them as prescribed in v 7.

u Nm 3, 45. v Nm 3, 12. 45. w Nm 3, 13; 13, 2; Lk 2, 23. x Nm 3, 9f. y Nm 4, 3. 23. z Ex 12, 6; Lv 23, 5. a 2 Chr 30, 2–15. b Ex 12, 46; Jn 19, 36.

the Passover, shall be cut off from his people, because he did not present the LORD's offering at the prescribed time. That man shall bear the consequences of his sin.

14“If an alien* who lives among you wishes to keep the LORD's Passover, he too shall observe the rules and regulations for the Passover. You shall have the same law for the resident alien as for the native of the land.”[c]

The Fiery Cloud 15On the day when the Dwelling was erected, the cloud* covered the Dwelling, the tent of the commandments; but from evening until morning it took on the appearance of fire over the Dwelling.[d] 16It was always so: during the day the Dwelling was covered by the cloud, which at night had the appearance of fire. 17Whenever the cloud rose from the tent, the Israelites would break camp; wherever the cloud came to rest, they would pitch camp.[e] 18At the bidding of the LORD the Israelites moved on, and at his bidding they encamped.[f] As long as the cloud stayed over the Dwelling, they remained in camp.

19Even when the cloud tarried many days over the Dwelling, the Israelites obeyed the LORD and would not move on; 20yet sometimes the cloud was over the Dwelling only for a few days. It was at the bidding of the LORD that they stayed in camp, and it was at his bidding that they departed. 21Sometimes the cloud remained there only from evening until morning; and when it rose in the morning, they would depart. Or if the cloud lifted during the day, or even at night, they would then set out. 22Whether the cloud tarried over the Dwelling for two days or for a month or longer, the Israelites remained in camp and did not depart; but when it lifted, they moved on. 23Thus, it was always at the bidding of the LORD that they encamped, and at his bidding that they set out; ever heeding the charge of the LORD, as he had bidden them through Moses.

CHAPTER 10

The Silver Trumpets 1The LORD said to Moses: 2“Make two trumpets of beaten silver, which you shall use in assembling the community and in breaking camp. 3When both are blown, the whole community shall gather round you at the entrance of the meeting tent; 4but when one of them is blown, only the princes, the chiefs of the troops of Israel, shall gather round you. 5When you sound the first alarm, those encamped on the east side shall set out; 6when you sound the second alarm, those encamped on the south side shall set out; when you sound the third alarm, those encamped on the west side shall set out; when you sound the fourth alarm, those encamped on the north side shall set out. Thus shall the alarm be sounded for them to depart. 7But in calling forth an assembly you are to blow an ordinary blast, without sounding the alarm.

8“It is the sons of Aaron, the priests, who shall blow the trumpets; and the use of them is prescribed by perpetual statute for you and your descendants. 9[g]When in your own land you go to war against an enemy that is attacking you, you shall sound the alarm on the trumpets, and the LORD, your God, will remember you and save you from your foes. 10On your days of celebration,* your festivals, and your new-moon feasts, you shall blow the trumpets over your holocausts and your peace offerings;[h] this will serve as a reminder of you before your God. I, the LORD, am your God.”

II: From Sinai to the Plains of Moab

Departure from Sinai 11In the second year, on the twentieth day of the second month, the cloud rose from the Dwelling of the commandments. 12The Israelites moved on from the

9, 14: An alien: this passage presupposes that he is already circumcised as prescribed in Ex 12, 48.

9, 15: The cloud: already mentioned at the departure from Egypt; cf Ex 13, 21f.

10, 10: Days of celebration: special holidays, such as the occasion of a victory. Festivals: the great annual feasts of the Passover, Pentecost and Booths described in Lv 23; Nm 28–29.

c Ex 12, 48f. d Ex 13, 21. e Wis 18, 3. f 1 Cor 10, 1. g 2 Chr 13, 14. h Nm 29, 1; 2 Chr 29, 26ff.

desert of Sinai by stages, until the cloud came to rest in the desert of Paran.

13 The first time that they broke camp at the bidding of the LORD through Moses, 14 [i]the camp of the Judahites, under its own standard and arranged in companies, was the first to set out. Nahshon, son of Amminadab, was over their host, 15 and Nethanel, son of Zuar, over the host of the tribe of Issachar, 16 and Eliab, son of Helon, over the host of the tribe of Zebulun. 17 Then, after the Dwelling was dismantled, the clans of Gershon and Merari set out, carrying the Dwelling. 18 The camp of the Reubenites, under its own standard and arranged in companies, was the next to set out, with Elizur, son of Shedeur, over their host, 19 and Shelumiel, son of Zurishaddai, over the host of the tribe of Simeon, 20 and Eliasaph, son of Reuel, over the host of the tribe of Gad. 21 The clan of Kohath then set out, carrying the sacred objects for the Dwelling, which was to be erected before their arrival. 22 The camp of the Ephraimites next set out, under its own standard and arranged in companies, with Elishama, son of Ammihud, over their host, 23 and Gamaliel, son of Pedahzur, over the host of the tribe of Manasseh, 24 and Abidan, son of Gideoni, over the host of the tribe of Benjamin. 25 Finally, as rear guard for all the camps, the camp of the Danites set out, under its own standard and arranged in companies, with Ahiezer, son of Amishaddai, over their host, 26 and Pagiel, son of Ochran, over the host of the tribe of Asher, 27 and Ahira, son of Enan, over the host of the tribe of Naphtali. 28 This was the order of departure for the Israelites, company by company.

Hobab as Guide As they were setting out, 29 Moses said to his brother-in-law Hobab, son of Reuel the Midianite, "We are setting out for the place which the LORD has promised to give us. Come with us, and we will be generous toward you, for the LORD has promised prosperity to Israel." 30 *But he answered, "No, I will not come. I am going instead to my own country and to my own kindred." 31 Moses said, "Please, do not leave us; you know where we can camp in the desert, and you will serve as eyes for us. 32 If you come with us, we will share with you the prosperity the LORD will bestow on us."

Into the Desert 33 [j]They moved on from the mountain of the LORD,* a three days' journey, and the ark of the covenant of the LORD which was to seek out their resting place went the three days' journey with them. 34 And when they set out from camp, the cloud of the LORD was over them by day.

35 Whenever the ark set out, Moses would say,

"Arise, O LORD, that your enemies may be
scattered,
and those who hate you may flee before
you."

36 And when it came to rest, he would say,

"Return, O LORD, you who ride upon the
clouds,
to the troops of Israel."

CHAPTER 11

Discontent of the People 1 Now the people complained in the hearing of the LORD;[k] and when he heard it his wrath flared up so that the fire of the LORD burned among them and consumed the outskirts of the camp. 2 But when the people cried out to Moses, he prayed to the LORD and the fire died out. 3 Hence that place was called Taberah,* because there the fire of the LORD burned among them.

4 The foreign elements among them were so greedy for meat that even the Israelites lamented again,[l] "Would that we had meat for food! 5 We remember the fish we used to eat without cost in Egypt, and the cucumbers, the melons, the leeks, the onions, and the garlic. 6 But now we are famished; we see nothing before us but this manna."[m]

10, 30ff: Hobab wished to be coaxed before granting the favor. From Jgs 1, 16 it seems probable that he did accede to Moses' request.

10, 33: The mountain of the Lord: Sinai (Horeb), elsewhere always called "the mountain of God."

11, 3: Taberah: means "the burning."

i 14ff: Nm 2, 3. 5. 7. j Dt 1, 33. k Dt 9, 22. l Ps 78, 18. m 5f: Nm 21, 5; Ex 16, 3; Acts 7, 39.

7 [n]Manna was like coriander seed* and had the appearance of bdellium. 8 When they had gone about and gathered it up, the people would grind it between millstones or pound it in a mortar, then cook it in a pot and make it into loaves, which tasted like cakes made with oil. 9 At night, when the dew fell upon the camp, the manna also fell.[o]

10 When Moses heard the people, family after family, crying at the entrance of their tents, so that the LORD became very angry, he was grieved. 11 "Why do you treat your servant so badly?" Moses asked the LORD. "Why are you so displeased with me that you burden me with all this people? 12 Was it I who conceived all this people? or was it I who gave them birth, that you tell me to carry them at my bosom, like a foster father carrying an infant, to the land you have promised under oath to their fathers? 13 Where can I get meat to give to all this people? For they are crying to me, 'Give us meat for our food.' 14 I cannot carry all this people by myself, for they are too heavy for me. 15 If this is the way you will deal with me, then please do me the favor of killing me at once, so that I need no longer face this distress."

The Seventy Elders 16 Then the LORD said to Moses, "Assemble for me seventy of the elders of Israel, men you know for true elders and authorities among the people, and bring them to the meeting tent. When they are in place beside you, 17 I will come down and speak with you there. I will also take some of the spirit that is on you and will bestow it on them, that they may share the burden of the people with you. You will then not have to bear it by yourself.

18 "To the people, however, you shall say: Sanctify yourselves for tomorrow, when you shall have meat to eat. For in the hearing of the LORD you have cried, 'Would that we had meat for food! Oh, how well off we were in Egypt!' Therefore the LORD will give you meat for food, 19 and you will eat it, not for one day, or two days, or five, or ten, or twenty days, 20 but for a whole month—until it comes out of your very nostrils and becomes loathsome to you. For you have spurned the LORD who is in your midst, and in his presence you have wailed, 'Why did we ever leave Egypt?' "

21 But Moses said, "The people around me include six hundred thousand soldiers; yet you say, 'I will give them meat to eat for a whole month.' 22 Can enough sheep and cattle be slaughtered for them? If all the fish of the sea were caught for them, would they have enough?" 23 The LORD answered Moses, "Is this beyond the LORD's reach? You shall see now whether or not what I have promised you takes place."

The Spirit on the Elders 24 So Moses went out and told the people what the LORD had said. Gathering seventy elders of the people, he had them stand around the tent. 25 The LORD then came down in the cloud and spoke to him. Taking some of the spirit that was on Moses, he bestowed it on the seventy elders; and as the spirit came to rest on them, they prophesied.*

26 Now two men, one named Eldad and the other Medad, were not in the gathering but had been left in the camp. They too had been on the list, but had not gone out to the tent; yet the spirit came to rest on them also, and they prophesied in the camp. 27 So, when a young man quickly told Moses, "Eldad and Medad are prophesying in the camp," 28 Joshua, son of Nun, who from his youth had been Moses' aide, said, "Moses, my lord, stop them." 29 But Moses answered him, "Are you jealous for my sake? Would that all the people of the LORD were prophets! Would that the LORD might bestow his spirit on them all!" 30 Then Moses retired to the camp, along with the elders of Israel.

The Quail 31 There arose a wind[p] sent by the

11, 7: Coriander seed: see note on Ex 16, 31. Bdellium: a transparent, amber-colored gum resin, which is also mentioned in Gn 2, 12.

11, 25: They prophesied: in the sense, not of foretelling the future, but of speaking in enraptured enthusiasm. Such manifestations of mystic exaltation occurred in the early days of Hebrew prophecy (1 Sm 10, 10ff; 19, 20ff) and in the first years of the Church (Acts 2, 6-11. 17; 19, 6; 1 Cor 12–14).

n 7f: Ex 16, 14f. 31; Ps 78, 24; Wis 16, 20; Jn 6, 31. o Ex 16, 14f. p Ps 78, 26ff.

LORD, that drove in quail from the sea and
brought them down over the camp site at a
height of two cubits from the ground* for the
distance of a day's journey all around the camp.
32 [q]All that day, all night, and all the next day the
people gathered in the quail. Even the one who
got the least gathered ten homers of them. Then
they spread them out* all around the camp.
33 But while the meat was still between their
teeth, before it could be consumed, the LORD's
wrath flared up against the people, and he struck
them with a very great plague. 34 So that place
was named Kibroth-hattaavah,* because it was
there that the greedy people were buried.

35 From Kibroth-hattaavah the people set out
for Hazeroth.

CHAPTER 12

Jealousy of Aaron and Miriam While they
were in Hazeroth, 1 Miriam and Aaron spoke
against Moses on the pretext of the marriage he
had contracted with a Cushite woman.* 2 They
complained,* "Is it through Moses alone that
the LORD speaks? Does he not speak through us
also?" And the LORD heard this. 3 [r]Now, Moses
himself was by far the meekest man on the face
of the earth. 4 So at once the LORD said to Moses
and Aaron and Miriam, "Come out, you three,
to the meeting tent." And the three of them
went. 5 Then the LORD came down in the
column of cloud, and standing at the entrance of
the tent, called Aaron and Miriam. When both
came forward, 6 he said, "Now listen to the
words of the LORD:

Should there be a prophet among you,
  in visions will I reveal myself to him,
  in dreams will I speak to him;
7 Not so with my servant Moses!
Throughout my house he bears my trust: [s]
8 face to face I speak to him, [t]
  plainly and not in riddles.
The presence of the LORD he beholds.

Why, then, did you not fear to speak against my
servant Moses?"

Miriam's Leprosy 9 So angry was the Lord
against them that when he departed, 10 and the
cloud withdrew from the tent, there was Mir-
iam, [u] a snow-white leper!* When Aaron turned
and saw her a leper, 11 "Ah, my lord!" he said to
Moses, "please do not charge us with the sin
that we have foolishly committed! 12 Let her not
thus be like the stillborn babe that comes forth
from its mother's womb with its flesh half
consumed." 13 Then Moses cried to the LORD,
"Please, not this! Pray, heal her!" 14 But the LORD
answered Moses, "Suppose her father had spit in
her face, would she not hide in shame for seven
days? Let her be confined outside the camp for
seven days; only then may she be brought
back." 15 So Miriam was confined outside the
camp for seven days, and the people did not start
out again until she was brought back.

16 After that the people set out from Hazeroth
and encamped in the desert of Paran.

CHAPTER 13

The Twelve Scouts 1 The LORD said to Moses,
2 "Send men to reconnoiter the land of Canaan,
which I am giving the Israelites. You shall send
one man from each ancestral tribe, all of them
princes." 3 [v]So Moses dispatched them from the
desert of Paran, as the LORD had ordered. All of
them were leaders among the Israelites; 4 by
name they were:

Shammua, son of Zaccur, of the tribe of
  Reuben;

11, 31: At a height of two cubits from the ground: exhausted by the storm, the quail could take but short, low flights, so that they were easily captured. To give food to the hungry people, God may have used the natural phenomenon of the annual migration of quail across the Sinai Peninsula. In the spring large flocks of these birds cross the Gulf of Aqabah flying toward the west; in the fall they fly back eastward from the Mediterranean. The sea mentioned here probably refers to the former body of water.

11, 32: They spread them out: to cure by drying.

11, 34: Kibroth-hattaavah: means "graves of greed."

12, 1: Cushite woman: apparently Zipporah, the Midianitess, is meant; cf Ex 2, 21. Perhaps the term is used here merely in the sense of "despised foreigner."

12, 2: The real reason for Miriam's quarrel with her brother Moses was her jealousy of his superior position; his Cushite wife served only as an occasion for the dispute. Aaron merely followed his sister in her rebellion; hence she alone was punished.

12, 10: A snow-white leper: afflicted with "white leprosy," a skin disease that generally is not serious or of long duration. Cf Lv 13, 3–6.

q 32f: 78, 26–31; 1 Cor 10, 6–7. r Sir 45, 1f. s Sir 45, 3; Heb 3, 2. 5. t Ex 33, 11; Dt 34, 10. u Dt 24, 9. v 3–33: Dt 1, 22–28.

5 Shaphat, son of Hori, of the tribe of Simeon;
6 Caleb, son of Jephunneh, of the tribe of Judah;
7 Igal [son of Joseph] of the tribe of Issachar;
10 Gaddiel, son of Sodi, of the tribe of Zebulun;
11 Gaddi, son of Susi, of the tribe of Manasseh,
for the Josephites, with
8 Hoshea, son of Nun, of the tribe of Ephraim;
9 Palti, son of Raphu, of the tribe of Benjamin;
12 Ammiel, son of Gemalli, of the tribe of Dan;
13 Sethur, son of Michael, of the tribe of Asher;
14 Nahbi, son of Vophsi, of the tribe of Naphtali;
15 Geuel, son of Machi, of the tribe of Gad.

16 These are the names of the men whom Moses
sent out to reconnoiter the land. But Hoshea,
son of Nun, Moses called Joshua.*
17 In sending them to reconnoiter the land of
Canaan, Moses said to them, "Go up here in the
Negeb, up into the highlands, 18 and see what
kind of land it is. Are the people living there
strong or weak, few or many? 19 Is the country in
which they live good or bad? Are the towns in
which they dwell open or fortified? 20 Is the soil
fertile or barren, wooded or clear? And do your
best to get some of the fruit of the land." It was
then the season for early grapes.
21 So they went up and reconnoitered the land
from the desert of Zin* as far as where Rehob
adjoins Labo of Hamath. 22 [w]Going up by way of
the Negeb, they reached Hebron, where Ahi-
man, Sheshai and Talmai, descendants of the
Anakim,* were living. [Hebron had been built
seven years before Zoan in Egypt.] 23 They also
reached the Wadi Eshcol,* where they cut down
a branch with a single cluster of grapes on it,
which two of them carried on a pole, as well as
some pomegranates and figs. 24 It was because of
the cluster the Israelites cut there that they
called the place Wadi Eshcol.[x]

Their Return 25 After reconnoitering the land
for forty days they returned, 26 [y]met Moses and
Aaron and the whole community of the Israelites
in the desert of Paran at Kadesh, made a report
to them all, and showed them the fruit of the
country. 27 They told Moses: "We went into the
land to which you sent us. It does indeed flow
with milk and honey, and here is its fruit.
28 However, the people who are living in the land
are fierce, and the towns are fortified and very
strong.[z] Besides, we saw descendants of the
Anakim there. 29 Amalekites live in the region of
the Negeb; Hittites, Jebusites and Amorites
dwell in the highlands, and Canaanites along the
seacoast and the banks of the Jordan."
30 Caleb, however, to quiet the people toward
Moses, said, "We ought to go up and seize the
land, for we can certainly do so." 31 But the men
who had gone up with him said, "We cannot
attack these people; they are too strong for us."
32 So they spread discouraging reports[a] among
the Israelites about the land they had scouted,
saying, "The land that we explored is a country
that consumes its inhabitants. And all the people
we saw there are huge men, 33 [b]veritable giants*
[the Anakim were a race of giants]; we felt like
mere grasshoppers, and so we must have
seemed to them."

CHAPTER 14

Threats of Revolt 1 At this, the whole commu-
nity broke out with loud cries, and even in the
night the people wailed. 2 [c]All the Israelites
grumbled against Moses and Aaron, the whole
community saying to them, "Would that we had
died in the land of Egypt, or that here in the
desert we were dead! 3 Why is the LORD bringing
us into this land only to have us fall by the
sword? Our wives and little ones will be taken as

13, 16: Joshua: in Hebrew, "Jehoshua," which was later modified to "Jeshua," the Hebrew pronunciation of the name "Jesus." Hoshea and Joshua are variants of one original name meaning "the LORD saves." Cf Mt 1, 21.

13, 21: The desert of Zin: north of Paran and southwest of the Dead Sea. It is quite distinct from "the desert of Sin" near the border of Egypt (Ex 16, 1; 17, 1; Nm 33, 11). Labo of Hamath: a town near Riblah (Jer 39, 5f) at the southern border of Hamath, an independent kingdom in southern Syria. David's conquests extended as far as Hamath (2 Sm 8, 9ff), and Labo thus formed the northern border of the ideal extent of Israel's possessions (Nm 34, 7ff; Ez 47, 15; 48, 1). Some commentators think that this verse is a later addition to the text; cf Dt 1, 24.

13, 22. 28: Anakim: an aboriginal race in southern Palestine, largely absorbed by the Canaanites before the Israelite invasion. Either because of their tall stature or because of the massive stone structures left by them the Israelites regarded them as giants.

13, 23: Eshcol: means "cluster."

13, 33: Giants: in Hebrew, "nephilim." Cf Gn 6, 4.

w Jos 11, 21f. x Nm 32, 9; Dt 1, 24f. y 26f: Ex 3, 8. 17. z 28f: Dt 9, 1f. a Nm 32, 9; Jos 14, 8. b Dt 2, 10. c Ex 16, 3; Ps 106, 25.

booty. Would it not be better for us to return to
Egypt?" 4 So they said to one another, "Let us
appoint a leader and go back to Egypt."

5 But Moses and Aaron fell prostrate before the
whole assembled community of the Israelites;
6 while Joshua, son of Nun, and Caleb, son of
Jephunneh, who had been in the party that
scouted the land, tore their garments 7 and said
to the whole community of the Israelites, [d] "The
country which we went through and explored is
a fine, rich land. 8 If the LORD is pleased with us,
he will bring us in and give us that land, a land
flowing with milk and honey. 9 [e]But do not rebel
against the LORD! You need not be afraid of the
people of that land; they are but food for us!*
Their defense has left them, but the LORD is with
us. Therefore, do not be afraid of them." 10 In
answer, the whole community threatened to
stone them.

The Lord's Sentence But then the glory of the
LORD appeared at the meeting tent to all the
Israelites. 11 And the LORD said to Moses, "How
long will this people spurn me? How long will
they refuse to believe in me, despite all the signs
I have performed among them? [f] 12 I will strike
them with pestilence and wipe them out. Then I
will make of you a nation greater and mightier
than they." [g]

13 [h]But Moses said to the LORD: "Are the
Egyptians to hear of this? For by your power you
brought out this people from among them.
14 And are they to tell of it to the inhabitants of
this land? It has been heard that you, O LORD,
are in the midst of this people; you, LORD, who
plainly reveal yourself! Your cloud stands over
them, and you go before them by day in a
column of cloud and by night in a column of
fire. [i] 15 If now you slay this whole people, the
nations who have heard such reports of you will
say, 16 'The LORD was not able to bring this
people into the land he swore to give them; that
is why he slaughtered them in the desert.' [j]
17 Now then, let the power of my Lord be
displayed in its greatness, even as you have said,
18 [k]'The LORD is slow to anger and rich in
kindness, forgiving wickedness and crime; yet
not declaring the guilty guiltless, but punishing
children to the third and fourth generation for
their fathers' wickedness.' 19 Pardon, then, the
wickedness of this people in keeping with your
great kindness, even as you have forgiven them
from Egypt until now." [l]

20 The LORD answered: "I pardon them as you
have asked. 21 Yet, by my life and the LORD's
glory that fills the whole earth, 22 of all the men
who have seen my glory and the signs I worked
in Egypt and in the desert, [m] and who neverthe-
less have put me to the test ten times already
and have failed to heed my voice, 23 not one shall
see the land which I promised on oath to their
fathers. None of these who have spurned me
shall see it. 24 But because my servant Caleb has
a different spirit and follows me unreservedly, [n] I
will bring him into the land where he has just
been, and his descendants shall possess it. 25 But
now, since the Amalekites and Canaanites are
living in the valleys,* turn away tomorrow and
set out in the desert on the Red Sea road."

26 The LORD also said to Moses and Aaron:
27 "How long will this wicked community grum-
ble against me? [o] I have heard the grumblings of
the Israelites against me. 28 Tell them:* By my
life, says the LORD, I will do to you just what I
have heard you say. 29 Here in the desert [p] shall
your dead bodies fall. Of all your men of twenty
years or more, registered in the census, who
grumbled against me, 30 not one shall enter the
land where I solemnly swore to settle you,
except Caleb, son of Jephunneh, and Joshua, son
of Nun. 31 Your little ones, however, who you
said would be taken as booty, I will bring in, and
they shall appreciate the land you spurned. [q]

14, 9: They are but food for us: that is, "we can easily consume and destroy them." This is the answer to the pessimistic report that this land "consumes its inhabitants" (Nm 13, 32).

14, 25: The valleys: the low-lying plains in the Negeb and along the seacoast and in the Jordan depression, as well as the higher valleys in the mountains farther north; cf Nm 14, 45.

14, 28f: God punished the malcontents by giving them their wish; cf v 2. Their lack of faith and of confidence in God is cited in 1 Cor 10, 10, and Heb 3, 12–18, as a warning for Christians.

d 7f: Dt 1, 25. e Dt 7, 18. f Ps 78, 22. 32. g Ex 32, 10. h 13–16: Ex 32, 12; Dt 9, 26ff; Ps 106, 23. i Ex 13, 21; Jos 2, 9f. j Ex 32, 12; Dt 9, 28. k Ex 20, 5; 34, 6f; Pss 103, 8; 145, 8. l Ps 78, 38. m 22f: Dt 1, 35. n Jos 14, 8f. o Ex 16, 7. 12. p Dt 1, 35; Heb 3, 17. q Dt 1, 39.

32But as for you, your bodies shall fall here in the desert, 33here where your children must wander for forty years, suffering for your faithlessness, till the last of you lies dead in the desert.[r] 34Forty days you spent in scouting the land; forty years shall you suffer for your crimes: one year for each day. Thus you will realize what it means to oppose me. 35I, the LORD, have sworn to do this to all this wicked community that conspired against me: here in the desert they shall die to the last man."

36And so it happened to the men whom Moses had sent to reconnoiter the land[s] and who on returning had set the whole community grumbling against him by spreading discouraging reports about the land; 37these men who had given out the bad report about the land were struck down by the LORD and died. 38Of all the men who had gone to reconnoiter the land, only Joshua, son of Nun, and Caleb, son of Jephunneh, survived.[t]

Unsuccessful Invasion 39When Moses repeated these words to all the Israelites, the people felt great remorse. 40Early the next morning they started up into the foothills, saying, "Here we are, ready to go up to the place that the LORD spoke of:[u] for we were indeed doing wrong." 41But Moses said, "Why are you again disobeying the LORD's orders? This cannot succeed. 42Do not go up, because the LORD is not in your midst; if you go, you will be beaten down before your enemies.[v] 43For there the Amalekites and Canaanites face you, and you will fall by the sword. You have turned back from following the LORD; therefore the LORD will not be with you."

44Yet they dared to go up into the foothills,[w] even though neither the ark of the covenant of the LORD nor Moses left the camp. 45And the Amalekites and Canaanites who dwelt in that hill country came down and defeated them, beating them back as far as Hormah.*

CHAPTER 15

Secondary Offerings 1The LORD said to Moses, 2*"Give the Israelites these instructions: When you have entered the land that I will give you for your homesteads, 3if you make to the LORD a sweet-smelling oblation from the herd or from the flock, in holocaust, in fulfillment of a vow, or as a freewill offering, or for one of your festivals, 4whoever does so shall also present to the LORD a cereal offering consisting of a tenth of an ephah of fine flour mixed with a fourth of a hin of oil, 5as well as a libation of a fourth of a hin of wine, with each lamb sacrificed in holocaust or otherwise. 6With each sacrifice of a ram you shall present a cereal offering of two tenths of an ephah of fine flour mixed with a third of a hin of oil, 7and a libation of a third of a hin of wine, thus making a sweet-smelling offering to the LORD. 8When you sacrifice an ox as a holocaust, or in fulfillment of a vow, or as a peace offering to the LORD, 9with it you shall present a cereal offering of three tenths of an ephah of fine flour mixed with half a hin of oil, 10and a libation of half a hin of wine, as a sweet-smelling oblation to the LORD. 11The same is to be done for each ox, ram, lamb or goat. 12Whatever the number you offer, do the same for each of them.

13"All the native-born shall make these offerings in the same way, whenever they present a sweet-smelling oblation to the LORD. 14Likewise, in any future generation, any alien residing with you permanently or for a time, who presents a sweet-smelling oblation to the LORD, shall do as you do. 15There is but one rule for you and for the resident alien, a perpetual rule for all your descendants. Before the LORD you and the alien are alike, 16with the same law and the same application of it for the alien residing among you as for yourselves."

17The LORD said to Moses, 18"Speak to the Israelites and tell them: When you enter the

14, 45: Hormah: one of the Canaanite royal cities in southern Judea (Jos 12, 14), known at this time as "Zephath"; the origin of the later name is told in Nm 21, 3; Jgs 1, 17.

15, 2–16: These laws on sacrifice are complementary to those of Lv 1–3. Since the food of the Israelites consisted not only of meat but also of bread, oil and wine, so, besides the animal oblations, they offered flour, wine and oil in sacrifice to the Lord.

r 33f: Nm 13, 26; 32, 13; Ps 95, 10; Ez 4, 6. s 36f: Nm 13, 17. 32f; 1 Cor 10, 10. t Nm 26, 65. u Nm 13, 18; Dt 1, 42. v Dt 1, 42. w Dt 1, 43.

land into which I will bring you 19and begin to eat of the food of that land, you shall offer the LORD a contribution 20consisting of a cake of your first batch of dough.* You shall offer it just as you offer a contribution from the threshing floor.[x] 21Throughout your generations you shall give a contribution to the LORD from your first batch of dough.

Sin Offerings 22*"When through inadvertence you fail to carry out any of these commandments which the LORD gives to Moses,[y] 23and through Moses to you, from the time the LORD first issues the commandment down through your generations: 24if the community itself unwittingly becomes guilty of the fault of inadvertence, the whole community shall offer the holocaust of one young bull as a sweet-smelling oblation pleasing to the LORD, along with its prescribed cereal offering and libation, as well as one he-goat as a sin offering. 25 [z]Then the priest shall make atonement for the whole Israelite community; thus they will be forgiven the inadvertence for which they have brought their holocaust as an oblation to the LORD. 26Not only the whole Israelite community, but also the aliens residing among you, shall be forgiven, since the fault of inadvertence affects all the people.

27"However, if it is an individual who sins inadvertently,[a] he shall bring a yearling she-goat as a sin offering, 28and the priest shall make atonement before the LORD for him who sinned inadvertently; when atonement has been made for him, he will be forgiven. 29You shall have but one law for him who sins inadvertently, whether he be a native Israelite or an alien residing with you.

30"But anyone who sins defiantly,[b] whether he be a native or an alien, insults the LORD, and shall be cut off from among his people. 31 [c]Since he has despised the word of the LORD and has broken his commandment, he must be cut off. He has only himself to blame."

The Sabbath-breaker 32While the Israelites were in the desert, a man was discovered gathering wood on the sabbath day. 33Those who caught him at it brought him to Moses and Aaron and the whole assembly. 34But they kept him in custody, for there was no clear decision* as to what should be done with him.[d] 35Then the LORD said to Moses, "This man shall be put to death; let the whole community stone him outside the camp." 36So the whole community led him outside the camp and stoned him to death, as the LORD had commanded Moses.

Tassels on the Cloak 37The LORD said to Moses, 38"Speak to the Israelites and tell them that they and their descendants must put tassels* on the corners of their garments, fastening each corner tassel with a violet cord.[e] 39When you use these tassels, let the sight of them remind you to keep all the commandments of the LORD, without going wantonly astray after the desires of your hearts and eyes. 40Thus you will remember to keep all my commandments and be holy to your God. 41I, the LORD, am your God who, as God, brought you out of Egypt that I, the LORD, may be your God."[f]

CHAPTER 16

Rebellion of Korah 1Korah, son of Izhar, son of Kohath, son of Levi,* [and Dathan and Abiram, sons of Eliab, son of Pallu, son of Reuben]

15, 20: Dough: some render, "barley grits." This word is used elsewhere only in Ez 44, 30 and Neh 10, 33; a related Hebrew word is used in Lv 2, 14.

15, 22ff: Although no moral guilt is incurred by an inadvertent violation of God's commandments, the sanctity of the law can require some reparation even for such violations.

15, 34: No clear decision: they already knew that a willful violation of the sabbath was a capital offense, but they did not yet know how the death penalty was to be inflicted.

15, 38: Tassels: at the time of Christ these tassels were worn by all pious Jews, including our Lord (Mt 9, 20f; Mk 6, 56); the Pharisees wore very large ones in ostentation of their zeal for the law (Mt 23, 5).

16, 1ff: The evidence seems to show that there were two distinct rebellions: one of Korah and his band (Nm 27, 3) and the other of Dathan and Abiram (Dt 11, 6); cf Ps 106. The present account combines both events into one narrative; but even here it is rather easy to separate the two, once certain proper names (vv 1. 6. 24. 32. 35) have been identified as glosses. The rebellion of the Reubenites, Dathan and Abiram, was of a political nature, against Moses alone as the civil leader; these rebels were punished by being swallowed alive in an earthquake. The rebellion of Korah was of a religious nature, against the religious leadership of both Moses and Aaron; about two hundred and fifty malcontents joined Korah's band; they were punished by fire. The parts of the present section which refer to the rebellion of Dathan and Abiram are vv 12–15 and vv 25–34 of chapter 16; the rest of chapter 16 and all of chapter 17 concern the rebellion of Korah.

x 19–20: Ez 44, 30. **y** 22f: Lv 4, 13f. **z** Lv 4, 20. **a** 27f: Lv 4, 27f. **b** Dt 17, 12. **c** Prv 13, 13. **d** Lv 24, 12. **e** Dt 22, 12. **f** Lv 22, 32f.

took 2 two hundred and fifty Israelites who were leaders in the community, members of the council and men of note. They stood before Moses, 3 and held an assembly against Moses and Aaron, to whom they said,[g] "Enough from you! The whole community, all of them, are holy; the LORD is in their midst. Why then should you set yourselves over the LORD's congregation?"

4 When Moses heard this, he fell prostrate. 5 Then he said to Korah and to all his band, "May the LORD make known tomorrow morning who belongs to him and who is the holy one and whom he will have draw near to him! Whom he chooses, he will have draw near him. 6 Do this: take your censers [Korah and all his band] 7 and put fire in them and place incense in them before the LORD tomorrow. He whom the LORD then chooses is the holy one. Enough from you Levites!"

8 Moses also said to Korah, "Listen to me, you Levites! 9 [h]Is it too little for you that the God of Israel has singled you out from the community of Israel, to have you draw near him for the service of the LORD's Dwelling and to stand before the community to minister for them? 10 He has allowed you and your kinsmen, the descendants of Levi, to approach him, and yet you now seek the priesthood too. 11 It is therefore against the LORD that you and all your band are conspiring. For what has Aaron done that you should grumble against him?"

Rebellion of Dathan and Abiram 12 Moses summoned Dathan and Abiram, sons of Eliab, but they answered, "We will not go.* 13 Are you not satisfied with having led us here away from a land flowing with milk and honey, to make us perish in the desert, that you must now lord it over us? 14 Far from bringing us to a land flowing with milk and honey, or giving us fields and vineyards for our inheritance, will you also gouge out our eyes?* No, we will not go."

15 Then Moses became very angry and said to the LORD, "Pay no heed to their offering. I have never taken a single ass from them, nor have I wronged any one of them."[i]

Korah 16 Moses said to Korah, "You and all your band shall appear before the LORD tomorrow—you and they and Aaron too. 17 Then each of your two hundred and fifty followers shall take his own censer, put incense in it, and offer it to the LORD; and you and Aaron, each with his own censer, shall do the same." 18 So they all took their censers, and laying incense on the fire they had put in them, they took their stand by the entrance of the meeting tent along with Moses and Aaron. 19 Then, when Korah had assembled all his band against them at the entrance of the meeting tent, the glory of the LORD appeared to the entire community, 20 and the LORD said to Moses and Aaron, 21 "Stand apart from this band, that I may consume them at once." 22 But they fell prostrate and cried out, "O God, God of the spirits of all mankind, will one man's sin make you angry with the whole community?" 23 The LORD answered Moses, 24 "Speak to the community and tell them: Withdraw from the space around the Dwelling" [of Korah, Dathan and Abiram].

Punishment of Dathan and Abiram 25 Moses, followed by the elders of Israel, arose and went to Dathan and Abiram.* 26 Then he warned the community, "Keep away from the tents of these wicked men and do not touch anything that is theirs: otherwise you too will be swept away because of all their sins." 27 When Dathan and Abiram had come out and were standing at the entrances of their tents with their wives and sons and little ones, 28 Moses said, "This is how you shall know that it was the LORD who sent me to do all I have done, and that it was not I who planned it: 29 if these men die an ordinary death, merely suffering the fate common to all mankind, then it was not the LORD who sent me. 30 But if the LORD does something entirely new, and the ground opens its mouth and swallows them alive down into

16, 12: We will not go: to appear before Moses' tribunal.
16, 14: Gouge out our eyes: blind us to the real state of affairs.
16, 25: Since Dathan and Abiram had refused to go to Moses (vv 12ff), he, with the elders as witnesses, was obliged to go to their tent.

g Ps 106, 16ff; Sir 45, 19; 1 Cor 10, 10. h Dt 10, 8. i I Sm 12, 3.

the nether world, with all belonging to them,
then you will know that these men have defied
the LORD." 31 [j] No sooner had he finished saying
all this than the ground beneath them split open,
32 and the earth opened its mouth and swallowed
them and their families [and all of Korah's men]
and all their possessions. 33 They went down
alive to the nether world with all belonging to
them; the earth closed over them, and they
perished from the community. 34 But all the
Israelites near them fled at their shrieks, saying,
"The earth might swallow us too!"
Punishment of Korah 35 So they withdrew
from the space around the Dwelling [of Korah,*
Dathan and Abiram]. And fire from the LORD
came forth which consumed the two hundred
and fifty men who were offering the incense.

CHAPTER 17

1 The LORD said to Moses, 2 "Tell Eleazar, son
of Aaron the priest, to remove the censers from
the embers; and scatter the fire some distance
away, 3 *for these sinners have consecrated the
censers at the cost of their lives. Have them
hammered into plates to cover the altar, because
in being presented before the LORD they have
become sacred. In this way they shall serve as a
sign to the Israelites." 4 So Eleazar the priest had
the bronze censers of those burned during the
offering hammered into a covering for the altar,
5 in keeping with the orders which the LORD had
given him through Moses. This cover was to be a
reminder to the Israelites that no layman, no one
who was not a descendant of Aaron, should
approach the altar to offer incense before the
LORD, lest he meet the fate of Korah and his
band.

6 The next day the whole Israelite community
grumbled against Moses and Aaron, saying, "It is
you who have slain the LORD's people." 7 But
while the community was deliberating against
them, Moses and Aaron turned toward the
meeting tent, and the cloud now covered it and
the glory of the LORD appeared. 8 Then Moses
and Aaron came to the front of the meeting tent,
9 and the LORD said to Moses and Aaron, 10 "Depart from this community, that I may consume
them at once." But they fell prostrate.

11 Then Moses said to Aaron, "Take your
censer, put fire from the altar in it, lay incense
on it, and bring it quickly to the community to
make atonement for them; for wrath has come
forth from the LORD and the blow is falling." [k]
12 Obeying the orders of Moses, Aaron took his
censer and ran in among the community, where
the blow was already falling on the people.
Then, as he offered the incense and made
atonement for the people, 13 standing there between the living and the dead, the scourge was
checked. 14 Yet fourteen thousand seven hundred died from the scourge, in addition to those
who died because of Korah. 15 When the scourge
had been checked, Aaron returned to Moses at
the entrance of the meeting tent.
Aaron's Staff 16 The LORD now said to Moses,
17 "Speak to the Israelites and get one staff* from
them for each ancestral house, twelve staffs in
all, one from each of their tribal princes. Mark
each man's name on his staff; 18 and mark
Aaron's name on Levi's staff,* for the head of
Levi's ancestral house shall also have a staff.
19 Then lay them down in the meeting tent, in
front of the commandments, where I meet you.
20 There the staff of the man of my choice shall
sprout. Thus will I suppress from my presence
the Israelites' grumbling against you."

21 So Moses spoke to the Israelites, and their
princes gave him staffs, twelve in all, one from
each tribal prince; and Aaron's staff was with

16, 35: This verse continues v 24; the first sentence is transposed from v 27.

17, 3: Whatever was brought into intimate contact with something sacred shared in its sacredness. See note on Nm 19, 20.

17, 17: The staff was not merely an article of practical use, but also a symbol of authority; cf Gn 49, 10; Nm 24, 17; Jer 48, 17. Hence, the staff of a leader of a tribe was considered the emblem of his tribe; in fact, certain Hebrew words for "staff" also means "tribe." Perhaps for this reason, to avoid confusion, the author here uses the term "ancestral house" instead of the ordinary word for "tribe."

17, 18: Levi's staff: it is not clear whether this is considered as one of the twelve mentioned in the preceding verse, or as a thirteenth staff. Sometimes Levi is reckoned as one of the twelve tribes (e.g., Dt 27, 12f), but more often the number twelve is arrived at by counting the two sub-tribes of Joseph, i.e., Ephraim and Manasseh, as distinct tribes. In this passage also it seems probable that the tribe of Levi is considered apart from the other twelve.

j 31ff: Nm 26, 10; Lv 10, 2; Dt 11, 6; Ps 106, 7f. k Wis 18, 20f.

them. 22 Then Moses laid the staffs down before
the LORD in the tent of the commandments.
23 The next day, when Moses entered the tent,
Aaron's staff, representing the house of Levi, had
sprouted and put forth not only shoots, but
blossoms as well, and even bore ripe almonds!
24 Moses thereupon brought out all the staffs
from the LORD's presence to the Israelites. After
each prince identified his own staff and took it,
25 the LORD said to Moses, "Put back Aaron's
staff in front of the commandments, to be kept
there as a warning to the rebellious, so that their
grumbling may cease before me; if it does not,
they will die." 26 And Moses did as the LORD had
commanded him.

Charge of the Sacred Things 27 *Then the
Israelites cried out to Moses, "We are perishing;
we are lost, we are all lost! 28 Every time anyone
approaches the Dwelling of the LORD, he dies!
Are we to perish to the last man?"

CHAPTER 18

1 The LORD said to Aaron,* "You and your
sons as well as the other members of your
ancestral house shall be responsible for the
sanctuary; but the responsibility of the priest-
hood shall rest on you and your sons alone.
2 Bring with you also your other kinsmen of the
tribe of Levi, your ancestral tribe, as your associ-
ates* and assistants, while you and your sons are
in front of the tent of the commandments. 3 They
shall look after your persons and the whole tent;
however, they shall not come near the sacred
vessels or the altar, lest both they and you die.
4 As your associates they shall have charge of all
the work connected with the meeting tent. But
no layman* shall come near you. 5 You shall have
charge of the sanctuary and of the altar, that
wrath may not fall again upon the Israelites.

6 "Remember, it is I who have taken your
kinsmen, the Levites, from the body of the
Israelites; they are a gift to you,[l] dedicated to
the LORD for the service of the meeting tent.
7 [m]But only you and your sons are to have charge
of performing the priestly functions in whatever
concerns the altar and the room within the
veil.* I give you the priesthood as a gift. Any
layman who draws near shall be put to death."

The Priests' Share of the Sacrifices 8 The
LORD said to Aaron,* "I myself have given you
charge of the contributions made to me in the
various sacred offerings of the Israelites;[n] by
perpetual ordinance I have assigned them to you
and to your sons as your priestly share. 9 You
shall have the right to share in the oblations that
are most sacred, in whatever they offer me as
cereal offerings or sin offerings or guilt offerings;
these shares shall accrue to you and to your
sons. 10 In eating them you shall treat them as
most sacred; every male among you may partake
of them. As sacred, they belong to you.

11 "You shall also have what is removed from
the gift in every wave offering* of the Israelites;
by perpetual ordinance I have assigned it to you
and to your sons and daughters.[o] All in your
family who are clean may partake of it. 12 I have
also assigned to you all the best[p] of the new oil
and of the new wine and grain that they give to
the LORD as their first fruits; 13 and likewise, of
whatever grows on their land, the first products
that they bring in to the LORD shall be yours; all
of your family who are clean may partake of
them. 14 Whatever is doomed* in Israel shall be
yours. 15 Every living thing that opens the womb,
whether of man or of beast, such as are to be
offered to the LORD, shall be yours;[q] but you
must let the first-born of man, as well as of
unclean animals, be redeemed. 16 The ransom for

17, 27f: Logically these two verses belong immediately after Nm 16, 35.

18, 1ff: This law, which kept unqualified persons from contact with sacred things, is the answer to the Israelites' cry in Nm 17, 28. It is followed by other laws concerning priests and Levites.

18, 2: Associates: in Hebrew this word alludes to the popular etymology of the name "Levi." Cf Gn 29, 34.

18, 4: Layman: here, "one who is not a Levite"; in v 7, "one who is not a priest."

18, 7: Veil: the outer veil, or "curtain," is probably meant.

18, 8ff: Two classes of offerings are here distinguished: the most sacred offering, which only the male members of the priestly families could eat (vv 8ff), and the other offerings, which even the women of the priestly families could eat (vv 11–19).

18, 11: Wave offering: this included the breast and right leg (v 18), the shoulder of the peace offering (Lv 7, 30–34), and portions of the nazirite sacrifice (Nm 6, 19f).

18, 14: Doomed: in Hebrew, herem, which means here "set aside from profane use and made sacred to the Lord." Cf Lv 27, 21. 28.

l Nm 3, 9; 8, 19. m Nm 3, 10. n Nm 5, 9. o Ex 29, 27f; Lv 7, 34; 10, 14. p 12f: Dt 18, 4; 26, 2. q Ex 13, 2.

a boy is to be paid when he is a month old; it is
fixed at five silver shekels according to the
sanctuary standard, twenty gerahs to the shekel.
17 But the first-born of cattle, sheep or goats shall
not be redeemed; they are sacred. Their blood
you must splash on the altar and their fat you
must burn as a sweet-smelling oblation to the
LORD. 18 [r]Their meat, however, shall be yours,
just as the breast and the right leg of the wave
offering belong to you. 19 By perpetual ordinance
I have assigned to you and to your sons and
daughters all the contributions from the sacred
gifts which the Israelites make to the LORD; this
is an inviolable covenant* to last forever before
the LORD, for you and for your descendants."
20 [s]Then the LORD said to Aaron,* "You shall not
have any heritage in the land of the Israelites nor
hold any portion among them; I will be your
portion and your heritage among them.

Tithes Due the Levites 21 "To the Levites,
however, I hereby assign all tithes in Israel as
their heritage in recompense for the service they
perform in the meeting tent.[t] 22 The Israelites
may no longer approach the meeting tent; else
they will incur guilt deserving death. 23 Only the
Levites are to perform the service of the meeting
tent, and they alone shall be held responsible;
this is a perpetual ordinance for all your genera-
tions. The Levites, therefore, shall not have any
heritage among the Israelites, 24 for I have as-
signed to them as their heritage the tithes which
the Israelites give as a contribution to the LORD.
That is why I have ordered that they are not to
have any heritage among the Israelites."

Tithes Paid by the Levites 25 The LORD said to
Moses, 26 "Give the Levites these instructions:
When you receive from the Israelites the tithes I
have assigned you from them as your heritage,
you are to make a contribution from them to the
LORD, a tithe of the tithes; 27 and your contribu-
tion will be credited to you as if it were grain
from the threshing floor or new wine from the
press. 28 Thus you too shall make a contribution
from all the tithes you receive from the Israelites,
handing over to Aaron the priest the part to be
contributed to the LORD. 29 From all the gifts that
you receive, and from the best parts, you are to
consecrate to the LORD your own full contribu-
tion.

30 "Tell them also: Once you have made your
contribution from the best part, the rest of the
tithes will be credited to you Levites as if it were
produce of the threshing floor or of the wine
press. 31 Your families, as well as you, may eat
them anywhere, since they are your recompense
for service at the meeting tent. 32 You will incur
no guilt so long as you make a contribution of
the best part. Do not profane the sacred gifts of
the Israelites and so bring death on yourselves."

CHAPTER 19

Ashes of the Red Heifer 1 The LORD said to
Moses and Aaron: 2 "This is the regulation which
the law of the LORD prescribes. Tell the Israelites
to procure for you a red heifer that is free from
every blemish and defect and on which no yoke
has ever been laid. 3 This is to be given to Eleazar
the priest, to be led outside the camp* and
slaughtered in his presence. 4 Eleazar the priest
shall take some of its blood on his finger and
sprinkle it seven times toward the front of the
meeting tent.* 5 Then the heifer shall be burned
in his sight, with its hide and flesh, its blood and
offal; 6 and the priest shall take some cedar
wood, hyssop and scarlet yarn and throw them
into the fire in which the heifer is being burned.
7 The priest shall then wash his garments and
bathe his body in water. He remains unclean

18, 19: An inviolable covenant: literally, "a covenant of salt." Cf 2 Chr 13, 5. The reference may perhaps be to the preservative power of salt (cf Mt 5, 13); but more likely the phrase refers to the custom of partaking of the same salt in common to render a contract unbreakable. See note on Lv 2, 13.

18, 20: The priests and Levites were forbidden to own hereditary land such as the other Israelites possessed; therefore in the allotment of the land they were not to receive any portion of it. Certain cities, however, were assigned to them for their residence; cf Nm 35, 1–8.

19, 3: Outside the camp: several Fathers of the Church saw in this a prefiguring of the sacrificial death of Christ outside the walls of Jerusalem; cf Jn 19, 20; Heb 13, 12; in the purifying water, into which the ashes of the red heifer were put, they saw a type of the water of Baptism.

19, 4: Toward the front of the meeting tent: since the tabernacle faced the east (Ex 26, 15–30), the killing of the heifer took place east of the camp; in later times it was done on the Mount of Olives, east of the Temple.

r Lv 7, 31–34. s Dt 10, 9; 18, 1f; Jos 13, 33; Ez 44, 28. t Heb 7, 5.

until the evening, and only afterward may he
return to the camp. 8 Likewise, he who burned
the heifer shall wash his garments, bathe his
body in water, and be unclean until evening.
9 Finally, a man who is clean shall gather up the
ashes of the heifer and deposit them in a clean
place outside the camp. There they are to be
kept for preparing lustral water for the Israelite
community. The heifer is a sin offering. 10 He
who has gathered up the ashes of the heifer shall
also wash his garments and be unclean until
evening. This is a perpetual ordinance, both for
the Israelites and for the aliens residing among
them.

Use of the Ashes 11 "Whoever touches the
dead body of any human being shall be unclean
for seven days; 12 he shall purify himself with the
water on the third and on the seventh day, and
then he will be clean again. But if he fails to purify
himself on the third and on the seventh day, he
will not become clean. 13 [u]Everyone who fails to
purify himself after touching the body of any de-
ceased person, defiles the Dwelling of the LORD
and shall be cut off from Israel. Since the lustral
water has not been splashed over him, he remains
unclean: his uncleanness still clings to him.

14 "This is the law: When a man dies in a tent,
everyone who enters the tent, as well as every-
one already in it, shall be unclean for seven days;
15 likewise, every vessel that is open, or with its
lid unfastened, shall be unclean. 16 Moreover,
everyone who in the open country touches a
dead person, whether he was slain by the sword
or died naturally, or who touches a human bone
or a grave, shall be unclean for seven days.
17 *For anyone who is thus unclean, ashes from
the sin offering shall be put in a vessel, and
spring water shall be poured on them. 18 Then a
man who is clean shall take some hyssop, dip it
in this water, and sprinkle it on the tent and on
all the vessels and persons that were in it, or on
him who touched a bone, a slain person or other
dead body, or a grave. 19 The clean man shall
sprinkle the unclean on the third and on the
seventh day; thus purified on the seventh day,
he shall wash his garments and bathe his body in
water, and in the evening he will be clean again.
20 *Any unclean man who fails to have himself
purified shall be cut off from the community,
because he defiles the sanctuary of the LORD. As
long as the lustral water has not been splashed
over him, he remains unclean. 21 This shall be a
perpetual ordinance for you.

"One who sprinkles the lustral water shall
wash his garments, and anyone who comes in
contact with this water shall be unclean until
evening. 22 Moreover, whatever the unclean per-
son touches becomes unclean itself, and anyone
who touches it becomes unclean until evening."

CHAPTER 20

Death of Miriam 1 The whole Israelite commu-
nity arrived in the desert of Zin in the first
month,* and the people settled at Kadesh. It was
here that Miriam died, and here that she was
buried.

Water Famine at Kadesh 2 As the community
had no water, they held a council against Moses
and Aaron. 3 The people contended with Moses,
exclaiming, "Would that we too had perished
with our kinsmen in the LORD's presence! 4 Why
have you brought the LORD's community into
this desert where we and our livestock are
dying? 5 Why did you lead us out of Egypt, only
to bring us to this wretched place which has
neither grain nor figs nor vines nor pomegran-
ates? Here there is not even water to drink!"
6 But Moses and Aaron went away from the
assembly to the entrance of the meeting tent,
where they fell prostrate.

Sin of Moses and Aaron Then the glory of the
LORD appeared to them, 7 and the LORD said to

19, 17ff: "If . . . the sprinkled ashes of a heifer sanctify the unclean unto the cleansing of the flesh, how much more will the blood of Christ . . . cleanse your conscience from dead works?" (Heb 9, 13f).

19, 20: Ritual uncleanness is, as it were, contagious; so also sacredness; see note on Nm 17, 3.

20, 1: The first month: we would expect the mention also of the day and of the year (after the exodus) when this took place; cf similar dates in Nm 1, 1; 10, 11; 33, 38; Dt 1, 3. Here the full date seems to have been lost. Probably the Israelites arrived in Kadesh in the third year after the exodus. Cf Dt 1, 46. The desert of Zin: a barren region with a few good oases, southwest of the Dead Sea. See note on Nm 13, 21.

u Lv 15, 31.

Moses, 8 "Take the staff and assemble the community, you and your brother Aaron, and in their presence order the rock to yield its waters. From the rock you shall bring forth water for the community and their livestock to drink." 9 So Moses took the staff from its place before the LORD, as he was ordered. 10 He and Aaron assembled the community in front of the rock, where he said to them,[v] "Listen to me, you rebels! Are we to bring water for you out of this rock?" 11 [w]Then, raising his hand, Moses struck the rock twice* with his staff, and water gushed out in abundance for the community and their livestock to drink. 12 *But the LORD said to Moses and Aaron, "Because you were not faithful to me in showing forth my sanctity before the Israelites, you shall not lead this community into the land I will give them."

13 These are the waters of Meribah,[x] where the Israelites contended against the LORD, and where he revealed his sanctity among them.

Edom's Refusal 14 From Kadesh Moses sent men to the king of Edom with the message: "Your brother Israel* has this to say: You know of all the hardships that have befallen us, 15 how our fathers went down to Egypt, where we stayed a long time, how the Egyptians maltreated us and our fathers, 16 and how, when we cried to the LORD,[y] he heard our cry and sent an angel who led us out of Egypt. Now here we are at the town of Kadesh at the edge of your territory. 17 Kindly let us pass through your country. We will not cross any fields or vineyards, nor drink any well water, but we will go straight along the royal road* without turning to the right or to the left, until we have passed through your territory."

18 But Edom answered him, "You shall not pass through here; if you do, I will advance against you with the sword." 19 The Israelites insisted, "We want only to go up along the highway. If we or our livestock drink any of your water, we will pay for it. Surely there is no harm in merely letting us march through." 20 But Edom still said, "No, you shall not pass through,"[z] and advanced against them with a large and heavily armed force. 21 Therefore, since Edom refused to let them pass through their territory, Israel detoured around them.

Death of Aaron 22 [a]Setting out from Kadesh, the whole Israelite community came to Mount Hor.* 23 There at Mount Hor, on the border of the land of Edom, the LORD said to Moses and Aaron, 24 "Aaron is about to be taken to his people; he shall not enter the land I am giving to the Israelites, because you both rebelled against my commandment at the waters of Meribah. 25 Take Aaron and his son Eleazar and bring them up on Mount Hor.[b] 26 Then strip Aaron of his garments and put them on his son Eleazar; for there Aaron shall be taken in death."

27 Moses did as the LORD commanded. When they had climbed Mount Hor in view of the whole community, 28 Moses stripped Aaron of his garments and put them on his son Eleazar. Then Aaron died there on top of the mountain.[c] When Moses and Eleazar came down from the mountain, 29 all the community understood that Aaron had passed away; and for thirty days the whole house of Israel mourned him.

CHAPTER 21

Victory over Arad 1 When the Canaanite king of Arad,* who lived in the Negeb,[d] heard that

20, 11: Twice: perhaps because he had not sufficient faith to work the miracle with the first blow. Cf v 12.

20, 12f: The sin of Moses and Aaron consisted in doubting God's mercy toward the ever-rebellious people. In showing forth my sanctity: God's sacred power and glory: an allusion to the name of the place, Kadesh, which means "sanctified, sacred." Meribah means "contention." Cf Ex 17, 7.

20, 14: Your brother Israel: the Edomites were descended from Esau, the brother of Jacob. Their country, to the southeast of the Dead Sea, was also known as Seir; cf Gn 25, 24ff; 36, 1. 8f.

20, 17: The royal road: an important highway, running north and south along the plateau east of the Dead Sea. In ancient times it was much used by caravans and armies; later it was improved by the Romans, and large stretches of it are still clearly recognizable.

20, 22: Mount Hor: not definitively identified, but probably to be sought in the vicinity of Kadesh. According to Dt 10, 6, Aaron died at Moserah (cf "Moseroth" in Nm 33, 30f), which is apparently the name of the region in which Mount Hor is situated.

21, 1–3: The account of this episode seems to be a later insertion here, for Nm 21, 4, belongs logically immediately after Nm 20, 29. Perhaps this is the same event as that mentioned in Jgs 1, 16f.

v Ex 17, 5f. w Ps 78, 15f; Wis 11, 4; 1 Cor 10, 4. x Nm 27, 14: Ex 17, 7. y Ex 2, 23. z Jgs 11, 17. a 21f: Nm 33, 37. b 25f: Dt 32, 50. c Nm 33, 38. d Nm 33, 40.

the Israelites were coming along the way of
Atharim, he engaged them in battle and took
some of them captive. 2Israel then made this
vow to the LORD: "If you deliver this people into
my hand, I will doom their cities."[e] 3Later,
when the LORD heeded Israel's prayer and
delivered up the Canaanites,[f] they doomed
them and their cities. Hence that place was
named Hormah.*

The Bronze Serpent 4From Mount Hor they
set out on the Red Sea road, to bypass the land of
Edom. But with their patience worn out by the
journey, 5the people complained[g] against God
and Moses, "Why have you brought us up from
Egypt to die in this desert, where there is no
food or water? We are disgusted with this
wretched food!"*

6In punishment the LORD sent among the
people saraph* serpents, which bit[h] the people
so that many of them died. 7Then the people
came to Moses and said, "We have sinned in
complaining against the LORD and you. Pray
the LORD to take the serpents from us." So
Moses prayed for the people, 8and the LORD
said to Moses, "Make a saraph and mount it on
a pole, and if anyone who has been bitten
looks at it, he will recover."* 9Moses accord-
ingly made a bronze serpent* and mounted it
on a pole, and whenever anyone who had been
bitten by a serpent looked at the bronze ser-
pent, he recovered.[i]

Journey around Moab 10The Israelites moved
on and encamped in Oboth.[j] 11Setting out from
Oboth, they encamped in Iye-abarim* in the
desert fronting Moab on the east. 12Setting out
from there, they encamped in the Wadi Zered.
13Setting out from there, they encamped on the
other side of the Arnon, in the desert that
extends from the territory of the Amorites; for
the Arnon forms Moab's boundary with the
Amorites. 14Hence it is said in the "Book of the
Wars of the LORD"* :

"Waheb in Suphah and the wadies,
15 Arnon and the wadi gorges
That reach back toward the site of Ar
and slant to the border of Moab."

16From there they went to Beer,* where there
was the well of which the LORD said to Moses,
"Bring the people together, and I will give them
water." 17Then it was that Israel sang this song:

"Spring up, O well!—so sing to it—
18 The well that the princes sank,
that the nobles of the people dug,
with their scepters and their staffs."

From Beer they went to Mattanah, 19from
Mattanah to Nahaliel, from Nahaliel to Bamoth,
20from Bamoth to the cleft in the plateau of
Moab at the headland of Pisgah that overlooks
Jeshimon.*

Victory over Sihon 21Now Israel sent men to
Sihon, king of the Amorites, with the message,
22"Let us pass through your country. We will not
turn aside into any field or vineyard, nor will we
drink any well water, but we will go straight
along the royal road until we have passed
through your territory." 23Sihon,[k] however,
would not let Israel pass through his territory,
but mustered all his forces and advanced into the
desert against Israel. When he reached Jahaz, he
engaged Israel in battle. 24But Israel defeated

21, 3: Hormah: related to the Hebrew word herem, meaning "doomed." See notes on Nm 14, 45; 18, 14.

21, 5: This wretched food: apparently the manna is meant.

21, 6: Saraph: the Hebrew name for a certain species of venomous snakes; the word probably signifies "the fiery one," these snakes being so called from the burning effect of their poisonous bite.

21, 8: If anyone who has been bitten looks at it, he will recover: "and as Moses lifted up the serpent in the desert, even so must the Son of Man be lifted up, that those who believe in him may not perish, but may have life everlasting" (Jn 3, 14f).

21, 9: King Hezekiah, in his efforts to abolish idolatry, "smashed the bronze serpent which Moses had made" (2 Kgs 18, 4).

21, 11: Iye-abarim: probably means "the ruins in the Abarim (Mountains)." See note on Nm 27, 12.

21, 14: The "Book of the Wars of the Lord": an ancient collection of Israelite songs, now lost. Waheb in Suphah: since neither place is mentioned elsewhere, it is quite uncertain whether these dubious Hebrew words are even to be considered as place names; some Hebrew words apparently lost must have preceded this phrase.

21, 16: Beer: means a well.

21, 20: Jeshimon: "the wasteland"; in 1 Sm 23, 19. 24, and 26, 1. 3, this is the desert of Judah, on the western side of the Dead Sea, but here and in Nm 23, 28, it seems to refer to the southern end of the Jordan valley where Beth-jeshimoth was situated.

e Jos 6, 17; Jgs 1, 17. f Nm 14, 45. g Nm 11, 6; Ex 16, 3. h Dt 8, 15; Wis 16, 5; 1 Cor 10, 9. i Wis 16, 6f. 10; Jn 3, 14f. j Nm 33, 43f. k Dt 2, 32; Jgs 11, 20.

him at the point of the sword, and took posses-
sion of his land from the Arnon to the Jabbok
and as far as the country of the Ammonites,
whose boundary was at Jazer. 25 [l]Israel seized all
the towns here and settled in these towns of the
Amorites, in Heshbon and all its dependencies.
26 Now Heshbon was the capital of Sihon, king of
the Amorites, who had fought against the former
king of Moab and had seized all his land from
Jazer to the Arnon. 27 That is why the poets say:

"Come to Heshbon, let it be rebuilt,
let Sihon's capital be firmly constructed.
28 For fire went forth from Heshbon
and a blaze from the city of Sihon;
It consumed the cities of Moab
and swallowed up the high places of the
Arnon.
29 Woe to you, O Moab!
You are ruined, O people of Chemosh!*
He let his sons become fugitives
and his daughters be taken captive
by the Amorite king Sihon.
30 Their plowland is ruined from Heshbon to
Dibon;
Ar is laid waste; fires blaze as far as
Medeba."

31 When Israel had settled in the land of the
Amorites, 32 Moses sent spies to Jazer; Israel then
captured it with its dependencies and dispos-
sessed the Amorites who were there.

Victory over Og 33 [m]Then they turned and
went up along the road to Bashan. But Og, king
of Bashan, advanced against them with all his
people to give battle at Edrei. 34 The LORD,
however, said to Moses, "Do not be afraid of
him; for into your hand I will deliver him with
all his people and his land. Do to him as you did
to Sihon, king of the Amorites, who lived in
Heshbon." [n] 35 So they struck him down with his
sons and all his people, until not a survivor was
left to him, and they took possession of his land.

CHAPTER 22

1 Then the Israelites moved on and encamped
in the plains of Moab* on the other side of the
Jericho stretch of the Jordan.

III: On the Plains of Moab

Balaam Summoned 2 Now Balak, son of Zip-
por, saw all that Israel did to the Amorites.
3 Indeed, Moab feared the Israelites greatly be-
cause of their numbers, and detested them. 4 So
Moab said to the elders of Midian, "Soon this
horde will devour all the country around us as
an ox devours the grass of the field." And Balak,
Zippor's son, who was king of Moab at that time,
5 sent messengers to Balaam, son of Beor, at
Pethor on the Euphrates, in the land of the
Amawites, summoning him with these words,
"A people has come here from Egypt who now
cover the face of the earth and are settling down
opposite us! 6 Please come and curse this people
for us;* they are stronger than we are. We may
then be able to defeat them and drive them out
of the country. For I know that whoever you
bless is blessed and whoever you curse is
cursed." 7 Then the elders of Moab and of
Midian left with the divination fee in hand and
went to Balaam. When they had given him
Balak's message, 8 he said to them in reply, "Stay
here overnight, and I will give you whatever
answer the LORD gives me." So the princes of
Moab lodged with Balaam.

9 Then God came to Balaam and said, "Who
are these men visiting you?" 10 Balaam answered
God, "Balak, son of Zippor, king of Moab, sent
me the message: 11 'This people that came here
from Egypt now cover the face of the earth.
Please come and lay a curse on them for us; we
may then be able to give them battle and drive
them out.' " 12 But God said to Balaam, "Do not
go with them and do not curse this people, for
they are blessed." 13 The next morning Balaam

21, 29: Chemosh: the chief god of the Moabites, and mentioned as such in the famous inscription of Mesha, king of Moab, who was the contemporary of the dynasty of Omri in Israel. Cf 1 Kgs 11, 7. 33; 2 Kgs 23, 13; Jer 48, 7. 13.

22, 1: The plains of Moab: the lowlands to the northeast of the Dead Sea, between the Jordan and the foothills below Mount Nebo. Here the Israelites remained until they crossed the Jordan, as told in Jos 1–4. Jericho lay to the west of the Jordan.

22, 6: Curse this people for us: Balak believed that if Balaam forecast an evil omen for Israel, this evil would come to pass, as if by magic. Balaam was a soothsayer or foreteller; cf Jos 13, 22.

l 25f: Jos 21, 39; Jgs 11, 26. m Dt 3, 1ff. n Ps 136, 17ff.

arose and told the princes of Balak, "Go back to your own country, for the LORD has refused to let me go with you." 14So the princes of Moab went back to Balak with the report, "Balaam refused to come with us."

Second Appeal to Balaam 15Balak again sent princes, who were more numerous and more distinguished than the others. 16On coming to Balaam they told him, "This is what Balak, son of Zippor, has to say: Please do not refuse to come to me. 17I will reward you very handsomely and will do anything you ask of me. Please come and lay a curse on this people for me." 18 [o]But Balaam replied to Balak's officials, "Even if Balak gave me his house full of silver and gold, I could not do anything, small or great, contrary to the command of the LORD, my God. 19But, you too shall stay here overnight, till I learn what else the LORD may tell me."

20That night God came to Balaam and said to him, "If these men have come to summon you, you may go with them; yet only on the condition that you do exactly as I tell you." 21So the next morning when Balaam arose, he saddled his ass, and went off with the princes of Moab.

The Talking Ass 22But now the anger of God flared up* at him for going, and the angel of the LORD stationed himself on the road to hinder him as he was riding along on his ass, accompanied by two of his servants. 23When the ass saw the angel of the LORD standing on the road with sword drawn, she turned off the road and went into the field, and Balaam had to beat her to bring her back on the road. 24Then the angel of the LORD took his stand in a narrow lane between vineyards with a stone wall on each side. 25When the ass saw the angel of the LORD there, she shrank against the wall; and since she squeezed Balaam's leg against it, he beat her again. 26The angel of the LORD then went ahead, and stopped next in a passage so narrow that there was no room to move either to the right or to the left. 27When the ass saw the angel of the LORD there, she cowered under Balaam. So, in anger, he again beat the ass with his stick.

28 [p]But now the LORD opened the mouth of the ass, and she asked Balaam, "What have I done to you that you should beat me these three times?" 29"You have acted so willfully against me," said Balaam to the ass, "that if I but had a sword at hand, I would kill you here and now." 30But the ass said to Balaam, "Am I not your own beast, and have you not always ridden upon me until now? Have I been in the habit of treating you this way before?" "No," replied Balaam.

31Then the LORD removed the veil from Balaam's eyes, so that he too saw the angel of the LORD standing on the road with sword drawn; and he fell on his knees and bowed to the ground. 32But the angel of the LORD said to him, "Why have you beaten your ass these three times? It is I who have come armed to hinder you because this rash journey of yours is directly opposed to me. 33When the ass saw me, she turned away from me these three times. If she had not turned away from me, I would have killed you; her I would have spared." 34Then Balaam said to the angel of the LORD, "I have sinned. Yet I did not know that you stood against me to oppose my journey. Since it has displeased you, I will go back home." 35But the angel of the LORD said to Balaam, "Go with the men; but you may say only what I tell you." So Balaam went on with the princes of Balak.

36When Balak heard that Balaam was coming, he went out to meet him at the boundary city Ir-Moab on the Arnon at the end of the Moabite territory. 37And he said to Balaam, "I sent an urgent summons to you! Why did you not come to me? Did you think I could not reward you?" 38Balaam answered him, "Well, I have come to you after all. But what power have I to say anything? I can speak only what God puts in my mouth." 39Then Balaam went with Balak, and they came to Kiriath-huzoth. 40Here Balak

22, 22: The anger of God flared up: not merely because Balaam was going to Balak, for he had God's permission for the journey (v 20), but perhaps because he was tempted by avarice to curse Israel against God's command. "They have followed the way of Balaam, son of Bosor, who loved the wages of wrongdoing" (2 Pt 2, 15); "and have rushed on thoughtlessly into the error of Balaam for the sake of gain" (Jude 11). Cf v 32 and compare Ex 4, 18–26.

o Nm 24, 13. p 2 Pt 2, 16.

slaughtered oxen and sheep, and sent portions to
Balaam and to the princes who were with him.
The First Oracle 41 The next morning Balak
took Balaam up on Bamoth-baal, and from there
he saw some of the clans.

CHAPTER 23

1 Then Balaam said to Balak, "Build me seven
altars, and prepare seven bullocks and seven
rams for me here." 2 So he did as Balaam had
ordered, offering a bullock and a ram on each
altar. And Balak said to him, "I have erected the
seven altars, and have offered a bullock and a
ram on each." 3 Balaam then said to him, "Stand
here by your holocaust while I go over there.
Perhaps the LORD will meet me, and then I will
tell you whatever he lets me see." He went out
on the barren height, 4 and God met him. 5 When
he had put an utterance in Balaam's mouth, the
LORD said to him, "Go back to Balak, and speak
accordingly." 6 So he went back to Balak, who
was still standing by his holocaust together with
all the princes of Moab. 7 Then Balaam gave
voice to his oracle:

From Aram* has Balak brought me here,
Moab's king, from the Eastern Mountains: [q]
"Come and lay a curse for me on Jacob,
come and denounce Israel."
8 How can I curse whom God has not cursed?
How denounce whom the LORD has not
denounced?
9 For from the top of the crags I see him,
from the heights I behold him.
Here is a people that lives apart*
and does not reckon itself among the
nations.
10 Who has ever counted the dust of Jacob,
or numbered Israel's wind-borne particles?*
May I die the death of the just,
may my descendants be as many as theirs!

11 "What have you done to me?" cried Balak
to Balaam. "It was to curse my foes that I
brought you here; instead, you have even
blessed them." 12 Balaam replied, "Is it not what
the LORD puts in my mouth that I must repeat
with care?"
The Second Oracle 13 Then Balak said to him,
"Please come with me to another place* from
which you can see only some and not all of
them, and from there curse them for me." 14 So
he brought him to the lookout field on the top of
Pisgah, where he built seven altars and offered a
bullock and a ram on each of them. 15 Balaam
then said to Balak, "Stand here by your holo-
caust, while I seek a meeting over there."
16 Then the LORD met Balaam, and having put an
utterance in his mouth, he said to him, "Go back
to Balak, and speak accordingly." 17 So he went
back to Balak, who was still standing by his
holocaust together with the princes of Moab.
When Balak asked him, "What did the LORD
say?" 18 Balaam gave voice to his oracle:

Be aroused, O Balak, and hearken;
give ear to my testimony, O son of Zippor!
19 God is not man that he should speak falsely,
nor human, that he should change his
mind.
Is he one to speak and not act,
to decree and not fulfill?
20 It is a blessing I have been given to pronounce;
a blessing which I cannot restrain.
21 Misfortune is not observed in Jacob,
nor misery* seen in Israel.
The LORD, his God, is with him;
with him is the triumph of his King.
22 It is God who brought him out of Egypt, [r]

23, 7: Aram: the ancient name of the region later known as Syria. The Eastern Mountains: the low ranges in the Syrian desert near the Euphrates and Balaam's town of Pethor; cf Nm 22, 5.

23, 9: A people that lives apart: Israel, as the chosen people of God, occupied a unique place among the nations, from which they kept themselves aloof.

23, 10: The dust of Jacob . . . Israel's wind-borne particles: the Israelites will be as numerous as dust in a desert sandstorm. May I . . . as many as theirs: a formula by which Balaam swears he is speaking the truth; he sees the reward of virtue in having numerous descendants.

23, 13: To another place: Balak thought that if Balaam would view Israel from a different site, he could forecast a different kind of omen.

23, 21: Misfortune . . . misery: Balaam admits that he is unable to predict any evils for Israel.

23, 22: A wild bull of towering might: the reference is to Israel, rather than to God.

q Nm 22, 6. r Nm 24, 8.

a wild bull of towering might.*
23 No, there is no sorcery against Jacob,
nor omen against Israel.
It shall yet be said of Jacob,
and of Israel, "Behold what God has
wrought!"
24 Here is a people that springs up like a lioness,
and stalks forth like a lion;
It rests not till it has devoured its prey
and has drunk the blood of the slain. [s]

25 "Even though you cannot curse them," said
Balak to Balaam, "at least do not bless them."
26 But Balaam answered Balak, "Did I not warn
you that I must do all that the LORD tells me?"
The Third Oracle 27 Then Balak said to Ba-
laam, "Come, let me bring you to another place;
perhaps God will approve of your cursing them
for me from there." 28 So he took Balaam to the
top of Peor, that overlooks Jeshimon. 29 Balaam
then said to him, "Here build me seven altars;
and here prepare for me seven bullocks and
seven rams." 30 And Balak did as Balaam had
ordered, offering a bullock and a ram on each
altar.

CHAPTER 24

1 Balaam, however, perceiving that the LORD
was pleased to bless Israel, did not go aside as
before to seek omens, but turned his gaze
toward the desert. 2 When he raised his eyes and
saw Israel encamped, tribe by tribe, the spirit of
God came upon him, 3 and he gave voice to his
oracle:

The utterance of Balaam, son of Beor,
the utterance of the man whose eye is true,
4 The utterance of one who hears what God
says,
and knows what the Most High knows,
Of one who sees what the Almighty sees,
enraptured, and with eyes unveiled:
5 How goodly are your tents, O Jacob;
your encampments, O Israel!
6 They are like gardens beside a stream,
like the cedars planted by the LORD.
7 His wells shall yield free-flowing waters,
he shall have the sea within reach;
His king shall rise higher than . . . .
and his royalty shall be exalted.
8 It is God who brought him out of Egypt,
a wild bull of towering might.
He shall devour the nations like grass,
their bones he shall strip bare. [t]
9 He lies crouching like a lion,
or like a lioness; who shall arouse him?
Blessed is he who blesses you,
and cursed is he who curses you! [u]

10 Balak beat his palms* together in a blaze of
anger at Balaam and said to him, "It was to curse
my foes that I summoned you here; yet three
times now you have even blessed them instead! [v]
11 Be off at once, then, to your home. I promised
to reward you richly, but the LORD has withheld
the reward from you!" 12 Balaam replied to
Balak, "Did I not warn the very messengers
whom you sent to me, 13 'Even if Balak gave me
his house full of silver and gold, I could not of
my own accord do anything, good or evil,
contrary to the command of the LORD'? What-
ever the LORD says I must repeat. [w]
The Fourth Oracle 14 "But now that I am
about to go to my own people, let me first warn
you what this people will do to your people in
the days to come." 15 Then Balaam gave voice to
his oracle:

The utterance of Balaam, son of Beor,
the utterance of the man whose eye is true,
16 The utterance of one who hears what God
says,
and knows what the Most High knows,
Of one who sees what the Almighty sees,
enraptured and with eyes unveiled.
17 I see him, though not now;
I behold him, though not near:
A star shall advance from Jacob,

24, 10: Balak beat his palms: a sign of disclaiming any responsibility for paying the promised reward.

s Nm 24, 9; Gn 49, 9. t Nm 23, 22. u Nm 23, 24; Gn 12, 3; 27, 29; 49, 9. v Nm 23, 11. w Nm 22, 18.

and a staff* shall rise from Israel,
That shall smite the brows of Moab,[x]
and the skulls of all the Shuthites,
18 Till Edom is dispossessed,
and no fugitive is left in Seir.
Israel shall do valiantly,
19 and Jacob shall overcome his foes.

20 Upon seeing Amalek, Balaam gave voice to his oracle:

First* of the peoples was Amalek,
but his end is to perish forever.[y]

21 Upon seeing the Kenites,* he gave voice to his oracle:

Your abode is enduring, O smith,
and your nest is set on a cliff;
22 Yet destined for burning—
even as I watch—are your inhabitants.

23 Upon seeing . . . he gave voice to his oracle:

*Alas, who shall survive of Ishmael,
24 to deliver his people from the hands of the Kittim?
When they have conquered Asshur and conquered Eber,
He too shall perish forever.

25 Then Balaam set out on his journey home; and Balak also went his way.

CHAPTER 25

Worship of Baal of Peor 1While Israel was
living at Shittim,* the people degraded them-
selves by having illicit relations with the Moabite
women.[z] 2These then invited the people to the
sacrifices of their god, and the people ate of the
sacrifices[a] and worshiped their god. 3When
Israel thus submitted to the rites of Baal of Peor,[b]
the LORD's anger flared up against Israel, 4 [c]and
he said to Moses, "Gather all the leaders of the
people, and hold a public execution* of the
guilty ones before the LORD, that his blazing
wrath may be turned away from Israel." 5So
Moses told the Israelite judges, "Each of you
shall kill those of his men who have submitted to
the rites of Baal of Peor."

Zeal of Phinehas 6Yet a certain Israelite came
and brought in a Midianite woman* to his
clansmen in the view of Moses and of the whole
Israelite community, while they were weeping at
the entrance of the meeting tent. 7 [d]When Phine-
has, son of Eleazar, son of Aaron the priest, saw
this, he left the assembly, and taking a lance in
hand, 8followed the Israelite into his retreat
where he pierced the pair of them, the Israelite
and the woman. Thus the slaughter of Israelites
was checked; 9but only after twenty-four thou-
sand had died.

10Then the LORD said to Moses, 11"Phinehas,
son of Eleazar, son of Aaron the priest, has
turned my anger from the Israelites by his zeal
for my honor* among them; that is why I did
not put an end to the Israelites for the offense to
my honor. 12 [e]Announce, therefore, that I hereby
give him my pledge of friendship, 13which shall
be for him and for his descendants after him the
pledge of an everlasting priesthood, because he

24, 17: A star . . . a staff: many of the Fathers have understood this as a Messianic prophecy, although it is not referred to anywhere in the New Testament; in this sense the star is Christ himself, just as he is the staff from Israel; cf Is 11, 1. But it is doubtful whether this passage is to be connected with the "star of the Magi" in Mt 2, 1–12. The Shuthites: mentioned in other documents of this period as nomads on the border of Palestine.

24, 20: First: literally "the beginning." Amalek was an aboriginal people in Palestine and therefore considered as of great antiquity. There is a deliberate contrast here between the words first and end.

24, 21: The Kenites lived in high strongholds in the mountains of southern Palestine and the Sinai Peninsula, and were skilled in working the various metals found in their territory. Their name is connected, at least by popular etymology, with the Hebrew word for "smith"; of similar sound is the Hebrew word for "nest"—hence the play on words in the present passage.

24, 23f: The translation of this short oracle is based on a reconstructed text and is rather uncertain. Ishmael: the survival of Ishmael is indicated in Gn 17, 20; 21, 13. 18.

25, 1: Shittim: the full name was Abel-shittim, a locality at the foot of the mountains in the northeastern corner of the plains of Moab (Nm 33, 49). Illicit relations: perhaps as part of the licentious worship of Baal of Peor.

25, 4: Hold a public execution: the same phrase occurs in 2 Sm 21, 6–14, where the context shows that at least a part of the penalty consisted in being denied honorable burial. In both passages, dismemberment as a punishment for the breaking of covenant pledges is a current understanding of the phrase.

25, 6: Midianite woman: at this time the Midianites were leagued with the Moabites in opposing Israel; cf Nm 22, 4. 7. Balaam had induced both the Midianites (Nm 31, 16) and the Moabites (Rv 2, 14) to lure the Israelites to the obscene rites of Baal of Peor. They were weeping: on account of the plague that had struck them; cf v 8.

25, 11: For my honor: by taking vengeance on those who had made Baal of Peor a rival of the Lord.

x 2 Sm 8, 2. y Ex 17, 14; 1 Sm 15, 3. z Nm 31, 16. a Ex 34, 15f. b Ps 106, 28; Hos 9, 10. c Dt 4, 3. d Ps 106, 30. e 12f: Sir 45, 23f; Ps 106, 31; 1 Mc 2, 26. 54.

was zealous on behalf of his God and thus made amends for the Israelites."

14*The Israelite slain with the Midianite woman was Zimri, son of Salu, prince of an ancestral house of the Simeonites. 15The slain Midianite woman was Cozbi, daughter of Zur, who was head of a clan, an ancestral house, in Midian.

Vengeance on the Midianites 16*The LORD then said to Moses, 17[f]"Treat the Midianites as enemies and crush them, 18for they have been your enemies by their wily dealings with you as regards Peor and as regards their kinswoman Cozbi, the daughter of the Midianite prince, who was killed at the time of the slaughter because of Peor."

CHAPTER 26

The Second Census 19After the slaughter* 1the LORD said to Moses and Eleazar, son of Aaron the priest, 2"Take a census, by ancestral houses, throughout the community of the Israelites of all those of twenty years or more who are fit for military service in Israel."[g] 3So on the plains of Moab along the Jericho stretch of the Jordan, Moses and the priest Eleazar registered 4those of twenty years or more, as the LORD had commanded Moses.

The Israelites who came out of the land of Egypt were as follows:

5[h]Of Reuben, the first-born of Israel, the Reubenites by clans were: through Hanoch the clan of the Hanochites, through Pallu the clan of the Palluites, 6through Hezron the clan of the Hezronites, through Carmi the clan of the Carmites. 7These were the clans of the Reubenites, of whom forty-three thousand seven hundred and thirty men were registered.

8From Pallu descended Eliab, 9and the descendants of Eliab were Dathan and Abiram[i]—the same Dathan and Abiram, councilors of the community, who revolted against Moses and Aaron [like Korah's band when it rebelled against the LORD]. 10The earth opened its mouth and swallowed them as a warning [Korah too and the band that died when the fire consumed two hundred and fifty men. 11The descendants of Korah, however, did not die out].

12The Simeonites by clans were: through Nemuel* the clan of the Nemuelites, through Jamin the clan of the Jaminites, through Jachin the clan of the Jachinites, 13through Sohar the clan of the Soharites, through Shaul the clan of the Shaulites. 14These were the clans of the Simeonites, of whom twenty-two thousand two hundred men were registered.

15The Gadites by clans were: through Zephon the clan of the Zephonites, through Haggi the clan of the Haggites, through Shuni the clan of the Shunites, 16through Ozni the clan of the Oznites, through Eri the clan of the Erites, 17through Arod the clan of the Arodites, through Areli the clan of the Arelites. 18These were the clans of the Gadites, of whom forty thousand five hundred men were registered.

19The sons of Judah who died in the land of Canaan were Er and Onan.[j] 20The Judahites by clans were: through Shelah the clan of the Shelahites, through Perez the clan of the Perezites, through Zerah the clan of the Zerahites. 21The Perezites were: through Hezron the clan of the Hezronites, through Hamul the clan of the Hamulites. 22These were the clans of Judah, of whom seventy-six thousand five hundred men were registered.

23The Issacharites by clans were: through Tola the clan of the Tolaites, through Puvah the clan of the Puvahites, 24through Jashub the clan of the Jashubites, through Shimron the clan of the Shimronites. 25These were the clans of Issachar, of whom sixty-four thousand three hundred men were registered.

26The Zebulunites by clans were: through Sered the clan of the Seredites, through Elon the

25, 14f: The nobility of the slain couple is mentioned in order to stress the courage of Phinehas in punishing them. The zeal of Phinehas became proverbial; cf Ps 106, 30; Sir 45, 23; 1 Mc 2, 26. 54.

25, 16ff: The account of the execution of this command is given in Nm 31, 1–18.

26, 19: This is the last verse of Ch 25.

26, 12: Nemuel: so also in Gn 46, 10; 1 Chr 4, 24. In Ex 6, 15, the same man is called "Jemuel"; it is uncertain which form is correct.

f 17f: Nm 31, 2–12. g Nm 1, 2f. h 5f: 1 Chr 5, 3. i 9f: Nm 16, 1. 32. j Gn 38, 7. 10; 46, 12; 1 Chr 2, 3.

clan of the Elonites, through Jahleel the clan of the Jahleelites. [27]These were the clans of the Zebulunites, of whom sixty thousand five hundred men were registered.

[28]The sons of Joseph were Manasseh, and Ephraim. [29]The Manassehites by clans were: through Machir the clan of the Machirites, through Gilead, a descendant of Machir, the clan of the Gileadites. [30]The Gileadites were: through Abiezer the clan of the Abiezrites, through Helek the clan of the Helekites, [31]through Asriel the clan of the Asrielites, through Shechem the clan of the Shechemites, [32]through Shemida the clan of the Shemidaites, through Hepher the clan of the Hepherites. [33] [k]Zelophehad, son of Hepher, had no sons, but only daughters, whose names were Mahlah, Noah, Hoglah, Milcah and Tirzah. [34]These were the clans of Manasseh, of whom fifty-two thousand seven hundred men were registered.

[35]The Ephraimites by clans were: through Shuthelah the clan of the Shuthelahites, through Becher the clan of the Bechrites, through Tahan the clan of the Tahanites. [36]The Shuthelahites were: through Eran the clan of the Eranites. [37]These were the clans of the Ephraimites, of whom thirty-two thousand five hundred men were registered.

These were the descendants of Joseph by clans.

[38]The Benjaminites by clans were: through Bela the clan of the Belaites, through Ashbel the clan of the Ashbelites, through Ahiram the clan of the Ahiramites, [39]through Shupham the clan of the Shuphamites, through Hupham the clan of the Huphamites. [40]The descendants of Bela were Arad and Naaman: through Arad the clan of the Aradites, through Naaman the clan of the Naamanites. [41]These were the Benjaminites by clans, of whom forty-five thousand six hundred men were registered.

[42]The Danites by clans were: through Shuham the clan of the Shuhamites. These were the clans of Dan, [43]of whom sixty-four thousand four hundred men were registered.

[44]The Asherites by clans were: through Imnah the clan of the Imnites, through Ishvi the clan of the Ishvites, through Beriah the clan of the Beriites, [45]through Heber the clan of the Heberites, through Malchiel the clan of the Malchielites. [46]The name of Asher's daughter was Serah. [47]These were the clans of Asher, of whom fifty-three thousand four hundred men were registered.

[48]The Naphtalites by clans were: through Jahzeel the clan of the Jahzeelites, through Guni the clan of the Gunites, [49]through Jezer the clan of the Jezerites, through Shillem the clan of the Shillemites. [50]These were the clans of Naphtali, of whom forty-five thousand four hundred men were registered.

[51]These six hundred and one thousand seven hundred and thirty were the Israelites who were registered.

Allotment of the Land [52]*The LORD said to Moses, [53] [l]"Among these groups the land shall be divided as their heritage in keeping with the number of individuals in each group. [54] [m]To a large group you shall assign a large heritage, to a small group a small heritage, each group receiving its heritage in proportion to the number of men registered in it. [55]But the land shall be divided by lot, as the heritage of the various ancestral tribes. [56]As the lot falls shall each group, large or small, be assigned its heritage."

Census of the Levites [57]The Levites registered by clans were: through Gershon the clan of the Gershonites, through Kohath the clan of the Kohathites, through Merari the clan of the Merarites. [58]These also were clans of Levi: the clan of the Libnites, the clan of the Hebronites, the clan of the Mahlites, the clan of the Mushites, the clan of the Korahites.

Among the descendants of Kohath was Am-

26, 52–56: The division of Canaan among the various tribes and clans and families was determined partly by the size of each group and partly by lot. Perhaps the lots determined the respective locality of each tribal land and the section reserved for each clan, while the relative size of the allotted locality and section depended on the numerical strength of each group. The Hebrews considered the outcome of the drawing of lots as an expression of God's will; cf Acts 1, 23–26.

k Nm 27, 1; 36, 11; Jos 17, 3. l Jos 11, 23. m Nm 33, 54; 35, 8.

ram, [59]whose wife was named Jochebed. She
also was of the tribe of Levi, born to the tribe in
Egypt. To Amram she bore Aaron and Moses and
their sister Miriam. [60]To Aaron were born Nadab
and Abihu, Eleazar and Ithamar. [61]But Nadab
and Abihu died when they offered profane fire
before the LORD.

[62]The total number of male Levites one
month or more of age, who were registered, was
twenty-three thousand.[n] They were not regis-
tered with the other Israelites, however, for no
heritage was given them among the Israelites.

[63]These, then, were the men registered by
Moses and the priest Eleazar in the census of the
Israelites taken on the plains of Moab along the
Jericho stretch of the Jordan. [64]Among them
there was not a man of those who had been
registered by Moses and the priest Aaron in the
census of the Israelites taken in the desert of
Sinai. [65] [o]For the LORD had told them that they
would surely die in the desert, and not one of
them was left except Caleb, son of Jephunneh,
and Joshua, son of Nun.

CHAPTER 27

Zelophehad's Daughters [1]Zelophehad, son of
Hepher, son of Gilead, son of Machir, son of
Manasseh, son of Joseph, had daughters named
Mahlah, Noah, Hoglah, Milcah and Tirzah.[p]
They came forward, [2]and standing in the pres-
ence of Moses, the priest Eleazar, the princes,
and the whole community at the entrance of the
meeting tent, said: [3]"Our father died in the
desert. Although he did not join those who
banded together against the LORD* [in Korah's
band], he died for his own sin without leaving
any sons. [4]But why should our father's name be
withdrawn from his clan merely because he had
no son? Let us, therefore, have property among
our father's kinsmen."

Laws Concerning Heiresses [5]*When Moses
laid their case before the LORD, [6]the LORD said to
him, [7]"The plea of Zelophehad's daughters is
just; you shall give them hereditary property
among their father's kinsmen, letting their fa-
ther's heritage pass on to them. [8]Therefore, tell
the Israelites: If a man dies without leaving a
son, you shall let his heritage pass on to his
daughter; [9]if he has no daughter, you shall give
his heritage to his brothers; [10]if he has no
brothers, you shall give his heritage to his
father's brothers; [11]if his father had no brothers,
you shall give his heritage to his nearest relative
in his clan, who shall then take possession of it."
This is the legal norm for the Israelites, as the
LORD commanded Moses.[q]

Joshua To Succeed Moses [12]The LORD said to
Moses, "Go up here into the Abarim Moun-
tains* and view the land that I am giving to the
Israelites.[r] [13]When you have viewed it, you too
shall be taken to your people, as was your
brother Aaron,[s] [14]because in the rebellion of the
community in the desert of Zin you both re-
belled against my order to manifest my sanctity
to them by means of the water."[t] [This is the
water of Meribah of Kadesh in the desert of Zin.]

[15]Then Moses said to the LORD, [16]"May the
LORD, the God of the spirits of all mankind,* set
over the community a man [17]who shall act as
their leader in all things, to guide them in all
their actions; that the LORD's community may
not be like sheep without a shepherd." [18]And
the LORD replied to Moses, "Take Joshua, son of
Nun,[u] a man of spirit,* and lay your hand upon
him. [19]Have him stand in the presence of the
priest Eleazar and of the whole community, and

27, 3: He did not join . . . against the Lord: had he done so, he and his heirs could have rightly been deprived of the privilege of receiving a portion in the Promised Land.

27, 5–11: The purpose of this law, as also that of the related laws in Nm 36, 2–10 (heiresses to marry within the same tribe), Dt 25, 5–10 (levirate marriage), and Lv 25, 10 (return of property in the jubilee year), was to keep the landed property within the proper domain of each tribe.

27, 12: The Abarim Mountains: the range on the eastern side of the Dead Sea.

27, 16: The God of the spirits of all mankind: the sense is either that God knows the character and abilities of all men and therefore knows best whom to appoint (cf Acts 1, 24), or, more probably, that God is Master of life and death and therefore can call Moses from this world whenever he wishes; cf the same phrase in Nm 16, 22, where "spirit" evidently means "the life principle."

27, 18: A man of spirit: literally, "a man in whom there is spirit": one who has the qualities of a good leader—courage, prudence, and strength of will. Cf Gn 41, 38; Dt 34, 9.

n Nm 3, 39. o Nm 14, 22ff. 29. p Nm 26, 33; Jos 17, 3. q Jer 32, 6–9. r Dt 3, 27; 32, 49; 34, 1. s 13f: Nm 20, 12. 24. t Dt 32, 51. u Dt 34, 9.

commission him before their eyes. 20Invest him with some of your own dignity, that the whole Israelite community may obey him. 21He shall present himself to the priest Eleazar, to have him seek out for him the decisions of the Urim* in the LORD's presence; and as he directs, Joshua, all the Israelites with him, and the community as a whole shall perform all their actions."

22Moses did as the LORD had commanded him. Taking Joshua and having him stand in the presence of the priest Eleazar and of the whole community, 23he laid his hands on him and gave him his commission, as the LORD had directed through Moses.

CHAPTER 28

General Sacrifices 1The LORD said to Moses, 2"Give the Israelites this commandment: At the times I have appointed, you shall be careful to present to me the food offerings that are offered to me as sweet-smelling oblations.

Each Morning and Evening 3 [v]"You shall tell them therefore: This is the oblation which you shall offer to the LORD: two unblemished yearling lambs each day as the established holocaust,* 4offering one lamb in the morning and the other during the evening twilight, 5each with a cereal offering of one tenth of an ephah of fine flour mixed with a fourth of a hin of oil of crushed olives.* 6This is the established holocaust that was offered at Mount Sinai as a sweet-smelling oblation to the LORD. 7And as the libation for the first lamb, you shall pour out to the LORD in the sanctuary* a fourth of a hin of wine. 8The other lamb, to be offered during the evening twilight, you shall offer with the same cereal offering and the same libation as in the morning, as a sweet-smelling oblation to the LORD.

On the Sabbath 9"On the sabbath day you shall offer two unblemished yearling lambs, with their cereal offering, two tenths of an ephah of fine flour mixed with oil, and with their libations. 10Each sabbath there shall be the sabbath holocaust in addition to the established holocaust and its libation.

At the New Moon Feast 11"On the first of each month* you shall offer as a holocaust to the LORD two bullocks, one ram, and seven unblemished yearling lambs, 12with three tenths of an ephah of fine flour mixed with oil as the cereal offering for each bullock, two tenths of an ephah of fine flour mixed with oil as the cereal offering for the ram, 13and one tenth of an ephah of fine flour mixed with oil as the cereal offering for each lamb, that the holocaust may be a sweet-smelling oblation to the LORD. 14Their libations shall be half a hin of wine for each bullock, a third of a hin for the ram, and a fourth of a hin for each lamb. This is the new moon holocaust for every new moon of the year. 15Moreover, one goat shall be sacrificed as a sin offering to the LORD. These are to be offered in addition to the established holocaust and its libation.

At the Passover 16"On the fourteenth day* of the first month falls the Passover of the LORD, [w] 17and the fifteenth day of this month is the pilgrimage feast. For seven days unleavened bread is to be eaten. 18On the first of these days you shall hold a sacred assembly, and do no sort of work. [x] 19As an oblation you shall offer a holocaust to the LORD, which shall consist of two bullocks, one ram, and seven yearling lambs that you are sure are unblemished, 20with their cereal offerings of fine flour mixed with oil, offering three tenths of an ephah for each bullock, two tenths for the ram, 21and one tenth for each of the seven lambs; 22and offer one goat

27, 21: The Urim: certain sacred objects which the Hebrew priests employed to ascertain the divine will, probably by obtaining a positive or negative answer to a given question. The full expression was "the Urim and Thummim"; cf Ex 28, 30; Lv 8, 8; Dt 33, 8; Ezr 2, 63; Neh 7, 65. Joshua was ordinarily not to receive direct revelations from God as Moses had received them.

28, 3: The established holocaust: "the tamid holocaust," the technical term for the daily sacrifice.

28, 5: Oil of crushed olives: this oil, made in a mortar, was purer and more expensive than oil extracted in the olive press.

28, 7: In the sanctuary: according to Sir 50, 15, it was at the base of the altar.

28, 11: On the first of each month: literally, "at the new moons"; beginning on the evening when the crescent of the new moon first appeared.

28, 16: On the fourteenth day: toward evening at the end of this day; cf Ex 12, 6. 18.

v 3–8: Ex 29, 38–42. w Ex 12, 18; Lv 23, 5; Dt 16, 1. x Ex 12, 16; Lv 23, 7.

as a sin offering in atonement for yourselves.
[23]These offerings you shall make in addition to
the established morning holocaust: [24]you shall
make exactly the same offerings each day for
seven days as food offerings, in addition to the
established holocaust with its libation, for a
sweet-smelling oblation to the LORD. [25]On the
seventh day you shall hold a sacred assembly,
and do no sort of work.[y]

At Pentecost [26]"On the day of first fruits,* on
your feast of Weeks,[z] when you present to the
LORD the new cereal offering, you shall hold a
sacred assembly, and do no sort of work. [27]You
shall offer as a sweet-smelling holocaust to the
LORD two bullocks, one ram, and seven yearling
lambs that you are sure are unblemished, [28]with
their cereal offerings of fine flour mixed with oil;
offering three tenths of an ephah for each
bullock, two tenths for the ram, [29]and one tenth
for each of the seven lambs. [30]Moreover, one
goat shall be offered as a sin offering in atone-
ment for yourselves. [31]You shall make these
offerings, together with their libations, in addi-
tion to the established holocaust with its cereal
offering.

CHAPTER 29

On New Year's Day [1]"On the first day of the
seventh month* you shall hold a sacred assem-
bly, and do no sort of work; it shall be a day on
which you sound the trumpet.[a] [2]You shall offer
as a sweet-smelling holocaust to the LORD one
bullock, one ram, and seven unblemished year-
ling lambs, [3]with their cereal offerings of fine
flour mixed with oil; offering three tenths of an
ephah for the bullock, two tenths for the ram,
[4]and one tenth for each of the seven lambs.
[5]Moreover, one goat shall be offered as a sin
offering in atonement for yourselves. [6]These are
to be offered in addition to the ordinary new
moon holocaust with its cereal offering, and in
addition to the established holocaust with its
cereal offering, together with the libations pre-
scribed for them, as a sweet-smelling oblation to
the LORD.

On the Day of Atonement [7]"On the tenth
day of this seventh month* you shall hold a
sacred assembly, and mortify yourselves, and do
no sort of work.[b] [8]You shall offer as a sweet-
smelling holocaust to the LORD one bullock, one
ram, and seven yearling lambs that you are sure
are unblemished, [9]with their cereal offerings of
fine flour mixed with oil; offering three tenths of
an ephah for the bullock, two tenths for the ram,
[10]and one tenth for each of the seven lambs.
[11]Moreover, one goat shall be sacrificed as a sin
offering. These are to be offered in addition to
the atonement sin offering,* the established
holocaust with its cereal offering, and their
libations.

On the Feast of Booths* [12]"On the fifteenth
day of the seventh month you shall hold a sacred
assembly,[c] and do no sort of work; then, for
seven days following, you shall celebrate a
pilgrimage feast to the LORD. [13]You shall offer as
a sweet-smelling holocaust to the LORD thirteen
bullocks,* two rams, and fourteen yearling
lambs that are unblemished, [14]with their cereal
offerings of fine flour mixed with oil; offering
three tenths of an ephah for each of the thirteen
bullocks, two tenths for each of the two rams,
[15]and one tenth for each of the fourteen lambs.
[16]Moreover, one goat shall be sacrificed as a sin
offering. These are to be offered in addition to
the established holocaust with its cereal offering
and libation.

[17]"On the second day you shall offer twelve
bullocks, two rams, and fourteen unblemished

28, 26: The day of first fruits: a unique term for this feast, which is usually called "the feast of Weeks"; it was celebrated as a thanksgiving for the wheat harvest seven weeks after the barley harvest (Passover). In the time of Christ it was commonly known by the Greek word "Pentecost," that is, "fiftieth" (day after the Passover); see note on Lv 23, 16.

29, 1: The first day of the seventh month: (about September-October) is now the Jewish New Year's Day. In the older calendar the year began with the first of Nisan (March-April); cf Ex 12, 2.

29, 7: The tenth day of this seventh month: the Day of Atonement. Mortify yourselves: literally, "afflict your souls," that is, with fasting.

29, 11: The atonement sin offering: the bullock prescribed in Lv 16, 11f.

29, 12: This feast of Booths celebrating the vintage harvest was the most popular of all and therefore had the most elaborate ritual. See note on Lv 23, 34.

29, 13: Thirteen bullocks: the number of bullocks sacrificed before the octave day was seventy, arranged on a descending scale so that the number on the seventh day was the sacred number seven.

y Ex 12, 16; 13, 6; Lv 23, 8. z Ex 34, 22. a Nm 10, 10; Lv 23, 24. b Lv 16, 29; 23, 27f. 32. c Lv 23, 34f.

yearling lambs, 18 with their cereal offerings and libations as prescribed for the bullocks, rams and lambs in proportion to their number, 19 as well as one goat for a sin offering, besides the established holocaust with its cereal offering and libation.

20 "On the third day you shall offer eleven bullocks, two rams, and fourteen unblemished yearling lambs, 21 with their cereal offerings and libations as prescribed for the bullocks, rams and lambs in proportion to their number, 22 as well as one goat for a sin offering, besides the established holocaust with its cereal offering and libation.

23 "On the fourth day you shall offer ten bullocks, two rams, and fourteen unblemished yearling lambs, 24 with their cereal offerings and libations as prescribed for the bullocks, rams and lambs in proportion to their number, 25 as well as one goat for a sin offering, besides the established holocaust with its cereal offering and libation.

26 "On the fifth day you shall offer nine bullocks, two rams, and fourteen unblemished yearling lambs, 27 [d]with their cereal offerings and libations as prescribed for the bullocks, rams and lambs in proportion to their number, 28 as well as one goat for a sin offering, besides the established holocaust with its cereal offering and libation.

29 "On the sixth day you shall offer eight bullocks, two rams, and fourteen unblemished yearling lambs, 30 with their cereal offerings and libations as prescribed for the bullocks, rams and lambs in proportion to their number, 31 as well as one goat for a sin offering, besides the established holocaust with its cereal offering and libation.

32 "On the seventh day you shall offer seven bullocks, two rams, and fourteen unblemished yearling lambs, 33 with their cereal offerings and libations as prescribed for the bullocks, rams and lambs in proportion to their number, 34 as well as one goat for a sin offering, besides the established holocaust with its cereal offering and libation.

35 "On the eighth day[e] you shall hold a solemn meeting,* and do no sort of work. 36 You shall offer up in holocaust as a sweet-smelling oblation to the LORD one bullock, one ram, and seven unblemished yearling lambs, 37 with their cereal offerings and libations as prescribed for the bullocks, rams and lambs in proportion to their number, 38 as well as one goat for a sin offering, besides the established holocaust with its cereal offering and libation.

39 "These are the offerings you shall make to the LORD on your festivals, besides whatever holocausts, cereal offerings, libations, and peace offerings you present as your votive or free-will offerings."

CHAPTER 30

1 Moses then gave the Israelites these instructions, just as the LORD had ordered him.

Validity and Annulment of Vows 2 Moses said to the heads of the Israelite tribes, "This is what the LORD has commanded: 3 When a man makes a vow to the LORD or binds himself under oath to a pledge* of abstinence, he shall not violate his word, but must fulfill exactly the promise he has uttered.[f]

4 "When a woman, while still a maiden in her father's house, makes a vow to the LORD, or binds herself to a pledge, 5 if her father learns of her vow or the pledge to which she bound herself and says nothing to her about it, then any vow or any pledge she has made remains valid. 6 But if on the day he learns of it her father expresses to her his disapproval, then any vow or any pledge she has made becomes null and void; and the LORD releases her from it, since her father has expressed to her his disapproval.

7 "If she marries while under a vow or under a

29, 35: A solemn meeting: the Hebrew word is the technical term for the closing celebration of the three major feasts of the Passover, Pentecost and Booths, or of other special feasts that lasted for a week. Cf Lv 23, 36; Dt 16, 8; 2 Chr 7, 9; Neh 8, 18.

30, 3: A vow . . . a pledge: here the former signifies the doing of some positive good deed, in particular the offering of some sacrifice; the latter signifies the abstaining from some otherwise licit action or pleasure; cf v 14.

d Nm 29, 30. 37. e Lv 23, 36; Jn 7, 37. f Dt 23, 22; Eccl 5, 3f.

rash pledge to which she bound herself, [8]and her husband learns of it, yet says nothing to her that day about it, then the vow or pledge she had made remains valid. [9]But if on the day he learns of it her husband expresses to her his disapproval, he thereby annuls the vow she had made or the rash pledge to which she had bound herself, and the LORD releases her from it. [10]The vow of a widow or of a divorced woman, or any pledge to which such a woman binds herself, is valid.

[11]"If it is in her husband's house* that she makes a vow or binds herself under oath to a pledge, [12]and her husband learns of it yet says nothing to express to her his disapproval, then any vow or any pledge she has made remains valid. [13]But if on the day he learns of them her husband annuls them, then whatever she has expressly promised in her vow or in her pledge becomes null and void; since her husband has annulled them, the LORD releases her from them.

[14]"Any vow or any pledge that she makes under oath to mortify herself, her husband can either allow to remain valid or render null and void. [15]But if her husband, day after day, says nothing at all to her about them, he thereby allows as valid any vow or any pledge she has made; he has allowed them to remain valid, because on the day he learned of them he said nothing to her about them. [16]If, however, he countermands them* some time after he first learned of them, he is responsible for her guilt."

[17]These are the statutes which the LORD prescribed through Moses concerning the relationship between a husband and his wife, as well as between a father and his daughter while she is still a maiden in her father's house.

CHAPTER 31

Extermination of the Midianites [1]The LORD said to Moses,* [2]"Avenge the Israelites on the Midianites, and then you shall be taken to your people." [3]So Moses told the people, "Select men from your midst and arm them for war, to attack the Midianites and execute the LORD's vengeance on them. [4]From each of the tribes of Israel you shall send a band of one thousand men to war." [5]From the clans of Israel, therefore, a thousand men of each tribe were levied, so that there were twelve thousand men armed for war. [6]Moses sent them out on the campaign, a thousand from each tribe, with Phinehas, son of Eleazar, the priest for the campaign, who had with him the sacred vessels and the trumpets for sounding the alarm. [7]They waged war against the Midianites, as the LORD had commanded Moses, and killed every male among them. [8]Besides those slain in battle, they killed the five Midianite kings:* Evi, Rekem, Zur, Hur and Reba; and they also executed Balaam, son of Beor, with the sword. [9]But the Israelites kept the women of the Midianites with their little ones as captives, and all their herds and flocks and wealth as spoil, [10]while they set on fire all the towns where they had settled and all their encampments. [11]Then they took all the booty, with the people and beasts they had captured, and brought the captives, together with the spoils and booty, [12]to Moses and the priest Eleazar and to the Israelite community at their camp on the plains of Moab, along the Jericho stretch of the Jordan.

Treatment of the Captives [13]When Moses and the priest Eleazar, with all the princes of the community, went outside the camp to meet them, [14]Moses became angry with the officers of the army, the clan and company commanders, who were returning from combat. [15]"So you have spared all the women!" he exclaimed. [16]"Why, they are the very ones who on Balaam's advice prompted the unfaithfulness of the Israelites toward the LORD in the Peor affair,[g] which began the slaughter of the LORD's community.

30, 11: In her husband's house: after her marriage. This contrasts with the case given in vv 7ff.

30, 16: He countermands them: he prevents their fulfillment. Since he has first allowed the vows to remain valid, he can no longer annul them.

31, 1ff: The narrative of Israel's relations with Midian, which was interrupted after Nm 25, 18, is now resumed.

31, 8: The five Midianite kings: they are called "Midianite princes, Sihon's vassals" in Jos 13, 21.

g 2 Pt 2, 15; Rv 2, 14.

17*Slay, therefore, every male child and every woman who has had intercourse with a man. 18But you may spare and keep for yourselves all girls who had no intercourse with a man.

Purification after Combat 19"Moreover, you shall stay outside the camp for seven days, and those of you who have slain anyone or touched anyone slain in battle shall purify yourselves on the third and on the seventh day. This applies both to you and to your captives. 20You shall also purify every article of cloth, leather, goats' hair, or wood."

21Eleazar the priest told the soldiers who had returned from combat: "This is what the law, as prescribed by the LORD to Moses, ordains: 22Whatever can stand fire, such as gold, silver, bronze, iron, tin and lead, 23you shall put into the fire, that it may become clean; however, it must also be purified with lustral water.* But whatever cannot stand fire you shall put into the water. 24On the seventh day you shall wash your clothes, and then you will again be clean. After that you may enter the camp."

Division of the Booty 25The LORD said to Moses: 26"With the help of the priest Eleazar and of the heads of the ancestral houses, count up all the human captives and the beasts that have been taken; 27then divide them evenly,* giving half to those who took active part in the war by going out to combat, and half to the rest of the community. 28You shall levy a tax for the LORD on the warriors who went out to combat: one out of every five hundred persons, oxen, asses and sheep 29in their half of the spoil you shall turn over to the priest Eleazar as a contribution to the LORD. 30From the Israelites' half you shall take one out of every fifty persons, and the same from the different beasts, oxen, asses and sheep, and give them to the Levites, who have charge of the LORD's Dwelling." 31So Moses and the priest Eleazar did this, as the LORD had commanded Moses.

Amount of Booty 32This booty, what was left of the loot which the soldiers had taken, amounted to six hundred and seventy-five thousand sheep, 33seventy-two thousand oxen, 34sixty-one thousand asses, 35and thirty-two thousand girls who were still virgins.

36The half that fell to those who had gone out to combat was: three hundred and thirty-seven thousand five hundred sheep, 37of which six hundred and seventy-five fell as tax to the LORD; 38thirty-six thousand oxen, of which seventy-two fell as tax to the LORD; 39thirty thousand five hundred asses, of which sixty-one fell as tax to the LORD; 40and sixteen thousand persons, of whom thirty-two fell as tax to the LORD. 41The taxes contributed to the LORD, Moses gave to the priest Eleazar, as the LORD had commanded him.

42The half for the other Israelites, which fell to the community when Moses had taken it from the soldiers, was: 43three hundred and thirty-seven thousand five hundred sheep, 44thirty-six thousand oxen, 45thirty thousand five hundred asses, 46and sixteen thousand persons. 47From this, the Israelites' share, Moses, as the LORD had ordered, took one out of every fifty, both of persons and of beasts, and gave them to the Levites, who had charge of the LORD's Dwelling.

Gifts of the Officers 48Then the officers who had been clan and company commanders of the army came up to Moses 49and said to him, "Your servants have counted up the soldiers under our command, and not one is missing. 50*So, to make atonement for ourselves before the LORD, each of us will bring as an offering to the LORD some gold article he has picked up, such as an anklet, a bracelet, a ring, an earring, or a necklace." 51Moses and the priest Eleazar accepted this gold from them, all of it in well-wrought articles. 52The gold that they gave as a contribution to the LORD amounted in all to

31, 17: There are later references to Midian in Jgs 6–8; 1 Kgs 11, 18; Is 60, 6. The present raid was only against those Midianites who were dwelling at this time near the encampment of the Israelites.

31, 23: Lustral water: water mixed with the ashes of the red heifer as prescribed in Nm 19, 9.

31, 27: Divide them evenly: for a similar division of the booty into two equal parts, between those who engaged in the fray and those who stayed with the baggage, cf 1 Sm 30, 24. But note that here the tax on the booty of the non-combatants is ten times as much as that on the soldier's booty.

31, 50: The precise nature and use of some of these articles of gold is not certain.

sixteen thousand seven hundred and fifty shekels. This was from the clan and company commanders; [53]what the common soldiers had looted each one kept for himself. [54]Moses, then, and the priest Eleazar accepted the gold from the clan and company commanders, and put it in the meeting tent as a memorial for the Israelites before the LORD.

CHAPTER 32

Request of Gad and Reuben [1]Now the Reubenites and Gadites had a very large number of livestock. Noticing that the land of Jazer and of Gilead* was grazing country, [2]they came to Moses and the priest Eleazar and to the princes of the community and said, [3]*"The region of Ataroth, Dibon, Jazer, Nimrah, Heshbon, Elealeh, Sebam, Nebo and Baal-meon, [4]which the LORD has laid low before the community of Israel, is grazing country. Now, since your servants have livestock," [5]they continued, "if we find favor with you, let this land be given to your servants as their property. Do not make us cross the Jordan."

Moses' Rebuke [6]But Moses answered the Gadites and Reubenites: "Are your kinsmen, then, to engage in war, while you remain here? [7]Why do you wish to discourage the Israelites from crossing to the land the LORD has given them? [8]That is just what your fathers did when I sent them from Kadesh-barnea to reconnoiter the land.[h] [9]They went up to the Wadi Eshcol and reconnoitered the land, then so discouraged the Israelites that they would not enter the land the LORD had given them. [10][i]At that time the wrath of the LORD flared up, and he swore, [11]'Because they have not followed me unreservedly, none of these men of twenty years or more who have come up from Egypt shall ever see this country I promised under oath to Abraham and Isaac and Jacob, [12][j]except the Kenizzite* Caleb, son of Jephunneh, and Joshua, son of Nun, who have followed the LORD unreservedly.' [13]So in his anger with the Israelites the LORD made them wander in the desert forty years, until the whole generation that had done evil in the sight of the LORD had died out. [14]And now here you are, a brood of sinners, rising up in your fathers' place to add still more to the LORD's blazing wrath against the Israelites. [15]If you turn away from following him, he will make them stay still longer in the desert, and so you will bring about the ruin of this whole nation."

Counter Proposal [16]But they were insistent with him: "We wish only to build sheepfolds here for our flocks, and towns for our families; [17]but we ourselves will march as troops in the van of the Israelites,[k] until we have led them to their destination. Meanwhile our families can remain here in the fortified towns, safe from attack by the natives. [18]We will not return to our homes until every one of the Israelites has taken possession of his heritage, [19][l]and will not claim any heritage with them once we cross the Jordan, so long as we receive a heritage for ourselves on this eastern side of the Jordan."

Agreement Reached [20]*Moses said to them in reply: "If you keep your word to march as troops in the LORD's vanguard [21]and to cross the Jordan in full force before the LORD until he has driven his enemies out of his way [22]and the land is subdued before him, then you may return here, quit of every obligation to the LORD and to Israel, and this region shall be your possession before the LORD.[m] [23]But if you do not do this, you will sin against the LORD, and you can be sure that you will not escape the consequences of your sin. [24]Build the towns, then, for your families, and the folds for your flocks, but also fulfill your express promise."

32, 1: Gilead: the name of the western part of the plateau east of the Jordan, sometimes signifying the whole region from the Yarmuk to the Jordan, sometimes only the northern part of this region, and sometimes, as here, only its southern part. Jazer lay to the east of southern Gilead.

32, 3: The places named in this verse, as well as the additional ones given in vv 34–38, were all in the former kingdom of Sihon, that is, in the region between the Jabbok and the Arnon. Cf Nm 21, 23f; Jos 13, 19–21. 24–27.

32, 12: Kenizzite: a member of the clan of Kenaz, which, according to Gn 36, 11. 15. 42, was Edomitic; hence, although Caleb belonged to the tribe of Judah (Nm 13, 6; 34, 19), he must have had Edomite blood in his veins; cf also Jos 14, 6. 14.

32, 20ff: Since the ark of the Lord was borne into battle with the Israelite army, the vanguard was said to march before the Lord.

h 8f: Nm 13, 31ff; Dt 1, 22. i 10f: Dt 1, 34f. j Nm 14, 24; Dt 1, 36. k Jos 4, 12f. l Jos 13, 8. m Jos 1, 15.

25 The Gadites and Reubenites answered Mo-
ses, "Your servants will do as you command, my
lord. 26 [n]While our wives and children, our herds
and other livestock remain in the towns of
Gilead, 27 all your servants will go across as
armed troops to battle before the LORD, just as
your lordship says."
28 Moses, therefore, gave this order in their
regard to the priest Eleazar, to Joshua, son of
Nun, and to the heads of the ancestral tribes of
the Israelites: 29 "If all the Gadites and Reuben-
ites cross the Jordan with you as combat troops
before the LORD, you shall give them Gilead as
their property when the land has been subdued
before you. 30 But if they will not go across with
you as combat troops before the LORD, you shall
bring their wives and children and livestock
across before you into Canaan, and they shall
have their property with you in the land of
Canaan."
31 To this the Gadites and Reubenites replied,
"We will do what the LORD has commanded us,
your servants. 32 We ourselves will go across into
the land of Canaan as troops before the LORD,
but we will retain our hereditary property on this
side of the Jordan." 33 So Moses gave them [* the
Gadites and Reubenites, as well as half the tribe
of Manasseh, son of Joseph, the kingdom of
Sihon, king of the Amorites, and the kingdom of
Og, king of Bashan,] the land with its towns and
the districts that surrounded them. [o]
34 The Gadites rebuilt the fortified towns of
Dibon, Ataroth, Aroer, 35 Atroth-shophan, Jazer,
Jogbehah, 36 Beth-nimrah and Beth-haran, and
they built sheepfolds. 37 The Reubenites rebuilt
Heshbon, Elealeh, Kiriathaim, 38 Nebo, Baal-
meon [names to be changed!],* and Sibmah.
These towns, which they rebuilt, they called by
their old names.

Other Conquests 39 The descendants of Ma-
chir, son of Manasseh, invaded Gilead and
captured it, driving out the Amorites who were
there. 40 [Moses gave Gilead to Machir, [p] son of
Manasseh, and he settled there.] 41 Jair, [q] a Manas-
sehite clan, campaigned against the tent villages,
captured them and called them Havvoth-jair.
42 Nobah also campaigned against Kenath, cap-
tured it with its dependencies and called it
Nobah after his own name.

CHAPTER 33

Stages on the Journey 1 The following are the
stages by which the Israelites journeyed up by
companies from the land of Egypt under the
guidance of Moses and Aaron.* 2 By the LORD's
command Moses recorded the starting places of
the various stages. The starting places of the
successive stages were:

3 *They set out from Rameses in the first
month,
on the fifteenth day of the first month.
On the Passover morrow the Israelites went
forth
in triumph, in view of all Egypt,
4 While the Egyptians buried their first-born
all of whom the LORD had struck down;
on their gods, too, the LORD executed
judgments. [r]

From Egypt to Sinai 5 Setting out from Rame-
ses, the Israelites camped at Succoth. 6 Setting
out from Succoth, they camped at Etham near
the edge of the desert. 7 Setting out from Etham,
they turned back to Pi-hahiroth, which is oppo-
site Baal-zephon, and they camped opposite

32, 33: The preceding is concerned solely with the two tribes of Gad and Reuben and with the land of the former kingdom of Sihon; hence it seems probable that the sudden reference here to the half-tribe of Manasseh and to their territory in Bashan, the former kingdom of Og, is a later addition to the text.

32, 38: The phrase in brackets is a gloss, warning the reader either to change the order of the preceding names, or, more probably, to read some other word, such as bosheth, "shame," for Baal. They called by their old names: literally, "they called by their names" (see Textual Notes); however, some understand the current Hebrew text to mean, "they called by new names."

33, 1ff: This list of camping sites was drawn up by Moses, as v 2 expressly states. However, in its present form it probably includes some glosses. Moreover, a comparison with the more detailed accounts of the journey as given elsewhere shows that this is not complete. It records just forty camping sites, not counting the starting place, Rameses, and the terminus, the plains of Moab. This number, which corresponds exactly to the forty years of wandering in the desert, is probably a schematic device. Besides, it seems that in its present form the order of some of these names has been disturbed. Several names listed here are not recorded elsewhere.

33, 3f: These two verses were probably borrowed from some ancient song celebrating the exodus from Egypt.

n Jos 1, 14. o Dt 3, 12; 29, 7; Jos 12, 6; 13, 8. p Dt 3, 15. q Dt 3, 14. r 4f: Ex 12, 12. 29. 37.

Migdol.[s] 8 Setting out from Pi-hahiroth, they
crossed over through the sea into the desert,[t]
and after a three days' journey in the desert of
Etham, they camped at Marah. 9 Setting out from
Marah, they came to Elim, where there were
twelve springs of water and seventy palm trees,
and they camped there.[u] 10 Setting out from
Elim, they camped beside the Red Sea. 11 Setting
out from the Red Sea, they camped in the desert
of Sin. 12 Setting out from the desert of Sin, they
camped at Dophkah. 13 Setting out from Doph-
kah, they camped at Alush. 14 Setting out from
Alush, they camped at Rephidim, where there
was no water for the people to drink.[v] 15 Setting
out from Rephidim, they camped in the desert of
Sinai.[w]

From Sinai to Kadesh 16 Setting out from the
desert of Sinai, they camped at Kibroth-
hattaavah. 17 Setting out from Kibroth-hattaavah,
they camped at Hazeroth.[x] 18 Setting out from
Hazeroth, they camped at Rithmah. 19 Setting
out from Rithmah, they camped at Rimmon-
perez. 20 Setting out from Rimmon-perez, they
camped at Libnah. 21 Setting out from Libnah,
they camped at Rissah. 22 Setting out from Ris-
sah, they camped at Kehelathah. 23 Setting out
from Kehelathah, they camped at Mount She-
pher. 24 Setting out from Mount Shepher, they
camped at Haradah. 25 Setting out from Haradah,
they camped at Makheloth. 26 Setting out from
Makheloth, they camped at Tahath. 27 Setting
out from Tahath, they camped at Terah. 28 Set-
ting out from Terah, they camped at Mithkah.
29 Setting out from Mithkah, they camped at
Hashmonah. 30 *Setting out from Hashmonah,—

From Mount Hor to Ezion-geber They
camped at Moseroth. 31 Setting out from Mose-
roth, they camped at Bene-jaakan. 32 Setting out
from Bene-jaakan, they camped at Mount
Gidgad. 33 Setting out from Mount Gidgad, they
camped at Jotbathah. 34 Setting out from Jotba-
thah, they camped at Abronah. 35 Setting out
from Abronah, they camped at Ezion-geber.
36 Setting out from Ezion-geber,—

From Kadesh to Mount Hor They camped in
the desert of Zin, at Kadesh.[y] 37 Setting out from
Kadesh, they camped at Mount Hor on the
border of the land of Edom. 38 [Aaron the priest
ascended Mount Hor[z] at the LORD's command,
and there he died in the fortieth year from the
departure of the Israelites from the land of
Egypt, on the first day of the fifth month.
39 Aaron was a hundred and twenty-three years
old when he died on Mount Hor. 40 *Now, when
the Canaanite king of Arad, who lived in the
Negeb in the land of Canaan, heard that the
Israelites were coming. . . .] 41 Setting out from
Mount Hor,—

From Ezion-geber to the Plains of Moab
*They camped at Zalmonah. 42 Setting out from
Zalmonah, they camped at Punon. 43 Setting out
from Punon, they camped at Oboth. 44 Setting
out from Oboth, they camped at Iye-abarim on
the border of Moab. 45 Setting out from Iye-
abarim, they camped at Dibon-gad. 46 Setting out
from Dibon-gad, they camped at Almon-
diblathaim. 47 Setting out from Almon-
diblathaim, they camped in the Abarim Moun-
tains opposite Nebo. 48 Setting out from the
Abarim Mountains, they camped on the plains of
Moab along the Jericho stretch of the Jordan.
49 Their camp along the Jordan on the plains of
Moab extended from Beth-jeshimoth to Abel-
shittim.

Conquest and Division of Canaan 50 The
LORD spoke to Moses on the plains of Moab
beside the Jericho stretch of the Jordan and said
to him: 51 "Tell the Israelites: When you go
across the Jordan into the land of Canaan,
52 drive out all the inhabitants of the land before
you; destroy all their stone figures and molten
images, and demolish all their high places.[a]

33, 30–36: Moseroth is mentioned in Dt 10, 6 (in the form of "Moserah"), as the place where Aaron died. It must therefore have been close to Mount Hor; cf Nm 20, 22ff. It seems very probable that the section vv 36b-41a stood originally immediately after v 30a.

33, 40: The verse begins the same account of the victory over Arad as is given in Nm 21, 1ff, where it also follows the account of Aaron's death.

33, 41b-49: It seems that this section stood originally immediately after v 36a.

s Ex 14, 2. t Ex 15, 22. u Ex 15, 27. v Ex 17, 1. w Ex 19, 2. x 17f: Nm 11, 34f. y 36f: Nm 20, 1. 22. z Nm 20, 25; Dt 32, 50. a Ex 23, 31; 34, 13; Dt 7, 5; 12, 3.

53“You shall take possession of the land and
settle in it, for I have given you the land as your
property. 54You shall apportion the land among
yourselves by lot, clan by clan, assigning a large
heritage to a large group and a small heritage to a
small group.[b] Wherever anyone’s lot falls, there
shall his property be within the heritage of his
ancestral tribe.

55“But if you do not drive out the inhabitants
of the land before you, those whom you allow to
remain will become as barbs in your eyes and
thorns in your sides, and they will harass you in
the country where you live,[c] 56and I will treat
you as I had intended to treat them.”

CHAPTER 34

The Boundaries 1The LORD said to Moses,
2“Give the Israelites this order: When you enter
the land of Canaan, this is the territory that shall
fall to you as your heritage—the land of Canaan
with its boundaries:

3“Your southern boundary shall be at the
desert of Zin along the border of Edom;[d] on the
east it shall begin at the end of the Salt Sea, 4and
turning south of the Akrabbim Pass, it shall cross
Zin, and extend south of Kadesh-barnea to
Hazar-addar; thence it shall cross to Azmon,[e]
5and turning from Azmon to the Wadi of Egypt,
shall terminate at the Sea.[f]

6“For your western boundary you shall have
the Great Sea* with its coast; this shall be your
western boundary.

7“The following shall be your boundary on
the north: from the Great Sea you shall draw a
line to Mount Hor,* 8and shall continue it from
Mount Hor to Labo in the land of Hamath, with
the boundary extending through Zedad.
9Thence the boundary shall reach to Ziphron
and terminate at Hazar-enan. This shall be your
northern boundary.

10“For your eastern boundary you shall draw
a line from Hazar-enan to Shepham. 11From
Shepham the boundary shall go down to Ar-Baal,
east of Ain, and descending further, shall strike
the ridge on the east side of the Sea of Chinne-
reth; 12thence the boundary shall continue along
the Jordan and terminate with the Salt Sea.

“This is the land that shall be yours, with the
boundaries that surround it.”

13Moses also gave this order to the Israelites:
“This is the land, to be apportioned among you
by lot, which the LORD has commanded to be
given to the nine and one half tribes. 14For all
the ancestral houses of the tribe of Reuben, and
the ancestral houses of the tribe of Gad, as well
as half of the tribe of Manasseh, have already
received their heritage; 15these two and one half
tribes have received their heritage on the eastern
side of the Jericho stretch of the Jordan, toward
the sunrise.”

Supervisors of the Allotment 16The LORD
said to Moses, 17“These are the names of the
men who shall apportion the land among you:
Eleazar the priest, and Joshua, son of Nun,
18[g]and one prince from each of the tribes whom
you shall designate for this task. 19These shall be
as follows:

from the tribe of Judah: Caleb, son of Jephunneh;
20from the tribe of Simeon: Samuel, son of Ammihud;
21from the tribe of Benjamin: Elidad, son of Chislon;
22from the tribe of Dan: Bukki, son of Jogli;
23from the tribe of Manasseh: Hanniel, son of Ephod; and
24from the tribe of Ephraim: Kemuel, son of Shiphtan, for the descendants of Joseph;
25from the tribe of Zebulun: Elizaphan, son of Parnach;
26from the tribe of Issachar: Paltiel, son of Azzan;
27from the tribe of Asher: Ahihud, son of Shelomi;
28from the tribe of Naphtali: Pedahel, son of Ammihud.”

29These are they whom the LORD com-

34, 6: The Great Sea: the Mediterranean.

34, 7f: Mount Hor: different from the one where Aaron died; cf Nm 20, 22; 33, 37f.

b Nm 26, 53ff. c Jos 23, 13; Jgs 2, 3. d Jos 15, 1f. e Jos 15, 3. f Jos 15, 4. g Nm 1, 4.

manded to assign the Israelites their heritage in the land of Canaan.

CHAPTER 35

Cities for the Levites 1 The LORD gave these instructions to Moses on the plains of Moab beside the Jericho stretch of the Jordan: 2 [h]"Tell the Israelites that out of their hereditary property they shall give the Levites cities for homes, as well as pasture lands around the cities. 3 The cities shall serve them to dwell in, and the pasture lands shall serve their herds and flocks and other animals. 4 The pasture lands of the cities to be assigned the Levites shall extend a thousand cubits from the city walls in each direction. 5 Thus you shall measure out two thousand cubits outside the city along each side—east, south, west and north—with the city lying in the center. This shall serve them as the pasture lands of their cities.

6 [i]"Now these are the cities you shall give to the Levites: the six cities of asylum which you must establish as places where a homicide can take refuge, and in addition forty-two other cities— 7 a total of forty-eight cities with their pasture lands to be assigned the Levites. 8 *In assigning the cities from the property of the Israelites, take more from a larger group and fewer from a smaller one, so that each group will cede cities to the Levites in proportion to its own heritage."

Cities of Asylum 9 The LORD said to Moses, 10 "Tell the Israelites: When you go across the Jordan into the land of Canaan, 11 select for yourselves cities[j] to serve as cities of asylum, where a homicide who has killed someone unintentionally may take refuge. 12 These cities shall serve you as places of asylum from the avenger of blood,* so that a homicide shall not be put to death unless he is first tried before the community. 13 Six cities of asylum shall you assign: 14 three beyond the Jordan, and three in the land of Canaan. 15 These six cities of asylum shall serve not only the Israelites but all the resident or transient aliens among them, so that anyone who has killed another unintentionally may take refuge there.

Murder and Manslaughter 16 *"If a man strikes another with an iron instrument and causes his death, he is a murderer and shall be put to death.[k] 17 If a man strikes another with a death-dealing stone in his hand and causes his death, he is a murderer and shall be put to death. 18 If a man strikes another with a death-dealing club in his hand and causes his death, he is a murderer and shall be put to death. 19 The avenger of blood may execute the murderer, putting him to death on sight.

20 "If a man pushes another out of hatred, or after lying in wait for him throws something at him, and causes his death,[l] 21 or if he strikes another out of enmity and causes his death, he shall be put to death as a murderer. The avenger of blood may execute the murderer on sight.

22 [m]"However, if a man pushes another accidentally and not out of enmity, or if without lying in wait for him he throws some object at him, 23 or without seeing him throws a death-dealing stone which strikes him and causes his death, although he was not his enemy nor seeking to harm him: 24 then the community, deciding the case between the slayer and the avenger of blood in accordance with these norms, 25 shall free the homicide from the avenger of blood and shall remand him to the city of asylum where he took refuge;[n] and he shall stay there until the death of the high priest who has been anointed with sacred oil. 26 If the homicide of his own accord leaves the bounds of the city of asylum where he has taken refuge, 27 and the avenger of blood finds him beyond these bounds and kills him, the avenger incurs no blood-guilt; 28 the homicide was bound to stay in his city of asylum until the death of the high priest. Only

35, 8: This provision was hardly observed in the actual assignment of the levitical cities as narrated in Jos 21.

35, 12: The avenger of blood: one of the close relatives of the slain (2 Sm 14, 7) who, as executor of public justice, had the right and duty to take the life of the murderer; cf Dt 19, 6. 12; Jos 20, 3. 5. 9.

35, 16–25: Here, as also in Dt 19, 1–13, there is a casuistic development of the original law as stated in Ex 21, 12ff.

h Jos 14, 3f; 21, 2. i Dt 4, 41f; Jos 20, 2. j 10ff: Dt 19, 2; Jos 20, 2ff. k Ex 21, 12; Lv 24, 17. l Ex 21, 14; Dt 19, 11. m Jos 20, 3. n Jos 20, 6.

after the death of the high priest may the homicide return to his own district.

29"These shall be norms for you and all your descendants, wherever you live, for rendering judgment.

Witnesses 30"Whenever someone kills another, the evidence of witnesses is required for the execution of the murderer.[o] The evidence of a single witness is not sufficient for putting a person to death.

No Indemnity 31"You shall not accept indemnity in place of the life of a murderer who deserves the death penalty; he must be put to death. 32Nor shall you accept indemnity to allow a refugee to leave his city of asylum and again dwell elsewhere in the land before the death of the high priest. 33You shall not desecrate the land where you live. Since bloodshed desecrates the land, the land can have no atonement for the blood shed on it except through the blood of him who shed it. 34Do not defile the land in which you live and in the midst of which I dwell;[p] for I am the LORD who dwells; in the midst of the Israelites."

CHAPTER 36

Property of Heiresses 1The heads of the ancestral houses in the clan of descendants of Gilead, son of Machir, son of Manasseh—one of the Josephite clans—came up and laid this plea before Moses and the priest Eleazar and before the princes who were the heads of the ancestral houses of the other Israelites. 2They said: "The LORD commanded you, my lord, to apportion the land by lot among the Israelites;[q] and you, my lord, were also commanded by the LORD to give the heritage of our kinsman Zelophehad to his daughters. 3But if they marry into one of the other Israelite tribes, their heritage will be withdrawn from our ancestral heritage and will be added to that of the tribe into which they marry; thus the heritage that fell to us by lot will be diminished. 4When the Israelites celebrate the jubilee year,* the heritage of these women will be permanently added to that of the tribe into which they marry and will be withdrawn from that of our ancestral tribe."

5*So Moses gave this regulation to the Israelites according to the instructions of the LORD: "The tribe of the Josephites are right in what they say. 6This is what the LORD commands with regard to the daughters of Zelophehad: They may marry anyone they please, provided they marry into a clan of their ancestral tribe, 7so that no heritage of the Israelites will pass from one tribe to another, but all the Israelites will retain their own ancestral heritage. 8Therefore, every daughter who inherits property in any of the Israelite tribes shall marry someone belonging to a clan of her own ancestral tribe, in order that all the Israelites may remain in possession of their own ancestral heritage. 9Thus, no heritage can pass from one tribe to another, but all the Israelite tribes will retain their own ancestral heritage."

10The daughters of Zelophehad obeyed the command which the LORD had given to Moses. 11Mahlah, Tirzah, Hoglah, Milcah and Noah, Zelophehad's daughters, married relatives on their father's side 12within the clans of the descendants of Manasseh, son of Joseph; hence their heritage remained in the tribe of their father's clan.

Conclusion 13These are the commandments and decisions which the LORD prescribed for the Israelites through Moses, on the plains of Moab beside the Jericho stretch of the Jordan.

36, 4: Before the jubilee year various circumstances, such as divorce, could make such property revert to its original tribal owners; but in the jubilee year it became irrevocably attached to its new owners.

36, 5–9: This is a supplement to the law given in Nm 27, 5–11.

o Dt 17, 6; 19, 15; Jn 8, 17; 2 Cor 13, 1; 1 Tm 5, 19. p Ex 29, 45. q Nm 26, 55; 27, 6; Jos 17, 3f.

THE BOOK OF DEUTERONOMY

The fifth and last book of the Pentateuch is called Deuteronomy, meaning "second law." In reality, what it contains is not a new law but a partial repetition, completion and explanation of the law proclaimed on Mount Sinai. The historical portions of the book are also a résumé of what is related elsewhere in the Pentateuch. The chief characteristic of this book is its vigorous oratorical style. In a series of eloquent discourses Moses presents the theme of covenant renewal in a vital religious framework. He exhorts, corrects and threatens his people, appealing to their past glory, their historic mission and the promise of future triumph. His aim is to enforce among the Israelites the Lord's claim to their obedience, loyalty and love. The events contained in the Book of Deuteronomy took place in the plains of Moab (Dt 1, 5) between the end of the wanderings in the desert (Dt 1, 3) and the crossing of the Jordan River (Jos 4, 19), a period of no more than forty days. The Book of Deuteronomy, written after the Israelites had for centuries been resident in the Land of Promise, takes the form of a testament of Moses, the great leader and legislator, to his people on the eve of his death. At the time of our Lord's coming, it shared with the Psalms a preeminent religious influence among the Old Testament books. The Savior quoted passages of Deuteronomy in overcoming the threefold temptation of Satan in the desert (Mt 4; Dt 6, 13. 16; 8, 3; 10, 20), and in explaining to the lawyer the first and greatest commandment (Mt 22, 35-39; Dt 6, 4).

The book is divided as follows:

I. Historical Review and Exhortation (Dt 1, 1—4, 43).
II. God and His Covenant (Dt 4, 44—11, 32).
III. Exposition of the Law (Dt 12, 1—26, 19).
IV. Final Words of Moses (Dt 27, 1—34, 12).

I: Historical Review and Exhortation

CHAPTER 1

Introduction 1These are the words which Mo-
ses spoke to all Israel beyond the Jordan [* in the
desert, in the Arabah, opposite Suph, between
Paran and Tophel, Laban, Hazeroth and Diza-
hab; 2it is a journey of eleven days from Horeb to
Kadesh-barnea by way of the highlands of Seir].
3In the fortieth year, on the first day of the
eleventh month, Moses spoke to the Israelites all
the commands that the LORD had given him in
their regard. 4After he had defeated Sihon, king
of the Amorites, who lived in Heshbon, [a] and
Og, king of Bashan, who lived in Ashtaroth and
in Edrei, 5Moses began to explain the law in the
land of Moab beyond the Jordan, as follows:
Departure from Horeb 6"The LORD, our
God, said to us at Horeb, 'You have stayed long
enough at this mountain. 7*Leave here and go
to the hill country of the Amorites and to all the
surrounding regions, [b] the land of the Canaan-
ites in the Arabah, the mountains, the foothills,
the Negeb and the seacoast; to Lebanon, and as
far as the Great River [the Euphrates]. 8I have
given that land over to you. [c] Go now and
occupy the land I swore to your fathers, Abra-
ham, Isaac and Jacob, I would give to them and
to their descendants.'
Appointment of Elders 9"At that time I said
to you, 'Alone, I am unable to carry you.* 10The

1, 1: The local setting of all these discourses is in the land of Moab beyond the Jordan (cf v 5), also known as the plains of Moab (Nm 36, 13).

1, 7: The Amorites and the Canaanites formed the principal part of the pre-Israelite population of Palestine. The foothills: the hills on the western slope of the Judean mountain range. The Arabah: the valley of the Jordan and the depression south of the Dead Sea. The Negeb: the arid land in southern Palestine.

1, 9: Carry you; cf v 31.

a Dt 3, 2; Nm 21, 21–35. b Nm 13, 29. c Gn 12, 7; 15, 18; 17, 7f; 28, 13f.

LORD, your God, has so multiplied you that you
are now as numerous as the stars in the sky.[d]
11 May the LORD, the God of your fathers,
increase you a thousand times over, and bless
you as he promised! 12 But how can I alone bear
the crushing burden that you are, along with
your bickering? 13 [e]Choose wise, intelligent and
experienced men from each of your tribes, that I
may appoint them as your leaders.' 14 You an-
swered me, 'We agree to do as you have
proposed.' 15 So I took outstanding men of your
tribes, wise and experienced, and made them
your leaders as officials over thousands, over
hundreds, over fifties and over tens, and other
tribal officers. 16 I charged your judges at that
time, 'Listen to complaints among your kinsmen,
and administer true justice to both parties even if
one of them is an alien.[f] 17 In rendering judg-
ment, do not consider who a person is; give ear
to the lowly and to the great alike, fearing no
man, for judgment is God's. Refer to me any case
that is too hard for you and I will hear it.'
18 Thereupon I gave you all the commands you
were to fulfill.

The Twelve Scouts 19 "Then, in obedience to
the command of the LORD, our God, we set out
from Horeb and journeyed through the whole
desert, vast and fearful as you have seen,[g] in the
direction of the hill country of the Amorites. We
had reached Kadesh-barnea 20 when I said to
you, 'You have come to the hill country of the
Amorites, which the LORD, our God, is giving us.
21 The LORD, your God, has given this land over
to you. Go up and occupy it, as the LORD, the
God of your fathers, commands you. Do not fear
or lose heart.' 22 [h]Then all of you came up to me
and said, 'Let us send men ahead to reconnoiter
the land for us and report to us on the road we
must follow and the cities we must take.'
23 Agreeing with the proposal, I chose twelve
men from your number, one from each tribe.
24 They set out into the hill country as far as the
Wadi Eshcol, and explored it. 25 Then, taking
along some of the fruit of the land, they brought
it down to us and reported, 'The land which the
LORD, our God, gives us is good.'

Threats of Revolt 26 "But you refused to go
up,[i] and after defying the command of the LORD,
your God, 27 you set to murmuring in your
tents,* 'Out of hatred for us the LORD has
brought us up out of the land of Egypt,[j] to
deliver us into the hands of the Amorites and
destroy us. 28 What shall we meet with up there?
Our kinsmen have made us fainthearted by
reporting that the people are stronger and taller
than we, and their cities are large and fortified to
the sky; besides, they saw the Anakim there.'[k]

29 "But I said to you, 'Have no dread or fear of
them. 30 The LORD, your God, who goes before
you, will himself fight for you, just as he took
your part before your very eyes in Egypt, 31 as
well as in the desert, where you saw how the
LORD, your God, carried you, as a man carries
his child, all along your journey until you ar-
rived at this place.' 32 Despite this, you would
not trust the LORD, your God, 33 who journeys
before you to find you a resting place—by day
in the cloud, and by night in the fire, to show
the way you must go.[l] 34 When the LORD heard
your words, he was angry; 35 and he swore,
'Not one man of this evil generation shall look
upon the good land I swore to give to your
fathers,[m] 36 except Caleb,* son of Jephunneh;
he shall see it. For to him and to his sons I will
give the land he trod upon, because he has
followed the LORD unreservedly.'

37 "The LORD was angered against me also on
your account, and said, 'Not even you shall enter
there,[n] 38 but your aide Joshua,[o] son of Nun,
shall enter. Encourage him, for he is to give
Israel its heritage. 39 Your little ones, who you
said would become booty, and your children,
who as yet do not know good from bad—they
shall enter; to them I will give it, and they shall

1, 27: In your tents: among yourselves.

1, 36: Except Caleb: Joshua also was allowed to enter, but he is not referred to here because special mention is made of him in v 38 as the successor of Moses.

d Dt 10, 22; Gn 15, 5. e 13ff: Ex 18, 21–25. f 16f: Ex 18, 26; 2 Chr 19, 6f; Prv 24, 23; Jn 7, 24; Jas 2, 9. g Dt 8, 15; 32, 10. h 22–28: Nm 13, 2–34. i Dt 9, 23. j Dt 9, 28; Nm 14, 1–4; Ps 106, 25. k Dt 9, 1f. l Ex 13, 21; Nm 10, 33f; 14, 14. m 34ff: Nm 14, 22f. 28–38; Jos 14, 9. n Dt 4, 21; 34, 4; Nm 20, 12. o Dt 31, 3. 7; Nm 27, 18ff; 34, 17.

occupy it.[p] 40But as for yourselves: turn about
and proceed into the desert on the Red Sea
road.'
Unsuccessful Invasion 41 [q]"In reply you said
to me, 'We have sinned against the LORD. We
will go up ourselves and fight, just as the LORD,
our God, commanded us.' And each of you
girded on his weapons, making light of going up
into the hill country. 42But the LORD said to me,
'Warn them: Do not go up and fight, lest you be
beaten down before your enemies, for I will not
be in your midst.' 43I gave you this warning but
you would not listen. In defiance of the LORD's
command you arrogantly marched off into the
hill country. 44Then the Amorites living there
came out against you and, like bees, chased you,
cutting you down in Seir as far as Hormah. 45On
your return you wept before the LORD, but he
did not listen to your cry or give ear to you.
46That is why you had to stay as long as you did
at Kadesh.

CHAPTER 2

Northward along Edom 1"When we did turn
and proceed into the desert on the Red Sea
road,[r] as the LORD had commanded me, we
circled around the highlands of Seir for a long
time. 2Finally the LORD said to me, 3'You have
wandered round these highlands long enough;
turn and go north. 4Give this order to the
people: You are now about to pass through the
territory of your kinsmen, the descendants of
Esau, who live in Seir. Though they are afraid of
you, be very careful 5not to come in conflict
with them, for I will not give you so much as a
foot of their land, since I have already given Esau
possession of the highlands of Seir. 6You shall
purchase from them with silver the food you eat
and the well water you drink. 7The LORD, your
God, has blessed you in all your undertakings;
he has been concerned about your journey
through this vast desert. It is now forty years that
he has been with you, and you have never been
in want.'[s]

Along Moab 8"Then we left behind us the
Arabah route, Elath, Ezion-geber, and Seir,
where our kinsmen, the descendants of Esau,
live; and we went on toward the desert of
Moab.[t] 9And the LORD said to me, 'Do not show
hostility to the Moabites or engage them in
battle, for I will not give you possession of any of
their land, since I have given Ar to the descen-
dants of Lot as their own.[u] 10[Formerly the
Emim lived there, a people strong and numerous
and tall like the Anakim;[v] 11like them they were
considered Rephaim. It was the Moabites who
called them Emim. 12In Seir, however, the
former inhabitants were the Horites;[w] the de-
scendants of Esau dispossessed them, clearing
them out of the way and taking their place, just
as the Israelites have done in the land of their
heritage which the LORD has given them.] 13Get
ready, then, to cross the Wadi Zered.'[x] So we
crossed it. 14Thirty-eight years had elapsed be-
tween our departure from Kadesh-barnea and
that crossing; in the meantime the whole genera-
tion of soldiers had perished from the camp, as
the LORD had sworn they should.[y] 15For it was
the LORD's hand that was against them, till he
wiped them out of the camp completely.
Along Ammon 16"When at length death had
put an end to all the soldiers among the people,
17the LORD said to me, 18'You are now about to
leave Ar and the territory of Moab behind. 19As
you come opposite the Ammonites,[z] do not
show hostility or come in conflict with them, for
I will not give you possession of any land of the
Ammonites, since I have given it to the descen-
dants of Lot as their own. 20[This also was
considered a country of the Rephaim from its
former inhabitants, whom the Ammonites called
Zamzummim, 21a people strong and numerous
and tall like the Anakim. But these, too, the
LORD cleared out of the way for the Ammonites,
who ousted them and took their place. 22He had
done the same for the descendants of Esau, who
dwell in Seir, by clearing the Horites out of their
way, so that the descendants of Esau have taken

p 39f: Nm 14, 31. q 41–45: Nm 14, 40. 42–45. r Dt 1, 40; Nm 14, 25; 21, 4. s Dt 8, 2ff. t Jgs 11, 18. u Gn 19, 36f. v Dt 1, 28. w Gn 36, 20f. x Nm 21, 12. y Nm 14, 29. 33. 35. z Gn 19, 38.

their place down to the present. 23 So also the Caphtorim,* migrating from Caphtor, cleared away the Avvim, who once dwelt in villages as far as Gaza, and took their place.]

Defeat of Sihon 24 " 'Advance now across the Wadi Arnon.[a] I now deliver into your hands Sihon, the Amorite king of Heshbon, and his land. Begin the occupation; engage him in battle. 25 This day I will begin to put a fear and dread of you into every nation under the heavens, so that at the mention of your name they will quake and tremble before you.'

26 "So I sent messengers from the desert of Kedemoth to Sihon, king of Heshbon, with this offer of peace: 27 'Let me pass through your country by the highway; I will go along it without turning aside to the right or to the left. 28 For the food I eat which you will supply, and for the water you give me to drink, you shall be paid in silver. Only let me march through, 29 as the descendants of Esau who dwell in Seir[b] and the Moabites who dwell in Ar have done, until I cross the Jordan into the land which the LORD, our God, is about to give us.' 30 But Sihon, king of Heshbon, refused to let us pass through his land, because the LORD, your God, made him stubborn in mind and obstinate in heart that he might deliver him up to you, as indeed he has now done.

31 "Then the LORD said to me, 'Now that I have already begun to hand over to you Sihon and his land, begin the actual occupation.' 32 So Sihon and all his people advanced against us to join battle at Jahaz; 33 but since the LORD, our God, had delivered him to us, we defeated him and his sons and all his people.[c] 34 At that time we seized all his cities and doomed* them all, with their men, women and children; we left no survivor.[d] 35 Our only booty was the livestock and the loot of the captured cities. 36 From Aroer on the edge of the Wadi Arnon and from the city in the wadi itself, as far as Gilead,[e] no city was too well fortified for us to whom the LORD had delivered them up. 37 However, in obedience to the command of the LORD, our God, you did not encroach upon any of the Ammonite land, neither the region bordering on the Wadi Jabbok, nor the cities of the highlands.[f]

CHAPTER 3

Defeat of Og 1 "Then we turned and proceeded toward Bashan. But Og, king of Bashan,[g] advanced against us with all his people to give battle at Edrei. 2 The LORD, however, said to me,[h] 'Do not be afraid of him, for I have delivered him into your hand with all his people and his land. Do to him as you did to Sihon, king of the Amorites, who lived in Heshbon.' 3 And thus the LORD, our God, delivered into our hands Og, king of Bashan, with all his people. We defeated him so completely that we left him no survivor. 4 At that time we captured all his cities, none of them eluding our grasp, the whole region of Argob, the kingdom of Og in Bashan: sixty cities in all, 5 to say nothing of the great number of unwalled towns. All the cities were fortified with high walls and gates and bars. 6 [i]As we had done to Sihon, king of Heshbon, so also here we doomed all the cities, with their men, women and children; 7 but all the livestock and the loot of each city we took as booty for ourselves.

8 "And so at that time we took from the two kings of the Amorites beyond the Jordan the territory from the Wadi Arnon to Mount Hermon 9 [which is called Sirion by the Sidonians and Senir by the Amorites], 10 comprising all the cities of the plateau and all Gilead and all the cities of the kingdom of Og in Bashan including Salecah and Edrei. 11 [Og, king of Bashan, was the last remaining survivor of the Rephaim. He had a bed of iron,* nine regular cubits long and four wide, which is still preserved in Rabbah of the Ammonites.]

2, 23: The Caphtorim: members of one of the groups of sea peoples who invaded the coast of Egypt and the southern part of Palestine about 1200 B.C. Caphtor: the ancient name of the island of Crete. Cf Am 9, 7.

2, 34: Doomed: see notes on Nm 18, 14; 21, 3.

3, 11: Bed of iron: some translate, "a sarcophagus of basalt."

a Nm 21, 13; Jgs 11, 19–22. b Dt 2, 5. 8f; Jgs 11, 17. c Dt 29, 7; Nm 21, 23–32. d Dt 3, 6; 29, 7f. e Dt 3, 12; Jos 13, 9. 16; Jgs 11, 26. f Nm 21, 24; Jos 12, 2. g Dt 29, 6; Nm 21, 33. h 2f: Nm 21, 34f. i Ps 135, 10ff.

Allotment of the Conquered Lands
12 [j]"When we occupied the land at that time, I
gave Reuben and Gad the territory from Aroer,
on the edge of the Wadi Arnon, halfway up into
the highlands of Gilead, with the cities therein.
13 The rest of Gilead and all of Bashan, the
kingdom of Og, the whole Argob region, I gave
to the half-tribe of Manasseh. [All this region of
Bashan was once called a land of the Rephaim.
14 Jair, a Manassehite clan, [k] took all the region of
Argob as far as the border of the Geshurites and
Maacathites, and called it after his own name
Bashan Havvoth-jair, the name it bears today.]
15 To Machir I gave Gilead, 16 and to Reuben and
Gad the territory from Gilead to the Wadi
Arnon—including the wadi bed and its banks—
and to the Wadi Jabbok, which is the border of
the Ammonites, 17 as well as the Arabah with the
Jordan and its eastern banks from Chinnereth to
the Salt Sea of the Arabah, under the slopes of
Pisgah. [l]

18 "At that time I charged them* as follows:
'The LORD, your God, has given you this land as
your own. But all you troops equipped for battle
must cross over in the vanguard of your brother
Israelites. [m] 19 Only your wives and children, as
well as your livestock, of which I know you have
a large number, shall remain behind in the
towns I have given you, [n] 20 until the LORD has
settled your kinsmen as well, and they too
possess the land which the LORD, your God, will
give them on the other side of the Jordan. [o] Then
you may all return to the possessions I have
given you.'

21 "It was then that I instructed Joshua, 'Your
eyes have seen all that the LORD, your God, has
done to both these kings; so, too, will the LORD
do to all the kingdoms which you will encounter
over there. 22 Fear them not, for the LORD, your
God, will fight for you.'

Refusal to Moses 23 "And it was then that I
besought the LORD, 24 'O Lord GOD, you have
begun to show to your servant your greatness
and might. For what god in heaven or on earth
can perform deeds as mighty as yours? 25 Ah, let
me cross over and see this good land beyond the
Jordan, this fine hill country, and the Lebanon!'
26 But the LORD was angry with me on your
account and would not hear me. [p] 'Enough!' the
LORD said to me. 'Speak to me no more of this.
27 Go up to the top of Pisgah and look out to the
west, and to the north, and to the south, and to
the east. Look well, for you shall not cross this
Jordan. [q] 28 Commission Joshua, [r] and encourage
and strengthen him, for he shall cross at the
head of this people and shall put them in
possession of the land you are to see.' 29 This was
while we were in the ravine opposite Beth-peor.

CHAPTER 4

Advantages of Fidelity 1 "Now, Israel, hear
the statutes and decrees which I am teaching
you to observe, that you may live, and may enter
in and take possession of the land which the
LORD, the God of your fathers, is giving you. 2 In
your observance of the commandments of the
LORD, your God, [s] which I enjoin upon you, you
shall not add to what I command you nor
subtract from it. 3 You have seen with your own
eyes what the LORD did at Baal-peor: [t] the LORD,
your God, destroyed from your midst everyone
that followed the Baal of Peor; 4 but you, who
clung to the LORD, your God, are all alive today.
5 Therefore, I teach you the statutes and decrees
as the LORD, my God, has commanded me, that
you may observe them in the land you are
entering to occupy. 6 Observe them carefully, for
thus will you give evidence of your wisdom and
intelligence to the nations, who will hear of all
these statutes and say, 'This great nation is truly
a wise and intelligent people.' 7 [u]For what great
nation is there that has gods so close to it as the
LORD, our God, is to us whenever we call upon
him? 8 Or what great nation has statutes and
decrees that are as just as this whole law which I
am setting before you today?

Revelation at Horeb 9 "However, take care
and be earnestly on your guard not to forget the

3, 18: I charged them: the words which follow were spoken to the men of Reuben and Gad (cf Nm 32).

j 12f: Nm 32, 29. 32f; Jos 13, 8. 29. k Nm 32, 41; Jos 13, 11. 13. l Dt 4, 49; Jos 12, 3. m Jos 1, 14; 4, 12. n Nm 32, 1. 4; Jos 1, 14. o Jos 22, 4. p Dt 4, 21. q Dt 34, 4; Nm 27, 12f. r Dt 1, 38; 31, 7; Nm 27, 22f. s Dt 13, 1. t Nm 25, 3–9. u 2 Sm 7, 23.

things which your own eyes have seen, nor let them slip from your memory as long as you live, but teach them to your children[v] and to your children's children: 10*There was the day on which you stood before the LORD, your God, at Horeb, and he said to me,[w] 'Assemble the people for me; I will have them hear my words, that they may learn to fear me as long as they live in the land and may so teach their children.' 11You came near and stood at the foot of the mountain,[x] which blazed to the very sky with fire and was enveloped in a dense black cloud. 12Then the LORD spoke to you from the midst of the fire.[y] You heard the sound of the words, but saw no form; there was only a voice. 13He proclaimed to you his covenant, which he commanded you to keep: the ten commandments, which he wrote on two tablets of stone. 14The LORD charged me at that time to teach you the statutes and decrees which you are to observe over in the land you will occupy.

Danger of Idolatry 15"You saw no form at all on the day the LORD spoke to you at Horeb from the midst of the fire.[z] Be strictly on your guard, therefore, 16not to degrade yourselves by fashioning an idol to represent any figure, whether it be the form of a man or of a woman,[a] 17of any animal on the earth or of any bird that flies in the sky, 18of anything that crawls on the ground or of any fish in the waters under the earth. 19And when you look up to the heavens and behold the sun or the moon or any star among the heavenly hosts, do not be led astray into adoring them and serving them.[b] These the LORD, your God, has let fall to the lot of all other nations under the heavens; 20but you he has taken and led out of that iron foundry,* Egypt, that you might be his very own people, as you are today.[c] 21Since the LORD was angered against me on your account[d] and swore that I should not cross the Jordan nor enter the good land which he is giving you as a heritage, 22I myself shall die in this country without crossing the Jordan; but you will cross over and take possession of that good land.[e] 23Take heed, therefore, lest, forgetting the covenant which the LORD, your God, has made with you, you fashion for yourselves against his command an idol in any form whatsoever.[f] 24For the LORD, your God, is a consuming fire, a jealous God.

God's Fidelity 25"When you have children and grandchildren, and have grown old* in the land, should you then degrade yourselves by fashioning an idol in any form and by this evil done in his sight provoke the LORD, your God, 26I call heaven and earth this day to witness against you, that you shall all quickly perish from the land which you will occupy when you cross the Jordan. You shall not live in it for any length of time but shall be promptly wiped out. 27The LORD will scatter you among the nations, and there shall remain but a handful of you among the nations to which the LORD will lead you.[g] 28There you shall serve gods fashioned by the hands of man out of wood and stone, gods which can neither see nor hear, neither eat nor smell.[h] 29Yet there too you shall seek the LORD, your God; and you shall indeed find him when you search after him with your whole heart and your whole soul.[i] 30In your distress, when all these things shall have come upon you, you shall finally return to the LORD, your God, and heed his voice. 31Since the LORD, your God, is a merciful God, he will not abandon and destroy you, nor forget the covenant which under oath he made with your fathers.[j]

Proofs of God's Love 32"Ask now of the days of old, before your time, ever since God created man upon the earth; ask from one end of the sky to the other: Did anything so great ever happen before? Was it ever heard of? 33Did a people ever hear the voice of God speaking from the midst of

4, 10: Beginning here and continuing on for several verses (at least to the end of v 14) is the "reminiscence," the account of the things that the Israelites should recall and teach their children.

4, 20: Egypt is called an iron foundry, or furnace for smelting iron, because God allowed the Israelites to be afflicted there for the sake of their spiritual purification; the same expression for Egypt occurs also in 1 Kgs 8, 51; Jer 11, 4; compare the expression, "the furnace of affliction," in Is 48, 10.

4, 25: Grown old: Israel will lose the freshness of its youthful fervor.

v Dt 11, 19; Ps 78, 3–6. w Heb 12, 18f. x Ex 19, 17f. y Dt 4, 33. 36; 5, 4. z Ex 24, 12; 31, 18; 34, 28. a Dt 5, 8; Ex 20, 4. b Dt 17, 3; Jb 31, 26ff. c 1 Kgs 8, 51; Jer 11, 4. d Dt 1, 37; 3, 26. e Dt 3, 27. f Dt 4, 16. g 27f: Dt 28, 36. 62. 64. h Ps 135, 15ff; Is 44, 9. i Jer 29, 13. j Dt 31, 8.

fire, as you did, and live?[k] 34Or did any god venture to go and take a nation for himself from the midst of another nation, by testings,* by signs and wonders,[l] by war, with his strong hand and outstretched arm, and by great terrors, all of which the LORD, your God, did for you in Egypt before your very eyes? 35All this you were allowed to see that you might know the LORD is God and there is no other. 36Out of the heavens he let you hear his voice to discipline you; on earth he let you see his great fire, and you heard him speaking out of the fire. 37For love of your fathers he chose their descendants and personally led you out of Egypt by his great power, 38driving out of your way nations greater and mightier than you, so as to bring you in and to make their land your heritage, as it is today. 39This is why you must now know, and fix in your heart, that the LORD is God in the heavens above and on earth below, and that there is no other.[m] 40You must keep his statutes and commandments which I enjoin on you today, that you and your children after you may prosper, and that you may have long life on the land which the LORD, your God, is giving you forever."[n]

Cities of Refuge 41[o]Then Moses set apart three cities in the region east of the Jordan, 42that a homicide might take refuge there if he unwittingly killed his neighbor to whom he had previously borne no malice, and that he might save his life by fleeing to one of these cities: 43Bezer in the desert, in the region of the plateau, for the Reubenites; Ramoth in Gilead for the Gadites; and Golan in Bashan for the Manassehites.

II: God and His Covenant

Introduction 44This is the law which Moses set before the Israelites. 45These are the ordinances, statutes and decrees which he proclaimed to them when they had come out of Egypt 46and were beyond the Jordan in the ravine opposite Beth-peor, in the land of Sihon, king of the Amorites, who dwelt in Hishbon and whom Moses and the Israelites defeated after coming out of Egypt. 47They occupied his land and the land of Og, king of Bashan, as well—the land of these two kings of the Amorites in the region east of the Jordan: 48from Aroer on the edge of the Wadi Arnon to Mount Sion* (that is, Hermon) 49and all the Arabah east of the Jordan, as far as the Arabah Sea under the slopes of Pisgah.[p]

CHAPTER 5

The Covenant at Horeb 1Moses summoned all Israel and said to them, "Hear, O Israel, the statutes and decrees which I proclaim in your hearing this day, that you may learn them and take care to observe them. 2The LORD, our God, made a covenant with us at Horeb;[q] 3not with our fathers did he make this covenant, but with us, all of us who are alive here this day. 4The LORD spoke with you face to face on the mountain from the midst of the fire. 5[r]Since you were afraid of the fire and would not go up the mountain, I stood between the LORD and you at that time, to announce to you these words of the LORD:

The Decalogue 6[s]'I, the LORD, am your God, who brought you out of the land of Egypt,[t] that place of slavery. 7[u]You shall not have other gods besides me. 8You shall not carve idols for yourselves[v] in the shape of anything in the sky above or on the earth below or in the waters beneath the earth; 9*you shall not bow down before them or worship them. For I, the LORD, your God, am a jealous God,[w] inflicting punishments for their fathers' wickedness on the children of those who hate me, down to the third

4, 34: Testings: the demonstrations of God's power as in the ten great plagues of Egypt; cf Dt 7, 19; 29, 2.

4, 48: Sion: another name for Mount Hermon, besides those mentioned in Dt 3, 9.

5, 9f: God does not punish us for another's sins, but because of the solidarity of human society, the good or evil deeds of one generation may make their effects felt even in later generations. Yet note how God's mercy allows the good effects of virtue to last much longer than the bad effects of vice: a thousand generations compared to three or four.

k Dt 4, 36; 5, 24. 26; Ex 20, 19. **l** Dt 7, 19; 26, 8; 29, 2; Ex 7, 3; 15, 3–10; Jer 32, 21. **m** Dt 4, 35. **n** Dt 6, 2f; 12, 28. **o** 41ff: Dt 19, 2–13; Nm 35, 6–29; Jos 20, 8; 21, 27. 36f; 1 Chr 6, 71. 80. **p** Dt 3, 17. **q** Dt 28, 69. **r** Ex 24, 2. **s** 6–21: Ex 20, 2–17. **t** Ps 81, 11. **u** Ps 81, 10. **v** Dt 27, 15; Lv 26, 1; Ps 97, 7. **w** Ex 34, 14.

and fourth generation 10 but bestowing mercy,
down to the thousandth generation,[x] on the
children of those who love me and keep my
commandments.

11 'You shall not take the name of the LORD,
your God, in vain.[y] For the LORD will not leave
unpunished him who takes his name in vain.

12 'Take care to keep holy the sabbath day as
the LORD, your God, commanded you. 13 Six
days you may labor and do all your work; 14 but
the seventh day is the sabbath of the LORD, your
God.[z] No work may be done then, whether by
you, or your son or daughter, or your male or
female slave, or your ox or ass or any of your
beasts, or the alien who lives with you. Your
male and female slave should rest as you do.
15 For remember that you too were once slaves in
Egypt,[a] and the LORD, your God, brought you
from there with his strong hand and out-
stretched arm. That is why the LORD, your God,
has commanded you to observe the sabbath day.

16 [b]'Honor your father and your mother, as the
LORD, your God, has commanded you, that you
may have a long life and prosperity in the land
which the LORD, your God, is giving you.

17 [c]'You shall not kill.

18 'You shall not commit adultery.

19 'You shall not steal.

20 'You shall not bear dishonest witness against
your neighbor.

21 'You shall not covet your neighbor's wife.

'You shall not desire your neighbor's house or
field, nor his male or female slave, nor his ox or
ass, nor anything that belongs to him.'

Moses as Mediator 22 "These words, and noth-
ing more, the LORD spoke with a loud voice to
your entire assembly on the mountain from the
midst of the fire and the dense cloud. He wrote
them upon two tablets of stone and gave them to
me. 23 But when you heard the voice from the
midst of the darkness, while the mountain was
ablaze with fire, you came to me in the person of
all your tribal heads and elders, 24 and said, 'The
LORD, our God, has indeed let us see his glory
and his majesty! We have heard his voice from
the midst of the fire[d] and have found out today
that a man can still live after God has spoken
with him. 25 But why should we die now? Surely
this great fire will consume us. If we hear the
voice of the LORD, our God, any more, we shall
die.[e] 26 For what mortal has heard, as we have,
the voice of the living God speaking from the
midst of fire, and survived? 27 Go closer, you, and
hear all that the LORD, our God, will say, and
then tell us what the LORD, our God, tells you;
we will listen and obey.'[f]

28 "The LORD heard your words as you were
speaking to me and said to me, 'I have heard the
words these people have spoken to you, which
are all well said.[g] 29 Would that they might
always be of such a mind, to fear me and to keep
all my commandments! Then they and their
descendants would prosper forever. 30 Go, tell
them to return to their tents. 31 Then you wait
here near me and I will give you all the
commandments, the statutes and decrees you
must teach them, that they may observe them in
the land which I am giving them to possess.'

32 "Be careful, therefore, to do as the LORD,
your God, has commanded you, not turning
aside to the right or to the left, 33 but following
exactly the way prescribed for you by the LORD,
your God, that you may live and prosper, and
may have long life in the land which you are to
occupy.[h]

CHAPTER 6

1 "These then are the commandments, the
statutes and decrees[i] which the LORD, your
God, has ordered that you be taught to observe
in the land into which you are crossing for
conquest, 2 so that you and your son and your
grandson may fear the LORD, your God, and
keep, throughout the days of your lives, all his
statutes and commandments[j] which I enjoin on
you, and thus have long life. 3 Hear then, Israel,
and be careful to observe them, that you may
grow and prosper the more, in keeping with the

x Dt 7, 9; Ex 20, 6. y Mt 5, 33. z Gn 2, 2; Ex 20, 8; 23, 12; Heb 4, 4. a Dt 15, 15; 16, 12; 24, 18. 22. b Sir 3, 2–16; Mt 15, 4; Mk 7, 10; Lk 18, 20; Eph 6, 2. c 17–20: Mt 5, 21. 27; Lk 18, 20; Jas 2, 11. d Dt 4, 33. e Dt 18, 16. f Ex 20, 19. g Dt 18, 17. h Dt 4, 40. i Dt 4, 1; 5, 31; 12, 1. j Dt 4, 40; 5, 29; 10, 12f.

promise of the LORD, the God of your fathers, to
give you a land flowing with milk and honey.
The Great Commandment 4*"Hear, O Israel!
The LORD is our God, the LORD alone![k] 5There-
fore, you shall love the LORD, your God, with all
your heart, and with all your soul, and with all
your strength.[l] 6Take to heart these words
which I enjoin on you today. 7Drill them into
your children.[m] Speak of them at home and
abroad, whether you are busy or at rest. 8Bind
them at your wrist as a sign* and let them be as
a pendant on your forehead.[n] 9Write them on
the doorposts of your houses and on your gates.[o]
Fidelity in Prosperity 10"When the LORD,
your God, brings you into the land which he
swore to your fathers, Abraham, Isaac and Jacob,
that he would give you, a land with fine, large
cities that you did not build,[p] 11with houses full
of goods of all sorts that you did not garner, with
cisterns that you did not dig, with vineyards and
olive groves that you did not plant; and when,
therefore, you eat your fill, 12 [q]take care not to
forget the LORD, who brought you out of the
land of Egypt, that place of slavery. 13 [r]The LORD,
your God, shall you fear; him shall you serve,*
and by his name shall you swear. 14You shall not
follow other gods, such as those of the surround-
ing nations, 15lest the wrath of the LORD, your
God, flare up against you and he destroy you
from the face of the land;[s] for the LORD, your
God, who is in your midst, is a jealous God.

16 [t]"You shall not put the LORD, your God, to
the test, as you did at Massah. 17But keep the
commandments of the LORD, your God, and the
ordinances and statutes he has enjoined on you.
18Do what is right and good in the sight of the
LORD, that you may, according to his word,
prosper, and may enter in and possess the good
land which the LORD promised on oath to your
fathers, 19thrusting all your enemies out of your
way.[u]
Instruction to Children 20"Later on, when
your son asks you what these ordinances, stat-
utes and decrees mean[v] which the LORD, our
God, has enjoined on you, 21you shall say to
your son, 'We were once slaves of Pharaoh in
Egypt, but the LORD brought us out of Egypt
with his strong hand[w] 22and wrought before our
eyes signs and wonders, great and dire, against
Egypt and against Pharaoh and his whole house.
23He brought us from there to lead us into the
land he promised on oath to our fathers, and to
give it to us. 24Therefore, the LORD commanded
us to observe all these statutes in fear of the
LORD, our God, that we may always have as
prosperous and happy a life as we have today;
25and our justice before the LORD, our God, is to
consist in carefully observing all these command-
ments he has enjoined on us.'

CHAPTER 7

Destruction of Pagans 1"When the LORD,
your God, brings you into the land which you
are to enter and occupy, and dislodges great
nations before you—the Hittites, Girgashites,
Amorites, Canaanites, Perizzites, Hivites and
Jebusites:[x] seven nations more numerous and
powerful than you— 2and when the LORD, your
God, delivers them up to you and you defeat
them, you shall doom them. Make no covenant
with them[y] and show them no mercy. 3You shall
not intermarry with them, neither giving your
daughters to their sons nor taking their daugh-
ters for your sons.[z] 4For they would turn your
sons from following me to serving other gods,
and then the wrath of the LORD would flare up
against you and quickly destroy you.

6, 4f: This passage contains the basic principle of the whole Mosaic law, the keynote of the Book of Deuteronomy: since the Lord alone is God, we must love him with an undivided heart. Christ cited these words as "the greatest and the first commandment," embracing in itself the whole law of God (Mt 22, 37f and parallels).

6, 8: Bind them . . . as a sign: these injunctions were probably meant merely in a figurative sense; cf Ex 13, 9. 16. However, the later Jews understood them literally, and tied on their wrists and foreheads "phylacteries," boxes containing strips of parchment on which the words were inscribed; cf Mt 23, 5.

6, 13: Him shall you serve: here, to "serve" God means especially to "worship" him; in this sense it is quoted by our Lord (Mt 4, 10) as an argument against worshiping the devil.

k Mk 12, 29. l Dt 10, 12; 11, 13; Mt 22, 37; Mk 12, 30; Lk 10, 27. m 6f: Dt 4, 9; 11, 18; 32, 46. n Dt 11, 18; Ex 13, 9. 16; Mt 23, 5. o Dt 11, 20. p 10f: Jos 24, 13. q Dt 5, 6. r Dt 10, 20; Mt 4, 10; Lk 4, 8. s 14f: Dt 8, 19; 11, 16. 28. t Nm 20, 1–13. u Ex 23, 27; 34, 11. v Ex 12, 26; 13, 14. w Ex 20, 2. x Ex 23, 23; 33, 2. y Ex 34, 12. z 3f: Ex 34, 16; 1 Kgs 11, 1f.

5“But this is how you must deal with them:[a]
Tear down their altars, smash their sacred pillars,
chop down their sacred poles,* and destroy their
idols by fire. 6For you are a people sacred to the
LORD, your God; he has chosen you from all the
nations on the face of the earth to be a people
peculiarly his own.[b] 7It was not because you are
the largest of all nations that the LORD set his
heart on you and chose you, for you are really
the smallest of all nations. 8It was because the
LORD loved you and because of his fidelity to the
oath he had sworn to your fathers, that he
brought you out with his strong hand from the
place of slavery, and ransomed you from the
hand of Pharaoh, king of Egypt. 9[c]Understand,
then, that the LORD, your God, is God indeed,
the faithful God who keeps his merciful cove-
nant down to the thousandth generation toward
those who love him and keep his command-
ments, 10but who repays with destruction the
person who hates him; he does not dally with
such a one, but makes him personally pay for it.
11You shall therefore carefully observe the com-
mandments, the statutes and the decrees which
I enjoin on you today.

Blessings of Obedience 12[d]“As your reward
for heeding these decrees and observing them
carefully, the LORD, your God, will keep with
you the merciful covenant which he promised
on oath to your fathers. 13He will love and bless
and multiply you; he will bless the fruit of your
womb and the produce of your soil, your grain
and wine and oil, the issue of your herds and the
young of your flocks, in the land which he swore
to your fathers he would give you.[e] 14You will
be blessed above all peoples; no man or woman
among you shall be childless nor shall your
livestock be barren. 15The LORD will remove all
sickness from you; he will not afflict you with
any of the malignant diseases that you know
from Egypt, but will leave them with all your
enemies.

16“You shall consume all the nations which
the LORD, your God, will deliver up to you. You
are not to look on them with pity, lest you be
ensnared into serving their gods. 17Perhaps you
will say to yourselves,[f] ‘These nations are
greater than we. How can we dispossess them?’
18But do not be afraid of them. Rather, call to
mind what the LORD, your God, did to Pharaoh
and to all Egypt: 19the great testings which your
own eyes have seen, the signs and wonders, his
strong hand and outstretched arm with which
the LORD, your God, brought you out.[g] The
same also will he do to all the nations of whom
you are now afraid. 20Moreover, the LORD, your
God, will send hornets among them, until the
survivors who have hidden from you are de-
stroyed.[h] 21Therefore, do not be terrified by
them, for the LORD, your God, who is in your
midst, is a great and awesome God. 22He will
dislodge these nations before you little by little.
You cannot exterminate them all at once, lest
the wild beasts become too numerous for you.[i]
23The LORD, your God, will deliver them up to
you and will rout them utterly until they are
annihilated.[j] 24He will deliver their kings into
your hand, that you may make their names
perish from under the heavens. No man will be
able to stand up against you,[k] till you have put
an end to them. 25The images of their gods you
shall destroy by fire. Do not covet the silver or
gold on them, nor take it for yourselves, lest you
be ensnared by it; for it is an abomination to the
LORD, your God. 26You shall not bring any
abominable thing into your house, lest you be
doomed with it; loathe and abhor it utterly as a
thing that is doomed.

CHAPTER 8

God’s Care 1“Be careful to observe all the
commandments[l] I enjoin on you today, that you
may live and increase, and may enter in and
possess the land which the LORD promised on
oath to your fathers. 2Remember how for forty
years now the LORD, your God, has directed all
your journeying in the desert,[m] so as to test you
by affliction and find out whether or not it was

7, 5: Sacred pillars . . . poles: see note on Ex 34, 13.

a Dt 12, 3; Ex 34, 13. b Dt 14, 2; 26, 18; Ex 19, 6. c 9f: Dt 5, 9f. d 12–16: Dt 28, 1–14; Ex 23, 22–26; Lv 26, 3–13. e Dt 30, 9. f 17f: Dt 1, 28ff. g Dt 4, 34. h Ex 23, 28ff. i Ex 23, 29f. j Dt 7, 2. k Dt 11, 25. l Dt 4, 1; 6, 1. m Dt 2, 7; 29, 4; Am 2, 10.

your intention to keep his commandments. 3He therefore let you be afflicted with hunger, and then fed you with manna,[n] a food unknown to you and your fathers, in order to show you that not by bread alone* does man live, but by every word that comes forth from the mouth of the LORD. 4The clothing did not fall from you in tatters, nor did your feet swell these forty years.[o] 5So you must realize that the LORD, your God, disciplines you even as a man disciplines his son.

Danger of Prosperity 6"Therefore, keep the commandments of the LORD, your God, by walking in his ways and fearing him. 7For the LORD, your God, is bringing you into a good country,[p] a land with streams of water, with springs and fountains welling up in the hills and valleys, 8a land of wheat and barley, of vines and fig trees and pomegranates, of olive trees and of honey, 9a land where you can eat bread without stint and where you will lack nothing, a land whose stones contain iron and in whose hills you can mine copper. 10But when you have eaten your fill, you must bless the LORD, your God, for the good country he has given you. 11Be careful not to forget the LORD, your God, by neglecting his commandments and decrees and statutes which I enjoin on you today: 12lest, when you have eaten your fill, and have built fine houses and lived in them, 13and have increased your herds and flocks, your silver and gold, and all your property, 14you then become haughty of heart and unmindful of the LORD, your God, who brought you out of the land of Egypt, that place of slavery; 15who guided you through the vast and terrible desert with its saraph serpents and scorpions, its parched and waterless ground; who brought forth water for you from the flinty rock[q] 16and fed you in the desert with manna, a food unknown to your fathers, that he might afflict you and test you, but also make you prosperous in the end. 17Otherwise, you might say to yourselves,[r] 'It is my own power and the strength of my own hand that has obtained for me this wealth.' 18Remember then, it is the LORD, your God, who gives you the power to acquire wealth, by fulfilling, as he has now done, the covenant which he swore to your fathers. 19But if you forget the LORD, your God, and follow other gods, serving and worshiping them,[s] I forewarn you this day that you will perish utterly. 20Like the nations which the LORD destroys before you, so shall you too perish for not heeding the voice of the LORD, your God.

CHAPTER 9

Unmerited Success 1"Hear, O Israel! You are now about to cross the Jordan to enter in and dispossess nations greater and stronger than yourselves, having large cities fortified to the sky,[t] 2the Anakim, a people great and tall.[u] You know of them and have heard it said of them, 'Who can stand up against the Anakim?' 3Understand, then, today that it is the LORD, your God, who will cross over before you as a consuming fire; he it is who will reduce them to nothing and subdue them before you, so that you can drive them out and destroy them quickly, as the LORD promised you.[v] 4After the LORD, your God, has thrust them out of your way, do not say to yourselves, 'It is because of my merits that the LORD has brought me in to possess this land';[w] for it is really because of the wickedness of these nations that the LORD is driving them out before you. 5No, it is not because of your merits or the integrity of your heart that you are going in to take possession of their land; but the LORD, your God, is driving these nations out before you on account of their wickedness and in order to keep the promise which he made on oath to your fathers, Abraham, Isaac and Jacob. 6Understand this, therefore: it is not because of your merits that the LORD, your God, is giving you this good land to possess, for you are a stiff-necked people.

The Golden Calf 7"Bear in mind and do not forget how you angered the LORD, your God, in the desert. From the day you left the land of Egypt until you arrived in this place, you have

8, 3: Not by bread alone, etc.: quoted by our Lord in Mt 4, 4. The sense is: God takes care of those who love him even when natural means seem to fail them.

n Ex 16, 12–15. 35; Nm 11, 6–9; Mt 4, 4; Lk 4, 4. o Dt 29, 4; Neh 9, 21. p Dt 11, 10ff. q Wis 11, 4. r Dt 9, 4. s Dt 4, 25f; 30, 18. t Dt 1, 28; 4, 38. u Nm 13, 33. v Dt 31, 3; Ex 23, 27. w Dt 8, 17.

been rebellious toward the LORD.[x] 8At Horeb you so provoked the LORD that he was angry enough to destroy you,[y] 9when I had gone up the mountain to receive the stone tablets of the covenant which the LORD made with you.[z] Meanwhile I stayed on the mountain forty days and forty nights without eating or drinking, 10till the LORD gave me the two tablets of stone inscribed, by God's own finger,[a] with a copy of all the words that the LORD spoke to you on the mountain from the midst of the fire on the day of the assembly. 11Then, at the end of the forty days and forty nights, when the LORD had given me the two stone tablets of the covenant, 12he said to me,[b] 'Go down from here now, quickly, for your people whom you have brought out of Egypt have become depraved; they have already turned aside from the way I pointed out to them and have made for themselves a molten idol. 13I have seen now how stiff-necked this people is,' the LORD said to me. 14'Let me be, that I may destroy them and blot out their name from under the heavens. I will then make of you a nation mightier and greater than they.'

15"When I had come down again from the blazing, fiery mountain, with the two tablets of the covenant in both my hands,[c] 16I saw how you had sinned against the LORD, your God: you had already turned aside from the way which the LORD had pointed out to you by making for yourselves a molten calf! 17Raising the two tablets with both hands I threw them from me and broke them before your eyes.[d] 18Then, as before, I lay prostrate before the LORD for forty days and forty nights without eating or drinking, because of all the sin you had committed in the sight of the LORD and the evil you had done to provoke him.[e] 19For I dreaded the fierce anger of the LORD against you: his wrath would destroy you.[f] Yet once again the LORD listened to me. 20With Aaron, too, the LORD was deeply angry, and would have killed him had I not prayed for him also at that time. 21Then, taking the calf, the sinful object you had made, and fusing it with fire, I ground it down to powder as fine as dust, which I threw into the wadi that went down the mountainside.[g]

22"At Taberah, at Massah, and at Kibroth-hattaavah likewise, you provoked the LORD to anger.[h] 23And when he sent you up from Kadesh-barnea to take possession of the land he was giving you, you rebelled against this command of the LORD, your God, and would not trust or obey him.[i] 24Ever since I have known you, you have been rebels against the LORD.

25"Those forty days, then, and forty nights, I lay prostrate before the LORD, because he had threatened to destroy you. 26This was my prayer to him: O Lord GOD, destroy not your people, the heritage which your majesty has ransomed and brought out of Egypt with your strong hand. 27Remember your servants, Abraham, Isaac and Jacob. Look not upon the stubbornness of this people nor upon their wickedness and sin, 28lest the people from whose land you have brought us say, 'The LORD was not able to bring them into the land he promised them'; or 'Out of hatred for them, he brought them out to slay them in the desert.'[j] 29They are, after all, your people and your heritage, whom you have brought out by your great power and with your outstretched arm.[k]

CHAPTER 10

1"At that time the LORD said to me, 'Cut two tablets of stone like the former;[l] then come up the mountain to me. Also make an ark of wood. 2I will write upon the tablets the commandments that were on the former tablets that you broke, and you shall place them in the ark.' 3So I made an ark of acacia wood, and cut two tablets of stone like the former, and went up the mountain carrying the two tablets.[m] 4[n]The LORD then wrote on them, as he had written before, the ten commandments which he spoke to you on the mountain from the midst of the fire on the day of the assembly. After the LORD had given them to me, 5I turned and came down the

x Dt 31, 27; Ex 14, 11; Nm 14, 11. y Ex 32, 4; Ps 106, 19. z Ex 24, 12. 18; 34, 28. a Ex 31, 18. b 12ff: Ex 32, 7–10. c Ex 32, 15. d 16f: Ex 32, 19. e Ex 32, 31; 34, 28. f Dt 10, 10; Ex 32, 10. g Ex 32, 20. h Ex 17, 7; Nm 11, 1ff. 34. i Nm 14, 1–4; Ps 106, 24f. j Nm 14, 14ff. k Dt 4, 20; Ex 6, 6f. l Ex 34, 1. m Ex 34, 4. n Ex 20, 1–17; 34, 28.

mountain, and placed the tablets in the ark I had
made.[o] There they have remained, in keeping
with the command the LORD gave me.

6[The Israelites set out from Beeroth Bene-
jaakan[p] for Moserah, where Aaron died and was
buried, his son Eleazar succeeding him in the
priestly office. 7From there they set out for
Gudgodah, and from Gudgodah for Jotbathah,[q] a
region where there is water in the wadies.]

8"At that time the LORD set apart the tribe of
Levi to carry the ark of the covenant of the
LORD,[r] to be in attendance before the LORD and
minister to him, and to give blessings in his
name, as they have done to this day. 9For this
reason, Levi has no share in the heritage with his
brothers;[s] the LORD himself is his heritage, as
the LORD, your God, has told him.

10"After I had spent these other forty days and
forty nights on the mountain, and the LORD had
once again heard me and decided not to destroy
you, 11he said to me, 'Go now and set out at the
head of your people,[t] that they may enter in and
occupy the land which I swore to their fathers I
would give them.'

The Lord's Majesty 12"And now, Israel, what
does the LORD, your God, ask of you but to fear
the LORD, your God, and follow his ways exactly,
to love and serve the LORD, your God, with all
your heart and all your soul,[u] 13to keep the
commandments and statutes of the LORD which
I enjoin on you today for your own good?
14Think! The heavens, even the highest heav-
ens,* belong to the LORD, your God, as well as
the earth and everything on it.[v] 15Yet in his love
for your fathers the LORD was so attached to
them as to choose you, their descendants, in
preference to all other peoples, as indeed he has
now done.[w] 16Circumcise your hearts,* there-
fore, and be no longer stiff-necked. 17For the
LORD, your God, is the God of gods, the LORD of
lords, the great God, mighty and awesome, who
has no favorites, accepts no bribes;[x] 18who
executes justice for the orphan and the widow,
and befriends the alien, feeding and clothing
him. 19So you too must befriend the alien, for
you were once aliens yourselves in the land of
Egypt.[y] 20The LORD, your God, shall you fear,
and him shall you serve; hold fast to him and
swear by his name.[z] 21He is your glory, he, your
God, who has done for you those great and
terrible things which your own eyes have seen.
22Your ancestors went down to Egypt seventy
strong,[a] and now the LORD, your God, has made
you as numerous as the stars of the sky.

CHAPTER 11

The Wonders of the Lord 1"Love the LORD,
your God, therefore, and always heed his
charge: his statutes, decrees and command-
ments. 2It is not your children, who have not
known it from experience, but you yourselves
who must now understand the discipline of the
LORD, your God; his majesty, his strong hand
and outstretched arm; 3the signs and deeds he
wrought among the Egyptians, on Pharaoh, king
of Egypt, and on all his land;[b] 4what he did to
the Egyptian army and to their horses and
chariots, engulfing them in the water of the Red
Sea as they pursued you,[c] and bringing ruin
upon them even to this day; 5what he did for
you in the desert until you arrived in this place;
6and what he did to the Reubenites Dathan and
Abiram, sons of Eliab, when the ground opened
its mouth and swallowed them up out of the
midst of Israel, with their families and tents and
every living thing that belonged to them.[d] 7With
your own eyes you have seen all these great
deeds that the LORD has done. 8Keep all the
commandments, then, which I enjoin on you
today, that you may be strong enough to enter in
and take possession of the land into which you
are crossing, 9and that you may have long life on

10, 14: Even the highest heavens: literally, "and the heavens of the heavens"; compare the phrase, "the third heaven," in 2 Cor 12, 2.

10, 16: Circumcise your hearts: cf Dt 30, 6; Jer 4, 4; Rom 2, 29. The "uncircumcised heart" (Lv 26, 41; Jer 9, 25; Ez 44, 7. 9) is closed and unreceptive to divine grace and guidance, just as "uncircumcised ears" (Jer 6, 10) are closed to sound, and "uncircumcised lips" (Ex 6, 12. 30) do not open well in speech.

o Ex 40, 20; 1 Kgs 8, 9. p Nm 33, 31. q Nm 33, 32f. r Nm 3, 6; 6, 23–27; 16, 9. s Nm 18, 20. t Ex 32, 34; 33, 1. u Dt 6, 2. 5. v Neh 9, 6. w Dt 7, 6ff. x 2 Chr 19, 7; Jb 34, 19; Wis 6, 7; Acts 10, 34; Rom 2, 11; Gal 2, 6. y Ex 22, 21; 23, 9; Lv 19, 33f. z Dt 6, 13; Mt 4, 10; Lk 4, 8. a Gn 46, 27; Ex 1, 5; Acts 7, 14. b Dt 6, 22; Ps 78, 42–51. c Ex 14, 26ff; 15, 9; Pss 78, 53; 106, 11. d Nm 16, 31ff.

the land which the LORD swore to your fathers he would give to them and their descendants, a land flowing with milk and honey.

The Gift of Rain 10“For the land which you are to enter and occupy is not like the land of Egypt from which you have come, where you would sow your seed and then water it by hand, as in a vegetable garden. 11 [e]No, the land into which you are crossing for conquest is a land of hills and valleys that drinks in rain from the heavens, 12a land which the LORD, your God, looks after; his eyes are upon it continually from the beginning of the year to the end. 13*If, then, you truly heed my commandments which I enjoin on you today, loving and serving the LORD, your God, with all your heart and all your soul,[f] 14I will give the seasonal rain to your land, the early rain* and the late rain, that you may have your grain, wine and oil to gather in; 15and I will bring forth grass in your fields for your animals.[g] Thus you may eat your fill. 16But be careful lest your heart be so lured away that you serve other gods and worship them.[h] 17For then the wrath of the LORD will flare up against you and he will close up the heavens, so that no rain will fall, and the soil will not yield its crops, and you will soon perish from the good land he is giving you.

Reward of Fidelity 18 [i]“Therefore, take these words of mine into your heart and soul. Bind them at your wrist as a sign, and let them be a pendant on your forehead. 19Teach them to your children, speaking of them at home and abroad, whether you are busy or at rest. 20And write them on the doorposts of your houses and on your gates, 21so that, as long as the heavens are above the earth, you and your children may live on in the land which the LORD swore to your fathers he would give them.

22“For if you are careful to observe all these commandments I enjoin on you, loving the LORD, your God, and following his ways exactly, and holding fast to him, 23the LORD will drive all these nations out of your way,[j] and you will dispossess nations greater and mightier than yourselves. 24 [k]Every place where you set foot shall be yours: from the desert and from Lebanon, from the Euphrates River to the Western Sea,* shall be your territory. 25None shall stand up against you; the LORD, your God, will spread the fear and dread of you through any land where you set foot, as he promised you.[l]

A Blessing and a Curse 26 [m]“I set before you here, this day, a blessing and a curse: 27a blessing for obeying the commandments of the LORD, your God, which I enjoin on you today; 28a curse if you do not obey the commandments of the LORD, your God, but turn aside from the way I ordain for you today, to follow other gods, whom you have not known. 29When the LORD, your God, brings you into the land which you are to enter and occupy, then you shall pronounce the blessing on Mount Gerizim,[n] the curse* on Mount Ebal. 30[Are they not beyond the Jordan, on the other side of the western road in the country of the Canaanites who live in the Arabah, opposite the Gilgal beside the terebinth of Moreh?] 31For you are about to cross the Jordan to enter and occupy the land which the LORD, your God, is giving you. When therefore, you take possession of it and settle there, 32be careful to observe all the statutes and decrees that I set before you today.

III: Exposition of the Law

CHAPTER 12

One Sanctuary 1“These are the statutes and decrees which you must be careful to observe in the land which the LORD, the God of your fathers, has given you to occupy, as long as you live on its soil. 2Destroy without fail every place on the high mountains, on the hills, and under

11, 13ff: As often in the Prophets, the discourse passes into the words of God himself. Cf Dt 7, 4; 17, 3; 28, 20; 29, 4f.

11, 14: The early rain: the rains which begin in October or November and continue intermittently throughout the winter. The late rain: the heavy showers of March and April. In Palestine the crops are sown in the autumn and reaped in the spring.

11, 24: The Western Sea: the Mediterranean.

11, 29: You shall pronounce the blessing . . . the curse: for the full ceremony, see chapters 27 and 28. Gerizim . . . Ebal: adjacent mountains in Samaria with a deep ravine between them. Their summits command an excellent view of the entire country.

e 11f: Dt 8, 7. f 13f: Dt 10, 12; Lv 26, 4. g Ps 104, 14. h 16f: Dt 4, 25f; 6, 14. i 18–21: Dt 6, 6–9. j Dt 7, 1; 9, 1. k Ex 23, 31. l Dt 2, 25; 7, 24; Ex 23, 27. m 26ff: Dt 28, 2–45; 30, 1. 15. 19. n Dt 27, 12f.

every leafy tree where the nations you are to dispossess worship their gods.[o] 3 Tear down their altars, smash their sacred pillars, destroy by fire their sacred poles, and shatter the idols of their gods, that you may stamp out the remembrance of them in any such place.

4 "That is not how you are to worship the LORD, your God. 5 Instead,[p] you shall resort to the place which the LORD, your God, chooses out of all your tribes and designates as his dwelling 6 and there you shall bring your holocausts and sacrifices, your tithes and personal contributions, your votive and freewill offerings, and the firstlings of your herds and flocks. 7 There, too, before the LORD, your God, you and your families shall eat and make merry over all your undertakings, because the LORD, your God, has blessed you. 8 You shall not do as we are now doing; here, everyone does what seems right to himself, 9 since you have not yet reached your resting place, the heritage which the LORD, your God, will give you. 10 But after you have crossed the Jordan and dwell in the land which the LORD, your God, is giving you as a heritage, when he has given you rest from all your enemies round about and you live there in security, 11 then to the place which the LORD, your God, chooses as the dwelling place for his name you shall bring all the offerings I command you: your holocausts and sacrifices, your tithes and personal contributions, and every special offering you have vowed to the LORD. 12 You shall make merry before the LORD, your God, with your sons and daughters, your male and female slaves, as well as with the Levite who belongs to your community but has no share of his own in your heritage. 13 Take care not to offer up your holocausts in any place you fancy, 14 but offer them up in the place which the LORD chooses from among your tribes; there you shall make whatever offerings I enjoin upon you.

Profane and Sacred Meals 15 "However, in any of your communities you may slaughter and eat to your heart's desire as much meat as the LORD, your God, has blessed you with; and the unclean as well as the clean may eat it, as they do the gazelle or the deer. 16 Only, you shall not partake of the blood, but must pour it out on the ground like water.[q] 17 Moreover, you shall not, in your own communities, partake of your tithe of grain or wine or oil, of the first-born of your herd or flock, of any offering you have vowed, of your freewill offerings, or of your personal contributions. 18 These you must eat before the LORD, your God, in the place he chooses, along with your son and daughter, your male and female slave, and the Levite who belongs to your community; and there, before the LORD, you shall make merry over all your undertakings. 19 Take care, also, that you do not neglect the Levite as long as you live in the land.[r]

20 "After the LORD, your God, has enlarged your territory, as he promised you,[s] when you wish meat for food,* you may eat it at will, to your heart's desire; 21 and if the place which the LORD, your God, chooses for the abode of his name is too far, you may slaughter in the manner I have told you any of your herd or flock that the LORD has given you, and eat it to your heart's desire in your own community. 22 You may eat it as you would the gazelle or the deer: the unclean and the clean eating it alike. 23 But make sure that you do not partake of the blood; for blood is life, and you shall not consume this seat of life with the flesh. 24 Do not partake of the blood, therefore, but pour it out on the ground like water. 25 Abstain from it, that you and your children after you may prosper for doing what is right in the sight of the LORD. 26 However, any sacred gifts or votive offerings that you may have, you shall bring with you to the place which the LORD chooses, 27 and there you must offer both the flesh and the blood of your holocausts on the altar of the LORD, your God; of your other sacrifices the blood indeed must be poured out against the altar of the LORD, your God,[t] but their flesh may be eaten. 28 Be careful to heed all these commandments I enjoin on

12, 20: Meat for food: as on special feasts. Meat was not eaten every day in Israel, even by the wealthy.

o 2f: Dt 7, 5; Ex 23, 24; 34, 13. p 5–7. 11f: Dt 14, 22–26; 15, 19f; 16, 2. 10f. 14f; 26, 2. q Dt 15, 23; Gn 9, 4; Lv 3, 17. r Dt 14, 27. s Dt 19, 8; Gn 28, 14; Ex 34, 24. t Lv 17, 11.

you, that you and your descendants may always prosper for doing what is good and right in the sight of the LORD, your God.

Pagan Rites 29“When the LORD, your God, removes the nations from your way as you advance to dispossess them, be on your guard! Otherwise, once they have been wiped out before you and you have replaced them and are settled in their land, 30you will be lured into following them. Do not inquire regarding their gods, ‘How did these nations worship their gods? I, too, would do the same.’ 31You shall not thus worship the LORD, your God, because they offered to their gods every abomination that the LORD detests, even burning their sons and daughters to their gods.[u]

CHAPTER 13

Penalties for Idolatry 1“Every command that I enjoin on you, you shall be careful to observe, neither adding to it nor subtracting from it.

2“If there arises among you a prophet or a dreamer* who promises you a sign or wonder, 3urging you to follow other gods, whom you have not known, and to serve them: even though the sign or wonder he has foretold you comes to pass, 4pay no attention to the words of that prophet or that dreamer; for the LORD, your God, is testing you to learn whether you really love him with all your heart and with all your soul. 5The LORD, your God, shall you follow, and him shall you fear; his commandment shall you observe, and his voice shall you heed, serving him and holding fast to him alone. 6[v]But that prophet or that dreamer shall be put to death, because, in order to lead you astray from the way which the LORD, your God, has directed you to take, he has preached apostasy from the LORD, your God, who brought you out of the land of Egypt and ransomed you from that place of slavery. Thus shall you purge the evil from your midst.

7“If your own full brother, or your son or daughter, or your beloved wife, or your intimate friend, entices you secretly to serve other gods, whom you and your fathers have not known, 8gods of any other nation, near at hand or far away, from one end of the earth to the other: 9do not yield to him or listen to him, nor look with pity upon him, to spare or shield him, 10but kill him. Your hand shall be the first raised to slay him; the rest of the people shall join in with you. 11You shall stone him to death, because he sought to lead you astray from the LORD, your God, who brought you out of the land of Egypt, that place of slavery. 12And all Israel, hearing of it, shall fear and never again do such evil as this in your midst.

13“If, in any of the cities which the LORD, your God, gives you to dwell in, you hear it said 14that certain scoundrels have sprung up among you and have led astray the inhabitants of their city to serve other gods whom you have not known, 15you must inquire carefully into the matter and investigate it thoroughly. If you find that it is true and an established fact that this abomination has been committed in your midst, 16[w]you shall put the inhabitants of that city to the sword, dooming the city and all life that is in it, even its cattle, to the sword. 17Having heaped up all its spoils in the middle of its square, you shall burn the city with all its spoils as a whole burnt offering to the LORD, your God. Let it be a heap of ruins forever, never to be rebuilt. 18You shall not retain anything that is doomed, that the blazing wrath of the LORD may die down and he may show you mercy and in his mercy for you may multiply you as he promised your fathers on oath; 19because you have heeded the voice of the LORD, your God, keeping all his commandments which I enjoin on you today, doing what is right in his sight.

CHAPTER 14

Pagan Mourning Rites 1“You are children of the LORD, your God. You shall not gash yourselves nor shave the hair above your foreheads for the dead.[x] 2For you are a people sacred to

13, 2. 4. 6: Dreamer: a false prophet who pretended to have received revelations from God in his dreams; cf Jer 23, 25–32; Zec 10, 2. But dreams could also be a channel of true prophecy (Nm 12, 6; Jl 3, 1) and of genuine revelations (Gn 20, 3. 6; 31, 10. 24; 37, 5. 9; Mt 1, 20; 2, 12f. 19; etc.).

u Lv 18, 21: Jer 7, 31. v 6–10. 14: Dt 6, 14; 17, 2–7. w 16f: Jos 6, 18. 24; 7, 26; 8, 28. x Lv 19, 28.

the LORD, your God, who has chosen you from
all the nations on the face of the earth to be a
people peculiarly his own.[y]
Clean and Unclean Animals 3“You shall not
eat any abominable thing.[z] 4[a]These are the
animals you may eat: the ox, the sheep, the
goat, 5the red deer, the gazelle, the roe deer, the
ibex, the addax, the oryx,* and the mountain
sheep. 6Any animal that has hoofs you may eat,
provided it is cloven-footed and chews the cud.
7But you shall not eat any of the following that
only chew the cud or only have cloven hoofs:
the camel, the hare and the rock badger, which
indeed chew the cud, but do not have hoofs and
are therefore unclean for you; 8and the pig,
which indeed has hoofs and is cloven-footed, but
does not chew the cud and is therefore unclean
for you. Their flesh you shall not eat, and their
dead bodies you shall not touch.[b]

9“Of the various creatures that live in the wa-
ter, whatever has both fins and scales you may
eat, 10but all those that lack either fins or scales
you shall not eat; they are unclean for you.

11“You may eat all clean birds. 12But you shall
not eat any of the following: the eagle, the
vulture, the osprey, 13the various kites and
falcons, 14all the various species of crows, 15the
ostrich, the nightjar, the gull, the various species
of hawks, 16the owl, the screech owl, the ibis,
17the desert owl, the buzzard, the cormorant,
18the stork, the various species of herons, the
hoopoe, and the bat. 19*All winged insects, too,
are unclean for you and shall not be eaten. 20But
you may eat any clean winged creatures.

21“You must not eat any animal that has died
of itself, for you are a people sacred to the LORD,
your God.[c] But you may give it to an alien who
belongs to your community, and he may eat it,
or you may sell it to a foreigner.

“You shall not boil a kid in its mother’s milk.*
Tithes 22“Each year you shall tithe all the
produce that grows in the field you have sown;[d]
23then in the place which the LORD, your God,
chooses as the dwelling place of his name[e] you
shall eat in his presence your tithe of the grain,
wine and oil, as well as the firstlings of your herd
and flock, that you may learn always to fear the
LORD, your God. 24If, however, the journey is
too much for you and you are not able to bring
your tithe, because the place which the LORD,
your God, chooses for the abode of his name is
too far for you, considering how the LORD has
blessed you,* 25you may exchange the tithe for
money and, with the purse of money in hand, go
to the place which the LORD, your God, chooses.
26You may then exchange the money for what-
ever you desire, oxen or sheep, wine or strong
drink, or anything else you would enjoy, and
there before the LORD, your God, you shall
partake of it and make merry with your family.
27But do not neglect the Levite who belongs to
your community, for he has no share in the
heritage with you.[f]

28“At the end of every third year you shall
bring out all the tithes of your produce for that
year and deposit them in community stores,
29that the Levite who has no share in the heritage
with you, and also the alien, the orphan and the
widow who belong to your community, may
come and eat their fill;[g] so that the LORD, your
God, may bless you in all that you undertake.

CHAPTER 15

Debts and the Poor 1“At the end of every
seven-year period* you shall have a relaxation of
debts,[h] 2which shall be observed as follows.
Every creditor shall relax his claim on what he
has loaned his neighbor; he must not press his

14, 5: The gazelle, the addax, the oryx: species of antelopes. The ibex: a species of wild goat.

14, 19f: The apparent contradiction is to be resolved in the light of Lv 11, 20–23; the unclean winged insects are those that walk on the ground; the clean winged creatures are those that leap on the ground, such as certain species of locusts.

14, 21: Boil a kid in its mother’s milk: see note on Ex 23, 19.

14, 24: Considering how the Lord has blessed you: should the Israelite farmer be blessed with an abundant harvest, a tenth of this would be too much to transport for a great distance.

15, 1: At the end of every seven-year period: in every seventh, or sabbatical, year. Cf Dt 15, 9; 31, 10; and compare Jer 34, 14 with Dt 15, 12. A relaxation of debts: it is uncertain whether a full cancellation of debts is meant, or merely a suspension of payment on them or on their interest among the Israelites. Cf Ex 23, 11 where the same Hebrew root is used of a field that is “let lie fallow” in the sabbatical year.

y Dt 7, 6. z Ez 4, 14; Acts 10, 14. a 4–20; Lv 11, 2–23. b Lv 11, 26. c Ex 22, 30; 23, 19; 34, 26. d Lv 27, 30. e 23f: Dt 12, 5ff. f Dt 12, 12. 19. g 28f: Dt 26, 12. h Neh 10, 31.

neighbor, his kinsman, because a relaxation in
honor of the LORD has been proclaimed. 3You
may press a foreigner, but you shall relax the
claim on your kinsman for what is yours.[i] 4Nay,
more! since the LORD, your God, will bless you
abundantly in the land he will give you to
occupy as your heritage, there should be no one
of you in need. 5If you but heed the voice of the
LORD, your God, and carefully observe all these
commandments which I enjoin on you today,
6you will lend to many nations, and borrow from
none;[j] you will rule over many nations, and
none will rule over you, since the LORD, your
God, will bless you as he promised. 7If one of
your kinsmen in any community is in need in
the land which the LORD, your God, is giving
you, you shall not harden your heart nor close
your hand to him in his need. 8Instead, you shall
open your hand to him and freely lend him
enough to meet his need.[k] 9Be on your guard
lest, entertaining the mean thought that the
seventh year, the year of relaxation, is near, you
grudge help to your needy kinsman and give him
nothing; else he will cry to the LORD against you
and you will be held guilty. 10When you give to
him, give freely and not with ill will; for the
LORD, your God, will bless you for this in all your
works and undertakings. 11The needy will never
be lacking* in the land; that is why I command
you to open your hand to your poor and needy
kinsman in your country.[l]

Hebrew Slaves 12"If your kinsman, a Hebrew
man or woman, sells himself to you, he is to
serve you for six years, but in the seventh year
you shall dismiss him from your service, a free
man.[m] 13When you do so, you shall not send
him away empty-handed, 14but shall weight him
down with gifts from your flock and threshing
floor and wine press, in proportion to the bless-
ing the LORD, your God, has bestowed on you.
15For remember that you too were once slaves in
the land of Egypt, and the LORD, your God,
ransomed you. That is why I am giving you this
command today.[n] 16If, however, he tells you
that he does not wish to leave you, because he is
devoted to you and your household, since he
fares well with you, 17you shall take an awl and
thrust it through his ear* into the door, and he
shall then be your slave forever.[o] Your female
slave, also, you shall treat in the same way.
18You must not be reluctant to let your slave go
free, since the service he has given you for six
years was worth twice a hired man's salary; then
also the LORD, your God, will bless you in
everything you do.

Firstlings 19[p]"You shall consecrate to the
LORD, your God, all the male firstlings of your
herd and of your flock. You shall not work the
firstlings of your cattle, nor shear the firstlings of
your flock. 20Year after year you and your family
shall eat them before the LORD, your God, in the
place he chooses.[q] 21If, however, a firstling is
lame or blind or has any other serious defect,
you shall not sacrifice it to the LORD, your God,
22but in your own communities you may eat it,
the unclean and the clean eating it alike, as you
would a gazelle or a deer. 23Only, you shall not
partake of its blood, which must be poured out
on the ground like water.[r]

CHAPTER 16

Feast of the Passover 1"Observe the month of
Abib* by keeping the Passover of the LORD, your
God,[s] since it was in the month of Abib that he
brought you by night out of Egypt. 2You shall
offer the Passover sacrifice from your flock or
your herd to the LORD, your God, in the place
which he chooses as the dwelling place of his
name. 3[t]You shall not eat leavened bread with
it. For seven days you shall eat with it only
unleavened bread, the bread of affliction, that
you may remember as long as you live the day of
your departure from the land of Egypt; for in
frightened haste you left the land of Egypt.

15, 11: The needy will never be lacking: compare the words of Christ, "The poor you have always with you" (Mt 26, 11).

15, 17: His ear: cf Ex 21, 6 and the note there.

16, 1: Abib: "ear of grain, ripe grain," the name of the month in which the barley harvest fell, corresponding to our March and April; at a later period this month received the Babylonian name of "Nisan."

i Dt 23, 20. j Dt 28, 12f. k Lv 25, 35; Sir 29, 1f; Mt 5, 42. l Dt 15, 8; Sir 29, 12. m Ex 21, 2; Jer 34, 14. n Dt 5, 15. o 16f: Ex 21, 5f. p Ex 13, 11. q Dt 14, 23. r 21ff: Dt 12, 15f; Lv 22, 20. s 1–8: Ex 12, 2–20; 23, 15; Nm 28, 16ff. 24f. t 3f: Ex 13, 6f; 34, 18.

4 Nothing leavened may be found in all your territory for seven days, and none of the meat which you sacrificed on the evening of the first day shall be kept overnight for the next day.

5 "You may not sacrifice the Passover in any of the communities which the LORD, your God, gives you; 6 only at the place which he chooses as the dwelling place of his name, and in the evening at sunset, on the anniversary of your departure from Egypt, shall you sacrifice the Passover. 7 You shall cook and eat it at the place the LORD, your God, chooses; then in the morning you may return to your tents. 8 For six days you shall eat unleavened bread, and on the seventh there shall be a solemn meeting in honor of the LORD, your God; on that day you shall not do any sort of work.

Feast of Weeks 9 [u]"You shall count off seven weeks, computing them from the day when the sickle is first put to the standing grain. 10 You shall then keep the feast of Weeks* in honor of the LORD, your God, and the measure of your own freewill offering shall be in proportion to the blessing the LORD, your God, has bestowed on you. 11 In the place which the LORD, your God, chooses as the dwelling place of his name,[v] you shall make merry in his presence together with your son and daughter, your male and female slave, and the Levite who belongs to your community, as well as the alien, the orphan and the widow among you. 12 Remember that you too were once slaves in Egypt, and carry out these statutes carefully.

Feast of Booths 13 [w]"You shall celebrate the feast of Booths for seven days, when you have gathered in the produce from your threshing floor and wine press.* 14 You shall make merry at your feast,[x] together with your son and daughter, your male and female slave, and also the Levite, the alien, the orphan and the widow who belong to your community. 15 For seven days you shall celebrate this pilgrim feast in honor of the LORD, your God, in the place which he chooses; since the LORD, your God, has blessed you in all your crops and in all your undertakings, you shall do naught but make merry.

16 "Three times a year,[y] then, every male among you shall appear before the LORD, your God, in the place which he chooses: at the feast of Unleavened Bread, at the feast of Weeks, and at the feast of Booths. No one shall appear before the LORD empty-handed, 17 but each of you with as much as he can give, in proportion to the blessings which the LORD, your God, has bestowed on you.

Judges 18 "You shall appoint judges and officials throughout your tribes to administer true justice for the people in all the communities which the LORD, your God, is giving you. 19 You shall not distort justice; you must be impartial.[z] You shall not take a bribe; for a bribe blinds the eyes even of the wise and twists the words even of the just. 20 Justice and justice alone shall be your aim, that you may have life and may possess the land which the LORD, your God, is giving you.

Pagan Worship 21 *"You shall not plant a sacred pole of any kind of wood beside the altar of the LORD, your God, which you will build;[a] 22 nor shall you erect a sacred pillar,* such as the LORD, your God, detests.

CHAPTER 17

1 "You shall not sacrifice to the LORD, your God, from the herd or from the flock an animal with any serious defect;[b] that would be an abomination to the LORD, your God.

2 [c]"If there is found among you, in any one of the communities which the LORD, your God, gives you, a man or a woman who does evil in the sight of the LORD, your God, and transgresses his covenant, 3 by serving other gods, or by worshiping the sun or the moon or any of the host of the sky, against my command;[d] 4 and if, on being informed of it, you find by careful

16, 10: Feast of Weeks: later known more commonly as "Pentecost."

16, 13: See note on Lv 23, 34.

16, 21—17, 7: This section seems to be out of its proper place, since it interrupts the natural sequence of the laws for the judges (Dt 16, 18–20 and 17, 8–13). It probably belongs to the similar section, Dt 12, 29—14, 2.

16, 21f: Sacred pole . . . sacred pillar: see note on Ex 34, 13.

u 9–12: Lv 23, 15–21. v Dt 12, 5. 7. 12. 18. w 13–15: Ex 23, 16; Lv 23, 34–43; Nm 29, 12–38. x Dt 16, 11. y Ex 23, 14f. 17; 34, 23; 2 Chr 8, 13. z Dt 1, 17; Ex 23, 8. a 1 Kgs 14, 15; 2 Chr 33, 3. b Lv 22, 20. c 2–7: Dt 13, 6–15. d Dt 4, 19.

investigation that it is true and an established fact that this abomination has been committed in Israel: [5]you shall bring the man (or woman) who has done the evil deed out to your city gates* and stone him to death. [6]The testimony of two or three witnesses is required for putting a person to death;[e] no one shall be put to death on the testimony of only one witness. [7]At the execution, the witnesses are to be the first to raise their hands against him; afterward all the people are to join in.[f] Thus shall you purge the evil from your midst.

Judges [8]"If in your own community there is a case at issue which proves too complicated for you to decide, in a matter of bloodshed or of civil rights or of personal injury, you shall then go up to the place which the LORD, your God, chooses, [9]to the levitical priests or to the judge who is in office at that time. They shall study the case and then hand down to you their decision.[g] [10]According to this decision that they give you in the place which the LORD chooses, you shall act, being careful to do exactly as they direct. [11]You shall carry out the directions they give you and the verdict they pronounce for you, without turning aside to the right or to the left from the decision they hand down to you. [12]Any man who has the insolence to refuse to listen to the priest* who officiates there in the ministry of the LORD, your God, or to the judge, shall die. Thus shall you purge the evil from your midst. [13]And all the people, on hearing of it, shall fear, and never again be so insolent.

The King [14]"When you have come into the land which the LORD, your God, is giving you, and have occupied it and settled in it, should you then decide to have a king over you like all the surrounding nations,[h] [15]you shall set that man over you as your king whom the LORD, your God, chooses.[i] He whom you set over you as king must be your kinsman; a foreigner, who is no kin of yours, you may not set over you. [16]But he shall not have a great number of horses;* nor shall he make his people go back again to Egypt to acquire them, against the LORD's warning that you must never go back that way again.[j] [17]Neither shall he have a great number of wives, lest his heart be estranged,[k] nor shall he accumulate a vast amount of silver and gold. [18]When he is enthroned in his kingdom, he shall have a copy of this law made from the scroll that is in the custody of the levitical priests.[l] [19]He shall keep it with him and read it all the days of his life that he may learn to fear the LORD, his God, and to heed and fulfill all the words of this law and these statutes. [20]Let him not become estranged from his countrymen through pride, nor turn aside to the right or to the left from these commandments. Then he and his descendants will enjoy a long reign in Israel.

CHAPTER 18

Priests [1]"The whole priestly tribe of Levi shall have no share in the heritage with Israel; they shall live on the oblations of the LORD and the portions due to him.[m] [2]Levi shall have no heritage among his brothers; the LORD himself is his heritage, as he has told him. [3]The priests shall have a right to the following things from the people: from those who are offering a sacrifice, whether the victim is from the herd or from the flock, the priest shall receive the shoulder, the jowls and the stomach. [4]You shall also give him the first fruits of your grain and wine and oil,[n] as well as the first fruits of the shearing of your flock; [5]for the LORD, your God, has chosen him and his sons out of all your tribes to be always in attendance to minister in the name of the LORD.

[6]"When a Levite goes from one of your

17, 5: Out to your city gates: outside the gates in an unclean place; cf Lv 24, 14; Nm 15, 36; Acts 7, 58; Heb 13, 12.

17, 12: The priest: the high priest; the judge: a layman. The former presided over the court in cases which directly concerned religion, the latter in cases of a more secular nature; cf 2 Chr 19, 8–11.

17, 16: Horses: chariotry for war. The Lord's warning: the same warning is also referred to in Dt 28, 68, although it is not mentioned explicitly elsewhere in the Pentateuch. We know from other sources that Egypt used to export war horses to Palestine. The danger envisioned here is that some king might make Israel a vassal of Egypt for the sake of such military aid.

e Dt 19, 15; Nm 35, 30; Mt 18, 16; Jn 8, 17; 2 Cor 13, 1. f Dt 13, 10. g Dt 21, 5; 2 Chr 19, 8. h 1 Sm 8, 5. 19f. i 1 Sm 9, 16; 10, 24; 16, 12. j Dt 28, 68; 1 Kgs 4, 26; 10, 26. k 1 Kgs 11; 3f; Neh 13, 26. l Dt 31, 9. 26. m Nm 18, 8f. 20–24; 1 Cor 9, 13. n Nm 18, 12; 2 Chr 31, 5.

communities anywhere in Israel in which he ordinarily resides, to visit, as his heart may desire, the place which the LORD chooses, [7]he may minister there in the name of the LORD, his God, like all his fellow Levites who are in attendance there before the LORD. [8]He shall then receive the same portions to eat as the rest, along with his monetary offerings and heirlooms.

Prophets [9]"When you come into the land which the LORD, your God, is giving you, you shall not learn to imitate the abominations of the peoples there.[o] [10]Let there not be found among you anyone who immolates his son or daughter[p] in the fire,* nor a fortune-teller, soothsayer, charmer, diviner, [11]or caster of spells, nor one who consults ghosts and spirits or seeks oracles from the dead. [12]Anyone who does such things is an abomination to the LORD, and because of such abominations the LORD, your God, is driving these nations out of your way.[q] [13]You, however, must be altogether sincere toward the LORD, your God. [14]Though these nations whom you are to dispossess listen to their soothsayers and fortune-tellers, the LORD, your God, will not permit you to do so.

[15]"A prophet like me* will the LORD, your God, raise up for you from among your own kinsmen; to him you shall listen.[r] [16]This is exactly what you requested of the LORD, your God, at Horeb on the day of the assembly, when you said, 'Let us not again hear the voice of the LORD, our God, nor see this great fire any more, lest we die.'[s] [17]And the LORD said to me, 'This was well said. [18]I will raise up for them a prophet like you from among their kinsmen, and will put my words into his mouth; he shall tell them all that I command him. [19]If any man will not listen to my words which he speaks in my name, I myself will make him answer for it.[t] [20]But if a prophet presumes to speak in my name[u] an oracle that I have not commanded him to speak, or speaks in the name of other gods, he shall die.'

[21]"If you say to yourselves, 'How can we recognize an oracle which the LORD has spoken?', [22]know that, even though a prophet speaks in the name of the LORD, if his oracle is not fulfilled or verified, it is an oracle which the LORD did not speak. The prophet has spoken it presumptuously, and you shall have no fear of him.

CHAPTER 19

Cities of Refuge [1]"When the LORD, your God, removes the nations whose land he is giving you, and you have taken their place and are settled in their cities and houses, [2][v]you shall set apart three cities* in the land which the LORD, your God, is giving you to occupy. [3]You shall thereby divide into three regions the land which the LORD, your God, will give you as a heritage, and so arrange the routes that every homicide will be able to find a refuge.

[4]"It is in the following case that a homicide may take refuge in such a place to save his life: when someone unwittingly kills his neighbor to whom he had previously borne no malice.[w] [5]For example, if he goes with his neighbor to a forest to cut wood, and as he swings his ax to fell a tree, its head flies off the handle and hits his neighbor a mortal blow, he may take refuge in one of these cities to save his life. [6]Should the distance be too great, the avenger of blood* may in the heat of his anger pursue the homicide and

18, 10f: Immolates his son or daughter in the fire: to Molech. See note on Lv 18, 21. Such human sacrifices are classed here with other pagan superstitions because they were believed to possess magical powers for averting a calamity; cf 2 Kgs 3, 27. Three other forms of superstition are listed here: augury (by a fortune-teller, a soothsayer or a diviner); black magic (by a charmer . . . or caster of spells); and necromancy (by one who consults ghosts and spirits or seeks oracles from the dead).

18, 15: A prophet like me: from the context (opposition to the pagan soothsayers) it seems that Moses is referring in general to all the true prophets who were to succeed him. But since Christ is the Great Prophet in whom the prophetic office finds its fulfillment and completion, this passage was understood in a special Messianic sense both by the Jews (Jn 6, 14; 7, 40) and by the Apostles (Acts 3, 22; 7, 37).

19, 2: Set apart three cities: the Israelites were to have at least six cities of refuge, three in the land east of the Jordan and three in the land of Canaan west of the Jordan (Nm 35, 9–34); but since the three cities east of the Jordan had now been appointed (Dt 4, 41–43), reference is made here only to the three west of the Jordan. The execution of this command is narrated in Jos 20.

19, 6: The avenger of blood: see note on Nm 35, 12.

o Dt 12, 29ff; Lv 18, 26–30. p 10f: Lv 18, 21; 19, 31; 20, 27; 1 Sm 28, 7; 2 Kgs 17, 17; 21, 6. q Dt 9, 4. r Jn 1, 45; 6, 14; Acts 3, 22; 7, 37. s Ex 20, 19. t Acts 3, 23. u 20. 22: Dt 13, 2ff. v Dt 4, 41ff; Ex 21, 13; Nm 35, 10–15; Jos 20, 2. 8. w Dt 4, 42; Nm 35, 15; Jos 20, 3. 5.

overtake him and strike him dead, even though he does not merit death since he had previously borne the slain man no malice. [7]That is why I order you to set apart three cities.

[8] [x]"But if the LORD, your God, enlarges your territory, as he swore to your fathers, and gives you all the land he promised your fathers he would give [9]in the event that you carefully observe all these commandments which I enjoin on you today, loving the LORD, your God, and ever walking in his ways: then add three cities to these three. [10]Thus, in the land which the LORD, your God, is giving you as a heritage, innocent blood will not be shed and you will not become guilty of bloodshed.

[11] [y]"However, if someone lies in wait for his neighbor out of hatred for him, and rising up against him, strikes him mortally, and then takes refuge in one of these cities, [12]the elders of his own city shall send for him and have him taken from there, and shall hand him over to be slain by the avenger of blood. [13]Do not look on him with pity, but purge from Israel the stain of shedding innocent blood, that you may prosper.

Removal of Landmarks [14]"You shall not move your neighbor's landmarks erected by your forefathers in the heritage you receive in the land which the LORD, your God, is giving you to occupy.[z]

False Witnesses [15]"One witness alone shall not take the stand against a man in regard to any crime or any offense of which he may be guilty; a judicial fact shall be established only on the testimony of two or three witnesses.[a]

[16]"If an unjust witness takes the stand against a man to accuse him of a defection from the law, [17]the two parties in the dispute shall appear before the LORD in the presence of the priests or judges in office at that time;[b] [18]and if after a thorough investigation the judges find that the witness is a false witness and has accused his kinsman falsely, [19]you shall do to him as he planned to do to his kinsman.[c] Thus shall you purge the evil from your midst. [20]The rest, on hearing of it, shall fear, and never again do a thing so evil among you. [21]Do not look on such a man with pity. Life for life, eye for eye, tooth for tooth, hand for hand, and foot for foot![d]

CHAPTER 20

Courage in War [1]"When you go out to war against your enemies and you see horses and chariots and an army greater than your own, do not be afraid of them, for the LORD, your God, who brought you up from the land of Egypt, will be with you.

[2]"When you are about to go into battle, the priest shall come forward and say to the soldiers: [3]'Hear, O Israel! Today you are going into battle against your enemies. Be not weakhearted or afraid; be neither alarmed nor frightened by them. [4]For it is the LORD, your God, who goes with you to fight for you against your enemies and give you victory.'[e]

[5]"Then the officials shall say to the soldiers,[f] 'Is there anyone who has built a new house and not yet had the housewarming? Let him return home, lest he die in battle and another dedicate it. [6]Is there anyone who has planted a vineyard and never yet enjoyed its fruits? Let him return home, lest he die in battle and another enjoy its fruits in his stead. [7]Is there anyone who has betrothed a woman and not yet taken her as his wife? Let him return home, lest he die in battle and another take her to wife.'[g] [8]In fine, the officials shall say to the soldiers, 'Is there anyone who is afraid and weakhearted?[h] Let him return home, lest he make his fellows as fainthearted as himself.'

[9]"When the officials have finished speaking to the soldiers, military officers shall be appointed over the army.

Cities of the Enemy [10]"When you march up to attack a city, first offer it terms of peace. [11]If it agrees to your terms of peace and opens its gates to you, all the people to be found in it shall serve you in forced labor. [12]But if it refuses to make peace with you and instead offers you battle, lay

x Gn 15, 18–21; 28, 14; Ex 23, 31; 34, 24. y 11ff: Ex 21, 12. 14; Nm 35, 20f. z Dt 27, 17; Prv 23, 10; Hos 5, 10. a Dt 17, 6; Nm 35, 30; Mt 18, 16; Jn 8, 17; 2 Cor 13, 1. b Dt 17, 8f. c 18f: Dn 13, 61f. d Ex 21, 23f; Lv 24, 20; Mt 5, 38. e Dt 1, 30; 3, 22; Jos 23, 10. f 5ff: 1 Mc 3, 56. g Dt 24, 5. h Jgs 7, 3.

siege to it, 13and when the LORD, your God, delivers it into your hand, put every male in it to the sword; 14but the women and children and livestock and all else in it that is worth plundering you may take as your booty, and you may use this plunder of your enemies which the LORD, your God, has given you.[i]

15"That is how you shall deal with any city at a considerable distance from you, which does not belong to the peoples of this land. 16But in the cities of those nations which the LORD, your God, is giving you as your heritage, you shall not leave a single soul alive. 17You must doom them all—the Hittites, Amorites, Canaanites, Perizzites, Hivites and Jebusites[j]—as the LORD, your God, has commanded you, 18lest they teach you to make any such abominable offerings as they make to their gods, and you thus sin against the LORD, your God.

Trees of a Besieged City 19"When you are at war with a city and have to lay siege to it for a long time before you capture it, you shall not destroy its trees by putting an ax to them. You may eat their fruit, but you must not cut down the trees. After all, are the trees of the field men, that they should be included in your siege? 20However, those trees which you know are not fruit trees you may destroy, cutting them down to build siegeworks with which to reduce the city that is resisting you.

CHAPTER 21

Expiation of Untraced Murder 1"If the corpse of a slain man* is found lying in the open on the land which the LORD, your God, is giving you to occupy, and it is not known who killed him, 2your elders and judges shall go out and measure the distances to the cities that are in the neighborhood of the corpse. 3When it is established which city is nearest the corpse, the elders of that city shall take a heifer that has never been put to work as a draft animal under a yoke, 4and bringing it down to a wadi with an ever-flowing stream at a place that has not been plowed or sown, they shall cut the heifer's throat there in the wadi.* 5The priests, the descendants of Levi, shall also be present, for the LORD, your God, has chosen them to minister to him and to give blessings in his name, and every case of dispute or violence must be settled by their decision.[k] 6Then all the elders of that city nearest the corpse shall wash their hands* over the heifer whose throat was cut in the wadi, 7and shall declare, 'Our hands did not shed this blood,* and our eyes did not see the deed. 8Absolve, O LORD, your people Israel, whom you have ransomed, and let not the guilt of shedding innocent blood remain in the midst of your people Israel.' Thus they shall be absolved from the guilt of bloodshed, 9and you shall purge from your midst the guilt of innocent blood, that you may prosper for doing what is right in the sight of the LORD.

Marriage with a Female Captive 10"When you go out to war against your enemies and the LORD, your God, delivers them into your hand, so that you take captives, 11if you see a comely woman among the captives and become so enamored of her that you wish to have her as wife, 12you may take her home to your house. But before she may live there, she must shave her head* and pare her nails 13and lay aside her captive's garb. After she has mourned her father and mother for a full month, you may have relations with her, and you shall be her husband and she shall be your wife. 14However, if later on you lose your liking for her, you shall give her her freedom, if she wishes it; but you shall not

21, 1–9: This paragraph is best read immediately after Dt 19, 21. The slain man may not necessarily have been murdered; he may have been killed by a wild beast. But the blood of the slain cries out to God from the soil where it was shed; cf Gn 4, 10. Therefore a religious ceremony of propitiation is here prescribed in order to avert God's anger on the community.

21, 4: They shall cut the heifer's throat there in the wadi: its blood is to be carried away by the stream, signifying thereby the removal of the human blood from the soil. This is not a sacrifice but a symbolic action; the priests are present merely as official witnesses.

21, 6: Wash their hands: a symbolic gesture in protestation of one's own innocence when human blood is unjustly shed; cf Mt 27, 24.

21, 7: This blood: the blood of the slain man as symbolized by the heifer's blood.

21, 12f: Shave her head . . . : these symbolic actions are meant to signify the purification of the woman from her pagan defilement or perhaps the end of her period of mourning for her previous husband.

i 13f: Nm 31, 7. 9. 11; Jos 22, 8. j 16f: Dt 7, 1f; Jos 10, 40; 11, 14. k Dt 19, 17.

sell her or enslave her, since she was married to you under compulsion.

Rights of the First-born 15"If a man with two wives loves one and dislikes the other; and if both bear him sons, but the first-born is of her whom he dislikes: 16when he comes to bequeath his property to his sons he may not consider as his first-born the son of the wife he loves, in preference to his true first-born, the son of the wife whom he dislikes. 17On the contrary, he shall recognize as his first-born the son of her whom he dislikes, giving him a double share of whatever he happens to own, since he is the first fruits of his manhood, and to him belong the rights of the first-born.

The Incorrigible Son 18"If a man has a stubborn and unruly son who will not listen to his father or mother, and will not obey them even though they chastise him, 19his father and mother shall have him apprehended and brought out to the elders at the gate* of his home city, 20where they shall say to those city elders, 'This son of ours is a stubborn and unruly fellow who will not listen to us; he is a glutton and a drunkard.' 21Then all his fellow citizens shall stone him to death. Thus shall you purge the evil from your midst, and all Israel, on hearing of it, shall fear.

Corpse of a Criminal 22"If a man guilty of a capital offense is put to death and his corpse hung on a tree,* 23it shall not remain on the tree overnight.[l] You shall bury it the same day; otherwise, since God's curse rests on him who hangs on a tree,* you will defile the land which the LORD, your God, is giving you as an inheritance.

CHAPTER 22

Care for Lost Animals 1"You shall not see your kinsman's ox or sheep driven astray without showing concern about it; see to it that it is returned to your kinsman.[m] 2If this kinsman does not live near you, or you do not know who he may be, take it to your own place and keep it with you until he claims it; then give it back to him. 3You shall do the same with his ass, or his garment, or anything else which your kinsman loses and you happen to find; you may not be unconcerned about them. 4You shall not see your kinsman's ass or ox foundering on the road without showing concern about it; see to it that you help him lift it up.

Various Precepts 5"A woman shall not wear an article proper to a man, nor shall a man put on a woman's dress; for anyone who does such things is an abomination to the LORD, your God.

6"If, while walking along, you chance upon a bird's nest with young birds or eggs in it, in any tree or on the ground, and the mother bird is sitting on them, you shall not take away the mother bird along with her brood; 7you shall let her go, although you may take her brood away. It is thus that you shall have prosperity and a long life.

8"When you build a new house, put a parapet around the roof; otherwise, if someone falls off, you will bring bloodguilt upon your house.

9[n]"You shall not sow your vineyard with two different kinds of seed; if you do, its produce shall become forfeit,* both the crop you have sown and the yield of the vineyard. 10You shall not plow with an ox and an ass harnessed together. 11You shall not wear cloth of two different kinds of thread, wool and linen, woven together.

12"You shall put twisted cords* on the four corners of the cloak that you wrap around you.[o]

Crimes against Marriage 13"If a man, after marrying a woman and having relations with her, comes to dislike her, 14and makes mon-

21, 19: The gate: in the city walls. This open space served as the forum for the administration of justice. Cf Dt 22, 15; 25, 7; Ru 4, 1f. 11; Is 29, 21; Am 5, 10. 12. 15.

21, 22: Hung on a tree: some understand, "impaled on a stake." In any case the hanging or impaling was not the means used to execute the criminal; he was first put to death by the ordinary means, stoning, and his corpse was then exposed on high as a salutary warning for others. Cf Jos 8, 29; 10, 26; 1 Sm 31, 10; 2 Sm 21, 9.

21, 23: God's curse rests on him who hangs on a tree: St. Paul quotes these words in Gal 3, 13, where he applies them to the crucified Savior, who "redeemed us from the curse of the law, becoming a curse for us."

22, 9: Become forfeit: to the sanctuary; cf Lv 19, 19; Jos 6, 19.

22, 12: Twisted cords: referred to as "tassels" on "violet cords" in Nm 15, 38. See note there.

l Gal 3, 13. m 1–4: Ex 23, 4f. n 9. 11: Lv 19, 19. o Nm 15, 38; Mt 23, 5.

strous charges against her and defames her by
saying, 'I married this woman, but when I first
had relations with her I did not find her a virgin,'
[15]the father and mother of the girl shall take the
evidence of her virginity* and bring it to the
elders at the city gate. [16]There the father of the
girl shall say to the elders, 'I gave my daughter to
this man in marriage, but he has come to dislike
her, [17]and now brings monstrous charges against
her, saying: I did not find your daughter a virgin.
But here is the evidence of my daughter's
virginity!' And they shall spread out the cloth
before the elders of the city. [18]Then these city
elders shall take the man and chastise him,*
[19]besides fining him one hundred silver shekels,
which they shall give to the girl's father, because
the man defamed a virgin in Israel. Moreover,
she shall remain his wife, and he may not
divorce her as long as he lives.

[20]"But if this charge is true, and evidence of
the girl's virginity is not found, [21]they shall bring
the girl to the entrance of her father's house and
there her townsmen shall stone her to death,
because she committed a crime against Israel by
her unchasteness in her father's house. Thus
shall you purge the evil from your midst.

[22]"If a man is discovered having relations with
a woman who is married to another, both the
man and the woman with whom he has had
relations shall die. [p] Thus shall you purge the evil
from your midst.

[23]"If within the city a man comes upon a
maiden who is betrothed,* and has relations
with her, [24]you shall bring them both out to the
gate of the city and there stone them to death:
the girl because she did not cry out for help
though she was in the city, and the man because
he violated his neighbor's wife. Thus shall you
purge the evil from your midst.

[25]"If, however, it is in the open fields that a
man comes upon such a betrothed maiden,
seizes her and has relations with her, the man
alone shall die. [26]You shall do nothing to the
maiden, since she is not guilty of a capital
offense. This case is like that of a man who rises
up against his neighbor and murders him: [27]it
was in the open fields that he came upon her,
and though the betrothed maiden may have
cried out for help, there was no one to come to
her aid.

[28] [q]"If a man comes upon a maiden that is not
betrothed, takes her and has relations with her,
and their deed is discovered, [29]the man who had
relations with her shall pay the girl's father fifty
silver shekels and take her as his wife, because
he has deflowered her. Moreover, he may not
divorce her as long as he lives.

CHAPTER 23

[1]"A man shall not marry his father's wife,*
nor shall he dishonor his father's bed.

Membership in the Community [2]"No one
whose testicles have been crushed or whose
penis has been cut off, may be admitted into the
community of the LORD. [3]No child of an incestu-
ous union may be admitted into the community
of the LORD, nor any descendant of his even to
the tenth generation. [4] [r]No Ammonite or Moab-
ite may ever be admitted into the community of
the LORD, nor any descendants of theirs even to
the tenth generation, [5] [s]because they would not
succor you with food and water on your journey
after you left Egypt, and because Moab hired
Balaam, son of Beor, from Pethor in Aram
Naharaim, to curse you; [6]though the LORD, your
God, would not listen to Balaam and turned his
curse into a blessing for you, because he loves
you. [7]Never promote their peace and prosperity
as long as you live. [8] [t]But do not abhor the
Edomite, since he is your brother, nor the
Egyptian, since you were an alien in his country.
[9]Children born to them may in the third genera-
tion be admitted into the community of the
LORD.

22, 15: The evidence of her virginity: the bridal garment or sheet stained with a little blood from the first nuptial relations.

22, 18: Chastise him: flog him, as prescribed in Dt 25, 1–3.

22, 23: A maiden who is betrothed: a girl who is married but not yet brought to her husband's home and whose marriage is therefore still unconsummated.

23, 1: Father's wife: stepmother. Dishonor: cf Dt 27, 20.

p Lv 20, 10; Jn 8, 4f. q 28f: Ex 22, 16. r Neh 13, 1f. s Nm 24, 10. t Gn 25, 24ff.

Cleanliness in Camp 10“When you are in camp during an expedition against your enemies, you shall keep yourselves from everything offensive. 11If one of you becomes unclean because of a nocturnal emission, he shall go outside the camp, and not return until, 12toward evening, he has bathed in water; then, when the sun has set, he may come back into the camp. 13Outside the camp you shall have a place set aside to be used as a latrine. 14You shall also keep a trowel in your equipment and with it, when you go outside to ease nature, you shall first dig a hole and afterward cover up your excrement. 15Since the LORD, your God, journeys along within your camp to defend you and to put your enemies at your mercy, your camp must be holy; otherwise, if he sees anything indecent in your midst, he will leave your company.

Various Precepts 16“You shall not hand over to his master a slave who has taken refuge from him with you. 17Let him live with you wherever he chooses, in any one of your communities* that pleases him. Do not molest him.

18*“There shall be no temple harlot among the Israelite women, nor a temple prostitute among the Israelite men.[u] 19You shall not offer a harlot's fee or a dog's price as any kind of votive offering in the house of the LORD, your God; both these things are an abomination to the LORD, your God.

20“You shall not demand interest from your countrymen on a loan of money or of food or of anything else on which interest is usually demanded.[v] 21You may demand interest from a foreigner, but not from your countryman, so that the LORD, your God, may bless you in all your undertakings on the land you are to enter and occupy.

22“When you make a vow to the LORD, your God, you shall not delay in fulfilling it; otherwise you will be held guilty, for the LORD, your God, is strict in requiring it of you. 23Should you refrain from making a vow, you will not be held guilty. 24But you must keep your solemn word and fulfill the votive offering you have freely promised to the LORD.

25“When you go through your neighbor's vineyard, you may eat as many of his grapes as you wish, but do not put them in your basket. 26When you go through your neighbor's grainfield, you may pluck some of the ears with your hand, but do not put a sickle to your neighbor's grain.

CHAPTER 24

Marriage Laws 1“When a man,* after marrying a woman and having relations with her, is later displeased with her because he finds in her something indecent,* and therefore he writes out a bill of divorce and hands it to her, thus dismissing her from his house: 2if on leaving his house she goes and becomes the wife of another man, 3and the second husband, too, comes to dislike her and dismisses her from his house by handing her a written bill of divorce; 4or if this second man who has married her, dies; then her former husband, who dismissed her, may not again take her as his wife after she has become defiled. That would be an abomination before the LORD, and you shall not bring such guilt upon the land which the LORD, your God, is giving you as a heritage.

5 [w]“When a man is newly wed, he need not

23, 17: In any one of your communities: from this it would seem that the slave in question is a fugitive from a foreign country.

23, 18f: The pagans believed that they could enter into special relationship with their gods and goddesses by having sexual relations with the pagan priests and priestesses who prostituted themselves for this purpose. The money paid for this was considered a sort of votive offering made to the pagan sanctuary. Such abominations were naturally forbidden in Israel. A dog's price: the money paid the pagan priest for his indecent service.

24, 1–4: This law is directly concerned only with forbidding divorced couples to remarry each other, and indirectly with checking hasty divorces, by demanding sufficient cause and certain legal formalities. Divorce itself is taken for granted and tolerated as an existing custom whose evils this law seeks to lessen. Cf Dt 22, 19. 29; Mal 2, 14ff. Christ gave the authentic interpretation of this law: “Moses, by reason of the hardness of your heart, permitted you to put away your wives; but it was not so from the beginning” (Mt 19, 8f).

24, 1: Something indecent: a rather indefinite phrase, meaning perhaps “immodest conduct.” At the time of Christ the rabbis differed in opinion concerning the sufficient grounds for divorce; cf Mt 19, 3.

u 1 Kgs 14, 24; 22, 46; 2 Kgs 23, 7. v Ex 22, 25; Lv 25, 37; Lk 6, 34f. w Dt 20, 7.

go out on a military expedition, nor shall any
public duty be imposed on him. He shall be
exempt for one year for the sake of his family, to
bring joy to the wife he has married.
Justice, Equity and Charity 6*"No one shall
take a hand mill or even its upper stone as a
pledge for debt, for he would be taking the
debtor's sustenance as a pledge.
7"If any man is caught kidnaping a fellow
Israelite in order to enslave him and sell him, the
kidnaper shall be put to death.[x] Thus shall you
purge the evil from your midst.
8[y]"In an attack of leprosy you shall be careful
to observe exactly and to carry out all the directions
of the levitical priests. Take care to act in
accordance with the instructions I have given
them. 9[z]Remember what the LORD, your God,
did to Miriam on the journey after you left Egypt.
10*"When you make a loan of any kind to
your neighbor, you shall not enter his house to
receive a pledge from him, 11but shall wait
outside until the man to whom you are making
the loan brings his pledge outside to you. 12If he
is a poor man, you shall not sleep in the mantle
he gives as a pledge, 13but shall return it to him
at sunset that he himself may sleep in it.[a] Then
he will bless you, and it will be a good deed of
yours before the LORD, your God.
14"You shall not defraud a poor and needy
hired servant, whether he be one of your own
countrymen or one of the aliens who live in your
communities. 15You shall pay him each day's
wages before sundown on the day itself, since he
is poor and looks forward to them.[b] Otherwise
he will cry to the LORD against you, and you will
be held guilty.
16"Fathers shall not be put to death for their
children, nor children for their fathers; only for
his own guilt shall a man be put to death.[c]
17"You shall not violate the rights of the alien
or of the orphan, nor take the clothing of a
widow as a pledge.[d] 18For, remember, you were
once slaves in Egypt, and the LORD, your God,
ransomed you from there; that is why I command
you to observe this rule.
19[e]"When you reap the harvest in your field
and overlook a sheaf there, you shall not go back
to get it; let it be for the alien, the orphan or the
widow, that the LORD, your God, may bless you in
all your undertakings. 20When you knock down
the fruit of your olive trees, you shall not go over
the branches a second time; let what remains be
for the alien, the orphan and the widow. 21When
you pick your grapes, you shall not go over the
vineyard a second time; let what remains be for
the alien, the orphan, and the widow. 22For remember
that you were once slaves in Egypt; that
is why I command you to observe this rule.

CHAPTER 25

1"When men have a dispute and bring it to
court, and a decision is handed down to them
acquitting the innocent party and condemning
the guilty party, 2if the latter deserves stripes, the
judge shall have him lie down and in his
presence receive the number of stripes his guilt
deserves. 3Forty stripes* may be given him, but
no more;[f] lest, if he were beaten with more
stripes than these, your kinsman should be
looked upon as disgraced because of the severity
of the beating.
4*"You shall not muzzle an ox when it is
treading out grain.[g]
Levirate Marriage 5"When brothers live together*
and one of them dies without a son, the
widow of the deceased shall not marry anyone
outside the family; but her husband's brother
shall go to her and perform the duty of a brother-

24, 6: Since the Israelites ground their grain into flour only in sufficient quantity for their current need, to deprive a debtor of his hand mill was virtually equivalent to condemning him to starve to death.

24, 10f: The debtor had the right to select the pledge that the creditor demanded as a guarantee for his loan.

25, 3: Forty stripes: a relatively mild punishment in ancient times. Later Jewish practice limited the number to thirty-nine; cf 2 Cor 11, 24.

25, 4: St. Paul argues from this verse that a laborer has the right to live on the fruits of his labor; cf 1 Cor 9, 9; 1 Tm 5, 18.

25, 5: When brothers live together: when relatives of the same clan, though married, hold their property in common. It was only in this case that the present law was to be observed, since one of its purposes was to keep the property of the deceased within the same clan. Such a marriage of a widow with her brother-in-law is known as a "levirate" marriage from the Latin word levir, meaning "a husband's brother."

x Ex 21, 16. y Lv 13, 1–14. z Nm 12, 10–15. a Ex 22, 26. b 14f: Lv 19, 13; Tb 4, 15; Sir 34, 25f; Jer 22, 13. c 2 Kgs 14, 6; 2 Chr 25, 4; Ez 18, 20. d Ex 22, 22; 23, 9. e 19ff: Lv 19, 9f; 23, 22. f 2 Cor 11, 24. g 1 Cor 9, 9; 1 Tm 5, 18.

in-law by marrying her.[h] 6[i]The first-born son she
bears shall continue the line of the deceased
brother, that his name may not be blotted out
from Israel. 7If, however, a man does not care to
marry his brother's wife, she shall go up to the
elders at the gate and declare, 'My brother-in-
law does not intend to perform his duty toward
me and refuses to perpetuate his brother's name
in Israel.' 8Thereupon the elders of his city shall
summon him and admonish him. If he persists in
saying, 'I am not willing to marry her,' 9*his
sister-in-law, in the presence of the elders, shall
go up to him and strip his sandal from his foot
and spit in his face, saying publicly, 'This is how
one should be treated who will not build up his
brother's family!' 10And his lineage shall be
spoken of in Israel as 'the family of the man
stripped of his sandal.'
Various Precepts 11"When two men are fight-
ing and the wife of one intervenes to save her
husband from the blows of his opponent, if she
stretches out her hand and seizes the latter by
his private parts, 12you shall chop off her hand
without pity.
13"You shall not keep two differing weights in
your bag, one large and the other small;[j] 14nor
shall you keep two different measures in your
house, one large and the other small. 15But use a
true and just weight, and a true and just
measure, that you may have a long life on the
land which the LORD, your God, is giving you.
16Everyone who is dishonest in any of these
matters is an abomination to the LORD, your
God.
17*"Bear in mind what Amalek did to you on
the journey after you left Egypt,[k] 18how without
fear of any god he harassed you along the way,
weak and weary as you were, and cut off at the
rear all those who lagged behind. 19Therefore,
when the LORD, your God, gives you rest from
all your enemies round about in the land which
he is giving you to occupy as your heritage, you
shall blot out the memory of Amalek from under
the heavens.[l] Do not forget!

CHAPTER 26

Thanksgiving for the Harvest 1"When you
have come into the land which the LORD, your
God, is giving you as a heritage, and have
occupied it and settled in it, 2you shall take some
first fruits[m] of the various products of the soil
which you harvest from the land which the
LORD, your God, gives you, and putting them in
a basket, you shall go to the place which the
LORD, your God, chooses for the dwelling place
of his name. 3There you shall go to the priest in
office at that time and say to him, 'Today I
acknowledge to the LORD, my God, that I have
indeed come into the land which he swore to
our fathers he would give us.' 4The priest shall
then receive the basket from you and shall set it
in front of the altar of the LORD, your God.
5Then you shall declare before the LORD, your
God, 'My father was a wandering Aramean*
who went down to Egypt with a small house-
hold and lived there as an alien.[n] But there he
became a nation great, strong and numerous.
6[o]When the Egyptians maltreated and oppressed
us, imposing hard labor upon us, 7we cried to
the LORD, the God of our fathers, and he heard
our cry and saw our affliction, our toil and our
oppression. 8He brought us out of Egypt with his
strong hand and outstretched arm, with terrify-
ing power, with signs and wonders;[p] 9and
bringing us into this country, he gave us this land
flowing with milk and honey.[q] 10Therefore, I
have now brought you the first fruits of the
products of the soil which you, O LORD, have

25, 9f: The penalty decreed for a man who refuses to comply with this law of family loyalty is public disgrace (the widow is to spit in his face) and the curse of poverty; sandals were proverbially a man's cheapest possession (cf Am 2, 6; 8, 6), and therefore "a man without sandals" was the poorest of the poor. Some commentators, however, connect this symbolic act with the ceremony mentioned in Ru 4, 7f.

25, 17–19: This attack on Israel by Amalek is not mentioned elsewhere in the Old Testament, although it probably was connected with the battle mentioned in Ex 17, 8. A campaign against Amalek was carried out by Saul; cf 1 Sm 15.

26, 5: Aramean: either in reference to the origin of the patriarchs from Aram Naharaim (cf Gn 24, 10; 25, 20; 28, 5; 31, 20. 24), or merely in the sense of "nomad," in the same way as "Arab" was later used; cf Jer 3, 2.

h Mt 22, 24; Mk 12, 19; Lk 20, 28. i 6–9; Ru 4, 5–10. j 13ff: Lv 19, 35f; Prv 16, 11; Ez 45, 10; Ml 6, 11. k Ex 17, 8. l Ex 17, 14; 1 Sm 15, 2f. m Ex 23, 19; 34, 26. n Gn 46, 6f; Acts 7, 14f. o 6f: Ex 1, 8–22; 2, 23ff; 3, 9; Nm 20, 15f. p Ex 12, 51. q Ex 3, 8.

given me.' And having set them before the
LORD, your God, you shall bow down in his
presence. 11 Then you and your family, together
with the Levite and the aliens who live among
you, shall make merry over all these good things
which the LORD, your God, has given you.[r]

Prayer with the Tithes 12 "When you have
finished setting aside all the tithes of your
produce in the third year,[s] the year of the tithes,
and you have given them to the Levite,* the
alien, the orphan and the widow, that they may
eat their fill in your own community, 13 you shall
declare before the LORD, your God, 'I have
purged my house of the sacred portion and I
have given it to the Levite,* the alien, the
orphan and the widow, just as you have com-
manded me. In this I have not broken or
forgotten any of your commandments: 14 *I have
not eaten any of the tithe as a mourner; I have
not brought any of it out as one unclean; I have
not offered any of it to the dead. I have thus
hearkened to the voice of the LORD, my God,
doing just as you have commanded me. 15 Look
down, then, from heaven, your holy abode, and
bless your people Israel and the soil you have
given us in the land flowing with milk and honey
which you promised on oath to our fathers.'

The Covenant 16 "This day the LORD, your
god, commands you to observe these statutes
and decrees. Be careful, then, to observe them
with all your heart and with all your soul.
17 Today you are making this agreement with the
LORD: he is to be your God and you are to walk
in his ways and observe his statutes, command-
ments and decrees, and to hearken to his voice.[t]
18 And today the LORD is making this agreement
with you: you are to be a people peculiarly his
own,[u] as he promised you; and provided you
keep all his commandments, 19 he will then raise
you high in praise and renown and glory above
all other nations he has made, and you will be a
people sacred to the LORD, your God, as he
promised."

IV: Final Words of Moses

CHAPTER 27

Ceremonies 1 Then Moses, with the elders of
Israel, gave the people this order: "Keep all these
commandments which I enjoin on you today.
2 On the day you cross the Jordan into the land
which the LORD, your God, is giving you, set up
some large stones and coat them with plaster.
3 Also write on them,[v] at the time you cross, all
the words of this law, that you may thus enter
into the land flowing with milk and honey,
which the LORD, your God, and the God of your
fathers, is giving you as he promised you.
4 When, moreover, you have crossed the Jordan,
besides setting up on Mount Ebal these stones
concerning which I command you today, and
coating them with plaster, 5 you shall also build
to the LORD, your God, an altar made of stones
that no iron tool has touched.[w] 6 You shall make
this altar of the LORD, your God, with undressed
stones, and shall offer on it holocausts to the
LORD, your God. 7 You shall also sacrifice peace
offerings and eat them there, making merry
before the LORD, your God. 8 On the stones* you
shall inscribe all the words of this law very
clearly."

9 Moses, with the levitical priests, then said to
all Israel: "Be silent, O Israel, and listen! This
day you have become the people of the LORD,
your God.[x] 10 You shall therefore hearken to the
voice of the LORD, your God, and keep his
commandments and statutes which I enjoin on
you today."

11 That same day Moses gave the people this
order: 12 "When you cross the Jordan, Simeon,
Levi, Judah, Issachar, Joseph and Benjamin shall
stand on Mount Gerizim[y] to pronounce bless-
ings over the people, 13 while Reuben, Gad,
Asher, Zebulun, Dan and Naphtali shall stand on
Mount Ebal to pronounce curses.

The Twelve Curses 14 "The Levites shall pro-
claim aloud to all the men of Israel: 15 'Cursed be
the man who makes a carved or molten idol[z]—

26, 12: And you have given them to the Levite . . . : as prescribed in Dt 14, 28f.
26, 14: These are allusions to pagan religious practices.
27, 8: On the stones: cf vv 3f; not the stones of the altar.

r Dt 12, 7. 12. s Dt 14, 28f. t Ex 24, 7. u 18f: Dt 7, 6; 14, 2; 28, 1; Ex 19, 5. v Jos 8, 32. w Ex 20, 25; Jos 8, 31. x Dt 26, 17ff. y 12f: Dt 11, 29; Jos 8, 33f. z Ex 20, 4. 23; Lv 19, 4; Wis 14, 8.

an abomination to the LORD, the product of a
craftsman's hands—and sets it up in secret!' And
all the people shall answer, 'Amen!'*
16'Cursed be he who dishonors his father or
his mother!' [a] And all the people shall answer,
'Amen!'
17'Cursed be he who moves his neighbor's
landmarks!' [b] And all the people shall answer,
'Amen!'
18'Cursed be he who misleads a blind man on
his way!' [c] And all the people shall answer,
'Amen!'
19'Cursed be he who violates the rights of the
alien, the orphan or the widow!' [d] And all the
people shall answer, 'Amen!'
20'Cursed be he who has relations with his
father's wife, for he dishonors his father's bed!' [e]
And all the people shall answer, 'Amen!'
21'Cursed be he who has relations with any
animal!' [f] And all the people shall answer,
'Amen!'
22'Cursed be he who has relations with his
sister or his half-sister!' [g] And all the people shall
answer, 'Amen!'
23'Cursed be he who has relations with his
mother-in-law!' [h] And all the people shall an-
swer, 'Amen!'
24'Cursed be he who slays his neighbor in
secret!' [i] And all the people shall answer,
'Amen!'
25'Cursed be he who accepts payment for
slaying an innocent man!' And all the people
shall answer, 'Amen!'
26'Cursed be he who fails to fulfill any of the
provisions of this law!' [j] And all the people shall
answer, 'Amen!'

CHAPTER 28*

Blessings for Obedience 1"Thus, then, [k] shall
it be: [l] if you continue to heed the voice of the
LORD, your God, and are careful to observe all
his commandments which I enjoin on you today,
the LORD, your God, will raise you high above all
the nations of the earth. [m] 2When you hearken to
the voice of the LORD, your God, all these
blessings will come upon you and overwhelm
you:

3"May you be blessed in the city,
and blessed in the country!
4"Blessed be the fruit of your womb,
the produce of your soil and the offspring of
your livestock,
the issue of your herds and the young of
your flocks! [n]
5"Blessed be your grain bin and your kneading
bowl!
6"May you be blessed in your coming in,
and blessed in your going out!*

Victory and Prosperity 7"The LORD will beat
down before you the enemies that rise up against
you; though they come out against you from but
one direction, they will flee before you in
seven.* 8The LORD will affirm his blessing upon
you, on your barns and on all your undertakings,
blessing you in the land that the LORD, your
God, gives you. 9Provided that you keep the
commandments of the LORD, your God, and
walk in his ways, he will establish you as a
people sacred to himself, as he swore to you; [o]
10so that, when all the nations of the earth see
you bearing the name of the LORD,* they will
stand in awe of you. [p] 11The LORD will increase
in more than goodly measure the fruit of your
womb, the offspring of your livestock, and the
produce of your soil, in the land which he swore
to your fathers he would give you. 12The LORD
will open up for you his rich treasure house of
the heavens, to give your land rain in due
season, blessing all your undertakings, so that

27, 15–26: Amen: see note on Nm 5, 22.

28, 1–69: This chapter would read better immediately after chapter 26.

28, 6: In your coming in . . . in your going out: at the beginning and end of every action, or in all actions in general.

28, 7. 25: From but one direction . . . in seven: in one compact mass, contrasted with many scattered groups.

28, 10: You bearing the name of the Lord: literally, "The LORD'S name is called over you," an expression signifying ownership and protection. Cf 2 Sm 12, 28; 1 Kgs 8, 43; Is 4, 1; 63, 19; Jer 7, 10f; 14, 9; 15, 16; 25, 29; Am 9, 12.

a Dt 21, 18–21; Ex 21, 17; Lv 20, 9. b Dt 19, 14. c Lv 19, 14. d Dt 24, 17; Ex 22, 21f. e Dt 22; 23, 1; Lv 18, 8; 20, 11. f Ex 22, 18; Lv 18, 23; 20, 15. g Lv 18, 9; 20, 17. h Lv 18, 17; 20, 14. i Ex 20, 13; 21, 12; Nm 35, 20f. j Gal 3, 10. k 1–68: Lv 26, 1–45. l 1–14: Dt 7, 12–16. m Dt 26, 19. n Dt 7, 13; 30. 9. o Dt 26, 18; Ex 19, 5f. p Dt 2, 25; 11, 25.

you will lend to many nations and borrow from none.[q] 13 The LORD will make you the head, not the tail,* and you will always mount higher and not decline, as long as you obey the commandments of the LORD, your God, which I order you today to observe carefully; 14 not turning aside to the right or to the left from any of the commandments which I now give you, in order to follow other gods and serve them.

Curses for Disobedience 15 "But if you do not hearken to the voice of the LORD, your God,[r] and are not careful to observe all his commandments which I enjoin on you today, all these curses shall come upon you and overwhelm you:

16 "May you be cursed in the city,
and cursed in the country!

17 "Cursed be your grain bin and your kneading bowl!

18 "Cursed be the fruit of your womb,
the produce of your soil and the offspring of your livestock,
the issue of your herds and the young of your flocks!

19 "May you be cursed in your coming in,
and cursed in your going out!

Sickness and Defeat 20 "The LORD will put a curse on you, defeat and frustration in every enterprise you undertake, until you are speedily destroyed and perish for the evil you have done in forsaking me. 21 The LORD will bring a pestilence upon you that will persist until he has exterminated you from the land you are entering to occupy. 22 The LORD will strike you with wasting and fever, with scorching, fiery drought, with blight and searing wind, that will plague you until you perish. 23 The sky over your heads will be like bronze and the earth under your feet like iron.[s] 24 For rain the LORD will give your land powdery dust, which will come down upon you from the sky until you are destroyed. 25 The LORD will let you be beaten down before your enemies; though you advance against them from one direction, you will flee before them in seven, so that you will become a terrifying example to all the kingdoms of the earth.[t] 26 Your carcasses will become food for all the birds of the air and for the beasts of the field, with no one to frighten them off. 27 The LORD will strike you with Egyptian boils[u] and with tumors, eczema and the itch, until you cannot be cured. 28 And the LORD will strike you with madness, blindness and panic, 29 so that even at midday you will grope like a blind man in the dark, unable to find your way.

Despoilment "You will be oppressed and robbed continually, with no one to come to your aid. 30 Though you betroth a wife, another man will have her. Though you build a house, you will not live in it. Though you plant a vineyard, you will not enjoy its fruits. 31 Your ox will be slaughtered before your eyes, and you will not eat of its flesh. Your ass will be stolen in your presence, but you will not recover it. Your flocks will be given to your enemies, with no one to come to your aid. 32 Your sons and daughters will be given to a foreign nation while you look on and grieve for them in constant helplessness. 33 A people whom you do not know will consume the fruit of your soil and of all your labor, and you will be oppressed and crushed at all times without surcease, 34 until you are driven mad by what your eyes must look upon. 35 *The LORD will strike you with malignant boils of which you cannot be cured, on your knees and legs, and from the soles of your feet to the crown of your head.

Exile 36 [v]"The LORD will bring you, and your king whom you have set over you, to a nation which you and your fathers have not known, and there you will serve strange gods of wood and stone, 37 and will call forth amazement, reproach and barbed scorn from all the nations to which the LORD will lead you.

Fruitless Labors 38 "Though you spend much seed on your field, you will harvest but little, for the locusts will devour the crop.[w] 39 Though you

28, 13: The head, not the tail: in the honorable position as leader. Cf Is 9, 14; 19, 15.
28, 35: This verse is best read with v 27.

q Dt 15, 6. r Bar 1, 20; Dn 9, 11; Mal 2, 2. s 22f: Lv 26, 19. t Lv 26, 17. 37. u Ex 9, 9ff. v 1 Kgs 9, 7ff; 2 Chr 7, 20ff; 33, 11; 36, 6. 20. w Ml 6, 15; Hg 1, 6.

plant and cultivate vineyards, you will not drink or store up the wine, for the grubs will eat the vines clean.[x] 40 Though you have olive trees throughout your country, you will have no oil for ointment, for your olives will drop off unripe.[y] 41 Though you beget sons and daughters, they will not remain with you, but will go into captivity.[z] 42 Buzzing insects will infest all your trees and the crops of your soil. 43 The alien residing among you will rise higher and higher above you, while you sink lower and lower. 44 He will lend to you, not you to him. He will become the head, you the tail.

45 "All these curses will come upon you, pursuing you and overwhelming you, until you are destroyed, because you would not hearken to the voice of the LORD, your God, nor keep the commandments and statutes he gave you. 46 They will light on you and your descendants as a sign and a wonder* for all time. 47 Since you would not serve the LORD, your God, with joy and gratitude for abundance of every kind, 48 therefore in hunger and thirst, in nakedness and utter poverty, you will serve the enemies whom the LORD will send against you. He will put an iron yoke on your neck, until he destroys you.

Invasion and Siege 49 [a]"The LORD will raise up against you a nation from afar, from the end of the earth, that swoops down like an eagle, a nation whose tongue you do not understand, 50 a nation of stern visage, that shows neither respect for the aged nor pity for the young. 51 They will consume the offspring of your livestock and the produce of your soil, until you are destroyed; they will leave you no grain or wine or oil, no issue of your herds or young of your flocks, until they have brought about your ruin. 52 They will besiege you in each of your communities, until the great, unscalable walls you trust in come tumbling down all over your land. They will so besiege you in every community throughout the land which the LORD, your God, has given you, 53 that in the distress of the siege to which your enemy subjects you, you will eat the fruit of your womb, the flesh of your own sons and daughters[b] whom the LORD, your God, has given you. 54 The most refined and fastidious man among you will begrudge his brother and his beloved wife and his surviving children 55 any share in the flesh of his children that he himself is using for food when nothing else is left him in the straits of the siege to which your enemy will subject you in all your communities. 56 The most refined and delicate woman among you, so delicate and refined that she would not venture to set the sole of her foot on the ground, will begrudge her beloved husband and her son and daughter 57 the afterbirth that issues from her womb and the infant she brings forth when she secretly uses them for food for want of anything else, in the straits of the siege to which your enemy will subject you in your communities.

Plagues 58 "If you are not careful to observe every word of the law which is written in this book, and to revere the glorious and awesome name of the LORD, your God, 59 he will smite you and your descendants with severe and constant blows, malignant and lasting maladies. 60 He will again afflict you with all the diseases of Egypt* which you dread, and they will persist among you.[c] 61 Should there be any kind of sickness or calamity not mentioned in this book of the law, that too the LORD will bring upon you until you are destroyed. 62 Of you who were numerous as the stars in the sky,[d] only a few will be left, because you would not hearken to the voice of the LORD, your God.

Exile 63 "Just as the LORD once took delight in making you grow and prosper,[e] so will he now take delight in ruining and destroying you, and you will be plucked out of the land you are now entering to occupy. 64 The LORD will scatter you among all the nations from one end of the earth to the other,[f] and there you will serve strange gods of wood and stone, such as you and your

28, 46: A sign and a wonder: an ominous example, attracting attention; cf Dt 29, 21–28.

28, 60: He will again afflict you with all the diseases of Egypt: such as the Lord had promised to remove from his people; cf Dt 7, 15.

x Zep 1, 13. y Mi 6, 15. z Lam 1, 5. a 49–52: Jer 5, 15ff; Bar 4, 15f. b Lv 26, 29; 2 Kgs 6, 28f; Jer 19, 9; Lam 4, 10; Bar 2, 3. c Dt 28, 27. d Dt 1, 10; Jer 42, 2. e Dt 30, 9. f Lv 26, 33.

fathers have not known. [65]Among these nations
you will find no repose, not a foot of ground to
stand upon, for there the LORD will give you an
anguished heart and wasted eyes* and a dis-
mayed spirit. [66]You will live in constant sus-
pense and stand in dread both day and night,
never sure of your existence. [67]In the morning
you will say, 'Would that it were evening!' and
in the evening you will say, 'Would that it were
morning!' for the dread that your heart must feel
and the sight that your eyes must see. [68]The
LORD will send you back in galleys* to Egypt, to
the region I told you that you were never to see
again;[g] and there you will offer yourselves for
sale to your enemies as male and female slaves,
but there will be no buyer."

[69]These are the words of the covenant which
the LORD ordered Moses to make with the
Israelites in the land of Moab, in addition to the
covenant which he made with them at Horeb.

CHAPTER 29

Past Favors Recalled [1]Moses summoned all
Israel and said to them, "You have seen all that
the LORD did in the land of Egypt before your
very eyes to Pharaoh and all his servants and to
all his land; [2]the great testings your own eyes
have seen, and those great signs and wonders.[h]
[3]But not even at the present day has the LORD
yet given you a mind to understand, or eyes to
see, or ears to hear.* [4]'I led you for forty years in
the desert.[i] Your clothes did not fall from you in
tatters nor your sandals from your feet; [5]bread
was not your food, nor wine or beer your drink.
Thus you should know that I, the LORD, am your
God.' [6][j]When we came to this place, Sihon, king
of Heshbon, and Og, king of Bashan, came out to
engage us in battle, but we defeated them [7]and
took over their land, which we then gave as a
heritage to the Reubenites, Gadites, and half the
tribe of Manasseh.[k] [8]Keep the terms of this
covenant, therefore, and fulfill them, that you
may succeed in whatever you do.

All Israel Bound to the Covenant [9]"You are
all now standing before the LORD, your God—
your chiefs and judges, your elders and officials,
and all of the men of Israel, [10]together with your
wives and children and the aliens who live in
your camp, down to those who hew wood and
draw water for you— [11]that you may enter into
the covenant of the LORD, your God, which he
concluded with you today under this sanction of
a curse;* [12]so that he may now establish you as
his people and he may be your God, as he
promised you and as he swore to your fathers
Abraham, Isaac and Jacob. [13]But it is not with
you alone that I am making this covenant, under
this sanction of a curse; [14]it is just as much with
those who are not here among us* today as it is
with those of us who are now here present
before the LORD, our God.

Warning against Idolatry [15]"You know in
what surroundings we lived in the land of Egypt
and what we passed by in the nations we
traversed, [16]and you saw the loathsome idols of
wood and stone, of gold and silver, that they
possess. [17]Let there be, then, no man or woman,
no clan or tribe among you, who would now
turn away their hearts from the LORD, our God,
to go and serve these pagan gods! Let there be
no root that would bear such poison and worm-
wood among you! [18]If any such person, upon
hearing the words of this curse, should beguile
himself into thinking that he can safely persist in
his stubbornness of heart, as though to sweep
away both the watered soil and the parched
ground,* [19]the LORD will never consent to
pardon him. Instead, the LORD's wrath and
jealousy will flare up against that man, and every
curse mentioned in this book will alight on him.
The LORD will blot out his name from under the
heavens [20]and will single him out from all the

28, 65: Wasted eyes: worn out and disappointed in their longing gaze.

28, 68: In galleys: in the ships of the Phoenician slave traders (Ez 27, 13; Jl 4, 6; Am 1, 9), who also dealt with Egypt (Is 23, 3).

29, 3: Eyes to see . . . ears to hear: with inner, spiritual discernment. Cf Mt 13, 43.

29, 11: Sanction of a curse: the present pact binds under penalty of the curses mentioned in this book. Cf v 20.

29, 14: Not here among us: this includes their descendants.

29, 18: To sweep away both the watered soil and the parched ground: apparently a proverb signifying that such an unfaithful Israelite will cause God to punish the good with the wicked, to root out the good plants growing in irrigated soil, together with the worthless plants growing in the dry ground.

g Hos 8, 13; 9, 3. h Dt 4, 34; Ex 19, 4. i Dt 8, 2. 4. j Dt 2, 24. 32; 3, 1; Nm 21, 33ff. k Dt 3, 16; Nm 32, 33.

tribes of Israel for doom, in keeping with all the curses of the covenant inscribed in this book of the law.

Punishment for Infidelity [21]"Future generations, your own descendants who will rise up after you, as well as the foreigners who will come here from far-off lands, when they see the calamities of this land and the ills with which the LORD has smitten it— [22]all its soil being nothing but sulphur and salt, a burnt-out waste, unsown and unfruitful, without a blade of grass, destroyed like Sodom and Gomorrah,[l] Admah and Zeboiim, which the LORD overthrew in his furious wrath— [23]they and all the nations will ask, 'Why has the LORD dealt thus with this land? Why this fierce outburst of wrath?'[m] [24]And the answer will be, 'Because they forsook the covenant which the LORD, the God of their fathers, had made with them when he brought them out of the land of Egypt, [25]and they went and served other gods and adored them, gods whom they did not know and whom he had not let fall to their lot: [26]that is why the LORD was angry with this land and brought on it all the imprecations listed in this book; [27]in his furious wrath and tremendous anger the LORD uprooted them from their soil and cast them out into a strange land,[n] where they are today.' [28][Both what is still hidden* and what has already been revealed concern us and our descendants forever, that we may carry out all the words of this law.]

CHAPTER 30

Mercy for the Repentant [1]"When all these things which I have set before you, the blessings and the curses, are fulfilled in you,[o] and from among whatever nations the LORD, your God, may have dispersed you, you ponder them in your heart: [2]then, provided that you and your children return to the LORD, your God, and heed his voice with all your heart and all your soul,[p] just as I now command you, [3]the LORD, your God, will change your lot; and taking pity on you, he will again gather you from all the nations wherein he has scattered you. [4]Though you may have been driven to the farthest corner of the world, even from there will the LORD, your God, gather you; even from there will he bring you back. [5]The LORD, your God, will then bring you into the land which your fathers once occupied, that you too may occupy it, and he will make you more prosperous and numerous than your fathers. [6]The LORD, your God, will circumcise your hearts* and the hearts of your descendants,[q] that you may love the LORD, your God, with all your heart and all your soul, and so may live. [7]But all those curses the LORD, your God, will assign to your enemies and the foes who persecuted you. [8]You, however, must again heed the LORD's voice and carry out all his commandments which I now enjoin on you. [9]Then the LORD, your God, will increase in more than goodly measure the returns from all your labors, the fruit of your womb, the offspring of your livestock, and the produce of your soil;[r] for the LORD, your God, will again take delight in your prosperity, even as he took delight in your fathers', [10]if only you heed the voice of the LORD, your God, and keep his commandments and statutes that are written in this book of the law, when you return to the LORD, your God, with all your heart and all your soul.

God's Command Clear [11]*"For this command which I enjoin on you today is not too mysterious and remote for you. [12]It is not up in the sky, that you should say, 'Who will go up in the sky to get it for us and tell us of it, that we may carry it out?' [13]Nor is it across the sea, that you should say, 'Who will cross the sea to get it for us and tell us of it, that we may carry it out?' [14]No, it is something very near to you, already in

29, 28: What is still hidden: the events of the future. What has already been revealed: God's law and the punishments in store for those who break it. Leave the future to God; our business is to keep his law.

30, 6: Circumcise your hearts: see note on Dt 10, 16.

30, 11–14: God has revealed his will so clearly that ignorance of his law can be no excuse. St. Paul in Rom 10, 6–10, applies these words to the ease with which we can come to faith and salvation in Christ.

30, 14: In your mouths: that you may readily talk about it; cf Dt 6, 7; 11, 19. And in your hearts: that you may easily remember it; cf Dt 6, 6; 11, 18.

l Gn 14, 10f; 19, 24f. m 23f: 1 Kgs 9, 8f; Jer 22, 8f. n Dn 9, 11–14. o Dt 11, 26ff. p 2f: Neh 1, 9. q Dt 6, 5. r Dt 28, 11.

your mouths* and in your hearts; you have only to carry it out.

The Choice before Israel 15"Here, then, I have today set before you life and prosperity, death and doom. 16If you obey the commandments of the LORD, your God, which I enjoin on you today, loving him, and walking in his ways, and keeping his commandments, statutes and decrees, you will live and grow numerous, and the LORD, your God, will bless you in the land you are entering to occupy. 17If, however, you turn away your hearts and will not listen, but are led astray and adore and serve other gods, 18I tell you now that you will certainly perish; you will not have a long life on the land which you are crossing the Jordan to enter and occupy. 19I call heaven and earth today to witness against you:[s] I have set before you life and death, the blessing and the curse.[t] Choose life, then, that you and your descendants may live, 20by loving the LORD, your God, heeding his voice, and holding fast to him. For that will mean life for you, a long life for you to live on the land which the LORD swore he would give to your fathers Abraham, Isaac and Jacob."

CHAPTER 31

The Lord's Leadership 1When Moses had finished speaking these words to all Israel, 2he said to them, "I am now one hundred and twenty years old[u] and am no longer able to move about freely; besides, the LORD has told me that I shall not cross this Jordan. 3It is the LORD your God, who will cross before you; he will destroy these nations before you, that you may supplant them.[v] [It is Joshua who will cross before you, as the LORD promised.] 4[w]The LORD will deal with them just as he dealt with Sihon and Og, the kings of the Amorites whom he destroyed, and with their country. 5When, therefore, the LORD delivers them up to you, you must deal with them exactly as I have ordered you.[x] 6Be brave and steadfast; have no fear or dread of them, for it is the LORD, your God, who marches with you; he will never fail you or forsake you."[y]

Call of Joshua 7Then Moses summoned Joshua and in the presence of all Israel said to him,[z] "Be brave and steadfast, for you must bring this people into the land which the LORD swore to their fathers he would give them; you must put them in possession of their heritage. 8It is the LORD who marches before you; he will be with you and will never fail you or forsake you. So do not fear or be dismayed."

The Reading of the Law 9When Moses had written down this law, he entrusted it to the levitical priests who carry the ark of the covenant of the LORD, and to all the elders of Israel, 10giving them this order: "On the feast of Booths,[a] at the prescribed time in the year of relaxation* which comes at the end of every seven-year period, 11when all Israel goes to appear before the LORD, your God, in the place which he chooses, you shall read this law* aloud in the presence of all Israel. 12Assemble the people—men, women and children, as well as the aliens who live in your communities—that they may hear it and learn it, and so fear the LORD, your God, and carefully observe all the words of this law. 13Their children also, who do not know it yet, must hear it and learn it, that they too may fear the LORD, your God, as long as you live on the land which you will cross the Jordan to occupy."

Commission of Joshua 14The LORD said to Moses, "The time is now approaching for you to die. Summon Joshua, and present yourselves at the meeting tent that I may give him his commission." So Moses and Joshua went and presented themselves at the meeting tent.* 15And the LORD appeared at the tent in a column of cloud, which stood still at the entrance of the tent.

A Command to Moses 16The LORD said to Moses, "Soon you will be at rest with your fathers, and then this people will take to render-

31, 10: The year of relaxation: cf Dt 15, 1ff and the note there.

31, 11ff: Reading the law not only instructed the people but also consoled them by the assurance of the divine goodness.

31, 14f. 23: V 23 is best read immediately after v 15; perhaps the original order was vv 7–8. 14–15. 23.

s Dt 4, 26. t Dt 11, 26ff; 28, 2. 15. u Dt 34, 7; Nm 20, 12. v Dt 9, 3. w Nm 21, 21–35. x Dt 7, 2. y Dt 20, 3f. z 7f: Jos 1, 6f. 9. a 10f: Dt 16, 13ff.

ing wanton worship to the strange gods among
whom they will live in the land they are about to
enter.[b] They will forsake me and break the
covenant which I have made with them. 17At
that time my anger will flare up against them; I
will forsake them and hide my face from them,
so that they will become a prey to be devoured,
and many evils and troubles will befall them. At
that time they will indeed say, 'Is it not because
our God is not among us that these evils have
befallen us?' 18Yet I will be hiding my face from
them at that time only because of all the evil
they have done in turning to other gods. 19Write
out this song,[c] then, for yourselves. Teach it to
the Israelites and have them recite it, so that this
song may be a witness for me against the
Israelites. 20For when I have brought them into
the land flowing with milk and honey which I
promised on oath to their fathers, and they have
eaten their fill and grown fat, if they turn to
other gods and serve them, despising me and
breaking my covenant; 21then, when many evils
and troubles befall them, this song, which their
descendants will not have forgotten to recite,
will bear witness against them. For I know what
they are inclined to do even at the present time,
before I have brought them into the land which I
promised on oath to their fathers." 22So Moses
wrote this song that same day, and he taught it
to the Israelites.

Commission of Joshua 23Then the LORD com-
missioned Joshua, son of Nun, and said to him,
"Be brave and steadfast, for it is you who must
bring the Israelites into the land which I prom-
ised them on oath.[d] I myself will be with you."

The Law Placed in the Ark 24When Moses
had finished writing out on a scroll the words of
the law in their entirety, 25he gave the Levites[e]
who carry the ark of the covenant of the LORD
this order: 26"Take this scroll of the law and put
it beside the ark of the covenant of the LORD,
your God, that there it may be a witness against
you. 27For I already know how rebellious and
stiff-necked you will be. Why, even now, while I
am alive among you, you have been rebels
against the LORD! How much more, then, after I
am dead! 28[f]Therefore, assemble all your tribal
elders and your officials before me, that I may
speak these words for them to hear, and so may
call heaven and earth to witness against them.
29[g]For I know that after my death you are sure
to become corrupt and to turn aside from the
way along which I directed you, so that evil will
befall you in some future age because you have
done evil in the LORD's sight, and provoked him
by your deeds."

The Song of Moses 30Then Moses recited the
words of this song from beginning to end, for the
whole assembly of Israel to hear:

CHAPTER 32

A

1 Give ear, O heavens, while I speak;*
    let the earth hearken to the words of my
        mouth!
2 May my instruction soak in like the rain,
    and my discourse permeate like the dew,
Like a downpour upon the grass,
    like a shower upon the crops:
3 For I will sing the LORD's renown.
    Oh, proclaim the greatness of our God!
4 The Rock—how faultless are his deeds,
    how right all his ways!
A faithful God, without deceit,
    how just and upright he is![h]
5 Yet basely has he been treated by his
        degenerate children,
    a perverse and crooked race![i]
6 Is the LORD to be thus repaid by you,
    O stupid and foolish people?
Is he not your father who created you?
    Has he not made you and established you?[j]
7 Think back on the days of old,

32, 1–43: In the style of the great prophets, the speaker is often God himself. The whole song is a poetic sermon, having for its theme God's benefits to Israel (vv 1–14) and Israel's ingratitude and idolatry in turning to the gods of the pagans, which sins will be punished by the pagans themselves (vv 15–29); in turn, the foolish pride of the pagans will be punished, and the Lord's honor will be vindicated (vv 30–43).

b Jgs 2, 12. 17. c Dt 31, 21; 32, 1–43. d Dt 31, 7f; Jos 1, 5ff. e 24f: Dt 31, 9. f Dt 32, 1–43. g Jgs 2, 19. h Ps 92, 15; Rv 15, 3. i Dt 31, 29; Ps 78, 8; Lk 9, 41. j Ex 4, 22; Is 63, 16; 64, 8; Jer 31, 9.

reflect on the years of age upon age.
Ask your father and he will inform you,
ask your elders and they will tell you: [k]
8 When the Most High assigned the nations their heritage,
when he parceled out the descendants of Adam, [l]
He set up the boundaries of the peoples
after the number of the sons of God;*
9 While the LORD's own portion was Jacob,
his hereditary share was Israel. [m]

10 He found them in a wilderness,
a wasteland of howling desert.
He shielded them and cared for them,
guarding them as the apple of his eye. [n]

11 As an eagle incites its nestlings forth
by hovering over its brood,
So he spread his wings to receive them
and bore them up on his pinions. [o]
12 The LORD alone was their leader,
no strange god was with him.
13 He had them ride triumphant over the summits of the land*
and live off the products of its fields,
Giving them honey to suck from its rocks
and olive oil from its hard, stony ground;

14 Butter from its cows and milk from its sheep,
with the fat of its lambs and rams;
Its Bashan* bulls and its goats,
with the cream of its finest wheat;
and the foaming blood of its grapes you drank.

B

15 [So Jacob ate his fill,]
the darling* grew fat and frisky;
you became fat and gross and gorged.
They spurned the God who made them
and scorned their saving Rock. [p]

16 They provoked him with strange gods
and angered him with abominable idols. [q]

17 They offered sacrifice to demons, to "no-gods,"
to gods whom they had not known before,
To newcomers just arrived,
of whom their fathers had never stood in awe.
18 You were unmindful of the Rock that begot you,
You forgot the God who gave you birth. [r]
19 When the LORD saw this, he was filled with loathing
and anger toward his sons and daughters.
20 "I will hide my face from them," he said,
"and see what will then become of them.
What a fickle race they are,
sons with no loyalty in them! [s]
21 "Since they have provoked me with their 'no-god'
and angered me with their vain idols,
I will provoke them with a 'no-people';
with a foolish nation I will anger them. [t]

22 "For by my wrath a fire is enkindled
that shall rage to the depths of the netherworld,
Consuming the earth with its yield,
and licking with flames the roots of the mountains. [u]
23 I will spend on them woe upon woe
and exhaust all my arrows against them:

24 "Emaciating hunger and consuming fever
and bitter pestilence,
And the teeth of wild beasts I will send among them,
with the venom of reptiles gliding in the dust.

25 "Snatched away by the sword in the street
and by sheer terror at home

32, 8: The sons of God: the angels; cf Jb 1, 6; 2, 1; 38, 7; Ps 89, 7f. Here the various nations are portrayed as having their respective guardian angels. Cf Dn 10, 20f; 12, 1.

32, 13: The land: Canaan.

32, 14: Bashan: a fertile grazing land east of the Jordan, famous for its strong cattle. Cf Ps 22, 13; Ez 39, 18; Am 4, 1.

32, 15: The darling: a probable meaning of the Hebrew word yeshurun, a term of endearment for "Israel." Cf Dt 33, 5. 26; Is 44, 2.

k Dt 4, 32; Ps 44, 2. l Gn 10, 1–32; Acts 17, 26. m Ex 19, 5; Ps 33, 12. n Dt 8, 15; Jer 2, 6; Zec 2, 8. o Ex 19, 4. p Dt 31, 20. q Nm 25, 2f; Ps 78, 58. r Jer 2, 32. s Dt 31, 17. t Rom 10, 19. u Lam 4, 11.

Shall be the youth and the maiden alike,
the nursing babe as well as the hoary old man.[v]

26 "I would have said, 'I will make an end of them
and blot out their name from men's memories,'
27 Had I not feared the insolence of their enemies,
feared that these foes would mistakenly boast,
'Our own hand won the victory;
the LORD had nothing to do with it.' "

28 For they are a people devoid of reason,*
having no understanding.
29 If they had insight they would realize what happened,
they would understand their future and say,

C

30 "How could one man rout a thousand,
or two men put ten thousand to flight,
Unless it was because their Rock sold them
and the LORD delivered them up?"
31 Indeed, their "rock" is not like our Rock,
and our foes are under condemnation.

32 They are a branch of Sodom's vine-stock,
from the vineyards of Gomorrah.
Poisonous are their grapes
and bitter their clusters.
33 Their wine is the venom of dragons
and the cruel poison of cobras.

34 "Is not this preserved in my treasury,
sealed up in my storehouse,
35 Against the day of vengeance and requital,
against the time they lose their footing?"
Close at hand is the day of their disaster,
and their doom is rushing upon them!

36 Surely, the LORD shall do justice for his people;
on his servants he shall have pity.
When he sees their strength failing,
and their protected and unprotected* alike disappearing,[w]
37 He will say, "Where are their gods[x]
whom they relied on as their 'rock'?
38 Let those who ate the fat of your sacrifices
and drank the wine of your libations
Rise up now and help you!
Let them be your protection!

39 "Learn then that I, I alone, am God,
and there is no god besides me.
It is I who bring both death and life,
I who inflict wounds and heal them,
and from my hand there is no rescue.[y]

40 "To the heavens I raise my hand and swear:
As surely as I live forever,

41 I will sharpen my flashing sword,
and my hand shall lay hold of my quiver.

"With vengeance I will repay my foes
and requite those who hate me.
42 I will make my arrows drunk with blood,
and my sword shall gorge itself with flesh—
With the blood of the slain and the captured,
Flesh from the heads of the enemy leaders."

43 Exult with him, you heavens,
glorify him, all you angels of God;
For he avenges the blood of his servants
and purges his people's land.

44 So Moses, together with Joshua, son of Nun,
went and recited all the words of this song for
the people to hear.

Final Appeal 45 When Moses had finished
speaking all these words to all Israel, 46 he said,[z]
"Take to heart all the warning which I have
now given you and which you must impress on
your children, that you may carry out carefully
every word of this law. 47 For this is no trivial
matter for you; rather, it means your very life,
since it is by this means that you are to enjoy a
long life on the land which you will cross the
Jordan to occupy."

32, 28–35: The reference is to the pagan nations, not to Israel.

32, 36: Their protected and unprotected: the meaning of the Hebrew is uncertain; according to some, the idea is "slaves and freemen."

v Lv 26, 25. w 2 Mc 7, 6. x 37f: Jgs 10, 14; Jer 2, 28. y Dt 4, 35; Tb 13, 2; Wis 16, 13. z Dt 4, 9.

Moses to View Canaan 48On that very day
the LORD said to Moses, 49"Go up on Mount
Nebo, here in the Abarim Mountains [it is in the
land of Moab facing Jericho], and view the land
of Canaan, which I am giving to the Israelites as
their possession. [a] 50Then you shall die on the
mountain you have climbed, and shall be taken
to your people, just as your brother Aaron died
on Mount Hor and there was taken to his
people; [b] 51because both of you broke faith with
me among the Israelites at the waters of
Meribath-kadesh in the desert of Zin by failing to
manifest my sanctity among the Israelites. [c]
52You may indeed view the land at a distance,
but you shall not enter that land which I am
giving to the Israelites." [d]

CHAPTER 33

Blessing upon the Tribes 1This is the blessing which Moses, the man of God, pronounced upon the Israelites before he died. 2He said:

"The LORD came from Sinai*
and dawned on his people from Seir;
He shone forth from Mount Paran
and advanced from Meribath-kadesh,
While at his right hand a fire blazed forth
and his wrath devastated the nations. [e]
3 But all his holy ones were in his hand;*
they followed at his feet
and he bore them up on his pinions.
4 A law he gave to us;
he made the community of Jacob his domain, [f]
5 and he became king of his darling,*
When the chiefs of the people assembled
and the tribes of Israel came together.
6 "May Reuben live and not die out, [g]
but let his men be few."*

7 The following is for Judah. He said:
"The LORD hears the cry of Judah;
you will bring him to his people.*
His own hands defend his cause
and you will be his help against his foes." [h]

8 Of Levi he said:
"To Levi belong your Thummim,
to the man of your favor your Urim;*
For you put him to the test at Massah
and you contended with him at the waters of Meribah. [i]
9 He said of his father, 'I regard him not';
his brothers he would not acknowledge,
and his own children he refused to recognize.
Thus the Levites keep your words,
and your covenant they uphold.*
10 They promulgate your decisions to Jacob
and your law to Israel.
They bring the smoke of sacrifice to your nostrils,
and burnt offerings to your altar. [j]
11 Bless, O LORD, his possessions
and accept the ministry of his hands.
Break the backs of his adversaries
and of his foes, that they may not rise."

12 Of Benjamin he said:
"Benjamin is the beloved of the LORD,
who shelters him all the day,
while he abides securely at his breast." [k]

13 Of Joseph he said: [l]
"Blessed by the LORD is his land
with the best of the skies above
and of the abyss crouching beneath;
14 With the best of the produce of the year,
and the choicest sheaves of the months;

33, 2–5. 26–29: These verses seem to form an independent hymn describing, in the form of a theophany, the conquest of Canaan. The first section of this hymn (vv 2–5) serves here as an introduction to the various "blessings"; the second section (vv 26–29), as their conclusion.

33, 3: His holy ones were in his hand: the Israelites were protected by the Lord.

33, 5. 26: The darling: see note on Dt 32, 15.

33, 6: In keeping with the other blessings, probably this verse was once introduced by the phrase, "Of Reuben he said." It is to be noted that there is no blessing here for Simeon.

33, 7: Bring him to his people: this probably refers to the isolated position of the tribe of Judah during the conquest of the Promised Land (cf Jgs 1, 17–19); according to some commentators the reference is to the divided kingdom.

33, 8: Thummim . . . Urim: see note on Ex 28, 30.

33, 9: The reference is probably to the Levites' slaughter of their brethren after the affair of the golden calf in the desert; cf Ex 32, 27–29.

a Nm 27, 12; 33, 47f. b Nm 20, 24ff. 28; 27, 13; 33, 38. c Nm 20, 12; 27, 14. d Dt 3, 27; 34, 4. e Ex 19, 18. 20; Jgs 5, 4f. f Jn 1, 17; 7, 19. g Gn 49, 3f. h Gn 49, 8–12. i Gn 49, 5; Ex 17, 7; 28, 30; Nm 20, 13. j Ex 30, 7f. k Gn 49, 27. l 13–17: Gn 49, 22–26.

15 With the finest gifts of the age-old mountains
and the best from the timeless hills;
16 With the best of the earth and its fullness,
and the favor of him who dwells in the bush.*
These shall come upon the head of Joseph
and upon the brow of the prince among his brothers,
17 The majestic bull, his father's first-born,
whose horns are those of the wild ox
With which to gore the nations,
even those at the ends of the earth."
[These are the myriads of Ephraim,
and these the thousands of Manasseh.]

18 Of Zebulun he said: [m]
"Rejoice, O Zebulun, in your pursuits,
and you, Issachar, in your tents!
19 You who invite the tribes to the mountains
where feasts are duly held,
Because you suck up the abundance of the seas*
and the hidden treasures of the sand."

20 Of Gad he said: [n]
"Blessed be he who has made Gad so vast!
He lies there like a lion
that has seized the arm and head of the prey.
21 He saw that the best should be his
when the princely portion* was assigned,
while the heads of the people were gathered.
He carried out the justice of the LORD
and his decrees respecting Israel." [o]

22 Of Dan he said:
"Dan is a lion's whelp, [p]
that springs forth from Bashan!"*

23 Of Naphtali he said:
"Naphtali is enriched with favors
and filled with the blessings of the LORD;
The lake* and south of it are his possession!" [q]

24 Of Asher he said: [r]
"More blessed than the other sons be Asher!
May he be the favorite among his brothers,
as the oil of his olive trees runs over his feet!*
25 May your bolts be of iron and bronze;
may your strength endure through all your days!"

26 "There is no god like the God of the darling,
who rides the heavens in his power,
and rides the skies in his majesty;
27 He spread out the primeval tent;
he extended the ancient canopy.
He drove the enemy out of your way
and the Amorite he destroyed.
28 Israel has dwelt securely,
and the fountain of Jacob has been undisturbed.
In a land of grain and wine,
where the heavens drip with dew. [s]
29 How fortunate you are, O Israel!
Where else is a nation victorious in the LORD?
The LORD is your saving shield,
and his sword is your glory.
Your enemies fawn upon you,
as you stride upon their heights." [t]

CHAPTER 34

Death and Burial of Moses 1 Then Moses
went up from the plains of Moab to Mount
Nebo, [u] the headland of Pisgah which faces
Jericho, and the LORD showed him all the land—
Gilead, and as far as Dan, 2 all Naphtali, the land
of Ephraim and Manasseh, all the land of Judah

33, 16: Him who dwells in the bush: a title given to the Lord because of his appearance to Moses in the burning bush; cf Ex 3.

33, 19: The abundance of the seas: perhaps the wealth that comes from sea-borne trade or from fishing. The hidden treasures of the sand: possibly an allusion to the valuable purple dye extracted from certain marine shells found on the coast of northern Palestine.

33, 21: The princely portion: Moses gave the tribe of Gad their land on the east of the Jordan only on condition that they would help the other tribes conquer the land west of the river; cf Nm 32; Jos 22.

33, 22: The sense is, "May he leap up like a lion of Bashan"; the heavily wooded hills of Bashan were notorious for their lions, but the tribe of Dan was not settled in this region.

33, 23: The lake: the Lake of Gennesaret on which the land of this tribe bordered.

33, 24: The land of the tribe of Asher was covered with olive groves.

m 18f: Gn 49, 13ff. n 20f: Gn 49, 19. o Nm 32, 1. 5. 16–19. 31f; Jos 1, 12–15; 1 Chr 5, 18–22. p Gn 49, 16f. q Gn 49, 21; Jos 19, 32–39. r 24f: Gn 49, 20. s Gn 27, 28. t Dt 4, 7f. u Dt 3, 27.

as far as the Western Sea, [3]the Negeb, the circuit
of the Jordan with the lowlands at Jericho, city of
palms, and as far as Zoar. [4]The LORD then said to
him, "This is the land[v] which I swore to
Abraham, Isaac and Jacob that I would give to
their descendants. I have let you feast your eyes
upon it, but you shall not cross over." [5]So there,
in the land of Moab, Moses, the servant of the
LORD, died[w] as the LORD had said; [6]and he was
buried in the ravine opposite Beth-peor in the
land of Moab, but to this day no one knows the
place of his burial. [7]Moses was one hundred and
twenty years old[x] when he died, yet his eyes
were undimmed and his vigor unabated. [8]For
thirty days the Israelites wept for Moses in the
plains of Moab, till they had completed the
period of grief and mourning for Moses.

[9]Now Joshua, son of Nun,[y] was filled with the
spirit of wisdom, since Moses had laid his hands
upon him; and so the Israelites gave him their
obedience, thus carrying out the LORD's com-
mand to Moses.

[10] [z]Since then no prophet has arisen in Israel
like Moses, whom the LORD knew face to face.
[11] [a]He had no equal in all the signs and wonders
the LORD sent him to perform in the land of
Egypt against Pharaoh and all his servants and
against all his land, [12]and for the might and the
terrifying power that Moses exhibited in the
sight of all Israel.

v Dt 3, 27; 32, 52; Gn 12, 7; 15, 18. w Dt 32, 50. x Dt 31, 2. y Nm 27, 18. 23; Jos 1, 17. z Ex 33, 11. a Dt 4, 34.

THE BOOK OF JOSHUA

The Book of Joshua derives its name from the successor of Moses, with whose deeds it is principally concerned. The purpose of the book is to demonstrate God's fidelity in giving to the Israelites the land he had promised them for an inheritance (Gn 15, 18ff; Jos 1, 2ff; 21, 41ff; 23, 14ff).

Their occupation of the country is begun with the crossing of the Jordan and the conquest of Jericho (ch 1—6), in both of which the Lord intervenes on their behalf. This is followed by a first foothold on the Palestinian mountain range, at Ai, Bethel and Gibeon (ch 7—9), and two sweeping campaigns against the city-states in the south of the country (ch 10) and in the north (ch 11), with a summary in ch 12. The broad claim to total sovereignty thus established is spelled out by a combined list of tribal boundaries and of the towns contained within each area or administrative district (ch 13—19), including cities of asylum and cities for the Levites (ch 20, 21). The book closes with a narrative about the tribes east of the Jordan (ch 22), a warning speech by Joshua (ch 23), and a renewal at Shechem (ch 24) of the covenant with the Lord, already affirmed there near the beginning (8, 30-35) of the conquest.

Like the books which precede it, the Book of Joshua was built up by a long and complex process of editing traditional materials. Both Jewish and Christian believers have always regarded it as inspired.

The entire history of the conquest of the Promised Land is a prophecy of the spiritual conquest of the world through the church under the leadership of Jesus the Messiah.

The Book of Joshua may be divided as follows:

I. Conquest of Canaan (Jos 1, 1—12, 24).
II. Division of the Land (Jos 13, 1—21, 45).
III. Return of the Transjordan Tribes and Joshua's Farewell (Jos 22, 1—24, 33).

I: Conquest of Canaan

CHAPTER 1

Divine Promise of Assistance 1After Moses, the servant of the LORD, had died, the LORD said to Moses' aide Joshua, son of Nun: 2"My servant Moses is dead. So prepare to cross the Jordan here, with all the people, into the land I will give the Israelites. 3As I promised Moses, I will deliver to you every place where you set foot. 4*Your domain is to be all the land of the Hittites, from the desert and from Lebanon east to the great river Euphrates and west to the Great Sea.[a] 5No one can withstand you while you live. I will be with you as I was with Moses:[b] I will not leave you nor forsake you. 6Be firm and steadfast, so that you may give this people possession of the land which I swore to their fathers I would give them. 7Above all, be firm and steadfast, taking care to observe the entire law which my servant Moses enjoined on you. Do not swerve from it either to the right or to the left, that you may succeed wherever you go. 8Keep this book of the law on your lips. Recite it by day and by night, that you may observe carefully all that is written in it; then you will successfully attain your goal. 9I command you: be firm and steadfast! Do not fear nor be dismayed, for the LORD, your God, is with you wherever you go."[c]

10So Joshua commanded the officers of the people: 11"Go through the camp and instruct the people, 'Prepare your provisions, for three days from now you shall cross the Jordan here, to march in and take possession of the land which the LORD, your God, is giving you.' "[d]

The Transjordan Tribes 12Joshua reminded the Reubenites, the Gadites, and the half-tribe of Manasseh: 13"Remember what Moses, the servant of the LORD, commanded you when he said, 'The LORD, your God, will permit you to settle in this land.' 14Your wives, your children, and your livestock shall remain in the land Moses gave you here beyond the Jordan.[e] But all the warriors among you must cross over armed ahead of your kinsmen and you must help them 15until the LORD has settled your kinsmen, and they like you possess the land which the LORD, your God, is giving them. Afterward you may return and occupy your own land, which Moses, the servant of the LORD, has given you east of the Jordan."[f] 16"We will do all you have commanded us," they answered Joshua, "and we will go wherever you send us. We will obey you as completely as we obeyed Moses. 17But may the LORD, your God, be with you as he was with Moses. 18If anyone rebels against your orders and does not obey every command you give him, he shall be put to death. But be firm and steadfast."

CHAPTER 2

Spies Saved by Rahab 1Then Joshua, son of Nun, secretly sent out two spies from Shittim, saying, "Go, reconnoiter the land and Jericho." When the two reached Jericho, they went into the house of a harlot* named Rahab,[g] where they lodged. 2But a report was brought to the king of Jericho that some Israelites had come there that night to spy out the land. 3So the king of Jericho sent Rahab the order, "Put out the visitors who have entered your house, for they have come to spy out the entire land." 4The woman[h] had taken the two men and hidden them, so she said, "True, the men you speak of came to me, but I did not know where they came from. 5At dark, when it was time for the gate to be shut, they left, and I do not know where they went. You will have to pursue them immediately to overtake them." 6Now, she had led them to the roof, and hidden them among her stalks of flax spread out* there. 7But the pursuers set out along the way to the fords of the

1, 4: The ideal frontiers are given: in the south the desert of Sinai, in the north the Lebanon range, in the east the Euphrates, and in the west the Great Sea, the Mediterranean.

2, 1: Harlot: this is the regular equivalent of the Hebrew word, but perhaps it is used here of Rahab in the broader sense of a woman who kept a public house. Joshua's spies hoped to remain undetected at such an inn.

2, 6: Stalks of flax spread out: to dry in the sun, after they had been soaked in water, according to the ancient process of preparing flax for linen-making. In the Near East the flax harvest occurs near the time of the feast of the Passover (Jos 4, 19; 5, 10); cf Ex 9, 31.

a 3f: Jos 14, 9; Gn 15, 18; Dt 11, 24. b Dt 31, 8; Heb 13, 5. c 7. 9: Dt 31, 7f. d Dt 11, 31. e Nm 32, 26. f Jos 22, 4; Dt 3, 20. g Mt 1, 5; Jas 2, 25. h Jos 6, 17.

Jordan, and once they had left, the gate was shut.

[8]Before the spies fell asleep, Rahab* came to them on the roof [9]and said: "I know that the LORD has given you the land, that a dread of you has come upon us, and that all the inhabitants of the land are overcome with fear of you.[i] [10]For we have heard how the LORD dried up the waters of the Red Sea before you when you came out of Egypt,[j] and how you dealt with Sihon and Og, the two kings of the Amorites beyond the Jordan, whom you doomed to destruction. [11]At these reports, we are disheartened; everyone is discouraged because of you, since the LORD, your God, is God in heaven above and on earth below.[k] [12]Now then, swear to me by the LORD that, since I am showing kindness to you, you in turn will show kindness to my family;[l] and give me an unmistakable token [13]that you are to spare my father and mother, brothers and sisters, and all their kin, and save us from death." [14]"We pledge our lives for yours," the men answered her. "If you do not betray this errand of ours, we will be faithful in showing kindness to you when the LORD gives us the land."

[15]Then she let them down through the window with a rope; for she lived in a house built into the city wall.* [16]"Go up into the hill country," she suggested to them, "that your pursuers may not find you. Hide there for three days, until they return; then you may proceed on your way." [17]The men answered her, "This is how we will fulfill the oath you made us take: [18]When we come into the land, tie this scarlet cord in the window through which you are letting us down; and gather your father and mother, your brothers and all your family into your house. [19]Should any of them pass outside the doors of your house, he will be responsible for his own death, and we shall be guiltless. But we shall be responsible if anyone in the house with you is harmed. [20]If, however, you betray this errand of ours, we shall be quit of the oath you have made us take." [21]"Let it be as you say," she replied, and bade them farewell. When they were gone, she tied the scarlet cord in the window.

[22]They went up into the hills, where they stayed three days until their pursuers, who had sought them all along the road without finding them, returned. [23]Then the two came back down from the hills, crossed the Jordan to Joshua, son of Nun, and reported all that had befallen them. [24]They assured Joshua, "The LORD has delivered all this land into our power; indeed, all the inhabitants of the land are overcome with fear of us."

CHAPTER 3

Preparations for Crossing the Jordan [1]Early the next morning, Joshua[m] moved with all the Israelites from Shittim to the Jordan, where they lodged before crossing over. [2]Three days later the officers went through the camp [3]and issued these instructions to the people: "When you see the ark of the covenant of the LORD, your God, which the levitical priests will carry, you must also break camp and follow it, [4]that you may know the way to take, for you have not gone over this road before. But let there be a space of two thousand cubits between you and the ark. Do not come nearer to it." [5]Joshua also said to the people, "Sanctify yourselves, for tomorrow the LORD will perform wonders among you." [6]And he directed the priests to take up the ark of the covenant and go on ahead of the people; and they did so.

[7]Then the LORD said to Joshua, "Today I will begin to exalt you in the sight of all Israel, that they may know I am with you, as I was with Moses.[n] [8]Now command the priests carrying the ark of the covenant to come to a halt in the Jordan when they reach the edge of the waters."

2, 8–11: Rahab's faith and good works are praised in the New Testament; cf Heb 11, 31; Jas 2, 25.

2, 15: A house built into the city wall: such houses, which used the city wall for their own inner walls, have been found at ancient sites. The upper story of Rahab's house was evidently higher than the city wall. It was through the window of such a house that St. Paul escaped from Damascus; cf Acts 9, 25; 2 Cor 11, 33.

i Ex 15, 15f; 23, 27. j Jos 4, 23; Ex 14, 21; Nm 21, 23–26. 33ff. k Dt 4, 39. l Jos 2, 18; 6, 23. 25. m Jos 2, 1. n Jos 1, 5; 4, 14.

9So Joshua said to the Israelites, "Come here and listen to the words of the LORD, your God." 10He continued: "This is how you will know that there is a living God in your midst, who at your approach will dispossess the Canaanites, Hittites, Hivites, Perizzites, Girgashites, Amorites and Jebusites.[o] 11The ark of the covenant of the LORD of the whole earth will precede you into the Jordan. 12[Now choose twelve men,[p] one from each of the tribes of Israel.] 13When the soles of the feet of the priests carrying the ark of the LORD, the Lord of the whole earth, touch the water of the Jordan, it will cease to flow; for the water flowing down from upstream will halt in a solid bank."

The Crossing Begun 14The people struck their tents to cross the Jordan, with the priests carrying the ark of the covenant ahead of them. 15No sooner had these priestly bearers of the ark waded into the waters at the edge of the Jordan, which overflows all its banks during the entire season of the harvest,* 16than the waters flowing from upstream halted, backing up in a solid mass[q] for a very great distance indeed, from Adam, a city in the direction of Zarethan; while those flowing downstream toward the Salt Sea of the Arabah disappeared entirely.* Thus the people crossed over opposite Jericho. 17While all Israel crossed over on dry ground, the priests carrying the ark of the covenant of the LORD remained motionless on dry ground in the bed of the Jordan[r] until the whole nation had completed the passage.

CHAPTER 4

Memorial Stones 1After the entire nation had crossed the Jordan, the LORD said to Joshua, 2"Choose twelve men[s] from the people, one from each tribe, 3and instruct them to take up twelve stones from this spot in the bed of the Jordan where the priests have been standing motionless.[t] Carry them over with you, and place them where you are to stay tonight."

4Summoning the twelve men whom he had selected from among the Israelites, one from each tribe, 5Joshua said to them: "Go to the bed of the Jordan in front of the ark of the LORD, your God; lift to your shoulders one stone apiece, so that they will equal in number the tribes of the Israelites. 6In the future, these are to be a sign among you. When your children ask you what these stones mean to you, 7you shall answer them, 'The waters of the Jordan ceased to flow before the ark of the covenant of the LORD when it crossed the Jordan.'[u] Thus these stones are to serve as a perpetual memorial to the Israelites." 8The twelve Israelites did as Joshua had commanded: they took up as many stones from the bed of the Jordan as there were tribes of the Israelites, and carried them along to the camp site, where they placed them, according to the LORD's direction. 9Joshua also had twelve stones set up in the bed of the Jordan on the spot where the priests stood who were carrying the ark of the covenant. They are there to this day.

10*The priests carrying the ark remained in the bed of the Jordan until everything had been done that the LORD had commanded Joshua to tell the people. The people crossed over quickly, 11and when all had reached the other side, the ark of the LORD, borne by the priests, also crossed to its place in front of them. 12The Reubenites, Gadites, and half-tribe of Manasseh, armed, marched in the vanguard of the Israelites, as Moses had ordered.[v] 13About forty thousand troops equipped for battle passed over before the LORD to the plains of Jericho.

14That day the LORD exalted Joshua in the sight of all Israel,[w] and thenceforth during his

3, 15: Season of the harvest: toward the end of March and the beginning of April, when the grain and other crops that grew during the rainy season of winter were reaped. The crossing took place "on the tenth day of the first month" of the Hebrew year, which began with the first new moon after the spring equinox; cf Jos 4, 19. At this time of the year the Jordan would be swollen as a result of the winter rains and the melting snow of Mount Hermon.

3, 16: The sudden damming of the river could have been caused by a landslide, as has happened on other occasions. The miraculous character of this event would not thereby be removed because God, who foretold it (Jos 3, 13), also caused it to take place at precisely the right moment (Jos 3, 15), whether or not he used natural forces to accomplish his will.

4, 10–18: After the digression about the two sets of memorial stones, the author resumes the narrative by briefly repeating the story of the crossing, which he had already told in Jos 3, 14–17.

o Ex 33, 2; Dt 7, 1. p Jos 4, 2. 4. q Ps 114, 3. r Jos 4, 7. 22. s Jos 3, 12. t Jos 3, 13; 4, 8f; Dt 27, 2. u Jos 3, 13. 16. v Dt 3, 18. w Jos 3, 7.

whole life they respected him as they had
respected Moses.
15 Then the LORD said to Joshua, 16 "Command
the priests carrying the ark of the command-
ments to come up from the Jordan."[x] 17 Joshua
did so, 18 and when the priests carrying the ark of
the covenant of the LORD had come up from the
bed of the Jordan, as the soles of their feet
regained the dry ground, the waters of the
Jordan resumed their course and as before over-
flowed all its banks.
19 The people came up from the Jordan on the
tenth day of the first month, and camped in
Gilgal on the eastern limits of Jericho. 20 At Gilgal
Joshua set up the twelve stones which had been
taken from the Jordan, 21 saying to the Israelites,
"In the future, when the children among you ask
their fathers what these stones mean, 22 you shall
inform them, 'Israel crossed the Jordan here on
dry ground.' 23 For the LORD, your God, dried up
the waters of the Jordan in front of you until you
crossed over, just as the LORD, your God, had
done at the Red Sea, which he dried up in front
of us until we crossed over;[y] 24 in order that all
the peoples of the earth may learn that the hand
of the LORD is mighty, and that you may fear the
LORD, your God, forever."

CHAPTER 5

Rites at Gilgal 1 When all the kings of the
Amorites to the west of the Jordan and all the
kings of the Canaanites by the sea heard that the
LORD had dried up the waters of the Jordan
before the Israelites until they crossed over, they
were disheartened and lost courage at their
approach.
2 On this occasion the LORD said to Joshua,
"Make flint knives and circumcise the Israelite
nation for the second time." 3 So Joshua made
flint knives and circumcised the Israelites at
Gibeath-haaraloth,* 4 under these circum-
stances: Of all the people who came out of
Egypt, every man of military age had died in the
desert[z] during the journey after they left Egypt.
5 Though all the men who came out were
circumcised, none of those born in the desert
during the journey after the departure from
Egypt were circumcised. 6 Now the Israelites had
wandered forty years in the desert, until all the
warriors among the people that came forth from
Egypt died off because they had not obeyed the
command of the LORD.[a] For the LORD swore[b]
that he would not let them see the land flowing
with milk and honey which he had promised
their fathers he would give us. 7 [c]It was the
children whom he raised up in their stead whom
Joshua circumcised, for these were yet with
foreskins, not having been circumcised on the
journey. 8 When the rite had been performed, the
whole nation remained in camp where they
were, until they recovered. 9 Then the LORD said
to Joshua, "Today I have removed the reproach
of Egypt from you."[d] Therefore the place is
called Gilgal* to the present day.
10 [e]While the Israelites were encamped at
Gilgal on the plains of Jericho, they celebrated
the Passover on the evening of the fourteenth of
the month.* 11 On the day after the Passover
they ate of the produce of the land in the form of
unleavened cakes and parched grain. On that
same day 12 after the Passover on which they ate
of the produce of the land, the manna ceased.
No longer was there manna for the Israelites,
who that year ate of the yield of the land of
Canaan.[f]
Siege at Jericho 13 *While Joshua was near
Jericho, he raised his eyes and saw one who
stood facing him, drawn sword in hand.[g] Joshua
went up to him and asked, "Are you one of us or
of our enemies?" 14 He replied, "Neither. I am

5, 3: Gibeath-haaraloth: "Hill of the Foreskins."

5, 9: The place is called Gilgal: by popular etymology, because of the similarity of sound with the Hebrew word gallothi, "I have removed." Gilgal probably means "(the place of) the circle of standing stones." Cf Jos 4, 4–8.

5, 10: The month: the first month of the year, later called Nisan; see note on Jos 3, 15. The crossing of the Jordan occurred, therefore, about the same time of the year as did the equally miraculous crossing of the Red Sea; cf Ex 12–14.

5, 13–6, 26: The account of the siege of Jericho embraces: (1) the command of the Lord, through his angel, to Joshua (Jos 5, 13—6, 5); (2) Joshua's instructions to the Israelites, with a brief summary of how these orders were carried out (Jos 6, 6–11); (3) a description of the action on each of the first six days (Jos 6, 12–14); (4) the events on the seventh day (Jos 6, 15–26).

x Jos 3, 6. y Ex 14, 21. z Nm 14, 29; 26, 64f; Dt 2, 16; Ps 106, 26; 1 Cor 10, 5. a Nm 14, 29. b Heb 3, 11. 17. c Dt 1, 39. d Jos 4, 19. e Ex 12, 6; Lv 23, 5; Nm 9, 3–5. f Ex 16, 35. g Ex 23, 20.

the captain of the host of the LORD and I have
just arrived." Then Joshua fell prostrate to the
ground in worship, and said to him, "What has
my lord to say to his servant?" 15 The captain of
the host of the LORD replied to Joshua, "Remove
your sandals from your feet, for the place on
which you are standing is holy."[h] And Joshua
obeyed.

CHAPTER 6

1 Now Jericho was in a state of siege because
of the presence of the Israelites, so that no one
left or entered. 2 And to Joshua the LORD said, "I
have delivered Jericho and its king into your
power. 3 Have all the soldiers circle the city,
marching once around it. Do this for six days,
4 [i]with seven priests carrying ram's horns ahead
of the ark. On the seventh day march around the
city seven times, and have the priests blow the
horns. 5 When they give a long blast on the ram's
horns and you hear that signal, all the people
shall shout aloud. The wall of the city will
collapse, and they will be able to make a frontal
attack."

6 Summoning the priests, Joshua, son of Nun,
then ordered them to take up the ark of the
covenant with seven of the priests carrying ram's
horns in front of the ark of the LORD. 7 And he
ordered the people to proceed in a circle around
the city, with the picked troops marching ahead
of the ark of the LORD. 8 At this order they
proceeded, with the seven priests who carried
the ram's horns before the LORD blowing their
horns, and the ark of the covenant of the LORD
following them. 9 In front of the priests with the
horns marched the picked troops; the rear guard
followed the ark, and the blowing of horns was
kept up continually as they marched. 10 But the
people had been commanded by Joshua not to
shout or make any noise or outcry until he gave
the word: only then were they to shout. 11 So he
had the ark of the LORD circle the city, going
once around it, after which they returned to
camp for the night.

12 Early the next morning, Joshua had the
priests take up the ark of the LORD. 13 The seven
priests bearing the ram's horns marched in front
of the ark of the LORD, blowing their horns.
Ahead of these marched the picked troops, while
the rear guard followed the ark of the LORD, and
the blowing of horns was kept up continually.
14 On this second day they again marched around
the city once before returning to camp; and for
six days in all they did the same.

15 On the seventh day, beginning at daybreak,
they marched around the city seven times in the
same manner; on that day only did they march
around the city seven times. 16 The seventh time
around, the priests blew the horns and Joshua
said to the people, "Now shout, for the LORD has
given you the city 17 and everything in it.[j] It is
under the LORD's ban. Only the harlot Rahab
and all who are in the house with her are to be
spared, because she hid the messengers we sent.
18 [k]But be careful not to take, in your greed,
anything that is under the ban;* else you will
bring upon the camp of Israel this ban and the
misery of it. 19 All silver and gold, and the articles
of bronze or iron, are sacred to the LORD. They
shall be put in the treasury of the LORD."

The Fall of Jericho 20 As the horns blew, the
people began to shout. When they heard the
signal horn, they raised a tremendous shout. The
wall collapsed,* and the people stormed the city
in a frontal attack and took it.[l] 21 They observed
the ban by putting to the sword all living
creatures[m] in the city: men and women, young
and old, as well as oxen, sheep and asses.

22 Joshua directed the two men who had spied
out the land, "Go into the harlot's house and
bring out the woman with all her kin, as you
swore to her you would do."[n] 23 The spies
entered and brought out Rahab, with her father,
mother, brothers, and all her kin.[o] Her entire

6, 18: That is under the ban: that is doomed to destruction; see notes on Lv 27, 29; Nm 18, 14; 21, 3.

6, 20: The wall collapsed: by the miraculous intervention of God. The blowing of the horns and the shouting of the people were a customary feature of ancient warfare, here intended by God as a test of the people's obedience and of their faith in his promise; cf Heb 11, 30.

h Ex 3, 5; Acts 7, 33. i Nm 10, 8f. j Jos 2, 4; Dt 20, 17; Heb 11, 31. k Jos 7, 12. 25; Dt 13, 18. 1 2 Mc 12, 15; Heb 11, 30. m Dt 7, 2. n Jos 2, 14. o Jos 2, 13; Heb 11, 31.

family they led forth and placed them outside the camp of Israel. 24 The city itself they burned with all that was in it,[p] except the silver, gold, and articles of bronze and iron, which were placed in the treasury of the house of the LORD. 25 *Because Rahab the harlot had hidden the messengers whom Joshua had sent to reconnoiter Jericho, Joshua spared her with her family and all her kin, who continue in the midst of Israel to this day.

26 [q]On that occasion Joshua imposed the oath: Cursed before the LORD be the man who attempts to rebuild this city, Jericho. He shall lose his first-born when he lays its foundation, and he shall lose his youngest son when he sets up its gates.*

27 Thus the LORD was with Joshua so that his fame spread throughout the land.[r]

CHAPTER 7

Defeat at Ai 1 But the Israelites violated the ban; Achan, son of Carmi, son of Zerah, son of Zara of the tribe of Judah, took goods that were under the ban,[s] and the anger of the LORD flared up against the Israelites.

2 Joshua next sent men from Jericho to Ai, which is near Bethel on its eastern side, with instructions to go up and reconnoiter the land. When they had explored Ai, 3 they returned to Joshua and advised, "Do not send all the people up; if only about two or three thousand go up, they can overcome Ai. The enemy there are few; you need not call for an effort from all the people." 4 About three thousand of the people made the attack, but they were defeated by those at Ai, 5 who killed some thirty-six of them. They pressed them back across the clearing in front of the city gate till they broke ranks, and defeated them finally on the descent, so that the confidence of the people melted away like water.

6 Joshua, together with the elders of Israel, rent his garments and lay prostrate before the ark of the LORD until evening; and they threw dust on their heads. 7 "Alas, O Lord GOD," Joshua prayed, "why did you ever allow this people to pass over the Jordan, delivering us into the power of the Amorites, that they might destroy us? Would that we had been content to dwell on the other side of the Jordan. 8 Pray, Lord, what can I say, now that Israel has turned its back to its enemies? 9 When the Canaanites and the other inhabitants of the land hear of it, they will close in around us and efface our name from the earth. What will you do for your great name?"

10 The LORD replied to Joshua: "Stand up. Why are you lying prostrate? 11 [t]Israel has sinned: they have violated the covenant which I enjoined on them. They have stealthily taken goods subject to the ban, and have deceitfully put them in their baggage. 12 If the Israelites cannot stand up to their enemies, but must turn their back to them, it is because they are under the ban.[u] I will not remain with you unless you remove from among you whoever has incurred the ban. 13 Rise, sanctify the people.[v] Tell them to sanctify themselves before tomorrow, for the LORD, the God of Israel, says: You are under the ban, O Israel. You cannot stand up to your enemies until you remove from among you whoever has incurred the ban. 14 In the morning you must present yourselves by tribes. The tribe which the LORD designates shall come forward by clans; the clan which the LORD designates shall come forward by families; the family which the LORD designates shall come forward one by one. 15 He who is designated as having incurred the ban shall be destroyed by fire, with all that is his, because he has violated the covenant of the LORD and has committed a shameful crime in Israel."

Achan's Guilt and Punishment 16 Early the next morning Joshua had Israel come forward by tribes, and the tribe of Judah was designated.*

6, 25: From Mt 1, 5, we learn that Rahab married Salmon of the tribe of Judah and thus became the great-great-grandmother of David, Christ's ancestor; cf Ru 4, 18–22.

6, 26: He shall lose his first-born . . . its gates: this curse was fulfilled when Hiel rebuilt Jericho as a fortified city during the reign of Ahab, king of Israel; cf 1 Kgs 16, 34. Till then Jericho was merely an unwalled village; cf Jos 18, 12. 21; Jgs 3, 13; 2 Sm 10, 5.

7, 16ff: Was designated: probably by means of the Urim and Thummim; cf 1 Sm 14, 38–42. See note on Ex 28, 30.

p Jos 8, 2. q 1 Kgs 16, 34. r Jos 1, 5. s Jos 6, 18; 22, 20; 1 Chr 2, 7. t Jos 6, 17–19. u Jos 6, 18. v Jos 3, 5; Lv 20, 7; 1 Sm 16, 5.

17 Then he had the clans of Judah come forward,
and the clan of Zerah was designated. He had
the clan of Zerah[w] come forward by families,
and Zabdi was designated. 18 Finally he had that
family come forward one by one, and Achan, son
of Carmi, son of Zabdi, son of Zerah of the tribe
of Judah, was designated. 19 Joshua said to
Achan, "My son, give to the LORD, the God of
Israel, glory and honor by telling me what you
have done; do not hide it from me." 20 Achan
answered Joshua, "I have indeed sinned against
the LORD, the God of Israel. This is what I have
done: 21 Among the spoils, I saw a beautiful
Babylonian mantle, two hundred shekels of
silver, and a bar of gold fifty shekels in weight; in
my greed I took them. They are now hidden in
the ground inside my tent, with the silver
underneath." 22 The messengers whom Joshua
sent hastened to the tent and found them hidden
there, with the silver underneath. 23 They took
them from the tent, brought them to Joshua and
all the Israelites, and spread them out before the
LORD.

24 Then Joshua and all Israel took Achan, son
of Zerah, with the silver, the mantle, and the bar
of gold, and with his sons and daughters, his ox,
his ass and his sheep, his tent, and all his
possessions, and led them off to the Valley of
Achor. 25 Joshua said, "The LORD bring upon you
today the misery with which you have afflicted
us!"[x] And all Israel stoned him to death 26 and
piled a great heap of stones over him, which
remains to the present day.[y] Then the anger of
the LORD relented. That is why the place is
called the Valley of Achor* to this day.

CHAPTER 8

Capture of Ai 1 The LORD then said to Joshua,
"Do not be afraid or dismayed. Take all the army
with you and prepare to attack Ai.[z] I have
delivered the king of Ai into your power, with
his people, city, and land. 2 Do to Ai and its king
what you did to Jericho and its king; except that
you may take its spoil and livestock as booty.[a]
Set an ambush behind the city." 3 So Joshua and
all the soldiers prepared to attack Ai. Picking out
thirty thousand warriors,* Joshua sent them off
by night 4 with these orders: "See that you
ambush the city from the rear, at no great
distance; then all of you be on the watch. 5 The
rest of the people and I will come up to the city,
and when they make a sortie against us as they
did the last time, we will flee from them. 6 They
will keep coming out after us until we have
drawn them away from the city, for they will
think we are fleeing from them as we did the last
time. When this occurs, 7 rise from ambush and
take possession of the city, which the LORD, your
God, will deliver into your power. 8 When you
have taken the city, set it afire in obedience to
the LORD's command. These are my orders to
you." 9 Then Joshua sent them away. They went
to the place of ambush, taking up their position
to the west of Ai, toward Bethel. Joshua, how-
ever, spent that night in the plain.

10 Early the next morning Joshua mustered the
army and went up to Ai at its head, with the
elders of Israel. 11 When all the troops he led
were drawn up in position before the city, they
pitched camp north of Ai, on the other side of
the ravine. 12 [He took about five thousand men
and set them in ambush between Bethel and Ai,
west of the city.] 13 Thus the people took up their
stations, with the main body north of the city
and the ambush west of it, and Joshua waited
overnight among his troops. 14 The king of Ai
saw this, and he and all his army came out very
early in the morning to engage Israel in battle at
the descent toward the Arabah, not knowing
that there was an ambush behind the city.
15 Joshua and the main body of the Israelites fled
in seeming defeat toward the desert, 16 till the
last of the soldiers in the city had been called out
to pursue them. 17 Since they were drawn away

7, 26: Achor: "misery, affliction." The reference is to the saying of Joshua in v 25, with an allusion also to the similar-sounding name of Achan.

8, 3: Thirty thousand warriors: this figure of the Hebrew text, which seems extremely high, may be due to a copyist's error; some manuscripts of the Septuagint have "three thousand," which is the number of the whole army in the first, unsuccessful attack (Jos 7, 4); the variant reading in v 12 mentions "five thousand."

w Nm 26, 20. x Jos 6, 18; 22, 20; 1 Chr 2, 7. y Jos 8, 29. z Jos 2, 24. a Jos 6, 21. 24; Dt 20, 14.

from the city, with every man engaged in this pursuit of Joshua and the Israelites, not a soldier remained in Ai [or Bethel], and the city was open and unprotected.

[18]Then the LORD directed Joshua, "Stretch out the javelin in your hand toward Ai, for I will deliver it into your power." Joshua stretched out the javelin in his hand toward the city, [19]and as soon as he did so, the men in ambush rose from their post, rushed in, captured the city, and immediately set it on fire. [20]By the time the men of Ai looked back, the smoke from the city was already sky-high. Escape in any direction was impossible, because the Israelites retreating toward the desert now turned on their pursuers; [21]for when Joshua and the main body of Israelites saw that the city had been taken from ambush and was going up in smoke, they struck back at the men of Ai. [22]Since those in the city came out to intercept them, the men of Ai were hemmed in by Israelites on either side, who cut them down without any fugitives or survivors[b] [23]except the king, whom they took alive and brought to Joshua.

[24]All the inhabitants of Ai who had pursued the Israelites into the desert were slain by the sword there in the open, down to the last man. Then all Israel returned and put to the sword those inside the city. [25]There fell that day a total of twelve thousand men and women, the entire population of Ai. [26] [c]Joshua kept the javelin in his hand stretched out until he had fulfilled the doom on all the inhabitants of Ai. [27]However, the Israelites took for themselves as booty the livestock and the spoil of that city, according to the command of the LORD issued to Joshua. [28]Then Joshua destroyed the place by fire, reducing it to an everlasting mound of ruins, as it remains today.[d] [29]He had the king of Ai hanged on a tree until evening;[e] then at sunset Joshua ordered the body removed from the tree and cast at the entrance of the city gate, where a great heap of stones was piled up over it, which remains to the present day.

Altar on Mount Ebal [30]*Later Joshua built an altar to the LORD, the God of Israel, on Mount Ebal, [31]of unhewn stones on which no iron tool had been used,[f] in keeping with the command to the Israelites of Moses, the servant of the LORD, as recorded in the book of the law. On this altar they offered holocausts and peace offerings to the LORD. [32]There, in the presence of the Israelites, Joshua inscribed upon the stones a copy of the law written by Moses.[g] [33]And all Israel, stranger and native alike, with their elders, officers and judges, stood on either side of the ark facing the levitical priests who were carrying the ark of the covenant of the LORD.[h] Half of them were facing Mount Gerizim and half Mount Ebal, thus carrying out the instructions of Moses, the servant of the LORD, for the blessing of the people of Israel on this first occasion. [34] [i]Then were read aloud all the words of the law, the blessings and the curses, exactly as written in the book of the law. [35] [j]Every single word that Moses had commanded, Joshua read aloud to the entire community, including the women and children, and the strangers who had accompanied Israel.

CHAPTER 9

Confederacy against Israel [1]When the news reached the kings west of the Jordan, in the mountain regions and in the foothills, and all along the coast of the Great Sea as far as Lebanon: Hittites, Amorites, Canaanites, Perizzites, Hivites and Jebusites,[k] [2]they all formed an alliance to launch a common attack against Joshua and Israel.

The Gibeonite Deception [3]On learning what Joshua had done to Jericho and Ai, the inhabitants of Gibeon[l] [4]put into effect a device of their own. They chose provisions for a journey, making use of old sacks for their asses, and old wineskins, torn and mended. [5]They wore old, patched sandals and shabby garments; and all the bread they took was dry and crumbly. [6]Thus they journeyed to Joshua in the camp at Gilgal,

8, 30–35: These ceremonies were prescribed in Dt 11, 29, and Dt 27, 2–26. See notes on those passages.

b Dt 7, 2. **c** Ex 17, 11ff. **d** Dt 13, 16. **e** Jos 10, 26f; Dt 21, 22f; Jn 19, 31. **f** Ex 20, 24f; Dt 27, 5f. **g** Dt 27, 2. 8. **h** Jos 3, 3; Dt 11, 27; 27, 12; 31, 9. 12. **i** Dt 28, 2–68; 30, 19; 31, 11; Neh 8, 2f. **j** Dt 31, 12. **k** Jos 3, 10; Ex 3, 8. 17; 23, 23; Dt 1, 7. **l** Jos 6, 21. 24; 11, 19.

where they said to him and to the men of Israel, "We have come from a distant land to propose that you make an alliance with us." [m] 7But the men of Israel replied to the Hivites,* "You may be living in land that is ours. How, then, can we make an alliance with you?" 8But they answered Joshua, "We are your servants." Then Joshua asked them, "Who are you? Where do you come from?" 9They answered him, "Your servants have come from a far-off land, because of the fame of the LORD, your God. For we have heard reports of all that he did in Egypt [n] 10and all that he did to the two kings of the Amorites beyond the Jordan, [o] Sihon, king of Heshbon, and Og, king of Bashan, who lived in Ashtaroth. 11So our elders and all the inhabitants of our country said to us, 'Take along provisions for the journey and go to meet them. Say to them: We are your servants; we propose that you make an alliance with us.' 12This bread of ours was still warm when we brought it from home as provisions the day we left to come to you, but now it is dry and crumbled. 13Here are our wineskins, which were new when we filled them, but now they are torn. Look at our garments and sandals, which are worn out from the very long journey." 14Then the Israelite princes partook of their provisions, without seeking the advice of the LORD. [p] 15So Joshua made an alliance with them and entered into an agreement to spare them, [q] which the princes of the community sealed with an oath.

Gibeonites Made Vassals 16Three days after the agreement was entered into, the Israelites learned that these people were from nearby, and would be living in Israel. 17The third day on the road, the Israelites came to their cities of Gibeon, Chephirah, Beeroth and Kiriath-jearim, 18but did not attack them, because the princes of the community had sworn to them by the LORD, the God of Israel. When the entire community grumbled against the princes, 19these all remonstrated with the people, "We have sworn to them by the LORD, the God of Israel, and so we cannot harm them. 20Let us therefore spare their lives and so deal with them that we shall not be punished for the oath we have sworn to them." 21Thus the princes recommended that they be let live, as hewers of wood and drawers of water* for the entire community; and the community did as the princes advised them.

22Joshua summoned the Gibeonites and said to them, "Why did you lie to us and say that you lived at a great distance from us, when you will be living in our very midst? 23For this are you accursed: every one of you shall always be a slave [hewers of wood and drawers of water] for the house of my God." 24They answered Joshua, "Your servants were fully informed of how the LORD, your God, commanded his servant Moses that you be given the entire land and that all its inhabitants be destroyed before you. Since, therefore, at your advance, we were in great fear for our lives, we acted as we did. [r] 25And now that we are in your power, do with us what you think fit and right." 26*Joshua did what he had decided: while he saved them from being killed by the Israelites, 27at the same time he made them, as they still are, hewers of wood and drawers of water for the community and for the altar of the LORD, in the place of the LORD's choice. [s]

CHAPTER 10

The Siege of Gibeon 1Now Adonizedek, king of Jerusalem, heard that, in the capture and destruction of Ai, Joshua had done to that city and its king as he had done to Jericho and its king. [t] He heard also that the inhabitants of Gibeon had made their peace with Israel, remaining among them, 2and that there was great fear abroad, because Gibeon was large enough for a royal city, larger even than the city of Ai, and all

9, 7: The Hivites: apparently the Gibeonites belonged to this larger ethnic group (cf also Jos 11, 19), although in 2 Sm 21, 2 they are classed as Amorites; both groups are listed among the seven nations in Canaan whom the Israelites were to exterminate; cf Dt 7, 1f.

9, 21: Hewers of wood and drawers of water: proverbial terms for the lowest social class in the Israelite community; cf Dt 29, 10f.

9, 26f: Later on, Saul violated the immunity of the Gibeonites, but David vindicated it; cf 2 Sm 21, 1–9.

m Ex 23, 32; Dt 7, 2. n Jos 2, 10. o Nm 21, 25. 33. p Nm 27, 21. q Jos 11, 19; 2 Sm 21, 2. r Ex 23, 27f; Dt 7, 1f. s Dt 12, 5. t Jos 9, 15; 6, 21. 24; 8, 26–29.

its men were brave. 3 So Adonizedek, king of Jerusalem, sent for Hoham, king of Hebron, Piram, king of Jarmuth, Japhia, king of Lachish, and Debir, king of Eglon, 4 to come to his aid for an attack on Gibeon, since it had concluded peace with Joshua and the Israelites.[u] 5 The five Amorite kings, of Jerusalem, Hebron, Jarmuth, Lachish and Eglon,* united all their forces and marched against Gibeon, where they took up siege positions. 6 Thereupon, the men of Gibeon sent an appeal to Joshua in his camp at Gilgal: "Do not abandon your servants. Come up here quickly and save us. Help us, because all the Amorite kings of the mountain country have joined forces against us."[v]

Joshua's Victory 7 So Joshua marched up from Gilgal with his picked troops and the rest of his soldiers. 8 Meanwhile the LORD said to Joshua, "Do not fear them, for I have delivered them into your power. Not one of them will be able to withstand you." 9 And when Joshua made his surprise attack upon them after an all-night march from Gilgal, 10 the LORD threw them into disorder before him. The Israelites inflicted a great slaughter on them at Gibeon and pursued them down the Beth-horon slope, harassing them as far as Azekah and Makkedah.

11 While they fled before Israel along the descent from Beth-horon, the LORD hurled great stones from the sky* above them all the way to Azekah, killing many.[w] More died from these hailstones than the Israelites slew with the sword. 12 On this day, when the LORD delivered up the Amorites to the Israelites,

Joshua prayed to the LORD,
and said in the presence of Israel:
Stand still, O sun, at Gibeon,
O moon, in the valley of Aijalon!
13 And the sun stood still,
and the moon stayed,
while the nation took vengeance on its foes.[x]

Is this not recorded* in the Book of Jashar? The sun halted in the middle of the sky; not for a whole day did it resume its swift course. 14 Never before or since was there a day like this, when the LORD obeyed the voice of a man; for the LORD fought for Israel. 15 [Then Joshua and all Israel returned to the camp at Gilgal.]

Execution of Amorite Kings 16 Meanwhile the five kings who had fled, hid in a cave at Makkedah. 17 When Joshua was told that the five kings had been discovered hiding in a cave at Makkedah, 18 he said, "Roll large stones to the mouth of the cave and post men over it to guard them. 19 But do not remain there yourselves. Pursue your enemies, and harry them in the rear. Do not allow them to escape to their cities, for the LORD, your God, has delivered them into your power."

20 Once Joshua and the Israelites had finally inflicted the last blows in this very great slaughter, and the survivors had escaped from them into the fortified cities, 21 all the army returned safely to Joshua and the camp at Makkedah, no man uttering a sound against the Israelites. 22 Then Joshua said, "Open the mouth of the cave and bring out those five kings to me." 23 Obediently, they brought out to him from the cave the five kings, of Jerusalem, Hebron, Jarmuth, Lachish and Eglon. 24 When they had done so, Joshua summoned all the men of Israel and said to the commanders of the soldiers who had marched with him, "Come forward and put your feet on the necks of these kings." They came forward and put their feet upon their necks. 25 Then Joshua said to them, "Do not be afraid or dismayed, be firm and steadfast. This is

10, 5: Hebron . . . Eglon: these four cities were to the south and southwest of Jerusalem.

10, 11: Great stones from the sky: the hailstones mentioned in the next sentence.

10, 13: Is this not recorded: the reference is to the preceding, poetic passage. Evidently the Book of Jashar, like the Book of the Wars of the Lord (Nm 21, 14), recounted in epic style the exploits of Israel's early heroes. The sun halted: though it is widely supposed that this passage describes in popular language and according to external appearances a miraculous lengthening of the day, it is equally probable that Joshua's prayer was rather for an abrupt obscuration of the sun, which would impede his enemies in their flight homeward and also prevent them from rallying their forces; this request would have been answered by the hailstorm (cf Sir 46, 5) and by a darkness relieved only twenty-four hours later, well into the next day.

u Jos 9, 15. v Jos 9, 6. w Jb 38, 22. x Sir 46, 4; Is 28, 21; Heb 3, 11.

what the LORD will do to all the enemies against whom you fight." 26 [y]Thereupon Joshua struck and killed them, and hanged them on five trees, where they remained hanging until evening. 27 At sunset they were removed from the trees at the command of Joshua and cast into the cave where they had hidden; over the mouth of the cave large stones were placed, which remain until this very day.

Conquest of Southern Canaan 28 [z]Makkedah, too, Joshua captured and put to the sword at that time. He fulfilled the doom on the city, on its king, and on every person in it, leaving no survivors. Thus he did to the king of Makkedah what he had done to the king of Jericho. 29 Joshua then passed on with all Israel from Makkedah to Libnah, which he attacked. 30 Libnah also, with its king, the LORD delivered into the power of Israel. He put it to the sword with every person there, leaving no survivors. Thus he did to its king what he had done to the king of Jericho. 31 Joshua next passed on with all Israel from Libnah to Lachish, where they set up a camp during the attack. 32 The LORD delivered Lachish into the power of Israel, so that on the second day Joshua captured it and put it to the sword with every person in it, just as he had done to Libnah. 33 At that time Horam, king of Gezer, came up to help Lachish, but Joshua defeated him and his people, leaving him no survivors. 34 From Lachish, Joshua passed on with all Israel to Eglon; encamping near it, they attacked it 35 and captured it the same day, putting it to the sword. He fulfilled the doom that day on every person in it, just as he had done at Lachish. 36 From Eglon, Joshua went up with all Israel to Hebron, which they attacked 37 and captured. They put it to the sword with its king, all its towns, and every person there, leaving no survivors, just as Joshua had done to Eglon. He fulfilled the doom on it and on every person there. 38 Then Joshua and all Israel turned back to Debir and attacked it, 39 capturing it with its king and all its towns. They put them to the sword and fulfilled the doom on every person there, leaving no survivors. Thus was done to Debir and its king what had been done to Hebron, as well as to Libnah and its king.

40 [a]Joshua conquered the entire country; the mountain regions, the Negeb, the foothills, and the mountain slopes, with all their kings. He left no survivors, but fulfilled the doom on all who lived there, just as the LORD, the God of Israel, had commanded. 41 Joshua conquered from Kadesh-barnea to Gaza, and all the land of Goshen* to Gibeon. 42 All these kings and their lands Joshua captured in a single campaign, for the LORD, the God of Israel, fought for Israel. 43 Thereupon Joshua with all Israel returned to the camp at Gilgal.

CHAPTER 11

Northern Confederacy 1 When Jabin, king of Hazor,* learned of this, he sent a message to Jobab, king of Madon, to the king of Shimron, to the king of Achshaph, 2 and to the northern kings in the mountain regions and in the Arabah near Chinneroth, in the foothills, and in Naphath-dor to the west. [b] 3 These were Canaanites to the east and west, Amorites, Hittites, Perizzites and Jebusites in the mountain regions, and Hivites at the foot of Hermon in the land of Mizpah. 4 They came out with all their troops, an army numerous as the sands on the seashore, and with a multitude of horses and chariots. 5 All these kings joined forces and marched to the waters of Merom,* where they encamped together to fight against Israel.

6 The LORD said to Joshua, "Do not fear them, for by this time tomorrow I will stretch them slain before Israel. You must hamstring their horses and burn their chariots." 7 Joshua with his

10, 41: Goshen: a town and its surrounding district at the southern end of the Judean mountains (cf Jos 11, 16; 15, 51); not to be confused with the land of Goshen in northeastern Egypt (Gen 45, 10), although in the current Hebrew Bible both names are spelled the same.

11, 1ff: Hazor, Madon, Shimron, and Chinneroth: cities and their surrounding districts in eastern Galilee. Achshaph and Naphathdor: southwest of Galilee. The mountain regions: in central and northern Galilee.

11, 5: The waters of Merom: a stream in central Galilee that flows southeast to water the fertile Arabah, or plain of Chinneroth on the western shore of the lake of Gennesaret.

y 26f: Jos 8, 29; Dt 21, 22f. z Jos 6, 21. a Dt 20, 16f. b Jos 12, 3; Jgs 1, 27.

whole army came upon them at the waters of Merom in a surprise attack. 8The LORD delivered them into the power of the Israelites, who defeated them and pursued them to Greater Sidon, to Misrephoth-maim,[c] and eastward to the valley of Mizpeh. They struck them all down, leaving no survivors. 9Joshua did to them as the LORD had commanded: he hamstrung their horses and burned their chariots.

Conquest of Northern Canaan 10At that time Joshua, turning back, captured Hazor and slew its king with the sword; for Hazor formerly was the chief of all those kingdoms. 11He also fulfilled the doom by putting every person there to the sword, till none was left alive. Hazor itself he burned. 12Joshua thus captured all those kings with their cities and put them to the sword, fulfilling the doom on them, as Moses, the servant of the LORD, had commanded.[d] 13However, Israel did not destroy by fire any of the cities built on raised sites, except Hazor, which Joshua burned. 14The Israelites took all the spoil and livestock of these cities as their booty; but the people they put to the sword, until they had exterminated the last of them, leaving none alive. 15As the LORD had commanded his servant Moses, so Moses commanded Joshua, and Joshua acted accordingly.[e] He left nothing undone that the LORD had commanded Moses should be done.

Survey of the Conquest 16So Joshua captured all this land: the mountain regions, the entire Negeb, all the land of Goshen, the foothills, the Arabah, as well as the mountain regions and foothills of Israel,[f] 17from Mount Halak that rises toward Seir[g] as far as Baal-gad in the Lebanon valley at the foot of Mount Hermon. All their kings he captured and put to death. 18Joshua waged war against all these kings for a long time. 19With the exception of the Hivites who lived in Gibeon, no city made peace with the Israelites; all were taken in battle.[h] 20For it was the design of the LORD to encourage them to wage war against Israel, that they might be doomed to destruction and thus receive no mercy, but be exterminated, as the LORD had commanded Moses.[i]

21*At that time Joshua penetrated the mountain regions and exterminated the Anakim in Hebron,[j] Debir, Anab, the entire mountain region of Judah, and the entire mountain region of Israel. Joshua fulfilled the doom on them and on their cities, 22so that no Anakim were left in the land of the Israelites. However, some survived in Gaza, in Gath, and in Ashdod. 23[k]Thus Joshua captured the whole country, just as the LORD had foretold to Moses. Joshua gave it to Israel as their heritage, apportioning it among the tribes. And the land enjoyed peace.*

CHAPTER 12*

Lists of Conquered Kings 1The kings of the land east of the Jordan, from the River Arnon to Mount Hermon, including all the eastern section of the Arabah, whom the Israelites conquered and whose lands they occupied, were: 2[l]First, Sihon, king of the Amorites, who lived in Heshbon. His domain extended from Aroer, which is on the bank of the Wadi Arnon, to include the wadi itself, and the land northward through half of Gilead to the Wadi Jabbok, 3as well as the Arabah from the eastern side of the Sea of Chinnereth, as far south as the eastern side of the Salt Sea of the Arabah in the direction of Beth-jeshimoth,[m] to a point under the slopes of Pisgah. 4Secondly, Og, king of Bashan, a survivor of the Rephaim, who lived at Ashtaroth and Edrei.[n] 5He ruled over Mount Hermon, Salecah, and all Bashan as far as the boundary of the Geshurites and Maacathites, and over half of

11, 21ff: Most of the land assigned to the tribe of Judah was not conquered by it till the early period of the Judges. See note on Jgs 1, 1–36.

11, 23: The land enjoyed peace: of a limited and temporary nature. Many of the individual tribes had still to fight against the remaining Canaanites; cf Jos 15, 13–17; 17, 12f. This verse forms the conclusion to the first part of the book. Cf note on Jos 12, 1–24.

12, 1–24: This chapter, inserted between the two principal parts of the book (chapters 1–11 and 13–21), resembles the lists of conquered cities which are inscribed on monuments of the Egyptian and Assyrian monarchs. Perhaps it was copied here from some such public Israelite record.

c Jos 13, 6. d Dt 7, 2; 20, 16f. e Dt 7, 2. f Jos 10, 41; 12, 8. g Jos 12, 7; Dt 7, 24. h Jos 9, 3. 7. 15. i Dt 2, 30; 20, 16f. j Jos 15, 13f; Nm 13, 22; Dt 1, 28. k Jos 14, 1–19, 51; Nm 34, 2–12. 12–5: Nm 21, 21–26. 33ff. m Jos 13, 20. n Jos 13, 11f.

Gilead as far as the territory of Sihon, king of
Heshbon. 6After Moses, the servant of the LORD,
and the Israelites conquered them, he assigned
their land to the Reubenites, the Gadites, and
the half-tribe of Manasseh, as their property.[o]
7This is a list of the kings whom Joshua and
the Israelites conquered west of the Jordan and
whose land, from Baal-gad in the Lebanon valley
to Mount Halak which rises toward Seir, Joshua
apportioned to the tribes of Israel. 8It included
the mountain regions and foothills, the Arabah,
the slopes, the desert, and the Negeb, belonging
to the Hittites, Amorites, Canaanites, Perizzites,
Hivites and Jebusites. 9They were the kings of
Jericho,[p] Ai (which is near Bethel), 10Jerusalem,
Hebron, 11Jarmuth, Lachish,[q] 12Eglon, Gezer,[r]
13Debir, Geder,[s] 14Hormah, Arad, 15Libnah,
Adullam,[t] 16Makkedah, Bethel,[u] 17Tappuah, He-
pher,[v] 18Aphek, Lasharon,[w] 19Madon, Hazor,[x]
20Shimron, Achshaph,[y] 21Taanach, Megiddo,[z]
22Kedesh, Jokneam (at Carmel),[a] 23and Dor (in
Naphath-dor), the foreign king at Gilgal,[b] 24and
the king of Tirzah, thirty-one kings in all.

II: Division of the Land

CHAPTER 13

Division of Land Commanded 1When Josh-
ua was old and advanced in years, the LORD
said to him:[c] "Though now you are old and
advanced in years, a very large part of the land
still remains to be conquered. 2This additional
land includes all Geshur* and all the districts of
the Philistines 3(from the stream adjoining
Egypt to the boundary of Ekron in the north is
reckoned Canaanite territory, though held by
the five lords of the Philistines in Gaza, Ashdod,
Ashkelon, Gath and Ekron); also where the Av-
vim are in the south;[d] 4all the land of the Ca-
naanites from Mearah of the Sidonians to
Aphek, and the boundaries of the Amorites;
5and the Gebalite territory; and all the Lebanon
on the east, from Baal-gad at the foot of Mount
Hermon to Labo in the land of Hamath. 6At the
advance of the Israelites I will drive out all the
Sidonian inhabitants of the mountain regions
between Lebanon and Misrephoth-maim;[e] at
least include these areas in the division of the
Israelite heritage, just as I have commanded
you. 7Now, therefore, apportion among the
nine tribes and the half-tribe of Manasseh the
land which is to be their heritage."

The Eastern Tribes 8[f]Now the other half of
the tribe of Manasseh, as well as the Reubenites
and Gadites, had received their heritage which
Moses, the servant of the LORD, had given them
east of the Jordan: 9from Aroer on the bank of
the Wadi Arnon and the city in the wadi itself,
through the tableland of Medeba and Dibon,
10with the rest of the cities of Sihon, king of the
Amorites, who reigned in Heshbon, to the
boundary of the Ammonites; 11also Gilead and
the territory of the Geshurites and Maacathites,
all Mount Hermon, and all Bashan as far as
Salecah, 12the entire kingdom in Bashan of Og, a
survivor of the Rephaim, who reigned at Ashta-
roth and Edrei. Though Moses conquered and
occupied these territories, 13the Israelites did not
dislodge the Geshurites and Maacathites, so that
Geshur and Maacath survive in the midst of
Israel to this day. 14[g]However, to the tribe of
Levi Moses assigned no heritage since, as the
LORD had promised them, the LORD, the God of
Israel, is their heritage.

Reuben 15[h]What Moses gave to the Reubenite
clans:[i] 16Their territory reached from Aroer, on
the bank of the Wadi Arnon, and the city in the
wadi itself, through the tableland about Medeba,
17to include Heshbon and all its towns which are
on the tableland, Dibon, Bamoth-baal, Beth-baal-
meon, 18Jahaz, Kedemoth, Mephaath, 19Kiria-
thaim, Sibmah, Zereth-shahar on the knoll
within the valley, 20Beth-peor, the slopes of
Pisgah, Beth-jeshimoth, 21 and the other cities of

13, 2: Geshur: not to be confused with the large Aramaean district of the same name in Bashan (vv 11–13; Dt 3, 14); here it is a region to the south of the Philistine country, since vv 2–5 list the unconquered lands along the coast from south to north; cf also 1 Sm 27, 8.

o Nm 32, 33; Dt 3, 12f. p Jos 6, 2; 8, 23. q 10f: Jos 10, 23. r Jos 10, 23. 33. s Jos 10, 38f; 15, 36. t Jos 10, 29f; 15, 35. u Jos 8, 17; 10, 28. v Jos 15, 34. w Jos 15, 53. x Jos 11, 1. 10. y Jos 11, 1. z Jos 17, 11. a Jos 19, 37. b Jos 11, 2. c Jos 23, 1. d Jgs 3, 3. e Jos 11, 8. f Jos 12, 6; Nm 32, 33. g Jos 14, 3f; Nm 18, 20–24. h 15–31; Dt 3, 12–17. i 15–23; Nm 21, 25–31; 32, 37f.

the tableland and, generally, of the kingdom of
Sihon. This Amorite king, who reigned in Hesh-
bon, Moses had killed, with his vassals, the
princes of Midian, who were settled in the land:
Evi, Rekem, Zur, Hur and Reba;[j] 22 and among
their slain followers the Israelites put to the
sword also the soothsayer Balaam, son of Beor.[k]
23 The boundary of the Reubenites was the bank
of the Jordan. These cities and their villages were
the heritage of the clans of the Reubenites.
Gad 24 [l]What Moses gave to the Gadite clans:
25 Their territory included Jazer, all the cities of
Gilead, and half the land of the Ammonites as far
as Aroer, toward Rabbah 26 (that is, from Hesh-
bon to Ramath-mizpeh and Betonim, and from
Mahanaim to the boundary of Lodebar); 27 and in
the Jordan valley: Beth-haram, Beth-nimrah, Suc-
coth, Zaphon, the other part of the kingdom of
Sihon, king of Heshbon, with the bank of the
Jordan to the southeastern tip of the Sea of
Chinnereth. 28 These cities and their villages
were the heritage of the clans of the Gadites.
Manasseh 29 [m]What Moses gave to the clans of
the half-tribe of Manasseh: 30 Their territory
included Mahanaim, all of Bashan, the entire
kingdom of Og, king of Bashan, and all the
villages of Jair, which are sixty cities in Bashan.[n]
31 Half of Gilead, with Ashtaroth and Edrei, once
the royal cities of Og in Bashan, fell to the
descendants of Machir, son of Manasseh, for half
the clans descended from Machir.
32 These are the portions which Moses gave
when he was in the plains of Moab, beyond the
Jordan east of Jericho. 33 However, Moses gave
no heritage to the tribe of Levi, since the LORD
himself, the God of Israel, is their heritage, as he
promised.[o]

CHAPTER 14

The Western Tribes 1 Here follow the portions
which the Israelites received in the land of
Canaan.[p] Eleazar the priest, Joshua, son of Nun,
and the heads of families in the tribes of the
Israelites determined 2 their heritage by lot, in
accordance with the instructions the LORD had
given through Moses concerning the remaining
nine and a half tribes.[q] 3 For to two and a half
tribes Moses had already given a heritage be-
yond the Jordan; and though the Levites were
given no heritage among the tribes,[r] 4 the descen-
dants of Joseph formed two tribes, Manasseh and
Ephraim. The Levites themselves received no
share of the land except cities to live in, with
their pasture lands for the cattle and flocks.[s]
5 Thus, in apportioning the land, did the
Israelites carry out the instructions of the LORD
to Moses.
Caleb's Portion 6 [t]When the Judahites came
up to Joshua in Gilgal, the Kenizzite Caleb, son
of Jephunneh, said to him: "You know what the
LORD said to the man of God, Moses, about you
and me in Kadesh-barnea. 7 [u]I was forty years old
when the servant of the LORD, Moses, sent me
from Kadesh-barnea to reconnoiter the land; and
I brought back to him a conscientious report.
8 [v]My fellow scouts who went up with me
discouraged the people, but I was completely
loyal to the LORD, my God. 9 On that occasion
Moses swore this oath, 'The land where you
have set foot shall become your heritage and that
of your descendants forever, because you have
been completely loyal to the LORD, my God.'
10 Now, as he promised, the LORD has preserved
me while Israel was journeying through the
desert, for the forty-five years since the LORD
spoke thus to Moses; and although I am now
eighty-five years old,[w] 11 I am still as strong today
as I was the day Moses sent me forth, with no
less vigor whether for war or for ordinary tasks.[x]
12 Give me, therefore, this mountain region
which the LORD promised me that day, as you
yourself heard. True, the Anakim are there, with
large fortified cities, but if the LORD is with me I
shall be able to drive them out, as the LORD
promised."[y] 13 Joshua blessed Caleb, son of Je-
phunneh, and gave him Hebron as his heritage.[z]
14 Therefore Hebron remains the heritage of the
Kenizzite Caleb, son of Jephunneh, to the pres-

j Nm 21, 24; 31, 8; Dt 3, 10. k Nm 31, 8. l 24–28: Nm 32, 34ff. m 29–31: Nm 32, 39ff. n Nm 32, 41. o Jos 18, 7; Nm 18, 20. p Jos 17, 4; 21, 1; Nm 34, 17f. q Nm 26, 55; 33, 54; 34, 13. r Jos 13, 8. 14. 33. s Jos 21, 3–40; Gn 48, 5. t Nm 14, 24. 30; 32, 12; Dt 1, 36. 38. u Nm 14, 6–9. v Nm 13, 31ff; 14, 24; 32, 12; Dt 1, 36. w Nm 14, 30. x Sir 46, 1ff. y Jos 11, 21. z Jos 10, 36f; 15, 13–19; 21, 11f.

ent day, because he was completely loyal to the LORD, the God of Israel. [15]Hebron was formerly called Kiriath-arba, for Arba, the greatest among the Anakim.[a] And the land enjoyed peace.

CHAPTER 15

Boundaries of Judah [1]The lot for the clans of the Judahite tribe fell in the extreme south toward the boundary of Edom, the desert of Zin in the Negeb.[b] [2][c]The boundary there ran from the bay that forms the southern end of the Salt Sea, [3]southward below the pass of Akrabbim, across through Zin, up to a point south of Kadesh-barnea, across to Hezron, and up to Addar; from there, looping around Karka, [4]it crossed to Azmon and then joined the Wadi of Egypt before coming out at the sea. [This is your southern boundary.] [5]The eastern boundary was the Salt Sea as far as the mouth of the Jordan.

[6][d]The northern boundary climbed from the bay where the Jordan meets the sea, up to Beth-hoglah, and ran north of Beth-arabah, up to Eben-Bohan-ben-Reuben. [7]Thence it climbed to Debir, north of the vale of Achor,[e] in the direction of the Gilgal that faces the pass of Adummim, on the south side of the wadi; from there it crossed to the waters of En-shemesh and emerged at En-rogel. [8]Climbing again to the Valley of Ben-Hinnom* on the southern flank of the Jebusites [that is, Jerusalem], the boundary rose to the top of the mountain at the northern end of the Valley of Rephaim,[f] which bounds the Valley of Hinnom on the west. [9]From the top of the mountain it ran to the fountain of waters of Nephtoah,[g] extended to the cities of Mount Ephron, and continued to Baalah, or Kiriath-jearim. [10]From Baalah the boundary curved westward to Mount Seir and passed north of the ridge of Mount Jearim (that is, Chesalon); thence it descended to Beth-shemesh, and ran across to Timnah. [11]It then extended along the northern flank of Ekron, continued through Shikkeron, and across to Mount Baalah, thence to include Jabneel, before it came out at the sea. [12]The western boundary was the Great Sea and its coast. This was the complete boundary of the clans of the Judahites.

Conquest by Caleb [13][h]As the LORD had commanded, Joshua gave Caleb, son of Jephunneh,[i] a portion among the Judahites, namely, Kiriath-arba (Arba was the father of Anak), that is, Hebron. [14][j]And Caleb drove out from there the three Anakim, the descendants of Anak: Sheshai, Ahiman and Talmai. [15]From there he marched up against the inhabitants of Debir,[k] which was formerly called Kiriath-sepher. [16]Caleb said, "I will give my daughter Achsah in marriage to the one who attacks Kiriath-sepher and captures it." [17]*Othniel, son of Caleb's brother Kenaz, captured it, and so Caleb gave him his daughter Achsah in marriage. [18]On the day of her marriage to Othniel, she induced him to ask her father for some land. Then, as she alighted from the ass, Caleb asked her, "What is troubling you?" [19]She answered, "Give me an additional gift! Since you have assigned to me land in the Negeb, give me also pools of water." So he gave her the upper and the lower pools.

Cities of Judah [20]*This is the heritage of the clans of the tribe of Judahites: [21]The cities of the tribe of the Judahites in the extreme southern district toward Edom were: Kabzeel, Eder, Jagur, [22]Kinah, Dimonah, Adadah, [23]Kedesh, Hazor and Ithnan; [24]Ziph, Telem, Bealoth, [25]Hazor-hadattah, and Kerioth-hezron (that is, Hazor); [26]Amam, Shema, Moladah, [27]Hazar-gaddah, Heshmon, Beth-pelet, [28]Hazar-shual, Beer-sheba, and Biziothiah, [29]Baalah, Iim, Ezem, [30]Eltolad, Chesil, Hormah, [31]Ziklag,[l] Madmannah, Sansannah, [32]Lebaoth, Shilhim and En-

15, 8: The Valley of Ben-hinnom: the southern limit of Jerusalem. Ben-hinnom means "son of Hinnom." The place was also called Valley of Hinnom, in Hebrew ge-hinnom, whence the word "Gehenna" is derived.

15, 17–19: The story of Othniel is told again in Jgs 1, 13–15; cf also Jgs 3, 9–11.

15, 20–62: This elaborate list of the cities of Judah was probably taken from a document made originally for administrative purposes; the cities are divided into four provincial districts, some of which have further subdivisions. For similar lists of the cities of Judah, cf Jos 19, 2–7; 1 Chr 4, 28–32; Neh 11, 25–30. This list has suffered in transmission, so that the totals given in vv 32 and 36 are not exact, and some of the names are probably misspelled; many of the cities cannot be identified.

a Jgs 1, 10. b Nm 34, 3. c 2–4: Nm 34, 3ff. d Jos 18, 18f. 22. e Jos 7, 26; 18, 16ff: 2 Sm 17, 17. f Jos 18, 16. g Jos 18, 15. h 13–19: Jgs 1, 10–15. i Jos 14, 13ff. j Nm 13, 22; Jgs 1, 20. k Jos 10, 38. l 1 Sm 27, 6.

rimmon; a total of twenty-nine cities with their villages.

33 In the foothills:* Eshtaol, Zorah, Ashnah, 34 Zanoah, Engannim, Tappuah, Enam, 35 Jarmuth, Adullam, Socoh, Azekah, 36 Shaaraim, Adithaim, Gederah, and Gederothaim; fourteen cities and their villages. 37 Zenan, Hadashah, Migdal-gad, 38 Dilean, Mizpeh, Joktheel, 39 Lachish, Bozkath, Eglon, 40 Cabbon, Lahmam, Chitlish, 41 Gederoth, Beth-dagon, Naamah and Makkedah; sixteen cities and their villages. 42 Libnah, Ether, Ashan, 43 Iphtah, Ashnah, Nezib, 44 Keilah, Achzib and Mareshah; nine cities and their villages. 45 Ekron and its towns and villages; 46 from Ekron to the sea, all the towns that lie alongside Ashdod and their villages; 47 Ashdod and its towns and villages; Gaza and its towns and villages, as far as the Wadi of Egypt and the coast of the Great Sea.

48 In the mountain regions: Shamir, Jattir, Socoh, 49 Dannah, Kiriath-sannah (that is, Debir), 50 Anab, Eshtemoh, Anim, 51 Goshen, Holon and Giloh; eleven cities and their villages. 52 Arab, Dumah, Eshan, 53 Janim, Beth-tappuah, Aphekah, 54 Humtah, Kiriath-arba (that is, Hebron), and Zior; nine cities and their villages. 55 Maon, Carmel, Ziph, Juttah, 56 Jezreel, Jokdeam, Zanoah, 57 Kain, Gibbeah and Timnah; ten cities and their villages. 58 Halhul, Beth-zur, Gedor, 59 Maarath, Beth-anoth and Eltekon; six cities and their villages. Tekoa, Ephrathah (that is, Bethlehem), Peor, Etam, Kulom, Tatam, Zores, Karim, Gallim, Bether and Manoko; eleven cities and their villages. 60 Kiriath-baal (that is, Kiriath-jearim) and Rabbah: two cities and their villages.[m]

61 In the desert:* Beth-arabah, Middin, Secacah, 62 Nibshan, Ir-hamelah and En-gedi; six cities and their villages. 63 [But the Jebusites who lived in Jerusalem the Judahites could not drive out; so the Jebusites dwell in Jerusalem beside the Judahites to the present day.[n]]

CHAPTER 16

The Joseph Tribes 1 The lot that fell to the Josephites* extended from the Jordan at Jericho to the waters of Jericho east of the desert; then the boundary went up from Jericho to the heights at Bethel.* 2 Leaving Bethel for Luz, it crossed the ridge to the border of the Archites at Ataroth, 3 and descended westward to the border of the Japhletites, to that of Lower Beth-horon, and to Gezer, ending thence at the sea.[o]

Ephraim 4 Within the heritage of Manasseh and Ephraim, sons of Joseph, 5 the dividing line* for the heritage of the clans of the Ephraimites ran from east of Ataroth-addar to Upper Beth-horon[p] 6 and thence to the sea. From Michmethath[q] on the north, their boundary curved eastward around Taanath-shiloh, and continued east of it to Janoah; 7 from there it descended to Ataroth and Naarah, and skirting Jericho, it ended at the Jordan. 8 From Tappuah[r] the boundary ran westward to the Wadi Kanah and ended at the sea. This was the heritage of the clans of the Ephraimites, 9 including the villages that belonged to each city set aside for the Ephraimites within the territory of the Manassehites.[s] 10 But they did not drive out the Canaanites living in Gezer,[t] who live on within Ephraim to the present day, though they have been impressed as laborers.

CHAPTER 17

Manasseh 1 Now as for the lot that fell to the tribe of Manasseh[u] as the first-born of Joseph: since his eldest son, Machir, the father of Gilead, was a warrior, who had already obtained Gilead and Bashan, 2 [v]the allotment was now made to the other descendants of Manasseh, the clans of Abiezer, Helek, Asriel, Shechem, Hepher and

15, 33: In the foothills: see note on Dt 1, 7.

15, 61: In the desert: in the Jordan rift near the Dead Sea.

16, 1—17, 18: The boundaries and cities of Judah, the most important tribe, having been given, the land of the next most important group, the two Josephite tribes of Ephraim and Manasseh, is now described, though it was separated from Judah by the territories of Benjamin (Jos 18, 11–20) and Dan (Jos 19, 40–48).

16, 1–3: This line formed the southern boundary of Ephraim and the northern boundaries of Benjamin and of Dan.

16, 5: The dividing line: separating Ephraim from Manasseh. Ephraim's northern border (v 5) is given in an east-to-west direction; its eastern border (v 6f) in a north-to-south direction.

m Jos 18, 14. n Jgs 1, 21; 2 Sm 5, 6. o Jos 10, 10. 33. p Jos 18, 13. q Jos 17, 7. r Jos 17, 7. s Jos 17, 9. t Jgs 1, 29. u Gn 41, 51; 46, 20; 48, 18; 50, 23; Nm 26, 29; Dt 3, 13. 15. v Nm 26, 29–32.

Shemida, the other male children of Manasseh,
son of Joseph.
3Furthermore, Zelophehad, son of Hepher,[w]
son of Gilead, son of Machir, son of Manasseh,
had had no sons, but only daughters, whose
names were Mahlah, Noah, Hoglah, Milcah, and
Tirzah. 4These presented themselves to Eleazar
the priest, to Joshua, son of Nun, and to the
princes, saying, "The LORD commanded Moses
to give us a heritage among our kinsmen." So in
obedience to the command of the LORD a
heritage was given to each of them among their
father's kinsmen.[x] 5Thus ten shares fell to Ma-
nasseh apart from the land of Gilead and Bashan
beyond the Jordan,[y] 6since these female descen-
dants of Manasseh received each a portion
among his sons. The land of Gilead fell to the
rest of the Manassehites.
7Manasseh bordered on Asher.* From Mich-
methath, near Shechem, another boundary ran
southward to include the natives of En-Tappuah,
8because the district of Tappuah belonged to
Manasseh, although Tappuah itself was an Ephra-
imite city on the border of Manasseh. 9This same
boundary continued down to the Wadi Kanah.[z]
The cities that belonged to Ephraim from among
the cities of Manasseh were those to the south of
the wadi; thus the territory of Manasseh ran
north of the wadi and ended at the sea. 10The
land on the south belonged to Ephraim and that
on the north to Manasseh; with the sea as their
common boundary, they reached Asher on the
north and Issachar on the east.
11 [a]Moreover, in Issachar and in Asher Manas-
seh was awarded Beth-shean[b] and its towns,
Ibleam and its towns, Dor and its towns and the
natives there, Endor and its towns and natives,
Taanach and its towns and natives, and Megiddo
and its towns and natives [the third is Naphath-
dor]. 12Since the Manassehites could not con-
quer these cities, the Canaanites persisted in this
region. 13When the Israelites grew stronger they
impressed the Canaanites as laborers, but they
did not drive them out.

Protest of Joseph Tribes 14The descendants
of Joseph said to Joshua, "Why have you given us
only one lot and one share as our heritage?[c] Our
people are too many, because of the extent to
which the LORD has blessed us." 15Joshua an-
swered them, "If you are too many, go up to the
forest and clear out a place for yourselves there
in the land of the Perizzites and Rephaim, since
the mountain regions of Ephraim are so narrow."
16For the Josephites said, "Our mountain regions
are not enough for us; on the other hand, the
Canaanites living in the valley region all have
iron chariots, in particular those in Beth-shean
and its towns, and those in the valley of Jez-
reel."[d] 17Joshua therefore said to Ephraim and
Manasseh, the house of Joseph, "You are a
numerous people and very strong. You shall have
not merely one share, 18for the mountain region
which is now forest shall be yours when you
clear it. Its adjacent land shall also be yours if,
despite their strength and iron chariots, you
drive out the Canaanites."

CHAPTER 18

1After they had subdued the land, the whole
community of the Israelites assembled at Shiloh,
where they set up the meeting tent.[e]

The Seven Remaining Portions 2Seven tribes
among the Israelites had not yet received their
heritage. 3Joshua therefore said to the Israelites,
"How much longer will you put off taking steps to
possess the land which the LORD, the God of your
fathers, has given you? 4Choose three men from
each of your tribes; I will commission them to
begin a survey of the land, which they shall de-
scribe for purposes of inheritance. When they re-
turn to me, 5you shall divide it into seven parts.
Judah is to retain its territory in the south,[f] and
the house of Joseph its territory in the north. 6You
shall bring here to me the description of the land

17, 7: Manasseh bordered on Asher: only at the extreme northwestern section of Manasseh's territory. The boundary given in the following sentences (vv 7–10) is a more detailed description of the one already mentioned in Jos 16, 5ff, as separating Manasseh from Ephraim.

w Nm 26, 33; 27, 1; 36, 2. x Nm 27, 6f; 36, 2. y Jos 13, 30f. z Jos 16, 8f. a 1 Chr 7, 29. b 11ff: Jgs 1, 27f. c Jos 16, 4; Gn 48, 19f. 22. d Jgs 6, 33. e Jos 19, 51. f Jos 15, 1—17, 18.

in seven sections. I will then cast lots for you here before the LORD, our God. 7For the Levites have no share among you,[g] because the priesthood of the LORD is their heritage; while Gad, Reuben, and the half-tribe of Manasseh have already received the heritage east of the Jordan which Moses, the servant of the LORD, gave them."

8When those who were to map out the land were ready for the journey, Joshua instructed them to survey the land, prepare a description of it, and return to him; then he would cast lots for them there before the LORD in Shiloh. 9So they went through the land, listed its cities in writing in seven sections, and returned to Joshua in the camp at Shiloh. 10Joshua then divided up the land for the Israelites into their separate shares, casting lots for them before the LORD in Shiloh.

Benjamin 11One lot fell to the clans of the tribe of Benjaminites. The territory allotted them lay between the descendants of Judah and those of Joseph. 12 [h]Their northern boundary* began at the Jordan and went over the northern flank of Jericho, up westward into the mountains, till it reached the desert of Beth-aven. 13From there it crossed over to the southern flank of Luz (that is, Bethel). Then it ran down to Ataroth-addar, on the mountaintop south of Lower Beth-horon.[i] 14For the western border, the boundary line swung south from the mountaintop opposite Beth-horon till it reached Kiriath-baal (that is, Kiriath-jearim), which city belonged to the Judahites. This was the western boundary. 15The southern boundary began at the limits of Kiriath-jearim and projected to the spring at Nephtoah. 16It went down to the edge of the mountain on the north of the Valley of Rephaim, where it faces the Valley of Ben-hinnom; and continuing down the Valley of Hinnom along the southern flank of the Jebusites, reached En-rogel.[j] 17Inclining to the north, it extended to En-shemesh, and thence to Geliloth, opposite the pass of Adummim. Then it dropped to Eben-Bohan-ben-Reuben, 18across the northern flank of the Arabah overlook, down into the Arabah.[k] 19From there the boundary continued across the northern flank of Beth-hoglah and extended to the northern tip of the Salt Sea, at the southern end of the Jordan. This was the southern boundary. 20The Jordan bounded it on the east. This was how the heritage of the clans of the Benjaminites was bounded on all sides.

21Now the cities belonging to the clans of the tribe of the Benjaminites were: Jericho, Beth-hoglah, Emek-keziz, 22Beth-arabah, Zemaraim, Bethel, 23Avvim, Parah, Ophra, 24Chephar-ammoni, Ophni and Geba; twelve cities and their villages. 25Also Gibeon, Ramah, Beeroth, 26Mizpeh, Chephirah, Mozah, 27Rekem, Irpeel, Taralah, 28Zela, Haeleph, the Jebusite city (that is, Jerusalem), Gibeah and Kiriath; fourteen cities and their villages. This was the heritage of the clans of Benjaminites.

CHAPTER 19

Simeon 1The second lot fell to Simeon. The heritage of the clans of the tribe of Simeonites lay within that of the Judahites. 2 [l]For their heritage they received Beer-sheba, Shema, Moladah, 3Hazar-shual, Balah, Ezem, 4Eltolad, Bethul, Hormah, 5Ziklag, Bethmar-caboth, Hazar-susah, 6Beth-lebaoth and Sharuhen; thirteen cities and their villages. 7Also En-rimmon, Ether and Ashan; four cities and their villages, 8besides all the villages around these cities as far as Baalath-beer (that is, Ramoth-negeb). This was the heritage of the clans of the tribe of the Simeonites. 9This heritage of the Simeonites was within the confines of the Judahites; for since the portion of the latter was too large for them, the Simeonites obtained their heritage within it.

Zebulun 10*The third lot fell to the clans of the Zebulunites. The limit of their heritage was at

18, 12–20: Benjamin's northern boundary (vv 12f) corresponded to part of the southern boundary of Ephraim (Jos 16, 1f). Their western border (v 14) was the eastern border of Dan (cf Jos 19, 40–47). Their southern boundary (vv 15–19) corresponded to part of the northern boundary of Judah (Jos 15, 6–9).

19, 10–16: Zebulun's territory was in the central section of the Plain of Esdraelon and of southern Galilee; it was bounded on the south by Manasseh, on the southeast by Issachar, on the northeast and north by Naphtali, and on the west by Asher. The site of the later city of Nazareth was within its borders. Bethlehem of Zebulun was, of course, distinct from the city of the same name in Judah. Twelve cities: apparently seven of the names are missing from v 15, unless some of the places mentioned in vv 12–14 are to be included in the number.

g Jos 13, 8. 33. h Jos 16, 1. i Jos 16, 2f. 5; Gn 28, 19. j Jos 15, 7f. k Jos 15, 6. 12–8: 1 Chr 4, 28–33.

Sarid. [11]Their boundary went up west . . . and
through Mareal, reaching Dabbesheth and the
wadi that is near Jokneam. [12]From Sarid east-
ward it ran to the district of Chisloth-tabor, on to
Daberath, and up to Japhia. [13]From there it
continued eastward to Gath-hepher and to Eth-
kazin, extended to Rimmon, and turned to
Neah. [14]Skirting north of Hannathon, the bound-
ary ended at the valley of Iphtahel. [15]Thus, with
Kattath, Nahalal, Shimron, Idalah and Bethle-
hem, there were twelve cities and their villages
[16]to comprise the heritage of the clans of the
Zebulunites.
Issachar [17]*The fourth lot fell to Issachar. The
territory of the clans of the Issacharites [18]in-
cluded Jezreel, Chesulloth, Shunem, [19]Hapha-
raim, Shion, Anaharath, [20]Rabbith, Kishion,
Ebez, [21]Remeth, En-gannim, En-haddah and
Beth-pazzez. [22]The boundary reached Tabor,
Shahazumah and Beth-shemesh, ending at the
Jordan. These sixteen cities and their villages
[23]were the heritage of the clans of the Issa-
charites.
Asher [24]*The fifth lot fell to the clans of the
tribe of the Asherites. [25]Their territory include
Helkath, Hali, Beten, Achshaph, [26]Allammelech,
Amad and Mishal, and reached Carmel on the
west, and Shihor-libnath. [27]In the other direc-
tion, it ran eastward of Beth-dagon, reached
Zebulun and the valley of Iphtahel; then north of
Beth-emek and Neiel, it extended to Cabul,
[28]Mishal, Abdon, Rehob, [m] Hammon and Kanah,
near Greater Sidon. [29]Then the boundary turned
back to Ramah and to the fortress city of Tyre;
thence it cut back to Hosah and ended at the
sea. Thus, with Mahalab, Achzib, [30]Ummah,
Acco, Aphek and Rehob, there were twenty-two
cities and their villages [31]to comprise the heri-
tage of the clans of the tribe of the Asherites.
Naphtali [32]*The sixth lot fell to the Naph-
talites. The boundary of the clans of the Naph-
talites [33]extended from Heleph, from the oak at
Zaanannim to Lakkum, including Adami-nekeb
and Jabneel, and ended at the Jordan. [34]In the
opposite direction, westerly, it ran through
Aznoth-tabor and from there extended to Huk-
kok; it touched Zebulun on the south, Asher on
the west, and the Jordan on the east. [35]The
fortified cities were Ziddim, Zer, Hammath, Rak-
kath, Chinnereth, [36]Adamah, Ramah, Hazor,
[37]Kedesh, Edrei, En-hazor, [38]Yiron, Migdal-el,
Horem, Beth-anath and Beth-shemesh; [n] nine-
teen cities and their villages, [39]to comprise the
heritage of the clans of the tribe of the Naph-
talites.
Dan [40]*The seventh lot fell to the clans of the
tribe of Danites. [41]Their heritage was the terri-
tory of Zorah, Eshtaol, Ir-shemesh, [42]Shaalabbin,
Aijalon, Ithlah, [o] [43]Elon, Timnah, Ekron,
[44]Eltekoh, Gibbethon, Baalath, [45]Jehud, Bene-
berak, Gath-rimmon, [46]Me-jarkon and Rakkon,
with the coast at Joppa. [47] [p]But the territory of
the Danites was too small for them; so the
Danites marched up and attacked Leshem,*
which they captured and put to the sword. Once
they had taken possession of Leshem, they
renamed the settlement after their ancestor Dan.
[48]These cities and their villages were the heri-
tage of the clans of the tribe of the Danites.
Joshua's City [49]When the last of them had
received the portions of the land they were to
inherit, the Israelites assigned a heritage in their
midst to Joshua, son of Nun. [50]In obedience to
the command of the LORD, they gave him the
city which he requested, Timnah-serah [q] in the
mountain region of Ephraim. He rebuilt the city
and made it his home.
[51]These are the final portions into which

19, 17–23: Issachar's land was on the eastern watershed of the Plain of Esdraelon, but also included the southeastern end of the Galilean mountains. It was surrounded by Manasseh on the south and east, by Naphtali on the north, and by Zebulun on the west. Jezreel (v 18) dominated the plain to which it gave its name, the later form of which was Esdraelon.

19, 24–31: Asher inherited the western slope of the Galilean hills as far as the sea, with Manasseh to the south, Zebulun and Naphtali to the east, and Phoenicia to the north.

19, 32–39: Naphtali received eastern Galilee; Asher was to the west and Zebulun and Issachar were to the south, while the upper Jordan and Mount Hermon formed the eastern border. Part of the tribe of Dan later on occupied the northern extremity of Naphtali's lands, at the sources of the Jordan (v 47).

19, 40–46: The original territory of Dan was a small enclave between Judah, Benjamin, Ephraim and the Philistines.

19, 47: Leshem: called Laish in Jgs 18, where the story of the migration of the Danites is told at greater length.

m 28f: Jgs 1, 31. n Jgs 1, 33. o Jgs 1, 35. p Jgs 18, 27–29. q Jos 24, 30; Jgs 2, 9.

Eleazar the priest, Joshua, son of Nun, and the heads of families in the tribes of the Israelites divided the land by lot in the presence of the LORD, at the door of the meeting tent in Shiloh.

CHAPTER 20

Cities of Asylum 1 The LORD said to Joshua:* 2 "Tell the Israelites to designate the cities of which I spoke to them through Moses,[r] 3 to which one guilty of accidental and unintended homicide may flee for asylum from the avenger of blood. 4 To one of these cities the killer shall flee, and standing at the entrance of the city gate, he shall plead his case before the elders, who must receive him and assign him a place in which to live among them. 5 Though the avenger of blood pursues him, they are not to deliver up the homicide who slew his fellow man unintentionally and not out of previous hatred. 6 Once he has stood judgment before the community, he shall live on in that city till the death of the high priest who is in office at the time. Then the killer may go back home to his own city from which he fled."[s]

List of Cities 7 So they set apart Kedesh in Galilee in the mountain region of Naphtali, Shechem in the mountain region of Ephraim, and Kiriath-arba (that is, Hebron) in the mountain region of Judah.[t] 8 And beyond the Jordan east of Jericho they designated Bezer on the open tableland in the tribe of Reuben, Ramoth in Gilead in the tribe of Gad, and Golan in Bashan in the tribe of Manasseh.[u] 9 These were the designated cities[v] to which any Israelite or stranger living among them who had killed a person accidentally might flee to escape death at the hand of the avenger of blood, until he could appear before the community.

CHAPTER 21

Levitical Cities 1 The heads of the Levite families* came up to Eleazar the priest, to Joshua, son of Nun, and to the heads of families of the other tribes of the Israelites[w] 2 at Shiloh in the land of Canaan, and said to them, "The LORD commanded, through Moses, that cities be given us to dwell in, with pasture lands for our livestock."[x] 3 Out of their own heritage, in obedience to this command of the LORD, the Israelites gave the Levites the following cities with their pasture lands.

4 When the first lot among the Levites fell to the clans of the Kohathites, the descendants of Aaron the priest obtained thirteen cities by lot from the tribes of Judah, Simeon and Benjamin. 5 The rest of the Kohathites obtained ten cities by lot from the clans of the tribe of Ephraim, from the tribe of Dan, and from the half-tribe of Manasseh. 6 The Gershonites obtained thirteen cities by lot from the clans of the tribe of Issachar, from the tribe of Asher, from the tribe of Naphtali, and from the half-tribe of Manasseh. 7 The clans of the Merarites obtained twelve cities from the tribes of Reuben, Gad and Zebulun. 8 These cities with their pasture lands the Israelites allotted to the Levites in obedience to the LORD's command through Moses.[y]

Cities of the Priests 9 [z]From the tribes of the Judahites and Simeonites they designated the following cities, 10 and assigned them to the descendants of Aaron in the Kohathite clan of the Levites, since the first lot fell to them: 11 first, Kiriath-arba (Arba was the father of Anak), that is, Hebron, in the mountain region of Judah, with the adjacent pasture lands, 12 although the open country and villages belonging to the city had been given to Caleb, son of Jephunneh, as his property.[a] 13 Thus to the descendants of Aaron the priest were given the city of asylum for homicides at Hebron, with its pasture lands; also, Libnah with its pasture lands, 14 Jattir with its pasture lands, Eshtemoa with its pasture lands, 15 Holon with its pasture lands, Debir with

20, 1–9: The laws concerning the cities of refuge are given in Nm 35, 9–28; Dt 19, 1–13; see notes on Nm 35, 16–25; Dt 19, 2.

21, 1: The order to establish special cities for the Levites is given in Nm 35, 1–8. The forty-eight cities listed here were hardly the exclusive possession of the Levites; at least the more important of them, such as Hebron, Shechem and Ramoth in Gilead, were certainly peopled for the most part by the tribe in whose territory they were situated. But in all these cities the Levites had special property rights which they did not possess in other cities; cf Lv 25, 32ff.

r Ex 21, 13; Nm 35, 10–14; Dt 4, 41–43; 19, 2–9. s Nm 35, 12. 24f. t Jos 15, 13; 19, 37; 21, 21. u Jos 21, 27. 36f. v Nm 35, 15. w Ex 6, 16–19; Nm 3, 17–20. x Nm 35, 2. y Nm 35, 2. z 9–19: 1 Chr 6, 54–60. a Jos 14, 14; 15, 13.

its pasture lands, 16 Ashan with its pasture lands,
Juttah with its pasture lands, and Beth-shemesh
with its pasture lands: nine cities from the two
tribes mentioned. 17 From the tribe of Benjamin
they obtained the four cities of Gibeon with its
pasture lands, Geba with its pasture lands,
18 Anathoth[b] with its pasture lands, and Almon
with its pasture lands. 19 These cities which with
their pasture lands belonged to the priestly
descendants of Aaron, were thirteen in all.

Cities of the Other Kohathites 20 [c]The rest of
the Kohathite clans among the Levites obtained
by lot, from the tribe of Ephraim, four cities.
21 They were assigned, with its pasture lands, the
city of asylum for homicides at Shechem in the
mountain region of Ephraim; also Gezer with its
pasture lands, 22 Kibzaim with its pasture lands,
and Beth-horon with its pasture lands. 23 From
the tribe of Dan they obtained the four cities of
Elteke with its pasture lands, Gibbethon with its
pasture lands, 24 Aijalon with its pasture lands,
and Gath-rimmon with its pasture lands; 25 and
from the half-tribe of Manasseh the two cities of
Taanach with its pasture lands and Ibleam with
its pasture lands. 26 These cities which with their
pasture lands belonged to the rest of the Kohath-
ite clans were ten in all.

Cities of the Gershonites 27 [d]The Gershonite
clan of the Levites received from the half-tribe of
Manasseh two cities: the city of asylum for
homicides at Golan with its pasture lands; and
also Beth-Astharoth with its pasture lands.
28 From the tribe of Issachar they obtained the
four cities of Kishion with its pasture lands,
Daberath with its pasture lands, 29 Jarmuth with
its pasture lands, and En-gannim with its pasture
lands; 30 from the tribe of Asher, the four cities of
Mishal with its pasture lands, Abdon with its
pasture lands, 31 Helkath with its pasture lands,
and Rehob with its pasture lands; 32 and from the
tribe of Naphtali, three cities: the city of asylum
for homicides at Kedesh in Galilee, with its
pasture lands; also Hammath with its pasture
lands, and Rakkath with its pasture lands.
33 These cities which with their pasture lands
belonged to the Gershonite clans were thirteen
in all.

Cities of the Merarites 34 [e]The Merarite clans,
the last of the Levites, received from the tribe of
Zebulun the four cities of Jokneam with its
pasture lands, Kartah with its pasture lands,
35 Rimmon with its pasture lands, and Nahalal
with its pasture lands; 36 also, across the Jordan,
from the tribe of Reuben, four cities: the city of
asylum for homicides at Bezer with its pasture
lands, Jahaz with its pasture lands, 37 Kedemoth
with its pasture lands, and Mephaath with its
pasture lands; 38 and from the tribe of Gad a total
of four cities: the city of asylum for homicides at
Ramoth in Gilead with its pasture lands, also
Mahanaim with its pasture lands, 39 Heshbon
with its pasture lands, and Jazer with its pasture
lands. 40 The cities which were allotted to the
Merarite clans, the last of the Levites, were
therefore twelve in all.

41 Thus the total number of cities[f] within the
territory of the Israelites which, with their pas-
ture lands, belonged to the Levites, was forty-
eight. 42 With each and every one of these cities
went the pasture lands round about it.

43 And so the LORD gave Israel all the land he
had sworn to their fathers he would give them.[g]
Once they had conquered and occupied it, 44 the
LORD gave them peace on every side, just as he
had promised their fathers. Not one of their
enemies could withstand them; the LORD
brought all their enemies under their power.
45 Not a single promise[h] that the LORD made to
the house of Israel was broken; every one was
fulfilled.

III: Return of the Transjordan Tribes and Joshua's Farewell

CHAPTER 22

The Eastern Tribes Dismissed 1 At that time
Joshua summoned the Reubenites, the Gadites,
and the half-tribe of Manasseh 2 and said to
them:[i] "You have done all that Moses, the
servant of the LORD, commanded you, and have

b Jer 1, 1. c 20–26: 1 Chr 6, 66–70. d 27–33: 1 Chr 6, 71–76. e 34–38: 1 Chr 6. 77–81. f Nm 35, 7. g Gn 12, 7; 13, 15; 15, 18; 26, 3; 28, 4. 13. h Jos 23, 14f. i Jos 1, 16f; Nm 32, 20ff; Dt 3, 18ff.

obeyed every command I gave you. 3For many
years now you have not once abandoned your
kinsmen, but have faithfully carried out the
commands of the LORD, your God. 4Since,
therefore, the LORD, your God, has settled your
kinsmen as he promised them, you may now
return to your tents beyond the Jordan; to your
own land, which Moses, the servant of the
LORD, gave you.[j] 5But be very careful to observe
the precept and law which Moses, the servant of
the LORD, enjoined upon you: love the LORD,
your God;[k] follow him faithfully; keep his com-
mandments; remain loyal to him; and serve him
with your whole heart and soul." 6Joshua then
blessed them and sent them away to their own
tents.

7(For, to half the tribe of Manasseh Moses had
assigned land in Bashan;[l] and to the other half
Joshua had given a portion along with their
kinsmen west of the Jordan.) What Joshua said
to them when he sent them off to their tents
with his blessing was, 8"Now that you are
returning to your own tents with great wealth,
with very numerous livestock, with silver, gold,
bronze and iron, and with a very large supply of
clothing, divide these spoils of your enemies
with your kinsmen there."[m] 9So the Reubenites,
the Gadites, and the half-tribe of Manasseh left
the other Israelites at Shiloh in the land of
Canaan and returned to the land of Gilead, their
own property, which they had received accord-
ing to the LORD's command through Moses.[n]

The Altar beside the Jordan 10When the
Reubenites, the Gadites, and the half-tribe of
Manasseh came to the region of the Jordan in
the land of Canaan, they built there at the Jordan
a conspicuously large altar. 11The other Israelites
heard the report[o] that the Reubenites, the Gad-
ites, and the half-tribe of Manasseh had built an
altar in the region of the Jordan facing the land of
Canaan,* across from them, 12and therefore
they assembled their whole community at Shiloh
to declare war on them.*

Accusation of the Western Tribes 13First,
however, they sent to the Reubenites, the Gad-
ites, and the half-tribe of Manasseh in the land of
Gilead an embassy consisting of Phinehas, son of
Eleazar the priest,[p] 14and ten princes, one from
every tribe of Israel, each one being both prince
and military leader of his ancestral house.
15When these came to the Reubenites, the
Gadites, and the half-tribe of Manasseh in the
land of Gilead, they said to them: 16[q]"The
whole community of the LORD sends this mes-
sage: What act of treachery is this you have
committed against the God of Israel? You have
seceded from the LORD this day, and rebelled
against him by building an altar of your own!
17For the sin of Peor, a plague came upon the
community of the LORD.[r] 18We are still not free
of that; must you now add to it? You are
rebelling against the LORD today and by tomor-
row he will be angry with the whole community
of Israel! 19If you consider the land you now
possess unclean,* cross over to the land the
LORD possesses, where the Dwelling of the LORD
stands,[s] and share that with us. But do not rebel
against the LORD, nor involve us in rebellion, by
building an altar of your own in addition to the
altar of the LORD, our God. 20When Achan, son
of Zerah,[t] violated the ban, did not wrath fall
upon the entire community of Israel? Though he
was but a single man, he did not perish alone*
for his guilt!"

Reply of the Eastern Tribes 21The Reuben-
ites, the Gadites, and the half-tribe of Manasseh
replied to the military leaders of the Israelites:
"The LORD is the God of gods. 22The LORD, the

22, 11: In the region of the Jordan facing the land of Canaan: on the eastern side of the Jordan valley. The river itself formed the boundary between these eastern tribes and the rest of the tribes who lived in what was formerly Canaan—though the term Canaan could also be used of both sides of the Jordan valley (cf v 10). The Transjordan tribes naturally built their altar in their own territory.

22, 12: To declare war on them: the western Israelites considered this altar, which seemed to violate the customary unity of the sanctuary (cf Lv 17, 1–9; Dt 12, 4–14), as a sign of secession and dangerous to national unity. The motives for the war were political as well as religious.

22, 19: Unclean: not sanctified by the Dwelling of the Lord.

22, 20: Achan . . . did not perish alone: his guilt caused the failure of the first attack on Ai (Jos 7, 4–23); this fact is adduced as an argument for the solidarity and mutual responsibility of all the Israelites.

j Jos 1, 13; 13, 8; Nm 32, 33. k Dt 6, 5f. 17; 10, 12; 11, 1. 13. 22. l Jos 17, 5. m Nm 31, 27. n Jos 18, 1; Nm 32, 1. 26. 29. o Dt 13, 13ff. p Ex 6, 25; Sir 45, 28. q Lv 17, 8f. r Nm 25, 3f; Dt 4, 3. s Jos 18, 1. t Jos 7, 1. 5.

God of gods,* knows and Israel shall know. If
now we have acted out of rebellion or treachery
against the LORD, our God, 23 and if we have
built an altar of our own to secede from the
LORD, or to offer holocausts, grain offerings or
peace offerings upon it, the LORD himself will
exact the penalty. 24 We did it rather out of our
anxious concern lest in the future your children
should say to our children: 'What have you to do
with the LORD, the God of Israel? 25 For the LORD
has placed the Jordan as a boundary between
you and us. You descendants of Reuben and Gad
have no share in the LORD.' Thus your children
would prevent ours from revering the LORD.
26 So we decided to guard our interests by
building this altar of our own: not for holocausts
or for sacrifices, 27 [u]but as evidence for you on
behalf of ourselves and our descendants, that we
have the right to worship the LORD in his
presence with our holocausts, sacrifices, and
peace offerings. Now in the future your children
cannot say to our children, 'You have no share in
the LORD.' 28 Our thought was, that if in the
future they should speak thus to us or to our
descendants, we could answer: 'Look at the
model of the altar of the LORD which our fathers
made, not for holocausts or for sacrifices, but to
witness* between you and us.' 29 Far be it from
us to rebel against the LORD or to secede now
from the LORD by building an altar for holocaust,
grain offering, or sacrifice in addition to the altar
of the LORD, our God, which stands before his
Dwelling."

30 When Phinehas the priest and the princes of
the community, the military leaders of the Israel-
ites, heard what the Reubenites, the Gadites and
the Manassehites had to say, they were satisfied.
31 Phinehas, son of Eleazar the priest, said to the
Reubenites, the Gadites and the Manassehites,
"Now we know that the LORD is with us. Since
you have not committed this act of treachery
against the LORD, you have kept the Israelites
free from punishment by the LORD."

32 Phinehas, son of Eleazar the priest, and the
princes returned from the Reubenites and the
Gadites in the land of Gilead to the Israelites in
the land of Canaan, and reported the matter to
them. 33 The report satisfied the Israelites, who
blessed God and decided against declaring war
on the Reubenites and Gadites or ravaging the
land they occupied.

34 The Reubenites and the Gadites gave the
altar its name* as a witness among them that the
LORD is God.

CHAPTER 23

Joshua's Final Plea 1 Many years later, after
the LORD had given the Israelites rest from all
their enemies round about them, and when
Joshua was old and advanced in years,[v] 2 he
summoned all Israel (including their elders,
leaders, judges and officers) and said to them: "I
am old and advanced in years. 3 You have seen all
that the LORD, your God, has done for you
against all these nations; for it has been the
LORD, your God, himself who fought for you.
4 [w]Bear in mind that I have apportioned among
your tribes as their heritage the nations that
survive [as well as those I destroyed] between
the Jordan and the Great Sea in the west. 5 The
LORD, your God, will drive them out and dis-
lodge them at your approach, so that you will
take possession of their land as the LORD, your
God, promised you. 6 Therefore strive hard to
observe and carry out all that is written in the
book of the law of Moses, not straying from it in
any way,[x] 7 or mingling with these nations while
they survive among you. You must not invoke
their gods, or swear by them, or serve them, or
worship them,[y] 8 but you must remain loyal to
the LORD, your God, as you have been to this
day. 9 At your approach the LORD has driven out

22, 22: The Lord, the God of gods: the Hebrew, which cannot be adequately rendered in English here, adds to the divine name Yahweh ("the LORD") two synonymous words for "God," el and elohim. The repetition of these three sacred words adds force to the protestations of fidelity and innocence.

22, 28: To witness: far from being destined to form a rival sanctuary, the model of the altar was intended by the eastern tribes solely as a means of teaching their children to be faithful to the one true sanctuary beyond the Jordan.

22, 34: The name of this altar was the Hebrew word for "witness," ᶜed.

u Dt 12, 5f. 17f. v Jos 13, 1. w Jos 13, 2-7; 14, 2; 18, 10; Ps 78, 55. x Jos 1, 7. y Dt 7, 2ff.

large and strong nations, and to this day no one
has withstood you. 10 One of you puts to flight a
thousand, because it is the LORD, your God,
himself who fights for you,[z] as he promised you.
11 Take great care, however, to love the LORD,
your God. 12 For if you ever abandon him and
ally yourselves with the remnant of these nations
while they survive among you, by intermarrying
and intermingling with them,[a] 13 know for cer-
tain that the LORD, your God, will no longer
drive these nations out of your way. Instead they
will be a snare and a trap for you, a scourge for
your sides and thorns for your eyes, until you
perish from this good land which the LORD, your
God, has given you.

14 "Today, as you see, I am going the way of all
men.* So now acknowledge with your whole
heart and soul that not one of all the promises
the LORD, your God, made to you has remained
unfulfilled. Every promise has been fulfilled for
you, with not one single exception. 15 [b]But just
as every promise the LORD, your God, made to
you has been fulfilled for you, so will he fulfill
every threat,* even so far as to exterminate you
from this good land which the LORD, your God,
has given you. 16 If you transgress the covenant
of the LORD, your God, which he enjoined on
you, serve other gods and worship them, the
anger of the LORD will flare up against you and
you will quickly perish from the good land
which he has given you."

CHAPTER 24

Reminder of the Divine Goodness 1 Joshua
gathered together all the tribes of Israel at
Shechem, summoning their elders, their leaders,
their judges and their officers. When they stood
in ranks before God, 2 Joshua addressed all the
people: "Thus says the LORD, the God of Israel:
In times past your fathers, down to Terah,[c]
father of Abraham and Nahor, dwelt beyond the
River* and served other gods. 3 But I brought
your father Abraham from the region beyond the
River and led him through the entire land of
Canaan.[d] I made his descendants numerous,
and gave him Isaac. 4 To Isaac I gave Jacob and
Esau.[e] To Esau I assigned the mountain region of
Seir in which to settle, while Jacob and his
children went down to Egypt.

5 "Then I sent Moses and Aaron, and smote
Egypt with the prodigies which I wrought in her
midst.[f] 6 Afterward I led you out of Egypt, and
when you reached the sea, the Egyptians pur-
sued your fathers to the Red Sea with chariots
and horsemen.[g] 7 Because they cried out to the
LORD,[h] he put darkness between your people
and the Egyptians, upon whom he brought the
sea so that it engulfed them. After you witnessed
what I did to Egypt, and dwelt a long time in the
desert, 8 [i]I brought you into the land of the
Amorites who lived east of the Jordan. They
fought against you, but I delivered them into
your power. You took possesion of their land,
and I destroyed them [the two kings of the
Amorites] before you. 9 [j]Then Balak, son of
Zippor, king of Moab, prepared to war against
Israel. He summoned Balaam, son of Beor, to
curse you; 10 [k]but I would not listen to Balaam.
On the contrary, he had to bless you, and I saved
you from him. 11 Once you crossed the Jordan[l]
and came to Jericho, the men of Jericho fought
against you, but I delivered them also into your
power. 12 And I sent the hornets* ahead of you
which drove them [the Amorites, Perizzites,
Canaanites, Hittites, Girgashites, Hivites and
Jebusites] out of your way; it was not your sword
or your bow.[m]

13 "I gave you a land which you had not tilled
and cities which you had not built, to dwell in;
you have eaten of vineyards and olive groves
which you did not plant.[n]

14 [o]"Now, therefore, fear the LORD and serve
him completely and sincerely. Cast out the gods
your fathers served beyond the River and in

23, 14: Going the way of all men: drawing near to death, the inevitable goal of all; cf 1 Kgs 2, 1f.

23, 15: Every threat: mentioned especially in Dt 28, 15–68.

24, 2: Beyond the River: east of the Euphrates; cf Gn 11, 28–31.

24, 12: The hornets: see note on Ex 23, 28.

z Ex 14, 14; Lv 26, 8; Dt 3, 22. a Ex 34, 16; Dt 7, 3. b Lv 26, 14–39; Dt 28, 15–68. c Gn 11, 26. 31; 31, 53. d Gn 12, 1; Acts 7, 2–4. e Gn 25, 24ff; 36, 8; 46, 1. 6; Acts 7, 15. f Ex 3, 10; 7, 14–12, 30. g Ex 12, 37. 51; 14, 9. h Ex 14, 10. 20. 27f. i Nm 21, 21–35. j Nm 22, 2–5. k Nm 23, 1–24, 25. l Jos 3, 14; 6, 1. m Jos 11, 20; Ex 23, 28; Dt 7, 20. n Dt 6, 10f. o Dt 10, 12; 1 Sm 7, 3; 12, 24; Tb 14, 9.

Egypt, and serve the LORD. 15 [p]If it does not please you to serve the LORD, decide today whom you will serve, the gods your fathers served* beyond the River or the gods of the Amorites in whose country you are dwelling. As for me and my household, we will serve the LORD."

Renewal of the Covenant 16 But the people answered, "Far be it from us to forsake the LORD for the service of other gods. 17 For it was the LORD, our God, who brought us and our fathers up out of the land of Egypt, out of a state of slavery. He performed those great miracles before our very eyes and protected us along our entire journey and among all the peoples through whom we passed. 18 At our approach the LORD drove out [all the peoples, including] the Amorites who dwelt in the land. Therefore we also will serve the LORD, for he is our God."

19 Joshua in turn said to the people, "You may not be able* to serve the LORD, for he is a holy God; he is a jealous God [q] who will not forgive your transgressions or your sins. 20 If, after the good he has done for you, you forsake the LORD and serve strange gods, he will do evil to you and destroy you."

21 But the people answered Joshua, "We will still serve the LORD." 22 Joshua therefore said to the people, "You are your own witnesses that you have chosen to serve the LORD." They replied, "We are, indeed!" 23 "Now, therefore, put away the strange gods that are among you and turn your hearts to the LORD, the God of Israel." 24 Then the people promised Joshua, "We will serve the LORD, our God, and obey his voice."

25 So Joshua made a covenant with the people that day and made statutes and ordinances for them at Shechem, 26 which he recorded in the book of the law of God. Then he took a large stone and set it up there under the oak that was in the sanctuary of the LORD. [r] 27 And Joshua said to all the people, "This stone shall be our witness, [s] for it has heard all the words which the LORD spoke to us. It shall be a witness against you, should you wish to deny your God." 28 Then Joshua dismissed the people, each to his own heritage. [t]

Death of Joshua 29 [u]After these events, Joshua, son of Nun, servant of the LORD, died at the age of a hundred and ten. 30 He was buried within the limits of his heritage at Timnath-serah [v] in the mountain region of Ephraim north of Mount Gaash. 31 Israel served the LORD during the entire lifetime of Joshua and that of the elders who outlived Joshua and knew all that the LORD had done for Israel. 32 [w]The bones of Joseph,* which the Israelites had brought up from Egypt, were buried in Shechem in the plot of ground Jacob had bought from the sons of Hamor, father of Shechem, for a hundred pieces of money. This was a heritage of the descendants of Joseph. 33 When Eleazar, son of Aaron, also died, he was buried on the hill which had been given to his son Phinehas [x] in the mountain region of Ephraim.

24, 15: The gods your fathers served: Abraham's ancestors were polytheists.

24, 19: You may not be able: fidelity to God's service is not easy, and therefore those who take such solemn obligations on themselves must be ever vigilant against human weakness.

24, 32: The bones of Joseph: the mummified body of Joseph (Gn 50, 25f), which the Israelites took with them as they left Egypt (Ex 13, 19), was fittingly buried at the ancient city of Shechem, near the border between the two Josephite tribes of Ephraim and Manasseh.

p Dt 30, 15–19. q Ex 20, 5; 23, 21; 34, 14; Lv 19, 2. r Gn 28, 18; 31, 45; Jgs 9, 6. s Gn 31, 48. 52; Dt 31, 19. 21. 26. t Jgs 2, 6. u 29ff: Jgs 2, 7ff. v Jos 19, 50: Jgs 2, 9. w Gn 33, 19; 50, 24; Ex 13, 19. x Jos 22, 13.

THE BOOK OF JUDGES

The Book of Judges derives its title from the twelve heroes of Israel whose deeds it records. They were not magistrates, but military leaders sent by God to aid and to relieve his people in time of external danger. They exercised their activities in the interval of time between the death of Joshua and the institution of the monarchy in Israel. Six of them—Othniel, Ehud, Barak, Gideon, Jephthah and Samson—are treated in some detail and have accordingly been styled the Major Judges. The other six, of whose activities this book preserves but a summary record, are called the Minor Judges. There were two other judges, whose judgeships are described in 1 Samuel—Eli and Samuel, who seem to have ruled the entire nation of Israel just before the institution of the monarchy. The twelve judges of the present book, however, very probably exercised their authority, sometimes simultaneously, over one or another tribe of Israel, never over the entire nation.

The purpose of the book is to show that the fortunes of Israel depended upon the obedience or disobedience of the people to God's law. Whenever they rebelled against him, they were oppressed by pagan nations; when they repented, he raised up judges to deliver them (cf Jgs 2, 10-23).

The accounts of various events, whether written shortly after their occurrence or orally transmitted, were later skillfully unified according to the moral purpose of the redactor sometime during the Israelite monarchy.

The book is divided as follows:

I. Palestine after the Death of Joshua (Jgs 1, 1—3, 6).
II. Stories of the Judges (Jgs 3, 7—16, 31).
III. The Tribes of Dan and Benjamin in the Days of the Judges (Jgs 17, 1—21, 25).

I: Palestine After the Death of Joshua

CHAPTER 1

Pagan Survivors in Palestine [1]After the death
of Joshua* the Israelites consulted the LORD,
asking, "Who shall be first among us to attack
the Canaanites and to do battle with them?" [a]
[2]The LORD answered, "Judah shall attack: I have
delivered the land into his power." [3]Judah then
said to his brother Simeon, "Come up with me
into the territory allotted to me, and let us
engage the Canaanites in battle. I will likewise
accompany you into the territory allotted to
you." So Simeon went with him.
[4]When the forces of Judah attacked, the LORD
delivered the Canaanites and Perizzites into
their power, and they slew ten thousand of them
in Bezek. [5]It was in Bezek that they came upon
Adonibezek and fought against him. When they
defeated the Canaanites and Perizzites, [6]Adoni-
bezek fled. They set out in pursuit, and when
they caught him, cut off his thumbs and his big
toes. [7]At this Adonibezek said, "Seventy kings,
with their thumbs and big toes cut off, used to
pick up scraps under my table. As I have done,
so has God repaid me." He was brought to
Jerusalem, and there he died. [8][The Judahites
fought against Jerusalem and captured it, putting
it to the sword; then they destroyed the city by
fire.]
[9] [b]Afterward the Judahites went down to fight
against the Canaanites who lived in the moun-
tain region, in the Negeb, and in the foothills,

1, 1–36: This chapter summarizes events most of which occurred shortly after the death of Joshua. Perhaps because they were planned and inaugurated by him, they are also attributed to him in the last half of the preceding book (Jos 14—22).

a Jgs 20, 18: Nm 27, 21. b Jos 10, 40; 11, 16; 12, 8.

10 [c]Judah also marched against the Canaanites who dwelt in Hebron, which was formerly called Kiriath-arba, and defeated Sheshai, Ahiman and Talmai.[d] 11 From there they marched against the inhabitants of Debir, which was formerly called Kiriath-sepher. 12 And Caleb said, "I will give my daughter Achsah in marriage to the one who attacks Kiriath-sepher and captures it." 13 [e]Othniel, son of Caleb's younger brother Kenaz, captured it; so Caleb gave him his daughter Achsah in marriage. 14 On the day of her marriage to Othniel she induced him to ask her father for some land. Then, as she alighted from the ass, Caleb asked her, "What is troubling you?" 15 "Give me an additional gift," she answered. "Since you have assigned land in the Negeb to me, give me also pools of water." So Caleb gave her the upper and the lower pool. 16 The descendants of the Kenite, Moses' father-in-law,* came up with the Judahites from the city of palms to the desert at Arad [which is in the Negeb]. But they later left and settled among the Amalekites.[f]

17 [g]Judah then went with his brother Simeon, and they defeated the Canaanites who dwelt in Zephath. After having doomed the city to destruction, they renamed it Hormah. 18 [h]Judah, however, did not occupy Gaza with its territory, Ashkelon with its territory, or Ekron with its territory. 19 [i]Since the LORD was with Judah, he gained possession of the mountain region. Yet he could not dislodge those who lived on the plain, because they had iron chariots. 20 As Moses had commanded, Hebron was given to Caleb, who then drove from it the three sons of Anak.[j]

21 *The Benjaminites did not dislodge the Jebusites who dwelt in Jerusalem, with the result that the Jebusites live in Jerusalem beside the Benjaminites to the present day.[k]

22 The house of Joseph, too, marched up against Bethel, and the LORD was with them. 23 The house of Joseph had a reconnaissance made of Bethel, which formerly was called Luz.[l] 24 The scouts saw a man coming out of the city and said to him, "Show us a way into the city, and we will spare you." 25 He showed them a way into the city, which they then put to the sword; but they let the man and his whole clan go free. 26 He then went to the land of the Hittites, where he built a city and called it Luz, as it is still called.

27 Manasseh did not take possession of Beth-shean with its towns or of Taanach with its towns. Neither did he dislodge the inhabitants of Dor and its towns, those of Ibleam and its towns, or those of Megiddo and its towns.[m] The Canaanites kept their hold in this district. 28 When the Israelites grew stronger, they impressed the Canaanites as laborers, but did not drive them out. 29 Similarly, the Ephraimites did not drive out the Canaanites living in Gezer, and so the Canaanites live in Gezer in their midst.[n]

30 Zebulun did not dislodge the inhabitants of Kitron or those of Nahalol; the Canaanites live among them, but have become forced laborers.

31 [o]Nor did Asher drive out the inhabitants of Acco or those of Sidon, or take possession of Mahaleb, Achzib, Helbah, Aphik or Rehob. 32 The Asherites live among the Canaanite natives of the land, whom they have not dislodged.

33 [p]Naphtali did not drive out the inhabitants of Beth-shemesh or those of Beth-anath, and so they live among the Canaanite natives of the land. However, the inhabitants of Beth-shemesh and Beth-anath have become forced laborers for them.

34 The Amorites hemmed in the Danites in the mountain region, not permitting them to go down into the plain.[q] 35 The Amorites had a firm hold in Harheres, Aijalon and Shaalbim, but as the house of Joseph gained the upper hand, they were impressed as laborers.

36 The territory of the Amorites extended from the Akrabbim pass to Sela and beyond.

1, 16: Moses' father-in-law: Reuel; cf Nm 10, 29–32 and note. City of palms: Jericho (cf Dt 34, 3), or a town in the Negeb.

1, 21: According to Jos 18, 16, Jerusalem was assigned to the tribe of Benjamin. But it was not actually taken from the Jebusites until David captured it (2 Sm 5, 6–9) and made it his capital, outside the tribal organization.

c Jos 15, 13–19. d Nm 13, 22; Jos 14, 15. e Jgs 3, 9. f Jgs 4, 11; Nm 10, 29–32. g Nm 21, 3. h Jos 11, 22. i Jos 17, 16ff. j Jos 14, 9. 13; 15, 14. k Jos 15, 63. l Gn 28, 19; 35, 6; 48, 3; Jos 18, 13. m 27f: Jos 17, 11ff. n Jos 16, 10. o 31f: Jos 19, 24–31. p Jos 19, 32–39. q Jos 19, 47f.

CHAPTER 2

Infidelities of the Israelites 1 [r]An angel of the LORD went up from Gilgal to Bochim and said, "It was I who brought you up from Egypt and led you into the land which I promised on oath to your fathers. I said that I would never break my covenant with you, 2 but that you were not to make a pact with the inhabitants of this land, and you were to pull down their altars. Yet you have not obeyed me.[s] What did you mean by this? 3 For now I tell you, I will not clear them out of your way; they shall oppose you and their gods shall become a snare for you."[t]

4 When the angel of the LORD had made these threats to all the Israelites, the people wept aloud; 5 and so that place came to be called Bochim.* They offered sacrifice there to the LORD.

6 [u]When Joshua dismissed the people, each Israelite went to take possession of his own hereditary land. 7 The people served the LORD during the entire lifetime of Joshua, and of those elders who outlived Joshua and who had seen all the great work which the LORD had done for Israel. 8 Joshua, son of Nun, the servant of the LORD, was a hundred and ten years old when he died; 9 and they buried him within the borders of his heritage at Timnath-heres in the mountain region of Ephraim north of Mount Gaash.[v]

10 But once the rest of that generation were gathered to their fathers, and a later generation arose that did not know the LORD, or what he had done for Israel, 11 the Israelites offended the LORD by serving the Baals.*[w] 12 Abandoning the LORD, the God of their fathers, who had led them out of the land of Egypt, they followed the other gods of the various nations around them, and by their worship of these gods provoked the LORD.

13 Because they had thus abandoned him and served Baal and the Ashtaroth,* 14 the anger of the LORD flared up against Israel, and he delivered them over to plunderers who despoiled them. He allowed them to fall into the power of their enemies round about whom they were no longer able to withstand. 15 Whatever they undertook, the LORD turned into disaster for them, as in his warning he had sworn he would do, till they were in great distress.[x] 16 Even when the LORD raised up judges to deliver them from the power of their despoilers, 17 they did not listen to their judges, but abandoned themselves to the worship of other gods. They were quick to stray from the way their fathers had taken, and did not follow their example of obedience to the commandments of the LORD. 18 Whenever the LORD raised up judges for them, he would be with the judge and save them from the power of their enemies as long as the judge lived; it was thus the LORD took pity on their distressful cries of affliction under their oppressors. 19 But when the judge died, they would relapse and do worse than their fathers, following other gods in service and worship, relinquishing none of their evil practices or stubborn conduct.[y]

20 [z]In his anger toward Israel the LORD said, "Inasmuch as this nation has violated my covenant which I enjoined on their fathers, and has disobeyed me, 21 I for my part will not clear away for them any more of the nations which Joshua left when he died." 22 Through these nations the Israelites were to be made to prove whether or not they would keep to the way of the LORD and continue in it as their fathers had done; 23 therefore the LORD allowed them to remain instead of expelling them immediately, or delivering them into the power of Israel.

CHAPTER 3

1 The following are the nations which the LORD allowed to remain, so that through them he might try all those Israelites who had no

2, 5: Bochim: the Hebrew word for "weepers."

2, 11: Baals: the chief god of the Canaanites and the Phoenicians was called "Baal," a word meaning "lord." He was honored by various titles, hence the plural form here, equivalent to "the pagan gods."

2, 13: Ashtaroth: the Canaanite Phoenician goddess of love and fertility was Astarte. The plural form used here refers to her various titles and images and is equivalent to "goddesses."

r 1ff: Jgs 6, 8ff. s Ex 34, 12f. 15; Dt 7, 2. 5; 21, 2f. t Nm 33, 55; Jos 23, 13. u 6–9: Jos 24, 28–31. v Jos 19, 50. w 11. 14; Jgs 3, 7f; 4, 1f; 6, 1; 10, 6f; 13, 1. x Dt 28, 15–68. y Jgs 3, 12; 4, 1; 6, 1; 8, 33. z 20f: Jos 23, 16.

experience of the battles with Canaan 2[just to instruct, by training them in battle, those generations only of the Israelites who would not have had that previous experience]: 3 [a]the five lords of the Philistines;* and all the Canaanites, the Sidonians, and the Hivites who dwell in the mountain region of Lebanon between Baal-hermon and the entrance to Hamath. 4These served to put Israel to the test, to determine whether they would obey the commandments the LORD had enjoined on their fathers through Moses. 5Besides, the Israelites were living among the Canaanites, Hittites, Amorites, Perizzites, Hivites and Jebusites. 6In fact, they took their daughters in marriage, and gave their own daughters to their sons in marriage, and served their gods.

II: Stories of the Judges

Othniel 7 [b]Because the Israelites had offended the LORD by forgetting the LORD, their God, and serving the Baals and the Asherahs,* 8the anger of the LORD flared up against them, and he allowed them to fall into the power of Cushan-rishathaim, king of Aram Naharaim, whom they served for eight years. 9But when the Israelites cried out to the LORD, he raised up for them a savior, Othniel, son of Caleb's younger brother Kenaz, who rescued them. 10The spirit of the LORD came upon him, and he judged Israel.[c] When he went out to war, the LORD delivered Cushan-rishathaim, king of Aram, into his power, so that he made him subject. 11The land then was at rest for forty years,[d] until Othniel, son of Kenaz, died.

Ehud 12Again the Israelites offended the LORD, who because of this offense strengthened Eglon, king of Moab, against Israel. 13In alliance with the Ammonites and Amalekites, he attacked and defeated Israel, taking possession of the city of palms. 14The Israelites then served Eglon, king of Moab, for eighteen years.

15But when the Israelites cried out to the LORD, he raised up for them a savior, the Benjaminite Ehud, son of Gera, who was left-handed. It was by him that the Israelites sent their tribute to Eglon, king of Moab. 16Ehud made himself a two-edged dagger a foot long, and wore it under his clothes over his right thigh. 17He presented the tribute to Eglon, king of Moab, who was very fat, 18and after the presentation went off with the tribute bearers. 19He returned, however, from where the idols are, near Gilgal, and said, "I have a private message for you, O king." And the king said, "Silence!" Then when all his attendants had left his presence, 20and Ehud went in to him where he sat alone in his cool upper room, Ehud said, "I have a message from God for you." So the king rose from his chair, 21and then Ehud with his left hand drew the dagger from his right thigh, and thrust it into Eglon's belly. 22The hilt also went in after the blade, and the fat closed over the blade because he did not withdraw the dagger from his body.

23Then Ehud went out into the hall, shutting the doors of the upper room on him and locking them. 24When Ehud had left and the servants came, they saw that the doors of the upper room were locked, and thought, "He must be easing himself in the cool chamber." 25They waited until they finally grew suspicious. Since he did not open the doors of the upper room, they took the key and opened them. There on the floor, dead, lay their lord!

26During their delay Ehud made good his escape and, passing the idols, took refuge in Seirah. 27On his arrival he sounded the horn in the mountain region of Ephraim, and the Israelites went down from the mountains with him as their leader. 28"Follow me," he said to them, "for the LORD has delivered your enemies the Moabites into your power." So they followed him down and seized the fords of the Jordan

3, 3: The Philistines: non-Semitic invaders, who gave their name to all Palestine, although they occupied only its southwestern plains. Their confederation embraced the five leading cities of Gaza, Ashkelon, Ashdod, Gath and Ekron.

3, 7: Asherahs: elsewhere rendered "sacred poles." See note on Ex 34, 13 and on Dt 7, 5. Here the word seems to mean "goddesses."

a Jos 13, 2–6. b Jgs 2, 11ff. c Jgs 6, 34; 11, 29; 13, 25; 14, 6. 19; 15, 14. d Jgs 5, 31; 8, 28.

leading to Moab, permitting no one to cross.[e] 29On that occasion they slew about ten thousand Moabites, all of them strong and valiant men. Not a man escaped. 30Thus was Moab brought under the power of Israel at that time; and the land had rest for eighty years.

Shamgar 31After him there was Shamgar, son of Anath, who slew six hundred Philistines with an oxgoad. He, too, rescued Israel.

CHAPTER 4

Deborah and Barak 1After Ehud's death, however, the Israelites again offended the LORD. 2So the LORD allowed them to fall into the power of the Canaanite king, Jabin, who reigned in Hazor.[f] The general of his army was Sisera, who dwelt in Harosheth-ha-goiim. 3But the Israelites cried out to the LORD; for with his nine hundred iron chariots he sorely oppressed the Israelites for twenty years.

4At this time the prophetess Deborah, wife of Lappidoth, was judging Israel. 5She used to sit under Deborah's palm tree, situated between Ramah and Bethel in the mountain region of Ephraim, and there the Israelites came up to her for judgment. 6She sent and summoned Barak, son of Abinoam,[g] from Kedesh of Naphtali. "This is what the LORD, the God of Israel, commands," she said to him; "go, march on Mount Tabor, and take with you ten thousand Naphtalites and Zebulunites. 7I will lead Sisera, the general of Jabin's army, out to you at the Wadi Kishon,[h] together with his chariots and troops, and will deliver them into your power." 8But Barak answered her, "If you come with me, I will go; if you do not come with me, I will not go." 9"I will certainly go with you," she replied, "but you shall not gain the glory in the expedition on which you are setting out, for the LORD will have Sisera fall into the power of a woman." So Deborah joined Barak and journeyed with him to Kedesh.

10Barak summoned Zebulun and Naphtali to Kedesh, and ten thousand men followed him. Deborah also went up with him.[i] 11*Now the Kenite Heber had detached himself from his own people, the descendants of Hobab, Moses' brother-in-law,[j] and had pitched his tent by the terebinth of Zaanannim, which was near Kedesh.

12It was reported to Sisera that Barak, son of Abinoam, had gone up to Mount Tabor. 13So Sisera assembled from Harosheth-ha-goiim at the Wadi Kishon all nine hundred of his iron chariots and all his forces. 14Deborah then said to Barak, "Be off, for this is the day on which the LORD has delivered Sisera into your power. The LORD marches before you." So Barak went down Mount Tabor, followed by his ten thousand men. 15And the LORD put Sisera[k] and all his chariots and all his forces to rout before Barak. Sisera himself dismounted from his chariot and fled on foot. 16Barak, however, pursued the chariots and the army as far as Harosheth-ha-goiim. The entire army of Sisera fell beneath the sword, not even one man surviving.

17*Sisera, in the meantime, had fled on foot to the tent of Jael, wife of the Kenite Heber, since Jabin, king of Hazor, and the family of the Kenite Heber were at peace with one another. 18Jael went out to meet Sisera and said to him, "Come in, my lord, come in with me; do not be afraid." So he went into her tent, and she covered him with a rug. 19He said to her, "Please give me a little water to drink. I am thirsty." But she opened a jug of milk for him to drink, and then covered him over.[l] 20"Stand at the entrance of the tent," he said to her. "If anyone comes and asks, 'Is there someone here?' say, 'No!' " 21Instead Jael, wife of Heber, got a tent peg and took a mallet in her hand. While Sisera was sound asleep, she stealthily approached him and drove the peg through his temple down into the ground, so that he perished in death.[m] 22Then when Barak came in pursuit of Sisera, Jael went out to meet him and said to him, "Come, I will

4, 11: Most of the Kenites occupied a district in the southern part of Judah (Jgs 1, 16). A group of them, however, had detached themselves and settled in lower Galilee.

4, 17–22: It is to be noted that the sacred author merely records the fact of the murder of Sisera. We must not construe this as approval of Jael's action.

e Jgs 4, 7. 14; 7, 9. 15. f Jos 11, 1. 10; Ps 83, 10; 1 Sm 12, 9. g Heb 11, 32. h Jgs 5, 21; Ps 83, 10. i Jgs 5, 18. j Nm 10, 29. k Ps 83, 10. l Jgs 5, 25. m Jgs 5, 26.

show you the man you seek." So he went in with her, and there lay Sisera dead, with the tent peg through his temple.

23 Thus on that day God humbled the Canaanite king, Jabin, before the Israelites; 24 their power weighed ever heavier upon him, till at length they destroyed the Canaanite king, Jabin.

CHAPTER 5

Canticle of Deborah 1 On that day Deborah [and Barak, son of Abinoam] sang this song:

2 Of chiefs who took the lead in Israel,*
of noble deeds by the people who bless the LORD,
3 Hear, O kings! Give ear, O princes!
I to the LORD will sing my song,
my hymn to the LORD, the God of Israel.

4 O LORD, when you went out from Seir,
when you marched from the land of Edom,
The earth quaked and the heavens were shaken,
while the clouds sent down showers.
5 Mountains trembled
in the presence of the LORD, the One of Sinai, [n]
in the presence of the LORD, the God of Israel. [o]
6 In the days of Shamgar, son of Anath, [p]
in the days of slavery caravans ceased;
Those who traveled the roads
went by roundabout paths.
7 Gone was freedom beyond the walls,
gone indeed from Israel.

When I, Deborah, rose,
when I rose, a mother in Israel,
8 New gods* were their choice;
then the war was at their gates.
Not a shield could be seen, nor a lance,
among forty thousand in Israel!

9 My heart is with the leaders of Israel,
nobles of the people who bless the LORD;
10 They who ride on white asses,
seated on saddlecloths as they go their way;
11 Sing of them to the strains of the harpers at the wells,
where men recount the just deeds of the LORD,
his just deeds that brought freedom to Israel.

12 Awake, awake, Deborah!
awake, awake, strike up a song.
Strength! arise, Barak,
make despoilers your spoil, son of Abinoam.
13 Then down came the fugitives with the mighty,
the people of the LORD came down for me as warriors.

14 From Ephraim, princes were in the valley;*
behind you was Benjamin, among your troops.
From Machir came down commanders,
from Zebulun wielders of the marshal's staff.
15 With Deborah were the princes of Issachar;
Barak, too, was in the valley, his course unchecked.

Among the clans of Reuben
great were the searchings of heart. [q]
16 Why do you stay beside your hearths
listening to the lowing of the herds?
Among the clans of Reuben
great were the searchings of heart!
17 Gilead, beyond the Jordan, rests;
why does Dan spend his time in ships?
Asher, who dwells along the shore,
is resting in his coves.
18 Zebulun is the people defying death;

5, 2–31: This canticle is an excellent example of early Hebrew poetry, even though some of its verses are now obscure.

5, 8: New gods: pagan deities; cf Dt 32, 16–18. God punished the idolatry of the Israelites by leaving them relatively unarmed before the attacks of their enemies, who had better weapons, made of iron; cf 1 Sm 13, 19–22.

5, 14–22: Praise for the tribes which formed the Israelite league against Sisera: Ephraim, Benjamin, Manasseh (represented by Machir), Zebulun, Issachar, and Naphtali (led by Barak). The tribes of Reuben, Gad (Gilead), Dan, and Asher are chided for their lack of co-operation. The more distant tribes of Judah and Simeon are not mentioned.

n Dt 33, 2; 2 Sm 22, 8; Pss 18, 8; 68, 9. o Ex 19, 16; Dt 4, 11; Ps 97, 5. p Jgs 3, 31. q Jgs 4, 14.

Naphtali, too, on the open heights![r]

19 The kings came and fought;
then they fought, those kings of Canaan,
At Taanach by the waters of Megiddo;
no silver booty did they take.[s]

20 From the heavens the stars, too, fought;*
from their courses they fought against
Sisera.[t]

21 The Wadi Kishon swept them away;
a wadi . . . , the Kishon.[u]

22 Then the hoofs of the horses pounded,
with the dashing, dashing of his steeds.

23 "Curse Meroz,"* says the LORD,
"hurl a curse at its inhabitants!
For they came not to my help,
as warriors to the help of the LORD."

24 Blessed among women be Jael,
blessed among tent-dwelling women.[v]

25 He asked for water, she gave him milk;[w]
in a princely bowl she offered curds.

26 With her left hand she reached for the peg,
with her right, for the workman's mallet.

She hammered Sisera, crushed his head;
she smashed, stove in his temple.

27 At her feet he sank down, fell, lay still;
down at her feet he sank and fell;
where he sank down, there he fell, slain.

28 From the window peered down and wailed
the mother of Sisera, from the lattice:
"Why is his chariot so long in coming?
why are the hoofbeats of his chariots
delayed?"

29 The wisest of her princesses answers her,
and she, too, keeps answering herself:

30 "They must be dividing the spoil they took:
there must be a damsel or two for each
man,
Spoils of dyed cloth as Sisera's spoil,
an ornate shawl or two for me in the spoil."

31 May all your enemies perish thus, O LORD![x]
but your friends be as the sun rising in its
might!

And the land was at rest for forty years.

CHAPTER 6

The Call of Gideon 1 The Israelites offended
the LORD, who therefore delivered them into the
power of Midian for seven years, 2 so that Midian
held Israel subject. For fear of Midian the
Israelites established the fire signals on the
mountains, the caves for refuge, and the strong-
holds. 3 And it used to be that when the Israelites
had completed their sowing, Midian, Amalek
and the Kedemites would come up,[y] 4 encamp
opposite them, and destroy the produce of the
land as far as the outskirts of Gaza, leaving no
sustenance in Israel, nor sheep, oxen or asses.
5 For they would come up with their livestock,
and their tents would become as numerous as
locusts; and neither they nor their camels could
be numbered, when they came into the land to
lay it waste. 6 Thus was Israel reduced to misery
by Midian, and so the Israelites cried out to the
LORD.

7 When Israel cried out to the LORD because of
Midian, 8 [z] he sent a prophet to the Israelites who
said to them, "The LORD, the God of Israel, says:
I led you up from Egypt; I brought you out of the
place of slavery. 9 I rescued you from the power
of Egypt and of all your other oppressors. I drove
them out before you and gave you their land.
10 And I said to you: I, the LORD, am your God;
you shall not venerate the gods of the Amorites
in whose land you are dwelling. But you did not
obey me."

11 Then the angel of the LORD came and sat
under the terebinth in Ophrah that belonged to
Joash the Abiezrite. While his son Gideon was
beating out wheat in the wine press to save it
from the Midianites, 12 the angel of the LORD
appeared to him and said, "The LORD is with

5, 20f: It would seem that nature aided the Hebrews in some way. Perhaps the torrential rains swelled the waters of Kishon, which then overwhelmed the Canaanites.

5, 23: Meroz: an unknown locality in which Hebrews probably resided, since its inhabitants are cursed for their failure to proffer aid.

r Jgs 4, 10. s Jgs 1, 27; Jos 17, 11. t Jgs 4, 15; Jos 10, 14. u Jgs 4, 7. 13. v Jgs 4, 17; Jdt 13, 17; Lk 1, 28. 42. w 25f: Jgs 4, 19. 21. x Ps 83, 10–19. y 3f: Jgs 7, 12; Dt 28, 30ff. z 8ff: Jgs 2, 1f; 10, 11–14.

you, O champion!" 13"My LORD," Gideon said
to him, "if the LORD is with us, why has all this
happened to us? Where are his wondrous deeds
of which our fathers told us when they said, 'Did
not the LORD bring us up from Egypt?' For now
the LORD has abandoned us and has delivered us
into the power of Midian." 14The LORD turned
to him and said, "Go with the strength you have
and save Israel from the power of Midian. It is I
who send you." 15But he answered him,
"Please, my lord, how can I save Israel? My
family is the meanest in Manasseh, and I am the
most insignificant in my father's house." 16"I
shall be with you," the LORD said to him, "and
you will cut down Midian to the last man." 17He
answered him, "If I find favor with you, give me
a sign that you are speaking with me. 18Do not
depart from here, I pray you, until I come back
to you and bring out my offering and set it before
you." He answered, "I will await your return."

19So Gideon went off and prepared a kid and
an ephah of flour in the form of unleavened
cakes. Putting the meat in a basket and the broth
in a pot, he brought them out to him under the
terebinth and presented them. 20The angel of
God said to him, "Take the meat and unleavened
cakes and lay them on this rock; then pour out
the broth." [a] When he had done so, 21the angel
of the LORD stretched out the tip of the staff he
held, and touched the meat and unleavened
cakes. Thereupon a fire came up from the rock
which consumed the meat and unleavened
cakes, and the angel of the LORD disappeared
from sight. 22 [b]Gideon, now aware that it had
been the angel of the LORD, said, "Alas, Lord
GOD, that I have seen the angel of the LORD face
to face!" 23The LORD answered him, "Be calm,
do not fear. You shall not die." 24So Gideon built
there an altar to the LORD and called it Yahweh-
shalom.* To this day it is still in Ophrah of the
Abiezrites.

25That same night the LORD said to him,
"Take the seven-year-old spare bullock and de-
stroy your father's altar to Baal and cut down the
sacred pole* that is by it. 26You shall build,
instead, the proper kind of altar to the LORD,
your God, on top of this stronghold. Then take
the spare bullock and offer it as a holocaust on
the wood from the sacred pole you have cut
down." 27So Gideon took ten of his servants and
did as the LORD had commanded him. But
through fear of his family and of the townspeo-
ple, he would not do it by day, but did it at night.
28Early the next morning the townspeople found
that the altar of Baal had been destroyed, the
sacred pole near it cut down, and the spare
bullock offered on the altar that was built.
29They asked one another, "Who did this?"
Their inquiry led them to the conclusion that
Gideon, son of Joash, had done it. 30So the
townspeople said to Joash, "Bring out your son
that he may die, for he has destroyed the altar of
Baal and has cut down the sacred pole that was
near it." 31But Joash replied to all who were
standing around him, "Do you intend to act in
Baal's stead, or be his champion? If anyone acts
for him, he shall be put to death by morning. If
he whose altar has been destroyed is a god, let
him act for himself!" 32So on that day Gideon
was called Jerubbaal,* because of the words,
"Let Baal take action against him, since he
destroyed his altar." [c]

33Then all Midian and Amalek and the
Kedemites mustered and crossed over into the
valley of Jezreel, where they encamped. 34The
spirit of the LORD enveloped Gideon; he blew
the horn that summoned Abiezer to follow him.
35He sent messengers, too, throughout Manas-
seh, which also obeyed his summons; through
Asher, Zebulun and Naphtali, likewise, he sent
messengers and these tribes advanced to meet
the others. 36Gideon said to God, "If indeed you
are going to save Israel through me, as you
promised, 37I am putting this woolen fleece on
the threshing floor. If dew comes on the fleece
alone, while all the ground is dry, I shall know
that you will save Israel through me, as you
promised." 38That is what took place. Early the

6, 24: Yahweh-shalom: Hebrew for "the LORD is peace," a reference to the Lord's words, "Be calm," literally, "Peace be to you!"

6, 25: The sacred pole: see note on Ex 34, 13.

6, 32: Jerubbaal: similar in sound to the Hebrew words meaning, "Let Baal take action."

a Jgs 13, 19. b 22f: Gn 32, 31; Dt 5, 24ff. c 1 Sm 12, 11.

next morning he wrung the dew from the fleece,
squeezing out of it a bowlful of water. 39 Gideon
then said to God, "Do not be angry with me if I
speak once more. Let me make just one more
test with the fleece. Let the fleece alone be dry,
but let there be dew on all the ground." 40 That
night God did so; the fleece alone was dry, but
there was dew on all the ground.

CHAPTER 7

Defeat of Midian 1 Early the next morning
Jerubbaal[d] (that is, Gideon) encamped by En-
harod with all his soldiers. The camp of Midian
was in the valley north of Gibeath-hammoreh.
2 The LORD said to Gideon, "You have too many
soldiers with you for me to deliver Midian into
their power, lest Israel vaunt itself against me
and say, 'My own power brought me the vic-
tory.' 3 Now proclaim to all the soldiers, 'If
anyone is afraid or fearful, let him leave.' "[e]
When Gideon put them to this test on the
mountain, twenty-two thousand of the soldiers
left, but ten thousand remained. 4 The LORD said
to Gideon, "There are still too many soldiers.
Lead them down to the water and I will test
them for you there. If I tell you that a certain
man is to go with you, he must go with you. But
no one is to go if I tell you he must not."
5 *When Gideon led the soldiers down to the
water, the LORD said to him, "You shall set to
one side everyone who laps up the water as a
dog does with its tongue; to the other, everyone
who kneels down to drink." 6 Those who lapped
up the water raised to their mouths by hand
numbered three hundred, but all the rest of the
soldiers knelt down to drink the water. 7 The
LORD said to Gideon, "By means of the three
hundred who lapped up the water I will save
you and will deliver Midian into your power. So
let all the other soldiers go home." 8 Their horns,
and such supplies as the soldiers had with them,
were taken up, and Gideon ordered the rest of
the Israelites to their tents, but kept the three
hundred men. Now the camp of Midian was
beneath him in the valley.
9 That night the LORD said to Gideon, "Go,
descend on the camp, for I have delivered it up
to you. 10 If you are afraid to attack, go down to
the camp with your aide Purah. 11 When you
hear what they are saying, you will have the
courage to descend on the camp." So he went
down with his aide Purah to the outposts of the
camp. 12 The Midianites, Amalekites, and all the
Kedemites lay in the valley, as numerous as
locusts. Nor could their camels be counted, for
these were as many as the sands on the sea-
shore. 13 *When Gideon arrived, one man was
telling another about a dream. "I had a dream,"
he said, "that a round loaf of barley bread was
rolling into the camp of Midian. It came to our
tent and struck it, and as it fell it turned the tent
upside down." 14 "This can only be the sword of
the Israelite Gideon, son of Joash," the other
replied. "God has delivered Midian and all the
camp into his power." 15 When Gideon heard the
description and explanation of the dream, he
prostrated himself. Then returning to the camp
of Israel, he said, "Arise, for the LORD has
delivered the camp of Midian into your power."
16 He divided the three hundred men into
three companies, and provided them all with
horns and with empty jars and torches inside the
jars. 17 "Watch me and follow my lead," he told
them. "I shall go to the edge of the camp, and as
I do, you must do also. 18 When I and those with
me blow horns, you too must blow horns all
around the camp and cry out, 'For the LORD and
for Gideon!' " 19 So Gideon and the hundred
men who were with him came to the edge of the
camp at the beginning of the middle watch,* just
after the posting of the guards. They blew the
horns and broke the jars they were holding. 20 All
three companies blew horns and broke their jars.

7, 5: The Lord desired not numerous but reliable soldiers. Those who drank from their hands were alert, standing ready to resist attack, whereas the others were careless and undependable. The cowardly soldiers had already been dismissed (v 3); cf Dt 20, 8.

7, 13: The barley loaf represents the agricultural Hebrews while the tent refers to the nomadic Midianites. The overthrow of the tent indicates the victory of the Hebrews over their Midianite oppressors.

7, 19: At the beginning of the middle watch: about two hours before midnight. The ancient Hebrews divided the night into three watches of about four hours each. At the beginning of a watch the sentinels were changed.

d Jgs 6, 32. e Dt 20, 8.

They held the torches in their left hands, and in their right the horns they were blowing, and cried out, "A sword for the LORD and Gideon!" [21]They all remained standing in place around the camp, while the whole camp fell to running and shouting and fleeing. [22]But the three hundred men kept blowing the horns, and throughout the camp the LORD set the sword of one against another.[f] The army fled as far as Beth-shittah in the direction of Zarethan, near the border of Abel-meholah at Tabbath.

[23]The Israelites were called to arms from Naphtali, from Asher, and from all Manasseh, and they pursued Midian. [24]Gideon also sent messengers throughout the mountain region of Ephraim to say, "Go down to confront Midian, and seize the water courses against them as far as Beth-barah, as well as the Jordan." So all the Ephraimites were called to arms, and they seized the water courses as far as Beth-barah, and the Jordan as well. [25] [g]They captured the two princes of Midian, Oreb and Zeeb, killing Oreb at the rock of Oreb and Zeeb at the wine press of Zeeb. Then they pursued Midian and carried the heads of Oreb and Zeeb to Gideon beyond the Jordan.

CHAPTER 8

[1]But the Ephraimites said to him, "What have you done to us, not calling us when you went to fight against Midian?" And they quarrelled bitterly with him. [2]"What have I accomplished now in comparison with you?" he answered them. "Is not the gleaning of Ephraim better than the vintage of Abiezer?[h] [3]Into your power God delivered the princes of Midian, Oreb and Zeeb. What have I been able to do in comparison with you?" When he said this, their anger against him subsided.

[4]When Gideon reached the Jordan and crossed it with his three hundred men, they were exhausted and famished. [5]So he said to the men of Succoth, "Will you give my followers some loaves of bread? They are exhausted, and I am pursuing Zebah and Zalmunna, kings of Midian." [6]But the princes of Succoth replied, "Are the hands of Zebah and Zalmunna already in your possession, that we should give food to your army?"* [7]Gideon said, "Very well; when the LORD has delivered Zebah and Zalmunna into my power, I will grind your flesh in with the thorns and briers of the desert." [8]He went up from there to Penuel and made the same request of them, but the men of Penuel answered him as had the men of Succoth. [9]So to the men of Penuel, too, he said, "When I return in triumph, I will demolish this tower."

[10]Now Zebah and Zalmunna were in Karkor with their force of about fifteen thousand men; these were all who were left of the whole Kedemite army, a hundred and twenty thousand swordsmen having fallen. [11]Gideon went up by the route of the nomads east of Nobah and Jogbehah, and attacked the camp when it felt secure. [12]Zebah and Zalmunna fled. He pursued them and took the two kings of Midian, Zebah and Zalmunna, captive, throwing the entire army into panic.

[13]Then Gideon, son of Joash, returned from battle by the pass of Heres. [14]He captured a young man of Succoth, who upon being questioned listed for him the seventy-seven princes and elders of Succoth. [15]So he went to the men of Succoth and said, "Here are Zebah and Zalmunna, with whom you taunted me, 'Are the hands of Zebah and Zalmunna already in your possession, that we should give food to your weary followers?' " [16]He took the elders of the city, and thorns and briers of the desert, and ground these men of Succoth into them. [17]He also demolished the tower of Penuel and slew the men of the city.

[18]Then he said to Zebah and Zalmunna, "Where now are the men you killed at Tabor?" "They all resembled you," they replied. "They appeared to be princes." [19]"They were my brothers, my mother's sons," he said. "As the LORD lives, if you had spared their lives, I should not kill you." [20]Then he said to his first-born,

8, 6: Are the hands . . . in your possession . . . ?: i.e., can you already boast of victory? The hands as well as the heads of slain enemies were cut off and counted as trophies; cf 2 Sm 4, 8; 2 Kgs 10, 7f; and the Ugaritic Anath Epic, V AB, II 10ff.

f 22f: Ps 83, 10; Is 9, 4. g Jgs 8, 3; Ps 83, 12; Is 10, 26. h Jg 6, 34.

Jether, "Go, kill them." Since Jether was still a boy, he was afraid and did not draw his sword. 21 Zebah and Zalmunna said, "Come, kill us yourself, for a man's strength is like the man." So Gideon stepped forward and killed Zebah and Zalmunna. He also took the crescents that were on the necks of their camels.

22 The Israelites then said to Gideon, "Rule over us—you, your son, and your son's son—for you rescued us from the power of Midian." 23 But Gideon answered them, "I will not rule over you, nor shall my son rule over you. The LORD must rule over you."

24 Gideon went on to say, "I should like to make a request of you. Will each of you give me a ring from his booty?" (For being Ishmaelites,* the enemy had gold rings.) 25 "We will gladly give them," they replied, and spread out a cloak into which everyone threw a ring from his booty. 26 The gold rings that he requested weighed seventeen hundred gold shekels, in addition to the crescents and pendants, the purple garments worn by the kings of Midian, and the trappings that were on the necks of their camels. 27 Gideon made an ephod out of the gold and placed it in his city Ophrah. However, all Israel paid idolatrous homage to it there, and caused the ruin of Gideon and his family.

28 Thus was Midian brought into subjection by the Israelites; no longer did they hold their heads high. And the land had rest for forty years, during the lifetime of Gideon.

Gideon's Son Abimelech 29 Then Jerubbaal, son of Joash, went back home to stay. 30 [i]Now Gideon had seventy sons, his direct descendants, for he had many wives. 31 His concubine* who lived in Shechem also bore him a son, whom he named Abimelech. 32 At a good old age Gideon, son of Joash, died and was buried in the tomb of his father Joash in Ophrah of the Abiezrites. 33 But after Gideon was dead, the Israelites again abandoned themselves to the Baals, making Baal of Berith* their god 34 and forgetting the LORD, their God, who had delivered them from the power of their enemies all around them. 35 Nor were they grateful to the family of Jerubbaal [Gideon] for all the good he had done for Israel.

CHAPTER 9

1 Abimelech, son of Jerubbaal, went to his mother's kinsmen in Shechem,[j] and said to them and to the whole clan to which his mother's family belonged, 2 "Put this question to all the citizens of Shechem: 'Which is better for you: that seventy men, or all Jerubbaal's sons, rule over you, or that one man rule over you?' You must remember that I am your own flesh and bone." 3 When his mother's kin repeated these words to them on his behalf, all the citizens of Shechem sympathized with Abimelech, thinking, "He is our kinsman." 4 They also gave him seventy silver shekels from the temple of Baal of Berith, with which Abimelech hired shiftless men and ruffians as his followers. 5 He then went to his ancestral house in Ophrah, and slew his brothers, the seventy sons of Jerubbaal, on one stone. Only the youngest son of Jerubbaal, Jotham, escaped, for he was hidden. 6 Then all the citizens of Shechem and all Beth-millo came together and proceeded to make Abimelech king by the terebinth at the memorial pillar in Shechem.

7 When this was reported to him, Jotham went to the top of Mount Gerizim, and standing there, cried out to them in a loud voice: "Hear me, citizens of Shechem, that God may then hear you! 8 Once the trees went to anoint a king over themselves. So they said to the olive tree, 'Reign over us.'[k] 9 But the olive tree answered them, 'Must I give up my rich oil, whereby men and gods are honored,* and go to wave over the trees?' 10 Then the trees said to the fig tree, 'Come; you reign over us!' 11 But the fig tree answered them, 'Must I give up my sweetness

8, 24: Ishmaelites: here as in Gn 37, 25–28, the designation is not ethnic; it refers rather to their status as nomads.

8, 31: Concubine: cf Gn 25, 1–11 and note.

8, 33: Baal of Berith: one of the titles of Baal as worshiped by the Canaanites of Shechem, meaning "the lord of the covenant."

9, 9: Whereby men and gods are honored: oil was used in the worship both of the true God and of false gods; it was prescribed in the worship of Yahweh (Lv 2, 1. 6. 15; 24, 2). It was also used to consecrate prophets, priests and kings (Ex 30, 25. 30; 1 Sm 10, 1; 16, 13).

i Jgs 9, 2. 5. j Jgs 8, 31. k Jgs 8, 22f.

and my good fruit, and go to wave over the
trees?' 12 Then the trees said to the vine, 'Come
you, and reign over us.' 13 But the vine answered
them, 'Must I give up my wine that cheers gods*
and men, and go to wave over the trees?' 14 Then
all the trees said to the buckthorn, 'Come; you
reign over us!' 15 But the buckthorn replied to
the trees, 'If you wish to anoint me king over
you in good faith, come and take refuge in my
shadow. Otherwise, let fire come from the
buckthorn and devour the cedars of Lebanon.'

16 *"Now then, if you have acted in good faith
and honorably in appointing Abimelech your
king, if you have dealt well with Jerubbaal and
with his family, and if you have treated him as he
deserved— 17 for my father fought for you at the
risk of his life when he saved you from the
power of Midian; 18 but you have risen against
his family this day and have killed his seventy
sons upon one stone, and have made Abimelech,
the son of his handmaid,[l] king over the citizens
of Shechem, because he is your kinsman— 19 if,
then, you have acted in good faith and with
honor toward Jerubbaal and his family this day,
rejoice in Abimelech and may he in turn rejoice
in you. 20 But if not, let fire come forth from
Abimelech to devour the citizens of Shechem
and Beth-millo, and let fire come forth from the
citizens and from Beth-millo to devour Abime-
lech." 21 Then Jotham went in flight to Beer,
where he remained for fear of his brother
Abimelech.

22 When Abimelech had ruled Israel for three
years, 23 God put bad feelings between Abime-
lech and the citizens of Shechem, who rebelled
against Abimelech. 24 This was to repay the
violence done to the seventy sons of Jerubbaal
and to avenge their blood upon their brother
Abimelech, who killed them, and upon the
citizens of Shechem, who encouraged him to kill
his brothers. 25 The citizens of Shechem then set
men in ambush for him on the mountaintops,
and these robbed all who passed them on the
road. But it was reported to Abimelech.

26 Now Gaal, son of Ebed, came over to
Shechem with his kinsmen. The citizens of
Shechem put their trust in him, 27 and went out
into the fields, harvested their grapes and trod
them out. Then they held a festival and went to
the temple of their god, where they ate and
drank and cursed Abimelech. 28 Gaal, son of
Ebed, said, "Who is Abimelech? And why
should we of Shechem serve him? Were not the
son of Jerubbaal and his lieutenant Zebul once
subject to the men of Hamor, father of She-
chem?[m] Why should we serve him? 29 Would
that this people were entrusted to my command!
I would depose Abimelech. I would say to
Abimelech, 'Get a larger army and come out!' "

30 At the news of what Gaal, son of Ebed, had
said, Zebul, the ruler of the city, was angry 31 and
sent messengers to Abimelech in Arumah with
the information: "Gaal, son of Ebed, and his
kinsmen have come to Shechem and are stirring
up the city against you. 32 Now rouse yourself;
set an ambush tonight in the fields, you and the
men who are with you. 33 Promptly at sunrise
tomorrow morning, make a raid on the city.
When he and his followers come out against
you, deal with him as best you can."

34 During the night Abimelech advanced with
all his soldiers and set up an ambush for She-
chem in four companies. 35 Gaal, son of Ebed,
went out and stood at the entrance of the city
gate. When Abimelech and his soldiers rose from
their place of ambush, 36 Gaal saw them and said
to Zebul, "There are men coming down from the
hilltops!" But Zebul answered him, "You see the
shadow of the hills as men." 37 But Gaal went on
to say, "Men are coming down from the region
of Tabbur-Haares, and one company is coming
by way of Elon-Meonenim." 38 Zebul said to him,
"Where now is the boast you uttered, 'Who is
Abimelech that we should serve him?' Are these
not the men for whom you expressed contempt?
Go out now and fight with them." 39 So Gaal
went out at the head of the citizens of Shechem
and fought against Abimelech. 40 But Abimelech

9, 13: Cheers gods: wine was used in the libations both of the Temple of Jerusalem and of pagan temples.

9, 16: Just as the noble trees refused the honor of royalty and were made subject to a mean plant, so did Abimelech of less noble birth than the seventy sons of Gideon now tyrannize over the people.

l Jgs 8, 31. m Gn 34, 2. 6.

routed him, and he fled before him; and many fell slain right up to the entrance of the gate. [41]Abimelech returned to Arumah, but Zebul drove Gaal and his kinsmen from Shechem, which they had occupied.

[42]The next day, when the people were taking the field, it was reported to Abimelech, [43]who divided the men he had into three companies, and set up an ambush in the fields. He watched till he saw the people leave the city, and then rose against them for the attack. [44]Abimelech and the company with him dashed in and stood by the entrance of the city gate, while the other two companies rushed upon all who were in the field and attacked them. [45]That entire day Abimelech fought against the city, and captured it. He then killed its inhabitants and demolished the city, sowing the site with salt.*

[46]When they heard of this, all the citizens of Migdal-shechem went into the crypt of the temple of El-berith. [47]It was reported to Abimelech that all the citizens of Migdal-shechem were gathered together. [48]So he went up Mount Zalmon with all his soldiers, took his ax in his hand, and cut down some brushwood. This he lifted to his shoulder, then said to the men with him, "Hurry! Do just as you have seen me do." [49]So all the men likewise cut down brushwood, and following Abimelech, placed it against the crypt. Then they set the crypt on fire over their heads, so that every one of the citizens of Migdal-shechem, about a thousand men and women, perished.

[50]Abimelech proceeded to Thebez, which he invested and captured. [51]Now there was a strong tower in the middle of the city, and all the men and women, in a word all the citizens of the city, fled there, shutting themselves in and going up to the roof of the tower. [52]Abimelech came up to the tower and fought against it, advancing to the very entrance of the tower to set it on fire. [53]But a certain woman cast the upper part of a millstone down on Abimelech's head, and it fractured his skull.[n] [54]He immediately called his armor-bearer and said to him, "Draw your sword and dispatch me, lest they say of me that a woman killed me."[o] So his attendant ran him through and he died. [55]When the Israelites saw that Abimelech was dead, they all left for their homes.

[56]Thus did God requite the evil Abimelech had done to his father in killing his seventy brothers. [57]God also brought all their wickedness home to the Shechemites, for the curse of Jotham, son of Jerubbaal, overtook them.

CHAPTER 10

Tola [1]After Abimelech there rose to save Israel the Issacharite Tola, son of Puah, son of Dodo, a resident of Shamir in the mountain region of Ephraim. [2]When he had judged Israel twenty-three years, he died and was buried in Shamir.

Jair [3]Jair the Gileadite came after him and judged Israel twenty-two years. [4]He had thirty sons who rode on thirty saddle-asses* and possessed thirty cities in the land of Gilead; these are called Havvoth-jair to the present day.[p] [5]Jair died and was buried in Kamon.

Oppression by the Ammonites [6]The Israelites again offended the LORD, serving the Baals and Ashtaroths, the gods of Aram, the gods of Sidon, the gods of Moab, the gods of the Ammonites, and the gods of the Philistines. Since they had abandoned the LORD and would not serve him, [7]the LORD became angry with Israel and allowed them to fall into the power of [the Philistines and] the Ammonites. [8]For eighteen years they afflicted and oppressed the Israelites in Bashan, and all the Israelites in the Amorite land beyond the Jordan in Gilead. [9]The Ammonites also crossed the Jordan to fight against Judah, Benjamin, and the house of Ephraim, so that Israel was in great distress.

[10]Then the Israelites cried out to the LORD, "We have sinned against you; we have forsaken our God and have served the Baals." [11][q]The

9, 45: Sowing the site with salt: a severe measure, which was a symbol of desolation, and even more, since it actually rendered the ground barren and useless.

10, 4: Saddle-asses: a sign of rank and wealth; cf Jgs 5, 10; 12, 14.

n 2 Sm 11, 21. o 1 Sm 31, 4; 1 Chr 10, 4. p Dt 3, 14. q 11–14: Jgs 2, 1ff; 6, 8ff.

LORD answered the Israelites: "Did not the
Egyptians, the Amorites,[r] the Ammonites, the
Philistines, 12the Sidonians, the Amalekites, and
the Midianites oppress you?[s] Yet when you cried
out to me, and I saved you from their grasp,
13you still forsook me and worshiped other gods.
Therefore I will save you no more. 14Go and cry
out to the gods you have chosen; let them save
you now that you are in distress." 15But the
Israelites said to the LORD, "We have sinned. Do
to us whatever you please. Only save us this
day." 16And they cast out the foreign gods from
their midst and served the LORD, so that he
grieved over the misery of Israel.

17The Ammonites had gathered for war and
encamped in Gilead, while the Israelites assem-
bled and encamped in Mizpah.[t] 18And among
the people the princes of Gilead said to one
another, "The one who begins the war against
the Ammonites shall be leader of all the inhabit-
ants of Gilead."[u]

CHAPTER 11

Jephthah 1There was a chieftain, the Gileadite
Jephthah, born to Gilead of a harlot. 2Gilead's
wife had also borne him sons, and on growing
up the sons of the wife had driven Jephthah
away, saying to him, "You shall inherit nothing
in our family, for you are the son of another
woman." 3So Jephthah had fled from his broth-
ers and had taken up residence in the land of
Tob. A rabble had joined company with him, and
went out with him on raids.

4Some time later, the Ammonites warred on
Israel. 5When this occurred the elders of Gilead
went to bring Jephthah from the land of Tob.
6"Come," they said to Jephthah, "be our com-
mander that we may be able to fight the
Ammonites." 7"Are you not the ones who hated
me and drove me from my father's house?"
Jephthah replied to the elders of Gilead. "Why
do you come to me now, when you are in
distress?" 8The elders of Gilead said to Jephthah,
"In any case, we have now come back to you; if
you go with us to fight against the Ammonites,
you shall be the leader of all of us who dwell in
Gilead." 9Jephthah answered the elders of Gil-
ead, "If you bring me back to fight against the
Ammonites and the LORD delivers them up to
me, I shall be your leader." 10The elders of
Gilead said to Jephthah, "The LORD is witness
between us that we will do as you say."

11So Jephthah went with the elders of Gilead,
and the people made him their leader and
commander.[v] In Mizpah, Jephthah settled all his
affairs before the LORD. 12Then he sent messen-
gers to the king of the Ammonites to say, "What
have you against me that you come to fight with
me in my land?" 13He answered the messengers
of Jephthah, "Israel took away my land from the
Arnon to the Jabbok and the Jordan when they
came up from Egypt.[w] Now restore the same
peaceably."

14Again Jephthah sent messengers to the king
of the Ammonites, 15saying to him, "This is what
Jephthah says: Israel did not take the land of
Moab or the land of the Ammonites.[x] 16For
when they came up from Egypt, Israel went
through the desert to the Red Sea and came to
Kadesh. 17Israel then sent messengers to the
king of Edom saying, 'Let me pass through your
land.' But the king of Edom did not give
consent. They also sent to the king of Moab, but
he too was unwilling. So Israel remained in
Kadesh.[y] 18Then they went through the desert,
and by-passing the land of Edom and the land of
Moab, went east of the land of Moab and
encamped across the Arnon.[z] Thus they did not
go through the territory of Moab, for the Arnon
is the boundary of Moab. 19 [a]Then Israel sent
messengers to Sihon, king of the Amorites, king
of Heshbon. Israel said to him, 'Let me pass
through your land to my own place.' 20But Sihon
refused to let Israel pass through his territory. On
the contrary, he gathered all his soldiers, who
encamped at Jahaz and fought Israel. 21But the
LORD, the God of Israel, delivered Sihon and all
his men into the power of Israel, who defeated
them and occupied all the land of the Amorites
dwelling in that region, 22the whole territory
from the Arnon to the Jabbok, from the desert to

r Nm 21, 21–32. s Jgs 6, 3. t Jgs 11, 29. u Jgs 11, 5–11. v Jgs 10, 18. w Nm 21, 13. 24ff. x Dt 2, 9. 19. y Nm 20, 1. 14. 18–21; Dt 1, 46. z Nm 21, 4. 11. 13; 22, 36; Dt 2, 8. a 19–22: Nm 21, 21–26; Dt 2, 26–36.

the Jordan. 23 If now the LORD, the God of Israel, has cleared the Amorites out of the way of his people, are you to dislodge Israel? 24 Should you not possess that which your god Chemosh* gave you to possess, and should we not possess all that the LORD, our God, has cleared out for us?[b] 25 Again, are you any better than Balak, son of Zippor, king of Moab? Did he ever quarrel with Israel, or did he war against them[c] 26 when Israel occupied Heshbon and its villages, Aroer and its villages, and all the cities on the banks of the Arnon?[d] Three hundred years have passed; why did you not recover them during that time? 27 I have not sinned against you, but you wrong me by warring against me. Let the LORD, who is judge, decide this day between the Israelites and the Ammonites!" 28 But the king of the Ammonites paid no heed to the message Jephthah sent him.

Jephthah's Vow 29 The spirit of the LORD came upon Jephthah. He passed through Gilead and Manasseh, and through Mizpah-Gilead as well, and from there he went on to the Ammonites. 30 *Jephthah made a vow to the LORD. "If you deliver the Ammonites into my power," he said, 31 "whoever comes out of the doors of my house to meet me when I return in triumph from the Ammonites shall belong to the LORD. I shall offer him up as a holocaust."

32 Jephthah then went on to the Ammonites to fight against them, and the LORD delivered them into his power, 33 so that he inflicted a severe defeat on them, from Aroer to the approach of Minnith (twenty cities in all) and as far as Abel-keramim. Thus were the Ammonites brought into subjection by the Israelites. 34 When Jephthah returned to his house in Mizpah, it was his daughter who came forth, playing the tambourines and dancing. She was an only child: he had neither son nor daughter besides her. 35 When he saw her, he rent his garments and said, "Alas, daughter, you have struck me down and brought calamity upon me. For I have made a vow to the LORD and I cannot retract."[e] 36 "Father," she replied, "you have made a vow to the LORD. Do with me as you have vowed, because the LORD has wrought vengeance for you on your enemies the Ammonites." 37 Then she said to her father, "Let me have this favor. Spare me for two months, that I may go off down the mountains to mourn my virginity* with my companions." 38 "Go," he replied, and sent her away for two months. So she departed with her companions and mourned her virginity on the mountains. 39 At the end of the two months she returned to her father, who did to her as he had vowed. She had not been intimate with man. It then became a custom in Israel 40 for Israelite women to go yearly to mourn the daughter of Jephthah the Gileadite for four days of the year.

CHAPTER 12

The Shibboleth Incident 1 The men of Ephraim gathered together and crossed over to Zaphon. They said to Jephthah, "Why do you go on to fight with the Ammonites without calling us to go with you? We will burn your house over you."[f] 2 Jephthah answered them, "My soldiers and I were engaged in a critical contest with the Ammonites. I summoned you, but you did not rescue me from their power. 3 When I saw that you would not effect a rescue, I took my life in my own hand and went on to the Ammonites, and the LORD delivered them into my power. Why, then, do you come up against me this day to fight with me?"

4 Then Jephthah called together all the men of Gilead and fought against Ephraim, whom they defeated; for the Ephraimites had said, "You of Gilead are Ephraimite fugitives in territory be-

11, 24: Chemosh: the chief god of the Moabites—not of the Ammonites, whose leading deity was called Molech or Milcom; cf Nm 21, 29; 1 Kgs 11, 7; 2 Kgs 23, 13. The error is probably due to an ancient copyist. Jephthah argues from the viewpoint of his adversaries, the Ammonites, that they were entitled to all the land they had conquered with the aid of their god. It does not necessarily follow that Jephthah himself believed in the actual existence of this pagan god.

11, 30–40: The text clearly implies that Jephthah vowed a human sacrifice, according to the custom of his pagan neighbors; cf 2 Kgs 3, 27. The inspired author merely records the fact; he does not approve of the action.

11, 37: Mourn my virginity: to bear children was woman's greatest pride; to be childless was regarded as a great misfortune. Hence Jephthah's daughter asks permission to mourn the fact that she will be put to death before she can bear children.

b Nm 21, 29; 1 Kgs 11, 7. c Nm 22, 2; Jos 24, 9; Mi 6, 5. d Nm 21, 25; Dt 2, 36. e Nm 30, 3. f Jgs 8, 1.

longing to Ephraim and Manasseh." 5The Gileadites took the fords of the Jordan toward Ephraim. When any of the fleeing Ephraimites said, "Let me pass," the men of Gilead would say to him, "Are you an Ephraimite?" If he answered, "No!" 6they would ask him to say "Shibboleth."* If he said "Sibboleth," not being able to give the proper pronunciation, they would seize him and kill him at the fords of the Jordan. Thus forty-two thousand Ephraimites fell at that time.

7After having judged Israel for six years, Jephthah the Gileadite died and was buried in his city in Gilead.

Ibzan 8After him Ibzan of Bethlehem judged Israel. 9He had thirty sons. He also had thirty daughters married outside the family, and he brought in as wives for his sons thirty young women from outside the family. After having judged Israel for seven years, 10Ibzan died and was buried in Bethlehem.

Elon 11After him the Zebulunite Elon judged Israel. When he had judged Israel for ten years, 12the Zebulunite Elon died and was buried in Elon in the land of Zebulun.

Abdon 13After him the Pirathonite Abdon, son of Hillel, judged Israel. 14He had forty sons and thirty grandsons who rode on seventy saddle-asses. After having judged Israel for eight years, 15the Pirathonite Abdon, son of Hillel, died and was buried in Pirathon in the land of Ephraim on the mountain of the Amalekites.

CHAPTER 13

The Birth of Samson 1The Israelites again offended the LORD, who therefore delivered them into the power of the Philistines for forty years.[g]

2There was a certain man from Zorah, of the clan of the Danites, whose name was Manoah. His wife was barren and had borne no children. 3An angel of the LORD appeared to the woman and said to her, "Though you are barren and have had no children, yet you will conceive and bear a son.[h] 4Now, then, be careful to take no wine or strong drink and to eat nothing unclean. 5As for the son you will conceive and bear, no razor shall touch his head,[i] for this boy is to be consecrated* to God from the womb. It is he who will begin the deliverance of Israel from the power of the Philistines."

6The woman went and told her husband, "A man of God came to me; he had the appearance of an angel of God, terrible indeed. I did not ask him where he came from, nor did he tell me his name. 7But he said to me, 'You will be with child and will bear a son. So take neither wine nor strong drink, and eat nothing unclean. For the boy shall be consecrated to God from the womb, until the day of his death.' " 8Manoah then prayed to the LORD. "O LORD, I beseech you," he said, "may the man of God whom you sent, return to us to teach us what to do for the boy who will be born."

9God heard the prayer of Manoah, and the angel of God came again to the woman as she was sitting in the field. Since her husband Manoah was not with her, 10the woman ran in haste and told her husband. "The man who came to me the other day has appeared to me," she said to him; 11so Manoah got up and followed his wife. When he reached the man, he said to him, "Are you the one who spoke to my wife?" "Yes," he answered. 12Then Manoah asked, "Now, when that which you say comes true, what are we expected to do for the boy?" 13The angel of the LORD answered Manoah, "Your wife is to abstain from all the things of which I spoke to her. 14She must not eat anything that comes from the vine, nor take wine or strong drink, nor eat anything unclean. Let her observe all that I have commanded her." 15Then Manoah said to the angel of the LORD, "Can we persuade you to stay, while we prepare a kid for you?" 16But the angel of the LORD answered Manoah, "Although you press me, I will not partake of your food. But if you will, you

12, 6: Shibboleth: "an ear of grain." But this Hebrew word can also mean "flood water" as in Ps 69, 3. 16. Apparently the Gileadites engaged the Ephraimites in conversation about the "flood water" of the Jordan. Differences in enunciating the initial sibilant of the Hebrew word betrayed different tribal affinities.

13, 5: Consecrated: In Hebrew, nazir. Samson therefore was for life to be under the nazirite vow, which obliged him to abstain from drinking wine or having his hair cut; cf Nm 6, 2–8.

g Jgs 10, 6. h 3f: 1 Sm 1, 20; Lk 1, 31. i Nm 6, 5.

may offer a holocaust to the LORD." Not knowing that it was the angel of the LORD, 17Manoah said to him, "What is your name, that we may honor you when your words come true?" 18The angel of the LORD answered him,[j] "Why do you ask my name, which is mysterious?"* 19 [k]Then Manoah took the kid with a cereal offering and offered it on the rock to the LORD, whose works are mysteries. While Manoah and his wife were looking on, 20as the flame rose to the sky from the altar, the angel of the LORD ascended in the flame of the altar. When Manoah and his wife saw this, they fell prostrate to the ground; 21but the angel of the LORD was seen no more by Manoah and his wife. Then Manoah, realizing that it was the angel of the LORD, 22said to his wife, "We will certainly die, for we have seen God." [l] 23But his wife pointed out to him, "If the LORD had meant to kill us, he would not have accepted a holocaust and cereal offering from our hands! Nor would he have let us see all this just now, or hear what we have heard."

24The woman bore a son and named him Samson.[m] The boy grew up and the LORD blessed him; 25the spirit of the LORD first stirred him in Mahaneh-dan, which is between Zorah and Eshtaol.

CHAPTER 14

Marriage of Samson 1Samson went down to Timnah and saw there one of the Philistine women.* 2On his return he told his father and mother, "There is a Philistine woman I saw in Timnah whom I wish you to get as a wife for me." 3His father and mother said to him, "Can you find no wife among your kinsfolk or among all our people, that you must go and take a wife from the uncircumcised Philistines?" But Samson answered his father, "Get her for me, for she pleases me." 4 [n]Now his father and mother did not know that this had been brought about by the LORD, who was providing an opportunity against the Philistines; for at that time they had dominion over Israel.

5*So Samson went down to Timnah with his father and mother. When they had come to the vineyards of Timnah, a young lion came roaring to meet him. 6But the spirit of the LORD came upon Samson, and although he had no weapons, he tore the lion in pieces as one tears a kid. 7However, on the journey to speak for the woman, he did not mention to his father or mother what he had done. 8Later, when he returned to marry the woman who pleased him, he stepped aside to look at the remains of the lion and found a swarm of bees and honey in the lion's carcass. 9So he scooped the honey out into his palms and ate it as he went along. When he came to his father and mother, he gave them some to eat, without telling them that he had scooped the honey from the lion's carcass.

10His father also went down to the woman, and Samson gave a banquet there, since it was customary for the young men to do this. 11When they met him, they brought thirty men to be his companions.* 12Samson said to them, "Let me propose a riddle to you. If within the seven days of the feast you solve it for me successfully, I will give you thirty linen tunics and thirty sets of garments. 13But if you cannot answer it for me, you must give me thirty tunics and thirty sets of garments." "Propose your riddle," they responded; "we will listen to it." 14So he said to them,

"Out of the eater came forth food,
 and out of the strong came forth
  sweetness."

After three days' failure to answer the riddle,

13, 18: Mysterious: incomprehensible, above human understanding. Hence, the angel speaks in the name of the Lord himself, to whom Manoah at once offers a sacrifice.

14, 1–3: Marriages were arranged by the parents of the bridegroom as well as of the bride; cf Gn 24, 2–8; 34, 3–6. The Mosaic law specified only seven pagan nations, not including the Philistines, in the prohibition against mixed marriages; cf Dt 7, 1–4. But national and religious sentiment was against any marriage with a non-Israelite; cf Gn 28, 1f; 1 Kgs 11, 1–10.

14, 5ff: Although Samson was accompanied by his parents on the journey to Timnah, v 7 implies that he was not near them when he tore the lion in pieces.

14, 11: Companions: known at a later period as "the friends of the bridegroom" (1 Mc 9, 39; Mk 2, 19), the best man and his fellows. Here they are Philistines (v 16), appointed by the family of the bride, who would also have several bridesmaids; cf Mt 25, 1–13.

j Gn 32, 29. k 19f: Jgs 6, 19ff. l 21f: Jgs 6, 22f. m Heb 11, 32. n Jgs 15, 11.

[15]they said on the fourth day to Samson's wife,
"Coax your husband to answer the riddle for us,
or we will burn you and your family. Did you
invite us here to reduce us to poverty?" [16]At
Samson's side, his wife wept and said, "You
must hate me; you do not love me, for you have
proposed a riddle to my countrymen, but have
not told me the answer." He said to her, "If I
have not told it even to my father or my mother,
must I tell it to you?" [17]But she wept beside him
during the seven days the feast lasted. On the
seventh day, since she importuned him, he told
her the answer, and she explained the riddle to
her countrymen.

[18]On the seventh day, before the sun set, the
men of the city said to him,

"What is sweeter than honey,
  and what is stronger than a lion?"

He replied to them,

"If you had not plowed with my heifer,
  you would not have solved my riddle."

[19]The spirit of the LORD came upon him, and
he went down to Ashkelon, where he killed
thirty of their men and despoiled them; he gave
their garments to those who had answered the
riddle. Then he went off to his own family in
anger, [20]and Samson's wife was married to the
one who had been best man at his wedding.[o]

CHAPTER 15

Samson Defeats the Philistines [1]After some
time, in the season of the wheat harvest, Samson
visited his wife, bringing a kid. But when he
said, "Let me be with my wife in private," her
father would not let him enter, [2]saying, "I
thought it certain you wished to repudiate her;
so I gave her to your best man. Her younger
sister is more beautiful than she; you may have
her instead." [3]Samson said to them, "This time
the Philistines cannot blame me if I harm them."
[4]So Samson left and caught three hundred foxes.
Turning them tail to tail, he tied between each
pair of tails one of the torches he had at hand.
[5]He then kindled the torches and set the foxes
loose in the standing grain of the Philistines, thus
burning both the shocks and the standing grain,
and the vineyards and olive orchards as well.

[6] [p]When the Philistines asked who had done
this, they were told, "Samson, the son-in-law of
the Timnite, because his wife was taken and
given to his best man." So the Philistines went
up and destroyed her and her family by fire.
[7]Samson said to them, "If this is how you act, I
will not stop until I have taken revenge on you."
[8]And with repeated blows, he inflicted a great
slaughter on them. Then he went down and
remained in a cavern of the cliff of Etam.

[9]The Philistines went up and, from a camp in
Judah, deployed against Lehi. [10]When the men
of Judah asked, "Why have you come up against
us?" they answered, "To take Samson prisoner;
to do to him as he has done to us." [11]Three
thousand men of Judah went down to the cavern
in the cliff of Etam and said to Samson, "Do you
not know that the Philistines are our rulers?
Why, then, have you done this to us?" He
answered them, "As they have done to me, so
have I done to them." [12]They said to him, "We
have come to take you prisoner, to deliver you
over to the Philistines." Samson said to them,
"Swear to me that you will not kill me your-
selves." [13]"No," they replied, "we will certainly
not kill you but will only bind you and deliver
you over to them."[q] So they bound him with
two new ropes and brought him up from the
cliff. [14]When he reached Lehi, and the Philis-
tines came shouting to meet him, the spirit of
the LORD came upon him: the ropes around his
arms became as flax that is consumed by fire and
his bonds melted away from his hands. [15]Near
him was the fresh jawbone of an ass; he reached
out, grasped it, and with it killed a thousand
men. [16]Then Samson said,

"With the jawbone of an ass
  I have piled them in a heap;
With the jawbone of an ass
  I have slain a thousand men."

[17]As he finished speaking he threw the jaw-
bone from him; and so that place was named

15, 17: Ramath-lehi: "heights of the jawbone."

o Jgs 15, 2. 6. p Jgs 14, 20. q Jgs 16, 11f.

Ramath-lehi.* [18]Being very thirsty, he cried to the LORD and said, "You have granted this great victory by the hand of your servant. Must I now die of thirst or fall into the hands of the uncircumcised?" [19]Then God split the cavity in Lehi, and water issued from it, which Samson drank till his spirit returned and he revived. Hence that spring in Lehi is called En-hakkore* to this day.

[20]Samson judged Israel for twenty years in the days of the Philistines.[r]

CHAPTER 16

[1]Once Samson went to Gaza, where he saw a harlot and visited her. [2]Informed that Samson had come there, the men of Gaza surrounded him with an ambush at the city gate all night long. And all the night they waited, saying, "Tomorrow morning we will kill him." [3]Samson rested there until midnight. Then he rose, seized the doors of the city gate and the two gateposts, and tore them loose, bar and all. He hoisted them on his shoulders and carried them to the top of the ridge opposite Hebron.

Samson and Delilah [4]After that he fell in love with a woman in the Wadi Sorek whose name was Delilah. [5]The lords of the Philistines came to her and said, "Beguile him and find out the secret of his great strength, and how we may overcome and bind him so as to keep him helpless. We will each give you eleven hundred shekels of silver."

[6]So Delilah said to Samson, "Tell me the secret of your great strength and how you may be bound so as to be kept helpless." [7]"If they bind me with seven fresh bowstrings which have not dried," Samson answered her, "I shall be as weak as any other man." [8]So the lords of the Philistines brought her seven fresh bowstrings which had not dried, and she bound him with them. [9]She had men lying in wait in the chamber and so she said to him, "The Philistines are upon you, Samson!" But he snapped the strings as a thread of tow is severed by a whiff of flame;[s] and the secret of his strength remained unknown.

[10]Delilah said to Samson, "You have mocked me and told me lies. Now tell me how you may be bound." [11]"If they bind me tight with new ropes, with which no work has been done," he answered her, "I shall be as weak as any other man."[t] [12]So Delilah took new ropes and bound him with them. Then she said to him, "The Philistines are upon you, Samson!" For there were men lying in wait in the chamber. But he snapped them off his arms like thread.

[13]Delilah said to Samson again, "Up to now you have mocked me and told me lies. Tell me how you may be bound." He said to her, "If you weave my seven locks of hair into the web and fasten them with the pin, I shall be as weak as any other man." [14]So while he slept, Delilah wove his seven locks of hair into the web, and fastened them in with the pin. Then she said, "The Philistines are upon you, Samson!" Awakening from his sleep, he pulled out both the weaver's pin and the web.

[15]Then she said to him, "How can you say that you love me when you do not confide in me? Three times already you have mocked me, and not told me the secret of your great strength!" [16]She importuned him continually and vexed him with her complaints till he was deathly weary of them. [17]So he took her completely into his confidence and told her, "No razor has touched my head,[u] for I have been consecrated to God from my mother's womb. If I am shaved, my strength will leave me, and I shall be as weak as any other man!" [18]When Delilah saw that he had taken her completely into his confidence, she summoned the lords of the Philistines, saying, "Come up this time, for he has opened his heart to me." So the lords of the Philistines came and brought up the money with them. [19]She had him sleep on her lap, and called for a man who shaved off his seven locks of hair. Then she began to mistreat him, for his strength had left him. [20]When she said, "The Philistines are upon you, Samson!", and he woke from his sleep, he thought he could make good his escape as he had done time and again, for he did not realize that the LORD had left him. [21]But the Philistines seized him and gouged out his

15, 19: En-hakkore: "the spring of him who cries out," an allusion to Samson's cry in v 18.

r Jgs 16, 31. s Jgs 15, 14. t Jgs 15, 13. u Jgs 13, 5.

eyes. Then they brought him down to Gaza and
bound him with bronze fetters, and he was put
to grinding in the prison. [22]But the hair of his
head began to grow as soon as it was shaved off.
The Death of Samson [23][v]The lords of the
Philistines assembled to offer a great sacrifice to
their god Dagon* and to make merry. They said,

"Our god has delivered into our power
  Samson our enemy."

[25]When their spirits were high, they said, "Call
Samson that he may amuse us." So they called
Samson from the prison, and he played the
buffoon before them. [24]When the people saw
him, they praised their god. For they said,

"Our god has delivered into our power
  our enemy, the ravager of our land,
  the one who has multiplied our slain."

Then they stationed him between the col-
umns. [26]Samson said to the attendant who was
holding his hand, "Put me where I may touch the
columns that support the temple and may rest
against them." [27]The temple was full of men and
women: all the lords of the Philistines were there,
and from the roof about three thousand men and
women looked on as Samson provided amuse-
ment. [28]Samson cried out to the LORD and said,
"O Lord GOD, remember me! Strengthen me, O
God, this last time that for my two eyes I may
avenge myself once and for all on the Philistines."
[29]Samson grasped the two middle columns on
which the temple rested and braced himself
against them, one at his right hand, the other at
his left. [30]And Samson said, "Let me die with the
Philistines!" He pushed hard, and the temple fell
upon the lords and all the people who were in it.
Those he killed at his death were more than those
he had killed during his lifetime.

[31]All his family and kinsmen went down and
bore him up for burial in the grave of his father
Manoah between Zorah and Eshtaol. He had
judged Israel for twenty years. [w]

III: The Tribes of Dan and Benjamin in the Days of the Judges

CHAPTER 17

Micah and the Levite [1]There was a man in
the mountain region of Ephraim whose name
was Micah. [2]He said to his mother, "The eleven
hundred shekels of silver over which you pro-
nounced a curse in my hearing when they were
taken from you, are in my possession. It was I
who took them; so now I will restore them to
you." [3]When he restored the eleven hundred
shekels of silver to his mother, she took two
hundred of them and gave them to the silver-
smith, who made of them a carved idol* over-
laid with silver. [x] [4]Then his mother said, "May
the LORD bless my son! I have consecrated the
silver to the LORD as my gift in favor of my son,
by making a carved idol overlaid with silver." It
remained in the house of Micah. [5]Thus the
layman Micah had a sanctuary. He also made an
ephod and household idols, [y] and consecrated
one of his sons, who became his priest. [6]In those
days there was no king in Israel; everyone did
what he thought best. [z]

[7]There was a young Levite who had resided
within the tribe of Judah at Bethlehem of Judah.
[8]From that city he set out to find another place
of residence. On his journey he came to the
house of Micah in the mountain region of
Ephraim. [9]Micah said to him, "Where do you
come from?" He answered him, "I am a Levite
from Bethlehem in Judah, and am on my way to
find some other place of residence." [10]"Stay with
me," Micah said to him. "Be father and priest to
me, [a] and I will give you ten silver shekels a year,
a set of garments, and your food." [11]So the
young Levite decided to stay with the man, to
whom he became as one of his own sons.
[12]*Micah consecrated the young Levite, who
became his priest, remaining in his house.
[13]Therefore Micah said, "Now I know that the

16, 23: Dagon was originally a Mesopotamian deity, whom the Philistines came to worship as their own god of grain.

17, 3: Idol: an image, not of a pagan god, but of the Lord. The Mosaic law forbade the making of an image even of the true God.

17, 12f: According to Nm 18, 1–7 only those Levites who were descended from Aaron could be consecrated as priests.

v 1 Sm 5, 2–5. w Jgs 15, 20. x Ex 20, 4; Lv 19, 4. y Jgs 18, 14. 17. z Jgs 18, 1; 21, 25. a Jgs 18, 19.

LORD will prosper me, since the Levite has become my priest."

CHAPTER 18

Migration of the Danites 1At that time there was no king in Israel.[b] Moreover the tribe of Danites were in search of a district to dwell in, for up to that time they had received no heritage among the tribes of Israel.*

2So the Danites sent from their clan a detail of five valiant men of Zorah and Eshtaol, to reconnoiter the land and scout it. With their instructions to go and scout the land, they traveled as far as the house of Micah in the mountain region of Ephraim, where they passed the night. 3Near the house of Micah, they recognized the voice* of the young Levite[c] and turned in that direction. "Who brought you here and what are you doing here?" they asked him. "What is your interest here?" 4"This is how Micah treats me," he replied to them. "He pays me a salary and I am his priest."[d] 5They said to him, "Consult God, that we may know whether the undertaking we are engaged in will succeed." 6The priest said to them, "Go and prosper: the LORD is favorable to the undertaking you are engaged in."

7So the five men went on and came to Laish. They saw that the people dwelling there lived securely after the manner of the Sidonians, quiet and trusting, with no lack of any natural resources. They were distant from the Sidonians and had no contact with other people. 8When the five returned to their kinsmen in Zorah and Eshtaol and were asked for a report, 9they replied, "Come, let us attack them, for we have seen the land and it is very good. Are you going to hesitate? Do not be slothful about beginning your expedition to possess the land. 10Those against whom you go are a trusting people, and the land is ample. God has indeed given it into your power: a place where no natural resource is lacking."

11So six hundred men of the clan of the Danites, fully armed with weapons of war, set out from where they were in Zorah and Eshtaol, 12and camped in Judah, up near Kiriath-jearim; hence to this day the place, which lies west of Kiriath-jearim, is called Mahaneh-dan.[e]

13From there they went on to the mountain region of Ephraim and came to the house of Micah. 14The five men who had gone to reconnoiter the land of Laish said to their kinsmen, "Do you know that in these houses there are an ephod, household idols, and a carved idol overlaid with silver?[f] Now decide what you must do!" 15So turning in that direction, they went to the house of the young Levite at the home of Micah and greeted him. 16The six hundred men girt with weapons of war, who were Danites, stood by the entrance of the gate, and the priest stood there also. 17Meanwhile, the five men who had gone to reconnoiter the land went up and entered the house of Micah. 18When they had gone in and taken the ephod, the household idols, and the carved idol overlaid with silver, the priest said to them, "What are you doing?" 19They said to him, "Be still: put your hand over your mouth. Come with us and be our father and priest.[g] Is it better for you to be priest for the family of one man or to be priest for a tribe and a clan in Israel?" 20The priest, agreeing, took the ephod, household idols, and carved idol and went off in the midst of the band. 21As they turned to depart, they placed their little ones, their livestock, and their goods at the head of the column.

22The Danites had already gone some distance, when those in the houses near that of Micah took up arms and overtook them. 23They called to the Danites, who turned about and said to Micah, "What do you want, that you have taken up arms?" 24"You have taken my god, which I made, and have gone off with my priest as well," he answered. "What is left for me? How, then, can you ask me what I want?" 25The Danites said to him, "Let us hear no further

18, 1: The tribe of Dan had been assigned a territory with definite limits in central Palestine. However they were unable to gain possession of the better portion of their land (Jgs 1, 34). So they now seek territory elsewhere in Palestine.

18, 3: Recognized the voice: perhaps they noticed the peculiar pronunciation of his south Hebrew dialect.

b Jos 19, 40–48. c Jgs 17, 7. d Jgs 17, 10. e Jgs 13, 25. f Jgs 17, 4f. g Jgs 17, 10.

sound from you, lest fierce men fall upon you and you and your family lose your lives." [26]The Danites then went on their way, and Micah, seeing that they were stronger than he, returned home.

[27]Having taken what Micah had made, and the priest he had had, they attacked Laish, a quiet and trusting people; they put them to the sword and destroyed their city by fire. [28]No one came to their aid, since the city was far from Sidon and they had no contact with other people. The Danites then rebuilt the city, which was in the valley that belongs to Beth-rehob, and lived there. [29]They named it Dan after their ancestor Dan, son of Israel. However, the name of the city was formerly Laish. [30]The Danites set up the carved idol for themselves, and Jonathan, son of Gershom, son of Moses, and his descendants were priests for the tribe of the Danites until the time of the captivity of the land.* [31]They maintained the carved idol Micah had made as long as the house of God was in Shiloh.

CHAPTER 19

The Levite from Ephraim [1]At that time, when there was no king in Israel,[h] there was a Levite residing in remote parts of the mountain region of Ephraim who had taken for himself a concubine from Bethlehem of Judah. [2]His concubine was unfaithful to him and left him for her father's house in Bethlehem of Judah, where she stayed for some four months. [3]Her husband then set out with his servant and a pair of asses, and went after her to forgive her and take her back. She brought him into her father's house, and on seeing him, the girl's father joyfully made him welcome. [4]He was detained by the girl's father, and so he spent three days with this father-in-law of his, eating and drinking and passing the night there. [5]*On the fourth day they rose early in the morning and he prepared to go. But the girl's father said to his son-in-law, "Fortify yourself with a little food; you can go later on." [6]So they stayed and the two men ate and drank together. Then the girl's father said to the husband, "Why not decide to spend the night here and enjoy yourself?" [7]The man still made a move to go, but when his father-in-law pressed him he went back and spent the night there.

[8]On the fifth morning he rose early to depart, but the girl's father said, "Fortify yourself and tarry until the afternoon." When he and his father-in-law had eaten, [9]and the husband was ready to go with his concubine and servant, the girl's father said to him, "It is already growing dusk. Stay for the night. See, the day is coming to an end. Spend the night here and enjoy yourself. Early tomorrow you can start your journey home." [10]The man, however, refused to stay another night; he and his concubine set out with a pair of saddled asses, and traveled till they came opposite Jebus, which is Jerusalem. [11]Since they were near Jebus with the day far gone, the servant said to his master, "Come, let us turn off to this city of the Jebusites and spend the night in it." [12]But his master said to him, "We will not turn off to a city of foreigners, who are not Israelites, but will go on to Gibeah.[i] [13]Come," he said to his servant, "let us make for some other place, either Gibeah or Ramah, to spend the night."[j] [14]So they continued on their way till the sun set on them when they were abreast of Gibeah of Benjamin.

[15]*There they turned off to enter Gibeah for the night.[k] The man waited in the public square of the city he had entered, but no one offered them the shelter of his home for the night. [16]In the evening, however, an old man came from his work in the field; he was from the mountain region of Ephraim, though he lived among the Benjaminite townspeople of Gibeah. [17]When he noticed the traveler in the public square of the city, the old man asked where he was going, and whence he had come. [18]He said to him, "We are traveling from Bethlehem of Judah far up into the mountain region of Ephraim, where I belong. I have been to Bethlehem of Judah and am now going back home; but no one has offered us

18, 30: Until . . . land: about the year 734 B.C., when the Assyrian emperor Tiglath-pileser III subjected northern Palestine.

19, 5–9: Such importuning of guests to prolong their stay at the home of their host is characteristic of Oriental hospitality.

19, 15: Private hospitality was the customary means of providing comfort to travelers where public facilities were so rare.

h Jgs 17, 6. i Jgs 1, 21. j Jos 18, 25. k Jgs 20, 4.

the shelter of his house. 19 We have straw and fodder for our asses, and bread and wine for the woman and myself and for our servant; there is nothing else we need." 20 "You are welcome," the old man said to him, "but let me provide for all your needs, and do not spend the night in the public square." 21 So he led them to his house and provided fodder for the asses. Then they washed their feet, and ate and drank.[l]

The Outrage at Gibeah 22 [m]While they were enjoying themselves, the men of the city, who were corrupt,* surrounded the house and beat on the door. They said to the old man whose house it was, "Bring out your guest, that we may abuse him." 23 The owner of the house went out to them and said, "No, my brothers; do not be so wicked. Since this man is my guest, do not commit this crime. 24 Rather let me bring out my maiden daughter or his concubine. Ravish them, or do whatever you want with them; but against the man you must not commit this wanton crime." 25 When the men would not listen to his host, the husband seized his concubine and thrust her outside to them. They had relations with her and abused her all night until the following dawn, when they let her go. 26 Then at daybreak the woman came and collapsed at the entrance of the house in which her husband was a guest, where she lay until the morning. 27 When her husband rose that day and opened the door of the house to start out again on his journey, there lay the woman, his concubine, at the entrance of the house with her hands on the threshold. 28 He said to her, "Come, let us go"; but there was no answer. So the man placed her on an ass and started out again for home.

29 *On reaching home, he took a knife to the body of his concubine, cut her into twelve pieces, and sent them throughout the territory of Israel. 30 [n]Everyone who saw this said, "Nothing like this has been done or seen from the day the Israelites came up from the land of Egypt to this day. Take note of it, and state what you propose to do."

CHAPTER 20

Assembly of Israelites 1 So all the Israelites came out as one man: from Dan to Beer-sheba,* and from the land of Gilead, the community was gathered to the LORD at Mizpah. 2 The leaders of all the people and all the tribesmen of Israel, four hundred thousand foot soldiers who were swordsmen, presented themselves in the assembly of the people of God. 3 Meanwhile, the Benjaminites heard that the Israelites had gone up to Mizpah. The Israelites asked to be told how the crime had taken place, 4 and the Levite, the husband of the murdered woman, testified: "My concubine and I went into Gibeah of Benjamin[o] for the night. 5 [p]But the citizens of Gibeah rose up against me by night and surrounded the house in which I was. Me they attempted to kill, and my concubine they abused so that she died. 6 [q]So I took my concubine and cut her up and sent her through every part of the territory of Israel, because of the monstrous crime they had committed in Israel. 7 *Now that you are all here, O Israelites, state what you propose to do."[r] 8 All the people rose as one man to say, "None of us is to leave for his tent or return to his home. 9 Now as for Gibeah, this is what we will do: We will proceed against it by lot, 10 taking from all the tribes of Israel ten men for every hundred, a hundred for every thousand, a thousand for every ten thousand, and procuring supplies for the soldiers who will go to deal fully and suitably with Gibeah of Benjamin for the crime it committed in Israel."

11 When, therefore, all the men of Israel without exception were leagued together against the city, 12 *the tribes of Israel sent men throughout

19, 22: Who were corrupt: literally "sons of Belial," indicating extreme perversion; cf Gn 19, 4–8. This crime and its punishment made the name Gibeah proverbial as a place of shameful wickedness; cf Hos 9, 9; 10, 9.

19, 29: A drastic means for arousing the tribes to avenge the unheard of crime of the Benjaminites.

20, 1: From Dan to Beer-sheba: from north to south. The land of Gilead: all the territory east of the Jordan.

20, 7: The Israelites were asked to decide at once what action to take concerning this crime; cf 2 Sm 16, 20. The Levite undoubtedly addressed the tribal heads who would speak in behalf of the multitude.

20, 12: Before the crime at Gibeah was punished, the Benjamin-

l Gn 18, 4; 24, 32; 43, 24. m 22–25: Gn 19, 4–9. n Hos 9, 9; 10, 9. o Jgs 19, 14f. p Jgs 19, 22–27. q Jgs 19, 29. r Jgs 19, 30.

the tribe of Benjamin to say, "What is this evil
which has occurred among you? 13 Now give up
these corrupt men of Gibeah, that we may put
them to death and thus purge the evil from
Israel." But the Benjaminites refused to accede
to the demand of their brothers, the Israelites.
14 Instead, the Benjaminites assembled from their
other cities to Gibeah, to do battle with the
Israelites. 15 The number of the Benjaminite
swordsmen from the other cities on that occa-
sion was twenty-six thousand, in addition to the
inhabitants of Gibeah. 16 Included in this total
were seven hundred picked men who were left-
handed, every one of them able to sling a stone
at a hair without missing. 17 Meanwhile, the
other Israelites who, without Benjamin, mus-
tered four hundred thousand swordsmen ready
for battle, 18 moved on to Bethel and consulted
God. When the Israelites asked who should go
first in the attack on the Benjaminites,[s] the LORD
said, "Judah shall go first."* 19 The next day the
Israelites advanced on Gibeah with their forces.

War with Benjamin 20 On the day the Israel-
ites drew up in battle array at Gibeah for the
combat with Benjamin, 21 the Benjaminites came
out of the city and felled twenty-two thousand
men of Israel. 23 Then the Israelites went up and
wept before the LORD until evening. "Shall I
again engage my brother Benjamin in battle?"
they asked the LORD; and the LORD answered
that they should. 22 But though the Israelite
soldiers took courage and again drew up for
combat in the same place as on the previous day,
24 when they met the Benjaminites for the sec-
ond time, 25 once again the Benjaminites who
came out of Gibeah against them felled eighteen
thousand Israelites, all of them swordsmen. 26 So
the entire Israelite army went up to Bethel,
where they wept and remained fasting before
the LORD until evening of that day, besides
offering holocausts and peace offerings before
the LORD. 27 [t]When the Israelites consulted the
LORD (for the ark of the covenant of God was
there in those days, 28 and Phinehas, son of
Eleazar, son of Aaron, was ministering to him in
those days), and asked, "Shall I go out again to
battle with Benjamin, my brother, or shall I
desist?" the LORD said, "Attack! for tomorrow I
will deliver him into your power." 29 [u]So Israel
set men in ambush around Gibeah.*

30 The Israelites went up against the Benjamin-
ites for the third time and formed their line of
battle at Gibeah as on other occasions. 31 The
Benjaminites went out to meet them, and in the
beginning they killed off about thirty of the
Israelite soldiers in the open field, just as on the
other occasions. 32 Therefore the Benjaminites
thought, "We are defeating them as before"; not
realizing that disaster was about to overtake
them. The Israelites, however, had planned the
flight so as to draw them away from the city onto
the highways. They were drawn away from the
city onto the highways, of which the one led to
Bethel, the other to Gibeon. 33 And then all the
men of Israel rose from their places. They re-
formed their ranks at Baal-tamar, and the Israel-
ites in ambush rushed from their place west of
Gibeah, 34 ten thousand picked men from all
Israel, and advanced against the city itself. In a
fierce battle, 35 the LORD defeated Benjamin
before Israel; and on that day the Israelites killed
twenty-five thousand one hundred men of Benja-
min, all of them swordsmen.

36 To the Benjaminites it had looked as though
the enemy were defeated, for the men of Israel
gave ground to Benjamin, trusting in the ambush
they had set at Gibeah. 37 But then the men in
ambush made a sudden dash into Gibeah, over-
ran it, and put the whole city to the sword.
38 Now, the other Israelites had agreed with the
men in ambush on a smoke signal they were to
send up from the city. 39 And though the men of

ites were invited to join their brethren, the Israelites, in punishing the crime. Since they failed to respond, special messengers were sent asking them to deliver up the guilty ones. They replied by gathering their forces for combat.

20, 18: Judah shall go first: the same response as in Jgs 1, 1f, but without the assurance of immediate success. Only after the Israelites were punished at the hands of the Benjaminites for their own grossness, and had performed penance, did they succeed in punishing the latter for their part in the crime of rape and murder, by gaining the victory over them.

20, 29–46: This stratagem proved more useful to the Israelites than force, as in the siege of Ai (Jos 8, 3–21). In the parallel accounts the first (vv 29–35) is a summary of the second (vv 36–46).

s Jgs 1, 1f. t 1 Sm 4, 3f. u 29–46: Jos 8, 4–24.

Benjamin had begun by killing off some thirty of the men of Israel, under the impression that they were defeating them as surely as in the earlier fighting, the Israelites wheeled about to resist 40as the smoke of the signal column began to rise up from the city. It was when Benjamin looked back and saw the whole city in flames against the sky 41that the men of Israel wheeled about. Therefore the men of Benjamin were thrown into confusion, for they realized the disaster that had overtaken them. 42They retreated before the men of Israel in the direction of the desert, with the fight being pressed against them. In their very midst, meanwhile, those who had been in the city were spreading destruction. 43The men of Benjamin had been surrounded, and were now pursued to a point east of Gibeah, 44while eighteen thousand of them fell, warriors to a man. 45The rest turned and fled through the desert to the rock Rimmon.[v] But on the highways the Israelites picked off five thousand men among them, and chasing them up to Gidom, killed another two thousand of them there. 46Those of Benjamin who fell on that day were in all twenty-five thousand swordsmen, warriors to a man. 47But six hundred others who turned and fled through the desert reached the rock Rimmon, where they remained for four months.

48The men of Israel withdrew through the territory of the Benjaminites, putting to the sword the inhabitants of the cities, the livestock, and all they chanced upon. Moreover they destroyed by fire all the cities they came upon.

CHAPTER 21

Wives for the Survivors 1Now the men of Israel* had sworn at Mizpah that none of them would give his daughter in marriage to anyone from Benjamin. 2So the people went to Bethel and remained there before God until evening, raising their voices in bitter lament.[w] 3They said, "LORD, God of Israel, why has it come to pass in Israel that today one tribe of Israel should be lacking?" 4Early the next day the people built an altar there and offered holocausts and peace offerings. 5Then the Israelites asked, "Are there any among all the tribes of Israel who did not come up to the LORD for the assembly?" For they had taken a solemn oath that anyone who did not go up to the LORD at Mizpah should be put to death without fail.[x]

6*The Israelites were disconsolate over their brother Benjamin and said, "Today one of the tribes of Israel has been cut off. 7What can we do about wives for the survivors, since we have sworn by the LORD not to give them any of our daughters in marriage?" 8And when they asked whether anyone among the tribes of Israel had not come up to the LORD in Mizpah, they found that none of the men of Jabesh-gilead had come to the encampment for the assembly. 9A roll call of the army established that none of the inhabitants of that city were present. 10The community, therefore, sent twelve thousand warriors with orders to go to Jabesh-gilead and put those who lived there to the sword, including the women and children. 11They were told to include under the ban* all males and every woman who was not still a virgin.[y] 12Finding among the inhabitants of Jabesh-gilead four hundred young virgins, who had had no relations with men, they brought them to the camp at Shiloh in the land of Canaan. 13 [z]Then the whole community sent a message to the Benjaminites at the rock Rimmon, offering them peace. 14When Benjamin returned at that time, they gave them as wives the women of Jabesh-gilead whom they had spared; but these proved to be not enough for them.

15The people were still disconsolate over Benjamin because the LORD had made a breach* among the tribes of Israel. 16And the elders of the community said, "What shall we do for wives for the survivors? For every woman in

21, 1–3: The anger of the Israelites led them to destroy their brethren, the Benjaminites. Having realized their goal, however, they were soon filled with dismay, and sought to restore the tribe they had all but exterminated.

21, 6–9: This account is summarized in the parallel passage in vv 2–5.

21, 11: Under the ban: see note on Nm 21, 3.

21, 15: Had made a breach: what is here attributed to God was in reality the free and deliberate act of the Israelites and happened only by the permissive will of God. The ancients attributed to the first primary cause what is more directly due to secondary causes.

v Jgs 21, 13. w Jgs 20, 26. x Jgs 20, 8ff. y Nm 31, 17. z Jgs 20, 47.

Benjamin has been put to death." 17They said,
"Those of Benjamin who survive must have
heirs, else one of the Israelite tribes will be
wiped out. 18*Yet we cannot give them any of
our daughters in marriage, because the Israelites
have sworn, 'Cursed be he who gives a woman
to Benjamin!' " 19Then they thought of the
yearly feast of the LORD at Shiloh, north of
Bethel, east of the highway that goes up from
Bethel to Shechem, and south of Lebonah.
20And they instructed the Benjaminites, "Go and
lie in wait in the vineyards. 21When you see the
girls of Shiloh come out to do their dancing,
leave the vineyards and each of you seize one of
the girls of Shiloh for a wife, and go to the land
of Benjamin. 22When their fathers or their broth-
ers come to complain to us, we shall say to
them, 'Release them to us as a kindness, since
we did not take a woman apiece in the war. Had
you yourselves given them these wives, you
would now be guilty.' "

23The Benjaminites did this; they carried off a
wife for each of them from their raid on the
dancers, and went back to their own territory,
where they rebuilt and occupied the cities.
24Also at that time the Israelites dispersed; each
of them left for his own heritage in his own clan
and tribe.

25*In those days there was no king in Israel;
everyone did what he thought best. [a]

21, 18: Regardless of the serious consequences of their vow, the Israelites considered themselves obliged to fulfill it; cf Jgs 11, 31. 35f. 39.

21, 25: Cf Jgs 17, 6; 18, 1; 19, 1. The verse gives the reason why the lawlessness of the period of judges, and the events described herein, were possible.

a Jgs 17, 6; 18, 1; 19, 1.

THE BOOK OF RUTH

The Book of Ruth is named after the Moabite woman who was joined to the Israelite people by her marriage with the influential Boaz of Bethlehem.

The book contains a beautiful example of filial piety, pleasing to the Hebrews especially because of its connection with King David, and useful both to Hebrews and to Gentiles. Its aim is to demonstrate the divine reward for such piety even when practiced by a stranger. Ruth's piety (Ru 2, 11), her spirit of self-sacrifice, and her moral integrity were favored by God with the gift of faith and an illustrious marriage whereby she became the ancestress of David and of Christ. In this, the universality of the messianic salvation is foreshadowed.

In the Greek and Latin canons the Book of Ruth is placed just after Judges, to which it is closely related because of the time of its action, and just before Samuel, for which it is an excellent introduction, since it traces the ancestry of the Davidic dynasty. One might characterize the literary form of this book as dramatic, since about two-thirds of it is in dialogue. Yet there is every indication that, as tradition has always held, it contains true history.

There is no certainty about the author of the book. It was written long after the events had passed (Ru 4, 7), which took place "in the time of the judges" (Ru 1, 1).

CHAPTER 1

Naomi in Moab [1]Once in the time of the
judges* there was a famine in the land; so a man
from Bethlehem of Judah departed with his wife
and two sons to reside on the plateau of Moab.
[2]The man was named Elimelech, his wife Na-
omi, and his sons Mahlon and Chilion; they
were Ephrathites from Bethlehem of Judah.
Some time after their arrival on the Moabite
plateau, [3]Elimelech, the husband of Naomi,
died, and she was left with her two sons, [4]who
married Moabite women, one named Orpah, the
other Ruth. When they had lived there about ten
years, [5]both Mahlon and Chilion died also, and
the woman was left with neither her two sons
nor her husband. [6]She then made ready to go
back from the plateau of Moab because word
reached her there that the LORD had visited his
people and given them food.
[7]She and her two daughters-in-law left the
place where they had been living. Then as they
were on the road back to the land of Judah,
[8]Naomi said to her two daughters-in-law, "Go
back, each of you, to your mother's house!*
May the LORD be kind to you as you were to the
departed and to me! [9]May the LORD grant each
of you a husband and a home in which you will
find rest." She kissed them good-by, but they
wept with loud sobs, [10]and told her they would
return with her to her people. [11]"Go back, my
daughters!" said Naomi. "Why should you come
with me? Have I other sons in my womb who
may become your husbands?* [12]Go back, my
daughters! Go, for I am too old to marry again.
And even if I could offer any hopes, or if tonight
I had a husband or had borne sons, [13]would you
then wait and deprive yourselves of husbands
until those sons grew up? No, my daughters! my
lot is too bitter for you, because the LORD has
extended his hand against me." [14]Again they
sobbed aloud and wept; and Orpah kissed her
mother-in-law good-by, but Ruth stayed with
her.
[15]"See now!" she said, "your sister-in-law has
gone back to her people and her god. Go back
after your sister-in-law!" [16]*But Ruth said, "Do
not ask me to abandon or forsake you! for
wherever you go I will go, wherever you lodge I
will lodge, your people shall be my people, and
your God my God. [17]Wherever you die I will
die, and there be buried. May the LORD do so
and so to me, and more besides, if aught but
death separates me from you!" [18]Naomi then
ceased to urge her, for she saw she was deter-
mined to go with her.

The Return to Bethlehem [19]So they went on
together till they reached Bethlehem. On their
arrival there, the whole city was astir over them,
and the women asked, "Can this be Naomi?"
[20][a]But she said to them, "Do not call me
Naomi.* Call me Mara, for the Almighty has
made it very bitter for me. [21]I went away with
an abundance, but the LORD has brought me
back destitute. Why should you call me Naomi,
since the LORD has pronounced against me and
the Almighty has brought evil upon me?" [22]Thus
it was that Naomi returned with the Moabite
daughter-in-law, Ruth, who accompanied her
back from the plateau of Moab. They arrived in
Bethlehem at the beginning of the barley har-
vest.*

CHAPTER 2

The Meeting [1]Naomi had a prominent kins-
man named Boaz,[b] of the clan of her husband
Elimelech. [2]Ruth the Moabite said to Naomi,

1, 1f: In the time of the judges: three generations before the end of the period of Judges; cf Ru 4, 21f. Bethlehem of Judah: to distinguish it from the town of the same name in the tribe of Zebulun (Jos 19, 15). Ephrathites from Bethlehem: belonging to a Judean clan which settled in Bethlehem; cf 1 Sm 17, 12; 1 Chr 2, 50f; 4, 4.

1, 8: Mother's house: the women's part of the dwelling; cf Jgs 4, 17; Song 3, 4.

1, 11: Have I other sons . . . husbands?: Naomi insisted that her daughters-in-law remain in their own country only for the sake of posterity. If she had had other sons, the levirate law would have obliged them to marry the widows of her deceased sons to perpetuate the names of the deceased; cf Gn 38, 8; Dt 25, 5f.

1, 16f: An example of heroic fidelity and piety. Ruth's decision, confirmed with an oath, to adhere to her mother-in-law impelled her to abandon her country and its pagan worship.

1, 20f: Naomi: means "amiable" or "pleasant," suggesting God's favor toward her. The Almighty has brought evil upon me: the ancients regarded adversity as a punishment from God for personal sin, as if good and evil were always repaid in a temporal and material manner.

1, 22: Barley harvest: early April. This circumstance favored the events of the narrative that follow.

a Ex 15, 23. b Ru 3, 2. 12; 4, 21; Mt 1, 5.

"Let me go and glean ears of grain* in the field of anyone who will allow me that favor."[c] Naomi said to her, "Go, my daughter," 3 and she went. The field she entered to glean after the harvesters happened to be the section belonging to Boaz of the clan of Elimelech. 4 Boaz himself came from Bethlehem and said to the harvesters, "The LORD be with you!"* and they replied, "The LORD bless you!" 5 Boaz asked the overseer of his harvesters, "Whose girl is this?" 6 The overseer of the harvesters answered, "She is the Moabite girl who returned from the plateau of Moab with Naomi.[d] 7 She asked leave to gather the gleanings into sheaves after the harvesters; and ever since she came this morning she has remained here until now, with scarcely a moment's rest."

8 Boaz said to Ruth, "Listen, my daughter! Do not go to glean in anyone else's field; you are not to leave here. Stay here with my women servants. 9 Watch to see which field is to be harvested, and follow them; I have commanded the young men to do you no harm. When you are thirsty, you may go and drink from the vessels the young men have filled." 10 Casting herself prostrate upon the ground, she said to him, "Why should I, a foreigner, be favored with your notice?" 11 [e]Boaz answered her: "I have had a complete account of what you have done for your mother-in-law after your husband's death; you have left your father and your mother and the land of your birth, and have come to a people whom you did not know previously. 12 May the LORD reward what you have done! May you receive a full reward from the LORD, the God of Israel, under whose wings you have come for refuge." 13 She said, "May I prove worthy of your kindness, my lord: you have comforted me, your servant, with your consoling words; would indeed that I were a servant of yours!" 14 At mealtime Boaz said to her, "Come here and have some food; dip your bread in the sauce." Then as she sat near the reapers, he handed her some roasted grain and she ate her fill and had some left over. 15 She rose to glean, and Boaz instructed his servants to let her glean among the sheaves themselves without scolding her, 16 and even to let drop some handfuls and leave them for her to glean without being rebuked.

17 She gleaned in the field until evening, and when she beat out what she had gleaned it came to about an ephah of barley, 18 which she took into the city and showed to her mother-in-law. Next she brought out and gave her what she had left over from lunch. 19 So her mother-in-law said to her, "Where did you glean today? Where did you go to work? May he who took notice of you be blessed!" Then she told her mother-in-law with whom she had worked. "The man at whose place I worked today is named Boaz," she said. 20 [f]"May he be blessed by the LORD, who is ever merciful to the living and to the dead," Naomi exclaimed to her daughter-in-law; and she continued, "He is a relative of ours, one of our next of kin."* 21 "He even told me," added Ruth the Moabite, "that I should stay with his servants until they complete his entire harvest." 22 "You would do well, my dear," Naomi rejoined, "to go out with his servants; for in someone else's field you might be insulted." 23 So she stayed gleaning with the servants of Boaz until the end of the barley and wheat harvests.

CHAPTER 3

Ruth Again Presents Herself When she was back with her mother-in-law, 1 Naomi said to her, "My daughter, I must seek a home for you that will please you. 2 [g]Now is not Boaz, with whose servants you were, a relative of ours? This evening he will be winnowing barley at the threshing floor. 3 So bathe and anoint yourself; then put on your best attire and go down to the threshing floor. Do not make yourself known to

2, 2: Let me go and glean . . . grain: even the poor, the widow, the stranger, and the orphan had a right to glean at harvest time; cf Lv 19, 9f; 23, 22; Dt 24, 19–22.

2, 4: The Lord be with you: courtesy and religious feeling characterize the salutations of the Hebrews. This greeting is used in the Christian liturgy.

2, 20: One of our next of kin: literally "our redeemer," a near relative of the same clan who had the right and duty to restore the land which an impoverished kinsman had alienated (Lv 25, 25–28), and to marry the widow of a relative who had died without male offspring so as to raise up posterity to his name (Dt 25, 5–10).

c Dt 24, 19. d Ru 1, 22. e Ru 1, 14–17. f Ru 3, 9. g Ru1.

the man before he has finished eating and drinking. [4]But when he lies down, take note of the place where he does so. Then go, uncover a place at his feet,* and lie down. He will tell you what to do." [5]"I will do whatever you advise," Ruth replied. [6]So she went down to the threshing floor and did just as her mother-in-law had instructed her.

[7]Boaz ate and drank to his heart's content. Then when he went and lay down at the edge of the sheaves, she stole up, uncovered a place at his feet, and lay down. [8]In the middle of the night, however, the man gave a start and turned around to find a woman lying at his feet. [9]He asked, "Who are you?" And she replied, "I am your servant Ruth. Spread the corner of your cloak over me,* for you are my next of kin." [10]He said, "May the LORD bless you, my daughter! You have been even more loyal now than before in not going after the young men, whether poor or rich.[h] [11]So be assured, daughter, I will do for you whatever you say; all my townspeople know you for a worthy woman. [12] [i]Now, though indeed I am closely related to you, you have another relative still closer.* [13]Stay as you are for tonight, and tomorrow, if he wishes to claim you, good! let him do so. But if he does not wish to claim you, as the LORD lives, I will claim you myself. Lie there until morning."[j] [14]So she lay at his feet until morning, but rose before men could recognize one another. Boaz said, "Let it not be known that this woman came to the threshing floor." [15]Then he said to her, "Take off your cloak and hold it out." When she did so, he poured out six measures of barley, helped her lift the bundle,[k] and left for the city.

[16]Ruth went home to her mother-in-law, who asked, "How have you fared, my daughter?" So she told her all the man had done for her, [17]and concluded, "He gave me these six measures of barley because he did not wish me to come back to my mother-in-law empty-handed!" [18]Naomi then said, "Wait here, my daughter, until you learn what happens, for the man will not rest, but will settle the matter today."

CHAPTER 4

Boaz Marries Ruth [1]Boaz went and took a seat at the gate;* and when he saw the closer relative[l] of whom he had spoken come along, he called to him by name, "Come and sit beside me!" And he did so. [2]Then Boaz picked out ten of the elders* of the city and asked them to sit nearby. When they had done this, [3]he said to the near relative: "Naomi, who has come back from the Moabite plateau, is putting up for sale the piece of land that belonged to our kinsman Elimelech. [4]*So I thought I would inform you, bidding you before those here present, including the elders of my people, to put in your claim for it if you wish to acquire it as next of kin.[m] But if you do not wish to claim it, tell me so, that I may be guided accordingly, for no one has a prior claim to yours, and mine is next." He answered, "I will put in my claim."

[5]*Boaz continued, "Once you acquire the field from Naomi, you must take also Ruth the Moabite,[n] the widow of the late heir, and raise up a family for the departed on his estate." [6]The near relative replied, "I cannot exercise my claim lest I depreciate my own estate. Put in a claim yourself in my stead, for I cannot exercise my claim." [7]Now it used to be the custom in

3, 4: Uncover a place at his feet . . . : confident of the virtue of Ruth and Boaz, Naomi advises this unusual expedient to her daughter-in-law for the purpose of introducing her claim.

3, 9: Spread the corner of your cloak over me: be my protector by marrying me according to the duty of a near kinsman; cf Dt 25, 5; Ez 16, 8.

3, 12: Relative still closer: who had a prior right and duty to marry Ruth.

4, 1: Took a seat at the gate: i.e., of the city, where business affairs were settled.

4, 2: Ten of the elders: to serve as judges in legal matters as well as witnesses of the settlement of business affairs; cf Dt 25, 7–9.

4, 4: Poverty had obliged Naomi to sell the land of her deceased husband. The law permitted the nearest kinsman to redeem the land and thus preserve the family patrimony; cf Lv 25, 25.

4, 5f: The heir of Elimelech's field had died without children (Ru 1, 5). The nearest of kin could now redeem the land but he must also take Ruth, the widow of the late heir, to wife to perpetuate the family of the deceased; cf Dt 25, 5f. The first male child of such a marriage would be the legal son of Mahlon and grandson of Elimelech.

h Dt 25, 5. i Ru 4, 1. j Ru 4, 5; Dt 25, 5. k Ru 2, 17. l Ru 3, 12. m Lv 25, 25. n Ru 3, 13; Dt 25, 5.

Israel that, to make binding a contract of redemption or exchange, one party would take off his sandal* and give it to the other. This was the form of attestation in Israel. 8So the near relative, in saying to Boaz, "Acquire it for yourself," drew off his sandal. 9Boaz then said to the elders and to all the people, "You are witnesses today that I have acquired from Naomi all the holdings of Elimelech, Chilion and Mahlon. 10I also take Ruth the Moabite, the widow of Mahlon, as my wife, in order to raise up a family for her late husband on his estate, so that the name of the departed may not perish among his kinsmen and fellow citizens. Do you witness this today?"
11 oAll those at the gate, including the elders, said, "We do so. May the LORD make this wife come into your house like Rachel and Leah, who between them built up the house of Israel. May you do well in Ephrathah and win fame in Bethlehem. 12 pWith the offspring the LORD will give you from this girl, may your house become like the house of Perez, whom Tamar bore to Judah."*

13Boaz took Ruth. When they came together as man and wife, the LORD enabled her to conceive and she bore a son. 14Then the women said to Naomi, "Blessed is the LORD who has not failed to provide you today with an heir! May he become famous in Israel! 15He will be your comfort and the support of your old age, for his mother is the daughter-in-law who loves you. She is worth more to you than seven sons!"
16Naomi took the child, placed him on her lap,* and became his nurse. 17And the neighbor women gave him his name, q at the news that a grandson had been born to Naomi. They called him Obed. He was the father of Jesse, the father of David.*
18 rThese are the descendants of Perez: Perez was the father of Hezron, s 19Hezron was the father of Ram, Ram was the father of Amminadab, 20 tAmminadab was the father of Nahshon, Nahshon was the father of Salmon, 21Salmon was the father of Boaz, Boaz was the father of Obed, 22 uObed was the father of Jesse, and Jesse became the father of David.

4, 7: Take off his sandal . . . : by this act the near relative renounced his legal right, both to the field of Elimelech and to the marriage with Ruth. The custom mentioned in Dt 25, 6 is somewhat different.

4, 12: Perez, whom Tamar bore to Judah: the right which Judah unwittingly satisfied for his daughter-in-law Tamar (Gn 38), Boaz willingly rendered to Ruth.

4, 16: Placed him on her lap: took him as her own; cf Gn 30, 3; 48, 12; Nm 11, 12.

4, 17: The father of Jesse, the father of David: indicating the place of Obed, Jesse and David in the line of Judah and the ancestry of Christ, the Messiah; cf Mt 1, 5f.

o Gn 29, 31–30, 24; 35, 19. p Gn 38, 29. q Lk 1, 58. r 18–22: 1 Chr 2, 4–15; Mt 1, 3–6. s Gn 46, 12; 1 Chr 4, 1. t Ex 6, 23; Nm 1, 7. u 1 Sm 16, 10–13.

THE HISTORICAL BOOKS

The historical books include 1 and 2 Samuel, 1 and 2 Kings, 1 and 2 Chronicles, Ezra, Nehemiah, 1 and 2 Maccabees. To these are added the special literary group of Tobit, Judith and Esther.

The books of Tobit, Judith, and 1 and 2 Maccabees, as well as parts of Esther, are called deuterocanonical: they are not contained in the Hebrew canon but have been accepted by the Catholic Church as canonical and inspired.

By means of a series of episodes involving the persons of Samuel, Saul, and David, a century of history unfolds in 1 and 2 Samuel from the close of the period of Judges to the rise and establishment of the monarchy in Israel. Most important is God's promise to David of a lasting dynasty (2 Sm 7), from which royal messianism in the Bible developed.

In 1 and 2 Kings the religious history of Israel extends another four centuries, from the last days of David to the Babylonian captivity and the destruction of Jerusalem (587 B.C.). The various sources for these books are woven into a uniform pattern based on the principle of fidelity to Yahweh for rulers and people alike. The sequence of regnal chronicles in both books is interrupted by a cycle of traditions surrounding the prophets Elijah (1 Kgs) and Elisha (2 Kgs).

Chronicles, Ezra and Nehemiah form a historical work, uniform in style and basic ideas. Chronicles records the long period from the reign of Saul to the return from exile, not so much with exactitude of detail as with concern for the meaning of the facts which demonstrate God's intervention in history. The Ezra-Nehemiah chronicle constitutes the most important source for the formation of the Jewish religious community after the Babylonian exile; the two persons most responsible for the reorganization of Jewish life were Ezra and Nehemiah.

1 and 2 Maccabees contain independent accounts of partially identical events which accompanied the attempted suppression of Judaism in Palestine in the second century B.C. Vigorous reaction to this attempt established for a time the religious and political independence of the Jews. 1 Maccabees portrays God as the eternal benefactor of the Jews and their unfailing source of help. The people are required to be devoted to his exclusive worship and to observe exactly the law he has given them. 2 Maccabees, besides supplementing the former volume, gives a theological interpretation of the history of the period and contains teaching on the resurrection from the dead, intercession of the saints, and suffrages for the dead.

Tobit, Judith, and Esther are examples of free composition—the religious novel used for purposes of edification and instruction. Interest in whatever historical data these books may contain is merely intensified by the addition of vivid details. Judith is a lesson in Providence: a pious reflection on the annual Passover observance to convey the reassurance that God is still the master of history who saves Israel from her enemies. Esther's purpose is the glorification of the Jewish people and the explanation of the origin, significance, and date of the feast of Purim. It is a literary development of the principle of reversal of fortune through punishment of the prosperous rich and reward for the virtuous who are oppressed.

Samuel to Maccabees demonstrates that before as well as during the millennium of history with which it is concerned, Israel was a covenanted people, bound to Yahweh, Lord of the universe, by the ties of faith and obedience. This required observance of the law and worship in his temple, the consequent rewards of which were divine favor and protection. In this way these books anticipate and prepare for the coming of him who would bring type and prophecy to fulfillment, history to term, and holiness to perfection: Christ, the Son of David and the promised Messiah.

THE BOOKS OF SAMUEL

Originally but one book, the scroll of Samuel was early divided into two. The Greek translators called these the first and second Books of Kingdoms, a title St. Jerome later modified to "Kings." The Hebrew title, "Samuel," alludes to the leading figure in the first book, who was responsible for the enthronement of David. It is David's history that the second book recounts.

This sacred work thus comprises the history of about a century, describing the close of the age of the Judges and the beginnings of monarchy in Israel under Saul and David. It is not a complete and continuous history, nor a systematic account of the period, but rather a series of episodes centered around the persons of Samuel, Saul and David, the principal figures leading up to the establishment of the royal dynasty of David.

The final editor is unknown, nor are we certain of the time at which the various strands of the narrative were put together, though one may think of the period, perhaps late in the seventh century B.C., when the other volumes of the "Former Prophets," from Joshua through Kings, were built into a more or less continuous historical corpus. The Samuel-Saul-David narratives clearly depend on several written sources: a Samuel cycle, two sets of stories about Saul and David, and a family history of David. This last (2 Sm 9—20; 1 Kgs 1—2), one of the most vivid historical narratives surviving from ancient times, probably originated early in the reign of Solomon.

One of the most significant theological contributions of the Old Testament is found in 2 Samuel 7, the oracle of Nathan. David is here promised an eternal dynasty, and this becomes the basis for the development of royal messianism throughout the Bible. With this promise to David one should compare 2 Chr 17; Pss 89, 20-38 and 132, 11ff; Acts 2, 30; and Heb 1, 5.

The contents of this work may be divided as follows:

I. History of the Last Judges, Eli and Samuel (1 Sm 1, 1—7, 17).
II. Establishment of the Monarchy in Israel (1 Sm 8, 1—12, 25).
III. Saul and David (1 Sm 13, 1—2 Sm 2, 7).
IV. The Reign of David (2 Sm 2, 8—20, 26).
V. Appendixes (2 Sm 21, 1—24, 25).

THE FIRST BOOK OF SAMUEL

I: History of the Last Judges, Eli and Samuel

CHAPTER 1

Elkanah and His Family at Shiloh 1 There was a certain man from Ramathaim, Elkanah by name, a Zuphite from the hill country of Ephraim. He was the son of Jeroham, son of Elihu, son of Tohu, son of Zuph, an Ephraimite.[a] 2 He had two wives, one named Hannah, the other Peninnah; Peninnah had children, but Hannah was childless. 3 This man regularly went on pilgrimage from his city to worship the LORD of hosts and to sacrifice to him at Shiloh, where the two sons of Eli, Hophni and Phinehas, were ministering as priests of the LORD.[b] 4 When the day came for Elkanah to offer sacrifice, he used to give a portion each to his wife Peninnah and to all her sons and daughters, 5 but a double portion to Hannah because he loved her, though the LORD had made her barren.[c] 6 Her rival, to upset her, turned it into a constant reproach to her that the LORD had left her barren.[d] 7 This went on year after year; each time they made their pilgrimage to the sanctuary of the LORD, Peninnah would approach her, and Hannah would weep and refuse to eat. 8 Her husband Elkanah used to ask her: "Hannah, why do you weep, and why do you refuse to eat? Why do you grieve? Am I not more to you than ten sons?"[e]

Hannah's Prayer 9 Hannah rose after one such meal at Shiloh, and presented herself before the LORD; at the time, Eli the priest was sitting on a chair near the doorpost of the LORD's temple. 10 In her bitterness she prayed to the LORD, weeping copiously, 11 and she made a vow, promising: "O LORD of hosts, if you look with pity on the misery of your handmaid, if you remember me and do not forget me, if you give your handmaid a male child, I will give him to the LORD* for as long as he lives; neither wine nor liquor shall he drink, and no razor shall ever touch his head."[f] 12 As she remained long at prayer before the LORD, Eli watched her mouth, 13 for Hannah was praying silently; though her lips were moving, her voice could not be heard. Eli, thinking her drunk, 14 said to her, "How long will you make a drunken show of yourself? Sober up from your wine!" 15 "It isn't that, my lord," Hannah answered. "I am an unhappy woman. I have had neither wine nor liquor; I was only pouring out my troubles to the LORD. 16 Do not think your handmaid a ne'er-do-well; my prayer has been prompted by my deep sorrow and misery." 17 Eli said, "Go in peace, and may the God of Israel grant you what you have asked of him." 18 She replied, "Think kindly of your maidservant," and left. She went to her quarters, ate and drank with her husband, and no longer appeared downcast. 19 Early the next morning they worshiped before the LORD, and then returned to their home in Ramah.

Hannah Bears a Son When Elkanah had relations with his wife Hannah, the LORD remembered her. 20 She conceived, and at the end of her term bore a son whom she called Samuel, since she had asked* the LORD for him. 21 The next time her husband Elkanah was going up with the rest of his household to offer the customary sacrifice to the LORD and to fulfill his vows, 22 Hannah did not go, explaining to her husband, "Once the child is weaned, I will take him to appear before the LORD and to remain there forever; I will offer him as a perpetual nazirite." 23 Her husband Elkanah answered her: "Do what you think best; wait until you have weaned him. Only, may the LORD bring your resolve to fulfillment!" And so she remained at home and nursed her son until she had weaned him.

1, 11: Give him to the Lord: some ancient texts call Samuel a nazir in this context; see note on Nm 6, 1ff.

1, 20: Since she had asked: this explanation would be more directly appropriate for the name Saul, which means "asked"; Samuel means "name of God."

a 1 Chr 6, 19f. b Ex 23, 14–17; 34, 23; Dt 16, 16; Jgs 21, 19. c Dt 21, 15ff. d Gn 16, 4f. e Ru 4, 15. f Nm 6, 1–5; Jgs 13, 2–5; 16, 17; Lk 1, 15.

Samuel Is Offered to God 24Once he was
weaned, she brought him up with her, along
with a three-year-old bull, an ephah* of flour,
and a skin of wine, and presented him at the
temple of the LORD in Shiloh. 25After the boy's
father had sacrificed the young bull, Hannah, his
mother, approached Eli 26and said: "Pardon, my
lord! As you live, my lord, I am the woman who
stood near you here, praying to the LORD. 27I
prayed for this child, and the LORD granted my
request. 28Now I, in turn, give him to the LORD;
as long as he lives, he shall be dedicated to the
LORD." She left him there;1*and as she wor-
shiped the LORD, she said:

CHAPTER 2

"My heart exults in the LORD,*
my horn* is exalted in my God.
I have swallowed up my enemies;
I rejoice in my victory.[g]
2 There is no Holy One like the LORD;
there is no Rock like our God.[h]

3 "Speak boastfully no longer,
nor let arrogance issue from your mouths.*
For an all-knowing God is the LORD,
a God who judges deeds.[i]
4 The bows of the mighty are broken,
while the tottering gird on strength.[j]
5 The well-fed hire themselves out for bread,
while the hungry batten on spoil.
The barren wife bears seven sons,
while the mother of many languishes.
6 "The LORD puts to death and gives life;
he casts down to the nether world;
he raises up again.[k]
7 The LORD makes poor and makes rich,
he humbles, he also exalts.
8 He raises the needy from the dust;
from the ash heap he lifts up the poor,
To seat them with nobles
and make a glorious throne their heritage.[l]
He gives to the vower his vow,
and blesses the sleep of the just.
"For the pillars of the earth are the LORD's,
and he has set the world upon them.
9 He will guard the footsteps of his faithful ones,
but the wicked shall perish in the darkness.
For not by strength does man prevail;
10 the LORD's foes shall be shattered.
The Most High in heaven thunders;
the LORD judges the ends of the earth.
Now may he give strength to his king
and exalt the horn of his anointed!"[m]

11When Elkanah returned home to Ramah,
the child remained in the service of the LORD
under the priest Eli.

Wickedness of Eli's Sons 12Now the sons of
Eli were wicked; they had respect neither for the
LORD 13nor for the priests' duties toward the
people. When someone offered a sacrifice, the
priest's servant would come with a three-
pronged fork, while the meat was still boiling,[n]
14and would thrust it into the basin, kettle,
caldron, or pot. Whatever the fork brought up,
the priest would keep. That is how all the
Israelites were treated who came to the sanctu-
ary at Shiloh. 15In fact, even before the fat was
burned, the priest's servant would come and say
to the man offering the sacrifice, "Give me some
meat to roast for the priest. He will not accept
boiled meat from you, only raw meat." 16And if
the man protested to him, "Let the fat be burned
first as is the custom, then take whatever you
wish," he would reply, "No, give it to me now,
or else I will take it by force."[o] 17Thus the young
men sinned grievously in the presence of the
LORD; they treated the offerings to the LORD
with disdain.

1, 24: An ephah: a little more than a bushel.

1, 1: And . . . said: this belongs to ch 2.

2, 1–10: A hymn attributed to Hannah, the mother of Samuel, as her thanksgiving to God because she has borne a son despite her previous sterility. She praises God as the helper of the weak (1ff), who casts down the mighty and raises up the lowly (3ff), and who alone is the source of true strength (8ff); the hymn ends with a prayer for the king (v 10). This canticle has several points of resemblance with our Lady's Magnificat.

2, 1: Horn: the symbol of strength; cf Pss 18, 3; 75, 5; 89, 18; 112, 9.

2, 3: Speak . . . mouths: addressed to the enemies mentioned in v 1.

g Dt 33, 17; 2 Sm 22, 3; Ps 18, 2; Is 61, 10; Lk 1, 47. 69 h 2 Sm 22, 3; Ps 18, 2. i Ps 75, 4. j Is 40, 29. k Dt 32, 39; Tb 4, 19; Jb 5, 11; Ps 30, 4; Wis 16, 13; Lk 1, 52. l Jb 9, 6; 38, 6; Ps 104, 5; 121, 3. m Ps 98, 9. n 13–15: Ex 29, 27f; Lv 7, 29–36; Dt 18, 3. o Lv 3, 3ff.

The Lord Rewards Hannah 18 Meanwhile,
the boy Samuel, girt with a linen apron,* was
serving in the presence of the LORD. 19 His
mother used to make a little garment for him,
which she would bring him each time she went
up with her husband to offer the customary
sacrifice. 20 And Eli would bless Elkanah and his
wife, as they were leaving for home. He would
say, "May the LORD repay you with children
from this woman for the gift she has made to the
LORD!" 21 The LORD favored Hannah so that she
conceived and gave birth to three more sons and
two daughters, while young Samuel grew up in
the service of the LORD.[p]

Eli's Futile Rebuke 22 When Eli was very old,
he heard repeatedly how his sons were treating
all Israel [and that they were having relations
with the women serving at the entry of the
meeting tent.]* 23 So he said to them: "Why are
you doing such things? 24 No, my sons, you must
not do these things! It is not a good report that I
hear the people of the LORD spreading about
you. 25 If a man sins against another man, one
can intercede for him with the LORD; but if a
man sins against the LORD, who can intercede
for him?" But they disregarded their father's
warning, since the LORD had decided on their
death. 26 Meanwhile, young Samuel was grow-
ing in stature and in worth in the estimation of
the LORD and of men.[q]

Doom of Eli's House* 27 A man of God came to
Eli and said to him: "This is what the LORD says: 'I
went so far as to reveal myself to your father's
family when they were in Egypt as slaves to the
house of Pharaoh. 28 I chose them out of all the
tribes of Israel to be my priests, to go up to my
altar, to burn incense, and to wear the ephod*
before me; and I assigned all the oblations of the
Israelites to your father's family.[r] 29 Why do you
keep a greedy eye on my sacrifices and on the
offerings which I have prescribed? And why do
you honor your sons in preference to me, fatten-
ing yourselves with the choicest part of every
offering of my people Israel?' 30 [s]This, therefore, is
the oracle of the LORD, the God of Israel: 'I said in
the past that your family and your father's family
should minister in my presence forever. But now,'
the LORD declares, 'away with this! for I will
honor those who honor me, but those who spurn
me shall be accursed. 31 Yes, the time is coming
when I will break your strength and the strength
of your father's family, so that no man in your
family shall reach old age. 32 You shall witness as a
disappointed rival all the benefits enjoyed by Is-
rael, but there shall never be an old man in your
family. 33 I will permit some of your family to re-
main at my altar, to wear out their eyes in consum-
ing greed; but the rest of the men of your family
shall die by the sword. 34 You shall have a sign in
what will happen to your two sons, Hophni and
Phinehas: both shall die on the same day.[t] 35 I will
choose a faithful priest who shall do what I have
in heart and mind. I will establish a lasting house
for him which shall function in the presence of
my anointed forever. 36 Then whoever is left of
your family will come to grovel before him for a
piece of silver or a loaf of bread, and will say:
Appoint me, I beg you, to a priestly function, that I
may have a morsel of bread to eat.' "[u]

CHAPTER 3

Revelation to Samuel 1 During the time young
Samuel was minister to the LORD under Eli, a
revelation of the LORD was uncommon* and
vision infrequent. 2 One day Eli was asleep in his
usual place. His eyes had lately grown so weak

2, 18: Linen apron: called in Hebrew "ephod," but not the same as the high priest's ephod (Ex 28, 6–14) or the ephod used in divination (v 28). Samuel wore a simple apron such as was worn by the priests (1 Sm 22, 18), and on one occasion also by David (2 Sm 6, 14).

2, 22: The bracketed words, which recall Ex 38, 8, are a gloss in the received text; they are lacking in the oldest Greek translation, and in a Hebrew manuscript from Qumran.

2, 27–36: These verses propose the punishment of Eli from a point of view contemporary with the reform of Josiah (2 Kgs 23, 9; cf v 36); they hint at the events recorded in 1 Sm 22, 18–23 and 1 Kgs 2, 27. The older story of this divine warning is that in 1 Sm 3, 11–14.

2, 28: Ephod: a portable container, presumably of cloth, for the lots used in ritual consultation of God during the days of the Judges (Jgs 17, 5; 18, 14–15) and down into the time of David (1 Sm 14, 3ff; 23, 6ff; 30, 7f). The ephod of the high priest described in Ex 28, 6ff becomes a garment upon which a breast-piece of decision symbolizes, but no longer serves for, such consultation. The Exodus text codifies a later form of the tradition.

3, 1: Uncommon: prophetic communications from God were almost unknown.

p 1 Sm 3, 19. q Lk 2, 52. r 1 Sm 23, 9; 30, 7f; Jgs 17, 5. s 30f: 2 Sm 22, 26; 1 Kgs 2, 27; Ps 18, 25. t 1 Sm 4, 11. u 2 Kgs 23, 9.

that he could not see. 3 The lamp of God was not
yet extinguished, and Samuel was sleeping in
the temple of the LORD where the ark of God
was.[v] 4 The LORD called to Samuel, who an-
swered, "Here I am." 5 He ran to Eli and said,
"Here I am. You called me." "I did not call you,"
Eli said. "Go back to sleep." So he went back to
sleep. 6 Again the LORD called Samuel, who rose
and went to Eli. "Here I am," he said. "You
called me." But he answered, "I did not call you,
my son. Go back to sleep."

7 At that time Samuel was not familiar with
the LORD, because the LORD had not revealed
anything to him as yet. 8 The LORD called Samuel
again, for the third time. Getting up and going to
Eli, he said, "Here I am. You called me." Then
Eli understood that the LORD was calling the
youth. 9 So he said to Samuel, "Go to sleep, and
if you are called, reply, 'Speak, LORD, for your
servant is listening.' " When Samuel went to
sleep in his place, 10 the LORD came and revealed
his presence, calling out as before, "Samuel,
Samuel!" Samuel answered, "Speak, for your
servant is listening." 11 The LORD said to Samuel:
"I am about to do something in Israel that will
cause the ears of everyone who hears it to ring.
12 On that day I will carry out in full against Eli
everything I threatened against his family. 13 I
announce to him that I am condemning his
family once and for all, because of this crime:
though he knew his sons were blaspheming
God, he did not reprove them.[w] 14 Therefore, I
swear to the family of Eli that no sacrifice or
offering will ever expiate its crime." 15 Samuel
then slept until morning, when he got up early
and opened the doors of the temple of the LORD.
He feared to tell Eli the vision, 16 but Eli called to
him, "Samuel, my son!" He replied, "Here I
am." 17 Then Eli asked, "What did he say to you?
Hide nothing from me! May God do thus and so
to you* if you hide a single thing he told you."
18 So Samuel told him everything, and held
nothing back. Eli answered, "He is the LORD. He
will do what he judges best."

Samuel Acknowledged as Prophet 19 Samuel
grew up, and the LORD was with him, not permit-
ting any word of his to be without effect.[x] 20 [y]Thus
all Israel from Dan to Beer-sheba came to know
that Samuel was an accredited prophet of the
LORD. 21 The LORD continued to appear at Shiloh;
he manifested himself to Samuel at Shiloh through
his word, 1 *and Samuel spoke to all Israel.

CHAPTER 4

Defeat of the Israelites At that time, the
Philistines gathered for an attack on Israel. Israel
went out to engage them in battle and camped at
Ebenezer, while the Philistines camped at
Aphek. 2 The Philistines then drew up in battle
formation against Israel. After a fierce struggle
Israel was defeated by the Philistines, who slew
about four thousand men on the battlefield.
3 When the troops retired to the camp, the elders
of Israel said, "Why has the LORD permitted us
to be defeated today by the Philistines? Let us
fetch the ark of the LORD from Shiloh that it may
go into battle among us and save us from the
grasp of our enemies."

Loss of the Ark 4 So the people sent to Shiloh
and brought from there the ark of the LORD of
hosts, who is enthroned upon the cherubim.*
The two sons of Eli, Hophni and Phinehas, were
with the ark of God.[z] 5 When the ark of the
LORD arrived in the camp, all Israel shouted so
loudly that the earth resounded. 6 The Philis-
tines, hearing the noise of shouting, asked,
"What can this loud shouting in the camp of the
Hebrews mean?" On learning that the ark of the
LORD had come into the camp, 7 the Philistines
were frightened. They said, "Gods have come to
their camp." They said also, "Woe to us! This has
never happened before. 8 Woe to us! Who can
deliver us from the power of these mighty
gods?* These are the gods that struck the

3, 17: May God do thus and so to you: the Biblical writers avoid repeating for us the specific terms of a curse as the speaker would have uttered it.

3, 1: And . . . Israel: this belongs to ch 4.

4, 4: Enthroned upon the cherubim: this title of the Lord seems to have originated in the sanctuary at Shiloh; it represents the divine Majesty as seated upon a throne on which he can be borne through the heavens by winged creatures somewhat as in the visions of Ez 1 and 10.

4, 8: These mighty gods: the Philistines, who were polytheists, are represented as supposing the Israelites honored several gods.

v Ex 25, 22; 27, 20f; Lv 24, 2. 4; 2 Chr 13, 11. w 1 Sm 2, 27–36. x 1 Sm 2, 21. y Jgs 20, 1. z Ex 25, 22.

Egyptians with various plagues and with pesti-
lence. [9]Take courage and be manly, Philistines;
otherwise you will become slaves to the He-
brews, as they were your slaves. So fight man-
fully!" [10]The Philistines fought and Israel was
defeated; every man fled to his own tent. It was
a disastrous defeat, in which Israel lost thirty
thousand foot soldiers.[a] [11]The ark of God was
captured, and Eli's two sons, Hophni and Phine-
has, were among the dead.[b]
Death of Eli [12]A Benjaminite fled from the
battlefield and reached Shiloh that same day,
with his clothes torn and his head covered with
dirt.[c] [13]When he arrived, Eli was sitting in his
chair beside the gate, watching the road, for he
was troubled at heart about the ark of God. The
man, however, went into the city to divulge his
news, which put the whole city in an uproar.
[14]Hearing the outcry of the men standing near
him, Eli inquired, "What does this commotion
mean?" [15](Eli was ninety-eight years old, and his
eyes would not focus, so that he could not see.)
[16]The man quickly came up to Eli and said, "It is
I who have come from the battlefield; I fled from
there today." He asked, "What happened, my
son?" [17]And the messenger answered: "Israel
fled from the Philistines; in fact, the troops
suffered heavy losses. Your two sons, Hophni
and Phinehas, are among the dead, and the ark
of God has been captured." [18]At this mention of
the ark of God, Eli fell backward from his chair
into the gateway; since he was an old man and
heavy, he died of a broken neck. He had judged
Israel for forty years.

[19]His daughter-in-law, the wife of Phinehas,
was with child and at the point of giving birth.
When she heard the news concerning the cap-
ture of the ark and the deaths of her father-in-
law and her husband, she was seized with the
pangs of labor, and gave birth. [20]She was about
to die when the women standing around her
said to her, "Never fear! You have given birth to
a son." Yet she neither answered nor paid any
attention.[d] [21][She named the child Ichabod,
saying, "Gone is the glory from Israel," with
reference to the capture of the ark of God and to
her father-in-law and her husband.] [22]She said,
"Gone is the glory from Israel," because the ark
of God had been captured.[e]

CHAPTER 5

The Ark in the Temple of Dagon [1][f]The
Philistines, having captured the ark of God,
transferred it from Ebenezer to Ashdod. [2]They
then took the ark of God and brought it into the
temple of Dagon, placing it beside Dagon.
[3]When the people of Ashdod rose early the next
morning, Dagon was lying prone on the ground
before the ark of the LORD. So they picked
Dagon up and replaced him. [4]But the next
morning early, when they arose, Dagon lay
prone on the ground before the ark of the LORD,
his head and hands broken off and lying on the
threshold, his trunk alone intact. [5]For this rea-
son, neither the priests of Dagon nor any others
who enter the temple of Dagon tread on the
threshold of Dagon in Ashdod to this very day;
they always step over it.
The Ark Is Carried About [6]Now the LORD
dealt severely with the people of Ashdod. He
ravaged and afflicted the city and its vicinity
with hemorrhoids; he brought upon the city a
great and deadly plague of mice* that swarmed
in their ships and overran their fields.[g] [7]On
seeing how matters stood, the men of Ashdod
decided, "The ark of the God of Israel must not
remain with us, for he is handling us and our god
Dagon severely." [8]So they summoned all the
Philistine lords and inquired of them, "What
shall we do with the ark of the God of Israel?"
The men of Gath replied, "Let them move the
ark of the God of Israel on to us." [9]So they
moved the ark of the God of Israel to Gath! But
after it had been brought there, the LORD threw
the city into utter turmoil: he afflicted its inhabit-
ants, young and old, and hemorrhoids broke out
on them. [10]The ark of God was next sent to
Ekron; but as it entered that city, the people

5, 6: Hemorrhoids . . . mice: a double calamity fell upon them—a plague of mice or rats, and a severe epidemic of pestilential tumors, probably the bubonic plague.

a Ps 78, 61. b 1 Sm 2, 34. c Jos 7, 6; 2 Sm 1, 2; Jer 7, 12. d 1 Sm 14, 3; Gn 35, 16ff. e Ps 78, 61. f 1–5: Jgs 16, 23–30; Is 45, 5f. 20f. g Ps 78, 66.

there cried out, "Why have they brought the ark
of the God of Israel here to kill us and our
kindred?" 11Then they, too, sent a summons to
all the Philistine lords and pleaded: "Send away
the ark of the God of Israel. Let it return to its
own place, that it may not kill us and our
kindred." A deadly panic had seized the whole
city, since the hand of God had been very heavy
upon it. 12Those who escaped death were af-
flicted with hemorrhoids, and the outcry from
the city went up to the heavens.

CHAPTER 6

The Ark To Be Returned 1The ark of the
LORD had been in the land of the Philistines
seven months 2when they summoned priests
and fortune-tellers to ask, "What shall we do
with the ark of the LORD? Tell us what we
should send back with it." 3They replied: "If you
intend to send away the ark of the God of Israel,
you must not send it alone, but must, by all
means, make amends to him through a guilt
offering.* Then you will be healed, and will
learn why he continues to afflict you." 4When
asked further, "What guilt offering should be our
amends to him?", they replied:
"Five golden hemorrhoids and five golden
mice to correspond to the number of Philistine
lords, since the same plague has struck all of you
and your lords. 5Therefore, make images of the
hemorrhoids and of the mice that are infesting
your land and give them as a tribute to the God
of Israel. Perhaps then he will cease to afflict
you, your gods, and your land. 6Why should you
become stubborn, as the Egyptians and Pharaoh
were stubborn? Was it not after he had dealt
ruthlessly with them that the Israelites were
released and departed?[h] 7So now set to work
and make a new cart. Then take two milch cows
that have not borne the yoke; hitch them to the
cart, but drive their calves indoors away from
them.[i] 8You shall next take the ark of the LORD
and place it on the cart, putting in a box beside it
the golden articles that you are offering, as
amends for your guilt. Start it on its way, and let
it go. 9Then watch! If it goes up to Beth-shemesh
along the route to his own territory, he has
brought this great calamity upon us; if not, we
will know it was not he who struck us, but that
an accident happened to us."
The Ark in Beth-shemesh 10They acted upon
this advice. Taking two milch cows, they hitched
them to the cart but shut up their calves indoors.
11Then they placed the ark of the LORD on the
cart, along with the box containing the golden
mice and the images of the hemorrhoids. 12The
cows went straight for the route to Beth-
shemesh and continued along this road, mooing
as they went, without turning right or left. The
Philistine lords followed them as far as the
border of Beth-shemesh. 13The people of Beth-
shemesh were harvesting the wheat in the
valley. When they looked up and spied the ark,
they greeted it with rejoicing. 14The cart came to
the field of Joshua the Beth-shemite and stopped
there. At a large stone in the field, the wood of
the cart was split up and the cows were offered
as a holocaust to the LORD.[j] 15The Levites,
meanwhile, had taken down the ark of God and
the box beside it, in which the golden articles
were, and had placed them on the great stone.
The men of Beth-shemesh also offered other
holocausts and sacrifices to the LORD that day.
16After witnessing this, the five Philistine lords
returned to Ekron the same day.
Guilt Offering 17The golden hemorrhoids the
Philistines sent back as a guilt offering to the
LORD were as follows: one for Ashdod, one for
Gaza, one for Ashkelon, one for Gath, and one
for Ekron. 18The golden mice, however, corre-
sponded to the number of all the cities of the
Philistines belonging to the five lords, including
fortified cities and open villages. The large stone
on which the ark of the LORD was placed is still
in the field of Joshua the Beth-shemite at the
present time.
Penalty for Irreverence 19The descendants of
Jeconiah did not join in the celebration with the
inhabitants of Beth-shemesh when they greeted

6, 3: A guilt offering: a propitiatory offering customary after unwitting transgression of the ordinances of God regarding holy things or property rights; cf Lv 6, 1ff.

h Ex 7, 14; 8, 15; 9, 34. i Nm 19, 2; Dt 21, 3; 2 Sm 6, 3. j 2 Sm 24, 21ff.

the ark of the LORD, and seventy of them were struck down. The people went into mourning at this great calamity with which the LORD had afflicted them. 20The men of Beth-shemesh asked, "Who can stand in the presence of this Holy One? To whom shall he go from us?" 21They then sent messengers to the inhabitants of Kiriath-jearim, saying, "The Philistines have returned the ark of the LORD; come down and get it."

CHAPTER 7

1So the inhabitants of Kiriath-jearim came for the ark of the LORD and brought it into the house of Abinadab on the hill, appointing his son Eleazar as guardian of the ark of the LORD.

Religious Reform 2From the day the ark came to rest in Kiriath-jearim a long time, twenty years, elapsed, and the whole Israelite population turned to the LORD. 3Samuel said to them: "If you wish with your whole heart to return to the LORD, put away your foreign gods and your Ashtaroth, devote yourselves to the LORD, and worship him alone. Then he will deliver you from the power of the Philistines." [k] 4So the Israelites put away their Baals and Ashtaroth, and worshiped the LORD alone. 5Samuel then gave orders, "Gather all Israel to Mizpah, that I may pray to the LORD for you." [l] 6When they were gathered at Mizpah, they drew water and poured it out on the ground* before the LORD, and they fasted that day, confessing, "We have sinned against the LORD." It was at Mizpah that Samuel began to judge the Israelites. [m]

Rout of the Philistines 7When the Philistines heard that the Israelites had gathered at Mizpah, their lords went up against Israel. Hearing this, the Israelites became afraid of the Philistines 8and said to Samuel, "Implore the LORD our God unceasingly for us, to save us from the clutches of the Philistines." [n] 9Samuel therefore took an unweaned lamb and offered it entire as a holocaust to the LORD. [o] He implored the LORD for Israel, and the LORD heard him. 10While Samuel was offering the holocaust, the Philistines advanced to join battle with Israel. That day, however, the LORD thundered loudly against the Philistines, and threw them into such confusion that they were defeated by Israel. 11Thereupon the Israelites sallied forth from Mizpah and pursued the Philistines, harrying them down beyond Beth-car. 12Samuel then took a stone and placed it between Mizpah and Jeshanah; he named it Ebenezer,* explaining, "To this point has the LORD helped us." 13Thus were the Philistines subdued, never again to enter the territory of Israel, for the LORD was severe with them as long as Samuel lived. [p] 14The cities from Ekron to Gath which the Philistines had taken from Israel were restored to them. Israel also freed the territory of these cities from the dominion of the Philistines. Moreover there was peace between Israel and the Amorites.

15Samuel judged Israel as long as he lived. 16He made a yearly journey, passing through Bethel, Gilgal and Mizpah and judging Israel at each of these sanctuaries. 17Then he used to return to Ramah, for that was his home. There, too, he judged Israel and built an altar to the LORD. [q]

II: Establishment of the Monarchy in Israel

CHAPTER 8*

Request for a King 1In his old age Samuel appointed his sons judges over Israel. 2His firstborn was named Joel, his second son, Abijah; they judged at Beer-sheba. 3His sons did not follow his example but sought illicit gain and accepted bribes, perverting justice. [r] 4Therefore all the elders of Israel came in a body to Samuel

7, 6: Poured it out on the ground: for the symbolism, cf 2 Sm 14, 14.

7, 12: Ebenezer: or eben ha-ezer, means "stone of help."

8, 1: From this chapter on, the First Book of Samuel gives us two and sometimes three viewpoints on most of the events with which it is concerned, such as the appointment of Saul as king, the reasons for his downfall, his relationship with David, even the circumstances of Saul's death (1 Sm 31; 2 Sm 1). The choice of Saul as king is seen, in ch 8, followed by 10, 17–24 and ch 12, as motivated by the people's defection from the proper service of God; this later editorial approach incorporates not only narratives with which it is consistent, but also early traditions (9, 1–10. 16; ch 11) which portray the events and their motivation quite differently.

k 1 Sm 12, 10. 20. 24; Jos 24, 23; Jgs 6, 6–10; 10, 10–16. l 1 Sm 10, 17; Jgs 20, 1. m Jgs 20, 26; Ps 22, 14; Lam 2, 19. n Ex 17, 9–13. o 9f: 2 Sm 22, 14f; Sir 46, 16ff. p Jgs 3, 30; 8, 28; 11, 33. q 1 Sm 9, 12; 14, 35. r Ex 23, 8; Dt 16, 19; Prv 17, 23.

at Ramah 5and said to him, "Now that you are old, and your sons do not follow your example, appoint a king over us, as other nations have, to judge us."[s]

God Grants the Request 6Samuel was displeased when they asked for a king to judge them. He prayed to the LORD, however, 7who said in answer: "Grant the people's every request. It is not you they reject, they are rejecting me as their king.[t] 8As they have treated me constantly from the day I brought them up from Egypt to this day, deserting me and worshiping strange gods, so do they treat you too. 9Now grant their request; but at the same time, warn them solemnly and inform them of the rights of the king who will rule them."

The Rights of a King 10Samuel delivered the message of the LORD in full to those who were asking him for a king. 11He told them: "The rights of the king who will rule you will be as follows: He will take your sons and assign them to his chariots and horses, and they will run before his chariot.[u] 12He will also appoint from among them his commanders of groups of a thousand and of a hundred soldiers. He will set them to do his plowing and his harvesting, and to make his implements of war and the equipment of his chariots.[v] 13He will use your daughters as ointment-makers, as cooks, and as bakers. 14He will take the best of your fields, vineyards, and olive groves, and give them to his officials.[w] 15He will tithe your crops and your vineyards, and give the revenue to his eunuchs and his slaves. 16He will take your male and female servants, as well as your best oxen and your asses, and use them to do his work. 17He will tithe your flocks and you yourselves will become his slaves.[x] 18When this takes place, you will complain against the king whom you have chosen, but on that day the LORD will not answer you."

Persistent Demand 19The people, however, refused to listen to Samuel's warning and said, "Not so! There must be a king over us.[y] 20We too must be like other nations, with a king to rule us and to lead us in warfare and fight our battles." 21When Samuel had listened to all the people had to say, he repeated it to the LORD, 22*who then said to him, "Grant their request and appoint a king to rule them." Samuel thereupon said to the men of Israel, "Each of you go to his own city."

CHAPTER 9

1There was a stalwart man from Benjamin named Kish, who was the son of Abiel, son of Zeror, son of Becorath, son of Aphiah, a Benjaminite.[z] 2He had a son named Saul, who was a handsome young man. There was no other Israelite handsomer than Saul; he stood head and shoulders above the people.[a]

The Lost Asses 3Now the asses of Saul's father, Kish, had wandered off. Kish said to his son Saul, "Take one of the servants with you and go out and hunt for the asses." 4Accordingly they went through the hill country of Ephraim, and through the land of Shalishah. Not finding them there, they continued through the land of Shaalim without success. They also went through the land of Benjamin, but they failed to find the animals. 5When they came to the land of Zuph, Saul said to the servant who was with him, "Come, let us turn back, lest my father forget about the asses and become anxious about us." 6The servant replied, "Listen! There is a man of God in this city, a man held in high esteem; all that he says is sure to come true. Let us go there now! Perhaps he can tell us how to accomplish our errand." 7 [b]But Saul said to his servant, "If we go, what can we offer the man? There is no bread in our bags, and we have no present to give the man of God. What have we?" 8Again the servant answered Saul, "I have a quarter of a silver shekel.* If I give that to the man of God, he will tell us our way." 10Saul then said to his servant, "Well said! Come on, let us

9, 8: A quarter of a silver shekel: about a tenth of an ounce of silver.

s 5f: Dt 17, 14f; Hos 13, 10; Acts 13, 21. t 7f: 1 Sm 12, 1. 12f; Jgs 8, 22f; 10, 13; 1 Kgs 9, 9. u 1 Sm 10, 25; Dt 17, 14–20; 1 Kgs 12. v 2 Sm 15, 1; 1 Kgs 1, 5. w 1 Sm 22, 7; 1 Kgs 21, 1–24; Ez 46, 18. x 1 Kgs 12, 4. y 1 Sm 10, 19. z 1 Sm 14, 51; 1 Chr 8, 33. a 1 Sm 10, 23. b 7f: Nm 22, 7; 1 Kgs 14, 3; 2 Kgs 4, 42; 5, 15; 8, 8f.

go!" And they went to the city where the man of
God lived.
Quest for Samuel's Aid 11 [c]As they were go-
ing up the ascent to the city, they met some girls
coming out to draw water and inquired of them,
"Is the seer in town?" 9 [d](In former times in
Israel, anyone who sent to consult God used to
say, "Come, let us go to the seer." For he who is
now called prophet was formerly called seer.)*
12 [e]The girls answered, "Yes, there—straight
ahead. Hurry now; just today he came to the
city, because the people have a sacrifice today on
the high place.* 13 When you enter the city, you
may reach him before he goes up to the high
place to eat. The people will not eat until he
arrives; only after he blesses the sacrifice will the
invited guests eat. Go up immediately, for you
should find him right now."
Samuel's Revelation about Saul 14 So they
went up to the city. As they entered it, Samuel
was coming toward them on his way to the high
place. 15 The day before Saul's arrival, the LORD
had given Samuel the revelation:[f] 16 "At this
time tomorrow I will send you a man from the
land of Benjamin whom you are to anoint as com-
mander of my people Israel. He shall save my
people from the clutches of the Philistines, for I
have witnessed their misery and accepted their
cry for help."[g] 17 When Samuel caught sight of
Saul, the LORD assured him, "This is the man of
whom I told you; he is to govern my people."
18 Saul met Samuel in the gateway and said,
"Please tell me where the seer lives." 19 Samuel
answered Saul: "I am the seer. Go up ahead of
me to the high place and eat with me today. In
the morning, before dismissing you, I will tell
you whatever you wish. 20 As for the asses you
lost three days ago, do not worry about them, for
they have been found. Whom does Israel desire
ardently if not you and your father's family?"
21 Saul replied: "Am I not a Benjaminite, of one of
the smallest tribes of Israel, and is not my clan
the least among the clans of the tribe of Benja-
min? Why say such things to me?"[h]
22 Samuel then took Saul and his servant and
brought them to the room, where he placed
them at the head of the guests, of whom there
were about thirty. 23 He said to the cook, "Bring
the portion I gave you and told you to put aside."
24 So the cook took up the leg and what went
with it,* and placed it before Saul. Samuel said:
"This is a reserved portion that has been set
before you. Eat, for it was kept for you until your
arrival; I explained that I was inviting some
guests." Thus Saul dined with Samuel that day.
25 When they came down from the high place
into the city, a mattress was spread for Saul on
the roof, 26 and he slept there.
Saul's Anointing At daybreak Samuel called to
Saul on the roof, "Get up, and I will start you on
your journey." Saul rose, and he and Samuel
went outside the city together. 27 As they were
approaching the edge of the town, Samuel said
to Saul, "Tell the servant to go on ahead of us,
but stay here yourself for the moment, that I
may give you a message from God."

CHAPTER 10

1 Then, from a flask he had with him, Samuel
poured oil on Saul's head; he also kissed him,
saying: "The LORD anoints you commander over
his heritage. You are to govern the LORD's people
Israel, and to save them from the grasp of their
enemies roundabout.[i]
"This will be the sign for you that the LORD
has anointed you commander over his heritage:
2 When you leave me today, you will meet two
men near Rachel's tomb* at Zelzah in the

9, 9: This verse is a later explanation of the term seer, first used in the text in 1 Sm 9, 11.

9, 12: On the high place: the local sanctuary on the top of a hill, where the sacrifice was offered and the sacrificial meal eaten.

9, 24: And what went with it: a slight change would give "and the fatty tail" as perhaps the original reading. Sheep in the Near East are exceptionally fat-tailed, and such a portion would be thought a special delicacy by the Hebrews. However, the ritual legislation as we know it (Lv 3, 9) would require that the fat tail be burned on the altar. If this general rule was later than the time of Samuel, the present text may have been retouched so as not to seem to contravene it. A Qumran text has "the festive (leg)" here.

10, 2: Here, as in Jer 31, 15, Rachel's tomb is placed north of Jerusalem. Later tradition understood Gn 35, 19f in the sense given by Mt 2, 16ff, and placed the tomb at Bethlehem, farther south.

c Gn 24, 11ff; Ex 2, 16. d Sir 46, 15. e 1 Sm 7, 17; 16, 2. 5; 20, 6. 29; Dt 12, 13; 1 Kgs 3, 2. 4. f Acts 13, 21. g 1 Sm 10, 1. h 1 Sm 15, 17. i 1 Sm 9, 16f; 24, 7; Jgs 9, 9; 1 Kgs 1, 39; Acts 13, 21.

territory of Benjamin, who will say to you, 'The asses you went to look for have been found. Your father is no longer worried about the asses, but is anxious about you and says, What shall I do about my son?'[j] 3Farther on, when you arrive at the terebinth of Tabor, you will be met by three men going up to God at Bethel; one will be bringing three kids, another three loaves of bread, and the third a skin of wine. 4They will greet you and offer you two wave offerings of bread, which you will take from them. 5 [k]After that you will come to Gibeath-elohim, where there is a garrison of the Philistines.* As you enter that city, you will meet a band of prophets, in a prophetic state, coming down from the high place preceded by lyres, tambourines, flutes and harps. 6The spirit of the LORD will rush upon you, and you will join them in their prophetic state and will be changed into another man.[l] 7When you see these signs fulfilled, do whatever you judge feasible, because God is with you. 8 [m]Now go down ahead of me to Gilgal, for I shall come down to you, to offer holocausts and to sacrifice peace offerings. Wait seven days until I come to you; I shall then tell you what you must do."*

Fulfillment of the Signs 9As Saul turned to leave Samuel, God gave him another heart. That very day all these signs came to pass . . . . 10*When they were going from there to Gibeah, a band of prophets met him, and the spirit of God rushed upon him, so that he joined them in their prophetic state.[n] 11When all who had known him previously saw him in a prophetic state among the prophets, they said to one another, "What has happened to the son of Kish? Is Saul also among the prophets?"[o] 12And some-one from that district added, "And who is their father?" Thus the proverb arose, "Is Saul also among the prophets?" 13When he came out of the prophetic state, he went home.

Silence about the Kingship 14Saul's uncle inquired of him and his servant, "Where have you been?" Saul replied, "To look for the asses. When we could not find them, we went to Samuel." 15Then Saul's uncle said, "Tell me, then, what Samuel said to you." 16Saul said to his uncle, "He assured us that the asses had been found." But he mentioned nothing to him of what Samuel had said about the kingship.

Saul Chosen King by Lot 17Samuel called the people together to the LORD at Mizpah[p] 18and addressed the Israelites: "Thus says the LORD, the God of Israel, 'It was I who brought Israel up from Egypt and delivered you from the power of the Egyptians and from the power of all the kingdoms that oppressed you.'[q] 19But today you have rejected your God, who delivers you from all your evils and calamities, by saying to him, 'Not so, but you must appoint a king over us.' Now, therefore, take your stand before the LORD according to tribes and families."[r] 20So Samuel had all the tribes of Israel come forward, and the tribe of Benjamin was chosen. 21Next he had the tribe of Benjamin come forward in clans, and the clan of Matri was chosen, and finally Saul, son of Kish, was chosen. But they looked for him in vain. 22 [s]Again they consulted the LORD, "Has he come here?" The LORD answered, "He is hiding among the baggage." 23They ran to bring him from there; and when he stood among the people, he was head and shoulders above all the crowd.[t] 24Samuel said to all the people, "Do you see the man whom the LORD has chosen? There is none like him among all the people!" Then all the people shouted, "Long live the king!"[u]

25Samuel next explained to the people the law of royalty* and wrote it in a book, which he

10, 5: A garrison of the Philistines: the Hebrew word for "garrison" has been explained alternatively to mean a pillar erected to mark the Philistine occupation, or an inspector or officer for the collection of taxes. In a prophetic state: in an ecstatic condition due to strong feelings of religious enthusiasm induced by a communal observance, possibly accompanied by music and dancing.

10, 8: By inserting this verse, with its seven days, an editor has prepared for one narrative of the rejection of Saul (1 Sm 13, 8–15) in the very context of Saul's anointing.

10, 10: The story has here been abridged by omitting the fulfillment of the first two signs given by Samuel (1 Sm 10, 2ff).

10, 25: The law of royalty: the charter defining the rights of the king.

j Jer 31, 15; Mk 14, 13. k 5f: 1 Sm 13, 3; 16, 13; 19, 20f. l 1 Sm 11, 6; 16, 13; Jgs 14, 6. 19; 15, 14; 2 Kgs 3, 15. m 1 Sm 13, 8; Lv 3, 1. n 1 Sm 19, 20–24; Nm 11, 25. o 1 Sm 19, 24. p 1 Sm 7, 5. q Ex 20, 2; Lv 11, 45; 25, 38; Nm 15, 41; Dt 5, 6; Jgs 6, 8f. r 1 Sm 8, 19. s 1 Sm 30, 24. t 1 Sm 9, 2; 16, 7. u 2 Sm 16, 16; 1 Kgs 1, 25; 2 Kgs 11, 12.

placed in the presence of the LORD. This done, Samuel dismissed the people, each to his own place.[v] [26]Saul also went home to Gibeah, accompanied by warriors whose hearts the LORD had touched. [27]But certain worthless men said, "How can this fellow save us?" They despised him and brought him no present.[w]

CHAPTER 11

Defeat of the Ammonites [1]About a month later,* Nahash the Ammonite went up and laid siege to Jabesh-gilead. All the men of Jabesh begged Nahash, "Make a treaty with us, and we will be your subjects."[x] [2]But Nahash the Ammonite replied, "This is my condition for a treaty with you: I must gouge out every man's right eye, that I may thus bring ignominy on all Israel." [3]The elders of Jabesh said to him: "Give us seven days to send messengers throughout the territory of Israel. If no one rescues us, we will surrender to you." [4]When the messengers arrived at Gibeah of Saul, they related the news to the people, all of whom wept aloud. [5]Just then Saul came in from the field, behind his oxen. "Why are the people weeping?" he asked. The message of the inhabitants of Jabesh was repeated to him. [6]As he listened to this report, the spirit of God rushed upon him and he became very angry.[y] [7]Taking a yoke of oxen, he cut them into pieces, which he sent throughout the territory of Israel by couriers with the message, "If anyone does not come out to follow Saul [and Samuel], the same as this will be done to his oxen!" In dread of the LORD, the people turned out to a man.[z] [8]When he reviewed them in Bezek, there were three hundred thousand Israelites and seventy thousand Judahites.

[9]To the messengers who had come he said, "Tell the inhabitants of Jabesh-gilead that tomorrow, while the sun is hot, they will be rescued." The messengers came and reported this to the inhabitants of Jabesh, who were jubilant, [10]and said to Nahash, "Tomorrow we will surrender to you, and you may do whatever you please with us." [11]On the appointed day, Saul arranged his troops in three companies and invaded the camp during the dawn watch. They slaughtered Ammonites until the heat of the day; by then the survivors were so scattered that no two were left together.

Saul Accepted as King [12]*The people then said to Samuel: "Who questioned whether Saul should rule over us? Hand over the men and we will put them to death."[a] [13]But Saul broke in to say, "No man is to be put to death this day, for today the LORD has saved Israel."[b] [14]Samuel said to the people, "Come, let us go to Gilgal to inaugurate the kingdom there." [15]So all the people went to Gilgal, where, in the presence of the LORD, they made Saul king. They also sacrificed peace offerings there before the LORD, and Saul and all the Israelites celebrated the occasion with great joy.

CHAPTER 12

Samuel's Integrity [1]Samuel addressed all Israel: "I have granted your request in every respect," he said. "I have set a king over you[c] [2]and now the king is your leader. As for me, I am old and gray, and have sons among you. I have lived with you from my youth to the present day. [3]Here I stand! Answer me in the presence of the LORD and of his anointed. Whose ox have I taken? Whose ass have I taken? Whom have I cheated? Whom have I oppressed? From whom have I accepted a bribe and overlooked his guilt? I will make restitution to you."[d] [4]They replied, "You have neither cheated us, nor oppressed us, nor accepted anything from anyone." [5]So he said to them, "The LORD is witness against you this day, and his anointed as well, that you have found nothing in my possession." "He is witness," they agreed.

11, 1: About a month later: there is ancient evidence for a longer introduction to this campaign. The time indication here may refer to its earlier stages rather than to the events of ch 10.

11, 12–14: With these verses, an editor has harmonized the account of the acknowledgment of Saul as king at Mizpah (1 Sm 10, 17–24) with the public acclamation at Gilgal (1 Sm 11, 15) after the defeat of the Ammonites (1 Sm 11, 1–11). The Greek text of 1 Sm 11, 15 reads "and Samuel anointed Saul as king," instead of they made Saul king.

v 1 Sm 8, 11; Dt 17, 14–20. w 1 Sm 11, 12. x 1 Sm 12, 12; 31, 11. y 1 Sm 16, 13; Jgs 14, 6. 19. z 1 Kgs 11, 30; 2 Kgs 13, 18. a 1 Sm 10, 27. b 2 Sm 19, 23. c 1 Sm 8, 7. 9. 22. d Ex 20, 17; 23, 8; Nm 16, 15; Dt 16, 19; Sir 46, 19.

Samuel Upbraids the People 6Continuing, Samuel said to the people: "The LORD is witness, who appointed Moses and Aaron, and who brought your fathers up from the land of Egypt.[e] 7Now, therefore, take your stand, and I shall arraign you before the LORD, and shall recount for you all the acts of mercy the LORD has done for you and your fathers. 8When Jacob and his sons went to Egypt and the Egyptians oppressed them, your fathers appealed to the LORD, who sent Moses and Aaron to bring them out of Egypt, and he gave them this place to live in.[f] 9But they forgot the LORD their God; and he allowed them to fall into the clutches of Sisera, the captain of the army of Jabin, king of Hazor, into the grasp of the Philistines, and into the grip of the king of Moab, who made war against them.[g] 10Each time they appealed to the LORD and said, 'We have sinned in forsaking the LORD and worshiping Baals and Ashtaroth; but deliver us now from the power of our enemies, and we will worship you.'[h] 11Accordingly, the LORD sent Jerubbaal, Barak, Jephthah, and Samson; he delivered you from the power of your enemies on every side, so that you were able to live in security.[i] 12Yet, when you saw Nahash, king of the Ammonites, advancing against you, you said to me, 'Not so, but a king must rule us,' even though the LORD your God is your king.[j]

Warnings for People and King 13"Now you have the king you want, a king the LORD has given you.[k] 14If you fear the LORD and worship him, if you are obedient to him and do not rebel against the LORD's command, if both you and the king who rules you follow the LORD your God—well and good. 15But if you do not obey the LORD and if you rebel against his command, the LORD will deal severely with you and your king, and destroy you. 16Now then, stand ready to witness the great marvel the LORD is about to accomplish before your eyes. 17Are we not in the harvest time for wheat? Yet I shall call to the LORD, and he will send thunder and rain. Thus you will see and understand how greatly the LORD is displeased that you have asked for a king."[l] 18Samuel then called to the LORD, and the LORD sent thunder and rain that day.

Assistance Promised As a result, all the people dreaded the LORD and Samuel. 19They said to Samuel, "Pray to the LORD your God for us, your servants, that we may not die for having added to all our other sins the evil of asking for a king." 20"Do not fear," Samuel answered them. "It is true you have committed all this evil; still, you must not turn from the LORD, but must worship him with your whole heart. 21Do not turn to meaningless idols which can neither profit nor save; they are nothing.[m] 22For the sake of his own great name the LORD will not abandon his people, since the LORD himself chose to make you his people.[n] 23As for me, far be it from me to sin against the LORD by ceasing to pray for you and to teach you the good and right way.[o] 24But you must fear the LORD and worship him faithfully with your whole heart; keep in mind the great things he has done among you. 25If instead you continue to do evil, both you and your king shall perish."

III: Saul and David

CHAPTER 13

1[Saul was . . . years old when he became king and he reigned . . . (two) years over Israel.]*

Saul Offers Sacrifice 2Saul chose three thousand men of Israel, of whom two thousand remained with him in Michmash and in the hill country of Bethel, and one thousand were with Jonathan in Gibeah of Benjamin. He sent the rest of the people back to their tents. 3Now Jonathan overcame the Philistine garrison* which was in Gibeah, and the Philistines got word of it. Then

13, 1: A formula like that of 2 Sm 5, 4 was introduced here at some time; but the age of Saul when he became king remains a blank, and the two years assigned for his reign in the received text cannot be correct. Tradition (Acts 13, 21) offers the round number, "forty years."

13, 3–4: The Philistine garrison: see note on 1 Sm 10, 5. Let the Hebrews hear: a different reading of these verses, based on the Greek, would yield: "And the Philistines heard that the Hebrews (or: the slaves) had revolted. Saul in the meantime sounded the trumpet throughout all the land (v 4), and all Israel heard that Saul. . . ."

e Mi 6, 4. f Gn 46, 5; Ex 1, 11; 2, 23ff. g Jgs 3, 12ff; 4, 2f; 10, 7; 13, 1. h 1 Sm 7, 3f. i Jgs 6, 14. 32; 11, 1. j 1 Sm 8, 6f. 19; 11, 1f; Jgs 8, 23. k 1 Sm 8, 7. l Ex 9, 23. 28ff; 1 Kgs 18, 1. m Dt 32, 37ff. n Jer 14, 21; Ex 20, 9; Dn 3, 34. o Ex 32, 11.

Saul sounded the horn throughout the land, with a proclamation, "Let the Hebrews hear!"[p] [4]Thus all Israel learned that Saul had overcome the garrison of the Philistines and that Israel had brought disgrace upon the Philistines; and the soldiers were called up to Saul in Gilgal. [5]The Philistines also assembled for battle, with three thousand chariots, six thousand horsemen, and foot soldiers as numerous as the sands of the seashore. Moving up against Israel, they encamped in Michmash, east of Beth-aven. [6]Some Israelites, aware of the danger and of the difficult situation, hid themselves in caves, in thickets, among rocks, in caverns, and in cisterns,[q] [7]and other Hebrews passed over the Jordan into the land of Gad and Gilead. Saul, however, held out at Gilgal, although all his followers were seized with fear.* [8]He waited seven days—the time Samuel had determined. When Samuel did not arrive at Gilgal, the men began to slip away from Saul.[r] [9]He then said, "Bring me the holocaust and peace offerings," and he offered up the holocaust.

King Saul Reproved [10]He had just finished this offering when Samuel arrived. Saul went out to greet him, [11]and Samuel asked him, "What have you done?" Saul replied: "When I saw that the men were slipping away from me, since you had not come by the specified time, and with the Philistines assembled at Michmash, [12]I said to myself, 'Now the Philistines will come down against me at Gilgal, and I have not yet sought the LORD's blessing.' So in my anxiety I offered up the holocaust." [13]Samuel's response was: "You have been foolish! Had you kept the command the LORD your God gave you, the LORD would now establish your kingship in Israel as lasting; [14]but as things are, your kingdom shall not endure. The LORD has sought out a man after his own heart and has appointed him commander of his people, because you broke the LORD's command."[s]

Philistine Invasion [15]Then Samuel set out from Gilgal and went his own way; but the rest of the people went up after Saul to meet the soldiers, going from Gilgal to Gibeah of Benjamin. Saul then numbered the soldiers he had with him, who were about six hundred.[t] [16]Saul, his son Jonathan, and the soldiers they had with them were now occupying Geba of Benjamin, and the Philistines were encamped at Michmash. [17]Meanwhile, raiders left the camp of the Philistines in three bands.[u] One band took the Ophrah road toward the district of Shual; [18]another turned in the direction of Beth-horon; and the third took the road for Geba that overlooks the Valley of the Hyenas toward the desert.

Disarmament of Israel [19]Not a single smith was to be found in the whole land of Israel, for the Philistines had said, "Otherwise the Hebrews will make swords or spears."[v] [20]All Israel, therefore, had to go down to the Philistines to sharpen their plowshares, mattocks, axes, and sickles. [21]The price for the plowshares and mattocks was two-thirds of a shekel, and a third of a shekel for sharpening the axes and for setting the ox-goads. [22]And so on the day of battle neither sword nor spear could be found in the possession of any of the soldiers with Saul or Jonathan. Only Saul and his son Jonathan had them.

Jonathan's Exploit [23]An outpost of the Philistines had pushed forward to the pass of Michmash.[w]

CHAPTER 14

[1]One day Jonathan, son of Saul, said to his armor-bearer, "Come, let us go over to the Philistine outpost on the other side." But he did not inform his father.[x] [2](Saul's command post was under the pomegranate tree near the threshing floor on the outskirts of Geba; those with him numbered about six hundred men. [3]Ahijah, son of Ahitub, brother of Ichabod, who was the son of Phinehas, son of Eli, the priest of the LORD at Shiloh, was wearing the ephod.) Nor did the soldiers know that Jonathan had gone.[y] [4]Flanking the ravine through which Jonathan intended

13, 7–15: These verses, like 1 Sm 10, 8, anticipate the rejection of Saul; a different occasion and motivation for this are given in ch 15, resumed in 1 Sm 28, 17f.

p 1 Sm 14, 1–15; Jgs 3, 27; 6, 34; 2 Sm 20, 1f. q 1 Sm 14, 22. r 1 Sm 10, 8. s 1 Sm 25, 30; 2 Sm 7, 15f; Ps 78, 70; Acts 13, 22. t 1 Sm 14, 2. u 1 Sm 14, 15. v Jgs 5, 8. w 1 Sm 14, 15. x 1 Sm 13, 3. y 1 Sm 2, 28; 4, 21; 14, 18; 23, 9; 30, 7.

to get over to the Philistine outpost there was a
rocky crag on each side, one called Bozez, the
other Seneh. 5One crag was to the north, toward
Michmash, the other to the south, toward Geba.
6Jonathan said to his armor-bearer: "Come, let
us go over to that outpost of the uncircumcised.
Perhaps the LORD will help us, because it is no
more difficult for the LORD to grant victory
through a few than through many."[z] 7His armor-
bearer replied, "Do whatever you are inclined to
do; I will match your resolve." 8Jonathan contin-
ued: "We shall go over to those men and show
ourselves to them. 9If they say to us, 'Stay there
until we can come to you,' we shall stop where
we are; we shall not go up to them. 10But if they
say, 'Come up to us,' we shall go up, because the
LORD has delivered them into our grasp. That
will be our sign." 11Accordingly, the two of them
appeared before the outpost of the Philistines,
who said, "Look, some Hebrews are coming out
of the holes where they have been hiding."
12The men of the outpost called to Jonathan and
his armor-bearer. "Come up here," they said,
"and we will teach you a lesson." So Jonathan
said to his armor-bearer, "Climb up after me, for
the LORD has delivered them into the grasp of
Israel." 13Jonathan clambered up with his armor-
bearer behind him; as the Philistines turned to
flee him, he cut them down, and his armor-
bearer followed him and finished them off. 14In
this first exploit Jonathan and his armor-bearer
slew about twenty men within half a furlong.
15Then panic spread to the army and to the
countryside, and all the soldiers, including the
outpost and the raiding parties, were terror-
stricken. The earth also shook, so that the panic
was beyond human endurance.

Rout of the Philistines 16The lookouts of Saul
in Geba of Benjamin saw that the enemy camp
had scattered and were running about in all
directions. 17Saul said to those around him,
"Count the troops and find out if any of us are
missing." When they had investigated, they
found Jonathan and his armor-bearer missing.
18Saul then said to Ahijah, "Bring the ephod*
here." (Ahijah was wearing the ephod in front of
the Israelites at that time.) 19While Saul was
speaking to the priest, the tumult in the Philis-
tine camp kept increasing. So he said to the
priest, "Withdraw your hand." 20And Saul and
all his men shouted and rushed into the fight,
where the Philistines, wholly confused, were
thrusting swords at one another.[a] 21In addition,
the Hebrews who had previously sided with the
Philistines and had gone up with them to the
camp, turned to join the Israelites under Saul
and Jonathan.[b] 22Likewise, all the Israelites who
were hiding in the hill country of Ephraim, on
hearing that the Philistines were fleeing, pursued
them in the rout.[c] 23Thus the LORD saved Israel
that day.

Saul's Oath The battle continued past Beth-
horon;* 24the whole people, about ten thousand
combatants, were with Saul, and there was
scattered fighting in every town in the hill
country of Ephraim. And Saul swore a very rash
oath that day, putting the people under this ban:
"Cursed be the man who takes food before
evening, before I am able to avenge myself on
my enemies." So none of the people tasted food.
25Indeed, there was a honeycomb lying on the
ground, 26and when the soldiers came to the
comb the swarm had left it; yet no one would
raise a hand to his mouth from it, because the
people feared the oath.

Violation of the Oath 27Jonathan, who had
not heard that his father had put the people
under oath, thrust out the end of the staff he was
holding and dipped it into the honey. Then he
raised it to his mouth and his eyes lit up. 28At
this one of the soldiers spoke up: "Your father
put the people under a strict oath, saying,
'Cursed be the man who takes food this day!' As
a result the people are weak." 29Jonathan re-
plied: "My father brings trouble to the land.
Look how bright my eyes are from this small

14, 18: Ephod: to be used in consulting God; see note on v 41, and that on 1 Sm 2, 28 above.

14, 23: Past Beth-horon: this is a textual correction influenced by 1 Sm 13, 18; the received Hebrew text refers to Bethel (Beth-aven), but the effect of the victory would seem to have been that the main ridge of mountains in the territories of Benjamin and Ephraim was cleared of Philistines.

z 1 Sm 17, 26. 36. 47; Sir 39, 18; 1 Mc 3, 19. a Jgs 7, 22. b 1 Sm 29, 4. c 1 Sm 13, 6.

taste of honey I have had. 30What is more, if the
people had eaten freely today of their enemy's
booty when they came across it, would not the
slaughter of the Philistines by now have been the
greater for it?"

Use of Flesh with Blood Forbidden 31After
the Philistines were routed that day from Mich-
mash to Aijalon, the people were completely
exhausted. 32So they pounced upon the spoil
and took sheep, oxen and calves, slaughtering
them on the ground and eating the flesh with
blood.[d] 33Informed that the people were sinning
against the LORD by eating the flesh with blood,
Saul said: "You have broken faith. Roll a large
stone here for me." 34He continued: "Mingle
with the people and tell each of them to bring
his ox or his sheep to me. Slaughter it here and
then eat, but you must not sin against the LORD
by eating the flesh with blood." So everyone
brought to the LORD whatever ox he had seized,
and they slaughtered them there; 35and Saul
built an altar to the LORD—this was the first time
he built an altar to the LORD.[e]

Jonathan in Danger of Death 36Then Saul
said, "Let us go down in pursuit of the Philistines
by night, to plunder among them until daybreak
and to kill them all off." They replied, "Do what
you think best." But the priest said, "Let us
consult God." 37So Saul inquired of God: "Shall I
go down in pursuit of the Philistines? Will you
deliver them into the power of Israel?" But he
received no answer on this occasion.[f] 38Saul
then said, "Come here, all officers of the army.
We must investigate and find out how this sin
was committed today. 39As the LORD lives who
has given victory to Israel, even if my son
Jonathan has committed it, he shall surely die!"
But none of the people answered him. 40So he
said to all Israel, "Stand on one side, and I and
my son Jonathan will stand on the other." The
people responded, "Do what you think best."[g]
41And Saul said to the LORD, the God of Israel:
"Why did you not answer your servant this
time? If the blame for this resides in me or my
son Jonathan, LORD, God of Israel, respond with
Urim; but if this guilt is in your people Israel,
respond with Thummim."* Jonathan and Saul
were designated, and the people went free.[h]
42Saul then said, "Cast lots between me and my
son Jonathan." And Jonathan was designated.
43Saul said to Jonathan, "Tell me what you have
done." Jonathan replied, "I only tasted a little
honey from the end of the staff I was holding.
Am I to die for this?" 44Saul said, "May God do
thus and so to me if you do not indeed die,
Jonathan!"[i]

Rescue of Jonathan 45But the army said to
Saul: "Is Jonathan to die, though it was he who
brought Israel this great victory? This must not
be! As the LORD lives, not a single hair of his
head shall fall to the ground, for God was with
him in what he did today!" Thus the soldiers
were able to rescue* Jonathan from death.[j]
46After that Saul gave up the pursuit of the
Philistines, who returned to their own territory.

Wars and Victories 47After taking over the
kingship of Israel, Saul waged war on all their
surrounding enemies—Moab, the Ammonites,
Aram, Beth-rehob, the king of Zobah, and the
Philistines. Wherever he turned, he was success-
ful[k] 48and fought bravely. He defeated Amalek
and delivered Israel from the hands of those who
were plundering them.

Saul's Family 49The sons of Saul were Jona-
than, Ishvi,* and Malchishua; his two daughters
were named, the elder, Merob, and the younger,
Michal.[l] 50Saul's wife, who was named Ahin-
oam, was the daughter of Ahimaaz. The name of
his general was Abner, son of Saul's uncle, Ner;
51Kish, Saul's father, and Ner, Abner's father,
were sons of Abiel.[m]

52An unremitting war was waged against the

14, 41: The Urim and Thummim, or sacred lots, were a device for ascertaining the will of God; they ceased to be used after the time of David. The material and the shape of these objects, and the manner in which they were used, are unknown. They gave a "yes" or "no" answer to specific questions.

14, 45: Rescue: the Hebrew word used is that for the "redemption" of the first-born (Ex 13, 13ff).

14, 49: Ishvi: known also as Ishbaal, in 2 Sm 2, 8 and elsewhere. The name may once have read "Ishyo" here.

d 1 Sm 15, 19. 21; Lv 3, 17; 7, 26f; 17, 10–14; Acts 15, 20. 29. e 1 Sm 7, 17; Jgs 6, 24. f 1 Sm 28, 6. 15. g Jos 7, 13ff. h 1 Sm 28, 6; Ex 28, 30; Dt 33, 8. i 1 Sm 3, 17; Ru 1, 17. j 2 Sm 14, 11; 1 Kgs 1, 52. k 2 Sm 1, 22; 8, 2–5. l 1 Sm 18, 20. 25; 31, 2; 1 Chr 8, 33; 9, 39; 10, 2. m 1 Sm 9, 1.

Philistines during Saul's lifetime. When Saul saw any strong or brave man, he took him into his service.

CHAPTER 15

1 Samuel said to Saul: "It was I the LORD sent to anoint you king over his people Israel. Now, therefore, listen to the message of the LORD. 2 This is what the LORD of hosts has to say: 'I will punish what Amalek did to Israel when he barred his way as he was coming up from Egypt.[n] 3 Go, now, attack Amalek, and deal with him and all that he has under the ban.* Do not spare him, but kill men and women, children and infants, oxen and sheep, camels and asses.' "[o]

Disobedience of Saul 4 Saul alerted the soldiers, and at Telaim reviewed two hundred thousand foot soldiers and ten thousand men of Judah.* 5 Saul went to the city of Amalek, and after setting an ambush in the wadi, 6 [p]warned the Kenites: "Come! Leave Amalek and withdraw, that I may not have to destroy you with them, for you were kind to the Israelites when they came up from Egypt." After the Kenites left, 7 Saul routed Amalek from Havilah to the approaches of Shur, on the frontier of Egypt.[q] 8 He took Agag, king of Amalek, alive, but on the rest of the people he put into effect the ban of destruction by the sword. 9 He and his troops spared Agag and the best of the fat sheep and oxen, and the lambs. They refused to carry out the doom on anything that was worthwhile, dooming only what was worthless and of no account.

Saul Is Reproved 10 Then the LORD spoke to Samuel: 11 "I regret* having made Saul king, for he has turned from me and has not kept my command." At this Samuel grew angry and cried out to the LORD all night. 12 Early in the morning he went to meet Saul, but was informed that Saul had gone to Carmel, where he erected a trophy in his own honor, and that on his return he had passed on and gone down to Gilgal. 13 When Samuel came to him, Saul greeted him: "The LORD bless you! I have kept the command of the LORD." 14 But Samuel asked, "What, then, is the meaning of this bleating of sheep that comes to my ears, and the lowing of oxen that I hear?" 15 Saul replied: "They were brought from Amalek. The men spared the best sheep and oxen to sacrifice to the LORD, your God; but we have carried out the ban on the rest." 16 Samuel said to Saul: "Stop! Let me tell you what the LORD said to me last night." "Speak!" he replied. 17 Samuel then said: "Though little in your own esteem, are you not leader of the tribes of Israel? The LORD anointed you king of Israel[r] 18 and sent you on a mission, saying, 'Go and put the sinful Amalekites under a ban of destruction. Fight against them until you have exterminated them.'[s] 19 Why then have you disobeyed the LORD? You have pounced on the spoil, thus displeasing the LORD."[t] 20 Saul answered Samuel: "I did indeed obey the LORD and fulfill the mission on which the LORD sent me. I have brought back Agag, and I have destroyed Amalek under the ban. 21 But from the spoil the men took sheep and oxen, the best of what had been banned, to sacrifice to the LORD their God in Gilgal."[u] 22 [v]But Samuel said:

"Does the LORD so delight in holocausts and
    sacrifices
  as in obedience to the command of the
    LORD?
Obedience is better than sacrifice,
  and submission than the fat of rams.*
23 For a sin like divination is rebellion,
  and presumption is the crime of idolatry.

15, 3: Under the ban: in such wars of extermination, all things (men, cities, beasts, etc.) were to be blotted out; nothing could be reserved for private use. The interpretation of God's will here attributed to Samuel is in keeping with the abhorrent practices of blood revenge prevalent among pastoral, seminomadic peoples such as the Hebrews had recently been. The slaughter of the innocent has never been in conformity with the will of God.

15, 4: The numbers here are not realistic; compare 1 Sm 14, 24 above.

15, 11: I regret: God manifests "regret" when, offended by men, he takes away his benefits, graces and favors. It is not God, but men, who change, to their own detriment.

15, 22: Samuel is disapproving, not of sacrifices in general, but of merely external sacrifices offered in defiance of God's commandment and without heartfelt obedience.

n Ex 17, 8–10. 16; Dt 25, 17ff. o 1 Sm 27, 8; 30, 17; Ex 17, 16; Nm 24, 20. p Nm 24, 21. q 1 Sm 27, 8. r 1 Sm 9, 21. s 1 Sm 28, 18. t 1 Sm 14, 32. u Lv 27, 28. v Prv 21, 3; Hos 6, 6; Am 5, 21–25; Zec 10, 2; Mt 9, 13; 12, 7; Heb 10, 9.

Because you have rejected the command of
the LORD,
he, too, has rejected you as ruler."

Saul Asks Forgiveness 24 Saul replied to Samuel: "I have sinned, for I have disobeyed the command of the LORD and your instructions. In my fear of the people, I did what they said.[w] 25 Now forgive my sin, and return with me, that I may worship the LORD." 26 But Samuel said to Saul, "I will not return with you, because you rejected the command of the LORD and the LORD rejects you as king of Israel."[x] 27 As Samuel turned to go, Saul seized a loose end of his mantle, and it tore off.[y] 28 So Samuel said to him: "The LORD has torn the kingdom of Israel from you this day, and has given it to a neighbor of yours, who is better than you.[z] 29 The Glory of Israel neither retracts nor repents, for he is not man that he should repent."[a] 30 But he answered: "I have sinned, yet honor me now before the elders of my people and before Israel. Return with me that I may worship the LORD your God." 31 And so Samuel returned with him, and Saul worshiped the LORD.

Agag Is Cut Down 32 Afterward Samuel commanded, "Bring Agag, king of Amalek, to me." Agag came to him struggling and saying, "So it is bitter death!" 33 And Samuel said,

"As your sword has made women childless,
so shall your mother be childless among
women."

Then he cut Agag down before the LORD in Gilgal.[b]

34 Samuel departed for Ramah, while Saul went up to his home in Gibeah of Saul. 35 Never again, as long as he lived, did Samuel see Saul. Yet he grieved over Saul, because the LORD regretted having made him king of Israel.[c]

CHAPTER 16

Samuel Sent to Bethlehem 1 [d]The LORD said to Samuel: "How long will you grieve for Saul, whom I have rejected as king of Israel? Fill your horn with oil, and be on your way. I am sending you to Jesse of Bethlehem, for I have chosen my king from among his sons."* 2 But Samuel replied: "How can I go? Saul will hear of it and kill me." To this the LORD answered: "Take a heifer along and say, 'I have come to sacrifice to the LORD.' 3 Invite Jesse to the sacrifice, and I myself will tell you what to do; you are to anoint for me the one I point out to you."

4 Samuel did as the LORD had commanded him. When he entered Bethlehem, the elders of the city came trembling to meet him and inquired, "Is your visit peaceful, O seer?" 5 He replied: "Yes! I have come to sacrifice to the LORD. So cleanse yourselves and join me today for the banquet." He also had Jesse and his sons cleanse themselves and invited them to the sacrifice.[e] 6 As they came, he looked at Eliab and thought, "Surely the LORD's anointed is here before him." 7 But the LORD said to Samuel: "Do not judge from his appearance or from his lofty stature, because I have rejected him. Not as man sees does God see, because man sees the appearance but the LORD looks into the heart."[f] 8 [g]Then Jesse called Abinadab and presented him before Samuel, who said, "The LORD has not chosen him." 9 Next Jesse presented Shammah, but Samuel said, "The LORD has not chosen this one either." 10 In the same way Jesse presented seven sons before Samuel, but Samuel said to Jesse, "The LORD has not chosen any one of these." 11 Then Samuel asked Jesse, "Are these all the sons you have?" Jesse replied, "There is still the youngest, who is tending the sheep." Samuel said to Jesse, "Send for him; we will not begin the sacrificial banquet until he arrives here."[h] 12 Jesse sent and had the young man brought to them. He was ruddy, a youth handsome to behold and making a splendid appearance. The LORD said, "There—anoint him, for this is he!"[i] 13 Then Samuel, with the horn of oil

16, 1: The anointing here prepared for is unknown to David's brother Eliab in the next chapter (1 Sm 17, 28), and David is twice anointed after Saul's death (2 Sm 2, 4; 5, 3).

w 1 Sm 26, 21. x 1 Kgs 11, 11. 30f. y 1 Sm 24, 6. z 1 Sm 28, 17; 2 Sm 7, 15f. a Nm 23, 19. b Ex 21, 23. c Gn 6, 6.

d 1 Kgs 1, 39; Ru 4, 17–22; 1 Chr 11, 3; Is 11, 1; Lk 2, 4. e 1 Sm 9, 12f; 20, 26; Ex 19, 10; Jb 1, 5. f 1 Sm 10, 23f; 1 Chr 28, 9; Prv 15, 11; Jer 17, 10; 20, 12; Lk 16, 15; Acts 1, 24. g 8ff: 1 Sm 17, 12f; 1 Chr 2, 13ff. h 1 Sm 17, 15. 28. 34; 2 Sm 7, 8. i 1 Sm 9, 2.

in hand, anointed him in the midst of his brothers; and from that day on, the spirit of the LORD rushed upon David. When Samuel took his leave, he went to Ramah.[j]

Saul's Spirit of Melancholy 14 [k]The spirit of the LORD had departed from Saul, and he was tormented by an evil spirit sent by the LORD.* 15 So the servants of Saul said to him: "Please! An evil spirit from God is tormenting you. 16 If your lordship will order it, we, your servants here in attendance on you, will look for a man skilled in playing the harp. When the evil spirit from God comes over you, he will play and you will feel better." 17 Saul then told his servants, "Find me a skillful harpist and bring him to me." 18 [l]A servant spoke up to say: "I have observed that one of the sons of Jesse of Bethlehem is a skillful harpist. He is also a stalwart soldier, besides being an able speaker, and handsome. Moreover, the LORD is with him."*

David Made Armor-Bearer 19 Accordingly, Saul dispatched messengers to ask Jesse to send him his son David, who was with the flock. 20 Then Jesse took five loaves of bread, a skin of wine, and a kid, and sent them to Saul by his son David.[m] 21 Thus David came to Saul and entered his service. Saul became very fond of him, made him his armor-bearer,[n] 22 and sent Jesse the message, "Allow David to remain in my service, for he meets with my approval." 23 Whenever the spirit from God seized Saul, David would take the harp and play, and Saul would be relieved and feel better, for the evil spirit would leave him.

CHAPTER 17

The Challenge of Goliath 1 The Philistines rallied their forces for battle at Socoh in Judah and camped between Socoh and Azekah at Ephes-dammim. 2 Saul and the Israelites also gathered and camped in the Vale of the Terebinth, drawing up their battle line to meet the Philistines. 3 The Philistines were stationed on one hill and the Israelites on an opposite hill, with a valley between them.

4 A champion named Goliath of Gath came out from the Philistine camp; he was six and a half feet tall. 5 He had a bronze helmet on his head and wore a bronze corselet of scale armor weighing five thousand shekels, 6 and bronze greaves, and had a bronze scimitar* slung from a baldric. 7 The shaft of his javelin was like a weaver's heddle-bar, and its iron head weighed six hundred shekels.* His shield-bearer went before him.[o] 8 He stood and shouted to the ranks of Israel: "Why come out in battle formation? I am a Philistine, and you are Saul's servants. Choose one of your men, and have him come down to me. 9 If he beats me in combat and kills me, we will be your vassals; but if I beat him and kill him, you shall be our vassals and serve us." 10 The Philistine continued: "I defy the ranks of Israel today. Give me a man and let us fight together." 11 Saul and all the men of Israel, when they heard this challenge of the Philistine, were dismayed and terror-stricken.

David Comes to the Camp* 12 [David was the son of an Ephrathite named Jesse, who was from Bethlehem in Judah. He had eight sons, and in the days of Saul was old and well on in years.[p] 13 The three oldest sons of Jesse had followed Saul to war; these three sons who had gone off to war were named, the first-born Eliab, the second son Abinadab, and the third Shammah. 14 David was the youngest. While the three oldest had joined Saul, 15 David would go and come from Saul to tend his father's sheep at Bethlehem.[q]

16, 14: An evil spirit sent by the Lord: the Lord permitted Saul to be tormented with violent fits of rage.

16, 18: Of the two traditions which describe the coming of David into Saul's service, the oldest Greek translation retains only the one comprised in 1 Sm 16, 14–23; 17, 1–11. 32–54. This effort at consistency is not in accord with the character of the rest of the book; see note on 1 Sm 8, 1. Though square brackets are used in this edition to indicate the passages lacking in the oldest translation, this is meant only to help the reader follow one account at a time. Both are equally a part of the inspired text, as are also the various amplifications and retouchings of the narrative given within brackets in chs 18 and 19.

17, 6: Scimitar: the Hebrew word for this is rather rare, and the nature of the weapon was in doubt until recent years. It is not the same as the sword of v 45.

17, 7: Six hundred shekels: over 15 pounds.

17, 12–31: An alternative account of how David came to undertake the combat with the Philistine is here inserted; it is continued in 1 Sm 17, 55—18, 6. See note on 1 Sm 16, 18.

j 1 Sm 10, 6; 11, 6; Jgs 3, 10; 9, 9; Sir 46, 13. k 1 Sm 18, 10f. l 2 Sm 17, 8. m 1 Sm 9, 7f; 10, 4. 27; 16, 1; 17, 27ff. n 1 Sm 18, 2. o 2 Sm 21, 19; 1 Chr 11, 23; 20, 5. p 1 Sm 16, 1. 10; Ru 1, 2. q 1 Sm 18, 2; 2 Sm 7, 8.

16[Meanwhile the Philistine came forward
and took his stand morning and evening for forty
days.
17[Now Jesse said to his son David: “Take this
ephah of roasted grain and these ten loaves for
your brothers, and bring them quickly to your
brothers in the camp. 18Also take these ten
cheeses for the field officer. Greet your brothers
and bring home some token from them. 19Saul,
and they, and all Israel are fighting against the
Philistines in the Vale of the Terebinth.” 20Early
the next morning, having left the flock with a
shepherd, David set out on his errand, as Jesse
had commanded him. He reached the barricade
of the camp just as the army, on their way to the
battleground, were shouting their battle cry.[r]
21The Israelites and the Philistines drew up
opposite each other in battle array. 22David
entrusted what he had brought to the keeper of
the baggage and hastened to the battle line
where he greeted his brothers.[s] 23While he was
talking with them, the Philistine champion, by
name Goliath of Gath, came up from the ranks
of the Philistines and spoke as before, and David
listened. 24When the Israelites saw the man,
they all retreated before him, very much afraid.
25The Israelites had been saying: “Do you see
this man coming up? He comes up to insult
Israel. If anyone should kill him, the king would
give him great wealth, and his daughter as well,
and would grant exemption to his father’s family
in Israel.”[t] 26David now said to the men stand-
ing by: “What will be done for the man who kills
this Philistine and frees Israel of the disgrace?
Who is this uncircumcised Philistine in any case,
that he should insult the armies of the living
God?”[u] 27They repeated the same words to him
and said, “That is how the man who kills him
will be rewarded.” 28When Eliab, his oldest
brother, heard him speaking with the men, he
grew angry with David and said: “Why did you
come down? With whom have you left those
sheep in the desert meanwhile? I know your
arrogance and your evil intent. You came down
to enjoy the battle!” 29David replied, “What
have I done now?—I was only talking.” 30Yet he
turned from him to another and asked the same
question; and everyone gave him the same
answer as before. 31The words that David had
spoken were overheard and reported to Saul,
who sent for him.]
David Fights Goliath 32Then David spoke to
Saul: “Let your majesty not lose courage. I am at
your service to go and fight this Philistine.”
33But Saul answered David, “You cannot go up
against this Philistine and fight with him, for you
are only a youth, while he has been a warrior
from his youth.” 34 [v]Then David told Saul: “Your
servant used to tend his father’s sheep, and
whenever a lion or bear came to carry off a
sheep from the flock, 35I would go after it and
attack it and rescue the prey from its mouth. If it
attacked me, I would seize it by the jaw, strike it,
and kill it. 36Your servant has killed both a lion
and a bear, and this uncircumcised Philistine will
be as one of them, because he has insulted the
armies of the living God.”
37David continued: “The LORD, who deliv-
ered me from the claws of the lion and the bear,
will also keep me safe from the clutches of this
Philistine.” Saul answered David, “Go! the LORD
will be with you.”[w]
Preparation for the Encounter 38Then Saul
clothed David in his own tunic, putting a bronze
helmet on his head and arming him with a coat
of mail. 39David also girded himself with Saul’s
sword over the tunic. He walked with difficulty,
however, since he had never tried armor before.
He said to Saul, “I cannot go in these, because I
have never tried them before.” So he took them
off. 40Then, staff in hand, David selected five
smooth stones from the wadi and put them in
the pocket of his shepherd’s bag. With his sling
also ready to hand, he approached the Philistine.
David’s Victory 41With his shield-bearer
marching before him, the Philistine also ad-
vanced closer and closer to David. 42When he
had sized David up, and seen that he was
youthful, and ruddy, and handsome in appear-
ance, he held him in contempt. 43The Philistine

r 1 Sm 26, 5. s 1 Sm 25, 13. t 1 Sm 18, 17; Jos 15, 16. u 1 Sm 18, 25; Jgs 15, 18; 2 Kgs 19, 4; Is 37, 4. v 34f: Jgs 14, 6; Sir 47, 3. w Prv 28, 1.

said to David, "Am I a dog that you come against me with a staff?" Then the Philistine cursed David by his gods 44and said to him, "Come here to me, and I will leave your flesh for the birds of the air and the beasts of the field." [x] 45David answered him: "You come against me with sword and spear and scimitar, but I come against you in the name of the LORD of hosts, the God of the armies of Israel that you have insulted. 46Today the LORD shall deliver you into my hand; I will strike you down and cut off your head. This very day I will leave your corpse and the corpses of the Philistine army for the birds of the air and the beasts of the field; thus the whole land shall learn that Israel has a God. 47All this multitude, too, shall learn that it is not by sword or spear that the LORD saves. For the battle is the LORD's, and he shall deliver you into our hands." [y]

48The Philistine then moved to meet David at close quarters, while David ran quickly toward the battle line in the direction of the Philistine. 49David put his hand into the bag and took out a stone, hurled it with the sling, and struck the Philistine on the forehead. The stone embedded itself in his brow, and he fell prostrate on the ground. 50[Thus David overcame the Philistine with sling and stone; he struck the Philistine mortally, and did it without a sword.] [z] 51Then David ran and stood over him; with the Philistine's own sword [which he drew from its sheath] he dispatched him and cut off his head. [a]

Flight of the Philistines When they saw that their hero was dead, the Philistines took to flight. 52Then the men of Israel and Judah, with loud shouts, went in pursuit of the Philistines to the approaches of Gath and to the gates of Ekron, and Philistines fell wounded along the road from Shaaraim as far as Gath and Ekron. 53On their return from the pursuit of the Philistines, the Israelites looted their camp. 54 [b]David took the head of the Philistine and brought it to Jerusalem; but he kept Goliath's armor in his own tent.*

David Presented to Saul 55[When Saul saw David go out to meet the Philistine, he asked his general Abner, "Abner, whose son is that youth?" Abner replied, "As truly as your majesty is alive, I have no idea." 56And the king said, "Find out whose son the lad is." 57So when David returned from slaying the Philistine, Abner took him and presented him to Saul. David was still holding the Philistine's head. 58Saul then asked him, "Whose son are you, young man?" David replied, "I am the son of your servant Jesse of Bethlehem."

CHAPTER 18

David and Jonathan 1[By the time David finished speaking with Saul, Jonathan had become as fond of David as if his life depended on him; he loved him as he loved himself. [c] 2Saul laid claim to David that day and did not allow him to return to his father's house. [d] 3And Jonathan entered into a bond with David, because he loved him as himself. 4Jonathan divested himself of the mantle he was wearing and gave it to David, along with his military dress, and his sword, his bow and his belt. [e] 5David then carried out successfully every mission on which Saul sent him. So Saul put him in charge of his soldiers, and this was agreeable to the whole army, even to Saul's own officers.]

Saul's Jealousy 6At the approach of Saul and David (on David's return after slaying the Philistine), women came out from each of the cities of Israel to meet King Saul, singing and dancing, with tambourines, joyful songs, and sistrums. [f] 7The women played and sang:

"Saul has slain his thousands,
and David his ten thousands." [g]

8Saul was very angry and resentful of the song, for he thought: "They give David ten thousands,

17, 54: At the time supposed by this narrative, Jerusalem was still Jebusite, and David had no military tent of his own; the verse is a later gloss.

x Dt 28, 26; Is 18, 6; Jer 15, 3. y 1 Sm 14, 6; Ps 33, 16. z Sir 47, 4; 1 Mc 4, 30. a 1 Sm 21, 10. b 1 Sm 31, 9. c 1 Sm 19, 1–7; 20, 17; 23, 16; 2 Sm 1, 26; 9, 1. d 1 Sm 16, 21; 17, 15. e 2 Sm 1, 22. f Ex 15, 20f; Jgs 11, 34; Jdt 15, 12. g 1 Sm 21, 12; 29, 5; Sir 47, 6f.

but only thousands to me. All that remains for
him is the kingship." 9[And from that day on,
Saul was jealous of David.

10[[h] The next day an evil spirit from God
came over Saul, and he raged in his house.
David was in attendance, playing the harp as at
other times, while Saul was holding his spear.
11Saul poised the spear, thinking to nail David to
the wall, but twice David escaped him.] 12Saul
then began to fear David, [because the LORD was
with him, but had departed from Saul himself.]
13Accordingly, Saul removed him from his pres-
ence by appointing him a field officer. So David
led the people on their military expeditions,
14and prospered in all his enterprises, for the
LORD was with him. 15Seeing how successful he
was, Saul conceived a fear of David; 16on the
other hand, all Israel and Judah loved him, since
he led them on their expeditions.[i]

17[Saul said to David, "There is my older
daughter, Merob, whom I will give you in
marriage if you become my champion and fight
the battles of the LORD." Saul had in mind, "I
shall not touch him; let the Philistines strike
him."[j] 18But David answered Saul: "Who am I?
And who are my kin or my father's clan in Israel
that I should become the king's son-in-law?"
19However, when it was time for Saul's daughter
Merob to be given to David, she was given in
marriage to Adriel the Meholathite instead.][k]

20Now Saul's daughter Michal loved David,
and it was reported to Saul, who was pleased at
this,[l] 21for he thought, "I will offer her to him to
become a snare for him, so that the Philistines
may strike him." [Thus for the second time Saul
said to David, "You shall become my son-in-law
today."] 22Saul then ordered his servants to
speak to David privately and to say: "The king is
fond of you, and all his officers love you. You
should become the king's son-in-law." 23But
when Saul's servants mentioned this to David,
he said: "Do you think it easy to become the
king's son-in-law? I am poor and insignificant."
24When his servants reported to him the nature
of David's answer, 25Saul commanded them to
say this to David: "The king desires no other
price for the bride than the foreskins of one
hundred Philistines, that he may thus take
vengeance on his enemies." Saul intended in this
way to bring about David's death through the
Philistines.[m] 26When the servants reported this
offer to David, he was pleased with the prospect
of becoming the king's son-in-law. [Before the
year was up,] 27David made preparations and
sallied forth with his men and slew two hundred
Philistines. He brought back their foreskins and
counted them out before the king, that he might
thus become the king's son-in-law. So Saul gave
him his daughter Michal in marriage. 28Saul thus
came to recognize that the LORD was with
David; besides, his own daughter Michal loved
David. 29Therefore Saul feared David all the
more [and was his enemy ever after].

30[The Philistine chiefs continued to make
forays, but each time they took the field, David
was more successful against them than any other
of Saul's officers, and as a result acquired great
fame.]

CHAPTER 19

Persecution of David 1Saul discussed his in-
tention of killing David with his son Jonathan
and with all his servants. But Saul's son Jona-
than, who was very fond of David,[n] 2told him:
"My father Saul is trying to kill you. Therefore,
please be on your guard tomorrow morning; get
out of sight and remain in hiding. 3I, however,
will go out and stand beside my father in the
countryside where you are, and will speak to
him about you. If I learn anything, I will let you
know."

4Jonathan then spoke well of David to his
father Saul, saying to him: "Let not your majesty
sin against his servant David, for he has commit-
ted no offense against you, but has helped you
very much by his deeds. 5When he took his life
in his hands and slew the Philistine, and the
LORD brought about a great victory for all Israel
through him, you were glad to see it. Why, then,
should you become guilty of shedding innocent

h 10f: 1 Sm 16, 14; 19, 9f; 20, 33; 22, 6; 26, 8. i 2 Sm 5, 2. j 1 Sm 14, 49; 17, 25. k 1 Sm 21, 8; 24, 16. l 1 Sm 14, 49; 25, 44; 26, 23; 2 Sm 3, 13. m 1 Sm 17, 26; Gn 34, 12. n 1 Sm 18, 1; 20, 1ff.

blood by killing David without cause?"[o] 6 Saul heeded Jonathan's plea and swore, "As the LORD lives, he shall not be killed." 7 So Jonathan summoned David and repeated the whole conversation to him. Jonathan then brought David to Saul, and David served him as before.

8 When war broke out again, David went out to fight against the Philistines and inflicted a great defeat upon them, putting them to flight. 9 [p]Then an evil spirit from the LORD came upon Saul as he was sitting in his house with spear in hand and David was playing the harp nearby. 10 Saul tried to nail David to the wall with the spear, but David eluded Saul, so that the spear struck only the wall, and David got away safe.

11 The same night, Saul sent messengers to David's house to guard it, that he might kill him in the morning. David's wife Michal informed him, "Unless you save yourself tonight, tomorrow you will be killed."* 12 Then Michal let David down through a window, and he made his escape in safety.[q] 13 Michal took the household idol and laid it in the bed, putting a net of goat's hair at its head and covering it with a spread.[r] 14 When Saul sent messengers to arrest David, she said, "He is sick." 15 Saul, however, sent the messengers back to see David and commanded them, "Bring him up to me in the bed, that I may kill him." 16 But when the messengers entered, they found the household idol in the bed, with the net of goat's hair at its head. 17 Saul therefore asked Michal: "Why did you play this trick on me? You have helped my enemy to get away!" Michal answered Saul: "He threatened me, 'Let me go or I will kill you.' "

David and Samuel in Ramah 18 Thus David got safely away; he went to Samuel in Ramah, informing him of all that Saul had done to him. Then he and Samuel went to stay in the sheds. 19 When Saul was told that David was in the sheds near Ramah, 20 he sent messengers to arrest David. But when they saw the band of prophets, presided over by Samuel, in a prophetic frenzy, they too fell into the prophetic state.[s] 21 Informed of this, Saul sent other messengers, who also fell into the prophetic state. For the third time Saul sent messengers, but they too fell into the prophetic state.

Saul among the Prophets 22 Saul then went to Ramah himself. Arriving at the cistern of the threshing floor on the bare hilltop, he inquired, "Where are Samuel and David?", and was told, "At the sheds near Ramah." 23 As he set out from the hilltop toward the sheds, the spirit of God came upon him also, and he continued on in a prophetic condition until he reached the spot. At the sheds near Ramah 24 he, too, stripped himself of his garments and he, too, remained in the prophetic state in the presence of Samuel; all that day and night he lay naked. That is why they say, "Is Saul also among the prophets?"[t]

CHAPTER 20

David Consults with Jonathan 1 David fled from the sheds near Ramah, and went to Jonathan. "What have I done?" he asked him. "What crime or what offense does your father hold against me that he seeks my life?"[u] 2 Jonathan answered him: "Heaven forbid that you should die! My father does nothing, great or small, without disclosing it to me. Why, then, should my father conceal this from me? This cannot be so!" 3 But David replied: "Your father is well aware that I am favored with your friendship, so he has decided, 'Jonathan must not know of this lest he be grieved.' Nevertheless, as the LORD lives and as you live, there is but a step between me and death." 4 Jonathan then said to David, "I will do whatever you wish." 5 David answered: "Tomorrow is the new moon, when I should in fact dine with the king. Let me go and hide in the open country until evening.[v] 6 If it turns out that your father misses me, say, 'David urged me to let him go on short notice to his city Bethlehem, because his whole clan is holding its seasonal sacrifice there.' 7 If he says, 'Very well,' your servant is safe. But if he becomes quite angry, you can be sure he has planned some

19, 11: This story in all probability originally followed 1 Sm 18, 29, placing the episode of David's escape on the night of his marriage with Michal.

o Dt 19, 10; Ps 119, 109. p 9f: 1 Sm 16, 14; 18, 10f. q Jos 2, 15; Acts 9, 25; 2 Cor 11, 33. r Gn 31, 19; Jos 17, 5; 18, 14, 18. 20. s 1 Sm 10, 5f. 10; Nm 11, 25. t 1 Sm 10, 10ff. u 1 Sm 19, 1–7, 11–17 v Nm 10, 10; 28, 11–15.

harm. 8[w]Do this kindness for your servant be-
cause of the LORD's bond between us, into
which you brought me: if I am guilty, kill me
yourself! Why should you give me up to your
father?" 9But Jonathan answered: "Not I! If ever
I find out that my father is determined to inflict
injury upon you, I will certainly let you know."
10David then asked Jonathan, "Who will tell me
if your father gives you a harsh answer?"

Mutual Agreement 11[Jonathan replied to Da-
vid, "Come, let us go out into the field." When
they were out in the open country together,
12Jonathan said to David: "As the LORD, the God
of Israel, lives, I will sound out my father about
this time tomorrow. Whether he is well disposed
toward David or not, I will send you the
information. 13[x]Should it please my father to
bring any injury upon you, may the LORD do
thus and so to Jonathan if I do not apprise you of
it and send you on your way in peace. May the
LORD be with you even as he was with my
father. 14Only this: if I am still alive, may you
show me the kindness of the LORD. But if I die,
15never withdraw your kindness from my house.
And when the LORD exterminates all the ene-
mies of David from the surface of the earth,
16the name of Jonathan must never be allowed
by the family of David to die out from among
you, or the LORD will make you answer for it."
17And in his love for David, Jonathan renewed
his oath to him, because he loved him as his very
self.]

18Jonathan then said to him: "Tomorrow is
the new moon; and you will be missed, since
your place will be vacant. 19On the following
day you will be missed all the more. Go to the
spot where you hid on the other occasion and
wait near the mound there.[y] 20On the third day
of the month I will shoot arrows, as though
aiming at a target. 21I will then send my
attendant to go and recover the arrows. If in fact
I say to him, 'Look, the arrow is this side of you;
pick it up,' come, for you are safe. As the LORD
lives, there will be nothing to fear. 22But if I say
to the boy, 'Look, the arrow is beyond you,' go,
for the LORD sends you away. 23However, in the
matter which you and I have discussed, the
LORD shall be between you and me forever."
24So David hid in the open country.

On the day of the new moon, when the king
sat at table to dine, 25taking his usual place
against the wall, Jonathan sat facing him, while
Abner sat at the king's side, and David's place
was vacant. 26[z]Saul, however, said nothing that
day, for he thought, "He must have become
unclean by accident, and not yet have been
cleansed."* 27On the next day, the second day
of the month, David's place was vacant. Saul
inquired of his son Jonathan, "Why has the son
of Jesse not come to table yesterday or today?"
28Jonathan answered Saul: "David urgently
asked me to let him go to his city, Bethlehem.
29'Please let me go,' he begged, 'for we are to
have a clan sacrifice in our city, and my brothers
insist on my presence. Now, therefore, if you
think well of me, give me leave to visit my
brothers.' That is why he has not come to the
king's table." 30But Saul was extremely angry
with Jonathan and said to him: "Son of a
rebellious woman, do I not know that, to your
own shame and to the disclosure of your
mother's shame, you are the companion of
Jesse's son? 31Why, as long as the son of Jesse
lives upon the earth, you cannot make good your
claim to the kingship! So send for him, and bring
him to me, for he is doomed."[a] 32But Jonathan
asked his father Saul: "Why should he die? What
has he done?" 33At this Saul brandished his
spear to strike him, and thus Jonathan learned
that his father was resolved to kill David.[b]
34Jonathan sprang up from the table in great
anger and took no food that second day of the
month, for he was grieved on David's account,
since his father had railed against him.

Jonathan's Farewell 35The next morning
Jonathan went out into the field with a little
boy for his appointment with David. 36There he
said to the boy, "Run and fetch the arrow." And

20, 26: The meal on the first day of the month would have religious overtones, and a ritual impurity (Lv 15, 16; Dt 23, 10ff) would bar David from sharing in it.

w 8f: 1 Sm 23, 17f. x 13–16: 1 Sm 24, 22f; 2 Sm 9, 1–13; 21, 7. y 1 Sm 19, 1–7. z 1 Sm 16, 5; Lv 7, 20f; 15, 1ff. a 2 Sm 12, 5. b 1 Sm 18, 11.

as the boy ran, he shot an arrow beyond him in
the direction of the city. 37When the boy made
for the spot where Jonathan had shot the arrow,
Jonathan called after him, "The arrow is farther
on!" 38Again he called to his lad, "Hurry, be
quick, don't delay!" Jonathan's boy picked up
the arrow and brought it to his master. 39The
boy knew nothing; only Jonathan and David
knew what was meant. 40Then Jonathan gave
his weapons to this boy of his and said to him,
"Go, take them to the city." 41When the boy
had left, David rose from beside the mound and
prostrated himself on the ground three times
before Jonathan in homage. They kissed each
other and wept aloud together. 42 [c]At length
Jonathan said to David, "Go in peace, in keep-
ing with what we two have sworn by the name
of the LORD: 'The LORD shall be between you
and me, and between your posterity and mine
forever.' "

CHAPTER 21

1Then David departed on his way, while Jona-
than went back into the city.
The Holy Bread 2David went to Ahimelech,
the priest of Nob, who came trembling to meet
him and asked, "Why are you alone? Is there no
one with you?"[d] 3David answered the priest:
"The king gave me a commission and told me to
let no one know anything about the business on
which he sent me or the commission he gave
me. For that reason I have arranged a meeting
place with my men. 4 [e]Now what have you on
hand? Give me five loaves, or whatever you can
find." 5But the priest replied to David, "I have
no ordinary bread on hand, only holy bread; if
the men have abstained from women, you may
eat some of that."* 6David answered the priest:
"We have indeed been segregated from women
as on previous occasions. Whenever I go on a
journey, all the young men are consecrated—
even for a secular journey. All the more so today,
when they are consecrated at arms!" 7So the
priest gave him holy bread, for no other bread
was on hand except the showbread which had
been removed from the LORD's presence and
replaced by fresh bread when it was taken
away.[f] 8One of Saul's servants was there that
day, detained before the LORD; his name was
Doeg the Edomite, and he was Saul's chief
henchman.
The Sword of Goliath 9David then asked
Ahimelech: "Do you have a spear or a sword on
hand? I brought along neither my sword nor my
weapons, because the king's business was ur-
gent." 10The priest replied: "The sword of
Goliath the Philistine, whom you killed in the
Vale of the Terebinth, is here [wrapped in a
mantle] behind an ephod. If you wish to take
that, take it; there is no sword here except that
one." David said: "There is none to match it.
Give it to me!"[g]
David a Fugitive 11That same day David took
to flight from Saul, going to Achish, king of
Gath.[h] 12But the servants of Achish said, "Is this
not David, the king of the land? During their
dances do they not sing,

'Saul has slain his thousands,
but David his ten thousands'?"[i]

13David took note of these remarks and became
very much afraid of Achish, king of Gath. 14So,
as they watched, he feigned insanity and acted
like a madman in their hands, drumming on the
doors of the gate and drooling onto his beard.
15Finally Achish said to his servants: "You see
the man is mad. Why did you bring him to me?
16Do I not have enough madmen, that you bring
in this one to carry on in my presence? Should
this fellow come into my house?"

CHAPTER 22

1David left Gath and escaped to the cave of
Adullam. When his brothers and the rest of his
family heard about it, they came down to him
there.[j] 2He was joined by all those who were in
difficulties or in debt, or who were embittered,

21, 5f: From women: the high priest, willing to distribute the holy bread to David and his men, requires that they be free from ritual uncleanness, associated in Old Testament times (Lv 15, 18) with the marriage act. David's answer supposes the discipline of a military campaign under the conditions of "holy war" (Dt 23, 10).

c 2 Sm 9, 1; 21, 7. d Is 10, 32; Mk 2, 26. e Lv 24, 5. 9. f 1 Sm 22, 9; Lv 24, 5–9; Mt 12, 3f; Mk 2, 26; Lk 6, 3ff. g 1 Sm 17, 51, 54. h 1 Sm 27, 2; 29, 5. i 1 Sm 18, 7; 29, 5. j 2 Sm 23, 13; Ps 63; Mi 1, 15.

and he became their leader. About four hundred
men were with him.
3 From there David went to Mizpeh of Moab
and said to the king of Moab, "Let my father and
mother stay with you, until I learn what God
will do for me." 4 He left them with the king of
Moab, and they stayed with him as long as
David remained in the refuge.*
5 But the prophet Gad said to David: "Do not
remain in the refuge. Leave, and go to the land
of Judah." And so David left and went to the
forest of Hereth.

Doeg Betrays Ahimelech 6 Now Saul heard
that David and his men had been located. At the
time he was sitting in Gibeah under a tamarisk
tree on the high place, holding his spear, while
all his servants were standing by.[k] 7 So he said to
them: "Listen, men of Benjamin! Will the son of
Jesse give all of you fields and vineyards? Will he
make each of you an officer over a thousand or a
hundred men,[l] 8 that you have all conspired
against me and no one tells me that my son has
made an agreement with the son of Jesse? None
of you shows sympathy for me or discloses to me
that my son has stirred up my servant to be an
enemy against me, as is the case today." 9 [m]Then
Doeg the Edomite, who was standing with the
officers of Saul, spoke up: "I saw the son of Jesse
come to Ahimelech, son of Ahitub, in Nob. 10 He
consulted the LORD for him and gave him
supplies, and the sword of Goliath the Philistine
as well."

Slaughter of the Priests 11 At this the king sent
a summons to Ahimelech the priest, son of
Ahitub, and to all his family who were priests in
Nob; and they all came to the king. 12 Then Saul
said, "Listen, son of Ahitub!" He replied, "Yes,
my lord." 13 Saul asked him, "Why did you
conspire against me with the son of Jesse by
giving him food and a sword and by consulting
God for him, that he might rebel against me and
become my enemy, as is the case today?"
14 Ahimelech answered the king: "And who
among all your servants is as loyal as David, the
king's son-in-law, captain of your bodyguard, and
honored in your own house? 15 Is this the first
time I have consulted God for him? No indeed!
Let not the king accuse his servant or anyone in
my family of such a thing. Your servant knows
nothing at all, great or small, about the whole
matter." 16 But the king said, "You shall die,
Ahimelech, with all your family." 17 The king
then commanded his henchmen standing by:
"Make the rounds and kill the priests of the
LORD, for they assisted David. They knew he
was a fugitive and yet failed to inform me." But
the king's servants refused to lift a hand to strike
the priests of the LORD.[n]
18 The king therefore commanded Doeg, "You
make the rounds and kill the priests!" So Doeg
the Edomite went from one to the next and
killed the priests himself, slaying on that day
eighty-five who wore the linen ephod. 19 Saul
also put the priestly city of Nob to the sword,
including men and women, children and infants,
and oxen, asses and sheep.

Abiathar Escapes 20 One son of Ahimelech,
son of Ahitub, named Abiathar, escaped and fled
to David.[o] 21 When Abiathar told David that Saul
had slain the priests of the LORD, 22 David said to
him: "I knew that day, when Doeg the Edomite
was there, that he would surely tell Saul. I am
responsible for the death of all your family.
23 Stay with me. Fear nothing; he that seeks your
life must seek my life also. You are under my
protection."

CHAPTER 23

Keilah Liberated 1 David received information
that the Philistines were attacking Keilah and
plundering the threshing floors.[p] 2 So he con-
sulted the LORD, inquiring, "Shall I go and defeat
these Philistines?" The LORD answered, "Go, for
you will defeat the Philistines and rescue Kei-
lah."[q] 3 But David's men said to him: "We are
afraid here in Judah. How much more so if we
go to Keilah against the forces of the Philistines!"
4 Again David consulted the LORD, who an-

22, 4–5: Refuge: seemingly connected with the cave complex spoken of in v 1.

k Ps 52. l 1 Sm 8, 14. m 9f: 1 Sm 21, 2–10. n 1 Sm 2, 31. 33; 21, 7. o 1 Sm 23, 6; 30, 7; 1 Kgs 2, 28f. p Jos 15, 44. q 1 Sm 28, 6.

swered, "Go down to Keilah, for I will deliver
the Philistines into your power." 5David then
went with his men to Keilah and fought with the
Philistines. He drove off their cattle and inflicted
a severe defeat on them, and thus rescued the
inhabitants of Keilah.
6Abiathar, son of Ahimelech, who had fled to
David, went down with David to Keilah, taking
the ephod with him.[r]
Flight from Keilah 7When Saul was told that
David had entered Keilah, he said: "God has put
him in my grip. Now he has shut himself in, for
he has entered a city with gates and bars." 8Saul
then called all the people to war, in order to go
down to Keilah and besiege David and his men.
9When David found out that Saul was planning
to harm him, he said to the priest Abiathar,
"Bring forward the ephod."[s] 10David then said:
"O LORD God of Israel, your servant has heard a
report that Saul plans to come to Keilah, to
destroy the city on my account. 11Will they hand
me over? And now: will Saul come down as
your servant has heard? O LORD God of Israel,
tell your servant." The LORD answered, "He will
come down." 12David then asked, "Will the
citizens of Keilah deliver me and my men into
the grasp of Saul?" And the LORD answered,
"Yes." 13So David and his men, about six hun-
dred in number, left Keilah and wandered from
place to place. When Saul was informed that
David had escaped from Keilah, he abandoned
the expedition.
David and Jonathan in Horesh 14David now
lived in the refuges in the desert, or in the barren
hill country near Ziph. Though Saul sought him
continually, the LORD did not deliver David into
his grasp. 15David was apprehensive because
Saul had come out to seek his life; but while he
was at Horesh in the barrens near Ziph, 16Saul's
son, Jonathan, came down there to David and
strengthened his resolve in the LORD.[t] 17He said
to him: "Have no fear, my father Saul shall not
lay a hand to you. You shall be king of Israel and
I shall be second to you. Even my father Saul
knows this." 18They made a joint agreement
before the LORD in Horesh, where David re-
mained, while Jonathan returned to his home.[u]
Treachery of the Ziphites 19Some of the Ziph-
ites went up to Saul in Gibeah and said, "David
is hiding among us, now in the refuges, and
again at Horesh, or on the hill of Hachilah, south
of the wasteland.[v] 20Therefore, whenever the
king wishes to come down, let him do so. It will
be our task to deliver him into the king's grasp."
21Saul replied: "The LORD bless you for your
sympathy toward me.[w] 22Go now and make
sure once more! Take note of the place where he
sets foot" (for he thought, perhaps they are
playing some trick on me). 23"Look around and
learn in which of all the various hiding places he
is holding out. Then come back to me with sure
information, and I will go with you. If he is in
the region, I will search him out among all the
families of Judah." 24So they went off to Ziph
ahead of Saul. At this time David and his men
were in the desert below Maon, in the Arabah
south of the wasteland.[x]
Escape from Saul 25When Saul and his men
came looking for him, David got word of it and
went down to the gorge in the desert below
Maon. Saul heard of this and pursued David into
the desert below Maon. 26As Saul moved along
one rim of the gorge, David and his men took to
the other. David was in anxious flight to escape
Saul, and Saul and his men were attempting to
outflank David and his men in order to capture
them, 27when a messenger came to Saul, saying,
"Come quickly, because the Philistines have
invaded the land." 28Saul interrupted his pursuit
of David and went to meet the Philistines. This is
how that place came to be called the Gorge of
Divisions.

CHAPTER 24

David Spares Saul 1David then went up from
there and stayed in the refuges behind Engedi.
2And when Saul returned from the pursuit of the
Philistines, he was told that David was in the
desert near Engedi. 3So Saul took three thousand
picked men from all Israel and went in search of

r 1 Sm 22, 20; 30, 7. s 1 Sm 2, 28. t 1 Sm 18, 1. u 1 Sm 18, 3; 20, 8. v 1 Sm 26, 1–3; Ps 54. w 2 Sm 2, 5. x 1 Sm 25, 2.

David and his men in the direction of the wild
goat crags. 4When he came to the sheepfolds
along the way, he found a cave, which he
entered to ease nature. David and his men were
occupying the inmost recesses of the cave.[y]
5David's servants said to him, "This is the day
of which the LORD said to you, 'I will deliver
your enemy into your grasp; do with him as you
see fit.' " So David moved up and stealthily cut
off an end of Saul's mantle. 6Afterward, how-
ever, David regretted that he had cut off an end
of Saul's mantle.[z] 7He said to his men, "The
LORD forbid that I should do such a thing to my
master, the LORD's anointed, as to lay a hand on
him, for he is the LORD's anointed."[a] 8With
these words David restrained his men and would
not permit them to attack Saul. Saul then left the
cave and went on his way. 9David also stepped
out of the cave, calling to Saul, "My lord the
king!" When Saul looked back, David bowed to
the ground in homage 10and asked Saul: "Why
do you listen to those who say, 'David is trying to
harm you'? 11You see for yourself today that the
LORD just now delivered you into my grasp in
the cave. I had some thought of killing you, but I
took pity on you instead. I decided, 'I will not
raise a hand against my lord, for he is the LORD's
anointed and a father to me.' 12Look here at this
end of your mantle which I hold. Since I cut off
an end of your mantle and did not kill you, see
and be convinced that I plan no harm and no
rebellion. I have done you no wrong, though you
are hunting me down to take my life.[b] 13The
LORD will judge between me and you, and the
LORD will exact justice from you in my case. I
shall not touch you. 14The old proverb says,
'From the wicked comes forth wickedness.' So I
will take no action against you. 15Against whom
are you on campaign, O king of Israel? Whom
are you pursuing? A dead dog, or a single flea!
16The LORD will be the judge; he will decide
between me and you. May he see this, and take
my part, and grant me justice beyond your
reach!"[c]

Saul's Remorse 17When David finished saying
these things to Saul, Saul answered, "Is that your
voice, my son David?" And he wept aloud.
18Saul then said to David: "You are in the right
rather than I; you have treated me generously,
while I have done you harm. 19Great is the
generosity you showed me today, when the
LORD delivered me into your grasp and you did
not kill me. 20For if a man meets his enemy, does
he send him away unharmed? May the LORD
reward you generously for what you have done
this day. 21And now, since I know that you shall
surely be king and that sovereignty over Israel
shall come into your possession,[d] 22swear to me
by the LORD that you will not destroy my
descendants and that you will not blot out my
name and family."[e] 23David gave Saul his oath
and Saul returned home, while David and his
men went up to the refuge.

CHAPTER 25

Death of Samuel 1Samuel died, and all Israel
gathered to mourn him; they buried him at his
home in Ramah.[f]

Nabal and Abigail 2Then David went down to
the desert of Maon. There was a man of Maon
who had property in Carmel; he was very
wealthy, owning three thousand sheep and a
thousand goats. At this time he was present for
the shearing of his flock in Carmel.[g] 3The man
was named Nabal, his wife, Abigail. The woman
was intelligent and attractive, but Nabal himself,
a Calebite, was harsh and ungenerous in his
behavior.[h] 4When David heard in the desert that
Nabal was shearing his flock, 5he sent ten young
men, instructing them: "Go up to Carmel. Pay
Nabal a visit and greet him in my name. 6Say to
him, 'Peace be with you, my brother, and with
your family, and with all who belong to you. 7I
have just heard that shearers are with you. Now,
when your shepherds were with us, we did
them no injury, neither did they miss anything
all the while they were in Carmel. 8Ask your
servants and they will tell you so. Look kindly on

y Ps 57. z 1 Sm 15, 27. a 1 Sm 10, 1; 31, 4; 2 Sm 1, 14. b Rom 12, 19. c 1 Sm 18, 19. 31; 26, 19; Pss 35, 1ff; 43, 1. d 1 Sm 26, 25. e 2 Sm 9, 1ff. f 1 Sm 28, 3; Sir 46, 13–20.

g 1 Sm 23, 24; Jos 15, 55. h 1 Sm 27, 3; Jos 14, 6; 1 Chr 2, 42. 45.

these young men, since we come at a festival
time. Please give your servants and your son
David whatever you can manage.' "
9 When David's young men arrived, they deliv-
ered this message fully to Nabal in David's name,
and then waited. 10 But Nabal answered the
servants of David: "Who is David? Who is the
son of Jesse? Nowadays there are many servants
who run away from their masters. 11 Must I take
my bread, my wine, my meat that I have
slaughtered for my own shearers, and give them
to men who come from I know not where?"
12 So David's young men retraced their steps and
on their return reported to him all that had been
said. 13 Thereupon David said to his men, "Let
everyone gird on his sword." And so everyone,
David included, girded on his sword. About four
hundred men went up after David, while two
hundred remained with the baggage.

14 But Nabal's wife Abigail was informed of
this by one of the servants, who said: "David
sent messengers from the desert to greet our
master, but he flew at them screaming. 15 Yet
these men were very good to us. We were done
no injury, neither did we miss anything all the
while we were living among them during our
stay in the open country. 16 For us they were like
a rampart night and day the whole time we were
pasturing the sheep near them. 17 Now, see what
you can do, for you must realize that otherwise
evil is in store for our master and for his whole
family. He is so mean that no one can talk to
him." 18 Abigail quickly got together two hun-
dred loaves, two skins of wine, five dressed
sheep, five seahs of roasted grain, a hundred
cakes of pressed raisins, and two hundred cakes
of pressed figs, and loaded them on asses. 19 She
then said to her servants, "Go on ahead; I will
follow you." But she did not tell her husband
Nabal.

20 As she came down through a mountain
defile riding on an ass, David and his men were
also coming down from the opposite direction.
When she met them, 21 David had just been
saying: "Indeed, it was in vain that I guarded all
this man's possessions in the desert, so that he
missed nothing. He has repaid good with evil.
22 May God do thus and so to David, if by
morning I leave a single male alive among all
those who belong to him." [i] 23 As soon as Abigail
saw David, she dismounted quickly from the ass
and, falling prostrate on the ground before
David, did him homage. 24 As she fell at his feet
she said:

"My lord, let the blame be mine. Please let
your handmaid speak to you, and listen to the
words of your handmaid. 25 Let not my lord pay
attention to that worthless man Nabal, for he is
just like his name. Fool is his name,* and he acts
the fool. I, your handmaid, did not see the young
men whom my lord sent. 26 Now, therefore, my
lord, as the LORD lives, and as you live, it is the
LORD who has kept you from shedding blood
and from avenging yourself personally. May your
enemies and those who seek to harm my lord
become as Nabal!* 27 Accept this present, then,
which your maidservant has brought for my
lord, and let it be given to the young men who
follow my lord. 28 Please forgive the transgres-
sion of your handmaid, for the LORD shall
certainly establish a lasting dynasty for my lord,
because your lordship is fighting the battles of
the LORD, and there is no evil to be found in you
your whole life long. 29 If anyone rises to pursue
you and to seek your life, may the life of my lord
be bound in the bundle of the living* in the care
of the LORD your God; but may he hurl out the
lives of your enemies as from the hollow of a
sling. [j] 30 And when the LORD carries out for my
lord the promise of success he has made concern-
ing you, and appoints you as commander over
Israel, [k] 31 you shall not have this as a qualm or
burden on your conscience, my lord, for having
shed innocent blood or for having avenged

25, 25: Fool is his name: Nabal in Hebrew means "a fool."
25, 26: Abigail anticipates that some misfortune will shortly overtake Nabal, as in fact it does (vv 37–38).
25, 29: The bundle of the living: the figure is perhaps taken from the practice of tying up valuables in a kerchief or bag for safekeeping. Abigail desires that David enjoy permanent peace and security, but that his enemies be subject to constant agitation and humiliation like a stone whirled about, cast out of the sling, and thereafter disregarded.

i 1 Kgs 16, 11; 21, 21; 2 Kgs 9, 8. j Ps 69, 28. k 1 Sm 13, 14; 2 Sm 3, 10.

yourself personally. When the LORD confers this benefit on your lordship, remember your handmaid." [32]David said to Abigail: "Blessed be the LORD, the God of Israel, who sent you to meet me today. [33]Blessed be your good judgment and blessed be you yourself, who this day have prevented me from shedding blood and from avenging myself personally. [34]Otherwise, as the LORD, the God of Israel, lives, who has restrained me from harming you, if you had not come so promptly to meet me, by dawn Nabal would not have had a single man or boy left alive." [35]David then took from her what she had brought him and said to her: "Go up to your home in peace! See, I have granted your request as a personal favor."

Nabal's Death [36]When Abigail came to Nabal, there was a drinking party in his house like that of a king, and Nabal was merry because he was very drunk. So she told him nothing at all before daybreak the next morning. [37]But then, when Nabal had become sober, his wife told him what had happened. At this his courage died within him, and he became like a stone. [38]About ten days later the LORD struck him and he died. [39]On hearing that Nabal was dead, David said: "Blessed be the LORD, who has requited the insult I received at the hand of Nabal, and who restrained his servant from doing evil, but has punished Nabal for his own evil deeds."

David Marries Abigail and Ahinoam David then sent a proposal of marriage to Abigail. [40]When David's servants came to Abigail in Carmel, they said to her, "David has sent us to you that he may take you as his wife." [41]Rising and bowing to the ground, she answered, "Your handmaid would become a slave to wash the feet of my lord's servants." [42]She got up immediately, mounted an ass, and followed David's messengers, with her five maids following in attendance upon her. She became his wife, [43] [l]and David also married Ahinoam of Jezreel. Thus both of them were his wives; but Saul gave David's wife Michal, Saul's own daughter, to Palti, son of Laish, who was from Gallim. [m]

CHAPTER 26

Saul's Life Again Spared [1] [n]Men from Ziph came to Saul in Gibeah, reporting that David was hiding on the hill of Hachilah at the edge of the wasteland. [2]So Saul went off down to the desert of Ziph with three thousand picked men of Israel, to search for David in the desert of Ziph. [3]Saul camped beside the road on the hill of Hachilah, at the edge of the wasteland. David, who was living in the desert, saw that Saul had come into the desert after him [4]and sent out scouts, who confirmed Saul's arrival. [5]David himself then went to the place where Saul was encamped and examined the spot where Saul and Abner, son of Ner, the general, had their sleeping quarters. Saul's were within the barricade, and all his soldiers were camped around him. [o] [6]David asked Ahimelech the Hittite, and Abishai, son of Zeruiah and brother of Joab, "Who will go down into the camp with me to Saul?" Abishai replied, "I will." [p] [7]So David and Abishai went among Saul's soldiers by night and found Saul lying asleep within the barricade, with his spear thrust into the ground at his head and Abner and his men sleeping around him.

[8]Abishai whispered to David: "God has delivered your enemy into your grasp this day. Let me nail him to the ground with one thrust of the spear; I will not need a second thrust!" [q] [9]But David said to Abishai, "Do not harm him, for who can lay hands on the LORD's anointed and remain unpunished? [10]As the LORD lives," David continued, "it must be the LORD himself who will strike him, whether the time comes for him to die, or he goes out and perishes in battle. [11]But the LORD forbid that I touch his anointed! Now take the spear which is at his head and the water jug, and let us be on our way." [12]So David took the spear and the water jug from their place at Saul's head, and they got away without anyone's seeing or knowing or awakening. All remained asleep, because the LORD had put them into a deep slumber.

David Taunts Abner [13]Going across to an opposite slope, David stood on a remote hilltop

l 1 Sm 27, 3. m 1 Sm 18, 20; 27, 3; 30, 5; 2 Sm 3, 2. 13ff; 1 Chr 3, 1. n 1f: 1 Sm 23, 19f; Ps 54. o 1 Sm 17, 20. p 1 Chr 2, 16. q 1 Sm 18, 11; 19, 10.

at a great distance from Abner, son of Ner, and the troops. 14He then shouted, "Will you not answer, Abner?" And Abner answered, "Who is it that calls me?" 15David said to Abner: "Are you not a man whose like does not exist in Israel? Why, then, have you not guarded your lord the king when one of his subjects went to kill the king, your lord? 16This is no creditable service you have performed. As the LORD lives, you people deserve death because you have not guarded your lord, the LORD's anointed. Go, look: where are the king's spear and the water jug that was at his head?"

Saul Admits His Guilt 17Saul recognized David's voice and asked, "Is that your voice, my son David?" David answered, "Yes, my lord the king." 18He continued: "Why does my lord pursue his servant? What have I done? What evil do I plan? 19Please, now, let my lord the king listen to the words of his servant. If the LORD has incited you against me, let an offering appease him; but if men, may they be cursed before the LORD, because they have exiled me so that this day I have no share in the LORD's inheritance,* but am told: 'Go, serve other gods!'[r] 20Do not let my blood flow to the ground far from the presence of the LORD. For the king of Israel has come out to seek a single flea as if he were hunting partridge in the mountains." 21Then Saul said: "I have done wrong. Come back, my son David, I will not harm you again, because you have held my life precious today. Indeed, I have been a fool and have made a serious mistake." 22But David answered: "Here is the king's spear. Let an attendant come over to get it. 23The LORD will reward each man for his justice and faithfulness. Today, though the LORD delivered you into my grasp, I would not harm the LORD's anointed.[s] 24As I valued your life highly today, so may the LORD value my life highly and deliver me from all difficulties." 25Then Saul said to David: "Blessed are you, my son David! You shall certainly succeed in whatever you undertake." David went his way, and Saul returned to his home.[t]

CHAPTER 27

Refuge among Philistines 1But David said to himself: "I shall perish some day at the hand of Saul. I have no choice but to escape to the land of the Philistines; then Saul will give up his continuous search for me throughout the land of Israel, and I shall be out of his reach." 2Accordingly, David departed with his six hundred men and went over to Achish, son of Maoch, king of Gath.[u] 3David and his men lived in Gath with Achish; each one had his family, and David had his two wives, Ahinoam from Jezreel and Abigail, the widow of Nabal from Carmel.[v] 4When Saul was told that David had fled to Gath, he no longer searched for him.

In Ziklag 5David said to Achish: "If I meet with your approval, let me have a place to live in one of the country towns. Why should your servant live with you in the royal city?" 6That same day Achish gave him Ziklag, which has, therefore, belonged to the kings of Judah* up to the present time.[w] 7In all, David lived a year and four months in the country of the Philistines.[x]

Raids on Israel's Foes 8David and his men went up and made raids on the Geshurites, Girzites, and Amalekites—peoples living in the land between Telam, on the approach to Shur, and the land of Egypt.[y] 9In attacking the land David would not leave a man or woman alive, but would carry off sheep, oxen, asses, camels, and clothes. On his return he brought these to Achish, 10who asked, "Whom did you raid this time?" And David answered, "The Negeb of Judah," or "The Negeb of Jarahmeel," or "The Negeb of the Kenites."[z] 11But David would not leave a man or woman alive to be brought to Gath, fearing that they would betray him by saying, "This is what David did." This was his

26, 19: The Lord's inheritance: the land of Israel (Dt 32, 8f), under the Lord's special protection, where he could be freely worshiped.

27, 6: Has . . . belonged to the kings of Judah: as a personal holding, outside the system of tribal lands; Jerusalem, when taken by David, had a similar status (2 Sm 5, 7–9).

r 1 Sm 24, 16. s 1 Sm 18, 20. t 1 Sm 24, 21. u 1 Sm 21, 11–16. v 1 Sm 25, 3. 44; 30, 3ff; 2 Sm 2, 3. w 1 Sm 30, 1. x 1 Sm 29, 3. y 1 Sm 15, 3, 7. z 1 Sm 30, 14, 29; 1 Chr 2, 9. 25. 42.

custom as long as he lived in the country of the Philistines. 12And Achish trusted David, thinking, "He must certainly be detested by his people Israel. I shall have him as my vassal forever."

CHAPTER 28

1In those days the Philistines mustered their military forces to fight against Israel. So Achish said to David, "You realize, of course, that you and your men must go out on campaign with me to Jezreel." 2David answered Achish, "Good! Now you shall learn what your servant can do." Then Achish said to David, "I shall appoint you my permanent bodyguard."

3Now Samuel had died and, after being mourned by all Israel, was buried in his city, Ramah. Meanwhile Saul had driven mediums and fortune-tellers out of the land.[a]

Saul in Dismay 4The Philistine levies advanced to Shunem and encamped. Saul, too, mustered all Israel; they camped on Gilboa. 5When Saul saw the camp of the Philistines, he was dismayed and lost heart completely. 6He therefore consulted the LORD; but the LORD gave no answer, whether in dreams or by the Urim or through prophets.[b] 7Then Saul said to his servants, "Find me a woman who is a medium, to whom I can go to seek counsel through her." His servants answered him, "There is a woman in Endor who is a medium."[c]

The Witch of Endor 8So he disguised himself, putting on other clothes, and set out with two companions. They came to the woman by night, and Saul said to her, "Tell my fortune through a ghost; conjure up for me the one I ask you to."[d] 9But the woman answered him, "You are surely aware of what Saul has done, in driving the mediums and fortune-tellers out of the land. Why, then, are you laying snares for my life, to have me killed?" 10But Saul swore to her by the LORD, "As the LORD lives, you shall incur no blame for this." 11Then the woman asked him, "Whom do you want me to conjure up?" and he answered, "Samuel."

Samuel Appears 12When the woman saw Samuel, she shrieked at the top of her voice and said to Saul, "Why have you deceived me? You are Saul!"* 13But the king said to her, "Have no fear. What do you see?" The woman answered Saul, "I see a preternatural being rising from the earth." 14"What does he look like?" asked Saul. And she replied, "It is an old man who is rising, clothed in a mantle." Saul knew that it was Samuel, and so he bowed face to the ground in homage.

Saul's Doom 15Samuel then said to Saul, "Why do you disturb me by conjuring me up?" Saul replied: "I am in great straits, for the Philistines are waging war against me and God has abandoned me. Since he no longer answers me through prophets or in dreams, I have called you to tell me what I should do."[e] 16To this Samuel said: "But why do you ask me, if the LORD has abandoned you and is with your neighbor?[f] 17The LORD has done to you what he foretold through me: he has torn the kingdom from your grasp and has given it to your neighbor David.

18"Because you disobeyed the LORD's directive and would not carry out his fierce anger against Amalek, the LORD has done this to you today.[g] 19Moreover, the LORD will deliver Israel, and you as well, into the clutches of the Philistines. By tomorrow you and your sons will be with me, and the LORD will have delivered the army of Israel into the hands of the Philistines."[h]

Saul's Despair 20Immediately Saul fell full length on the ground, for he was badly shaken by Samuel's message. Moreover, he had no bodily strength left, since he had eaten nothing all that day and night. 21Then the woman came to Saul, and seeing that he was quite terror-stricken, said to him: "Remember, your maidservant obeyed you: I took my life in my hands and fulfilled the request you made of me. 22Now

28, 12: Human beings cannot communicate at will with the souls of the dead. God may, however, permit a departed soul to appear to the living and even to disclose things unknown to them. Saul's own prohibition of necromancy and divination (v 3) was in keeping with the consistent teaching of the Old Testament. If we are to credit the reality of the apparition to Saul, it was due, not to the summons of the witch, but to God's will; the woman merely furnished the occasion.

a 1 Sm 25, 1; Sir 46, 20. b 1 Sm 14, 37. 41; Ex 28, 30; Lv 8, 8. c Lv 19, 31; 20, 27; Dt 18, 10ff; 1 Chr 10, 13f; Acts 16, 16. d 1 Kgs 14, 2. e Sir 46, 20. f 1 Sm 15, 27f. g 1 Sm 15, 18f. 26. h 1 Sm 31, 2–6; Sir 46, 20.

you, in turn, please listen to your maidservant. Let me set something before you to eat, so that you may have strength when you go on your way." 23But he refused, saying, "I will not eat." However, when his servants joined the woman in urging him, he listened to their entreaties, got up from the ground, and sat on a couch. 24The woman had a stall-fed calf in the house, which she now quickly slaughtered. Then taking flour, she kneaded it and baked unleavened bread. 25She set the meal before Saul and his servants, and they ate. Then they stood up and left the same night.

CHAPTER 29

David's Aid Rejected 1Now the Philistines had mustered all their forces in Aphek, and the Israelites were encamped at the spring of Harod near Jezreel.[i] 2As the Philistine lords were marching their groups of a hundred and a thousand, David and his men were marching in the rear guard with Achish. 3The Philistine chiefs asked, "What are those Hebrews doing here?" And Achish answered them: "Why, that is David, the officer of Saul, king of Israel. He has been with me now for a year or two, and I have no fault to find with him from the day he came over to me until the present."[j] 4But the Philistine chiefs were angered at this and said to him: "Send that man back! Let him return to the place you picked out for him. He must not go down into battle with us, lest during the battle he become our enemy. For how else can he win back his master's favor, if not with the heads of these men of ours?[k] 5Is this not the David of whom they sing during their dances,

'Saul has slain his thousands,
but David his ten thousands'?"[l]

6So Achish summoned David and said to him: "As the LORD lives, you are honest, and I should be pleased to have you active with me in the camp, for I have found nothing wrong with you from the day of your arrival to this day. But you are not welcome to the lords. 7Withdraw peaceably, now, and do nothing that might displease the Philistine lords." 8But David said to Achish: "What have I done? Or what have you against your servant from the first day I have been with you to this day, that I cannot go to fight against the enemies of my lord the king?" 9"You know," Achish answered David, "that you are acceptable to me. But the Philistine chiefs have determined you are not to go up with us to battle. 10So the first thing tomorow, you and your lord's servants who came with you, go to the place I picked out for you. Do not decide to take umbrage at this; you are as acceptable to me as an angel of God. But make an early morning start, as soon as it grows light, and be on your way." 11So David and his men left early in the morning to return to the land of the Philistines. The Philistines, however, went on up to Jezreel.

CHAPTER 30

Ziklag in Ruins 1Before David and his men reached Ziklag on the third day, the Amalekites had raided the Negeb and Ziklag, had stormed the city, and had set it on fire.[m] 2They had taken captive the women and all who were in the city, young and old, killing no one; they had carried them off when they left. 3David and his men arrived at the city to find it burned to the ground and their wives, sons and daughters taken captive. 4Then David and those who were with him wept aloud until they could weep no more. 5David's two wives, Ahinoam of Jezreel and Abigail, the widow of Nabal from Carmel, had also been carried off with the rest.[n] 6Now David found himself in great difficulty, for the men spoke of stoning him, so bitter were they over the fate of their sons and daughters. But with renewed trust in the LORD his God, 7 [o]David said to Abiathar, the priest, son of Ahimelech, "Bring me the ephod!" When Abiathar brought him the ephod, 8David inquired of the LORD, "Shall I pursue these raiders? Can I overtake them?" The LORD answered him, "Go in pursuit, for you shall surely overtake them and effect a rescue."

Raid of the Amalekites 9So David went off with his six hundred men and came as far as the Wadi Besor, where those who were to remain

i 1 Sm 4, 1. j 1 Sm 27, 7. k 1 Chr 12, 19f. l 1 Sm 18, 6f; 21, 11. m 1 Sm 27, 6. 10; 1 Chr 12, 21. n 1 Sm 25, 42; 27, 3; 30, 5. o 7f: 1 Sm 2, 28; 23, 6; Ex 28, 30.

behind halted. 10David continued the pursuit
with four hundred men, but two hundred were
too exhausted to cross the Wadi Besor and
remained behind. 11An Egyptian was found in
the open country and brought to David. He was
provided with food, which he ate, and given
water to drink; 12a cake of pressed figs and two
cakes of pressed raisins were also offered to him.
When he had eaten, he revived; he had not
taken food nor drunk water for three days and
three nights. 13Then David asked him, "To
whom do you belong, and where do you come
from?" He replied: "I am an Egyptian, the slave
of an Amalekite. My master abandoned me
because I fell sick three days ago today. 14We
raided the Negeb of the Cherethites, the territory
of Judah, and the Negeb of Caleb; and we set
Ziklag on fire."[p] 15David then asked him, "Will
you lead me down to this raiding party?" He
answered, "Swear to me by God that you will
not kill me or deliver me to my master, and I will
lead you to the raiding party." 16He did lead
them, and there were the Amalekites scattered
all over the ground, eating, drinking, and in a
festive mood because of all the rich booty they
had taken from the land of the Philistines and
from the land of Judah.

The Booty Recovered 17From dawn to sun-
down David attacked them, putting them under
the ban so that none escaped except four hun-
dred young men, who mounted their camels and
fled.[q] 18David recovered everything the Amalek-
ites had taken, and rescued his two wives.
19Nothing was missing, small or great, booty or
sons or daughters, of all that the Amalekites had
taken. David brought back everything. 20More-
over, David took all the sheep and oxen, and as
they drove them before him, they shouted, "This
is David's spoil."

Division of the Spoils 21When David came to
the two hundred men who had been too ex-
hausted to follow him, and whom he had left
behind at the Wadi Besor, they came out to meet
David and the men with him. On nearing them
David greeted them. 22But all the stingy and
worthless men among those who had accompa-
nied David spoke up to say, "Since they did not
accompany us, we will not give them anything
from the booty, except to each man his wife and
children. Let them take those along and be on
their way." 23But David said: "You must not do
this, my brothers, after what the LORD has given
us. He has protected us and delivered into our
grip the band that came against us. 24Who could
agree with this proposal of yours? Rather, the
share of the one who goes down to battle and
that of the one who remains with the baggage
shall be the same; they shall share alike."[r] 25And
from that day forward he made it a law and a
custom in Israel, as it still is today.[s]

David's Gifts to Judah 26When David came to
Ziklag, he sent part of the spoil to the elders of
Judah, city by city, saying, "This is a gift to you
from the spoil of the enemies of the LORD": 27to
those in Bethel, to those in Ramoth-negeb, to
those in Jattir, 28to those in Aroer, to those in
Siphmoth, to those in Eshtemoa, 29to those in
Racal, to those in the Jerahmeelite cities, to those
in the Kenite cities,[t] 30to those in Hormah, to
those in Borashan, to those in Athach, 31to those
in Hebron, and to all the places frequented by
David and his men.

CHAPTER 31

Death of Saul and His Sons 1 [u]As they pressed
their attack on Israel, with the Israelites fleeing
before them and falling mortally wounded on
Mount Gilboa, 2the Philistines pursued Saul and
his sons closely, and slew Jonathan, Abinadab,
and Malchishua, sons of Saul.[v] 3The battle raged
around Saul, and the archers hit him; he was
pierced through the abdomen. 4Then Saul said
to his armor-bearer, "Draw your sword and run
me through, lest these uncircumcised come and
make sport of me." But his armor-bearer, badly
frightened, refused to do it. So Saul took his own
sword and fell upon it.[w] 5 [x]When the armor-
bearer saw that Saul was dead, he too fell upon
his sword and died with him.* 6Thus Saul, his

31, 5: This report of the suicidal act of Saul is presented as a part of his downfall, to be judged accordingly.

p 1 Sm 27, 10; Ez 25, 16. q 1 Sm 15, 3; Jos 6, 17; Jgs 7, 12. r 1 Sm 17, 22; 25, 13. s Nm 31, 27. t 1 Sm 27, 10. u 1–13: 1 Chr 10, 1–12; 2 Sm 1, 1–16; 4, 4. v 1 Sm 14, 49; 28, 19; 1 Chr 10, 2f. w 1 Sm 24, 7; Jgs 9, 54; 1 Chr 10, 4. x 1 Sm 10, 1; 26, 9; 2 Mc 14, 42.

three sons, and his armor-bearer died together
on that same day.
7When the Israelites on the slope of the valley
and those along the Jordan saw that the men of
Israel had fled and that Saul and his sons were
dead, they too abandoned their cities and fled.
Then the Philistines came and lived in those
cities.
8The day after the battle the Philistines came
to strip the slain, and found Saul and his three
sons lying on Mount Gilboa. 9They cut off Saul's
head and stripped him of his armor, and then
sent the good news throughout the land of the
Philistines to their idols and to the people.[y]
10They put his armor in the temple of Astarte,
but impaled his body on the wall of Beth-shan.
Burial of Saul 11 [z]When the inhabitants of
Jabesh-gilead heard what the Philistines had
done to Saul, 12all their warriors set out, and
after marching throughout the night, removed
the bodies of Saul and his sons from the wall of
Beth-shan, and brought them to Jabesh, where
they cremated them.* 13Then they took their
bones and buried them under the tamarisk tree
in Jabesh, and fasted for seven days.

31, 12: Cremated them: cremation was not normally practiced in Israel, though it was known in the country from pre-Israelite times.

y 1 Sm 17, 54; 2 Sm 1, 20; 2 Mc 15, 35. z 11ff: 1 Sm 11, 1–11; 2 Sm 2, 4–7.

THE SECOND BOOK OF SAMUEL

CHAPTER 1

Report of Saul's Death 1After the death of
Saul, David returned from his defeat of the
Amalekites and spent two days in Ziklag.[a] 2On
the third day a man came from Saul's camp,
with his clothes torn and dirt on his head. Going
to David, he fell to the ground in homage.
3David asked him, "Where do you come from?"
He replied, "I have escaped from the Israelite
camp." 4"Tell me what happened," David bade
him. He answered that the soldiers had fled the
battle and that many of them had fallen and
were dead, among them Saul and his son Jona-
than. 5Then David said to the youth who was
reporting to him, "How do you know that Saul
and his son Jonathan are dead?" 6 [b]The youthful
informant replied: "It was by chance that I found
myself on Mount Gilboa and saw Saul leaning on
his spear, with chariots and horsemen closing in
on him. 7He turned around and, seeing me,
called me to him. When I said, 'Here I am,' 8he
asked me, 'Who are you?' and I replied, 'An
Amalekite.' 9Then he said to me, 'Stand up to
me, please, and finish me off, for I am in great
suffering, yet fully alive.' 10So I stood up to him
and dispatched him, for I knew that he could not
survive his wound. I removed the crown from
his head and the armlet from his arm and
brought them here to my lord."
11David seized his garments and rent them,
and all the men who were with him did like-
wise.[c] 12They mourned and wept and fasted
until evening for Saul and his son Jonathan, and
for the soldiers of the LORD of the clans of Israel,
because they had fallen by the sword.[d] 13Then
David said to the young man who had brought
him the information, "Where are you from?" He
replied, "I am the son of an Amalekite immi-
grant." 14David said to him, "How is it that you
were not afraid to put forth your hand to
desecrate the LORD's anointed?"[e] 15David then
called one of the attendants and said to him,
"Come, strike him down"; and the youth struck
him a mortal blow. 16Meanwhile David said to
him, "You are responsible for your own death,
for you testified against yourself when you said,
'I dispatched the LORD's anointed.' "
Elegy for Saul and Jonathan 17Then David
chanted this elegy for Saul and his son Jonathan,

a 1 Sm 30, 17–20; 31, 1–13. b 6–10: 2 Sm 4, 10; 1 Sm 31, 1–4; 1 Chr 10, 1–4. c 2 Sm 13, 31. d 1 Sm 31, 13. e 1 Sm 10, 1; 24, 7; Ps. 105, 15.

18 which is recorded in the Book of Jashar to be
taught to the Judahites. He sang:[f]

19 "Alas! the glory of Israel, Saul,
slain upon your heights;
how can the warriors have fallen!

20 "Tell it not in Gath,
herald it not in the streets of Ashkelon,
Lest the Philistine maidens rejoice,
lest the daughters of the strangers exult![g]
21 Mountains of Gilboa,
may there be neither dew nor rain upon
you,
nor upsurgings of the deeps!*
Upon you lie begrimed the warriors' shields,
the shield of Saul, no longer anointed with
oil.[h]

22 "From the blood of the slain,
from the bodies of the valiant,
The bow of Jonathan did not turn back,
or the sword of Saul return unstained.[i]
23 Saul and Jonathan, beloved and cherished,
separated neither in life nor in death,
swifter than eagles, stronger than lions!
24 Women of Israel, weep over Saul,
who clothed you in scarlet and in finery,
who decked your attire with ornaments of
gold.

25 "How can the warriors have fallen—
in the thick of the battle,
slain upon your heights!
26 "I grieve for you, Jonathan my brother!
most dear have you been to me;
More precious have I held love for you
than love for women.[j]

27 "How can the warriors have fallen,
the weapons of war have perished!"

CHAPTER 2

David Anointed King 1 After this David in-
quired of the LORD, "Shall I go up into one of the
cities of Judah?" The LORD replied to him, "Yes."
Then David asked, "Where shall I go?" He
replied, "To Hebron." 2 So David went up there
accompanied by his two wives, Ahinoam of
Jezreel and Abigail, the widow of Nabal of
Carmel.[k] 3 David also brought up his men with
their families, and they dwelt in the cities near
Hebron. 4 Then the men of Judah came there and
anointed David king of the Judahites.[l]

A report reached David that the men of
Jabesh-gilead had buried Saul. 5 So David sent
messengers to the men of Jabesh-gilead and said
to them: "May you be blessed by the LORD for
having done this kindness to your lord Saul in
burying him. 6 And now may the LORD be kind
and faithful to you. I, too, will be generous to
you for having done this. 7 Take courage, there-
fore, and prove yourselves valiant men, for
though your lord Saul is dead, the Judahites have
anointed me their king."

IV: The Reign of David

Ishbaal King of Israel 8 Abner, son of Ner,
Saul's general, took Ishbaal, son of Saul, and
brought him over to Mahanaim,[m] 9 where he
made him king over Gilead, the Ashurites,
Jezreel, Ephraim, Benjamin, and the rest of
Israel. 10 Ishbaal, son of Saul, was forty years old
when he became king over Israel, and he
reigned for two years. The Judahites alone fol-
lowed David. 11 In all, David spent seven years
and six months in Hebron as king of the Ju-
dahites.[n]

Combat near Gibeon 12 Now Abner, son of
Ner, and the servants of Ishbaal, Saul's son, left
Mahanaim for Gibeon. 13 Joab, son of Zeruiah,
and David's servants also set out and met them
at the pool of Gibeon. And they sat down, one
group on one side of the pool and the other on
the opposite side. 14 Then Abner said to Joab,
"Let the young men rise and perform for us."
Joab replied, "All right!" 15 So they rose and were
counted off: twelve of the Benjaminites of
Ishbaal, son of Saul, and twelve of David's

1, 21: Upsurgings of the deeps: this reading attempts to recover from an unintelligible Hebrew phrase the poetic parallel to dew and rain. The sense would be a wish that the mountain should have neither moisture from above nor water from springs or wells.

f Jos 10, 13. g Jgs 16, 23; 1 Sm 31, 9; Mi 1, 10. h Gn 27, 28. i 1 Sm 14, 47. j 1 Sm 18, 1; 1 Mc 9, 21. k 1 Sm 25, 42f. l 1 Sm 31, 11ff. m 1 Sm 14, 50. n 2 Sm 5, 5; 1 Kgs 2, 11.

servants. [16]Then each one grasped his oppo-
nent's head and thrust his sword into his oppo-
nent's side, and all fell down together.* And so
that place, which is in Gibeon, was named the
Field of the Sides.
Death of Asahel [17]After a very fierce battle
that day, Abner and the men of Israel were
defeated by David's servants. [18]The three sons of
Zeruiah were there—Joab, Abishai, and Asahel.
Asahel, who was as fleet of foot as a gazelle in
the open field,[o] [19]set out after Abner, turning
neither right nor left in his pursuit.[p] [20]Abner
turned around and said, "Is that you, Asahel?"
He replied, "Yes." [21]Abner said to him, "Turn
right or left; seize one of the young men and
take what you can strip from him." But Asahel
would not desist from his pursuit. [22]Once more
Abner said to Asahel: "Stop pursuing me! Why
must I strike you to the ground? How could I
face your brother Joab?"[q] [23]Still he refused to
stop. So Abner struck him in the abdomen with
the heel of his javelin, and the weapon pro-
truded from his back. He fell there and died on
the spot. And all who came to the place where
Asahel had fallen and died, came to a halt.
[24]Joab and Abishai, however, continued the
pursuit of Abner. The sun had gone down when
they came to the hill of Ammah which lies east
of the valley toward the desert near Geba.
Truce between Joab and Abner [25]Here the
Benjaminites rallied around Abner, forming a
single group, and made a stand on the hilltop.
[26]Then Abner called to Joab and said: "Must the
sword destroy to the utmost? Do you not know
that afterward there will be bitterness? How
much longer will you refrain from ordering the
people to stop the pursuit of their brothers?"
[27]Joab replied, "As God lives, if you had not
spoken, the soldiers would not have been with-
drawn from the pursuit of their brothers until
morning." [28]Joab then sounded the horn, and all
the soldiers came to a halt, pursuing Israel no
farther and fighting no more. [29]Abner and his
men marched all night long through the Arabah,
crossed the Jordan, marched all through the
morning, and came to Mahanaim. [30]Joab, after
interrupting the pursuit of Abner, assembled all
the men. Besides Asahel, nineteen other ser-
vants of David were missing. [31]But David's
servants had fatally wounded three hundred and
sixty men of Benjamin, followers of Abner.
[32]They took up Asahel and buried him in his
father's tomb in Bethlehem. Joab and his men
made an all-night march, and dawn found them
in Hebron.

CHAPTER 3

[1]There followed a long war between the
house of Saul and that of David, in which David
grew stronger, but the house of Saul weaker.
Sons Born in Hebron [2][r]Sons were born to
David in Hebron: his first-born, Amnon, of
Ahinoam from Jezreel; [3]the second, Chileab, of
Abigail the widow of Nabal of Carmel; the third,
Absalom, son of Maacah the daughter of Talmai,
king of Geshur;[s] [4]the fourth, Adonijah, son of
Haggith; the fifth, Shephatiah, son of Abital;[t]
[5]and the sixth, Ithream, of David's wife Eglah.
These were born to David in Hebron.
Ishbaal and Abner Quarrel [6]During the war
between the house of Saul and of David, Abner
was gaining power in the house of Saul. [7]Now
Saul had had a concubine, Rizpah, the daughter
of Aiah. And Ishbaal, son of Saul, said to Abner,
"Why have you been intimate with my father's
concubine?"[u] [8]Enraged at the words of Ishbaal,
Abner said, "Am I a dog's head in Judah? At
present I am doing a kindness to the house of
your father Saul, to his brothers and his friends,
by keeping you out of David's clutches; yet this
day you charge me with a crime involving a
woman! [9]May God do thus and so to Abner if I
do not carry out for David what the LORD swore
to him[v] — [10]that is, take away the kingdom
from the house of Saul and establish the throne
of David over Israel and over Judah from Dan to
Beer-sheba."[w] [11]In his fear of Abner, Ishbaal was
no longer able to say a word to him.

2, 16: The nature of this gruesome game is not clear, and the place name is variously given in the older texts.

o 2 Sm 23, 24: 1 Chr 2, 16. p 1 Chr 27, 7. q 2 Sm 3, 27f. 30. r 2–5: 1 Chr 3, 14. s 2 Sm 13, 37; 15, 8. t 1 Kgs 1, 5. u 2 Sm 21, 8ff. v Ru 1, 17. w 2 Sm 5, 2; 1 Sm 25, 30.

Abner and David Reconciled 12 Then Abner
sent messengers to David in Telam, where he
was at the moment, to say, "Make an agreement
with me, and I will aid you by bringing all Israel
over to you." 13 He replied, "Very well, I will
make an agreement with you. But one thing I
require of you. You must not appear before me
unless you bring back Michal, Saul's daughter,
when you come to present yourself to me."[x]
14 At the same time David sent messengers to
Ishbaal, son of Saul, to say, "Give me my wife
Michal, whom I espoused by paying a hundred
Philistine foreskins." 15 Ishbaal sent for her and
took her away from her husband Paltiel, son of
Laish,[y] 16 who followed her weeping as far as
Bahurim. But Abner said to him, "Go back!"
And he turned back.

17 Abner then said in discussion with the
elders of Israel: "For a long time you have been
seeking David as your king. 18 Now take action,
for the LORD has said of David, 'By my servant
David I will save my people Israel from the grasp
of the Philistines and from the grasp of all their
enemies.' " 19 Abner also spoke personally to
Benjamin, and then went to make his own
report to David in Hebron concerning all that
would be agreeable to Israel and to the whole
house of Benjamin. 20 When Abner, accompa-
nied by twenty men, came to David in Hebron,
David prepared a feast for Abner and for the men
who were with him. 21 Then Abner said to
David, "I will now go to assemble all Israel for
my lord the king, that they may make an
agreement with you; you will then be king over
all whom you wish to rule." So David bade
Abner farewell, and he went away in peace.

Death of Abner 22 Just then David's servants
and Joab were coming in from an expedition,
bringing much plunder with them. Abner, hav-
ing been dismissed by David, was no longer with
him in Hebron but had gone his way in peace.
23 When Joab and the whole force he had with
him arrived, he was informed, "Abner, son of
Ner, came to David; he has been sent on his way
in peace." 24 So Joab went to the king and said:
"What have you done? Abner came to you. Why
did you let him go peacefully on his way? 25 Are
you not aware that Abner came to deceive you
and to learn the ins and outs of all that you are
doing?" 26 Joab then left David, and without
David's knowledge sent messengers after Abner,
who brought him back from the cistern of Sirah.
27 When Abner returned to Hebron, Joab took
him aside within the city gate as though to speak
with him privately. There he stabbed him in the
abdomen, and he died in revenge for the killing
of Joab's brother Asahel.[z] 28 Later David heard of
it and said: "Before the LORD, I and my kingdom
are forever innocent.[a] 29 May the full responsibil-
ity for the death of Abner, son of Ner, be laid to
Joab and to all his family. May the men of Joab's
family never be without one suffering from a
discharge, or a leper, or one unmanly, one falling
by the sword, or one in need of bread!" 30 [Joab
and his brother Abishai had lain in wait for
Abner because he killed their brother Asahel in
battle at Gibeon.]

David Mourns Abner 31 Then David said to
Joab and to all the people who were with him,
"Rend your garments, gird yourselves with sack-
cloth, and mourn over Abner." King David
himself followed the bier.[b] 32 When they had
buried Abner in Hebron, the king wept aloud at
the grave of Abner, and the people also wept.
33 And the king sang this elegy over Abner:

"Would Abner have died like a fool?
34 Your hands were not bound with chains,
nor your feet placed in fetters;
As men fall before the wicked, you fell."

And all the people continued to weep for him.
35 Then they went to console David with food
while it was still day. But David swore, "May
God do thus and so to me if I eat bread or
anything else before sunset."[c] 36 All the people
noted this with approval, just as they were
pleased with everything that the king did. 37 So
on that day all the people and all Israel came to
know that the king had no part in the killing of
Abner, son of Ner. 38 The king then said to his
servants: "You must recognize that a great

x 1 Sm 18, 20–27. y 1 Sm 25, 44. z 1 Kgs 2, 5. 32. a 28.
30: 2 Sm 2, 22f. b 2 Sm 21, 10. c Ru 1, 17.

general has fallen today in Israel. [39]Although I am the anointed king, I am weak this day, and these men, the sons of Zeruiah, are too ruthless for me. May the LORD requite the evildoer in accordance with his evil deed."[d]

CHAPTER 4

Death of Ishbaal [1]When Ishbaal, son of Saul, heard that Abner had died in Hebron, he ceased to resist and all Israel was alarmed. [2]Ishbaal, son of Saul, had two company leaders named Baanah and Rechab, sons of Rimmon the Beerothite, of the tribe of Benjamin. [Beeroth, too, was ascribed to Benjamin:[e] [3]the Beerothites fled to Gittaim, where they have been resident aliens to this day.[f] [4]Jonathan, son of Saul, had a son named Meribbaal* with crippled feet. He was five years old when the news about Saul and Jonathan came from Jezreel, and his nurse took him up and fled. But in their hasty flight, he fell and became lame.][g] [5]The sons of Rimmon the Beerothite, Rechab and Baanah, came into the house of Ishbaal during the heat of the day, while he was taking his siesta. [6]The portress of the house had dozed off while sifting wheat, and was asleep. So Rechab and his brother Baanah slipped past [7]and entered the house while Ishbaal was lying asleep in his bedroom. They struck and killed him, and cut off his head. Then, taking the head, they traveled on the Arabah road all night long.

The Murder Avenged [8]They brought the head of Ishbaal to David in Hebron and said to the king: "This is the head of Ishbaal, son of your enemy Saul, who sought your life. Thus has the LORD this day avenged my lord the king on Saul and his posterity." [9]But David replied to Rechab and his brother Baanah, sons of Rimmon the Beerothite: "As the LORD lives, who rescued me from all difficulty, [10]in Ziklag I seized and put to death the man who informed me of Saul's death, thinking himself the bearer of good news for which I ought to give him a reward.[h] [11]How much more now, when wicked men have slain an innocent man in bed at home, must I hold you responsible for his death and destroy you from the earth!" [12]So at a command from David, the young men killed them and cut off their hands and feet, hanging them up near the pool in Hebron. But he took the head of Ishbaal and buried it in Abner's grave in Hebron.[i]

CHAPTER 5

David King of Israel [1][j]All the tribes of Israel came to David in Hebron and said: "Here we are, your bone and your flesh. [2]In days past, when Saul was our king, it was you who led the Israelites out and brought them back. And the LORD said to you, 'You shall shepherd my people Israel and shall be commander of Israel.' "[k] [3]When all the elders of Israel came to David in Hebron, King David made an agreement with them there before the LORD, and they anointed him king of Israel. [4]David was thirty years old when he became king, and he reigned for forty years: [5]seven years and six months in Hebron over Judah, and thirty-three years in Jerusalem over all Israel and Judah.[l]

Capture of Zion* [6][m]Then the king and his men set out for Jerusalem against the Jebusites who inhabited the region. David was told, "You cannot enter here: the blind and the lame will drive you away!" which was their way of saying, "David cannot enter here."[n] [7]But David did take the stronghold of Zion, which is the City of David. [8]On that day David said: "All who wish to attack the Jebusites must strike at them through the water shaft. The lame and the blind shall be the personal enemies of David." That is why it is said, "The blind and the lame shall not enter the palace."[o] [9]David then dwelt in the stronghold, which was called the City of David;

4, 4: Saul's grandson Meribbaal is the subject of ch 9 below. The text of this verse may owe its present place to the fact that pre-Christian copies of the Books of Samuel tended to confuse his name with that of his uncle Ishbaal, Saul's son and successor, a principal figure in chapters 2–4.

5, 6–12: David's most important military exploit, the taking of Jerusalem, is here presented before his battles with the Philistines, vv 17–25, which were earlier in time. The sense of vv 6 and 8 is in doubt.

d Ps 28, 4; Is 3, 11. e 2 Sm 9, 3; Jos 9, 17f. f Jos 18, 25. g 2 Sm 9, 3; 19, 25. h 2 Sm 1, 6–10. 14. 16. i Dt 21, 22f; 1 Sm 31, 10. j 1ff: 1 Chr 11, 1ff. k 2 Sm 3, 10; Dt 17, 15; 1 Sm 18, 16. l 2 Sm 2, 11; 1 Kgs 2, 11; 1 Chr 3, 4. m 6–10: 1 Chr 11, 4–9. n Jos 15, 63; Jgs 1, 19. 21; Is 29, 3. o Lv 21, 18; Mt 21, 14f.

he built up the area from Millo to the palace.[p]
10 David grew steadily more powerful, for the
LORD of hosts was with him.[q] 11 [r]Hiram, king of
Tyre, sent ambassadors to David; he furnished
cedar wood, as well as carpenters and masons,
who built a palace for David.[s] 12 And David
knew that the LORD had established him as king
of Israel and had exalted his rule for the sake of
his people Israel.

David's Family in Jerusalem 13 [t]David took
more concubines and wives in Jerusalem after he
had come from Hebron, and more sons and
daughters were born to him in Jerusalem.
14 These are the names of those who were born
to him in Jerusalem: Shammua, Shobab, Nathan,
Solomon, 15 Ibhar, Elishua, Nepheg, Japhia,
16 Elishama, Baaliada, and Eliphelet.

Rout of the Philistines 17 When the Philistines
heard that David had been anointed king of
Israel, they all took the field in search of him. On
hearing this, David went down to the refuge.*
18 The Philistines came and overran the valley of
Rephaim.* 19 David inquired of the LORD, "Shall
I attack the Philistines—will you deliver them
into my grip?" The LORD replied to David,
"Attack, for I will surely deliver the Philistines
into your grip." 20 David then went to Baal-
perazim,* where he defeated them. He said,
"The LORD has scattered my enemies before me
like waters that have broken free." That is why
the place is called Baal-perazim. 21 They aban-
doned their gods there, and David and his men
carried them away. 22 But the Philistines came up
again and overran the valley of Rephaim. 23 So
David inquired of the LORD, who replied: "You
must not attack frontally, but circle their rear
and meet them before the mastic trees. 24 When
you hear a sound of marching* in the tops of the
mastic trees, act decisively, for the LORD will
have gone forth before you to attack the camp of
the Philistines." 25 David obeyed the LORD's
command and routed the Philistines from Gib-
eon as far as Gezer.

CHAPTER 6

The Ark Brought to Jerusalem 1 [u]David again
assembled all the picked men of Israel, thirty
thousand in number. 2 Then David and all the
people who were with him set out for Baala of
Judah to bring up from there the ark of God,
which bears the name of the LORD of hosts
enthroned above the cherubim.[v] 3 The ark of
God was placed on a new cart and taken away
from the house of Abinadab on the hill. Uzzah
and Ahio, sons of Abinadab, guided the cart,[w]
4 with Ahio walking before it, 5 while David and
all the Israelites made merry before the LORD
with all their strength, with singing and with
citharas, harps, tambourines, sistrums and cym-
bals.[x] 6 When they came to the threshing floor of
Nodan, Uzzah reached out his hand to the ark of
God and steadied it, for the oxen were making it
tip. 7 But the LORD was angry with Uzzah; God
struck him on that spot, and he died there before
God. 8 David was disturbed because the LORD
had vented his anger on Uzzah. (The place has
been called Perez-uzzah down to the present
day.)[y] 9 David feared the LORD that day and said,
"How can the ark of the LORD come to me?"
10 So David would not have the ark of the LORD
brought to him in the City of David, but diverted
it to the house of Obed-edom the Gittite.

11 The ark of the LORD remained in the house
of Obed-edom the Gittite for three months, and
the LORD blessed Obed-edom and his whole
house.[z] 12 [a]When it was reported to King David
that the LORD had blessed the family of Obed-
edom and all that belonged to him, David went
to bring up the ark of God from the house of
Obed-edom into the City of David amid festivi-

5, 17: Refuge: probably near Adullam (1 Sm 22, 1–5).

5, 18–25: The successive defeats of the Philistines in the valley of Rephaim southwest of Jerusalem had the effect of blocking their access to the mountain ridge near Gibeon, and confining them to their holdings on the coast and in the foothills beyond Gezer to the west and south.

5, 20: Baal-perazim: means approximately "the lord of scatterings."

5, 24: Sound of marching: the wind in the treetops suggestive of the Lord's footsteps.

p 1 Kgs 3, 1; 11, 27. q Pss 78, 70ff. 89; 132, 13. r 11–25: 1 Chr 14, 1–16. s 11f: 1 Kgs 5, 15; 1 Chr 14, 1f. t 13–16: 1 Chr 3, 5–8; 14, 3–7. u 1–11: 1 Chr 13, 1–14. v Ex 25, 10; Jos 15, 9; Ps 132, 8ff; 1 Chr 1, 4. w 1 Sm 4, 3f; 6, 7f; 7, 1; Dn 3, 55. x Pss 68, 25f; 150, 3. 5. y 1 Kgs 8, 1. z 1 Chr 26. 4. a 12–23: 1 Chr 15, 1–29; Ps 24, 7–10.

ties. 13As soon as the bearers of the ark of the LORD had advanced six steps, he sacrificed an ox and a fatling. 14Then David, girt with a linen apron, came dancing before the LORD with abandon,[b] 15as he and all the Israelites were bringing up the ark of the LORD with shouts of joy and to the sound of the horn. 16As the ark of the LORD was entering the City of David, Saul's daughter Michal looked down through the window and saw King David leaping and dancing before the LORD, and she despised him in her heart. 17[c]The ark of the LORD was brought in and set in its place within the tent David had pitched for it. Then David offered holocausts and peace offerings before the LORD. 18When he finished making these offerings, he blessed the people in the name of the LORD of hosts. 19He then distributed among all the people, to each man and each woman in the entire multitude of Israel, a loaf of bread, a cut of roast meat, and a raisin cake. With this, all the people left for their homes.

20When David returned to bless his own family, Saul's daughter Michal came out to meet him and said, "How the king of Israel has honored himself today, exposing himself to the view of the slave girls of his followers, as a commoner might do!"[d] 21But David replied to Michal: "I was dancing before the LORD. As the LORD lives, who preferred me to your father and his whole family when he appointed me commander of the LORD's people, Israel, not only will I make merry before the LORD,[e] 22but I will demean myself even more. I will be lowly in your esteem, but in the esteem of the slave girls you spoke of I will be honored." 23And so Saul's daughter Michal was childless to the day of her death.

CHAPTER 7

David's Concern for the Ark 1[f]When King David was settled in his palace, and the LORD had given him rest from his enemies on every side,[g] 2he said to Nathan the prophet, "Here I am living in a house of cedar, while the ark of God dwells in a tent!"[h] 3Nathan answered the king, "Go, do whatever you have in mind, for the LORD is with you."[i] 4But that night the LORD spoke to Nathan and said: 5"Go, tell my servant David, 'Thus says the LORD: Should you build me a house to dwell in?[j] 6I have not dwelt in a house from the day on which I led the Israelites out of Egypt to the present, but I have been going about in a tent under cloth. 7In all my wanderings everywhere among the Israelites, did I ever utter a word to any one of the judges whom I charged to tend my people Israel, to ask: Why have you not built me a house of cedar?'

The Lord's Promises 8"Now then, speak thus to my servant David, 'The LORD of hosts has this to say:* It was I who took you from the pasture and from the care of the flock to be commander of my people Israel.[k] 9I have been with you wherever you went, and I have destroyed all your enemies before you. And I will make you famous like the great ones of the earth.[l] 10I will fix a place for my people Israel; I will plant them so that they may dwell in their place without further disturbance. Neither shall the wicked continue to afflict them as they did of old, 11since the time I first appointed judges over my people Israel. I will give you rest from all your enemies. The LORD also reveals to you that he will establish a house for you.[m] 12[n]And when your time comes and you rest with your ancestors, I will raise up your heir after you, sprung from your loins, and I will make his kingdom firm. 13It is he who shall build a house for my name. And I will make his royal throne firm

7, 8–16: The prophecy to David contained in these verses is cited again, in poetic form, in Ps 89, 20–38, and alluded to in Ps 132. The promise regarding the people of Israel, vv 10–11, is a part of the promise to David at least as old as the composition of this chapter of Samuel, where it is anticipated in vv 6–7, and alluded to in David's thanksgiving, vv 23–24; it applies to the people an expression used of David in Ps 89, 23. The prophecy to David is the basis for Jewish expectation of a messiah, son of David, which Jesus Christ fulfilled in a transcendent way; cf Acts 2, 30; Heb 1, 5.

b 1 Sm 2, 18. c 17ff: Lv 1, 1–17; 3, 1–17; 1 Chr 16, 1ff. d 1 Chr 16, 43. e 1 Sm 13, 14; 15, 28. f 1–29: 1 Chr 17, 1–27. g 1 Kgs 5, 4. h Dt 12, 10; 25, 19. i Ps 132, 1–5. j 1 Kgs 5, 17; 8, 16. 27; 1 Chr 22, 8; 28, 3; Is 66, 1; Acts 7, 48. k 1 Sm 16, 13; 17, 15–20; Ps 78, 70f; Am 7, 14. l Ps 89, 27. m 2 Sm 23, 5; 1 Kgs 2, 4–24. n 12ff: 1 Kgs 5, 19, 8, 19; 1 Chr 22, 10; 2 Chr 7, 18; Ps 89, 5, 27f. 30. 37f; Lk 1, 32; Heb 1, 5.

forever. 14I will be a father to him, and he shall be a son to me. And if he does wrong, I will correct him with the rod of men and with human chastisements; 15but I will not withdraw my favor from him as I withdrew it from your predecessor Saul, whom I removed from my presence.[o] 16Your house and your kingdom shall endure forever before me; your throne shall stand firm forever.' "[p] 17Nathan reported all these words and this entire vision to David.

King David's Prayer 18Then King David went in and sat before the LORD and said, "Who am I, Lord GOD, and who are the members of my house, that you have brought me to this point?[q] 19Yet even this you see as too little, Lord GOD; you have also spoken of the house of your servant for a long time to come: this too you have shown to man,* Lord GOD! 20What more can David say to you? You know your servant, Lord GOD! 21For your servant's sake and as you have had at heart, you have brought about this entire magnificent disclosure to your servant. 22And so—

"Great are you, Lord GOD! There is none like you and there is no God but you, just as we have heard it told.[r] 23What other nation on earth is there like your people Israel, which God has led, redeeming it as his people; so that you have made yourself renowned by doing this magnificent deed, and by doing awe-inspiring things as you have cleared nations and their gods out of the way of your people, which you redeemed for yourself from Egypt?[s] 24[t]You have established for yourself your people Israel as yours forever, and you, LORD, have become their God. 25And now, LORD God, confirm for all time the prophecy you have made concerning your servant and his house, and do as you have promised. 26Your name will be forever great, when men say, 'The LORD of hosts is God of Israel,' and the house of your servant David stands firm before you. 27It is you, LORD of hosts, God of Israel, who said in a revelation to your servant, 'I will build a house for you.' Therefore your servant now finds the courage to make this prayer to you. 28And now, Lord GOD, you are God and your words are truth; you have made this generous promise to your servant.[u] 29Do, then, bless the house of your servant that it may be before you forever; for you, Lord GOD, have promised, and by your blessing the house of your servant shall be blessed forever."

CHAPTER 8

Summary of David's Wars 1 [v]After this David attacked the Philistines and conquered them, wresting . . . * from the Philistines. 2He also defeated Moab and then measured them with a line, making them lie down on the ground. He told off two lengths of line for execution, and a full length* to be spared. Thus the Moabites became tributary to David. 3 [w]Next David defeated Hadadezer, son of Rehob, king of Zobah, when he went to reestablish his dominion at the Euphrates River.[x] 4David captured from him one thousand seven hundred horsemen and twenty thousand foot soldiers. And he hamstrung all the chariot horses, preserving only enough for a hundred chariots.[y] 5When the Arameans of Damascus came to the aid of Hadadezer, king of Zobah, David slew twenty-two thousand of them. 6David then placed garrisons in Aram of Damascus, and the Arameans became subjects, tributary to David. The LORD brought David victory in all his undertakings. 7David also took away the golden shields used by Hadadezer's servants and brought them to Jerusalem. [These Shishak, king of Egypt, took away when he came to Jerusalem in the days of Rehoboam, son of Solomon.] 8From Tebah and Berothai, towns

7, 19: This too you have shown to man: the text as transmitted has, rather, "and this is instruction for (or: the law of) mankind." The author of Chronicles (1 Chr 17, 17) saw approximately the same phrase, which he endeavored to fit into the context in a quite different sense. The above is conjectural; cf Dt 5, 24.

8, 1: Wresting . . . : the Hebrew text here gives "the bridle of the cubit"; 1 Chr 18, 1 understood "Gath and its dependent villages"; others implausibly read "dominion of the capital city."

8, 2: Two lengths . . . a full length: usually taken to mean that two-thirds of them were executed; but it could mean that two-thirds were spared, if the line was used full length in their case but doubled on itself to make "two lines" for those to be put to death.

o 2 Sm 23, 5; 1 Sm 13, 14; 15, 26. 28; 2 Kgs 19, 34; 1 Chr 17, 11–14; Ps 89, 34. p 2 Sm 23, 5; Dn 2, 45; 1 Mc 2, 57; Mk 11, 10; Lk 1, 32f; Heb 1, 8. q 1 Chr 17, 16. r Ex 15, 11; Is 45, 5. s Dt 4, 7. 34. t 24f: Ex 6, 7; Dt 7, 6; 26, 17; 29, 12. u Nm 23, 19; Jn 17, 17. v 1–18: 1 Chr 18, 1–17. w 3–8: 2 Sm 10, 15–19. x 2 Sm 10, 6; 1 Kgs 11, 23. y Jos 11, 6. 9.

of Hadadezer, King David removed a very large quantity of bronze. 9When Toi, king of Hamath, heard that David had defeated all the forces of Hadadezer, 10he sent his son Hadoram to King David to greet him and to congratulate him for his victory over Hadadezer in battle, because Toi had been in many battles with Hadadezer. Hadoram also brought with him articles of silver, gold, and bronze. 11These, too, King David consecrated to the LORD, together with the silver and gold he had taken from every nation he had conquered: 12from Edom and Moab, from the Ammonites, from the Philistines, from the Amalekites, and from the plunder of Hadadezer, son of Rehob, king of Zobah.

13On his return,* David became famous for having slain eighteen thousand Edomites in the Salt Valley;[z] 14after which he placed garrisons in Edom. Thus all the Edomites became David's subjects, and the LORD brought David victory in all his undertakings.

David's Officials 15[a]David reigned over all Israel, judging and administering justice to all his people. 16Joab, son of Zeruiah, was in command of the army. Jehoshaphat, son of Ahilud, was chancellor. 17Zadok, son of Ahitub, and Ahimelech, son of Abiathar, were priests. Shawsha was scribe. 18Benaiah, son of Jehoiada, was in command of the Cherethites and Pelethites. And David's sons were priests.[b]

CHAPTER 9

David and Meribbaal 1David asked, "Is there any survivor of Saul's house to whom I may show kindness for the sake of Jonathan?"[c] 2Now there was a servant of the family of Saul named Ziba. He was summoned to David, and the king asked him, "Are you Ziba?" He replied, "Your servant."[d] 3Then the king inquired, "Is there any survivor of Saul's house to whom I may show God's kindness?" Ziba answered the king, "There is still Jonathan's son, whose feet are crippled."[e] 4The king said to him, "Where is he?" and Ziba answered, "He is in the house of Machir, son of Ammiel, in Lodebar."[f] 5So King David sent for him and had him brought from the house of Machir, son of Ammiel, in Lodebar. 6When Meribbaal, son of Jonathan, son of Saul, came to David, he fell prostrate in homage. David said, "Meribbaal," and he answered, "Your servant." 7"Fear not," David said to him, "I will surely be kind to you for the sake of your father Jonathan. I will restore to you all the lands of your grandfather Saul, and you shall always eat at my table." 8Bowing low, he answered, "What is your servant that you should pay attention to a dead dog like me?"[g] 9The king then called Ziba, Saul's attendant, and said to him: "I am giving your lord's son all that belonged to Saul and to all his family. 10You and your sons and servants must till the land for him. You shall bring in the produce, which shall be food for your lord's family to eat. But Meribbaal, your lord's son, shall always eat at my table." Ziba, who had fifteen sons and twenty servants, 11said to the king, "Your servant shall do just as my lord the king has commanded him." And so Meribbaal ate at David's table like one of the king's sons.[h] 12Meribbaal had a young son whose name was Mica; and all the tenants of Ziba's family worked for Meribbaal.[i] 13But Meribbaal lived in Jerusalem, because he always ate at the king's table. He was lame in both feet.[j]

CHAPTER 10

Insult of the Ammonites 1[k]Some time later* the king of the Ammonites died, and his son Hanun succeeded him as king. 2David thought, "I will be kind to Hanun, son of Nahash, as his father was kind to me." So David sent his servants with condolences to Hanun for the loss of his father. But when David's servants entered the country of the Ammonites, 3the Ammonite princes said to their lord Hanun: "Do you think

8, 13: On his return: possibly to Jerusalem, after the revolt of Absalom, a circumstance which this catalogue of victories would avoid mentioning. 1 Chr 18, 13 attributes the defeat of the Edomites to Abishai.

10, 1: Some time later: early in the reign of David, since Hanun's father had been ruling in Ammon at the beginning of Saul's reign (1 Sm 11) and Solomon was as yet unborn (2 Sm 11, 1; 12, 24).

z 2 Kgs 14, 7. a 15–18: 2 Sm 20, 23–26; 1 Kgs 4, 1–6; 1 Chr 18, 14–17. b 2 Sm 15, 18; 20, 7. 23; 23, 20. c 2 Sm 21, 7; 1 Sm 18, 1–4; 20, 8ff. 15f. 42. d 2 Sm 16, 1–4; 19, 27. e 2 Sm 4, 4. f 2 Sm 17, 27. g 1 Sm 24, 15. h 2 Sm 19, 29. i 1 Chr 8, 34. j 2 Sm 21, 7. k 1–19: 1 Chr 19, 1–19.

that David is honoring your father by sending men with condolences? Is it not rather to explore the city, to spy on it, and to overthrow it, that David has sent his messengers to you?" 4 Hanun, therefore, seized David's servants and, after shaving off half their beards and cutting away the lower halves of their garments at the buttocks, sent them away.[l] 5 When he was told of it, King David sent out word to them, since the men were quite ashamed. "Stay in Jericho until your beards grow," he said, "and then come back."

Ammonites Defeated 6 *In view of the offense they had given to David, the Ammonites sent for and hired twenty thousand Aramean foot soldiers from Beth-rehob and Zobah, as well as the king of Maacah with one thousand men, and twelve thousand men from Tob.[m] 7 On learning this, David sent out Joab with the entire levy of trained soldiers.[n] 8 The Ammonites came out and drew up in battle formation at the entrance of their city gate, while the Arameans of Zobah and Rehob and the men of Tob and Maacah remained apart in the open country. 9 When Joab saw the battle lines drawn up against him, both front and rear, he made a selection from all the picked troops of Israel and arrayed them against the Arameans. 10 He placed the rest of the soldiers under the command of his brother Abishai, who arrayed them against the Ammonites. 11 Joab said, "If the Arameans are stronger than I, you shall help me. But if the Ammonites are stronger than you, I will come to help you. 12 Be brave; let us prove our valor for the sake of our people and the cities of our God; the LORD will do what he judges best." 13 When Joab and the soldiers who were with him approached the Arameans for battle, they fled before him. 14 The Ammonites, seeing that the Arameans had fled, also fled from Abishai and withdrew into the city. Joab then ceased his attack on the Ammonites and returned to Jerusalem.

Arameans Defeated 15 [o]Then the Arameans responded to their defeat by Israel with a full mustering of troops; 16 Hadadezer sent for and enlisted Arameans from beyond the Euphrates. They came to Helam, with Shobach, general of Hadadezer's army, at their head. 17 On receiving this news, David assembled all Israel, crossed the Jordan, and went to Helam. The Arameans drew up in formation against David and fought with him. 18 But the Arameans gave way before Israel, and David's men killed seven hundred charioteers and forty thousand of the Aramean foot soldiers. Shobach, general of the army, was struck down and died on the field. 19 All of Hadadezer's vassal kings, in view of their defeat by Israel, then made peace with the Israelites and became their subjects. And the Arameans were afraid to give further aid to the Ammonites.

CHAPTER 11

David's Sin 1 At the turn of the year,* when kings go out on campaign, David sent out Joab along with his officers and the army of Israel, and they ravaged the Ammonites and besieged Rabbah. David, however, remained in Jerusalem.[p] 2 One evening David rose from his siesta and strolled about on the roof of the palace. From the roof he saw a woman bathing, who was very beautiful. 3 David had inquiries made about the woman and was told, "She is Bathsheba, daughter of Eliam, and wife of [Joab's armor-bearer] Uriah the Hittite."[q] 4 Then David sent messengers and took her. When she came to him, he had relations with her, at a time when she was just purified after her monthly period. She then returned to her house.[r] 5 But the woman had conceived, and sent the information to David, "I am with child."

6 David therefore sent a message to Joab, "Send me Uriah the Hittite." So Joab sent Uriah to David. 7 When he came, David questioned him about Joab, the soldiers, and how the war

10, 6–9: A Hebrew text from Qumran (4Q Sam[a]) comes closer in these verses to what is given in 1 Chr 19, 6–9. The scene of the conflict is more likely Rabbath-Ammon, with Josephus (Ant., vii, 123), than Madeba, as in 1 Chr; compare ch 11.

11, 1: At the turn of the year: in the spring.

l Is 20, 4. m 2 Sm 8, 3; 1 Sm 14, 47. n 2 Sm 11, 1. o 15–19: 2 Sm 8, 3–8; 1 Chr 9, 16–19. p 2 Sm 10, 7; 1 Chr 20, 1. q 2 Sm 23, 39. r Lv 15, 19.

was going, and Uriah answered that all was well. 8David then said to Uriah, "Go down to your house and bathe your feet." Uriah left the palace, and a portion was sent out after him from the king's table. 9But Uriah slept at the entrance of the royal palace with the other officers of his lord, and did not go down to his own house. 10David was told that Uriah had not gone home. So he said to Uriah, "Have you not come from a journey? Why, then, did you not go down to your house?" 11Uriah answered David, "The ark and Israel and Judah are lodged in tents, and my lord Joab and your majesty's servants are encamped in the open field. Can I go home to eat and to drink and to sleep with my wife? As the LORD lives and as you live, I will do no such thing."[s] 12Then David said to Uriah, "Stay here today also, I shall dismiss you tomorrow." So Uriah remained in Jerusalem that day. On the day following, 13David summoned him, and he ate and drank with David, who made him drunk. But in the evening he went out to sleep on his bed among his lord's servants, and did not go down to his home. 14The next morning David wrote a letter to Joab which he sent by Uriah. 15In it he directed: "Place Uriah up front, where the fighting is fierce. Then pull back and leave him to be struck down dead." 16So while Joab was besieging the city, he assigned Uriah to a place where he knew the defenders were strong. 17When the men of the city made a sortie against Joab, some officers of David's army fell, and among them Uriah the Hittite died.

18Then Joab sent David a report of all the details of the battle, 19instructing the messenger, "When you have finished giving the king all the details of the battle, 20the king may become angry and say to you: 'Why did you go near the city to fight? Did you not know that they would shoot from the wall above? 21Who killed Abimelech, son of Jerubbaal? Was it not a woman who threw a millstone down on him from the wall above, so that he died in Thebez? Why did you go near the wall?' Then you in turn shall say, 'Your servant Uriah the Hittite is also dead.' "[t] 22The messenger set out, and on his arrival he relayed to David all the details as Joab had instructed him.* 23He told David: "The men had us at a disadvantage and came out into the open against us, but we pushed them back to the entrance of the city gate. 24Then the archers shot at your servants from the wall above, and some of the king's servants died, among them your servant Uriah." 25David said to the messenger: "This is what you shall convey to Joab: 'Do not be chagrined at this, for the sword devours now here and now there. Strengthen your attack on the city and destroy it.' Encourage him."

26When the wife of Uriah heard that her husband had died, she mourned her lord. 27But once the mourning was over, David sent for her and brought her into his house. She became his wife and bore him a son. But the LORD was displeased with what David had done.

CHAPTER 12

Nathan's Parable 1*The LORD sent Nathan to David, and when he came to him, he said: "Judge this case for me! In a certain town there were two men, one rich, the other poor.[u] 2The rich man had flocks and herds in great numbers. 3But the poor man had nothing at all except one little ewe lamb that he had bought. He nourished her, and she grew up with him and his children. She shared the little food he had and drank from his cup and slept in his bosom. She was like a daughter to him. 4Now, the rich man received a visitor, but he would not take from his own flocks and herds to prepare a meal for the wayfarer who had come to him. Instead he took the poor man's ewe lamb and made a meal of it for his visitor." 5David grew very angry with that man and said to Nathan: "As the LORD lives, the man who has done this merits death! 6He shall

11, 22: After this verse, the Greek text, which is here the older form, has David, angry with Joab, repeat exactly the questions Joab had foreseen in vv 20ff. In v 24 of our oldest Greek text, the messenger specifies that about eighteen men were killed.

12, 1–4: This utterance of Nathan is in regular lines in Hebrew, resembling English blank verse.

s 1 Sm 4, 3f. t Jgs 9, 50–54. u Sir 47, 1.

restore the ewe lamb fourfold because he has done this and has had no pity."[v]

David's Punishment 7 Then Nathan said to David: "You are the man! Thus says the LORD God of Israel: 'I anointed you king of Israel. I rescued you from the hand of Saul.[w] 8 I gave you your lord's house and your lord's wives for your own. I gave you the house of Israel and of Judah. And if this were not enough, I could count up for you still more. 9 Why have you spurned the LORD and done evil in his sight? You have cut down Uriah the Hittite with the sword; you took his wife as your own, and him you killed with the sword of the Ammonites. 10 Now, therefore, the sword shall never depart from your house, because you have despised me and have taken the wife of Uriah to be your wife.'[x] 11 Thus says the LORD: 'I will bring evil upon you out of your own house. I will take your wives while you live to see it, and will give them to your neighbor. He shall lie with your wives in broad daylight.[y] 12 You have done this deed in secret, but I will bring it about in the presence of all Israel, and with the sun looking down.' "

David's Repentance 13 Then David said to Nathan, "I have sinned against the LORD." Nathan answered David: "The LORD on his part has forgiven your sin: you shall not die.[z] 14 But since you have utterly spurned the LORD by this deed, the child born to you must surely die." 15 Then Nathan returned to his house.

The LORD struck the child that the wife of Uriah had borne to David, and it became desperately ill. 16 David besought God for the child. He kept a fast, retiring for the night to lie on the ground clothed in sackcloth. 17 The elders of his house stood beside him urging him to rise from the ground; but he would not, nor would he take food with them. 18 On the seventh day, the child died. David's servants, however, were afraid to tell him that the child was dead, for they said: "When the child was alive, we spoke to him, but he would not listen to what we said. How can we tell him the child is dead? He may do some harm!" 19 But David noticed his servants whispering among themselves and realized that the child was dead. He asked his servants, "Is the child dead?" They replied, "Yes, he is." 20 Rising from the ground, David washed and anointed himself, and changed his clothes. Then he went to the house of the LORD and worshiped. He returned to his own house, where at his request food was set before him, and he ate. 21 His servants said to him: "What is this you are doing? While the child was living, you fasted and wept and kept vigil; now that the child is dead you rise and take food." 22 He replied: "While the child was living, I fasted and wept, thinking, 'Perhaps the LORD will grant me the child's life.' 23 But now he is dead. Why should I fast? Can I bring him back again? I shall go to him, but he will not return to me."[a] 24 Then David comforted his wife Bathsheba. He went and slept with her; and she conceived and bore him a son, who was named Solomon. The LORD loved him 25 and sent the prophet Nathan to name him Jedidiah, on behalf of the LORD.

Ammonite War Ends 26 [b]Joab fought against Rabbah of the Ammonites and captured this royal city. 27 He sent messengers to David with the word: "I have fought against Rabbah and have taken the water-city. 28 Therefore, assemble the rest of the soldiers, join the siege against the city and capture it, lest it be I that capture the city and it be credited to me." 29 So David assembled the rest of the soldiers and went to Rabbah. When he had fought against it and captured it, 30 he took the crown from Milcom's head. It weighed a talent,* of gold and precious stones; it was placed on David's head. He brought out immense booty from the city, 31 and also led away the inhabitants, whom he assigned to work with saws, iron picks, and iron axes, or put to work at the brickmold. This is what he did to all the Ammonite cities. David and all the soldiers then returned to Jerusalem.

12, 30: Weighed a talent: since this would be more than 75 pounds, some commentators picture the idol's crown as displaying a single precious stone of large size, which David took to wear; but the text does not say this.

v Ex 21, 37; Lk 19, 8. w 1 Sm 16, 13. x 2 Sm 13, 28f; 18, 14. y 2 Sm 16, 11. 22. z 1 Kgs 21, 29; Pss 32, 5; 50, 6; Sir 47, 11. a Jb 7, 9. b 26–31: 1 Chr 20, 1–3.

CHAPTER 13

The Crime of Amnon 1 Some time later the following incident occurred. David's son Absalom had a beautiful sister named Tamar, and David's son Amnon loved her.[c] 2 He was in such straits over his sister Tamar that he became sick; since she was a virgin, Amnon thought it impossible to carry out his designs toward her. 3 Now Amnon had a friend named Jonadab, son of David's brother Shimeah, who was very clever.[d] 4 He asked him, "Prince, why are you so dejected morning after morning? Why not tell me?" So Amnon said to him, "I am in love with Tamar, my brother Absalom's sister." 5 Then Jonadab replied, "Lie down on your bed and pretend to be sick. When your father comes to visit you, say to him, 'Please let my sister Tamar come and encourage me to take food. If she prepares something appetizing in my presence, for me to see, I will eat it from her hand.' " 6 So Amnon lay down and pretended to be sick. When the king came to visit him, Amnon said to the king, "Please let my sister Tamar come and prepare some fried cakes before my eyes, that I may take nourishment from her hand."

7 David then sent home a message to Tamar, "Please go to the house of your brother Amnon and prepare some nourishment for him." 8 Tamar went to the house of her brother Amnon, who was in bed. Taking dough and kneading it, she twisted it into cakes before his eyes and fried the cakes. 9 Then she took the pan and set out the cakes before him. But Amnon would not eat; he said, "Have everyone leave me." When they had all left him, 10 Amnon said to Tamar, "Bring the nourishment into the bedroom, that I may have it from your hand." So Tamar picked up the cakes she had prepared and brought them to her brother Amnon in the bedroom. 11 But when she brought them to him to eat, he seized her and said to her, "Come! Lie with me, my sister!" 12 But she answered him, "No, my brother! Do not shame me! That is an intolerable crime in Israel. Do not commit this insensate deed.[e] 13 Where would I take my shame? And you would be a discredited man in Israel. So please, speak to the king; he will not keep me from you."[f]

14 Not heeding her plea, he overpowered her; he shamed her and had relations with her. 15 Then Amnon conceived an intense hatred for her, which far surpassed the love he had had for her. "Get up and leave," he said to her. 16 She replied, "No, brother, because to drive me out would be far worse than the first injury you have done me." He would not listen to her, 17 but called the youth who was his attendant and said, "Put her outside, away from me, and bar the door after her." 18 Now she had on a long tunic, for that is how maiden princesses dressed in olden days. When his attendant put her out and barred the door after her, 19 Tamar put ashes on her head and tore the long tunic in which she was clothed. Then, putting her hands to her head, she went away crying loudly. 20 Her brother Absalom said to her: "Has your brother Amnon been with you? Be still now, my sister; he is your brother. Do not take this affair to heart." But Tamar remained grief-stricken and forlorn in the house of her brother Absalom. 21 King David, who got word of the whole affair, became very angry. He did not, however, spark the resentment of his son Amnon, whom he favored because he was his first-born. 22 Absalom, moreover, said nothing at all to Amnon, although he hated him for having shamed his sister Tamar.

Absalom's Plot 23 After a period of two years Absalom had shearers in Baal-hazor near Ephraim, and he invited all the princes. 24 Absalom went to the king and said: "Your servant is having shearers. Please, your majesty, come with all your retainers to your servant." 25 But the king said to Absalom, "No, my son, all of us should not go lest we be a burden to you." And though Absalom urged him, he refused to go and began to bid him goodbye. 26 Absalom then said, "If you will not come yourself, please let my brother Amnon come to us." The king asked him, "Why should he go to you?" 27 At Absalom's urging, however, he sent Amnon and all the other princes with him. Absalom prepared a

c 2 Sm 3, 2f; 1 Chr 3, 9. d 1 Sm 21, 21. e Lv 18, 9; 20, 17; Dt 27, 22. f Gn 34, 7.

banquet fit for royalty. 28 [g]But he had instructed his servants: "Now watch! When Amnon is merry with wine and I say to you, 'Kill Amnon,' put him to death. Do not be afraid, for it is I who order you to do it. Be resolute and act manfully."

Death of Amnon 29When the servants did to Amnon as Absalom had commanded, all the other princes rose, mounted their mules, and fled. 30While they were still on the road, a report reached David that Absalom had killed all the princes and that not one of them had survived. 31The king stood up, rent his garments, and then lay on the ground. All his servants standing by him also rent their garments.[h] 32But Jonadab, son of David's brother Shimeah, spoke up: "Let not my lord think that all the young princes have been killed! Amnon alone is dead, for Absalom was determined on this ever since Amnon shamed his sister Tamar. 33So let not my lord the king put faith in the report that all the princes are dead. Amnon alone is dead." 34Meanwhile, Absalom had taken flight. Then the servant on watch looked about and saw a large group coming down the slope from the direction of Bahurim. He came in and reported this, telling the king that he had seen some men coming down the mountainside from the direction of Bahurim. 35So Jonadab said to the king: "There! The princes have come. It is as your servant said." 36No sooner had he finished speaking than the princes came in, weeping aloud. The king, too, and all his servants wept very bitterly. 37But Absalom, who had taken flight, went to Talmai, son of Ammihud, king of Geshur,[i] 38and stayed in Geshur for three years.

Efforts for Absalom's Return 39The king continued during all that time to mourn over his son; but his longing reached out for Absalom as he became reconciled to the death of Amnon.

CHAPTER 14

1When Joab, son of Zeruiah, observed how the king felt toward Absalom, 2he sent to Tekoa and brought from there a gifted woman, to whom he said: "Pretend to be in mourning. Put on mourning apparel and do not anoint yourself with oil, that you may appear to be a woman who has been long in mourning for a departed one. 3Then go to the king and speak to him in this manner." And Joab instructed her what to say.

4So the woman of Tekoa went to the king and fell prostrate to the ground in homage, saying, "Help, your majesty!" 5 [j]The king said to her, "What do you want?" She replied: "Alas, I am a widow; my husband is dead. 6Your servant had two sons, who quarreled in the field. There being no one to part them, one of them struck his brother and killed him. 7Then the whole clan confronted your servant and demanded: 'Give up the one who killed his brother. We must put him to death for the life of his brother whom he has slain; we must extinguish the heir also.' Thus they will quench my remaining hope* and leave my husband neither name nor posterity upon the earth."[k] 8The king then said to the woman: "Go home. I will issue a command on your behalf." 9The woman of Tekoa answered him, "Let me and my family be to blame, my lord king; you and your throne are innocent." 10Then the king said, "If anyone says a word to you, have him brought to me, and he shall not touch you again." 11But she went on to say, "Please, your majesty, keep in mind the LORD your God, that the avenger of blood may not go too far in destruction and that my son may not be done away with." He replied, "As the LORD lives, not a hair of your son shall fall to the ground."

12The woman continued, "Please let your servant say still another word to my lord the king." He replied, "Speak." 13So the woman said: "Why, then, do you think of this same kind of thing against the people of God? In pronouncing as he has, the king shows himself guilty, for not bringing back his own banished son. 14We

14, 7: Hope: literally, "glowing coal." The image is similar to that of the lighted lamp, e.g., Ps 89, 17, to keep alive the ancestral name.

g 28f: 2 Sm 12, 10. h 2 Sm 1, 11. i 2 Sm 3, 3; 15, 8. j 5f: 2 Kgs 6, 26f. k Nm 35, 19.

must indeed die; we are then like water that is poured out on the ground and cannot be gathered up. Yet, though God does not bring back life, he does take thought how not to banish* anyone from him.[l] 15And now, if I have presumed to speak of this matter to your majesty, it is because the people have given me cause to fear. And so your servant thought: 'Let me speak to the king. Perhaps he will grant the petition of his maidservant. 16For the king must surely consent to free his servant from the grasp of one who would seek to destroy me and my son as well from God's inheritance.' " 17And the woman concluded: "Let the word of my lord the king provide a resting place;* indeed, my lord the king is like an angel of God, evaluating good and bad. The LORD your God be with you." [m]

18The king answered the woman, "Now do not conceal from me anything I may ask you!" The woman said, "Let my lord the king speak." 19So the king asked, "Is Joab involved with you in all this?" And the woman answered: "As you live, my lord the king, it is just as your majesty has said, and not otherwise. It was your servant Joab who instructed me and told your servant all these things she was to say. 20Your servant Joab did this to come at the issue in a roundabout way. But my lord is as wise as an angel of God, so that he knows all things on earth."

Absalom's Return 21Then the king said to Joab: "I hereby grant this request. Go, therefore, and bring back young Absalom." 22Falling prostrate to the ground in homage and blessing the king, Joab said, "This day I know that I am in good favor with you, my lord the king, since the king has granted the request of his servant." 23Joab then went off to Geshur and brought Absalom to Jerusalem. 24But the king said, "Let him go to his own house; he shall not appear before me." So Absalom went off to his house and did not appear before the king.

25In all Israel there was not a man who could so be praised for his beauty as Absalom, who was without blemish from the sole of his foot to the crown of his head. 26When he shaved his head—which he used to do at the end of every year, because his hair became too heavy for him—the hair weighed two hundred shekels according to the royal standard. 27Absalom had three sons born to him, besides a daughter named Tamar, who was a beautiful woman.[n]

Absalom Is Pardoned 28Absalom lived in Jerusalem for two years without appearing before the king. 29Then he summoned Joab to send him to the king, but Joab would not come to him. Although he summoned him a second time, Joab refused to come. 30He therefore instructed his servants: "You see Joab's field that borders mine, on which he has barley. Go, set it on fire." And so Absalom's servants set the field on fire.[o] Joab's farmhands came to him with torn garments and reported to him what had been done. 31At this, Joab went to Absalom in his house and asked him, "Why have your servants set my field on fire?" 32Absalom answered Joab: "I was summoning you to come here, that I may send you to the king to say: 'Why did I come back from Geshur? I would be better off if I were still there!' Now, let me appear before the king. If I am guilty, let him put me to death." 33Joab went to the king and reported this. The king then called Absalom, who came to him and in homage fell on his face to the ground before the king. Then the king kissed him.

CHAPTER 15

Absalom's Plot 1After this Absalom provided himself with chariots, horses, and fifty henchmen.[p] 2Moreover, Absalom used to rise early and stand alongside the road leading to the gate. If someone had a lawsuit to be decided by the king, Absalom would call to him and say, "From what city are you?" And when he replied, "Your servant is of such and such a tribe of Israel," 3Absalom would say to him, "Your suit is good and just, but there is no one to hear you in the king's name." 4And he would continue: "If only I could be appointed judge in the land! Then

14, 14: How not to banish: a possible allusion to the religious institution of cities of refuge for involuntary murderers; see Nm 35, 9–15.

14, 17: A resting place: cf Ps 95, 11; Heb 3, 7—4, 11. The reference here is to a return home for Absalom to Israel.

l Jb 7, 9; 14, 7–12; Ps 88, 5, 11ff. m 17. 20: 1 Sm 29, 9. n 2 Sm 18, 18. o Jgs 15, 4f. p 1 Sm 8, 11; 1 Kgs 1, 5.

everyone who has a lawsuit to be decided might
come to me and I would render him justice."
[5]Whenever a man approached him to show
homage, he would extend his hand, hold him,
and kiss him. [6]By behaving in this way toward
all the Israelites who came to the king for
judgment, Absalom was stealing away the loyal-
ties of the men of Israel.
Conspiracy in Hebron [7]After a period of four
years, Absalom said to the king: "Allow me to go
to Hebron and fulfill a vow I made to the LORD.
[8]For while living in Geshur in Aram, your
servant made this vow: 'If the LORD ever brings
me back to Jerusalem, I will worship him in
Hebron.' "[q] [9]The king wished him a safe jour-
ney, and he went off to Hebron. [10]Then Absalom
sent spies throughout the tribes of Israel to say,
"When you hear the sound of the horn, declare
Absalom king in Hebron." [11]Two hundred men
had accompanied Absalom from Jerusalem. They
had been invited and went in good faith, know-
ing nothing of the plan. [12]Absalom also sent to
Ahithophel the Gilonite, David's counselor, an
invitation to come from his town, Giloh, for the
sacrifices he was about to offer. So the conspir-
acy gained strength, and the people with Absa-
lom increased in numbers.[r]
David Flees Jerusalem [13]An informant came
to David with the report, "The Israelites have
transferred their loyalty to Absalom."[s] [14]At this,
David said to all his servants who were with him
in Jerusalem: "Up! Let us take flight, or none of
us will escape from Absalom. Leave quickly, lest
he hurry and overtake us, then visit disaster
upon us and put the city to the sword." [15]The
king's officers answered him, "Your servants are
ready, whatever our lord the king chooses to
do." [16]Then the king set out, accompanied by
his entire household, except for ten concubines
whom he left behind to take care of the palace.[t]
[17]As the king left the city, with all his officers
accompanying him, they halted opposite the
ascent of the Mount of Olives, at a distance,
[18]while the whole army marched past him.[u]
David and Ittai As all the Cherethites and
Pelethites, and the six hundred men of Gath
who had accompanied him from that city, were
passing in review before the king, [19]he said to
Ittai the Gittite: "Why should you also go with
us? Go back and stay with the king, for you are a
foreigner and you, too, are an exile from your
own country. [20]You came only yesterday, and
shall I have you wander about with us today,
wherever I have to go? Return and take your
brothers with you, and may the LORD be kind
and faithful to you." [21]But Ittai answered the
king, "As the LORD lives, and as my lord the king
lives, your servant shall be wherever my lord the
king may be, whether for death or for life."[v] [22]So
the king said to Ittai, "Go, then, march on." And
Ittai the Gittite, with all his men and all the
dependents that were with him, marched on.
[23]Everyone in the countryside wept aloud as the
last of the soldiers went by, and the king crossed
the Kidron Valley with all the soldiers moving on
ahead of him by way of the Mount of Olives,
toward the desert.
David and the Priests [24]Zadok, too [with all
the Levite bearers of the ark of the covenant of
God], and Abiathar brought the ark of God to a
halt until the soldiers had marched out of the
city. [25]Then the king said to Zadok: "Take the
ark of God back to the city. If I find favor with
the LORD, he will bring me back and permit me
to see it and its lodging. [26]But if he should say, 'I
am not pleased with you,' I am ready; let him do
to me as he sees fit."[w] [27]The king also said to the
priest Zadok: "See to it that you and Abiathar
return to the city in peace, and both your sons
with you, your own son Ahimaaz, and Abia-
thar's son Jonathan. [28]Remember, I shall be
waiting at the fords near the desert until I
receive information from you." [29]So Zadok and
Abiathar took the ark of God back to Jerusalem
and remained there.

[30]As David went up the Mount of Olives, he
wept without ceasing. His head was covered,
and he was walking barefoot. All those who
were with him also had their heads covered and

q 2 Sm 3, 3; 13, 37. r 2 Sm 16, 23. s Ps 3. t 2 Sm 16, 21f; 20, 3. u 2 Sm 8, 18. v Ru 1, 16. w 2 Sm 16, 10.

were weeping as they went.[x] [31]When David was informed that Ahithophel was among the conspirators with Absalom, he said, "O LORD, turn the counsel of Ahithophel to folly!"[y]

David and Hushai [32]When David reached the top, where men used to worship God, Hushai the Archite was there to meet him, with rent garments and dirt upon his head.[z] [33]David said to him: "If you come with me, you will be a burden to me. [34]But if you return to the city and say to Absalom, 'Let me be your servant, O king; I was formerly your father's servant, but now I will be yours,' you will undo for me the counsel of Ahithophel.[a] [35]You will have the priests Zadok and Abiathar there with you. If you hear anything from the royal palace, you shall report it to the priests Zadok and Abiathar, [36]who have there with them both Zadok's son Ahimaaz and Abiathar's son Jonathan. Through them you shall send on to me whatever you hear." [37]So David's friend Hushai went into the city of Jerusalem as Absalom was about to enter it.

CHAPTER 16

David and Ziba [1]David had gone a little beyond the top when Ziba, the servant of Meribbaal, met him with saddled asses laden with two hundred loaves of bread, an ephah of cakes of pressed raisins, an ephah of summer fruits, and a skin of wine.[b] [2]The king said to Ziba, "What do you plan to do with these?" Ziba replied: "The asses are for the king's household to ride on. The bread and summer fruits are for your servants to eat, and the wine for those to drink who are weary in the desert." [3]Then the king said, "And where is your lord's son?" Ziba answered the king, "He is staying in Jerusalem, for he said, 'Now the Israelites will restore to me my father's kingdom.' "[c] [4]The king therefore said to Ziba, "So! Everything Meribbaal had is yours." Then Ziba said: "I pay you homage, my lord the king. May I find favor with you!"[d]

David and Shimei [5]As David was approaching Bahurim, a man named Shimei, the son of Gera of the same clan as Saul's family, was coming out of the place, cursing as he came.[e] [6]He threw stones at David and at all the king's officers, even though all the soldiers, including the royal guard, were on David's right and on his left. [7]Shimei was saying as he cursed: "Away, away, you murderous and wicked man! [8]The LORD has requited you for all the bloodshed in the family of Saul,* in whose stead you became king, and the LORD has given over the kingdom to your son Absalom. And now you suffer ruin because you are a murderer." [9]Abishai, son of Zeruiah, said to the king: "Why should this dead dog curse my lord the king? Let me go over, please, and lop off his head."[f] [10]But the king replied: "What business is it of mine or of yours, sons of Zeruiah, that he curses? Suppose the LORD has told him to curse David; who then will dare to say, 'Why are you doing this?' "[g] [11]Then the king said to Abishai and to all his servants: "If my own son, who came forth from my loins, is seeking my life, how much more might this Benjaminite do so? Let him alone and let him curse, for the LORD has told him to.[h] [12]Perhaps the LORD will look upon my affliction and make it up to me with benefits for the curses he is uttering this day." [13]David and his men continued on the road, while Shimei kept abreast of them on the hillside, all the while cursing and throwing stones and dirt as he went.[i] [14]The king and all the soldiers with him arrived at the Jordan tired out, and stopped there for a rest.

Absalom's Counselors [15]In the meantime Absalom, accompanied by Ahithophel, entered Jerusalem with all the Israelites. [16]When David's friend Hushai the Archite came to Absalom, he said to him: "Long live the king! Long live the king!"[j] [17]But Absalom asked Hushai: "Is this your devotion to your friend? Why did you not go with your friend?" [18]Hushai replied to Absalom: "On the contrary, I am his whom the LORD and all this people and all Israel have chosen, and with him I will stay. [19]Furthermore, as I was in attendance upon your father, so will I be

16, 8: Bloodshed . . . Saul: refers to the episode recounted in 2 Sm 21, 1–14.

x 2 Sm 19, 5; Mi 1, 8. y 2 Sm 16, 23; 17, 14. 23. z 2 Sm 16, 16. a 2 Sm 16, 19. b 2 Sm 4, 4; 9, 1–13; 19, 18. 25. c 2 Sm 19, 26f. d 2 Sm 19, 30. e 2 Sm 3, 16; 19, 17. 22f; 1 Kgs 2, 8. f 2 Sm 19, 23. 29; 1 Sm 24, 15; 26, 6. g 2 Sm 15, 25f; 19, 23. h 2 Sm 12, 11. i 2 Sm 19, 19–24. j 2 Sm 15, 32–37.

before you. Whom should I serve, if not his son?"[k] [20]Then Absalom said to Ahithophel, "Offer your counsel on what we should do." [21]Ahithophel replied to Absalom: "Have relations with your father's concubines, whom he left behind to take care of the palace. When all Israel hears how odious you have made yourself to your father, all your partisans will take courage."[l] [22]So a tent was pitched on the roof for Absalom, and he visited his father's concubines in view of all Israel.[m]

Counsel of Ahithophel [23]Now the counsel given by Ahithophel at that time was as though one had sought divine revelation. Such was all his counsel both to David and to Absalom.[n]

CHAPTER 17

[1]Ahithophel went on to say to Absalom: "Please let me choose twelve thousand men, and be off in pursuit of David tonight. [2]If I come upon him when he is weary and discouraged, I shall cause him to panic. When all the people with him flee, I shall strike down the king alone. [3]Then I can bring back the rest of the people to you, as a bride returns to her husband. It is the death of only one man you are seeking; then all the people will be at peace." [4]This plan was agreeable to Absalom and to all the elders of Israel.

Counsel of Hushai [5]Then Absalom said, "Now call Hushai the Archite also; let us hear what he too has to say." [6]When Hushai came to Absalom, Absalom said to him: "This is what Ahithophel proposed. Shall we follow his proposal? If not, speak up." [7]Hushai replied to Absalom, "This time Ahithophel has not given good counsel." [8]And he went on to say: "You know that your father and his men are warriors, and that they are as fierce as a bear in the wild robbed of her cubs. Moreover, since your father is skilled in warfare, he will not spend the night with the people.[o] [9]Even now he lies hidden in one of the caves or in some other place. And if some of our soldiers should fall at the first attack, whoever hears of it will say, 'Absalom's followers have been slaughtered.' [10]Then even the brave man with the heart of a lion will lose courage. For all Israel knows that your father is a warrior and that those who are with him are brave.

[11]"This is what I counsel: Let all Israel from Dan to Beer-sheba, who are as numerous as the sands by the sea, be called up for combat; and go with them yourself. [12]We can then attack him wherever we find him, settling down upon him as dew alights on the ground. None shall survive—neither he nor any of his followers. [13]And if he retires into a city, all Israel shall bring ropes to that city and we can drag it into the gorge, so that not even a pebble of it can be found." [14]Then Absalom and all the Israelites pronounced the counsel of Hushai the Archite better than that of Ahithophel. For the LORD had decided to undo Ahithophel's good counsel, in order thus to bring Absalom to ruin.[p]

David Told of the Plan [15]Then Hushai said to the priests Zadok and Abiathar: "This is the counsel Ahithophel gave Absalom and the elders of Israel, and this is what I counseled. [16]So send a warning to David immediately, not to spend the night at the fords near the desert, but to cross over without fail. Otherwise the king and all the people with him will be destroyed." [17]Now Jonathan and Ahimaaz were staying at En-rogel, since they could not risk being seen entering the city. A maidservant was to come with information for them, and they in turn were to go and report to King David. [18]But an attendant saw them and informed Absalom. They sped on their way and reached the house of a man in Bahurim who had a cistern in his courtyard. They let themselves down into this, [19]and the housewife took the cover and spread it over the cistern, strewing ground grain on the cover so that nothing could be noticed. [20]When Absalom's servants came to the woman at the house, they asked, "Where are Ahimaaz and Jonathan?" The woman replied, "They went by a short while ago toward the water." They searched, but found no one, and so returned to Jerusalem. [21]As soon as they left, Ahimaaz and Jonathan came up out of the cistern and went on to inform King David. They said to him: "Leave!

k 2 Sm 15, 34. l 2 Sm 15, 16; 20, 3. m 2 Sm 12, 11f. n 2 Sm 15, 12. 31; 17, 23. o Hos 13, 8. p 2 Sm 15, 31.

Cross the water at once, for Ahithophel has
given the following counsel in regard to you."
22 So David and all his people moved on and
crossed the Jordan. By daybreak, there was no
one left who had not crossed.

23 When Ahithophel saw that his counsel was
not acted upon, he saddled his ass and departed,
going to his home in his own city. Then, having
left orders concerning his family, he hanged
himself. And so he died and was buried in his
father's tomb.[q]

24 Now David had gone to Mahanaim when
Absalom crossed the Jordan accompanied by all
the Israelites. 25 Absalom had put Amasa in
command of the army in Joab's place. Amasa
was the son of an Ishmaelite named Ithra, who
had married Abigail, daughter of Jesse and sister
of Joab's mother Zeruiah.[r] 26 Israel and Absalom
encamped in the territory of Gilead.

27 When David came to Mahanaim, Shobi, son
of Nahash from Rabbah of the Ammonites,
Machir, son of Ammiel from Lodebar, and Barzil-
lai, the Gileadite from Rogelim,[s] 28 brought
couches, coverlets, basins and earthenware, as
well as wheat, barley, flour, roasted grain, beans,
lentils,[t] 29 honey, butter and cheese from the
flocks and herds, for David and those who were
with him to eat; for they said, "The people have
been hungry and tired and thirsty in the desert."

CHAPTER 18

Preparation for Battle 1 After mustering the
troops he had with him, David placed officers in
command of groups of a thousand and groups of
a hundred. 2 David then put a third part of the
soldiers under Joab's command, a third under
command of Abishai, son of Zeruiah and brother
of Joab, and a third under command of Ittai the
Gittite. The king then said to the soldiers, "I
intend to go out with you myself." 3 But they
replied: "You must not come out with us. For if
we should flee, we shall not count; even if half
of us should die, we shall not count. You are
equal to ten thousand of us. Therefore it is better
that we have you to help us from the city." 4 So
the king said to them, "I will do what you think
best"; and he stood by the gate as all the soldiers
marched out in units of a hundred and of a
thousand. 5 But the king gave this command to
Joab, Abishai and Ittai: "Be gentle with young
Absalom for my sake." All the soldiers heard the
king instruct the various leaders with regard to
Absalom.

Defeat of Absalom 6 David's army then took
the field against Israel, and a battle was fought in
the forest near Mahanaim. 7 The forces of Israel
were defeated by David's servants, and the
casualties there that day were heavy—twenty
thousand men. 8 The battle spread out over that
entire region, and the thickets consumed more
combatants that day than did the sword.

Death of Absalom 9 Absalom unexpectedly
came up against David's servants. He was
mounted on a mule, and, as the mule passed
under the branches of a large terebinth, his hair
caught fast in the tree. He hung between heaven
and earth while the mule he had been riding ran
off. 10 Someone saw this and reported to Joab
that he had seen Absalom hanging from a
terebinth. 11 Joab said to his informant: "If you
saw him, why did you not strike him to the
ground on the spot? Then it would have been
my duty to give you fifty pieces of silver and a
belt." 12 But the man replied to Joab: "Even if I
already held a thousand pieces of silver in my
two hands, I would not harm the king's son, for
the king charged you and Abishai and Ittai in our
hearing to protect the youth Absalom for his
sake. 13 Had I been disloyal and killed him, the
whole matter would have come to the attention
of the king, and you would stand aloof." 14 Joab
replied, "I will not waste time with you in this
way." And taking three pikes in hand, he thrust
for the heart of Absalom, still hanging from the
tree alive.[u] 15 Next, ten of Joab's young armor-
bearers closed in on Absalom, and killed him
with further blows. 16 Joab then sounded the
horn, and the soldiers turned back from the
pursuit of the Israelites, because Joab called on
them to halt.[v] 17 Absalom was taken up and cast
into a deep pit in the forest, and a very large

q 2 Sm 15, 31; 16, 23. r 2 Sm 19, 14; 20, 4–13. s 2 Sm 9, 4; 19, 32; 1 Kgs 2, 7. t 2 Sm 19, 32; Ezr 2, 61. u 2 Sm 12, 10; 13, 28f. v 2 Sm 20, 23–26.

mound of stones was erected over him. And all
the Israelites fled to their own tents.[w]
18 During his lifetime Absalom had taken a
pillar and erected it for himself in the King's
Valley, for he said, "I have no son to perpetuate
my name." The pillar which he named for
himself is called Yad-abshalom to the present
day.[x]

David Told of Absalom's Death 19 Then Ahim-
aaz, son of Zadok, said, "Let me run to take the
good news to the king that the LORD has set him
free from the grasp of his enemies." 20 But Joab
said to him: "You are not the man to bring the
news today. On some other day you may take
the good news, but today you would not be
bringing good news, for in fact the king's son is
dead." 21 Then Joab said to a Cushite, "Go, tell
the king what you have seen." The Cushite
bowed to Joab and sped away. 22 But Ahimaaz,
son of Zadok, said to Joab again, "Come what
may, permit me also to run after the Cushite."
Joab replied: "Why do you want to run, my son?
You will receive no reward." 23 But he insisted,
"Come what may, I want to run." Joab said to
him, "Very well." Ahimaaz sped off by way of
the Jordan plain and outran the Cushite.
24 Now David was sitting between the two
gates, and a lookout mounted to the roof of the
gate above the city wall, where he looked about
and saw a man running all alone. 25 The lookout
shouted to inform the king, who said, "If he is
alone, he has good news to report." As he kept
coming nearer, 26 the lookout spied another run-
ner. From his place atop the gate he cried out,
"There is another man running by himself." And
the king responded, "He, too, is bringing good
news." 27 Then the lookout said, "I notice that
the first one runs like Ahimaaz, son of Zadok."
The king replied, "He is a good man; he comes
with good news."[y] 28 Then Ahimaaz called out
and greeted the king. With face to the ground he
paid homage to the king and said, "Blessed be
the LORD your God, who has delivered up the
men who rebelled against my lord the king."
29 But the king asked, "Is the youth Absalom
safe?" And Ahimaaz replied, "I saw a great
disturbance when the king's servant Joab sent
your servant on, but I do not know what it was."
30 The king said, "Step aside and remain in
attendance here." So he stepped aside and
remained there. 31 When the Cushite came in,
he said, "Let my lord the king receive the good
news that this day the LORD has taken your part,
freeing you from the grasp of all who rebelled
against you." 32 But the king asked the Cushite,
"Is young Absalom safe?" The Cushite replied,
"May the enemies of my lord the king and all
who rebel against you with evil intent be as that
young man!"

CHAPTER 19

1 The king was shaken, and went up to the
room over the city gate to weep. He said as he
wept, "My son Absalom! My son, my son
Absalom! If only I had died instead of you,
Absalom, my son, my son!"

Joab Reproves David 2 Joab was told that the
king was weeping and mourning for Absalom;
3 and that day's victory was turned into mourn-
ing for the whole army when they heard that the
king was grieving for his son. 4 The soldiers stole
into the city that day like men shamed by flight
in battle. 5 Meanwhile the king covered his face
and cried out in a loud voice, "My son Absalom!
Absalom! My son, my son!"[z] 6 Then Joab went
to his residence and said: "Though they saved
your life and your sons' and daughters' lives, also
the lives of your wives and those of your
concubines, you have put all your servants to
shame today 7 by loving those who hate you and
hating those who love you. For you have shown
today that officers and servants mean nothing to
you. Indeed I am now certain that if Absalom
were alive today and all of us dead, you would
think that more suitable. 8 Now then, get up! Go
out and speak kindly to your servants. I swear by
the LORD that if you do not go out, not a single
man will remain with you overnight, and this
will be a far greater disaster for you than any that
has afflicted you from your youth until now."
9 So the king stepped out and sat at the gate.
When all the people were informed that the king

w Jos 7, 26; 8, 29; 10, 27. x 2 Sm 14, 27. y 2 Kgs 9, 20.
z 2 Sm 15, 30.

was sitting at the gate, they came into his presence.

The Reconciliation Now the Israelites had fled to their separate tents, [10]but throughout the tribes of Israel all the people were arguing among themselves, saying to one another: "The king delivered us from the clutches of our enemies, and it was he who rescued us from the grip of the Philistines. But now he has fled from the country before Absalom, [11]and Absalom, whom we anointed over us, died in battle. Why, then, should you remain silent about restoring the king to his palace?" When the talk of all Israel reached the king, [12]David sent word to the priests Zadok and Abiathar: "Say to the elders of Judah: 'Why should you be last to restore the king to his palace? [13]You are my brothers, you are my bone and flesh. Why should you be last to restore the king?' [14]Also say to Amasa: 'Are you not my bone and flesh? May God do thus and so to me, if you do not become my general permanently in place of Joab.' "[a] [15]He won over all the Judahites as one man, and so they summoned the king to return, with all his servants.

David and Shimei [16]When the king, on his return, reached the Jordan, Judah had come to Gilgal to meet him and to escort him across the Jordan. [17]Shimei, son of Gera, the Benjaminite from Bahurim, hurried down with the Judahites to meet King David,[b] [18]accompanied by a thousand men from Benjamin. Ziba, too, the servant of the house of Saul, accompanied by his fifteen sons and twenty servants, hastened to the Jordan before the king.[c] [19] [d]They crossed over the ford to bring the king's household over and to do whatever he wished. When Shimei, son of Gera, crossed the Jordan, he fell down before the king [20]and said to him: "May my lord not hold me guilty, and may he not remember and take to heart the wrong that your servant did the day my lord the king left Jerusalem. [21]For your servant knows that he has done wrong. Yet realize that I have been the first of the whole house of Joseph to come down today to meet my lord the king." [22]But Abishai, son of Zeruiah, countered: "Shimei must be put to death for this. He cursed the LORD's anointed." [23]David replied: "What has come between you and me, sons of Zeruiah, that you would create enmity for me this day? Should anyone die today in Israel? Am I not aware that today I am king of Israel?"[e] [24]Then the king said to Shimei, "You shall not die." And the king gave him his oath.

David and Meribbaal [25]Meribbaal, son of Saul, also went down to meet the king. He had not washed his feet nor trimmed his mustache nor washed his clothes from the day the king left until he returned safely. [26]When he came from Jerusalem to meet the king, the king asked him, "Why did you not go with me, Meribbaal?"[f] [27]He replied: "My lord the king, my servant betrayed me. For your servant, who is lame, said to him, 'Saddle the ass for me, that I may ride on it and go with the king.'[g] [28]But he slandered your servant before my lord the king. But my lord the king is like an angel of God. Do what you judge best. [29]For though my father's entire house deserved only death from my lord the king, yet you placed your servant among the guests at your table. What right do I still have to make further appeal to the king?"[h] [30]But the king said to him: "Why do you go on talking? I say, 'You and Ziba shall divide the property.' "[i] [31]Meribbaal answered the king, "Indeed let him have it all, now that my lord the king has returned safely to his palace."

David and Barzillai [32]Barzillai the Gileadite also came down from Rogelim and escorted the king to the Jordan for his crossing, taking leave of him there.[j] [33]It was Barzillai, a very old man of eighty and very wealthy besides, who had provisioned the king during his stay in Mahanaim. [34]The king said to Barzillai, "Cross over with me, and I will provide for your old age as my guest in Jerusalem." [35]But Barzillai answered the king: "How much longer have I to live, that I should go up to Jerusalem with the king? [36]I am

a 2 Sm 17, 25; 20, 4. b 2 Sm 16, 5–13. c 2 Sm 16, 1–4; 19, 25–31. d 19ff: 2 Sm 16, 13; Ex 22, 27; 1 Kgs 2, 8. e 2 Sm 16, 9f; 1 Sm 11, 13; 1 Kgs 2, 8. 38. 46. f 2 Sm 16, 3. g 2 Sm 9, 2–13; Dt 21, 12f. h 2 Sm 9, 9ff. i 2 Sm 16, 4. j 2 Sm 17, 27ff; 1 Kgs 2, 7; Ezr 2, 61.

now eighty years old. Can I distinguish between
good and bad? Can your servant taste what he
eats and drinks, or still appreciate the voices of
singers and songstresses? Why should your ser-
vant be any further burden to my lord the king?
[37]In escorting the king across the Jordan, your
servant is doing little enough! Why should the
king give me this reward? [38]Please let your
servant go back to die in his own city by the
tomb of his father and mother. Here is your
servant Chimham. Let him cross over with my
lord the king. Do for him whatever you will."
[39]Then the king said to him, "Chimham shall
come over with me, and I will do for him as you
would wish. And anything else you would like
me to do for you, I will do." [40]Then all the
people crossed over the Jordan, but the king
remained; he kissed Barzillai and bade him
Godspeed as he returned to his own district.
[41]Finally the king crossed over to Gilgal, accom-
panied by Chimham.
Israel and Judah Quarrel All the people of
Judah and half of the people of Israel had
escorted the king across. [42]But all these Israelites
began coming to the king and saying, "Why did
our brothers the Judahites steal you away and
escort the king and his household across the
Jordan, along with all David's men?" [43]All the
Judahites replied to the men of Israel: "Because
the king is our relative. Why are you angry over
this affair? Have we had anything to eat at the
king's expense? Or have portions from his table
been given to us?" [44]The Israelites answered the
Judahites: "We have ten shares in the king. Also,
we are the first-born rather than you. Why do
you slight us? Were we not first to speak of
restoring the king?" Then the Judahites in turn
spoke even more fiercely than the Israelites. [k]

CHAPTER 20

Sheba's Rebellion [1]Now a rebellious individ-
ual from Benjamin named Sheba, the son of
Bichri, happened to be there. He sounded the
horn and cried out,

"We have no portion in David,
nor any share in the son of Jesse.
Every man to his tent, O Israel!" [l]

[2]So all the Israelites left David for Sheba, son of
Bichri. But from the Jordan to Jerusalem the
Judahites remained loyal to their king. [3]When
King David came to his palace in Jerusalem, he
took the ten concubines whom he had left
behind to take care of the palace and placed
them in confinement. He provided for them, but
had no further relations with them. And so they
remained in confinement to the day of their
death, lifelong widows. [m]
Amasa's Death [4]Then the king said to Amasa:
"Summon the Judahites for me within three
days. Then present yourself here." [n] [5]Accord-
ingly Amasa set out to summon Judah, but
delayed beyond the time set for him by David.
[6]Then David said to Abishai: "Sheba, son of
Bichri, may now do us more harm than Absalom
did. Take your lord's servants and pursue him,
lest he find fortified cities and take shelter while
we look on." [7]So Joab and the Cherethites and
Pelethites and all the warriors marched out
behind Abishai from Jerusalem to campaign in
pursuit of Sheba, son of Bichri. [o] [8]*They were at
the great stone in Gibeon when Amasa met
them. Now Joab had a belt over his tunic, from
which was slung, in its sheath near his thigh, a
sword that could be drawn with a downward
movement. [p] [9]And Joab asked Amasa, "How are
you, my brother?" With his right hand Joab held
Amasa's beard as if to kiss him. [10]And since
Amasa was not on his guard against the sword in
Joab's other hand, Joab stabbed him in the
abdomen with it, so that his entrails burst forth
to the ground, and he died without receiving a
second thrust. Then Joab and his brother Abishai
pursued Sheba, son of Bichri. [q] [11]One of Joab's
attendants stood by Amasa and said, "Let him
who favors Joab and is for David follow Joab."
[12]Amasa lay covered with blood in the middle of
the highroad, and the man noticed that all the

20, 8: The text of this verse is quite uncertain.

k 1 Kgs 11, 31. l 1 Kgs 12, 16. m 2 Sm 15, 16; 16, 20ff.
n 2 Sm 17, 25; 19, 14. o 2 Sm 8, 18. p 2 Sm 2, 13. q 1 Kgs 2, 5.

soldiers were stopping. So he removed Amasa
from the road to the field and placed a garment
over him, because all who came up to him were
stopping. 13When he had been removed from
the road, everyone went on after Joab in pursuit
of Sheba, son of Bichri.
Joab Pursues Sheba 14Sheba passed through
all the tribes of Israel to Abel Beth-maacah. Then
all the Bichrites assembled and they too entered
the city after him. 15So David's servants came
and besieged him in Abel Beth-maacah. They
threw up a mound against the city, and all the
soldiers who were with Joab began battering the
wall to throw it down. 16Then a wise woman
from the city stood on the outworks and called
out, "Listen, listen! Tell Joab to come here, that I
may speak with him." 17When Joab had come
near her, the woman said, "Are you Joab?" And
he replied, "Yes." She said to him, "Listen to
what your maidservant has to say." He replied,
"I am listening." 18Then she went on to say:
"There is an ancient saying,* 'Let them ask if
they will in Abel[r] 19or in Dan whether loyalty is
finished or ended in Israel.' You are seeking to
beat down a city that is a mother in Israel. Why
do you wish to destroy the inheritance of the
LORD?" 20Joab answered, "Not at all, not at all! I
do not wish to destroy or to ruin anything.
21That is not the case at all. A man named
Sheba, son of Bichri, from the hill country of
Ephraim has rebelled against King David. Surren-
der him alone, and I will withdraw from the
city." Then the woman said to Joab, "His head
shall be thrown to you across the wall." 22She
went to all the people with her advice, and they
cut off the head of Sheba, son of Bichri, and
threw it out to Joab. He then sounded the horn,
and they scattered from the city to their own
tents, while Joab returned to Jerusalem to the
king.
David's Officials 23Joab was in command of
the whole army of Israel. Banaiah, son of Jehoi-
ada, was in command of the Cherethites and
Pelethites.[s] 24Adoram was in charge of the
forced labor. Jehoshaphat, son of Ahilud, was the
chancellor. 25Shawsha was the scribe. Zadok and
Abiathar were priests.[t] 26Ira the Jairite was also
David's priest.

V: APPENDIXES

CHAPTER 21

Gibeonite Vengeance 1During David's reign
there was a famine for three successive years.
David had recourse to the LORD, who said,
"There is bloodguilt on Saul and his family
because he put the Gibeonites to death."[u] 2So
the king called the Gibeonites and spoke to
them. (Now the Gibeonites were not Israelites,
but survivors of the Amorites; and although the
Israelites had given them their oath, Saul had
attempted to kill them off in his zeal for the men
of Israel and Judah.)[v] 3David said to the Gibeon-
ites, "What must I do for you and how must I
make atonement, that you may bless the inheri-
tance of the LORD?" 4The Gibeonites answered
him, "We have no claim against Saul and his
house for silver or gold, nor is it our place to put
any man to death in Israel." Then he said, "I will
do for you whatever you propose." 5They said to
the king, "As for the man who was exterminat-
ing us and who intended to destroy us that we
might have no place in all the territory of Israel,
6let seven men from among his descendants be
given to us, that we may dismember them before
the LORD in Gibeon, on the LORD's mountain."
The king replied, "I will give them up." 7The
king, however, spared Meribbaal, son of Jona-
than, son of Saul, because of the LORD's oath
that formed a bond between David and Saul's
son Jonathan.[w] 8But the king took Armoni and
Meribbaal, the two sons that Aiah's daughter
Rizpah had borne to Saul, and the five sons of
Saul's daughter Merob that she had borne to
Adriel, son of Barzillai the Meholathite,[x] 9and
surrendered them to the Gibeonites. They then
dismembered them on the mountain before the
LORD. The seven fell at the one time; they were

20, 18f: The proverbial expression here has been poorly transmitted, and its sense is doubtful.

r Gn 49, 16. s 2 Sm 8, 16ff; 23, 20. t 2 Sm 8, 17f. u 2 Sm 24, 13. v Jos 9, 3–27. w 2 Sm 9, 13; 1 Sm 18, 3; 20, 8ff. 15f. 42. x 2 Sm 3, 7.

put to death during the first days of the
harvest—that is, at the beginning of the barley
harvest.
10 Then Rizpah, Aiah's daughter, took sack-
cloth and spread it out for herself on the rock
from the beginning of the harvest until rain came
down on them from the sky, fending off the birds
of the sky from settling on them by day, and the
wild animals by night.[y] 11 When David was
informed of what Rizpah, Aiah's daughter, the
concubine of Saul, had done, 12 he went and
obtained the bones of Saul and of his son
Jonathan from the citizens of Jabesh-gilead, who
had carried them off secretly from the public
square of Beth-shan, where the Philistines had
hanged them at the time they killed Saul on
Gilboa.[z] 13 When he had brought up from there
the bones of Saul and of his son Jonathan, the
bones of those who had been dismembered were
also gathered up. 14 Then the bones of Saul and
of his son Jonathan were buried in the tomb of
his father Kish at Zela in the territory of Benja-
min. After all that the king commanded had
been carried out, God granted relief to the land.[a]
Exploits in Philistine Wars 15 There was an-
other battle between the Philistines and Israel.
David went down with his servants and fought
the Philistines, but David grew tired. 16 Dadu,
one of the Rephaim, whose bronze spear
weighed three hundred shekels, was about to
take him captive. Dadu was girt with a new
sword and planned to kill David, 17 but Abishai,
son of Zeruiah, came to his assistance and struck
and killed the Philistine. Then David's men
swore to him, "You must not go out to battle
with us again, lest you quench the lamp of
Israel."[b]
18 [c]After this there was another battle with the
Philistines in Gob. On that occasion Sibbecai,
from Husha, killed Saph, one of the Rephaim.[d]
19 [e]There was another battle with the Philistines
in Gob, in which Elhanan, son of Jair from
Bethlehem, killed Goliath of Gath, who had a
spear with a shaft like a weaver's heddle-bar.
20 There was another battle at Gath in which
there was a man of large stature with six fingers
on each hand and six toes on each foot—twenty-
four in all. He too was one of the Rephaim.
21 And when he insulted Israel, Jonathan, son of
David's brother Shimei, killed him.[f] 22 These
four were Rephaim in Gath, and they fell at the
hands of David and his servants.

CHAPTER 22

Song of Thanksgiving* 1 David sang the
words of this song to the LORD when the LORD
had rescued him from the grasp of all his
enemies and from the hand of Saul.[g] 2 This is
what he sang:[h]

A

I

"O LORD, my rock, my fortress, my deliverer,
3 my God, my rock of refuge!
My shield, the horn of my salvation,*
my stronghold, my refuge,
my savior, from violence you keep me safe.[i]
4 'Praised be the LORD,' I exclaim,
and I am safe from my enemies.

II

5 "The breakers of death surged round about
me,*
the floods of perdition overwhelmed me;
6 The cords of the nether world enmeshed me,
the snares of death overtook me.
7 In my distress I called upon the LORD
and cried out to my God;

22, 1–51: This song of thanksgiving is also given, with a few small variants, in Ps 18. In both places it is attributed to David. Two main sections can be distinguished. In the first part, after an introductory stanza of praise to God (2–4), David describes the peril he was in (5–7), and then poetically depicts, under the form of a theophany, God's intervention in his behalf (8–20), concluding with an acknowledgment of God's justice (21–31). In the second part, God is praised for having prepared the psalmist for war (32–35), given him victory over his enemies (36–39), whom he put to flight (40–43), and bestowed on him dominion over many peoples (44–46). The entire song ends with paean of grateful praise (47–51).

22, 3: The horn of my salvation: my strong savior. The horn, the dreadful weapon of an enraged bull, was a symbol of strength; cf Lk 1, 69.

22, 5f: These verses are to be understood figuratively.

y 2 Sm 3, 31; 12, 16. z 1 Sm 31, 10–13. a 2 Sm 24, 25. b 1 Kgs 11, 36; 15, 4; 2 Kgs 8, 19. c 18–22: 1 Chr 20, 4–8. d 2 Sm 23, 27. e 19f: 1 Sm 17, 4. 7. f 2 Sm 13, 3. g Ps 18, 1. h 2–51: Ps 18, 3–51. i 1 Sm 2, 1f.

From his temple* he heard my voice,
and my cry reached his ears.

III

8 "The earth swayed and quaked;*
the foundations of the heavens trembled
and shook when his wrath flared up.
9 Smoke rose from his nostrils,
and a devouring fire from his mouth;
he kindled coals into flame.
10 He inclined the heavens and came down,
with dark clouds under his feet.[j]
11 He mounted a cherub* and flew,
borne on the wings of the wind.[k]
12 He made darkness the shelter about him,
with spattering rain and thickening clouds.
13 From the brightness of his presence
coals were kindled to flame.
14 "The LORD thundered from heaven;
the Most High gave forth his voice.
15 He sent forth arrows to put them to flight;
he flashed lightning and routed them.[l]
16 Then the wellsprings of the sea appeared,
the foundations of the earth were laid bare,
At the rebuke of the LORD,
at the blast of the wind of his wrath.
17 "He reached out from on high and grasped me;
he drew me out of the deep waters.[m]
18 He rescued me from my mighty enemy,
from my foes, who were too powerful for me.
19 They attacked me on my day of calamity,
but the LORD came to my support.
20 He set me free in the open,
and rescued me, because he loves me.

IV

21 "The LORD rewarded me according to my justice;
according to the cleanness of my hands he requited me.
22 For I kept the ways of the LORD
and was not disloyal to my God.
23 For his ordinances were all present to me,
and his statutes I put not from me;
24 But I was wholehearted toward him,
and I was on my guard against guilt.
25 And the LORD requited me according to my justice,
according to my innocence in his sight.
26 [n]"Toward the faithful you are faithful;*
toward the wholehearted you are wholehearted;
27 Toward the sincere you are sincere;
but toward the crooked you are astute.
28 You save lowly people,
though on the lofty your eyes look down.
29 You are my lamp,* O LORD!
O my God, you brighten the darkness about me.
30 For with your aid I run against an armed band,
and by the help of my God I leap over a wall.
31 God's way is unerring;
the promise of the LORD is fire-tried;
he is a shield to all who take refuge in him."[o]

B

I

32 "For who is God except the LORD?
Who is a rock save our God?
33 The God who girded me with strength
and kept my way unerring;
34 Who made my feet swift as those of hinds

22, 7: His temple: his heavenly abode.

22, 8ff: God's intervention is graphically portrayed under the figures of an earthquake (vv 8. 16) and a thunderstorm (vv 9–15); cf Jgs 5, 4f; Pss 29; 97, 2–6; Hb 3.

22, 11: He mounted a cherub: since God makes the winds his messengers, or "angels" (Ps 104, 4), he is spoken of poetically as riding on the clouds, or on the angelic creatures called "cherubim." His earthly throne above the ark of the covenant was likewise associated with two winged cherubim; cf Ex 37, 7ff. In both senses the Lord is enthroned upon the cherubim; cf Pss 79, 2; 99, 1.

22, 26f: Men are treated by God in the same way they treat him and their fellow men.

22, 29: My lamp: a figure of life and happiness; cf 1 Kgs 11, 36.

j Ps 144, 5. k Ex 25, 18. l Ps 144, 6. m Ps 144, 7. n 26f: 1 Sm 2, 30. o Prv 30, 5.

and set me on the heights;*
35 Who trained my hands for war
till my arms could bend a bow of brass.

II

36 "You have given me your saving shield,
and your help has made me great.
37 You made room for my steps;
unwavering was my stride.
38 I pursued my enemies and destroyed them,
nor did I turn again till I made an end of them.
39 I smote them and they did not rise;
they fell beneath my feet.

III

40 "You girded me with strength for war;
you subdued my adversaries beneath me.
41 My enemies you put to flight before me
and those who hated me I destroyed.
42 They cried for help—but no one saved them;
to the LORD—but he answered them not.
43 I ground them fine as the dust of the earth;
like the mud in the streets I trampled them down.

IV

44 "You rescued me from the strife of my people;
you made me head over nations.
A people I had not known became my slaves;
45 as soon as they heard me, they obeyed.
46 The foreigners fawned and cringed before me;
they staggered forth from their fortresses."

C

47 "The LORD live! And blessed be my Rock!
Extolled be my God, Rock of my salvation.
48 O God, who granted me vengeance,
who made peoples subject to me
49 and helped me escape from my enemies,
Above my adversaries you exalt me
and from the violent man you rescue me.
50 Therefore will I proclaim you, O LORD, among the nations,
and I will sing praise to your name, [p]
51 You who gave great victories to your king
and showed kindness to your anointed,
to David and his posterity forever."

CHAPTER 23

The Last Words of David*

1 These are the last words of David:
"The utterance of David, son of Jesse;
the utterance of the man God raised up,
Anointed of the God of Jacob,
favorite of the Mighty One of Israel. [q]
2 The spirit of the LORD spoke through me;
his word was on my tongue. [r]
3 The God of Israel spoke;
of me the Rock of Israel said,
'He that rules over men in justice,
that rules in the fear of God, [s]
4 Is like the morning light at sunrise
on a cloudless morning,
making the greensward sparkle after rain.' [t]
5 Is not my house firm before God?
He has made an eternal covenant with me,
set forth in detail and secured. [u]
Will he not bring to fruition
all my salvation and my every desire?
6 But the wicked are all like thorns to be cast away;
they cannot be taken up by hand. [v]
7 He who wishes to touch them
must arm himself with iron and the shaft of a spear,
and they must be consumed by fire."

David's Warriors 8 These are the names of Da-
vid's warriors.* Ishbaal, son of Hachamoni, was
the first of the Three. It was he who brandished
his battle-ax over eight hundred slain in a single
encounter. [w] 9 Next to him, among the Three

22, 34: The heights: a natural stronghold safe from attack; cf Ps 62, 3; Hb 3, 19.

23, 1–7: The text of this short composition in the spirit of the wisdom writers (Prv 30, 1–6) is difficult in places; it views David's career in retrospect.

23, 8ff: There are thirty-seven warriors in all mentioned in this list. First there are the Three warriors most noted for singlehanded exploits (vv 8–12). Then comes the story of a daring adventure by three unnamed members of the larger group (vv 13–17). Next come the commanders of the king's bodyguard, Abishai (vv 18–19) and Benaiah (vv 20–23), with whom must be counted Asahel (v 24) and Joab (vv 18. 24. 37), and finally the group of the Thirty (vv 24–39).

p Ps 22, 23; Rom 15, 9. q 1 Kgs 2, 3–9; Sir 47, 8. r Is 59, 21; Jer 1, 9. s Ps 72, 1–4. t Jgs 5, 31; Ps 72, 6. u 2 Sm 7, 11. 15f; Ps 89, 30; Is 55, 3. v Dt 13, 14. w 8–39: 1 Chr 11, 41; 27, 1–15.

warriors, was Eleazar, son of Dodo the Ahohite.
He was with David at Ephesdammim when the
Philistines assembled there for battle. The Israel-
ites had retreated,[x] 10but he stood his ground
and fought the Philistines until his hand grew
tired and became cramped, holding fast to the
sword. The LORD brought about a great victory
on that day; the soldiers turned back after Elea-
zar, but only to strip the slain. 11Next to him was
Shammah, son of Agee the Hararite. The Philis-
tines had assembled at Lehi, where there was a
plot of land full of lentils. When the soldiers fled
from the Philistines,[y] 12he took his stand in the
middle of the plot and defended it. He slew the
Philistines, and the LORD brought about a great
victory. Such were the deeds of the Three war-
riors.

13During the harvest three of the Thirty went
down to David in the cave of Adullam, while a
Philistine clan was encamped in the Vale of
Rephaim.[z] 14At that time David was in the
refuge, and there was a garrison of Philistines in
Bethlehem. 15Now David had a strong craving
and said, "Oh, that someone would give me a
drink of water from the cistern that is by the gate
of Bethlehem!" 16So the Three warriors broke
through the Philistine camp and drew water
from the cistern that is by the gate of Bethlehem.
But when they brought it to David he refused to
drink it, and instead poured it out to the LORD,
17saying: "The LORD forbid that I do this! Can I
drink the blood of these men who went at the
risk of their lives?" So he refused to drink it.

18Abishai, brother of Joab, son of Zeruiah, was
at the head of the Thirty. It was he who bran-
dished his spear over three hundred slain. He was
listed among the Thirty 19and commanded
greater respect than the Thirty, becoming their
leader. However, he did not attain to the Three.

20Benaiah, son of Jehoiada, a stalwart from
Kabzeel, was a man of great achievements. It
was he who slew the two lions in Moab. He also
went down and killed the lion in the cistern at
the time of the snow.[a] 21It was he, too, who
slew an Egyptian of large stature. Although the
Egyptian was armed with a spear, he went
against him with a club and wrested the spear
from the Egyptian's hand, then killed him with
his own spear. 22Such were the deeds performed
by Benaiah, son of Jehoiada. He was listed
among the Thirty warriors 23and commanded
greater respect than the Thirty. However, he did
not attain to the Three. David put him in
command of his bodyguard.[b] 24Asahel,* brother
of Joab . . . .[c]

Among the Thirty were: Elhanan, son of Dodo,
from Bethlehem; 25Shammah from En-harod;
Elika from En-harod; 26Helez from Beth-pelet;
Ira, son of Ikkesh, from Tekoa; 27Abiezer from
Anathoth; Sibbekai from Hushah;[d] 28Zalmon
from Ahoh; Maharai from Netophah; 29Heled,
son of Baanath, from Netophah; Ittai, son of Ribai,
from Gibeah of the Benjaminites; 30Benaiah from
Pirathon; Hiddai from Nahale-gaash; 31Abibaal
from Beth-arabah; Azmaveth from Bahurim;
32Eliahba from Shaalbon; Jashen the Gunite; Jona-
than, 33son of Shammah the Hararite; Ahiam, son
of Sharar the Hararite; 34Eliphelet, son of Ahas-
bai, from Beth-maacah; Eliam, son of Ahithophel,
from Gilo; 35Hezrai from Carmel; Paarai the Ar-
bite; 36Igal, son of Nathan, from Zobah; Bani the
Gadite; 37Zelek the Ammonite; Naharai from Bee-
roth, armor-bearer of Joab, son of Zeruiah; 38Ira
from Jattir; Gareb from Jattir; 39Uriah the
Hittite—thirty-seven in all.[e]

CHAPTER 24

Census of the People 1*The LORD's anger
against Israel flared again,[f] and he incited David
against the Israelites by prompting him to num-
ber Israel and Judah. 2Accordingly the king said
to Joab and the leaders of the army who were
with him, "Tour all the tribes in Israel from Dan
to Beer-sheba and register the people, that I may
know their number." 3But Joab said to the king:
"May the LORD your God increase the number of

23, 24: A more complete notice about Asahel, who died early in his career (2 Sm 2, 16–23), is to be presumed lost at this point. Elhanan is the first of the Thirty.

24, 1ff: This story was probably joined at one time to 2 Sm 21, 1–14.

x 1 Sm 17, 1. y Jgs 15, 9. z 1 Sm 22, 1; Mi 1, 15. a 2 Sm 8, 18; 20, 23; Jgs 14, 6; 1 Kgs 2, 29f. b 1 Sm 22, 14. c 2 Sm 2, 18–23. d 2 Sm 21, 18. e 2 Sm 11, 3f. f 1–25: 1 Chr 21, 1–27.

people a hundredfold for your royal majesty to
see it with his own eyes. But why does it please
my lord the king to order a thing of this kind?"
4 The king, however, overruled Joab and the lead-
ers of the army, so they left the king's presence
in order to register the people of Israel. 5 Crossing
the Jordan, they began near Aroer, south of the
city in the wadi, and went in the direction of
Gad, toward Jazer. 6 They continued on to Gilead
and to the district below Mount Hermon. Then
they proceeded to Dan; from there they turned
toward Sidon, 7 going to the fortress of Tyre and
to all the cities of the Hivites and Canaanites,
and ending up at Beer-sheba in the Negeb of
Judah. 8 Thus they toured the whole country,
reaching Jerusalem again after nine months and
twenty days. 9 Joab then reported to the king the
number of people registered: in Israel, eight hun-
dred thousand men fit for military service; in
Judah, five hundred thousand.
The Pestilence 10 Afterward, however, David
regretted having numbered the people, and said
to the LORD: "I have sinned grievously in what I
have done.[g] But now, LORD, forgive the guilt of
your servant, for I have been very foolish."*
11 When David rose in the morning, the LORD had
spoken to the prophet Gad, David's seer, saying:
12 "Go and say to David, 'This is what the LORD
says: I offer you three alternatives; choose one of
them, and I will inflict it on you.' " 13 Gad then
went to David to inform him. He asked: "Do you
want a three years' famine to come upon your
land, or to flee from your enemy three months
while he pursues you, or to have a three days'
pestilence in your land? Now consider and decide
what I must reply to him who sent me."[h] 14 David
answered Gad: "I am in very serious difficulty.
Let us fall by the hand of God, for he is most
merciful; but let me not fall by the hand of man."
15 Thus David chose the pestilence. Now it was
the time of the wheat harvest when the plague
broke out among the people. [The LORD then sent
a pestilence over Israel from morning until the
time appointed, and seventy thousand of the peo-
ple from Dan to Beer-sheba died.] 16 But when the
angel stretched forth his hand toward Jerusalem
to destroy it, the LORD regretted the calamity and
said to the angel causing the destruction among
the people, "Enough now! Stay your hand." The
angel of the LORD was then standing at the thresh-
ing floor of Araunah the Jebusite.[i] 17 When David
saw the angel who was striking the people, he
said to the LORD: "It is I who have sinned; it is I,
the shepherd, who have done wrong. But these
are sheep; what have they done? Punish me and
my kindred."*
Sacrifice of Atonement 18 On the same day
Gad went to David and said to him, "Go up and
build an altar to the LORD on the threshing floor
of Araunah the Jebusite." 19 Following Gad's
bidding, David went up as the LORD had com-
manded. 20 Now Araunah looked down and
noticed the king and his servants coming toward
him while he was threshing wheat. So he went
out and paid homage to the king, with face to
the ground. 21 Then Araunah asked, "Why does
my lord the king come to his servant?" David
replied, "To buy the threshing floor from you, to
build an altar to the LORD, that the plague may
be checked among the people." 22 [j]But Araunah
said to David: "Let my lord the king take and
offer up whatever he may wish. Here are oxen
for holocausts, and threshing sledges and the
yokes of the oxen for wood. 23 All this does
Araunah give to the king." Araunah then said to
the king, "May the LORD your God accept your
offering." 24 The king, however, replied to Arau-
nah, "No, I must pay you for it, for I cannot offer
to the LORD my God holocausts that cost noth-
ing." So David bought the threshing floor and
the oxen for fifty silver shekels. 25 Then David
built an altar there to the LORD, and offered
holocausts and peace offerings. The LORD
granted relief to the country, and the plague was
checked in Israel.

24, 10: The narrative supposes that since the people belonged to the Lord rather than to the king, only the Lord should know their exact number.

24, 17: Before this verse a Qumran manuscript (4Q Sam^a) gives the fuller text of 1 Chr 21, 16, an alternative to the words "When David saw the angel who was striking the people."

g 1 Sm 24, 6; 1 Chr 21, 7. h 2 Sm 21, 1. i Ex 12, 23; 2 Kgs 19, 35. j 22f: 1 Sm 6, 14; 1 Kgs 19, 21.

THE BOOKS OF KINGS

The two Books of Kings were originally, like 1 and 2 Samuel, a single historical work. In conjunction with the Books of Samuel, they extend the consecutive history of Israel from the birth of Samuel to the destruction of Jerusalem in 587 B.C. This combined work is designed as a religious history; hence in Kings the temple, which is the chosen site for the worship of Yahweh, occupies the center of attention.

The Books of Kings show clearly the theological bent of a Deuteronomic editor. In them, as already in Judges, material from various sources, such as the "book of the acts of Solomon" (1 Kgs 11, 41) and the "book of the chronicles of the kings of Israel" (1 Kgs 14, 19), is forged into structural unity by an editor whose principal interest is in the fidelity to Yahweh of rulers and people. The reigns of individual kings are adapted to an editorial framework consisting of a presentation and an obituary notice for each, in stereotyped formulas. In between, the achievements of the king are reported—above all, his fidelity or lack of fidelity to Yahweh. The faithful prosper; the unfaithful pay for their defections. Since this is basically a narrative of sin and retribution, it would not be inappropriate to entitle the Books of Kings "The Rise and Fall of the Israelite Monarchy."

Without minimizing the complexity of the process by which this material was transmitted for many centuries, one may speak of two editions of the Books: the first at some time between 621 B.C. and 597 B.C. and the second, final edition during the Exile; probably shortly after Jehoiachin was released from his Babylonian prison (561 B.C.).

1 Kings carries the history of Israel from the last days and death of David to the accession in Samaria of Ahaziah, son of Ahab, near the end of the reign of Jehoshaphat, king of Judah. Judgment is passed on Ahaziah's reign but the details are given only later, in 2 Kings. We should note the two large cycles of traditions which grew up around the great prophetic figures of Elijah and Elisha, the former in 1 Kings and the latter chiefly in 2 Kings. These cycles, which interrupt the sequence of regnal chronicles, were very probably preserved and transmitted by the prophetic communities to which there are references in the same traditions. The Elijah cycle is the more important since it dramatically underscores Israel's critical struggle with the religion of Canaan.

The principal divisions of the Books of Kings are:

I. The Reign of Solomon (1 Kgs 1, 1—11, 43).
II. Judah and Israel to the Time of Ahab (1 Kgs 12, 1—16, 34).
III. Stories of the Prophets (1 Kgs 17, 1—22, 54).
IV. The Kingdoms of Israel and Judah (2 Kgs 1, 1—17, 41).
V. The Kingdom of Judah after 721 B.C. (2 Kgs 18, 1—25, 30).

THE FIRST BOOK OF KINGS

I: The Reign of Solomon

CHAPTER 1

1When King David was old and advanced in
years, though they spread covers over him he
could not keep warm. 2His servants therefore
said to him, "Let a young virgin be sought to
attend you, lord king, and to nurse you. If she
sleeps with your royal majesty, you will be kept
warm." 3So they sought for a beautiful girl
throughout the territory of Israel, and found
Abishag the Shunamite, whom they brought to
the king. 4The maiden, who was very beautiful,
nursed the king and cared for him, but the king
did not have relations with her.

Ambition of Adonijah 5Adonijah, son of Hag-
gith, began to display his ambition to be king. He
acquired chariots, drivers, and fifty henchmen.
6Yet his father never rebuked him or asked why
he was doing this. Adonijah was also very
handsome, and next in age to Absalom by the
same mother. 7He conferred with Joab, son of
Zeruiah, and with Abiathar the priest, and they
supported him. 8However, Zadok the priest,
Benaiah, son of Jehoiada, Nathan the prophet,
and Shimei and his companions, the pick of
David's army, did not side with Adonijah.
9When he slaughtered sheep, oxen, and fatlings
at the stone Zoheleth, near En-rogel,* Adonijah
invited all his brothers, the king's sons, and all
the royal officials of Judah. 10But he did not
invite the prophet Nathan, or Benaiah, or the
pick of the army, or his brother Solomon.

Solomon Proclaimed King 11Then Nathan
said to Bathsheba, Solomon's mother: "Have
you not heard that Adonijah, son of Haggith, has
become king without the knowledge of our lord
David? 12Come now, let me advise you so that
you may save your life and that of your son
Solomon. 13Go, visit King David, and say to him,
'Did you not, lord king, swear to your hand-
maid: Your son Solomon shall be king after me
and shall sit upon my throne? Why, then, has
Adonijah become king?' 14And while you are
still there speaking to the king, I will come in
after you and confirm what you have said."

15So Bathsheba visited the king in his room,
while Abishag the Shunamite was attending him
because of his advanced age. 16Bathsheba bowed
in homage to the king, who said to her, "What
do you wish?" 17She answered him: "My lord,
you swore to me your handmaid by the Lord,
your God, that my son Solomon should reign
after you and sit upon your throne. 18But now
Adonijah has become king, and you, my lord
king, do not know it. 19He has slaughtered oxen,
fatlings, and sheep in great numbers; he has
invited all the king's sons, Abiathar the priest,
and Joab, the general of the army, but not your
servant Solomon. 20Now, my lord king, all Israel
is waiting for you to make known to them who
is to sit on the throne after your royal majesty.*
21If this is not done, when my lord the king
sleeps with his fathers, I and my son Solomon
will be considered criminals."

22While she was still speaking to the king, the
prophet Nathan came in. 23When he had been
announced, the prophet entered the king's pres-
ence and, bowing to the floor, did him homage.
24Then Nathan said: "Have you decided, my lord
king, that Adonijah is to reign after you and sit on
your throne? 25He went down today and slaugh-
tered oxen, fatlings, and sheep in great numbers;
he invited all the king's sons, the commanders of
the army, and Abiathar the priest, and they are
eating and drinking in his company and saying,
'Long live King Adonijah!' 26But me, your ser-
vant, he did not invite; nor Zadok the priest, nor
Benaiah, son of Jehoiada, nor your servant Solo-
mon. 27Was this done by my royal master's order
without my being told who was to succeed to
your majesty's kingly throne?"

28King David answered, "Call Bathsheba
here." When she re-entered the king's presence

1, 9: En-rogel: the modern Job's Well southeast of Jerusalem. It marked the ancient boundary between the tribes of Benjamin and Judah (Jos 15, 7; 18, 16). Here David's men sought information about Absalom's revolt (2 Sm 17, 17).

1, 20: At this time, neither law nor the right of primogeniture, but the will of the ruling monarch, determined succession to the throne.

and stood before him, 29 the king swore, "As the LORD lives, who has delivered me from all distress, 30 this very day I will fulfill the oath I swore to you by the LORD, the God of Israel, that your son Solomon should reign after me and should sit upon my throne in my place." 31 Bowing to the floor in homage to the king, Bathsheba said, "May my lord, King David, live forever!" 32 Then King David summoned Zadok the priest, Nathan the prophet, and Benaiah, son of Jehoiada. When they had entered the king's presence, 33 he said to them: "Take with you the royal attendants. Mount my son Solomon upon my own mule and escort him down to Gihon. 34 There Zadok the priest and Nathan the prophet are to anoint him king of Israel, and you shall blow the horn and cry, 'Long live King Solomon!' 35 When you come back in his train, he is to go in and sit upon my throne and reign in my place. I designate him ruler of Israel and of Judah." 36 In answer to the king, Benaiah, son of Jehoiada, said: "So be it! May the LORD, the God of my lord the king, so decree! 37 As the LORD has been with your royal majesty, so may he be with Solomon, and exalt his throne even more than that of my lord, King David!"

38 So Zadok the priest, Nathan the prophet, Benaiah, son of Jehoiada, and the Cherethites and Pelethites* went down, and mounting Solomon on King David's mule, escorted him to Gihon. 39 Then Zadok the priest took the horn of oil from the tent and anointed Solomon. They blew the horn and all the people shouted, "Long live King Solomon!" 40 Then all the people went up after him, playing flutes and rejoicing so much as to split open the earth with their shouting.

41 Adonijah and all the guests who were with him heard it, just as they ended their banquet. When Joab heard the sound of the horn, he asked, "What does this uproar in the city mean?" 42 As he was speaking, Jonathan, son of Abiathar the priest, arrived. "Come," said Adonijah, "you are a man of worth and must bring good news." 43 "On the contrary!" Jonathan answered him. "Our lord, King David, has made Solomon king. 44 The king sent with him Zadok the priest, Nathan the prophet, Benaiah, son of Jehoiada, and the Cherethites and Pelethites, and they mounted him upon the king's own mule. 45 Zadok the priest and Nathan the prophet anointed him king at Gihon, and they went up from there rejoicing, so that the city is in an uproar. That is the noise you heard. 46 Besides, Solomon took his seat on the royal throne, 47 and the king's servants went in and paid their respects to our lord, King David, saying, 'May God make Solomon more famous than you and exalt his throne more than your own!' And the king in his bed worshiped God, 48 and this is what he said: 'Blessed be the LORD, the God of Israel, who has this day seated one of my sons upon my throne, so that I see it with my own eyes.' "

49 All the guests of Adonijah left in terror, each going his own way. 50 Adonijah, in fear of Solomon, also left; he went and seized the horns of the altar.* 51 It was reported to Solomon that Adonijah, in his fear of King Solomon, had seized the horns of the altar and said, "Let King Solomon first swear that he will not kill me, his servant, with the sword." 52 Solomon answered, "If he proves himself worthy, not a hair shall fall from his head. But if he is found guilty of crime, he shall die." 53 King Solomon sent to have him brought down from the altar, and he came and paid homage to the king. Solomon then said to him, "Go to your home."

CHAPTER 2

David's Last Instructions and Death 1 When the time of David's death drew near,* he gave these instructions to his son Solomon: 2 "I am going the way of all mankind. Take courage and

1, 38: Cherethites and Pelethites: mercenaries in David's bodyguard. They became part of his retinue after he defeated the Philistines and established himself in Jerusalem; cf 2 Sm 8, 18; 15, 18; 20, 23.

1, 50: Horns of the altar: the protuberances on each of the four corners of the altar were surrounded with a special degree of holiness (Ex 27, 2; 29, 12), and constituted a place of asylum for transgressors of the law (Ex 21, 13f; 1 Kgs 2, 28).

2, 1–6. 8–9: Solomon is expected to remove from his father's family the imputation of blood guilt brought upon it by Joab in the unwarranted killings of Abner (2 Sm 3, 27–29) and Amasa (2 Sm 19, 9–10); and likewise to punish Shimei for his curse, the effects of which David had pledged himself not to avenge in person (2 Sm 19, 21–23). The standards of morality presumed in these verses are far from the Christian ones.

be a man. [3]Keep the mandate of the LORD, your God, following his ways and observing his statutes, commands, ordinances, and decrees as they are written in the law of Moses, that you may succeed in whatever you do, wherever you turn,[a] [4]and the LORD may fulfill the promise he made on my behalf when he said, 'If your sons so conduct themselves that they remain faithful to me with their whole heart and with their whole soul, you shall always have someone of your line on the throne of Israel.'[b] [5]You yourself know what Joab, son of Zeruiah, did to me when he slew the two generals of Israel's armies, Abner, son of Ner, and Amasa, son of Jether. He took revenge for the blood of war in a time of peace, and put blood shed without provocation on the belt about my waist and on the sandal on my foot.[c] [6]Act with the wisdom you possess; you must not allow him to go down to the grave in peaceful old age.

[7]"But be kind to the sons of Barzillai the Gileadite, and have them eat at your table. For they received me kindly when I was fleeing your brother Absalom.[d]

[8]"You also have with you Shimei, son of Gera, the Benjaminite of Bahurim, who cursed me balefully when I was going to Mahanaim. Because he came down to meet me at the Jordan, I swore to him by the LORD that I would not put him to the sword.[e] [9]But you must not let him go unpunished. You are a prudent man and will know how to deal with him to send down his hoary head in blood to the grave."

[10]David rested with his ancestors and was buried in the City of David.[f] [11]The length of David's reign over Israel was forty years: he reigned seven years in Hebron and thirty-three years in Jerusalem.[g]

The Kingdom Made Secure [12]When Solomon was seated on the throne of his father David, with his sovereignty firmly established, [13]Adonijah, son of Haggith, went to Bathsheba, the mother of Solomon. "Do you come as a friend?" she asked. "Yes," he answered, [14]and added, "I have something to say to you." She replied, "Say it." [15]So he said: "You know that the kingdom was mine, and all Israel expected me to be king. But the kingdom escaped me and became my brother's, for the LORD gave it to him. [16]But now there is one favor I would ask of you. Do not refuse me." And she said, "Speak on." [17]He said, "Please ask King Solomon, who will not refuse you, to give me Abishag the Shunamite for my wife."* [18]"Very well," replied Bathsheba, "I will speak to the king for you."

[19]Then Bathsheba went to King Solomon to speak to him for Adonijah, and the king stood up to meet her and paid her homage. Then he sat down upon his throne, and a throne was provided for the king's mother, who sat at his right. [20]"There is one small favor I would ask of you," she said. "Do not refuse me." "Ask it, my mother," the king said to her, "for I will not refuse you." [21]So she said, "Let Abishag the Shunamite be given to your brother Adonijah for his wife." [22]"And why do you ask Abishag the Shunamite for Adonijah?" King Solomon answered his mother. "Ask the kingdom for him as well, for he is my elder brother and has with him Abiathar the priest and Joab, son of Zeruiah." [23]And King Solomon swore by the LORD: "May God do thus and so to me, and more besides, if Adonijah has not proposed this at the cost of his life. [24]And now, as the LORD lives, who has seated me firmly on the throne of my father David and made of me a dynasty as he promised, this day shall Adonijah be put to death." [25]Then King Solomon sent Benaiah, son of Jehoiada, who struck him dead.

[26]The king said to Abiathar the priest: "Go to your land in Anathoth. Though you deserve to die, I will not put you to death this time, because you carried the ark of the Lord GOD before my father David and shared in all the hardships my

2, 17. 22–25: Abishag had been the concubine of King David (1 Kgs 1, 4). His successor, Solomon, inherited his father's harem. When Adonijah requested Abishag as his wife, he was subtly undermining the security of Solomon's throne and exposing himself to the suspicion of insurrection that would cost him his life; cf 2 Sm 3, 6–11; 16, 22.

a Dt 17, 19. b 2 Sm 7, 11–16; Ps 132, 11f. c 2 Sm 3, 27; 20, 10. d 2 Sm 19, 33ff. e 2 Sm 16, 5; 19, 19. f Acts 2, 29. g 1 Chr 29, 27.

father endured." 27So Solomon deposed Abiathar from his office of priest of the LORD, thus fulfilling the prophecy which the LORD had made in Shiloh about the house of Eli.[h]

28When the news came to Joab, who had sided with Adonijah, though not with Absalom, he fled to the tent of the LORD and seized the horns of the altar. 29King Solomon was told that Joab had fled to the tent of the LORD and was at the altar. He sent Benaiah, son of Jehoiada, with the order, "Go, strike him down." 30Benaiah went to the tent of the LORD and said to him, "The king says, 'Come out.' " But he answered, "No! I will die here." Benaiah reported to the king, "This is what Joab said to me in reply." 31The king answered him: "Do as he has said. Strike him down and bury him, and you will remove from me and from my family the blood which Joab shed without provocation. 32The LORD will hold him responsible for his own blood, because he struck down two men better and more just than himself, and slew them with the sword without my father David's knowledge: Abner, son of Ner, general of Israel's army, and Amasa, son of Jether, general of Judah's army.[i] 33Joab and his descendants shall be responsible forever for their blood. But there shall be the peace of the LORD forever for David, and his descendants, and his house, and his throne." 34Benaiah, son of Jehoiada, went back, struck him down and killed him; he was buried in his house in the desert. 35The king appointed Benaiah, son of Jehoiada, over the army in his place, and put Zadok the priest in place of Abiathar.

36Then the king summoned Shimei and said to him: "Build yourself a house in Jerusalem and live there. Do not go anywhere else. 37For if you leave, and cross the Kidron Valley, be certain you shall die without fail. You shall be responsible for your own blood." 38Shimei answered the king: "I accept. Your servant will do just as the king's majesty has said." So Shimei stayed in Jerusalem for a long time. 39But three years later, two of Shimei's servants ran away to Achish, son of Maacah, king of Gath, and Shimei was informed that his servants were in Gath. 40So Shimei rose, saddled his ass, and went to Achish in Gath in search of his servants, whom he brought back. 41When Solomon was informed that Shimei had gone from Jerusalem to Gath, and had returned, 42the king summoned Shimei and said to him: "Did I not have you swear by the LORD to your clear understanding of my warning that, if you left and went anywhere else, you should die without fail? And you answered, 'I accept and obey.' 43Why, then, have you not kept the oath of the LORD and the command that I gave you?" 44And the king said to Shimei: "You know in your heart the evil that you did to my father David. Now the LORD requites you for your own wickedness. 45But King Solomon shall be blessed, and David's throne shall endure before the LORD forever." 46The king then gave the order to Benaiah, son of Jehoiada, who struck him dead as he left.

CHAPTER 3

Wisdom of Solomon 1With the royal power firmly in his grasp, Solomon allied himself by marriage with Pharaoh, king of Egypt. The daughter of Pharaoh, whom he married, he brought to the City of David, until he should finish building his palace, and the temple of the LORD, and the wall around Jerusalem.[j]

2However, the people were sacrificing on the high places, for up to that time no temple had been built to the name of the LORD. 3Solomon loved the LORD, and obeyed the statutes of his father David; yet he offered sacrifice and burned incense on the high places.

4The king went to Gibeon to sacrifice there, because that was the most renowned high place. Upon its altar Solomon offered a thousand holocausts. 5In Gibeon the LORD appeared to Solomon in a dream at night. God said, "Ask something of me and I will give it to you." 6Solomon answered: "You have shown great favor to your servant, my father David, because he behaved faithfully toward you, with justice and an upright heart; and you have continued this great favor toward him, even today, seating a son of his on his throne. 7O LORD, my God, you have made me, your servant, king to suc-

h 1 Sm 2, 31. i 2 Sm 3, 27; 20, 10. j 1 Kgs 7, 8; 2 Chr 1, 1.

ceed my father David; but I am a mere youth,
not knowing at all how to act. 8I serve you in the
midst of the people whom you have chosen, a
people so vast that it cannot be numbered or
counted. 9Give your servant, therefore, an under-
standing heart to judge your people and to
distinguish right from wrong. For who is able to
govern this vast people of yours?"[k]

10The LORD was pleased that Solomon made
this request. 11So God said to him: "Because you
have asked for this—not for a long life for your-
self, nor for riches, nor for the life of your ene-
mies, but for understanding so that you may
know what is right— 12I do as you requested. I
give you a heart so wise and understanding that
there has never been anyone like you up to now,
and after you there will come no one to equal you.
13In addition, I give you what you have not asked
for, such riches and glory that among kings there
is not your like.[l] 14And if you follow me by keep-
ing my statutes and commandments, as your fa-
ther David did, I will give you a long life."

15When Solomon awoke from his dream, he
went to Jerusalem, stood before the ark of the
covenant of the LORD, offered holocausts and
peace offerings, and gave a banquet for all his
servants.

Solomon's Judgment 16Later, two harlots
came to the king and stood before him. 17One
woman said: "By your leave, my lord, this
woman and I live in the same house, and I gave
birth in the house while she was present. 18On
the third day after I gave birth, this woman also
gave birth. We were alone in the house; there
was no one there but us two. 19This woman's
son died during the night; she smothered him by
lying on him. 20Later that night she got up and
took my son from my side, as I, your handmaid,
was sleeping. Then she laid him in her bosom,
after she had laid her dead child in my bosom.
21I rose in the morning to nurse my child, and I
found him dead. But when I examined him in
the morning light, I saw it was not the son
whom I had borne."

22The other woman answered, "It is not so!
The living one is my son, the dead one is yours."
But the first kept saying, "No, the dead one is
your child, the living one is mine!" Thus they
argued before the king.

23Then the king said: "One woman claims,
'This, the living one, is my child, and the dead
one is yours.' The other answers, 'No! The dead
one is your child; the living one is mine.' "
24The king continued, "Get me a sword." When
they brought the sword before him, 25he said,
"Cut the living child in two, and give half to one
woman and half to the other." 26The woman
whose son it was, in the anguish she felt for it,
said to the king, "Please, my lord, give her the
living child—please do not kill it!" The other,
however, said, "It shall be neither mine nor
yours. Divide it!" 27The king then answered,
"Give the first one the living child! By no means
kill it, for she is the mother."

28When all Israel heard the judgment the king
had given, they were in awe of him, because
they saw that the king had in him the wisdom of
God for giving judgment.

CHAPTER 4

Chief Officers of the Kingdom 1Solomon
was king over all Israel, 2and these were the
officials he had in his service:

Azariah, son of Zadok, priest;
3Elihoreph and Ahijah, sons of Shisha, scribes;
Jehoshaphat, son of Ahilud, chancellor;
4[Benaiah, son of Jehoiada, commander of the army;
Zadok and Abiathar, priests;]
5Azariah, son of Nathan, chief of the commissaries;
Zabud, son of Nathan, companion to the king;
6Ahishar, major-domo of the palace; and
Adoniram, son of Abda, superintendent of the forced labor.

Solomon's Royal State 7*Solomon had twelve
commissaries for all Israel who supplied food for
the king and his household, each having to

4, 7–19: The administration of the kingdom thus initiated by Solomon continued in its main features for the duration of the monarchy in Israel and Judah.

k 2 Chr 1, 10. l Wis 7, 11; Mt 6, 29.

provide for one month in the year. [8]Their names were:

the son of Hur in the hill country of Ephraim;
[9]the son of Deker in Makaz, Shaalbim, Beth-shemesh, Elon and Beth-hanan;
[10]the son of Hesed in Arubboth, as well as in Socoh and the whole region of Hepher;
[11]the son of Abinadab, who was married to Solomon's daughter Taphath, in all the Naphath-dor;
[12]Baana, son of Ahilud, in Taanach and Megiddo, and beyond Jokmeam, and in all Beth-shean, and in the country around Zarethan below Jezreel from Beth-shean to Abel-meholah;
[13]the son of Geber in Ramoth-Gilead, having charge of the villages of Jair, son of Manasseh, in Gilead; and of the district of Argob in Bashan—sixty large walled cities with gates barred with bronze;
[14]Ahinadab, son of Iddo, in Mahanaim;
[15]Ahimaaz, who was married to Basemath, another daughter of Solomon, in Naphtali;
[16]Baana, son of Hushai, in Asher and along the rocky coast;
[17]Jehoshaphat, son of Paruah, in Issachar;
[18]Shimei, son of Ela, in Benjamin;
[19]Geber, son of Uri, in the land of Gilead, the land of Sihon, king of the Amorites, and of Og, king of Bashan.

There was one prefect besides, in the king's own land.*

CHAPTER 5

[7]These commissaries, one for each month, provided food for King Solomon and for all the guests at the royal table. They left nothing unprovided. [8]For the chariot horses and draft animals also, each brought his quota of barley and straw to the required place.

[20]* Judah and Israel were as numerous as the sands by the sea; they ate and drank and made merry. [1]Solomon ruled over all the kingdoms from the River to the land of the Philistines, down to the border of Egypt; they paid Solomon tribute and were his vassals as long as he lived. [m]

[2]Solomon's supplies for each day were thirty kors of fine flour, sixty kors of meal, [3]ten fatted oxen, twenty pasture-fed oxen, and a hundred sheep, not counting harts, gazelles, roebucks, and fatted fowl.

[4]He ruled over all the land west of the Euphrates, from Tiphsah to Gaza, and over all its kings, and he had peace on all his borders round about. [5]Thus Judah and Israel lived in security, every man under his vine or under his fig tree from Dan to Beer-sheba, as long as Solomon lived.

[6]Solomon had four thousand stalls for his twelve thousand chariot horses. [n]

[9] [o]Moreover, God gave Solomon wisdom and exceptional understanding and knowledge, as vast as the sand on the seashore. [10]Solomon surpassed all the Cedemites and all the Egyptians in wisdom. [11]He was wiser than all other men—than Ethan the Ezrahite, or Heman, Chalcol, and Darda, the musicians—and his fame spread throughout the neighboring nations. [12]Solomon also uttered three thousand proverbs, and his songs numbered a thousand and five. [p] [13]He discussed plants, from the cedar on Lebanon to the hyssop growing out of the wall, and he spoke about beasts, birds, reptiles, and fishes. [14]Men came to hear Solomon's wisdom from all nations, sent by all the kings of the earth who had heard of his wisdom.

Preparations for the Temple [15]When Hiram, king of Tyre, heard that Solomon had been anointed king in place of his father, he sent an embassy to him; for Hiram had always been David's friend. [16]Solomon sent back this message to Hiram: [17]"You know that my father David, because of the enemies surrounding him on all sides, could not build a temple in honor of the LORD, his God, until such a time as the LORD should put these enemies under the soles of his feet. [18]But now the LORD, my God, has

4, 19: One prefect . . . in the king's own land: the royal territory of Judah had its own peculiar administration different from that of the twelve districts which had to supply the king and his household with a month's provisions of food each year (v 7).

5, 20: This verse belongs to ch 4.

m Sir 47, 15f; 2 Chr 9, 26. n 2 Chr 9, 25f. o 9–14; Sir 47, 16f. p 1 Kgs 3, 12.

given me peace on all sides. There is no enemy or threat of danger. [19]So I propose to build a temple in honor of the LORD, my God, as the LORD predicted to my father David when he said: 'It is your son whom I will put upon your throne in your place who shall build the temple in my honor.'[q] [20]Give orders, then, to have cedars from the Lebanon cut down for me. My servants shall accompany yours, since you know that there is no one among us who is skilled in cutting timber like the Sidonians, and I will pay you whatever you say for your servants' salary."

[21]When he had heard the words of Solomon, Hiram was pleased and said, "Blessed be the LORD this day, who has given David a wise son to rule this numerous people." [22]Hiram then sent word to Solomon, "I agree to the proposal you sent me, and I will provide all the cedars and fir trees you wish. [23]My servants shall bring them down from the Lebanon to the sea, and I will arrange them into rafts in the sea and bring them wherever you say. There I will break up the rafts, and you shall take the lumber. You, for your part, shall furnish the provisions I desire for my household."

[24]So Hiram continued to provide Solomon with all the cedars and fir trees he wished; [25]while Solomon every year gave Hiram twenty thousand kors of wheat to provide for his household, and twenty thousand measures of pure oil. [26]The LORD, moreover, gave Solomon wisdom as he promised him, and there was peace between Hiram and Solomon, since they were parties to a treaty.

[27]King Solomon conscripted thirty thousand workmen from all Israel. [28]He sent them to the Lebanon each month in relays of ten thousand, so that they spent one month in the Lebanon and two months at home. Adoniram was in charge of the draft. [29]Solomon had seventy thousand carriers and eighty thousand stonecutters in the mountain, [30]in addition to three thousand three hundred overseers, answerable to Solomon's prefects for the work, directing the people engaged in the work. [31]By order of the king, fine, large blocks were quarried to give the temple a foundation of hewn stone. [32]Solomon's and Hiram's builders, along with the Gebalites, hewed them out, and prepared the wood and stones for building the temple.

CHAPTER 6

Building of the Temple [1]In the four hundred and eightieth year from the departure of the Israelites from the land of Egypt, in the fourth year of Solomon's reign over Israel, in the month of Ziv, which is the second month, the construction of the temple of the LORD* was begun.[r]

[2]The temple which King Solomon built for the LORD was sixty cubits long, twenty wide, and twenty-five high. [3]The porch in front of the temple was twenty cubits from side to side, along the width of the nave, and ten cubits deep in front of the temple. [4]Splayed windows with trellises were made for the temple, [5]and adjoining the wall of the temple, which enclosed the nave and the sanctuary, an annex of several stories was built. [6]Its lowest story was five cubits wide, the middle one six cubits wide, the third seven cubits wide, because there were offsets along the outside of the temple so that the beams would not be fastened into the walls of the temple. [7](The temple was built of stone dressed at the quarry, so that no hammer, axe, or iron tool was to be heard in the temple during its construction.) [8]The entrance to the lowest floor of the annex was at the right side of the temple, and stairs with intermediate landings led up to the middle story and from the middle story to the third. [9]When the temple was built to its full height, it was roofed in with rafters and boards of cedar. [10]The annex, with its lowest story five cubits high, was built all along the outside of the temple, to which it was joined by cedar beams.

[11]This word of the LORD* came to Solomon:

6, 1: Construction of the temple of the Lord is here paralleled in importance with the founding of the nation after the departure from Egypt. In both, God is the central figure who chose Israel as his people, and now chooses the place where his temple should be built (Dt 12, 4–18. 26). The year is given in a round number, 480, which corresponds to twelve generations. The fourth year of Solomon's reign: c. 968 B.C.

6, 11ff: The word of the Lord . . . my people Israel: the oracle,

q 2 Sm 7, 13; 1 Chr 22, 10. r 2 Chr 3, 1.

12"As to this temple you are building—if you observe my statutes, carry out my ordinances, keep and obey all my commands, I will fulfill toward you the promise I made to your father David.[s] 13 [t]I will dwell in the midst of the Israelites and will not forsake my people Israel."

14When Solomon finished building the temple, 15its walls were lined from floor to ceiling beams with cedar paneling, and its floor was laid with fir planking. 16At the rear of the temple a space of twenty cubits was set off by cedar partitions from the floor to the rafters, enclosing the sanctuary, the holy of holies. 17The nave, or part of the temple in front of the sanctuary, was forty cubits long. 18The cedar in the interior of the temple was carved in the form of gourds and open flowers; all was of cedar, and no stone was to be seen.

19In the innermost part of the temple* was located the sanctuary to house the ark of the LORD's covenant, 20twenty cubits long, twenty wide, and twenty high.* 21Solomon overlaid the interior of the temple with pure gold. He made in front of the sanctuary a cedar altar, overlaid it with gold, and looped it with golden chains. 22The entire temple was overlaid with gold so that it was completely covered with it; the whole altar before the sanctuary was also overlaid with gold. 23In the sanctuary were two cherubim, each ten cubits high, made of olive wood. 24Each wing of a cherub measured five cubits so that the space from wing tip to wing tip of each was ten cubits. 25The cherubim were identical in size and shape, 26and each was exactly ten cubits high. 27The cherubim were placed in the inmost part of the temple, with their wings spread wide, so that one wing of each cherub touched a side wall while the other wing, pointing toward the middle of the room, touched the corresponding wing of the second cherub. 28The cherubim, too, were overlaid with gold.

29The walls on all sides of both the inner and the outer rooms had carved figures of cherubim, palm trees, and open flowers. 30The floor of both the inner and the outer rooms was overlaid with gold. 31At the entrance of the sanctuary, doors of olive wood were made; the doorframes had beveled posts. 32The two doors were of olive wood, with carved figures of cherubim, palm trees, and open flowers. The doors were overlaid with gold, which was also molded to the cherubim and the palm trees. 33The same was done at the entrance to the nave, where the doorposts of olive wood were rectangular. 34The two doors were of fir wood; each door was banded by a metal strap, front and back, 35and had carved cherubim, palm trees, and open flowers, over which gold was evenly applied.

36The inner court was walled off by means of three courses of hewn stones and one course of cedar beams.

37The foundations of the LORD's temple were laid in the month of Ziv 38in the fourth year, and it was completed in all particulars, exactly according to plan, in the month of Bul, the eighth month, in the eleventh year. Thus it took Solomon seven years to build it.

CHAPTER 7

Building of the Palace 1His own palace Solomon completed after thirteen years of construction.[u] 2He built the hall called the Forest of Lebanon one hundred cubits long, fifty wide, and thirty high; it was supported by four rows of cedar columns, with cedar capitals upon the columns. 3Moreover, it had a ceiling of cedar above the beams resting on the columns; these beams numbered forty-five, fifteen to a row. 4There were three window frames at either end,

---

which came as a climax at the completion of the work, was an expression of God's acceptance and approval. Nevertheless the fulfillment of God's promises to David and his royal descendants will depend on their observance of his ordinances and commands.

6, 19: The innermost part of the temple: the sanctuary or holy of holies reserved exclusively for the Lord. Here through his presence he dwelt as on a throne between the cherubim above the ark of the covenant (2 Kgs 6, 23–28; 2 Chr 3, 10–13). See note on Ex 25, 18ff.

6, 20: Twenty (cubits) high: it is usually supposed that the holy of holies was of this height because it had a raised floor, five cubits above the floor level of the nave, rather than a dropped ceiling. The building was twenty-five cubits high (v 2) according to the reading here followed.

s 2 Sm 7, 13. t 1 Chr 22, 9f. u 1 Kgs 9, 10.

with windows in strict alignment. [5]The posts of all the doorways were rectangular, and the doorways faced each other, three at either end. [6]The porch of the columned hall he made fifty cubits long and thirty wide. The porch extended the width of the columned hall, and there was a canopy in front. [7]He also built the vestibule of the throne where he gave judgment—that is, the tribunal; it was paneled with cedar from floor to ceiling beams. [8]His living quarters were in another court, set in deeper than the tribunal and of the same construction. A palace like this tribunal was built for Pharaoh's daughter, whom Solomon had married.[v]

[9]All these buildings were of fine stones, hewn to size and trimmed front and back with a saw, from the foundation to the bonding course. [10](The foundation was made of fine, large blocks, some ten cubits and some eight cubits. [11]Above were fine stones hewn to size, and cedar wood.) [12]The great court was enclosed by three courses of hewn stones and a bonding course of cedar beams. So also were the inner court of the temple of the LORD and the temple porch.

Furnishing of the Temple [13]King Solomon had Hiram brought from Tyre. [14]He was a bronze worker, the son of a widow from the tribe of Naphtali; his father had been from Tyre. He was endowed with skill, understanding, and knowledge of how to produce any work in bronze. He came to King Solomon and did all his metal work.

[15]Two hollow bronze columns* were cast, each eighteen cubits high and twelve cubits in circumference; their metal was of four fingers' thickness.[w] [16]There were also two capitals cast in bronze, to place on top of the columns, each of them five cubits high. [17]Two pieces of network with a chainlike mesh were made to cover the (nodes of the) capitals on top of the columns, one for each capital. [18]Four hundred pomegranates were also cast; two hundred of them in a double row encircled the piece of network on each of the two capitals. [19]The capitals on top of the columns were finished wholly in a lotus pattern [20]above the level of the nodes and their enveloping network. [21]The columns were then erected adjacent to the porch of the temple, one to the right, called Jachin, and the other to the left, called Boaz. [22]Thus the work on the columns was completed.

[23]*The sea was then cast; it was made with a circular rim, and measured ten cubits across, five in height, and thirty in circumference.[x] [24]Under the brim, gourds encircled it, ten to the cubit all the way around; the gourds were in two rows and were cast in one mold with the sea. [25]This rested on twelve oxen,* three facing north, three facing west, three facing south, and three facing east, with their haunches all toward the center, where the sea was set upon them. [26]It was a handbreadth thick, and its brim resembled that of a cup, being lily-shaped. Its capacity was two thousand measures.

[27]Ten stands were also made of bronze, each four cubits long, four wide, and three high. [28]When these stands were constructed, panels were set within the framework. [29]On the panels between the frames there were lions, oxen, and cherubim; and on the frames likewise, above and below the lions and oxen, there were wreaths in relief.

[30]Each stand had four bronze wheels and bronze axles. [32]The four wheels were below the paneling, and the axletrees of the wheels and the stand were of one piece. Each wheel was a cubit and a half high. [33]The wheels were constructed like chariot wheels; their axles, fellies, spokes, and hubs were all cast.

The four legs of each stand had cast braces, which were under the basin; they had wreaths on each side. [34]These four braces, extending to the corners of each stand, were of one piece with the stand.

[35]On top of the stand there was a raised collar half a cubit high, with supports and panels which were of one piece with the top of the

7, 15–21: The two hollow bronze columns, Jachin and Boaz (2 Chr 3, 17), stood free to the right and left of the temple porch. The names are related to God's power (Boaz) founding (Jachin) the temple and his people.

7, 23–26: The sea . . . rested on twelve oxen: this was a large circular tank containing about twelve thousand gallons of water.

v 1 Kgs 3, 1. w Jer 52, 21. x 2 Chr 4, 2.

stand. 31 This was surmounted by a crown one
cubit high within which was a rounded opening
to provide a receptacle a cubit and a half in
depth. There was carved work at the opening,
on panels that were angular, not curved. 36 On
the surfaces of the supports and on the panels,
wherever there was a clear space, cherubim,
lions, and palm trees were carved, as well as
wreaths all around. 37 This was how the ten
stands were made, all of the same casting, the
same size, the same shape. 38 Ten bronze basins
were then made, each four cubits in diameter
with a capacity of forty measures, one basin for
the top of each of the ten stands. 39 The stands
were placed, five on the south side of the
temple and five on the north. The sea was
placed off to the southeast from the south side
of the temple.
40 When Hiram made the pots, shovels, and
bowls, he therewith completed all his work for
King Solomon in the temple of the LORD: 41 two
columns, two nodes for the capitals on top of
the columns, two pieces of network covering
the nodes for the capitals on top of the col-
umns, 42 four hundred pomegranates in double
rows on both pieces of network that covered
the two nodes of the capitals where they met
the columns, 43 ten stands, ten basins on the
stands, 44 one sea, twelve oxen supporting the
sea, 45 pots, shovels, and bowls. All these arti-
cles which Hiram made for King Solomon in
the temple of the LORD were of burnished
bronze. 46 The king had them cast in the neigh-
borhood of the Jordan, in the clayey ground
between Succoth and Zarethan. 47 Solomon did
not weigh all the articles because they were so
numerous; the weight of the bronze, therefore,
was not determined.
48 Solomon had all the articles made for the
interior of the temple of the LORD: the golden
altar; the golden table on which the showbread
lay; 49 the lampstands of pure gold, five to the
right and five to the left before the sanctuary,
with their flowers, lamps, and tongs of gold;
50 basins, snuffers, bowls, cups, and fire pans of
pure gold; and hinges of gold for the doors of the
inner room, or holy of holies, and for the doors
of the outer room, the nave.
51 When all the work undertaken by King
Solomon in the temple of the LORD was com-
pleted, he brought in the dedicated offerings of
his father David, putting the silver, gold, and
other articles in the treasuries of the temple of
the LORD.[y]

CHAPTER 8

Dedication of the Temple 1 At the order of
Solomon, the elders of Israel and all the leaders
of the tribes, the princes in the ancestral houses
of the Israelites, came to King Solomon in
Jerusalem, to bring up the ark of the LORD's
covenant from the City of David [which is
Zion].[z] 2 All the men of Israel assembled before
King Solomon during the festival in the month of
Ethanim (the seventh month). 3 When all the
elders of Israel had arrived, the priests took up
the ark; 4 they carried the ark of the LORD and
the meeting tent with all the sacred vessels that
were in the tent. (The priests and Levites carried
them.)
5 King Solomon and the entire community of
Israel present for the occasion sacrificed before
the ark sheep and oxen too many to number or
count. 6 *The priests brought the ark of the
covenant of the LORD to its place beneath the
wings of the cherubim in the sanctuary, the holy
of holies of the temple. 7 The cherubim had their
wings spread out over the place of the ark,
sheltering the ark and its poles from above. 8 The
poles were so long that their ends could be seen
from that part of the holy place adjoining the
sanctuary; however, they could not be seen
beyond. (They have remained there to this day.)
9 There was nothing in the ark but the two stone
tablets which Moses had put there at Horeb,
when the LORD made a covenant with the

8, 6–9: The transfer of the ark of the covenant into the newly constructed temple building, and the oracle of God's acceptance (1 Kgs 9, 3–9), and his act of possession (1 Kgs 8, 10–13), constituted the temple's solemn dedication, and made of it the abiding dwelling of God among his people for which David had hoped (2 Sm 6, 12–15; 7, 1–3). The concurrence of the feast of Booths marks an appropriate transition of God's dwelling among nomadic tribes to his permanent abode among a settled people.

y 2 Chr 5, 1. z 2 Chr 5, 2.

Israelites at their departure from the land of Egypt.[a]

10When the priests left the holy place, the cloud filled the temple of the LORD 11so that the priests could no longer minister because of the cloud, since the LORD's glory had filled the temple of the LORD. 12Then Solomon said, "The LORD intends to dwell in the dark cloud;[b] 13I have truly built you a princely house, a dwelling where you may abide forever."

14The king turned and greeted the whole community of Israel as they stood. 15He said to them: "Blessed be the LORD, the God of Israel, who with his own mouth made a promise to my father David and by his hand has brought it to fulfillment. It was he who said, 16'Since the day I brought my people Israel out of Egypt, I have not chosen a city out of any tribe of Israel for the building of a temple to my honor; but I choose David to rule my people Israel.' 17When my father David wished to build a temple to the honor of the LORD, the God of Israel,[c] 18the Lord said to him, 'In wishing to build a temple to my honor, you do well. 19It will not be you, however, who will build the temple; but the son who will spring from you, he shall build the temple to my honor.' 20And now the LORD has fulfilled the promise that he made: I have succeeded my father David and sit on the throne of Israel, as the LORD foretold, and I have built this temple to honor the LORD, the God of Israel. 21I have provided in it a place for the ark in which is the covenant of the LORD, which he made with our fathers when he brought them out of the land of Egypt."

Solomon's Prayer 22Solomon stood before the altar of the LORD in the presence of the whole community of Israel, and stretching forth his hands toward heaven, 23he said, "LORD, God of Israel, there is no God like you in heaven above or on earth below; you keep your covenant of kindness with your servants who are faithful to you with their whole heart. 24You have kept the promise you made to my father David, your servant. You who spoke that promise, have this day, by your own power, brought it to fulfillment. 25Now, therefore, LORD, God of Israel, keep the further promise you made to my father David, your servant, saying, 'You shall always have someone from your line to sit before me on the throne of Israel, provided only that your descendants look to their conduct so that they live in my presence, as you have lived in my presence.'[d] 26Now, LORD, God of Israel, may this promise which you made to my father David, your servant, be confirmed.

27"Can it indeed be that God dwells among men on earth? If the heavens and the highest heavens cannot contain you, how much less this temple which I have built! 28Look kindly on the prayer and petition of your servant, O LORD, my God, and listen to the cry of supplication which I, your servant, utter before you this day. 29May your eyes watch night and day over this temple, the place where you have decreed you shall be honored; may you heed the prayer which I, your servant, offer in this place. 30Listen to the petitions of your servant and of your people Israel which they offer in this place. Listen from your heavenly dwelling and grant pardon.

31"If a man sins against his neighbor and is required to take an oath sanctioned by a curse, when he comes and takes the oath before your altar in this temple, 32listen in heaven; take action and pass judgment on your servants. Condemn the wicked and punish him for his conduct, but acquit the just and establish his innocence.

33*"If your people Israel sin against you and are defeated by an enemy, and if then they return to you, praise your name, pray to you, and entreat you in this temple, 34listen in heaven and forgive the sin of your people Israel, and bring them back to the land you gave their fathers.

35"If the sky is closed, so that there is no rain, because they have sinned against you and you afflict them, and if then they repent of their sin,

8, 33–34. 46–53: These references to deportation of Israelites to a hostile land are an expansion of Solomon's prayer dating from the Babylonian exile four centuries later.

a Ex 34, 27; Heb 9, 4. b 2 Chr 6, 1. c 2 Sm 7, 5. d 2 Sm 7, 12.

and pray, and praise your name in this place,
36 listen in heaven and forgive the sin of your
servant and of your people Israel, teaching them
the right way to live and sending rain upon this
land of yours which you have given to your
people as their heritage.

37 "If there is famine in the land or pestilence;
or if blight comes, or mildew, or a locust swarm,
or devouring insects; if an enemy of your people
besieges them in one of their cities; whatever
plague or sickness there may be, 38 if then any
one [of your entire people Israel] has remorse of
conscience and offers some prayer or petition,
stretching out his hands toward this temple,
39 listen from your heavenly dwelling place and
forgive. You who alone know the hearts of all
men, render to each one of them according to
his conduct; knowing their hearts, so treat them
40 that they may fear you as long as they live on
the land you gave our fathers.

41 "To the foreigner, likewise, who is not of
your people Israel, but comes from a distant land
to honor you 42 (since men will learn of your
great name and your mighty hand and your
outstretched arm), when he comes and prays
toward this temple, 43 listen from your heavenly
dwelling. Do all that the foreigner asks of you,
that all the peoples of the earth may know your
name, may fear you as do your people Israel, and
may acknowledge that this temple which I have
built is dedicated to your honor.

44 "Whatever the direction in which you may
send your people forth to war against their
enemies, if they pray to you, O LORD, toward the
city you have chosen and the temple I have built
in your honor, 45 listen in heaven to their prayer
and petition, and defend their cause.

46 "When they sin against you (for there is no
man who does not sin), and in your anger
against them you deliver them to the enemy, so
that their captors deport them to a hostile land,
far or near,[e] 47 may they repent in the land of
their captivity and be converted. If then they
entreat you in the land of their captors and say,
'We have sinned and done wrong; we have been
wicked'; 48 if with their whole heart and soul
they turn back to you in the land of the enemies
who took them captive, pray to you toward the
land you gave their fathers, the city you have
chosen, and the temple I have built in your
honor, 49 listen from your heavenly dwelling.
50 Forgive your people their sins and all the
offenses they have committed against you, and
grant them mercy before their captors, so that
these will be merciful to them. 51 For they are
your people and your inheritance, whom you
brought out of Egypt, from the midst of an iron
furnace.

52 "Thus may your eyes be open to the petition
of your servant and to the petition of your people
Israel. Hear them whenever they call upon you,
53 because you have set them apart among all the
peoples of the earth for your inheritance, as you
declared through your servant Moses when you
brought our fathers out of Egypt, O Lord GOD."

54 When Solomon finished offering this entire
prayer of petition to the LORD, he rose from
before the altar of the LORD, where he had been
kneeling with his hands outstretched toward
heaven. 55 He stood and blessed the whole
community of Israel, saying in a loud voice:
56 "Blessed be the LORD who has given rest to his
people Israel, just as he promised. Not a single
word has gone unfulfilled of the entire generous
promise he made through his servant Moses.
57 May the LORD, our God, be with us as he was
with our fathers and may he not forsake us nor
cast us off. 58 May he draw our hearts to himself,
that we may follow him in everything and keep
the commands, statutes, and ordinances which
he enjoined on our fathers. 59 May this prayer I
have offered to the LORD, our God, be present to
him day and night, that he may uphold the cause
of his servant and of his people Israel as each day
requires, 60 that all the peoples of the earth may
know the LORD is God and there is no other.
61 You must be wholly devoted to the LORD, our
God, observing his statutes and keeping his
commandments, as on this day."

62 The king and all Israel with him offered
sacrifices before the LORD. 63 Solomon offered as
peace offerings to the LORD twenty-two thou-

e 2 Chr 6, 36; Eccl 7, 20; 1 Jn 1, 8.

sand oxen and one hundred twenty thousand
sheep. Thus the king and all the Israelites
dedicated the temple of the LORD. [64]On that day
the king consecrated the middle of the court
facing the temple of the LORD; he offered there
the holocausts, the cereal offerings, and the fat of
the peace offerings, because the bronze altar
before the LORD was too small to hold these
offerings.
[65]On this occasion Solomon and all the Israel-
ites, who had assembled in large numbers from
Labo of Hamath to the wadi of Egypt, celebrated
the festival before the LORD, our God, for seven
days. [66]On the eighth day he dismissed the
people, who bade the king farewell and went to
their homes, rejoicing and happy over all the
blessings the LORD had given to his servant
David and to his people Israel.

CHAPTER 9

Promise and Warning to Solomon [1]After
Solomon finished building the temple of the
LORD, the royal palace, and everything else that
he had planned, [2]the LORD appeared to him a
second time, as he had appeared to him in
Gibeon.[f] [3]The LORD said to him: "I have heard
the prayer of petition which you offered in my
presence. I have consecrated this temple which
you have built; I confer my name upon it
forever, and my eyes and my heart shall be there
always. [4]As for you, if you live in my presence as
your father David lived, sincerely and uprightly,
doing just as I have commanded you, keeping
my statutes and decrees, [5]I will establish your
throne of sovereignty over Israel forever, as I
promised your father David when I said, 'You
shall always have someone from your line on the
throne of Israel.'[g] [6]But if you and your descen-
dants ever withdraw from me, fail to keep the
commandments and statutes which I set before
you, and proceed to venerate and worship
strange gods, [7]I will cut off Israel from the land I
gave them and repudiate the temple I have
consecrated to my honor. Israel shall become a
proverb and a byword among all nations, [8]and
this temple shall become a heap of ruins. Every
passerby shall catch his breath in amazement,
and ask, 'Why has the LORD done this to the
land and to this temple?'[h] [9]Men will answer:
'They forsook the LORD, their God, who brought
their fathers out of the land of Egypt; they
adopted strange gods which they worshiped and
served. That is why the LORD has brought down
upon them all this evil.' "
Other Acts of the King [10]After the twenty
years during which Solomon built the two
houses, the temple of the LORD and the palace of
the king— [11]Hiram, king of Tyre, supplying
Solomon with all the cedar wood, fir wood, and
gold he wished—King Solomon gave Hiram
twenty cities in the land of Galilee. [12]Hiram left
Tyre to see the cities Solomon had given him,
but was not satisfied with them. [13]So he said,
"What are these cities you have given me, my
brother?" And he called them the land of Cabul,
as they are called to this day. [14]Hiram, however,
had sent King Solomon one hundred and twenty
talents of gold.*
[15]This is an account of the forced labor which
King Solomon levied in order to build the tem-
ple of the LORD, his palace, Millo,* the wall of
Jerusalem, Hazor, Megiddo, Gezer [16](Pharaoh
king of Egypt, had come up and taken Gezer
and, after destroying it by fire and slaying all
the Canaanites living in the city, had given it as
dowry to his daughter, Solomon's wife; [17]Solo-
mon then rebuilt Gezer), Lower Beth-horon,
[18]Baalath, Tamar in the desert of Judah, [19]all
his cities for supplies, cities for chariots and for
horses, and whatever else Solomon decided
should be built in Jerusalem, in Lebanon, and in
the entire land under his dominion. [20]All the
non-Israelite people who remained in the land,
descendants of the Amorites, Hittites, Periz-
zites, Hivites, and Jebusites [21]whose doom the
Israelites had been unable to accomplish, Solo-
mon conscripted as forced laborers, as they are

9, 14: One hundred and twenty talents of gold: approximately three million six hundred thousand dollars.

9, 15: Millo: probably means a filling, and may refer to an artificial earthwork or platform of stamped ground south of the temple area. It was begun by David (2 Sm 5, 9); cf 1 Kgs 9, 24; 11, 27.

f 1 Kgs 3, 5; 11, 9; 2 Chr 7, 12. g 2 Sm 7, 12–16. h Dt 29, 23; Jer 22, 8.

to this day. 22 But Solomon enslaved none of the Israelites, for they were his fighting force, his ministers, commanders, adjutants, chariot officers, and charioteers. 23 The supervisors of Solomon's works who policed the people engaged in the work numbered five hundred and fifty.

24 As soon as Pharaoh's daughter went up from the City of David to her palace, which he had built for her, Solomon built Millo.

25 Three times a year Solomon used to offer holocausts and peace offerings on the altar which he had built to the LORD, and to burn incense before the LORD; and he kept the temple in repair.

26 King Solomon also built a fleet at Ezion-geber, which is near Elath on the shore of the Red Sea in the land of Edom.* 27 In this fleet Hiram placed his own expert seamen with the servants of Solomon. 28 They went to Ophir, and brought back four hundred and twenty talents of gold to King Solomon.

CHAPTER 10

Visit of the Queen of Sheba 1 The queen of Sheba,* having heard of Solomon's fame, came to test him with subtle questions.[i] 2 She arrived in Jerusalem with a very numerous retinue, and with camels bearing spices, a large amount of gold, and precious stones. She came to Solomon and questioned him on every subject in which she was interested. 3 King Solomon explained everything she asked about, and there remained nothing hidden from him that he could not explain to her.

4 When the queen of Sheba witnessed Solomon's great wisdom, the palace he had built, 5 the food at his table, the seating of his ministers, the attendance and garb of his waiters, his banquet service, and the holocausts he offered in the temple of the LORD, she was breathless. 6 "The report I heard in my country about your deeds and your wisdom is true," she told the king. 7 "Though I did not believe the report until I came and saw with my own eyes, I have discovered that they were not telling me the half. Your wisdom and prosperity surpass the report I heard. 8 Happy are your men, happy these servants of yours, who stand before you always and listen to your wisdom. 9 Blessed be the LORD, your God, whom it has pleased to place you on the throne of Israel. In his enduring love for Israel, the LORD has made you king to carry out judgment and justice." 10 Then she gave the king one hundred and twenty gold talents, a very large quantity of spices, and precious stones. Never again did anyone bring such an abundance of spices as the queen of Sheba gave to King Solomon.

11 Hiram's fleet, which used to bring gold from Ophir, also brought from there a large quantity of cabinet* wood and precious stones. 12 With the wood the king made supports for the temple of the LORD and for the palace of the king, and harps and lyres for the chanters. No more such wood was brought or seen to the present day.

13 King Solomon gave the queen of Sheba everything she desired and asked for, besides such presents as were given her from Solomon's royal bounty. Then she returned with her servants to her own country.

Solomon's Wealth 14 The gold that Solomon received every year weighed six hundred and sixty-six gold talents, 15 in addition to what came from the Tarshish fleet, from the traffic of merchants, and from all the kings of Arabia and the governors of the country. 16 Moreover, King Solomon made two hundred shields of beaten gold (six hundred gold shekels went into each shield)[j] 17 and three hundred bucklers of beaten gold (three minas of gold went into each buckler); and he put them in the hall of the Forest of Lebanon. 18 The king also had a large ivory throne made, and overlaid it with refined gold. 19 The throne had six steps, a back with a round top, and an arm on each side of the seat.

9, 26: Ezion-geber . . . Edom: the first mention of maritime commerce in the Israelite kingdom (to which the land of Edom was subject after its conquest by King David; cf 2 Sm 8, 14).

10, 1: Queen of Sheba: women rulers among the Arabs are recorded in eighth-century-B.C. Assyrian inscriptions. Sheba was for centuries the leading principality in what is now the Yemen.

10, 11f: Cabinet: an unknown wood, probably fragrant.

i 2 Chr 9, 1; Mt 12, 42; Lk 11, 31. j 1 Kgs 14, 26.

Next to each arm stood a lion; 20and twelve
other lions stood on the steps, two to a step,
one on either side of each step. Nothing like
this was produced in any other kingdom. 21In
addition, all King Solomon's drinking vessels
were of gold, and all the utensils in the hall of
the Forest of Lebanon were of pure gold. There
was no silver, for in Solomon's time it was
considered worthless. 22The king had a fleet of
Tarshish ships* at sea with Hiram's fleet. Once
every three years the fleet of Tarshish ships
would come with a cargo of gold, silver, ivory,
apes, and monkeys. 23Thus King Solomon sur-
passed in riches and wisdom all the kings of
the earth. 24And the whole world sought audi-
ence with Solomon, to hear from him the wis-
dom which God had put in his heart. 25Each
one brought his yearly tribute: silver or gold
articles, garments, weapons, spices, horses and
mules.

26Solomon collected chariots and drivers; he
had one thousand four hundred chariots and
twelve thousand drivers; these he allocated
among the chariot cities and to the king's service
in Jerusalem.[k] 27The king made silver as com-
mon in Jerusalem as stones, and cedars as
numerous as the sycamores of the foothills.
28Solomon's horses were imported from Cilicia,
where the king's agents purchased them. 29A
chariot imported from Egypt cost six hundred
shekels, a horse one hundred and fifty shekels;
they were exported at these rates to all the
Hittite and Aramean kings.

CHAPTER 11

The Sins of Solomon 1*King Solomon loved
many foreign women besides the daughter of
Pharaoh (Moabites, Ammonites, Edomites, Sido-
nians, and Hittites),[l] 2from nations with which
the LORD had forbidden the Israelites to inter-
marry, "because," he said, "they will turn your
hearts to their gods."[m] 3But Solomon fell in love
with them. He had seven hundred wives of
princely rank and three hundred concubines,
and his wives turned his heart.

4When Solomon was old his wives had turned
his heart to strange gods, and his heart was not
entirely with the LORD, his God, as the heart of
his father David had been. 5By adoring Astarte,
the goddess of the Sidonians, and Milcom, the
idol of the Ammonites, 6Solomon did evil in the
sight of the LORD; he did not follow him
unreservedly as his father David had done.
7Solomon then built a high place to Chemosh,
the idol of Moab, and to Molech, the idol of the
Ammonites, on the hill opposite Jerusalem. 8He
did the same for all his foreign wives who
burned incense and sacrificed to their gods. 9The
LORD, therefore, became angry with Solomon,
because his heart was turned away from the
LORD, the God of Israel, who had appeared to
him twice[n] 10(for though the LORD had forbid-
den him this very act of following strange gods,
Solomon had not obeyed him).

11So the LORD said to Solomon: "Since this is
what you want, and you have not kept my
covenant and my statutes which I enjoined on
you, I will deprive you of the kingdom and give
it to your servant. 12I will not do this during your
lifetime, however, for the sake of your father
David; it is your son whom I will deprive.[o]
13Nor will I take away the whole kingdom. I will
leave your son one tribe for the sake of my
servant David and of Jerusalem, which I have
chosen."

14The LORD then raised up an adversary to
Solomon: Hadad the Edomite, who was of the
royal line in Edom. 15Earlier, when David had

10, 22: Tarshish ships: large, strong vessels for long voyages. Tarshish was the ancient Tartessus, a Phoenician colony in southern Spain, the name of which denotes a center for smelting metallic ore.

11, 1–3. 7: The glorious rise of Solomon, his piety and wisdom, administrative skill and wealth, the extension of his kingdom, his prestige among neighboring rulers, his reign of peace, above all his friendship with God—these are now eclipsed by his sins of intermarriage with great numbers of pagan wives and the consequent forbidden worship of their gods (Ex 34, 11–16; Dt 7, 1–5). His construction of temples in their honor merited the punishment of loss of a united kingdom to his posterity, and the opposition of adversaries to himself (vv 14. 23–27). Hadad the Edomite rebelled against Solomon at the beginning of his reign (v 25). Rezon of Syria established a new kingdom in Dàmascus; Jeroboam of Israel constituted the greatest threat because of his revolt from within. This threefold threat culminated in the breakup of Solomon's kingdom.

k 2 Chr 1, 14. l Dt 17, 17; Sir 47, 19f. m Ex 34, 16. n 1 Kgs 9, 2. o 1 Kgs 12, 15.

conquered Edom, Joab, the general of the army,
while going to bury the slain, put to death every
male in Edom.[p] 16Joab and all Israel remained
there six months until they had killed off every
male in Edom. 17Meanwhile, Hadad, who was
only a boy, fled toward Egypt with some Edom-
ite servants of his father. 18They left Midian and
passing through Paran, where they picked up
additional men, they went into Egypt to Pha-
raoh, king of Egypt, who gave Hadad a house,
appointed him rations, and assigned him land.

19Hadad won great favor with Pharaoh, so
that he gave him in marriage the sister of Queen
Tahpenes, his own wife. 20Tahpenes' sister bore
Hadad a son, Genubath. After his weaning, the
queen kept him in Pharaoh's palace, where he
then lived with Pharaoh's own sons. 21When
Hadad in Egypt heard that David rested with his
ancestors and that Joab, the general of the army,
was dead, he said to Pharaoh, "Give me leave to
return to my own country." 22Pharaoh said to
him, "What do you lack with me, that you are
seeking to return to your own country?" "Noth-
ing," he said, "but please let me go!"

23God raised up against Solomon another
adversary, in Rezon, the son of Eliada, who had
fled from his lord, Hadadezer, king of Zobah,
24when David defeated them with slaughter.
Rezon gathered men about him and became
leader of a band, went to Damascus, settled
there, and became king in Damascus. 25He was
an enemy of Israel as long as Solomon lived; this
added to the harm done by Hadad, who made a
rift in Israel by becoming king over Edom.

26Solomon's servant Jeroboam, son of Nebat,
an Ephraimite from Zeredah with a widowed
mother, Zeruah, also rebelled against the king.[q]
27This is why he rebelled. King Solomon was
building Millo, closing up the breach of his
father's City of David. 28Jeroboam was a man of
means, and when Solomon saw that he was also
an industrious young man, he put him in charge
of the entire labor force of the house of Joseph.
29At that time Jeroboam left Jerusalem, and the
prophet Ahijah the Shilonite met him on the
road. The two were alone in the area, and the
prophet was wearing a new cloak.[r] 30Ahijah
took off his new cloak, tore it into twelve pieces,
31and said to Jeroboam:

"Take ten pieces for yourself; the LORD, the
God of Israel, says: 'I will tear away the kingdom
from Solomon's grasp and will give you ten of
the tribes.[s] 32One tribe shall remain to him for
the sake of David my servant, and of Jerusalem,
the city I have chosen out of all the tribes of
Israel. 33The ten I will give you because he has
forsaken me and has worshiped Astarte, goddess
of the Sidonians, Chemosh, god of Moab, and
Milcom, god of the Ammonites; he has not
followed my ways or done what is pleasing to
me according to my statutes and my decrees, as
his father David did. 34Yet I will not take any of
the kingdom from Solomon himself, but will
keep him a prince as long as he lives for the sake
of my servant David, whom I chose, who kept
my commandments and statutes. 35But I will
take the kingdom from his son and will give it to
you—that is, the ten tribes. 36I will give his son
one tribe, that my servant David may always
have a lamp before me in Jerusalem, the city in
which I choose to be honored. 37I will take you;
you shall reign over all that you desire and shall
become king of Israel. 38If, then, you heed all
that I command you, follow my ways, and please
me by keeping my statutes and my command-
ments like my servant David, I will be with you.
I will establish for you, as I did for David, a
lasting dynasty; I will give Israel to you. 39I will
punish David's line for this, but not forever.' "

40When Solomon tried to have Jeroboam
killed for his rebellion, he escaped to King
Shishak, in Egypt, where he remained until
Solomon's death.

41The rest of the acts of Solomon, with all his
deeds and his wisdom, are recorded in the book
of the chronicles of Solomon. 42The time that
Solomon reigned in Jerusalem over all Israel was
forty years. 43Solomon rested with his ancestors;
he was buried in his father's City of David, and
his son Rehoboam succeeded him as king.

p 2 Sm 8, 14. q 2 Chr 13, 6. r 1 Kgs 14, 2; 2 Chr 10, 15 s 1 Kgs 12, 15.

II: Judah and Israel to the Time of Ahab

CHAPTER 12

Secession of Israel 1 Rehoboam went to Shechem,* where all Israel had come to proclaim him king.[t] 3 They said to Rehoboam: 4 "Your father put on us a heavy yoke. If you now lighten the harsh service and the heavy yoke your father imposed on us, we will serve you." 5 "Come back to me in three days," he answered them. When the people had departed, 6 King Rehoboam consulted the elders who had been in his father's service while he was alive, and asked, "What answer do you advise me to give this people?" 7 They replied, "If today you will be the servant of this people and submit to them, giving them a favorable answer, they will be your servants forever." 8 But he ignored the advice the elders had given him, and consulted the young men who had grown up with him and were in his service. 9 He said to them, "What answer do you advise me to give this people, who have asked me to lighten the yoke my father imposed on them?" 10 The young men who had grown up with him replied, "This is what you must say to this people who have asked you to lighten the yoke your father put on them: 'My little finger is thicker than my father's body. 11 Whereas my father put a heavy yoke on you, I will make it heavier. My father beat you with whips, but I will beat you with scorpions.' "

12 On the third day all Israel came back to King Rehoboam, as he had instructed them to do. 13 Ignoring the advice the elders had given him, the king gave the people a harsh answer. 14 He said to them, as the young men had advised: "My father put on you a heavy yoke, but I will make it heavier. My father beat you with whips, but I will beat you with scorpions." 15 The king did not listen to the people, for the LORD brought this about to fulfill the prophecy he had uttered to Jeroboam, son of Nebat, through Ahijah the Shilonite.[u]

16 When all Israel saw that the king did not listen to them, the people answered the king:

"What share have we in David?*
We have no heritage in the son of Jesse.
To your tents, O Israel!
Now look to your own house, David."

So Israel went off to their tents, 17 but Rehoboam reigned over the Israelites who lived in the cities of Judah. 18 King Rehoboam then sent out Adoram, superintendent of the forced labor, but all Israel stoned him to death. Rehoboam managed to mount his chariot to flee to Jerusalem, 19 and Israel went into rebellion against David's house to this day. 2 Jeroboam, son of Nebat, who was still in Egypt, where he had fled from King Solomon, returned from Egypt as soon as he learned this. 20 When all Israel heard that Jeroboam had returned, they summoned him to an assembly and made him king over all Israel. None remained loyal to David's house except the tribe of Judah alone.

21 On his arrival in Jerusalem, Rehoboam gathered together all the house of Judah and the tribe of Benjamin—one hundred eighty thousand seasoned warriors—to fight against the house of Israel, to restore the kingdom to Rehoboam, son of Solomon. 22 [v]However, the LORD spoke to Shemaiah, a man of God: 23 "Say to Rehoboam, son of Solomon, king of Judah, and to the house of Judah and to Benjamin, and to the rest of the people: 24 'Thus says the LORD: You must not march out to fight against your brother Israelites. Let every man return home, for I have brought this about.' " They accepted this message of the LORD and gave up the expedition accordingly.

25 Jeroboam built up Shechem in the hill country of Ephraim and lived there. Then he left it and built up Penuel.

12, 1: Shechem: chief city of the northern tribes, where a covenant of fidelity had previously been made between the Lord and his people and a stone of witness had been erected in memory of the event (Jos 24, 25ff).

12, 16: What share have we in David: even in David's time the northern tribes seemed ready to withdraw from Judah (2 Sm 20, 1). The unreasonable attitude of Rehoboam toward them intensified the discontent caused by the oppression of Solomon (v 4) and thus precipitated the establishment of a rival monarchy (v 20).

t 2 Chr 10, 1. u 1 Kgs 11, 12. 31. v 22–24; 2 Chr 11, 2ff.

Religious Rebellion* 26Jeroboam thought to
himself: "The kingdom will return to David's
house. 27If now this people go up to offer
sacrifices in the temple of the LORD in Jerusalem,
the hearts of this people will return to their
master, Rehoboam, king of Judah, and they will
kill me." 28After taking counsel, the king made
two calves of gold and said to the people: "You
have been going up to Jerusalem long enough.
Here is your God, O Israel, who brought you up
from the land of Egypt."[w] 29And he put one in
Bethel, the other in Dan.* 30This led to sin,
because the people frequented these calves in
Bethel and in Dan. 31He also built temples on
the high places and made priests from among the
people who were not Levites.[x] 32Jeroboam estab-
lished a feast in the eighth month on the
fifteenth day of the month to duplicate in Bethel
the pilgrimage feast of Judah, with sacrifices to
the calves he had made; and he stationed in
Bethel priests of the high places he had built.

Message of the Prophet from Judah
33Jeroboam ascended the altar he built in Bethel
on the fifteenth day of the eighth month, the
month in which he arbitrarily chose to establish
a feast for the Israelites; he was going to offer
sacrifice.

CHAPTER 13

1A man of God came from Judah to Bethel by the
word of the LORD, while Jeroboam was standing
at the altar to offer sacrifice. 2He cried out
against the altar the word of the LORD: "O altar,
altar, the LORD says, 'A child shall be born to the
house of David, Josiah by name, who shall
slaughter upon you the priests of the high places
who offer sacrifice upon you, and he shall burn
human bones upon you.' "[y] 3He gave a sign that
same day and said: "This is the sign that the
LORD has spoken: The altar shall break up and
the ashes on it shall be strewn about."

4When King Jeroboam heard what the man of
God was crying out against the altar, he
stretched forth his hand from the altar and said,
"Seize him!" But the hand he stretched forth
against him withered, so that he could not draw
it back. 5Moreover, the altar broke up and the
ashes from it were strewn about—the sign the
man of God had given as the word of the LORD.
6Then the king appealed to the man of God.
"Entreat the LORD, your God," he said, "and
intercede for me that I may be able to withdraw
my hand." So the man of God entreated the
LORD, and the king recovered the normal use of
his hand. 7"Come home with me for some
refreshment," the king invited the man of God,
"and I will give you a present." 8"If you gave me
half your kingdom," the man of God said to the
king, "I would not go with you, nor eat bread or
drink water in this place. 9For I was instructed
by the word of the LORD not to eat bread or
drink water and not to return by the way I
came." 10So he departed by another road and
did not go back the way he had come to Bethel.

11There was an old prophet living in the city,
whose sons came and told him all that the man
of God had done that day in Bethel. When they
repeated to their father the words he had spoken
to the king, 12the father asked them, "Which
way did he go?" And his sons pointed out to him
the road taken by the man of God who had
come from Judah. 13Then he said to his sons,
"Saddle the ass for me." When they had saddled
it, he mounted 14and followed the man of God,
whom he found seated under a terebinth. When
he asked him, "Are you the man of God who
came from Judah?" he answered, "Yes." 15Then
he said, "Come home with me and have some
bread." 16"I cannot go back with you, and I
cannot eat bread or drink water with you in this
place," he answered, 17"for I was told by the

12, 26–32: Jeroboam feared reunification of the divided kingdom through worship in the single temple in Jerusalem. To prevent this he encouraged shrines on the high places, and appointed false priests to supplement those of levitical descent. The golden bullocks he installed in two of his sanctuaries, though probably intended as bearers of the invisible Divine Majesty, quickly became occasions for idolatry. Thus Jeroboam caused Israel to sin, and sealed his doom and that of his royal house (1 Kgs 13, 34; 14, 7–14).

12, 29: Bethel and Dan: at the southern and northern boundaries of the separate kingdom of Israel, where sanctuaries had existed in the past (Gn 12, 8; 13, 3; 18, 10–22; 25, 1–16; Jgs 18, 1–31).

w Tb 1, 5; Ex 32, 8. x 2 Chr 11, 15. y 2 Kgs 23, 16.

word of the LORD neither to eat bread nor drink
water here, and not to go back the way I came."
18But he said to him, "I, too, am a prophet like
you, and an angel told me in the word of the
LORD to bring you back with me to my house
and to have you eat bread and drink water." He
was lying to him, however.
19So he went back with him, and ate bread
and drank water in his house. 20But while they
were sitting at table, the LORD spoke to the
prophet who had brought him back, 21and he
cried out to the man of God who had come from
Judah: "The LORD says, 'Because you rebelled
against the command of the LORD and did not
keep the command which the LORD, your God,
gave you, 22but returned and ate bread and
drank water in the place where he told you to do
neither, your corpse shall not be brought to the
grave of your ancestors.' "
23After he had eaten bread and drunk water,
the ass was saddled for him, and he again 24set
out. But a lion met him on the road, and killed
him. His corpse lay sprawled on the road, and
the ass remained standing by it, and so did the
lion. 25Some passers-by saw the body lying in the
road, with the lion standing beside it, and
carried the news to the city where the old
prophet lived. 26On hearing it, the prophet who
had brought him back from his journey said: "It
is the man of God who rebelled against the
command of the LORD. He has delivered him to
a lion, which mangled and killed him, as the
LORD predicted to him." 27Then he said to his
sons, "Saddle the ass for me." When they had
saddled it, 28he went off and found the body
lying in the road with the ass and the lion
standing beside it. The lion had not eaten the
body nor had it harmed the ass. 29The prophet
lifted up the body of the man of God and put it
on the ass, and brought it back to the city to
mourn over it and to bury it. 30He laid the man's
body in his own grave, and they mourned over
it: "Alas, my brother!" 31After he had buried
him, he said to his sons, "When I die, bury me in
the grave where the man of God is buried. Lay
my remains beside his. 32For the word of the
LORD which he proclaimed against the altar in
Bethel and against all the shrines on the high
places in the cities of Samaria shall certainly
come to pass."
33Jeroboam did not give up his evil ways after
this event, but again made priests for the high
places from among the common people. Who-
ever desired it was consecrated and became a
priest of the high places. 34This was a sin on the
part of the house of Jeroboam for which it was to
be cut off and destroyed from the earth.

CHAPTER 14

Death of Abijah 1At that time Abijah, son of
Jeroboam, took sick. 2So Jeroboam said to his
wife, "Get ready and disguise yourself so that
none will recognize you as Jeroboam's wife.
Then go to Shiloh, where you will find the
prophet Ahijah. It is he who predicted my reign
over this people.[z] 3Take along ten loaves, some
cakes, and a jar of preserves, and go to him. He
will tell you what will happen to the child."
4The wife of Jeroboam obeyed. She made the
journey to Shiloh and entered the house of
Ahijah who could not see because age had
dimmed his sight.
5The LORD had said to Ahijah: "Jeroboam's
wife is coming to consult you about her son, for
he is sick. This is what you must tell her. When
she comes, she will be in disguise." 6So Ahijah,
hearing the sound of her footsteps as she entered
the door, said, "Come in, wife of Jeroboam. Why
are you in disguise? I have been commissioned
to give you bitter news. 7Go, tell Jeroboam, 'This
is what the LORD, the God of Israel, says: I
exalted you from among the people and made
you ruler of my people Israel. 8I deprived the
house of David of the kingdom and gave it to
you. Yet you have not been like my servant
David, who kept my commandments and fol-
lowed me with his whole heart, doing only what
pleased me. 9You have done worse than all who
preceded you: you have gone and made for
yourself strange gods and molten images to
provoke me; but me you have cast behind your
back. 10Therefore, I am bringing evil upon the

z 1 Kgs 11, 29.

house of Jeroboam: I will cut off every male in
Jeroboam's line, whether slave or freeman in
Israel, and will burn up the house of Jeroboam
completely, as though dung were being burned.[a]
11 When one of Jeroboam's line dies in the city,
dogs will devour him; when one of them dies in
the field, he will be devoured by the birds of the
sky. For the LORD has spoken!'[b] 12 So leave; go
home! As you step inside the city, the child will
die, 13 and all Israel will mourn him and bury
him, for he alone of Jeroboam's line will be laid
in the grave, since in him alone of Jeroboam's
house has something pleasing to the LORD, the
God of Israel, been found. 14 Today, at this very
moment, the LORD will raise up for himself a
king of Israel who will destroy the house of
Jeroboam. 15 The LORD will strike Israel like a
reed tossed about in the water and will pluck out
Israel from this good land which he gave their
fathers, scattering them beyond the River, be-
cause they made sacred poles for themselves and
thus provoked the LORD. 16 He will give up Israel
because of the sins Jeroboam has committed and
caused Israel to commit."

17 So Jeroboam's wife started back; when she
reached Tirzah and crossed the threshold of her
house, the child died. 18 He was buried with all
Israel mourning him, as the LORD had prophe-
sied through his servant the prophet Ahijah.

19 The rest of the acts of Jeroboam, with his
warfare and his reign, are recorded in the book
of the chronicles of the kings of Israel. 20 The
length of Jeroboam's reign was twenty-two
years. He rested with his ancestors, and his son
Nadab succeeded him as king.

Reign of Rehoboam 21 Rehoboam, son of Solo-
mon, reigned in Judah. He was forty-one years
old when he became king, and he reigned
seventeen years in Jerusalem, the city in which,
out of all the tribes of Israel, the LORD chose to
be honored. His mother was the Ammonite
named Naamah.[c]

22 Judah did evil in the sight of the LORD, and
by their sins angered him even more than their
fathers had done. 23 They, too, built for them-
selves high places, pillars, and sacred poles, upon
every high hill and under every green tree.
24 There were also cult prostitutes in the land.
Judah imitated all the abominable practices of
the nations whom the LORD had cleared out of
the Israelites' way.

25 In the fifth year of King Rehoboam, Shishak,
king of Egypt, attacked Jerusalem.* 26 He took
everything, including the treasures of the temple
of the LORD and those of the royal palace, as well
as all the gold shields made under Solomon.[d]
27 To replace them, King Rehoboam had bronze
shields made, which he entrusted to the officers
of the guard on duty at the entrance of the royal
palace. 28 Whenever the king visited the temple
of the LORD, those on duty would carry the
shields, and then return them to the guardroom.

29 The rest of the acts of Rehoboam, with all
that he did, are recorded in the book of the
chronicles of the kings of Judah. 30 There was
constant warfare between Rehoboam and Jero-
boam. 31 Rehoboam rested with his ancestors; he
was buried with them in the City of David. His
mother was the Ammonite named Naamah. His
son Abijam succeeded him as king.

CHAPTER 15

Reign of Abijam 1 In the eighteenth year of
King Jeroboam, son of Nebat, Abijam became
king of Judah;[e] 2 he reigned three years in
Jerusalem. His mother's name was Maacah,
daughter of Abishalom. 3 He imitated all the sins
his father had committed before him, and his
heart was not entirely with the LORD, his God,
like the heart of his grandfather David. 4 Yet for
David's sake the LORD, his God, gave him a lamp
in Jerusalem, raising up his son after him and
permitting Jerusalem to endure; 5 because David
had pleased the LORD and did not disobey any of

14, 25: In the fifth year . . . Shishak, king of Egypt, attacked Jerusalem: c. 926 B.C. According to 2 Chr 12, 1–12, the repentance of King Rehoboam and of the princes of Israel after the warning of the prophet Shemaiah diverted the actual attack on Jerusalem. Shishak, however, carried off the treasures of the temple of the Lord and of the king's palace (2 Chr 12, 9). A bas-relief of this Pharaoh in the temple of Aman at Karnak commemorates his conquest of some hundred and fifty Palestinian and Trans-Jordanian cities and towns.

a 1 Kgs 15, 29. b 1 Kgs 16, 4. c 2 Chr 12, 13. d 1 Kgs 10, 16. e 2 Chr 13, 1f.

his commands as long as he lived, except in the
case of Uriah the Hittite.[f]
7The rest of Abijam's acts, with all that he did,
are written in the book of the chronicles of the
kings of Judah.[g] 6There was war between Abi-
jam and Jeroboam. 8Abijam rested with his
ancestors; he was buried in the City of David,
and his son Asa succeeded him as king.
Reign of Asa 9In the twentieth year of Jero-
boam, king of Israel, Asa, king of Judah, began to
reign; 10he reigned forty-one years in Jerusalem.
His grandmother's name was Maacah, daughter
of Abishalom. 11Asa pleased the LORD like his
forefather David, 12banishing the temple prosti-
tutes from the land and removing all the idols his
father had made. 13He also deposed his grand-
mother Maacah from her position as queen
mother, because she had made an outrageous
object for Asherah. Asa cut down this object and
burned it in the Kidron Valley. 14The high places
did not disappear; yet Asa's heart was entirely
with the LORD as long as he lived. 15He brought
into the temple of the LORD his father's and his
own votive offerings of silver, gold, and various
utensils.
16There was war between Asa and Baasha,
king of Israel, as long as they both reigned.
17Baasha, king of Israel, attacked Judah and
fortified Ramah to prevent communication with
Asa, king of Judah.[h] 18Asa then took all the silver
and gold remaining in the treasuries of the
temple of the LORD and of the royal palace.
Entrusting them to his ministers, King Asa sent
them to Ben-hadad, son of Tabrimmon, son of
Hezion, king of Aram,* resident in Damascus.
He said: 19"There is a treaty between you and
me, as there was between your father and my
father. I am sending you a present of silver and
gold. Go, break your treaty with Baasha, king of
Israel, that he may withdraw from me." 20Ben-
hadad agreed with King Asa and sent the leaders
of his troops against the cities of Israel. They
attacked Ijon, Dan, Abel-beth-maacah, and all
Chinnereth, besides all the land of Naphtali.
21When Baasha heard of it, he left off fortifying
Ramah, and stayed in Tirzah. 22Then King Asa
summoned all Judah without exception, and
they carried away the stones and beams with
which Baasha was fortifying Ramah. With them
King Asa built Geba of Benjamin and Mizpeh.
23The rest of the acts of Asa, with all his valor
and accomplishments, and the cities he built, are
written in the book of the chronicles of the kings
of Judah. In his old age, Asa had an infirmity in
his feet. 24He rested with his ancestors; he was
buried in his forefather's City of David, and his
son Jehoshaphat succeeded him as king.[i]
Reign of Nadab 25In the second year of Asa,
king of Judah, Nadab, son of Jeroboam, became
king of Israel; he reigned over Israel two years.
26He did evil in the LORD's sight, imitating his
father's conduct and the sin which he had
caused Israel to commit. 27Baasha, son of Ahijah,
of the house of Issachar, plotted against him and
struck him down at Gibbethon of the Philistines,
which Nadab and all Israel were besieging.
28Baasha killed him in the third year of Asa, king
of Judah, and reigned in his stead. 29Once he
was king, he killed off the entire house of
Jeroboam, not leaving a single soul to Jeroboam
but destroying him utterly, according to the
warning which the LORD had pronounced
through his servant, Ahijah the Shilonite,[j] 30be-
cause of the sins Jeroboam committed and
caused Israel to commit, by which he provoked
the LORD, the God of Israel, to anger.
31The rest of the acts of Nadab, with all that
he did, are written in the book of the chronicles
of the kings of Israel. 32[There was war between
Asa and Baasha, king of Israel, as long as they
lived.]
Reign of Baasha 33In the third year of Asa,
king of Judah, Baasha, son of Ahijah, began his
twenty-four-year reign over Israel in Tirzah.
34He did evil in the LORD's sight, imitating the
conduct of Jeroboam and the sin he had caused
Israel to commit.

15, 18: Ben-hadad . . . king of Aram: Ben-hadad I, third successor of Rezon, who had thrown off the yoke of the Israelites during the reign of Solomon and become king of Aram (11, 23f).

f 2 Sm 11, 4. g 2 Chr 13, 2. h 2 Chr 16, 1. i 2 Chr 17, 1. j 1 Kgs 14, 10; 21, 22.

CHAPTER 16

[1]The LORD spoke against Baasha to Jehu, son of Hanani, and said: [2]"Inasmuch as I lifted you up from the dust and made you ruler of my people Israel, but you have imitated the conduct of Jeroboam and have caused my people Israel to sin, provoking me to anger by their sins, [3]I will destroy you, Baasha, and your house;[k] [4]I will make your house like that of Jeroboam, son of Nebat. If anyone of Baasha's line dies in the city, dogs shall devour him; if he dies in the field, he shall be devoured by the birds of the sky."[l]

[5]The rest of the acts of Baasha, with all his valor and accomplishments, are written in the book of the chronicles of the kings of Israel.[m] [6]Baasha rested with his ancestors; he was buried in Tirzah, and his son Elah succeeded him as king. [7][Through the prophet Jehu, son of Hanani, the LORD had threatened Baasha and his house, because of all the evil Baasha did in the sight of the LORD, provoking him to anger by his evil deeds, so that he became like the house of Jeroboam; and because he killed Nadab.]

Reign of Elah [8]In the twenty-sixth year of Asa, king of Judah, Elah, son of Baasha, began his two-year reign over Israel in Tirzah. [9]His servant Zimri, commander of half his chariots, plotted against him. As he was in Tirzah, drinking to excess in the house of Arza, superintendent of his palace in Tirzah, [10]Zimri entered; he struck and killed him in the twenty-seventh year of Asa, king of Judah, and reigned in his place.[n] [11]Once he was seated on the royal throne, he killed off the whole house of Baasha, not sparing a single male relative or friend of his. [12]Zimri destroyed the entire house of Baasha, as the LORD had prophesied to Baasha through the prophet Jehu, [13]because of all the sins which Baasha and his son Elah committed and caused Israel to commit, provoking the LORD, the God of Israel, to anger by their idols.

[14]The rest of the acts of Elah, with all that he did, are written in the book of the chronicles of the kings of Israel.

Reign of Zimri [15]In the twenty-seventh year of Asa, king of Judah, Zimri reigned seven days in Tirzah. The army was besieging Gibbethon of the Philistines [16]when they heard that Zimri had formed a conspiracy and had killed the king. So that day in the camp all Israel proclaimed Omri, general of the army, king of Israel. [17]Omri marched up from Gibbethon, accompanied by all Israel, and laid siege to Tirzah. [18]When Zimri saw the city was captured, he entered the citadel of the royal palace and burned down the palace over him. He died [19]because of the sins he had committed, doing evil in the sight of the LORD by imitating the sinful conduct of Jeroboam, thus causing Israel to sin.

[20]The rest of the acts of Zimri, with the conspiracy he carried out, are written in the book of the chronicles of the kings of Israel.

[21]At that time the people of Israel were divided, half following Tibni, son of Ginath, to make him king, and half for Omri. [22]The partisans of Omri prevailed over those of Tibni, son of Ginath. Tibni died and Omri became king.

Reign of Omri [23]In the thirty-first year of Asa, king of Judah, Omri became king; he reigned over Israel twelve years, the first six of them in Tirzah. [24]He then bought the hill of Samaria from Shemer for two silver talents and built upon the hill, naming the city he built Samaria after Shemer, the former owner. [25]But Omri did evil in the LORD's sight beyond any of his predecessors. [26]He closely imitated the sinful conduct of Jeroboam, son of Nebat, causing Israel to sin and to provoke the LORD, the God of Israel, to anger by their idols.

[27]The rest of the acts of Omri, with all his valor and accomplishments, are written in the book of the chronicles of the kings of Israel. [28]Omri rested with his ancestors; he was buried in Samaria, and his son Ahab succeeded him as king.

Reign of Ahab [29]In the thirty-eighth year of Asa, king of Judah, Ahab, son of Omri, became king of Israel; he reigned over Israel in Samaria for twenty-two years. [30]Ahab, son of Omri, did evil in the sight of the LORD more than any of his predecessors. [31]It was not enough for him to imitate the sins of Jeroboam, son of Nebat. He

k 1 Kgs 21, 22. l 1 Kgs 14, 11. m 2 Chr 16, 1. n 2 Kgs 9,31.

even married Jezebel, daughter of Ethbaal, king of the Sidonians, and went over to the veneration and worship of Baal. [32]Ahab erected an altar to Baal in the temple of Baal which he built in Samaria, [33]and also made a sacred pole. He did more to anger the LORD, the God of Israel, than any of the kings of Israel before him.

[34] [o]During his reign, Hiel from Bethel rebuilt Jericho. He lost his first-born son, Abiram, when he laid the foundation, and his youngest son, Segub, when he set up the gates, as the LORD had foretold through Joshua, son of Nun.

III: Stories of the Prophets

CHAPTER 17

Drought Predicted by Elijah [1]Elijah the Tishbite,* from Tishbe in Gilead, said to Ahab: "As the LORD, the God of Israel, lives, whom I serve, during these years there shall be no dew or rain except at my word." [p] [2]The LORD then said to Elijah: [3]"Leave here, go east and hide in the Wadi Cherith, east of the Jordan. [4]You shall drink of the stream, and I have commanded ravens to feed you there." [5]So he left and did as the LORD had commanded. He went and remained by the Wadi Cherith, east of the Jordan. [6]Ravens brought him bread and meat in the morning, and bread and meat in the evening, and he drank from the stream.

Elijah and the Widow [7]After some time, however, the brook ran dry, because no rain had fallen in the land. [8]So the LORD said to him: [9]"Move on to Zarephath of Sidon and stay there. I have designated a widow there to provide for you." [10]He left and went to Zarephath. As he arrived at the entrance of the city, a widow was gathering sticks there; he called out to her, "Please bring me a small cupful of water to drink." [q] [11]She left to get it, and he called out after her, "Please bring along a bit of bread." [12]"As the LORD, your God, lives," she answered, "I have nothing baked; there is only a handful of flour in my jar and a little oil in my jug. Just now I was collecting a couple of sticks, to go in and prepare something for myself and my son; when we have eaten it, we shall die." [13]"Do not be afraid," Elijah said to her. "Go and do as you propose. But first make me a little cake and bring it to me. Then you can prepare something for yourself and your son. [14]For the LORD, the God of Israel, says, 'The jar of flour shall not go empty, nor the jug of oil run dry, until the day when the LORD sends rain upon the earth.' " [15]She left and did as Elijah had said. She was able to eat for a year, and he and her son as well; [16]the jar of flour did not go empty, nor the jug of oil run dry, as the LORD had foretold through Elijah.

[17]Some time later the son of the mistress of the house fell sick, and his sickness grew more severe until he stopped breathing. [18]So she said to Elijah, "Why have you done this to me, O man of God? Have you come to me to call attention to my guilt and to kill my son?" [19]"Give me your son," Elijah said to her. Taking him from her lap, he carried him to the upper room where he was staying, and laid him on his own bed. [20]He called out to the LORD: "O LORD, my God, will you afflict even the widow with whom I am staying by killing her son?" [21]Then he stretched himself out upon the child three times and called out to the LORD: "O LORD, my God, let the life breath return to the body of this child." [22]The LORD heard the prayer of Elijah; the life breath returned to the child's body and he revived. [23]Taking the child, Elijah brought him down into the house from the upper room and gave him to his mother. "See!" Elijah said to her, "your son is alive." [24]"Now indeed I know that you are a man of God," the woman replied to Elijah. "The word of the LORD comes truly from your mouth."

17, 1: Elijah the Tishbite: one of the most important figures in Old Testament history. As his name indicates ("Yahweh is my God"), Elijah was the successful leader in the struggle to preserve the knowledge and worship of Yahweh against the encroaching worship of Baal introduced into Israel by Jezebel, the Tyrian wife of Ahab. The Elijah cycle of narratives includes, besides the above struggle, miracle stories, denunciations of kings, and a preparation for the prophet's role as eschatological forerunner of the "great day of the Lord"; cf Mal 3, 23–24; Mt 17, 10–13; Lk 1, 17.

o Jos 6, 26. p Sir 48, 3; Jas 5, 17. q Lk 4, 26.

CHAPTER 18

Elijah and the Prophets of Baal 1Long after-
ward, in the third year, the LORD spoke to Elijah.
“Go, present yourself to Ahab,” he said, “that I
may send rain upon the earth.” 2So Elijah went
to present himself to Ahab.
3Now the famine in Samaria was bitter, 4and
Ahab had summoned Obadiah, his vizier, who
was a zealous follower of the LORD. When
Jezebel was murdering the prophets of the LORD,
Obadiah took a hundred prophets, hid them
away fifty each in two caves, and supplied them
with food and drink. 5Ahab said to Obadiah,
“Come, let us go through the land to all sources
of water and to all the streams. We may find
grass and save the horses and mules, so that we
shall not have to slaughter any of the beasts.”
6Dividing the land to explore between them,
Ahab went one way by himself, Obadiah another
way by himself.
7As Obadiah was on his way, Elijah met him.
Recognizing him, Obadiah fell prostrate and
asked, “Is it you, my lord Elijah?” 8“Yes,” he
answered. “Go tell your master, ‘Elijah is
here!’ ” 9But Obadiah said, “What sin have I
committed, that you are handing me over to
Ahab to have me killed? 10As the LORD, your
God, lives, there is no nation or kingdom where
my master has not sent in search of you. When
they replied, ‘He is not here,’ he made each
kingdom and nation swear they could not find
you. 11And now you say, ‘Go tell your master:
Elijah is here!’ 12After I leave you, the spirit of
the LORD will carry you to some place I do not
know, and when I go to inform Ahab and he
does not find you, he will kill me. Your servant
has revered the LORD from his youth. 13Have
you not been told, my lord, what I did when
Jezebel was murdering the prophets of the
LORD—that I hid a hundred of the prophets of
the LORD, fifty each in two caves, and supplied
them with food and drink? 14And now you say,
‘Go tell your master: Elijah is here!’ He will kill
me!” 15Elijah answered, “As the LORD of hosts
lives, whom I serve, I will present myself to him
today.”
16So Obadiah went to meet Ahab and in-
formed him. Ahab came to meet Elijah, 17and
when he saw Elijah, said to him, “Is it you, you
disturber of Israel?” 18“It is not I who disturb
Israel,” he answered, “but you and your family,
by forsaking the commands of the LORD and
following the Baals. 19Now summon all Israel to
me on Mount Carmel, as well as the four
hundred and fifty prophets of Baal and the four
hundred prophets of Asherah who eat at Jeze-
bel’s table.” 20So Ahab sent to all the Israelites
and had the prophets assemble on Mount Car-
mel.
21Elijah appealed to all the people and said,
“How long will you straddle the issue? If the
LORD is God, follow him; if Baal, follow him.”
The people, however, did not answer him. 22So
Elijah said to the people, “I am the only surviv-
ing prophet of the LORD, and there are four
hundred and fifty prophets of Baal. 23Give us
two young bulls. Let them choose one, cut it
into pieces, and place it on the wood, but start
no fire. I shall prepare the other and place it on
the wood, but shall start no fire. 24You shall call
on your gods, and I will call on the LORD. The
God who answers with fire is God.” All the
people answered, “Agreed!”
25Elijah then said to the prophets of Baal,
“Choose one young bull and prepare it first, for
there are more of you. Call upon your gods, but
do not start the fire.” 26Taking the young bull
that was turned over to them, they prepared it
and called on Baal from morning to noon,
saying, “Answer us, Baal!” But there was no
sound, and no one answering. And they hopped
around the altar they had prepared. 27When it
was noon, Elijah taunted them: “Call louder, for
he is a god and may be meditating, or may have
retired, or may be on a journey. Perhaps he is
asleep and must be awakened.” 28They called
out louder and slashed themselves with swords
and spears, as was their custom, until blood
gushed over them. 29Noon passed and they
remained in a prophetic state until the time for
offering sacrifice. But there was not a sound; no
one answered, and no one was listening.
30Then Elijah said to all the people, “Come
here to me.” When they had done so, he

repaired the altar of the LORD which had been destroyed. 31He took twelve stones, for the number of tribes of the sons of Jacob, to whom the LORD had said, "Your name shall be Israel." 32He built an altar in honor of the LORD with the stones, and made a trench around the altar large enough for two seahs of grain. 33When he had arranged the wood, he cut up the young bull and laid it on the wood. 34"Fill four jars with water," he said, "and pour it over the holocaust and over the wood." "Do it again," he said, and they did it again. "Do it a third time," he said, and they did it a third time. 35The water flowed around the altar, and the trench was filled with the water.

36At the time for offering sacrifice, the prophet Elijah came forward and said, "LORD, God of Abraham, Isaac, and Israel, let it be known this day that you are God in Israel and that I am your servant and have done all these things by your command. 37Answer me, LORD! Answer me, that this people may know that you, LORD, are God and that you have brought them back to their senses." 38The LORD's fire came down and consumed the holocaust, wood, stones, and dust, and it lapped up the water in the trench. 39Seeing this, all the people fell prostrate and said, "The LORD is God! The LORD is God!" 40Then Elijah said to them, "Seize the prophets of Baal. Let none of them escape!" They were seized, and Elijah had them brought down to the brook Kishon and there he slit their throats.

41Elijah then said to Ahab, "Go up, eat and drink, for there is the sound of a heavy rain." 42So Ahab went up to eat and drink, while Elijah climbed to the top of Carmel, crouched down to the earth, and put his head between his knees. 43"Climb up and look out to sea," he directed his servant, who went up and looked, but reported, "There is nothing." Seven times he said, "Go, look again!" 44And the seventh time the youth reported, "There is a cloud as small as a man's hand rising from the sea." Elijah said, "Go and say to Ahab, 'Harness up and leave the mountain before the rain stops you.' " 45In a trice, the sky grew dark with clouds and wind, and a heavy rain fell. Ahab mounted his chariot and made for Jezreel. 46But the hand of the LORD was on Elijah, who girded up his clothing and ran before Ahab as far as the approaches to Jezreel.

CHAPTER 19

Flight to Horeb 1Ahab told Jezebel all that Elijah had done—that he had put all the prophets to the sword. 2Jezebel then sent a messenger to Elijah and said, "May the gods do thus and so to me if by this time tomorrow I have not done with your life what was done to each of them." 3Elijah was afraid and fled for his life, going to Beer-sheba of Judah. He left his servant there 4and went a day's journey into the desert, until he came to a broom tree and sat beneath it. He prayed for death: "This is enough, O LORD! Take my life, for I am no better than my fathers." 5He lay down and fell asleep under the broom tree, but then an angel touched him and ordered him to get up and eat. 6He looked and there at his head was a hearth cake and a jug of water. After he ate and drank, he lay down again, 7but the angel of the LORD came back a second time, touched him, and ordered, "Get up and eat, else the journey will be too long for you!" 8He got up, ate and drank; then strengthened by that food, he walked forty days and forty nights to the mountain of God, Horeb.

9There he came to a cave, where he took shelter. But the word of the LORD came to him, "Why are you here, Elijah?" 10He answered: "I have been most zealous for the LORD, the God of hosts, but the Israelites have forsaken your covenant, torn down your altars, and put your prophets to the sword. I alone am left, and they seek to take my life." 11*Then the LORD said, "Go outside and stand on the mountain

19, 11ff: Compare these divine manifestations to Elijah with those to Moses (Ex 19, 1–23; 33, 21ff; 34, 5) on the same Mount Horeb (Sinai) (Dt 4, 10–15). Though various phenomena, such as wind, storms, earthquakes, fire (Ex 19, 18f), herald the divine presence, they do not constitute the presence itself which, like the tiny whispering sound, is imperceptible and bespeaks the spirituality of God. It was fitting that Elijah, whose mission it was to reestablish the covenant and restore the pure faith, should have returned to Horeb where the covenant was revealed to Moses and through him to the Israelite people (Ex 3, 1–4. 17; 33, 18–34, 9). Moses and Elijah appeared with Christ at the time of his transfiguration (Mt 17, 1–9; Mk 9, 1–7; Lk 9, 28–36).

before the LORD; the LORD will be passing by." A strong and heavy wind was rending the mountains and crushing rocks before the LORD—but the LORD was not in the wind. After the wind there was an earthquake—but the LORD was not in the earthquake. 12After the earthquake there was fire—but the LORD was not in the fire. After the fire there was a tiny whispering sound. 13When he heard this, Elijah hid his face in his cloak and went and stood at the entrance of the cave. A voice said to him, "Elijah, why are you here?" 14He replied, "I have been most zealous for the LORD, the God of hosts. But the Israelites have forsaken your covenant, torn down your altars, and put your prophets to the sword. I alone am left, and they seek to take my life."[r] 15*"Go, take the road back to the desert near Damascus," the LORD said to him. "When you arrive, you shall anoint Hazael as king of Aram. 16Then you shall anoint Jehu, son of Nimshi, as king of Israel, and Elisha, son of Shaphat of Abel-meholah, as prophet to succeed you.[s] 17If anyone escapes the sword of Hazael, Jehu will kill him. If he escapes the sword of Jehu, Elisha will kill him. 18Yet I will leave seven thousand men in Israel—all those who have not knelt to Baal or kissed him."[t]

Call of Elisha* 19Elijah set out, and came upon Elisha, son of Shaphat, as he was plowing with twelve yoke of oxen; he was following the twelfth. Elijah went over to him and threw his cloak over him. 20Elisha left the oxen, ran after Elijah, and said, "Please, let me kiss my father and mother goodbye, and I will follow you." "Go back!" Elijah answered. "Have I done anything to you?" 21Elisha left him and, taking the yoke of oxen, slaughtered them; he used the plowing equipment for fuel to boil their flesh, and gave it to his people to eat. Then he left and followed Elijah as his attendant.

CHAPTER 20

Ahab's Victories over Ben-hadad 1Ben-hadad, king of Aram, gathered all his forces, and accompanied by thirty-two kings with horses and chariotry, proceeded to invest and attack Samaria. 2He sent couriers to Ahab, king of Israel, within the city, 3and said to him, "This is Ben-hadad's message: 'Your silver and gold are mine, and your wives and your promising sons are mine.' " 4The king of Israel answered, "As you say, my lord king, I and all I have are yours." 5But the couriers came again and said, "This is Ben-hadad's message: 'I sent you word to give me your silver and gold, your wives and your sons. 6Now, however, at this time tomorrow I will send my servants to you, and they shall ransack your house and the houses of your servants. They shall seize and take away whatever they consider valuable.' "

7The king of Israel then summoned all the elders of the land and said: "Understand clearly that this man wants to ruin us. When he sent to me for my wives and sons, my silver and my gold, I did not refuse him." 8All the elders and all the people said to him, "Do not listen. Do not give in." 9Accordingly he directed the couriers of Ben-hadad, "Say to my lord the king, 'I will do all that you demanded of your servant the first time. But this I cannot do.' " The couriers left and reported this. 10Ben-hadad then sent him the message, "May the gods do thus and so to me if there is enough dust in Samaria to make handfuls for all my followers." 11The king of Israel replied, "Tell him, 'It is not for the man who is buckling his armor to boast as though he were taking it off.' " 12Ben-hadad was drinking in the pavilions with the kings when he heard this reply. "Prepare the assault," he commanded his servants; and they made ready to storm the city.

13Then a prophet came up to Ahab, king of Israel, and said: "The LORD says, 'Do you see all

19, 15–17: Elijah himself carried out only the third of the commissions entrusted to him (vv 19–21); Elisha was deputed to perform the first in person (2 Kgs 8, 7–19), and the second through one of his followers (2 Kgs 9, 1–10).

19, 19–21: Elijah's act of throwing his mantle over the shoulders of Elisha expressed the divine call to share the prophetic mission. Elisha's prompt response through destruction of his plow and oxen is an example of total obedience and detachment from his former manner of living in order to promote the glory of God.

r Rom 11, 3. s 2 Kgs 9, 2. t Rom 11, 4.

this huge army? When I deliver it up to you
today, you will know that I am the Lord.' "
14But Ahab asked, "Through whom will it be
delivered up?" He answered, "The Lord says,
'Through the retainers of the governors of the
provinces.' " Then Ahab asked, "Who is to
attack?" He replied, "You are." 15So Ahab called
up the retainers of the governors of the prov-
inces, two hundred thirty-two of them. Behind
them he mustered all the Israelite soldiery, who
numbered seven thousand. 16They marched out
at noon, while Ben-hadad was drinking heavily
in the pavilions with the thirty-two kings who
were his allies. 17When the retainers of the
governors of the provinces marched out first,
Ben-hadad received word that some men had
marched out of Samaria. 18He answered,
"Whether they have come out for peace or for
war, in any case take them alive." 19But when
these had come out of the city—the soldiers of
the governors of the provinces with the army
following them— 20each of them struck down
his man. The Arameans fled with Israel pursuing
them, while Ben-hadad, king of Aram, escaped
on a chariot steed. 21The king of Israel went out,
took the horses and chariots, and inflicted a
severe defeat on Aram.

22Then the prophet went up to the king of
Israel and said to him: "Go, regroup your forces.
Mark well what you do, for at the beginning of
the year* the king of Aram will attack you."
23On the other hand, the servants of the king of
Aram said to him: "Their gods are gods of
mountains. That is why they defeated us. But if
we fight them on level ground, we shall be sure
to defeat them. 24This is what you must do: Take
the kings from their posts and put prefects in
their places. 25Mobilize an army as large as the
army that has deserted you, horse for horse,
chariot for chariot. Let us fight them on level
ground, and we shall surely defeat them." He
took their advice and did this.

26At the beginning of the year, Ben-hadad
mobilized Aram and went up to Aphek to fight
against Israel. 27The Israelites, too, were called
to arms and supplied with provisions; then they
went out to engage the foe. The Israelites,
encamped opposite them, seemed like a couple
of small flocks of goats, while Aram covered the
countryside. 28A man of God came up and said
to the king of Israel: "The Lord says, 'Because
Aram has said the Lord is a god of mountains,
not a god of plains, I will deliver up to you all
this large army, that you may know I am the
Lord.' " 29They were encamped opposite each
other for seven days. On the seventh day battle
was joined, and the Israelites struck down one
hundred thousand foot soldiers of Aram in one
day. 30The survivors, twenty-seven thousand of
them, fled into the city of Aphek, and there the
wall collapsed. Ben-hadad, too, fled, and took
refuge within the city, in an inside room.

31His servants said to him: "We have heard
that the kings of the land of Israel are merciful
kings. Allow us, therefore, to garb ourselves in
sackcloth, with cords around our heads, and go
out to the king of Israel. Perhaps he will spare
your life." 32So they dressed in sackcloth girded
at the waist, and wearing cords around their
heads, they went to the king of Israel. "Your
servant Ben-hadad pleads for his life," they said.
"Is he still alive?" the king asked. "He is my
brother." 33Hearing this as a good omen, the
men quickly took him at his word and said,
"Ben-hadad is your brother." He answered, "Go
and get him." When Ben-hadad came out to
him, the king had him mount his chariot. 34Ben-
hadad said to him, "I will restore the cities
which my father took from your father, and you
may make yourself bazaars in Damascus, as my
father did in Samaria." "On these terms," Ahab
replied, "I will set you free." So he made an
agreement with him and then set him free.

35One of the guild prophets was prompted by
the Lord to say to his companion, "Strike me."
But he refused to strike him. 36Then he said to
him, "Since you did not obey the voice of the
Lord, a lion will kill you when you leave me."
When they parted company, a lion came upon
him and killed him. 37The prophet met another
man and said, "Strike me." The man struck him
a blow and wounded him. 38The prophet went

20, 22: At the beginning of the year: in the spring.

on and waited for the king on the road, having disguised himself with a bandage over his eyes. 39As the king was passing, he called out to the king and said, "Your servant went into the thick of the battle, and suddenly someone turned and brought me a man and said, 'Guard this man. If he is missing, you shall have to pay for his life with your life or pay out a talent of silver.' 40But while your servant was looking here and there, the man disappeared." The king of Israel said to him, "That is your sentence. You have decided it yourself." 41He immediately removed the bandage from his eyes, and the king of Israel recognized him as one of the prophets. 42He said to him: "The LORD says, 'Because you have set free the man I doomed to destruction, your life shall pay for his life, your people for his people.' " Disturbed and angry, the king of Israel went off homeward and entered Samaria.[u]

CHAPTER 21

Seizure of Naboth's Vineyard 1Some time after this, as Naboth the Jezreelite had a vineyard in Jezreel next to the palace of Ahab, king of Samaria, 2Ahab said to Naboth, "Give me your vineyard to be my vegetable garden, since it is close by, next to my house. I will give you a better vineyard in exchange, or, if you prefer, I will give you its value in money." 3"The LORD forbid," Naboth answered him, "that I should give you my ancestral heritage." 4Ahab went home disturbed and angry at the answer Naboth the Jezreelite had made to him: "I will not give you my ancestral heritage." Lying down on his bed, he turned away from food and would not eat.

5His wife Jezebel came to him and said to him, "Why are you so angry that you will not eat?" 6He answered her, "Because I spoke to Naboth the Jezreelite and said to him, 'Sell me your vineyard, or, if you prefer, I will give you a vineyard in exchange.' But he refused to let me have his vineyard." 7"A fine ruler over Israel you are indeed!" his wife Jezebel said to him. "Get up. Eat and be cheerful. I will obtain the vineyard of Naboth the Jezreelite for you."

8So she wrote letters in Ahab's name and, having sealed them with his seal, sent them to the elders and to the nobles who lived in the same city with Naboth. 9This is what she wrote in the letters: "Proclaim a fast and set Naboth at the head of the people. 10Next, get two scoundrels to face him and accuse him of having cursed God and king. Then take him out and stone him to death." 11His fellow citizens—the elders and the nobles who dwelt in his city—did as Jezebel had ordered them in writing, through the letters she had sent them. 12They proclaimed a fast and placed Naboth at the head of the people. 13Two scoundrels came in and confronted him with the accusation, "Naboth has cursed God and king." And they led him out of the city and stoned him to death. 14Then they sent the information to Jezebel that Naboth had been stoned to death.

15When Jezebel learned that Naboth had been stoned to death, she said to Ahab, "Go on, take possession of the vineyard of Naboth the Jezreelite which he refused to sell you, because Naboth is not alive, but dead." 16On hearing that Naboth was dead, Ahab started off on his way down to the vineyard of Naboth the Jezreelite, to take possession of it.

17But the LORD said to Elijah the Tishbite: 18"Start down to meet Ahab, king of Israel, who rules in Samaria. He will be in the vineyard of Naboth, of which he has come to take possession. 19*[v] This is what you shall tell him, 'The LORD says: After murdering, do you also take possession? For this, the LORD says: In the place where the dogs licked up the blood of Naboth, the dogs shall lick up your blood, too.' " 20*"Have you found me out, my enemy?" Ahab

21, 19: The response of Ahab to this divine judgment is described in v 27, and the consequences are given in vv 28–29, and in 2 Kgs 9, 21–26.

21, 20–26: In these verses the Judean editor of the Books of Kings substitutes, for the message of Elijah prepared for in v 19, a sweeping and definitive judgment against the whole family of Ahab in the same terms as were used against the families of Jeroboam I (1 Kgs 14, 9–11) and Baasha (1 Kgs 16, 2–4). This judgment is the fruit of later theological reflection; it is not occasioned directly by the crime against Naboth, but by the idolatry of Ahab and Jezebel. The judgment on Jezebel herself (v 23) may have been uttered by Elijah during the Naboth episode; it finds its fulfillment in 2 Kgs 9, 36–37. Still another theological explanation for the death of Ahab is given by the north Israelite writer of 1 Kgs 20, 35–42 above.

u 1 Kgs 22, 35. v 1 Kgs 22, 38.

said to Elijah. "Yes," he answered. "Because you have given yourself up to doing evil in the LORD's sight, 21I am bringing evil upon you: I will destroy you and will cut off every male in Ahab's line, whether slave or freeman, in Israel.[w] 22I will make your house like that of Jeroboam, son of Nebat, and like that of Baasha, son of Ahijah, because of how you have provoked me by leading Israel into sin."[x] 23(Against Jezebel, too, the LORD declared, "The dogs shall devour Jezebel in the district of Jezreel.")[y] 24"When one of Ahab's line dies in the city, dogs will devour him; when one of them dies in the field, the birds of the sky will devour him." 25Indeed, no one gave himself up to the doing of evil in the sight of the LORD as did Ahab, urged on by his wife Jezebel. 26He became completely abominable by following idols, just as the Amorites had done, whom the LORD drove out before the Israelites.

27When Ahab heard these words, he tore his garments and put on sackcloth over his bare flesh. He fasted, slept in the sackcloth, and went about subdued. 28Then the LORD said to Elijah the Tishbite, 29"Have you seen that Ahab has humbled himself before me? Since he has humbled himself before me, I will not bring the evil in his time. I will bring the evil upon his house during the reign of his son."[z]

CHAPTER 22

Campaign against Ramoth-gilead 1Three years passed without war between Aram and Israel.[a] 2In the third year, however, King Jehoshaphat of Judah came down to the king of Israel, 3who said to his servants, "Do you not know that Ramoth-gilead is ours and we are doing nothing to take it from the king of Aram?" 4He asked Jehoshaphat, "Will you come with me to fight against Ramoth-gilead?" Jehoshaphat answered the king of Israel, "You and I are as one, and your people and my people, your horses and my horses as well." 5Jehoshaphat also said to the king of Israel, "Seek the word of the LORD at once."

6The king of Israel gathered together the prophets, about four hundred of them, and asked, "Shall I go to attack Ramoth-gilead or shall I refrain?" "Go up," they answered. "The LORD will deliver it over to the king." 7But Jehoshaphat said, "Is there no other prophet of the LORD here whom we may consult?" 8The king of Israel answered, "There is one other through whom we might consult the LORD, Micaiah, son of Imlah; but I hate him because he prophesies not good but evil about me." Jehoshaphat said, "Let not your majesty speak of evil against you."

9So the king of Israel called an official and said to him, "Get Micaiah, son of Imlah, at once." 10The king of Israel and King Jehoshaphat of Judah were seated, each on his throne, clothed in their robes of state on a threshing floor at the entrance of the gate of Samaria, and all the prophets were prophesying before them. 11Zedekiah, son of Chenaanah, made himself horns of iron and said, "The LORD says, 'With these you shall gore Aram until you have destroyed them.' " 12The other prophets prophesied in a similar vein, saying: "Go up to Ramoth-gilead; you shall succeed. The LORD will deliver it over to the king."

13The messenger who had gone to call Micaiah said to him, "Look now, the prophets are unanimously predicting good for the king. Let your word be the same as any of theirs; predict good." 14"As the LORD lives," Micaiah answered, "I shall say whatever the LORD tells me."

15When he came to the king, the king said to him, "Micaiah, shall we go to fight against Ramoth-gilead, or shall we refrain?" "Go up," he answered, "you shall succeed! The LORD will deliver it over to the king." 16But the king answered him, "How many times must I adjure you to tell me nothing but the truth in the name of the LORD?" 17So Micaiah said:

"I see all Israel
scattered on the mountains,

w 2 Kgs 9, 8. x 1 Kgs 15, 29; 16, 3. y 2 Kgs 9, 36. z 2 Kgs 9, 26. a 2 Chr 18, 1.

like sheep without a shepherd,
and the LORD saying, 'These have no master!
Let each of them go back home in peace.' "

18 The king of Israel said to Jehoshaphat, "Did
I not tell you he prophesies not good but evil
about me?" 19 *Micaiah continued: "Therefore
hear the word of the LORD: I saw the LORD
seated on his throne, with the whole host of
heaven standing by to his right and to his left.
20 The LORD asked, 'Who will deceive Ahab, so
that he will go up and fall at Ramoth-gilead?'
And one said this, another that, 21 until one of
the spirits came forth and presented himself to
the LORD, saying, 'I will deceive him.' The LORD
asked, 'How?' 22 He answered, 'I will go forth
and become a lying spirit in the mouths of all his
prophets.' The LORD replied, 'You shall succeed
in deceiving him. Go forth and do this.' 23 So
now, the LORD has put a lying spirit in the
mouths of all these prophets of yours, but the
LORD himself has decreed evil against you."
24 Thereupon Zedekiah, son of Chenaanah,
came up and slapped Micaiah on the cheek,
saying, "Has the spirit of the LORD, then, left me
to speak with you?" 25 "You shall find out,"
Micaiah replied, "on that day when you retreat
into an inside room to hide." 26 The king of Israel
then said, "Seize Micaiah and take him back to
Amon, prefect of the city, and to Joash, the king's
son, 27 and say, 'This is the king's order: Put this
man in prison and feed him scanty rations of
bread and water until I return in safety.' " 28 But
Micaiah said, "If ever you return in safety, the
LORD has not spoken through me."*
29 The king of Israel and King Jehoshaphat of
Judah went up to Ramoth-gilead, 30 and the king
of Israel said to Jehoshaphat, "I will disguise
myself and go into battle, but you put on your
own clothes." So the king of Israel disguised
himself and entered the fray. 31 In the meantime
the king of Aram had given his thirty-two chariot
commanders the order, "Do not fight with
anyone at all except the king of Israel." 32 When
the chariot commanders saw Jehoshaphat, they
cried out, "That must be the king of Israel!" and
shifted to fight him. But Jehoshaphat shouted his
battle cry, 33 and the chariot commanders, aware
that he was not the king of Israel, gave up
pursuit of him. 34 Someone, however, drew his
bow at random, and hit the king of Israel
between the joints of his breastplate. He ordered
his charioteer, "Rein about and take me out of
the ranks, for I am disabled." 35 The battle grew
fierce during the day, and the king, who was
propped up in his chariot facing the Arameans,
died in the evening. The blood from his wound
flowed to the bottom of the chariot.[b] 36 At sunset
a cry went through the army, "Every man to his
city, every man to his land, 37 for the king is
dead!" So they went to Samaria, where they
buried the king. 38 When the chariot was washed
at the pool of Samaria, the dogs licked up his
blood and harlots bathed there, as the LORD had
prophesied.[c]
39 The rest of the acts of Ahab, with all that he
did, including the ivory palace and all the cities
he built, are recorded in the book of the chroni-
cles of the kings of Israel. 40 Ahab rested with his
ancestors, and his son Ahaziah succeeded him as
king.

Reign of Jehoshaphat 41 Jehoshaphat, son of
Asa, began to reign over Judah in the fourth year
of Ahab, king of Israel. 42 Jehoshaphat was thirty-
five years old when he began to reign, and he
reigned twenty-five years in Jerusalem. His
mother's name was Azubah, daughter of Shilhi.
43 He followed all the ways of his father Asa
unswervingly, doing what was right in the
LORD's sight. 44 Nevertheless, the high places did
not disappear, and the people continued to
sacrifice and to burn incense on the high places.
45 Jehoshaphat also made peace with the king of
Israel. 46 The rest of the acts of Jehoshaphat, with
his prowess, what he did and how he fought, are

22, 19–23: The prophet Micaiah uses as a last resort to deter Ahab from his foolhardy design of fighting against Ramoth-gilead the literary device of describing false prophets as messengers of a lying spirit which God, after holding counsel with his angels, permits to deceive them.

22, 28: A note in the Hebrew text after this verse attributes to Micaiah ben Imlah the first words of the book of a different Micaiah, the minor prophet of Moreshet.

b 1 Kgs 20, 42. c 1 Kgs 21, 19.

recorded in the book of the chronicles of the
kings of Judah.
47He removed from the land the rest of the
cult prostitutes who had remained in the reign of
his father Asa. 48There was no king in Edom, but
an appointed regent. 49Jehoshaphat made Tar-
shish ships to go to Ophir for gold; but in fact the
ships did not go, because they were wrecked at
Ezion-geber. 50Then Ahaziah, son of Ahab, said
to Jehoshaphat, "Let my servants accompany
your servants in the ships." But Jehoshaphat
would not agree. 51Jehoshaphat rested with his
ancestors; he was buried in his forefathers' City
of David. His son Jehoram succeeded him as
king.
Reign of Ahaziah 52Ahaziah, son of Ahab,
began to reign over Israel in Samaria in the
seventeenth year* of Jehoshaphat, king of Judah;
he reigned two years over Israel. 53He did evil in
the sight of the LORD, behaving like his father,
his mother, and Jeroboam, son of Nebat, who
caused Israel to sin. 54He served and worshiped
Baal, thus provoking the LORD, the God of Israel,
just as his father had done.

22, 52: Seventeenth year: so the present Hebrew text. More consistent with 2 Kgs 1, 17 would be a date in the twenty-fourth year of Jehoshaphat for Ahab's death; see note on 2 Kgs 1, 1.

THE SECOND BOOK OF KINGS

I: The Kingdoms of Israel and Judah

CHAPTER 1

Ahaziah Consults Baalzebub 1After Ahab's
death, Moab rebelled against Israel.[a] 2Ahaziah
had fallen through the lattice of his roof terrace
at Samaria and had been injured. So he sent out
messengers with the instructions: "Go and in-
quire of Baalzebub,* the god of Ekron, whether I
shall recover from this injury."
3Meanwhile, the angel of the LORD said to
Elijah the Tishbite: "Go, intercept the messen-
gers of Samaria's king, and ask them, 'Is it
because there is no God in Israel that you are
going to inquire of Baalzebub, the god of Ekron?'
4For this, the LORD says: 'You shall not leave the
bed upon which you lie; instead, you shall
die.' " And with that, Elijah departed. 5The
messengers then returned to Ahaziah, who
asked them, "Why have you returned?" 6"A
man came up to us," they answered, "who said
to us, 'Go back to the king who sent you and tell
him: The LORD says, Is it because there is no
God in Israel that you are sending to inquire of
Baalzebub, the god of Ekron? For this you shall
not leave the bed upon which you lie; instead,
you shall die.' " 7The king asked them, "What
was the man like who came up to you and said
these things to you?" 8"Wearing a hairy gar-
ment,"* they replied, "with a leather girdle
about his loins." "It is Elijah the Tishbite!" he
exclaimed.[b]
Death of Two Captains 9Then the king sent a
captain with his company of fifty men after
Elijah. The prophet was seated on a hilltop when
he found him. "Man of God," he ordered, "the
king commands you to come down." 10"If I am a
man of God," Elijah answered the captain, "may
fire come down from heaven and consume you
and your fifty men." And fire came down from
heaven and consumed him and his fifty men.[c]
11Ahaziah sent another captain with his com-
pany of fifty men after Elijah. "Man of God," he
called out to Elijah, "the king commands you to
come down immediately." 12"If I am a man of

1, 2: Baalzebub: in this form, "Baal of flies." The name in the Hebrew text is a derisive alteration of Baalzebul, "Prince Baal." The best New Testament evidence supports the latter form in Mt 10, 25; Lk 11, 15. Later associations with Aramaic beeldebaba, "enemy," gave the ancient name its connotation of "devil."

1, 8: Hairy garment: a sign of ascetical and prophetic calling, imitated by John the Baptizer; see Mt 3, 4; Mk 1, 6.

a 2 Kgs 3, 4–27. b Zec 13, 4. c Lv 10, 2; Sir 48, 3f; Lk 9, 54f.

God," Elijah answered him, "may fire come
down from heaven and consume you and your
fifty men." And divine fire* came down from
heaven, consuming him and his fifty men.
Death of the King 13 Again, for the third time,
Ahaziah sent a captain with his company of fifty
men. When the third captain arrived, he fell to
his knees before Elijah, pleading with him. "Man
of God," he implored him, "let my life and the
lives of these fifty men, your servants, count for
something in your sight! 14 Already fire has come
down from heaven, consuming two captains
with their companies of fifty men. But now, let
my life mean something to you!" 15 Then the
angel of the LORD said to Elijah, "Go down with
him; you need not be afraid of him."

16 So Elijah left and went down with him and
stated to the king: "Thus says the LORD: 'Be-
cause you sent messengers to inquire of Baalze-
bub, the god of Ekron, you shall not leave the
bed upon which you lie; instead you shall die."[d]

17 Ahaziah died in fulfillment of the prophecy
of the LORD spoken by Elijah. Since he had no
son, his brother Joram* succeeded him as king,
in the second year of Jehoram, son of Jehosha-
phat, king of Judah. 18 The rest of the acts of
Ahaziah are recorded in the book of chronicles
of the kings of Israel.

CHAPTER 2

Elijah and Elisha 1 When the LORD was about
to take Elijah up to heaven in a whirlwind, he
and Elisha were on their way from Gilgal.*
2 "Stay here, please," Elijah said to Elisha. "The
LORD has sent me on to Bethel." "As the LORD
lives, and as you yourself live," Elisha replied, "I
will not leave you." So they went down to
Bethel, 3 where the guild prophets went out to
Elisha and asked him, "Do you know that the
LORD will take your master from over you
today?" "Yes, I know it," he replied. "Keep still."

4 Then Elijah said to him, "Stay here, please,
Elisha, for the LORD has sent me on to Jericho."
"As the LORD lives, and as you yourself live,"
Elisha replied, "I will not leave you." 5 They
went on to Jericho, where the guild prophets
approached Elisha and asked him, "Do you
know that the LORD will take your master from
over you today?" "Yes, I know it," he replied.
"Keep still."

6 Elijah said to Elisha, "Please stay here; the
LORD has sent me on to the Jordan." "As the
LORD lives, and as you yourself live," Elisha
replied, "I will not leave you." And so the two
went on together. 7 Fifty of the guild prophets
followed, and when the two stopped at the
Jordan, stood facing them at a distance. 8 Elijah
took his mantle, rolled it up and struck the
water, which divided, and both crossed over on
dry ground.[e]
Elisha Succeeds Elijah 9 When they had
crossed over, Elijah said to Elisha, "Ask for
whatever I may do for you, before I am taken
from you." Elisha answered, "May I receive a
double portion of your spirit."* 10 "You have
asked something that is not easy," he replied.
"Still, if you see me taken up from you, your
wish will be granted; otherwise not."[f] 11 As they
walked on conversing, a flaming chariot and
flaming horses came between them, and Elijah
went up to heaven in a whirlwind.[g] 12 When
Elisha saw it happen he cried out, "My father!*

1, 12: Divine fire: literally, "fire of God," which in Hebrew sounds quite like man of God. The play on words is the basis for Elijah's alleged retort. This story was told among the people to enhance the dignity of the prophet and to reflect the power of God whom he served. The mercy which God extends even to the wicked is described in Wis 11, 17—12, 22, and the prophet Elijah was well aware of it (1 Kgs 21, 28f).

1, 17: Joram: in the Second Book of Kings the name Joram (yoram), alternately Jehoram (yehoram), appears in numerous passages to designate both the king of Judah, son and successor of Jehoshaphat (848–841 B.C.), and the contemporary king of Israel, son of Ahab (852–841 B.C.). For the convenience of the reader in distinguishing these two kings, the longer form, Jehoram, is used to designate the king of Judah and the shorter form, Joram, to designate the king of Israel. See note on 2 Kgs 3, 1.

2, 1: Gilgal: commonly identified with Jiljulieh, about seven miles north of Bethel, and different from the Gilgal in Dt 11, 30 near Shechem, and that in Jos 4 and 5, passim, near Jericho.

2, 9: Double portion of your spirit: as the first-born son inherited a double portion of his father's property (Dt 21, 17), so Elisha asks to inherit from Elijah his spirit of prophecy in the degree befitting his principal disciple. In Nm 11, 17. 25, God bestows some of the spirit of Moses on others.

2, 12: My father: a religious title accorded prophetic leaders; cf 2 Kgs 6, 21; 8, 9. Israel's chariots and drivers: Elijah was worth more than a whole army in defending Israel and the true religion. King Joash of Israel uses the same phrase of Elisha himself (2 Kgs 13, 14).

d Sir 48, 6. e Ex 14, 16. 22. f Nm 11, 17. 25. g Gn 5, 24; 1 Mc 2, 58; Acts 1, 9.

my father! Israel's chariots and drivers!" But
when he could no longer see him, Elisha gripped
his own garment and tore it in two.[h]
13 Then he picked up Elijah's mantle which
had fallen from him, and went back and stood at
the bank of the Jordan.[i] 14 Wielding the mantle
which had fallen from Elijah, he struck the water
in his turn and said, "Where is the LORD, the
God of Elijah?" When Elisha struck the water it
divided and he crossed over.
15 The guild prophets in Jericho, who were on
the other side, saw him and said, "The spirit of
Elijah rests on Elisha." They went to meet him,
bowing to the ground before him. 16 "Among
your servants are fifty brave men," they said.
"Let them go in search of your master. Perhaps
the spirit of the LORD has carried him away to
some mountain or some valley." "Do not send
them," he answered.[j] 17 However, they kept
urging him, until he was embarrassed and said,
"Send them." So they sent the fifty men, who
searched for three days without finding him.
18 When they returned to Elisha in Jericho,
where he was staying, he said to them, "Did I
not tell you not to go?"
Healing of the Water 19 Once the inhabitants
of the city complained to Elisha, "The site of
the city is fine indeed, as my lord can see, but
the water is bad and the land unfruitful."
20 "Bring me a new bowl," Elisha said, "and put
salt into it." When they had brought it to him,
21 he went out to the spring and threw salt into
it, saying, "Thus says the LORD, 'I have purified
this water. Never again shall death or miscar-
riage spring from it.' " 22 And the water has
stayed pure even to this day, just as Elisha
prophesied.
The Prophet's Curse 23 *From there Elisha
went up to Bethel. While he was on the way,
some small boys came out of the city and jeered
at him. "Go up, baldhead," they shouted, "go
up, baldhead!" 24 The prophet turned and saw
them, and he cursed them in the name of the
LORD. Then two she-bears came out of the
woods and tore forty-two of the children to
pieces.
25 From there he went to Mount Carmel, and
thence he returned to Samaria.

CHAPTER 3

Campaign of Joram against Moab 1 Joram,
son of Ahab, became king of Israel in Samaria [in
the eighteenth year of Jehoshaphat, king of
Judah, and he reigned for twelve years].* 2 He
did evil in the LORD's sight, though not as much
as his father and mother. He did away with the
pillar of Baal, which his father had made, 3 but he
still clung to the sin to which Jeroboam, son of
Nebat, had lured Israel; this he did not give up.
4 Now Mesha, king of Moab, who raised
sheep, used to pay the king of Israel as tribute a
hundred thousand lambs and the wool of a
hundred thousand rams. 5 But when Ahab died,
the king of Moab had rebelled against the king of
Israel. 6 Joram as king mustered all Israel, and
when he set out on a campaign from Samaria,
7 he sent the king of Judah the message: "The
king of Moab is in rebellion against me. Will you
join me in battle against Moab?" "I will," he
replied. "You and I shall be as one, your people

2, 23f: This story, like the one about Elijah and the captains (ch 1), is preserved for us in Scripture to convey a popular understanding of the dignity of the prophet. Told in popular vein, it becomes a caricature, in which neither Elisha nor the bears behave in character. See note on 2 Kgs 1, 12 and the contrasting narrative in ch 4.

3, 1: The sequence of the reigns between Ahab and Jehu of Israel may be reconstructed as follows: Jehoshaphat of Judah outlived Ahab by a short time, so that Ahaziah of Israel was his contemporary. Jehoram of Judah succeeded his father Jehoshaphat while Ahaziah of Israel was still alive. Jehoram (Joram) of Israel became king, following his brother Ahaziah, in the second year of Jehoram of Judah (2 Kgs 1, 17); this is one datum on which the earliest Greek evidence and the standard Hebrew text are in agreement.

The two Jehorams were contemporary for much of their reigns; Jehoram of Judah was succeeded by Ahaziah something more than a year before Jehu did away with the rulers of both kingdoms (2 Kgs 9, 1–29).

The Moabite campaign of 2 Kgs 3, 4–27 is thus best placed under the two Kings Jehoram, before the Edomite rebellion mentioned in 2 Kgs 8, 20. In the received Hebrew text, Jehoshaphat has been made the Judahite protagonist in the campaign against Moab as a tribute to his piety; this assimilates the story of 2 Kgs 3 to that of 1 Kgs 22, but creates difficulties in the chronology which the extant data leave party unresolved. An older practice for stories of the Israelite kings was to leave them and their fellow kings without identification by name; cf 2 Kgs 6, 8—7, 20. The name of Jehoshaphat has been omitted from a number of places in 2 Kgs 3—8, in this translation; cf 1 Kgs 22, 51.

h 2 Kgs 13, 14; Sir 48, 9. 12. i 1 Kgs 19, 19. j 1 Kgs 18, 12.

and mine, and your horses and mine as well."[k] 8They discussed the route for their attack, and settled upon the route through the desert of Edom.

9So the king of Israel set out, accompanied by the king of Judah and the king of Edom. After their roundabout journey of seven days the water gave out for the army and for the animals with them. 10"Alas!" exclaimed the king of Israel. "The LORD has called together these three kings to put them in the grasp of Moab." 11But the king of Judah asked, "Is there no prophet of the LORD here through whom we may inquire of the LORD?" One of the officers of the king of Israel replied, "Elisha, son of Shaphat, who poured water on the hands of Elijah, is here."[l] 12"He has the word of the LORD," the king of Judah agreed. So the kings of Israel, Judah, and Edom went down to Elisha. 13"What do you want with me?" Elisha asked the king of Israel. "Go to the prophets of your father and to the prophets of your mother." "No," the king of Israel replied. "The LORD has called these three kings together to put them in the grasp of Moab." 14Then Elisha said, "As the LORD of hosts lives, whom I serve, were it not that I respect the king of Judah, I should neither look at you nor notice you at all.[m] 15Now get me a minstrel."

When the minstrel played, the power of the LORD came upon Elisha 16and he announced: "Thus says the LORD, 'Provide many catch basins in this wadi.' 17For the LORD says, 'Though you will see neither wind nor rain, yet this wadi will be filled with water for you, your livestock, and your pack animals to drink.' 18And since the LORD does not consider this enough, he will also deliver Moab into your grasp. 19You shall destroy every fortified city, fell every fruit tree, stop up all the springs, and ruin every fertile field with stones."[n]

20In the morning, at the time of the sacrifice, water came from the direction of Edom and filled the land.[o] 21Meanwhile, all Moab heard that the kings had come to give them battle; every man capable of bearing arms was called up and stationed at the border. 22Early that morning, when the sun shone on the water, the Moabites saw the water at a distance as red as blood.* 23"This is blood!" they exclaimed. "The kings have fought among themselves and killed one another. Quick! To the spoils, Moabites!" 24But when they reached the camp of Israel, the Israelites rose up and attacked the Moabites, who fled from them. They ranged through the countryside striking down the Moabites, and 25destroying the cities; each of them cast stones onto every fertile field till they had loaded it down; all the springs they stopped up and every useful tree they felled. Finally only Kir-hareseth* was left behind its stone walls, and the slingers had surrounded it and were attacking it.[p] 26When he saw that he was losing the battle, the king of Moab took seven hundred swordsmen to break through to the king of Aram, but he failed. 27So he took his first-born, his heir apparent, and offered him as a holocaust upon the wall. The wrath against Israel* was so great that they gave up the siege and returned to their own land.[q]

CHAPTER 4

The Widow's Oil 1[r]A certain woman, the widow of one of the guild prophets, complained to Elisha: "My husband, your servant, is dead. You know that he was a God-fearing man, yet now his creditor has come to take my two children as his slaves."* 2"How can I help you?" Elisha answered her. "Tell me what you have in the house." "This servant of yours has nothing in the house but a jug of oil," she replied. 3"Go out," he said, "borrow vessels from all your neighbors—as many empty vessels as you can. 4Then come back and close the door on yourself and your children; pour the oil into all the

3, 22: Red as blood: possibly caused by the red sandstone of the Wadi Zered (Dt 2, 13), south of Moab.

3, 25: Kir-hareseth: modern Kerak, east of the Dead Sea; cf Is 16, 7. 11; Jer 48, 31. 36.

3, 27: The wrath against Israel: probably the wrath of Chemosh, the Moabite god to whom the child was offered. He was feared by the Israelites who lost heart on foreign soil.

4, 1: His creditor . . . slaves: Hebrew law permitted the selling of wife and children as chattels for debt; cf Ex 21, 7; Am 2, 6; 8, 6; Is 50.

k 1 Kgs 22, 4. l 1 Kgs 22, 7. m 1 Kgs 18, 15. n Dt 20, 19. o 1 Kgs 18, 29. p Jb 5, 23. q Jgs 11, 30f. r 1 Kgs 17, 8–16.

vessels, and as each is filled, set it aside." 5She went and did so, closing the door on herself and her children. As they handed her the vessels, she would pour in oil. 6When all the vessels were filled, she said to her son, "Bring me another vessel." "There is none left," he answered her. And then the oil stopped. 7She went and told the man of God, who said, "Go and sell the oil to pay off your creditor; with what remains, you and your children can live."

Elisha and the Shunammite 8One day Elisha came to Shunem, where there was a woman of influence, who urged him to dine with her. Afterward, whenever he passed by, he used to stop there to dine. 9So she said to her husband, "I know that he is a holy man of God. Since he visits us often, 10let us arrange a little room on the roof and furnish it for him with a bed, table, chair, and lamp, so that when he comes to us he can stay there." 11Some time later Elisha arrived and stayed in the room overnight. 12Then he said to his servant Gehazi, "Call this Shunammite woman." He did so, and when she stood before Elisha, 13he told Gehazi, "Say to her, 'You have lavished all this care on us; what can we do for you? Can we say a good word for you to the king or to the commander of the army?' " She replied, "I am living among my own people." 14Later Elisha asked, "Can something be done for her?" "Yes!" Gehazi answered. "She has no son, and her husband is getting on in years." 15"Call her," said Elisha. When she had been called, and stood at the door, 16Elisha promised, "This time next year you will be fondling a baby son." "Please, my lord," she protested, "you are a man of God; do not deceive your servant."[s] 17Yet the woman conceived, and by the same time the following year she had given birth to a son, as Elisha promised.

18The day came when the child was old enough to go out to his father among the reapers.[t] 19"My head hurts!" he complained to his father. "Carry him to his mother," the father said to a servant. 20The servant picked him up and carried him to his mother; he stayed with her until noon, when he died in her lap. 21The mother took him upstairs and laid him on the bed of the man of God. Closing the door on him, she went out 22and called to her husband, "Let me have a servant and a donkey. I must go quickly to the man of God, and I will be back." 23"Why are you going to him today?" he asked. "It is neither the new moon nor the sabbath." But she bade him good-bye, 24and when the donkey was saddled, said to her servant: "Lead on! Do not stop my donkey unless I tell you to." 25She kept going till she reached the man of God on Mount Carmel. When he spied her at a distance, the man of God said to his servant Gehazi: "There is the Shunammite! 26Hurry to meet her, and ask if all is well with her, with her husband, and with the boy." "Greetings,"* she replied. 27But when she reached the man of God on the mountain, she clasped his feet. Gehazi came near to push her away, but the man of God said: "Let her alone, she is in bitter anguish; the LORD hid it from me and did not let me know." 28"Did I ask my lord for a son?" she cried out. "Did I not beg you not to deceive me?" 29"Gird your loins," Elisha said to Gehazi, "take my staff with you and be off; if you meet anyone, do not greet him,* and if anyone greets you, do not answer. Lay my staff upon the boy." 30But the boy's mother cried out: "As the LORD lives and as you yourself live, I will not release you." So he started to go back with her.

31 [u]Meanwhile, Gehazi had gone on ahead and had laid the staff upon the boy, but there was no sound or sign of life. He returned to meet Elisha and informed him that the boy had not awakened. 32When Elisha reached the house, he found the boy lying dead. 33He went in, closed the door on them both, and prayed to the LORD.[v] 34Then he lay upon the child on the bed, placing his mouth upon the child's mouth, his eyes upon the eyes, and his hands upon the

4, 26: Greetings: the conventional answer to Gehazi's question, which tells him nothing.

4, 29: Do not greet him: the profuse exchange of compliments among Orientals meeting and greeting one another consumed time. Urgency necessitated their omission, as our Lord counseled his disciples (Lk 10, 4).

s Gn 18, 10. t 1 Kgs 17, 17–24. u 31–36; Acts 20, 10ff. v 1 Kgs 17, 21–23.

hands. As Elisha stretched himself over the
child, the body became warm. 35He arose, paced
up and down the room, and then once more lay
down upon the boy, who now sneezed seven
times and opened his eyes.[w] 36Elisha summoned
Gehazi and said, "Call the Shunammite." She
came at his call, and Elisha said to her, "Take
your son." 37She came in and fell at his feet in
gratitude; then she took her son and left the
room.
The Poisoned Stew 38When Elisha returned
to Gilgal, there was a famine in the land. Once,
when the guild prophets were seated before
him, he said to his servant, "Put the large pot on,
and make some vegetable stew for the guild
prophets." 39Someone went out into the field to
gather herbs and found a wild vine, from which
he picked a clothful of wild gourds. On his
return he cut them up into the pot of vegetable
stew without anybody's knowing it. 40The stew
was poured out for the men to eat, but when
they began to eat it, they exclaimed, "Man of
God, there is poison in the pot!" And they could
not eat it. 41"Bring some meal," Elisha said. He
threw it into the pot and said, "Serve it to the
people to eat." And there was no longer any-
thing harmful in the pot.
Multiplication of Loaves 42A man came from
Baal-shalishah bringing the man of God twenty
barley loaves made from the first-fruits, and fresh
grain in the ear. "Give it to the people to eat,"
Elisha said. 43But his servant objected, "How can
I set this before a hundred men?" "Give it to the
people to eat," Elisha insisted. "For thus says the
LORD, 'They shall eat and there shall be some left
over.' " 44And when they had eaten, there was
some left over, as the LORD had said.

CHAPTER 5

Cure of Naaman 1Naaman, the army com-
mander of the king of Aram, was highly es-
teemed and respected by his master, for through
him the LORD had brought victory to Aram. But
valiant as he was, the man was a leper. 2Now the
Arameans had captured from the land of Israel in
a raid a little girl, who became the servant of
Naaman's wife. 3"If only my master would
present himself to the prophet in Samaria," she
said to her mistress, "he would cure him of his
leprosy." 4Naaman went and told his lord just
what the slave girl from the land of Israel had
said. 5"Go," said the king of Aram. "I will send
along a letter to the king of Israel." So Naaman
set out, taking along ten silver talents, six
thousand gold pieces, and ten festal garments.
6To the king of Israel he brought the letter,
which read: "With this letter I am sending my
servant Naaman to you, that you may cure him
of his leprosy."

7When he read the letter, the king of Israel
tore his garments and exclaimed: "Am I a god
with power over life and death, that this man
should send someone to me to be cured of
leprosy? Take note! You can see he is only
looking for a quarrel with me!"[x] 8When Elisha,
the man of God, heard that the king of Israel had
torn his garments, he sent word to the king:
"Why have you torn your garments? Let him
come to me and find out that there is a prophet
in Israel."

9Naaman came with his horses and chariots
and stopped at the door of Elisha's house. 10The
prophet sent him the message: "Go and wash
seven times in the Jordan, and your flesh will
heal, and you will be clean."[y] 11But Naaman
went away angry, saying, "I thought that he
would surely come out and stand there to invoke
the LORD his God, and would move his hand
over the spot, and thus cure the leprosy. 12Are
not the rivers of Damascus, the Abana and the
Pharpar, better than all the waters of Israel?
Could I not wash in them and be cleansed?"*
With this, he turned about in anger and left.

13But his servants came up and reasoned with
him. "My father," they said, "if the prophet had
told you to do something extraordinary, would
you not have done it? All the more now, since he
said to you, 'Wash and be clean,' should you do

5, 12: Wash in them and be cleansed: typical of the ambiguity in ritual healing or cleanliness. The muddy waters of the Jordan are no match hygienically for the mountain spring waters of Damascus; ritually, it is the other way around.

w Heb 11, 35. x Gn 30, 2; 1 Sm 2, 6; Jn 5, 21. y Jn 9, 7.

as he said." [14]So Naaman went down and plunged into the Jordan seven times at the word of the man of God. His flesh became again like the flesh of a little child, and he was clean.[z]

[15]He returned with his whole retinue to the man of God. On his arrival he stood before him and said, "Now I know that there is no God in all the earth, except in Israel. Please accept a gift from your servant."

[16]"As the LORD lives whom I serve, I will not take it," Elisha replied; and despite Naaman's urging, he still refused. [17]Naaman said: "If you will not accept, please let me, your servant, have two mule-loads of earth,* for I will no longer offer holocaust or sacrifice to any other god except to the LORD. [18]But I trust the LORD will forgive your servant this: when my master enters the temple of Rimmon to worship there, then I, too, as his adjutant, must bow down in the temple of Rimmon. May the LORD forgive your servant this." [19]"Go in peace,"* Elisha said to him.

[20]Naaman had gone some distance when Gehazi, the servant of Elisha, the man of God, thought to himself: "My master was too easy with this Aramean Naaman, not accepting what he brought. As the LORD lives, I will run after him and get something out of him." [21]So Gehazi hurried after Naaman. Aware that someone was running after him, Naaman alighted from his chariot to wait for him. "Is everything all right?" he asked. [22]"Yes," Gehazi replied, "but my master sent me to say, 'Two young men have just come to me, guild prophets from the hill country of Ephraim. Please give them a talent of silver and two festal garments.' " [23]"Please take two talents," Naaman said, and pressed them upon him. He tied up these silver talents in bags and gave them, with the two festal garments, to two of his servants, who carried them before Gehazi. [24]When they reached the hill, Gehazi took what they had, carried it into the house, and sent the men on their way.

[25]He went in and stood before Elisha his master, who asked him, "Where have you been, Gehazi?" He answered, "Your servant has not gone anywhere." [26]But Elisha said to him: "Was I not present in spirit when the man alighted from his chariot to wait for you? Is this a time to take money or to take garments, olive orchards or vineyards, sheep or cattle, male or female servants? [27]The leprosy of Naaman shall cling to you and your descendants forever." And Gehazi left Elisha, a leper white as snow.[a]

CHAPTER 6

Recovery of the Lost Ax [1]The guild prophets once said to Elisha: "There is not enough room for us to continue to live here with you. [2]Let us go to the Jordan, where by getting one beam apiece we can build ourselves a place to live." "Go," Elisha said. [3]"Please agree to accompany your servants," one of them requested. "Yes, I will come," he replied.

[4]So he went with them, and when they arrived at the Jordan they began to fell trees. [5]While one of them was felling a tree trunk, the iron axhead slipped into the water. "O master," he cried out, "it was borrowed!" [6]"Where did it fall?" asked the man of God. When he pointed out the spot, Elisha cut off a stick, threw it into the water, and brought the iron to the surface. [7]"Pick it up," he said. And the man reached down and grasped it.

Aramean Ambush [8]When the king of Aram was waging war on Israel, he would make plans with his servants to attack a particular place. [9]But the man of God would send word to the king of Israel, "Be careful! Do not pass by this place, for Aram will attack there." [10]So the king of Israel would send word to the place which the man of God had indicated, and alert it; then they would be on guard. This happened several times.

[11]Greatly disturbed over this, the king of Aram called together his officers. "Will you not tell me," he asked them, "who among us is for the king of Israel?" [12]"No one, my lord king," answered one of the officers. "The Israelite

5, 17: Two mule-loads of earth: Israelite earth on which to erect in Aram an altar to the God of Israel.

5, 19: Go in peace: Elisha understands and approves the situation of Naaman who, though a proselyte as regards belief in and worship of the God of Israel, is required by his office to assist his master, the king, worshiping in the pagan temple of Rimmon.

z Lk 4, 27. a Ex 4, 6; Nm 12, 10.

prophet Elisha can tell the king of Israel the very words you speak in your bedroom.” 13“Go, find out where he is,” he said, “so that I may take him captive.”

Blinded Aramean Soldiers Informed that Elisha was in Dothan, 14he sent there a strong force with horses and chariots. They arrived by night and surrounded the city. 15Early the next morning, when the attendant of the man of God arose and went out, he saw the force with its horses and chariots surrounding the city. “Alas!” he said to Elisha. “What shall we do, my lord?” 16“Do not be afraid,” Elisha answered. “Our side outnumbers theirs.” 17Then he prayed, “O LORD, open his eyes, that he may see.” And the LORD opened the eyes of the servant, so that he saw the mountainside filled with horses and fiery chariots around Elisha.[b]

18When the Arameans came down to get him, Elisha prayed to the LORD, “Strike this people blind, I pray you.” And in answer to the prophet’s prayer the LORD struck them blind. 19Then Elisha said to them: “This is the wrong road, and this is the wrong city. Follow me! I will take you to the man you want.” And he led them to Samaria. 20When they entered Samaria, Elisha prayed, “O LORD, open their eyes that they may see.” The LORD opened their eyes, and they saw that they were inside Samaria. 21When the king of Israel saw them, he asked, “Shall I kill them, my father?” 22“You must not kill them,” replied Elisha. “Do you slay those whom you have taken captive with your sword or bow?* Serve them bread and water. Let them eat and drink, and then go back to their master.” 23The king spread a great feast for them. When they had eaten and drunk he sent them away, and they went back to their master. No more Aramean raiders came into the land of Israel.

Siege of Samaria 24After this, Ben-hadad, king of Aram, mustered his whole army and laid seige to Samaria. 25Because of the seige the famine in Samaria was so severe that an ass’s head sold for eighty pieces of silver, and a fourth of a kab of wild onion for five pieces of silver.

26One day, as the king of Israel was walking on the city wall, a woman cried out to him, “Help, my lord king!” 27“No,” he replied, “the LORD help you! Where could I find help for you: from the threshing floor or the winepress?” 28Then the king asked her, “What is your trouble?” She replied: “This woman said to me, ‘Give up your son that we may eat him today; then tomorrow we will eat my son.’[c] 29So we boiled my son and ate him. The next day I said to her, ‘Now give up your son that we may eat him.’ But she hid her son.” 30When the king heard the woman’s words, he tore his garments. And as he was walking on the wall, the people saw that he was wearing sackcloth underneath, next to his skin.[d]

31“May God do thus and so to me,” the king exclaimed, “if the head of Elisha, son of Shaphat, stays on him today!” 32Meanwhile, Elisha was sitting in his house in conference with the elders. The king had sent a man ahead before he himself should come to him. Elisha had said to the elders: “Do you know that this son of a murderer is sending someone to cut off my head? When the messenger comes, see that you close the door and hold it fast against him. His master’s footsteps are echoing behind him.” 33While Elisha was still speaking, the king came down to him and said, “This evil is from the LORD. Why should I trust in the LORD any longer?”

CHAPTER 7

1Elisha said: “Hear the word of the LORD! Thus says the LORD, ‘At this time tomorrow a seah of fine flour will sell for a shekel, and two seahs of barley for a shekel, in the market* of Samaria.’ ” 2But the adjutant on whose arm the king leaned, answered the man of God, “Even if the LORD were to make windows in heaven, how could this happen?” “You shall see it with

6, 22: With your sword or bow: since the king would not slay prisoners who had surrendered to his power, much less should he slay prisoners captured by God’s power. By Oriental custom they became guests within Samaria’s walls.

7, 1: Market: literally “gate,” the principal place of trading in ancient walled cities in time of peace.

b 2 Kgs 7, 6; Ps 67, 18. c Dt 28, 53–57. d 1 Kgs 20, 31; 21, 27.

your own eyes," Elisha said, "but you shall not eat of it." [e]

The Lepers at the Gate [3]At the city gate were four lepers who were deliberating, "Why should we sit here until we die?[f] [4]If we decide to go into the city, we shall die there, for there is famine in the city. If we remain here, we shall die too. Come, let us desert to the camp of the Arameans. If they spare us, we live; if they kill us, we die." [5]At twilight they left for the Arameans; but when they reached the edge of the camp, no one was there. [6][g]The LORD had caused the army of the Arameans to hear the sound of chariots and horses, the din of a large army, and they had reasoned among themselves, "The king of Israel has hired the kings of the Hittites and the kings of the borderlands* to fight us." [7]Then in the twilight they fled, abandoning their tents, their horses, and their asses, the whole camp just as it was, and fleeing for their lives.

[8]After the lepers reached the edge of the camp, they went first into one tent, ate and drank, and took silver, gold, and clothing from it, and went out and hid them. Back they came into another tent, took things from it, and again went out and hid them. [9]Then they said to one another: "We are not doing right. This is a day of good news, and we are keeping silent. If we wait until morning breaks, we shall be blamed. Come, let us go and inform the palace."

[10]They came and summoned the city gatekeepers. "We went to the camp of the Arameans," they said, "but no one was there—not a human voice, only the horses and asses tethered, and the tents just as they were left." [11]The gatekeepers announced this and it was reported within the palace. [12]Though it was night, the king got up; he said to his servants: "Let me tell you what the Arameans have done to us. Knowing that we are in famine, they have left their camp to hide in the field, hoping to take us alive and enter our city when we leave it." [13]One of his servants, however, suggested: "Since those who are left in the city are no better off than all the throng that has perished, let some of us take five of the abandoned horses and send scouts to investigate."

End of the Siege [14]They took two chariots, and horses, and the king sent them to reconnoiter the Aramean army. "Go and find out," he ordered. [15]They followed the Arameans as far as the Jordan, and the whole route was strewn with garments and other objects that the Arameans had thrown away in their haste. The messengers returned and told the king.

[16]The people went out and plundered the camp of the Arameans; and then a seah of fine flour sold for a shekel and two seahs of barley for a shekel, as the LORD had said.

[17]The king put in charge of the gate the officer who was his adjutant; but the people trampled him to death at the gate, just as the man of God had predicted when the king visited him. [18]Thus was fulfilled the prophecy of the man of God to the king, "Two seahs of barley will sell for a shekel, and one seah of fine flour for a shekel at this time tomorrow at the gate of Samaria." [19]The adjutant had answered the man of God, "Even if the LORD were to make windows in heaven, how could this happen?" And Elisha had replied, "You shall see it with your own eyes, but you shall not eat of it." [20]And that is what happened to him, for the people trampled him to death at the gate.

CHAPTER 8

Prediction of Famine [1]Elisha once said to the woman whose son he had restored to life: "Get ready! Leave with your family and settle wherever you can, because the LORD has decreed a seven-year famine which is coming upon the land." [h] [2]The woman got ready and did as the man of God said, setting out with her family and settling in the land of the Philistines for seven years. [3]At the end of the seven years, the woman returned from the land of the Philistines and went out to the king to claim her house and her field. [4]The king was talking with Gehazi, the servant of the man of God. "Tell me," he said,

7, 6: Kings of the borderlands: from Musur in Anatolia rather than Egypt.

e 2 Kgs 7, 17; Ps 78, 23; Is 24, 18. f Lv 13, 46. g 6f: 2 Kgs 6, 17; 19, 35f; 2 Sm 5. 24. h 2 Kgs 4, 36.

"all the great things that Elisha has done." [5]Just as he was relating to the king how his master had restored a dead person to life, the very woman whose son Elisha had restored to life came to the king to claim her house and field. "My lord king," Gehazi said, "this is the woman, and this is that son of hers whom Elisha restored to life." [6]The king questioned the woman, and she told him her story. With that the king placed an official* at her disposal, saying, "Restore all her property to her, with all that the field produced from the day she left the land until now."

Death of Ben-hadad Foretold [7]Elisha came to Damascus at a time when Ben-hadad, king of Aram, lay sick. When he was told that the man of God had come there, [8]the king said to Hazael, "Take a gift with you and go call on the man of God. Have him consult the LORD as to whether I shall recover from this sickness." [9]Hazael went to visit him, carrying a present, and with forty camel loads of the best goods of Damascus. On his arrival, he stood before the prophet and said, "Your son Ben-hadad, king of Aram, has sent me to ask you whether he will recover from his sickness." [10]"Go and tell him," Elisha answered, "that he will surely recover. However, the LORD has showed me that he will in fact die." [11]Then he stared him down until Hazael became ill at ease. The man of God wept, [12]and Hazael asked, "Why are you weeping, my lord?" Elisha replied, "Because I know the evil that you will inflict upon the Israelites. You will burn their fortresses, you will slay their youth with the sword, you will dash their little children to pieces, you will rip open their pregnant women." [i]

[13]Hazael exclaimed, "How can a dog like me, your servant,* do anything so important?" "The LORD has showed you to me as king over Aram," replied Elisha. [j]

[14]Hazael left Elisha and returned to his master. "What did Elisha tell you?" asked Ben-hadad. "He told me that you would surely recover," replied Hazael. [15]The next day, however, Hazael took a cloth, dipped it in water, and spread it over the king's face, so that he died. And Hazael reigned in his stead.

Reign of Jehoram of Judah [16]In the fifth year of Joram, son of Ahab, king of Israel, Jehoram,* son of Jehoshaphat, king of Judah, became king. [17] [k]He was thirty-two years old when he began to reign, and he reigned eight years in Jerusalem. [18]He conducted himself like the kings of Israel of the line of Ahab, since the sister of Ahab was his wife; and he did evil in the LORD's sight. [19]Even so, the LORD was unwilling to destroy Judah, because of his servant David. For he had promised David that he would leave him a lamp in the LORD's presence for all time. [l] [20]During Jehoram's reign, Edom revolted against the sovereignty of Judah and chose a king of its own. [21]Thereupon Jehoram with all his chariots crossed over to Zair. He arose by night and broke through the Edomites when they had surrounded him and the commanders of his chariots. Then his army fled homeward. [22]To this day Edom has been in revolt against the rule of Judah. Libnah also revolted at that time. [m] [23]The rest of the acts of Jehoram, with all that he did, are recorded in the book of the chronicles of the kings of Judah. [24]Jehoram rested with his ancestors and was buried with them in the City of David. His son Ahaziah succeeded him as king.

Accession of Ahaziah [25]Ahaziah, son of Jehoram, king of Judah, became king in the twelfth year of Joram,* son of Ahab, king of Israel. [26]He was twenty-two years old when he began his reign, and he reigned one year in Jerusalem. His mother's name was Athaliah; she was the daughter of Omri, king of Israel. [27]He conducted himself like the house of Ahab, doing evil in the LORD's sight as they did, since he was related to

8, 6: An official: Literally "eunuch," and perhaps actually so in this instance.

8, 13: A dog . . . your servant: Hazael feigns humility (1 Sm 24, 14; 2 Sm 9, 8), without attending to the crimes he would commit after usurping the royal power as the prophet predicts. Anything so important: literally "a great deed" for a patriotic Syrian.

8, 16: Jehoram of Judah succeeded his father Jehoshaphat during the reign of Ahaziah of Israel. See note on 2 Kgs 3, 1.

8, 25: Twelfth year of Joram: i.e., of Israel, who probably reigned only eight years.

i 2 Kgs 13, 7. j 2 Kgs 15, 16; 1 Kgs 19, 15. k 17ff: 2 Chr 21, 5ff. l 2 Sm 7, 11–16; 21, 17; 1 Kgs 11, 36; 15, 4; 2 Chr 21, 7. m Gn 27, 40; 2 Chr 21, 8ff.

them by marriage. 28He joined Joram, son of
Ahab, in battle against Hazael, king of Aram, at
Ramoth-gilead, where the Arameans wounded
Joram.[n] 29King Joram returned to Jezreel to be
healed of the wounds which the Arameans had
inflicted on him at Ramah in his battle against
Hazael, king of Aram. Then Ahaziah, son of
Jehoram, king of Judah, went down to Jezreel to
visit him there in his illness.

CHAPTER 9

Anointing of Jehu 1The prophet Elisha called
one of the guild prophets and said to him: "Gird
your loins, take this flask of oil with you, and go
to Ramoth-gilead.[o] 2When you get there, look
for Jehu, son of Jehoshaphat, son of Nimshi.
Enter and take him away from his companions
into an inner chamber.[p] 3From the flask you
have, pour oil on his head, and say, 'Thus says
the LORD: I anoint you king over Israel.' Then
open the door and flee without delay."[q] 4The
young man (the guild prophet) went to Ramoth-
gilead. 5When he arrived, the commanders of
the army were in session. "I have a message for
you, commander," he said. "For which one of
us?" asked Jehu. "For you, commander," he
answered. 6Jehu got up and went into the house.
Then the young man poured the oil on his head
and said, "Thus says the LORD, the God of Israel:
'I anoint you king over the people of the LORD,
over Israel. 7*You shall destroy the house of
Ahab your master; thus will I avenge the blood
of my servants the prophets, and the blood of all
the other servants of the LORD shed by Jezebel,
8[r]and by all the rest of the family of Ahab. I will
cut off every male in Ahab's line, whether slave
or freeman in Israel. 9I will deal with the house
of Ahab as I dealt with the house of Jeroboam,
son of Nebat, and with the house of Baasha, son
of Ahijah. 10Dogs shall devour Jezebel at the
confines of Jezreel, so that no one can bury
her.' " Then he opened the door and fled.
11When Jehu rejoined his master's servants,
they asked him, "Is all well? Why did that
madman come to you?" "You know that kind of
man and his talk," he replied. 12But they said,
"Not at all! Come, tell us." So he told them what
the young man had said to him, and finally,
"Thus says the LORD: 'I anoint you king over
Israel.' " 13At once each took his garment,
spread it under Jehu on the bare steps, blew the
trumpet, and cried out, "Jehu is king!"[s]
14[t]Thus Jehu, son of Jehoshaphat, son of
Nimshi, formed a conspiracy against Joram.
Joram, with all Israel, had been besieging
Ramoth-gilead against Hazael, king of Aram,
15but had returned to Jezreel to be healed of the
wounds the Arameans had inflicted on him in
the battle against Hazael, king of Aram.

Murder of Joram "If you are truly with me,"
Jehu said, "see that no one escapes from the city to
report in Jezreel." 16Then Jehu mounted his char-
iot and drove to Jezreel, where Joram lay ill and
Ahaziah, king of Judah, had come to visit him.
17The watchman standing on the tower in
Jezreel saw the troop of Jehu coming and re-
ported, "I see chariots." "Get a driver," Joram
said, "and send him to meet them and to ask
whether all is well." 18So a driver went out to
meet him and said, "The king asks whether all is
well." "What does it matter to you how things
are?" Jehu said. "Get behind me." The watch-
man reported to the king, "The messenger has
reached them, but is not returning."
19Joram sent a second driver, who went to
them and said, "The king asks whether all is
well." "What does it matter to you how things
are?" Jehu replied. "Get behind me."
20The watchman reported, "The messenger
has reached them, but is not returning. The
driving is like that of Jehu, son of Nimshi, in its
fury." 21"Prepare my chariot," said Joram.
When they had done so, Joram, king of Israel,
and Ahaziah, king of Judah, set out, each in his
own chariot, to meet Jehu. They reached him
near the field of Naboth the Jezreelite. 22When

9, 7–10: The editors of the Books of Kings have here added to the prophet's message the same type of indictment and sanctions against the family of Ahab as were invoked against the dynasties of Jeroboam (1 Kgs 14, 10f), Baasha (1 Kgs 16, 3f), and Ahab on a previous occasion (1 Kgs 21, 21–24).

n 2 Kgs 9, 14f. o 1 Kgs 21, 29; Hos 1, 4. p 1 Kgs 19, 16; q 1 Kgs 19, 16. r 8ff: 1 Kgs 14, 10f; 16, 3f: 21, 21–24. s Mt 21, 8. t 14f: 2 Kgs 8, 28f; 1 Kgs 22, 3f.

Joram recognized Jehu, he asked, "Is all well, Jehu?" "How can all be well," Jehu replied, "as long as the many fornications and witchcrafts* of your mother Jezebel continue?" 23Joram reined about and fled, crying to Ahaziah, "Treason, Ahaziah!" 24But Jehu drew his bow and shot Joram between the shoulders, so that the arrow went through his heart and he collapsed in his chariot. 25 [u]Then Jehu said to his adjutant Bidkar, "Take him and throw him into the field of Naboth the Jezreelite. For I remember that when we were driving teams behind his father Ahab, the LORD delivered this oracle against him: 26'As surely as I saw yesterday the blood of Naboth and the blood of his sons,' says the LORD, 'I will repay you for it in that very plot of ground, says the LORD.' So now take him into this plot of ground, in keeping with the word of the LORD."

Death of Ahaziah 27 [v]Seeing what was happening, Ahaziah, king of Judah, fled toward Beth-haggan. Jehu pursued him, shouting, "Kill him too!" And they pierced him as he rode through the pass of Gur near Ibleam. He continued his flight as far as Megiddo and died there. 28His servants brought him in a chariot to Jerusalem and buried him in the tomb of his ancestors in the City of David. 29Ahaziah had become king of Judah in the eleventh year of Joram, son of Ahab.

Death of Jezebel 30When Jezebel learned that Jehu had arrived in Jezreel, she shadowed her eyes, adorned her hair, and looked down from her window. 31As Jehu came through the gate, she cried out, "Is all well, Zimri, murderer of your master?" [w] 32Jehu looked up to the window and shouted, "Who is on my side? Anyone?" At this, two or three eunuchs looked down toward him. 33"Throw her down," he ordered. They threw her down, and some of her blood spurted against the wall and against the horses. Jehu rode in over her body 34and, after eating and drinking, he said: "Attend to that accursed woman and bury her; after all, she was a king's daughter." 35But when they went to bury her, they found nothing of her but the skull, the feet, and the hands. 36They returned to Jehu, and when they told him, he said, "This is the sentence which the LORD pronounced through his servant Elijah the Tishbite: 'In the confines of Jezreel dogs shall eat the flesh of Jezebel. [x] 37The corpse of Jezebel shall be like dung in the field in the confines of Jezreel, so that no one can say: This was Jezebel.' "

CHAPTER 10

Killing of Ahab's Descendants 1Ahab had seventy descendants in Samaria. Jehu prepared letters and sent them to the city rulers, to the elders, and to the guardians of Ahab's descendants in Samaria. [y] 2"Since your master's sons are with you," he wrote, "and you have the chariots, the horses, a fortified city, and the weapons, when this letter reaches you 3decide which is the best and the fittest of your master's offspring, place him on his father's throne, and fight for your master's house." 4They were overcome with fright and said, "If two kings could not withstand him, how can we?" 5So the vizier and the ruler of the city, along with the elders and the guardians, sent this message to Jehu: "We are your servants, and we will do everything you tell us. We will proclaim no one king; do whatever you think best." 6So Jehu wrote them a second letter: "If you are on my side and will obey me, count the heads of your master's sons and come to me in Jezreel at this time tomorrow." [The seventy princes were in the care of prominent men of the city, who were rearing them.]

7When the letter arrived, they took the princes and slew all seventy of them, put their heads in baskets, and sent them to Jehu in Jezreel. 8"They have brought the heads of the princes," a messenger came in and told him. "Pile them in two heaps at the entrance of the city until morning," he ordered. 9Going out in the morning, he stopped and said to all the people: "You are not responsible, and although I conspired against my lord and slew him, yet who

9, 22: Fornications and witchcrafts: the worship of foreign gods.

u 25f: 1 Kgs 21, 9–16. v 27ff: 2 Chr 22, 7ff. w 1 Kgs 16, 9ff. x 1 Kgs 21, 23. y Jgs 9, 5; 1 Kgs 15, 29; 16, 11.

killed all these? [10]Know that not a single word which the LORD has spoken against the house of Ahab shall go unfulfilled. The LORD has accomplished all that he foretold through his servant Elijah." [z] [11]Thereupon Jehu slew all who were left of the family of Ahab in Jezreel, as well as all his powerful supporters, intimates, and priests, leaving him no survivor. [a]

Ahaziah's Kinsmen [12] [b]Then he set out for Samaria, and at Beth-eked-haroim on the way, [13]he came across kinsmen of Ahaziah, king of Judah. "Who are you?" he asked. "We are kinsmen of Ahaziah," they replied. "We are going down to visit the princes and the family of the queen mother." [14]"Take them alive," Jehu ordered. They were taken alive, forty-two in number, then slain at the pit of Beth-eked. Not one of them was spared.

Jehu in Samaria [15]When he had left there, Jehu met Jehonadab, son of Rechab, on the road. He greeted him and asked, "Are you sincerely disposed toward me, as I am toward you?" "Yes," replied Jehonadab. "If you are," continued Jehu, "give me your hand." Jehonadab gave him his hand, and Jehu drew him up into his chariot. [c] [16]"Come with me," he said, "and see my zeal for the LORD." And he took him along in his own chariot.

[17]When he arrived in Samaria, Jehu slew all who remained there of Ahab's line, doing away with them completely and thus fulfilling the prophecy which the LORD had spoken to Elijah.

Baal's Temple Destroyed [18]Jehu gathered all the people together and said to them: "Ahab served Baal to some extent, but Jehu will serve him yet more. [d] [19]Now summon for me all Baal's prophets, all his worshipers, and all his priests. See that no one is absent, for I have a great sacrifice for Baal. Whoever is absent shall not live." This Jehu did as a ruse, so that he might destroy the worshipers of Baal. [20]Jehu said further, "Proclaim a solemn assembly in honor of Baal." They did so, [21]and Jehu sent word of it throughout the land of Israel. All the worshipers of Baal without exception came into the temple of Baal, which was filled to capacity. [22]Then Jehu said to the custodian of the wardrobe, "Bring out the garments for all the worshipers of Baal." When he had brought out the garments for them, [e] [23]Jehu, with Jehonadab, son of Rechab, entered the temple of Baal and said to the worshipers of Baal, "Search and be sure that there is no worshiper of the LORD here with you, but only worshipers of Baal." [24]Then they proceeded to offer sacrifices and holocausts. Now Jehu had stationed eighty men outside with this warning, "If one of you lets anyone escape of those whom I shall deliver into your hands, he shall pay life for life." [25]As soon as he finished offering the holocaust, Jehu said to the guards and officers, "Go in and slay them. Let no one escape." So the guards and officers put them to the sword and cast them out. Afterward they went into the inner shrine of the temple of Baal, [26]took out the stele of Baal, and burned the shrine. [27]Then they smashed the stele of Baal, tore down the building, and turned it into a latrine, as it remains today.

[28]Thus Jehu rooted out the worship of Baal from Israel. [29]However, he did not desist from the sins which Jeroboam, son of Nebat, had caused Israel to commit, as regards the golden calves at Bethel and at Dan. [f] [30]The LORD said to Jehu, "Because you have done well what I deem right, and have treated the house of Ahab as I desire, your sons to the fourth generation shall sit upon the throne of Israel." [g] [31]But Jehu was not careful to observe wholeheartedly the law of the LORD, the God of Israel, since he did not desist from the sins which Jeroboam caused Israel to commit.

[32] [h]At that time the LORD began to dismember Israel. Hazael defeated the Israelites throughout their territory [33]east of the Jordan (all the land of Gilead, of the Gadites, Reubenites and Manassehites), from Aroer on the river Arnon up through Gilead and Bashan.

[34]The rest of the acts of Jehu, his valor and all his accomplishments, are written in the book of the chronicles of the kings of Israel. [35]Jehu

z 1 Kgs 21, 17–24. 29. a Hos 1, 4. b 12ff: 2 Chr 22, 8f. c 1 Chr 2, 55; Jer 35, 1–11. d 1 Kgs 16, 30ff. e 1 Kgs 16, 32.

f 1 Kgs 12, 28f. g 2 Kgs 15, 12ff. h Am 1, 3.

rested with his ancestors and was buried in Samaria. His son Jehoahaz succeeded him as king. 36The length of Jehu's reign over Israel in Samaria was twenty-eight years.

CHAPTER 11

Rule of Athaliah 1When Athaliah, the mother of Ahaziah, saw that her son was dead, she began to kill off the whole royal family.[i] 2But Jehosheba,* daughter of King Jehoram and sister of Ahaziah, took Joash, his son, and spirited him away, along with his nurse, from the bedroom where the princes were about to be slain. She concealed him from Athaliah, and so he did not die. 3For six years he remained hidden in the temple of the LORD, while Athaliah ruled the land.

4[j]But in the seventh year, Jehoiada summoned the captains of the Carians and of the guards. He had them come to him in the temple of the LORD, exacted from them a sworn commitment, and then showed them the king's son. 5He gave them these orders: "This is what you must do: the third of you who come on duty on the sabbath shall guard the king's palace; 6another third shall be at the gate Sur; and the last third shall be at the gate behind the guards. 7The two of your divisions who are going off duty that week shall keep guard over the temple of the LORD for the king. 8You shall surround the king, each with drawn weapons, and if anyone tries to approach the cordon, kill him; stay with the king, whatever he may do."

9[k]The captains did just as Jehoiada the priest commanded. Each one with his men, both those going on duty for the sabbath and those going off duty that week, came to Jehoiada the priest. 10[l]He gave the captains King David's spears and shields, which were in the temple of the LORD. 11And the guards, with drawn weapons, lined up from the southern to the northern limit of the enclosure, surrounding the altar and the temple on the king's behalf. 12Then Jehoiada led out the king's son and put the crown and the insignia upon him. They proclaimed him king and anointed him, clapping their hands and shouting, "Long live the king!"[m]

13[n]Athaliah heard the noise made by the people, and appeared before them in the temple of the LORD. 14When she saw the king standing by the pillar,* as was the custom, and the captains and trumpeters near him, with all the people of the land rejoicing and blowing trumpets, she tore her garments and cried out, "Treason, treason!" 15Then Jehoiada the priest instructed the captains in command of the force: "Bring her outside through the ranks. If anyone follows her," he added, "let him die by the sword." He had given orders that she should not be slain in the temple of the LORD. 16She was led out forcibly to the horse gate of the royal palace, where she was put to death.

17[o]Then Jehoiada made a covenant between the LORD as one party and the king and the people as the other, by which they would be the LORD's people; and another covenant, between the king and the people. 18Thereupon all the people of the land went to the temple of Baal and demolished it. They shattered its altars and images completely, and slew Mattan, the priest of Baal, before the altars. After appointing a detachment for the temple of the LORD, Jehoiada 19with the captains, the Carians, the guards, and all the people of the land, led the king down from the temple of the LORD through the guards' gate to the palace, where Joash took his seat on the royal throne. 20All the people of the land rejoiced and the city was quiet, now that Athaliah had been slain with the sword at the royal palace.

CHAPTER 12

Reign of Joash 1Joash was seven years old when he became king.[p] 2Joash began to reign in the seventh year of Jehu, and he reigned forty years in Jerusalem. His mother, who was named Zibiah, was from Beer-sheba. 3Joash did what was pleasing to the LORD as long as he lived, because the priest Jehoiada guided him. 4Still,

11, 2: Jehosheba was the wife of Jehoida, the high priest; cf 2 Chr 22, 11.

11, 14: By the pillar: see note on 2 Chr 23, 13.

i Jgs 9, 5. j 4–8: 2 Chr 23, 1–7. k 9–12: 2 Chr 23, 8–11. l 10ff: 2 Sm 8, 7; 1 Kgs 1, 33f. m 2 Sm 1, 10. n 13–16: 2 Chr 23, 12–15. o 17–20: 2 Chr 23, 16–21. p 1f: 2 Chr 24, 1f.

the high places did not disappear; the people
continued to sacrifice and to burn incense there.
5 [q]For the priests Joash made this rule: "All the
funds for sacred purposes that are brought to the
temple of the LORD—the census tax, personal
redemption money, and whatever funds are
freely brought to the temple of the LORD— 6the
priests may take for themselves, each from his
own clients. However, they must make what-
ever repairs on the temple may prove neces-
sary." 7Nevertheless, as late as the twenty-third
year of the reign of King Joash, the priests had
not made needed repairs on the temple. 8Accord-
ingly, King Joash summoned the priest Jehoiada
and the other priests. "Why do you not repair
the temple?" he asked them. "You must no
longer take funds from your clients, but you shall
turn them over for the repairs." 9 [r]So the priests
agreed that they would neither take funds from
the people nor make the repairs on the temple.
10The priest Jehoiada then took a chest, bored
a hole in its lid, and set it beside the stele, on the
right as one entered the temple of the LORD. The
priests who guarded the entry would put into it
all the funds that were brought to the temple of
the LORD. 11When they noticed that there was a
large amount of silver in the chest, the royal
scribe [and the priest] would come up, and they
would melt down all the funds that were in the
temple of the LORD, and weigh them. 12The
amount thus realized they turned over to the
master workmen in the temple of the LORD.
They in turn would give it to the carpenters and
builders working in the temple of the LORD,
13and to the lumbermen and stone cutters, and
for the purchase of the wood and hewn stone
used in repairing the breaches, and for any other
expenses that were necessary to repair the
temple. 14None of the funds brought to the
temple of the LORD were used there to make
silver cups, snuffers, basins, trumpets, or any
gold or silver article. 15Instead, they were given
to the workmen, and with them they repaired
the temple of the LORD. 16Moreover, no reckon-
ing was asked of the men who were provided
with the funds to give to the workmen, because
they held positions of trust. 17The funds from
guilt-offerings and from sin-offerings, however,
were not brought to the temple of the LORD;
they belonged to the priests.
18 [s]Then King Hazael of Aram mounted a
siege against Gath. When he had taken it,
Hazael decided to go on to attack Jerusalem.[t]
19But King Jehoash of Judah took all the dedi-
cated offerings presented by his forebears, Je-
hoshaphat, Jehoram, and Ahaziah, kings of Ju-
dah, as well as his own, and all the gold there
was in the treasuries of the temple and the
palace, and sent them to King Hazael of Aram,
who then led his forces away from Jerusalem.
20The rest of the acts of Joash, with all that he
did, are recorded in the book of the chronicles of
the kings of Judah. 21Certain of his officials
entered into a plot against him and killed him at
Beth-millo. 22Jozacar, son of Shimeath, and Je-
hozabad, son of Shomer, were the officials who
killed him. He was buried in his forefathers' City
of David, and his son Amaziah succeeded him as
king.

CHAPTER 13

Reign of Jehoahaz of Israel 1In the twenty-
third year of Joash, son of Ahaziah, king of
Judah, Jehoahaz, son of Jehu, began his
seventeen-year reign over Israel in Samaria. 2He
did evil in the LORD's sight, conducting himself
like Jeroboam, son of Nebat, and not renouncing
the sin he had caused Israel to commit. 3The
LORD was angry with Israel and for a long time
left them in the power of Hazael, king of Aram,
and of Ben-hadad, son of Hazael. 4Then Jehoa-
haz entreated the LORD, who heard him, since
he saw the oppression to which the king of Aram
had subjected Israel.[u] 5So the LORD gave Israel a
savior,* and the Israelites, freed from the power
of Aram, dwelt in their own homes as formerly.
6Nevertheless, they did not desist from the sins
which the house of Jeroboam had caused Israel

13, 5: A savior: by this language, typical of the Book of Judges (Jgs 3, 9. 15), Jeroboam II of Israel is meant; cf 2 Kgs 14, 27.

q 5–8: 2 Chr 24, 5–10. r 9–16: 2 Chr 24, 11–14. s 2 Kgs 8, 12. t 18–22: 2 Chr 24, 23–27. u 2 Kgs 14, 26f.

to commit, but persisted in them. The sacred
pole* also remained standing in Samaria.[v] [7]No
soldiers were left to Jehoahaz, except fifty horse-
men with ten chariots and ten thousand foot
soldiers, since the king of Aram had destroyed
them and trampled them like dust. [8]The rest of
the acts of Jehoahaz, with all his valor and
accomplishments, are recorded in the book of
the chronicles of the kings of Israel. [9]Jehoahaz
rested with his ancestors and was buried in
Samaria. His son Joash succeeded him as king.

Reign of Joash of Israel [10]In the thirty-
seventh year of Joash, king of Judah, Jehoash,
son of Jehoahaz, began his sixteen-year reign
over Israel in Samaria. [11]He did evil in the sight
of the LORD; he did not desist from any of the
sins which Jeroboam, son of Nebat, had caused
Israel to commit, but persisted in them. [12]*[The
rest of the acts of Joash, the valor with which he
fought against Amaziah, king of Judah, and all
his accomplishments, are recorded in the book
of the chronicles of the kings of Israel.[w] [13]Joash
rested with his ancestors, and Jeroboam occu-
pied the throne. Joash was buried with the kings
of Israel in Samaria.]

[14]When Elisha was suffering from the sickness
of which he was to die, King Joash of Israel went
down to visit him. "My father, my father!"* he
exclaimed, weeping over him. "Israel's chariots
and horsemen!"[x] [15]"Take a bow and some
arrows," Elisha said to him. When he had done
so, [16]*Elisha said to the king of Israel, "Put your
hand on the bow." As the king held the bow,
Elisha placed his hands over the king's hands
[17]and said, "Open the window toward the east."
He opened it, Elisha said, "Shoot," and he shot.
The prophet exclaimed, "The LORD's arrow of
victory! The arrow of victory over Aram! You
will completely conquer Aram at Aphec."

[18]Then he said to the king of Israel, "Take the
arrows," which he did. Elisha said to him,
"Strike the ground!" He struck the ground three
times and stopped. [19]Angry with him, the man
of God said: "You should have struck five or six
times; you would have defeated Aram com-
pletely. Now, you will defeat Aram only three
times."

[20]Elisha died and was buried. At the time,
bands of Moabites used to raid the land each
year. [21]Once some people were burying a man,
when suddenly they spied such a raiding band.
So they cast the dead man into the grave of
Elisha, and everyone went off. But when the
man came in contact with the bones of Elisha,
he came back to life and rose to his feet.[y]

[22]King Hazael of Aram oppressed Israel during
the entire reign of Jehoahaz. [23]But the LORD was
merciful with Israel and looked on them with
compassion because of his covenant with Abra-
ham, Isaac, and Jacob. He was unwilling to
destroy them or to cast them out from his
presence.[z] [24]So when King Hazael of Aram died
and his son Ben-hadad succeeded him as king,
[25]Joash, son of Jehoahaz, took back from Ben-
hadad, son of Hazael, the cities which Hazael
had taken in battle from his father Jehoahaz.
Joash defeated Ben-hadad three times, and thus
recovered the cities of Israel.

CHAPTER 14

Amaziah of Judah* [1]In the second year of
Joash, son of Jehoahaz, king of Israel, Amaziah,
son of Joash, king of Judah, began to reign. [2][a]He
was twenty-five years old when he became king,
and he reigned twenty-nine years in Jerusalem.
His mother, whose name was Jehoaddin, was
from Jerusalem. [3]He pleased the LORD, yet not
like his forefather David, since he did just as his
father Joash had done. [4]Thus the high places did
not disappear, but the people continued to

13, 6: Sacred pole: see note on Ex 34, 13.

13, 12f: The conclusion to the reign of Joash is given again in 2 Kgs 14, 15f, where it is more appropriate.

13, 14: My father, my father: the king expresses here the same sentiments as those with which Elisha addressed Elijah.

13, 16–19: Symbolic acts similar to these are seen in Ex 17, 8ff; Jos 8, 18ff; Ez 4, 1ff.

14, 1f: In the second year . . . twenty-nine years in Jerusalem: the reigns of the kings of Judah between Athaliah and Ahaz are assigned too many years in all to correspond to the reigns in Israel from Jehu to the fall of Samaria. It seems probable that Amaziah was murdered as soon as his son Azariah was old enough to rule, and that Amaziah's reign was nearer nineteen than twenty-nine years. The correlation, in 2 Kgs 15, 1, of the beginning of Azariah's reign with the 27th year of Jeroboam II can hardly be correct; and the sixteen-year reign of Jotham of Judah (2 Kgs 15, 33) consisted for the most part of a regency during the illness of his father (2 Kgs 15, 5).

v Ex 34, 13. w 2 Kgs 14, 8–16. x 2 Kgs 2, 12. y Sir 48, 14. z Dt 9, 27. a 2f: 2 Chr 25, 1f.

sacrifice and to burn incense on them. 5 [b]When Amaziah had the kingdom firmly in hand, he slew the officials who had murdered the king, his father. 6But the children of the murderers he did not put to death, obeying the LORD's command written in the book of the law of Moses, "Fathers shall not be put to death for their children, nor shall children be put to death for their fathers; each one shall die for his own sin." [c]

7Amaziah slew ten thousand Edomites in the Salt Valley, and took Sela in battle. He renamed it Joktheel, the name it has to this day. [d]

8Then Amaziah sent messengers to Jehoash, son of Jehoahaz, son of Jehu, king of Israel, with this challenge, "Come, let us meet face to face." [e] 9King Jehoash of Israel sent this reply to the king of Judah: "The thistle of Lebanon sent word to the cedar of Lebanon, 'Give your daughter to my son in marriage,' but an animal of Lebanon passed by and trampled the thistle underfoot. 10You have indeed conquered Edom, and you have become ambitious. Enjoy your glory, but stay at home! Why involve yourself and Judah with you in misfortune and failure?"

11But Amaziah would not listen. King Jehoash of Israel then advanced, and he and King Amaziah of Judah met in battle at Beth-shemesh of Judah. 12Judah was defeated by Israel, and all the Judean soldiery fled homeward. 13King Jehoash of Israel captured Amaziah, son of Jehoash, son of Ahaziah, king of Judah, at Beth-shemesh. He went on to Jerusalem where he tore down four hundred cubits of the city wall, from the Gate of Ephraim to the Corner Gate. 14He took all the gold and silver and all the utensils there were in the temple of the LORD and in the treasuries of the palace, and hostages as well. Then he returned to Samaria. 15The rest of the acts of Jehoash, his valor, and how he fought Amaziah, king of Judah, are recorded in the book of the chronicles of the kings of Israel. [f] 16Jehoash rested with his ancestors; he was buried in Samaria with the kings of Israel. His son Jeroboam succeeded him as king.

17Amaziah, son of Joash, king of Judah, survived Jehoash, son of Jehoahaz, king of Israel, by fifteen years.* 18The rest of the acts of Amaziah are written in the book of the chronicles of the kings of Judah. 19When a conspiracy was formed against him in Jerusalem, he fled to Lachish. But he was pursued to Lachish and killed there. 20He was brought back on horses and buried with his ancestors in the City of David in Jerusalem. 21Thereupon all the people of Judah took the sixteen-year-old Azariah* and proclaimed him king to succeed his father Amaziah. [g] 22It was Azariah who rebuilt Elath and restored it to Judah, after King Amaziah rested with his ancestors.

Jeroboam II of Israel 23In the fifteenth year of Amaziah, son of Joash, king of Judah, Jeroboam, son of Joash, king of Israel, began his forty-one-year reign in Samaria. 24He did evil in the sight of the LORD; he did not desist from any of the sins which Jeroboam, son of Nebat, had caused Israel to commit. 25He restored the boundaries of Israel from Labo-of-Hamath to the sea of the Arabah,* just as the LORD, the God of Israel, had prophesied through his servant, the prophet Jonah, son of Amittai, from Gath-hepher. 26For the LORD saw the very bitter affliction of Israel, where there was neither slave nor freeman, no one at all to help Israel. [h] 27Since the LORD had not determined to blot out the name of Israel from under the heavens, he saved them through Jeroboam, son of Joash. 28The rest of the acts of Jeroboam, his valor and all his accomplishments, how he fought with Damascus and turned back Hamath from Israel, are recorded in the book of the chronicles of the kings of Israel. 29Jeroboam rested with his ancestors, the kings of Israel, and his son Zechariah succeeded him as king.

14, 17: See note on 2 Kgs 14, 1f.
14, 21: Azariah: also called Uzziah in many texts.
14, 25: Sea of the Arabah: the Dead Sea. Jonah: see note on Jon 1, 1.

b 5f: 2 Chr 25, 3f. c Dt 24, 16; Ez 18, 20. d 2 Sm 8, 13f; 2 Chr 25, 11. e 2 Kgs 13, 12; Jgs 9, 8-15. f 2 Kgs 13, 12f. g 2 Chr 26, 1f. h 2 Kgs 13, 4f; 1 Kgs 14, 10.

CHAPTER 15

Azariah of Judah [1] [i]Azariah, son of Amaziah, king of Judah, became king in the twenty-seventh year* of Jeroboam, king of Israel. [2]He was sixteen years old when he began to reign, and he reigned fifty-two years in Jerusalem. His mother, whose name was Jecholiah, was from Jerusalem. [3]He pleased the LORD just as his father Amaziah had done. [4]Yet the high places did not disappear; the people continued to sacrifice and to burn incense on them. [5] [j]The LORD afflicted the king, and he was a leper to the day of his death. He lived in a house apart, while Jotham, the king's son, was vizier and regent for the people of the land. [6]The rest of the acts of Azariah, and all his accomplishments, are recorded in the book of the chronicles of the kings of Judah. [7]Azariah rested with his ancestors, and was buried with them in the City of David. His son Jotham succeeded him as king.

Zechariah of Israel [8]In the thirty-eighth year of Azariah, king of Judah, Zechariah, son of Jeroboam, was king of Israel in Samaria for six months. [9]He did evil in the sight of the LORD as his fathers had done, and did not desist from the sins which Jeroboam, son of Nebat, had caused Israel to commit. [10]Shallum, son of Jabesh, conspired against Zechariah, attacked and killed him at Ibleam, and reigned in his place. [11]The rest of the acts of Zechariah are recorded in the book of the chronicles of the kings of Israel. [12]Thus the LORD's promise to Jehu, "Your descendants to the fourth generation shall sit upon the throne of Israel," was fulfilled. [k]

Shallum of Israel [13]Shallum, son of Jabesh, became king in the thirty-ninth year of Uzziah, king of Judah; he reigned one month in Samaria. [14]Menahem, son of Gadi, came up from Tirzah to Samaria, where he attacked and killed Shallum, son of Jabesh, and reigned in his place. [15]The rest of the acts of Shallum, and the fact of his conspiracy, are recorded in the book of the chronicles of the kings of Israel. [16]At that time, Menahem punished Tappuah, all the inhabitants of the town and of its whole district, because on his way from Tirzah they did not let him in. He punished them even to ripping open all the pregnant women.

Menahem of Israel [17]In the thirty-ninth year of Azariah, king of Judah, Menahem, son of Gadi, began his ten-year reign over Samaria. [18]He did evil in the sight of the LORD, not desisting from the sins which Jeroboam, son of Nebat, had caused Israel to commit. During his reign, [19]Pul,* king of Assyria, invaded the land, and Menahem gave him a thousand talents of silver to have his assistance in strengthening his hold on the kingdom. [20]Menahem secured the money to give to the king of Assyria by exacting it from all the men of substance in the country, fifty silver shekels from each. The king of Assyria did not remain in the country but withdrew. [21]The rest of the acts of Menahem, and all his accomplishments, are recorded in the book of the chronicles of the kings of Israel. [22]Menahem rested with his ancestors, and his son Pekahiah succeeded him as king.

Pekahiah of Israel [23]In the fiftieth year of Azariah, king of Judah, Pekahiah, son of Menahem, began his two-year reign over Israel in Samaria. [24]He did evil in the sight of the LORD, not desisting from the sins which Jeroboam, son of Nebat, had caused Israel to commit. [25]His adjutant Pekah, son of Remaliah, who had with him fifty men from Gilead, conspired against him, killed him within the palace stronghold in Samaria, and reigned in his place. [26]The rest of the acts of Pekahiah, and all his accomplishments, are recorded in the book of the chronicles of the kings of Israel.

Pekah of Israel [27]In the fifty-second year of Azariah, king of Judah, Pekah, son of Remaliah, began his twenty-year reign over Israel in Samaria.* [28]He did evil in the sight of the LORD, not desisting from the sins which Jeroboam, son of Nebat, had caused Israel to commit. [29]During

15, 1: Twenty-seventh year: see note on 2 Kgs 14, 1f.

15, 19: Pul: the Babylonian throne name of the Assyrian Tiglath-pileser III; cf 2 Kgs 15, 29.

15, 27: The twenty years here ascribed to Pekah are an impossibility; the calculation which made his reign, of five years at most, appear so long may have been based on the attempt to give Jotham of Judah a full sixteen-year reign independently of his regency. See 2 Kgs 16, 1 and the note on 2 Kgs 14, 1f.

i 1ff: 2 Chr 26, 3f. j 5ff: 2 Chr 26, 21ff. k 2 Kgs 10, 30.

the reign of Pekah, king of Israel, Tiglath-pileser, king of Assyria, came and took Ijon, Abel-beth-maacah, Janoah, Kedesh, Hazor, all the territory of Naphtali, Gilead, and Galilee, deporting the inhabitants to Assyria. 30 Hoshea, son of Elah, conspired against Pekah, son of Remaliah; he attacked and killed him, and reigned in his place [in the twentieth year of Jotham, son of Uzziah]. 31 The rest of the acts of Pekah, and all his accomplishments, are recorded in the book of the chronicles of the kings of Israel.

Jotham of Judah 32 [l] In the second year of Pekah, son of Remaliah, king of Israel, Jotham, son of Uzziah, king of Judah, began to reign. 33 He was twenty-five years old when he became king, and he reigned sixteen years in Jerusalem. His mother's name was Jerusha, daughter of Zadok. 34 He pleased the LORD, just as his father Uzziah had done. 35 Nevertheless the high places did not disappear and the people continued to sacrifice and to burn incense on them. It was he who built the Upper Gate* of the temple of the LORD. 36 The rest of the acts of Jotham, and all his accomplishments, are recorded in the book of the chronicles of the kings of Judah. 37 It was at that time that the LORD first loosed Rezin, king of Aram, and Pekah, son of Remaliah, against Judah. 38 Jotham rested with his ancestors and was buried with them in his forefather's City of David. His son Ahaz succeeded him as king.

CHAPTER 16

Ahaz of Judah 1 [m] In the seventeenth year of Pekah, son of Remaliah, Ahaz, son of Jotham, king of Judah, began to reign. 2 Ahaz was twenty years old when he became king, and he reigned sixteen years in Jerusalem. He did not please the LORD, his God, like his forefather David, 3 but conducted himself like the kings of Israel, and even immolated his son by fire, in accordance with the abominable practice of the nations whom the LORD had cleared out of the way of the Israelites. [n] 4 Further, he sacrificed and burned incense on the high places, on hills, and under every leafy tree. [o]

5 Then Rezin, king of Aram, and Pekah, son of Remaliah, king of Israel, came up to Jerusalem to attack it. Although they besieged Ahaz, they were unable to conquer him. [p] 6 At the same time the king of Edom recovered Elath for Edom, driving the Judeans out of it. The Edomites then entered Elath, which they have occupied until the present. [q]

7 Meanwhile, Ahaz sent messengers to Tiglath-pileser, king of Assyria, with the plea: "I am your servant and your son. Come up and rescue me from the clutches of the king of Aram and the king of Israel, who are attacking me." [r] 8 Ahaz took the silver and gold that were in the temple of the LORD and in the palace treasuries and sent them as a present to the king of Assyria, [s] 9 who listened to him and moved against Damascus, which he captured. He deported its inhabitants to Kir and put Rezin to death.*

10 King Ahaz went to Damascus to meet Tiglath-pileser, king of Assyria. When he saw the altar in Damascus, King Ahaz sent to Uriah the priest a model of the altar and a detailed design of its construction. 11 Uriah the priest built an altar according to the plans which King Ahaz sent him from Damascus, and had it completed by the time the king returned home. 12 On his arrival from Damascus, the king inspected this altar, then went up to it and offered sacrifice on it, 13 burning his holocaust and cereal-offering, pouring out his libation, and sprinkling the blood of his peace-offerings on the altar. [t] 14 The bronze altar that stood before the LORD he brought from the front of the temple—that is, from the space

15, 35: The Upper Gate: also the Gate of Benjamin; cf Jer 20, 2; Ez 9, 2.

16, 9: Firmly dated events bearing on chapters 16 through 20 are: the fall of Damascus (16, 9) in 732 B.C., the fall of Samaria (18, 9–11) in 721 B.C., and Sennacherib's invasion of Judah (18, 3) in 701 B.C., which is equated both in Kgs and in Is 36, 1 with the 14th year of Hezekiah. These data make it necessary to credit Ahaz with at least a twenty-year reign, between 735 and c. 715 B.C., and to exclude the correlations between Hoshea of Israel and Hezekiah in chapter 18. If the 14th-year correspondence for 701 B.C. is given up, other arrangements are possible. The alleged ages of Jotham (15, 33), Ahaz (16, 2), and Hezekiah (18, 2) at their successive accessions to the throne do not argue for an early date for Hezekiah; but one or more of these may be artificial. Azariah (15, 1–7; Is 6, 1) was still on the throne of Judah in 743 B.C.

l 32–38: 2 Chr 27, 1–4. 7–9. m 1–4: 2 Chr 28, 1–4. n Lv 18, 21. o Dt 12, 2. p 2 Chr 28, 5f. q 2 Chr 28, 17. r 2 Chr 28, 16. s 2 Chr 28, 21. t 2 Chr 28, 23.

between the new altar and the temple of the
Lord—and set it on the north side of his altar.
15 [u]"Upon the large altar," King Ahaz com-
manded Uriah the priest, "burn the morning
holocaust and the evening cereal-offering, the
royal holocaust and cereal-offering, as well as the
holocausts, cereal-offerings, and libations of the
people. You must also sprinkle on it all the blood
of holocausts and sacrifices. But the old bronze
altar shall be mine for consultation."* 16 Uriah
the priest did just as King Ahaz had commanded.
17 King Ahaz detached the frames from the bases
and removed the lavers from them; he also took
down the bronze sea from the bronze oxen that
supported it, and set it on a stone pavement.[v]
18 In deference to the king of Assyria he removed
from the temple of the LORD the emplacement
which had been built in the temple for a throne,
and the outer entrance for the king.* 19 The rest
of the acts of Ahaz are recorded in the book of
the chronicles of the kings of Judah.[w] 20 Ahaz
rested with his ancestors and was buried with
them in the City of David. His son Hezekiah
succeeded him as king.

CHAPTER 17

Hoshea of Israel 1 In the twelfth year of Ahaz,
king of Judah, Hoshea, son of Elah, began his
nine-year reign over Israel in Samaria. 2 He did
evil in the sight of the LORD, yet not to the
extent of the kings of Israel before him. 3 Shal-
maneser,* king of Assyria, advanced against
him, and Hoshea became his vassal and paid him
tribute.[x] 4 But the king of Assyria found Hoshea
guilty of conspiracy for sending envoys to the
king of Egypt at Sais, and for failure to pay the
annual tribute to his Assyrian overlord. 5 For this,
the king of Assyria arrested and imprisoned
Hoshea; he then occupied the whole land and
attacked Samaria, which he besieged for three
years. 6 In the ninth year of Hoshea, the king of
Assyria* took Samaria, and deported the Israel-
ites to Assyria, settling them in Halah, at the
Habor, a river of Gozan, and in the cities of the
Medes.[y]

7 This came about because the Israelites
sinned against the LORD, their God, who had
brought them up from the land of Egypt, from
under the domination of Pharaoh, king of Egypt,
and because they venerated other gods. 8 They
followed the rites of the nations whom the LORD
had cleared out of the way of the Israelites [and
the kings of Israel whom they set up]. 9 They
adopted unlawful practices toward the LORD,
their God. They built high places in all their
settlements, the watchtowers as well as the
walled cities. 10 They set up pillars and sacred
poles for themselves on every high hill and
under every leafy tree.[z] 11 There, on all the high
places, they burned incense like the nations
whom the LORD had sent into exile at their
coming. They did evil things that provoked the
LORD, 12 and served idols, although the LORD had
told them, "You must not do this."

13 And though the LORD warned Israel and
Judah by every prophet and seer, "Give up your
evil ways and keep my commandments and
statutes, in accordance with the entire law
which I enjoined on your fathers and which I
sent you by my servants the prophets," 14 [a]they
did not listen, but were as stiff-necked as their
fathers, who had not believed in the LORD, their
God. 15 They rejected his statutes, the covenant
which he had made with their fathers, and the
warnings which he had given them. The vanity
they pursued, they themselves became: they
followed the surrounding nations whom the
LORD had commanded them not to imitate.[b]
16 They disregarded all the commandments of
the LORD, their God, and made for themselves
two molten calves; they also made a sacred pole
and worshiped all the host of heaven, and served
Baal.[c] 17 [d]They immolated their sons and daugh-
ters by fire, practiced fortune-telling and divina-

16, 15: For consultation: perhaps the introduction into Judah of the Babylonian practice of omen sacrifices; cf Ez 21, 16.

16, 18: Emplacement . . . for a throne, and the outer entrance for the king: signs of sovereignty for the Hebrew kings.

17, 3: Shalmaneser: son and successor of Tiglath-pileser.

17, 6: The king of Assyria: Shalmaneser's successor and usurper, Sargon II.

u Ex 29, 38f; Nm 28, 3f. v 2 Chr 28, 24. w 2 Chr 28, 26f. x 2 Kgs 18, 9; Tb 1, 2. y 2 Kgs 18, 10f. z Ex 23, 24; 34, 13; Dt 12, 2. a Jer 25, 5; Dt 9, 13. b Jer 2, 5. c 1 Kgs 12, 28; Ex 34, 13; Dt 4, 19; 17, 2f. d Lv 18, 21; Dt 18, 10.

tion, and sold themselves into evildoing in the LORD's sight, provoking him 18 till, in his great anger against Israel, the LORD put them away out of his sight. Only the tribe of Judah was left.

19 Even the people of Judah, however, did not keep the commandments of the LORD, their God, but followed the rites practiced by Israel. 20 So the LORD rejected the whole race of Israel. He afflicted them and delivered them over to plunderers, finally casting them out from before him. 21 When he tore Israel away from the house of David, they made Jeroboam, son of Nebat, king: he drove the Israelites away from the LORD, causing them to commit a great sin.[e] 22 The Israelites imitated Jeroboam in all the sins he committed, nor would they desist from them. 23 Finally, the LORD put Israel away out of his sight as he had foretold through all his servants, the prophets; and Israel went into exile from their native soil to Assyria, an exile lasting to the present.[f]

24 The king of Assyria brought people from Babylon, Cuthah, Avva, Hamath, and Sepharvaim, and settled them in the cities of Samaria in place of the Israelites. They took possession of Samaria and dwelt in its cities. 25 When they first settled there, they did not venerate the LORD, so he sent lions among them that killed some of their number. 26 A report reached the king of Assyria: "The nations whom you deported and settled in the cities of Samaria do not know how to worship the God of the land, and he has sent lions among them that are killing them, since they do not know how to worship the God of the land." 27 The king of Assyria gave the order, "Send back one of the priests whom I deported, to go there and settle, to teach them how to worship the God of the land." 28 So one of the priests who had been deported from Samaria returned and settled in Bethel, and taught them how to venerate the LORD.

29 But these peoples began to make their own gods in the various cities in which they were living; in the shrines on the high places which the Samaritans had made, each people set up gods.[g] 30 Thus the Babylonians made Marduk and his consort; the men of Cuth made Nergal; the men of Hamath made Ashima; 31 the men of Avva made Nibhaz and Tartak; and the men of Sepharvaim immolated their children by fire to their city gods, King Hadad and his consort Anath. 32 They also venerated the LORD, choosing from their number priests for the high places, who officiated for them in the shrines on the high places.[h] 33 But, while venerating the LORD, they served their own gods, following the worship of the nations from among whom they had been deported.

34 To this day they worship according to their ancient rites.* [They did not venerate the LORD nor observe the statutes and regulations, the law and commandments, which the LORD enjoined on the descendants of Jacob, whom he had named Israel.[i] 35 When he made a covenant with them, he commanded them: "You must not venerate other gods, nor worship them, nor serve them, nor offer sacrifice to them.[j] 36 The LORD, who brought you up from the land of Egypt with great power and outstretched arm: him shall you venerate, him shall you worship, and to him shall you sacrifice. 37 You must be careful to observe forever the statutes and regulations, the law and commandment, which he wrote for you, and you must not venerate other gods. 38 The covenant which I made with you, you must not forget; you must not venerate other gods. 39 But the LORD, your God, you must venerate; it is he who will deliver you from the power of all your enemies." 40 They did not listen, however, but continued in their earlier manner.] 41 Thus these nations venerated the LORD, but also served their idols. And their sons and grandsons, to this day, are doing as their fathers did.

17, 34–40: They did not . . . earlier manner: this passage is an adaptation of language denouncing the Israelites to make it applicable to the later Samaritan sect of postexilic times. The original bearing of the discourse (vv 13–15) can be seen by reading it between vv 22 and 23. Cf also 2 Kgs 18, 12.

e 1 Kgs 12, 19f; 12, 26–33. f Jer 25, 9. g Jn 4, 9. h 1 Kgs 12, 31. i Gn 32, 29. j Ex 20, 3ff.

II: The Kingdom of Judah after 721 B.C.

CHAPTER 18

Hezekiah 1 [k]In the third year of Hoshea, son of Elah, king of Israel, Hezekiah, son of Ahaz, king of Judah, began to reign. 2He was twenty-five years old when he became king, and he reigned twenty-nine years in Jerusalem. His mother's name was Abi, daughter of Zechariah. 3He pleased the LORD, just as his forefather David had done. 4It was he who removed the high places, shattered the pillars, and cut down the sacred poles. He smashed the bronze serpent called Nehushtan which Moses had made, because up to that time the Israelites were burning incense to it.[l] 5He put his trust in the LORD, the God of Israel; and neither before him nor after him was there anyone like him among all the kings of Judah. 6Loyal to the LORD, Hezekiah never turned away from him, but observed the commandments which the LORD had given Moses. 7The LORD was with him, and he prospered in all that he set out to do. He rebelled against the king of Assyria and did not serve him. 8He also subjugated the watchtowers and walled cities of the Philistines, all the way to Gaza and its territory.

9In the fourth year of King Hezekiah, which was the seventh year of Hoshea, son of Elah, king of Israel, Shalmaneser, king of Assyria, attacked Samaria, laid siege to it,* 10 [m]and after three years captured it. In the sixth year of Hezekiah, the ninth year of Hoshea, king of Israel, Samaria was taken. 11The king of Assyria then deported the Israelites to Assyria and settled them in Halah, at the Habor, a river of Gozan, and in the cities of the Medes. 12This came about because they had not heeded the warning of the LORD, their God, but violated his covenant, not heeding and not fulfilling the commandments of Moses, the servant of the LORD.[n]

Invasion of Sennacherib 13*In the fourteenth year of King Hezekiah, Sennacherib,* king of Assyria, went on an expedition against all the fortified cities of Judah and captured them.[o] 14Hezekiah, king of Judah, sent this message to the king of Assyria at Lachish: "I have done wrong. Leave me, and I will pay whatever tribute you impose on me." The king of Assyria exacted three hundred talents of silver and thirty talents of gold from Hezekiah, king of Judah. 15Hezekiah paid him all the funds there were in the temple of the LORD and in the palace treasuries. 16He broke up the door panels and the uprights of the temple of the LORD which he himself had ordered to be overlaid with gold, and gave the gold to the king of Assyria.[p]

17The king of Assyria sent the general, the lord chamberlain, and the commander* from Lachish with a great army to King Hezekiah at Jerusalem. They went up, and on their arrival in Jerusalem, stopped at the conduit of the upper pool on the highway of the fuller's field.[q] 18They called for the king, who sent out to them Eliakim, son of Hilkiah, the master of the palace; Shebnah the scribe; and the herald Joah, son of Asaph.[r] 19The commander said to them, "Tell Hezekiah, 'Thus says the great king, the king of Assyria: On what do you base this confidence of yours? 20Do you think mere words substitute for strategy and might in war? On whom, then, do you rely, that you rebel against me? 21This Egypt, the staff on which you rely, is in fact a broken reed which pierces the hand of anyone who leans on it. That is what Pharaoh, king of Egypt, is to all who rely on him.[s] 22But if you say to me, We rely on the LORD, our God, is not he the one whose high places and altars Hezekiah has removed, commanding Judah and Jerusalem to worship before this altar in Jerusalem?'

18, 9: See note on 2 Kgs 16, 9.

18, 13—20, 11: Duplication of Is 36, 1—38, 8. 21. 22.

18, 13: Sennacherib succeeded Sargon II as king of Assyria. His Judean campaign was waged in 701 B.C. See note on 2 Kgs 16, 9.

18, 17: General, the lord chamberlain . . . commander: the text lists three major functionaries by their Assyrian titles, of which only the first, more nearly "lord lieutenant," is military in origin; the commander was technically the king's chief butler.

k 1ff: 2 Chr 28, 27; 29, 1f. l Ex 23, 24; 34, 13; Nm 21, 9; Dt 12, 2; 2 Chr 31, 1; Wis 16, 6; Jn 3, 14. m 10f: 2 Kgs 17. 6; Tb 1, 2. n 2 Kgs 17, 7–18. o 2 Chr 32, 1ff; Sir 48, 18; Is 36, 1. p 1 Kgs 6, 20–22. q 2 Chr 32, 9; Is 36, 1ff. r Is 22, 13–25. s Is 30, 1–7; 31, 1–3; Ez 29, 6–7.

23 "Now, make a wager with my lord, the king of Assyria: I will give you two thousand horses if you can put riders on them. 24 How then can you repulse even one of the least servants of my lord, relying as you do on Egypt for chariots and horsemen? 25 Was it without the LORD's will that I have come up to destroy this place? The LORD said to me, 'Go up and destroy that land!' "

26 Then Eliakim, son of Hilkiah, and Shebnah and Joah said to the commander: "Please speak to your servants in Aramaic; we understand it. Do not speak to us in Judean within earshot of the people who are on the wall."

27 But the commander replied: "Was it to your master and to you that my lord sent me to speak these words? Was it not rather to the men sitting on the wall, who, with you, will have to eat their own excrement and drink their urine?" 28 Then the commander stepped forward and cried out in a loud voice in Judean, "Listen to the words of the great king, the king of Assyria. 29 Thus says the king: 'Do not let Hezekiah deceive you, since he cannot deliver you out of my hand. 30 Let not Hezekiah induce you to rely on the LORD, saying, The LORD will surely save us; this city will not be handed over to the king of Assyria. 31 Do not listen to Hezekiah, for the king of Assyria says: Make peace with me and surrender! Then each of you will eat of his own vine and of his own fig-tree, and drink the water of his own cistern, 32 until I come to take you to a land like your own, a land of grain and wine, of bread and orchards, of olives, oil and fruit syrup. Choose life, not death. Do not listen to Hezekiah when he would seduce you by saying, The LORD will rescue us. 33 Has any of the gods of the nations ever rescued his land from the hand of the king of Assyria? 34 Where are the gods of Hamath and Arpad? Where are the gods of Sepharvaim, Hena, and Avva? Where are the gods of the land of Samaria?[t] 35 Which of the gods for all these lands ever rescued his land from my hand? Will the LORD then rescue Jerusalem from my hand?' " 36 But the people remained silent and did not answer him one word, for the king had ordered them not to answer him.

37 Then the master of the palace, Eliakim, son of Hilkiah, Shebnah the scribe, and the herald Joah, son of Asaph, came to Hezekiah with their garments torn, and reported to him what the commander had said.

CHAPTER 19

Hezekiah and Isaiah 1 [u]When King Hezekiah heard this, he tore his garments, wrapped himself in sackcloth, and went into the temple of the LORD. 2 He sent Eliakim, the master of the palace, Shebnah the scribe, and the elders of the priests, wrapped in sackcloth, to tell the prophet Isaiah, son of Amoz, 3 "Thus says Hezekiah: 'This is a day of distress, of rebuke, and of disgrace. Children are at the point of birth, but there is no strength to bring them forth.* 4 Perhaps the LORD, your God, will hear all the words of the commander, whom his master, the king of Assyria, sent to taunt the living God, and will rebuke him for the words which the LORD, your God, has heard. So send up a prayer for the remnant that is here.' " 5 When the servants of King Hezekiah had come to Isaiah, 6 he said to them, "Tell this to your master: 'Thus says the LORD: Do not be frightened by the words you have heard, with which the servants of the king of Assyria have blasphemed me.[v] 7 I am about to put in him such a spirit that, when he hears a certain report, he will return to his own land, and there I will cause him to fall by the sword.' "

8 When the commander, on his return, heard that the king of Assyria had withdrawn from Lachish, he found him besieging Libnah. 9 The king of Assyria heard a report that Tirhakah, king of Ethiopia, had come out to fight against him. Again he sent envoys to Hezekiah with this message: 10 "Thus shall you say to Hezekiah, king of Judah: 'Do not let your God on whom you rely deceive you by saying that Jerusalem will not be handed over to the king of Assyria. 11 You have heard what the kings of Assyria have done to all other countries: they doomed them!

19, 3: See note on Is 37, 3.

t 2 Kgs 17, 24. u 1–7: Is 37, 1–7. v Is 10, 5–19.

Will you, then, be saved? 12Did the gods of the
nations whom my fathers destroyed save them?
Gozan, Haran, Rezeph, or the Edenites in Telas-
sar?[w] 13Where are the king of Hamath, the king
of Arpad, or the kings of the cities Sepharvaim,
Hena and Avva?' "[x]
14 [y]Hezekiah took the letter from the hand of
the messengers and read it; then he went up to
the temple of the LORD, and spreading it out
before him, 15he prayed in the LORD's presence:
"O LORD, God of Israel, enthroned upon the
cherubim! You alone are God over all the
kingdoms of the earth. You have made the
heavens and the earth.[z] 16Incline your ear, O
LORD, and listen! Open your eyes, O LORD, and
see! Hear the words of Sennacherib which he
sent to taunt the living God. 17Truly, O LORD,
the kings of Assyria have laid waste the nations
and their lands, 18and cast their gods into the
fire; they destroyed them because they were not
gods, but the work of human hands, wood and
stone.[a] 19Therefore, O LORD, our God, save us
from the power of this man, that all the king-
doms of the earth may know that you alone, O
LORD, are God."[b]
Punishment of Sennacherib 20Then Isaiah,
son of Amoz, sent this message to Hezekiah:
"Thus says the LORD, the God of Israel, in
answer to your prayer for help against Sennach-
erib, king of Assyria: I have listened! 21This is
the word the LORD has spoken concerning him:*

" 'She despises you, laughs you to scorn,
the virgin daughter Zion!
Behind you she wags her head,
daughter Jerusalem.
22 Whom have you insulted and blasphemed,
against whom have you raised your voice
And lifted up your eyes on high?
Against the Holy One of Israel!
23 Through your servants you have insulted the
LORD.
You said: With my many chariots
I climbed the mountain heights,
the recesses of Lebanon;
I cut down its lofty cedars,
its choice cypresses;
I reached the remotest heights,
its forest park.
24 I dug wells and drank water in foreign lands;
I dried up with the soles of my feet
all the rivers of Egypt.

25 " 'Have you not heard?
Long ago I prepared it,
From days of old I planned it.
Now I have brought it to pass:
That you should reduce fortified cities
into heaps of ruins,
26 While their inhabitants, shorn of power,
are dismayed and ashamed,
Becoming like the plants of the field, like the
green growth,
like the scorched grass on the housetops.
27 I am aware whether you stand or sit;
I know whether you come or go,[c]
28 and also your rage against me.
Because of your rage against me
and your fury which has reached my ears,
I will put my hook in your nose
and my bit in your mouth,
and make you return the way you came.

29 " 'This shall be a sign for you:
this year you shall eat the aftergrowth,
next year, what grows of itself;
But in the third year, sow and reap,
plant vineyards and eat their fruit!
30 The remaining survivors of the house of Judah
shall again strike root below
and bear fruit above.
31 For out of Jerusalem shall come a remnant,
and from Mount Zion, survivors.
The zeal of the LORD of hosts shall do this.'

32"Therefore, thus says the LORD concerning
the king of Assyria: 'He shall not reach this city,
nor shoot an arrow at it, nor come before it with
a shield, nor cast up siege-works against it. 33He
shall return by the same way he came, without
entering the city, says the LORD. 34I will shield

19, 21–31: vv 21–28 are addressed to Sennacherib, vv 29–31 to Judah.

w 2 Kgs 17, 6. x 2 Kgs 18, 34. y 14–19: 2 Chr 32, 20; Is 37, 14–20. z Ex 25, 18. a Jer 10, 3. b 1 Kgs 18, 24. c Ps 139, 2f.

and save this city for my own sake, and for the
sake of my servant David.' "[d]
35 That night the angel of the LORD went forth
and struck down one hundred and eighty-five
thousand men in the Assyrian camp. Early the
next morning, there they were, all the corpses of
the dead.[e] 36 So Sennacherib, the king of Assyria,
broke camp, and went back home to Nineveh.
37 When he was worshiping in the temple of
his god Nisroch, his sons Adrammelech and
Sharezer slew him with the sword and fled into
the land of Ararat. His son Esar-haddon reigned
in his stead.

CHAPTER 20

Hezekiah's Illness 1 [f]In those days, when
Hezekiah was mortally ill, the prophet Isaiah,
son of Amoz, came and said to him: "Thus says
the LORD: 'Put your house in order, for you are
about to die; you shall not recover.' " 2 He
turned his face to the wall and prayed to the
LORD: 3 "O LORD, remember how faithfully and
wholeheartedly I conducted myself in your pres-
ence, doing what was pleasing to you!" And
Hezekiah wept bitterly.
4 Before Isaiah had left the central courtyard,
the word of the LORD came to him: 5 "Go back
and tell Hezekiah, the leader of my people:
'Thus says the LORD, the God of your forefather
David: I have heard your prayer and seen your
tears. I will heal you. In three days you shall go
up to the LORD's temple; 6 I will add fifteen years
to your life. I will rescue you and this city from
the hand of the king of Assyria; I will be a shield
to this city for my own sake, and for the sake of
my servant David.' "
7 Isaiah then ordered a poultice of figs to be
brought and applied to the boil, that he might
recover. 8 Then Hezekiah asked Isaiah, "What is
the sign that the LORD will heal me and that I
shall go up to the temple of the LORD on the
third day?" 9 Isaiah replied, "This will be the sign
for you from the LORD that he will do what he
has promised: Shall the shadow go forward or
back ten steps?"
10 "It is easy for the shadow to advance ten
steps," Hezekiah answered. "Rather, let it go
back ten steps." 11 So the prophet Isaiah invoked
the LORD, who made the shadow retreat the ten
steps it had descended on the staircase to the
terrace of Ahaz.
12 *At that time, when Merodach-baladan, son
of Baladan, king of Babylon, heard that Hezekiah
had been ill, he sent letters and gifts to him.[g]
13 Hezekiah was pleased at this, and therefore
showed the messengers his whole treasury, his
silver, gold, spices and fine oil, his armory, and
all that was in his storerooms; there was nothing
in his house or in all his realm that Hezekiah did
not show them.
14 Then Isaiah the prophet came to King Heze-
kiah and asked him: "What did these men say
to you? Where did they come from?" "They
came from a distant land, from Babylon," re-
plied Hezekiah. 15 "What did they see in your
house?" the prophet asked. "They saw every-
thing in my house," answered Hezekiah.
"There is nothing in my storerooms that I did
not show them."
16 Then Isaiah said to Hezekiah: "Hear the
word of the LORD: 17 The time is coming when
all that is in your house, and everything that
your fathers have stored up until this day, shall
be carried off to Babylon; nothing shall be left,
says the LORD. 18 Some of your own bodily
descendants shall be taken and made servants in
the palace of the king of Babylon."
19 Hezekiah replied to Isaiah, "The word of
the LORD which you have spoken is favorable."
For he thought, "There will be peace and
security in my lifetime."
20 The rest of the acts of Hezekiah, all his
valor, and his construction of the pool and
conduit* by which water was brought into the
city, are written in the book of the chronicles of
the kings of Judah.[h] 21 Hezekiah rested with his
ancestors and his son Manasseh succeeded him
as king.

20, 12–19: Duplication of Is 39, 1–8.
20, 20: Pool and conduit: Hezekiah's tunnel; cf 2 Chr 32, 30.

d 2 Sm 7, 12; Hos 1, 7. e Sir 48, 21; 2 Chr 32, 21f; Is 37, 36–38; 1 Mc 7, 41; 2 Mc 8, 19. f 1–9: 2 Chr 32, 24; Is 38, 1–8. g 12f: Is 39, 1f; 2 Chr 32, 27ff. h 2 Chr 32, 30; Sir 48, 17.

CHAPTER 21

Reign of Manasseh 1 [i]Manasseh was twelve years old when he began to reign, and he reigned fifty-five years in Jerusalem. His mother's name was Hephzibah. 2 He did evil in the sight of the LORD, following the abominable practices of the nations whom the LORD had cleared out of the way of the Israelites. 3 He rebuilt the high places which his father Hezekiah had destroyed. He erected altars to Baal, and also set up a sacred pole, as Ahab, king of Israel, had done. He worshiped and served the whole host of heaven.[j] 4 He built altars in the temple of the LORD, about which the LORD had said, "I will establish my name in Jerusalem"— 5 altars for the whole host of heaven, in the two courts of the temple.[k]

6 He immolated his son by fire. He practiced soothsaying and divination, and reintroduced the consulting of ghosts and spirits. He did much evil in the LORD's sight and provoked him to anger.

7 The Asherah idol he had made, he set up in the temple, of which the LORD had said to David and to his son Solomon: "In this temple and in Jerusalem, which I have chosen out of all the tribes of Israel, I shall place my name forever.[l] 8 I will not in future allow Israel to be driven off the land I gave their fathers, provided that they are careful to observe all I have commanded them, the entire law which my servant Moses enjoined upon them." 9 But they did not listen, and Manasseh misled them into doing even greater evil than the nations whom the LORD had destroyed at the coming of the Israelites.

10 Then the LORD spoke through his servants the prophets: 11 "Because Manasseh, king of Judah, has practiced these abominations and has done greater evil than all that was done by the Amorites before him, and has led Judah into sin by his idols,[m] 12 therefore thus says the LORD, the God of Israel: 'I will bring such evil on Jerusalem and Judah that, whenever anyone hears of it, his ears shall ring. 13 I will measure Jerusalem with the same cord as I did Samaria, and with the plummet I used for the house of Ahab. I will wipe Jerusalem clean as one wipes a dish, wiping it inside and out.[n] 14 I will cast off the survivors of my inheritance and deliver them into enemy hands, to become a prey and a booty for all their enemies, 15 because they have done evil in my sight and provoked me from the day their fathers came forth from Egypt until today.' "

16 In addition to the sin which he caused Judah to commit, Manasseh did evil in the sight of the LORD, shedding so much innocent blood as to fill the length and breadth of Jerusalem. 17 The rest of the acts of Manasseh, the sin he committed and all that he did, are written in the book of the chronicles of the kings of Judah.[o] 18 Manasseh rested with his ancestors and was buried in his palace garden, the garden of Uzza. His son Amon succeeded him as king.

Reign of Amon 19 [p]Amon was twenty-two years old when he began to reign, and he reigned two years in Jerusalem. His mother's name was Meshullemeth, daughter of Haruz of Jotbah. 20 He did evil in the sight of the LORD, as his father Manasseh had done. 21 He followed exactly the path his father had trod, serving and worshiping the idols his father had served. 22 He abandoned the LORD, the God of his fathers, and did not follow the path of the LORD. 23 Subjects of Amon conspired against him and slew the king in his palace, 24 but the people of the land then slew all who had conspired against King Amon, and proclaimed his son Josiah king in his stead. 25 The rest of the acts that Amon did are written in the book of the chronicles of the kings of Judah. 26 He was buried in his own grave in the garden of Uzza, and his son Josiah succeeded him as king.

CHAPTER 22

Reign of Josiah 1 [q]Josiah was eight years old when he began to reign, and he reigned thirty-one years in Jerusalem. His mother's name was Jedidah, daughter of Adaiah of Bozkath. 2 He pleased the LORD and conducted himself unswervingly just as his ancestor David had done.

i 1–10: 2 Chr 33, 1–10. j 2 Kgs 17, 16; 1 Kgs 18, 4; 16, 32f. k Lv 18, 21. l 2 Sm 7, 13; 1 Kgs 8, 16: 9, 3. m 1 Kgs 21, 26; Jer 15, 4. n Is 34, 11; Am 7, 7–9; Lam 2, 8. o 2 Chr 33, 18ff. p 19–26: 2 Chr 33, 21–25. q 1f: 2 Chr 34, 1f.

3 [r]In his eighteenth year, King Josiah sent the
scribe Shaphan,* son of Azaliah, son of Meshul-
lam, to the temple of the LORD with orders to
4 [s]go to the high priest Hilkiah and have him
smelt down the precious metals that had been
donated to the temple of the Lord, which the
doorkeepers had collected from the people.
5 They were to be consigned to the master
workmen in the temple of the LORD, who should
then pay them out to the carpenters, builders,
and lumbermen making repairs on the temple,
6 and for the purchase of wood and hewn stone
for the temple repairs. 7 No reckoning was asked
of them regarding the funds consigned to them,
because they held positions of trust.

The Book of the Law 8 The high priest Hil-
kiah informed the scribe Shaphan, "I have
found the book of the law in the temple of the
LORD." Hilkiah gave the book to Shaphan, who
read it. 9 Then the scribe Shaphan went to the
king and reported, "Your servants have smelted
down the metals available in the temple and
have consigned them to the master workmen in
the temple of the LORD." 10 The scribe Shaphan
also informed the king that the priest Hilkiah
had given him a book, and then read it aloud to
the king. 11 When the king had heard the con-
tents of the book of the law, he tore his gar-
ments[t] 12 and issued this command to Hilkiah
the priest, Ahikam, son of Shaphan, Achbor,
son of Micaiah, the scribe Shaphan, and the
king's servant Asaiah: 13 "Go, consult the LORD
for me, for the people, for all Judah, about the
stipulations of this book that has been found,
for the anger of the LORD has been set furiously
ablaze against us, because our fathers did not
obey the stipulations of this book, nor fulfill our
written obligations."

14 So Hilkiah the priest, Ahikam, Achbor, Sha-
phan, and Asaiah betook themselves to the
Second Quarter in Jerusalem, where the prophet-
ess Huldah resided. She was the wife of Shallum,
son of Tikvah, son of Harhas, keeper of the
wardrobe. When they had spoken to her, 15 she
said to them, "Thus says the LORD, the God of
Israel: 'Say to the man who sent you to me,
16 Thus says the LORD: I will bring upon this
place and upon its inhabitants all the evil that is
threatened in the book which the king of Judah
has read. 17 Because they have forsaken me and
have burned incense to other gods, provoking
me by everything to which they turn their
hands, my anger is ablaze against this place and
it cannot be extinguished.'

18 "But to the king of Judah who sent you to
consult the LORD, give this response: 'Thus says
the LORD, the God of Israel: As for the threats
you have heard, 19 because you were heartsick
and have humbled yourself before the LORD
when you heard my threats that this place and
its inhabitants would become a desolation and a
curse; because you tore your garments and wept
before me; I in turn have listened, says the
LORD. 20 I will therefore gather you to your
ancestors; you shall go to your grave in peace,
and your eyes shall not see all the evil I will bring
upon this place.' " This they reported to the
king.

CHAPTER 23

1 [u]The king then had all the elders of Judah
and of Jerusalem summoned together before
him. 2 The king went up to the temple of the
LORD with all the men of Judah and all the
inhabitants of Jerusalem: priests, prophets, and
all the people, small and great. He had the entire
contents of the book of the covenant that had
been found in the temple of the LORD, read out
to them. 3 Standing by the column, the king
made a covenant before the LORD that they
would follow him and observe his ordinances,
statutes and decrees with their whole hearts and
souls, thus reviving the terms of the covenant
which were written in this book. And all the
people stood as participants in the covenant.

4 Then the king commanded the high priest

22, 3: Shaphan: head of a prominent family in the reign of Josiah, secretary to the king, bearer and reader of the newfound book of the law (vv 3–13; 2 Chr 34, 8f. 15–20). He and his sons favored the reform of King Josiah and supported the prophet Jeremiah; cf Jer 26, 24.

r 3–13: 2 Chr 34, 8–21. s 4–7: 2 Kgs 12, 11–16. t 11–20: 2 Chr 34, 19–28. u 1–5: 2 Chr 34, 29–33.

Hilkiah, his vicar, and the doorkeepers to re-
move from the temple of the LORD all the objects
that had been made for Baal, Asherah, and the
whole host of heaven. He had these burned
outside Jerusalem on the slopes of the Kidron
and their ashes carried to Bethel.[v] 5He also put
an end to the pseudo-priests whom the kings of
Judah had appointed to burn incense on the high
places in the cities of Judah and in the vicinity of
Jerusalem, as well as those who burned incense
to Baal, to the sun, moon, and signs of the
Zodiac, and to the whole host of heaven.[w]
6From the temple of the LORD he also removed
the sacred pole, to the Kidron Valley, outside
Jerusalem; there he had it burned and beaten to
dust, which was then scattered over the com-
mon graveyard.[x] 7He tore down the apartments
of the cult prostitutes* which were in the temple
of the LORD, and in which the women wove
garments for the Asherah.[y]

8He brought in all the priests from the cities of
Judah, and then defiled, from Geba to Beer-
sheba, the high places where they had offered
incense. He also tore down the high place of the
satyrs, which was at the entrance of the Gate of
Joshua, governor of the city, to the left as one
enters the city gate.[z] 9The priests of the high
places could not function at the altar of the LORD
in Jerusalem; but they, along with their relatives,
ate the unleavened bread.

10The king also defiled Topheth in the Valley
of Ben-hinnom, so that there would no longer be
any immolation of sons or daughters by fire* in
honor of Molech.[a] 11He did away with the
horses which the kings of Judah had dedicated to
the sun; these were at the entrance of the
temple of the LORD, near the chamber of
Nathan-melech the eunuch, which was in the
large building.* The chariots of the sun he
destroyed by fire. 12He also demolished the
altars made by the kings of Judah on the roof
(the roof terrace of Ahaz), and the altars made by
Manasseh in the two courts of the temple of the
LORD. He pulverized them and threw the dust
into the Kidron Valley.[b] 13The king defiled the
high places east of Jerusalem, south of the
Mount of Misconduct,* which Solomon, king of
Israel, had built in honor of Astarte, the Sidonian
horror, of Chemosh, the Moabite horror, and of
Milcom, the idol of the Ammonites.[c] 14He broke
to pieces the pillars, cut down the sacred poles,
and filled the places where they had been with
human bones.[d] 15Likewise the altar which was
at Bethel, the high place built by Jeroboam, son
of Nebat, who caused Israel to sin—this same
altar and high place he tore down, breaking up
the stones and grinding them to powder, and
burning the Asherah.[e]

16When Josiah turned and saw the graves
there on the mountainside, he ordered the bones
taken from the graves and burned on the altar,
and thus defiled it in fulfillment of the word of
the LORD which the man of God had proclaimed
as Jeroboam was standing by the altar on the
feast day. When the king looked up and saw the
grave of the man of God who had proclaimed
these words, 17he asked, "What is that tomb-
stone I see?" The men of the city replied, "It is
the grave of the man of God who came from
Judah and predicted the very things you have
done to the altar of Bethel." 18[f]"Let him be," he
said, "let no one move his bones." So they left
his bones undisturbed together with the bones of
the prophet who had come from Samaria.*

19Josiah also removed all the shrines on the
high places near the cities of Samaria which the
kings of Israel had erected, thereby provoking
the LORD; he did the very same to them as he
had done in Bethel.[g] 20He slaughtered upon the
altars all the priests of the high places that were

23, 7: Cult prostitutes: of both sexes; cf 1 Kgs 14, 24.

23, 10: Topheth . . . by fire: condemned by Deuteronomic law and denounced by Jeremiah (Dt 12, 31; Jer 7, 29ff; Jer 19).

23, 11: Large building: to the west of the temple area (1 Chr 26, 18), named in the Hebrew by an Egyptian name for a similar construction.

23, 13: Mount of Misconduct: a paranomasia on "Mount of Olives" (in Hebrew Maschit/mishcheh) as suggested by the Targum. Cf Vulgate, "Mount of Offense." Horror . . . idol: in all three phrases here the Hebrew uses a pejorative designation meaning "abomination."

23, 18: From Samaria: more narrowly, from Bethel; cf 1 Kgs 13, 31f.

v 2 Chr 34, 3-5; Sir 49, 3. w Dt 17, 3ff. x Dt 16, 21; 1 Kgs 14, 23. y 1 Kgs 14, 24; Dt 23, 18f. z Dt 12, 2f. a Lv 18, 21. b 2 Kgs 21, 5. c 1 Kgs 11, 7. d Dt 16, 21f; 1 Kgs 14, 23. e 1 Kgs 12, 31f; 13, 32. f 1 Kgs 13, 31. g 2 Chr 34, 6f.

at the shrines, and burned human bones upon
them. Then he returned to Jerusalem.
21 The king issued a command to all the
people to observe the Passover of the LORD, their
God, as it was prescribed in that book of the
covenant.[h] 22 No Passover such as this had been
observed during the period when the Judges
ruled Israel, or during the entire period of the
kings of Israel and the kings of Judah, 23 until the
eighteenth year of King Josiah, when this Pass-
over of the LORD was kept in Jerusalem.
24 Further, Josiah did away with the consulta-
tion of ghosts and spirits, with the household
gods, idols,* and all the other horrors to be seen
in the land of Judah and in Jerusalem, so that he
might carry out the stipulations of the law
written in the book that the priest Helkiah had
found in the temple of the LORD.[i]
25 Before him there had been no king who
turned to the LORD as he did, with his whole
heart, his whole soul, and his whole strength, in
accord with the entire law of Moses; nor could
any after him compare with him.[j]
26 Yet, because of all the provocations that
Manasseh had given, the LORD did not desist
from his fiercely burning anger against Judah.
27 The LORD said: "Even Judah will I put out of
my sight as I did Israel. I will reject this city,
Jerusalem, which I chose, and the temple of
which I said, 'There shall my name be.' "[k]

28 The rest of the acts of Josiah, with all that he
did, are written in the book of the chronicles of
the kings of Judah.[l] 29 In his time Pharaoh Neco,
king of Egypt, went up toward the river Euphra-
tes to the king of Assyria. King Josiah set out to
confront him, but was slain at Megiddo at the
first encounter.[m] 30 His servants brought his body
on a chariot from Megiddo to Jerusalem, where
they buried him in his own grave. Then the
people of the land* took Jehoahaz, son of Josiah,
anointed him, and proclaimed him king to
succeed his father.

Reign of Jehoahaz 31 Jehoahaz was twenty-
three years old when he began to reign, and he
reigned three months in Jerusalem. His mother,
whose name was Hamutal, daughter of Jere-
miah, was from Libnah.[n] 32 He did evil in the
sight of the LORD, just as his forebears had done.
33 Pharaoh Neco took him prisoner at Riblah in
the land of Hamath, thus ending his reign in
Jerusalem. He imposed a fine upon the land of a
hundred talents of silver and a talent of gold.*
34 Pharaoh Neco then appointed Eliakim, son of
Josiah, king in place of his father Josiah; he
changed his name to Jehoiakim. Jehoahaz he
took away with him to Egypt, where he died.
35 Jehoiakim gave the silver and gold to Pharaoh,
but taxed the land to raise the amount Pharaoh
demanded. He exacted the silver and gold from
the people of the land, from each proportion-
ately, to pay Pharaoh Neco.
Reign of Jehoiakim 36 [o]Jehoiakim was twenty-
five years old when he began to reign, and he
reigned eleven years in Jerusalem. His mother's
name was Zebidah, daughter of Pedaiah, from
Rumah. 37 He did evil in the sight of the LORD,
just as his forebears had done.

CHAPTER 24

1 [p]During his reign Nebuchadnezzar, king of
Babylon, moved against him, and Jehoiakim
became his vassal for three years. Then Jehoia-
kim turned and rebelled against him. 2 The LORD
loosed against him bands of Chaldeans, Arame-
ans, Moabites, and Ammonites; he loosed them
against Judah to destroy it, as the LORD had
threatened through his servants the prophets.[q]
3 This befell Judah because the LORD had stated
that he would inexorably put them out of his
sight for the sins Manasseh had committed in all
that he did; 4 and especially because of the
innocent blood he shed, with which he filled
Jerusalem, the LORD would not forgive.[r]
5 The rest of the acts of Jehoiakim, with all that

23, 24: Household gods . . . idols: teraphim. See note on Gn 31, 19.

23, 30. 35: People of the land: in this period, the phrase referred to "landed gentry"; in later times it meant "the poor." Cf 2 Kgs 24, 14.

23, 33: A talent of gold: some manuscripts of the Greek and Syriac texts have "ten talents."

h Dt 16, 1–8; 2 Chr 35, 1ff. 18f. i 2 Kgs 21, 6; Gn 31, 19; Dt 18, 11; Jgs 18, 14. j Dt 6, 5. k 2 Kgs 24, 2. l 2 Chr 35, 26f. m 2 Chr 35, 20–24. n 2 Chr 36, 2f. o 36f: 2 Chr 36, 4f. p 1–5: 2 Chr 36, 6ff. q 2 Kgs 23, 27. r 2 Kgs 21, 16.

he did, are written in the book of the chronicles of the kings of Judah.[s] 6Jehoiakim rested with his ancestors, and his son Jehoiachin succeeded him as king. 7The king of Egypt did not again leave his own land, for the king of Babylon had taken all that belonged to the king of Egypt from the wadi of Egypt to the Euphrates River.

Reign of Jehoiachin 8Jehoiachin was eighteen years old when he began to reign, and he reigned three months* in Jerusalem. His mother's name was Nehushta, daughter of Elnathan of Jerusalem. 9He did evil in the sight of the LORD, just as his forebears had done.

10At that time the officials of Nebuchadnezzar, king of Babylon, attacked Jerusalem, and the city came under siege.[t] 11Nebuchadnezzar, king of Babylon, himself arrived at the city while his servants were besieging it. 12Then Jehoiachin, king of Judah, together with his mother, his ministers, officers, and functionaries, surrendered to the king of Babylon, who, in the eighth year of his reign, took him captive. 13He carried off all the treasures of the temple of the LORD and those of the palace, and broke up all the gold utensils that Solomon, king of Israel, had provided in the temple of the LORD, as the LORD had foretold.[u] 14He deported all Jerusalem: all the officers and men of the army, ten thousand in number, and all the craftsmen and smiths. None were left among the people of the land except the poor. 15He deported Jehoiachin to Babylon, and also led captive from Jerusalem to Babylon the king's mother and wives, his functionaries, and the chief men of the land.[v] 16The king of Babylon also led captive to Babylon all seven thousand men of the army, and a thousand craftsmen and smiths, all of them trained soldiers. 17In place of Jehoiachin, the king of Babylon appointed his uncle Mattaniah king, and changed his name to Zedekiah.

Reign of Zedekiah 18Zedekiah was twenty-one years old when he became king, and he reigned eleven years in Jerusalem. His mother's name was Hamutal, daughter of Jeremiah of Libnah.[w] 19He also did evil in the sight of the LORD, just as Jehoiakim had done. 20The LORD's anger befell Jerusalem and Judah till he cast them out from his presence. Thus Zedekiah rebelled against the king of Babylon.[x]

CHAPTER 25

1*[y] In the tenth month of the ninth year of Zedekiah's reign, on the tenth day of the month, Nebuchadnezzar, king of Babylon, and his whole army advanced against Jerusalem, encamped around it, and built siege walls on every side. 2The siege of the city continued until the eleventh year of Zedekiah. 3On the ninth day of the fourth month, when famine had gripped the city, and the people had no more bread, 4the city walls were breached. Then the king and all the soldiers left the city by night through the gate between the two walls which was near the king's garden. Since the Chaldeans had the city surrounded, they went in the direction of the Arabah. 5But the Chaldean army pursued the king and overtook him in the desert near Jericho, abandoned by his whole army.

6The king was therefore arrested and brought to Riblah to the king of Babylon, who pronounced sentence on him. 7He had Zedekiah's sons slain before his eyes. Then he blinded Zedekiah, bound him with fetters, and had him brought to Babylon.

8On the seventh day of the fifth month (this was in the nineteenth year of Nebuchadnezzar, king of Babylon), Nebuzaradan, captain of the bodyguard, came to Jerusalem as the representative of the king of Babylon. 9He burned the house of the LORD, the palace of the king, and all the houses of Jerusalem; every large building was destroyed by fire.[z] 10Then the Chaldean troops who were with the captain of the guard tore down the walls that surrounded Jerusalem.

11Then Nebuzaradan, captain of the guard, led into exile the last of the people remaining in

24, 8: He reigned three months: in the year 597 B.C.

25, 1–30: This chapter parallels Jer 39 and 52; see notes to those parts of Jeremiah.

25, 11: Those who had deserted: perhaps on the advice of Jeremiah; cf Jer 38, 2f.

s 2 Chr 36, 8. t 2 Chr 36, 10; Dn 1, 1f. u 2 Kgs 20, 17; Is 39, 6. v Est A, 3; 2, 6. w 2 Chr 36, 9; Jer 37, 1f; 52, 1ff. x 2 Kgs 22, 17; 23, 27. y 1–21: Jer 39, 1–10; 52, 4–28. z 2 Chr 36, 19; Ps 74, 7.

the city, and those who had deserted* to the king of Babylon, and the last of the artisans. 12 But some of the country's poor, Nebuzaradan, captain of the guard, left behind as vinedressers and farmers.

13 The bronze pillars that belonged to the house of the LORD, and the wheeled carts and the bronze sea in the house of the LORD, the Chaldeans broke into pieces; they carried away the bronze to Babylon.[a] 14 They took also the pots, the shovels, the snuffers, the bowls, the pans and all the bronze vessels used for service.[b] 15 The fire-holders and the bowls which were of gold or silver the captain of the guard also carried off. 16 The weight in bronze of the two pillars, the bronze sea, and the wheeled carts, all of them furnishings which Solomon had made for the house of the LORD, was never calculated. 17 Each of the pillars was eighteen cubits high; a bronze capital five cubits high surmounted each pillar, and a network with pomegranates encircled the capital, all of bronze; and so for the other pillar, as regards the network.[c]

18 The captain of the guard also took Seraiah the high priest, Zephaniah the second priest, and the three keepers of the entry. 19 And from the city he took one courtier, a commander of soldiers, five men in the personal service of the king who were still in the city, the scribe of the army commander, who mustered the people of the land, and sixty of the common people still remaining in the city. 20 The captain of the guard, Nebuzaradan, arrested these and brought them to the king of Babylon at Riblah; 21 the king had them struck down and put to death in Riblah, in the land of Hamath. Thus was Judah exiled from her land.

Governorship of Gedaliah 22 [d]As for the people whom he had allowed to remain in the land of Judah, Nebuchadnezzar, king of Babylon, appointed as their governor Gedaliah, son of Ahikam, son of Shaphan. 23 Hearing that the king of Babylon had appointed Gedaliah governor, all the army commanders with their men came to him at Mizpah: Ishmael, son of Nethaniah, Johanan, son of Kareah, Seraiah, son of Tanhumeth the Netophathite, and Jaazaniah, from Beth-maacah. 24 Gedaliah gave the commanders and their men his oath. "Do not be afraid of the Chaldean officials," he said to them. "Remain in the country and serve the king of Babylon, and all will be well with you."

25 But in the seventh month Ishmael, son of Nethaniah, son of Elishama, of royal descent, came with ten men, attacked Gedaliah and killed him, along with the Jews and Chaldeans who were in Mizpah with him. 26 Then all the people, great and small, left with the army commanders and went to Egypt for fear of the Chaldeans.

Release of Jehoiachin 27 [e]In the thirty-seventh year of the exile of Jehoiachin, king of Judah, on the twenty-seventh day of the twelfth month, Evil-merodach, king of Babylon, in the inaugural year of his own reign, raised up Jehoiachin, king of Judah, from prison. 28 He spoke kindly to him and gave him a throne higher than that of the other kings who were with him in Babylon. 29 Jehoiachin took off his prison garb and ate at the king's table as long as he lived. 30 The allowance granted him by the king was a perpetual allowance, in fixed daily amounts, for as long as he lived.

a 2 Kgs 16, 17; 1 Kgs 7, 15–39; 2 Chr 3, 15; 36, 18; Jer 27, 19. b 1 Kgs 7, 48ff. c 1 Kgs 7, 15; Jer 52, 21ff. d 22–26: Jer 40, 5. 7–41, 1–3. e 27–30: Jer 52, 31–34.

THE FIRST BOOK OF CHRONICLES

Originally the two books of Chronicles formed, with the Books of Ezra and Nehemiah, a single historical work, uniform in style and basic ideas. The Greek title, paraleipomena, means "things omitted, or passed over (in Samuel and Kings)." The Books of Chronicles, however, are more than a supplement to Samuel and Kings; a comparison of the two histories discloses striking differences in scope and purpose. The Books of Chronicles record in some detail the lengthy span from the reign of Saul to the return from the Exile. Unlike the exact science of history today, wherein factual accuracy and impartiality of judgment are the standards for estimating what is of permanent worth, ancient biblical history, with rare exceptions, was less concerned with reporting in precise detail all the facts of a situation than with explaining the meaning of those facts. Such history was primarily interpretative and, in the Old Testament, its purpose was to disclose the action of the living God in the affairs of men. For this reason we speak of it as "sacred history"; its writer's first concern was to bring out the divine or supernatural dimension in history.

This is apparent when we examine the primary objective of the Chronicler in compiling his work. In view of the situation which confronted the Jewish people at this time (the end of the fifth century B.C.), the Chronicler realized that Israel's political greatness was a thing of the past. It would be a people under God, or nothing. Yet Israel's past held the key to her future. The Chronicler proposed to establish and defend the legitimate claims of the Davidic monarchy in Israel's history, and to underscore the place of Jerusalem and its divinely established temple worship as the center of religious life for the Jewish community of his day. If Judaism was to survive and prosper, it would have to heed the lessons of the past and devoutly serve Yahweh in the place where he had chosen to dwell, the temple of Jerusalem. From the Chronicler's point of view, David's reign was the ideal to which all subsequent rule in Judah must aspire.

The Chronicler was much more interested in David's religious and cultic influence than in his political power. There is little of royal messianism in his book. He apparently regarded as something of the distant past the prophet Zechariah's abortive attempt to have the Davidic kingdom reestablished in the time of Zerubbabel at the end of the sixth century B.C. (Zec 6, 9-15). He saw David's primary importance as deriving from the establishment of Jerusalem and its temple as the center of the true worship of the Lord. Furthermore, he presented David as the one who had authorized the elaborate ritual (which, in point of fact, only gradually evolved in the temple built by Zerubbabel) and who had also appointed Levites to supervise the liturgical services there.

There are good reasons for believing that originally the Books of Ezra and Nehemiah formed the last part of a single literary work that began with 1 and 2 Chronicles. Some authors even regard Ezra himself as having been the anonymous Chronicler. In any case, the Chronicler's Hebrew as well as his religious and political outlook points to c. 400 B.C. as the time of composition of this work.

The Chronicler used sources in writing his history. Besides the canonical Books of Genesis, Exodus, Numbers, Joshua and Ruth, and especially the Books of Samuel and Kings, he cites the titles of many other works no longer extant. "The books of the kings of Israel," or "the books of the kings of Israel and Judah," "the history of Samuel the seer," "the history of Nathan the prophet," "the history of Gad the seer," "the commentary of the Books of Kings," are some of the documents mentioned as historical sources.

In addition, the Chronicler's work contains early preexilic material not found in the Books of Kings. At one time scholars discounted the value of this material, but modern research has shown that, even though the Chronicler may have at times treated the material rather freely, he derived it from authentic and reliable sources.

The principal divisions of 1 Chronicles are as follows:

I. Genealogical Tables (1, 1—9, 34).
II. The History of David (9, 35—29, 30).

I: Genealogical Tables

CHAPTER 1

From Adam to Abraham 1 [a]* Adam, Seth,
Enosh, 2 [b]Kenan, Mahalalel, Jared, 3 Enoch, Me-
thuselah, Lamech, [c] 4 Noah, Shem, Ham, and
Japheth. [d] 5 [e]The descendants of Japheth were
Gomer, Magog, Madai, Javan, Tubal, Meshech,
and Tiras. 6 The descendants of Gomer were
Ashkenaz, Riphath, and Togarmah. 7 The descen-
dants of Javan were Elishah, Tarshis, the Kittim,
and the Rodanim.

8 [f]The descendants of Ham were Cush,
Mesraim, Put, and Canaan. 9 The descendants of
Cush were Seba, Havilah, Sabta, Raama, and
Sabteca. The descendants of Raama were Sheba
and Dedan. 10 Cush became the father of Nim-
rod, who was the first to be a conqueror on the
earth. 11 [g]Mesraim became the father of the
Ludim, Anamim, Lehabim, Naphtuhim, 12 Path-
rusim, Casluhim, and Caphtorim, from whom
the Philistines sprang. 13 Canaan became the
father of Sidon, his first-born, and Heth, 14 and
the Jebusite, the Amorite, the Girgashite, 15 the
Hivite, the Arkite, the Sinite, 16 the Arvadite, the
Zemarite, and the Hamathite.

17 [h]The descendants of Shem were Elam,
Asshur, Arpachshad, Lud, and Aram. The descen-
dants of Aram were Uz, Hul, Gether, and Mash.
18 Arpachshad became the father of Shelah, and
Shelah became the father of Eber. 19 Two sons
were born to Eber; the first was named Peleg
(for in his time the world was divided), and his
brother was Joktan. 20 Joktan became the father
of Almodad, Sheleph, Hazarmaveth, Jerah, 21 Ha-
doram, Uzal, Diklah, 22 Ebal, Abimael, Sheba,
23 Ophir, Havilah, and Jobab; all these were the
sons of Joktan.

24 [i]Shem, Arpachshad, Shelah, 25 Eber, Peleg,
Reu, 26 Serug, Nahor, Terah, 27 Abram, who was
Abraham. [j]

From Abraham to Jacob 28 The sons of Abra-
ham were Isaac and Ishmael. [k] 29 These were
their descendants: [l]

Nebaioth, the first-born of Ishmael, then Ke-
dar, Adbeel, Mibsam, 30 Mishma, Dumah,
Massa, Hadad, Tema, 31 Jetur, Naphish, and Kede-
mah. These were the descendants of Ishmael.

32 [m]The descendants of Keturah, Abraham's
concubine: she bore Zimran, Jokshan, Medan,
Midian, Ishbak, and Shuah. The sons of Jokshan
were Sheba and Dedan. 33 The descendants of
Midian were Ephah, Epher, Hanoch, Abida, and
Eldaah. All these were the descendants of Ketu-
rah.

34 Abraham became the father of Isaac. The
sons of Isaac were Esau and Israel. [n]

35 [o]The sons of Esau were Eliphaz, Reuel,
Jeush, Jalam, and Korah. 36 The sons of Eliphaz
were Teman, Omar, Zephi, Gatam, Kenaz,
[Timna,] and Amalek. 37 The sons of Reuel were
Nahath, Zerah, Shammah, and Mizzah.

1, 1—9, 34: The Chronicler set as his task the retelling, from his particular viewpoint, of the story of God's people from the beginning to his own day. Since his primary interest was the history of David and the Davidic dynasty of Judah, he presents through mere genealogical lists a summary of what preceded the reign of Saul, David's predecessor in the kingdom. The sources for these genealogies are mostly the canonical Hebrew Scriptures that were already in their present form in his time. The cross references in this book indicate in each case the scriptural sources used.

a 1 Chr 4, 25f; Gn 5, 3. 6. 9. b 2ff: Gn 5, 9–32; 10, 2ff. c Gn 4, 25. d Gn 5, 32; 6, 10; 9, 18. e 5ff: Gn 10, 2ff. f Gn 10, 8. g 11–16: Gn 10, 13–18. h 17–23: Gn 10, 22–29; 11, 10–18. i 24–27: Gn 11, 10–26; Lk 3, 34ff. j Gn 17, 5; Neh 9, 7. k Gn 16, 11. 15; 21, 2f; Gal 4, 22f; Heb 11, 11. l 29ff: Gn 25, 13–16. m 32f: Gn 25, 1–4. n Gn 21, 2f; 25, 19. 25f: 32, 28f; Mt 1, 2; Lk 3, 34. o 35ff: Gn 36, 4f. 10–13. 15ff.

38 [p]The descendants of Seir* were Lotan, Sho-
bal, Zibeon, Anah, Dishon, Ezer, and Dishan.
39 The sons of Lotan were Hori and Homam;
Timna was the sister of Lotan. 40 The sons of
Shobal were Alian, Manahath, Ebal, Shephi,
and Onam. The sons of Zibeon were Aiah and
Anah. 41 The sons of Anah: Dishon. The sons of
Dishon were Hemdan, Eshban, Ithran, and Che-
ran. 42 The sons of Ezer were Bilhan, Zaavan,
and Jaakan. The sons of Dishan were Uz and
Aran.

43 [q]The kings who reigned in the land of Edom
before they had Israelite kings were the follow-
ing: Bela, son of Beor, the name of whose city
was Ninhabah. 44 When Bela died, Jobab, son of
Zerah, from Bozrah, succeeded him.[r] 45 When
Jobab died, Husham, from the land of the
Temanites, succeeded him.[s] 46 Husham died and
Hadad, son of Bedad, succeeded him. He over-
threw the Midianites on the Moabite plateau,
and the name of his city was Avith. 47 Hadad died
and Samlah of Masrekah succeeded him. 48 Sam-
lah died and Shaul from Rehoboth-han-nahar
succeeded him. 49 When Shaul died, Baal-hanan,
son of Achbor, succeeded him. 50 Baal-hanan
died and Hadad succeeded him. The name of his
city was Pai, and his wife's name was Meheta-
bel. She was the daughter of Matred, who was
the daughter of Mezahab. 51 [t]After Hadad
died . . . .

These were the chiefs of Edom: the chiefs of
Timna, Aliah, Jetheth, 52 Oholibamah, Elah, Pi-
non, 53 Kenaz, Teman, Mibzar, 54 Magdiel, and
Iram were the chiefs of Edom.

CHAPTER 2

1 These were the sons of Israel: Reuben,
Simeon, Levi, Judah, Issachar, Zebulun,[u] 2 Dan,
Joseph, Benjamin, Naphtali, Gad, and Asher.[v]
Judah 3 The sons of Judah* were: Er, Onan, and
Shelah; these three were born to him of Bath-
shua, a Canaanite woman. But Judah's first-born,
Er, was wicked in the sight of the LORD, so he
killed him.[w] 4 Judah's daughter-in-law Tamar
bore him Perez and Zerah, so that he had five
sons in all.[x]

5 The sons of Perez were Hezron and Hamul.[y]
6 The sons of Zerah were Zimri, Ethan, Heman,
Calcol, and Darda—five in all.[z] 7 The sons of
Zimri: Carmi. The sons of Carmi: Achar, who
brought trouble upon Israel by violating the
ban.[a] 8 The sons of Ethan: Azariah. 9 The sons
born to Hezron were Jerahmeel, Ram, and
Chelubai.[b] *

10 *Ram became the father of Amminadab,
and Amminadab became the father of Nahshon,
a prince of the Judahites.[c] 11 [d]Nahshon became
the father of Salma. Salma became the father of
Boaz. 12 Boaz became the father of Obed. Obed
became the father of Jesse. 13 [e]Jesse became the
father of Eliab, his first-born, of Abinadab, the
second son, Shimea, the third,[f] 14 Nethanel, the
fourth, Raddai, the fifth, 15 Ozem, the sixth, and
David, the seventh. 16 Their sisters were Zeruiah
and Abigail. Zeruiah had three sons: Abishai,
Joab, and Asahel.[g] 17 Abigail bore Amasa, whose
father was Jether the Ishmaelite.[h]

18 *By his wife Azubah, Caleb, son of Hezron,
became the father of a daughter, Jerioth. Her
sons were Jesher, Shobab, and Ardon.[i] 19 When
Azubah died, Caleb married Ephrath, who bore
him Hur.[j] 20 Hur became the father of Uri, and

1, 38: Seir: another name for Esau (v 35) or Edom (v 43).

2, 3—4, 23: For two reasons, the Chronicler places the genealogy of the tribe of Judah before that of the other tribes, giving it also at greater length than the others: because of his interest in David and because in the Chronicler's time the people of God were almost exclusively Jews. Both David and the Jews were of the tribe of Judah.

2, 9: Chelubai: a variant form of the name Caleb (vv 18. 42), distinct from Chelub of 1 Chr 4, 11.

2, 10–17: Immediate ancestors of David. A similar list is given in Ru 4, 19–22; each list, independent of the other, derives from a common source.

2, 18–24: Descendants of Caleb. In 1 Chr 4, 15, as is often the case in the Pentateuch (Nm 13, 6; 14, 6. 30; 26, 65; etc.), Caleb is called son of Jephunneh. Here he is called son of Hezron, perhaps because the Calebites were reckoned as part of the clan of the Hezronites.

p 38–42; Gn 36, 20–28. q 43–54: Gn 36, 31–43. r Is 34, 6; 63, 1; Jer 49, 13. 22. s Gn 36, 11; Jb 2, 11; Jer 49, 7. 20. t 51–54: Gn 36, 40–43. u Gn 29, 32–35; 30, 18. 20; 35, 23. v Gn 30, 6. 8. 11. 13. 24; 35, 18. 24ff. w 1 Chr 4, 21; Gn 38, 1–5; 46, 12. x Gn 38, 7. 13–30; 46, 12; Rv 4, 12. 18; Mt 1, 3. y Gn 46, 12. z 1 Kgs 5, 11. a Jos 7, 1. 18ff. 24f; 22, 20. b Rv 4, 19; Mt 1, 3. c Rv 4, 19; Mt 1, 4. d 11f: Nm 1, 7; Rv 4, 20f; Mt 1, 4f. e 13ff: 1 Sm 16, 6–13; 17, 13f. f 2 Chr 11, 18. g 2 Sm 2, 18. h 2 Sm 17, 25; 19, 14; 20, 4–13. i 1 Chr 2, 24. j 1 Chr 2, 24.

Uri became the father of Bezalel.[k] 21 Then Hez-
ron had relations with the daughter of Machir,
the father of Gilead, having married her when he
was sixty years old. She bore him Segub.[l]
22 Segub became the father of Jair,[m] who pos-
sessed twenty-three cities in the land of Gilead.
23 Geshur and Aram took from them the villages
of Jair, that is, Kenath and its towns, sixty cities
in all, which had belonged to the sons of Machir,
the father of Gilead.[n] 24 After the death of
Hezron, Caleb had relations with Ephrathah, the
widow of his father Hezron, and she bore him
Ashhur, the father of Tekoa.[o]
25 The sons of Jerahmeel,* the first-born of
Hezron, were Ram, the first-born, then Bunah,
Oren, and Ozem, his brothers.[p] 26 Jerahmeel also
had another wife, Atarah by name, who was the
mother of Onam. 27 The sons of Ram, the first-
born of Jerahmeel, were Maaz, Jamin, and Eker.
28 The sons of Onam were Shammai and Jada.
The sons of Shammai were Nadab and Abishur.
29 Abishur's wife, who was named Abihail, bore
him Ahban and Molid. 30 The sons of Nadab
were Seled and Appaim. Seled died without
sons. 31 The sons of Appaim: Ishi. The sons of
Ishi: Sheshan. The sons of Sheshan: Ahlai.[q]
32 The sons of Jada, the brother of Shammai,
were Jether and Jonathan. Jether died without
sons. 33 The sons of Jonathan were Peleth and
Zaza. These were the descendants of Jerahmeel.
34 Sheshan, who had no sons, only daughters,
had an Egyptian slave named Jarha. 35 Sheshan
gave his daughter in marriage to his slave Jarha,
and she bore him Attai. 36 Attai became the
father of Nathan. Nathan became the father of
Zabad. 37 Zabad became the father of Ephlal.
Ephlal became the father of Obed. 38 Obed
became the father of Jehu. Jehu became the
father of Azariah. 39 Azariah became the father of
Helez. Helez became the father of Eleasah.
40 Eleasah became the father of Sismai. Sismai
became the father of Shallum. 41 Shallum be-
came the father of Jekamiah. Jekamiah became
the father of Elishama.
42 The descendants of Caleb,* the brother of
Jerahmeel: [Mesha] his first-born, who was the
father of Ziph. Then the sons of Mareshah, who
was the father of Hebron. 43 The sons of Hebron
were Korah, Tappuah, Rekem, and Shema.
44 Shema became the father of Raham, who was
the father of Jorkeam. Rekem became the father
of Shammai. 45 The sons of Shammai: Maon,
who was the father of Beth-zur. 46 Ephah, Ca-
leb's concubine, bore Haran, Moza, and Gazez.
Haran became the father of Gazez. 47 The sons of
Jahdai were Regem, Jotham, Geshan, Pelet,
Ephah, and Shaaph. 48 Maacah, Caleb's concu-
bine, bore Sheber and Tirhanah. 49 She also bore
Shaaph, the father of Madmannah, Sheva, the
father of Machbenah, and the father of Gibea.
Achsah was Caleb's daughter.[r]
50 These were descendants of Caleb, sons of
Hur,* the first-born of Ephrathah: Shobal, the
father of Kiriath-jearim, 51 Salma, the father of
Bethlehem, and Hareph, the father of Beth-
gader. 52 The sons of Shobal, the father of Kiriath-
jearim, were Reaiah, half the Manahathites,
53 and the clans of Kiriath-jearim: the Ithrites, the
Puthites, the Shumathites, and the Mishraites.
From these the people of Zorah and the Eshtao-
lites derived.[s] 54 The descendants of Salma were
Bethlehem, the Netophathites, Atroth-beth-Joab,
half the Manahathites, and the Zorites. 55 [t]The
clans of the Sopherim dwelling in Jabez were the
Tirathites, the Shimeathites, and the Sucathites.
They were the Kenites, who came from Ham-
math of the ancestor of the Rechabites.

CHAPTER 3

1 [u]The following* were the sons of David who
were born to him in Hebron: the first-born,
Amnon, by Ahinoam of Jezreel; the second,
Daniel,* by Abigail of Carmel; 2 the third, Absa-
lom, son of Maacah, who was the daughter of

2, 25–41: The Jerahmeelites were a clan in the Negeb of Judah.
2, 42–49: Another list, dating from preexilic times, of the Calebites, a clan that inhabited the south of Judah.
2, 50–55: The Hurites, a clan dwelling to the south and west of Jerusalem and related to the Calebites.
3, 1–9: David's sons.
3, 1: Daniel: called Chileab in 2 Sm 3, 3.

k Ex 24, 14; 31, 2; 35, 30; 2 Chr 1, 5. l Nm 26, 29; 27, 1; 32, 32; Jos 13, 31; Jgs 5, 14. m Nm 32, 41; 1 Kgs 4, 13. n Dt 3, 14; Jos 13, 30; Jgs 10, 4. o 1 Chr 2, 19; 2 Sm 14, 2; 2 Chr 11, 6. p 1 Sm 27, 10; 30, 29; Jb 32, 2. q 1 Chr 4, 20. r Jos 15, 16; Jgs 1, 12. s Jgs 18, 2. t Nm 24, 21; Jgs 1, 16; 4, 11; 1 Sm 15, 6. u 1–4: 2 Sm 3, 2–5.

Talmai, king of Geshur; the fourth, Adonijah,
son of Haggith; 3 the fifth, Shephatiah, by Abital;
the sixth, Ithream, by his wife Eglah. 4 Six in all
were born to him in Hebron, where he reigned
seven years and six months. Then he reigned
thirty-three years in Jerusalem,[v] 5 [w]where the
following were born to him: Shimea,* Shobab,
Nathan, Solomon—four by Bathsheba, the
daughter of Ammiel,[x] 6 Ibhar, Elishua, Eliphelet,
7 Nogah, Nepheg, Japhia, 8 Elishama, Eliada, and
Eliphelet—nine. 9 All these were sons of David,
in addition to other sons by concubines; and
Tamar was their sister.[y]

10 [z]* The son of Solomon was Rehoboam,
whose son was Abijah, whose son was Asa,
whose son was Jehoshaphat,[a] 11 whose son was
Joram, whose son was Ahaziah, whose son was
Joash,[b] 12 whose son was Amaziah, whose son
was Azariah, whose son was Jotham,[c] 13 whose
son was Ahaz, whose son was Hezekiah, whose
son was Manasseh,[d] 14 whose son was Amon,
whose son was Josiah.[e] 15 The sons of Josiah
were: the first-born, Johanan; the second, Jehoia-
kim; the third, Zedekiah; the fourth, Shallum.*[f]
16 The sons of Jehoiakim were: Jeconiah, his son;
Zedekiah, his son.[g]

17 The sons of Jeconiah* the captive were:
Shealtiel,[h] 18 Malchiram, Pedaiah, Shenazzar,*
Jekamiah, Shama, and Nedabiah. 19 The sons of
Pedaiah were Zerubbabel* and Shimei. The sons
of Zerubbabel were Meshullam and Hananiah;
Shelomith was their sister. 20 The sons of Meshul-
lam were Hashubah, Ohel, Berechiah, Hasadiah,
Jushab-hesed—five. 21 The sons of Hananiah
were Pelatiah, Jeshaiah, Rephaiah, Arnan, Oba-
diah, and Shecaniah. 22 [i]The sons of Shecaniah
were Shemiah, Hattush, Igal, Bariah, Neariah,
Shaphat—six. 23 The sons of Neariah were Elioe-
nai, Hizkiah, and Azrikam—three. 24 The sons of
Elioenai were Hodaviah, Eliashib, Pelaiah, Ak-
kub, Johanan, Delaiah, and Anani—seven.

CHAPTER 4

1 *The descendants of Judah were: Perez,
Hezron, Carmi, Hur, and Shobal.[j] 2 Reaiah, the
son of Shobal, became the father of Jahath, and
Jahath became the father of Ahumai and Lahad.
These were the clans of the Zorathites.

3 These were the descendants of Hareph, the
father of Etam: Jezreel, Ishma, and Idbash; their
sister was named Hazzelelponi. 4 Penuel was the
father of Gedor, and Ezer the father of Hushah.
These were the descendants of Hur, the first-
born of Ephrathah, the father of Bethlehem.

5 Ashhur, the father of Tekoa, had two wives,
Helah and Naarah.[k] 6 Naarah bore him Ahuz-
zam, Hepher, the Temenites and the
Ahashtarites. These were the descendants of
Naarah. 7 The sons of Helah were Zereth, Izhar,
Ethnan, and Koz. 8 Koz became the father of
Anub and Zobebah, as well as of the clans of
Aharhel, son of Harum. 9 Jabez was the most
distinguished of the brothers. His mother had
named him Jabez, saying, "I bore him with
pain." 10 Jabez prayed to the God of Israel: "Oh,
that you may truly bless me and extend my
boundaries! Help me and make me free of
misfortune, without pain!" And God granted his
prayer.

11 Chelub, the brother of Shuhah, became the

3, 5: Shimea: called Shammua in 2 Sm 5, 14. Ammiel: called Eliam in 2 Sm 11, 3.

3, 10–16: The kings of Judah from Solomon to the destruction of Jerusalem by the Babylonians.

3, 15: Shallum: the same as Jehoahaz, Josiah's successor; cf Jer 22, 11.

3, 17–24: The descendants of King Jechoniah up to the time of the Chronicler. If twenty-five years are allowed to each generation, the ten generations between Jechoniah and Anani (the last name on the list) would bring the birth of the latter to about 405 B.C.—an important item in establishing the approximate date of the Chronicler.

3, 18: Shenazzar: presumably the same as Sheshbazzar of Ezr 1, 8. 11; 5, 14ff, the prince of Judah who was the first Jewish governor of Judah after the exile. Both forms of the name probably go back to the Babylonian name Sin-ab-ussar signifying, "O [god] Sin, protect [our] father!"

3, 19: Zerubbabel: here called the son of Pedaiah, though elsewhere (Hg 1, 12. 14; 2, 2. 23; Ezr 3, 2. 8; 5, 2; Neh 12, 1) called son of Shealtiel. The latter term may merely mean that Zerubbabel succeeded Shealtiel as head of the house of David.

4, 1–43: The southern tribes.

v 2 Sm 2, 11; 5, 5. w 5–8: 2 Sm 5, 14ff. x 2 Sm 5, 5. y 2 Sm 13, 1f. z 10–17: Mt 1, 7–12. a 1 Kgs 11, 43; 14, 31; 15, 1. 8. 24; 2 Chr 9, 31; 12, 16; 13, 23; 17, 1. b 1 Kgs 22, 51; 2 Chr 21, 1; 22, 1; 24, 1. 27. c 2 Kgs 12, 21; 14, 21; 15, 7; 2 Chr 25, 1; 26, 1. 23; 27, 1. d 2 Kgs 15, 38; 16, 20; 20, 21; 2 Chr 28, 1. 27; 32, 33. e 2 Kgs 21, 18. 26; 2 Chr 33, 20. 25. f 2 Kgs 23, 34; 24, 17; 2 Chr 36, 4. 10. g 2 Kgs 24, 6. 17; 2 Chr 36, 8. 10. h 17. 19; Ezr 2, 2; 3, 2. 8; 5, 2; Sir 49, 11; Hg 1, 1. 12. 14; Mt 1, 12f; Lk 3, 27. i Neh 3, 29. j 1 Chr 2, 4f. 7. 9. 50; Gn 38, 29; 46, 12; Mt 1, 3. k 1 Chr 2, 24.

father of Mehir, who was the father of Eshton.
[12]Eshton became the father of Beth-rapha, Pa-
seah, and Tehinnah, the father of the city of
Nahash. These were the men of Recah.

[13]The sons of Kenaz were Othniel and Sera-
iah. The sons of Othniel were Hathath and
Meonothai;[l] [14]Meonothai became the father of
Ophrah. Seraiah became the father of Joab, the
father of Geharashim, so called because they
were craftsmen. [15]The sons of Caleb, son of
Jephunneh, were Ir, Elah, and Naam. The sons
of Elah were . . . and Kenaz.[m] [16]The sons of
Jehallelel were Ziph, Ziphah, Tiria, and Asarel.
[17]The sons of Ezrah were Jether, Mered, Epher,
and Jalon. Jether became the father of Miriam,
Shammai, and Ishbah, the father of Eshtemoa.
[. . . . . .][n] [18]His (Mered's) Egyptian wife bore
Jared, the father of Gedor, Heber, the father of
Soco, and Jekuthiel, the father of Zanoah. These
were the sons of Bithiah, the daughter of Pha-
raoh, whom Mered married. [19]The sons of his
Jewish wife, the sister of Naham, the father of
Keilah, were Shimon the Garmite and Ishi the
Maacathite. [20]The sons of Shimon were Amnon,
Rinnah, Ben-hanan, and Tilon. The son of Ishi
was Zoheth and the son of Zoheth . . . .

[21]The descendants of Shelah, son of Judah,
were: Er, the father of Lecah; Laadah, the father
of Mareshah; the clans of the linen weavers'
guild in Beth-ashbea;[o] [22]Jokim; the men of
Cozeba; and Joash and Saraph, who held prop-
erty in Moab, but returned to Bethlehem. [These
are events of old.] [23]They were potters and
inhabitants of Netaim and Gederah, where they
lived in the king's service.

Simeon [24]The sons of Simeon were Nemuel,
Jamin, Jachin, Zerah, and Shaul,[p] [25]whose son
was Shallum, whose son was Mibsam, whose
son was Mishma. [26]The descendants of Mishma
were his son Hammuel, whose son was Zaccur,
whose son was Shimei. [27]Shimei had sixteen
sons and six daughters. His brothers, however,
did not have many sons, and as a result all their
clans did not equal the number of the Judahites.

[28][q]They dwelt in Beer-sheba, Moladah,
Hazar-shual, [29]Bilhah, Ezem, Tolad, [30]Bethuel,
Hormah, Ziklag, [31]Beth-marcaboth, Hazar-
susim, Beth-biri, and Shaaraim. Until David
came to reign, these were their cities [32]and their
villages. Etam, also, and Ain, Rimmon, Tochen,
and Ashan—five cities, [33]together with all their
outlying villages as far as Baal. Here is where
they dwelt, and so it was inscribed of them in
their family records.

[34]Meshobab, Jamlech, Joshah, son of Ama-
ziah, [35]Joel, Jehu, son of Joshibiah, son of Sera-
iah, son of Asiel, [36]Elioenai, Jaakobath, Jeshoha-
iah, Asaiah, Adiel, Jesimiel, Benaiah, [37]Ziza, son
of Shiphi, son of Allon, son of Jedaiah, son of
Shimri, son of Shemaiah— [38]these just named
were princes in their clans, and their ancestral
houses spread out to such an extent[r] [39]that they
went to the approaches of Gedor,* east of the
valley, seeking pasture for their flocks. [40]They
found abundant and good pastures, and the land
was spacious, quiet, and peaceful. [41]They who
have just been listed by name set out during the
reign of Hezekiah, king of Judah, and attacked
the tents of Ham (for Hamites dwelt there
formerly) and also the Meunites who were
there. They pronounced against them the ban
that is still in force and dwelt in their place
because they found pasture there for their
flocks.[s]

[42]Five hundred of them (the Simeonites) went
to Mount Seir under the leadership of Pelatiah,
Neariah, Rephaiah, and Uzziel, sons of Ishi.
[43]They attacked the surviving Amalekites who
had escaped, and have resided there to the
present day.[t]

CHAPTER 5

Reuben [1]*The sons of Reuben, the first-born
of Israel. (He was indeed the first-born, but

4, 39: Gedor: in the Greek, Gerar, no doubt correct.
5, 1–26: The Transjordan tribes.

l Jos 15, 17; Jgs 1, 13; 3, 9. 11. m Nm 13, 6; 14, 6; 32, 12; Jos 14, 6. 14. n 1 Sm 30, 28. o 1 Chr 2, 3; Gn 38, 5; 46, 12; Nm 26, 20. p Gn 46, 10; Ex 6, 15; Nm 26, 12f. q 28–32: Jos 19, 2–8. r Nm 1, 2. s 2 Kgs 18, 1f; 2 Chr 29, 1. t Ex 17, 8. 14; Dt 25, 17ff; 1 Sm 14, 48; 15, 3. 7f; 2 Sm 8, 12.

because he disgraced the couch of his father his birthright was given to the sons of Joseph, son of Israel, so that he is not listed in the family records according to birthright.[u] [2]Judah, in fact, became powerful among his brothers, so that the ruler came from him, though the birthright had been Joseph's.)[v] [3]The sons of Reuben, the first-born of Israel, were Hanoch, Pallu, Hezron, and Carmi.[w] [4]His son was Joel, whose son was Shemaiah, whose son was Gog, whose son was Shimei, [5]whose son was Micah, whose son was Reaiah, whose son was Baal, [6]whose son was Beerah, whom Tiglath-pileser, the king of Assyria, took into exile; he was a prince of the Reubenites.[x] [7]His brothers who belonged to his clans, when they were listed in the family records according to their descendants, were: Jeiel, the chief, and Zechariah, [8]and Bela, son of Azaz, son of Shema, son of Joel. The Reubenites lived in Aroer and as far as Nebo and Baal-meon;[y] [9]toward the east they dwelt as far as the desert which extends from the Euphrates River, for they had much livestock in the land of Gilead.[z] [10]During the reign of Saul they waged war with the Hagrites, and when they had defeated them they occupied their tents throughout the region east of Gilead.[a]

Gad [11]The Gadites lived alongside them in the land of Bashan as far as Salecah.[b] [12]Joel was chief, Shapham was second in command, and Janai was judge in Bashan.[c] [13]Their brothers, corresponding to their ancestral houses, were: Michael, Meshullam, Sheba, Jorai, Jacan, Zia, and Eber—seven. [14]These were the sons of Abihail, son of Huri, son of Jaroah, son of Gilead, son of Michael, son of Jeshishai, son of Jahdo, son of Buz. [15]Ahi, son of Abdiel, son of Guni, was the head of their ancestral houses. [16]They dwelt in Gilead, in Bashan and its towns, and in all the pasture lands of Sirion to the borders. [17]All were listed in the family records in the time of Jotham, king of Judah, and of Jeroboam, king of Israel.

[18]The Reubenites, Gadites, and half-tribe of Manasseh were warriors, men who bore shield and sword and who drew the bow, trained in warfare—forty-four thousand seven hundred and sixty men fit for military service. [19]When they waged war against the Hagrites and against Jetur, Naphish, and Nodab,[d] [20]they received help so that they mastered the Hagrites and all who were with them. For during the battle they called on God, and he heard them because they had put their trust in him.[e] [21]Along with one hundred thousand men they also captured their livestock: fifty thousand camels, two hundred fifty thousand sheep, and two thousand asses. [22]Many had fallen in battle, for victory is from God; and they took over their dwelling place until the time of the exile.[f]

East Manasseh [23]The numerous members of the half-tribe of Manasseh lived in the land of Bashan as far as Baal-hermon, Senir, and Mount Hermon. [24]The following were the heads of their ancestral houses: Epher, Ishi, Eliel, Azriel, Jeremiah, Hodaviah, and Jahdiel—men who were warriors, famous men, and heads over their ancestral houses.

[25]However, they offended the God of their fathers by lusting after the gods of the natives of the land, whom God had cleared out of their way.[g] [26]Therefore the God of Israel incited against them the anger of Pul,* king of Assyria, and of Tiglath-pileser, king of Assyria, who deported the Reubenites, the Gadites, and the half-tribe of Manasseh and brought them to Halah, Habor, and Hara, and to the river Gozan, where they have remained to this day.[h]

Levi* [27]The sons of Levi were Gershon, Kohath, and Merari.[i] [28]The sons of Kohath were Amram, Izhar, Hebron, and Uzziel.[j] [29]The children of Amram were Aaron, Moses, and Miriam. The sons of Aaron were Nadab, Abihu,

5, 26: Pul: the name which the Assyrian king Tiglath-pileser III (745–727 B.C.) took as king of Babylon.

5, 27—6, 66: The tribe of Levi. The list gives special prominence to Levi's son Kohath, from whom were descended both the Aaronite priests (1 Chr 5, 28–41) and the leading group of temple singers (1 Chr 6, 18–23).

u Gn 35, 22; 48, 5. 15–22; 49, 3f; Dt 33, 6. v 1 Chr 28, 4; Gn 49, 8ff. w Gn 46, 9; Ex 6, 14; Nm 26, 5f. x 2 Kgs 15, 29. y Jos 13, 9. 16f; Nm 32, 3. 38. z Jos 22, 9. a Ps 83, 6. b Jos 13, 11. 24–28. c Gn 46, 16. d 1 Chr 1, 31; 5, 10; Gn 25, 15; Ps 83, 6. e Dt 33, 20f. f Nm 32, 39; Dt 3, 8ff; Jgs 3, 3. g Ex 34, 14ff; 2 Kgs 17, 7. h 2 Kgs 15, 9. 29; 17, 6. i 1 Chr 6, 1; 23, 6; Gn 46, 11; Ex 6, 16; Nm 26, 57. j 1 Chr 6, 3; Ex 6, 18.

Eleazar, and Ithamar.[k] 30*Eleazar became the
father of Phinehas. Phinehas became the father
of Abishua. 31Abishua became the father of
Bukki. Bukki became the father of Uzzi. 32Uzzi
became the father of Zerahiah. Zerahiah be-
came the father of Meraioth. 33Meraioth be-
came the father of Amariah. Amariah became
the father of Ahitub. 34Ahitub became the fa-
ther of Zadok. Zadok became the father of
Ahimaaz. 35Ahimaaz became the father of Aza-
riah. Azariah became the father of Johanan.
36Johanan became the father of Azariah, who
served as priest in the temple Solomon built in
Jerusalem. 37Azariah became the father of Ama-
riah. Amariah became the father of Ahitub.
38Ahitub became the father of Zadok. Zadok
became the father of Shallum. 39Shallum be-
came the father of Hilkiah. Hilkiah became the
father of Azariah. 40Azariah became the father
of Seraiah. Seraiah became the father of Jehoza-
dak. 41Jehozadak was one of those who went
into the exile which the LORD inflicted on Ju-
dah and Jerusalem through Nebuchadnezzar.

CHAPTER 6

1The sons of Levi were Gershon, Kohath, and
Merari.[l] 2The sons of Gershon were named
Libni and Shimei.[m] 3The sons of Kohath were
Amram, Izhar, Hebron, and Uzziel.[n] 4 [o]The sons
of Merari were Mahli and Mushi.

The following were the clans of Levi, distrib-
uted according to their ancestors: 5of Gershon:
his son Libni, whose son was Jahath, whose son
was Zimmah, 6whose son was Joah, whose son
was Iddo, whose son was Zerah, whose son was
Jetherai.

7The descendants of Kohath were: his son
Amminadab, whose son was Korah, whose son
was Assir, 8whose son was Elkanah, whose son
was Ebiasaph, whose son was Assir, 9whose son
was Tahath, whose son was Uriel, whose son
was Uzziah, whose son was Shaul. 10The sons of
Elkanah were Amasai and Ahimoth, 11whose
son was Elkanah, whose son was Zophai, whose
son was Nahath, 12whose son was Eliab, whose
son was Jeroham, whose son was Elkanah,
whose son was Samuel. 13The sons of Samuel
were Joel, the first-born, and Abijah, the second.

14The descendants of Merari were Mahli,
whose son was Libni, whose son was Shimei,
whose son was Uzzah,[p] 15whose son was
Shimea, whose son was Haggiah, whose son was
Asaiah.

16The following were entrusted by David with
the choir services* in the LORD's house from the
time when the ark had obtained a permanent
resting place. 17They served as singers before the
Dwelling of the meeting tent until Solomon built
the temple of the LORD in Jerusalem, and they
performed their services in an order prescribed
for them. 18Those who so performed are the
following, together with their descendants.

Among the Kohathites: Heman, the chanter,
son of Joel, son of Samuel, 19son of Elkanah, son
of Jeroham, son of Eliel, son of Toah, 20son of
Zuth, son of Elkanah, son of Mahath, son of
Amasi, 21son of Elkanah, son of Joel, son of
Azariah, son of Zephaniah, 22son of Tahath, son
of Assir, son of Ebiasaph, son of Korah,[q] 23son of
Izhar, son of Kohath, son of Levi, son of Israel.
24His brother Asaph stood at his right hand.
Asaph was the son of Berechiah, son of Shimea,
25son of Michael, son of Baaseiah, son of Malchi-
jah, 26son of Ethni, son of Zerah, son of Adaiah,
27son of Ethan, son of Zimmah,[r] son of Shimei,
28son of Jahath, son of Gershon, son of Levi.

29Their brothers, the Merarites, stood at the
left: Ethan, son of Kishi, son of Abdi, son of
Malluch, 30son of Hashabiah, son of Amaziah,
son of Hilkiah, 31son of Amzi, son of Bani, son of
Shemer, 32son of Mahli, son of Mushi, son of
Merari, son of Levi.[s]

5, 30–41: The line of preexilic priests. The list seems to be confused in vv 36ff, which repeat the names, mostly in inverse order, that occur in vv 34f. A similar but shorter list is given, with variations, in Ezr 7, 1–5.

6, 16–32: The origin of the choir services performed by the levitical families in the postexilic temple at the time of the Chronicler is here attributed to David, somewhat as all the laws in the Pentateuch are attributed to Moses.

k Ex 6, 20; Nm 26, 59f. **l** 1 Chr 5, 27; 23, 6; Gn 46, 11; Ex 6, 16; Nm 26, 57. **m** Ex 6, 17. **n** Ex 6, 18; Nm 3, 19; 26, 59. **o** 1 Chr 6, 14; Ex 6, 19; Nm 3, 20; 26, 58. **p** 1 Chr 6, 4; Ex 6, 19; Nm 3, 20; 26, 58. **q** Ex 6, 24. **r** 1 Chr 6, 2. 5. **s** Ex 6, 19; Nm 26, 58.

33 Their brother Levites were appointed to all other services of the Dwelling of the house of God.[t] 34 However, it was Aaron and his descendants who burnt the offerings on the altar of holocausts and on the altar of incense; they alone had charge of the holy of holies and of making atonement for Israel, as Moses, the servant of God, had ordained.[u]

35 These were the descendants of Aaron: his son Eleazer, whose son was Phinehas, whose son was Abishua, 36 whose son was Bukki, whose son was Uzzi, whose son was Zerahiah, 37 whose son was Meraioth, whose son was Amariah, whose son was Ahitub, 38 whose son was Zadok, whose son was Ahimaaz.

39 *The following were their dwelling places to which their encampment was limited. To the descendants of Aaron who belonged to the clan of the Kohathites, since the first lot fell to them, 40 was assigned Hebron with its adjacent pasture lands in the land of Judah, 41 although the open country and the villages belonging to the city had been given to Caleb, the son of Jephunneh. 42 There were assigned to the descendants of Aaron: Hebron, a city of asylum, Libnah with its pasture lands, Jattir with its pasture lands, Eshtemoa with its pasture lands, 43 Holon with its pasture lands, Debir with its pasture lands, 44 Ashan with its pasture lands, Jetta with its pasture lands, and Beth-shemesh with its pasture lands. 45 Also from the tribe of Benjamin: Gibeon with its pasture lands, Geba with its pasture lands, Almon with its pasture lands, Anathoth with its pasture lands. In all, they had thirteen cities with their pasture lands. 49 The Israelites assigned these cities with their pasture lands to the Levites, 50 designating them by name and assigning them by lot from the tribes of the Judahites, Simeonites, and Benjaminites.

46 The other Kohathites obtained ten cities by lot for their clans from the tribe of Ephraim, from the tribe of Dan, and from the half-tribe of Manasseh. 47 The clans of the Gershonites obtained thirteen cities from the tribes of Issachar, Asher, and Naphtali, and from the half-tribe of Manasseh in Bashan. 48 The clans of the Merarites obtained twelve cities by lot from the tribes of Reuben, Gad, and Zebulun.

51 The clans of the Kohathites obtained cities by lot from the tribe of Ephraim. 52 They were assigned: Shechem in the mountain region of Ephraim, a city of asylum, with its pasture lands, Gezer with its pasture lands, 53 Kibzaim with its pasture lands, and Beth-horon with its pasture lands. 54 From the tribe of Dan: Elteke with its pasture lands, Gibbethon with its pasture lands, Aijalon with its pasture lands, and Gath-rimmon with its pasture lands. 55 From the half-tribe of Manasseh: Taanach with its pasture lands and Ibleam with its pasture lands. These belonged to the rest of the Kohathite clan.

56 The clans of the Gershonites received from the half-tribe of Manasseh: Golan in Bashan with its pasture lands and Ashtaroth with its pasture lands. 57 From the tribe of Issachar: Kedesh with its pasture lands, Daberath with its pasture lands, 58 Ramoth with its pasture lands, and En-gannim with its pasture lands. 59 From the tribe of Asher: Mashal with its pasture lands, Abdon with its pasture lands, 60 Hilkath with its pasture lands, and Rehob with its pasture lands. 61 From the tribe of Naphtali: Kedesh in Galilee with its pasture lands, Hammon with its pasture lands, and Kiriathaim with its pasture lands.

62 The rest of the Merarites received from the tribe of Zebulun: Jokneam with its pasture lands, Kartah with its pasture lands, Rimmon with its pasture lands, and Tabor with its pasture lands. 63 Across the Jordan at Jericho [that is, east of the Jordan] they received from the tribe of Reuben: Bezer in the desert with its pasture lands, Jahzah with its pasture lands, 64 Kedemoth with its pasture lands, and Mephaath with its pasture lands. 65 From the tribe of Gad: Ramoth in Gilead with its pasture lands, Mahanaim with its pasture lands, 66 Heshbon with its pasture lands, and Jazer with its pasture lands.

6, 39–66: Regarding the nature of the rights of Levites in the cities assigned to them, see note on Jos 21, 1.

t 1 Chr 15, 17. 19; 16, 41f; 2 Chr 5, 12. u 1 Chr 16, 39f.

CHAPTER 7

Issachar* 1The sons of Issachar were Tola,
Puah, Jashub, and Shimron: four.[v] 2The sons of
Tola were Uzzi, Rephaiah, Jeriel, Jahmai, Ibsam,
and Shemuel, warrior heads of the ancestral
houses of Tola. Their kindred numbered twenty-
two thousand six hundred in the time of Da-
vid.[w] 3The sons of Uzzi: Izarahiah. The sons of
Izarahiah were Michael, Obadiah, Joel, and
Isshiah. All five of these were chiefs. 4Their
kindred, by ancestral houses, numbered thirty-
six thousand men in organized military troops,
since they had more wives and sons 5than their
fellow tribesmen. In all the clans of Issachar
there was a total of eighty-seven thousand war-
riors in their family records.

Benjamin 6The sons of Benjamin were Bela,
Becher, and Jediael—three.[x] 7The sons of Bela
were Ezbon, Uzzi, Uzziel, Jerimoth, and Iri—
five. They were heads of their ancestral houses
and warriors. Their family records listed twenty-
two thousand and thirty-four. 8The sons of
Becher were Zemirah, Joash, Eliezer, Elioenai,
Omri, Jeremoth, Abijah, Anathoth, and
Alemeth—all these were sons of Becher.[y] 9Their
family records listed twenty thousand two hun-
dred of their kindred who were heads of their
ancestral houses and warriors. 10The sons of
Jediael: Bilhan. The sons of Bilhan were Jeush,
Benjamin, Ehud, Chenaanah, Zethan, Tarshish,
and Ahishahar. 11All these were descendants of
Jediael, heads of ancestral houses and warriors.
They numbered seventeen thousand two hun-
dred men fit for military service . . . Shupham
and Hupham.[z]

Dan, Naphtali and Manasseh 12 [a]The sons of
Dan: Hushim. 13The sons of Naphtali were
Jahziel, Guni, Jezer, and Shallum. These were
descendants of Bilhah. 14The sons of Manasseh,
whom his Aramean concubine bore:[b] she bore
Machir, the father of Gilead.[c] 15Machir took a
wife whose name was Maacah; his sister's name
was Molecheth. Manasseh's second son was
named Zelophehad, but to Zelophehad only
daughters were born.[d] 16Maacah, Machir's wife,
bore a son whom she named Peresh. He had a
brother named Sheresh, whose sons were Ulam
and Rakem. 17The sons of Ulam: Bedan. These
were the descendants of Gilead, the son of
Machir, the son of Manasseh. 18His sister Mo-
lecheth bore Ishhod, Abiezer, and Mahlah.
19The sons of Shemida were Ahian, Shechem,
Likhi, and Aniam.

Ephraim 20 [e]The sons of Ephraim: Shuthelah,
whose son was Bered, whose son was Tahath,
whose son was Eleadah, whose son was Tahath,
21whose son was Zabad. Ephraim's son Shuthe-
lah, and Ezer and Elead, who were born in the
land, were slain by the inhabitants of Gath
because they had gone down to take away their
livestock. 22Their father Ephraim mourned a
long time, but after his kinsmen had come and
comforted him, 23he visited his wife, who con-
ceived and bore a son whom he named Beriah,
since evil had befallen his house.[f] 24He had a
daughter, Sheerah, who built lower and upper
Beth-horon and Uzzen-sheerah. 25Zabad's son
was Rephah, whose son was Resheph, whose
son was Telah, whose son was Tahan, 26whose
son was Ladan, whose son was Ammihud,
whose son was Elishama,[g] 27whose son was
Nun, whose son was Joshua.

28Their property and their dwellings were in
Bethel and its towns, Naaran to the east, Gezer
and its towns to the west, and also Shechem and
its towns as far as Ayyah and its towns.[h]
29Manasseh, however, had possession of Beth-
shean and its towns, Taanach and its towns,
Megiddo and its towns, and Dor and its towns.
In these dwelt the descendants of Joseph, the
son of Israel.[i]

Asher 30The sons of Asher were Imnah,
Ishvah, Ishvi, and Beriah; their sister was Se-
rah.[j] 31Beriah's sons were Heber and Malchiel,
who was the father of Birzaith. 32Heber became
the father of Japhlet, Shomer, Hotham, and their
sister Shua. 33The sons of Japhlet were Pasach,
Bimhal, and Ashvath; these were the sons of

7, 1–40: The northern tribes.

v Gn 46, 13. w Nm 26, 23f; Jgs 10, 1. x 1 Chr 7, 6; Gn 46, 21; Nm 26, 38. y 1 Chr 7, 8. z Nm 26, 39. a 12f: Gn 46, 24; Nm 26, 48f. b 14–19: Nm 26, 29–32. c Nm 26, 29; Jos 17, 1. d Nm 26, 33; Jos 17, 3. e Nm 26, 35. f 1 Chr 8, 13. g Nm 1, 10; 2, 18; 7, 48; 10, 22. h Gn 12, 8; 1 Kgs 9, 16. i Jos 17, 11. j Gn 46, 17; Nm 26, 44ff.

Japhlet. 34The sons of Shomer were Ahi, Roh-
gah, Jehubbah, and Aram. 35The sons of his
brother Hotham were Zophah, Imna, Shelesh,
and Amal. 36The sons of Zophah were Suah,
Harnepher, Shual, Beri, Imrah, 37Bezer, Hod,
Shamma, Shilshah, Ithran, and Beera. 38The
sons of Jether were Jephunneh, Pispa, and Ara.
39The sons of Ulla were Arah, Hanniel, and
Rizia. 40All these were descendants of Asher,
heads of ancestral houses, distinguished men,
warriors, and chiefs among the princes. Their
family records numbered twenty-six thousand
men fit for military service.

CHAPTER 8

Benjamin* 1Benjamin became the father of
Bela, his first-born, Ashbel, the second son,
Aharah, the third,[k] 2Nohah, the fourth, and
Rapha, the fifth. 3The sons of Bela were Addar
and Gera, the father of Ehud. 4The sons of Ehud
were Abishua, Naaman, Ahoah,[l] 5Gera, Shephu-
phan, and Huram. 6These were the sons of
Ehud, family heads over those who dwelt in
Geba and were deported to Manahath. 7Also
Naaman, Ahijah, and Gera. The last, who led
them into exile, became the father of Uzza and
Ahihud. 8Shaharaim became a father on the
Moabite plateau after he had put away his wives
Hushim and Baara. 9By his wife Hodesh he
became the father of Jobab, Zibia, Mesha, Mal-
cam, 10Jeuz, Sachia, and Mirmah. These were
his sons, family heads. 11By Hushim he became
the father of Abitub and Elpaal. 12The sons of
Elpaal were Eber, Misham, Shemed, who built
Ono and Lod with its nearby towns,[m] 13Beriah,
and Shema. They were family heads of those
who dwelt in Aijalon, and they put the inhabit-
ants of Gath to flight. 14Their brethren were
Elpaal, Shashak, and Jeremoth. 15Zebadiah,
Arad, Eder, 16Michael, Ishpah, and Joha were
the sons of Beriah. 17Zebadiah, Meshullam,
Hizki, Heber, 18Ishmerai, Izliah, and Jobab were
the sons of Elpaal. 19Jakim, Zichri, Zabdi, 20Elie-
nai, Zillethai, Eliel, 21Adaiah, Beraiah, and Shim-
rath were the sons of Shimei. 22Ishpan, Eber,
Eliel, 23Abdon, Zichri, Hanan, 24Hananiah,
Elam, Anthothijah, 25Iphdeiah, and Penuel were
the sons of Shashak. 26Shamsherai, Shehariah,
Athaliah, 27Jaareshiah, Elijah, and Zichri were
the sons of Jeroham. 28These were family heads
over their kindred, chiefs who dwelt in Jerusa-
lem.

29[n]In Gibeon dwelt Jeiel, the founder of
Gibeon, whose wife's name was Maacah; 30also
his first-born son, Abdon, and Zur, Kish, Baal,
Ner, Nadab, 31Gedor, Ahio, Zecher, and Mik-
loth. 32Mikloth became the father of Shimeah.
These, too, dwelt with their relatives in Jerusa-
lem, opposite their fellow tribesmen. 33[o]Ner
became the father of Kish, and Kish became the
father of Saul. Saul became the father of Jona-
than, Malchishua, Abinadab, and Eshbaal.[p]
34The son of Jonathan was Meribbaal, and Merib-
baal became the father of Micah.[q] 35The sons of
Micah were Pithon, Melech, Tarea, and Ahaz.
36Ahaz became the father of Jehoaddah, and
Jehoaddah became the father of Alemeth, Azma-
veth, and Zimri. Zimri became the father of
Moza.[r] 37Moza became the father of Binea,
whose son was Raphah, whose son was Eleasah,
whose son was Azel.[s] 38Azel had six sons,
whose names were Azrikam, his first-born, Ish-
mael, Sheariah, Azariah, Obadiah, and Hanan;
all these were the sons of Azel. 39The sons of
Eshek, his brother, were Ulam, his first-born,
Jeush, the second son, and Eliphelet, the third.
40The sons of Ulam were combat archers, and
many were their sons and grandsons: one hun-
dred and fifty. All these were the descendants of
Benjamin.

CHAPTER 9

1Thus all Israel was inscribed in its family
records which are recorded in the book of the
kings of Israel.[t]

Now Judah had been carried in captivity to

8, 1–40: A second, variant list of the Benjaminites, with special prominence given to Saul's family (vv 33–40).

k 1 Chr 7, 6; Gn 46, 21; Nm 26, 38ff. l Jgs 3, 15. m Neh 11, 35. n 29–32: 1 Chr 9, 35–38. o 33–38: 1 Chr 9, 39–44. p 1 Chr 10, 2; 1 Sm 9, 1; 14, 49. 51; 31, 2. q 2 Sm 4, 4; 9, 6. 10. 12. r 1 Chr 9, 42. s 1 Chr 9, 43. t 2 Chr 16, 11; 20, 34; 25, 26; 27, 7; 33, 18; 36, 8.

Babylon because of its rebellion. 2 [u]*The first to settle again in their cities and dwell there were certain lay Israelites, the priests, the Levites, and the temple slaves.[v]

Jerusalemites 3In Jerusalem lived Judahites and Benjaminites; also Ephraimites and Manassehites. 4Among the Judahites was Uthai, son of Ammihud, son of Omri, son of Imri, son of Bani, one of the descendants of Perez, son of Judah. 5Among the Shelanites were Asaiah, the first-born, and his sons. 6Among the Zerahites were Jeuel and six hundred and ninety of their brethren. 7Among the Benjaminites were Sallu, son of Meshullam, son of Hodaviah, son of Hassenuah; 8Ibneiah, son of Jeroham; Elah, son of Uzzi, son of Michri; Meshullam, son of Shephatiah, son of Reuel, son of Ibnijah. 9Their kindred of various families were nine hundred and fifty-six. All those named were heads of their ancestral houses.

10Among the priests were Jedaiah; Jehoiarib; Jachin; 11Azariah, son of Hilkiah, son of Meshullam, son of Zadok, son of Meraioth, son of Ahitub, the ruler of the house of God; 12Adaiah, son of Jeroham, son of Pashhur, son of Malchijah; Maasai, son of Adiel, son of Jahzerah, son of Meshullam, son of Meshillemith, son of Immer. 13Their brethren, heads of their ancestral houses, were one thousand seven hundred and sixty, valiant for the work of the service of the house of God.

14Among the Levites were Shemaiah, son of Hasshub, son of Azrikam, son of Hashabiah, one of the descendants of Merari; 15Bakbakkar; Heresh; Galal; Mattaniah, son of Mica, son of Zichri, a descendant of Asaph; 16Obadiah, son of Shemaiah, son of Galal, a descendant of Jeduthun; and Berechiah, son of Asa, son of Elkanah, whose family lived in the villages of the Netophathites.

17The gatekeepers were Shallum, Akkub, Talmon, Ahiman, and their brethren; Shallum was the chief. 18Previously they had stood guard at the king's gate on the east side; now they became gatekeepers for the encampments of the Levites. 19Shallum, son of Kore, son of Ebiasaph, a descendant of Korah, and his brethren of the same ancestral house of the Korahites had as their assigned task the guarding of the threshold of the tent, just as their fathers had guarded the entrance to the encampment of the LORD. 20Phinehas, son of Eleazar, had been their chief in times past—the LORD be with him![w] 21Zechariah, son of Meshelemiah, guarded the gate of the meeting tent.[x] 22In all, those who were chosen for gatekeepers at the threshold were two hundred and twelve. They were inscribed in the family records of their villages. David and Samuel the seer had established them in their position of trust. 23Thus they and their sons kept guard over the gates of the house of the LORD, the house which was then a tent. 24The gatekeepers were stationed at the four sides, to the east, the west, the north, and the south.[y] 25Their kinsmen who lived in their own villages took turns in assisting them for seven-day periods,[z] 26while the four chief gatekeepers were on constant duty. These were the Levites who also had charge of the chambers and treasures of the house of God. 27At night they lodged about the house of God, for it was in their charge and they had the duty of opening it each morning.

28Some of them had charge of the liturgical equipment, tallying it as it was brought in and taken out. 29Others were appointed to take care of the utensils and all the sacred vessels, as well as the fine flour, the wine, the oil, the frankincense, and the spices. 30It was the sons of priests, however, who mixed the spiced ointments.[a] 31 [b]Mattithiah, one of the Levites, the first-born of Shallum the Koreite, was entrusted with preparing the cakes. 32Benaiah the Kohathite, one of their brethren, was in charge of setting out the showbread each sabbath.[c]

33These were the chanters and the gatekeepers, family heads over the Levites. They stayed in the chambers when free of duty, for day and night they had to be ready for service. 34These

9, 2–34: The inhabitants of Jerusalem after the exile. A similar list, with many variants in the names, is given in Neh 11, 3–24.

u 2–22: Neh 11, 3–19. v Ezr 2, 70; 7, 7; Neh 11, 3. w Ex 6, 25; Nm 25, 7. 11; Jgs 20, 28. x 1 Chr 26, 2. 14. y 1 Chr 26, 13. z 2 Chr 23, 4f. a Ex 30, 22–33. b 31f: 1 Chr 23, 29; Lv 2, 1ff; 6, 13ff; 7, 11. c Ex 25, 30; Lv 24, 5–8.

were the levitical family heads over their kin-
dred, chiefs who dwelt in Jerusalem.

II: The History of David

Genealogy of Saul 35 [d]In Gibeon dwelt Jeiel,
the founder of Gibeon, whose wife's name was
Maacah. 36His first-born son was Abdon; then
came Zur, Kish, Baal, Ner, Nadab, 37Gedor,
Ahio, Zechariah, and Mikloth. 38Mikloth be-
came the father of Shimeam. These, too, with
their brethren, dwelt opposite their brethren in
Jerusalem. 39Ner became the father of Kish, and
Kish became the father of Saul. Saul became the
father of Jonathan, Malchishua, Abinadab, and
Eshbaal. 40The son of Jonathan was Meribbaal,
and Meribbaal became the father of Micah.
41The sons of Micah were Pithon, Melech,
Tahrea, and Ahaz. 42Ahaz became the father of
Jehoaddah, and Jehoaddah became the father of
Alemeth, Azmaveth, and Zimri. Zimri became
the father of Moza. 43Moza became the father of
Binea, whose son was Rephaiah, whose son was
Eleasah, whose son was Azel. 44Azel had six
sons, whose names were Azrikam, his first-born,
Ishmael, Sheariah, Azariah, Obadiah, and Ha-
nan; these were the sons of Azel.

CHAPTER 10

His Death and Burial 1 [e]Now the Philistines
were at war with Israel; the Israelites fled before
the Philistines, and a number of them fell, slain
on Mount Gilboa. 2The Philistines pressed hard
after Saul and his sons. When the Philistines had
killed Jonathan, Abinadab, and Malchishua, sons
of Saul, 3the whole fury of the battle descended
upon Saul. Then the archers found him, and
wounded him with their arrows.

4Saul said to his armor-bearer, "Draw your
sword and thrust me through with it, that these
uncircumcised may not come and maltreat me."
But the armor-bearer, in great fear, refused. So
Saul took his own sword and fell on it; 5and
seeing him dead, the armor-bearer also fell on his
sword and died. 6Thus, with Saul and his three
sons, his whole house died at one time. 7When
all the Israelites who were in the valley saw that
Saul and his sons had died in the rout, they left
their cities and fled; thereupon the Philistines
came and occupied them.

8On the following day, when the Philistines
came to strip the slain, they found Saul and his
sons where they had fallen on Mount Gilboa.
9They stripped him, cut off his head, and took
his armor; these they sent throughout the land
of the Philistines to convey the good news to
their idols and their people. 10His armor they put
in the house of their gods, but his skull they
impaled on the temple of Dagon.

11When all the inhabitants of Jabesh-gilead
had heard what the Philistines had done to Saul,
12its warriors rose to a man, recovered the
bodies of Saul and his sons, and brought them to
Jabesh. They buried their bones under the oak of
Jabesh, and fasted seven days.[f]

13*Thus Saul died because of his rebellion
against the LORD in disobeying his command,
and also because he had sought counsel of a
necromancer,[g] 14and had not rather inquired of
the LORD. Therefore the LORD slew him, and
transferred his kingdom to David, the son of
Jesse.[h]

CHAPTER 11

David Is Made King 1 [i]Then all Israel gathered
about David in Hebron, and they said: "Surely,
we are of the same bone and flesh as you. 2Even
formerly, when Saul was still the king, it was you
who led Israel in all its battles. And now the
LORD, your God, has said to you, 'You shall
shepherd my people Israel and be ruler over
them.' "[j] 3Then all the elders of Israel came to
the king at Hebron, and there David made a
covenant with them in the presence of the
LORD; and they anointed him king over Israel, in
accordance with the word of the LORD as
revealed through Samuel.[k]

10, 13f: The Chronicler's comment on why Saul met his tragic end: he had disobeyed the Lord's command given through the prophet Samuel (1 Sm 15, 3–9), and had sought counsel of a necromancer (1 Sm 28, 6–19), contrary to the Mosaic law against necromancy (Dt 18, 10f).

d 35–44: 1 Chr 8, 29–38. e 1–12: 1 Sm 31, 1–13. f 2 Sm 2, 5. g Dt 18, 10ff; 1 Sm 13, 13f; 15, 3. 11. 26. h 1 Sm 15, 28; 2 Sm 3, 9f. i 1–9: 2 Sm 5, 1–10. j 1 Sm 18, 5. 13–16. 30; 19, 8. k 1 Sm 16, 1. 13; 2 Sm 2, 4.

Jerusalem Captured [4]Then David and all Is-
rael went to Jerusalem, that is, Jebus, where the
natives of the land were called Jebusites.[l] [5]The
inhabitants of Jebus said to David, "You shall not
enter here." David nevertheless captured the
fortress of Sion, which is the City of David.
[6]David said, "Whoever strikes the Jebusites first
shall be made the chief commander." Joab, the
son of Zeruiah, was the first to go up; and so he
became chief.[m] [7]David took up his residence in
the fortress, which thenceforth was called the
City of David. [8]He rebuilt the city on all sides,
from the Millo all the way around, while Joab
restored the rest of the city.[n] [9]David became
more and more powerful, for the LORD of hosts
was with him.

David's Warriors [10][o]These were David's chief
warriors who, together with all Israel, supported
him in his reign in order to make him true king,
even as the LORD had commanded concerning
Israel. [11]Here is the list of David's warriors:

Ishbaal, the son of Hachamoni, chief of the
Three.* He brandished his spear against three
hundred, whom he slew in a single encounter.

[12]Next to him Eleazar, the son of Dodo the
Ahohite, one of the Three warriors.[p] [13]He was
with David at Pas-dammim, where the Philis-
tines had massed for battle. The plowland was
fully planted with barley, but its defenders were
retreating before the Philistines.[q] [14]He made a
stand on the sown ground, kept it safe, and cut
down the Philistines. Thus the LORD brought
about a great victory.

[15]Three of the Thirty chiefs went down to the
rock, to David, who was in the cave of Adullam
while the Philistines were encamped in the
valley of Rephaim.[r] [16]David was then in the
stronghold, and a Philistine garrison was at
Bethlehem. [17]David expressed a desire: "Oh,
that someone would give me a drink from the
cistern that is by the gate at Bethlehem!"
[18]Thereupon the Three broke through the en-
campment of the Philistines, drew water from
the cistern by the gate at Bethlehem, and carried
it back to David. But David refused to drink it.
Instead, he poured it out as a libation to the
LORD, [19]saying, "God forbid that I should do
such a thing! Could I drink the blood of these
men who risked their lives?" For at the risk of
their lives they brought it; and so he refused to
drink it. Such deeds as these the Three warriors
performed.

[20][s]Abishai, the brother of Joab. He was the
chief of the Thirty;* he brandished his spear
against three hundred, and slew them. Thus he
had a reputation like that of the Three.[t] [21]He
was twice as famous as any of the Thirty and
became their commander, but he did not attain
to the Three.

[22]Benaiah, the son of Jehoiada, a valiant man
of mighty deeds, from Kabzeel. He killed the two
sons of Ariel of Moab, and also, on a snowy day,
he went down and killed the lion in the cistern.
[23]He likewise slew the Egyptian, a huge man
five cubits tall. The Egyptian carried a spear that
was like a weaver's heddle-bar, but he came
against him with a staff, wrested the spear from
the Egyptian's hand, and killed him with his
own spear. [24]Such deeds as these of Benaiah, the
son of Jehoiada, gave him a reputation like that
of the Three. [25]He was more famous than any of
the Thirty, but he did not attain to the Three.
David put him in charge of his bodyguard.[u]

[26]Also these warriors: Asahel, the brother of
Joab; Elhanan, son of Dodo, from Bethlehem;[v]
[27]Shammoth, from En-harod; Helez, from Palti;
[28]Ira, son of Ikkesh, from Tekoa; Abiezer, from
Anathoth; [29]Sibbecai, from Husha; Ilai, from
Ahoh;[w] [30]Maharai, from Netophah; Heled, son
of Baanah, from Netophah;[x] [31]Ithai, son of Ribai,
from Gibeah of Benjamin; Benaiah, from Pira-
thon;[y] [32]Hurai, from the valley of Gaash; Abiel,
from Beth-arabah; [33]Azmaveth, from Bahurim;
Eliahba, from Shaalbon; [34]Jashen the Gunite;

11, 11f: The Three: the Chronicler names only two of them: Ishbaal and Eleazar. According to 2 Sm 23, 8–12, the Three were Ishbaal, Eleazar, and Shammah.

11, 20: The Thirty: listed by name in vv 26–47. The list given in 2 Sm 23, 8–39 often differs in names and spellings; for the numbers, see the note there.

l Jos 15, 8; Jgs 1, 21; 19, 10f. m 2 Sm 2, 13ff; 8, 16. n 1 Kgs 9, 15. 24; 11, 27; 2 Chr 32, 5. o 10–41: 2 Sm 23, 8–39. p 1 Chr 27, 4. q 1 Sm 17, 1. r 1 Chr 14, 9; 2 Sm 5, 18. 22. s 20f: 2 Sm 23, 18f. t 1 Chr 18, 12; 1 Sm 26, 6ff; 2 Sm 16, 9; 18, 2; 21, 17. u 2 Sm 8, 18; 20, 23. v 1 Chr 2, 16; 27, 7. w 1 Chr 27, 11. x 1 Chr 27, 13. y 1 Chr 27, 14.

Jonathan, son of Shagee, from En-harod;
35 Ahiam, son of Sachar, from En-harod; Eliphe-
leth, son of 36 Ahasabi, from Beth-maacah; Ahi-
jah, from Gilo; 37 Hezro, from Carmel; Naarai,
the son of Ezbai; 38 Joel, brother of Nathan, from
Rehob, the Gadite; 39 Zelek the Ammonite; Naha-
rai, from Beeroth, the armor-bearer of Joab, son
of Zeruiah; 40 Ira, from Jattir; Gareb, from Jattir;
41 Uriah the Hittite; Zabad, son of Ahlai, 42 and,
in addition to the Thirty, Adina, son of Shiza, the
Reubenite, chief of the tribe of Reuben; 43 Ha-
nan, from Beth-maacah; Joshaphat the Mithnite;
44 Uzzia, from Ashterath; Shama and Jeiel, sons
of Hotham, from Aroer; 45 Jediael, son of Shimri,
and Joha, his brother, the Tizite; 46 Eliel the
Mahavite; Jeribai and Joshaviah, sons of Elnaam;
Ithmah, from Moab; 47 Eliel, Obed, and Jaasiel
the Mezobian.

CHAPTER 12

David's Early Followers 1 The following men
came to David in Ziklag while he was still under
banishment from Saul, son of Kish; they, too,
were among the warriors who helped him in his
battles.[z] 2 They were archers who could use
either the right or the left hand, both in slinging
stones and in shooting arrows with the bow.
They were some of Saul's kinsmen, from Benja-
min. 3 Ahiezer was their chief, along with Joash,
both sons of Shemaah of Gibeah; also Jeziel and
Pelet, sons of Azmaveth; Beracah; Jehu, from
Anathoth;[a] 4 Ishmaiah the Gibeonite, a warrior
on the level of the Thirty, and in addition to their
number: 5 Jeremiah; Jahaziel; Johanan; Jozabad,
from Gederah; 6 Eluzai; Jerimoth; Bealiah;
Shemariah; Shephatiah the Haruphite; 7 Elka-
nah, Isshiah, Azarel, Joezer, and Ishbaal, who
were Korahites; 8 Joelah, finally, and Zebadiah,
sons of Jeroham, from Gedor.

9 Some of the Gadites also went over to David
when he was at the stronghold in the wilder-
ness. They were valiant warriors, experienced
soldiers equipped with shield and spear, who
bore themselves like lions, and were as swift as
the gazelles on the mountains.[b] 10 Ezer was their
chief, Obadiah was second, Eliab third, 11 Mish-
mannah fourth, Jeremiah fifth, 12 Attai sixth, Eliel
seventh, 13 Johanan eighth, Elzabad ninth, 14 Jere-
miah tenth, and Machbannai eleventh. 15 These
Gadites were army commanders, the lesser
placed over hundreds and the greater over
thousands. 16 It was they who crossed over the
Jordan when it was overflowing both its banks in
the first month, and dispersed all who were in
the valleys to the east and to the west.

17 Some Benjaminites and Judahites also came
to David at the stronghold. 18 David went out to
meet them and addressed them in these words:
"If you come peacefully, to help me, I am of a
mind to have you join me. But if you have come
to betray me to my enemies though my hands
have done no wrong, may the God of our fathers
see and punish you."

19 Then spirit enveloped Amasai, the chief of
the Thirty, who spoke:

"We are yours, O David,
we are with you, O son of Jesse.
Peace, peace to you,
and peace to him who helps you;
your God it is who helps you."

So David received them and placed them among
the leaders of his troops.

20 Men from Manasseh also deserted to David
when he came with the Philistines to battle
against Saul. However, he did not help the
Philistines, for their lords took counsel and sent
him home, saying, "At the cost of our heads he
will desert to his master Saul." 21 As he was
returning to Ziklag, therefore, these deserted to
him from Manasseh: Adnah, Jozabad, Jediael,
Michael, Jozabad, Elihu, and Zillethai, chiefs of
thousands of Manasseh. 22 They helped David by
taking charge of his troops, for they were all
warriors and became commanders of his army.
23 And from day to day men kept coming to
David's help until there was a vast encampment,
like an encampment of angels.

The Assembly at Hebron 24 This is the muster
of the detachments of armed troops that came to
David at Hebron to transfer to him Saul's king-
dom, as the LORD had ordained. 25 *Judahites

12, 25–38: The Chronicler fills out the pageantry of joyous

z 1 Sm 27, 1–7. a 1 Chr 27, 12. b Dt 33, 20.

bearing shields and spears: six thousand eight hundred armed troops. 26Of the Simeonites, warriors fit for battle: seven thousand one hundred. 27Of the Levites: four thousand six hundred, 28along with Jehoiada, leader of the line of Aaron, with another three thousand seven hundred, 29and Zadok, a young warrior, with twenty-two princes of his father's house. 30Of the Benjaminites, the brethren of Saul: three thousand—until this time, most of them had held their allegiance to the house of Saul. 31Of the Ephraimites: twenty thousand eight hundred warriors, men renowned in their ancestral houses. 32Of the half-tribe of Manasseh: eighteen thousand, designated by name to come and make David king. 33Of the Issacharites, their chiefs who were endowed with an understanding of the times and who knew what Israel had to do: two hundred chiefs, together with all their brethren under their command. 34From Zebulun, men fit for military service, set in battle array with every kind of weapon for war: fifty thousand men rallying with a single purpose. 35From Naphtali: one thousand captains, and with them, armed with shield and lance, thirty-seven thousand men. 36Of the Danites, set in battle array: twenty-eight thousand six hundred. 37From Asher, fit for military service and set in battle array: forty thousand. 38From the other side of the Jordan, of the Reubenites, Gadites, and the half-tribe of Manasseh, men equipped with every kind of weapon of war: one hundred and twenty thousand.

39All these soldiers, drawn up in battle order, came to Hebron with the resolute intention of making David king over all Israel. The rest of Israel was likewise of one mind to make David king. 40They remained with David for three days, feasting and drinking, for their brethren had prepared for them. 41Moreover, their neighbors from as far as Issachar, Zebulun, and Naphtali came bringing food on asses, camels, mules, and oxen—provisions in great quantity of meal, pressed figs, raisins, wine, oil, oxen, and sheep. For there was rejoicing in Israel.

CHAPTER 13

Transfer of the Ark 1 [c]After David had taken counsel with his commanders of thousands and of hundreds, that is to say, with every one of his leaders, 2he said to the whole assembly of Israel: "If it seems good to you, and is so decreed by the LORD our God, let us summon the rest of our brethren from all the districts of Israel, and also the priests and the Levites from their cities with pasture lands, that they may join us; [d] 3and let us bring the ark of our God here among us, for in the days of Saul we did not visit it." 4And the whole assembly agreed to do this, for the idea was pleasing to all the people.

5Then David assembled all Israel, from Shihor of Egypt* to Labo of Hamath, to bring the ark of God from Kiriath-jearim. [e] 6David and all Israel went up to Baalah, that is, to Kiriath-jearim, of Judah, to bring back the ark of God, which was known by the name "LORD enthroned upon the cherubim." [f] 7They transported the ark of God on a new cart from the house of Abinadab; Uzzah and Ahio were guiding the cart, 8while David and all Israel danced before God with great enthusiasm, amid songs and music on lyres, harps, tambourines, cymbals, and trumpets.

9As they reached the threshing floor of Chidon,* Uzzah stretched out his hand to steady the ark, for the oxen were upsetting it. 10Then the LORD became angry with Uzzah and struck him; he died there in God's presence, because he had laid his hand on the ark. 11David was disturbed because the LORD's anger had broken

occasions in keeping with his much later appreciation of the significance of the event in the history of God's people: the numbers in attendance at David's crowning in Hebron (cf 2 Sm 5, 1ff) are recounted in the same spirit of enthusiasm which in v 23 compares David's band of desert freebooters to a numerous encampment of angels.

13, 5: Shihor of Egypt: the eastern branch of the Nile delta. Labo of Hamath: in southern Syria.

13, 9: Chidon: in 2 Sm 6, 6, Nodan.

c 1–14: 2 Sm 6, 1–11. d Nm 35, 1ff; Jos 14, 4; 21, 2ff. e 1 Chr 15, 3; Jos 13, 3. 5; 1 Sm 6, 21; 7, 1f; 2 Sm 6, 1–11. f Jos 15, 9; 18, 14; 1 Sm 4, 4; 7, 1.

out against Uzzah. Therefore that place has been
called Perez-uzza* even to this day.
12David was now afraid of God, and he said,
"How can I bring the ark of God with me?"
13Therefore he did not take the ark back with
him to the City of David, but he took it instead
to the house of Obed-edom the Gittite. 14The ark
of God remained in the house of Obed-edom
with his family for three months, and the LORD
blessed Obed-edom's household and all that he
possessed.[g]

CHAPTER 14

David in Jerusalem 1[h]Hiram, king of Tyre,
sent envoys to David along with masons and
carpenters, and cedar wood to build him a
house.[i] 2David now understood that the LORD
had truly confirmed him as king over Israel, for
his kingdom was greatly exalted for the sake of
his people Israel. 3[j]David took other wives in
Jerusalem and became the father of more sons
and daughters. 4These are the names of those
who were born to him in Jerusalem: Shammua,
Shobab, Nathan, Solomon, 5Ibhar, Elishua, Elpe-
let, 6Nogah, Nepheg, Japhia, 7Elishama, Beeli-
ada, and Eliphelet.
The Philistine Wars 8When the Philistines had
heard that David was anointed king over all Is-
rael, they went up in unison to seek him out. But
when David heard of this, he marched out against
them. 9Meanwhile the Philistines had come and
raided the valley of Rephaim.[k] 10David inquired
of God, "Shall I advance against the Philistines,
and will you deliver them into my power?" The
LORD answered him, "Advance, for I will deliver
them into your power." 11They advanced, there-
fore, to Baal-perazim, and David defeated them
there. Then David said, "God has used me to
break through my enemies just as water breaks
through a dam." Therefore that place was called
Baal-perazim. 12The Philistines had left their gods
there, and David ordered them to be burnt.[l]
13Once again the Philistines raided the valley,
14and again David inquired of God. But God
answered him: "Do not try to pursue them, but
go around them and come upon them from the
direction of the mastic trees. 15When you hear
the sound of marching in the tops of the mastic
trees, then go forth to battle, for God has already
gone before you to strike the army of the
Philistines." 16David did as God commanded
him, and they routed the Philistine army from
Gibeon to Gezer.
17Thus David's fame was spread abroad
through every land, and the LORD made all the
nations fear him.

CHAPTER 15

The Ark Brought to Jerusalem 1David built
houses for himself in the City of David and pre-
pared a place for the ark of God, pitching a tent for
it there. 2At that time he said, "No one may carry
the ark of God except the Levites, for the LORD
chose them to carry the ark of the LORD and to
minister to him forever."[m] 3Then David assem-
bled all Israel in Jerusalem to bring the ark of the
LORD to the place which he had prepared for it.[n]
4David also called together the sons of Aaron and
the Levites: 5of the sons of Kohath, Uriel, their
chief, and one hundred and twenty of his breth-
ren; 6of the sons of Merari, Asaiah, their chief,
and two hundred and twenty of his brethren; 7of
the sons of Gershon, Joel, their chief, and one
hundred and thirty of his brethren; 8of the sons of
Elizaphan, Shemaiah, their chief, and two hun-
dred of his brethren; 9of the sons of Hebron, Eliel,
their chief, and eighty of his brethren; 10of the
sons of Uzziel, Amminadab, their chief, and one
hundred and twelve of his brethren.
11David summoned the priests Zadok and
Abiathar, and the Levites Uriel, Asaiah, Joel,
Shemaiah, Eliel, and Amminadab,[o] 12and said to
them: "You, the heads of the levitical families,
must sanctify yourselves along with your breth-
ren and bring the ark of the LORD, the God of
Israel, to the place which I have prepared for it.[p]
13Because you were not with us the first time,
the wrath of the LORD our God burst upon us,

13, 11: Perez-uzza: A Hebrew term meaning "the breaking out against Uzza."

g 1 Chr 26, 4f. h 1–16: 2 Sm 5, 11–25. i 1 Kgs 5, 1; 2 Chr 2, 3. j 3–7: 1 Chr 3, 5–8; 2 Sm 5, 13–16. k 1 Chr 11, 15. l Dt 7, 5. 25. m Nm 1, 50; 7, 9; Dt 10, 8; 31, 25; 1 Sm 6, 15; Jos 3, 8. n 1 Chr 13, 5; 2 Sm 6, 15. 17. o 1 Chr 16, 39; 2 Sm 8, 17; 15, 29. 35. p 2 Chr 29, 5. 15. 34; 30, 3. 15. 24.

for we did not seek him aright."[q] 14 Accordingly, the priests and the Levites sanctified themselves to bring up the ark of the LORD, the God of Israel. 15 The Levites bore the ark of God on their shoulders with poles, as Moses had ordained according to the word of the LORD[r].

16 David commanded the chiefs of the Levites to appoint their brethren as chanters, to play on musical instruments, harps, lyres, and cymbals, to make a loud sound of rejoicing.[s] 17 Therefore the Levites appointed Heman, son of Joel, and, among his brethren, Asaph, son of Berechiah; and among the sons of Merari, their brethren, Ethan, son of Kushaiah;[t] 18 and, together with these, their brethren of the second rank: the gatekeepers Zechariah, Uzziel, Shemiramoth, Jehiel, Unni, Eliab, Benaiah, Maaseiah, Mattithiah, Eliphelehu, Mikneiah, Obed-edom, and Jeiel. 19 The chanters, Heman, Asaph, and Ethan, sounded brass cymbals. 20 Zechariah, Uzziel, Shemiramoth, Jehiel, Unni, Eliab, Maaseiah, and Benaiah played on harps set to "Alamoth."* 21 But Mattithiah, Eliphelehu, Mikneiah, Obed-edom, and Jeiel led the chant on lyres set to "the eighth." 22 Chenaniah was the chief of the Levites in the chanting; he directed the chanting, for he was skillful.[u] 23 Berechiah and Elkanah were gatekeepers before the ark. 24 The priests, Shebaniah, Joshaphat, Nethanel, Amasai, Zechariah, Benaiah, and Eliezer, sounded the trumpets before the ark of God. Obed-edom and Jeiel were also gatekeepers before the ark.[v]

25 [w]Thus David, the elders of Israel, and the commanders of thousands went to bring up the ark of the covenant of the LORD with joy from the house of Obed-edom. 26 While the Levites, with God's help, were bearing the ark of the covenant of the LORD, seven bulls and seven rams were sacrificed.[x] 27 David was clothed in a robe of fine linen, as were all the Levites who carried the ark, the singers, and Chenaniah, the leader of the chant; David was also wearing a linen ephod.[y] 28 Thus all Israel brought back the ark of the covenant of the LORD with joyful shouting, and to the sound of horns, trumpets, and cymbals, and the music of harps and lyres. 29 But as the ark of the covenant of the LORD was entering the City of David, Michal, daughter of Saul, looked down from her window, and when she saw King David leaping and dancing, she despised him in her heart.[z]

CHAPTER 16

1 [a]They brought in the ark of God and set it within the tent which David had pitched for it. Then they offered up holocausts and peace offerings to God.[b] 2 When David had finished offering up the holocausts and peace offerings, he blessed the people in the name of the LORD, 3 and distributed to every Israelite, to every man and to every woman, a loaf of bread, a piece of meat, and a raisin cake.

The Ministering Levites 4 He now appointed certain Levites to minister before the ark of the LORD, to celebrate, thank, and praise the LORD, the God of Israel.[c] 5 Asaph was their chief, and second to him were Zechariah, Uzziel, Shemiramoth, Jehiel, Mattithiah, Eliab, Benaiah, Obed-edom, and Jeiel. These were to play on harps and lyres, while Asaph was to sound the cymbals, 6 and the priests Benaiah and Jahaziel were to be the regular trumpeters before the ark of the covenant of God.

7 Then, on that same day, David appointed Asaph and his brethren to sing for the first time these praises of the LORD:

8 *Give thanks to the LORD, invoke his name;[d]
 make known among the nations his deeds.
9 Sing to him, sing his praise,
 proclaim all his wondrous deeds.
10 Glory in his holy name;
 rejoice, O hearts that seek the LORD!

15, 20: Alamoth: a musical term (literally, "young women") of uncertain meaning, occurring also in Ps 46, 1, where it is rendered as virgins. Perhaps it may mean something like "soprano," whereas the term "eighth" (Hebrew sheminith, v 21) may then mean "bass"; cf Pss 6, 1; 12, 1.

16, 8–36: A hymn composed of parts, with textual variants, from several Psalms; vv 8–22 = Ps 105, 1–15; vv 23–33 = Ps 96, 1–13; vv 34–36 = Ps 106, 1. 47f.

q 1 Chr 13, 3. r Ex 25, 13ff; Nm 1, 50; 7, 9; 2 Chr 35, 3. s 1 Chr 13, 8; 16, 5; 2 Chr 5, 12; 29, 25; Neh 12, 27. t 1 Chr 6, 31–47; 25, 1–8. u 1 Chr 26, 29. v Nm 10, 8; Jos 6, 4ff. w 25–29: 2 Sm 6, 12–16. x 2 Sm 6, 17; 2 Chr 29, 21. y 1 Sm 2, 18; 2 Sm 6, 14. z 2 Sm 6, 20ff. a 1–3: 2 Sm 6, 17ff. b 1 Chr 15, 1. c Sir 47, 9. d 8–22: Ps 105, 1–15.

11 Look to the LORD in his strength;
seek to serve him constantly.
12 Recall the wondrous deeds that he has wrought,
his portents, and the judgments he has uttered,
13 You descendants of Israel, his servants,
sons of Jacob, his chosen ones!

14 He, the LORD, is our God;
throughout the earth his judgments prevail.
15 He remembers forever his covenant
which he made binding for a thousand generations—
16 Which he entered into with Abraham
and by his oath to Isaac;
17 Which he established for Jacob by statute,
for Israel as an everlasting covenant,
18 Saying, "To you will I give the land of Canaan
as your alloted inheritance."

19 When they were few in number,
a handful, and strangers there,
20 Wandering from nation to nation,
from one kingdom to another people,
21 He let no one oppress them,
and for their sake he rebuked kings:
22 "Touch not my anointed,
and to my prophets do no harm."

23 [e]Sing to the LORD, all the earth,
announce his salvation, day after day.
24 Tell his glory among the nations;
among all peoples, his wondrous deeds.
25 For great is the LORD and highly to be praised;
and awesome is he, beyond all gods.
26 For all the gods of the nations are things of nought,
but the LORD made the heavens.
27 Splendor and majesty go before him;
praise and joy are in his holy place.

28 Give to the LORD, you families of nations,
give to the LORD glory and praise;
29 Give to the LORD the glory due his name!
Bring gifts, and enter his presence;
worship the LORD in holy attire.

30 Tremble before him, all the earth;
he has made the world firm, not to be moved.
31 Let the heavens be glad and the earth rejoice;
let them say among the nations: The LORD is king.
32 Let the sea and what fills it resound;
let the plains rejoice and all that is in them!
33 Then shall all the trees of the forest exult
before the LORD, for he comes:
he comes to rule the earth.
34 [f]Give thanks to the LORD, for he is good,
for his kindness endures forever;
35 And say, "Save us, O God, our savior,
gather us and deliver us from the nations,
That we may give thanks to your holy name
and glory in praising you."
36 Blessed be the LORD, the God of Israel,
through all eternity!
Let all the people say, Amen! Alleluia.

37 Then David left Asaph and his brethren
there before the ark of the covenant of the LORD
to minister before the ark regularly according to
the daily ritual; 38 he also left there Obed-edom
and sixty-eight of his brethren, including Obed-
edom, son of Jeduthun, and Hosah, to be gate-
keepers.[g]
39 But the priest Zadok and his priestly breth-
ren he left before the Dwelling of the LORD on
the high place at Gibeon,[h] 40 to offer holocausts
to the LORD on the altar of holocausts regularly,
morning and evening, and to do all that is
written in the law of the LORD which he has
decreed for Israel.[i] 41 With them were Heman
and Jeduthun and the others who were chosen
and designated by name to give thanks to the
LORD, "because his kindness endures forever,"[j]
42 with trumpets and cymbals for accompani-
ment, and instruments for the sacred chant. The
sons of Jeduthun kept the gate.[k]
43 Then all the people departed, each to his
own home, and David returned to bless his
household.[l]

e 23–33: Ps 96, 1–13. f 34ff: Ps 106, 1. 47f. g 1 Chr 15, 24. h 1 Kgs 3, 4. i Ex 29, 38–42; Lv 6, 9; Nm 28, 3. 6; 2 Chr 13, 11. j 2 Chr 5, 12; 7, 3. 6; 20, 21; Ezr 3, 11. k 2 Chr 29, 27. l 2 Sm 6, 19f.

CHAPTER 17

The Oracle of Nathan 1 [m]After David had
taken up residence in his house, he said to
Nathan the prophet, "See, I am living in a house
of cedar, but the ark of the covenant of the LORD
dwells under tentcloth." [n] 2 Nathan replied to
David, "Do, therefore, whatever you desire, for
God is with you."
3 But that same night the word of God came to
Nathan: 4 "Go and tell my servant David, Thus
says the LORD: It is not you who are to build a
house for me to dwell in. [o] 5 For I have never
dwelt in a house, from the time when I led Israel
onward, even to this day, but I have been
lodging in tent or pavilion 6 as long as I have
wandered about with all of Israel. Did I ever say
a word to any of the judges of Israel whom I
commanded to guide my people, such as, 'Why
have you not built me a house of cedar?'
7 Therefore, tell my servant David, Thus says the
LORD of hosts: I took you from the pasture, from
following the sheep, that you might become
ruler over my people Israel. [p] 8 I was with you
wherever you went, and I cut down all your
enemies before you. I will make your name great
like that of the greatest on the earth. 9 I will
assign a place for my people Israel and I will
plant them in it to dwell there henceforth
undisturbed; nor shall wicked men ever again
oppress them, as they did at first, 10 and during
all the time when I appointed judges over my
people Israel. And I will subdue all your ene-
mies. Moreover, I declare to you that I, the
LORD, will build you a house; 11 so that when
your days have been completed and you must
join your fathers, I will raise up your offspring
after you who will be one of your own sons, and
I will establish his kingdom. [q] 12 He it is who shall
build me a house, and I will establish his throne
forever. [r] 13 I will be a father to him, and he shall
be a son to me, and I will not withdraw my favor
from him as I withdrew it from him who
preceded you; [s] 14 but I will maintain him in my
house and in my kingdom forever, and his
throne shall be firmly established forever."
15 All these words and this whole vision Na-
than related exactly to David.

David's Thanksgiving 16 Then David came in
and sat in the LORD's presence, saying: "Who
am I, O LORD God, and what is my family, that
you should have brought me as far as I have
come? 17 And yet, even this you now consider
too little, O God! For you have made a promise
regarding your servant's family reaching into the
distant future, and you have looked on me as
henceforth the most notable of men, O LORD
God. [t] 18 What more can David say to you? You
know your servant. 19 O LORD, for your servant's
sake and in keeping with your purpose, you have
done this great thing. 20 O LORD, there is no one
like you and there is no God but you, just as we
have always understood. [u]
21 "Is there, like your people Israel, whom you
redeemed from Egypt, another nation on earth
whom a god went to redeem as his people? You
won for yourself a name for great and awesome
deeds by driving out the nations before your
people. [v] 22 You made your people Israel your
own forever, and you, O LORD, became their
God. 23 Therefore, O LORD, may the promise that
you have uttered concerning your servant and
his house remain firm forever. Bring about what
you have promised, 24 that your renown as LORD
of hosts, God of Israel, may be great and abide
forever, while the house of David, your servant,
is established in your presence.
25 "Because you, O my God, have revealed to
your servant that you will build him a house,
your servant has made bold to pray before you. [w]
26 Since you, O LORD, are truly God and have
promised this good thing to your servant, 27 and
since you have deigned to bless the house of
your servant, so that it will remain forever—
since it is you, O LORD, who blessed it, it is
blessed forever." [x]

m 1–27: 2 Sm 7, 1–29. n 1 Chr 15, 1; 2 Sm 5, 11. o 1 Chr 28, 3; 1 Kgs 8, 19. p 1 Sm 16, 11. q 2 Sm 7, 12f. r 1 Chr 22, 10; 28, 6. 10. s 2 Sm 7, 14. t 2 Sm 7, 19. u Sir 36, 4. v Dt 4, 7; 2 Sm 7, 23. w 2 Sm 7, 27. x Nm 22, 6.

CHAPTER 18

David's Victories 1[y]After this, David defeated
the Philistines and subdued them; and he took
Gath and its towns away from the control of the
Philistines. 2He also defeated Moab, and the
Moabites became his subjects, paying tribute.
3David then defeated Hadadezer, king of
Zobah toward Hamath, when the latter was on
his way to set up his victory stele at the river
Euphrates. 4David took from him twenty thou-
sand foot soldiers, one thousand chariots, and
seven thousand horsemen. Of the chariot horses,
David hamstrung all but one hundred.[z] 5The
Arameans of Damascus came to the aid of
Hadadezer, king of Zobah, but David also slew
twenty-two thousand of their men. 6Then David
set up garrisons in the Damascus region of Aram,
and the Arameans became his subjects, paying
tribute. Thus the LORD made David victorious in
all his campaigns.
7David took the golden shields that were
carried by Hadadezer's attendants and brought
them to Jerusalem. 8He likewise took away from
Tibhath and Cun, cities of Hadadezer, large
quantities of bronze, which Solomon later used
to make the bronze sea and the pillars and the
vessels of bronze.[a]
9When Tou, king of Hamath, heard that David
had defeated the entire army of Hadadezer, king
of Zobah, 10he sent his son Hadoram to wish
King David well and to congratulate him on
having waged a victorious war against Hadade-
zer; for Hadadezer had been at war with Tou.
He also sent David gold, silver and bronze
utensils of every sort.[b] 11These also King David
consecrated to the LORD along with all the silver
and gold that he had taken from the nations:
from Edom, Moab, the Ammonites, the Philis-
tines, and Amalek.
12Abishai, the son of Zeruiah, also slew eigh-
teen thousand Edomites in the Valley of Salt.[c]
13He set up garrisons in Edom, and all the
Edomites became David's subjects. Thus the
LORD made David victorious in all his cam-
paigns.

David's Officials 14[d]David reigned over all
Israel and dispensed justice and right to all his
people. 15Joab, son of Zeruiah, was in command
of the army; Jehoshaphat, son of Ahilud, was
herald;[e] 16Zadok, son of Ahitub, and Ahime-
lech, son of Abiathar, were priests;* Shavsha
was scribe;[f] 17Benaiah, son of Jehoiada, was in
command of the Cherethites and the Pelethites;
and David's sons were the chief assistants to the
king.*[g]

CHAPTER 19

Campaigns against Ammon 1[h]Afterward Na-
hash, king of the Ammonites, died and his son
succeeded him as king. 2David said, "I will show
kindness to Hanun, the son of Nahash, for his
father treated me with kindness." Therefore he
sent envoys to him to comfort him over the
death of his father. But when David's servants
had entered the land of the Ammonites to
comfort Hanun, 3the Ammonite princes said to
Hanun, "Do you think David is doing this—
sending you these consolers—to honor your
father? Have not his servants rather come to you
to explore the land, spying it out for its over-
throw?" 4Thereupon Hanun seized David's ser-
vants and had them shaved and their garments
cut off half-way at the hips. Then he sent them
away. 5When David was informed of what had
happened to his men, he sent messengers to
meet them, for the men had been greatly dis-
graced. "Remain at Jericho," the king told them,

18, 16: Zadok . . . and Ahimelech, son of Abiathar, were priests: as in the Chronicler's source, 2 Sm 8, 17. But according to 2 Sm 15, 24. 29. 35; 17, 15; 19, 11; 20, 25, and even 1 Chr 15, 11, it was Abiathar who shared the priestly office with Zadok, and he remained in this office even during the early years of Solomon's reign (1 Kgs 2, 26; 4, 4). Moreover, according to 1 Sm 22, 20; 23, 6; 30, 7, Ahimelech was the father, not the son, of Abiathar. If the text Ahimelech, son of Abiathar, is not due to a scribal change, one must assume that Abiathar had a son who was named after his grandfather and who shared the priestly office with his father during the last years of David's reign.

18, 17: David's sons were the chief assistants to the king: in the parallel passage, 2 Sm 8, 18, which was the Chronicler's source, David's sons were priests. The change is characteristic of the Chronicler, for whom only Aaron's descendants could be priests.

y 1–13: 2 Sm 8, 1–14. z 2 Sm 8, 14; Jos 11, 6. 9. a 2 Sm 8, 8; 1 Kgs 7, 15. 23. 27. b 2 Sm 8, 10. c 2 Sm 8, 13; 2 Kgs 14, 7. d 14–17: 2 Sm 8, 15–18. e 1 Chr 11, 6; 2 Sm 8, 16; 1 Kgs 4, 3. f 1 Chr 24, 3. 6. 31; 2 Sm 8, 17. g 1 Chr 11, 22; 2 Sm 8, 18; 1 Kgs 1, 38. 44. h 1–19: 2 Sm 10, 1–19.

"until your beards have grown again; and then you may come back here."

6 When the Ammonites realized that they had put themselves in bad odor with David, Hanun and the Ammonites sent a thousand talents of silver to hire chariots and horsemen from Aram Naharaim, from Aram-maacah, and from Zobah. 7 They hired thirty-two thousand chariots along with the king of Maacah and his army, who came and encamped before Medeba. The Ammonites also assembled from their cities and came out for war.

8 When David heard of this, he sent Joab and his whole army of warriors against them. 9 The Ammonites marched out and lined up for battle at the gate of the city, while the kings who had come to their help remained apart in the open field. 10 When Joab saw that there was a battle line both in front of and behind him, he chose some of the best fighters among the Israelites and set them in array against the Arameans;[i] 11 the rest of the army, which he placed under the command of his brother Abishai, then lined up to oppose the Ammonites.[j] 12 And he said: "If the Arameans prove too strong for me, you must come to my help; and if the Ammonites prove too strong for you, I will save you. 13 Hold steadfast and let us show ourselves courageous for the sake of our people and the cities of our God; then may the LORD do what seems best to him." 14 Joab therefore advanced with his men to engage the Arameans in battle; but they fled before him. 15 And when the Ammonites saw that the Arameans had fled, they also took to flight before his brother Abishai, and reentered the city. Joab then returned to Jerusalem.

16 Seeing themselves vanquished by Israel, the Arameans sent messengers to bring out the Arameans from the other side of the River, with Shophach, the general of Hadadezer's army, at their head. 17 When this was reported to David, he gathered all Israel together, crossed the Jordan, and met them. With the army of David drawn up to fight the Arameans, they gave battle. 18 But the Arameans fled before Israel, and David slew seven thousand of their chariot fighters and forty thousand of their foot soldiers; he also killed Shophach, the general of the army. 19 When the vassals of Hadadezer saw themselves vanquished by Israel, they made peace with David and became his subjects. After this, the Arameans refused to come to the aid of the Ammonites.

CHAPTER 20

1 At the beginning of the following year, the time when kings go to war, Joab led the army out in force, laid waste the land of the Ammonites, and went on to besiege Rabbah, while David himself remained in Jerusalem. When Joab had attacked Rabbah and destroyed it, 2 [k]David took the crown of Milcom from the idol's head. It was found to weigh a talent of gold; and it contained precious stones, which David wore on his own head. He also brought out a great amount of booty from the city. 3 He deported the people of the city and set them to work with saws, iron picks, and axes. Thus David dealt with all the cities of the Ammonites. Then he and his whole army returned to Jerusalem.

Victories over the Philistines 4 [l]Afterward there was another battle with the Philistines, at Gezer. At that time, Sibbecai the Hushathite slew Sippai, one of the descendants of the Raphaim, and the Philistines were subdued.[m] 5 Once again there was war with the Philistines, and Elhanan, the son of Jair, slew Lahmi, the brother of Goliath* of Gath, whose spear shaft was like a weaver's heddle-bar.[n]

6 In still another battle, at Gath, they encountered a giant, also a descendant of the Raphaim, who had six fingers to each hand and six toes to each foot; twenty-four in all. 7 He defied Israel, and Jonathan, the son of Shimea, David's brother, slew him. 8 These were the descendants of the Raphaim of Gath who died at the hands of David and his servants.

20, 5: Elhanan . . . slew Lahmi, the brother of Goliath: the Chronicler thus solves the difficulty of the apparent contradiction between 1 Sm 17, 49ff (David killed Goliath) and 2 Sm 21, 19 (Elhanan killed Goliath).

i 1 Chr 20, 23; 1 Kgs 2, 28. 34. j 1 Chr 23, 18f. k 2f: 2 Sm 12, 30f. l 4–8: 2 Sm 21, 18–22. m 1 Chr 11, 29; 27, 11. n 1 Chr 11, 26; 1 Sm 17, 4. 23.

CHAPTER 21

David's Census; the Plague [1] [o]A satan* rose up against Israel, and he enticed David into taking a census of Israel.[p] [2]David therefore said to Joab and to the other generals of the army, "Go, find out the number of the Israelites from Beer-sheba to Dan, and report back to me that I may know their number." [3]But Joab replied: "May the LORD increase his people a hundredfold! My lord king, are not all of them my lord's subjects? Why does my lord seek to do this thing? Why will he bring guilt upon Israel?" [4]However, the king's command prevailed over Joab, who departed and traversed all of Israel, and then returned to Jerusalem. [5]Joab reported the result of the census to David: of men capable of wielding a sword, there were in all Israel one million one hundred thousand, and in Judah four hundred and seventy thousand. [6]Levi and Benjamin, however, he did not include in the census, for the king's command was repugnant to Joab.[q] [7]This command displeased God, who began to punish Israel. [8]Then David said to God, "I have sinned greatly in doing this thing. Take away your servant's guilt, for I have acted very foolishly."

[9]Then the LORD spoke to Gad, David's seer, in these words:[r] [10]"Go, tell David: Thus says the LORD: I offer you three alternatives; choose one of them, and I will inflict it on you." [11]Accordingly, Gad went to David and said to him: "Thus says the LORD: Decide now— [12]will it be three years of famine; or three months of fleeing your enemies, with the sword of your foes ever at your back; or three days of the LORD's own sword, a pestilence in the land, with the LORD's destroying angel in every part of Israel? Therefore choose: What answer am I to give him who sent me?" [13]Then David said to Gad: "I am in dire straits. But I prefer to fall into the hand of the LORD, whose mercy is very great, than into the hands of men."

[14]Therefore the LORD sent pestilence upon Israel, and seventy thousand men of Israel died. [15]God also sent an angel to destroy Jerusalem; but as he was on the point of destroying it, the LORD saw and decided against the calamity, and said to the destroying angel, "Enough now! Stay your hand!"[s]

Ornan's Threshing Floor The angel of the LORD was then standing by the threshing floor of Ornan the Jebusite. [16]When David raised his eyes, he saw the angel of the LORD standing between earth and heaven, with a naked sword in his hand stretched out against Jerusalem. David and the elders, clothed in sackcloth, prostrated themselves face to the ground, [17]and David prayed to God: "Was it not I who ordered the census of the people? I am the one who sinned, I did this wicked thing. But these sheep, what have they done? O LORD, my God, strike me and my father's family, but do not afflict your people with this plague!"

[18]Then the angel of the LORD commanded Gad to tell David to go up and erect an altar to the LORD on the threshing floor of Ornan the Jebusite.[t] [19]David went up at Gad's command, given in the name of the LORD. [20]While Ornan was threshing wheat, he turned around and saw the king, and his four sons who were with him, without recognizing them. [21]But as David came on toward him, he looked up and saw that it was David. Then he left the threshing floor and bowed down before David, his face to the ground. [22]David said to Ornan: "Sell me the ground of this threshing floor, that I may build on it an altar to the LORD. Sell it to me at its full price, that the plague may be stayed from the people." [23]But Ornan said to David: "Take it as your own, and let my lord the king do what seems best to him. See, I also give you the oxen for the holocausts, the threshing sledges for the wood, and the wheat for the cereal offering. I give it all to you." [24]But King David replied to

21, 1: A satan: in the parallel passage of 2 Sm 24, 1, the Lord's anger. The change in the term reflects the changed theological outlook of postexilic Israel, when evil could no longer be attributed directly to God. At an earlier period the Hebrew word satan ("adversary," or, especially in a court of law, "accuser"), when not used of men, designated an angel who accused men before God (Jb 1, 6–12; 2, 1–7; Zec 3, 1f). Here, as in later Judaism (Wis 2, 24) and in the New Testament, satan, or the "devil" (from the Greek translation of the word), designates an evil spirit who tempts men to wrongdoing.

o 1–7: 2 Sm 24, 1–25. p Zec 3, 1f. q 1 Chr 27, 24; Nm 1, 49. r 1 Chr 29, 29; 1 Sm 9, 9; 2 Chr 29, 25. s Gn 6, 6; Ex 32, 14; 2 Sm 24, 16; Jon 3, 10. t 2 Chr 3, 1.

Ornan: "No! I will buy it from you properly, at its full price. I will not take what is yours for the LORD, nor offer up holocausts that cost me nothing." 25 So David paid Ornan six hundred shekels of gold* for the place.

Altar of Holocausts 26 David then built an altar there to the LORD, and offered up holocausts and peace offerings. When he called upon the LORD, he answered him by sending down fire from heaven upon the altar of holocausts.[u] 27 Then the LORD gave orders to the angel to return his sword to its sheath.

28 Once David saw that the LORD had heard him on the threshing floor of Ornan the Jebusite, he continued to offer sacrifices there. 29 The Dwelling of the LORD, which Moses had built in the desert, and the altar of holocausts were at that time on the high place at Gibeon.[v] 30 But David could not go there to worship God, for he was fearful of the sword of the angel of the LORD. 1 Therefore David said, "This is the house of the LORD God, and this is the altar of holocausts for Israel."*[w]

CHAPTER 22

Material for the Temple 2 *David then ordered that all the aliens who lived in the land of Israel be brought together, and he appointed them stonecutters to hew out stone blocks for building the house of God.[x] 3 He also laid up large stores of iron to make nails for the doors of the gates, and clamps, together with so much bronze that it could not be weighed,[y] 4 and cedar trees without number. The Sidonians and Tyrians brought great stores of cedar logs to David,[z] 5 who said: "My son Solomon is young and immature; but the house that is to be built for the LORD must be made so magnificent that it will be renowned and glorious in all countries. Therefore I will make preparations for it." Thus before his death David laid up materials in abundance.[a]

Charge to Solomon 6 Then he called for his son Solomon and commanded him to build a house for the LORD, the God of Israel. 7 [b]David said to Solomon: "My son, it was my purpose to build a house myself for the honor of the LORD, my God. 8 But this word of the LORD came to me: 'You have shed much blood, and you have waged great wars. You may not build a house in my honor, because you have shed too much blood upon the earth in my sight. 9 However, a son is to be born to you. He will be a peaceful man, and I will give him rest from all his enemies on every side. For Solomon shall be his name, and in his time I will bestow peace* and tranquility on Israel.[c] 10 It is he who shall build a house in my honor; he shall be a son to me, and I will be a father to him, and I will establish the throne of his kingship over Israel forever.'[d] 11 Now, my son, the LORD be with you, and may you succeed in building the house of the LORD your God, as he has said you shall. 12 May the LORD give you prudence and discernment when he brings you to rule over Israel, so that you keep the law of the LORD, your God. 13 Only then shall you succeed, if you are careful to observe the precepts and decrees which the LORD gave Moses for Israel. Be brave and steadfast; do not fear or lose heart.[e] 14 See, with great effort I have laid up for the house of the LORD a hundred thousand talents of gold,* a million talents of

21, 25: Six hundred shekels of gold: about 10,000 dollars. According to 2 Sm 24, 24, David paid 50 shekels of silver, about 20 dollars, for Ornan's threshing floor; but for the Chronicler the site of the temple was much more precious than that.

21, 1: This belongs to ch 22.

22, 2ff: According to 1 Kgs 5, 15–32, it was Solomon who made the material preparations for building the temple, even though David had wished to do so (1 Kgs 5, 17ff). The Chronicler, however, sought to have David, who was Israel's ideal king, more closely connected with Israel's most sacred sanctuary, the temple of Jerusalem.

22, 9: The Hebrew word for peace, shalom, is reflected in the name Solomon, in Hebrew, Shelomo. A contrast is drawn here between Solomon, the peaceful man, and David, who waged great wars (v 8). David was prevented from building the temple, not only because all his time was taken up in waging war (1 Kgs 5, 17), but also because he shed much blood (v 8), and in the eyes of the Chronicler this made him ritually unfit for the task.

22, 14: A hundred thousand talents of gold: about 3,775 tons of gold. A million talents of silver: about 37,750 tons of silver. The fantastically exaggerated figures are intended merely to stress the inestimable value of the temple as the center of Israelite worship. More modest figures are given in 1 Kgs 9, 14. 28; 10, 10. 14.

u Lv 9, 24; Jgs 6, 21; 1 Kgs 18. 38; 2 Chr 7, 1; 2 Mc 2, 10ff. v 1 Chr 16, 39; 1 Kgs 8, 4; 2 Chr 1, 8. w 1 Chr 21, 18. 26. 28; 2 Chr 3, 1. x 1 Kgs 5, 31f; 9, 20f; 2 Chr 2, 16f. y 1 Chr 18, 8; 1 Kgs 7, 47. z 1 Chr 10, 27; Ezr 3, 7. a 1 Chr 29, 1. b 7-10: 1 Chr 17, 1–14; 28, 2–7; 2 Sm 7, 1–16; 1 Kgs 5, 3ff; 8, 17–21. c 2 Sm 12, 24. d Heb 1, 5. e 1 Chr 28, 7. 20; Dt 31, 6. 23; Jos 1, 6f. 9; 1 Kgs 2, 2f.

silver, and bronze and iron in such great quantities that they cannot be weighed. I have also stored up wood and stones, to which you must add.[f] 15Moreover, you have available an unlimited supply of workmen, stonecutters, masons, carpenters, and every kind of craftsman 16skilled in gold, silver, bronze, and iron. Set to work, therefore, and the LORD be with you!"

Charge to the Leaders 17David also commanded all of Israel's leaders to help his son Solomon: 18"Is not the LORD your God with you? Has he not given you rest on every side? Indeed, he has delivered the occupants of the land into my power, and the land is subdued before the LORD and his people.[g] 19Therefore, devote your hearts and souls to seeking the LORD your God. Proceed to build the sanctuary of the LORD God, that the ark of the covenant of the LORD and God's sacred vessels may be brought into the house built in honor of the LORD."[h]

CHAPTER 23

The Levitical Classes 1When David had grown old and was near the end of his days, he made his son Solomon king over Israel.[i] 2He then gathered together all the leaders of Israel, together with the priests and the Levites.

3The Levites thirty years old and above were counted, and their total number was found to be thirty-eight thousand men.[j] 4Of these, twenty-four thousand were to direct the service of the house of the LORD, six thousand were to be officials and judges, 5four thousand were to be gatekeepers, and four thousand were to praise the LORD with the instruments which David had devised for praise.[k] 6David divided them into classes according to the sons of Levi: Gershon, Kohath, and Merari.[l]

7To the Gershonites belonged Ladan and Shimei. 8The sons of Ladan: Jehiel the chief, then Zetham and Joel; three in all.[m] 9The sons of Shimei were Shelomoth, Haziel, and Haran; three. These were the heads of the families of Ladan. 10The sons of Shimei were Jahath, Zizah, Jeush, and Beriah; these were the sons of Shimei, four in all. 11Jahath was the chief and Zizah was second to him; but Jeush and Beriah had not many sons, and therefore they were classed as a single family, fulfilling a single office.

12The sons of Kohath: Amram, Izhar, Hebron, and Uzziel; four in all.[n] 13The sons of Amram were Aaron and Moses. Aaron was set apart to be consecrated as most holy, he and his sons forever, to offer sacrifice before the LORD, to minister to him, and to bless his name forever.[o] 14As for Moses, however, the man of God, his sons were counted as part of the tribe of Levi. 15The sons of Moses were Gershon and Eliezer.[p] 16The sons of Gershon: Shubael the chief.[q] 17The sons of Eliezer were Rehabiah the chief—Eliezer had no other sons, but the sons of Rehabiah were very numerous. 18The sons of Izhar: Shelomith the chief. 19The sons of Hebron: Jeriah, the chief, Amariah, the second, Jahaziel, the third, and Jekameam, the fourth.[r] 20The sons of Uzziel: Micah, the chief, and Isshiah, the second.[s]

21The sons of Merari: Mahli and Mushi. The sons of Mahli: Eleazar and Kish.[t] 22Eleazar died leaving no sons, only daughters; the sons of Kish, their kinsmen, married them.[u] 23The sons of Mushi: Mahli, Eder, and Jeremoth; three in all.[v]

24These were the sons of Levi according to their ancestral houses, the family heads as they were enrolled one by one according to their names. They performed the work of the service of the house of the LORD from twenty years of age upward,[w] 27for David's final orders were to enlist the Levites from the time they were twenty years old.

25David said: "The LORD, the God of Israel, has given rest to his people, and has taken up his dwelling in Jerusalem.[x] 26Henceforth the Levites need not carry the Dwelling or any of its

f 1 Chr 29, 2ff. g 1 Chr 23, 25; Jos 21, 44; 23, 1; 2 Sm 7, 1. h 1 Kgs 8, 6. 21; 2 Chr 5, 7; 6, 11. i 1 Chr 28, 5; 1 Kgs 1, 30. j Nm 4, 3. 23. 30. 35. 39. 43. 47; 8, 23–26; 2 Chr 31, 17. k 1 Chr 9, 22. l 1 Chr 6, 1. 16–30; 26, 1–19; Ex 6, 16; Nm 3, 17; 26, 57. m 1 Chr 26, 21f; 29, 8. n 1 Chr 26, 23; Ex 6, 18; Nm 3, 19; 26, 23ff. o 1 Chr 6, 49; Ex 6, 20; 28, 1; Nm 6, 23. p Ex 2, 22; 18, 3f. q 1 Chr 26, 24. r 1 Chr 24, 23. s 1 Chr 24, 24f. t 1 Chr 6, 29; 24, 26. 28f; Ex 6, 19; Nm 3, 20. 33. u 1 Chr 24, 28f. v 1 Chr 6, 47; 24, 30. w 2 Chr 31, 17; Ezr 3, 8. x 1 Chr 22, 18; Ps 132, 13.

furnishings or equipment.[y] 28 Rather, their duty shall be to assist the sons of Aaron in the service of the house of the LORD, having charge of the courts, the chambers, and the preservation of everything holy: they shall take part in the service of the house of God. 29 They shall also have charge of the showbread, of the fine flour for the cereal offering, of the wafers of unleavened bread, and of the baking and mixing, and of all measures of quantity and size.[z] 30 They must be present every morning to offer thanks and to praise the LORD, and likewise in the evening;[a] 31 and at every offering of holocausts to the LORD on sabbaths, new moons, and feast days, in such numbers as are prescribed, they must always be present before the LORD.[b] 32 They shall observe what is prescribed for them concerning the meeting tent, the sanctuary, and the sons of Aaron, their brethren, in the service of the house of the LORD."[c]

CHAPTER 24

The Priestly Classes 1 The descendants of Aaron also were divided into classes. The sons of Aaron were Nadab, Abihu, Eleazar, and Ithamar.[d] 2 Nadab and Abihu died before their father, leaving no sons; therefore only Eleazar and Ithamar served as priests.[e] 3 David, with Zadok, a descendant of Eleazar, and Ahimelech, a descendant of Ithamar, assigned the functions for the priestly service.[f] 4 But since the descendants of Eleazar were found to be more numerous than those of Ithamar, the former were divided into sixteen groups, and the latter into eight groups, each under its family head. 5 Their functions were assigned impartially by lot, for there were officers of the holy place, and officers of the divine presence, descended both from Eleazar and from Ithamar. 6 The scribe Shemaiah, son of Nethanel, a Levite, made a record of it in the presence of the king, and of the leaders, of Zadok the priest, and of Ahimelech, son of Abiathar,* and of the heads of the ancestral houses of the priests and of the Levites, listing two successive family groups from Eleazar before each one from Ithamar.[g]

7 [h] The first lot fell to Jehoiarib, the second to Jedaiah, 8 the third to Harim, the fourth to Seorim, 9 the fifth to Malchijah, the sixth to Mijamin, 10 the seventh to Hakkoz, the eighth to Abijah,[i] 11 the ninth to Jeshua, the tenth to Shecaniah, 12 the eleventh to Eliashib, the twelfth to Jakim, 13 the thirteenth to Huppah, the fourteenth to Ishbaal, 14 the fifteenth to Bilgah, the sixteenth to Immer, 15 the seventeenth to Hezir, the eighteenth to Happizzez, 16 the nineteenth to Pethahiah, the twentieth to Jehezkel, 17 the twenty-first to Jachin, the twenty-second to Gamul, 18 the twenty-third to Delaiah, the twenty-fourth to Maaziah. 19 This was the appointed order of their service when they functioned in the house of the LORD in keeping with the precepts given them by Aaron, their father, as the LORD, the God of Israel, had commanded him.[j]

Other Levites 20 [k] Of the remaining Levites, there were Shubael, of the descendants of Amram, and Jehdeiah, of the descendants of Shubael; 21 Isshiah, the chief, of the descendants of Rehabiah; 22 Shelomith of the Izharites, and Jahath of the descendants of Shelomith. 23 The descendants of Hebron were Jeriah, the chief, Amariah, the second, Jahaziel, the third, Jekameam, the fourth. 24 The descendants of Uzziel were Micah; Shamir, of the descendants of Micah; 25 Isshiah, the brother of Micah; and Zechariah, a descendant of Isshiah. 26 The descendants of Merari were Mahli, Mushi, and the descendants of his son Uzziah. 27 The descendants of Merari through his son Uzziah: Shoham, Zaccur, and Ibri. 28 Descendants of Mahli were Eleazar, who had no sons, 29 and Jerahmeel, of the descendants of Kish. 30 The descendants of Mushi were Mahli, Eder, and Jerimoth.

These were the descendants of the Levites according to their ancestral houses. 31 They too, in the same manner as their relatives, the

24, 6: Ahimelech, son of Abiathar: see note on 1 Chr 18, 16.

y 1 Chr 15, 15; 2 Chr 35, 3. z 1 Chr 9, 29. 31f; Lv 2, 1. 4f; 24, 5–8. a Nm 28, 3–8. b Nm 28, 2–29. 39. c Nm 3, 6–9; 18, 2–5. d Ex 6, 23; Nm 3, 2ff; 26, 60. e Lv 10, 1–7. 12; Nm 3, 2. 4. f 1 Chr 18, 16; 2 Sm 8, 17; 2 Chr 8, 14. g 1 Chr 18, 16; 2 Sm 8, 17. h 7–10: 1 Chr 9, 10ff; Ezr 2, 36ff; Neh 7, 39ff; 11, 10ff. i Lk 1, 5. j 2 Chr 23, 8. k 20–31: 1 Chr 23, 7–23.

descendants of Aaron, cast lots in the presence of King David, Zadok, Ahimelech, and the heads of the priestly and levitical families; the more important family did so in the same way as the less important one.[l]

CHAPTER 25

The Singers [1]David and the leaders of the liturgical cult set apart for service the descendants of Asaph, Heman, and Jeduthun, as singers of inspired song to the accompaniment of lyres and harps and cymbals.[m]

This is the list of those who performed this service: [2]*Of the sons of Asaph: Zaccur, Joseph, Nethaniah, and Asharelah, sons of Asaph, under the direction of Asaph, who sang inspired songs under the guidance of the king. [3]Of Jeduthun, these sons of Jeduthun: Gedaliah, Zeri, Jeshaiah, Shimei, Hashabiah, and Mattithiah; six, under the direction of their father Jeduthun, who sang inspired songs to the accompaniment of a lyre, to give thanks and praise to the LORD. [4]Of Heman, these sons of Heman: Bukkiah, Mattaniah, Uzziel, Shubael, and Jerimoth; Hananiah, Hanani, Eliathah, Giddalti, Romamti-ezer, Joshbekashah, Mallothi, Hothir, and Mahazioth. [5]All these were the sons of Heman, the king's seer in divine matters; to enhance his prestige, God gave Heman fourteen sons and three daughters.[n] [6]All these, whether of Asaph, Jeduthun, or Heman, were under their fathers' direction in the singing in the house of the LORD to the accompaniment of cymbals, harps and lyres, serving in the house of God, under the guidance of the king.[o] [7]Their number, together with that of their brethren who were trained in singing to the LORD, all of them skilled men, was two hundred and eighty-eight. [8]They cast lots for their functions equally, young and old, master and pupil alike.[p]

[9]The first lot fell to Asaph, the family of Joseph; he and his sons and his brethren were twelve. Gedaliah was the second; he and his brethren and his sons were twelve. [10]The third was Zaccur, his sons, and his brethren: twelve. [11]The fourth fell to Izri, his sons, and his brethren: twelve. [12]The fifth was Nethaniah, his sons, and his brethren: twelve. [13]The sixth was Bukkiah, his sons, and his brethren: twelve. [14]The seventh was Jesarelah, his sons, and his brethren: twelve. [15]The eighth was Jeshaiah, his sons, and his brethren: twelve. [16]The ninth was Mattaniah, his sons, and his brethren: twelve. [17]The tenth was Shimei, his sons, and his brethren: twelve. [18]The eleventh was Uzziel, his sons, and his brethren: twelve. [19]The twelfth fell to Hashabiah, his sons, and his brethren: twelve. [20]The thirteenth was Shubael, his sons, and his brethren: twelve. [21]The fourteenth was Mattithiah, his sons, and his brethren: twelve. [22]The fifteenth fell to Jeremoth, his sons, and his brethren: twelve. [23]The sixteenth fell to Hananiah, his sons, and his brethren: twelve. [24]The seventeenth fell to Joshbekashah, his sons, and his brethren: twelve. [25]The eighteenth fell to Hanani, his sons, and his brethren: twelve. [26]The nineteenth fell to Mallothi, his sons, and his brethren: twelve. [27]The twentieth fell to Eliathah, his sons, and his brethren: twelve. [28]The twenty-first fell to Hothir, his sons, and his brethren: twelve. [29]The twenty-second fell to Giddalti, his sons, and his brethren: twelve. [30]The twenty-third fell to Mahazioth, his sons, and his brethren: twelve. [31]The twenty-fourth fell to Romamti-ezer, his sons, and his brethren: twelve.

CHAPTER 26

Classes of Gatekeepers [1][q]As for the classes of gatekeepers. Of the Korahites was Meshelemiah, the son of Kore, one of the sons of Abiasaph. [2]Meshelemiah's sons: Zechariah, the first-born, Jediael, the second son, Zebadiah, the third, Jathniel, the fourth, [3]Elam, the fifth,

25, 2–31: This list of twenty-four classes of temple singers balances the list of the twenty-four classes of priests (1 Chr 24, 4–19). The last nine names in 1 Chr 25, 4, which seem to form a special group, appear to have been originally fragments or incipits of hymns. With some slight changes in the vocalization, the names would mean: "Have mercy on me, O Lord," "Have mercy on me," "You are my God," "I magnify," "I extol the help of . . . ," "Sitting in adversity," "I have fulfilled," "He made abundant," and "Visions."

l 1 Chr 25, 8; 26, 13. m 1 Chr 6, 31ff; 15, 16f. 19; 16, 37; 2 Chr 5, 12; 35, 15; Neh 12, 27. 45. n 2 Chr 35, 15. o 1 Chr 15, 16. p 1 Chr 24, 31. q 1 Chr 9, 19; 2 Chr 8, 14; 23, 19; 35, 15; Neh 12, 45.

Jehohanan, the sixth, Eliehoenai, the seventh. 4 Obed-edom's sons: Shemaiah, the first-born, Jehozabad, a second son, Joah, the third, Sachar, the fourth, Nethanel, the fifth, 5 Ammiel, the sixth, Issachar, the seventh, Peullethai, the eighth, for God blessed him. 6 To his son Shemaiah were born sons who ruled over their family, for they were warriors. 7 The sons of Shemaiah were Othni, Rephael, Obed, and Elzabad; also his brethren who were men of might, Elihu and Semachiah. 8 All these were of the sons of Obed-edom, who, together with their sons and their brethren, were mighty men, fit for the service. Of Obed-edom, sixty-two. 9 Of Meshelemiah, eighteen sons and brethren, mighty men.

10 Hosah, a descendant of Merari, had these sons: Shimri, the chief (for though he was not the first-born, his father made him chief),[r] 11 Hilkiah, the second son, Tebaliah, the third, Zechariah, the fourth. All the sons and brethren of Hosah were thirteen.

12 To these classes of gatekeepers, under their chief men, were assigned watches in the service of the house of the LORD, for each group in the same way. 13 They cast lots for each gate, the small and the large families alike. 14 When the lot was cast for the east side, it fell to Meshelemiah. Then they cast lots for his son Zechariah, a prudent counselor, and the north side fell to his lot.[s] 15 To Obed-edom fell the south side, and to his sons the storehouse. 16 To Hosah fell the west side with the Shallecheth gate at the ascending highway. For each family, watches were established. 17 On the east, six watched each day, on the north, four each day, on the south, four each day, and at the storehouse they were two and two; 18 as for the large building* on the west, there were four at the highway and two at the large building. 19 These were the classes of the gatekeepers, descendants of Kore and Merari.

Treasurers 20 Their brother Levites superintended the stores for the house of God and the stores of votive offerings.[t] 21 Among the descendants of Ladan the Gershonite, the family heads were descendants of Jehiel: the descendants of Jehiel,[u] 22 [v]Zetham and his brother Joel, who superintended the treasures of the house of the LORD. 23 From the Amramites, Izharites, Hebronites, and Uzzielites, 24 Shubael, son of Gershon, son of Moses, was chief superintendent over the treasures. 25 [w]His associate pertained to Eliezer, whose son was Rehabiah, whose son was Jeshaiah, whose son was Joram, whose son was Zichri, whose son was Shelomith. 26 This Shelomith and his brethren superintended all the stores of the votive offerings dedicated by King David, the heads of the families, the commanders of thousands and of hundreds, and the commanders of the army,[x] 27 from the booty they had taken in the wars, for the enhancement of the house of the LORD. 28 Also, whatever Samuel the seer, Saul, son of Kish, Abner, son of Ner, Joab, son of Zeruiah, and all others had consecrated, was under the charge of Shelomith and his brethren.

Magistrates 29 Among the Izharites, Chananiah and his sons were in charge of Israel's civil affairs as officials and judges.[y] 30 Among the Hebronites, Hashabiah and his brethren, one thousand seven hundred police officers, had the administration of Israel on the western side of the Jordan in all the work of the LORD and in the service of the king.[z] 31 Among the Hebronites, Jerijah was their chief according to their family records. In the fortieth year of David's reign search was made, and there were found among them outstanding officers at Jazer of Gilead.[a] 32 His brethren were also police officers, two thousand seven hundred heads of families. King David appointed them to the administration of the Reubenites, the Gadites, and the half-tribe of Manasseh in everything pertaining to God and to the king.

26, 18: The large building (in the Hebrew text Parbar): see note on 2 Kgs 23, 11.

r 1 Chr 16, 38. s 1 Chr 9, 24. t 1 Chr 28, 12; 1 Kgs 7, 51. u 1 Chr 23, 7f; 29, 8. v 22ff: 1 Chr 23, 8. 12. 16. w 1 Chr 23, 17f; 24, 21. x 2 Sm 8, 11. y 1 Chr 23, 4. z 1 Chr 27, 17; Neh 11, 15f. a 1 Chr 23, 19; 29, 27; Jos 13, 25.

CHAPTER 27

Army Commanders* 1This is the list of the Israelite family heads, commanders of thousands and of hundreds, and other officers who served the king in all that pertained to the divisions, of twenty-four thousand men each, that came and went month by month throughout the year.

2Over the first division for the first month was Ishbaal, son of Zabdiel, and in his division were twenty-four thousand men; 3a descendant of Perez, he was chief over all the commanders of the army for the first month. 4Over the division of the second month was Eleazar, son of Dodo, from Ahoh, and in his division were twenty-four thousand men.[b] 5[c]The third army commander, chief for the third month, was Benaiah, son of Jehoiada the priest, and in his division were twenty-four thousand men. 6This Benaiah was a warrior among the Thirty and over the Thirty. His son Ammizabad was over his division. 7Fourth, for the fourth month, was Asahel, brother of Joab, and after him his son Zebadiah, and in his division were twenty-four thousand men.[d] 8Fifth, for the fifth month, was the commander Shamhuth, a descendant of Zerah, and in his division were twenty-four thousand men. 9Sixth, for the sixth month, was Ira, son of Ikkesh, from Tekoa, and in his division were twenty-four thousand men. 10Seventh, for the seventh month, was Helles, from Beth-pheleth, of the sons of Ephraim, and in his division were twenty-four thousand men. 11Eighth, for the eighth month, was Sibbecai the Hushathite, a descendant of Zerah, and in his division were twenty-four thousand men.[e] 12Ninth, for the ninth month, was Abiezer from Anathoth, of Benjamin, and in his division were twenty-four thousand men. 13Tenth, for the tenth month, was Maharai from Netophah, a descendant of Zerah, and in his division were twenty-four thousand men. 14Eleventh, for the eleventh month, was Benaiah the Pirathonite, of Ephraim, and in his division were twenty-four thousand men. 15Twelfth, for the twelfth month, was Heldai the Netophathite, of the family of Othniel, and in his division were twenty-four thousand men.

Tribal Heads 16Over the tribes of Israel, for the Reubenites the leader was Eliezer, son of Zichri; for the Simeonites, Shephatiah, son of Maacah; 17for Levi, Hashabiah, son of Kemuel; for Aaron, Zadok; 18for Judah, Eliab, one of David's brothers; for Issachar, Omri, son of Michael;[f] 19for Zebulun, Ishmaiah, son of Obadiah; for Naphtali, Jeremoth, son of Azriel; 20for the sons of Ephraim, Hoshea, son of Azaziah; for the half-tribe of Manasseh, Joel, son of Pedaiah; 21for the half-tribe of Manasseh in Gilead, Iddo, son of Zechariah; for Benjamin, Jaasiel, son of Abner; 22for Dan, Azarel, son of Jeroham. These were the commanders of the tribes of Israel.

23David did not count those who were twenty years of age or younger, for the LORD had promised to multiply Israel like the stars of the heavens.[g] 24Joab, son of Zeruiah, began to take the census, but he did not complete it, for because of it wrath fell upon Israel. Therefore the number did not enter into the book of chronicles of King David.[h]

Overseers 25Over the treasures of the king was Azmaveth, the son of Adiel. Over the stores in the country, the cities, the villages, and the towers was Jonathan, son of Uzziah.[i] 26Over the farm workers who tilled the soil was Ezri, son of Chelub. 27Over the vineyards was Shimei from Ramah, and over their produce for the wine cellars was Zabdi the Shiphmite. 28Over the olive trees and sycamores of the foothills was Baal-hanan the Gederite, and over the stores of oil was Joash. 29Over the cattle that grazed in Sharon was Shitrai the Sharonite, and over the cattle in the valleys was Shaphat, the son of Adlai; 30over the camels was Obil the Ishmaelite; over the she-asses was Jehdeiah the Merono-

27, 1–15: This list of army commanders is similar to, but distinct from, the list of David's warriors as given in 1 Chr 11, 10–47. The schematic enumeration of the soldiers as presented here is, no doubt, artificial and grossly exaggerated (12 × 24,000 = 288,000 men!), unless the Hebrew word (eleph) for thousand is understood as designating a military unit of much smaller size; see note on 1 Chr 12, 25–38.

b 1 Chr 9, 37; 11, 12; 2 Sm 23, 9. c 5f: 1 Chr 11, 22ff; 18, 17; 2 Sm 23, 20ff. d 2 Sm 2, 18; 23, 24. e 1 Chr 11, 29; 20, 4; 2 Sm 21, 18. f 1 Chr 2, 13. g 1 Chr 22, 17. h 2 Sm 24, 10. i 2 Sm 23, 31.

thite; 31 and over the flocks was Jaziz the Hag-
rite. All these were the overseers of King David's
possessions.
David's Court 32 Jonathan, David's uncle and a
man of intelligence, was counselor and scribe;
he and Jehiel, the son of Hachmoni, were tutors
of the king's sons. 33 Ahithophel was also the
king's counselor, and Hushai the Archite was the
king's confidant.[j] 34 After Ahithophel* came Je-
hoiada, the son of Benaiah, and Abiathar. The
commander of the king's army was Joab.

CHAPTER 28

The Assembly at Jerusalem 1 David assem-
bled at Jerusalem all the leaders of Israel, the
heads of the tribes, the commanders of the
divisions who were in the service of the king,
the commanders of thousands and of hundreds,
the overseers of all the king's estates and posses-
sions, and his sons, together with the courtiers,
the warriors, and every important man.[k] 2 [l]King
David rose to his feet and said: "Hear me, my
brethren and my people. It was my purpose to
build a house of repose myself for the ark of the
covenant of the LORD, the footstool for the feet
of our God;* and I was preparing to build it.
3 But God said to me, 'You may not build a house
in my honor, for you are a man who fought wars
and shed blood.' 4 However, the LORD, the God
of Israel, chose me from all my father's family to
be king over Israel forever. For he chose Judah as
leader, then one family of Judah, that of my
father; and finally, among all the sons of my
father, it pleased him to make me king over all
Israel.[m] 5 And of all my sons—for the LORD has
given me many sons—he has chosen my son
Solomon to sit on the LORD's royal throne over
Israel.[n] 6 For he said to me: 'It is your son
Solomon who shall build my house and my
courts, for I have chosen him for my son, and I
will be a father to him.[o] 7 I will establish his
kingdom forever, if he perseveres in keeping my
commandments and decrees as he keeps them
now.' 8 Therefore in the presence of all Israel, the
assembly of the LORD, and in the hearing of our
God, I exhort you to keep and to carry out all the
commandments of the LORD, your God, that you
may continue to possess this good land and
afterward leave it as an inheritance to your
children forever.[p]
9 "As for you, Solomon, my son, know the
God of your father and serve him with a perfect
heart and a willing soul, for the LORD searches
all hearts and understands all the mind's
thoughts. If you seek him, he will let himself be
found by you; but if you abandon him, he will
cast you off forever.[q] 10 See, then! The LORD has
chosen you to build a house as his sanctuary.
Take courage and set to work."
Temple Plans Given to Solomon 11 Then Da-
vid gave to his son Solomon the pattern of the
portico and of the building itself, with its store-
rooms, its upper rooms and inner chambers, and
the room with the propitiatory.[r] 12 He provided
also the pattern for all else that he had in mind
by way of courts for the house of the LORD, with
the surrounding compartments for the stores for
the house of God and the stores of the votive
offerings, 13 as well as for the divisions of the
priests and Levites, for all the work of the service
of the house of the LORD, and for all the liturgical
vessels of the house of the LORD. 14 He specified
the weight of gold to be used in the golden
vessels for the various services and the weight of
silver to be used in the silver vessels for the
various services; 15 likewise for the golden
lampstands and their lamps he specified the
weight of gold for each lampstand and its lamps,
and for the silver lampstands he specified the
weight of silver for each lampstand and its

27, 34: After Ahithophel: after his suicide (2 Sm 17, 23). Jehoiada then succeeded him as the king's counselor. Abiathar: the priest. The Chronicler does not mention his office because he regards only the Zadokites as legitimate high priests.

28, 2: The ark . . . the footstool . . . of our God: the Lord, who was invisibly enthroned upon the cherubim that were associated with the ark of the covenant at Shiloh and later in the Jerusalem temple, had the ark as his footstool; cf Pss 99, 5; 132, 7. The propitiatory (1 Chr 28, 11) and the chariot throne (1 Chr 28, 18) reflect the different circumstances of the postexilic community, for whom only the place of the ark was a focal point of worship, though the ark itself was no longer present.

j 2 Sm 15, 12. 32–37; 16, 16–19. 23; 17, 5–16. 23. k 1 Chr 27, 2–22. 25–31; 11, 10ff. l 2f: 1 Chr 17, 4; 22, 7ff; 2 Sm 7, 5; 1 Kgs 5, 3; Ps 132, 3–7. m 1 Chr 17, 23; Gn 49, 8ff; 1 Sm 16, 6–13. n 1 Chr 3, 1–9; 14, 3–7; 22, 9; 23, 1; Wis 9, 7. o 1 Chr 17, 11ff; 22, 9f; 2 Sm 7, 12f. p Dt 4, 5. q 1 Chr 29, 17; 2 Chr 15, 2; 1 Kgs 8, 61. r Ex 25, 9. 40; 26, 30.

lamps, depending on the use to which each
lampstand was to be put.[s] [16]He specified the
weight of gold for each table to hold the show-
bread, and the silver for the silver tables; [17]the
pure gold to be used for the forks and pitchers;
the amount of gold for each golden bowl and the
silver for each silver bowl; [18]the refined gold,
and its weight, to be used for the altar of
incense; and, finally, gold for what would sug-
gest a chariot throne:* the cherubim that spread
their wings and covered the ark of the covenant
of the LORD.[t] [19]He had successfully committed
to writing the exact specifications of the pattern,
because the hand of the LORD was upon him.

[20]Then David said to his son Solomon: "Be
firm and steadfast; go to work without fear or
discouragement, for the LORD God, my God, is
with you. He will not fail you or abandon you
before you have completed all the work for the
service of the house of the LORD.[u] [21]The classes
of the priests and Levites are ready for all the
service of the house of God; they will help you
in all your work with all those who are eager to
show their skill in every kind of craftsmanship.
Also the leaders and all the people will do
everything that you command."[v]

CHAPTER 29

Offerings for the Temple [1]King David then
said to the whole assembly: "My son Solomon,
whom alone God has chosen, is still young and
immature; the work, however, is great, for this
castle is not intended for man, but for the LORD
God.[w] [2]For this reason I have stored up for the
house of my God, as far as I was able, gold for
what will be made of gold, silver for what will be
made of silver, bronze for what will be made of
bronze, iron for what will be made of iron, wood
for what will be made of wood, onyx stones and
settings for them, carnelian and mosaic stones,
every other kind of precious stone, and great
quantities of marble.[x] [3]But now, because of the
delight I take in the house of my God, in
addition to all that I stored up for the holy house,
I give to the house of my God my personal
fortune in gold and silver: [4]three thousand
talents of Ophir gold, and seven thousand talents
of refined silver, for overlaying the walls of the
rooms,[y] [5]for the various utensils to be made of
gold and silver, and for every work that is to be
done by artisans. Now, who else is willing to
contribute generously this day to the LORD?"[z]

[6]Then the heads of the families, the leaders of
the tribes of Israel, the commanders of thousands
and of hundreds, and the overseers of the king's
affairs came forward willingly[a] [7]and contributed
for the service of the house of God five thousand
talents and ten thousand darics of gold, ten thou-
sand talents of silver, eighteen thousand talents of
bronze, and one hundred thousand talents of
iron.[b] [8]Those who had precious stones gave
them into the keeping of Jehiel the Gershonite for
the treasury of the house of the LORD.[c] [9]The
people rejoiced over these free-will offerings,
which had been contributed to the LORD whole-
heartedly. King David also rejoiced greatly.[d]

David's Prayer [10]Then David blessed the LORD
in the presence of the whole assembly, praying
in these words:

"Blessed may you be, O LORD,
God of Israel our father,
from eternity to eternity.

[11]"Yours, O LORD, are grandeur and power,
majesty, splendor, and glory.
For all in heaven and on earth is yours;
yours, O LORD, is the sovereignty;
you are exalted as head over all.

[12]"Riches and honor are from you,
and you have dominion over all.
In your hand are power and might;
it is yours to give grandeur and strength to
all.[e]

[13]Therefore, our God, we give you thanks
and we praise the majesty of your name.

[14]"But who am I, and who are my people,
that we should have the means to contribute so

28, 18: Chariot throne: probably suggested by Ez 1, 4–24; 10, 1–22.

s Ex 25, 31–37. t Ex 25, 18–22; 30, 1–10; 1 Kgs 6, 23–28. u 1 Chr 22, 13. 16; Jos 1, 5. v Ex 36, 1–5. w 1 Chr 22, 5; 28, 5. x 1 Chr 22, 14. y 2 Chr 9, 10; 1 Kgs 9, 28; 10, 11. z Ex 25, 2; 35, 5f. a 1 Chr 27, 1. 25–31; 28, 1. b Ezr 2, 69; 8, 27; Neh 7, 70ff. c 1 Chr 23, 8; 26, 21. d 2 Kgs 12, 4. e 2 Chr 20, 6; Wis 6, 3.

freely? For everything is from you, and we only
give you what we have received from you. 15 For
we stand before you as aliens: we are only your
guests, like all our fathers. Our life on earth is
like a shadow that does not abide.[f] 16 O LORD
our God, all this wealth that we have brought
together to build you a house in honor of your
holy name comes from you and is entirely yours.
17 I know, O my God, that you put hearts to the
test and that you take pleasure in uprightness.
With a sincere heart I have willingly given all
these things, and now with joy I have seen your
people here present also giving to you gener-
ously. 18 O LORD, God of our fathers Abraham,
Isaac, and Israel, keep such thoughts in the
hearts and minds of your people forever, and
direct their hearts toward you.[g] 19 Give to my
son Solomon a wholehearted desire to keep your
commandments, precepts, and statutes, that he
may carry out all these plans and build the castle
for which I have made preparation."

20 Then David besought the whole assembly,
"Now bless the LORD your God!" And the whole
assembly blessed the LORD, the God of their
fathers, bowing down and prostrating them-
selves before the LORD and before the king. 21 On
the following day they offered sacrifices and
holocausts to the LORD, a thousand bulls, a
thousand rams, and a thousand lambs, together
with their libations and many other sacrifices for
all Israel; 22 and on that day they ate and drank
in the LORD's presence with great rejoicing.
Solomon Anointed Then for a second time*
they proclaimed David's son Solomon king, and
they anointed him as the LORD's prince, and
Zadok as priest. 23 Thereafter Solomon sat on the
throne of the LORD as king in place of his father
David; he prospered, and all Israel obeyed him.[h]
24 All the leaders and warriors, and also all the
other sons of King David, swore allegiance to
King Solomon. 25 And the LORD exalted Solomon
greatly in the eyes of all Israel, giving him a
glorious reign such as had not been enjoyed by
any king over Israel before him.[i]
Death of David 26 Thus David, the son of Jesse,
had reigned over all Israel. 27 The time that he
reigned over Israel was forty years: in Hebron he
reigned seven years, and in Jerusalem thirty-
three.[j] 28 He died at a ripe old age, rich in years
and wealth and glory, and his son Solomon
succeeded him as king.[k]

29 Now the deeds of King David, first and last,
can be found written in the history of Samuel the
seer, the history of Nathan the prophet, and the
history of Gad the seer,[l] 30 together with the
particulars of his reign and valor, and of the
events that affected him and all Israel and all the
kingdoms of the surrounding lands.

29, 22: For a second time: the first time is referred to in 1 Chr 23, 1. Here there is a solemn public ratification of David's earlier appointment of Solomon as his successor.

f Lv 25, 23; Wis 2, 5; 5, 9. g Ex 3, 6. 15f; 4. 5; 1 Kgs 18, 36. h 1 Chr 28, 5; 2 Chr 9, 8; 1 Kgs 2, 10ff. i 2 Chr 1, 12; 1 Kgs 3, 13. j 2 Sm 5, 5; 1 Kgs 2, 11. k 1 Chr 23, 1. l 1 Chr 21, 9; 1 Sm 22, 5.

THE SECOND BOOK OF CHRONICLES

The Second Book of Chronicles takes up the history of the monarchy where the First Book breaks off. It begins with the account of the reign of Solomon from the special viewpoint of the Chronicler. The portrait of Solomon is an idealized one; he appears as second only to David. The great achievement of the building of the temple and the magnificence of Solomon's court are described in detail while the serious defects of his reign are passed over without comment. All this is in keeping with the Chronicler's purpose of stressing the supreme importance of the temple and its worship. He wishes to impress on his readers the splendor of God's dwelling and the magnificence of the liturgy of sacrifice, prayer and praise offered there. Judah's kings are judged by their attitude toward the temple and its cult. To this ideal of one people, united in the worship of the one true God at the temple of Jerusalem founded by David and Solomon, the restored community would have to conform.

In treating the period of divided monarchy, the Chronicler gives practically all his attention to the kingdom of Judah. His omission of the northern Israelite kings is significant. In his view, the northern tribes of Israel were in religious schism as long as they worshiped Yahweh in a place other than the temple of Jerusalem. The Chronicler makes no mention of the important sanctuaries of Yahweh at Dan and Bethel—as though they had never existed. Nevertheless he retains the ancient ideal of "all Israel" (a phrase occurring forty-one times in Chronicles) as the people of God. The condition he places for a united people is that "the whole congregation of Israel" worship the Lord only in his temple at Jerusalem. This explains his praise of Kings Hezekiah and Josiah for striving, after the fall of Samaria, to unite the remnants of the northern tribes of Israel into the kingdom of Judah.

At the end of the fifth century B.C., during the Chronicler's own time, "the people of the land" were the descendants of the people of all the tribes (including Judah) who had not gone into exile. These had become intermingled with aliens and had evolved a religion of Yahweh very different from the Judaism that developed during the Babylonian exile. Thus, religious and political cooperation between the returned exiles and these "people of the land" was out of the question for the Chronicler. This he clearly shows in the last part of his work, the Books of Ezra and Nehemiah.

The Second Book of Chronicles is divided as follows:

I. The Reign of Solomon (1, 1—9, 31).
II. The Monarchy before Hezekiah (10, 1—27, 9).
III. Reforms of Hezekiah and Josiah (28, 1—36, 1).
IV. End of the Kingdom (36, 2-23).

I: The Reign of Solomon

CHAPTER 1

Solomon at Gibeon 1 Solomon, son of David,
strengthened his hold on the kingdom, for the
LORD, his God, was with him, constantly making
him more renowned. 2 He sent a summons to all
Israel, to the commanders of thousands and of
hundreds, the judges, the princes of all Israel,
and the family heads; 3 [a]and, accompanied by
the whole assembly, he went to the high place at
Gibeon, because the meeting tent of God, made
in the desert by Moses, the LORD's servant, was
there. 4 (The ark of God, however, David had
brought up from Kiriath-jearim to Jerusalem,
where he had provided a place and pitched a
tent for it.) 5 The bronze altar made by Bezalel,
son of Uri, son of Hur, he put in front of the
LORD's Dwelling* on the high place. There
Solomon and the assembly consulted the LORD, [b]
6 and Solomon offered sacrifice in the LORD's
presence on the bronze altar at the meeting tent;
he offered a thousand holocausts upon it.

7 That night God appeared to Solomon and
said to him, "Make a request of me, and I will
grant it to you." 8 Solomon answered God: "You
have shown great favor to my father David, and
you have allowed me to succeed him as king.
9 Now, LORD God, may your promise to my
father David be fulfilled, for you have made me

1, 5: The bronze altar . . . the Lord's Dwelling: the Chronicler justifies Solomon's worship at the high place of Gibeon. He pictures the Lord's Dwelling, i.e., the Mosaic meeting tent, and the bronze altar made at Moses' command (Ex 31, 1–9) as still at Gibeon after David had removed the ark of the covenant from there to a new tent in Jerusalem (1 Chr 15, 1. 25; 16, 1). The altar made by Bezalel is described as being of acacia wood plated with bronze (Ex 27, 1f). Solomon later made an all-bronze altar for the temple in Jerusalem (2 Chr 4, 1).

a 3–12: 1 Kgs 3, 4–15; 1 Chr 21, 29. b Ex 27, 1f; 31, 2; 1 Chr 2, 20.

king over a people as numerous as the dust of the earth. [10]Give me, therefore, wisdom and knowledge to lead this people, for otherwise who could rule this great people of yours?" [11]God then replied to Solomon: "Since this has been your wish and you have not asked for riches, treasures and glory, nor for the life of those who hate you, nor even for a long life for yourself, but have asked for wisdom and knowledge in order to rule my people over whom I have made you king, [12]wisdom and knowledge are given you; but I will also give you riches, treasures and glory, such as kings before you never had, nor will those have them who come after you."

Solomon's Wealth [13]Solomon returned to Jerusalem from the high place at Gibeon, from the meeting tent, and became king over Israel. [14]He gathered together chariots and drivers, so that he had one thousand four hundred chariots and twelve thousand drivers he could station in the chariot cities and with the king in Jerusalem.[c] [15]The king made silver and gold as common in Jerusalem as stones, while cedars became as numerous as the sycamores of the foothills.[d] [16]Solomon also imported horses from Egypt and Cilicia.[e] The king's agents would acquire them by purchase from Cilicia,* [17]and would then bring up chariots from Egypt and export them at six hundred silver shekels, with the horses going for a hundred and fifty shekels. At these rates they served as middlemen for all the Hittite and Aramean kings.[f]

Preparations for the Temple [18]Solomon gave orders for the building of a house to honor the LORD and also of a house for his own royal estate.

CHAPTER 2

[1]He conscripted seventy thousand men to carry stone and eighty thousand to cut the stone in the mountains, and over these he placed three thousand six hundred overseers.[g] [2][h]Moreover, Solomon sent this message to Huram, king of Tyre: "As you dealt with my father David, sending him cedars to build a house for his dwelling, so deal with me. [3]I intend to build a house for the honor of the LORD, my God, and to consecrate it to him, for the burning of fragrant incense in his presence, for the perpetual display of the showbread, for holocausts morning and evening, and for the sabbaths, new moons, and festivals of the LORD, our God: such is Israel's perpetual obligation.[i] [4]And the house I intend to build must be large, for our God is greater than all other gods. [5]Yet who is really able to build him a house, since the heavens and even the highest heavens cannot contain him? And who am I that I should build him a house, unless it be to offer incense in his presence?[j] [6]Now, send me men skilled at work in gold, silver, bronze and iron, in purple, crimson, and violet fabrics, and who know how to do engraved work, to join the craftsmen who are with me in Judah and Jerusalem, whom my father David appointed. [7]Also send me boards of cedar, cypress and cabinet wood from Lebanon, for I realize that your servants know how to cut the wood of the Lebanon. My servants will labor with yours [8]in order to prepare for me a great quantity of wood, since the house I intend to build must be lofty and wonderful. [9]I will furnish as food for your servants, the hewers who cut the wood, twenty thousand kors of wheat, twenty thousand kors of barley, twenty thousand measures of wine, and twenty thousand measures of oil."[k]

[10]Huram, king of Tyre, wrote an answer which he sent to Solomon: "Because the LORD loves his people, he has placed you over them as king." [11]He added: "Blessed be the LORD, the God of Israel, who made heaven and earth, for having given King David a wise son of intelligence and understanding, who will build a house for the LORD and also a house for his royal estate.[l] [12]I am now sending you a craftsman of

1, 16f: Egypt . . . Cilicia: it seems likely that the horses came from Cilicia and the chariots from Egypt. Some read the source of these data in 1 Kgs 10, 28f as containing the name (Musur) of a mountain district north of Cilicia, rather than of Egypt; but the author of Chronicles surely understood Egypt; cf 2 Chr 9, 28.

c 2 Chr 9, 25; 10, 26–29. d 1 Kgs 10, 27. e 1 Kgs 10, 28. f 1 Kgs 10, 29. g 2 Chr 2, 17; 5, 29f. h 2–9: 1 Kgs 5, 15–20; 1 Chr 14, 1. i Lv 24, 5–8; Nm 28–29. j 2 Chr 6, 18. k 1 Kgs 5, 25; Ezr 3, 7. l 1 Kgs 5, 21.

great skill, Huram-abi,[m] 13son of a Danite woman* and of a father from Tyre; he knows how to work with gold, silver, bronze and iron, with stone and wood, with purple, violet, fine linen and crimson, and also how to do all kinds of engraved work and to devise every type of artistic work that may be given him and your craftsmen and the craftsmen of my lord David your father. 14 [n]And now, let my lord send to his servants the wheat, barley, oil and wine which he has promised. 15For our part, we will cut trees on Lebanon, as many as you need, and float them down to you at the port of Joppa, whence you may take them up to Jerusalem."[o]

16 [p]Thereupon Solomon took a census of all the alien men who were in the land of Israel (following the census David his father had taken of them), who were found to number one hundred fifty-three thousand six hundred. 17Of these he made seventy thousand carriers and eighty thousand cutters in the mountains, and three thousand six hundred overseers to keep the people working.[q]

CHAPTER 3

Building of the Temple 1 [r]Then Solomon began to build the house of the LORD in Jerusalem on Mount Moriah,* which had been pointed out to his father David, on the spot which David had selected, the threshing-floor of Ornan the Jebusite. 2He began to build in the second month of the fourth year of his reign. 3These were the specifications laid down by Solomon for building the house of God: the length was sixty cubits according to the old measure, and the width was twenty cubits;[s] 4the porch which lay before the nave along the width of the house was also twenty cubits, and it was twenty cubits high.* He overlaid its interior with pure gold.[t] 5The nave he overlaid with cypress wood which he covered with fine gold, embossing on it palms and chains.[u] 6He also decorated the building with precious stones. 7The house; its beams and thresholds, as well as its walls and its doors, he overlaid with gold, and he engraved cherubim upon the walls. (The gold was from Parvaim.) 8He also made the room of the holy of holies. Its length corresponded to the width of the house, twenty cubits, and its width was also twenty cubits. He overlaid it with fine gold to the amount of six hundred talents.[v] 9The weight of the nails was fifty gold shekels. The upper chambers he likewise covered with gold.

10 [w]For the room of the holy of holies he made two cherubim of carved workmanship, which were then overlaid with gold. 11The wings of the cherubim spanned twenty cubits: 12one wing of each cherub, five cubits in length, extended to a wall of the building, while the other wing, also five cubits in length, touched the corresponding wing of the second cherub. 13The combined wingspread of the two cherubim was thus twenty cubits. They stood upon their own feet, facing toward the nave. 14He made the veil* of violet, purple, crimson and fine linen, and had cherubim embroidered upon it.[x]

15 [y]In front of the building he set two columns thirty-five cubits high; the capital topping each was of five cubits. 16He worked out chains in the form of a collar with which he encircled the capitals of the columns, and he made a hundred pomegranates which he set on the chains. 17He set up the columns to correspond with the nave, one for the right side and the other for the left, and he called the one to the right Jachin and the one to the left Boaz.

2, 13: A Danite woman: a widow of the tribe of Naphtali (1 Kgs 7, 14). The Danites had settled in the northern section of Naphtali's territory (Jgs 18, 27ff). Bezalel's fellow craftsman was of the tribe of Dan (Ex 31, 6).

3, 1: Mount Moriah: the height in the land of Moriah (Gn 22, 2). This is the only place in the Bible where the temple mount is identified with the site where Abraham was to sacrifice Isaac.

3, 4: The porch . . . twenty cubits high: this measurement, not given in the Books of Kings, is here based on a variant Greek text that may be a later revision. The received Hebrew text says, "one hundred and twenty cubits high." The height of the two free-standing columns adjacent to the porch (1 Kgs 7, 15–16) is nearly doubled by the Chronicler (2 Chr 3, 15).

3, 14: The veil: at the entrance of the holy of holies, as also in the Mosaic meeting tent (Ex 26, 31f). Solomon's temple had doors at this place (1 Kgs 6, 31). Apparently there was a veil here in the temple of the Chronicler's time as there was also in Herod's temple (Mt 27, 51; Mk 15, 38; Lk 23, 45).

m 12f: 1 Kgs 7, 13f; Ex 31, 1–5. n 14f: 1 Kgs 5, 22–26. o Ezr 3, 7. p 16f: 1 Chr 22, 2. q 2 Chr 2, 1. r 1f: Gn 22, 2; 1 Kgs 6, 1; 1 Chr 21, 22–26. s 1 Kgs 6, 2; Ez 40, 5. t 1 Kgs 6, 3; Ez 40, 48. u 1 Kgs 6, 15; Ez 41, 1. v 1 Kgs 6, 16f. 20; Ez 41, 3. w 10–13: 1 Kgs 6, 23–27. x Mt 27, 51. y 15ff: 1 Kgs 7, 15–22; Ez 40, 49.

CHAPTER 4

1 Then he made a bronze altar twenty cubits long, twenty cubits wide and ten cubits high.[z] 2 [a]He also made the molten sea. It was perfectly round, ten cubits in diameter, five in depth, and thirty in circumference; 3 below the rim a ring of figures of oxen* encircled the sea, ten to the cubit, all the way around; there were two rows of these cast in the same mold with the sea. 4 It rested on twelve oxen, three facing north, three west, three south, and three east, with their haunches all toward the center; the sea rested on their backs. 5 It was a handbreadth thick, and its brim was made like that of a cup, being lily-shaped. It had a capacity of three thousand measures.*

6 Then he made ten basins for washing, placing five of them to the right and five to the left. Here were cleansed the victims for the holocausts; but the sea was for the priests to wash in.[b]

7 He made the lampstands of gold, ten of them as was prescribed, and placed them in the nave, five to the right and five to the left.[c] 8 He made ten tables and had them set in the nave, five to the right and five to the left; and he made a hundred golden bowls.[d] 9 He made the court of the priests and the great courtyard and the gates of the courtyard; the gates he overlaid with bronze.[e] 10 The sea was placed off to the southeast from the right side of the temple.[f]

11 [g]Huram also made the pots, the shovels and the bowls. Huram thus completed the work he had to do for King Solomon in the house of God: 12 two columns, two nodes for the capitals topping these two columns, and two networks covering the nodes of the capitals topping the columns; 13 also four hundred pomegranates for the two networks, with two rows of pomegranates to each network, to cover the two nodes of the capitals topping the columns. 14 He made the stands, and the basins on the stands; 15 one sea, and the twelve oxen under it; 16 likewise the pots, the shovels and the forks. Huram-abi made all these articles for King Solomon from polished bronze for the house of the LORD. 17 The king had them cast in the Jordan region, in the clayey ground between Succoth and Zeredah. 18 Solomon made all these vessels, so many in number that the weight of the bronze was not ascertained.

19 Solomon had all these articles made for the house of God: the golden altar, the tables on which the showbread lay, 20 the lampstands and their lamps of pure gold which were to burn according to prescription before the sanctuary, 21 flowers, lamps and gold tongs [this was the purest gold], 22 snuffers, bowls, cups and firepans of pure gold. As for the entry to the house, its inner doors to the holy of holies, as well as the doors to the nave, were of gold.

CHAPTER 5

Dedication of the Temple 1 [h]When all the work undertaken by Solomon for the temple of the LORD had been completed, he brought in the dedicated offerings of his father David, putting the silver, the gold and all the other articles in the treasuries of the house of God. 2 At Solomon's order the elders of Israel and all the leaders of the tribes, the princes of the Israelite ancestral houses, came to Jerusalem to bring up the ark of the LORD's covenant from the City of David (which is Zion). 3 All the men of Israel assembled before the king during the festival of the seventh month. 4 [i]When all the elders of Israel had arrived, the Levites* took up the ark, 5 and they carried the ark and the meeting tent with all the sacred vessels that were in the tent; it was the levitical priests who carried them.

6 King Solomon and the entire community of

4, 3: Oxen: in 1 Kgs 7, 24 this double row of ornaments is described as being gourds. The text of Kings available to the Chronicler may have been faulty on this point as the words are similar in sound. In 2 Chr 4, 16 the forks correspond in a similar way to bowls in the text of 1 Kings (7, 40).

4, 5: Three thousand measures: according to 1 Kgs 7, 26, "two thousand measures."

5, 4: The Levites: The parallel passage in 1 Kgs 8, 3 has the priests; but see 2 Chr 5, 5, where the Deuteronomic term levitical priests is used, as also in 2 Chr 23, 18; 30, 27.

z Ez 43, 13–17. a 2–5: 1 Kgs 7, 23–26; Ez 43, 13. b 1 Kgs 7, 38f; Ez 40, 38. c 1 Kgs 7, 49. d 1 Kgs 7, 50; 1 Chr 28, 16. e 1 Kgs 7, 12. f 1 Kgs 7, 39. g 11–22; 1 Kgs 7, 40–51. h 1–14: 1 Kgs 7, 51–8, 13. i 4f: 2 Chr 35, 3.

Israel gathered about him before the ark were sacrificing sheep and oxen so numerous that they could not be counted or numbered. 7 The priests brought the ark of the covenant of the LORD to its place beneath the wings of the cherubim in the sanctuary, the holy of holies of the temple. 8 The cherubim had their wings spread out over the place of the ark, sheltering the ark and its poles from above. 9 The poles were long enough so that their ends could be seen from that part of the holy place nearest the sanctuary; however, they could not be seen beyond. The ark has remained there to this day.* 10 There was nothing in it but the two tablets which Moses put there on Horeb, the tablets of the covenant which the LORD made with the Israelites at their departure from Egypt.

11 When the priests came out of the holy place (all the priests who were present had purified themselves without reference to the rotation of their various classes), 12 the Levites who were singers, all who belonged to Asaph, Heman, Jeduthun, and their sons and brothers, clothed in fine linen, with cymbals, harps and lyres, stood east of the altar, and with them a hundred and twenty priests blowing trumpets.

13 When the trumpeters and singers were heard as a single voice praising and giving thanks to the LORD, and when they raised the sound of the trumpets, cymbals and other musical instruments to "give thanks to the LORD, for he is good, for his mercy endures forever," the building of the LORD's temple was filled with a cloud. 14 The priests could not continue to minister because of the cloud, since the LORD's glory filled the house of God.[j]

CHAPTER 6

1 [k]Then Solomon said: "The LORD intends to dwell in the dark cloud. 2 I have truly built you a princely house and dwelling, where you may abide forever." 3 [l]Turning about, the king greeted the whole community of Israel as they stood. 4 He said: "Blessed be the LORD, the God of Israel, who with his own mouth made a promise to my father David and by his own hands brought it to fulfillment. He said: 5 'Since the day I brought my people out of the land of Egypt, I have not chosen any city from among all the tribes of Israel for the building of a temple to my honor, nor have I chosen any man to be commander of my people Israel; 6 but now I choose Jerusalem, where I shall be honored, and I choose David to rule my people Israel.' 7 My father David wished to build a temple to the honor of the LORD, the God of Israel, 8 but the LORD said to him: 'In wishing to build a temple to my honor, you do well. 9 However, you shall not build the temple; rather, your son whom you will beget shall build the temple to my honor.'

10 "Now the LORD has fulfilled the promise that he made. I have succeeded my father David and have taken my seat on the throne of Israel, as the LORD foretold, and I have built the temple to the honor of the LORD, the God of Israel. 11 And I have placed there the ark, in which abides the covenant of the LORD which he made with the Israelites."

Solomon's Prayer 12 [m]Solomon then took his place before the altar of the LORD in the presence of the whole community of Israel and stretched forth his hands. 13 He had made a bronze platform five cubits long, five cubits wide, and three cubits high, which he had placed in the middle of the courtyard. Having ascended it, Solomon knelt in the presence of the whole of Israel and stretched forth his hands toward heaven.* 14 Thus he prayed: "LORD, God of Israel, there is no god like you in heaven or on earth; you keep your covenant and show kindness to your servants who are wholeheartedly faithful to you. 15 You have kept the promise you made to my father David, your servant. With your own mouth you spoke it, and by your own hand you have brought it to fulfillment this day. 16 Now,

5, 9: The ark has remained there to this day: the Chronicler must have copied this from his source (1 Kgs 8, 8) without reflecting that the ark was lost in the Babylonian destruction of Jerusalem; cf 2 Mc 2, 4–8.

6, 13: This verse is not found in the Chronicler's source; cf 1 Kgs 8, 22f. He has Solomon praying on a bronze platform . . . in the middle of the courtyard because at the time of the Chronicler only the priests prayed before the altar.

j 2 Chr 7, 2; 1 Kgs 8, 10f. k 1f: 1 Kgs 8, 12f. 13–11: 1 Kgs 8, 14–21. m 12–41: 1 Kgs 8, 22–53.

therefore, LORD, God of Israel, keep the further
promise you made to my father David, your
servant, when you said, 'You shall always have
someone from your line to sit before me on the
throne of Israel, provided only that your descen-
dants look to their conduct so as always to live
according to my law, even as you have lived in
my presence.' 17Now, LORD, God of Israel, may
this promise which you made to your servant
David be confirmed.

18"Can it indeed be that God dwells with
mankind on earth? If the heavens and the
highest heavens cannot contain you, how much
less this temple which I have built! 19Look
kindly on the prayer and petition of your ser-
vant, O LORD, my God, and listen to the cry of
supplication your servant makes before you.
20May your eyes watch day and night over this
temple, the place where you have decreed you
shall be honored; may you heed the prayer
which I your servant offer toward this place.
21Listen to the petitions of your servant and of
your people Israel which they direct toward this
place. Listen from your heavenly dwelling, and
when you have heard, pardon.

22"When any man sins against his neighbor
and is required to take an oath of execration
against himself, and when he comes for the oath
before your altar in this temple, 23listen from
heaven: take action and pass judgment on your
servants, requiting the wicked man and holding
him responsible for his conduct, but absolving
the innocent and rewarding him according to his
virtue. 24When your people Israel have sinned
against you and are defeated by the enemy, but
afterward they return and praise your name, and
they pray to you and entreat you in this temple,
25listen from heaven and forgive the sin of your
people Israel, and bring them back to the land
which you gave them and their fathers. 26When
the sky is closed so that there is no rain, because
they have sinned against you, but then they pray
toward this place and praise your name, and
they withdraw from sin because you afflict them,
27listen in heaven and forgive the sin of your
servants and of your people Israel. But teach
them the right way to live, and send rain upon
your land which you gave your people as their
heritage. 28When there is famine in the land,
when there is pestilence, or blight, or mildew, or
locusts, or caterpillars; when their enemies be-
siege them at any of their gates; whenever there
is a plague or sickness of any kind; 29when any
Israelite of all your people offers a prayer or
petition of any kind, and in awareness of his
affliction and pain, stretches out his hands to-
ward this temple, 30listen from your heavenly
dwelling place, and forgive. Knowing his heart,
render to everyone according to his conduct, for
you alone know the hearts of men. 31So may
they fear you and walk in your ways as long as
they live on the land you gave our fathers.

32"For the foreigner, too, who is not of your
people Israel, when he comes from a distant land
to honor your great name, your mighty power,
and your outstretched arm, when they come in
prayer to this temple, 33listen from your heav-
enly dwelling place, and do whatever the for-
eigner entreats you, that all the peoples of the
earth may know your name, fearing you as do
your people Israel, and knowing that this house
which I have built is dedicated to your honor.

34"When your people go forth to war against
their enemies, wherever you send them, and
pray to you in the direction of this city and of the
house I have built to your honor, 35listen from
heaven to their prayer and petition, and defend
their cause. 36When they sin against you (for
there is no man who does not sin), and in your
anger against them you deliver them to the
enemy, so that their captors deport them to
another land, far or near, 37when they repent in
the land where they are captive and are con-
verted, when they entreat you in the land of
their captivity and say, 'We have sinned and
done wrong; we have been wicked,' 38and with
their whole heart and with their whole soul they
turn back to you in the land of those who hold
them captive, when they pray in the direction of
their land which you gave their fathers, and of
the city you have chosen, and of the house
which I have built to your honor, 39listen from
your heavenly dwelling place, hear their prayer
and petitions, and uphold their cause. Forgive

your people who have sinned against you. 40My
God, may your eyes be open and your ears
attentive to the prayer of this place. 41And now,

"Advance, LORD God, to your resting place,
you and the ark of your majesty.
May your priests, LORD God, be clothed with
salvation,
may your faithful ones rejoice in good
things.
42 LORD God, reject not the plea of your
anointed,
remember the devotion of David, your
servant."

CHAPTER 7

1 [n]When Solomon had ended his prayer, fire
came down from heaven and consumed the
holocaust and the sacrifices, and the glory of the
LORD filled the house. 2But the priests could not
enter the house of the LORD, for the glory of the
LORD had filled the house of the LORD. [o] 3All the
Israelites looked on while the fire came down
and the glory of the LORD was upon the house,
and they fell down upon the pavement with
their faces to the earth and adored, praising the
LORD, "for he is good, for his mercy endures
forever." 4The king and all the people were
offering sacrifices before the LORD. [p] 5King Solo-
mon offered as sacrifice twenty-two thousand
oxen, and one hundred twenty thousand
sheep. [q]

End of the Dedication 6Thus the king and all
the people dedicated the house of God. The
priests were standing at their stations, as were
the Levites, with the musical instruments of the
LORD which King David had made for "praising
the LORD, for his mercy endures forever," when
David used them to accompany the hymns.
Across from them the priests blew the trumpets
and all Israel stood. [r]

7Then Solomon consecrated the middle part
of the court which lay before the house of the
LORD; there he offered the holocausts and the fat
of the peace offerings, since the bronze altar
which Solomon had made could not hold the
holocausts, the cereal offerings and the fat. [s]

8On this occasion Solomon and with him all
Israel, who had assembled in very large numbers
from Labo of Hamath to the Wadi of Egypt,
celebrated the festival for seven days. [t] 9 [u]On the
eighth day they held a special meeting, for they
had celebrated the dedication of the altar for
seven days and the feast* for seven days. 10On
the twenty-third day of the seventh month he
sent the people back to their tents, rejoicing and
glad at heart at the good things the LORD had
done for David, for Solomon, and for his people
Israel. 11 [v]Solomon completed the house of the
LORD and the royal palace; he successfully
accomplished everything he had planned to do
in regard to the house of the LORD and his own
house.

God's Promise to Solomon 12The LORD ap-
peared to Solomon during the night and said to
him: "I have heard your prayer, and I have
chosen this place for my house of sacrifice. 13If I
close heaven so that there is no rain, if I
command the locust to devour the land, if I send
pestilence among my people, 14and if my people,
upon whom my name has been pronounced,
humble themselves and pray, and seek my
presence and turn from their evil ways, I will
hear them from heaven and pardon their sins
and revive their land. 15Now my eyes shall be
open and my ears attentive to the prayer of this
place. 16And now I have chosen and consecrated
this house that my name may be there forever;
my eyes and my heart also shall be there always.

17"As for you, if you live in my presence as
your father David did, doing all that I have
commanded you and keeping my statutes and
ordinances, 18I will establish your royal throne as

7, 9f: The feast: of Booths, celebrated on the fifteenth day of the seventh month and followed by a solemn octave lasting through the twenty-second day (Lv 23, 33–36; Nm 29, 12–35); the people are therefore sent home on the twenty-third day (v 10). The festival (v 8) for the dedication of the altar and of the temple lasted for seven days before the feast of Booths, from the seventh to the fourteenth day. According to 1 Kgs 8, 65f, the people are dismissed at the end of these seven days.

n 1–10: 1 Kgs 8, 54–66; Jgs 6, 21; 1 Chr 21, 26; 2 Mc 2, 10. o 2 Chr 5, 14; Ex 24, 16; 1 Kgs 8, 10f. p 2 Chr 5, 13; 1 Kgs 8, 62; Ps 136, 1. q 1 Kgs 8, 62f. r Nm 10, 8. 10; Ps 136, 1. s 1 Kgs 8, 64. t 1 Kgs 8, 65. u 9f: 1 Kgs 8, 66. v 11–22: 1 Kgs 9, 1–9.

I covenanted with your father David when I said, 'There shall never be lacking someone of yours as ruler in Israel.' 19But if you turn away and forsake my statutes and commands which I placed before you, if you proceed to venerate and worship strange gods, 20then I will uproot the people from the land I gave them; I will cast from my sight this house which I have consecrated to my honor, and I will make it a proverb and a byword among all peoples. 21This temple which is so exalted—everyone passing by it will be amazed and ask: 'Why has the LORD done this to this land and to this house?' 22And men will answer: 'They forsook the LORD, the God of their fathers, who brought them out of the land of Egypt, and they adopted strange gods and worshiped them and served them. That is why he has brought down upon them all this evil.' "

CHAPTER 8

Public Works 1 [w]After the twenty years during which Solomon built the house of the LORD and his own house, 2he built up the cities which Huram had given him,* and settled Israelites there. 3Then Solomon went to Hamath of Zoba and conquered it. 4He built Tadmor* in the desert region and all the supply cities, which he built in Hamath. 5 [x]He built Upper Beth-horon and Lower Beth-horon, fortified cities with walls, gates and bars; 6also Baalath, all the supply cities belonging to Solomon, and all the cities for the chariots, the cities for the horsemen, and whatever else Solomon decided should be built in Jerusalem, in the Lebanon, and in the entire land under his dominion. 7All the people that remained of the Hittites, Amorites, Perizzites, Hivites, and Jebusites, who were not of Israel— 8that is, their descendants remaining in the land, whom the Israelites had not destroyed—Solomon subjected to forced labor, as they continue to this day. 9But Solomon did not enslave the Israelites for his works. They became soldiers, commanders of his warriors, and commanders of his chariots and his horsemen. 10They were also King Solomon's two hundred and fifty overseers who had charge of the people.

Solomon's Piety 11Solomon brought the daughter of Pharaoh up from the City of David to the palace which he had built for her, for he said, "No wife of mine shall dwell in the house of David, king of Israel, for the places where the ark of the LORD has come are holy."

12In those times Solomon offered holocausts to the LORD upon the altar of the LORD which he had built in front of the porch, 13as was required day by day according to the command of Moses, and in particular on the sabbaths, at the new moons, and on the fixed festivals three times a year: on the feast of the Unleavened Bread, the feast of Weeks and the feast of Booths.[y]

14And according to the ordinance of his father David he appointed the various classes of the priests for their service, and the Levites according to their functions of praise and ministry alongside the priests, as the daily duty required. The gatekeepers of the various classes stood guard at each gate, since such was the command of David, the man of God.[z] 15There was no deviation from the king's command in any respect relating to the priests and Levites or the treasuries. 16All of Solomon's work was carried out successfully from the day the foundation of the house of the LORD was laid until the house of the LORD had been completed in every detail.

Glories of the Court 17In those times Solomon went to Ezion-geber and to Elath on the seashore of the land of Edom.[a] 18Huram, through his servants, sent him ships and crewmen acquainted with the sea, who accompanied Solomon's servants to Ophir and brought back from there four hundred and fifty talents of gold to King Solomon.[b]

8, 2: The cities which Huram had given him: according to 1 Kgs 9, 10–14, Solomon had ceded the cities as payment for the timber and gold received from Tyre. But since Huram was dissatisfied, he may have returned the cities to Solomon.

8, 4: Tadmor: later known as Palmyra, an important caravan city in the Syrian desert. The parallel passage in 1 Kgs 9, 18 has Tamar, in southern Judah; cf Ez 47, 19; 48, 28. But Solomon may well have fortified Tadmor against the Arameans.

w 1f: 1 Kgs 9, 10f. x 5–12: 1 Kgs 9, 18–25. y 1 Kgs 9, 25; Ex 23, 14; Nm 28—29. z 1 Chr 23—26; Neh 12, 46. a 1 Kgs 9, 26; Mt 12, 42; Lk 11, 31. b 1 Kgs 9, 27f.

CHAPTER 9

[1]When the queen of Sheba heard of Solomon's fame, she came to Jerusalem to test him with subtle questions, accompanied by a very numerous retinue and by camels bearing spices, much gold, and precious stones. She came to Solomon and questioned him on every subject in which she was interested.[c] [2]Solomon explained to her everything she asked about, and there remained nothing hidden from Solomon that he could not explain to her.

[3]When the queen of Sheba witnessed Solomon's wisdom, the palace he had built, [4]the food at his table, the seating of his ministers, the attendance of his servants and their dress, his cupbearers and their dress, and the holocausts he offered in the house of the LORD, it took her breath away. [5]"The account I heard in my country about your deeds and your wisdom is true," she told the king. [6]"Yet I did not believe the report until I came and saw with my own eyes. I have discovered that they did not tell me the half of your great wisdom; you have surpassed the stories I heard. [7]Happy are your men, happy these servants of yours, who stand before you always and listen to your wisdom. [8]Blessed be the LORD, your God, who has been so pleased with you as to place you on his throne as king for the LORD, your God. Because your God has so loved Israel as to will to make it last forever, he has appointed you over them as king to administer right and justice." [9]Then she gave the king one hundred and twenty gold talents and a very large quantity of spices, as well as precious stones. There was no other spice like that which the queen of Sheba gave to King Solomon.

[10]The servants of Huram and of Solomon who brought gold from Ophir also brought cabinet wood and precious stones. [11]With the cabinet wood the king made stairs for the temple of the LORD and the palace of the king; also lyres and harps for the chanters. The like of these had not been seen before in the land of Judah.

[12]King Solomon gave the queen of Sheba everything she desired and asked him for, more than she had brought to the king. Then she returned to her own country with her servants.

[13] [d]The gold that Solomon received each year weighed six hundred and sixty-six gold talents, [14]in addition to what was collected from travelers and what the merchants brought. All the kings of Arabia also, and the governors of the country, brought gold and silver to Solomon.

[15]Moreover, King Solomon made two hundred large shields of beaten gold, six hundred shekels of beaten gold going into each shield, [16]and three hundred bucklers of beaten gold, three hundred shekels of gold going into each buckler; these the king put in the hall of the Forest of Lebanon.

[17]King Solomon also made a large ivory throne which he overlaid with fine gold. [18]The throne had six steps; a footstool of gold was fastened to it, and there was an arm on each side of the seat, with two lions standing beside the arms. [19]Twelve other lions also stood there, one on either side of each step. Nothing like this had ever been produced in any other kingdom. [20]Furthermore, all of King Solomon's drinking vessels were of gold, and all the utensils in the hall of the Forest of Lebanon were of pure gold; silver was not considered of value in Solomon's time. [21]For the king had ships that went to Tarshish with the servants of Huram. Once every three years the fleet of Tarshish would return with a cargo of gold and silver, ivory, apes and monkeys. [22]Thus King Solomon surpassed all the other kings of the earth in riches as well as in wisdom.

[23]All the kings of the earth sought audience with Solomon, to hear from him the wisdom which God had put in his heart. [24]Year in and year out, each one would bring his tribute—silver and gold articles, garments, weapons, spices, horses and mules. [25]Solomon also had four thousand stalls of horses, chariots, and twelve thousand horsemen, which he assigned to the chariot cities and to the king in Jerusalem. [26]He was ruler over all the kings from the River to the land of the Philistines and down to the

c 1 Kgs 10, 1f; Mt 12, 42; Lk 11, 31. d 13–28: 1 Kgs 10, 14–28.

border of Egypt. 27The king made silver as
common in Jerusalem as stones, while cedars
became as numerous as the sycamores of the
foothills. 28Horses were imported for Solomon
from Egypt and from all the lands.*
The Death of Solomon 29 [e]The rest of the acts
of Solomon, first and last, are written, as is well
known, in the acts of Nathan the prophet, in the
prophecy of Ahijah the Shilonite, and in the
visions of Iddo the seer which concern Jero-
boam, son of Nebat. 30Solomon reigned in
Jerusalem over all Israel for forty years. 31He
rested with his ancestors; he was buried in his
father's City of David, and his son Rehoboam
succeeded him as king.

II: The Monarchy before Hezekiah

CHAPTER 10

Division of the Kingdom 1 [f]Rehoboam went
to Shechem, for all Israel* had come to Shechem
to proclaim him king. 2When Jeroboam, son of
Nebat, heard of this in Egypt where he had fled
from King Solomon, he returned from Egypt.
3Jeroboam was summoned to the assembly, and
he and all Israel said to Rehoboam: 4"Your father
laid a heavy yoke upon us. If you now lighten
the harsh service and the heavy yoke that your
father imposed on us, we will serve you." 5"In
three days," he answered them, "come back to
me."
When the people had departed, 6King Reho-
boam consulted the elders who had been in the
service of his father during Solomon's lifetime,
asking, "What answer do you advise me to give
this people?" 7They replied, "If you will deal
kindly with this people and give in to them,
acceding to their request, they will be your
servants forever." 8But he ignored the advice the
elders had given him and consulted the young
men who had grown up with him and were in
his service. 9He said to them, "What answer do
you advise me to give this people, who have
asked me to lighten the yoke my father imposed
on them?" 10The young men who had grown up
with him replied: "This is the answer you should
give to this people who have said to you, 'Your
father laid a heavy yoke upon us, but do you
lighten our yoke'; this you should say to them:
'My little finger is thicker than my father's body.
11Whereas my father put a heavy yoke on you, I
will make it heavier! My father beat you with
whips, but I will beat you with scorpions!"
12On the third day, Jeroboam and all the
people came back to King Rehoboam as he had
instructed them to do. 13Ignoring the advice the
elders had given him, the king gave them a harsh
answer, 14speaking to them according to the
advice of the young men: "My father laid a
heavy yoke on you, but I will make it heavier.
My father beat you with whips, but I will beat
you with scorpions." 15The king would not listen
to the people, for this turn of events was divinely
ordained to fulfill the prophecy the LORD had
uttered to Jeroboam, the son of Nebat, through
Ahijah the Shilonite.[g]
16 [h]When all Israel saw that the king would
not listen to them, the people answered the
king,

"What share have we in David?
We have no heritage in the son of Jesse.
Everyone to your tents, O Israel!
Now look to your own house, David!"

So all Israel went off to their tents. 17Reho-
boam, therefore, reigned over only those Israel-
ites who lived in the cities of Judah. 18King
Rehoboam then sent out Hadoram, who was
superintendent of the forced labor, but the
Israelites stoned him to death. Rehoboam him-
self managed to mount his chariot and flee to
Jerusalem. 19Thus Israel has been in rebellion
against David's house to this day.

9, 28: See note on 2 Chr 1, 16f.
10, 1: All Israel: as in the original source (1 Kgs 12, 1), the northern tribes, distinct from Judah and Benjamin. Contrast the Chronicler's own terms, those Israelites who lived in the cities of Judah (v 17), and all the Israelites [literally, all Israel] in Judah and Benjamin (2 Chr 11, 3).

e 29ff: 1 Kgs 11, 41ff. f 1–14: 1 Kgs 12, 1–14. g 1 Kgs 11, 29–39; 12, 15. h 16–19: 1 Kgs 12, 16–19.

CHAPTER 11

1 [i]On his arrival in Jerusalem Rehoboam gath-
ered together the house of Judah and Benjamin,
a hundred and eighty thousand seasoned war-
riors, to have them fight against Israel and
restore the kingdom to him. 2 However, the
word of the LORD came to Shemiah, a man of
God: 3 "Say to Rehoboam, son of Solomon, king
of Judah, and to all the Israelites in Judah and
Benjamin: 4 'Thus says the LORD: You must not
march out to fight against your brothers. Let
every man return home, for what has occurred I
have brought about.' " They obeyed this mes-
sage of the LORD and gave up the expedition
against Jeroboam.

Rehoboam's Works* 5 Rehoboam took up resi-
dence in Jerusalem and built fortified cities in
Judah. 6 He built up Bethlehem, Etam, Tekoa,
7 Beth-zur, Soco, Adullam, 8 Gath, Mareshah,
Ziph, 9 Adoraim, Lachish, Azekah, 10 Zorah, Aija-
lon, and Hebron; these were fortified cities in
Judah and Benjamin. 11 Then he strengthened
the fortifications and put commanders in them,
with supplies of food, oil and wine. 12 In every
city were shields and spears, and he made them
very strong. Thus Judah and Benjamin remained
his.

Refugees from the North 13 Now the priests
and Levites throughout Israel presented them-
selves to him from all parts of their land, 14 for
the Levites left their assigned pasture lands and
their holdings and came to Judah and Jerusalem,
because Jeroboam and his sons repudiated them
as priests of the LORD.[j] 15 In their place, he
himself appointed priests for the high places and
satyrs and calves he had made.[k] 16 After them, all
those of the Israelite tribes who firmly desired to
seek the LORD, the God of Israel, came to
Jerusalem to sacrifice to the LORD, the God of
their fathers. 17 Thus they strengthened the king-
dom of Judah and made Rehoboam, son of
Solomon, prevail for three years; for they walked
in the way of David and Solomon three years.

Rehoboam's Family 18 Rehoboam took to him-
self as wife Mahalath, daughter of Jerimoth, son
of David and of Abihail, daughter of Eliab, son of
Jesse. 19 She bore him sons: Jehush, Shemariah
and Zaham. 20 After her, he married Maacah,
daughter of Absalom, who bore him Abijah,
Attai, Ziza and Shelomith.[l] 21 Rehoboam loved
Maacah, daughter of Absalom, more than all his
other wives and concubines; he had taken
eighteen wives and sixty concubines, and he
fathered twenty-eight sons and sixty daughters.
22 Rehoboam constituted Abijah, son of Maacah,
commander among his brothers, for he intended
to make him king. 23 He acted prudently, distrib-
uting various of his sons throughout all the
districts of Judah and Benjamin, in all the
fortified cities; and he furnished them with
copious provisions and sought an abundance of
wives for them.

CHAPTER 12

His Apostasy 1 After Rehoboam had consoli-
dated his rule and had become powerful, he
abandoned the law of the LORD, he and all Israel
with him.[m] 2 Thus it happened that in the fifth
year of King Rehoboam, Shishak, king of Egypt,
attacked Jerusalem, for they had been unfaithful
to the LORD.[n] 3 He came up with twelve hun-
dred chariots and sixty thousand horsemen, and
there was no counting the army that came with
him from Egypt—Libyans, Sukkites* and Ethiopi-
ans. 4 They captured the fortified cities of Judah
and came as far as Jerusalem. 5 Then Shemaiah
the prophet came to Rehoboam and the com-
manders of Judah who had gathered at Jerusalem
because of Shishak, and said to them: "Thus says
the LORD: 'You have abandoned me, and there-
fore I have abandoned you to the power of
Shishak.' "[o]

6 However, the commanders of Israel and the
king humbled themselves, saying, "The LORD is
just." 7 When the LORD saw that they had
humbled themselves, the word of the LORD

11, 5–12: These verses, though not found in 1 Kgs, are apparently based on a reliable, ancient source.

12, 3: Sukkites: foreign mercenaries in the Egyptian army.

i 1–4: 1 Kgs 12, 21–24. j 1 Kgs 12, 32. k 1 Kgs 12, 32; Lv 17, 7. l 1 Kgs 15, 2. m 1 Kgs 11, 4; 14, 22. n 1 Kgs 14, 25. o 2 Chr 11, 2.

came to Shemaiah: "Because they have humbled
themselves, I will not destroy them; I will give
them some deliverance, and my wrath shall not
be poured out upon Jerusalem through Shishak.
8But they shall be his servants, that they may
know what it is to serve me and what it is to
serve earthly kingdoms." 9 [p]Therefore Shishak,
king of Egypt, attacked Jerusalem and carried off
the treasures of the temple of the LORD and of
the king's palace. He took everything, including
the gold bucklers that Solomon had made. 10(To
replace them, King Rehoboam made bronze
bucklers, which he entrusted to the officers of
the guard on duty at the entrance of the royal
palace. 11Whenever the king visited the temple
of the LORD, the troops would come bearing
them, and then they would return them to the
guardroom.) 12Because he had humbled himself,
the anger of the LORD turned from him so that it
did not destroy him completely; and in Judah,
moreover, good deeds were found.

13King Rehoboam consolidated his power in
Jerusalem and continued to rule; he was forty-
one years old when he became king, and he
reigned seventeen years in Jerusalem, the city in
which, out of all the tribes of Israel, the LORD
chose to be honored. Rehoboam's mother was
named Naamah, an Ammonite.[q] 14He did evil,
for he had not truly resolved to seek the LORD.
15 [r]The acts of Rehoboam, first and last, are
written, as is well known, in the history of
Shemaiah the prophet and of Iddo the seer [his
family record]. There was war continually be-
tween Rehoboam and Jeroboam. 16Rehoboam
rested with his ancestors; he was buried in the
City of David. His son Abijah succeeded him as
king.

CHAPTER 13

War between Abijah and Jeroboam 1 [s]In the
eighteenth year of King Jeroboam, Abijah be-
came king of Judah; 2he reigned three years in
Jerusalem. His mother was named Michaiah,
daughter of Uriel of Gibeah. There was war
between Abijah and Jeroboam.

3Abijah joined battle with a force of four
hundred thousand picked warriors, while Jero-
boam lined up against him in battle with eight
hundred thousand picked and valiant warriors.
4*Abijah stood on Mount Zemaraim, which is in
the highlands of Ephraim, and said: "Listen to
me, Jeroboam and all Israel! 5Do you not know
that the LORD, the God of Israel, has given the
kingdom of Israel to David forever, to him and to
his sons, by a covenant made in salt? 6Yet
Jeroboam, son of Nebat, the servant of Solomon,
son of David, has stood up and rebelled against
his lord![t] 7Worthless men, scoundrels, joined
him and overcame Rehoboam, son of Solomon,
when Rehoboam was young and unthinking,
and no match for them. 8But now, do you think
you are a match for the kingdom of the LORD
commanded by the sons of David, simply be-
cause you are a huge multitude and have with
you the golden calves which Jeroboam made you
for gods?

9"Have you not expelled the priests of the
LORD, the sons of Aaron, and the Levites, and
made for yourselves priests like the peoples of
foreign lands? Everyone who comes to conse-
crate himself with a young bull and seven rams
becomes a priest of no-gods. 10But as for us, the
LORD is our God, and we have not forsaken him.
The priests ministering to the LORD are sons of
Aaron, and the Levites also have their offices.
11They burn holocausts to the LORD and fragrant
incense morning after morning and evening after
evening; they display the showbread on the pure
table, and the lamps of the golden lampstand
burn evening after evening; for we observe our
duties to the LORD, our God, but you have
abandoned him. 12See, God is with us, at our
head, and his priests are here with trumpets to
sound the attack against you. Do not battle
against the LORD, the God of your fathers, O
Israelites, for you will not succeed!"

13But Jeroboam had an ambush go around
them to come at them from the rear; so that
while his army faced Judah, his ambush lay
behind them. 14When Judah turned and saw
that they had to battle on both fronts, they cried

13, 4–12: This is a free composition of the Chronicler to show that this was a religious, rather than a political, war.

p 9ff: 1 Kgs 14, 25–28. q 1 Kgs 14, 21. r 15f: 1 Kgs 14, 29ff. s 1f: 1 Kgs 15, 1f. t 1 Kgs 11, 26.

out to the LORD and the priests sounded the trumpets. 15 Then the men of Judah shouted; and when they did so, God defeated Jeroboam and all Israel before Abijah and Judah. 16 The Israelites fled before Judah, and God delivered them into their hands. 17 Abijah and his people inflicted a severe defeat upon them; five hundred thousand picked men of Israel fell slain. 18 The Israelites were subdued on that occasion and the Judahites were victorious because they relied on the LORD, the God of their fathers. 19 Abijah pursued Jeroboam and took cities from him: Bethel and its dependencies, Jeshanah and its dependencies, and Ephron and its dependencies. 20 Jeroboam did not regain power during the time of Abijah; the LORD struck him down and he died, 21 while Abijah continued to grow stronger. He took to himself fourteen wives and fathered twenty-two sons and sixteen daughters.

Death of Abijah 22 [u]The rest of Abijah's acts, his deeds and his words, are written in the midrash of the prophet Iddo. 23 Abijah rested with his ancestors; they buried him in the City of David. His son Asa succeeded him as king. During his time, ten years of peace began in the land.

CHAPTER 14

Asa the Reformer 1 [v]Asa did what was good and pleasing to the LORD, his God, 2 removing the heathen altars and the high places, breaking to pieces the sacred pillars, and cutting down the sacred poles. 3 He commanded Judah to seek the LORD, the God of their fathers, and to observe the law and its commands. 4 He removed the high places and incense stands from all the cities of Judah, and under him the kingdom had peace. 5 He built fortified cities in Judah, for the land had peace and no war was waged against him during these years, because the LORD had given him peace. 6 He said to Judah: "Let us build these cities and surround them with walls, towers, gates and bars. The land is still ours, for we have sought the LORD, our God; we sought him, and he has given us rest on every side." So they built and prospered.

The Ethiopian Invasion* 7 Asa had an army of three hundred thousand shield- and lance-bearers from Judah, and two hundred and eighty thousand from Benjamin who carried bucklers and were archers, all of them valiant warriors. 8 Zerah the Ethiopian moved against them with a force of one million men and three hundred chariots, and he came as far as Mareshah.[w] 9 Asa went out to meet him and set himself in battle array in the valley of Zephathah, near Mareshah. 10 Asa called upon the LORD, his God, praying: "O LORD, there is none like you to help the powerless against the strong. Help us, O LORD, our God, for we rely on you, and in your name we have come against this multitude. You are the LORD, our God; let no man prevail against you."[x] 11 And so the LORD defeated the Ethiopians before Asa and Judah, and they fled.[y] 12 Asa and those with him pursued them as far as Gerar, and the Ethiopians fell until there were no survivors, for they were crushed before the LORD and his army, which carried away enormous spoils. 13 Then the Judahites conquered all the cities around Gerar, for the fear of the LORD was upon them; they despoiled all the cities, for there was much booty in them. 14 They attacked also the tents of the cattle-herders and carried off a great number of sheep and camels. Then they returned to Jerusalem.

CHAPTER 15

Cult Reform 1 Upon Azariah, son of Oded, came the spirit of God. 2 He went forth to meet Asa and said to him: "Hear me, Asa and all Judah and Benjamin! The LORD is with you when you are with him, and if you seek him he will be present to you; but if you abandon him, he will abandon you.[z] 3 For a long time Israel had no true God, no priest-teacher and no law, 4 but when in their distress they turned to the LORD, the God of Israel, and sought him, he was present to them.[a] 5 In that former time there was

14, 7-14: An Ethiopian invasion of Judah is mentioned only in 1 Chronicles. This account may be a legend contrived to show how the pious King Asa was rewarded through divine assistance. There may, however, have been an incursion of nomads from the Negeb at this time; cf vv 13f.

u 22f: 2 Chr 12, 15; 1 Kgs 7ff. v 1f: 2 Chr 33, 15; Ex 23, 24; 34, 13; 1 Kgs 15, 11f. w 2 Chr 16, 8. x 2 Chr 32, 8. y Pss 20, 7f; 60, 11f. z Jer 29, 13f; Hos 3, 4f. a Dt 4, 29f.

no place for anyone to go or come, but there
were many terrors upon the inhabitants of the
lands. 6Nation crushed nation and city crushed
city, for God destroyed them by every kind of
adversity.[b] 7But as for you, be strong and do not
relax, for your work shall be rewarded."[c]
8When Asa heard these words and the proph-
ecy [Oded the prophet], he was encouraged to
remove the detestable idols from the whole land
of Judah and Benjamin and from the cities he
had taken in the highlands of Ephraim, and to
restore the altar of the LORD which was before
the vestibule of the LORD. 9Then he convened all
Judah and Benjamin, together with those of
Ephraim, Manasseh and Simeon who sojourned
with them; for many had fled to him from Israel
when they saw that the LORD, his God, was with
him. 10*They gathered at Jerusalem in the third
month of the fifteenth year of Asa's reign, 11and
sacrificed to the LORD at that time seven hun-
dred oxen and seven thousand sheep of the
booty they had brought. 12They entered into a
covenant to seek the LORD, the God of their
fathers, with all their heart and soul; 13and
everyone who would not seek the LORD, the
God of Israel, was to be put to death, whether
small or great, whether man or woman.[d] 14They
swore to the LORD with a loud voice, with
shouting and with trumpets and horns. 15All
Judah rejoiced over the oath, for they had sworn
with their whole heart and sought him with
complete desire, so that he was present to them.
And the LORD gave them rest on every side.[e]
16[f]Maacah, the mother of King Asa, he de-
posed as queen mother because she had made
an outrageous object for Asherah; Asa cut this
down, smashed it, and burnt it in the Kidron
Valley. 17Although the high places did not disap-
pear from Israel, yet Asa's heart was undivided
as long as he lived. 18He brought into the house
of God his father's votive offerings and his own:
silver, gold, and various utensils. 19There was no
war until the thirty-fifth year of Asa's reign.

CHAPTER 16

Asa's Infidelity 1[g]In the thirty-sixth year of
Asa's reign, Baasha, king of Israel, attacked
Judah and fortified Ramah to prevent any com-
munication with Asa, king of Judah. 2Asa then
brought out silver and gold from the treasuries of
the temple of the LORD and of the royal palace
and sent them to Ben-hadad, king of Aram, who
lived in Damascus, with this message: 3"There is
a treaty between you and me, as there was
between your father and my father. See, I am
sending you silver and gold. Go, break your
treaty with Baasha, king of Israel, that he may
withdraw from me." 4Ben-hadad agreed to King
Asa's request and sent the leaders of his troops
against the cities of Israel. They attacked Ijon,
Dan, Abel-maim, and all the store cities of
Naphtali. 5When Baasha heard of it, he left off
fortifying Ramah; he stopped his work. 6Then
King Asa commandeered all of Judah to carry
away the stone and wood with which Baasha
had been fortifying Ramah, and with them he
fortified Geba and Mizpah.
7At that time Hanani the seer came to Asa,
king of Judah, and said to him: "Because you
relied on the king of Aram and did not rely on
the LORD, your God, the army of the king of
Aram has escaped* your hand. 8Were not the
Ethiopians and Libyans a vast army, with great
numbers of chariots and drivers? And yet, be-
cause you relied on the LORD, he delivered
them into your power.[h] 9The eyes of the LORD
roam over the whole earth, to encourage those
who are devoted to him wholeheartedly. You
have acted foolishly in this matter, for from
now on you will have wars."[i] 10But Asa be-
came angry with the seer and imprisoned him
in the stocks, so greatly was he enraged at him

15, 10ff: With this description of a covenant ceremony in the third month of a year beginning in the spring, the Chronicler lays a foundation for celebrating the ancient feast of Pentecost (Weeks) as the time for a solemn renewal of the people's covenant with God on Mount Sinai; see Ex 19, 1ff; Lv 23, 16 and the note there. This is also the background for Pentecost as the "birthday of the Church."

16, 7: The king of Aram . . . escaped: according to the Lucianic recension, "the king of Israel escaped": this may well be the original reading; Asa was friendly with Aram.

b Is 19, 2. c Is 7, 4; Jer 31, 16. d Neh 10, 30. e Dt 4, 29. f 16ff: 1 Kgs 15, 13ff. g 1-6: 1 Kgs 15, 16-21. h 2 Chr 14, 8-14. i Ps 33, 13ff.

over this. Asa also oppressed some of his people at this time.

11 [j]Now the acts of Asa, first and last, can be found recorded in the book of the kings of Judah and Israel. 12In the thirty-ninth year of his reign, Asa contracted a serious disease in his feet. But even in his sickness he did not seek the LORD, but only the physicians. 13Asa rested with his ancestors; he died in the forty-first year of his reign. 14They buried him in the tomb he had hewn for himself in the City of David, having laid him upon a couch which was filled with spices and various kinds of aromatics compounded into an ointment. They also burned a very great funeral pyre for him.

CHAPTER 17

Zeal of Jehoshaphat for the Law 1His son Jehoshaphat succeeded him as king and strengthened his hold against Israel.[k] 2He placed armed forces in all the fortified cities of Judah, and put garrisons in the land of Judah and in the cities of Ephraim which his father Asa had taken. 3The LORD was with Jehoshaphat,* for he walked in the ways his father had pursued in the beginning, and he did not consult the Baals. 4Rather, he sought the God of his father and observed his commands, and not the practices of Israel. 5As a result, the LORD made his kingdom secure, and all Judah gave Jehoshaphat gifts, so that he enjoyed great wealth and glory. 6Thus he was encouraged to follow the LORD's ways, and again he removed the high places and the sacred poles from Judah.[l]

7In the third year of his reign he sent his leading men, Ben-hail, Obadiah, Zechariah, Nethanel and Micaiah, to teach in the cities of Judah. 8With them he sent the Levites Shemaiah, Nethaniah, Zebadiah, Asahel, Shemiramoth, Jehonathan, Adonijah and Tobijah, together with the priests Elishama and Jehoram.[m] 9They taught in Judah, having with them the book containing the law of the LORD; they traveled through all the cities of Judah and taught among the people.[n]

His Power 10Now the fear of the LORD was upon all the kingdoms of the countries surrounding Judah, so that they did not war against Jehoshaphat. 11Some of the Philistines brought Jehoshaphat gifts and a tribute of silver; and the Arabs also brought him a flock of seven thousand seven hundred rams and seven thousand seven hundred he-goats.

12Jehoshaphat grew steadily greater. He built strongholds and store cities in Judah. 13He carried out many works in the cities of Judah, and he had soldiers, valiant warriors, in Jerusalem. 14This was their mustering according to their ancestral houses. Of Judah, the commanders of thousands: Adnah the commander, and with him three hundred thousand valiant warriors. 15Next to him, Jehohanan the commander, and with him two hundred eighty thousand. 16Next to him, Amasiah, son of Zichri, who offered himself to the LORD, and with him two hundred thousand valiant warriors. 17From Benjamin: Eliada, a valiant warrior, and with him two hundred thousand armed with bow and buckler. 18Next to him, Jozabad, and with him one hundred and eighty thousand equipped for war. 19These were at the service of the king; in addition were those whom the king had placed in the fortified cities throughout all Judah.

CHAPTER 18

Alliance with Israel 1 [o]Jehoshaphat therefore had wealth and glory in abundance; but he became related to Ahab by marriage. 2After some years he went down to Ahab at Samaria; Ahab offered numerous sheep and oxen for him and the people with him, and persuaded him to go up against Ramoth-gilead. 3Ahab, king of Israel, asked Jehoshaphat, king of Judah, "Will you come with me to Ramoth-gilead?" "You and I are as one," was his answer; "your people and my people as well. We will be with you in the battle." 4But Jehoshaphat also said to the king of Israel, "Seek the word of the LORD at once."

The Prophets 5The king of Israel gathered his prophets, four hundred in number, and asked them, "Shall we go to attack Ramoth-gilead, or

17, 3: The Lord was with Jehoshaphat: along with Hezekiah and Josiah, Jehoshaphat was one of the Chronicler's favorite kings.

j 11–14: 1 Kgs 15, 23f. k 1 Kgs 15, 24. l 2 Chr 20, 33; Ex 34, 13. m 2 Chr 19, 8. n Ezr 7, 25. o 1–34: 1 Kgs 22, 1–35.

shall I refrain?" "Go up," they answered. "God
will deliver it over to the king." 6But Jehosha-
phat said, "Is there no other prophet of the LORD
here whom we may consult?" 7The king of Israel
answered Jehoshaphat, "There is still another
through whom we may consult the LORD, but I
hate him, for he prophesies not good but always
evil about me. That is Micaiah, son of Imlah."
Jehoshaphat said, "Let not your Majesty speak of
evil against you." 8So the king of Israel called an
official, to whom he said, "Get Micaiah, son of
Imlah, at once." 9The king of Israel and King
Jehoshaphat of Judah were seated each on his
throne, clothed in their robes of state on a
threshing floor at the entrance of the gate of
Samaria, and all the prophets were prophesying
before them.

10Zedekiah, son of Chenaanah, made iron
horns for himself and said: "The LORD says,
'With these you shall gore Aram until you have
destroyed them.' " 11The other prophets prophe-
sied in the same vein, saying: "Go up to Ramoth-
gilead. You shall succeed; the LORD will deliver
it over to the king." 12*The messenger who had
gone to call Micaiah said to him: "Look now, the
prophets unanimously predict good for the king.
Let your word, like each of theirs, predict good."
13"As the LORD lives," Micaiah answered, "I will
say what my God tells me."

14When he came to the king, the king said to
him, "Micaiah, shall we go to fight against
Ramoth-gilead, or shall I refrain?" "Go up," he
answered, "and succeed; they will be delivered
into your power." 15But the king said to him,
"How many times must I adjure you to tell me
nothing but the truth in the name of the LORD?"
16Then Micaiah answered:

"I see all Israel
scattered on the mountains,
Like sheep without a shepherd,
and the LORD saying, 'These have no
master!
Let each of them go back home in peace.' "

17The king of Israel said to Jehoshaphat, "Did I
not tell you that he prophesies no good about
me, but only evil?" 18But Micaiah continued:
"Therefore hear the word of the LORD: I saw the
LORD seated on his throne, with the whole host
of heaven standing by to his right and to his left.
19The LORD asked, 'Who will deceive Ahab, king
of Israel, so that he will go up and fall at Ramoth-
gilead?' And one said this, another that, 20until a
spirit came forward and presented himself to the
LORD, saying, 'I will deceive him.' The LORD
asked, 'How?' 21He answered, 'I will go forth
and become a lying spirit in the mouths of all his
prophets.' The LORD agreed: 'You shall succeed
in deceiving him. Go forth and do this.' 22So
now the LORD has put a lying spirit in the
mouths of these your prophets, but the LORD
himself has decreed evil against you."

23Thereupon Zedekiah, son of Chenaanah,
came up and slapped Micaiah on the cheek,
saying, "Which way did the spirit of the LORD go
when he left me to speak to you?" 24"You shall
find out," Micaiah replied, "on that day when
you enter an innermost chamber to hide." 25The
king of Israel then said: "Seize Micaiah and take
him back to Amon, prefect of the city, and to
Joash the king's son, 26and say, 'This is the king's
order: Put this man in prison and feed him
scanty rations of bread and water until I return
in safety!' " 27But Micaiah said, "If ever you
return in safety, the LORD has not spoken
through me." And he said, "Hear, O peoples, all
of you!"*

Ahab's Death 28The king of Israel and King
Jehoshaphat of Judah went up to Ramoth-gilead
29and the king of Israel said to Jehoshaphat, "I
will go into battle disguised, but you put on your
own clothes." So the king of Israel disguised
himself and they entered the fray. 30Meanwhile,
the king of Aram had given his chariot command-
ers the order, "Fight with no one, small or great,
except the king of Israel." 31When the command-
ers saw Jehoshaphat, they exclaimed, "That
must be the king of Israel!" and shifted to fight

18, 12–22: See note on 1 Kgs 22, 19–23.

18, 27: "Hear, O peoples, all of you!": this quotation, which appears in some texts of 1 Kgs 22, 28, ascribes to the prophets Micaiah ben Imlah the opening words of the prophetic utterance of Micah of Moresheth (Mi 1, 2), a century later.

him. But Jehoshaphat cried out and the LORD
helped him; God induced them to leave him.
32The chariot commanders became aware that
he was not the king of Israel and gave up their
pursuit of him. 33Someone, however, drew his
bow at random and hit the king of Israel
between the joints of his breastplate. He ordered
his charioteer, "Rein about and take me out of
the ranks, for I am disabled." [p] 34The battle grew
fierce during the day, and the king of Israel
braced himself up on his chariot facing the
Arameans until evening. He died as the sun was
setting.

CHAPTER 19

Jehoshaphat Rebuked 1King Jehoshaphat of
Judah returned in safety to his house in Jerusa-
lem. 2Jehu the seer, son of Hanani,* met King
Jehoshaphat and said to him: "Should you help
the wicked and love those who hate the LORD?
For this reason, wrath is upon you from the
LORD. 3Yet some good things are to be found in
you, since you have removed the sacred poles
from the land and have been determined to seek
God."

Judges Appointed 4Jehoshaphat dwelt in Jeru-
salem; but he went out again among the people
from Beer-sheba to the highlands of Ephraim and
brought them back to the LORD, the God of their
fathers. 5He appointed judges in the land, in all
the fortified cities of Judah, city by city, 6and he
said to them: "Take care what you do, for you
are judging, not on behalf of man, but on behalf
of the LORD; he judges with you. [q] 7And now, let
the fear of the LORD be upon you. Act carefully,
for with the LORD, our God, there is no injustice,
no partiality, no bribe-taking." [r] 8In Jerusalem
also, Jehoshaphat appointed some Levites and
priests and some of the family heads of Israel to
judge in the name of the LORD and to settle
quarrels among the inhabitants of Jerusalem. [s]
9He gave them this command: "You shall act
faithfully and wholeheartedly in the fear of the
LORD. 10And in every dispute that your brethren
living in their cities bring to you, whether it
concerns bloodguilt or questions of law, com-
mand, statutes, or judgments, warn them lest
they become guilty before the LORD and his
wrath come upon you and your brethren. Do
that and you shall be guiltless. [t] 11See now,
Amariah is high priest over you in everything
that pertains to the LORD, and Zebadiah, son of
Ishmael, is leader of the house of Judah in all
that pertains to the king; and the Levites will be
your officials. Act firmly, and the LORD will be
with the good."

CHAPTER 20

Invasion from Edom* 1After this the Moab-
ites, the Ammonites, and with them some Meu-
nites came to fight against Jehoshaphat. 2The
message was brought to Jehoshaphat: "A great
multitude is coming against you from across the
sea, from Edom; they are already in Hazazon-
tamar" (which is En-gedi). 3Jehoshaphat was
frightened, and he hastened to consult the LORD.
He proclaimed a fast for all Judah. 4Then Judah
gathered to seek help from the LORD; from every
one of the cities of Judah they came to seek the
LORD. [u]

Prayer of Jehoshaphat 5Jehoshaphat stood up
in the assembly of Judah and Jerusalem in the
house of the LORD before the new court, 6and he
said: "LORD, God of our fathers, are you not the
God in heaven, and do you not rule over all the
kingdoms of the nations? In your hand is power
and might, and no one can withstand you. [v]
7Was it not you, our God, who drove out the
inhabitants of this land before your people Israel
and gave it forever to the descendants of Abra-
ham, your friend? [w] 8They have dwelt in it and
they built in it a sanctuary to your honor, saying,
9'When evil comes upon us, the sword of
judgment, or pestilence, or famine, we will

19, 2: Jehu the seer, son of Hanani: hardly the same seer as Jehu, son of Hanani, who prophesied against Baasha almost 50 years earlier (1 Kgs 16–1).

20, 1–30: Although the account here seems to be a free composition of the Chronicler, there is probably a basis in fact for it; there could well have been a raid of nomads against Judah in the reign of Jehoshaphat, similar to Zerah's attack on Asa (2 Chr 14, 8–14). The story may also, in some way, be connected with the campaign of Israel and Judah against Moab through the territory of Edom (2 Kgs 3, 4–27).

p 2 Chr 35, 23; 1 Kgs 22, 34. q Dt 1, 16ff; 16, 19f. r Dt 10, 17. s 2 Chr 17, 8f; Dt 17, 8–13; Ps 122, 3ff. t Nm 35, 19. u Jer 36, 6; Jb 1, 14. v 2 Chr 32, 7; Dt 4, 39. w Dn 3, 35.

stand before this house and before you, for your name is in this house, and we will cry out to you in our affliction, and you will hear and save!' [10]And now, see the Ammonites, Moabites, and those of Mount Seir whom you did not allow Israel to invade when they came from the land of Egypt, but instead they passed them by and did not destroy them.[x] [11]See how they are now repaying us by coming to drive us out of the possession you have given us. [12]O our God, will you not pass judgment on them? We are powerless before this vast multitude that comes against us. We are at a loss what to do, hence our eyes are turned toward you."

Victory Prophesied [13]All Judah was standing before the LORD, with their little ones, their wives, and their young sons. [14]And the spirit of the LORD came upon Jahaziel, son of Zechariah, son of Benaiah, son of Jeiel, son of Mattaniah, a Levite of the clan of Asaph, in the midst of the assembly, [15]and he said: "Listen, all of Judah, inhabitants of Jerusalem, and King Jehoshaphat! The LORD says to you: 'Do not fear or lose heart at the sight of this vast multitude, for the battle is not yours but God's. [16]Go down against them tomorrow. You will see them coming up by the ascent of Ziz, and you will come upon them at the end of the wadi which opens on the wilderness of Jeruel. [17]You will not have to fight in this encounter. Take your places, stand firm, and see how the LORD will be with you to deliver you, Judah and Jerusalem. Do not fear or lose heart. Tomorrow go out to meet them, and the LORD will be with you.' "[y] [18]Then Jehoshaphat knelt down with his face to the ground, and all Judah and the inhabitants of Jerusalem fell down before the LORD in worship. [19]Levites from among the Kohathites and Korahites rose to sing the praises of the LORD, the God of Israel, in a resounding chorus.

The Invaders Destroyed [20]In the early morning they hastened out to the wilderness of Tekoa. As they were going out, Jehoshaphat halted and said: "Listen to me, Judah and inhabitants of Jerusalem! Trust in the LORD, your God, and you will be found firm. Trust in his prophets and you will succeed."[z] [21]After consulting with the people, he appointed some to sing to the LORD and some to praise the holy Appearance* as it went forth at the head of the army. They sang: "Give thanks to the LORD, for his mercy endures forever."[a] [22]At the moment they began their jubilant hymn, the LORD laid an ambush against the Ammonites, Moabites, and those of Mount Seir who were coming against Judah, so that they were vanquished. [23]For the Ammonites and Moabites set upon the inhabitants of Mount Seir and completely exterminated them. And when they had finished with the inhabitants of Seir, they began to destroy each other.[b]

[24]When Judah came to the watchtower of the desert and looked toward the throng, they saw only corpses fallen on the ground, with no survivors. [25]Jehoshaphat and his people came to take plunder, and they found an abundance of cattle and personal property, garments and precious vessels. They took so much that they were unable to carry it all; they were three days taking the spoil, so great was it. [26]On the fourth day they held an assembly in the Valley of Beracah—for there they blessed the LORD; therefore that place has ever since been called the Valley of Beracah.* [27]Then all the men of Judah and Jerusalem, with Jehoshaphat at their head, turned back toward Jerusalem celebrating the joyful victory the LORD had given them over their enemies. [28]They came to Jerusalem, to the house of the LORD, with harps, lyres and trumpets. [29]And the fear of God came upon all the kingdoms of the surrounding lands when they heard how the LORD had fought against the enemies of Israel. [30]Thereafter Jehoshaphat's kingdom enjoyed peace, for his God gave him rest on every side.

Jehoshaphat's Other Deeds [31] [c]Thus Jehoshaphat reigned over Judah. He was thirty-five years old when he became king, and he reigned

20, 21: Holy Appearance: the Lord, who is with the Israelite army (v 17), manifests himself (the same language is in Ps 29, 2) in bringing Israel the victory (Ex 14, 14. 24).

20, 26: Beracah: the Hebrew word for "blessing."

x Dt 2, 4f. 9f. 18f. **y** Is 8, 10. **z** Is 7, 9. **a** Ps 136, 1. **b** Jos 6, 17; Ez 38, 21. **c** 31–34: 1 Kgs 22, 41–45.

twenty-five years in Jerusalem. His mother was named Azubah, daughter of Shilhi. [32]He followed the path of his father Asa unswervingly, doing what was right in the LORD's sight. [33]But the high places were not removed, nor as yet had the people fixed their hearts on the God of their fathers.

[34]The rest of the acts of Jehoshaphat, first and last, can be found written in the chronicle of Jehu, son of Hanani, which is inserted in the book of the kings of Israel. [35]After this, King Jehoshaphat of Judah allied himself with King Ahaziah of Israel, who did evil. [36] [d]He joined with him in building ships to sail to Tarshish; the fleet was built at Ezion-geber. [37]But Eliezer, son of Dodavahu from Mareshah, prophesied against Jehoshaphat, saying, "Because you have joined with Ahaziah, the LORD will shatter your work." And the ships were wrecked and were unable to sail to Tarshish.

CHAPTER 21

[1]Jehoshaphat rested with his ancestors; he was buried with them in the City of David. Jehoram, his son, succeeded him as king.[e] [2]His brothers, sons of Jehoshaphat, were Azariah, Jehiel, Zechariah, Azariah, Michael and Shephatiah; all these were sons of King Jehoshaphat of Judah. [3]Their father gave them numerous gifts of silver, gold and precious objects, together with fortified cities in Judah, but the kingship he gave to Jehoram because he was the first-born.

Evil Deeds of Jehoram [4]When Jehoram had come into his father's kingdom and had consolidated his power, he put to the sword all his brothers and also some of the princes of Israel. [5] [f]Jehoram was thirty-two years old when he became king, and he reigned eight years in Jerusalem. [6]He conducted himself like the kings of Israel of the line of Ahab, because one of Ahab's daughters* was his wife. He did evil in the sight of the LORD, [7]but the LORD would not destroy the house of David because of the covenant he had made with David and because of his promise to give him and his sons a lamp for all time.[g]

[8] [h]During his time Edom revolted against the sovereignty of Judah; they chose a king of their own. [9]Thereupon Jehoram crossed over with his officers and all the chariots he had. He arose by night and broke through the Edomites when they had surrounded him and the commanders of his chariots. [10]However, Edom has continued in revolt against the sovereignty of Judah down to the present time. Libnah also revolted at that time against Jehoram's sovereignty because he had forsaken the LORD, the God of his fathers. [11]He also set up high places in the mountains of Judah; he led the inhabitants of Jerusalem into idolatry and seduced Judah.

Retribution [12]He received a letter from the prophet Elijah* with this message: Thus says the LORD, the God of your ancestor David: 'Because you have not followed the path of your father Jehoshaphat, nor of Asa, king of Judah, [13]but instead have walked in the way of the kings of Israel and have led Judah and the inhabitants of Jerusalem into idolatry, as did the house of Ahab, and also because you have murdered your brothers of your father's house who were better than you, [14]the LORD will strike your people, your children, your wives, and all that is yours with a great plague; [15]and you shall have severe pains from a disease in your bowels, while your bowels issue forth because of the disease, day after day.' "

[16]Then the LORD stirred up against Jehoram the animosity of the Philistines and of the Arabs who bordered on the Ethiopians. [17]They came up against Judah, invaded it, and carried away all the wealth found in the king's palace, along with his sons and his wives; there was left to him only one son, Jehoahaz, his youngest. [18]After these events, the LORD afflicted him with an incurable disease of the bowels. [19]As time went on until a

21, 6: One of Ahab's daughters: Athaliah. In 2 Chr 22, 2 (and its source, 2 Kgs 8, 26) she is called Omri's daughter; but this should probably be understood in the sense of granddaughter.

21, 12: Elijah: the only mention by the Chronicler of this prophet of the northern kingdom of Israel. It is doubtful that Elijah was still living in the reign of Jehoram of Judah; in any case, the attribution of the letter to him is most likely an imaginative filling out of the narration.

d 36f: 1 Kgs 22, 48f. e 1 Kgs 22, 51. f 5ff: 2 Kgs 8, 17ff. g 1 Kgs 11, 36; 2 Kgs 8, 19. h 8ff: Gn 27, 40; 2 Kgs 8, 20ff.

period of two years had elapsed, his bowels
issued forth because of the disease and he died in
great pain. His people did not make a pyre for
him like that of his fathers. 20He was thirty-two
years old when he became king, and he reigned
eight years in Jerusalem. He departed unloved
and was buried in the City of David, but not in
the tombs of the kings.[i]

CHAPTER 22

Ahaziah 1 [j]Then the inhabitants of Jerusalem
made Ahaziah, his youngest son, king in his
stead, since all the older sons had been slain by
the band that had come into the fort with the
Arabs. Thus Ahaziah, son of Jehoram, reigned as
king of Judah. 2He was twenty-two years old
when he became king, and he reigned one year
in Jerusalem. His mother was named Athaliah,
daughter of Omri. 3He, too, followed the ways of
the house of Ahab, because his mother coun-
seled him to act sinfully. 4To his own destruc-
tion, he did evil in the sight of the LORD, as did
the house of Ahab, since they were his counsel-
ors after the death of his father.

5He was also following their counsel when he
accompanied Jehoram, son of Ahab, king of
Israel, to battle against Hazael, king of Aram, at
Ramoth-gilead. There Jehoram was wounded by
the Arameans. 6He returned to Jezreel to be
healed of the wounds he had received at Rama
in his battle against Hazael, king of Aram.
Because of this illness, Ahaziah, son of Jehoram,
king of Judah, went down to visit Jehoram, son
of Ahab, in Jezreel. 7Now it was willed by God
for Ahaziah's downfall that he should join Jeho-
ram, for after his arrival he rode out with
Jehoram to Jehu, son of Nimshi, whom the LORD
had anointed to cut down the house of Ahab.[k]
8While Jehu was executing judgment on the
house of Ahab, he also encountered the princes
of Judah and the nephews of Ahaziah who were
his attendants, and he slew them.[l] 9Then he
looked for Ahaziah himself. They caught him
where he was hiding in Samaria and brought
him to Jehu, who put him to death. They buried
him, for they said, "He was the grandson of
Jehoshaphat, who sought the LORD with his
whole heart."[m] There remained in Ahaziah's
house no one powerful enough to wield the
kingship.*

Usurpation of Athaliah 10 [n]When Athaliah,
mother of Ahaziah, learned that her son was
dead, she proceeded to kill off all the royal
offspring of the house of Judah. 11But Jehosheba,
a royal princess, secretly took Ahaziah's son
Joash from among the king's sons who were
about to be slain, and put him and his nurse in a
bedroom. In this way Jehosheba, who was the
daughter of King Jehoram, a sister of Ahaziah,
and wife of Jehoiada the priest, hid the child
from Athaliah's sight, so that she did not put him
to death. 12For six years he remained hidden
with them in the house of God, while Athaliah
ruled over the land.

CHAPTER 23

Athaliah Overthrown 1 [o]In the seventh year,
Jehoiada took courage and entered a conspiracy
with certain captains: Azariah, son of Jehoram;
Ishmael, son of Jehohanan; Azariah, son of
Obed; Masseiah, son of Adaiah; and Elishaphat,
son of Zichri. 2They journeyed about Judah,
gathering the Levites from all the cities of Judah
and also the heads of the Israelite families. When
they had come to Jerusalem, 3the whole assem-
bly made a covenant with the king in the house
of God. Jehoiada said to them: "Here is the
king's son who must reign, as the LORD prom-
ised concerning the sons of David. 4This is what
you must do: a third of your number, both
priests and Levites, who come in on the sabbath
must guard the thresholds, 5another third must
be at the king's palace, and the final third at the
Foundation Gate, when all the people will be in
the courts of the LORD's temple. 6Let no one
enter the LORD's house except the priests and
those Levites who are ministering. They may
enter because they are holy; but all the other
people must observe the prescriptions of the
LORD. 7The Levites shall surround the king on all

22, 9: This account of the death of Ahaziah of Judah is not derived from 2 Kgs 9, 27f, with which it is at variance.

i 2 Kgs 8, 24. j 1–6: 2 Kgs 8, 24–29. k 2 Kgs 9, 21; 10, 12ff. l 2 Kgs 10, 12ff. m 2 Kgs 9, 27f. n 10ff: 2 Kgs 11, 1ff. o 1–17. 19ff: 2 Kgs 11, 4–20.

sides, each with his weapon drawn. Whoever tries to enter the house must be slain. Stay with the king wherever he goes."

8The Levites and all Judah did just as Jehoiada the priest commanded. Each brought his men, those who were to come in on the sabbath as well as those who were to depart on the sabbath, since Jehoiada the priest had not dismissed any of the divisions.[p] 9Jehoiada the priest gave the captains the spears, shields and bucklers of King David which were in the house of God. 10He stationed all the people, each with his spear in hand, from the southern to the northern extremity of the enclosure, around the altar and the temple on the king's behalf. 11Then they brought out the king's son, set the crown and the insignia upon him, and made him king. Jehoiada and his sons anointed him, and they cried, "Long live the king!"

12When Athaliah heard the din of the people running and acclaiming the king, she went to the people in the temple of the LORD. 13She looked, and there was the king standing beside his pillar* at the entrance, the officers and the trumpeters around him, and all the people of the land rejoicing and blowing trumpets, while the singers with their musical instruments were leading the acclaim. Athaliah tore her garments and cried out, "Treason! treason!" 14Then Jehoiada the priest sent out the captains who were in command of the army; he said to them: "Take her outside through the ranks, and if anyone tries to follow her, let him die by the sword. For," the priest continued, "you must not put her to death in the LORD's temple." 15So they seized her, and when she arrived at the entrance to the Horse Gate of the palace, they put her to death there.

16Then Jehoiada made a covenant between himself and all the people and the king, that they should be the LORD's people. 17And all the people went to the temple of Baal and tore it down. They smashed its altars and images, and they slew Mattan, the priest of Baal, before the altars. 18Then Jehoiada gave the charge of the LORD's temple into the hands of the levitical priests, to whom David had assigned turns in the temple for offering the holocausts of the LORD, as is written in the law of Moses, with rejoicing and song, as David had provided.[q] 19Moreover, he stationed guards at the gates of the LORD's temple, so that no one unclean in any respect might enter. 20Then he took the captains, the nobles, the rulers among the people, and all the people of the land, and led the king out of the LORD's house. When they had come within the upper gate of the king's house, they seated the king upon the royal throne. 21All the people of the land rejoiced and the city was quiet, now that Athaliah had been put to death by the sword.

CHAPTER 24

The Temple Restored 1[r]Joash was seven years old when he became king, and he reigned forty years in Jerusalem. His mother, named Zibiah, was from Beer-sheba. 2Joash did what was pleasing to the LORD as long as Jehoiada the priest lived. 3Jehoiada provided him with two wives, and he became the father of sons and daughters.

4After some time, Joash decided to restore the LORD's temple. 5He called together the priests and Levites and said to them: "Go out to all the cities of Judah and collect money* from all Israel that you may repair the house of your God over the years. You must hasten this affair." But the Levites did not hasten. 6Then the king summoned Jehoiada, who was in charge, and said to him: "Why have you not required the Levites to bring in from Judah and Jerusalem the tax levied by Moses, the servant of the LORD, and by the

23, 13: Beside his pillar: the king had a special place in the eastern gateway of the temple court that contained the altar of holocausts. He occupied this place on feasts and sabbaths at the time of the statutory offerings, or when he made freewill offerings of his own; cf 2 Kgs 11, 4 and also Ez 46, 1–8 for a later reflection of this.

24, 5: Collect money: according to 2 Kgs 12, 5, the people themselves brought the money to the temple; it consisted, at least in part, of voluntary contributions. At the time of the Chronicler (see Neh 10, 32) there was a fixed head tax for the upkeep of the temple (2 Chr 34, 9), based on Ex 30, 12–16. This was still in force in New Testament times (Mt 17, 24f).

p 2 Kgs 11, 9; 1 Chr 24, 19. q 1 Chr 23, 13. r 1–14: 2 Kgs 12, 1–13.

assembly of Israel, for the tent of the testimony?"[s] 7 For the wicked Athaliah and her sons had damaged the house of God and had even turned over to the Baals the dedicated resources of the LORD's temple.

8 At the king's command, therefore, they made a chest, which they put outside the gate of the LORD's temple.[t] 9 They had it proclaimed throughout Judah and Jerusalem that the tax which Moses, the servant of God, had imposed on Israel in the desert should be brought to the LORD.[u] 10 All the princes and the people rejoiced; they brought what was asked and cast it into the chest until it was filled. 11 Whenever the chest was brought to the royal officials by the Levites and they saw that it contained much money, the royal scribe and an overseer for the high priest came, emptied the chest, then took it back and returned it to its place. This they did day after day until they had collected a large sum of money. 12 Then the king and Jehoiada gave it to the workmen in charge of the labor on the LORD's temple, who hired masons and carpenters to restore the temple, and also iron- and bronze-smiths to repair it. 13 The workmen labored, and the task of restoration progressed under their hands. They restored the house of God according to its original form, and reinforced it. 14 After they had finished, they brought the rest of the money to the king and to Jehoiada, who had it made into utensils for the LORD's temple, utensils for the service and the holocausts, and basins and other gold and silver utensils. They offered holocausts in the LORD's temple continually throughout the lifetime of Jehoiada. 15 Jehoiada lived to a ripe old age; he was a hundred and thirty years old when he died. 16 He was buried in the City of David with the kings, because he had done good in Israel, in particular with respect to God and his temple.

Apostasy of King Joash 17 After the death of Jehoiada, the princes of Judah came and paid homage to the king, and the king then listened to them. 18 They forsook the temple of the LORD, the God of their fathers, and began to serve the sacred poles and the idols; and because of this crime of theirs, wrath came upon Judah and Jerusalem.[v] 19 Although prophets were sent to them to convert them to the LORD, the people would not listen to their warnings. 20 Then the spirit of God possessed Zechariah, son of Jehoiada the priest. He took his stand above the people and said to them: "God says, 'Why are you transgressing the LORD's commands, so that you cannot prosper? Because you have abandoned the LORD, he has abandoned you.' " 21 But they conspired against him, and at the king's order they stoned him to death in the court of the LORD's temple. 22 Thus King Joash was unmindful of the devotion shown him by Jehoiada, Zechariah's father, and slew his son. And as he was dying, he said, "May the LORD see and avenge."

Retribution 23 At the turn of the year a force of Arameans came up against Joash. They invaded Judah and Jerusalem, did away with all the princes of the people, and sent all their spoil to the king of Damascus.[w] 24 Though the Aramean force came with few men, the LORD surrendered a very large force into their power, because Judah had abandoned the LORD, the God of their fathers. So punishment was meted out to Joash.[x] 25 [y]After the Arameans had departed from him, leaving him in grievous suffering, his servants conspired against him because of the murder of the son of Jehoiada the priest. They killed him on his sickbed. He was buried in the City of David, but not in the tombs of the kings.

26 These conspired against him: Zabad, son of Shimeath from Ammon, and Jehozabad, son of Shimrith from Moab. 27 Of his sons, and the great tribute imposed on him, and of his rebuilding of the house of God, there is a written account in the midrash of the book of the kings. His son Amaziah succeeded him as king.[z]

CHAPTER 25

Campaign in Edom 1 [a]Amaziah was twenty-five years old when he became king, and he reigned twenty-nine years in Jerusalem. His

s Ex 25, 1–9; Neh 10, 33. t 2 Chr 34, 9. u Ex 30, 13. v Ex 34, 13. w 2 Kgs 12, 17f. x Dt 32, 30. y 25f: 2 Kgs 12, 21f. z 2 Kgs 12, 19. 22. a 1–4: 2 Kgs 14, 1–6.

mother, named Jehoaddan, was from Jerusalem. 2He did what was pleasing in the sight of the LORD, though not wholeheartedly. 3After he had strengthened his hold on the kingdom, he slew those of his servants who had killed the king, his father; 4but he did not put their children to death, for he acted according to what is written in the law, in the Book of Moses, as the LORD commanded: "Fathers shall not be put to death for their children, nor children for their fathers; but only for his own guilt shall a man be put to death."[b]

5Amaziah mustered Judah and placed them, out of all Judah and Benjamin according to their ancestral houses, under leaders of thousands and of hundreds. When he had counted those of twenty years and over, he found them to be three hundred thousand picked men fit for war, capable of handling lance and shield. 6He also hired a hundred thousand valiant warriors from Israel for a hundred talents of silver. 7But a man of God came to him and said: "O king, let not the army of Israel go with you, for the LORD is not with Israel, with any Ephraimite. 8Instead, go on your own, strongly prepared for the conflict; otherwise the LORD will defeat you in the face of the enemy. It is God who has the power to reinforce or to defeat." 9Amaziah answered the man of God, "But what is to be done about the hundred talents that I paid for the troops of Israel?" The man of God replied, "The LORD can give you much more than that." 10Amaziah then disbanded the troops that had come to him from Ephraim, and sent them home. They, however, became furiously angry with Judah, and returned home blazing with resentment.

11Amaziah now assumed command of his army. They proceeded to the Valley of Salt, and there they killed ten thousand men of Seir.[c] 12The Judahites also brought back another ten thousand alive, whom they led to the summit of the Rock and then cast down, so that they were all crushed. 13Meanwhile, the mercenaries whom Amaziah had dismissed from battle service with him raided the cities of Judah from Samaria to Beth-horon. They killed three thousand of the inhabitants and took away much booty.

Infidelity of Amaziah 14When Amaziah returned from his conquest of the Edomites he brought back with him the gods of the people of Seir, which he set up as his own gods; he bowed down before them and offered sacrifice to them. 15Then the anger of the LORD blazed out against Amaziah, and he sent a prophet to him who said: "Why have you had recourse to this people's gods that could not save their own people from your hand?" 16While he was still speaking, however, the king said to him: "Have you been made the king's counselor? Be silent! Why should it be necessary to kill you?" Therefore the prophet desisted. "I know, however," he said, "that God has let you take counsel to your own destruction, because you have done this thing and have refused to hear my counsel."

Retribution 17[d]Having taken counsel, King Amaziah of Judah sent messengers to Joash, son of Jehoahaz, son of Jehu, the king of Israel, saying, "Come, let us meet each other face to face." 18King Joash of Israel sent this reply to King Amaziah of Judah: "The thistle of the Lebanon sent a message to the cedar of the Lebanon, saying, 'Give your daughter to my son for his wife.' But the wild beasts of the Lebanon passed by and trampled the thistle down.[e] 19You are thinking, 'See, I have beaten Edom!', and thus ambition makes you proud. Remain at home. Why involve yourself, and Judah with you, in misfortune and failure?" 20But Amaziah would not listen, for God had determined to hand them over because they had had recourse to the gods of Edom.

21Therefore King Joash of Israel advanced and he and King Amaziah met in battle at Beth-shemesh of Judah. 22There Judah was defeated by Israel, and all the Judean soldiers fled homeward. 23King Joash of Israel captured Amaziah, king of Judah, son of Joash, son of Jehoahaz, at Beth-shemesh and brought him to Jerusalem. Then he tore down the wall of Jerusalem from the Ephraim Gate to the Corner Gate, a distance

b Dt 24, 16; 2 Kgs 14, 5f; Ez 18, 20. c 2 Kgs 14, 7. d 17–24: 2 Kgs 14, 8–14. e Jgs 9, 7–15; 2 Kgs 14, 9.

of four hundred cubits. 24He took away all the gold and silver and all the vessels he found in the house of God with Obed-edom,* together with the treasures of the palace, and hostages as well. Then he returned to Samaria.

25[f]Amaziah, son of Joash, king of Judah, survived Joash, son of Jehoahaz, king of Israel, by fifteen years. 26The rest of the acts of Amaziah, first and last, can be found written, as is well known, in the book of the kings of Judah and Israel. 27Now from the time that Amaziah ceased to follow the LORD, a conspiracy was formed against him in Jerusalem; hence he fled to Lachish. But they pursued him to Lachish and put him to death there. 28They brought him back on horses and buried him with his ancestors in the City of Judah.*

CHAPTER 26

The Works of Uzziah 1[g]All the people of Judah chose Uzziah, though he was but sixteen years of age, and proclaimed him king to succeed his father Amaziah. 2He rebuilt Elath and restored it to Judah; this was after King Amaziah had gone to rest with his ancestors. 3Uzziah was sixteen years old when he became king, and he reigned fifty-two years in Jerusalem. His mother, named Jecoliah, was from Jerusalem. 4He pleased the LORD, just as his father Amaziah had done.

5He was prepared to seek God as long as Zechariah* lived, who taught him to fear God; and as long as he sought the LORD, God made him prosper.[h] 6He went out and fought the Philistines and razed the walls of Gath, Jabneh and Ashdod [and built cities in the district of Ashdod and in Philistia].[i] 7God helped him against the Philistines, against the Arabs who dwelt in Gurbaal, and against the Meunites. 8The Ammonites paid tribute to Uzziah and his fame spread as far as Egypt, for he grew stronger and stronger. 9Moreover, Uzziah built towers in Jerusalem at the Corner Gate, at the Valley Gate, and at the Angle, and he fortified them. 10He built towers in the desert and dug numerous cisterns, for he had many cattle. He had plowmen in the foothills and the plains, and vinedressers in the highlands and the garden land. He was a lover of the soil.

11Uzziah also had a standing army of fit soldiers divided into bands according to the number in which they were mustered by Jeiel the scribe and Maaseiah the recorder, under the command of Hananiah, one of the king's officials. 12The entire number of family heads over these valiant warriors was two thousand six hundred, 13and at their disposal was a mighty army of three hundred seven thousand five hundred fighting men of great valor to help the king against his enemies. 14Uzziah provided for them—for the entire army—bucklers, lances, helmets, breastplates, bows and slingstones. 15He also built machines in Jerusalem, devices contrived to stand on the towers and at the angles of the walls to shoot arrows and cast large stones. His fame spread far and wide, and his power was ascribed to the marvelous help he had received.

Pride and Fall 16But after he had become strong, he became proud to his own destruction and broke faith with the LORD, his God. He entered the temple of the LORD to make an offering on the altar of incense. 17But Azariah the priest, and with him eighty other priests of the LORD, courageous men, followed him. 18They opposed King Uzziah, saying to him: "It is not for you, Uzziah, to burn incense to the LORD, but for the priests, the sons of Aaron, who have been consecrated for this purpose. Leave the sanctuary, for you have broken faith and no longer have a part in the glory that comes from the LORD God."[j] 19Uzziah, who was holding a censer for burning the incense, became angry, but at the moment he showed his anger to the priests, while they were looking at him in the

25, 24: With Obed-edom: possibly a reference to the priest of an Edomite false worship (cf v 14), if not to a levitical family of gatekeepers; cf 1 Chr 15, 18; 26, 12–15.

25, 28: The City of Judah: in the parallel passage of 2 Kgs 14, 20, the City of David. The Chronicler is referring, by this term, to the capital of Judah, Jerusalem.

26, 5: Zechariah: this person, not otherwise identified, is referred to in language suggesting a pious layman rather than a priest or prophet; cf 2 Chr 29, 1.

f 25–28: 2 Kgs 14, 17–20. g 1–4: 2 Kgs 14, 21f; 15, 1ff. h 2 Chr 24, 2. i Am 1, 8. j Ex 30, 7.

house of the LORD beside the altar of incense, leprosy broke out on his forehead.[k] 20Azariah the chief priest and all the other priests examined him, and when they saw that his forehead was leprous, they expelled him from the temple. He himself fled willingly, for the LORD had afflicted him. 21 [l]King Uzziah remained a leper to the day of his death. As a leper he dwelt in a segregated house, for he was excluded from the house of the LORD. Therefore his son Jotham was regent of the palace and ruled the people of the land.

22The prophet Isaiah, son of Amos, wrote the rest of the acts of Uzziah, first and last. 23Uzziah rested with his ancestors; he was buried with them in the field adjoining the royal cemetery, for they said, "He was a leper." His son Jotham succeeded him as king.

CHAPTER 27

Jotham 1 [m]Jotham was twenty-five years old when he became king, and he reigned sixteen years in Jerusalem. His mother was named Jerusa, daughter of Zadok. 2He pleased the LORD just as his father Uzziah had done, though he did not enter the temple of the LORD; the people, however, continued to act sinfully.

3He built the upper gate of the LORD's house and had much construction done on the wall of Ophel. 4Moreover, he built cities in the hill country of Judah, and in the forest land he set up fortresses and towers. 5He fought with the king of the Ammonites and conquered them. That year the Ammonites paid him one hundred talents of silver, together with ten thousand kors of wheat and ten thousand of barley. They brought the same to him also in the second and in the third year. 6Thus Jotham continued to grow strong because he lived resolutely in the presence of the LORD, his God. 7 [n]The rest of the acts of Jotham, his wars and his activities, can be found written in the book of the kings of Israel and Judah. 8He was twenty-five years old when he became king, and he reigned sixteen years in Jerusalem. 9Jotham rested with his ancestors and was buried in the City of David, and his son Ahaz succeeded him as king.

III: Reforms of Hezekiah and Josiah

CHAPTER 28

Impiety of Ahaz 1 [o]Ahaz was twenty years old when he became king, and he reigned sixteen years in Jerusalem. He did not please the LORD as his forefather David had done, 2but conducted himself like the kings of Israel and even made molten idols of the Baals. 3Moreover, he offered sacrifice in the Valley of Ben-hinnom, and immolated his sons by fire according to the abominable practice of the nations which the LORD had cleared out before the Israelites.[p] 4He offered sacrifice and incense on the high places, on hills, and under every leafy tree.

Retribution 5Therefore the LORD, his God, delivered him into the power of the king of Aram. The Arameans defeated him and carried away captive a large number of his people, whom they brought to Damascus. He was also delivered into the power of the king of Israel, who defeated him with great slaughter.[q] 6For Pekah, son of Remaliah, slew one hundred and twenty thousand of Judah in a single day, all of them valiant men, because they had abandoned the LORD, the God of their fathers. 7Zichri, an Ephraimite warrior, killed Maaseiah, the king's son, and Azrikam, the master of the palace, and also Elkanah, who was second to the king. 8The Israelites took away as captives two hundred thousand of their brethren's wives, sons and daughters; they also took from them much plunder, which they brought to Samaria.

The Prophecy of Oded 9In Samaria there was a prophet of the LORD by the name of Oded. He went out to meet the army returning to Samaria and said to them: "It was because the LORD, the God of your fathers, was angry with Judah that he delivered them into your hands. You, however, have slaughtered them with a fury that has reached up to heaven. 10And now you are

k Nm 12, 10. l 21ff: 2 Kgs 15, 5ff; Lv 13, 46; Nm 19, 20. m 1–3; 2 Kgs 15, 32–35. n 7–9: 2 Kgs 15, 36ff. o 1–4: 2 Kgs 16, 1–4. p 2 Kgs 16, 3; Lv 18, 21. q 2 Kgs 16, 5; Is 7, 1–9.

planning to make the children of Judah and Jerusalem your slaves and bondwomen. Are not you yourselves, therefore, guilty of a crime against the LORD, your God? 11Now listen to me: send back the captives you have carried off from among your brethren, for the burning anger of the LORD is upon you."

12At this, some of the Ephraimite leaders, Azariah, son of Johanan, Berechiah, son of Meshillemoth, Jehizkiah, son of Shallum, and Amasa, son of Hadlai, themselves stood up in opposition to those who had returned from the war. 13They said to them: "Do not bring the captives here, for what you propose will make us guilty before the LORD and increase our sins and our guilt. Our guilt is already great, and there is a burning anger upon Israel." 14Therefore the soldiers left their captives and the plunder before the princes and the whole assembly. 15Then the men just named proceeded to help the captives. All of them who were naked they clothed from the booty; they clothed them, put sandals on their feet, gave them food and drink, anointed them, and all who were weak they set on asses. They brought them to Jericho, the city of palms, to their brethren. Then they returned to Samaria.[r]

Further Sins of Ahaz 16At that time King Ahaz sent an appeal for help to the kings of Assyria.[s] 17The Edomites had returned, attacked Judah, and carried off captives.[t] 18The Philistines too had raided the cities of the foothills and the Negeb of Judah; they captured Beth-shemesh, Aijalon, Gederoth, Soco and its dependencies, Timnah and its dependencies, and Gimzo and its dependencies, and occupied them. 19For the LORD had brought Judah low because of Ahaz, king of Israel,* who let Judah go its own way and proved utterly faithless to the LORD. 20Tilgath-pilneser, king of Assyria, did indeed come to him, but to oppress him rather than to help him.[u] 21Though Ahaz plundered the LORD's house and the houses of the king and the princes to make payment to the king of Assyria, it availed him nothing.[v]

22While he was already in distress, the same King Ahaz became even more unfaithful to the LORD. 23He sacrificed to the gods of Damascus who had defeated him, saying, "Since it was the gods of the kings of Aram who helped them, I will sacrifice to them that they may help me also." However, they only caused further disaster to him and to all Israel.[w] 24Ahaz gathered up the utensils of God's house and broke them in pieces. He closed the doors of the LORD's house and had altars made for himself in every corner of Jerusalem.[x] 25In every city throughout Judah he set up high places to offer sacrifice to other gods. Thus he angered the LORD, the God of his fathers.

26[y]The rest of his deeds and his activities, first and last, can be found written in the book of the kings of Judah and Israel. 27Ahaz rested with his ancestors and was buried in Jerusalem—in the city, for they did not bring him to the tombs of the kings of Israel. His son Hezekiah succeeded him as king.

CHAPTER 29

Reforms of Hezekiah 1[z]Hezekiah was twenty-five years old when he became king, and he reigned twenty-nine years in Jerusalem. His mother was named Abia, daughter of Zechariah. 2He pleased the LORD just as his forefather David had done. 3It was he who, in the first month of the first year of his reign, opened the doors of the LORD's house and repaired them.[a] 4He summoned the priests and Levites, gathered them in the open space to the east, 5and said to them: "Listen to me, you Levites! Sanctify yourselves now and sanctify the house of the LORD, the God of your fathers, and clean out the filth from the sanctuary. 6Our fathers acted faithlessly and did evil in the eyes of the LORD, our God. They abandoned him, turned away their faces from the LORD's dwelling, and turned their backs on

28, 19: Ahaz, king of Israel: in the period of the divided kingdom the term king of Israel would elsewhere mean "king of the northern Kingdom of Israel."

r Lk 10, 25–37. s 2 Kgs 16, 7. t 2 Kgs 16, 6. u 2 Kgs 16, 10; Is 7, 17–20; 8, 5–8. v 2 Kgs 16, 8. w 2 Kgs 16, 12f; Is 10, 20. x 2 Chr 29, 3; 30, 14; 2 Kgs 16, 17. y 26f: 2 Kgs 16, 19f. z 1ff: 2 Kgs 18, 1ff. a 2 Chr 28, 24.

him. [7]They also closed the doors of the vestibule, extinguished the lamps, and refused to burn incense and offer holocausts in the sanctuary to the honor of the God of Israel.[b] [8] [c]Therefore the anger of the LORD has come upon Judah and Jerusalem; he has made them an object of terror, astonishment and mockery, as you see with your own eyes. [9]For our fathers, as you know, fell by the sword, and our sons, our daughters and our wives have been taken captive because of this. [10]Now, I intend to make a covenant with the LORD, the God of Israel, that his burning anger may withdraw from us. [11]My sons, be not negligent any longer, for it is you whom the LORD has chosen to stand before him, to minister to him, to be his ministers and to offer incense."

[12]Then the Levites arose: Mahath, son of Amasai, and Joel, son of Azariah, descendants of the Kohathites; of the sons of Merari: Kish, son of Abdi, and Azariah, son of Jehallel; of the Gershonites: Joah, son of Zimmah, and Eden, son of Joah; [13]of the sons of Elizaphan: Shimri and Jeuel; of the sons of Asaph: Zechariah and Mattaniah; [14]of the sons of Heman: Jehuel and Shimei; of the sons of Jeduthun: Shemiah and Uzziel. [15]They gathered their brethren together and sanctified themselves; then they came as the king had ordered, to cleanse the LORD's house in keeping with his words.

[16]The priests entered the interior of the LORD's house to cleanse it; and whatever they found in the LORD's temple that was unclean they brought out to the court of the LORD's house, where the Levites took it from them and carried it out to the Kidron Valley. [17]They began the work of consecration on the first day of the first month, and on the eighth day of the month they arrived at the vestibule of the LORD; they consecrated the LORD's house during eight days, and on the sixteenth day of the first month, they had finished.

[18]Then they went inside to King Hezekiah and said: "We have cleansed the entire house of the LORD, the altar of holocausts with all its utensils, and the table for the showbread with all its utensils. [19]All the articles which King Ahaz during his reign had thrown away because of his apostasy, we have restored and consecrated, and they are now before the LORD's altar."

The Rite of Expiation [20]Then King Hezekiah hastened to convoke the princes of the city and went up to the LORD's house. [21]Seven bulls, seven rams, seven lambs and seven he-goats were brought for a sin offering for the kingdom, for the sanctuary, and for Judah, and he ordered the sons of Aaron, the priests, to offer them on the altar of the LORD. [22]They slaughtered the bulls, and the priests collected the blood and cast it on the altar. Then they slaughtered the rams and cast the blood on the altar; then they slaughtered the lambs and cast the blood on the altar. [23]Then the he-goats for the sin offering were led before the king and the assembly, who laid their hands upon them. [24]The priests then slaughtered them and offered their blood on the altar to atone for the sin of all Israel; for "The holocaust and the sin offering," the king had said, "is for all Israel."

[25]He stationed the Levites in the LORD's house with cymbals, harps and lyres according to the prescriptions of David, of Gad the king's seer, and of Nathan the prophet; for the prescriptions were from the LORD through his prophets. [26]The Levites were stationed with the instruments of David, and the priests with the trumpets. [27]Then Hezekiah ordered the holocaust to be sacrificed on the altar, and in the same instant that the holocaust began, they also began the song of the LORD, to the accompaniment of the trumpets and the instruments of David, king of Israel. [28]The entire assembly prostrated itself, and they continued to sing the song and to sound the trumpets until the holocaust had been completed. [29]As the holocaust was completed, the king and all who were with him knelt and prostrated themselves. [30]King Hezekiah and the princes then commanded the Levites to sing the praises of the LORD in the words of David and of Asaph the seer. They sang praises till their joy was full, then fell down and prostrated themselves.

b 2 Kgs 16, 15. c 8f: Lv 26, 32f; Dt 28, 25; Jer 25, 18.

[31]Hezekiah now spoke out this command: "You have undertaken a work for the LORD. Approach, and bring forward the sacrifices and thank offerings for the house of the LORD." Then the assembly brought forward the sacrifices and thank offerings and all the holocausts which were free-will offerings. [32]The number of holocausts that the assembly brought forward was seventy oxen, one hundred rams, and two hundred lambs: all of these as a holocaust to the LORD. [33]As consecrated gifts there were six hundred oxen and three thousand sheep. [34]Since the priests were too few in number to be able to skin all the victims for the holocausts, their brethren the Levites assisted them until the task was completed and the priests had sanctified themselves; the Levites, in fact, were more willing than the priests to sanctify themselves.[d] [35]Also, the holocausts were many, along with the fat of the peace offerings and the libations for the holocausts. Thus the service of the house of the LORD was reestablished. [36]Hezekiah and all the people rejoiced over what God had reestablished for the people, and at how suddenly this had been done.

CHAPTER 30

Invitation to the Passover [1]Hezekiah sent a message to all Israel and Judah, and even wrote letters to Ephraim and Manasseh saying that they should come to the house of the LORD in Jerusalem to celebrate the Passover in honor of the LORD, the God of Israel.[e] [2][f]The king, his princes, and the entire assembly in Jerusalem had agreed to celebrate the Passover during the second month, [3]for they could not celebrate it at the time of the restoration: the priests had not sanctified themselves in sufficient numbers, and the people were not gathered at Jerusalem. [4]When this proposal had been approved by the king and the entire assembly, [5]they issued a decree to be proclaimed throughout all Israel from Beer-sheba to Dan, that everyone should come to Jerusalem to celebrate the Passover in honor of the LORD, the God of Israel; for not many had kept it in the manner prescribed. [6]Accordingly the couriers, with the letters written by the king and his princes, traversed all Israel and Judah, and at the king's command they said: "Israelites, return to the LORD, the God of Abraham, Isaac and Israel, that he may return to you, the remnant left from the hands of the Assyrian kings. [7]Be not like your fathers and your brethren who proved faithless to the LORD, the God of their fathers, so that he delivered them over to desolation, as you yourselves now see.[g] [8]Be not obstinate, as your fathers were; extend your hands to the LORD and come to his sanctuary that he has consecrated forever, and serve the LORD, your God, that he may turn away his burning anger from you. [9]For when you return to the LORD, your brethren and your children will find mercy with their captors and return to this land; for merciful and compassionate is the LORD, your God, and he will not turn away his face from you if you return to him."[h]

[10]So the couriers passed from city to city in the land of Ephraim and Manasseh and as far as Zebulun, but they were derided and scoffed at. [11]Nevertheless, some from Asher, Manasseh and Zebulun humbled themselves and came to Jerusalem. [12]In Judah, however, the power of God brought it about that the people were of one mind to carry out the command of the king and the princes in accordance with the word of the LORD. [13]Thus many people gathered in Jerusalem to celebrate the feast of Unleavened Bread in the second month; it was a very great assembly.

The Passover Celebrated [14]They proceeded to take down the altars that were in Jerusalem; also they removed all the altars of incense and cast them into the Kidron Valley.[i] [15]They slaughtered the Passover on the fourteenth day of the second month. The priests and Levites, touched with shame, sanctified themselves and brought holocausts into the house of the LORD. [16]They stood in the places prescribed for them according to the law of Moses, the man of God. The priests sprinkled the blood given them by the Levites; [17]for many in the assembly had not sanctified themselves, and the Levites were in charge of

d 1 Chr 15, 12. e Ex 12, 1–28. f 2ff: Nm 9, 6–13. g Acts 7, 51. h 1 Kgs 8, 50. i 2 Chr 28, 42f.

slaughtering the Passover victims for all who were unclean and therefore could not consecrate them to the LORD.[j] 18 The greater part of the people, in fact, chiefly from Ephraim, Manasseh, Issachar and Zebulun, had not cleansed themselves. Nevertheless they ate the Passover, contrary to the prescription; for Hezekiah prayed for them, saying, "May the LORD, who is good, grant pardon to 19 everyone who has resolved to seek God, the LORD, the God of his fathers, though he be not clean as holiness requires." 20 The LORD heard Hezekiah and spared the people.

21 Thus the Israelites who were in Jerusalem celebrated the feast of Unleavened Bread with great rejoicing for seven days, and the Levites and the priests sang the praises of the LORD day after day with all their strength. 22 Hezekiah spoke encouragingly to all the Levites who had shown themselves well skilled in the service of the LORD. And when they had completed the seven days of festival, slaying peace offerings and singing praises to the LORD, the God of their fathers, 23 the whole assembly agreed to celebrate another seven days. With joy, therefore, they continued the festivity seven days longer. 24 King Hezekiah of Judah had contributed a thousand bulls and seven thousand sheep to the assembly, and the princes had contributed to the assembly a thousand bulls and ten thousand sheep. The priests sanctified themselves in great numbers, 25 and the whole assembly of Judah rejoiced, together with the priests and Levites and the rest of the assembly that had come from Israel, as well as the sojourners from the land of Israel and those that lived in Judah. 26 There was great rejoicing in Jerusalem, for since the days of Solomon, son of David, king of Israel, there had not been the like in the city. 27 Then the levitical priests rose and blessed the people; their voice was heard and their prayer reached heaven, God's holy dwelling.

CHAPTER 31

Liturgical Reform 1 After all this was over, those Israelites who had been present went forth to the cities of Judah and smashed the sacred pillars, cut down the sacred poles, and tore down the high places and altars throughout Judah, Benjamin, Ephraim and Manasseh, until all were destroyed. Then the Israelites returned to their various cities, each to his own possession.[k]

2 Hezekiah reestablished the classes of the priests and the Levites according to their former classification, assigning to each priest and Levite his proper service, whether in regard to holocausts or peace offerings, thanksgiving or praise, or ministering in the gates of the encampment of the LORD. 3 From his own wealth the king allotted a portion for holocausts, those of morning and evening and those on sabbaths, new moons and festivals, as prescribed in the law of the LORD.[l] 4 He also commanded the people living in Jerusalem to provide the support of the priests and Levites, that they might devote themselves entirely to the law of the LORD.

5 As soon as the order was promulgated, the Israelites brought, in great quantities, the best of their grain, wine, oil and honey, and all the produce of the fields; they gave a generous tithe of everything.[m] 6 Israelites and Judahites living in other cities of Judah also brought in tithes of oxen, sheep, and things that had been consecrated to the LORD, their God; these they brought in and set out in heaps.[n] 7 It was in the third month that they began to establish these heaps, and they completed them in the seventh month.* 8 When Hezekiah and the princes had come and seen the heaps, they blessed the LORD and his people Israel. 9 Then Hezekiah questioned the priests and the Levites concerning the heaps, 10 and the priest Azariah, head of the house of Zadoc, answered him, "Since they began to bring the offerings to the house of the LORD, we have eaten to the full and have had

31, 7: Third month . . . seventh month: between the feast of Pentecost and that of Booths, an interval without rain in Palestine, at the end of which the problem of storage (v 11) would become more urgent.

j 2 Chr 35, 6. k 2 Chr 34, 3f; 2 Kgs 18, 4. l 1 Chr 29, 3; Ez 45, 17; Nm 28—29. m Nm 18, 8–24; Dt 14, 22f. n Nm 12, 44–47; 13, 10–13.

much left over, for the LORD has blessed his people. This great supply is what was left over."[o]

[11]Hezekiah then gave orders that chambers should be constructed in the house of the LORD. When this had been done, [12]the offerings, tithes and consecrated things were deposited there in safekeeping. The overseer of these things was Conaniah the Levite, and his brother Shimei was second in charge. [13]Jehiel, Azaziah, Nathan, Asahel, Jerimoth, Jozabad, Eliel, Ismachiah, Mahath and Benaiah were supervisors subject to Conaniah and his brother Shimei by appointment of King Hezekiah and of Azariah, the prefect of the house of God. [14]Kore, the son of Imnah, a Levite and the keeper of the eastern gate, was in charge of the free-will gifts made to God; he distributed the offerings made to the LORD and the most holy of the consecrated things. [15]Under him in the priestly cities were Eden, Miniamin, Jeshua, Shemaiah, Amariah and Shecaniah, who faithfully made the distribution to their brethren, great and small alike, according to their classes.

[16]There was also a register by ancestral houses of males thirty years of age and over, for all priests who were eligible to enter the house of the LORD according to the daily rule to fulfill their service in the order of their classes.[p] [17]The priests were inscribed in their family records according to their ancestral houses, and the Levites of twenty years and over according to their various offices and classes.[q] [18]A distribution was also made to all who were inscribed in the family records, for their little ones, wives, sons and daughters—thus for the entire assembly, since they were to sanctify themselves by sharing faithfully in the consecrated things. [19]The sons of Aaron, the priests who lived on the lands attached to their cities, had in every city men designated by name to distribute portions to every male among the priests and to every Levite listed in the family records.

[20]This Hezekiah did in all Judah. He did what was good, upright and faithful before the LORD, his God. [21]Everything that he undertook, for the service of the house of God or for the law and the commandments, was to do the will of his God. He did this wholeheartedly, and he prospered.[r]

CHAPTER 32

Invasion of Sennacherib [1]But after he had proved his fidelity by such deeds, Sennacherib, king of Assyria, came. He invaded Judah, besieged the fortified cities, and proposed to take them by storm.[s] [2]When Hezekiah saw that Sennacherib was coming with the intention of attacking Jerusalem, [3]he decided in counsel with his princes and warriors to stop the waters of the springs outside the city. When they had pledged him their support, [4] [t]a large crowd was gathered which stopped all the springs and also the running stream in the valley nearby. For they said, "Why should the kings of Assyria come and find an abundance of water?" [5]He then looked to his defenses: he rebuilt the wall where it was broken down, raised towers upon it, and built another wall outside. He strengthened the Millo of the City of David and had a great number of spears and shields prepared.[u] [6]Then he appointed army commanders over the people. He gathered them together in his presence in the open space at the gate of the city and encouraged them with these words: [7]"Be brave and steadfast; do not be afraid or dismayed because of the king of Assyria and all the throng that is coming with him, for there is more with us than with him.[v] [8]For he has only an arm of flesh, but we have the LORD, our God, to help us and to fight our battles." And the people took confidence from the words of King Hezekiah of Judah.[w]

Threat of Sennacherib [9] [x]After this, while Sennacherib, king of Assyria, himself remained at Lachish with all his forces, he sent his officials to Jerusalem with this message for King Hezekiah of Judah, and all the Judahites who were in Jerusalem: [10]"King Sennacherib of Assyria has this to say: On what are you relying, while you remain under siege in Jerusalem? [11]Has not

o Lv 25, 19–22. p 1 Chr 23, 3f. q 1 Chr 23, 6–24. r Ps 119, 2f. s 2 Kgs 18, 13. t Is 22, 9. 11. u Neh 2, 17f. v 2 Chr 14, 10; 20, 6–12. w Is 31, 3. x 9–20: 2 Kgs 18, 17–37; Is 36, 1–22.

Hezekiah deceived you, delivering you over to a death of famine and thirst, by his claim that 'the LORD, our God, will save us from the grasp of the king of Assyria'? 12 Has not this same Hezekiah removed his high places and altars and commanded Judah and Jerusalem, 'You shall prostrate yourselves before one altar only, and on it alone you shall offer incense'? 13 Do you not know what my fathers and I have done to all the peoples of other lands? Were the gods of the nations in those lands able to save their lands from my hand? 14 Who among all the gods of those nations which my fathers put under the ban was able to save his people from my hand? Will your god, then, be able to save you from my hand? 15 Let not Hezekiah mislead you further and deceive you in any such way. Do not believe him! Since no other god of any other nation or kingdom has been able to save his people from my hand or the hands of my fathers, how much the less shall your god save you from my hand!"

16 His officials said still more against the LORD God and against his servant Hezekiah, 17 for he had written letters to deride the LORD, the God of Israel, speaking of him in these terms: "As the gods of the nations in other lands have not saved their people from my hand, neither shall Hezekiah's god save his people from my hand."[y] 18 In a loud voice they shouted in the Judean language to the people of Jerusalem who were on the wall, to frighten and terrify them so that they might capture their city. 19 They spoke of the God of Israel as though he were one of the gods of the other peoples of the earth, a work of human hands. 20 But because of this, King Hezekiah and the prophet Isaiah, son of Amos, prayed and called out to heaven.[z]

Defeat of Sennacherib 21 Then the LORD sent an angel, who destroyed every valiant warrior, leader and commander in the camp of the Assyrian king, so that he had to return shamefaced to his own country. And when he entered the temple of his god, some of his own offspring struck him down there with the sword.[a] 22 Thus the LORD saved Hezekiah and the inhabitants of Jerusalem from the hand of Sennacherib, king of Assyria, as from every other power; he gave them rest on every side. 23 Many brought gifts for the LORD to Jerusalem and costly objects for King Hezekiah of Judah, who thereafter was exalted in the eyes of all the nations.[b]

Hezekiah's Other Deeds 24 In those days Hezekiah became mortally ill. He prayed to the LORD, who answered him by giving him a sign.[c] 25 Hezekiah, however, did not then discharge his debt of gratitude, for he had become proud. Therefore anger descended upon him and upon Judah and Jerusalem. 26 [d]But then Hezekiah humbled himself for his pride—both he and the inhabitants of Jerusalem; and therefore the LORD did not vent his anger on them during the time of Hezekiah.

27 [e]Hezekiah possessed very great wealth and glory. He had treasuries made for his silver, gold, precious stones, spices, jewels, and other precious things of all kinds; 28 also storehouses for the harvest of grain, for wine and oil, and barns for the various kinds of cattle and for the flocks. 29 He built cities for himself, and he acquired sheep and oxen in great numbers, for God gave him very great riches. 30 This same Hezekiah stopped the upper outflow of water from Gihon and led it underground westward to the City of David. Hezekiah prospered in all his undertakings.[f] 31 Nevertheless, in respect to the ambassadors [princes] sent to him from Babylon to investigate the sign that had occurred in the land, God forsook him to test him, that he might know all that was in his heart.

32 The rest of Hezekiah's acts, including his pious works, can be found written in the Vision of the Prophet Isaiah, son of Amos, and in the book of the kings of Judah and Israel. 33 Hezekiah rested with his ancestors; he was buried at the approach to the tombs* of the descendants of David. All Judah and the inhabitants of Jerusalem paid him honor at his death. His son Manasseh succeeded him as king.

32, 33: The approach to the tombs: literally, "the ascent of the tombs," which may mean "the upper section of the tombs," their most prominent and honored place.

y 2 Kgs 19, 9–13; Is 37, 9–13. z 2 Kgs 19, 14–19; Is 37, 14–20. a 2 Kgs 19, 35ff; Is 37, 36ff. b 2 Chr 14, 6. c 2 Kgs 20, 1–11; Is 38, 1–8. d 26. 31: 2 Kgs 20, 12–19; Is 39, 1–8. e 27f: 2 Kgs 20, 13; Is 39, 2. f 2 Kgs 20, 20f.

CHAPTER 33

Impiety of Manasseh 1 [g]Manasseh was twelve years old when he became king, and he reigned fifty-five years in Jerusalem. 2 He did evil in the sight of the LORD, following the abominable practices of the nations whom the LORD had cleared out of the way of the Israelites. 3 He rebuilt the high places which his father Hezekiah had torn down, erected altars for the Baals, made sacred poles, and prostrated himself before the whole host of heaven and worshiped them. 4 He even built altars in the temple of the LORD, of which the LORD had said, "In Jerusalem shall my name be forever": 5 he built altars to the whole host of heaven in the two courts of the LORD's house. 6 It was he, too, who immolated his sons by fire in the Valley of Ben-hinnom. He practiced augury, divination and magic, and appointed necromancers and diviners of spirits, so that he provoked the LORD with the great evil that he did in his sight. 7 He placed an idol that he had carved in the house of God, of which God had said to David and his son Solomon: "In this house and in Jerusalem which I have chosen from all the tribes of Israel I shall place my name forever. 8 I will not again allow Israel's feet to leave the land which I assigned to your fathers, provided they are careful to observe all that I commanded them, keeping the whole law and the statutes and the ordinances given by Moses." 9 Manasseh misled Judah and the inhabitants of Jerusalem into doing even greater evil than the nations which the LORD had destroyed at the coming of the Israelites. 10 The LORD spoke to Manasseh and his people, but they paid no attention.

His Conversion 11 [h]Therefore the LORD brought against them the army commanders of the Assyrian king; they took Manasseh with hooks, shackled him with chains, and transported him to Babylon.* 12 In this distress, he began to appease the LORD, his God. He humbled himself abjectly before the God of his fathers 13 and prayed to him.* The LORD let himself be won over: he heard his prayer and restored him to his kingdom in Jerusalem. Then Manasseh understood that the LORD is indeed God.

14 Afterward he built an outer wall for the City of David to the west of Gihon in the valley, extending to the Fish Gate and encircling Ophel; he built it very high. He stationed army officers in all the fortified cities of Judah. 15 He removed the foreign gods and the idol from the LORD's house and all the altars he had built on the mount of the LORD's house and in Jerusalem, and he cast them outside the city.[i] 16 He restored the altar of the LORD, and sacrificed on it peace offerings and thank offerings, and commanded Judah to serve the LORD, the God of Israel. 17 Though the people continued to sacrifice on the high places, they now did so to the LORD, their God.

18 [j]The rest of the acts of Manasseh, his prayer to his God, and the words of the seers who spoke to him in the name of the LORD, the God of Israel, can be found written in the chronicles of the kings of Israel. 19 His prayer and how his supplication was heard, all his sins and his infidelity, the sites where he built high places and erected sacred poles and carved images before he humbled himself, all can be found written down in the history of his seers. 20 Manasseh rested with his ancestors and was buried in his own palace. His son Amon succeeded him as king.

Amon 21 [k]Amon was twenty-two years old when he became king, and he reigned two years in Jerusalem. 22 He did evil in the sight of the LORD, just as his father Manasseh had done. Amon offered sacrifice to all the idols which his father Manasseh had made, and worshiped them. 23 Moreover, he did not humble himself before the LORD as his father Manasseh had

33, 11: There is no evidence elsewhere for an imprisonment of King Manasseh in Babylon. However, according to the Assyrian inscriptions, he paid tribute to the Assyrian kings Esarhaddon (680–669 B.C.) and Asshurbanipal (668–627 B.C.). He may well have been obliged to go to Nineveh to take the oath of allegiance as vassal to the king of Assyria.

33, 13: And prayed to him: these words led an unknown writer to compose the apocryphal "Prayer of Manasseh," which is added as an appendix to many editions of the Vulgate Bible and is used in the public prayers of the church.

g 1–10: 2 Kgs 21, 1–9. h Jb 36, 7f; Ez 19, 9. i 2 Chr 14, 2. j 18. 20: 2 Kgs 21, 17f. k 21–25: 2 Kgs 21, 19–26.

done; on the contrary, Amon only increased his guilt. 24 His servants conspired against him and put him to death in his own house. 25 But the people of the land slew all those who had conspired against King Amon, and then they, the people of the land, made his son Josiah king in his stead.

CHAPTER 34

Reforms of Josiah 1 [l]Josiah was eight years old when he became king, and he reigned thirty-one years in Jerusalem. 2 He pleased the LORD, following the path of his ancestor David. 3 [m]In the eighth year of his reign, while he was still a youth, he began to seek after the God of his forefather David, and in his twelfth year* he began to purge Judah and Jerusalem of the high places, the sacred poles and the carved and molten images. 4 In his presence, the altars of the Baals were destroyed; the incense stands erected above them were torn down; the sacred poles and the carved and molten images were shattered and beaten into dust, which was strewn over the tombs of those who had sacrificed to them; 5 and the bones of the priests he burned upon their altars. Thus he purged Judah and Jerusalem. 6 He did likewise in the cities of Manasseh, Ephraim, Simeon, and in the ruined villages of the surrounding country as far as Naphtali; 7 he destroyed the altars, broke up the sacred poles and carved images and beat them into dust, and tore down the incense stands throughout the land of Israel. Then he returned to Jerusalem.

The Temple Restored 8 [n]In the eighteenth year of his reign, in order to cleanse the temple as well as the land, he sent Shaphan, son of Azaliah, Maaseiah, the ruler of the city, and Joah, son of Joahaz, the chamberlain, to restore the house of the LORD, his God. 9 They came to Hilkiah the high priest and turned over the money brought to the house of God which the Levites, the guardians of the threshold, had collected from Manasseh, Ephraim, and all the remnant of Israel, as well as from all of Judah, Benjamin, and the inhabitants of Jerusalem.[o] 10 They turned it over to the master workmen in the house of the LORD, and these in turn used it to pay the workmen in the LORD's house who were restoring and repairing the temple. 11 They also gave it to the carpenters and the masons to buy hewn stone and timber for the tie beams and rafters of the buildings which the kings of Judah had allowed to fall into ruin. 12 The men worked faithfully at their tasks; their overseers were Jahath and Obadiah, Levites of the line of Merari, and Zechariah and Meshullam, of the Kohathites, who directed them. All those Levites who were skillful with musical instruments 13 were in charge of the men who carried the burdens, and they directed all the workers in every kind of labor. Some of the other Levites were scribes, officials and gatekeepers.

The Finding of the Law 14 [p]When they brought out the money that had been deposited in the house of the LORD, Hilkiah the priest found the book of the law of the LORD given through Moses. 15 He reported this to Shaphan the scribe, saying, "I have found the book of the law in the house of the LORD." Hilkiah gave the book to Shaphan, 16 who brought it to the king at the same time that he was making his report to him. He said, "Your servants are doing everything that has been entrusted to them; 17 they have turned into bullion the metals deposited in the LORD's house and have handed it over to the overseers and the workmen." 18 Then Shaphan the scribe announced to the king, "Hilkiah the priest has given me a book." And Shaphan read from it before the king.

19 When the king heard the words of the law, he tore his garments 20 and issued this command to Hilkiah, to Ahikam, son of Shaphan, to Abdon, son of Michah, to Shaphan the scribe,

34, 3: In his twelfth year: c. 628 B.C., the year after Ashurbanipal's death, when Judah could free itself from Assyrian domination. From 2 Kgs 22, 1—23, 25 alone, one might think that Josiah's reform began only after the discovery of the book of the law in the temple, in the eighteenth year of his reign. But the Chronicler is no doubt right in placing the beginning of the reform at an earlier period. The very repair of the temple, which led to the finding of the book of the law, must have been occasioned by a cultic reform.

l 1f: 2 Kgs 22, 1f. m 3–7: 2 Chr 14, 1–4; 31, 1; 2 Kgs 23, 4–20. n 8–13: 2 Kgs 22, 3–7. o 2 Chr 24, 8f. p 14–28: 2 Kgs 22, 8–20.

and to Asaiah, the king's servant: [21]"On behalf
of myself and those who are left in Israel and
Judah, go, consult the LORD concerning the
words of the book that has been found. For the
anger of the LORD has been set furiously ablaze
against us, since our fathers have not kept the
word of the LORD and have not done all that is
written in this book." [22]Then Hilkiah and the
other men from the king went to the prophetess
Huldah, the wife of Shallum, son of Tokhath, son
of Hasrah, the guardian of the wardrobe; she
dwelt in Jerusalem, in the new quarter. They
spoke to her as they had been instructed, [23]and
she said to them: "Thus says the LORD, the God
of Israel: 'Tell the one who sent you to me,
[24]The LORD says: I am prepared to bring evil
upon this place and upon its inhabitants, all the
curses written in the book that has been read
before the king of Judah. [25]Because they have
abandoned me and have offered incense to other
gods, provoking me by every deed that they have
performed, my anger is ablaze against this place
and cannot be extinguished.'

[26]"But to the king of Judah who sent you to
consult the LORD, give this response: 'Thus says
the LORD, the God of Israel, concerning the
threats you have heard: [27]Because you were
heartsick and have humbled yourself before God
on hearing his words spoken against this place
and its inhabitants; because you have humbled
yourself before me, have torn your garments,
and have wept before me, I in turn have
listened—so declares the LORD. [28]I will gather
you to your ancestors and you shall be taken to
your grave in peace. Your eyes shall not see all
the evil I will bring upon this place and upon its
inhabitants.' "

They brought back this message to the king.

Renewal of the Covenant [29] [q]The king now
convened all the elders of Judah and Jerusalem.
[30]He went up to the house of the LORD with all
the men of Judah and the inhabitants of Jerusa-
lem, the priests, the Levites, and all the people,
great and small; and he had read aloud to them
the entire text of the book of the covenant that
had been found in the house of the LORD.
[31]Standing at his post,* the king made a cove-
nant before the LORD to follow the LORD and to
keep his commandments, decrees, and statutes
with his whole heart and soul, thus observing
the terms of the covenant written in this book.
[32]He thereby committed all who were of Jerusa-
lem and Benjamin, and the inhabitants of Jerusa-
lem conformed themselves to the covenant of
God, the God of their fathers. [33]Josiah removed
every abominable thing from all the territory
belonging to the Israelites, and he obliged all
who were in Israel to serve the LORD, their God.
During his lifetime they did not desert the LORD,
the God of their fathers. [r]

CHAPTER 35

The Passover [1] [s]Josiah celebrated in Jerusalem
a Passover to honor the LORD; the Passover
sacrifice was slaughtered on the fourteenth day
of the first month. [t] [2]He reappointed the priests
to their duties and encouraged them in the
service of the LORD's house. [3]He said to the
Levites who were to instruct all Israel, and who
were consecrated to the LORD: "Put the holy ark
in the house built by Solomon, son of David,
king of Israel. It shall no longer be a burden on
your shoulders. Serve now the LORD, your God,
and his people Israel. [u] [4]Prepare yourselves in
your ancestral houses and your classes according
to the prescriptions of King David of Israel and
his son Solomon. [5]Stand in the sanctuary accord-
ing to the divisions of the ancestral houses of
your brethren, the common people, so that the
distribution of the Levites and the families may
be the same. [v] [6]Slay the Passover sacrifice, sanc-
tify yourselves, and be at the disposition of your
brethren, that all may be carried out according to
the word of the LORD given through Moses." [w]

[7]Josiah contributed to the common people a
flock of lambs and kids, thirty thousand in
number, each to serve as a Passover victim for
any who were present, and also three thousand

34, 31: Standing at his post: see note on 2 Chr 23, 13.

q 29–32: 2 Kgs 23, 1ff. r 2 Kgs 23, 4–20. s 1–19: 2 Kgs 23, 21ff. t Ex 12, 1–28; 2 Kgs 23, 21. u 2 Chr 5, 4; 1 Chr 15, 12. 15. v 1 Chr 24—26. w 2 Chr 30, 17.

oxen; these were from the king's property.[x] 8His
princes also gave a free-will gift to the people,
the priests and the Levites. Hilkiah, Zechariah
and Jehiel, prefects of the house of God, gave to
the priests two thousand six hundred Passover
victims together with three hundred oxen.[y]
9Conaniah and his brothers Shemaiah, Nethanel,
Hashabiah, Jehiel and Jozabad, the rulers of the
Levites, contributed to the Levites five thousand
Passover victims, together with five hundred
oxen.
10When the service had been arranged, the
priests took their places, as did the Levites in
their classes according to the king's command.
11The Passover sacrifice was slaughtered, where-
upon the priests sprinkled some of the blood and
the Levites proceeded to the skinning. 12They
separated what was destined for the holocaust
and gave it to various groups of the ancestral
houses of the common people to offer to the
LORD, as is prescribed in the book of Moses.
They did the same with the oxen. 13They
cooked the Passover on the fire as prescribed,
and also cooked the sacred meals in pots,
cauldrons and pans, then brought them quickly
to all the common people.[z] 14Afterward they
prepared the Passover for themselves and for the
priests. Indeed the priests, the sons of Aaron,
were busy offering holocausts and the fatty
portions until night; therefore the Levites pre-
pared for themselves and for the priests, the sons
of Aaron. 15The singers, the sons of Asaph, were
at their posts as prescribed by David: Asaph,
Heman and Jeduthun, the king's seer. The
gatekeepers were at every gate; there was no
need for them to leave their stations, for their
brethren, the Levites, prepared for them. 16Thus
the entire service of the LORD was arranged that
day so that the Passover could be celebrated and
the holocausts offered on the altar of the LORD,
as King Josiah had commanded. 17The Israelites
who were present on that occasion kept the
Passover and the feast of the Unleavened Bread
for seven days. 18 [a]No such Passover had been
observed in Israel since the time of the prophet
Samuel, nor had any king of Israel kept a
Passover like that of Josiah, the priests and
Levites, all of Judah and Israel that were present,
and the inhabitants of Jerusalem. 19It was in the
eighteenth year of Josiah's reign that this Pass-
over was observed.

Josiah's Reign Ends 20After Josiah had done
all this to restore the temple, Neco, king of
Egypt, came up to fight at Carchemish on the
Euphrates, and Josiah went out to intercept him.
21Neco sent messengers to him, saying: "What
quarrel is between us, king of Judah? I have not
come against you this day, for my war is with
another kingdom, and God has told me to
hasten. Do not interfere with God who is with
me, as otherwise he will destroy you." 22But
Josiah would not withdraw from him, for he had
sought a pretext for fighting with him. Therefore
he would not listen to the words of Neco that
came from the mouth of God, but went out to
fight in the plain of Megiddo. 23Then the archers
shot King Josiah, who said to his servants, "Take
me away, for I am seriously wounded."[b] 24His
servants removed him from his own chariot,
placed him in another he had in reserve, and
brought him to Jerusalem, where he died. He
was buried in the tombs of his ancestors, and all
Judah and Jerusalem mourned him. 25Jeremiah
also composed a lamentation over Josiah,*
which is recited to this day by all the male and
female singers in their lamentations over Josiah.
These have been made obligatory for Israel, and
can be found written in the Lamentations.
26 [c]The rest of the chronicle of Josiah, his
pious deeds in regard to what is written in the
law of the LORD, and his acts, first and last, can
be found written in the book of the kings of
Israel and Judah.

CHAPTER 36

1 [d]The people of the land took Jehoahaz, son
of Josiah, and made him king in Jerusalem in his
father's stead.

35, 25: The reference to a lamentation over Josiah composed by Jeremiah is not found either in 2 Kgs or Jer; but see note on Zec 12, 11. Their lamentations: probably a reference to the canonical Book of Lamentations.

x Ex 12, 5. y Nm 7, 1–83. z Nm 12, 8f. a 18f: 2 Kgs 23, 22f. b 2 Chr 18, 33f. c 2 Kgs 23, 28. d 1–4: 2 Kgs 23, 30–34; 1 Chr 3, 15f.

IV: End of the Kingdom

Jehoahaz [2]Jehoahaz was twenty-three years old when he became king, and he reigned three months in Jerusalem. [3]The king of Egypt deposed him in Jerusalem and fined the land one hundred talents of silver and a talent of gold. [4]Then the king of Egypt made his brother Eliakim king over Judah and Jerusalem, and changed his name to Jehoiakim. Neco took his brother Jehoahaz away and brought him to Egypt.

Jehoiakim [5]Jehoiakim was twenty-five years old when he became king, and he reigned eleven years in Jerusalem. He did evil in the sight of the LORD, his God.[e] [6][f]Nebuchadnezzar, king of Babylon, came up against him and bound him with chains to take him to Babylon.* [7]Nebuchadnezzar also carried away to Babylon some of the vessels of the house of the LORD and put them in his palace in Babylon. [8]The rest of the acts of Jehoiakim, the abominable things that he did, and what therefore happened to him, can be found written in the book of the kings of Israel and Judah. His son Jehoiachin succeeded him as king.[g]

Jehoiachin [9]Jehoiachin was eighteen years old when he became king, and he reigned three months [and ten days] in Jerusalem. He did evil in the sight of the LORD.[h] [10]At the turn of the year, King Nebuchadnezzar sent for him and had him brought to Babylon, along with precious vessels from the temple of the LORD. He made his brother Zedekiah* king over Judah and Jerusalem.[i]

Zedekiah [11]Zedekiah was twenty-one years old when he became king, and he reigned eleven years in Jerusalem.[j] [12]He did evil in the sight of the LORD, his God, and he did not humble himself before the prophet Jeremiah, who spoke the word of the LORD.[k] [13]He also rebelled against King Nebuchadnezzar, who had made him swear by God. He became stiff-necked and hardened his heart rather than return to the LORD, the God of Israel.[l] [14]Likewise all the princes of Judah, the priests and the people added infidelity to infidelity, practicing all the abominations of the nations and polluting the LORD's temple which he had consecrated in Jerusalem.

Dissolution of Judah [15]Early and often did the LORD, the God of their fathers, send his messengers to them, for he had compassion on his people and his dwelling place.[m] [16]But they mocked the messengers of God, despised his warnings, and scoffed at his prophets, until the anger of the LORD against his people was so inflamed that there was no remedy.[n] [17]Then he brought up against them the king of the Chaldeans, who slew their young men in their own sanctuary building, sparing neither young man nor maiden, neither the aged nor the decrepit; he delivered all of them over into his grip.[o] [18]All the utensils of the house of God, the large and the small, and the treasures of the LORD's house and of the king and his princes, all these he brought to Babylon.[p] [19]They burnt the house of God, tore down the walls of Jerusalem, set all its palaces afire, and destroyed all its precious objects.[q] [20]Those who escaped the sword he carried captive to Babylon, where they became his and his sons' servants until the kingdom of the Persians came to power. [21]All this was to fulfill the word of the LORD spoken by Jeremiah: "Until the land has retrieved its lost sabbaths, during all the time it lies waste it shall have rest while seventy years are fulfilled."

Decree of Cyrus [22]*In the first year of Cyrus,

36, 6: Nebuchadnezzar . . . bound him with chains to take him to Babylon: the Chronicler does not say that Jehoiakim was actually taken to Babylon. According to 2 Kgs 24, 1–6, Jehoiakim revolted after being Nebuchadnezzar's vassal for three years; he died in Jerusalem before the Babylonian king could reach the city. However, Dn 1, 1f, apparently based on 2 Chr 36, 6f, speaks of Jehoiakim's deportation to Babylon.

36, 10: His brother Zedekiah: Zedekiah was actually the brother of Jehoiakim and the uncle of Jehoiachin (2 Kgs 24, 17; Jer 37, 1), though scarcely older than his nephew (2 Kgs 24, 8. 18; 2 Chr 36, 9. 11).

36, 22f: The words of these verses are identical with those of Ezr 1, 1–3a. Originally Ezra-Nehemiah formed the last part of the single work of the Chronicler, of which 1 and 2 Chronicles formed the first part. But when Ezra-Nehemiah was regarded as a natural sequence to the Books of Samuel and of Kings, it was separated from 1 and 2 Chronicles and placed before them. Thus, 1 and 2 Chronicles became the last part of the Hebrew Bible. To

e 2 Kgs 23, 36f; Jer 22, 18f. f 2 Kgs 24, 1f. g 2 Kgs 24, 5. h 2 Kgs 24, 8f. i 2 Kgs 24, 10–16. j 2 Kgs 24, 18ff; Jer 52, 1ff. k Jer 37, 1ff. l 2 Kgs 25, 1; Jer 52, 4; Ex 17, 13–16. m Jer 7, 25; Heb 1, 1. n Mt 23, 34ff. o Lam 1, 15; 5, 11–14. p 2 Kgs 25, 14f. q 2 Kgs 25, 9f; Lam 2, 8.

king of Persia, in order to fulfill the word of the LORD spoken by Jeremiah, the LORD inspired King Cyrus of Persia to issue this proclamation throughout his kingdom, both by word of mouth and in writing: [r] 23 "Thus says Cyrus, king of Persia: 'All the kingdoms of the earth the LORD, the God of heaven, has given to me, and he has also charged me to build him a house in Jerusalem, which is in Judah. Whoever, therefore, among you belongs to any part of his people, let him go up, and may his God be with him!' "

prevent this work from ending on a note of doom, Ezr 1, 1-3a was repeated as 2 Chr 36, 22f.

r Ezr 1, 1ff.

THE BOOK OF EZRA

The last four books of the Hebrew canon are Ezra, Nehemiah, 1 and 2 Chronicles, in that order. Originally, however, Ezra and Nehemiah followed the Books of Chronicles, and formed with them a unified historical work so homogeneous in spirit that one usually speaks of a single author for the four books. He is called "the Chronicler." The treatment of Ezra-Nehemiah as a single book by the earliest chroniclers was undoubtedly due to the fact that in ancient times the two books were put under the one name—Ezra. The combined work Ezra-Nehemiah is our most important literary source for the formation of the Jewish religious community after the Babylonian exile. This is known as the period of the Restoration, and the two men most responsible for the reorganization of Jewish life at this time were Ezra and Nehemiah.

In the present state of the Ezra-Nehemiah text, there are several dislocations of large sections so that the chronological or logical sequence is disrupted. The major instances are pointed out in the footnotes. Although Ezra appears before Nehemiah in this work, it seems probable that Nehemiah's activity preceded his.

What is known of Ezra and his work is due almost exclusively to Ezra 7—10 (the "Ezra Memoirs") and to Neh 8—9. Strictly speaking, the term "Ezra Memoirs" should be used only of that section in which Ezra speaks in the first person, i.e., 7, 27—9, 15. Compare the "Nehemiah Memoirs" in Neh 1, 1—7, 72a; 11, 1f; 12, 27-43; 13, 4-31. The Chronicler combined this material with other sources at his disposal. The personality of Ezra is less known than that of Nehemiah. Ben Sirach, in his praise of the fathers, makes no mention of Ezra. The genealogy of Ezra (7, 1-5) traces his priesthood back to Aaron, brother of Moses. This was the accepted way of establishing the legality of one's priestly office. He is also called *a scribe, well-versed in the law of Moses* (7, 6), indicating Ezra's dedication to the study of the Torah, which he sought to make the basic rule of life in the restored community. It was in religious and cultic reform rather than in political affairs that Ezra made his mark as a postexilic leader. Jewish tradition holds him in great honor; the Talmud even regards him as a second Moses, claiming that the Torah would have been given to Israel through Ezra had not Moses preceded him.

Ezra is sometimes accused of having been a mere legalist who gave excessive attention to the letter of the law. His work, however, should be seen and judged within a specific historical context. He gave to his people a cohesion and spiritual unity which prevented the disintegration of the small Jewish community. Had it not been for the intransigence of Ezra and of those who adopted his ideal, it is doubtful that Judaism would have so effectively resisted Hellenism, then or in later centuries. Ezra set the tone of the postexilic community, and it was characterized by fidelity to the Torah, Judaism's authentic way of life. It is in this light that we can judge most fairly the work of Ezra during the Restoration.

The Book of Ezra is divided as follows:

I. The Return from Exile (1, 1—6, 22).
II. The Deeds of Ezra (7, 1—10, 44).

The following list of the kings of Persia, with the dates of their reigns, will be useful for dating the events mentioned in Ezra-Nehemiah:

Cyrus	538–529 B.C.
Cambyses	529–521 B.C.
Darius I	521–485 B.C.
Xerxes	485–464 B.C.
Artaxerxes I	464–423 B.C.
Darius II	423–404 B.C.
Artaxerxes II	404–358 B.C.
Artaxerxes III	358–337 B.C.
End of the Persian Empire (Defeat of Darius III)	331 B.C.

I: The Return from Exile

CHAPTER 1

The Decree of Cyrus 1 [a]In the first year of
Cyrus,* king of Persia, in order to fulfill the
word of the LORD spoken by Jeremiah, the LORD
inspired King Cyrus of Persia to issue this
proclamation throughout his kingdom, both by
word of mouth and in writing: 2"Thus says
Cyrus, king of Persia: 'All the kingdoms of the
earth the LORD, the God of heaven, has given to
me, and he has also charged me to build him a
house in Jerusalem, which is in Judah. 3Who-
ever, therefore, among you belongs to any part of
his people, let him go up, and may his God be
with him! 4Let everyone who has survived, in
whatever place he may have dwelt, be assisted
by the people of that place with silver, gold,
goods, and cattle, together with free-will offer-
ings for the house of God in Jerusalem.'"
5Then the family heads of Judah and Benja-
min and the priests and Levites—everyone, that
is, whom God had inspired to do so—prepared
to go up to build the house of the LORD in
Jerusalem. 6All their neighbors gave them help
in every way, with silver, gold, goods, and cattle,
and with many precious gifts besides all their
free-will offerings. [b] 7King Cyrus, too, had the
utensils of the house of the LORD brought forth
which Nebuchadnezzar had taken away from
Jerusalem and placed in the house of his god.
8Cyrus, king of Persia, had them brought forth
by the treasurer Mithredath, and counted out to
Sheshbazzar,* the prince of Judah. 9This was the
inventory: sacks of goldware, thirty; sacks of
silverware, one thousand and twenty-nine;
10golden bowls, thirty; silver bowls, four hun-
dred and ten; other ware, one thousand pieces.
11Total of the gold- and silverware: five thousand
four hundred pieces.* All these Sheshbazzar
took with him when the exiles were brought
back from Babylon to Jerusalem.

1, 1: In the first year of Cyrus: as sovereign over the world empire which began with his conquest of Babylon; that is, 538 B.C.

1, 8: Sheshbazzar: very probably the fourth son of Jehoiachin, king of Judah, taken captive to Babylon in 598 B.C., listed in 1 Chr 3, 18 as Senneser; if so, he was the uncle of Zerubbabel (Ezr 3, 2ff); see note on 1 Chr 3, 18.

1, 11: Total . . . five thousand four hundred pieces: either this figure or the figures given for one or more of the items listed (vv 9f) have been corrupted in the transmission of the text.

a 1ff: Ezr 36, 22f; Jer 25, 11f; 29, 10; Zec 1, 12. b Ex 3, 22; 11, 2; 12, 35.

CHAPTER 2

Census of the Province [1]*These are the inhabitants of the province who returned from the captivity of the exiles, whom Nebuchadnezzar, king of Babylon, had carried away to Babylon,[c] and who came back to Jerusalem and Judah, each man in his own city* [2](those who returned with Zerubbabel, Jeshua, Nehemiah, Seraiah, Reelaiah, Mordecai, Bilshan, Mispereth, Bigvai, Rehum, and Baanah):

The census of the men of Israel: [3]sons of Parosh, two thousand one hundred and seventy-two; [4]sons of Shephatiah, three hundred and seventy-two; [5]sons of Arah, seven hundred and seventy-five; [6]sons of Pahath-moab, who were sons of Jeshua and Joab, two thousand eight hundred and twelve; [7]sons of Elam, one thousand two hundred and fifty-four; [8]sons of Zattu, nine hundred and forty-five; [9]sons of Zaccai, seven hundred and sixty; [10]sons of Bani, six hundred and forty-two; [11]sons of Bebai, six hundred and twenty-three; [12]sons of Azgad, one thousand two hundred and twenty-two; [13]sons of Adonikam, six hundred and sixty-six; [14]sons of Bigvai, two thousand and fifty-six; [15]sons of Adin, four hundred and fifty-four; [16]sons of Ater, who were sons of Hezekiah, ninety-eight; [17]sons of Bezai, three hundred and twenty-three; [18]sons of Jorah, one hundred and twelve; [19]sons of Hashum, two hundred and twenty-three; [20]sons of Gibeon, ninety-five; [21]sons of Bethlehem, one hundred and twenty-three; [22]men of Netophah, fifty-six; [23]men of Anathoth, one hundred and twenty-eight; [24]men of Beth-azmaveth, forty-two; [25]men of Kiriath-jearim, Chephirah, and Beeroth, seven hundred and forty-three; [26]men of Ramah and Geba, six hundred and twenty-one; [27]men of Michmas, one hundred and twenty-two; [28]men of Bethel and Ai, two hundred and twenty-three; [29]sons of Nebo, fifty-two; [30]sons of Magbish, one hundred and fifty-six; [31]sons of the other Elam, one thousand two hundred and fifty-four; [32]sons of Harim, three hundred and twenty; [33]sons of Lod, Hadid, and Ono, seven hundred and twenty-five; [34]sons of Jericho, three hundred and forty-five; [35]sons of Senaah, three thousand six hundred and thirty.

[36]The priests: sons of Jedaiah, who were of the house of Jeshua, nine hundred and seventy-three; [37]sons of Immer, one thousand and fifty-two; [38]sons of Pashhur, one thousand two hundred and forty-seven; [39]sons of Harim, one thousand and seventeen.

[40]The Levites: sons of Jeshua, Kadmiel, Binnui, and Hodaviah, seventy-four.[d]

[41]The singers: sons of Asaph, one hundred and twenty-eight.

[42]The gatekeepers: sons of Shallum, sons of Ater, sons of Talmon, sons of Akkub, sons of Hatita, sons of Shobai, one hundred and thirty-nine in all.

[43]The temple slaves: sons of Ziha, sons of Hasupha, sons of Tabbaoth, [44]sons of Keros, sons of Siaha, sons of Padon, [45]sons of Lebanah, sons of Hagabah, sons of Akkub, [46]sons of Hagab, sons of Shamlai, sons of Hanan, [47]sons of Giddel, sons of Gahar, sons of Reaiah, [48]sons of Rezin, sons of Nekoda, sons of Gazzam, [49]sons of Uzza, sons of Paseah, sons of Besai, [50]sons of Asnah, sons of the Meunites, sons of the Nephusites, [51]sons of Bakbuk, sons of Hakupha, sons of Harhur, [52]sons of Bazluth, sons of Mehida, sons of Harsha, [53]sons of Barkos, sons of Sisera, sons of Temah, [54]sons of Neziah, sons of Hatipha.

[55]Descendants of the slaves of Solomon: sons of Sotai, sons of Hassophereth, sons of Peruda, [56]sons of Jaalah, sons of Darkon, sons of Giddel, [57]sons of Shephatiah, sons of Hattil, sons of Pochereth-hazzebaim, sons of Ami. [58]The total of the temple slaves and the descendants of the slaves of Solomon was three hundred and ninety-two.

[59]The following who returned from Tel-melah, Tel-harsha, Cherub, Addan, and Immer were unable to prove that their ancestral houses and their descent were Israelite: [60]sons of Delaiah, sons of Tobiah, sons of Nekoda, six hundred

2, 1–67: As it now stands, this list is an expanded form of the lists of returned captives from the sixth century B.C.; see Neh 7, 6–72, where it reappears.

c Neh 7, 6–67. d Neh 12, 24.

and fifty-two. 61 Also, of the priests: sons of Habaiah, sons of Hakkoz, sons of Barzillai (he had married one of the daughters of Barzillai the Gileadite and became known by his name).[e] 62 These men searched their family records, but their names could not be found written there; hence they were degraded from the priesthood, 63 and His Excellency* ordered them not to partake of the most holy foods until there should be a priest bearing the Urim and Thummim.

64 The entire assembly taken together came to forty-two thousand three hundred and sixty, 65 not counting their male and female slaves, who were seven thousand three hundred and thirty-seven. They also had two hundred male and female singers. 66 Their horses were seven hundred and thirty-six, their mules two hundred and forty-five, 67 their camels four hundred and thirty-five, their asses six thousand seven hundred and twenty.

68 When they arrived at the house of the LORD in Jerusalem, some of the family heads made free-will offerings for the house of God, to rebuild it in its place. 69 According to their means they contributed to the treasury for the temple service: sixty-one thousand drachmas of gold, five thousand minas of silver, and one hundred garments for the priests. 70 The priests, the Levites, and some of the common people took up residence in Jerusalem; but the singers, the gatekeepers, and the temple slaves dwelt in their cities. Thus all the Israelites dwelt in their cities.

CHAPTER 3

Restoration of the Altar 1 Now when the seventh month* came, after the Israelites had settled in their cities, the people gathered at Jerusalem as one man.[f] 2 Then Jeshua, son of Jozadak, together with his brethren the priests, and Zerrubbabel, son of Shealtiel, together with his brethren, set about rebuilding the altar of the God of Israel in order to offer on it the holocausts prescribed in the law of Moses, the man of God. 3 Despite their fear of the peoples of the land, they replaced the altar on its foundations and offered holocausts to the LORD on it, both morning and evening.[g] 4 They also kept the feast of Booths in the manner prescribed, and they offered the daily holocausts in the proper number required for each day.[h] 5 Thereafter they offered the established holocaust, the sacrifices prescribed for the new moons and all the festivals sacred to the LORD, and those which anyone might offer as a free-will gift to the LORD. 6 From the first day of the seventh month they began to offer holocausts to the LORD, though the foundation of the temple of the LORD had not yet been laid.

Founding of the Temple 7 Then they hired stonecutters and carpenters, and sent food and drink and oil to the Sidonians and Tyrians that they might ship cedar trees from the Lebanon to the port of Joppa, as Cyrus, king of Persia, had authorized.[i] 8 In the year after their coming to the house of God in Jerusalem, in the second month, Zerubbabel, son of Shealtiel, and Jeshua, son of Jozadak, together with the rest of their brethren, the priests and Levites and all who had come from the captivity to Jerusalem, began by appointing the Levites twenty years of age and over to supervise the work on the house of the LORD. 9 Jeshua and his sons and brethren, with Kadmiel and Binnui, son of Henadad, and their sons and their brethren, the Levites, stood as one man to supervise those who were engaged in the work on the house of God. 10 When the builders had laid the foundation of the LORD's temple, the vested priests with the trumpets and the Levites, sons of Asaph, were stationed there with the cymbals to praise the LORD in the manner

2, 63: His Excellency: the deputy of the Persian government; from the context, he was one of the Jewish exile leaders. Nehemiah as governor receives the same title (Neh 8, 9; 10, 2). Urim and Thummim: see note on Ex 28, 30.

3, 1f: The seventh month: Tishri (September–October), apparently of 538 B.C.; cf Ezr 1, 1; 4, 5. In this case, it was Sheshbazzar who erected the first altar, since he began the work on the foundations of the temple in Jerusalem; cf Ezr 5, 16. It was in the second year of Darius I, i.e., in 520 B.C., that Jeshua and Zerubbabel resumed the work on the temple that had been temporarily interrupted (Ezr 4, 24—5, 1; Hg 1, 1; 2, 1). The Chronicler or a later editor of the text here attributes to them the beginning of the work which, in reality, they merely completed. Shealtiel: the oldest son of King Jehoiachin of Judah and the brother of Sheshbazzar (1 Chr 3, 18f); Zerubbabel was therefore the grandson of Jehoiachin; see note on Ezr 1, 8.

e 2 Sm 17, 27; 19, 32f; 1 Kgs 2, 7. f Neh 7, 73—8, 1. g 1 Kgs 8, 64; Dn 9, 25. h Ex 23, 16; Nm 28, 3–8. i 1 Chr 22, 4; 2 Chr 2, 9.

laid down by David, king of Israel.[j] 11They alternated in songs of praise and thanksgiving to the LORD, "for he is good, for his kindness to Israel endures forever"; and all the people raised a great shout of joy, praising the LORD because the foundation of the LORD's house had been laid.[k] 12Many of the priests, Levites, and family heads, the old men who had seen the former house, cried out in sorrow as they watched the foundation of the present house being laid.[l] Many others, however, lifted up their voices in shouts of joy, 13and no one could distinguish the sound of the joyful shouting from the sound of those who were weeping; for the people raised a mighty clamor which was heard afar off.[m]

CHAPTER 4

Samaritan Interference 1When the enemies of Judah and Benjamin heard that the exiles were building a temple for the LORD, the God of Israel, 2they approached Zerubbabel and the family heads and said to them, "Let us build with you, for we seek your God just as you do, and we have sacrificed to him since the days of Esarhaddon, king of Assyria, who had us brought here." 3But Zerubbabel, Jeshua, and the rest of the family heads of Israel answered them, "It is not your responsibility to build with us a house for our God, but we alone must build it for the LORD, the God of Israel, as King Cyrus of Persia has commanded us." 4Thereupon the people of the land set out to intimidate and dishearten the people of Judah so as to keep them from building. 5They also suborned counselors to work against them and thwart their plans during the remaining years of Cyrus, king of Persia, and until the reign of Darius,* king of Persia.

Later Hostility 6Also at the beginning of the reign of Ahashuerus they prepared a written accusation against the inhabitants of Judah and Jerusalem.

7Again, in the time of Artaxerxes, Mithredath wrote in concert with Tabeel and the rest of his fellow officials to Artaxerxes, king of Persia. The document was written in Aramaic* and was accompanied by a translation. [Aramaic:]

8*Then Rehum, the governor, and Shimshai, the scribe, wrote the following letter against Jerusalem to King Artaxerxes: 9"Rehum, the governor, Shimshai, the scribe, and their fellow judges, officials, and agents from among the Persian, Urukian, Babylonian, Susian (that is, Elamite), 10and the other peoples whom the great and illustrious Assurbanipal transported and settled in the city of Samaria and elsewhere in the province West-of-Euphrates, as follows . . . ." 11This is a copy of the letter that they sent to him:

"To King Artaxerxes, your servants, the men of West-of-Euphrates, as follows: 12Let it be known to the king that the Jews who came up from you to us have arrived at Jerusalem and are now rebuilding this rebellious and evil city. They are raising up its walls, and the foundations have already been laid. 13Now let it be known to the king that if this city is rebuilt and its walls are raised up again, they will no longer pay taxes, tributes, or tolls; thus it can only result in harm to the throne. 14Now, since we partake of the salt of the palace, we ought not simply to look on while the king is being dishonored. Therefore we have sent this message to inform you, O king, 15so that inquiry may be made in the historical records of your fathers. In the historical records you can discover and verify that this city is a rebellious city which has proved fatal to kings and provinces, and that sedition has been fostered there since ancient times. For that reason this city was destroyed. 16We inform you, O king, that if this city is rebuilt and its walls are raised up again, by that

4, 5: Darius: Darius I (521–485 B.C.). The temple-building narrative continues in Ezr 4, 24. In between (Ezr 4, 6–23) is a series of notes about the opposition to the returned exiles voiced at the Persian court in the early fifth century B.C., after the temple had been reestablished.

4, 7: Aramaic: this word in the original text seems to be a note indicating a change of language from Hebrew to Aramaic, which in fact takes place here. The Aramaic section ends with Ezr 6, 18, but again in Ezr 7, 12–26 a royal letter is cited in Aramaic.

4, 8–23: The central question here is the rebuilding of the fortification walls of Jerusalem, not the building of the temple. The interruption of work on the city wall some time before 445 B.C. was the occasion for the coming of Nehemiah to Palestine (Neh 1, 1–4; 2, 1–5). Artaxerxes: Artaxerxes I (464–423 B.C.).

j Ezr 2, 41. k Pss 100, 5; 136; Jer 33, 11. l Hg 2, 3. m Tb 14, 5.

very fact you will no longer own any part of West-of-Euphrates."

17The king sent this answer: "To Rehum, the governor, Shimshai, the scribe, and their fellow officials living in Samaria and elsewhere in the province West-of-Euphrates, greetings and the following: 18The communication which you sent us has been read plainly in my presence. 19When at my command inquiry was made, it was verified that from ancient times this city has risen up against kings and that rebellion and sedition have been fostered there. 20Powerful kings were once in Jerusalem who ruled over all West-of-Euphrates, and taxes, tributes, and tolls were paid to them. 21Give orders, therefore, that will stop the work of these men. This city may not be rebuilt until a further decree has been issued by me. 22Take care that you do not neglect this matter, lest the evil grow to the detriment of the throne."

23As soon as a copy of King Artaxerxes' letter had been read before Rehum, the governor, Shimshai, the scribe, and their fellow officials, they went in all haste to the Jews in Jerusalem and stopped their work by force of arms.[n]

Rebuilding of the Temple 24Thus it was that the work on the house of God in Jerusalem was halted. This inaction lasted until the second year of the reign of Darius,* king of Persia.

CHAPTER 5

1Then the prophets Haggai and Zechariah,* son of Iddo, began to prophesy to the Jews in Judah and Jerusalem in the name of the God of Israel.[o] 2Thereupon Zerubbabel, son of Shealtiel, and Jeshua, son of Jozadak, began again to build the house of God in Jerusalem, with the prophets of God giving them support. 3At that time there came to them Tattenai, governor of West-of-Euphrates, and Shethar-bozenai, and their fellow officials, who asked of them: "Who issued the decree for you to build this house and raise this edifice? 4What are the names of the men who are building this structure?" 5But their God watched over the elders of the Jews so that they were not hindered, until a report could go to Darius and then a written order be sent back concerning this matter.

6A copy of the letter sent to King Darius by Tattenai, governor of West-of-Euphrates, and Shethar-bozenai, and their fellow officials from West-of-Euphrates; 7they sent him a report in which was written the following:

"To King Darius, all good wishes! 8Let it be known to the king that we have visited the province of Judah and the house of the great God: it is being rebuilt of cut stone and the walls are being reinforced with timber; the work is being carried on diligently and is making good progress under their hands. 9We then questioned the elders, addressing to them the following words: 'Who issued the decree for you to build this house and raise this edifice?' 10We also asked them their names, to report them to you in a list of the men who are their leaders. 11This was their answer to us: 'We are the servants of the God of heaven and earth, and we are rebuilding the house built here long years ago, which a great king of Israel built and finished. 12But because our fathers provoked the wrath of the God of heaven, he delivered them into the power of the Chaldean, Nebuchadnezzar, king of Babylon, who destroyed this house and led the people captive to Babylon. 13However, in the first year of Cyrus, king of Babylon, King Cyrus issued a decree for the rebuilding of this house of God. 14Moreover, the gold and silver utensils of the house of God which Nebuchadnezzar had taken from the temple in Jerusalem and carried off to the temple in Babylon, King Cyrus ordered to be removed from the temple in Babylon and consigned to a certain Sheshbazzar, whom he named governor. 15And he commanded him: Take these utensils and deposit them in the temple of Jerusalem, and let the house of God be rebuilt on its former site. 16Then this same Sheshbazzar came and laid the foundations of

4, 24: The second year . . . of Darius: 520 B.C.; it marks the beginning of the successful restoration of the temple, which was accomplished within the five years following (Ezr 5, 1—6, 18).

5, 1: The prophets Haggai and Zechariah: two of the Minor Prophets, whose books record their role in the encouragement of this work.

n Neh 1, 3. o Hg 1, 14—2, 9; Zec 4, 9.

the house of God in Jerusalem. Since that time
the building has been going on, and it is not yet
completed.' [17]Now, if it please the king, let a
search be made in the royal archives of Babylon
to discover whether a decree really was issued
by King Cyrus for the rebuilding of this house of
God in Jerusalem. And may the king's pleasure
in this matter be communicated to us."

CHAPTER 6

The Decree of Darius [1]Thereupon King Da-
rius issued an order to search the archives in
which the Babylonian records were stored away;
[2] [p]and in Ecbatana, the stronghold in the prov-
ince of Media, a scroll was found containing the
following text: "Memorandum. [3]In the first year
of King Cyrus, King Cyrus issued a decree: The
house of God in Jerusalem. The house is to be
rebuilt as a place for offering sacrifices and bring-
ing burnt offerings. Its height is to be sixty cubits
and its width sixty cubits. [4]It shall have three
courses of cut stone for each one of timber. The
costs are to be borne by the royal palace. [5]Also,
the gold and silver utensils of the house of God
which Nebuchadnezzar took from the temple of
Jerusalem and brought to Babylon are to be sent
back: to be returned to their place in the temple
of Jerusalem and deposited in the house of God.

[6]"Now, therefore, Tattenai, governor of West-
of-Euphrates, and Shethar-bozenai, and you,
their fellow officials in West-of-Euphrates, do not
interfere in that place. [7]Let the governor and the
elders of the Jews continue the work on that
house of God; they are to rebuild it on its former
site. [8]I also issue this decree concerning your
dealing with these elders of the Jews in the
rebuilding of that house of God: From the royal
revenue, the taxes of West-of-Euphrates, let
these men be repaid for their expenses, in full
and without delay. [9]Whatever else is required—
young bulls, rams, and lambs for holocausts to
the God of heaven, wheat, salt, wine, and oil,
according to the requirements of the priests who
are in Jerusalem—is to be delivered to them day
by day without fail, [10]that they may continue to
offer sacrifices of pleasing odor to the God of
heaven and pray for the life of the king and his
sons. [11]I also issue this decree: If any man
violates this edict, a beam is to be taken from his
house, and he is to be lifted up and impaled on
it; and his house is to be reduced to rubble for
this offense. [12]And may the God who causes his
name to dwell there overthrow every king or
people who may undertake to alter this or to
destroy this house of God in Jerusalem. I, Darius,
have issued this decree; let it be carefully
executed."

[13]Then Tattenai, the governor of West-of-
Euphrates, and Shethar-bozenai, and their fellow
officials carried out fully the instructions King
Darius had sent them. [14]The elders of the Jews
continued to make progress in the building,
supported by the message of the prophets, Hag-
gai and Zechariah, son of Iddo. They finished the
building according to the command of the God
of Israel and the decrees of Cyrus and Darius
[and of Artaxerxes, king of Persia]. [15]They com-
pleted this house on the third day of the month
Adar, in the sixth year of the reign of King
Darius. [16]The Israelites—priests, Levites, and
the other returned exiles—celebrated the dedica-
tion of this house of God with joy. [17]For the
dedication of this house of God, they offered one
hundred bulls, two hundred rams, and four
hundred lambs, together with twelve he-goats as
a sin-offering for all Israel, in keeping with the
number of the tribes of Israel. [18]Finally, they set
up the priests in their classes and the Levites in
their divisions for the service of God in Jerusa-
lem, as is prescribed in the book of Moses.

The Passover [19] [q]The exiles kept the Passover
on the fourteenth day of the first month. [20]The
Levites, every one of whom had purified himself
for the occasion, sacrificed the Passover for the
rest of the exiles, for their brethren the priests,
and for themselves. [21]The Israelites who had
returned from the exile partook of it together
with all those who had separated themselves
from the uncleanness of the peoples of the land
to join them in seeking the LORD, the God of
Israel. [r] [22]They joyfully kept the feast of Un-

p 2–12; Ezr 1, 4–11. q 19–22; Ex 12, 1–20. r Ps 47, 9.

leavened Bread for seven days, for the LORD had filled them with joy by making the king of Assyria* favorable to them, so that he gave them help in their work on the house of God, the God of Israel.

II: The Deeds of Ezra

CHAPTER 7

Ezra the Scribe [1]After these events,* during
the reign of Artaxerxes, king of Persia, Ezra, son
of Seraiah, son of Azariah, son of Hilkiah, [2]son of
Shallum, son of Zadok, son of Ahitub, [3]son of
Amariah, son of Azariah, son of Meraioth, [4]son
of Zerahiah, son of Uzzi, son of Bukki, [5]son of
Abishua, son of Phinehas, son of Eleazar, son of
the high priest Aaron— [6]this Ezra came up from
Babylon. He was a scribe, well-versed in the law of Moses which was given by the LORD, the God of Israel. Because the hand of the LORD, his God, was upon him, the king granted him all that he requested.[s]

[7]Some of the Israelites and some priests, Levites, singers, gatekeepers, and temple slaves also came up to Jerusalem in the seventh year of
King Artaxerxes. [8]Ezra came to Jerusalem in the
fifth month of that seventh year of the king. [9]On
the first day of the first month he resolved on the journey up from Babylon, and on the first day of the fifth month he arrived at Jerusalem, for the
favoring hand of his God was upon him. [10]Ezra
had set his heart on the study and practice of the law of the LORD and on teaching statutes and ordinances in Israel.[t]

The Decree of Artaxerxes [11]This is a copy of
the rescript which King Artaxerxes gave to Ezra the priest-scribe, the scribe of the text of the LORD's commandments and statutes for Israel:

[12] [u]"Artaxerxes, king of kings, to Ezra the
priest, scribe of the law of the God of heaven
(then, after greetings): [13]I have issued this de-
cree, that anyone in my kingdom belonging to the people of Israel, its priests or Levites, who is minded to go up to Jerusalem with you, may do
so. [14]You are the envoy from the king and his
seven counselors to supervise Judah and Jerusalem in respect of the law of your God which is in
your possession, [15]and to bring with you the
silver and gold which the king and his counselors have freely contributed to the God of Israel,
whose dwelling is in Jerusalem, [16]as well as all
the silver and gold which you may receive throughout the province of Babylon, together with the free-will offerings which the people and priests freely contribute for the house of their
God in Jerusalem. [17]You must take care, there-
fore, to use this money to buy bulls, rams, lambs, and the cereal offerings and libations proper to these, and offer them on the altar of the house of
your God in Jerusalem. [18]You and your brethren
may do whatever seems best to you with the remainder of the silver and gold, conformably to
the will of your God. [19]The utensils consigned to
you for the service of the house of your God you are to deposit before the God of Jerusalem.
[20]Whatever else you may be required to supply
for the needs of the house of your God, you may
draw from the royal treasury. [21]I, Artaxerxes the
king, issue this decree to all the treasurers of West-of-Euphrates: Whatever Ezra the priest, scribe of the law of the God of heaven, requests
of you, dispense to him accurately, [22]within
these limits: silver, one hundred talents; wheat, one hundred kors; wine, one hundred baths; oil,
one hundred baths; salt, without limit. [23]Let
everything that is ordered by the God of heaven be carried out exactly for the house of the God of heaven, that wrath may not come upon the
realm of the king and his sons. [24]We also inform
you that it is not permitted to impose taxes, tributes, or tolls on any priest, Levite, singer, gatekeeper, temple slave, or any other servant of that house of God.

[25]"As for you, Ezra, in accordance with the

6, 22: Assyria: used here in a broad sense for the Persian Empire.

7, 1–8: The date of Ezra's journey to Palestine is not known with certainty. The seventh year of King Artaxerxes I would be 458 B.C., and the present order of the text suggests that date. The narratives of Ezra and Nehemiah make it seem to many, however, that the arrival of Nehemiah in 445 B.C. should precede that of Ezra. If so, Ezra may be thought to have come in 398 B.C., the seventh year of King Artaxerxes II. Others argue for the thirty seventh year of Artaxerxes I, that is, 428 B.C.; this would suppose that the date given in the text has suffered in transmission.

s Ezr 7, 28; 8, 18; Neh 2, 8. 18. t Ps 119, 45. u 12–17: Ezr 1, 2ff.

wisdom of your God* which is in your posses-
sion, appoint magistrates and judges to adminis-
ter justice to all the people in West-of-Euphrates,
to all, that is, who know the laws of your God.
Instruct those who do not know these laws.[v]
[26]Whoever does not obey the law of your God
and the law of the king, let strict judgment be
executed upon him, whether death, or corporal
punishment, or a fine on his goods, or imprison-
ment."

Ezra and His Companions [27]Blessed be the
LORD, the God of our fathers, who thus disposed
the mind of the king to glorify the house of the
LORD in Jerusalem, [28]and who let me find favor
with the king, with his counselors, and with all
the most influential royal officials. I therefore
took courage and, with the hand of the LORD,
my God, upon me, I gathered together Israelite
family heads to make the return journey with
me.[w]

CHAPTER 8

[1]This is the list of the family heads who
returned with me from Babylon during the reign
of King Artaxerxes:
[2]Of the sons of Phinehas, Gershon; of the
sons of Ithamar, Daniel; of the sons of David,
Hattush, [3]son of Shecaniah; of the sons of
Parosh, Zechariah, and with him one hundred
and fifty males were enrolled; [4]of the sons of
Pahath-moab, Eliehoenai, son of Zerahiah, and
with him two hundred males; [5]of the sons of
Zattu, Shecaniah, son of Jahaziel, and with him
three hundred males; [6]of the sons of Adin, Ebed,
son of Jonathan, and with him fifty males; [7]of
the sons of Elam, Jeshaiah, son of Athaliah, and
with him seventy males; [8]of the sons of Shepha-
tiah, Zebadiah, son of Michael, and with him
eighty males; [9]of the sons of Joab, Obadiah, son
of Jehiel, and with him two hundred and eigh-
teen males; [10]of the sons of Bani, Shelomith, son
of Josiphiah, and with him one hundred and
sixty males; [11]of the sons of Bebai, Zechariah,
son of Bebai, and with him twenty-eight males;
[12]of the sons of Azgad, Johanan, son of Hakka-
tan, and with him one hundred and ten males;
[13]of the sons of Adonikam, younger sons, whose
names were Eliphelet, Jeiel, and Shemaiah, and
with them sixty males; [14]of the sons of Bigvai,
Uthai, son of Zakkur, and with him seventy
males.

The Journey to Jerusalem [15]I had them as-
semble by the river that flows toward Ahava,*
where we made camp for three days. There I
perceived that both laymen and priests were
present, but I could not discover a single Levite.
[16]Therefore I sent Eliezer, Ariel, Shemaiah, Jarib,
Elnathan, Nathan, Zechariah, and Meshullam,
wise leaders, [17]with a command for Iddo, the
leader in the place Casiphia, instructing them
what to say to Iddo and his brethren, and to the
temple slaves in Casiphia, in order to procure for
us ministers for the house of our God. [18]They
sent to us—for the favoring hand of our God was
upon us—a well-instructed man, one of the sons
of Mahli, son of Levi, son of Israel, namely
Sherebiah, with his sons and brethren, eighteen
men.[x] [19]They also sent us Hashabiah, and with
him Jeshaiah, sons of Merari, and their brethren
and their sons, twenty men. [20]Of the temple
slaves (those whom David and the princes
appointed to serve the Levites) there were two
hundred and twenty. All these men were en-
rolled by name.[y]

[21]Then I proclaimed a fast, there by the river
of Ahava, that we might humble ourselves
before our God to petition from him a safe
journey for ourselves, our children, and all our
possessions. [22]For I would have been ashamed
to ask the king for troops and horsemen to
protect us against enemies along the way, since
we had said to the king, "The favoring hand of
our God is upon all who seek him, but his
mighty wrath is against all who forsake him."[z]
[23]So we fasted, and prayed to our God for this,
and our petition was granted. [24]Next I selected
twelve of the priestly leaders along with Shere-
biah, Hashabiah, and ten of their brethren, [25]and
I weighed out before them the silver and the

7, 25: The wisdom of your God: the Mosaic law; cf vv 6, 14.
8, 15: Ahava: a town at an unidentified site in Babylonia. The river that flowed toward it was probably a branch or canal of the Euphrates.

v 2 Chr 17, 9. w Ezr 7, 6. x Ezr 7, 6. y Ezr 2, 43. z Neh 2, 9.

gold and the utensils offered for the house of our God by the king, his counselors, his officials, and all the Israelites of that region. I consigned it to them in these amounts: 26 silver, six hundred and fifty talents; silver utensils, one hundred; gold, one hundred talents; 27 twenty golden bowls valued at a thousand darics; two vases of excellent polished bronze, as precious as gold. 28 I addressed them in these words: "You are consecrated to the LORD, and the utensils are also consecrated; the silver and the gold are a free-will offering to the LORD, the God of your fathers. 29 Keep good watch over them till you weigh them out in Jerusalem in the presence of the chief priests and Levites and the family leaders of Israel, in the chambers of the house of the LORD." 30 The priests and the Levites then took over the silver, the gold, and the utensils that had been weighed out, to bring them to Jerusalem, to the house of our God.

31 We set out for Jerusalem from the river of Ahava on the twelfth day of the first month. The hand of our God remained upon us, and he protected us from enemies and bandits along the way. 32 Thus we arrived at Jerusalem, where we first rested for three days. 33 On the fourth day, the silver, the gold, and the utensils were weighed out in the house of our God and consigned to the priest Meremoth, son of Uriah, who was assisted by Eleazar, son of Phinehas; they were assisted by the Levites Jozabad, son of Jeshua, and Noadiah, son of Binnui. 34 Everything was in order as to number and weight, and the total weight was registered. At that same time, 35 those who had returned from the captivity, the exiles, offered as holocausts to the God of Israel twelve bulls for all Israel, ninety-six rams, seventy-seven lambs, and twelve goats as sin-offerings: all these as a holocaust to the LORD. 36 Finally, the orders of the king were presented to the king's satraps and to the governors in West-of-Euphrates, who gave their support to the people and to the house of God.*

CHAPTER 9

Denunciation of Mixed Marriages 1 [a]When these matters had been concluded, the leaders approached me with this report: "Neither the Israelite laymen nor the priests nor the Levites have kept themselves aloof from the peoples of the land and their abominations [Canaanites, Hittites, Perizzites, Jebusites, Ammonites, Moabites, Egyptians, and Amorites]; 2 for they have taken some of their daughters as wives for themselves and their sons, and thus they have desecrated the holy race with the peoples of the land. Furthermore, the leaders and rulers have taken a leading part in this apostasy!"

Ezra's Exhortation 3 When I had heard this thing, I tore my cloak and my mantle, plucked hair from my head and beard, and sat there stupefied.[b] 4 Around me gathered all who were in dread of the sentence of the God of Israel on this apostasy of the exiles, while I remained motionless until the evening sacrifice.[c] 5 Then, at the time of the evening sacrifice, I rose in my wretchedness, and with cloak and mantle torn I fell on my knees, stretching out my hands to the LORD, my God.

6 I said: "My God, I am too ashamed and confounded to raise my face to you, O my God, for our wicked deeds are heaped up above our heads and our guilt reaches up to heaven.[d] 7 *From the time of our fathers even to this day great has been our guilt, and for our wicked deeds we have been delivered over, we and our kings and our priests, to the will of the kings of foreign lands, to the sword, to captivity, to pillage, and to disgrace, as is the case today.

8 "And now, but a short time ago, mercy came to us from the LORD, our God, who left us a remnant and gave us a stake in his holy place; thus our God has brightened our eyes and given us relief in our servitude.[e] 9 For slaves we are, but in our servitude our God has not abandoned us; rather, he has turned the good will of the kings of Persia toward us. Thus he has given us

8, 30: The story of Ezra's mission is seemingly continued from this point by Neh 7, 72b—8, 18, which may be read before Ezr 9, 1.

9, 7: After this verse, the next part of the prayer attributed to Ezra is perhaps to be found in Neh 9, 6–37, which may be read as leading up to Ezr 9, 8–15.

a 1f: Dt 7, 1; Neh 9, 2. b Ps 119, 136. c Is 66, 2. d Ps 38, 4. e Is 4, 3.

new life to raise again the house of our God and restore its ruins, and has granted us a fence in Judah and Jerusalem.[f] 10But now, O our God, what can we say after all this? For we have abandoned your commandments, 11which you gave through your servants the prophets: the land which you are entering to take as your possession is a land unclean with the filth of the peoples of the land, with the abominations with which they have filled it from one end to the other in their uncleanness.[g] 12Do not, then, give your daughters to their sons in marriage, and do not take their daughters for your sons. Never promote their peace and prosperity; thus you will grow strong, enjoy the produce of the land, and leave it as an inheritance to your children forever.[h]

13"After all that has come upon us for our evil deeds and our great guilt—though you, our God, have made less of our sinfulness than it deserved and have allowed us to survive as we do— 14shall we again violate your commandments by intermarrying with these abominable peoples? Would you not become so angered with us as to destroy us without remnant or survivor? 15O LORD, God of Israel, you are just; yet we have been spared, the remnant we are today. Here we are before you in our sins. Because of all this, we can no longer stand in your presence."

CHAPTER 10

The People's Response 1While Ezra prayed and acknowledged their guilt, weeping and prostrate before the house of God, a very large assembly of Israelites gathered about him, men, women, and children; and the people wept profusely. 2Then Shecaniah, the son of Jehiel, one of the sons of Elam, made this appeal to Ezra: "We have indeed betrayed our God by taking as wives foreign women of the peoples of the land. Yet even now there remains a hope for Israel. 3Let us therefore enter into a covenant before our God to dismiss all our foreign wives and the children born of them, in keeping with what you, my lord, advise, and those who fear the commandments of our God. Let the law be observed! 4Rise, then, for this is your duty! We will stand by you, so have courage and take action!"

5Ezra rose to his feet and demanded an oath from the chiefs of the priests, from the Levites and from all Israel that they would do as had been proposed; and they swore it. 6Then Ezra retired from his place before the house of God and entered the chamber of Johanan, son of Eliashib,* where he spent the night neither eating food nor drinking water, for he was in mourning over the betrayal by the exiles. 7A proclamation was made throughout Judah and Jerusalem that all the exiles should gather together in Jerusalem, 8and that whoever failed to appear within three days would, according to the judgment of the leaders and elders, suffer the confiscation of all his possessions, and himself be excluded from the assembly of the exiles.

9All the men of Judah and Benjamin gathered together in Jerusalem within the three-day period: it was in the ninth month,* on the twentieth day of the month. All the people, standing in the open place before the house of God, were trembling both over the matter at hand and because it was raining. 10Then Ezra, the priest, stood up and said to them: "Your unfaithfulness in taking foreign women as wives has added to Israel's guilt. 11But now, give praise to the LORD, the God of your fathers, and do his will: separate yourselves from the peoples of the land and from these foreign women."[i] 12In answer, the whole assembly cried out with a loud voice: "Yes, it is our duty to do as you say! 13But the people are numerous and it is the rainy season, so that we cannot remain out-of-doors; besides, this is not a task that can be performed in a single day or even two, for those of us who

10, 6: Johanan, son of Eliashib: actually, the grandson of Eliashib; the father of Johanan was Eliashib's son Joiada (Neh 12, 10f. 22). Since Eliashib was high priest at the time of Nehemiah (Neh 3, 1. 20f; 13, 4. 7) and Johanan, if not yet high priest, was at least old enough to have his own separate quarters (chamber) in the temple at the time of Ezra, it is practically certain that Nehemiah's activity in Jerusalem must have preceded that of Ezra.

10, 9: Ninth month: Chislev (November–December), during the "early rains" in Palestine. Since the assembly took place in the open . . . all the people . . . were trembling . . . because it was raining.

f Ps 106, 46. g Lv 18, 24f; Ez 36, 17. h Dt 7, 3. i Neh 9, 2.

have sinned in this regard are many. 14Let our leaders represent the whole assembly; then let all those in our cities who have taken foreign women for wives appear at appointed times, accompanied by the elders and magistrates of each city in question, till we have turned away from us our God's burning anger over this affair." 15Only Jonathan, son of Asahel, and Jahzeiah, son of Tikvah, were against this proposal, with Meshullam and Shabbethai the Levite supporting them.

The Guilty 16*The exiles did as agreed. Ezra appointed as his assistants men who were family heads, one for each family, all of them designated by name. They held sessions to examine the matter, beginning with the first day of the tenth month. 17By the first day of the first month they had passed judgment on all the men who had taken foreign women for wives.

18Among the priests, the following were found to have taken foreign women for wives: Of the sons of Jeshua, son of Jozadak, and his brethren: Maaseiah, Eliezer, Jarib, and Gedaliah. 19They pledged themselves to dismiss their wives, and as a guilt-offering for their guilt they gave a ram from the flock. 20Of the sons of Immer: Hanani and Zebadiah; 21of the sons of Harim: Maaseiah, Elijah, Shemaiah, Jehiel, and Uzziah; 22of the sons of Pashhur: Elioenai, Maaseiah, Ishmael, Nethanel, Jozabad, and Elasah.

23Of the Levites: Jozabad, Shemei, Kelaiah (also called Kelita), Pethahiah, Judah, and Eliezer.[j]

24Of the singers: Eliashib and Zakkur; of the gatekeepers: Shallum, Telem, and Uri.

25Among the other Israelites: Of the sons of Parosh: Ramiah, Izziah, Malchijah, Mijamin, Eleazar, Malchijah, and Benaiah; 26of the sons of Elam: Mattaniah, Zechariah, Jehiel, Abdi, Jeremoth, and Elijah; 27of the sons of Zattu: Elioenai, Eliashib, Mattaniah, Jeremoth, Zabad, and Aziza; 28of the sons of Bebai: Jehohanan, Hananiah, Zabbai, and Athlai; 29of the sons of Bani: Meshullam, Malluch, Adaiah, Jashub, Sheal, and Jeremoth; 30of the sons of Pahath-moab: Adna, Chelal, Benaiah, Maaseiah, Mattaniah, Bezalel, Binnui, and Manasseh; 31of the sons of Harim: Eliezer, Isshijah, Malchijah, Shemaiah, Shimeon, 32Benjamin, Malluch, Shemariah; 33of the sons of Hashum: Mattenai, Mattattah, Zabad, Eliphelet, Jeremai, Manasseh, Shimei; 34of the sons of Begui: Maadai, Amram, Uel, 35Benaiah, Bedeiah, Cheluhi, 36Vaniah, Meremoth, Eliashib, 37Mattaniah, Mattenai, and Jaasu; 38of the sons of Binnui: Shimei, 39Shelemiah, Nathan, and Adaiah; 40of the sons of Zachai: Shashai, Sharai, 41Azarel, Shelemiah, Shemariah, 42Shallum, Amariah, Joseph; 43of the sons of Nebo: Jeiel, Mattithiah, Zabad, Zebina, Jaddai, Joel, Benaiah.

44All these had taken foreign wives; but they sent them away, both the women and their children.*

10, 16f: The work of the committee lasted three months, from the first day of the tenth month, Tebet (December–January), to the first day of the first month, Nisan (March–April), of the following Jewish year.

10, 44: The account of the problem of mixed marriages at the time of Ezra is continued in Neh 9, 1–5; this may be read immediately after Ezr 10, 44, though the date given in Neh 9, 1 fits more precisely after Ezr 10, 15; cf Hg 2, 10–14.

j Neh 8, 7; 10, 11.

THE BOOK OF NEHEMIAH

Problems common to the combined Books Ezra-Nehemiah have been pointed out in the Introduction to the Book of Ezra. The achievements of the two men were complementary; each helped to make it possible for Judaism to maintain its identity during the difficult days of the Restoration. Nehemiah was the man of action who rebuilt the walls of Jerusalem and introduced necessary administrative reforms. Ezra in turn was the great religious reformer who succeeded in establishing the Torah as the constitution of the returned community.

The biblical sources for Nehemiah's life and work are the autobiographical portions scattered through the book. They are called the "Memoirs of Nehemiah," and have been used more extensively and effectively by "the Chronicler" than the "Memoirs of Ezra." No competent scholar questions the authenticity of Nehemiah's memoirs. From these and other sources, the picture emerges of a man dedicated to the single purpose of the welfare of his people. Despite temperamental shortcomings, Nehemiah was a man of good practical sense combined with deep faith in God. In view of his selfless service to a community capable of severely testing any leader, we can be indulgent toward his numerous appeals to God to credit him with the work he had done. Nehemiah was a layman, and his generous dedication of talents to the service of God and of God's people remains an example of undiminished force for laymen today.

The Book of Nehemiah is divided as follows:

I. The Deeds of Nehemiah (1, 1—7, 72).
II. Promulgation of the Law (8, 1—13, 31).

I: The Deeds of Nehemiah

CHAPTER 1

Nehemiah's Vocation 1The words of Nehe-
miah, the son of Hacaliah.*

In the month Chislev of the twentieth year, I
was in the citadel of Susa 2when Hanani, one of
my brothers, came with other men from Judah. I
asked them about the Jews, the remnant pre-
served after the captivity, and about Jerusalem,
3and they answered me: "The survivors of the
captivity there in the province are in great
distress and under reproach. Also, the wall of
Jerusalem lies breached, and its gates have been
gutted with fire." 4When I heard this report, I
began to weep and continued mourning for
several days; I fasted and prayed before the God
of heaven.

5I prayed: "O LORD, God of heaven, great and
awesome God, you who preserve your covenant
of mercy toward those who love you and keep
your commandments,[a] 6may your ear be atten-
tive, and your eyes open, to heed the prayer
which I, your servant, now offer in your pres-
ence day and night for your servants the Israel-
ites, confessing the sins which we of Israel have
committed against you, I and my father's house
included.[b] 7Grievously have we offended you,
not keeping the commandments, the statutes,
and the ordinances which you committed to
your servant Moses.[c] 8But remember, I pray, the
promise which you gave through Moses, your
servant, when you said:[d] 'Should you prove
faithless, I will scatter you among the nations;
9but should you return to me and carefully keep
my commandments, even though your outcasts
have been driven to the farthest corner of the
world, I will gather them from there, and bring
them back to the place which I have chosen as
the dwelling place for my name.' 10They are
your servants, your people, whom you freed by
your great might and your strong hand.[e] 11O
LORD, may your ear be attentive to my prayer
and that of all your willing servants who revere
your name. Grant success to your servant this
day, and let him find favor with this man"—for I
was cupbearer to the king.*[f]

1, 1: The first mission of Nehemiah, from the twentieth year of Artaxerxes I, lasted from the spring (Neh 2, 1) of 445 B.C. until 433 B.C. (Neh 5, 14). It is recounted in Neh 1, 1—6, 15; 12, 27–43; 6, 16—7, 5; 11, 1–21, which may be read in that order.

1, 11: Cupbearer to the king: an important official in the royal household. Because Nehemiah could appear in the queen's presence (Neh 2, 6), it is commonly presumed that he was a eunuch; but this is not necessarily so.

a Dt 7, 9. 12; Dn 9, 4. b 2 Chr 6, 40. c Dn 3, 29f. d 8f: Dt 30, 1–5. e Dt 9, 29. f Ps 118, 25.

CHAPTER 2

Appointment by the King [1]In the month Nisan of the twentieth year of King Artaxerxes, when the wine was in my charge, I took some and offered it to the king. As I had never before been sad in his presence, [2]the king asked me, "Why do you look sad? If you are not sick, you must be sad at heart." Though I was seized with great fear, [3]I answered the king: "May the king live forever! How could I not look sad when the city where my ancestors are buried lies in ruins, and its gates have been eaten out by fire?" [4]The king asked me, "What is it, then, that you wish?" I prayed to the God of heaven [5]and then answered the king: "If it please the king, and if your servant is deserving of your favor, send me to Judah, to the city of my ancestors' graves, to rebuild it." [6]Then the king, and the queen seated beside him, asked me how long my journey would take and when I would return. I set a date that was acceptable to him, and the king agreed that I might go.

[7]I asked the king further: "If it please the king, let letters be given to me for the governors of West-of-Euphrates, that they may afford me safe-conduct till I arrive in Judah; [8]also a letter for Asaph, the keeper of the royal park, that he may give me wood for timbering the gates of the temple-citadel and for the city wall and the house that I shall occupy." The king granted my requests, for the favoring hand of my God was upon me.[g] [9]Thus I proceeded to the governors of West-of-Euphrates and presented the king's letters to them. The king also sent with me army officers and cavalry.[h]

[10]When Sanballat the Horonite* and Tobiah the Ammonite slave had heard of this, they were very much displeased that someone had come to seek the welfare of the Israelites.

Circuit of the City [11]When I had arrived in Jerusalem, I first rested there for three days. [12]Then I set out by night with only a few other men (for I had not told anyone what my God had inspired me to do for Jerusalem) and with no other animals but my own mount. [13]*I rode out at night by the Valley Gate, passed by the Dragon Spring, and came to the Dung Gate, observing how the walls of Jerusalem lay in ruins and its gates had been eaten out by fire. [14]Then I passed over to the Spring Gate and to the King's Pool. Since there was no room here for my mount to pass with me astride, [15]I continued on foot up the wadi by night, inspecting the wall all the while till I once more reached the Valley Gate, by which I went back in. [16]The magistrates knew nothing of where I had gone or what I was doing, for as yet I had disclosed nothing to the Jews, neither to the priests, nor to the nobles, nor to the magistrates, nor to the others who would be concerned about the matter.

Rebuilding Jerusalem's Walls [17]Afterward I said to them: "You see the evil plight in which we stand: how Jerusalem lies in ruins and its gates have been gutted by fire. Come, let us rebuild the wall of Jerusalem, so that we may no longer be an object of derision!" [18]Then I explained to them how the favoring hand of my God had rested upon me, and what the king had said to me. They replied, "Let us be up and building!" And they undertook the good work with vigor.[i]

[19]On hearing of this, Sanballat the Horonite, Tobiah the Ammonite slave, and Geshem the Arab mocked us and ridiculed us. "What is this

2, 10: Sanballat the Horonite: the governor of the province of Samaria (Neh 3, 33f), apparently a native of one of the Bethhorons. A letter from the Jews living at Elephantine in southern Egypt, dated 408–407 B.C., mentions "Delayah and Shelemyah, the sons of Sanballat, the governor of Samaria." Although his own name was Babylonian—Sin-uballit, i.e., "Sin (the moon god) has given life"—two sons had names referring to Yahweh. Tobiah, the Ammonite slave: the governor of the province of Ammon in Transjordan. His honorary title, "servant" (in Hebrew, ebed), i.e., of the king, could also be understood as slave, and Nehemiah no doubt meant it in this derogatory sense. The Tobiads remained a powerful family even in Maccabean times (2 Mc 3, 11). Sanballat and Tobiah together with Geshem the Arab (Neh 2, 19; 6, 1f), who was probably in charge of Edom and the regions to the south and southeast of Judah, opposed the rebuilding of Jerusalem's walls on policital grounds; the city was the capital of a rival province.

2, 13ff: Nehemiah left Jerusalem by the Valley Gate near the northwestern end of the old City of David and went south down the Tyropoean Valley toward the Dragon Spring (or the En-rogel of Jos 15, 7; 18, 16; 2 Sm 17, 17; 1 Kgs 1, 9, now known as Job's Well) at the juncture of the Valley of Hinnom and the Kidron Valley; he then turned north at the Dung Gate (or the Potsherd Gate of Jer 19, 2) at the southern end of the city and proceeded up the wadi, that is, the Kidron Valley, passing the Spring Gate (at the Spring of Gihon) and the King's Pool (unidentified); finally he turned west and then south to his starting point.

g Ezr 7, 6. h Ezr 8, 22. i Ezr 7, 6.

that you are about?" they asked. "Are you
rebelling against the king?" [20]My answer to
them was this: "It is the God of heaven who will
grant us success. We, his servants, shall set about
the rebuilding; but for you there is to be neither
share nor claim nor memorial* in Jerusalem."

CHAPTER 3

List of Workers* [1]Eliashib the high priest and
his priestly brethren took up the task of rebuild-
ing the Sheep Gate. They timbered it and set up
its doors, its bolts, and its bars, then continued
the rebuilding to the Tower of Hananel.[j] [2]At
their side the men of Jericho were rebuilding,
and next to them was Zaccur, son of Imri. [3]The
Fish Gate was rebuilt by the sons of Hassenaah;
they timbered it and set up its doors, its bolts,
and its bars.[k] [4]At their side Meremoth, son of
Uriah, son of Hakkoz, carried out the work of
repair; next to him was Meshullam, son of
Berechiah, son of Meshezabel; and next to him
was Zadok, son of Baana. [5]Next to him the
Tekoites carried out the work of repair; how-
ever, some of their outstanding men would not
submit to the labor asked by their lords. [6]The
New City Gate was repaired by Joiada, son of
Paseah; and Meshullam, son of Besodeiah; they
timbered it and set up its doors, its bolts, and its
bars. [7]At their side were Melatiah the Gibeonite,
Jadon the Meronothite, and the men of Gibeon
and of Mizpah, who were under the jurisdiction
of the governor of West-of-Euphrates. [8]Next to
them the work of repair was carried out by
Uzziel, son of Harhaiah, a member of the
goldsmiths' guild, and at his side was Hananiah,
one of the perfumers' guild. They restored
Jerusalem as far as the wall of the public square.*
[9]Next to them the work of repair was carried out
by Rephaiah, son of Hur, leader of half the
district of Jerusalem, [10]and at his side was
Jedaiah, son of Harumaph, who repaired oppo-
site his own house. Next to him Hattush, son of
Hashabneiah, carried out the work of repair.
[11]The adjoining sector, as far as the Oven Tower,
was repaired by Malchijah, son of Harim, and
Hasshub, of Pahath-moab. [12]At their side the
work of repair was carried out by Shallum, son
of Hallohesh, leader of half the district of Jerusa-
lem, by himself and his daughters. [13]The Valley
Gate was repaired by Hanun and the inhabitants
of Zanoah; they rebuilt it and set up its doors, its
bolts, and its bars. They also repaired a thousand
cubits of the wall up to the Dung Gate. [14]The
Dung Gate was repaired by Malchijah, son of
Rechab, leader of the district of Beth-haccherem;
he rebuilt it and set up its doors, its bolts, and its
bars. [15]The Spring Gate was repaired by Shal-
lum, son of Colhozeh, leader of the district of
Mizpah; he rebuilt it, roofed it over, and set up
its doors, its bolts, and its bars. He also repaired
the wall of the Aqueduct Pool near the king's
garden as far as the steps that lead down from
the City of David. [16]After him, the work of repair
was carried out by Nehemiah, son of Azbuk,
leader of half the district of Beth-zur, to a place
opposite the tombs of David, as far as the
artificial pool and the barracks.

[17]After him, the Levites carried out the work
of repair: Rehum, son of Bani. Next to him, for
his own district, was Hashabiah, leader of half
the district of Keilah. [18]After him, their brethren
carried out the work of repair: Binnui, son of
Henadad, leader of half the district of Keilah;
[19]next to him Ezer, son of Jeshua, leader of
Mizpah, who repaired the adjoining sector, the
Corner, opposite the ascent to the arsenal.
[20]After him, Baruch, son of Zabbai, repaired the
adjoining sector from the Corner to the entrance
of the house of Eliashib, the high priest. [21]After
him, Meremoth, son of Uriah, son of Hakkoz,
repaired the adjoining sector from the entrance
of Eliashib's house to the end of the house.

[22]After him, the work of repair was carried
out by the priests, men of the surrounding

2, 20: Neither share nor claim nor memorial: although Sanballat and Tobiah were Yahwist, Nehemiah would not let them participate in any of the rights of the religious community in Jerusalem.

3, 1–32: The construction work on the gates and walls of the city is described in counterclockwise direction, beginning and ending at the Sheep Gate (to the north of the temple). The exact sites of many of the topographical points mentioned are uncertain.

3, 8: Wall of the public square: that is, the section of wall bounding the place of assembly outside the Gate of Ephraim, or New City Gate; cf Neh 3, 6; 8, 16.

j Jer 31, 38. k Ezr 2, 35; Zep 1, 10.

country. 23After them, Benjamin and Hasshub carried out the repair in front of their houses; after them, Azariah, son of Maaseiah, son of Ananiah, made the repairs alongside his house. 24After him, Binnui, son of Henadad, repaired the adjoining sector from the house of Azariah to the Corner [that is, to the Angle]. 25After him, Palal, son of Uzai, carried out the work of repair opposite the Corner and the tower projecting from the Upper Palace at the quarters of the guard. After him, Pedaiah, son of Parosh, carried out the work of repair 26to a point opposite the Water Gate on the east, and the projecting tower. 27After him, the Tekoites repaired the adjoining sector opposite the great projecting tower, to the wall of Ophel [the temple slaves were dwelling on Ophel].

28Above the Horse Gate the priests carried out the work of repair, each before his own house. 29After them Zadok, son of Immer, carried out the repair before his house, and after him the repair was carried out by Shemaiah, son of Shecaniah, keeper of the East Gate.[l] 30After him, Hananiah, son of Shelemiah, and Hanun, the sixth son of Zalaph, repaired the adjoining sector; after them, Meshullam, son of Berechiah, repaired the place opposite his own lodging. 31After him, Malchijah, a member of the goldsmiths' guild, carried out the work of repair as far as the quarters of the temple slaves and the merchants, before the Gate of Inspection and as far as the upper chamber of the Angle. 32Between the upper chamber of the Angle and the Sheep Gate, the goldsmiths and the merchants carried out the work of repair.

Opposition from Judah's Foes 33When Sanballat heard that we were rebuilding the wall, it roused his anger and he became very much incensed. He ridiculed the Jews, 34saying in the presence of his brethren and the troops of Samaria: "What are these miserable Jews trying to do? Will they complete their restoration in a single day? Will they recover these stones, burnt as they are, from the heaps of dust?" 35Tobiah the Ammonite was beside him, and he said: "It is a rubble heap they are building. Any fox that attacked it would breach their wall of stones!" 36Take note, O our God, how we were mocked! Turn back their derision upon their own heads and let them be carried away to a land of captivity! 37Hide not their crime and let not their sin be blotted out in your sight, for they insulted the builders to their face![m] 38We, however, continued to build the wall, which was soon filled in and completed up to half its height. The people worked with a will.

CHAPTER 4

1When Sanballat, Tobiah, the Arabs, the Ammonites, and the Ashdodites heard that the restoration of the walls of Jerusalem was progressing—for the gaps were beginning to be closed up—they became extremely angry. 2Thereupon they all plotted together to come and fight against Jerusalem and thus to throw us into confusion. 3We prayed to our God and posted a watch against them day and night for fear of what they might do. 4Meanwhile the Judahites were saying:

"Slackened is the bearers' strength,
  there is no end to the rubbish;
Never shall we be able
  the wall to rebuild."

5Our enemies thought, "Before they are aware of it or see us, we shall come into their midst, kill them, and put an end to the work."

6When the Jews who lived near them had come to us from one place after another, and had told us ten times over that they were about to attack us, 7I stationed guards down below, behind the wall, near the exposed points, assigning them by family groups with their swords, their spears, and their bows. 8I made an inspection, then addressed these words to the nobles, the magistrates, and the rest of the people: "Have no fear of them! Keep in mind the LORD, who is great and to be feared, and fight for your brethren, your sons and daughters, your wives and your homes." 9When our enemies became aware that we had been warned and that God

l Ezr 40, 6. m Jer 18, 23.

had upset their plan, we all went back, each to his own task at the wall.

[10]From that time on, however, only half my able men took a hand in the work, while the other half, armed with spears, bucklers, bows, and breastplates, stood guard behind the whole house of Judah[n] [11]as they rebuilt the wall. The load carriers, too, were armed; each did his work with one hand and held a weapon with the other. [12]Every builder, while he worked, had his sword girt at his side. Also, a trumpeter stood beside me, [13]for I had said to the nobles, the magistrates, and the rest of the people: "Our work is scattered and extensive, and we are widely separated from one another along the wall; [14]wherever you hear the trumpet sound, join us there; our God will fight with us." [15]Thus we went on with the work, half of the men with spears at the ready, from daybreak till the stars came out.

[16]At the same time I told the people to spend the nights inside Jerusalem, each man with his own attendant, so that they might serve as a guard by night and a working force by day. [17]Neither I, nor my kinsmen, nor any of my attendants, nor any of the bodyguard that accompanied me took off his clothes; everyone kept his weapon at his right hand.

CHAPTER 5

Antisocial Conduct [1] [o]Then there rose a great outcry of the common people and their wives against certain of their fellow Jews. [2]Some said: "We are forced to pawn our sons and daughters in order to get grain to eat that we may live." [3]Others said: "We are forced to pawn our fields, our vineyards, and our houses, that we may have grain during the famine." [4]Still others said: "To pay the king's tax we have borrowed money on our fields and our vineyards. [5]And though these are our own kinsmen and our children are as good as theirs, we have had to reduce our sons and daughters to slavery, and violence has been done to some of our daughters! Yet we can do nothing about it, for our fields and our vineyards belong to others."[p]

Nehemiah's Action [6]I was extremely angry when I heard the reasons they had for complaint. [7]After some deliberation, I called the nobles and magistrates to account, saying to them, "You are exacting interest from your own kinsmen!"* I then rebuked them severely, [8]saying to them: "As far as we were able, we bought back our fellow Jews who had been sold to Gentiles; you, however, are selling your own brothers, to have them bought back by us." They remained silent, for they could find no answer.[q] [9]I continued: "What you are doing is not good. Should you not walk in the fear of our God, and put an end to the derision of our Gentile enemies? [10]I myself, my kinsmen, and my attendants have lent the people money and grain without charge. Let us put an end to this usury! [11]I ask that you return to them this very day their fields, their vineyards, their olive groves, and their houses, together with the interest on the money, the grain, the wine, and the oil that you have lent them." [12]They answered: "We will return everything and exact nothing further from them. We will do just what you ask." Then I called for the priests and had them administer an oath to these men that they would do as they had promised. [13]I also shook out the folds of my garment, saying, "Thus may God shake from his home and his fortune every man who fails to keep this promise, and may he thus be shaken out and emptied!" And the whole assembly answered, "Amen," and praised the LORD. Then the people did as they had promised.

Nehemiah's Lack of Self-Interest [14]Moreover, from the time that King Artaxerxes appointed me governor in the land of Judah, from his twentieth to his thirty-second year—during these twelve years neither I nor my brethren lived from the governor's allowance. [15]The earlier governors, my predecessors, had laid a heavy burden on the people, taking from them each day forty silver shekels for their food; then too, their men oppressed the people. But I, because I feared God, did not act thus. [16]Moreover, though I had acquired no land of my own, I did

5, 7: You are exacting interest from your own kinsmen!: contrary to the Mosaic law (Dt 23, 20).

n Ps 149, 6. o 1f: Jer 34, 8–22. p Ez 21, 7; Lv 25, 39. q Lv 25, 48.

my part in this work on the wall, and all my men were gathered there for the work. 17Though I set my table for a hundred and fifty persons, Jews and magistrates, as well as those who came to us from the nations round about, 18and though the daily preparations were made at my expense—one beef, six choice muttons, poultry—besides all kinds of wine in abundance every ten days, despite this I did not claim the governor's allowance, for the labor lay heavy upon this people. 19Keep in mind, O my God, in my favor all that I did for this people.

CHAPTER 6

Plots against Nehemiah 1When it had been reported to Sanballat, Tobiah, Geshem the Arab, and our other enemies that I had rebuilt the wall and that there was no breach left in it (though up to that time I had not yet set up the doors in the gates), 2Sanballat and Geshem sent me this message: "Come, let us hold council together at Caphirim in the plain of Ono." They were planning to do me harm. 3However, I sent messengers to them with this reply: "I am engaged in a great enterprise and am unable to come down; why should the work stop, while I leave it to come down to you?" 4Four times they sent me this same proposal, and each time I gave the same reply. 5Then, the fifth time, Sanballat sent me the same message by one of his servants, who bore an unsealed letter 6containing this text: "Among the nations it has been reported—Geshem is witness to this—that you and the Jews are planning a rebellion; that for this reason you are rebuilding the wall; and that you are to be their king"—and so on. 7"Also, that you have set up prophets in Jerusalem to proclaim you king of Judah. Now, since matters like these must reach the ear of the king, come, let us hold council together." 8I sent him this answer: "Nothing of what you report has taken place; rather, it is the invention of your own mind." 9They were all trying to frighten us, thinking, "Their hands will slacken in the work, and it will never be completed." But instead, I now redoubled my efforts.

10I went to the house of Shemaiah, son of Delaiah, son of Mehetabel, who was unable to go about, and he said:

"Let us meet in the house of God,
 inside the temple building;
 let us lock the doors of the temple.
For men are coming to kill you;
 by night they are coming to kill you."

11My answer was: "A man like me take flight? Can a man like me enter the temple to save his life? I will not go!" 12For on consideration it was plain to me that God had not sent him; rather, because Tobiah and Sanballat had bribed him, he voiced this prophecy concerning me 13that I might act on it out of fear and commit this sin. Then they would have had a shameful story with which to discredit me. 14Keep in mind Tobiah and Sanballat, O my God, because of these things they did; keep in mind as well Noadiah the prophetess and the other prophets who were trying to frighten me.[r]

Conclusion of the Work 15The wall was finished on the twenty-fifth day of Elul;* it had taken fifty-two days. 16When all our enemies had heard of this, and all the nations round about had taken note of it, our enemies lost much face in the eyes of the nations, for they knew that it was with our God's help that this work had been completed.[s] 17*At that same time, however, many letters were going to Tobiah from the nobles of Judah, and Tobiah's letters were reaching them, 18for many in Judah were in league with him, since he was the son-in-law of Shecaniah, son of Arah, and his son Jehohanan had married the daughter of Meshullam, son of Berechiah. 19Thus they would praise his good deeds in my presence and relate to him whatever I said; and Tobiah sent letters trying to frighten me.

6, 15: Elul: the sixth month (August–September). Fifty-two days: according to Josephus (Antiquities XI, v 8), the rebuilding of the walls of Jerusalem by Nehemiah took two years and four months, which seems more probable.

6, 17ff: These verses should be read immediately after v 14.

r Jer 23, 9–40; Zec 13, 3. s Ps 118, 22f; 127, 1.

CHAPTER 7

[1]When the wall had been rebuilt, I had the
doors set up, and the gatekeepers [and the
singers and the Levites] were put in charge of
them. [2]Over Jerusalem I placed Hanani, my
brother, and Hananiah, the commander of the
citadel, who was a more trustworthy and God-
fearing man than most. [3]I said to them: "The
gates of Jerusalem are not to be opened until the
sun is hot, and while the sun is still shining they
shall shut and bar the doors. Appoint as watch-
men the inhabitants of Jerusalem, some at their
watch posts, and others before their own
houses."

Census of the Province [4]Now the city was
quite wide and spacious, but its population was
small, and none of the houses had been rebuilt.
[5]When my God had put it into my mind to
gather together the nobles, the magistrates, and
the common people, and to examine their family
records, I came upon the family list of those who
had returned in the earliest period. There I
found the following written:

[6] [t]* These are the inhabitants of the province
who returned from the captivity of the exiles
whom Nebuchadnezzar, king of Babylon, had
carried away, and who came back to Jerusalem
and Judah, each man to his own city [7](those
who returned with Zerubbabel, Jeshua, Nehe-
miah, Azariah, Raamiah, Nahamani, Mordecai,
Bilshan, Mispereth, Bigvai, Nehum, and Baa-
nah).

The census of the men of Israel: [8]sons of
Parosh, two thousand one hundred and seventy-
two; [9]sons of Shephatiah, three hundred and
seventy-two; [10]sons of Arah, six hundred and
fifty-two; [11]sons of Pahath-moab who were sons
of Jeshua and Joab, two thousand eight hundred
and eighteen; [12]sons of Elam, one thousand two
hundred and fifty-four; [13]sons of Zattu, eight
hundred and forty-five; [14]sons of Zaccai, seven
hundred and sixty; [15]sons of Binnui, six hundred
and forty-eight; [16]sons of Bebai, six hundred and
twenty-eight; [17]sons of Azgad, two thousand
three hundred and twenty-two; [18]sons of Adoni-
kam, six hundred and sixty-seven; [19]sons of
Bigvai, two thousand and sixty-seven; [20]sons of
Adin, six hundred and fifty-five; [21]sons of Ater
who were sons of Hezekiah, ninety-eight; [22]sons
of Hashum, three hundred and twenty-eight;
[23]sons of Bezai, three hundred and twenty-four;
[24]sons of Hariph, one hundred and twelve;
[25]sons of Gibeon, ninety-five; [26]men of Bethle-
hem and Netophah, one hundred and eighty-
eight; [27]men of Anathoth, one hundred and
twenty-eight; [28]men of Beth-azmaveth, forty-
two; [29]men of Kiriath-jearim, Chephirah, and
Beeroth, seven hundred and forty-three; [30]men
of Ramah and Geba, six hundred and twenty-
one; [31]men of Michmas, one hundred and
twenty-two; [32]men of Bethel and Ai, one hun-
dred and twenty-three; [33]men of Nebo, fifty-
two; [34]sons of another Elam, one thousand two
hundred and fifty-four; [35]sons of Harim, three
hundred and twenty; [36]sons of Jericho, three
hundred and forty-five; [37]sons of Lod, Hadid,
and Ono, seven hundred and twenty-one; [38]sons
of Senaah, three thousand nine hundred and
thirty.

[39]The priests: sons of Jedaiah who were of the
house of Jeshua, nine hundred and seventy-
three; [40]sons of Immer, one thousand and fifty-
two; [41]sons of Pashhur, one thousand two
hundred and forty-seven; [42]sons of Harim, one
thousand and seventeen.

[43]The Levites: sons of Jeshua, Kadmiel, Bin-
nui, Hodeviah, seventy-four.

[44]The singers: sons of Asaph, one hundred
and forty-eight.

[45]The gatekeepers: sons of Shallum, sons of
Ater, sons of Talmon, sons of Akkub, sons of
Hatita, sons of Shobai, one hundred and thirty-
eight.

[46]The temple slaves: sons of Ziha, sons of
Hasupha, sons of Tabbaoth, [47]sons of Keros, sons
of Sia, sons of Padon, [48]sons of Lebana, sons of
Hagaba, sons of Shalmai, [49]sons of Hanan, sons
of Giddel, sons of Gahar, [50]sons of Reaiah, sons
of Rezin, sons of Nekoda, [51]sons of Gazzam,
sons of Uzza, sons of Paseah, [52]sons of Besai,
sons of the Meunites, sons of the Nephusites,
[53]sons of Bakbuk, sons of Hakupha, sons of

7, 6–72a: See note on Ezr 2, 1–67.

t 6–72: Ezr 2, 1–70.

Harhur, 54 sons of Bazlith, sons of Mehida, sons of Harsha, 55 sons of Barkos, sons of Sisera, sons of Temah, 56 sons of Neziah, sons of Hatipha.

57 Descendants of the slaves of Solomon: sons of Sotai, sons of Sophereth, sons of Perida, 58 sons of Jaala, sons of Darkon, sons of Giddel, 59 sons of Shephatiah, sons of Hattil, sons of Pochereth-hazzebaim, sons of Amon. 60 The total of the temple slaves and the descendants of the slaves of Solomon was three hundred and ninety-two.

61 The following who returned from Tel-melah, Tel-harsha, Cherub, Addon, and Immer were unable to prove that their ancestral houses and their descent were Israelite: 62 sons of Delaiah, sons of Tobiah, sons of Nekoda, six hundred and forty-two. 63 Also, of the priests: sons of Hobaiah, sons of Hakkoz, sons of Barzillai (he had married one of the daughters of Barzillai the Gileadite and became known by his name). 64 These men searched their family records, but their names could not be found written there; hence they were degraded from the priesthood, 65 and His Excellency* ordered them not to partake of the most holy foods until there should be a priest bearing the Urim and Thummim.

66 The entire assembly taken together came to forty-two thousand three hundred and sixty, 67 not counting their male and female slaves, who were seven thousand three hundred and thirty-seven. They also had two hundred male and female singers. Their horses were seven hundred and thirty-six, their mules two hundred and forty-five, 68 their camels four hundred and thirty-five, their asses six thousand seven hundred and twenty.

69 Certain of the family heads contributed to the service. His Excellency put into the treasury one thousand drachmas of gold, fifty basins, thirty garments for priests, and five hundred minas of silver. 70 Some of the family heads contributed to the treasury for the temple service: twenty thousand drachmas of gold and two thousand two hundred minas of silver. 71 The contributions of the rest of the people amounted to twenty thousand drachmas of gold, two thousand minas of silver, and sixty-seven garments for priests.

72 The priests, the Levites, the gatekeepers, the singers, the temple slaves, and all Israel took up residence in their cities.

II: Promulgation of the Law

CHAPTER 8

Ezra Reads the Law* Now when the seventh month came, 1 the whole people gathered as one man in the open space before the Water Gate, and they called upon Ezra the scribe to bring forth the book of the law of Moses which the LORD prescribed for Israel. [u] 2 On the first day of the seventh month, therefore, Ezra the priest brought the law before the assembly, which consisted of men, women, and those children old enough to understand. 3 Standing at one end of the open place that was before the Water Gate, he read out of the book from daybreak till midday, in the presence of the men, the women, and those children old enough to understand; and all the people listened attentively to the book of the law. 4 Ezra the scribe stood on a wooden platform that had been made for the occasion; at his right side stood Mattithiah, Shema, Anaiah, Uriah, Hilkiah, and Maaseiah, and on his left Pedaiah, Mishael, Malchijah, Hashum, Hashbaddanah, Zechariah, Meshullam. 5 Ezra opened the scroll so that all the people might see it (for he was standing higher up than any of the people); and, as he opened it, all the people rose. 6 Ezra blessed the LORD, the great God, and all the people, their hands raised high, answered, "Amen, amen!" Then they bowed down and prostrated themselves before the LORD, their faces to the ground. 7 [The Levites Jeshua, Bani, Sherebiah, Jamin, Akkub, Shabbethai, Hodiah, Maaseiah, Kelita, Azariah, Jozabad, Hanan, and Pelaiah explained the law to the people, who remained in their places.] [v] 8 Ezra

7, 65. 69: His Excellency: see note on Ezr 2, 63.

7, 72b—8, 18: to be read after Ezr 8, 36. The gloss mentioning Nehemiah in v 9 was inserted in this Ezra section after the dislocation of several parts of Ezra-Nehemiah had occurred. There is no clear evidence of a simultaneous presence of Nehemiah and Ezra in Jerusalem; Neh 12, 26 and 12, 36 are also scribal glosses.

u Ezr 3, 1. v Neh 10, 11.

read plainly from the book of the law of God,
interpreting it so that all could understand what
was read.[w] 9Then [Nehemiah, that is, His Excel-
lency, and] Ezra the priest-scribe [and the Levites
who were instructing the people] said to all the
people: "Today is holy to the LORD your God. Do
not be sad, and do not weep"—for all the people
were weeping as they heard the words of the
law. 10He said further: "Go, eat rich foods and
drink sweet drinks, and allot portions to those
who had nothing prepared; for today is holy to
our LORD. Do not be saddened this day, for
rejoicing in the LORD must be your strength!"[x]
11[And the Levites quieted all the people, saying,
"Hush, for today is holy, and you must not be
saddened."] 12Then all the people went to eat
and drink, to distribute portions, and to cele-
brate with great joy, for they understood the
words that had been expounded to them.
The Feast of Booths 13On the second day, the
family heads of the whole people and also the
priests and the Levites gathered around Ezra the
scribe and examined the words of the law more
closely. 14They found it written in the law
prescribed by the LORD through Moses that the
Israelites must dwell in booths during the feast
of the seventh month;[y] 15and that they should
have this proclamation made throughout their
cities and in Jerusalem: "Go out into the hill
country and bring in branches of olive trees,
oleasters, myrtle, palm, and other leafy trees, to
make booths, as the law prescribes."[z] 16The
people went out and brought in branches with
which they made booths for themselves, on the
roofs of their houses, in their courtyards, in the
courts of the house of God, and in the open
spaces of the Water Gate and the Gate of
Ephraim. 17Thus the entire assembly of the
returned exiles made booths and dwelt in them.
Now the Israelites had done nothing of this sort
from the days of Jeshua, son of Nun, until this
occasion; therefore there was very great joy.
18Ezra read from the book of the law of God day
after day, from the first day to the last. They kept
the feast for seven days, and the solemn assem-
bly on the eighth day, as was required.

CHAPTER 9

Confession of the People 1[a]* On the twenty-
fourth day of this month, the Israelites gathered
together fasting and in sackcloth, their heads
covered with dust. 2Those of Israelite descent
separated themselves from all who were of
foreign extraction, then stood forward and con-
fessed their sins and the guilty deeds of their
fathers.[b] 3When they had taken their places,
they read from the book of the law of the LORD
their God, for a fourth part of the day, and during
another fourth part they made their confession
and prostrated themselves before the LORD their
God. 4Standing on the platform of the Levites
were Jeshua, Binnui, Kadmiel, Shebaniah,
Bunni, Sherebiah, Bani, and Chenani, who cried
out to the LORD their God with a loud voice.
5The Levites Jeshua, Kadmiel, Bani, Hashabne-
iah, Sherebiah, Hodiah, Shebaniah, and Petha-
hiah said,

"Arise, bless the LORD, your God,
from eternity to eternity!"

The Israelites answered with the blessing,

"Blessed is your glorious name,
and exalted above all blessing and praise."[c]

6*Then Ezra said: "It is you, O LORD, you are
the only one; you made the heavens, the highest
heavens and all their host, the earth and all that
is upon it, the seas and all that is in them. To all
of them you give life, and the heavenly hosts
bow down before you.
7"You, O LORD, are the God who chose
Abram, who brought him out from Ur of the
Chaldees, and named him Abraham.[d] 8When
you had found his heart faithful in your sight,
you made the covenant with him to give to him
and his posterity the land of the Canaanites,

9, 1–5: This is a continuation of the account concerning the problem of mixed marriages at the time of Ezra; it should be read immediately after Ezr 10, 44.

9, 6–37: The prayer of Ezra which began in Ezr 9, 6f is here continued; see note on Ezr 9, 7.

w Ezr 7, 6. x Est 9, 19. y Ex 23, 14; Lv 23, 33–36. z Ps 118, 27. a Dn 9, 3. b Ezr 9, 1f; 10, 11. c Dn 2, 20; 3, 52. d Gn 12, 1; 17, 5.

Hittites, Amorites, Perizzites, Jebusites, and Gir-
gashites. These promises of yours you fulfilled,
for you are just. [e]

9 "You saw the affliction of our fathers in Egypt,
you heard their cry by the Red Sea; [f]
10 You worked signs and wonders against
Pharoah,
against all his servants and the people of his
land,
Because you knew of their insolence toward
them;
thus you made for yourself a name even to
this day. [g]
11 The sea you divided before them,
on dry ground they passed through the
midst of the sea;
Their pursuers you hurled into the depths,
like a stone into the mighty waters. [h]
12 With a column of cloud you led them by day,
and by night with a column of fire,
To light the way of their journey,
the way in which they must travel. [i]
13 On Mount Sinai you came down,
you spoke with them from heaven;
You gave them just ordinances, firm laws,
good statutes, and commandments; [j]
14 Your holy sabbath you made known to them,
commandments, statutes, and law you
prescribed for them,
by the hand of Moses your servant. [k]
15 Food from heaven you gave them in their
hunger,
water from a rock you sent them in their
thirst.
You bade them enter and occupy the land
which you had sworn with upraised hand to
give them. [l]

16 "But they, our fathers, proved to be inso-
lent; they held their necks stiff and would not
obey your commandments. 17 They refused to
obey and no longer remembered the miracles
you had worked for them. They stiffened their
necks and turned their heads to return to their
slavery in Egypt. But you are a God of pardons,
gracious and compassionate, slow to anger and
rich in mercy; you did not forsake them. [m]
18 Though they made for themselves a molten
calf, and proclaimed, 'Here is your God who
brought you up out of Egypt,' and were guilty of
great effronteries, [n] 19 yet in your great mercy you
did not forsake them in the desert. The column
of cloud did not cease to lead them by day on
their journey, nor did the column of fire by night
cease to light for them the way by which they
were to travel.

20 "Your good spirit you bestowed on them, to
give them understanding; your manna you did
not withhold from their mouths, and you gave
them water in their thirst. [o] 21 Forty years in the
desert you sustained them: they did not want;
their garments did not become worn, and their
feet did not become swollen. [p] 22 You gave them
kingdoms and peoples, which you divided up
among them as border lands. They possessed the
land of Sihon, king of Heshbon, and the land of
Og, king of Bashan. [q]

23 "You made their children as numerous as
the stars of the heavens, and you brought them
into the land which you had commanded their
fathers to enter and possess. [r] 24 The sons went in
to take possession of the land, and you humbled
before them the Canaanite inhabitants of the
land and delivered them over into their power,
their kings as well as the peoples of the land, to
do with them as they would. 25 They captured
fortified cities and fertile land; they took posses-
sion of houses filled with all good things, cisterns
already dug, vineyards, olive groves, and fruit
trees in abundance. They could eat and have
their fill, fatten and feast themselves on your
immense good gifts. [s]

26 "But they were contemptuous and rebel-
lious: they cast your law behind their backs, they
slew your prophets who bore witness against
them in order to bring them back to you, and
they were guilty of great effronteries. [t] 27 There-
fore you delivered them into the power of their

e Gn 15, 18f. f Ex 2, 23f. g Ex 7—11; 14. h Ex 15, 5. 10. i Ex 13, 21f. j Ex 19—20. k Ex 20, 8. l Ex 16, 4; 17, 1f. m Nm 14, 1–4; Ex 34, 6; Dn 9, 9. n Ex 32, 4. o Dt 2, 7. p Dt 8, 4. q Nm 21, 21—35; Dt 1, 4; 2, 26–3, 11. r Dt 1, 10. s Dt 3, 5; 6, 10f; 11, 11; 32, 15. t Wis 2, 10–20.

enemies, who oppressed them. But in the time of their oppression they would cry out to you, and you would hear them from heaven, and according to your great mercy give them saviors to deliver them from the power of their enemies.[u]

28“As soon as they had relief, they would go back to doing evil in your sight. Then again you abandoned them to the power of their enemies, who crushed them. Then they cried out to you, and you heard them from heaven and delivered them according to your mercy, many times over. 29You bore witness against them, in order to bring them back to your law. But they were insolent and would not obey your commandments; they sinned against your ordinances, from which men draw life when they practice them. They turned stubborn backs, stiffened their necks, and would not obey.[v] 30You were patient with them for many years, bearing witness against them through your spirit, by means of your prophets; still they would not listen. Thus you delivered them over into the power of the peoples of the lands. 31Yet in your great mercy you did not completely destroy them and you did not forsake them, for you are a kind and merciful God.

32“Now, therefore, O our God, great, mighty, and awesome God, you who in your mercy preserve the covenant, take into account all the disasters that have befallen us, our kings, our princes, our priests, our prophets, our fathers, and your entire people, from the time of the kings of Assyria until this day![w] 33In all that has come upon us you have been just, for you kept faith while we have done evil.[x] 34Yes, our kings, our princes, our priests, and our fathers have not kept your law; they paid no attention to your commandments and the obligations of which you reminded them. 35While they were yet in their kingdom, in the midst of the many good things that you had given them and in the wide and fertile land that you had spread out before them, they did not serve you nor did they turn away from their evil deeds. 36But, see, we today are slaves; and as for the land which you gave our fathers that they might eat its fruits and good things—see, we have become slaves upon it! 37Its rich produce goes to the kings whom you set over us because of our sins, who rule over our bodies and our cattle as they please. We are in great distress!”

CHAPTER 10

Agreement of the People 1*In view of all this, we are entering into a firm pact, which we are putting into writing. On the sealed document appear the names of our princes, our Levites, and our priests.[y]

2On the sealed document: His Excellency Nehemiah, son of Hacaliah, and Zedekiah.

3Seraiah, Azariah, Jeremiah, 4Pashhur, Amariah, Malchijah, 5Hattush, Shebaniah, Malluch, 6Harim, Meremoth, Obadiah, 7Daniel, Ginnethon, Baruch, 8Meshullam, Abijah, Mijamin, 9Maaziah, Bilgai, Shemaiah: these are the priests.

10The Levites: Jeshua, son of Azaniah; Binnui, of the sons of Henadad; Kadmiel; 11and their brethren Shebaniah, Hodiah, Kelita, Pelaiah, Hanan,[z] 12Mica, Rehob, Hashabiah, 13Zaccur, Sherebiah, Shebaniah, 14Hodiah, Bani, Beninu.

15The leaders of the people: Parosh, Pahath-moab, Elam, Zattu, Bani, 16Bunni, Azgad, Bebai, 17Adonijah, Bigvai, Adin, 18Ater, Hezekiah, Azzur, 19Hodiah, Hashum, Bezai, 20Hariph, Anathoth, Nebai, 21Magpiash, Meshullam, Hazir, 22Meshezabel, Zadok, Jaddua, 23Pelatiah, Hanan, Anaiah, 24Hoshea, Hananiah, Hasshub, 25Hallohesh, Pilha, Shobek, 26Rehum, Hashabnah, Maaseiah, 27Ahiah, Hanan, Anan, 28Malluch, Harim, Baanah.

Provisions of the Pact 29The rest of the people, priests, Levites, gatekeepers, singers, temple slaves, and all others who have separated themselves from the peoples of the lands in favor of the law of God, with their wives, their sons, their daughters, all who are of the age of

10, 1–40: This section belongs to the Nehemiah narrative rather than to that of Ezra. It is best read after Neh 13, 31. In view of all this: considering the situation described in Neh 13, 4–31.

u Dn 9, 19. v Lv 18, 5; 30. 16; 32, 47. w Lam 5. x Dn 3, 27; 9, 14. y Neh 12, 12–26. z Ezr 10, 23.

discretion, [30]join with their brethren who are
their princes, and with the sanction of a curse
take this oath to follow the law of God which
was given through Moses, the servant of God,
and to observe carefully all the commandments
of the LORD, our Lord, his ordinances and his
statutes.[a]

[31]Agreed, that we will not marry our daugh-
ters to the peoples of the land, and that we will
not take their daughters for our sons.[b]

[32]When the peoples of the land bring in
merchandise or any kind of grain for sale on the
sabbath day, we will not buy from them on the
sabbath or on any other holy day. We will forgo
the seventh year, as well as every kind of debt.[c]

[33]We impose these commandments on our-
selves: to give a third of a shekel each year for
the service of the house of our God,[d] [34]for the
showbread, for the daily cereal offering, for the
daily holocaust, for the sabbaths, new moons,
and festivals, for the holy offerings, for sin
offerings to make atonement for Israel, and for
every service of the house of our God. [35]We,
priests, Levites, and people, have determined by
lot concerning the procurement of wood: it is to
be brought to the house of our God by each of
our family houses at stated times each year, to be
burnt on the altar of the LORD, our God, as the
law prescribes.[e] [36][f]We have agreed to bring
each year to the house of the LORD the first fruits
of our fields and of our fruit trees, of whatever
kind; [37]also, as is prescribed in the law, to bring
to the house of our God, to the priests who serve
in the house of our God, the first-born of our
children and our animals, including the first-
born of our flocks and herds. [38]The first batch of
our dough, and our offerings of the fruit of every
tree, of wine and of oil, we will bring to the
priests, to the chambers of the house of our God.
The tithe of our fields we will bring to the
Levites; they, the Levites, shall take the tithe in
all the cities of our service.[g] [39]An Aaronite priest
shall be with the Levites when they take the
tithe, and the Levites shall bring the tithe of the
tithes to the house of our God, to the chambers
of the treasury. [40]For to these chambers the
Israelites and Levites bring the offerings of grain,
wine, and oil; there also are housed the utensils
of the sanctuary, and the ministering priests, the
gatekeepers, and the singers. We will not neglect
the house of our God.

CHAPTER 11

Repeopling of Jerusalem [1]*The leaders of the
people took up residence in Jerusalem, and the
rest of the people cast lots to bring one man in
ten to reside in Jerusalem, the holy city, while
the other nine would remain in the other cities.[h]
[2]The people applauded all those men who
willingly agreed to take up residence in Jerusa-
lem.

The Residents of Jerusalem [3][i]These are the
heads of the province who took up residence in
Jerusalem. (In the cities of Judah dwelt lay
Israelites, priests, Levites, temple slaves, and the
descendants of the slaves of Solomon, each man
on the property he owned in his own city.)

[4]In Jerusalem dwelt both Judahites and Benja-
minites. Of the Judahites: Athaiah, son of Uz-
ziah, son of Zechariah, son of Amariah, son of
Shephatiah, son of Mehallalel, of the sons of
Perez; [5]Maaseiah, son of Baruch, son of Colho-
zeh, son of Hazaiah, son of Adaiah, son of
Joiarib, son of Zechariah, a son of the Shelanites.
[6]The total of the sons of Perez who dwelt in
Jerusalem was four hundred and sixty-eight
valiant men.

[7]These were the Benjaminites: Sallu, son of
Meshullam, son of Joed, son of Pedaiah, son of
Kolaiah, son of Maaseiah, son of Ithiel, son of
Jeshaiah, [8]and his brethren, warriors, nine hun-
dred and twenty-eight in number. [9]Joel, son of
Zichri, was their commander, and Judah, son of
Hassenuah, was second in charge of the city.

[10]Among the priests were: Jedaiah; Joiarib;
Jachin; [11]Seraiah, son of Hilkiah, son of Meshul-
lam, son of Zadok, son of Meraioth, son of
Ahitub, the ruler of the house of God, [12]and

11, 1–19: This list of the family heads who lived in Jerusalem at the time of Nehemiah is best read after Neh 7, 72a. It is basically the same as that given in 1 Chr 9, 2–17, but there are many differences between the two lists.

a Neh 13, 23–27. b Neh 13, 15–22. c Neh 5, 1–13; Ex 20, 8; Lv 25, 2–7. d 2 Chr 24, 6, 9f; Lv 24, 5–9. e Neh 13, 31. f 36f: Ex 13, 1. 11ff; Dt 26, 1. g Neh 13, 10–14; Nm 18, 21. 24ff. h Neh 7, 4. i 3–19: 1 Chr 9, 2–34.

their brethren who carried out the temple service, eight hundred and twenty-two; Adaiah, son of Jeroham, son of Pelaliah, son of Amzi, son of Zechariah, son of Pashhur, son of Malchijah, 13 and his brethren, family heads, two hundred and forty-two; and Amasai, son of Azarel, son of Ahzai, son of Meshillemoth, son of Immer, 14 and his brethren, warriors, one hundred and twenty-eight. Their commander was Zabdiel, son of Haggadol.

15 Among the Levites were Shemaiah, son of Hasshub, son of Azrikam, son of Hashabiah, son of Bunni; 16 Shabbethai and Jozabad, levitical chiefs who were placed over the external affairs of the house of God; 17 Mattaniah, son of Micah, son of Zabdi, son of Asaph, director of the psalms, who led the thanksgiving at prayer; Bakbukiah, second in rank among his brethren; and Abda, son of Shammua, son of Galal, son of Jeduthun. 18 The total of the Levites in the holy city was two hundred and eighty-four.

19 The gatekeepers were Akkub, Talmon, and their brethren, who kept watch over the gates; one hundred and seventy-two in number.

20 The rest of Israel, including priests and Levites, were in all the other cities of Judah, each man in his inheritance.

21 The temple slaves lived on Ophel. Ziha and Gishpa were in charge of the temple slaves.

22 The prefect of the Levites in Jerusalem was Uzzi, son of Bani, son of Hashabiah, son of Mattaniah, son of Mica; he was one of the sons of Asaph, the singers appointed to the service of the house of God[j] — 23 for they had been appointed by royal decree, and there was a fixed schedule for the singers assigning them their daily duties.

24 Pethahiah, son of Meshezabel, a descendant of Zerah, son of Judah, was royal deputy in all affairs that concerned the people.

The Other Cities 25 As concerns their villages in the country: Judahites lived in Kiriath-arba and its dependencies, in Dibon and its dependencies, in Jekabzeel and its villages, 26 in Jeshua, Moladah, Beth-pelet, 27 in Hazar-shual, in Beer-sheba and its dependencies, 28 in Ziklag, in Meconah and its dependencies, 29 in En-rimmon, Zorah, Jarmuth, 30 Zanoah, Adullam, and their villages, Lachish and its countryside, Azekah and its dependencies. They were settled from Beer-sheba to Ge-hinnom.

31 Benjaminites were in Geba, Michmash, Aija, Bethel and its dependencies, 32 Anathoth, Nob, Ananiah, 33 Hazor, Ramah, Gittaim, 34 Hadid, Zeboim, Neballat, 35 Lod, Ono, and the Valley of the Artisans.

36 Some sections of the Levites from Judah settled in Benjamin.

CHAPTER 12

Priests and Levites under Zerubbabel

1 [k]The following are the priests and Levites who returned with Zerubbabel, son of Shealtiel, and Jeshua: Seraiah, Jeremiah, Ezra, 2 Amariah, Malluch, Hattush, 3 Shecaniah, Rehum, Meremoth, 4 Iddo, Ginnethon, Abijah, 5 Mijamin, Maadiah, Bilgah, 6 Shemaiah, and Joiarib, Jedaiah, 7 Sallu, Amok, Hilkiah, Jedaiah. These were the priestly heads and their brethren in the days of Jeshua.

8 The Levites were Jeshua, Binnui, Kadmiel, Sherebiah, Judah, Mattaniah; the last-mentioned, together with his brethren, was in charge of the hymns, 9 while Bakbukiah and Unno and their brethren ministered opposite them by turns.

High Priests* 10 Jeshua became the father of Joiakim, Joiakim became the father of Eliashib, and Eliashib became the father of Joiada. 11 Joiada became the father of Johanan, and Johanan became the father of Jaddua.

12, 10f: Jeshua, the high priest when Zerubbabel was governor, i.e., the last decades of the sixth century B.C. (Hg 1, 1. 12. 14; 2, 2. 4). He was the grandfather of Eliashib, the high priest at least in the early period of Nehemiah's governorship, i.e., 445–433 B.C. (Ezr 10, 6; Neh 3, 1. 20f; 13, 4. 7). Eliashib, in turn, was the grandfather of Johanan, a grown man, if not yet a high priest, at the time of Ezra, i.e., c. 400 B.C. (Ezr 10, 6, and note). According to Josephus (Antiquities XI, v), whose testimony here is doubtful, Jaddua, son of Johanan, died as an old man about the same time that Alexander the Great died, i.e., 323 B.C. If this list of the postexilic high priests, at least as far as Johanan, comes, as seems probable (cf v 23), from the Chronicler himself and not from a later scribe, it is of prime importance for dating the Chronicler's work in the first decades of the fourth century B.C.

j 2 Chr 20, 14. k 1–6; Neh 12, 12–22.

Priests and Levites under Joiakim 12 [l]In the days of Joiakim these were the priestly family heads: for Seraiah, Meraiah; for Jeremiah, Hananiah; 13 for Ezra, Meshullam; for Amariah, Jehohanan; 14 for Malluch, Jonathan; for Shebaniah, Joseph; 15 for Harim, Adna; for Meremoth, Helkai; 16 for Iddo, Zechariah; for Ginnethon, Meshullam; 17 for Abijah, Zichri; for Miamin, . . . ; for Maadiah, Piltai; 18 for Bilgah, Shammua; for Shemaiah, Jehonathan; 19 and for Joiarib, Mattenai; for Jedaiah, Uzzi; 20 for Sallu, Kallai; for Amok, Eber; 21 for Hilkiah, Hashabiah; for Jedaiah, Nethanel.

22 In the time of Eliashib, Joiada, Johanan, and Jaddua, the family heads of the priests were written down in the Book of Chronicles, up until the reign of Darius the Persian. 23 The sons of Levi: the family heads were written down in the Book of Chronicles, up until the time of Johanan, the son of Eliashib.

24 The heads of the Levites were Hashabiah, Sherebiah, Jeshua, Binnui, Kadmiel. Their brethren who stood opposite them to sing praises and thanksgiving in fulfillment of the command of David, the man of God, one section opposite the other, [m] 25 were Mattaniah, Bakbukiah, Obadiah.

Meshullam, Talmon, and Akkub were gatekeepers. They kept watch over the storerooms at the gates. [n]

26 All these lived in the time of Joiakim, son of Jeshua, son of Jozadak [and in the time of Nehemiah the governor and of Ezra the priest-scribe].

Dedication of the City Wall 27 *At the dedication of the wall of Jerusalem, the Levites were sought out wherever they lived and were brought to Jerusalem to celebrate a joyful dedication with thanksgiving hymns and the music of cymbals, harps, and lyres. 28 The levitical singers gathered together from the region about Jerusalem, from the villages of the Netophathites, 29 from Beth-gilgal, and from the plains of Geba and Azmaveth (for the singers had built themselves settlements about Jerusalem). 30 The priests and Levites first purified themselves, then they purified the people, the gates, and the wall.

31 I had the princes of Judah mount the wall, and I arranged two great choirs. The first of these proceeded to the right, along the top of the wall, in the direction of the Dung Gate, 32 followed by Hoshaiah and half the princes of Judah, 33 along with Azariah, Ezra, Meshullam, 34 Judah, Benjamin, Shemaiah, and Jeremiah, 35 priests with the trumpets, and also Zechariah, son of Jonathan, son of Shemaiah, son of Mattaniah, son of Micaiah, son of Zaccur, son of Asaph, 36 and his brethren Shemaiah, Azarel, Milalai, Gilalai, Maai, Nethanel, Judah, and Hanani, with the musical instruments of David, the man of God. [Ezra the scribe was at their head.] 37 At the Spring Gate they went straight up by the steps of the City of David and continued along the top of the wall above the house of David until they came to the Water Gate on the east.

38 The second choir proceeded to the left, followed by myself and the other half of the princes of the people, along the top of the wall past the Oven Tower as far as the Broad Wall, 39 then past the Ephraim Gate [the New City Gate], the Fish Gate, the Tower of Hananel, and the Hundred Tower, as far as the Sheep Gate [and they came to a halt at the Prison Gate].

40 The two choirs took up a position in the house of God; I, too, who had with me half the magistrates, 41 the priests Eliakim, Maaseiah, Minjamin, Micaiah, Elioenai, Zechariah, Hananiah, with the trumpets, 42 and Maaseiah, Shemaiah, Eleazar, Uzzi, Jehohanan, Malchijah, Elam, and Ezer. The singers were heard under the leadership of Jezrahiah. 43 Great sacrifices were offered on that day, and there was rejoicing over the great feast of the LORD in which they shared. The women and the children joined in, and the rejoicing at Jerusalem could be heard from afar off.

12, 27–43: The dedication of the wall of Jerusalem took place, no doubt, soon after the restoration of the wall and its gates had been completed. Therefore, this section is best read after Neh 6, 15.

l 12–22: Neh 10, 3–9; 12, 1–6. m Ezr 2, 40. n Neh 11, 17.

Offerings for Priests and Levites* 44 [o]At that time men were appointed over the chambers set aside for stores, offerings, first fruits, and tithes; in them they were to collect from the fields of the various cities the portions legally assigned to the priests and Levites. For Judah rejoiced in its appointed priests and Levites 45who carried out the ministry of their God and the ministry of purification (as did the singers and the gatekeepers) in accordance with the prescriptions of David and of Solomon, his son. 46For the heads of the families of the singers and the hymns of praise and thanksgiving to God came down from the days of David and Asaph in times of old.[p] 47Thus all Israel, in the days of Zerubbabel [and in the days of Nehemiah], gave the singers and the gatekeepers their portions, according to their daily needs. They made their consecrated offering to the Levites, and the Levites made theirs to the sons of Aaron.[q]

CHAPTER 13

Separation from Aliens 1 [r]* At that time, when there was reading from the book of Moses in the hearing of the people, it was found written there that "no Ammonite or Moabite may ever be admitted into the assembly of God; 2for they would not succor the Israelites with food and water, but they hired Balaam to curse them, though our God turned the curse into a blessing."[s] 3When they had heard the law, they separated from Israel every foreign element.[t]

Reform in the Temple 4*Before this, the priest Eliashib, who had been placed in charge of the chambers of the house of our God and who was an associate of Tobiah, 5had set aside for the latter's use a large chamber in which had previously been stored the cereal offerings, incense and utensils, the tithes in grain, wine, and oil allotted to the Levites, singers, and gatekeepers, and the offerings due the priests.[u] 6During all this time I had not been in Jerusalem, for in the thirty-second year of Artaxerxes, king of Babylon, I had gone back to the king. After due time,* however, I asked leave of the king 7and returned to Jerusalem, where I discovered the evil thing that Eliashib had done for Tobiah, in setting aside for him a chamber in the courts of the house of God. 8This displeased me very much, and I had all of Tobiah's household goods thrown outside the chamber. 9Then I gave orders to purify the chambers, and I had them replace there the utensils of the house of God, the cereal offerings, and the incense.

10I learned, too, that the portions due the Levites were no longer being given, so that the Levites and the singers who should have been carrying out the services had deserted, each man to his own field. 11I took the magistrates to task, demanding, "Why is the house of God abandoned?" Then I brought the Levites together and had them resume their stations. 12All Judah once more brought in the tithes of grain, wine, and oil to the storerooms;[v] 13and in charge of the storerooms I appointed the priest Shelemiah, Zadok the scribe, and Pedaiah, one of the Levites, together with Hanan, son of Zaccur, son of Mattaniah, as their assistant; for these men were held to be trustworthy. It was their duty to make the distribution to their brethren. 14Remember this to my credit, O my God! Let not the devotion which I showed for the house of my God and its services be forgotten!

Sabbath Observance 15In those days I perceived that men in Judah were treading the winepresses on the sabbath; that they were bringing in sheaves of grain, loading them on their asses, together with wine, grapes, figs, and every other

12, 44–47: This account of the provisions made for the temple services is apparently a composition of the Chronicler. At that time: a mere connective; no particular time is meant, but the account fits best after that of the restoration of the temple (Ezr 6, 13–18) in the days of Zerubbabel (v 47). The gloss mentioning Nehemiah is not in the ancient Greek version.

13, 1ff: These verses were composed by the Chronicler to serve as an introduction to the reforms that Nehemiah instituted during his second mission in Jerusalem (vv 4–31). The part of the book of Moses read to the people is freely quoted here from Dt 23, 3–6.

13, 4–31: This is part of the "Memoirs of Nehemiah"; it is continued in Neh 10, 1–40.

13, 6: After due time: it is not known when Nehemiah returned to Jerusalem or how long his second period of activity there lasted, but it probably ended before Ezra came to Palestine; see note on Ezr 7, 1–8.

o 44f: 1 Chr 23—26; 2 Chr 8, 14. p 2 Chr 29, 30; 35, 15. q Neh 13, 10f; 10, 39; Nm 18, 26. r 1ff: Dt 23, 3–6. s Nm 22—24. t Neh 13, 23–28. u Neh 12, 44. v Neh 10, 38f; 12, 44f. 47; 2 Chr 31, 6.

kind of burden, and bringing them to Jerusalem on the sabbath day. I warned them to sell none of these victuals.[w] [16]In Jerusalem itself the Tyrians who were resident there were importing fish and every other kind of merchandise and selling it to the Judahites on the sabbath. [17]I took the nobles of Judah to task, demanding of them: "What is this evil thing that you are doing, profaning the sabbath day? [18]Did not your fathers act in this same way, with the result that our God has brought all this evil upon us and upon this city? Would you add to the wrath against Israel by once more profaning the sabbath?"

[19]When the shadows were falling on the gates of Jerusalem before the sabbath, I ordered the doors to be closed and forbade them to be reopened till after the sabbath. I posted some of my own men at the gates so that no burden might enter on the sabbath day. [20]The merchants and sellers of various kinds of merchandise spent the night once or twice outside Jerusalem, [21]but then I warned them, saying to them: "Why do you spend the night alongside the wall? If you keep this up, I will lay hands on you!" From that time on, they did not return on the sabbath. [22]Then I ordered the Levites to purify themselves and to go and watch the gates, so that the sabbath day might be kept holy. This, too, remember in my favor, O my God, and have mercy on me in accordance with your great mercy!

Mixed Marriages [23]Also in those days I saw Jews who had married Ashdodite, Ammonite, or Moabite wives.[x] [24]Of their children, half spoke Ashdodite,* and none of them knew how to speak Jewish; and so it was in regard to the languages of the various other peoples. [25]I took them to task and cursed them; I had some of them beaten and their hair pulled out; and I adjured them by God: "You shall not marry your daughters to their sons nor take any of their daughters for your sons or for yourselves! [26]Did not Solomon, the king of Israel, sin because of them? Though among the many nations there was no king like him, and though he was beloved of his God and God had made him king over all Israel, yet even he was made to sin by foreign women.[y] [27]Must it also be heard of you that you have done this same very great evil, betraying our God by marrying foreign women?"

[28]One of the sons of Joiada, son of Eliashib the high priest, was the son-in-law of Sanballat the Horonite! I drove him from my presence.[z] [29]Remember against them, O my God, how they defiled the priesthood and the covenant of the priesthood and the Levites!

[30]Thus I cleansed them of all foreign contamination. I established the various functions for the priests and Levites, so that each had his appointed task. [31]I also provided for the procurement of wood at stated times and for the first fruits. Remember this in my favor, O my God![a]

13, 24: Ashdodite: the language spoken at Ashdod, more likely an Aramaic rather than a Philistine dialect. Jewish: Hebrew as spoken in postexilic Judah.

w Neh 10, 32; Ex 20, 8. x Neh 10, 31; 13, 1ff; Dt 23, 3. y 1 Kgs 11, 1–13. z Neh 2, 10; 13, 4f. 7ff. a Neh 10, 35f.

THE BOOK OF TOBIT

The Book of Tobit, named after its principal hero, combines specifically Jewish piety and morality with oriental folklore in a fascinating story that has enjoyed wide popularity in both Jewish and Christian circles. Prayers, psalms, and words of wisdom, as well as the skillfully constructed story itself, provide valuable insights into the faith and the religious milieu of its unknown author. The book was probably written early in the second century B.C.; it is not known where.

Tobit, a devout and wealthy Israelite living among the captives deported to Nineveh, from the northern kingdom of Israel in 721 B.C., suffers severe reverses and is finally blinded. Because of his misfortunes he begs the Lord to let him die. But recalling the large sum he had formerly deposited in far-off Media, he sends his son Tobiah there to bring back the money. In Media, at this same time, a young woman, Sarah, also prays for death, because she has lost seven husbands, each killed in turn on his wedding night by the demon Asmodeus. God hears the prayers of Tobit and Sarah, and sends the angel Raphael in disguise to aid them both.

Raphael makes the trip to Media with Tobiah. When Tobiah is attacked by a large fish as he bathes, Raphael orders him to seize it and to remove its gall, heart, and liver because they make "useful medicines." Later, at Raphael's urging, Tobiah marries Sarah, and uses the fish's heart and liver to drive Asmodeus from the bridal chamber. Returning to Nineveh with his wife and his father's money, Tobiah rubs the fish's gall into his father's eyes and cures them. Finally, Raphael reveals his true identity and returns to heaven. Tobit then utters his beautiful hymn of praise. Before dying, Tobit tells his son to leave Nineveh because God will destroy that wicked city. After Tobiah buries his father and mother, he and his family depart for Media, where he later learns that the destruction of Nineveh has taken place.

The inspired author of the book used the literary form of religious novel (as in Jonah and Judith) for the purpose of instruction and edification. There may have been a historical nucleus around which the story was composed, but this possibility has nothing to do with the teaching of the book. The seemingly historical data—names of kings, cities, etc.—are used merely as vivid details to create interest and charm.

Although the Book of Tobit is usually listed with the historical books, it more correctly stands midway between them and the wisdom literature. It contains numerous maxims like those found in the wisdom books (cf 4, 3-19. 21; 12, 6-10; 14, 7.9) as well as the customary sapiential themes: fidelity to the law, the intercessory function of angels, piety toward parents, the purity of marriage, reverence for the dead, and the value of almsgiving, prayer, and fasting. The book makes Tobit a relative of *Ahiqar,* a hero of ancient Near Eastern folklore.

Written in Aramaic, the original of the book was lost for centuries. The Greek translation, existing in three different recensions, is our primary source. In 1955, fragments of the book in Aramaic and in Hebrew were recovered from Cave IV at Qumran. These texts are in substantial agreement with the Greek recension that has served as the basis for the present translation.

The divisions of the Book of Tobit are:

I. Tobit's Ordeals (1, 3—3, 6).
II. Sarah's Plight (3, 7-17).
III. Tobiah's Journey and Marriage to Sarah (4, 1—9, 6).
IV. Tobiah's Return; Cure of Tobit's Blindness (10, 1—11, 18).
V. Raphael Reveals His Identity (12, 1-22).
VI. Tobit's Song of Praise (13, 1-18).
VII. Epilogue (14, 1-15).

CHAPTER 1

Tobit 1 This book tells the story of Tobit,* son of Tobiel, son of Hananiel, son of Aduel, son of Gabael of the family of Asiel, of the tribe of Naphtali, 2 who during the reign of Shalmaneser,* king of Assyria, was taken captive

1, 1: Tobit: in the fragments of the book found at Qumran, is given as Tobi, an abbreviated form of Tobiyah (v 9; Ezr 2, 60) or of Tobiyabu (2 Chr 17, 8), a name which means "Yahweh is good." Tobiel, "God is good"; Hananiel, "God is merciful." The book abounds in theophoric names.

1, 2: Shalmaneser V (727–722 B.C.): began the siege of Samaria; the inhabitants of the northern kingdom were taken into captivity by his successor, Sargon II (722–705). Thisbe and Phogor: towns of Galilee that have not been identified; Thisbe in Gilead was perhaps the birthplace of Elijah. Kedesh: cf Jos 20, 7. Asser: Hazor (Jos 11, 1).

from Thisbe, which is south of Kedesh Naphtali
in upper Galilee, above and to the west of Asser,
north of Phogor.[a]

I: Tobit's Ordeals

His Virtue 3 I, Tobit, have walked all the days
of my life on the paths of truth and righteous-
ness. I performed many charitable works for my
kinsmen and my people who had been deported
with me to Nineveh, in Assyria. 4 When I lived as
a young man in my own country, Israel, the
entire tribe of my forefather Naphtali had broken
away from the house of David and from Jerusa-
lem. This city had been singled out of all Israel's
tribes, so that they all might offer sacrifice in the
place where the temple, God's dwelling, had
been built and consecrated for all generations to
come. 5 [b]All my kinsmen, like the rest of the
tribe of my forefather Naphtali, used to offer
sacrifice on all the mountains of Galilee as well
as to the young bull which Jeroboam, king of
Israel, had made in Dan.*

6 [c]I, for my part, would often make the
pilgrimage alone to Jerusalem for the festivals, as
is prescribed for all Israel by perpetual decree.*
Bringing with me the first fruits of the field and
the firstlings of the flock, together with a tenth
of my income and the first shearings of the
sheep,[d] I would hasten to Jerusalem 7 [e]and
present them to the priests, Aaron's sons, at the
altar. To the Levites who were doing service in
Jerusalem I would give the tithe of grain, wine,
olive oil, pomegranates, figs, and other fruits.
And except for sabbatical years, I used to give a
second tithe in money, which each year I would
go and disburse in Jerusalem. 8 The third tithe I
gave to orphans and widows, and to converts
who were living with the Israelites. Every third
year I would bring them this offering, and we ate
it in keeping with the decree of the Mosaic law
and the commands of Deborah, the mother of
my father Tobiel; for when my father died, he
left me an orphan.

9 When I reached manhood, I married Anna, a
woman of our own lineage. By her I had a son
whom I named Tobiah. 10 Now after I had been
deported to Nineveh, all my brothers and rela-
tives ate the food of heathens,[f] 11 but I refrained
from eating that kind of food. 12 Because of this
wholehearted service of God, 13 the Most High
granted me favor and status with Shalmaneser,
so that I became purchasing agent for all his
needs.[g] 14 Every now and then until his death I
would go to Media to buy goods for him. I also
deposited several pouches containing a great
sum of money* with my kinsman Gabael, son of
Gabri, who lived at Rages, in Media. 15 But when
Shalmaneser died and his son Sennacherib*
succeeded him as king, the roads to Media
became unsafe, so I could no longer go there.

Courage in Burying the Dead 16 During Shal-
maneser's reign I performed many charitable
works for my kinsmen and my people. 17 [h]I
would give my bread to the hungry and my
clothing to the naked. If I saw one of my people
who had died and been thrown outside the walls
of Nineveh, I would bury him.* 18 I also buried
anyone whom Sennacherib slew when he re-
turned as a fugitive from Judea during the days
of judgment decreed against him by the heav-
enly King because of the blasphemies he had
uttered. In his rage he killed many Israelites, but
I used to take their bodies by stealth and bury
them; so when Sennacherib looked for them, he
could not find them. 19 But a certain citizen of

1, 5: Jeroboam established sanctuaries in Dan and Bethel so that the people would no longer go to Jerusalem for the festivals. The gold statues of bulls which he placed in the sanctuaries were considered the throne of Yahweh; but the people soon came to worship the images themselves. Jeroboam also encouraged the high places or hilltop shrines (1 Kgs 12, 26–33).

1, 6ff: Perpetual decree: Dt 12, 11. 13–14. Refusing to worship at Jeroboam's shrines, the faithful Tobit continued to bring his offerings to Jerusalem; see 2 Chr 11, 16. For the various tithes, cf Nm 18, 20–32; 2 Chr 31, 4–6; Dt 14, 22–29; 26, 12f.

1, 14: A great sum of money: literally, "ten silver talents," about ten thousand dollars. Rages: modern Rai, about five miles southeast of Teheran. Media: the northwestern part of modern Iran.

1, 15: Sennacherib (705–681 B.C.): the son of Sargon (722–705 B.C.); neither was descended from Shalmaneser. Inconsistencies such as this point to the fact that the Book of Tobit is a religious novel (see Introduction; also notes on 5, 6 and 14, 15).

1, 17–18: Tobit risked his own life to bury the dead. Deprivation of burial was viewed with horror by the Jews. Cf Tb 4, 3–4; 6, 15; 14, 12–13.

a 2 Kgs 17, 3; 18, 9ff. b 1 Kgs 12, 26–32. c Ex 23, 14f. 17; 34, 23. d Dt 16, 16. e 7f: Nm 18, 12f. 24; Dt 14, 22–29; 18, 4f. f Lv 11: Dt 14, 3–21; Acts 15, 29; 1 Cor 8, 7ff. g Dn 2, 48f. h Jb 31, 16–20.

Nineveh informed the king that it was I who buried the dead. When I found out that the king knew all about me and wanted to put me to death, I went into hiding; then in my fear I took to flight. [20]Afterward, all my property was confiscated; I was left with nothing. All that I had was taken to the king's palace, except for my wife Anna and my son Tobiah.

[21]But less than forty days later the king was assassinated by two of his sons, who then escaped into the mountains of Ararat. His son Esarhaddon,* who succeeded him as king, placed Ahiqar, my brother Anael's son, in charge of all the accounts of his kingdom, so that he took control over the entire administration.[i] [22]Then Ahiqar interceded on my behalf, and I was able to return to Nineveh. For under Sennacherib, king of Assyria, Ahiqar had been chief cupbearer, keeper of the seal, administrator, and treasurer; and Esarhaddon reappointed him. He was a close relative—in fact, my nephew.

CHAPTER 2

[1]Thus under King Esarhaddon I returned to my home, and my wife Anna and my son Tobiah were restored to me. Then on our festival of Pentecost, the feast of Weeks,* a fine dinner was prepared for me, and I reclined to eat.[j] [2]The table was set for me, and when many different dishes were placed before me, I said to my son Tobiah: "My son, go out and try to find a poor man from among our kinsmen exiled here in Nineveh. If he is a sincere worshiper of God, bring him back with you, so that he can share this meal with me. Indeed, son, I shall wait for you to come back."*

[3]Tobiah went out to look for some poor kinsman of ours. When he returned he exclaimed, "Father!" I said to him, "What is it, son?" He answered, "Father, one of our people has been murdered! His body lies in the market place where he was just strangled!" [4]I sprang to my feet, leaving the dinner untouched; and I carried the dead man from the street and put him in one of the rooms, so that I might bury him after sunset. [5]Returning to my own quarters, I washed myself* and ate my food in sorrow.[k] [6]I was reminded of the oracle pronounced by the prophet Amos against Bethel:[l]

"Your festivals shall be returned into
mourning,
And all your songs into lamentation."

[7]And I wept. Then at sunset I went out, dug a grave, and buried him.

[8]The neighbors mocked me, saying to one another: "Will this man never learn! Once before he was hunted down for execution because of this very thing; yet now that he has escaped, here he is again burying the dead!"

Tobit's Blindness [9]That same night I bathed, and went to sleep next to the wall of my courtyard. Because of the heat I left my face uncovered. [10]I did not know there were birds perched on the wall above me, till their warm droppings settled in my eyes, causing cataracts.* I went to see some doctors for a cure, but the more they anointed my eyes with various salves, the worse the cataracts became, until I could see no more. For four years I was deprived of eyesight, and all my kinsmen were grieved at my condition. Ahiqar, however, took care of me for two years, until he left for Elymais.

[11]At that time my wife Anna worked for hire at weaving cloth, the kind of work women do. [12]When she sent back the goods to their owners,

1, 21: Esarhaddon: 681–669 B.C. Ahiqar: a hero of ancient folklore, known for his outstanding wisdom. The Story (or Wisdom) of Ahiqar was very popular in antiquity and is extant in many different forms: Aramaic, Syriac, Armenian, Arabic (Arabian Nights), Greek (Aesop's Fables), Slavonic, Ethiopic, and Romanian. The sacred author makes Tobit the uncle of the famous Ahiqar in order to enhance Tobit's own prestige. See note on Tb 14, 10.

2, 1: The feast of Weeks: also called by its Greek name Pentecost, was celebrated fifty days after the Passover. Cf Lv 23, 15–21; Dt 16, 9–12.

2, 2: Almsgiving and charity to the poor are important virtues taught by the book (Tb 4, 7–11. 16f; 12, 8f; 14, 10f).

2, 5: I washed myself: because of ritual defilement from touching a corpse (Nm 19, 11–13).

2, 10: Cataracts: literally, "white scales, or films." Elymais: the Greek name of ancient Elam, a district northeast of the head of the Persian Gulf.

i 2 Kgs 19, 37; 2 Chr 32, 21; Sir 48, 21; Is 37, 38; 2 Mc 8, 19. j Lv 23, 15–21; Nm 28, 26–31; Dt 16, 9–12. k Nm 19, 11–22. l Am 8, 10; 1 Mc 1, 39.

they would pay her. Late in winter* she finished
the cloth and sent it back to the owners. They
paid her the full salary, and also gave her a young
goat for the table. 13 On entering my house the
goat began to bleat. I called to my wife and said:
"Where did this goat come from? Perhaps it was
stolen! Give it back to its owners; we have no
right to eat stolen food!" 14 [m]But she said to me,
"It was given to me as a bonus over and above
my wages." Yet I would not believe her; and told
her to give it back to its owners. I became very
angry with her over this. So she retorted:
"Where are your charitable deeds now? Where
are your virtuous acts? See! Your true character
is finally showing itself!"*

CHAPTER 3

1 Grief-stricken in spirit, I groaned and wept aloud. Then with sobs I began to pray:

Tobit's Prayer for Death

2 "You are righteous, O Lord,
and all your deeds are just;
All your ways are mercy and truth;
you are the judge of the world. [n]
3 And now, O Lord, may you be mindful of me,
and look with favor upon me.
Punish me not for my sins,
nor for my inadvertent offenses,
nor for those of my fathers. [o]

"They sinned against you,
4 and disobeyed your commandments.
So you handed us over to plundering, exile,
and death,
till we were an object lesson, a byword, a
reproach
in all the nations among whom you
scattered us. [p]

5 "Yes, your judgments are many and true
in dealing with me as my sins
and those of my fathers deserve.
For we have not kept your commandments,
nor have we trodden the paths of truth
before you.

6 "So now, deal with me as you please,
and command my life breath to be taken
from me,
that I may go from the face of the earth into
dust.
It is better for me to die than to live,*
because I have heard insulting calumnies,
and I am overwhelmed with grief. [q]

"Lord, command me to be delivered from such
anguish;
let me go to the everlasting abode;
Lord, refuse me not.
For it is better for me to die
than to endure so much misery in life,
and to hear these insults!"

II: Sarah's Plight

Sarah Falsely Accused 7 *On the same day, at
Ecbatana in Media, it so happened that Raguel's
daughter Sarah also had to listen to abuse, from
one of her father's maids. 8 For she had been
married to seven husbands, but the wicked
demon Asmodeus* killed them off before they
could have intercourse with her, as it is pre-
scribed for wives. So the maid said to her: "You
are the one who strangles your husbands! Look
at you! You have already been married seven
times, but you have had no joy with any one of
your husbands. 9 Why do you beat us? Because
your husbands are dead? Then why not join

2, 12: Late in winter: literally, "seventh of Dystros," the Macedonian month which corresponds to the Jewish month of Shebat (January–February). For the table: literally, "for the hearth"; the gift had probably been made in view of some springtime festival like the Jewish Purim.

2, 14: Anna's sharp rebuke calls to mind the words of Job's wife (Jb 2, 9).

3, 6: It is better for me to die than to live: in his distress Tobit uses the words of the petulant Jonah (Jon 4, 3. 8), who wished to die because God did not destroy the hated Ninevites. In similar circumstances, Moses (Nm 11, 15), Elijah (1 Kgs 19, 4), and Job (Jb 7, 15) also prayed for death. Everlasting abode: a reference to Sheol, the dismal abode of the dead from which no one returns (Jb 7, 9–10; 14, 12; Is 26, 14). The revelation of a blessed immortality had not yet been made. See note on Tb 4, 6.

3, 7: From here on, the story is told in the third person. V 7 relates one of the several marvelous coincidences which the storyteller uses to heighten interest; see also vv 16. 17; 4, 1; 5, 4. Ecbatana: Hamadan in modern Iran; this was the capital of ancient Media. Raguel: "friend of God."

3, 8: Asmodeus: in Persian aeshma daeva, "demon of wrath," adopted into Aramaic with the sense of "the Destroyer." He will be subdued (Tb 8, 3) by Raphael (v 17), "God heals."

m Jb 2, 9. n Pss 25, 10; 119, 137; Dn 3, 27. o Ex 34, 7. p Dt 28, 15; Bar 1, 16–22; 2, 4f; 3, 8; Dn 9, 5f. q Nm 11, 15; 1 Kgs 19, 4; Jb 7, 15; Jon 4, 3. 8.

them! May we never see a son or daughter of yours!"

10 That day she was deeply grieved in spirit. She went in tears to an upstairs room in her father's house with the intention of hanging herself. But she reconsidered, saying to herself: "No! People would level this insult against my father: 'You had only one beloved daughter, but she hanged herself because of ill fortune!' And thus would I cause my father in his old age to go down to the nether world laden with sorrow. It is far better for me not to hang myself, but to beg the Lord to have me die, so that I need no longer live to hear such insults."[r]

11 At that time, then, she spread out her hands, and facing the window,* poured out this prayer:

Sarah's Prayer for Death

"Blessed are you, O Lord, merciful God!
Forever blessed and honored is your holy name;
may all your works forever bless you.[s]
12 And now, O Lord, to you I turn my face
and raise my eyes.
13 Bid me to depart from the earth,
never again to hear such insults.

14 "You know, O Master, that I am innocent
of any impure act with a man,
15 And that I have never defiled my own name
or my father's name in the land of my exile.
"I am my father's only daughter,
and he has no other child to make his heir,
Nor does he have a close kinsman or other relative
whom I might bide my time to marry.
I have already lost seven husbands;
why then should I live any longer?
But if it please you, Lord, not to slay me,
look favorably upon me and have pity on me;
never again let me hear these insults!"

An Answer to Prayer 16 At that very time, the prayer of these two suppliants was heard in the glorious presence of Almighty God. 17 [t]So Raphael was sent to heal them both: to remove the cataracts from Tobit's eyes, so that he might again see God's sunlight; and to marry Raguel's daughter Sarah to Tobit's son Tobiah, and then drive the wicked demon Asmodeus from her. For Tobiah had the right* to claim her before any other who might wish to marry her.

In the very moment that Tobit returned from the courtyard to his house, Raguel's daughter Sarah came downstairs from her room.*

III: Tobiah's Journey and Marriage to Sarah

CHAPTER 4

A Father's Instruction 1 That same day Tobit remembered the money he had deposited with Gabael at Rages in Media, and he thought, 2 "Now that I have asked for death, why should I not call my son Tobiah and let him know about this money before I die?" 3 So he called his son Tobiah; and when he came, he said to him:* "My son, when I die, give me a decent burial. Honor your mother, and do not abandon her as long as she lives. Do whatever pleases her, and do not grieve her spirit in any way.[u] 4 Remember, my son, that she went through many trials for your sake while you were in her womb. And when she dies, bury her in the same grave with me.

5 "Through all your days, my son, keep the Lord in mind, and suppress every desire to sin or to break his commandments. Perform good

3, 11: Facing the window: that is, looking toward Jerusalem; cf Dn 6, 11. Blessed are you and "Blessed be God" are traditional openings of Jewish prayers (Tb 8, 5, 15; 11, 14; 13, 1).

3, 17: Tobiah had the right: according to the patriarchal custom of marriage within the family group. Tobiah was Sarah's closest eligible relative (Tb 6, 12). Cf Tb 4, 12–13; Gn 24.

4, 3–19: A collection of maxims which parallel those in the wisdom literature, especially Prv and Sir (see Introduction): duties toward parents (3–4); cf also Tb 14, 13; perseverance in virtue and avoidance of evil (5–6. 14b); necessity and value of almsgiving and charity (7–11. 16–17); marriage to a kinsman (12–13a); industry (13b); prompt payment of wages (14a); the golden rule (15a); temperance (15b); docility (18); prayer (19).

r Tb 6, 15; Gn 37, 35; 42, 38; 44, 29. 31. s 1 Kgs 8, 44, 48; Pss 28, 2; 134, 2; Dn 6, 11. t Tb 4, 12f; 6, 12f; Gn 24, 3f. u Ex 20, 12; Prv 23, 22; Sir 7, 27.

works all the days of your life, and do not tread
the paths of wrongdoing. 6 [v]For if you are stead-
fast in your service, your good works will bring
success, not only to you, but also to all those
who live uprightly.*

7 "Give alms from your possessions. Do not
turn your face away from any of the poor, and
God's face will not be turned away from you.[w]
8 Son, give alms in proportion to what you own.
If you have great wealth, give alms out of your
abundance; if you have but little, distribute even
some of that. But do not hesitate to give alms;
9 you will be storing up a goodly treasure for
yourself against the day of adversity.[x]
10 Almsgiving frees one from death, and keeps
one from going into the dark abode. 11 Alms are a
worthy offering in the sight of the Most High for
all who give them.[y]

12 "Be on your guard, son, against every form
of immorality, and above all, marry a woman of
the lineage of your forefathers. Do not marry a
stranger who is not of your father's tribe, be-
cause we are sons of the prophets. My boy, keep
in mind Noah, Abraham, Isaac, and Jacob, our
fathers from of old: all of them took wives from
among their own kinsmen and were blessed in
their children. Remember that their posterity
shall inherit the land.[z] 13 Therefore, my son, love
your kinsmen. Do not be so proudhearted to-
ward your kinsmen, the sons and daughters of
your people, as to refuse to take a wife for
yourself from among them. For in such arro-
gance there is ruin and great disorder. Likewise,
in worthlessness there is decay and dire poverty,
for worthlessness is the mother of famine.

14 "Do not keep with you overnight the wages
of any man who works for you, but pay him
immediately. If you thus behave as God's ser-
vant, you will receive your reward. Keep a close
watch on yourself, my son, in everything you do,
and discipline yourself in all your conduct.[a]
15 Do to no one what you yourself dislike. Do not
drink wine till you become drunk, nor let
drunkenness accompany you on your way.[b]

16 [c]"Give to the hungry some of your bread,
and to the naked some of your clothing. What-
ever you have left over, give away as alms; and
do not begrudge the alms you give. 17 [d]Be lavish
with your bread and wine at the burial of the
virtuous, but do not share them with sinners.*

18 "Seek counsel from every wise man, and do
not think lightly of any advice that can be useful.
19 [e]At all times bless the Lord God, and ask him
to make all your paths straight and to grant
success to all your endeavors and plans. For no
pagan nation possesses good counsel, but the
Lord himself gives all good things. If the Lord
chooses, he raises a man up; but if he should
decide otherwise, he casts him down to the
deepest recesses of the nether world. So now,
my son, keep in mind my commandments, and
never let them be erased from your heart.*

20 "And now, son, I wish to inform you that I
have deposited a great sum of money with
Gabri's son Gabael at Rages in Media. 21 Do not
be discouraged, my child, because of our pov-
erty. You will be a rich man if you fear God,
avoid all sin, and do what is right before the Lord
your God."[f]

CHAPTER 5

The Angel Raphael 1 Then Tobiah replied to
his father Tobit: "Everything that you have
commanded me, father, I will do. 2 But how
shall I be able to obtain the money from him,
since he does not know me nor do I know him?
What can I show him to make him recognize
me and trust me, so that he will give me the
money? I do not even know which roads to
take for the journey into Media!" 3 Tobit an-

4, 6: Before the revelation of retribution for all men in the afterlife—a doctrine taught in the Book of Wisdom—Old Testament man believed that virtue guaranteed earthly prosperity, and sin earthly disaster (cf Dt 28).

4, 17: Tobit counsels his son either to give alms in honor of the dead, or, more probably, to give the "bread of consolation" to the family of the deceased. Cf Jer 16, 7; Ez 24, 17.

4, 19: Prayer is the foundation of a moral life.

v Tb 13, 6; Jn 3, 21; Eph 4, 15. w 7f: Tb 12, 8ff; Dt 15, 7f. 11; Prv 19, 17; Sir 4, 1–6; 14, 13; Lk 14, 13; 1 Jn 3, 17. x Mt 6, 20f. y Sir 3, 30; 29, 12. z Tb 3, 15. 17; 6, 12; Gn 11, 29. 31; 25, 20; 28, 1–4; 29, 15–30; Ex 34, 16; Dt 7, 3; Jgs 14, 3. a Lv 19, 13; Dt 24, 15. b Mt 7, 12; Lk 6, 31. c Dt 15, 10; Is 58, 7; Mt 25, 35f; 2 Cor 9, 7. d Jer 16, 7; Lk 14, 13. e Dt 4, 6; Ps 119, 10. f 1 Tm 6, 6ff.

swered his son Tobiah: "We exchanged signatures on a document* written in duplicate; I divided it into two parts, and each of us kept one; his copy I put with the money. Think of it, twenty years have already passed since I deposited that money! So now, my son, find yourself a trustworthy man who will make the journey with you. We will, of course, give him a salary when you return; but get back that money from Gabael."

4 Tobiah went to look for someone acquainted with the roads who would travel with him to Media. As soon as he went out, he found the angel Raphael standing before him, though he did not know* that this was an angel of God.[g] 5 Tobiah said to him, "Who are you, young man?" He replied, "I am an Israelite, one of your kinsmen. I have come here to work." Tobiah said, "Do you know the way to Media?" 6 The other replied: "Yes, I have been there many times. I know the place well and I know all the routes. I have often traveled to Media; I used to stay with our kinsman Gabael, who lives at Rages in Media. It is a good two days' travel from Ecbatana to Rages,* for Rages is situated at the mountains, Ecbatana out on the plateau." 7 Tobiah said to him, "Wait for me, young man, till I go back and tell my father; for I need you to make the journey with me. I will, of course, pay you."[h] 8 Raphael replied, "Very well, I will wait for you; but do not be long."

9 Tobiah went back to tell his father Tobit what had happened. He said to him, "I have just found a man who is one of our own Israelite kinsmen!" Tobit said, "Call the man, so that I may find out what family and tribe he comes from, and whether he is trustworthy enough to travel with you, son." Tobiah went out to summon the man saying, "Young man, my father would like to see you."

10 When Raphael entered the house, Tobit greeted him first. Raphael said, "Hearty greetings* to you!" Tobit replied: "What joy is left for me any more? Here I am, a blind man who cannot see God's sunlight, but must remain in darkness, like the dead who no longer see the light! Though alive, I am among the dead. I can hear a man's voice, but I cannot see him." Raphael said, "Take courage! God has healing in store for you; so take courage!" Tobit then said: "My son Tobiah wants to go to Media. Can you go with him to show him the way? I will of course pay you, brother." Raphael answered: "Yes, I can go with him, for I know all the routes. I have often traveled to Media and crossed all its plains and mountains; so I know every road well." 11 Tobit asked, "Brother, tell me, please, what family and tribe are you from?" 12 Raphael said: "Why? Do you need a tribe and a family? Or are you looking for a hired man to travel with your son?" Tobit replied, "I wish to know truthfully whose son you are, brother, and what your name is."[i]

13 Raphael answered, "I am Azariah,* son of Hananiah the elder, one of your own kinsmen." 14 Tobit exclaimed: "Welcome! God save you, brother! Do not be provoked with me, brother, for wanting to learn the truth about your family. So it turns out that you are a kinsman, and from a noble and good line! I knew Hananiah and Nathaniah, the two sons of Shemaiah the elder; with me they used to make the pilgrimage to Jerusalem, where we would worship together. No, they did not stray from the right path; your kinsmen are good men. You are certainly of good lineage, and welcome!"

5, 3: Document: in Greek cheirographon. In the Middle Ages, notably in England, a deed and its duplicate were written on one piece of parchment, with the Latin word chirographum inscribed across the top of the sheet or between the two copies of the text. The document was then cut in two in either a straight or a wavy line, the parts being given to the persons concerned. Perhaps this procedure derived from the present verse of Tobit. Duplicate documents, usually one open and the other sealed, are well known from the ancient Near East.

5, 4: He did not know: the theme of an angel in disguise occurs frequently in folklore as well as in the Old Testament (Gn 18; cf Heb 13, 2).

5, 6: It is a good two days' travel from Echatana to Rages: Alexander's army took eleven days in forced marches to cover this distance, about 180 miles. The author is merely using popular impressions about faraway places; he is not teaching geography. (See notes on Tb 1, 15; 3, 7 and Introduction.)

5, 10: Hearty greetings and what joy form a wordplay on the Greek verb chairein, "to greet" and "to be joyful."

5, 13–14: Azariah, "Yahweh helps"; Hananiah, "Yahweh is merciful"; Nathaniah, "Yahweh gives"; Shemaiah, "Yahweh hears."

g Heb 13, 2. h Tb 12, 2. i Jgs 13, 17f.

15 Then he added: “For each day you are away I will give you the normal wages,* plus expenses for you and for my son. If you go with my son, 16 I will even add a bonus to your wages!” Raphael replied: “I will go with him; have no fear. In good health we shall leave you, and in good health we shall return to you, for the way is safe.” 17 Tobit said, “God bless you, brother.” Then he called his son and said to him: “My son, prepare whatever you need for the journey, and set out with your kinsman. May God in heaven protect you on the way and bring you back to me safe and sound; and may his angel accompany you for safety, my son.”

Before setting out on his journey, Tobiah kissed his father and mother. Tobit said to him, “Have a safe journey.” 18 But his mother began to weep. She said to Tobit: “Why have you decided to send my child away? Is he not the staff to which we cling, ever there with us in all that we do? 19 I hope more money is not your chief concern! Rather let it be a ransom for our son! 20 What the Lord has given us to live on is certainly enough for us.” 21 Tobit reassured her: “Have no such thought. Our son will leave in good health and come back to us in good health. Your own eyes will see the day when he returns to you safe and sound. 22 So, no such thought; do not worry about them, my love.* For a good angel will go with him, his journey will be successful, and he will return unharmed.” 1 Then she stopped weeping.*

CHAPTER 6

Journey to Rages 2 When the boy left home, accompanied by the angel, the dog followed Tobiah out of the house and went with him. The travelers walked till nightfall, and made camp beside the Tigris River. 3 Now when the boy went down to wash his feet in the river, a large fish suddenly leaped out of the water and tried to swallow his foot. He shouted in alarm. 4 But the angel said to him, “Take hold of the fish and don’t let it get away!” The boy seized the fish and hauled it up on the shore. 5 The angel then told him: “Cut the fish open and take out its gall, heart, and liver, and keep them with you; but throw away the entrails. Its gall, heart, and liver make useful medicines.”* 6 After the lad had cut the fish open, he put aside the gall, heart, and liver. Then he broiled and ate part of the fish; the rest he salted and kept for the journey.

Raphael’s Instructions 7 Afterward they traveled on together till they were near Media. The boy asked the angel this question: “Brother Azariah, what medicinal value is there in the fish’s heart, liver, and gall?” 8 He answered: “As regards the fish’s heart and liver, if you burn them so that the smoke surrounds a man or a woman who is afflicted by a demon or evil spirit, the affliction will leave him completely, and no demons will ever return to him again. 9 And as for the gall, if you rub it on the eyes of a man who has cataracts, blowing into his eyes right on the cataracts, his sight will be restored.”

10 When they had entered Media and were getting close to Ecbatana, 11 Raphael said to the boy, “Brother Tobiah!” He answered, “Yes, what is it?” Raphael continued: “Tonight we must stay with Raguel, who is a relative of yours. He has a daughter named Sarah, 12 but no other child. Since you are Sarah’s closest relative, you before all other men have the right to marry her. Also, her father’s estate is rightfully yours to inherit. Now the girl is sensible, courageous, and very beautiful; and her father loves her dearly.”[j] 13 He continued: “Since you have the right to marry her, listen to me, brother. Tonight I will ask the girl’s father to let us have her as your bride. When we return from Rages, we will hold the wedding feast for her. I know that Raguel cannot keep her from you or let her become engaged to another man; that would be

5, 15: The normal wages: literally, “a drachma,” about seventeen cents, a day’s wage for a workingman.

5, 22: My love: literally, “sister,” a term of endearment applied to one’s wife; cf Tb 7, 11. 15; 8, 4. 21; 10, 6. 13; Song 4, 9. 10. 12; 5, 1f. A good angel: a reference to the guardian angel, though Tobit does not know, of course, that Raphael himself, disguised as Azariah, is the good angel in this case.

5, 1: Then . . . weeping: this verse belongs to ch 6.

6, 5: Its gall . . . medicines: belief in the healing power of these organs was common among even the physicians of antiquity.

j Tb 4, 12f; Nm 36, 8.

a capital crime according to the decree in the Book of Moses,* and he knows that it is your right, before all other men, to marry his daughter. So heed my words, brother; tonight we must speak for the girl, so that we may have her engaged to you. And when we return from Rages, we will take her and bring her back with us to your house."

14Tobiah objected, however: "Brother Azariah, I have heard that this woman has already been married seven times, and that her husbands died in their bridal chambers. On the very night they approached her, they dropped dead. And I have heard it said that it was a demon who killed them. 15So now I too am afraid of this demon. Because he loves her, he does not harm her; but he does slay any man who wishes to come close to her. I am my father's only child. If I should die, I would bring my father and mother down to their grave in sorrow over me. And they have no other son to bury them!"[k]

16Raphael said to him: "Do you not remember your father's orders? He commanded you to marry a woman from your own family. So now listen to me, brother; do not give another thought to this demon, but marry Sarah. I know that tonight you shall have her for your wife! 17When you go into the bridal chamber, take the fish's liver and heart, and place them on the embers for the incense. 18As soon as the demon smells the odor they give off, he will flee and never again show himself near her. Then when you are about to have intercourse with her, both of you first rise up to pray.* Beg the Lord of heaven to show you mercy and grant you deliverance. But do not be afraid, for she was set apart for you before the world existed. You will save her, and she will go with you. And I suppose that you will have children by her, who will take the place of brothers for you. So do not worry."

When Tobiah heard Raphael say that she was his kinswoman, of his own family's lineage, he fell deeply in love with her, and his heart became set on her.

CHAPTER 7

At the House of Raguel 1When they entered Ecbatana, Tobiah said, "Brother Azariah, lead me straight to our kinsman Raguel." So he brought him to the house of Raguel, whom they found seated by his courtyard gate. They greeted him first. He said to them, "Greetings to you too, brothers! Good health to you, and welcome!" When he brought them into his home, 2he said to his wife Edna, "This young man looks just like my kinsman Tobit!" 3So Edna asked them, "Who are you, brothers?" They answered, "We are of the exiles from Naphtali at Nineveh." 4She said, "Do you know our kinsman Tobit?" They answered, "Indeed we do!" She asked, "Is he well?" 5They answered, "Yes, he is alive and well." Then Tobiah exclaimed, "He is my father!" 6Raguel sprang up and kissed him, shedding tears of joy. 7But when he heard that Tobit had lost his eyesight, he was grieved and wept aloud. He said to Tobiah: "My child, God bless you! You are the son of a noble and good father. But what a terrible misfortune that such a righteous and charitable man should be afflicted with blindness!" He continued to weep in the arms of his kinsman Tobiah. 8His wife Edna also wept for Tobit; and even their daughter Sarah began to weep.

Marriage of Tobiah and Sarah 9Afterward, Raguel slaughtered a ram from the flock and gave them a cordial reception. When they had bathed and reclined to eat, Tobiah said to Raphael, "Brother Azariah, ask Raguel to let me marry my kinswoman Sarah." 10Raguel overheard the words; so he said to the boy: "Eat and drink and be merry tonight, for no man is more entitled to marry my daughter Sarah than you, brother. Besides, not even I have the right to give her to anyone but you, because you are my closest relative. But I will explain the situation to you very frankly. 11I have given her in marriage to seven men, all of whom were kinsmen of ours, and all died on the very night they approached her. But now, son, eat and drink. I am sure the Lord will look after you both." Tobiah

6, 13: Raguel . . . Book of Moses: Nm 36, 6–8 prescribed marriage within the ancestral tribe, but no death penalty is mentioned.

6, 18: Rise up to pray: prayer is needed to drive out the demon.

k Tb 3, 10.

answered, "I will eat or drink nothing until you set aside what belongs to me."

Raguel said to him: "I will do it. She is yours according to the decree of the Book of Moses. Your marriage to her has been decided in heaven! Take your kinswoman; from now on you are her love, and she is your beloved. She is yours today and ever after. And tonight, son, may the Lord of heaven prosper you both. May he grant you mercy and peace." [12]Then Raguel called his daughter Sarah, and she came to him. He took her by the hand and gave her to Tobiah with the words: "Take her according to the law. According to the decree written in the Book of Moses she is your wife. Take her and bring her back safely to your father. And may the God of heaven grant both of you peace and prosperity." [l] [13]He then called her mother and told her to bring a scroll, so that he might draw up a marriage contract stating that he gave Sarah to Tobiah as his wife according to the decree of the Mosaic law. Her mother brought the scroll, and he drew up the contract, to which they affixed their seals. [m]

[14]Afterward they began to eat and drink. [15]Later Raguel called his wife Edna and said, "My love, prepare the other bedroom and bring the girl there." [16]She went and made the bed in the room, as she was told, and brought the girl there. After she had cried over her, she wiped away the tears and said: [17]"Be brave, my daughter. May the Lord of heaven grant you joy in place of your grief. Courage, my daughter." Then she left.

CHAPTER 8

Expulsion of the Demon [1]When they had finished eating and drinking, the girl's parents wanted to retire. They brought the young man out of the dining room and led him into the bedroom. [2]At this point Tobiah, mindful of Raphael's instructions, took the fish's liver and heart from the bag which he had with him, and placed them on the embers for the incense.* [3]The demon, repelled by the odor of the fish, fled into Upper Egypt;* Raphael pursued him there and bound him hand and foot. Then Raphael returned immediately.

[4]When the girl's parents left the bedroom and closed the door behind them, Tobiah arose from bed and said to his wife, "My love, get up. Let us pray and beg our Lord to have mercy on us and to grant us deliverance." [5]She got up, and they started to pray and beg that deliverance might be theirs. He began with these words:

"Blessed are you, O God of our fathers;
praised be your name forever and ever.
Let the heavens and all your creation
praise you forever. [n]
[6]You made Adam and you gave him his wife Eve
to be his help and support;
and from these two the human race descended.
You said, 'It is not good for the man to be alone;
let us make him a partner like himself.' [o]
[7]Now, Lord, you know that I take this wife of mine
not because of lust,
but for a noble purpose.
Call down your mercy on me and on her,
and allow us to live together to a happy old age."

[8]They said together, "Amen, amen," [9]and went to bed for the night.

But Raguel got up and summoned his servants. With him they went out to dig a grave, [10]for he said, "I must do this, because if Tobiah should die, we would be subjected to ridicule and insult." [11]When they had finished digging the grave, Raguel went back into the house and called his wife, [12]saying, "Send one of the maids in to see whether Tobiah is alive or dead, so that

8, 2f: The manner of coping with demonic influences among the ancients seems quaint to us. However, the fish here is part of the story, and not a recipe for exorcism. It is clear that the author places primary emphasis on the value of prayer to God (Tb 6, 18; 8, 4–8), on the role of the angel as God's agent, and on the pious dispositions of Tobiah.

8, 3: Into Upper Egypt: to the desert there. The desert was considered the dwelling place of demons. Cf Is 13, 21; 34, 14; Mt 4, 1; 12, 43.

l Gn 24, 50f. m Tb 6, 12. n Dn 3, 26. o Gn 2, 18–23.

if necessary we may bury him without anyone's knowing about it." [13]She sent the maid, who lit a lamp, opened the bedroom door, went in, and found them sound asleep together. [14]The maid went out and told the girl's parents that Tobiah was alive, and that there was nothing wrong. [15]Then Raguel praised the God of heaven in these words:

"Blessed are you, O God, with every holy and
pure blessing!
Let all your chosen ones praise you;
let them bless you forever!
[16]Blessed are you, who have made me glad;
what I feared did not happen.
Rather you have dealt with us
according to your great mercy.
[17]Blessed are you, for you were merciful
toward two only children.
Grant them, Master, mercy and deliverance,
and bring their lives to fulfillment
with happiness and mercy."

[18]Then he told his servants to fill in the grave before dawn.

Wedding Feast [19]He asked his wife to bake many loaves of bread; he himself went out to the herd and picked out two steers and four rams which he ordered to be slaughtered. So the servants began to prepare the feast. [20]He summoned Tobiah and made an oath in his presence, saying: "For fourteen days* you shall not stir from here, but shall remain here eating and drinking with me; and you shall bring joy to my daughter's sorrowing spirit. [21]Take, to begin with, half of whatever I own when you go back in good health to your father; the other half will be yours when I and my wife die. Be of good cheer, my son! I am your father, and Edna is your mother; and we belong to you and to your beloved now and forever. So be happy, son!"

CHAPTER 9

The Money Recovered [1]Then Tobiah called Raphael and said to him: [2]"Brother Azariah, take along with you four servants and two camels and travel to Rages. Go to Gabael's house and give him this bond. Get the money and then bring him along with you to the wedding celebration. [4]For you know that my father is counting the days. If I should delay my return by a single day, I would cause him intense grief. [3]You witnessed the oath that Raguel has sworn; I cannot violate his oath." [5]So Raphael, together with the four servants and two camels, traveled to Rages in Media, where they stayed at Gabael's house. Raphael gave Gabael his bond and told him about Tobit's son Tobiah, and that he had married and was inviting him to the wedding celebration. Gabael promptly checked over the sealed moneybags, and they placed them on the camels.

[6]The following morning they got an early start and traveled to the wedding celebration. When they entered Raguel's house, they found Tobiah reclining at table. He sprang up and greeted Gabael, who wept and blessed him, exclaiming: "O noble and good child, son of a noble and good, upright and charitable man, may the Lord grant heavenly blessing to you and to your wife, and to your wife's father and mother. Blessed be God, because I have seen the very image of my cousin Tobit!"

IV: Tobiah's Return; Cure of Tobit's Blindness

CHAPTER 10

Anxiety of the Parents [1]Meanwhile, day by day, Tobit was keeping track of the time Tobiah would need to go and to return. When the number of days was reached and his son did not appear, [2]he said, "I wonder what has happened. Perhaps he has been detained there; or perhaps Gabael is dead, and there is no one to give him the money." [3]And he began to worry. [4]His wife Anna said, "My son has perished and is no longer among the living!" And she began to weep aloud and to wail over her son: [5]"Alas, my child, light of my eyes, that I let you make this journey!" [6]But Tobit kept telling her: "Hush, do not think about it, my love; he is safe! Probably

8, 20: For fourteen days: because of the happy, and unexpected, turn of events, Raguel doubles the time of the wedding feast. When Tobiah returns home, the usual seven-day feast is held (Tb 11, 18). Cf Jgs 14, 12.

they have to take care of some unexpected business there. The man who is traveling with him is trustworthy, and is one of our own kinsmen. So do not worry over him, my love. He will be here soon." 7But she retorted, "Stop it, and do not lie to me! My child has perished!" She would go out and keep watch all day at the road her son had taken, and she ate nothing. At sunset she would go back home to wail and cry the whole night through, getting no sleep at all.[p]

Departure from Ecbatana Now at the end of the fourteen-day wedding celebration which Raguel had sworn to hold for his daughter, Tobiah went to him and said: "Please let me go, for I know that my father and mother do not believe they will ever see me again. So I beg you, father, let me go back to my father. I have already told you how I left him." 8Raguel said to Tobiah: "Stay, my child, stay with me. I am sending messengers to your father Tobit, and they will give him news of you." 9But Tobiah insisted, "No, I beg you to let me go back to my father."

10Raguel then promptly handed over to Tobiah Sarah his wife, together with half of all his property: male and female slaves, oxen and sheep, asses and camels, clothing, money, and household goods. 11Bidding them farewell, he let them go. He embraced Tobiah and said to him: "Good-bye, my son. Have a safe journey. May the Lord of heaven grant prosperity to you and to your wife Sarah. And may I see children of yours before I die!" 12Then he kissed his daughter Sarah and said to her: "My daughter, honor your father-in-law and your mother-in-law, because from now on they are as much your parents as the ones who brought you into the world. Go in peace, my daughter; let me hear good reports about you as long as I live." Finally he said good-bye to them and sent them away.

13Then Edna said to Tobiah: "My child and beloved kinsman, may the Lord bring you back safely, and may I live long enough to see children of you and of my daughter Sarah before I die. Before the Lord, I entrust my daughter to your care. Never cause her grief at any time in your life. Go in peace, my child. From now on I am your mother, and Sarah is your beloved. May all of us be prosperous all the days of our lives." She kissed them both and sent them away in peace.

14When Tobiah left Raguel, he was full of happiness and joy, and he blessed the Lord of heaven and earth, the King of all, for making his journey so successful. Finally he said good-bye to Raguel and his wife Edna, and added, "May I honor you all the days of my life!"

CHAPTER 11

Homeward Journey 1Then they left and began their return journey. When they were near Kaserin, just before Nineveh, 2Raphael said: "You know how we left your father. 3Let us hurry on ahead of your wife to prepare the house while the rest of the party are still on the way." 4So they both went on ahead and Raphael said to Tobiah, "Have the gall in your hand!" And the dog ran along behind them.

5Meanwhile, Anna sat watching the road by which her son was to come. 6When she saw him coming, she exclaimed to his father, "Tobit, your son is coming, and the man who traveled with him!"

7Raphael said to Tobiah before he reached his father: "I am certain that his eyes will be opened. 8Smear the fish gall on them. This medicine will make the cataracts shrink and peel off from his eyes; then your father will again be able to see the light of day."

Sight Restored 9Then Anna ran up to her son, threw her arms around him, and said to him, "Now that I have seen you again, son, I am ready to die!" And she sobbed aloud.[q] 10Tobit got up and stumbled out through the courtyard gate. Tobiah went up to him 11with the fish gall in his hand, and holding him firmly, blew into his eyes. "Courage, father," he said. 12Next he smeared the medicine on his eyes, 13and it made them smart. Then, beginning at the corners of Tobit's eyes, Tobiah used both hands to peel off the cataracts. When Tobit saw his son, he threw his arms around him 14and wept. He exclaimed, "I can see you, son, the light of my eyes!" Then he said:

p Gn 45, 26. q Gn 33, 4; 45, 14; 46, 29f; Lk 15, 20.

"Blessed be God,
  and praised be his great name,
  and blessed be all his holy angels.
May his holy name be praised
  throughout all the ages,
15 Because it was he who scourged me,
  and it is he who has had mercy on me.
  Behold, I now see my son Tobiah!"

Then Tobit went back in, rejoicing and praising
God with full voice. Tobiah told his father that
his journey had been a success; that he had
brought back the money; and that he had
married Raguel's daughter Sarah, who would
arrive shortly, for she was approaching the gate
of Nineveh.[r]
16 Rejoicing and praising God, Tobit went out
to the gate of Nineveh to meet his daughter-in-
law. When the people of Nineveh saw him
walking along briskly, with no one leading him
by the hand, they were amazed. 17 Before them
all Tobit proclaimed how God had mercifully
restored sight to his eyes. When Tobit reached
Sarah, the wife of his son Tobiah, he greeted her:
"Welcome, my daughter! Blessed be your God
for bringing you to us, daughter! Blessed are
your father and your mother. Blessed is my son
Tobiah, and blessed are you, daughter! Welcome
to your home with blessing and joy. Come in,
daughter!" That day there was joy for all the
Jews who lived in Nineveh. 18 Ahiqar and his
nephew Nadab also came to rejoice with Tobit.
They celebrated Tobiah's wedding feast for
seven happy days, and he received many gifts.

V: Raphael Reveals His Identity

CHAPTER 12

Raphael's Wages* 1 When the wedding cele-
bration came to an end, Tobit called his son
Tobiah and said to him, "Son, see to it that you
give what is due to the man who made the
journey with you; give him a bonus too."
2 Tobiah said: "Father, how much shall I pay
him? It would not hurt me at all to give him half
of all the wealth he brought back with me.[s] 3 He
led me back safe and sound; he cured my wife;
he brought the money back with me; and he
cured you. How much of a bonus should I give
him?" 4 Tobit answered, "It is only fair, son, that
he should receive half of all that he brought
back." 5 So Tobiah called Raphael and said, "Take
as your wages half of all that you have brought
back, and go in peace."
Exhortation* 6 Raphael called the two men
aside privately and said to them: "Thank God!
Give him the praise and the glory. Before all the
living, acknowledge the many good things he has
done for you, by blessing and extolling his name
in song. Before all men, honor and proclaim
God's deeds, and do not be slack in praising him.*
7 A king's secret it is prudent to keep, but the
works of God are to be declared and made
known. Praise them with due honor. Do good,
and evil will not find its way to you. 8 Prayer and
fasting are good, but better than either is
almsgiving accompanied by righteousness.* A lit-
tle with righteousness is better than abundance
with wickedness. It is better to give alms than to
store up gold;[t] 9 for almsgiving saves one from
death and expiates every sin. Those who regularly
give alms shall enjoy a full life;[u] 10 but those ha-
bitually guilty of sin are their own worst enemies.
Raphael's Identity 11 "I will now tell you the
whole truth; I will conceal nothing at all from
you. I have already said to you, 'A king's secret it
is prudent to keep, but the works of God are to
be made known with due honor.' 12 [v]I can now
tell you that when you, Tobit, and Sarah prayed,

12, 1–5: Tobit and his son generously agree to give Azariah far more than the wages agreed upon in Tb 5, 15–16.

12, 6–10: In the fashion of a wisdom teacher, Raphael gives the two men a short exhortation similar to the one Tobit gave his son in Tb 4, 3–19.

12, 6f: The Jews considered the duty of praising God their most esteemed privilege. Without praise of God, life was meaningless. Cf Is 38, 16–20.

12, 8: Prayer . . . fasting . . . almsgiving . . . righteousness: these, together with the proper attitude toward wealth, are treated in great detail by Christ our Lord in the Sermon on the Mount (Mt 6).

12, 12. 15: Raphael is one of the seven specially designated intercessors who present man's prayers to God. Angelology was developing in this period. The names of two other angels are given in the Bible: Gabriel (Dn 8, 16; 9, 21; Lk 1, 19. 26) and Michael (Dn 10, 13. 21; 12, 1; Jude 9; Rv 12, 7).

r Tb 13, 2; Dt 32, 39; 1 Sm 2, 6. s Tb 5, 3. 7. 15f. t Tb 4, 7–11; Sir 29, 8–13. u Dn 4, 24. v Jb 33, 23f; Acts 10, 4; Rv 8, 3f.

it was I who presented and read the record of
your prayer before the Glory of the Lord; and I
did the same thing when you used to bury the
dead.* 13 When you did not hesitate to get up
and leave your dinner in order to go and bury
the dead, 14 I was sent to put you to the test.* At
the same time, however, God commissioned me
to heal you and your daughter-in-law Sarah. 15 I
am Raphael, one of the seven angels who enter
and serve before the Glory of the Lord." [w]

16 Stricken with fear, the two men fell to the
ground. 17 But Raphael said to them: "No need
to fear; you are safe. Thank God now and
forever. 18 As for me, when I came to you it was
not out of any favor on my part, but because it
was God's will. So continue to thank him every
day; praise him with song. 19 Even though you
watched me eat and drink, I did not really do so;
what you were seeing was a vision. 20 So now get
up from the ground and praise God. Behold, I
am about to ascend to him who sent me; write
down all these things that have happened to
you." [x] 21 When Raphael ascended, they rose to
their feet and could no longer see him. 22 They
kept thanking God and singing his praises; and
they continued to acknowledge these marvelous
deeds which he had done when the angel of God
appeared to them.

VI: Tobit's Song of Praise

CHAPTER 13

1 Then Tobit composed this joyful prayer:*

Blessed be God who lives forever,
because his kingdom lasts for all ages. [y]
2 For he scourges and then has mercy;
he casts down to the depths of the netherworld,
and he brings up from the great abyss.
No one can escape his hand. [z]

3 Praise him, you Israelites, before the Gentiles,
for though he has scattered you among them,
4 he has shown you his greatness even there.
Exalt him before every living being,
because he is the Lord our God,
our Father and God forever.
5 He scourged you for your iniquities,
but will again have mercy on you all.
He will gather you from all the Gentiles
among whom you have been scattered. [a]

6 When you turn back to him with all your heart,
to do what is right before him,
Then he will turn back to you,
and no longer hide his face from you. [b]

So now consider what he has done for you,
and praise him with full voice.
Bless the Lord of righteousness,
and exalt the King of the ages.

In the land of my exile I praise him,
and show his power and majesty to a sinful nation.
"Turn back, you sinners! do the right before him:
perhaps he may look with favor upon you
and show you mercy.

7 "As for me, I exalt my God,
and my spirit rejoices in the King of heaven.
8 Let all men speak of his majesty,
and sing his praises in Jerusalem."

9 O Jerusalem, holy city,
he scourged you for the works of your hands,*
but will again pity the children of the righteous. [c]
10 Praise the Lord for his goodness,
and bless the King of the ages,
so that his tent may be rebuilt in you with joy.

12, 14: I was sent . . . test: God often sends trials to purify his faithful servants further. Cf Jb 1—2.

13, 1–18: Tobit's hymn of praise (cf Ex 15, 1–18; Jdt 16, 1–17) is divided into two parts. The first part (vv 1–8) is a song of praise that echoes themes from the hymns and psalms of the kingdom; the second (vv 9–18) is addressed to Jerusalem in the style of the prophets who spoke of a new and ideal Jerusalem (Is 60); cf Rv 21.

13, 9: Works of your hands: idols.

w Lk 1, 19; Rv 8, 2. x Jgs 13, 20. y Tb 3, 11; 8, 5. 15; 1 Chr 29, 10; Dn 3, 26. z Tb 11, 15; 13, 9; Dt 32, 39; 1 Sm 2, 6; Wis 16, 13. a Dt 30, 3; Neh 1, 9. b Dt 30, 2. c Tb 11, 15; Mi 7, 19; Rv 21.

May he gladden within you all who were captives;
all who were ravaged may he cherish within you
for all generations to come. [d]

11 A bright light will shine to all parts of the earth;
many nations shall come to you from afar,
And the inhabitants of all the limits of the earth,
drawn to you by the name of the Lord God,
Bearing in their hands their gifts for the King of heaven.
Every generation shall give joyful praise in you,
and shall call you the chosen one,
through all ages forever. [e]

12 Accursed are all who speak a harsh word against you;
accursed are all who destroy you
and pull down your walls,
And all who overthrow your towers
and set fire to your homes;
but forever blessed are all those who build you up. [f]

13 Go, then, rejoice over the children of the righteous,
who shall all be gathered together
and shall bless the Lord of the ages.
14 Happy are those who love you,
and happy those who rejoice in your prosperity.

Happy are all the men who shall grieve over you,
over all your chastisements,
For they shall rejoice in you
as they behold all your joy forever. [g]

15 My spirit blesses the Lord, the great King;
16 Jerusalem shall be rebuilt as his home forever.

Happy for me if a remnant of my offspring survive
to see your glory and to praise the King of heaven!

The gates of Jerusalem shall be built with sapphire and emerald,
and all your walls with precious stones.
The towers of Jerusalem shall be built with gold,
and their battlements with pure gold. [h]
17 The streets of Jerusalem shall be paved
with rubies and stones of Ophir;
18 The gates of Jerusalem shall sing hymns of gladness,
and all her houses shall cry out, "Alleluia!"
"Blessed be God who has raised you up!
may he be blessed for all ages!"
For in you they shall praise his holy name forever.

The end of Tobit's hymn of praise

VII: Epilogue

CHAPTER 14

Parting Advice 1 Tobit died peacefully at the age of a hundred and twelve, and received an honorable burial in Nineveh. 2 He was sixty-two years old when he lost his eyesight, and after he recovered it he lived in prosperity, giving alms and continually blessing God and praising the divine Majesty.

3 Just before he died, he called his son Tobiah and Tobiah's seven sons, and gave him this command: "Son, take your children [i] 4 and flee into Media, for I believe God's word which was spoken by Nahum* against Nineveh. It shall all happen, and shall overtake Assyria and Nineveh; indeed, whatever was said by Israel's prophets, whom God commissioned, shall occur. Not one of all the oracles shall remain unfulfilled, but everything shall take place in the time appointed

14, 4f: Nahum: one of the minor prophets, whose book contains oracles of doom against Nineveh. Here, in keeping with the period to which he assigns his story, the sacred author makes Tobit speak as if the punishment of Nineveh, the destruction of Jerusalem (587 B.C.), the exile from Judah and the return, would all take place in the future. The technique of using the facts of past history as seemingly future predictions, is a frequent device of apocalyptic writers. The Good Land: a favorite name for the promised land. Cf Dt 1, 35; 3, 25; 4, 21. 22.

d Is 44, 26, 28; Am 9, 11; Zec 1, 16. e Is 2, 3f; 9, 1; 49, 6; 60, 1; Mi 4, 2; Zec 8, 22. f Bar 4, 31f. g Ps 122, 6; Is 66, 10. h Tb 14, 5; Is 54, 11–13; 62, 2; Rv 21, 10–21. i Gn 47, 29f.

for it. So it will be safer in Media than in Assyria or Babylon. For I know and believe that whatever God has spoken will be accomplished. It shall happen, and not a single word of the prophecies shall prove false.

"As for our kinsmen who dwell in Israel, they shall all be scattered and led away into exile from the Good Land. The entire country of Israel shall become desolate; even Samaria and Jerusalem shall become desolate! God's temple there shall be burnt to the ground and shall be desolate for a while.[j] 5But God will again have mercy on them and bring them back to the land of Israel. They shall rebuild the temple, but it will not be like the first one, until the era when the appointed times shall be completed.* Afterward all of them shall return from their exile, and they shall rebuild Jerusalem with splendor. In her the temple of God shall also be rebuilt; yes, it will be rebuilt for all generations to come, just as the prophets of Israel said of her.[k] 6[l]All the nations of the world shall be converted and shall offer God true worship; all shall abandon their idols which have deceitfully led them into error,* 7and shall bless the God of the ages in righteousness. Because all the Israelites who are to be saved in those days will truly be mindful of God, they shall be gathered together and go to Jerusalem; in security shall they dwell forever in the land of Abraham, which will be given over to them. Those who sincerely love God shall rejoice, but those who become guilty of sin shall completely disappear from the land.[m]

9"Now, children, I give you this command: serve God faithfully and do what is right before him; you must tell your children to do what is upright and to give alms, to be mindful of God and at all times to bless his name sincerely and with all their strength.

8"Now, as for you, my son, depart from Nineveh; do not remain here. 10The day you bury your mother next to me, do not even stay overnight within the confines of the city. For I see that people here shamelessly commit all sorts of wickedness and treachery. Think, my son, of all that Nadab* did to Ahiqar, the very one who brought him up: Ahiqar went down alive into the earth! Yet God made Nadab's disgraceful crime rebound against him. Ahiqar came out again into the light, but Nadab went into the everlasting darkness, for he had tried to kill Ahiqar. Because Ahiqar had given alms to me, he escaped from the deadly trap Nadab had set for him. But Nadab himself fell into the deadly trap, and it destroyed him.[n] 11So, my children, note well what almsgiving does, and also what wickedness does—it kills! But now my spirit is about to leave me."

Death of Tobit and Tobiah 12They placed him on his bed and he died; and he received an honorable burial. When Tobiah's mother died, he buried her next to his father. He then departed with his wife and children for Media, where he settled in Ecbatana with his father-in-law Raguel.[o] 13He took respectful care of his aging father-in-law and mother-in-law; and he buried them at Ecbatana in Media. Then he inherited Raguel's estate as well as that of his father Tobit. 14He died at the venerable age of a hundred and seventeen. 15But before he died, he heard of the destruction of Nineveh and saw its effects. He witnessed the exile of the city's inhabitants when Cyaxares,* king of Media, led them captive into Media. Tobiah praised God for all that he had done against the citizens of Nineveh and Assyria. Before dying he rejoiced over Nineveh's destruction, and he blessed the Lord God forever and ever. Amen.

14, 5: Until the era . . . completed: a reference to the advent of messianic times, in which a new, more perfect temple was to be expected. Cf Heb 9, 1–14.

14, 6: Conversion of the Gentiles is also to come in the messianic era.

14, 10: Nadab: In the story of Ahiqar, the hero Ahiqar, chancellor under the Assyrian kings Sennacherib and Esarhaddon, adopts his nephew Nadab and prepares him to become his successor. But Nadab treacherously plots to have his uncle put to death. Ahiqar hides in a friend's house, and is finally vindicated (came out again into the light) when Nadab's scheme is discovered. Thereupon Nadab is thrown into a dungeon where he dies (went into everlasting darkness). It was Ahiqar's almsgiving that delivered him from death; see note on Tb 2, 2.

14, 15: Cyaxares: Nabopolassar, king of Babylon, and Cyaxares conquered and destroyed Nineveh in 612 B.C.; see note on Tb 1, 15.

j Na 2, 2—3, 19. k Neh 12, 27; Jer 31, 38. l Tb 45, 14; Is 60, 1–4. m Is 60, 21; Jer 32, 37; Ex 34, 28; 37, 25; 39, 26. n Tb 1, 21f. o Tb 4, 4.

THE BOOK OF JUDITH

The Book of Judith is a vivid story relating how, in a grave crisis, God delivered the Jewish people through the instrumentality of a woman. The unknown author composed this edifying narrative of divine providence at the end of the second or the beginning of the first century B.C. The original was almost certainly written in Hebrew, but the Greek text shows so much freedom in adapting from the Septuagint the language of older biblical books that it must be regarded as having a literary character of its own. It is this Greek form of the book, accepted as canonical by the Catholic Church, which is translated here. St. Jerome, who prepared (with some reluctance) a Latin text of Judith, based his work on a secondary Aramaic text available to him in Palestine, combined with an older Latin rendering from the Greek. The long hymn of chapter 16 he took in its entirety from that earlier Latin text.

Since it is no longer possible to determine with any precision the underlying events which may have given rise to this narrative, it is enough to note that the author sought to strengthen the faith of his people in God's abiding presence among them. The Book of Judith is a tract for difficult times; the reader, it was hoped, would take to heart the lesson that God was still the Master of history, who could save Israel from her enemies. Note the parallel with the time of the Exodus: as God had delivered his people by the hand of Moses, so he could deliver them by the hand of the pious widow Judith (see note on 2, 12).

The story can be divided into two parts. In the first (cc 1—7), Holofernes, commander-in-chief of the armies of Nebuchadnezzar, leads an overwhelming Assyrian force in a punitive campaign against the vassals who refused to help in the Assyrian war against the Medes. The Jewish people stubbornly resist the enemy at Bethulia, guarding the route of access to Jerusalem. Despite the warning of Achior that the Jews cannot be conquered unless they sin against God, the proud general lays siege to the town and cuts off its water supply. After a siege of thirty-four days, the exhausted defenders are desperate and ready to surrender.

At this point, the climax of the story, Judith (the name means "Jewess") appears and promises to defeat the Assyrians. The rest of the story is too well known to repeat in detail. Having fasted and prayed, Judith dresses in her finest garments and proceeds to the Assyrian camp, where she succeeds in killing Holofernes while he lies in a drunken stupor. The Assyrians panic when they discover this, and the Jews are able to rout and slaughter them. The beautiful hymn of the people honoring Judith (15, 9-10) is often applied to Mary in the liturgy.

Any attempt to read the book directly against the backdrop of Jewish history in relation to the empires of the ancient world is bound to fail. The story was written as a pious reflection on the meaning of the yearly Passover observance. It draws its inspiration from the Exodus narrative (especially Ex 14, 31) and from the texts of Isaiah and the Psalms portraying the special intervention of God for the preservation of Jerusalem. The theme of God's hand as the agent of this providential activity, reflected of old in the hand of Moses and now in the hand of Judith, is again exemplified at a later time in Jewish synagogue art. God's hand reaching down from heaven appears as part of the scene at Dura-Europos (before A.D. 256) in paintings of the Exodus, of the sacrifice of Isaac (Gn 22), and of Ezekiel's valley of dry bones (Ez 37).

The Book of Judith is divided as follows:

I. Peril of the Jews (1, 1—7, 32).
II. Deliverance of the Jews (8, 1—14, 10).
III. Victory (14, 11—16, 25).

I: Peril of the Jews

CHAPTER 1

War against the Medes 1 It was the twelfth
year of the reign of Nebuchadnezzar, king of the
Assyrians in the great city of Nineveh. At that
time Arphaxad ruled over the Medes in Ecbat-
ana. 2 Around this city he built a wall of blocks of
stone, each three cubits in height and six in
length. He made the wall seventy cubits high
and fifty thick. 3 At the gates he raised towers of
a hundred cubits, with a thickness of sixty cubits
at the base. 4 The gateway he built to a height of
seventy cubits, with an opening forty cubits
wide for the passage of his chariot forces and the
marshaling of his infantry. 5 Then King Nebuchad-
nezzar waged war against King Arphaxad in the
vast plain, in the district of Ragae. 6 To him there
rallied all the inhabitants of the mountain region,
all who dwelt along the Euphrates, the Tigris,
and the Hydaspes, and King Arioch of the
Elamites, in the plain. Thus many nations came
together to resist the people of Cheleoud.*

Ultimatum to the West 7 Now Nebuchadnez-
zar, king of the Assyrians, sent messengers to all
the inhabitants of Persia, and to all those who
dwelt in the West: to the inhabitants of Cilicia
and Damascus, Lebanon and Anti-Lebanon, to
all who dwelt along the seacoast, 8 to the peoples
of Carmel, Gilead, Upper Galilee, and the vast
plain of Esdraelon, 9 to all those in Samaria and
its cities, and west of the Jordan as far as
Jerusalem, Bethany, Chelous, Kadesh, and the
River of Egypt; to Tahpanhes, Raamses, all the
land of Goshen, 10 Tanis, Memphis and beyond,
and to all the inhabitants of Egypt as far as the
borders of Ethiopia.

11 But the inhabitants of all that land disre-
garded the summons of Nebuchadnezzar, king of
the Assyrians, and would not go with him to the
war. They were not afraid of him but regarded
him as a lone individual opposed to them, and
turned away his envoys empty-handed, in dis-
grace. 12 Then Nebuchadnezzar fell into a violent
rage against all that land, and swore by his
throne and his kingdom that he would avenge
himself on all the territories of Cilicia and
Damascus and Syria, and also destroy with his
sword all the inhabitants of Moab, Ammon, the
whole of Judea, and those living anywhere in
Egypt as far as the borders of the two seas.*

Defeat of Arphaxad 13 In the seventeenth year
he proceeded with his army against King Ar-
phaxad, and was victorious in his campaign. He
routed the whole force of Arphaxad, his entire
cavalry and all his chariots, 14 and took posses-
sion of his cities. He pressed on to Ecbatana and
took its towers, sacked its marketplaces, and
turned its glory into shame. 15 Arphaxad himself
he overtook in the mountains of Ragae, ran him
through with spears, and utterly destroyed him.
16 Then he returned home with all his numerous,
motley horde of warriors; and there he and his
army relaxed and feasted for a hundred and
twenty days. [a]

CHAPTER 2

Council of War against the West 1 In the
eighteenth year, on the twenty-second day of the
first month, there was a discussion in the palace
of Nebuchadnezzar, king of the Assyrians, about
taking revenge on the whole world, as he had
threatened. 2 He summoned all his ministers and
nobles, laid before them his secret plan, and
urged the total destruction of those countries.
3 They decided to do away with all those who
had refused to comply with the order he had
issued.

4 When he had completed his plan, Nebuchad-
nezzar, king of the Assyrians, summoned Holo-
fernes, general in chief of his forces, second to
himself in command, and said to him: 5 [b]"Thus
says the great king, the lord of all the earth: Go
forth from my presence, take with you men of
proven valor, a hundred and twenty thousand
infantry and twelve thousand cavalry, 6 and pro-
ceed against all the land of the West, because
they did not comply with the order I issued.

1, 6: Cheleoud: probably the Chaldeans are meant.

1, 12: The two seas: the ancient rulers in Mesopotamia often designated the limits of their realm as extending from the Upper Sea (the Mediterranean) to the Lower Sea (the Persian Gulf).

a Est 1, 3f. b 5f: Est 3, 8f.

[7]Tell them to have earth and water* ready, for I will come against them in my wrath; I will cover all the land with the feet of my soldiers, to whom I will deliver them as spoils. [8]Their slain shall fill their ravines and wadies, the swelling torrent shall be choked with their dead; [9]and I will deport them as exiles to the very ends of the earth.

[10]"You go before me and take possession of all their territories for me. If they surrender to you, guard them for me till the day of their punishment. [11]As for those who resist, show them no quarter, but deliver them up to slaughter and plunder in each country you occupy. [12]For as I live,* and by the strength of my kingdom, what I have spoken I will accomplish by my power. [13]Do not disobey a single one of the orders of your lord; fulfill them exactly as I have commanded you, and do it without delay."

Campaign of Holofernes [14]So Holofernes left the presence of his lord, and summoned all the princes, and the generals and officers of the Assyrian army. [15]He mustered a hundred and twenty thousand picked troops, as his lord had commanded, and twelve thousand mounted archers, [16]and grouped them into a complete combat force. [17]He took along a very large number of camels, asses, and mules for their baggage; innumerable sheep, cattle, and goats for their food supply; [18]abundant provisions for each man, and much gold and silver from the royal palace.

[19]Then he and his whole army proceeded on their expedition in advance of King Nebuchadnezzar, to cover all the western region with their chariots and cavalry and regular infantry. [20]A huge, irregular force, too many to count, like locusts or the dust of the earth, went along with them.[c]

[21]After a three-day march from Nineveh, they reached the plain of Bectileth, and from Bectileth they next encamped near the mountains to the north of Upper Cilicia. [22]From there Holofernes took his whole force, the infantry, cavalry, and chariots, and marched into the mountain region. [23]He devastated Put and Lud,* and plundered all the Rassisites and the Ishmaelites on the border of the desert toward the south of Chaldea.

[24]Then, following the Euphrates, he went through Mesopotamia, and battered down every fortified city along the Wadi Abron, until he reached the sea. [25]He seized the territory of Cilicia, and cut down everyone who resisted him. Then he proceeded to the southern borders of Japheth, toward Arabia. [26]He surrounded all the Midianites, burned their tents, and plundered their sheepfolds. [27]Descending to the plain of Damascus at the time of the wheat harvest, he set fire to all their fields, destroyed their flocks and herds, despoiled their cities, devastated their plains, and put all their youths to the sword.

[28]The fear and dread of him fell upon all the inhabitants of the coastland, upon those in Sidon and Tyre, and those who dwelt in Sur and Ocina, and the inhabitants of Jamnia. Those in Azotus and Ascalon also feared him greatly.

CHAPTER 3

Submission of the West [1]They therefore sent messengers to him to sue for peace in these words: [2]"We, the servants of Nebuchadnezzar the great king, lie prostrate before you; do with us as you will. [3]Our dwellings and all our wheat fields, our flocks and herds, and all our encampments are at your disposal; make use of them as you please. [4]Our cities and their inhabitants are also at your service; come and deal with them as you see fit."

2, 7: Earth and water: in the Persian period, the offering of these to a conqueror was a symbolic gesture of unconditional surrender.

2, 12: As I live: in the Old Testament, an oath proper to divinity; cf Dt 32, 40. Nebuchadnezzar is making himself equal to God; see Jdt 6, 2. By my power: literally "by my hand." The hand of Nebuchadnezzar raised in opposition to God and to his people is the occasion for Judith's intervention by a woman's hand; cf Jdt 9, 9f; Is 10, 5–14.

2, 23: Put and Lud: the same as the "Put and Lud" mentioned in Ez 30, 5 as allies of Egypt, and in Ez 27, 10 as supplying mercenary soldiers to Tyre. Here they seem inserted to embellish the narrative with assonance and prophetic associations rather than to indicate definite localities.

c Jgs 7, 12.

5 After the spokesmen had reached Holofernes and given him this message, 6 he went down with his army to the seacoast, and stationed garrisons in the fortified cities; from them he impressed picked troops as auxiliaries. 7 The people of these cities and all the inhabitants of the countryside received him with garlands and dancing to the sound of timbrels. 8 Nevertheless, he devastated their whole territory and cut down their sacred groves, for he had been commissioned to destroy all the gods of the earth, so that every nation might worship Nebuchadnezzar alone, and every people and tribe invoke him as a god.[d] 9 At length Holofernes reached Esdraelon in the neighborhood of Dothan, the approach to the main ridge of the Judean mountains; 10 he set up his camp between Geba* and Scythopolis, and stayed there a whole month to refurbish all the equipment of his army.

CHAPTER 4

Israelite Defense 1 When the Israelites who dwelt in Judea heard of all that Holofernes, commander in chief of Nebuchadnezzar, king of the Assyrians, had done to the nations, and how he had despoiled all their temples and destroyed them, 2 they were in extreme dread of him, and greatly alarmed for Jerusalem and the temple of the LORD, their God. 3 Now, they had lately returned from exile, and only recently had all the people of Judea been gathered together, and the vessels, the altar, and the temple been purified from profanation.* 4 So they sent word to the whole region of Samaria, to Kona, Beth-horon, Belmain, and Jericho, to Choba and Aesora, and to the valley of Salem. 5 The people there posted guards on all the summits of the high mountains, fortified their villages, and since their fields had recently been harvested, stored up provisions in preparation for war.

6 Joakim, who was high priest* in Jerusalem in those days, wrote to the inhabitants of Bethulia [and Betomesthaim], which is on the way to Esdraelon, facing the plain near Dothan, 7 and instructed them to keep firm hold of the mountain passes, since these offered access to Judea. It would be easy to ward off the attacking forces, as the defile was only wide enough for two abreast. 8 The Israelites carried out the orders given them by Joakim, the high priest, and the senate of the whole people of Israel, which met in Jerusalem.*

Prayer and Penance 9 All the men of Israel cried to God with great fervor and did penance— 10 [e]they, along with their wives, and children, and domestic animals.* All their resident aliens, hired laborers, and slaves also girded themselves with sackcloth. 11 And all the Israelite men, women, and children who lived in Jerusalem prostrated themselves in front of the temple building,* with ashes strewn on their heads, displaying their sackcloth covering before the LORD. 12 The altar, too, they draped in sackcloth; and with one accord they cried out fervently to the God of Israel not to allow their children to be seized, their wives to be taken captive, the cities of their inheritance to be ruined, or the sanctuary to be profaned and mocked for the nations to gloat over.[f]

13 The LORD heard their cry and had regard for their distress. For the people observed a fast of many days' duration throughout Judea, and before the sanctuary of the LORD Almighty in Jerusalem.[g] 14 The high priest Joakim, and all the priests in attendance on the LORD who served his altar, were also girded with sackcloth as they offered the daily holocaust, the votive offerings, and the free-will offerings of the people. 15 With

3, 10: Geba: perhaps originally "Gelboe," the mountain range near the eastern end of which lay Scythopolis, the Greek name for ancient Beth-shean (Jos 17, 11).

4, 3: Returned from exile . . . profanation: these allusions are variously attributed—to the Persian period (538–323 B.C.), or even to a condition in the days of Antiochus Epiphanes (175–164 B.C.).

4, 6: Joakim, who was high priest: see Bar 1, 7 and the footnote on Bar 1, 8f; this name for a high priest cannot be used in dating the events in Jdt.

4, 8: The organization of the Jewish nation as subject to a high priest and a senate, or council of elders, was proper to the Greek period (after 323 B.C.), and is reflected in the coinage of John Hyrcanus (135–104 B.C.).

4, 10: Domestic animals: see note on Jon 3, 8.

4, 11: Prostrated themselves in front of the temple building: for a parallel to this ceremony of entreaty, see Jl 1, 13f; 2, 15ff, and the note on Jl 2, 17.

d Ex 34, 13. e 10f: Jon 3, 7f. f Est 4, 1f. g Est 4, 16.

ashes upon their turbans, they cried to the LORD with all their strength to look with favor on the whole house of Israel.

CHAPTER 5

Council against the Israelites 1 It was reported to Holofernes, commander in chief of the Assyrian army, that the Israelites were ready for battle, and had blocked the mountain passes, fortified the summits of all the higher peaks, and placed roadblocks in the plains. 2 In great anger he summoned all the rulers of the Moabites, the generals of the Ammonites, and all the satraps of the seacoast 3 and said to them: "Now tell me, you Canaanites, what sort of people is this that dwells in the mountains? Which cities do they inhabit? How large is their army? In what does their power and strength consist? Who has set himself up as their king and the leader of their army? 4 Why have they refused to come out to meet me along with all the other inhabitants of the West?"

Achior's Speech 5 Then Achior, the leader of all the Ammonites, said to him: "My lord, hear this account from your servant; I will tell you the truth about this people that lives near you [that inhabits this mountain region]; no lie shall escape your servant's lips.[h]

6 *"These people are descendants of the Chaldeans. 7 They formerly dwelt in Mesopotamia, for they did not wish to follow the gods of their forefathers who were born in the land of the Chaldeans.[i] 8 Since they abandoned the way of their ancestors, and acknowledged with divine worship the God of heaven, their forefathers expelled them from the presence of their gods. So they fled to Mesopotamia and dwelt there a long time. 9 Their God bade them leave their abode and proceed to the land of Canaan. Here they settled, and grew very rich in gold, silver, and a great abundance of livestock.[j] 10 Later, when famine had gripped the whole land of Canaan, they went down into Egypt. They stayed there as long as they found sustenance, and grew into such a great multitude that the number of their race could not be counted.[k] 11 [l]The king of Egypt, however, rose up against them, shrewdly forced them to labor at brickmaking, oppressed and enslaved them. 12 But they cried to their God, and he struck the land of Egypt with plagues for which there was no remedy. When the Egyptians expelled them, 13 [m]God dried up the Red Sea before them, 14 and led them along the route to Sinai and Kadesh-barnea. First they drove out all the inhabitants of the desert; 15 then they settled in the land of the Amorites, destroyed all the Heshbonites by main force, crossed the Jordan, and took possession of the whole mountain region.[n] 16 They expelled the Canaanites, the Perizzites, the Jebusites, the Shechemites, and all the Gergesites; and they lived in these mountains a long time.[o]

17 [p]"As long as the Israelites did not sin in the sight of their God, they prospered, for their God, who hates wickedness, was with them. 18 But when they deviated from the way he prescribed for them, they were ground down steadily, more and more, by frequent wars, and finally taken as captives into foreign lands. The temple of their God was razed to the ground, and their cities were occupied by their enemies.[q] 19 But now that they have returned to their God, they have come back from the Dispersion wherein they were scattered, and have repossessed Jerusalem, where their sanctuary is, and have settled again in the mountain region which was unoccupied.

20 [r]"So now, my lord and master, if these people are at fault, and are sinning against their God, and if we verify this offense of theirs, then we shall be able to go up and conquer them. 21 But if they are not a guilty nation, then your lordship should keep his distance; otherwise their LORD and God will shield them, and we shall become the laughingstock of the whole world."

5, 6–9: Achior outlines the early history of the Hebrews, whose forefather, Abraham, first lived in Ur of the Chaldeans (Gn 11, 28) and then migrated to Haran (Gn 11, 31) in Aram Naharaim (Gn 24, 10), which was called Mesopotamia by the Greeks. The gods of their forefathers were the pagan deities worshiped by Abraham's relatives (Jos 24, 2).

h Jdt 11, 9–19. i Gn 11, 31. j Gn 11, 31—12, 5. k Gn 42, 1–5; 46, 1–7; Ex 1, 7. l 11f: Ex 5, 4–21; 7, 1–9. m 13f: Ex 14, 21f. 29. n Nm 21, 21–32; Jos 2, 10. o Dt 7, 1. p 17f: Dt 28—30; Ps 106, 40–46; Is 59, 7. q 2 Kgs 25. r 20f: Jdt 8, 18ff; 11, 10.

22Now when Achior had concluded his recom-
mendation, all the people standing round about
the tent murmured; and the officers of Holofer-
nes and all the inhabitants of the seacoast and of
Moab alike said he should be cut to pieces.
23"We are not afraid of the Israelites," they said,
"for they are a powerless people, incapable of a
strong defense. 24Let us therefore attack them;
your great army, Lord Holofernes, will swallow
them up."[s]

CHAPTER 6

Holofernes' Answer 1When the noise of the
crowd surrounding the council had subsided,
Holofernes, commander in chief of the Assyrian
army, said to Achior, in the presence of the
whole throng of coastland peoples, of the Moab-
ites, and of the Ammonite mercenaries: 2"Who
are you, Achior, to prophesy among us as you
have done today, and to tell us not to fight
against the Israelites because their God protects
them? What god is there beside Nebuchadnez-
zar? He will send his force and destroy them
from the face of the earth. Their God will not
save them;[t] 3but we, the servants of Nebuchad-
nezzar, will strike them down as one man, for
they will be unable to withstand the force of our
cavalry.[u] 4We will overwhelm them with it, and
the mountains shall be drunk with their blood,
and their plains filled with their corpses. Not a
trace of them shall survive our attack: they shall
utterly perish, says King Nebuchadnezzar, lord
of all the earth; for he has spoken, and his words
shall not remain unfulfilled.[v] 5As for you,
Achior, you Ammonite mercenary, for saying
these things in a moment of perversity you shall
not see my face after today, until I have taken
revenge on this race of people from Egypt.
6Then at my return, the sword of my army or the
spear of my servants will pierce your sides, and
you shall fall among their slain.[w] 7My servants
will now conduct you to the mountain region,
and leave you at one of the towns along the
ascent. 8You shall not die till you are destroyed
together with them. 9If you still cherish the hope
that they will not be taken, then there is no need
for you to be downcast. I have spoken, and my
words shall not prove false in any respect."

Achior in Bethulia 10Then Holofernes ordered
the servants who were standing by in his tent to
seize Achior, conduct him to Bethulia, and hand
him over to the Israelites. 11So the servants took
him in custody and brought him out of the camp
into the plain. From there they led him into the
mountain region till they reached the springs
below Bethulia. 12When the men of the city saw
them, they seized their weapons and ran out of
the city to the crest of the ridge; and all the
slingers blocked the ascent of Holofernes' ser-
vants by hurling stones upon them. 13So they
took cover below the mountain, where they
bound Achior and left him lying at the foot of the
mountain; then they returned to their lord.

14The Israelites came down to him from their
city, loosed him, and brought him into Bethulia.
They haled him before the rulers of the city,
15who in those days were Uzziah, son of Micah
of the tribe of Simeon, Chabris, son of
Gothoniel, and Charmis, son of Melchiel.
16They then convened all the elders of the city;
and all their young men, as well as the women,
gathered in haste at the place of assembly. They
placed Achior in the center of the throng, and
Uzziah questioned him about what had hap-
pened. 17He replied by giving them an account
of what was said in the council of Holofernes,
and of all his own words among the Assyrian
officers, and of all the boasting threats of Holofer-
nes against the house of Israel.

18At this the people fell prostrate and wor-
shiped God; and they cried out: 19"LORD, God of
heaven, behold their arrogance! Have pity on the
lowliness of our people, and look with favor this
day on those who are consecrated to you."*
20Then they reassured Achior and praised him
highly. 21Uzziah brought him from the assembly
to his home, where he gave a banquet for the

6, 19: The Latin Vulgate (6, 15) has a longer form of this prayer: "Lord, God of heaven and earth, behold their arrogance; regard our lowliness and look with favor on your holy ones; show that you do not abandon those who trust in you, but that you humble those who trust in themselves and glory in their own strength."

s Jdt 6. 2; 9, 7; 16, 2. t Jdt 3, 8; 9, 7. u Is 36, 18ff. v Jdt 6, 17. w Jdt 5, 22.

elders. That whole night they called upon the God of Israel for help.

CHAPTER 7

Siege of Bethulia 1 The following day Holofernes ordered his whole army, and all the allied troops that had come to his support, to move against Bethulia, seize the mountain passes, and engage the Israelites in battle. 2 That same day all their fighting men went into action. Their forces numbered a hundred and seventy thousand infantry and twelve thousand horsemen, not counting the baggage train or the men who accompanied it on foot—a very great army. 3 They encamped at the spring in the valley near Bethulia, and spread out in breadth toward Dothan as far as Balbaim, and in length from Bethulia to Cyamon, which faces Esdraelon.

4 When the Israelites saw how many there were, they said to one another in great dismay: "Soon they will devour the whole country. Neither the high mountains nor the valleys and hills can support the mass of them." 5 Yet they all seized their weapons, lighted fires on their bastions,* and kept watch throughout the night.

6 On the second day Holofernes led out all his cavalry in the sight of the Israelites who were in Bethulia. 7 He reconnoitered the approaches to their city and located their sources of water; these he seized, stationing armed detachments around them, while he himself returned to his troops.

8 All the commanders of the Edomites and all the leaders of the Ammonites, together with the generals of the seacoast, came to Holofernes and said: 9 "Sir, listen to what we have to say, that there may be no losses among your troops. 10 These Israelites do not rely on their spears, but on the height of the mountains where they dwell; it is not easy to reach the summit of their mountains.[x] 11 Therefore, sir, do not attack them in regular formation; thus not a single one of your troops will fall. 12 Stay in your camp, and spare all your soldiers. Have some of your servants keep control of the source of water that flows out at the base of the mountain, 13 for that is where the inhabitants of Bethulia get their water. Then thirst will begin to carry them off, and they will surrender their city. Meanwhile, we and our men will go up to the summits of the nearby mountains, and encamp there to guard against anyone's leaving the city.[y] 14 They and their wives and children will languish with hunger, and even before the sword strikes them they will be laid low in the streets of their city. 15 Thus you will render them dire punishment for their rebellion and their refusal to meet you peacefully."

16 Their words pleased Holofernes and all his ministers, and he ordered their proposal to be carried out. 17 Thereupon the Moabites moved camp, together with five thousand Assyrians. They encamped in the valley, and held the water supply and the springs of the Israelites. 18 The Edomites and the Ammonites went up and encamped in the mountain region opposite Dothan; and they sent some of their men to the south and to the east opposite Egrebel, near Chusi, which is on Wadi Mochmur. The rest of the Assyrian army was encamped in the plain, covering the whole countryside. Their enormous store of tents and equipment was spread out in profusion everywhere.

19 The Israelites cried to the LORD, their God, for they were disheartened, since all their enemies had them surrounded, and there was no way of slipping through their lines.[z] 20 The whole Assyrian camp, infantry, chariots, and cavalry, kept them thus surrounded for thirty-four days. All the reservoirs of water failed the inhabitants of Bethulia, 21 and the cisterns ran dry, so that on no day did they have enough to drink, but their drinking water was rationed. 22 Their children fainted away, and the women and youths were consumed with thirst and were collapsing in the streets and gateways of the city, with no strength left in them.

23 All the people, therefore, including youths,

7, 5: Lighted fires on their bastions: to serve as signals for alerting the neighboring towns. Reference to fire signals in time of siege is made in the Lachish ostraca at the beginning of the sixth century B.C. Kept watch throughout the night: to prevent a surprise attack.

x 1 Kgs 20, 23. 28. y Ex 5, 21. z Ps 106, 6.

women, and children, went in a crowd to Uzziah and the rulers of the city. They set up a great clamor and said before the elders: 24“God judge between you and us! You have done us grave injustice in not making peace with the Assyrians. 25There is no help for us now! Instead, God has sold us into their power by laying us prostrate before them in thirst and utter exhaustion. 26Therefore, summon them and deliver the whole city as booty to the troops of Holofernes and to all his forces; 27we would be better off to become their prey. We should indeed be made slaves, but at least we should live, and not have to behold our little ones dying before our eyes and our wives and children breathing out their souls. 28We adjure you by heaven and earth, and by our God, the LORD of our forefathers, who is punishing us for our sins and those of our forefathers, to do as we have proposed, this very day.”

29All in the assembly with one accord broke into shrill wailing and loud cries to the LORD their God. 30But Uzziah said to them, “Courage, my brothers! Let us wait five days more for the LORD our God, to show his mercy toward us; he will not utterly forsake us. 31But if those days pass without help coming to us, I will do as you say.” 32Then he dispersed the men to their posts, and they returned to the walls and towers of the city; the women and children he sent to their homes. Throughout the city they were in great misery.

II: Deliverance of the Jews

CHAPTER 8

Judith 1Now in those days Judith, daughter of Merari, son of Joseph, son of Oziel, son of Elkiah, son of Ananias, son of Gideon, son of Raphain, son of Ahitob, son of Elijah, son of Hilkiah, son of Eliab, son of Nathanael, son of Salamiel, son of Sarasadai,* son of Simeon, son of Israel, heard of this. 2Her husband, Manasseh, of her own tribe and clan, had died at the time of the barley harvest. 3While he was in the field supervising those who bound the sheaves, he suffered sunstroke; and he died of this illness in Bethulia, his native city. He was buried with his forefathers in the field between Dothan and Balamon. 4The widowed Judith remained three years and four months at home, 5where she set up a tent* for herself on the roof of her house. She put sackcloth about her loins and wore widow’s weeds. 6She fasted all the days of her widowhood, except sabbath eves and sabbaths, new moon eves and new moons, feastdays and holidays of the house of Israel.[a] 7She was beautifully formed and lovely to behold. Her husband, Manasseh, had left her gold and silver, servants and maids, livestock and fields, which she was maintaining. 8No one had a bad word to say about her, for she was a very God-fearing woman.

Her Words to the Elders 9When Judith, therefore, heard of the harsh words which the people, discouraged by their lack of water, had spoken against their ruler, and of all that Uzziah had said to them in reply, swearing that he would hand over the city to the Assyrians at the end of five days, 10she sent the maid who was in charge of all her things to ask Uzziah, Chabris, and Charmis, the elders of the city, to visit her. 11When they came, she said to them: “Listen to me, you rulers of the people of Bethulia. What you said to the people today is not proper. When you promised to hand over the city to our enemies at the end of five days unless within that time the LORD comes to our aid, you interposed between God and yourselves this oath which you took. 12Who are you, then, that you should have put God to the test this day, setting yourselves in the place of God in human affairs?[b] 13It is the LORD Almighty for whom you are laying down conditions; will you never understand anything? 14You cannot plumb the depths of the human heart or grasp the workings of the human mind; how then can you fathom

8, 1: Salamiel, son of Sarasadai: head of the tribe of Simeon during the wanderings of the Israelites in the desert (Nm 1, 6).
8, 5: A tent: erected by Judith on the roof of her house (v 5); it was here that the elders came to confer with her (v 11).

a Lk 2, 37. b Jb 38, 2; 40, 2. 7f; 42, 3.

God, who has made all these things, discern his mind, and understand his plan? [c]

"No, my brothers, do not anger the LORD our God. [15]For if he does not wish to come to our aid within the five days, he has it equally within his power to protect us at such time as he pleases, or to destroy us in the face of our enemies. [16]It is not for you to make the LORD our God give surety for his plans.

"God is not man that he should be moved by threats,
nor human, that he may be given an ultimatum.

[17]"So while we wait for the salvation that comes from him, let us call upon him to help us, and he will hear our cry if it is his good pleasure. [18]For there has not risen among us in recent generations, nor does there exist today, any tribe, or clan, or town, or city of ours that worships gods made by hands, as happened in former days. [d] [19]It was for such conduct that our forefathers were handed over to the sword and to pillage, and fell with great destruction before our enemies. [e] [20]But since we acknowledge no other god but the LORD, we hope that he will not disdain us or any of our people. [21]If we are taken, all Judea will fall, our sanctuary will be plundered, and God will make us pay for its profanation with our life's blood. [22]For the slaughter of our kinsmen, for the taking of exiles from the land, and for the devastation of our inheritance, he will lay the guilt on our heads. Wherever we shall be enslaved among the nations, we shall be a mockery and a reproach in the eyes of our masters. [23]Our enslavement will not be turned to our benefit, but the LORD our God will maintain it to our disgrace.

[24]"Therefore, my brothers, let us set an example for our kinsmen. Their lives depend on us, and the defense of the sanctuary, the temple, and the altar rests with us. [25][f]Besides all this, we should be grateful to the LORD our God, for putting us to the test, as he did our forefathers. [26]Recall how he dealt with Abraham, and how he tried Isaac, and all that happened to Jacob in Syrian Mesopotamia while he was tending the flocks of Laban, his mother's brother. [27]Not for vengeance did the LORD put them in the crucible to try their hearts, nor has he done so with us. It is by way of admonition that he chastises those who are close to him." [g]

Uzziah's Response [28]Then Uzziah said to her: "All that you have said was spoken with good sense, and no one can gainsay your words. [29]Not today only is your wisdom made evident, but from your earliest years all the people have recognized your prudence, which corresponds to the worthy dispositions of your heart. [30]The people, however, were so tortured with thirst that they forced us to speak to them as we did, and to bind ourselves by an oath that we cannot break. [31]But now, God-fearing woman that you are, pray for us that the LORD may send rain to fill up our cisterns, lest we be weakened still further."

[32]Then Judith said to them: "Listen to me! I will do something that will go down from generation to generation among the descendants of our race. [33]Stand at the gate tonight to let me pass through with my maid; and within the days you have specified before you will surrender the city to our enemies, the LORD will rescue Israel by my hand. [34]You must not inquire into what I am doing, for I will not tell you until my plan has been accomplished." [35]Uzziah and the rulers said to her, "Go in peace, and may the LORD God go before you to take vengeance upon our enemies!" [36]Then they withdrew from the tent and returned to their posts.

CHAPTER 9

The Prayer of Judith [1]Judith threw herself down prostrate, with ashes strewn upon her head, and wearing nothing over her sackcloth. While the incense was being offered in the temple of God in Jerusalem that evening, Judith prayed to the LORD with a loud voice: [h] [2]"LORD,

9, 2: The maiden: Dinah, Jacob's daughter, who was violated by Shechem, the Hivite (Gn 34, 2).

c Jb 41, 3; Prv 14, 10; Wis 9, 13; Is 40, 13; Rom 11, 33f; 1 Cor 2, 11 d Jdt 5, 20f; 11, 10. e Pss 78, 56f; 106, 13f; Jer 7, 16–20; 14, 7. f 25f: Gn 22, 1–12; 29, 22–30. g Dt 4, 7. h Ex 30, 7f; Ps 141, 2.

God of my forefather Simeon! You put a sword
into his hand to take revenge upon the foreign-
ers who had immodestly loosened the maiden's*
girdle, shamefully exposed her thighs, and dis-
gracefully violated her body. This they did,
though you forbade it.[i] 3Therefore you had their
rulers slaughtered; and you covered with their
blood the bed in which they lay deceived, the
same bed that had felt the shame of their own
deceiving. You smote the slaves together with
their princes, and the princes together with their
servants.* 4Their wives you handed over to
plunder, and their daughters to captivity; and all
the spoils you divided among your favored sons,
who burned with zeal for you, and in their
abhorrence of the defilement of their kins-
woman, called on you for help.

5"O God, my God, hear me also, a widow. It
is you who were the author of those events and
of what preceded and followed them. The pres-
ent, also, and the future you have planned.
Whatever you devise comes into being;[j] 6the
things you decide on come forward and say,
'Here we are!' All your ways are in readiness,
and your judgment is made with foreknowl-
edge.[k]

7 [l]"Here are the Assyrians, a vast force, prid-
ing themselves on horse and rider, boasting of
the power of their infantry, trusting in shield and
spear, bow and sling. They do not know that

8" 'You, the LORD, crush warfare;
Lord is your name.'

"Shatter their strength in your might, and
crush their force in your wrath; for they have
resolved to profane your sanctuary, to defile the
tent where your glorious name resides, and to
overthrow with iron the horns of your altar. 9See
their pride, and send forth your wrath upon their
heads. Give me, a widow, the strong hand to
execute my plan.[m] 10With the guile of my lips,
smite the slave together with the ruler, the ruler
together with his servant; crush their pride by
the hand of a woman.

11"Your strength is not in numbers, nor does
your power depend upon stalwart men; but you
are the God of the lowly, the helper of the
oppressed, the supporter of the weak, the protec-
tor of the forsaken, the savior of those without
hope.

12"Please, please, God of my forefather, God
of the heritage of Israel, LORD of heaven and
earth, Creator of the waters, King of all you have
created, hear my prayer! 13Let my guileful
speech bring wound and wale on those who
have planned dire things against your covenant,
your holy temple, Mount Zion, and the homes
your children have inherited.[n] 14Let your whole
nation and all the tribes know clearly that you
are the God of all power and might, and that
there is no other who protects the people of
Israel but you alone."

CHAPTER 10

Judith's Departure 1As soon as Judith had
thus concluded, and ceased her invocation to
the God of Israel, 2she rose from the ground. She
called her maid and they went down into the
house, which she used only on sabbaths and
feast days. 3She took off the sackcloth she had
on, laid aside the garments of her widowhood,
washed her body with water, and anointed it
with rich ointment. She arranged her hair and
bound it with a fillet, and put on the festive
attire she had worn while her husband, Manas-
seh, was living.[o] 4She chose sandals for her feet,
and put on her anklets, bracelets, rings, earrings,
and all her other jewelry. Thus she made herself
very beautiful, to captivate the eyes of all the
men who should see her.[p]

5She gave her maid a leather flask of wine and
a cruse of oil. She filled a bag with roasted grain,
fig cakes, bread and cheese; all these provisions
she wrapped up and gave to the maid to carry.[q]

6Then they went out to the gate of the city of
Bethulia and found Uzziah and the elders of the
city, Chabris and Charmis, standing there.
7When these men saw Judith transformed in

9, 3: Because Shechem had deceived and violated Dinah, her brothers, Simeon and Levi, tricked Shechem and the men of his city into being circumcised, and then slew them while they were confined to bed from the circumcision; cf Gn 34, 13–29.

i Gn 34. j Is 44, 7. k Jb 38, 35; Is 46, 9–13; Bar 3, 35. l 7f: Jdt 5, 23; 6, 2; 16, 2. m Ps 33, 16. n Jdt 10, 4; 11, 20. 23; 16, 6. 9. o Jdt 8, 6ff. p Jdt 9, 13. q Jdt 12, 2.

looks and differently dressed, they were very much astounded at her beauty and said to her, 8“May the God of our fathers bring you to favor, and make your undertaking a success, for the glory of the Israelites and the exaltation of Jerusalem.”

Judith bowed down to God. Then she said to them, 9“Order the gate of the city opened for me, that I may go to carry out the business we discussed.” So they ordered the youths to open the gate for her as she requested. 10When they did so, Judith and her maid went out. The men of the city kept her in view as she went down the mountain and crossed the valley; then they lost sight of her.

Judith Captured 11As Judith and her maid walked directly across the valley, they encountered the Assyrian outpost. 12The men took her in custody and asked her, “To what people do you belong? Where do you come from, and where are you going?” She replied: “I am a daughter of the Hebrews, and I am fleeing from them, because they are about to be delivered up to you as prey.* 13I have come to see Holofernes, the general in chief of your forces, to give him a trustworthy report; I will show him the route by which he can ascend and take possession of the whole mountain district without a single one of his men suffering injury or loss of life.” [r]

14When the men heard her words and gazed upon her face, which appeared wondrously beautiful to them, they said to her, 15“By coming down thus promptly to see our master, you have saved your life. Now go to his tent; some of our men will accompany you to present you to him. 16When you stand before him, have no fear in your heart; give him the report you speak of, and he will treat you well.” 17So they detailed a hundred of their men as an escort for her and her maid, and these conducted them to the tent of Holofernes.

18When the news of her arrival spread among the tents, a crowd gathered in the camp. They came and stood around her as she waited outside the tent of Holofernes, while he was being informed about her. 19They marveled at her beauty, regarding the Israelites with wonder because of her, and they said to one another, “Who can despise this people that has such women among them? It is not wise to leave one man of them alive, for if any were to be spared they could beguile the whole world.”

Judith Meets Holofernes 20The guard of Holofernes and all his servants came out and ushered her into the tent. 21Now Holofernes was reclining on his bed under a canopy with a netting of crimson and gold, emeralds and other precious stones. 22When they announced her to him, he came out to the antechamber, preceded by silver lamps; 23and when Holofernes and his servants beheld Judith, they all marveled at the beauty of her face. She threw herself down prostrate before him, but his servants raised her up.

CHAPTER 11

1Then Holofernes said to her: “Take courage, lady; have no fear in your heart! Never have I harmed anyone who chose to serve Nebuchadnezzar, king of all the earth. 2Nor would I have raised my spear against your people who dwell in the mountain region, had they not despised me and brought this upon themselves. 3But now tell me why you fled from them and came to us. In any case, you have come to safety. Take courage! Your life is spared tonight and for the future. 4No one at all will harm you. Rather, you will be well treated, as are all the servants of my lord, King Nebuchadnezzar.”

5 [s]Judith answered him: “Listen to the words of your servant, and let your handmaid speak in your presence! I will tell no lie to my lord this night, 6and if you follow out the words of your handmaid, God will give you complete success, and my lord will not fail in any of his undertakings. 7By the life of Nebuchadnezzar, king of all the earth, and by the power of him who has sent you to set all creatures aright! not only do men serve him through you; but even the wild beasts

10, 12f: The deceitful means used by Judith against Holofernes, here and in Jdt 11, 5–19, are to be judged in the light of the moral concepts of Old Testament times; cf Gn 27, 1–25; 34, 13–29; 37, 32ff; Jos 2, 1–7; Jgs 4, 17–22.

r Jdt 11, 5f. s 5f: Jdt 10, 13.

and the cattle and the birds of the air, because of your strength, will live for Nebuchadnezzar and his whole house.[t] [8]Indeed, we have heard of your wisdom and sagacity, and all the world is aware that throughout the kingdom you alone are competent, rich in experience, and distinguished in military strategy.

[9][u]"As for Achior's speech in your council, we have heard of it. When the men of Bethulia spared him, he told them all he had said to you. [10]So then, my lord and master, do not disregard his word, but bear it in mind, for it is true. For our people are not punished, nor does the sword prevail against them, except when they sin against their God.[v] [11]But now their guilt has caught up with them by which they bring the wrath of their God upon them whenever they do wrong; so that my lord will not be repulsed and fail, but death will overtake them. [12]Since their food gave out and all their water ran low, they decided to kill their animals, and determined to consume all the things which God in his laws forbade them to eat. [13]They decreed that they would use up the first fruits of grain and the tithes of wine and oil which they had sanctified and reserved for the priests who minister in the presence of our God in Jerusalem: things which no layman should even touch with his hands. [14]They have sent messengers to Jerusalem to bring back to them authorization from the council of the elders; for the inhabitants there have also done these things. [15]On the very day when the response reaches them and they act upon it, they will be handed over to you for destruction.

[16]"As soon as I, your handmaid, learned all this, I fled from them. God has sent me to perform with you such deeds that people throughout the world will be astonished on hearing of them. [17]Your handmaid is, indeed, a God-fearing woman, serving the God of heaven night and day. Now I will remain with you, my lord; but each night your handmaid will go out to the ravine and pray to God. He will tell me when the Israelites have committed their crimes. [18]Then I will come and let you know, so that you may go out with your whole force, and not one of them will be able to withstand you. [19]I will lead you through Judea, till you come to Jerusalem, and there I will set up your judgment seat. You will drive them like sheep that have no shepherd, and not even a dog will growl at you. This was told me, and announced to me in advance, and I in turn have been sent to tell you."

[20]Her words pleased Holofernes and all his servants; they marveled at her wisdom and exclaimed,[w] [21]"No other woman from one end of the world to the other looks so beautiful and speaks so wisely!" [22]Then Holofernes said to her: "God has done well in sending you ahead of your people, to bring victory to our arms, and destruction to those who have despised my lord. [23]You are fair to behold, and your words are well spoken. If you do as you have said, your God will be my God; you shall dwell in the palace of King Nebuchadnezzar, and shall be renowned throughout the earth."[x]

CHAPTER 12

Judith's Conduct [1]Then he ordered them to lead her into the room where his silverware was kept, and bade them set a table for her with his own delicacies to eat and his own wine to drink. [2]But Judith said, "I will not partake of them, lest it be an occasion of sin; but I shall be amply supplied from the things I brought with me."[y] [3]Holofernes asked her: "But if your provisions give out, where shall we get more of the same to provide for you? None of your people are with us." [4]Judith answered him, "As surely as you, my lord, live, your handmaid will not use up her supplies till the LORD accomplishes by my hand what he has determined."

[5]Then the servants of Holofernes led her into the tent, where she slept till midnight. In the night watch just before dawn, she rose [6]and sent this message to Holofernes, "Give orders, my lord, to let your handmaid go out for prayer." [7]So Holofernes ordered his bodyguard not to hinder her. Thus she stayed in the camp three

t Jer 27, 6; Bar 3, 16f; Dn 2, 38. u 9f: Jdt 5, 5. v Jdt 5, 21; 8, 18. w Jdt 9, 13. x Jdt 9, 13. y Jdt 10, 5; Dn 1, 8.

days. Each night she went out to the ravine of Bethulia, where she washed herself at the spring of the camp. [8]After bathing, she besought the LORD, the God of Israel, to direct her way for the triumph of his people. [9]Then she returned purified to the tent, and remained there until her food was brought to her toward evening.

Holofernes' Banquet [10]On the fourth day Holofernes gave a banquet for his servants alone, to which he did not invite any of the officers.* [11]And he said to Bagoas, the eunuch in charge of his household: "Go and persuade this Hebrew woman in your care to come and to eat and drink with us. [12]It would be a disgrace for us to have such a woman with us without enjoying her company. If we do not entice her, she will laugh us to scorn."

[13]So Bagoas left the presence of Holofernes, and came to Judith and said, "So fair a maiden should not be reluctant to come to my lord to be honored by him, to enjoy drinking wine with us, and to be like one of the Assyrian women who live in the palace of Nebuchadnezzar." [14]She replied, "Who am I to refuse my lord? Whatever is pleasing to him I will promptly do. This will be a joy for me till the day of my death."

[15]Thereupon she proceeded to put on her festive garments and all her feminine adornments. Meanwhile her maid went ahead and spread out on the ground for her in front of Holofernes the fleece Bagoas had furnished for her daily use in reclining at her dinner. [16]Then Judith came in and reclined on it. The heart of Holofernes was in rapture over her, and his spirit was shaken. He was burning with the desire to possess her, for he had been biding his time to seduce her from the day he saw her. [17]Holofernes said to her, "Drink and be merry with us!" [18]Judith replied, "I will gladly drink, my lord, for at no time since I was born have I ever enjoyed life as much as I do today." [19]She then took the things her maid had prepared, and ate and drank in his presence. [20]Holofernes, charmed by her, drank a great quantity of wine, more than he had ever drunk on one single day in his life.

CHAPTER 13

[1]When it grew late, his servants quickly withdrew. Bagoas closed the tent from the outside and excluded the attendants from their master's presence. They went off to their beds, for they were all tired from the prolonged banquet. [2]Judith was left alone in the tent with Holofernes, who lay prostrate on his bed, for he was sodden with wine. [3]She had ordered her maid to stand outside the bedroom and wait, as on the other days, for her to come out; she said she would be going out for her prayer. To Bagoas she had said this also.

Beheading of Holofernes [4]When all had departed, and no one, small or great, was left in the bedroom, Judith stood by Holofernes' bed and said within herself: "O LORD, God of all might, in this hour look graciously on my undertaking for the exaltation of Jerusalem; [5]now is the time for aiding your heritage and for carrying out my design to shatter the enemies who have risen against us." [6]She went to the bedpost near the head of Holofernes, and taking his sword from it, [7]drew close to the bed, grasped the hair of his head, and said, "Strengthen me this day, O God of Israel!" [8]Then with all her might she struck him twice in the neck and cut off his head.[z] [9]She rolled his body off the bed and took the canopy from its supports. Soon afterward, she came out and handed over the head of Holofernes to her maid, [10]who put it into her food pouch; and the two went off together as they were accustomed to do for prayer.

The Return to Bethulia They passed through the camp, and skirting the ravine, reached Bethulia on the mountain. As they approached its gates, [11]Judith shouted to the guards from a distance: "Open! Open the gate! God, our God, is with us. Once more he has made manifest his strength in Israel and his power against our enemies; he has done it this very day." [12]When

12, 10: Banquet for his servants alone . . . officers: Holofernes invited the officials of his household, but not the officers of his army who were needed for military duty.

z Jgs 4, 21.

the citizens heard her voice, they quickly descended to their city gate and summoned the city elders. [13]All the people, from the least to the greatest, hurriedly assembled, for her return seemed unbelievable. They opened the gate and welcomed the two women. They made a fire for light; and when they gathered around the two, [14]Judith urged them with a loud voice: "Praise God, praise him! Praise God, who has not withdrawn his mercy from the house of Israel, but has shattered our enemies by my hand this very night." [15]Then she took the head out of the pouch, showed it to them, and said: "Here is the head of Holofernes, general in charge of the Assyrian army, and here is the canopy under which he lay in his drunkenness. The LORD struck him down by the hand of a woman. [a] [16]As the LORD lives, who has protected me in the path I have followed, I swear that it was my face that seduced Holofernes to his ruin, and that he did not sin with me to my defilement or disgrace."

[17]All the people were greatly astonished. They bowed down and worshiped God, saying with one accord, "Blessed are you, our God, who today have brought to nought the enemies of your people." [18]Then Uzziah said to her: "Blessed are you, daughter, by the Most High God, above all the women on earth; and blessed be the LORD God, the creator of heaven and earth, who guided your blow at the head of the chief of our enemies. [b] [19]Your deed of hope will never be forgotten by those who tell of the might of God. [20]May God make this redound to your everlasting honor, rewarding you with blessings, because you risked your life when your people were being oppressed, and you averted our disaster, walking uprightly before our God." And all the people answered, "Amen! Amen!"

CHAPTER 14

Judith's Counsel [1]Then Judith said to them: "Listen to me, my brothers. Take this head and hang it on the parapet of your wall. [2]At daybreak, when the sun rises on the earth, let each of you seize his weapons, and let all the able-bodied men rush out of the city under command of a captain, as if about to go down into the plain against the advance guard of the Assyrians, but without going down. [3]They will seize their armor and hurry to their camp to awaken the generals of the Assyrian army. When they run to the tent of Holofernes and do not find him, panic will seize them, and they will flee before you. [4]Then you and all the other inhabitants of the whole territory of Israel will pursue them and strike them down in their tracks. [5]But before doing this, summon for me Achior the Ammonite, that he may see and recognize the one who despised the house of Israel and sent him here to meet his death."

Achior Summoned* [6]So they called Achior from the house of Uzziah. When he came and saw the head of Holofernes in the hand of one of the men in the assembly of the people, he fell forward in a faint. [7]Then, after they lifted him up, he threw himself at the feet of Judith in homage, saying: "Blessed are you in every tent of Judah; and in every foreign nation, all who hear of you will be struck with terror. [8]But now, tell me all that you did during these days." So Judith told him, in the presence of the people, all that she had been doing from the day she left till the time she began speaking to them. [9]When she finished her account, the people cheered loudly, and their city resounded with shouts of joy. [10]Now Achior, seeing all that the God of Israel had done, believed firmly in him. He had the flesh of his foreskin circumcised, and he has been united with the house of Israel to the present day.

III: Victory

Consternation in the Camp [11]At daybreak they hung the head of Holofernes on the wall. Then all the Israelite men took up their arms and went to the slopes of the mountain. [12]When the

14, 6–10: In recognizing the head of Holofernes, whom he had known personally, Achior was so overcome with the evidence of the Lord's power exerted through a woman that he believed in the God of Israel.

a Jdt 14, 18. b Jgs 5, 24; Lk 1, 28. 42.

Assyrians saw them, they notified their captains; these, in turn, went to the generals and division leaders and all their other commanders. [13]They came to the tent of Holofernes and said to the one in charge of all his things, "Waken our master, for the slaves have dared come down to give us battle, to their utter destruction." [14]Bagoas went in, and knocked at the entry of the tent, presuming that he was sleeping with Judith. [15]As no one answered, he parted the curtains, entered the bedroom, and found him lying on the floor, a headless corpse. [16]He broke into a loud clamor of weeping, groaning, and howling, and rent his garments. [17]Then he entered the tent where Judith had her quarters; and, not finding her, he rushed out to the troops and cried: [18]"The slaves have duped us! A single Hebrew woman has brought disgrace on the house of King Nebuchadnezzar. Here is Holofernes headless on the ground!" [c]

[19]When the commanders of the Assyrian army heard these words, they rent their tunics and were seized with consternation. Loud screaming and howling arose in the camp.

CHAPTER 15

[1]On hearing what had happened, those still in their tents were amazed, [2]and overcome with fear and trembling. No one kept ranks any longer; they scattered in all directions, and fled along every road, both through the valley and in the mountains. [3]Those also who were stationed in the mountain district around Bethulia took to flight. Then all the Israelite warriors overwhelmed them.

Pursuit [4]Uzziah sent messengers to Betomasthaim, to Choba and Kona, and to the whole country of Israel to report what had happened, that all might fall upon the enemy and destroy them. [5]On hearing this, all the Israelites, with one accord, attacked them and cut them down as far as Choba. Even those from Jerusalem and the rest of the mountain region took part in this, for they too had been notified of the happenings in the camp of their enemies. The Gileadites and the Galileans struck the enemy's flanks with great slaughter, even beyond Damascus and its territory. [6]The remaining inhabitants of Bethulia swept down on the camp of the Assyrians, plundered it, and acquired great riches. [7]The Israelites who returned from the slaughter took possession of what was left, till the towns and villages in the mountains and on the plain were crammed with the enormous quantity of booty they had seized. [d]

[8]The high priest Joakim and the elders of the Israelites, who dwelt in Jerusalem, came to see for themselves the good things that the LORD had done for Israel, and to meet and congratulate Judith. [e] [9]When they had visited her, all with one accord blessed her, saying:

"You are the glory of Jerusalem,
the surpassing joy of Israel;
you are the splendid boast of our people.*
[10]With your own hand you have done all this;
you have done good to Israel,
and God is pleased with what you have wrought.
May you be blessed by the LORD Almighty
forever and ever!"

And all the people answered, "Amen!"

[11]For thirty days the whole populace plundered the camp, giving Judith the tent of Holofernes, with all his silver, his couches, his dishes, and all his furniture, which she accepted. She harnessed her mules, hitched her wagons to them, and loaded these things on them.

[12]All the women of Israel gathered to see her; and they blessed her and performed a dance in her honor. She took branches in her hands and distributed them to the women around her,[f] [13]and she and the other women crowned themselves with garlands of olive leaves. At the head of all the people, she led the women in the dance, while the men of Israel followed in their armor, wearing garlands and singing hymns.

15, 9: You are the glory of Jerusalem, the surpassing joy of Israel; you are the splendid boast of our people: these words are used in the liturgy of the Church in regard to the Blessed Virgin Mary.

c Jdt 13, 15; 16, 5–9; Jgs 9, 54. d Est 9, 5. 16. e Est 9, 10. f Ex 15, 20f; Jgs 11, 34; 1 Sm 18, 6; Jer 31, 4. 13.

Hymn of Praise [14]Judith led all Israel in this song of thanksgiving, and the people swelled this hymn of praise:

CHAPTER 16

1 "Strike up the instruments,
a song to my God with timbrels,
chant to the LORD with cymbals;
Sing to him a new song,
exalt and acclaim his name. [g]
2 For the LORD is God; he crushes warfare,
and sets his encampment among his people;
he snatched me from the hands of my persecutors. [h]

3 "The Assyrian came from the mountains of the north,
with the myriads of his forces he came;
Their numbers blocked the torrents, their horses covered the hills.
4 He threatened to burn my land,
put my youths to the sword,
Dash my babes to the ground,
make my children a prey,
and seize my virgins as spoil.

5 "But the LORD Almighty thwarted them,
by a woman's hand he confounded them. [i]
6 Not by youths was their mighty one struck down,
nor did titans bring him low,
nor huge giants attack him;
But Judith, the daughter of Merari,
by the beauty of her countenance disabled him. [j]
7 She took off her widow's garb
to raise up the afflicted in Israel.
She anointed her face with fragrant oil;
8 with a fillet she fastened her tresses
and put on a linen robe to beguile him.
9 Her sandals caught his eyes,
and her beauty captivated his mind.
The sword cut through his neck. [k]

10 "The Persians were dismayed at her daring,
the Medes appalled at her boldness.
11 When my lowly ones shouted, they were terrified;
when my weaklings cried out, they trembled;
at the sound of their war cry, they took to flight.
12 The sons of slave girls pierced them through;
the supposed sons of rebel mothers cut them down;
they perished before the ranks of my LORD.

13 "A new hymn I will sing to my God.
O LORD, great are you and glorious,
wonderful in power and unsurpassable. [l]
14 Let your every creature serve you;
for you spoke, and they were made,
You sent forth your spirit, and they were created;
no one can resist your word. [m]
15 The mountains to their bases, and the seas, are shaken;
the rocks, like wax, melt before your glance. [n]

"But to those who fear you,
you are very merciful.
16 Though the sweet odor of every sacrifice is a trifle,
and the fat of all holocausts but little in your sight,
one who fears the LORD is forever great. [o]

17 "Woe to the nations that rise against my people!
The LORD Almighty will requite them;
in the day of judgment he will punish them:
He will send fire and worms into their flesh,*
and they shall burn and suffer forever." [p]

Thanksgiving [18]The people then went to Jeru-
salem to worship God; when they were purified,
they offered their holocausts, free-will offerings,
and gifts. [19]Judith dedicated, as a votive offering
to God, all the things of Holofernes that the
people had given her, as well as the canopy that
she herself had taken from his bedroom. [q] [20]For

16, 17: Fire and worms into their flesh: see footnote on Is 66, 24.

g Pss 81, 2f; 135, 1ff; 149, 1ff. h Jdt 5, 23; 6, 2; 9, 7f; Ex 15, 3; Ps 46, 10. i Jdt 14, 8. j Jdt 9, 13. k Jdt 9, 13. l Ps 144, 9. m Pss 33, 9; 104, 30; 148, 5. n Jgs 5, 5; Ps 97, 5. o Ps 86, 11; Sir 34, 13–17. p Is 66, 24. q Nm 31, 48–54; Dt 13, 13–18; Jos 6, 18f.

three months the people continued their celebration in Jerusalem before the sanctuary, and Judith remained with them.

Judith's Renown 21 When those days were over, each one returned to his inheritance. Judith went back to Bethulia and remained on her estate. For the rest of her life she was renowned throughout the land. 22 Many wished to marry her, but she gave herself to no man all the days of her life from the time of the death and burial of her husband, Manasseh. 23 She lived to be very old in the house of her husband, reaching the advanced age of a hundred and five. She died in Bethulia, where they buried her in the tomb of her husband, Manasseh;[r] 24 and the house of Israel mourned her for seven days. Before she died, she distributed her goods to the relatives of her husband, Manasseh, and to her own relatives; and to the maid she gave her freedom.

25 [s]During the life of Judith and for a long time after her death, no one again disturbed the Israelites.*

16, 25: The Vulgate adds: "The feast day of this victory was adopted by the Hebrews into the calendar of their holy days, and has been celebrated by the Jews from that time to the present." However, there is no other evidence of such a festivity; and it is the ancient feast of Passover to which the narrative is especially suited.

r Gn 23, 19; 49, 29–32. s Jgs 3, 11. 30; 5, 31; 8, 28.

THE BOOK OF ESTHER

The Book of Esther is named after its Jewish heroine. It tells the story of the plot of Haman the Agagite, jealous and powerful vizier of King Xerxes (Ahasuerus) of Persia (485–464 B.C.), to destroy in a single day all the Jews living in the Persian Empire. He is moved to this out of hatred for the Jewish servant Mordecai, who for religious motives refuses to render him homage. The day of the proposed massacre is determined by lot. Meanwhile Esther, niece and adopted daughter of Mordecai, is chosen queen by King Xerxes in place of Vashti. She averts the pogrom planned against her people and has the royal decree of extermination reversed against Haman and the enemies of the Jews. Mordecai replaces Haman, and together with Esther, works for the welfare of their people. The event is celebrated with feasting and great joy, and the memory of it is to be perpetuated by the annual observance of the feast of Purim (lots), when the lot of destruction for the Jews was reversed for one of deliverance and triumph by Queen Esther and her uncle Mordecai.

The purpose of the book is didactic: the glorification of the Jewish people and the explanation of the origin, significance and date of the feast of Purim on the fourteenth and fifteenth of Adar (February–March). The book was intended as a consolation for Israel, a reminder that God's providence continually watches over them, never abandoning them when they serve him faithfully or turn to him in sincere repentance. There is no justification for interpreting the story in mythological or cultic terms, as though Mordecai and Esther represented Marduk and Ishtar in their mythological triumph over two Elamite deities.

The Hebrew text of Esther is found in the Hebrew Bible, where it is the last of the five megilloth (scrolls) read on special feasts of the Jewish liturgical year.

The book is a free composition—not a historical document, despite the Achaemenian coloring of the narrative. Its time of composition may well have been at the end of the Persian Empire, toward the close of the fourth century B.C. The author shows skill in developing his story and in using the art of contrast for instruction and edification. The solution to the difficulties of the book is to be found in its literary presentation rather than in a forced attempt to square detailed data of the narrative with facts. The evident literary motif of the reversal of fortune of the prosperous wicked and the oppressed virtuous through eventual punishment of the former and triumph of the latter finds parallels in the story of Joseph (Gn 37; 39—45) and of Judith (8—16). The book is vindictive, but it should be remembered that the precept of love of enemies had not yet been taught by the word and example of Christ.

The text of Esther, written originally in Hebrew, was transmitted in two forms: a short Hebrew form and a longer Greek version. The latter contains 107 additional verses, inserted at appropriate places within the Hebrew form of the text. A few of these seem to have a Hebrew origin while the rest are Greek in original composition. It is possible that the Hebrew form of the text is original throughout. If it systematically omits reference to God and his Providence over Israel, this is perhaps due to fear of irreverent response (see note on 4, 14). The Greek text with the above-mentioned additions is probably a later literary paraphrase in which the author seeks to have the reader share his sentiments. This standard Greek text is pre-Christian in origin. The church has accepted the additions as equally inspired with the rest of the book.

In the present translation, the portions preceded by the letters A through F indicate the underlying Greek additions referred to above. The regular chapter numbers apply to the Hebrew text.

The book may be divided as follows:

I. Prologue (A, 1-17).
II. Elevation of Esther (1, 1—2, 23).
III. Haman's Plot against the Jews (3, 1-13; B, 1-7; 3, 14—4, 8; B, 8; 4, 9-16; C, 1—D, 16; 5, 1-14).
IV. Vindication of the Jews (6, 1—8, 12; E, 1-24; 8, 13—10, 3).
V. Epilogue (F, 1-11).

The order of the Vulgate text in relation to the order of the Greek text is as follows:

Vulg. 11, 2—12, 6 = A, 1-17 at the beginning of the book.
13, 1-7 = B, 1-7 after 3, 13.
13, 8—15, 3-19 = C, 1—D, 16 after 4, 16.
15, 1-2 = B, 8.9 after 4, 8.
16, 1-24 = E, 1-24 after 8, 12.
10, 4—10, 13 = F, 1-10 after 10, 3.

I: Prologue

CHAPTER A

Dream of Mordecai 1 In the second year of the reign of the great King Ahasuerus,* on the first day of Nisan, Mordecai, son of Jair, son of Shimei, son of Kish, of the tribe of Benjamin, had a dream. [a] 2 He was a Jew residing in the city of Susa, a prominent man who served at the king's

A, 1: King Ahasuerus: Xerxes I (485–464 B.C.). Mordecai: a Babylonian name, after the god Marduk. The genealogy of Mordecai is designed to reflect opposition to Israel's enemy, as narrated in 1 Sm 15, 7ff, where Saul (whose father's name was Kish, of the Tribe of Benjamin) conquered Agag the Amalekite; in A, 17 Haman is said to be the son of an Agagite. Further emphasis on the Benjaminite-Agagite opposition can be seen in Shimei, the Benjaminite who reviled David (2 Sm 16, 5ff). Jair appears to be the minor Judge, a Transjordan Manassehite (Jgs 10, 3). The chronology of the book would make Mordecai well over one hundred years old, since he was deported with Jehoiachin about 598 B.C.; cf Est 2, 5f.

a Est 2, 5.

court, [3]and one of the captives whom Nebuchadnezzar, king of Babylon, had taken from Jerusalem with Jeconiah, king of Judah.[b]

[4] [c]This was his dream.* There was noise and tumult, thunder and earthquake—confusion upon the earth. [5]Two great dragons came on, both poised for combat. They uttered a mighty cry, [6]and at their cry every nation prepared for war, to fight against the race of the just. [7]It was a dark and gloomy day. Tribulation and distress, evil and great confusion, lay upon the earth. [8]The whole race of the just were dismayed with fear of the evils to come upon them, and were at the point of destruction. [9] [d]Then they cried out to God, and as they cried, there appeared to come forth a great river, a flood of water from a little spring. [10]The light of the sun broke forth; the lowly were exalted and they devoured the nobles.

[11]Having seen this dream and what God intended to do, Mordecai awoke. He kept it in mind, and tried in every way, until night, to understand its meaning.

The Plot Discovered [12] [e]Mordecai lodged at the court with Bagathan and Thares, two eunuchs of the king who were court guards. [13]He overheard them plotting, investigated their plans, and discovered that they were preparing to lay hands on King Ahasuerus. So he informed the king about them, [14]and the king had the two eunuchs questioned and, upon their confession, put to death. [15]Then the king had these things recorded; Mordecai, too, put them into writing. [16]The king also appointed Mordecai to serve at the court, and rewarded him* for his actions.[f]

[17]Haman, however, son of Hammedatha the Agagite,* who was in high honor with the king, sought to harm Mordecai and his people because of the two eunuchs of the king.[g]

II: Elevation of Esther

CHAPTER 1

The Banquet of Ahasuerus [1]During the reign of Ahasuerus—this was the Ahasuerus who ruled over a hundred and twenty-seven provinces from India to Ethiopia *— [2]while he was occupying the royal throne in the stronghold of Susa,* [3]in the third year of his reign, he presided over a feast for all his officers and ministers: the Persian and Median aristocracy, the nobles, and the governors of the provinces.[h] [4]For as many as a hundred and eighty days, he displayed the glorious riches of his kingdom and the resplendent wealth of his royal estate.

[5]At the end of this time the king gave a feast of seven days in the garden court of the royal palace for all the people, great and small, who were in the stronghold of Susa. [6]There were white cotton draperies and violet hangings, held by cords of crimson byssus from silver rings on marble pillars. Gold and silver couches were on the pavement, which was of porphyry, marble, mother-of-pearl, and colored stones. [7]Liquor was served in a variety of golden cups, and the royal wine flowed freely, as befitted the king's munificence. [8]By ordinance of the king the drinking was unstinted, for he had instructed all the stewards of his household to comply with the good pleasure of everyone.

[9]Queen Vashti* also gave a feast for the women inside the royal palace of King Ahasuerus.

Deposal of Vashti [10]On the seventh day, when the king was merry with wine, he instructed Mehuman, Biztha, Harbona, Bigtha, Abagtha, Zethar, and Carkas, the seven eunuchs who attended King Ahasuerus,[i] [11]to bring Queen Vashti into his presence wearing the royal crown, that he might display her beauty to the

A, 4: The interpretation of this dream is given in Est F, 1–6.

A, 16: Rewarded him: this reward comes only later; see the sequence of events from the Hebrew text of Esther at 2, 22f, and 6, 3, below.

A, 17: Haman . . . the Agagite: opposed Mordecai the Benjaminite, by whom, however, he was overcome (Est 7, 9f), just as King Agag the Amalekite, was conquered by King Saul ancestor of Mordecai (1 Sm 15, 7ff).

1, 1: From India to Ethiopia: from western India to Upper Egypt, the greatest extent of the Persian Empire achieved under Darius the Great, father of Ahasuerus.

1, 2: Susa: ancient capital of Elam (Gn 14, 1); under the Achamenid kings, one of the two capitals of the Persian Empire. The other was Persepolis, the summer palace of the kings.

1, 9: Queen Vashti: Herodotus (Histories 7, 61) relates that the wife of Ahasuerus was Amestris.

b Est 2, 6; 2 Kgs 24, 15; 2 Chr 36, 9f; Jer 22, 24ff; 24, 1; 29, 1f. c 4ff: Est F, 2. 4ff. d gf: Est F, 3. e 12–15: Est 2, 21ff; 6, 1ff. f Est 6, 3. g Est 3, 1–15; B, 1–7; E, 13. h Jdt 1, 16. i Dn 5, 1.

populace and the officials, for she was lovely to
behold. 12But Queen Vashti refused to come at
the royal order issued through the eunuchs. At
this the king's wrath flared up, and he burned
with fury. 13He conferred with the wise men
versed in the law, because the king's business
was conducted in general consultation with
lawyers and jurists. 14He summoned Carshena,
Shethar, Admatha, Tarshish, Meres, Marsena
and Memucan, the seven Persian and Median
officials who were in the king's personal service
and held first rank in the realm,[j] 15and asked
them, "What is to be done by law with Queen
Vashti for disobeying the order of King Ahasue-
rus issued through the eunuchs?"

16In the presence of the king and of the
officials, Memucan answered: "Queen Vashti
has not wronged the king alone, but all the
officials and the populace throughout the prov-
inces of King Ahasuerus. 17For the queen's
conduct will become known to all the women,
and they will look with disdain upon their
husbands when it is reported, 'King Ahasuerus
commanded that Queen Vashti be ushered into
his presence, but she would not come.' 18This
very day the Persian and Median ladies who
hear of the queen's conduct will rebel against all
the royal officials, with corresponding disdain
and rancor. 19If it please the king, let an irrevoca-
ble royal decree* be issued by him and inscribed
among the laws of the Persians and Medes,
forbidding Vashti to come into the presence of
King Ahasuerus and authorizing the king to give
her royal dignity to one more worthy than she.[k]
20Thus, when the decree which the king will
issue is published throughout his realm, vast as it
is, all wives will honor their husbands, from the
greatest to the least."

21This proposal found acceptance with the
king and the officials, and the king acted on the
advice of Memucan. 22He sent letters to all the
royal provinces, to each province in its own
script and to each people in its own language,*
to the effect that every man should be lord in his
own home.

CHAPTER 2

Esther Made Queen 1After this, when King
Ahasuerus' wrath had cooled, he thought over
what Vashti had done and what had been
decreed against her. 2Then the king's personal
attendants suggested: "Let beautiful young vir-
gins be sought for the king. 3Let the king appoint
commissaries in all the provinces of his realm to
bring together all beautiful young virgins to the
harem in the stronghold of Susa. Under the care
of the royal eunuch Hegai, custodian of the
women, let cosmetics be given them. 4Then the
girl who pleases the king shall reign in place of
Vashti." This suggestion pleased the king, and he
acted accordingly.

5There was in the stronghold of Susa a certain
Jew named Mordecai, son of Jair, son of Shimei,
son of Kish, a Benjaminite, 6who had been
exiled from Jerusalem with the captives taken
with Jeconiah, king of Judah, whom Nebuchad-
nezzar, king of Babylon, had deported.[l] 7He was
foster father to Hadassah,* that is, Esther, his
cousin; for she had lost both father and mother.
The girl was beautifully formed and lovely to
behold. On the death of her father and mother,
Mordecai had taken her as his own daughter.[m]

8When the king's order and decree had been
obeyed and many maidens brought together to
the stronghold of Susa under the care of Hegai,
Esther also was brought in to the royal palace
under the care of Hegai, custodian of the
women. 9The girl pleased him and won his
favor. So he promptly furnished her with cosmet-
ics and provisions. Then picking out seven maids
for her from the royal palace, he transferred both
her and her maids to the best place in the harem.
10Esther did not reveal her nationality or family,
for Mordecai had commanded her not to do so.

1, 19: Irrevocable royal decree: the historian Siculus indicates that such a concept of irrevocable laws existed in the time of Darius III (335–331 B.C.), the last of the Persian kings; cf Est 8, 8.

1, 22: To each province . . . script and to each people . . . language: many languages were spoken in the Persian Empire, the principal ones being Persian, Elamite, Babylonian, Aramaic, Phoenician, Egyptian, and Greek. Each of them had its own script.

2, 7: Hadassah (the feminine form of hadas, myrtle), was the name by which this woman would be known among her Jewish compatriots. Esther is a variant of the name of the Babylonian goddess Ishtar.

j Ezr 7, 14. k Est 8, 5. 8; Dn 6, 8f. l Est A, 3; 2 Kgs 24, 15; 2 Chr 36, 9f; Jer 22, 24ff; 24, 1; 29, 1f. m Est 2, 15.

[11]Day by day Mordecai would walk about in front of the court of the harem, to learn how Esther was faring and what was to become of her.

[12]Each girl went in turn to visit King Ahasuerus after the twelve months' preparation decreed for the women. Of this period of beautifying treatment, six months were spent with oil of myrrh, and the other six months with perfumes and cosmetics. [13]Then, when the girl was to visit the king, she was allowed to take with her from the harem to the royal palace whatever she chose. [14]She would go in the evening and return in the morning to a second harem under the care of the royal eunuch Shaashgaz, custodian of the concubines. She could not return to the king unless he was pleased with her and had her summoned by name.[n]

[15]As for Esther, daughter of Abihail and adopted daughter of his nephew Mordecai, when her turn came to visit the king, she did not ask for anything but what the royal eunuch Hegai, custodian of the women, suggested. Yet she won the admiration of all who saw her. [16]Esther was led to King Ahasuerus in his palace in the tenth month, Tebeth, in the seventh year of his reign. [17]The king loved Esther more than all other women, and of all the virgins she won his favor and benevolence. So he placed the royal diadem on her head and made her queen in place of Vashti. [18]Then the king gave a great feast in honor of Esther to all his officials and ministers, granting a holiday* to the provinces and bestowing gifts with royal bounty.

The Plot Discovered* [19][o][To resume: From the time the virgins had been brought together,and while Mordecai was passing his time at the king's gate, [20]Esther had not revealed her family or nationality, because Mordecai had told her not to; and Esther continued to follow Mordecai's instructions, just as she had when she was being brought up by him. [21][p]And during the time that Mordecai spent at the king's gate,*Bagathan and Thares, two of the royal eunuchs who guarded the entrance, had plotted in anger to lay hands on King Ahasuerus. [22]When the plot became known to Mordecai, he told Queen Esther, who in turn informed the king for Mordecai. [23]The matter was investigated and verified, and both of them were hanged on a gibbet.* This was written in the annals for the king's use.]

III: Haman's Plot Against the Jews

CHAPTER 3

Mordecai Refuses To Honor Haman [1]After these events King Ahasuerus raised Haman, son of Hammedatha the Agagite, to high rank, seating him above all his fellow officials.[q] [2]All the king's servants who were at the royal gate would kneel and bow down to Haman, for that is what the king had ordered in his regard.[r] Mordecai, however, would not kneel and bow down.* [3]The king's servants who were at the royal gate said to Mordecai, "Why do you disobey the king's order?"[s] [4]When they had reminded him day after day and he would not listen to them, they informed Haman, to see whether Mordecai's explanation was acceptable, since he had told them that he was a Jew.

Haman's Reprisal [5]When Haman observed that Mordecai would not kneel and bow down to him, he was filled with anger. [6]Moreover, he thought it was not enough to lay hands on Mordecai alone. Since they had told Haman of Mordecai's nationality, he sought to destroy all the Jews, Mordecai's people, throughout the realm of King Ahasuerus. [7]In the first month,

2, 18: A holiday: or perhaps, "a remission of taxes."

2, 19–23: This is a resumption, in a slightly different form, of the story already told in Est A, 12–15.

2, 21: Mordecai . . . at the king's gate: to exercise watchful care for Esther. Some understand this to mean that Mordecai was stationed at the gate to render royal service; cf Est A, 2.

2, 23: Hanged on a gibbet: impaled, perhaps, after the Babylonian manner.

3, 2: Mordecai . . . would not kneel and bow down: in order not to render to man, the homage which he regarded as belonging to God alone; cf Est C, 5ff.

3, 7: Pur: a Babylonian word which the Hebrew translates as goral, "lot." This word is preserved in the text because its plural, purim, became the name of the feast of Purim commemorating the deliverance of the Jews; cf Est 9, 24. 26.

n Est 2, 19f; 4, 11. 16. o 19f: Est 2, 14. p 21ff: Est A, 12–15; 6, 1ff. q Est B, 3; 5, 11; E, 11. r Est C, 5; 5, 9. 13; 6, 10. 12. s Est 4, 16.

Nisan, in the twelfth year of King Ahasuerus, the
*pur,** or lot, was cast in Haman's presence, to
determine the day and the month for the destruc-
tion of Mordecai's people on a single day, and
the lot fell on the thirteenth day of the twelfth
month, Adar.[t]
Decree against the Jews 8Then Haman said
to King Ahasuerus: "Dispersed among the na-
tions throughout the provinces of your kingdom,
there is a certain people living apart, with laws
differing from those of every other people. They
do not obey the laws of the king, and so it is not
proper for the king to tolerate them.[u] 9If it please
the king, let a decree be issued to destroy them;
and I will deliver to the procurators ten thou-
sand silver talents for deposit in the royal trea-
sury."[v] 10The king took the signet ring* from his
hand and gave it to Haman, son of Hammedatha
the Agagite, the enemy of the Jews.[w] 11"The
silver you may keep," the king said to Haman,
"but as for this people, do with them whatever
you please."
12So the royal scribes were summoned; and
on the thirteenth day of the first month they
wrote, at the dictation of Haman, an order to the
royal satraps, the governors of every province,
and the officials of every people, to each prov-
ince in its own script and to each people in its
own language. It was written in the name of
King Ahasuerus and sealed with the royal signet
ring. 13Letters were sent by couriers to all the
royal provinces, that all the Jews, young and old,
including women and children, should be killed,
destroyed, wiped out in one day, the thirteenth
day of the twelfth month, Adar, and that their
goods should be seized as spoil.[x]

CHAPTER B

1This is a copy of the letter:
"The great King Ahasuerus writes to the
satraps of the hundred and twenty-seven prov-
inces from India to Ethiopia, and the governors
subordinate to them, as follows: 2When I came
to rule many peoples and to hold sway over the
whole world, I determined not to be carried
away with the sense of power, but always to deal
fairly and with clemency; to provide for my
subjects a life of complete tranquillity; and by
making my government humane and effective as
far as the borders, to restore the peace desired by
all men.[y] 3When I consulted my counselors as to
how this might be accomplished, Haman, who
excels among us in wisdom, who is outstanding
for constant devotion and steadfast loyalty, and
who has gained the second rank in the king-
dom,[z] 4brought it to our attention that, mixed in
with all the races throughout the world, there is
one people of bad will, which by its laws is
opposed to every other people and continually
disregards the decrees of kings, so that the unity
of empire blamelessly designed by us cannot be
established.[a]
5"Having noted, therefore, that this most
singular people is continually at variance with all
men, lives by divergent and alien laws, is inimi-
cal to our interests, and commits the worst
crimes, so that stability of government cannot be
obtained, 6we hereby decree that all those who
are indicated to you in the letters of Haman,
who is in charge of the administration and is a
second father to us, shall, together with their
wives and children, be utterly destroyed by the
swords of their enemies, without any pity or
mercy, on the fourteenth day* of the twelfth
month, Adar, of the current year;[b] 7so that
when these people, whose present ill will is of
long standing, have gone down into the nether
world by a violent death on one same day, they
may at last leave our affairs stable and undis-
turbed for the future."

3, 10: Signet ring: a ring containing a seal which was impressed on documents to authenticate them. By giving this ring to Haman, the king bestowed on him the power to authenticate royal decrees.

B, 6: Fourteenth day: the Hebrew text, as in Est 2, 13 above, and the Greek text here translated do not agree on the day of the month specified by the king; in fact, a two-day celebration is decreed in chapter 9, and the 13th, 14th and 15th of Adar are all mentioned; see Est 9, 15. 18.

t Est 9, 24ff; F, 10. u Est 3, 13; B, 4; E, 24; Dn 3, 8-12; Wis 2, 14f. v Est 7, 4. w Gn 41, 42. x Est B, 6; 7, 4. y Est E, 8f. z Est 3, 1; 5, 11; E, 11. a Est 3, 8; E, 24. b Est 3, 13; 7, 4; E, 11ff.

(CHAPTER 3)

14A copy of the decree to be promulgated as
law in every province was published to all the
peoples, that they might be prepared for that
day. 15The couriers set out in haste at the king's
command; meanwhile, the decree was promul-
gated in the stronghold of Susa. The king and
Haman then sat down to feast, but the city of
Susa was thrown into confusion.

CHAPTER 4

Esther's Aid Sought by Mordecai 1When
Mordecai learned all that was happening, he tore
his garments, put on sackcloth and ashes, and
walked through the city, crying out loudly and
bitterly,[c] 2till he came before the royal gate,
which no one clothed in sackcloth might enter.
3(Likewise in each of the provinces, wherever
the king's legal enactment reached, the Jews
went into deep mourning, with fasting, weeping,
and lament; they all slept on sackcloth and
ashes.)

4Queen Esther's maids and eunuchs came
and told her. Overwhelmed with anguish, she
sent garments for Mordecai to put on, so that he
might take off his sackcloth; but he refused.
5Esther then summoned Hathach, one of the
king's eunuchs whom he had placed at her
service, and commanded him to find out what
this action of Mordecai meant and the reason for
it. 6So Hathach went out to Mordecai in the
public square in front of the royal gate, 7and
Mordecai told him all that had happened, as well
as the exact amount of silver Haman had prom-
ised to pay to the royal treasury for the slaughter
of the Jews. 8He also gave him a copy of the
written decree for their destruction which had
been promulgated in Susa, to show and explain
to Esther. He was to instruct her to go to the
king; she was to plead and intercede with him in
behalf of her people. 8*"Remember the days of
your lowly estate," Mordecai had him say,
"when you were brought up in my charge; for
Haman, who is second to the king, has asked for
our death. 9Invoke the LORD and speak to the
king for us; save us from death."

Hathach returned to Esther and told her what
Mordecai had said. 10Then Esther replied to
Hathach and gave him this message for Morde-
cai: 11"All the servants of the king and the
people of his provinces know that any man or
woman who goes to the king in the inner court
without being summoned, suffers the automatic
penalty of death, unless the king extends to him
the golden scepter, thus sparing his life. Now as
for me, I have not been summoned to the king
for thirty days."[d]

12When Esther's words were reported to
Mordecai, 13he had this reply brought to her:
"Do not imagine that because you are in the
king's palace, you alone of all the Jews will
escape. 14Even if you now remain silent, relief
and deliverance will come to the Jews from
another source;* but you and your father's
house will perish. Who knows but that it was for
a time like this that you obtained the royal
dignity?"

15Esther sent back to Mordecai the response:
16"Go and assemble all the Jews who are in
Susa; fast on my behalf, all of you, not eating or
drinking, night or day, for three days. I and my
maids will also fast in the same way. Thus
prepared, I will go to the king, contrary to the
law. If I perish, I perish!"[e]

CHAPTER C

Prayer of Mordecai Mordecai went away and
did exactly as Esther had commanded. 1Recall-
ing all that the LORD had done, he prayed to him
2and said: "O Lord God, almighty King, all
things are in your power, and there is no one to
oppose you in your will to save Israel. 3You
made heaven and earth and every wonderful
thing under the heavens. 4You are LORD of all,
and there is no one who can resist you, LORD.
5[f]You know all things. You know, O LORD, that
it was not out of insolence or pride or desire for
fame that I acted thus in not bowing down to the
proud Haman. 6Gladly would I have kissed the

4, 8: This verse belongs to ch B.
4, 14: From another source: very probably Mordecai refers to divine aid; the Greek additions (C) are explicit about this.

c Jdt 4, 12. d Est 2, 14; 4, 12; D, 12. e Est C, 12f. f 5ff: Est 3, 2; 5, 9.

soles of his feet for the salvation of Israel. 7But I acted as I did so as not to place the honor of man above that of God. I will not bow down to anyone but you, my LORD. It is not out of pride that I am acting thus. 8And now, LORD God, King, God of Abraham, spare your people, for our enemies plan our ruin and are bent upon destroying the inheritance that was yours from the beginning. 9Do not spurn your portion, which you redeemed for yourself out of Egypt. 10Hear my prayer; have pity on your inheritance and turn our sorrow into joy: thus we shall live to sing praise to your name, O LORD. Do not silence those who praise you."

11All Israel, too, cried out with all their strength, for death was staring them in the face.

Prayer of Esther 12 [g]Queen Esther, seized with mortal anguish, likewise had recourse to the LORD. 13Taking off her splendid garments, she put on garments of distress and mourning. In place of her precious ointments she covered her head with dirt and ashes. She afflicted her body severely; all her festive adornments were put aside, and her hair was wholly disheveled.

14Then she prayed to the LORD, the God of Israel, saying: "My LORD, our King, you alone are God. Help me, who am alone and have no help but you, 15for I am taking my life in my hand.[h] 16As a child I was wont to hear from the people of the land of my forefathers that you, O LORD, chose Israel from among all peoples, and our fathers from among all their ancestors, as a lasting heritage, and that you fulfilled all your promises to them.[i] 17But now we have sinned in your sight, and you have delivered us into the hands of our enemies, 18because we worshiped their gods. You are just, O LORD. 19But now they are not satisfied with our bitter servitude, but have undertaken 20to do away with the decree you have pronounced, and to destroy your heritage; to close the mouths of those who praise you, and to extinguish the glory of your temple and your altar; 21to open the mouths of the heathen to acclaim their false gods, and to extol an earthly king forever.

22"O LORD, do not relinquish your scepter to those that are nought. Let them not gloat over our ruin, but turn their own counsel against them and make an example of our chief enemy. 23Be mindful of us, O LORD. Manifest yourself in the time of our distress and give me courage, King of gods and Ruler of every power. 24Put in my mouth persuasive words in the presence of the lion and turn his heart to hatred for our enemy, so that he and those who are in league with him may perish. 25Save us by your power, and help me, who am alone and have no one but you, O LORD.

"You know all things. 26You know that I hate the glory of the pagans, and abhor the bed of the uncircumcised or of any foreigner. 27You know that I am under constraint, that I abhor the sign of grandeur which rests on my head when I appear in public; abhor it like a polluted rag, and do not wear it in private. 28I, your handmaid, have never eaten at the table of Haman, nor have I graced the banquet of the king or drunk the wine of libations.* 29From the day I was brought here till now, your handmaid has had no joy except in you, O LORD, God of Abraham. 30O God, more powerful than all, hear the voice of those in despair. Save us from the power of the wicked, and deliver me from my fear."

CHAPTER D

Esther Is Received by the King 1On the third day, putting an end to her prayers, she took off her penitential garments and arrayed herself in her royal attire. 2In making her state appearance, after invoking the all-seeing God and savior, she took with her two maids; 3on the one she leaned gently for support, 4while the other followed her, bearing her train. 5She glowed with the perfection of her beauty and her countenance was as joyous as it was lovely, though her heart was shrunk with fear. 6She passed through all the portals till she stood face to face with the king, who was seated on his royal throne, clothed in full robes of state, and covered with gold and precious stones, so that he inspired

C, 28: Wine of libations: offered in sacrifice to the gods.

g 12f: Est 4, 16. h Est 4, 16. i Dt 4, 20; 7, 6; 9, 29; 14, 2; 26, 18; 32, 9.

great awe. 7As he looked up, his features ablaze with the height of majestic anger, the queen staggered, changed color, and leaned weakly against the head of the maid in front of her. 8But God changed the king's anger to gentleness. In great anxiety he sprang from his throne, held her in his arms until she recovered, and comforted her with reassuring words. 9"What is it, Esther?" he said to her. "I am your brother. Take courage! 10You shall not die because of this general decree of ours. 11Come near!" 12Raising the golden scepter, he touched her neck with it, embraced her, and said, "Speak to me."[j]

13She replied: "I saw you, my lord, as an angel of God, and my heart was troubled with fear of your majesty. 14For you are awesome, my lord, though your glance is full of kindness." 15As she said this, she fainted. 16The king became troubled and all his attendants tried to revive her.

CHAPTER 5

1*[Now on the third day, Esther put on her royal garments and stood in the inner courtyard, looking toward the royal palace, while the king was seated on his royal throne in the audience chamber, facing the palace doorway. 2He saw Queen Esther standing in the courtyard, and made her welcome by extending toward her the golden staff which he held. She came up to him, and touched the top of the staff.]

3Then the king said to her, "What is it, Queen Esther? What is your request? Even if it is half of my kingdom, it shall be granted you."[k] 4"If it please your majesty," Esther replied, "come today with Haman to a banquet I have prepared." 5And the king ordered, "Have Haman make haste to fulfill the wish of Esther."

First Banquet of Esther So the king went with Haman to the banquet Esther had prepared. 6During the drinking of the wine, the king said to Esther, "Whatever you ask for shall be granted, and whatever request you make shall be honored, even if it is for half my kingdom."[l] 7Esther replied: "This is my petition and request: 8if I have found favor with the king and if it pleases your majesty to grant my petition and honor my request, come with Haman tomorrow to a banquet which I shall prepare for you; and then I will do as you ask."

Haman's Plot against Mordecai 9That day Haman left happy and in good spirits. But when he saw that Mordecai at the royal gate did not rise, and showed no fear of him, he was filled with anger toward him.[m] 10Haman restrained himself, however, and went home, where he summoned his friends and his wife Zeresh. 11He recounted the greatness of his riches, the large number of his sons, and just how the king had promoted him and placed him above the officials and royal servants.[n] 12"Moreover," Haman added, "Queen Esther invited no one but me to the banquet with the king; again tomorrow I am to be her guest, with the king. 13Yet none of this satisfies me as long as I continue to see the Jew Mordecai sitting at the royal gate."[o] 14His wife Zeresh and all his friends said to him, "Have a gibbet set up, fifty cubits in height, and in the morning ask the king to have Mordecai hanged on it. Then go to the banquet with the king in good cheer." This suggestion pleased Haman, and he had the gibbet erected.[p]

IV: Vindication of the Jews

CHAPTER 6

Mordecai's Reward from the King 1That night the king, unable to sleep, asked that the chronicle of notable events be brought in. While this was being read to him, 2the passage occurred in which Mordecai reported Bagathan and Teresh, two of the royal eunuchs who guarded the entrance, for seeking to lay hands on King Ahasuerus.[q] 3The king asked, "What was done to reward and honor Mordecai for this?" The king's attendants replied, "Nothing was done for him."[r]

4"Who is in the court?" the king asked. Now

5, 1f: The Hebrew text here translated is a short form of the account already given in Greek.

j Est 4, 11. k Est 5, 6; 7, 2; 9, 12. l Est 5, 3. m Est 3, 2f; C, 5ff; 6, 10. 12. n Est 3, 1; B, 3; E, 11; 9, 6–10. o Est 3, 2f; 6, 10, 12. p Est 6, 4; 7, 9f. q Est A, 12ff; 2, 21ff. r Est A, 16.

Haman had entered the outer court of the king's palace to suggest to the king that Mordecai should be hanged on the gibbet he had raised for him.[s] 5 The king's servants answered him, "Haman is waiting in the court." "Let him come in," the king said. 6 When Haman entered, the king said to him, "What should be done for the man whom the king wishes to reward?" Now Haman thought to himself, "Whom would the king more probably wish to reward than me?" 7 So he replied to the king: "For the man whom the king wishes to reward 8 there should be brought the royal robe which the king wore and the horse on which the king rode when the royal crown was placed on his head. 9 The robe and the horse should be consigned to one of the noblest of the king's officials, who must clothe the man the king wishes to reward, have him ride on the horse in the public square of the city, and cry out before him, 'This is what is done for the man whom the king wishes to reward.' "[t] 10 Then the king said to Haman: "Hurry! Take the robe and horse as you have proposed, and do this for the Jew Mordecai, who is sitting at the royal gate. Do not omit anything you proposed."[u] 11 So Haman took the robe and horse, clothed Mordecai, had him ride in the public square of the city, and cried out before him, "This is what is done for the man whom the king wishes to reward."

12 Mordecai then returned to the royal gate, while Haman hurried home, his head covered in grief.[v] 13 When he told his wife Zeresh and all his friends everything that had happened to him, his advisers and his wife Zeresh said to him, "If Mordecai, before whom you are beginning to decline, is of the Jewish race, you will not prevail against him, but will surely be defeated by him."

Esther's Second Banquet 14 While they were speaking with him, the king's eunuchs arrived and hurried Haman off to the banquet Esther had prepared.

CHAPTER 7

1 So the king and Haman went to the banquet with Queen Esther. 2 Again, on this second day, during the drinking of the wine, the king said to Esther, "Whatever you ask, Queen Esther, shall be granted you. Whatever request you make shall be honored, even for half the kingdom."[w] 3 Queen Esther replied: "If I have found favor with you, O king, and if it pleases your majesty, I ask that my life be spared, and I beg that you spare the lives of my people. 4 For my people and I have been delivered to destruction, slaughter, and extinction. If we were to be sold into slavery I would remain silent, but as it is, the enemy will be unable to compensate for the harm done to the king."[x] 5 "Who and where," said King Ahasuerus to Queen Esther, "is the man who has dared to do this?"[y] 6 Esther replied, "The enemy oppressing us is this wicked Haman." At this, Haman was seized with dread of the king and queen.

7 The king left the banquet in anger and went into the garden of the palace, but Haman stayed to beg Queen Esther for his life, since he saw that the king had decided on his doom. 8 When the king returned from the garden of the palace to the banquet hall, Haman had thrown himself on the couch on which Esther was reclining; and the king exclaimed, "Will he also violate the queen while she is with me in my own house!" Scarcely had the king spoken, when the face of Haman was covered over.

Punishment of Haman 9 [z]Harbona, one of the eunuchs who attended the king, said, "At the house of Haman stands a gibbet fifty cubits high. Haman prepared it for Mordecai, who gave the report that benefited the king." The king answered, "Hang him on it." 10 So they hanged Haman on the gibbet which he had made ready for Mordecai, and the anger of the king abated.

CHAPTER 8

1 That day King Ahasuerus gave the house of Haman, enemy of the Jews, to Queen Esther; and Mordecai was admitted to the king's presence, for Esther had revealed his relationship to her.[a] 2 The king removed his signet ring from

s Est 5, 14; 7, 9f. t Gn 41, 42f; 1 Kgs 1, 33; Dn 5, 29. u Est 2, 21; 3, 2f; 5, 9. 13. v Est 2, 21; 3, 2f; 5, 9. 13. w Est 5, 3.

x Est 3, 13; B, 6. y Est 3, 8f. z 9f: Est 5, 14; 6, 4. a Est 9, 1; Prv 11, 8; 26, 27; Mt 7, 2.

Haman, and transferred it into the keeping of Mordecai; and Esther put Mordecai in charge of the house of Haman. [b]

The Second Royal Decree 3In another audience with the king, Esther fell at his feet and tearfully implored him to revoke the harm done by Haman the Agagite, and the plan he had devised against the Jews. 4The king stretched forth the golden scepter to Esther. So she rose and, standing in his presence, 5said: "If it pleases your majesty and seems proper to you, and if I have found favor with you and you love me, let a document be issued to revoke the letters which that schemer Haman, son of Hammedatha the Agagite, wrote for the destruction of the Jews in all the royal provinces. [c] 6For how can I witness the evil that is to befall my people, and how can I behold the destruction of my race?"

7King Ahasuerus then said to Queen Esther and to the Jew Mordecai: "Now that I have given Esther the house of Haman, and they have hanged him on the gibbet because he attacked the Jews, 8 [d]you in turn may write in the king's name what you see fit concerning the Jews and seal the letter with the royal signet ring." For whatever is written in the name of the king and sealed with the royal signet ring cannot be revoked.*

9At that time, on the twenty-third day of the third month, Sivan, the royal scribes were summoned. Exactly as Mordecai dictated, they wrote to the Jews and to the satraps, governors, and officials of the hundred and twenty-seven provinces from India to Ethiopia: to each province in its own script and to each people in its own language, and to the Jews in their own script and language. 10These letters, which he wrote in the name of King Ahasuerus and sealed with the royal signet ring, he sent by mounted couriers riding thoroughbred royal steeds. 11 [e]In these letters the king authorized the Jews in each and every city to group together and defend their lives, and to kill, destroy, wipe out, along with their wives and children, every armed group of any nation or province which should attack them, and to seize their goods as spoil 12throughout the provinces of King Ahasuerus, on a single day, the thirteenth of the twelfth month, Adar.

CHAPTER E

1The following is a copy of the letter:

"King Ahasuerus the Great to the governors of the provinces in the hundred and twenty-seven satrapies from India to Ethiopia, and to those responsible for our interests: Greetings!

2"Many have become the more ambitious the more they were showered with honors through the bountiful generosity of their patrons. 3Not only do they seek to do harm to our subjects; incapable of bearing such greatness, they even begin plotting against their own benefactors. 4Not only do they drive out gratitude from among men; with the arrogant boastfulness of those to whom goodness has no meaning, they suppose they will escape the vindictive judgment of the all-seeing God.

5"Often, too, the fair speech of friends entrusted with the administration of affairs has induced many placed in authority to become accomplices in the shedding of innocent blood, and has involved them in irreparable calamities 6by deceiving with malicious slander the sincere good will of rulers. 7This can be verified in the ancient stories that have been handed down to us, but more fully when one considers the wicked deeds perpetrated in your midst by the pestilential influence of those undeserving of authority. 8 [f]We must provide for the future, so as to render the kingdom undisturbed and peaceful for all men, 9taking advantage of changing conditions and deciding always with equitable treatment matters coming to our attention.

8, 8: Whatever is written . . . cannot be revoked: the king cannot directly grant Esther's request (v 5) to revoke the previous decree against the Jews because of the irrevocable character of the laws of the Medes and Persians (Est 1, 19; Dn 6, 9); but he empowers Esther to issue a new decree in his name which renders the earlier decree without effect; cf Est 3, 12f.

b Prv 13, 22; Dn 2, 48f. c Est 1, 19. d Est 1, 19. e 11f: Est 9, 1–4. f 8f: Est B, 2.

[10]"For instance, Haman, son of Hammedatha, a Macedonian,* certainly not of Persian blood, and very different from us in generosity, was hospitably received by us. [11]He so far enjoyed the good will which we have toward all peoples that he was proclaimed 'father of the king,' before whom everyone was to bow down; he attained the rank second to the royal throne.[g] [12]But, unequal to this dignity, he strove to deprive us of kingdom and of life; [13]and by weaving intricate webs of deceit, he demanded the destruction of Mordecai, our savior and constant benefactor, and of Esther, our blameless royal consort, together with their whole race.[h] [14]For by such measures he hoped to catch us defenseless and to transfer the rule of the Persians to the Macedonians. [15]But we find that the Jews, who were doomed to extinction by this arch-criminal, are not evildoers, but rather are governed by very just laws [16]and are the children of the Most High, the living God of majesty, who has maintained the kingdom in a flourishing condition for us and for our forebears.

[17]"You will do well, then, to ignore the letter sent by Haman, son of Hammedatha, [18]for he who composed it has been hanged, together with his entire household, before the gates of Susa. Thus swiftly has God, who governs all, brought just punishment upon him.[i]

[19]"You shall exhibit a copy of this letter publicly in every place, to certify that the Jews may follow their own laws, [20]and that you may help them on the day set for their ruin, the thirteenth day of the twelfth month, Adar, to defend themselves against those who attack them. [21]For God, the ruler of all, has turned that day for them from one of destruction of the chosen race into one of joy. [22]Therefore, you too must celebrate this memorable day among your designated feasts with all rejoicing, [23]so that both now and in the future it may be, for us and for loyal Persians, a celebration of victory, and for those who plot against us a reminder of destruction.

[24]"Every city and province, without exception, that does not observe this decree shall be ruthlessly destroyed with fire and sword, so that it will be left not merely untrodden by men, but even shunned by wild beasts and birds forever."[j]

(CHAPTER 8)

[13]A copy of the letter to be promulgated as law in each and every province was published among all the peoples, so that the Jews might be prepared on that day to avenge themselves on their enemies.* [14]Couriers mounted on royal steeds sped forth in haste at the king's order, and the decree was promulgated in the stronghold of Susa.

[15]Mordecai left the king's presence clothed in a royal robe of violet and of white cotton, with a large crown of gold and a cloak of crimson byssus. The city of Susa shouted with joy,[k] [16]and there was splendor and merriment for the Jews, exultation and triumph. [17]In each and every province and in each and every city, wherever the king's order arrived, there was merriment and exultation, banqueting and feasting for the Jews. And many of the peoples of the land embraced Judaism, for they were seized with a fear of the Jews.[l]

CHAPTER 9

Victory of the Jews [1] [m]When the day arrived on which the order decreed by the king was to be carried out, the thirteenth day of the twelfth month, Adar, on which the enemies of the Jews had expected to become masters of them, the situation was reversed: the Jews became masters of their enemies. [2]The Jews mustered in their cities throughout the provinces of King Ahasuerus to attack those who sought to do them harm, and no one could withstand them, but all peoples were seized with a fear of them. [3]More-

E, 10: Macedonian: a redactor of the book in the Hellenistic period used the designation Macedonian, here and in v 14, to express, after Macedonia's conquest of Persia, the most odious kind of man that a Persian ruler could be supposed to think of; the Hebrew text, for a similar reason, called Haman an Agagite. See note on Est A, 17.

8, 13: Avenge themselves on their enemies: partly in self-defense (Est E, 20), and partly to express the fact that the extreme cruelty designed against the Jews by their enemies now recoiled upon the latter as a punishment. Cf 9, 1f.

g Est B, 3. 6. h Est A, 17. i Est 7, 10; 9, 14. j Est 3, 8f; B, 4. k Dn 5, 7. l Est 9, 27. m 1f: Est 8, 11f.

over, all the officials of the provinces, the satraps, governors, and royal procurators supported the Jews from fear of Mordecai; [4]for Mordecai was powerful in the royal palace, and the report was spreading through all the provinces that he was continually growing in power.

[5]The Jews struck down all their enemies with the sword, killing and destroying them; they did to their enemies as they pleased.[n] [6][o]In the stronghold of Susa, the Jews killed and destroyed five hundred men. [7]They also killed Parshandatha, Dalphon, Aspatha, [8]Porathai, Adalia, Aridatha, [9]Parmashta, Arisai, Aridai, and Vaizatha, [10][p]the ten sons of Haman, son of Hammedatha, the foe of the Jews. However, they did not engage in plundering.*

[11]On the same day, when the number of those killed in the stronghold of Susa was reported to the king, [12]he said to Queen Esther: "In the stronghold of Susa the Jews have killed and destroyed five hundred men, as well as the ten sons of Haman. What must they have done in the other royal provinces! You shall again be granted whatever you ask, and whatever you request shall be honored." [13]So Esther said, "If it pleases your majesty, let the Jews in Susa be permitted again tomorrow to act according to today's decree, and let the ten sons of Haman be hanged on gibbets." [14]The king then gave an order to this effect, and the decree was published in Susa. So the ten sons of Haman were hanged,[q] [15]and the Jews in Susa mustered again on the fourteenth of the month of Adar and killed three hundred men in Susa.* However, they did not engage in plundering.[r]

[16]The other Jews, who dwelt in the royal provinces, also mustered and defended themselves, and obtained rest from their enemies. They killed seventy-five thousand* of their foes, without engaging in plunder,[s] [17]on the thirteenth day of the month of Adar. On the fourteenth of the month they rested, and made it a day of feasting and rejoicing.

[18](The Jews in Susa, however, mustered on the thirteenth and fourteenth of the month. But on the fifteenth they rested, and made it a day of feasting and rejoicing.) [19]That is why the rural Jews, who dwell in villages, celebrate the fourteenth of the month of Adar as a day of rejoicing and feasting, a holiday on which they send gifts of food to one another.

The Feast of Purim [20]Mordecai recorded these events and sent letters to all the Jews, both near and far, in all the provinces of King Ahasuerus. [21]He ordered them to celebrate every year both the fourteenth and the fifteenth of the month of Adar [22]as the day on which the Jews obtained rest from their enemies and as the month which was turned for them from sorrow into joy, from mourning into festivity. They were to observe these days with feasting and gladness, sending food to one another and gifts to the poor. [23]The Jews took upon themselves for the future this observance which they instituted at the written direction of Mordecai.[t]

[24][u]Haman, son of Hammedatha the Agagite, the foe of all the Jews, had planned to destroy them and had cast the *pur,* or lot, for the time of their defeat and destruction. [25]Yet, when Esther entered the royal presence, the king ordered in writing that the wicked plan Haman had devised against the Jews should instead be turned against Haman and that he and his sons should be hanged on gibbets.[v] [26]And so these days have been named Purim after the word *pur.*

Thus, because of all that was contained in this letter, and because of what they had witnessed and experienced in this affair, [27]the Jews established and took upon themselves, their descendants, and all who should join them, the inviolable obligation of celebrating these two days every year in the manner prescribed by this letter, and at the time appointed.[w] [28]These days

9, 10: They did not engage in plundering: in contrast to the Israelites who fought Agag (1 Sm 15, 9); cf also vv 15f.

9, 15: This second slaughter explains the two dates (13th and 14th) of the Purim celebration by Jews in Susa (v 18).

9, 16: Seventy-five thousand: according to the Greek text this number was fifteen thousand.

n Jdt 15, 6. o 6–10: Est 5, 11; B, 3; E, 11. p Est 9, 15; Jdt 15, 7. 11. q Est 7, 10; E, 18. r Est 9, 10. s Jdt 15, 6. t Est 9, 29. u 24ff: Est 3, 7; F, 10. v Est 6, 5–13. w Est 8, 12. 17.

were to be commemorated and kept in every generation, by every clan, in every province, and in every city. These days of Purim were never to fall into disuse among the Jews, nor into oblivion among their descendants.

29 Queen Esther, daughter of Abihail and of Mordecai* the Jew, wrote to confirm with full authority this second letter about Purim, 30 when Mordecai sent documents concerning peace and security to all the Jews in the hundred and twenty-seven provinces of Ahasuerus' kingdom.[x] 31 Thus were established, for their appointed time, these days of Purim which Mordecai the Jew and Queen Esther had designated for the Jews, just as they had previously enjoined upon themselves and upon their race the duty of fasting and supplication.* 32 The command of Esther confirmed these prescriptions for Purim and was recorded in the book.

CHAPTER 10

1 King Ahasuerus laid tribute on the land and on the islands of the sea. 2 All the acts of his power and valor, as well as a detailed account of the greatness of Mordecai, whom the king promoted, are recorded in the chronicles of the kings of Media and Persia. 3 The Jew Mordecai was next in rank to King Ahasuerus, in high standing among the Jews, and was regarded with favor by his many brethren, as the promoter of his people's welfare and the herald of peace for his whole race.[y]

V: Epilogue

CHAPTER F

Mordecai's Dream Fulfilled 1 [z]Then Mordecai said: "This is the work of God. 2 I recall the dream I had about these very things, and not a single detail has been left unfulfilled— 3 the tiny spring that grew into a river, the light of the sun, the many waters. The river is Esther, whom the king married and made queen. 4 The two dragons are myself and Haman. 5 The nations are those who assembled to destroy the name of the Jews, 6 but my people is Israel, who cried to God and was saved.

"The LORD saved his people and delivered us from all these evils. God worked signs and great wonders, such as have not occurred among the nations. 7 For this purpose he arranged two lots:* one for the people of God, the second for all the other nations. 8 These two lots were fulfilled in the hour, the time, and the day of judgment before God and among all the nations. 9 God remembered his people and rendered justice to his inheritance.[a]

10 "Gathering together with joy and happiness before God, they shall celebrate these days on the fourteenth and fifteenth of the month Adar throughout all future generations of his people Israel."*

9, 29: Queen Esther, daughter of Abihail and of Mordecai: the natural offspring of Abihail and adopted daughter of Mordecai; cf Est 2, 15. This second letter: for the burden of this letter see Est 9, 20ff. It was endorsed by Queen Esther. The first letter, written in the king's name, is referred to in Est 8, 9.

9, 31: Fasting and supplication: as the Jews had previously undertaken the duty of fasting and supplication to prevent the impending disaster, they now observe days of festival to commemorate their deliverance—in both cases (cf Est 4, 3. 15f) at the request of Mordecai and Esther.

F, 7: Two lots: in this passage of the Greek text, which gives a more religious interpretation of the feast, the two lots are drawn by God to determine, respectively, the destiny of Israel and that of the nations. In Est 3, 7 above, translated from the Hebrew text, the feast is called Purim because of the lots which Aman cast to determine the day for the extinction of the Jews.

F, 10: The Greek text of Esther contains a postscript as follows: In the fourth year of the reign of Ptolemy and Cleopatra, Dositheus, who said he was a priest and Levite, and his son Ptolemy brought the present letter of Purim, saying that it was genuine and that Lysimachus, son of Ptolemy, of the community of Jerusalem, had translated it. The date referred to in this postscript is most probably 78–77 B.C., in the reign of Ptolemy XII and Cleopatra V.

x Est 9, 23–26. **y** 2 Mc 15, 14. **z** 1–6: Est A, 4–10. **a** Est 3, 7; 9, 17f. 21. 24–28.

THE FIRST BOOK OF MACCABEES

The name Maccabee, probably meaning "hammer," is actually applied in the Books of Maccabees to only one man, Judas, third son of the priest Mattathias and first leader of the revolt against the Seleucid kings who persecuted the Jews (1 Mc 2, 4. 66; 2 Mc 8, 5. 16; 10, 1. 16). Traditionally the name has come to be applied to the brothers of Judas, his supporters, and even to other Jewish heroes of the period, such as the seven brothers (2 Mc 7).

The two Books of Maccabees, placed last in the Douai version of the Old Testament, contain independent accounts of events in part identical which accompanied the attempted suppression of Judaism in Palestine in the second century B.C. The vigorous reaction to this attempt established for a time the religious and political independence of the Jews.

1 Maccabees was written about 100 B.C., in Hebrew, but the original has not come down to us. Instead, we have an early, pre-Christian, Greek translation full of Hebrew idioms. The author, probably a Palestinian Jew, is unknown. He was familiar with the traditions and sacred books of his people and had access to much reliable information on their recent history (from 175 to 134 B.C.). He may well have played some part in it himself in his youth. His purpose in writing is to record the salvation of Israel which God worked through the family of Mattathias (5, 62)—especially through his three sons, Judas, Jonathan, and Simon, and his grandson, John Hyrcanus. Implicitly the writer compares their virtues and their exploits with those of the ancient heroes, the Judges, Samuel, and David.

There are seven poetic sections in the book which imitate the style of classical Hebrew poetry: four laments (1, 25-28. 36-40; 2, 8-13; 3, 45), and three hymns of praise of "our fathers" (2, 51-64), of Judas (3, 3-9), and of Simon (14, 4-15).

The doctrine expressed in the book is the customary belief of Israel, without the new developments which appear in 2 Maccabees and Daniel. The people of Israel have been specially chosen by the one true God as his covenant-partner, and they alone are privileged to know him and worship him. He is their eternal benefactor and their unfailing source of help. The people, in turn, must be loyal to his exclusive worship and must observe exactly the precepts of the law he has given them.

There is no doctrine of individual immortality except in the survival of one's name and fame, nor does the book express any messianic expectation, though messianic images are applied historically to "the days of Simon" (14, 4-17). In true deuteronomic tradition, the author insists on fidelity to the law as the expression of Israel's love for God. The contest which he describes is a struggle, not simply between Jew and Gentile, but between those who would uphold the law and those, Jews or Gentiles, who would destroy it. His severest condemnation goes, not to the Seleucid politicians, but to the lawless apostates among his own people, adversaries of Judas and his brothers, who are models of faith and loyalty.

1 Maccabees has importance also for the New Testament. Salvation is paralleled with Jewish national aspirations (1 Mc 4, 46—14, 41), in contrast to the universal reign of God taught by Christ in the Gospel (Mt 13, 47-50; 22, 1-14). Also, destruction of the wall of the temple separating Jew from Gentile is an act of desecration in 1 Mc 9, 54, but in Eph 2, 14, an act of redemption and unification of both through Christ. On the other hand, association, in 1 Mc 2, 52, of Abraham's offering up of Isaac (Gn 22) with his justification by God (Gn 15, 6) is reflected in Jn 2, 21f, just as the Scriptures are regarded as a source of consolation in 1 Mc 12, 9 and in Rom 15, 4.

The Books of Maccabees, though regarded by Jews and Protestants as apocryphal, i.e., not inspired Scripture, because not contained in the Palestinian Canon or list of books drawn up at the end of the first century A.D., have nevertheless always been accepted by the Catholic Church as inspired, on the basis of apostolic tradition.

1 Maccabees is divided as follows:

I. Introduction: Hellenism in Asia Minor (1, 1-9).
II. The Maccabean Revolt (1, 10—2, 70).
III. Leadership of Judas Maccabeus (3, 1—9, 22).
IV. Leadership of Jonathan (9, 23—12, 54).
V. Simon, High Priest and Ethnarch (13, 1—16, 24).

I: Introduction: Hellenism In Asia Minor

CHAPTER 1

Conquests and Death of Alexander 1 [a]After Alexander the Macedonian, Philip's son, who came from the land of Kittim,* had defeated Darius, king of the Persians and Medes, he became king in his place, having first ruled in Greece. 2 He fought many campaigns, captured fortresses, and put kings to death. 3 He advanced to the ends of the earth, gathering plunder from many nations; the earth fell silent before him, and his heart became proud and arrogant. 4 He collected a very strong army and conquered provinces, nations, and rulers, and they became his tributaries. 5 But after all this he took to his bed, realizing that he was going to die. 6 He therefore summoned his officers, the nobles, who had been brought up with him from his youth, to divide his kingdom among them while he was still alive. 7 Alexander had reigned twelve years* when he died.

8 So his officers took over his kingdom, each in his own territory, 9 and after his death they all put on royal crowns, and so did their sons after them for many years, causing much distress over the earth.

II: The Maccabean Revolt

Pact between Jews and Gentiles 10 There sprang from these a sinful offshoot, Antiochus Epiphanes, son of King Antiochus, once a hostage at Rome. He became king in the year one hundred and thirty-seven* of the kingdom of the Greeks. [b]

11 In those days there appeared in Israel men who were breakers of the law, and they seduced many people, saying: "Let us go and make an alliance with the Gentiles all around us; since we separated from them, many evils have come upon us." [c] 12 The proposal was agreeable; 13 [d]some from among the people promptly went to the king, and he authorized them to introduce the way of living of the Gentiles. 14 Thereupon they built a gymnasium* in Jerusalem according to the Gentile custom. 15 They covered over the mark of their circumcision and abandoned the holy covenant; they allied themselves with the Gentiles and sold themselves to wrongdoing. [e]

1, 1: Land of Kittim: Greece. The name referred originally to inhabitants of Kiti, capital of the isle of Cyprus, then to any Cypriots (Is 23, 1; Jer 2, 10), later to Greeks in general, and finally even to Romans. See note on Dn 11, 30. Darius: Darius III, Codoman (336–331 B.C.).

1, 7: Twelve years: 336–323 B.C.

1, 10: The year one hundred and thirty-seven: Antiochus IV seized the throne in September, 175 B.C. Dates are given in this book according to the Seleucid era, which however was reckoned in two different ways. Antiochians considered this date to be October, 312 B.C. (Syrian calendar), while Babylonians and Jewish priests accepted April, 311 B.C. as the commencement of the era (temple calendar). The author of 1 Mc dates political events by the Syrian calendar but religious events by the temple calendar. Accordingly, the civil New Year occurred variously in September or October, the religious New Year in March or April.

1, 14: Gymnasium: symbol and center of athletic and intellectual life, it was the chief instrument of Hellenistic propaganda. Jewish youth were attracted by sports and encouraged to join youth clubs. They received training in military skills and in the duties of citizens. Through participation in the intellectual life, many were gradually won over to paganism.

a 1–10: Dn 8, 20ff; 11, 3f. 21. b 2 Mc 4, 7. c 2 Mc 4, 9–17. d 13ff: 2 Mc 4, 7–17. e 1 Cor 7, 18.

Egyptian Campaign of Antiochus [16]When his kingdom seemed secure, Antiochus proposed to become king of Egypt, so as to rule over both kingdoms. [17]He invaded Egypt with a strong force, with chariots and elephants,* and with a large fleet,[f] [18]to make war on Ptolemy, king of Egypt. Ptolemy was frightened at his presence and fled, leaving many casualties. [19]The fortified cities in the land of Egypt were captured, and Antiochus plundered the land of Egypt.

Persecution of the Jews [20][g]After Antiochus had defeated Egypt in the year one hundred and forty-three,* he returned and went up to Israel and to Jerusalem with a strong force. [21]He insolently invaded the sanctuary and took away the golden altar, the lampstand for the light with all its fixtures, [22]the offering table, the cups and the bowls, the golden censers, the curtain, the crowns, and the golden ornament on the façade of the temple. He stripped off everything, [23]and took away the gold and silver and the precious vessels; he also took all the hidden treasures he could find. [24]Taking all this, he went back to his own country, after he had spoken with great arrogance and shed much blood.

25 And there was great mourning for Israel, in
every place where they dwelt,
26 and the rulers and the elders groaned.
Virgins and young men languished,
and the beauty of the women was
disfigured.
27 Every bridegroom took up lamentation,
she who sat in the bridal chamber mourned,
28 And the land was shaken on account of its
inhabitants,
and all the house of Jacob was covered with
shame.

[29][h]Two years later, the king sent the Mysian commander to the cities of Judah, and he came to Jerusalem with a strong force. [30]He spoke to them deceitfully in peaceful terms, and won their trust. Then he attacked the city suddenly, in a great onslaught, and destroyed many of the people in Israel. [31]He plundered the city and set fire to it, demolished its houses and its surrounding walls, [32]took captive the women and children, and seized the cattle. [33]Then they built up the City of David* with a high, massive wall and strong towers, and it became their citadel.[i] [34]There they installed a sinful race, perverse men, who fortified themselves inside it, [35]storing up weapons and provisions, and depositing there the plunder they had collected from Jerusalem. And they became a great threat.

36 The citadel became an ambush against the
sanctuary,
and a wicked adversary to Israel at all times.
37 And they shed innocent blood around the
sanctuary;
they defiled the sanctuary.
38 Because of them the inhabitants of Jerusalem
fled away,
and she became the abode of strangers.
She became a stranger to her own offspring,
and her children forsook her.
39 Her sanctuary was as desolate as a
wilderness;[j]
her feasts were turned into mourning,
Her sabbaths to shame,
her honor to contempt.
40 Her dishonor was as great as her glory had
been,
and her exaltation was turned into
mourning.

Prohibitions against Religion [41]Then the king wrote to his whole kingdom that all should be one people, [42]each abandoning his particular customs. All the Gentiles conformed to the command of the king, [43]and many Israelites

1, 17: Elephants: an important part of Seleucid armament. About 300 B.C. Seleucus I, founder of the dynasty, procured five hundred of them from India; cf 1 Mc 6, 34–37.

1, 20: Defeated Egypt in the year one hundred and forty-three: 169 B.C. No mention is made in 1 Mc of the second expedition to Egypt a year later, described in 2 Mc 5, 1. 11. Dn 11, 25. 29 records both.

1, 33: City of David: not Mount Zion on the eastern hill of Jerusalem, which David captured from the Jebusites (2 Sm 5, 7), but a new fortress built on the western hill and overlooking the temple and its courts on Mount Zion. It was occupied for twenty-six years by the Syro-Macedonian garrison, together with apostate Jews, and was a continual threat to the temple and the Jewish people (v 36); cf 1 Mc 13, 49ff.

f 2 Mc 5, 1; Dn 11, 25–28. g 20–24: 2 Mc 5, 11–21. h 29–32: 2 Mc 5, 24ff. i 1 Mc 6, 18. j 39f: Tb 2, 6; Am 8, 10.

were in favor of his religion; they sacrificed to
idols and profaned the sabbath.
44 [k]The king sent messengers with letters to
Jerusalem and to the cities of Judah, ordering
them to follow customs foreign to their land:
45 to prohibit holocausts, sacrifices, and libations
in the sanctuary, to profane the sabbaths and
feast days, 46 [l]to desecrate the sanctuary and the
sacred ministers, to build pagan altars and tem-
ples and shrines, 47 to sacrifice swine and un-
clean animals, 48 to leave their sons uncircum-
cised, and to let themselves be defiled with
every kind of impurity and abomination, 49 so
that they might forget the law and change all
their observances. 50 Whoever refused to act
according to the command of the king should be
put to death.[m]
51 Such were the orders he published through-
out his kingdom. He appointed inspectors over
all the people, and he ordered the cities of Judah
to offer sacrifices, each city in turn. 52 Many of
the people, those who abandoned the law,
joined them and committed evil in the land.
53 Israel was driven into hiding, wherever places
of refuge could be found.
54 On the fifteenth day of the month Chislev,
in the year one hundred and forty-five,* the king
erected the horrible abomination upon the altar of
holocausts, and in the surrounding cities of Judah
they built pagan altars.[n] 55 They also burnt in-
cense at the doors of houses and in the streets.
56 Any scrolls of the law* which they found they
tore up and burnt. 57 Whoever was found with a
scroll of the covenant, and whoever observed the
law, was condemned to death by royal decree.[o]
58 So they used their power against Israel, against
those who were caught, each month, in the cit-
ies. 59 On the twenty-fifth day of each month they
sacrificed on the altar erected over the altar of
holocausts. 60 [p]Women who had had their chil-
dren circumcised were put to death, in keeping
with the decree, 61 with the babies hung from
their necks; their families also and those who had
circumcised them were killed. 62 But many in Is-
rael were determined and resolved in their hearts
not to eat anything unclean; 63 they preferred to
die rather than to be defiled with unclean food or
to profane the holy covenant; and they did die.
Terrible affliction was upon Israel.[q]

CHAPTER 2

Mattathias and His Sons 1 In those days Matta-
thias, son of John, son of Simeon, a priest of the
family of Joarib, left Jerusalem and settled in
Modein.* 2 He had five sons: John, who was
called Gaddi;[r] 3 Simon, who was called Thassi;
4 Judas, who was called Maccabeus; 5 Eleazar,
who was called Avaran; and Jonathan, who was
called Apphus. 6 When he saw the sacrileges that
were being committed in Judah and in Jerusa-
lem, 7 he said: "Woe is me! Why was I born to
see the ruin of my people and the ruin of the
holy city, and to sit idle while it is given into the
hands of enemies, and the sanctuary into the
hands of strangers?

8 "Her temple has become like a man disgraced,
9 her glorious ornaments have been carried
off as spoils,
Her infants have been murdered in her streets,
her young men by the sword of the enemy.[s]
10 What nation has not taken its share of her
realm,
and laid its hand on her possessions?
11 All her adornment has been taken away.
From being free, she has become a slave.
12 We see our sanctuary and our beauty
and our glory laid waste,
And the Gentiles have defiled them!
13 Why are we still alive?"

14 Then Mattathias and his sons tore their gar-
ments, put on sackcloth, and mourned bitterly.

1, 54: Fifteenth day of the month Chislev in the year one hundred and forty-five: early December, 167 B.C. Horrible abomination: in the original Hebrew, a contemptuous pun on the title "Lord of heaven" given to the god Zeus Olympios, to whom an image or perhaps an altar was erected upon the altar of holocausts in the temple of Jerusalem; cf Dn 9, 27; 11, 31.

1, 56f: Scrolls of the law: one or more of the first five books of the Old Testament.

2, 1: Modein: a village twenty miles northwest of Jerusalem.

k 44–63: 2 Mc 6, 1–11. l 2 Mc 6, 2; Dn 9, 27. m 2 Mc 6, 18—7, 41. n 1 Mc 6, 7; Dn 9, 27; 11, 31. o 2 Mc 2, 14. p 60f: 2 Mc 6, 10. q 2 Mc 6, 10. r 1 Chr 24, 7. s Lam 2, 11, 21.

Pagan Worship Refused [15]The officers of the
king in charge of enforcing the apostasy came to
the city of Modein to organize the sacrifices.
[16]Many of Israel joined them, but Mattathias and
his sons gathered in a group apart. [17]Then the
officers of the king addressed Mattathias: "You
are a leader, an honorable and great man in this
city, supported by sons and kinsmen. [18]Come
now, be the first to obey the king's command, as
all the Gentiles and the men of Judah and those
who are left in Jerusalem have done. Then you
and your sons shall be numbered among the
King's Friends,* and shall be enriched with
silver and gold and many gifts." [19]But Mattathias
answered in a loud voice: "Although all the
Gentiles in the king's realm obey him, so that
each forsakes the religion of his fathers and
consents to the king's orders, [20]yet I and my
sons and my kinsmen will keep to the covenant
of our fathers. [21]God forbid that we should
forsake the law and the commandments. [22]We
will not obey the words of the king nor depart
from our religion in the slightest degree."

[23]As he finished saying these words, a certain
Jew came forward in the sight of all to offer
sacrifice on the altar in Modein according to the
king's order. [24]When Mattathias saw him, he
was filled with zeal; his heart was moved and his
just fury was aroused; he sprang forward and
killed him upon the altar. [25]At the same time, he
also killed the messenger of the king who was
forcing them to sacrifice, and he tore down the
altar. [26]Thus he showed his zeal for the law, just
as Phinehas did with Zimri, son of Salu. [t]

[27]Then Mattathias went through the city
shouting, "Let everyone who is zealous for the
law and who stands by the covenant follow after
me!" [28]Thereupon he fled to the mountains with
his sons, leaving behind in the city all their
possessions. [u] [29]Many who sought to live accord-
ing to righteousness and religious custom went
out into the desert* to settle there, [30]they and
their sons, their wives and their cattle, because
misfortunes pressed so hard on them.

[31]It was reported to the officers and soldiers of
the king who were in the City of David, in
Jerusalem, that certain men who had flouted the
king's order had gone out to the hiding places in
the desert. [32] [v]Many hurried out after them, and
having caught up with them, camped opposite
and prepared to attack them on the sabbath.
[33]"Enough of this!" the pursuers said to them.
"Come out and obey the king's command, and
your lives will be spared." [34]But they replied,
"We will not come out, nor will we obey the
king's command to profane the sabbath."
[35]Then the enemy attacked them at once; [36]but
they did not retaliate; they neither threw stones,
nor blocked up their own hiding places. [37]They
said, "Let us all die without reproach; heaven
and earth are our witnesses that you destroy us
unjustly." [38]So the officers and soldiers attacked
them on the sabbath, and they died with their
wives, their children and their cattle, to the
number of a thousand persons.

[39]When Mattathias and his friends heard of it,
they mourned deeply for them. [40]"If we all do as
our kinsmen have done," they said to one an-
other, "and do not fight against the Gentiles for
our lives and our traditions, they will soon destroy
us from the earth." [41]On that day they came to
this decision: "Let us fight against anyone who
attacks us on the sabbath, so that we may not all
die as our kinsmen died in the hiding places."

[42]Then they were joined by a group of
Hasideans,* valiant Israelites, all of them devout
followers of the law. [43]And all those who were
fleeing from the disaster joined them and sup-
ported them. [44]They gathered an army and
struck down sinners in their anger and lawbreak-
ers in their wrath, and the survivors fled to the
Gentiles for safety. [w] [45]Mattathias and his friends

2, 18: The King's Friends: a regular order of nobility at Hellenistic courts. The various grades are frequently mentioned in this book: Friends, Chief Friends, Kinsmen.

2, 29: The desert: the sparsely inhabited mountain country southward from Jerusalem and west of the Dead Sea. It was an arid region with some perennial springs and a fair amount of rain in winter.

2, 42: Hasideans: in Hebrew hasidim, "pious ones," a religious group devoted to the strict observance of the law. They were the forerunners of both the Pharisees and the Essenes. They first supported the Maccabean movement, but subsequently opposed it, regarding it as too political.

t 1 Mc 2, 54; Nm 25, 6–14. u 2 Mc 5, 27. v 32–38: 2 Mc 6, 11. w Is 63, 3.

went about and tore down the pagan altars;
46they also forcibly circumcised any uncircum-
cised boys whom they found in the territory of
Israel. 47They put to flight the arrogant, and the
work prospered in their hands. 48They saved the
law from the hands of the Gentiles and of the
kings and did not let the sinner triumph.
Death of Mattathias 49When the time came
for Mattathias to die, he said to his sons:
"Arrogance and scorn have now grown strong; it
is a time of disaster and violent anger. 50There-
fore, my sons, be zealous for the law and give
your lives for the covenant of our fathers.

51 "Remember the deeds that our fathers did in their times,
and you shall win great glory and an everlasting name.
52 Was not Abraham found faithful in trial,
and it was reputed to him as uprightness? [x]
53 Joseph, when in distress, kept the commandment,
and he became master of Egypt. [y]
54 Phinehas our father, for his burning zeal,
received the covenant of an everlasting priesthood. [z]
55 Joshua, for executing his commission,
became a judge in Israel. [a]
56 Caleb, for bearing witness before the assembly,
received an inheritance in the land. [b]
57 David, for his piety,
received as a heritage a throne of everlasting royalty. [c]
58 Elijah, for his burning zeal for the law,
was taken up to heaven. [d]
59 Hananiah, Azariah and Mishael, for their faith,
were saved from the fire. [e]
60 Daniel, for his innocence,
was delivered from the jaws of lions. [f]
61 And so, consider this from generation to generation,
that none who hope in him shall fail in strength.
62 Do not fear the words of a sinful man,
for his glory ends in corruption and worms.
63 Today he is exalted, and tomorrow he is not to be found,
because he has returned to his dust,
and his schemes have perished.
64 Children! be courageous and strong in keeping the law,
for by it you shall be glorified.

65"Here is your brother Simeon who I know is a
wise man; listen to him always, and he will be a
father to you. 66And Judas Maccabeus, a warrior
from his youth, shall be the leader of your army
and direct the war against the nations. 67You
shall also gather about you all who observe the
law, and you shall avenge the wrongs of your
people. 68Pay back the Gentiles what they de-
serve, and observe the precepts of the law."
69Then he blessed them, and he was united
with his fathers. 70He died in the year one
hundred and forty-six,* and was buried in the
tombs of his fathers in Modein, and all Israel
mourned him greatly.

III: Leadership of Judas Maccabeus

CHAPTER 3

Defeat of Apollonius and Seron 1Then his
son Judas, who was called Maccabeus, took his
place. 2All his brothers and all who had joined
his father supported him, and they carried on
Israel's war joyfully.

3 He spread abroad the glory of his people,
and put on his breastplate like a giant.
He armed himself with weapons of war;
he planned battles and protected the camp with his sword. [g]
4 In his actions he was like a lion,
like a young lion roaring for prey.
5 He pursued the wicked, hunting them out,
and those who troubled his people he destroyed by fire.
6 The lawbreakers were cowed by fear of him,
and all evildoers were dismayed.

2, 70: In the year one hundred and forty-six: 166 B.C.

x Gn 15, 6; 22, 1ff. y Gn 39, 7–10; 41, 39–43. z Nm 25, 10–13; Sir 45, 28ff. a Jos 1, 2, 5. b Nm 13, 30; 14, 6–9. 24; Jos 14, 14. c 2 Sm 2, 4; 7, 16. d 1 Kgs 19, 10. 14; 2 Kgs 2, 11. e Dn 3, 50. f Dn 6, 23; 14, 31–42. g 2 Mc 8, 5.

By his hand redemption was happily achieved,
7 and he afflicted many kings;
He made Jacob glad by his deeds,
and his memory is blessed forever.
8 He went about the cities of Judah
destroying the impious there.
He turned away wrath from Israel
9 and was renowned to the ends of the earth;
he gathered together those who were
perishing.

10 Then Apollonius* gathered the Gentiles,
together with a large army from Samaria, to fight
against Israel. 11 When Judas learned of it, he
went out to meet him and defeated and killed
him. Many fell wounded, and the rest fled.
12 Their possessions were seized and the sword
of Apollonius was taken by Judas, who fought
with it the rest of his life.

13 But Seron, commander of the Syrian army,
heard that Judas had gathered many about him,
an assembly of faithful men ready for war. 14 So
he said, "I will make a name for myself and win
glory in the kingdom by defeating Judas and his
followers, who have despised the king's com-
mand." 15 And again a large company of rene-
gades advanced with him to help him take
revenge on the Israelites. 16 When he reached
the ascent of Beth-horon,* Judas went out to
meet him with a few men. 17 But when they saw
the army coming against them, they said to
Judas: "How can we, few as we are, fight such a
mighty host as this? Besides, we are weak today
from fasting." 18 But Judas said: "It is easy for
many to be overcome by a few; in the sight of
Heaven there is no difference between deliver-
ance by many or by few; 19 for victory in war
does not depend upon the size of the army, but
on strength that comes from Heaven.[h] 20 With
great presumption and lawlessness they come
against us to destroy us and our wives and
children and to despoil us; 21 but we are fighting
for our lives and our laws. 22 He himself* will
crush them before us; so do not be afraid of
them." 23 When he finished speaking, he rushed
suddenly upon Seron and his army, who were
crushed before him. 24 He pursued Seron down
the descent of Beth-horon into the plain. About
eight hundred* of their men fell, and the rest
fled to the country of the Philistines.[i] 25 Then
Judas and his brothers began to be feared, and
dread fell upon the Gentiles about them. 26 His
fame reached the king, and all the Gentiles
talked about the battles of Judas.

Regency of Lysias 27 When Antiochus heard
about these events, he was angry; so he ordered
a muster of all the forces of his kingdom, a very
strong army. 28 He opened his treasure chests,
gave his soldiers a year's pay, and commanded
them to be prepared for anything. 29 He then
found that this exhausted the money in his
treasury; moreover the income from the prov-
ince was small, because of the dissension and
distress he had brought upon the land by abolish-
ing the laws which had been in effect from of
old. 30 He feared that, as had happened more
than once, he would not have enough for his
expenses and for the gifts that he had previously
given with a more liberal hand than the preced-
ing kings. 31 Greatly perplexed, he decided to go
to Persia and levy tribute on those provinces,
and so raise a large sum of money. 32 He left
Lysias, a nobleman of royal blood, in charge of
the king's affairs from the Euphrates River to the
frontier of Egypt, 33 and commissioned him to
take care of his son Antiochus until his own
return. 34 He entrusted to him half of the army,
and the elephants, and gave him instructions
concerning everything he wanted done. As for
the inhabitants of Judea and Jerusalem, 35 Lysias
was to send an army against them to crush and
destroy the power of Israel and the remnant of

3, 10: Apollonius: the Mysian commander mentioned in 1 Mc 1, 29 and in 2 Mc 5, 24.

3, 16: Beth-horon: the famous pass leading up from the coastal plain to the Judean hill country. Here Joshua won an important battle (Jos 10, 10f), and in 66 A.D. a Roman force under Cestius was trapped and massacred.

3, 22: He himself: out of reverence for God, the author of 1 Mc prefers to use this and other expressions, such as "Heaven," instead of the divine name. Cf 1 Mc 3, 50.

3, 24: About eight hundred: the figures given in this book for strength of armies and number of casualties are not to be taken literally. In accordance with biblical usage, they indicate rather the importance of the battle described or the greatness of the victory.

h 1 Sm 14, 16. i Jos 10, 10.

Jerusalem and efface their memory from the
land. 36He was to settle foreigners in all their
territory and distribute their land by lot.
37The king took the remaining half of the
army and set out from Antioch, his capital, in the
year one hundred and forty-seven; he crossed
the Euphrates River and advanced inland.*
The Victories of Judas 38[j]Lysias chose Ptol-
emy, son of Dorymenes, and Nicanor* and Gor-
gias, capable men among the King's Friends,[k]
39and with them he sent forty thousand men and
seven thousand cavalry to invade the land of Ju-
dah and ravage it according to the king's orders.
40Setting out with all their forces, they came and
pitched their camp near Emmaus* in the plain.
41When the merchants of the country heard of
their fame, they came to the camp, bringing fet-
ters and a large sum of silver and gold, to buy the
Israelites as slaves. A force from Idumea and from
Philistia joined with them.
42Judas and his brothers saw that the situation
had become critical now that armies were en-
camped within their territory; they knew of the
orders which the king had given to destroy and
utterly wipe out the people. 43So they said to
one another, "Let us restore our people from
their ruined estate, and fight for our people and
our sanctuary!"
44The assembly gathered together to prepare
for battle and to pray and implore mercy and
compassion.
45Jerusalem was uninhabited, like a desert;
not one of her children entered or came
out.
The sanctuary was trampled on,
and foreigners were in the citadel;
it was a habitation of Gentiles.
Joy had disappeared from Jacob,
and the flute and the harp were silent.
46[l]Thus they assembled and went to Mizpah
near Jerusalem, because there was formerly at
Mizpah a place of prayer for Israel.* 47That day
they fasted and wore sackcloth; they sprinkled
ashes on their heads and tore their clothes.
48They unrolled the scroll of the law, to learn
about the things for which the Gentiles con-
sulted the images of their idols.* 49They brought
with them the priestly vestments, the first fruits,
and the tithes; and they brought forward the
nazirites* who had completed the time of their
vows.[m] 50And they cried aloud to Heaven:
"What shall we do with these men, and where
shall we take them? 51For your sanctuary has
been trampled on and profaned, and your priests
are in mourning and humiliation. 52Now the
Gentiles are gathered together against us to
destroy us. You know what they plot against us.
53How shall we be able to resist them unless you
help us?" 54Then they blew the trumpets and
cried out loudly.
55After this Judas appointed officers among
the people, over thousands, over hundreds, over
fifties, and over tens. 56He proclaimed that those
who were building houses, or were just married,
or were planting vineyards, and those who were
afraid, could each return to his home, according
to the law.[n] 57Then the army moved off, and
they camped to the south of Emmaus. 58Judas
said: "Arm yourselves and be brave; in the
morning be ready to fight these Gentiles who
have assembled against us to destroy us and our
sanctuary. 59It is better for us to die in battle
than to witness the ruin of our nation and our
sanctuary. Whatever Heaven wills, he will do."[o]

CHAPTER 4

1Now Gorgias took five thousand infantry and
a thousand picked cavalry, and this detachment
set out at night 2in order to attack the camp of

3, 37: This expedition, in the spring of 165 B.C., resulted in failure; cf ch 6.

3, 38: Nicanor: the leader of another attack against the Jews four years later. He was finally killed by Judas; cf 1 Mc 7, 26–46.

3, 40: Emmaus: probably not the village mentioned in Lk 24, 13, but a settlement about twenty miles west of Jerusalem at the edge of the hill country.

3, 46: . . . Mizpah a place of prayer for Israel: a holy place established of old eight miles north and slightly west of Jerusalem. It was here that Samuel began to judge the Israelites (1 Sm 7, 5–11; 10, 17).

3, 48: To learn . . . idols: favorable omens for the coming battle. A contrast is intended between the idol worship of the pagans and the consultation of the word of God by the Jews; cf 2 Mc 8, 23.

3, 49: Nazirites: see note on Nm 6, 1ff.

j 38–44: 2 Mc 8, 8–15. k 38f: 1 Mc 7, 26; 2 Mc 4, 45; 8, 8f; 10, 14. l 46ff: 1 Sm 7, 5f; 2 Mc 8, 16–23. m Nm 6, 2–5. n Dt 20, 5–8; Jgs 7, 3. o 1 Mc 2, 21f.

the Jews and take them by surprise. Some men
from the citadel were their guides. 3Judas heard
of it, and himself set out with his soldiers to
attack the king's army at Emmaus, 4while the
latter's forces were still scattered away from the
camp. 5During the night Gorgias came into the
camp of Judas, and found no one there; so he
began to hunt for them in the mountains, saying,
"They are fleeing from us."

6But at daybreak Judas appeared in the plain
with three thousand men, who lacked such
armor and swords as they would have wished.
7They saw the army of the Gentiles, strong and
breastplated, flanked with cavalry, and made up
of expert soldiers. 8Judas said to the men with
him: "Do not be afraid of their numbers or dread
their attack. 9Remember how our fathers were
saved in the Red Sea, when Pharaoh pursued
them with an army.[p] 10So now let us cry to
Heaven in the hope that he will favor us,
remember his covenant with our fathers, and
destroy this army before us today.[q] 11All the
Gentiles shall know that there is One who
redeems and delivers Israel."

12When the foreigners looked up and saw
them marching toward them, 13they came out of
their camp for battle, and the men with Judas
blew the trumpet. 14The battle was joined and
the Gentiles were defeated and fled toward the
plain. 15Their whole rearguard fell by the sword,
and they were pursued as far as Gazara* and the
plains of Judea, to Azotus and Jamnia. About
three thousand of their men fell.

16When Judas and the army returned from the
pursuit, 17he said to the people: "Do not be
greedy for the plunder, for there is a fight ahead
of us, 18and Gorgias and his army are near us on
the mountain. But now stand firm against our
enemies and overthrow them. Afterward you
can freely take the plunder."

19As Judas was finishing this speech, a detach-
ment appeared, looking down from the moun-
tain. 20They saw that their army had been put to
flight and their camp was being burned. The
smoke that could be seen indicated what had
happened. 21When they realized this, they were
terrified; and when they also saw the army of
Judas in the plain ready to attack, 22they all fled
to Philistine territory.*

23Then Judas went back to plunder the camp,
and his men collected much gold and silver,
violet and crimson cloth, and great treasure.
24As they returned, they were singing hymns
and glorifying Heaven, "for he is good, for his
mercy endures forever."[r] 25Thus Israel had a
great deliverance that day.

Victory over Lysias 26[s]But those of the foreign-
ers who had escaped went and told Lysias all
that had occurred. 27When he heard it he was
disturbed and discouraged, because things in
Israel had not turned out as he intended and as
the king had ordered.

28So the following year he gathered together
sixty thousand picked men and five thousand
cavalry, to subdue them. 29They came into
Idumea and camped at Beth-zur,* and Judas met
them with ten thousand men. 30Seeing that the
army was strong, he prayed thus:

"Blessed are you, O Savior of Israel, who
broke the rush of the mighty one by the hand of
your servant David and delivered the camp of
the Philistines into the hand of Jonathan, the son
of Saul, and his armor-bearer.[t] 31Give this army
into the hands of your people Israel; make them
ashamed of their troops and their cavalry.
32Strike them with fear, weaken the boldness of
their strength, and let them tremble at their own
destruction. 33Strike them down by the sword of
those who love you, that all who know your
name may hymn your praise."

34Then they engaged in battle, and about five
thousand of Lysias' men fell in hand-to-hand

4, 15: Gazara: Gezer of the Hebrew Bible, five miles northwest of Emmaus: Azotus, Hebrew Ashdod, lay to the southwest; and Jamnia, Hebrew Jabneel (Jos 15, 11) or Jabneh (2 Chr 26, 6), to the west of Gazara.

4, 22: Philistine territory: the coastal cities of southern Palestine, traditionally hostile to Jerusalem. Jamnia in particular was an important base for the Seleucid power.

4, 29: Beth-zur: an important frontier city in the mountain area, fifteen miles southwest of Jerusalem. Its inhabitants were sympathetic to the Maccabees and refused to receive Lysias.

p Ex 14, 21ff. q 1 Mc 2, 21. r Ps 118, 1ff. 29. s 26–35: 2 Mc 11, 1–12. t 1 Sm 17, 48ff.

fighting. [35]When Lysias saw his ranks beginning to give way, and the increased boldness of Judas, whose men were ready either to live or to die bravely, he withdrew to Antioch and began to recruit mercenaries so as to return to Judea with greater numbers.*

Purification of the Temple [36] [u]Then Judas and his brothers said, "Now that our enemies have been crushed, let us go up to purify the sanctuary* and rededicate it." [37]So the whole army assembled, and went up to Mount Zion. [38]They found the sanctuary desolate, the altar desecrated, the gates burnt, weeds growing in the courts as in a forest or on some mountain, and the priests' chambers demolished. [v] [39]Then they tore their clothes and made great lamentation; they sprinkled their heads with ashes [40]and fell with their faces to the ground. And when the signal was given with trumpets, they cried out to Heaven.

[41]Judas appointed men to attack those in the citadel, while he purified the sanctuary. [42]He chose blameless priests, devoted to the law; [43]these purified the sanctuary and carried away the stones of the Abomination to an unclean place. [44]They deliberated what ought to be done with the altar of holocausts that had been desecrated. [w] [45]The happy thought came to them to tear it down, lest it be a lasting shame to them that the Gentiles had defiled it; so they tore down the altar. [x] [46]They stored the stones in a suitable place on the temple hill, until a prophet should come and decide what to do with them. [47]Then they took uncut stones, according to the law, and built a new altar like the former one. [y] [48]They also repaired the sanctuary and the interior of the temple and purified the courts. [49]They made new sacred vessels and brought the lampstand, the altar of incense, and the table into the temple. [z] [50]Then they burned incense on the altar and lighted the lamps on the lampstand, and these illuminated the temple. [a] [51]They also put loaves on the table and hung up the curtains. Thus they finished all the work they had undertaken.

[52]Early in the morning on the twenty-fifth day of the ninth month, that is, the month of Chislev, in the year one hundred and forty-eight,* [53]they arose and offered sacrifice according to the law on the new altar of holocausts that they had made. [b] [54]On the anniversary of the day on which the Gentiles had defiled it, on that very day it was reconsecrated with songs, harps, flutes, and cymbals. [55]All the people prostrated themselves and adored and praised Heaven, who had given them success.

[56]For eight days they celebrated the dedication of the altar and joyfully offered holocausts and sacrifices of deliverance and praise. [57]They ornamented the façade of the temple with gold crowns and shields; they repaired the gates and the priests' chambers and furnished them with doors. [58]There was great joy among the people now that the disgrace of the Gentiles was removed. [59]Then Judas and his brothers and the entire congregation of Israel decreed that the days of the dedication* of the altar should be observed with joy and gladness on the anniversary every year for eight days, from the twenty-fifth day of the month Chislev. [c]

[60]At that time they built high walls and strong towers around Mount Zion, to prevent the Gentiles from coming and trampling over it as they had done before. [61]Judas also placed a garrison there to protect it, and likewise fortified Beth-zur, that the people might have a stronghold facing Idumea.

CHAPTER 5*

Punishment of Hostile Acts [1] [d]When the Gentiles round about heard that the altar had been

4, 35: According to 2 Mc 11, 13–15, peace negotiations followed between Lysias and Judas.

4, 36: The sanctuary: the whole temple area with its walls, courts and outbuildings, to be distinguished from the temple proper, the oblong edifice with porch, main room and inner shrine.

4, 52: Twenty-fifth day of the ninth month . . . in the year one hundred and forty-eight: December 14, 164 B.C.

4, 59: Days of the dedication . . . Chislev: institution of the feast of Hannukah, also called the feast of Dedication (Jn 10, 22). Josephus Flavius calls it the feast of Lights.

5, 1: The events of this chapter occurred within the year 163 B.C.

u 36–59: 2 Mc 10, 1–8. v Ps 74, 2–7. w 1 Kgs 8, 64. x 1 Mc 6, 7. y Ex 20, 25. z Ex 25, 23–39; 30, 1–6. a Ex 30, 7ff. b 53. 56: Ex 30, 10; Ez 43, 18–27. c Jn 10, 22. d 1f: 1 Mc 13, 6.

rebuilt and the sanctuary consecrated as before, they were very angry. 2 So they decided to destroy the descendants of Jacob who were among them, and they began to massacre and persecute the people. 3 [e]Then Judas attacked the sons of Esau at Akrabattene* in Idumea, because they were blockading Israel; he defeated them heavily, overcame and despoiled them. 4 He also remembered the malice of the sons of Baean,* who had become a snare and a stumblingblock to the people by ambushing them along the roads. 5 He forced them to take refuge in towers, which he besieged; he vowed their annihilation and burned down the towers along with all the persons in them. 6 *Then he crossed over to the Ammonites, where he found a strong army and a large body of people with Timothy as their leader. 7 He fought many battles with them, routed them, and struck them down. 8 After seizing Jazer and its villages, he returned to Judea.

Liberation of Galilean Jews 9 The Gentiles in Gilead assembled to attack and destroy the Israelites who were in their territory; these then fled to the stronghold of Dathema. 10 They sent a letter to Judas and his brothers saying: "The Gentiles around us have combined against us to destroy us, 11 and they are preparing to come and seize this stronghold to which we have fled. Timothy is the leader of their army. 12 Come at once and rescue us from them, for many of us have fallen. 13 All our kinsmen who were among the Tobiads have been killed; the Gentiles have carried away their wives and children and their goods, and they have slain there about a thousand men."[f]

14 While they were reading this letter, suddenly other messengers, in torn clothes, arrived from Galilee to deliver a similar message: 15 that the inhabitants of Ptolemais,* Tyre, and Sidon, and the whole of Gentile Galilee had joined forces to destroy them. 16 When Judas and the people heard this, a great assembly convened to consider what they should do for their unfortunate kinsmen who were being attacked by enemies.

17 Judas said to his brother Simon: "Choose men for yourself, and go, rescue your kinsmen in Galilee; I and my brother Jonathan will go to Gilead."

18 In Judea he left Joseph, son of Zechariah, and Azariah, leader of the people, with the rest of the army to guard it. 19 "Take charge of these people," he commanded them, "but do not fight against the Gentiles until we return." 20 Three thousand men were allotted to Simon, to go into Galilee, and eight thousand men to Judas, for Gilead.

21 Simon went into Galilee and fought many battles with the Gentiles. They were crushed before him, 22 and he pursued them to the very gate of Ptolemais. About three thousand men of the Gentiles fell, and he gathered their spoils. 23 He took with him the Jews who were in Galilee and in Arbatta, with their wives and children and all that they had, and brought them to Judea with great rejoicing.

Rescue in Gilead 24 [g]Judas Maccabeus and his brother Jonathan crossed the Jordan and marched for three days through the desert. 25 There they met some Nabateans,* who received them peacefully and told them all that had happened to the Jews in Gilead: 26 "Many of them have been imprisoned in Bozrah, in Bosor near Alema, in Chaspho, Maked, and Carnaim"—all of these are large, fortified cities— 27 "and some have been imprisoned in the other cities of Gilead. Tomorrow their enemies plan to attack the strongholds and to seize and destroy all these people in one day."

5, 3: Akrabattene: a district southwest of the Dead Sea.

5, 4: Sons of Baean: 2 Mc 10, 15–23 calls them simply Idumeans.

5, 6ff: This summary anticipates the order of events and would fit better between vv 36 and 37. It corresponds to 2 Mc 12, 17–23. The action was probably a reprisal for the massacre referred to in v 13. Timothy was the Seleucid governor of Transjordan. Jazer: a town on the road from the Jordan to Amman.

5, 15: Ptolemais: Hebrew Acco (Jgs 1, 31), modern Acre, on the coast north of Haifa.

5, 25: Nabateans: an Arab people who acquired wealth and power as caravan merchants in the final two centuries B.C. They settled down, established Petra as their capital, and for a time controlled all of Transjordan, even as far as Damascus. It was from a Nabatean governor that St. Paul escaped about 38 A.D. (2 Cor 11, 32f).

e 3ff: 2 Mc 10, 15–23. f 2 Mc 12, 17. g 24–36: 2 Mc 12, 10ff.

28 Thereupon Judas suddenly changed direction with his army, marched across the desert to Bozrah, and captured the city. He slaughtered all the male population, took all their possessions, and set fire to the city. 29 He led his army from that place by night, and they marched toward the stronghold of Dathema. 30 When morning came, they looked ahead and saw a countless multitude of people, with ladders and devices for capturing the stronghold, and beginning to attack the people within. 31 When Judas perceived that the struggle had begun and that the noise of the battle was resounding to heaven with trumpet blasts and loud shouting, 32 he said to the men of his army, "Fight for our kinsmen today."

33 He came up behind them with three columns blowing their trumpets and shouting in prayer. 34 When the army of Timothy realized that it was Maccabeus, they fell back before him, and he inflicted on them a crushing defeat. About eight thousand of their men fell that day. 35 Then he turned toward Alema and attacked and captured it; he killed all the male population, plundered the place, and burned it down. 36 From there he moved on and took Chaspho, Maked, Bosor, and the other cities of Gilead.

37 [h]After these events Timothy assembled another army and camped opposite Raphon, on the other side of the stream. 38 Judas sent men to spy on the camp, and they reported to him: "All the Gentiles around us have rallied to him, making a very large force; 39 they have also hired Arabs to help them, and have camped beyond the stream, ready to attack you." So Judas went forward to attack them.

40 As Judas and his army were approaching the running stream, Timothy said to the officers of his army: "If he crosses over to us first, we shall not be able to resist him; he will certainly defeat us.[i] 41 But if he is afraid and camps on the other side of the river, we will cross over to him and defeat him."

42 But when Judas reached the running stream, he stationed the officers of the people beside the stream and gave them this order: "Do not allow any man to pitch a tent; all must go into battle." 43 He was the first to cross to the attack, with all the people behind him, and the Gentiles were crushed before them; they threw away their arms and fled to the temple enclosure at Carnaim. 44 The Jews captured that city and burnt the enclosure with all who were in it. So Carnaim was subdued, and Judas met with no more resistance.[j]

45 Then he assembled all the Israelites, great and small, who were in Gilead, with their wives and children and their goods, a great crowd of people, to go into the land of Judah. 46 [k]When they reached Ephron,* a large and strongly fortified city along the way, they found it impossible to encircle it on either the right or the left; they would have to march right through it. 47 But the men in the city shut them out and blocked up the gates with stones.[l] 48 Then Judas sent them his peaceful message: "We wish to cross your territory in order to reach our own; no one will harm you; we will only march through." But they would not open to him.

49 So Judas ordered a proclamation to be made in the camp that everyone make an attack from the place where he was. 50 When the men of the army took up their positions, he assaulted the city all that day and night, and it was delivered to him. 51 He slaughtered every male, razed and plundered the city, and passed through it over the slain.

52 Then they crossed the Jordan to the great plain in front of Beth-shan; 53 and Judas kept rounding up the stragglers and encouraging the people the whole way, until he reached the land of Judah. 54 They ascended Mount Zion in joy and gladness and offered holocausts, because not one of them had fallen; they returned in safety.

Joseph and Azariah Defeated 55 During the time that Judas and Jonathan were in the land of Gilead, and Simon his brother was in Galilee opposite Ptolemais, 56 Joseph, son of Zechariah, and Azariah, the leaders of the army, heard

5, 46: Ephron: a city in Transjordan opposite Beth-shan, about five miles east of the Jordan River. Situated on a height, it dominated the valleys of the two tributaries of the Jordan.

h 37–44; 2 Mc 12, 20–26. i 1 Sm 14, 9f. j 2 Mc 12, 21. k 46–54; 2 Mc 12, 27–31. l Nm 20, 17–21; 21, 21–25.

about the brave deeds and the fighting that they were doing. 57 They said, "Let us also make a name for ourselves by going out and fighting against the Gentiles around us."

58 They gave orders to the men of their army who were with them, and marched toward Jamnia. 59 But Gorgias and his men came out of the city to meet them in battle. 60 Joseph and Azariah were beaten, and were pursued to the frontiers of Judea, and about two thousand Israelites fell that day. 61 It was a bad defeat for the people, because they had not obeyed Judas and his brothers, thinking that they would do brave deeds. 62 But they did not belong to the family of those men to whom it was granted to achieve Israel's salvation. 63 The valiant Judas and his brothers were greatly renowned in all Israel and among all the Gentiles, wherever their name was heard; 64 and men gathered about them and praised them.

65 Then Judas and his brothers went out and attacked the sons of Esau* in the country toward the south; he took Hebron and its villages, and he destroyed its strongholds and burned the towers around it. 66 He then set out for the land of the Philistines and passed through Marisa. 67 At that time some priests fell in battle who had gone out rashly to fight in their desire to distinguish themselves. 68 Judas then turned toward Azotus in the land of the Philistines. He destroyed their altars and burned the statues of their gods; and after plundering their cities he returned to the land of Judah.

CHAPTER 6

Defeat and Death of Antiochus IV 1 [m]As King Antiochus was traversing the inland provinces, he heard that in Persia there was a city called Elymais,* famous for its wealth in silver and gold, 2 and that its temple was very rich, containing gold helmets, breastplates, and weapons left there by Alexander, son of Philip, king of Macedon, the first king of the Greeks. 3 He went therefore and tried to capture and pillage the city. But he could not do so, because his plan became known to the people of the city 4 who rose up in battle against him. So he retreated and in great dismay withdrew from there to return to Babylon.

5 While he was in Persia, a messenger brought him news that the armies sent into the land of Judah had been put to flight; 6 that Lysias had gone at first with a strong army and been driven back by the Israelites; that they had grown strong by reason of the arms, men, and abundant possessions taken from the armies they had destroyed; 7 that they had pulled down the Abomination which he had built upon the altar in Jerusalem; and that they had surrounded with high walls both the sanctuary, as it had been before, and his city of Beth-zur.[n]

8 When the king heard this news, he was struck with fear and very much shaken. Sick with grief because his designs had failed, he took to his bed. 9 There he remained many days, overwhelmed with sorrow, for he knew he was going to die.

10 So he called in all his Friends and said to them: "Sleep has departed from my eyes, for my heart is sinking with anxiety. 11 I said to myself: 'Into what tribulation have I come, and in what floods of sorrow am I now! 12 Yet I was kindly and beloved in my rule.' But I now recall the evils I did in Jerusalem, when I carried away all the vessels of gold and silver that were in it, and for no cause gave orders that the inhabitants of Judah be destroyed. 13 I know that this is why these evils have overtaken me; and now I am dying, in bitter grief, in a foreign land."

14 Then he summoned Philip, one of his Friends, and put him in charge of his whole kingdom. 15 He gave him his crown, his robe, and his signet ring, so that he might guide the king's son Antiochus and bring him up to be

5, 65: Sons of Esau: Idumeans.

6, 1: Elymais: the mountainous region of Elam, north of the Persian Gulf. This section continues the story from 1 Mc 3, 37 and pertains to events preceding those in 1 Mc 4, 37ff.

m 1–13: 2 Mc 1, 12–17; 9, 1–29. n 1 Mc 1, 54; 4, 41ff.60f.

king. 16 King Antiochus died in Persia in the year one hundred and forty-nine.*

The Citadel Besieged 17 When Lysias learned that the king was dead, he set up the king's son Antiochus,* whom he had reared as a child, to be king in his place; and he gave him the title Eupator.[o]

18 The men in the citadel were hemming in Israel around the sanctuary, continually trying to harm them and to strengthen the Gentiles.[p] 19 But Judas planned to destroy them, and called all the people together to besiege them. 20 So in the year one hundred and fifty* they assembled and stormed the citadel, for which purpose he constructed catapults and other devices. 21 Some of the besieged escaped, joined by impious Israelites; 22 they went to the king and said:

"How long will you fail to do justice and avenge our kinsmen? 23 We agreed to serve your father and to follow his orders and obey his edicts. 24 And for this the sons of our people have become our enemies; they have put to death as many of us as they could find and have plundered our estates. 25 They have acted aggressively not only against us, but throughout their whole territory. 26 Look! They have now besieged the citadel in Jerusalem in order to capture it, and they have fortified the sanctuary and Beth-zur. 27 Unless you quickly forestall them, they will do even worse things than these, and you will not be able to stop them."

Campaign against Judas 28 [q]When the king heard this he was angry, and he called together all his Friends, the officers of his army, and the commanders of the cavalry.[r] 29 Mercenary forces also came to him from other kingdoms and from the islands of the seas. 30 His army numbered a hundred thousand foot-soldiers, twenty thousand cavalry, and thirty-two elephants trained for war. 31 They passed through Idumea and camped before Beth-zur. For many days they attacked it; they constructed siege-devices, but the besieged made a sortie and burned these, and they fought bravely.

32 Then Judas marched away from the citadel and moved his camp to Beth-zechariah, on the way to the king's camp. 33 The king, rising before dawn, moved his force hastily along the road to Beth-zechariah; and the armies prepared for battle, while the trumpets sounded. 34 They made the elephants drunk on grape and mulberry wine to provoke them to fight. 35 The beasts were distributed along the phalanxes, each elephant having assigned to it a thousand men in coats of mail, with bronze helmets, and five hundred picked cavalry. 36 These anticipated the beast wherever it was; and wherever it moved, they moved too and never left it. 37 A strong wooden tower covering each elephant, and fastened to it by a harness, held, besides the Indian mahout, three soldiers who fought from it. 38 The remaining cavalry were stationed on one or the other of the two flanks of the army, to harass the enemy and to be protected from the phalanxes. 39 When the sun shone on the gold and bronze shields, the mountains gleamed with their brightness and blazed like flaming torches. 40 Part of the king's army extended over the heights, while some were on low ground, but they marched forward steadily and in good order. 41 All who heard the noise of their numbers, the tramp of their marching, and the clashing of the arms, trembled; for the army was very great and strong.

42 Judas with his army advanced to fight, and six hundred men of the king's army fell. 43 Eleazar, called Avaran, saw one of the beasts bigger than any of the others and covered with royal armor, and he thought the king must be on it.[s] 44 So he gave up his life to save his people and win an everlasting name for himself. 45 He dashed up to it in the middle of the phalanx, killing men right and left, so that they fell back from him on both sides. 46 He ran right under the

6, 16: The year one hundred and forty-nine: September 22, 164, to October 9, 163 B.C. A Babylonian list of the Seleucid kings indicates that Antiochus died in November or early December of 164.

6, 17: The king's son Antiochus: Antiochus V Eupator, then about nine years old. He was in Antioch, still in the charge of Lysias, who proceeded to govern and wage wars in his name. Both were put to death two years later, when Demetrius, brother of Antiochus IV, arrived to claim the kingship; cf 1 Mc 7, 1ff.

6, 20: The year one hundred and fifty: October, 163, to September, 162 B.C.

o 2 Mc 10, 10f. p 1 Mc 1, 33ff. q 28–54: 2 Mc 13, 1–23. r 28ff: 2 Mc 13, 1f. s 2 Mc 13, 15.

elephant and stabbed it in the belly, killing it. The beast fell to the ground on top of him, and he died there.

[47]When the Jews saw the strength of the royal army and the ardor of its forces, they retreated from them. [48] [t]A part of the king's army went up to Jerusalem to attack them, and the king established camps in Judea and at Mount Zion. [49] [u]He made peace with the men of Beth-zur, and they evacuated the city, because they had no food there to enable them to stand a siege, for that was a sabbath year in the land.* [50]The king took Beth-zur and stationed a garrison there to hold it. [51]For many days he besieged the sanctuary, setting up artillery and machines, fire-throwers, catapults and mechanical bows for shooting arrows and slingstones. [52]The Jews countered by setting up machines of their own, and kept up the fight a long time. [53]But there were no provisions in the storerooms, because it was the seventh year, and the tide-over provisions had been eaten up by those who had been rescued from the Gentiles and brought to Judea. [54]Few men remained in the sanctuary; the rest scattered, each to his own home, for the famine was too much for them.

Peace Treaty [55] [v]Lysias heard that Philip, whom King Antiochus, before his death, had appointed to train his son Antiochus to be king, [56]had returned from Persia and Media with the army that accompanied the king, and that he was seeking to take over the government. [57]So he hastily resolved to withdraw. He said to the king, the leaders of the army, and the soldiers: "We are growing weaker every day, our provisions are scanty, the place we are besieging is strong, and it is our duty to take care of the affairs of the kingdom. [w] [58]Therefore let us now come to terms with these men, and make peace with them and all their nation. [59]Let us grant them freedom to live according to their own laws as formerly; it was on account of their laws, which we abolished, that they became angry and did all these things."

[60]The proposal found favor with the king and the leaders; he sent peace terms to the Jews, and they accepted. [61]So the king and the leaders swore an oath to them, and on these terms they evacuated the fortification. [62]But when the king entered Mount Zion and saw how the place was fortified, he broke the oath he had sworn and gave orders for the encircling wall to be destroyed. [63]Then he departed in haste and returned to Antioch, where he found Philip in possession of the city. He fought against him and took the city by force.

CHAPTER 7

Expedition of Bacchides and Alcimus [1] [x]In the year one hundred and fifty-one,* Demetrius, son of Seleucus, set out from Rome, arrived with a few men in a city on the seacoast, and began to rule there. [2]As he was preparing to enter the royal palace of his ancestors, the soldiers seized Antiochus and Lysias to bring them to him. [3]When he was informed of this, he said, "Do not show me their faces." [4]So the soldiers killed them, and Demetrius sat on the royal throne.

[5]Then all the lawless and impious men of Israel came to him. They were led by Alcimus,* who desired to be high priest. [6]They made this accusation to the king against the people: "Judas and his brothers have destroyed all your friends and have driven us out of our country. [7]So now, send a man whom you trust to go and see all the havoc Judas has done to us and to the king's land, and let him punish them and all their supporters."

6, 49: A sabbath year in the land: when sowing and reaping were prohibited (Ex 23, 10f; Lv 25, 2–7). The year without a harvest (autumn of 164 to autumn of 163) was followed by a food shortage.

7, 1ff: The year one hundred and fifty-one: the spring of 161 B.C. Demetrius, son of Seleucus, was the lawful heir to the kingdom; but when only nine years old, he was taken as a hostage at Rome in place of his uncle, who ruled as Antiochus IV Epiphanes. At the age of twenty-five Demetrius fled secretly from Rome and, with the support of the Syrians, overcame his rival Antiochus V and put him to death. The royal palace: at Antioch.

7, 5f: Alcimus: a renegade Jew hostile to the Maccabees, who became high priest after the death of Menelaus (2 Mc 14, 3). He received confirmation in his office from the new King Demetrius (v 9), and brought malicious charges against Judas and his brothers and the people (v 6). He wrought more evils on the Israelites than the Gentiles had done (v 23).

t 48f: 2 Mc 13, 22–23. u Lv 25, 2. v 55–63: 2 Mc 13, 23–26. w 2 Mc 11, 13ff. x 1–7: 2 Mc 14, 1–11.

[8]Then the king chose Bacchides, one of the
King's Friends, governor of West-of-Euphrates, a
great man in the kingdom, and faithful to the
king. [9][y]He sent him and the impious Alcimus, to
whom he granted the high priesthood, with
orders to take revenge on the Israelites. [10]They
set out and, on arriving in the land of Judah with
a great army, sent messengers who spoke deceit-
fully to Judas and his brothers in peaceful terms.
[11]But these paid no attention to their words,
seeing that they had come with a great army. [12]A
group of scribes, however, gathered about Alci-
mus and Bacchides to ask for a just agreement.
[13][z]The Hasideans were the first among the
Israelites to seek peace with them, [14]for they
said, "A priest of the line of Aaron has come with
the army, and he will not do us any wrong."
[15]He spoke with them peacefully and swore to
them, "We will not try to injure you or your
friends." [16]So they trusted him. But he arrested
sixty of them and killed them in one day,
according to the text of Scripture:

[17]"The flesh of your saints they have strewn,
and their blood they have shed round about
Jerusalem,
and there was no one to bury them. [a]

[18]Then fear and dread of them came upon all the
people, who said: "There is no truth or justice
among them; they violated the agreement and
the oath that they swore."

[19]Bacchides withdrew from Jerusalem and
pitched his camp in Beth-zaith.* He had many of
the men arrested who deserted to him, throwing
them into the great pit. [20]He handed the prov-
ince over to Alcimus, leaving troops to help him,
while he himself returned to the king.

[21]Alcimus spared no pains to maintain his
high priesthood, [22]and all those who were
disturbing their people gathered about him.
They took possession of the land of Judah and
caused great distress in Israel. [23]When Judas saw
all the evils that Alcimus and his men were
bringing upon the Israelites, more than even the
Gentiles had done, [24]he went about all the
borders of Judea and took revenge on the men
who had deserted, preventing them from going
out into the country. [25]But when Alcimus saw
that Judas and his followers were gaining
strength and realized that he could not oppose
them, he returned to the king and accused them
of grave crimes.

Defeat of Nicanor [26][b]Then the king sent Nica-
nor, one of his famous officers, who was a bitter
enemy of Israel, with orders to destroy the
people. [27]Nicanor came to Jerusalem with a
large force and deceitfully sent to Judas* and his
brothers this peaceable message: [28]"Let there be
no fight between me and you. I will come with a
few men to meet you peaceably."

[29]So he came to Judas, and they greeted one
another peaceably. But Judas' enemies were
prepared to seize him. [30]When he became aware
that Nicanor had come to him with treachery in
mind, Judas was afraid and would not meet him
again. [c] [31]When Nicanor saw that his plan had
been discovered, he went out to fight Judas near
Caphar-salama.* [32]About five hundred men of
Nicanor's army fell; the rest fled to the City of
David.

[33][d]After this, Nicanor went up to Mount
Zion. Some of the priests from the sanctuary and
some of the elders of the people came out to
greet him peaceably and to show him the
holocaust that was being offered for the king.
[34]But he mocked and ridiculed them, defiled
them,* and spoke disdainfully. [35]In a rage he
swore: "If Judas and his army are not delivered
to me at once, when I return victorious I will
burn this temple down." He went away in great
anger. [36]The priests, however, went in and stood
before the altar and the sanctuary. [e] They wept

7, 19: Beth-zaith: about three miles north of Beth-zur and twelve miles south of Jerusalem.

7, 27: Nicanor . . . deceitfully sent to Judas: a more favorable picture of Nicanor, as an honest man who became a personal friend of Judas, is given in 2 Mc 14, 17–25. Their friendship was broken by the intrigues of Alcimus (2 Mc 14, 26–30).

7, 31: Caphar-salama: a village seven miles north-northwest of Jerusalem, on the road leading to Beth-horon.

7, 34: Defiled them: spitting on the priests caused them to become legally defiled.

y 9ff: 2 Mc 14, 46. z 13f: 1 Mc 2, 42. a Ps 79, 1ff. b 26f: 1 Mc 3, 38; 2 Mc 8, 9; 14, 12f. c 2 Mc 14, 30. d 33–38: 2 Mc 14, 31–36. e Jl 2, 17.

and said: 37“You have chosen this house to bear your name, to be a house of prayer and petition for your people. 38Take revenge on this man and his army, and let them fall by the sword. Remember their blasphemies, and do not let them continue.”

39Nicanor left Jerusalem and pitched his camp at Beth-horon, where the Syrian army joined him. 40But Judas camped in Adasa* with three thousand men. Here Judas uttered this prayer: 41“When they who were sent by the king blasphemed, your angel went out and killed a hundred and eighty-five thousand of them.[f] 42In the same way, crush this army before us today, and let the rest know that Nicanor spoke wickedly against your sanctuary; judge him according to his wickedness.”[g]

43The armies met in battle on the thirteenth day of the month Adar. Nicanor's army was crushed, and he himself was the first to fall in the battle.[h] 44When his army saw that Nicanor was dead, they threw down their arms and fled. 45The Jews pursued them a day's journey, from Adasa to near Gazara, blowing the trumpets behind them as signals. 46From all the surrounding villages of Judea people came out and closed in on them. They hemmed them in, and all the enemies fell by the sword; not a single one escaped.

47Then the Jews collected the spoils and the booty; they cut off Nicanor's head and his right arm, which he had lifted up so arrogantly. These they brought to Jerusalem and displayed there. 48The people rejoiced greatly, and observed that day as a great festival. 49They decreed that it should be observed every year on the thirteenth of Adar.* 50And for a short time* the land of Judah was quiet.

CHAPTER 8

Treaty with the Romans* 1Judas had heard of the reputation of the Romans. They were valiant fighters and acted amiably to all who took their side. They established a friendly alliance with all who applied to them. 2He was also told of their battles and the brave deeds that they had performed against the Gauls,* conquering them and forcing them to pay tribute. 3They had gotten possession of the silver and gold mines in Spain, 4and by planning and persistence had conquered the whole country, although it was very remote from their own. They had crushed the kings who had come against them from the far corners of the earth and had inflicted on them severe defeat, and the rest paid tribute to them every year. 5Philip* and Perseus, king of the Macedonians, and the others who opposed them in battle had been overwhelmed and subjugated. 6Antiochus* the Great, king of Asia, who had fought against them with a hundred and twenty elephants and with cavalry and chariots and a very great army, had been defeated by them. 7They had taken him alive and obliged him and the kings who succeeded him to pay a heavy tribute, to give hostages and a section of 8Lycia,

7, 40: Adasa: a village southeast of Caphar-salama.

7, 49: The thirteenth of Adar: March 27, 160 B.C. This day in the Jewish calendar was called the “Day of Nicanor” (2 Mc 15, 36), but it was not long celebrated by the Jews.

7, 50: A short time: about one month following the death of Nicanor. After that began the attack of Bacchides resulting in the death of Judas (1 Mc 9, 1–18).

8, 1: This chapter contains the account of the embassy which Judas sent to Rome, probably before the death of Nicanor, to conclude a treaty of alliance between Rome and the Jewish nation. Without precise chronology, the pertinent data are gathered into a unified theme.

The image of the Roman Republic greatly impressed the smaller Eastern peoples seeking support against their overlords (1–16), because of Roman success in war (2–11) and effective aid to their allies (12–13). Numerous interventions by Rome in the politics of the Near East bear witness to its power and prestige in the second century B.C. Cf 1 Mc 1, 10; 7, 2; 12, 3; 15, 15–24; 2 Mc 11, 34. With the Roman control of Palestine in 63 B.C., the Republic and later the Empire became heartily detested. The eulogy of Rome in this chapter is one of the reasons why 1 Maccabees was not preserved by the Palestinian Jews of the century that followed.

8, 2: Gauls: probably the Celts of northern Italy and southern France, subdued by the Romans in 222 B.C., and again in 200–191 B.C.; but perhaps also those in Asia Minor (the Galatians), whom the Romans defeated in 189 B.C.

8, 5: Philip: Philip V of Macedonia, defeated by a Graeco-Roman alliance at Cynoscephalae in 197 B.C. Perseus, his son, was defeated at Pydna in 168 B.C., and died a prisoner. With this, the kingdom of Macedonia came to an end.

8, 6: Antiochus: Antiochus III, greatest of the Seleucid kings. He was defeated at Magnesia in 190 B.C. By the Treaty of Apamea in 189, he was obliged to pay Rome a crushing indemnity of 15,000 talents. It was the weakening of Antiochene power and the growing military and economic influence of Rome that led Antiochus IV to adopt the policy of political, religious and cultural unification of Syria and Palestine.

8, 8: Lycia, Mysia: regions in western Asia Minor. These names are restored here by conjectural emendation; the Greek text has “India, Media,” most likely through scribal error. Eumenes: Eumenes II (197–158), king of Pergamum, an ally of Rome who benefited greatly from Antiochus' losses.

f 41f: 2 Mc 8, 19; 15, 22ff. g Is 37, 36ff. h 2 Mc 15, 25–35.

Mysia,* and Lydia from among their best provinces. The Romans took these from him and gave them to King Eumenes. 9*When the men of Greece had planned to come and destroy them, 10the Romans discovered it, and sent against the Greeks a single general who made war on them. Many were wounded and fell, and the Romans took their wives and children captive. They plundered them, took possession of their land, tore down their strongholds and reduced them to slavery even to this day. 11All the other kingdoms and islands that had ever opposed them they destroyed and enslaved; 12with their friends, however, and those who relied on them, they maintained friendship. They had conquered kings both far and near, and all who heard of their fame were afraid of them. 13In truth, those whom they desired to help to a kingdom became kings, and those whom they wished to depose they deposed; and they were greatly exalted. 14Yet with all this, none of them put on a crown or wore purple as a display of grandeur. 15They had made for themselves a senate house, and every day three hundred and twenty men took counsel, deliberating on all that concerned the people and their well-being. 16They entrusted their government to one man* every year, to rule over their entire country, and they all obeyed that one, and there was no envy or jealousy among them.

17So Judas chose Eupolemus, son of John, son of Accos, and Jason, son of Eleazar, and sent them to Rome to establish an alliance of friendship with them.[i] 18He did this to get rid of the yoke, for it was obvious that the kingdom of the Greeks was subjecting Israel to slavery. 19After making a very long journey to Rome, the envoys entered the senate and spoke as follows: 20"Judas, called Maccabeus, and his brothers, with the Jewish people, have sent us to you to make a peaceful alliance with you, and to enroll ourselves among your allies and friends." 21The proposal pleased the Romans, 22and this is a copy of the reply they inscribed on bronze tablets and sent to Jerusalem,* to remain there with the Jews as a record of peace and alliance:[j]

23"May it be well with the Romans and the Jewish nation at sea and on land forever; may sword and enemy be far from them. 24But if war is first made on Rome, or any of its allies in any of their dominions, 25the Jewish nation will help them wholeheartedly, as the occasion shall demand; 26and to those who wage war they shall not give nor provide grain, arms, money, or ships; this is Rome's decision. They shall fulfill their obligations without receiving any recompense. 27In the same way, if war is made first on the Jewish nation, the Romans will help them willingly, as the occasion shall demand, 28and to those who are attacking them there shall not be given grain, arms, money, or ships; this is Rome's decision. They shall fulfill their obligations without deception. 29On these terms the Romans have made an agreement with the Jewish people. 30But if both parties hereafter decide to add or take away anything, they shall do as they choose, and whatever they shall add or take away shall be valid.

31"Moreover, concerning the wrongs that King Demetrius has done to them, we have written to him thus: 'Why have you made your yoke heavy upon our friends and allies the Jews? 32If they complain about you again, we will do them justice and make war on you by land and sea.' "

CHAPTER 9

Invasion of Judah 1When Demetrius heard that Nicanor and his army had fallen in battle, he

8, 9f: The revolt of the Achaean League, inserted here, occurred in 146 B.C., after Judas' time. It was crushed by the Roman consul Lucius Mummius and marked the end of Greek independence. The author regards all Greeks as the enemies of God.

8, 16: They entrusted their government to one man: actually the Roman Republic always had two consuls as joint heads of the government. Presumably, a single one dealt with embassies and answered letters, hence the impression the Jews received; cf 1 Mc 15, 16.

8, 22: The reply . . . on bronze tablets and sent to Jerusalem: the decree of the Senate would be inscribed on bronze and kept in the Roman Capitol, with only a copy in letter form sent to Jerusalem. The translation of the decree into Hebrew and then into Greek, as found here in 1 Mc, may have occasioned this error.

i 1 Mc 12, 1f; 15, 15–22. j 1 Mc 14, 18.

again sent Bacchides and Alcimus into the land of Judah, along with the right wing of his army. 2They took the road to Galilee, and camping opposite the ascent at Arbela, they captured it* and killed many people. 3In the first month of the year one hundred and fifty-two,* they encamped against Jerusalem. 4Then they set out for Berea with twenty thousand men and two thousand cavalry. 5Judas, with three thousand picked men, had camped at Elasa. 6When his men saw the great number of the troops, they were very much afraid, and many slipped away from the camp, until only eight hundred men remained.

7As Judas saw that his army was melting away just when the battle was imminent, he was panic-stricken, because he had no time to gather them together. 8But in spite of his discouragement, he said to those who remained: "Let us go forward to meet our enemies; perhaps we can put up a good fight against them." 9They tried to dissuade him, saying: "We certainly cannot. Let us save our lives now, and come back with our kinsmen, and then fight against them. Now we are too few." 10But Judas said: "Far be it from me to do such a thing as to flee from them! If our time has come, let us die bravely for our kinsmen and not leave a stain upon our glory!"

Death of Judas 11Then the army of Bacchides moved out of camp and took its position for combat. The cavalry were divided into two squadrons, and the slingers and the archers came on ahead of the army, and all the valiant men were in the front line. 12Bacchides was on the right wing. Flanked by the two squadrons, the phalanx attacked as they blew their trumpets. Those who were on Judas' side also blew their trumpets. 13The earth shook with the noise of the armies, and the battle raged from morning until evening. 14Seeing that Bacchides was on the right, with the main force of his army, Judas, with all the most stouthearted rallying to him, 15drove back the right wing and pursued them as far as the mountain slopes.* 16But when the men on the left wing saw that the right wing was driven back, they turned and followed Judas and his men, taking them in the rear. 17The battle was fought desperately, and many on both sides fell wounded. 18Then Judas fell, and the rest fled.

19Jonathan and Simon took their brother Judas and buried him in the tomb of their fathers at Modein. 20All Israel bewailed him in great grief. They mourned for him many days, and they said, 21"How the mighty one has fallen, the savior of Israel!" [k] 22The other acts of Judas, his battles, the brave deeds he performed, and his greatness have not been recorded; but they were very many.

IV: Leadership of Jonathan

Bacchides and Jonathan 23After the death of Judas, the transgressors of the law raised their heads in every part of Israel, and all kinds of evildoers appeared. 24In those days there was a very great famine, and the country deserted to them. 25Bacchides chose impious men and made them masters of the country. 26These sought out and hunted down the friends of Judas and brought them to Bacchides, who punished and derided them. 27There had not been such great distress in Israel since the time prophets ceased to appear among the people.

28Then all the friends of Judas came together and said to Jonathan: 29"Since your brother Judas died, there has been no one like him to oppose our enemies, Bacchides and those who are hostile to our nation. 30Now therefore we have chosen you today to be our ruler and leader

9, 2: They took the road . . . Arbela, they captured it: this passage is restored, in part, by conjectural emendation. The present Greek text could be translated, "They took the road to Gilgal, and camping opposite Mesaloth at Arbela, they captured it." But Arbela (modern Khirbet Irbid) was in Galilee—on a high hill overlooking the western shore of the Sea of Galilee. Gilgal, on the contrary, was in the Jordan valley near Jericho. "Mesaloth" is probably a corrupt form of a Hebrew word meaning "steps, ascent."

9, 3: The first month of the year one hundred and fifty-two: April/May 160 B.C., by the temple calendar.

9, 15: As far as the mountain slopes: conjectural emendation. The Greek text has "as far as Mount Azotus"; this is most unlikely. Apparently the Greek translator mistook the Hebrew word ashdot, "slopes," for asdod, "Azotus."

k 2 Sam 1, 27.

in his place, and to fight our battle." 31 From that moment Jonathan accepted the leadership, and took the place of Judas his brother.

32 When Bacchides learned of it, he sought to kill him. 33 But Jonathan and his brother Simon and all the men with him discovered this, and they fled to the desert of Tekoa* and camped by the waters of the pool of Asphar.*

35 Jonathan sent his brother* as leader of the convoy to ask permission of his friends, the Nabateans, to deposit with them their great quantity of baggage.[l] 36 But the sons of Jambri from Medaba* made a raid and seized and carried off John and everything he had. 37 After this, word was brought to Jonathan and his brother Simon: "The sons of Jambri are celebrating a great wedding, and with a large escort they are bringing the bride, the daughter of one of the great princes of Canaan, from Nadabath." 38 Remembering the blood of John their brother, they went up and hid themselves under cover of the mountain. 39 They watched, and suddenly saw a noisy crowd with baggage; the bridegroom and his friends and kinsmen had come out to meet the bride's party with tambourines and musicians and much equipment. 40 The Jews rose up against them from their ambush and killed them. Many fell wounded, and after the survivors fled toward the mountain, all their spoils were taken. 41 Thus the wedding was turned into mourning, and the sound of music into lamentation. 42 Having taken their revenge for the blood of their brother, the Jews returned to the marshes of the Jordan.

43 When Bacchides heard of it, he came on the sabbath to the banks of the Jordan with a large force. 44 Then Jonathan said to his companions, "Let us get up now and fight for our lives, for today is not like yesterday and the day before. 45 The battle is before us, and behind us are the waters of the Jordan on one side, marsh and thickets on the other, and there is no way of escape.* 46 Cry out now to Heaven for deliverance from our enemies." 47 When they joined battle, Jonathan raised his arm to strike Bacchides, but Bacchides backed away from him. 48 Jonathan and his men jumped into the Jordan and swam across to the other side, but the enemy did not pursue them across the Jordan. 49 A thousand men on Bacchides' side fell that day.

50 On returning to Jerusalem, Bacchides built strongholds in Judea: the Jericho fortress, as well as Emmaus, Beth-horon, Bethel, Timnath, Pharathon, and Tephon, with high walls and gates and bars.* 51 In each he put a garrison to oppose Israel. 52 He fortified the city of Beth-zur, Gazara and the citadel, and put soldiers in them and stores of provisions. 53 He took as hostages the sons of the leaders of the country and put them in custody in the citadel at Jerusalem.[m]

54 In the year one hundred and fifty-three, in the second month,* Alcimus ordered the wall of the inner court of the sanctuary to be torn down, thus destroying the work of the prophets. But he only began to tear it down. 55 Just at that time he had a stroke, and his work was interrupted; his mouth was closed and he was paralyzed, so that he could no longer utter a word to give orders concerning his house. 56 Finally he died in great agony. 57 Seeing that Alcimus was dead, Bacchides returned to the king, and the land of Judah was quiet for two years.

58 Then all the transgressors of the law held a council and said: "Jonathan and his companions are living in peace and security. Now then, let us have Bacchides return, and he will capture all of them in a single night." 59 So they went and took counsel with him. 60 When Bacchides was setting out with a large force, he sent letters secretly to all his allies in Judea, telling them to seize Jonathan and his companions. They were

9, 33: Tekoa: Home of the prophet Amos in the wild country above the Dead Sea, southeast of Jerusalem.

9, 34: Omitted, it is a dittography of verse 43.

9, 35: Jonathan sent his brother: this was John who was called Gaddi (1 Mc 2, 2; cf 9, 36. 38).

9, 36: Medaba: northeast of the Dead Sea.

9, 45: Jonathan's force was apparently trapped in one of the many oxbows of the lower Jordan. Bacchides had crossed and caught them still on the east bank.

9, 50: These sites constitute a ring on the edges of the province of Judea.

9, 54: In the year . . . second month: May 159 B.C.

l 1 Mc 5, 25. m 1 Mc 10, 9.

not able to do this, however, because their plot became known. 61 In fact, Jonathan's men seized about fifty of the men of the country who were ringleaders in the mischief and put them to death. 62 Then Jonathan and Simon and their companions withdrew to Bethbasi* in the desert; they rebuilt and strengthened its fortifications that had been demolished. 63 When Bacchides learned of this, he gathered together his whole force and sent word to those who were in Judea. 64 He came and pitched his camp before Bethbasi, and constructing siege-machines, he fought against it for many days.

65 Leaving his brother Simon in the city, Jonathan, accompanied by a small group of men, went out into the field. 66 He struck down Odomera and his kinsmen and the sons of Phasiron in their encampment; these men had set out to go up to the siege with their forces. 67 Simon and his men then sallied forth from the city and set fire to the machines. 68 They fought against Bacchides, and he was beaten. This caused him great distress. Because the enterprise he had planned came to naught, 69 he was angry with the lawless men who had advised him to invade the province. He killed many of them and resolved to return to his own country.

70 Jonathan learned of this and sent ambassadors to make peace with him and to obtain the release of the prisoners. 71 He agreed to do as Jonathan had asked. He swore an oath to him that he would never try to injure him for the rest of his life; 72 and he released the prisoners he had previously taken from the land of Judah. He returned to his own country and never came into their territory again.

73 Then the sword ceased in Israel. Jonathan settled in Michmash; he began to judge* the people, and he destroyed the impious in Israel.

CHAPTER 10

Revolt of Alexander 1 In the year one hundred and sixty,* Alexander, who was called Epiphanes, son of Antiochus, came up and took Ptolemais. He was accepted and began to reign there. 2 When King Demetrius heard of it, he mustered a very large army and marched out to engage him in combat. 3 Demetrius sent a letter to Jonathan written in peaceful terms, to pay him honor; 4 for he said: "Let us be the first to make peace with him, before he makes peace with Alexander against us, 5 since he will remember all the wrongs we have done to him, his brothers, and his nation."

6 So Demetrius authorized Jonathan, as his ally, to gather an army and procure arms; and he ordered that the hostages in the citadel be released to him. 7 Accordingly Jonathan went up to Jerusalem and read the letter to all the people. The men in the citadel 8 were struck with fear when they heard that the king had given him authority to gather an army. 9 They released the hostages to Jonathan, and he gave them back to their parents.[n] 10 Thereafter Jonathan dwelt in Jerusalem, and began to build and restore the city. 11 He ordered the workmen to build the walls and encircle Mount Zion with square stones for its fortification, which they did. 12 The foreigners in the strongholds that Bacchides had built, took flight; 13 each one of them left his place and returned to his own country. 14 Only in Beth-zur did some remain of those who had abandoned the law and the commandments, for they used it as a place of refuge.

Jonathan Supports Alexander 15 King Alexander heard of the promises that Demetrius had made to Jonathan; he was also told of the battles and valiant deeds of Jonathan and his brothers and the troubles that they had endured. 16 He

9, 62: Bethbasi: two miles east of Bethlehem, and six miles north of Tekoa.

9, 73: Began to judge: exercise the governing authority as in the book of Judges. With Jerusalem and the garrison towns (v 50) firmly in Seleucid hands, Jonathan's freedom of action was greatly restricted. Michmash, southeast of Bethel, famous for the exploit of the former Jonathan, son of Saul; cf 1 Sm 14.

10, 1: The year one hundred and sixty: 152 B.C. Alexander . . . Antiochus: Alexander Balas claimed to be a son of Antiochus IV. He had the backing of the Romans, who had never forgiven Demetrius for becoming king without their permission. The latter meanwhile had become unpopular with his own people as well as with the Jews.

n 1 Mc 9, 53.

said, "Shall we ever find another man like him?
Let us now make him our friend and ally." 17 So
he sent Jonathan a letter written in these terms:
18 "King Alexander sends greetings to his brother
Jonathan. 19 We have heard of you, that you are a
mighty warrior and worthy to be our friend.
20 We have therefore appointed you today to be
high priest of your nation; you are to be called
the King's Friend, and you are to look after our
interests and preserve amity with us." He also
sent him a purple robe and a crown of gold.[o]
21 Jonathan put on the sacred vestments in the
seventh month of the year one hundred and
sixty at the feast of Booths,* and he gathered
an army and procured many arms. 22 When
Demetrius heard of these things, he was dis-
tressed and said: 23 Why have we allowed Alex-
ander to get ahead of us by gaining the friend-
ship of the Jews and thus strengthening him-
self? 24 I too will write them conciliatory words
and offer dignities and gifts, so that they may
be an aid to me."
25 So he sent them this message: "King Deme-
trius sends greetings to the Jewish nation. 26 We
have heard how you have kept the treaty with us
and continued in our friendship and not gone
over to our enemies, and we are glad. 27 Con-
tinue, therefore, to keep faith with us, and we
will reward you with favors in return for what
you do in our behalf. 28 We will grant you many
exemptions and will bestow gifts on you.
29 "I now free you, as I also exempt all the
Jews, from the tribute, the salt tax, and the
crown levies.[p] 30 [q]Instead of collecting the third
of the grain and the half of the fruit of the trees
that should be my share, I renounce the right
from this day forward. Neither now nor in the
future will I collect them from the land of Judah
or from the three districts annexed from Sa-
maria.* 31 Let Jerusalem and her territory, her
tithes and her tolls, be sacred and free from tax.
32 I also yield my authority over the citadel in
Jerusalem, and I transfer it to the high priest,
that he may put in it such men as he shall choose
to guard it. 33 Every one of the Jews who has
been carried into captivity from the land of Judah
into any part of my kingdom I set at liberty
without ransom; and let all their taxes, even
those on their cattle, be canceled. 34 Let all feast
days, sabbaths, new moon festivals, appointed
days, and the three days that precede each feast
day, and the three days that follow, be days of
immunity and exemption for every Jew in my
kingdom. 35 Let no man have authority to exact
payment from them or to molest any of them in
any matter.
36 "Let thirty thousand Jews be enrolled in the
king's army and allowances be given them, as is
due to all the king's soldiers. 37 Let some of them
be stationed in the king's principal strongholds,
and of these let some be given positions of trust
in the affairs of the kingdom. Let their superiors
and their rulers be taken from among them, and
let them follow their own laws, as the king has
commanded in the land of Judah.
38 "Let the three districts that have been added
to Judea from the province of Samaria be incorpo-
rated with Judea so that they may be under one
man and obey no other authority than the high
priest. 39 Ptolemais and its confines I give as a
present to the sanctuary in Jerusalem for the
necessary expenses of the sanctuary. 40 I make a
yearly personal grant of fifteen thousand silver
shekels out of the royal revenues, from appropri-
ate places. 41 All the additional funds that the
officials did not hand over as they had done in
the first years, shall henceforth be handed over
for the services of the temple. 42 Moreover, the
dues of five thousand silver shekels that used to
be taken from the revenue of the sanctuary
every year shall be canceled, since these funds
belong to the priests who perform the services.
43 Whoever takes refuge in the temple of Jerusa-
lem or in any of its precincts, because of money

10, 21: Jonathan . . . feast of Booths: Jonathan began to discharge the office of high priest October 23–30, 152 B.C. For seven years after the death of Alcimus there had been no high priest in Jerusalem. It was taken for granted that the king, though a Gentile, had the power to appoint one. The Maccabees, though a priestly family, were not of the line of Zadok, and some in Israel regarded Jonathan's tenure as a usurpation.

10, 30: The three districts annexed from Samaria: mentioned by name in 1 Mc 11, 34. The present Greek text, by a scribal error, has added "and Galilee" after "Samaria."

o 1 Mc 2, 18. p 1 Mc 11, 28f. 35. q 1 Mc 11, 28, 34.

he owes the king, or because of any other debt, shall be released, together with all the goods he possesses in my kingdom. 44The cost of rebuilding and restoring the structures of the sanctuary shall be covered out of the royal revenue. 45Likewise the cost of building the walls of Jerusalem and fortifying it all around, and of building walls in Judea, shall be donated from the royal revenue."

46When Jonathan and the people heard these words, they neither believed nor accepted them, for they remembered the great evil that Demetrius had done in Israel, and how sorely he had afflicted them. 47They therefore decided in favor of Alexander, for he had been the first to address them peaceably, and they remained his allies for the rest of his life.

48King Alexander gathered together a large army and encamped opposite Demetrius. 49The two kings joined battle, and when the army of Demetrius fled, Alexander pursued him, and overpowered his soldiers. 50He pressed the battle hard until sunset, and Demetrius fell that day.

Treaty of Ptolemy and Alexander 51Alexander sent ambassadors to Ptolemy, king of Egypt, with this message: 52"Now that I have returned to my realm, taken my seat on the throne of my fathers, and established my rule by crushing Demetrius and gaining control of my country— 53for I engaged him in battle, defeated him and his army, and recovered the royal throne— 54let us now establish friendship with each other. Give me your daughter for my wife; and as your son-in-law, I will give to you and to her gifts worthy of you."

55King Ptolemy answered in these words: "Happy the day on which you returned to the land of your fathers and took your seat on their royal throne! 56I will do for you what you have written; but meet me in Ptolemais, so that we may see each other, and I will become your father-in-law as you have proposed."

57So Ptolemy with his daughter Cleopatra* set out from Egypt and came to Ptolemais in the year one hundred and sixty-two. 58There King Alexander met him, and Ptolemy gave him his daughter Cleopatra in marriage. Their wedding was celebrated at Ptolemais with great splendor according to the custom of kings.

59King Alexander also wrote to Jonathan to come and meet him. 60So he went with pomp to Ptolemais, where he met the two kings and gave them and their friends silver and gold and many gifts and thus won their favor.[r] 61Some pestilent Israelites, transgressors of the law, united against him to accuse him, but the king paid no heed to them. 62He ordered Jonathan to be divested of his ordinary garments and to be clothed in royal purple; and so it was done. 63The king also had him seated at his side. He said to his magistrates: "Go with him to the center of the city and make a proclamation that no one is to bring charges against him on any grounds or be troublesome to him in any way."

64[s]When his accusers saw the honor paid to him in the proclamation, and the purple with which he was clothed, they all fled. 65The king also honored him by numbering him among his Chief Friends and made him military commander and governor of the province. 66So Jonathan returned in peace and happiness to Jerusalem.

Victory over Apollonius 67In the year one hundred and sixty-five,* Demetrius, son of Demetrius, came from Crete to the land of his fathers. 68When King Alexander heard of it he was greatly troubled, and returned to Antioch. 69Demetrius appointed Apollonius governor of Coelesyria. Having gathered a large army, Apollonius pitched his camp at Jamnia. From there he sent this message to Jonathan the high priest: 70"You are the only one who resists us. I am laughed at and put to shame on your account. Why are you displaying power against us in the mountains? 71If you have confidence in your forces, come down now to us in the plain, and let us test each other's strength there; the city forces are on my side. 72Inquire and learn who I

10, 57: Cleopatra: Cleopatra Thea, then about fifteen years old. She later married Demetrius II, and later still, his brother Antiochus VII. The year one hundred and sixty-two. 151/150 B.C.

10, 67: The year one hundred and sixty-five: 147 B.C. Demetrius: Demetrius II Nicator.

r 1 Mc 2, 18. s 64f: 1 Mc 2, 18; 11, 27.

am and who the others are who are helping me. Men say that you cannot make a stand against us because your fathers were twice put to flight in their own land. [73]Now you too will be unable to withstand our cavalry and such a force as this in the plain, where there is not a stone or a pebble or a place to flee."

[74]When Jonathan heard the message of Apollonius, he was roused. Choosing ten thousand men, he set out from Jerusalem, and Simon his brother joined him to help him. [75]He pitched camp near Joppa, but the men in the city shut him out because Apollonius had a garrison there. When the Jews besieged it, [76]the men of the city became afraid and opened the gates, and so Jonathan took possession of Joppa.*

[77]When Apollonius heard of it, he drew up three thousand horsemen and an innumerable infantry. He marched on Azotus as though he were going on through the country, but at the same time he advanced into the plain, because he had such a large number of horsemen to rely on. [78]Jonathan followed him to Azotus, and they engaged in battle. [79]Apollonius, however, had left a thousand cavalry in hiding behind them. [80]When Jonathan discovered that there was an ambush behind him, his army was surrounded. From morning until evening they showered his men with arrows. [81]But his men held their ground, as Jonathan had commanded, whereas the enemy's horses became tired out. [82]When the horsemen were exhausted, Simon attacked the phalanx, overwhelmed it and put it to flight. [83]The horsemen too were scattered over the plain. The enemy fled to Azotus and entered Beth-dagon, the temple of their idol, to save themselves. [84]But Jonathan burned and plundered Azotus with its neighboring towns, and destroyed by fire both the temple of Dagon and the men who had taken refuge in it.[t] [85]Those who fell by the sword, together with those who were burned alive, came to about eight thousand men. [86]Then Jonathan left there and pitched his camp at Ashkalon, and the people of that city came out to meet him with great pomp. [87]He and his men then returned to Jerusalem, laden with much booty. [88]When King Alexander heard of these events, he accorded new honors to Jonathan. [89]He sent him a gold buckle, such as is usually given to King's Kinsmen;* he also gave him Ekron and all its territory as a possession.

CHAPTER 11

Alliance of Demetrius and Ptolemy [1]The king of Egypt gathered his forces, as numerous as the sands of the seashore, and many ships; and he sought by deceit to take Alexander's kingdom and add it to his own. [2]He entered Syria with peaceful words, and the people in the cities opened their gates to welcome him, as King Alexander had ordered them to do, since Ptolemy was his father-in-law. [3]But when Ptolemy entered the cities, he stationed garrison troops in each one. [4]When he reached Azotus, he was shown the temple of Dagon destroyed by fire, Azotus and its suburbs demolished, corpses lying about, and the charred bodies of those burned by Jonathan in the war and stacked up along his route.[u] [5]To prejudice the king against Jonathan, he was told what the latter had done; but the king said nothing. [6]Jonathan met the king with pomp at Joppa, and they greeted each other and spent the night there. [7]Jonathan accompanied the king as far as the river called Eleutherus* and then returned to Jerusalem.

[8]Plotting evil against Alexander, King Ptolemy took possession of the cities along the seacoast as far as Seleucia-by-the-Sea.* [9]He sent ambassadors to King Demetrius, saying: "Come, let us make a pact with each other; I will give you my daughter whom Alexander has married, and you shall reign over your father's kingdom. [10]I regret

10, 76: Joppa: about forty miles northwest of Jerusalem. For the first time the Maccabees took possession of a seaport; nominally it was on behalf of King Alexander.

10, 89: Kinsmen: a class higher than Chief Friends.

11, 7: Eleutherus: modern Nahr el-Kebir, the northern border of modern Lebanon; in the second century B.C. the northern limit of Coelesyria.

11, 8: Seleucia-by-the-Sea: at the mouth of the Orontes, the port city of Antioch.

t 1 Mc 11, 4; 1 Sm 5, 2–5. u 1 Mc 10, 84.

that I gave him my daughter, for he has sought to kill me."* [11]His real reason for accusing Alexander, however, was that he coveted Alexander's kingdom. [12]After taking his daughter away and giving her to Demetrius, Ptolemy broke with Alexander; their enmity became open. [13]Then Ptolemy entered Antioch and assumed the crown of Asia; he thus wore two crowns on his head, that of Egypt and that of Asia.

Deaths of Alexander and Ptolemy [14]King Alexander was in Cilicia at that time, because the people of that region had revolted. [15]When Alexander heard the news, he came to challenge Ptolemy in battle. Ptolemy marched out and met him with a strong force and put him to flight. [16]Alexander fled to Arabia to seek protection. King Ptolemy's triumph was complete [17]when the Arab Zabdiel cut off Alexander's head and sent it to Ptolemy. [18]But three days later King Ptolemy himself died, and his men in the fortified cities were killed by the inhabitants of the strongholds. [19]Thus Demetrius became king in the year one hundred and sixty-seven.*

Pact with Demetrius [20]At that time Jonathan gathered together the men of Judea to attack the citadel in Jerusalem, and they set up many machines against it. [21]Some transgressors of the law, enemies of their own nation, went to the king and informed him that Jonathan was besieging the citadel. [22]When Demetrius heard this, he was furious, and set out immediately for Ptolemais. He wrote to Jonathan to discontinue the siege and to meet him for a conference at Ptolemais as soon as possible.

[23]On hearing this, Jonathan ordered the siege to continue. He selected some elders and priests of Israel and exposed himself to danger [24]by going to the king at Ptolemais. He brought with him silver, gold apparel, and many other presents, and found favor with the king. [25]Although some impious men of his own nation brought charges against him, [26]the king treated him just as his predecessors had done and showed him great honor in the presence of all his Friends. [27]He confirmed him in the high priesthood and in all the honors he had previously held, and had him enrolled among his Chief Friends.

[28]Jonathan asked the king to exempt Judea and the three districts of Samaria from tribute, promising him in return three hundred talents.[v] [29]The king agreed and wrote the following letter to Jonathan about all these matters:

[30] [w]"King Demetrius sends greetings to his brother* Jonathan and to the Jewish nation. [31]We are sending you, for your information, a copy of the letter that we wrote to Lasthenes* our kinsman concerning you. [32]'King Demetrius sends greetings to his father Lasthenes. [33]Because of the good will they show us, we have decided to bestow benefits on the Jewish nation, who are our friends and who observe their obligations to us. [34] [x]Therefore we confirm their possession, not only of the territory of Judea, but also of the three districts of Aphairema,* Lydda, and Ramathaim. These districts, together with all their dependencies, were transferred from Samaria to Judea in favor of all those who offer sacrifices for us in Jerusalem instead of paying the royal taxes that formerly the king received from them each year from the produce of the soil and the fruit of the trees. [35]From this day on we grant them release from payment of all other things that would henceforth be due to us, that is, of tithes and tribute and of the tax on the salt pans and the crown tax. [36]Henceforth none of these provisions shall ever be revoked. [37]Be sure, therefore, to have a copy of these instructions made and given to Jonathan, that it may be displayed in a conspicuous place on the holy hill.' "

11, 10: I regret . . . to kill me: according to Josephus, Ammonius, a friend of Alexander, had tried to assassinate Ptolemy, and the latter claimed that Alexander was the instigator, thus calumniating him to gain his kingdom (v 11).

11, 19: The year one hundred and sixty-seven: 146/145 B.C. The two deaths (vv 17–18) occurred in the summer of 145 B.C.

11, 30: Brother: this title and father in v 32 are honorific titles used of the Kinsmen.

11, 31: Lasthenes: leader of the mercenary troops who had come with Demetrius from Crete. He was now the young king's chief minister and was apparently responsible for the disastrous policy (v 38) of disbanding the national army.

11, 34: Aphairema: the Ophrah of Jos 18, 23; 1 Sm 23, 6; the Ephron of 2 Chr 13, 19; and the Ephraim of Jn 11, 54—modern et-Taiyibeh, five miles northeast of Bethel. Lydda: the Lod of the postexilic Jews (Ez 2, 33; Neh 11, 35) and the hometown of Aeneas, who was cured by Peter (Acts 9, 32ff). It is ten miles southeast of Joppa. Ramathaim: the Ramathaim-zophim of 1 Sm 1, 1, and the Arimathea of Mt 27, 57—modern Rentis, nine miles northeast of Lydda.

v 1 Mc 10, 29; 11, 34. w 30–37: 1 Mc 10, 26–45. x 34f: 1 Mc 10, 29; 11, 28.

The Intrigue of Trypho 38When King Demetrius saw that the land was peaceful under his rule and that he had no opposition, he dismissed his entire army, every man to his home, except the foreign troops which he had hired from the islands of the nations. So all the soldiers who had served under his predecessors hated him. 39When a certain Trypho, who had previously belonged to Alexander's party, saw that all the troops were grumbling at Demetrius, he went to Imalkue the Arab, who was bringing up Alexander's young son Antiochus.[y] 40Trypho kept urging Imalkue to hand over the boy to him, that he might make him king in his father's place. During his stay there of many days, he told him of all that Demetrius had done and of the hatred that his soldiers had for him.

Jonathan Aids Demetrius 41Meanwhile Jonathan sent the request to King Demetrius to withdraw his troops from the citadel of Jerusalem and from the other strongholds, for they were constantly hostile to Israel. 42Demetrius, in turn, sent this word to Jonathan: "I will not only do this for you and your nation, but I will greatly honor you and your nation when I find the opportunity. 43Do me the favor, therefore, of sending men to fight for me, because all my troops have revolted."

44So Jonathan sent three thousand good fighting men to him at Antioch. When they came to the king, he was delighted over their arrival, 45for the populace, one hundred and twenty thousand strong, had massed in the center of the city in an attempt to kill him. 46But he took refuge in the palace, while the populace gained control of the main streets and began to fight. 47So the king called the Jews to his aid. They all rallied around him and spread out through the city. On that day they killed about a hundred thousand men in the city, 48which, at the same time, they set on fire and plundered on a large scale. Thus they saved the king's life. 49When the populace saw that the Jews held the city at their mercy, they lost courage and cried out to the king in supplication, 50"Give us your terms and let the Jews stop attacking us and our city." So they threw down their arms and made peace. 51The Jews thus gained glory in the eyes of the king and all his subjects, and they became renowned throughout his kingdom. Finally they returned to Jerusalem with much spoil.

52But when King Demetrius was sure of his royal throne, and the land was peaceful under his rule, 53he broke all his promises and became estranged from Jonathan. Instead of rewarding Jonathan for all the favors he had received from him, he caused him much trouble.

Alliance with Trypho 54After this, Trypho returned and brought with him the young boy Antiochus, who became king and wore the royal crown.[z] 55All the soldiers whom Demetrius had discharged rallied around Antiochus and fought against Demetrius, who was routed and fled. 56Trypho captured the elephants and occupied Antioch. 57Then young Antiochus wrote to Jonathan: "I confirm you in the high priesthood and appoint you ruler over the four districts and wish you to be one of the King's Friends." 58He also sent him gold dishes and a dinner service, gave him the right to drink from gold cups, to dress in royal purple, and to wear a gold buckle.[a] 59Likewise, he made Jonathan's brother Simon governor of the region from the Ladder of Tyre* to the frontier of Egypt.

60Jonathan set out and traveled through West-of-Euphrates* and its cities, and all the forces of Syria espoused his cause as allies. When he arrived at Ashkalon, the citizens welcomed him with pomp. 61But when he set out for Gaza, the people of Gaza locked their gates against him. So he besieged it and burned and plundered its suburbs. 62Then the people of Gaza appealed to him for mercy, and he granted them peace. He took the sons of their chief men as hostages and sent them to Jerusalem. He then traveled on through the province as far as Damascus.

War with Demetrius 63Jonathan heard that the generals of Demetrius had come with a

11, 59: Laddir of Tyre: modern Ras en-Naqurah, on the border between Lebanon and Israel, where the mountains reach the sea, so that the coastal road must ascend in a series of steps.

11, 60: West-of-Euphrates: refers here to the territory of Palestine and Coelesyria, but not Upper Syria; cf 1 Mc 3, 32; 7, 8.

y 1 Mc 12, 39. z 1 Mc 11, 39; 12, 39. a 1 Mc 2, 18.

strong force to Kadesh in Galilee, intending to
remove him from office. 64So he went to meet
them, leaving his brother Simon in the province.
65Simon besieged Beth-zur, attacked it for many
days, and blockaded the inhabitants. 66When
they sued for peace, he granted it to them. He
expelled them from the city, took possession of
it, and put a garrison there.

67Meanwhile, Jonathan and his army pitched
their camp near the waters of Gennesaret, and at
daybreak they went to the plain of Hazor.*
68There, in front of him on the plain, was the
army of the foreigners. This army attacked him
in the open, having first detached an ambush
against him in the mountains. 69Then the men in
ambush rose out of their places and joined in the
battle. 70All of Jonathan's men fled; no one
stayed except the army commanders Mattathias,
son of Absalom, and Judas, son of Chalphi.
71Jonathan tore his clothes, threw earth on his
head, and prayed. 72Then he went back to the
combat and so overwhelmed the enemy that
they took to flight. 73Those of his men who were
running away saw it and returned to him; and
with him they pursued the enemy as far as their
camp in Kadesh, where they pitched their own
camp. 74Three thousand of the foreign troops fell
on that day. Then Jonathan returned to Jerusalem.

CHAPTER 12

Alliances with Rome and Sparta 1When Jona-
than saw that the times favored him, he sent
selected men to Rome to confirm and renew his
friendship with the Romans.[b] 2He also sent
letters to Sparta and other places for the same
purpose.

3After reaching Rome, the men entered the
senate chamber and said, "The high priest Jonathan and the Jewish people have sent us to
renew the earlier friendship and alliance between you and them." 4The Romans gave them
letters addressed to the authorities in the various
places, requesting them to provide the envoys
with safe conduct to the land of Judah.

5This is a copy of the letter that Jonathan
wrote to the Spartans: 6"Jonathan the high
priest, the senate of the nation, the priests, and
the rest of the Jewish people send greetings to
their brothers the Spartans. 7Long ago a letter
was sent to the high priest Onias* from Arius,
who then reigned over you, stating that you are
our brothers, as the attached copy shows.[c]
8Onias welcomed the envoy with honor and
received the letter, which clearly referred to
alliance and friendship. 9 [d]Though we have no
need of these things, since we have for our
encouragement the sacred books that are in our
possession,* 10we have ventured to send word
to you for the renewal of brotherhood and
friendship, so as not to become strangers to you
altogether; a long time has passed since your
mission to us. 11We, on our part, have never
ceased to remember you in the sacrifices and
prayers that we offer on our feasts and other
appropriate days, as it is right and proper to
remember brothers. 12We likewise rejoice in
your renown. 13But many hardships and wars
have beset us, and the kings around us have
attacked us. 14We did not wish to be troublesome to you and to the rest of our allies and
friends in these wars; 15with the help of Heaven
for our support, we have been saved from our
enemies, and they have been humbled. 16So we
have chosen Numenius, son of Antiochus, and
Antipater, son of Jason, and we have sent them
to the Romans to renew our former friendship
and alliance with them.[e] 17We have also ordered
them to come to you and greet you, and to
deliver to you our letter about the renewal of our
brotherhood. 18Therefore kindly send us an
answer on this matter."

19This is a copy of the letter that was sent to
Onias: 20[f]"Arius, king of the Spartans, sends
greetings to Onias the high priest. 21A document

11, 67: Plain of Hazor: the site of the ancient Canaanite city (Jos 11, 10), ten miles north of the Lake of Gennesaret.

12, 7: Onias: Onias I, high priest from 323–300 or 290 B.C. Arius: Arius I, king from 309 to 265 B.C. The letter was sent long ago, i.e., a century and a half before.

12, 9: The sacred books . . . in our possession: a reference to "the law, the prophets and other books," as mentioned in the Prologue to Sirach (v 1), after 132 B.C.

b 1 Mc 8, 17. c 1 Mc 12, 20–23. d Rom 15, 4. e 1 Mc 14, 22; 15, 15. f 20–23: 1 Mc 12, 6f.

has been found stating that the Spartans and the Jews are brothers; both nations descended from Abraham. 22Now that we have learned this, kindly write to us about your welfare. 23We, on our part, are informing you that your cattle and your possessions are ours, and ours are yours. We have, therefore, given orders that you should be told of this."

Demetrius Repelled 24Jonathan heard that the generals of Demetrius had returned to attack him with a stronger army than before. 25He set out from Jerusalem and went into the country of Hamath* to meet them, giving them no time to enter his province. 26The spies he had sent into their camp came back and reported that the enemy had made ready to attack the Jews that very night. 27Therefore, when the sun set, Jonathan ordered his men to be on guard and to remain armed, ready for combat, throughout the night. He also set outposts all around the camp. 28When the enemy heard that Jonathan and his men were ready for battle, their hearts sank with fear and dread. They lighted fires and then withdrew. 29But because Jonathan and his men were watching the lights burning, they did not know what had happened until morning. 30Then Jonathan pursued them, but he could not overtake them, for they had crossed the river Eleutherus. 31So Jonathan turned aside against the Arabs who are called Zabadeans, overwhelming and plundering them. 32Then he marched on to Damascus and traversed that whole region.

33Simon also set out and went as far as Ashkalon and its neighboring strongholds. He then turned to Joppa and occupied it, 34for he heard that its men had intended to hand over this stronghold to the supporters of Demetrius. He left a garrison there to guard it.

35When Jonathan returned, he assembled the elders of the people, and with them he made plans for building strongholds in Judea, 36for making the walls of Jerusalem still higher, and for erecting a high barrier between the citadel and the city, that would isolate the citadel and so prevent its garrison from commerce with the city. 37The people therefore worked together on building up the city, for part of the east wall above the ravine had collapsed. The quarter called Chaphenatha was also repaired. 38Simon likewise built up Adida in the Shephelah, and strengthened its fortifications by providing them with gates and bars.

Capture of Jonathan 39Trypho was determined to become king of Asia, assume the crown, and do away with King Antiochus.[g] 40But he was afraid that Jonathan would not permit him, but would fight against him. Looking for a way to seize and kill him, he set out and reached Beth-shan. 41Jonathan marched out against him with forty thousand picked fighting men and came to Beth-shan. 42But when Trypho saw that Jonathan had arrived with a large army, he was afraid to offer him violence. 43Instead, he received him with honor, introduced him to all his friends, and gave him presents. He also ordered his friends and soldiers to obey him as they would himself. 44Then he said to Jonathan: "Why have you put all your soldiers to so much trouble when we are not at war? 45Pick out a few men to stay with you, send the rest back home, and then come with me to Ptolemais. I will hand it over to you together with other strongholds and their garrisons, as well as the officials, then I will leave and go home. That is why I came here."

46Jonathan believed him and did as he said. He dismissed his troops, and they returned to the land of Judah. 47But he kept with him three thousand men, of whom he sent two thousand to Galilee while one thousand accompanied him. 48Then as soon as Jonathan had entered Ptolemais, the men of the city closed the gates and seized him; all who had entered with him, they killed with the sword.

49Trypho sent soldiers and cavalry to Galilee and the Great Plain* to destroy all Jonathan's men. 50These, upon learning that Jonathan had been captured and his companions killed, en-

12, 25: Country of Hamath: the Seleucid territory of Upper Syria northeast of Coelesyria and separated from it by the Eleutherus River. The latter territory was under the command of Jonathan (1 Mc 11, 59f).

12, 49: The Great Plain: of Beth-shan (v 41), where Jonathan's disbanded troops remained.

g 1 Mc 11, 39f. 54f.

couraged one another and went out in compact body ready to fight. [51]As their pursuers saw that they were ready to fight for their lives, they turned back. [52]Thus all these men of Jonathan came safely into the land of Judah. They mourned over Jonathan and his men, and were in great fear, and all Israel fell into deep mourning.

[53]All the nations round about sought to destroy them. They said, "Now that they have no leader to help them, let us make war on them and wipe out their memory from among men." [h]

V: Simon, High Priest and Ethnarch

CHAPTER 13

Simon, Leader of the Jews [1]When Simon heard that Trypho was gathering a large army to invade and ravage the land of Judah, [2]and saw that the people were in dread and terror, he went up to Jerusalem. There he assembled the people [3]and exhorted them in these words: "You know what I, my brothers, and my father's house have done for the laws and the sanctuary; what battles and disasters we have been through. [4]It was for the sake of these, for the sake of Israel, that all my brothers have perished, and I alone am left. [5]Far be it from me, then, to save my own life in any time of distress, for I am not better than my brothers. [6]Rather will I avenge my nation and the sanctuary, as well as your wives and children, for all the nations out of hatred have united to destroy us." [i]

[7]As the people heard these words, their spirit was rekindled. [8]They shouted in reply: "You are our leader in place of your brothers Judas and Jonathan. [9]Fight our battles, and we will do everything that you tell us." [10]So Simon mustered all the men able to fight, and quickly completing the walls of Jerusalem, fortified it on every side. [11]He sent Jonathan, son of Absalom, to Joppa with a large force; Jonathan drove out the occupants and remained there.

Deceit and Treachery of Trypho [12]Then Trypho moved from Ptolemais with a large army to invade the land of Judah, bringing Jonathan with him as prisoner. [13]But Simon pitched his camp at Adida, facing the plain. [14]When Trypho learned that Simon had succeeded his brother Jonathan, and that he intended to fight him, he sent envoys to him with this message: [15]"We have detained your brother Jonathan on account of the money that he owed the royal treasury in connection with the offices that he held. [16]Therefore, if you send us a hundred talents of silver, and two of his sons as hostages to guarantee that when he is set free he will not revolt against us, we will release him."

[17]Although Simon knew that they were speaking deceitfully to him, he gave orders to get the money and the boys, for fear of provoking much hostility among the people, who might say [18]that Jonathan perished because Simon would not send Trypho the money and the boys. [19]So he sent the boys and the hundred talents; but Trypho broke his promise and would not let Jonathan go. [20]*Next he began to invade and ravage the country. His troops went around by the road that leads to Adora, but Simon and his army moved along opposite him everywhere he went. [21]The men in the citadel sent messengers to Trypho, urging him to come to them by way of the desert, and to send them provisions. [22]Although Trypho got all his cavalry ready to go, there was a heavy fall of snow that night, and he could not go. So he left for Gilead. [23]When he was approaching Baskama,* he had Jonathan killed and buried there. [24]Then Trypho returned to his own country.

Jonathan's Tomb [25]Simon sent for the remains of his brother Jonathan, and buried him in Modein, the city of his fathers. [26]All Israel bewailed him with solemn lamentation, mourning over him for many days. [27]Then Simon erected over the tomb of his father and his brothers a monument of stones, polished front and back, and raised high enough to be seen at a distance.

13, 20f: The invaders made a wide flanking movement to invade Judea from the south. Adora was a few miles southwest of Beth-zur. They would avoid Beth-zur itself and other strongholds of the Maccabees by following the way of the desert.

13, 23: Baskama: northeast of the Sea of Galilee.

h 1 Mc 5, 2; 13, 6. i 1 Mc 5, 2; 12, 53.

28 He set up seven pyramids facing one another for his father and his mother and his four brothers. 29 For the pyramids he devised a setting of big columns, on which he carved suits of armor as a perpetual memorial, and next to the armor he placed carved ships, which could be seen by all who sailed the sea. 30 This tomb which he built at Modein is there to the present day.

Pact between Simon and Demetrius 31 Trypho dealt treacherously with the young King Antiochus. He killed him 32 and assumed the kingship in his place, putting on the crown of Asia. Thus he brought much evil on the land. 33 Simon, on his part, built up the strongholds of Judea, strengthening their fortifications with high towers, thick walls, and gates with bars, and he stored up provisions in the fortresses. 34 Simon also sent chosen men to King Demetrius with the request that he grant the land a release from taxation, for all that Trypho did was to plunder the land. 35 In reply, King Demetrius sent him the following letter:

36 "King Demetrius sends greetings to Simon the high priest, the friend of kings, and to the elders and the Jewish people. 37 We have received the gold crown and the palm branch that you sent. We are willing to be on most peaceful terms with you and to write to our official to grant you release from tribute. 38 Whatever we have guaranteed to you remains in force, and the strongholds that you have built shall remain yours. 39 We remit any oversights and defaults incurred up to now, as well as the crown tax that you owe. Any other tax that may have been collected in Jerusalem shall no longer be collected there. 40 If any of you are qualified for enrollment in our service, let them be enrolled. Let there be peace between us."

41 Thus in the year one hundred and seventy,* the yoke of the Gentiles was removed from Israel, 42 and the people began to write in their records and contracts, "In the first year of Simon, high priest, governor, and leader of the Jews."

Capture of Gazara and the Citadel 43 In those days Simon besieged Gazara* and surrounded it with troops. He made a siege machine, pushed it up against the city, and attacked and captured one of the towers.[j] 44 The men who had been on the siege machine jumped down into the city and caused a great tumult there. 45 The men of the city, joined by their wives and children, went up on the wall, with their garments rent, and cried out in loud voices, begging Simon to grant them peace. 46 "Do not treat us according to our evil deeds," they said, "but according to your mercy."

47 So Simon came to terms with them and did not destroy them. He made them leave the city, however, and he purified the houses in which there were idols. Then he entered the city with hymns and songs of praise. 48 After removing from it everything that was impure, he settled there men who observed the law. He improved its fortifications and built himself a residence.

49 The men in the citadel in Jerusalem were prevented from going out into the country and back for the purchase of food; they suffered greatly from hunger, and many of them died of starvation. 50 They finally cried out to Simon for peace, and he gave them peace. He expelled them from the citadel and cleansed it of impurities. 51 On the twenty-third day of the second month,* in the year one hundred and seventy-one, the Jews entered the citadel with shouts of jubilation, waving of palm branches, the music of harps and cymbals and lyres, and the singing of hymns and canticles, because a great enemy of Israel had been destroyed.[k] 52 Simon decreed that this day should be celebrated every year with rejoicing. He also strengthened the fortifications of the temple hill alongside the citadel, and he and his companions dwelt there. 53 Seeing that his son John* was now a grown man, Simon

13, 41: The year one hundred and seventy: March, 142, to April, 141 B.C., by the temple calendar.

13, 43: Gazara: a key position in the Shephelah, fortified by Bacchides in 160 B.C.; cf 1 Mc 9, 52.

13, 51: The twenty-third day of the second month: June 3, 141 B.C.

13, 53: John: John Hyrcanus, who was to succeed his father as ruler and high priest; cf 1 Mc 16, 23f.

j 2 Mc 10, 32–38. k 1 Mc 1, 36.

made him commander of all his soldiers, with
his residence in Gazara.

CHAPTER 14

Capture of Demetrius 1In the year one hun-
dred and seventy-two,* King Demetrius assem-
bled his army and marched into Media to obtain
help so that he could fight Trypho. 2When
Arsaces,* king of Persia and Media, heard that
Demetrius had invaded his territory, he sent one
of his generals to take him alive. 3The general
went forth and defeated the army of Demetrius;
he captured him and brought him to Arsaces,
who put him in prison.

Glory of Simon

4 The land was at rest all the days of Simon,
who sought the good of his nation.
His people were delighted with his power
and his magnificence throughout his reign.[l]
5 As his crowning glory he captured the port of
Joppa
and made it a gateway to the isles of the sea.
6 He enlarged the borders of his nation
and gained control of the country.[m]
7 He took many enemies prisoners of war
and made himself master of Gazara, Beth-
zur, and the citadel.

He cleansed the citadel of its impurities;
there was no one to withstand him.
8 The people cultivated their land in peace;
the land yielded its produce
and the trees of the field their fruit.[n]
9 Old men sat in the squares,
all talking about the good times,
while the young men wore the glorious
apparel of war.[o]
10 He supplied the cities with food
and equipped them with means of defense,
till his glorious name reached the ends of
the earth.
11 He brought peace to the land,
and Israel was filled with happiness.[p]
12 Every man sat under his vine and his fig tree,
with no one to disturb him.[q]
13 No one was left to attack them in their land;
the kings in those days were crushed.
14 He strengthened all the lowly among his
people
and was zealous for the law;
he suppressed all the lawless and the
wicked.
15 He made the temple splendid
and enriched its equipment.

Alliance with Rome and Sparta 16When peo-
ple heard in Rome and even in Sparta that
Jonathan had died, they were deeply grieved.*
17But when the Romans heard that his brother
Simon had been made high priest in his place
and was master of the country and the cities,
18they sent him inscribed tablets of bronze to
renew with him the friendship and alliance that
they had established with his brothers Judas and
Jonathan.[r] 19These were read before the assem-
bly in Jerusalem.

20This is a copy of the letter that the Spartans
sent: "The rulers and the citizens of Sparta send
greetings to Simon the high priest, the elders,
the priests, and the rest of the Jewish people, our
brothers. 21The envoys you sent to our people
have informed us of your glory and fame, and we
were happy that they came. 22In accordance
with what they said we have recorded the
following in the public decrees: Since Nume-
nius, son of Antiochus, and Antipater, son of
Jason, envoys of the Jews, have come to us to
renew their friendship with us,[s] 23the people
have voted to receive the men with honor, and
to deposit a copy of their words in the public
archives, so that the people of Sparta may have a
record of them. A copy of this decree has been
made for Simon the high priest."

24After this, Simon sent Numenius to Rome

14, 1: The year one hundred and seventy-two: 141–140 B.C. The expedition began most probably in the spring of 140.

14, 2: Arsaces: Arsaces VI, also called Mithridates I, the Parthian king (171–138 B.C.). Parthians had overrun Persia and now held Babylonia, both of which had hitherto belonged to the Seleucid empire. The Greeks and Macedonians in these countries had appealed to Demetrius for help.

14, 16: The embassy to Rome and Sparta was sent soon after Simon's accession to power, and the replies were received before Demetrius' expedition (vv 1–3)—probably in 142 B.C.

l 1 Mc 3, 3–9. m Ex 34, 24. n Zec 8, 12. o Zec 8, 4f. p Lv 26, 6. q Mi 4, 4; Zec 3, 10. r Mc 8, 22. s 1 Mc 12, 16; 15, 15.

with a great gold shield weighing a thousand minas, to confirm the alliance with the Romans.[t]

Decree of Honor 25 When the people heard of these things, they said, "How can we thank Simon and his sons? 26 He and his brothers and his father's house have stood firm and repulsed Israel's enemies. They have thus preserved its liberty." So they made an inscription on bronze tablets, which they affixed to pillars on Mount Zion. 27 The following is a copy of the inscription:

"On the eighteenth day of Elul,* in the year one hundred and seventy-two, that is, the third year under Simon the high priest in Asaramel, 28 in a great assembly of priests, people, rulers of the nation, and elders of the country, the following proclamation was made:

29 " 'Since there have often been wars in our country, Simon, son of the priest Mattathias, descendant of Joarib, and his brothers have put themselves in danger and resisted the enemies of their nation, so that their sanctuary and law might be maintained, and they have thus brought great glory to their nation. 30 After Jonathan had rallied his nation and become their high priest, he was gathered to his kinsmen. 31 When the enemies of the Jews sought to invade and devastate their country and to lay hands on their temple, 32 Simon rose up and fought for his nation, spending large sums of his own money to equip the men of his nation's armed forces and giving them their pay. 33 He fortified the cities of Judea, especially the frontier city of Beth-zur, where he stationed a garrison of Jewish soldiers, and where previously the enemy's arms had been stored. 34 He also fortified Joppa by the sea and Gazara on the border of Azotus, a place previously occupied by the enemy; these cities he resettled with Jews, and furnished them with all that was necessary for their restoration. 35 When the Jewish people saw Simon's loyalty and the glory he planned to bring to his nation, they made him their leader and high priest because of all he had accomplished and the loyalty and justice he had shown his nation. In every way he sought to exalt his people.

36 " 'In his time and under his guidance they succeeded in driving the Gentiles out of their country, especially those in the City of David in Jerusalem, who had built for themselves a citadel from which they used to sally forth to defile the environs of the temple and inflict grave injury on its purity. 37 In this citadel he stationed Jewish soldiers, and he strengthened its fortifications for the defense of the land and the city, while he also raised the wall of Jerusalem to a greater height. 38 Consequently, King Demetrius confirmed him in the high priesthood, 39 [u]made him one of his Friends, and conferred the highest honors on him. 40 He had indeed heard that the Romans had addressed the Jews as friends, allies, and brothers and that they had received Simon's envoys with honor.

41 " 'The Jewish people and their priest have, therefore, made the following decisions. Simon shall be their permanent leader and high priest until a true prophet arises. 42 He shall act as governor general over them, and shall have charge of the temple, to make regulations concerning its functions and concerning the country, its weapons and strongholds; 43 he shall be obeyed by all. All contracts made in the country shall be dated by his name. He shall have the right to wear royal purple and gold ornaments. 44 It shall not be lawful for any of the people or priests to nullify any of these decisions, or to contradict the orders given by him, or to convene an assembly in the country without his consent, to be clothed in royal purple or wear an official gold brooch. 45 Whoever acts otherwise or violates any of these prescriptions shall be liable to punishment.

46 " 'All the people approved of granting Simon the right to act in accord with these decisions, 47 and Simon accepted and agreed to act as high priest, governor general, and ethnarch* of the Jewish people and priests and to exercise supreme authority over all.' "

48 It was decreed that this inscription should be engraved on bronze tablets, to be set up in a

14, 27: Eighteenth day of Elul: September 13, 140 B.C. Asaramel: a Hebrew name meaning "court of the people of God."

14, 47: Ethnarch: a subaltern ruler over a racial group whose office needed confirmation by a higher authority within the empire.

t 1 Mc 12, 16; 15, 15. u 39f: 1 Mc 2, 18.

conspicuous place in the precincts of the temple, [49]and that copies of it should be deposited in the treasury, where they would be available to Simon and his sons.

CHAPTER 15

Letter of Antiochus [1]Antiochus,* son of King Demetrius, sent a letter from the islands of the sea to Simon, the priest and ethnarch of the Jews, and to all the nation, [2]which read as follows:

"King Antiochus sends greetings to Simon, the priest and ethnarch, and to the Jewish nation. [3]Whereas certain villains have gained control of the kingdom of my ancestors, I intend to reclaim it, that I may restore it to its former state. I have recruited a large number of mercenary troops and equipped warships [4]to make a landing in my country and take revenge on those who have ruined it and laid waste many cities in my realm.

[5]"Now, therefore, I confirm to you all the tax exemptions that the kings before me granted you and whatever other privileges they conferred on you. [6]I authorize you to coin your own money, as legal tender in your country. [7]Jerusalem and its temple shall be free. All the weapons you have prepared and all the strongholds you have built and now occupy shall remain in your possession. [8]All debts, present or future, due to the royal treasury shall be canceled for you, now and for all time. [9]When we recover our kingdom, we will greatly honor you and your nation and the temple, so that your glory will be manifest in all the earth."

[10]In the year one hundred and seventy-four,* Antiochus invaded the land of his ancestors, and all the troops rallied to him, so that few were left with Trypho. [11]Pursued by Antiochus, Trypho fled to Dor, by the sea,* [12]realizing what a mass of troubles had come upon him now that his soldiers had deserted him. [13]Antiochus encamped before Dor with a hundred and twenty thousand infantry and eight thousand horsemen. [14]While he invested the city, his ships closed in along the coast, so that he blockaded it by land and sea and let no one go in or out.

Roman Alliance Renewed [15]Meanwhile, Numenius and his companions left Rome with letters such as this addressed to various kings and countries: [v]

[16]"Lucius,* Consul of the Romans, sends greetings to King Ptolemy. [17]Certain envoys of the Jews, our friends and allies, have come to us to renew their earlier alliance of friendship. They had been sent by Simon the high priest and the Jewish people, [18]and they brought with them a gold shield worth a thousand minas. [w] [19]Therefore we have decided to write to various kings and countries, that they are not to harm them, or wage war against them or their cities or their country, and are not to assist those who fight against them. [20]We have also decided to accept the shield from them. [21]If, then, any troublemakers from their country take refuge with you, hand them over to Simon the high priest, so that he may punish them according to their law."

[22]The consul sent similar letters to Kings Demetrius, Attalus,* Ariarthes and Arsaces; [23]to all the countries—Sampsames, Sparta, Delos, Myndos, Sicyon, Caria, Samos, Pamphylia, Lycia, Halicarnassus, Rhodes, Phaselis, Cos, Side, Aradus, Gortyna, Cnidus, Cyprus, and Cyrene. [24]A copy of the letter was also sent to Simon the high priest.

Hostility of Antiochus [25]When King Antiochus was encamped before Dor, he assaulted it continuously both with troops and with the siege machines he had made. He blockaded Trypho by preventing anyone from going in or out. [26]Simon sent to Antiochus' support two thousand elite troops, together with gold and silver and much equipment. [27]But he refused to

15, 1: Antiochus: Antiochus VII Sidetes, son of Demetrius I, and younger brother of Demetrius II, now a prisoner of the Parthians. At the age of twenty he set out from the island of Rhodes to take his brother's place and drive out the usurper Trypho.

15, 10: The year one hundred and seventy-four: 138 B.C.

15, 11: Dor, by the sea: a fortress on the Palestinian coast, fifteen miles south of Carmel.

15, 16: Lucius: perhaps Lucius Caecilius Metellus, consul in 142 B.C., or Lucius Calpurnicus Piso, consul in 140–139 B.C. This document pertains to Simon's first year as leader.

15, 22: Attalus: Attalus II of Pergamum, reigned 159–138 B.C. Ariarthes: Ariarthes V of Cappadocia, reigned 162–130 B.C. Arsaces: see note on 1 Mc 14, 2.

v 1 Mc 8, 17; 12, 16; 14, 22, 24. w 1 Mc 14, 24.

accept the aid; in fact, he broke all the agreements he had previously made with Simon and became hostile toward him.

28He sent Athenobius, one of his Friends, to confer with Simon and say: "You are occupying Joppa and Gazara and the citadel of Jerusalem; these are cities of my kingdom. 29You have laid waste their territories, done great harm to the land, and taken possession of many districts in my realm. 30Therefore, give up the cities you have seized and the tribute money of the districts outside the territory of Judea of which you have taken possession; 31or instead, pay me five hundred talents of silver for the devastation you have caused and five hundred talents more for the tribute money of the cities. If you do not do this, we will come and make war on you."

32So Athenobius, the king's Friend, came to Jerusalem, and on seeing the splendor of Simon's court, the gold and silver plate on the sideboard, and the rest of his rich display, he was amazed. When he gave him the king's message, 33Simon said to him in reply:

"We have not seized any foreign land; what we took is not the property of others, but our ancestral heritage which for a time had been unjustly held by our enemies. 34Now that we have the opportunity, we are holding on to the heritage of our ancestors. 35As for Joppa and Gazara, which you demand, the men of these cities were doing great harm to our people and laying waste our country; however, we are willing to pay you a hundred talents for these cities."

36Athenobius made no reply, but returned to the king in anger. When he told him of Simon's words, of his splendor, and of all he had seen, the king fell into a violent rage.

Victory over Cendebeus 37Trypho had gotten aboard a ship and escaped to Orthosia.* 38Then the king appointed Cendebeus commander in chief of the seacoast, and gave him infantry and cavalry forces. 39He ordered him to move his troops against Judea and to fortify Kedron* and strengthen its gates, so that he could launch attacks against the Jewish people. Meanwhile the king went in pursuit of Trypho. 40When Cendebeus came to Jamnia, he began to harass the people and to make incursions into Judea, where he took people captive or massacred them. 41As the king ordered, he fortified Kedron and stationed horsemen and infantry there, so that they could go out and patrol the roads of Judea.

CHAPTER 16

1John then went up from Gazara and told his father Simon what Cendebeus was doing. 2Simon called his two oldest sons, Judas and John, and said to them: "I and my brothers and my father's house have fought the battles of Israel from our youth until today, and many times we succeeded in saving Israel. 3I have now grown old, but you, by the mercy of Heaven, have come to man's estate. Take my place and my brother's, and go out and fight for our nation; and may the help of Heaven be with you!"

4John then mustered in the land twenty thousand warriors and horsemen. Setting out against Cendebeus, they spent the night at Modein, 5rose early, and marched into the plain. There, facing them, was an immense army of foot soldiers and horsemen, and between the two armies was a stream. 6John and his men took their position against the enemy. Seeing that his men were afraid to cross the stream, John crossed first. When his men saw this, they crossed over after him. 7Then he divided his infantry into two corps and put his cavalry between them, for the enemy's horsemen were very numerous. 8They blew the trumpets, and Cendebeus and his army were put to flight; many of them fell wounded, and the rest fled toward the stronghold. 9It was then that John's brother Judas fell wounded; but John pursued them until Cendebeus reached Kidron, which he had fortified. 10Some took refuge in the towers on the plain of Azotus, but John set fire to these, and about two thousand of the enemy perished. He then returned to Judea in peace.

15, 37: Orthosia: a port between Tripoli and the Eleutherus River.

15, 39: Kedron: a few miles southeast of Jamnia and facing the fortress of Gazara held by John Hyrcanus.

Murder of Simon and His Sons [11]Ptolemy, son of Abubus, had been appointed governor of the plain of Jericho, and he had much silver and gold, [12]being the son-in-law of the high priest. [13]But he became ambitious and sought to get control of the country. So he made treacherous plans to do away with Simon and his sons. [14]As Simon was inspecting the cities of the country and providing for their needs, he and his sons Mattathias and Judas went down to Jericho in the year one hundred and seventy-seven, in the eleventh month* (that is, the month Shebat). [15]The son of Abubus gave them a deceitful welcome in the little stronghold called Dok* which he had built. While serving them a sumptuous banquet, he had his men hidden there. [16]Then, when Simon and his sons had drunk freely, Ptolemy and his men sprang up, weapons in hand, rushed upon Simon in the banquet hall, and killed him, his two sons, and some of his servants. [17]By this vicious act of treason he repaid good with evil.

[18]Then Ptolemy wrote an account of this and sent it to the king, asking that troops be sent to help him and that the country be turned over to him. [19]He sent other men to Gazara to do away with John. To the army officers he sent letters inviting them to come to him so that he might present them with silver, gold, and gifts. [20]He also sent others to seize Jerusalem and the mount of the temple. [21]But someone ran ahead and brought word to John at Gazara that his father and his brothers had perished, and that Ptolemy had sent men to kill him also. [22]On hearing this, John was utterly astounded. When the men came to kill him, he had them arrested and put to death, for he knew what they meant to do. [23]*Now the rest of the history of John, his wars and the brave deeds he performed, his rebuilding of the walls, and his other achievements— [24]these things are recorded in the chronicle of his pontificate, from the time that he succeeded his father as high priest.

16, 14: In the year one hundred and seventy-seven, in the eleventh month: January-February, 134 B.C., by the temple calendar.

16, 15: Dok: a fortress built on a cliff three miles northwest of Jericho, near modern Ain Duq.

16, 23f: John Hyrcanus was ruler and high priest from 134 B.C. till his death in 104 B.C. These verses suggest that the book was written, or at least completed, only after he died.

THE SECOND BOOK OF MACCABEES

Although this book, like the preceding one, receives its title from its protagonist, Judas Maccabee (or Maccabeus), it is not a sequel to 1 Maccabees. The two differ in many respects. Whereas the first covers the period from the beginning of the reign of Antiochus IV (175 B.C.) to the accession of John Hyrcanus I (134 B.C.), this present book treats of the events in Jewish history from the time of the high priest Onias III and King Seleucus IV (c. 180 B.C.) to the defeat of Nicanor's army (161 B.C.).

The author of 2 Maccabees states (2, 23) that his one-volume work is an abridgment of a certain five-volume work by Jason of Cyrene; but since this latter has not survived, it is difficult to determine its relationship to the present epitome. One does not know how freely the anonymous epitomizer may have rewritten his shorter composition, or how closely he may have followed the wording of the original in the excerpts he made. Some parts of the text here, clearly not derived from Jason's work, are the Preface (2, 19-32), the Epilogue (15, 37-39), and probably also certain moralizing reflections (e.g., 5, 17-20; 6, 12-17). It is certain, however, that both works were written in Greek, which explains why the Second Book of Maccabees was not included in the canon of the Hebrew Bible.

The book is not without genuine historical value in supplementing 1 Maccabees, and it contains some apparently authentic documents (11, 16-38). Its purpose, whether intended by Jason himself or read into it by the compiler, is to give a theological interpretation to the history of the period. There is less interest, therefore, in the actual exploits of Judas Maccabeus than in God's marvelous interventions. These direct the course of events, both to punish the sacrilegious and blasphemous pagans, and to purify God's holy temple and restore it to his faithful people. The author sometimes effects his purpose by transferring events from their proper chronological order, and giving exaggerated figures for the size of armies and the numbers killed in battle; he also places long, edifying discourses and prayers in the mouths of his heroes, and inclines to elaborate descriptions of celestial apparitions (3, 24-34; 5, 2ff; 10, 29f; 15, 11-16). He is the earliest known composer of stories that glorify God's holy martyrs (6, 18—7, 42; 14, 37-46).

Of theological importance are the author's teachings on the resurrection of the just on the last day (7, 9. 11. 14. 23; 14, 46), the intercession of the saints in heaven for people living on earth (15, 11-16), and the power of the living to offer prayers and sacrifices for the dead (12, 39-46).

The beginning of 2 Maccabees consists of two letters sent by the Jews of Jerusalem to their coreligionists in Egypt. They deal with the observance of the feast commemorating the central event of the book, the purification of the temple. It is uncertain whether the author or a later scribe prefixed these letters to the narrative proper. If the author is responsible for their insertion, he must have written his book some time after 124 B.C., the date of the more recent of the two letters. In any case, Jason's five-volume work very likely continued the history of the Jews well into the Hasmonean period, so that 2 Maccabees would probably not have been produced much before the end of the second century B.C.

The main divisions of 2 Maccabees are:

I. Letters to the Jews in Egypt (1, 1—2, 18).
II. Author's Preface (2, 19-32).
III. Heliodorus' Attempt To Profane the Temple (3, 1-40).
IV. Profanation and Persecution (4, 1—7, 42).
V. Victories of Judas and Purification of the Temple (8, 1—10, 8).
VI. Renewed Persecution (10, 9—15, 36).
VII. Epilogue (15, 37-39).

I: Letters to the Jews In Egypt

CHAPTER 1

First Letter 124 B.C. 1The Jews in Jerusalem
and in the land of Judea send greetings to their
brethren, the Jews in Egypt, and wish them true
peace! 2May God bless you and remember his
covenant with his faithful servants, Abraham,
Isaac and Jacob. 3May he give to all of you a
heart to worship him and to do his will readily
and generously. 4May he open your heart to his
law and his commandments and grant you
peace. 5May he hear your prayers, and be
reconciled to you, and never forsake you in time
of adversity. 6Even now we are praying for you
here.

[7]In the reign of Demetrius,* the year one
hundred and sixty-nine, we Jews wrote to you
during the trouble and violence that overtook us
in those years after Jason and his followers had
revolted against the holy land and the kingdom, [a]
[8]setting fire to the gatehouse and shedding
innocent blood. But we prayed to the LORD, and
our prayer was heard;* we offered sacrifices and
fine flour; we lighted the lamps and set out the
loaves of bread. [b] [9]We are now reminding you to
celebrate the feast of Booths in the month of
Chislev.* [10]Dated in the year one hundred and
eighty-eight.*

Festival Letter 164 B.C. The people of Jerusa-
lem and Judea, the senate, and Judas send
greetings and good wishes to Aristobulus, coun-
selor of King Ptolemy and member of the family
of the anointed priests, and to the Jews in Egypt.
[11]Since we have been saved by God from grave
dangers, we give him great thanks for having
fought on our side against the king;* [12] [c]it was
he who drove out those who fought against the
holy city. [13]When their leader arrived in Persia
with his seemingly irresistible army, they were
cut to pieces in the temple of the goddess
Nanea* through a deceitful stratagem employed
by Nanea's priests. [14]*On the pretext of marry-
ing the goddess, Antiochus with his Friends had
come to the place to get its great treasures by
way of dowry. [15]When the priests of the
Nanaeon had displayed the treasures, Antiochus
with a few attendants came to the temple
precincts. As soon as he entered the temple, the
priests locked the doors. [16]Then they opened a
hidden trapdoor in the ceiling, hurled stones at
the leader and his companions and struck them
down. They dismembered the bodies, cut off
their heads and tossed them to the people
outside. [17]Forever blessed be our God, who has
thus punished the wicked!

[18]*We shall be celebrating the purification of
the temple on the twenty-fifth day of the month
Chislev, so we thought it right to inform you that
you too may celebrate the feast of Booths and of
the fire that appeared when Nehemiah, the
rebuilder of the temple* and the altar, offered
sacrifices. [19]When our fathers were being exiled
to Persia,* devout priests of the time took some
of the fire from the altar and hid it secretly in the
hollow of a dry cistern, making sure that the
place would be unknown to anyone. [20]Many
years later, when it so pleased God, Nehemiah,
commissioned by the king of Persia, sent the
descendants of the priests who had hidden the
fire to look for it. [21]When they informed us that
they could not find any fire, but only muddy
water, he ordered them to scoop some out and
bring it. After the material for the sacrifices had
been prepared, Nehemiah ordered the priests to
sprinkle with the water the wood and what lay
on it. [22]When this was done and in time the sun,
which had been clouded over, began to shine, a
great fire blazed up, so that everyone marveled.
[23]While the sacrifice was being burned, the

1, 7: Demetrius: Demetrius II, king of Syria (145–139, 129–125 B.C.). The year one hundred and sixty-nine of the Seleucid era, 143 B.C. Regarding the dates in 1 and 2 Mc, see note on 1 Mc 1, 10. On the troubles caused by Jason and his revolt against the kingdom, i.e., the rule of the legitimate high priest, see 2 Mc 4, 7–22.

1, 8: Our prayer was heard: in the ultimate victory of the Maccabees.

1, 9: Feast of Booths in the month of Chislev: really the feast of the Dedication of the temple (2 Mc 10, 1–8), celebrated on the twenty-fifth of Chislev (Nov.-Dec.). Its solemnity resembles that of the true feast of Booths (Lv 23, 33–43), celebrated on the fifteenth of Tishri (Sept.-Oct.); cf 2 Mc 1, 18.

1, 10: 124 B.C. The date pertains to the preceding, not the following letter. King Ptolemy: Ptolemy VI Philometor, ruler of Egypt from 180 to 145 B.C.; he is mentioned also in 1 Mc 1, 18; 10, 51–59.

1, 11f: The king: Antiochus IV of Syria, the bitter persecutor of the Jews, who, as leader of the Syrian army that invaded Persia, perished there in 164 B.C.

1, 13: Nanea: an oriental goddess comparable to Artemis of the Greeks.

1, 14–17: A different account of the death of Antiochus IV is given in 2 Mc 9, 1–29, and another variant account in 1 Mc 6, 1–16. The writer of this letter had probably heard a distorted rumor of the king's death. This fact and other indications show that the letter was written very soon after Antiochus IV died, hence in 164 B.C.

1, 18–36: This purely legendary account of Nehemiah's miraculous fire is incorporated in the letter because of its connection with the temple and its rededication.

1, 18: Nehemiah, the rebuilder of the temple: he rebuilt the walls of Jerusalem, but the temple had been rebuilt by Zerubbabel almost a century before.

1, 19: Persia: actually Babylonia, which later became part of the Persian Empire.

a 2 Mc 4, 7–20. b 1 Mc 4, 38. c 12–17: 2 Mc 9, 1–29; 1 Mc 6, 1–13.

priests recited a prayer, and all present joined in with them, Jonathan leading and the rest responding with Nehemiah.

[24]The prayer was as follows: "LORD, LORD God, creator of all things, awesome and strong, just and merciful, the only king and benefactor, [25]who alone are gracious, just, almighty, and eternal, Israel's savior from all evil, who chose our forefathers and sanctified them: [26]accept this sacrifice on behalf of all your people Israel and guard and sanctify your heritage. [27]Gather together our scattered people, free those who are the slaves of the Gentiles, look kindly on those who are despised and detested, and let the Gentiles know that you are our God. [28]Punish those who tyrannize over us and arrogantly mistreat us. [29]Plant your people in your holy place, as Moses promised."[d]

[30]Then the priests began to sing hymns. [31]After the sacrifice was burned, Nehemiah ordered the rest of the liquid to be poured upon large stones. [32]As soon as this was done, a flame blazed up, but its light was lost in the brilliance cast from a light on the altar. [33]When the event became known and the king of the Persians was told that, in the very place where the exiled priests had hidden the fire, a liquid was found with which Nehemiah and his people had burned the sacrifices, [34]the king, after verifying the fact, fenced the place off and declared it sacred. [35]To those on whom the king wished to bestow favors he distributed the large revenues he received there. [36]Nehemiah and his companions called the liquid nephthar, meaning purification, but most people name it naphtha.*

CHAPTER 2

[1]*You will find in the records, not only that Jeremiah the prophet ordered the deportees to take some of the aforementioned fire with them, [2]but also that the prophet, in giving them the law, admonished them not to forget the commandments of the LORD or be led astray in their thoughts, when seeing the gold and silver idols and their ornaments.[e] [3]With other similar words he urged them not to let the law depart from their hearts. [4][f]The same document also tells how the prophet, following a divine revelation, ordered that the tent and the ark should accompany him and how he went off to the mountain* which Moses climbed to see God's inheritance. [5]When Jeremiah arrived there, he found a room in a cave in which he put the tent, the ark, and the altar of incense; then he blocked up the entrance. [6]Some of those who followed him came up intending to mark the path, but they could not find it. [7]When Jeremiah heard of this, he reproved them: "The place is to remain unknown until God gathers his people together again and shows them mercy. [8]Then the LORD will disclose these things, and the glory of the LORD will be seen in the cloud, just as it appeared in the time of Moses and when Solomon prayed that the Place* might be gloriously sanctified."[g]

[9]It is also related how Solomon in his wisdom offered a sacrifice at the dedication and the completion of the temple. [10]Just as Moses prayed to the LORD and fire descended from the sky and consumed the sacrifices, so Solomon also prayed and fire came down and burned up the holocausts.[h] [11]Moses had said,[i] "Because it had not been eaten, the sin offering was burned up."* [12]Solomon also celebrated the feast in the same way for eight days.

[13]Besides these things, it is also told in the records and in Nehemiah's Memoirs* how he collected the books about the kings, the writings of the prophets and of David, and the royal letters about sacred offerings. [14]In like manner Judas also collected for us the books that had been scattered because of the war, and we now

1, 36: By a play on words, the Greek term naphtha (petroleum) is assimilated to some Semitic word, perhaps nephthar, meaning "loosened."

2, 1–8: This legendary account of how Jeremiah hid the sacred tent (which was not mentioned after the time of Solomon!), the ark, and the altar is given for the purpose of explaining why the postexilic temple was the legitimate place of worship even without these sacred objects.

2, 4: The mountain: Nebo; cf Dt 34, 1.

2, 8: The place: the temple of Jerusalem.

2, 11: The statement attributed here to Moses seems to be based on Lv 10, 16–20.

2, 13: Nehemiah's Memoirs: a lost apocryphal work.

d 2 Mc 2, 18; Dt 30, 3ff. e Bar 6, 3–72. f 4f: Dt 32, 49; 34, 1; Rv 11, 19. g 1 Kgs 8, 11. h Lv 9, 23f; 2 Chr 7, 1. i Lv 10, 16–20.

have them in our possession.[j] [15]If you need them, send messengers to get them for you.

[16]As we are about to celebrate the feast of the purification of the temple, we are writing to you requesting you also to please celebrate the feast. [17]It is God who has saved all his people and has restored to all of them their heritage, the kingdom, the priesthood, and the sacred rites, [18]as he promised through the law. We trust in God, that he will soon have mercy on us and gather us together from everywhere under the heavens to his holy Place, for he has rescued us from great perils and has purified his Place.[k]

II: Author's Preface

[19]This is the story of Judas Maccabeus and his brothers, of the purification of the great temple, the dedication of the altar, [20]the campaigns against Antiochus Epiphanes and his son Eupator,* [21]and of the heavenly manifestations accorded to the heroes who fought bravely for Judaism, so that, few as they were, they seized the whole land, put to flight the barbarian hordes, [22]regained possession of the world-famous temple, liberated the city, and reestablished the laws that were in danger of being abolished, while the LORD favored them with all his generous assistance. [23]All this, which Jason of Cyrene set forth in detail in five volumes, we will try to condense into a single book.

Purpose and Method [24]In view of the flood of statistics, and the difficulties encountered by those who wish to plunge into historical narratives where the material is abundant, [25]we have aimed to please those who prefer simple reading, as well as to make it easy for the studious who wish to commit things to memory, and to be helpful to all. [26]For us who have taken upon ourselves the labor of making this digest, the task, far from being easy, is one of sweat and of sleepless nights, [27]just as the preparation of a festive banquet is no light matter for one who thus seeks to give enjoyment to others. Similarly, to win the gratitude of many we will gladly endure these inconveniences, [28]while we leave the responsibility for exact details to the original author, and confine our efforts to giving only a summary outline. [29]As the architect of a new house must give his attention to the whole structure, while the man who undertakes the decoration and the frescoes has only to concern himself with what is needed for ornamentation, so I think it is with us. [30]To enter into questions and examine them thoroughly from all sides is the task of the professional historian; [31]but the man who is making an adaptation should be allowed to aim at brevity of expression and to omit detailed treatment of the matter. [32]Here, then, we shall begin our account without further ado; it would be nonsense to write a long preface to a story and then abbreviate the story itself.

III: Heliodorus' Attempt to Profane the Temple*

CHAPTER 3

Treachery of Simon [1][l]While the holy city lived in perfect peace and the laws were strictly observed because of the piety of the high priest Onias* and his hatred of evil, [2]the kings themselves honored the Place and glorified the temple with the most magnificent gifts. [3]Thus Seleucus,* king of Asia, defrayed from his own revenues all the expenses necessary for the sacrificial services. [4]But a certain Simon, of the priestly course of Bilgah,* who had been appointed superintendent of the temple, had a quarrel with the high priest about the supervision of the city market.[m] [5]Since he could not prevail against Onias, he went to Apollonius of Tarsus, who at that time was governor of Coele-

2, 20: For the account of the campaigns against Antiochus IV Epiphanes, see 2 Mc 4, 7—10, 9; and for the account of those against his son Antiochus V Eupator, see 2 Mc 10, 10—13, 26.

3, 1-40: This legendary episode about Heliodorus is recounted here for the purpose of stressing the inviolability of the temple of Jerusalem; its later profanation was allowed by God because of the people's sins; cf 2 Mc 5, 17f.

3, 1: The high priest Onias: Onias III, who was priest from 196 to 175 B.C., and died in 171 B.C. He was the son of Simon, whose praises are sung in Sir 50, 1-21.

3, 3: Seleucus: Seleucus IV Philopator, who reigned from 187 to 175 B.C.

3, 4: Bilgah: a priestly family mentioned in Neh 12, 5. 18.

j 1 Mc 1, 57. k Dt 30, 3ff. l 1ff: 2 Mc 5, 19f; 15, 12. m 2 Mc 4, 23.

syria and Phoenicia, [6]and reported to him that the treasury in Jerusalem was so full of untold riches that the total sum of money was incalculable and out of all proportion to the cost of the sacrifices, and that it would be possible to bring it all under the control of the king.

Mission of Heliodorus [7]When Apollonius had an audience with the king, he informed him about the riches that had been reported to him. The king chose his minister Heliodorus and sent him with instructions to expropriate the aforesaid wealth. [8]So Heliodorus immediately set out on his journey, ostensibly to visit the cities of Coelesyria and Phoenicia, but in reality to carry out the king's purpose. [9]When he arrived in Jerusalem and had been graciously received by the high priest of the city, he told him about the information that had been given, and explained the reason for his presence, and he asked if these things were really true. [10]The high priest explained that part of the money was a care fund for widows and orphans,[n] [11]and a part was the property of Hyrcanus, son of Tobias,* a man who occupied a very high position. Contrary to the calumnies of the impious Simon, the total amounted to four hundred talents of silver and two hundred of gold. [12]He added that it was utterly unthinkable to defraud those who had placed their trust in the sanctity of the Place and in the sacred inviolability of a temple venerated all over the world. [13]But because of the orders he had from the king, Heliodorus said that in any case the money must be confiscated for the royal treasury. [14]So on the day he had set he went in to take an inventory of the funds.

Anguish of the Faithful There was great distress throughout the city. [15]Priests prostrated themselves in their priestly robes before the altar, and loudly begged him in heaven who had given the law about deposits to keep the deposits safe for those who had made them. [16]Whoever saw the appearance of the high priest was pierced to the heart, for the changed color of his face manifested the anguish of his soul. [17]The terror and bodily trembling that had come over the man clearly showed those who saw him the pain that lodged in his heart. [18]People rushed out of their houses in crowds to make public supplication, because the Place was in danger of being profaned. [19]Women, girded with sackcloth below their breasts, filled the streets; maidens secluded indoors ran together, some to the gates, some to the walls, others peered through the windows, [20]all of them with hands raised toward heaven, making supplication. [21]It was pitiful to see the populace variously prostrated in prayer and the high priest full of dread and anguish.

Divine Intervention [22]While they were imploring the almighty LORD to keep the deposits safe and secure for those who had placed them in trust, [23]Heliodorus went on with his plan. [24]But just as he was approaching the treasury with his bodyguards, the LORD of spirits who holds all power manifested himself in so striking a way that those who had been bold enough to follow Heliodorus were panic-stricken at God's power and fainted away in terror. [25]There appeared to them a richly caparisoned horse, mounted by a dreadful rider. Charging furiously, the horse attacked Heliodorus with its front hoofs. The rider was seen to be wearing golden armor. [26]Then two other young men, remarkably strong, strikingly beautiful, and splendidly attired, appeared before him. Standing on each side of him, they flogged him unceasingly until they had given him innumerable blows. [27]Suddenly he fell to the ground, enveloped in great darkness. Men picked him up and laid him on a stretcher. [28]The man who a moment before had entered that treasury with a great retinue and his whole bodyguard was carried away helpless, having clearly experienced the sovereign power of God. [29]While he lay speechless and deprived of all hope of aid, due to an act of God's

3, 11: Son of Tobias: a member of the Tobiad family of Transjordan (Neh 2, 10; 6, 17ff; 13, 4–8). Hyrcanus' father was Joseph, whose mother was the sister of the high priest Onias II.

n Dt 14, 29.

power, [30]the Jews praised the LORD who had marvelously glorified his holy Place; and the temple, charged so shortly before with fear and commotion, was filled with joy and gladness, now that the almighty LORD had manifested himself.

[31]Soon some of the companions of Heliodorus begged Onias to invoke the Most High, praying that the life of the man who was about to expire might be spared. [32]Fearing that the king might think that Heliodorus had suffered some foul play at the hands of the Jews, the high priest offered a sacrifice for the man's recovery. [33]While the high priest was offering the sacrifice of atonement, the same young men in the same clothing again appeared and stood before Heliodorus. "Be very grateful to the high priest Onias," they told him. "It is for his sake that the LORD has spared your life. [34]Since you have been scourged by Heaven, proclaim to all men the majesty of God's power." When they had said this, they disappeared.

Testimony of Heliodorus [35]After Heliodorus had offered a sacrifice to the LORD and made most solemn vows to him who had spared his life, he bade Onias farewell, and returned with his soldiers to the king. [36]Before all men he gave witness to the deeds of the most high God that he had seen with his own eyes. [37]When the king asked Heliodorus who would be a suitable man to be sent to Jerusalem next, he answered: [38]"If you have an enemy or a plotter against the government, send him there, and you will receive him back well-flogged, if indeed he survives at all; for there is certainly some special divine power about the Place. [39]He who has his dwelling in heaven watches over that Place and protects it, and he strikes down and destroys those who come to harm it." [40]This was how the matter concerning Heliodorus and the preservation of the treasury turned out.

IV: Profanation and Persecution

CHAPTER 4

Onias Appeals to the King [1]The Simon mentioned above as the informer about the funds against his own country, made false accusations that it was Onias who threatened Heliodorus and instigated the whole miserable affair. [2]He dared to brand as a plotter against the government the man who was a benefactor of the city, a protector of his compatriots, and a zealous defender of the laws. [3]When Simon's hostility reached such a point that murders were being committed by one of his henchmen, [4]Onias saw that the opposition was serious and that Apollonius, son of Menestheus, the governor of Coelesyria and Phoenicia, was abetting Simon's wickedness. [5]So he had recourse to the king, not as an accuser of his countrymen, but as a man looking to the general and particular good of all the people. [6]He saw that, unless the king intervened, it would be impossible to have a peaceful government, and that Simon would not desist from his folly.

Jews Led by Jason To Apostatize [7]But Seleucus died,* and when Antiochus surnamed Epiphanes succeeded him on the throne, Onias' brother Jason obtained the high priesthood by corrupt means:^{o} [8]in an interview, he promised the king three hundred and sixty talents of silver, as well as eighty talents from another source of income. [9]Besides this he agreed to pay a hundred and fifty more, if he were given authority to establish a gymnasium and a youth club* for it and to enroll men in Jerusalem as Antiochians.

[10]When Jason received the king's approval and came into office, he immediately initiated his countrymen into the Greek way of life. [11]He set aside the royal concessions granted to the Jews through the mediation of John, father of Eupolemus* (that Eupolemus who would later go on an embassy to the Romans to establish a

4, 7: Seleucus died: he was murdered by Heliodorus. Antiochus Epiphanes was his younger brother. Onias' brother showed his love for the Greek way of life (v 10) by changing his Hebrew name Joshua, or Jesus, to the Greek name Jason.

4, 9: Youth club: an educational institution in which young men were trained both in Greek intellectual culture and in physical fitness. Antiochians: honorary citizens of Antioch, a Hellenistic city of the Seleucid Kingdom that had a corporation of such Antiochians, who enjoyed certain political and commercial privileges.

4, 11: Eupolemus: one of the two envoys sent to Rome by Judas Maccabeus (1 Mc 8, 17).

o 2 Mc 1, 7; 1 Mc 1, 10.

treaty of friendship with them); he abrogated the lawful institutions and introduced customs contrary to the law.[p] 12He quickly established a gymnasium* at the very foot of the acropolis, where he induced the noblest young men to wear the Greek hat.[q] 13The craze for Hellenism and foreign customs reached such a pitch, through the outrageous wickedness of the ungodly pseudo-high-priest Jason, 14that the priests no longer cared about the service of the altar. Disdaining the temple and neglecting the sacrifices, they hastened, at the signal for the discus-throwing, to take part in the unlawful exercises on the athletic field. 15They despised what their ancestors had regarded as honors, while they highly prized what the Greeks esteemed as glory. 16Precisely because of this, they found themselves in serious trouble: the very people whose manner of life they emulated, and whom they desired to imitate in everything, became their enemies and oppressors. 17It is no light matter to flout the laws of God, as the following period will show.

18When the quinquennial games were held at Tyre in the presence of the king, 19the vile Jason sent envoys as representatives of the Antiochians of Jerusalem, to bring there three hundred silver drachmas for the sacrifice to Hercules. But the bearers themselves decided that the money should not be spent on a sacrifice, as that was not right, but should be used for some other purpose. 20So the contribution destined by the sender for the sacrifice to Hercules was in fact applied, by those who brought it, to the construction of triremes.*

21When Apollonius, son of Menestheus, was sent to Egypt for the coronation of King Philometor,* Antiochus learned that the king was opposed to his policies; so he took measures for his own security. 22After going to Joppa, he proceeded to Jerusalem. There he was received with great pomp by Jason and the people of the city, who escorted him with torchlights and acclamations; following this, he led his army into Phoenicia.

Menelaus Supplants Jason 23Three years later Jason sent Menelaus,* brother of the aforementioned Simon, to deliver the money to the king, and to obtain decisions on some important matters. 24When he had been introduced to the king, he flattered him with such an air of authority that he secured the high priesthood for himself, outbidding Jason by three hundred talents of silver. 25He returned with the royal commission, but with nothing that made him worthy of the high priesthood; he had the temper of a cruel tyrant and the rage of a wild beast. 26Then Jason, who had cheated his own brother and now saw himself cheated by another man, was driven out as a fugitive to the country of the Ammonites.

27Although Menelaus had obtained the office, he did not make any payments of the money he had promised to the king, 28in spite of the demand of Sostratus, the commandant of the citadel, whose duty it was to collect the taxes. For this reason, both were summoned before the king. 29Menelaus left his brother Lysimachus as his substitute in the high priesthood, while Sostratus left Crates, commander of the Cypriots, as his substitute.

Murder of Onias 30While these things were taking place, the people of Tarsus and Mallus* rose in revolt, because their cities had been given as a gift to Antiochis, the king's mistress. 31The king, therefore, went off in haste to settle the affair, leaving Andronicus, one of his nobles, as his deputy. 32Then Menelaus, thinking this a good opportunity, stole some gold vessels from the temple and presented them to Andronicus; he had already sold some other vessels in Tyre and in the neighboring cities. 33When Onias had

4, 12: Since the gymnasium, where the youth exercised naked (Greek gymnos), lay in the Tyropoeon Valley to the east of the citadel, it was directly next to the temple on its eastern side. The Greek hat: a wide-brimmed hat, traditional headgear of Hermes, the patron god of athletic contests; it formed part of the distinctive costume of the members of the "youth club."

4, 20: Triremes: war vessels with three banks of oars.

4, 21: Philometor: Ptolemy VI, king of Egypt, c. 172 to c. 145 B.C.

4, 23: Menelaus: Jewish high priest from c. 172 to his execution in 162 B.C. (2 Mc 13, 3–8).

4, 30: Mallus: a city of Cilicia (v 36) in southeastern Asia Minor, about thirty miles east of Tarsus.

p 1 Mc 8, 17. q 1 Mc 1, 14.

clear evidence of the facts, he made a public protest, after withdrawing to the inviolable sanctuary at Daphne, near Antioch. [34]Thereupon Menelaus approached Andronicus privately and asked him to lay hands on Onias. So Andronicus went to Onias, and by treacherously reassuring him through sworn pledges with right hands joined, persuaded him, in spite of his suspicions, to leave the sanctuary. Then, without any regard for justice, he immediately put him to death.

[35]As a result, not only the Jews, but many people of other nations as well, were indignant and angry over the unjust murder of the man. [36]When the king returned from the region of Cilicia, the Jews of the city,* together with the Greeks who detested the crime, went to see him about the murder of Onias. [37]Antiochus was deeply grieved and full of pity; he wept as he recalled the prudence and noble conduct of the deceased. [38]Inflamed with anger, he immediately stripped Andronicus of his purple robe, tore off his other garments, and had him led through the whole city to the very place where he had committed the outrage against Onias; and there he put the murderer to death. Thus the LORD rendered him the punishment he deserved.

Riot against Lysimachus [39]Many sacrilegious thefts had been committed by Lysimachus in the city* with the connivance of Menelaus. When word was spread that a large number of gold vessels had been stolen, the people assembled in protest against Lysimachus. [40]As the crowds, now thoroughly enraged, began to riot, Lysimachus launched an unjustified attack against them with about three thousand armed men under the leadership of Auranus, a man as advanced in folly as he was in years. [41]Reacting against Lysimachus' attack, the people picked up stones or pieces of wood or handfuls of the ashes lying there and threw them in wild confusion at Lysimachus and his men. [42]As a result, they wounded many of them and even killed a few, while they put all the rest to flight. The sacrilegious thief himself they slew near the treasury.

[43]Charges about this affair were brought against Menelaus. [44]When the king came to Tyre, three men sent by the senate* presented to him the justice of their cause. [45]But Menelaus, seeing himself on the losing side, promised Ptolemy, son of Dorymenes, a substantial sum of money if he would win the king over.[r] [46]So Ptolemy retired with the king under a colonnade, as if to get some fresh air, and persuaded him to change his mind. [47]Menelaus, who was the cause of all the trouble, the king acquitted of the charges, while he condemned to death those poor men who would have been declared innocent even if they had pleaded their case before Scythians. [48]Thus, those who had prosecuted the case for the city, for the people, and for the sacred vessels, quickly suffered unjust punishment. [49]For this reason, even some Tyrians were indignant over the crime and provided sumptuously for their burial. [50]But Menelaus, thanks to the covetousness of the men in power, remained in office, where he grew in wickedness and became the chief plotter against his fellow citizens.

CHAPTER 5

Sedition and Death of Jason [1]About this time Antiochus sent his second expedition* into Egypt.[s] [2][t]It then happened that all over the city, for nearly forty days, there appeared horsemen charging in midair, clad in garments interwoven with gold—companies fully armed with lances [3]and drawn swords; squadrons of cavalry in battle array, charges and countercharges on this side and that, with brandished shields and bristling spears, flights of arrows and flashes of gold ornaments, together with armor of every sort. [4]Therefore all prayed that this vision might be a good omen.

4, 36: The city: Antioch. But some understand the Greek to mean "each city."

4, 39: The city: Jerusalem. Menelaus was still in Syria.

4, 44: The senate: the council of Jewish elders at Jerusalem; cf 1 Mc 12, 6.

5, 1: Second expedition: the first invasion of Egypt by Antiochus in 169 B.C. (1 Mc 1, 16–20) is not mentioned in 2 Mc, unless the coming of the Syrian army to Palestine (2 Mc 4, 21f) is regarded as the first invasion. The author of 2 Mc apparently combines the first pillage of Jerusalem in 169 B.C. after Antiochus' first invasion of Egypt (1 Mc 1, 20–28; cf 2 Mc 5, 5ff) with the second pillage of the city two years later (167 B.C.), following the king's second invasion of Egypt in 168 B.C. (1 Mc 1, 29–35; cf 2 Mc 5, 24ff).

r 2 Mc 8, 8; 1 Mc 3, 38. s 1 Mc 1, 17. t 2f: 2 Mc 3, 24ff; 10, 29f; 11, 8.

[5]But when a false rumor circulated that Antiochus was dead, Jason* gathered fully a thousand men and suddenly attacked the city. As the defenders on the walls were forced back and the city was finally being taken, Menelaus took refuge in the citadel. [6]Jason then slaughtered his fellow citizens without mercy, not realizing that triumph over one's own kindred was the greatest failure, but imagining that he was winning a victory over his enemies, not his fellow countrymen. [7]Even so, he did not gain control of the government, but in the end received only disgrace for his treachery, and once again took refuge in the country of the Ammonites. [8]At length he met a miserable end. Called to account before Aretas,* king of the Arabs, he fled from city to city, hunted by all men, hated as a transgressor of the laws, abhorred as the butcher of his country and his countrymen. After being driven into Egypt, [9]he crossed the sea to the Spartans, among whom he hoped to find protection because of his relations with them. There he who had exiled so many from their country perished in exile; [10]and he who had cast out so many to lie unburied went unmourned himself with no funeral of any kind or any place in the tomb of his ancestors.

The City Ravaged [11] [u]When these happenings were reported to the king, he thought that Judea was in revolt. Raging like a wild animal, he set out from Egypt and took Jerusalem by storm. [12]He ordered his soldiers to cut down without mercy those whom they met and to slay those who took refuge in their houses. [13]There was a massacre of young and old, a killing of women and children, a slaughter of virgins and infants. [14]In the space of three days, eighty thousand were lost, forty thousand meeting a violent death, and the same number being sold into slavery. [15]Not satisfied with this, the king dared to enter the holiest temple in the world; Menelaus, that traitor both to the laws and to his country, served as guide. [16]He laid his impure hands on the sacred vessels and gathered up with profane hands the votive offerings made by other kings for the advancement, the glory, and the honor of the Place. [17]Puffed up in spirit, Antiochus did not realize that it was because of the sins of the city's inhabitants that the LORD was angry for a little while and hence disregarded the holy Place. [v] [18]If they had not become entangled in so many sins, this man, like Heliodorus, who was sent by King Seleucus to inspect the treasury, would have been flogged and turned back from his presumptuous action as soon as he approached. [19] [w]The LORD, however, had not chosen the people for the sake of the Place, but the Place for the sake of the people.* [20]Therefore, the Place itself, having shared in the people's misfortunes, afterward participated in their good fortune; and what the Almighty had forsaken in his anger was restored in all its glory, once the great Sovereign became reconciled.

[21]Antiochus carried off eighteen hundred talents from the temple, and hurried back to Antioch. In his arrogance he planned to make the land navigable and the sea passable on foot, so carried away was he with pride. [x] [22]But he left governors to harass the nation: at Jerusalem, Philip, a Phrygian by birth,* and in character more cruel than the man who appointed him; [23]at Mount Gerizim,* Andronicus; and besides these, Menelaus, who lorded it over his fellow citizens worse than the others did. Out of hatred for the Jewish citizens, [24] [y]the king sent Apollonius,* commander of the Mysians, at the head of an army of twenty-two thousand men, with orders to kill all the grown men and sell the women and young men into slavery. [25]When this man arrived in Jerusalem, he pretended to

5, 5: Jason: brother of Onias III, was claimant of the high priesthood (2 Mc 4, 7–10). Later he was supplanted by Menelaus who drove him into Transjordan (2 Mc 4, 26).

5, 8: Aretas: King Aretas I of the Nabateans; cf 1 Mc 5, 25.

5, 19: Man is more important than even the most sacred institutions; cf Mk 2, 27.

5, 22: Philip, a Phrygian by birth: the Philip of 2 Mc 6, 11 and 8, 8, but probably not the same as Philip the regent of 2 Mc 9, 29 and 1 Mc 6, 14.

5, 23: Mount Gerizim: the sacred mountain of the Samaritans at Shechem; cf 2 Mc 6, 2.

5, 24: Apollonius: the Mysian commander of 1 Mc 1, 29; mentioned also in 2 Mc 3, 5; 4, 4.

u 11–21: 1 Mc 1, 20–24. v 2 Mc 6, 12–16; 7, 16–19. 32–38. w 19ff: 2 Mc 3, 1ff; 1 Chr 17, 9; Mk 2, 27. x 1 Mc 1, 23f. y 24ff: 1 Mc 1, 29f.

be peacefully disposed and waited until the holy day of the sabbath; then, finding the Jews refraining from work, he ordered his men to parade fully armed. 26 All those who came out to watch, he massacred, and running through the city with armed men, he cut down a large number of people.

27 But Judas Maccabeus with about nine others withdrew to the wilderness where he and his companions lived like wild animals in the hills, continuing to eat what grew wild to avoid sharing the defilement. [z]

CHAPTER 6

The Temple Desecrated 1 [a]Not long after this the king sent an Athenian senator to force the Jews to abandon the customs of their ancestors and live no longer by the laws of God; 2 also to profane the temple in Jerusalem and dedicate it to Olympian Zeus,* and that on Mount Gerizim to Zeus the Hospitable, as the inhabitants of the place requested. [b] 3 This intensified the evil in an intolerable and utterly disgusting way. 4 The Gentiles filled the temple with debauchery and revelry; they amused themselves with prostitutes* and had intercourse with women even in the sacred court. They also brought into the temple things that were forbidden, 5 so that the altar was covered with abominable offerings prohibited by the laws.

Abolition of the Law 6 A man could not keep the sabbath or celebrate the traditional feasts, nor even admit that he was a Jew. 7 Moreover, at the monthly celebration of the king's birthday the Jews had, from bitter necessity, to partake of the sacrifices, and when the festival of Dionysus* was celebrated, they were compelled to march in his procession, wearing wreaths of ivy.

8 At the suggestion of the citizens of Ptolemais, a decree was issued ordering the neighboring Greek cities to act in the same way against the Jews: oblige them to partake of the sacrifices, 9 and put to death those who would not consent to adopt the customs of the Greeks. It was obvious, therefore, that disaster impended. 10 Thus, two women who were arrested for having circumcised their children were publicly paraded about the city with their babies hanging at their breasts and then thrown down from the top of the city wall. [c] 11 Others, who had assembled in nearby caves to observe the sabbath in secret, were betrayed to Philip and all burned to death. In their respect for the holiness of that day, they had scruples about defending themselves. [d]

Purpose of Divine Judgment 12 [e]Now I beg those who read this book not to be disheartened by these misfortunes, but to consider that these chastisements were meant not for the ruin but for the correction of our nation. 13 It is, in fact, a sign of great kindness to punish sinners promptly instead of letting them go for long. 14 [f]Thus, in dealing with other nations, the LORD patiently waits until they reach the full measure of their sins before he punishes them; but with us he has decided to deal differently, 15 in order that he may not have to punish us more severely later, when our sins have reached their fullness. 16 He never withdraws his mercy from us. Although he disciplines us with misfortunes, he does not abandon his own people. 17 Let these words suffice for recalling this truth. Without further ado we must go on with our story.

Martyrdom of Eleazar* 18 Eleazar, one of the foremost scribes, a man of advanced age and noble appearance, was being forced to open his mouth to eat pork. [g] 19 But preferring a glorious death to a life of defilement, he spat out the meat, and went forward of his own accord to the instrument of torture, 20 as men ought to do who

6, 2: Olympain Zeus: equated with the Syrian Baal shomem ("the lord of the heavens"), a term which the Jews rendered as "Shiqqus shomem," horrible abomination (Dn 9, 27; 11, 31; 12, 11; 1 Mc 1, 54).

6, 4: Amused themselves with prostitutes: as in the fertility cults of the ancient Near East; see notes on Bar 6, 10. 42f.

6, 7: Dionysus: called also Bacchus the god of the grape harvest and of wine; ivy was one of his symbols.

6, 18—7, 42: The stories of Eleazar and of the mother and her seven sons, among the earliest models of "martyrology," were understandably popular among the Christians of the early centuries. Written originally to encourage God's people in times of persecution, they add gruesome details to the record of tortures, and place long speeches in the mouths of the martyrs.

z 1 Mc 2, 28. a 1–11: 1 Mc 1, 44–63. b 1 Mc 1, 46; Dn 9, 27. c 1 Mc 1, 60f. d 1 Mc 2, 32–38. e 12–16: 2 Mc 5, 17; 7, 16–19. 32–38. f Wis 11, 9f; 12, 2, 22. g Lv 11, 7f; Heb 11, 35.

have the courage to reject the food which it is unlawful to taste even for love of life. [21]Those in charge of that unlawful ritual meal took the man aside privately, because of their long acquaintance with him, and urged him to bring meat of his own providing, such as he could legitimately eat, and to pretend to be eating some of the meat of the sacrifice prescribed by the king; [22]in this way he would escape the death penalty, and be treated kindly because of their old friendship with him. [23]But he made up his mind in a noble manner, worthy of his years, the dignity of his advanced age, the merited distinction of his gray hair, and of the admirable life he had lived from childhood; and so he declared that above all he would be loyal to the holy laws given by God.

He told them to send him at once to the abode of the dead, explaining: [24]"At our age it would be unbecoming to make such a pretense; many young men would think the ninety-year-old Eleazar had gone over to an alien religion. [25]Should I thus dissimulate for the sake of a brief moment of life, they would be led astray by me, while I would bring shame and dishonor on my old age. [26]Even if, for the time being, I avoid the punishment of men, I shall never, whether alive or dead, escape the hands of the Almighty. [27]Therefore, by manfully giving up my life now, I will prove myself worthy of my old age, [28]and I will leave to the young a noble example of how to die willingly and generously for the revered and holy laws."

He spoke thus, and went immediately to the instrument of torture. [29]Those who shortly before had been kindly disposed, now became hostile toward him because what he had said seemed to them utter madness. [30]When he was about to die under the blows, he groaned and said: "The LORD in his holy knowledge knows full well that, although I could have escaped death, I am not only enduring terrible pain in my body from this scourging, but also suffering it with joy in my soul because of my devotion to him." [31]This is how he died, leaving in his death a model of courage and an unforgettable example of virtue not only for the young but for the whole nation.

CHAPTER 7

Martyrdom of a Mother and Her Sons [1]It also happened that seven brothers with their mother were arrested and tortured with whips and scourges by the king, to force them to eat pork in violation of God's law.[h] [2]One of the brothers, speaking for the others, said: "What do you expect to achieve by questioning us? We are ready to die rather than transgress the laws of our ancestors." [3]At that the king, in a fury, gave orders to have pans and caldrons heated. [4]While they were being quickly heated, he commanded his executioners to cut out the tongue of the one who had spoken for the others, to scalp him and cut off his hands and feet, while the rest of his brothers and his mother looked on. [5]When he was completely maimed but still breathing, the king ordered them to carry him to the fire and fry him. As a cloud of smoke spread from the pan, the brothers and their mother encouraged one another to die bravely, saying such words as these: [6]"The LORD God is looking on, and he truly has compassion on us, as Moses declared in his canticle, when he protested openly with the words, 'And he will have pity on his servants.' "[i]

[7]When the first brother had died in this manner, they brought the second to be made sport of. After tearing off the skin and hair of his head, they asked him, "Will you eat the pork rather than have your body tortured limb by limb?" [8]Answering in the language of his forefathers, he said, "Never!" So he too in turn suffered the same tortures as the first. [9]At the point of death he said: "You accursed fiend, you are depriving us of this present life, but the King of the world will raise us up* to live again forever. It is for his laws that we are dying."[j]

[10]After him the third suffered their cruel sport. He put out his tongue at once when told to do so, and bravely held out his hands, [11]as he

7, 9: The King of the world will raise us up: here, and in vv 11. 14. 23. 29. 36, belief in the future resurrection of the body, at least for the just, is clearly stated; cf also 2 Mc 12, 44; 14, 46; Dn 12, 2.

h Jer 15, 9. **i** Dt 32, 36. **j** 2 Mc 12, 44; 14, 46.

spoke these noble words: "It was from Heaven
that I received these; for the sake of his laws I
disdain them; from him I hope to receive them
again."[k] 12 Even the king and his attendants
marveled at the young man's courage, because
he regarded his sufferings as nothing.
13 After he had died, they tortured and mal-
treated the fourth brother in the same way.
14 When he was near death, he said, "It is my
choice to die at the hands of men with the God-
given hope of being restored to life by him; but
for you, there will be no resurrection to life."
15 They next brought forward the fifth brother
and maltreated him. 16 Looking at the king, he
said:[l] "Since you have power among men,
mortal though you are, do what you please. But
do not think that our nation is forsaken by God.
17 Only wait, and you will see how his great
power will torment you and your descendants."
18 After him they brought the sixth brother.
When he was about to die, he said: "Have no
vain illusions. We suffer these things on our own
account, because we have sinned against our
God; that is why such astonishing things have
happened to us. 19 Do not think, then, that you
will go unpunished for having dared to fight
against God."[m]
20 Most admirable and worthy of everlasting
remembrance was the mother, who saw her
seven sons perish in a single day, yet bore it
courageously because of her hope in the LORD.
21 Filled with a noble spirit that stirred her
womanly heart with manly courage, she ex-
horted each of them in the language of their
forefathers with these words: 22 "I do not know
how you came into existence in my womb; it
was not I who gave you the breath of life, nor
was it I who set in order the elements of which
each of you is composed. 23 Therefore, since it is
the Creator of the universe who shapes each
man's beginning, as he brings about the origin of
everything, he, in his mercy, will give you back
both breath and life, because you now disregard
yourselves for the sake of his law."
24 Antiochus, suspecting insult in her words,
thought he was being ridiculed. As the youngest
brother was still alive, the king appealed to him,
not with mere words, but with promises on
oath, to make him rich and happy if he would
abandon his ancestral customs: he would make
him his Friend and entrust him with high office.
25 When the youth paid no attention to him at
all, the king appealed to the mother, urging her
to advise her boy to save his life. 26 After he had
urged her for a long time, she went through the
motions of persuading her son. 27 In derision of
the cruel tyrant, she leaned over close to her son
and said in their native language: "Son, have pity
on me, who carried you in my womb for nine
months, nursed you for three years, brought you
up, educated and supported you to your present
age. 28 I beg you, child, to look at the heavens
and the earth and see all that is in them; then
you will know that God did not make them out
of existing things;* and in the same way the
human race came into existence. 29 Do not be
afraid of this executioner, but be worthy of your
brothers and accept death, so that in the time of
mercy I may receive you again with them."
30 She had scarcely finished speaking when
the youth said: "What are you waiting for? I will
not obey the king's command. I obey the com-
mand of the law given to our forefathers through
Moses. 31 But you, who have contrived every
kind of affliction for the Hebrews, will not
escape the hands of God. 32 [n]We, indeed, are
suffering because of our sins. 33 Though our
living LORD treats us harshly for a little while to
correct us with chastisements, he will again be
reconciled with his servants. 34 But you, wretch,
vilest of all men! do not, in your insolence,
concern yourself with unfounded hopes, as you
raise your hand against the children of Heaven.
35 You have not yet escaped the judgment of the
almighty and all-seeing God. 36 My brothers,
after enduring brief pain, have drunk of never-
failing life, under God's covenant, but you, by
the judgment of God, shall receive just punish-

7, 28: God did not make them out of existing things: that is, God made all things solely by his omnipotent will and his creative word; cf Heb 11, 3.

k 2 Mc 12, 43ff. l 16–19: 2 Mc 5, 17; 6, 12–16. m Acts 5, 39. n 32. 38: 2 Mc 5, 17; 6, 12–16; 17, 16–19.

ments for your arrogance. 37 Like my brothers, I offer up my body and my life for our ancestral laws, imploring God to show mercy soon to our nation, and by afflictions and blows to make you confess that he alone is God. 38 Through me and my brothers, may there be an end to the wrath of the Almighty that has justly fallen on our whole nation." 39 At that, the king became enraged and treated him even worse than the others, since he bitterly resented the boy's contempt. 40 [o]Thus he too died undefiled, putting all his trust in the LORD. 41 The mother was last to die, after her sons.

42 Enough has been said about the sacrificial meals and the excessive cruelties.

V: Victories of Judas and Purification of the Temple

CHAPTER 8

Judas Maccabeus 1 [p]Judas Maccabeus and his companions entered the villages secretly, summoned their kinsmen, and by also enlisting others who remained faithful to Judaism, assembled about six thousand men. 2 They implored the LORD to look kindly upon his people, who were being oppressed on all sides; to have pity on the temple, which was profaned by godless men; 3 to have mercy on the city, which was being destroyed and about to be leveled to the ground; to hearken to the blood that cried out to him; 4 to remember the criminal slaughter of innocent children and the blasphemies uttered against his name; and to manifest his hatred of evil. 5 [q]Once Maccabeus got his men organized, the Gentiles could not withstand him, for the LORD's wrath had now changed to mercy. 6 Coming unexpectedly upon towns and villages, he would set them on fire. He captured strategic positions, and put to flight a large number of the enemy. 7 He preferred the nights as being especially helpful for such attacks. Soon the fame of his valor spread everywhere.

First Victory over Nicanor* 8 When Philip saw that Judas was gaining ground little by little and that his successful advances were becoming more frequent, he wrote to Ptolemy, governor of Coelesyria and Phoenicia, to come to the aid of the king's government.[r] 9 Ptolemy promptly selected Nicanor, son of Patroclus, one of the Chief Friends, and sent him at the head of at least twenty thousand armed men of various nations to wipe out the entire Jewish race. With him he associated Gorgias, a professional military commander, well-versed in the art of war.[s] 10 Nicanor planned to raise the two thousand talents of tribute owed by the king to the Romans by selling captured Jews into slavery. 11 So he immediately sent word to the coastal cities, inviting them to buy Jewish slaves and promising to deliver ninety slaves for a talent—little did he dream of the punishment that was to fall upon him from the Almighty.

12 When Judas learned of Nicanor's advance and informed his companions about the approach of the army, 13 the cowardly and those who lacked faith in God's justice deserted and got away. 14 But the others sold everything they had left, and at the same time besought the LORD to deliver those whom the ungodly Nicanor had sold before even meeting them. 15 They begged the LORD to do this, if not for their sake, at least for the sake of the covenants made with their forefathers, and because they themselves bore his holy, glorious name. 16 Maccabeus assembled his men, six thousand strong, and exhorted them not to be panicstricken before the enemy, nor to fear the large number of the Gentiles attacking them unjustly, but to fight courageously, 17 keeping before their eyes the lawless outrage perpetrated by the Gentiles against the holy Place and the affliction of the humiliated city, as well as the subversion of their ancestral way of life. 18 "They trust in weapons and acts of daring," he said, "but we trust in almighty God, who can by a mere nod destroy not only those who attack us, but the whole world." 19 He went on to tell them of the times when help had been given their ancestors: both

8, 8–29. 34ff: This account of the campaign of Nicanor and Gorgias against Judas is paralleled, with certain differences, in 1 Mc 3, 38—4, 24.

o 40f: Heb 11, 35. p 1–7: 2 Mc 5, 27; 1 Mc 3, 10–26. q 5ff: 1 Mc 3, 3–9. r 2 Mc 4, 45; 1 Mc 3, 38. s 1 Mc 7, 26.

the time of Sennacherib, when a hundred and eighty-five thousand of his men were destroyed,[t] [20]and the time of the battle in Babylonia against the Galatians, when only eight thousand Jews fought along with four thousand Macedonians; yet when the Macedonians were hard pressed, the eight thousand routed one hundred and twenty thousand and took a great quantity of booty, because of the help they received from Heaven. [21]With such words he encouraged them and made them ready to die for their laws and their country.

Then Judas divided his army into four, [22]placing his brothers, Simon, Joseph,* and Jonathan, each over a division, assigning to each fifteen hundred men. [23](There was also Eleazar.) After reading to them from the holy book and giving them the watchword, "The Help of God," he himself took charge of the first division and joined in battle with Nicanor.[u] [24]With the Almighty as their ally, they killed more than nine thousand of the enemy, wounded and disabled the greater part of Nicanor's army, and put all of them to flight. [25]They also seized the money of those who had come to buy them as slaves. When they had pursued the enemy for some time, [26]they were obliged to return by reason of the late hour. It was the day before the sabbath, and for that reason they could not continue the pursuit. [27]They collected the enemy's arms and stripped them of their spoils, and then observed the sabbath with fervent praise and thanks to the LORD who kept them safe for that day on which he let descend on them the first dew of his mercy. [28]After the sabbath, they gave a share of the booty to the persecuted and to widows and orphans; the rest they divided among themselves and their children. [29]When this was done, they made supplication in common, imploring the merciful LORD to be completely reconciled with his servants.

Timothy and Bacchides Defeated [30]They also challenged the forces of Timothy and Bacchides, killed more than twenty thousand of them, and captured some very high fortresses. They divided the enormous plunder, allotting half to themselves and the rest to the persecuted, to orphans, widows, and the aged. [31]They collected the enemies' weapons and carefully stored them in suitable places; the rest of the spoils they carried to Jerusalem. [32]They also killed the commander of Timothy's forces, a most wicked man, who had done great harm to the Jews. [33]While celebrating the victory in their ancestral city, they burned both those who had set fire to the sacred gates and Callisthenes, who had taken refuge in a little house; so he received the reward his wicked deeds deserved.

Humiliation of Nicanor [34] [v]The accursed Nicanor, who had brought the thousand slave dealers to buy the Jews, [35]after being humbled through the LORD's help by those whom he had thought of no account, laid aside his fine clothes and fled alone across country like a runaway slave, until he reached Antioch. He was eminently successful in destroying his own army. [36]So he who had promised to provide tribute for the Romans by the capture of the people of Jerusalem testified that the Jews had a champion, and that they were invulnerable for the very reason that they followed the laws laid down by him.

CHAPTER 9

Punishment and Death of Antiochus*

[1] [w]About that time Antiochus retreated in disgrace from the region of Persia. [2]He had entered the city called Persepolis and attempted to rob the temple and gain control of the city. Thereupon the people had swift recourse to arms, and Antiochus' men were routed, so that in the end Antiochus was put to flight by the natives and forced to beat a shameful retreat. [3]On his arrival

8, 22: Joseph: called John in 1 Mc 2, 2; 9, 36. 38. This paragraph interrupts the story of Nicanor's defeat, which is resumed in v 34. The purpose of the author apparently is to group together the defeats suffered by the Syrians on various occasions. Battles against Timothy are recounted in 1 Mc 5, 37–44 and 2 Mc 12, 10–25; against Bacchides in 1 Mc 7, 8–20.

9, 1–28: In order to keep together the various accounts of God's punishment of the persecutors of his people, the author places here the stories of Antiochus' illness and death (in actuality the king died only after the purification of the temple; cf 1 Mc 4, 36–59; 6, 1–16; 2 Mc 10, 1–8); of Judas' campaigns in Idumea and Transjordan (cf 2 Mc 5, 1–51; 2 Mc 10, 14–38); and of the first expedition of Lysias (1 Mc 4, 26–35; 2 Mc 11, 1–15).

t 2 Mc 15, 22; 2 Kgs 19, 35; Is 37, 36. u 1 Mc 3, 48. v 34f: 2 Mc 8, 23f; 1 Mc 7, 26. w 1–29: 2 Mc 1, 12–17; 1 Mc 6, 1–13.

in Ecbatana, he learned what had happened to Nicanor and to Timothy's forces. 4 Overcome with anger, he planned to make the Jews suffer for the injury done by those who had put him to flight. Therefore he ordered his charioteer to drive without stopping until he finished the journey.

Yet the condemnation of Heaven rode with him, since he said in his arrogance, "I will make Jerusalem the common graveyard of the Jews as soon as I arrive there." 5 So the all-seeing LORD, the God of Israel, struck him down with an unseen but incurable blow; for scarcely had he uttered those words when he was seized with excruciating pains in his bowels and sharp internal torment,[x] 6 a fit punishment for him who had tortured the bowels of others with many barbarous torments. 7 Far from giving up his insolence, he was all the more filled with arrogance. Breathing fire in his rage against the Jews, he gave orders to drive even faster. As a result he hurtled from the dashing chariot, and every part of his body was racked by the violent fall. 8 [y]Thus he who previously, in his superhuman presumption, thought he could command the waves of the sea, and imagined he could weigh the mountaintops in his scales, was now thrown to the ground and had to be carried on a litter, clearly manifesting to all the power of God. 9 [z]The body of this impious man swarmed with worms, and while he was still alive in hideous torments, his flesh rotted off, so that the entire army was sickened by the stench of his corruption. 10 Shortly before, he had thought that he could reach the stars of heaven, and now, no one could endure to transport the man because of this intolerable stench.

11 At last, broken in spirit, he began to give up his excessive arrogance, and to gain some understanding, under the scourge of God, for he was racked with pain unceasingly. 12 When he could no longer bear his own stench, he said, "It is right to be subject to God, and not to think one's mortal self divine." 13 Then this vile man vowed to the LORD, who would no longer have mercy on him, 14 that he would set free the holy city, toward which he had been hurrying with the intention of leveling it to the ground and making it a common graveyard; 15 he would put on perfect equality with the Athenians all the Jews, whom he had judged not even worthy of burial, but fit only to be thrown out with their children to be eaten by vultures and wild animals; 16 he would adorn with the finest offerings the holy temple which he had previously despoiled; he would restore all the sacred vessels many times over; and would provide from his own revenues the expenses required for the sacrifices. 17 Besides all this, he would become a Jew himself and visit every inhabited place to proclaim there the power of God. 18 But since God's punishment had justly come upon him, his sufferings were not lessened, so he lost hope for himself and wrote the following letter to the Jews in the form of a supplication. It read thus:

19 *"To my esteemed Jewish citizens, Antiochus, their king and general, sends hearty greetings and best wishes for their health and happiness. 20 If you and your children are well and your affairs are going as you wish, I thank God very much, for my hopes are in heaven. 21 Now that I am ill, I recall with affection the esteem and good will you bear me. On returning from the regions of Persia, I fell victim to a troublesome illness; so I thought it necessary to form plans for the general welfare of all. 22 Actually, I do not despair about my health, since I have great hopes of recovering from my illness. 23 Nevertheless, I know that my father, whenever he went on campaigns in the hinterland, would name his successor, 24 so that, if anything unexpected happened or any unwelcome news came, the people throughout the realm would know to whom the government had been entrusted, and

9, 19–27: Despite the statement in v 18, this letter is not really a supplication. It is rather a notification to all the king's subjects of the appointment of his son as his successor and a request that they be loyal to the new king. Apparently the same letter, which has every appearance of being authentic, was sent to the various peoples throughout the kingdom, with only a few words of address changed for each group.

x Acts 12, 20–23. y Jb 38, 8–11; Ps 65, 6f; Is 40, 12. z Acts 12, 23.

so not be disturbed. [25]I am also bearing in mind that the neighboring rulers, especially those on the borders of our kingdom, are on the watch for opportunities and waiting to see what will happen. I have therefore appointed as king my son Antiochus, whom I have often before entrusted and commended to most of you, when I made hurried visits to the outlying provinces. I have written to him the letter copied below.* [26]Therefore I beg and entreat each of you to remember the general and individual benefits you have received, and to continue to show good will toward me and my son. [27]I am confident that, following my policy, he will treat you with mildness and kindness in his relations with you."

[28]So this murderer and blasphemer, after extreme sufferings, such as he had inflicted on others, died a miserable death in the mountains of a foreign land. [29]His foster brother Philip brought the body home; but fearing Antiochus' son, he later withdrew into Egypt, to Ptolemy Philometor.

CHAPTER 10

Purification of Temple and City [1] [a]When Maccabeus and his companions, under the LORD's leadership, had recovered the temple and the city, [2]they destroyed the altars erected by the Gentiles in the marketplace and the sacred enclosures. [3]After purifying the temple, they made a new altar. Then, with fire struck from flint, they offered sacrifice for the first time in two years,* burned incense, and lighted lamps. They also set out the showbread. [4]When they had done this, they prostrated themselves and begged the LORD that they might never again fall into such misfortunes, and that if they should sin at any time, he might chastise them with moderation and not hand them over to blasphemous and barbarous Gentiles. [5]On the anniversary of the day on which the temple had been profaned by the Gentiles, that is, the twenty-fifth of the same month Chislev, the purification of the temple took place. [6]The Jews celebrated joyfully for eight days as on the feast of Booths, remembering how, a little while before, they had spent the feast of Booths living like wild animals in caves on the mountains. [7]Carrying rods entwined with leaves, green branches and palms, they sang hymns of grateful praise to him who had brought about the purification of his own Place. [8]By public edict and decree they prescribed that the whole Jewish nation should celebrate these days every year.

VI: Renewed Persecution

Death of Ptolemy [9]Such was the end of Antiochus surnamed Epiphanes.[b] [10]Now we shall relate what happened under Antiochus Eupator, the son of that godless man, and shall give a summary of the chief evils caused by the wars. [11]When Eupator succeeded to the kingdom, he put a certain Lysias in charge of the government as commander in chief of Coelesyria and Phoenicia. [12]Ptolemy, surnamed Macron,* had taken the lead in treating the Jews fairly because of the previous injustice that had been done them, and he endeavored to have peaceful relations with them. [13]As a result, he was accused before Eupator by the King's Friends. In fact, on all sides he heard himself called a traitor for having abandoned Cyprus, which Philometor had entrusted to him, and for having gone over to Antiochus Epiphanes. Since he could not command the respect due to his high office, he ended his life by taking poison.

Victory over the Idumeans* [14]When Gorgias became governor of the region, he employed foreign troops and used every opportunity to attack the Jews. [15] [c]At the same time the Idumeans, who held some important strongholds, were harassing the Jews; they welcomed fugitives from Jerusalem and endeavored to continue the war. [16]Maccabeus and his companions, after public prayers asking God to be their ally, moved

9, 25: The letter copied below: not included in the text of 2 Mc.

10, 3: Two years: three years according to 1 Mc 1, 54 and 4, 52.

10, 12: Ptolemy Macron: son of Dorymenes (2 Mc 4, 45), was formerly hostile to the Jews (2 Mc 6, 8).

10, 14–23: Probably the same campaign of Judas against the Idumeans that is mentioned in 1 Mc 5, 1–3.

a 1–8: 1 Mc 4, 36–59. b 2 Mc 2, 21; 1 Mc 6, 17. c 15–23: 1 Mc 5, 3ff.

quickly against the strongholds of the Idumeans.
17 Attacking vigorously, they gained control of
the places, drove back all who manned the
walls, and cut down those who opposed them,
killing as many as twenty thousand men.
18 When at least nine thousand took refuge in
two very strong towers, containing everything
necessary to sustain a siege, 19 Maccabeus left
Simon and Joseph, along with Zacchaeus and his
men, in sufficient numbers to besiege them,
while he himself went off to places where he
was more urgently needed. 20 But some of the
men in Simon's force who were money lovers let
themselves be bribed by some of the men in the
towers; on receiving seventy thousand
drachmas, they allowed a number of them to
escape. 21 When Maccabeus was told what had
happened, he assembled the rulers of the people
and accused those men of having sold their
kinsmen for money by setting their enemies free
to fight against them. 22 So he put them to death
as traitors, and without delay captured the two
towers. 23 As he was successful at arms in all his
undertakings, he destroyed more than twenty
thousand men in the two strongholds.
Victory over Timothy 24 Timothy, who had
previously been defeated by the Jews,* gathered
a tremendous force of foreign troops and col-
lected a large number of cavalry from Asia; then
he appeared in Judea, ready to conquer it by
force. 25 At his approach, Maccabeus and his
men made supplication to God, sprinkling earth
upon their heads and girding their loins in
sackcloth. 26 Lying prostrate at the foot of the
altar, they begged him to be gracious to them,
and to be an enemy to their enemies, and a foe
to their foes, as the law declares.[d]
27 After the prayer, they took up their arms
and advanced a considerable distance from the
city, halting when they were close to the enemy.
28 As soon as dawn broke,* the armies joined
battle, the one having as pledge of success and
victory not only their valor but also their reliance
on the LORD, and the other taking fury as their
leader in the fight.
29 [e]In the midst of the fierce battle, there
appeared to the enemy from the heavens five
majestic men riding on golden-bridled horses,
who led the Jews on. 30 They surrounded
Maccabeus, and shielding him with their own
armor, kept him from being wounded. They shot
arrows and hurled thunderbolts at the enemy,
who were bewildered and blinded, thrown into
confusion and routed. 31 Twenty-five hundred of
their foot soldiers and six hundred of their
horsemen were slain. 32 Timothy, however, fled
to a well-fortified stronghold called Gazara,
where Chaereas was in command.[f] 33 For four
days Maccabeus and his men eagerly besieged
the fortress. 34 Those inside, relying on the
strength of the place, kept repeating outrageous
blasphemies and uttering abominable words.
35 When the fifth day dawned, twenty young
men in the army of Maccabeus, angered over
such blasphemies, bravely stormed the wall and
with savage fury cut down everyone they en-
countered. 36 Others who climbed up the same
way swung around on the defenders, taking the
besieged in the rear; they put the towers to the
torch, spread the fire and burned the blasphem-
ers alive. Still others broke down the gates and
let in the rest of the troops, who took possession
of the city. 37 Timothy had hidden in a cistern,
but they killed* him, along with his brother
Chaereas, and Apollophanes. 38 On completing
these exploits, they blessed, with hymns of
grateful praise, the LORD who shows great kind-
ness to Israel and grants them victory.

CHAPTER 11

Defeat of Lysias* 1 [g]Very soon afterward, Lys-
ias, guardian and kinsman of the king and head
of the government, being greatly displeased at
what had happened, 2 mustered about eighty

10, 24: Timothy . . . previously . . . defeated by the Jews: as recounted in 2 Mc 8, 30ff.

10, 28: As soon as dawn broke: the same battle at dawn as in 1 Mc 5, 30–34.

10, 37: Timothy . . . they killed: apparently, the same Timothy is still alive in 2 Mc 12, 2. 18–25. The present passage is not in chronological order; Gazara, v 32 (Gezer) was not captured by the Jews until much later (cf 1 Mc 9, 50ff; 13, 53).

11, 1–12: The defeat of Lysias at Beth-zur probably occurred before the purification of the temple; cf 1 Mc 4, 26–35.

d Ex 23, 22. e 29f: 2 Mc 3, 24ff; 5, 2f: 10, 29f; 11, 8. f 1 Mc 13, 43–48. g 1–12: 1 Mc 4, 26–35.

thousand infantry and all his cavalry and
marched against the Jews. His plan was to make
Jerusalem a Greek settlement; [3]to levy tribute on
the temple, as he did on the sanctuaries of the
other nations; and to put the high priesthood up
for sale every year. [4]He did not take God's
power into account at all, but felt exultant
confidence in his myriads of foot soldiers, his
thousands of horsemen, and his eighty ele-
phants. [5]So he invaded Judea, and when he
reached Beth-zur, a fortified place about twenty
miles from Jerusalem, launched a strong attack
against it. [6]When Maccabeus and his men
learned that Lysias was besieging the strong-
holds, they and all the people begged the LORD
with lamentations and tears to send a good angel
to save Israel.[h] [7]Maccabeus himself was the first
to take up arms, and he exhorted the others to
join him in risking their lives to help their
kinsmen. Then they resolutely set out together.
[8]Suddenly, while they were still near Jerusalem,
a horseman appeared at their head, clothed in
white garments and brandishing gold weapons.[i]
[9]Then all of them together thanked God for his
mercy, and their hearts were filled with such
courage that they were ready to assault not only
men, but the most savage beasts, yes, even walls
of iron. [10]Now that the LORD had shown his
mercy toward them, they advanced in battle
order with the aid of their heavenly ally. [11]Hurl-
ing themselves upon the enemy like lions, they
laid low eleven thousand foot soldiers and six-
teen hundred horsemen, and put all the rest to
flight. [12]Most of those who got away were
wounded and stripped of their arms, while
Lysias himself escaped only by shameful flight.

Peace with the Syrians [13][j]But Lysias was not
a stupid man. He reflected on the defeat he had
suffered, and came to realize that the Hebrews
were invincible because the mighty God was
their ally. He therefore sent a message [14]persuad-
ing them to settle everything on just terms, and
promising to persuade the king also, and to
induce him to become their friend.
[15]Maccabeus, solicitous for the common good,
agreed to all that Lysias proposed; and the king,
on his part, granted in behalf of the Jews all the
written requests of Maccabeus to Lysias.

Official Letters [16]These are the terms of the
letter which Lysias wrote to the Jews: "Lysias
sends greetings to the Jewish people. [17]John and
Absalom, your envoys, have presented your
signed communication and asked about the
matters contained in it. [18]Whatever had to be
referred to the king I called to his attention, and
the things that were acceptable he has granted.
[19]If you maintain your loyalty to the govern-
ment, I will endeavor to further your interests in
the future. [20]On the details of these matters I
have authorized my representatives, as well as
your envoys, to confer with you. [21]Farewell."
The year one hundred and forty-eight,* the
twenty-fourth of Dioscorinthius.

[22]The king's letter read thus: "King Antiochus
sends greetings to his brother Lysias. [23]Now that
our father has taken his place among the gods,
we wish the subjects of our kingdom to be
undisturbed in conducting their own affairs.
[24]We understand that the Jews do not agree with
our father's policy concerning Greek customs
but prefer their own way of life. They are
petitioning us to let them retain their own
customs. [25]Since we desire that this people too
should be undisturbed, our decision is that their
temple be restored to them and that they live in
keeping with the customs of their ancestors.
[26]Accordingly, please send them messengers to
give them our assurances of friendship, so that,
when they learn of our decision, they may have
nothing to worry about but may contentedly go
about their own business."

[27]The king's letter to the people was as fol-
lows: "King Antiochus sends greetings to the Jew-
ish senate and to the rest of the Jews. [28]If you are
well, it is what we desire. We too are in good
health. [29]Menelaus has told us of your wish to
return home and attend to your own affairs.
[30]Therefore, those who return by the thirtieth of

11, 21: The year one hundred and forty-eight: 164 B.C. The reading of the name of the month and its position in the calendar are uncertain.

h Ex 23, 20. i 2 Mc 3, 24ff; 5, 2f; 10, 29f. j 13–33: 1 Mc 6, 57–61.

Xanthicus will have our assurance of full permission [31]to observe their dietary laws and other laws, just as before, and none of the Jews shall be molested in any way for faults committed through ignorance. [32]I have also sent Menelaus to reassure you. [33]Farewell." In the year one hundred and forty-eight, the fifteenth of Xanthicus.*

[34]The Romans also sent them a letter as follows: "Quintus Memmius and Titus Manius, legates of the Romans, send greetings to the Jewish people. [35]Whatever Lysias, kinsman of the king, has granted you, we also approve. [36]But the matters on which he passed judgment should be submitted to the king. As soon as you have considered them, send someone to us with your decisions so that we may present them to your advantage, for we are on our way to Antioch. [37]Make haste, then, to send us those who can inform us of your intentions. [38]Farewell." In the year one hundred and forty-eight, the fifteenth of Xanthicus.*

CHAPTER 12

Persecution Renewed [1]After these agreements were made, Lysias returned to the king, and the Jews went about their farming. [2]But some of the local governors, Timothy and Apollonius, son of Gennaeus,* as also Hieronymus and Demophon, to say nothing of Nicanor, the commander of the Cyprians, would not allow them to live in peace.

[3]Some people of Joppa also committed this outrage: they invited the Jews who lived among them, together with their wives and children, to embark on boats which they had provided. There was no hint of enmity toward them: [4]this was done by public vote of the city. When the Jews, not suspecting treachery and wishing to live on friendly terms, accepted the invitation, the people of Joppa took them out to sea and drowned at least two hundred of them.

Activity of Judas [5]As soon as Judas heard of the barbarous deed perpetrated against his countrymen, he summoned his men; [6]and after calling upon God, the just judge, he marched against the murderers of his kinsmen. In a night attack he set the harbor on fire, burnt the boats, and put to the sword those who had taken refuge there. [7]When the gates of the town were shut, he withdrew, intending to come back later and wipe out the entire population of Joppa.

[8]On hearing that the men of Jamnia planned to give like treatment to the Jews who lived among them, [9]he attacked the Jamnian populace by night, setting fire to the harbor and the fleet, so that the glow of the flames was visible as far as Jerusalem, thirty miles away.

[10] [k]When the Jews had gone about a mile from there* in the campaign against Timothy, they were attacked by Arabs numbering at least five thousand foot soldiers, and five hundred horsemen. [11]After a hard fight, Judas and his companions, with God's help, were victorious. The defeated nomads begged Judas to make friends with them and promised to supply the Jews with cattle and to help them in every other way. [12]Realizing that they could indeed be useful in many respects, Judas agreed to make peace with them. After the pledge of friendship had been exchanged, the Arabs withdrew to their tents.

[13]He also attacked a certain city called Caspin, fortified with earthworks and ramparts and inhabited by a mixed population of Gentiles. [14]Relying on the strength of their walls and their supply of provisions, the besieged treated Judas and his men with contempt, insulting them and even uttering blasphemies and profanity. [15]But Judas and his men invoked the aid of the great Sovereign of the world, who, in the day of Joshua, overthrew Jericho without battering-ram or siege machine; then they furiously stormed the ramparts. [l] [16]Capturing the city by the will of

11, 33: The date, which is the same as the date of the Romans' letter (v 38), cannot be correct. The king's letter must be connected with the peace treaty of the year 149 of the Seleucid era, i.e., 163 B.C. Perhaps the mention of the month of Xanthicus in the body of the letter (v 30) caused the date of the Romans' letter to be transferred to this one.

11, 38: The date is April 12, 164 B.C.

12, 2: Apollonius, son of Gennaeus: not the Apollonius who was the son of Menestheus (2 Mc 4, 21). Nicanor: probably distinct from the Nicanor of 2 Mc 14, 2.

12, 10: From there: not from the aforesaid Jamnia (vv 8f) or Joppa (vv 3–7), but from a place in Transjordan; vv 10–26 parallel the account given in 1 Mc 5, 9–13. 24–54 of Judas' campaign in northern Transjordan.

k 10–16: 1 Mc 5, 24–36. **l** Jos 6, 1–21.

God, they inflicted such indescribable slaughter on it that the adjacent pool, which was about a quarter of a mile wide, seemed to be filled with the blood that flowed into it.

17 [m]When they had gone on some ninety miles, they reached Charax,[n] where there were certain Jews known as Toubiani.* 18But they did not find Timothy in that region, for he had already departed from there without having done anything except to leave behind in one place a very strong garrison. 19But Dositheus and Sosipater, two of Maccabeus' captains, marched out and destroyed the force of more than ten thousand men that Timothy had left in the stronghold. 20Meanwhile, Maccabeus divided his army into cohorts, with a commander over each cohort, and went in pursuit of Timothy, who had a force of a hundred and twenty thousand foot soldiers and twenty-five hundred horsemen. 21When Timothy learned of the approach of Judas, he sent on ahead of him the women and children, as well as the baggage, to a place called Karnion, which was hard to besiege and even hard to reach because of the difficult terrain of that region. 22But when Judas' first cohort appeared, the enemy was overwhelmed with fear and terror at the manifestation of the All-seeing. Scattering in every direction, they rushed away in such headlong flight that in many cases they wounded one another, pierced by the swords of their own men. 23Judas pressed the pursuit vigorously, putting the sinners to the sword and destroying as many as thirty thousand men.

24Timothy himself fell into the hands of the men under Dositheus and Sosipater; but with great cunning, he asked them to spare his life and let him go, because he had in his power the parents and relatives of many of them, and could make these suffer. 25When he had fully confirmed his solemn pledge to restore them unharmed, they let him go for the sake of saving their brethren.

Further Successes 26Judas then marched to Karnion and the shrine of Atargatis,* where he killed twenty-five thousand people. 27 [o]After the defeat and destruction of these, he moved his army to Ephron, a fortified city inhabited by people of many nationalities. Robust young men took up their posts in defense of the walls, from which they fought valiantly; inside were large supplies of machines and missiles. 28But the Jews, invoking the Sovereign who forcibly shatters the might of his enemies, got possession of the city and slaughtered twenty-five thousand of the people in it. 29Then they set out from there and hastened on to Scythopolis,* seventy-five miles from Jerusalem. 30But when the Jews who lived there testified to the good will shown by the Scythopolitans and to their kind treatment even in times of adversity, 31Judas and his men thanked them and exhorted them to be well disposed to their race in the future also. Finally they arrived in Jerusalem, shortly before the feast of Weeks.

32After this feast called Pentecost, they lost no time in marching against Gorgias, governor of Idumea, 33who opposed them with three thousand foot soldiers and four hundred horsemen. 34In the ensuing battle, a few of the Jews were slain. 35A man called Dositheus, a powerful horseman and one of Bacenor's men,* caught hold of Gorgias, grasped his military cloak and dragged him along by main strength, intending to capture the vile wretch alive, when a Thracian horseman attacked Dositheus and cut off his arm at the shoulder. Then Gorgias fled to Marisa. 36After Esdris and his men had been fighting for a long time and were weary, Judas called upon the LORD to show himself their ally and leader in the battle. 37Then, raising a battle cry in his ancestral language, and with songs, he

12, 17: Certain Jews known as Toubiani: because they lived "in the land of Tob" (1 Mc 5, 13).

12, 26: Atargatis: a Syrian goddess, represented by the body of a fish.

12, 29: Scythopolis: the Greek name of the city of Beth-shan; cf 1 Mc 5, 52.

12, 35: One of Bacenor's men: certain ancient witnesses to the text have "one of the Toubiani"; cf v 17.

m 17–26: 1 Mc 5, 37–44. n 1 Mc 5, 13. o 27–31: 2 Mc 5, 45–54.

charged Gorgias' men when they were not expecting it and put them to flight.

Expiation for the Dead [38]Judas rallied his army and went to the city of Adullam. As the week was ending, they purified themselves according to custom and kept the sabbath there. [39]On the following day, since the task had now become urgent, Judas and his men went to gather up the bodies of the slain and bury them with their kinsmen in their ancestral tombs. [40]But under the tunic of each of the dead they found amulets sacred to the idols of Jamnia, which the law forbids the Jews to wear. So it was clear to all that this was why these men had been slain.[p] [41]They all therefore praised the ways of the LORD, the just judge who brings to light the things that are hidden. [42]*Turning to supplication, they prayed that the sinful deed might be fully blotted out. The noble Judas warned the soldiers to keep themselves free from sin, for they had seen with their own eyes what had happened because of the sin of those who had fallen. [43]He then took up a collection among all his soldiers, amounting to two thousand silver drachmas, which he sent to Jerusalem to provide for an expiatory sacrifice. In doing this he acted in a very excellent and noble way, inasmuch as he had the resurrection of the dead in view; [44]for if he were not expecting the fallen to rise again, it would have been useless and foolish to pray for them in death. [45]But if he did this with a view to the splendid reward that awaits those who had gone to rest in godliness, it was a holy and pious thought. [46]Thus he made atonement for the dead that they might be freed from this sin.

CHAPTER 13

The Syrians Invade Judea [1]In the year one hundred and forty-nine,* Judas and his men learned that Antiochus Eupator was invading Judea with a large force, [2]and that with him was Lysias, his guardian, who was in charge of the government. They led* a Greek army of one hundred and ten thousand foot soldiers, fifty-three hundred horsemen, twenty-two elephants, and three hundred chariots armed with scythes.[q]

Death of Menelaus [3]Menelaus also joined them, and with great duplicity kept urging Antiochus on, not for the welfare of his country, but in the hope of being established in office. [4]But the King of kings aroused the anger of Antiochus against the scoundrel. When the king was shown by Lysias that Menelaus was to blame for all the trouble, he ordered him to be taken to Beroea* and executed there in the customary local method.[r] [5]There is at that place a tower seventy-five feet high, full of ashes,* with a circular rim sloping down steeply on all sides toward the ashes. [6]A man guilty of sacrilege or notorious for certain other crimes is brought up there and then hurled down to destruction. [7]In such a manner was Menelaus, the transgressor of the law, fated to die; he was deprived even of decent burial. [8]It was altogether just that he who had committed so many sins against the altar with its pure fire and ashes should meet his death in ashes.

Skirmish near Modein [9]The king was advancing, his mind full of savage plans for inflicting on the Jews worse things than those they suffered in his father's time. [10]When Judas learned of this, he urged the people to call upon the LORD night and day, to help them now, if ever, [11]when they were about to be deprived of their law, their country, and their holy temple; and not to allow this nation, which had just begun to revive, to be subjected again to blasphemous Gentiles. [12]When they had all joined in doing this, and

12, 42–46: This is the earliest statement of the doctrine that prayers (v 42) and sacrifices (v 43) for the dead are beneficial. The statement is made here, however, only for the purpose of proving that Judas believed in the resurrection of the just (2 Mc 7, 9. 14. 23. 36). That is, he believed that expiation could be made for certain sins of otherwise good men—soldiers who had given their lives for God's cause. Thus, they could share in the resurrection. His belief was similar to, but not quite the same as, the Catholic doctrine of purgatory.

13, 1: In the year one hundred and forty-nine: 163–162 B.C.

13, 2: They led: the Greek means literally "Each (of them) led," but it is unlikely that the author meant the already immense numbers to be doubled; the numbers are similar to those in 1 Mc 6, 30.

13, 4: Beroea: the Greek name of Aleppo.

13, 5: Ashes: probably smoldering ashes; the tower resembles the ancient Persian fire towers.

p Dt 7, 25. q 1 Mc 6, 30. r 1 Tm 6, 15; Rv 17, 14; 19, 16.

had implored the merciful LORD continuously with weeping and fasting and prostrations for three days, Judas encouraged them and told them to stand ready. 13 After a private meeting with the elders, he decided that, before the king's army could invade Judea and take possession of the city, the Jews should march out and settle the matter with God's help. 14 Leaving the outcome to the Creator of the world, and exhorting his followers to fight nobly to death for the laws, the temple, the city, the country, and the government, he pitched his camp near Modein. 15 Giving his men the battle cry "God's Victory," he made a night attack on the king's pavilion with a picked force of the bravest young men and killed about two thousand in the camp. They also slew* the lead elephant and its rider.[s] 16 Finally they withdrew in triumph,* having filled the camp with terror and confusion. 17 Day was just breaking when this was accomplished with the help and protection of the LORD.

Treaty with Antiochus V 18 [t]The king, having had a taste of the Jews' daring, tried to take their positions by a stratagem. 19 So he marched against Beth-zur, a strong fortress of the Jews; but he was driven back, checked, and defeated. 20 Judas then sent supplies to the men inside, 21 but Rhodocus, of the Jewish army, betrayed military secrets* to the enemy. He was found out, arrested, and imprisoned. 22 The king made a second attempt by negotiating with the men of Beth-zur. After giving them his pledge and receiving theirs, he withdrew 23 and attacked Judas and his men. But he was defeated. Next he heard that Philip, who was left in charge of the government in Antioch, had rebelled. Dismayed, he parleyed with the Jews, submitted to their terms, and swore to observe their rights. Having come to this agreement, he offered a sacrifice, and honored the temple with a generous donation. 24 He approved of Maccabeus and left him as military and civil governor of the territory from Ptolemais to the region of the Gerrenes.* 25 When he came to Ptolemais, the people of that city were angered by the peace treaty; in fact they were so indignant that they wanted to annul its provisions. 26 But Lysias took the platform, defended the treaty as well as he could, and won them over by persuasion. After calming them and gaining their good will, he returned to Antioch.

That is how the king's attack and withdrawal went.

CHAPTER 14

Antagonism of Alcimus 1 [u]Three years later,* Judas and his men learned that Demetrius, son of Seleucus, had sailed into the port of Tripolis with a powerful army and a fleet, 2 and that he had occupied the country, after doing away with Antiochus and his guardian Lysias.

3 A certain Alcimus, a former high priest, who had willfully incurred defilement at the time of the revolt, realized that there was no way for him to salvage his position and regain access to the holy altar. 4 So he went to King Demetrius in the year one hundred and fifty-one and presented him with a gold crown and a palm branch, as well as some of the customary olive branches from the temple. On that occasion he kept quiet.[v] 5 But he found an opportunity to further his mad scheme when he was invited to the council by Demetrius and questioned about the dispositions and intentions of the Jews. He replied: 6 "Those Jews called Hasideans, led by Judas Maccabeus, are warmongers, who stir up sedition and keep the kingdom from enjoying peace and quiet. 7 For this reason, now that I am deprived of my ancestral dignity, that is to say, the high priesthood, I have come here— 8 first, out of my genuine concern for the king's interests, and secondly, out of consideration for my

13, 15: Slew: literally "stabbed"; the deed was done by Eleazar (1 Mc 6, 43–46).

13, 16: They withdrew in triumph: according to 1 Mc 6, 47 they fled.

13, 21: Military secrets: probably about the lack of provisions in the besieged city; cf 1 Mc 6, 49.

13, 24: The Greek text is uncertain and may be rendered: "He approved of Maccabeus, then left Hegemonides as governor of the territory . . ." Gerrenes: probably the inhabitants of Gerar, southeast of Gaza.

14, 1: Three years later: actually, Demetrius (I Soter), son of Seleucus (IV), landed at Tripolis in the year 151 of the Seleucid era (v 4), i.e., 162–161 B.C.; cf 1 Mc 7, 1–7.

s 1 Mc 6, 43–46. t 18–23: 1 Mc 6, 48–53. u 1–11: 1 Mc 7, 1–7. v 1 Mc 7, 7. 25.

own countrymen, since our entire nation is suffering great affliction from the unreasonable conduct of the people just mentioned. [9]When you have informed yourself in detail on these matters, O king, act in the interest of our country and its hard-pressed people with the same gracious consideration that you show toward all. [10]As long as Judas is around, it is impossible for the state to enjoy peace." [11]When he had said this, the other Friends who were hostile to Judas quickly added fuel to Demetrius' indignation.

Dealings with Nicanor [12] [w]The king immediately chose Nicanor, who had been in command of the elephants, and appointed him governor of Judea. He sent him off [13]with orders to put Judas to death, to disperse his followers, and to set up Alcimus as high priest of the great temple. [14]The Gentiles from Judea, who would have banished Judas,* came flocking to Nicanor, thinking that the misfortunes and calamities of the Jews would mean prosperity for themselves. [15] [x]When the Jews heard of Nicanor's coming, and that the Gentiles were rallying to him, they sprinkled themselves with earth and prayed to him who established his people forever, and who always comes to the aid of his heritage. [16]At their leader's command, they set out at once and came upon the enemy at the village of Adasa. [17]Judas' brother Simon had engaged Nicanor, but because of the sudden appearance of the enemy suffered a slight repulse. [18]However, when Nicanor heard of the valor of Judas and his men, and the great courage with which they fought for their country, he shrank from deciding the issue by bloodshed. [19]So he sent Posidonius, Theodotus and Mattathias to arrange an agreement. [20]After a long discussion of the terms, each leader communicated them to his troops; and when general agreement was expressed, they assented to the treaty. [21]A day was set on which the leaders would meet by themselves. From each side a chariot came forward and thrones were set in place. [22]Judas had posted armed men in readiness at suitable points for fear that the enemy might suddenly carry out some treacherous plan. But the conference was held in the proper way. [23]Nicanor stayed on in Jerusalem, where he did nothing out of place. He got rid of the throngs of ordinary people who gathered around him; [24]but he always kept Judas in his company, for he had a cordial affection for the man. [25]He urged him to marry and have children; so Judas married, settled down, and shared the common life.

Threats against Judas [26]When Alcimus saw their friendship for each other, he took the treaty that had been made, went to Demetrius, and said that Nicanor was plotting against the state, and that he had appointed Judas, the conspirator against the kingdom, to be his successor. [27]Stirred up by the villain's calumnies, the king became enraged. He wrote to Nicanor, stating that he was displeased with the treaty, and ordering him to send Maccabeus as a prisoner to Antioch without delay. [28]When this message reached Nicanor he was dismayed, for he hated to break his agreement with a man who had done no wrong. [29]However, there was no way of opposing the king, so he watched for an opportunity to carry out this order by a stratagem. [30]But Maccabeus noticed that Nicanor was becoming cool in his dealings with him, and acting with unaccustomed rudeness when they met; he concluded that this coldness betokened no good. So he gathered together a large number of his men, and went into hiding from Nicanor.

[31] [y]When Nicanor realized that he had been disgracefully outwitted by the man, he went to the great and holy temple, at a time when the priests were offering the customary sacrifices, and ordered them to surrender Judas. [32]As they declared under oath that they did not know where the wanted man was, [33]he raised his right hand toward the temple and swore this oath: "If you do not hand Judas over to me as prisoner, I will level this shrine of God to the ground; I will tear down the altar, and erect here a splendid temple to Dionysus." [34]With these words he went away. The priests stretched out their hands

14, 14: Who would have banished Judas: the meaning of the Greek is uncertain; some render it: "who had fled before Judas."

w 12f: 2 Mc 8, 9; 1 Mc 3, 38f. x 15–19: 1 Mc 7, 26–32. y 31–36: 1 Mc 7, 33–38.

toward heaven, calling upon the unfailing defender of our nation in these words: [35]“LORD of all, though you are in need of nothing, you have approved of a temple for your dwelling place among us.[z] [36]Therefore, O holy One, LORD of all holiness, preserve forever undefiled this house, which has been so recently purified.”

The Story of Razis* [37]A certain Razis, one of the elders of Jerusalem, was denounced to Nicanor as a patriot. A man highly regarded, he was called a father of the Jews because of his love for them. [38]In the early days of the revolt, he had been convicted of Judaism, and had risked body and life in his ardent zeal for it. [39]Nicanor, to show his detestation of the Jews, sent more than five hundred soldiers to arrest him. [40]He thought that by arresting such a man he would deal the Jews a hard blow. [41]But when these troops, on the point of capturing the tower, were forcing the outer gate and calling for fire to set the door ablaze, Razis, now caught on all sides, turned his sword against himself, [42]preferring to die nobly rather than fall into the hands of vile men and suffer outrages unworthy of his noble birth. [43]In the excitement of the struggle he failed to strike exactly. So while the troops rushed in through the doors, he gallantly ran up to the top of the wall and with manly courage threw himself down into the crowd. [44]But as they quickly drew back and left an opening, he fell into the middle of the empty space. [45]Still breathing, and inflamed with anger, he got up and ran through the crowd, with blood gushing from his frightful wounds. [46]Then, standing on a steep rock, as he lost the last of his blood, he tore out his entrails and flung them with both hands into the crowd, calling upon the LORD of life and of spirit to give these back to him again. Such was the manner of his death.[a]

CHAPTER 15

Nicanor's Blasphemy [1]When Nicanor learned that Judas and his companions were in the territory of Samaria, he decided to attack them in all safety on the day of rest. [2]The Jews who were forced to follow him pleaded, “Do not massacre them in that way, like a savage barbarian, but show respect for the day which the All-seeing has exalted with holiness above all other days.” [3]At this the thrice-sinful wretch asked if there was a ruler in heaven who prescribed the keeping of the sabbath day.[b] [4]When they replied that there was indeed such a ruler in heaven, the living LORD himself, who commanded the observance of the sabbath day, [5]he said, “I, on my part, am ruler on earth, and my orders are that you take up arms and carry out the king's business.” Nevertheless he did not succeed in carrying out his cruel plan.

Fresh Hope [6]In his utter boastfulness and arrogance Nicanor had determined to erect a public monument of victory* over Judas and his men. [7]But Maccabeus remained confident, fully convinced that he would receive help from the LORD. [8]He urged his men not to fear the enemy, but mindful of the help they had received from Heaven in the past, to expect that now, too, victory would be given them by the Almighty. [9]By encouraging them with words from the law and the prophets,* and by reminding them of the battles they had already won, he filled them with fresh enthusiasm. [10]Having stirred up their courage, he gave his orders and pointed out at the same time the perfidy of the Gentiles and their violation of oaths. [11]When he had armed each of them, not so much with the safety of shield and spear as with the encouragement of noble words, he cheered them all by relating a dream, a kind of vision, worthy of belief.

[12]What he saw was this: Onias, the former high priest,* a good and virtuous man, modest in appearance, gentle in manners, distinguished in speech, and trained from childhood in every virtuous practice, was praying with outstretched arms for the whole Jewish community.[c] [13]Then

14, 37–46: The story of Razis belongs to the “martyrology” class of literature; it is similar to the stories in 2 Mc 6, 18—7, 42.

15, 6: Public monument of victory: a heap of stones covered with the arms and armor of the fallen enemy.

15, 9: The law and the prophets: the first of the three parts of the Hebrew Scriptures, called the sacred books (1 Mc 12, 9).

15, 12: Onias, the former high priest: Onias III (2 Mc 3, 1–40). Evidently the author believed that the departed just were in some way alive even before the resurrection.

z Acts 17, 25. a 2 Mc 7, 9ff. b 1 Mc 7, 34. c 2 Mc 3, 1ff.

in the same way another man appeared, distinguished by his white hair and dignity, and with an air about him of extraordinary, majestic authority. [14]Onias then said of him, "This is God's prophet Jeremiah,* who loves his brethren and fervently prays for his people and their holy city." [15]Stretching out his right hand, Jeremiah presented a gold sword to Judas. As he gave it to him he said, [16]"Accept this holy sword as a gift from God; with it you shall crush your adversaries."

Defeat and Death of Nicanor [17]Encouraged by Judas' noble words, which had power to instill valor and stir young hearts to courage, the Jews determined not to delay, but to charge gallantly and decide the issue by hand-to-hand combat with the utmost courage, since their city and its temple with the sacred vessels were in danger. [18]They were not so much concerned about their wives and children or their brothers and kinsmen; their first and foremost fear was for the consecrated sanctuary.[d] [19]Those who remained in the city suffered a like agony, anxious as they were about the battle in the open country.

[20]Everyone now awaited the decisive moment. The enemy were already drawing near with their troops drawn up in battle line, their elephants placed in strategic positions, and their cavalry stationed on the flanks. [21]Maccabeus, contemplating the hosts before him, their elaborate equipment, and the fierceness of their elephants, stretched out his hands toward heaven and called upon the LORD who works miracles; for he knew that it is not through arms but through the LORD's decision that victory is won by those who deserve it. [22][e]He prayed to him thus: "You, O LORD, sent your angel in the days of King Hezekiah of Judea, and he slew a hundred and eighty-five thousand men of Sennacherib's army. [23]Sovereign of the heavens, send a good angel now to spread fear and dread before us. [24]By the might of your arm may those be struck down who have blasphemously come against your holy people!" With this he ended his prayer.

[25][f]Nicanor and his men advanced to the sound of trumpets and battle songs. [26]But Judas and his men met the army with supplication and prayers. [27]Fighting with their hands and praying to God with their hearts, they laid low at least thirty-five thousand, and rejoiced greatly over this manifestation of God's power. [28]When the battle was over and they were joyfully departing, they discovered Nicanor lying there in all his armor; [29]so they raised tumultuous shouts in their native tongue in praise of the divine Sovereign.

[30]Then Judas, who was ever in body and soul the chief defender of his fellow citizens, and had maintained from youth his affection for his countrymen, ordered Nicanor's head and whole right arm to be cut off and taken to Jerusalem. [31]When he arrived there, he assembled his countrymen, stationed the priests before the altar, and sent for those in the citadel.* [32]He showed them the vile Nicanor's head and the wretched blasphemer's arm that had been boastfully stretched out against the holy dwelling of the Almighty. [33]He cut out the tongue of the godless Nicanor, saying he would feed it piecemeal to the birds and would hang up the other wages of his folly opposite the temple. [34]At this, everyone looked toward heaven and praised the LORD who manifests his divine power, saying, "Blessed be he who has kept his own Place undefiled!"

[35]Judas hung up Nicanor's head on the wall of the citadel, a clear and evident proof to all of the Lord's help.[g] [36]By public vote it was unanimously decreed never to let this day pass unobserved,[h] but to celebrate it on the thirteenth day of the twelfth month, called Adar in Aramaic, the eve of Mordecai's Day.*

15, 14: Jeremiah: regarded by the postexilic Jews as one of the greatest figures in their history; cf 2 Mc 2, 1; Mt 16, 14. Who . . . prays for his people: a clear belief in the intercession of the saints.

15, 31: Those in the citadel: presumably Jewish soldiers; actually, the citadel was still in the possession of the Syrians.

15, 36: Mordecai's Day: the feast of Purim, celebrated on the fourteenth and fifteenth days of Adar (Est 9, 17–22).

d 1 Mc 4, 36. e 22f: 2 Mc 8, 19; 2 Kgs 19, 35; Is 37, 36; 1 Mc 7, 40f. f 25–36: 2 Mc 8, 39–50. g 1 Sm 31, 9f. h 1 Mc 7, 49.

VII: Epilogue

Author's Apology [37]Since Nicanor's doings ended in this way, with the city remaining in possession of the Hebrews from that time on, I will bring my own story to an end here too. [38]If it is well written and to the point, that is what I wanted; if it is poorly done and mediocre, that is the best I could do. [39]Just as it is harmful to drink wine alone or water alone, whereas mixing wine with water makes a more pleasant drink that increases delight, so a skillfully composed story delights the ears of those who read the work. Let this, then, be the end.

THE WISDOM BOOKS

The Books of Job, Psalms, Proverbs, Ecclesiastes, the Song of Songs, Wisdom, and Sirach, are all versified by the skillful use of parallelism, that is, of the balanced and symmetrical phrases peculiar to Hebrew poetry. With the exception of the Psalms, the majority of which are devotional lyrics, and the Song of Songs, a nuptial hymn, these books belong to the general class of wisdom or didactic literature, strictly so called because their chief purpose is instruction.

The wisdom literature of the Bible is the fruit of a movement among ancient oriental people to gather, preserve and express, usually in aphoristic style, the results of human experience as an aid toward understanding and solving the problems of life. In Israel especially, the movement concerned itself with such basic and vital problems as man's origin and destiny, his quest for happiness, the problem of suffering, of good and evil in human conduct, of death, and the state beyond the grave. Originating with oral tradition, these formulations found their way into the historical books of the Old Testament in the shape of proverbs, odes, chants, epigrams, and also into those psalms intended for instruction.

The developed compositions of this literature form the sapiential books. The Book of Proverbs is a collection of sentences or practical norms for moral conduct. The Book of Job is an artistic dialogue skillfully handling the problem of suffering though only from the standpoint of temporal life. Ecclesiastes examines a wide range of human experience only to conclude that all things are vanity except the fear of the Lord and observance of his commandments, and that God requites man in his own good time. Sirach gathers and presents the fruits of past experience, thus preparing for the Book of Wisdom, which sees for the just man seeking happiness the full hope of immortality (Wis 3, 4).

Those who cultivated wisdom were called sages. Men of letters, scribes, skilled in the affairs of government, and counselors to rulers, they were instructors of the people, especially of youth (Sir 51, 13-30). In times of crisis they guided the people by revaluating tradition, thus helping to preserve unity, peace and good will. The most illustrious of the sages, and the originator of wisdom literature in Israel, was Solomon. Because of his fame, some of the wisdom books of which he was not the author bear his name.

Despite numerous resemblances, sometimes exaggerated, between the sapiential literature of pagan nations and the wisdom books of the Bible, the former are often replete with vagaries and abound in polytheistic conceptions; the latter remained profoundly human, universal, fundamentally moral, and essentially religious and monotheistic. Under the influence of the law and the prophets, wisdom became piety and virture; impiety and vice were folly. The teachers of wisdom were regarded as men of God, and their books were placed beside the law and the prophets. The highest wisdom became identified with the spirit of God through which the world was created and preserved (Prv 8, 22-31), and mankind was enlightened.

The limitations of Old Testament wisdom served to crystallize the problems of human life and destiny, thus preparing for their solution through New Testament revelation. Ecclesiastes' vain search for success and happiness on earth ends when the Savior assures these things to his followers, not in this world but in the bliss of heaven. The anxiety in the Book of Job over reconciling God's justice and wisdom with the suffering of the innocent is relieved by the account of the crucified and risen Redeemer in the gospel. By fulfilling all that the Psalms foretold concerning him, Jesus makes the Psalter his prayer book and that of the church for all time. The love of God for the chosen people which underlies the Song of Songs is perfected in the union of Christ with his church. The personification of the wisdom of Proverbs, Wisdom and Sirach shines forth in resplendent reality in the Word who was with God, and who was God, and who became incarnate to dwell among us; cf Jn 1, 2. 14.

THE BOOK OF JOB

The Book of Job, named after its protagonist, is an exquisite dramatic poem which treats of the problem of the suffering of the innocent, and of retribution. The contents of the book, together with its artistic structure and elegant style, place it among the literary masterpieces of all time.

Job, an oriental chieftain, pious and upright, richly endowed in his own person and in domestic prosperity, suffers a sudden and complete reversal of fortune. He loses his property and his children; a loathsome disease afflicts his body; and sorrow oppresses his soul. Nevertheless, Job does not complain against God. When some friends visit him to condole with him, Job protests his innocence and does not understand why he is afflicted. He curses the day of his birth and longs for death to bring an end to his sufferings. The debate which ensues consists of three cycles of speeches. Job's friends insist that his plight can only be a punishment for personal wrongdoing and an invitation from God to repentance. Job rejects their inadequate explanation and calls for a response from God himself. At this point the speeches of a youth named Elihu (ch 32–37) interrupt the development.

In response to Job's plea that he be allowed to see God and hear from him the cause of his suffering, God answers, not by justifying his action before men, but by referring to his own omniscience and almighty power. Job is content with this. He recovers his attitude of humility and trust in God, which is deepened now and strengthened by his experience of suffering.

The author of the book is not known; it was composed some time between the 7th and 5th centuries; B.C. Its literary form, with speeches, prologue and epilogue disposed according to a studied plan, indicates that the purpose of the writing is didactic. The lesson is that even the just may suffer here, and their sufferings are a test of their fidelity. They shall be rewarded in the end. Man's finite mind cannot probe the depths of the divine omniscience that governs the world. The problems we encounter can be solved by a broader and deeper awareness of God's power, presence (42, 5) and wisdom.

The divisions of the Book of Job are as follows:

I. Prologue (1, 1—2, 13).
II. First Cycle of Speeches (3, 1—14, 22).
III. Second Cycle of Speeches (15, 1—21, 34).
IV. Third Cycle of Speeches (22, 1—28, 28).
V. Job's Final Summary of His Cause (29, 1—31, 37)
VI. Elihu's Speeches (32, 1—37, 24).
VII. The Lord's Speech (38, 1—42, 6).
VIII. Epilogue (42, 7-17).

I: Prologue

CHAPTER 1

Job's Wealth and Piety 1 In the land of Uz*
there was a blameless and upright man named
Job,[a] who feared God and avoided evil. 2 *Seven
sons and three daughters were born to him; 3 and
he had seven thousand sheep, three thousand
camels, five hundred yoke of oxen, five hundred
she-asses, and a great number of work animals, so
that he was greater than any of the men of the
East.* 4 His sons used to take turns giving feasts,
sending invitations to their three sisters to eat and
drink with them. 5 And when each feast had run
its course, Job would send for them and sanctify
them, rising early and offering holocausts for ev-
ery one of them. For Job said, "It may be that my
sons have sinned and blasphemed God in their
hearts." This Job did habitually.
6 [b]One day, when the sons of God* came to
present themselves before the LORD, Satan also
came among them.[c] 7 And the LORD said to Satan,
"Whence do you come?" Then Satan answered
the LORD and said,[d] "From roaming the earth and
patrolling it." 8 And the LORD said to Satan, "Have
you noticed my servant Job, and that there is no
one on earth like him, blameless and upright,
fearing God and avoiding evil?" 9 But Satan an-
swered the LORD and said, "Is it for nothing that
Job is God-fearing? 10 Have you not surrounded
him and his family and all that he has with your
protection? You have blessed the work of his
hands, and his livestock are spread over the land.
11 [e]But now put forth your hand and touch any-
thing that he has, and surely he will blaspheme
you to your face." 12 And the LORD said to Satan,
"Behold, all that he has is in your power; only do
not lay a hand upon his person." So Satan went
forth from the presence of the LORD.

The First Trial 13 And so one day, while his
sons and his daughters were eating and drinking
wine in the house of their eldest brother, 14 a
messenger came to Job and said, "The oxen
were plowing and the asses grazing beside them,
15 and the Sabeans* carried them off in a raid.
They put the herdsmen to the sword, and I alone
have escaped to tell you." 16 While he was yet
speaking, another came and said, "Lightning*
has fallen from heaven and struck the sheep and
their shepherds and consumed them; and I
alone have escaped to tell you." 17 While he was
yet speaking, another came and said, "The
Chaldeans formed three columns, seized the
camels, carried them off, and put those tending
them to the sword, and I alone have escaped to
tell you." 18 While he was yet speaking, another
came and said, "Your sons and daughters were
eating and drinking wine in the house of their
eldest brother, 19 when suddenly a great wind
came across the desert and smote the four
corners of the house. It fell upon the young
people and they are dead; and I alone have
escaped to tell you." 20 Then Job began to tear his
cloak and cut off his hair. He cast himself
prostrate upon the ground, 21 and said,

"Naked I came forth from my mother's
 womb,[f]
and naked shall I go back again.*
The LORD gave and the LORD has taken away;
 blessed be the name of the LORD!"

22 In all this Job did not sin,[g] nor did he say
anything disrespectful of God.

CHAPTER 2

The Second Trial 1 Once again the sons of
God[h] came to present themselves before the
LORD, and Satan also came with them. 2 And the
LORD said to Satan, "Whence do you come?"
And Satan answered the LORD and said, "From
roaming the earth and patrolling it." 3 And the
LORD said to Satan, "Have you noticed my
servant Job, and that there is no one on earth
like him, faultless and upright, fearing God and

1, 1: Uz: somewhere in Edom or Arabia. Job: a not uncommon name in ancient Semitic circles; its original meaning was "enemy."

1, 2f: The numbers mentioned here indicate Job's great wealth and happiness, external proof of God's friendship.

1, 3: Men of the East: that is, east of Palestine.

1, 6: Sons of God: angels. Satan: literally, "adversary."

1, 15: Sabeans: from southern Arabia.

1, 16: Lightning: literally, "God's fire."

1, 21: Go back again: to the earth; cf Gn 2, 7; Sir 40, 1.

a Jb 2, 3. b 6ff: Jb 2. 1ff. c Gn 6, 2, 4; Zec 3, 1; Lk 22, 31; Rv 12, 9. d 1 Pt 5, 8. e Jb 2, 5. f Eccl 5, 14; 1 Tm 6, 7. g Jb 2, 10; Jas 5, 11. h Jb 1, 6.

avoiding evil?[i] He still holds fast to his inno-
cence although you incited me against him to
ruin him without cause." 4 And Satan answered
the LORD and said, "Skin for skin!* All that a
man has will he give for his life. 5 [j]But now put
forth your hand and touch his bone and his flesh,
and surely he will blaspheme you to your face."
6 And the LORD said to Satan, "He is in your
power; only spare his life." 7 So Satan went forth
from the presence of the LORD and smote Job
with severe boils from the soles of his feet to the
crown of his head. 8 And he took a potsherd to
scrape himself, as he sat among the ashes. 9 Then
his wife said to him,[k] "Are you still holding to
your innocence? Curse God and die."* 10 But he
said to her, "Are even you going to speak as
senseless women do? We accept good things
from God; and should we not accept evil?"
Through all this, Job said nothing sinful.[l]

Job's Three Friends 11 Now when three of
Job's friends heard of all the misfortune that had
come upon him, they set out each one from his
own place: Eliphaz from Teman, Bildad from
Shuh, and Zophar from Naamath.* They met and
journeyed together to give him sympathy and
comfort. 12 But when, at a distance, they lifted up
their eyes and did not recognize him, they began
to weep aloud; they tore their cloaks and threw
dust upon their heads. 13 Then they sat down
upon the ground with him seven days and seven
nights, but none of them spoke a word to him; for
they saw how great was his suffering.

II: First Cycle of Speeches

CHAPTER 3

Job's Plaint 1 After this, Job opened his mouth
and cursed his day. 2 Job spoke out and said:

3 Perish the day on which I was born,[m]
the night when they said, "The child is a
boy!"
4 May that day be darkness:
let not God above call for it,
nor light shine upon it!
5 May darkness and gloom claim it,
clouds settle upon it,
the blackness of night affright it!
6 May obscurity seize that day;
let it not occur among the days of the year,
nor enter into the count of the months!
7 May that night be barren;
let no joyful outcry greet it!
8 Let them curse it who curse the sea,
the appointed disturbers of Leviathan!*
9 May the stars of its twilight be darkened;
may it look for daylight, but have none,
nor gaze on the eyes of the dawn,
10 Because it kept not shut the doors of the
womb
to shield my eyes from trouble!
11 Why did I not perish at birth,[n]
come forth from the womb and expire?
16 Or why was I not buried away like an
untimely birth,*
like babes that have never seen the light?
12 Wherefore did the knees receive me?
or why did I suck at the breasts?
13 For then I should have lain down and been
tranquil;
had I slept, I should then have been at rest
14 With kings and counselors of the earth
who built where now there are ruins
15 Or with princes who had gold
and filled their houses with silver.
17 There* the wicked cease from troubling,
there the weary are at rest.

2, 4: Skin for skin: an expression which, as applied to Job, means that he has borne his suffering patiently thus far only because he seeks to avoid greater suffering and to receive greater favors from God.

2, 9: Curse God and die: you have nothing to hope for from God and therefore nothing to live for.

2, 11: The names of Job's friends suggest Edomite origin. The Edomites (Ob 8f) and more specifically the Temanites (Jer 49, 7) enjoyed a reputation for wisdom.

3, 8: Leviathan: in Jb 40, 25, the crocodile; here the reference is probably to a mythological sea monster symbolizing primeval chaos. Cf Jb 9, 13; 26, 13; Pss 74, 13f; 104, 26; Is 27, 1.

3, 16: This verse has been placed between vv 11 and 12 where it probably stood originally. There is reason to believe that here, as well as in several other places in Job, the original order of the poetic lines was accidentally disturbed in the early transmission of the text; so in chapters 12–15; 19–21; 24–31; 34; 36; 38–42. The verse numbers given in such cases are always those of the current Hebrew text, though the arrangement may differ. The footnotes will advise the reader of the difficulties and provide him with further indications for following the progress of thought in the book.

3, 17: There: in death.

i Jb 1, 1. j Jb 1, 11. k Jb 19, 17. l Jb 1, 22; Sir 2, 4; Jas 5, 11. m Jer 20, 14. n Jb 10, 18f.

[18] There the captives are at ease together,
and hear not the voice of the slave driver.
[19] Small and great are there the same,
and the servant is free from his master.
[20] Why is light given to the toilers,
and life to the bitter in spirit?
[21] They wait for death and it comes not;
they search for it rather than for hidden treasures,
[22] Rejoice in it exultingly,
and are glad when they reach the grave:
[23] Men whose path is hidden from them,
and whom God has hemmed in!
[24] For sighing comes more readily to me than food,
and my groans well forth like water.
[25] For what I fear overtakes me,
and what I shrink from comes upon me.
[26] I have no peace nor ease;
I have no rest, for trouble comes!

CHAPTER 4

Eliphaz's First Speech [1] Then spoke Eliphaz the Temanite, who said:

[2] If someone attempts a word with you, will you mind?
For how can anyone refrain from speaking?
[3] Behold, you have instructed many,
and have made firm their feeble hands.
[4] Your words have upheld the stumbler;
you have strengthened his faltering knees.
[5] But now that it comes to you, you are impatient;
when it touches yourself, you are dismayed.
[6] Is not your piety a source of confidence,
and your integrity of life your hope?
[7] Reflect now, what innocent person perishes? [o]
Since when are the upright destroyed?
[8] As I see it, those who plow for mischief
and sow trouble, reap the same.
[9] By the breath of God they perish, [p]
and by the blast of his wrath they are consumed.
[10] Though the lion* roars, though the king of beasts cries out,
yet the teeth of the young lions are broken;
[11] The old lion perishes for lack of prey,
and the cubs of the lioness are scattered.
[12] For a word was stealthily brought to me,*
and my ear caught a whisper of it.
[13] In my thoughts during visions of the night, [q]
when deep sleep falls on men,
[14] Fear came upon me, and shuddering,
that terrified me to the bones.
[15] Then a spirit passed before me,
and the hair of my flesh stood up.
[16] It paused, but its likeness I could not discern;
a figure was before my eyes,
and I heard a still voice:
[17] "Can a man be righteous as against God? [r]
Can a mortal be blameless against his Maker?
[18] Lo, he puts no trust in his servants, [s]
and with his angels he can find fault.
[19] How much more with those that dwell in houses of clay,
whose foundation is in the dust,
who are crushed more easily than the moth!
[20] Morning or evening they may be shattered;
with no heed paid to it, they perish forever.
[21] The pegs of their tent are plucked up;
they die without knowing wisdom."

CHAPTER 5

[1] Call now! Will anyone respond to you?
To which of the holy ones will you appeal?
[2] Nay, impatience kills the fool
and indignation slays the simpleton.
[3] I have seen a fool spreading his roots, [t]
but his household suddenly decayed.
[4] His children shall be far from safety;
they shall be crushed at the gate* without a rescuer.
[5] What they have reaped the hungry shall eat up;
[or God shall take it away by blight;]

4, 10: The lion: used figuratively here for the violent, rapacious sinner who cannot prevail against God.
4, 12–21: A dramatic presentation of the idea of man's nothingness in contrast to God's greatness.
5, 4: At the gate: of the city, where justice was administered.

o Ps 37, 25. p Ps 18, 16; Is 11, 4; 2; Thes 2, 8. q Jb 33, 15. r Jb 9, 2; 15, 14ff; 25, 4; Pss 130, 3; 143, 2. s Jb 15, 15; 2 Pt 2, 4; Jude 6. t Ps 37, 35f.

and the thirsty shall swallow their
substance.
6 For mischief comes not out of the earth,
nor does trouble spring out of the ground;
7 But man himself begets mischief,
as sparks* fly upward.
8 In your place, I would appeal to God,
and to God I would state my plea.*
10 He gives rain upon the earth
and sends water upon the fields;
11 [u]He sets up on high the lowly,
and those who mourn he exalts to safety.
12 He frustrates the plans of the cunning,
so that their hands achieve no success;
13 He catches the wise in their own ruses,[v]
and the designs of the crafty are routed.
14 They meet with darkness in the daytime,
and at noonday they grope as though it
were night.
15 But the poor from the edge of the sword
and from the hand of the mighty, he saves.
16 Thus the unfortunate have hope,
and iniquity closes her mouth.
17 Happy is the man whom God reproves!
The Almighty's chastening do not reject.
18 For he wounds, but he binds up;[w]
he smites, but his hands give healing.
19 Out of six troubles he will deliver you,
and at the seventh* no evil shall touch you.
20 In famine he will deliver you from death,
and in war from the threat of the sword;
21 From the scourge of the tongue you shall be
hidden,
and shall not fear approaching ruin.
22 At destruction and want you shall laugh;
the beasts of the earth you need not dread.
23 You shall be in league with the stones of the
field,
and the wild beasts shall be at peace with
you.
24 And you shall know that your tent is secure;
taking stock of your household, you shall
miss nothing.
25 You shall know that your descendants are
many,
and your offspring as the grass of the earth.
26 You shall approach the grave in full vigor,
as a shock of grain comes in at its season.
27 Lo, this we have searched out; so it is!
This we have heard, and you should know.

CHAPTER 6

Job's First Reply 1 Then Job answered and
said:

2 Ah, could my anguish but be measured
and my calamity laid with it in the scales,
3 They would now outweigh the sands of the
sea!
Because of this I speak without restraint.
4 For the arrows of the Almighty pierce me,[x]
and my spirit drinks in their poison;
the terrors of God are arrayed against me.
5 Does the wild ass bray when he has grass?*
Does the ox low over his fodder?
6 Can a thing insipid be eaten without salt?
Is there flavor in the white of an egg?
7 I refuse to touch them;
they are loathsome food to me.
8 Oh, that I might have my request,
and that God would grant what I long for:
9 Even that God would decide to crush me,
that he would put forth his hand and cut me
off!
10 Then I should still have consolation
and could exult through unremitting pain,
because I have not transgressed the
commands of the Holy One.
11 What strength have I that I should endure,
and what is my limit that I should be
patient?
12 Have I the strength of stones,
or is my flesh of bronze?

5, 7: Sparks: in Hebrew, "sons of resheph," which the ancient versions took as the name of a bird.
5, 9: Omitted here; it is a duplicate of Jb 9, 10.
5, 19: Six . . . the seventh: proverbial expression for any large number; cf Prv 24, 16; Lk 17, 4.
6, 5f: Job would not complain if his life were as pleasant to him as fodder to a hungry animal; but his life is as disagreeable as insipid food. White of an egg: thus the obscure Hebrew has been understood in Jewish tradition; some render it "mallow juice."

u 1 Sm 2, 7f; Ps 113, 7; Lk 1, 52. v 1 Cor 3, 19. w Hos 6, 1f. x Ps 88, 17.

13 Have I no helper,[y]
and has advice deserted me?
14 A friend owes kindness to one in despair,
though he have forsaken the fear of the
Almighty.
15 My brethren are undependable as a brook,
as watercourses that run dry in the wadies;
16 Though they may be black with ice,
and with snow heaped upon them,
17 Yet once they flow, they cease to be;
in the heat, they disappear from their place.
18 Caravans turn aside from their routes;
they go into the desert and perish.
19 The caravans of Tema* search,
the companies of Sheba have hopes;
20 They are disappointed, though they were
confident;
they come there and are frustrated.
21 It is thus that you have now become for me;
you see a terrifying thing and are afraid.
22 Have I asked you to give me anything,
to offer a gift for me from your possessions,
23 Or to deliver me from the enemy,
or to redeem me from oppressors?
24 Teach me, and I will be silent;
prove to me wherein I have erred.
25 How agreeable are honest words;
yet how unconvincing is your argument!
26 Do you consider your words as proof,
but the sayings of a desperate man as wind?
27 You would even cast lots for the orphan,
and would barter away your friend!
28 Come, now, give me your attention;
surely I will not lie to your face.
29 Think it over; let there be no injustice.
Think it over; I still am right.
30 Is there insincerity on my tongue,
or cannot my taste discern falsehood?

CHAPTER 7

1 [z]Is not man's life on earth a drudgery?*
Are not his days those of a hireling?
2 He is a slave who longs for the shade,
a hireling who waits for his wages.
3 So I have been assigned months of misery,
and troubled nights have been told off for
me.
4 If in bed I say, "When shall I arise?"
then the night drags on;
I am filled with restlessness until the dawn.
5 My flesh is clothed with worms and scabs;[a]
my skin cracks and festers;
6 My days are swifter than a weaver's shuttle;
they come to an end without hope.
7 Remember that my life is like the wind;[b]
I shall not see happiness again.
8 The eye that now sees me shall no more
behold me;
as you look at me, I shall be gone.
9 As a cloud dissolves and vanishes,[c]
so he who goes down to the nether world
shall come up no more.
10 He shall not again return to his house;
his place shall know him no more.
11 My own utterance I will not restrain;
I will speak in the anguish of my spirit;
I will complain in the bitterness of my soul.
12 *Am I the sea, or a monster of the deep,
that you place a watch over me?*
Why have you set me up as an object of
attack?
or why should I be a target for you?
13 When I say, "My bed shall comfort me,
my couch shall ease my complaint,"
14 Then you affright me with dreams
and with visions terrify me,
15 So that I should prefer choking
and death rather than my pains.
16 I waste away: I cannot live forever;[d]
let me alone, for my days are but a breath.
17 What is man, that you make much of him,
or pay him any heed?
18 You observe him with each new day[e]
and try him at every moment!
19 How long will it be before you look away from
me,

6, 19: Tema: in northwest Arabia. Sheba: see note on Jb 1, 15.
7, 1: Drudgery: taken by some to refer to military service; cf also Jb 14, 14.
7, 12: An allusion in poetic imagery to primeval chaos as a monstrous ocean vanquished by God at the world's creation.
7, 12–21: Job now speaks, not to his friends, but to God.

y Jb 19, 14f. z Jb 14, 14. a Jb 2, 7f. b Pss 8, 5; 144, 3. c 9f: Jb 10. 21; 14, 10ff; 2 Sm 12, 23; 14, 14; Wis 2, 1. d Jb 14, 1ff, 5. e Ps 17, 3.

and let me alone long enough to swallow
my spittle?
20 Though I have sinned, what can I do to you,
O watcher of men?
21 Why do you not pardon my offense,
or take away my guilt?
For soon I shall lie down in the dust;
and should you seek me I shall then be
gone.

CHAPTER 8

Bildad's First Speech 1 Bildad the Shuhite spoke out and said:

2 How long will you utter such things?
The words from your mouth are like a
mighty wind!
3 Does God pervert judgment,[f]
and does the Almighty distort justice?
4 If your children have sinned against him
and he has left them in the grip of their
guilt,
5 Still, if you yourself have recourse to God
and make supplication to the Almighty,
6 Should you be blameless and upright,
surely now he will awake for you
and restore your rightful domain;
7 Your former state will be of little moment,
for in time to come you will flourish indeed.
8 If you inquire of the former generations,
and give heed to the experience of the
fathers[g]
9 (As we are but of yesterday and have no
knowledge,
because our days on earth are but a
shadow),[h]
10 Will they not teach you and tell you
and utter their words of understanding?
11 Can the papyrus grow up without mire?*
Can the reed grass flourish without water?
12 While it is yet green and uncut,
it withers quicker than any grass.
13 So is the end of everyone who forgets God,
and so shall the hope of the godless man
perish.
14 His confidence is but a gossamer thread
and his trust is a spider's web.
15 He shall rely upon his family, but it shall not
last;
he shall cling to it, but it shall not endure.
16 He is full of sap before sunrise,
and beyond his garden his shoots go forth;
17 About a heap of stones are his roots entwined;
among the rocks he takes hold.
18 Yet if one tears him from his place,
it will disown him: "I have never seen
you!"
19 There he lies rotting beside the road,
and out of the soil another sprouts.
20 Behold, God will not cast away the upright;
neither will he take the hand of the wicked.
21 Once more will he fill your mouth with
laughter,
and your lips with rejoicing.
22 They that hate you shall be clothed with
shame,
and the tent of the wicked shall be no more.

CHAPTER 9

Job's Second Reply 1 Then Job answered and said:

2 I know well that it is so;
but how can a man be justified before God?
3 Should one wish to contend with him,
he could not answer him once in a
thousand times.
4 God is wise in heart and mighty in strength;
who has withstood him and remained
unscathed?
5 He removes the mountains before they know
it;
he overturns them in his anger.
6 He shakes the earth out of its place,[i]
and the pillars beneath it tremble.
7 He commands the sun, and it rises not;
he seals up the stars.
8 He alone stretches out the heavens[j]
and treads upon the crests of the sea.
9 He made the Bear and Orion,

8, 11ff: As marsh plants need water, so man needs God. These verses are taken by some as a quotation from the teaching of the forefathers; cf v 10.

f Jb 34, 10ff. g Dt 4, 32; 32, 7. h Jb 14, 2; Pss 102, 12; 109, 23; 144, 4; Wis 2, 5. i Jb 26, 11. j Ps 104, 2; Is 40, 22.

the Pleiades and the constellations of the
south;
10 He does great things past finding out,
marvelous things beyond reckoning.
11 Should he come near me, I see him not;
should he pass by, I am not aware of him;
12 Should he seize me forcibly, who can say him
nay?
Who can say to him, "What are you doing?"
13 He is God and he does not relent;
the helpers of Rahab* bow beneath him.
14 How much less shall I give him any answer,
or choose out arguments against him!
15 Even though I were right, I could not answer
him, [k]
but should rather beg for what was due me.
16 If I appealed to him and he answered my call,
I could not believe that he would hearken
to my words;
17 With a tempest he might overwhelm me,
and multiply my wounds without cause;
18 He need not suffer me to draw breath,
but might fill me with bitter griefs.
19 If it be a question of strength, he is mighty;
and if of judgment, who will call him to
account?
20 Though I were right, my own mouth might
condemn me; [l]
were I innocent, he might put me in the
wrong.
21 Though I am innocent, I myself cannot know
it;
I despise my life.
22 It is all one! therefore I say:
Both the innocent and the wicked he
destroys. [m]
23 When the scourge slays suddenly,
he laughs at the despair of the innocent.
24 The earth is given into the hands of the
wicked;
he covers the faces of its judges.
If it is not he, who then is it?
25 My days are swifter than a runner,
they flee away; they see no happiness; [n]
26 They shoot by like skiffs of reed,
like an eagle swooping upon its prey.
27 If I say: I will forget my complaining,
I will lay aside my sadness and be of good
cheer,
28 Then I am in dread of all my pains;
I know that you* will not hold me
innocent.
29 If I must be accounted guilty,
why then should I strive in vain?
30 If I should wash myself with snow
and cleanse my hands with lye,
31 Yet you would plunge me in the ditch,
so that my garments would abhor me.
32 For he is not a man like myself, that I should
answer him,
that we should come together in judgment.
33 Would that there were an arbiter between us,
who could lay his hand upon us both
34 and withdraw his rod from me.
Would that his terrors did not frighten me;
35 that I might speak without being afraid of
him.
Since this is not the case with me,
1 *I loathe my life. [o]

CHAPTER 10

I will give myself up to complaint;
I will speak from the bitterness of my soul.
2 I will say to God: Do not put me in the wrong!
Let me know why you oppose me.
3 Is it a pleasure for you to oppress,
to spurn the work of your hands,
and smile on the plan of the wicked?
4 Have you eyes of flesh?
Do you see as man sees?
5 Are your days as the days of a mortal, [p]
and are your years as a man's lifetime,
6 That you seek for guilt in me
and search after my sins,
7 Even though you know that I am not wicked, [q]
and that none can deliver me out of your
hand?

9, 13: Rahab: cf Jb 26, 12. See note on Ps 89, 11.
9, 28–31: You: refers to God.
10, 1: I loathe my life: this is the first verse of ch 10.

k Jb 10, 15. l Jb 15, 6. m Eccl 9, 2. n Jb 7, 6. o Jb 9, 21. p Jb 36, 26. q Jb 2, 3. 9; Dt 32, 39; Wis 16, 15.

8 Your hands have formed me and fashioned
me;
will you then turn and destroy me?
9 Oh, remember that you fashioned me from
clay! [r]
Will you then bring me down to dust again?
10 Did you not pour me out as milk,
and thicken me like cheese?
11 With skin and flesh you clothed me,
with bones and sinews knit me together.
12 Grace and favor you granted me,
and your providence has preserved my
spirit.
13 Yet these things you have hidden in your
heart;
I know that they are your purpose:
14 If I should sin, you would keep a watch against
me,
and from my guilt you would not absolve
me.
15 If I should be wicked, alas for me!
if righteous, I dare not hold up my head,
filled with ignominy and sodden with
affliction!
16 Should it lift up, you hunt me like a lion:
repeatedly you show your wondrous power
against me,
17 You renew your attack upon me
and multiply your harassment of me;
in waves your troops come against me.
18 Why then did you bring me forth from the
womb? [s]
I should have died and no eye have seen
me.
19 I should be as though I had never lived;
I should have been taken from the womb to
the grave.
20 Are not the days of my life few?
Let me alone, that I may recover a little
21 Before I go whence I shall not return, [t]
to the land of darkness and of gloom,
22 The black, disordered land
where darkness is the only light.

CHAPTER 11

Zophar's First Speech 1 And Zophar the Naamathite spoke out and said:

2 Should not the man of many words be
answered,
or must the garrulous man necessarily be
right?
3 Shall your babblings keep men silent,
and shall you deride and no one give
rebuke?
4 Shall you say: "My teaching is pure,
and I am clean in your sight"?
5 But oh, that God would speak,
and open his lips against you,
6 And tell you that the secrets of wisdom
are twice as effective:
So you might learn that God
will make you answer for your guilt.
7 Can you penetrate the designs of God? [u]
Dare you vie with the perfection of the
Almighty?
8 It is higher than the heavens; what can you
do?
It is deeper than the nether world; what can
you know?
9 It is longer than the earth in measure,
and broader than the sea.
10 If he seize and imprison
or call to judgment, who then can say him
nay?
11 For he knows the worthlessness of men
and sees iniquity; will he then ignore it?
12 Will empty man then gain understanding,
and the wild jackass [v] be made docile?
13 If you set your heart aright
and stretch out your hands toward him,
14 If you remove all iniquity from your conduct,
and let not injustice dwell in your tent,
15 Surely then you may lift up your face in
innocence;
you may stand firm and unafraid.
16 For then you shall forget your misery,
or recall it like waters that have ebbed
away.

r Jb 4, 19; 33, 6; Gn 2, 7; 3, 19; Ps 146, 4. s Jb 3, 3, 11. t Jb 7, 9f; 16, 22. u Rom 11, 33. v Jb 39, 5–8.

17 Then your life shall be brighter than the
noonday;
its gloom shall become as the morning,
18 And you shall be secure, because there is
hope;
you shall look round you and lie down in
safety,[w]
19 and you shall take your rest with none to
disturb.
Many shall entreat your favor,
20 but the wicked, looking on, shall be
consumed with envy.
Escape shall be cut off from them,
they shall wait to expire.

CHAPTER 12

Job's Third Reply 1 Then Job replied and said:

2 No doubt you are the intelligent folk,
and with you wisdom shall die!
3 But I have intelligence as well as you;[x]
for who does not know such things as
these?
4 I have become the sport of my neighbors:*
"The one whom God answers when he calls
upon him,
the just, the perfect man," is a
laughingstock;[y]
5 The undisturbed esteem my downfall a
disgrace
such as awaits unsteady feet;
6 Yet the tents of robbers are prosperous,
and those who provoke God are secure.
7 But now ask the beasts to teach you,
and the birds of the air to tell you;
8 Or the reptiles on earth to instruct you,
and the fish of the sea to inform you.
9 Which of all these does not know
that the hand of God has done this?
10 In his hand is the soul of every living thing,[z]
and the life breath of all mankind.
11 Does not the ear judge words
as the mouth tastes food?[a]
12 So with old age is wisdom,[b]
and with length of days understanding.
13 With him are wisdom and might;
his are counsel and understanding.
14 If he breaks a thing down, there is no
rebuilding;[c]
if he imprisons a man, there is no release.
15 He holds back the waters and there is
drought;[d]
he sends them forth and they overwhelm
the land.
18 He loosens the bonds imposed by kings
and leaves but a waistcloth to bind the
king's own loins.*
21 He breaks down the barriers of the streams
19 and lets their never-failing waters flow
away.
16 With him are strength and prudence;
the misled and the misleaders are his.
17 He sends counselors away barefoot,
and of judges he makes fools.
20 He silences the trusted adviser,
and takes discretion from the aged.
22 The recesses of the darkness he discloses,
and brings the gloom forth to the light.
23 He makes nations great and he destroys them;
he spreads peoples abroad and he abandons
them.
24 He takes understanding from the leaders of the
land,
25 till they grope in the darkness without light;
he makes them stagger like drunken men.

CHAPTER 13

1 Lo, all this my eye has seen;
my ear has heard and perceived it.
2 What you know, I also know;[e]
I fall not short of you.
3 But I would speak with the Almighty;[f]
I wish to reason with God.
4 You are glossing over falsehoods
and offering vain remedies, every one of
you!
5 Oh, that you would be altogether silent!
This for you would be wisdom.

12, 4f: The Hebrew is somewhat obscure, but the general sense is that the wicked mock at the pious when the latter appear to be abandoned by God; cf Ps 22, 7ff; Mt 27, 39–43.

12, 18: Waistcloth . . . loins: he reduces kings to the condition of slaves, who wear only a cloth wrapped about the waist.

w Lv 26, 6; Ps 4, 9. x Jb 13, 2; 15, 9. y Jb 21, 3; 30, 1. z Acts 17, 28. a Jb 34, 3. b Jb 32, 7. c Rv 3, 7. d Gn 7, 11–24. e Jb 12, 3; 15, 9. f Jb 23, 4.

[6] Hear now the rebuke I shall utter
and listen to the reproof from my lips.
[7] Is it for God that you speak falsehood?
Is it for him that you utter deceit?
[8] Is it for him that you show partiality?
Do you play advocate on behalf of God?
[9] Will it be well when he shall search you out?
Would you impose on him as one does on men?
[10] He will openly rebuke you
if even in secret you show partiality.
[11] Surely will his majesty affright you
and the dread of him fall upon you.
[12] Your reminders are ashy maxims,
your fabrications are mounds of clay.
[13] Be silent, let me alone! that I may speak
and give vent to my feelings.
[14] I will carry my flesh between my teeth,
and take my life in my hand.*
[15] Slay me though he might,[g] I will wait for him;
I will defend my conduct before him.
[16] And this shall be my salvation,
that no impious man can come into his presence.
[17] Pay careful heed to my speech,
and give my statement a hearing.
[18] Behold, I have prepared my case,[h]
I know that I am in the right.
[19] If anyone can make a case against me,
then I shall be silent and die.
[20] These things only do not use against me,*
then from your presence I need not hide:
[21] Withdraw your hand far from me,
and let not the terror of you frighten me.
[22] Then call me, and I will respond;
or let me speak first, and answer me.
[23] What are my faults and my sins?
My misdeeds and my sins make known to me!
[24] Why do you hide your face[i]
and consider me your enemy?
[25] Will you harass a wind-driven leaf,
or pursue a withered straw?
[26] For you draw up bitter indictments against me,
and punish in me the faults of my youth.
[27] You put my feet in the stocks;
you watch all my paths
and trace out all my footsteps.

CHAPTER 14

[1] Man born of woman
is short-lived and full of trouble,[j]
[2] Like a flower that springs up and fades,[k]
swift as a shadow that does not abide.
[3] Upon such a one will you cast your eyes
so as to bring him into judgment before you,
[28] Though he wears out like a leather bottle,
like a garment that the moth has consumed?*
[4] Can a man be found who is clean of defilement?[l]
There is none, [5]however short his days.
You know the number of his months;
you have fixed the limit which he cannot pass.
[6] Look away from him and let him be,
while, like a hireling, he completes his day.
[7] For a tree there is hope,
if it be cut down, that it will sprout again
and that its tender shoots will not cease.
[8] Even though its root grow old in the earth,
and its stump die in the dust,
[9] Yet at the first whiff of water it may flourish again
and put forth branches like a young plant.
[10] But when a man dies, all vigor leaves him;[m]
when man expires, where then is he?
[11] As when the waters of a lake fail,
or a stream grows dry and parches,
[12] So men lie down and rise not again.
Till the heavens are no more, they shall not awake,
nor be roused out of their sleep.[n]

13, 14: The second half of the verse is a common biblical expression for risking one's life; cf Jgs 12, 3; 1 Sm 19, 5; 28, 21; Ps 119, 109; the first half of the verse must have a similar meaning. Job is so confident of his innocence that he is willing to risk his life by going to judgment with God.

13, 20: From here to the end of chapter 14, Job pleads his case, addressing God rather than his three friends.

14, 28: This verse has been transposed from ch 13.

g Jb 27, 5. h Jb 33, 9. i Jb 19, 11; 33, 10. j Jb 10, 20; 15, 14; Pss 39, 5f; 89, 46; Wis 2, 1. k Jb 8, 9; Pss 90:6; 102, 12; 103, 15; 109, 23; 144, 4; Is 40, 6f; Jas 1, 10. l Ps 51, 4, 7. m Jb 20, 7. n Jb 7, 10.

13 Oh, that you would hide me in the nether world
and keep me sheltered till your wrath is past;
would fix a time for me, and then remember me!
14 When a man has died, were he to live again,
all the days of my drudgery I would wait,[o]
until my relief should come.
15 You would call, and I would answer you;
you would esteem the work of your hands.
16 Surely then you would count my steps,[p]
and not keep watch for sin in me.
17 My misdeeds would be sealed up in a pouch,*
and you would cover over my guilt.
18 But as a mountain falls at last
and its rock is moved from its place,
19 As waters wear away the stones
and floods wash away the soil of the land,
so you destroy the hope of man.
20 You prevail once for all against him and he passes on;
with changed appearance you send him away.
21 If his sons are honored, he is not aware of it;
if they are in disgrace, he does not know about them.
22 Only his own flesh pains him,
and his soul grieves for him.

III: Second Cycle of Speeches

CHAPTER 15

Second Speech of Eliphaz 1 Then Eliphaz the Temanite spoke and said:

2 Should a wise man answer with airy opinions,
or puff himself up with wind?
3 Should he argue in speech which does not avail,
and in words which are to no profit?
4 You in fact do away with piety,
and you lessen devotion toward God,
5 Because your wickedness instructs your mouth,
and you choose to speak like the crafty.
6 Your own mouth condemns you, not I;[q]
your own lips refute you.
7 Are you indeed the first-born of mankind,
or were you brought forth before the hills?
8 Are you privy to the counsels of God,[r]
and do you restrict wisdom to yourself?
9 What do you know that we do not know?[s]
What intelligence have you which we have not?
10 There are gray-haired old men among us
more advanced in years than your father.
11 Are the consolations of God not enough for you,
and speech that deals gently with you?
12 Why do your notions carry you away,
and why do your eyes blink,
13 So that you turn your anger against God
and let such words escape your mouth!
14 What is a man that he should be blameless,[t]
one born of woman that he should be righteous?[u]
15 If in his holy ones God places no confidence,[v]
and if the heavens are not clean in his sight,
16 How much less so is the abominable, the corrupt:
man, who drinks in iniquity like water!
17 I will show you, if you listen to me;
what I have seen I will tell—
18 What wise men relate
and have not contradicted since the days of their fathers,
19 To whom alone the land was given,
when no foreigner moved among them.
20 The wicked man is in torment all his days,
and limited years are in store for the tyrant;
21 The sound of terrors is in his ears;
when all is prosperous, the spoiler comes upon him.
22 He despairs of escaping the darkness,
and looks ever for the sword;
23 A wanderer, food for the vultures,
he knows that his destruction is imminent.
24 By day the darkness fills him with dread;

14, 17: Sealed up in a pouch: hidden away and forgotten.

o Jb 7, 1. p Jb 31, 4; 34, 21. q Jb 9, 20. r Jb 11, 7; Wis 9, 13; Jer 23, 18; Rom 11, 34; 1 Cor 2, 11, 16. s Jb 12, 3; 13 2. t 14ff: Jb 25, 4ff. u Jb 14, 4. v Jb 4, 18f.

distress and anguish overpower him.
25 Because he has stretched out his hand against God
and bade defiance to the Almighty,
26 One shall rush sternly upon him
with the stout bosses of his shield,
like a king prepared for the charge.
27 Because he has blinded himself with his crassness,
padding his loins with fat,
28 He shall dwell in ruinous cities,
in houses that are deserted,
That are crumbling into clay
29 with no shadow to lengthen over the ground.
He shall not be rich, and his possessions shall not endure;
31 for vain shall be his bartering.
30 A flame shall wither him up in his early growth,
and with the wind his blossoms shall disappear.
32 His stalk shall wither before its time,
and his branches shall be green no more.
33 He shall be like a vine that sheds its grapes unripened,
and like an olive tree casting off its bloom.
34 For the breed of the impious shall be sterile,[w]
and fire shall consume the tents of extortioners.
35 They conceive malice and bring forth emptiness;[x]
they give birth to failure.*

CHAPTER 16

Job's Fourth Reply 1 Then Job answered and said:

2 I have heard this sort of thing many times.[y]
Wearisome comforters are you all!
3 Is there no end to windy words?
Or what sickness have you that you speak on?
4 I also could talk as you do,
were you in my place.
I could declaim over you,
or wag my head at you;
5 I could strengthen you with talk,
or shake my head with silent lips.
6 If I speak, this pain I have will not be checked;
if I leave off, it will not depart from me.
7 But now that I am exhausted and stunned,
all my company has closed in on me.
8 As a witness there rises up
my traducer, speaking openly against me;
9 I am the prey his wrath assails,
he gnashes his teeth against me.
My enemies lord it over me;
10 their mouths are agape to bite me.
They smite me on the cheek insultingly;
they are all enlisted against me.
11 God has given me over to the impious;
into the clutches of the wicked he has cast me.
12 I was in peace, but he dislodged me;
he seized me by the neck and dashed me to pieces.
He has set me up for a target;
13 his arrows strike me from all directions,
He pierces my sides without mercy,
he pours out my gall upon the ground.
14 He pierces me with thrust upon thrust;
he attacks me like a warrior.
15 I have fastened sackcloth over my skin,
and have laid my brow in the dust.
16 My face is inflamed with weeping
and there is darkness over my eyes,
17 Although my hands are free from violence,
and my prayer is sincere.
18 O earth, cover not my blood,
nor let my outcry come to rest!*
19 Even now, behold, my witness* is in heaven,
and my spokesman is on high.
20 My friends it is who wrong me;
before God my eyes drop tears,
21 That he may do justice for a mortal in his presence

15, 35: They give birth to failure: their wicked plans yield nothing but futile results. Cf Ps 7, 15; Is 59, 4.

16, 18: As the blood of those who were unjustly slain cries to heaven for vengeance (Gn 4, 10; Ez 24, 6–9), so Job's sufferings demand redress.

16, 19: Witness: refers either to God or, more probably, to Job's prayer.

w Wis 3, 11, 18. x Ps 7, 15; Is 59, 4. y Jb 12, 3.

and decide between a man and his
neighbor.
22 For my years are numbered now,
and I am on a journey from which I shall
not return.

CHAPTER 17

1 My spirit is broken, my lamp of life
extinguished;
my burial is at hand.
2 I am indeed mocked,
and, as their provocation mounts, my eyes
grow dim.
3 Grant me one to offer you a pledge on my
behalf:*
who is there that will give surety for me?
4 You darken their minds to knowledge;
therefore they do not understand.
5 My lot is described as evil,
6 and I am made a byword of the people; [z]
their object lesson I have become.
7 My eye has grown blind with anguish,
and all my frame is shrunken to a shadow.
8 Upright men are astonished at this,
and the innocent aroused against the
wicked.
9 Yet the righteous shall hold to his way,
and he who has clean hands increase in
strength.
10 But turn now, and come on again;
for I shall not find a wise man among you!
11 My days are passed away, my plans are at an
end,
the cherished purposes of my heart.
12 Such men change the night into day;
where there is darkness they talk of
approaching light.
13 If I look for the nether world as my dwelling,
if I spread my couch in the darkness,
14 If I must call corruption "my father,"
and the maggot "my mother" and "my
sister,"
15 Where then is my hope,
and my prosperity, who shall see?
16 Will they descend with me into the nether
world?
Shall we go down together into the dust?

CHAPTER 18

Bildad's Second Speech 1 Then Bildad the
Shuhite replied and said:

2 When will you put an end to words?
Reflect, and then we can have discussion.
3 Why are we accounted like the beasts,
their equals in your sight?
4 You who tear yourself in your anger,*
shall the earth be neglected on your account
[or the rock be moved out of its place]?
5 Truly, the light of the wicked is extinguished;
no flame brightens his hearth.
6 The light is darkened in his tent;
in spite of him, his lamp goes out. [a]
7 His vigorous steps are hemmed in,
and his own counsel casts him down.
8 For he rushes headlong into a net,
and he wanders into a pitfall.
9 A trap seizes him by the heel,
and a snare lays hold of him.
10 A noose for him is hid on the ground,
and the toils for him on the way.
11 On every side terrors affright him; [b]
they harry him at each step.
12 Disaster is ready at his side,
13 the first-born of death* consumes his limbs.
14 Fiery destruction lodges in his tent,
and marches him off to the king of terrors.*
He is plucked from the security of his tent;
15 over his abode brimstone is scattered.
16 Below, his roots dry up,
and above, his branches wither.
17 His memory perishes from the land, [c]
and he has no name on the earth.
18 He is driven from light into darkness,
and banished out of the world.
19 He has neither son nor grandson among his
people,
nor any survivor where once he dwelt.

17, 3: Addressed to God; v 10 to Job's friends.

18, 4: Job himself is portrayed as having the heedless rage of wild beasts, despite which God does not forsake the usual course of Divine Providence.

18, 13: First-born of death: that is, disease, plague.

18, 14: The king of terrors: of the nether world, death; however, the Hebrew is obscure.

z Jb 30, 9. a Jb 21, 17; Prv 13, 9; 24, 20. b Jb 15, 20-24; 27, 20. c Ps 34, 17; Prv 2, 22; 10, 7.

[20] They who come after shall be appalled at his fate;
they who went before are struck with horror.
[21] So is it then with the dwelling of the impious man,
and such is the place of him who knows not God!

CHAPTER 19

Job's Fifth Reply [1] Then Job answered and said:

[2] How long will you vex my soul,
grind me down with words?
[3] These ten times you have reviled me,
have assailed me without shame!
[4] Be it indeed that I am at fault
and that my fault remains with me.
[5] Even so, if you would vaunt yourselves against me
and cast up to me my reproach,
[6] Know then that God has dealt unfairly with me,
and compassed me round with his net.
[7] If I cry out "Injustice!" I am not heard. [d]
I cry for help, but there is no redress.
[8] He has barred my way and I cannot pass;
he has veiled my path in darkness;
[9] He has stripped me of my glory,
and taken the diadem from my brow.
[10] He breaks me down on every side, and I am gone;
my hope he has uprooted like a tree.
[11] His wrath he has kindled against me;
he counts me among his enemies. [e]
[12] His troops advance as one man;
they build up their road to attack me,
and they encamp around my tent.
[13] My brethren have withdrawn from me, [f]
and my friends are wholly estranged.
[14] My kinsfolk and companions neglect me,
and my guests have forgotten me.
[15] Even my handmaids treat me as a stranger;
I am an alien in their sight.
[16] I call my servant, but he gives no answer,
though in my speech I plead with him.
[17] My breath is abhorred by my wife; [g]
I am loathsome to the men of my family.
[18] The young children, too, despise me;
when I appear, they speak against me.
[19] All my intimate friends hold me in horror;
those whom I loved have turned against me! [h]
[20] My bones cleave to my skin,
and I have escaped with my flesh between my teeth.*
[21] Pity me, pity me, O you my friends,
for the hand of God has struck me!
[22] Why do you hound me as though you were divine,*
and insatiably prey upon me?
[23] Oh, would that my words were written down! [i]
Would that they were inscribed in a record:*
[24] That with an iron chisel and with lead
they were cut in the rock forever!
[25] But as for me, I know that my Vindicator lives,*
and that he will at last stand forth upon the dust; [j]
[27] Whom I myself shall see:
my own eyes, not another's, shall behold him,
[26] And from my flesh I shall see God;
my inmost being is consumed with longing.
[28] But you who say, "How shall we persecute him,
seeing that the root of the matter is found in him?"

19, 20: With my flesh between my teeth: meaning perhaps that Job has been reduced to such an extremity that he scarcely has thin lips over his teeth. But the current Hebrew text of this line is probably corrupt.

19, 22: Divine: possessing God's attributes of judgment and authority to punish.

19, 23f: Job regards what he is about to say as so important that he wishes it recorded in a permanent manner.

19, 25. 27: The meaning of this passage is obscure because the original text has been poorly preserved and the ancient versions do not agree among themselves. It is certain that Job expresses his belief in a future vindication by God (called here in the Hebrew "Goel"), but the time and manner of this vindication are undefined. In the Vulgate Job is made to indicate a belief in physical resurrection after death, but the Hebrew and the other ancient versions are less specific.

d Jb 30, 20. e Jb 13, 24; 33, 10. f Jb 6, 13. g Jb 2, 9. h Sir 6, 8. i Jb 31, 35. j 25ff: Phil 3, 20; Ti 2, 13.

29 Be afraid of the sword for yourselves,
for these crimes deserve the sword;
that you may know that there is a judgment.

CHAPTER 20

Zophar's Second Speech 1 Then Zophar the Naamathite spoke and said:

3 A rebuke which puts me to shame I hear,
2 and because of this I am disturbed.
So now my thoughts provide me with an answer,
and from my understanding a spirit gives me a reply.
4 Do you not know this from olden time,
since man was placed upon the earth,
5 That the triumph of the wicked is short
and the joy of the impious but for a moment? [k]
6 Though his pride mount up to the heavens
and his head reach to the clouds,
7 Yet he perishes forever like the fuel of his fire,
and the onlookers say, "Where is he?" [l]
8 Like a dream he takes flight and is not found again;
he fades away like a vision of the night.
9 The eye which saw him does so no more;
nor shall his dwelling again behold him.
11 Though his frame is full of youthful vigor,
this shall lie with him in the dust.
12 Though wickedness is sweet in his mouth,
and he hides it under his tongue,
13 Though he retains it and will not let it go
but keeps it still within his mouth,
14 Yet in his stomach the food shall turn;
it shall be venom of asps inside him.
15 The riches he swallowed he shall disgorge;
God shall compel his belly to disown them.
16 The poison of asps he shall drink in;
the viper's fangs shall slay him.
17 He shall see no streams of oil,*
no torrents of honey or milk.
18 Restoring his gains, he shall not enjoy them;
though his wealth increases, he shall not rejoice.
19 Because he has oppressed the poor,
and stolen a patrimony he had not built up,
21 Therefore his prosperity shall not endure,
10 and his hands shall yield up his riches. [m]
20 Though he has known no quiet in his greed,
his treasures shall not save him. [n]
22 [o] When he abounds to overflowing, he shall be brought into straits,
and nought shall be left of his goods.
23 God shall send against him the fury of his wrath
and rain down his missiles of war upon him.
24 Should he escape the iron weapon,
the bow of bronze shall pierce him through;
25 The dart shall come out of his back;
terrors shall fall upon him.
26 Complete darkness is in store for him;
the fire which shall consume him needs not to be fanned. [p]
27 The heavens shall reveal his guilt,
and the earth shall rise up against him.
28 The flood shall sweep away his house
with the waters that run off in the day of God's anger.
29 This is the portion of a wicked man,
and the heritage appointed him by God. [q]

CHAPTER 21

Job's Sixth Reply 1 Then Job said in reply:

2 At least listen to my words, [r]
and let that be the consolation you offer.
3 Bear with me while I speak;
and after I have spoken, you can mock!
4 Is my complaint toward man?
And why should I not be impatient?
5 Look at me and be astonished,
put your hands over your mouths.
6 When I think of it, I am dismayed,
and horror takes hold on my flesh.

7 Why do the wicked survive,
grow old, become mighty in power? [s]

20, 17: Oil: olive oil, one of the main agricultural products of Palestine, a land proverbially rich in honey and milk.

k Jb 21, 13; Ps 37, 35f. l Jb 14, 10; Ps 37, 10, 36. m Jb 27, 14. n Eccl 5, 9; Lk 12, 20. o Jb 15, 20–35. p Dt 32, 22. q Jb 27, 13. r Jb 13, 17. s Jb 12, 6; Pss 37, 35; 73, 3; Eccl 8, 14; Jer 12, 1f; Mal 3, 14f.

8 Their progeny is secure in their sight;
they see before them their kinsfolk and their offspring.
9 Their homes are safe and without fear,
nor is the scourge of God upon them.
10 Their bulls gender without fail;
their cows calve and do not miscarry.
11 These folk have infants numerous as lambs,
and their children dance.
12 They sing to the timbrel and harp,
and make merry to the sound of the flute.
13 They live out their days in prosperity,
and tranquilly go down to the nether world.[t]
14 Yet they say to God, "Depart from us,[u]
for we have no wish to learn your ways!
15 What is the Almighty that we should serve him?
And what gain shall we have if we pray to him?"[v]
16 If their happiness is not in their own hands
and if the counsel of the wicked is repulsive to God,[w]
17 How often is the lamp of the wicked put out?
How often does destruction come upon them,
the portion he allots in his anger?
18 Let them be like straw before the wind,
and like chaff which the storm snatches away!
19 May God not store up the man's misery for his children;
let him requite the man himself so that he feels it,
20 Let his own eyes see the calamity,
and the wrath of the Almighty let him drink!
21 For what interest has he in his family after him,
when the number of his months is finished?
23 One dies in his full vigor,
wholly at ease and content;
24 His figure is full and nourished,
and his bones are rich in marrow.
25 Another dies in bitterness of soul,
having never tasted happiness.
26 Alike they lie down in the dust,
and worms cover them both.

27 Behold, I know your thoughts,
and the arguments you rehearse against me.
28 For you say, "Where is the house of the magnate,
and where the dwelling place of the wicked?"
29 Have you not asked the wayfarers
and do you not recognize their monuments?
30 Nay, the evil man is spared calamity when it comes;
32 and on the day he is carried to the grave
31 Who will charge him with his conduct to his face,
and for what he has done who will repay him?
33 Sweet to him are the clods of the valley,
and over him the funeral mound keeps watch,
While all the line of mankind follows him,
and the countless others who have gone before.
34 How then can you offer me vain comfort,
while in your answers perfidy remains?

IV: Third Cycle of Speeches

CHAPTER 22

Eliphaz's Third Speech 1 Then Eliphaz the Temanite answered and said:

2 Can a man be profitable to God?[x]
Though to himself a wise man be profitable!
22 Can anyone teach God knowledge,
seeing that he judges those on high?*
3 Is it of advantage to the Almighty if you are just?[y]
Or is it a gain to him if you make your ways perfect?
4 Is it because of your piety that he reproves you—

22, 22: Those on high: the angels. (This verse has been transposed from ch 21.)

t Jb 34, 20. u Jb 22, 17. v Mal 3, 14. w Jb 22, 18. x Jb 9, 2. y Jb 35, 7.

that he enters with you into judgment?
5 Is not your wickedness manifold?
Are not your iniquities endless?

6 You have unjustly kept your kinsmen's goods in pawn,*
left them stripped naked of their clothing.[z]
7 To the thirsty you have given no water to drink,
and from the hungry you have withheld bread;
8 As if the land belonged to the man of might,
and only the privileged were to dwell in it.
9 You have sent widows away empty-handed,
and the resources of orphans you have destroyed.[a]
10 Therefore snares are round about you,[b]
and a sudden terror causes you dismay,
11 Or darkness, in which you cannot see;
a deluge of waters covers you.

12 Does not God, in the heights of the heavens,[c]
behold the stars, high though they are?
13 Yet you say, "What does God know?[d]
Can he judge through the thick darkness?
14 Clouds hide him so that he cannot see;
he walks upon the vault of the heavens!"

15 Do you indeed keep to the ancient way
trodden by worthless men,
16 Who were snatched away before their time;
whose foundations a flood swept away?
17 These men said to God, "Depart from us!"
and, "What can the Almighty do to us?"
18 [Yet he had filled their houses with good things![e]
But far be from me the mind of the impious!]*
19 The just look on and are gladdened,
and the innocent deride them:[f]
20 "Truly these have been destroyed where they stood,
and such as were left, fire has consumed!"

21 Come to terms with him to be at peace.
In this shall good come to you:
22 Receive instruction from his mouth,
and lay up his words in your heart.
23 If you return to the Almighty, you will be restored;
if you put iniquity far from your tent,
24 And treat raw gold like dust,
and the fine gold of Ophir* as pebbles from the brook,
25 Then the Almighty himself shall be your gold
and your sparkling silver.

26 For then you shall delight in the Almighty
and you shall lift up your face toward God.
27 You shall entreat him and he will hear you,[g]
and your vows you shall fulfill.
28 When you make a decision, it shall succeed for you,
and upon your ways the light shall shine.
29 For he brings down the pride of the haughty,
but the man of humble mien he saves.[h]
30 God delivers him who is innocent;
you shall be delivered through cleanness of hands.[i]

CHAPTER 23

Job's Seventh Reply 1 Again Job answered and said:

2 Though I know my complaint is bitter,
his hand is heavy upon me in my groanings.
3 Oh, that today I might find him,
that I might come to his judgment seat!
4 I would set out my cause before him,
and fill my mouth with arguments;
5 I would learn the words with which he would answer,
and understand what he would reply to me.
6 Even should he contend against me with his great power,
yet, would that he himself might heed me!
7 There the upright man might reason with him,
and I should once and for all preserve my rights.

22, 6ff: This criticism of Job by Eliphaz is altogether untrue, but it is made to dramatize the latter's argument that God always acts justly when he causes someone to suffer. Verse 8 is misplaced.
22, 18: A gloss, taken partly from Jb 21, 16.
22, 24: Ophir: cf note to Ps 45, 10.

z Jb 24, 3; Dt 24, 6, 17; Ez 18, 12, 16. a Dt 24, 17; 27, 19. b Jb 18, 8ff. c Jb 11, 8. d 13f: Pss 10, 11; 73, 11; 94, 7; Is 29, 15; Ez 8, 12: 9, 9. e Jb 21, 16. f Ps 107, 42. g Jb 33, 26. h Ps 138, 6; Prv 29, 23; Mt 23, 12; Lk 1, 52; Jas 4, 10; 1 Pt 5, 5. i Jb 17.9; Ps 18, 21, 25.

8 But if I go to the east, he is not there;
or to the west, I cannot perceive him;
9 Where the north enfolds him, I behold him not;
by the south he is veiled, and I see him not.
10 Yet he knows my way;
if he proved me, I should come forth as gold.[j]
11 My foot has always walked in his steps;
his way I have kept and have not turned aside.
12 From the commands of his lips I have not departed;
the words of his mouth I have treasured in my heart.
13 But he has decided, and who can say him nay?
What he desires, that he does.[k]
14 For he will carry out what is appointed for me;
and many such things may yet be in his mind.
15 Therefore am I dismayed before him;
when I take thought, I fear him.
16 Indeed God has made my courage fail;
the Almighty has put me in dismay.
17 Yes, would that I had vanished in darkness,
and that thick gloom were before me to conceal me.

CHAPTER 24

1 Why are not times set by the Almighty,
and why do his friends not see his days?*
2 The wicked remove landmarks;
they steal away herds and pasture them.
3 The asses of orphans they drive away;
they take the widow's ox for a pledge.
4 They force the needy off the road;
all the poor of the land are driven into hiding.
5 Like wild asses in the desert, these go forth
to their task of seeking food;
The steppe provides food for the young among them;
6 they harvest at night in the untilled land.
7 They pass the night naked, without clothing,
for they have no covering against the cold;
8 They are drenched with the rain of the mountains,
and for want of shelter they cling to the rock.
11 Between the rows they press out the oil;
they glean in the vineyard of the wicked.
They tread the wine presses, yet suffer thirst,
10 and famished are those who carry the sheaves.
12 From the dust the dying groan,
and the souls of the wounded cry out
[yet God does not treat it as unseemly].
13 There are those who are rebels against the light;[l]
they know not its ways;
they abide not in its paths.
14 When there is no light the murderer rises,
to kill the poor and needy.
15 The eye of the adulterer watches for the twilight;[m]
he says, "No eye will see me."
In the night the thief roams about,
and he puts a mask over his face;
16 in the dark he breaks into houses.
By day they shut themselves in;
none of them know the light,
17 for daylight they regard as darkness.*

* * *

18 Their portion in the land is accursed,
20 and wickedness is splintered like wood.
19.21. . . . .
22 To him who rises without assurance of his life

24, 1: Why does not God favor his friends by the speedy punishment of his enemies? (The text and order of verses in this chapter are not certain; note the omission of v 9 which duplicates words of vv 2–4.)

24, 17: The asterisks which follow this verse mark off a passage (vv 18–24) which cannot be ascribed to Job with certainty. Vv 17–24 are in general poorly preserved; and much of vv 18–21 has not been translated because these verses are obscure. St. Jerome renders them as follows: (18) "He is light upon the face of the water, cursed be his portion on the earth; let him not walk by the way of vineyards. (19) Let him pass from the snow waters to excessive heat, and his sin even to hell. (20) Let mercy forget him; may worms be his sweetness; let him be remembered no more, but be broken in pieces as an unfruitful tree. (21) For he has fed the barren that bears not, and to the widow he has done no good."

j Ps 66, 10; Prv 17, 3; Mal 3, 3; 1 Pt 1, 7. k Jb 42, 2; Pss 115, 3; 135, 6. l Jn 3, 19f. m Prv 7, 9f.

23 he gives safety and support.
He sustains the mighty by his strength,
and his eyes are on their ways.
24 They are exalted for a while, and then they are gone;
they are laid low and, like all others, are gathered up;
like ears of grain they shrivel.

* * *

25 If this be not so, who will confute me,
and reduce my argument to nought?

CHAPTER 25

Bildad's Third Speech 1 Then Bildad the Shuhite answered and said:

2 Dominion and awesomeness are his
who brings about harmony in his heavens.
3 Is there any numbering of his troops?*
Yet to which of them does not his light extend?
4 How can a man be just in God's sight, [n]
or how can any woman's child be innocent?
5 Behold, even the moon is not bright
and the stars are not clear in his sight.
6 How much less man, who is but a maggot,
the son of man, who is only a worm? [o]

CHAPTER 26

Job's Reply 1 Then Job spoke again and said:*

2 What help you give to the powerless,
what strength to the feeble arm!
3 How you counsel, as though he had no wisdom;
how profuse is the advice you offer!
4 With whose help have you uttered those words,
and whose is the breath that comes forth from you? [p]
5 The shades* beneath writhe in terror, [q]
the waters, and their inhabitants.
6 Naked before him is the nether world,*
and Abaddon has no covering. [r]
7 He stretches out the North* over empty space,
and suspends the earth over nothing at all;
8 He binds up the waters in his clouds,
yet the cloud is not rent by their weight;
9 He holds back the appearance of the full moon
by spreading his clouds before it.

10 He has marked out a circle* on the surface of the deep [s]
as the boundary of light and darkness.
11 The pillars of the heavens tremble [t]
and are stunned at his thunderous rebuke;
12 By his power he stirs up the sea,
and by his might he crushes Rahab;*
13 With his angry breath he scatters the water,
and he hurls the lightning against it relentlessly;
His hand pierces the fugitive dragon*
as from his hand it strives to flee. [u]
14 Lo, these are but the outlines of his ways,
and how faint is the word we hear!

CHAPTER 27

Job's Reply

1 1 I will teach you the manner of God's dealings,
and the way of the Almighty I will not conceal.
2 As God lives,* who withholds my deserts, [v]
the Almighty, who has made bitter my soul,
3 So long as I still have life in me
and the breath of God is in my nostrils,

25, 3: His troops: the heavenly hosts, the stars or the angels. His light: compare the wording in Jb 24, 13: those who are rebels against the light.

26, 1–14: Probably to be read as Job's reply to Bildad's short speech. Some, however, would make it the reply to Zophar (Jb 27, 13–21); it would thus lead up to the poem of ch 28.

26, 5: Shades: the dead in Sheol, the nether world; cf Pss 6, 6; 88, 11.

26, 6: Nether world: cf note to Ps 6, 6. Abaddon: Hebrew for "(place of) destruction," a synonym for nether world; cf Jb 28, 22; Rv 9, 11.

26, 7: The North: used here as a synonym for the firmament, the heavens; cf Is 14, 13.

26, 10: Circle: the horizon of the ocean which serves as the boundary for the activity of light and darkness.

26, 12: Rahab: cf Jb 9, 13; see note on Ps 89, 11.

26, 13: The fugitive dragon: the same term occurs in Is 27, 1 in apposition to Leviathan; see note on Jb 3, 8. This is actually Jb 27, 22.

27, 2–12: This is probably to be read as Job's reply to Zophar's speech of Jb 27, 13–21. In the current Hebrew text the heading for this chapter (Jb 27, 1, here omitted) is identical with Jb 29, 1; we should expect rather such a heading as is Jb 21, 1; 23, 1; 26, 1.

n Jb 4, 17ff; 9, 2. o Jb 4, 19; 15, 16. p Gn 2, 7. q Prv 9, 18. r Ps 139, 7–12. s Jb 38, 8–11; Prv 8, 29. t Jb 9, 6. u Is 27, 1. v Jb 34, 5.

4 My lips shall not speak falsehood,
nor my tongue utter deceit!
5 Far be it from me to account you right;
till I die I will not renounce my innocence.[w]
6 My justice I maintain and I will not relinquish it;
my heart does not reproach me for any of my days.
7 Let my enemy be as the wicked
and my adversary as the unjust!
8 For what can the impious man expect when he is cut off,
when God requires his life?
9 Will God then attend to his cry
when calamity comes upon him?
10 Will he then delight in the Almighty
and call upon him constantly?
12 Behold, you yourselves have all seen it;
why then do you spend yourselves in idle words!

* * *

13 *This is the portion of a wicked man from God,
the inheritance an oppressor receives from the Almighty:[x]
14 Though his children be many, the sword is their destiny.
His offspring shall not be filled with bread.
15 His survivors, when they die, shall have no burial,
and their widows shall not be mourned.
16 Though he heap up silver like dust
and store away mounds of clothing,
17 What he has stored the just man shall wear,
and the innocent shall divide the silver.
18 He builds his house as of cobwebs,
or like a booth put up by the vinekeeper.
19 He lies down a rich man, one last time;
he opens his eyes and nothing remains to him.[y]
20 Terrors rush upon him by day;
at night the tempest carries him off.
21 The storm wind seizes him and he disappears;
it sweeps him out of his place.*

* * *

CHAPTER 28

The Inaccessibility of Wisdom

1 There is indeed a mine for silver,*
and a place for gold which men refine.
2 Iron is taken from the earth,
and copper is melted out of stone.
4 . . . .
5 The earth, though out of it comes forth bread,
is in fiery upheaval underneath.
6 Its stones are the source of sapphires,
and there is gold in its dust.

12 But whence can wisdom be obtained,
and where is the place of understanding?[z]
13 Man knows nothing to equal it,
nor is it to be had in the land of the living.
15 Solid gold cannot purchase it,
nor can its price be paid with silver.[a]
16 It cannot be bought with gold of Ophir,*
with the precious onyx or the sapphire.
17 Gold or crystal cannot equal it,
nor can golden vessels reach its worth.
18 Neither coral nor jasper should be thought of;
it surpasses pearls and 19 Arabian topaz.

20 Whence, then, comes wisdom,
and where is the place of understanding?
21 It is hid from the eyes of any beast;
from the birds of the air it is concealed.
7 The path to it no bird of prey knows,
nor has the hawk's eye seen that path.

27, 13–21: This is probably to be read as Zophar's third speech. The asterisks are present to indicate it is not likely that the sacred writer intended these words to be ascribed to Job.

27, 21: The Hebrew has two more verses: v 22 (read above with Jb 26, 13); and v 23, which is a variant form of v 21.

28, 1–28: Note the changed order of verses; v 4 is uncertain. This chapter contains a beautifully vivid description of that Wisdom which is beyond the attainment of creatures; known only to God, it is reflected in the order and majesty of his creation. Man, however, can, in a way, participate in this Wisdom by fearing the Lord and avoiding evil. Scholars are not agreed regarding the authorship of this poem, though it is altogether worthy of the author of the Book of Job. Used here as a counterpoise to ch 3 at the beginning of the dialogue, it may have been first conceived as an independent poem.

28, 16: Ophir: cf note to Ps 45, 10.

w Jb 2, 3, 9; 13, 15; 33, 9. x Jb 20, 4–29. y Pss 49, 18; 76, 6. z Eccl 7, 24f; Bar 3, 14f. 29–33. a Prv 3, 14; 8, 10f, 19; 16, 16; Wis 7, 7–11.

[8] The proud beasts have not trodden it,
nor has the lion gone that way.
[14] The abyss declares, "It is not in me";
and the sea says, "I have it not."
[22] Abaddon* and Death say,
"Only by rumor have we heard of it."

[23] God knows the way to it; [b]
it is he who is familiar with its place. [c]
[24] For he beholds the ends of the earth
and sees all that is under the heavens.
[3] He has set a boundary for the darkness;
to the farthest confines he penetrates.
[9] He sets his hand to the flinty rock,
and overturns the mountains at their foundations.
[10] He splits channels in the rocks;
his eyes behold all that is precious.
[11] He probes the wellsprings of the streams,
and brings hidden things to light.
[25] He has weighed out the wind,
and fixed the scope of the waters;
[26] When he made rules for the rain
and a path for the thunderbolts, [d]
[27] Then he saw wisdom and appraised it,
gave it its setting, knew it through and through.
[28] And to man he said:
Behold, the fear of the LORD is wisdom;
and avoiding evil is understanding. [e]

V: Job's Final Summary of His Cause

CHAPTER 29

[1] Job took up his theme anew and said:

[2] Oh, that I were as in the months past!
as in the days when God watched over me, [f]
[3] While he kept his lamp shining above my head,
and by his light I walked through darkness;
[4] As I was in my flourishing days,
when God sheltered my tent;
[5] When the Almighty was yet with me,
and my children were round about me;
[6] When my footsteps were bathed in milk,
and the rock flowed with streams of oil;*
[7] When I went forth to the gate of the city
and set up my seat in the square—

[8] Then the young men saw me and withdrew,
while the elders rose up and stood;
[9] The chief men refrained from speaking
and covered their mouths with their hands; [g]
[10] The voice of the princes was silenced,
and their tongues stuck to the roofs of their mouths.

[21] For me they listened and waited;
they were silent for my counsel.
[22] Once I spoke, they said no more,
but received my pronouncement drop by drop.
[23] They waited for me as for the rain;
they drank in my words like the spring rains.

[24] When I smiled on them they were reassured;
[25] mourners took comfort from my cheerful glance.
I chose out their way and presided;
I took a king's place in the armed forces.
[11] Whoever heard of me blessed me;
those who saw me commended me.

[12] For I rescued the poor who cried out for help,
the orphans, and the unassisted;
[13] The blessing of those in extremity came upon me,
and the heart of the widow I made joyful.
[14] I wore my honesty like a garment;
justice was my robe and my turban.
[15] I was eyes to the blind,
and feet to the lame was I;
[16] I was a father to the needy;
the rights of the stranger I studied,
[17] And I broke the jaws of the wicked man;
from his teeth I forced the prey.

28, 22: Abaddon: cf note to Jb 26, 6.
29, 6: Hyperbole to express abundance; see note on Jb 20, 17.

b 23–27: Prv 8, 22–31. c Prv 2, 6; Sir 1, 1; Jas 1, 5. d Jb 38, 25; Prv 3, 20. e Ps 111, 10; Prv 1, 7; 9, 10; Sir 1, 16. f Jb 1, 10. g Wis 8, 10ff.

18 Then I said: "In my own nest I shall grow old;
I shall multiply years like the phoenix.*
19 My root is spread out to the waters;
the dew rests by night on my branches.
20 My glory is fresh within me,
and my bow is renewed in my hand!"

CHAPTER 30

1 But now they hold me in derision
who are younger in years than I; [h]
Whose fathers I should have disdained
to rank with the dogs of my flock.
2 Such strength as they had, to me meant nought;
they were utterly destitute.

3 In want and hunger was their lot, [i]
they who fled to the parched wastelands:
4 They plucked saltwort* and shrubs;
the roots of the broom plant were their food.
5 They were banished from among men,
with an outcry like that against a thief—
6 To dwell on the slopes of the wadies,
in caves of sand and stone;
7 Among the bushes they raised their raucous cry;
under the nettles they huddled together.
8 Irresponsible, nameless men,
they were driven out of the land.

9 Yet now they sing of me in mockery;
I am become a byword among them. [j]
10 They abhor me, they stand aloof from me,
they do not hesitate to spit in my face!
11 Indeed, they have loosed their bonds; they lord it over me,
and have thrown off restraint in my presence.

12 To subvert my paths they rise up;
they build their approaches for my ruin.
13 To destroy me, they attack with none to stay them;
14 as through a wide breach they advance.
Amid the uproar they come on in waves;
15 over me rolls the terror.
My dignity is borne off on the wind,
and my welfare vanishes like a cloud.
18 One with great power lays hold of my clothing;*
by the collar of my tunic he seizes me:
19 He has cast me into the mire;
I am leveled with the dust and ashes.

20 I cry to you, but you do not answer me; [k]
you stand off and look at me,
21 Then you turn upon me without mercy
and with your strong hand you buffet me.
22 You raise me up and drive me before the wind;
I am tossed about by the tempest.
23 Indeed I know you will turn me back in death
to the destined place of everyone alive. [l]
24 Yet should not a hand be held out
to help a wretched man in his calamity?
25 Or have I not wept for the hardships of others;
was not my soul grieved for the destitute? [m]
26 Yet when I looked for good, then evil came;
when I expected light, then came darkness.

16 My soul ebbs away from me;
27 days of affliction have overtaken me.
17 My frame takes no rest by night;
my inward parts seethe and will not be stilled.
28 I go about in gloom, without the sun;
I rise up in public to voice my grief.

29 I have become the brother of jackals,
companion to the ostrich.
30 My blackened skin falls away from me;
the heat scorches my very frame.
31 My harp is turned to mourning,
and my reed pipe to sounds of weeping.

CHAPTER 31

2 But what is man's lot from God above,
his inheritance from the Almighty on high?

29, 18: Phoenix: a legendary bird which, after several centuries of life, consumed itself in fire, then rose from its ashes in youthful freshness. This meaning, originally intended in the Greek, later came to mean "palm tree." Some render the Hebrew as "sand."

30, 4: Saltwort: found in salt marshes and very sour to the taste; eaten by the extremely poor as a cooked vegetable. Broom plant: the juniper or brushwood; cf Ps 120, 4; a figure of bitterness and poverty, because of its bitter-tasting roots which are practically inedible.

30, 18–23: Job here refers to God's stern treatment of him.

h Jb 12, 4; 19, 18. i 3–8: Jb 24, 5f. j Jb 17, 6. k Jb 19, 7. l Heb 9, 27. m Jb 29, 12–16.

3 Is it not calamity for the unrighteous,
and woe for evildoers?
4 Does he not see my ways,
and number all my steps? [n]
6 Let God weigh me in the scales of justice;
thus will he know my innocence! [o]

5 If I have walked in falsehood*
and my foot has hastened to deceit;
7 If my steps have turned out of the way,
and my heart has followed my eyes,
or any stain clings to my hands,
8 Then may I sow, but another eat of it,
or may my planting be rooted up!

38 If my land has cried out against me
till its very furrows complained;
39 If I have eaten its produce without payment
and grieved the hearts of its tenants;
40 Then let the thistles grow instead of wheat
and noxious weeds instead of barley!

1 If I have made an agreement with my eyes*
and entertained any thoughts against a maiden;
9 If my heart has been enticed toward a woman,
and I have lain in wait at my neighbor's door;
10 Then may my wife grind for another,
and may others cohabit with her!
11 For that would be heinous,
a crime to be condemned; [p]
12 A fire that should burn down to the abyss
till it consumed all my possessions to the roots. [q]
13 Had I refused justice to my manservant
or to my maid, when they had a claim against me,
14 What then should I do when God rose up;
what could I answer when he demanded an account?
15 Did not he who made me in the womb make him?
Did not the same One fashion us before our birth?
16 If I have denied anything to the poor, [r]
or allowed the eyes of the widow to languish
17 While I ate my portion alone,
with no share in it for the fatherless,
18 Though like a father God has reared me from my youth,
guiding me even from my mother's womb—
19 If I have seen a wanderer without clothing,
or a poor man without covering,
20 Whose limbs have not blessed me
when warmed with the fleece of my sheep;
21 If I have raised my hand against the innocent
because I saw that I had supporters at the gate—*
22 Then may my arm fall from the shoulder,
my forearm be broken at the elbow!
23 For the dread of God will be upon me,
and his majesty will overpower me.
24 Had I put my trust in gold
or called fine gold my security;
25 Or had I rejoiced that my wealth was great,
or that my hand had acquired abundance—
26 Had I looked upon the sun as it shone, [s]
or the moon in the splendor of its progress,*
27 And had my heart been secretly enticed
to waft them a kiss with my hand;
28 This too would be a crime for condemnation,
for I should have denied God above. [t]

29 Had I rejoiced at the destruction of my enemy
or exulted when evil fell upon him, [u]
30 Even though I had not suffered my mouth to sin
by uttering a curse against his life—
31 Had not the men of my tent exclaimed,
"Who has not been fed with his meat!"*
32 Because no stranger lodged in the street,

31, 5–34: Job's final protestation of his innocence.
31, 1. 9: Note the gradation: avoidance of sinful glances and thoughts against a maiden; desire for another's wife.
31, 21: Gate: cf notes on Jb 5, 4; Ru 4, 1.
31, 26ff: Job never sinned by worshiping the sun or the moon; waft them a kiss: an act of idolatrous worship.
31, 31: The members of his household will testify to his hospitality.

n Jb 14, 16; 34, 21; Ps 139, 3; Prv 5, 21. o Jb 23, 10. p Ex 20, 14; Lv 20, 10; Dt 22, 22. q Sir 9, 8f. r 16–23: Jb 29, 12–16. s 26f: Dt 4, 19. t Dt 17, 2–7. u Prv 24, 17.

but I opened my door to wayfarers—
33 Had I, out of human weakness, hidden my sins
and buried my guilt in my bosom*
34 Because I feared the noisy multitude
and the scorn of the tribes terrified me—
then I should have remained silent, and not come out of doors!

35 Oh, that I had one to hear my case,
and that my accuser would write out his indictment! [v]
36 Surely, I should wear it on my shoulder*
or put it on me like a diadem;
37 Of all my steps I should give him an account;
like a prince* I should present myself before him.

This is my final plea; let the Almighty answer me!

The words of Job are ended.

VI: Elihu's Speeches

CHAPTER 32

1 Then the three men ceased to answer Job,
because he was righteous [w] in his own eyes.
2 [x] But the anger of Elihu,* son of Barachel the
Buzite, of the family of Ram, was kindled. He
was angry with Job for considering himself
rather than God to be in the right. 3 [y] He was
angry also with the three friends because they
had not found a good answer and had not
condemned Job. 4 But since these men were
older than he, Elihu bided his time before
addressing Job. 5 When, however, Elihu saw that
there was no reply in the mouths of the three
men, his wrath was inflamed. 6 So Elihu, son of
Barachel the Buzite, spoke out and said:

I am young and you are very old;
therefore I held back and was afraid
to declare to you my knowledge.
7 Days should speak, I thought,
and many years teach wisdom! [z]
8 But it is a spirit in man, [a]
the breath of the Almighty, that gives him understanding.
9 It is not those of many days who are wise,
nor the aged who understand the right.
10 Therefore I say, hearken to me;
let me too set forth my knowledge!

11 Behold, I have waited for your discourses,
and have given ear to your arguments.
12 Yes, I followed you attentively
as you searched out what to say;
And behold, there is none who has convicted Job,
not one of you who could refute his statements.
13 Yet do not say, "We have met wisdom.*
God may vanquish him but not man!"
14 For had he addressed his words to me,
I should not then have answered him as you have done.

15 They are dismayed, they make no more reply;
words fail them.
16 Must I wait? Now that they speak no more,
and have ceased to make reply,
17 I too will speak my part;
I also will show my knowledge!
18 For I am full of matters to utter;
the spirit within me compels me.
19 Like a new wineskin with wine under pressure,
my bosom is ready to burst.
20 Let me speak and obtain relief;
let me open my lips, and make reply.

31, 33f: Job's present protest is made, not in spite of hidden sins which he had been unwilling to disclose, but out of genuine innocence.

31, 36: On my shoulder: i.e., boldly, proudly.

31, 37: Like a prince: not as a frightened criminal. Final plea: literally, "tau," the last letter of the Hebrew alphabet; in the current Hebrew text this line is in v 35, while the following one ends v 40.

32, 2: Elihu means "My God is he." This speaker was from Buz, which, according to Jer 25, 23, was near Tema and Dedan. A young man, he impetuously and impatiently upbraids Job for his boldness toward God, and the three friends for not successfully answering Job. He undertakes to defend God's absolute justice and to explain more clearly why there is suffering. While fundamentally his position is the same as that of the three friends, he does locate more definitely, though not perfectly, the place of suffering in the divine plan.

32, 13: Met wisdom: in Job's arguments.

v Jb 19, 23; 23, 3-7. w Jb 33, 9. x Jb 13, 18; 27, 6; 34, 5; 35, 2. y Jb 22, 5. z Jb 12, 12. a Jb 33, 4.

21 I would not be partial to anyone,
nor give flattering titles to any.
22 For I know nought of flattery;
if I did, my Maker would soon take me away.

CHAPTER 33

1 Therefore, O Job, hear my discourse,
and hearken to all my words.
2 Behold, now I open my mouth;
my tongue and my voice form words.
3 I will state directly what is in my mind,
my lips shall utter knowledge sincerely;
4 For the spirit of God has made me,
the breath of the Almighty keeps me alive. [b]

5 If you are able, refute me;
draw up your arguments and stand forth.
6 Behold I, like yourself, have been taken
from the same clay by God. [c]
7 Therefore no fear of me should dismay you,
nor should my presence weigh heavily upon you.

8 But you have said in my hearing,
as I listened to the sound of your words:
9 "I am clean and without transgression;
I am innocent; there is no guilt in me. [d]
10 Yet he invents pretexts against me
and reckons me as his enemy. [e]
11 He puts my feet in the stocks;
he watches all my ways!"[f]

12 In this you are not just, let me tell you;
for God is greater than man.
13 Why, then, do you make complaint against him
that he gives no account of his doings? [g]
14 For God does speak, perhaps once,
or even twice, though one perceive it not.

15 In a dream, in a vision of the night,
[when deep sleep falls upon men]
as they slumber in their beds,
16 It is then he opens the ears of men
and as a warning to them, terrifies them;
17 By turning man from evil
and keeping pride away from him,
18 He withholds his soul from the pit
and his life from passing to the grave.

19 Or a man is chastened on his bed by pain
and unceasing suffering within his frame,
20 So that to his appetite food becomes repulsive,
and his senses reject the choicest nourishment. [h]
21 His flesh is wasted so that it cannot be seen,
and his bones, once invisible, appear;
22 His soul draws near to the pit,
his life to the place of the dead.

23 If then there be for him an angel,*
one out of a thousand, a mediator,
To show him what is right for him
and bring the man back to justice,
24 He will take pity on him and say,
"Deliver him from going down to the pit;
I have found him a ransom."

25 Then his flesh shall become soft as a boy's;
he shall be again as in the days of his youth.
26 He shall pray and God will favor him;
he shall see God's face with rejoicing. [i]
27 He shall sing before men and say,
"I sinned and did wrong,
yet he has not punished me accordingly.
28 He delivered my soul from passing to the pit,
and I behold the light of life."

29 Lo, all these things God does,
twice, or thrice, for a man,
30 Bringing back his soul from the pit
to the light, in the land of the living.
31 Be attentive, O Job; listen to me!
Be silent and I will speak.
32 If you have aught to say, then answer me.
Speak out! I should like to see you justified.
33 If not, then do you listen to me;
be silent while I teach you wisdom.

CHAPTER 34

1 Then Elihu continued and said:
2 Hear, O wise men, my discourse,
and you that have knowledge, hear me!

33, 23: Angel: one of the thousands who stand between God and man as intermediaries, reminding man of his duties and giving God an account of their fulfillment.

b Jb 32, 8. c Jb 31, 15. d Jb 10, 7; 13, 18; 27, 5f; 29, 14; 32, 1; 34, 5. e Jb 13, 24; 19, 11. f Jb 13, 27; 31, 4. g Jb 31, 35. h Jb 6, 7. i Jb 22, 26–29.

[3] For the ear tests words,
as the taste does food.[j]
[4] Let us discern for ourselves what is right;
let us learn between us what is good.
[5] For Job has said, "I am innocent,
but God has taken what is my due.[k]
[6] Notwithstanding my right I am set at nought;
in my wound the arrow rankles, sinless
though I am."[l]

[7] What man is like Job?
He drinks in blasphemies like water,
[8] Keeps company with evildoers
and goes along with wicked men,
[9] When he says, "It profits a man nought
that he is pleasing to God."[m]

[10] Therefore, men of understanding, hearken to
me:
far be it from God to do wickedness;
far from the Almighty to do wrong![n]
[11] Rather, he requites men for their conduct,
and brings home to a man his way of life.[o]
[12] Surely, God cannot act wickedly,
the Almighty cannot violate justice.[p]
[13] Who gave him government over the earth,
or who else set all the land in its place?[q]
[14] If he were to take back his spirit to himself,
withdraw to himself his breath,
[15] All flesh would perish together,
and man would return to the dust.[r]

[16] Now, do you, O Job, hear this!
Hearken to the words I speak!
[17] Can an enemy of justice indeed be in control,
or will you condemn the supreme Just One,
[18] Who says to a king, "You are worthless!"
and to nobles, "You are wicked!"
[19] Who neither favors the person of princes,
nor respects the rich more than the poor?
For they are all the work of his hands;[s]
20 in a moment they die, even at midnight.[t]
He brings on nobles, and takes them away,
removing the powerful without lifting a
hand;

[21] For his eyes are upon the ways of man,
and he beholds all his steps.

[22] There is no darkness so dense
that evildoers can hide in it.
[25] Therefore he discerns their works;
he turns at night and crushes them.
[23] For he forewarns no man of his time
to come before God in judgment.
[24] Without a trial he breaks the mighty,[u]
and sets others in their stead,
[27] Because they turned away from him
and heeded none of his ways,
[28] But caused the cries of the poor to reach him,
so that he heard the plea of the afflicted.

[29] If he remains tranquil, who then can
condemn?*
If he hides his face, who then can behold
him?
30
. . . .
[31] When anyone says to God,
"I was misguided; I will offend no more.
[32] Teach me wherein I have sinned;
if I have done wrong, I will do so no more,"
[33] Would you then say that God must punish,
since you reject what he is doing?
It is you who must choose, not I;
speak, therefore, what you know.

[34] Men of understanding will say to me,
every wise man who hears my views:
[35] "Job speaks without intelligence,
and his words are without sense."[v]
[36] Let Job be tried to the limit,
since his answers are those of the impious;
[37] For he is adding rebellion to his sin
by brushing off our arguments
and addressing many words to God.

CHAPTER 35

[1] Then Elihu proceeded and said:

[2] Do you think it right to say,

34, 26. 29f: The extant Hebrew text of these verses contains several added phrases which either represent duplication or are very obscure.

j Jb 12, 11. k Jb 33, 9f. l Jb 9, 20. m Jb 9, 22f. 30f; 21, 15; 35, 3. n Jb 36, 23. o Ps 62, 13; Prv 24, 12; Mt 16, 27; Rom 2, 6; 2 Cor 5, 10; Rv 22, 12. p Jb 8, 3. q Jb 38, 4–7. r Jb 10, 9. s Dt 10, 17; 2 Chr 19, 7; Wis 6, 7; Acts 10, 34; Rom 2, 11; Eph 6, 9; Col 3, 25; 1 Pt 1, 17. t Jb 21, 3. u Ps 2, 9. v Jb 35, 16; 38, 2; 42, 3.

"I am just rather than God"?[w]
3 To say, "What does it profit me;
what advantage have I more than if I had sinned?"[x]
4 I have words for a reply to you*
and your three companions as well.
5 Look up to the skies and behold;
regard the heavens high above you.
6 If you sin, what injury do you do to God?
Even if your offenses are many, how do you hurt him?
7 If you are righteous, what do you give him,
or what does he receive from your hand?[y]
8 Your wickedness can affect only a man like yourself;
and your justice only a fellow human being.

9 In great oppression men cry out;
they call for help because of the power of the mighty,
10 Saying, "Where is God, my Maker,
who has given visions in the night,
11 Taught us rather than the beasts of the earth,
and made us wise rather than the birds of the heavens?"
12 Though thus they cry out, he answers not
against the pride of the wicked.
13 But it is idle to say God does not hear
or that the Almighty does not take notice.
14 Even though you say that you see him not,*
the case is before him; with trembling should you wait upon him.
15 But now that you have done otherwise, God's anger punishes,
nor does he show concern that a man will die.
16 Yet Job to no purpose opens his mouth,
and without knowledge multiplies words.[z]

CHAPTER 36

1 Elihu proceeded further and said:

2 Wait yet a little and I will instruct you,
for there are still words to be said on God's behalf.
3 I will bring my knowledge from afar,
and to my Maker I will accord the right.
4 For indeed, my theme cannot fail me:
the one perfect in knowledge I set before you.

5 Behold, God rejects the obstinate in heart;*
he preserves not the life of the wicked,
6 He withholds not the just man's rights,
but grants vindication to the oppressed[a]
7 And with kings upon thrones
he sets them, exalted forever.[b]

8 Or if they are bound with fetters
and held fast by bonds of affliction,
9 Then he makes known to them what they have done
and their sins of boastful pride.
10 He opens their ears to correction
and exhorts them to turn back from evil.

11 If they obey and serve him,
they spend their days in prosperity,
their years in happiness.
12 But if they obey not, they perish;
they die for lack of knowledge.*

13 The impious in heart lay up anger for themselves;
they cry not for help when he enchains them;
14 Therefore they expire in youth,
and perish among the reprobate.*
15 But he saves the unfortunate through their affliction,
and instructs them through distress.
16-20 . . . .*

35, 4: A reply to you: Elihu refers to Job's statement that the innocent suffer as much as the wicked, and especially to Eliphaz's words in Jb 22, 2f.

35, 14f: The text here is uncertain. It seems to indicate that Job should have realized God's indifference is only apparent, and that, because he has not done so, God will punish him.

36, 5–21: Perhaps this section should be read between vv 6 and 7 of chapter 34.

36, 12: Knowledge: practical wisdom in serving God, which they lack because they refused it when warned (cf v 10).

36, 14: Reprobate: cf Dt 23, 18f.

36, 16–20: The Hebrew text here is in disorder. The Vulgate has: "(16) Therefore he will give you most ample salvation from the narrow mouth which has no foundations beneath it; but the repose of your table will be filled with fatness. (17) Your case has been judged as that of the wicked; case and judgment you will receive. (18) Let no wrath, then, overcome you, that you oppress anyone; nor let numerous gifts mislead you. (19) Lay down your greatness without tribulation, and all who are mighty in strength. (20) Do not draw out the night, that people may go in place of them."

w Jb 32, 2. x Jb 34, 9. y Jb 22, 3; 41, 2; Lk 17, 10; Rom 11, 35. z Jb 34, 35; 38, 2; 42, 3. a Ps 72, 4. 12f. b Ps 113, 7f.

21 Take heed, turn not to evil;
for you have preferred carousal to affliction.

22 Behold, God is sublime in his power.
What teacher is there like him?
23 Who prescribes for him his conduct,
or who can say, "You have done wrong"? [c]
24 Remember, you should extol his work,
which men have praised in song.
25 All men contemplate it;
man beholds it from afar.

26 Lo, God is great beyond our knowledge;
the number of his years is past searching out.
27 He holds in check the waterdrops
that filter in rain through his mists,
28 Till the skies run with them
and the showers rain down on mankind.
31 For by these* he nourishes the nations,
and gives them food in abundance.
29.30 Lo! he spreads the clouds in layers
as the carpeting of his tent.*
32 In his hands he holds the lightning,
and he commands it to strike the mark.
33 His thunder speaks for him
and incites the fury of the storm.

CHAPTER 37

1 At this my heart trembles
and leaps out of its place,
2 To hear his angry voice*
as it rumbles forth from his mouth!
3 Everywhere under the heavens he sends it,
with his lightning, to the ends of the earth.
4 Again his voice roars—
the majestic sound of his thunder.
5 He does great things beyond our knowing;
wonders past our searching out.
6 For he says to the snow, "Fall to the earth";
likewise to his heavy, drenching rain.
7 He shuts up all mankind indoors;
8 the wild beasts take to cover
and remain quietly in their dens.

9 Out of its chamber* comes forth the tempest;
from the north winds, the cold.
10 With his breath God brings the frost,
and the broad waters become congealed. [d]
11 With hail, also, the clouds are laden,
as they scatter their flashes of light.
12 He it is who changes their rounds,* according to his plans,
in their task upon the surface of the earth,
13 whether for punishment or mercy, as he commands.

14 Hearken to this, O Job!
Stand and consider the wondrous works of God!
15 Do you know how God lays his commands upon them,
and makes the light shine forth from his clouds?
16 Do you know how the clouds are banked,
the wondrous work of him who is perfect in knowledge?
17 You, whom the streams of water fail
when a calm from the south comes over the land,
18 Do you spread out with him the firmament of the skies,
hard as a brazen mirror?*

19 Teach us then what we shall say to him;
we cannot, for the darkness, make our plea.
20 Will he be told about it when I speak,
or when a man says he is being destroyed?*
21 Nay, rather, it is as the light which men see not
while it is obscured among the clouds,
till the wind comes by and sweeps the clouds away.*

36, 31: These: refers to the showers of v 28, if the verse order indicated above is correct.

36, 29f: Because of the uncertainty of the text, no translation of these verses has received unanimous approval from exegetes.

37, 2: Voice: the thunder.

37, 9: Chamber: where it was popularly believed storms were kept enclosed.

37, 12: Their rounds: of rain (Jb 36, 27), of clouds (Jb 36, 29f), of lightning and thunder (Jb 36, 32f), of snow (Jb 37, 6), of winds (Jb 37, 9).

37, 18: The firmament . . . mirror: the ancients thought of the sky as a ceiling above which were the "upper waters" (cf Gn 1, 6f; 7, 11); when this ceiling became as hard as metal, the usual rain failed to fall on the earth (cf Lv 26, 19; Dt 28, 23).

37, 20: Will an angel bring this to God's attention?

37, 21: Even though God seems not to know our circumstances, he does know them, just as surely as the sun shines, unseen by man, behind the clouds.

c Jb 34, 10; Is 40, 13. d Ps 148, 17.

22 From the North the splendor comes,*
surrounding God's awesome majesty!
23 The Almighty! we cannot discover him,
pre-eminent in power and judgment;
his great justice owes no one an accounting.
24 Therefore men revere him,
though none can see him, however wise
their hearts.

VII: The Lord's Speech

CHAPTER 38

1 Then the LORD* addressed Job out of the
storm and said:

2 Who is this that obscures divine plans
with words of ignorance?
3 Gird up your loins* now, like a man;
I will question you, and you tell me the
answers! [e]
4 Where were you when I founded the earth?
Tell me, if you have understanding.
5 Who determined its size; do you know?
Who stretched out the measuring line for it?
6 Into what were its pedestals sunk,
and who laid the cornerstone,
7 While the morning stars sang in chorus
and all the sons of God* shouted for joy?

8 And who shut within doors the sea,
when it burst forth from the womb; [f]
9 When I made the clouds its garment
and thick darkness its swaddling bands?
10 When I set limits for it
and fastened the bar of its door,
11 And said: Thus far shall you come but no
farther,
and here shall your proud waves be stilled!

12 Have you ever in your lifetime commanded
the morning
and shown the dawn its place
13 For taking hold of the ends of the earth,
till the wicked are shaken from its surface?
14 The earth is changed as is clay by the seal,
and dyed as though it were a garment;
15 But from the wicked the light is withheld,
and the arm of pride is shattered.

16 Have you entered into the sources of the sea,
or walked about in the depths of the abyss?
17 Have the gates of death been shown to you,
or have you seen the gates of darkness?
18 Have you comprehended the breadth of the
earth?
Tell me, if you know all:
19 Which is the way to the dwelling place of
light,
and where is the abode of darkness,
20 That you may take them to their boundaries
and set them on their homeward paths?
21 You know, because you were born before
them,
and the number of your years is great!*
22 Have you entered the storehouse of the snow,
and seen the treasury of the hail
23 Which I have reserved for times of stress,
for the days of war* and of battle?
24 Which way to the parting of the winds,
whence the east wind spreads over the
earth?
25 Who has laid out a channel for the downpour
and for the thunderstorm a path
26 To bring rain to no man's land,
the unpeopled wilderness;
27 To enrich the waste and desolate ground
till the desert blooms with verdure?
28 Has the rain a father;
or who has begotten the drops of dew?
29 Out of whose womb comes the ice,
and who gives the hoarfrost its birth in the
skies,

37, 22: Now the storms of doubt and ignorance disappear, and from the North, used here as a symbol for God's mysterious abode, comes the splendor of the manifestation of God's majestic ways.

38, 1: Now the Lord enters the debate and addresses two discourses (38—39 and 40—41) to Job, in which he speaks of his wisdom and power, which are altogether beyond the capacity of Job, who therefore should never dare to demand a reason for the divine actions. Out of the storm: frequently the background of the appearances of the Lord in the Old Testament; cf Pss 18; 50; Na 1, 3; Hb 3.

38, 3: Gird up your loins: prepare for combat—figuratively, be ready to defend yourself in debate.

38, 7: Sons of God: angels; cf Jb 1, 6.

38, 21: Divine irony.

38, 22f: Hail . . . of war: thus God used a hailstorm to rout Joshua's foes in the battle of Gibeon; cf Jos 10, 11; Sir 46, 5.

e Jb 40, 1. f Gn 1, 9.

30 When the waters lie covered as though with stone
that holds captive the surface of the deep?
31 Have you fitted a curb to the Pleiades,*
or loosened the bonds of Orion?
32 Can you bring forth the Mazzaroth in their season,
or guide the Bear with its train?
33 Do you know the ordinances of the heavens;
can you put into effect their plan on the earth?
34 Can you raise your voice among the clouds,
or veil yourself in the waters of the storm?*
35 Can you send forth the lightnings on their way,
or will they say to you, "Here we are"?*
37 Who counts the clouds in his wisdom?
Or who tilts the water jars of heaven
38 So that the dust of earth is fused into a mass
and its clods made solid?
39 Do you hunt the prey for the lioness
or appease the hunger of her cubs,
40 While they crouch in their dens,
or lie in wait in the thicket?
36 Who puts wisdom in the heart,
and gives the cock its understanding?*
41 Who provides nourishment for the ravens
when their young ones cry out to God,[g]
and they rove abroad without food?

CHAPTER 39

1 Do you know about the birth of the mountain goats,
watch for the birth pangs of the hinds,
2 Number the months that they must fulfill,
and fix the time of their bringing forth?
3 They crouch down and bear their young;
they deliver their progeny in the desert.
4 When their offspring thrive and grow,
they leave and do not return.
5 Who has given the wild ass his freedom,
and who has loosed him from bonds?
6 I have made the wilderness his home
and the salt flats his dwelling.
7 He scoffs at the uproar of the city,
and hears no shouts of a driver.
8 He ranges the mountains for pasture,
and seeks out every patch of green.

9 Will the wild ox consent to serve you,
and to pass the nights by your manger?
10 Will a rope bind him in the furrow,
and will he harrow the valleys after you?
11 Will you trust him for his great strength
and leave to him the fruits of your toil?
12 Can you rely on him to thresh out your grain
and gather in the yield of your threshing floor?
13 The wings of the ostrich* beat idly;
her plumage is lacking in pinions.
14 When she leaves her eggs on the ground*
and deposits them in the sand,
15 Unmindful that a foot may crush them,
that the wild beasts may trample them,
16 She cruelly disowns her young
and ruthlessly makes nought of her brood;
17 For God has withheld wisdom from her
and has given her no share in understanding.
18 Yet in her swiftness of foot
she makes sport of the horse and his rider.

19 Do you give the horse his strength,*
and endow his neck with splendor?
20 Do you make the steed to quiver
while his thunderous snorting spreads terror?
21 He jubilantly paws the plain
and rushes in his might against the weapons.
22 He laughs at fear and cannot be deterred;
he turns not back from the sword.
23 Around him rattles the quiver,

38, 31f: Pleiades . . . Orion . . . Bear: cf Jb 9, 9. Mazzaroth: it is uncertain what astronomical group is meant by this Hebrew word; perhaps a southern constellation (cf Jb 9, 9).
38, 34: Veil yourself . . . storm: wrap yourself in a cloud, as God comes in a theophany; cf Ps 18, 12.
38, 35: Here we are: at your service.
38, 36: Understanding: the reflection of divine Wisdom discernible in the created animal instincts of the cock.
39, 13: The wings of the ostrich cannot raise her from the ground, but they help her to run swiftly.
39, 14ff: It was popularly believed that, because the ostrich laid her eggs on the sand, she was thereby cruelly abandoning them; cf Lam 4, 3.
39, 19–25: The famous description of a war horse.
g Ps 147, 9.

angry with you and with your two friends;* for you have not spoken rightly concerning me, as has my servant Job. 8 Now, therefore, take seven bullocks and seven rams, and go to my servant Job, and offer up a holocaust for yourselves; and let my servant Job pray for you;* for his prayer I will accept, not to punish you severely. For you have not spoken rightly concerning me, as has my servant Job." 9 Then Eliphaz the Temanite, and Bildad the Shuhite, and Zophar the Naamathite, went and did as the LORD had commanded them. And the LORD accepted the intercession of Job.

10 Also, the LORD restored the prosperity of Job, after he had prayed for his friends; the LORD even gave to Job twice as much as he had before. 11 Then all his brethren and his sisters came to him, and all his former acquaintances, and they dined with him in his house. They condoled with him and comforted him for all the evil which the LORD had brought upon him; and each one gave him a piece of money* and a gold ring.

12 [k]Thus the LORD blessed the latter days of Job more than his earlier ones. For he had fourteen thousand sheep, six thousand camels, a thousand yoke of oxen, and a thousand she-asses. 13 And he had seven sons and three daughters, 14 of whom* he called the first Jemimah, the second Keziah, and the third Keren-happuch. 15 In all the land no other women were as beautiful as the daughters of Job; and their father gave them an inheritance* among their brethren. 16 After this, Job lived a hundred and forty years;* and he saw his children, his grandchildren, and even his great-grandchildren.[l] 17 Then Job died, old and full of years.

42, 8: Job becomes the intercessor for his friends, as were other great Old Testament characters, e.g., Abraham and Moses, and as our Lord would be, whom he prefigured. Seven: a symbolic number.

42, 11: A piece of money: the term is the same as that used in Gn 33, 19; Jos 24, 32. Gold ring: for the nose or ear.

42, 14: Job's daughters had names symbolic of their charms: Jemimah, dove; Keziah, precious perfume (cf Ps 45, 9); Keren-happuch, cosmetic jar—more precisely, a container for a black powder that was used like modern mascara.

42, 15: Ordinarily daughters did not inherit property unless there were no sons; cf Nm 27, 1–11.

42, 16: As his other rewards were twice as much as he had before (v 10), so Job's hundred and forty years were double the expected span of human life; cf Ps 90, 10.

k Jb 1, 3. l Jb 5, 25f.

THE BOOK OF PSALMS

The Hebrew Psalter numbers 150 songs. The corresponding number in the LXX differs because of a different division of certain psalms. Hence the numbering in the Greek Psalter (which was followed by the Latin Vulgate) is usually one digit behind the Hebrew. In *The New American Bible* the numbering of the verses follows the Hebrew numbering; many of the traditional English translations are often a verse number behind the Hebrew because they do not count the superscriptions as a verse.

The superscriptions derive from pre-Christian Jewish tradition, and they contain technical terms, many of them apparently liturgical, which are no longer known to us. Seventy-three psalms are attributed to David, but there is no sure way of dating any psalm. Some are preexilic (before 587), and others are postexilic (after 539), but not as late as the Maccabean period (ca 165). The psalms are the product of many individual collections (e.g., Songs of Ascents, Pss 120–134), which were eventually combined into the present work in which one can detect five "books," because of the doxologies which occur at 41, 14; 72, 18–19; 89, 53; 106, 48.

Two important features of the psalms deserve special notice. First, the majority were composed originally precisely for liturgical worship. This is shown by the frequent indication of liturgical leaders interacting with the community (e.g., 118, 1–4). Secondly, they follow certain distinct patterns or literary forms. Thus, the hymn is a song of praise, in which a community is urged joyfully to sing out the praise of God. Various reasons are given for this praise (often introduced by "for" or "because"): the divine work of creation and sustenance (Pss 8; 104), or the divine acts in Israel's favor (Pss 135, 1–12; 136). Some of the hymns have received a more specific classification, based on content. The "Songs of Zion" are so called because they exalt Zion, the city in which God dwells among the people (Pss 46; 48). Others are termed "enthronement" psalms because they re-enact or re-present in the liturgy the kingship of the Lord (Pss 47; 96–99). Characteristic of the songs of praise is the joyful summons to get involved in the activity; Ps 104 is an exception to this, although it remains universal in its thrust.

Another type of psalm is similar to the hymn: the thanksgiving psalm. This too is a song of praise acknowledging the Lord as the rescuer of the psalmist from a desperate situation. Very often the psalmist will give a flash-back, recounting the past distress, and the plea that was uttered (Pss 30; 116). The setting for such prayers seems to have been the offering of a *todah* (a "praise" sacrifice) with friends in the Temple.

There are more psalms of lament than of any other type. They may be individual (e.g., Pss 3–7; 22) or communal (e.g., Ps 44). Although they usually begin with a cry for help, they develop in various ways. The description of the distress is couched in the broad imagery typical of the Bible (one is in Sheol, the Pit, or is afflicted by enemies or wild beasts, etc.)—in such a way that one cannot pinpoint the exact nature of the psalmist's plight. However, Ps 51 (cf also Ps 130) seems to refer clearly to deliverance from sin. Several laments end on a note of certainty that the Lord has heard the prayer (cf Ps 7, but contrast Ps 88), and the Psalter has been characterized as a movement from lament to praise. If this is somewhat of an exaggeration, it serves at least to emphasize the frequent expressions of trust which characterize the lament. In some cases it would seem as if the theme of trust has been lifted out to form a literary type all its own; cf Pss 23; 62; 91. Among the communal laments can be counted Pss 74 and 79. They complain to the Lord about some national disaster, and try to motivate God to intervene in favor of the suffering people.

Other psalms are clearly classified on account of content, and they may be in themselves laments or psalms of thanksgiving. Among the "royal" psalms, that deal directly with the currently reigning king, are Pss 20; 21; and 72. Many of the royal psalms were given a messianic interpretation by Christians. In Jewish tradition they were preserved, even after kingship had disappeared, because they were read in the light of the Davidic covenant reported in 2 Samuel 7. Certain psalms are called wisdom psalms because they seem to betray the influence of the concerns of the sages (cf Pss 37; 49), but there is no general agreement as to the number of these prayers. Somewhat related to the wisdom psalms are the "torah" psalms, in which the torah (instruction or law) of the Lord is glorified (Pss 1; 19, 8–14; 119). Pss 78; 105 and 106 can be considered as "historical" psalms. Although the majority of the psalms have a liturgical setting, there are certain prayers that may be termed "liturgies," so clearly does their structure reflect a liturgical incident (e.g., Pss 15; 24).

It is obvious that not all of the psalms can be pigeon-holed into neat classifications, but even a brief sketch of these types help us to catch the structure and spirit of the psalms we read. It has been rightly said that the psalms are "a school of prayer." They not only provide us with models to follow, but inspire us to voice our own deepest feelings and aspirations.

FIRST BOOK—PSALMS 1–41

PSALM 1*

True Happiness in God's Law

I

1 Happy those* who do not follow
the counsel of the wicked,
Nor go the way* of sinners,
nor sit in company with scoffers. [a]
2 Rather, the law of the LORD* is their joy;
God's law they study day and night. [b]
3 They are like a tree [c]
planted near streams of water,
that yields its fruit in season;
Its leaves never wither;
whatever they do prospers.

II

4 But not the wicked!*
They are like chaff driven by the wind. [d]
5 Therefore the wicked will not survive
judgment,
nor will sinners in the assembly of the just.
6 The LORD watches over the way of the just, [e]
but the way of the wicked leads to ruin.

PSALM 2*

A Psalm for a Royal Coronation

1 Why do the nations protest
and the peoples grumble in vain? [f]

Ps 1: A preface to the whole Book of Psalms, contrasting with striking similes the destiny of the good and the wicked. The psalm views life as activity, as choosing either the good or the bad. Each "way" brings its inevitable consequences. The wise through their good actions will experience rootedness and life, and the wicked, rootlessness and death.

1, 1: Those: literally, "the man." That word is used here and in many of the Psalms as typical, and therefore is translated "they." **The way**: a common biblical term for manner of living or moral conduct (Pss 32, 8; 101, 2. 6; Prv 2, 20; 1 Kgs 8, 36).

1, 2: The law of the LORD: either the Torah, the first five books of the Bible, or, more probably, divine teaching or instruction.

1, 4: The wicked: those who by their actions distance themselves from God's life-giving presence.

Ps 2: A royal psalm. To rebellious kings (1–3) God responds vigorously (4–6). A speaker proclaims the divine decree (in the legal adoption language of the day), making the Israelite king the earthly representative of God (7–9) and warning kings to obey (10–11). The psalm has a messianic meaning for the Church; the New Testament understands it of Christ (Acts 4, 25–27; 13, 33; Heb 1, 5).

a Pss 26, 4–5; 40, 5. b Jos 1, 8; Ps 119; Sir 39, 1. c Pss 52, 10; 92, 13–15; Jer 17, 8. d Pss 35, 5; 83, 14–16; Jb 21, 18. e Ps 37, 18. f Rv 11, 18.

2 Kings on earth rise up
and princes plot together
against the LORD and his anointed: [g]*
3 "Let us break their shackles
and cast off their chains!" [h]
4 The one enthroned in heaven laughs;
the LORD derides them, [i]
5 Then speaks to them in anger,
terrifies them in wrath:
6 "I myself have installed my king
on Zion, my holy mountain."
7 I will proclaim the decree of the LORD,
who said to me, "You are my son;
today I am your father. [j]
8 Only ask it of me,
and I will make your inheritance the nations,
your possession the ends of the earth.
9 With an iron rod you shall shepherd them,
like a clay pot you will shatter them." [k]
10 And now, kings, give heed;
take warning, rulers on earth.
11 Serve the LORD with fear;
with trembling bow down in homage,
Lest God be angry and you perish from the way
in a sudden blaze of anger.
Happy are all who take refuge in God! [l]

PSALM 3*

Threatened but Trusting

1 A psalm of David, when he fled from his son Absalom. [m]*

I

2 How many are my foes, LORD!
How many rise against me!
3 How many say of me,
"God will not save that one." [n] *Selah**
4 But you, LORD, are a shield around me;
my glory, you keep my head high. [o]

II

5 Whenever I cried out to the LORD,
I was answered from the holy mountain. *Selah*
6 Whenever I lay down and slept,
the LORD preserved me to rise again. [p]
7 I do not fear, then, thousands of people
arrayed against me on every side.

III

8 Arise, LORD! Save me, my God!
You will shatter the jaws of all my foes;
you will break the teeth of the wicked. [q]
9 Safety comes from the LORD!
Your blessing for your people! [r] *Selah*

PSALM 4*

Trust in God

1 For the leader;* with stringed instruments.
A psalm of David.

I

2 Answer when I call, my saving God.
In my troubles, you cleared a way;
show me favor; hear my prayer. [s]

II

3 How long will you people mock my honor,
love what is worthless, chase after lies? [t] *Selah*
4 Know that the LORD works wonders for the faithful;
the LORD hears when I call out.

2, 2: **Anointed**: in Hebrew *mashiah*, "anointed"; in Greek *christos*, whence English Messiah and Christ. In Israel kings (Jgs 9, 8; 1 Sm 9, 16; 16, 12–13) and high priests (Lv 8, 12; Nm 3, 3) received the power of their office through anointing.

Ps 3: An individual lament complaining of enemies who deny that God will come to the rescue (2–3). Despite such taunts the psalmist hopes for God's protection even in sleep (4–7). The psalm prays for an end to the enemies' power to speak maliciously (8) and closes peacefully with an expression of trust (9).

3, 1: The superscription, added later, relates the psalm to an incident in the life of David.

3, 3. 5. 9: **Selah**: the term is generally considered a direction to the cantor or musicians but its exact meaning is not known. It occurs 71 times in 39 psalms.

Ps 4: An individual lament emphasizing trust in God. The petition is based upon the psalmist's vivid experience of God as savior (2). That experience of God is the basis for the warning to the wicked: revere God who intervenes on the side of the faithful (3–6). The faithful psalmist exemplifies the blessings given to the just (7–9).

4, 1: **For the leader**: many psalm headings contain this rubric. Its exact meaning is unknown but may signify that such psalms once stood together in a collection of "the choirmaster." Cf 1 Chr 15, 21.

g Ps 83, 6. h Ps 149, 8. i Pss 37, 13; 59, 9; Wis 4, 18. j Pss 89, 27; 110, 2–3; Is 49, 1. k Rv 2, 27; 12, 5; 19, 15. l Pss 34, 9; 146, 5; Prv 16, 20. m 2 Sm 15, 13ff. n Ps 71, 11. o Pss 7, 11; 18, 3; 62, 7–8; Dt 33, 29; Is 60, 19. p Ps 4, 9; Prv 3, 24. q Ps 58, 7. r Ps 28, 9; Jon 2, 10. s Ps 118, 5. t Ps 62, 4.

5 Tremble* and do not sin;
upon your beds ponder in silence. [u]
6 Offer fitting sacrifice
and trust in the LORD. [v]

III

7 Many say, "May we see better times!
LORD, show us the light of your face!" [w] *Selah*
8 But you have given my heart more joy
than they have when grain and wine
abound.
9 In peace I shall both lie down and sleep, [x]
for you alone, LORD, make me secure.

PSALM 5*

Prayer for Divine Help

1 For the leader; with wind instruments.
A psalm of David.

I

2 Hear my words, O LORD;
listen to my sighing. [y]
3 Hear my cry for help,
my king, my God!
To you I pray, O LORD;
4 at dawn you will hear my cry;
at dawn I will plead before you and wait. [z]

II

5 You are not a god who delights in evil;
no wicked person finds refuge with you;
6 the arrogant cannot stand before you.
You hate all who do evil;
7 you destroy all who speak falsely. [a]
Murderers and deceivers
the LORD abhors.

III

8 But I can enter your house
because of your great love.
I can worship in your holy temple
because of my reverence for you, LORD. [b]
9 Guide me in your justice because of my foes;
make straight your way before me. [c]

IV

10 For there is no sincerity in their mouths;
their hearts are corrupt.
Their throats* are open graves; [d]
on their tongues are subtle lies.
11 Declare them guilty, God;
make them fall by their own devices. [e]
Drive them out for their many sins;
they have rebelled against you.

V

12 Then all who take refuge in you will be glad
and forever shout for joy. [f]
Protect them that you may be the joy
of those who love your name.
13 For you, LORD, bless the just;
you surround them with favor like a shield.

PSALM 6*

Prayer in Distress

1 For the leader; with stringed instruments, "upon
the eighth."* A psalm of David.

I

2 Do not reprove me in your anger, LORD,
nor punish me in your wrath. [g]
3 Have pity on me, LORD, for I am weak;
heal me, LORD, for my bones are
trembling. [h]

4, 5: Tremble: be moved deeply with religious awe. The Greek translation understood the emotion to be anger, and it is so cited in Eph 4, 26.

Ps 5: A lament contrasting the security of the house of God (8–9. 12–13) with the danger of the company of evildoers (5–7. 10–11). The psalmist therefore prays that God will hear (2–4) and grant the protection and joy of the temple.

5, 10: Their throats: their speech brings harm to their hearers (cf Jer 5, 16). The verse mentions four parts of the body, each a source of evil to the innocent.

Ps 6: The first of the seven Penitential Psalms (Pss 6; 32; 38; 51; 102; 130; 143), a designation dating from the seventh century A.D. for psalms suitable to express repentance. The psalmist does not, as in many laments, claim to be innocent but appeals to God's mercy (5). Sin here, as often in the Bible, is both the sinful act and its injurious consequences; here it is physical sickness (3–4. 7–8) and the attacks of enemies (8. 9. 11). The psalmist prays that the effects of personal and social sin be taken away.

6, 1: Upon the eighth: apparently a musical notation, now lost.

u Eph 4, 26. v Ps 51, 19. w Pss 31, 17; 44, 4; 67, 1; 80, 4; Jb 13, 24; Nm 6, 25; Dn 9, 17. x Ps 3, 6. y Pss 86, 6; 130, 1–2. z Wis 16, 28. a Ps 101, 7; Wis 14, 9; Hb 1, 13. b Ps 138, 2; Jon 2, 5. c Ps 23, 3; Prv 4, 11; Is 26, 7. d Rom 3, 13. e Ps 141, 10. f Ps 64, 11. g Ps 38, 2. h Jer 17, 14–15.

4 In utter terror is my soul—
and you, LORD, how long . . . ?[i]*
5 Turn, LORD, save my life;
in your mercy* rescue me.
6 For who among the dead remembers you?
Who praises you in Sheol?[j]*

II

7 I am wearied with sighing;
all night long tears drench my bed;
my couch is soaked with weeping.
8 My eyes are dimmed with sorrow,
worn out because of all my foes.[k]

III

9 Away from me, all who do evil![l]
The LORD has heard my weeping.
10 The LORD has heard my prayer;
the LORD takes up my plea.
11 My foes will be terrified and disgraced;
all will fall back in sudden shame.[m]

PSALM 7*

God the Vindicator

1 A plaintive song of David, which he sang to the LORD concerning Cush, the Benjaminite.

I

2 LORD my God, in you I take refuge;
rescue me; save me from all who pursue me,[n]
3 Lest they maul me like lions,
tear me to pieces with none to save.

II

4 LORD my God, if I am at fault in this,*
if there is guilt on my hands,
5 If I have repaid my friend with evil—
I spared even those who hated me without cause—
6 Then let my enemy pursue and overtake me,
trample my life to the ground,
and leave me dishonored in the dust.[o]
Selah

III

7 Rise up, LORD, in your anger;
rise against the fury of my foes.[p]
Wake to judge as you have decreed.
8 Have the assembly of the peoples gather about you;
sit on your throne high above them,
9 O LORD, judge of the nations.
Grant me justice, LORD, for I am blameless,
free of any guilt.
10 Bring the malice of the wicked to an end;
uphold the innocent,
O God of justice,
who tries hearts and minds.[q]

IV

11 A shield before me is God
who saves the honest heart.[r]
12 God is a just judge,
who rebukes in anger every day.
13 If sinners do not repent,
God sharpens his sword,
strings and readies the bow,[s]
14 Prepares his deadly shafts,
makes arrows blazing thunderbolts.[t]

V

15 Sinners conceive iniquity;
pregnant with mischief,
they give birth to failure.[u]
16 They open a hole and dig it deep,
but fall into the pit they have dug.[v]
17 Their mischief comes back upon themselves;
their violence falls on their own heads.

6, 4: **How long?**: elliptical for "How long will it be before you answer my prayer?" Cf Ps 13, 2–3.

6, 5: **Mercy**: Hebrew *hesed*, translated as "mercy" or "love," describes God's affectionate fidelity to human beings, which is rooted in divine and not human integrity.

6, 6: A motive for God to preserve the psalmist from death: in the shadowy world of the dead no one offers you praise. Sheol is the biblical term for the underworld where the insubstantial souls of dead human beings dwelt. It was similar to the Hades of Greek and Latin literature. In the second century B.C., biblical books begin to speak positively of life with God after death (Dn 12, 1–3; Wis 3).

Ps 7: An individual lament. The psalmist flees to God's presence in the sanctuary for justice and protection (2–3) and takes an oath that only the innocent can swear (4–6). The innocent psalmist can thus hope for the just God's protection (7–14) and be confident that the actions of the wicked will come back upon their own heads (15–17). The justice of God leads the psalmist to praise (18).

7, 4: **At fault in this**: in the accusation the enemies have made against the psalmist.

i Pss 13, 2–3; 74, 10; 89, 47. j Pss 30, 10; 88, 11; 115, 17; Is 38, 18. k Pss 31, 10; 38, 11; 40, 13. l Ps 119, 115; Mt 7, 23; Lk 13, 27. m Pss 35, 4. 26; 40, 15; 71, 13. n Pss 6, 5; 22, 21. o Ps 143, 3. p Pss 9, 4; 19, 20. q Pss 17, 3; 26, 2; 35, 24; 43, 1; 139, 23; Jer 17, 10; 20, 12. r Ps 3, 4. s Ps 11, 2. t Is 50, 11. u Jb 15, 35; Is 59, 4. v Pss 9, 16; 35, 8; 57, 7; Prv 26, 27; Eccl 10, 8; Sir 27, 26.

VI

18 I praise the justice of the LORD;
I celebrate the name of the LORD Most High.[w]

PSALM 8*

Divine Majesty and Human Dignity

1 For the leader; "upon the *gittith.*"*
A psalm of David.

2 O LORD, our Lord,
how awesome is your name through all the earth!
You have set your majesty above the heavens!
3 Out of the mouths of babes[x] and infants*
you have drawn a defense* against your foes,
to silence enemy and avenger.*
4 When I see your heavens, the work of your fingers,
the moon and stars that you set in place—
5 What are humans that you are mindful of them,[y]
mere mortals* that you care for them?[z]
6 Yet you have made them little less than a god,*
crowned them with glory and honor.
7 You have given them rule over the works of your hands,[a]
put all things at their feet:
8 All sheep and oxen,
even the beasts of the field,
9 The birds of the air, the fish of the sea,
and whatever swims the paths of the seas.
10 O LORD, our Lord,
how awesome is your name through all the earth!

PSALMS 9–10*

Thanksgiving for Victory and Prayer for Justice

1 For the leader; according to *Muth Labben.**
A psalm of David.

A

I

2 I will praise you, LORD, with all my heart;
I will declare all your wondrous deeds.
3 I will delight and rejoice in you;
I will sing hymns to your name, Most High.
4 For my enemies turn back;
they stumble and perish before you.

II

5 You upheld my right and my cause,
seated on your throne, judging justly.
6 You rebuked the nations, you destroyed the wicked;
their name you blotted out for all time.[b]
7 The enemies have been ruined forever;
you destroyed their cities;
their memory has perished.

Ps 8: While marvelling at the limitless grandeur of God (2–3), the psalmist is struck first by the smallness of human beings in creation (4–5), and then by the royal dignity and power that God has graciously bestowed upon them (6–10).

8, 1: **Upon the gittith**: probably the title of the melody to which the psalm was to be sung or a musical instrument.

8, 3: **Babes and infants**: the text is obscure. Some join this line to the last line of 2 (itself obscure) to read: "(you) whose majesty is exalted above the heavens / by the mouths of babes and infants." **Drawn a defense**: some prefer the Septuagint's "fashioned praise," which is quoted in Mt 21, 16. **Enemy and avenger**: probably cosmic enemies. The primeval powers of watery chaos are often personified in poetic texts (Pss 74, 13–14; 89, 11; Jb 9, 13; 26, 12–13; Is 51, 9).

8, 5: **Humans . . . mere mortals**: literally, "(mortal) person" . . . "son of man (in sense of a human being, Hebrew *'adam*)." The emphasis is on the fragility and mortality of human beings to whom God has given great dignity.

8, 6: **Little less than a god**: Hebrew *'elohim,* the ordinary word for "God" or "the gods" or members of the heavenly court. The Greek version translated *'elohim* by "angel, messenger"; several ancient and modern versions so translate. The meaning seems to be that God created human beings almost at the level of the beings in the heavenly world. Heb 2, 9 finds the eminent fulfillment of this verse in Jesus Christ, who was humbled before being glorified. Cf also 1 Cor 15, 27, where St. Paul applies to Christ the closing words of v 7.

Pss 9–10: Pss 9 and 10 in the Hebrew text have been transmitted as separate poems but they actually form a single acrostic poem and are so transmitted in the Greek and Latin tradition. Each verse of the two psalms begins with a successive letter of the Hebrew alphabet (though several letters have no corresponding stanza). The psalm states loosely connected themes: the rescue of the helpless poor from their enemies, God's worldwide judgment and rule over the nations, the psalmist's own concern for rescue (14–15).

9, 1: **Muth Labben**: probably the melodic accompaniment of the psalm, now lost.

w Pss 18, 50; 30, 5; 135, 3; 146, 2. x Mt 21, 16; Wis 10, 21. y Ps 144, 3; Jb 7, 17. z Heb 2, 6ff. a 7ff: Gn 1, 26. 28; Wis 9, 2; 1 Cor 15, 27. b Jb 18, 17.

III

8 The LORD rules forever,
has set up a throne for judgment.
9 It is God who governs the world with justice, [c]
who judges the peoples with fairness.
10 The LORD is a stronghold for the oppressed,
a stronghold in times of trouble. [d]
11 Those who honor your name trust in you;
you never forsake those who seek you,
LORD.

IV

12 Sing hymns to the LORD enthroned on Zion;
proclaim God's deeds among the nations!
13 For the avenger of bloodshed remembers,
does not forget the cry of the afflicted. [e]

V

14 Have mercy on me, LORD;
see how my foes afflict me!
You alone can raise me from the gates of
death. [f]
15 Then I will declare all your praises,
sing joyously of your salvation
in the gates of daughter Zion.*

VI

16 The nations fall into the pit they dig;
in the snare they hide, their own foot is
caught.
17 The LORD is revealed in this divine rule:
by the deeds they do the wicked are
trapped. [g]* *Higgaion. Selah*

VII

18 To Sheol the wicked will depart,
all the nations that forget God.
19 The needy will never be forgotten,
nor will the hope of the afflicted ever
fade. [h]
20 Arise, LORD, let no mortal prevail;
let the nations be judged in your presence.
21 Strike them with terror, LORD;
show the nations they are mere mortals.
Selah

B

I

1 Why, LORD, do you stand at a distance
and pay no heed to these troubled times?
2 Arrogant scoundrels pursue the poor;
they trap them by their cunning schemes. [i]

II

3 The wicked even boast of their greed;
these robbers curse and scorn the LORD. [j]
4 In their insolence the wicked boast:
"God doesn't care, doesn't even exist." [k]
5 Yet their affairs always succeed;
they ignore your judgment on high;
they sneer at all who oppose them.
6 They say in their hearts, "We will never fall;
never will we see misfortune."
7 Their mouths are full of oaths, violence, and
lies;
discord and evil are under their tongues. [l]
8 They wait in ambush near towns;
their eyes watch for the helpless,
to murder the innocent in secret. [m]
9 They lurk in ambush like lions in a thicket,
hide there to trap the poor,
snare them and close the net. [n]
10 The helpless are crushed, laid low;
they fall into the power of the wicked,
11 Who say in their hearts, "God pays no
attention,
shows no concern, never bothers to
look." [o]

III

12 Rise up, LORD God! Raise your arm!
Do not forget the poor!
13 Why should the wicked scorn God,
say in their hearts, "God doesn't care"?
14 But you do see;
you do observe this misery and sorrow; [p]
you take the matter in hand.
To you the helpless can entrust their cause;
you are the defender of orphans. [q]

9, 15: Daughter Zion: an ancient Near Eastern city could sometimes be personified as a woman or a queen, the spouse of the god of the city.

9, 17: The LORD is revealed in this divine rule: God has so made the universe that the wicked are punished by the very actions they perform.

c Pss 96, 10; 98, 9. d Ps 37, 39; Is 25, 4. e Jb 16, 18. f Wis 16, 13. g Sir 27, 26. h Prv 23, 18. i Is 32, 7. j Ps 36, 2. k Ps 14, 1; Jb 22, 13; Is 29, 15; Jer 5, 12; Zep 1, 12. l Is 32, 7; Rom 3, 14. m Ps 11, 2; Jb 24, 14. n Ps 17, 12; Prv 1, 11; Jer 5, 26. o Pss 44, 25; 64, 6; 73, 11; 94, 7; Ez 9, 9. p Pss 31, 8; 56, 9; 2 Kgs 20, 5; Is 25, 8; Rv 7, 17. q Ex 22, 21–22.

15 Break the arms of the wicked and depraved;
make them account for their crimes;
let none of them survive.

IV

16 The LORD is king forever;[r]
the nations have vanished from God's land.
17 You listen, LORD, to the needs of the poor;
you encourage them and hear their prayers.
18 You win justice for the orphaned and
oppressed;[s]
no one on earth will cause terror again.

PSALM 11*

Confidence in the Presence of God

1 For the leader. Of David.

I

In the LORD I take refuge;
how can you say to me,
"Flee like a bird to the mountains![t]
2 See how the wicked string their bows,
fit their arrows to the string
to shoot from the shadows at the upright.[u]
3 When foundations* are being destroyed,
what can the upright do?"

II

4 The LORD is in his holy temple;
the LORD's throne is in heaven.[v]
God's eyes keep careful watch;
they test all peoples.
5 The LORD tests the good and the bad,
hates those who love violence,
6 And rains upon the wicked
fiery coals and brimstone,
a scorching wind their allotted cup.[w]*
7 The LORD is just and loves just deeds;
the upright shall see his face.

PSALM 12*

Prayer against Evil Tongues

1 For the leader; "upon the eighth." A psalm of David.

I

2 Help, LORD, for no one loyal remains;
the faithful have vanished from the human
race.[x]
3 Those who tell lies to one another
speak with deceiving lips and a double
heart.[y]

II

4 May the LORD cut off all deceiving lips,
and every boastful tongue,
5 Those who say, "By our tongues we prevail;
when our lips speak, who can lord it over
us?"[z]

III

6 "Because they rob the weak, and the needy
groan,
I will now arise," says the LORD;
"I will grant safety to whoever longs for
it."[a]

IV

7 The promises of the LORD are sure,
silver refined in a crucible,*
silver purified seven times.[b]
8 LORD, protect us always;
preserve us from this generation.
9 On every side the wicked strut;
the shameless are extolled by all.

PSALM 13*

Prayer in Time of Illness

1 For the leader. A psalm of David.

I

2 How long, LORD? Will you utterly forget me?

Ps 11: A song of trust. Though friends counsel flight to the mountain country (a traditional hideout) to escape trouble (1–3), the innocent psalmist reaffirms confidence in God, who protects those who seek asylum in the temple (4–7).

11, 3: Foundations: usually understood of public order. Cf Ps 82, 5.

11, 6: Their allotted cup: the cup that God gives people to drink is a common figure for their destiny. Cf Pss 16, 5; 75, 9; Mt 20, 22; 26, 39; Rv 14, 10.

Ps 12: A lament. The psalmist, thrown into a world where lying and violent people persecute the just (2–3), prays that the wicked be punished (4–5). The prayer is not simply for vengeance but arises from a desire to see God's justice appear on earth. V 6 preserves the word of assurance spoken by the priest to the lamenter; it is not usually transmitted in such psalms. In vv 7–9 the psalmist affirms the intention to live by the word of assurance.

12, 7: A crucible: literally, "in a crucible in the ground." The crucible was placed in the ground for support.

Ps 13: A lament in which the psalmist, seriously ill (4), expresses fear that enemies will interpret his or her death as a divine

r Ps 145, 13; Jer 10, 10. s Dt 10, 18. t Pss 55, 7; 91, 4. u Pss 7, 13; 37, 14; 57, 5; 64, 4. v Pss 14, 2; 102, 20; Hb 2, 20; Dt 26, 15; Is 66, 1; Mt 5, 34. w Pss 120, 4; 140, 11; Prv 16, 27; Ez 38, 22; Rv 8, 5; 20, 10. x Pss 14, 3; 116, 11; Is 59, 15; Mi 7, 2. y Pss 28, 3; 55, 22; Is 59, 3–4; Jer 9, 7. z Sir 5, 3. a Is 33, 10. b Pss 18, 31; 19, 8; Prv 30, 5.

How long will you hide your face from
me? [c]
3 How long must I carry sorrow in my soul,
grief in my heart day after day?
How long will my enemy triumph over me?
II
4 Look upon me, answer me, LORD, my God!
Give light to my eyes lest I sleep in death,
5 Lest my enemy say, "I have prevailed,"
lest my foes rejoice at my downfall. [d]
III
6 I trust in your faithfulness.
Grant my heart joy in your help,
That I may sing of the LORD,
"How good our God has been to me!" [e]

PSALM 14*

A Lament over Widespread Corruption

1 For the leader. Of David.

I
Fools* say in their hearts,
"There is no God." [f]
Their deeds are loathsome and corrupt;
not one does what is right.
2 The LORD looks down from heaven
upon the human race, [g]
To see if even one is wise, [h]
if even one seeks God.
3 All have gone astray;
all alike are perverse.
Not one does what is right,
not even one. [i]
II
4 Will these evildoers never learn?
They devour my people as they devour
bread; [j]
they do not call upon the LORD. [k]
5 They have good reason, then, to fear;
God is with the company of the just.
6 They would crush the hopes of the poor,
but the poor have the LORD as their refuge.
III
7 Oh, that from Zion might come
the deliverance of Israel,
That Jacob may rejoice, and Israel be glad
when the LORD restores his people! [l]*

PSALM 15*

The Righteous Israelite

1 A psalm of David.

I
LORD, who may abide in your tent?
Who may dwell on your holy mountain? [m]*
II
2 Whoever walks without blame, [n]
doing what is right,
speaking truth from the heart;
3 Who does not slander a neighbor,
does no harm to another,
never defames a friend;
4 Who disdains the wicked,
but honors those who fear the LORD;
Who keeps an oath despite the cost,
5 lends no money at interest,*
accepts no bribe against the innocent. [o]
III
Whoever acts like this
shall never be shaken.

---

judgment. Hence the heartfelt prayer (2–3) is for healing that will signal to those enemies that the psalmist enjoys God's favor (4–5). The poem ends with a confession of trust in God and a statement of praise (6).

Ps 14: The lament (duplicated in Ps 53) depicts the world as consisting of two types of people: "the fools" (= the wicked, 1–3) and "the company of the just" (4–6; also called "my people," and "the poor"). The wicked persecute the just, but the psalm expresses the hope that God will punish the wicked and reward the good.

14, 1: Fools: literally, "the fool." The singular is used typically, hence the plural translation.

14, 7: Israel . . . Jacob . . . his people: the righteous poor are identified with God's people.

Ps 15: The psalm records a liturgical scrutiny at the entrance to the temple court (cf Ps 24, 3–6; Is 33, 14b–16). The Israelite wishing to be admitted had to ask the temple official what conduct was appropriate to God's precincts. Note the emphasis on virtues relating to one's neighbor.

15, 1: Your tent . . . your holy mountain: the temple could be referred to as "tent" (Ps 61, 5; Is 33, 20), a reference to the tent of the wilderness period and the tent of David (2 Sm 6, 17; 7, 2), predecessors of the temple. **Holy mountain:** a venerable designation of the divine abode (Pss 2, 6; 3, 5; 43, 3; 48, 2, etc.).

15, 5: Lends no money at interest: lending money in the Old Testament was often seen as assistance to the poor in their distress, not as an investment; making money off the poor by charging interest was thus forbidden (Ex 22, 24; Lv 25, 36–37; Dt 23, 20).

c Pss 6, 4; 44, 25; 77, 8; 79, 5; 89, 47; 94, 3; Lam 5, 20. d Ps 38, 17. e Ps 116, 7. f Pss 10, 4; 36, 2; Is 32, 6; Jer 5, 12. g Pss 11, 4; 102, 20. h 2b–3: Rom 3, 11–12. i Ps 12, 1. j Ps 27, 2; Is 9, 11. k Ps 79, 6. l Ps 85, 2. m Is 56, 7. n Ps 119, 1. o Ex 22, 24; 23, 8.

PSALM 16*

God the Supreme Good

1 A *miktam** of David.

I

Keep me safe, O God;
in you I take refuge.[p]
2 I say to the LORD,
you are my Lord,
you are my only good.
3 Worthless are all the false gods of the land.
Accursed are all who delight in them.
4 They multiply their sorrows
who court other gods.
Blood libations to them I will not pour out,
nor will I take their names* upon my lips.
5 LORD, my allotted portion and my cup,
you have made my destiny secure.[q]
6 Pleasant places were measured out for me;*
fair to me indeed is my inheritance.

II

7 I bless the LORD who counsels me;
even at night my heart exhorts me.
8 I keep the LORD always before me;
with the Lord at my right, I shall never be
shaken.[r]
9 Therefore my heart is glad, my soul rejoices;
my body also dwells secure,
10 For you will not abandon me to Sheol,
nor let your faithful servant see the pit.[s]*
11 You will show me the path to life,
abounding joy in your presence,
the delights at your right hand forever.

PSALM 17*

Prayer for Rescue from Persecutors

1 A prayer of David.

I

Hear, LORD, my plea for justice;
pay heed to my cry;
Listen to my prayer
spoken without guile.
2 From you let my vindication come;
your eyes see what is right.
3 You have tested my heart,
searched it in the night.[t]
You have tried me by fire,
but find no malice in me.
My mouth has not transgressed
4 as humans often do.
As your lips have instructed me,
I have kept the way of the law.
5 My steps have kept to your paths;
my feet have not faltered.[u]

II

6 I call upon you; answer me, O God.
Turn your ear to me; hear my prayer.
7 Show your wonderful love,
you who deliver with your right arm
those who seek refuge from their foes.
8 Keep me as the apple of your eye;
hide me in the shadow of your wings*
9 from the violence of the wicked.[v]

III

My ravenous enemies press upon me;[w]
10 they close their hearts,*

Ps 16: In the first section, the psalmist rejects the futile worship of false gods (2–5), preferring Israel's God (1), the giver of the land (6). The second section reflects on the wise and life-giving presence of God (7–11).

16,1: Miktam: a term occurring six times in psalm superscriptions, always with "David." Its meaning is unknown.

16, 4: Take their names: to use the gods' names in oaths and hence to affirm them as one's own gods.

16, 6: Pleasant places were measured out for me: the psalmist is pleased with the plot of land measured out to the family, which was to be passed on to succeeding generations ("my inheritance").

16, 10: Nor let your faithful servant see the pit: Hebrew *shahath* means here the pit, a synonym for Sheol, the underworld. The Greek translation derives the word here and elsewhere from the verb *shahath*, "to be corrupt." On the basis of the Greek, Acts 2, 25–32 and 13, 35–37 apply the verse to Christ's resurrection, "Nor will you suffer your holy one to see corruption."

Ps 17: A lament of an individual unjustly attacked who has taken refuge in the temple. Confident of being found innocent, the psalmist cries out for God's just judgment (1–5) and requests divine help against enemies (6–9a). Those ravenous lions (9b–12) should be punished (13–14). The psalm ends with a serene statement of praise (15). The Hebrew text of vv 3–4 and 14 is uncertain.

17, 8: Apple of your eye . . . shadow of your wings: images of God's special care. Cf Dt 32, 10; Prv 7, 2; Is 49, 2.

17, 10–12. 14: An extended metaphor: the enemies are lions.

p Ps 25, 20. q Pss 23, 5; 73, 26; Nm 18, 20; Lam 3, 24. r Pss 73, 23; 121, 5. 8–12; Acts 2, 25–28. s Pss 28, 1; 30, 4; 49, 16; 86, 13; Jon 2, 7; Acts 13, 35. t Pss 26, 2; 139, 23. u Ps 18, 36; Jb 23, 11–12. v Pss 36, 8; 57, 2; 61, 5; 63, 8; 91, 4; Dt 32, 10; Ru 2, 12; Zec 2, 12; Mt 23, 37. w 9b–12: Pss 10, 9; 22, 14. 22; 35, 17; 58, 7; Jb 4, 10–11.

fill their mouths with proud roaring.
11 Their steps even now encircle me;
they watch closely, keeping low to the ground,
12 Like lions eager for prey,
like young lions lurking in ambush.
13 Rise, O LORD, confront and cast them down;
rescue me so from the wicked.
14 Slay them with your sword;
with your hand, LORD, slay them;
snatch them from the world in their prime.
Their bellies are being filled with your friends;
their children are satisfied too,
for they share what is left with their young.
15 I am just—let me see your face;
when I awake,* let me be filled with your presence.[x]

PSALM 18*

A King's Thanksgiving for Victory

1 For the leader. Of David, the servant of the LORD, who sang to the LORD the words of this song after the LORD had rescued him from the clutches of all his enemies and from the hand of Saul. 2 He said:

I

I love you, LORD, my strength,
3 LORD, my rock, my fortress, my deliverer,[y]
My God, my rock of refuge,
my shield, my saving horn,* my stronghold![z]
4 Praised be the LORD, I exclaim!
I have been delivered from my enemies.

II

5 The breakers of death surged round about me;
the menacing floods terrified me.
6 The cords* of Sheol tightened;
the snares of death lay in wait for me.[a]
7 In my distress I called out: LORD!
I cried out to my God.[b]
From his temple* he heard my voice;
my cry to him reached his ears.
8 The earth rocked and shook;*
the foundations of the mountains trembled;
they shook as his wrath flared up.[c]
9 Smoke rose in his nostrils,
a devouring fire poured from his mouth;
it kindled coals into flame.
10 He parted the heavens and came down,
a dark cloud under his feet.[d]
11 Mounted on a cherub* he flew,
borne along on the wings of the wind.
12 He made darkness the cover about him;
his canopy, heavy thunderheads.
13 Before him scudded his clouds,
hail and lightning too.[e]
14 The LORD thundered from heaven;
the Most High made his voice resound.[f]
15 He let fly his arrows* and scattered them;
shot his lightning bolts and dispersed them.[g]
16 Then the bed of the sea appeared;
the world's foundations lay bare,[h]
At the roar of the LORD,
at the storming breath of his nostrils.
17 He reached down from on high and seized me;
drew me out of the deep waters.[i]
18 He rescued me from my mighty enemy,

17, 15: When I awake: probably the psalmist has spent the night in the sanctuary (cf 3) and hopes to wake to an oracle assuring God's protective presence.

Ps 18: A royal thanksgiving for a military victory, duplicated in 2 Sm 22. Thanksgiving psalms are in essence reports of divine rescue. The psalm has two parallel reports of rescue, the first told from a heavenly perspective (5–20), and the second from an earthly perspective (36–46). The first report adapts old mythic language of a cosmic battle between sea and rainstorm in order to depict God's rescue of the Israelite king from his enemies. Each report has a short hymnic introduction (2–4. 32–35) and conclusion (21–31. 47–51).

18, 3: My saving horn: my strong savior. The horn referred to is the weapon of a bull and the symbol of fertility. Cf 1 Sm 2, 10; Ps 132, 17; Lk 1, 69.

18, 6: Cords: hunting imagery, the cords of a snare.

18, 7: His temple: his heavenly abode.

18, 8–16: God appears in the storm, which in Palestine comes from the west. The introduction to the theophany (vv 8–9) is probably a description of a violent, hot, and dry east-wind storm. In the fall transition period from the rainless summer to the rainy winter such storms regularly precede the rains. Cf Ex 14, 21–22.

18, 11: Cherub: a winged creature, derived from myth, in the service of the deity (Gn 3, 24; Ex 25, 18–20; 37, 6–9). Cherubim were the throne bearers of the deity (Pss 80, 2; 99, 1; 1 Kgs 6, 23–28; 8, 6–8).

18, 15: Arrows: lightning.

x Pss 4, 7; 31, 17; 67, 2; 80, 4; Nm 6, 25; Dn 9, 17. y 2–51: 2 Sm 22, 2–51. z Pss 3, 4; 31, 3–4; 42, 10; Gn 49, 24; Dt 32, 4. a Pss 88, 8; 93, 3–4; 116, 3–4. b Jon 2, 3. c Pss 97, 3–4; 99, 1; Jgs 5, 4–5; Is 64, 1; Hab 3, 9–11. d Pss 104, 3; 144, 5; Is 63, 19. e Ex 13, 21; 19, 16. f Pss 29; 77, 19; Ex 19, 19; Jb 37, 3–4. g Ps 144, 6; Wis 5, 21. h Ps 77, 17; Zec 9, 14. i Ps 144, 7.

from foes too powerful for me.
19 They attacked me on a day of distress,
but the LORD came to my support.
20 He set me free in the open;
he rescued me because he loves me.

III

21 The LORD acknowledged my righteousness,
rewarded my clean hands.[j]
22 For I kept the ways of the LORD;
I was not disloyal to my God.
23 His laws were all before me,
his decrees I did not cast aside.
24 I was honest toward him;
I was on guard against sin.
25 So the LORD rewarded my righteousness,
the cleanness of my hands in his sight.
26 Toward the faithful you are faithful;
to the honest you are honest;[k]
27 Toward the sincere, sincere;
but to the perverse you are devious.
28 Humble people you save;
haughty eyes you bring low.[l]
29 You, LORD, give light to my lamp;
my God brightens the darkness about me.[m]
30 With you I can rush an armed band,
with my God to help I can leap a wall.
31 God's way is unerring;
the LORD's promise is tried and true;
he is a shield for all who trust in him.[n]

IV

32 Truly, who is God except the LORD?
Who but our God is the rock?[o]
33 This God who girded me with might,
kept my way unerring,
34 Who made my feet swift as a deer's,
set me safe on the heights,[p]
35 Who trained my hands for war,
my arms to bend even a bow of bronze.[q]*

V

36 You have given me your protecting shield;
your right hand has upheld me;
you stooped to make me great.
37 You gave me room to stride;
my feet never stumbled.[r]
38 I pursued my enemies and overtook them;
I did not turn back till I destroyed them.
39 I struck them down; they could not rise;
they fell dead at my feet.
40 You girded me with strength for war,
subdued adversaries at my feet.
41 My foes you put to flight before me;
those who hated me I destroyed.
42 They cried for help, but no one saved them;
cried to the LORD but got no answer.
43 I ground them fine as dust in the wind;
like mud in the streets I trampled them
down.
44 You rescued me from the strife of peoples;
you made me head over nations.
A people I had not known became my slaves;
45 as soon as they heard of me they obeyed.
Foreigners cringed before me;
46 their courage failed;
they came trembling from their fortresses.[s]

VI

47 The LORD lives! Blessed be my rock![t]
Exalted be God, my savior!
48 O God who granted me vindication,
made peoples subject to me,[u]
49 and preserved me from my enemies,
Truly you have exalted me above my
adversaries,
from the violent you have rescued me.
50 Thus I will proclaim you, LORD, among the
nations;
I will sing the praises of your name.[v]
51 You have given great victories to your king,
and shown kindness to your anointed,
to David and his posterity forever.[w]

PSALM 19*

God's Glory in the Heavens and in the Law

1 For the leader. A psalm of David.

I

2 The heavens declare the glory of God;

18, 35: Bow of bronze: hyperbole for a bow difficult to bend and therefore capable of propelling an arrow with great force.

Ps 19: The heavenly elements of the world, now beautifully

j Ps 26; 1 Sm 26, 23. k Ps 125, 4. l Jb 22, 29; Prv 3, 34. m Pss 27, 1; 36, 10; 43, 3; 119, 105; Jb 29, 3; Mi 7, 8. n Pss 12, 6; 77, 13; Prv 30, 5. o Is 44, 8; 45, 21. p Hb 3, 19. q Ps 144, 1. r Ps 17, 5. s Mi 7, 17. t Ps 144, 1. u Ps 144, 2. v Pss 7, 18; 30, 5; 57, 9; 135, 3; 146, 2; Rom 15, 9. w Pss 89, 28–37; 144, 10; 1 Sm 2, 10.

the sky proclaims its builder's craft. [x]
3 One day to the next conveys that message;
one night to the next imparts that
knowledge.
4 There is no word or sound;*
no voice is heard;
5 Yet their report goes forth through all the
earth,
their message, to the ends of the world.
God has pitched there a tent for the sun;*
6 it comes forth like a bridegroom from his
chamber,
and like an athlete joyfully runs its course.
7 From one end of the heavens it comes forth;
its course runs through to the other;
nothing escapes its heat.

II

8 The law of the LORD is perfect,
refreshing the soul.
The decree of the LORD is trustworthy,
giving wisdom to the simple. [y]
9 The precepts of the LORD are right,
rejoicing the heart.
The command of the LORD is clear,
enlightening the eye.
10 The fear of the LORD is pure,
enduring forever.
The statutes of the LORD are true,
all of them just;
11 More desirable than gold,
than a hoard of purest gold,
Sweeter also than honey
or drippings from the comb. [z]
12 By them your servant is instructed;*
obeying them brings much reward.

III

13 Who can detect heedless failings?
Cleanse me from my unknown faults.
14 But from willful sins keep your servant;
let them never control me.
Then shall I be blameless,
innocent of grave sin.
15 Let the words of my mouth meet with your
favor,
keep the thoughts of my heart before you,
LORD, my rock and my redeemer.

PSALM 20*

Prayer for the King in Time of War

1 For the leader. A psalm of David.

I

2 The LORD answer you in time of distress;
the name of the God of Jacob defend you!
3 May God send you help from the temple,
from Zion be your support. [a]
4 May God remember* your every offering,
graciously accept your holocaust, *Selah*
5 Grant what is in your heart,
fulfill your every plan.
6 May we shout for joy at your victory,*
raise the banners in the name of our God.
The LORD grant your every prayer!

II

7 Now I know victory is given
to the anointed of the LORD. [b]
God will answer him from the holy heavens
with a strong arm that brings victory.
8 Some rely on chariots, others on horses,
but we on the name of the LORD our God. [c]

---

arranged, bespeak the power and wisdom of their creator (2–7). The creator's wisdom is available to human beings in the law (8–11), toward which the psalmist prays to be open (12–15). The themes of light and speech unify the poem.

19, 4: **No word or sound**: the regular functioning of the heavens and the alternation of day and night inform humans without words of the creator's power and wisdom.

19, 5: **The sun**: in other religious literature the sun is a judge and lawgiver since it sees all in its daily course; 5b–7 form a transition to the law in 8–11. The six synonyms for God's revelation (8–11) are applied to the sun in comparable literature.

19, 12: **Instructed**: the Hebrew verb means both to shine and to teach. Cf Dn 12, 3.

Ps 20: The people pray for the king before battle. The people ask for divine help (2–6) and express confidence that such help will be given (7–10). A solemn assurance of divine help may well have been given between the two sections in the liturgy, something like the promises of Pss 12, 6 and 21, 9–13. The final verse (10) echoes the opening verse.

20, 4: **Remember**: God's remembering implies readiness to act. Cf Gn 8, 1; Ex 2, 24.

20, 6: **Victory**: the Hebrew root is often translated "salvation," "to save," but in military contexts it can have the specific meaning of "victory."

x Pss 8, 1; 50, 6; 97, 6. y Pss 12, 7; 119. z Sir 24, 19. a Pss 128, 5; 134, 3. b Pss 18, 51; 144, 10; 1 Sm 2, 10. c Ps 147, 10–11; 2 Chr 14, 10; Prv 21, 31; 1 Sm 17, 45; Is 31, 1; 36, 9.

9 They collapse and fall,
but we stand strong and firm. [d]
10 LORD, grant victory to the king;
answer when we call upon you.

PSALM 21*

Thanksgiving and Assurances for the King

1 For the leader. A psalm of David.

I

2 LORD, the king finds joy in your power; [e]
in your victory how greatly he rejoices!
3 You have granted him his heart's desire;
you did not refuse the prayer of his lips.
Selah
4 For you welcomed him with goodly blessings;
you placed on his head a crown of pure gold.
5 He asked life of you;
you gave it to him,
length of days forever.[f]
6 Great is his glory in your victory;
majesty and splendor you confer upon him.
7 You make him the pattern of blessings forever,
you gladden him with the joy of your presence.
8 For the king trusts in the LORD,
stands firm through the love of the Most High.

II

9 Your hand will reach all your enemies;
your right hand will reach your foes!
10 At the time of your coming
you will drive them into a furnace.
Then the LORD's anger will consume them,
devour them with fire.
11 Even their descendants you will wipe out from the earth,
their offspring from the human race.
12 Though they intend evil against you,
devising plots, they will not succeed,
13 For you will put them to flight;
you will aim at them with your bow.

III

14 Arise, LORD, in your power! [g]
We will sing and chant the praise of your might.

PSALM 22*

The Prayer of an Innocent Person

1 For the leader; according to "The deer of the dawn."* A psalm of David.

I

2 My God, my God, why have you abandoned me?
Why so far from my call for help,
from my cries of anguish? [h]
3 My God, I call by day, but you do not answer;
by night, but I have no relief. [i]
4 Yet you are enthroned as the Holy One;
you are the glory of Israel.[j]
5 In you our ancestors trusted;
they trusted and you rescued them.
6 To you they cried out and they escaped;
in you they trusted and were not disappointed. [k]
7 But I am a worm, hardly human,*
scorned by everyone, despised by the people. [l]
8 All who see me mock me;
they curl their lips and jeer;
they shake their heads at me: [m]
9 "You relied on the LORD—let him deliver you;
if he loves you, let him rescue you." [n]
10 Yet you drew me forth from the womb,

Ps 21: The first part of this royal psalm is a thanksgiving (2–8), and the second is a promise that the king will triumph over his enemies (9–14). The king's confident prayer (3. 5) and trust in God (8) enable him to receive the divine gifts of vitality, peace, and military success. V 14 reprises v 1. When kings ceased in Israel after the sixth century B.C., the psalm was sung of a future Davidic king.

Ps 22: A lament unusual in structure and in intensity of feeling. The psalmist's present distress is contrasted with God's past mercy in vv 2–12. In vv 13–22 enemies surround the psalmist. The last third is an invitation to praise God (23–27), becoming a universal chorus of praise (28–32). The psalm is important in the New Testament. Its opening words occur on the lips of the crucified Jesus (Mk 15, 34; Mt 27, 46), and several other verses are quoted, or at least alluded to, in the accounts of Jesus' passion (Mt 27, 35. 43; Jn 19, 24).

22, 1: The deer of the dawn: apparently the title of the melody.

22, 7: I am a worm, hardly human: the psalmist's sense of isolation and dehumanization, an important motif of Ps 22, is vividly portrayed here.

d Is 40, 30. e Ps 63, 12. f 1 Kgs 3, 14. g Nm 10, 35. h Is 49, 14; 54, 7; Mt 27, 46; Mk 15, 34. i Sir 2, 10. j Is 6, 3. k Ps 25, 3; Is 49, 23; Dn 3, 40. l Is 53, 3. m Ps 109, 25; Mt 27, 39; Mk 15, 29; Lk 23, 35. n Ps 71, 11; Wis 2, 18–20; Mt 27, 43.

made me safe at my mother's breast.
11 Upon you I was thrust from the womb;
since birth you are my God.[o]
12 Do not stay far from me,
for trouble is near,
and there is no one to help.[p]

II

13 Many bulls* surround me;
fierce bulls of Bashan* encircle me.
14 They open their mouths against me,
lions that rend and roar.[q]
15 Like water my life drains away;
all my bones grow soft.
My heart has become like wax,
it melts away within me.
16 As dry as a potsherd is my throat;
my tongue sticks to my palate;
you lay me in the dust of death.*
17 Many dogs surround me;
a pack of evildoers closes in on me.
So wasted are my hands and feet
18 that I can count all my bones.[r]
They stare at me and gloat;
19 they divide my garments among them;
for my clothing they cast lots.[s]
20 But you, LORD, do not stay far off;
my strength, come quickly to help me.
21 Deliver me from the sword,
my forlorn life from the teeth of the dog.
22 Save me from the lion's mouth,
my poor life from the horns of wild bulls.[t]

III

23 Then I will proclaim your name to the assembly;
in the community I will praise you:[u]*
24 "You who fear the LORD, give praise!
All descendants of Jacob, give honor;
show reverence, all descendants of Israel!
25 For God has not spurned or disdained
the misery of this poor wretch,
Did not turn away* from me,
but heard me when I cried out.
26 I will offer praise in the great assembly;
my vows I will fulfill before those who fear him.
27 The poor* will eat their fill;
those who seek the LORD will offer praise.
May your hearts enjoy life forever!"[v]

IV

28 All the ends of the earth
will worship and turn to the LORD;
All the families of nations
will bow low before you.[w]
29 For kingship belongs to the LORD,
the ruler over the nations.[x]
30 All who sleep in the earth
will bow low before God;
All who have gone down into the dust*
will kneel in homage.
31 And I will live for the LORD;
my descendants will serve you.
32 The generation to come will be told of the Lord,
that they may proclaim to a people yet unborn
the deliverance you have brought.[y]

PSALM 23*

The Lord, Shepherd and Host

1 A psalm of David.

I

The LORD is my shepherd;*
there is nothing I lack.[z]

22, 13–14: Bulls: the enemies of the psalmist are also portrayed in less-than-human form, as wild animals (cf 17. 21–22). **Bashan**: a grazing land east of the Jordan, famed for its cattle. Cf Dt 32, 14; Ez 39, 18; Am 4, 1.

22, 16: The dust of death: the netherworld, the domain of the dead.

22, 23: In the community I will praise you: the person who offered a thanksgiving sacrifice in the temple recounted to the other worshipers the favor received from God and invited them to share in the sacrificial banquet. The final section (24–32) may be a summary or a citation of the psalmist's poem of praise.

22, 25: Turn away: literally, "hides his face from me," an important metaphor for God withdrawing from someone, e.g., Mi 3, 4; Is 8, 17; Pss 27, 9; 69, 18; 88, 15.

22, 27: The poor: originally the poor, who were dependent on God; the term (*'anawim*) came to include the religious sense of "humble, pious, devout."

22, 30: Hebrew unclear. The translation assumes that all on earth (28–29) and under the earth (30) will worship God.

o Ps 71, 6; Is 44, 2; 46, 3. p Pss 35, 22; 38, 22; 71, 12. q Ps 17, 12; Jb 4, 10; 1 Pt 5, 8. r Ps 109, 24. s Mt 27, 35; Mk 15, 24; Lk 23, 34; Jn 19, 24. t Pss 7, 2–3; 17, 12; 35, 17; 57, 5; 58, 7; 2 Tm 4, 17. u Pss 26, 12; 35, 18; 40, 10; 109, 30; 149, 1; 2 Sm 22, 50; Heb 2, 12. v Pss 23, 5; 69, 33. w Ps 86, 9; Tb 13, 11; Is 45, 22; 52, 10; Zec 14, 16. x Ps 103, 19; Ob 21; Zec 14, 9. y Pss 48, 14–15; 71, 18; 78, 6; 102, 19; Is 53, 10. z Pss 80, 2; 95, 7; 100, 3; Dt 2, 7.

2 In green pastures you let me graze;
to safe waters you lead me;
3 you restore my strength.
You guide me along the right path*
for the sake of your name. [a]
4 Even when I walk through a dark valley, [b]*
I fear no harm for you are at my side;
your rod and staff give me courage.

II

5 You set a table before me*
as my enemies watch;*
You anoint my head with oil; [c]*
my cup overflows. [d]
6 Only goodness and love* will pursue me
all the days of my life;
I will dwell in the house of the LORD [e]
for years to come.

PSALM 24*

The Glory of God in Procession to Zion

1 A psalm of David.

I

The earth is the LORD's and all it holds, [f]
the world and those who live there.
2 For God founded it on the seas,
established it over the rivers. [g]

II

3 Who may go up the mountain of the LORD? [h]
Who can stand in his holy place?
4 "The clean of hand and pure of heart,*
who are not devoted to idols,
who have not sworn falsely.
5 They will receive blessings from the LORD,
and justice from their saving God.
6 Such are the people that love the LORD,
that seek the face of the God of Jacob."
Selah

III

7 Lift up your heads, O gates;
rise up, you ancient portals,*
that the king of glory may enter. [i]
8 Who is this king of glory?
The LORD, a mighty warrior,
the LORD, mighty in battle.
9 Lift up your heads, O gates;
rise up, you ancient portals,
that the king of glory may enter.
10 Who is this king of glory?
The LORD of hosts is the king of glory. *Selah*

PSALM 25*

Confident Prayer for Forgiveness and Guidance

1 Of David.

I

I wait for you, O LORD;
I lift up my soul 2 to my God. [j]
In you I trust; do not let me be disgraced; [k]
do not let my enemies gloat over me.
3 No one is disgraced who waits for you, [l]
but only those who lightly break faith.

Ps 23: God's loving care for the psalmist is portrayed under the figures of a shepherd for the flock (1–4) and a host's generosity toward a guest (5–6). The imagery of both sections is drawn from traditions of the exodus (Is 40, 11; 49, 10; Jer 31, 10).

23, 1: My shepherd: God as good shepherd is common in both the Old Testament and the New Testament (Ez 34, 11–16 and Jn 10, 11–18).

23, 3: The right path: connotes "right way" and "way of righteousness."

23, 4: A dark valley: a different division of the Hebrew consonants yields the translation "the valley of the shadow of death."

23, 5: You set a table before me: this expression occurs in an exodus context in Ps 78, 19. **As my enemies watch:** my enemies see that I am God's friend and guest. **Oil:** a perfumed ointment made from olive oil, used especially at banquets (Ps 104, 15; Mt 26, 7; Lk 7, 37. 46; Jn 12, 2).

23, 6: Goodness and love: the blessings of God's covenant with Israel.

Ps 24: The psalm apparently accompanied a ceremony of the entry of God (invisibly enthroned upon the ark), followed by the people, into the temple. The temple commemorated the creation of the world (1–2). The people had to affirm their fidelity before being admitted into the sanctuary (3–6; cf Ps 15). A choir identifies the approaching God and invites the very temple gates to bow down in obeisance (7–10).

24, 4–5: Literally, "the one whose hands are clean." The singular is used for the entire class of worshipers, hence the plural translation.

24, 7. 9: Lift up your heads, O gates . . . you ancient portals: the literal meaning is impossible since the portcullis (a gate that moves up and down) was unknown in the ancient world. Extra-biblical parallels suggest a full personification of the circle of gate towers: they are like a council of elders, bowed down and anxious, awaiting the return of the army and the Great Warrior gone to battle.

Ps 25: A lament. Each verse begins with a successive letter of the Hebrew alphabet. Such acrostic psalms are often a series of statements only loosely connected. The psalmist mixes ardent pleas (1–2. 16–22) with expressions of confidence in God who forgives and guides.

a Prv 4, 11. b Jb 10, 21–22; Is 50, 10. c Ps 92, 11. d Ps 16, 5. e Ps 27, 4. f Pss 50, 12; 89, 12; Dt 10, 14; 1 Cor 10, 26. g Ps 136, 6; Is 42, 5. h Ps 15, 1. i Ps 118, 19–20. j Pss 86, 4; 143, 8. k Ps 71, 1. l Ps 22, 6; Is 49, 23; Dn 3, 40.

4 Make known to me your ways, LORD;
teach me your paths. [m]
5 Guide me in your truth and teach me,
for you are God my savior.
For you I wait all the long day,
because of your goodness, LORD.*
6 Remember your compassion and love, O LORD;
for they are ages old. [n]
7 Remember no more the sins of my youth; [o]
remember me only in light of your love.

II

8 Good and upright is the LORD,
who shows sinners the way,
9 Guides the humble rightly,
and teaches the humble the way.
10 All the paths of the LORD are faithful love
toward those who honor the covenant demands.
11 For the sake of your name, LORD,
pardon my guilt, though it is great.
12 Who are those who fear the LORD?
God shows them the way to choose. [p]
13 They live well and prosper,
and their descendants inherit the land. [q]
14 The counsel of the LORD belongs to the faithful;
the covenant instructs them.
15 My eyes are ever upon the LORD,
who frees my feet from the snare. [r]

III

16 Look upon me, have pity on me,
for I am alone and afflicted. [s]
17 Relieve the troubles of my heart;
bring me out of my distress.
18 Put an end to my affliction and suffering;
take away all my sins.
19 See how many are my enemies,
see how fiercely they hate me.
20 Preserve my life and rescue me;
do not let me be disgraced, for I trust in you.
21 Let honesty and virtue preserve me;
I wait for you, O LORD.
22 Redeem Israel, God,*
from all its distress!

PSALM 26*

Prayer of Innocence

1 Of David.

I

Grant me justice, LORD!
I have walked without blame. [t]
In the LORD I have trusted;
I have not faltered.
2 Test me, LORD, and try me;
search my heart and mind. [u]
3 Your love is before my eyes;
I walk guided by your faithfulness. [v]

II

4 I do not sit with deceivers,
nor with hypocrites do I mingle.
5 I hate the company of evildoers;
with the wicked I do not sit.
6 I will wash my hands* in innocence [w]
and walk round your altar, LORD,
7 Lifting my voice in thanks,
recounting all your wondrous deeds.
8 LORD, I love the house where you dwell,
the tenting-place of your glory. [x]

III

9 Do not take me away with sinners,
nor my life with the violent. [y]
10 Their hands carry out their schemes;
their right hands are full of bribes.
11 But I walk without blame; [z]
redeem me, be gracious to me! [a]

25, 5: Because of your goodness, LORD: these words have been transposed from the end of 7 to preserve the pattern of two lines per letter of the Hebrew alphabet in the acrostic poem.

25, 22: A final verse beginning with the Hebrew letter *pe* is added to the normal 22-letter alphabet. Thus the letters *aleph, lamed,* and *pe* open the first, middle (v 11), and last lines of the psalm. Together, they spell *aleph,* the first letter of the alphabet.

Ps 26: Like a priest washing before approaching the altar (Ex 30, 17–21), the psalmist seeks God's protection upon entering the temple. 1–3, matched by 11–12, remind God of past integrity while asking for purification; 4–5, matched by 9–10, pray for inclusion among the just; 6–8, the center of the poem, express the joy in God at the heart of all ritual.

26, 6: I will wash my hands: the washing of hands was a liturgical act (Ex 30, 19. 21; 40, 31–32), symbolic of inner as well as outer cleanness. Cf Is 1, 16.

m Pss 27, 11; 86, 11; 119, 12. 35; 143, 8. 10. n Sir 51, 8. o Jb 13, 26; Is 64, 8. p Prv 19, 23. q Ps 37, 9. 29. r Pss 123, 1. 2; 141, 8. s Pss 86, 16; 119, 132. t Ps 7, 9. u Pss 17, 3; 139, 23. v Ps 86, 11. w Ps 73, 13. x Pss 29, 9; 63, 3; Ex 24, 16; 25, 8. y Ps 28, 3. z Ps 101, 6. a Ps 25, 16.

I cried out to you and you healed* me.
4 LORD, you brought me up from Sheol;
you kept me from going down to the pit. [v]*

II

5 Sing praise to the LORD, you faithful;
give thanks to God's holy name.
6 For divine anger lasts but a moment;
divine favor lasts a lifetime.
At dusk weeping comes for the night;
but at dawn there is rejoicing.

III

7 Complacent,* I once said,
"I shall never be shaken."
8 LORD, when you showed me favor
I stood like the mighty mountains.
But when you hid your face
I was struck with terror. [w]
9 To you, LORD, I cried out;
with the Lord I pleaded for mercy:
10 "What gain is there from my lifeblood,
from my going down to the grave?
Does dust give you thanks
or declare your faithfulness?*
11 Hear, O LORD, have mercy on me;
LORD, be my helper."

IV

12 You changed my mourning into dancing;
you took off my sackcloth
and clothed me with gladness. [x]
13 With my whole being I sing
endless praise to you.
O LORD, my God,
forever will I give you thanks.

PSALM 31*

Prayer in Distress and Thanksgiving for Escape

1 For the leader. A psalm
of David.

I

2 In you, LORD, I take refuge; [y]
let me never be put to shame.
In your justice deliver me;
3 incline your ear to me;
make haste to rescue me!
Be my rock of refuge,
a stronghold to save me.
4 You are my rock and my fortress; [z]
for your name's sake lead and guide me.
5 Free me from the net they have set for me,
for you are my refuge.
6 Into your hands I commend my spirit; [a]*
you will redeem me, LORD, faithful God.
7 You hate those who serve worthless idols,
but I trust in the LORD.
8 I will rejoice and be glad in your love,
once you have seen my misery,
observed my distress. [b]
9 You will not abandon me into enemy hands,
but will set my feet in a free and open space.

II

10 Be gracious to me, LORD, for I am in distress;
with grief my eyes are wasted,
my soul and body spent.
11 My life is worn out by sorrow,
my years by sighing.
My strength fails in affliction;

29, 10: The flood: God defeated the primordial waters and made them part of the universe. Cf Pss 89, 10–13 and 93, 3–4.

29, 11: His people: God's people, Israel.

Ps 30: An individual thanksgiving in four parts: praise and thanks for deliverance and restoration (2–4); an invitation to others to join in (5–6); a flashback to the time before deliverance (7–11); a return to praise and thanks (12–13). Two sets of images recur: 1) going down, death, silence; 2) coming up, life, praising. God has delivered the psalmist from one state to the other.

30, 1: For the dedication of the temple: a later adaptation of the psalm to celebrate the purification of the temple in 164 B.C. during the Maccabean Revolt.

30, 3: Healed: for God as healer, see also Pss 103, 3; 107, 20; Hos 6, 1; 7, 1; 11, 3; 14, 5.

30, 4: Sheol . . . pit: the shadowy underworld residence of the spirits of the dead, here a metaphor for near death.

30, 7: Complacent: untroubled existence is often seen as a source of temptation to forget God. Cf Dt 8, 10–18; Hos 13, 6; Prv 30, 9.

30, 10: In the stillness of Sheol no one gives you praise; let me live and be among your worshipers. Cf Pss 6, 6; 88, 11–13; 115, 17; Is 38, 18.

Ps 31: A lament (2–19) with a strong emphasis on trust (4. 6. 15–16), ending with an anticipatory thanksgiving (20–25). As is usual in laments, the affliction is couched in general terms. The psalmist feels overwhelmed by evil people but trusts in the "faithful God" (6).

31, 6: Into your hands I commend my spirit: in Lk 23, 46 Jesus breathes his last with this psalm verse. Stephen in Acts 7, 59 alludes to these words as he is attacked by enemies. The verse is used as an antiphon in the Divine Office at Compline, the last prayer of the day.

v Ps 28, 1; Jon 2, 7. w Ps 104, 29. x Is 61, 3; Jer 31, 13. y 2–4: Ps 71, 1–3. z Ps 18, 2. a Lk 23, 46; Acts 7, 59. b Ps 10, 14.

my bones are consumed. [c]
12 To all my foes I am a thing of scorn,
to my neighbors, a dreaded sight,
a horror to my friends.
When they see me in the street,
they quickly shy away. [d]
13 I am forgotten, out of mind like the dead;
I am like a shattered dish.*
14 I hear the whispers of the crowd;
terrors are all around me.*
They conspire against me;
they plot to take my life.
15 But I trust in you, LORD;
I say, "You are my God." [e]
16 My times are in your hands;
rescue me from my enemies,
from the hands of my pursuers.
17 Let your face shine on your servant;[f]
save me in your kindness.
18 Do not let me be put to shame,
for I have called to you, LORD.
Put the wicked to shame;
reduce them to silence in Sheol.
19 Strike dumb their lying lips,
proud lips that attack the just
in contempt and scorn. [g]

III

20 How great is your goodness, LORD,
stored up for those who fear you.
You display it for those who trust you,
in the sight of all the people.
21 You hide them in the shelter of your presence,
safe from scheming enemies.
You keep them in your abode,
safe from plotting tongues. [h]
22 Blessed be the LORD,
who has shown me wondrous love,
and been for me a city most secure.
23 Once I said in my anguish,
"I am shut out from your sight." [i]
Yet you heard my plea,
when I cried out to you.
24 Love the LORD, all you faithful.
The LORD protects the loyal,
but repays the arrogant in full.
25 Be strong and take heart,
all you who hope in the LORD.

PSALM 32*

Remission of Sin

1 Of David. A *maskil.*

I

Happy the sinner whose fault is removed,
whose sin is forgiven. [j]
2 Happy those to whom the LORD imputes no guilt,
in whose spirit is no deceit.

II

3 As long as I kept silent,* my bones wasted away;
I groaned all the day. [k]
4 For day and night your hand was heavy upon me;
my strength withered as in dry summer heat. *Selah*
5 Then I declared my sin to you;
my guilt I did not hide. [l]
I said, "I confess my faults to the LORD,"
and you took away the guilt of my sin. *Selah*
6 Thus should all your faithful pray
in time of distress.
Though flood waters* threaten,
they will never reach them. [m]
7 You are my shelter; from distress you keep me;
with safety you ring me round. *Selah*

31, 13: **Like a shattered dish**: a common comparison for something ruined and useless. Cf Is 30, 14; Jer 19, 11; 22, 28.

31, 14: **Terrors are all around**: a cry used in inescapable danger. Cf Jer 6, 25; 20, 10; 46, 5; 49, 29.

Ps 32: An individual thanksgiving and the second of the seven Penitential Psalms (cf Ps 6). The opening declaration—the forgiven are blessed (1–2)—arises from the psalmist's own experience. At one time the psalmist was stubborn and closed, a victim of sin's power (3–4), and then became open to the forgiving God (5–7). Sin here, as often in the Bible, is not only the personal act of rebellion against God but also the consequences of that act—frustration and waning of vitality. Having been rescued, the psalmist can teach others the joys of justice and the folly of sin (8–11).

32, 3: **I kept silent**: did not confess the sin before God.

32, 6: **Flood waters**: the untamed waters surrounding the earth, a metaphor for danger.

c Pss 32, 3; 38, 10–11. d Jb 19, 13–19. e Ps 140, 7; Is 25, 1. f Ps 67, 1; Nm 6, 24. g Ps 12, 4. h Ps 27, 5. i Jon 2, 5. j Is 1, 18; Ps 65, 3; Rom 4, 7–8. k Ps 31, 11. l Pss 38, 19; 51, 5. m Ps 18, 5.

III

8 I will instruct you and show you the way you
should walk,
give you counsel and watch over you.
9 Do not be senseless like horses or mules;
with bit and bridle their temper is curbed,
else they will not come to you.

IV

10 Many are the sorrows of the wicked,
but love surrounds those who trust in the
LORD.
11 Be glad in the LORD and rejoice, you just;
exult, all you upright of heart. [n]

PSALM 33*

Praise of the Lord's Power and Providence

I

1 Rejoice, you just, in the LORD;
praise from the upright is fitting. [o]
2 Give thanks to the LORD on the harp;
on the ten-stringed lyre offer praise. [p]
3 Sing to God a new song;
skillfully play with joyful chant.
4 For the LORD's word is true;
all his works are trustworthy.
5 The LORD loves justice and right
and fills the earth with goodness. [q]

II

6 By the LORD's word the heavens were made;
by the breath of his mouth all their host. [r]*
7 The waters of the sea were gathered as in a
bowl;*
in cellars the deep was confined. [s]

III

8 Let all the earth fear the LORD;
let all who dwell in the world show
reverence.
9 For he spoke, and it came to be,
commanded, and it stood in place. [t]
10 The LORD foils the plan of nations,
frustrates the designs of peoples.
11 But the plan of the LORD stands forever,
wise designs through all generations. [u]
12 Happy the nation whose God is the LORD,
the people chosen as his very own. [v]

IV

13 From heaven the LORD looks down
and observes the whole human race, [w]
14 Surveying from the royal throne
all who dwell on earth.
15 The one who fashioned the hearts of them all
knows all their works.

V

16 A king is not saved by a mighty army,
nor a warrior delivered by great strength.
17 Useless is the horse for safety;
its great strength, no sure escape.
18 But the LORD's eyes are upon the reverent,
upon those who hope for his gracious help,
19 Delivering them from death,
keeping them alive in times of famine.

VI

20 Our soul waits for the LORD,
who is our help and shield. [x]
21 For in God our hearts rejoice;
in your holy name we trust.
22 May your kindness, LORD, be upon us;
we have put our hope in you.

PSALM 34*

Thanksgiving to God Who Delivers the Just

1 Of David, when he feigned madness before
Abimelech,* who forced him to depart.

I

2 I will bless the LORD at all times;

Ps 33: A hymn in which the just are invited (1–3) to praise God, who by a mere word (4–5) created the three-tiered universe of the heavens, the cosmic waters, and the earth (6–9). Human words, in contrast, effect nothing (10–11). The greatness of human beings consists in God's choosing them as a special people and their faithful response (12–22).

33, 6: All their host: the stars of the sky are commonly viewed as a vast army, e.g., Neh 9, 6; Is 40, 26; 45, 12; Jer 33, 22.

33, 7: The waters . . . as in a bowl: ancients sometimes attributed the power keeping the seas from overwhelming land to a primordial victory of the storm-god over personified Sea. God confines the seas as easily as one puts water in a bowl.

Ps 34: A thanksgiving in acrostic form, each line beginning with a successive letter of the Hebrew alphabet. In this psalm one letter is missing and two are in reverse order. The psalmist, fresh from the experience of being rescued (5. 7), can teach the "poor," those who are defenseless, to trust in God alone (4. 12). God will make them powerful (5–11) and give them protection (12–23).

34, 1: Abimelech: a scribal error for Achish. In 1 Sm 21, 13–16, David feigned madness before Achish, not Abimelech.

n Ps 33, 1. o Pss 32, 11; 147, 1. p Pss 92, 4; 144, 9. q Ps 119, 64. r Gn 2, 1. s Ps 78, 13; Gn 1, 9–10; Ex 15, 8. t Ps 148, 5; Gn 1, 3f; Jdt 16, 14. u Prv 19, 21; Is 40, 8. v Ps 144, 15; Ex 19, 6; Dt 7, 6. w Jb 34, 21; Sir 15, 19; Jer 16, 17; 32, 19. x Ps 115, 9.

praise shall be always in my mouth.[y]
3 My soul will glory in the LORD
that the poor may hear and be glad.
4 Magnify the LORD with me;
let us exalt his name together.

II

5 I sought the LORD, who answered me,
delivered me from all my fears.
6 Look to God that you may be radiant with joy
and your faces may not blush for shame.
7 In my misfortune I called,
the LORD heard and saved me from all
distress.
8 The angel of the LORD, who encamps with
them,
delivers all who fear God.[z]
9 Learn to savor how good the LORD is;
happy are those who take refuge in him.[a]
10 Fear the LORD, you holy ones;
nothing is lacking to those who fear him.[b]
11 The powerful* grow poor and hungry,
but those who seek the LORD lack no good
thing.

III

12 Come, children,* listen to me;[c]
I will teach you the fear of the LORD.
13 Who among you loves life,[d]
takes delight in prosperous days?
14 Keep your tongue from evil,
your lips from speaking lies.
15 Turn from evil and do good;[e]
seek peace and pursue it.
16 The LORD has eyes for the just[f]
and ears for their cry.
17 The LORD's face is against evildoers
to wipe out their memory from the earth.
18 When the just cry out, the LORD hears
and rescues them from all distress.
19 The LORD is close to the brokenhearted,
saves those whose spirit is crushed.
20 Many are the troubles of the just,
but the LORD delivers from them all.
21 God watches over all their bones;
not a one shall be broken.[g]
22 Evil will slay the wicked;
those who hate the just are condemned.
23 The LORD redeems loyal servants;
no one is condemned whose refuge is God.

PSALM 35*

Prayer for Help against Unjust Enemies

1 Of David.

I

Oppose, LORD, those who oppose me;*
war upon those who make war upon me.
2 Take up the shield and buckler;
rise up in my defense.
3 Brandish lance and battle-ax
against my pursuers.
Say to my heart,
"I am your salvation."
4 Let those who seek my life
be put to shame and disgrace.
Let those who plot evil against me[h]
be turned back and confounded.
5 Make them like chaff before the wind,[i]
with the angel of the LORD driving them on.
6 Make their way slippery and dark,
with the angel of the LORD pursuing them.

II

7 Without cause they set their snare for me;
without cause they dug a pit for me.
8 Let ruin overtake them unawares;
let the snare they have set catch them;
let them fall into the pit they have dug.[j]
9 Then I will rejoice in the LORD,
exult in God's salvation.
10 My very bones shall say,

34, 11: The powerful: literally, "lions." Fierce animals were sometimes metaphors for influential people.

34, 12: Children: the customary term for students in Wisdom literature.

Ps 35: A lament of a person betrayed by friends. The psalmist prays that the evildoers be publicly exposed as unjust (1–8), and gives thanks in anticipation of vindication (9–10). Old friends are the enemies (11–16). May their punishment come quickly (17–21)! The last part (22–26) echoes the opening in praying for the destruction of the psalmist's persecutors. The psalm may appear vindictive, but one must keep in mind that the psalmist is praying for *public* redress now of a *public* injustice. There is at this time no belief in an afterlife in which justice will be redressed.

35, 1–6: The mixture of judicial, martial, and hunting images shows that the language is figurative. The actual injustice is false accusation of serious crimes (11. 15. 20–21). The psalmist seeks lost honor through a trial before God.

y Ps 145, 2. z Ex 14, 19. a Ps 2, 12. b Prv 3, 7. c Prv 1, 8; 4, 1. d 13–17: 1 Pt 3, 10–12. e Ps 37, 27. f Ps 33, 18. g Jn 19, 36. h Pss 40, 15; 71, 13. i Pss 1, 4; 83, 14; Jb 21, 18. j Pss 7, 16; 9, 16; 57, 7; Prv 26, 27; Eccl 10, 8; Sir 27, 26.

"O LORD, who is like you,[k]
Who rescue the afflicted from the powerful,
the afflicted and needy from the despoiler?"

III

11 Malicious witnesses come forward,
accuse me of things I do not know.
12 They repay me evil for good
and I am all alone.[l]
13 Yet I, when they were ill, put on sackcloth,*
afflicted myself with fasting,
sobbed my prayers upon my bosom.
14 I went about in grief as for my brother,
bent in mourning as for my mother.
15 Yet when I stumbled they gathered with glee,
they gathered against me like strangers.
They slandered me without ceasing;
16 without respect they mocked me,
gnashed their teeth against me.

IV

17 LORD, how long will you look on?
Save me from roaring beasts,
my precious life from lions![m]
18 Then I will thank you in the great assembly;
I will praise you before the mighty throng.[n]
19 Do not let lying foes smirk at me,
my undeserved enemies wink knowingly.[o]
20 They speak no words of peace,
but against the quiet in the land
they fashion deceitful speech.[p]
21 They open wide their mouths against me.
They say, "Aha! Good!
Our eyes relish the sight!"[q]
22 You see this, LORD; do not be silent;[r]
Lord, do not withdraw from me.
23 Awake, be vigilant in my defense,
in my cause, my God and my Lord.
24 Defend me because you are just, LORD;
my God, do not let them gloat over me.
25 Do not let them say in their hearts,
"Aha! Just what we wanted!"
Do not let them say,
"We have devoured that one!"
26 Put to shame and confound
all who relish my misfortune.
Clothe with shame and disgrace
those who lord it over me.
27 But let those who favor my just cause
shout for joy and be glad.
May they ever say, "Exalted be the LORD
who delights in the peace of his loyal
servant."
28 Then my tongue shall recount your justice,
declare your praise, all the day long.[s]

PSALM 36*

Human Wickedness and Divine Providence

1 For the leader. Of David, the servant of the LORD.

I

2 Sin directs the heart of the wicked;
their eyes are closed to the fear of God.[t]
3 For they live with the delusion:
their guilt will not be known and hated.*
4 Empty and false are the words of their mouth;
they have ceased to be wise and do good.
5 In their beds they hatch plots;
they set out on a wicked way;
they do not reject evil.[u]

II

6 LORD, your love reaches to heaven;
your fidelity, to the clouds.[v]
7 Your justice is like the highest mountains;
your judgments,* like the mighty deep;
all living creatures you sustain, LORD.
8 How precious is your love, O God!
We take refuge in the shadow of your
wings.[w]*
9 We feast on the rich food of your house;
from your delightful stream[x] you give us
drink.

35, 13. 15–17: The Hebrew is obscure.

Ps 36: A psalm with elements of wisdom (2–5), the hymn (6–10), and the lament (11–13). The rule of sin over the wicked (2–5) is contrasted with the rule of divine love and mercy over God's friends (6–10). The psalm ends with a prayer that God's guidance never cease (11–13).

36, 3: Hated: punished by God.

36, 6–7: Love . . . judgments: God actively controls the entire world.

36, 8: The shadow of your wings: metaphor for divine protection. It probably refers to the winged cherubim in the holy of holies in the temple. Cf 1 Kgs 6, 23–28. 32; 2 Chr 3, 10–13; Ez 1, 4–9.

k Ps 86, 8; 89, 7. 9; Ex 15, 11. l Pss 27, 12; 38, 20–21; 109, 5; Jer 18, 20. m Pss 17, 12; 22, 22; 58, 7. n Pss 22, 23; 26, 12; 35, 18; 40, 10; 149, 1. o Ps 38, 17. p Ps 120, 6–7. q Ps 40, 16; Lam 2, 16. r Pss 22, 12; 38, 21; 109, 1. s Ps 71, 15–16. t Rom 3, 18. u Mi 2, 1. v Pss 57, 11; 71, 19. w Ps 17, 8. x Gn 2, 8. 10.

10 For with you is the fountain of life,[y]
and in your light we see light.[z]
11 Continue your kindness toward your friends,
your just defense of the honest heart.
12 Do not let the foot of the proud overtake me,
nor the hand of the wicked disturb me.
13 There make the evildoers fall;
thrust them down, never to rise.

PSALM 37*

The Fate of Sinners and the Reward of the Just

1 Of David.

ALEPH

Do not be provoked by evildoers;
do not envy those who do wrong.[a]
2 Like grass they wither quickly;
like green plants they wilt away.[b]

BETH

3 Trust in the LORD and do good
that you may dwell in the land* and live secure.[c]
4 Find your delight in the LORD
who will give you your heart's desire.[d]

GIMEL

5 Commit your way to the LORD;
trust that God will act[e]
6 And make your integrity shine like the dawn,
your vindication like noonday.[f]

DALETH

7 Be still before the LORD;
wait for God.
Do not be provoked by the prosperous,
nor by malicious schemers.

HE

8 Give up your anger, abandon your wrath;
do not be provoked; it brings only harm.
9 Those who do evil will be cut off,
but those who wait for the LORD will possess the land.[g]

WAW

10 Wait a little, and the wicked will be no more;
look for them and they will not be there.
11 But the poor will possess the land,[h]
will delight in great prosperity.

ZAYIN

12 The wicked plot against the just
and grind their teeth at them;
13 But the LORD laughs at them,[i]
knowing their day is coming.

HETH

14 The wicked draw their swords;
they string their bows
To fell the poor and oppressed,
to slaughter those whose way is honest.[j]
15 Their swords will pierce their own hearts;
their bows will be broken.

TETH

16 Better the poverty of the just
than the great wealth of the wicked.[k]
17 The arms of the wicked will be broken;
the LORD will sustain the just.

YODH

18 The LORD watches over the days of the blameless;
their heritage lasts forever.
19 They will not be disgraced when times are hard;
in days of famine they will have plenty.

KAPH

20 The wicked perish,
the enemies of the LORD;

Ps 37: The psalm responds to the problem of evil, which the Old Testament often expresses as a question: Why do the wicked prosper and the good suffer? The psalm answers that the situation is only temporary. God will reverse things, rewarding the good and punishing the wicked here on earth. The perspective is concrete and earthbound: people's very actions place them among the ranks of the good or wicked. Each group or "way" has its own inherent dynamism—eventual frustration for the wicked, eventual reward for the just. The psalm is an acrostic, i.e., each section begins with a successive letter of the Hebrew alphabet. Each section has its own imagery and logic.

37, 3. 9. 11. 22. 27. 29. 34: The land: the promised land, Israel, which became for later interpreters a type or figure of heaven. Cf Heb 11, 9–10. 13–16. The New Testament Beatitudes (Mt 5, 3–12; Lk 6, 20–26) have been influenced by the psalm, especially their total reversal of the present and their interpretation of the happy future as possession of the land.

y Is 55, 1; Jn 4, 14. z Ps 80, 4. 8. 20. a Prv 3, 31; 23, 17; 24, 1. 19. b Pss 90, 5–6; 102, 12; 103, 15–16; Jb 14, 2; Is 40, 7. c Ps 128, 2. d Prv 10, 24. e Ps 55, 23; Prv 3, 5; 16, 3. f Wis 5, 6; Is 58, 10. g Ps 25, 13; Prv 2, 21; Is 57, 13. h Mt 5, 4. i Pss 2, 4; 59, 9; Wis 4, 18. j Pss 11, 2; 57, 5; 64, 4. k Prv 15, 16; 16, 8.

Like the beauty of meadows they vanish;
like smoke they disappear. [l]

LAMEDH

21 The wicked borrow but do not repay;
the just are generous in giving.
22 For those blessed by the Lord will possess the land,
but those accursed will be cut off.

MEM

23 Those whose steps are guided by the LORD; [m]
whose way God approves,
24 May stumble, but they will never fall,
for the LORD holds their hand.

NUN

25 Neither in my youth, nor now in old age
have I ever seen the just abandoned [n]
or their children begging bread.
26 The just always lend generously,
and their children become a blessing.

SAMEKH

27 Turn from evil and do good,
that you may inhabit the land forever. [o]
28 For the LORD loves justice
and does not abandon the faithful.

AYIN

When the unjust are destroyed,
and the children of the wicked cut off,
29 The just will possess the land
and live in it forever. [p]

PE

30 The mouths of the just utter wisdom; [q]
their tongues speak what is right.
31 God's teaching is in their hearts; [r]
their steps do not falter.

SADHE

32 The wicked spy on the just
and seek to kill them.
33 But the LORD does not leave the just in their power,
nor let them be condemned when tried.

QOPH

34 Wait eagerly for the LORD,
and keep to the way; [s]
God will raise you to possess the land;
you will gloat when the wicked are cut off.

RESH

35 I have seen ruthless scoundrels,
strong as flourishing cedars. [t]
36 When I passed by again, they were gone;
though I searched, they could not be found.

SHIN

37 Observe the honest, mark the upright;
those at peace with God have a future. [u]
38 But all sinners will be destroyed;
the future of the wicked will be cut off.

TAW

39 The salvation of the just is from the LORD,
their refuge in time of distress. [v]
40 The LORD helps and rescues them,
rescues and saves them from the wicked,
because in God they take refuge.

PSALM 38*

Prayer of an Afflicted Sinner

1 A psalm of David. For remembrance.

I

2 LORD, punish me no more in your anger;
in your wrath do not chastise me! [w]
3 Your arrows have sunk deep in me; [x]
your hand has come down upon me.
4 My flesh is afflicted because of your anger;
my frame aches because of my sin. [y]
5 My iniquities overwhelm me,
a burden beyond my strength. [z]

II

6 Foul and festering are my sores
because of my folly.
7 I am stooped and deeply bowed; [a]
all day I go about mourning.

Ps 38: In this lament, one of the Penitential Psalms (cf Ps 6), the psalmist acknowledges the sin that has brought physical and mental sickness and social ostracism. There is no one to turn to for help; only God can undo the past and restore the psalmist.

l Wis 5, 14. m Prv 20, 24. n Jb 4, 7; Sir 2, 10. o Ps 34, 14–15; Am 5, 14. p Ps 25, 13; Prv 2, 21; Is 57, 13. q Prv 10, 31. r Ps 40, 9; Dt 6, 6; Is 51, 7; Jer 31, 33. s Ps 31, 24. t Ps 92, 8–9; Is 2, 13; Ez 31, 10–11. u Prv 23, 18; 24, 14. v Ps 9, 10; Is 25, 4. w Ps 6, 2. x Jb 6, 4; Lam 3, 12; Pss 31, 11; 64, 7. y Is 1, 5–6. z Ps 40, 13; Ezr 9, 6. a Ps 35, 14.

8 My loins burn with fever;
my flesh is afflicted.
9 I am numb and utterly crushed;
I wail with anguish of heart. [b]
10 My Lord, my deepest yearning is before you;
my groaning is not hidden from you.
11 My heart shudders, my strength forsakes me;
the very light of my eyes has failed. [c]
12 Friends and companions shun my pain;
my neighbors stand far off.
13 Those who seek my life lay snares for me;
they seek my misfortune, they speak of ruin;
they plot treachery all the day.

III

14 But I am like the deaf, hearing nothing,
like the dumb, saying nothing,
15 Like someone who does not hear,
who has no answer ready.
16 LORD, I wait for you;
O Lord, my God, answer me. [d]
17 For I fear they will gloat,
exult over me if I stumble.

IV

18 I am very near to falling;
my pain is with me always.
19 I acknowledge my guilt
and grieve over my sin. [e]
20 But many are my foes without cause,
a multitude of enemies without reason,
21 Repaying me evil for good,
harassing me for pursuing good. [f]
22 Forsake me not, O LORD;
my God, be not far from me! [g]
23 Come quickly to help me, [h]
my Lord and my salvation!

PSALM 39*

The Vanity of Life

1 For the leader, for Jeduthun. [i] A psalm of David.

I

2 I said, "I will watch my ways,
lest I sin with my tongue;
I will set a curb on my mouth."
3 Dumb and silent before the wicked,
I refrained from any speech.
But my sorrow increased;
4 my heart smoldered within me. [j]
In my thoughts a fire blazed up,
and I broke into speech:

II

5 LORD, let me know my end, the number of my days,
that I may learn how frail I am.
6 You have given my days a very short span;
my life is as nothing before you.
All mortals are but a breath. [k] *Selah*
7 Mere phantoms, we go our way;
mere vapor, our restless pursuits;
we heap up stores without knowing for whom.
8 And now, Lord, what future do I have?
You are my only hope.
9 From all my sins deliver me;
let me not be the taunt of fools.

III

10 I was silent and did not open my mouth
because you were the one who did this.
11 Take your plague away from me;
I am ravaged by the touch of your hand.
12 You rebuke our guilt and chasten us;
you dissolve all we prize like a cobweb.
All mortals are but a breath. *Selah*
13 Listen to my prayer, LORD, hear my cry;
do not be deaf to my weeping!
I sojourn with you like a passing stranger,
a guest, like all my ancestors. [l]
14 Turn your gaze from me, that I may find peace
before I depart to be no more.

PSALM 40*

Gratitude and Prayer for Help

1 For the leader. A psalm of David.

A

I

2 I waited, waited for the LORD;

Ps 39: The lament of a mortally ill person who at first had resolved to remain silently submissive (2–4). But the grief was too much and now the psalmist laments the brevity and vanity of life (5–7), yet remaining hopeful (8–10). The psalmist continues to express both acceptance of the illness and hope for healing in 11–14.

b Ps 102, 4–6. c Pss 6, 8; 31, 10. d Ps 13, 4. e Pss 32, 5; 51, 5. f Ps 109, 5. g Pss 22, 2. 12. 20; 35, 22. h Ps 40, 14. i 1 Chr 16, 41; Pss 62, 1; 77, 1. j Jer 20, 9. k Pss 62, 10; 90, 9–10; 144, 4; Jb 7, 6. 16; 14, 1. 5; Eccl 6, 12; Wis 2, 5. l Ps 119, 19; Gn 23, 4; Heb 11, 13; 1 Pt 2, 11.

who bent down and heard my cry, [m]
3 Drew me out of the pit of destruction,
out of the mud of the swamp, [n]
Set my feet upon rock,
steadied my steps,
4 And put a new song* in my mouth, [o]
a hymn to our God.
Many shall look on in awe
and they shall trust in the LORD.

II

5 Happy those whose trust is the LORD,
who turn not to idolatry
or to those who stray after falsehood. [p]
6 How numerous, O LORD, my God,
you have made your wondrous deeds!
And in your plans for us
there is none to equal you. [q]
Should I wish to declare or tell them,
too many are they to recount. [r]

III

7 Sacrifice and offering you do not want; [s]*
but ears open to obedience you gave me.
Holocausts and sin-offerings you do not
require;
8 so I said, "Here I am;
your commands for me are written in the
scroll.
9 To do your will is my delight;
my God, your law is in my heart!" [t]
10 I announced your deed to a great assembly;
I did not restrain my lips;
you, LORD, are my witness. [u]
11 Your deed I did not hide within my heart;
your loyal deliverance I have proclaimed.
I made no secret of your enduring kindness
to a great assembly.

B

I

12 LORD, do not withhold your compassion from
me;
may your enduring kindness ever preserve
me. [v]
13 For all about me are evils beyond count;
my sins so overcome me I cannot see.
They are more than the hairs of my head;
my courage fails me. [w]

II

14 LORD, graciously rescue me! [x]
Come quickly to help me, LORD!
15 Put to shame and confound
all who seek to take my life.
Turn back in disgrace
those who desire my ruin. [y]
16 Let those who say "Aha!" [z]
know dismay and shame.
17 But may all who seek you
rejoice and be glad in you.
May those who long for your help
always say, "The LORD be glorified." [a]
18 Though I am afflicted and poor,
the Lord keeps me in mind.
You are my help and deliverer;
my God, do not delay!

PSALM 41*

Thanksgiving after Sickness

1 For the leader. A psalm of David.

I

2 Happy those concerned for the lowly and
poor;*

Ps 40: A thanksgiving (2–13) has been combined with a lament (14–18), that appears also in Ps 70. The psalmist describes the rescue in spatial terms—being raised up from the swampy underworld to firm earth where one can praise God (2–4). All who trust God will experience like protection (5–6)! The psalm stipulates the precise mode of thanksgiving: not animal sacrifice but open and enthusiastic proclamation of the salvation just experienced (7–11). A prayer for protection concludes (12–18).

40, 4: A new song: a song in response to the new action of God (cf Pss 33, 3; 96, 1; 144, 9; 149, 1; Is 42, 10). Giving thanks is not purely a human response but is itself a divine gift.

40, 7–9: Obedience is better than sacrifice (cf 1 Sm 15, 22; Is 1, 10–20; Hos 6, 6; Am 5, 22–25; Mi 6, 6–8; Acts 7, 42–43 [quoting Am 5, 25–26 LXX]). Heb 10, 5–9 quotes the somewhat different Greek version and interprets it as Christ's self-oblation.

Ps 41: A thanksgiving for rescue from illness (4. 5. 9). Many people, even friends, have interpreted the illness as a divine punishment for sin and have ostracized the psalmist (5–11). The healing shows the return of God's favor and rebukes the psalmist's detractors (12–13).

41, 2: Happy those concerned for the lowly and poor: other psalms use the same formula ("Happy those") for those whom God favors. Cf Pss 32, 1–2; 34, 9; 40, 5; 65, 5. The psalmist's

m Lam 3, 25. n Pss 28, 1; 30, 4; 69, 3. 15–16; 88, 5; Prv 1, 12; Jon 2, 7. o Ps 33, 3. p Ps 1, 1; Prv 16, 20; Jer 17, 7. q Ps 35, 10. r Pss 71, 15; 139, 17–18. s 7–9: Heb 10, 5–7; Ps 51, 18–19; Am 5, 22; Hos 6, 6; Is 1, 11–15. t Ps 37, 31. u Pss 22, 23; 26, 12; 35, 18; 149, 1. v Ps 89, 34. w Ps 38, 5. 11; Ezr 9, 6. x 14–18: Pss 70, 2–6; 71, 12. y Ps 35, 4. 26. z Ps 35, 21. 25. a Ps 35, 27.

when misfortune strikes, the LORD delivers
them. [b]
3 The LORD keeps and preserves them,
makes them happy in the land,
and does not betray them to their enemies.
4 The LORD sustains them on their sickbed,
allays the malady when they are ill.

II

5 Once I prayed, "LORD, have mercy on me;
heal me, I have sinned against you.
6 My enemies say the worst of me:
'When will that one die and be forgotten?'
7 When people come to visit me,
they speak without sincerity.
Their hearts store up malice;
they leave and spread their vicious lies. [c]
8 My foes all whisper against me;
they imagine the worst about me:
9 I have a deadly disease, they say;
I will never rise from my sickbed.
10 Even the friend who had my trust,
who shared my table, has scorned me. [d]*
11 But you, LORD, have mercy and raise me up
that I may repay them as they deserve."*

III

12 By this I know you are pleased with me,
that my enemy no longer jeers at me.
13 For my integrity you have supported me
and let me stand in your presence forever.

* * *

14 Blessed be the LORD, the God of Israel,
from all eternity and forever.
Amen. Amen. [e]*

SECOND BOOK—PSALMS 42–72

PSALMS 42–43*

Longing for God's Presence in the Temple

1 For the leader. A *maskil* of the Korahites.*

I

2 As the deer longs for streams of water, [f]
so my soul longs for you, O God.
3 My being thirsts for God, the living God.
When can I go and see the face of God? [g]*
4 My tears have been my food day and night, [h]
as they ask daily, "Where is your God?" [i]
5 Those times I recall
as I pour out my soul, [j]
When I went in procession with the crowd,
I went with them to the house of God,
Amid loud cries of thanksgiving,
with the multitude keeping festival. [k]
6 Why are you downcast, my soul;
why do you groan within me?
Wait for God, whom I shall praise again,
my savior and my God.

II

7 My soul is downcast within me;
therefore I will remember you
From the land of the Jordan* and Hermon,
from the land of Mount Mizar. [l]
8 Here deep calls to deep* in the roar of your
torrents.
All your waves and breakers sweep over
me. [m]
9 At dawn may the LORD bestow faithful love

---

statement about God's love of the poor is based on the experience of being rescued (1–3).

41, 10: Even the friend . . . has scorned me: Jn 13, 18 cites this verse to characterize Judas as a false friend. **Scorned me:** an interpretation of the unclear Hebrew, "made great the heel against me."

41, 11: That I may repay them as they deserve: the healing itself is an act of judgment through which God decides for the psalmist and against the false friends. The prayer is not necessarily for strength to punish enemies.

41, 14: The doxology, not part of the psalm, marks the end of the first of the five books of the Psalter. Compare Pss 72, 18–20; 89, 53; 106, 48.

Pss 42–43: Pss 42–43 form a single lament of three sections, each section ending in an identical refrain (42, 6. 12; 43, 5). The psalmist is in the extreme north of Israel, far from Jerusalem, and longs for the divine presence that Israel experienced in the temple liturgy. Despite sadness, the psalmist hopes once again to join the worshiping crowds.

42, 1: The Korahites: a major guild of temple singers (2 Chr 20, 19) whose name appears in the superscriptions of Pss 42; 44–49; 84–85; 87–88.

42, 3: See the face of God: "face" designates a personal presence (Gn 33, 10; Ex 10, 28–29; 2 Sm 17, 11). The expressions "see God/God's face" occur elsewhere (Pss 11, 7; 17, 15; 63, 3; cf Ex 24, 10; 33, 7–11; Jb 33, 26) for the presence of God in the temple.

42, 7: From the land of the Jordan: the sources of the Jordan are in the foothills of Mount Hermon in present-day southern Lebanon. Mount Mizar is presumed to be a mountain in the same range.

42, 8: Here deep calls to deep: to the psalmist, the waters arising in the north are overwhelming and far from God's presence, like the waters of chaos (Pss 18, 5; 69, 2–3. 15; Jon 2, 3–6).

b Tb 4, 7–11. c Pss 31, 12; 38, 12–13; 88, 8; Jb 19, 13–19; Jer 20, 10. d Ps 55, 14–15; Jn 13, 18. e Neh 9, 5. f 2–3: Pss 63, 2; 84, 3; 143, 6; Is 26, 9. g Ps 27, 4. h Pss 80, 6; 102, 10. i Ps 79, 10; Jl 2, 17. j Lam 3, 20. k Ps 122, 5. l Ps 43, 3. m Pss 18, 5; 32, 6; 69, 2; 88, 8; Jon 2, 4.

that I may sing praise through the night,
praise to the God of my life.
10 I say to God, "My rock,
why do you forget me? [n]
Why must I go about mourning
with the enemy oppressing me?"
11 It shatters my bones, when my adversaries
reproach me.
They say to me daily: "Where is your God?"
12 Why are you downcast, my soul,
why do you groan within me?
Wait for God, whom I shall praise again,
my savior and my God.

III

1 Grant me justice, God;
defend me from a faithless people;
from the deceitful and unjust rescue me. [o]
2 You, God, are my strength.
Why then do you spurn me?
Why must I go about mourning,
with the enemy oppressing me?
3 Send your light and fidelity,*
that they may be my guide [p]
And bring me to your holy mountain,
to the place of your dwelling, [q]
4 That I may come to the altar of God,
to God, my joy, my delight.
Then I will praise you with the harp,
O God, my God.
5 Why are you downcast, my soul?
Why do you groan within me?
Wait for God, whom I shall praise again,
my savior and my God.

PSALM 44*

God's Past Favor and Israel's Present Need

1 For the leader. A *maskil* of the Korahites.

I

2 O God, we have heard with our own ears;
our ancestors have told us [r]
The deeds you did in their days,
with your own hand in days of old:
3 You rooted out nations to plant them, [s]
crushed peoples to make room for them.
4 Not with their own swords did they conquer
the land, [t]
nor did their own arms bring victory;
It was your right hand, your own arm,
the light of your face, for you favored
them. [u]
5 You are my king and my God, [v]
who bestows victories on Jacob.
6 Through you we batter our foes;
through your name, trample our
adversaries.
7 Not in my bow do I trust,
nor does my sword bring me victory.
8 You have brought us victory over our enemies,
shamed those who hate us.
9 In God we have boasted all the day long;
your name we will praise forever. *Selah*

II

10 But now you have rejected and disgraced us; [w]
you do not march out with our armies. [x]
11 You make us retreat* before the foe;
those who hate us plunder us at will. [y]
12 You hand us over like sheep to be slaughtered,
scatter us among the nations. [z]
13 You sell your people for nothing;
you make no profit from their sale. [a]
14 You make us the reproach of our neighbors, [b]
the mockery and scorn of those around us.
15 You make us a byword among the nations;
the peoples shake their heads at us.
16 All day long my disgrace is before me;
shame has covered my face
17 At the sound of those who taunt and revile,
at the sight of the spiteful enemy.

43, 3: Your light and fidelity: a pair of divine attributes personified as guides for the pilgrimage. The psalmist seeks divine protection for the journey to Jerusalem.

Ps 44: In this lament the community reminds God of past favors which it has always acknowledged (2–9). But now God has abandoned Israel to defeat and humiliation (10–17), though the people are not conscious of any sin against the covenant (18–23). They struggle with being God's special people amid divine silence; yet they continue to pray (24–27).

44, 11: You make us retreat: the corollary of v 4. Defeat, like victory, is God's doing; neither Israel nor its enemies can claim credit (23).

n Pss 18, 2; 31, 3–4. o Ps 119, 154. p Pss 18, 29; 27, 1; 36, 10; Mi 7, 8. q Ps 122, 1. r Ps 78, 3. s Pss 78, 55; 80, 9f. t Dt 8, 17f; Jos 24, 12. u Pss 4, 7; 31, 17; 67, 2; 80, 4; Nm 6, 25; Dn 9, 17. v Ps 145, 1. w 10–27: Ps 89, 39–52. x Ps 60, 12. y Lv 26, 17; Dt 28, 25. z Lv 26, 33; Dt 28, 64. a Dt 32, 30; Is 52, 3. b 14–17: Pss 79, 4; 80, 7; 123, 3–4; Jb 12, 4; Dn 9, 16.

III

18 All this has come upon us,
though we have not forgotten you,
nor been disloyal to your covenant.
19 Our hearts have not turned back,*
nor have our steps strayed from your path.
20 Yet you have left us crushed,
desolate in a place of jackals; [c]*
you have covered us with darkness.
21 If we had forgotten the name of our God,
stretched out our hands to another god,
22 Would not God have discovered this,
God who knows the secrets of the heart?
23 For you we are slain all the day long,
considered only as sheep to be
slaughtered. [d]

IV

24 Awake! Why do you sleep, O Lord?
Rise up! Do not reject us forever! [e]
25 Why do you hide your face;[f]
why forget our pain and misery?
26 We are bowed down to the ground; [g]
our bodies are pressed to the earth.
27 Rise up, help us!
Redeem us as your love demands.

PSALM 45*

Song for a Royal Wedding

1 For the leader; according to "Lilies." A *maskil* of the Korahites. A love song.

I

2 My heart is stirred by a noble theme,
as I sing my ode to the king.
My tongue is the pen of a nimble scribe.

II

3 You are the most handsome of men;
fair speech has graced your lips,
for God has blessed you forever. [h]
4 Gird your sword upon your hip, mighty
warrior!
In splendor and majesty ride on
triumphant! [i]
5 In the cause of truth and justice
may your right hand show you wondrous
deeds.
6 Your arrows are sharp;
peoples will cower at your feet;
the king's enemies will lose heart.
7 Your throne, O god,* stands forever; [j]
your royal scepter is a scepter for justice.
8 You love justice and hate wrongdoing;
therefore God, your God, has anointed you
with the oil of gladness above your fellow
kings.
9 With myrrh, aloes, and cassia
your robes are fragrant.
From ivory-paneled palaces*
stringed instruments bring you joy.
10 Daughters of kings are your lovely wives;
a princess arrayed in Ophir's gold*
comes to stand at your right hand.

III

11 Listen, my daughter, and understand;
pay me careful heed.
Forget your people and your father's house,*
12 that the king might desire your beauty.
He is your lord;

44, 19: Our hearts have not turned back: Israel's defeat was not caused by its lack of fidelity.

44, 20: A place of jackals: following Israel's defeat and exile (11–12), the land lies desolate, inhabited only by jackals. Cf Is 13, 22; Jer 9, 10; 10, 22. Others take *tannim* as "sea monster" (cf Ez 29, 3; 32, 2) and render: "you crushed us as you did the sea monster."

Ps 45: A song for the Davidic king's marriage to a foreign princess from Tyre in Phoenicia. The court poet sings (2. 18) of God's choice of the king (3. 8), of his role in establishing divine rule (4–8), and of his splendor as he waits for his bride (9–10). The woman is to forget her own house when she becomes wife to the king (11–13). Her majestic beauty today is a sign of the future prosperity of the royal house (14–18). The psalm was retained in the collection when there was no reigning king, and came to be applied to the king who was to come, the messiah.

45, 7: O god: the king, in courtly language, is called "god," i.e., more than human, representing God to the people. Heb 1, 8–9 applies 7–8 to Christ.

45, 9: Ivory-paneled palaces: literally, "palaces of ivory." Ivory paneling and furniture decoration have been found in Samaria and other ancient Near Eastern cities. Cf Am 3, 15.

45, 10: Ophir's gold: uncertain location, possibly a region on the coast of southern Arabia or eastern Africa, famous for its gold. Cf 1 Kgs 9, 28; 10, 11; Jb 22, 24.

45, 11: Forget your people and your father's house: the bride should no longer consider herself a daughter of her father's house, but the wife of the king—the queen.

c Jer 9, 10. d Rom 8, 36. e Pss 10, 1; 74, 1; 77, 8; 79, 5; 83, 2. f Pss 10, 11; 89, 47; Jb 13, 24. g Ps 119, 25. h Song 5, 10–16. i Ps 21, 5. j 7–8: Heb 1, 8–9.

13 honor him, daughter of Tyre.
Then the richest of the people
will seek your favor with gifts. [k]
14 All glorious is the king's daughter as she
enters, [l]
her raiment threaded with gold;
15 In embroidered apparel she is led to the king.
The maids of her train are presented to the
king.
16 They are led in with glad and joyous acclaim;
they enter the palace of the king.

IV

17 The throne of your fathers your sons will have;
you shall make them princes through all the
land. [m]
18 I will make your name renowned through all
generations;
thus nations shall praise you forever. [n]

PSALM 46*

God, the Protector of Zion

1 For the leader. A song of the Korahites.
According to *alamoth.**

I

2 God is our refuge and our strength,
an ever-present help in distress. [o]
3 Thus we do not fear, though earth be shaken*
and mountains quake to the depths of the
sea,
4 Though its waters rage and foam
and mountains totter at its surging. [p]
The LORD of hosts is with us;*
our stronghold is the God of Jacob. *Selah*

II

5 Streams of the river gladden the city of God,
the holy dwelling of the Most High. [q]*
6 God is in its midst; it shall not be shaken;
God will help it at break of day. [r]
7 Though nations rage and kingdoms totter,
God's voice thunders and the earth
trembles. [s]
8 The LORD of hosts is with us;
our stronghold is the God of Jacob. *Selah*

III

9 Come and see the works of the LORD,
who has done fearsome deeds on earth; [t]
10 Who stops wars to the ends of the earth,
breaks the bow, splinters the spear,
and burns the shields with fire; [u]
11 Who says:
"Be still and confess that I am God!
I am exalted among the nations,
exalted on the earth." [v]
12 The LORD of hosts is with us;
our stronghold is the God of Jacob. *Selah*

PSALM 47*

The Ruler of All the Nations

1 For the leader. A psalm of the Korahites.

I

2 All you peoples, clap your hands;
shout to God with joyful cries. [w]
3 For the LORD, the Most High, inspires awe,
the great king over all the earth, [x]
4 Who made people subject to us,
brought nations under our feet, [y]
5 Who chose a land for our heritage,
the glory* of Jacob, the beloved. [z] *Selah*

II

6 God mounts the throne* amid shouts of joy;

Ps 46: A song of confidence in God's protection of Zion with close parallels to Ps 48. The dominant note in Ps 46 is sounded by the refrain, **The LORD of hosts is with us** (4. 8. 12). The first strophe (2–4) sings of the security of God's presence even in utter chaos; the second (5–8), of divine protection of the city from its enemies; the third (9–12), of God's imposition of imperial peace.

46, 1: Alamoth: the melody of the psalm, now lost.

46, 3–4: Figurative ancient Near Eastern language to describe social and political upheavals.

46, 4b: The first line of the refrain is similar in structure and meaning to Isaiah's name for the royal child, Immanuel, **With us is God** (Is 7, 14; 8, 8. 10).

46, 5: Jerusalem is not situated on a river. This description derives from mythological descriptions of the divine abode and symbolizes the divine presence as the source of all life (cf Is 33, 21; Ez 47, 1–12; Jl 4, 18; Zec 14, 8; Rv 22, 1–2).

Ps 47: A hymn calling on the nations to acknowledge the universal rule of Israel's God (2–5) who is enthroned as king over Israel and the nations (6–10).

47, 5: Our heritage . . . the glory: the land of Israel (cf Is 58, 14), which God has given Israel in an act of sovereignty.

47, 6: God mounts the throne: "has gone up to the throne," according to the context (9). Christian liturgical tradition has applied the verse to the ascension of Christ.

k Ps 72, 10–11; Is 60, 5f. 114–16: Ez 16, 10–13. m Gn 17, 6. n Is 60, 15. o Ps 48, 4; Is 33, 2. p Ps 93, 3–4; Jb 9, 5–6; Is 24, 18–20; 54, 10. q Pss 48, 2–3; 76, 3. r Is 7, 14. s Pss 2, 1–5; 48, 5–8; 76, 7–9; Is 17, 12–14. t Ps 48, 9–10. u Ps 76, 4. v Ps 48, 11. w Ps 89, 16; Zep 3, 14. x Ps 95, 3; Ex 15, 18; Is 24, 23; 52, 7. y Ps 2, 8. z Is 58, 14.

the LORD, amid trumpet blasts.[a]
7 Sing praise to God, sing praise;
sing praise to our king, sing praise.

III

8 God is king over all the earth;[b]
sing hymns of praise.
9 God rules over the nations;
God sits upon his holy throne.
10 The princes of the peoples assemble
with the people of the God of Abraham.
For the rulers of the earth belong to God,
who is enthroned on high.[c]

PSALM 48*

The Splendor of the Invincible City

1 A psalm of the Korahites.* A song.

I

2 Great is the LORD and highly praised
in the city of our God:[d]
The holy mountain, 3 fairest of heights,
the joy of all the earth,[e]
Mount Zion, the heights of Zaphon,[f]*
the city of the great king.

II

4 God is its citadel,
renowned as a stronghold.
5 See! The kings assembled,
together they invaded.
6 When they looked* they were astounded;
terrified, they were put to flight![g]
7 Trembling seized them there,
anguish, like a woman's labor,[h]
8 As when the east wind wrecks
the ships of Tarshish!*

III

9 What we had heard we now see*
in the city of the LORD of hosts,
In the city of our God,
founded to last forever. *Selah*
10 O God, within your temple
we ponder your steadfast love.
11 Like your name, O God,
your praise reaches the ends of the earth.[i]
Your right hand is fully victorious.
12 Mount Zion is glad!
The cities of Judah rejoice
because of your saving deeds![j]

IV

13 Go about Zion, walk all around it,
note the number of its towers.
14 Consider the ramparts, examine its citadels,
that you may tell future generations:[k]
15 "Yes, so mighty is God,*
our God who leads us always!"

PSALM 49*

Confidence in God rather than in Riches

1 For the leader. A psalm of the Korahites.*

2 Hear this, all you peoples!
Give ear, all who inhabit the world,
3 You of lowly birth or high estate,

Ps 48: A Zion hymn, praising the holy city as the invincible dwelling place of God. Unconquerable, it is an apt symbol of God who has defeated all enemies. After seven epithets describing the city (2–3), the psalm describes the victory by the Divine Warrior over hostile kings (4–8). The second half proclaims the dominion of the God of Zion over all the earth (9–12) and invites pilgrims to announce that God is eternally invincible like Zion itself (13–15).

48, 1: **Korahites**: see note on Ps 42, 1.

48, 3: **The heights of Zaphon**: the mountain abode of the Canaanite storm-god Baal in comparable texts. To speak of Zion as if it were Zaphon was to claim for Israel's God what Canaanites claimed for Baal. Though topographically speaking Zion is only a hill, viewed religiously it towers over other mountains as the home of the supreme God (cf Ps 68, 16–17).

48, 6: **When they looked**: the kings are stunned by the sight of Zion, touched by divine splendor. The language is that of holy war, in which the enemy panics and flees at the sight of divine glory.

48, 8: **The ships of Tarshish**: large ships, named after the distant land or port of Tarshish, probably ancient Tartessus in southern Spain, although other identifications have been proposed. Cf Is 2, 16; 60, 9; Jon 1, 3.

48, 9: **What we had heard we now see**: the glorious things that new pilgrims had heard about the holy city—its beauty and awesomeness—they now see with their own eyes. The seeing here contrasts with the seeing of the hostile kings in 6.

48, 15: **So mighty is God**: Israel's God is like Zion in being eternal and invincible. The holy city is therefore a kind of "sacrament" of God.

Ps 49: The psalm affirms confidence in God (cf Pss 23; 27, 1–6; 62) in the face of the apparent good fortune of the unjust rich. Cf Pss 37; 73. Reliance on wealth is misplaced (8–10) for it is of no avail in the face of death (18–20). After inviting all to listen to this axiom of faith (2–5), the psalmist depicts the self-delusion of

a Pss 24, 8. 10; 68, 18–19; 98, 6. b 8–9: Pss 72, 11; 93, 1; 96, 10; 97, 1; 99, 1; Jer 10, 7. c Ps 89, 19; Ex 3, 6; Is 2, 2–4. d Pss 96, 4; 145, 3. e Ps 50, 2; Lam 2, 15. f Is 14, 13. g Jgs 5, 19. h Ex 15, 14; Jer 4, 31. i Mal 1, 11. j Ps 97, 8. k Pss 22, 31–32; 71, 18.

rich and poor alike.
4 My mouth shall speak wisdom,
my heart shall offer insight. [l]
5 I will turn my attention to a problem,*
expound my question* to the music of a lyre.

I

6 Why should I fear in evil days,
when my wicked pursuers ring me round,
7 Those who trust in their wealth
and boast of their abundant riches? [m]
8 One cannot redeem oneself,*
pay to God a ransom. [n]
9 Too high the price to redeem a life;
one would never have enough
10 To stay alive forever
and never see the pit.
11 Anyone can see that the wisest die,
the fool and the senseless pass away too, [o]
and must leave their wealth to others. [p]
12 Tombs are their homes forever,
their dwellings through all generations,
though they gave their names to their lands.
13 For all their riches
mortals do not abide;
they perish like the beasts. [q]

II

14 This is the destiny of those who trust in folly,
the end of those so pleased with their wealth. *Selah*
15 Like sheep they are herded into Sheol,
where death will be their shepherd.
Straight to the grave they descend,
where their form will waste away,
Sheol will be their palace.
16 But God will redeem my life, *Selah*
will take me* from the power of Sheol. [r]
17 Do not fear when others become rich,
when the wealth of their houses grows great.
18 When they die they will take nothing with them,
their wealth will not follow them down. [s]
19 When living, they congratulate themselves and say:
"All praise you, you do so well."
20 But they will join the company of their forebears,
never again to see the light. [t]
21 For all their riches,
if mortals do not have wisdom,
they perish like the beasts.

PSALM 50*

The Acceptable Sacrifice

1 A psalm of Asaph.

I

The LORD, the God of gods,
has spoken and summoned the earth
from the rising of the sun to its setting. [u]
2 From Zion God shines forth, [v]
perfect in beauty.
3 Our God comes and will not be silent!
Devouring fire precedes,
storming fiercely round about. [w]
4 God summons the heavens above
and the earth to the judgment of his people:
5 "Gather my faithful ones before me,
those who made a covenant with me by sacrifice."
6 The heavens proclaim divine justice,
for God alone is the judge. [x] *Selah*

---

the ungodly (6–13), whose destiny is to die like ignorant beasts (13. 18; cf Prv 7, 21–23). Their wealth should occasion no alarm, for they will come to nought, whereas God will save the just (14–21).

49,1: Korahites: see note on Ps 42, 1.

49, 5: Problem: the psalmist's personal solution to the perennial biblical problem of the prosperity of the wicked. **Question**: parallel in meaning to **problem**; in Wisdom literature it means the mysterious way of how the world works.

49, 8: One cannot redeem oneself: an axiom. For the practice of redemption, cf Jb 6, 21–23. A play on the first Hebrew word of v 8 and v 16 relates the two verses.

49, 16: Will take me: the same Hebrew verb is used of God "taking up" a favored servant: Enoch in Gn 5,24; Elijah in 2 Kgs 2, 11–12; the righteous person in Ps 73, 24. The verse apparently states the hope that God will rescue the faithful psalmist in the same manner.

Ps 50: A covenant lawsuit stating that the sacrifice God really wants is the sacrifice of praise accompanied by genuine obedience (cf Mi 6, 1–8). It begins with a theophany and the summoning of the court (1–6). Then in direct address God explains what is required of the faithful (7–15), rebukes the hypocritical worshiper

l Ps 78, 2; Mt 13, 35. m Jb 31, 24. n Prv 10, 15; 11, 4; Ez 7, 19; Mt 16, 26. o Eccl 2, 16. p Ps 39, 7; Sir 11, 18–19. q Eccl 3, 18–21. r Pss 16, 10; 86, 13; 103, 4; 116, 8. s Sir 11, 18–19; Eccl 5, 15; 1 Tm 6, 7. t Jb 10, 21–22. u Dt 10, 17; Jos 22, 22. v Ps 48, 2. w Ps 97, 3; Dn 7, 10. x Pss 19, 2; 97, 6.

II

7 "Listen, my people, I will speak;
Israel, I will testify against you;
God, your God, am I.
8 Not for your sacrifices do I rebuke you,
nor for your holocausts, set before me daily.
9 I need no bullock from your house,
no goats from your fold. [y]
10 For every animal of the forest is mine,
beasts by the thousands on my mountains.
11 I know every bird of the heavens;
the creatures of the field belong to me.
12 Were I hungry, I would not tell you,
for mine is the world and all that fills it. [z]
13 Do I eat the flesh of bulls
or drink the blood of goats?
14 Offer praise as your sacrifice to God; [a]
fulfill your vows to the Most High.
15 Then call on me in time of distress; [b]
I will rescue you, and you shall honor me."

III

16 But to the wicked God says:
"Why do you recite my commandments
and profess my covenant with your lips?
17 You hate discipline;
you cast my words behind you!
18 When you see thieves, you befriend them;
with adulterers you throw in your lot.
19 You give your mouth free rein for evil;
you harness your tongue to deceit.
20 You sit maligning your own kin,
slandering the child of your own mother.
21 When you do these things should I be silent?
Or do you think that I am like you?
I accuse you, I lay the charge before you.

IV

22 "Understand this, you who forget God,
lest I attack you with no one to rescue.
23 Those who offer praise as a sacrifice honor me;
to the obedient I will show the salvation of
God." [c]

PSALM 51*

The Miserere: Prayer of Repentance

1 For the leader. A psalm of David,
2 when Nathan the prophet came to him
after his affair with Bathsheba. [d]

I

3 Have mercy on me, God, in your goodness;
in your abundant compassion blot out my
offense.
4 Wash away all my guilt;
from my sin cleanse me.
5 For I know my offense;
my sin is always before me. [e]
6 Against you alone have I sinned;
I have done such evil in your sight
That you are just in your sentence,
blameless when you condemn. [f]
7 True, I was born guilty,
a sinner, even as my mother conceived
me. [g]*
8 Still, you insist on sincerity of heart;
in my inmost being teach me wisdom.
9 Cleanse me with hyssop,* that I may be pure;
wash me, make me whiter than snow. [h]
10 Let me hear sounds of joy and gladness;
let the bones you have crushed rejoice.

II

11 Turn away your face from my sins;

(16–21), and concludes with a threat and a promise (22–23; cf Is 1, 19–20).

Ps 51: A lament, the most famous of the seven Penitential Psalms, prays for the removal of the personal and social disorders that sin has brought. The poem has two parts of approximately equal length: 3–10 and 11–19, and a conclusion in 20–21. The two parts interlock by repetition of "blot out" in the first verse of each section (3. 11), of "wash (away)" just after the first verse of each section (4) and just before the last verse (9) of the first section, and of "heart," "God," and "spirit" in 12 and 19. The first part (3–10) asks deliverance from sin, which is not just a past act but its emotional, physical, and social consequences. The second part (11–19) seeks something more profound than wiping the slate clean: nearness to God, living by the spirit of God (12–13), like the relation between God and people described in Jer 31, 33–34. Nearness to God brings joy and the authority to teach sinners (15–16). Such proclamation is better than offering sacrifice (17–19). The last two verses ask for the rebuilding of Jerusalem (20–21).

51, 7: A sinner, even as my mother conceived me: literally, "In iniquity was I conceived," an instance of hyperbole: at no time was the psalmist ever without sin. Cf Ps 88, 16, "I am mortally afflicted since youth," i.e., I have always been afflicted. The verse does not imply that the sexual act of conception is sinful.

51, 9: Hyssop: a small bush whose many woody twigs make a natural sprinkler. It was prescribed in the Mosaic law as an instrument for sprinkling sacrificial blood or lustral water for cleansing. Cf Ex 12, 22; Lv 14, 4; Nm 19, 18.

y Ps 69, 32; Am 5, 21–22. z Pss 24, 1; 89, 12; Dt 10, 14; 1 Cor 10, 26. a Heb 13, 15. b Ps 77, 3. c Ps 91, 16. d 2 Sm 12. e Pss 32, 5; 38, 19; Is 59, 12. f Rom 3, 4. g Jb 14, 4. h Jb 9, 30; Is 1, 18; Ez 36, 25.

blot out all my guilt.
12 A clean heart create for me, God;
renew in me a steadfast spirit.[i]
13 Do not drive me from your presence,
nor take from me your holy spirit.[j]
14 Restore my joy in your salvation;
sustain in me a willing spirit.
15 I will teach the wicked your ways,
that sinners may return to you.
16 Rescue me from death, God, my saving God,
that my tongue may praise your healing
power.[k]
17 Lord, open my lips;
my mouth will proclaim your praise.
18 For you do not desire sacrifice;*
a burnt offering you would not accept.[l]
19 My sacrifice, God, is a broken spirit;
God, do not spurn a broken, humbled heart.

III

20 Make Zion prosper in your good pleasure;*
rebuild the walls of Jerusalem.[m]
21 Then you will be pleased with proper sacrifice,
burnt offerings and holocausts;
then bullocks will be offered on your altar.

PSALM 52*

The Deceitful Tongue

1 For the leader. A *maskil* of David,
2 when Doeg the Edomite went and told Saul,
"David went to the house of Ahimelech."[n]

I

3 Why do you glory in evil,
you scandalous liar?
All day long 4 you plot destruction;
your tongue is like a sharpened razor,
you skillful deceiver.[o]
5 You love evil rather than good,
lies rather than honest speech.[p] *Selah*
6 You love any word that destroys,
you deceitful tongue.[q]

II

7 Now God will strike you down,
leave you crushed forever,
Pluck you from your tent,
uproot you from the land of the living.[r]
Selah
8 The righteous will look on with awe;
they will jeer and say:[s]
9 "That one did not take God as a refuge,
but trusted in great wealth,
relied on devious plots."[t]

III

10 But I, like an olive tree in the house of God,[u]*
trust in God's faithful love forever.
11 I will praise you always
for what you have done.
I will proclaim before the faithful[v]
that your name is good.

PSALM 53*

A Lament over Widespread Corruption

1 For the leader; according to *Mahalath*.
A *maskil* of David.

I

2 Fools say in their hearts,[w]
"There is no God."[x]
Their deeds are loathsome and corrupt;
not one does what is right.
3 God looks down from heaven
upon the human race,[y]
To see if even one is wise,[z]
if even one seeks God.
4 All have gone astray;
all alike are perverse.

51, 18: For you do not desire sacrifice: the mere offering of the ritual sacrifice apart from good dispositions is not acceptable to God. Cf Ps 50.

51, 20–21: Most scholars think that these verses were added to the psalm some time after the destruction of the temple in 587 B.C. The verses assume that the rebuilt temple will be an ideal site for national reconciliation.

Ps 52: A condemnation of the powerful and arrogant (3–6), who bring down upon themselves God's judgment (7). The just, those who trust in God alone, are gladdened and strengthened by the downfall of their traditional enemies (8–11).

52, 10: Like a green olive tree: the righteous will flourish in the house of God like a well-watered olive tree. Cf Pss 92, 14; 128, 3.

Ps 53: A lament of an individual, duplicated in Ps 14, except that "God" is used for "the LORD," and v 6 is different. See under Ps 14.

i Ez 11, 19. j Wis 1, 5; 9, 17; Is 63, 11; Hg 2, 5; Rom 8, 9. k Ps 30, 10. l Pss 40, 7; 50, 8; Am 5, 21–22; Hos 6, 6; Is 1, 11–15; Heb 10, 5–7. m Jer 31, 4; Ez 36, 33. n 1 Sm 21, 8; 22, 6ff. o Pss 12, 3; 59, 8; 120, 2–3; Sir 51, 3. p Jer 4, 22; Jn 3, 19–20. q Jer 9, 4. r Pss 27, 13; 28, 5; 56, 14; Jb 18, 14; Prv 2, 22; Is 38, 11. s Pss 44, 14; 64, 9. t Jb 31, 24; Prv 11, 28. u Pss 1, 3; 92, 12–14; Jer 11, 16; 17, 8. v Pss 22, 23; 26, 12; 35, 18; 149, 1. w 2–6a: Ps 14, 1–5a. x Pss 10, 4; 36, 2; Is 32, 6; Jer 5, 12. y Pss 11, 4; 102, 20. z 2b–3: Rom 3, 11–12.

Not one does what is right, not even one.[a]

II

5 Will these evildoers never learn?
They devour my people as they devour bread;[b]
they do not call upon God.[c]
6 They have good reason to fear,
though now they do not fear.
For God will certainly scatter
the bones of the godless.
They will surely be put to shame,
for God has rejected them.

III

7 Oh, that from Zion might come
the deliverance of Israel,
That Jacob may rejoice and Israel be glad[d]
when God restores the people!

PSALM 54*

Confident Prayer in Great Peril

1 For the leader. On stringed instruments.
A *maskil* of David,
2 when the Ziphites came and said to Saul,
"David is hiding among us."[e]

I

3 O God, by your name* save me.
By your strength defend my cause.
4 O God, hear my prayer.
Listen to the words of my mouth.
5 The arrogant have risen against me;
the ruthless seek my life;
they do not keep God before them.[f] *Selah*

II

6 God is present as my helper;[g]
the Lord sustains my life.
7 Turn back the evil upon my foes;
in your faithfulness, destroy them.[h]
8 Then I will offer you generous sacrifice
and praise your gracious name, LORD,
9 Because it has rescued me from every trouble,
and my eyes look down on my foes.[i]

PSALM 55*

A Lament over Betrayal

1 For the leader. On stringed instruments.
A *maskil* of David.

I

2 Listen, God, to my prayer;[j]
do not hide from my pleading;
3 hear me and give answer.
I rock with grief; I groan
4 at the uproar of the enemy,
the clamor of the wicked.
They heap trouble upon me,
savagely accuse me.
5 My heart pounds within me;
death's terrors fall upon me.
6 Fear and trembling overwhelm me;
shuddering sweeps over me.
7 I say, "If only I had wings like a dove
that I might fly away and find rest.[k]
8 Far away I would flee;
I would stay in the desert.[l] *Selah*
9 I would soon find a shelter
from the raging wind and storm."

II

10 Lord, check and confuse their scheming.
I see violence and strife in the city
11 making rounds on its walls day and night.
Within are mischief and evil;
12 treachery is there as well;
oppression and fraud never leave its streets.[m]
13 If an enemy had reviled me,

Ps 54: A lament in which the person under attack calls directly upon God for help (3–5). Refusing to despair, the psalmist hopes in God, who is active in history and just (6–7). The psalm ends with a serene promise to return thanks (8–9).

54, 3: By your name: one is present in one's name, hence God as revealed to humans.

Ps 55: The psalmist, betrayed by intimate friends (14–15. 21–22), prays that God punish those oath breakers and thus be acknowledged as the protector of the wronged. The sufferings of the psalmist include both ostracism (4) and mental turmoil (5–6), culminating in the wish to flee society (7–9). The wish for a sudden death for one's enemies (16) occurs elsewhere in the psalms; an example of such a death is the earth opening under the wicked Dathan and Abiram (Nm 16, 31–32). The psalmist, confident of vindication, exhorts others to a like trust in the God of justice (23–24). The psalm is not so much for personal vengeance as for a public vindication of God's righteousness now. There was no belief in an afterlife where such vindication could take place.

a Ps 12, 2. b Ps 27, 2; Is 9, 11. c Ps 79, 6. d Ps 85, 2. e 1 Sm 23, 19; 26, 1. f Ps 86, 14. g Ps 118, 7. h Ps 143, 12. i Pss 59, 11; 91, 8; 92, 12. j 2–3: Pss 5, 2–3; 55, 2–3; 86, 6; 130, 1–2; Lam 3, 56; Jon 2, 3. k Ps 11, 1. l Jer 9, 1; Rv 12, 6. m Jer 5, 1; 6, 6; Ez 22, 2; Hb 1, 3; Zep 3, 1.

that I could bear;
If my foe had viewed me with contempt,
from that I could hide.
14 But it was you, my other self,
my comrade and friend, [n]
15 You, whose company I enjoyed,
at whose side I walked
in procession in the house of God.

III

16 Let death take them by surprise;
let them go down alive to Sheol, [o]
for evil is in their homes and hearts.
17 But I will call upon God,
and the LORD will save me.
18 At dusk, dawn, and noon
I will grieve and complain,
and my prayer will be heard. [p]
19 God will give me freedom and peace
from those who war against me,
though there are many who oppose me.
20 God, who sits enthroned forever, [q]
will hear me and humble them.
For they will not mend their ways;
they have no fear of God.
21 They strike out at friends
and go back on their promises.
22 Softer than butter is their speech,
but war is in their hearts.
Smoother than oil are their words,
but they are unsheathed swords. [r]
23 Cast your care upon the LORD,
who will give you support.
God will never allow
the righteous to stumble. [s]
24 But you, God, will bring them down
to the pit of destruction. [t]
These bloodthirsty liars
will not live half their days,
but I put my trust in you. [u]

PSALM 56*

Trust in God

1 For the director. According to *Yonath elem rehoqim.** A *miktam* of David, when the Philistines seized him at Gath. [v]

I

2 Have mercy on me, God,
for I am treated harshly;
attackers press me all the day.
3 My foes treat me harshly all the day;
yes, many are my attackers.
O Most High, 4 when I am afraid,
in you I place my trust.
5 God, I praise your promise;
in you I trust, I do not fear. [w]
What can mere flesh do to me? [x]

II

6 All the day they foil my plans;
their every thought is of evil against me.
7 They hide together in ambush;
they watch my every step;
they lie in wait for my life. [y]
8 They are evil; watch them, God!
Cast the nations down in your anger!
9 My wanderings you have noted;
are my tears not stored in your vial,*
recorded in your book? [z]
10 My foes turn back when I call on you.
This I know: God is on my side.
11 God, I praise your promise;
12 in you I trust, I do not fear.
What can mere mortals do to me?

III

13 I have made vows to you, God;
with offerings I will fulfill them, [a]
14 Once you have snatched me from death,
kept my feet from stumbling,
That I may walk before God
in the light of the living.

Ps 56: Beset physically (2–3) and psychologically (6–7), the psalmist maintains a firm confidence in God (5. 9–10). Nothing will prevent the psalmist from keeping the vow to give thanks for God's gift of life (13–14). A refrain (5. 11–12) divides the psalm in two equal parts.

56, 1: Yonath elem rehoqim: Hebrew words probably designating the melody to which the psalm was to be sung.

56, 9: Are my tears not stored in your vial: a unique saying in the Old Testament. The context suggests that the tears are saved because they are precious; God puts a high value on each of the psalmist's troubles.

n Ps 41, 10; Jer 9, 3; Mt 26, 21–24 par. o Ps 49, 15; Nm 16, 33; Prv 1, 2; Is 5, 14. p Dn 6, 11. q Pss 29, 10; 93, 2; Bar 3, 3. r Pss 12, 3; 28, 3; 57, 5; 62, 5; 64, 4; Prv 26, 24–28; Jer 9,7. s Ps 37, 5; Prv 3, 5; 16, 3; 1 Pt 5, 7. t Pss 28, 1; 30, 4; 40, 3; 88, 5; 143, 7; Prv 1, 12; Jon 2, 7. u Pss 25, 2; 56, 4; 130, 5. v 1 Sm 21, 10. w Ps 130, 5. x Ps 118, 6; Heb 13, 6. y Ps 140, 5–6. z Ps 10, 14; 2 Kgs 20, 5; Is 25, 8; Rv 7, 17. a Nm 30, 3.

PSALM 57*

Confident Prayer for Deliverance

1 For the director. Do not destroy.* A *miktam* of David, when he fled from Saul into a cave.[b]

I

2 Have mercy on me, God,
have mercy on me.
In you I seek shelter.
In the shadow of your wings* I seek shelter
till harm pass by.[c]
3 I call to God Most High,
to God who provides for me.
4 May God send help from heaven to save me,
shame those who trample upon me.
May God send fidelity and love. *Selah*
5 I must lie down in the midst of lions
hungry for human prey.[d]
Their teeth are spears and arrows;
their tongue, a sharpened sword.[e]
6 Show yourself over the heavens, God;
may your glory appear above all the earth.[f]

II

7 They have set a trap for my feet;
my soul is bowed down;
They have dug a pit before me.
May they fall into it themselves![g] *Selah*
8 My heart is steadfast, God,
my heart is steadfast.
I will sing and chant praise.[h]
9 Awake, my soul;
awake, lyre and harp!
I will wake the dawn.[i]*
10 I will praise you among the peoples, Lord;
I will chant your praise among the nations.[j]
11 For your love towers to the heavens;
your faithfulness, to the skies.[k]
12 Show yourself over the heavens, God;
may your glory appear above all the earth.

PSALM 58*

The Dethroning of Unjust Rulers

1 For the leader. Do not destroy.*
A *miktam* of David.

I

2 Do you indeed pronounce justice, O gods;*
do you judge mortals fairly?[l]
3 No, you freely engage in crime;
your hands dispense violence to the earth.

II

4 The wicked have been corrupt since birth;
liars from the womb, they have gone astray.
5 Their poison is like the poison of a snake,*
like that of a serpent stopping its ears,[m]
6 So as not to hear the voice of the charmer
who casts such cunning spells.

III

7 O God, smash the teeth in their mouths;
break the jaw-teeth of these lions, LORD![n]
8 Make them vanish like water flowing away;[o]
trodden down, let them wither like grass.[p]
9 Let them dissolve like a snail that oozes
away,*
like an untimely birth that never sees the
sun.[q]
10 Suddenly, like brambles or thistles,

Ps 57: Each of the two equal strophes contains a prayer for rescue from enemies, accompanied by joyful trust in God (2–5. 7–11). The refrain prays that God be manifested as saving (6. 12). Ps 108 is nearly identical to part of this psalm (57, 8–12 = 108, 2–6).

57, 1: Do not destroy: probably the title of the melody to which the psalm was to be sung.

57, 2: The shadow of your wings: probably refers to the wings of the cherubim (powerful winged animals) whose wings spread over the ark in the inner chamber of the temple (1 Kgs 6, 23–28).

57, 9: I will wake the dawn: by a bold figure the psalmist imagines the sound of music and singing will waken a new day.

Ps 58: A lament expressing trust in God's power to dethrone all powers obstructing divine rule of the world. First condemned are "the gods," the powers that were popularly imagined to control human destinies (2–3), then "the wicked," the human instruments of these forces (4–6). The psalmist prays God to prevent them from harming the just (7–10). The manifestation of justice will gladden the just; they will see that their God is with them (11–12). The psalm is less concerned with personal vengeance than with public vindication of God's justice now.

58, 1: Do not destroy: probably the title of the melody to which the psalm was to be sung.

58, 2: Gods: the Bible sometimes understands pagan gods to be lesser divine beings who are assigned by Israel's God to rule the foreign nations. Here they are accused of injustice, permitting the human judges under their patronage to abuse the righteous. Cf Ps 82.

58, 5–6: The image is that of a poisonous snake that is controlled by the voice or piping of its trainer.

58, 9: A snail that oozes away: empty shells suggested to ancients that snails melted away as they left a slimy trail.

b 1 Sm 22, 1. c Pss 17, 8; 36, 8. d Pss 17, 11–12; 22, 22; 58, 7. e Pss 11, 2; 64, 4. f Ps 72, 19; Nm 14, 21. g Pss 7, 15; 140, 5–6. h Ps 108, 2. i Jb 38, 12. j Pss 9, 12; 18, 50. k Pss 36, 6; 71, 19. l Ps 82, 2; Dt 16, 19. m Pss 64, 4; 140, 3; Rom 3, 13. n Ps 3, 7. o Wis 16, 29. p Ps 37, 2. q Jb 3, 16.

have the whirlwind snatch them away. [r]
11 Then the just shall rejoice to see the
vengeance
and bathe their feet in the blood of the
wicked. [s]
12 Then it will be said:
"Truly there is a reward for the just;
there is a God who is judge on earth!"

PSALM 59*

Complaint against Bloodthirsty Enemies

1 For the director. Do not destroy.* A *miktam* of David, when Saul sent people to watch his house and kill him. [t]

I

2 Rescue me from my enemies, my God;
lift me out of reach of my foes.
3 Deliver me from evildoers;
from the bloodthirsty save me.
4 They have set an ambush for my life;
the powerful conspire against me.
For no offense or misdeed of mine, LORD,
5 for no fault they hurry to take up arms.
Come near and see my plight!
6 You, LORD of hosts, are the God of Israel!
Awake! Punish all the nations.
Have no mercy on these worthless traitors.
Selah
7 Each evening they return,
growling like dogs, prowling the city. [u]
8 Their mouths pour out insult;
sharp words are on their lips.
They say: "Who is there to hear?"*
9 You, LORD, laugh at them;
you deride all the nations. [v]
10 My strength, for you I watch;
you, God, are my fortress, 11 my loving
God.

II

May God go before me,
and show me my fallen foes.
12 Slay them, God,
lest they deceive my people.
Shake them by your power;
Lord, our shield, bring them down.
13 For the sinful words of their mouths and lips
let them be caught in their pride.
For the lies they have told under oath [w]
14 destroy them in anger,
destroy till they are no more.
Then people will know God rules over Jacob,
yes, even to the ends of the earth. [x] *Selah*
15 Each evening they return,
growling like dogs, prowling the city.
16 They roam about as scavengers;
if they are not filled, they howl.

III

17 But I shall sing of your strength,
extol your love at dawn,
For you are my fortress,
my refuge in time of trouble.
18 My strength, your praise I will sing;
you, God, are my fortress, my loving God.

PSALM 60*

Lament after Defeat in Battle

1 For the leader; according to "The Lily of. . . ." A *miktam* of David (for teaching),
2 when he fought against Aram-Naharaim and Aram-Zobah; and Joab, coming back, killed twelve thousand Edomites in the Valley of Salt. [y]

I

3 O God, you rejected us, broke our defenses;
you were angry but now revive us.
4 You rocked the earth, split it open; [z]
repair the cracks for it totters.
5 You made your people go through hardship,
made us stagger from the wine you gave
us. [a]
6 Raise up a flag for those who revere you,

Ps 59: A lament in two parts (2–9. 11b–17), each ending in a refrain (10. 18). Both parts alternate prayer for vindication (2–3. 5b–6. 11b–14) with vivid depictions of the psalmist's enemies (4–5a. 7–8. 15–16). The near curse in 12–13 is not a crude desire for revenge but a wish that God's just rule over human affairs be recognized now.

59, 1: Do not destroy: probably the title of the melody to which the psalm was to be sung.

59, 8: Who is there to hear?: a sample of the enemies' godless reflection. The answer is that God hears their blasphemies.

Ps 60: The community complains that God has let the enemy win the battle (3–5) and asks for an assurance of victory (6–7). In the oracle God affirms ownership of the land; the invasion of other nations is not permanent and will be reversed ultimately (8–10).

r Jb 21, 18; Hos 13, 3; Na 1, 10. s Ps 68, 24; Is 63, 1–6. t 1 Sm 19, 11. u Ps 55, 11. v Pss 2, 4; 37, 13; Wis 4, 18. w Prv 12, 13; 18, 7. x Ps 83, 18–19; Ez 5, 13. y 2 Sm 8, 2. 3. 13; 1 Chr 18, 2. 3. 12. z Ps 75, 4; Is 24, 19. a Ps 75, 9; Is 51, 17. 21–22; Jer 25, 15.

a refuge for them out of bowshot. *Selah*
7 Help with your right hand and answer us*
that your loved ones may escape.

II

8 In the sanctuary God promised:
"I will exult, will apportion Shechem;
the valley of Succoth* I will measure out.*
9 Gilead is mine, mine is Manasseh;
Ephraim is the helmet for my head,
Judah, my own scepter.*
10 Moab is my washbowl;*
upon Edom I cast my sandal.[b]*
I will triumph over Philistia."

III

11 Who will bring me to the fortified city?*
Who will lead me into Edom?
12 Was it not you who rejected us, God?
Do you no longer march with our armies?[c]
13 Give us aid against the foe;
worthless is human help.
14 We will triumph with the help of God,
who will trample down our foes.

PSALM 61*

Prayer of the King in Time of Danger

1 For the leader; with stringed instruments. Of David.

I

2 Hear my cry, O God,
listen to my prayer!
3 From the brink of Sheol* I call;
my heart grows faint.
Raise me up, set me on a rock,
4 for you are my refuge,
a tower of strength against the foe.[d]
5 Then I will ever dwell in your tent,
take refuge in the shelter of your wings.[e]
Selah

II

6 O God, when you accept my vows
and hear the plea of those
who revere your name in prayer:*
7 "Add to the days of the king's life;
may his years be many generations;[f]
8 May he reign before God forever;[g]
may your love and fidelity preserve
him"—[h]
9 Then* I will sing your name forever,
fulfill my vows day after day.

PSALM 62*

Trust in God Alone

1 For the leader; *'al Jeduthun.** A psalm of David.

I

2 My soul rests in God alone,[i]
from whom comes my salvation.
3 God alone is my rock and salvation,
my secure height; I shall never fall.
4 How long will you set upon people,
all of you beating them down,
As though they were a sagging fence
or a battered wall?
5 Even from my place on high
they plot to dislodge me.
They delight in lies;
they bless with their mouths,
but inwardly they curse.[j] *Selah*

With renewed confidence, the community resolves to fight again (11). The opening lament is picked up again (12–14), but this time with new awareness of God's power and human limitation.

60, 7–14: These verses occur again as the second half of Ps 108.

60, 8: I will apportion . . . measure out: God lays claim to these places. **The valley of Succoth:** probably the lower stretch of the Jabbok valley.

60, 9: Judah, my own scepter: an allusion to the Testament of Jacob, Gn 49, 10.

60, 10: Moab is my washbowl: Moab borders the Dead Sea, hence a metaphor for the country. **Upon Edom I cast my sandal:** an ancient legal gesture of taking possession of land.

60, 11: The fortified city: perhaps Bozrah, the fortified capital of Edom. Cf Is 34, 6; 63, 1; Am 1, 12.

Ps 61: A lament of the king who feels himself at the brink of death (3) and cries out for the strong and saving presence of God (3b–5). The king cites the prayer being made for him (7–8), and promises to give thanks to God.

61, 3: Brink of Sheol: literally, "edge of the earth," "earth" being taken in its occasional meaning "the underworld." Cf Jon 2, 3.

61, 6: In prayer: added for sense. Vv 7–8 express **the plea** of v 6.

61, 9: Then: Hebrew "just as," i.e., in accord with the vows referred to in v 6.

Ps 62: A song of trust displaying serenity from experiencing God's power (the refrains of 2–3 and 6–7) and anger toward unjust enemies (4–5). From the experience of being rescued, the psalmist can teach others to trust in God (10–13).

62, 1: 'Al Jeduthun: apparently the Hebrew name for the melody.

b Ru 4, 7–8. c Ps 44, 10. d Ps 46, 2. e Pss 17, 8; 36, 8; 57, 2. f Ps 21, 5. g Pss 72, 5; 89, 5. 30. 37. h Pss 85, 11; 89, 15. 25; Prv 20, 28. i 2–3. 6–7: Pss 18, 3; 31, 3–4; 42, 10; 118, 8; 146, 3. j Pss 12, 3; 28, 3; 55, 22; Prv 26, 24–25.

II

6 My soul, be at rest in God alone,
from whom comes my hope.
7 God alone is my rock and my salvation,
my secure height; I shall not fall.
8 My safety and glory are with God, [k]
my strong rock and refuge.
9 Trust God at all times, my people!
Pour out your hearts to God our refuge!
Selah

III

10 Mortals are a mere breath,
the powerful but an illusion; [l]
On a balance they rise;*
together they are lighter than air.
11 Do not trust in extortion;
in plunder put no empty hope.
Though wealth increase,
do not set your heart upon it. [m]
12 One thing God has said;
two things* I have heard: [n]
Power belongs to God;
13 so too, Lord, does kindness,
And you render to each of us
according to our deeds. [o]

PSALM 63*

Ardent Longing for God

1 A psalm of David, when he was in the wilderness of Judah. [p]

I

2 O God, you are my God—
for you I long!
For you my body yearns;
for you my soul thirsts,
Like a land parched, lifeless,
and without water. [q]
3 So I look to you in the sanctuary
to see your power and glory.
4 For your love is better than life;*
my lips offer you worship!

II

5 I will bless you as long as I live;
I will lift up my hands, calling on your name.
6 My soul shall savor the rich banquet of praise,
with joyous lips my mouth shall honor you!
7 When I think of you upon my bed,
through the night watches I will recall
8 That you indeed are my help,
and in the shadow of your wings I shout for joy. [r]
9 My soul clings fast to you;
your right hand upholds me.

III

10 But those who seek my life will come to ruin;
they shall go down to the depths of the earth!
11 They shall be handed over to the sword
and become the prey of jackals!
12 But the king shall rejoice in God;
all who swear by the Lord* shall exult,
for the mouths of liars will be shut! [s]

PSALM 64*

Treacherous Conspirators Punished by God

1 For the leader. A psalm of David.

I

2 O God, hear my anguished voice;
from the foes I dread protect my life.

62, 10: On a balance they rise: precious objects were weighed by balancing two pans suspended from a beam. The lighter pan rises.

62, 12: One thing . . . two things: parallelism of numbers for the sake of variation, a common device in Semitic poetry. One should not literally add up the numbers. Cf Am 1, 3; Prv 6, 16–19; 30, 15. 18. 21.

Ps 63: A psalm expressing the intimate relationship between God and the worshiper. Separated from God (2), the psalmist longs for the divine life given in the temple (3–6), which is based on a close relationship with God (7–9). May all my enemies be destroyed and God's true worshipers continue in giving praise (10–12)!

63, 4: For your love is better than life: only here in the Old Testament is anything prized above life—in this case God's love.

63, 12: All who swear by the Lord: to swear by a particular god meant that one was a worshiper of that god (Is 45, 23; 48. 1; Zep 1, 5).

Ps 64: A lament of a person overwhelmed by the malice of the wicked who are depicted in the psalms as the enemies of the righteous (2–7). When people see God bringing upon the wicked the evil they intended against others, they will know who is the true ruler of the world (8–10). The final verse is a vow of praise (11).

k Ps 3, 3; Is 26, 4; 60, 19. l Pss 39, 6–7; 144, 4; Jb 7, 16; Wis 2, 5. m Jb 31, 25; Eccl 5, 9; Jer 17, 11; Mt 6, 19–21. 24. n Jb 40, 5. o Pss 28, 4; 31, 24; 2 Sm 3, 39; Jb 34, 11; Jer 17, 10; Mt 16, 27; Rom 2, 6; 2 Tm 4, 14. p 1 Sm 24. q Pss 42, 2; 143, 6; Is 26, 9. r Pss 17, 8; 36, 8. s Ps 107, 42.

3 Hide me from the malicious crowd,
the mob of evildoers.
4 They sharpen their tongues like swords,
ready their bows for arrows of poison words. [t]
5 They shoot at the innocent from ambush,
shoot without risk, catch them unawares.*
6 They resolve on their wicked plan;
they conspire to set snares;
they say: "Who will see us?"
7 They devise wicked schemes,
conceal the schemes they devise;
the designs of their hearts are hidden. [u]

II

8 But God will shoot arrows at them
and strike them unawares. [v]
9 They will be brought down by their own tongues;
all who see them will shake their heads. [w]
10 Then all will fear and proclaim God's deed,
pondering what has been done.
11 The just will rejoice and take refuge in the LORD;
all the upright will glory in their God. [x]

PSALM 65*

Thanksgiving for God's Blessings

1 For the leader. A psalm of David. A song.

I

2 To you we owe our hymn of praise,
O God on Zion;
To you our vows* must be fulfilled,
3 you who hear our prayers.
To you all flesh must come [y]*
4 with its burden of wicked deeds.
We are overcome by our sins;
only you can pardon them. [z]
5 Happy the chosen ones you bring
to dwell in your courts.
May we be filled with the good things of your house,
the blessings of your holy temple!

II

6 You answer us with awesome deeds* of justice,
O God our savior,
The hope of all the ends of the earth
and of far distant islands. [a]
7 You are robed in power,
you set up the mountains by your might.
8 You still the roaring of the seas, [b]
the roaring of their waves,
the tumult of the peoples. [c]
9 Distant peoples stand in awe of your marvels;
east and west you make resound with joy.
10 You visit the earth and water it,*
make it abundantly fertile. [d]
God's stream* is filled with water;
with it you supply the world with grain.
Thus do you prepare the earth:
11 you drench plowed furrows,
and level their ridges.
With showers you keep the ground soft,
blessing its young sprouts.
12 You adorn the year with your bounty;
your paths* drip with fruitful rain.
13 The untilled meadows also drip;
the hills are robed with joy.
14 The pastures are clothed with flocks,
the valleys blanketed with grain;
they cheer and sing for joy. [e]

64, 5: Catch them unawares: literally, "suddenly," i.e., "unexpectedly."

Ps 65: The community, aware of its unworthiness (3–4), gives thanks for divine bounty (5), a bounty resulting from God's creation victory (6–9). At God's touch the earth comes alive with vegetation and flocks (10–14).

65, 2: Vows: the Israelites were accustomed to promising sacrifices in the temple if their prayers were heard.

65, 3: To you all flesh must come: all must have recourse to God's mercy.

65, 6: Awesome deeds: the acts of creating—installing mountains, taming seas, restraining nations (7–8)—that are visible worldwide (6. 9).

65, 10–14: Apparently a description of the agricultural year, beginning with the first fall rains that soften the hard sun-baked soil (10–11).

65, 10: God's stream: the fertile waters of the earth derive from God's fertile waters in the heavenly world.

65, 12: Paths: probably the tracks of God's storm chariot dropping rain upon earth.

t Pss 11, 2; 37, 14; 55, 22; 57, 5. u Ps 140, 3; Prv 6, 14. v Pss 7, 13–14; 38, 3; Dt 32, 42. w Pss 5, 11; 44, 14; 52, 6. x Pss 36, 8; 57, 2. y Is 66, 23. z Pss 32, 1–2; 78, 38; Is 1, 18. a Is 66, 19. b Pss 89, 10; 107, 29; Jb 38, 11; Mt 8, 26. c Is 17, 12. d Lv 26, 4; Is 30, 23. 25; Jl 2, 22–23. e Is 44, 23.

PSALM 66*

Praise of God, Israel's Deliverer

1 For the leader. A song; a psalm.

I

Shout joyfully to God, all you on earth;
2 sing of his glorious name;
give him glorious praise.[f]
3 Say to God: "How awesome your deeds!
Before your great strength your enemies
cringe.
4 All on earth fall in worship before you;[g]
they sing of you, sing of your name!" *Selah*

II

5 Come and see the works of God,*
awesome in the deeds done for us.
6 He changed the sea to dry land;
through the river they passed on foot.[h]
Therefore let us rejoice in him,
7 who rules by might forever,
Whose eyes are fixed upon the nations.
Let no rebel rise to challenge! *Selah*
8 Bless our God, you peoples;
loudly sound his praise,
9 Who has kept us alive
and not allowed our feet to slip.[i]
10 You tested us, O God,
tried us as silver tried by fire.[j]
11 You led us into a snare;
you bound us at the waist as captives.
12 You let captors set foot on our neck;*
we went through fire and water;
then you led us out to freedom.[k]

III

13 I will bring holocausts* to your house;
to you I will fulfill my vows,
14 The vows my lips pronounced
and my mouth spoke in distress.
15 Holocausts of fatlings I will offer you
and burnt offerings of rams;
I will sacrifice oxen and goats. *Selah*
16 Come and hear, all you who fear God,
while I recount what has been done
for me.
17 I called to the Lord with my mouth;
praise was upon my tongue.
18 Had I cherished evil in my heart,
the Lord would not have heard.
19 But God did hear
and listened to my voice in prayer.
20 Blessed be God, who did not refuse me
the kindness I sought in prayer.

PSALM 67*

Harvest Thanks and Petition

1 For the leader; with stringed instruments.
A psalm; a song.

I

2 May God be gracious to us* and bless us;
may God's face shine upon us.[l] *Selah*
3 So shall your rule be known upon the earth,
your saving power among all the nations.[m]
4 May the peoples praise you, God;
may all the peoples praise you!

II

5 May the nations be glad and shout for joy;
for you govern the peoples justly,
you guide the nations upon the earth.[n]
Selah
6 May the peoples praise you, God;
may all the peoples praise you!

Ps 66: In the first part (1–12), the community praises God for powerful acts for Israel, both in the past (the exodus from Egypt and the entry into the land [6]) and in the present (deliverance from a recent but unspecified calamity [8–12]). In the second part (13–20), an individual from the rescued community fulfills a vow to offer a sacrifice of thanksgiving. As often in thanksgivings, the rescued person steps forward to teach the community what God has done (16–20).

66, 5–6: Cf the events described in Ex 14, 1—15, 21; Jos 3, 11—4, 24, and Ps 114.

66, 12: You let captors set foot on our neck: literally, "you let men mount our head." Conquerors placed their feet on the neck of their enemies as a sign of complete defeat. Cf Jos 10, 24. A ceremonial footstool of the Egyptian king Tutankhamen portrays bound and prostrate bodies of enemies ready for the king's feet on their heads, and one of Tutankhamen's ceremonial chariots depicts the king as a sphinx standing with paw atop the neck of an enemy.

66, 13: Holocausts: wholly burnt offerings. Cf Lv 1, 3–13; 6, 1–4; 22, 17–20.

Ps 67: A petition for a bountiful harvest (7), made in the awareness that Israel's prosperity will persuade the nations to worship its God.

67, 2: May God be gracious to us: the people's petition echoes the blessing pronounced upon them by the priests. Cf Nm 6, 22–27.

f Ps 65, 14; Is 44, 23. g 3–4: Ps 18, 45; Mi 7, 17. h Pss 74, 15; 114, 3; Ex 14, 21f; Jos 3, 14ff; Is 44, 27; 50, 2. i Pss 91, 12; 121, 3; 1 Sm 2, 9; Prv 3, 23. j Is 48, 10. k Is 43, 2. l Pss 4, 7; 31, 17; 44, 4; 80, 4; Dn 9, 17. m Jer 33, 9. n Ps 98, 9.

III

7 The earth has yielded its harvest;
God, our God, blesses us. [o]
8 May God bless us still;
that the ends of the earth may revere our God.

PSALM 68*

The Exodus and Conquest, Pledge of Future Help

1 For the leader. A psalm of David; a song.

I

2 God will arise for battle;*
the enemy will be scattered;
those who hate God will flee. [p]
3 The wind will disperse them like smoke;
as wax is melted by fire,
so the wicked will perish before God. [q]
4 Then the just will be glad;
they will rejoice before God;
they will celebrate with great joy.

II

5 Sing to God, praise the divine name;
exalt the rider of the clouds.*
Rejoice before this God
whose name is the LORD. [r]
6 Father of the fatherless, defender of widows— [s]
this is the God whose abode is holy,
7 Who gives a home to the forsaken,
who leads prisoners out to prosperity,
while rebels live in the desert.*

III

8 God, when you went forth before your people, [t]
when you marched through the desert, *Selah*
9 The earth quaked, the heavens shook,
before God, the One of Sinai,
before God, the God of Israel.
10 You claimed a land as your own, O God;
11 your people settled there.
There you poured abundant rains, God,
graciously given to the poor in their need.

IV

12a The Lord announced the news of victory:*
13a "The kings and their armies are in desperate flight. [u]
12b All you people so numerous,
14a will you stay by the sheepfolds? [v]
13b Every household will share the booty,
14b perhaps a dove sheathed with silver,
14c its wings covered with yellow gold."
15 When the Almighty routed the kings there,
the spoils were scattered like snow on Zalmon.*

Ps 68: The psalm is extremely difficult because the Hebrew text is badly preserved and the ceremony that it describes is uncertain. The translation assumes the psalm accompanied the early autumn Feast of Tabernacles (Sukkoth), which included a procession of the tribes (25–28). Israel was being oppressed by a foreign power, perhaps Egypt (31–32)—unless Egypt stands for any oppressor. The psalm may have been composed from segments of ancient poems, which would explain why the transitions are implied rather than explicitly stated. At any rate, v 2 is based on Nm 10, 35–36, and vv 8–9 are derived from Jgs 5, 4–5.

The argument develops in nine stanzas (each of three to five poetic lines): 1) confidence that God will destroy Israel's enemies (2–4); 2) call to praise God as savior (5–7); 3) God's initial rescue of Israel from Egypt (8), the Sinai encounter (9), and the settlement in Canaan (10–11); 4) the defeat of the Canaanite kings (12–15); 5) the taking of Jerusalem, where Israel's God will rule the world (16–19); 6) praise for God's past help and for the future interventions that will be modeled on the ancient exodus-conquest (20–24); 7) procession at the Feast of Tabernacles (25–28); 8) prayer that the defeated enemies bring tribute to the temple (29–32); 9) invitation for all kingdoms to praise Israel's God (33–36).

68, 2: The opening line alluding to Nm 10, 35 makes clear that God's assistance in the period of the exodus and conquest is the model and assurance of all future divine help.

68, 5: Exalt the rider of the clouds: God's intervention is in the imagery of Canaanite myth in which the storm-god mounted the storm clouds to ride to battle. Such theophanies occur throughout the psalm: 2–3. 8–10. 12–15. 18–19. 22–24. 29–32. 34–35. See Dt 33, 26; Ps 18, 8–16; Is 19, 1.

68, 7: While rebels live in the desert: rebels must live in the arid desert, whereas God's people will live in the well-watered land (vv 8–11).

68, 12–15: The Hebrew text upon which the translation is based has apparently suffered dislocation and has been substantially rearranged for sense. The version of the defeat of the kings differs from that in the Book of Joshua, where the people play a significant role. Here God alone is responsible for the victory (though the actual battle is not described); Israel only gathers the spoils. God alone is the source of Israel's success; human effort is not important.

68, 15: Zalmon: generally taken as the name of a mountain where snow is visible in winter, perhaps to be located in the Golan Heights or in the mountains of Bashan or Hauran east of the Sea of Galilee.

o Ps 85, 13; Lv 26, 4; Ez 34, 27; Hos 2, 23–24. p Nm 10, 35. q Ps 97, 5; Jdt 16, 15; Wis 5, 14; Mi 1, 4. r Pss 18, 10; 104, 3; Dt 33, 26; Is 19, 1. s 6–7: Pss 103, 6; 146, 7. 9; Ex 22, 20–22; Bar 6, 37. t 8–9: Pss 44, 10; 114, 4. 7; Jgs 5, 4–5; Heb 12, 26. u Jgs 5, 19. 22. v Jgs 5, 16.

V

16 You high mountains of Bashan,
you rugged mountains of Bashan,
17 You rugged mountains, why look with envy
at the mountain* where God has chosen to dwell,
where the LORD resides forever? [w]
18 God's chariots were myriad, thousands upon thousands;
from Sinai the Lord entered the holy place.
19 You went up to its lofty height;
you took captives, received slaves as tribute. [x]
No rebels can live in the presence of God.

VI

20 Blessed be the Lord day by day,
God, our salvation, who carries us. [y]
Selah
21 Our God is a God who saves;
escape from death is in the LORD God's hands.
22 God will crush the skulls of the enemy,
the hairy heads of those who walk in sin. [z]
23 The Lord has said:
"Even from Bashan I will fetch them,
fetch them even from the depths of the sea.*
24 You will wash your feet in your enemy's blood;
the tongues of your dogs will lap it up." [a]

VII

25 Your procession* comes into view, O God,
your procession into the holy place, my God and king.
26 The singers go first, the harpists follow;
in their midst girls sound the timbrels. [b]
27 In your choirs, bless God;
bless the LORD, you from Israel's assemblies.
28 In the lead is Benjamin, few in number;
there the princes of Judah, a large throng,
the princes of Zebulun, the princes of Naphtali, too. [c]

VIII

29 Summon again, O God, your power,
the divine power you once showed for us.
30 Show it from your temple on behalf of Jerusalem,
that kings may bring you tribute.
31 Roar at the wild beast of the reeds,*
the herd of mighty bulls, the lords of nations;
scatter the nations that delight in war.
32 Exact rich tribute from lower Egypt, [d]*
from upper Egypt,* gold and silver;
make Ethiopia* extend its hands to God. [e]

IX

33 You kingdoms of the earth, sing to God; [f]
chant the praises of the Lord, *Selah*
34 Who rides the heights of the ancient heavens,
whose voice is thunder, mighty thunder.
35 Confess the power of God,
whose majesty protects Israel,
whose power is in the sky.
36 Awesome is God in his holy place,
the God of Israel,
who gives power and strength to his people. [g]
Blessed be God!

68, 17: **The mountain**: Mount Zion, the site of the temple.
68, 23: **Even from Bashan . . . from the depths of the sea**: the heights and the depths, the farthest places where enemies might flee.
68, 25-28: **Your procession**: the procession renews God's original taking up of residence on Zion, described in 16-19.
68, 31: **The wild beast of the reeds**: probably the Nile crocodile, a symbol for Egypt; see 32 and Ez 29, 2-5.
68, 31-32: **Lower Egypt** is the delta area north of Cairo. **Upper Egypt** is the Nile Valley from Cairo to Aswan. **Ethiopia** is still further south.

w Ps 132, 13-14; Ez 43, 7. x Ps 47, 8; Eph 4, 8-10. y Pss 34, 2; 145, 2; Is 46, 3-4; 63, 9. z Dt 32, 42. a Pss 58, 11; 1 Kgs 21, 19; 22, 38; Is 63, 1-6. b Pss 81, 2-3; 87, 7; 149, 3; 150, 3-5; 2 Sm 6, 5. c Is 8, 23. d Ez 29, 2ff. e Is 18, 7; 45, 14. f Ps 138, 4. g Pss 28, 8; 29, 11.

PSALM 69*

A Cry of Anguish in Great Distress

1 For the leader; according to "Lilies."* Of David.

I

2 Save me, God,
for the waters* have reached my neck. [h]
3 I have sunk into the mire of the deep,
where there is no foothold.
I have gone down to the watery depths;
the flood overwhelms me. [i]
4 I am weary with crying out;
my throat is parched.
My eyes have failed,
looking for my God. [j]
5 More numerous than the hairs of my head
are those who hate me without cause. [k]
Too many for my strength
are my treacherous enemies.
Must I now restore
what I did not steal?*

II

6 God, you know my folly;
my faults are not hidden from you.
7 Let those who wait for you, LORD of hosts,
not be shamed through me.
Let those who seek you, God of Israel, [l]
not be disgraced through me.
8 For your sake I bear insult,
shame covers my face. [m]
9 I have become an outcast to my kin,
a stranger to my mother's children. [n]
10 Because zeal for your house consumes me,*
I am scorned by those who scorn you. [o]*
11 I have wept and fasted, [p]
but this led only to scorn.
12 I clothed myself in sackcloth;
I became a byword for them.
13 They who sit at the gate gossip about me;
drunkards make me the butt of their songs.

III

14 But I pray to you, LORD,
for the time of your favor.
God, in your great kindness answer me
with your constant help. [q]
15 Rescue me from the mire; [r]
do not let me sink.
Rescue me from my enemies
and from the watery depths.
16 Do not let the floodwaters overwhelm me,
nor the deep swallow me,
nor the mouth of the pit close over me.
17 Answer me, LORD, in your generous love;
in your great mercy turn to me.
18 Do not hide your face from your servant;
in my distress hasten to answer me! [s]
19 Come and ransom my life;
because of my enemies redeem me.
20 You know my reproach, my shame, my disgrace;
before you stand all my foes.
21 Insult has broken my heart, and I am weak;
I looked for compassion, but there was none,
for comforters, but found none. [t]
22 Instead they put gall in my food;
for my thirst they gave me vinegar. [u]

IV

23 Make their own table a snare for them,
a trap for their friends. [v]
24 Make their eyes so dim they cannot see;

Ps 69: A lament complaining of suffering in language both metaphorical (2–3 and 15–16, the waters of chaos) and literal (4. 5. 9. 11–13, exhaustion, alienation from family and community, false accusation). In the second part the psalmist prays with special emphasis that the enemies be punished for all to see (23–29). Despite the pain, the psalmist does not lose hope that all be set right, and promises public praise (30–37). The psalm, which depicts the suffering of the innocent just person vividly, is cited often by the New Testament especially in the passion accounts, e.g., v 5 in Jn 15, 25; v 22 in Mk 15, 23. 36 and parallels and in Jn 19, 29. The psalm prays not so much for personal vengeance as for public vindication of God's justice. There was, at this time, no belief in an afterlife where such vindication could take place. Redress had to take place now, in the sight of all.

69, 1: "Lilies": apparently the name of the melody.

69, 2: Waters: the waters of chaos from which God created the world are a common metaphor for extreme distress. Cf Pss 18, 5; 42, 8; 88, 8; Jon 2, 3–6.

69, 5: What I did not steal: the psalmist, falsely accused of theft, is being forced to make restitution.

69, 10: Zeal for your house consumes me: the psalmist's commitment to God's cause brings only opposition. Cf Jn 2, 17. I

h Pss 18, 5; 93, 3–4; Jb 22, 11. i Pss 40, 2; 124, 4–5. j Pss 25, 15; 119, 82; 123, 2; 141, 8; Is 38, 14. k Ps 40, 13; Lam 3, 52; Jn 15, 25. l Ps 40, 17. m Jer 15, 15. n Jb 19, 13–15. o Ps 119, 139; Jn 2, 17; Rom 15, 3. p 11–13: Ps 109, 24–25; Jb 30, 9; Lam 3, 14. q Is 49, 8. r 15–16: Pss 28, 1; 30, 4; 32, 6; 40, 3; 88, 5; Prv 1, 12. s Pss 102, 3; 143, 7. t Lam 1, 2. u Lam 3, 15; Mt 27, 34. 48; Mk 15, 23. v Rom 11, 9–10.

keep their backs ever feeble.
25 Pour out your wrath upon them;
let the fury of your anger overtake them.
26 Make their camp desolate,
with none to dwell in their tents. [w]
27 For they pursued the one you struck,
added to the pain of the one you wounded.
28 Add that to their crimes;
let them not attain to your reward.
29 Strike them from the book of the living;
do not count them among the just! [x]

V

30 But I am afflicted and in pain;
let your saving help protect me, God,
31 That I may praise God's name in song*
and glorify it with thanksgiving.
32 My song will please the LORD more than oxen,
more than bullocks with horns and hooves: [y]
33 "See, you lowly ones, and be glad;
you who seek God, take heart! [z]
34 For the LORD hears the poor,
does not spurn those in bondage.
35 Let the heavens and the earth sing praise,
the seas and whatever moves in them!"

VI

36 God will rescue Zion,
rebuild the cities of Judah. [a]
God's servants shall dwell in the land and possess it;
37 it shall be the heritage of their descendants;
those who love God's name shall dwell there. [b]

PSALM 70*

Prayer for Divine Help

1 For the leader; of David. For remembrance.

2 Graciously rescue me, God! [c]
Come quickly to help me, LORD! [d]
3 Confound and put to shame
those who seek my life. [e]
Turn back in disgrace
those who desire my ruin.
4 Let those who say "Aha!" [f]
turn back in their shame.
5 But may all who seek you
rejoice and be glad in you.
May those who long for your help
always say, "God be glorified!" [g]
6 Here I am, afflicted and poor.
God, come quickly!
You are my help and deliverer.
LORD, do not delay!

PSALM 71*

Prayer in Time of Old Age

I

1 In you, LORD, I take refuge; [h]
let me never be put to shame. [i]
2 In your justice rescue and deliver me;
listen to me and save me!
3 Be my rock and refuge,
my secure stronghold;
for you are my rock and fortress. [j]
4 My God, rescue me from the power of the wicked,
from the clutches of the violent. [k]
5 You are my hope, Lord;
my trust, GOD, from my youth.
6 On you I depend since birth;
from my mother's womb you are my strength; [l]
my hope in you never wavers.
7 I have become a portent to many,*
but you are my strong refuge!
8 My mouth shall be filled with your praise,

am scorned by those who scorn you: Rom 15, 3 uses the verse as an example of Jesus' unselfishness.

69, 31: That I may praise God's name in song: the actual song is cited in 33–35, the word "praise" in 35 referring back to "praise" in 31.

Ps 70: A lament of a poor and afflicted person (6) who has no resource except God, and who cries out to be saved from the enemy. The psalm is almost identical to Ps 40, 14–18.

Ps 71: A lament of an old person (9. 18) whose afflictions are interpreted by enemies as a divine judgment (11). The first part of the psalm pleads for help (1–4) on the basis of a hope learned from a lifetime's experience of God; the second part describes the menace (9–13) yet remains buoyant (14–16); the third develops the theme of hope and praise.

71, 7: A portent to many: the afflictions of the sufferer are taken as a manifestation of God's anger. Cf Dt 28, 46; Ps 31, 12.

w Acts 1, 20. x Ps 139, 16; Ex 32, 32; Is 4, 3; Dn 12, 1; Mal 3, 16; Rv 3, 5. y Pss 40, 7; 50, 8–9. 14; 51, 18; Is 1, 11–15; Hos 6, 6; Am 5, 21–22; Heb 10, 5–8. z Pss 22, 27; 35, 27; 70, 5. a Is 44, 26; Ez 36, 10. b Ps 102, 29; Is 65, 9. c 2–6: Ps 40, 14–18. d Ps 71, 12. e Ps 35, 4. 26. f Ps 35, 21. 25. g Ps 35, 27. h 1–3: Ps 31, 2–4. i Ps 25, 2. j Ps 18, 3. k Ps 140, 2. l Ps 22, 11.

shall sing your glory every day.

II

9 Do not cast me aside in my old age;
as my strength fails, do not forsake me.
10 For my enemies speak against me;
they watch and plot against me. [m]
11 They say, "God has abandoned that one.
Pursue, seize the wretch!
No one will come to the rescue!"
12 God, do not stand far from me;
my God, hasten to help me. [n]
13 Bring to a shameful end
those who attack me;
Cover with contempt and scorn
those who seek my ruin. [o]
14 I will always hope in you
and add to all your praise.
15 My mouth shall proclaim your just deeds,
day after day your acts of deliverance,
though I cannot number them all. [p]
16 I will speak of the mighty works of the Lord;
O GOD, I will tell of your singular justice.

III

17 God, you have taught me from my youth;
to this day I proclaim your wondrous deeds.
18 Now that I am old and gray, [q]
do not forsake me, God,
That I may proclaim your might
to all generations yet to come, [r]
Your power 19 and justice, God,
to the highest heaven.
You have done great things; [s]
O God, who is your equal? [t]
20 You have sent me many bitter afflictions,
but once more revive me.
From the watery depths of the earth
once more raise me up.
21 Restore my honor;
turn and comfort me,
22 That I may praise you with the lyre
for your faithfulness, my God,
And sing to you with the harp,
O Holy One of Israel!
23 My lips will shout for joy as I sing your praise;
my soul, too, which you have redeemed.
24 Yes, my tongue shall recount
your justice day by day.
For those who sought my ruin
will have been shamed and disgraced.

PSALM 72*

A Prayer for the King

1 Of Solomon.

I

O God, give your judgment to the king;
your justice to the son of kings; [u]*
2 That he may govern your people with justice,
your oppressed with right judgment, [v]
3 That the mountains may yield their bounty for
the people,
and the hills great abundance, [w]
4 That he may defend the oppressed among the
people,
save the poor and crush the oppressor.

II

5 May he live as long as the sun endures,
like the moon, through all generations. [x]
6 May he be like rain coming down upon the
fields,
like showers watering the earth, [y]
7 That abundance may flourish in his days,
great bounty, till the moon be no more.

III

8 May he rule from sea to sea,
from the river to the ends of the earth. [z]*
9 May his foes kneel before him,
his enemies lick the dust. [a]

Ps 72: A royal psalm in which the Israelite king, as the representative of God, is the instrument of divine justice (1–4. 12–14) and blessing (5–7. 15–17) for the whole world. The king is human, giving only what he has received from God. Hence intercession must be made for him. The extravagant language is typical of oriental royal courts.

72, 1: The king . . . the son of kings: the crown prince is the king's son; the prayer envisages the dynasty.

72, 8: From sea to sea . . . the ends of the earth: the boundaries of the civilized world known at the time: from the Mediterranean Sea (the western sea) to the Persian Gulf (the eastern sea), and from the Euphrates (the river) to the islands and lands of southwestern Europe, "the ends of the earth." The words may also have a mythic nuance—the earth surrounded by cosmic waters, hence everywhere.

m Pss 3, 2; 22, 8. n Ps 22, 20. o Pss 35, 4; 40, 15; 70, 3. p Ps 35, 28. q Is 46, 3–4. r Pss 22, 31–32; 48, 14–15; 145, 4. s Ps 72, 18. t Ps 86, 8. u Ps 99, 4; Jer 23, 5. v Prv 31, 8–9. w Is 52, 7; 55, 12. x Ps 89, 37–38; Jer 31, 35. y Dt 32, 2; Is 45, 8; Hos 6, 3. z Dt 11, 24; Zec 9, 10. a Is 49, 23; Mi 7, 17.

10 May the kings of Tarshish and the islands*
bring tribute,
the kings of Arabia and Seba* offer
gifts. [b]
11 May all kings bow before him,
all nations serve him. [c]
12 For he rescues the poor when they cry out,
the oppressed who have no one to help.
13 He shows pity to the needy and the poor [d]
and saves the lives of the poor.
14 From extortion and violence he frees them,
for precious is their blood* in his sight.

IV

15 Long may he live, receiving gold from
Arabia,
prayed for without cease, blessed day
by day.
16 May wheat abound in the land,
flourish even on the mountain heights.
May his fruit increase like Lebanon's,
his wheat like the grasses of the land. [e]*
17 May his name be blessed forever;
as long as the sun, may his name endure.[f]
May the tribes of the earth give blessings with
his name;*
may all the nations regard him as favored. [g]

* * *

18 Blessed be the LORD, the God of Israel,*
who alone does wonderful deeds. [h]
19 Blessed be his glorious name forever;
may all the earth be filled with the LORD's
glory. [i]
Amen and amen.

20 The end of the psalms of David, son of
Jesse.

THIRD BOOK —PSALMS 73–89

PSALM 73*

The Trial of the Just

1 A psalm of Asaph.

How good God is to the upright,
the Lord, to those who are clean of heart!

I

2 But, as for me, I lost my balance;
my feet all but slipped,
3 Because I was envious of the arrogant
when I saw the prosperity of the wicked.[j]
4 For they suffer no pain;
their bodies are healthy and sleek.
5 They are free of the burdens of life;
they are not afflicted like others.
6 Thus pride adorns them as a necklace;
violence clothes them as a robe.
7 Out of their stupidity comes sin;
evil thoughts flood their hearts. [k]
8 They scoff and spout their malice;
from on high they utter threats. [l]
9 They set their mouths against the heavens,*
their tongues roam the earth.
10 So my people turn to them
and drink deeply of their words.*
11 They say, "Does God really know?"
"Does the Most High have any
knowledge?" [m]
12 Such, then, are the wicked,
always carefree, increasing their wealth.

II

13 Is it in vain that I have kept my heart
clean,

72, 10: Tarshish and the islands: the far west (Ps 48, 6); **Arabia and Seba**: the far south (1 Kgs 10, 1).

72, 14: Their blood: cf Ps 116, 15.

72, 16: The translation of the difficult Hebrew is tentative.

72, 17: May the tribes of the earth give blessing with his name: an echo of the promise to the ancestors (Gn 12, 3; 26, 4; 28, 14), suggesting that the monarchy in Israel fulfilled the promise to Abraham, Isaac, and Jacob.

72, 18–19: A doxology marking the end of Book II of the Psalter.

Ps 73: The opening verse of this probing poem (cf Pss 37; 49) is actually the psalmist's hard-won conclusion from personal experience: God is just and good! The psalmist describes near loss of faith (2–3), occasioned by observing the wicked who blasphemed God with seeming impunity (4–12). Feeling abandoned despite personal righteousness, the psalmist could not bear the injustice until an experience of God's nearness in the temple made clear how deluded the wicked were. Their sudden destruction shows their impermanence (13–20). The just can thus be confident, for, as the psalmist now knows, their security is from God (1. 23–28).

73, 9: They set their mouths against the heavens: in an image probably derived from mythic stories of half-divine giants, the monstrous speech of the wicked is likened to enormous jaws gaping wide, devouring everything in sight.

73, 10: The Hebrew is obscure.

b Ps 68, 30; Is 60, 5–6; 1 Kgs 10, 1ff. c Pss 47, 8. d Prv 31, 9. e Is 27, 6; Hos 14, 6–8; Am 9, 13. f Ps 21, 7. g Gn 12, 3; Zec 8, 13. h Pss 41, 14; 89, 53; 106, 48; 136, 4. i Ps 57, 5; Nm 14, 21. j Ps 37, 1; Jb 21, 13. k Jb 15, 27. l Ps 17, 10. m Ps 10, 11; Jb 22, 13.

washed my hands in innocence? [n]
14 For I am afflicted day after day,
chastised every morning.
15 Had I thought, "I will speak as they do,"
I would have betrayed your people.
16 Though I tried to understand all this,
it was too difficult for me,
17 Till I entered the sanctuary of God
and came to understand their end.*

III

18 You set them, indeed, on a slippery road;
you hurl them down to ruin.
19 How suddenly they are devastated;
undone by disasters forever!
20 They are like a dream after waking, Lord,
dismissed like shadows when you arise. [o]

IV

21 Since my heart was embittered
and my soul deeply wounded,
22 I was stupid and could not understand;
I was like a brute beast in your presence.
23 Yet I am always with you;
you take hold of my right hand. [p]
24 With your counsel you guide me,
and at the end receive me with honor.*
25 Whom else have I in the heavens?
None beside you delights me on earth.
26 Though my flesh and my heart fail,
God is the rock of my heart, my portion
forever.
27 But those who are far from you perish;
you destroy those unfaithful to you.
28 As for me, to be near God is my good,
to make the Lord GOD my refuge.
I shall declare all your works
in the gates of daughter Zion.

PSALM 74*

Prayer at the Destruction of the Temple

1 A *maskil* of Asaph.

I

Why, God, have you cast us off forever? [q]*
Why does your anger burn against the
sheep of your pasture? [r]
2 Remember your flock that you gathered of old,
the tribe you redeemed as your very own.
Remember Mount Zion where you dwell. [s]
3 Turn your steps toward the utter ruins,
toward the sanctuary devastated by the
enemy.
4 Your foes roared triumphantly in your shrine;
they set up their own tokens of victory.
5 They hacked away like foresters gathering
boughs,
swinging their axes in a thicket of trees.
6 They smashed all your engraved work,
pounded it with hammer and pick.
7 They set your sanctuary on fire;
the abode of your name they razed and
profaned. [t]
8 They said in their hearts, "Destroy
them all!
Burn all the shrines of God in the land!"
9 Now we see no signs,*
we have no prophets, [u]
no one who knows how long.
10 How long, O God, shall the enemy jeer? [v]

73, 17: And came to understand their end: the psalmist receives a double revelation in the temple: 1) the end of the wicked comes unexpectedly (18–20); 2) God is with me.

73, 24: And at the end receive me with honor: a perhaps deliberately enigmatic verse. It is understood by some commentators as reception into heavenly glory, hence the traditional translation, "receive me into glory." The Hebrew verb can indeed refer to mysterious divine elevation of a righteous person into God's domain: Enoch in Gn 5, 24; Elijah in 2 Kgs 2, 11–12; the righteous psalmist in Ps 49, 16. Personal resurrection in the Old Testament, however, is clearly attested only in the second century B.C. The verse is perhaps best left unspecified as a reference to God's nearness and protection.

Ps 74: A communal lament sung when the enemy invaded the temple; it would be especially appropriate at the destruction of Jerusalem in 587 B.C. Israel's God is urged to look upon the ruined sanctuary and remember the congregation who worshiped there (1–11). People and sanctuary are bound together; an attack on Zion is an attack on Israel. In the second half of the poem, the community brings before God the story of their origins—their creation (12–17)—in order to move God to reenact that deed of creation now. Will God allow a lesser power to destroy the divine project (18–23)?

74, 1: Forever: the word implies that the disaster is already of long duration. Cf 74, 9 and note.

74, 9: Now we see no signs: ancients often asked prophets to say for how long a divine punishment was to last. Cf 2 Sm 24, 13. Here no prophet has arisen to indicate the duration.

n Ps 26, 6; Mal 3, 14. o Jb 20, 8. p Ps 121, 5. q Pss 10, 1; 44, 24; 77, 8. r Ps 80, 5. s Pss 68, 17; 132, 13; Ex 15, 17; Jer 10, 16; 51, 19. t Is 64, 10; Ps 79, 1. u Lam 2, 9. v Ps 89, 47.

Shall the foe revile your name forever?
11 Why draw back your right hand,
why keep it idle beneath your cloak?

II

12 Yet you, God, are my king from of old,*
winning victories throughout the earth.
13 You stirred up the sea in your might; [w]
you smashed the heads of the dragons on the waters. [x]
14 You crushed the heads of Leviathan, [y]
tossed him for food to the sharks.
15 You opened up springs and torrents,
brought dry land out of the primeval waters.
16 Yours the day and yours the night;
you set the moon and sun in place.
17 You fixed all the limits of the earth;
summer and winter you made. [z]
18 Remember how the enemy has jeered, O LORD,
how a foolish people has reviled your name.
19 Do not surrender to beasts those who praise you;
do not forget forever the life of your afflicted.
20 Look to your covenant,
for the land is filled with gloom;
the pastures, with violence.
21 Let not the oppressed turn back in shame;
may the poor and needy praise your name.
22 Arise, God, defend your cause;
remember the constant jeers of the fools.
23 Do not ignore the clamor of your foes,
the unceasing uproar of your enemies.

PSALM 75*

God the Judge of the World

1 For the leader. Do not destroy! A psalm of Asaph; a song.

I

2 We thank you, God, we give thanks;
we call upon your name,
declare your wonderful deeds.
You said:*
3 "I will choose the time;
I will judge fairly.
4 The earth and all its inhabitants will quake,
but I have firmly set its pillars." [a] *Selah*

II

5 So I say to the boastful: "Do not boast!" [b]
to the wicked: "Do not raise your horns!*
6 Do not raise your horns against heaven!
Do not speak arrogantly against the Rock!" [c]
7 For judgment comes not from east or from west,
not from the desert or from the mountains, [d]
8 But from God who decides,
who brings some low and raises others high. [e]
9 Yes, a cup* is in the LORD's hand,
foaming wine, fully spiced.*
When God pours it out,
they will drain it even to the dregs;
all the wicked of the earth must drink. [f]
10 But I will rejoice forever;
I will sing praise to the God of Jacob,
11 Who has said:
"I will break off all the horns of the wicked,
but the horns of the just shall be lifted up." [g]

74, 12–17: Comparable Canaanite literature describes the storm-god's victory over all-encompassing Sea and its allies (dragons and Leviathan) and the subsequent peaceful arrangement of the universe, sometimes through the placement of paired cosmic elements (day and night, sun and moon). Cf Ps 89, 12–13. The psalm apparently equates the enemies attacking the temple with the destructive cosmic forces already tamed by God. Why then are those forces now raging untamed against your own people?

Ps 75: The psalmist gives thanks and rejoices (2. 10) for the direct intervention of God, which is promised in two oracles (3–4. 11). Expecting that divine intervention, the psalmist warns evildoers to repent (5–9).

75, 2: You said: supplied for clarity here and in v 11. The translation assumes in both places that the psalmist is citing an oracle of God.

75, 5: Do not raise your horns!: the horn is the symbol of strength; to raise one's horn is to exalt one's own power as v 6 explains.

75, 9: A cup: "the cup of God's wrath" is the punishment inflicted on the wicked. Cf Is 51, 17; Jer 25, 15–29; 49, 12; Ez 23, 31–33. **Spiced:** literally, "a mixed drink"; spices or drugs were added to wine. Cf Prv 9, 2. 5.

w Ps 89, 10. x Is 51, 9–10. y Jb 3, 8; 40, 25; Is 27, 1. z 16–17: Gn 1. a Pss 46, 3; 60, 4; 93, 1; 96, 10; 104, 5; 1 Sm 2, 8; Is 24, 19. b 1 Sm 2, 3; Zec 2, 1–4. c Jb 15, 25. d Mt 24, 23–27. e Jb 5, 11; 1 Sm 2, 7. f Ps 60, 5; Jb 21, 20; Is 51, 17. 21–22; Jer 25, 15ff; Hb 2, 16. g Ps 92, 11.

PSALM 76*

God Defends Zion

1 For the leader; a psalm with stringed instruments.
A song of Asaph.

I

2 Renowned in Judah is God,[h]
whose name is great in Israel.
3 On Salem* is God's tent, a shelter on Zion.
4 There the flashing arrows were shattered,
shield, sword, and weapons of war.[i] *Selah*

II

5 Terrible and awesome are you,
stronger than the ancient mountains.*
6 Despoiled are the bold warriors;
they sleep their final sleep;
the hands of all the mighty have failed.[j]
7 At your roar, O God of Jacob,
chariots and steeds lay still.
8 So terrible and awesome are you;
who can stand before you and your great
anger?[k]
9 From the heavens you pronounced sentence;
the earth was terrified and reduced to
silence,
10 When you arose, O God, for judgment
to deliver the afflicted of the land. *Selah*
11 Even wrathful Edom praises you;
the remnant of Hamath* keeps your feast.

III

12 Make and keep vows to the LORD your God.[l]
May all present bring gifts to this awesome
God,
13 Who checks the pride of princes,
inspires awe among the kings of earth.

PSALM 77*

Confidence in God during National Distress

1 For the leader; *'al Jeduthun.* A psalm of Asaph.

I

2 I cry aloud to God,
cry to God to hear me.
3 On the day of my distress I seek the Lord;
by night my hands are raised unceasingly;[m]
I refuse to be consoled.
4 When I think of God, I groan;
as I ponder, my spirit grows faint.[n] *Selah*
5 My eyes cannot close in sleep;
I am troubled and cannot speak.
6 I consider the days of old;
the years long past 7 I remember.[o]
In the night I meditate in my heart;
I ponder and my spirit broods:
8 "Will the Lord reject us forever,[p]
never again show favor?
9 Has God's love ceased forever?
Has the promise failed for all ages?
10 Has God forgotten mercy,
in anger withheld compassion?" *Selah*
11 I conclude:* "My sorrow is this,
the right hand of the Most High has left
us."[q]

II

12 I will remember* the deeds of the LORD;
yes, your wonders of old I will remember.[r]
13 I will recite all your works;
your exploits I will tell.
14 Your way, O God, is holy;
what god is as great as our God?[s]
15 You alone are the God who did wonders;

Ps 76: A song glorifying Zion, the mountain of Jerusalem where God destroyed Israel's enemies. Zion is thus the appropriate site to celebrate the victory (3–4), a victory described in parallel scenes (5–7. 8–11). Israel is invited to worship its powerful patron deity (12–13).

76, 3: Salem: an ancient name for Jerusalem, used here perhaps on account of its allusion to the Hebrew word for peace, *shalom.* Cf Gn 14, 18; Heb 7, 1–3.

76, 5: Ancient mountains: conjectural translation of a difficult Hebrew phrase on the basis of Gn 49, 26. The mountains are part of the structure of the universe (Ps 89, 12–13).

76, 11: Edom . . . Hamath: conjectural translation. Israel's neighbors to the southeast and north.

Ps 77: A community lament in which the speaker ("I") describes the anguish of Israel at God's silence when its very existence is at stake (2–11). In response the speaker recites the story of how God brought the people into existence (12–21). The question is thus posed to God: Will you allow the people you created to be destroyed?

77, 11: I conclude: literally, "I said." The psalmist, after pondering the present distress and God's promises to Israel, has decided that God has forgotten the people.

77, 12: I will remember: the verb sometimes means to make present the great deeds of Israel's past by reciting them. Cf Pss 78, 42; 105, 5; 106, 7.

h Hb 3, 2. i Pss 46, 10; 122, 6–9. j 2 Kgs 19, 35; Jer 51, 39; Na 3, 18. k Dt 7, 21; 1 Sm 6, 20; Na 1, 6; Mal 3, 2. l Nm 30, 3. m Pss 50, 15; 88, 2. n Jon 2, 8. o Ps 143, 5; Dt 32, 7. p 8–10: Pss 13, 2; 44, 24; 74, 1; 80, 5; 89, 47; Lam 3, 31. q Ex 15, 6. 12; Pss 17, 7; 18, 36. r Ps 143, 5. s Ps 18, 31; Ex 15, 11.

among the peoples you revealed your
might. [t]
16 With your arm you redeemed your people,
the descendants of Jacob and Joseph. [u]
Selah
17 The waters saw you, God;
the waters saw you and lashed about,
trembled even to their depths. [v]
18 The clouds poured down their rains;
the thunderheads rumbled;
your arrows flashed back and forth. [w]
19 The thunder of your chariot wheels
resounded;
your lightning lit up the world;
the earth trembled and quaked. [x]
20 Through the sea was your path;
your way, through the mighty waters,
though your footsteps were unseen. [y]
21 You led your people like a flock
under the care of Moses and Aaron. [z]

PSALM 78*

A New Beginning in Zion and David

1 A *maskil* of Asaph.

I

Attend, my people, to my teaching;
listen to the words of my mouth.
2 I will open my mouth in story,*
drawing lessons from of old. [a]
3 We have heard them, we know them;
our ancestors have recited them to us. [b]
4 We do not keep them from our children;
we recite them to the next generation,
The praiseworthy and mighty deeds of the
LORD,
the wonders that he performed. [c]
5 God set up a decree in Jacob,
established a law in Israel: [d]
What he commanded our ancestors,
they were to teach their children;
6 That the next generation might come to know,
children yet to be born. [e]
In turn they were to recite them to their
children,
7 that they too might put their trust in God,
And not forget the works of God,
keeping his commandments.
8 They were not to be like their ancestors,
a rebellious and defiant generation,[f]
A generation whose heart was not constant,[g]
whose spirit was not faithful to God,
9 Like the ranks of Ephraimite archers,*
who retreated on the day of battle.
10 They did not keep God's covenant;
they refused to walk by his law.
11 They forgot his works,
the wondrous deeds he had shown them.

II

A

12 In the sight of their ancestors God did
wonders,
in the land of Egypt, the plain of Zoan. [h]*
13 He split the sea and led them across,[i]
piling up the waters rigid as walls.[j]
14 God led them with a cloud by day,
all night with the light of fire. [k]
15 He split rock in the desert,

Ps 78: A recital of history to show that past generations did not respond to God's gracious deeds and were punished by God making the gift into a punishment. Will Israel now fail to appreciate God's new act—the choosing of Zion and of David? The tripartite introduction invites Israel to learn the lessons hidden in its traditions (1–4. 5–7. 8–11); each section ends with the mention of God's acts. There are two distinct narratives of approximately equal length: the wilderness events (12–39) and the movement from Egypt to Canaan (40–72). The structure of both is parallel: gracious act (12–16. 40–55), rebellion (17–20. 56–58), divine punishment (21–31. 59–64), God's readiness to forgive and begin anew (32–39. 65–72). The psalm may reflect the reunification program of either King Hezekiah (late eighth century) or King Josiah (late seventh century) in that the Northern Kingdom (Ephraim, Joseph) is especially invited to accept Zion and the Davidic king.

78, 2: Story: Hebrew *mashal* literally means "comparison" and can signify a story with a hidden meaning. Mt 13, 35 cites the verse to explain Jesus' use of parables.

78, 9: Ephraimite archers: Ephraim was the most important tribe of the Northern Kingdom. Its military defeat (here unspecified) demonstrates its infidelity to God, who otherwise would have protected it.

78, 12. 43: Zoan: a city on the arm of the Nile, a former capital of Egypt.

t Pss 86, 10; 89, 6. u Gn 46, 26–27; Neh 1, 10. v Pss 18, 16; 114, 3; Na 1, 4. w Pss 18, 14–15; 29; 144, 6; Jb 37, 3–4; Wis 5, 21; Hb 3, 10–11; Zec 9, 14. x Pss 18, 8; 97, 4; 99, 1; Ex 19, 16; Jgs 5, 4–5. y Neh 9, 11; Wis 14, 3; Is 51, 10; Hb 3, 15. z Ps 78, 52; Is 63, 11–14; Hos 12, 14; Mi 6, 4. a Ps 49, 5; Mt 13, 35. b Ps 44, 2. c Ex 10, 2; Dt 4, 9; Jb 8, 8. d Ps 147, 19; Dt 33, 4. e Ps 22, 31–32; Dt 4, 9; 6, 7. f Dt 31, 27; 32, 5. g Ps 95, 10. h Ps 106, 7. i 13–14: Ex 14–15; Ps 136, 13. j Ex 14, 22; 15, 8. k Ps 105, 39; Ex 13, 21; Wis 18, 3.

gave water to drink, abounding as the
deep. [l]
16 He made streams flow from crags,
drew out rivers of water.

B

17 But they went on sinning against him,
rebelling against the Most High in the
desert. [m]
18 They tested God in their hearts,
demanding the food they craved. [n]
19 They spoke against God, and said,
"Can God spread a table in the desert? [o]
20 True, when he struck the rock,
water gushed forth,
the wadis flooded.
But can he also provide bread,
give meat to his people?"

C

21 The LORD heard and grew angry; [p]
fire blazed up against Jacob;
anger flared up against Israel.
22 For they did not believe in God,
did not trust in his saving power.
23 So he commanded the skies above;*
the doors of heaven he opened.
24 God rained manna upon them for food;
bread from heaven he gave them. [q]
25 All ate a meal fit for heroes;
food he sent in abundance.
26 He stirred up the east wind in the heavens;
by his power God brought on the south
wind.
27 He rained meat upon them like dust,
winged fowl like the sands of the sea,
28 Brought them down in the midst of the camp,
round about their tents.
29 They ate and were well filled;
he gave them what they had craved.
30 But while they still wanted more,
and the food was still in their mouths,
31 God's anger attacked them,
killed their best warriors,
laid low the youth of Israel. [r]
32 In spite of all this they went on sinning,
they did not believe in his wonders.

D

33 God ended their days abruptly,
their years in sudden death.
34 When he slew them, they began to seek him;
they again inquired of their God. [s]
35 They remembered* that God was their rock,
God Most High, their redeemer.
36 But they deceived him with their mouths,
lied to him with their tongues.
37 Their hearts were not constant toward him;
they were not faithful to his covenant. [t]
38 But God is merciful and forgave their sin;
he did not utterly destroy them.
Time and again he turned back his anger,
unwilling to unleash all his rage. [u]*
39 He was mindful that they were flesh,
a breath that passes and does not return.

III

A

40 How often they rebelled against God in the
desert,
grieved him in the wasteland.
41 Again and again they tested God,
provoked the Holy One of Israel.
42 They did not remember his power,
the day he redeemed them from the foe, [v]
43 When he displayed his wonders in Egypt,*
his marvels in the plain of Zoan. [w]
44 God changed their rivers to blood;
their streams they could not drink.
45 He sent insects that devoured them, [x]
frogs that destroyed them.
46 He gave their harvest to the caterpillar,
the fruits of their labor to the locust.
47 He killed their vines with hail, [y]

78, 23–31: On the manna and the quail, see Ex 16 and Nm 11. Unlike Ex 16, here both manna and quail are instruments of punishment, showing that a divine gift can become deadly because of Israel's apostasy.

78, 35: Remembered: invoked God publicly in worship. Their words were insincere (36).

78, 38: God is always ready to forgive and begin anew, as in choosing Zion and David (65–72).

78, 43–55: Ex 7–12 records ten plagues. Here there are six

l Pss 105, 41; 114, 8; Ex 17, 1–7; Nm 20, 2–13; Dt 8, 15; Wis 11, 4; Is 48, 21. m Dt 9, 7; Ez 20, 13. n Ps 106, 14; Ex 16, 2–36. o Ps 23, 5. p 21f: Nm 11; Dt 32, 22. q Ps 105, 40; Ex 16, 4. 14; Dt 8, 3; Wis 16, 20; Jn 6, 31. r Nm 14, 29. s Dt 32, 15. 18; Is 26, 16. t Ps 95, 10; Is 29, 13. u Ps 85, 4; Ex 32, 14; Is 48, 9; Ez 20, 22. v Ps 106, 21. w 43f: Pss 105, 27–36; 135, 9; Ex 7, 14—11, 10; 12, 29–36; Wis 16–18. x Ex 8, 17. y Wis 16, 16.

their sycamores with frost.
48 He exposed their flocks to deadly hail,
their cattle to lightning. [z]
49 He unleashed against them his fiery breath,
roar, fury, and distress,
storming messengers of death.
50 He cleared a path for his anger;
he did not spare them from death;
he delivered their beasts to the plague.
51 He struck all the firstborn of Egypt, [a]
love's first child in the tents of Ham.
52 God led forth his people like sheep;
he guided them through the desert like a flock. [b]
53 He led them on secure and unafraid,
but the sea enveloped their enemies. [c]
54 He brought them to his holy land,
the mountain his right hand had won. [d]
55 God drove out the nations before them,
apportioned them a heritage by lot,
settled the tribes of Israel in their tents.

B

56 But they tested, rebelled against God Most High,
his decrees they did not observe.
57 They turned back, deceitful like their ancestors;
they proved false like a bow with no tension.
58 They enraged him with their high places;
with their idols they goaded him. [e]

C

59 God heard and grew angry;
he rejected Israel completely.
60 He forsook the shrine at Shiloh, [f] *
the tent where he dwelt with humans.
61 He gave up his might into captivity,
his glorious ark into the hands of the foe. [g]
62 God abandoned his people to the sword;
he was enraged against his heritage.
63 Fire consumed their young men;
their young women heard no wedding songs. [h]
64 Their priests fell by the sword;
their widows made no lamentation.

D

65 Then the Lord awoke as from sleep,
like a warrior from the effects of wine.
66 He put his enemies to flight;
everlasting shame he dealt them.
67 He rejected the tent of Joseph,
chose not the tribe of Ephraim.
68 God chose the tribe of Judah,*
Mount Zion which he favored. [i]
69 He built his shrine like the heavens,
like the earth which he founded forever.
70 He chose David his servant,
took him from the sheepfold. [j]
71 From tending sheep God brought him,
to shepherd Jacob, his people,
Israel, his heritage. [k]
72 He shepherded them with a pure heart;
with skilled hands he guided them.

PSALM 79*

A Prayer for Jerusalem

1 A psalm of Asaph.

I

O God, the nations have invaded your heritage;
they have defiled your holy temple,
have laid Jerusalem in ruins. [l]
2 They have left the corpses of your servants
as food for the birds of the heavens,
the flesh of your faithful for the beasts of the earth. [m]

---

divine attacks upon Egypt; the seventh climactic act is God's bringing Israel to the holy land.

78, 60: Shiloh: an important shrine in the north prior to Jerusalem. Despite its holy status, it was destroyed (60–64; cf Jer 7, 12. 14).

78, 68. 70: God's ultimate offer of mercy to the sinful helpless people is Zion and the Davidic king.

Ps 79: A communal lament complaining that the nations have defiled the temple and murdered the holy people, leaving their corpses unburied (1–4). The occasion is probably the destruction of Jerusalem by the Babylonian army in 587 B.C. The people ask how long the withdrawal of divine favor will last (5), pray for action now (6–7), and admit that their own sins have brought about the catastrophe (8–9). They seek to persuade God to act for reasons of honor: the nations who do not call upon the Name are running amok (6); the divine honor is compromised (1. 10. 12); God's own servants suffer (2–4. 11).

z Ex 9, 3. a Pss 105, 36; 136, 10; Ex 12, 29. b Ps 77, 21. c Ex 14, 26–28. d Ex 15, 17. e Dt 32, 16. 21. f Jos 18, 1; 1 Sm 1, 3; Jer 7, 12; 26, 6. g 1 Sm 4, 11. 22. h Dt 32, 25; Jer 7, 34. i Pss 48, 2; 50, 2; Lam 2, 15. j Ps 89, 21; Ez 34, 23; 37, 24; 2 Chr 6, 6. k 1 Sm 16, 11–13; 2 Sm 7, 8. l 2 Kgs 25, 9–10; Lam 1, 10. m Jer 7, 33.

3 They have spilled their blood like water
all around Jerusalem,
and no one is left to bury them.[n]
4 We have become the reproach of our
neighbors,
the scorn and derision of those around us.[o]

II

5 How long, LORD? Will you be angry forever?
Will your rage keep burning like fire?[p]
6 Pour out your wrath on nations that reject
you,
on kingdoms that do not call on your
name,[q]
7 For they have devoured Jacob,
laid waste his home.
8 Do not hold past iniquities against us;
may your compassion come quickly,
for we have been brought very low.[r]

III

9 Help us, God our savior,
for the glory of your name.
Deliver us, pardon our sins
for your name's sake.[s]
10 Why should the nations say,
"Where is their God?"[t]
Before our eyes make clear to the nations
that you avenge the blood of your servants.[u]

IV

11 Let the groans of prisoners come before you;
by your great power free those doomed to
death.[v]
12 Lord, inflict on our neighbors sevenfold
the disgrace they inflicted on you.[w]
13 Then we, your people, the sheep of your
pasture,
will give thanks to you forever;
through all ages we will declare your praise.

PSALM 80*

Prayer to Restore God's Vineyard

1 For the leader; according to "Lilies." *Eduth*.*
A psalm of Asaph.

I

2 Shepherd of Israel, listen,
guide of the flock of Joseph!
From your throne upon the cherubim reveal
yourself[x]
3 to Ephraim, Benjamin, and Manasseh.
Stir up your power, come to save us.
4 O LORD of hosts, restore us;
Let your face shine upon us,
that we may be saved.[y]

II

5 LORD of hosts,
how long will you burn with anger
while your people pray?[z]
6 You have fed them the bread of tears,
made them drink tears in abundance.[a]
7 You have left us to be fought over by our
neighbors;
our enemies deride us.[b]
8 O LORD of hosts, restore us;
let your face shine upon us,
that we may be saved.

III

9 You brought a vine* out of Egypt;
you drove away the nations and planted it.
10 You cleared the ground;
it took root and filled the land.
11 The mountains were covered by its shadow,
the cedars of God by its branches.
12 It sent out boughs as far as the sea,*
shoots as far as the river.*
13 Why have you broken down the walls,
so that all who pass by pluck its fruit?[c]

Ps 80: A community lament in time of military defeat. Using the familiar image of Israel as a vineyard, the people complain that God has broken down the wall protecting the once splendid vine brought from Egypt (9–14). They pray that God will again turn to them and use the Davidic king to lead them to victory (15–20).

80, 1: Lilies . . . . Eduth: the first term is probably the title of the melody to which the psalm was to be sung; the second is unexplained.

80, 9: A vine: a frequent metaphor for Israel. Cf Is 5, 1–7; 27, 2–5; Jer 2, 21; Hos 10, 1; Mt 21, 33.

80, 12: The sea: the Mediterranean. **The river:** the Euphrates. Cf Gn 15, 18; 1 Kgs 5, 1. The terms may also have a mythic nuance—the seas that surround the earth; sea and river are sometimes paralleled in poetry.

n 1 Mc 7, 17; Jer 14, 16. o Pss 44, 14; 80, 7; 123, 3–4; Jb 12, 4; Dn 9, 16; Zep 2, 8. p Pss 13, 2; 44, 24; 89, 47; Dt 4, 24. q Ps 14, 4; Jer 10, 25. r Ps 142, 7. s Ez 20, 44; 36, 22. t Pss 42, 4; 115, 2; Jl 2, 17. u Jl 4, 21. v Ps 102, 21. w Ps 89, 51–52. x Pss 23, 1–3; 95, 7; 100, 3; Gn 48, 15; Ex 25, 22; 1 Sm 4, 4; 2 Sm 6, 2; Mi 7, 14. y 4. 8. 20: Pss 4, 7; 31, 17; 67, 2; 85, 5; Nm 6, 25; Dn 9, 17. z Pss 13, 2; 44, 24; 74, 1; 79, 5; 89, 47; Dt 4, 24. a Pss 42, 4; 102, 10. b Pss 44, 14; 79, 4; 123, 3–4; Jb 12, 4; Dn 9, 16; Zep 2, 8. c Ps 89, 41.

14 The boar from the forest strips the vine;
the beast of the field feeds upon it. [d]
15 Turn again, LORD of hosts;
look down from heaven and see;
Attend to this vine,
16 the shoot your right hand has planted.
17 Those who would burn or cut it down—
may they perish at your rebuke.
18 May your help be with the man at your right hand,
with the one* whom you once made strong.
19 Then we will not withdraw from you;
revive us, and we will call on your name.
20 LORD of hosts, restore us;
let your face shine upon us,
that we may be saved.

PSALM 81*

An Admonition to Fidelity

1 For the leader; "upon the *gittith.*" * Of Asaph.

I

2 Sing joyfully to God our strength; [e]
shout in triumph to the God of Jacob!
3 Take up a melody, sound the timbrel,
the sweet-sounding harp and lyre.
4 Blow the trumpet at the new moon,
at the full moon,* on our solemn feast.[f]
5 For this is a law in Israel,
an edict of the God of Jacob, [g]
6 Who made it a decree for Joseph
when he came out of the land of Egypt.

II

I hear a new oracle:*
7 "I relieved their shoulders of the burden;*
their hands put down the basket. [h]*
8 In distress you called and I rescued you;
unseen, I spoke to you in thunder;
At the waters of Meribah* I tested you and said: [i] *Selah*
9 'Listen, my people, I give you warning!
If only you will obey me, Israel! [j]
10 There must be no foreign god among you; [k]*
you must not worship an alien god.
11 I, the LORD, am your God,
who brought you up from the land of Egypt.
Open wide your mouth that I may fill it.'
12 But my people did not listen to my words;
Israel did not obey me.
13 So I gave them over to hardness of heart;
they followed their own designs. [l]
14 But even now if my people would listen,
if Israel would walk in my paths, [m]
15 In a moment I would subdue their foes,
against their enemies unleash my hand. [n]
16 Those who hate the LORD would tremble,
their doom sealed forever.
17 But Israel I would feed with the finest wheat,
satisfy them with honey from the rock." [o]

PSALM 82*

The Downfall of Unjust Gods

1 A psalm of Asaph.

I

God rises in the divine council,

80, 18: The man at your right hand . . . the one: the Davidic king who will lead the army in battle.

Ps 81: At a pilgrimage feast, probably harvest in the fall, the people assemble in the temple in accord with the Sinai ordinances (2–6a). They hear a divine word (mediated by a temple speaker) telling how God rescued them from slavery in Egypt (7–9), gave them the fundamental commandment of fidelity (9–11), which would bring punishment if they refused to obey (12–13). But if Israel repents, God will be with them once again, bestowing protection and fertility (14–17).

81, 1: Upon the gittith: probably the title of the melody to which the psalm was to be sung or a musical instrument.

81, 4: New moon . . . full moon: the pilgrimage feast of harvest began with a great assembly (Lv 23, 24; Nm 29, 1), used the new moon as a sign (Nm 29, 6), and included trumpets (Lv 23, 24).

81, 6: I hear a new oracle: literally, "a tongue I do not know I hear." A temple official speaks the word of God (6b–17), which is authoritative and unlike merely human words (cf Nm 24, 4. 16).

81, 7: I relieved their shoulders of the burden: literally, "his [Israel's] shoulder," hence the plural translation. A reference to the liberation of Israel from slavery in Egypt. **The basket**: for carrying clay to make bricks. Cf Ex 1, 14.

81, 8: Meribah: place of rebellion in the wilderness; cf Ex 17, 7; Nm 20, 13.

81, 10: There must be no foreign god among you: as in Pss 50 and 95, Israel is challenged to obey the first commandment of fidelity to God after the proclamation of the exodus.

Ps 82: As in Ps 58, the pagan gods are seen as subordinate divine beings to whom Israel's God had delegated oversight of the foreign countries in the beginning (Dt 32, 8–9 LXX). Now God

d Hos 2, 14. e Pss 43, 4; 68, 26; 149, 3; 150, 3–4; Jdt 16, 1. f Lv 23, 24; Nm 29, 1. g Ex 23, 14ff. h Ex 1, 14; 6, 6. i Ps 95, 8; Ex 2, 23ff; 17, 7; 19, 16; Nm 20, 13; 27, 14. j Ex 15, 26; Is 55, 2–3. k 10–11: Ex 20, 2–6; Dt 5, 6–10. l Jer 3, 17; 7, 24. m Is 48, 18. n Lv 26, 7–8. o Ps 147, 14; Dt 32, 13–14.

gives judgment in the midst of the gods. [p]
2 "How long will you judge unjustly
and favor the cause of the wicked? [q] *Selah*
3 Defend the lowly and fatherless;
render justice to the afflicted and needy.
4 Rescue the lowly and poor;
deliver them from the hand of the
wicked." [r]

II

5 The gods neither know nor understand,
wandering about in darkness,
and all the world's foundations shake.*
6 I declare: "Gods though you be,*
offspring of the Most High all of you,
7 Yet like any mortal you shall die;
like any prince you shall fall."
8 Arise, O God, judge the earth,*
for yours are all the nations.

PSALM 83*

Prayer against a Hostile Alliance

1 A song; a psalm of Asaph.

I

2 God, do not be silent;
God, be not still and unmoved! [s]
3 See how your enemies rage;
your foes proudly raise their heads.
4 They conspire against your people,
plot against those you protect. [t]
5 They say, "Come, let us wipe out their nation;
let Israel's name be mentioned no more!"
6 They scheme with one mind,
in league against you: [u]
7 The tents of Ishmael and Edom,*
the people of Moab and Hagar, [v]*
8 Gebal,* Ammon, and Amalek, [w]
Philistia and the inhabitants of Tyre. [x]
9 Assyria, too, in league with them
gives aid to the descendants of Lot.* *Selah*

II

10 Deal with them as with Midian;*
as with Sisera and Jabin at the torrent
Kishon, [y]
11 Those destroyed at Endor,
who became dung for the ground. [z]
12 Make their nobles like Oreb and Zeeb,
all their princes like Zebah and Zalmunna,
13 Who made a plan together,
"Let us seize the pastures of God."
14 My God, turn them into withered grass,
into chaff flying before the wind. [a]
15 As a fire raging through a forest,
a flame setting mountains ablaze, [b]
16 Pursue them with your tempest;
terrify them with your storm. [c]
17 Cover their faces with shame,
till they pay you homage, LORD.
18 Let them be dismayed and shamed forever;
let them perish in disgrace.
19 Show them you alone are the LORD,
the Most High over all the earth. [d]

PSALM 84*

Prayer of a Pilgrim to Jerusalem

1 For the leader; "upon the *gittith*." A psalm
of the Korahites.

I

2 How lovely your dwelling,

arises in the heavenly assembly (1) to rebuke the unjust "gods" (2–4), who are stripped of divine status and reduced in rank to mortals (5–7). They are accused of misruling the earth by not upholding the poor. A short prayer for universal justice concludes the psalm (8).

82, 5: The gods are blind and unable to declare what is right. Their misrule shakes earth's foundations (cf Pss 11, 3; 75, 4), which God made firm in creation (Ps 96, 10).

82, 6: I declare: "Gods though you be": in Jn 10, 34 Jesus uses the verse to prove that those to whom the word of God is addressed can fittingly be called "gods."

82, 8: Judge the earth: according to Dt 32, 8–9 LXX, Israel's God had originally assigned jurisdiction over the foreign nations to the subordinate deities, keeping Israel as a personal possession. Now God will directly take over the rulership of the whole world.

Ps 83: The community lament complains to God of the nations' attempts to wipe out the name of Israel (2–9). The psalmist sees all Israel's enemies throughout its history united in a conspiracy (3–9). May God destroy the current crop of enemies as the enemies of old were destroyed (10–13), and may they be pursued until they acknowledge the name of Israel's God (14–19).

83, 7–9: Apart from the Assyrians, all the nations listed here were neighbors of Israel. **The people of . . . Hagar:** a tribe of the desert regions east of **Ammon** and **Moab** (1 Chr 5, 10. 19–22). **Gebal** is the Phoenician city of Byblos or perhaps a mountain region south of the Dead Sea. **The descendants of Lot** are Moab and Edom (Gn 19, 36–38 and Dt 2, 9). These nations were never united against Israel in the same period; the psalm has lumped them all together.

83, 10–13: For the historical events, see Jgs 4–8.

Ps 84: Israelites celebrated three pilgrimage feasts in Jerusalem

p Is 3, 13–14. q Ps 58, 2. r Dt 1, 17. s Pss 10, 1; 44, 24; 109, 1. t Jer 11, 9. u Ps 2, 2. v Nm 20, 23; 1 Chr 5, 10. 19. w Ex 17, 8. x Jos 13, 2. y Ex 2, 15; Is 9, 3; 10, 26. z Jer 8, 2. a Pss 1, 4; 35, 5; 58, 10; Is 5, 24; 10, 17; 17, 13; 29, 5; Ez 21, 3. b Ps 50, 3. c Jb 25, 32; 27, 21. d Ps 97, 9; Dt 4, 39; Dn 3, 45.

O LORD of hosts! [e]
3 My soul yearns and pines
for the courts of the LORD.[f]
My heart and flesh cry out
for the living God.
4 As the sparrow finds a home
and the swallow a nest to settle her young,*
My home is by your altars,
LORD of hosts, my king and my God! [g]
5 Happy are those who dwell in your house!
They never cease to praise you.
Selah

II

6 Happy are those who find refuge in you,
whose hearts are set on pilgrim roads.
7 As they pass through the Baca valley,*
they find spring water to drink.
Also from pools the Lord provides water
for those who lose their way.
8 They pass through outer and inner wall
and see the God of gods on Zion.

III

9 LORD of hosts, hear my prayer;
listen, God of Jacob.
Selah
10 O God, look kindly on our shield;
look upon the face of your anointed. [h]*

IV

11 Better one day in your courts
than a thousand elsewhere.
Better the threshold of the house of my God
than a home in the tents of the wicked.
12 For a sun and shield is the LORD God,
bestowing all grace and glory.
The LORD withholds no good thing
from those who walk without reproach.
13 O LORD of hosts,
happy are those who trust in you!

PSALM 85*

Prayer for Divine Favor

1 For the leader. A psalm of the Korahites.

I

2 You once favored, LORD, your land,
restored the good fortune of Jacob. [i]
3 You forgave the guilt of your people,
pardoned all their sins.
Selah
4 You withdrew all your wrath,
turned back your burning anger. [j]

II

5 Restore us once more, God our savior;
abandon your wrath against us. [k]
6 Will you be angry with us forever,
drag out your anger for all generations? [l]
7 Please give us life again,
that your people may rejoice in you.
8 Show us, LORD, your love;
grant us your salvation.

III

9 I will listen for the word of God;
surely the LORD will proclaim peace
To his people, to the faithful,
to those who trust in him.*
10 Near indeed is salvation for the loyal;
prosperity will fill our land.
11 Love and truth will meet;*
justice and peace will kiss. [m]
12 Truth will spring from the earth;
justice will look down from heaven. [n]
13 The LORD will surely grant abundance;
our land will yield its increase. [o]
14 Prosperity will march before the LORD,
and good fortune will follow behind.

---

annually. The psalm expresses the sentiments of the pilgrims eager to enjoy the divine presence.

84, 4: The desire of a restless bird for a secure home is an image of the desire of a pilgrim for the secure house of God. Cf Ps 42, 2–3, where the image for the desire of the pilgrim is the thirst of the deer for water.

84, 7: Baca valley: Hebrew obscure; probably a valley on the way to Jerusalem.

84, 10: Our shield . . . your anointed: the king had a role in the liturgical celebration. For the king as shield, cf Ps 89, 19.

Ps 85: A national lament reminding God of past favors and forgiveness (2–4) and begging for forgiveness and grace now (5–8). A speaker represents the people who wait humbly with open hearts (9–10): God will be active on their behalf (11–14). The situation suggests the conditions of Judea during the early post-exilic period, the fifth century B.C.; the thoughts are similar to those of postexilic prophets (Hg 1, 5–11; 2, 6–9).

85, 9: The prophet listens to God's revelation. Cf Hb 2, 1.

85, 11–14: Divine activity is personified as pairs of virtues.

e Pss 43, 3–4; 122, 1. f Pss 42, 2–3; 63, 2–3; 143, 6; Is 26, 9. g Ps 5, 3. h Ps 89, 19. i Pss 14, 7; 126, 4. j Ps 78, 38; Ex 32, 14; Is 48, 9. k Ps 80, 4. l Pss 79, 5; 89, 47. m Pss 89, 15; 97, 2. n Is 45, 8. o Ps 67, 7; Lv 26, 4; Ez 34, 27; Hos 2, 23–24; Zec 8, 12.

PSALM 86*

Prayer in Time of Distress

1 A prayer of David.

I

Hear me, LORD, and answer me,
for I am poor and oppressed.
2 Preserve my life, for I am loyal;
save your servant who trusts in you.
3 You are my God; pity me, Lord;
to you I call all the day.
4 Gladden the soul of your servant;
to you, Lord, I lift up my soul. [p]
5 Lord, you are kind and forgiving,
most loving to all who call on you. [q]
6 LORD, hear my prayer;
listen to my cry for help. [r]
7 In this time of trouble I call,
for you will answer me.

II

8 None among the gods can equal you, O Lord;
nor can their deeds compare to yours. [s]
9 All the nations you have made shall come
to bow before you, Lord,
and give honor to your name. [t]
10 For you are great and do wondrous deeds;
and you alone are God.

III

11 Teach me, LORD, your way
that I may walk in your truth, [u]
single-hearted and revering your name.
12 I will praise you with all my heart,
glorify your name forever, Lord my God.
13 Your love for me is great;
you have rescued me from the depths of
Sheol. [v]
14 O God, the arrogant have risen against me;
a ruthless band has sought my life;
to you they pay no heed.
15 But you, Lord, are a merciful and gracious
God,
slow to anger, most loving and true. [w]
16 Turn to me, have pity on me;
give your strength to your servant;
save this child of your handmaid. [x]
17 Give me a sign of your favor:
make my enemies see, to their confusion,
that you, LORD, help and comfort me.

PSALM 87*

Zion the True Birthplace of Diaspora Pilgrims

1 A psalm of the Korahites. A song.

I

The LORD loves the city [y]
founded on holy mountains,
2 Loves the gates* of Zion
more than any dwelling in Jacob.
3 Glorious things are said of you,
O city of God! *Selah*

II

4 From Babylon and Egypt I count
those who acknowledge the LORD.
Philistia, Ethiopia, Tyre,
of them it can be said:
"This one was born there."
5 But of Zion it must be said:*
"They all were born here." [z]
The Most High confirms this; [a]
6 the LORD notes in the register of the
peoples:
"This one was born here." [b] *Selah*
7 So all sing in their festive dance:
"Within you is my true home." [c]

Ps 86: An individual lament. The psalmist, "poor and oppressed" (1), "devoted" (2), "your servant" (2. 4. 16), "rescued from the depths of Sheol" (13), attacked by the ruthless (14), desires only God's protection (1–7. 11–17).

Ps 87: A song of Zion, like Psalms 46; 48; 76; and 132. After the exile of the sixth century B.C., diaspora Jews from all over the world (4) made the long pilgrimage to Jerusalem, the city of God (1–3). Such Jews may have hailed from distant lands, but the psalm sees them as children of Zion (5–7). The original occasion may have been Pentecost, which always attracted a large number of diaspora Jews.

87, 2: The gates: the city itself, a common Hebrew idiom.

87, 5–6: The bond between the exile and the holy city was so strong as to override the exile's citizenship of lesser cities.

p Pss 25, 1; 143, 8. q Jl 2, 13. r Pss 5, 2; 130, 1–2. s Pss 35, 10; 89, 9; Ex 15, 11; Dt 3, 24; Jer 10, 6. t Ps 22, 28; Zec 14, 16; Rv 15, 4. u Pss 25, 4; 26, 3; 27, 11; 119, 12. 35; 143, 8. 10. v Pss 30, 4; 40, 3; Jon 2, 7. w Pss 103, 8; 130, 7; 145, 8; Ex 34, 6. x Pss 25, 16; 116, 16; Wis 9, 5. y 1–2: Pss 76, 2–3; 78, 68–69. z Gal 4, 26. a Ps 48, 9. b Is 4, 3. c Pss 68, 26; 149, 3.

PSALM 88*

A Despairing Lament

1 A song; a psalm of the Korahites. For the leader; according to *Mahalath.* For singing; a *maskil* of Heman the Ezrahite.

I

2 LORD, my God, I call out by day;
at night I cry aloud in your presence. [d]
3 Let my prayer come before you;
incline your ear to my cry. [e]
4 For my soul is filled with troubles;[f]*
my life draws near to Sheol.
5 I am reckoned with those who go down to the pit;
I am weak, without strength.
6 My couch is among the dead,
with the slain who lie in the grave.
You remember them no more;
they are cut off from your care.
7 You plunged me into the bottom of the pit,
into the darkness of the abyss.
8 Your wrath lies heavy upon me;
all your waves crash over me. [g]
Selah
9 Because of you my friends shun me;
you make me loathsome to them; [h]
Caged in, I cannot escape;
10 my eyes grow dim from trouble.

II

All day I call on you, LORD;
I stretch out my hands to you.
11 Do you work wonders for the dead?*
Do the shades arise and praise you? [i]
Selah
12 Is your love proclaimed in the grave,
your fidelity in the tomb?
13 Are your marvels declared in the darkness,
your righteous deeds in the land of oblivion?

III

14 But I cry out to you, LORD;
in the morning my prayer comes before you.
15 Why do you reject me, LORD?
Why hide your face from me?
16 I am mortally afflicted since youth;
lifeless, I suffer your terrible blows.
17 Your wrath has swept over me;
your terrors have reduced me to silence. [j]
18 All the day they surge round like a flood;
from every side they close in on me.
19 Because of you companions shun me; [k]
my only friend is darkness.

PSALM 89*

A Lament over God's Promise to David

1 A *maskil* of Ethan the Ezrahite.

I

2 The promises of the LORD I will sing forever, [l]
proclaim your loyalty through all ages.
3 For you said, "My love is established forever;*
my loyalty will stand as long as the heavens.
4 I have made a covenant with my chosen one;
I have sworn to David my servant:
5 I will make your dynasty stand forever
and establish your throne through all ages." [m]
Selah

II

6 The heavens praise your marvels, LORD,
your loyalty in the assembly of the holy ones. [n]
7 Who in the skies ranks with the LORD?

Ps 88: A lament in which the psalmist prays for rescue from the alienation of approaching death. Each of the three stanzas begins with a call to God (2. 10b. 14) and complains of the death that separates one from God. The tone is persistently grim.

88, 4–8: In imagination the psalmist already experiences the alienation of Sheol.

88, 11–13: The psalmist seeks to persuade God to act out of concern for divine honor: the shades give you no worship, so keep me alive to offer you praise.

Ps 89: The community laments the defeat of the Davidic king, to whom God promised kingship as enduring as the heavens (2–5). The psalm narrates how God became king of the divine beings (6–9) and how the Davidic king became king of earthly kings (20–38). Since the defeat of the king calls into question God's promise, the community ardently prays God to be faithful to the original promise to David (39–52).

89, 3–5: David's dynasty is to be as long-lasting as the heavens, a statement reinforced by using the same verbs (establish, stand) both of the divine love and loyalty and of the Davidic dynasty and throne. Cf 29–30.

d Ps 77, 3. e Ps 119, 170. f 4–7: Pss 28, 1; 30, 4; 40, 3; 86, 13; 143, 7; Nm 16, 33; Jb 17, 1; Jon 2, 7. g Pss 18, 5; 32, 6; 42, 8; 69, 2; Jon 2, 4. h Pss 38, 12; 79, 4; 80, 7; 123, 3–4; 142, 8; Jb 12, 4; 19, 13; Lam 3, 7; Dn 9, 16. i Pss 6, 6; 30, 10; 38, 18; 115, 17. j Jb 6, 4; 20, 25. k Jb 19, 13. l Is 63, 7. m Pss 61, 7–8; 132, 11; 2 Sm 7, 8–16. n Pss 29, 1; 82, 1; Jb 1, 6; 5, 1.

Who is like the LORD among the gods? [o]*
8 A God dreaded in the council of the holy ones,
greater and more awesome than all who sit there!
9 LORD, God of hosts, who is like you?
Mighty LORD, your loyalty is always present.
10 You rule the raging sea; [p]
you still its swelling waves.
11 You crushed Rahab* with a mortal blow;
your strong arm scattered your foes.
12 Yours are the heavens, yours the earth;
you founded the world and everything in it. [q]
13 Zaphon and Amanus* you created;
Tabor* and Hermon* rejoice in your name.
14 Mighty your arm, strong your hand,
your right hand is ever exalted.
15 Justice and judgment are the foundation of your throne;
love and loyalty march before you. [r]
16 Happy the people who know you, LORD,
who walk in the radiance of your face.
17 In your name they sing joyfully all the day;
at your victory they raise the festal shout. [s]
18 You are their majestic strength;
by your favor our horn* is exalted. [t]
19 Truly the LORD is our shield,
the Holy One of Israel, our king! [u]

III

20 Once you spoke in vision; [v]
to your faithful ones you said:
"I have set a leader over the warriors;
I have raised up a hero from the army.
21 I have chosen David, my servant;
with my holy oil I have anointed him.
22 My hand will be with him; [w]
my arm will make him strong.
23 No enemy shall outwit him,
nor shall the wicked defeat him.
24 I will crush his foes before him,
strike down those who hate him.
25 My loyalty and love will be with him;
through my name his horn will be exalted.
26 I will set his hand upon the sea,
his right hand upon the rivers.*
27 He shall cry to me, 'You are my father, [x]
my God, the Rock that brings me victory!'
28 I myself make him firstborn,
Most High* over the kings of the earth.
29 Forever I will maintain my love for him; [y]
my covenant with him stands firm.
30 I will establish his dynasty forever,
his throne as the days of the heavens.
31 If his descendants forsake my law, [z]
do not follow my decrees,
32 If they fail to observe my statutes,
do not keep my commandments,
33 I will punish their crime with a rod
and their guilt with lashes.
34 But I will not take my love from him,
nor will I betray my bond of loyalty. [a]
35 I will not violate my covenant;
the promise of my lips I will not alter. [b]
36 By my holiness I swore once for all: [c]
I will never be false to David.
37 His dynasty will continue forever, [d]
his throne, like the sun before me.
38 Like the moon it will stand eternal,
forever firm like the sky!"* *Selah*

89, 7: The gods: literally, "the sons of gods," "the holy ones" and "courtiers" of 6 and 8. These heavenly spirits are members of God's court.

89, 11: Rahab: a mythological sea monster whose name is used in the Bible mainly as a personification of primeval chaos. Cf Jb 9, 13; 26, 12; Ps 74, 13–14; Is 51, 9.

89, 13: Zaphon and Amanus: two sacred mountains in northern Syria. **Tabor**: a high hill in the valley of Jezreel in northern Israel. **Hermon**: a mountain in Lebanon, forming the southern spur of the Anti-Lebanon range.

89, 18. 25: Horn: a concrete noun for an abstract quality; horn is a symbol of strength.

89, 26: The sea . . . the rivers: geographically the limits of the Davidic Empire (the Mediterranean and the Euphrates); mythologically, the traditional forces of chaos. See note on v 11.

89, 28: Most High: a divine title, which is here extended to David as God's own king. Cf Ps 2, 7–9; Is 9, 5. As God rules over the members of the heavenly council (6–9), so David, God's surrogate, rules over earthly kings.

89, 37–38: Like the sun before me . . . like the sky: as enduring as the heavenly lights. Cf 2–5 and Ps 72, 5. 17.

o 7–9: Pss 35, 10; 86, 8; 113, 5; Ex 15, 11; Jer 10, 6. p 10–11: Pss 65, 8; 74, 13–15; 107, 29; Jb 7, 12; Is 51, 9–10. q Pss 24, 1–2; 50, 12; Dt 10, 14; 1 Cor 10, 26. r Pss 85, 11–12; 97, 2. s Ps 47, 2; Zep 3, 14. t Pss 112, 9; 148, 14. u Pss 47, 9; 96, 10; 97, 1; 99, 1; Is 6, 3. v 20–21: Pss 78, 70; 132, 11–12; 2 Sm 7, 4. 8–16; 1 Chr 17, 3. 7–14; Is 42, 1; Acts 13, 22. w 22–25: 1 Sm 2, 9–10. x 27–28: Pss 2, 7; 110, 2–3; 2 Sm 7, 9. 14; Col 1, 15. 18; Rv 1, 5. y 29–30: Pss 18, 51; 61, 8; 144, 10; 2 Sm 7, 11; Is 55, 3. z 31–33: Lv 26, 14–33. a Ps 40, 12; Sir 47, 22. b Jer 33, 20–21. c Am 4, 2. d 37–38: Pss 61, 8; 72, 5; Sir 43, 6.

IV

39 But now you have rejected and spurned,[e]
been enraged at your anointed.
40 You renounced the covenant with your servant,
defiled his crown in the dust.
41 You broke down all his defenses,[f]
left his strongholds in ruins.
42 All who pass through seize plunder;
his neighbors deride him.
43 You have exalted the right hand of his foes,
have gladdened all his enemies.[g]
44 You turned back his sharp sword,
did not support him in battle.
45 You brought to an end his splendor,
hurled his throne to the ground.
46 You cut short the days of his youth,
covered him with shame. *Selah*
47 How long, LORD?
Will you stay hidden forever?
Must your wrath smolder like fire?[h]
48 Remember how brief is my life,
how frail the race you created![i]
49 What mortal can live and not see death?
Who can escape the power of Sheol?[j] *Selah*
50 Where are your promises of old, Lord,
the loyalty sworn to David?
51 Remember, Lord, the insults to your servants,
how I bear all the slanders of the nations.[k]
52 Your enemies, LORD, insult your anointed;
they insult my every endeavor.

* * *

53 Blessed be the LORD forever! Amen and amen![l]*

FOURTH BOOK—PSALMS 90–106

PSALM 90*

God's Eternity and Human Frailty

1 A prayer of Moses, the man of God.

I

Lord, you have been our refuge
through all generations.
2 Before the mountains were born,
the earth and the world brought forth,
from eternity to eternity you are God.[m]
4* A thousand years in your eyes
are merely a yesterday,[n]
3 But humans you return to dust,
saying, "Return,* you mortals!"[o]
4c Before a watch passes in the night,*
5 you have brought them to their end;[p]*
They disappear like sleep at dawn;
they are like grass that dies.
6 It sprouts green in the morning;
by evening it is dry and withered.[q]*

II

7 Truly we are consumed by your anger,
filled with terror by your wrath.
8 You have kept our faults before you,
our hidden sins exposed to your sight.[r]
9 Our life ebbs away under your wrath;[s]
our years end like a sigh.
10 Seventy is the sum of our years,
or eighty, if we are strong;
Most of them are sorrow and toil;
they pass quickly, we are all but gone.
11 Who comprehends your terrible anger?
Your wrath matches the fear it inspires.

89, 53: The doxology at the end of the third book of the Psalms; it is not part of Ps 89.

Ps 90: A communal lament that describes only in general terms the cause of the community's distress. After confidently invoking God (1), the psalm turns to a complaint contrasting God's eternity with the brevity of human life (2–6) and sees in human suffering the punishment for sin (7–12). The psalm concludes with a plea for God's intervention (13–17).

90, 3: Return: one word of God is enough to return mortals to the dust from which they were created. Humans were created from earth in Gn 2, 7; 3, 19.

90, 4: The translation reverses the order of the difficult Hebrew verses 3 and 4 to get the probable original order. **A watch in the night**: the night was divided into three sentry periods or watches. Cf Jgs 7, 19.

90, 5: You have brought them to their end: an interpretation of the unclear Hebrew.

90, 6: It is dry and withered: the transitory nature of the grass under the scorching sun was proverbial. Cf Ps 129, 6; Is 40, 6–8.

e 39–47: Ps 44, 10–25. f 41–42: Ps 80, 13–14. g Lam 1, 5. h Pss 13, 2; 44, 25; 74, 10; 79, 5; Dt 4, 24. i Pss 39, 5–6; 62, 10; 90, 9–10; 144, 4; Jb 7, 6. 16; 14, 1. 5; Eccl 6, 12; Wis 2, 5. j Ps 90, 3. k Ps 79, 12. l Pss 41, 14; 72, 18; 106, 48. m Pss 48, 15; 55, 20; 93, 2; 102, 13; Hb 1, 12. n 2 Pt 3, 8. o Pss 103, 14; 104, 29; 146, 4; Gn 3, 19; 1 Mc 2, 63; Jb 34, 14–15; Eccl 3, 20; 12, 7; Sir 40, 11. p Ps 89, 48. q Pss 37, 2; 102, 11; 103, 15–16; Jb 14, 1–2; Is 40, 6–8. r Ps 109, 14–15; Hos 7, 2. s 9–10: Pss 39, 5–7; 62, 10; 102, 24–25; 144, 4; Gn 6, 3; Jb 7, 6. 16; 14, 5; Prv 10, 27; Eccl 6, 12; Wis 2, 5; Sir 18, 8; Is 65, 20.

[12] Teach us to count our days aright,
that we may gain wisdom of heart.
[13] Relent, O LORD! How long?
Have pity on your servants!
[14] Fill us at daybreak with your love, [t]
that all our days we may sing for joy.
[15] Make us glad as many days as you humbled us,
for as many years as we have seen trouble. [u]
[16] Show your deeds to your servants,
your glory to their children.
[17] May the favor of the Lord our God be ours. [v]
Prosper the work of our hands!
Prosper the work of our hands!

PSALM 91*

Security Under God's Protection

I

[1] You who dwell in the shelter of the Most High,*
who abide in the shadow of the Almighty,*
[2] Say to the LORD, "My refuge and fortress,
my God in whom I trust." [w]
[3] God will rescue you from the fowler's snare,
from the destroying plague,
[4] Will shelter you with pinions,
spread wings that you may take refuge; [x]
God's faithfulness is a protecting shield.
[5] You shall not fear the terror of the night
nor the arrow that flies by day, [y]
[6] Nor the pestilence that roams in darkness,
nor the plague that ravages at noon. [z]
[7] Though a thousand fall at your side,
ten thousand at your right hand,
near you it shall not come.
[8] You need simply watch;
the punishment of the wicked you will see. [a]
[9] You have the LORD for your refuge;
you have made the Most High your stronghold.
[10] No evil shall befall you,
no affliction come near your tent. [b]
[11] For God commands the angels [c]*
to guard you in all your ways. [d]
[12] With their hands they shall support you,
lest you strike your foot against a stone. [e]
[13] You shall tread upon the asp and the viper,
trample the lion and the dragon. [f]

II

[14] Whoever clings to me I will deliver;
whoever knows my name I will set on high. [g]
[15] All who call upon me I will answer; [h]
I will be with them in distress; [i]
I will deliver them and give them honor.
[16] With length of days I will satisfy them
and show them my saving power. [j]

PSALM 92*

A Hymn of Thanksgiving for God's Fidelity

[1] A psalm. A sabbath song.

I

[2] It is good to give thanks to the LORD,
to sing praise to your name, Most High, [k]
[3] To proclaim your love in the morning,
your faithfulness in the night,
[4] With the ten-stringed harp,
with melody upon the lyre. [l]
[5] For you make me jubilant, LORD, by your deeds;
at the works of your hands I shout for joy.

II

[6] How great are your works, LORD! [m]
How profound your purpose!

Ps 91: A prayer of someone who has taken refuge in the security of the temple (1–2). The psalmist is confident that God's presence will protect the people in every dangerous situation (3–13). The final verses are an oracle of salvation promising salvation to those who trust in God (14–16).

91, 1: The shelter of the Most High: basically "hiding place" but in the psalms a designation for the protected temple precincts. Cf Pss 27, 5; 31, 21; 61, 5. **The shadow of the Almighty:** literally, "the shadow of the wings of the Almighty." Cf Pss 17, 8; 36, 8; 57, 2; 63, 8. V 4 makes clear that the shadow is an image of the safety afforded by the outstretched wings of the cherubim in the holy of holies.

91, 11–12: The words are cited in Lk 4, 10–11; Mt 4, 6, as Jesus' reply to Satan in the desert.

Ps 92: A hymn of praise and thanks for God's faithful deeds (2–5). The wicked, deluded by their prosperity (6–9), are punished (10), whereas the psalmist has already experienced God's protection (11–16).

t Ps 17, 15. u Nm 14, 34; Jer 31, 13. v Ps 33, 22. w Pss 18, 3; 31, 3–4; 42, 10; 142, 6; 2 Sm 22, 3. x Pss 17, 8; 36, 8; 57, 2; 63, 8; Dt 32, 11; Ru 2, 12; Mt 23, 37. y Prv 3, 25; Song 3, 8. z Dt 32, 24. a Ps 92, 12. b Prv 12, 21; Dt 7, 15. c 11–12: Mt 4, 6; Lk 4, 10f. d Heb 1, 14. e Ps 121, 3; Prv 3, 23. f Is 11, 8; Lk 10, 19. g Pss 9, 11; 119, 132. h Jer 33, 3; Zec 13, 9. i Is 43, 2. j Prv 3, 2. k Pss 33, 1; 147, 1. l Pss 33, 2; 144, 9. m 6–7: Pss 131, 1; 139, 6. 17; Wis 13, 1; 17, 1.

7 A senseless person cannot know this;
a fool cannot comprehend.
8 Though the wicked flourish like grass
and all sinners thrive,[n]
They are destined for eternal destruction;
9 for you, LORD, are forever on high.
10 Indeed your enemies, LORD,
indeed your enemies shall perish;
all sinners shall be scattered.[o]

III

11 You have given me the strength of a wild bull;[p]
you have poured rich oil upon me.[q]
12 My eyes look with glee on my wicked enemies;
my ears delight in the fall of my foes.[r]
13 The just shall flourish like the palm tree,
shall grow like a cedar of Lebanon.[s]
14 Planted* in the house of the LORD,
they shall flourish in the courts of our God.
15 They shall bear fruit even in old age,
always vigorous and sturdy,
16 As they proclaim: "The LORD is just;
our rock, in whom there is no wrong."[t]

PSALM 93*

God is a Mighty King

1 The LORD is king,* robed with majesty;
the LORD is robed, girded with might.[u]
The world will surely stand in place,
never to be moved.[v]
2 Your throne stands firm from of old;
you are from everlasting, LORD.[w]
3 The flood* has raised up, LORD;
the flood has raised up its roar;
the flood has raised its pounding waves.
4 More powerful than the roar of many waters,
more powerful than the breakers of the sea,
powerful in the heavens is the LORD.
5 Your decrees are firmly established;
holiness belongs to your house, LORD,
for all the length of days.

PSALM 94*

A Prayer for Deliverance from the Wicked

I

1 LORD, avenging God,
avenging God, shine forth![x]
2 Rise up, judge of the earth;
give the proud what they deserve.[y]

II

3 How long, LORD, shall the wicked,
how long shall the wicked glory?[z]
4 How long will they mouth haughty speeches,
go on boasting, all these evildoers?[a]
5 They crush your people, LORD,
torment your very own.
6 They kill the widow and alien;
the fatherless they murder.[b]
7 They say, "The LORD does not see;
the God of Jacob takes no notice."[c]

III

8 Understand, you stupid people!
You fools, when will you be wise?[d]
9 Does the one who shaped the ear not hear?
The one who formed the eye not see?[e]
10 Does the one who guides nations not rebuke?
The one who teaches humans not have knowledge?

92, 14: Planted: the just are likened to trees growing in the sacred precincts of the temple, which is often seen as the source of life and fertility because of God's presence. Cf Ps 36, 9. 10; Ez 47, 1–12.

Ps 93: A hymn celebrating the kingship of God, who created the world (1–2) by defeating the sea (3–4). In the ancient myth that is alluded to here, Sea completely covered the land, making it impossible for the human community to live. Sea, or Flood, roars in anger against God, who is personified in the storm. God's utterances or decrees are given authority by the victory over Sea (5).

93, 1: The LORD is king: literally, "the LORD reigns." This psalm, and Pss 47 and 96–99, are sometimes called enthronement psalms. They may have been used in a special liturgy during which God's ascent to the throne was ritually reenacted. They have also been interpreted eschatologically, pointing to the coming of God as king at the end-time.

93, 3: The flood: the primordial sea was tamed by God in the act of creation. It is a figure of chaos and rebellion. Cf Ps 46, 4.

Ps 94: A lament of an individual who is threatened by wicked people. The danger affects the whole community. Calling upon God as judge (1–2), the psalm complains about oppression of the holy community by people within (3–7). Bold declarations of faith follow: denunciation of evildoers (8–11) and assurance to the just (12–15). The psalm continues with further lament (16–19) and ends with strong confidence in God's response (20–23).

n Ps 37, 35. o Pss 68, 1–2; 125, 5. p Ps 75, 10; Dt 33, 17. q Ps 23, 5. r Ps 91, 8. s Pss 1, 3; 52, 10; Jer 17, 8. t Dt 32, 4. u Pss 47, 8; 96, 10; 97, 1; 99, 1. v Pss 75, 2–3; 104, 5. w Pss 55, 20; 90, 2; 102, 13; Hb 1, 12. x Na 1, 2. y Jer 51, 56; Lam 3, 64. z Pss 13, 2; 75, 5; Jer 12, 1. a Ps 73; Mal 2, 17; 3, 14. b Ex 22, 21–22; Dt 24, 17–22. c Pss 10, 11; 64, 6; 73, 11; Jb 22, 13–14; Ez 9, 9. d Prv 1, 22; 8, 5. e Ex 4, 11; Prv 20, 12.

11 The LORD does know human plans;
they are only puffs of air.[f]

IV

12 Happy those whom you guide, LORD,[g]
whom you teach by your instruction.
13 You give them rest from evil days,
while a pit is being dug for the wicked.
14 You, LORD, will not forsake your people,
nor abandon your very own.[h]
15 Judgment shall again be just,
and all the upright of heart will follow it.

V

16 Who will rise up for me against the wicked?
Who will stand up for me against evildoers?
17 If the LORD were not my help,
I would long have been silent in the grave.[i]
18 When I say, "My foot is slipping,"
your love, LORD, holds me up.[j]
19 When cares increase within me,
your comfort gives me joy.

VI

20 Can unjust judges be your allies,
those who create burdens in the name of law,
21 Those who conspire against the just
and condemn the innocent to death?
22 No, the LORD is my secure height,
my God, the rock where I find refuge,
23 Who will turn back their evil upon them[k]
and destroy them for their wickedness.
Surely the LORD our God will destroy them![l]

PSALM 95*

A Call to Praise and Obedience

I

1 Come, let us sing joyfully to the LORD;
cry out to the rock of our salvation.[m]
2 Let us greet him with a song of praise,
joyfully sing out our psalms.
3 For the LORD is the great God,
the great king over all gods,[n]
4 Whose hand holds the depths of the earth;
who owns the tops of the mountains.
5 The sea and dry land belong to God,
who made them, formed them by hand.[o]

II

6 Enter, let us bow down in worship;
let us kneel before the LORD who made us.
7 For this is our God,
whose people we are,
God's well-tended flock.[p]

III

Oh, that today you would hear his voice:[q]
8 Do not harden your hearts as at Meribah,*
as on the day of Massah* in the desert.
9 There your ancestors tested me;
they tried me though they had seen my works.[r]
10 Forty years I loathed that generation;
I said: "This people's heart goes astray;
they do not know my ways."[s]
11 Therefore I swore in my anger:
"They shall never enter my rest."*

PSALM 96*

God of the Universe

I

1 Sing to the LORD a new song;[t]
sing to the LORD, all the earth.
2 Sing to the LORD, bless his name;
announce his salvation day after day.
3 Tell God's glory among the nations;
among all peoples, God's marvelous deeds.[u]

Ps 95: Twice the psalm calls the people to praise and worship God (1–2. 6), the king of all creatures (3–5) and shepherd of the flock (7ab). The last strophe warns the people to be more faithful than were their ancestors in the journey to the promised land (7c–11). This invitation to praise God regularly opens the Church's official prayer, the Liturgy of the Hours.

95, 8: Meribah: literally, "contention"; the place where the Israelites quarreled with God. **Massah**: "testing," the place where they put God to the trial. Cf Ex 17, 7; Nm 20, 13.

95, 11: My rest: the promised land as in Dt 12, 9. Heb 4 applies the verse to the eternal rest of heaven.

Ps 96: A hymn inviting all humanity to praise the glories of Israel's God (1–3), who is the sole God (4–6). To the just ruler of all belongs worship (7–10); even inanimate creation is to offer praise (11–13). This psalm has numerous verbal and thematic contacts with Is 40–55, as does Ps 98. Another version of the psalm is 1 Chr 16, 23–33.

f Ps 33, 15; 1 Cor 3, 20. g Ps 119, 71; Jb 5, 17. h 1 Sm 12, 22; Sir 47, 22. i Ps 115, 17. j Ps 145, 14. k Pss 7, 16; 9, 16; 35, 8; 57, 7; Prv 26, 27; Eccl 10, 8; Sir 27, 26. l Ps 107, 42. m Dt 32, 15. n Pss 47, 2; 135, 5. o Ps 24, 1–2. p Pss 23, 1–3; 100, 3; Mi 7, 14. q 7c–11: Pss 81, 8; 106, 32; Heb 3, 7–11. 15; 4, 3. 5. 7. r Nm 14, 22; 20, 2–13; Dt 6, 16; 33, 8. s Ps 78, 8; Nm 14, 34; Dt 32, 5. t Ps 98, 1; Is 42, 10. u Pss 98, 4; 105, 1.

II

4 For great is the LORD and highly to be praised,
to be feared above all gods.[v] *
5 For the gods of the nations all do nothing,
but the LORD made the heavens.[w]
6 Splendor and power go before him;
power and grandeur are in his holy place.

III

7 Give to the LORD, you families of nations,
give to the LORD glory and might;
8 give to the LORD the glory due his name![x]
Bring gifts and enter his courts;
9 bow down to the LORD, splendid in
holiness.
Tremble before God, all the earth;
10 say among the nations: The LORD is king.[y]
The world will surely stand fast, never to be
moved.
God rules the peoples with fairness.

IV

11 Let the heavens be glad and the earth rejoice;
let the sea and what fills it resound;[z]
12 let the plains be joyful and all that is in
them.
Then let all the trees of the forest rejoice
13 before the LORD who comes,
who comes to govern the earth,[a]
To govern the world with justice
and the peoples with faithfulness.

PSALM 97*

The Divine Ruler of All

I

1 The LORD is king; let the earth rejoice;
let the many islands be glad.[b]
2 Cloud and darkness surround the Lord;
justice and right are the foundation of his
throne.[c]
3 Fire goes before him;
everywhere it consumes the foes.
4 Lightning illumines the world;
the earth sees and trembles.[d]
5 The mountains melt like wax before the LORD,
before the Lord of all the earth.[e]
6 The heavens proclaim God's justice;
all peoples see his glory.[f]

II

7 All who serve idols are put to shame,
who glory in worthless things;
all gods* bow down before you.[g]
8 Zion hears and is glad,
and the cities of Judah rejoice
because of your judgments, O LORD.[h]
9 You, LORD, are the Most High over all the
earth,[i]
exalted far above all gods.
10 The LORD loves those who hate evil,
protects the lives of the faithful,[j]
rescues them from the hand of the wicked.
11 Light dawns for the just;
gladness, for the honest of heart.[k]
12 Rejoice in the LORD, you just,
and praise his holy name.[l]

PSALM 98*

The Coming of God

1 A psalm.

I

Sing a new song to the LORD,
who has done marvelous deeds,[m]
Whose right hand and holy arm*
have won the victory.[n] *

96, 4: For references to other gods, see comments on Pss 58 and 82.

Ps 97: The hymn begins with God appearing in a storm, a traditional picture of some ancient Near Eastern gods (1–6); cf Ps 18, 8–16; Mi 1, 3–4; Hb 3, 3–15. Israel rejoices in the overthrowing of idol worshipers and their gods (7–9) and the rewarding of the faithful righteous (10–12).

97, 7: **All gods**: divine beings thoroughly subordinate to Israel's God. The Greek translates "angels," an interpretation adopted by Heb 1, 6.

Ps 98: A hymn, similar to Ps 96, extolling God for Israel's victory (1–3). All nations (4–6) and even inanimate nature (7–8) are summoned to welcome God's coming to rule over the world (9).

98, 1: **Marvelous deeds . . . victory**: the conquest of all threats to the peaceful existence of Israel, depicted in the psalms variously as a cosmic force such as sea, or nations bent on Israel's destruction, or evildoers seemingly triumphant. **Whose right hand and holy arm**: God is pictured as a powerful warrior.

v Pss 48, 2; 95, 3; 145, 3. w Ps 97, 7; Is 40, 17; 1 Cor 8, 4. x Ps 29, 2. y Pss 75, 4; 93, 1. z Ps 98, 7. a Ps 98, 9. b Pss 75, 4; 93, 1; 96, 10. c Pss 85, 11; 89, 15; Ex 19, 6; Dt 4, 11; 5, 22; 1 Kgs 8, 12. d Pss 18, 8; 50, 3; 77, 18; 99, 1; Jgs 5, 4–5. e Jdt 16, 15; Mi 1, 4. f Ps 50, 6. g Ps 96, 5. h Ps 48, 12. i Ps 83, 19. j Ps 121, 7. k Ps 112, 4. l Ps 30, 5. m Ps 96, 1; Is 42, 10. n Is 59, 16; 63, 5.

2 The LORD has made his victory known;
has revealed his triumph for the nations to see,
3 Has remembered faithful love
toward the house of Israel.
All the ends of the earth have seen
the victory of our God.

II

4 Shout with joy to the LORD, all the earth;
break into song; sing praise.
5 Sing praise to the LORD with the harp,
with the harp and melodious song.
6 With trumpets and the sound of the horn
shout with joy to the King, the LORD. [o]

III

7 Let the sea and what fills it resound, [p]
the world and those who dwell there.
8 Let the rivers clap their hands,
the mountains shout with them for joy, [q]
9 Before the LORD who comes,
who comes to govern the earth, [r]
To govern the world with justice
and the peoples with fairness. [s]

PSALM 99*

The Holy King

I

1 The LORD is king, the peoples tremble;
God is enthroned on the cherubim,* the earth quakes. [t]
2 The LORD is great on Zion,
exalted above all the peoples.
3 Let them praise your great and awesome name:
holy is God! [u]

II

4 O mighty king, lover of justice,
you alone have established fairness;
you have created just rule in Jacob. [v]
5 Exalt the LORD, our God;
bow down before his footstool; [w]*
holy is God!

III

6 Moses and Aaron were among his priests,
Samuel among those who called on God's name;
they called on the LORD, who answered them. [x]
7 From the pillar of cloud God spoke to them;
they kept the decrees, the law they received. [y]
8 O LORD, our God, you answered them;
you were a forgiving God,
though you punished their offenses. [z]
9 Exalt the LORD, our God;
bow down before his holy mountain;
holy is the LORD, our God.

PSALM 100*

Processional Hymn

1 A psalm of thanksgiving.

Shout joyfully to the LORD, all you lands;
2 worship the LORD with cries of gladness;
come before him with joyful song.
3 Know that the LORD is God,
our maker to whom we belong,
whose people we are, God's well-tended flock. [a]*
4 Enter the temple gates with praise,
its courts with thanksgiving.
Give thanks to God, bless his name; [b]
5 good indeed is the LORD,

Ps 99: A hymn to God as the king whose grandeur is most clearly seen on Mount Zion (2) and in the laws given to Israel (4). Israel is special because of God's word of justice, which was mediated by the revered speakers, Moses, Aaron, and Samuel (6–8). The poem is structured by the threefold statement that God is holy (3. 5. 9) and by the twice-repeated command to praise (5. 9).

99, 1: Enthroned on the cherubim: cherubim were composite beings with animal and human features, common in ancient Near Eastern art. Two cherubim were placed on the ark (or box) of the covenant in the holy of holies. Upon them God was believed to dwell invisibly. Cf Ex 25, 20–22; 1 Sm 4, 4; 2 Sm 6, 2; Ps 80, 2.

99, 5: Footstool: a reference to the ark. Cf 1 Chr 28, 2; Ps 132, 7.

Ps 100: A hymn inviting the people to enter the temple courts with thank offerings for the God who created them.

100, 3: Although the people call on all the nations of the world to join in their hymn, they are conscious of being the chosen people of God.

o Ps 47, 6–7. p Ps 96, 11. q Is 44, 23; 55, 12. r Ps 96, 13. s Ps 67, 5. t Pss 18, 8–11; 80, 2; 93, 1; Ex 25, 22; 1 Sm 4, 4; 2 Sm 6, 2. u Is 6, 3. v Pss 72, 1; 99, 4; Jer 23, 5. w Ps 132, 7. x Jer 15, 1. y Ex 33, 9; Nm 12, 5. z Ex 32, 11; Nm 20, 12. a Pss 23, 1; 95, 7; Mi 7, 14; Is 64, 7. b 4–5: Pss 106, 1; 107, 1; 118, 1; 136, 1; 138, 8; Jer 33, 11.

Whose love endures forever,
whose faithfulness lasts through every age.

PSALM 101*

Norm of Life for Rulers

1 A psalm of David.

I

I sing of love and justice;
to you, LORD, I sing praise.
2 I follow the way of integrity;[c]
when will you come to me?
I act with integrity of heart
within my royal court.[d]*
3 I do not allow into my presence
anyone who speaks perversely.
Whoever acts shamefully I hate;
no such person can be my friend.[e]
4 I shun the devious of heart;
the wicked I do not tolerate.
5 Whoever slanders another in secret
I reduce to silence.[f]
Haughty eyes and arrogant hearts[g]
I cannot endure.

II

6 I look to the faithful of the land;*
they alone can be my companions.
Those who follow the way of integrity,[h]
they alone can enter my service.
7 No one who practices deceit
can hold a post in my court.
No one who speaks falsely
can be among my advisors.[i]
8 Each morning* I clear the wicked from the land,*
and rid the LORD's city of all evildoers.

PSALM 102*

Prayer in Time of Distress

1 The prayer of one afflicted and wasting away whose anguish is poured out before the LORD.

I

2 LORD, hear my prayer;
let my cry come to you.
3 Do not hide your face from me
now that I am in distress.[j]
Turn your ear to me;
when I call, answer me quickly.
4 For my days vanish like smoke;[k]
my bones burn away as in a furnace.
5 I am withered, dried up like grass,
too wasted to eat my food.
6 From my loud groaning
I become just skin and bones.
7 I am like a desert owl,
like an owl among the ruins.
8 I lie awake and moan,
like a lone sparrow on the roof.
9 All day long my enemies taunt me;
in their rage, they make my name a curse.*
10 I eat ashes like bread,
mingle my drink with tears.[l]
11 Because of your furious wrath,
you lifted me up just to cast me down.
12 My days are like a lengthening shadow;[m]
I wither like the grass.[n]

II

13 But you, LORD, are enthroned forever;
your renown is for all generations.[o]
14 You will again show mercy to Zion;
now is the time for pity;
the appointed time has come.

Ps 101: The king, grateful at being God's chosen (1), promises to be a ruler after God's own heart (2–3), allowing into the royal service only the God-fearing (3–8).

101, 2: Within my royal court: the king promises to make his own household a model for Israel, banning all officials who abuse their power.

101, 6: I look to the faithful of the land: the king seeks companions only among those faithful to God.

101, 8: Each morning: the normal time for the administration of justice (2 Sm 15, 2; Jer 21, 12) and for the arrival of divine aid (Pss 59, 17; 143, 8; Is 33, 2). **I clear the wicked from the land:** the king, as God's servant, is responsible for seeing that divine justice is carried out.

Ps 102: A lament, one of the Penitential Psalms. The psalmist, experiencing psychic and bodily disintegration (4–12), cries out to God (1–3). In the temple precincts where God has promised to be present, the psalmist recalls God's venerable promises to save the poor (13–23). The final part (24–29) restates the original complaint and prayer, and emphasizes God's eternity.

102, 9: They make my name a curse: enemies use the psalmist's name in phrases such as, "May you be as wretched as this person!"

c Ps 26, 11. d 1 Kgs 9, 4; Is 33, 15. e Prv 11, 20. f Prv 17, 20; 30, 10. g Prv 21, 4. h Ps 26, 11; Prv 20, 7. i Ps 5, 5; Prv 25, 5. j Pss 69, 18; 143, 7. k 4–6: Ps 38, 7–9. l Pss 42, 4; 80, 6. m Pss 109, 23; 144, 4; Jb 8, 9; 14, 2; Eccl 6, 12; Wis 2, 5. n Ps 90, 5–6. o Pss 55, 20; 90, 2; 93, 2; 102, 13; 135, 13; 145, 13; Lam 5, 19; Hb 1, 12.

15 Its stones are dear to your servants;
its dust moves them to pity.
16 The nations shall revere your name, LORD,
all the kings of the earth, your glory, [p]
17 Once the LORD has rebuilt Zion
and appeared in glory,
18 Heeding the plea of the lowly,
not scorning their prayer.
19 Let this be written for the next generation,
for a people not yet born,
that they may praise the LORD: [q]
20 "The LORD looked down from the holy heights,*
viewed the earth from heaven, [r]
21 To attend to the groaning of the prisoners,
to release those doomed to die." [s]
22 Then the LORD's name will be declared on Zion,
the praise of God in Jerusalem,
23 When all peoples and kingdoms gather
to worship the LORD. [t]

III

24 God has shattered my strength in mid-course,
has cut short my days.
25 I plead, O my God,
do not take me in the midst of my days. [u]*
Your years last through all generations.
26 Of old you laid the earth's foundations; [v]
the heavens are the work of your hands.
27 They perish, but you remain;
they all wear out like a garment;
Like clothing you change them and they are changed,
28 but you are the same, your years have no end.
29 May the children of your servants live on;
may their descendants live in your presence. [w]

PSALM 103*

Praise of Divine Goodness

1 Of David.

I

Bless the LORD, my soul;
all my being, bless his holy name!
2 Bless the LORD, my soul;
do not forget all the gifts of God,
3 Who pardons all your sins,
heals all your ills,
4 Delivers your life from the pit, [x]
surrounds you with love and compassion,
5 Fills your days with good things;
your youth is renewed like the eagle's.*

II

6 The LORD does righteous deeds,
brings justice to all the oppressed. [y]
7 His ways were revealed to Moses,
mighty deeds to the people of Israel.
8 Merciful and gracious is the LORD,
slow to anger, abounding in kindness. [z]
9 God does not always rebuke,
nurses no lasting anger,
10 Has not dealt with us as our sins merit,
nor requited us as our deeds deserve.

III

11 As the heavens tower over the earth,
so God's love towers over the faithful. [a]
12 As far as the east is from the west,
so far have our sins been removed from us.
13 As a father has compassion on his children,
so the LORD has compassion on the faithful.
14 For he knows how we are formed,
remembers that we are dust. [b]
15 Our days are like the grass;
like flowers of the field we blossom. [c]
16 The wind sweeps over us and we are gone;
our place knows us no more.

102, 20–23: Both 20–21 and 22–23 depend on 19.

102, 25: In the midst of my days: when the normal span of life is but half completed. Cf Is 38, 10; Jer 17, 11.

Ps 103: The speaker in this hymn begins by praising God for personal benefits (1–5), then moves on to God's mercy toward all the people (6–18). Even sin cannot destroy that mercy (11–13), for the eternal God is well aware of the people's human fragility (14–18). The psalmist invites the heavenly beings to join in praise (19–22).

103, 5: Your youth is renewed like the eagle's: because of the eagle's long life it was a symbol of perennial youth and vigor. Cf Is 40, 31.

p Is 59, 19; 66, 18. q Ps 22, 31–32. r Pss 11, 4; 14, 2. s Ps 79, 11. t Is 60, 3–4; Zec 2, 15; 8, 22. u Pss 39, 5; 90, 10; Jb 14, 5. v 26–28: Heb 1, 10–12. w Ps 69, 36–37. x Pss 28, 1; 30, 4; 40, 3; 69, 16; 88, 5; 143, 7; Prv 1, 12; Jon 2, 7. y Ps 146, 6–7. z Pss 86, 15; 145, 8; Ex 34, 6–7; Nm 14, 18; Jer 3, 12; Jl 2, 13; Jon 4, 2. a Is 55, 9. b Ps 90, 3. c Pss 37, 2; 90, 5–6; Is 40, 7.

17 But the LORD's kindness is forever,
toward the faithful from age to age.
He favors the children's children
18 of those who keep his covenant,
who take care to fulfill its precepts.

IV

19 The LORD's throne is established in heaven;
God's royal power rules over all.
20 Bless the LORD, all you angels, [d]
mighty in strength and attentive,
obedient to every command.
21 Bless the LORD, all you hosts,
ministers who do God's will.
22 Bless the LORD, all creatures,
everywhere in God's domain.
Bless the LORD, my soul!

PSALM 104*

Praise of God the Creator

I

1 Bless the LORD, my soul!
LORD, my God, you are great indeed!
You are clothed with majesty and glory,
2 robed in light as with a cloak.
You spread out the heavens like a tent; [e]
3 you raised your palace upon the waters.*
You make the clouds your chariot;
you travel on the wings of the wind.
4 You make the winds your messengers;
flaming fire, your ministers. [f]

II

5 You fixed the earth on its foundation,*
never to be moved.
6 The ocean covered it like a garment;
above the mountains stood the waters.
7 At your roar they took flight;
at the sound of your thunder they fled. [g]
8 They rushed up the mountains, down the valleys
to the place you had fixed for them.
9 You set a limit they cannot pass;
never again will they cover the earth. [h]

III

10 You made springs flow into channels
that wind among the mountains.
11 They give drink to every beast of the field; [i]
here wild asses quench their thirst.
12 Beside them the birds of heaven nest;
among the branches they sing.
13 You water the mountains from your palace;
by your labor the earth abounds.
14 You raise grass for the cattle
and plants for our beasts of burden.
You bring bread from the earth,
15 and wine to gladden our hearts,
Oil to make our faces gleam,
food to build our strength.
16 The trees of the LORD drink their fill,*
the cedars of Lebanon, which you planted.
17 There the birds build their nests;
junipers are the home of the stork. [j]
18 The high mountains are for wild goats;
the rocky cliffs, a refuge for badgers.

IV

19 You made the moon to mark the seasons, [k]
the sun that knows the hour of its setting.
20 You bring darkness and night falls,
then all the beasts of the forest roam abroad.
21 Young lions roar for prey;
they seek their food from God. [l]
22 When the sun rises, they steal away
and rest in their dens.
23 People go forth to their work,
to their labor till evening falls.

V

24 How varied are your works, LORD!
In wisdom you have wrought them all;
the earth is full of your creatures. [m]

Ps 104: A hymn praising God who easily and skillfully made rampaging waters and primordial night into a world vibrant with life. The psalmist describes God's splendor in the heavens (1–4), how the chaotic waters were tamed to fertilize and feed the world (5–18), and how primordial night was made into a gentle time of refreshment (19–23). The picture is like Gn 1, 1–2: a dark and watery chaos is made dry and lighted so that creatures might live. The psalmist reacts to the beauty of creation with awe (24–34). May sin not deface God's work (35)!

104, 3: Your palace upon the waters: God's heavenly dwelling above the upper waters of the sky. Cf Gn 1, 6–7; Ps 29, 10.

104, 5–9: God places the gigantic disk of the earth securely on its foundation and then, as a warrior, chases away the enveloping waters and confines them under, above, and around the earth.

104, 16–18: Even the exotic flora and fauna of the high mountains of the Lebanon range receive adequate water.

d Ps 148, 2; Dn 3, 58. e Prv 8, 27–28; Jb 9, 8; Is 40, 22; Gn 1, 6–7; Am 9, 6. f Heb 1, 7. g Ps 29, 3. h Jer 5, 22; Gn 9, 11–15. i 11–14: Ps 147, 8–9. j Ez 31, 6. k Sir 43, 6. l Jb 38, 39. m Ps 92, 6; Sir 39, 16.

25 Look at the sea, great and wide!
It teems with countless beings,
living things both large and small. [n]
26 Here ships ply their course;
here Leviathan,* your creature, plays. [o]

VI

27 All of these look to you
to give them food in due time. [p]
28 When you give to them, they gather;
when you open your hand, they are well filled.
29 When you hide your face, they are lost.*
When you take away their breath, they perish
and return to the dust from which they came. [q]
30 When you send forth your breath, they are created,
and you renew the face of the earth.

VII

31 May the glory of the LORD endure forever;
may the LORD be glad in these works!
32 If God glares at the earth, it trembles;
if God touches the mountains, they smoke! [r]
33 I will sing to the LORD all my life;
I will sing praise to my God while I live. [s]
34 May my theme be pleasing to God;
I will rejoice in the LORD.
35 May sinners vanish from the earth,
and the wicked be no more.
Bless the LORD, my soul! Hallelujah!*

PSALM 105*

God's Fidelity to the Promise

I

1 Give thanks to the LORD, invoke his name; [t]
make known among the peoples his deeds! [u]
2 Sing praise, play music;
proclaim all his wondrous deeds!
3 Glory in his holy name;
rejoice, O hearts that seek the LORD!
4 Rely on the mighty LORD;
constantly seek his face. [v]
5 Recall the wondrous deeds he has done,
his signs and his words of judgment,
6 You descendants of Abraham his servant,
offspring of Jacob the chosen one!

II

7 The LORD is our God
who rules the whole earth.
8 He remembers forever his covenant,
the pact imposed for a thousand generations,
9 Which was made with Abraham,
confirmed by oath to Isaac, [w]
10 And ratified as binding for Jacob,
an everlasting covenant for Israel:
11 "To you I give the land of Canaan,
your own allotted heritage." [x]

III

12 When they were few in number, [y]
a handful, and strangers there,
13 Wandering from nation to nation,
from one kingdom to another,
14 He let no one oppress them;
for their sake he rebuked kings:*
15 "Do not touch my anointed,
to my prophets* do no harm."

IV

16 Then he called down a famine on the land,
destroyed the grain that sustained them. [z]
17 He had sent a man ahead of them,

104, 26: Leviathan: a sea monster symbolizing primeval chaos. Cf Ps 74, 14; Is 27, 1; Jb 40, 25. God does not destroy chaos but makes it part of the created order.

104, 29–30: On one level, the spirit (or wind) of God is the fall and winter rains that provide food for all creatures. On another, it is the breath (or spirit) of God that makes beings live.

104, 35: Hallelujah: a frequent word in the last third of the Psalter. The word combines the plural imperative of praise (*hallelu*) with an abbreviated form of the divine name Yah(weh).

Ps 105: A hymn to God who promised the land of Canaan to the holy people. Cf Pss 78; 106; 136. Israel is invited to praise and seek the presence of God (1–6), who is faithful to the promise of land to the ancestors (7–11). In every phase of the national story—the ancestors in the land of Canaan (12–15), Joseph in Egypt (16–22), Israel in Egypt (23–38), Israel in the desert on the way to Canaan (39–45)—God remained faithful, reiterating the promise of the land to successive servants.

105, 14: Kings: Pharaoh and Abimelech of Gerar. Cf Gn 12, 17; 20, 6–7.

105, 15: My anointed . . . my prophets: the patriarchs Abraham, Isaac, and Jacob, who were "anointed" in the sense of being consecrated and recipients of God's revelation.

n Sir 43, 26. o Jb 3, 8; 40, 25. p Pss 136, 25; 145, 15–16. q Jb 34, 14–15; Eccl 3, 20; Ps 90, 3. r Ps 144, 5. s Ps 146, 2. t 1–15: 1 Chr 16, 8–22. u Pss 18, 50; 96, 3; 145, 5; Is 12, 4–5. v Pss 24, 6; 27, 8. w Gn 15, 1ff; 26, 3. x Gn 12, 7; 15, 18. y 12–13: Dt 4, 27; 26, 5. z Gn 41, 54. 57.

Joseph, sold as a slave. [a]
18 They shackled his feet with chains;
collared his neck in iron, [b]
19 Till his prediction came to pass,
and the word of the LORD proved him true. [c]
20 The king sent and released him;
the ruler of peoples set him free. [d]
21 He made him lord over his palace,
ruler over all his possessions, [e]
22 To instruct his princes by his word,
to teach his elders wisdom.

V

23 Then Israel entered Egypt;[f]
Jacob lived in the land of Ham.*
24 God greatly increased his people,
made them too many for their foes. [g]
25 He turned their hearts to hate his people,
to treat his servants unfairly. [h]
26 He sent his servant Moses,
Aaron whom he had chosen. [i]
27 They worked his signs in Egypt[j]*
and wonders in the land of Ham.
28 He sent darkness and it grew dark,
but they rebelled against his word.
29 He turned their waters into blood
and killed all their fish.
30 Their land swarmed with frogs,
even the chambers of their kings.
31 He spoke and there came swarms of flies,
gnats through all their country.
32 For rain he gave them hail,
flashes of lightning throughout their land.
33 He struck down their vines and fig trees,
shattered the trees of their country.
34 He spoke and the locusts came,
grasshoppers without number. [k]
35 They devoured every plant in the land;
they ravaged the crops of their fields.
36 He struck down every firstborn in the land,
the first fruits of all their vigor.
37 He brought his people out,
laden with silver and gold; [l]
no stragglers among the tribes.
38 Egypt rejoiced when they left,
for panic had seized them.

VI

39 He spread a cloud as a cover,
and made a fire to light up the night. [m]
40 They asked and he brought them quail;
with bread from heaven he filled them. [n]
41 He split the rock and water gushed forth;
it flowed through the desert like a river. [o]
42 For he remembered his sacred word
to Abraham his servant.
43 He brought his people out with joy,
his chosen ones with shouts of triumph.
44 He gave them the lands of the nations,
the wealth of the peoples to own, [p]
45 That they might keep his laws
and observe his teachings. [q]
Hallelujah!

PSALM 106*

Israel's Confession of Sin

1 Hallelujah!

A

Give thanks to the LORD, who is good,
whose love endures forever. [r]
2 Who can tell the mighty deeds of the LORD,

105, 23. 27: The land of Ham: a synonym for Egypt. Cf Gn 10, 6.

105, 27–38: This psalm and Ps 78, 43–51 have an account of the plagues differing in number or in order from Ex 7, 14–12, 30. Several versions of the exodus story were current.

Ps 106: Israel is invited to praise the God whose mercy has always tempered judgment of Israel (1–3). The speaker, on behalf of all, seeks solidarity with the people, who can always count on God's fidelity despite their sin (4–5). Confident of God's mercy, the speaker invites national repentance (6) by reciting from Israel's history eight instances of sin, judgment, and forgiveness. The sins are the rebellion at the Red Sea (6–12; see Ex 14–15), the craving for meat in the desert (13–15; see Nm 11), the challenge to Moses' authority (16–18; see Nm 16), the golden calf episode (19–23; see Ex 32–34), the refusal to take Canaan by the southern route (24–27; see Nm 13–14 and Dt 1–2), the rebellion at Baal-Peor (28–31; see Nm 25, 1–10), the anger of Moses (32–33; see Nm 20, 1–13), and mingling with the nations (34–47). The last, as suggested by its length and generalized language, may be the sin that invites the repentance of the present generation. The text gives the site of each sin: Egypt (7), the desert (14), the camp (16), Horeb (19), in their tents (25), Baal-Peor (28), the waters of Meribah (32), Canaan (38).

a Gn 37, 28. 36; 45, 5. b Gn 39, 20. c Gn 40–41. d Gn 41, 14. e Gn 41, 41–44. f Gn 46, 1–47, 12; Acts 7, 15. g Ex 1, 7; Acts 7, 17. h Ex 1, 8–14. i Ex 3, 10; 4, 27. j 27–36: Ps 78, 43–51; Ex 7–12. k Jl 1, 4. l Ex 12, 33–36. m Ps 78, 14; Ex 13, 21–22; Wis 18, 3. n Ps 78, 24–28; Ex 16, 13–15; Nm 11, 31ff; Wis 16, 20. o Ps 78, 15–16; Ex 17, 1–7; Nm 20, 11. p Dt 4, 37–40. q Dt 6, 20–25; 7, 8–11. r Pss 100, 5; 107, 1; 1 Chr 16, 34; Jer 33, 11; Dn 3, 89.

proclaim in full God's praise?
3 Happy those who do what is right,
whose deeds are always just. [s]
4 Remember me, LORD, as you favor your people;
come to me with your saving help, [t]
5 That I may see the prosperity of your chosen,
rejoice in the joy of your people,
and glory with your heritage.

B

6 We have sinned like our ancestors; [u]
we have done wrong and are guilty.

I

7 Our ancestors in Egypt
did not attend to your wonders.
They did not remember your great love;
they defied the Most High at the Red Sea.
8 Yet he saved them for his name's sake
to make his power known. [v]
9 He roared at the Red Sea and it dried up.
He led them through the deep as through a desert. [w]
10 He rescued them from hostile hands,
freed them from the power of the enemy.
11 The waters covered their oppressors;
not one of them survived.
12 Then they believed his words
and sang songs of praise. [x]

II

13 But they soon forgot all he had done;
they had no patience for his plan.
14 In the desert they gave way to their cravings,
tempted God in the wasteland. [y]
15 So he gave them what they asked
and sent among them a wasting disease. [z]

III

16 In the camp they challenged Moses [a]
and Aaron, the holy one of the LORD.
17 The earth opened and swallowed Dathan,
it closed on the followers of Abiram.
18 Against that company the fire blazed;
flames consumed the wicked.

IV

19 At Horeb they fashioned a calf, [b]
worshiped a metal statue.
20 They exchanged their glorious God
for the image of a grass-eating bull.
21 They forgot the God who saved them,
who did great deeds in Egypt, [c]
22 Amazing deeds in the land of Ham,
fearsome deeds at the Red Sea.
23 He would have decreed their destruction,
had not Moses, the chosen leader,
Withstood him in the breach*
to turn back his destroying anger. [d]

V

24 Next they despised the beautiful land; [e]
they did not believe the promise.
25 In their tents they complained;
they did not obey the LORD.
26 So with raised hand he swore
to destroy them in the desert,
27 To scatter their descendants among the nations,
disperse them in foreign lands.

VI

28 They joined in the rites of Baal of Peor, [f]
ate food sacrificed to dead gods.
29 They provoked him by their actions,
and a plague broke out among them.
30 Then Phinehas rose to intervene,
and the plague was brought to a halt.
31 This was counted for him as a righteous deed
for all generations to come.

VII

32 At the waters of Meribah they angered God, [g]
and Moses suffered because of them.*
33 They so embittered his spirit

106, 23: Withstood him in the breach: the image is that of Moses standing in a narrow break made in the wall to keep anyone from entering.

106, 32: Moses suffered because of them: Moses was not allowed to enter the promised land because of his rash words (Nm 20, 12). According to Dt 1, 37, Moses was not allowed to cross because of the people's sin, not his own.

s Is 56, 1–2. t Ps 25, 7; Neh 5, 19. u 6–7: Ps 78, 11–17; Ex 14, 11; Lv 26, 40; 1 Kgs 8, 47; Bar 2, 12; Dn 9, 5. v Ez 36, 20–22. w Ex 14, 21–31; Is 50, 2; 63, 11–14; Na 1, 4. x Ex 15, 1–21. y Ps 78, 18; Ex 15, 24; 16, 3; Nm 11, 1–6. z Ps 78, 26–31; Nm 11, 33. a 16–18: Nm 16; Dt 11, 6; Is 26, 11. b 19–20: Ex 32; Dt 9, 8–21; Jer 2, 11; Acts 7, 41; Rom 1, 23. c Ps 78, 42–58; Dt 32, 18; Jer 2, 32. d Ex 32, 11; Dt 9, 25; Ez 22, 30. e 24–27: Lv 26, 33; Nm 14; Dt 1, 25–36; Ez 20, 15. 23. f 28–31: Nm 25; Dt 26, 14; Sir 45, 23–24. g 32–33: Ps 95, 8–9; Ex 17, 1–7; Nm 20, 2–13; Dt 6, 16; 33, 8.

that rash words crossed his lips.

VIII

34 They did not destroy the peoples
as the LORD had commanded them, [h]
35 But mingled with the nations
and imitated their ways. [i]
36 They worshiped their idols
and were ensnared by them. [j]
37 They sacrificed to the gods*
their own sons and daughters,
38 Shedding innocent blood,
the blood of their own sons and daughters,
Whom they sacrificed to the idols of Canaan,
desecrating the land with bloodshed.
39 They defiled themselves by their actions,
became adulterers by their conduct.
40 So the LORD grew angry with his people,
abhorred his own heritage.
41 He handed them over to the nations,
and their adversaries ruled them. [k]
42 Their enemies oppressed them,
kept them under subjection.
43 Many times did he rescue them,
but they kept rebelling and scheming
and were brought low by their own guilt. [l]
44 Still God had regard for their affliction
when he heard their wailing.
45 For their sake he remembered his covenant
and relented in his abundant love, [m]
46 Winning for them compassion
from all who held them captive.

C

47 Save us, LORD, our God;
gather us from among the nations
That we may give thanks to your holy name
and glory in praising you. [n]

* * *

48 Blessed be the LORD, the God of Israel,
from everlasting to everlasting!
Let all the people say, Amen! [o]
Hallelujah!*

FIFTH BOOK—PSALMS 107–150

PSALM 107*

God the Savior of Those in Distress

1 "Give thanks to the LORD who is good,
whose love endures forever!" [p]
2 Let that be the prayer of the LORD's redeemed,
those redeemed from the hand of the foe, [q]
3 Those gathered from foreign lands,
from east and west, from north and south. [r]

I

4 Some had lost their way in a barren desert;
found no path toward a city to live in.
5 They were hungry and thirsty;
their life was ebbing away. [s]
6 In their distress they cried to the LORD,
who rescued them in their peril,
7 Guided them by a direct path [t]
so they reached a city to live in. [u]
8 Let them thank the LORD for such kindness,
such wondrous deeds for mere mortals.
9 For he satisfied the thirsty,
filled the hungry with good things. [v]

II

10 Some lived in darkness and gloom,
in prison, bound with chains,
11 Because they rebelled against God's word,
scorned the counsel of the Most High, [w]
12 Who humbled their hearts through hardship;
they stumbled with no one to help. [x]
13 In their distress they cried to the LORD,
who saved them in their peril,

106, 37: The gods: Hebrew *shedim,* customarily translated "demons," occurs in parallelism with "gods" in an important inscription from Transjordan and hence is translated "gods."

106, 48: A doxology ending Book IV of the Psalter. It is not part of the psalm.

Ps 107: A hymn inviting those who have been rescued by God to give praise (1–3). Four archetypal divine rescues are described, each ending in thanksgiving: from the sterile desert (4–9), from imprisonment in gloom (10–16), from mortal illness (17–22), and from the angry sea (23–32). The number four connotes totality, all the possible varieties of rescue. The same saving activity of God is shown in Israel's history (33–41); whenever the people were endangered God rescued them. The last verses invite people to ponder the persistent saving acts of God (42–43).

h Dt 7, 1; Jgs 2, 1–5. i Lv 18, 3; Jgs 1, 27–35; 3, 5. j 36–38: Lv 18, 21; Nm 35, 33; Dt 32, 17; Jgs 2, 11–13. 17. 19; 2 Kgs 16, 3; Bar 4, 7; 1 Cor 10, 20. k Jgs 2, 14–23. l Is 63, 7–9. m Lv 26, 42. n 1 Chr 16, 35. o Pss 41, 14; 72, 18; 89, 53; 1 Chr 16, 36; Neh 9, 5. p Pss 100, 4–5; 106, 1; Jer 33, 11. q Is 63, 12. r Is 43, 5–6; 49, 12; Zec 8, 7. s Dt 8, 15; 32, 10; Is 49, 10. t Is 35, 8; 40, 3; 43, 19. u Dt 6, 10. v Lk 1, 53. w Is 42, 7. 22; Jb 36, 8–9; Prv 1, 25. x Ps 106, 43.

14 Led them forth from darkness and gloom
and broke their chains asunder.[y]
15 Let them thank the LORD for such kindness,
such wondrous deeds for mere mortals.
16 For he broke down the gates of bronze
and snapped the bars of iron.

III

17 Some fell sick from their wicked ways,
afflicted because of their sins.
18 They loathed all manner of food;[z]
they were at the gates of death.
19 In their distress they cried to the LORD,
who saved them in their peril,
20 Sent forth the word to heal them,[a]
snatched them from the grave.
21 Let them thank the LORD for such kindness,
such wondrous deeds for mere mortals.
22 Let them offer a sacrifice in thanks,
declare his works with shouts of joy.

IV

23 Some went off to sea in ships,
plied their trade on the deep waters.[b]
24 They saw the works of the LORD,
the wonders of God in the deep.
25 He spoke and roused a storm wind;
it tossed the waves on high.[c]
26 They rose up to the heavens, sank to the
depths;
their hearts trembled at the danger.
27 They reeled, staggered like drunkards;
their skill was of no avail.[d]
28 In their distress they cried to the LORD,
who brought them out of their peril,
29 Hushed the storm to a murmur;
the waves of the sea were stilled.[e]
30 They rejoiced that the sea grew calm,
that God brought them to the harbor they
longed for.
31 Let them thank the LORD for such kindness,
such wondrous deeds for mere mortals.
32 Let them praise him in the assembly of the
people,
give thanks in the council of the elders.

V

33 God changed rivers into desert,*
springs of water into thirsty ground,[f]
34 Fruitful land into a salty waste,
because of the wickedness of its people.[g]
35 He changed the desert into pools of water,
arid land into springs of water,[h]
36 And settled the hungry there;
they built a city to live in.[i]
37 They sowed fields and planted vineyards,
brought in an abundant harvest.[j]
38 God blessed them, they became very many,
and their livestock did not decrease.[k]
40 But he poured out contempt on princes,
made them wander the trackless wastes,[l]
39 Where they were diminished and brought low
through misery and cruel oppression,
41 While the poor were released from their
affliction;
their families increased like their flocks.[m]
42 The upright saw this and rejoiced;[n]
all wickedness shut its mouth.
43 Whoever is wise will take note of these
things,[o]
will ponder the merciful deeds of the LORD.

PSALM 108*

Prayer for Victory

1 A song; a psalm of David.

I

2 My heart is steadfast, God;[p]
my heart is steadfast.
I will sing and chant praise.
3 Awake, my soul; awake, lyre and harp!
I will wake the dawn.[q]
4 I will praise you among the peoples, LORD;

107, 33–41: God destroyed Sodom and Gomorrah in Gn 18–19, which the psalm sees as the destruction of the wicked inhabitants of Canaan to prepare the way for Israel (33–34). God then led Israel through the desert to give them a fertile land (35–38) and protected them from every danger (39–41).

Ps 108: A prayer compiled from two other psalms: 2–6 are virtually the same as Ps 57, 8–12; 7–14 are the same as Ps 60, 7–14. An old promise of salvation (8–10) is combined with a confident assurance (1–6. 14) and petition (7. 12–13).

y Is 42, 7; 49, 9; 51, 14. z Jb 6, 6–7; 33, 20. a Ps 147, 15; Wis 16, 12; Is 55, 11; Mt 8, 8. b Sir 43, 25. c Jon 1, 4. d Is 29, 9. e Pss 65, 8; 89, 10; Mt 8, 26 par. f Is 35, 7; 42, 15; 50, 2. g Gn 19, 23–28; Dt 29, 22; Sir 39, 23. h Ps 114, 8; Is 41, 8. i Ez 36, 35. j Is 65, 21; Jer 31, 5. k Dt 7, 13–14. l Jb 12, 23–25. m Ps 113, 7. n Pss 58, 11; 63, 12. o Hos 14, 10. p 2–6: Ps 57, 8–12. q Jb 38, 12.

I will chant your praise among the nations.[r]
5 For your love towers to the heavens;
your faithfulness, to the skies.[s]
6 Appear on high over the heavens, God;
may your glory appear above all the earth.
7 Help with your right hand and answer us
that your loved ones may escape.

II

8 God promised in the sanctuary:[t]
"I will exult, I will apportion Shechem;
the valley of Succoth I will measure out.
9 Gilead is mine, mine is Manasseh;
Ephraim is the helmet for my head,
Judah, my own scepter.
10 Moab is my washbowl;
upon Edom I cast my sandal;[u]
I will triumph over Philistia."

III

11 Who will bring me to the fortified city?
Who will lead me into Edom?
12 Was it not you who rejected us, God?
Do you no longer march with our armies?[v]
13 Give us aid against the foe;
worthless is human help.
14 We will triumph with the help of God,
who will trample down our foes.

PSALM 109*

Prayer of a Person Falsely Accused

1 For the leader. A psalm of David.

I

O God, whom I praise, do not be silent,[w]
2 for wicked and treacherous mouths attack me.
They speak against me with lying tongues;
3 with hateful words they surround me,
attacking me without cause.
4 In return for my love they slander me,
even though I prayed for them.
5 They repay me evil for good,
hatred for my love.[x]

II

My enemies say of me:
6 "Find a lying witness,
an accuser* to stand by his right hand,
7 That he may be judged and found guilty,
that his plea may be in vain.
8 May his days be few;
may another take his office.[y]
9 May his children be fatherless,
his wife, a widow.[z]
10 May his children be vagrant beggars,
driven from their hovels.
11 May the usurer snare all he owns,
strangers plunder all he earns.
12 May no one treat him kindly
or pity his fatherless children.
13 May his posterity be destroyed,[a]
his name cease in the next generation.
14 May the LORD remember his fathers' guilt;
his mother's sin not be canceled.[b]
15 May their guilt be always before the LORD,[c]
till their memory is banished from the earth,[d]
16 For he did not remember to show kindness,
but hounded the wretched poor
and brought death to the brokenhearted.
17 He loved cursing; may it come upon him;
he hated blessing; may none come to him.
18 May cursing clothe him like a robe;
may it enter his belly like water,
seep into his bones like oil.
19 May it be near as the clothes he wears,
as the belt always around him."

III

20 May the LORD bring all this* upon my accusers,
upon those who speak evil against me.

Ps 109: A lament notable for the length and vehemence of its prayer against evildoers (6–20); the cry to God (1) and the complaint (22–25) are brief in comparison. The psalmist is apparently the victim of a slander campaign, potentially devastating in a society where reputation and honor are paramount. In the emotional perspective of the psalm, there are only two types of people: the wicked and their poor victims. The psalmist is a poor victim (22. 31) and by that fact a friend of God and enemy of the wicked. The psalmist seeks vindication not on the basis of personal virtue but because of God's promise to protect the poor.

109, 6: An accuser: Hebrew *satan*, a word occurring in Jb 1–2 and Zec 3, 1–2. In the latter passage Satan stands at the right hand of the high priest to bring false accusations against him before God. Here the accuser is human.

109, 20: May the LORD bring all this: the psalmist prays that God ratify the curses of 6–19 and bring them upon the wicked.

r Pss 9, 12; 18, 50; 148, 13. s Pss 36, 6; 71, 19. t 8–14: Ps 60, 8–14. u Ru 4, 7–8. v Ps 44, 10. w Pss 35, 22; 83, 1. x Pss 35, 12; 38, 21; Prv 17, 13; Jer 18, 20. y Acts 1, 20. z Ex 22, 23; Jer 18, 21. a Ps 21, 11; Prv 10, 7. b Ex 20, 5. c Ps 90, 8. d Ps 34, 16.

21 But you, LORD, my God,
deal kindly with me for your name's sake;
in your great mercy rescue me.
22 For I am sorely in need;
my heart is pierced within me.
23 Like a lengthening shadow I near my end,
all but swept away like the locust.
24 My knees totter from fasting; [e]
my flesh has wasted away.
25 I have become a mockery to them;
when they see me, they shake their heads.
26 Help me, LORD, my God;
save me in your kindness.
27 Make them know this is your hand,
that you, LORD, have acted.
28 Though they curse, may you bless;
shame my foes, that your servant may
rejoice.
29 Clothe my accusers with disgrace;
make them wear shame like a mantle.
30 I will give fervent thanks to the LORD;
before all I will praise my God.[f]
31 For God stands at the right hand of the poor
to defend them against unjust accusers.

PSALM 110*

God Appoints the King both King and Priest

1 A psalm of David.

The LORD says to you, my lord:*
"Take your throne at my right hand,
while I make your enemies your
footstool." [g]*
2 The scepter of your sovereign might
the LORD will extend from Zion.
The LORD says: "Rule over your enemies!
3 Yours is princely power from the day of your
birth.
In holy splendor before the daystar,*
like the dew I begot you." [h]*
4 The LORD has sworn and will not waver:
"Like Melchizedek* you are a priest
forever." [i]
5 At your right hand is the Lord,
who crushes kings on the day of wrath, [j]
6 Who, robed in splendor, judges nations,
crushes heads across the wide earth,
7 Who drinks from the brook by the wayside*
and thus holds high the head. [k]

PSALM 111*

Praise of God for Goodness to Israel

1 Hallelujah.

I will praise the LORD with all my heart [l]
in the assembled congregation of the
upright.*
2 Great are the works of the LORD,
to be treasured for all their delights.
3 Majestic and glorious is your* work,
your wise design endures forever.
4 You won renown for your wondrous deeds;
gracious and merciful is the LORD. [m]
5 You gave food to those who fear you,*
mindful of your covenant forever.
6 You showed powerful deeds to your people,

Ps 110: A royal psalm in which a court singer recites three oracles in which God assures the king that his enemies are conquered (1–2), makes the king "son" in traditional adoption language (3), gives priestly status to the king and promises to be with him in future military ventures (4–7).

110, 1: The LORD says to you, my lord: literally, "The LORD says to my lord," a polite form of address of an inferior to a superior. Cf 1 Sm 25, 25; 2 Sm 1, 10. The court singer refers to the king. Jesus in the synoptic gospels (Mt 22, 41–46 and parallels) takes the psalmist to be David and hence "my lord" refers to the messiah, who must be someone greater than David. **Your footstool:** in ancient times victorious kings put their feet on the prostrate bodies of their enemies.

110, 3: Before the daystar: possibly an expression for before the world began (Prv 8, 22). **Like the dew I begot you:** an adoption formula as in Pss 2, 7; 89, 27–28.

110, 4: Like Melchizedek: Melchizedek was the ancient king of Salem (Jerusalem) who blessed Abraham (Gn 14, 18–20); like other kings of the time he performed priestly functions. Heb 7 sees in Melchizedek a type of Christ.

110, 7: Who drinks from the brook by the wayside: the meaning is uncertain. Some see an allusion to a rite of royal consecration at the Gihon spring (cf 1 Kgs 1, 33. 38). Others find here an image of the divine warrior (or king) pursuing enemies so relentlessly that he does not stop long enough to eat and drink.

Ps 111: A temple singer (1) tells how God is revealed in Israel's history (2–10). The deeds reveal God's very self, powerful, merciful, faithful. The poem is an acrostic, each verse beginning with a successive letter of the Hebrew alphabet.

111, 1: In the assembled congregation of the upright: in the temple. Cf Ps 149, 1.

111, 3: Your: the psalm refers to God in the third person throughout; the shift to the second person is for the sake of inclusive language.

111, 5: Food to those who fear you: probably a reference to the manna in the desert, which elsewhere is seen as a type of the Eucharist. Cf Jn 6, 31–33. 49–51.

e 24–25: Ps 69, 11–13. f Ps 111, 1. g Mt 22, 44; Acts 2, 34–35; 1 Cor 15, 25; Heb 1, 13; 8, 1; 10, 12–13; 1 Pt 3, 22. h Pss 2, 7; 89, 27; Is 49, 1. i Pss 89, 35; 132, 11; Gn 14, 18; Heb 5, 6; 7, 21. j Ps 2, 9; Rv 2, 27; 12, 5; 19, 15. k Ps 3, 4. l Ps 138, 1. m Pss 103, 8; 112, 4.

giving them the lands* of the nations.
7 The works of your hands are right and true,
reliable all your decrees,
8 Established forever and ever,
to be observed with loyalty and care.
9 You sent deliverance to your people,
ratified your covenant forever;
holy and awesome is your name.
10 The fear of the LORD* is the beginning of wisdom; [n]
prudent are all who live by it.
Your praise endures forever.

PSALM 112*

The Blessings of the Just

1 Hallelujah!

Happy are those* who fear the LORD,
who greatly delight in God's commands. [o]
2 Their descendants shall be mighty in the land,
a generation upright and blessed.
3 Wealth and riches shall be in their homes;
their prosperity* shall endure forever.
4 They shine through the darkness, a light for the upright; [p]
they are gracious, merciful, and just.
5 All goes well for those gracious in lending,
who conduct their affairs with justice.
6 They shall never be shaken;
the just shall be remembered forever. [q]
7 They shall not fear an ill report;
their hearts are steadfast, trusting the LORD.
8 Their hearts are tranquil, without fear,
till at last they look down on their foes.
9 Lavishly they give to the poor;
their prosperity shall endure forever; [r]
their horn* shall be exalted in honor.
10 The wicked shall be angry to see this;
they will gnash their teeth and waste away;
the desires of the wicked come to nothing.

PSALM 113*

Praise of God's Care of the Poor

1 Hallelujah!

I

Praise, you servants of the LORD,
praise the name of the LORD. [s]
2 Blessed be the name of the LORD
both now and forever.
3 From the rising of the sun to its setting
let the name of the LORD be praised.

II

4 High above all nations is the LORD;
above the heavens God's glory. [t]
5 Who is like the LORD,
our God enthroned on high,
6 looking down on heaven and earth? [u]
7 The LORD raises the needy from the dust,
lifts the poor from the ash heap, [v]
8 Seats them with princes,
the princes of the people,
9 Gives the childless wife a home,
the joyful mother of children. [w]
Hallelujah!

PSALM 114*

The Lord's Wonders at the Exodus

1 When Israel came forth from Egypt,
the house of Jacob from an alien people,
2 Judah became God's holy place,

111, 6: Lands: literally, "inheritance, heritage."

111, 10: The fear of the LORD: reverence for God, the Hebrew term for religion.

Ps 112: An acrostic poem detailing the blessings received by those who remain close to God by obedience to the commandments. Among their blessings are children (2), wealth that enables them to be magnanimous (3. 5. 9), and virtue by which they encourage others (4). The just person is an affront to the wicked, whose hopes remain unfulfilled (10). The logic resembles Pss 1 and 111.

112, 1: Happy are those: literally, "Happy the person." "Person" is used typically, hence the plural translation.

112, 3: Prosperity: literally, "justice." In the Second Temple Period the word acquired the nuance of liberality and almsgiving. Cf Sir 3, 30; 7, 10; Mt 6, 1–4.

112, 9: Their horn: the symbol for vitality and honor.

Ps 113: A hymn exhorting the congregation to praise God's name, i.e., the way in which God is present in the world; the name is mentioned three times in 1–3. The divine name is especially honored in the temple (1) but its recognition is not limited by time (2) and space (3), for God is everywhere active (4–5) especially in rescuing the lowly faithful (7–9).

Ps 114: A hymn celebrating Israel's escape from Egypt, journey through the wilderness, and entry into the promised land, and the miracles of nature that bore witness to God's presence in their midst. In the perspective of the psalm, the people proceed directly from Egypt into the promised land (1–2). Sea and Jordan, which stood like soldiers barring the people from their land, flee before the mighty God as the earth recoils from the battle (3–4). The poet taunts the natural elements as one taunts defeated enemies (5–6).

n Prv 1, 7; 9, 10; Sir 1, 16. o Pss 1, 1–2; 119, 1–2; 128, 1. p Pss 37, 6; 97, 11; Prv 13, 9; Is 58, 10. q Prv 10, 7; Wis 8, 13. r Prv 22, 9; 2 Cor 9, 9. s Ps 135, 1. t Ps 148, 13. u Ps 89, 7–9. v Ps 107, 41; 1 Sm 2, 7–8. w 1 Sm 2, 5; Is 54, 1.

Israel, God's domain.[x]
3 The sea beheld and fled;*
the Jordan turned back.[y]
4 The mountains skipped like rams;
the hills, like lambs of the flock.[z]
5 Why was it, sea, that you fled?
Jordan, that you turned back?
6 You mountains, that you skipped like rams?
You hills, like lambs of the flock?
7 Tremble, earth, before the Lord,[a]
before the God of Jacob,
8 Who turned rock into pools of water,
stone into flowing springs.[b]*

PSALM 115*

The Greatness of the True God

I

1 Not to us, LORD, not to us
but to your name give glory
because of your faithfulness and love.[c]
2 Why should the nations say,
"Where is their God?"[d]*
3 Our God is in heaven;
whatever God wills is done.[e]

II

4 Their idols are silver and gold,[f]
the work of human hands.[g]
5 They have mouths but do not speak,
eyes but do not see.
6 They have ears but do not hear,
noses but do not smell.
7 They have hands but do not feel,
feet but do not walk,
and no sound rises from their throats.
8 Their makers shall be like them,
all who trust in them.

III

9 The house of Israel trusts in the LORD,[h]
who is their help and shield.[i]
10 The house of Aaron trusts in the LORD,
who is their help and shield.
11 Those who fear the LORD* trust in the LORD,
who is their help and shield.
12 The LORD remembers us and will bless us,
will bless the house of Israel,
will bless the house of Aaron,
13 Will bless those who fear the LORD,
small and great alike.
14 May the LORD increase your number,
you and your descendants.
15 May you be blessed by the LORD,
who made heaven and earth.
16 The heavens* belong to the LORD,
but the earth is given to us.[j]
17 The dead do not praise the LORD,
all those gone down into silence.[k]*
18 It is we who bless the LORD,
both now and forever.
Hallelujah!

PSALM 116*

Thanksgiving to God Who Saves from Death

I

1 I love the LORD, who listened
to my voice in supplication,
2 Who turned an ear to me

114, 3–4: Pairs of cosmic elements such as sea and rivers, mountains and hills, are sometimes mentioned in creation accounts. Personified here as warriors, the pairs tremble in fear before the Divine Warrior. The quaking also recalls the divine appearance in the storm at Sinai (Ex 19, 16–19) and elsewhere (Jgs 5, 4–5; Ps 18, 8–16).

114, 8: The miracles of giving drink to the people in the arid desert. Cf Ex 17, 1–7; Is 41, 17–18.

Ps 115: A response to the enemy taunt, "Where is your God?" This hymn to the glory of Israel's God (1–3) ridicules the lifeless idols of the nations (4–8), expresses in a litany the trust of the various classes of the people in God (9–11), invokes God's blessing on them as they invoke the divine name (12–15), and concludes as it began with praise of God. Ps 135, 15–18 similarly mocks the Gentile gods and has a similar litany and hymn (Ps 135, 19–21).

115, 2: Where is their God?: implies that God cannot help them.

115, 9–11: The house of Israel . . . the house of Aaron . . . those fear the LORD: the laity of Israelite birth, the priests, and the converts to Judaism. Cf Pss 118, 2–4; 135, 19–21. In the New Testament likewise "those who fear the Lord" means converts to Judaism (cf Acts 10, 2. 22. 35; 13, 16. 26).

115, 16: The heavens: literally, "the heaven of heavens" or "the highest heavens," i.e., above the firmament. See note on Ps 148, 4.

115, 17: See note on Ps 6, 6.

Ps 116: A thanksgiving in which the psalmist responds to divine rescue from mortal danger (3–4) and from near despair (10–11) with vows and temple sacrifices (13–14. 17–19). The Greek and Latin versions divide the psalm into two parts: 1–9 and 10–19, corresponding to its two major divisions.

x Ex 19, 6. y Ex 14, 21f; Jos 3, 14ff; Pss 66, 6; 74, 15. z Ps 29, 6; Wis 19, 9. a Ps 68, 9. b Ex 17, 6; Nm 20, 11. c Ez 36, 22–23. d Ps 79, 10. e Ps 135, 6. f 4–10: Ps 135, 15–19; Wis 15, 15–16; Is 44, 9f; Jer 10, 1–5. g Is 40, 19. h Ps 118, 2–4. i Ps 33, 20. j Gn 1, 28. k Pss 6, 6; 88, 11ff; Sir 17, 22f; Is 38, 18.

on the day I called.
3 I was caught by the cords of death;[l]*
the snares of Sheol had seized me;
I felt agony and dread.
4 Then I called on the name of the LORD,
"O LORD, save my life!"

II

5 Gracious is the LORD and just;
yes, our God is merciful.[m]
6 The LORD protects the simple;
I was helpless, but God saved me.
7 Return, my soul, to your rest;
the LORD has been good to you.[n]
8 For my soul has been freed from death,
my eyes from tears, my feet from
stumbling.[o]
9 I shall walk before the LORD
in the land of the living.[p]*

III

10 I kept faith, even when I said,*
"I am greatly afflicted!"[q]
11 I said in my alarm,
"No one can be trusted!"[r]
12 How can I repay the LORD
for all the good done for me?
13 I will raise the cup of salvation*
and call on the name of the LORD.
14 I will pay my vows to the LORD
in the presence of all his people.
15 Too costly in the eyes of the LORD*
is the death of his faithful.[s]
16 LORD, I am your servant,
your servant, the child of your
maidservant;[t]
you have loosed my bonds.
17 I will offer a sacrifice of thanksgiving
and call on the name of the LORD.[u]
18 I will pay my vows to the LORD[v]
in the presence of all his people,
19 In the courts of the house of the LORD,
in your midst, O Jerusalem.
Hallelujah!

PSALM 117*

The Nations Called to Praise

1 Praise the LORD, all you nations!
Give glory, all you peoples![w]
2 The LORD's love for us is strong;
the LORD is faithful forever.
Hallelujah!

PSALM 118*

Hymn of Thanksgiving

I

1 Give thanks to the LORD, who is good,[x]
whose love endures forever.
2 Let the house of Israel say:
God's love endures forever.
3 Let the house of Aaron say,
God's love endures forever.
4 Let those who fear the LORD say,[y]
God's love endures forever.

II

5 In danger I called on the LORD;
the LORD answered me and set me free.
6 The LORD is with me; I am not afraid;
what can mortals do against me?[z]
7 The LORD is with me as my helper;
I shall look in triumph on my foes.

116, 3: The cords of death: death is personified here; it attempts to capture the psalmist with snares and nets. Cf Ps 18, 6.

116, 9: The land of the living: the phrase elsewhere is an epithet of the Jerusalem temple (cf Pss 27, 13; 52, 7; Is 38, 11). Hence the psalmist probably refers to being present to God in the temple.

116, 10: I kept faith, even when I said: even in the days of despair, the psalmist did not lose all hope.

116, 13: The cup of salvation: probably the libation of wine poured out in gratitude for rescue. Cf Ex 25, 29; Nm 15, 5. 7. 10.

116, 15: Too costly in the eyes of the LORD: the meaning is that the death of God's faithful is grievous to God, not that God is pleased with the death. Cf Ps 72, 14. In Wis 3, 5–6 God accepts the death of the righteous as a sacrificial burnt offering.

Ps 117: This shortest of hymns calls on the nations to acknowledge God's supremacy. The supremacy of Israel's God has been demonstrated to them by the people's secure existence, which is owed entirely to God's gracious fidelity.

Ps 118: A thanksgiving liturgy accompanying a victory procession of the king and the people into the temple precincts. After an invocation in the form of a litany (1–4), the psalmist (very likely speaking in the name of the community) describes how the people confidently implored God's help (5–9) when hostile peoples threatened its life (10–14); vividly God's rescue is recounted (15–18). Then follows a dialogue at the temple gates between the priests and the psalmist as the latter enters to offer the thanksgiving sacrifice (19–25). Finally, the priests impart their blessing (26–27), and the psalmist sings in gratitude (28–29).

l Ps 18, 5; Jon 2, 3. m Ex 34, 6. n Ps 13, 6. o Ps 56, 14; Is 25, 8; Rv 21, 4. p Pss 27, 13; 56, 14; Is 38, 11. q 2 Cor 4, 13. r Ps 12, 2. s Ps 72, 14; Is 43, 4. t Pss 86, 16; 143, 12; Wis 9, 5. u Lv 7, 12ff. v Jon 2, 10. w Rom 15, 11. x Pss 100, 5; 136, 1f. y Ps 115, 9–11. z Ps 27, 1; Heb 13, 6.

[8] Better to take refuge in the LORD [a]
than to put one's trust in mortals.
[9] Better to take refuge in the LORD
than to put one's trust in princes.

III

[10] All the nations surrounded me;
in the LORD's name I crushed them.
[11] They surrounded me on every side;
in the LORD's name I crushed them.
[12] They surrounded me like bees; [b]
they blazed like fire among thorns;
in the LORD's name I crushed them.
[13] I was hard pressed and falling,
but the LORD came to my help. [c]
[14] The LORD, my strength and might,
came to me as savior. [d]

IV

[15] The joyful shout of deliverance
is heard in the tents of the victors:
"The LORD's right hand strikes with power;
[16] the LORD's right hand is raised;
the LORD's right hand strikes with power."
[17] I shall not die but live
and declare the deeds of the LORD.
[18] The LORD chastised me harshly,
but did not hand me over to death.

V

[19] Open the gates of victory;
I will enter and thank the LORD. [e]
[20] This is the LORD's own gate,
where the victors enter.*
[21] I thank you for you answered me;
you have been my savior.
[22] The stone the builders rejected*
has become the cornerstone. [f]
[23] By the LORD has this been done;
it is wonderful in our eyes.
[24] This is the day the LORD has made;
let us rejoice in it and be glad.
[25] LORD, grant salvation!*
LORD, grant good fortune!

VI

[26] Blessed is he
who comes in the name of the LORD. [g]
We bless you from the LORD's house.
[27] The LORD is God and has given us light.
Join in procession with leafy branches
up to the horns of the altar.

VII

[28] You are my God, I give you thanks;
my God, I offer you praise.
[29] Give thanks to the LORD, who is good,
whose love endures forever.

PSALM 119*

A Prayer to God, the Lawgiver

ALEPH

[1] Happy those whose way is blameless,
who walk by the teaching of the LORD. [h]
[2] Happy those who observe God's decrees,
who seek the LORD with all their heart. [i]
[3] They do no wrong;
they walk in God's ways.
[4] You have given them the command
to keep your precepts with care.

118, 20: Where the victors enter: their victory has demonstrated that God favors them; they are "just" in the biblical sense.

118, 22: The stone the builders rejected: a proverb: what is insignificant to human beings has become great through divine election. The "stone" may originally have meant the foundation stone or capstone of the temple. The New Testament interpreted the verse as referring to the death and resurrection of Christ (Mt 21, 42; Acts 4, 11; cf Is 28, 16 and Rom 9, 33; 1 Pt 2, 7).

118, 25: Grant salvation: the Hebrew for this cry has come into English as "Hosanna." This cry and the words in 26 were used in the gospels to welcome Jesus entering the temple on Palm Sunday (Mk 11, 9–10).

Ps 119: This psalm, the longest by far in the Psalter, praises God for giving such splendid laws and instruction for people to live by. The author glorifies and thanks God for the Torah, prays for protection from sinners enraged by others' fidelity to the law, laments the cost of obedience, delights in the law's consolations, begs for wisdom to understand the precepts, and asks for the rewards of keeping them. Several expected elements do not appear in the psalm: Mount Sinai with its story of God's revelation and gift to Israel of instruction and commandments, the temple and other institutions related to revelation and laws (frequent in other psalms). The psalm is fascinated with God's word directing and guiding human life.

The poem is an acrostic; its twenty-two stanzas (of eight verses each) are in the order of the Hebrew alphabet. Each of the eight verses within a stanza begins with the same letter. Each verse contains one word for "instruction." The translation here given attempts to translate each Hebrew word for "instruction" with the same English word. There are, however, nine words for "instruction," not eight, so the principle of a different word for "instruction" in each verse cannot be maintained with perfect consistency. The nine words for "instruction" in the translation are: law, edict, command, precept, word, utterance, way, decree, and teaching.

a 8f: Ps 146, 3. b Dt 1, 44. c Ps 129, 1–2. d Ex 15, 2; Is 12, 2. e Is 26, 2. f Mt 21, 42; Lk 20, 17; Acts 4, 11; Rom 9, 33; 1 Pt 2, 7. g Mt 21, 9; 23, 39. h Pss 1, 1–2; 15, 2; 112, 1. i Dt 4, 29.

5 May my ways be firm
in the observance of your laws!
6 Then I will not be ashamed
to ponder all your commands.
7 I will praise you with sincere heart
as I study your just edicts.
8 I will keep your laws;
do not leave me all alone.

BETH

9 How can the young walk without fault?
Only by keeping your words.
10 With all my heart I seek you;
do not let me stray from your commands.
11 In my heart I treasure your promise,
that I may not sin against you.
12 Blessed are you, O LORD;
teach me your laws.[j]
13 With my lips I recite
all the edicts you have spoken.
14 I find joy in the way of your decrees
more than in all riches.
15 I will ponder your precepts
and consider your paths.
16 In your laws I take delight;
I will never forget your word.

GIMEL

17 Be kind to your servant that I may live,
that I may keep your word.
18 Open my eyes to see clearly
the wonders of your teachings.
19 I am a sojourner in the land;[k]*
do not hide your commands from me.
20 At all times my soul is stirred
with longing for your edicts.
21 With a curse you rebuke the proud
who stray from your commands.
22 Free me from disgrace and contempt,
for I observe your decrees.
23 Though princes meet and talk against me,
your servant studies your laws.
24 Your decrees are my delight;
they are my counselors.

DALETH

25 I lie prostrate in the dust;[l]
give me life in accord with your word.
26 I disclosed my ways and you answered me;
teach me your laws.
27 Make me understand the way of your precepts;
I will ponder your wondrous deeds.
28 I weep in bitter pain;
in accord with your word to strengthen me.
29 Lead me from the way of deceit;
favor me with your teaching.
30 The way of loyalty I have chosen;
I have set your edicts before me.
31 I cling to your decrees, LORD;
do not let me come to shame.
32 I will run the way of your commands,
for you open my docile heart.*

HE

33 LORD, teach me the way of your laws;
I shall observe them with care.[m]
34 Give me insight to observe your teaching,
to keep it with all my heart.
35 Lead me in the path of your commands,[n]
for that is my delight.
36 Direct my heart toward your decrees
and away from unjust gain.
37 Avert my eyes from what is worthless;
by your way give me life.
38 For your servant fulfill your promise
made to those who fear you.
39 Turn away from me the taunts I dread,
for your edicts bring good.
40 See how I long for your precepts;
in your justice give me life.

WAW

41 Let your love come to me, LORD,
salvation in accord with your promise.
42 Let me answer my taunters with a word,
for I trust in your word.
43 Do not take the word of truth from my mouth,
for in your edicts is my hope.

119, 19: A sojourner in the land: like someone without the legal protection of a native inhabitant, the psalmist has a special need for the guidance of God's teaching.

119, 32: For you open my docile heart: literally, "you make broad my heart."

j Pss 25, 4; 27, 11; 86, 11; 143, 8. 10. k Ps 39, 13. l Ps 44, 26. m Ps 19, 12. n Pss 25, 4; 27, 11; 86, 11; 143, 8. 10.

44 I will keep your teachings always,
for all time and forever.
45 I will walk freely in an open space
because I cherish your precepts.
46 I will speak openly of your decrees
without fear even before kings.
47 I delight in your commands,
which I dearly love.
48 I lift up my hands to your commands;*
I study your laws, which I love.

ZAYIN

49 Remember your word to your servant
by which you give me hope.
50 This is my comfort in affliction,
your promise that gives me life.
51 Though the arrogant utterly scorn me,
I do not turn from your teaching.
52 When I recite your edicts of old
I am comforted, LORD.
53 Rage seizes me because of the wicked;
they forsake your teaching.
54 Your laws become my songs
wherever I make my home.
55 Even at night I remember your name
in observance of your teaching, LORD.
56 This is my good fortune,
for I have observed your precepts.

HETH

57 My portion is the LORD;
I promise to keep your words.
58 I entreat you with all my heart:
have mercy on me in accord with your
promise.
59 I have examined my ways
and turned my steps to your decrees.
60 I am prompt, I do not hesitate
in keeping your commands.
61 Though the snares of the wicked surround me,
your teaching I do not forget.
62 At midnight I rise to praise you
because your edicts are just.
63 I am the friend of all who fear you,
of all who keep your precepts.
64 The earth, LORD, is filled with your love;[o]
teach me your laws.

TETH

65 You have treated your servant well,
according to your word, O LORD.
66 Teach me wisdom and knowledge,
for in your commands I trust.
67 Before I was afflicted I went astray,
but now I hold to your promise.
68 You are good and do what is good;
teach me your laws.
69 The arrogant smear me with lies,
but I observe your precepts with all my
heart.
70 Their hearts are gross and fat;[p]
as for me, your teaching is my delight.
71 It was good for me to be afflicted,
in order to learn your laws.
72 Teaching from your lips is more precious to me
than heaps of silver and gold.

YODH

73 Your hands made me and fashioned me;
give me insight to learn your commands.
74 Those who fear you rejoice to see me,
because I hope in your word.
75 I know, LORD, that your edicts are just;
though you afflict me, you are faithful.
76 May your love comfort me
in accord with your promise to your
servant.
77 Show me compassion that I may live,
for your teaching is my delight.
78 Shame the proud for oppressing me unjustly,
that I may study your precepts.
79 Let those who fear you turn to me,
those who acknowledge your decrees.
80 May I be wholehearted toward your laws,
that I may not be put to shame.

KAPH

81 My soul longs for your salvation;
I put my hope in your word.[q]
82 My eyes long to see your promise.[r]
When will you comfort me?

119, 48: I lift up my hands to your commands: to lift up the hands was an ancient gesture of reverence to God. Here the picture is applied to God's law.

o Ps 33, 5. p Pss 17, 10; 73, 7; Jb 15, 27. q Ps 130, 6. r Pss 25, 15; 123, 1–2; 141, 8.

83 I am like a wineskin shriveled by smoke,[s]
but I have not forgotten your laws.
84 How long can your servant survive?
When will your edict doom my foes?
85 The arrogant have dug pits for me;
defying your teaching.
86 All your commands are steadfast.
Help me! I am pursued without cause.
87 They have almost ended my life on earth,
but I do not forsake your precepts.
88 In your kindness give me life,
to keep the decrees you have spoken.

LAMEDH

89 Your word, LORD, stands forever;[t*]
it is firm as the heavens.
90 Through all generations your truth endures;
fixed to stand firm like the earth.
91 By your edicts they stand firm to this day,
for all things are your servants.
92 Had your teaching not been my delight,
I would have perished in my affliction.
93 I will never forget your precepts;
through them you give me life.
94 I am yours; save me,
for I cherish your precepts.
95 The wicked hope to destroy me,
but I pay heed to your decrees.
96 I have seen the limits of all perfection,
but your command is without bounds.

MEM

97 How I love your teaching, LORD!
I study it all day long.
98 Your command makes me wiser than my foes,
for it is always with me.
99 I have more understanding than all my
teachers,
because I ponder your decrees.
100 I have more insight than my elders,
because I observe your precepts.[u]
101 I keep my steps from every evil path,
that I may obey your word.
102 From your edicts I do not turn,
for you have taught them to me.
103 How sweet to my tongue is your promise,
sweeter than honey to my mouth![v]
104 Through your precepts I gain insight;
therefore I hate all false ways.

NUN

105 Your word is a lamp for my feet,
a light for my path.[w]
106 I make a solemn vow
to keep your just edicts.
107 I am very much afflicted, LORD;
give me life in accord with your word.
108 Accept my freely offered praise;[x]
LORD, teach me your decrees.
109 My life is always at risk,
but I do not forget your teaching.
110 The wicked have set snares for me,
but from your precepts I do not stray.
111 Your decrees are my heritage forever;
they are the joy of my heart.
112 My heart is set on fulfilling your laws;
they are my reward forever.

SAMEKH

113 I hate every hypocrite;
your teaching I love.
114 You are my refuge and shield;
in your word I hope.
115 Depart from me, you wicked,[y]
that I may observe the commands of my
God.
116 Sustain me by your promise that I may live;
do not disappoint me in my hope.
117 Strengthen me that I may be safe,
ever to contemplate your laws.
118 You reject all who stray from your laws,
for vain is their deceit.
119 Like dross you regard all the wicked on earth;
therefore I love your decrees.
120 My flesh shudders with dread of you;
I hold your edicts in awe.

AYIN

121 I have fulfilled your just edict;
do not abandon me to my oppressors.
122 Guarantee your servant's welfare;

119, 89–91: God's word creates the world, which manifests that word by its permanence and reliability.

s Jb 30, 30. t Is 40, 8. u Jb 32, 6; Wis 4, 8–9. v Ps 19, 11. w Ps 18, 29; Prv 6, 23. x Ps 50, 14. 23; Heb 13, 15. y Pss 6, 9; 139, 19; Jb 21, 14.

do not let the arrogant oppress me.
123 My eyes long to see your salvation
and the justice of your promise.
124 Act with kindness toward your servant;
teach me your laws.
125 I am your servant; give me discernment
that I may know your decrees.
126 It is time for the LORD to act;
they have disobeyed your teaching.
127 Truly I love your commands
more than the finest gold.
128 Thus I follow all your precepts;
every wrong way I hate.

PE

129 Wonderful are your decrees;
therefore I observe them.
130 The revelation of your words sheds light,
gives understanding to the simple.
131 I sigh with open mouth,
yearning for your commands.
132 Turn to me and be gracious, [z]
your edict for lovers of your name.
133 Steady my feet in accord with your promise;
do not let iniquity lead me.
134 Free me from human oppression,
that I may keep your precepts.
135 Let your face shine upon your servant;
teach me your laws.
136 My eyes shed streams of tears
because your teaching is not followed.

SADHE

137 You are righteous, LORD,
and just are your edicts. [a]
138 You have issued your decrees in justice
and in surpassing faithfulness.
139 I am consumed with rage,
because my foes forget your words.
140 Your servant loves your promise;
it has been proved by fire.
141 Though belittled and despised,
I do not forget your precepts.
142 Your justice is forever right,
your teaching forever true.
143 Though distress and anguish come upon me,
your commands are my delight.
144 Your decrees are forever just;
give me discernment that I may live.

QOPH

145 I call with all my heart, O LORD;
answer me that I may observe your laws.
146 I call to you to save me
that I may keep your decrees.
147 I rise before dawn and cry out;
I put my hope in your words.
148 My eyes greet the night watches
as I meditate on your promise. [b]
149 Hear my voice in your love, O LORD;
by your edict give me life.
150 Malicious persecutors draw near me;
they are far from your teaching.
151 You are near, O LORD;
reliable are all your commands.
152 Long have I known from your decrees
that you have established them forever.

RESH

153 Look at my affliction and rescue me,
for I have not forgotten your teaching.
154 Take up my cause and redeem me; [c]
for the sake of your promise give me life.
155 Salvation is far from sinners
because they do not cherish your laws.
156 Your compassion is great, O LORD;
in accord with your edicts give me life.
157 Though my persecutors and foes are many
I do not turn from your decrees.
158 I view the faithless with loathing, [d]
because they do not heed your promise.
159 See how I love your precepts, LORD;
in your kindness give me life.
160 Your every word is enduring;
all your just edicts are forever.

SHIN

161 Princes persecute me without reason,
but my heart reveres only your word.
162 I rejoice at your promise,
as one who has found rich spoil.

z Pss 25, 16; 86, 16. a Tb 3, 2. b Pss 63, 7; 77, 7. c Ps 43, 1. d Ps 139, 22.

163 Falsehood I hate and abhor;
your teaching I love.
164 Seven times a day I praise you
because your edicts are just.
165 Lovers of your teaching have much peace; [e]
for them there is no stumbling block.
166 I look for your salvation, LORD,
and I fulfill your commands.
167 I observe your decrees;
I love them very much.
168 I observe your precepts and decrees;
all my ways are before you.

TAW

169 Let my cry come before you, LORD;[f]
in keeping with your word give me
discernment.
170 Let my prayer come before you;
rescue me according to your promise.
171 May my lips pour forth your praise,
because you teach me your laws.
172 May my tongue sing of your promise,
for all your commands are just.
173 Keep your hand ready to help me,
for I have chosen your precepts.
174 I long for your salvation, LORD;
your teaching is my delight.
175 Let me live to praise you;
may your edicts give me help.
176 I have wandered like a lost sheep;
seek out your servant,
for I do not forget your commands. [g]

PSALM 120*

Prayer of a Returned Exile

1 A song of ascents.*

I

The LORD answered me
when I called in my distress: [h]
2 LORD, deliver me from lying lips,
from treacherous tongues. [i]

II

3 What will the Lord inflict on you,
O treacherous tongue,
and what more besides?*
4 A warrior's sharpened arrows
and fiery coals of brushwood! [j]*

III

5 Alas, I was an alien in Meshech,*
I lived near the tents of Kedar!
6 Too long did I live
among those who hated peace.
7 When I spoke of peace,
they were for war. [k]

PSALM 121*

The Lord My Guardian

1 A song of ascents.

I

I raise my eyes toward the mountains.*
From where will my help come? [l]
2 My help comes from the LORD,
the maker of heaven and earth. [m]

Ps 120: A thanksgiving, reporting divine rescue (1) yet with fervent prayer for further protection against lying attackers (2–4). The psalmist is acutely conscious of living away from God's own land where divine peace prevails (5–7).

120, 1: Song of ascents: Pss 120–134 all begin with this superscription. Most probably these fifteen psalms once formed a collection of psalms sung when pilgrims went to Jerusalem, since one "ascended" to Jerusalem (1 Kgs 12, 28; Pss 24, 3; 122, 4; Lk 2, 42) or to the house of God or to an altar (1 Kgs 12, 33; 2 Kgs 23, 2; Ps 24, 3). Less probable is the explanation that these psalms were sung by the exiles when they "ascended" to Jerusalem from Babylonia (cf Ezr 7, 9). The idea, found in the Mishnah, that the fifteen steps on which the Levites sang corresponded to these fifteen psalms (*Middot* 2, 5) must underlie the Vulgate translation *canticum graduum*, "song of the steps" or "gradual song."

120, 3: More besides: a common curse formula in Hebrew was "May the Lord do such and such evils to you [the evils being specified], and add *still more* to them." Cf 1 Sm 3, 17; 14, 44; 25, 22. Here the psalmist is at a loss for a suitable malediction.

120, 4: Coals of brushwood: coals made from the stalk of the broom plant burn with intense heat. The psalmist thinks of lighted coals cast at his enemies.

120, 5: Meshech was in the far north (Gn 10, 2) and **Kedar** was a tribe of the north Arabian desert (Gn 25, 13). The psalmist may be thinking generally of all aliens living among inhospitable peoples.

Ps 121: A blessing given to someone embarking on a dangerous journey, whether a soldier going on a campaign or a pilgrim returning home from the temple. People look anxiously at the wooded hills. Will God protect them on their journey (1)? The speaker declares that God is not confined to a place or a time (2), that every step is guarded (3–4); night and day (5–6) God watches over their every movement (7–8).

121, 1: The mountains: possibly Mount Zion, the site of the temple and hence of safety, but more probably mountains as a place of dangers, causing anxiety to the psalmist.

e Ps 72, 7. f Ps 88, 3. g Is 53, 6; Jer 50, 6; Lk 15, 1–7. h Jon 2, 3. i Ps 12, 3–5; Sir 51, 3. j Pss 11, 6; 140, 11; Prv 16, 27. k Pss 35, 20; 140, 3–4. l Jer 3, 23. m Pss 124, 8; 146, 6.

II

3 God will not allow your foot to slip; [n]
your guardian does not sleep.
4 Truly, the guardian of Israel
never slumbers nor sleeps.
5 The LORD is your guardian; *
the LORD is your shade
at your right hand. [o]
6 By day the sun cannot harm you,
nor the moon by night. [p]
7 The LORD will guard you from all evil,
will always guard your life. [q]
8 The LORD will guard your coming and going
both now and forever. [r]

PSALM 122*

A Pilgrim's Prayer for Jerusalem

1 A song of ascents. Of David.

I

I rejoiced when they said to me,
"Let us go to the house of the LORD." [s]
2 And now our feet are standing
within your gates, Jerusalem.
3 Jerusalem, built as a city,
walled round about. [t] *
4 Here the tribes have come,
the tribes of the LORD,
As it was decreed for Israel,
to give thanks to the name of the LORD. [u]
5 Here are the thrones of justice,
the thrones of the house of David.

II

6 For the peace of Jersusalem pray:
"May those who love you prosper!
7 May peace be within your ramparts,
prosperity within your towers." [v]
8 For family and friends I say,
"May peace be yours."
9 For the house of the LORD, our God, I pray,
"May blessings be yours."

PSALM 123*

Reliance on the Lord

1 A song of ascents.

To you I raise my eyes,
to you enthroned in heaven. [w]
2 Yes, like the eyes of a servant
on the hand of his master,
Like the eyes of a maid
on the hand of her mistress,
So our eyes are on the LORD our God,
till we are shown favor.
3 Show us favor, LORD, show us favor,
for we have our fill of contempt. [x]
4 We have our fill of insult from the insolent,
of disdain from the arrogant.

PSALM 124*

God, the Rescuer of the People

1 A song of ascents. Of David.

I

Had not the LORD been with us,
let Israel say, [y]
2 Had not the LORD been with us,
when people rose against us,
3 They would have swallowed us alive, [z]
for their fury blazed against us.
4 The waters would have engulfed us,

121, 5–6: The image of shade, a symbol of protection, is apt: God as shade protects from the harmful effects that ancients believed were caused by the sun and moon.

Ps 122: A song of Zion, sung by pilgrims obeying the law to visit Jerusalem three times on a journey. The singer anticipates joining the procession into the city (1–3). Jerusalem is a place of encounter, where the people praise God (4) and hear the divine justice mediated by the king (5). The very buildings bespeak God's power (cf Ps 48, 13–15). May the grace of this place transform the people's lives (6–9)!

122, 3: Walled round about: literally, "which is joined to it," probably referring both to the density of the buildings and to the dense population.

Ps 123: A lament that begins as a prayer of an individual (1), who expresses by a touching comparison exemplary confidence in God (2). The psalm ends in prayer that God relieve the people's humiliation at the hands of the arrogant (3–4).

Ps 124: A thanksgiving which teaches that Israel's very existence is owed to God who rescues them. In the first part Israel's enemies are compared to the mythic sea dragon (2b–3a; cf Jer 51, 34) and Flood (3b–5; cf Is 51, 9–10). The psalm heightens the malice of human enemies by linking them to the primordial enemies of God's creation. Israel is a bird freed from the trapper's snare (6–8)—freed originally from Pharaoh and now from the current danger.

124, 8: Our help is the name: for the idiom, see Ex 18, 4.

Ps 125: In response to exilic anxieties about the ancient promises of restoration, the psalm expresses confidence that God will

n Pss 66, 9; 91, 12; 1 Sm 2, 9; Prv 3, 23. o Pss 16, 8; 73, 23. p Wis 18, 3; Is 25, 4; 49, 10. q Ps 97, 10. r Dt 28, 6. s Pss 43, 3–4; 84, 2–5. t Ps 48, 13–14. u Dt 16, 16. v Ps 128, 5. w Pss 25, 15; 119, 82; 141, 8. x Ps 44, 13–14; Jb 12, 4. y Ps 129, 1. z Prv 1, 12.

the torrent overwhelmed us; [a]
5 seething waters would have drowned us.

II

6 Blessed be the LORD, who did not leave us
to be torn by their fangs.
7 We escaped with our lives
like a bird from the fowler's snare;
the snare was broken and we escaped.
8 Our help is the name* of the LORD,
the maker of heaven and earth. [b]

PSALM 125*

Israel's Protector

1 A song of ascents.

I

Like Mount Zion are they
who trust in the LORD,
unshakable, forever enduring. [c]
2 As mountains surround Jerusalem,
the LORD surrounds his people
both now and forever. [d]

II

3 The scepter of the wicked will not prevail
in the land given to the just,*
Lest the just themselves
turn their hands to evil.

III

4 Do good, LORD, to the good,
to those who are upright of heart. [e]
5 But those who turn aside to crooked ways
may the LORD send down with the wicked. [f]
Peace upon Israel! [g]

PSALM 126*

The Reversal of Zion's Fortunes

1 A song of ascents.

I

When the LORD restored the fortunes of Zion, [h]
then we thought we were dreaming.
2 Our mouths were filled with laughter;
our tongues sang for joy. [i]
Then it was said among the nations,
"The LORD has done great things for them."
3 The LORD had done great things for us;
Oh, how happy we were!
4 Restore again our fortunes, LORD,
like the dry stream beds of the Negeb.*

II

5 Those who sow in tears
will reap with cries of joy. [j]
6 Those who go forth weeping,
carrying sacks of seed,
Will return with cries of joy,
carrying their bundled sheaves.

PSALM 127*

The Need of God's Blessing

1 A song of ascents. Of Solomon.

I

Unless the LORD build the house,
they labor in vain who build.
Unless the LORD guard the city,
in vain does the guard keep watch.
2 It is vain for you to rise early
and put off your rest at night,
To eat bread earned by hard toil—
all this God gives to his beloved in sleep. [k]

II

3 Children too are a gift from the LORD,
the fruit of the womb, a reward. [l]
4 Like arrows in the hand of a warrior
are the children born in one's youth.
5 Blessed are they whose quivers are full.
They will never be shamed
contending with foes at the gate.*

---

surround the people as the mountains surround Zion (1–2). The just will not be contaminated by the wicked (3). May God judge between the two groups (4–5).

125, 3: **The land given to the just**: literally, "the lot of the just." The promised land was divided among the tribes of Israel by lot (Nm 26, 55; Jos 18). **The just** are the members of the people who are obedient to God. If the domination of the wicked were to continue in the land, even the just would be infected by their evil attitudes.

Ps 126: A lament probably sung shortly after Israel's return from exile. The people rejoice that they are in Zion (1–3) but mere presence in the holy city is not enough; they must pray for the prosperity and the fertility of the land (4). The last verses are probably an oracle of promise: the painful work of sowing will be crowned with life (5–6).

126, 4: **Like the dry stream beds of the Negeb**: the psalmist prays for rain in such abundance that the dry riverbeds will run.

Ps 127: The psalm puts together two proverbs (1–2 and 3–5) on God establishing "houses" or families. The prosperity of human groups is not the work of humans but the gift of God.

127, 5: **At the gate**: the reference is not to enemies besieging

a Pss 18, 5; 69, 2. b Pss 121, 2; 146, 6. c Prv 10, 25. d Dt 32, 11. e Ps 18, 25ff. f Prv 3, 32. g Ps 128, 6. h Ps 14, 7. i Jb 8, 21. j Bar 4, 23; Is 65, 19. k Eccl 2, 24. l Pss 115, 14; 128, 3; Dt 28, 11; Prv 17, 6.

PSALM 128*

The Happy Home of the Just

1 A song of ascents.

I

Happy are all who fear the LORD,*
who walk in the ways of God. [m]
2 What your hands provide you will enjoy;
you will be happy and prosper: [n]
3 Like a fruitful vine
your wife within your home,
Like olive plants
your children around your table. [o]
4 Just so will they be blessed
who fear the LORD.

II

5 May the LORD bless you from Zion,
all the days of your life [p]
That you may share Jerusalem's joy
6 and live to see your children's children. [q]
Peace upon Israel! [r]

PSALM 129*

Against Israel's Enemies

1 A song of ascents.

I

Much have they oppressed me from my youth,
now let Israel say. [s]
2 Much have they oppressed me from my
youth, [t]
yet they have not prevailed.
3 Upon my back the plowers plowed,
as they traced their long furrows. [u]
4 But the just LORD cut me free
from the ropes of the yoke of the wicked.*

II

5 May they be scattered in disgrace,
all who hate Zion.
6 May they be like grass on the rooftops*
withered in early growth, [v]
7 Never to fill the reaper's hands,
nor the arms of the binders of sheaves,
8 With none passing by to call out:
"The blessing of the LORD be upon you!*
We bless you in the name of the LORD!" [w]

PSALM 130*

Prayer for Pardon and Mercy

1 A song of ascents.

I

Out of the depths* I call to you, LORD;
2 Lord, hear my cry!
May your ears be attentive
to my cry for mercy. [x]
3 If you, LORD, mark our sins,
Lord, who can stand? [y]
4 But with you is forgiveness
and so you are revered.*

II

5 I wait with longing for the LORD,
my soul waits for his word. [z]

---

the walls of a city but to adversaries in litigation. Law courts functioned in the open area near the main city gate. The more adult sons a man had, the more forceful he would appear in disputes. Cf Prv 31, 23.

Ps 128: A statement that the ever-reliable God will bless the reverent (1). God's blessing is concrete: satisfaction and prosperity, a fertile spouse and abundant children (2–4). The perspective is that of the adult male, ordinarily the ruler and representative of the household to the community. The last verses extend the blessing to all the people for generations to come (5–6).

128, 1: **All who fear the LORD**: literally, singular: "the one fearing," is used in a typical sense and so is translated by the plural.

Ps 129: A psalm giving thanks for God's many rescues of Israel over the long course of their history (1–4); the people pray that their oppressors never know the joy of harvest (5–8).

129, 4: **The ropes of the yoke of the wicked**: usually understood as the rope for yoking animals to the plow. If it is severed, the plowing (cf 3) comes to a halt.

129, 6: **Like grass on the rooftops**: after the spring rains, grass would sprout from the coat of mud with which the flat roofs of simple houses were covered, but when the dry summer began there was no moisture in the thin roof-covering to sustain the grass.

129, 8: **The blessing of the LORD be upon you**: harvesters greeted one another with such blessings. Cf Ru 2, 4.

Ps 130: This lament, a Penitential Psalm, is the *De profundis* used in liturgical prayers for the faithful departed. In deep sorrow the psalmist cries to God (1–2), asking for mercy (3–4). The psalmist's trust (5–6) becomes a model for the people (7–8).

130, 1: **The depths**: Sheol here is a metaphor of total misery. Deep anguish makes the psalmist feel "like those descending to the pit" (Ps 143, 7).

130, 4: **And so you are revered**: the experience of God's mercy leads one to a greater sense of God.

m Ps 112, 1. n Ps 112, 3. o Jb 29, 5; Ps 144, 12. p Pss 20, 3; 134, 3. q Jb 42, 16; Prv 17, 6. r Ps 125, 5. s Ps 124, 1. t Ps 118, 13. u Is 51, 23. v Is 37, 27. w Ps 118, 26. x Pss 5, 2–3; 55, 2–3; 86, 6; Lam 3, 55–56; Jon 2, 3. y Na 1, 6. z Ps 119, 81.

6 My soul looks for the Lord
more than sentinels for daybreak. [a]
More than sentinels for daybreak,
7 let Israel look for the LORD,
For with the LORD is kindness,
with him is full redemption, [b]
8 And God will redeem Israel
from all their sins. [c]

PSALM 131*

Humble Trust in God

1 A song of ascents. Of David.

LORD, my heart is not proud;
nor are my eyes haughty.
I do not busy myself with great matters,
with things too sublime for me. [d]
2 Rather, I have stilled my soul,
hushed it like a weaned child.
Like a weaned child on its mother's lap,
so is my soul within me. [e]
3 Israel, hope in the LORD,
now and forever.

PSALM 132*

The Covenant between David and God

1 A song of ascents.

I

LORD, remember David
and all his anxious care;*
2 How he swore an oath to the LORD,
vowed to the Mighty One of Jacob:*
3 "I will not enter the house where I live, [f]
nor lie on the couch where I sleep;
4 I will give my eyes no sleep,
my eyelids no rest,
5 Till I find a home for the LORD,
a dwelling for the Mighty One of Jacob."
6 "We have heard of it in Ephrathah;*
we have found it in the fields of Jaar.*
7 Let us enter God's dwelling;
let us worship at God's footstool." [g]
8 "Arise, LORD, come to your resting place, [h]
you and your majestic ark.
9 Your priests will be clothed with justice;
your faithful will shout for joy."
10 For the sake of David your servant,
do not reject your anointed.

II

11 The LORD swore an oath to David,
a pledge never to be broken: [i]
"Your own offspring [j] I will set upon your throne.
12 If your sons observe my covenant,
the laws I shall teach them,
Their sons, in turn,
shall sit forever on your throne."
13 Yes, the LORD has chosen Zion,
desired it for a dwelling:
14 "This is my resting place forever;
here I will dwell, for I desire it.
15 I will bless Zion with meat;
its poor I will fill with bread.
16 I will clothe its priests with blessing;
its faithful shall shout for joy. [k]
17 There I will make a horn sprout for David's line; [l]*
I will set a lamp for my anointed.

Ps 131: A song of trust, in which the psalmist gives up self-sufficiency (1), like a babe enjoying the comfort of its mother's lap (2), thus providing a model for Israel's faith (3).

Ps 132: A song for a liturgical ceremony in which the ark, the throne of Israel's God, was carried in procession to the temple. The singer asks that David's care for the proper housing of the ark be regarded with favor (1–5), and tells how it was brought to Jerusalem (6–10). There follows God's promise of favor to the Davidic dynasty (11–12) and to Zion (13–17). The transfer of the ark to the tent in Jerusalem is described in 2 Sm 6.

132, 1: All his anxious care: to build the temple. Cf 2 Sm 7, 1–17 and 1 Kgs 8, 17.

132, 2. 5: Mighty One of Jacob: one of the titles of Israel's God. Cf Gn 49, 24; Is 49, 26; 60, 16.

132, 6: Ephrathah: the homeland of David. Cf Ru 4, 11. **The fields of Jaar**: poetic for Kiriath-jearim, a town west of Jerusalem, where the ark remained for several generations. Cf 1 Sm 7, 1–2 ; 2 Sm 6, 2; 1 Chr 13, 5–6.

132, 17: A horn sprout for David's line: the image of the horn, a symbol of strength, is combined with that of a "sprout," a term used for the Davidic descendant (cf Jer 23, 5; 33, 15; Zec 3, 8; 6, 12). Early Christians referred the latter designation to Christ as son of David (Lk 1, 69).

a Is 21, 11; 26, 9. b Pss 86, 15; 100, 5; 103, 8. c Ps 25, 22; Mt 1, 21. d Ps 139, 6. e Is 66, 12–13. f 2 Sm 7; 1 Chr 28, 2. g Ps 99, 5. h 8–10: Pss 2, 2; 89, 21; 95, 11; Nm 10, 35; 2 Chr 6, 41–42; Sir 24, 7. i Ps 110, 4; 2 Sm 7, 12. j 11–14: Ps 68, 17; 1 Kgs 8, 13; Sir 24, 7. k 2 Chr 6, 41; Is 61, 10. l Is 11, 1; Jer 33, 15; Ez 29, 21; Zec 3, 8; Lk 1, 69.

18 His foes I will clothe with shame,
but on him my crown shall gleam."

PSALM 133*

A Vision of a Blessed Community

1 A song of ascents. Of David.

How good it is, how pleasant,
where the people* dwell as one!
2 Like precious ointment* on the head, [m]
running down upon the beard,
Upon the beard of Aaron,
upon the collar of his robe.
3 Like dew* of Hermon* coming down
upon the mountains of Zion. [n]
There the LORD has lavished blessings,
life for evermore! [o]

PSALM 134*

Exhortation to the Night Watch to Bless God

1 A song of ascents.

Come, bless the LORD,
all you servants of the LORD*
Who stand in the house of the LORD
through the long hours of night. [p]
2 Lift up your hands toward the sanctuary, [q]
and bless the LORD.
3 May the LORD who made heaven and earth [r]
bless you from Zion.

PSALM 135*

Praise of God, the Ruler and Benefactor of Israel

1 Hallelujah!

I

Praise the name of the LORD!
Praise, you servants of the LORD, [s]
2 Who stand in the house of the LORD,
in the courts of the house of our God! [t]
3 Praise the LORD; the LORD is good!
Sing to God's name; it is gracious!
4 For the LORD has chosen Jacob,
Israel as a treasured possession. [u]*

II

5 I know that the LORD is great,
our Lord is greater than all gods. [v]
6 Whatever the LORD wishes
he does in heaven and on earth,
in the seas and in all the deeps. [w]
7 He raises storm clouds from the end of the earth,
makes lightning and rain,
brings forth wind from the storehouse. [x]

III

8 He struck down Egypt's firstborn, [y]
human and beast alike,
9 And sent signs and portents against you, Egypt,
against Pharaoh and all his servants.
10 The Lord struck down many nations, [z]
slew mighty kings—

Ps 133: A benediction over a peaceful community, most probably the people Israel, but appropriate too for Israelite families (1). The history of Israel, whether of its ancestors in the book of Genesis or of later periods, was a history of distinct groups struggling to live in unity. Here that unity is declared blessed, like the holy oils upon the priest Aaron or the dew of the rainless summer that waters the crops (2–3).

133, 1: The people: literally, "brothers," i.e., male and female members of a kin group or people—most probably, the people Israel.

133, 2: Ointment: oil was used at the consecration of the high priest (Ex 30, 22–33).

133, 3: Dew: dew was an important source of moisture in the dry climate (Gn 27, 28; Hos 14, 6). **Hermon:** the majestic snow-capped mountain visible in the north of Palestine.

Ps 134: A brief liturgy exhorting the temple singers to acknowledge the great deeds of God at a night service (cf Is 30, 29). Mount Zion is the place from which blessings affect the lives of humans, for there Israel's God dwells.

134, 1: Servants of the LORD: priests and Levites. Cf Dt 10, 8; Pss 113, 1; 135, 1; Dn 3, 84–85.

Ps 135: The hymn begins and ends with an invitation to praise God (1–3. 19–20) for the great act of choosing Israel (4). The story of Israel's emergence as a people is told in 5–14; God created and redeemed the people, easily conquering all opposition. God's defeat of hostile powers means that the powers themselves and their images are useless (15–18). The last three verses appear also in Ps 115, 4–8.

135, 4: Though all nations are God's, Israel has a special status as God's "treasured" people: Ex 19, 5; Dt 7, 6; 14, 2; 26, 18; Mal 3, 17.

m Ex 30, 25. 30. n Hos 14, 6. o Dt 28, 8; 30, 20. p Ps 135, 1–2; 1 Chr 9, 33. q Pss 28, 2; 141, 2. r Pss 20, 3; 128, 5; Nm 6, 24. s Ps 113, 1. t Ps 134, 1. u Pss 33, 12; 144, 15; Ex 19, 6; Dt 7, 6. v Ps 95, 3; Ex 18, 11. w Ps 115, 3. x Ps 148, 8; Jer 10, 13; 51, 16; Jb 37, 9. y 8–9: Pss 78, 51; 105, 27. 36; 136, 10; Ex 12, 29. z 10–12: Nm 21, 21–35; Dt 2, 24—3, 17; Ps 136, 17–22.

11 Sihon, king of the Amorites,
Og, king of Bashan,
all the kings of Canaan—
12 And made their land a heritage,
a heritage for Israel his people.
13 O LORD, your name is forever,
your renown, from age to age! [a]
14 For the LORD defends his people,
shows mercy to his servants. [b]

IV

15 The idols of the nations are silver and gold, [c]
the work of human hands.
16 They have mouths but speak not;
they have eyes but see not;
17 They have ears but hear not;
no breath is in their mouths.
18 Their makers shall be like them,
all who trust in them.

V

19 House of Israel, bless the LORD! [d]
House of Aaron, bless the LORD!
20 House of Levi, bless the LORD!
You who fear the LORD, bless the LORD!
21 Blessed from Zion be the LORD,
who dwells in Jerusalem!
Hallelujah!

PSALM 136*

Hymn of Thanksgiving for God's Everlasting Love

I

1 Praise the LORD, who is so good; [e]
God's love endures forever;
2 Praise the God of gods;
God's love endures forever;
3 Praise the Lord of lords;
God's love endures forever;

II

4 Who alone has done great wonders, [f]
God's love endures forever;
5 Who skillfully made the heavens, [g]
God's love endures forever;
6 Who spread the earth upon the waters, [h]
God's love endures forever;
7 Who made the great lights,
God's love endures forever;
8 The sun to rule the day,
God's love endures forever;
9 The moon and stars to rule the night, [i]
God's love endures forever;

III

10 Who struck down the firstborn of Egypt, [j]
God's love endures forever;
11 And led Israel from their midst,
God's love endures forever;
12 With mighty hand and outstretched arm, [k]
God's love endures forever;
13 Who split in two the Red Sea,
God's love endures forever;
14 And led Israel through,
God's love endures forever;
15 But swept Pharaoh and his army into the Red
Sea, [l]
God's love endures forever;
16 Who led the people through the desert, [m]
God's love endures forever;

IV

17 Who struck down great kings, [n]
God's love endures forever;
18 Slew powerful kings,
God's love endures forever;
19 Sihon, king of the Amorites,
God's love endures forever;
20 Og, king of Bashan,
God's love endures forever;
21 And made their lands a heritage,
God's love endures forever;
22 A heritage for Israel,* God's servant,
God's love endures forever.

Ps 136: The hymn praises Israel's God ("the God of gods," 2), who has created the world in which Israel lives. The refrain occurring after every line suggests that a speaker and chorus sang the psalm in antiphonal fashion. A single act of God is described in 4–25: God arranges the heavens and the earth as the environment for human community, and then creates the community by freeing them and giving them land. In the final section (23–25) God, who created the people and gave them land, continues to protect and nurture them.

136, 22: A heritage for Israel: the land was given to Israel by God to be handed on to future generations.

a Ps 102, 13; Ex 3, 15. b Dt 32, 36. c 15–18: Ps 115, 4–6. 8. d 19–20: Ps 118, 2–4. e Pss 100, 5; 118, 1. f Ps 72, 18. g Gn 1, 9–19. h Ps 24, 2. i Jer 31, 35. j Ex 12, 29. 51; 14, 22. 27; 15, 22; Pss 78, 51–52; 135, 8. k Dt 4, 34. l Ex 14, 21f. m Dt 8, 2. 15. n 17–22: Ps 135, 10–12.

V

23 The LORD remembered us in our misery,
God's love endures forever;
24 Freed us from our foes,
God's love endures forever;
25 And gives food to all flesh,
God's love endures forever.

VI

26 Praise the God of heaven,
God's love endures forever.

PSALM 137*

Sorrow and Hope in Exile

I

1 By the rivers of Babylon
we sat mourning and weeping
when we remembered Zion. [o]
2 On the poplars* of that land
we hung up our harps. [p]
3 There our captors asked us
for the words of a song;
Our tormentors, for a joyful song:
"Sing for us a song of Zion!"
4 But how could we sing a song of the LORD
in a foreign land?

II

5 If I forget you, Jerusalem,
may my right hand wither. [q]
6 May my tongue stick to my palate
if I do not remember you,
If I do not exalt Jerusalem
beyond all my delights.

III

7 Remember, LORD, against Edom
that day at Jerusalem.
They said: "Level it, level it
down to its foundations!" [r]
8 Fair Babylon, you destroyer,
happy those who pay you back
the evil you have done us! [s]
9 Happy those who seize your children
and smash them against a rock. [t]*

PSALM 138*

Hymn of a Grateful Heart

1 Of David.

I

I thank you, LORD, with all my heart; [u]
before the gods* to you I sing.
2 I bow low toward your holy temple;
I praise your name for your fidelity and love.
For you have exalted over all
your name and your promise.
3 When I cried out, you answered;
you strengthened my spirit.

II

4 All the kings of earth will praise you, LORD,
when they hear the words of your mouth.
5 They will sing of the ways of the LORD:
"How great is the glory of the LORD!"
6 The LORD is on high, but cares for the lowly [v]
and knows the proud from afar.
7 Though I walk in the midst of dangers,
you guard my life when my enemies rage.
You stretch out your hand;
your right hand saves me.
8 The LORD is with me to the end.
LORD, your love endures forever.
Never forsake the work of your hands!

Ps 137: A temple singer refuses to sing the people's sacred songs in an alien land despite demands from Babylonian captors (1–4). The singer swears an oath by what is most dear to a musician—hands and tongue—to exalt Jerusalem always (5–6). The psalm ends with a prayer that the old enemies of Jerusalem, Edom and Babylon, be destroyed (7–9).

137, 2: Poplars: sometimes incorrectly translated "willow." The Euphrates poplar is a high tree common on riverbanks in the Orient.

137, 9: Happy those who seize your children and smash them against a rock: the infants represent the future generations, and so must be destroyed if the enemy is truly to be eradicated.

Ps 138: A thanksgiving to God, who came to the rescue of the psalmist. Divine rescue was not the result of the psalmist's virtues but of God's loving fidelity (1–3). The act is not a private transaction but a public act that stirs the surrounding nations to praise God's greatness and care for the people (4–6). The psalmist, having experienced salvation, trusts that God will always be there in moments of danger (7–8).

138, 1: Before the gods: i.e., heavenly beings, who were completely subordinate to Israel's God. The earthly temple represents the heavenly palace of God.

o Ez 3, 15; Lam 3, 48. p Is 24, 8; Lam 5, 14. q Jer 51, 50. r Jer 49, 7; Lam 4, 21–22; Ez 25, 12–14. s Is 47, 1–3; Jer 50–51. t Hos 14, 1. u Ps 9, 1. v Lk 1, 51–52.

PSALM 139*

The All-knowing and Ever-present God

1 For the leader. A psalm of David.

I

LORD, you have probed me, you know me:
2 you know when I sit and stand; [w]*
you understand my thoughts from afar.
3 My travels and my rest you mark;
with all my ways you are familiar.
4 Even before a word is on my tongue,
LORD, you know it all.
5 Behind and before you encircle me
and rest your hand upon me.
6 Such knowledge is beyond me,
far too lofty for me to reach. [x]

II

7 Where can I hide from your spirit?
From your presence, where can I flee?
8 If I ascend to the heavens, you are there;
if I lie down in Sheol, you are there too. [y]
9 If I fly with the wings of dawn*
and alight beyond the sea,*
10 Even there your hand will guide me,
your right hand hold me fast.
11 If I say, "Surely darkness shall hide me,
and night shall be my light" —*
12 Darkness is not dark for you,
and night shines as the day.
Darkness and light are but one. [z]

III

13 You formed my inmost being;
you knit me in my mother's womb. [a]
14 I praise you, so wonderfully you made me;
wonderful are your works!
My very self you knew;
15 my bones were not hidden from you,
When I was being made in secret,
fashioned as in the depths of the earth.*
16 Your eyes foresaw my actions;
in your book all are written down; [b]
my days were shaped, before one came to be.

IV

17 How precious to me are your designs, O God;
how vast the sum of them!
18 Were I to count, they would outnumber the sands;
to finish, I would need eternity. [c]
19 If only you would destroy the wicked, O God,
and the bloodthirsty would depart from me! [d]
20 Deceitfully they invoke your name;
your foes swear faithless oaths.
21 Do I not hate, LORD, those who hate you?
Those who rise against you, do I not loathe? [e]
22 With fierce hatred I hate them,
enemies I count as my own.

V

23 Probe me, God, know my heart;
try me, know my concerns. [f]
24 See if my way is crooked,
then lead me in the ancient paths.*

PSALM 140*

Prayer for Deliverance from the Wicked

1 For the leader. A psalm of David.

I

2 Deliver me, LORD, from the wicked;
preserve me from the violent, [g]

Ps 139: A hymnic meditation on God's omnipresence and omniscience. The psalmist is keenly aware of God's all-knowing gaze (1–6), of God's presence in every part of the universe (7–12), and of God's control over the psalmist's very self (13–16). Summing up 1–16, 17–18 express wonder. There is only one place hostile to God's rule—wicked people. The psalmist prays to be removed from their company (19–24).

139, 2: When I sit and stand: in all my physical movement.

139, 9: Fly with the wings of dawn: go to the extremities of the east. **Beyond the sea:** uttermost bounds of the west; the sea is the Mediterranean.

139, 11: Night shall be my light: night to me is what day is to others.

139, 15: The depths of the earth: figurative language for the womb, stressing the hidden and mysterious operations that occur there.

139, 24: My way . . . the ancient paths: the manner of living of our ancestors, who were faithful to God's will. Cf Jer 6, 16.

Ps 140: A lament seeking rescue from violent and treacherous foes (2–6). The psalmist remains trusting (7–8), vigorously praying that the plans of the wicked recoil upon themselves (9–12). A serene statement of praise ends the psalm (13–14). The psalmist is content to be known as one of "the needy," "the poor," "the just," "the upright" (13–14), a class of people expecting divine protection.

w 2 Kgs 19, 27; Jb 12, 13. x Ps 131, 1. y Jb 23, 8–9; Jer 23, 23–24. z Jb 12, 22. a Wis 7, 1; Eccl 11, 5; Jb 1, 21. b Mal 3, 16. c Jb 11, 7. d Jb 21, 14. e Ps 119, 158. f Pss 17, 3; 26, 2. g Ps 71, 4.

3 From those who plan evil in their hearts,
who stir up conflicts every day,
4 Who sharpen their tongues like serpents,
venom of asps upon their lips. [h]* *Selah*

II

5 Keep me, LORD, from the clutches of the wicked;
preserve me from the violent,
who plot to trip me up. [i]
6 The arrogant have set a trap for me;
villains have spread a net,*
laid snares for me by the wayside. *Selah*
7 I say to the LORD: You are my God; [j]
listen, LORD, to the words of my prayer.
8 My revered LORD, my strong helper,
my helmet on the day of battle.
9 LORD, do not grant the desires of the wicked;
do not let their plots succeed. *Selah*
10 Around me they raise their proud heads;
may the mischief they threaten overwhelm them.
11 May God rain burning coals upon them, [k]
cast them into the grave never more to rise.

III

12 Slanderers will not survive on earth;
evil will quickly entrap the violent.
13 For I know the LORD will secure
justice for the needy, their rights for the poor.
14 Then the just will give thanks to your name;
the upright will dwell in your presence. [l]

PSALM 141*

Prayer for Deliverance from the Wicked

1 A psalm of David.

LORD, I call to you;
come quickly to help me;
listen to my plea when I call.
2 Let my prayer be incense* before you;
my uplifted hands* an evening sacrifice. [m]
3 Set a guard, LORD, before my mouth,
a gatekeeper at my lips. [n]
4 Do not let my heart incline to evil,
or yield to any sin.
I will never feast upon
the fine food of evildoers.
5 Let the just strike me; that is kindness;*
let them rebuke me; that is oil for my head. [o]
All this I shall not refuse,
but will pray despite these trials.
6 When their leaders are cast over the cliff,
all will learn that my prayers were heard.
7 As when a farmer plows a field into broken clods,
so their bones will be strewn at the mouth of Sheol.
8 My eyes are upon you, O GOD, my Lord; [p]
in you I take refuge; do not strip me of life.
9 Guard me from the trap they have set for me,
from the snares of evildoers. [q]
10 Into their own nets let all the wicked fall,
while I make good my own escape.

PSALM 142*

A Prayer in Time of Trouble

1 A *maskil* of David, when he was in the cave.*
A prayer.

2 With full voice I cry to the LORD;
with full voice I beseech the LORD.
3 Before God I pour out my complaint,
lay bare my distress.
4 My spirit is faint within me, [r]
but you know my path. [s]

140, 4: Similar metaphors for a wicked tongue are used in Pss 52, 4; 55, 22; 58, 5.

140, 6: **Have set a trap . . . have spread a net**: the same figure, of hunters setting traps, occurs in Pss 9, 16; 31, 5; 35, 7; 64, 6. Cf Mt 22, 15; Lk 11, 54.

Ps 141: A lament of an individual (1–2) who is keenly aware that only the righteous can worship God properly and who therefore prays to be protected from the doomed wicked (3–10).

141, 2: **Incense**: literally, "smoke," i.e., the fragrant fumes arising from the altar at the burning of sacrificial animals or of aromatic spices; also used in Rv 5, 8 as a symbol of prayer. **My uplifted hands**: the gesture of supplication. Cf Pss 28, 2; 63, 5; 88, 10; 119, 48; 134, 2; 143, 6.

141, 5–7: The Hebrew text is obscure.

Ps 142: In this lament imploring God for help (2–4b), the psalmist tells how enemies have set a trap (4c–5), and prays for rescue (6–8). The speaker feels utterly alone (5), exhausted (7), and may even be imprisoned (8a). Prison is possibly a metaphor for general distress. The last two verses are the vow of praise, made after receiving an assurance of divine help (8cd).

142, 1: **In the cave**: cf 1 Sm 22, 1; 24, 1–3; Ps 57, 1.

h Ps 64, 4; Rom 3, 13. i Jer 18, 22; Pss 56, 7; 57, 7. j Ps 31, 15. k Pss 11, 6; 120, 4; Gn 19, 24. l Pss 11, 7; 16, 11; 17, 15. m Ps 134, 2; Ex 30, 8. n Sir 22, 27. o Prv 9, 8; 25, 12. p Pss 25, 15; 123, 1–2. q Ps 142, 4. r Ps 143, 4. s Ps 139, 24.

Along the way I walk
they have hidden a trap for me. [t]
5 I look to my right hand, [u]
but no friend is there.
There is no escape for me;
no one cares for me.
6 I cry out to you, LORD,
I say, You are my refuge, [v]
my portion in the land of the living. [w]
7 Listen to my cry for help,
for I am brought very low. [x]
Rescue me from my pursuers,
for they are too strong for me.
8 Lead me out of my prison,
that I may give thanks to your name.
Then the just shall gather around me*
because you have been good to me.

PSALM 143*

A Prayer in Distress

1 A psalm of David.

LORD, hear my prayer;
in your faithfulness listen to my pleading;
answer me in your justice.
2 Do not enter into judgment with your servant;
before you no living being can be just. [y]
3 The enemy has pursued me;
they have crushed* my life to the ground. [z]
They have left me in darkness
like those long dead. [a]
4 My spirit is faint within me;
my heart is dismayed. [b]
5 I remember the days of old;
I ponder all your deeds;
the works of your hands I recall. [c]
6 I stretch out my hands to you;
I thirst for you like a parched land. [d] *Selah*
7 Hasten to answer me, LORD;
for my spirit fails me.
Do not hide your face from me,
lest I become like those descending to the pit. [e]
8 At dawn let me hear of your kindness,
for in you I trust.
Show me the path I should walk,
for to you I entrust my life. [f]
9 Rescue me, LORD, from my foes,
for in you I hope.
10 Teach me to do your will,
for you are my God.
May your kind spirit guide me
on ground that is level.
11 For your name's sake, LORD, give me life;
in your justice lead me out of distress.
12 In your kindness put an end to my foes;
destroy all who attack me,
for I am your servant. [g]

PSALM 144*

A Prayer for Victory and Prosperity

1 Of David.

I

Blessed be the LORD, my rock,*
who trains my hands for battle,
my fingers for war;
2 My safeguard and my fortress,
my stronghold, my deliverer,
My shield, in whom I trust,

142, 8: Then the just shall gather around me: in the temple, when the psalmist offers a thanksgiving sacrifice.

Ps 143: One of the Church's seven Penitential Psalms, this lament is a prayer to be freed from death-dealing enemies. The psalmist addresses God, aware that there is no equality between God and humans; salvation is a gift (1–2). Victimized by evil people (3–4), the psalmist recites ("remembers") God's past actions on behalf of the innocent (5–6). The psalm continues with fervent prayer (7–9) and a strong desire for guidance and protection (10–12).

143, 3: They have crushed: literally, "he crushed"; the singular is used typically, hence the plural translation.

Ps 144: The psalm may reflect a ceremony in which the king, as leader of the army, asked God's help (1–8). In 9 the poem shifts abruptly from pleading to thanksgiving, and (except for 11) shifts again to prayer for the people. The first section (1–2) is a prayer of thanks for victory; the second (3–7a), a humble acknowledgment of human nothingness and a supplication that God show forth saving power; the third (9–11), a promise of future thanksgiving; the fourth (12–15), a wish for prosperity and peace. A prayer for deliverance from treacherous foes serves as a refrain after the second and third sections (7b–8. 11). Except for its final section, the psalm is made up almost entirely of verses from other psalms.

144, 1–2: Composed of phrases from Ps 18, 3. 35. 47–48.

t Ps 141, 9. u Pss 16, 8; 73, 23; 121, 5. v Ps 91, 2. 9. w Pss 16, 5; 27, 13; 116, 9; Is 38, 11. x Ps 79, 8. y Eccl 7, 20; Jb 4, 17; Rom 3, 20. z Ps 7, 6. a Lam 3, 6. b Ps 142, 4; Jb 17, 1. c Ps 77, 6. 12. d Pss 42, 2; 63, 2. e Pss 28, 1; 30, 4; 88, 5; Prv 1, 12. f Pss 25, 4; 27, 11; 86, 11; 119, 12. 35. g Ps 116, 16.

who subdues peoples under me.

II

3 LORD, what are mortals that you notice
them;
human beings, that you take thought of
them?[h]*
4 They are but a breath;
their days are like a passing shadow.[i]*
5 LORD, incline your heavens and come;*
touch the mountains and make them
smoke.[j]
6 Flash forth lightning and scatter my foes;
shoot your arrows and rout them.
7 Reach out your hand from on high;
deliver me from the many waters;
rescue me from the hands of foreign foes.
8 Their mouths speak untruth;
their right hands are raised in lying oaths.*
9 O God, a new song I will sing to you;
on a ten-stringed lyre I will play for you.[k]
10 You give victory to kings;
you delivered David your servant.[l]
From the menacing sword 11 deliver me;
rescue me from the hands of foreign foes.
Their mouths speak untruth;
their right hands are raised in lying oaths.

III

12 May our sons be like plants[m]
well nurtured from their youth,
Our daughters, like carved columns,
shapely as those of the temple.
13 May our barns be full
with every kind of store.
May our sheep increase by thousands,
by tens of thousands in our fields;
may our oxen be well fattened.
14 May there be no breach in the walls,
no exile, no outcry in our streets.[n]
15 Happy the people so blessed;
happy the people whose God is the LORD.[o]

PSALM 145*

The Greatness and Goodness of God

1 Praise. Of David.

I will extol you, my God and king;
I will bless your name forever.
2 Every day I will bless you;
I will praise your name forever.[p]
3 Great is the LORD and worthy of high praise;[q]
God's grandeur is beyond understanding.
4 One generation praises your deeds to the next
and proclaims your mighty works.[r]
5 They speak of the splendor of your majestic
glory,
tell of your wonderful deeds.[s]
6 They speak of your fearsome power
and attest to your great deeds.[t]
7 They publish the renown of your abounding
goodness
and joyfully sing of your justice.
8 The LORD is gracious and merciful,
slow to anger and abounding in love.[u]
9 The LORD is good to all,
compassionate to every creature.[v]
10 All your works give you thanks, O LORD
and your faithful bless you.[w]
11 They speak of the glory of your reign
and tell of your great works,
12 Making known to all your power,
the glorious splendor of your rule.
13 Your reign is a reign for all ages,
your dominion for all generations.[x]
The LORD is trustworthy in every word,
and faithful in every work.
14 The LORD supports all who are falling

144, 3: Similar to Ps 8, 5.
144, 4: Composed of phrases from Pss 39, 6; 102, 12.
144, 5–7: Adapted in large part from Pss 18, 10. 15. 17; 104, 32.
144, 8b. 11b: Their right hands are raised in lying oaths: the psalmist's enemies give false testimony.
Ps 145: A hymn in acrostic form; every verse begins with a successive letter of the Hebrew alphabet. Acrostic poems usually do not develop ideas but consist rather of loosely connected statements. The singer invites all to praise God (1–3. 21). The "works of God" make God present and invite human praise (4–7); they climax in a confession (8–9). God's mighty acts show forth divine kingship (10–20), a major theme in the literature of early Judaism and in Christianity.

h Jb 7, 17. i Pss 62, 10; 90, 9–10; Jb 7, 16; Eccl 6, 12; Wis 2, 5. j Is 63, 19. k Ps 33, 2–3. l Ps 18, 51. m Ps 128, 3. n Is 65, 19. o Ps 33, 12. p Ps 34, 2. q Pss 48, 2; 95, 3; 96, 4; Jb 36, 26. r Pss 22, 31–32; 48, 14–15; 71, 18; 78, 4; Ex 10, 2; Dt 4, 9. s Pss 96, 3; 105, 2. t Ps 66, 3. u Pss 86, 5. 15; 103, 8; Ex 34, 6; Sir 2, 11. v Ps 103, 13; Wis 11, 24. w Dn 3, 57. x Pss 10, 16; 102, 13; 146, 10; Lam 5, 19; Dn 3, 100; Rv 11, 15.

and raises up all who are bowed down.[y]
15 The eyes of all look hopefully to you;
you give them their food in due season.[z]
16 You open wide your hand
and satisfy the desire of every living thing.
17 You, LORD, are just in all your ways,
faithful in all your works.[a]
18 You, LORD, are near to all who call upon you,
to all who call upon you in truth.[b]
19 You satisfy the desire of those who fear you;
you hear their cry and save them.[c]
20 You, LORD, watch over all who love you,
but all the wicked you destroy.[d]
21 My mouth will speak your praises, LORD;
all flesh will bless your holy name forever.[e]

PSALM 146*

Trust in God the Creator and Redeemer

1 Hallelujah!

2 Praise the LORD, my soul;
I shall praise the LORD all my life,
sing praise to my God while I live.[f]

I

3 Put no trust in princes,
in mere mortals powerless to save.[g]
4 When they breathe their last, they return to the earth;
that day all their planning comes to nothing.[h]

II

5 Happy those whose help is Jacob's God,
whose hope is in the LORD, their God,
6 The maker of heaven and earth,
the seas and all that is in them,[i]
Who keeps faith forever,
7 secures justice for the oppressed,[j]
gives food to the hungry.
The LORD sets prisoners free;[k]
8 the LORD gives sight to the blind.
The LORD raises up those who are bowed down;[l]
the LORD loves the righteous.
9 The LORD protects the stranger,
sustains the orphan and the widow,[m]
but thwarts the way of the wicked.
10 The LORD shall reign forever,
your God, Zion, through all generations![n]
Hallelujah!

PSALM 147*

God's Word Restores Jerusalem

1 Hallelujah!

I

How good to celebrate our God in song;
how sweet to give fitting praise.[o]
2 The LORD rebuilds Jerusalem,
gathers the dispersed of Israel,[p]
3 Heals the brokenhearted,
binds up their wounds,[q]
4 Numbers all the stars,
calls each of them by name.[r]
5 Great is our Lord, vast in power,
with wisdom beyond measure.[s]
6 The LORD sustains the poor,
but casts the wicked to the ground.[t]

II

7 Sing to the LORD with thanksgiving;
with the lyre celebrate our God,[u]
8 Who covers the heavens with clouds,*
provides rain for the earth,
makes grass sprout on the mountains,[v]
9 Who gives animals their food
and ravens what they cry for.[w]

Ps 146: A hymn of someone who has learned there is no other source of strength except the merciful God. Only God, not mortal humans (3–4), can help vulnerable and oppressed people (5–9). The first of the five hymns that conclude the Psalter.

Ps 147: The hymn is divided into three sections by the calls to praise in 1, 7, and 12. The first section praises the powerful creator who restores exiled Judah (1–6); the second section, the creator who provides food to animals and humans; the third and climactic section exhorts the holy city to recognize it has been re-created and made the place of disclosure for God's word, a word as life-giving as water.

147, 8–9: God clothes the fields and feeds the birds. Cf Mt 6, 26. 30.

y Pss 94, 18; 146, 8. z Pss 136, 25; 104, 27–28; Mt 6, 25–26. a Dt 32, 4. b Dt 4, 7; Is 55, 6; 58, 9. c Ps 34, 18. d Jgs 5, 31. e Sir 40, 35. f Pss 103, 1; 104, 33. g Ps 118, 8–9. h Pss 90, 3; 104, 29; 1 Mc 2, 63; Jb 34, 14–15; Eccl 3, 20; 12, 7; Sir 40, 11; Is 2, 22. i Ex 20, 11; Pss 121, 2; 124, 8; Acts 14, 15; Rv 14, 7. j Ps 103, 6. k Ps 68, 7; Is 49, 9; 61, 1. l Ps 145, 14. m Ps 68, 6; Dt 10, 18. n Ps 145, 13; Lam 5, 19. o Pss 33, 1; 92, 2. p Is 11, 12; 56, 8; Jer 31, 10. q Jb 5, 18; Is 30, 26; 61, 1; Jer 33, 6. r Is 40, 26. s Jdt 16, 13; Jer 51, 15. t Ps 146, 9; 1 Sm 2, 7–8. u Ps 71, 22. v Ps 104, 13f; Jb 5, 10; Jer 14, 22; Jl 2, 23. w Jb 38, 41; Mt 6, 26.

10 God takes no delight in the strength of
horses,*
no pleasure in the runner's stride.[x]
11 Rather the LORD takes pleasure in the devout,
those who await his faithful care.

III

12 Glorify the LORD, Jerusalem;
Zion, offer praise to your God,
13 Who has strengthened the bars of your gates,
blessed your children within you,[y]
14 Brought peace to your borders,
and filled you with finest wheat.[z]
15 The LORD sends a command to earth;*
his word runs swiftly![a]
16 Thus snow is spread like wool,
frost is scattered like ash,[b]
17 Hail is dispersed like crumbs;
before such cold the waters freeze.
18 Again he sends his word and they melt;
the wind is unleashed and the waters flow.
19 The LORD also proclaims his word to Jacob,
decrees and laws to Israel.[c]
20 God has not done this for other nations;
of such laws they know nothing.
Hallelujah!

PSALM 148*

All Creation Summoned to Praise

1 Hallelujah!

I

Praise the LORD from the heavens;
give praise in the heights.
2 Praise him, all you angels;
give praise, all you hosts.[d]
3 Praise him, sun and moon;
give praise, all shining stars.
4 Praise him, highest heavens,*
you waters above the heavens.
5 Let them all praise the LORD's name;
for the LORD commanded and they were
created,[e]
6 Assigned them duties forever,
gave them tasks that will never change.

II

7 Praise the LORD from the earth,
you sea monsters and all deep waters;[f]
8 You lightning and hail, snow and clouds,
storm winds that fulfill his command;
9 You mountains and all hills,
fruit trees and all cedars;[g]
10 You animals wild and tame,
you creatures that crawl and fly;[h]
11 You kings of the earth and all peoples,
princes and all who govern on earth;
12 Young men and women too,
old and young alike.
13 Let them all praise the LORD's name,
for his name alone is exalted,
majestic above earth and heaven.[i]
14 The LORD has lifted high the horn of his
people;*
to the glory of all the faithful,
of Israel, the people near to their God.
Hallelujah!

PSALM 149*

Praise God with Song and Sword

1 Hallelujah!

Sing to the LORD a new song,
a hymn in the assembly of the faithful.[j]

147, 10–11: Acknowledging one's dependence upon God rather than claiming self-sufficiency pleases God. Cf Pss 20, 8; 33, 16–19.

147, 15–19: God speaks through the thunder of nature and the word of revealed law. Cf Is 55, 10–11. The weather phenomena are well known in Jerusalem: a blizzard of snow and hail followed by a thunderstorm that melts the ice.

Ps 148: A hymn inviting the beings of heaven (1–6) and of earth (7–14) to praise God. The hymn does not distinguish between inanimate and animate (and rational) nature.

148, 4: **Highest heavens:** literally, "the heavens of the heavens," i.e., the space above the firmament, where the "upper waters" are stored. Cf Gn 1, 6–7; Dt 10, 14; 1 Kgs 8, 27; Ps 104, 3. 13.

148, 14: **The LORD has lifted high the horn of his people:** horn = strength, the concrete noun for the abstract. Of all peoples God has chosen Israel to return praise and thanks in a special way.

Ps 149: A hymn inviting the people of Israel to celebrate their God in song and festive dance (1–3. 5) because God has chosen them and given them victory (4). The exodus and conquest are the defining acts of Israel; the people must be ready to do again those acts in the future at the divine command (6–9).

x Pss 20, 8; 33, 16–18. y Ps 48, 14. z Ps 81, 17. a Ps 33, 9. b Jb 6, 16; 37, 10; 38, 22. c Ps 78, 5; Bar 3, 37; Dt 4, 7–8. d Dn 3, 58–63; Ps 103, 20f. e Ps 33, 9; Gn 1, 3f; Jdt 16, 14. f Gn 1, 21; Ps 135, 6. g Is 44, 23. h Gn 1, 21. 24f; Ps 30, 5; Dt 4, 7. i Ps 30, 5; Dt 4, 7. j Pss 22, 23; 26, 12; 35, 18; 40, 10; Jdt 16, 1.

[2] Let Israel be glad in their maker,
the people of Zion rejoice in their king.
[3] Let them praise his name in festive dance,
make music with tambourine and lyre. [k]*
[4] For the LORD takes delight in his people,
honors the poor with victory.
[5] Let the faithful rejoice in their glory,
cry out for joy at their banquet,*
[6] With the praise of God in their mouths,
and a two-edged sword in their hands, [l]
[7] To bring retribution on the nations,
punishment on the peoples, [m]
[8] To bind their kings with chains,
shackle their nobles with irons,
[9] To execute the judgments decreed for them—
such is the glory* of all God's faithful.
Hallelujah!

PSALM 150*

Final Doxology

[1] Hallelujah!

Praise God in his holy sanctuary; [n]*
give praise in the mighty dome of heaven.*
[2] Give praise for his mighty deeds, [o]
praise him for his great majesty.
[3] Give praise with blasts upon the horn, [p]
praise him with harp and lyre.
[4] Give praise with tambourines and dance,
praise him with flutes and strings. [q]
[5] Give praise with crashing cymbals,
praise him with sounding cymbals.
[6] Let everything that has breath
give praise to the LORD! [r]
Hallelujah!

149, 3: **Make music with tambourine and lyre**: the verse recalls the great exodus hymn of Ex 15, 20.

149, 5: **At their banquet**: literally, "upon their couches." The people reclined to banquet.

149, 9: **The glory**: what brings honor to the people is their readiness to carry out the divine will, here conceived as punishing injustice done by the nations.

Ps 150: The psalm is a closing doxology both for the fifth book of the Psalms (107–149) and for the Psalter as a whole. Temple musicians and dancers are called to lead all beings on earth and in heaven in praise of God. The psalm proclaims to whom praise shall be given, and where (1); what praise shall be given, and why (2); how praise shall be given (3–5), and by whom (6).

150, 1: **His holy sanctuary**: God's temple on earth. **The mighty dome of heaven**: literally, "[God's] strong vault"; heaven is here imagined as a giant plate separating the inhabited world from the waters of the heavens.

k Pss 68, 26; 81, 2–3; 87, 7; 150, 3–4. l Neh 4, 10–12; 2 Mc 15, 27. m Wis 3, 8. n Dn 3, 53. o Dt 3, 24. p 3ff: Pss 81, 3–4; 149, 3; 2 Sm 6, 5; 1 Chr 13, 8; 16, 5. 42; 2 Chr 5, 12–13; 7, 6. q Ps 68, 26; Ex 15, 20. r Rv 5, 13.

THE BOOK OF PROVERBS

The first word of this book, *Mishle,* has provided the title by which it is generally designated in Jewish and Christian circles. The name "Proverbs," while not an exact equivalent of *Mishle,* describes the main contents satisfactorily, even though it is hardly an adequate designation for such parts as 1, 1—9, 18 or 31, 10-31. Among some early Christian writers the book was also known by the name of "Wisdom," and in the Roman Missal it was for many centuries referred to as a "Book of Wisdom."

The Book of Proverbs is an anthology of didactic poetry forming part of the sapiential literature of the Old Testament. Its primary purpose, indicated in the first sentence (1, 2f), is to teach wisdom. It is thus directed particularly to the young and inexperienced (1, 4); but also to those who desire advanced training in wisdom (1, 5f). The wisdom which the book teaches covers a wide field of human and divine activity, ranging from matters purely secular to most lofty moral and religious truths, such as God's omniscience (5, 21; 15, 3-11), power (19, 21; 21, 30), providence (20, 1-24), goodness (15, 29), and the joy and strength resulting from abandonment to him (3, 5; 16, 20; 18, 10). The teaching of the entire book is placed on a firm religious foundation by the principle that "the fear of the Lord is the beginning of knowledge" (1, 7; cf 9, 10).

To Solomon are explicitly ascribed parts II and V of the book; he is the patron of Hebrew wisdom. Of Agur (part VI) and Lemuel (part VIII), nothing further is known. Parts III and IV are attributed to "the wise." The remaining parts are anonymous.

The manner of compilation is conjectural. Parts II and V may have circulated first as independent collections, compiled before the fall of Jerusalem, as the references to Solomon (10, 1) and Hezekiah (25, 1) suggest. Parts III, IV and VII would seem to belong together as a third collection of a similar kind. The author of the first nine chapters, a religious sage familiar with the earlier sacred books, was the editor of the whole as we have it, probably in the early part of the fifth century B.C.

Christ and the Apostles often expressly quoted the Proverbs (Jn 7, 38; Rom 12, 20; Jas 4, 6) or repeated their teaching; compare Lk 10, 14, and Prv 25, 7; 1 Pt 4, 8; Jas 5, 20 and Prv 10, 12. The book has an important place in the Latin and Greek liturgies.

On the basis of titles, subject matter, and poetic structure the Book of Proverbs may be divided as follows:

I. Introduction: The Value of Wisdom (1, 1—9, 18).
II. First Collection of the Proverbs of Solomon (10, 1—22, 16).
III. Sayings of the Wise (22, 17—24, 22).
IV. Other Sayings of the Wise (24, 23-34).
V. Second Collection of the Proverbs of Solomon (25, 1—29, 27).
VI. The Words of Agur (30, 1-6).
VII. Numerical Proverbs (30, 7-33).
VIII. The Words of Lemuel (31, 1-9).
IX. The Ideal Wife (31, 10–31).

I: Introduction: The Value Of Wisdom

CHAPTER 1

Purpose of the Proverbs of Solomon*

1 The proverbs of Solomon,[a] the son of David,
king of Israel:
2 That men may appreciate wisdom and
discipline,*
may understand words of intelligence;
3 May receive training in wise conduct,
in what is right, just and honest;
4 That resourcefulness may be imparted to the
simple,*
to the young man knowledge and
discretion.
5 A wise man by hearing them will advance in
learning,
an intelligent man will gain sound guidance,
6 That he may comprehend proverb and
parable,
the words of the wise and their riddles.

7 The fear of the LORD* is the beginning of
knowledge;[b]
wisdom and instruction fools despise.

The Path of the Wicked: Greed and Violence*

8 Hear, my son, your father's instruction,
and reject not your mother's teaching;
9 A graceful diadem will they be for your head;
a torque for your neck.
10 My son, should sinners entice you, 11 and say,
"Come along with us!
Let us lie in wait for the honest man,
let us, unprovoked, set a trap for the
innocent;
12 Let us swallow them up, as the nether world
does, alive,
in the prime of life, like those who go down
to the pit!
13 All kinds of precious wealth shall we gain,
we shall fill our houses with booty;
14 Cast in your lot with us,
we shall all have one purse!"—

15 My son, walk not in the way with them,
hold back your foot from their path!
16 [For their feet run to evil,
they hasten to shed blood.[c]]
17 It is in vain that a net is spread*
before the eyes of any bird—
18 These men lie in wait for their own blood,
they set a trap for their own lives.
19 This is the fate of everyone greedy of loot:
unlawful gain takes away the life of him
who acquires it.

Wisdom in Person Gives Warning*

20 Wisdom cries aloud in the street,
in the open squares she raises her voice;[d]
21 Down the crowded ways she calls out,
at the city gates she utters her words:
22 "How long, you simple ones, will you love
inanity,
23 how long will you turn away at my reproof?
Lo! I will pour out to you my spirit,
I will acquaint you with my words.

24 "Because I called and you refused,
I extended my hand and no one took
notice;[e]
25 Because you disdained all my counsel,
and my reproof you ignored—
26 I, in my turn, will laugh at your doom;
I will mock when terror overtakes you;

1, 1–6: This prologue explains the purpose of the book: to educate the inexperienced in knowledge and right conduct, and to increase the learning of the wise man by proverbs, parables and riddles.

1, 2: Discipline: education or formation which dispels ignorance and corrects vice.

1, 4: Simple: immature and inexperienced, hence easily influenced for good or evil.

1, 7: Fear of the Lord: reverential fear and respect for God on account of his sovereignty, goodness and justice toward men. This is the foundation of religion.

1, 8–19: A warning against association with the greedy and the violent who seek to destroy the honest man and to steal his possessions (11–14). The trap which the wicked set for the innocent (11), in the end (19) takes away the life of the wicked themselves.

1, 17: Instructed by the wise man, the youth (of v 4) will recognize the invitation of the wicked (11–14) as a net spread before him, and he will thus, like the bird, be protected against falling into it.

1, 20–33: Wisdom is here personified: with divine authority she sets forth and proclaims the moral order, instructing and threatening (24–33) the multitudes in the streets and places of assembly.

a Prv 10, 1; 25, 1; 1 Kgs 4, 32. b Prv 9, 10; Jb 28, 28; Ps 111, 10; Sir 1, 16. c Is 59, 7. d Prv 8, 1–3; 9, 3. e Is 65, 2. 12; 66, 4; Jer 7, 13.

27 When terror comes upon you like a storm,
and your doom approaches like a
whirlwind;
when distress and anguish befall you.

28 "Then they call me, but I answer not;
they seek me, but find me not;*
29 Because they hated knowledge,
and chose not the fear of the LORD;
30 They ignored my counsel,
they spurned all my reproof;
And in their arrogance they preferred
arrogance,
and like fools they hated knowledge:
31 "Now they must eat the fruit of their own way,
and with their own devices be glutted.*
32 For the self-will of the simple kills them,
the smugness of fools destroys them.
33 But he who obeys me dwells in security,
in peace, without fear of harm."[f]

CHAPTER 2*

The Blessings of Wisdom*

1 My son, if you receive my words
and treasure my commands,
2 Turning your ear to wisdom,*
inclining your heart to understanding;
3 Yes, if you call to intelligence,
and to understanding raise your voice;
4 If you seek her like silver,
and like hidden treasures search her out:

5 Then will you understand the fear of the
LORD;
the knowledge of God you will find;
6 For the LORD gives wisdom,
from his mouth come knowledge and
understanding;[g]
7 He has counsel in store for the upright,
he is the shield of those who walk
honestly,
8 Guarding the paths of justice,
protecting the way of his pious ones.

9 Then you will understand rectitude and
justice,
honesty, every good path;
10 For wisdom will enter your heart,
knowledge will please your soul,
11 Discretion will watch over you,
understanding will guard you;

12 Saving you from the way of evil men,
from men of perverse speech,
13 Who leave the straight paths
to walk in ways of darkness,
14 Who delight in doing evil,
rejoice in perversity;
15 Whose ways are crooked,
and devious their paths;

16 Saving you from the wife of another,
from the adulteress with her smooth
words,[h]
17 Who forsakes the companion of her youth
and forgets the pact with her God;
18 For her path sinks down to death,
and her footsteps lead to the shades;[i]
19 None who enter thereon come back again,
or gain the paths of life.

20 Thus you may walk in the way of good men,
and keep to the paths of the just.
21 For the upright will dwell in the land,[j]
the honest will remain in it;
22 But the wicked will be cut off from the land,
the faithless will be rooted out of it.

1, 28: Overtaken by doom, the foolish seek wisdom, but in vain because they do so too late. Cf Jn 7, 34; 8, 21.

1, 31: Sinners are punished by the bad fruits which their sins produce. Cf Wis 11, 16.

2—7: These chapters form an ordered discourse in seven "columns" of twenty-two verses each. Chapter 2 introduces the four topics about which the sage instructs his pupil: the service of God (3, 1–12. 25–34), the search for wisdom (3, 13–24. 35; 4, 1–9), the avoidance of evil companions among men (4, 10–27; 5, 21–23), and among women (5, 1–20; 6, 20—7, 27). The last topic is treated at a length equal to the first three because the discourse is meant especially for youths (cf Prv 1, 4).

2, 1–22: The search for wisdom (1–4) leads to the protection of God (5–8) and of wisdom herself (9ff; cf Prv 1, 20–33) and to deliverance from evil men (12–15) and evil women (16–19), and so to lasting happiness (20ff).

2, 2f: Wisdom, understanding, intelligence: various names or aspects of the same gift.

f Prv 8, 33f. g Jb 32, 8; Wis 7, 25; Sir 1, 1; Jas 1, 5. h Prv 5, 3. 20; 6, 24; 7, 5; 22, 14. i Prv 5, 5f; 7, 27. j 21f: Prv 10, 7, 30; Jb 18, 17; Pss 21, 9–13; 37, 22. 28.

CHAPTER 3

Attitude toward the Lord*

1 My son, forget not my teaching,
keep in mind my commands;
2 For many days, and years of life, [k]
and peace, will they bring you.

3 Let not kindness and fidelity leave you;
bind them around your neck;
4 Then will you win favor and good esteem
before God and man.

5 Trust in the LORD with all your heart,
on your own intelligence rely not;
6 In all your ways be mindful of him,
and he will make straight your paths.

7 Be not wise in your own eyes, [l]
fear the LORD and turn away from evil;
8 This will mean health for your flesh
and vigor for your bones.

9 Honor the LORD with your wealth,
with first fruits of all your produce; [m]
10 Then will your barns be filled with grain,
with new wine your vats will overflow.
11 The discipline of the LORD, my son, disdain
not; [n]
spurn not his reproof;
12 For whom the LORD loves he reproves,
and he chastises the son he favors. [o]

The Value of Wisdom*

13 Happy the man who finds wisdom,
the man who gains understanding! [p]
14 For her profit is better than profit in silver,
and better than gold is her revenue;
15 She is more precious than corals,*
and none of your choice possessions can
compare with her. [q]

16 Long life is in her right hand,
in her left are riches and honor;
17 Her ways are pleasant ways,
and all her paths are peace;
18 She is a tree of life* to those who grasp her, [r]
and he is happy who holds her fast.

19 The LORD by wisdom founded the earth,
established the heavens by understanding;
20 By his knowledge the depths break open,
and the clouds drop down dew.*
21 My son, let not these slip out of your sight:
keep advice and counsel in view;
22 So will they be life to your soul,
and an adornment for your neck.
23 Then you may securely go your way;
your foot will never stumble;
24 When you lie down, you need not be afraid,
when you rest, your sleep will be sweet.
35 Honor is the possession of wise men,
but fools inherit shame.

Attitude toward Fellow Men*

25 Be not afraid of sudden terror,
of the ruin of the wicked* when it comes;
26 For the LORD will be your confidence,
and will keep your foot from the snare.

27 Refuse no one the good on which he has a
claim
when it is in your power to do it for him.
28 Say not to your neighbor, "Go, and come
again,
tomorrow I will give," when you can give at
once.

3, 1–12: Many are the rewards for fidelity and trust in God, and for diffidence of self (1–8). Cf Dt 30, 20; Is 38, 19. The offering of material things for divine worship is blessed by an increase of such goods (9f). Even correction and chastisement are a mark of God's love and favor (11f).

3, 13–24: Wisdom, or understanding, is more valuable than silver and gold. Its fruit is long life, riches, honor and happiness (13–18). Even the creation of the universe and its adornment (Gn 1) were not done without wisdom (19f). It is the life of the soul and gives security in work and in repose (21–24).

3, 15: Corals: some precious stone may be intended.

3, 18: A tree of life: cf Prv 11, 30; 13, 12; Gn 2, 9.

3, 20: For the Hebrews, the depths enclosed the great subterranean ocean; the rain and dew descended from the celestial ocean above the firmament; cf Gn 1, 6–10; Jb 26, 8. 12; Pss 18, 16; 24, 2.

3, 25–34: Serving God with confidence in him (25f) requires serving one's neighbor through kindness (27f), peace with the good (29ff), no envy of the wicked (31), because the Lord's friendship and kindness are with the just; his curse is with the wicked.

3, 25: The ruin of the wicked: i.e., the ruin that comes upon the wicked.

k Prv 4, 10; 9, 11; 10, 27. l Rom 11, 25; 12, 16. m Ex 34, 26; Lv 27, 30; Dt 26, 2; Sir 7, 31; 35, 7. n Heb 12, 5f. o Jdt 8, 27; Rv 3, 19. p Prv 8, 34f. q Prv 8, 11. 19; Wis 7, 8–11. r Prv 4, 13; 8, 35; 11, 30; Gn 2, 9; 3, 22.

29 Plot no evil against your neighbor,
against him who lives at peace with you.
30 Quarrel not with a man without cause,
with one who has done you no harm.
31 Envy not the lawless man
and choose none of his ways: [s]
32 To the LORD the perverse man is an abomination,
but with the upright is his friendship.

33 The curse of the LORD is on the house of the wicked,
but the dwelling of the just he blesses;
34 When he is dealing with the arrogant, he is stern, [t]
but to the humble he shows kindness.

CHAPTER 4

Wisdom: the Supreme Guide of Men*

1 Hear, O children, a father's instruction,
be attentive, that you may gain understanding!
2 Yes, excellent advice I give you;
my teaching do not forsake.
3 When I was my father's child,
frail, yet the darling of my mother,
4 He taught me, and said to me:
"Let your heart hold fast my words: [u]
keep my commands, that you may live!

5 "Get wisdom, get understanding!
Do not forget or turn aside from the words I utter.
6 Forsake her not, and she will preserve you;
love her, and she will safeguard you;
7 The beginning of wisdom is: get wisdom;
at the cost of all you have, get understanding.
8 Extol her, and she will exalt you;
she will bring you honors if you embrace her;
9 She will put on your head a graceful diadem;
a glorious crown will she bestow on you."

The Good and the Evil Way*

10 Hear, my son, and receive my words,
and the years of your life shall be many. [v]
11 On the way of wisdom I direct you,
I lead you on straightforward paths.
12 When you walk, your step will not be impeded,
and should you run, you will not stumble.
13 Hold fast to instruction, never let her go;
keep her, for she is your life.

14 The path of the wicked enter not,
walk not on the way of evil men;
15 Shun it, cross it not,
turn aside from it, and pass on.
16 For they cannot rest unless they have done evil;
to have made no one stumble steals away their sleep.
17 For they eat the bread of wickedness
and drink the wine of violence.
19 The way of the wicked is like darkness;
they know not on what they stumble.
18 But the path of the just is like shining light,
that grows in brilliance till perfect day.*

20 My son, to my words be attentive,
to my sayings incline your ear;
21 Let them not slip out of your sight,
keep them within your heart;
22 For they are life to those who find them, [w]
to man's whole being they are health.

23 With closest custody, guard your heart,
for in it are the sources of life.
24 Put away from you dishonest talk,
deceitful speech put far from you.
25 Let your eyes look straight ahead
and your glance be directly forward.
26 Survey the path for your feet,
and let all your ways be sure.
27 Turn neither to right nor to left,
keep your foot far from evil.

4, 1–9: The sage speaks as a father admonishing his children to secure wisdom at any cost.

4, 10–27: The way of wisdom leads directly to life (10–13); it is a light that grows brighter (18). The wise man is bound to shun (14–17) the dark and violent path of the wicked (19). Singleness of purpose and right conduct proceed from the heart of a wise man as from the source of life (23–26); they save him from destruction on evil paths (4, 27; 5, 21ff).

4, 18: Till perfect day: literally, "till the day is established"; this may refer to full daylight or to noonday.

s Prv 23, 17; 24, 1. 19; Ps 37, 1. t Prv 1, 26. u 1 Kgs 2, 2ff. v Prv 3, 2. w Prv 8, 35.

CHAPTER 5

Warning against Adultery*

1 My son, to my wisdom be attentive,
to my knowledge incline your ear,
2 That discretion may watch over you,
and understanding may guard you.
3 The lips of an adulteress drip with honey,
and her mouth is smoother than oil; [x]
4 But in the end she is as bitter as wormwood,
as sharp as a two-edged sword.
5 Her feet go down to death,
to the nether world her steps attain; [y]
6 Lest you see before you the road to life,
her paths will ramble, you know not where.

7 So now, O children, listen to me,
go not astray from the words of my mouth.
8 Keep your way far from her, [z]
approach not the door of her house,
9 Lest you give your honor* to others, [a]
and your years to a merciless one;
10 Lest strangers have their fill of your wealth,
your hard-won earnings go to an alien's
house;
11 And you groan in the end,
when your flesh and your body are
consumed;
12 And you say, "Oh, why did I hate instruction,
and my heart spurn reproof!
13 Why did I not listen to the voice of my
teachers,
nor to my instructors incline my ear!
14 I have all but come to utter ruin,
condemned by the public assembly!"

15 Drink water from your own cistern,
running water from your own well.
16 How may your water sources be dispersed
abroad,
streams of water in the streets?
17 Let your fountain be yours alone,
not one shared with strangers;
18 And have joy of the wife of your youth,
19 your lovely hind, your graceful doe.*
Her love will invigorate you always,
through her love you will flourish
continually,
22 When you lie down she will watch over you,
and when you wake, she will share your
concerns;
wherever you turn, she will guide you.*
20 Why then, my son, should you go astray for
another's wife
and accept the embraces of an adulteress?

21 For each man's ways are plain to the LORD's
sight;*
all their paths he surveys; [b]
22 By his own iniquities the wicked man will be
caught,
in the meshes of his own sin he will be held
fast;
23 He will die from lack of discipline,
through the greatness of his folly he will be
lost.

CHAPTER 6

Miscellaneous Proverbs*

1 My son, if you have become surety to your
neighbor, [c]
given your hand in pledge* to another,
2 You have been snared by the utterance of your
lips,
caught by the words of your mouth;
3 So do this, my son, to free yourself,
since you have fallen into your neighbor's
power:
Go, hurry, stir up your neighbor!
4 Give no sleep to your eyes,

5, 1–20: Understanding and discretion guard a man against the wiles of an adulteress, which lead astray and beget bitterness, bloodshed and death (1–6). They destroy honor, waste the years of life, despoil hard-earned wealth, consume the flesh, and bring remorse in the end (7–14). Conjugal fidelity and love for one wife only bring happiness and security (15–20). Cf Prv 6, 20—7, 27.

5, 9: Honor: the words "life" and "wealth" have also been read in this place. A merciless one: the offended husband; cf Prv 6, 34f.

5, 19: Lovely hind . . . graceful doe: oriental symbols of feminine beauty and charm; cf Song 2, 7. 9. 17.

5, 22: This is transposed from chapter 6, 22.

5, 21–23: These verses are best read after Prv 4, 27.

6, 1–19: These verses interrupt the discourse of chapters 2—7, which should be read apart from them; they contain four shorter proverbs akin to those in chapter 30.

6, 1: Given your hand in pledge: literally, "struck your hands"; this was probably the legal method for closing a contract.

x Prv 7, 5. y Prv 2, 18; 7, 27. z Prv 7, 25. a 9f: Sir 9, 6. b Jb 14, 16; 31, 4; 34, 21. c 1f: Prv 11, 15; 22, 26; Sir 8, 13; 29, 19.

nor slumber to your eyelids;
5 Free yourself as a gazelle from the snare,
or as a bird from the hand of the fowler.

6 Go to the ant,[d] O sluggard,
study her ways and learn wisdom;
7 For though she has no chief,
no commander or ruler,
8 She procures her food in the summer,
stores up her provisions in the harvest.
9 How long, O sluggard, will you rest?
when will you rise from your sleep?
10 A little sleep, a little slumber,
a little folding of the arms to rest—*
11 Then will poverty come upon you like a
highwayman,
and want like an armed man.

12 A scoundrel, a villain, is he
who deals in crooked talk.
13 He winks his eyes,
shuffles his feet,
makes signs with his fingers;
14 He has perversity in his heart,
is always plotting evil,
sows discord.
15 Therefore suddenly ruin comes upon him;
in an instant he is crushed beyond cure.

16 There are six things the LORD hates,
yes, seven are an abomination to him;*
17 Haughty eyes, a lying tongue,
and hands that shed innocent blood;
18 A heart that plots wicked schemes,
feet that run swiftly to evil,
19 The false witness who utters lies,
and he who sows discord among brothers.

Warning against Adultery*

20 Observe, my son, your father's bidding,
and reject not your mother's teaching;
21 Keep them fastened over your heart always,
put them around your neck;

23 For the bidding is a lamp, and the teaching a
light,
and a way to life are the reproofs of
discipline;
24 To keep you from your neighbor's wife,
from the smooth tongue of the adulteress.[e]
25 Lust not in your heart after her beauty,
let her not captivate you with her glance![f]
26 For the price of a loose woman
may be scarcely a loaf of bread,
But if she is married,
she is a trap for your precious life.*
27 Can a man take fire to his bosom,
and his garments not be burned?
28 Or can a man walk on live coals,
and his feet not be scorched?
29 So with him who goes in to his neighbor's
wife—
none who touches her shall go
unpunished.[g]

30 Men despise not the thief if he steals
to satisfy his appetite when he is hungry;
31 Yet if he be caught he must pay back
sevenfold;
all the wealth of his house he may yield up.
32 But he who commits adultery is a fool;
he who would destroy himself does it.
33 A degrading beating will he get,
and his disgrace will not be wiped away;
34 For vindictive is the husband's wrath,
he will have no pity on the day of
vengeance;
35 He will not consider any restitution,
nor be satisfied with the greatest gifts.

CHAPTER 7

1 My son, keep my words,
and treasure my commands.
2 Keep my commands and live,
my teaching as the apple of your eye;

6, 10: This verse may be regarded as the sluggard's reply or as a continuation of the remonstrance.

6, 16–19: The seven vices symbolized for the most part by bodily organs are pride, lying, murder, intrigue, readiness to do evil, false witness, and the stirring up of discord.

6, 20—7, 27: Parental training and the love of wisdom are an invaluable and constant help for the young (6, 20–23; 7, 1–4). They are the best defense against adultery (6, 24; 7, 5. 24f), which involves the guilty in many dangers and punishments (6, 26–35; 7, 6–27). Cf Prv 5, 1–20.

6, 26: Some interpret the verse in a progressive sense, i.e., to satisfy the increasing demands of a courtesan a man is reduced to poverty; if the woman is married, even his very life is endangered.

d Prv 30, 25. e Prv 2, 16; 7, 5. f Ex 20, 17; Dt 5, 21; Sir 9, 8; 25, 20; Mt 5, 28. g Sir 9, 9.

3 Bind them on your fingers,
write them on the tablet of your heart. [h]
4 Say to Wisdom, "You are my sister!"
call Understanding, "Friend!"
5 That they may keep you from another's wife,
from the adulteress with her smooth words. [i]
6 For at the window of my house,
through my lattice I looked out—

7 And I saw among the simple ones,
I observed among the young men,
a youth with no sense,
8 Going along the street near the corner,
then walking in the direction of her house—
9 In the twilight, at dusk of day,
at the time of the dark of night.
10 And lo! the woman comes to meet him,
robed like a harlot, with secret designs—
11 She is fickle and unruly,
in her home her feet cannot rest;
12 Now she is in the streets, now in the open squares,
and at every corner she lurks in ambush—
13 When she seizes him, she kisses him,
and with an impudent look says to him:

14 "I owed peace offerings,
and today I have fulfilled my vows;*
15 So I came out to meet you,
to look for you, and I have found you!
16 With coverlets I have spread my couch,
with brocaded cloths of Egyptian linen;
17 I have sprinkled my bed with myrrh,
with aloes, and with cinnamon.

18 "Come, let us drink our fill of love,
until morning, let us feast on love!
19 For my husband is not at home,
he has gone on a long journey;
20 A bag of money he took with him,
not till the full moon will he return home."

21 She wins him over by her repeated urging,
with her smooth lips she leads him astray; [j]
22 He follows her stupidly,
like an ox that is led to slaughter;
Like a stag that minces toward the net,
23 till an arrow pierces its liver;
Like a bird that rushes into a snare,
unaware that its life is at stake.

24 So now, O children, listen to me,
be attentive to the words of my mouth!
25 Let not your heart turn to her ways,
go not astray in her paths;
26 For many are those she has struck down dead,
numerous, those she has slain.
27 Her house is made up of ways to the nether world,
leading down into the chambers of death. [k]

CHAPTER 8

The Discourse of Wisdom*

1 Does not Wisdom call,
and Understanding raise her voice? [l]
2 On the top of the heights along the road,
at the crossroads she takes her stand;
3 By the gates at the approaches of the city,
in the entryways she cries aloud:
4 "To you, O men, I call;
my appeal is to the children of men.
5 You simple ones, gain resource,
you fools,* gain sense.
6 "Give heed! for noble things I speak;
honesty opens my lips.
7 Yes, the truth my mouth recounts,*
but wickedness my lips abhor.
8 Sincere are all the words of my mouth,
no one of them is wily or crooked;

7, 14: "Peace offerings . . . vows": a portion of the sacrifice reverted to the donor and had to be eaten on the same day at a family festival (Lv 7, 11–15). In this figure, the adulteress offers to share with the foolish young man the deadly feast of her sensuality.

8, 1–36: Wisdom is here personified as in Prv 1, 20–33, to confirm the words of the teacher of wisdom. She exalts her grandeur and origin, and invites all (1–11) to be attentive to her salutary influence in human society (12–21), for she was privileged to be present at the creation of the world (22–31). Finally, she promises life and the favor of God to those who find her, death to those who despise her.

8, 5: Simple ones . . . fools: see note on Prv 1, 4.

8, 7f: The truth and sincerity of wisdom are absolute because they are divine. They can neither deceive nor tolerate deception. An intelligent man understands and accepts them.

h Dt 6, 8. i Prv 2, 16; 6, 24. j Prv 5, 3; 6, 24. k Prv 2, 18f; 5, 5. l Prv 1, 20f; 9, 3.

9 All of them are plain to the man of intelligence,
and right to those who attain knowledge.
10 Receive my instruction in preference to silver,
and knowledge rather than choice gold.
11 [For Wisdom is better than corals,
and no choice possession can compare with her. [m]]

12 "I, Wisdom, dwell with experience,
and judicious knowledge I attain.
13 [The fear of the LORD is to hate evil;]
Pride, arrogance, the evil way,
and the perverse mouth I hate. [n]
14 Mine are counsel and advice;
mine is strength; I am understanding.*
15 By me kings reign,
and lawgivers establish justice;
16 By me princes govern,
and nobles; all the rulers of earth.

17 "Those who love me I also love,
and those who seek me find me.
18 With me are riches and honor, [o]
enduring wealth and prosperity.
19 My fruit is better than gold, yes, than pure gold,
and my revenue than choice silver. [p]
20 On the way of duty I walk,
along the paths of justice,
21 Granting wealth to those who love me,
and filling their treasuries.

22 "The LORD begot me, the first-born of his ways,*
the forerunner of his prodigies of long ago; [q]
23 From of old I was poured forth,*
at the first, before the earth. [r]
24 When there were no depths I was brought forth,*
when there were no fountains or springs of water;
25 Before the mountains were settled into place,
before the hills, I was brought forth;
26 While as yet the earth and the fields were not made,
nor the first clods of the world.

27 "When he established the heavens I was there, [s]
when he marked out the vault over the face of the deep;
28 When he made firm the skies above,
when he fixed fast the foundations of the earth;
29 When he set for the sea its limit,
so that the waters should not transgress his command;
30 Then was I beside him as his craftsman,*
and I was his delight day by day, [t]
Playing before him all the while,
31 playing on the surface of his earth;
and I found delight in the sons of men.

32 "So now, O children, listen to me;
33 instruction and wisdom do not reject!
Happy the man who obeys me,
and happy those who keep my ways,
34 Happy the man watching daily at my gates,
waiting at my doorposts;
35 For he who finds me finds life, [u]
and wins favor from the LORD;
36 But he who misses me harms himself;
all who hate me love death."

8, 14: What is here predicated of wisdom is elsewhere attributed to God (Jb 12, 13–16).

8, 22–31: Wisdom is of divine origin. It is here represented as a being which existed before all things (22–26) and concurred with God when he planned and executed the creation of the universe, adorned it with beauty and variety, and established its wonderful order (27–30). Here that plurality of divine Persons is foreshadowed which was afterward to be fully revealed when Wisdom in the Person of Jesus Christ became incarnate.

8, 23: Poured forth: the exact meaning of the Hebrew is uncertain; the expression must imply the equivalent of "born." The Hebrews likened the movement of air and of spirit to that of liquids.

8, 24–26: The formless mass from which God created the heavens and the earth; cf Gn 1, 1f; 2, 4ff.

8, 30: His craftsman: furnishing God with the plan, as it were, for the creation of all things; cf Jb 38, 1f; Wis 7, 22—8, 1. I was his delight: the ever-present object of God's complacency.

m Prv 3, 15; Wis 7, 8. n Prv 6, 16f; 16, 5. o Prv 3, 16. p Prv 3, 14. q Wis 9, 9; Sir 1, 1; 24, 9. r Sir 1, 4. s Prv 3, 19; Sir 24, 4f. t Wis 9, 9. u Prv 3, 13–18; 4, 22.

CHAPTER 9

The Two Banquets*

1 Wisdom has built her house,
she has set up her seven columns;
2 She has dressed her meat, mixed her wine,
yes, she has spread her table.
3 She has sent out her maidens; she calls*
from the heights out over the city: [v]
4 "Let whoever is simple turn in here;
to him who lacks understanding, I say,
5 Come, eat of my food,
and drink of the wine I have mixed!
6 Forsake foolishness that you may live;
advance in the way of understanding.
11 For by me your days will be multiplied
and the years of your life increased." [w]

7 He who corrects an arrogant man earns insult;
and he who reproves a wicked man incurs opprobrium.
8 Reprove not an arrogant man, lest he hate you;
reprove a wise man, and he will love you. [x]
9 Instruct a wise man, and he becomes still wiser;
teach a just man, and he advances in learning.

10 The beginning of wisdom is the fear of the LORD,
and knowledge of the Holy One is understanding. [y]
12 If you are wise, it is to your own advantage;
and if you are arrogant, you alone shall bear it.

13 The woman Folly is fickle, [z]
she is inane, and knows nothing.
14 She sits at the door of her house
upon a seat on the city heights,
15 Calling to passers-by
as they go on their straight way:
16 "Let whoever is simple turn in here,
or who lacks understanding; for to him I say,
17 Stolen water is sweet,
and bread gotten secretly is pleasing!"*
18 Little he knows that the shades are there,
that in the depths of the nether world are her guests!*

II: First Collection Of The Proverbs Of Solomon*

CHAPTER 10

1 The Proverbs of Solomon:

A wise son makes his father glad,
but a foolish son is a grief to his mother. [a]

2 Ill-gotten treasures profit nothing,
but virtue saves from death. [b]

3 The LORD permits not the just to hunger,
but the craving of the wicked he thwarts.

4 The slack hand impoverishes,
but the hand of the diligent enriches. [c]

5 A son who fills the granaries in summer is a credit;
a son who slumbers during harvest, a disgrace.

6 Blessings are for the head of the just,
but a rod for the back of the fool.

7 The memory of the just will be blessed,
but the name of the wicked will rot.

8 A wise man heeds commands,
but a prating fool will be overthrown.

9, 1–6. 13–18: Wisdom and folly are represented as matrons, each inviting people to her banquet. Wisdom offers the food and drink of divine doctrine and virtue which give life (1–6). Unstable and senseless folly furnishes the stolen bread and water of deceit and vice which bring death to her guests.

9, 3: She calls: i.e., indirectly, through her maidens; but the text could also mean that wisdom herself publicly proclaims her invitation.

9, 17: The secrecy implies wrongdoing.

9, 18: The banquet chamber of folly is a tomb from which no one who enters it is released.

10, 1—22, 16: The varied contents of this first collection of Solomon's proverbs apply mostly to individual life. Each of its three hundred and seventy-five proverbs is meant to be distinct from the others, developing one idea through contrasting parallelism in chapters 10—15, and a climactic treatment in 16—22.

v Prv 8, 1f. w Prv 3, 2. 16; 4, 10; 10, 27. x Sir 10, 27. y Prv 1, 7; Jb 28, 28; Ps 111, 10; Sir 1, 16. z 13–18; Prv, 7, 7–27. a Prv 1, 1; 15, 20; 17, 25; 19, 13; 25, 1; 29, 15. b Prv 11, 4. 6. c Prv 6, 11; 12, 24; 13, 4; 20, 13; 28, 19.

9 He who walks honestly walks securely,
but he whose ways are crooked will fare badly.

10 He who winks at a fault causes trouble,
but he who frankly reproves promotes peace.

11 A fountain of life is the mouth of the just,
but the mouth of the wicked conceals violence.

12 Hatred stirs up disputes,
[d]but love covers all offenses.*

13 On the lips of the intelligent is found wisdom,
[but the mouth of the wicked conceals violence].

14 Wise men store up knowledge,
but the mouth of a fool is imminent ruin.

15 The rich man's wealth is his strong city;
the ruination of the lowly is their poverty.*

16 The just man's recompense leads to life,
the gains of the wicked, to sin.[e]

17 A path to life is his who heeds admonition,
but he who disregards reproof goes astray.[f]

18 It is the lips of the liar that conceal hostility;
but he who spreads accusations is a fool.

19 Where words are many, sin is not wanting;
but he who restrains his lips does well.[g]

20 Like choice silver is the just man's tongue;
the heart of the wicked is of little worth.

21 The just man's lips nourish many,
but fools die for want of sense.

22 It is the LORD's blessing that brings wealth,[h]
and no effort can substitute for it.*

23 Crime is the entertainment of the fool;
so is wisdom for the man of sense.

24 What the wicked man fears will befall him,
but the desire of the just will be granted.

25 When the tempest passes, the wicked man is no more;
but the just man is established forever.

26 As vinegar to the teeth, and smoke to the eyes,
is the sluggard to those who use him as a messenger.

27 The fear of the LORD prolongs life,
but the years of the wicked are brief.[i]

28 The hope of the just brings them joy,
but the expectation of the wicked comes to nought.

29 The LORD is a stronghold to him who walks honestly,
but to evildoers, their downfall.

30 The just man will never be disturbed,
but the wicked will not abide in the land.

31 The mouth of the just yields wisdom,
but the perverse tongue will be cut off.

32 The lips of the just know how to please,
but the mouth of the wicked, how to pervert.

CHAPTER 11

1 False scales are an abomination to the LORD,
but a full weight is his delight.[j]

2 When pride comes, disgrace comes;
but with the humble is wisdom.

3 The honesty of the upright guides them;
the faithless are ruined by their duplicity.

4 Wealth is useless on the day of wrath,[k]
but virtue saves from death.*

5 The honest man's virtue makes his way straight,

10, 12: Love covers all offenses: a favorite maxim of the Apostles; cf 1 Cor 13, 7; Jas 5, 20; 1 Pt 4, 8; also Prv 17, 9.

10, 15: The inspired author reflects upon the reality of the power of money and the defeat of poverty, without approving these things.

10, 22: The blessing of God rather than our own industry crowns our efforts with success; cf Ps 127, 1f; Mt 6, 25–34.

11, 4: Wealth . . . death: not what a man is worth but what he is, counts before God.

d 1 Cor 13, 4–7; 1 Pt 4, 8. e Prv 11, 18f. f Prv 15, 10. g Prv 17, 27; Sir 20, 17; Jas 1, 19. h Sir 11, 22. i Prv 3, 2; 4, 10; 9, 11; 14, 27. j Prv 16, 11; 20, 10; Lv 19, 35f. k Prv 10, 2.

but by his wickedness the wicked man
falls. [l]

6 The virtue of the upright saves them,
but the faithless are caught in their own
intrigue.

7 When a wicked man dies his hope perishes, [m]
and what is expected from strength comes
to nought.

8 The just man escapes trouble,
and the wicked man falls into it in his stead.

9 With his mouth the impious man would ruin
his neighbor, [n]
but through their knowledge the just make
their escape.

10 When the just prosper, the city rejoices; [o]
and when the wicked perish, there is
jubilation.

11 Through the blessing of the righteous the city
is exalted,
but through the mouth of the wicked it is
overthrown.

12 He who reviles his neighbor has no sense,
but the intelligent man keeps silent.

13 A newsmonger reveals secrets, [p]
but a trustworthy man keeps a confidence.

14 For lack of guidance a people falls;
security lies in many counselors. [q]

15 He is in a bad way who becomes surety for
another, [r]
but he who hates giving pledges is safe.

16 A gracious woman wins esteem,
but she who hates virtue is covered with
shame.

[The slothful become impoverished,
but the diligent gain wealth.]

17 A kindly man benefits himself,
but a merciless man harms himself.

18 The wicked man makes empty profits,
but he who sows virtue has a sure reward. [s]

19 Virtue directs toward life,
but he who pursues evil does so to his
death.

20 The depraved in heart are an abomination to
the LORD,
but those who walk blamelessly are his
delight.

21 Truly the evil man shall not go unpunished,
but those who are just shall escape.

22 Like a golden ring in a swine's snout
is a beautiful woman with a rebellious
disposition.

23 The desire of the just ends only in good;
the expectation of the wicked is wrath.

24 One man is lavish yet grows still richer;
another is too sparing, yet is the poorer.

25 He who confers benefits will be amply
enriched,
and he who refreshes others will himself be
refreshed.

26 Him who monopolizes grain, the people
curse—
but blessings upon the head of him who
distributes it!

27 He who seeks the good commands favor,
but he who pursues evil will have evil befall
him.

28 He who trusts in his riches will fall,
but like green leaves the just flourish. [t]

29 He who upsets his household has empty air for
a heritage;
and the fool will become slave to the wise
man.

30 The fruit of virtue is a tree of life,
but violence takes lives away.

31 If the just man is punished on earth,
how much more the wicked and the
sinner! [u]

l Prv 28, 18. m Prv 10, 28; Wis 3, 18. n Prv 29, 5. o Prv 28, 12; 29, 2. p Prv 20, 19. q Prv 15, 22; 20, 18; 24, 6. r Prv 6, 1f. s Prv 10, 16. t Ps 52, 9f. u 1 Pt 4, 18.

CHAPTER 12

1 He who loves correction loves knowledge,
but he who hates reproof is stupid.[v]

2 The good man wins favor from the LORD,
but the schemer is condemned by him.

3 No man is built up by wickedness,
but the root of the just will never be disturbed.

4 A worthy wife is the crown of her husband,[w]
but a disgraceful one is like rot in his bones.

5 The plans of the just are legitimate;
the designs of the wicked are deceitful.

6 The words of the wicked are a deadly ambush,
but the speech of the upright saves them.

7 The wicked are overthrown and are no more,
but the house of the just stands firm.

8 According to his good sense a man is praised,
but one with a warped mind is despised.

9 Better a lowly man who supports himself
than one of assumed importance who lacks bread.[x]

10 The just man takes care of his beast,
but the heart of the wicked is merciless.

11 He who tills his own land has food in plenty,
but he who follows idle pursuits is a fool.[y]

12 The stronghold of evil men will be demolished,
but the root of the just is enduring.

13 In the sin of his lips the evil man is ensnared,
but the just comes free of trouble.

14 From the fruit of his words a man has his fill of good things,[z]
and the work of his hands comes back to reward him.*

15 The way of the fool seems right in his own eyes,
but he who listens to advice is wise.

16 The fool immediately shows his anger,
but the shrewd man passes over an insult.

17 He tells the truth who states what he is sure of,
but a lying witness speaks deceitfully.[a]

18 The prating of some men is like sword thrusts,
but the tongue of the wise is healing.

19 Truthful lips endure forever,
the lying tongue, for only a moment.

20 Deceit is in the hands of those who plot evil,
but those who counsel peace have joy.

21 No harm befalls the just,
but the wicked are overwhelmed with misfortune.

22 Lying lips are an abomination to the LORD,[b]
but those who are truthful are his delight.

23 A shrewd man conceals his knowledge,
but the hearts of fools gush forth folly.

24 The diligent hand will govern,
but the slothful will be enslaved.[c]

25 Anxiety in a man's heart depresses it,
but a kindly word makes it glad.[d]

26 The just man surpasses his neighbor,
but the way of the wicked leads them astray.

27 The slothful man catches not his prey,
but the wealth of the diligent man is great.

28 In the path of justice there is life,
but the abominable way leads to death.

CHAPTER 13

1 A wise son loves correction,
but the senseless one heeds no rebuke.

2 From the fruit of his words a man eats good things,[e]
but the treacherous one craves violence.

3 He who guards his mouth protects his life;
to open wide one's lips brings downfall.[f]

12, 14: Cf Mt 7, 17; Gal 6, 8.

v Prv 15, 5. 10; 29, 1; Sir 19, 5; 21, 6. w Sir 26, 1. 16. x Sir 10, 26. y Prv 28, 19; Sir 20, 27. z Prv 13, 2; 18, 20. a Prv 14, 5. b Prv 6, 17. c Prv 10, 4; 13, 4. d Prv 15, 13; 17, 22. e Prv 12, 14; 18, 20. f Prv 18, 7; 21, 23.

4 The soul of the sluggard craves in vain,
but the diligent soul is amply satisfied.

5 Anything deceitful the just man hates,
but the wicked brings shame and disgrace.

6 Virtue guards one who walks honestly,
but the downfall of the wicked is sin. [g]

7 One man pretends to be rich, yet has nothing;
another pretends to be poor, yet has great wealth.

8 A man's riches serve as ransom for his life,
but the poor man heeds no rebuke.

9 The light of the just shines gaily,
but the lamp* of the wicked goes out. [h]

10 The stupid man sows discord by his insolence,
but with those who take counsel is wisdom.

11 Wealth quickly gotten dwindles away,
but amassed little by little, it grows. [i]

12 Hope deferred makes the heart sick,
but a wish fulfilled is a tree of life.

13 He who despises the word* must pay for it,
but he who reveres the commandment will be rewarded.

14 The teaching of the wise is a fountain of life,
that a man may avoid the snares of death.

15 Good sense brings favor,
but the way of the faithless is their ruin.

16 The shrewd man does everything with prudence,
but the fool peddles folly.

17 A wicked messenger brings on disaster,
but a trustworthy envoy is a healing remedy.

18 Poverty and shame befall the man who disregards correction,
but he who heeds reproof is honored.

19 Lust indulged starves the soul,
but fools hate to turn from evil.

20 Walk with wise men and you will become wise,
but the companion of fools will fare badly. [j]

21 Misfortune pursues sinners,
but the just shall be recompensed with good.

22 The good man leaves an inheritance to his children's children,
but the wealth of the sinner is stored up for the just.

23 A lawsuit devours the tillage of the poor,
but some men perish for lack of a law court.

24 He who spares his rod hates his son,
but he who loves him takes care to chastise him. [k]

25 When the just man eats, his hunger is appeased;
but the belly of the wicked suffers want.

CHAPTER 14

1 Wisdom builds her house,
but Folly tears hers down with her own hands.

2 He who walks uprightly fears the LORD,
but he who is devious in his ways spurns him.

3 In the mouth of the fool is a rod for his back,
but the lips of the wise preserve them.

4 Where there are no oxen, the crib remains empty;
but large crops come through the strength of the bull.

5 A truthful witness does not lie,
but a false witness utters lies. [l]

6 The senseless man seeks in vain for wisdom,
but knowledge is easy to the man of intelligence.

7 To avoid the foolish man, take steps!

13, 9: Light . . . lamp: symbols of life and prosperity; cf Prv 4, 18f.
13, 13: Word: advice, or God's law.

g Prv 11, 3. 5f. h Prv 24, 20. i Prv 28, 20. 22. j Sir 6, 34; 8, 8. 17. k Prv 19, 18; 22, 15; 23, 13f; 29, 15; Sir 30, 1. 8–13. l Prv 12. 17.

But knowing lips one meets with by
surprise.

8 The shrewd man's wisdom gives him
knowledge of his way,
but the folly of fools is their deception.

9 Guilt lodges in the tents of the arrogant,
but favor in the house of the just.

10 The heart knows its own bitterness,
and in its joy no one else shares.

11 The house of the wicked will be destroyed,
but the tent of the upright will flourish. [m]

12 Sometimes a way seems right to a man,
but the end of it leads to death! [n]

13 Even in laughter the heart may be sad
and the end of joy may be sorrow.

14 The scoundrel suffers the consequences of his
ways,
and the good man reaps the fruit of his
paths.

15 The simpleton believes everything,
but the shrewd man measures his steps.

16 The wise man is cautious and shuns evil;
the fool is reckless and sure of himself.

17 The quick-tempered man makes a fool of
himself,
but the prudent man is at peace.

18 The adornment of simpletons is folly,
but shrewd men gain the crown of
knowledge.

19 Evil men must bow down before the good,
and the wicked, at the gates of the just.

20 Even by his neighbor the poor man is hated,
but the friends of the rich are many. [o]

21 He sins who despises the hungry;
but happy is he who is kind to the poor!

22 Do not those who plot evil go astray?
But those intent on good gain kindness and
constancy.

23 In all labor there is profit,
but mere talk tends only to penury.

24 The crown of the wise is resourcefulness;
the diadem of fools is folly.

25 The truthful witness saves lives,
but he who utters lies is a betrayer.

26 In the fear of the LORD is a strong defense;
even for one's children he will be a refuge.

27 The fear of the LORD is a fountain of life,
that a man may avoid the snares of death.

28 In many subjects lies the glory of the king;
but if his people are few, it is the prince's
ruin.

29 The patient man shows much good sense,
but the quick-tempered man displays folly at
its height. [p]

30 A tranquil mind gives life to the body,
but jealousy rots the bones.

31 He who oppresses the poor blasphemes his
Maker,
but he who is kind to the needy glorifies
him. [q]

32 The wicked man is overthrown by his
wickedness,
but the just man finds a refuge in his
honesty.

33 In the heart of the intelligent wisdom abides,
but in the bosom of fools it is unknown.

34 Virtue exalts a nation,
but sin is a people's disgrace.

35 The king favors the intelligent servant,
but the worthless one incurs his wrath.

CHAPTER 15

1 A mild answer calms wrath, [r]
but a harsh word stirs up anger.

2 The tongue of the wise pours out knowledge,
but the mouth of fools spurts forth folly.

m Prv 3, 33; 12, 7; 15, 25. n Prv 16, 25. o Prv 19, 4. 7; Sir 6, 8, 12. p Prv 16, 32; 19, 11; Jas 1, 19. q Prv 17, 5. r Prv 25, 15; Sir 6, 5.

[3]The eyes of the LORD are in every place,
keeping watch on the evil and the good.

[4]A soothing tongue is a tree of life,
but a perverse one crushes the spirit.

[5]The fool spurns his father's admonition,
but prudent is he who heeds reproof.[s]

[6]In the house of the just there are ample
resources,
but the earnings of the wicked are in
turmoil.

[7]The lips of the wise disseminate knowledge,
but the heart of fools is perverted.

[8]The sacrifice of the wicked is an abomination
to the LORD,[t]
but the prayer of the upright is his delight.

[9]The way of the wicked is an abomination to
the LORD,
but he loves the man who pursues virtue.[u]

[10]Severe punishment is in store for the man who
goes astray;
he who hates reproof will die.

[11]The nether world and the abyss* lie open
before the LORD;
how much more the hearts of men!

[12]The senseless man loves not to be reproved;
to wise men he will not go.

[13]A glad heart lights up the face,
but by mental anguish the spirit is broken.[v]

[14]The mind of the intelligent man seeks
knowledge,
but the mouth of fools feeds on folly.

[15]Every day is miserable for the depressed,
but a lighthearted man has a continual feast.

[16]Better a little with fear of the LORD*
than a great fortune with anxiety.

[17]Better a dish of herbs where love is
than a fatted ox and hatred with it.

[18]An ill-tempered man stirs up strife,[w]
but a patient man allays discord.

[19]The way of the sluggard is hemmed in as with
thorns,
but the path of the diligent is a highway.

[20]A wise son makes his father glad,
but a fool of a man despises his mother.[x]

[21]Folly is joy to the senseless man,
but the man of understanding goes the
straight way.

[22]Plans fail when there is no counsel,
but they succeed when counselors are
many.[y]

[23]There is joy for a man in his utterance;
a word in season, how good it is![z]

[24]The path of life leads the prudent man
upward,
that he may avoid the nether world below.

[25]The LORD overturns the house of the proud,
but he preserves intact the widow's
landmark.

[26]The wicked man's schemes are an
abomination to the LORD,[a]
but the pure speak what is pleasing to him.

[27]He who is greedy of gain brings ruin on his
own house,
but he who hates bribes will live.

[28]The just man weighs well his utterance,
but the mouth of the wicked pours out evil.

[29]The LORD is far from the wicked,
but the prayer of the just he hears.

[30]A cheerful glance brings joy to the heart;
good news invigorates the bones.

[31]He who listens to salutary reproof[b]
will abide among the wise.

15, 11: Nether world . . . abyss: the abode of the dead, signifying the profound obscurity which is open nevertheless to the sight and power of God.

15, 16f: Not the amount of temporal goods but the virtue of their possessor makes them a source of happiness.

s Prv 12, 1; 13, 18. t Prv 21, 27; Eccl 4, 17; Sir 34, 18ff; Is 1, 11–15. u Prv 11, 20; 21, 21. v Prv 12, 25; 17, 22; Sir 30, 22. w Prv 26, 21; 29, 22; Sir 28, 11. x Prv 10, 1; 29, 3. y Prv 11, 14. z Prv 25, 11; Sir 20, 6. a Prv 6, 18. b Prv 25, 12.

32 He who rejects admonition despises his own soul,
but he who heeds reproof gains understanding.

33 The fear of the LORD is training for wisdom,
and humility goes before honors. [c]

CHAPTER 16

1 Man may make plans in his heart,
but what the tongue utters is from the LORD.*

2 All the ways of a man may be pure in his own eyes,
but it is the LORD who proves the spirit. [d]

3 Entrust your works to the LORD,
and your plans will succeed.

4 The LORD has made everything for his own ends,
even the wicked for the evil day.*

5 Every proud man is an abomination to the LORD; [e]
I assure you that he will not go unpunished.

6 By kindness and piety guilt is expiated,
and by the fear of the LORD man avoids evil.

7 When the LORD is pleased with a man's ways,
he makes even his enemies be at peace with him.

8 Better a little with virtue,
than a large income with injustice.

9 In his mind a man plans his course,
but the LORD directs his steps. [f]

10 The king's lips are an oracle;
no judgment he pronounces is false.*

11 Balance and scales belong to the LORD;
all the weights used with them are his concern. [g]

12 Kings have a horror of wrongdoing,
for by righteousness the throne endures. [h]

13 The king takes delight in honest lips,
and the man who speaks what is right he loves. [i]

14 The king's wrath is like messengers of death, [j]
but a wise man can pacify it.

15 In the light of the king's countenance is life,
and his favor is like a rain cloud in spring.

16 How much better to acquire wisdom than gold!
To acquire understanding is more desirable than silver. [k]

17 The path of the upright avoids misfortune;
he who pays attention to his way safeguards his life.

18 Pride goes before disaster,
and a haughty spirit before a fall.

19 It is better to be humble with the meek
than to share plunder with the proud. [l]

20 He who plans a thing will be successful;
happy is he who trusts in the LORD!

21 The wise man is esteemed for his discernment,
yet pleasing speech increases his persuasiveness.

22 Good sense is a fountain of life to its possessor,
but folly brings chastisement on fools.

23 The mind of the wise man makes him eloquent,
and augments the persuasiveness of his lips.

24 Pleasing words are a honeycomb,
sweet to the taste and healthful to the body.

25 Sometimes a way seems right to a man,
but the end of it leads to death! [m]

16, 1: Words, like actions, often produce results different from those which were planned.
16, 4: Even the wicked, in their punishment, cannot escape glorifying God's justice.
16, 10: Decisions of supreme judicial authority were presumed disinterested and correct.

c Prv 1, 7; Sir 1, 24. d Prv 21, 2. e Prv 6, 16f; 8, 13. f Prv 19, 21; 20, 24. g Prv 11, 1. h Prv 25, 5. i Prv 14, 35; 22, 11. j Prv 19, 12; 20, 2. k Prv 8, 10f. 19. l Prv 11, 2. m Prv 14, 12.

26 The laborer's appetite labors for him,
for his mouth urges him on. [n]

27 A scoundrel is a furnace of evil,
and on his lips there is a scorching fire.

28 An intriguer sows discord,
and a talebearer separates bosom friends. [o]

29 A lawless man allures his neighbor,
and leads him into a way that is not good.

30 He who winks his eye is plotting trickery;
he who compresses his lips has mischief ready.

31 Gray hair is a crown of glory; [p]
it is gained by virtuous living.

32 A patient man is better than a warrior,
and he who rules his temper, than he who takes a city. [q]

33 When the lot is cast into the lap,
its decision depends entirely on the LORD.*

CHAPTER 17

1 Better a dry crust with peace
than a house full of feasting with strife.

2 An intelligent servant will rule over a worthless son,
and will share the inheritance with the brothers.*

3 The crucible for silver, and the furnace for gold,
but the tester of hearts is the LORD.

4 The evil man gives heed to wicked lips,
and listens to falsehood from a mischievous tongue.*

5 He who mocks the poor blasphemes his Maker; [r]
he who is glad at calamity will not go unpunished.

6 Grandchildren are the crown of old men,
and the glory of children is their parentage.

7 Fine words are out of place in a fool;
how much more, lying words in a noble!

8 A man who has a bribe to offer rates it a magic stone;
at every turn it brings him success.

9 He who covers up a misdeed fosters friendship,
but he who gossips about it separates friends.

10 A single reprimand does more for a man of intelligence
than a hundred lashes for a fool.

11 On rebellion alone is the wicked man bent,
but a merciless messenger will be sent against him.

12 Face a bear robbed of her cubs,
but never a fool in his folly!

13 If a man returns evil for good,
from his house evil will not depart. [s]

14 The start of strife is like the opening of a dam;
therefore, check a quarrel before it begins!

15 He who condones the wicked, [t] he who condemns the just,
are both an abomination to the LORD.

16 Of what use in the fool's hand are the means
to buy wisdom, since he has no mind for it?

17 He who is a friend is always a friend,
and a brother is born for the time of stress. [u]

18 Senseless is the man who gives his hand in pledge,
who becomes surety for his neighbor. [v]

19 He who loves strife loves guilt; [w]
he who builds his gate high* courts disaster.

16, 33: The favorable or unfavorable result of chance depends on God. Deciding strifes and doubts by lot was practiced by the ancient Hebrews; cf Ex 28, 15–30; Lv 16, 8; Jos 7, 14; 1 Sm 10, 20f.

17, 2: Intelligence and ability are esteemed more highly than nobility of blood.

17, 4: To justify his own evil ways, a wicked man judges evil of others. Cf Mt 7, 1–5.

17, 19: Builds . . . high: a symbol of arrogance.

n Prv 10, 4. o Prv 6, 14. 19; 17, 9; 26, 22; Sir 28, 15. p Prv 20, 29. q Prv 14, 29. r Prv 14, 31. s Mt 5, 39; Rom 12, 17; 1 Thes 5, 15; 1 Pt 3, 9. t Prv 24, 24; Is 5, 23. u Prv 18, 24. v Prv 6, 1f; 11, 15. w Prv 15, 18.

20 He who is perverse in heart finds no good,
and a double-tongued man falls into trouble.

21 To be a fool's parent is grief for a man;
the father of a numskull has no joy.

22 A joyful heart is the health of the body,
but a depressed spirit dries up the bones.[x]

23 The wicked man accepts a concealed bribe
to pervert the course of justice.

24 The man of intelligence fixes his gaze on wisdom,[y]
but the eyes of a fool are on the ends of the earth.

25 A foolish son is vexation to his father,
and bitter sorrow to her who bore him.[z]

26 It is wrong to fine an innocent man,
but beyond reason to scourge princes.

27 He who spares his words is truly wise,
and he who is chary of speech is a man of intelligence.[a]

28 Even a fool, if he keeps silent, is considered wise;
if he closes his lips, intelligent.

CHAPTER 18

1 In estrangement one seeks pretexts:
with all persistence he picks a quarrel.

2 The fool takes no delight in understanding,
but rather in displaying what he thinks.

3 With wickedness comes contempt,
and with disgrace comes scorn.

4 The words from a man's mouth are deep waters,
but the source of wisdom is a flowing brook.[b]

5 It is not good to be partial to the guilty,
and so to reject a rightful claim.[c]

6 The fool's lips lead him into strife,
and his mouth provokes a beating.

7 The fool's mouth is his ruin;
his lips are a snare to his life.[d]

8 The words of a talebearer are like dainty morsels
that sink into one's inmost being.[e]

9 The man who is slack in his work
is own brother to the man who is destructive.

10 The name of the LORD is a strong tower;*
the just man runs to it and is safe.

11 The rich man's wealth is his strong city;[f]
he fancies it a high wall.

12 Before his downfall a man's heart is haughty,[g]
but humility goes before honors.*

13 He who answers before he hears[h] —
his is the folly and the shame.*

14 A man's spirit sustains him in infirmity—
but a broken spirit who can bear?

15 The mind of the intelligent gains knowledge,
and the ear of the wise seeks knowledge.

16 A man's gift clears the way for him,
and gains him access to great men.[i]

17 The man who pleads his case first seems to be in the right;
then his opponent comes and puts him to the test.

18 The lot puts an end to disputes,
and is decisive in a controversy between the mighty.*

19 A brother is a better defense than a strong city,
and a friend is like the bars of a castle.

18, 10f: Religion is a strong support and sure refuge in the struggle of life. The rich foolishly rely on their wealth for such support.

18, 12: Compare the Savior's words: "Whoever exalts himself shall be humbled, but whoever humbles himself shall be exalted" (Mt 23, 12).

18, 13: To speak without first listening is characteristic of a fool; cf Prv 10, 14; Sir 11, 8.

18, 18: See note on Prv 16, 33.

x Prv 12, 25; 15, 13. y Eccl 8, 1. z Prv 10, 1; 29, 15. a Prv 10, 19; Sir 1, 21; Jas 1, 19. b Prv 20, 5; Jn 7, 38. c Prv 24, 23; 28, 21. d Prv 10, 14; 12, 13; 13, 3; Eccl 10, 12. e Prv 26, 22. f Prv 10, 15. g Prv 11, 2; 16, 18; Sir 10, 15. h Sir 11, 8. i Prv 21, 14.

20 From the fruit of his mouth a man has his fill;*
with the yield of his lips he sates himself.[j]

21 Death and life are in the power of the tongue;[k]
those who make it a friend shall eat its fruit.

22 He who finds a wife finds happiness;
it is a favor he receives from the LORD.[l]

23 The poor man implores,
but the rich man answers harshly.

24 Some friends bring ruin on us,
but a true friend is more loyal than a brother.[m]

CHAPTER 19

1 Better a poor man who walks in his integrity
than he who is crooked in his ways and rich.[n]

2 Without knowledge even zeal is not good;
and he who acts hastily, blunders.

3 A man's own folly upsets his way,
but his heart is resentful against the LORD.

4 Wealth adds many friends,
but the friend of the poor man deserts him.[o]

5 The false witness will not go unpunished,
and he who utters lies will not escape.[p]

6 Many curry favor with a noble;
all are friends of the man who has something to give.

7 All the poor man's brothers hate him;
how much more do his friends shun him!

8 He who gains intelligence is his own best friend;
he who keeps understanding will be successful.

9 The false witness will not go unpunished,
and he who utters lies will perish.

10 Luxury is not befitting a fool;
much less should a slave rule over princes.

11 It is good sense in a man to be slow to anger,
and it is his glory to overlook an offense.

12 The king's wrath is like the roaring of a lion,
but his favor, like dew on the grass.[q]

13 The foolish son is ruin to his father,[r]
and the nagging of a wife is a persistent leak.

14 Home and possessions are an inheritance from parents,
but a prudent wife is from the LORD.[s]

15 Laziness plunges a man into deep sleep,
and the sluggard must go hungry.[t]

16 He who keeps the precept keeps his life,
but the despiser of the word will die.[u]

17 He who has compassion on the poor lends to the LORD,[v]
and he will repay him for his good deed.*

18 Chastise your son, for in this there is hope;
but do not desire his death.[w]

19 The man of violent temper pays the penalty;
even if you rescue him, you will have it to do again.

20 Listen to counsel and receive instruction,
that you may eventually become wise.

21 Many are the plans in a man's heart,
but it is the decision of the LORD that endures.[x]

22 From a man's greed comes his shame;
rather be a poor man than a liar.

23 The fear of the LORD is an aid to life;
one eats and sleeps without being visited by misfortune.

24 The sluggard loses his hand in the dish;
he will not even lift it to his mouth.[y]

18, 20f: Everyone must accept the consequences, of benefit or harm to himself, which his words produce.

19, 17: Cf Mt 25, 34–40.

j Prv 12, 14; 13, 2. k Sir 37, 18. l Prv 12, 4; 19, 14; Sir 7, 26. m Prv 17, 17. n Prv 28, 6. o Prv 14, 20; Sir 13, 20ff. p Dt 19, 16–20; Dn 13, 61. q Prv 20, 2. r Prv 10, 1; 17, 25. s Prv 18, 22. t Prv 6, 9ff. u Prv 13, 13; 16, 17. v Prv 14, 21; 22, 9; 28, 27. w Prv 13, 24; 23, 13f. x Prv 16, 9. y Prv 26, 15.

25 If you beat an arrogant man, the simple learn a lesson;
if you rebuke an intelligent man, he gains knowledge. [z]

26 He who mistreats his father, or drives away his mother,
is a worthless and disgraceful son. [a]

27 If a son ceases to hear instruction,
he wanders from words of knowledge.

28 An unprincipled witness perverts justice,
and the mouth of the wicked pours out iniquity.

29 Rods are prepared for the arrogant,
and blows for the backs of fools. [b]

CHAPTER 20

1 Wine is arrogant, strong drink is riotous;
none who goes astray for it is wise. [c]

2 The dread of the king is as when a lion roars; [d]
he who incurs his anger forfeits his life.

3 It is honorable for a man to shun strife,
while every fool starts a quarrel.

4 In seedtime the sluggard plows not;
when he looks for the harvest, it is not there.

5 The intention in the human heart is like water far below the surface,
but the man of intelligence draws it forth. [e]

6 Many are declared to be men of virtue:
but who can find one worthy of trust?

7 When a man walks in integrity and justice,
happy are his children after him!

8 A king seated on the throne of judgment
dispels all evil with his glance.

9 Who can say, "I have made my heart clean, [f]
I am cleansed of my sin"?*

10 Varying weights, varying measures,
are both an abomination to the LORD. [g]

11 Even by his manners the child betrays
whether his conduct is innocent and right.

12 The ear that hears, and the eye that sees—
the LORD has made them both.

13 Love not sleep, lest you be reduced to poverty;
eyes wide open mean abundant food.

14 "Bad, bad!" says the buyer;
but once he has gone his way, he boasts.*

15 Like gold or a wealth of corals,
wise lips are a precious ornament.

16 Take his garment who becomes surety for another, [h]
and for strangers yield it up!*

17 The bread of deceit is sweet to a man,
but afterward his mouth will be filled with gravel.

18 Plans made after advice succeed;
so with wise guidance wage your war.

19 A newsmonger reveals secrets;
so have nothing to do with a babbler!

20 If one curses his father or mother,
his lamp will go out* at the coming of darkness. [i]

21 Possessions gained hastily at the outset
will in the end not be blessed.

22 Say not, "I will repay evil!"
Trust in the LORD and he will help you. [j]

23 Varying weights are an abomination to the LORD,
and false scales are not good. [k]

20, 9: Man can be free of sin only by the power of God. Cf 1 Kgs 8, 46ff; Jb 4, 17; 14, 4; Pss 51, 2ff; 130, 3f; Rom 3, 23f; 1 Jn 1, 8.

20, 14: What one wishes to buy is valued cheaply in order that it may be obtained at a low price; once purchased, it is deemed more valuable.

20, 16: Caution is again advised in the matter of becoming surety; cf Prv 6, 1ff.

20, 20: His lamp will go out: misfortune, even death, awaits him; cf Prv 13, 9; Ex 21, 17.

z Prv 17, 10; 21, 11. a Sir 3, 16. b Prv 26, 3. c Prv 23, 29–35. d Prv 19, 12. e Prv 18, 4. f 1 Kgs 8, 46; 2 Chr 6, 36; Eccl 7, 20; 1 Jn 1, 8. g Prv 11, 1; 20, 23. h Prv 27, 13. i Prv 30, 11. 17; Ex 21, 17; Lv 20, 9; Mt 15, 4. j Prv 24, 29; Sir 28, 1; Mt 5, 39; Rom 12, 17. 19; 1 Thes 5, 15; 1 Pt 3, 9. k Prv 11, 1; 20, 10.

24 Man's steps are from the LORD; [l]
how, then, can a man understand his way?*

25 Rashly to pledge a sacred gift is a trap for a man,
or to regret a vow once made.*

26 A wise king winnows the wicked,
and threshes them under the cartwheel.

27 A lamp from the LORD is the breath of man;
it searches through all his inmost being.

28 Kindness and piety safeguard the king,
and he upholds his throne by justice. [m]

29 The glory of young men is their strength,
and the dignity of old men is gray hair. [n]

30 Evil is cleansed away by bloody lashes,
and a scourging to the inmost being.

CHAPTER 21

1 Like a stream is the king's heart in the hand of the Lord;
wherever it pleases him, he directs it.

2 All the ways of a man may be right in his own eyes,
but it is the LORD who proves hearts. [o]

3 To do what is right and just [p]
is more acceptable to the LORD than sacrifice.*

4 Haughty eyes and a proud heart—
the tillage of the wicked is sin.

5 The plans of the diligent are sure of profit,
but all rash haste leads certainly to poverty.

6 He who makes a fortune by a lying tongue
is chasing a bubble over deadly snares.

7 The oppression of the wicked will sweep them away,
because they refuse to do what is right.

8 The way of the culprit is crooked,
but the conduct of the innocent is right.

9 It is better to dwell in a corner of the housetop
than in a roomy house with a quarrelsome woman. [q]

10 The soul of the wicked man desires evil;
his neighbor finds no pity in his eyes.

11 When the arrogant man is punished, the simple are the wiser;
when the wise man is instructed, he gains knowledge. [r]

12 The just man appraises the house of the wicked:
there is one who brings down the wicked to ruin.

13 He who shuts his ear to the cry of the poor
will himself also call and not be heard.

14 A secret gift allays anger,
and a concealed present, violent wrath.

15 To practice justice is a joy for the just,
but terror for evildoers. [s]

16 The man who strays from the way of good sense
will abide in the assembly of the shades.*

17 He who loves pleasure will suffer want;
he who loves wine and perfume will not be rich.

18 The wicked man serves as ransom for the just,*
and the faithless man for the righteous. [t]

19 It is better to dwell in a wilderness
than with a quarrelsome and vexatious wife.

20 Precious treasure remains in the house of the wise,

20, 24: Man is dependent upon God and cannot fully foresee his own course.
20, 25: This verse cautions against making vows without proper reflection; cf Dt 23, 22ff; Eccl 5, 4f.
21, 3: External rites or sacrifices do not please God unless accompanied by internal worship and right moral conduct; cf Prv 15, 8; 21, 27; Is 1, 11–15; Am 5, 22; Mal 1, 12.
21, 16: Assembly of the shades: cf note on Jb 26, 5.
21, 18: Wicked . . . ransom for the just: exemplified in the history of God's chosen people whom he ransomed from Egypt at the cost of the life of Pharaoh and his army (Ex 14, 23–31), and from Babylon by giving to Cyrus, the Persian conqueror, Egypt, Ethiopia and Seba, the richest lands of the world (Is 43, 1ff).

l Prv 16, 9. m Prv 16, 12. n Prv 16, 31. o Prv 16, 2. p 1 Sm 15, 22; Hos 6, 6. q Prv 21, 19; 25, 24; 27, 15; Sir 25, 23. r Prv 19, 25. s Prv 10, 29. t Prv 11, 8.

but the fool consumes it.

21 He who pursues justice and kindness
will find life and honor.

22 The wise man storms a city of the mighty,
and overthrows the stronghold in which it trusts.

23 He who guards his mouth and his tongue
keeps himself from trouble. [u]

24 Arrogant is the name for the man of overbearing pride
who acts with scornful effrontery.

25 The sluggard's propensity slays him,
for his hands refuse to work.

26 Some are consumed with avarice all the day,
but the just man gives unsparingly.

27 The sacrifice of the wicked is an abomination,
the more so when they offer it with a bad intention. [v]

28 The false witness will perish, [w]
but he who listens will finally have his say.

29 The wicked man is brazenfaced,
but the upright man pays heed to his ways.

30 There is no wisdom, no understanding,
no counsel, against the LORD.

31 The horse is equipped for the day of battle,
but victory is the LORD's.

CHAPTER 22

1 A good name is more desirable than great riches,
and high esteem, than gold and silver. [x]

2 Rich and poor have a common bond:
the LORD is the maker of them all. [y]

3 The shrewd man perceives evil and hides,
while simpletons continue on and suffer the penalty. [z]

4 The reward of humility and fear of the LORD
is riches, honor and life.

5 Thorns and snares are on the path of the crooked;
he who would safeguard his life will shun them.

6 Train a boy in the way he should go;
even when he is old, he will not swerve from it.

7 The rich rule over the poor,
and the borrower is the slave of the lender.

8 He who sows iniquity reaps calamity, [a]
and the rod destroys his labors.

9 The kindly man will be blessed,
for he gives of his sustenance to the poor.

10 Expel the arrogant man and discord goes out;
strife and insult cease.

11 The LORD loves the pure of heart; [b]
the man of winning speech has the king for his friend.

12 The eyes of the LORD safeguard knowledge,
but he defeats the projects of the faithless.

13 The sluggard says, "A lion is outside; [c]
in the streets I might be slain."*

14 The mouth of the adulteress is a deep pit; [d]
he with whom the LORD is angry will fall into it.

15 Folly is close to the heart of a child,
but the rod of discipline will drive it far from him.

16 He who oppresses the poor to enrich himself
will yield up his gains to the rich as sheer loss.*

22, 13: To avoid the effort required for doing good, the sluggard exaggerates the difficulties that must be overcome.

22, 16: Money gained by exploiting the poor is in turn lost to those who are more wealthy.

u Prv 13, 3. v Prv 15, 8; Sir 34, 18ff. w Prv 19, 5. 9. x Eccl 7, 1. y Prv 29, 13. z Prv 27, 12. a Jb 4, 8; Sir 7, 3; Hos 8, 7. b Mt 5, 8. c Prv 26, 13. d Prv 23, 27.

III: Sayings of the Wise*

17 The sayings of the wise:*

Incline your ear, and hear my words, [e]
and apply your heart to my doctrine;
18 For it will be well if you keep them in your bosom,
if they all are ready on your lips.
19 That your trust may be in the LORD,
I make known to you the words of Amen-em-Ope.*
20 Have I not written for you the "Thirty,"
with counsels and knowledge,
21 To teach you truly
how to give a dependable report to one who sends you?

22 Injure not the poor because they are poor,
nor crush the needy at the gate;
23 For the LORD will defend their cause,[f]
and will plunder the lives of those who plunder them.

24 Be not friendly with a hotheaded man,
nor the companion of a wrathful man,
25 Lest you learn his ways,
and get yourself into a snare.

26 Be not one of those who give their hand in pledge,
of those who become surety for debts; [g]
27 For if you have not the means to pay,
your bed will be taken from under you.

28 Remove not the ancient landmark
which your fathers set up. [h]

29 You see a man skilled at his work?
He will stand in the presence of kings;
he will not stand in the presence of obscure men.

CHAPTER 23

1 When you sit down to dine with a ruler,
keep in mind who is before you;
2 And put a knife to your throat*
if you have a ravenous appetite.
3 Do not desire his delicacies;
they are deceitful food.
4 Toil not to gain wealth,
cease to be concerned about it;
5 While your glance flits to it, it is gone!
for assuredly it grows wings,
like the eagle that flies toward heaven.

6 Do not take food with a grudging man,
and do not desire his dainties;
7 For in his greed he is like a storm.
"Eat and drink," he says to you,
though his heart is not with you;
8 The little you have eaten you will vomit up,
and you will have wasted your agreeable words.
9 Speak not for the fool's hearing;
he will despise the wisdom of your words. [i]

10 Remove not the ancient landmark,[j]
nor invade the fields of orphans;
11 For their redeemer is strong;
he will defend their cause against you. [k]

12 Apply your heart to instruction,
and your ears to words of knowledge.

13 Withhold not chastisement from a boy;
if you beat him with the rod, he will not die. [l]
14 Beat him with the rod, [m]
and you will save him from the nether world.

15 My son, if your heart be wise,
my own heart also will rejoice;

22, 17—24, 22: This collection of proverbs, introduced as sayings of the wise, is given in the more intimate and personal form of an address to a pupil called the son and is arranged in strophes instead of couplets.

22, 17—23, 35: The maxims warn against: oppression of the poor and defenseless (22, 22f), anger (24f), giving surety for debts (26f), bad manners at a king's table (23, 1f), anxiety for riches (4f), a grudging host (6ff), intemperance in food and drink (19ff. 29–35), and adultery (26ff). They exhort to: careful workmanship (22, 29), respect for the rights of orphans (23, 10f), correction of the young (13f), filial piety (15f. 22–25), and fear of the Lord (17f).

22, 19f: Amen-em-Ope: an Egyptian scribe to whom is attributed a collection of maxims in Thirty chapters (v 20) composed for the instruction of his children and addressed to a young man who wishes to enter upon a career. The inspired editor of Proverbs does not translate these, but uses their materials in constructing a similar collection of proverbs.

23, 2: Put a knife to your throat: a proverbial metaphor for self-restraint.

e Prv 5, 1. f Prv 23, 11. g Prv 6, 1f; 11, 15; 17, 18. h Prv 23, 10; Dt 19, 14; 27, 17. i Prv 9, 7. j Prv 22, 28. k Prv 22, 23. l Prv 13, 24; 19, 18; Sir 30, 1. m Prv 29, 15. 17.

16 And my inmost being will exult,
when your lips speak what is right.

17 Let not your heart emulate sinners, [n]
but be zealous for the fear of the LORD
always;
18 For you will surely have a future,
and your hope will not be cut off. [o]

19 Hear, my son, and be wise,
and guide your heart in the right way.
20 Consort not with winebibbers,
nor with those who eat meat to excess;
21 For the drunkard and the glutton come to
poverty,
and torpor clothes a man in rags.

22 Listen to your father who begot you,
and despise not your mother when she is
old.
23 Get the truth, and sell it not—
wisdom, instruction and understanding.
24 The father of a just man will exult with glee;
he who begets a wise son will have joy in
him. [p]
25 Let your father and mother have joy;
let her who bore you exult.

26 My son, give me your heart,
and let your eyes keep to my ways.
27 For the harlot is a deep ditch,
and the adulteress a narrow pit;
28 Yes, she lies in wait like a robber, [q]
and increases the faithless among men.

29 Who scream? Who shriek?*
Who have strife? Who have anxiety?
Who have wounds for nothing?
Who have black eyes?
30 Those who linger long over wine,
those who engage in trials of blended
wine. [r]
31 Look not on the wine when it is red,
when it sparkles in the glass.
It goes down smoothly;
32 but in the end it bites like a serpent,
or like a poisonous adder.
33 Your eyes behold strange sights,
and your heart utters disordered thoughts;
34 You are like one now lying in the depths of the
sea,
now sprawled at the top of the mast.
35 "They struck me, but it pained me not;
they beat me, but I felt it not;
When shall I awake
to seek wine once again?"*

CHAPTER 24

1 Be not emulous of evil men,*
and desire not to be with them; [s]
2 For their hearts plot violence,
and their lips speak of foul play.

3 By wisdom is a house built,
by understanding is it made firm;
4 And by knowledge are its rooms filled
with every precious and pleasing
possession.
5 A wise man is more powerful than a strong
man,
and a man of knowledge than a man of
might; [t]
6 For it is by wise guidance that you wage your
war,
and the victory is due to a wealth of
counselors. [u]

7 For a fool, to be silent is wisdom; [v]
not to open his mouth at the gate.*
8 He who plots evil doing—
men call him an intriguer.
9 Beyond intrigue and folly and sin,
it is arrogance that men find abominable.

10 If you remain indifferent* in time of adversity,

23, 29–35: A vivid description of the evil effects, physical and psychological, of drunkenness.

23, 35: Wine makes the drunkard insensible to bodily and moral harm. His one desire is to indulge again.

24, 1–22: These verses continue an exhortation to wisdom (vv 3–7. 13f), and against: violence (1f), pride and intrigue (8f), callousness (10–12), injustice (15f), joy in the failure of others (17f) or scandal at their success (19f), and rebellion against authority (21f).

24, 7: At the gate: of the city, where justice was administered and public affairs discussed; see note on Ru 4, 1. Cf also Pss 69, 13; 127, 5; Prv 22, 22; 31, 23. 31.

24, 10: Indifferent: to those who suffer unjustly.

n Prv 3, 31; 24, 1.19. o Prv 24, 14. p Prv 10, 1. q Prv 7, 10–27. r Prv 20, 1; Sir 19, 2; Hos 4, 11. s Prv 3, 31; 23, 17. t Prv 21, 22. u Prv 20, 18. v Sir 6, 21.

your strength will depart from you.
11 Rescue those who are being dragged to
death,*
and from those tottering to execution
withdraw not.
12 If you say, "I know not this man!"
does not he who tests hearts perceive it?
He who guards your life knows it,
and he will repay each one according to his
deeds. [w]

13 If you eat honey, my son, because it is good,
if virgin honey is sweet to your taste;
14 Such, you must know, is wisdom to your soul.
If you find it, you will have a future,
and your hope will not be cut off. [x]

15 Lie not in wait against the home of the just
man,
ravage not his dwelling place;
16 For the just man* falls seven times and rises
again,
but the wicked stumble to ruin.

17 Rejoice not when your enemy falls,
and when he stumbles, let not your heart
exult,
18 Lest the LORD see it, be displeased with you,
and withdraw his wrath from your enemy.

19 Be not provoked with evildoers,
nor envious of the wicked;
20 For the evil man has no future,
the lamp of the wicked will be put out. [y]

21 My son, fear the LORD and the king;*
have nothing to do with those who rebel
against them;
22 For suddenly arises the destruction they send,
and the ruin from either one, who can
measure?

IV: Other Sayings of the Wise*

23 These also are sayings of the wise:

To show partiality in judgment is not good. [z]
24 He who says to the wicked man, "You are
just"—
men will curse him, people will denounce
him;
25 But those who convict the evildoer will fare
well,
and on them will come the blessing of
prosperity.
26 He gives a kiss on the lips*
who makes an honest reply.

27 Complete your outdoor tasks,
and arrange your work in the field;
afterward you can establish your house.*

28 Be not a witness against your neighbor
without just cause, [a]
thus committing folly with your lips.
29 Say not, "As he did to me, so will I do to
him; [b]
I will repay the man according to his
deeds."*

30 I passed by the field of the sluggard,
by the vineyard of the man without sense;
31 And behold! it was all overgrown with
thistles;
its surface was covered with nettles,
and its stone wall broken down.
32 And as I gazed at it, I reflected;
I saw and learned the lesson:
33 A little sleep, a little slumber, [c]
a little folding of the arms to rest—
34 Then will poverty come upon you like a
highwayman,
and want like an armed man.

24, 11: Rescue . . . death: most probably refers to the legal rescue of those unjustly condemned to death.

24, 16: The just man overcomes every misfortune which oppresses him. Seven times: i.e., an indefinite number; cf Mt 18, 21f; Lk 17, 4.

24, 21f: One owes obedience to God and to supreme civil authority (Mt 22, 21; Rom 13, 1ff; 1 Pt 2, 13f). The punishments for failure in either duty transcend the limits of private justice.

24, 23–34: This collection of sayings continues in the same vein as the preceding: it instructs in fairness (23–26) and preparation for the future (27); and warns against vengeance (28f) and slothfulness (30–34).

24, 26: He gives a kiss on the lips: shows himself a true friend.

24, 27: This verse is commonly interpreted as advocating careful and practical preparation for marriage.

24, 29: This verse indicates great progress from the principle on the law of Talion (see note on Ex 21, 23ff) toward the teaching found in Rom 12, 17ff. Cf also Prv 25, 21ff.

w Ps 62, 13; Sir 16, 12; Mt 16, 27; Rom 2, 6. x Prv 23, 18. y Prv 13, 9. z Prv 18, 5; 28, 21; Lv 19, 15; Dt 1, 17; 16, 19. a Prv 19, 5; 25, 18. b Prv 20, 22. c 33f: Prv 6, 10f.

V: Second Collection Of The Proverbs Of Solomon

CHAPTER 25

1 These also are proverbs of Solomon.[d] The men of Hezekiah,* king of Judah, transmitted them.

2 God has glory in what he conceals,
kings have glory in what they fathom.
3 As the heavens in height, and the earth in depth,
the heart of kings is unfathomable.

4 Remove the dross from silver,
and it comes forth perfectly purified;
5 Remove the wicked from the presence of the king,
and his throne is made firm through righteousness.

6 Claim no honor in the king's presence,*
nor occupy the place of great men;
7 For it is better that you be told, "Come up closer!"
than that you be humbled before the prince.[e]

8 What your eyes have seen
bring not forth hastily against an opponent;
For what will you do later on
when your neighbor puts you to shame?
9 Discuss your case with your neighbor,
but another man's secret do not disclose;
10 Lest, hearing it, he reproach you,
and your ill repute cease not.

11 Like golden apples in silver settings
are words spoken at the proper time.

12 Like a golden earring, or a necklace of fine gold,
is a wise reprover to an obedient ear.

13 Like the coolness of snow in the heat of the harvest
is a faithful messenger for the one who sends him.
[He refreshes the soul of his master.]

14 Like clouds and wind when no rain follows
is the man who boastfully promises what he never gives.

15 By patience is a ruler persuaded,[f]
and a soft tongue will break a bone.

16 If you find honey, eat only what you need,
lest you become glutted with it and vomit it up.

17 Let your foot be seldom in your neighbor's house,
lest he have more than enough of you, and hate you.

18 Like a club, or a sword, or a sharp arrow,
is the man who bears false witness against his neighbor.

19 Like an infected tooth or an unsteady foot
is [dependence on] a faithless man in time of trouble.

20 Like a moth in clothing, or a maggot in wood,
sorrow gnaws at the human heart.[g]

21 If your enemy be hungry, give him food to eat,*
if he be thirsty, give him to drink;[h]

22 For live coals you will heap on his head,
and the LORD will vindicate you.

23 The north wind brings rain,
and a backbiting tongue an angry countenance.

24 It is better to dwell in a corner of the housetop
than in a roomy house with a quarrelsome woman.[i]

25 Like cool water to one faint from thirst
is good news from a far country.

25, 1: The men of Hezekiah: literary men at the royal court of Hezekiah who are represented as transcribing the proverbs from other collections. Hezekiah was a reformer of national religious life (2 Chr 29, 25–30).

25, 6f: Compare the lesson on humility which was taught by Christ (Lk 14, 7–11).

25, 21f: Charity is invaluable in resolving enmities and restoring peace. Live coals: i.e., either remorse and embarrassment for the harm done, or increased punishment for refusing reconciliation. Cf Mt 5, 44; Rom 12, 20.

d Prv 1, 1. e Lk 14, 8ff. f Prv 15, 1. 4. g Sir 30, 24. h Rom 12, 20. i Prv 21, 9.

26 Like a troubled fountain or a polluted spring
is a just man who gives way before the wicked.

27 To eat too much honey is not good;
nor to seek honor after honor.*

28 Like an open city with no defenses
is the man with no check on his feelings.

CHAPTER 26*

1 Like snow in summer, or rain in harvest,
honor for a fool is out of place.

2 Like the sparrow in its flitting, like the swallow in its flight,
a curse uncalled-for arrives nowhere.

3 The whip for the horse, the bridle for the ass,
and the rod for the back of fools.[j]

4 Answer not the fool according to his folly,*
lest you too become like him.

5 Answer the fool according to his folly,
lest he become wise in his own eyes.

6 He cuts off his feet, he drinks down violence,
who sends messages by a fool.

7 A proverb in the mouth of a fool*
hangs limp, like crippled legs.

8 Like one who entangles the stone in the sling
is he who gives honor to a fool.

9 Like a thorn stick brandished by the hand of a drunkard
is a proverb in the mouth of fools.

10 Like an archer wounding all who pass by
is he who hires a drunken fool.

11 As the dog returns to his vomit,
so the fool repeats his folly.[k]

12 You see a man wise in his own eyes?
There is more hope for a fool than for him.

13 The sluggard says, "There is a lion in the street,
a lion in the middle of the square!"[l]

14 The door turns on its hinges,
the sluggard, on his bed!

15 The sluggard loses his hand in the dish;
he is too weary to lift it to his mouth.[m]

16 The sluggard imagines himself wiser
than seven men who answer with good sense.

17 Like the man who seizes a passing dog by the ears
is he who meddles in a quarrel not his own.

18 Like a crazed archer
scattering firebrands and deadly arrows

19 Is the man who deceives his neighbor,
and then says, "I was only joking."

20 For lack of wood, the fire dies out;
and when there is no talebearer, strife subsides.

21 What a bellows is to live coals, what wood is to fire,
such is a contentious man in enkindling strife.[n]

22 The words of a talebearer are like dainty morsels
that sink into one's inmost being.[o]

23 Like a glazed finish on earthenware
are smooth lips with a wicked heart.

24 With his lips an enemy pretends,
but in his inmost being he maintains deceit;

25 When he speaks graciously, trust him not,[p]
for seven abominations* are in his heart.

26 A man may conceal hatred under dissimulation,

25, 27: Nor . . . honor after honor: the text is uncertain.
26, 1–28: Concrete images describe the vices of fools (1–12), of sluggards (13–16), of meddlers (17–19), of talebearers (20ff), and of flatterers (23–28).
26, 4f: There is no contradiction between these two proverbs. In any answer the wise man gives he must protect his own interest against the fool.
26, 7ff: The fool abuses whatever knowledge he possesses.
26, 25: Seven abominations: many evil intentions.

j Pv 19, 29; Sir 33, 25. k 2 Pt 2, 22. l Prv 22, 13. m Prv 19, 24. n Prv 15, 18; 29, 22. o Prv 18, 8. p Sir 12, 10; 27, 23.

but his malice will be revealed in the assembly.

27 He who digs a pit falls into it;
and a stone comes back upon him who rolls it. [q]

28 The lying tongue is its owner's enemy,
and the flattering mouth works ruin.

CHAPTER 27

1 Boast not of tomorrow,
for you know not what any day may bring forth.

2 Let another praise you—not your own mouth;
someone else—not your own lips.

3 Stone is heavy, and sand a burden,
but a fool's provocation is heavier than both. [r]

4 Anger is relentless, and wrath overwhelming—
but before jealousy who can stand?

5 Better is an open rebuke
than a love that remains hidden.

6 Wounds from a friend may be accepted as well meant,
but the greetings of an enemy one prays against.

7 One who is full, tramples on virgin honey;
but to the man who is hungry, any bitter thing is sweet.

8 Like a bird that is far from its nest
is a man who is far from his home.

9 Perfume and incense gladden the heart,
but by grief the soul is torn asunder.

10 Your own friend and your father's friend forsake not;
but if ruin befalls you, enter not a kinsman's house.
Better is a neighbor near at hand
than a brother far away.

11 If you are wise, my son, you will gladden my heart,
and I will be able to rebut him who taunts me.

12 The shrewd man perceives evil and hides;
simpletons continue on and suffer the penalty. [s]

13 Take his garment who becomes surety for another, [t]
and for the sake of a stranger, yield it up!*

14 When one greets his neighbor with a loud voice in the early morning,
a curse can be laid to his charge.*

15 For a persistent leak on a rainy day
the match is a quarrelsome woman. [u]

16 He who keeps her stores up a stormwind;
he cannot tell north from south.

17 As iron sharpens iron,
so man sharpens his fellow man.

18 He who tends a fig tree eats its fruit,
and he who is attentive to his master will be enriched.

19 As one face differs from another,
so does one human heart from another.

20 The nether world and the abyss are never satisfied; [v]
so too the eyes of men.

21 As the crucible tests silver and the furnace gold,
so a man is tested by the praise he receives.

22 Though you should pound the fool to bits
with the pestle, amid the grits in a mortar,
his folly would not go out of him.

23 Take good care of your flocks,*
give careful attention to your herds;

24 For wealth lasts not forever,
nor even a crown from age to age.

27, 13: See note on Prv 20, 16.
27, 14: The loud voice suggests hypocrisy in the greeting.
27, 23–27: The land of Palestine was very suitable for flocks and herds, which formed the principal source of wealth for their owners.

q Eccl 10, 8; Sir 27, 25f. r Sir 22, 14f. s Prv 22, 3. t Prv 20, 16. u Prv 21, 9; 25, 24. v Prv 30, 16; Eccl 4, 8.

25 When the grass is taken away and the
aftergrowth appears,
and the mountain greens are gathered in,

26 The lambs will provide you with clothing,
and the goats will bring the price of a field,

27 And there will be ample goat's milk to supply
you,
to supply your household,
and maintenance for your maidens.

CHAPTER 28

1 The wicked man flees although no one
pursues him;
but the just man, like a lion, feels sure of
himself.

2 If a land is rebellious, its princes will be many;
but with a prudent man it knows security.*

3 A rich man who oppresses the poor
is like a devastating rain that leaves no food.

4 Those who abandon the law* praise the
wicked man,
but those who keep the law war against
him.

5 Evil men understand nothing of justice,
but those who seek the LORD understand
all.

6 Better a poor man who walks in his integrity
than he who is crooked in his ways and
rich. [w]

7 He who keeps the law is a wise son,
but the gluttons' companion disgraces his
father.

8 He who increases his wealth by interest and
overcharge*
gathers it for him who is kind to the
poor.

9 When one turns away his ear from hearing the
law, [x]
even his prayer is an abomination.*

10 He who seduces the upright into an evil way
will himself fall into his own pit.
[And blameless men will gain prosperity.]

11 The rich man is wise in his own eyes,
but a poor man who is intelligent sees
through him.

12 When the just are triumphant, there is great
jubilation;
but when the wicked gain pre-eminence,
people hide.

13 He who conceals his sins prospers not,
but he who confesses and forsakes them
obtains mercy.

14 Happy the man who is always on his guard;
but he who hardens his heart will fall into
evil.

15 Like a roaring lion or a ravenous bear
is a wicked ruler over a poor people.

16 The less prudent the prince, the more his
deeds oppress.
He who hates ill-gotten gain prolongs his
days.

17 Though a man burdened with human blood
were to flee to the grave, none should
support him.

18 He who walks uprightly is safe,
but he whose ways are crooked falls into
the pit.

19 He who cultivates his land will have plenty of
food,
but from idle pursuits a man has his fill of
poverty. [y]

20 The trustworthy man will be richly blessed;

28, 2: The meaning of this poorly preserved verse seems to be that frequent changes of rulers often result from moral corruption and political disorder.

28, 4: The law: religious and moral teaching.

28, 8: Interest and overcharge were strictly forbidden in the old law among Israelites because it was presumed that the borrower was in distress; cf Ex 22, 25; Lv 25, 35ff; Dt 23, 19; Ps 15, 5; Ez 18, 8. Civil and divine law will take the offender's wealth from him.

28, 9: Prayers offered in bad faith are displeasing to God.

w Prv 19, 1. x Prv 21, 27. y Prv 12, 11.

he who is in haste to grow rich will not go
unpunished.[z]

21 To show partiality is never good:[a]
for even a morsel of bread a man may do
wrong.

22 The avaricious man is perturbed about his
wealth,
and he knows not when want will come
upon him.

23 He who rebukes a man gets more thanks in
the end
than one with a flattering tongue.

24 He who defrauds father or mother and calls it
no sin,[b]
is a partner of the brigand.

25 The greedy man stirs up disputes,
but he who trusts in the LORD will prosper.

26 He who trusts in himself is a fool,
but he who walks in wisdom is safe.

27 He who gives to the poor suffers no want,[c]
but he who ignores them gets many a curse.

28 When the wicked gain pre-eminence, other
men hide;
but at their fall the just flourish.

CHAPTER 29

1 The man who remains stiff-necked and hates
rebuke
will be crushed suddenly beyond cure.

2 When the just prevail, the people rejoice;
but when the wicked rule, the people
groan.[d]

3 He who loves wisdom makes his father glad,
but he who consorts with harlots squanders
his wealth.[e]

4 By justice a king gives stability to the land;
but he who imposes heavy taxes ruins it.

5 The man who flatters his neighbor
is spreading a net under his feet.

6 The wicked man steps into a snare,
but the just man runs on joyfully.

7 The just man has a care for the rights of the
poor;
the wicked man has no such concern.

8 Arrogant men set the city ablaze,
but wise men calm the fury.[f]

9 If a wise man disputes with a fool,
he may rage or laugh but can have no
peace.

10 Bloodthirsty men hate the honest man,
but the upright show concern for his life.

11 The fool gives vent to all his anger;
but by biding his time, the wise man calms
it.[g]

12 If a ruler listens to lying words,
his servants all become wicked.

13 The poor and the oppressor* have a common
bond:[h]
the Lord gives light to the eyes of
both.

14 If a king is zealous for the rights of the
poor,
his throne stands firm forever.

15 The rod of correction gives wisdom,
but a boy left to his whims disgraces his
mother.[i]

16 When the wicked prevail, crime increases;
but their downfall the just will behold.

17 Correct your son, and he will bring you
comfort,
and give delight to your soul.

18 Without prophecy the people become
demoralized;
but happy is he who keeps the law.

19 By words no servant can be trained;[j]
for he understands what is said, but obeys
not.

29, 13: God gives life to all classes of people; cf Prv 22, 2.

z Prv 13, 11. a Prv 24, 23. b Mk 7, 11ff. c Prv 19, 17; Sir 4, 3–8. d Prv 11, 10. e Prv 5, 10; 10, 1. f Prv 11, 11. g Prv 12, 16; 25, 28; Sir 21, 26. h Prv 22, 2. i Prv 13, 24; 22, 15; 23, 13f; Sir 22. 6; 30, 1. j Sir 33, 25f.

20 Do you see a man hasty in his words? [k]
More can be hoped for from a fool!

21 If a man pampers his servant from childhood,
he will turn out to be stubborn.

22 An ill-tempered man stirs up disputes,
and a hotheaded man is the cause of many sins. [l]

23 Man's pride causes his humiliation,
but he who is humble of spirit obtains honor. [m]

24 The accomplice of a thief is his own enemy:*
he hears himself put under a curse, yet discloses nothing.

25 The fear of man brings a snare,
but he who trusts in the LORD is safe.

26 Many curry favor with the ruler,
but the rights of each are from the LORD.

27 The evildoer is an abomination to the just,
and he who walks uprightly is an abomination to the wicked.

VI: The Words of Agur

CHAPTER 30

1 The words of Agur,* son of Jakeh the Massaite:

The pronouncement of mortal man: "I am not God;*
I am not God, that I should prevail.
2 Why, I am the most stupid of men,
and have not even human intelligence;
3 Neither have I learned wisdom,
nor have I the knowledge of the Holy One.
4 Who has gone up to heaven and come down again—
who has cupped the wind in his hands?
Who has bound up the waters in a cloak—
who has marked out all the ends of the earth?
What is his name, what is his son's name,
if you know it?"
5 Every word of God is tested; [n]
he is a shield to those who take refuge in him.
6 Add nothing to his words, [o]
lest he reprove you, and you be exposed as a deceiver.

VII: Numerical Proverbs

7 Two things I ask of you,
deny them not to me before I die:
8 Put falsehood and lying far from me,
give me neither poverty nor riches;
[provide me only with the food I need;]
9 Lest, being full, I deny you,
saying, "Who is the Lord?"
Or, being in want, I steal,
and profane the name of my God.

10 Slander not a servant to his master,
lest he curse you, and you have to pay the penalty.

11 There is a group of people that curses its father,*
and blesses not its mother. [p]
12 There is a group that is pure in its own eyes,
yet is not purged of its filth.
13 There is a group—how haughty their eyes!
how overbearing their glance!
14 There is a group whose incisors are swords,
whose teeth are knives,
Devouring the needy from the earth,
and the poor from among men.

29, 24: Is his own enemy: because he not only incurs guilt as an accomplice but, by his silence, brings down on himself the curse invoked on the unknown guilty partner.

30, 1: Agur: an unknown person. Massaite: from Massa in northern Arabia, elsewhere referred to as an encampment of the Ishmaelites (Gn 25, 14). But the word may not be intended as a place name; it might signify "an oracle," "a prophecy."

30, 1ff: Agur wishes to stress man's insignificance when he is compared to God; cf Jb 38—39.

30, 11–14: Perverted people are here classified as unfilial (11), self-righteous (12), proud (13) and rapacious (14).

k Eccl 5, 1. l Prv 15, 18; 26, 21. m Prv 11, 2; 16, 18; 18, 12; Jb 22, 29. n Ps 12, 7. o Dt 4, 2. p Prv 20. 20.

15 The two daughters of the leech are, "Give,
Give."*
Three things are never satisfied,
four never say, "Enough!"
16 The nether world, and the barren womb; [q]
the earth, that is never saturated with
water,
and fire, that never says, "Enough!"
17 The eye that mocks a father,
or scorns an aged mother,
Will be plucked out by the ravens in the
valley;
the young eagles will devour it.

18 Three things are too wonderful for me,*
yes, four I cannot understand:
19 The way of an eagle in the air,
the way of a serpent upon a rock,
The way of a ship on the high seas,
and the way of a man with a maiden.
20 Such is the way of an adulterous woman:
she eats, wipes her mouth,
and says, "I have done no wrong."*

21 Under three things the earth trembles,
yes, under four it cannot bear up:
22 Under a slave when he becomes king,
and a fool when he is glutted with food; [r]
23 Under an odious woman when she is wed,
and a maidservant when she displaces her
mistress.

24 Four things are among the smallest on the
earth,
and yet are exceedingly wise:
25 Ants—a species not strong,
yet they store up their food in the summer;
26 Rock-badgers*—a species not mighty,
yet they make their home in the crags;
27 Locusts—they have no king,
yet they migrate all in array;
28 Lizards—you can catch them with your
hands,
yet they find their way into kings' palaces.
29 Three things are stately in their stride,
yes, four are stately in their carriage:
30 The lion, mightiest of beasts,
who retreats before nothing;
31 The strutting cock, and the he-goat,
and the king at the head of his people.

32 If you have foolishly been proud*
or presumptuous—put your hand on your
mouth;
33 For the stirring of milk brings forth curds,
and the stirring of anger brings forth blood.

VIII: The Words of Lemuel

CHAPTER 31

1 The words of Lemuel, king of Massa. The advice which his mother gave him:

2 What, my son, my first-born!
what, O son of my womb;
what, O son of my vows!
3 Give not your vigor to women,
nor your strength to those who ruin kings. [s]
4 It is not for kings, O Lemuel,
not for kings to drink wine;
strong drink is not for princes! [t]
5 Lest in drinking they forget what the law
decrees,
and violate the rights of all who are in need.
6 Give strong drink to one who is perishing,
and wine to the sorely depressed;
7 When they drink, they will forget their misery,
and think no more of their burdens.
8 Open your mouth in behalf of the dumb,
and for the rights of the destitute;

30, 15f: The two daughters . . . "Give, Give": the text is obscure but the sense seems to be that the leech is insatiable in its desire for blood, just as are the nether world for victims, the barren womb for offspring, the parched earth for water, and fire for fuel (16).

30, 18f: The soaring flight of the eagle, the mysterious movement upon a rock of the serpent which has no feet, the path of the ship through the trackless deep, and the marvelous procreation of human life, excite great wonderment.

30, 20: This verse portrays the indifference of an adulterous woman who thinks there is no trace of her wicked act.

30, 26: Rock-badgers: cf note on Ps 104, 18.

30, 32f: The anger aroused by overweening pride threatens an awesome punishment.

q Prv 27, 20. r Prv 19, 10; Eccl 10, 6f. s Prv 5, 9. t Prv 20, 1.

[9] Open your mouth, decree what is just,
defend the needy and the poor!

IX: The Ideal Wife

[10] When one finds a worthy wife, [u]
her value is far beyond pearls.
[11] Her husband, entrusting his heart to her,
has an unfailing prize.
[12] She brings him good, and not evil,*
all the days of her life.
[13] She obtains wool and flax
and makes cloth with skillful hands.
[14] Like merchant* ships,
she secures her provisions from afar.
[15] She rises while it is still night,
and distributes food to her household.
[16] She picks out a field to purchase;
out of her earnings she plants a vineyard.
[17] She is girt about with strength,
and sturdy are her arms.
[18] She enjoys the success of her dealings;
at night her lamp is undimmed.*
[19] She puts her hands to the distaff,
and her fingers ply the spindle.
[20] She reaches out her hands to the poor,
and extends her arms to the needy.
[21] She fears not the snow for her household;
all her charges are doubly clothed.
[22] She makes her own coverlets;
fine linen and purple are her clothing.
[23] Her husband is prominent at the city gates
as he sits with the elders of the land.
[24] She makes garments and sells them,
and stocks the merchants with belts.
[25] She is clothed with strength and dignity,
and she laughs at the days to come.*
[26] She opens her mouth in wisdom,
and on her tongue is kindly counsel.
[27] She watches the conduct of her household,
and eats not her food in idleness.
[28] Her children rise up and praise her;
her husband, too, extols her:
[29] "Many are the women of proven worth,
but you have excelled them all."
[30] Charm is deceptive and beauty fleeting;
the woman who fears the LORD is to be praised.*
[31] Give her a reward of her labors,
and let her works praise her at the city gates.

31, 12: Good and not evil: i.e., prosperity, not adversity.

31, 14: Merchant: literally, "Canaanite" (cf v 24), probably because the merchant class had been composed chiefly of Canaanites.

31, 18: Her lamp is undimmed: indicates abundance of productive work and its accompanying prosperity; cf Prv 20, 20; Jb 18, 6.

31, 25: Laughs at the days to come: anticipates the future with gladness free from anxiety.

31, 30: The true charm of the ideal wife is her religious spirit, for she fears the Lord; cf note on Prv 1, 7.

u 10–31: Sir 26, 1ff. 13–18.

THE BOOK OF ECCLESIASTES

The title *ECCLESIASTES* given to this book is the Greek translation of the Hebrew name *QOHELETH* meaning, perhaps, "one who convokes an assembly." The book, however, does not consist of public addresses, but is a treatise, more or less logically developed, on the vanity of all things. Reflections in prose and aphorisms in verse are intermingled in Ecclesiastes, which contains, besides, an introduction and an epilogue.

The book is concerned with the purpose and value of human life. While admitting the existence of a divine plan, it considers such a plan to be hidden from man, who seeks happiness without ever finding it here below (3, 11; 8, 7. 17). Ecclesiastes applies his "Vanity of vanities" to everything "under the sun," even to that wisdom which seeks to find at last a semblance of good in the things of the world. Merit does not yield happiness for it is often tried by suffering. Riches and pleasures do not avail. Existence is monotonous, enjoyment

fleeting and vain; darkness quickly follows. Life, then, is an enigma beyond human ability to solve.

While Ecclesiastes concedes that there is an advantage for man in the enjoyment of certain legitimate pleasures lest he lapse into pessimism and despair, he nevertheless considers this indulgence also vanity unless man returns due thanks to the Creator who has given him all. Under this aspect, earthly wisdom would rise to the higher level of true spiritual wisdom. This true wisdom is not found "under the sun" but is perceived only by the light of faith, inasmuch as it rests with God, who is the final Judge of the good and the bad, and whose reign endures forever. The Epilogue gives the clue to this thought (12, 13f).

The moral teaching of the book is imperfect, like the Old Testament itself (Heb 7, 19), yet it marks an advance in the development of the doctrine of divine retribution. While rejecting the older solution of earthly rewards and punishments, Ecclesiastes looks forward to a more lasting one. The clear answer to the problem was to come with the light of Christ's teaching concerning future life.

The author of the book was a teacher of popular wisdom (12, 9). Qoheleth was obviously only his literary name. Because he is called "David's son, king in Jerusalem," it was commonly thought that he was King Solomon. Such personation, however, was but a literary device to lend greater dignity and authority to the book—a circumstance which does not in any way impugn its inspired character. The Epilogue seems to have been written by an editor, probably a disciple of Qoheleth. The entire work differs considerably in language and style from earlier books of the Old Testament. It reflects a late period of Hebrew, and was probably written about three centuries before Christ.

CHAPTER 1

1 The words of David's son, Qoheleth,* king in Jerusalem: [a]

Vanity of Toil without Profit

2 Vanity of vanities,* says Qoheleth,
vanity of vanities! All things are vanity! [b]
3 What profit has man from all the labor [c]
which he toils at under the sun?*
4 One generation passes and another comes,
but the world forever stays.
5 The sun rises and the sun goes down;
then it presses on to the place where it rises.
6 Blowing now toward the south, then toward the north,
the wind turns again and again, resuming its rounds.
7 All rivers go to the sea,
yet never does the sea become full.
To the place where they go,
the rivers keep on going.
8 All speech is labored;
there is nothing man can say.*
The eye is not satisfied with seeing
nor is the ear filled with hearing. [d]

9 What has been, that will be; what has been
done, that will be done. Nothing is new under
the sun. [e] 10 Even the thing of which we say,
"See, this is new!" has already existed in the
ages that preceded us. [f] 11 There is no remem-
brance of the men of old; [g] nor of those to come
will there be any remembrance among those
who come after them.*

1, 1: Qoheleth: see Introduction.

1, 2: Vanity of vanities: a Hebrew superlative expressing the supreme degree of futility and emptiness.

1, 3: Under the sun: used throughout this book to signify "on the earth."

1, 8: All speech . . . man can say: or "All things are wearisome beyond man's power to tell."

1, 11: Men remember nothing long; God, however, never forgets.

a Eccl 7, 27; 12, 8f. b Eccl 12, 8. c Eccl 2, 11. 22; 3, 9; 5, 15. d Eccl 8, 17. e Eccl 3, 15; 6, 10. f Eccl 3, 15. g Eccl 2, 16.

I: Qoheleth's Investigation of Life

Twofold Introduction 12 I, Qoheleth, was king over Israel in Jerusalem, 13 and I applied my mind to search and investigate in wisdom all things that are done under the sun.[h]

A thankless task God has appointed
for men to be busied about.

14 I have seen all things that are done under the sun,[i] and behold, all is vanity and a chase after wind.*

15 What is crooked cannot be made straight,
and what is missing cannot be supplied.

16 [j]Though I said to myself, "Behold, I have become great and stored up wisdom beyond all who were before me in Jerusalem, and my mind has broad experience of wisdom and knowledge"; 17 yet when I applied my mind to know wisdom and knowledge, madness and folly, I learned that this also is a chase after wind.[k]

18 For in much wisdom there is much sorrow,
and he who stores up knowledge stores up grief.

CHAPTER 2

Study of Pleasure-seeking 1 I said to myself,* "Come, now, let me try you with pleasure and the enjoyment of good things."[l] But behold, this too was vanity. 2 Of laughter I said: "Mad!" and of mirth: "What good does this do?" 3 I thought of beguiling my senses with wine, though my mind was concerned with wisdom,* and of taking up folly, until I should understand what is best for men to do under the heavens during the limited days of their life.

4 I undertook great works; I built myself houses and planted vineyards; 5 I made gardens and parks, and set out in them fruit trees of all sorts. 6 And I constructed for myself reservoirs to water a flourishing woodland. 7 I acquired male and female slaves, and slaves were born in my house. I also had growing herds of cattle and flocks of sheep, more than all who had been before me in Jerusalem. 8 I amassed for myself silver and gold, and the wealth of kings and provinces. I got for myself male and female singers and all human luxuries. 9 I became great, and I stored up more than all others before me in Jerusalem; my wisdom, too, stayed with me. 10 [m]Nothing that my eyes desired did I deny them, nor did I deprive myself of any joy, but my heart rejoiced in the fruit of all my toil. This was my share for all my toil. 11 [n]But when I turned to all the works that my hands had wrought, and to the toil at which I had taken such pains, behold! all was vanity and a chase after wind, with nothing gained under the sun. 12 For what will the man do who is to come after the king? What men have already done!

Study of Wisdom and Folly I went on to the consideration of wisdom, madness and folly. 13 And I saw that wisdom has the advantage over folly as much as light has the advantage over darkness.

14 The wise man has eyes in his head,
but the fool walks in darkness.[o]

Yet I knew that one lot befalls both of them. 15 So I said to myself, if the fool's lot is to befall me also, why then should I be wise? Where is the profit for me? And I concluded in my heart that this too is vanity. 16 [p]Neither of the wise man nor of the fool will there be an abiding remembrance, for in days to come both will have been forgotten. How is it that the wise man dies as well as the fool! 17 Therefore I loathed life, since for me the work that is done under the sun is evil; for all is vanity and a chase after wind.

1, 14: Chase after wind: futility, like an attempt to corral the winds. Cf Hos 12, 2. The ancient versions understood "affliction of spirit." These words are used to conclude sections of the discourse, as far as Eccl 6, 9.

2, 1–11: The author here assumes the role of Solomon.

2, 3: Though my mind . . . wisdom: while indulging in pleasure the author hopes to discover wherein man's true happiness consists.

h Eccl 8, 9. i Eccl 2, 11. 17. j Eccl 2, 9. k Eccl 2, 3; 7, 25. l Wis 2, 6. m Eccl 3, 22; 5, 18. n Eccl 1, 17; Sir 44, 9. o 14f: Eccl 6, 8; 9, 2f. p Eccl 1, 11; Wis 2, 4.

Study of the Fruits of Toil

To Others the Profits 18 And I detested all the
fruits of my labor under the sun, because I must
leave them to a man who is to come after me.
19 And who knows whether he will be a wise
man or a fool? Yet he will have control over all
the fruits of my wise labor under the sun. This
also is vanity. 20 So my feelings turned to despair
of all the fruits of my labor under the sun. 21 For
there is a man who has labored with wisdom
and knowledge and skill, and to another, who
has not labored over it, he must leave his
property. This also is vanity and a great misfor-
tune. 22 [q]For what profit comes to a man from all
the toil and anxiety of heart with which he has
labored under the sun? 23 All his days sorrow and
grief are his occupation; even at night his mind
is not at rest. This also is vanity.

24 [r]There is nothing better for man than to eat
and drink and provide himself with good things
by his labors. Even this, I realized, is from the
hand of God.* 25 For who can eat or drink apart
from him? 26 [s]For to whatever man he sees fit he
gives wisdom and knowledge and joy; but to the
sinner he gives the task of gathering possessions
to be given to whatever man God sees fit. This
also is vanity and a chase after wind.

CHAPTER 3

Man Cannot Hit on the Right Time To Act

1 There is an appointed time for everything,
and a time for every affair under the
heavens.
2 A time to be born, and a time to die;
a time to plant, and a time to uproot the
plant.
3 A time to kill, and a time to heal;
a time to tear down, and a time to build.
4 A time to weep, and a time to laugh;
a time to mourn, and a time to dance.
5 A time to scatter stones, and a time to gather
them;
a time to embrace, and a time to be far from
embraces.
6 A time to seek, and a time to lose;
a time to keep, and a time to cast away.
7 A time to rend, and a time to sew;
a time to be silent, and a time to speak.
8 A time to love, and a time to hate;
a time of war, and a time of peace.

9 [t]What advantage has the worker from his
toil? 10 I have considered the task which God has
appointed for men to be busied about. 11 [u]He has
made everything appropriate to its time, and has
put the timeless into their hearts, without men's
ever discovering, from beginning to end, the
work which God has done. 12 I recognized that
there is nothing better than to be glad and to do
well during life. 13 [v]For every man, moreover, to
eat and drink and enjoy the fruit of all his labor is
a gift of God. 14 I recognized that whatever God
does will endure forever; there is no adding to it,
or taking from it. Thus has God done that he
may be revered. 15 [w]What now is has already
been; what is to be, already is; and God re-
stores* what would otherwise be displaced.

The Problem of Retribution 16 [x]And still un-
der the sun in the judgment place I saw wicked-
ness, and in the seat of justice, iniquity. 17 [y]And I
said to myself, both the just and the wicked God
will judge, since there is a time for every affair
and on every work a judgment. 18 I said to
myself: As for the children of men, it is God's
way of testing them and of showing that they are
in themselves like beasts. 19 For the lot of man
and of beast is one lot; the one dies as well as the
other. Both have the same life-breath, and man
has no advantage over the beast; but all is vanity.
20 [z]Both go to the same place; both were made
from the dust, and to the dust they both return.
21 [a]Who knows if the life-breath of the children
of men goes upward and the life-breath of beasts
goes earthward? 22 [b]And I saw that there is
nothing better for a man than to rejoice in his

2, 24: Unrestrained indulgence is not advocated here, but legitimate pleasure and the cheerfulness it begets.

3, 15: God restores: the meaning is probably that God allows no part of his creation to drop out of existence.

q Eccl 1, 3. r Eccl 3, 12f. 22; 5, 17f; 8, 15. s Prv 13, 22. t Eccl 1, 3. u Eccl 8, 17; 11, 5; Gn 1, 31. v Eccl 2, 24. w Eccl 1, 9. x Eccl 4, 1. y Eccl 12, 14. z Eccl 12, 7; Gn 2, 7; 3, 19; Ps 103, 14; Wis 2, 3; Sir 10, 9; 17, 1; 40, 11. a Wis 2, 2. b Eccl 8, 7; 10, 14.

work; for this is his lot. Who will let him see
what is to come after him?

CHAPTER 4

Vanity of Toil 1Again I considered all the
oppressions that take place under the sun: the
tears of the victims with none to comfort them!
From the hand of their oppressors comes vio-
lence, and there is none to comfort them! [c] 2And
those now dead, I declared more fortunate in
death than are the living to be still alive. [d] 3And
better off than both is the yet unborn, who has
not seen the wicked work that is done under the
sun. 4Then I saw that all toil and skillful work is
the rivalry of one man for another. This also is
vanity and a chase after wind.

5 "The fool folds his arms
  and consumes his own flesh"*—
6 Better is one handful with tranquility
  than two with toil and a chase after wind!

Companions and Successors 7Again I found
this vanity under the sun: 8a solitary man with
no companion; with neither son nor brother. Yet
there is no end to all his toil, and riches do not
satisfy his greed. "For whom do I toil and
deprive myself of good things?" This also is
vanity and a worthless task. 9Two are better
than one: they get a good wage for their labor.
10If the one falls, the other will lift up his
companion. Woe to the solitary man! For if he
should fall, he has no one to lift him up. 11So
also, if two sleep together, they keep each other
warm. How can one alone keep warm? 12Where
a lone man may be overcome, two together can
resist. A three-ply cord is not easily broken.

13Better is a poor but wise youth than an old
but foolish king who no longer knows caution;
14for from a prison house* one comes forth to
rule, since even in his royalty he was poor at
birth. 15Then I saw all those who are to live and
move about under the sun with the heir appar-
ent who will succeed to his place.* 16There is no
end to all these people, to all over whom he
takes precedence; yet the later generations will
not applaud him. This also is vanity and a chase
after wind.

Vanity of Many Words 17 [e]Guard your step
when you go to the house of God. Let your
approach be obedience, rather than the fools'
offering of sacrifice;* for they know not how to
keep from doing evil.

CHAPTER 5

1Be not hasty in your utterance and let not
your heart be quick to make a promise in God's
presence. God is in heaven and you are on earth;
therefore let your words be few.

2 For nightmares* come with many cares,
  and a fool's utterance with many words.

3 [f]When you make a vow to God, delay not its
fulfillment. For God has no pleasure in fools;
fulfill what you have vowed. 4You had better not
make a vow than make it and not fulfill it. 5Let
not your utterances make you guilty, and say not
before his representative, "It was a mistake," lest
God be angered by such words and destroy the
works of your hands. 6 [g]Rather, fear God!

Gain and Loss of Goods 7 [h]If you see oppres-
sion of the poor, and violation of rights and
justice in the realm, do not be shocked by the
fact, for the high official has another higher than
he watching him and above these are others
higher still—. 8Yet an advantage for a country in
every respect is a king for the arable land.*

9 [i]The covetous man is never satisfied with
money, and the lover of wealth reaps no fruit
from it; so this too is vanity. 10Where there are
great riches, there are also many to devour
them. Of what use are they to the owner except
to feast his eyes upon? 11Sleep is sweet to the

4, 5: Consumes his own flesh: refuses to work for the necessities of life and consequently suffers hunger and impairs his bodily health.

4, 14: Prison house: probably his mother's womb, from which the king issues without possessions. Cf Eccl 5, 14.

4, 15: The king is no sooner dead than the people transfer their allegiance to his successor.

4, 17: The fools' . . . sacrifice: unacceptable to God because of their disobedience; cf 1 Sm 15, 22; Hos 6, 6.

5, 2: Nightmares: literally, "dreams."

5, 8: The wording of this verse has perhaps never been adequately explained.

c Eccl 5, 7. d Eccl 7, 2. e 1 Sm 15, 22; Hos 6, 6. f Nm 30, 3; Dt 23, 23; Ps 50, 14. g Eccl 12, 13; Dt 10, 12. h Eccl 3, 16; 4, 1. i Prv 28, 22.

laboring man, whether he eats little or much, but the rich man's abundance allows him no sleep.

12 [j]This is a grievous evil which I have seen under the sun: riches kept by their owner to his hurt. 13 Should the riches be lost through some misfortune, he may have a son when he is without means. 14 [k]As he came forth from his mother's womb, so again shall he depart, naked as he came, having nothing from his labor that he can carry in his hand. 15 This too is a grievous evil, that he goes just as he came. What then does it profit him to toil for wind? 16 All the days of his life are passed in gloom and sorrow, under great vexation, sickness and wrath.

17 [l]Here is what I recognize as good: it is well for a man to eat and drink and enjoy all the fruits of his labor under the sun during the limited days of the life which God gives him; for this is his lot. 18 Any man to whom God gives riches and property, and grants power to partake of them, so that he receives his lot and finds joy in the fruits of his toil, has a gift from God. 19 For he will hardly dwell on the shortness of his life, because God lets him busy himself with the joy of his heart.*

CHAPTER 6

Limited Worth of Enjoyment 1 There is another evil which I have seen under the sun, and it weighs heavily upon man: 2 [m]there is the man to whom God gives riches and property and honor, so that he lacks none of all the things he craves; yet God does not grant him power to partake of them, but a stranger devours them. This is vanity and a dire plague. 3 Should a man have a hundred children and live many years, no matter to what great age, still if he has not the full benefit of his goods, or if he is deprived of burial, of this man I proclaim that the child born dead is more fortunate than he.* 4 Though it came in vain and goes into darkness and its name is enveloped in darkness; 5 though it has not seen or known the sun, yet the dead child is at rest rather than such a man. 6 Should he live twice a thousand years and not enjoy his goods, do not both go to the same place?*

7 All man's toil is for his mouth,* yet his desire is not fulfilled. 8 For what advantage has the wise man over the fool, or what advantage has the poor man in knowing how to conduct himself in life? 9 "What the eyes see is better than what the desires wander after."* This also is vanity and a chase after wind.

II: Qoheleth's Conclusions

10 Whatever is, was long ago given its name, and the nature of man is known, and that he cannot contend in judgment with one who is stronger than he.* 11 For though there are many sayings that multiply vanity, what profit is there for a man? 12 [n]For who knows what is good for a man in life, the limited days of his vain life (which God has made like a shadow)? Because—who is there to tell a man what will come after him under the sun?

A. Man Cannot Find Out What Is Good for Him To Do

CHAPTER 7

Critique of Sages on the Day of Adversity

1 A good name is better than good ointment,*
  and the day of death than the day of birth. [o]
2 It is better to go to the house of mourning
  than to the house of feasting,
For that is the end of every man,
  and the living should take it to heart. [p]
3 Sorrow is better than laughter,
  because when the face is sad the heart
  grows wiser.

5, 19: The meaning is that the joys of life, though temporary, keep a man from dwelling on the ills which afflict humanity.

6, 3: A large family, a long life, an honorable burial, all were highly esteemed by the Hebrews, and it was considered a great misfortune to be deprived of them.

6, 6: Same place: the grave.

6, 7: Mouth: appetite, and therefore, body.

6, 9: Better . . . wander after: the good that is present to us is better than that which is absent and, perhaps, unattainable.

6, 10: The one who is stronger than man is God.

7, 1: Ointment: applied to the child at birth; a good name remains even after death.

j Jb 20, 20. k Jb 1, 21; 1 Tm 6, 7. l 17f: Eccl 2, 24. m Eccl 2, 18f. n Jb 8, 9; 14, 2; Ps 102, 12. o Eccl 4, 2; Prv 22, 1; Sir 41, 13. p Eccl 4, 2.

4 The heart of the wise is in the house of
mourning,
but the heart of fools is in the house of
mirth.
5 It is better to hearken to the wise man's
rebuke
than to hearken to the song of fools;
6 For as the crackling of thorns under a pot,
so is the fool's laughter.
This also is vanity,
7 For oppression can make a fool of a wise man,
and a bribe corrupts the heart.
8 Better is the end of speech than its beginning;
better is the patient spirit than the lofty
spirit.
9 Do not in spirit become quickly discontented,
for discontent lodges in the bosom of a fool.

10 Do not say: How is it that former times
were better than these? For it is not in wisdom
that you ask about this.

11 Wisdom and an inheritance are good,
and an advantage to those that see the sun.

12 For the protection of wisdom is as the protec-
tion of money; and the advantage of knowledge
is that wisdom preserves the life of its owner.
13 Consider the work of God. Who can make
straight what he has made crooked? 14 On a good
day enjoy good things, and on an evil day
consider: Both the one and the other God has
made, so that man cannot find fault with him in
anything.
**Critique of Sages on Justice and
Wickedness** 15 I have seen all manner of things
in my vain days: a just man perishing in his
justice, and a wicked one surviving in his
wickedness. 16 [q]"Be not just to excess, and be
not overwise, lest you be ruined.* 17 Be not
wicked to excess, and be not foolish. Why
should you die before your time?"* 18 It is good
to hold to this rule, and not to let that one* go;
but he who fears God will win through at all
events.
19 Wisdom is a better defense for the wise man
than would be ten princes in the city, 20 [r]yet
there is no man on earth so just as to do good
and never sin.* 21 [s]Do not give heed to every
word that is spoken lest you hear your servant
speaking ill of you, 22 for you know in your heart
that you have many times spoken ill of others.
23 All these things I probed in wisdom. I said,
"I will acquire wisdom"; but it was beyond me.
24 What exists is far-reaching; it is deep, very
deep: who can find it out? 25 [t]I turned my
thoughts toward knowledge; I sought and pur-
sued wisdom and reason, and I recognized that
wickedness is foolish and folly is madness.
Critique of Sages on Women 26 [u]More bitter
than death I find the woman who is a hunter's
trap, whose heart is a snare and whose hands are
prison bonds. He who is pleasing to God will
escape her, but the sinner will be entrapped by
her. 27 Behold, this have I found, says Qoheleth,
adding one thing to another that I might dis-
cover the answer 28 which my soul still seeks and
has not found: One man out of a thousand have
I come upon, but a woman among them all I
have not found.* 29 Behold, only this have I
found out: God made mankind straight, but men
have had recourse to many calculations.*

CHAPTER 8

Critique of Sages on the Wise Man and the King

1 Who is like the wise man,
and who knows the explanation of things?

7, 16: St. Jerome explains the warning against excessive justice in reference to the self-righteous man who is so stern that he is never willing to forgive sin in others; cf vv 20ff.

7, 17: Untimely death was traditionally recognized as a divine punishment of the wicked; cf 1 Sm 2, 31–34; Jer 17, 11; Ps 55, 24; Prv 10, 27. This warning against presumptuous wickedness is not an endorsement of any lesser degree of misconduct.

7, 18: This rule . . . that one: the sayings cited in vv 16f. Others refer this and that to riches and wisdom (cf 7, 12), justice and wisdom, or justice and wickedness. This last supposition makes the author's thought hard to follow.

7, 20: This is to be understood in the sense of Rom 5, 12. See note there.

7, 28: The author found sincerity rare among men, but among women still more rare.

7, 29: Calculations: the many vain attempts and schemes of men to attain happiness by their own efforts.

q 16f: Eccl 8, 12ff. r Jb 25, 4; Prv 20, 9; 1 Kgs 8, 46; Rom 3, 23; Jas 3, 2; 1 Jn 1, 8. s 21f: 1 Kgs 8, 46. t Eccl 1, 17. u Prv 5, 4.

A man's wisdom illumines his face,
but an impudent look is resented.

2 Observe the precept of the king, and in view
of your oath to God, 3 be not hasty to withdraw
from the king; do not join in with a base plot, for
he does whatever he pleases, 4 because his word
is sovereign, and who can say to him, "What are
you doing?"

5 "He who keeps the commandment experi-
ences no evil, and the wise man's heart knows
times and judgments; 6 for there is a time and a
judgment for everything."—Yet it is a great
affliction for man 7 [v]that he is ignorant of what is
to come; for who will make known to him how
it will be? 8 There is no man who is master of the
breath of life so as to retain it, and none has
mastery of the day of death. There is no exemp-
tion from the struggle, nor are the wicked saved
by their wickedness. 9 [w]All these things I consid-
ered and I applied my mind to every work that is
done under the sun, while one man tyrannizes
over another to his hurt.

The Problem of Retribution 10 Meanwhile I
saw wicked men approach and enter; and as
they left the sacred place, they were praised in
the city for what they had done. This also is
vanity.* 11 Because the sentence against evildo-
ers is not promptly executed, therefore the
hearts of men are filled with the desire to
commit evil— 12 because the sinner does evil a
hundred times and survives. Though indeed I
know that it shall be well with those who fear
God, for their reverence toward him; 13 and that
it shall not be well with the wicked man, and he
shall not prolong his shadowy* days, for his lack
of reverence toward God.

14 This is a vanity which occurs on earth: there
are just men treated as though they had done
evil and wicked men treated as though they had
done justly. This, too, I say is vanity.
15 [x]Therefore I commend mirth, because there is
nothing good for man under the sun except
eating and drinking and mirth: for this is the
accompaniment of his toil during the limited
days of the life which God gives him under the
sun.*

16 [y]When I applied my heart to know wisdom
and to observe what is done on earth, 17 [z]I
recognized that man is unable to find out all
God's work that is done under the sun, even
though neither by day nor by night do his eyes
find rest in sleep. However much man toils in
searching, he does not find it out; and even if the
wise man says that he knows, he is unable to
find it out.

B. Man Does Not Know What Is To Come

CHAPTER 9

1 All this I have kept in mind and recognized:*
the just, the wise, and their deeds are in the
hand of God. Love from hatred* man cannot
tell; both appear equally vain, 2 [a]in that there is
the same lot for all, for the just and the wicked,
for the good and the bad, for the clean and the
unclean, for him who offers sacrifice and him
who does not. As it is for the good man, so it is
for the sinner; as it is for him who swears rashly,
so it is for him who fears an oath. 3 Among all the
things that happen under the sun, this is the
worst, that things turn out the same for all.
Hence the minds of men are filled with evil, and
madness is in their hearts during life; and
afterward they go to the dead.

4 Indeed, for any among the living there is
hope; a live dog is better off than a dead lion.
5 [b]For the living know that they are to die, but
the dead no longer know anything. There is no
further recompense for them, because all mem-
ory of them is lost. 6 For them, love and hatred
and rivalry have long since perished. They will

8, 10: The text is obscure. The Latin has "wicked men buried, who, while still alive, were in the holy place, and were praised in the city as if their works were just."

8, 13: Shadowy: perhaps an addition here; cf Eccl 6, 12.

8, 15: See notes on Eccl 2, 24; 5, 19.

9, 1–10: These statements are based on a very imperfect concept of life beyond the grave. With Christian revelation about the future life came the only satisfactory solution of the problem which so perplexed the author.

9, 1: Love from hatred: divine favor or disfavor.

v Eccl 3, 22; 10, 14. w Eccl 1, 13f. x Eccl 2, 24; 9, 7. y Eccl 1, 13; 3, 10. z Eccl 3, 11. a Eccl 2, 14. b Eccl 1, 11.

never again have part in anything that is done
under the sun.
7 [c]Go, eat your bread with joy and drink your
wine with a merry heart, because it is now that
God favors your works. 8At all times let your
garments be white, and spare not the perfume
for your head. 9Enjoy life with the wife whom
you love, all the days of the fleeting life that is
granted you under the sun. This is your lot in
life, for the toil of your labors under the sun.
10Anything you can turn your hand to, do with
what power you have; for there will be no work,
nor reason, nor knowledge, nor wisdom in the
nether world where you are going.
The Evil Time Not Known 11Again I saw
under the sun that the race is not won by the
swift, nor the battle by the valiant, nor a
livelihood by the wise, nor riches by the shrewd,
nor favor by the experts; for a time of calamity
comes to all alike. 12Man no more knows his
own time* than fish taken in the fatal net, or
birds trapped in the snare; like these the chil-
dren of men are caught when the evil time falls
suddenly upon them.
The Uncertain Future and the Sages 13On
the other hand I saw this wise deed under the
sun, which I thought sublime. 14Against a small
city with few men in it advanced a mighty king,
who surrounded it and threw up great
siegeworks about it. 15But in the city lived a man
who, though poor, was wise, and he delivered it
through his wisdom. Yet no one remembered
this poor man. 16 [d]Though I had said, "Wisdom
is better than force," yet the wisdom of the poor
man is despised and his words go unheeded.

17 "The quiet words of the wise are better
heeded
than the shout of a ruler of fools"—!

18 "A fly that dies can spoil the perfumer's
ointment,
and a single slip can ruin much that is
good."

CHAPTER 10

1 More weighty than wisdom or wealth is a little
folly!
2 The wise man's understanding turns him to
his right;
the fool's understanding turns him to his
left.*

3When the fool walks through the street, in
his lack of understanding he calls everything
foolish.
4Should the anger of the ruler burst upon you,
forsake not your place; for mildness abates great
offenses.
5I have seen under the sun another evil, like a
mistake that proceeds from the ruler: 6a fool put
in lofty position while the rich sit in lowly places.
7I have seen slaves on horseback, while princes
walked on the ground like slaves.

8 He who digs a pit may fall into it, [e]
and he who breaks through a wall may be
bitten by a serpent.

9 He who moves stones may be hurt by them,
and he who chops wood is in danger from
it.

10If the iron becomes dull, though at first he
made easy progress, he must increase his efforts;
but the craftsman has the advantage of his skill.

11 If the serpent bites because it has not been
charmed,
then there is no advantage for the charmer.

12 Words from the wise man's mouth win favor,
but the fool's lips consume him.[f]
13 The beginning of his words is folly,
and the end of his talk is utter madness;
14 yet the fool multiplies words.
Man knows not what is to come,
for who can tell him what is to come after
him?[g]
15 When will the fool be weary of his labor,
he who knows not the way to the city?*

9, 12: His own time: the time of death or sudden disaster.
10, 2: It is doubtful whether the author is endorsing either direction; cf Prv 4, 25ff.
10, 15: He who . . . city: perhaps a proverbial expression for supreme stupidity.

c Eccl 2, 1. 24; 8, 15; 11, 9. d Prv 24, 5. e 8f: Prv 26, 27; Sir 27, 29. f Sir 21, 19. g Eccl 5, 2; 8, 7.

Man Does Not Know What Evil Will Come

16 Woe to you, O land, whose king was a servant,
and whose princes dine in the morning!
17 Blessed are you, O land, whose king is of noble birth,
and whose princes dine at the right time
(for vigor and not in drinking bouts).
18 When hands are lazy, the rafters sag;
when hands are slack, the house leaks.
19 Bread and oil call forth merriment
and wine makes the living glad,
but money answers for everything.
20 Even in your thoughts do not make light of the king,
nor in the privacy of your bedroom revile the rich,
Because the birds of the air may carry your voice,
a winged creature may tell what you say.

CHAPTER 11

1 Cast your bread upon the waters;*
after a long time you may find it again.
2 Make seven or eight portions;*
you know not what misfortune may come upon the earth.

Man Does Not Know What Good Will Come

3 When the clouds are full,
they pour out rain upon the earth.
Whether a tree falls to the south or to the north,
wherever it falls, there shall it lie.
4 One who pays heed to the wind will not sow,
and one who watches the clouds will never reap.
5 Just as you know not how the breath of life
fashions the human frame in the mother's womb,
So you know not the work of God
which he is accomplishing in the universe.[h]
6 In the morning sow your seed,
and at evening let not your hand be idle:
For you know not which of the two will be successful,
or whether both alike will turn out well.

Poem on Youth and Old Age 7 Light is sweet!
and it is pleasant for the eyes to see the sun.
8 However many years a man may live, let him,
as he enjoys them all, remember that the days of
darkness will be many. All that is to come is
vanity.

9 Rejoice, O young man, while you are young,
and let your heart be glad in the days of your youth.
Follow the ways of your heart,
the vision of your eyes;
Yet understand that as regards all this
God will bring you to judgment.
10 Ward off grief from your heart
and put away trouble from your presence,
though the dawn of youth is fleeting.*

CHAPTER 12

1 Remember your Creator in the days of your youth,
before the evil days come
And the years approach of which you will say,
I have no pleasure in them;
2 Before the sun is darkened,
and the light, and the moon, and the stars,
while the clouds return* after the rain;
3 When the guardians* of the house tremble,
and the strong men are bent,
And the grinders are idle because they are few,
and they who look through the windows grow blind;
4 When the doors* to the street are shut,
and the sound of the mill is low;
When one waits for the chirp of a bird,
but all the daughters of song are suppressed;

11, 1: This may refer to a spirit of adventure in business or to generosity in almsgiving. Waters: of the ocean, which sometimes carry lost treasures to the shore.

11, 2: This verse refers either to almsgiving or to the wisdom of not putting all one's cargo into a single vessel.

11, 10: Dawn . . . fleeting: literally, "youth and the dawn [of life] are vanity."

12, 2: The sun . . . return: the cloudy and rainy Palestinian winter, a natural symbol of old age.

12, 3: Guardians: the arms; strong men: the legs; grinders; the teeth; they who . . . windows: the eyes.

12, 4: Doors: the tightly compressed lips; sound of the mill: perhaps the sound of mastication; daughters of song: the voice.

h Eccl 8, 17.

5 And one fears heights,
and perils in the street;
When the almond tree blooms,*
and the locust grows sluggish
and the caper berry is without effect,
Because man goes to his lasting home,
and mourners go about the streets;
6 Before the silver cord is snapped
and the golden bowl* is broken,
And the pitcher is shattered at the spring,
and the broken pulley falls into the well,
7 And the dust returns to the earth as it once
was,
and the life breath returns to God who gave
it.[i]

8 Vanity of vanities, says Qoheleth,
all things are vanity![j]

Epilogue 9 Besides being wise, Qoheleth
taught the people knowledge, and weighed,
scrutinized and arranged many proverbs.
10 Qoheleth sought to find pleasing sayings, and
to write down true sayings with precision.
11 The sayings of the wise are like goads; like
fixed spikes are the topics given by one collec-
tor.* 12 [k]As to more than these, my son, be-
ware. Of the making of many books there is no
end, and in much study there is weariness for
the flesh.
13 [l]The last word, when all is heard: Fear God
and keep his commandments, for this is man's
all;* 14 [m]because God will bring to judgment
every work, with all its hidden qualities,
whether good or bad.

12, 5: The almond tree blooms: resembling the white hair of age. The locust . . . sluggish: an image of the stiffness in movement of the aged. The caper berry: a stimulant for appetite.

12, 6: The golden bowl suspended by the silver cord was a symbol of life; the snapping of the cord and the breaking of the bowl, a symbol of death. The pitcher . . . the broken pulley: another pair of metaphors for life and its ending.

12, 11: Goads . . . one collector: the sayings were stimulants to thought and also spikes or centers around which to group correlated pronouncements of the wise.

12, 13: Man's all: St. Jerome explains: "Unto this is every man born, that, knowing his Maker, he may revere him in fear, honor, and the observance of his commandments."

i Eccl 3, 20f; Jb 34, 15. j Eccl 1, 2. k Eccl 1, 18. l Eccl 5, 6. m Eccl 11, 9.

THE SONG OF SONGS

The Song of Songs, meaning the greatest of songs (1, 1), contains in exquisite poetic form the sublime portrayal and praise of the mutual love of the Lord and his people. The Lord is the Lover and his people are the beloved. Describing this relationship in terms of human love, the author simply follows Israel's tradition. Isaiah (5, 1-7; 54, 4-8), Jeremiah (2, 2f. 32), and Ezekiel (16; 23) all characterize the covenant between the Lord and Israel as a marriage. Hosea the prophet sees the idolatry of Israel in the adultery of Gomer (1—3). He also represents the Lord speaking to Israel's heart (2, 16) and changing her into a new spiritual people, purified by the Babylonian captivity and betrothed anew to her divine Lover "in justice and uprightness, in love and mercy" (2, 21).

The author of the Song, using the same literary figure, paints a beautiful picture of the ideal Israel, the chosen people of the Old and New Testaments, whom the Lord led by degrees to an exalted spiritual union with himself in the bond of perfect love. When the Song is thus interpreted there is no reason for surprise at the tone of the poem, which employs in its descriptions the courtship and marriage customs of the author's time. Moreover, the poem is not an allegory in which each remark, e.g., in the dialogue of the lovers, has a higher meaning. It is a parable in which the true meaning of mutual love comes from the poem as a whole.

While the Song is thus commonly understood by most Catholic scholars, it is also possible to see in it an inspired portrayal of ideal human love. Here we would have from God a description of the sacredness and the depth of married union.

Although the poem is attributed to Solomon in the traditional title (1, 1), the language and style of the work, among other considerations, point to a time after the end of the Babylonian Exile (538 B.C.) as that in which an unknown poet composed this masterpiece. The structure of the Song is difficult to analyze; here it is regarded as a lyric dialogue, with dramatic movement and interest.

The use of marriage as a symbol, characteristic of the Song, is found extensively also in the New Testament (Mt 9, 15; 25, 1-13; Jn 3; 29; 2 Cor 11, 2; Eph 5, 23-32; Rv 19, 7ff; 21, 9ff). In Christian tradition, the Song has been interpreted in terms of the union between Christ and the Church and, particularly by St. Bernard, of the union between Christ and the individual soul. Throughout the liturgy, especially in the Little Office, there is a consistent application of the Song of Songs to the Blessed Virgin Mary.

I: The Song Of Songs By Solomon*

CHAPTER 1

Love's Desires

2 B Let him kiss me with kisses of his mouth!*
More delightful is your love than wine! [a]
3 Your name spoken is a spreading perfume—
that is why the maidens love you.
4 Draw me!—
D We will follow you eagerly!
B Bring me, O king, to your chambers.

D With you we rejoice and exult,
we extol your love; it is beyond
wine: [b]
how rightly you are loved!

Love's Boast

5 B I am as dark—but lovely,
O daughters of Jerusalem*—
As the tents of Kedar,
as the curtains of Salma.
6 Do not stare at me because I am swarthy,*
because the sun has burned me.
My brothers have been angry with me;
they charged me with the care of the
vineyards:
my own vineyard I have not cared for.

Love's Inquiry

7 B Tell me, you whom my heart loves,*
where you pasture your flock,
where you give them rest at midday,
Lest I be found wandering
after the flocks of your companions.

8 G If you do not know,
O most beautiful among women,
Follow the tracks of the flock
and pasture the young ones
near the shepherds' camps.

Love's Vision

9 G To the steeds of Pharaoh's chariots*
would I liken you, my beloved:
10 Your cheeks lovely in pendants,

1, 1: This title is actually the first verse of chapter 1.

1, 2ff: The marginal letters indicate the speaker of the verses: B—Bride; D—Daughters of Jerusalem; G—Bridegroom. In vv 2–7 the bride and the daughters address the bridegroom who appears here as a king, but more often in the poem as a shepherd. King and shepherd are familiar figures of the Lord in the Sacred Scriptures. Cf Ps 23, 1; Is 40, 11; Jn 10, 1–16.

1, 5: Daughters of Jerusalem: the chorus whom the bride addresses and who ask her questions (Song 5, 9; 6, 1), thus developing action within the poem. Kedar: a Syrian desert region whose name suggests blackness; tents were often made of black goat hair. Curtains: tent coverings of Salma, a region close to Kedar.

1, 6: Swarthy: tanned by the sun from working in her brothers' vineyards. My own vineyard: the bride herself; cf Is 5, 1–7, where Israel is designated as the vineyard and the Lord is the Lover.

1, 7: Here and elsewhere in the Song (3, 1; 5, 8; 6, 1), the bride expresses her desire to be in the company of her lover. These verses point to a certain tension in the poem. Only at the end (Song 8, 5ff) does mutual possession of the lovers become final.

1, 9ff: The bridegroom compares the girl's beauty to the rich adornment of the royal chariot of Pharaoh.

a 2f: Song 4, 10. b Song 4, 10.

your neck in jewels.
11 We will make pendants of gold for you,
and silver ornaments.

Love's Union

12 **B** For the king's banquet
my nard* gives forth its fragrance.
13 My lover is for me a sachet of myrrh*
to rest in my bosom.
14 My lover is for me a cluster of henna*
from the vineyards of Engedi.

15 **G** Ah, you are beautiful, my beloved, [c]
ah, you are beautiful; your eyes are doves!*

16 **B** Ah, you are beautiful, my lover—
yes, you are lovely.
Our couch, too, is verdant;*
17 the beams of our house are cedars,
our rafters, cypresses.

CHAPTER 2

1 I am a flower of Sharon,*
a lily of the valley.

2 **G** As a lily among thorns,
so is my beloved among women.
3 **B** As an apple tree among the trees of the woods,
so is my lover among men.
I delight to rest in his shadow,
and his fruit is sweet to my mouth.
4 He brings me into the banquet hall*
and his emblem over me is love. [d]
5 Strengthen me with raisin cakes,
refresh me with apples,
for I am faint with love. [e]
6 His left hand is under my head
and his right arm embraces me.[f]
7 I adjure you, daughters of Jerusalem, [g]
by the gazelles and hinds* of the field,
Do not arouse, do not stir up love
before its own time.

A Tryst in the Spring

8 **B** Hark! my lover—here he comes*
springing across the mountains,
leaping across the hills.
9 My lover is like a gazelle
or a young stag.
Here he stands behind our wall,
gazing through the windows,
peering through the lattices.
10 My lover speaks; he says to me,
"Arise, my beloved, my beautiful one,
and come!
11 "For see, the winter is past,
the rains are over and gone.
12 The flowers appear on the earth,
the time of pruning the vines has come,
and the song of the dove is heard in our land.
13 The fig tree puts forth its figs,
and the vines, in bloom, give forth fragrance.
Arise, my beloved, my beautiful one,
and come!

14 "O my dove in the clefts of the rock,*
in the secret recesses of the cliff,
Let me see you,
let me hear your voice,
For your voice is sweet,
and you are lovely."

15 **B** Catch us the foxes, the little foxes*
that damage the vineyards; for our vineyards are in bloom!

1, 12: Nard: a precious perfume, a figure of the bride; cf Song 4, 14.

1, 13: Myrrh: produced from aromatic resin of balsam or roses.

1, 14: Henna: a plant which bears white scented flowers.

1, 15: Doves: suggesting innocence and charm.

1, 16f: Though the meeting place of the lovers is but a shepherd's hut of green branches, it becomes a palace with beams of cedar and rafters of cypress when adorned with their love.

2, 1: Flower of Sharon: probably the narcissus, which grows in the fertile Plain of Sharon lying between Mount Carmel and Jaffa on the Mediterranean coast.

2, 4ff: The banquet hall, the sweet things of the table, the embrace of the bride and bridegroom, express the delicacy of their affection and the intimacy of their love.

2, 7: By the gazelles and hinds: the swiftness of these animals and the luster and soft expression of their eyes are suggestive of love; cf Prv 5, 19.

2, 8ff: In this sudden change of scene, the bride pictures her lover hastening toward her dwelling until his voice is heard bidding her come to him.

2, 14: The bride is addressed as though she were a dove in a mountain fastness out of sight and reach.

2, 15: A snatch of song in answer to the request of v 14; cf Song 8, 13f. Foxes: all who threaten to disturb the security of love symbolized by the vineyard; cf v 16.

c Song 4, 1. 7. d Song 1, 4. e Song 5, 8. f Song 8, 3. g Song 3, 5; 8, 4.

16 My lover belongs to me and I to him;
he browses among the lilies. [h]
17 Until the day breathes cool* and the shadows lengthen,
roam, my lover,
Like a gazelle or a young stag
upon the mountains of Bether. [i]

CHAPTER 3

Loss and Discovery

1 B On my bed at night I sought him*
whom my heart loves—
I sought him but I did not find him. [j]
2 I will rise then and go about the city;
in the streets and crossings I will seek
Him whom my heart loves.
I sought him but I did not find him.
3 The watchmen came upon me,
as they made their rounds of the city:
Have you seen him whom my heart loves?
4 I had hardly left them
when I found him whom my heart loves.
I took hold of him and would not let him go
till I should bring him to the home of my mother, [k]
to the room of my parent.
5 I adjure you, daughters of Jerusalem,
by the gazelles and hinds of the field,
Do not arouse, do not stir up love
before its own time. [l]

Regal State of the Bridegroom

6 D What is this coming up from the desert,*
like a column of smoke
Laden with myrrh, with frankincense,
and with the perfume of every exotic dust? [m]
7 Ah, it is the litter of Solomon;
sixty valiant men surround it,
of the valiant men of Israel:
8 All of them expert with the sword,
skilled in battle,
Each with his sword at his side
against danger in the watches of the night.

9 King Solomon made himself a carriage
of wood from Lebanon.
10 He made its columns of silver,
its roof of gold,
Its seat of purple cloth,
its framework inlaid with ivory.
11 Daughters of Jerusalem, come forth
and look upon King Solomon
In the crown with which his mother has crowned him
on the day of his marriage,
on the day of the joy of his heart.

CHAPTER 4

The Charms of the Beloved

1 G Ah, you are beautiful, my beloved, [n]
ah, you are beautiful!
Your eyes are doves [o]
behind your veil.
Your hair is like a flock of goats
streaming down the mountains of Gilead.
2 Your teeth* are like a flock of ewes to be shorn,
which come up from the washing,
All of them big with twins,
none of them thin and barren.
3 Your lips are like a scarlet strand;
your mouth is lovely.
Your cheek is like a half-pomegranate*
behind your veil.

4 Your neck is like David's tower [p]
girt with battlements;
A thousand bucklers hang upon it,
all the shields of valiant men.*
5 Your breasts are like twin fawns, [q]
the young of a gazelle
that browse among the lilies.

2, 17: Breathes cool: in the evening when the sun is going down. Cf Gn 3, 8. Bether: a very obscure word; some interpret it in the sense of ruggedness; others, of spices; still others, of sacrifice (Gn 15, 10).
3, 1ff: See the parallel in Song 5, 2–8.
3, 6ff: The lover is portrayed as King Solomon, escorted by sixty armed men, coming in royal procession to meet his bride.
4, 2: Teeth: praised for whiteness and regularity.
4, 3: Pomegranate: a fruit somewhat like an orange, with a firm skin and deep red color. The girl's cheek is compared, in roundness and tint, to a half-pomegranate.
4, 4: The ornaments about her neck are compared to the trophies on the city walls. Cf 1 Kgs 10, 10; 14, 26ff; Ez 27, 10.

h Song 6, 3; 7, 10. i Song 4, 6; 8, 14. j 1ff: Song 5, 2ff. k Song 8, 2. l Song 2, 7; 8, 4. m Song 6, 10; 8, 5. n Song 1, 15. o 1ff: Song 6, 5ff. p Song 7, 5. q Song 7, 4.

6 Until the day breathes cool and the shadows
lengthen,[r]
I will go to the mountain of myrrh,
to the hill of incense.*
7 You are all-beautiful, my beloved,
and there is no blemish in you.*

8 Come from Lebanon, my bride,
come from Lebanon, come!
Descend from the top of Amana,
from the top of Senir and Hermon,*
From the haunts of lions,
from the leopards' mountains.
9 You have ravished my heart, my sister,* my
bride;[s]
you have ravished my heart with one glance
of your eyes,
with one bead of your necklace.
10 How beautiful is your love, my sister, my
bride,[t]
how much more delightful is your love than
wine,
and the fragrance of your ointments than all
spices!
11 Your lips drip honey,* my bride,
sweetmeats and milk are under your
tongue;
And the fragrance of your garments
is the fragrance of Lebanon.

The Lover and His Garden

12 G You are an enclosed garden, my sister, my
bride,[u]
an enclosed garden, a fountain sealed.*
13 You are a park that puts forth pomegranates,
with all choice fruits;
14 Nard and saffron, calamus and cinnamon,
with all kinds of incense;
Myrrh and aloes,
with all the finest spices.*
15 You are a garden fountain, a well of water
flowing fresh from Lebanon.
16 Arise, north wind! Come, south wind!
blow upon my garden*
that its perfumes may spread abroad.
B Let my lover come to his garden
and eat its choice fruits.

CHAPTER 5

1 G I have come to my garden, my sister, my
bride;[v]
I gather my myrrh and my spices,
I eat my honey and my sweetmeats,
I drink my wine and my milk.
D Eat, friends; drink!* Drink freely of love!

A Fruitless Search

2 B I was sleeping, but my heart kept vigil;*
I heard my lover knocking:
"Open to me, my sister, my beloved,
my dove, my perfect one![w]
For my head is wet with dew,
my locks with the moisture of the night."
3 I have taken off my robe,*
am I then to put it on?
I have bathed my feet,
am I then to soil them?

4 My lover put his hand through the opening;
my heart trembled within me,
and I grew faint when he spoke.
5 I rose to open to my lover,
with my hands dripping myrrh:
With my fingers dripping choice myrrh
upon the fittings of the lock.
6 I opened to my lover—
but my lover had departed, gone.[x]

4, 6: Mountain of myrrh . . . hill of incense: spoken figuratively of the bride; cf Song 8, 14.
4, 7: Cf St. Paul's description of the church in Eph 5, 27. This verse is also applied to Our Lady, especially in the liturgy of the feast of the Immaculate Conception.
4, 8: Amana . . . Senir and Hermon: these rugged heights symbolize obstacles that would separate the lovers; cf Song 2, 14.
4, 9: Sister: a term of endearment; it forms part of the conventional language of love used in this canticle.
4, 11: Honey: sweet words. Cf Prv 5, 3.
4, 12: Enclosed garden . . . fountain sealed: reserved for the bridegroom alone. The bride's fidelity is implied. Cf Prv 5, 15–19.
4, 14: These plants are all known for their sweet scent.
4, 16: The last two lines of the verse are spoken by the girl, inviting her lover to herself, the garden.
5, 1: Eat, friends; drink!: the lovers are encouraged to enjoy the delights of their love, symbol of Christ's union with the church.
5, 2–8: A trial similar to that in Song 3, 1ff.
5, 3f: The bride's hesitation is due, not to levity, but to strong emotion.

r Song 2, 17. s Song 6, 5. t Song 1, 2f. u Song 6, 2. 11. v Song 6, 2. w 2ff: Song 3, 1f. x Song 3, 1.

I sought him but I did not find him;
I called to him but he did not answer me.*

7 The watchmen came upon me[y]
as they made their rounds of the city;
They struck me, and wounded me,
and took my mantle from me,
the guardians of the walls.*
8 I adjure you, daughters of Jerusalem,[z]
if you find my lover—
What shall you tell him?—
that I am faint with love.

The Charms of the Lost Lover

9 D How does your lover differ from any other,
O most beautiful among women?
How does your lover differ from any other,
that you adjure us so?

10 B My lover is radiant and ruddy;*
he stands out among thousands.
11 His head is pure gold;
his locks are palm fronds,
black as the raven.
12 His eyes are like doves
beside running waters,
His teeth would seem bathed in milk,
and are set like jewels.
13 His cheeks are like beds of spice
with ripening aromatic herbs.
His lips are red blossoms;
they drip choice myrrh.

14 His arms are rods of gold
adorned with chrysolites.
His body is a work of ivory
covered with sapphires.
15 His legs are columns of marble
resting on golden bases.
His stature is like the trees on Lebanon,
imposing as the cedars.
16 His mouth is sweetness itself;
he is all delight.
Such is my lover, and such my friend,
O daughters of Jerusalem.

CHAPTER 6

Discovery

1 D Where has your lover gone,
O most beautiful among women?
Where has your lover gone
that we may seek him with you?*
2 B My lover has come down to his garden,*
to the beds of spice,
To browse in the garden[a]
and to gather lilies.
3 My lover belongs to me and I to him;
he browses among the lilies.[b]

The Charms of the Beloved

4 G You are as beautiful as Tirzah, my beloved,*
as lovely as Jerusalem,
as awe-inspiring as bannered troops.
5 Turn your eyes from me,[c]
for they torment me.
Your hair is like a flock of goats
streaming down from Gilead.
6 Your teeth are like a flock of ewes[d]
which come up from the washing,
All of them big with twins,
none of them thin and barren.
7 Your cheek is like a half-pomegranate
behind your veil.
8 There are sixty queens, eighty concubines,
and maidens without number—
9 One alone is my dove, my perfect one,
her mother's chosen,
the dear one of her parent.
The daughters saw her and declared her
fortunate,
the queens and concubines, and they sang
her praises;

5, 6: The disappearance of the lover seems to be a deliberate trial and test inflicted on the girl.

5, 7: The watchmen do not know the reason for the girl's appearance in the city streets; cf Song 3, 2ff.

5, 10f: In answer to the question of v 9, the girl sings her lover's praises (vv 10–16). Gold: indicates how precious the lover is. Palm fronds: his thick, luxuriant growth of hair.

6, 1: The daughters of Jerusalem are won by this description of the lover and offer their aid in seeking him.

6, 2f: Determined to share her lover with no one, the girl refuses the aid offered by the daughters in seeking him. She implies that she had never really lost him, for he has come down to his garden.

6, 4–9: The lover again celebrates her beauty. Tirzah: probably meaning "pleasant"; it was the early capital of the northern kingdom of Israel (1 Kgs 16).

y Song 3, 3. z Song 2, 5. a Song 4, 12; 5, 1. b Song 2, 16; 7, 11. c Song 4, 9. d 6f: Song 4, 1ff.

10 D Who is this that comes forth like the dawn,[e]
as beautiful as the moon, as resplendent as the sun,
as awe-inspiring as bannered troops?

Love's Meeting

11 B I came down to the nut garden[f]
to look at the fresh growth of the valley,
To see if the vines were in bloom,
if the pomegranates had blossomed.
12 Before I knew it, my heart had made me
the blessed one of my kinswomen.*

CHAPTER 7

The Beauty of the Bride

1 D Turn, turn, O Shulammite,*
turn, turn, that we may look at you!

B Why would you look at the Shulammite
as at the dance of the two companies?

2 D How beautiful are your feet in sandals,*
O prince's daughter!
Your rounded thighs are like jewels,
the handiwork of an artist.
3 Your navel is a round bowl
that should never lack for mixed wine.
Your body is a heap of wheat
encircled with lilies.
4 Your breasts are like twin fawns,
the young of a gazelle.[g]
5 Your neck is like a tower of ivory.[h]
Your eyes are like the pools in Heshbon
by the gate of Bath-rabbim.
Your nose is like the tower on Lebanon
that looks toward Damascus.*
6 Your head rises like Carmel;
your hair is like draperies of purple;
a king is held captive in its tresses.

Love's Desires

7 G How beautiful you are, how pleasing,
my love, my delight!
8 Your very figure is like a palm tree,*
your breasts are like clusters.
9 I said: I will climb the palm tree,
I will take hold of its branches.
Now let your breasts be like clusters of the vine
and the fragrance of your breath like apples,
10 And your mouth like an excellent wine—

Love's Union

B that flows smoothly for my lover,
spreading over the lips and the teeth.*
11 I belong to my lover*
and for me he yearns.[i]
12 Come, my lover, let us go forth to the fields
and spend the night among the villages.
13 Let us go early to the vineyards, and see
if the vines are in bloom,
If the buds have opened,
if the pomegranates have blossomed;[j]
There will I give you my love.
14 The mandrakes* give forth fragrance,
and at our doors are all choice fruits;
Both fresh and mellowed fruits, my lover,
I have kept in store for you.

CHAPTER 8

1 Oh, that you were my brother,
nursed at my mother's breasts!

6, 12: The text is obscure in Hebrew and in the ancient versions. The Vulgate reads: "I did not know; my soul disturbed me because of the chariots of Aminadab."

7, 1: Shulammite: so called either because the girl is considered to be from Shulam in the plain of Esdraelon (cf 1 Kgs 1, 3) or because the name may mean "the peaceful one," and thus recall the name of Solomon. As at the dance of the two companies: the meaning is uncertain. The question in this verse could be construed as a refusal to dance; more probably, however, the girl accedes, as the following verses suggest.

7, 2–6: A flattering description of the girl's charms. Rounded . . . jewels: the meaning of these Hebrew words is not certain. Wine and wheat are symbolic of fertility; they are here associated with parts of the body which have a close relation to fruitfulness.

7, 5: The comparison emphasizes the stateliness and whiteness of the neck, and the limpidity of the eyes. Bath-rabbim: a proper name which occurs only here; there was a city of Rabbah north-east of Heshbon in Transjordan. Cf Jer 49, 3.

7, 8f: Palm tree: a figure of stateliness. The bridegroom is eager to enjoy the possession of his bride.

7, 10: The bride delicately turns his compliment into an expression of the love and tenderness she feels for him.

7, 11–14: The girl's answer assures him of her affection and invites him to return with her to the rural delights which are associated with their love and which recall the meeting described in Song 6, 11f.

7, 14: Mandrakes: herbs believed to have power to arouse love and promote fertility; cf Gn 30, 14ff.

e Song 3, 6; 8, 5. f Song 4, 12ff; 7, 13. g Song 4, 5. h Song 4, 4. i Song 2, 16; 6, 3. j Song 6, 11.

If I met you out of doors, I would kiss you
and none would taunt me.
2 I would lead you, bring you in
to the home of my mother.[k]
There you would teach me to give you
spiced wine to drink, and pomegranate juice.
3 His left hand is under my head
and his right arm embraces me.[l]
4 I adjure you, daughters of Jerusalem,
by the gazelles and hinds of the field,
Do not arouse, do not stir up love,
before its own time.[m]

Homecoming

5 D Who is this coming up from the desert,[n]
leaning upon her lover?*
G Under the apple tree I awakened you;
it was there that your mother conceived you,
it was there that your parent conceived.

True Love

6 B Set me as a seal* on your heart,
as a seal on your arm;
For stern as death is love,
relentless as the nether world is devotion;
its flames are a blazing fire.
7 Deep waters cannot quench love,
nor floods sweep it away.
Were one to offer all he owns to purchase love,
he would be roundly mocked.

Chastity and Its Welcome

8 "Our sister is little*
and she has no breasts as yet.
What shall we do for our sister
when her courtship begins?
9 If she is a wall,
we will build upon it a silver parapet;
If she is a door,
we will reinforce it with a cedar plank."

10 I am a wall,
and my breasts are like towers.
So now in his eyes I have become
one to be welcomed.

The Bride and Her Dowry

11 B Solomon had a vineyard at Baal-hamon;*
he gave over the vineyard to caretakers.
For its fruit one would have to pay
a thousand silver pieces.
12 My vineyard is at my own disposal;
the thousand pieces are for you,
O Solomon,
and two hundred for the caretakers of its fruit.

Life Together

13 G O garden-dweller,*
my friends are listening for your voice,
let me hear it!

14 B Be swift, my lover,
like a gazelle or a young stag
on the mountains of spices![o]

8, 5: The lovers are pictured walking homeward, enjoying the fulfillment of the desire which the girl expressed in vv 1f. The groom speaks of their first meeting.

8, 6f: Seal: this could be worn bound to the arm, as here, or suspended at the neck, or as a ring (Jer 22, 24). It was used for identification and signatures. Stern . . . relentless: in human experience, death and the nether world are inevitable, unrelenting; in the end they always triumph. Love, which is just as certain of its victory, matches its strength against the natural enemies of life; waters cannot extinguish it nor floods carry it away. It is more priceless than all riches.

8, 8ff: The bride affirms her chastity. In 8, 9 she quotes the course of action which her elder brothers had decided on. While she is yet immature, they will shelter her in view of eventual marriage. If she is virtuous, she will be honored; if she is unchaste, she will be kept under strict vigilance. In reply to this she proclaims her virtue and boasts of having found welcome from her lover.

8, 11f: These enigmatic verses have been variously interpreted. In v 11 the girl alludes to a vineyard of great value which is compared to her own self in v 12. Her enormous dowry, a thousand silver pieces, is in keeping with her intrinsic worth. She has been the generous lover, giving herself and a dowry to her lover, referred to as Solomon, and also smaller gifts to her brothers, the caretakers (cf vv 8ff).

8, 13f: As in Song 2, 14f, her lover asks for a word or a song and she replies in words similar to those found in Song 2, 17.

k Song 3, 4. l Song 2, 6. m Song 2, 7; 3, 5. n Song 3, 6; 6, 10. o Song 2, 9. 17; 4, 6.

THE BOOK OF WISDOM

The Book of Wisdom was written about a hundred years before the coming of Christ. Its author, whose name is not known to us, was a member of the Jewish community at Alexandria, in Egypt. He wrote in Greek, in a style patterned on that of Hebrew verse. At times he speaks in the person of Solomon, placing his teachings on the lips of the wise king of Hebrew tradition in order to emphasize their value. His profound knowledge of the earlier Old Testament writings is reflected in almost every line of the book, and marks him, like Ben Sira, as an outstanding representative of religious devotion and learning among the sages of postexilic Judaism.

The primary purpose of the sacred author was the edification of his co-religionists in a time when they had experienced suffering and oppression, in part at least at the hands of apostate fellow Jews. To convey his message he made use of the most popular religious themes of his time, namely the splendor and worth of divine wisdom (6, 22—11, 1), the glorious events of the Exodus (11, 2-16; 12, 23-27; 15, 18—19, 22), God's mercy (11, 17—12, 22), the folly of idolatry (13, 1—15, 17), and the manner in which God's justice is vindicated in rewarding or punishing the individual soul (1, 1—6, 21). The first ten chapters especially form a preparation for the fuller teachings of Christ and his church. Many passages from this section of the book, notably 3, 1-8, are used by the church in her liturgy.

The principal divisions of the Book of Wisdom are:

I. The Reward of Justice (1, 1—6, 21).
II. Praise of Wisdom by Solomon (6, 22—11, 1).
III. Special Providence of God during the Exodus (11, 2-16; 12, 23-27; 15, 18—19, 22) with digressions on God's mercy (11, 17—12, 22) and on the folly and shame of idolatry (13, 1—15, 17).

I: The Reward Of Justice

CHAPTER 1

Exhortation to Justice, the Key to Life

1 Love justice,* you who judge the earth; [a]
think of the LORD in goodness,
and seek him in integrity of heart; [b]
2 Because he is found by those who test him not,
and he manifests himself to those who do not disbelieve him. [c]
3 For perverse counsels separate a man from God,
and his power, put to the proof, rebukes the foolhardy; [d]
4 Because into a soul that plots evil wisdom enters not,
nor dwells she in a body under debt of sin. [e]
5 For the holy spirit of discipline* flees deceit
and withdraws from senseless counsels;
and when injustice occurs it is rebuked. [f]
6 For wisdom is a kindly spirit,
yet she acquits not the blasphemer of his guilty lips;
Because God is the witness of his inmost self [g]
and the sure observer of his heart
and the listener to his tongue. [h]
7 For the spirit of the LORD fills the world, [i]
is all-embracing, and knows what man says.*

1, 1: Justice: not merely the cardinal virtue of that name (cf Wis 8, 7), but the universal moral quality which is the application of Wisdom to moral conduct.

1, 5: Discipline: here and elsewhere, another name for Wisdom; injustice: the opposite of the virtue in Wis 1, 1.

1, 7: This verse is applied to the Holy Spirit in the liturgy at Pentecost.

a 1 Chr 29, 17; Ps 2, 10; Is 26, 9. b 1f: Sir 1, 25. c 1 Chr 28, 9. d Is 59, 2. e Sir 15, 7f; Rom 7, 14. f Is 63, 10. g Jer 17, 10. h 6f: Jer 23, 24f. i Wis 12, 1.

8 Therefore no one who utters wicked things
can go unnoticed,
nor will chastising condemnation pass him
by.[j]
9 For the devices of the wicked man shall be
scrutinized,
and the sound of his words shall reach the
LORD,
for the chastisement of his transgressions;
10 Because a jealous ear hearkens to everything,[k]
and discordant grumblings are no secret.
11 Therefore guard against profitless grumbling,
and from calumny* withhold your tongues;
For a stealthy utterance does not go
unpunished,
and a lying mouth slays the soul.
12 Court not death by your erring way of life,
nor draw to yourselves destruction by the
works of your hands.
13 Because God did not make death,[l]
nor does he rejoice in the destruction of the
living.
14 For he fashioned all things that they might
have being;
and the creatures of the world are
wholesome,
And there is not a destructive drug among
them
nor any domain of the nether world on
earth,
15 For justice is undying.[m]

The Wicked Reject Immortality and Justice Alike

16 It was the wicked who with hands and words
invited death,
considered it a friend, and pined for it,
and made a covenant with it,
Because they deserve to be in its possession,[n]

CHAPTER 2

1 they who said among themselves, thinking
not aright:
"Brief and troublous is our lifetime;[o]
neither is there any remedy for man's dying,
nor is anyone known to have come back
from the nether world.
2 For haphazard were we born,
and hereafter we shall be as though we had
not been;
Because the breath in our nostrils is a smoke
and reason is a spark at the beating of our
hearts,
3 And when this is quenched, our body will be
ashes
and our spirit will be poured abroad like
unresisting air.[p]
4 Even our name will be forgotten in time,
and no one will recall our deeds.
So our life will pass away like the traces of a
cloud,
and will be dispersed like a mist
pursued by the sun's rays
and overpowered by its heat.
5 For our lifetime is the passing of a shadow;
and our dying cannot be deferred
because it is fixed with a seal; and no one
returns.[q]
6 Come, therefore, let us enjoy the good things
that are real,
and use the freshness of creation avidly.[r]
7 Let us have our fill of costly wine and
perfumes,
and let no springtime blossom pass us by;
8 let us crown ourselves with rosebuds ere
they wither.
9 Let no meadow be free from our
wantonness;*
everywhere let us leave tokens of our
rejoicing,
for this our portion is, and this our lot.[s]
10 Let us oppress the needy just man;
let us neither spare the widow
nor revere the old man for his hair grown
white with time.[t]
11 But let our strength be our norm of justice;
for weakness proves itself useless.

1, 11: Calumny: speech against God and his providence is meant.

2, 9: Let no meadow . . . wantonness: the extant Greek Mss have "Let none of us be without part in our wanton doings." Most Latin Mss have both forms of this line.

j Prv 19, 5. k 10f: Nm 14, 27f. l 13f: Ez 18, 32; 33, 11; 2 Pt 3, 9. m Is 51, 6ff. n Is 28, 15. o Jb 14, 1; 7, 9. p Jb 7, 9; Jas 4, 14. q Ps 144, 4. r Is 22, 13; 1 Cor 15, 32. s Jer 13, 25. t Ex 22, 22ff; Lv 19, 32.

12 *Let us beset the just one, because he is
obnoxious to us;
he sets himself against our doings,
Reproaches us for transgressions of the law*
and charges us with violations of our
training.[u]
13 He professes to have knowledge of God
and styles himself a child of the
LORD.[v]
14 To us he is the censure of our thoughts;
merely to see him is a hardship for us,[w]
15 Because his life is not like other men's,
and different are his ways.
16 He judges us debased;
he holds aloof from our paths as from things
impure.
He calls blest the destiny of the just
and boasts that God is his Father.[x]
17 Let us see whether his words be true;
let us find out what will happen to him.[y]
18 For if the just one be the son of God, he will
defend him
and deliver him from the hand of his foes.[z]
19 With revilement and torture let us put him to
the test
that we may have proof of his gentleness
and try his patience.
20 Let us condemn him to a shameful death;
for according to his own words, God will
take care of him."[a]
21 These were their thoughts, but they erred;
for their wickedness blinded them,[b]
22 And they knew not the hidden counsels of
God;
neither did they count on a recompense of
holiness
nor discern the innocent souls' reward.[c]
23 For God formed man to be imperishable;
the image of his own nature he made him.[d]
24 But by the envy of the devil, death entered the
world,
and they who are in his possession
experience it.[e]

CHAPTER 3

The Hidden Counsels of God

A. On Suffering

1 But the souls of the just are in the hand of
God,[f]
and no torment shall touch them.*
2 They seemed, in the view of the foolish, to be
dead;
and their passing away was thought an
affliction
3 and their going forth from us, utter
destruction.
But they are in peace.[g]
4 For if before men, indeed, they be punished,
yet is their hope full of immortality;
5 Chastised a little, they shall be greatly blessed,
because God tried them
and found them worthy of himself.[h]
6 As gold in the furnace, he proved them,
and as sacrificial offerings* he took them to
himself.[i]
7 In the time of their visitation* they shall shine,
and shall dart about as sparks through
stubble;[j]
8 They shall judge nations and rule over peoples,
and the LORD shall be their King forever.[k]
9 Those who trust in him shall understand truth,
and the faithful shall abide with him in love:
Because grace and mercy are with his holy
ones,[l]
and his care is with his elect.

2, 12–20: Often applied to the Passion of our Lord; many have understood these verses as a direct prophecy. Cf Mt 27, 41–44.

2, 12: Law: the law of Moses; training has the same meaning.

3, 1–8: Verses frequently applied to the martyrs.

3, 6: Offerings: the image is that of the holocaust, in which the victim is completely consumed by fire.

3, 7: Visitation: God's loving judgment of those who have been faithful to him; the same word is used in Wis 14, 11 for the punishment of the wicked at God's final judgment. Cf also Wis 3, 13.

u Hos 8, 1. v Mt 27, 43; Jn 8, 55; 10, 36–39. w Mt 9, 4. x Jer 6, 30. y Gn 37, 20. z Ps 22, 9; Is 42, 1; Mt 27, 43; Jn 5, 18. a Jas 5, 6. b Rom 1, 21. c Ps 18, 24f; Prv 11, 18; Mt 11, 25. d Gn 1, 26f; Is 54, 16 LXX. e Gn 3, 1–24; Rom 5, 12. f Jb 12, 10; 5, 19. g Is 57, 2. h Tb 12, 13; 2 Cor 4, 17; 1 Pt 1, 6f. i Ps 51, 19; Prv 17, 3; Sir 2, 5; Is 48, 10. j Dn 12, 3; Ob 18; Mal 3, 3; Mt 13, 43. k Wis 8, 14; Prv 8, 16; Dn 7, 22; 1 Cor 6, 2; Rv 20, 4. l Wis 3, 9; 4, 15; Jb 10, 12; Jn 15, 10.

10 But the wicked shall receive a punishment to
match their thoughts,*
since they neglected justice and forsook the
LORD.
11 For he who despises wisdom and instruction is
doomed.[m]
Vain is their hope, fruitless are their labors,
and worthless are their works.[n]
12 Their wives are foolish and their children
wicked;
accursed is their brood.[o]

B. On Childlessness

13 Yes, blessed is she who, childless and
undefiled,
knew not transgression of the marriage bed;
she shall bear fruit at the visitation of
souls.*
14 So also the eunuch whose hand wrought no
misdeed,
who held no wicked thoughts against the
LORD—
For he shall be given fidelity's choice reward*
and a more gratifying heritage in the LORD's
temple.[p]
15 For the fruit of noble struggles is a glorious
one;
and unfailing is the root of understanding.[q]
16 But the children of adulterers will remain
without issue,
and the progeny of an unlawful bed will
disappear.[r]
17 For should they attain long life, they will be
held in no esteem,
and dishonored will their old age be at last;
18 While should they die abruptly, they have no
hope
nor comfort in the day of scrutiny;
19 for dire is the end of the wicked
generation.[s]

CHAPTER 4

1 Better is childlessness with virtue;
for immortal is its memory:*
because both by God is it acknowledged,
and by men.[t]
2 When it is present men imitate it,
and they long for it when it is gone;
And forever it marches crowned in triumph,
victorious in unsullied deeds of valor.
3 But the numerous progeny of the wicked shall
be of no avail;
their spurious offshoots shall not strike deep
root
nor take firm hold.[u]
4 For even though their branches flourish for a
time,
they are unsteady and shall be rocked by the
wind
and, by the violence of the winds,
uprooted;[v]
5 Their twigs shall be broken off untimely,
and their fruit be useless, unripe for eating,
and fit for nothing.
6 For children born of lawless unions
give evidence of the wickedness of their
parents, when they are examined.

C. On Early Death

7 But the just man, though he die early, shall be
at rest.[w]
8 For the age that is honorable comes not with
the passing of time,[x]
nor can it be measured in terms of years.
9 Rather, understanding is the hoary crown for
men,
and an unsullied life, the attainment of old
age.
10 He who pleased God was loved;[y]
he who lived among sinners was
transported—*

3, 10: To match their thoughts: a fate as empty as that which they describe; cf Wis 2, 1–5.

3, 13: Visitation of souls: that is, the last judgment. Cf Wis 3, 7–9.

3, 14: Fidelity's choice reward: cf Is 56, 1–8. More gratifying: better than sons and daughters; cf Is 56, 5.

4, 1: The Latin form of this line, "Oh, how fair is the chaste generation in its glory!" is a later adaptation, which is applied in the liturgy to the splendor of virginity.

4, 10f: There are allusions here to Enoch (Gn 5, 21–24), who was young by patriarchal standards, and to Lot (Gn 19, 10f; 2 Pt 2, 7f). Cf also Is 57, 1f.

m Prv 1, 7. n 11f: Sir 41, 8. o Dt 28, 18ff. p Is 56, 2–5. q Sir 1, 18. r 2 Sm 12, 14. s Ps 34, 22. t Sir 16, 1ff; Prv 3, 3f. u Sir 23, 25. v Sir 40, 15; Is 40, 24. w Wis 3, 3. x 8f: Jb 12, 12; 32, 9; Sir 25, 4ff. y Gn 5, 24; Sir 44, 16; Heb 11, 5.

[11] Snatched away, lest wickedness pervert his
mind
or deceit beguile his soul; [z]
[12] For the witchery of paltry things obscures
what is right
and the whirl of desire transforms the
innocent mind. [a]
[13] Having become perfect in a short while,
he reached the fullness of a long career;
[14] for his soul was pleasing to the LORD,
therefore he sped him out of the midst of
wickedness. [b]
But the people saw and did not understand,
nor did they take this into account.*
[16] Yes, the just man dead condemns the sinful
who live,
and youth swiftly completed
condemns the many years of the wicked
man grown old. [c]
[17] For they see the death of the wise man
and do not understand what the LORD
intended for him,
or why he made him secure.
[18] They see, and hold him in contempt;
but the LORD laughs them to scorn. [d]
[19] And they shall afterward become dishonored
corpses [e]
and an unceasing mockery among the dead.
For he shall strike them down speechless and
prostrate [f]
and rock them to their foundations;
They shall be utterly laid waste
and shall be in grief
and their memory shall perish.

The Final Judgment of the Wicked

[20] Fearful shall they come, at the counting up* of
their sins,
and their lawless deeds shall convict them
to their face.

CHAPTER 5

[1] Then shall the just one with great assurance
confront [g]
his oppressors who set at nought his
labors. [h]
[2] Seeing this, they shall be shaken with dreadful
fear,
and amazed at the unlooked-for salvation.
[3] They shall say among themselves, rueful
and groaning through anguish of spirit:
"This is he whom once we held as a
laughingstock
and as a type for mockery, [4] fools that we
were!
His life we accounted madness,
and his death dishonored.
[5] See how he is accounted among the sons of
God;
how his lot is with the saints! [i]
[6] We, then, have strayed from the way of truth, [j]
and the light of justice did not shine for us,
and the sun did not rise for us. [k]
[7] We had our fill of the ways of mischief and of
ruin;
we journeyed through impassable deserts,
but the way of the LORD we knew not.
[8] What did our pride avail us?
What have wealth and its boastfulness
afforded us? [l]
[9] All of them passed like a shadow
and like a fleeting rumor; [m]
[10] Like a ship traversing the heaving water,
of which, when it has passed, no trace can
be found,
no path of its keel in the waves.
[11] Or like a bird flying through the air;
no evidence of its course is to be found—
But the fluid air, lashed by the beat of pinions,
and cleft by the rushing force
Of speeding wings, is traversed:
and afterward no mark of passage can be
found in it.
[12] Or as, when an arrow has been shot at a mark,
the parted air straightway flows together
again

4, 15: The verse here omitted repeats the last two lines of Wis 3, 9.
4, 20: Counting up: the last judgment.

z Is 57, 1f. a Wis 2, 21; Dn 13, 9. b Gn 19, 22. 29; 2 Pt 2, 7. c Mt 12, 41f. d Ps 37, 13. e Neh 1, 10 LXX; Ps 18, 8; Is 14, 19; Jer 23, 39f. f 2 Mc 3, 29. g 1f: 2 Thes 1, 6f. h Col 2, 15. i Acts 26, 18; Col 1, 12. j Prv 4, 18f; Jn 12, 35. k 6f. Is 59, 6–14. l Ps 49, 7; Prv 10, 2. m 9ff. 1 Chr 20, 15; Ps 144, 4; Jb 9, 25f LXX.

so that none discerns the way it went
through—
13 Even so we, once born, abruptly came to
nought
and held no sign of virtue to display,
but were consumed in our wickedness."[n]
14 Yes, the hope of the wicked is like thistledown
borne on the wind,
and like fine, tempest-driven foam;
Like smoke scattered by the wind,
and like the passing memory of the nomad
camping for a single day.[o]
15 But the just live forever,
and in the LORD is their recompense,
and the thought of them is with the Most
High.[p]
16 Therefore shall they receive the splendid
crown,
the beauteous diadem, from the hand of the
LORD—
For he shall shelter them with his right
hand,
and protect them with his arm.[q]
17 He shall take his zeal for armor[r]
and he shall arm creation to requite the
enemy;
18 He shall don justice for a breastplate
and shall wear sure judgment for a helmet;
19 He shall take invincible rectitude as a shield[s]
20 and whet his sudden anger for a sword,
And the universe shall war with him against
the foolhardy.
21 Well-aimed shafts of lightnings shall go forth
and from the clouds as from a well-drawn
bow shall leap to the mark;[t]
22 and as from his sling, wrathful hailstones
shall be hurled.
The water of the sea shall be enraged against
them
and the streams shall abruptly overflow;[u]
23 A mighty wind shall confront them
and a tempest winnow them out;
Thus lawlessness shall lay the whole earth
waste
and evildoing overturn the thrones of
potentates.[v]

CHAPTER 6

Exhortation To Seek Wisdom

1 Hear, therefore, kings, and understand;[w]
learn, you magistrates of the earth's
expanse!
2 Hearken, you who are in power over the
multitude
and lord it over throngs of peoples!
3 Because authority was given you by the LORD
and sovereignty by the Most High,
who shall probe your works and scrutinize
your counsels![x]
4 Because, though you were ministers of his
kingdom, you judged not rightly,
and did not keep the law,*
nor walk according to the will of God,
5 Terribly and swiftly shall he come against you,
because judgment is stern for the exalted—
6 For the lowly may be pardoned out of mercy[y]
but the mighty shall be mightily put to the
test.
7 For the Lord of all shows no partiality,
nor does he fear greatness,[z]
Because he himself made the great as well as
the small,
and he provides for all alike;
8 but for those in power a rigorous scrutiny
impends.
9 To you, therefore, O princes, are my words
addressed[a]
that you may learn wisdom and that you
may not sin.
10 For those who keep the holy precepts
hallowed shall be found holy,
and those learned in them will have ready a
response.*

6, 4: Law: that of Moses; cf v 10; Wis 2, 12.
6, 10: Response: a suitable plea before the great Judge. Cf Prv 22, 21; Jb 31, 14; Hb 2, 1; Sir 8, 9.

n Ez 33, 10. o Jb 21, 18; Ps 1, 4; 37, 20; Is 17, 13. p Is 62, 11; Ez 18, 9. q Ex 33, 22; Is 62, 3; 2 Tm 4, 8; 1 Pt 5, 4. r 17: Is 59, 16. s 19f: Dt 32, 40ff. t Hb 3, 9ff. u Dt 11, 4. v Wis 11, 20; Sir 10, 13f. w 1f: Wis 1, 1; Sir 33, 19; Mi 3, 1. 9. x 2 Chr 36, 23; Prv 8, 15f; Jn 19, 11; Rom 13, 1ff. y 6ff: Lk 12, 48. z Dt 1, 17; Prv 22, 2. a 9ff: Dt 4, 10; Ps 2, 12; Sir 32, 14; 1 Jn 3, 7.

11 Desire therefore my words;
long for them and you shall be instructed.
12 Resplendent and unfading is Wisdom,
and she is readily perceived by those who love her,
and found by those who seek her.[b]
13 She hastens to make herself known in anticipation of men's desire;[c]
14 he who watches for her at dawn shall not be disappointed,
for he shall find her sitting by his gate.
15 For taking thought of her is the perfection of prudence,
and he who for her sake keeps vigil shall quickly be free from care;
16 Because she makes her own rounds, seeking those worthy of her,
and graciously appears to them in the ways,
and meets them with all solicitude.[d]
17 For the first step toward discipline is a very earnest desire for her;[e]
then, care for discipline is love of her;
18 love means the keeping of her laws;
To observe her laws is the basis for incorruptibility;
19 and incorruptibility makes one close to God;
20 thus the desire for Wisdom leads up to a kingdom.
21 If, then, you find pleasure in throne and scepter, you princes of the peoples,
honor Wisdom, that you may reign as kings forever.

II: Praise Of Wisdom By Solomon

Introduction

22 Now what Wisdom is, and how she came to be, I shall relate;
and I shall hide no secrets from you,
But from the very beginning I shall search out
and bring to light knowledge of her,
nor shall I diverge from the truth.[f]
23 Neither shall I admit consuming jealousy to my company,
because that can have no fellowship with Wisdom.[g]
24 A great number of wise men is the safety of the world,
and a prudent king, the stability of his people;[h]
25 so take instruction from my words, to your profit.

CHAPTER 7

Solomon Is Like All Other Men

1 I too am a mortal man, the same as all the rest,[i]
and a descendant of the first man formed of earth.*
And in my mother's womb I was molded into flesh
2 in a ten-months' period*—body and blood,
from the seed of man, and the pleasure that accompanies marriage.
3 And I too, when born, inhaled the common air,
and fell upon the kindred earth;
wailing, I uttered that first sound common to all.
4 In swaddling clothes and with constant care I was nurtured.
5 For no king has any different origin or birth,
6 but one is the entry into life for all; and in one same way they leave it.[j]

Solomon Prayed and Wisdom and Riches Came to Him

7 Therefore I prayed, and prudence was given me;
I pleaded, and the spirit of Wisdom came to me.[k]
8 I preferred her to scepter and throne,[l]

7, 1: First man formed of earth: Adam. The author omits throughout the book the proper names of the characters in sacred history of whom he speaks; see especially chapter 10.

7, 2: In a ten-months' period: thus the ancients were accustomed to reckon the period of pregnancy.

b Wis 7, 10; Prv 8, 17; Jer 29, 13. c 13ff: Prv 8, 3. 17. 34. d Prv 8, 20f; Sir 15, 1ff. e 17–21; Ps 2, 10ff; Prv 4, 4–9; 7, 1–4; 8, 15f; Dn 7, 27; Jn 14, 15. 21; 1 Jn 5, 3. f Tb 12, 7. 11; Mt 13, 11; Jn 15, 15. g Wis 7, 13; Jas 3, 14f. h Prv 24, 6; 29, 4; Sir 10, 1ff. i 1f: Wis 10, 1; Gn 2, 7; Jb 10, 9–12; 33, 6; 1 Cor 15, 47ff. j Jb 1, 21; 1 Tm 6, 7f. k 1 Kgs 3, 5–15; Prv 2, 3–11. l 8f: Wis 8, 5; 1 Kgs 10, 21; Prv 3, 14ff; 8, 10. 18f; Jb 28, 15–19.

And deemed riches nothing in comparison
with her,
9 nor did I liken any priceless gem to her;
Because all gold, in view of her, is a little sand,
and before her, silver is to be accounted
mire.
10 Beyond health and comeliness I loved her,
And I chose to have her rather than the light,
because the splendor of her never yields to
sleep.[m]
11 Yet all good things together came to me in her
company,[n]
and countless riches at her hands;
12 And I rejoiced in them all, because Wisdom is
their leader,
though I had not known that she is the
mother of these.[o]

Solomon Prays for Help To Speak of Wisdom

13 Simply I learned about her, and ungrudgingly
do I share—
her riches I do not hide away;[p]
14 For to men she is an unfailing treasure;
those who gain this treasure win the
friendship of God,
to whom the gifts they have from
discipline* commend them.
15 Now God grant I speak suitably
and value these endowments at their
worth:
For he is the guide of Wisdom
and the director of the wise.
16 For both we and our words are in his hand,
as well as all prudence and knowledge of
crafts.[q]
17 For he gave me sound knowledge of existing
things,
that I might know the organization of the
universe and the force of its elements,
18 The beginning and the end and the midpoint
of times,
the changes in the sun's course and the
variations of the seasons.
19 Cycles of years, positions of the stars,
20 natures of animals, tempers of beasts,
Powers of the winds and thoughts of men,
uses of plants and virtues of roots—
21 Such things as are hidden I learned, and such
as are plain;
22 for Wisdom, the artificer of all, taught me.[r]

Nature and Incomparable Dignity of Wisdom

For in her is a spirit
intelligent, holy, unique,
Manifold, subtle, agile,
clear, unstained, certain,
Not baneful, loving the good, keen,[s]
unhampered, beneficent, 23 kindly,
Firm, secure, tranquil,
all-powerful, all-seeing,
And pervading all spirits,
though they be intelligent, pure and very
subtle.
24 For Wisdom is mobile beyond all motion,
and she penetrates and pervades all things
by reason of her purity.[t]
25 For she is an aura of the might of God
and a pure effusion of the glory of the
Almighty;
therefore nought that is sullied enters into
her.
26 For she is the refulgence of eternal light,
the spotless mirror of the power of God,
the image of his goodness.[u]
27 And she, who is one, can do all things,
and renews everything while herself
perduring;
And passing into holy souls from age to age,
she produces friends of God and prophets.[v]
28 For there is nought God loves, be it not one
who dwells with Wisdom.
29 For she is fairer than the sun[w]
and surpasses every constellation of the
stars.
Compared to light, she takes precedence;

7, 14: Discipline: cf note on Wis 1, 5.

m Prv 6, 23. n Prv 8, 21. o Prv 8, 14f. p Wis 6, 23. q Wis 3, 1. r Wis 14, 2; Prv 8, 30. s 22f: Heb 4, 12f; Jas 3, 17. t Wis 8, 1. u 2 Cor 4, 4; Col 1, 15; Heb 1, 3. v Ex 33, 11; Jb 42, 2; Ps 104, 29; Jl 3, 1. w 29f: Song 6, 3. 9.

30 for that, indeed, night supplants,
but wickedness prevails not over Wisdom.

CHAPTER 8

1 Indeed, she reaches from end to end* mightily
and governs all things well. [x]

Solomon Sought Wisdom, the Source of Blessings

2 Her I loved and sought after from my youth;
I sought to take her for my bride
and was enamored of her beauty. [y]
3 She adds to nobility the splendor of
companionship with God;
even the LORD of all loved her.
4 For she is instructress in the understanding of
God,
the selector of his works. [z]
5 And if riches be a desirable possession in life,
what is more rich than Wisdom, who
produces all things? [a]
6 And if prudence renders service, [b]
who in the world is a better craftsman than
she?
7 Or if one loves justice,
the fruits of her works are virtues;
For she teaches moderation and prudence,
justice and fortitude,*
and nothing in life is more useful for men
than these.
8 Or again, if one yearns for copious learning,
she knows the things of old, and infers
those yet to come.
She understands the turns of phrases and the
solutions of riddles;
signs and wonders she knows in advance
and the outcome of times and ages. [c]

Solomon Sought Wisdom as His Counselor and Comfort

9 So I determined to take her to live with me,
knowing that she would be my counselor
while all was well,
and my comfort in care and grief.
10 For her sake I should have glory among the
masses, [d]
and esteem from the elders, though I be but
a youth.
11 I should become keen in judgment,
and should be a marvel before rulers.
12 They would abide my silence and attend my
utterance;
and as I spoke on further,
they would place their hands upon their
mouths.*
13 For her sake I should have immortality
and leave to those after me an everlasting
memory. [e]
14 I should govern peoples, and nations would be
my subjects— [f]
15 terrible princes, hearing of me, would be
afraid;
in the assembly I should appear noble, and
in war courageous.
16 Within my dwelling, I should take my repose
beside her;
For association with her involves no bitterness
and living with her no grief,
but rather joy and gladness. [g]

Solomon Realizes That Wisdom Is a Gift of God

17 Thinking thus within myself,
and reflecting in my heart
That there is immortality in kinship with
Wisdom, [h]
18 and good pleasure in her friendship,
and unfailing riches in the works of her
hands,
And that in frequenting her society there is
prudence,
and fair renown in sharing her discourses,
I went about seeking to take her for my
own.
19 Now, I was a well-favored child,*

8, 1: End to end: from one end of the heavens to the other.
8, 7: Moderation . . . fortitude: what are now known as the cardinal virtues.
8, 12: Hands upon their mouths: an oft-mentioned sign of respect among the ancients for unanswerable wisdom; cf Jb 40, 4.
8, 19f: Here the sacred writer mentions first bodily, then spiritual, excellence. To make it plain that the latter is the governing factor in the harmonious development of the human person, he then reverses the order.

x Wis 7, 24; 15, 1. y 1 Kgs 3, 7ff; Ps 45, 12; Prv 5, 18; 8, 17. z Prv 8, 27–31. a Prv 8, 18f. b 6f: Prv 8, 14f. c Prv 1, 6; Sir 39, 1ff; 42, 19f; Dn 2, 21. d 10ff: 1 Kgs 3, 28; Jb 29, 8ff. 21f. e Sir 15, 6; 41, 12f; Is 56, 5. f Wis 3, 8; Ps 18, 48; 47, 4. g Prv 29, 6; Sir 15, 6; Bar 3, 38. h Prv 3, 18.

and I came by a noble nature;
20 or rather, being noble, I attained an unsullied body.
21 And knowing that I could not otherwise possess her* except God gave it—
and this, too, was prudence, to know whose is the gift—
I went to the LORD and besought him, [i]
and said with all my heart:

CHAPTER 9

Solomon's Prayer

1 God of my fathers, LORD of mercy, [j]
you who have made all things by your word [k]
2 And in your wisdom have established man
to rule the creatures produced by you, [l]
3 To govern the world in holiness and justice,
and to render judgment in integrity of heart: [m]
4 Give me Wisdom, the attendant at your throne,
and reject me not from among your children; [n]
5 For I am your servant, the son of your handmaid,
a man weak and short-lived
and lacking in comprehension of judgment and of laws. [o]
6 Indeed, though one be perfect among the sons of men,
if Wisdom, who comes from you, be not with him,
he shall be held in no esteem. [p]
7 You have chosen me king over your people
and magistrate for your sons and daughters. [q]
8 You have bid me build a temple on your holy mountain
and an altar in the city that is your dwelling place,
a copy of the holy tabernacle which you had established from of old. [r]
9 Now with you is Wisdom, who knows your works
and was present when you made the world;
Who understands what is pleasing in your eyes
and what is conformable with your commands. [s]
10 Send her forth from your holy heavens
and from your glorious throne dispatch her
That she may be with me and work with me,
that I may know what is your pleasure. [t]
11 For she knows and understands all things,
and will guide me discreetly in my affairs
and safeguard me by her glory; [u]
12 Thus my deeds will be acceptable,
and I shall judge your people justly
and be worthy of my father's throne. [v]
13 For what man knows God's counsel,
or who can conceive what the LORD intends? [w]
14 For the deliberations of mortals are timid,
and unsure are our plans.
15 For the corruptible body burdens the soul
and the earthen shelter weighs down the mind that has many concerns. [x]
16 And scarce do we guess the things on earth,
and what is within our grasp we find with difficulty;
but when things are in heaven, who can search them out? [y]
17 Or who ever knew your counsel, except you had given Wisdom
and sent your holy spirit from on high? [z]
18 And thus were the paths of those on earth made straight,
and men learned what was your pleasure,
and were saved by Wisdom. [a]

8, 21: Possess her: in the Latin, "be continent." Though this verse has often been cited in connection with the virtue of chastity, the original must certainly mean "be possessed of Wisdom."

i 1 Kgs 3, 9; 4, 29; Prv 2, 6; Jas 1, 5. j Ps 86, 15. k 1f: Gn 1; Ps 33, 6; Prv 3, 19; Jer 10, 12; Jn 1, 3. 10. l Ps 8, 7ff; Sir 17, 2ff. m 1 Kgs 3, 6; 9 4f; Ps 9, 8f. n 2 Chr 1, 10. o 1 Kgs 3, 7; Ps 116, 16. p Wis 3, 17; 1 Kgs 11, 4; 1 Cor 3, 18ff. q 1 Chr 28, 5. r Ex 25, 8f; 2 Sm 7, 13; 1 Chr 28, 5; 2 Chr 6, 1f; 7, 7; Tb 1, 4; Pss 15. 1; 48, 2f. s Dt 6, 17f; Prv 8, 22–31; Jn 1, 1ff. 10. t Wis 18, 15; Mt 5, 34; Jn 3, 17; 20, 21. u Wis 8, 8. v 1 Kgs 3, 6–9. w Is 40, 13; Bar 3, 31. x Jb 4, 19. y Sir 1. 3; Jn 3, 12. z Jn 14, 26. a Wis 10, 9; Prv 28, 26.

CHAPTER 10*

Wisdom Preserves Her Followers

1 She preserved the first-formed father* of the world [b]
when he alone had been created; [c]
And she raised him up from his fall,
2 and gave him power to rule all things. [d]
3 But when the unjust man* withdrew from her in his anger,
he perished through his fratricidal wrath. [e]
4 When on his account the earth was flooded,
Wisdom again saved it,
piloting the just man* on frailest wood. [f]
5 She, when the nations were sunk in universal wickedness,
knew the just man,* kept him blameless before God,
and preserved him resolute against pity for his child. [g]
6 She delivered the just man* from among the wicked who were being destroyed, [h]
when he fled as fire descended upon Pentapolis—
7 Where as a testimony to its wickedness,
there yet remain a smoking desert,
Plants bearing fruit that never ripens,
and the tomb of a disbelieving soul,* a standing pillar of salt. [i]
8 For those who forsook Wisdom
first were bereft of knowledge of the right,
And then they left mankind a memorial of their folly—
so that they could not even be hidden in their fall.
9 But Wisdom delivered from tribulations those who served her. [j]
10 She, when the just man fled from his brother's anger, [k]
guided him in direct ways,*
Showed him the kingdom of God
and gave him knowledge of holy things;
She prospered him in his labors
and made abundant the fruit of his works,
11 Stood by him against the greed of his defrauders,
and enriched him; [l]
12 She preserved him from foes,
and secured him against ambush,
And she gave him the prize for his stern struggle
that he might know that devotion to God* is mightier than all else. [m]
13 She did not abandon the just man* when he was sold, [n]
but delivered him from sin. [o]
14 She went down with him into the dungeon,
and did not desert him in his bonds,
Until she brought him the scepter of royalty
and authority over his oppressors,
Showed those who had defamed him false,
and gave him eternal glory.
15 The holy people and blameless race—it was she
who delivered them from the nation that oppressed them. [p]
16 She entered the soul of the LORD's servant,*
and withstood fearsome kings with signs and portents; [q]
17 she gave the holy ones the recompense of their labors, [r]
Conducted them by a wondrous road,
and became a shelter for them by day
and a starry flame by night.

10, 1–21: This chapter prepares for the following section (11, 2—19, 22) on the history of Israel in the Exodus, by reviewing the dealings of Wisdom with the patriarchs. It has a parallel in Sir 44–50; cf also Wis 18, 9.
10, 1f: Adam.
10, 3: Cain.
10, 4: Noah.
10, 5: Abraham.
10, 6: Lot. Pentapolis: the five cities, including Sodom; cf Gn 14, 2.
10, 7: Disbelieving soul: Lot's wife; cf Gn 19, 26.
10, 10ff: Jacob.
10, 12: Devotion to God: in the Greek this signifies "piety" or "religion," and is the equivalent of the Hebrew "fear of the Lord"; cf Prv 1, 7.
10, 13f: Joseph.
10, 16: Moses.

b 1–16: Heb 11, 17–27. c Wis 7, 1. d Gn 1, 28. e Gn 4, 1–16. f Wis 14, 5f; Gn 6, 5–9. g Gn 22, 7–10. h Gn 18, 22–33; 19, 15–25; 2 Pt 2, 6f. i Gn 19, 26; Lk 17, 32. j Wis 16, 8. k Gn 27, 43ff; 28, 12–15. l Gn 30, 29f; 31, 5–12. m Gn 32, 24–29; 1 Tm 4, 8. n 13f: Gn 37–45. o Gn 39, 7–10. p Ex 3, 9; 14, 30; 19, 6. q Wis 1, 4; 7, 27; Ex 4, 10; Ps 76, 13. r 17ff; Wis 14, 3; 19, 7; Ex 13, 21f; 14—15; Pss 77, 20f; 78, 13. 53; Is 4, 5f.

18 She took them across the Red Sea
and brought them through the deep waters—
19 But their enemies she overwhelmed,
and cast them up* from the bottom of the depths.
20 Therefore the just despoiled the wicked;
and they sang, O LORD, your holy name
and praised in unison your conquering hand [s]—
21 Because Wisdom opened the mouths of the dumb,
and gave ready speech to infants. [t]

CHAPTER 11

1 She made their affairs prosper through the holy prophet. [u]

III: Special Providence Of God During The Exodus

Introduction

2 They journeyed through the uninhabited desert,*
and in solitudes they pitched their tents; [v]
3 they withstood enemies and took vengeance on their foes. [w]
4 When they thirsted, they called upon you,
and water was given them from the sheer rock,
assuagement for their thirst from the hard stone.
5 For by the things through which their foes were punished
they in their need were benefited. [x]

First Example: Water Punishes the Egyptians and Benefits the Israelites

6 Instead of a spring, when the perennial river*
was troubled with impure blood [y]
7 as a rebuke to the decree for the slaying of infants,
You gave them abundant water in an unhoped-for way,
8 once you had shown by the thirst they then had
how you punished their adversaries.
9 For when they had been tried, though only mildly chastised, [z]
they recognized how the wicked, condemned in anger, were being tormented.
11 Both those afar off and those close by were afflicted: [a]
10 the latter you tested, admonishing them as a father;
the former as a stern king you probed and condemned.
12 For a twofold grief took hold of them [b]
and a groaning at the remembrance of the ones who had departed.
13 For when they heard that the cause of their own torments
was a benefit to these others, they recognized the Lord.
14 Him who of old had been cast out in exposure
they indeed mockingly rejected;
but in the end of events, they marveled at him,
since their thirst proved unlike that of the just. [c]

Second Example: Animals Punish the Egyptians and Benefit the Israelites

15 And in return for their senseless, wicked thoughts,
which misled them into worshiping dumb*
serpents and worthless insects,
You sent upon them swarms of dumb creatures for vengeance; [d]
16 that they might recognize that a man is punished by the very things through which he sins. [e]

10, 19: Cast them up: their bodies, on the shore.

11, 2ff: Few verses in these later chapters can be fully understood without consulting the passages in the Mosaic books which are indicated in the cross references. The theme of this part of the book is expressed in Wis 11, 5, and is illustrated in the following chapters by five examples drawn from Exodus events.

11, 6ff: The perennial river: the Nile; the contrast is between the first plague of Egypt (Ex 7, 17–24) and the water drawn from the rock in Horeb (Ex 17, 5–7; Nm 20, 8–11).

11, 15: Dumb: that is, irrational.

s Ex 12, 35f; 15, 1–21. t Ex 4, 10–15; Ps 8, 3; Mt 11, 25. u Dt 2, 7; Hos 12, 14. v 2ff: Ex 17, 2–6; Nm 20, 1–13; Pss 63, 2; 107, 4–7; Jer 2, 6. w Ex 17, 8–16; Nm 21, 1ff. 21–35; 31, 1–12; Ps 118, 10ff. x Wis 16, 1f. y 6ff: Wis 18, 5; Ex 1, 22; 7, 17–24. z 9ff: Wis 3, 5; 16, 3f; Dt 8, 2–5; Ps 6, 2; Prv 3, 12; 2 Mc 6, 12–11.11 a Ps 6, 2. b 12f: Wis 16, 8; Ex 14, 4. 18. c Ex 2, 3. d Wis 12, 23f; 15, 18—16, 1; Ex 7, 26ff. e Wis 12, 23. 27; Ex 10, 16; Prv 1, 31f; 26, 27.

Digression on God's Mercy

17 For not without means was your almighty hand,[f]
that had fashioned the universe from formless matter,
to send upon them a drove of bears or fierce lions,
18 Or new-created, wrathful, unknown beasts
to breathe forth fiery breath,
Or pour out roaring smoke,
or flash terrible sparks from their eyes.
19 Not only could these attack and completely destroy them;
even their frightful appearance itself could slay.
20 Even without these, they could have been killed at a single blast,
pursued by retribution
and winnowed out by your mighty spirit;
But you have disposed all things by measure and number and weight.[g]
21 For with you great strength abides always;
who can resist the might of your arm?[h]
22 Indeed, before you the whole universe is as a grain from a balance,*
or a drop of morning dew come down upon the earth.[i]
23 But you have mercy on all, because you can do all things;
and you overlook the sins of men that they may repent.[j]
24 For you love all things that are
and loathe nothing that you have made;
for what you hated, you would not have fashioned.[k]
25 And how could a thing remain, unless you willed it;
or be preserved, had it not been called forth by you?[l]
26 But you spare all things, because they are yours, O LORD and lover of souls,[m]

CHAPTER 12

1 for your imperishable spirit is in all things![n]
2 Therefore you rebuke offenders little by little,
warn them, and remind them of the sins they are committing,
that they may abandon their wickedness
and believe in you, O LORD!
3 For, truly, the ancient inhabitants of your holy land,[o]
4 whom you hated for deeds most odious—
Works of witchcraft and impious sacrifices;
5 a cannibal feast of human flesh
and of blood, from the midst of . . .*—
These merciless murderers of children,
6 and parents who took with their own hands defenseless lives,[p]
You willed to destroy by the hands of our fathers,
7 that the land that is dearest of all to you
might receive a worthy colony of God's children.[q]
8 But even these, as they were men, you spared,
and sent wasps as forerunners of your army
that they might exterminate them by degrees.[r]
9 Not that you were without power to have the wicked vanquished in battle by the just,
or wiped out at once by terrible beasts or by one decisive word;[s]
10 But condemning them bit by bit, you gave them space for repentance.
You were not unaware that their race was wicked
and their malice ingrained,[t]
And that their dispositions would never change;
11 for they were a race accursed from the beginning.
Neither out of fear for anyone
did you grant amnesty for their sins.[u]

11, 22: Grain from a balance: a tiny particle used for weighing on sensitive scales.

12, 5: And of blood, from the midst of . . . : this line is obscure in the current Greek text and in all extant translations. Either one or two words would complete it. The horrible crimes here spoken of (cf Wis 14, 23) were not unheard of in the ancient pagan world.

f 17ff: Wis 12, 8f; 16, 1. 5; Gn 1, 1f; Dt 32, 24; 2 Kgs 17, 25f; Hos 13, 4–8. g Jb 4, 9. h Wis 12, 12; 2 Chr 20, 6. i Hos 13, 3. j Wis 12, 10; Dt 9, 27; Acts 17, 30; Rom 2, 4; 11, 32; 2 Pt 3, 9. k Ps 145, 9. l Is 41, 4. m Wis 12, 16; Is 63, 9. n Wis 1, 7. o 3ff: Wis 14, 23; Dt 18, 9–12; Pss 5, 6; 106, 28. 34–39; Jer 19, 4f; Ez 16, 3. 20f. 36. p Nm 33, 52. q Dt 11, 12. r Ex 23, 28ff; Dt 7, 17–24. s Wis 11, 18; 18, 15; Nm 16, 21. t Wis 11, 23; Ps 55, 20; Sir 16, 9. u Gn 9, 25.

12 For who can say to you, "What have you
done?"
or who can oppose your decree?
Or when peoples perish, who can challenge
you, their maker;
or who can come into your presence as
vindicator of unjust men? [v]
13 For neither is there any god besides you who
have the care of all,
that you need show you have not unjustly
condemned; [w]
14 Nor can any king or prince confront you on
behalf of those you have punished. [x]
15 But as you are just, you govern all things
justly;
you regard it as unworthy of your power
to punish one who has incurred no blame. [y]
16 For your might is the source of justice;
your mastery over all things makes you
lenient to all. [z]
17 For you show your might when the perfection
of your power is disbelieved;*
and in those who know you, you rebuke
temerity. [a]
18 But though you are master of might, you judge
with clemency,
and with much lenience you govern us;
for power, whenever you will, attends you.
19 And you taught your people, by these deeds, [b]
that those who are just must be kind;
And you gave your sons good ground for hope
that you would permit repentance for their
sins.
20 For these were enemies of your servants,
doomed to death;
yet, while you punished them with such
solicitude and pleading,
granting time and opportunity to abandon
wickedness,
21 With what exactitude you judged your sons,
to whose fathers you gave the sworn
covenants of goodly promises! [c]
22 Us, therefore, you chastise, and our enemies
with a thousand blows you punish,
that we may think earnestly of your
goodness when we judge,
and, when being judged, may look for
mercy.

Second Example Resumed

23 Hence those unjust also, who lived a life of
folly,
you tormented through their own
abominations. [d]
24 For they went far astray in the paths of error,
taking for gods the worthless and disgusting
among beasts,
deceived like senseless infants. [e]
25 Therefore as though upon unreasoning
children,
you sent your judgment on them as a
mockery; [f]
26 But they who took no heed of punishment
which was but child's play
were to experience a condemnation worthy
of God.
27 For in the things through which they suffered
distress,
since they were tortured by the very things
they deemed gods,
They saw and recognized the true God
whom before they had refused to know;
with this, their final condemnation came
upon them. [g]

Digression on False Worship

CHAPTER 13

A. Nature Worship

1 For all men were by nature foolish who were
in ignorance of God,
and who from the good things seen did not
succeed in knowing him who is,*
and from studying the works did not discern
the artisan; [h]

12, 17: The brunt of God's anger and vindictive justice is borne by those who know him and yet defy his authority and might. Cf Wis 1, 2; 15, 2, but also Wis 12, 27; 18. 13.

13, 1: Him who is: the Hebrew sacred name of God; cf Ex 3, 14.

v 2 Sm 16, 10; Eccl 8, 4; Sir 46, 19; Is 45, 9; Dn 4, 32; Rom 9, 19ff. w Wis 6, 7; Dt 3, 24; 32, 39; Is 44, 6. 8. x Jer 49, 19; 50, 44. y Gn 18, 23ff; Dt 32, 4. z Wis 2, 11; 11, 26; Ps 103, 19. a Wis 15, 2f; Ex 9, 16. b 19f: Wis 11, 23; Sir 17, 24. c Wis 18, 22; Gn 50, 24; Dt 7, 6–14; Ps 105, 8ff. d Wis 11, 16; 16, 1. e Dt 11, 28; Jer 5, 28; Rom 1, 23. f Jer 4, 22. g Wis 16, 16; Ex 14, 4. 28. h Acts 14, 17; Eph 4, 17ff.

2 But either fire, or wind, or the swift air,
or the circuit of the stars, or the mighty water,
or the luminaries of heaven,* the governors of the world, they considered gods. [i]
3 Now if out of joy in their beauty they thought them gods,
let them know how far more excellent is the Lord than these;
for the original source of beauty fashioned them. [j]
4 Or if they were struck by their might and energy,
let them from these things realize how much more powerful is he who made them. [k]
5 For from the greatness and the beauty of created things
their original author, by analogy, is seen.
6 But yet, for these the blame is less;*
For they indeed have gone astray perhaps,
though they seek God and wish to find him.
7 For they search busily among his works,
but are distracted by what they see, because the things seen are fair.
8 But again, not even these are pardonable.
9 For if they so far succeeded in knowledge
that they could speculate about the world,
how did they not more quickly find its LORD?

B. IDOLATRY

10 But doomed are they, and in dead things are their hopes,
who termed gods things made by human hands:
Gold and silver, the product of art, and likenesses of beasts,
or useless stone, the work of an ancient hand. [l]

The Carpenter and Wooden Idols

11 A carpenter may saw out a suitable tree [m]
and skillfully scrape off all its bark,
And deftly plying his art,
produce something fit for daily use, [n]
12 and use up the refuse from his handiwork in preparing his food, and have his fill;
13 Then the good-for-nothing refuse from these remnants,
crooked wood grown full of knots,
he takes and carves to occupy his spare time. [o]
This wood he models with listless skill,
and patterns it on the image of a man
14 or makes it resemble some worthless beast.
When he has daubed it with red and crimsoned its surface with red stain,
and daubed over every blemish in it, [p]
15 He makes a fitting shrine for it
and puts it on the wall, fastening it with a nail. [q]
16 Thus lest it fall down he provides for it,
knowing that it cannot help itself;
for, truly, it is an image and needs help. [r]
17 But when he prays about his goods or marriage or children, [s]
he is not ashamed to address the thing without a soul.
And for vigor he invokes the powerless;
18 and for life he entreats the dead;
And for aid he beseeches the wholly incompetent,
and about travel, something that cannot even walk.
19 And for profit in business and success with his hands
he asks facility of a thing with hands completely inert.

CHAPTER 14

1 Again, one preparing for a voyage and about to traverse the wild waves
cries out to wood more unsound than the boat that bears him. [t]

13, 2: Luminaries of heaven: the Latin interprets, "sun and moon"; governors: cf Gn 1, 16.

13, 6: The blame is less: the greater blame is incurred by those mentioned in Wis 13, 10 and 15, 14ff.

i Gn 1, 14–19; Dt 4, 19; Jb 31, 26ff. j Ps 8, 4. k Jer 10, 2; Bar 6, 39. l Wis 3, 11; 15, 5. 17; Dt 4, 25–28; 7, 25; 27, 15; Ps 115, 4; Hos 14, 4; Acts 17, 29. m 11–19: Is 44, 9–20. n Wis 15, 7; Bar 6, 58. o Dt 4, 16. p Jer 10, 9. q Is 40, 20; 41, 7; 44, 13. r 1 Sm 5, 3ff; Bar 6, 57. s 17ff: Wis 15, 15. t Is 46, 7.

2 For the urge for profits devised this latter,
and Wisdom the artificer produced it.
3 But your providence, O Father! guides it,
for you have furnished even in the sea a road,
and through the waves a steady path, [u]
4 Showing that you can save from any danger,
so that even one without skill may embark. [v]
5 But you will that the products of your Wisdom be not idle;
therefore men trust their lives even to frailest wood,
and have been safe crossing the surge on a raft. [w]
6 For of old, when the proud giants were being destroyed,
the hope of the universe, who took refuge on a raft,*
left to the world a future for his race, under the guidance of your hand. [x]
7 For blest is the wood through which justice comes about;*
8 but the handmade idol is accursed, and its maker as well:
he for having produced it, and it, because though corruptible, it was termed a god. [y]
9 Equally odious to God are the evildoer and his evil deed;
10 and the thing made shall be punished with its contriver.
11 Therefore upon even the idols of the nations shall a visitation come,
since they have become abominable amid God's works,
Snares for the souls of men
and a trap for the feet of the senseless. [z]

The Origin and Evils of Idolatry

12 For the source of wantonness is the devising of idols;
and their invention was a corruption of life. [a]
13 For in the beginning they were not,
nor shall they continue forever; [b]
14 for by the vanity of men they came into the world,
and therefore a sudden end is devised for them.
15 For a father, afflicted with untimely mourning,
made an image of the child so quickly taken from him,
And now honored as a god what was formerly a dead man
and handed down to his subjects mysteries and sacrifices.
16 Then, in time, the impious practice gained strength and was observed as law,
and graven things were worshiped by princely decrees. [c]
17 Men who lived so far away that they could not honor him in his presence
copied the appearance of the distant king
And made a public image of him they wished to honor,
out of zeal to flatter him when absent, as though present.
18 And to promote this observance among those to whom it was strange,
the artisan's ambition provided a stimulus.
19 For he, mayhap in his determination to please the ruler,
labored over the likeness to the best of his skill; [d]
20 And the masses, drawn by the charm of the workmanship,
soon thought he should be worshiped who shortly before was honored as a man. [e]
21 And this became a snare for mankind,
that men enslaved to either grief or tyranny
conferred the incommunicable Name on stocks and stones.
22 Then it was not enough for them to err in their knowledge of God; [f]
but even though they live in a great war of ignorance,
they call such evils peace. [g]

14, 6: Noah.
14, 7: Often applied to the Cross of our Lord.

u Ps 107, 23–30; Is 43, 16. v Wis 16, 8. w Wis 10, 4. x Gn 6, 4; 17, 1ff. 21f. y Rom 1, 23. z Wis 3, 7; 23, 33; Nm 33, 4; Jos 23, 13; Ps 115, 4; Jer 6, 15; 10, 15; 46, 25; Hos 9, 15. a Rom 1, 23ff. b Is 2, 18. c Dn 3, 4ff; 1 Mc 1, 47–50. d Is 44, 12f LXX. e Wis 15, 4. f 22–31: Jer 2, 20; 3, 1–25; Hos 4, 1f. 9–19; Rom 1, 26–31; Gal 5, 19ff; 1 Tm 1, 9f. g Jer 6, 14; Ez 13, 10.

23 For while they celebrate either child-slaying
sacrifices or clandestine mysteries,
or frenzied carousals in unheard-of rites, [h]
24 They no longer safeguard either lives or pure
wedlock;
but each either waylays and kills his
neighbor, or aggrieves him by adultery.
25 And all is confusion—blood and murder, theft
and guile, [i]
corruption, faithlessness, turmoil, perjury,
26 Disturbance of good men, neglect of gratitude,
besmirching of souls, unnatural lust,
disorder in marriage, adultery and
shamelessness.
27 For the worship of infamous idols
is the reason and source and extremity of all
evil. [j]
28 For they either go mad with enjoyment, or
prophesy lies,
or live lawlessly or lightly forswear
themselves. [k]
29 For as their trust is in soulless idols,
they expect no harm when they have sworn
falsely.
30 But on both counts shall justice overtake
them:
because they thought ill of God and devoted
themselves to idols, [l]
and because they deliberately swore false
oaths, despising piety.*
31 For not the might of those that are sworn by
but the retribution of sinners
ever follows upon the transgression of the
wicked.*

CHAPTER 15

1 But you, our God, are good and true,
slow to anger, and governing all with
mercy. [m]
2 For even if we sin, we are yours, and know
your might;
but we will not sin, knowing that we belong
to you. [n]
3 For to know you well is complete justice,
and to know your might is the root of
immortality. [o]
4 For neither did the evil creation of men's fancy
deceive us,
nor the fruitless labor of painters, [p]
A form smeared with varied colors,
5 the sight of which arouses yearning in the
senseless man,
till he longs for the inanimate form of a dead
image.
6 Lovers of evil things, and worthy of such
hopes
are they who make them and long for them
and worship them. [q]

The Potter's Clay Idols

7 For truly the potter, laboriously working the
soft earth,
molds for our service each several article:
Both the vessels that serve for clean purposes
and their opposites, all alike;
As to what shall be the use of each vessel of
either class
the worker in clay is the judge. [r]
8 And with misspent toil he molds a
meaningless god from the selfsame clay;
though he himself shortly before was made
from the earth
And after a little, is to go whence he was
taken,
when the life that was lent him is
demanded back. [s]
9 But his concern is not that he is to die
nor that his span of life is brief;
Rather, he vies with goldsmiths and
silversmiths
and emulates molders of bronze,
and takes pride in modeling counterfeits. [t]
10 Ashes his heart is! more worthless than earth
is his hope, [u]
and more ignoble than clay his life;
11 Because he knew not the one who fashioned
him,

14, 30: Piety: the sanctity of oaths.
14, 31: Perjury is a form of deceit which calls for punishment even though it be practiced in the name of a lifeless idol.

h Wis 12, 4f; 14, 15; Is 57, 5. i 25f: Jer 7, 8f; 22, 17. j Ex 23, 13. k Jer 5, 31; 29, 26. l Wis 1, 1. 8; 11, 20; Jer 5, 2. 7. m Ex 34, 6f; Pss 86, 5. 15; 145, 8. 9. 14. n Jb 10, 14f LXX. o Wis 3, 15; Jn 17, 3. p Wis 13, 14. q Ps 115, 8. r Wis 13, 11; Jer 18, 3f; Rom 9, 21; 2 Tm 2, 20f. s Gn 3, 19; Eccl 12, 7. t Bar 6, 46. u Jb 13, 12 LXX.

and breathed into him a quickening soul,
and infused a vital spirit. [v]
12 Instead, he esteemed our life a plaything,
and our span of life a holiday for gain;
"For one must," says he, "make profit every way, be it even out of evil." [w]
13 For this man more than any knows that he is sinning,
when out of earthen stuff he creates fragile vessels and idols alike.
14 But all quite senseless, and worse than childish in mind,
are the enemies of your people who enslaved them. [x]
15 For they esteemed all the idols of the nations, gods,
which have no use of the eyes for vision,
nor nostrils to snuff the air,
Nor ears to hear,
nor fingers on their hands for feeling;
even their feet are useless to walk with. [y]
16 For a man made them; [z]
one whose spirit has been lent him fashioned them.
For no man succeeds in fashioning a god like himself;
17 being mortal, he makes a dead thing with his lawless hands.
For he is better than the things he worships;
he at least lives, but never they.

Second Example Resumed

18 And besides, they worship* the most loathsome beasts— [a]
for compared as to folly, these are worse than the rest,*
19 Nor for their looks are they good or desirable beasts,
but they have escaped both the approval of God and his blessing. [b]

CHAPTER 16

1 Therefore they* were fittingly punished by similar creatures,
and were tormented by a swarm of insects. [c]
2 Instead of this punishment, you benefited your people
with a novel dish, the delight they craved,
by providing quail for their food; [d]
3 That those others, when they desired food,
since the creatures sent to plague them were so loathsome,
should be turned from even the craving of necessities,
While these, after a brief period of privation,
partook of a novel dish. [e]
4 For upon those oppressors, inexorable want had to come;
but these needed only be shown how their enemies were being tormented. [f]
5 For when the dire venom of beasts came upon them [g]
and they were dying from the bite of crooked serpents,
your anger endured not to the end.
6 But as a warning, for a short time they were terrorized,
though they had a sign* of salvation, to remind them of the precept of your law.
7 For he who turned toward it was saved,
not by what he saw,
but by you, the savior of all.
8 And by this also you convinced our foes
that you are he who delivers from all evil. [h]
9 For the bites of locusts and of flies slew them,
and no remedy was found to save their lives
because they deserved to be punished by such means; [i]
10 But not even the fangs of poisonous reptiles overcame your sons,
for your mercy brought the antidote to heal them. [j]

15, 18ff: The author here returns to the main theme of chapters 11—19, which was interrupted by the digression 13, 1—15, 17.
15, 18: For . . . rest: this may mean that the creatures worshiped by the Egyptians (e.g., crocodiles, serpents, scarabs, etc.) were more patently lacking in intelligence than the general run of beasts; cf Wis 11, 15; 12, 24.
16, 1: They: the Egyptian idolaters.
16, 6: Sign: the brazen serpent; cf Nm 21, 9.

v Gn 2, 7; Zec 12, 1. w Jas 4, 13f. x Ex 1, 13. y Wis 14, 11; Dt 4, 28; Pss 115, 4–7; 135, 15ff. z 16f: Wis 13. 10. a Wis 11, 15; 12, 24. b Gn 1, 25; 3, 14. c Wis 11, 15f; 12, 23. 27; Ex 7, 27; 8, 12. 17. d Wis 11, 13; 19, 11f; Ex 16, 13; Nm 11, 31f; Ps 105, 40. e Wis 11, 15; Ex 8, 10; 16, 3. f Wis 11, 8f. g 5f: Nm 21, 4–9; Dt 32, 24; Jer 8, 7 LXX. h Gn 48, 16; 2 Mc 1, 24f. i Ex 8, 16–28; 10, 4–19; Pss 78, 45f; 105, 31. 34; Rv 9, 1–11. j Dt 32, 33.

11 For as a reminder of your injunctions, they
were stung,
and swiftly they were saved,
Lest they should fall into deep forgetfulness
and become unresponsive to your
beneficence. [k]
12 For indeed, neither herb nor application cured
them,
but your all-healing word, O LORD! [l]
13 For you have dominion over life and death; [m]
you lead down to the gates of the nether
world, and lead back.
14 Man, however, slays in his malice,
but when the spirit has come away, it does
not return,
nor can he bring back the soul once it is
confined.*
15 But your hand none can escape.

Third Example: A Rain of Manna for Israel instead of the Plague of Storms

16 For the wicked who refused to know you
were punished by the might of your arm,
Pursued by unwonted rains and hailstorms
and unremitting downpours,
and consumed by fire. [n]
17 For against all expectation, in water which
quenches anything,
the fire grew more active;
For the universe fights on behalf of the just. [o]
18 For now the flame was tempered [p]
so that the beasts might not be burnt up that
were sent upon the wicked,
but that these might see and know they
were struck by the judgment of God;
19 And again, even in the water, fire blazed
beyond its strength
so as to consume the produce of the wicked
land.
20 Instead of this, you nourished your people
with food of angels
and furnished them bread from heaven,
ready to hand, untoiled-for,
endowed with all delights and conforming
to every taste. [q]
21 For this substance of yours revealed your
sweetness toward your children,
and serving the desire of him who received
it,
was blended to whatever flavor each one
wished. [r]
22 Yet snow and ice* withstood fire and were not
melted,
that they might know that their enemies'
fruits
Were consumed by a fire that blazed in the
hail
and flashed lightning in the rain. [s]
23 But this fire, again, that the just might be
nourished,
forgot even its proper strength; [t]
24 For your creation, serving you, its maker,
grows tense for punishment against the
wicked,
but is relaxed in benefit for those who trust
in you. [u]
25 Therefore at that very time, transformed in all
sorts of ways,
it was serving your all-nourishing bounty
according to what they needed and desired;
26 That your sons whom you loved might learn,
O LORD,
that it is not the various kinds of fruits that
nourish man,
but it is your word that preserves those who
believe you! [v]
27 For what was not destroyed by fire,
when merely warmed by a momentary
sunbeam, melted; [w]
28 So that men might know that one must give
you thanks before the sunrise,
and turn to you at daybreak. [x]
29 For the hope of the ingrate melts like a wintry
frost
and runs off like useless water. [y]

16, 14: Confined: in the nether world, in limbo.
16, 22: Snow and ice: the manna; cf Wis 16, 27; 19, 21.

k Ps 78, 11. **l** Ex 15, 26. **m** 13ff: Dt 32, 39; 1 Sm 2, 6; Tb 13, 2; Ps 78, 34. 39; Eccl 8, 8; Dn 5, 19; 2 Mc 6, 26; 7, 23. **n** Wis 11, 21; 12, 27; Ex 5, 2; 9, 29–34. **o** Wis 10, 20; 19, 20; Ex 9, 23–28; 2 Mc 8, 36; 14, 34. **p** 18f: Wis 19, 20f. **q** Ex 16, 4; Nm 11, 8; Ps 78, 24f; Jn 6, 31. **r** Ps 34, 9. **s** Ex 9, 25–31; 10, 12; Ps 148, 8. **t** Wis 19, 21. **u** Wis 5, 17. 20; 19, 6; Sir 39, 25ff. **v** Dt 8, 3; Mt 4, 4. **w** Ex 16, 21. **x** Pss 57, 9f; 92, 3. **y** Wis 5, 14; 2 Sm 14, 14.

CHAPTER 17

Fourth Example: Darkness Afflicts the Egyptians, While the Israelites Have Light

[1] For great are your judgments, and hardly to be described;
therefore the unruly souls were wrong. [z]
[2] For when the lawless thought to enslave the holy nation,
shackled with darkness, fettered by the long night,
they lay confined beneath their own roofs as exiles from the eternal providence. [a]
[3] For they who supposed their secret sins were hid [b]
under the dark veil of oblivion
Were scattered in fearful trembling,
terrified by apparitions.
[4] For not even their inner chambers kept them fearless,
for crashing sounds on all sides terrified them,
and mute phantoms with somber looks appeared.
[5] No force, even of fire, was able to give light,
nor did the flaming brilliance of the stars
succeed in lighting up that gloomy night. [c]
[6] But only intermittent, fearful fires*
flashed through upon them;
And in their terror they thought beholding these was worse
than the times when that sight was no longer to be seen. [d]
[7] And mockeries of the magic art were in readiness,
and a jeering reproof of their vaunted shrewdness. [e]
[8] For they who undertook to banish fears and terrors from the sick soul
themselves sickened with a ridiculous fear.
[9] For even though no monstrous thing frightened them,
they shook at the passing of insects and the hissing of reptiles, [f]
[10] And perished trembling,
reluctant to face even the air that they could nowhere escape.
[11] For wickedness, of its nature cowardly,
testifies in its own condemnation,
and because of a distressed conscience,
always magnifies misfortunes. [g]
[12] For fear is nought but the surrender of the helps that come from reason;
[13] and the more one's expectation is of itself uncertain,
the more one makes of not knowing the cause that brings on torment.
[14] So they, during that night, powerless though it was,
that had come upon them from the recesses of a powerless* nether world,
while all sleeping the same sleep,
[15] Were partly smitten by fearsome apparitions
and partly stricken by their soul's surrender;
for fear came upon them, sudden and unexpected. [h]
[16] Thus, then, whoever was there fell
into that unbarred prison and was kept confined. [i]
[17] For whether one was a farmer, or a shepherd,
or a worker at tasks in the wasteland,
Taken unawares, he served out the inescapable sentence;
[18] for all were bound by the one bond of darkness. [j]
And were it only the whistling wind,
or the melodious song of birds in the spreading branches,
Or the steady sound of rushing water,
[19] or the rude crash of overthrown rocks,
Or the unseen gallop of bounding animals,
or the roaring cry of the fiercest beasts,
Or an echo resounding from the hollow of the hills,
these sounds, inspiring terror, paralyzed them.

17, 6: Fires: that is, lightnings.
17, 14: Powerless: the nether world, the home of darkness, has no power against God, nor even against such men as do not submit to it of themselves; cf Wis 1, 14ff.

z Ex 6, 6 LXX. a Wis 18, 4; Ex 1, 13f; 19, 6; 10, 21ff. b 3f: Wis 1, 7f; 10, 8; 18, 17. c Wis 10, 17; Jer 23, 24 LXX. d Ex 9, 23f. e Wis 12, 25f; Ex 7, 11f. 22; 8, 3; 9, 11; 10, 2. f Wis 16, 1; Jer 26, 22 LXX. g Wis 4, 6; 10, 7; Rom 2, 15. h Ex 11, 9f. i Wis 18, 4; Ex 10, 23. j 18f: Lv 26, 36.

20 For the whole world shone with brilliant light [k]
and continued its works without
interruption;
21 Over them alone was spread oppressive night,
an image of the darkness that next should
come upon them;
yet they were to themselves more
burdensome than the darkness.

CHAPTER 18

1 But your holy ones had very great light;
And those others, who heard their voices but
did not see their forms,
since now they themselves had suffered,
called them blest;
2 And because they who formerly had been
wronged did not harm them, they
thanked them,
and pleaded with them, for the sake of the
difference between them.*
3 Instead of this, you furnished the flaming pillar
which was a guide on the unknown way,
and the mild sun for an honorable
migration. [l]
4 For those deserved to be deprived of light and
imprisoned by darkness,
who had kept your sons confined
through whom the imperishable light of the
law was to be given to the world. [m]

Fifth Example: Death of the Egyptian First-born; the Israelites Are Spared

5 When they determined to put to death the
infants of the holy ones,
and when a single boy* had been cast forth
but saved,
As a reproof you carried off their multitude of
sons
and made them perish all at once in the
mighty water. [n]
6 That night was known beforehand to our
fathers,
that, with sure knowledge of the oaths in
which they put their faith, they might
have courage. [o]
7 Your people awaited
the salvation of the just and the destruction
of their foes. [p]
8 For when you punished our adversaries,
in this you glorified us whom you had
summoned. [q]
9 For in secret the holy children of the good
were offering sacrifice
and putting into effect with one accord the
divine institution,
That your holy ones should share alike the
same good things and dangers, [r]
having previously sung the praises of the
fathers.*
10 But the discordant cry of their enemies
responded,
and the piteous wail of mourning for
children was borne to them. [s]
11 And the slave was smitten with the same
retribution as his master;
even the plebeian suffered the same as the
king. [t]
12 And all alike by a single death
had countless dead;
For the living were not even sufficient for the
burial,
since at a single instant their nobler
offspring were destroyed. [u]
13 For though they disbelieved at every turn on
account of sorceries,
at the destruction of the first-born they
acknowledged that the people* was
God's son. [v]
14 For when peaceful stillness compassed
everything
and the night in its swift course was half
spent,
15 Your all-powerful word from heaven's royal
throne

18, 2: The difference between them: God's distinctive manner of treating the Israelites and the Egyptians according to their respective merits.
18, 5: Single boy: Moses.
18, 9: Praises of the fathers: cf Sir 44—50; Wis 10.
18, 13: People: the Hebrews.

k 20f: Ex 10, 23; Is 9, 1; 60, 1ff; 2 Pt 2, 17. l Ex 13, 21. m Wis 17, 2; Ps 119, 105; Is 2, 3. 5. n Wis 11, 7. 14; Ex 1, 16. 22; 2, 3. 6–10; 15, 10; Neh 9, 11. o Wis 12, 21; Ex 6, 8; 13, 5. p Ex 14, 13. q Wis 19, 22; Ex 3, 18; Is 43, 3f. r Ex 12, 21–28; Sir 44—50. s Ex 12, 30; Jer 9, 17. 19. t Ex 11, 5; 12, 29. u Nm 33, 4. v Wis 17, 7; Ex 4, 22f; 12, 12. 29; 13, 2. 13. 15.

bounded, a fierce warrior, into the doomed land,[w]
16 bearing the sharp sword of your inexorable decree.
And as he alighted, he filled every place with death;
he still reached to heaven, while he stood upon the earth.[x]
17 Then, forthwith, visions in horrible dreams perturbed them[y]
and unexpected fears assailed them;
18 And cast half-dead, one here, another there,
each was revealing the reason for his dying.
19 For the dreams that disturbed them had proclaimed this beforehand,
lest they perish unaware of why they suffered ill.
20 But the trial of death touched at one time even the just,
and in the desert a plague struck the multitude;
Yet not for long did the anger last.[z]
21 For the blameless man* hastened to be their champion,
bearing the weapon of his special office,
prayer and the propitiation of incense;
He withstood the wrath and put a stop to the calamity,
showing that he was your servant.[a]
22 And he overcame the bitterness
not by bodily strength, not by force of arms;
But by word he overcame the smiter,*
recalling the sworn covenants with their fathers.[b]
23 For when corpses had already fallen one on another in heaps,
he stood in the midst and checked the anger,
and cut off the way to the living.[c]
24 For on his full-length robe was the whole world,
and the glories of the fathers were carved in four rows upon the stones,
and your grandeur* was on the crown upon his head.[d]
25 To these names the destroyer yielded, and these he feared;
for the mere trial of anger was enough.[e]

CHAPTER 19

1 But the wicked, merciless wrath assailed until the end.
For he* knew beforehand what they were yet to do:[f]
2 That though they themselves had agreed to the departure
and had anxiously sent them* on their way,
they would regret it and pursue them.[g]
3 For while they* were still engaged in funeral rites
and were mourning at the burials of the dead,
They adopted another senseless plan;
and those whom they had sent away with entreaty,
they pursued as fugitives.[h]
4 For a compulsion suited to this ending drew them on,
and made them forgetful of what had befallen them,
That they might fill out the torments of their punishment,
5 and your people might experience a glorious* journey
while those others met an extraordinary death.
6 For all creation, in its several kinds, was being made over anew,
serving its natural laws,
that your children might be preserved unharmed.[i]
7 The cloud overshadowed their camp;

18, 21: Blameless man: Aaron acting according to his office of high priest and intercessor.
18, 22: Smiter: the destroying angel; cf v 25.
18, 24: Glories . . . grandeur: the name of God and the names of the tribes were inscribed on the high priest's apparel.
19, 1: He: i.e., God.
19, 2: Them: the Hebrews.
19, 3: They: the Egyptians.
19, 5: Glorious: more precisely, "wondrous," but the word reflects glorified in Wis 18, 8 and 19, 22.

w Wis 9, 10; Ex 15, 3. x 1 Chr 21, 16; Heb 4, 12; Rv 1, 16. y 17ff: Wis 17, 3f. z Wis 16, 5; Nm 17, 9–15. a Wis 12, 21; Ex 32, 12f; Ps 20, 8. b 12, 21; Ex 32, 12f. c Nm 14, 29f. d Ex 28, 15–21. 31–38; Sir 45, 8–12; 50, 11. e 1 Chr 21, 15. f Ex 14, 4. g Ex 12, 33; 14, 5. 8. h Wis 18, 10. 12; Ex 12, 30ff. i Wis 5, 17; 16, 24.

and out of what had before been water, dry
land was seen emerging:
Out of the Red Sea an unimpeded road,
and a grassy plain out of the mighty flood.[j]
8 Over this crossed the whole nation sheltered
by your hand,
after they beheld stupendous wonders.
9 For they ranged about like horses,
and bounded about like lambs,
praising you, O Lord! their deliverer.[k]
10 For they were still mindful of what had
happened in their sojourn:
how instead of the young of animals the
land brought forth gnats,
and instead of fishes the river swarmed with
countless frogs.[l]
11 And later they saw also a new kind of bird[m]
when, prompted by desire, they asked for
pleasant foods;
12 For to appease them quail came to them from
the sea.
13 And the punishments came upon the sinners
only after forewarnings from the violence of
the thunderbolts.
For they justly suffered for their own
misdeeds,
since indeed they treated their guests with
the more grievous* hatred.[n]
14 For those others did not receive unfamiliar
visitors,[o]
but these were enslaving beneficent guests.
15 And not that only; but what punishment was
to be theirs*
since they received strangers unwillingly!
16 Yet these, after welcoming them with
festivities,
oppressed with awful toils
those who now shared with them the same
rights.[p]
17 And they were struck with blindness,
as those others had been at the portals of
the just—
When, surrounded by yawning darkness,
each sought the entrance of his own gate.[q]
18 For the elements, in variable harmony among
themselves,
like strings of the harp, produce new
melody,
while the flow of music steadily persists.
And this can be perceived exactly from a
review of what took place.
19 For land creatures were changed into water
creatures,
and those that swam went over on to the
land.
20 Fire in water maintained its own strength,[r]
and water forgot its quenching nature;
21 Flames, by contrast, neither consumed the
flesh
of the perishable animals that went about in
them,
nor melted the icelike, quick-melting kind
of ambrosial food.
22 For every way, O LORD! you magnified and
glorified your people;
unfailing, you stood by them in every time
and circumstance.[s]

19, 13: More grievous: than that of the people of Sodom; cf Gn 19.
19, 15: Theirs: the people of Sodom.

j Ex 14, 21–29. k Wis 10, 20; 16, 8; Ex 15, 1–18; Ps 114, 4–6. l Ex 7, 27ff; 8, 12–15; Ps 105, 30f. m 11f: Wis 16, 2; Ps 78, 18. n 2 Mc 7, 18. 32. o 14f: Gn 15, 13; Ex 2, 22. p Gn 45, 17–20; 47, 4ff; Ex 1, 11. q Wis 17, 2; Gn 19, 11. r 20f: Wis 16, 17ff. 22f. 27. s Wis 18, 8; Lv 26, 44; Ps 126, 3.

THE BOOK OF SIRACH

(Ecclesiasticus)

The Book of Sirach derives its name from the author, Jesus, son of Eleazar, son of Sirach (50, 27). Its earliest title seems to have been "Wisdom of the Son of Sirach." The designation "Liber Ecclesiasticus," meaning "Church Book," appended to some Greek and Latin manuscripts was due to the extensive use which the church made of this book in presenting moral teaching to catechumens and to the faithful.

The author, a sage who lived in Jerusalem, was thoroughly imbued with love for the law, the priesthood, the temple, and divine worship. As a wise and experienced observer of life he addressed himself to his contemporaries with the motive of helping them to maintain religious faith and integrity through study of the holy books, and through tradition.

The book contains numerous maxims formulated with care, grouped by affinity, and dealing with a variety of subjects such as the individual, the family, and the community in their relations with one another and with God. It treats of friendship, education, poverty and wealth, the law, religious worship, and many other matters which reflect the religious and social customs of the time.

Written in Hebrew between 200 and 175 B.C., the text was translated into Greek sometime after 132 B.C. by the author's grandson, who also wrote a Foreword which contains information about the book, the author, and the translator himself. Until the close of the nineteenth century Sirach was known only in translations, of which this Greek rendering was the most important. From it the Latin version was made. Between 1896 and 1900, again in 1931, and several times since 1956, manuscripts were discovered containing in all about two thirds of the Hebrew text, which agrees substantially with the Greek. One such text, from Masada, is pre-Christian in date.

Though not included in the Hebrew Bible after the first century A.D., nor accepted by Protestants, the Book of Sirach has always been recognized by the Catholic Church as divinely inspired and canonical. The Foreword, though not inspired, is placed in the Bible because of its antiquity and importance.

The contents of Sirach are of a discursive nature not easily divided into separate parts. Chapters 1—43 deal largely with moral instruction; chapters 44, 1—50, 24 contain a eulogy of the heroes of Israel and some of the patriarchs. There are two appendices in which the author expresses his gratitude to God, and appeals to the unlearned to acquire true wisdom.

The church uses the Book of Sirach extensively in her liturgy.

FOREWORD

Many important truths have been handed down to us through the law, the prophets, and the later authors; and for these the instruction and wisdom of Israel merit praise. Now, those who are familiar with these truths must not only understand them themselves but, as lovers of wisdom, be able, in speech and in writing, to help others less familiar. Such a one was my grandfather, Jesus, who, having devoted himself for a long time to the diligent study of the law, the prophets, and the rest of the books[1] of our ancestors, and having developed a thorough

[1] The law, the prophets and the rest of the books: the Sacred Scriptures of the Old Testament written before the time of Sirach, according to the threefold division of the present Hebrew Bible.

familiarity with them, was moved to write something himself in the nature of instruction and wisdom, in order that those who love wisdom might, by acquainting themselves with what he too had written, make even greater progress in living in conformity with the divine law.

You therefore are now invited to read it in a spirit of attentive good will, with indulgence for any apparent failure on our part, despite earnest efforts, in the interpretation of particular passages. For words spoken originally in Hebrew are not as effective when they are translated into another language. That is true not only of this book but of the law itself, the prophets and the rest of the books, which differ no little when they are read in the original.

I arrived in Egypt in the thirty-eighth year of the reign of King Euergetes,[2] and while there, I found a reproduction of our valuable teaching.[3] I therefore considered myself in duty bound to devote some diligence and industry to the translation of this book. Many sleepless hours of close application have I devoted in the interval to finishing the book for publication, for the benefit of those living abroad who wish to acquire wisdom and are disposed to live their lives according to the standards of the law.

[2] Thirty-eighth . . . Euergetes: 132 B.C. The reference is to Ptolemy VII, Physkon Euergetes II (170–163; 145, 117 B.C.).
[3] Reproduction . . . teaching: may refer to the Septuagint (Greek) translation of Hebrew wisdom writings predating Sirach.

THE WISDOM OF SIRACH

CHAPTER 1

Praise of Wisdom*

1 All wisdom* comes from the LORD
and with him it remains forever. [a]
2 The sand of the seashore, the drops of rain,
the days of eternity: who can number these?
3 Heaven's height, earth's breadth,
the depths of the abyss: who can explore these?
4 Before all things else wisdom was created;
and prudent understanding, from eternity.
5 To whom has wisdom's root been revealed?
Who knows her subtleties? [b]
6 There is but one, wise and truly awe-inspiring,
seated upon his throne:
7 It is the LORD; he created her,
has seen her and taken note of her. [c]
8 He has poured her forth upon all his works,
upon every living thing according to his bounty;
he has lavished her upon his friends.
9 *Fear of the LORD* is glory and splendor,
gladness and a festive crown.
10 Fear of the LORD warms the heart,
giving gladness and joy and length of days.
11 He who fears the LORD will have a happy end;
even on the day of his death he will be blessed.
12 The beginning of wisdom is fear of the LORD,
which is formed with the faithful in the womb. [d]
13 With devoted men was she created from of old,
and with their children her beneficence abides.
14 Fullness of wisdom is fear of the LORD;
she inebriates men with her fruits. [e]
15 Her entire house she fills with choice foods,

1, 1–8: The Lord is the source and preserver of wisdom (1); he created her from eternity, before all things else (4–7); all his works reflect wisdom (2f. 8).

1, 1: Wisdom: here the author speaks of true wisdom, namely God's external revelation of himself. Throughout the book he describes in great detail just what wisdom is; sometimes it is divine; sometimes it is a synonym for God's law; sometimes it is human. But the author makes clear that even human wisdom, properly understood, comes from God.

1, 9–18: Here are described the spiritual and temporal blessings that come during the lifetime of him who fears the Lord, i.e., practices true religion.

1, 9: Fear of the Lord: see note on Ps 111, 10.

a 1 Kgs 3, 9. b Bar 3, 15. c Jb 28, 27. d Jb 28, 28; Ps 111, 10; Prv 1, 7; 9, 10. e Eccl 12, 13.

her granaries with her harvest.
16 Wisdom's garland is fear of the LORD,
with blossoms of peace and perfect health.[f]
17 Knowledge and full understanding she
showers down;
she heightens the glory of those who
possess her.
18 The root of wisdom is fear of the LORD;
her branches are length of days.

19 One cannot justify unjust anger;*
anger plunges a man to his downfall.
20 A patient man need stand firm but for a time,
and then contentment comes back to him.
21 For a while he holds back his words,
then the lips of many herald his wisdom.
22 Among wisdom's treasures is the paragon of
prudence;
but fear of the LORD is an abomination to
the sinner.
23 If you desire wisdom, keep the
commandments,
and the LORD will bestow her upon you;
24 For fear of the LORD is wisdom and culture;
loyal humility is his delight.
25 Be not faithless to the fear of the LORD,*
nor approach it with duplicity of heart.
26 Play not the hypocrite before men;
over your lips keep watch.
27 Exalt not yourself lest you fall
and bring upon you dishonor;
28 For then the LORD will reveal your secrets
and publicly cast you down,
29 Because you approached the fear of the LORD
with your heart full of guile.

CHAPTER 2

Duties toward God

1 My son, when you come to serve the LORD,*
prepare yourself for trials.[g]
2 Be sincere of heart and steadfast,
undisturbed in time of adversity.
3 Cling to him, forsake him not;
thus will your future be great.
4 Accept whatever befalls you,
in crushing misfortune be patient;
5 For in fire gold is tested,
and worthy men in the crucible of
humiliation.[h]
6 Trust God and he will help you;
make straight your ways and hope in him.

7 You who fear the LORD, wait for his mercy,
turn not away lest you fall.
8 You who fear the LORD, trust him,
and your reward will not be lost.
9 You who fear the LORD, hope for good things,
for lasting joy and mercy.
10 Study the generations long past and
understand;
has anyone hoped in the LORD and been
disappointed?
Has anyone persevered in his fear and been
forsaken?
has anyone called upon him and been
rebuffed?[i]
11 Compassionate and merciful is the LORD;
he forgives sins, he saves in time of trouble.

12 Woe to craven hearts and drooping hands,*
to the sinner who treads a double path!
13 Woe to the faint of heart who trust not,
who therefore will have no shelter!
14 Woe to you who have lost hope!
what will you do at the visitation of the
LORD?
15 Those who fear the LORD disobey not his
words;
those who love him keep his ways.[j]
16 Those who fear the LORD seek to please him,
those who love him are filled with his law.

1, 19–22: The disciple of wisdom shuns unjust anger which brings downfall. By patience and self-control he preserves calm, recovers contentment, and receives public praise. The sinner, on the contrary, despises the restraints which religion imposes.

1, 25–29: Infidelity to religion, or the use of it for any but the single purpose of serving God, is hypocrisy and self-exaltation, deserving of public disgrace.

2, 1–11: Serving God is not without its trials (1); moreover, it must be done with sincerity, steadfastness and fidelity (2f). Misfortune and humiliation merely purify man and prove his worth (4f). Patience and unwavering trust in God are always rewarded with the benefits of God's mercy and of lasting joy (6–11).

2, 12–18: A warning to those who compromise their religion in time of affliction; they fail in courage and trust and therefore have no security (12ff). But those who fear the Lord through obedience, reverence, love and humility find his mercy equal to his majesty (15–18).

f Sir 21, 11. g 2 Tm 3, 12. h Prv 17, 3; Wis 3, 6; 1 Pt 1, 7. i Pss 31, 2; 145, 18f. j Jn 14, 23.

[17] Those who fear the LORD prepare their hearts
and humble themselves before him.
[18] Let us fall into the hands of the LORD
and not into the hands of men,
For equal to his majesty
is the mercy that he shows. [k]

CHAPTER 3

Duties toward Parents*

[1] Children, pay heed to a father's right;
do so that you may live.
[2] For the LORD sets a father in honor over his children;
a mother's authority he confirms over her sons.
[3] He who honors his father atones for sins;
[4] he stores up riches who reveres his mother.
[5] He who honors his father is gladdened by children,
and when he prays he is heard.
[6] He who reveres his father will live a long life;
he obeys the LORD who brings comfort to his mother.

[7] He who fears the LORD honors his father,
and serves his parents as rulers.
[8] In word and deed honor your father
that his blessing may come upon you; [l]
[9] For a father's blessing gives a family firm roots,
but a mother's curse uproots the growing plant. [m]
[10] Glory not in your father's shame,
for his shame is no glory to you!
[11] His father's honor is a man's glory;
disgrace for her children, a mother's shame.
[12] My son, take care of your father when he is old;
grieve him not as long as he lives. [n]
[13] Even if his mind fail, be considerate with him;
revile him not in the fullness of your strength.
[14] For kindness to a father will not be forgotten,
it will serve as a sin offering—it will take lasting root.
[15] In time of tribulation it will be recalled to your advantage,
like warmth upon frost it will melt away your sins.
[16] A blasphemer is he who despises his father;
accursed of his Creator, he who angers his mother. [o]

Humility*

[17] My son, conduct your affairs with humility,
and you will be loved more than a giver of gifts.
[18] Humble yourself the more, the greater you are,
and you will find favor with God. [p]
[19] For great is the power of God;
by the humble he is glorified.*
[20] What is too sublime for you, seek not,
into things beyond your strength search not. [q]
[21] What is committed to you, attend to;
for what is hidden is not your concern.
[22] With what is too much for you meddle not,
when shown things beyond human understanding.
[23] Their own opinion has misled many,
and false reasoning unbalanced their judgment.
[24] Where the pupil of the eye is missing, there is no light,
and where there is no knowledge, there is no wisdom.

[25] A stubborn man will fare badly in the end,
and he who loves danger will perish in it.
[26] A stubborn man will be burdened with sorrow;
a sinner will heap sin upon sin.

3, 1–16: Besides the virtues that must characterize our conduct toward God, special duties toward our neighbor are enjoined, such as honor and respect toward parents, with corresponding blessings (1–9). Even to old and infirm parents this respect is due (10–13); through it, the sins of children are pardoned (14f). Failure to render respect is blasphemy and merits a curse from God (16). Cf Ex 20, 12; Eph 6, 2f.

3, 17–27: Humility gives a true estimate of self (17ff). Through it a man performs duty, avoids what is beyond his understanding and strength (20ff). Pride, however, begets false greatness, misjudgment, stubbornness, sorrow, affliction and perdition (23–27).

3, 19: An alternate or additional line would read: "For though many have been great in the course of time, it is to the humble he reveals his secrets." Cf Mt 11, 25f; 1 Cor 1, 26–29.

k Sir 18, 3. **l** Ex 20, 12; Dt 5, 16; Mt 15, 4; Mk 7, 10; Eph 6, 2. **m** Gn 27, 29; 49, 2–27. **n** Prv 23, 22. **o** Prv 19, 26; 30, 11. 14. 17. **p** Mt 23, 12. **q** Ps 131, 1.

27 For the affliction of the proud man there is no cure;
he is the offshoot of an evil plant.[r]
28 The mind of a sage appreciates proverbs,
and an attentive ear is the wise man's joy.

Alms for the Poor*

29 Water quenches a flaming fire,
and alms atone for sins.[s]
30 He who does a kindness is remembered afterward;
when he falls, he finds a support.

CHAPTER 4

1 My son, rob not the poor man of his livelihood:
force not the eyes of the needy* to turn away.[t]
2 A hungry man grieve not,
a needy man anger not;
3 Do not exasperate the downtrodden;
delay not to give to the needy.
4 A beggar in distress do not reject;
avert not your face from the poor.
5 From the needy turn not your eyes,
give no man reason to curse you;
6 For if in the bitterness of his soul he curse you,
his Creator will hear his prayer.
7 Endear yourself to the assembly;
before a ruler bow your head.
8 Give a hearing to the poor man,
and return his greeting with courtesy;
9 Deliver the oppressed from the hand of the oppressor;
let not justice be repugnant to you.
10 To the fatherless be as a father,
and help their mother as a husband would;
Thus will you be like a son to the Most High,
and he will be more tender to you than a mother.

The Rewards of Wisdom*

11 Wisdom instructs her children
and admonishes those who seek her.
12 He who loves her loves life;
those who seek her out win her favor.
13 He who holds her fast inherits glory;
wherever he dwells, the LORD bestows blessings.
14 Those who serve her serve the Holy One;
those who love her the LORD loves.[u]
15 He who obeys her judges nations;
he who hearkens to her dwells in her inmost chambers.
16 If one trusts her, he will possess her;
his descendants too will inherit her.
17 She walks with him as a stranger,
and at first she puts him to the test;
Fear and dread she brings upon him
and tries him with her discipline;
With her precepts she puts him to the proof,
until his heart is fully with her.
18 Then she comes back to bring him happiness
and reveal her secrets to him.
19 But if he fails her, she will abandon him
and deliver him into the hands of despoilers.

Sincerity and Justice*

20 Use your time well; guard yourself from evil,
and bring upon yourself no shame.
21 There is a sense of shame laden with guilt,
and a shame that merits honor and respect.
22 Show no favoritism to your own discredit;
let no one intimidate you to your own downfall.
23 Refrain not from speaking at the proper time,
and hide not away your wisdom;
24 For it is through speech that wisdom becomes known,
and knowledge through the tongue's rejoinder.

3, 29—4, 10: Mercy and kindness toward those in misfortune atone for sin and endear a man to God and to his fellow men.

4, 1: Eyes of the needy: when they look for help; cf Sir 18, 17.

4, 11–19: The Hebrew text presents wisdom speaking in the first person, as in ch 24. The precious fruits of wisdom: life, favor, glory, blessings, God's love, are intended to arouse desire for her (11–14). Her disciples are like priests (14) and judges (15), even partners who possess her for themselves and their descendants (16). They enjoy happiness and penetrate her profound secrets after surviving her tests (17f). Those who fail her are abandoned to destruction (19).

4, 20–31: Besides the interior trials of discipline and precept, the disciple of wisdom is warned against external dangers to his sincerity and justice, namely evil, human respect (20f), compromise of liberty in speech and action (22–25), false shame, and ignorance (26). He must fight for the truth (28), and avoid cynicism and laziness (29), and inconsistency in his conduct (30).

r Dt 32, 32; Wis 12, 10. s Dn 4, 27. t Tb 4, 7–11. u Wis 7, 28.

25 Never gainsay the truth,
and struggle not against the rushing stream.
26 Be not ashamed to acknowledge your guilt,
but of your ignorance rather be ashamed.
27 Do not abase yourself before an impious man,
nor refuse to do so before rulers.
28 Even to the death fight for truth,
and the LORD your God will battle for you.
29 Be not surly in your speech,
nor lazy and slack in your deeds.
30 Be not a lion at home,
nor sly and suspicious at work.
31 Let not your hand be open to receive
and clenched when it is time to give.

CHAPTER 5

Against Presumption*

1 Rely not on your wealth;
say not: "I have the power." [v]
2 Rely not on your strength
in following the desires of your heart.
3 Say not: "Who can prevail against me?"
for the LORD will exact the punishment.
4 Say not: "I have sinned, yet what has befallen
me?"
for the LORD bides his time.
5 Of forgiveness be not overconfident,
adding sin upon sin.
6 Say not: "Great is his mercy;
my many sins he will forgive."
7 For mercy and anger alike are with him;
upon the wicked alights his wrath.
8 Delay not your conversion to the LORD,
put it not off from day to day;
9 For suddenly his wrath flames forth;
at the time of vengeance, you will be
destroyed.
10 Rely not upon deceitful wealth,
for it will be no help on the day of wrath. [w]

Sincerity in Speech

11 Winnow not in every wind,
and start not off in every direction.*
12 Be consistent in your thoughts;
steadfast be your words.*
13 Be swift to hear,
but slow to answer. [x]
14 If you have the knowledge, answer your
neighbor;
if not, put your hand over your mouth.
15 Honor and dishonor through talking!
A man's tongue can be his downfall.
16 Be not called a detractor;
use not your tongue for calumny;
17 For shame has been created for the thief,
and the reproach of his neighbor for the
double-tongued.

CHAPTER 6

1 Say nothing harmful, small or great;
be not a foe instead of a friend;
A bad name and disgrace will you acquire:
"That for the evil man with double
tongue!"*
2 Fall not into the grip of desire, [y]
lest, like fire, it consume your strength;
3 Your leaves it will eat, your fruits destroy,
and you will be left a dry tree,
4 For contumacious desire destroys its owner
and makes him the sport of his enemies.

True Friendship*

5 A kind mouth multiplies friends,
and gracious lips prompt friendly greetings.
6 Let your acquaintances be many,
but one in a thousand your confidant.
7 When you gain a friend, first test him, [z]
and be not too ready to trust him.
8 For one sort of friend is a friend when it suits
him,

5, 1–10: The vices of the rich are pride and independence (1f), presumption (3), false security (4–7), and impenitence (8), which cannot escape the divine wrath (9f). Cf Prv 18, 23; 19, 1; 28, 6.

5, 11: A proverbial expression condemning inconstancy and advocating sincerity and honesty.

5, 12—6, 1: Proper use of the tongue requires constancy in speech (5, 12), prudence (13f), reserve (15), charity (6, 1), as well as the avoidance of detraction, calumny (16) and double talk, which bring shame and disgrace (5, 17; 6, 1).

6, 1: "That . . . double tongue!": people will say this against the man whose deceitful tongue has brought him to disgrace.

6, 5–17: True friends are discerned not by prosperity (11) but through the trials of adversity: distress, quarrels (9), sorrow (10) and misfortune (12). Such friends are rare and their value is beyond estimation, a gift from God (14–17).

v Lk 12, 19. w Prv 10, 2; 11, 4. 28. x Prv 29, 20; Jas 1, 19. y 2–3: Sir 9, 8; 23, 17; Jb 31, 12; Is 56, 3. z 7ff: Sir 12, 8f; 37, 1–5; Prv 19, 4.

but he will not be with you in time of
distress.
9 Another is a friend who becomes an enemy,
and tells of the quarrel to your shame.
10 Another is a friend, a boon companion,
who will not be with you when sorrow
comes.
11 When things go well, he is your other self,
and lords it over your servants;
12 But if you are brought low, he turns against
you
and avoids meeting you.
13 Keep away from your enemies;
be on your guard with your friends.
14 A faithful friend is a sturdy shelter;
he who finds one finds a treasure.
15 A faithful friend is beyond price,
no sum can balance his worth.
16 A faithful friend is a life-saving remedy,
such as he who fears God finds;
17 For he who fears God behaves accordingly,
and his friend will be like himself.

Blessings of Wisdom*

18 My son, from your youth embrace discipline;
thus will you find wisdom with graying hair.
19 As though plowing and sowing, draw close to
her;
then await her bountiful crops.
20 For in cultivating her you will labor but little,
and soon you will eat of her fruits.
21 How irksome she is to the unruly!
The fool cannot abide her.
22 She will be like a burdensome stone to test
him,
and he will not delay in casting her aside.
23 For discipline* is like her name,
she is not accessible to many.

24 Listen, my son, and heed my advice;
refuse not my counsel.
25 Put your feet into her fetters,
and your neck under her yoke.
26 Stoop your shoulders and carry her
and be not irked at her bonds.
27 With all your soul draw close to her;
with all your strength keep her ways.
28 Search her out, discover her; seek her and you
will find her.
Then when you have her, do not let her go;
29 Thus will you afterward find rest in her,
and she will become your joy.
30 Her fetters will be your throne of majesty;
her bonds, your purple cord.
31 You will wear her as your robe of glory, [a]
bear her as your splendid crown.*

32 My son, if you wish, you can be taught;
if you apply yourself, you will be shrewd.
33 If you are willing to listen, you will learn;
if you give heed, you will be wise.
34 Frequent the company of the elders;
whoever is wise, stay close to him.
35 Be eager to hear every godly discourse;
let no wise saying escape you. [b]
36 If you see a man of prudence, seek him out;
let your feet wear away his doorstep!
37 Reflect on the precepts of the LORD,
let his commandments be your constant
meditation;
Then he will enlighten your mind,
and the wisdom you desire he will grant. [c]

CHAPTER 7

Conduct in Public Life*

1 Do no evil, and evil will not overtake you;
2 avoid wickedness, and it will turn aside
from you.
3 Sow not in the furrows of injustice,
lest you harvest it sevenfold. [d]
4 Seek not from the LORD authority,

6, 18–37: The various figures in each of the three strophes urge the search for wisdom through patience (19–23), docility (32–37), and perseverance in trials (25ff), promising rich rewards (28–31). Cf 4, 11–19.

6, 23: Discipline (musar, in the sense of wisdom) is a perfect homonym for musar, "removed, withdrawn"; thus the path of discipline is inaccessible to many.

6, 31: Some forms of the text speak also of the "yoke" of wisdom under the imagery of golden ornaments.

7, 1–17: In the conduct of social relations wisdom forbids evil and injustice (1ff), pride (5. 15ff), ambition and human respect (4, 6), public disorder (7), presumption and impatience toward God (9f), ridicule (11), mischief and deceit toward one's neighbor (8. 12f).

a Is 62, 3. b Sir 8, 9. c Ps 1, 2. d Prv 22, 8.

nor from the king a place of honor.
5 Parade not your justice before the LORD,
and before the king flaunt not your wisdom.[e]
6 Seek not to become a judge
if you have not strength to root out crime,
Or you will show favor to the ruler
and mar your integrity.
7 Be guilty of no evil before the city's populace,
nor disgrace yourself before the assembly.
8 Do not plot to repeat a sin;
not even for one will you go unpunished.
9 Say not: "He will appreciate my many gifts;
the Most High will accept my offerings."[f]
10 Be not impatient in prayers,
and neglect not the giving of alms.
11 Laugh not at an embittered man;
be mindful of him who exalts and humbles.*
12 Plot no mischief against your brother,
nor against your friend and companion.
13 Delight not in telling lie after lie,
for it never results in good.
14 Thrust not yourself into the deliberations of princes,[g]
and repeat not the words of your prayer.*
15 Hate not laborious tasks,
nor farming, which was ordained by the Most High.[h]
16 Do not esteem yourself better than your fellows;
remember, his wrath will not delay.
17 More and more, humble your pride;
what awaits man is worms.[i]

Duties of Family Life, Religion and Charity*

18 Barter not a friend for money,
nor a dear brother for the gold of Ophir.*
19 Dismiss not a sensible wife;
a gracious wife is more precious than corals.
20 Mistreat not a servant who faithfully serves,
nor a laborer who devotes himself to his task.[j]
21 Let a wise servant be dear to you as your own self;
refuse him not his freedom.*
22 If you have livestock, look after them;
if they are dependable, keep them.
23 If you have sons, chastise them;
bend their necks* from childhood.[k]
24 If you have daughters, keep them chaste,
and be not indulgent to them.[l]
25 Giving your daughter in marriage ends a great task;
but give her to a worthy man.[m]
26 If you have a wife, let her not seem odious to you;
but where there is ill-feeling, trust her not.
27 With your whole heart honor your father;
your mother's birthpangs forget not.[n]
28 Remember, of these parents you were born;
what can you give them for all they gave you?
29 With all your soul, fear God,
revere his priests.
30 With all your strength, love your Creator,
forsake not his ministers.
31 Honor God and respect the priest;
give him his portion as you have been commanded:[o]
First fruits and contributions,
due sacrifices and holy offerings.*
32 To the poor man also extend your hand,
that your blessing may be complete;
33 Be generous to all the living,

7, 11: Him who exalts and humbles: God; cf 1 Sm 2, 7; Ps 75, 8; Lk 1, 52.

7, 14: Repeat not . . . prayer: brevity of speech in dealings with superiors and more especially with God is a sign of reverence and respect; cf Eccl 5, 1; Mt 6, 7.

7, 18–36: The duties of respect and appreciation, justice and kindness should characterize relations toward members of the household (18–28), and also toward God and his priests (29ff), the poor and afflicted, the living and the dead (32–36).

7, 18: Ophir was the port, at present unidentified, to which the ships of Solomon sailed and from which they brought back gold and silver; cf note on Ps 45, 10.

7, 21: After six years of service a Hebrew slave was entitled to freedom; cf Ex 21, 2; Dt 15, 12–15.

7, 23: Bend their necks: keep them from rebellious pride; so with the Greek. Cf Sir 30, 12. The present Hebrew text, which is probably not original here, reads: "Choose wives for them while they are young."

7, 31: First fruits . . . holy offerings: cf Ex 29, 27; Lv 7, 31–34; Nm 18, 8–20; Dt 18, 1–5.

7, 33: This seems to refer to the observances ordained toward the dead, that is, proper mourning and burial. Cf 2 Sm 21, 12ff; Tb 1, 20; 12, 12. When this verse is read in the light of later teaching, prayers for the souls of the deceased would also be recommended. Cf 2 Mc 12, 43ff.

e Jb 9, 2; Ps 143, 2; Prv 25, 6; 1 Cor 4, 4. f Sir 34, 18; 35, 12. g Sir 32, 7ff; Mt 6, 7. h Gn 2, 15; 3, 17. i Is 66, 24. j Lv 19, 13; Dt 24, 14f; Jas 5, 4. k Sir 30, 8–13; Prv 13, 24. l Sir 42, 9ff. m 1 Cor 7, 36ff. n Ex 20, 12. o Lv 7, 31; Nm 18, 18.

and withhold not your kindness from the
dead.*
34 Avoid not those who weep,
but mourn with those who mourn; [p]
35 Neglect not to visit the sick—
for these things you will be loved. [q]
36 In whatever you do, remember your last
days,
and you will never sin.

CHAPTER 8

Prudence in Dealing with Other Men*

1 Contend not with an influential man,
lest you fall into his power.
2 Quarrel not with a rich man,
lest he pay out the price of your downfall;
For gold has dazzled many,
and perverts the character of princes. [r]
3 Dispute not with a man of railing speech,
heap no wood upon his fire. [s]
4 Be not too familiar with an unruly man,
lest he speak ill of your forebears.
5 Shame not a repentant sinner; [t]
remember, we all are guilty.*
6 Insult no man when he is old,
for some of us, too, will grow old.
7 Rejoice not when a man dies;
remember, we are all to die.
8 Spurn not the discourse of the wise, [u]
but acquaint yourself with their proverbs;
From them you will acquire the training
to serve in the presence of princes.
9 Reject not the tradition of old men
which they have learned from their
fathers;
From it you will obtain the knowledge
how to answer in time of need.
10 Kindle not the coals of a sinner,
lest you be consumed in his flaming fire.
11 Let not the impious man intimidate you;
it will set him in ambush against you.*
12 Lend not to one more powerful than yourself;
and whatever you lend, count it as lost. [v]
13 Go not surety beyond your means;
think any pledge a debt you must pay.
14 Contend not at law with a judge,
for he will settle it according to his whim.
15 Travel not with a ruthless man,
lest he weigh you down with calamity;
For he will go his own way straight,
and through his folly you will perish with
him.
16 Provoke no quarrel with a quick-tempered
man
nor ride with him through the desert;
For bloodshed is nothing to him;
when there is no one to help you, he will
destroy you.
17 Take no counsel with a fool,
for he can keep nothing to himself.
18 Before a stranger do nothing that should be
kept secret,
for you know not what it will engender. [w]
19 Open your heart to no man,
and banish not your happiness.

CHAPTER 9

Advice concerning Women*

1 Be not jealous of the wife of your bosom,
lest you teach her to do evil against you.*
2 Give no woman power over you
to trample upon your dignity. [x]
3 Be not intimate with a strange woman,
lest you fall into her snares.
4 With a singing girl be not familiar,
lest you be caught in her wiles.
5 Entertain no thoughts against a virgin,

8, 1–19: A prudent man will be circumspect, avoiding conflict with the powerful, the rich and insolent, the impious, the irascible, and with judges (1ff. 10ff. 14. 16). He will seek friendship not with the undisciplined (4. 12f) and the ruthless (15), nor with fools and strangers (17ff), but with the wise and the ancients of the people (8f).

8, 5: We all are guilty: cf 1 Kgs 8, 46; 2 Chr 6, 36; Eccl 7, 20; Rom 3, 9f; 1 Jn 1, 8.

8, 11: To give in to the wicked in one instance becomes an occasion of sin for the future.

9, 1–9: Prudence and reserve in dealing with women are the best defense of morality. To preserve the liberty and dignity of his person and the integrity of his possessions, a man must avoid jealousy toward his own wife and familiarity toward all other women. Cf Sir 25, 12—26, 18.

9, 1: Unjust suspicions often engender hatred between husband and wife and may prompt a wife to commit those faults of which heretofore she had been innocent.

p Rom 12, 15. q Mt 25, 36. r Sir 31, 6; Dt 16, 19. s Prv 26, 20. t 1 Kgs 8, 46; 1 Jn 1, 8. u 8f: Sir 6, 35. v Sir 29, 4–7; Prv 17, 18. w Prv 25, 9f. x Sir 25, 21.

lest you be enmeshed in damages for her.*
6 Give not yourself to harlots,
lest you surrender your inheritance.[y]
7 Gaze not about the lanes of the city
and wander not through its squares;
8 Avert your eyes from a comely woman;
gaze not upon the beauty of another's wife—
Through woman's beauty many perish,
for lust for it burns like fire.[z]
9 With a married woman dine not,
recline not at table to drink by her side,
Lest your heart be drawn to her
and you go down in blood to the grave.

Choice of Friends*

10 Discard not an old friend,
for the new one cannot equal him.
A new friend is like new wine
which you drink with pleasure only when it has aged.
11 Envy not a sinner's fame,
for you know not what disaster awaits him.
12 Rejoice not at a proud man's success;
remember he will not reach death unpunished.
13 Keep far from the man who has power to kill,
and you will not be filled with the dread of death.
But if you approach him, offend him not,
lest he take away your life;
Know that you are stepping among snares
and walking over a net.
14 As best you can, take your neighbors' measure,
and associate with the wise.
15 With the learned be intimate;
let all your conversation be about the law of the LORD.
16 Have just men for your table companions;
in the fear of God be your glory.

Concerning Rulers*

17 Skilled artisans are esteemed for their deftness;
but the ruler of his people is the skilled sage.
18 Feared in the city is the man of railing speech,
and he who talks rashly is hated.

CHAPTER 10

1 A wise magistrate lends stability to his people,
and the government of a prudent man is well ordered.[a]
2 As the people's judge, so are his ministers;[b]
as the head of a city, its inhabitants.
3 A wanton king destroys his people,
but a city grows through the wisdom of its princes.[c]
4 Sovereignty over the earth is in the hand of God,
who raises up on it the man of the hour;
5 Sovereignty over every man is in the hand of God,
who imparts his majesty to the ruler.

The Sin of Pride*

6 No matter the wrong, do no violence to your neighbor,
and do not walk the path of arrogance.[d]
7 Odious to the LORD and to men is arrogance,
and the sin of oppression they both hate.
8 Dominion is transferred from one people to another
because of the violence of the arrogant.
9 Why are dust and ashes proud?*
even during life man's body decays;
10 A slight illness—the doctor jests,
a king today—tomorrow he is dead.
11 When a man dies, he inherits corruption;

9, 5: Cf Ex 22, 15f; Dt 22, 28f; Jb 31, 1.

9, 10–16: In social relations, adherence to the law of the Lord should serve as a guide (15). Associate with true friends (10), with the just and the learned (14ff); avoid the company of the mighty and of sinners doomed to punishment (11ff). Cf Sir 8, 1–19.

9, 17—10, 5: Public office as conducted justly or unjustly benefits or destroys the people, according to the axiom, "as the prince, so the people." Cf Is 24, 2. God, however, has sovereignty over both.

10, 6–18: Glory displayed through arrogance and pride is false and displeasing to God and men, because founded on dust and ashes (6–11). It is the denial of the glory due to God, and therefore the source of all sin (12f). Even the memory of the proud is destroyed and God transfers their power to the lowly (14–18).

10, 9f: The text is uncertain. Its general implication is that man deteriorates physically even while alive: a slight illness today may be followed by death tomorrow. The uncertainty of life leaves no room for pride.

y Prv 5, 3–11; 6, 24; 29, 3. z Sir 25, 20; 41, 21. a Wis 6, 24. b 2f: Prv 29, 12. c Prv 29, 4. 8. d Lv 19, 18.

worms and gnats and maggots.[e]
12 The beginning of pride is man's stubbornness
in withdrawing his heart from his Maker;
13 For pride is the reservoir of sin,
a source which runs over with vice;
Because of it God sends unheard-of afflictions
and brings men to utter ruin.[f]
14 The thrones of the arrogant God overturns
and establishes the lowly in their stead.
15 The roots of the proud God plucks up,
to plant the humble in their place:
16 He breaks down their stem to the level of the ground,
then digs their roots from the earth.
17 The traces of the proud God sweeps away
and effaces the memory of them from the earth.
18 Insolence is not allotted to a man,
nor stubborn anger to one born of woman.

True Glory*

19 Whose offspring can be in honor? Those of men.
Which offspring are in honor? Those who fear God.
Whose offspring can be in disgrace? Those of men.
Which offspring are in disgrace? Those who transgress the commandments.
20 Among brethren their leader is in honor;
he who fears God is in honor among his people.
21 Be it tenant or wayfarer, alien or pauper,
his glory is the fear of the LORD.
22 It is not just to despise a man who is wise but poor,
nor proper to honor any sinner.[g]
23 The prince, the ruler, the judge are in honor;
but none is greater than he who fears God.
24 When free men serve a prudent slave,
the wise man does not complain.[h]
25 Flaunt not your wisdom in managing your affairs,
and boast not in your time of need.
26 Better the worker who has plenty of everything
than the boaster who is without bread.[i]
27 My son, with humility have self-esteem;
prize yourself as you deserve.
28 Who will acquit him who condemns himself?
who will honor him who discredits himself?
29 The poor man is honored for his wisdom
as the rich man is honored for his wealth;
30 Honored in poverty, how much more so in wealth!
Dishonored in wealth, in poverty how much the more!

CHAPTER 11

1 The poor man's wisdom lifts his head high
and sets him among princes.
2 Praise not a man for his looks;
despise not a man for his appearance.
3 Least is the bee among winged things,
but she reaps the choicest of all harvests.
4 Mock not the worn cloak
and jibe at no man's bitter day:
For strange are the works of the LORD,
hidden from men his deeds.
5 The oppressed often rise to a throne,
and some that none would consider wear a crown.*
6 The exalted often fall into utter disgrace;
the honored are given into enemy hands.

Moderation*

7 Before investigating, find no fault;
examine first, then criticize.
8 Before hearing, answer not,
and interrupt no one in the middle of his speech.[j]
9 Dispute not about what is not your concern;

10, 19—11, 6: Regardless of social barriers, genuine honor among men comes from fear of the Lord and a true estimate of self. The Lord exalts the lowly and oppressed; transgressors of the commandments merit dishonor and disgrace.

11, 5: Cf 1 Sm 2, 8; Ps 105, 17–22; Lk 1, 52.

11, 7–25: Discretion regulates a man's conduct toward others and their affairs (7ff); as regards his own interests, a man should avoid solicitude for the passing external benefits of life and property (10–14. 18f. 21. 23ff), and cultivate the lasting inward gifts of wisdom and virtue (15. 17. 20. 22).

e Jb 17, 14. f Prv 18, 12. g Jas 2, 1–4. h Prv 17, 2. i Prv 12, 9. j Prv 18, 13.

in the strife of the arrogant take no part.
10 My son, why increase your cares,
since he who is avid for wealth will not be blameless?
Even if you run after it, you will never overtake it;
however you seek it, you will not find it.
11 One may toil and struggle and drive,
and fall short all the more.[k]
12 Another goes his way a weakling and a failure,
with little strength and great misery—
Yet the eyes of the LORD look favorably upon him;
he raises him free of the vile dust,
13 Lifts up his head and exalts him
to the amazement of the many.
14 Good and evil, life and death,[l]
poverty and riches, are from the LORD.*
15 Wisdom and understanding and knowledge of affairs,*
love and virtuous paths are from the LORD.
16 Error and darkness were formed with sinners from their birth,
and evil grows old with evildoers.
17 The LORD's gift remains with the just;
his favor brings continued success.
18 A man may become rich through a miser's life,
and this is his allotted reward:
19 When he says: "I have found rest,[m]
now I will feast on my possessions,"
He does not know how long it will be
till he dies and leaves them to others.*

20 My son, hold fast to your duty, busy yourself with it,
grow old while doing your task.
21 Admire not how sinners live,
but trust in the LORD and wait for his light;
For it is easy with the LORD
suddenly, in an instant, to make a poor man rich.
22 God's blessing is the lot of the just man,
and in due time his hopes bear fruit.
23 Say not: "What do I need?
What further pleasure can be mine?"
24 Say not: "I am independent.
What harm can come to me now?"
25 The day of prosperity makes one forget adversity;
the day of adversity makes one forget prosperity.[n]
26 For it is easy with the LORD on the day of death*
to repay man according to his deeds.
27 A moment's affliction brings forgetfulness of past delights;
when a man dies, his life is revealed.
28 Call no man happy before his death,
for by how he ends, a man is known.

Care in Choosing Friends

29 Bring not every man into your house,
for many are the snares of the crafty one;
30 Though he seem like a bird confined in a cage,
yet like a spy he will pick out the weak spots.
31 The talebearer turns good into evil;
with a spark he sets many coals afire.
32 The evil man lies in wait for blood,
and plots against your choicest possessions.
33 Avoid a wicked man, for he breeds only evil,
lest you incur a lasting stain.
34 Lodge a stranger with you, and he will subvert your course,
and make a stranger of you to your own household.

CHAPTER 12

1 If you do good, know for whom you are doing it,*
and your kindness will have its effect.
2 Do good to the just man and reward will be yours,
if not from him, from the LORD.

11, 14: Divine Providence ultimately governs the lives of men. Evil: misfortune and calamity sent by God either in punishment or as an incentive to repentance or to greater virtue.

11, 15f: Some ancient witnesses omit these two verses.

11, 19: Cf the parable of the rich man, Lk 12, 16–21.

11, 26ff: Sirach, writing before Christian revelation, did not go beyond the hour of death to find full divine retribution.

12, 1–7: The limitations to the practice of charity here reflected were removed by Christ, who requires that good be done even to enemies and to those who hate, persecute and calumniate us (Mt 5, 43–48).

k Ps 127, 2; Eccl 4, 8. l Jb 1, 21; 2, 10. m Eccl 4, 8; 6, 2; Lk 12, 19. n Sir 18, 25.

[3]No good comes to him who gives comfort to
the wicked,*
nor is it an act of mercy that he does.
[4]Give to the good man, refuse the sinner;[o]
refresh the downtrodden, give nothing to
the proud man.
[5]No arms for combat should you give him,
lest he use them against yourself;
[6]With twofold evil you will meet
for every good deed you do for him.
[7]The Most High himself hates sinners,
and upon the wicked he takes vengeance.

[8]In our prosperity we cannot know our
friends;*
in adversity an enemy will not remain
concealed.[p]
[9]When a man is successful even his enemy is
friendly;
in adversity even his friend disappears.[q]
[10]Never trust your enemy,
for his wickedness is like corrosion in
bronze.
[11]Even though he acts humbly and peaceably
toward you,
take care to be on your guard against him.
Rub him as one polishes a brazen mirror,*
and you will find that there is still corrosion.
[12]Let him not stand near you,
lest he oust you and take your place.
Let him not sit at your right hand,
lest he then demand your seat,
And in the end you appreciate my advice,
when you groan with regret, as I warned
you.
[13]Who pities a snake charmer when he is bitten,
or anyone who goes near a wild beast?
[14]So is it with the companion of the proud man,
who is involved in his sins:
[15]While you stand firm, he makes no bold move;
but if you slip, he cannot hold back.
[16]With his lips an enemy speaks sweetly,
but in his heart he schemes to plunge you
into the abyss.
Though your enemy has tears in his eyes,
if given the chance, he will never have
enough of your blood.
[17]If evil comes upon you, you will find him at
hand;
feigning to help, he will trip you up,
[18]Then he will nod his head and clap his hands
and hiss repeatedly, and show his true face.

CHAPTER 13

Caution Regarding Associates*

[1]He who touches pitch blackens his hand;
he who associates with an impious man
learns his ways.
[2]Bear no burden too heavy for you;
go with no one greater or wealthier than
yourself.
How can the earthen pot go with the metal
cauldron?
When they knock together, the pot will be
smashed:
[3]The rich man does wrong and boasts of it,
the poor man is wronged and begs
forgiveness.
[4]As long as the rich man can use you he will
enslave you,
but when you are exhausted, he will
abandon you.
[5]As long as you have anything he will speak fair
words to you,
and with smiles he will win your
confidence;
[6]When he needs something from you he will
cajole you,
then without regret he will impoverish you.
[7]While it serves his purpose he will beguile
you,
then twice or three times he will terrify
you;

12, 3ff: The author advises against generosity to those who would abuse it.

12, 8–18: Through adversity friends are distinguished from enemies; to trust the latter or permit them intimacy is to invite disaster. Cf note on Sir 6, 5–17.

12, 11: Brazen mirror: see note on Ex 38, 8.

13, 1—14, 2: By means of various figures Sirach indicates the practical impossibility of genuine and sincere companionship between the poor and the proud rich. He lays down the principle of associating with equals (13, 15).

o 4f: Gal 6, 10. p Prv 17, 17. q Prv 19, 4–7.

When later he sees you he will pass you by,
and shake his head over you.
8 Guard against being presumptuous;
be not as those who lack sense.
9 When invited by a man of influence, keep your distance;
then he will urge you all the more.
10 Be not bold with him lest you be rebuffed,
but keep not too far away lest you be forgotten.
11 Engage not freely in discussion with him,
trust not his many words;
For by prolonged talk he will test you,
and though smiling he will probe you.
12 Mercilessly he will make of you a laughingstock,
and will not refrain from injury or chains.
13 Be on your guard and take care
never to accompany men of violence.

14 Every living thing loves its own kind,
every man a man like himself.
15 Every being is drawn to its own kind;
with his own kind every man associates.
16 Is a wolf ever allied with a lamb?
So it is with the sinner and the just.[r]
17 Can there be peace between the hyena and the dog?
Or between the rich and the poor can there be peace?*
18 Lion's prey are the wild asses of the desert;
so too the poor are feeding grounds for the rich.
19 A proud man abhors lowliness;
so does the rich man abhor the poor.
20 When a rich man stumbles he is supported by a friend;
when a poor man trips he is pushed down by a friend.
21 Many are the supporters for a rich man when he speaks;
though what he says is odious, it wins approval.
When a poor man speaks they make sport of him;
he speaks wisely and no attention is paid him.
22 A rich man speaks and all are silent,
his wisdom they extol to the clouds.
A poor man speaks and they say: "Who is that?"
If he slips they cast him down.
23 Wealth is good when there is no sin;
but poverty is evil by the standards of the proud.
24 The heart of a man changes his countenance,
either for good or for evil.[s]
25 The sign of a good heart is a cheerful countenance;
withdrawn and perplexed is the laborious schemer.

CHAPTER 14

1 Happy the man whose mouth brings him no grief,
who is not stung by remorse for sin.[t]
2 Happy the man whose conscience does not reproach him,
who has not lost hope.

The Use of Wealth

3 Wealth ill becomes the mean man;*
and to the miser, of what use is gold?
4 What he denies himself he collects for others,
and in his possessions a stranger will revel.[u]
5 To whom will he be generous who is stingy with himself
and does not enjoy what is his own?
6 None is more stingy than he who is stingy with himself;
he punishes his own miserliness.
7 If ever he is generous, it is by mistake;
and in the end he displays his greed.
8 In the miser's opinion his share is too small;
9 he refuses his neighbor and brings ruin on himself.

13, 17: The hostility between the dogs which guard the flocks at night and the rapacious hyenas is proverbial in Palestine.

14, 3–16: The miser does no good even to himself (3–10); wealth should be wisely used during life, for it must be left behind at death (11–16). In the light of the gospel, generosity has a higher motivation and promise of reward than the Old Testament writer could propose. Cf Mt 6, 19ff; Lk 12, 32ff.

r 2 Cor 6, 14ff. s Prv 15, 13. t Sir 19, 15; 25, 8; Jas 3, 2. u Eccl 6, 2.

10 The miser's eye is rapacious for bread,
but on his own table he sets it stale.
11 My son, use freely whatever you have
and enjoy it as best you can; [v]
12 Remember that death does not tarry,
nor have you been told the grave's
appointed time.
13 Before you die, be good to your friend,
and give him a share in what you possess. [w]
14 Deprive not yourself of present good things,
let no choice portion escape you.
15 Will you not leave your riches to others,
and your earnings to be divided by lot?
16 Give, take, and treat yourself well,
for in the nether world there are no joys to
seek.
17 All flesh grows old, like a garment;
the age-old law is: All must die. [x]
18 As with the leaves that grow on a vigorous
tree:
one falls off and another sprouts—
So with the generations of flesh and blood:
one dies and another is born. [y]
19 All man's works will perish in decay,
and his handiwork will follow after him.

The Search for Wisdom and Its Blessings*

20 Happy the man who meditates on wisdom,
and reflects on knowledge; [z]
21 Who ponders her ways in his heart,
and understands her paths;
22 Who pursues her like a scout,
and lies in wait at her entry way;
23 Who peeps through her windows,
and listens at her doors;
24 Who encamps near her house,
and fastens his tent pegs next to her walls;
25 Who pitches his tent beside her,
and lives as her welcome neighbor;
26 Who builds his nest in her leafage,
and lodges in her branches;
27 Who takes shelter with her from the heat,
and dwells in her home.

CHAPTER 15

1 He who fears the LORD will do this;
he who is practiced in the law will come to
wisdom.
2 Motherlike she will meet him,
like a young bride she will embrace him,
3 Nourish him with the bread of understanding,
and give him the water of learning to
drink. [a]
4 He will lean upon her and not fall,
he will trust in her and not be put to shame.
5 She will exalt him above his fellows;
in the assembly she will make him
eloquent.
6 Joy and gladness he will find,
an everlasting name inherit. [b]
7 Worthless men will not attain to her,
haughty men will not behold her.
8 Far from the impious is she,
not to be spoken of by liars.
9 Unseemly is praise on a sinner's lips,
for it is not accorded to him by God.
10 But praise is offered by the wise man's tongue;
its rightful steward will proclaim it.

Man's Free Will

11 Say not: "It was God's doing that I fell away";
for what he hates he does not do.
12 Say not: "It was he who set me astray";
for he has no need of wicked man. [c]
13 Abominable wickedness the LORD hates,
he does not let it befall those who fear him.
14 When God, in the beginning, created man,
he made him subject to his own free
choice. [d]
15 If you choose you can keep the
commandments;
it is loyalty to do his will.
16 There are set before you fire and water;
to whichever you choose, stretch forth your
hand.
17 Before man are life and death,
whichever he chooses shall be given him. [e]

14, 20—15, 20: From his social teaching the sage now turns to consider individual responsibility. Happiness is to be found in the pursuit and possession of wisdom (14, 20—15, 5). Joy and honor are given, not to the sinner (7ff), but to him who fears God and observes his law (1–6. 10). The sinner is fully responsible for his conduct because God, who sees all things (18f), is not the author of wickedness (11ff. 20): he gives to every man the liberty to choose between good and evil (14–17).

v Prv 3, 9. w Sir 4, 1; Tb 4, 7. x Ps 103; 14ff; Is 40, 6; Jas 1, 10; 1 Pt 1, 24. y Eccl 1, 4. z Ps 1, 2. a Jn 4, 10; 6, 31ff. b Sir 6, 29–32. c Jas 1, 13. d Gn 1, 27. e Dt 30, 15.

18 Immense is the wisdom of the LORD;
he is mighty in power, and all-seeing.
19 The eyes of God see all he has made;
he understands man's every deed.[f]
20 No man does he command to sin,
to none does he give strength for lies.

CHAPTER 16

God's Punishment of Sinners*

1 Desire not a brood of worthless children,
nor rejoice in wicked offspring.
2 Many though they be, exult not in them
if they have not the fear of the LORD.
3 Count not on their length of life,[g]
have no hope in their future.
For one can be better than a thousand;
rather die childless than have godless
children!
4 Through one wise man can a city be peopled;
through a clan of rebels it becomes desolate.
5 Many such things has my eye seen,
even more than these has my ear heard.
6 Against a sinful band fire is enkindled,[h]
upon a godless people wrath flames out.*
7 He forgave not the leaders of old*
who rebelled long ago in their might;[i]
8 He spared not the neighbors of Lot[j]
whom he detested for their pride;*
9 Nor did he spare the doomed people*
who were uprooted because of their sin;
10 Nor the six hundred thousand foot soldiers[k]
who perished for the impiety of their
hearts.*
11 And had there been but one stiffnecked man,
it were a wonder had he gone unpunished.
For mercy and anger alike are with him
who remits and forgives, though on the
wicked alights his wrath.
12 Great as his mercy is his punishment;
he judges men, each according to his deeds.
13 A criminal does not escape with his plunder;
a just man's hope God does not leave
unfulfilled.
14 Whoever does good has his reward,
which each receives according to his deeds.
15 Say not: "I am hidden from God;
in heaven who remembers me?
Among so many people I cannot be known;
what am I in the world of spirits?
16 Behold, the heavens, the heaven of heavens,
the earth and the abyss tremble at his
visitation;
17 The roots of the mountains, the earth's
foundations,
at his mere glance, quiver and quake.
18 Of me, therefore, he will take no thought;
with my ways who will concern himself?
19 If I sin, no eye will see me;
if all in secret I am disloyal, who is to
know?[l]
20 Who tells him of just deeds
and what could I expect for doing my
duty?"
21 Such are the thoughts of senseless men,
which only the foolish knave will
think.

Divine Wisdom Seen in Creation*

22 Hearken to me, my son, take my advice,
apply your mind to my words,
23 While I propose measured wisdom,
and impart accurate knowledge.
24 When at the first God created his works
and, as he made them, assigned their
tasks,[m]
25 He ordered for all time what they were to do

16, 1–21: Sinful offspring are a great misfortune (1–4), for history and experience show how God punishes sin (5–10). He judges everyone according to his deeds (11ff); no one is hidden from him or escapes retribution at his hand (15–21).

16, 6: For Korah and his band (6a), see Nm 16, 35; Ps 106, 18; for the disgruntled Israelites (6b), Ps 78, 21f.

16, 7: The leaders of old: the "mighty men of old" who were destroyed by the flood: Gn 6, 4; Wis 14, 6; Bar 3, 26ff.

16, 8: The people of Sodom and Gomorrah: Gn 19, 24f; Ez 16, 49f.

16, 9: The Canaanites: Ex 23, 23f. 27–31; 33, 2; Dt 7, 1; Wis 12, 3.

16, 10: The Israelites who murmured against Moses: Nm 11, 20; 14, 12. 22ff.

16, 22—17, 18: In harmony with Gn 1—2, the author describes God's wisdom in creating the universe and all things in it (22–28), endowing man with a moral nature, with wisdom and knowledge and freedom of will according to his own image (17, 1. 6), so that man may govern the earth (3f), praise God's name (8), obey his law (9–12), and render to him an account of his deeds (18). Cf Pss 19; 104.

f Pss 33, 18; 34, 16; Heb 4, 13. g 3f: Wis 4, 1f. h Sir 21, 9. i Gn 6, 4; Wis 14, 6; Bar 3, 26ff. j Gn 19, 24ff. k Nm 14, 29. l Sir 23, 18. m Gn 1, 4ff.

and their domains from generation to
generation.
They were not to hunger, nor grow weary,
nor ever cease from their tasks.
26 Not one should ever crowd its neighbor,
nor should they ever disobey his word.
27 Then the LORD looked upon the earth,
and filled it with his blessings. [n]
28 Its surface he covered with all manner of life
which must return into it again.

CHAPTER 17

1 The LORD from the earth created man,
and in his own image he made him. [o]
2 Limited days of life he gives him [p]
and makes him return to earth again.
3 He endows man with a strength of his own,
and with power over all things else on
earth.
4 He puts the fear of him in all flesh,
and gives him rule over beasts and birds.
5 He forms men's tongues and eyes and ears,
and imparts to them an understanding
heart.
6 With wisdom and knowledge he fills them;
good and evil he shows them.
7 He looks with favor upon their hearts,
and shows them his glorious works,
8 That they may describe the wonders of his
deeds
and praise his holy name.
9 He has set before them knowledge,
a law of life as their inheritance;
10 An everlasting covenant* he has made with
them,
his commandments he has revealed to
them.
11 His majestic glory their eyes beheld,
his glorious voice their ears heard.
12 He says to them, "Avoid all evil";
each of them he gives precepts about his
fellow men.
13 Their ways are ever known to him,
they cannot be hidden from his eyes.
14 Over every nation he places a ruler,*
but the LORD's own portion is Israel. [q]
15 All their actions are clear as the sun to him,
his eyes are ever upon their ways.
16 Their wickedness cannot be hidden from him;
all of their sins are before the LORD.
17 A man's goodness God cherishes like a signet
ring,
a man's virtue, like the apple of his eye.
18 Later he will rise up and repay them,
and requite each one of them as they
deserve. [r]

Appeal for a Return to God*

19 But to the penitent he provides a way back,
he encourages those who are losing hope!
20 Return to the LORD and give up sin,
pray to him and make your offenses few.
21 Turn again to the Most High and away from
sin,
hate intensely what he loathes;
22 Who in the nether world can glorify the Most
High [s]
in place of the living who offer their praise?
23 No more can the dead give praise than those
who have never lived;
they glorify the LORD who are alive and
well.
24 How great the mercy of the LORD,
his forgiveness of those who return to him!
25 The like cannot be found in men,
for not immortal is any son of man.
26 Is anything brighter than the sun? Yet it can be
eclipsed.
How obscure* then the thoughts of flesh
and blood!

17, 10: An everlasting covenant . . . his commandments: the various covenants which God entered into with mankind, e.g., Gn 2, 15ff; 17, 1–22, especially on Mount Sinai where the people saw God's glory and heard his voice (Ex 19, 16—24, 18).

17, 14: Ruler: this may refer to civil authority or to angels placed over nations as guardians; see note on Dt 32, 8, and the cross references above.

17, 19–27: Exhorting the sinner to return to God (19ff. 24ff), the author implies that the Lord will postpone death for a repentant sinner so that he may fulfill his destiny of praising God on earth (22f). In the light of Christian teaching, the gift of final penitence extends this divine purpose into life everlasting. See note on Ps 6, 6; cf also Ez 18, 23; 33, 11–16.

17, 26: Obscure: literally, evil; compare Gn 6, 5. Though moral fault is not excluded, the thought here is the inability to understand the merciful designs of God. Cf Wis 9, 14–18.

n Gn 1, 20ff. o Gn 2, 7; 3. 19. p 2ff: Gn 1, 26ff; Ps 8, 4–8. q Ex 19, 5; Dt 4, 19f; 32, 8f; Dn 10, 13–21; 12, 1; Rom 13, 1. r Jb 19, 25; Jl 3, 4. s 22f: Pss 6, 6; 115, 17; Is 38, 18.

[27] God watches over the hosts of highest heaven,
while all men are dust and ashes.

CHAPTER 18

The Divine Power and Mercy*

[1] The Eternal is the judge of all things without exception;
the LORD alone is just.
[2] Whom has he made equal to describing his works,
and who can probe his mighty deeds?
[3] Who can measure his majestic power,
or exhaust the tale of his mercies?
[4] One cannot lessen, nor increase,
nor penetrate the wonders of the LORD.
[5] When a man ends he is only beginning,
and when he stops he is still bewildered.
[6] What is man, of what worth is he?
the good, the evil in him, what are these?
[7] The sum of a man's days is great
if it reaches a hundred years: [t]
[8] Like a drop of sea water, like a grain of sand,
so are these few years among the days of eternity.
[9] That is why the LORD is patient with men
and showers upon them his mercy.
[10] He sees and understands that their death is grievous,
and so he forgives them all the more.
[11] Man may be merciful to his fellow man,
but the LORD's mercy reaches all flesh,
[12] Reproving, admonishing, teaching,
as a shepherd guides his flock; [u]
[13] Merciful to those who accept his guidance,
who are diligent in his precepts.

The Necessity of Prudence

[14] My son, to your charity add no reproach,*
nor spoil any gift by harsh words.
[15] Like dew that abates a burning wind,
so does a word improve a gift.
[16] Sometimes the word means more than the gift;
both are offered by a kindly man.
[17] Only a fool upbraids before giving;
a grudging gift wears out the expectant eyes. [v]
[18] Be informed before speaking;
before sickness prepare the cure.
[19] Before you are judged, seek merit for yourself,
and at the time of visitation you will have a ransom.*
[20] Before you have fallen, humble yourself;
when you have sinned, show repentance.
[21] Delay not to forsake sins,
neglect it not till you are in distress.
[22] Let nothing prevent the prompt payment of your vows;*
wait not to fulfill them when you are dying. [w]
[23] Before making a vow have the means to fulfill it;
be not one who tries the LORD.
[24] Think of wrath and the day of death,
the time of vengeance when he will hide his face. [x]
[25] Remember the time of hunger in the time of plenty,
poverty and want in the day of wealth. [y]
[26] Between morning and evening the weather changes;
before the LORD all things are fleeting.
[27] A wise man is circumspect in all things;
when sin is rife he keeps himself from wrongdoing.
[28] Any learned man should make wisdom known,*
and he who attains to her should declare her praise;

18, 1–13: Not only are God's justice and power beyond man's understanding (1–5), his mercy also is boundless and surpasses all human compassion (6–13).

18, 14–27: The practice of charity is an art which avoids every offense to the recipient (14–18). Prudence directs the changing circumstances of daily life toward the attainment of its reward at the time of visitation, i.e., the day of reckoning (19–27).

18, 19: Merit . . . ransom: almsgiving is often portrayed in the Bible as a means of approach to the forgiving mercy of God. Cf Sir 3, 29f; 29, 11f; Tb 12, 12f; Dn 4, 24; Lk 16, 9; Acts 10, 31.

18, 22f: The usual object of a vow in Old Testament times was the offering of a bloody sacrifice.

18, 28f: A general statement on the teaching of wisdom, serving either as a conclusion to the preceding section or as an introduction to the following one. The neighbors of the wise man are regarded as the field into which he channels the waters of wisdom to encourage growth. Cf Sir 24, 28–31.

t Ps 90, 10. u Jn 10, 11. v Sir 20, 13. w Nm 30, 3; Dt 23, 22; Ps 50, 14; Prv 20, 25; Eccl 5, 4. x Sir 7, 16. y Sir 11, 25.

29 Those trained in her words must show their
wisdom,
dispensing sound proverbs like life-giving
waters.

Self-Control*

30 Go not after your lusts, [z]
but keep your desires in check.
31 If you satisfy your lustful appetites
they will make you the sport of your
enemies.
32 Have no joy in the pleasures of a moment
which bring on poverty redoubled;
33 Become not a glutton and a winebibber
with nothing in your purse.

CHAPTER 19

1 He who does so grows no richer;
he who wastes the little he has will be
stripped bare.
2 Wine and women make the mind giddy,
and the companion of harlots becomes
reckless. [a]
4 He who lightly trusts in them has no sense,
and he who strays after them sins against
his own life.
3 Rottenness and worms will possess him,
for contumacious desire destroys its owner.

The Proper Use of Speech*

5 He who gloats over evil will meet with evil,
and he who repeats an evil report has no
sense.
6 Never repeat gossip,
and you will not be reviled. [b]
7 Tell nothing to friend or foe;
if you have a fault, reveal it not, [c]
8 For he who hears it will hold it against you,
and in time become your enemy.
9 Let anything you hear die within you;
be assured it will not make you burst.
10 When a fool hears something, he is in labor,
like a woman giving birth to a child.
11 Like an arrow lodged in a man's thigh
is gossip in the breast of a fool.
12 Admonish your friend—he may not have done
it;
and if he did, that he may not do it again. [d]
13 Admonish your neighbor—he may not have
said it;
and if he did, that he may not say it again.
14 Admonish your friend—often it may be
slander;
every story you must not believe.
15 Then, too, a man can slip and not mean it;
who has not sinned with his tongue? [e]
16 Admonish your neighbor before you break
with him;
thus will you fulfill the law of the Most
High. [f]

How To Recognize True Wisdom*

17 All wisdom is fear of the LORD;
perfect wisdom is the fulfillment of the
law. [g]
18 The knowledge of wickedness is not wisdom,
nor is there prudence in the counsel of
sinners.
19 There is a shrewdness that is detestable,
while the simple man may be free from
sin.
20 There are those with little understanding who
fear God,
and those of great intelligence who violate
the law.
21 There is a shrewdness keen but dishonest,
which by duplicity wins a judgment.
22 There is the wicked man who is bowed in
grief,
but is full of guile within;
23 He bows his head and feigns not to hear,

18, 30—19, 4: Inordinate gratification of the senses makes a man unreasonable, the slave of passion, the sport of his enemies. In the end it destroys him physically and spiritually.

19, 5–16: An excellent commentary on the eighth commandment of the Decalogue, forbidding intemperance in speech through calumny, rash judgment, and detraction (5f), and inculcating discreet silence in defense of self and of neighbor (7–11). Justice requires that an accused neighbor be given a hearing, and charity urges fraternal correction; both together fulfill the law of the Most High (12–16); cf Mt 7, 1f; 18, 15f.

19, 17–26: True and false wisdom as here described are synonymous with virtue and vice, with the fulfillment of the law and the violation of it.

z Rom 6, 12; 13, 14. a Prv 20, 1; 23, 20ff. b Prv 25, 10. c Sir 8, 18f. d Lv 19, 17; Mt 18, 15; Lk 17, 3. e Sir 14, 1; Jas 3, 2. f Lv 19, 17. g Sir 1, 1. 12. 14; Jb 28, 28; Ps 111, 10; Prv 1, 7; 9, 10.

but when not observed, he will take
advantage of you:
24 Even though his lack of strength keeps him
from sinning,
when he finds the opportunity, he will do
harm.
25 One can tell a man by his appearance;
a wise man is known as such when first
met.
26 A man's attire, his hearty laughter and his gait,
proclaim him for what he is.

CHAPTER 20

Conduct of the Wise and the Foolish

1 An admonition can be inopportune,*
and a man may be wise to hold his peace.
2 It is much better to admonish than to lose
one's temper,
for one who admits his fault will be kept
from disgrace.
3 Like a eunuch lusting for intimacy with a
maiden
is he who does right under compulsion.*
4 One man is silent and is thought wise,
another is talkative and is disliked.
5 One man is silent because he has nothing to
say;
another is silent, biding his time. [h]
6 A wise man is silent till the right time comes,
but a boasting fool ignores the proper time.
7 He who talks too much is detested;
he who pretends to authority is hated.

8 Some misfortunes bring success;*
some things gained are a man's loss.
9 Some gifts do one no good,
and some must be paid back double.*
10 Humiliation can follow fame,
while from obscurity a man can lift up his
head.
11 A man may buy much for little,
but pay for it seven times over.
12 A wise man makes himself popular by a few
words,
but fools pour forth their blandishments in
vain.
13 A gift from a rogue will do you no good,
for in his eyes his one gift is equal to
seven.
14 He gives little and criticizes often,
and like a crier he shouts aloud.
He lends today, he asks it back tomorrow;
hateful indeed is such a man.
15 A fool has no friends,
nor thanks for his generosity;
16 Those who eat his bread have an evil tongue.
How many times they laugh him to scorn!

17 A fall to the ground is less sudden than a slip of
the tongue;*
that is why the downfall of the wicked
comes so quickly.
18 Insipid food is the untimely tale;
the unruly are always ready to offer it.
19 A proverb when spoken by a fool is
unwelcome,
for he does not utter it at the proper time.
20 A man through want may be unable to sin,
yet in this tranquility he cannot rest.
21 One may lose his life through shame,
and perish through a fool's intimidation.
22 A man makes a promise to a friend out of
shame,
and has him for his enemy needlessly.
23 A lie is a foul blot in a man,
yet it is constantly on the lips of the
unruly.
24 Better a thief than an inveterate liar,
yet both will suffer disgrace;
25 A liar's way leads to dishonor,
his shame remains ever with him.

20, 1–7: Wisdom indicates the proper times for speech and silence, that is, the occasions when the most benefit can be gained from them.

20, 3: The sense is that violence or force against a person can prevent an external act of sin or compel a good deed without eliminating the internal sin or desire of wrongdoing. Cf Sir 20, 20.

20, 8–16: In a series of paradoxes the author indicates how much true and lasting values differ from apparent ones.

20, 9: And some . . . double: or perhaps, "but some are doubly precious."

20, 17–25: The ill-timed speech of the wicked, the unruly and a fool is repulsive (17ff); human respect exposes one to intimidation, rash promises and enmity (21f); lies bring dishonor and lasting disgrace (23ff).

h Sir 20, 1; Prv 10, 19; 17, 28.

26 A wise man advances himself by his words,*
a prudent man pleases the great.
27 He who works his land has abundant crops,
he who pleases the great is pardoned his faults.
28 Favors and gifts blind the eyes;
like a muzzle over the mouth they silence reproof.[i]
29 Hidden wisdom and unseen treasure—
of what value is either?
30 Better the man who hides his folly
than the one who hides his wisdom.

CHAPTER 21

Sin Must Be Avoided*

1 My son, if you have sinned, do so no more,
and for your past sins pray to be forgiven.
2 Flee from sin as from a serpent
that will bite you if you go near it;
Its teeth are lion's teeth,
destroying the souls of men.
3 Every offense is a two-edged sword;
when it cuts, there can be no healing.
4 Violence and arrogance wipe out wealth;
so too a proud man's home is destroyed.
5 Prayer from a poor man's lips is heard at once,
and justice is quickly granted him.
6 He who hates correction walks the sinner's path,
but he who fears the LORD repents in his heart.
7 Widely known is the boastful speaker,
but the wise man knows his own faults.
8 He who builds his house with another's money
is collecting stones for his funeral mound.
9 A band of criminals is like a bundle of tow;
they will end in a flaming fire.[j]
10 The path of sinners is smooth stones
that end in the depths of the nether world.*

The Wise and the Foolish Differ*

11 He who keeps the law controls his impulses;
he who is perfect in fear of the LORD has wisdom.
12 He can never be taught who is not shrewd,
but one form of shrewdness is thoroughly bitter.
13 A wise man's knowledge wells up in a flood,
and his counsel, like a living spring;[k]
14 A fool's mind is like a broken jar—
no knowledge at all can it hold.
15 When an intelligent man hears words of wisdom,
he approves them and adds to them;
The wanton hears them with scorn
and casts them behind his back.
16 A fool's chatter is like a load on a journey,
but there is charm to be found upon the lips of the wise.
17 The views of a prudent man are sought in an assembly,
and his words are considered with care.
18 Like a house in ruins is wisdom to a fool;
the stupid man knows it only as inscrutable words.
19 Like fetters on the legs is learning to a fool,
like a manacle on his right hand.
20 A fool raises his voice in laughter,
but a prudent man at the most smiles gently.[l]
21 Like a chain of gold is learning to a wise man,
like a bracelet on his right arm.

22 The fool steps boldly into a house,

20, 26–30: Unlike the fool who invites disaster through misuse of his tongue, the sage through prudent speech gains in honor and esteem among the great (26f). He must beware, however, of accepting bribes, lest he share in evil through silence when he should reprove (28ff).

21, 1–10: Under various figures the consequences of sin are described as destructive of wealth, and even of bodily life, and deserving of death and a place in the depths of the nether world (2ff. 6a. 8ff). Through prayer, forgiveness can be sought (1), and through fear of the Lord, repentance is achieved (1, 5. 6b).

21, 10: The path of sinners . . . nether world: eternal retribution is not yet proposed in this reference. It became clearly revealed through the teaching of Christ; cf Mt 7, 13f; 25, 41–46; Lk 16, 19–31.

21, 11–28: The mind of the wise man is a fountain of knowledge (13. 15); his will is trained to keep the law (11); his words are gracious, valued, carefully weighed, sincere (16f. 25f); his conduct is respectful, cultured and restrained (20. 22ff). The fool's mind is devoid of knowledge and impenetrable to it (12. 14. 18f); his will rejects it (15); his talk is burdensome (16), his laughter unrestrained (20), his conversation shallow and meddlesome (25f); his conduct is bold and rude (22ff); his abuse of others redounds on himself (27f).

i Ex 23, 8; Dt 16, 19. j Ps 21, 9. k Prv 13, 14; 16, 22. l Eccl 7, 6.

while the well-bred man remains outside; [m]
23 A boor peeps through the doorway of a house,
but a cultured man keeps his glance cast down.
24 It is rude for one to listen at a door;
a cultured man would be overwhelmed by the disgrace of it.
25 The lips of the impious talk of what is not their concern,
but the words of the prudent are carefully weighed.
26 Fools' thoughts are in their mouths,
wise men's words are in their hearts.
27 When a godless man curses his adversary,*
he really curses himself.
28 A slanderer besmirches himself,
and is hated by his neighbors.

CHAPTER 22

On Laziness and Foolishness

1 The sluggard is like a stone in the mud;*
everyone hisses at his disgrace.
2 The sluggard is like a lump of dung;
whoever touches him wipes his hands.
3 An unruly child is a disgrace to its father;
if it be a daughter, she brings him to poverty. [n]
4 A thoughtful daughter becomes a treasure to her husband,
a shameless one is her father's grief.
5 A hussy shames her father and her husband;
by both she is despised.
6 Like a song in time of mourning is inopportune talk,*
but lashes and discipline are at all times wisdom.
7 Teaching a fool is like gluing a broken pot, [o]
or like disturbing a man in the depths of sleep;
8 He talks with a slumberer who talks with a fool,
for when it is over, he will say, "What was that?"
9 Weep over the dead man, for his light has gone out;
weep over the fool, for sense has left him.
10 Weep but a little over the dead man, for he is at rest;
but worse than death is the life of a fool.
11 Seven days of mourning for the dead,
but for the wicked fool a whole lifetime. [p]

12 Speak but seldom with the stupid man,
be not the companion of a brute;
13 Beware of him lest you have trouble
and be spattered when he shakes himself;
Turn away from him and you will find rest
and not be wearied by his lack of sense.
14 What is heavier than lead,
and what is its name but "Fool"?
15 Sand and salt and an iron mass
are easier to bear than a stupid man. [q]

16 Masonry bonded with wooden beams*
is not loosened by an earthquake;
Neither is a resolve constructed with careful deliberation
shaken in a moment of fear.
17 A resolve that is backed by prudent understanding
is like the polished surface of a smooth wall.
18 Small stones lying on an open height
will not remain when the wind blows;
Neither can a timid resolve based on foolish plans
withstand fear of any kind.

21, 27: Adversary: this can be understood in the sense that, if a man curses one who led him into sin, he implicitly curses himself for having yielded to the sin; or in the sense that the enemy is the man's own sinful nature; or even in the sense that the enemy is the devil, since the Hebrew word used here is satan. Cf 1 Chr 21, 1; Zec 3, 2; 2 Pt 2, 12f; Jude 9.

22, 1–15: To Sirach, a lazy person and an unruly child are a cause of shame and disgrace; everyone wishes to be rid of them (1–5). A wicked fool is as senseless as a man asleep or dead, but the grief he causes others lasts a lifetime (7–11). He is like a brute, troublesome and intolerable (12–15).

22, 6: Like a song . . . is . . . talk: some understand talk in the sense of a rebuke unheeded by the unruly as a joyful song is out of place among mourners. Corporal punishment, however, is always effective.

22, 16ff: A prudent mind firmly resolved is undisturbed by violent and conflicting thoughts, whereas a foolish person is tossed about by the winds of fear, like small stones whipped about by high winds.

m Prv 25, 17. n Prv 17, 21; 19, 13. o 7–11: Prv 23, 9. p Gn 50, 10. q Prv 27, 3.

The Preservation of Friendship*

19 One who jabs the eye brings tears:
he who pierces the heart bares its feelings.
20 He who throws stones at birds drives them away,
and he who insults a friend breaks up the friendship.
21 Should you draw a sword against a friend,
despair not, it can be undone.
22 Should you speak sharply to a friend,
fear not, you can be reconciled.
But a contemptuous insult, a confidence broken,
or a treacherous attack will drive away any friend.

23 Make fast friends with a man while he is poor;
thus will you enjoy his prosperity with him.
In time of trouble remain true to him,
so as to share in his inheritance when it comes.
24 Before flames burst forth an oven smokes;
so does abuse come before bloodshed.
25 From a friend in need of support
no one need hide in shame;
26 But from him who brings harm to his friend
all will stand aloof who hear of it.

Prayer*

27 Who will set a guard over my mouth,
and upon my lips an effective seal,
That I may not fail through them,
that my tongue may not destroy me? [r]

CHAPTER 23

1 LORD, Father and Master of my life,*
permit me not to fall by them!
2 Who will apply the lash to my thoughts,
to my mind the rod of discipline,
That my failings may not be spared,
nor the sins of my heart overlooked;
3 Lest my failings increase,
and my sins be multiplied;
Lest I succumb to my foes,
and my enemy rejoice over me?
4 LORD, Father and God of my life,
abandon me not into their control!
5 A brazen look allow me not;
ward off passion from my heart,
6 Let not the lustful cravings of the flesh master me,
surrender me not to shameless desires.

The Proper Use of the Tongue*

7 Give heed, my children, to the instruction that I pronounce,
for he who keeps it will not be enslaved.
8 Through his lips is the sinner ensnared;
the railer and the arrogant man fall thereby.
9 Let not your mouth form the habit of swearing,
or becoming too familiar with the Holy Name. [s]
10 Just as a slave that is constantly under scrutiny*
will not be without welts,
So one who swears continually by the Holy Name
will not remain free from sin.
11 A man who often swears heaps up obligations;
the scourge will never be far from his house.
If he swears in error, he incurs guilt;
if he neglects his obligation, his sin is doubly great. [t]
If he swears without reason he cannot be found just,
and all his house will suffer affliction.
12 There are words which merit death;

22, 19–26: As disputes and violence weaken friendship, and disloyalty and abuse of confidence destroy it utterly (19–22. 24. 26), so kindness to a poor man in time of poverty and adversity builds up friendship and merits a share in his prosperity and inheritance (23. 25).

22, 27—23, 6: The sage implores the divine assistance to preserve him through stern discipline from sins of the tongue (22, 27; 23, 1); ignorance of mind and weakness of will (2f); and inclinations of the senses and the flesh, lest he fall into the hands of his enemies, or become a prey of shameful desires (3–6).

23, 1: Lord, Father and Master of my life: these words express the tender personal relationship between the author's soul and God, the need of his assistance, and the truth of his providence.

23, 7–15: A warning against sins of the tongue through misuse of the Holy Name, thoughtless swearing which involves obligation and incurs guilt (7–11), blasphemy (12), talk that is coarse and blundersome (13f), and the incorrigible habit of abusive language (15).

23, 10: As a slave . . . under scrutiny, so is he who calls on God to witness the truth of what he says.

r Ps 141, 3. s Ex 20, 7; Lv 19, 12; Dt 5, 11; Mt 5, 33ff. t Lv 5, 4ff.

may they never be heard among Jacob's
heirs.
For all such words are foreign to the devout,
who do not wallow in sin.
13 Let not your mouth become used to coarse
talk,
for in it lies sinful matter.
14 Keep your father and mother in mind
when you sit among the mighty,
Lest in their presence you commit a blunder
and disgrace your upbringing,
By wishing you had never been born
or cursing the day of your birth. [u]
15 A man who has the habit of abusive language
will never mature in character as long as he
lives.

Sins of the Flesh*

16 Two types of men multiply sins,
a third* draws down wrath;
For burning passion is a blazing fire,
not to be quenched till it burns itself out:
A man given to sins of the flesh,
who never stops until the fire breaks forth;
17 The rake to whom all bread is sweet
and who is never through till he dies; [v]
18 And the man who dishonors his marriage bed
and says to himself, "Who can see me?
Darkness surrounds me, walls hide me;
no one sees me; why should I fear to sin?" [w]
Of the Most High he is not mindful,
19 fearing only the eyes of men;
He does not understand that the eyes of the
LORD,
ten thousand times brighter than the sun,
Observe every step a man takes
and peer into hidden corners.
20 He who knows all things before they exist
still knows them all after they are made.
21 Such a man will be punished in the streets of
the city; [x]
when he least expects it, he will be
apprehended.*
22 So also with the woman who is unfaithful to
her husband
and offers as heir her son by a stranger.
23 First, she has disobeyed the law of the Most
High;
secondly, she has wronged her husband;
Thirdly, in her wanton adultery
she has borne children by another man.*
24 Such a woman will be dragged before the
assembly,*
and her punishment will extend to her
children;
25 Her children will not take root;
her branches will not bring forth fruit.
26 She will leave an accursed memory;
her disgrace will never be blotted out.
27 Thus all who dwell on the earth shall know,
and all who inhabit the world shall
understand,
That nothing is better than the fear of the
LORD,
nothing more salutary than to obey his
commandments. [y]

CHAPTER 24

Praise of Wisdom

1 Wisdom sings her own praises,*
before her own people she proclaims her
glory;

23, 16–27: From sins of the tongue the author proceeds to treat of sins of the flesh and their dire consequences. The passion of lust tyrannizes over its victims and, like fire, consumes and utterly destroys them (16f. 22–26). The false security of the adulterer serves but to aggravate his inevitable fate (18–21). Only the fear of the Lord and observance of his commandments can assure moral safety (27).

23, 16: Two types . . . a third: three kinds of sins of impurity, with increasing degrees of gravity: solitary sins (16), fornication (17) and adultery (18–21).

23, 21: Cf Lv 20, 10; Dt 22, 22.

23, 23: The detailed evil of adultery includes disobedience to God's law (Ex 20, 14), injustice to a partner in marriage, and disgraceful offspring.

23, 24f: The judgment of the assembly determined the illegitimacy of children born of adultery or incest and excluded them from the "community of the Lord" (Dt 23, 3). Cf Wis 3, 16–19; 4, 3–6.

24, 1–27: In this chapter Wisdom speaks in the first person, describing her origin, her dwelling place in Israel, and the reward she gives her followers. As in Prv 8, Wisdom is described as a being who comes from God and is distinct from him. While we do not say with certainty that this description applies to a personal being, it does foreshadow the beautiful doctrine of the Word of God later developed in St. John's Gospel (Jn 1, 1–14). In the liturgy this chapter is applied to the Blessed Virgin because of her constant and intimate association with Christ, the Incarnate Wisdom.

u Sir 7, 27; Ex 20, 12; Dt 5, 16. v Prv 9, 17. w Is 29, 15. x 21f: Lv 20, 10; Dt 22, 21. y Sir 1, 10–18. 24; Prv 3, 1f.

2 In the assembly of the Most High she opens
her mouth,
in the presence of his hosts she declares her
worth:
3 "From the mouth of the Most High I came
forth, [z]
and mistlike covered the earth.
4 In the highest heavens did I dwell,
my throne on a pillar of cloud.
5 The vault of heaven I compassed alone,
through the deep abyss I wandered.
6 Over waves of the sea, over all the land,
over every people and nation I held sway.
7 Among all these I sought a resting place;
in whose inheritance should I abide?

8 "Then the Creator of all gave me his
command,
and he who formed me chose the spot for
my tent,
Saying, 'In Jacob make your dwelling,
in Israel your inheritance.'
9 Before all ages, in the beginning, he created
me,
and through all ages I shall not cease to be.
10 In the holy tent I ministered before him,
and in Zion I fixed my abode.
11 Thus in the chosen city he has given me rest,
in Jerusalem is my domain.
12 I have struck root among the glorious people,
in the portion of the LORD, his heritage.

13 "Like a cedar on Lebanon I am raised aloft,
like a cypress on Mount Hermon,
14 Like a palm tree in Engedi,
like a rosebush in Jericho,
Like a fair olive tree in the field,
like a plane tree growing beside the water.
15 Like cinnamon, or fragrant balm, or precious
myrrh,
I give forth perfume; [a]
Like galbanum and onycha and sweet spices,
like the odor of incense in the holy place.*
16 I spread out my branches like a terebinth,
my branches so bright and so graceful.
17 I bud forth delights like the vine,
my blossoms become fruit fair and rich.
18 Come to me, all you that yearn for me,
and be filled with my fruits;*
19 You will remember me as sweeter than honey,
better to have than the honeycomb.
20 He who eats of me will hunger still,*
he who drinks of me will thirst for more; [b]
21 He who obeys me will not be put to shame,
he who serves me will never fail."

22 All this is true of the book of the Most High's
covenant, [c]
the law which Moses commanded us
as an inheritance for the community of
Jacob.*
23 It overflows, like the Pishon, with wisdom— [d]
like the Tigris in the days of the new
fruits.
24 It runs over, like the Euphrates, with
understanding,
like the Jordan at harvest time.
25 It sparkles like the Nile with knowledge,
like the Gihon* at vintage time.
26 The first man never finished comprehending
wisdom,
nor will the last succeed in fathoming her.
27 For deeper than the sea are her thoughts;
her counsels, than the great abyss.

28 Now I, like a rivulet from her stream,*
channeling the waters into a garden,
29 Said to myself, "I will water my plants,
my flower bed I will drench";
And suddenly this rivulet of mine became a
river,
then this stream of mine, a sea.

24, 15: These substances were associated with worship, being mentioned in Ex 30, 22f. 34 as the ingredients of the anointing oil and the sacred incense. Israel was a priestly nation.

24, 18: Compare the words of the Savior in Mt 11, 28ff.

24, 20: So pleasing is wisdom to man that, far from being satiated, he will always desire more.

24, 22: Here the author begins to speak once more, Wisdom having ended her discourse in the preceding verse. Wisdom and the law of Moses are now identified.

24, 25: Gihon: understood by some to have been a name for the Nile; cf Gn 2, 13.

24, 28–31: Spoken by the author. He had at first drawn a small portion of the water of wisdom for his own private benefit, but finding it so useful, he soon began to let others share in this boon by teaching them the lessons of wisdom.

z 3ff: Sir 1, 1; Prv 2, 6; 8, 22–36; Wis 7, 24f. a Ex 30, 22–25. b Is 55, 1; Jn 6, 35. c Ex 24, 7. d 23ff: Gn 2, 11–14.

30 Thus do I send my teachings forth shining like
the dawn,
to become known afar off.
31 Thus do I pour out instruction like prophecy
and bestow it on generations to come.

CHAPTER 25

Those Who Are Worthy of Praise*

1 With three things I am delighted,
for they are pleasing to the LORD and to
men:
Harmony among brethren, friendship among
neighbors,
and the mutual love of husband and wife.
2 Three kinds of men I hate;
their manner of life I loathe indeed:
A proud pauper, a rich dissembler,
and an old man lecherous in his dotage.

3 What you have not saved in your youth,
how will you acquire in your old age?
4 How becoming to the gray-haired is judgment,
and a knowledge of counsel to those on in
years!
5 How becoming to the aged is wisdom,
understanding and prudence to the
venerable!
6 The crown of old men is wide experience;
their glory, the fear of the LORD.

7 There are nine who come to my mind as
blessed,
a tenth whom my tongue proclaims:
The man who finds joy in his children,
and he who lives to see his enemies'
downfall.
8 Happy is he who dwells with a sensible wife,
and he who plows not like a donkey yoked
with an ox.*
Happy is he who sins not with his tongue,
and he who serves not his inferior.
9 Happy is he who finds a friend
and he who speaks to attentive ears.
10 He who finds wisdom is great indeed,
but not greater than he who fears the LORD.
11 Fear of the LORD surpasses all else,
its possessor is beyond compare.

Wicked and Virtuous Women*

12 Worst of all wounds is that of the heart,
worst of all evils is that of a woman.
13 Worst of all sufferings is that from one's foes,
worst of all vengeance is that of one's
enemies:
14 No poison worse than that of a serpent,
no venom greater than that of a woman.
15 With a dragon or a lion I would rather dwell
than live with an evil woman.
16 Wickedness changes a woman's looks,
and makes her sullen as a female bear.
17 When her husband sits among his neighbors,
a bitter sigh escapes him unawares.

18 There is scarce any evil like that in a woman;
may she fall to the lot of the sinner!
19 Like a sandy hill to aged feet
is a railing wife to a quiet man.
20 Stumble not through woman's beauty,
nor be greedy for her wealth;
21 The man is a slave, in disgrace and shame,
when a wife supports her husband.
22 Depressed mind, saddened face,
broken heart—this from an evil wife.
Feeble hands and quaking knees—
from a wife who brings no happiness to her
husband.
23 In woman was sin's beginning,
and because of her we all die.*

25, 1–11: While praising brotherly love, love of neighbor, and conjugal love, the sage condemns their opposites in the arrogant pauper who despises his brother, the fraudulent rich man who cheats his neighbor, and the lecherous old man unfaithful to his wife (1f). This last, sensual from his youth, lacks the mature blessings of judgment and wisdom in old age (3–6), and the joy of a peaceful household, where honesty and dignity, friendship, wisdom and fear of God prevail (7–11).

25, 8: Like a donkey yoked with an ox: incompatibility between husband and wife.

25, 12–25: Wickedness in a woman is most grievous, painful and bitter to her husband. Through it she becomes vengeful, dangerous and intolerable, jealous, talkative, intemperate and unchaste. Even her very appearance is changed (12–17). The worst of all evils, a source of grief, a snare and a disgrace to her husband, she depresses his mind, saddens and breaks his heart, destroys his strength (18–22). She must not be indulged but made obedient or punished (24f).

25, 23: According to the account in Gn 3, to which Ben Sirach refers, sin, the cause of death, originated in woman: Eve, the first human being to sin, induced Adam to follow her example. But it is through Adam, as head of the race, that original sin and its punishment of spiritual death are presented by St. Paul (Rom 5) as having entered the world, to become the occasion for the redemptive work of Christ our Lord.

24 Allow water no outlet,
and be not indulgent to an erring wife.
25 If she walks not by your side,
cut her away from you.

CHAPTER 26

1 Happy the husband of a good wife,*
twice-lengthened are his days; [e]
2 A worthy* wife brings joy to her husband,
peaceful and full is his life.
3 A good wife is a generous gift
bestowed upon him who fears the LORD;[f]
4 Be he rich or poor, his heart is content,
and a smile is ever on his face.

5 There are three things at which my heart quakes,
a fourth before which I quail:
Though false charges in public, trial before all the people,
and lying testimony are harder to bear than death,
6 A jealous wife is heartache and mourning*
and a scourging tongue like the other three.
7 A bad wife is a chafing yoke;
he who marries her seizes a scorpion.
8 A drunken wife arouses great anger,
for she does not hide her shame.
9 By her eyelids and her haughty stare
an unchaste wife can be recognized.
10 Keep a strict watch over an unruly wife,
lest, finding an opportunity, she make use of it; [g]
11 Follow close if her eyes are bold,
and be not surprised if she betrays you:
12 As a thirsty traveler with eager mouth
drinks from any water that he finds,
So she settles down before every tent peg
and opens her quiver for every arrow.
13 A gracious wife delights her husband,
her thoughtfulness puts flesh on his bones;
14 A gift from the LORD is her governed speech,
and her firm virtue is of surpassing worth.
15 Choicest of blessings is a modest wife,
priceless her chaste person.
16 Like the sun rising in the LORD's heavens,
the beauty of a virtuous wife is the radiance of her home.
17 Like the light which shines above the holy lampstand,*
are her beauty of face and graceful figure.
18 Golden columns on silver bases
are her shapely limbs and steady feet.*

Dangers to Integrity and Friendship

19 These two bring grief to my heart,
and the third arouses my horror:
A wealthy man reduced to want;
illustrious men held in contempt;
And the man who passes from justice to sin,
for whom the LORD makes ready the sword. [h]

20 A merchant can hardly remain upright,*
nor a shopkeeper free from sin;

CHAPTER 27

1 For the sake of profit many sin,
and the struggle for wealth blinds the eyes. [i]
2 Like a peg driven between fitted stones,

26, 1–4. 13–18: A good wife is as a gift from God, bringing joy and peace, happiness and contentment to her husband (1–4) through her thoughtfulness, reserve, modesty and chastity, beauty, grace and virtue (13–18).

26, 2: Worthy: gifted spiritually, mentally and physically. Cf Prv 31, 10.

26, 6–12: A repetition of the thought expressed in Sir 25, 12–25.

26, 17f: The holy lampstand and the golden columns stood in the holy place of the ancient Tabernacle (Ex 25, 31–40; 26, 32).

26, 18: Among the additions found here in some manuscripts are the following lines:

"My son, take care in the prime of life
not to surrender your strength to strangers;
Single out from the land a goodly field
and there with confidence sow the seed of your increase;
So shall you have your offspring around you,
and in confidence shall they grow up.
"Though a woman for hire be thought of as a trifle,
a married woman is a deadly snare for those who embrace her. [Cf Prv 6, 26.]
"A wife's complaint should be made in meekness,
and show itself in a slight flush;
But a loud-mouthed, scolding wife
is a trumpet signaling for battle:
Any human being who answers that challenge
will spend his life amid the turbulence of war."

26, 20—27, 15: From proper conduct in family life, the author proceeds to social morality, warning especially against injustice in commerce (26, 20—27, 3), and perversity of speech in business (4–7). The pursuit of justice in these matters is all the more meritorious as it is difficult (8ff). The discourses of the devout are marked with wisdom, but the conversations of the wicked, with offense, swearing, cursing, quarrels and even bloodshed (11–15).

e Sir 25, 8; Prv 18, 22; 31, 10ff. f Sir 36, 24. g Sir 42, 11. h Ez 18, 24ff. i Sir 7, 18; 31, 6; Prv 30, 8f.

between buying and selling sin is wedged
in.
3 Unless you earnestly hold fast to the fear of the
LORD,
suddenly your house will be thrown down.
4 When a sieve is shaken, the husks appear;
so do a man's faults when he speaks.
5 As the test of what the potter molds is in the
furnace,
so in his conversation is the test of a man.[j]
6 The fruit of a tree shows the care it has had;
so too does a man's speech disclose the bent
of his mind.[k]
7 Praise no man before he speaks,
for it is then that men are tested.
8 If you strive after justice you will attain it,
and put it on like a splendid robe.
9 Birds nest with their own kind,
and fidelity comes to those who live by it.
10 As a lion crouches in wait for prey,
so do sins for evildoers.
11 Ever wise are the discourses of the devout,
but the godless man, like the moon, is
inconstant.
12 Limit the time you spend among fools,
but frequent the company of thoughtful
men.
13 The conversation of the wicked is offensive,
their laughter is wanton guilt.
14 Their oath-filled talk makes the hair stand on
end,
their brawls make one stop one's ears.
15 Wrangling among the haughty ends in
bloodshed,
their cursing is painful to hear.[l]
16 He who betrays a secret cannot be trusted,*
he will never find an intimate friend.[m]
17 Cherish your friend, keep faith with him;
but if you betray his confidence, follow him
not;
18 For as an enemy might kill a man,
you have killed your neighbor's friendship.
19 Like a bird released from the hand,
you have let your friend go and cannot
recapture him;
20 Follow him not, for he is far away,
he has fled like a gazelle from the trap.
21 A wound can be bound up, and an insult
forgiven,
but he who betrays secrets does hopeless
damage.[n]

Malice, Anger and Vengeance

22 He who has shifty eyes plots mischief
and no one can ward him off;
23 In your presence he uses honeyed talk,
and admires your every word,
But later he changes his tone
and twists your words to your ruin.[o]
24 There is nothing that I hate so much,
and the LORD hates him as well.[p]
25 As a stone falls back on him who throws it
up,[q]
so a blow struck in treachery injures more
than one.
26 As he who digs a pit falls into it,
and he who lays a snare is caught in it,
27 Whoever does harm will be involved in it
without knowing how it came upon him.
28 Mockery and abuse will be the lot of the
proud,
and vengeance lies in wait for them like a
lion.
29 The trap seizes those who rejoice in pitfalls,
and pain will consume them before they
die;
30 Wrath and anger are hateful things,
yet the sinner hugs them tight.

CHAPTER 28

1 The vengeful will suffer the LORD's vengeance,
for he remembers their sins in detail.[r]
2 Forgive your neighbor's injustice;
then when you pray, your own sins will be
forgiven.[s]

27, 16—28, 11: Betrayal of confidence through indiscretion destroys friendship and does irreparable harm (16–21); cf Sir 22, 22. False friendship based on hypocrisy and deceit is hateful to God and man (22ff); it soon becomes a victim of its own treachery (25ff). The same fate awaits the malicious and vengeful (27, 28—28, 1). They can obtain mercy and forgiveness only by first forgiving their neighbor, being mindful of death and of the commandments of the Most High (28, 2–7). And they must avoid quarrels and strife (8–11).

j 1 Pt 1, 7. k Mt 7, 20. l Sir 23, 9–15. m Prv 11, 13; 20, 19. n Sir 22, 20. o Prv 26, 24ff. p Prv 6, 13. 16. q 25f: Ps 7, 16f; Prv 26, 27: Eccl 10, 8. r Dt 32, 35; Rom 12, 19. s Mt 6, 14.

3 Should a man nourish anger against his fellows
and expect healing from the LORD? [t]
4 Should a man refuse mercy to his fellows,
yet seek pardon for his own sins?
5 If he who is but flesh cherishes wrath,
who will forgive his sins?
6 Remember your last days, set enmity aside;
remember death and decay, and cease from sin! [u]
7 Think of the commandments, hate not your neighbor;
of the Most High's covenant, and overlook faults.
8 Avoid strife and your sins will be fewer,
for a quarrelsome man kindles disputes,
9 Commits the sin of disrupting friendship
and sows discord among those at peace. [v]
10 The more wood, the greater the fire, [w]
the more underlying it, the fiercer the fight;
The greater a man's strength, the sterner his anger,
the greater his power, the greater his wrath.
11 Pitch and resin make fires flare up,
and insistent quarrels provoke bloodshed.

The Evil Tongue*

12 If you blow upon a spark, it quickens into flame,
if you spit on it, it dies out;
yet both you do with your mouth!
13 Cursed be gossips and the double-tongued,
for they destroy the peace of many. [x]
14 A meddlesome tongue subverts many,
and makes them refugees among the peoples;
It destroys walled cities,
and overthrows powerful dynasties.
15 A meddlesome tongue can drive virtuous women from their homes
and rob them of the fruit of their toil;
16 Whoever heeds it has no rest,
nor can he dwell in peace.

17 A blow from a whip raises a welt,
but a blow from the tongue smashes bones;
18 Many have fallen by the edge of the sword,
but not as many as by the tongue. [y]
19 Happy he who is sheltered from it,
and has not endured its wrath;
Who has not borne its yoke
nor been fettered with its chains;
20 For its yoke is a yoke of iron
and its chains are chains of bronze!
21 Dire is the death it inflicts,
besides which even the nether world is a gain;
22 It will not take hold among the just
nor scorch them in its flame,
23 But those who forsake the LORD will fall victims to it,
as it burns among them unquenchably!
It will hurl itself against them like a lion;
like a panther, it will tear them to pieces.
24 As you hedge round your vineyard with thorns,
set barred doors over your mouth; [z]
25 As you seal up your silver and gold,
so balance and weigh your words.
26 Take care not to slip by your tongue
and fall victim to your foe waiting in ambush.

CHAPTER 29

Loans, Alms and Surety*

1 He does a kindness who lends to his neighbor,
and he fulfills the precepts who holds out a helping hand. [a]
2 Lend to your neighbor in his hour of need,

28, 12–26: Further treatment of sins of the tongue and their havoc; cf Sir 5, 12—6, 1; 19, 5–16; 20, 17–25; 23, 7–15. Gossips and the double-tongued destroy domestic peace (12–16). The whip, the sword, chains, even the nether world, are not so cruel as the suffering inflicted by an evil tongue (17–21). Not the just but those who forsake the Lord are victims of their evil tongues (22f). Therefore, guard your mouth and tongue as you would guard treasure against an enemy (24ff).

29, 1–20: Some practical maxims concerning the use of wealth. Give to a poor man (8f), lend to a needy neighbor, but repay when a loan falls due lest the lender's burden be increased (1–5) and his kindness abused (6f); through charity build up defense against evil (10–13). Go surety for your neighbor according to your means, but take care (20) not to fall, for the shameless play false and bring their protectors and themselves to misfortune and ruin (14–19).

t Mt 18, 23ff. u Sir 7, 36; 38, 20. v Prv 15, 18. w 10ff: Prv 26, 20f. x Sir 5, 16f. y Jas 3, 5ff. z Sir 22, 27; Ps 141, 3. a Dt 15, 8; Ps 112, 5; Prv 19, 17.

and pay back your neighbor when a loan
falls due; [b]
3 Keep your promise, be honest with him,
and you will always come by what you
need.
4 Many a man who asks for a loan
adds to the burdens of those who help him;
5 When he borrows, he kisses the lender's hand
and speaks with respect of his creditor's
wealth;
But when payment is due he disappoints him
and says he is helpless to meet the claim.
6 If the lender is able to recover barely half,
he considers this an achievement;
If not, he is cheated of his wealth
and acquires an enemy at no extra charge;
With curses and insults the borrower pays him
back,
with abuse instead of honor.
7 Many refuse to lend, not out of meanness,
but from fear of being cheated.

8 To a poor man, however, be generous;
keep him not waiting for your alms;
9 Because of the precept, help the needy,
and in their want, do not send them away
empty-handed. [c]

10 Spend your money for your brother and friend,
and hide it not under a stone to
perish;
11 Dispose of your treasure as the Most High
commands,
for that will profit you more than the
gold. [d]
12 Store up almsgiving in your treasure house,
and it will save you from every evil;
13 Better than a stout shield and a sturdy spear
it will fight for you against the foe.

14 A good man goes surety for his neighbor,
and only the shameless would play him
false; [e]
15 Forget not the kindness of your backer,
for he offers his very life for you.
16 The wicked turn a pledge on their behalf into
misfortune,
and the ingrate abandons his protector;
17 Going surety has ruined many prosperous men
and tossed them about like waves of the
sea, [f]
18 Has exiled men of prominence
and sent them wandering through foreign
lands.
19 The sinner through surety comes to grief,
and he who undertakes too much falls into
lawsuits.
20 Go surety for your neighbor according to your
means,
but take care lest you fall thereby.

Frugality and Its Rewards*

21 Life's prime needs are water, bread, and
clothing,
a house, too, for decent privacy. [g]
22 Better a poor man's fare under the shadow of
one's own roof
than sumptuous banquets among
strangers. [h]
23 Be it little or much, be content with what you
have,
and pay no heed to him who would
disparage your home;
24 A miserable life it is to go from house to
house,
for as a guest you dare not open your
mouth.
25 The visitor has no thanks for filling the cups;
besides, you will hear these bitter
words:
26 "Come here, stranger, set the table,
give me to eat the food you have!
27 Away, stranger, for one more worthy;
for my brother's visit I need the room!"
28 Painful things to a sensitive man
are abuse at home and insults from his
creditors.

29, 21–28: The man who provides his own basic needs of food, clothing and dwelling, and is content with what he has, preserves his freedom and self-respect (21ff). But if he lives as a guest, even among the rich, he exposes himself to insult and abuse (24–28).

b Ex 22, 24ff; Lv 25, 36; Mt 5, 42. c Sir 4, 1ff; Lv 19, 9f; 23, 22; Dt 15, 8. d Sir 17, 17; Tb 4, 7ff. e Sir 8, 13. f Prv 6, 1f; 11, 15. g Sir 39, 26. h Sir 40, 29.

CHAPTER 30

The Training of Children*

1 He who loves his son chastises him often,
that he may be his joy when he grows up. [i]
2 He who disciplines his son will benefit from him,
and boast of him among his intimates.
3 He who educates his son makes his enemy jealous,
and shows his delight in him among his friends.
4 At the father's death, he will seem not dead,
since he leaves after him one like himself,
5 Whom he looks upon through life with joy,
and even in death, without regret:
6 The avenger he leaves against his foes,
and the one to repay his friends with kindness.

7 He who spoils his son will have wounds to bandage,
and will quake inwardly at every outcry.
8 A colt untamed turns out stubborn;
a son left to himself grows up unruly.
9 Pamper your child and he will be a terror for you,
indulge him and he will bring you grief.
10 Share not in his frivolity lest you share in his sorrow,
when finally your teeth are clenched in remorse.
11 Give him not his own way in his youth,
and close not your eyes to his follies.
12 Bend him to the yoke when he is young,
thrash his sides while he is still small,
Lest he become stubborn, disobey you,
and leave you disconsolate. [j]
13 Discipline your son, make heavy his yoke,
lest his folly humiliate you.

Health of Soul and Body*

14 Better a poor man strong and robust,
than a rich man with wasted frame.
15 More precious than gold is health and well-being,
contentment of spirit than coral.
16 No treasure greater than a healthy body;
no happiness, than a joyful heart!
17 Preferable is death to a bitter life, [k]
unending sleep to constant illness.*
18 Dainties set before one who cannot eat
are like the offerings placed before a tomb. [l]
19 What good is an offering to an idol
that can neither taste nor smell?
20 So it is with the afflicted man
who groans at the good things his eyes behold!

21 Do not give in to sadness,
torment not yourself with brooding; [m]
22 Gladness of heart is the very life of man,
cheerfulness prolongs his days.
23 Distract yourself, renew your courage,
drive resentment far away from you;
For worry has brought death to many,
nor is there aught to be gained from resentment. [n]
24 Envy and anger shorten one's life,
worry brings on premature old age.
25 One who is cheerful and gay while at table
benefits from his food. [o]

CHAPTER 31

The Proper Attitude toward Riches*

1 Keeping watch over riches wastes the flesh,
and the care of wealth drives away rest.

30, 1-13: Sound discipline and careful education of children correct frivolity and stubbornness, prevent remorse and humiliation, and bring to parents lasting joy and delight, prestige among friends, jealousy of enemies, perpetuation and vindication of themselves through their offspring (1–6). Lack of discipline and overindulgence of children bring sorrow and disappointment, terror and grief (7–13).

30, 14-25: Health of mind and body and joy of heart are judged more precious than wealth (14ff); bitterness, constant illness and affliction more difficult to bear than death (17–20). Sadness, resentment, anxiety, envy and anger shorten . . . life; they should be dispelled by cheerfulness and gladness of heart, which help to prolong one's days (21–25).

30, 17: Preferable is death . . . constant illness: the true value of human suffering was revealed through the passion and death of Christ. It serves as reparation for sin, and when united with Christ's suffering, as merit for eternal life.

31, 1-11: Solicitude for acquiring wealth and anxiety over preserving it disturb repose and easily lead to sin and ruin (1–7). Cf Mt 6, 25–34. A rich man who has not sinned or been seduced by wealth is worthy of praise (8–11).

i Prv 13, 24; 23, 13; 29, 15; Heb 12, 7. j Sir 7, 23. k Sir 41, 2. l Tb 4, 17. m Sir 38, 20; Prv 12, 25; 15, 13; 17, 22. n Sir 38, 18f. o Prv 15, 15.

2 Concern for one's livelihood banishes slumber;
more than a serious illness it disturbs repose.*
3 The rich man labors to pile up wealth,
and his only rest is wanton pleasure;
4 The poor man toils for a meager subsistence,
and if ever he rests, he finds himself in want.
5 The lover of gold will not be free from sin,
for he who pursues wealth is led astray by it.
6 Many have been ensnared by gold,
though destruction lay before their eyes; [p]
7 It is a stumbling block to those who are avid for it,
a snare for every fool.
8 Happy the rich man found without fault,*
who turns not aside after gain! [q]
9 Who is he, that we may praise him?
he, of all his kindred, has done wonders,
10 For he has been tested by gold and come off safe,
and this remains his glory;
He could have sinned but did not,
could have done evil but would not,
11 So that his possessions are secure,
and the assembly recounts his praises. [r]

Table Etiquette*

12 If you are dining with a great man,
bring not a greedy gullet to his table,
Nor cry out, "How much food there is here!"
13 Remember that gluttony is evil.
No creature is greedier than the eye:
therefore it weeps for any cause. [s]
15 Recognize that your neighbor feels as you do,
and keep in mind your own dislikes:
14 Toward what he eyes, do not put out a hand;
nor reach when he does for the same dish.
16 Behave at table like a favored guest,
and be not greedy, lest you be despised.
17 Be the first to stop, as befits good manners;
gorge not yourself, lest you give offense. [t]
18 If there are many with you at table,
be not the first to reach out your hand.
19 Does not a little suffice for a well-bred man?
When he lies down, it is without discomfort. [u]
20 Distress and anguish and loss of sleep,
and restless tossing for the glutton!
Moderate eating ensures sound slumber
and a clear mind next day on rising.
21 If perforce you have eaten too much,
once you have emptied your stomach,* you will have relief.
22 Listen to me, my son, and scorn me not;
later you will find my advice good.
In whatever you do, be moderate,
and no sickness will befall you.
23 On a man generous with food, blessings are invoked,
and this testimony to his goodness is lasting; [v]
24 He who is miserly with food is denounced in public,
and this testimony to his stinginess is lasting.
25 Let not wine-drinking be the proof of your strength,
for wine has been the ruin of many.
26 As the furnace probes the work of the smith,
so does wine the hearts of the insolent.
27 Wine is very life to man
if taken in moderation.
Does he really live who lacks the wine
which was created for his joy? [w]
28 Joy of heart, good cheer and merriment
are wine drunk freely at the proper time.
29 Headache, bitterness and disgrace

31, 2: The Hebrew adds a verse that seems out of place here: "A faithful comrade drives away reproach, and the friend who keeps secrets is as dear as life."

31, 8ff: The church in her liturgy applies this passage to holy confessors of the Faith.

31, 12—32, 13: A man observing etiquette at table avoids greed and selfishness (31, 12f), is considerate of a neighbor's likes and dislikes and generous toward him (14f. 23f), observes proper manners (16ff), is moderate in eating and drinking (19–22. 25–30). A good host makes himself one with his guests, is solicitous for them (32, 1f), provides conversation and diversion (3–6), is modest in speech (7f. 10), is respectful of elders (9), polite in comportment and grateful to God for his favors (11ff).

31, 21: Emptied your stomach: the practice of induced vomiting, well-known among pagan Romans, and less well-known among the Jews, seems to be referred to here.

p Sir 8, 2. q Sir 5, 1. 10. r Prv 29, 14. s Sir 37, 28ff; Prv 23, 1f. t Sir 37, 29. u Eccl 5, 11. v Prv 22, 9. w Ps 104, 15; 1 Tm 5, 23.

is wine drunk amid anger and strife.
30 More and more wine is a snare for the fool;
it lessens his strength and multiplies his wounds.
31 Rebuke not your neighbor when wine is served,
nor put him to shame while he is merry;
Use no harsh words with him
and distress him not in the presence of others.

CHAPTER 32

1 If you are chosen to preside at dinner, be not puffed up,
but with the guests be as one of themselves;
Take care of them first before you sit down;
2 when you have fulfilled your duty, then take your place,
To share in their joy
and win praise for your hospitality.
3 Being older, you may talk; that is only your right,
but temper your wisdom, not to disturb the singing.
4 When wine is present, do not pour out discourse,
and flaunt not your wisdom at the wrong time.
5 Like a seal of carnelian in a setting of gold
is a concert when wine is served.
6 Like a gold mounting with an emerald seal
is string music with delicious wine.
7 Young man, speak only when necessary,[x]
when they have asked you more than once;
8 Be brief, but say much in those few words,
be like the wise man, taciturn.
9 When among your elders be not forward,
and with officials be not too insistent.
10 Like the lightning that flashes before a storm
is the esteem that shines on modesty.
11 When it is time to leave, tarry not;
be off for home! There take your ease,
12 And there enjoy doing as you wish,
but without sin or words of pride.
13 Above all, give praise to your Creator,
who showers his favors upon you.

The Providence of God

14 He who would find God must accept discipline;*
he who seeks him obtains his request.[y]
15 He who studies the law masters it,
but the hypocrite finds it a trap.[z]
16 His judgment is sound who fears the LORD;
out of obscurity he draws forth a clear plan.[a]
17 The sinner turns aside reproof
and distorts the law to suit his purpose.[b]
18 The thoughtful man will not neglect direction;
the proud and insolent man is deterred by nothing.
19 Do nothing without counsel,
and then you need have no regrets.[c]
20 Go not on a way that is set with snares,
and let not the same thing trip you twice.
21 Be not too sure even of smooth roads,
22 be careful on all your paths.
23 Whatever you do, be on your guard,
for in this way you will keep the commandments.
24 He who keeps the law preserves himself;
and he who trusts in the LORD shall not be put to shame.

CHAPTER 33

1 No evil can harm the man who fears the LORD;
through trials, again and again he is safe.[d]
2 He who hates the law is without wisdom,
and is tossed about like a boat in a storm.
3 The prudent man trusts in the word of the LORD,
and the law is dependable for him as a divine oracle.*
4 Prepare your words and you will be listened to;

32, 14—33, 4: God is shown to reveal himself through the discipline of his law, a clear and safe plan of life for the pious Jew of old. Direction and counsel are aids in following it (14ff. 18–24; 33, 1. 3f). Sinners and hypocrites, hating the law or distorting it, fail in wisdom and are devoid of security (32, 15. 17f; 33, 2).

33, 3: Oracle: as the answer given through the Urim and Thummim to the high priest is true, so the law proves itself true to him who obeys it. Cf Ex 28, 30; Nm 27, 21.

x 7ff: Sir 7, 14. y Sir 4, 13. z Sir 2, 16. a Ps 37, 6. b Sir 21, 6; Prv 12, 1. c Sir 37, 16; Tb 4, 18. d Ps 91, 10.

draw upon your training, and then give
your answer.
5 Like the wheel of a cart is the mind of a fool;*
his thoughts revolve in circles.
6 A fickle friend is like the stallion
that neighs, no matter who the rider.
7 Why is one day more important than another,
when it is the sun that lights up every day?
8 It is due to the LORD's wisdom that they
differ;
it is through him the seasons and feasts
come and go. [e]
9 Some he dignifies and sanctifies,
and others he lists as ordinary days.[f]
10 So too, all men are of clay,
for from earth man was formed; [g]
11 Yet with his great knowledge the LORD makes
men unlike;
in different paths he has them walk.
12 Some he blesses and makes great,
some he sanctifies and draws to himself.
Others he curses and brings low,
and expels them from their place.
13 Like clay in the hands of a potter,
to be molded according to his pleasure,
So are men in the hands of their Creator,
to be assigned by him their function. [h]
14 As evil contrasts with good, and death with
life,
so are sinners in contrast with the just; [i]
15 See now all the works of the Most High:
they come in pairs, the one the opposite of
the other.

16 Now I am the last to keep vigil,*
like a gleaner after the vintage;
17 Since by the LORD's blessing I have made
progress
till like a vintager I have filled my
winepress,
18 I would inform you that not for myself only
have I toiled,
but for every seeker after wisdom.

Property and Servants*

19 Listen to me, O leaders of the multitude;
O rulers of the assembly, give ear! [j]
20 Let neither son nor wife, neither brother nor
friend,
have power over you as long as you live.
21 While breath of life is still in you,
let no man have dominion over you.
Give not to another your wealth,
lest then you have to plead with him;
22 Far better that your children plead with you
than that you should look to their
generosity.
23 Keep control over all your affairs;
let no one tarnish your glory.
24 When your few days reach their limit,
at the time of death distribute your
inheritance.

25 Fodder and whip and loads for an ass;
the yoke and harness and the rod of his
master.
27 Food, correction and work for a slave;
and for a wicked slave, punishment in the
stocks.
26 Make a slave work and he will look for his
rest;
let his hands be idle and he will seek to be
free. [k]
28 Force him to work that he be not idle,
for idleness is an apt teacher of mischief.
29 Put him to work, for that is what befits him;
if he becomes unruly, load him with chains.
30 But never lord it over any human being,
and do nothing unjust.
31 If you have but one slave, treat him like
yourself,

33, 5–15: Contrasts observable in the physical universe as well as in the moral order serve the purposes of divine wisdom (5–9). All creatures are like clay . . . in the hands of their Creator—the fool and the wise man, the sinner, and the just (10–15). This does not imply that man is created to be a sinner: God is not the author of wickedness. Cf Jas 1, 13f.

33, 16ff: Here the author refers to himself as the most recent of the writers who have endeavored to present true wisdom to their readers.

33, 19–33: Public officials should reject every influence that would restrict their freedom in the management of their affairs. They must make their own household subservient to them rather than be subservient to it (19–24). Slaves are to be given food and work and correction but never to be treated unjustly (25–29). Great care should be taken of good slaves (30–33).

e Gn 1, 14. f Ex 20, 11. g Gn 2, 7. h Wis 15, 7; Jer 18, 1–6; Rom 9, 20f. i Sir 42, 25. j Wis 6, 1f. k Prv 29, 19.

for you have acquired him with your life's
blood; [l]
32 If you have but one slave, deal with him as a
brother,
for you need him as you need your life:
33 If you mistreat him and he runs away,
in what direction will you look for
him?

CHAPTER 34

Trust in the Lord and Not in Dreams*

1 Empty and false are the hopes of the senseless,
and fools are borne aloft by dreams.
2 Like a man who catches at shadows or chases
the wind,
is the one who believes in dreams.
3 What is seen in dreams is to reality
what the reflection of a face is to the face
itself.
4 Can the unclean produce the clean?
can the liar ever speak the truth? [m]
5 Divination, omens and dreams all are unreal;
what you already expect, the mind depicts.
6 Unless it be a vision specially sent by the Most
High,
fix not your heart on it;
7 For dreams have led many astray,
and those who believed in them have
perished.
8 The law is fulfilled without fail,
and perfect wisdom is found in the mouth
of the faithful man.
9 A man with training gains wide knowledge;
a man of experience speaks sense.
10 One never put to the proof knows little,
whereas with travel a man adds to his
resourcefulness.
11 I have seen much in my travels,
learned more than ever I could say.
12 Often I was in danger of death,
but by these attainments I was saved.
13 Lively is the courage of those who fear the
LORD,
for they put their hope in their savior;
14 He who fears the LORD is never alarmed,
never afraid; for the LORD is his hope. [n]
15 Happy the soul that fears the LORD!
In whom does he trust, and who is his
support?
16 The eyes of the LORD are upon those who love
him;
he is their mighty shield and strong support,
A shelter from the heat, a shade from the
noonday sun,
a guard against stumbling, a help against
falling. [o]
17 He buoys up the spirits, brings a sparkle to the
eyes,
gives health and life and blessing.

True Worship of God*

18 Tainted his gifts who offers in sacrifice
ill-gotten goods!
Mock presents from the lawless win not
God's favor. [p]
19 The Most High approves not the gifts of the
godless,
nor for their many sacrifices does he forgive
their sins.
20 Like the man who slays a son in his father's
presence
is he who offers sacrifice from the
possessions of the poor.
21 The bread of charity is life itself for the
needy; [q]
he who withholds it is a man of blood.
22 He slays his neighbor who deprives him of his
living;
he sheds blood who denies the laborer his
wages.
23 If one man builds up and another tears down,
what do they gain but trouble?
24 If one man prays and another curses,

34, 1–17: Confidence placed in dreams, divinations and omens is false because these are devoid of reality (1–8). True confidence is founded on knowledge and experience (9–12), and above all on the fear of the Lord, with its accompanying blessings of divine assistance and protection (13–17).

34, 18–26: To be acts of true religion, sacrifice and penance must be accompanied by the proper moral dispositions. To offer to God goods taken from the poor (18–22), or to practice penance without interior reform, is a mockery, worthless in the sight of God (23–26). Cf Mt 15, 4–7; Mk 7, 9–13.

l Sir 7, 21. m Jb 14, 4. n Pss 23, 4; 112, 7f; Prv 3, 23ff; 28, 1. o Pss 33, 18; 34, 16. p Sir 35, 11; Prv 21, 27. q 21f: Lv 19, 13; Dt 24, 14f; Tb 4, 14.

whose voice will the LORD hear?
25 If a man again touches a corpse after he has bathed,
what did he gain by the purification? [r]
26 So with a man who fasts for his sins,
but then goes and commits them again:
Who will hear his prayer,
and what has he gained by his mortification?

CHAPTER 35*

1 To keep the law is a great oblation, [s]
and he who observes the commandments sacrifices a peace offering.
2 In works of charity one offers fine flour,*
and when he gives alms he presents his sacrifice of praise.
3 To refrain from evil pleases the LORD,
and to avoid injustice is an atonement.
4 Appear not before the LORD empty-handed,
for all that you offer is in fulfillment of the precepts. [t]
5 The just man's offering enriches the altar
and rises as a sweet odor before the Most High.
6 The just man's sacrifice is most pleasing,
nor will it ever be forgotten.
7 In generous spirit pay homage to the LORD,
be not sparing of freewill gifts. [u]
8 With each contribution show a cheerful countenance,
and pay your tithes in a spirit of joy. [v]
9 Give to the Most High as he has given to you,
generously, according to your means.

10 For the LORD is one who always repays,
and he will give back to you sevenfold. [w]
11 But offer no bribes, these he does not accept!
Trust not in sacrifice of the fruits of extortion, [x]
12 For he is a God of justice,
who knows no favorites. [y]
13 Though not unduly partial toward the weak,
yet he hears the cry of the oppressed.*
14 He is not deaf to the wail of the orphan, [z]
nor to the widow when she pours out her complaint;

15 Do not the tears that stream down her cheek
cry out against him that causes them to fall?
16 He who serves God willingly is heard;
his petition reaches the heavens.
17 The prayer of the lowly pierces the clouds;
it does not rest till it reaches its goal,
18 Nor will it withdraw till the Most High responds,
judges justly and affirms the right.

19 God indeed will not delay,
and like a warrior, will not be still [a]
20 Till he breaks the backs of the merciless
and wreaks vengeance upon the proud;
21 Till he destroys the haughty root and branch,
and smashes the scepter of the wicked;
22 Till he requites mankind according to its deeds,
and repays men according to their thoughts;
23 Till he defends the cause of his people,
and gladdens them by his mercy.
24 Welcome is his mercy in time of distress
as rain clouds in time of drought.

CHAPTER 36

A Prayer for God's People*

1 Come to our aid, O God of the universe,
and put all the nations in dread of you!
2 Raise your hand against the heathen,
that they may realize your power.
3 As you have used us to show them your holiness,

35, 1–24: Keeping the commandments of the law and avoiding injustice constitute sacrifice pleasing and acceptable to God (1ff). Offerings also should be made to him, cheerfully and generously; these he repays . . . sevenfold (4–10). Extortion from widows and orphans is injustice, which God quickly repays (11–18). Punishing the proud and the merciless and coming to the aid of the distressed, he requites all according to their deeds (19–24).

35, 2: Fine flour, together with oil and frankincense, was a prescribed offering to God; cf Lv 2, 1ff.

35, 13: Cf Lv 19, 15.

36, 1–17: Making an act of faith and hope in the supreme Lord of the universe, the author begs God to continue manifesting his holiness and mercy through Israel, his people (1ff. 10–13), and his power and justice through the punishment of the nations (2. 5–9), that all the earth may acknowledge him the eternal God (4. 14–17).

r Nm 19, 11f; Prv 26, 11; 2 Pt 2, 22. s 1ff: 1 Sm 15, 22; Ps 51, 18f; Is 1, 11–18; Hos 6, 6; Am 5, 21–24. t Ex 23, 15; 34, 20; Dt 16, 16. u Sir 7, 31. v 2 Cor 9, 7. w Prv 19, 17. x Sir 34, 18f; Prv 21, 27. y Dt 10, 17; 2 Chr 19, 7; Jb 34, 19; Wis 6, 7; Acts 10, 34; Rom 2, 11; Gal 2, 6; 1 Pt 1, 17. z 14f: Ex 22, 22. a Is 42, 13ff: 2 Pt 3, 9.

so now use them to show us your glory.
4 Thus they will know, as we know,
that there is no God but you.

5 Give new signs and work new wonders;
show forth the splendor of your right hand
and arm;
6 Rouse your anger, pour out wrath,
humble the enemy, scatter the foe. [b]
7 Hasten the day, bring on the time;
9 crush the heads of the hostile rulers.
8 Let raging fire consume the fugitive,
and your people's oppressors meet
destruction.
10 Gather all the tribes of Jacob,
that they may inherit the land as of old.
11 Show mercy to the people called by your
name;
Israel, whom you named your first-born. [c]
12 Take pity on your holy city,
Jerusalem, your dwelling place. [d]
13 Fill Zion with your majesty,
your temple with your glory.

14 Give evidence of your deeds of old;
fulfill the prophecies spoken in your name,
15 Reward those who have hoped in you,
and let your prophets be proved true.
16 Hear the prayer of your servants,
for you are ever gracious to your people;
17 Thus it will be known to the very ends of the
earth
that you are the eternal God.

Choice of Associates*

18 The throat can swallow any food,
yet some foods are more agreeable than
others;
19 As the palate tests meat by its savor,
so does a keen mind insincere words.
20 A deceitful character causes grief,
but an experienced man can turn the tables
on him.
21 Though any man may be accepted as a
husband,
yet one girl will be more suitable than
another:
22 A woman's beauty makes her husband's face
light up,
for it surpasses all else that charms the eye; [e]
23 And if, besides, her speech is kindly,
his lot is beyond that of mortal men.
24 A wife is her husband's richest treasure,
a helpmate, a steadying column. [f]
25 A vineyard with no hedge will be overrun;
a man with no wife becomes a homeless
wanderer.
26 Who will trust an armed band
that shifts from city to city?
27 Or a man who has no nest,
but lodges where night overtakes him? [g]

CHAPTER 37

1 Every friend declares his friendship,
but there are friends who are friends in
name only. [h]
2 Is it not a sorrow unto death
when your bosom companion becomes
your enemy?
3 "Alas, my companion! Why were you created
to blanket the earth with deceit?"
4 A false friend will share your joys,
but in time of trouble he stands afar off.
5 A true friend will fight with you against the
foe,
against your enemies he will be your
shield-bearer.
6 Forget not your comrade during the battle,
and neglect him not when you distribute
your spoils.

7 Every counselor points out a way,
but some counsel ways of their own;
8 Be on the alert when one proffers advice,
find out first of all what he wants.

36, 18—37, 15: In the choice of wife, friend or associate, experience is a discerner of character (18–21). Beauty and kindly speech make a woman desirable as wife (22f). The good wife becomes her husband's richest treasure, his helpmate in establishing his household (24–27). A true friend fights for his comrade and shares his spoils with him (37, 5f); a false one deceives and abandons him in time of need (1–4). A true counselor and associate should be sought among those who keep the commandments, not among those who break them and seek their own advantage (7–12). In all things pray to God for light and follow conscience (13ff).

b Ps 79, 6. c Ex 4, 22. d 2 Chr 6, 41; Ps 132, 8. 14; Is 2, 1ff; Mi 4, 1ff. e Sir 26, 13ff. f Gn 2, 18; Prv 18, 22. g Prv 27, 8. h Sir 6, 7ff.

For he may be thinking of himself alone;
why should the profit fall to him?
9 He may tell you how good your way will be,
and then stand by to watch your misfortune.
10 Seek no advice from one who regards you with hostility;
from those who envy you, keep your intentions hidden.
11 Speak not to a woman about her rival,
nor to a coward about war,
to a merchant about business,
to a buyer about value,
to a miser about generosity,
to a cruel man about mercy,
to a lazy man about work,
to a seasonal laborer about the harvest,
to an idle slave about a great task:
pay no attention to any advice they give.
12 Instead, associate with a religious man,
who you are sure keeps the commandments;
Who is like-minded with yourself
and will feel for you if you fall.
13 Then, too, heed your own heart's counsel;
for what have you that you can depend on more?
14 A man's conscience can tell him his situation
better than seven watchmen in a lofty tower.
15 Most important of all, pray to God
to set your feet in the path of truth.

Wisdom and Temperance

16 A word is the source of every deed;*
a thought, of every act. [i]
17 The root of all conduct is the mind;
four branches it shoots forth:
18 Good and evil, death and life,
their absolute mistress is the tongue. [j]
19 A man may be wise and benefit many,
yet be of no use to himself.
20 Though a man may be wise, if his words are rejected
he will be deprived of all enjoyment.
21 When a man is wise to his own advantage,
the fruits of his knowledge are seen in his own person;
22 When a man is wise to his people's advantage,
the fruits of his knowledge are enduring: [k]
23 Limited are the days of one man's life,
but the life of Israel is days without number.
24 One wise for himself has full enjoyment,
and all who see him praise him;
25 One wise for his people wins a heritage of glory,
and his name endures forever. [l]

26 My son, while you are well, govern your appetite*
so that you allow it not what is bad for you;
27 For not every food is good for everyone,
nor is everything suited to every taste. [m]
28 Be not drawn after every enjoyment, [n]
neither become a glutton for choice foods,
29 For sickness comes with overeating,
and gluttony brings on biliousness.
30 Through lack of self-control many have died,
but the abstemious man prolongs his life.

CHAPTER 38

Sickness and Death

1 Hold the physician in honor, for he is essential to you,*
and God it was who established his profession.
2 From God the doctor has his wisdom,
and the king provides for his sustenance.
3 His knowledge makes the doctor distinguished,

37, 16–25: Thoughts determine action. Wisdom is the source of good and life; folly, of evil and death (16ff). If the fruits of a man's wisdom benefit himself, he may be praised in his own lifetime; if they benefit his people, his praise endures after him, in their lives (19–25).

37, 26–30: Temperance and self-control should govern a man's appetite for food, which is intended not to destroy but to preserve life.

38, 1–15: The profession of medicine comes from God, who makes the earth yield healing herbs and gives the physician knowledge of their virtue (1–8). In illness the sick man should cleanse his soul from sin and petition God for help through an offering of sacrifice; the physician, too, does well to invoke God that he may understand the illness and apply the proper remedy (9–14). The sinner, in contrast, defies both his Maker and the doctor (15).

i Sir 32, 19. j Prv 18, 21. k Sir 15, 1ff. l Sir 39, 9; 44, 13f. m 1 Cor 6, 12; 10, 23. n 28f: Sir 31, 13. 16ff.

and gives him access to those in authority.
[4]God makes the earth yield healing herbs
which the prudent man should not neglect;
[5]Was not the water sweetened by a twig
that men might learn his power? [o]
[6]He endows men with the knowledge
to glory in his mighty works,
[7]Through which the doctor eases pain
and the druggist prepares his medicines;
[8]Thus God's creative work continues without cease
in its efficacy on the surface of the earth.

[9]My son, when you are ill, delay not,
but pray to God, who will heal you: [p]
[10]Flee wickedness; let your hands be just,
cleanse your heart of every sin;
[11]Offer your sweet-smelling oblation and petition,
a rich offering according to your means. [q]
[12]Then give the doctor his place
lest he leave; for you need him too.
[13]There are times that give him an advantage,
[14]and he too beseeches God
That his diagnosis may be correct
and his treatment bring about a cure.
[15]He who is a sinner toward his Maker
will be defiant toward the doctor.

[16]My son, shed tears for one who is dead*
with wailing and bitter lament;
As is only proper, prepare the body,
absent not yourself from his burial: [r]
[17]Weeping bitterly, mourning fully,
pay your tribute of sorrow, as he deserves,
[18]One or two days, to prevent gossip;
then compose yourself after your grief,
[19]For grief can bring on an extremity
and heartache destroy one's health. [s]
[20]Turn not your thoughts to him again;
cease to recall him; think rather of the end. [t]
[21]Recall him not, for there is no hope of his return;
it will not help him, but will do you harm. [u]
[22]Remember that his fate will also be yours;
for him it was yesterday, for you today. [v]
[23]With the departed dead, let memory fade;
rally your courage, once the soul has left.

Vocations of the Craftsman and the Scribe*

[24]The scribe's profession increases his wisdom;
whoever is free from toil can become a wise man.
[25]How can he become learned who guides the plow,
who thrills in wielding the goad like a lance,
Who guides the ox and urges on the bullock,
and whose every concern is for cattle?
[26]His care is for plowing furrows,
and he keeps a watch on the beasts in the stalls.

[27]So with every engraver and designer
who, laboring night and day,
Fashions carved seals,
and whose concern is to vary the pattern.
His care is to produce a vivid impression,
and he keeps watch till he finishes his design.

[28]So with the smith standing near his anvil,
forging crude iron.
The heat from the fire sears his flesh,
yet he toils away in the furnace heat.
The clang of the hammer deafens his ears,
his eyes are fixed on the tool he is shaping.
His care is to finish his work,
and he keeps watch till he perfects it in detail.

[29]So with the potter sitting at his labor
revolving the wheel with his feet.
He is always concerned for his products,

38, 16–23: A period of mourning for the deceased and care for their burial is becoming (16ff). But grief should not be excessive, for it neither helps the dead, who cannot return, nor fails to harm the living. The mourner's own end will quickly follow, and the time to prepare for it is now (19–23).

38, 24—39, 11: More excellent than the useful service of craftsmen—farmer, engraver, smith, potter (25–34)—is the profession of the scribe (24), who studies and meditates on the law of the Most High, seeks him in prayer of thanksgiving, petition and repentance for sin (39, 1. 6f), explores the wisdom of the past and present, travels abroad to observe the conduct of many peoples, and attends rulers and great men. Through the spirit of understanding granted by God, he will show forth his wisdom to the glory of God's law, gaining renown for generations to come (2–5. 8–11).

o Ex 15, 25. p Is 38, 2f. q Lv 2, 1ff. r Sir 22, 9f. s Prv 12, 25; 15, 13; 17, 22. t Sir 7, 36; 18, 24; 30, 21. u 2 Sm 12, 23; Wis 2, 1. v Jas 4, 13ff.

and turns them out in quantity.
30 With his hands he molds the clay,
and with his feet softens it.
His care is for proper coloring,
and he keeps watch on the fire of his kiln.
31 All these men are skilled with their hands,
each one an expert at his own task;
32 Without them no city could be lived in,
and wherever they stay, they need not hunger.
33 They do not occupy the judge's bench,
nor are they prominent in the assembly;
They set forth no decisions or judgments,
nor are they found among the rulers;
34 Yet they maintain God's ancient handiwork,
and their concern is for exercise of their skill.

CHAPTER 39

1 How different the man who devotes himself
to the study of the law of the Most High!
He explores the wisdom of the men of old
and occupies himself with the prophecies;
2 He treasures the discourses of famous men,
and goes to the heart of involved sayings;
3 He studies obscure parables,
and is busied with the hidden meanings of the sages.
4 He is in attendance on the great,
and has entrance to the ruler.
5 He travels among the peoples of foreign lands
to learn what is good and evil among men.
6 His care is to seek the LORD, his Maker,
to petition the Most High,
To open his lips in prayer,
to ask pardon for his sins.
Then, if it pleases the LORD Almighty,
he will be filled with the spirit of understanding;
He will pour forth his words of wisdom
and in prayer give thanks to the LORD,
7 Who will direct his knowledge and his counsel,
as he meditates upon his mysteries.
8 He will show the wisdom of what he has learned
and glory in the law of the LORD's covenant.
9 Many will praise his understanding;
his fame can never be effaced;
Unfading will be his memory,
through all generations his name will live; [w]
10 Peoples will speak of his wisdom,
and in assembly sing his praises.
11 While he lives he is one out of a thousand,
and when he dies his renown will not cease.

Praise of God the Creator*

12 Once more I will set forth my theme
to shine like the moon in its fullness!
13 Listen, my faithful children: open up your petals,
like roses planted near running waters;
14 Send up the sweet odor of incense,
break forth in blossoms like the lily.
Send up the sweet odor of your hymn of praise;
bless the LORD for all he has done!
15 Proclaim the greatness of his name,
loudly sing his praises,
With music on the harp and all stringed instruments;
sing out with joy as you proclaim:
16 The works of God are all of them good;
in its own time every need is supplied. [x]
17 At his word the waters become still as in a flask;
he had but to speak and the reservoirs were made. [y]
18 He has but to command and his will is done;
nothing can limit his achievement.
19 The works of all mankind are present to him;
not a thing escapes his eye. [z]
20 His gaze spans all the ages;
to him there is nothing unexpected.

39, 12–35: The sage invites his disciples to join him in joyfully proclaiming his favorite theme: The works of God are all of them good; in its own time every need is supplied (12–16. 32–35). He describes God's omniscience, supreme power and wisdom, whereby all created things, good in themselves, are ever present to him, obey him, and fulfill their intended purpose (17–21), bringing blessing to the virtuous, but evil and punishment to the wicked who misuse them (22–31). Cf similar hymns of praise, Sir 36, 1–17; 42, 15—43, 35.

w Sir 37, 25; 44, 14. x Gn 1, 31; Eccl 3, 11. y Gn 1, 6–10; Ex 14, 21f; Jos 3, 16. z Sir 15, 19; 42, 20.

21 No cause then to say: "What is the purpose of
this?"
Everything is chosen to satisfy a need.
22 His blessing overflows like the Nile;
like the Euphrates it enriches the surface of
the earth.
23 Again, his wrath expels the nations
and turns fertile land into a salt marsh. [a]
24 For the virtuous his paths are level,
to the haughty they are steep;
25 Good things for the good he provided from the
beginning,
but for the wicked good things and bad.
26 Chief of all needs for human life
are water and fire, iron and salt,
The heart of the wheat, milk and honey,
the blood of the grape, and oil, and cloth; [b]
27 For the good all these are good,
but for the wicked they turn out evil.
28 There are storm winds created to punish,
which in their fury can dislodge mountains;
When destruction must be, they hurl all their
force
and appease the anger of their Maker.
29 In his treasury also, kept for the proper time,
are fire and hail, famine, disease,
30 Ravenous beasts, scorpions, vipers,
and the avenging sword to exterminate the
wicked;
31 In doing his bidding they rejoice,
in their assignments they disobey not his
command.
32 So from the first I took my stand,
and wrote down as my theme:
33 The works of God are all of them good;
every need when it comes he fills. [c]
34 No cause then to say: "This is not as good as
that";
for each shows its worth at the proper time.
35 So now with full joy of heart proclaim
and bless the name of the Holy One.

CHAPTER 40

Joys and Miseries of Life

1 A great anxiety has God allotted,*
and a heavy yoke, to the sons of men; [d]
From the day one leaves his mother's womb
to the day he returns to the mother of all the
living,*
2 His thoughts, the fear in his heart,
and his troubled forebodings till the day he
dies—
3 Whether he sits on a lofty throne
or grovels in dust and ashes,
4 Whether he bears a splendid crown
or is wrapped in the coarsest of cloaks—
5 Are of wrath and envy, trouble and dread,
terror of death, fury and strife.
Even when he lies on his bed to rest,
his cares at night disturb his sleep.
6 So short is his rest it seems like none,
till in his dreams he struggles as he did by
day,
Terrified by what his mind's eye sees,
like a fugitive being pursued;
7 As he reaches safety, he wakes up
astonished that there was nothing to fear.
8 So it is with all flesh, with man and with beast,
but for sinners seven times more.
9 Plague and bloodshed, wrath and the sword,
plunder and ruin, famine and death: [e]
10 For the wicked, these were created evil,
and it is they who bring on destruction.
11 All that is of earth returns to earth,
and what is from above returns above.*
12 All that comes from bribes or injustice will be
wiped out,

40, 1–16: The former idyllic description of the universe is contrasted with the picture of the evils afflicting humanity. Every man, high or low, is burdened from birth to death with fears, anxieties and troubles, by day and often by night, the time appointed for rest (1–7). For sinners, the suffering is much greater (8ff). What they gained by violence and injustice is quickly destroyed; but justice endures forever (14ff).

40, 1: Mother of all the living: the earth from which man was taken. Cf Gn 2, 7; 3, 19f; Jb 1, 21; Ps 139, 15.

40, 11: All that is of earth . . . returns above: a reference to bodily mortality and to the divine origin of life from the Spirit of God. Cf Sir 41, 10; Gn 2, 7; 3, 19; Jb 34, 14f; Pss 104, 29f; 146, 4; Eccl 12, 7. The Greek and the Latin render the second half of the verse: "all waters shall return to the sea."

a Jos 1, 2–6. b Sir 29, 21. c Sir 39, 16; Gn 1, 31; Eccl 3, 11. d Gn 3, 17; Jb 7, 1; 14, 1; Eccl 2, 23. e Sir 39, 28ff.

but loyalty remains for ages.
13 Wealth out of wickedness is like a wadi in spate:
like a mighty stream with lightning and thunder,
14 Which, in its rising, rolls along the stones,
but suddenly, once and for all, comes to an end.[f]
15 The offshoot of violence will not flourish,
for the root of the godless is on sheer rock;
16 Or they are like reeds on the riverbank,
withered before all other plants.
17 But goodness will never be cut off,
and justice endures forever.

Wealth or wages can make life sweet,*
but better than either is finding a treasure.
18 A child or a city will preserve one's name,
but better than either, attaining wisdom.[g]
19 Sheepfolds and orchards bring flourishing health;
but better than either, a devoted wife;
20 Wine and music delight the soul,
but better than either, conjugal love.[h]
21 The flute and the harp offer sweet melody,
but better than either, a voice that is true.
22 Charm and beauty delight the eye,
but better than either, the flowers of the field.[i]
23 A friend, a neighbor, are timely guides,
but better than either, a prudent wife.
24 A brother, a helper, for times of stress;
but better than either, charity that rescues.
25 Gold and silver make one's way secure,
but better than either, sound judgment.
26 Wealth and vigor build up confidence,
but better than either, fear of God.
Fear of the LORD leaves nothing wanting;
he who has it need seek no other support:
27 The fear of God is a paradise of blessings;
its canopy, all that is glorious.[j]
28 My son, live not the life of a beggar,*
better to die than to beg;
29 When one has to look to another's table,
his life is not really a life.
His neighbor's delicacies bring revulsion of spirit
to one who understands inward feelings:[k]
30 In the mouth of the shameless man begging is sweet,
but within him it burns like fire.

CHAPTER 41

1 O death! how bitter the thought of you*
for the man at peace amid his possessions,
For the man unruffled and always successful,
who still can enjoy life's pleasures.
2 O death! how welcome your sentence
to the weak man of failing strength,
Tottering and always rebuffed,
with no more sight, with vanished hope.[l]
3 Fear not death's decree for you;
remember, it embraces those before you,
and those after.[m]
4 Thus God has ordained for all flesh;
why then should you reject the will of the Most High?
Whether one has lived a thousand years, a hundred, or ten,
in the nether world he has no claim on life.

5 A reprobate line are the children of sinners,[n]
and witless offspring are in the homes of the wicked.
6 Their dominion is lost to sinners' children,
and reproach abides with their descendants.
7 Children curse their wicked father,
for they suffer disgrace through him.
8 Woe to you, O sinful men,
who forsake the law of the Most High.
9 If you have children, calamity will seize them;
you will beget them only for groaning.

40, 17–27: Of the many treasures making life sweet, such as health, children, friends, music, vigor, the best are called true conjugal love, wisdom, and above all, fear of God; cf Sir 25, 6–11.

40, 28ff: Among the Jews, beggary was considered degrading to human dignity; it was agreeable only to the shameless, who had lost their sense of honor. Cf Sir 29, 22f.

41, 1–13: Whether death seems bitter to one who enjoys peace, success and pleasure, or welcome to one who is weak and in despair, it comes to all and must be accepted as the will of God (1–4). As the human body passes away (11), so do those who have sinned through the body and their offspring alike, who, needy and accursed, pass on with their parents as if they had never been (5–10). Only the good name of the virtuous endures (11ff).

f Sir 23, 25; Wis 4, 3ff. g Prv 19, 14. h Ps 104, 15. i Mt 6, 28f. j Is 4, 5. k Sir 29, 24. l Sir 30, 17. m Sir 38, 20ff. n 5ff: Sir 3, 9ff; Wis 3, 16–19.

When you stumble, there is lasting joy;
at death, you become a curse.
10 Whatever is of nought returns to nought,
so too the godless from void to void. [o]
11 Man's body is a fleeting thing,
but a virtuous name will never be annihilated. [p]
12 Have a care for your name, for it will stand by you
better than precious treasures in the thousands; [q]
13 The boon of life is for limited days,
but a good name, for days without number.*

True and False Shame*

14 My children, heed my instruction about shame;
judge of disgrace only according to my rules,
For it is not always well to be ashamed,
nor is it always the proper thing to blush:
15 Before father and mother be ashamed of immorality,
before master and mistress, of falsehood;
16 Before prince and ruler, of flattery;
before the public assembly, of crime;
17 Before friend and companion, of disloyalty,
and of breaking an oath or agreement.
18 Be ashamed of theft from the people where you settle,
and of stretching out your elbow when you dine;
19 Of refusing to give when asked,
of defrauding another of his appointed share,
20 Of failing to return a greeting,
and of rebuffing a friend;
21 Of gazing at a married woman,
and of entertaining thoughts about another's wife; [r]
Of trifling with a servant girl you have,
and of violating her couch;
22 Of using harsh words with friends,
and of following up your gifts with insults; [s]
23 Of repeating what you hear,
and of betraying secrets— [t]
24 These are the things you should rightly avoid as shameful
if you would be looked upon by everyone with favor.

CHAPTER 42

1 But of these things be not ashamed,
lest you sin through human respect: [u]
2 Of the law of the Most High and his precepts,
or of the sentence to be passed upon the sinful;
3 Of sharing the expenses of a business or a journey,
or of dividing an inheritance or property;
4 Of accuracy of scales and balances,
or of tested measures and weights; [v]
5 Of acquiring much or little,
or of bargaining in dealing with a merchant;
Of constant training of children,
or of beating the sides of a disloyal servant; [w]
6 Of a seal to keep an erring wife at home,
or of a lock placed where there are many hands;
7 Of numbering every deposit,
or of recording all that is given or received;
8 Of chastisement of the silly and the foolish,
or of the aged and infirm answering for wanton conduct.
Thus you will be truly cautious
and recognized by all men as discreet.

A Father's Care for His Daughter*

9 A daughter is a treasure that keeps her father wakeful,
and worry over her drives away rest: [x]
Lest she pass her prime unmarried,
or when she is married, lest she be disliked;

41, 13: After this verse many texts repeat Sir 20, 29f.

41, 14—42, 8: The author illustrates the subject of true and false shame with numerous and detailed examples of sin (14–24) and virtue (42, 1–8), following the norm of the commandments.

42, 9–14: The author considers a daughter to be a source of anxiety to her father, lest she fail to marry, or be seduced, or lest, marrying, she be disliked, prove unfaithful, or find herself sterile (9f). He is advised to keep a close watch on her at home, and on her companionship while abroad, lest he suffer on her account among the people (11–14).

o Sir 40, 11; Wis 4, 19. p Prv 10, 7. q Prv 22, 1; Eccl 7, 1. r Sir 9, 8; Mt 5, 28. s Sir 18, 14; 20, 13. t Sir 27, 16. u Prv 24, 23; Jas 2, 1. v Prv 11, 1. w Sir 30, 1–13; 33, 25–33. x Sir 7, 24f.

10 While unmarried, lest she be seduced,
or, as a wife, lest she prove unfaithful;
Lest she conceive in her father's home,
or be sterile in that of her husband.
11 Keep a close watch on your daughter,
lest she make you the sport of your enemies,
A byword in the city, a reproach among the people,
an object of derision in public gatherings.
See that there is no lattice in her room,
no place that overlooks the approaches to the house.[y]
12 Let her not parade her charms before men,[z]
or spend her time with married women;
13 For just as moths come from garments,
so harm to women comes from women:
14 Better a man's harshness than a woman's indulgence,
and a frightened daughter than any disgrace.

The Works of God in Nature*

15 Now will I recall God's works;
what I have seen, I will describe.
At God's word were his works brought into being;
they do his will as he has ordained for them.[a]
16 As the rising sun is clear to all,
so the glory of the LORD fills all his works;
17 Yet even God's holy ones must fail
in recounting the wonders of the LORD,
Though God has given these, his hosts, the strength
to stand firm before his glory.
18 He plumbs the depths and penetrates the heart;
their innermost being he understands.
The Most High possesses all knowledge,
and sees from of old the things that are to come:
19 He makes known the past and the future,
and reveals the deepest secrets.
20 No understanding does he lack;
no single thing escapes him.[b]
21 Perennial is his almighty wisdom;
he is from all eternity one and the same,
22 With nothing added, nothing taken away;
no need of a counselor for him![c]
23 How beautiful are all his works!
even to the spark and fleeting vision!
24 The universe lives and abides forever;
to meet each need, each creature is preserved.
25 All of them differ, one from another,
yet none of them has he made in vain,
For each in turn, as it comes, is good;
can one ever see enough of their splendor?[d]

CHAPTER 43

1 The clear vault of the sky shines forth[e]
like heaven itself, a vision of glory.
2 The orb of the sun, resplendent at its rising:
what a wonderful work of the Most High!
3 At noon it seethes the surface of the earth,
and who can bear its fiery heat?
4 Like a blazing furnace of solid metal,
it sets the mountains aflame with its rays;
By its fiery darts the land is consumed;
the eyes are dazzled by its light.
5 Great indeed is the LORD who made it,
at whose orders it urges on its steeds.
6 The moon, too, that marks the changing times,
governing the seasons, their lasting sign,[f]
7 By which we know the feast days and fixed dates,
this light-giver which wanes in its course:
8 As its name says, each month it renews itself;
how wondrous in this change!
9 The beauty, the glory, of the heavens are the stars
that adorn with their sparkling the heights of God,[g]
10 At whose command they keep their place

42, 15—43, 35: These verses comprise a new section. In them the author contemplates God's power, beauty and goodness as manifested in the mighty work of creating and preserving the universe (42, 15ff. 23. 25; 43, 1–27), his omniscience (42, 18ff), his perfect wisdom (21f), his eternity (24). The conclusion is a fervent hymn of praise (43, 28–35). Cf Sir 16, 22—18, 13.

y Sir 26, 10. z 12f: Sir 9, 1–9. a Ps 77, 12f. b Sir 39, 19; Wis 1, 6–10. c Is 40, 13; Rom 11, 34. d Sir 33, 15. e 1ff: Ps 19, 2f. f Lv 23, 5; Nm 28, 11–14; Ps 81, 4. g Ps 8, 4.

and never relax in their vigils.
A weapon against the flood waters stored on high,
lighting up the firmament by its brilliance,
11 Behold the rainbow! Then bless its Maker,
for majestic indeed is its splendor; [h]
12 It spans the heavens with its glory,
this bow bent by the mighty hand of God.

13 His rebuke marks out the path for the lightning,
and speeds the arrows of his judgment to their goal.
14 At it the storehouse is opened,
and like vultures the clouds hurry forth.
15 In his majesty he gives the storm its power
and breaks off the hailstones.
16 The thunder of his voice makes the earth writhe;
before his might the mountains quake.
17 A word from him drives on the south wind,
the angry north wind, the hurricane and the storm.
18 He sprinkles the snow like fluttering birds;
it comes to settle like swarms of locusts.
19 Its shining whiteness blinds the eyes,
the mind is baffled by its steady fall.
20 He scatters frost like so much salt;
it shines like blossoms on the thornbush.
21 Cold northern blasts he sends
that turn the ponds to lumps of ice.
He freezes over every body of water,
and clothes each pool with a coat of mail.
22 When the mountain growth is scorched with heat,
and the flowering plains as though by flames,
23 The dripping clouds restore them all,
and the scattered dew enriches the parched land.
24 His is the plan that calms the deep,
and plants the islands in the sea.
25 Those who go down to the sea tell part of its story,
and when we hear them we are thunderstruck; [i]
26 In it are his creatures, stupendous, amazing,
all kinds of life, and the monsters of the deep.
27 For him each messenger succeeds,
and at his bidding accomplishes his will. [j]
28 More than this we need not add;
let the last word be, he is all in all!*
29 Let us praise him the more, since we cannot fathom him,
for greater is he than all his works;
30 Awful indeed is the LORD's majesty,
and wonderful is his power.
31 Lift up your voices to glorify the LORD,
though he is still beyond your power to praise;
32 Extol him with renewed strength,
and weary not, though you cannot reach the end:
33 For who can see him and describe him?
or who can praise him as he is? [k]
34 Beyond these, many things lie hid;
only a few of his works have we seen.
35 It is the LORD who has made all things,
and to those who fear him he gives wisdom. [l]

CHAPTER 44

Praise of Israel's Great Ancestors

1 Now will I praise those godly men,*
our ancestors, each in his own time:*
2 The abounding glory of the Most High's portion,
his own part, since the days of old.
Subduers of the land in kingly fashion,
men of renown for their might, [m]

43, 28: All in all: the perfections reflected in creation are found in a transcendent way in God, who alone is their source.

44, 1—50, 24: As in the previous section God's wisdom shone forth in the works of nature, so in these chapters it is also revealed through the history of God's people as seen in the lives of their patriarchs, prophets, priests and rulers. The example of these great men, whose virtues are here recalled, constitutes a high point of the author's teaching and illustrates his belief in the canonical Scriptures.

44, 1–15: The reader is here introduced to those men of Israel, later mentioned by name, who through various achievements and beneficial social activities have acquired great renown (1–8. 14f); and also to those who, though forgotten, endure through the fruit of their virtues and through their families because of God's covenant with them (9–13).

h Gn 9, 13. i Ps 104, 25–30. j Ps 33, 6. k Ps 106, 2. l Jb 28, 28. m Dt 32, 8f.

3 Or counselors in their prudence,
or seers of all things in prophecy; [n]
4 Resolute princes of the folk,
and governors with their staves;
Authors skilled in composition,
and forgers of epigrams with their spikes;
5 Composers of melodious psalms,
or discoursers on lyric themes;
6 Stalwart men, solidly established
and at peace in their own estates—
7 All these were glorious in their time,
each illustrious in his day.
8 Some of them have left behind a name
and men recount their praiseworthy deeds;
9 But of others there is no memory,
for when they ceased, they ceased.
And they are as though they had not lived,
they and their children after them.
10 Yet these also were godly men
whose virtues have not been forgotten;
11 Their wealth remains in their families,
their heritage with their descendants;
12 Through God's covenant with them their family endures,
their posterity for their sake.
13 And for all time their progeny will endure,
their glory will never be blotted out;
14 Their bodies are peacefully laid away,
but their name lives on and on. [o]
15 At gatherings their wisdom is retold,
and the assembly proclaims their praise.

The Early Patriarchs

16 [ENOCH* walked with the LORD and was taken up, [p]
that succeeding generations might learn by his example.]
17 NOAH, found just and perfect,
renewed the race in the time of devastation. [q]
Because of his worth there were survivors,
and with a sign to him the deluge ended;
18 A lasting agreement was made with him,
that never should all flesh be destroyed.
19 ABRAHAM, father of many peoples,
kept his glory without stain: [r]
20 He observed the precepts of the Most High,
and entered into an agreement with him;
In his own flesh he incised the ordinance,*
and when tested he was found loyal. [s]
21 For this reason, God promised him with an oath
that in his descendants the nations would be blessed,
That he would make him numerous as the grains of dust,
and exalt his posterity like the stars;
That he would give them an inheritance from sea to sea,
and from the River* to the ends of the earth.
22 And for ISAAC he renewed the same promise
because of Abraham, his father.
The covenant with all his forebears was confirmed,
and the blessing rested upon the head of JACOB. [t]
23 God acknowledged him as the first-born,
and gave him his inheritance.
He fixed the boundaries for his tribes,
and their division into twelve.

CHAPTER 45

Praise of Moses, Aaron and Phinehas

1 From him was to spring the man*
who won the favor of all: [u]

44, 16: Enoch: because of his friendship with God and also by reason of his unusual disappearance from the earth, this prophet's renown was great among the chosen people, particularly in the two centuries just before the coming of Christ; cf Gn 5, 21–24; Heb 11, 5. The present verse is an expansion of the original text; cf Sir 49, 14.

44, 20: In his own flesh . . . ordinance: the covenant of circumcision; cf Gn 17, 10–14. And when tested . . . loyal: Abraham's willingness to sacrifice his son Isaac at the Lord's command; cf Gn 22, 9–12.

44, 21: The River: the Euphrates; cf Gn 2, 14.

45, 1–5: Moses manifested God's power through miracles (1ff), God's authority through the promulgation of the commandments and the law (5), and God's mercy through the intimacy granted him by the Lord for his own faithfulness and meekness (4f). The very personification of the old covenant, Moses was also a type of Christ, the Prophet and Legislator of the new; cf Dt 18, 15.

n Sir 39, 1. o Wis 3, 3. p Sir 49, 14; Gn 5, 18–24; Heb 11, 5. q Gn 6, 8—9, 29; Heb 11, 7. r Gn 12, 1—25, 10; Gal 3, 6; Heb 11, 8–19. s Gn 17, 10; 22, 1. t Gn 26, 3. 5. 24; 27, 28f; 28, 14. u Ex 2, 2; 11, 3; 33, 11; Nm 12, 7.

Dear to God and men,
Moses, whose memory is held in benediction.
2 God's honor [v] devolved upon him,*
and the Lord strengthened him with fearful powers; [w]
3 God wrought swift miracles at his words
and sustained him in the king's presence.
He gave him the commandments for his people,
and revealed to him his glory. [x]
4 For his trustworthiness and meekness
God selected him from all mankind; [y]
5 He permitted him to hear his voice,
and led him into the cloud,
Where, face to face,* he gave him the commandments,
the law of life and understanding,
That he might teach his precepts to Jacob,
his judgments and decrees to Israel.

6 He raised up also, like Moses in holiness,*
his brother Aaron, of the tribe of Levi. [z]
7 He made him perpetual in his office
when he bestowed on him the priesthood* of his people;
He established him in honor
and crowned him with lofty majesty;
8 He clothed him with splendid apparel,
and adorned him with the glorious vestments:
Breeches and tunic and robe
with pomegranates around the hem,
9 And a rustle of bells round about,
through whose pleasing sound at each step
He would be heard within the sanctuary,
and the children of his race would be remembered;
10 The sacred vestments of gold, of violet,
and of crimson, wrought with embroidery;
The breastpiece for decision, the ephod and cincture
11 with scarlet yarn, the work of the weaver;
Precious stones with seal engravings
in golden settings, the work of the jeweler,
To commemorate in incised letters
each of the tribes of Israel;
12 On his turban the diadem of gold,
its plate wrought with the insignia of holiness,
Majestic, glorious, renowned for splendor,
a delight to the eyes, beauty supreme.
13 Before him, no one was adorned with these,
nor may they ever be worn by any
Except his sons and them alone,
generation after generation, for all time.
14 His cereal offering is wholly burnt
with the established sacrifice twice each day;
15 For Moses ordained him
and anointed him with the holy oil,
In a lasting covenant with him
and with his family, as permanent as the heavens,
That he should serve God in his priesthood
and bless his people in his name.
16 He chose him from all mankind
to offer holocausts and choice offerings,
To burn sacrifices of sweet odor for a memorial,
and to atone for the people of Israel.
17 He gave to him his laws,
and authority to prescribe and to judge:
To teach the precepts to his people,
and the ritual to the descendants of Israel.
18 Men of other families were inflamed against him,
were jealous of him in the desert,
The followers of Dathan and Abiram,

45, 2: God's honor devolved upon him: Moses was actually God's substitute in dealing with Pharaoh, hence God entrusted his own honor to Moses.

45, 5: Face to face: on God's intimacy with Moses, see Ex 33, 11; Nm 12, 8. St. Paul alluded to this in 1 Cor 13, 12.

45, 6–21: The author here expresses his reverence and esteem for the priesthood of the old covenant. He recalls God's choice of Aaron and his sons for this sublime office (6f), and describes in detail the beauty of the high priest's vestments (8–13). He relates the ordination of Aaron at the hands of Moses, his brother (15), and describes the priestly functions, of offering sacrifice to God (16), and of blessing (15), teaching, governing and judging the people (17); the inheritance of the high priest (20ff); the punishment of those families who were jealous of Aaron (18f); and the confirmation of the covenant of the priesthood with Aaron's descendants through Phinehas (23ff).

45, 7: The priesthood of Aaron was superseded by the priesthood of Christ; cf Heb 7, 18–28.

v Ex 7, 1—13, 22. w 2–5: Ex 7—Dt 34. x Ex 4, 17; 7, 1. y Nm 12, 3. 7. z 6ff: Ex 28f; Wis 18, 24. a Nm 16, 1ff.

and the band of Korah in their defiance.[a]
19 But the LORD saw this and became angry,
he destroyed them in his burning wrath.
He brought down upon them a miracle,
and consumed them with his flaming fire.
20 Then he increased the glory of Aaron[b]
and bestowed upon him his inheritance:
The sacred offerings he allotted to him,
with the showbread as his portion;
21 The oblations of the LORD are his food,
a gift to him and his descendants.
22 But he holds no land among the people
nor shares with them their heritage;
For the LORD himself is his portion,
his inheritance in the midst of Israel.

23 PHINEHAS too, the son of Eleazar,
was the courageous third of his line
When, zealous for the God of all,
he met the crisis of his people[c]
And, at the prompting of his noble heart,
atoned for the children of Israel.
24 Therefore on him again God conferred the right,
in a covenant of friendship, to provide for the sanctuary,
So that he and his descendants
should possess the high priesthood forever.
25 For even his covenant with David,
the son of Jesse of the tribe of Judah,
Was an individual heritage through one son alone;
but the heritage of Aaron is for all his descendants.[d]

26 And now bless the LORD
who has crowned you with glory!
May he grant you wisdom of heart
to govern his people in justice,
Lest their welfare should ever be forgotten,
or your authority, throughout all time.

CHAPTER 46

Joshua, Caleb and the Judges

1 Valiant leader was JOSHUA, son of Nun*
assistant to Moses in the prophetic office,
Formed to be, as his name implies,
the great savior of God's chosen ones,
To punish the enemy
and to win the inheritance for Israel.[e]
2 What glory was his when he raised his arm,
to brandish his javelin against the city![f]
3 And who could withstand him
when he fought the battles of the LORD?*
4 Did he not by his power stop the sun,
so that one day became two?[g]
5 He called upon the Most High God
when his enemies beset him on all sides,
And God Most High gave answer to him
in hailstones of tremendous power,
6 Which he rained down upon the hostile army
till on the slope he destroyed the foe;
That all the doomed nations might know
that the LORD was watching over his people's battles.
And because he was a devoted follower of God
7 and in Moses' lifetime showed himself loyal,
He and CALEB,* son of Jephunneh,
when they opposed the rebel assembly,
Averted God's anger from the people
and suppressed the wicked complaint—[h]
8 Because of this, they were the only two spared
from the six hundred thousand infantry,
To lead the people into their inheritance,
the land flowing with milk and honey.[i]
9 And the strength he gave to Caleb
remained with him even in his old age
Till he won his way onto the summits of the land;
his family too received an inheritance,[j]
10 That all the people of Jacob might know

46, 1–6: Joshua: whose name means "the LORD is savior" (1), was the instrument through which God delivered his people in miraculous ways (2–6) by destroying their enemies, whose land he gave to the Israelites as an inheritance (1).

46, 3: The battles of the Lord: cf Jos 6—10.

46, 7–10: Caleb, who with Joshua advised Moses and the people in the desert to conquer Canaan, despite the counsel of their companion scouts and the rebellion of the people, merited to lead the Israelites of the succeeding generation into the Promised Land. Caleb in his old age received as his inheritance a portion of land which he himself had previously conquered; cf Jos 15, 13f.

b 20f: Nm 18, 11–21; Dt 10, 9. c Nm 25, 7–13; Ps 106, 30f; 1 Mc 2, 26. 54. d 2 Sm 7, 12–16. e Ex 17, 9; Nm 27, 18; Dt 34, 9; Jos 1, 1–4. f Jos 8, 18. g Jos 10, 13. h Nm 13, 30; 14, 6. i Nm 14, 22–38. j Jos 14, 6; 15, 13.

how good it is to be a devoted follower of
the LORD.
11 The JUDGES,* too, each one of them,
whose hearts were not deceived,
Who did not abandon God:
may their memory be ever blessed, [k]
12 Their bones return to life from their resting
place,
and their names receive fresh luster in their
children!
13 Beloved of his people, dear to his Maker,
dedicated from his mother's womb,
Consecrated to the LORD as a prophet,
was SAMUEL, the judge and priest.
At God's word he established the kingdom
and anointed princes to rule the people. [l]
14 By the law of the LORD he judged the nation,
when he visited the encampments of Jacob.
15 As a trustworthy prophet he was sought out
and his words proved him true as a seer.
16 He, too, called upon God,
and offered him a suckling lamb; [m]
17 Then the LORD thundered forth from heaven,
and the tremendous roar of his voice was
heard. [n]
18 He brought low the rulers of the enemy
and destroyed all the lords of the
Philistines.
19 When Samuel approached the end of his life,
he testified before the LORD and his
anointed prince,
"No bribe or secret gift have I taken from any
man!"
and no one dared gainsay him. [o]
20 Even when he lay buried, his guidance was
sought;
he made known to the king his fate,
And from the grave he raised his voice
as a prophet, to put an end to wickedness. [p]

CHAPTER 47

Nathan, David and Solomon

1 After him came NATHAN*
who served in the presence of David. [q]
2 Like the choice fat of the sacred offerings,
so was DAVID in Israel. [r]
3 He made sport of lions as though they were
kids,
and of bears, like lambs of the flock. [s]
4 As a youth he slew the giant
and wiped out the people's disgrace,
When his hand let fly the slingstone
that crushed the pride of Goliath. [t]
5 Since he called upon the Most High God,
who gave strength to his right arm
To defeat the skilled warrior
and raise up the might of his people,
6 Therefore the women sang his praises
and ascribed to him tens of thousands.
When he assumed the royal crown, he
battled [u]
7 and subdued the enemy on every side.
He destroyed the hostile Philistines
and shattered their power till our own day. [v]
8 With his every deed he offered thanks
to God Most High, in words of praise.
With his whole being he loved his Maker
and daily had his praises sung;
9 He added beauty to the feasts
and solemnized the seasons of each year
With string music before the altar,
providing sweet melody for the psalms [w]
10 So that when the Holy Name was praised,
before daybreak the sanctuary would
resound.
11 The LORD forgave him his sins
and exalted his strength forever;
He conferred on him the rights of royalty
and established his throne in Israel. [x]

46, 11–20: Of the Judges praised and blessed for their fidelity to God in opposing idolatry, Samuel, a man of spotless integrity, was the greatest (11f. 19). He was judge of the entire nation, and was also a prophet and priest who through his sacrificial offering obtained victory over the Philistines. He established the kingdom, anointed kings (13–18), and even after his death foretold the king's fate and put an end to wickedness (20).

47, 1–11: David, a youthful and fearless warrior, the favorite of all Israel, by defeating Goliath, the boastful Philistine giant, removed the people's disgrace and greatly strengthened their power (1–7). With his whole being he loved and praised God, and his devotion to divine worship led him to develop liturgical cult. David fell into sin, but repenting, received pardon from God and the promise of an everlasting kingdom (8–11).

k Jgs 1, 1—16, 31. **l** 1 Sm 1, 10ff; 8, 4ff; 10, 1; 16, 13. **m** 1 Sm 7, 9. **n** Sir 12, 18. **o** 1 Sm 12, 3. **p** 1 Sm 28, 14. **q** 2 Sm 7, 2. **r** 1 Sm 16, 11. **s** 1 Sm 17, 35. **t** 1 Sm 17, 49. **u** 1 Sm 18, 7. **v** 2 Sm 5, 6–25. **w** 1 Chr 16, 4ff; 23, 2ff; 25, 1–7. **x** 2 Sm 12, 13; 7, 12–16.

12 Because of his merits he had as his successor*
a wise son, who lived in security: [y]
13 SOLOMON reigned during an era of peace,
for God made tranquil all his borders.
He built a house to the name of God,
and established a lasting sanctuary. [z]
14 How wise you were when you were young,
overflowing with instruction, like the Nile
in flood! [a]
15 Your understanding covered the whole earth,
and, like a sea, filled it with knowledge.
16 Your fame reached distant coasts,
and their peoples came to hear you;
17 With song and story and riddle,
and with your answers, you astounded the
nations.
18 You were called by that glorious name
which was conferred upon Israel.*
Gold you gathered like so much iron,
you heaped up silver as though it were lead;
19 But you abandoned yourself to women
and gave them dominion over your body. [b]
20 You brought dishonor upon your reputation,
shame upon your marriage,
Wrath upon your descendants,
and groaning upon your domain;
21 Thus two governments came into being,
when in Ephraim kingship was usurped. [c]
22 But God does not withdraw his mercy,
nor permit even one of his promises to fail.
He does not uproot the posterity of his chosen
one,
nor destroy the offspring of his friend.
So he gave to Jacob a remnant,
to David a root from his own family. [d]
23 Solomon finally slept with his fathers,
and left behind him one of his sons,
Expansive* in folly, limited in sense,
REHOBOAM, who by his policy made the
people rebel;
Until one arose who should not be
remembered,
the sinner who led Israel into sin, [e]
Who brought ruin to Ephraim
24 and caused them to be exiled from their
land.

Elijah and Elisha

Their sinfulness grew more and more,
25 and they lent themselves to every evil,*

CHAPTER 48

1 Till like a fire there appeared the prophet
whose words were as a flaming furnace. [f]
2 Their staff of bread he shattered,
in his zeal he reduced them to straits;
3 By God's word he shut up the heavens
and three times brought down fire. [g]
4 How awesome are you, ELIJAH!
Whose glory is equal to yours?
5 You brought a dead man back to life
from the nether world, by the will of the
LORD. [h]
6 You sent kings down to destruction,
and nobles, from their beds of sickness. [i]
7 You heard threats at Sinai,
at Horeb avenging judgments. [j]
8 You anointed kings who should inflict
vengeance,
and a prophet as your successor. [k]
9 You were taken aloft in a whirlwind,
in a chariot with fiery horses. [l]

47, 12–24: Solomon, son and successor of David, inherited peace through his father's conquests. He built the magnificent temple of Jerusalem (12f) and received from God the favor of unparalleled wisdom, through which he obtained great fame (14–17). Luxury and sensuality, however, brought disgrace upon him, and because of his oppressive burdens, he disposed the kingdom for division after his death (19–21. 23f). Nevertheless God did not withdraw his promise of establishing his throne in the descendants of David (22).

47, 18: Cf 2 Sm 12, 25, where Solomon is called Jedidiah, "beloved of the Lord." The same term is used of Israel in Jer 11, 15.

47, 23: Expansive: the name Rehoboam means "the people is expansive," that is, widespread. The sinner: Jeroboam; cf 1 Kgs 12, 2. 20. 26–32.

47, 25—48, 11: The prophetic ministry of Elijah amid widespread idolatry is here described as a judgment by fire (47, 25f). Through his preaching, miracles and vengeance against God's enemies within and without Israel, the prophet succeeded for a time in destroying idols and in restoring faith and the worship of the true God (48, 2–8). His miraculous departure from this life gave rise to the belief that he did not die but would return before the end of the world to put an end to wrath and restore the tribes of Israel (9ff). Cf Mt 17, 9–13.

y 1 Kgs 2, 12. z 1 Kgs 5, 1. 5. a 14–18: 1 Kgs 5, 9–14; 10, 14–28. b 1 Kgs 11, 1ff. c 1 Kgs 12, 1ff. d 2 Sm 7, 15; Ps 89, 34ff. e 1 Kgs 11, 43; 12, 13. 21; 13, 34; 2 Kgs 17, 6ff. f 1 Kgs 17, 1. g 1 Kgs 17, 1; 2 Kgs 1, 9–14. h 1 Kgs 17, 22. i 1 Kgs 21, 19; 2 Kgs 1, 17. j 1 Kgs 19, 8ff. k 1 Kgs 19, 15ff. l 2 Kgs 2, 11.

10 You are destined, it is written, in time to come
to put an end to wrath before the day of the
LORD,
To turn back the hearts of fathers toward their
sons,
and to re-establish the tribes of Jacob. [m]
11 Blessed is he who shall have seen you before
he dies,
12 O Elijah, enveloped in the whirlwind! [n]

Then ELISHA, filled with a twofold portion of
his spirit,*
wrought many marvels by his mere word.
During his lifetime he feared no one,
nor was any man able to intimidate his will.
13 Nothing was beyond his power; [o]
beneath him flesh was brought back into
life.
14 In life he performed wonders,
and after death, marvelous deeds.
15 Despite all this the people did not repent,
nor did they give up their sins,
Until they were rooted out of their land
and scattered all over the earth.
But Judah remained, a tiny people,
with its rulers from the house of David. [p]
16 Some of these did what was right,
but others were extremely sinful.

Hezekiah and Isaiah*

17 HEZEKIAH fortified his city
and had water brought into it; [q]
With iron tools he cut through the rock
and he built reservoirs for water.
18 During his reign Sennacherib led an invasion,
and sent his adjutant;
He shook his fist at Zion
and blasphemed God in his pride. [r]
19 The people's hearts melted within them,
and they were in anguish like that of
childbirth.
20 But they called upon the Most High God
and lifted up their hands to him;
He heard the prayer they uttered,
and saved them through ISAIAH. [s]
21 God struck the camp of the Assyrians
and routed them with a plague. [t]
22 For Hezekiah did what was right
and held fast to the paths of David,
As ordered by the illustrious prophet
Isaiah, who saw the truth in visions.
23 In his lifetime he turned back the sun
and prolonged the life of the king. [u]
24 By his powerful spirit he looked into the
future [v]
and consoled the mourners of Zion;
25 He foretold what should be till the end of time,
hidden things yet to be fulfilled.

CHAPTER 49

Josiah and the Prophets*

1 The name JOSIAH is like blended incense,
made lasting by a skilled perfumer. [w]
Precious is his memory, like honey to the taste,
like music at a banquet.
2 For he grieved over our betrayals
and destroyed the abominable idols.
3 He turned to God with his whole heart,
and, though times were evil, he practiced
virtue.
4 Except for David, Hezekiah and Josiah,
they all were wicked;
They abandoned the law of the Most High,
these kings of Judah, right to the very end.
5 So he gave over their power to others,
their glory to a foolish foreign nation
6 Who burned the holy city

48, 12–16: Elisha fearlessly continued the work of his predecessor by numerous miracles (12ff), but the obstinacy of the people eventually brought on the destruction of the kingdom of Israel and the dispersion of its subjects. Judah, however, survived under the rule of Davidic kings, both good and bad (15f).

48, 17–25: The fidelity, trust and courage of King Hezekiah (17. 22), the zeal of the prophet Isaiah, and the prayer of the people (20) availed with God. The Assyrian oppressors were routed (18f. 21), the king's life was prolonged, and consolations were granted the people through Isaiah's prophecies concerning the future (23ff), especially the coming of the Messiah and the establishment of his kingdom; cf Is 7, 14; 9, 6f; 40—65.

49, 1–10: The author's praise of King Josiah (1–3), of the prophets Jeremiah and Ezekiel and likewise the minor prophets (7–10) derives from their spirit of fidelity to the Lord and his law amid the infidelity of kings and people (4ff. 10).

m Mal 3, 23f; Mt 17, 10. n 2 Kgs 2, 9; 3, 13. o 13f: 2 Kgs 13, 21. p 2 Kgs 15, 29; 18, 11. q 2 Kgs 20, 20; 2 Chr 32, 3ff. 30. r 2 Kgs 18, 13ff; Is 36, 1ff. s 2 Kgs 19, 20. t 2 Kgs 19, 35; Is 37, 36. u 2 Kgs 20, 11; Is 38, 8. v 24f: 2 Kgs 20, 17; Is 40, 1ff; 42, 9; 46, 10; 48, 6; 61, 2. w 2 Kgs 22, 1; 2 Chr 34, 1.

and left its streets desolate,
As Jeremiah had foretold;[x] 7 for they had treated him badly
who even in the womb had been made a prophet,
To root out, pull down, and destroy,
and then to build and to plant.[y]
8 Ezekiel beheld the vision
and described the different creatures of the chariot;[z]
9 He also referred to Job,
who always persevered in the right path.[a]
10 Then, too, the Twelve Prophets—
may their bones return to life from their resting place!—
Gave new strength to Jacob
and saved him by their faith and hope.

The Heroes after the Exile

11 How can we fittingly praise Zerubbabel,*
who was like a signet ring on God's right hand,[b]
12 And Jeshua, Jozadak's son?
In their time they built the house of God;
They erected the holy temple,
destined for everlasting glory.
13 Extolled be the memory of Nehemiah!
He rebuilt our ruined walls,
Restored our shattered defenses,
and set up gates and bars.[c]

The Earliest Patriarchs

14 Few on earth have been made the equal of Enoch,*
for he was taken up bodily.[d]
15 Was ever a man born like Joseph?
Even his dead body was provided for.[e]
16 Glorious, too, were Shem and Seth and Enos;
but beyond that of any living being
was the splendor of Adam.[f]

CHAPTER 50

Simon, Son of Jochanan

1 The greatest among his brethren, the glory of his people,
was Simon the priest, son of Jochanan,*
In whose time the house of God was renovated,
in whose days the temple was reinforced.
2 In his time also the wall was built
with powerful turrets for the temple precincts;
3 In his time the reservoir was dug,
the pool with a vastness like the sea's.
4 He protected his people against brigands
and strengthened his city against the enemy.
5 How splendid he was as he appeared from the tent,
as he came from within the veil!
6 Like a star shining among the clouds,
like the full moon at the holyday season;
7 Like the sun shining upon the temple,
like the rainbow appearing in the cloudy sky;
8 Like the blossoms on the branches in springtime,
like a lily on the banks of a stream;
Like the trees of Lebanon in summer,
9 like the fire of incense at the sacrifice;
Like a vessel of beaten gold,
studded with precious stones;
10 Like a luxuriant olive tree thick with fruit,
like a cypress standing against the clouds;
11 Vested in his magnificent robes,
and wearing his garments of splendor,[g]

49, 11ff: Zerubbabel and Jeshua, in rebuilding the temple, and Nehemiah, the governor, in repairing the walls of the Holy City, also restored what these constructions signify, namely, religious worship and civil authority as prescribed in the law.

49, 14ff: The patriarchs here mentioned were glorious because of their spirit of religion, i.e., their profound reverence for God and obedience to him. The splendor of Adam, moreover, was due to his direct origin from God.

50, 1–21: The son of Jochanan here mentioned was Simon II, in whose time as high priest (219–196 B.C.) great works were accomplished for the benefit of public worship and welfare (1–4). The author, a contemporary of this high priest, describes in great detail and by numerous comparisons the impression of awful majesty received, the lofty joy aroused, at sight of the high priest fully vested entering the sanctuary, ascending the altar (6–11), and, in the presence of the whole assembly of Israel, encircled by assistant priests bearing offerings, sacrificing the burnt offering on the Day of Atonement, while the trumpets blast and the people bow down in adoration of the Most High (12–17). The hymnody, the joyful shouts of the multitude, and finally the high priest's blessing, in which he pronounces—once only in the year, on this occasion—the holy name of Yahweh, climax the description of this most solemn Jewish liturgical function (18–21).

x 2 Kgs 25, 9; 2 Chr 36, 19. y Jer 1, 5, 10. z Ez 1, 4ff. a Ez 14, 14. 20. b 11f: Ezr 3, 2; Hg 1, 12; Zec 3, 1. c Neh 1, 1; 3, 1. d Sir 44, 16; Gn 5, 18–24. e Gn 37—50; Ex 13, 19; Jos 24, 32. f Gn 1, 27; 4, 25f. g Sir 45, 8–12; Ex 28, 2–5; 39, 1–21.

As he ascended the glorious altar
and lent majesty to the court of the sanctuary.
12 When he received the sundered victims from the priests
while he stood before the sacrificial wood,
His brethren ringed him about like a garland,
like a stand of cedars on Lebanon;
13 All the sons of Aaron in their dignity
clustered around him like poplars,
With the offerings to the LORD in their hands,
in the presence of the whole assembly of Israel.
14 Once he had completed the services at the altar
with the arranging of the sacrifices for the Most High,
15 And had stretched forth his hand for the cup,[h]
to offer blood of the grape,
And poured it out at the foot of the altar,
a sweet-smelling odor to the Most High God,
16 The sons of Aaron would sound a blast,
the priests, on their trumpets of beaten metal;
A blast to resound mightily
as a reminder before the Most High.[i]
17 Then all the people with one accord
would quickly fall prostrate to the ground
In adoration before the Most High,
before the Holy One of Israel.
18 Then hymns would re-echo,
and over the throng sweet strains of praise resound.
19 All the people of the land would shout for joy,
praying to the Merciful One,
As the high priest completed the services at the altar
by presenting to God the sacrifice due;
20 Then coming down he would raise his hands
over all the congregation of Israel.[j]
The blessing of the LORD would be upon his lips,
the name of the LORD would be his glory.
21 Then again the people would lie prostrate
to receive from him the blessing of the Most High.

22 And now, bless the God of all,*
who has done wondrous things on earth;
Who fosters men's growth from their mother's womb,
and fashions them according to his will!
23 May he grant you joy of heart
and may peace abide among you;
24 May his goodness toward us endure in Israel
as long as the heavens are above.

Epilogue and Canticles

25 My whole being loathes two nations,*
the third is not even a people:*
26 Those who live in Seir* and Philistia,
and the degenerate folk who dwell in Shechem.[k]

27 Wise instruction, appropriate proverbs,*
I have written in this book,
I, Jesus, son of Eleazar, son of Sirach,
as they gushed forth from my heart's understanding.
28 Happy the man who meditates upon these things,
wise the man who takes them to heart!
29 If he puts them into practice, he can cope with anything,
for the fear of the LORD is his lamp.

CHAPTER 51

1 I give you thanks, O God of my father;*
I praise you, O God my savior!

50, 22ff: Praise and thanksgiving are given to God for his wondrous works, and a blessing is invoked on man that he may enjoy peace and gladness of heart and the abiding goodness of the Most High.

50, 25f: The author's abhorrence of the pagan Edomites (Idumeans), Philistines and Samaritans can be understood in the light of Old Testament thinking, which does not always distinguish between hatred of evildoers and hatred of the evil they do.

50, 25: Not even a people: the Samaritans.

50, 26: Seir: Mount Seir in the territory of the Edomites. Shechem: a city in Samaria.

50, 27ff: These verses contain the subscription of the author, Jesus, son of Eleazar, son of Sirach, to his long and beautiful treatise on wisdom as applying to all of human life, integrating it under the direction of the fear of the Lord.

51, 1-12: A canticle of praise and thanks to God for delivering the author from slander, dangers, destruction, death, the nether world, and evil of every kind.

h 15f: Nm 15, 5; 28, 7. i Nm 10, 10. j Nm 6, 23-26. k 2 Kgs 17, 24; Jn 4, 9.

I will make known your name, refuge of my
life; [l]
2 you have been my helper against my
adversaries.
You have saved me from death,
and kept back my body from the pit,
From the clutches of the nether world you
have snatched my feet; [m]
3 you have delivered me, in your great mercy,
From the scourge of a slanderous tongue,
and from lips that went over to falsehood;
From the snare of those who watched for my
downfall,
and from the power of those who sought
my life; [n]
From many a danger you have saved me,
4 from flames that hemmed me in on every
side; [o]
From the midst of unremitting fire,
5 from the deep belly of the nether world;
From deceiving lips and painters of lies,
6 from the arrows of dishonest tongues.
I was at the point of death,
my soul was nearing the depths of the
nether world; [p]
7 I turned every way, but there was no one to
help me,
I looked for one to sustain me, but could
find no one. [q]
8 But then I remembered the mercies of the
LORD,
his kindness through ages past;
For he saves those who take refuge in him,
and rescues them from every evil.
9 So I raised my voice from the very earth,
from the gates of the nether world, my cry.
10 I called out: O Lord, you are my father,
you are my champion and my savior;
Do not abandon me in time of trouble,
in the midst of storms and dangers. [r]
11 I will ever praise your name
and be constant in my prayers to you.
Thereupon the LORD heard my voice,
he listened to my appeal;
12 He saved me from evil of every kind
and preserved me in time of trouble.
For this reason I thank him and I praise him;
I bless the name of the LORD.*

13 *When I was young and innocent,*
I sought wisdom. [s]
14 She came to me in her beauty,
and until the end I will cultivate her.
15 As the blossoms yielded to ripening grapes,
the heart's joy,
My feet kept to the level path
because from earliest youth I was familiar
with her.

51, 12: After this verse the Hebrew text gives the litany of praise contained below. It is similar to Ps 136. Though not found in any versions, and therefore of doubtful authenticity, the litany seems from internal evidence to go back to the time of Sirach:

Give thanks to the Lord, for he is good, for his mercy endures forever;
Give thanks to the God of glory, for his mercy endures forever;
Give thanks to the guardian of Israel, for his mercy endures forever;
Give thanks to the creator of the universe, for his mercy endures forever;
Give thanks to the redeemer of Israel, for his mercy endures forever;
Give thanks to him who gathers the dispersed of Israel, for his mercy endures forever;
Give thanks to him who builds his city and his sanctuary, for his mercy endures forever;
Give thanks to him who makes a horn to sprout forth, for the house of David, for his mercy endures forever;
Give thanks to him who has chosen for his priests the sons of Zadok, for his mercy endures forever;
Give thanks to the shield of Abraham, for his mercy endures forever;
Give thanks to the rock of Isaac, for his mercy endures forever;
Give thanks to the mighty one of Jacob, for his mercy endures forever;
Give thanks to him who has chosen Zion, for his mercy endures forever;
Give thanks to the king over kings of kings, for his mercy endures forever;
He has lifted up the horn of his people, be this his praise from all his faithful ones,
From the children of Israel, the people close to him. Alleluia! (Cf Ps 148, 14.)

51, 13–30: An alphabetic canticle describing: a) the approach to wisdom through prayer, persistent study and instruction (13–17), purification from sin, enlightenment and ardent desire; b) the possession of wisdom (18–22). The author concludes with an urgent invitation to men to receive instruction in wisdom from him, and to live by it, because wisdom gives herself to those who seek her (23–26); and for their labor. God will reward them in the end (27–30). Cf Mt 11, 28; Eccl 12, 14.

In the Greek of 13f there is an expansion introducing Solomon as the speaker. This deviates from the original author's intent. It reads, "Publicly, in my prayer, facing the temple, I asked for her."

l Ps 138, 1. m Ps 91, 3. n Pss 40, 5; 91, 3. o Ps 66, 12. p Pss 88, 4; 94, 17. q Pss 22, 12; 142, 5. r Ps 89, 27. s Sir 34, 11.

16 In the short time I paid heed,
I met with great instruction.
17 Since in this way I have profited,
I will give my teacher grateful praise.

18 I became resolutely devoted to her—
the good I persistently strove for.
19 I burned with desire for her,
never turning back.
I became preoccupied with her,
never weary of extolling her.
My hand opened her gate
and I came to know her secrets.
20 For her I purified my hands;
in cleanness I attained to her.
At first acquaintance with her, I gained
understanding
such that I will never forsake her. [t]
21 My whole being was stirred as I learned about
her;
therefore I have made her my prize
possession.
22 The LORD has granted me my lips as a reward,
and my tongue will declare his praises.

23 Come aside to me, you untutored,
and take up lodging in the house of
instruction; [u]
24 How long will you be deprived of wisdom's
food,
how long will you endure such bitter thirst?
25 I open my mouth and speak of her:
gain, at no cost, wisdom for yourselves. [v]
26 Submit your neck to her yoke,
that your mind may accept her teaching.
For she is close to those who seek her,
and the one who is in earnest finds her. [w]
27 See for yourselves! I have labored only a little,
but have found much.
28 Acquire but a little instruction;
you will win silver and gold through her.
29 Let your spirits rejoice in the mercy of God,
and be not ashamed to give him praise.
30 Work at your tasks in due season,
and in his own time God will give you your
reward. [x]

t Prv 4, 6. u Prv 8, 5. v Sir 6, 20. w Sir 6, 25. x Sir 2, 8; Jb 34, 11; Jn 9, 4.

THE PROPHETIC BOOKS

The prophetic books bear the names of the four major and twelve minor prophets, besides Lamentations and Baruch. The terms "major" and "minor" refer merely to the length of the respective compositions and not to any distinction in the prophetic office. Jonah is a story of the mission of the prophet rather than a collection of prophecies. Lamentations and Daniel are listed among the hagiographa in the Hebrew Bible, not among the prophetic books. The former contains a series of elegies on the fate of Jerusalem; the latter is apocalyptic in character. Daniel, who lived far removed from Palestine, was not called by God to preach; yet the book is counted as prophecy. Baruch, though excluded from the Hebrew canon, is found in the Septuagint version, and the church has always acknowledged it to be sacred and inspired.

The prophetic books, together with the oral preaching of the prophets, were the result of the institution of prophetism, in which a succession of Israelites chosen by God and appointed by him to be prophets received communications from him and transmitted them to the people in his name (Dt 18, 15-20). The prophets were spokesmen of God, intermediaries between him and his people. The communications they received from God came through visions, dreams, and ecstasies and were transmitted to the people through sermons, writings, and symbolic actions.

The office of prophet was due to a direct call from God. It was not the result of heredity, just as it was not a permanent gift but a transient one, subject entirely to the divine will. The prophets preserved and developed revealed religion (1 Sm 12, 6-25), denounced idolatry (1 Kgs 14, 1-13), defended the moral law (2 Sm 12, 1-15), gave counsel in political matters (Is 31, 1ff), and often also in matters of private life (1 Sm 9, 6-9). At times miracles confirmed their preaching, and their predictions of the future intensified the expectation of the Messiah and of his kingdom.

The prophetic literature in this volume contains the substance of the prophets' authentic preaching, resumes, and genuine samples of such preaching. Some parts were recorded by the prophets themselves, some by persons other than the prophets who uttered them.

The prophecies express judgments of the people's moral conduct, on the basis of the Mosaic alliance between God and Israel. They teach sublime truths and lofty morals. They contain exhortations, threats, announcements of punishment, promises of deliverance, made with solemn authority and in highly imaginative language. In the affairs of men, their prime concern is the interests of God, especially in what pertains to the chosen people through whom the Messiah is to come; hence their denunciations of idolatry and of that externalism in worship which excludes the interior spirit of religion. They are concerned also with the universal nature of the moral law, with personal responsibility, with the person and office of the Messiah, and with the conduct of foreign nations.

In content, the literary genre of prophecy uses warning and threat besides exhortation and promise to declare in God's name events of the near and distant future (Is 8–9). In form, the divine source of prophetic declaration appears in: "The word (or oracle) of the Lord," or "Thus says the Lord," followed by the announcement of a coming event and its moral cause (Hos 4, 7-10). Divine exhortation and promise are introduced by such forms as: "Hear this word, O men of Israel, that the Lord pronounces over you" (Am 3, 1). Kindly and persuasive tones pervade the promises of reward and even the threats of punishment (Am 5, 14-15).

Disregard for exact chronological perspective in the prophecies is an additional characteristic.

Predictions of the immediate and distant future are often interrelated, not on the basis of years separating the events but on the analogy of the pattern joining present with very distant, though similar, conditions and circumstances. This is prophetic compenetration, idealization in which persons and things of the more immediate present, in the prophet's day, fade into a wider and more perfect order of persons and things of the future; the former are figures and types of the latter. Thus, some details of what the Psalmist said of the kingdom of David and Solomon (Ps 72) went beyond what was fulfilled in these men, as St. Thomas points out, and found their realization only in the kingdom of Christ. St. Jerome before him, and still earlier the apostles themselves—Peter (Acts 2, 14-36) and Paul (Gal 4, 21-31)—taught us that through anticipation in types we discover in Sacred Scripture the truth of things to come.

Thus the universal blessing for mankind, often promised by God through the mouths of his prophets in figures and types, was in time to become personalized and to confer its full benefit on us through the Word made flesh, who became for us the New Covenant through his life, death, and resurrection, as the prophets had foretold.

THE BOOK OF ISAIAH

The greatest of the prophets appeared at a critical moment of Israel's history. The second half of the eighth century B.C. witnessed the collapse of the northern kingdom under the hammerlike blows of Assyria (722), while Jerusalem itself saw the army of Sennacherib drawn up before its walls (701). In the year that Uzziah, king of Judah, died (742), Isaiah received his call to the prophetic office in the Temple of Jerusalem. Close attention should be given to chapter 6, where this divine summons to be the ambassador of the Most High is circumstantially described.

The vision of the Lord enthroned in glory stamps an indelible character on Isaiah's ministry and provides the key to the understanding of his message. The majesty, holiness and glory of the Lord took possession of his spirit and, conversely, he gained a new awareness of human pettiness and sinfulness. The enormous abyss between God's sovereign holiness and man's sin overwhelmed the prophet. Only the purifying coal of the seraphim could cleanse his lips and prepare him for acceptance of the call: "Here I am, send me!"

The ministry of Isaiah may be divided into three periods, covering the reigns of Jotham (742–735), Ahaz (735–715), and Hezekiah (715–687). To the first period belong, for the most part, the early oracles (1—5) which exposed the moral breakdown of Judah and its capital, Jerusalem. With the accession of Ahaz, the prophet became adviser to the king, whose throne was threatened by the Syro-Ephraimite coalition. Rejecting the plea of Isaiah for faith and courage, the weak Ahaz turned to Assyria for help. From this period came the majority of messianic oracles found in the section of Immanuel prophecies (6—12).

Hezekiah succeeded his father and undertook a religious reform which Isaiah undoubtedly supported. But the old intrigues began again, and the king was soon won over to the pro-Egyptian party. Isaiah denounced this "covenant with death" and again summoned Judah to faith in Yahweh as her only hope. But it was too late; the revolt had already begun. Assyria acted quickly and her army, after ravaging Judah, laid siege to Jerusalem (701). "I shut up Hezekiah like a bird in his cage," boasts the famous inscription of Sennacherib. But Yahweh delivered the

city, as Isaiah had promised: God is the Lord of history, and Assyria but an instrument in his hands.

Little is known about the last days of this great religious leader, whose oracles, of singular poetic beauty and power constantly reminded his wayward people of their destiny and the fidelity of Yahweh to his promises.

The complete Book of Isaiah is an anthology of poems composed chiefly by the great prophet, but also by disciples, some of whom came many years after Isaiah. In 1—39 most of the oracles come from Isaiah and faithfully reflect the situation in eighth-century Judah. To disciples deeply influenced by the prophet belong sections such as the Apocalypse of Isaiah (24—27), the oracles against Babylon (13—14), and probably the poems of 34—35.

Chapters 40—55, sometimes called the Deutero-Isaiah, are generally attributed to an anonymous poet who prophesied toward the end of the Babylonian exile. From this section come the great messianic oracles known as the songs of the Servant, whose mysterious destiny of suffering and glorification is fulfilled in the passion and glorification of Christ. Chapters 56—66 contain oracles from a later period and were composed by disciples who inherited the spirit and continued the work of the great prophet.

The principal divisions of the Book of Isaiah are the following:

A. The Book of Judgment:
I. Indictment of Israel and Judah (1, 1—5, 30).
II. Immanuel Prophecies (6, 1—12, 6).
III. Oracles against the Pagan Nations (13, 1—23, 18).
IV. Apocalypse of Isaiah (24, 1—27, 13).
V. The Lord Alone, Israel's and Judah's Salvation (28, 1—33, 24).
VI. The Lord, Zion's Avenger (34, 1—35, 10).
VII. Historical Appendix (36, 1—39, 8).
B. The Book of Consolation:
I. The Lord's Glory in Israel's Liberation (40, 1—48, 21).
II. Expiation of Sin, Spiritual Liberation of Israel (49, 1—55, 13).
III. Return of the First Captives (56, 1—66, 24).

A. THE BOOK OF JUDGMENT

I: Indictment of Israel and Judah

CHAPTER 1

Israel's Sinfulness 1 The vision* which Isaiah, son of Amoz, had concerning Judah and Jerusalem in the days of Uzziah, Jotham, Ahaz and Hezekiah, kings of Judah.

2 Hear, O heavens, and listen, O earth,
for the LORD speaks:
Sons have I raised and reared,
but they have disowned me! [a]
3 An ox knows its owner,
and an ass, its master's manger;
But Israel* does not know,
my people has not understood.
4 Ah! sinful nation, people laden with wickedness,
evil race, corrupt children!

1, 1: The title of the book: an editorial addition. Isaiah: meaning "the salvation of the Lord," or "The Lord is salvation." Amoz: not the minor prophet. Judah: the southern kingdom of the tribes of Judah and Benjamin. Uzziah: also called Azariah; cf 2 Kgs 15, 1; 2 Chr 26, 1.

1, 3: Israel, not the northern kingdom, as in Is 9, 11, exclusively, which Isaiah usually calls "Ephraim" from the tribe bordering on the southern kingdom, but the entire chosen people; cf Is 8, 14.

a Dt 32, 1. 5f.

They have forsaken the LORD,
spurned the Holy One of Israel,*
apostatized. [b]
5 Where would you yet be struck,*
you that rebel again and again?
The whole head is sick,
the whole heart faint.
6 From the sole of the foot to the head
there is no sound spot:
Wound and welt and gaping gash,
not drained, or bandaged,
or eased with salve.
7 Your country is waste,
your cities burnt with fire;
Your land before your eyes
strangers devour
[a waste, like Sodom overthrown]—
8 And daughter Zion* is left
like a hut in a vineyard,
Like a shed in a melon patch,
like a city blockaded.

9 Unless the LORD of hosts*
had left us a scanty remnant,
We had become as Sodom,
we should be like Gomorrah. [c]
10 Hear the word of the LORD,
princes of Sodom!
Listen to the instruction of our God,
people of Gomorrah!
11 What care I for the number of your
sacrifices?*
says the LORD.
I have had enough of whole-burnt rams
and fat of fatlings;
In the blood of calves, lambs and goats
I find no pleasure. [d]

12 When you come in to visit me,
who asks these things of you?
13 Trample my courts no more!
Bring no more worthless offerings;
your incense is loathsome to me.
New moon and sabbath, calling of assemblies,
octaves with wickedness:* these I cannot
bear. [e]
14 Your new moons and festivals I detest;
they weigh me down, I tire of the load.
15 When you spread out your hands,*
I close my eyes to you;
Though you pray the more,
I will not listen.
Your hands are full of blood![f]
16 Wash yourselves clean!
Put away your misdeeds from before my eyes;
cease doing evil; 17 learn to do good.
Make justice your aim: redress the wronged,
hear the orphan's plea, defend the widow. [g]

18 Come now, let us set things right,
says the LORD:
Though your sins be like scarlet,
they may become white as snow;
Though they be crimson red,
they may become white as wool. [h]
19 If you are willing, and obey,
you shall eat the good things of the land;
20 But if you refuse and resist,
the sword shall consume you:
for the mouth of the LORD has spoken!

21 How has she turned adulteress,
the faithful city, so upright!*
Justice used to lodge within her,
but now, murderers. [i]
22 Your silver is turned to dross,
your wine is mixed with water.
23 Your princes are rebels
and comrades of thieves;
Each one of them loves a bribe

1, 4: Holy One of Israel: a title used frequently by Isaiah, rarely by other writers.
1, 5–8: Sufferings inflicted upon God's people for their sins.
1, 8: Daughter Zion: Jerusalem. Hut . . . shed: for the shelter of watchmen and laborers.
1, 9: Lord of hosts: God, who is the Creator and Ruler of the heavenly armies of the angels, stars, etc. Remnant: St. Paul uses this text in Rom 9, 29, where he speaks of God's saving mercy toward the Jews and Gentiles. Sodom . . . Gomorrah: cf Gn 19.
1, 11: The number of your sacrifices: however numerous, they are not acceptable without the right dispositions on the part of the worshipers.
1, 13: Octaves with wickedness: the solemnity of the feasts marred by evil deeds.
1, 15: Spread out your hands: in prayer.
1, 21: A picture of Jerusalem, once so faithful to God. Apostasy from the covenant is often likened by the prophets to unfaithfulness to the marriage vow.

b Is 5, 24; Dt 32, 15. c Rom 9, 29. d Ps 50, 8–13; Sir 34, 19; Mi 6, 7. e Prv 15, 8; Jer 6, 20. f Prv 1, 28; Sir 34, 21–25. g Ex 23, 6; Dt 24, 17; Sir 4, 9f; Jer 22, 3; Ez 22, 7; Zec 7, 9f. h Ps 51, 9. i Jer 3, 8; Hos 2, 7.

and looks for gifts.
The fatherless they defend not,
and the widow's plea does not reach them. [j]
24 Now, therefore, says the Lord,
the LORD of hosts, the Mighty One of Israel:
Ah! I will take vengeance on my foes
and fully repay my enemies! [k]
25 I will turn my hand against you,
and refine your dross in the furnace,
removing all your alloy.
26 I will restore your judges as at first,
and your counselors as in the beginning;
After that you shall be called
city of justice, faithful city. [l]

27 Zion shall be redeemed by judgment,
and her repentant ones by justice.*
28 Rebels and sinners alike shall be crushed,
those who desert the LORD shall be consumed.
29 You shall be ashamed of the terebinths which you prized,
and blush for the groves which you chose.*
30 You shall become like a tree with falling leaves,
like a garden that has no water.
31 The strong man shall turn to tow,
and his work shall become a spark;
Both shall burn together,
and there shall be none to quench the flames.

CHAPTER 2

Zion, the Messianic Capital 1 This is what Isaiah, son of Amoz, saw concerning Judah and Jerusalem.*

2 In days to come,*
The mountain of the LORD's house [m]
shall be established as the highest mountain
and raised above the hills.
All nations shall stream toward it; [n]
3 many peoples shall come and say:
"Come, let us climb the LORD's mountain,
to the house of the God of Jacob,
That he may instruct us in his ways,
and we may walk in his paths." [o]
For from Zion shall go forth instruction,
and the word of the LORD from Jerusalem.*
4 He shall judge between the nations,
and impose terms on many peoples.
They shall beat their swords into plowshares
and their spears into pruning hooks;
One nation shall not raise the sword against another,
nor shall they train for war again. [p]

5 O house of Jacob, come,
let us walk in the light of the LORD!

The Lord's Judgment against Idols

6 You have abandoned your people,
the house of Jacob,
Because they are filled with fortune-tellers
and soothsayers,* like the Philistines;
they covenant with strangers. [q]
7 Their land is full of silver and gold,
and there is no end to their treasures;
Their land is full of horses,
and there is no end to their chariots.
8 Their land is full of idols;
they worship the works of their hands,
that which their fingers have made. [r]

9 But man is abased,
each one brought low.
[Do not pardon them!]
10 Get behind the rocks,
hide in the dust,

1, 27: This verse is the key to the whole Book of Isaiah. Zion's defiant persistence in sin has demanded a divine judgment, by which her survivors will be cleansed and will return to God in justice; cf Is 40, 2.

1, 29: Terebinths which you prized . . . groves which you chose: as popular shrines for idolatrous worship.

2, 1: An editorial addition introducing chapters 2–5.

2, 2–4: The messianic destiny which ensures Judah's later restoration. In the messianic kingdom the prophets generally see the Lord's house as the seat of authority and the source of clear and certain doctrine; also, its rule willingly accepted by all peoples, maintained by spiritual sanctions, and tending to universal peace. This passage is found substantially unchanged in Mi 4, 1–3; it probably, although not certainly, has Isaiah as its author.

2, 3: Zion . . . Jerusalem: types of the earthly center of the messianic kingdom.

2, 6: Fortunetellers and soothsayers: divination was strictly forbidden; cf Dt 18, 9–14.

j Ex 23, 8; Dt 16, 19. k Dt 32, 41. l Jer 33, 7ff; Zec 8, 3. m 2ff: Mi 4, 1ff. n Is 56, 7. o Zec 8, 20–23. p Is 9, 7; 11, 4; Ps 72, 3f; Zec 9, 10. q Is 8, 19; 19, 3. r Is 31, 1ff.

From the terror of the LORD
and the splendor of his majesty! [s]
11 The haughty eyes of man will be lowered,
the arrogance of men will be abased,
and the LORD alone will be exalted, on that day.*
12 For the LORD of hosts will have his day
against all that is proud and arrogant,
all that is high, and it will be brought low;
13 Yes, against all the cedars of Lebanon*
and all the oaks of Bashan,
14 Against all the lofty mountains
and all the high hills,
15 Against every lofty tower
and every fortified wall,
16 Against all the ships of Tarshish*
and all stately vessels.
17 Human pride will be abased,
the arrogance of men brought low,
And the LORD alone will be exalted, on that day.

18 The idols will perish forever.

19 Men will go into caves in the rocks
and into holes in the earth,
From the terror of the LORD
and the splendor of his majesty,
when he arises to overawe the earth.

20 On that day men will throw to the moles and the bats the idols of silver and gold which they made for worship.

21 They go into caverns in the rocks
and into crevices in the cliffs,
From the terror of the LORD
and the splendor of his majesty,
when he arises to overawe the earth.

22 As for you, let man alone,
in whose nostrils is but a breath;
for what is he worth?

CHAPTER 3

Judgment of Judah and Jerusalem

1 The Lord, the LORD of hosts,*
shall take away from Jerusalem and from Judah
support and prop [all supplies of bread and water]: [t]
2 Hero and warrior,
judge and prophet, fortune-teller and elder,
3 The captain of fifty and the nobleman,
counselor, skilled magician, and expert charmer.
4 I will make striplings their princes;
the fickle shall govern them,
5 And the people shall oppress one another,
yes, every man his neighbor.
The child shall be bold toward the elder,
and the base toward the honorable.
6 When a man seizes his brother
in his father's house, saying,
"You have clothes! Be our ruler,
and take in hand this ruin!"—
7 Then shall he answer in that day:
"I will not undertake to cure this,
when in my own house there is no bread or clothing!
You shall not make me ruler of the people."

8 Jerusalem is crumbling, Judah is falling;
for their speech and their deeds are before the LORD,
a provocation in the sight of his majesty.
9 Their very look bears witness against them;
their sin like Sodom they vaunt,
They hide it not. Woe to them!
they deal out evil to themselves.
10 Happy the just, for it will be well with them,
the fruit of their works they will eat.
11 Woe to the wicked man! All goes ill,
with the work of his hands he will be repaid.

2, 11: That day: the day of the Lord, a day of retribution, often referred to, especially by the minor prophets, and described in terms of natural phenomena: earthquake, fire, storm.

2, 13: Lebanon: Mount Lebanon in Syria, famed for its cedars. Bashan: the wooded uplands east of the Jordan River.

2, 16: Tarshish: cf note on Ps 48, 8.

3, 1–12: Anarchy will reign in Jerusalem and Judah. In the prevailing desperation, even the most unworthy and the least qualified will be sought as rulers.

s 2 Thes 1, 9. t Lv 26, 26; Ez 4, 16.

12 My people—a babe in arms will be their tyrant,
and women will rule them!
O my people, your leaders mislead,
they destroy the paths you should follow.

13 The LORD rises to accuse,
standing to try his people.
14 The Lord enters into judgment
with his people's elders and princes:
It is you who have devoured the vineyard;
the loot wrested from the poor is in your houses.
15 What do you mean by crushing my people,
and grinding down the poor when they look to you?
says the Lord, the God of hosts. [u]
16 The LORD said: [v]
Because the daughters of Zion are haughty,
and walk with necks outstretched
Ogling and mincing as they go,
their anklets tinkling with every step,
17 The Lord shall cover the scalps of Zion's daughters with scabs,
and the LORD shall bare their heads.*

18 On that day the LORD will do away with the
finery of the anklets, sunbursts, and crescents;
19 the pendants, bracelets, and veils; 20 the head-
dresses, bangles, cinctures, perfume boxes, and
amulets; 21 the signet rings, and the nose rings;*
22 the court dresses, wraps, cloaks, and purses;
23 the mirrors, linen tunics, turbans, and shawls.

24 Instead of perfume there will be stench,
instead of the girdle, a rope,
And for the coiffure, baldness;
for the rich gown, a sackcloth skirt.
Then, instead of beauty:
25 Your men will fall by the sword,
and your champions, in war;
26 Her gates will lament and mourn,
as the city sits desolate on the ground.

CHAPTER 4

1 Seven women will take hold of one man*
on that day, saying:
"We will eat our own food
and wear our own clothing;
Only let your name be given us,
put an end to our disgrace!"

The Messianic Branch

2 On that day,
The branch of the LORD* will be luster and glory,
and the fruit of the earth will be honor and splendor
for the survivors of Israel. [w]
3 He who remains in Zion
and he that is left in Jerusalem
Will be called holy:
every one marked down for life* in Jerusalem. [x]
4 When the Lord washes away
the filth of the daughters of Zion,
And purges Jerusalem's blood from her midst
with a blast of searing judgment,
5 Then will the LORD create,
over the whole site of Mount Zion
and over her place of assembly,
A smoking cloud by day
and a light of flaming fire by night. [y]
6 For over all, his glory will be shelter and protection:
shade from the parching heat of day,
refuge and cover from storm and rain.

CHAPTER 5

The Vineyard Song

1 Let me now sing of my friend,
my friend's song concerning his vineyard.
My friend had a vineyard*
on a fertile hillside;
2 He spaded it, cleared it of stones,
and planted the choicest vines;

3, 17: Bare their heads: a mark of social disgrace; cf Nm 5, 18.
3, 21: Nose rings: of gold, a feminine ornament in the East; cf note on Gn 24, 22.
4, 1: Seven women . . . one man: the disproportion of the sexes due to war leaves the female population almost without male partners. The women are eager to marry, not for support, but to avoid the disgrace of being childless.
4, 2: Branch of the Lord: divine blessings in general, which later culminated in the Messiah; cf Jer 23, 5; Zec 3, 8; 6, 12.
4, 3: Marked down for life: in God's list of his elect; cf Ex 32, 32.
5, 1: My friend had a vineyard: the Lord and his chosen people.

u Lv 25, 42. 55. v 16ff: Is 32, 11f. w Is 11, 1; Jer 23, 5; 33, 15. x Is 6, 13; 10, 20; Ob 17. y Ex 13, 21.

Within it he built a watchtower,
and hewed out a wine press.
Then he looked for the crop of grapes,
but what it yielded was wild grapes.

3 Now, inhabitants of Jerusalem and men of Judah,
judge between me and my vineyard:
4 What more was there to do for my vineyard
that I had not done?
Why, when I looked for the crop of grapes,
did it bring forth wild grapes?
5 Now, I will let you know
what I mean to do to my vineyard:
Take away its hedge, give it to grazing,
break through its wall, let it be trampled!
6 Yes, I will make it a ruin:
it shall not be pruned or hoed,
but overgrown with thorns and briers;
I will command the clouds
not to send rain upon it.
7 The vineyard of the LORD of hosts is the house of Israel,
and the men of Judah are his cherished plant;
He looked for judgment, but see, bloodshed!
for justice, but hark, the outcry!*

Doom of the Unjust

8 Woe to you who join house to house,*
who connect field with field,
Till no room remains, and you are left to dwell
alone in the midst of the land! [z]
9 In my hearing the LORD of hosts has sworn:
Many houses shall be in ruins,
large ones and fine, with no one to live in them. [a]
10 Ten acres* of vineyard
shall yield but one liquid measure,
And a homer of seed
shall yield but an ephah.
17 Lambs shall graze there at pasture,
and kids shall eat in the ruins of the rich.
11 Woe to those who demand strong drink
as soon as they rise in the morning,
And linger into the night
while wine inflames them!
12 With harp and lyre, timbrel and flute,
they feast on wine;
But what the LORD does, they regard not,
the work of his hands they see not. [b]
13 Therefore my people go into exile,
because they do not understand;
Their nobles die of hunger,
and their masses are parched with thirst.
14 Therefore the nether world* enlarges its throat
and opens its maw without limit;
Down go their nobility and their masses,
their throngs and their revelry. [c]
15 Men shall be abased, each one brought low,
and the eyes of the haughty lowered,
16 But the LORD of hosts shall be exalted by his judgment,
and God the Holy shall be shown holy by his justice.
18 Woe to those who tug at guilt with cords of perversity,
and at sin as if with cart ropes!
19 To those who say, "Let him make haste
and speed his work, that we may see it;
On with the plan of the Holy One of Israel!
let it come to pass, that we may know it!" [d]
20 Woe to those who call evil good, and good evil,
who change darkness into light, and light into darkness,
who change bitter into sweet, and sweet into bitter!
21 Woe to those who are wise in their own sight,
and prudent in their own esteem! [e]
22 Woe to the champions at drinking wine,
the valiant at mixing strong drink! [f]
23 To those who acquit the guilty for bribes,
and deprive the just man of his rights! [g]

5, 7: Judgment . . . bloodshed . . . justice . . . outcry: in Hebrew, these adversative terms constitute a play on words.
5, 8–10: Land-grabbers who unjustly acquire property will be impoverished instead of enriched.
5, 10: Ten acres: a field requiring ten days of plowing by a yoke of oxen. Liquid measure: in Hebrew, a "bath," i.e., about ten gallons. Homer: a dry measure of about ten bushels. Ephah: a dry measure of about one bushel.
5, 14: Nether world: cf note on Ps 6, 6.

z Mi 2, 2. a Is 6, 12. b Am 6, 5f. c Hb 2, 5. d Jer 5, 12: 2 Pt 3, 4. e Prv 3, 7; Rom 12, 16. f Sir 31, 3. g Ex 23, 8; Prv 17, 15.

24 Therefore, as the tongue of fire licks up
stubble,
as dry grass shrivels in the flame,
Even so their root shall become rotten
and their blossom scatter like dust;
For they have spurned the law of the LORD of
hosts,
and scorned the word of the Holy One of
Israel.
25 Therefore the wrath of the LORD blazes against
his people,
he raises his hand to strike them;
When the mountains quake,
their corpses shall be like refuse in the
streets.
For all this, his wrath is not turned back,
and his hand is still outstretched.

Invasion*

26 He will give a signal to a far-off nation,
and whistle to them from the ends of the
earth;
speedily and promptly will they come.
27 None of them will stumble with weariness,
none will slumber and none will sleep.
None will have his waist belt loose,
nor the thong of his sandal broken.
28 Their arrows are sharp,
and all their bows are bent.
The hoofs of their horses seem like flint,
and their chariot wheels like the hurricane.
29 Their roar is that of the lion,
like the lion's whelps they roar;
They growl and seize the prey,
they carry it off and none will rescue it.
30 [They will roar over it, on that day,
with a roaring like that of the sea.] [h]

II: Immanuel Prophecies

CHAPTER 6

Call of Isaiah 1 In the year king Uzziah died,* I
saw the Lord seated on a high and lofty throne, [i]
with the train of his garment filling the temple.*
2 Seraphim were stationed above; each of them
had six wings: with two they veiled their faces,
with two they veiled their feet, and with two
they hovered aloft. [j]
3 "Holy, holy, holy is the LORD of hosts!" they
cried one to the other. "All the earth is filled
with his glory!" 4 [k] At the sound of that cry, the
frame of the door shook and the house was filled
with smoke.*
5 Then I said, "Woe is me, I am doomed!* For
I am a man of unclean lips, living among a
people of unclean lips; yet my eyes have seen
the King, the LORD of hosts!" [l] 6 Then one of the
seraphim flew to me, holding an ember which
he had taken with tongs from the altar.
7 He touched my mouth with it. "See," he
said, "now that this has touched your lips,* your
wickedness is removed, your sin purged." [m]
8 Then I heard the voice of the Lord saying,
"Whom shall I send? Who will go for us?" "Here
I am;" I said; "send me!" 9 And he replied: Go
and say to this people:*

Listen carefully, but you shall not understand!
Look intently, but you shall know nothing! [n]
10 You are to make the heart of this people
sluggish,
to dull their ears and close their eyes;
Else their eyes will see, their ears hear,
their heart understand,
and they will turn and be healed. [o]

5, 26–30: A description of the invading Assyrian army, God's instrument for punishing his people.

6, 1: In the year King Uzziah died: 742 B.C.

6, 1ff: Temple: the holy place, just in front of the holy of holies. Seraphim: literally "the burning ones," are celestial beings who surround the throne of God. Each has six wings. Reverence for the divine majesty causes them to veil their faces with two wings; modesty, to veil their extremities in similar fashion; alacrity in God's service, to extend two wings in preparation for flight. Holy, holy, holy: God's perfect interior holiness whose exterior manifestation is his glory. These words are found in the Roman liturgy just before the Canon of the Mass.

6, 4: Smoke: reminiscent of the clouds which surrounded God at Mount Sinai; cf Ex 19, 16–19; Dt 4, 11f.

6, 5: Doomed: it was popularly believed that to see God would lead to one's death; cf Gn 32, 31; Ex 33, 20; Jgs 13, 22.

6, 7: Touched your lips: Isaiah is thus symbolically purified to be worthy of his vocation as God's prophet. In the Roman liturgy, the celebrant at Mass makes reference to this incident just before he reads the gospel.

6, 9f: The truth that the nation will remain impenitent is vividly foretold, as if its obstinacy would be caused, instead of merely occasioned, by the prophet's warning. Cf Mt 13, 13ff; Mk 4, 12; Lk 8, 10.

h Is 8, 22. i Jn 12, 41. j Rv 4, 8. k 1 Kgs 8, 10f; Rv 15, 8. l Gn 32, 3; Ex 20, 19; 33, 20; Jgs 6, 22; 13, 22. m Jer 1, 9; Dn 10, 16. n Mt 13, 14f; Mk 4, 12; Lk 8, 10; Acts 28, 26f. o Jer 5, 21; Jn 12, 40.

11 “How long, O Lord?” I asked. And he
replied:

Until the cities are desolate,
without inhabitants,
Houses, without a man,
and the earth is a desolate waste.
12 Until the LORD removes men far away,
and the land is abandoned more and more.*
13 If there be still a tenth part in it,
then this in turn shall be laid waste;
As with a terebinth or an oak
whose trunk remains when its leaves have
fallen.
[Holy offspring is the trunk.] [p]

CHAPTER 7

Birth of Immanuel 1 In the days of Ahaz,* king
of Judah, son of Jotham, son of Uzziah, Rezin,
king of Aram, and Pekah, king of Israel, son of
Remaliah, went up to attack Jerusalem,[q] but
they were not able to conquer it. 2 When word
came to the house of David that Aram was
encamped in Ephraim, the heart of the king and
the heart of the people trembled, as the trees of
the forest tremble in the wind.
3 [r]Then the LORD said to Isaiah: Go out to
meet Ahaz, you and your son Shear-jashub,* at
the end of the conduit of the upper pool, on the
highway of the fuller’s field, 4 and say to him:
Take care you remain tranquil and do not fear;
let not your courage fail before these two stumps
of smoldering brands [the blazing anger of Rezin
and the Arameans, and of the son of Remaliah],
5 because of the mischief that Aram [Ephraim and
the son of Remaliah] plots against you, saying,
6 “Let us go up and tear Judah asunder, make it
our own by force, and appoint the son of Tabeel*
king there.”
7 Thus says the LORD:

This shall not stand, it shall not be!
8 Damascus is the capital of Aram,
and Rezin the head of Damascus;
Samaria is the capital of Ephraim,
and Remaliah’s son the head of Samaria.
9 But within sixty years and five,*
Ephraim shall be crushed, no longer a
nation.
Unless your faith is firm
you shall not be firm! [s]

10 Again the LORD spoke to Ahaz: 11 Ask for a
sign from the LORD, your God; let it be deep as
the nether world, or high as the sky!* 12 But
Ahaz answered, “I will not ask! I will not tempt
the LORD!”* 13 Then he said: Listen, O house of
David! Is it not enough for you to weary men,
must you also weary my God!? 14 Therefore the
Lord himself will give you this sign:* the virgin
shall be with child, and bear a son, and shall
name him Immanuel. 15 He shall be living on
curds and honey* by the time he learns to reject
the bad and choose the good. 16 For before the
child learns to reject the bad and choose the
good, the land of those two kings whom you
dread shall be deserted.
17 The LORD shall bring upon you and your

6, 12: Several limited deportations in the time of Isaiah would later culminate in the Babylonian Exile.

7, 1: Days of Ahaz: who ruled from 735 to 715 B.C. This attack against Jerusalem by the kings of Aram (Syria) and Israel was occasioned by Ahaz’ refusal to enter with them into an anti-Assyrian alliance; cf 2 Kgs 16.

7, 3: Shear-jashub: this name means “a remnant will return.”

7, 6: Son of Tabeel: an adherent of Jerusalem’s enemies. His appointment would interrupt the lawful succession from David.

7, 9: Within sixty years and five: if the text is correct, its reference is unknown.

7, 11: Deep . . . sky: an extraordinary or miraculous sign that would prove God’s firm will to save the royal house of David from its oppressors.

7, 12: Tempt the Lord: Ahaz expresses in this hypocritical way his preference for depending upon the might of Assyria rather than upon God.

7, 14: The sign proposed by Isaiah was concerned with the preservation of Judah in the midst of distress (cf Is 7, 15. 17), but more especially with the fulfillment of God’s earlier promise to David (2 Sm 7, 12–16) in the coming of Immanuel (meaning, “With us is God”) as the ideal king (cf Is 9, 5–6; 11, 1–5). The church has always followed St. Matthew in seeing the transcendent fulfillment of this verse in Christ and his Virgin Mother. The prophet need not have known the full force latent in his own words; and some Catholic writers have sought a preliminary and partial fulfillment in the conception and birth of the future King Hezekiah, whose mother, at the time Isaiah spoke, would have been a young, unmarried woman (Hebrew, almah). The Holy Spirit was preparing, however, for another Nativity which alone could fulfill the divinely given terms of Immanuel’s mission, and in which the perpetual virginity of the Mother of God was to fulfill also the words of this prophecy in the integral sense intended by the divine Wisdom.

7, 15: Curds and honey: the restricted diet of those who remain after devastation has changed the once fertile fields of Judah into grazing land; cf Is 7, 21–25.

p Is 10, 22. q 2 Kgs 16, 5; 2 Chr 28, 5–15. r Is 36, 2; 2 Chr 32, 3. s Is 8, 6ff.

people and your father's house days worse than
any since Ephraim seceded from Judah. [This
means the king of Assyria.] 18 On that day

The LORD shall whistle
for the fly that is in the farthest streams of
Egypt,
and for the bee in the land of Assyria.
19 All of them shall come and settle
in the steep ravines and in the rocky clefts,
on all thornbushes and in all pastures.

20 On that day the LORD shall shave with the
razor hired from across the River [with the king
of Assyria] the head, and the hair between the
legs. It shall also shave off the beard.*
21 On that day a man shall keep a heifer or a
couple of sheep, 22 and from their abundant yield
of milk he shall live on curds; curds and honey
shall be the food of all who remain in the land.
23 On that day every place where there used to
be a thousand vines, worth a thousand pieces of
silver, shall be turned to briers and thorns.
24 Men shall go there with bow and arrows; for
all the country shall be briers and thorns. 25 For
fear of briers and thorns you shall not go upon
any mountainside which used to be hoed with
the mattock; they shall be grazing land for cattle
and shall be trampled upon by sheep.

CHAPTER 8

The Son of Isaiah 1 The LORD said to me: Take
a large cylinder-seal, and inscribe on it in ordi-
nary letters:* "Belonging to Maher-shalal-hash-
baz." 2 And I took reliable witnesses,* Uriah the
priest, and Zechariah, son of Jeberechiah. 3 Then
I went to the prophetess* and she conceived and
bore a son. The LORD said to me: Name him
Maher-shalal-hash-baz, 4 for before the child
knows how to call his father or mother by name,
the wealth of Damascus and the spoil of Samaria
shall be carried off by the king of Assyria.
5 Again the LORD spoke to me:

6 Because this people* has rejected
the waters of Shiloah that flow gently,[t]
And melts with fear before the loftiness of
Rezin and Remaliah's son,
7 Therefore the LORD raises against them
the waters of the River, great and mighty
[the king of Assyria and all his power].
It shall rise above all its channels,
and overflow all its banks;
8 It shall pass into Judah, and flood it all
throughout:
up to the neck it shall reach;
It shall spread its wings
the full width of your land, Immanuel!
9 Know, O peoples, and be appalled!
Give ear, all you distant lands!
Arm, but be crushed! Arm, but be crushed!
10 Form a plan,* and it shall be thwarted;
make a resolve, and it shall not be carried
out,
for "With us is God!"

Disciples of Isaiah 11 For thus said the LORD to
me, taking hold of me and warning me not to
walk in the way of this people:[u]

12 Call not alliance what this people calls
alliance,
and fear not, nor stand in awe of what they
fear.
13 But with the LORD of hosts make your
alliance—
for him be your fear and your awe.
14 Yet he shall be a snare, an obstacle and a
stumbling stone
to both the houses of Israel,
A trap and a snare

7, 20: God will use the Assyrians from across the River (the Euphrates) as his instrument (razor) to inflict disgrace and suffering upon his people.

8, 1: Ordinary letters: easily read by all. Maher-shalal-hash-baz: a symbolic name to be given to another son of Isaiah (v 3); it means "quick spoils; speedy plunder," and describes what the Assyrians will do.

8, 2: Reliable witnesses: who would testify that Isaiah had indeed prophesied the future destruction. Uriah the priest: cf 2 Kgs 16, 10.

8, 3: The prophetess: wife of Isaiah.

8, 6ff: This people: Judah. Waters of Shiloah: the stream that flows into the pool of Shiloah in Jerusalem, its slow current symbolizing the silent, divine protection which Judah has rejected. God will therefore summon the mighty Assyrian army, symbolized by the River (Euphrates), to devastate Judah, which, however, will not be entirely destroyed, because it is the land of Immanuel.

8, 10: The plan of Israel's enemies will be thwarted because, as the name "Immanuel" signifies, With us is God.

t Jn 9, 7. 11. u Ez 3, 14.

to those who dwell in Jerusalem;[v]
15 And many among them shall stumble and fall,
broken, snared, and captured.

16 The record is to be folded and the sealed
instruction kept among my disciples.* 17 For I
will trust in the LORD, who is hiding his face
from the house of Jacob; yes, I will wait for him.
18 Look at me and the children whom the Lord
has given me: we are signs* and portents in
Israel from the LORD of hosts who dwells on
Mount Zion. 19 [w]And when they say to you,
"Inquire of mediums and fortune-tellers (who
chirp and mutter!*); should not a people inquire
of their gods, apply to the dead on behalf of the
living?"— 20 then this document will furnish its
instruction. That kind of thing they will surely
say.*

The Prince of Peace 23 First he degraded the
land of Zebulun and the land of Naphtali;* but in
the end he has glorified the seaward road, the
land west of the Jordan, the District of the
Gentiles.

Anguish has taken wing, dispelled is darkness:
for there is no gloom where but now there
was distress.

CHAPTER 9

1 The people who walked in darkness[x]
have seen a great light;
Upon those who dwelt in the land of gloom
a light has shone.
2 You have brought them abundant joy
and great rejoicing,
As they rejoice before you as at the harvest,
as men make merry when dividing spoils.
3 For the yoke that burdened them,
the pole on their shoulder,
And the rod of their taskmaster
you have smashed, as on the day of Midian.
4 For every boot that tramped in battle,
every cloak rolled in blood,
will be burned as fuel for flames.[y]
5 For a child* is born to us, a son is given us;
upon his shoulder dominion rests.
They name him Wonder-Counselor,
God-Hero,
Father-Forever, Prince of Peace.[z]
6 His dominion is vast
and forever peaceful,
From David's throne, and over his kingdom,
which he confirms and sustains
By judgment and justice,
both now and forever.
The zeal of the LORD of hosts will do this![a]

Fall of the Northern Kingdom

7 The Lord has sent word against Jacob,
it falls upon Israel;
8 And all the people know it,
Ephraim and those who dwell in Samaria,
those who say in arrogance and pride of
heart,
9 "Bricks have fallen,
but we will build with cut stone;
Sycamores are felled,
but we will replace them with cedars."
10 But the LORD raises up their foes against them
and stirs up their enemies to action:
11 Aram* on the east and the Philistines on the
west
devour Israel with open mouth.
For all this, his wrath is not turned back,
and his hand is still outstretched!

8, 16: Kept among my disciples: for preservation and transmission.

8, 18: Signs: Isaiah and his sons had symbolic names.

8, 19: Chirp and mutter: a mocking reference to the sounds uttered by necromancers, as if the dead were speaking; all such practices were forbidden.

8, 21f: These verses have been transposed and placed within Is 14, 25, which affords the context in which they can be understood.

8, 23: Zebulun . . . Naphtali: northern Palestine, which was first to be attacked by the Assyrians; God, however, redeems it, as he redeems all his people. Seaward road: from Damascus, across southern Galilee to the Mediterranean Sea. District of the Gentiles: northern Galilee, inhabited by pagans; cf Jos 20, 7; Is 9, 1. Mt 4, 15f refers to this, since Jesus began his public mission in Galilee.

9, 5: A child: the Immanuel of Is 7, 14 and 8, 8; cf Is 11, 1. 2. 9. In Christian tradition and liturgy, this passage is used to refer to Christ. Upon his shoulder dominion rests: authority. Wonder-Counselor: remarkable for his wisdom and prudence. God-Hero: a warrior and a defender of his people, like God himself. Father-Forever: ever devoted to his people. Prince of Peace: his reign will be characterized by peace.

9, 11: Aram: the Syrian kingdom, with its capital at Damascus.

v Rom 9, 33; 1 Pt 2, 8. w Lv 19, 31; Dt 18, 10ff. x 1f: Mt 4, 15f. y Sir 39, 9. z Ps 72, 7; Lk 2, 11. 14. a Jer 23, 5; Lk 1, 32f.

12 The people do not turn to him who struck
them,
nor seek the LORD of hosts.
13 So the LORD severs from Israel head and tail,
palm branch and reed in one day.
14 [The elder and the noble are the head,
the prophet who teaches falsehood is the
tail.]
15 The leaders of this people mislead them
and those to be led are engulfed. [b]
16 For this reason, the Lord does not spare their
young men,
and their orphans and widows he does not
pity;
They are wholly profaned and sinful,
and every mouth gives vent to folly.
For all this, his wrath is not turned back,
his hand is still outstretched!

17 For wickedness burns like fire,
devouring brier and thorn;
It kindles the forest thickets,
which go up in columns of smoke.
18 At the wrath of the LORD of hosts the land
quakes,
and the people are like fuel for fire;
No man spares his brother,
each devours the flesh of his neighbor.
19 Though they hack on the right, they are
hungry;
though they eat on the left, they are not
filled.
20 Manasseh devours Ephraim,* and Ephraim
Manasseh;
together they turn on Judah.
For all this, his wrath is not turned back,
his hand is still outstretched!

CHAPTER 10

Social Injustice

1 Woe to those who enact unjust statutes
and who write oppressive decrees, [c]
2 Depriving the needy of judgment
and robbing my people's poor of their rights,
Making widows their plunder,
and orphans their prey! [d]
3 What will you do on the day of punishment,
when ruin comes from afar?
To whom will you flee for help?
Where will you leave your wealth,
4 Lest it sink beneath the captive
or fall beneath the slain?
For all this, his wrath is not turned back,
his hand is still outstretched!

Assyria the Unconscious Instrument of God

5 Woe to Assyria! My rod in anger,
my staff in wrath.
6 Against an impious nation* I send him,
and against a people under my wrath I order
him
To seize plunder, carry off loot,
and tread them down like the mud of the
streets.
7 But this is not what he intends,
nor does he have this in mind;
Rather, it is in his heart to destroy,
to make an end of nations not a few.
8 "Are not my commanders all kings?" he says,
9 "Is not Calno like Carchemish, [e]
Or Hamath like Arpad,
or Samaria like Damascus?*
10 Just as my hand reached out to idolatrous
kingdoms
that had more images than Jerusalem and
Samaria,
11 Just as I treated Samaria and her idols,
shall I not do to Jerusalem and her graven
images?" [f]

12 *[But when the LORD has brought to an end
all his work on Mount Zion and in Jerusalem,

I will punish the utterance
of the king of Assyria's proud heart,
13 and the boastfulness of his haughty eyes.
For he says:]

"By my own power I have done it,

9, 20: Manasseh . . . Ephraim: two of the leading tribes of the northern kingdom.

10, 6f: Impious nation: Israel. It was God's intention to use Assyria merely to punish, not to destroy, his people.

10, 9: Calno . . . Damascus: cities captured by the Assyrians.

b Is 28, 7; Jer 2, 8; 5, 31; 20, 6; 23, 13f; 29, 30ff; Ez 13, 1–7; 22, 28; Mi 3, 11. c Jer 8, 8. d Is 1, 23. e Is 36, 19; Am 6, 2. f Is 36, 20.

and by my wisdom, for I am shrewd.
I have moved the boundaries of peoples,
their treasures I have pillaged,
and, like a giant, I have put down the enthroned.
14 My hand has seized like a nest
the riches of nations;
As one takes eggs left alone,
so I took in all the earth;
No one fluttered a wing,
or opened a mouth, or chirped!"

15 Will the axe boast against him who hews with it?
Will the saw exalt itself above him who wields it?
As if a rod could sway him who lifts it,
or a staff him who is not wood!
16 Therefore the Lord, the LORD of hosts,
will send among his fat ones* leanness,
And instead of his glory there will be kindling
like the kindling of fire.
17 The Light of Israel will become a fire,
Israel's Holy One a flame,
That burns and consumes his briers
and his thorns in a single day.
18 His splendid forests and orchards
will be consumed, soul and body;
19 And the remnant of the trees in his forest
will be so few,
Like poles set up for signals,
that any boy can record them.
20 On that day
The remnant of Israel,
the survivors of the house of Jacob,
will no more lean upon him who struck them;
But they will lean upon the LORD,
the Holy One of Israel, in truth.
21 A remnant will return,* the remnant of Jacob,
to the mighty God.
22 For though your people, O Israel,
were like the sand of the sea,
Only a remnant of them will return;
their destruction is decreed
as overwhelming justice demands.[g]

23 Yes, the destruction he has decreed, the
Lord, the GOD of hosts, will carry out within the
whole land. 24 Therefore thus says the Lord, the
GOD of hosts: O my people, who dwell in Zion,
do not fear the Assyrian, though he strikes you
with a rod, and raises his staff against you. 25 For
only a brief moment more, and my anger shall be
over; but them I will destroy in wrath. 26 Then
the LORD of hosts will raise against them a
scourge such as struck Midian at the rock of
Oreb; and he will raise his staff over the sea as
he did against Egypt.[h] 27 On that day,*

His burden shall be taken from your shoulder,
and his yoke shattered from your neck.

Sennacherib's Invasion

He has come up from the direction of Rimmon,
28 he has reached Aiath, passed through Migron,
at Michmash his supplies are stored.
29 They cross the ravine:
"We will spend the night at Geba."
Ramah is in terror,
Gibeah of Saul has fled.
30 Cry and shriek, O daughter of Gallim!
Hearken, Laishah! Answer her, Anathoth!
31 Madmenah is in flight,
the inhabitants of Gebim seek refuge.
32 Even today he will halt at Nob,*
he will shake his fist at the mount of daughter Zion,
the hill of Jerusalem!
33 Behold, the Lord, the LORD of hosts,
lops off the boughs with terrible violence;
The tall of stature are felled,
and the lofty ones brought low;
34 The forest thickets are felled with the axe,
and Lebanon in its splendor falls.

10, 16: His fat ones: the strong men of the king of Assyria.

10, 21: A remnant will return: in Hebrew, shear-jashub, an allusion to the name of Isaiah's son, Shear-jashub; cf Is 7, 3.

10, 27–32: A poetic description of the progress of the Assyrian army, advancing from the north through Judah to the gates of Jerusalem.

10, 32ff: Just when the enemy is about to capture Jerusalem, God intervenes and destroys the hostile army.

g Rom 9, 27f. h Jgs 7, 25.

CHAPTER 11

The Rule of Immanuel

[1] But a shoot shall sprout from the stump of Jesse,*
and from his roots a bud shall blossom.[i]
[2] The spirit of the LORD shall rest upon him:[j]
a spirit of wisdom and of understanding,
A spirit of counsel and of strength,
a spirit of knowledge and of fear of the LORD,*
[3] and his delight shall be the fear of the LORD.
Not by appearance shall he judge,
nor by hearsay shall he decide,
[4] But he shall judge the poor with justice,
and decide aright for the land's afflicted.[k]
He shall strike the ruthless with the rod of his mouth,
and with the breath of his lips he shall slay the wicked.
[5] Justice shall be the band around his waist,
and faithfulness a belt upon his hips.

[6] Then the wolf shall be a guest of the lamb,*
and the leopard shall lie down with the kid;
The calf and the young lion shall browse together,
with a little child to guide them.[l]
[7] The cow and the bear shall be neighbors,
together their young shall rest;
the lion shall eat hay like the ox.
[8] The baby shall play by the cobra's den,
and the child lay his hand on the adder's lair.
[9] There shall be no harm or ruin on all my holy mountain;
for the earth shall be filled with knowledge of the LORD,
as water covers the sea.[m]

Union of Ephraim and Judah

[10] On that day,
The root of Jesse,
set up as a signal for the nations,
The Gentiles shall seek out,
for his dwelling shall be glorious.[n]
[11] On that day,
The Lord shall again take it in hand[o]
to reclaim the remnant of his people
that is left from Assyria and Egypt,
Pathros, Ethiopia, and Elam,
Shinar, Hamath, and the isles of the sea.*
[12] He shall raise a signal to the nations
and gather the outcasts of Israel;
The dispersed of Judah he shall assemble
from the four corners of the earth.
[13] The envy of Ephraim shall pass away,
and the rivalry of Judah be removed;
Ephraim shall not be jealous of Judah,
and Judah shall not be hostile to Ephraim;[p]
[14] But they shall swoop down on the foothills
of the Philistines to the west,
together they shall plunder the Kedemites;*
Edom and Moab shall be their possessions,
and the Ammonites their subjects.
[15] The LORD shall dry up the tongue of the Sea of Egypt,*
and wave his hand over the Euphrates in his fierce anger
And shatter it into seven streamlets,
so that it can be crossed in sandals.[q]
[16] There shall be a highway for the remnant of his people
that is left from Assyria,
As there was for Israel
when he came up from the land of Egypt.

11, 1: Jesse: David's father. Shoot . . . stump: after the Babylonian exile only a stump of the Davidic dynasty will remain; from it will arise the new shoot, the messianic King.

11, 2f: The source of the traditional names of the gifts of the Holy Spirit. The Septuagint and the Vulgate read "piety" for fear of the Lord in its first occurrence, thus listing seven gifts.

11, 6–9: This picture of the idyllic harmony of paradise is a dramatic symbol of the universal peace and justice of messianic times.

11, 11: Pathros . . . sea: where God's people lived in exile. Pathros: upper Egypt. Elam: east of Babylonia. Shinar: Babylonia. Hamath: on the Orontes River in Syria. Isles: or coastlands, in the Mediterranean.

11, 14: Kedemites: tribes in the Arabian Desert.

11, 15: Tongue . . . Egypt: the body of water between Egypt and Palestine.

i Lk 3, 32. j Mt 3, 16; Mk 1, 10. k Pss 72, 2. 4; 98, 9; 2 Thes 2, 8. l Is 65, 25. m Hb 2, 14. n Is 49, 22; Rom 15, 12. o Is 27, 13; Mi 7, 12; Zec 10, 10. p Ex 37, 16–17. q Ex 14, 29.

CHAPTER 12

Song of Thanksgiving*

1 On that day, you will say:
I give you thanks, O LORD;
though you have been angry with me,
your anger has abated, and you have
consoled me.
2 God indeed is my savior;
I am confident and unafraid.
My strength and my courage is the LORD,
and he has been my savior. [r]
3 With joy you will draw water
at the fountain of salvation, 4 and say on that
day:
Give thanks to the LORD, acclaim his name;
among the nations make known his deeds,
proclaim how exalted is his name.
5 Sing praise to the LORD for his glorious
achievement;
let this be known throughout all the earth. [s]
6 Shout with exultation, O city of Zion,
for great in your midst
is the Holy One of Israel! [t]

III: Oracles Against the Pagan Nations

CHAPTER 13

Babylon 1 An oracle concerning Babylon; a vi-
sion of Isaiah, son of Amoz.

2 Upon the bare mountains set up a signal;
cry out to them,*
Wave for them to enter
the gates of the volunteers. [u]

3 I have commanded my dedicated soldiers,*
I have summoned my warriors,
eager and bold to carry out my anger.
4 Listen! the rumble on the mountains:
that of an immense throng!
Listen! the noise of kingdoms,
nations assembled!
The LORD of hosts is mustering
an army for battle. [v]
5 They come from a far-off country,
and from the end of the heavens,
The LORD and the instruments of his wrath,
to destroy all the land.

6 Howl, for the day of the LORD* is near;
as destruction from the Almighty it comes. [w]
7 Therefore all hands fall helpless,[x]
the bows of the young men fall from their
hands.
Every man's heart melts 8 in terror.
Pangs and sorrows take hold of them,
like a woman in labor they writhe;
They look aghast at each other,
their faces aflame. [y]
9 Lo, the day of the LORD comes,
cruel, with wrath and burning anger;
To lay waste the land
and destroy the sinners within it!
10 The stars and constellations of the heavens
send forth no light;
The sun is dark when it rises,
and the light of the moon does not shine. [z]
11 Thus I will punish the world for its evil
and the wicked for their guilt.
I will put an end to the pride of the arrogant,
the insolence of tyrants I will humble. [a]
12 I will make mortals more rare than pure gold,
men, than gold of Ophir.*
13 For this I will make the heavens tremble
and the earth shall be shaken from its place,
At the wrath of the LORD of hosts
on the day of his burning anger.

14 Like a hunted gazelle,
or a flock that no one gathers,
Every man shall turn to his kindred

12, 1–6: Israel's thanksgiving to the Lord, expressed in language like that of the Psalms.

13, 2: To them: the Medes (v 17) and Persians, who would destroy Babylon. Gates of the volunteers: the mustering places of Babylon's enemies for war against her.

13, 3: Dedicated soldiers: in the sense that they will wage a "holy war" and carry out God's plan.

13, 6ff: Day of the Lord: described often in prophetical writings, it generally signified the coming of the Lord in power and majesty to destroy his enemies and inaugurate his kingdom. Here it refers to the overthrow of Babylon. The figures used convey the idea of horror and destruction. Read vv 6–8 with vv 14–16.

13, 12: Ophir: cf note to Ps 45, 10.

r Ex 15, 2; Ps 118, 14. s Ex 15, 1. t Is 41, 14. 16; 54, 1; Zep 3, 14; Zec 2, 10. u Is 5, 26. v Jer 50, 9. w Jer 46, 10; Jl 1, 15. x Ez 7, 17. y Is 21, 3; Ps 48, 7; Mi 4, 9. z Is 24, 23. a Is 2, 17; Jer 50. 32.

and flee to his own land. [b]
15 Everyone who is caught shall be run through;
to a man, they shall fall by the sword.
16 Their infants shall be dashed to pieces in their sight;
their houses shall be plundered
and their wives ravished. [c]

17 I am stirring up against them the Medes,
who think nothing of silver
and take no delight in gold. [d]
18 The fruit of the womb they shall not spare,
nor shall they have eyes of pity for children.
19 And Babylon, the jewel of kingdoms,
the glory and pride of the Chaldeans,
Shall be overthrown by God
like Sodom and like Gomorrah.
20 She shall never be inhabited,
nor dwelt in, from age to age;
The Arab shall not pitch his tent there,
nor shepherds couch their flocks. [e]
21 But wildcats shall rest there
and owls shall fill the houses;
There ostriches shall dwell,
and satyrs* shall dance. [f]
22 Desert beasts shall howl in her castles,
and jackals in her luxurious palaces.
Her time is near at hand
and her days shall not be prolonged.

CHAPTER 14

The King of Babylon 1 When the LORD has
pity on Jacob and again chooses Israel and settles
them on their own soil, the aliens will join them
and be counted with the house of Jacob. [g] 2 The
house of Israel will take them and bring them
along to its place, and possess them as male and
female slaves on the Lord's soil, making captives
of its captors and ruling over its oppressors. [h]
3 On the day the LORD relieves you of sorrow and
unrest and the hard service in which you have
been enslaved, [i] 4 you will take up this taunt-
song* against the king of Babylon: [j]

How the oppressor has reached his end!
how the turmoil is stilled!
5 The LORD has broken the rod of the wicked,
the staff of the tyrants
6 That struck the peoples in wrath
relentless blows;
That beat down the nations in anger,
with oppression unchecked.
7 The whole earth rests peacefully,
song breaks forth;
8 The very cypresses rejoice over you,
and the cedars of Lebanon:
"Now that you are laid to rest,
there will be none to cut us down." [k]

9 The nether world below is all astir
preparing for your coming;
It awakens the shades to greet you,
all the leaders of the earth;
It has the kings of all nations
rise from their thrones.
10 All of them speak out
and say to you,
"You too have become weak like us,
you are the same as we.
11 Down to the nether world your pomp is brought,
the music of your harps.
The couch beneath you is the maggot,
your covering, the worm." [l]
12 How have you fallen from the heavens,
O morning star,* son of the dawn!
How are you cut down to the ground,
you who mowed down the nations!
13 You said in your heart: [m]
"I will scale the heavens;
Above the stars of God
I will set up my throne;
I will take my seat on the Mount of Assembly,
in the recesses of the North.*
14 I will ascend above the tops of the clouds;
I will be like the Most High!" [n]

13, 21: Satyrs: in the popular mind, demons of goatlike form dwelling in ruins, symbols of immorality; cf Lv 17, 7.

14, 4–21: This taunt-song, or satire, is one of the finest in the Bible.

14, 12: Morning star: the king of Babylon. The Vulgate has "Lucifer," a name applied by the church Fathers to Satan.

14, 13: Recesses of the North: see note on Ps 48, 3.

b Jer 50, 16. c Na 3, 10. d Is 21, 2; Jer 51, 11. 28. e Jer 51, 62. f Is 34, 13f; 35, 7. g Is 56, 3; 60, 4; Ps 102, 14; Jer 24, 6; Zec 1, 17. h Is 66, 20. i Jer 30, 10. j Hb 2, 6. k Ez 31, 16. l Sir 10, 13. m Jer 51, 53; Am 9, 2. n Ez 28, 2.

15 Yet down to the nether world you go
to the recesses of the pit!
16 When they see you they will stare,
pondering over you:
"Is this the man who made the earth tremble,
and kingdoms quake?
17 Who made the world a desert,
razed its cities,
and gave his captives no release?
18 All the kings of the nations lie in glory,
each in his own tomb;
19 But you are cast forth without burial,
loathsome and corrupt,
Clothed as those slain at sword-point,
a trampled corpse.
Going down to the pavement of the
pit,
20 you will never be one with them in the
grave."
For you have ruined your land,
you have slain your people!

Let him not be named forever,
that scion of an evil race!
21 Make ready to slaughter his sons
for the guilt of their fathers;
Lest they rise and possess the earth,
and fill the breadth of the world with
tyrants.

22 I will rise up against them, says the LORD of
hosts, and cut off from Babylon name and
remnant, progeny and offspring, says the LORD.[o]
23 I will make it a haunt of hoot owls and a
marshland; I will sweep it with the broom of
destruction, says the LORD of hosts.

Assyria

24 The LORD of hosts has sworn:
As I have resolved,
so shall it be;
As I have proposed,
so shall it stand:

25 I will break the Assyrian in my land
and trample him on my mountains;
21 *He shall pass through it hard-pressed and
hungry,
and in his hunger he shall become enraged,
and curse his king and his gods.
He shall look upward,
but there shall be strict darkness
without any dawn;
22 He shall gaze at the earth,
but there shall be distress and darkness,
with the light blacked out by its
clouds.
(25) Then his yoke shall be removed from them,
and his burden from their shoulder.
26 This is the plan proposed for the whole earth,
and this the hand outstretched over all
nations.
27 The LORD of hosts has planned;
who can thwart him?
His hand is stretched out;
who can turn it back?

Philistia 28 In the year that King Ahaz died,*
there came this oracle:

29 Rejoice not, O Philistia, not a man of you,
that the rod* which smote you is broken;
For out of the serpent's root shall come an
adder,
its fruit shall be a flying saraph.
30 In my pastures the poor shall eat,
and the needy lie down in safety;
But I will kill your root with famine
that shall slay even your remnant.
31 Howl, O gate; cry out, O city!
Philistia, all of you melts away!
For there comes a smoke from the north,
without a straggler in the ranks.
32 What will one answer the messengers of the
nation?
"The LORD has established Zion,
and in her the afflicted of his people find
refuge."[p]

14, 21f: He . . . clouds: the two verses have been transposed from chap. 8.
14, 28: The year that King Ahaz died: 715 B.C.

14, 29: Rod: an Assyrian oppressor whose identity is uncertain. Flying saraph: a poisonous serpent, distinguished by its speedy movement; cf note on Nm 21, 6.

o Jer 51, 62. p Pss 87, 5; 102, 17f; Zep 3, 12.

CHAPTER 15

Moab

1 Oracle on Moab:
Laid waste in a night,
Ar of Moab is destroyed;
Laid waste in a night,
Kir of Moab is destroyed. [q]
2 Up goes daughter Dibon [r]
to the high places to weep;
Over Nebo and over Medeba
Moab wails.
Every head is shaved,
every beard sheared off.*
3 In the streets they wear sackcloth,
lamenting and weeping;
On rooftops and in the squares
everyone wails.
4 Heshbon and Elealeh cry out,
they are heard as far as Jahaz.
At this the loins of Moab tremble,
his soul quivers within him; [s]
5 The heart of Moab cries out,
his fugitives reach Zoar
[Eglath-shelishiyah].
The ascent of Luhith
they climb weeping;
On the way to Horonaim [t]
they utter rending cries.

6 The waters of Nimrim
have become a waste;
The grass is withered,
new growth is gone,
nothing is green.
7 So now whatever they have acquired or stored away
they carry across the Gorge of the Poplars,
8 For the cry has gone round
the land of Moab;
As far as Eglaim the wailing,
and to Beer-elim, the wail.
9 The waters of Dimon were filled with blood,*
but I will bring still more upon Dimon:
Lions for those who are fleeing from Moab
and for those who remain in the land!

CHAPTER 16

1 Send them forth, hugging the earth like reptiles,
from Sela across the desert,
to the mount of daughter Zion.
2 Like flushed birds,
like startled nestlings,
Are the daughters of Moab
at the fords of the Arnon.*
3 Offer counsel, take their part:*
at high noon let your shadow be like the night,
To hide the outcasts,
to conceal the fugitives.
4 Let the outcasts of Moab live with you,
be their shelter from the destroyer.
When the struggle is ended, the ruin complete,
and they have done with trampling the land,
5 A throne shall be set up in mercy,
and on it shall sit in fidelity
[in David's tent]
A judge upholding right
and prompt to do justice. [u]

6 We have heard of the pride of Moab,
how very proud he is,
With his haughty, arrogant insolence
that his empty words do not match. [v]

7 Therefore Moab wails for Moab,*
everywhere they wail;
For the raisin cakes* of Kir-hareseth
they sigh, stricken with grief. [w]
8 The terraced slopes of Heshbon languish,

15, 2: Every head . . . sheared off: traditional signs of grief.

15, 9: There is in the Hebrew a play on words: Dimon and dam, the latter signifying "blood."

16, 2: The Arnon: principal river of Moab.

16, 3–5: Directed to Jerusalem, which should receive the suffering Moabites with mercy, as befits the city of David's family, who were partly descended from Ruth the Moabite.

16, 7–14: Moab had been prosperous; now it has become a desert.

16, 7: Raisin cakes: masses of dried compressed grapes used as food (cf 2 Sm 6, 19; 1 Chr 16, 3; Ct 2, 5), and also in pagan cult (Hos 3, 1).

q Is 16, 7. r Jer 48, 38f. s Jer 48, 34. t Is 16, 9; Jer 48, 3. u Is 32, 1. v Jer 48, 29. w Is 15, 3.

the vines of Sibmah,
Whose clusters overpowered
the lords of nations,
While they reached as far as Jazer
and scattered over the desert,*
And whose branches spread forth
and extended over the sea.
9 Therefore I weep with Jazer
for the vines of Sibmah;
I water you with tears,
Heshbon and Elealeh;
For on your summer fruits and harvests
the battle cry has fallen.[x]
10 From the orchards are taken away
joy and gladness,
In the vineyards there is no singing,
no shout of joy;
In the wine presses no one treads grapes,
the vintage shout is stilled.[y]
11 Therefore for Moab
my breast moans like a lyre,
and my heart for Kir-hareseth.[z]
12 When Moab grows weary on the high places,[a]
he shall enter his sanctuary to pray,
but it shall avail him nothing.*

13 *This is the word the LORD spoke against
Moab in times past. 14 But now the LORD has
spoken: In three years, like those of a hireling,
the glory of Moab shall be degraded despite all
its great multitude; there shall be a remnant,
very small and weak.

CHAPTER 17

Damascus

1 Oracle on Damascus:*
Lo, Damascus shall cease to be a city
and become a ruin;[b]
2 Her cities shall be forever abandoned,
given over to flocks to lie in undisturbed.
3 The fortress shall be lost to Ephraim*
and the kingdom to Damascus;
The remnant of Aram shall have the same
glory
as the Israelites,
says the LORD of hosts.
4 On that day
The glory of Jacob shall fade,
and his full body grow thin,[c]
5 Like the reaper's mere armful of stalks
when he gathers the standing grain;
Or as when one gleans the ears
in the Valley of Rephaim.*
6 Only a scattering of grapes shall be left!
As when an olive tree has been beaten,
Two or three olives remain at the very top,
four or five on its fruitful branches,*
says the LORD, the God of Israel.[d]

7 On that day man shall look to his maker,
his eyes turned toward the Holy One of
Israel.[e]
8 He shall not look to the altars, his handiwork,
nor shall he regard what his fingers have
made:
the sacred poles* or the incense stands.
9 On that day his strong cities shall be
like those abandoned by the Hivites and
Amorites
When faced with the children of Israel:
they shall be laid waste.[f]
10 For you have forgotten God, your savior,
and remembered not the Rock, your
strength.
Therefore, though you plant your pagan
plants*
and set out your foreign vine slips,[g]

16, 8: Desert: to the east. Sea: the Dead Sea.
16, 12: In vain do the Moabites appeal to their god Chemosh.
16, 13f: A prose application of the preceding poetic oracle against Moab (15, 1—16, 12); cf Jer 4, 8. Like those of a hireling: who fulfills his period of service according to the shortest manner of reckoning; cf Is 21, 16.
17, 1: Damascus: capital of Syria, destroyed in 732 B.C.
17, 3: Ephraim: Israel, leagued with Syria against Assyria and Judah; destroyed in 721 B.C. Aram: Syria.
17, 5: Valley of Rephaim: a fertile plain to the southwest of Jerusalem; cf Jos 15, 8; 2 Sm 5, 18.
17, 6: Olives not easily picked by hand were knocked from the tree by means of a long stick; cf Is 24, 13.
17, 8: Sacred poles: see note on Ex 34, 13. Incense stands: small altars on which incense was burned in idolatrous worship; cf Is 27, 9; Lv 26, 30.
17, 10: Pagan plants: literally, "plants of delights," understood by some as planted in honor of the god of fertility.

x Is 15, 5; Jer 48, 32. y Is 24, 8. z Is 15, 5; Jer 48, 36. a Jer 48, 13. b Jer 49, 23. c Is 10, 16. d Is 24, 13. e Mi 5, 12. f Is 27, 10. g Jer 2, 32; Hos 8, 14.

11 Though you make them grow the day you
plant them
and make your sprouts blossom on the next
morning,
The harvest shall disappear on the day of the
grievous blow,
the incurable blight.

12 Ah! the roaring of many peoples*
that roar like the roar of the seas!
The surging of nations
that surge like the surging of mighty waves!
13 But God shall rebuke them,
and they shall flee far away;
Windswept, like chaff on the mountains,
like tumbleweed in a storm.
14 In the evening, they spread terror,
before morning, they are gone!
Such is the portion of those who despoil us,
the lot of those who plunder us.

CHAPTER 18

Ethiopia

1 Ah, land of buzzing insects,*
beyond the rivers of Ethiopia,*
2 Sending ambassadors by sea,
in papyrus boats on the waters!
Go, swift messengers,
to a nation tall and bronzed,
To a people dreaded near and far,
a nation strong and conquering,
whose land is washed by rivers.[h]
3 All you who inhabit the world,
who dwell on earth,
When the signal is raised on the mountain,
look!
When the trumpet blows, listen!
4 For thus says the LORD to me:
I will quietly look on from where I dwell,
Like the glowing heat of sunshine,
like a cloud of dew at harvest time.
5 Before the vintage, when the flowering is
ended,
and the blooms are succeeded by ripening
grapes,
Then comes the cutting of branches with
pruning hooks
and the discarding of the lopped-off shoots.
6 They shall all be left to the mountain birds of
prey,
and to the beasts in the land;
The birds of prey shall summer on them
and on them all the beasts of the earth shall
winter.

7 Then will gifts be brought to the LORD of
hosts from a people tall and bronzed, from a
people dreaded near and far, a nation strong and
conquering, whose land is washed by rivers—to
Mount Zion where dwells the name of the LORD
of hosts.[i]

CHAPTER 19

Egypt

1 Oracle on Egypt:
See, the LORD is riding on a swift cloud
on his way to Egypt;
The idols of Egypt tremble before him,
the hearts of the Egyptians melt within
them.
2 I will rouse Egypt against Egypt:
brother will war against brother,
Neighbor against neighbor,
city against city, kingdom against kingdom.
3 The courage of the Egyptians ebbs away
within them,
and I will bring to nought their counsel;
They shall consult idols and charmers,
ghosts and spirits.[j]
4 I will deliver Egypt
into the power of a cruel master,*
A harsh king who shall rule over them,
says the Lord, the LORD of hosts.[k]

17, 12f: Many peoples: the hordes that accompanied the invading Assyrians, whom God repels just as he vanquished the primeval waters of chaos; see notes on Jb 3, 8; 7, 12; Ps 89, 11.

18, 1: Land of buzzing insects: the region of the Upper Nile where these multiplied with great rapidity.

18, 1f: Papyrus boats: light and serviceable vessels made of bundles of papyrus stalks and sealed with pitch. Egypt, ruled by a dynasty from Ethiopia, had invited Judah to join a coalition against Assyria, but Isaiah bade the ambassadors return to their own people.

19, 4: Cruel master: the king of Assyria.

h Is 18, 7. i Is 45, 14; Zep 3, 10; Mal 1, 11. j Is 44, 25. k Ez 29, 19; 30, 10.

[5] The waters shall be drained from the sea,
the river shall shrivel and dry up; [l]
[6] Its streams shall become foul,
and the canals of Egypt shall dwindle and dry up.
Reeds and rushes shall wither away,
[7] and bulrushes on the bank of the Nile;
All the sown land along the Nile
shall dry up and blow away, and be no more.
[8] The fishermen shall mourn and lament,
all who cast hook in the Nile;
Those who spread their nets in the water
shall pine away.
[9] The linen-workers shall be disappointed,
the combers and weavers shall turn pale; [m]
[10] The spinners shall be crushed,
all the hired laborers shall be despondent.
[11] Utter fools are the princes of Zoan!*
the wisest of Pharaoh's advisers give stupid counsel.
How can you say to Pharaoh,
"I am a disciple of wise men, of ancient kings"?
[12] Where then are your wise men?
Let them tell you and make known
What the LORD of hosts has planned
against Egypt.
[13] The princes of Zoan have become fools,
the princes of Memphis have been deceived.
The chiefs of her tribes
have led Egypt astray.
[14] The LORD has prepared among them
a spirit of dizziness,
And they have made Egypt stagger in
whatever she does,
as a drunkard staggers in his vomit.
[15] Egypt shall have no work to do [n]
for head or tail, palm branch or reed.*

[16] On that day the Egyptians shall be like
women, trembling with fear, because of the
LORD of hosts shaking his fist at them. [o] [17] And
the land of Judah shall be a terror to the
Egyptians. Every time they remember Judah,
they shall stand in dread because of the plan
which the LORD of hosts has in mind for them. [p]

[18] On that day there shall be five cities* in the
land of Egypt speaking the language of Canaan
and swearing by the LORD of hosts; one shall be
called "City of the Sun."

[19] On that day there shall be an altar to the
LORD in the land of Egypt, and a sacred pillar to
the LORD near the boundary. [20] It shall be a sign
and a witness to the LORD of hosts in the land of
Egypt, when they cry out to the LORD against
their oppressors, and he sends them a savior to
defend and deliver them. [21] The LORD shall make
himself known to Egypt, and the Egyptians shall
know the LORD in that day; they shall offer
sacrifices and oblations, and fulfill the vows they
make to the LORD. [q] [22] Although the LORD shall
smite Egypt severely, he shall heal them; they
shall turn to the LORD and he shall be won over
and heal them.

[23] On that day there shall be a highway from
Egypt to Assyria; the Assyrians shall enter Egypt,
and the Egyptians enter Assyria, and Egypt shall
serve Assyria.

[24] On that day Israel shall be a third party with
Egypt and Assyria, a blessing in the midst of the
land, [r] [25] when the LORD of hosts blesses it:
"Blessed be my people Egypt, and the work of
my hands Assyria, and my inheritance, Israel."

CHAPTER 20

Captivity of Egypt and Ethiopia [1] In the year
the general sent by Sargon, king of Assyria,
fought against Ashdod and captured it, [2] the
LORD gave a warning through Isaiah,* the son of
Amoz: Go and take off the sackcloth from your
waist, and remove the sandals from your feet.
This he did, walking naked and barefoot. [3] Then

19, 11. 13: Zoan: later known as Tanis, and Memphis (in Hebrew Noph) were the key cities of the Nile Delta.

19, 15: Head or tail, palm branch or reed: the leaders or the people; cf Is 9, 13f.

19, 18: Five cities: colonies of Jews living together and speaking their languages, Hebrew and Aramaic; cf Jer, chap. 43. City of the Sun: the meaning is uncertain, but the reference seems to be to the city known later as Heliopolis.

20, 2–6: The symbolic act of the prophet conveyed the idea that Assyria would lead captive the Egyptians and Ethiopians. The Judeans and their allies would then realize the folly of having trusted in them.

l Ez 30, 12; 32, 2. m Ez 27, 7. n Is 9, 14. o Na 3, 13. p Ex 14, 25. q Zec 14, 16. 18. r Gn 12, 2.

the LORD said: Just as my servant Isaiah has gone
naked and barefoot for three years as a sign and
portent against Egypt and Ethiopia, 4 so shall the
king of Assyria lead away captives from Egypt,
and exiles from Ethiopia, young and old, naked
and barefoot, with buttocks uncovered [the
shame of Egypt]. 5 They shall be dismayed and
ashamed because of Ethiopia, their hope, and
because of Egypt, their boast.[s] 6 The inhabitants
of this coastland shall say on that day, "Look at
our hope! We have fled here for help and
deliverance from the king of Assyria; where can
we flee now?"[t]

CHAPTER 21

Fall of Babylon

1 Oracle on the wastelands by the sea:*
Like whirlwinds sweeping in waves through
the Negeb,
there comes from the desert,
from the fearful land,
2 A cruel sight, revealed to me:
the traitor betrays,
the despoiler spoils.
"Go up, Elam; besiege, O Media;*
I will put an end to all groaning!"[u]
3 Therefore my loins are filled with anguish,
pangs have seized me like those of a woman
in labor;
I am too bewildered to hear,
too dismayed to look.[v]
4 My mind reels,
shuddering assails me;
My yearning for twilight
has turned into dread.
5 They set the table,
spread out the rugs;
they eat, they drink.*
Rise up, O princes,
oil the shield!
6 For thus says my Lord to me:
Go, station a watchman,
let him tell what he sees.
7 If he sees a chariot,
a pair of horses,
Someone riding an ass,
someone riding a camel,
Then let him pay heed,
very close heed.
8 Then the watchman cried,
"On the watchtower, O my Lord,
I stand constantly by day;
And I stay at my post
through all the watches of the night.[w]
9 Here he comes now:
a single chariot,
a pair of horses;
He calls out and says,
'Fallen, fallen is Babylon,
And all the images of her gods
are smashed to the ground.' "[x]
10 O my people who have been threshed,
beaten on my threshing floor!
What I have heard
from the LORD of hosts,
The God of Israel,
I have announced to you.[y]

Edom

11 Oracle on Edom:
They call to me from Seir,*
"Watchman, how much longer the night?
Watchman, how much longer the night?"
12 The watchman replies,
"Morning has come, and again night.
If you will ask, ask; come back again."

Arabia

13 Oracle on Arabia:*
In the thicket in the nomad country spend the
night,

21, 1: Wastelands by the sea: Babylonia. Negeb: the desert south of Judah.

21, 2: Elam . . . Media: nations which, under the leadership of Cyrus, captured Babylon in 538 B.C. End to all groaning: those who were captives of Babylon shall be freed.

21, 5: Babylon is destroyed while its leaders are feasting; cf Dn 5. Oil the shield: shields were oiled and greased so as to divert blows more easily.

21, 11f: Seir: another name for Edom. The Edomites ask the prophet how much longer they must suffer (the night of suffering); he answers ambiguously: "Liberation (morning) and further suffering (night)," but perhaps they will later receive a more encouraging answer (ask; come back again).

21, 13f: Arabia: that is, the nomad country. Dedanites: an Arab tribe associated with Edom and Tema, and living east of the Red Sea; cf Gn 10, 7; 25, 3; Jer 25, 23.

s Is 30, 3. 5. t Is 31, 3; 36. 6. u Is 13, 17. v Ps 38, 8. w Hb 2, 1. x Is 46, 1; Jer 50, 2: 51, 8; Rv 14, 8. y Is 51, 23.

O caravans of Dedanites.
14 Meet the thirsty, bring them water;
you who dwell in the land of Tema,
greet the fugitives with bread.
15 They flee from the sword,
from the whetted sword;
From the taut bow,
from the fury of battle.

16 For thus says the Lord to me: In another year, like those of a hireling,* all the glory of Kedar shall come to an end. 17 Few of Kedar's stalwart archers shall remain, for the LORD, the God of Israel, has spoken.

CHAPTER 22

Jerusalem

1 Oracle of the Valley of Vision:*
What is the matter with you now, that you
have gone up,
all of you, to the housetops,
2 O city full of noise and chaos,
O wanton town!
Your slain are not slain with the sword,
nor killed in battle.[z]
3 All your leaders fled away together,
fled afar off;
All who were in you were captured together,
captured without the use of a bow.[a]
4 At this I say: Turn away from me,
let me weep bitterly;
Do not try to comfort me
for the ruin of the daughter of my people.[b]
5 It is a day of panic, rout and confusion,
from the Lord, the GOD of hosts, in the
Valley of Vision.
Walls crash;
they cry for help to the mountains.[c]
6 Elam* takes up the quivers,
Aram mounts the horses,
and Kir uncovers the shields.
7 Your choice valleys are filled with chariots,
and horses are posted at the gates,
8 and shelter over Judah is removed.

*On that day you looked to the weapons in
the House of the Forest; 9 you saw that the
breaches in the City of David were many; you
collected the water of the lower pool. 10 You num-
bered the houses of Jerusalem, tearing some
down to strengthen the wall; 11 you made a reser-
voir between the two walls for the water of the
old pool. But you did not look to the city's Maker,
nor did you consider him who built it long ago.

12 On that day the Lord,
the GOD of hosts, called on you
To weep and mourn,
to shave your head and put on sackcloth.[d]
13 But look! you feast and celebrate,
you slaughter oxen and butcher sheep,
You eat meat and drink wine:
"Eat and drink, for tomorrow we die!"[e]
14 This reaches the ears of the LORD of hosts—
You shall not be pardoned this wickedness
till you die,
says the Lord, the GOD of hosts.

Shebna and Eliakim

15 Thus says the Lord, the GOD of hosts:
Up, go to that official,
Shebna,* master of the palace,
16 Who has hewn for himself a sepulcher on a
height
and carved his tomb in the rock:
"What are you doing here, and what people
have you here,
that here you have hewn for yourself a
tomb?"
17 The LORD shall hurl you down headlong,
mortal man!
He shall grip you firmly
18 And roll you up and toss you like a ball

21, 16: Year . . . of a hireling: see note on Is 16, 14. Kedar: a nomad tribe in Arabia; cf Is 42, 11; 60, 7; Ps 120, 5.
22, 1–8: Valley of Vision: while the people live in revelry and disorder, the prophet foresees the impending doom of the city.
22, 6: Elam, Aram, Kir: all allies of Assyria. Kir: perhaps the same people referred to in Am 1, 5.
22, 8–11: Defense measures, in which the inhabitants of Jerusalem placed their trust instead of relying on God. House of the Forest: an armory built by Solomon; its columns of wood suggested the trees of a forest; cf 1 Kgs 7, 2; 10, 17.
22, 15: Shebna: referred to as the scribe in Is 36, 3.

z Is 32. 13. a 2 Kgs 25, 4. b Jer 6, 26; 9, 1; 14, 17. c Is 37, 3. d Jl 2, 17. e Is 56, 12; Wis 2, 6; 1 Cor 15, 32.

into an open land
To perish there, you and the chariots you glory in,
you disgrace to your master's house!
19 I will thrust you from your office
and pull you down from your station.

20 On that day I will summon my servant
Eliakim,* son of Hilkiah;[f]
21 I will clothe him with your robe,
and gird him with your sash,
and give over to him your authority.
He shall be a father to the inhabitants of Jerusalem,
and to the house of Judah.
22 I will place the key* of the House of David on his shoulder;
when he opens, no one shall shut,
when he shuts, no one shall open.[g]
23 I will fix him like a peg in a sure spot,
to be a place of honor for his family;
24 On him shall hang all the glory of his family:*
descendants and offspring,
all the little dishes, from bowls to jugs.

25 On that day, says the LORD of hosts, the peg fixed in a sure spot shall give way, break off and fall, and the weight that hung on it shall be done away with; for the LORD has spoken.

CHAPTER 23

Tyre and Sidon

1 Oracle on Tyre:
Wail, O ships of Tarshish,*
for your port is destroyed;
From the land of the Kittim*
the news reaches them.
2 Silence! you who dwell on the coast,
you merchants of Sidon,
Whose messengers crossed the sea
3 over the deep waters.
The grain of Shihor,* the harvest of the Nile,
was her revenue,
and she the merchant among nations.
4 Shame, O Sidon, fortress on the sea,
for the sea has spoken:*
"I have not been in labor, nor given birth,
nor raised young men,
nor reared virgins."
5 When it is heard in Egypt
they shall be in anguish at the news of Tyre.
6 Pass over to Tarshish, wailing,
you who dwell on the coast!
7 Is this your wanton city,
whose origin is from of old,
Whose feet have taken her
to dwell in distant lands?
8 Who has planned such a thing
against Tyre, the bestower of crowns,
Whose merchants are princes,
whose traders are the earth's honored men?
9 The LORD of hosts has planned it,
to disgrace all pride of majesty,
to degrade all the earth's honored men.[h]
10 Cross to your own land,
O ship of Tarshish;
the harbor is no more.
11 His hand he stretches out over the sea,
he shakes kingdoms;
The LORD has ordered the destruction
of Canaan's strongholds.*
12 You shall exult no more, he says,
you who are now oppressed, virgin daughter Sidon.
Arise, pass over to the Kittim,
even there you shall find no rest.[i]
13 *[This people is the land of the Chaldeans, not Assyria.]
She whom the impious founded,
setting up towers for her,
Has had her castles destroyed,
and has been turned into a ruin.[j]

22, 20: Eliakim: also referred to in Is 36, 3; he is described as loyal to God.
22, 22: Key: symbol of authority; cf Mt 16, 19; Rv 3, 7.
22, 24f: If Eliakim should anger God, he and his family (compared here to dishes, bowls and jugs) will suffer disaster.
23, 1–4. 12ff: These verses refer to Sidon, vv 5–11 to Tyre.
23, 1: Kittim: Cyprus.
23, 3: Shihor: a synonym for the Nile.
23, 4: The sea brings to distant coasts the news that Sidon must disown her children; her people are dispersed.
23, 11: Canaan's strongholds: the fortresses of Phoenicia.
23, 13: The gloss here identifies she whom the impious founded with the land of the Chaldeans.

f 2 Kgs 18, 18. 37. g Rv 3, 7. h Ez 28, 7. i Ez 28, 21f. j Ez 26, 7.

14 Lament, O ships of Tarshish,
for your haven is destroyed.

15 On that day, Tyre shall be forgotten for seventy years. With the days of another king, at the end of seventy years,* it shall be for Tyre as in the song about the harlot: [k]

16 Take a harp, go about the city,
O forgotten harlot;
Pluck the strings skillfully, sing many songs,
that they may remember you.

17 At the end of the seventy years the LORD shall visit Tyre. She shall return to her hire and deal with all the world's kingdoms on the face of the earth. [l] 18 But her merchandise and her hire shall be sacred to the LORD. It shall not be stored up or laid away, but from her merchandise those who dwell before the LORD shall eat their fill and clothe themselves in choice attire.*

IV: Apocalypse of Isaiah*

CHAPTER 24

Devastation of the World: A Remnant Saved

1 Lo, the LORD empties the land and lays it waste;
he turns it upside down,
scattering its inhabitants: [m]
2 Layman and priest alike,
servant and master,
The maid as her mistress,
the buyer as the seller,
The lender as the borrower,
the creditor as the debtor.
3 The earth is utterly laid waste, utterly stripped,
for the LORD has decreed this thing.
4 The earth mourns and fades,
the world languishes and fades;
both heaven and earth languish.
5 The earth is polluted because of its inhabitants,
who have transgressed laws, violated statutes,
broken the ancient covenant.*
6 Therefore a curse devours the earth,
and its inhabitants pay for their guilt;
Therefore they who dwell on earth turn pale,
and few men are left.
7 The wine mourns, the vine languishes,
all the merry-hearted groan. [n]
8 Stilled are the cheerful timbrels,
ended the shouts of the jubilant,
stilled is the cheerful harp. [o]
9 They cannot sing and drink wine;
strong drink is bitter to those who partake of it.
10 Broken down is the city of chaos,*
shut against entry, every house. [p]
11 In the streets they cry out for lack of wine;
all joy has disappeared
and cheer has left the land. [q]
12 In the city nothing remains but ruin;
its gates are battered and desolate.
13 Thus it is within the land,
and among the peoples,
As with an olive tree after it is beaten,
as with a gleaning when the vintage is done. [r]
14 These* lift up their voice in acclaim;
from the sea they proclaim the majesty of the LORD:
15 "For this, in the coastlands,
give glory to the LORD!
In the coastlands of the sea,
to the name of the LORD, the God of Israel!" [s]
16 From the end of the earth we hear songs:
"Splendor to the Just One!"
But I said, "I am wasted, wasted away.
Woe is me! The traitors betray:
with treachery have the traitors betrayed!

23, 15: Seventy years: a conventional period of time indicating simply a long disaster; cf Jer 25, 11 and 29, 10.
23, 18: Describes the conversion of Tyre.
24, 1—27, 13: This section, probably composed at a later date, contains oracles on the day of the Lord, combined with hymns of thanksgiving and of supplication.
24, 5: Ancient covenant: God's commandments to all mankind.
24, 10: City of chaos: a symbol of godlessness as opposed to Jerusalem, the city of God.
24, 14: These: the saved.

k Jer 25, 11. l Ez 27, 12. m Is 13, 9; Hos 4, 9. n Jl 1, 10. o Jer 7, 34; Hos 2, 13. p Is 25, 2. q Jer 48, 33; Lam 5, 14f. r Is 17, 6; Mi 7, 1. s Is 42. 10. 12; Zep 2, 11.

17 Terror, pit, and trap [t]
are upon you, inhabitant of the earth;
18 He who flees at the sound of terror
will fall into the pit;
He who climbs out of the pit
will be caught in the trap.
For the windows on high will be opened
and the foundations of the earth will shake.
19 The earth will burst asunder,
the earth will be shaken apart,
the earth will be convulsed.
20 The earth will reel like a drunkard,
and it will sway like a hut;
Its rebellion will weigh it down,
until it falls, never to rise again." [u]

21 On that day the LORD will punish
the host of the heavens* in the heavens,
and the kings of the earth on the earth. [v]
22 They will be gathered together
like prisoners into a pit;
They will be shut up in a dungeon,
and after many days they will be punished.
23 Then the moon will blush [w]
and the sun grow pale,
For the LORD of hosts will reign
on Mount Zion and in Jerusalem,
glorious in the sight of his elders.*

CHAPTER 25

1 O LORD, you are my God,*
I will extol you and praise your name;
For you have fulfilled your wonderful plans of old,
faithful and true. [x]
2 For you have made the city a heap,
the fortified city a ruin;
The castle of the insolent is a city no more,
nor ever to be rebuilt. [y]
3 Therefore a strong people will honor you,
fierce nations will fear you.
4 For you are a refuge to the poor,
a refuge to the needy in distress;
Shelter from the rain,
shade from the heat. [z]
As with the cold rain,
5 as with the desert heat,
even so you quell the uproar of the wanton.
6 On this mountain* the LORD of hosts
will provide for all peoples
A feast of rich food and choice wines,
juicy, rich food and pure, choice wines.
7 On this mountain he will destroy
the veil that veils all peoples,
The web that is woven over all nations; [a]
8 he will destroy death forever.
The Lord GOD will wipe away
the tears from all faces;
The reproach of his people he will remove
from the whole earth; for the LORD has spoken.

9 On that day it will be said:
"Behold our God, to whom we looked to save us!
This is the LORD for whom we looked;
let us rejoice and be glad that he has saved us!" [b]
10 For the hand of the LORD will rest on this mountain,
but Moab* will be trodden down
as a straw is trodden down in the mire. [c]
11 He will stretch forth his hands in Moab
as a swimmer extends his hands to swim;
He will bring low their pride
as his hands sweep over them. [d]
12 The high-walled fortress he will raze,
and strike it down level with the earth, with the very dust. [e]

CHAPTER 26

The Divine Vindicator 1 On that day they will sing this song in the land of Judah:

"A strong city have we;
he sets up walls and ramparts to protect us.
2 Open up the gates

24, 21: Host of the heavens: the stars, which were regarded by the pagans as gods; cf Dt 4, 19; Jer 8, 2.
24, 23: His elders: the heavenly courtiers surrounding the throne of God.
25, 1–8: Victory in messianic times.
25, 6: This mountain: Zion, symbol of the heavenly Jerusalem.
25, 10: Moab: symbol of God's enemies.

t 17f. Jer 48, 43f. u Is 9, 14. v Ps 76, 13. w Is 13, 10; Jl 3, 3f; 4, 15. x Ex 15, 2. y Jer 9, 11. z Is 14, 32; 32, 2; Na 1, 7. a Is 60, 1. 3; 1 Cor 15, 53ff; Rv 7, 17; 21, 4. b Is 30, 18f. c Zep 2, 9f. d Is 16, 6f. 14. e Is 26, 5.

to let in a nation that is just,
one that keeps faith.[f]
3 A nation of firm purpose you keep in peace;
in peace, for its trust in you."[g]

4 Trust in the LORD forever!
For the LORD is an eternal Rock.[h]
5 He humbles those in high places,
and the lofty city he brings down;
He tumbles it to the ground,
levels it with the dust.[i]
6 It is trampled underfoot by the needy,
by the footsteps of the poor.
7 The way of the just is smooth;
the path of the just you make level.[j]
8 Yes, for your way and your judgments,
O LORD,
we look to you;
Your name and your title
are the desire of our souls,
9 My soul yearns for you in the night,
yes, my spirit within me keeps vigil for you;
When your judgment dawns upon the earth,
the world's inhabitants learn justice.[k]
10 The wicked man, spared, does not learn
justice;
in an upright land he acts perversely,
and sees not the majesty of the LORD.[l]
11 O LORD, your hand is uplifted,
but they behold it not;
Let them be shamed when they see your zeal
for your people:
let the fire prepared for your enemies
consume them.
12 O LORD, you mete out peace to us,
for it is you who have accomplished all we
have done.[m]
13 O LORD, our God, other lords than you have
ruled us;
it is from you only that we can call upon
your name.

14 Dead they are, they have no life,
shades that cannot rise;
For you have punished and destroyed them,
and wiped out all memory of them.
15 You have increased the nation, O LORD,
increased the nation to your own glory,
and extended far all the borders of the
land.[n]
16 O LORD, oppressed by your punishment,
we cried out in anguish under your
chastising.[o]
17 As a woman about to give birth
writhes and cries out in her pains,
so were we in your presence, O LORD.[p]
18 We conceived and writhed in pain,
giving birth to wind;
Salvation we have not achieved for the earth,
the inhabitants of the world cannot bring it
forth.
19 But your dead shall live, their corpses shall
rise;
awake and sing, you who lie in the dust.[q]
For your dew is a dew of light,
and the land of shades gives birth.*

Day of the Lord: Reward and Punishment

20 Go, my people, enter your chambers,
and close your doors behind you;
Hide yourselves for a brief moment,
until the wrath is past.
21 See, the LORD goes forth from his place,
to punish the wickedness of the earth's
inhabitants;
The earth will reveal the blood upon her,
and no longer conceal her slain.[r]

CHAPTER 27

1 On that day,
The LORD will punish with his sword
that is cruel, great, and strong,
Leviathan the fleeing serpent,
Leviathan the coiled serpent;
and he will slay the dragon* that is in the
sea.[s]

26, 19: This verse refers to the restoration of Israel in messianic times under the figure of the resurrection of the dead; cf Ez, chap. 37.

27, 1: Leviathan . . . dragon: symbols of the forces of evil which God vanquishes even as he overcame primeval chaos; cf notes on Jb 3, 8; 7, 12.

f Ps 118, 19f. g Is 32, 17f; 54, 13. h Is 30, 29; Ps 62, 8. i Is 25, 12; 32, 19. j Ps 23, 3f; Prv 11, 3. 5. k Ps 94, 15. l Is 5, 12. m Jer 29, 11. n Is 54, 2f; Neh 9, 23. o Hos 6, 1. p Mi 4, 10. q Ez 37, 5f; Dn 12. 2; Hos 6, 2. r Mi 1, 3. s Jb 40, 25–32; Ez 32, 2.

2 On that day—
The pleasant vineyard, sing about it! [t]
3 I, the LORD, am its keeper,
I water it every moment;
Lest anyone harm it,
night and day I guard it. [u]
4 I am not angry,
but if I were to find briers and thorns,
In battle I should march against them;
I should burn them all. [v]
8 Expunging and expelling, I should strive
against them,
carrying them off with my cruel wind in
time of storm. [w]
6 In days to come Jacob shall take root,
Israel shall sprout and blossom,
covering all the world with fruit.
7 Is he to be smitten as his smiter was smitten?
or slain as his slayer was slain?*
5 Or shall he cling to me for refuge?*
He must make peace with me;
peace shall he make with me! [x]
9 This, then, shall be the expiation of Jacob's
guilt,
this the whole fruit of the removal of his
sin:
He shall pulverize all the stones of the altars
like pieces of chalk;
no sacred poles or incense altars shall stand.
10 For the fortified city* shall be
desolate,
an abandoned pasture, a forsaken
wilderness,
where calves shall browse and lie. [y]
Its boughs shall be destroyed,
11 its branches shall wither and be broken off,
and women shall come to build a fire with
them.
This is not an understanding people;
therefore their maker shall not spare them,
nor shall he who formed them have mercy
on them. [z]
12 On that day,
The LORD shall beat out the grain
between the Euphrates and the Wadi of
Egypt,*
and you shall be gleaned one by one, O sons
of Israel.
13 On that day,*
A great trumpet shall blow,
and the lost in the land of Assyria
and the outcasts in the land of Egypt
Shall come and worship the LORD
on the holy mountain, in Jerusalem. [a]

V: The Lord Alone, Israel's and Judah's Salvation

CHAPTER 28

The Fate of Samaria

1 Woe to the majestic garland
of the drunkard Ephraim,*
To the fading blooms of his glorious beauty,
on the head of him who is stupefied with
wine. [b]
2 Behold, the LORD has a strong one and a
mighty,*
who, like a downpour of hail, a destructive
storm,
Like a flood of water, great and overflowing,
levels to the ground with violence; [c]
3 With feet that will trample
the majestic garland of the drunkard
Ephraim.
4 The fading blooms of his glorious beauty
on the head of the fertile valley
Will be like an early fig before summer:

27, 7: God's people will not be treated as sternly as were their enemies.

27, 5. 9: Israel will make peace with God and destroy all signs of idolatrous worship.

27, 10f: The fortified city: symbol of the powers of evil; see note on Is 24, 10.

27, 12: The Euphrates and the Wadi of Egypt: the ideal borders of Israel; cf Gn 15, 18; 2 Kgs 24, 7.

27, 13: The triumph of God's people is described in eschatological language; they will gather in Jerusalem from Assyria and Egypt.

28, 1: Ephraim: the northern kingdom. Its capital, Samaria, was built upon a hill, suggestive of a majestic garland adorning the head of the drunken kingdom.

28, 2: A strong one and a mighty: Assyria.

t Is 5, 1. u Is 5, 2ff; Ps 121, 4f. v Is 10, 17. w Jer 18, 17. x Is 37, 31; Rom 11, 12. y Is 6, 11. z Jer 4, 22. a Hos 11, 11. b Hos 7, 5; Am 6, 6. c Is 30, 30.

when a man sees it,
he picks and swallows it at once.
5 On that day the LORD of hosts
will be a glorious crown
And a brilliant diadem
to the remnant of his people,
6 A spirit of justice
to him who sits in judgment,
And strength to those
who turn back the battle at the gate.

Against Judah

7 But these also stagger from wine
and stumble from strong drink:
Priest and prophet stagger from strong drink,
overpowered by wine;
Led astray by strong drink,
staggering in their visions,
tottering when giving judgment. [d]
8 Yes, all the tables
are covered with filthy vomit,
with no place left clean.
9 "To whom would he impart knowledge?*
To whom would he convey the message?
To those just weaned from milk,
those taken from the breast? 10 For he says,
'Command on command, command on
command,
rule on rule, rule on rule,
here a little, there a little!' "
11 Yes, with stammering lips and in a strange
language*
he will speak to this people [e]
12 to whom he said:
This is the resting place,
give rest to the weary;
Here is repose—
but they would not listen.
13 So for them the word of the LORD shall be:
"Command on command, command on
command,
Rule on rule, rule on rule,
here a little, there a little!"
So that when they walk, they stumble
backward,
broken, ensnared, and captured.

14 Therefore, hear the word of the LORD, you
arrogant,
who rule this people in Jerusalem:
15 Because you say, "We have made a covenant
with death,
and with the nether world* we have made
a pact;
When the overwhelming scourge passes,
it will not reach us;
For we have made lies our refuge,
and in falsehood we have found a hiding
place,"—[f]
16 Therefore, thus says the Lord GOD:
See, I am laying a stone in Zion,*
a stone that has been tested,
A precious cornerstone as a sure
foundation;
he who puts his faith in it shall not be
shaken. [g]
17 I will make of right a measuring line,
of justice a level.—
Hail shall sweep away the refuge of lies,
and waters shall flood the hiding place.
18 Your covenant with death shall be canceled
and your pact with the nether world shall
not stand.
When the overwhelming scourge passes,
you shall be trampled down by it.
19 Whenever it passes, it shall take you;

28, 9f: The words of those who ridicule Isaiah. The Hebrew of v 10, by its very sound, conveys the idea of mocking imitation of what the prophet says, as though he spoke like a stammering child: SAU LASAU, SAU LASAU, CAU LACAU, CAU LACAU, ZE'ER SHAM, ZE'ER SHAM. But in v 13 God repeats these words in deadly earnest, putting them in the mouth of the victorious pagan army.

28, 11: God will answer the mockers and defend Isaiah. Strange language: spoken by the invading army.

28, 15. 18: A covenant with death, and with the nether world: an alliance with foreign powers, such as Egypt and Babylon, to prevent death and destruction. Have made lies . . . a hiding place: this confidence in human aid proves to be false and deceitful, incapable of averting the dreaded disaster. Overwhelming scourge: the flood of the Assyrian invasion; cf Is 8, 7f.

28, 16: A stone in Zion: the true and sure foundation of salvation promised by God to the Davidic dynasty (cf Is 7, 13–16; 9, 1–6), which the Apostles saw fulfilled in Christ the universal Savior; cf 1 Pt 2, 6–8; Rom 9, 33; 10, 9ff. Cornerstone: the assurance of salvation rejected by Israel in the prophet's time, is reflected by the psalmist (Ps 118, 22) and fulfilled in the Person of Christ; cf Mt 21, 42; Lk 20, 17; Acts 4, 11; Rom 9. 33; 1 Pt 2, 7.

d Is 56, 10. 12. e Jer 5, 15; 1 Cor 14, 21; Dt 28, 49; Bar 4, 15. f Wis 1, 16; Jer 5, 12. g Ps 118, 22; Mt 21, 42; Acts 4, 11; Rom 9, 33; 1 Pt 2, 6.

morning after morning it shall pass,
By day and by night;
terror alone shall convey the message.
20 For the bed shall be too short to stretch out in,
and the cover too narrow to wrap in.
21 For the LORD shall rise up as on Mount Perazim,*
bestir himself as in the Valley of Gibeon,
To carry out his work, his singular work,
to perform his deed, his strange deed. [h]
22 Now, be arrogant no more
lest your bonds be tightened,
For I have heard from the Lord, the GOD of hosts,
the destruction decreed for the whole earth. [i]
23 Give ear and hear my voice,*
pay attention and listen to what I say:
24 Is the plowman forever plowing,
always loosening and harrowing his land for planting?
25 When he has leveled the surface,
does he not scatter gith and sow cumin,*
Put in wheat and barley,
with spelt as its border?
26 He has learned this rule,
instructed by his God.
27 Gith is not threshed with a sledge,
nor does a cartwheel roll over cumin.
But gith is beaten out with a staff,
and cumin crushed for food with a rod.
28 No, he does not thresh it unendingly,
nor does he crush it
with his noisy cartwheels and horses.
29 This too comes from the LORD of hosts;
wonderful is his counsel and great his wisdom.

CHAPTER 29

The Fall of Jerusalem

1 Woe to Ariel, Ariel,*
the city where David encamped!
Add year to year,
let the feasts come round. [j]
2 But I will bring distress upon Ariel,
with mourning and grief.
You shall be to me like Ariel, [k]
3 I will encamp like David against you;
I will encircle you with outposts
and set up siege works against you. [l]
4 Prostrate you shall speak from the earth,
and from the base dust your words shall come.
Your voice shall be like a ghost's from the earth,
and your words like chirping* from the dust.
5 The horde of your arrogant shall be like fine dust,
the horde of the tyrants like flying chaff.
Then suddenly, in an instant, [m]
6 you shall be visited by the LORD of hosts,
With thunder, earthquake, and great noise,
whirlwind, storm, and the flame of consuming fire.
7 Then like a dream,*
a vision in the night,
Shall be the horde of all the nations
who war against Ariel
with all the earthworks of her besiegers.
8 As when a hungry man dreams he is eating
and awakens with an empty stomach,
Or when a thirsty man dreams he is drinking
and awakens faint and dry,
So shall the horde of all the nations be,
who make war against Zion.

28, 21: Mount Perazim . . . Valley of Gibeon: where David defeated the Philistines; cf 2 Sm 5, 20. 25; 1 Chr 14, 11. 16.

28, 23–29: The practical variation of the farmer's work taught him by God reflects God's dealing with his people, wisely adapted to circumstances; he does not crush their weakness altogether; cf ch 29.

28, 25: Gith . . . cumin: herbs used in seasoning food. Spelt: a variety of wheat.

29, 1f: Ariel: variously interpreted to mean "lion of God" or "hearth (altar) of God," a poetic name for Jerusalem; or perhaps to be read as Uru-el, "foundation of God," an archaic name for the Jebusite city of Jerusalem; like that Ariel, against which David encamped, it will be besieged by God.

29, 4: Chirping: see note on Is 8, 19.

29, 7f: Just when the Assyrians think their capture of Jerusalem to be certain, the Lord will snatch victory from their hands and save his city.

h Jos 10, 10; 2 Sm 5, 20; 1 Chr 14, 11. i Is 10, 23. j 2 Sm 5, 9. k Is 33, 7. l 2 Kgs 25, 1; Ez 4, 2. m Is 17, 13; Ps 18, 43; Jb 21, 18.

Blindness and Perversity

9 Be irresolute, stupefied;*
blind yourselves and stay blind!
Be drunk, but not from wine,
stagger, but not from strong drink! [n]
10 For the LORD has poured out on you
a spirit of deep sleep.
He has shut your eyes [the prophets]
and covered your heads [the seers]. [o]

11 For you the revelation of all this has become
like the words of a sealed scroll. When it is
handed to one who can read, with the request,
"Read this," he replies, "I cannot; it is sealed." [p]
12 When it is handed to one who cannot read,
with the request, "Read this," he replies, "I
cannot read."

13 The Lord said:
Since this people draws near with words only
and honors me with their lips alone,
though their hearts are far from me,
And their reverence for me has become
routine observance of the precepts of
men, [q]
14 Therefore I will again deal with this people
in surprising and wondrous fashion:
The wisdom of its wise men shall perish
and the understanding of its prudent men
be hid. [r]
15 Woe to those who would hide their plans
too deep for the LORD!
Who work in the dark, saying,
"Who sees us, or who knows us?" [s]
16 Your perversity is as though the potter
were taken to be the clay:
As though what is made should say of its
maker,
"He made me not!"
Or the vessel should say of the
potter,
"He does not understand." [t]

Redemption*

17 But a very little while,
and Lebanon shall be changed into an
orchard,
and the orchard be regarded as a forest! [u]
18 On that day the deaf shall hear
the words of a book;
And out of gloom and darkness,
the eyes of the blind shall see. [v]
19 The lowly will ever find joy in the LORD,
and the poor rejoice in the Holy One of
Israel. [w]
20 For the tyrant will be no more
and the arrogant will have gone;
All who are alert to do evil will be cut off, [x]
21 those whose mere word condemns a man,
Who ensnare his defender at the gate,
and leave the just man with an empty
claim. [y]
22 Therefore thus says the LORD,
the God of the house of Jacob,
who redeemed Abraham:*
Now Jacob shall have nothing to be ashamed
of,
nor shall his face grow pale. [z]
23 When his children see
the work of my hands in his midst,
They shall keep my name holy;
they shall reverence the Holy One of Jacob,
and be in awe of the God of Israel.
24 Those who err in spirit shall acquire
understanding,
and those who find fault shall receive
instruction.

CHAPTER 30

Futile Alliance with Egypt

1 Woe to the rebellious children,
says the LORD,
Who carry out plans that are not
mine,

29, 9–12: Jerusalem in her blindness refuses to believe God's revelation that she will be saved.

29, 17–24: The prophet presents God's plan of redemption in terms of unheard-of natural phenomena as if such changes in nature took place, e. g., the change of the cedars of Lebanon into an orchard (v 17).

29, 22: Who redeemed Abraham: by freeing him from the idolatry of his native land.

n Is 19, 14; 28, 7f. o Is 6, 10; Rom 11, 8. p Dn 12, 4. q Ez 33, 31; Mt 15, 8f; Mk 7, 6f. r Jer 49, 7; 1 Cor 1, 19. s Is 30, 1; Ez 8, 12; Jn 3, 19f. t Is 45, 9; Jer 18, 6; Rom 9, 20. u Is 32, 15. v Is 35, 5; 42, 6f. w Is 61, 1. x Is 28, 22. y Am 5, 10. 12. z Is 45, 17.

who weave webs that are not inspired by
me,
adding sin upon sin. [a]
2 They go down to Egypt,
but my counsel they do not seek.
They find their strength in Pharaoh's
protection
and take refuge in Egypt's shadow; [b]
3 Pharaoh's protection shall be your shame,
and refuge in Egypt's shadow your
disgrace. [c]
4 When their princes are at Zoan
and their messengers reach Hanes, [d]
5 All shall be ashamed
of a people that gain them nothing,
Neither help nor benefit,
but only shame and reproach. [e]

6 [Oracle on the Beasts of the Negeb]

Through the distressed and troubled land
of the lioness and roaring lion,
of the viper and flying saraph,*
They carry their riches on the backs of asses
and their treasures on the humps of camels
To a people good for nothing,
7 to Egypt whose help is futile and vain.
Therefore I call her
"Rahab* quelled."
8 Now come, write it on a tablet they can keep,
inscribe it in a record;*
That it may be in future days
an eternal witness: [f]
9 This is a rebellious people,
deceitful children,
Children who refuse
to obey the law of the LORD. [g]
10 They say to the seers, "Have no visions" ;
to the prophets, "Do not descry for us what
is right;
speak flatteries to us, conjure up illusions. [h]
11 Out of the way! Out of our path!
Let us hear no more
of the Holy One of Israel." [i]
12 Therefore, thus says the Holy One of Israel:
Because you reject this word,
And put your trust in what is crooked and
devious,
and depend on it,
13 This guilt of yours shall be
like a descending rift
Bulging out in a high wall
whose crash comes suddenly, in an instant. [j]
14 It crashes like a potter's jar
smashed beyond rescue,
And among its fragments cannot be found
a sherd to scoop fire from the hearth
or dip water from the cistern. [k]

15 For thus said the Lord GOD,
the Holy One of Israel:
By waiting and by calm you shall be saved,
in quiet and in trust your strength lies.
But this you did not wish. [l]
16 "No," you said,
"Upon horses we will flee."
—Very well, flee!
"Upon swift steeds we will ride."
—Not so swift as your pursuers. [m]
17 A thousand shall tremble at the threat of one;
if five threaten you, you shall flee,
Until you are left like a flagstaff on the
mountaintop,
like a flag on the hill.
18 Yet the LORD is waiting to show you favor,
and he rises to pity you;
For the LORD is a God of justice:
blessed are all who wait for him! [n]

19 O people of Zion, who dwell in Jerusalem,
no more will you weep;
He will be gracious to you when you cry out,
as soon as he hears he will answer you. [o]
20 The Lord will give you the bread you need

30, 6: Flying saraph: see note on Nm 21, 6.
30, 7: Rahab: Egypt, here as elsewhere (cf Ps 87, 4), is compared to the stormy, impetuous sea monster (cf Is 51, 9; Jb 26, 12; Ps 89, 11), which yet, when asked for aid by Judah, becomes silent, quelled.
30, 8: Isaiah will write down his condemnation of the people so that (vv 12–18) its fulfillment may afterward be admitted.

a Is 1, 4. b Is 31, 1; 36, 6. c Is 20, 5; Jer 2, 26f. d Is 19, 11. e 36, 6. f Is 8, 1. 16; Jer 36, 2; Heb 2, 2. g Is 1, 4; Jer 7, 28. h Jer 5, 31. i Jb 21, 14f. j Ez 13, 14. k Jer 19, 11. l Is 7, 4; Mi 7, 7. m Is 31, 3. n Ps 34, 9; Jer 17, 7. o Is 58, 9.

and the water for which you thirst.
No longer will your Teacher* hide himself,
but with your own eyes you shall see your Teacher,
21 While from behind, a voice shall sound in your ears:
"This is the way; walk in it,"
when you would turn to the right or to the left. [p]
22 And you shall consider unclean your silver-plated idols
and your gold-covered images;
You shall throw them away like filthy rags
to which you say, "Begone!" [q]

Zion's Future Prosperity

23 He will give rain for the seed
that you sow in the ground,
And the wheat that the soil produces
will be rich and abundant.
On that day your cattle will graze
in spacious meadows; [r]
24 The oxen and the asses that till the ground
will eat silage tossed to them
with shovel and pitchfork.
25 Upon every high mountain and lofty hill
there will be streams of running water.
On the day of the great slaughter,
when the towers fall, [s]
26 The light of the moon will be like that of the sun
and the light of the sun will be seven times greater
[like the light of seven days].
On the day the LORD binds up the wounds of his people,
he will heal the bruises left by his blows. [t]

Divine Judgment on Assyria*

27 See the name of the LORD coming from afar
in burning wrath, with lowering clouds!
His lips are filled with fury,
his tongue is like a consuming fire;
28 His breath, like a flood in a ravine
that reaches suddenly to the neck,
Will winnow the nations with a destructive winnowing,
and with repeated winnowings will he battle against them
[and a bridle on the jaws of the peoples to send them astray].
30 The LORD will make his glorious voice heard,
and let it be seen how his arm descends
In raging fury and flame of consuming fire,
in driving storm and hail.
31 When the LORD speaks, Assyria will be shattered,
as he strikes with the rod;
32 While at every sweep of the rod
which the LORD will bring down on him in punishment,
29 You will sing
as on a night when a feast is observed,
And be merry of heart,
as one marching along with a flute
Toward the mountain of the LORD,
toward the Rock of Israel,
accompanied by the timbrels and lyres.
33 For the pyre* has long been ready,
prepared for the king;
Broad and deep it is piled
with dry grass and wood in abundance,
And the breath of the LORD, like a stream of sulphur,
will set it afire.

CHAPTER 31

Against the Egyptian Alliance

1 Woe to those who go down to Egypt for help,
who depend upon horses;
Who put their trust in chariots because of their number,
and in horsemen because of their combined power,
But look not to the Holy One of Israel
nor seek the LORD! [u]
2 Yet he too is wise and will bring disaster;

30, 20: Teacher: God, who in the past taught in a veiled manner through his prophets, will in future help them to understand his teaching clearly. This was eminently true when the Son of God became Man.

30, 27–33: God's punishment of Assyria. The name of the Lord: God himself; cf Ps 20, 2.

30, 29–33: Pyre: on which the corpse of the king of Assyria is burned. This is the occasion of festal rejoicing for the Israelites, who are now free from his yoke.

p Jer 31, 33f. q Is 31, 7. r Lv 26, 3. 5. s Jl 4, 18. t Jer 30, 17. u Is 30, 2; 36, 6.

he will not turn from what he has
threatened to do.
He will rise up against the house of the
wicked
and against those who help evildoers.
3 The Egyptians are men, not God,
their horses are flesh, not spirit;
When the LORD stretches forth his
hand,
the helper shall stumble, the one helped
shall fall,
and both of them shall perish together. [v]

4 Thus says the LORD to me:
As a lion or a lion cub
growling over its prey,
With a band of shepherds
assembled against it,
Is neither frightened by their shouts
nor disturbed by their noise,
So shall the LORD of hosts come down
to wage war upon the mountain and hill of
Zion.
5 Like hovering birds, so the LORD of hosts
shall shield Jerusalem,
To protect and deliver,
to spare and rescue it. [w]

6 Return, O children of Israel, to him whom
you have utterly deserted. [x] 7 On that day each
one of you shall spurn his sinful idols of silver
and gold, which he made with his hands. [y]

Downfall of Assyria

8 Assyria shall fall by a sword not wielded by
man,
no mortal sword shall devour him;
He shall flee before the sword,
and his young men shall be impressed as
laborers. [z]
9 He shall rush past his crag* in panic,
and his princes shall flee in terror from his
standard,
Says the LORD who has a fire in Zion
and a furnace in Jerusalem.

CHAPTER 32

The Kingdom of Justice

1 See, a king will reign justly
and princes will rule rightly. [a]
2 Each of them will be a shelter from the wind,
a retreat from the rain.
They will be like streams of water in a dry
country,
like the shade of a great rock in a parched
land. [b]
3 The eyes of those who see will not be closed;
the ears of those who hear will be attentive.
4 The flighty will become wise and capable,
and the stutterers will speak fluently and
clearly.
5 No more will the fool be called noble,
nor the trickster be considered honorable.
6 For the fool speaks foolishly,
planning evil in his heart:
How to do wickedness,
to speak perversely against the LORD,
To let the hungry go empty
and the thirsty be without drink. [c]
7 And the trickster uses wicked trickery,
planning crimes:
How to ruin the poor with lies,
and the needy when they plead their case.
8 But the noble man plans noble things,
and by noble things he stands.

The Women of Jerusalem

9 O complacent ladies, rise up and hear my
voice,
overconfident women, give heed to my
words.
10 In a little more than a year
you overconfident ones will be shaken;
The vintage will fail,
there will be no harvest. [d]
11 Tremble, you who are complacent!
Shudder, you who are overconfident!
Strip yourselves bare,
with only a loincloth to cover you. [e]
12 Beat your breasts

31, 9: Crag: the king as the rallying point of the princes.

v Ps 146, 3ff. w Ps 91, 4. x Jer 3, 12. y Is 30, 22. z Is 37,
36. a Is 16, 5; Ps 72, 2ff; Jer 23, 5. b Is 4, 6; 25, 4. c Prv 10,
32; Eccl 10, 12f. d Zep 1, 13. e Jer 4, 8.

for the pleasant fields, the fruitful vine,
13 And the soil of my people,
overgrown with thorns and briers;
For all the joyful houses,
the wanton city.[f]
14 Yes, the castle* will be forsaken,
the noisy city deserted;[g]
19 Down it comes, as trees come down in the forest!
The city will be utterly laid low.
Hill and tower will become wasteland forever
for wild asses to frolic in, and flocks to pasture,
15 Until the spirit from on high*
is poured out on us.
Then will the desert become an orchard
and the orchard be regarded as a forest.[h]

16 Right will dwell in the desert
and justice abide in the orchard.
17 Justice will bring about peace;
right will produce calm and security.[i]
18 My people will live in peaceful country,
in secure dwellings and quiet resting places.[j]
20 Happy are you who sow beside every stream,
and let the ox and the ass go freely![k]

CHAPTER 33

Overthrow of Assyria

1 Woe, O destroyer never destroyed,
O traitor never betrayed!
When you finish destroying, you will be destroyed;
when wearied with betraying, you will be betrayed.
2 O LORD, have pity on us, for you we wait.
Be our strength every morning,
our salvation in time of trouble![l]
3 At the roaring sound, peoples flee;
when you rise in your majesty, nations are scattered.
4 Men gather spoil as caterpillars are gathered up;
they rush upon it like the onrush of locusts.[m]
5 The LORD is exalted, enthroned on high;
he fills Zion with right and justice.[n]
6 That which makes her seasons lasting,
the riches that save her, are wisdom and knowledge;
the fear of the LORD is her treasure.[o]

7 See, the men of Ariel cry out in the streets,
the messengers of Shalem* weep bitterly.
8 The highways are desolate,
travelers have quit the paths,
Covenants are broken, their terms are spurned;
yet no man gives it a thought.[p]
9 The country languishes in mourning,
Lebanon withers with shame;
Sharon* is like the steppe,
Bashan and Carmel are stripped bare.[q]
10 Now will I rise up, says the LORD,
now will I be exalted, now be lifted up.
11 You conceive dry grass, bring forth stubble;
my spirit shall consume you like fire.
12 The peoples shall be as in a limekiln,
like brushwood cut down for burning in the fire.[r]
13 Hear, you who are far off, what I have done;
you who are near, acknowledge my might.
14 On Zion sinners are in dread,
trembling grips the impious:
"Who of us can live with the consuming fire?
who of us can live with the everlasting flames?"[s]
15 He who practices virtue and speaks honestly,
who spurns what is gained by oppression,
Brushing his hands free of contact with a bribe,
stopping his ears lest he hear of bloodshed,
closing his eyes lest he look on evil—[t]

32, 14. 19: The castle: the citadel of Jerusalem. Hill and tower: the fortified hill, in Hebrew Ophel, with its stronghold called "the great projecting tower" in Neh 3, 27.
32, 15–18. 20: Extraordinary peace and prosperity will come to Israel under just rulers.
33, 7: Ariel . . . Shalem: Jerusalem; cf Is 29, 1; Gn 14, 18.
33, 9: Sharon: the fertile plain near the Mediterranean.

f Is 7, 23; 34, 13. g Is 27, 10. h Is 35, 1; 44, 3. i Is 54, 13f; Ps 72, 7; Jas 3, 18. j Mi 4, 4. k Is 30, 23. l Is 25, 9. m 2 Chr 20, 25. n Is 1, 26. o Prv 9, 10. p Jgs 5, 6. q Na 1, 4. r Is 10, 17. s Na 1, 6. t Pss 15, 2–6; 24, 4f.

16 He shall dwell on the heights,
his stronghold shall be the rocky fastness,
his food and drink in steady supply.

Restoration of Zion

17 Your eyes will see a king* in his splendor,
they will look upon a vast land.
18 Your mind will dwell on the terror:
"Where is he who counted, where is he who weighed?
Where is he who counted the towers?"
19 To the people of alien tongue you will look no more,
the people of obscure speech,
stammering in a language not understood.
20 Look to Zion, the city of our festivals;
let your eyes see Jerusalem
as a quiet abode, a tent not to be struck,
Whose pegs will never be pulled up,
nor any of its ropes severed.
22 Indeed the LORD will be there with us, majestic;
yes, the LORD our judge, the LORD our lawgiver,
the LORD our king, he it is who will save us.
21 In a place of rivers and wide streams
on which no boat is rowed,
where no majestic ship* passes,
23 The rigging hangs slack;
it cannot hold the mast in place,
nor keep the sail spread out.
Then the blind will divide great spoils
and the lame will carry off the loot.
24 No one who dwells there will say, "I am sick";
the people who live there will be forgiven their guilt.

VI: The Lord, Zion's Avenger

CHAPTER 34

Judgment upon Edom

1 Come near, O nations, and hear;
be attentive, O peoples!
Let the earth and what fills it listen,
the world and all it produces. [u]
2 The LORD is angry with all the nations
and is wrathful against all their host;
he has doomed them and given them over to slaughter.
3 Their slain shall be cast out,
their corpses shall send up a stench;
The mountains shall run with their blood, [v]
4 and all the hills shall rot;
The heavens shall be rolled up like a scroll,
and all their host shall wither away,
As the leaf wilts on the vine,
or as the fig withers on the tree. [w]
5 When my sword has drunk its fill in the heavens,
lo, it shall come down in judgment
upon Edom, a people I have doomed. [x]
6 The LORD has a sword filled with blood, [y]
greasy with fat,
With the blood of lambs and goats,
with the fat of rams' kidneys;
For the LORD has a sacrifice in Bozrah,
a great slaughter in the land of Edom.
7 Wild oxen shall be struck down with fatlings,
and bullocks with bulls;
Their land shall be soaked with blood,
and their earth greasy with fat.
8 For the LORD has a day of vengeance,
a year of requital by Zion's defender. [z]
9 Edom's streams shall be changed into pitch
and her earth into sulphur,
and her land shall become burning pitch;
10 Night and day it shall not be quenched,
its smoke shall rise forever.
From generation to generation she shall lie waste,
never again shall anyone pass through her.
11 But the desert owl and hoot owl shall possess her,
the screech owl and raven shall dwell in her.
The LORD will measure her with line and plummet
to be an empty waste
for satyrs* to dwell in. [a]

33, 17: King: the messianic King, or God; cf v 22.
33, 21. 23: Boat . . . majestic ship: of a foreign oppressor.
34, 11: Satyrs: see note on Is 13, 21; cf Is 34, 14.

u Dt 32, 1. v Ez 32, 4. 6. w Is 13, 10; Ez 32, 7f; 4, 15. x Jer 46, 10. y 6f: Jer 49, 12f. z Is 13, 9; 63, 4. a Is 14, 23; Zep 2, 14.

12 Her nobles shall be no more,
nor shall kings be proclaimed there;
all her princes are gone. [b]
13 Her castles shall be overgrown with thorns,
her fortresses with thistles and briers.
She shall become an abode for jackals
and a haunt for ostriches. [c]
14 Wildcats shall meet with desert beasts,
satyrs shall call to one another;
There shall the lilith* repose,
and find for herself a place to rest.
15 There the hoot owl shall nest and lay eggs,
hatch them out and gather them in her shadow;
There shall the kites assemble,
none shall be missing its mate.
16 Look in the book of the LORD* and read:
No one of these shall be lacking,
For the mouth of the LORD has ordered it,
and his spirit shall gather them there. [d]
17 It is he who casts the lot for them,
and with his hand he marks off their shares of her;
They shall possess her forever,
and dwell there from generation to generation.

CHAPTER 35

Israel's Deliverance*

1 The desert and the parched land will exult;
the steppe will rejoice and bloom. [e]
2 They will bloom with abundant flowers,
and rejoice with joyful song.
The glory of Lebanon will be given to them,
the splendor of Carmel and Sharon;
They will see the glory of the LORD,
the splendor of our God. [f]
3 Strengthen the hands that are feeble,
make firm the knees that are weak, [g]
4 Say to those whose hearts are frightened:
Be strong, fear not!
Here is your God,
he comes with vindication;
With divine recompense
he comes to save you. [h]
5 Then will the eyes of the blind be opened,
the ears of the deaf be cleared; [i]
6 Then will the lame leap like a stag,
then the tongue of the dumb will sing. [j]

Streams will burst forth in the desert,
and rivers in the steppe.
7 The burning sands will become pools,
and the thirsty ground, springs of water;
The abode where jackals lurk
will be a marsh for the reed and papyrus.
8 A highway will be there,
called the holy way;
No one unclean may pass over it,
nor fools go astray on it.
9 No lion will be there,
nor beast of prey go up to be met upon it.
It is for those with a journey to make,
and on it the redeemed will walk. [k]
10 Those whom the LORD has ransomed will return
and enter Zion singing,
crowned with everlasting joy;
They will meet with joy and gladness,
sorrow and mourning will flee. [l]

VII: Historical Appendix

CHAPTER 36

Invasion of Sennacherib* 1 In the fourteenth year of King Hezekiah, Sennacherib, king of Assyria, went on an expedition against all the fortified cities of Judah and captured them. [m]
2 From Lachish the king of Assyria sent his commander with a great army to King Hezekiah in Jerusalem. When he stopped at the conduit of the upper pool, on the highway of the fuller's

34, 14: Lilith: a female demon thought to roam about the desert.

34, 16: Book of the Lord: God's list of all his creatures; cf Ps 69, 29, "the book of the living"; Ps 139, 16, "your book."

35, 1–10: Similar to the description of the return from the Exile, as found in chaps. 40–55.

36, 1—39, 8: Except for 38, 9–20, this historical appendix describing the siege, etc., is paralleled in 2 Kgs 18, 13—20, 19, which, however, has certain details proper to itself. The events are also recorded in substantially the same way in the cuneiform inscriptions of Sennacherib.

b Ob 18. c Is 13, 21; Hos 9, 6. d Jos 18, 10; Ps 78, 55. e Is 55, 12f. f Is 60, 13; Ps 96, 12. g Jb 4, 3f; Heb 12, 12. h Is 41, 10; Zec 8, 13. i Is 29, 18; 32, 3. j Is 41, 18; 43, 10. 19. k Is 62, 10; Lv 26, 6. l Is 51, 11. m 2 Kgs 18, 13; 2 Chr 32, 1.

field, 3there came out to him the master of the
palace, Eliakim, son of Hilkiah, and Shebna the
scribe, and the herald Joah, son of Asaph. 4The
commander said to them, "Tell King Hezekiah:
Thus says the great king, the king of Assyria, 'On
what do you base this confidence of yours? 5Do
you think mere words substitute for strategy and
might in war? On whom, then, do you rely, that
you rebel against me? 6This Egypt, the staff on
which you rely, is in fact a broken reed which
pierces the hand of anyone who leans on it. That
is what Pharaoh, king of Egypt, is to all who rely
on him.[n] 7But if you say to me: "We rely on the
LORD, our God," is not he the one whose high
places and altars Hezekiah removed,* command-
ing Judah and Jerusalem to worship before this
altar?'[o]

8"Now, make a wager with my lord the king
of Assyria: 'I will give you two thousand horses,
if you can put riders on them.' 9How then can
you repulse even one of the least servants of my
lord? And yet you rely on Egypt for chariots and
horsemen! 10'Was it without the LORD's will that
I have come up to destroy this land? The LORD
said to me, "Go up and destroy that land!" ' "[p]

11Then Eliakim and Shebna and Joah said to
the commander, "Please speak to your servants
in Aramaic; we understand it. Do not speak to
us in Judean within earshot of the people who
are on the wall."*

12But the commander replied, "Was it to you
and your master that my lord sent me to speak
these words? Was it not rather to the men sitting
on the wall, who, with you, will have to eat their
own excrement and drink their own urine?"
13Then the commander stepped forward and
cried out in a loud voice in Judean, "Listen to the
words of the great king, the king of Assyria.
14Thus says the king: 'Do not let Hezekiah
deceive you, since he cannot deliver you. 15Let
not Hezekiah induce you to rely on the LORD,
saying, "The LORD will surely save us; this city
will not be handed over to the king of Assyria." '
16Do not listen to Hezekiah, for the king of
Assyria says: 'Make peace with me and surren-
der! Then each of you will eat of his own vine
and of his own fig tree, and drink the water of
his own cistern,[q] 17until I come to take you to a
land like your own, a land of grain and wine, of
bread and vineyards. 18Do not let Hezekiah
seduce you by saying, "The LORD will save us."
Has any of the gods of the nations ever rescued
his land from the hand of the king of Assyria?[r]
19Where are the gods of Hamath and Arpad?
Where are the gods of Sepharvaim? Where are
the gods of Samaria? Have they saved Samaria
from my hand?[s] 20Which of all the gods of these
lands ever rescued his land from my hand? Will
the LORD then save Jerusalem from my hand?' "
21But they remained silent and did not answer
him one word, for the king had ordered them
not to answer him.

22Then the master of the palace, Eliakim, son
of Hilkiah, Shebna the scribe, and the herald
Joah, son of Asaph, came to Hezekiah with their
garments torn, and reported to him what the
commander had said.

CHAPTER 37

1When King Hezekiah heard this, he tore his
garments, wrapped himself in sackcloth, and
went into the temple of the LORD. 2He sent
Eliakim, the master of the palace, and Shebna
the scribe, and the elders of the priests, wrapped
in sackcloth, to tell the prophet Isaiah, son of
Amoz: 3"Thus says Hezekiah: 'This is a day of
distress, of rebuke, and of disgrace. Children are
at the point of birth, but there is no strength to
bring them forth.* 4Perhaps the LORD, your
God, will hear the words of the commander,
whom his master, the king of Assyria, sent to
taunt the living God, and will rebuke him for the

36, 7: The Assyrians pretend that Hezekiah's removal of the high places and altars (illegal sanctuaries) was taken by the Lord as an insult. They declare to Jerusalem's emissaries that the city therefore no longer has a right to the Lord's protection and that they are the ones who truly carry out his will (cf v 10).

36, 11: The Jewish emissaries ask that the conversation be carried on in Aramaic, not in Judean, for they fear the effect of the Assyrian claims upon the morale of the people.

37, 3: A proverbial expression. In the Bible the pangs of childbirth often typify extreme anguish; cf Is 13, 8; Jer 6, 24; Mi 4, 9f. In this instance there is reference to the desperate situation of Hezekiah from which he was scarcely able to free himself.

n Is 30, 2. o 2 Kgs 18, 4. p Is 10, 5f. q 1 Kgs 4, 25; Zec 3, 10. r Is 37, 11. s Is 10, 9; 37, 13.

words which the LORD, your God, has heard. Send up a prayer for the remnant that is here.' "

5When the servants of King Hezekiah had come to Isaiah, 6he said to them: "Tell this to your master: 'Thus says the LORD: Do not be frightened by the words you have heard, with which the servants of the king of Assyria have blasphemed me.[t] 7I am about to put in him such a spirit that, when he hears a certain report, he will return to his own land, and there I will cause him to fall by the sword.' "

8When the commander returned to Lachish and heard that the king of Assyria had left there, he found him besieging Libnah. 9The king of Assyria heard a report that Tirhakah,* king of Ethiopia, had come out to fight against him. Again he sent envoys to Hezekiah with this message: "Thus shall you say to Hezekiah, king of Judah: 10'Do not let your God on whom you rely deceive you by saying that Jerusalem will not be handed over to the king of Assyria.[u] 11You yourself have heard what the kings of Assyria have done to all the countries: They doomed them! Will you, then, be saved? 12Did the gods of the nations whom my fathers destroyed save them? Gozen, Haran, Rezeph, and the Edenites in Telassar? 13Where is the king of Hamath, the king of Arpad, or a king of the cities of Sepharvaim, Hena or Ivvah?' "

14Hezekiah took the letter from the hand of the messengers and read it; then he went up to the temple of the LORD, and spreading it out before him, 15he prayed to the LORD: 16"O LORD of hosts, God of Israel, enthroned upon the cherubim! You alone are God over all the kingdoms of the earth. You have made the heavens and the earth.* 17Incline your ear, O LORD, and listen! Open your eyes, O LORD, and see! Hear all the words of the letter that Sennacherib sent to taunt the living God. 18Truly, O LORD, the kings of Assyria have laid waste all the nations and their lands, 19and cast their gods into the fire; they destroyed them because they were not gods but the work of human hands, wood and stone.[v] 20Therefore, O LORD, our God, save us from his hand, that all the kingdoms of the earth may know that you, O LORD, alone are God."

Punishment of Sennacherib 21Then Isaiah, son of Amoz, sent this message to Hezekiah: Thus says the LORD, the God of Israel: In answer to your prayer for help against Sennacherib, king of Assyria, 22this is the word the LORD has spoken concerning him:[w]

She despises you, laughs you to scorn,
  the virgin daughter Zion;
Behind you she wags her head,
  daughter Jerusalem.
23 Whom have you insulted and blasphemed,
  against whom have you raised your voice
And lifted up your eyes on high?
  Against the Holy One of Israel![x]
24 Through your servants you have insulted the
    Lord:
  You said, "With my many chariots
I climbed the mountain heights,
  the recesses of Lebanon;
I cut down its lofty cedars,
  its choice cypresses;
I reached the remotest heights,
  its forest park.
25 I dug wells and drank water in foreign lands;
  I dried up with the soles of my feet
  all the rivers of Egypt."

26 Have you not heard?
  Long ago I prepared it,
From days of old I planned it,
  now I have brought it to pass:
That you should reduce fortified cities
  into heaps of ruins,
27 While their inhabitants, shorn of power,
  are dismayed and ashamed,
Becoming like the plants of the field,

37, 9: Tirhakah: may have been general of the Egyptian army in 701 B.C.; later he became king, one of the Ethiopian dynasty of Egyptian kings (c. 690–664 B.C.). Many consider that this account in Isaiah combines features of two originally distinct sieges of Jerusalem by Sennacherib.

37, 16: In contrast to the empty boasting of the Assyrians, Hezekiah proclaims the Lord as God over all the kingdoms of the earth.

t Is 41, 10–14; 51, 7. u Is 36, 14. v Jer 16, 20. w 2 Kgs 19, 21. x Is 1, 4.

like the green growth,
like the scorched grass on the housetops.
28 I am aware whether you stand or sit;
I know whether you come or go,
and also your rage against me.
29 Because of your rage against me
and your fury which has reached my ears,
I will put my hook in your nose
and my bit in your mouth,
and make you return the way you came.

30 This shall be a sign for you:*
this year you shall eat the aftergrowth,
next year, what grows of itself;
But in the third year, sow and reap,
plant vineyards and eat their fruit!
31 The remaining survivors of the house of Judah
shall again strike root below
and bear fruit above.[y]
32 For out of Jerusalem shall come a remnant,
and from Mount Zion, survivors.
The zeal of the LORD of hosts shall do this.

33 Therefore, thus says the LORD concerning
the king of Assyria: He shall not reach this city,
nor shoot an arrow at it, nor come before it with
a shield, nor cast up siegeworks against it. 34 He
shall return by the same way he came, without
entering the city, says the LORD.[z] 35 I will shield
and save this city for my own sake, and for the
sake of my servant David.[a]
36 The angel of the LORD went forth and struck
down one hundred and eighty-five thousand in
the Assyrian camp.[b] Early the next morning,
there they were, all the corpses of the dead.*
37 So Sennacherib, the king of Assyria, broke
camp and went back home to Nineveh.[c]
38 When he was worshiping in the temple of
his god Nisroch, his sons Adrammelech and
Sharezer slew him with the sword and fled into
the land of Ararat.* His son Esarhaddon reigned
in his stead.

CHAPTER 38

Sickness and Recovery of Hezekiah* 1 In
those days,* when Hezekiah was mortally ill,
the prophet Isaiah, son of Amoz, came and said
to him: "Thus says the LORD: Put your house in
order, for you are about to die; you shall not
recover."[d] 2 Then Hezekiah turned his face to
the wall and prayed to the LORD:
3 "O LORD, remember how faithfully and
wholeheartedly I conducted myself in your pres-
ence, doing what was pleasing to you!" And
Hezekiah wept bitterly.[e]
4 Then the word of the LORD came to Isaiah:
5 "Go, tell Hezekiah:* Thus says the LORD, the
God of your father David: I have heard your
prayer and seen your tears. I will heal you: in
three days you shall go up to the LORD's temple;
I will add fifteen years to your life. 6 I will rescue
you and this city from the hand of the king of
Assyria; I will be a shield to this city."[f]
21 Isaiah then ordered a poultice of figs to be
taken and applied to the boil, that he might
recover. 22 Then Hezekiah asked, "What is the
sign that I shall go up to the temple of the
LORD?"
7 [Isaiah answered:] "This will be the sign for
you from the LORD that he will do what he has
promised: 8 See, I will make the shadow cast by
the sun on the stairway to the terrace of Ahaz*
go back the ten steps it has advanced." So the
sun came back the ten steps it had advanced.[g]

37, 30: You: Hezekiah. A sign: it is difficult to know the nature of this sign. Either it is merely a proverbial expression to signify that prosperity follows adversity, or it indicates that after two years the normal conditions of life will be resumed.

37, 36: The destruction of Sennacherib's army is also recorded by Herodotus, a Greek historian of the fifth century B.C. It was probably due to the bubonic plague, but the sacred author attributes it to its ultimate cause, God through his angel.

37, 38: The violent death of Sennacherib (681 B.C.) is also mentioned in non-biblical sources. It occurred twenty years after his invasion of Judea.

38, 1—39, 8: The events of this section—sickness and recovery of Hezekiah, embassy of Merodach-baladan—point forward to Babylon (cc 40–66). They occurred prior to the events of Is 36, 1—37, 38, which point back to Assyria (Is 1, 1—35, 10).

38, 1: In those days: a time prior to the siege of Jerusalem in 701 B.C.

38, 5: Since Hezekiah died in 687 B.C. this sickness of his seems to have been in 702 B.C., that is, fifteen years before.

38, 8: Stairway to the terrace of Ahaz: this interpretation is based on a reading of the Hebrew text revised according to the Dead Sea Scroll of Isaiah; cf 2 Kgs 23, 12. Many translate the phrase as "steps of Ahaz" and understand this as referring to a sundial.

y Is 27, 6. z Is 37, 29. a 1 Kgs 15, 4f. b Is 10, 12; 17, 14. c 2 Kgs 19, 35f. d 2 Kgs 20, 1. e 2 Kgs 18, 5f. f Is 37, 35. g 2 Kgs 20, 9. 11.

Hezekiah's Hymn of Thanksgiving 9The song of Hezekiah, king of Judah, after he had been sick and had recovered from his illness:

10 Once I said,
"In the noontime of life* I must depart!
To the gates of the nether world I shall be consigned
for the rest of my years." [h]
11 I said, "I shall see the LORD* no more
in the land of the living.
No longer shall I behold my fellow men
among those who dwell in the world."
12 My dwelling, like a shepherd's tent,
is struck down and borne away from me;
You have folded up my life, like a weaver
who severs the last thread.*
Day and night you give me over to torment; [i]
13 I cry out until the dawn.
Like a lion he breaks all my bones;
[day and night you give me over to torment].
14 Like a swallow I utter shrill cries;
I moan like a dove.
My eyes grow weak, gazing heavenward:
O Lord, I am in straits; be my surety!

15 What am I to say or tell him?*
He has done it!
I shall go on through all my years
despite the bitterness of my soul.
16 Those live whom the LORD protects;
yours . . . the life of my spirit.*
You have given me health and life;
17 thus is my bitterness transformed into peace.
You have preserved my life
from the pit of destruction,
When you cast behind your back
all my sins.*
18 For it is not the nether world that gives you thanks,*
nor death that praises you;
Neither do those who go down into the pit
await your kindness. [j]
19 The living, the living give you thanks,
as I do today.
Fathers declare to their sons,
O God, your faithfulness.
20 The LORD is our savior;
we shall sing to stringed instruments
In the house of the LORD
all the days of our life.

CHAPTER 39

Embassy from Merodach-baladan 1At that
time when Merodach-baladan,* son of Baladan,
king of Babylon, heard that Hezekiah had recov-
ered from his sickness, he sent letters and gifts to
him. [k] 2Hezekiah was pleased at this, and there-
fore showed the messengers his treasury, the
silver and gold, the spices and fine oil, his whole
armory, and everything that was in his store-
rooms; there was nothing in his house or in his
whole realm that he did not show them. [l]
3Then Isaiah the prophet came to King Heze-
kiah and asked him, "What did these men say to
you? Where did they come from?" Hezekiah
answered, "They came to me from a distant
land, from Babylon." 4"What did they see in
your house?" he asked. Hezekiah replied, "They
saw everything in my house; there is nothing in
my storerooms that I did not show them."
5Then Isaiah said to Hezekiah, "Hear the
word of the LORD of hosts: 6Behold, the days

38, 10: In the noontime of life: long before the end of a full span of life; cf Pss 55, 24; 102, 25.

38, 11: See the Lord: go to the temple and take part in its service.

38, 12: These two metaphors emphasize the suddenness and finality of death.

38, 15: What am I to say or tell him?: a rhetorical question, as if the poet were at a loss in giving fitting expression to his gratitude; cf Ps 116, 12. He has done it: accomplished the cure. Despite the bitterness: even though the one praying was previously so dejected.

38, 16: Yours . . . the life of my spirit: the current Hebrew text is corrupt. The revised Latin psalter renders it: "You have revived my soul."

38, 17: You cast behind your back all my sins: figurative language to express the divine forgiveness of sins, as if God no longer saw or cared about them. This expression is ordinarily used of men forgetting God; cf 1 Kgs 14, 9; Ez 23, 35; Ps 50, 17.

38, 18f: See note on Ps 6, 6.

39, 1: Merodach-baladan: twice king of Babylon, probably from 721 to 710 B.C., and again for nine months, in 704–703. This visit of his messengers, certainly before 701, was in reality a political one. Babylon hoped to lead an anti-Assyrian confederation composed of neighboring states.

h Jb 17, 11; Ps 102, 25. i Jb 7, 6. j Pss 6, 6; 88, 11–13. k 1–8: 2 Kgs 20, 12. l 2 Chr 32, 25ff.

shall come when all that is in your house, and everything that your fathers have stored up until this day, shall be carried off to Babylon;* nothing shall be left, says the LORD.[m] 7 Some of your own bodily descendants shall be taken and made servants in the palace of the king of Babylon."[n] 8 Hezekiah replied to Isaiah, "The word of the LORD which you have spoken is favorable."* For he thought, "There will be peace and security in my lifetime."[o]

B. THE BOOK OF CONSOLATION

I: The Lord's Glory in Israel's Liberation

CHAPTER 40

Promise of Salvation

1 Comfort, give comfort to my people,
says your God.
2 Speak tenderly to Jerusalem, and proclaim to her
that her service* is at an end,
her guilt is expiated;
Indeed, she has received from the hand of the LORD
double for all her sins.[p]

3 A voice cries out:*
In the desert prepare the way of the LORD!
Make straight in the wasteland a highway for our God![q]
4 Every valley shall be filled in,
every mountain and hill shall be made low;
The rugged land shall be made a plain,
the rough country, a broad valley.
5 Then the glory of the LORD shall be revealed,
and all mankind shall see it together;
for the mouth of the LORD has spoken.

6 A voice says, "Cry out!"
I answer, "What shall I cry out?"
"All mankind is grass,
and all their glory like the flower of the field.[r]
7 The grass withers, the flower wilts,
when the breath of the LORD blows upon it.
[So then, the people is the grass.]
8 Though the grass withers and the flower wilts,
the word of our God stands forever."

9 Go up onto a high mountain,
Zion, herald of glad tidings;
Cry out at the top of your voice,
Jerusalem, herald of good news!
Fear not to cry out
and say to the cities of Judah:
Here is your God!
10 Here comes with power
the Lord GOD,
who rules by his strong arm;
Here is his reward with him,
his recompense before him.
11 Like a shepherd he feeds his flock;
in his arms he gathers the lambs,
Carrying them in his bosom,
and leading the ewes with care.[s]

Power of the Creator To Save His People

12 Who has cupped in his hand the waters of the sea,
and marked off the heavens with a span?*
Who has held in a measure the dust of the earth,
weighed the mountains in scales
and the hills in a balance?
13 Who has directed the spirit of the LORD,
or has instructed him as his counselor?[t]
14 Whom did he consult to gain knowledge?
Who taught him the path of judgment,
or showed him the way of understanding?

39, 6: Because Judah preferred to follow a pro-Babylonian policy, instead of trusting in God, it would later be exiled to Babylon.

39, 8: Favorable: for the Exile would not occur in his lifetime.

40, 2: Service: servitude and exile.

40, 3–5: The figurative language here describes the actual return of the exiles from Babylon to Jerusalem. It is the Lord who leads them; their road is made easy for them. Mt 3, 3 and parallels see in these verses a prophecy of the Baptizer and Christ.

40, 12: Span: the distance between the extended little finger and the thumb. Measure: literally, "third"; here a small container.

m 2 Kgs 24, 13; 25, 13ff. n 2 Chr 33, 11; Dn 1, 2f. o 2 Chr 32, 26. p Is 50, 21. q Mt 3, 3; Jn 1, 23. r Jb 8, 12; 14, 2; Ps 37, 2; Sir 14, 18; Jas 1, 10; 1 Pt 1, 24. s Is 49, 9f; 63, 11; Ez 34, 23; 37, 24; Jn 10, 11. t Wis 9, 13; Rom 11, 34; 1 Cor 2, 16; Jb 38, 1ff.

15 Behold, the nations count as a drop of the bucket,
as dust on the scales;
the coastlands weigh no more than powder.
16 Lebanon would not suffice for fuel,*
nor its animals be enough for holocausts.
17 Before him all the nations are as nought,
as nothing and void he accounts them.

18 To whom can you liken God? [u]
With what equal can you confront him?
19 An idol, cast by a craftsman,
which the smith plates with gold
and fits with silver chains? [v]
20 Mulberry wood, the choice portion
which a skilled craftsman picks out for himself,
Choosing timber that will not rot,
to set up an idol that will not be unsteady? [w]
6 One man helps another,*
one says to the other, "Keep on!"
7 The craftsman encourages the goldsmith,
the one who beats with the hammer, him who strikes on the anvil;
He says the soldering is good,
and he fastens it with nails to steady it.

21 Do you not know? Have you not heard?
Was it not foretold you from the beginning?
Have you not understood? Since the earth was founded
22 He sits enthroned above the vault of the earth,
and its inhabitants are like grasshoppers;
He stretches out the heavens like a veil,
spreads them out like a tent to dwell in. [x]
23 He brings princes to nought
and makes the rulers of the earth as nothing.
24 Scarcely are they planted or sown,
scarcely is their stem rooted in the earth,
When he breathes upon them and they wither,
and the stormwind carries them away like straw.
25 To whom can you liken me as an equal?
says the Holy One.
26 Lift up your eyes on high
and see who has created* these:
He leads out their army and numbers them,
calling them all by name.
By his great might and the strength of his power
not one of them is missing! [y]
27 Why, O Jacob, do you say,*
and declare, O Israel,
"My way is hidden from the LORD,
and my right is disregarded by my God"?
28 Do you not know
or have you not heard?
The LORD is the eternal God,
creator of the ends of the earth.
He does not faint nor grow weary,
and his knowledge is beyond scrutiny.
29 He gives strength to the fainting;
for the weak he makes vigor abound.
30 Though young men faint and grow weary,
and youths stagger and fall,
31 They that hope in the LORD will renew their strength,
they will soar as with eagles' wings;
They will run and not grow weary,
walk and not grow faint.

CHAPTER 41

The Liberator of Israel

1 Keep silence before me, O coastlands;*
you peoples, wait for my words!
Let them draw near and speak;
let us come together for judgment.

2 Who has stirred up from the East the champion of justice,*

40, 16: Lebanon . . . fuel: the famed cedars would not be enough to keep the fires of sacrifice burning.
40, 6–7: These two verses have been transposed from chap. 41.
40, 26: Created: see note on Gn 1, 1. By name: for he is their Creator.
40, 27f: God's people, here called Jacob and Israel, must not give way to discouragement: their Lord is the eternal God.
41, 1–4: It is generally agreed that these verses describe the vocation and victory of Cyrus, whom the Lord used as his instrument to redeem Israel.
41, 2: Cyrus is the champion of justice and God's attendant.

u 18f: Acts 17, 29. v Ps 115, 4–7. w Is 44, 13. x Ps 104, 2. y Ps 147, 4f.

and summoned him to be his attendant?
To him he delivers the nations
and subdues the kings;
With his sword he reduces them to dust,
with his bow, to driven straw.
3 He pursues them, passing on without loss,
by a path his feet do not even tread.
4 Who has performed these deeds?
He who has called forth the generations
since the beginning. [z]

I, the LORD, am the first,
and with the last I will also be.
5 The coastlands see, and fear;
the ends of the earth tremble:
these things are near, they come to pass.
8 But you, Israel, my servant, [a]
Jacob, whom I have chosen,
offspring of Abraham my friend—
9 You whom I have taken from the ends of the earth
and summoned from its far-off places,
You whom I have called my servant,
whom I have chosen and will not cast off—
10 Fear not, I am with you;
be not dismayed; I am your God.
I will strengthen you, and help you,
and uphold you with my right hand of justice.

11 Yes, all shall be put to shame and disgrace
who vent their anger against you;
Those shall perish and come to nought
who offer resistance.
12 You shall seek out, but shall not find,
those who strive against you;
They shall be as nothing at all
who do battle with you.

13 For I am the LORD, your God,
who grasp your right hand;
It is I who say to you, "Fear not,
I will help you."
14 Fear not, O worm Jacob,
O maggot Israel;
I will help you, says the LORD;
your redeemer* is the Holy One of Israel.
15 I will make of you a threshing sledge,
sharp, new, and double-edged,
To thresh the mountains and crush them,
to make the hills like chaff.
16 When you winnow them, the wind shall carry them off
and the storm shall scatter them.
But you shall rejoice in the LORD,
and glory in the Holy One of Israel.
17 The afflicted and the needy seek water in vain,
their tongues are parched with thirst.
I, the LORD, will answer them;
I, the God of Israel, will not forsake them.
18 I will open up rivers on the bare heights,
and fountains in the broad valleys;
I will turn the desert into a marshland,
and the dry ground into springs of water.
19 I will plant in the desert the cedar,
acacia, myrtle, and olive;
I will set in the wasteland the cypress,
together with the plane tree and the pine,
20 That all may see and know,
observe and understand,
That the hand of the LORD has done this,
the Holy One of Israel has created it.

21 Present your case, says the LORD;*
bring forward your reasons, says the King of Jacob.
22 Let them come near and foretell to us
what it is that shall happen!
What are the things of long ago?
Tell us, that we may reflect on them
And know their outcome;
or declare to us the things to come!
23 Foretell the things that shall come afterward,
that we may know that you are gods!
Do something, good or evil,
that will put us in awe and in fear.
24 Why, you are nothing and your work is nought!
To choose you is an abomination.

41, 14: Redeemer: in Hebrew, goel, one who frees another from slavery and avenges his sufferings; cf Lv 25, 48; Dt 19, 6. 12.

41, 21–24: An indictment of idols.

z Is 44, 7; 46, 10. a 8f: Is 44, 1f. 21; 45, 4.

25 I have stirred up one from the north, and he comes;
from the east I summon him* by name;
He shall trample the rulers down like red earth,
as the potter treads the clay.
26 Who announced this from the beginning, that we might know;
beforehand, that we might say it is true?
Not one of you foretold it, not one spoke;
no one heard you say,
27 "The first news for Zion: they are coming now,"
or, "For Jerusalem I will pick out a bearer of the glad tidings."
28 When I look, there is not one,
no one of them to give counsel,
to make an answer when I question them.
29 Ah, all of them are nothing,
their works are nought,
their idols are empty wind!

CHAPTER 42

The Servant of the Lord

1 Here is my servant* whom I uphold,
my chosen one with whom I am pleased,
Upon whom I have put my spirit;
he shall bring forth justice to the nations, [b]
2 Not crying out, not shouting,
not making his voice heard in the street.
3 A bruised reed he shall not break,
and a smoldering wick he shall not quench,*
4 Until he establishes justice on the earth;
the coastlands* will wait for his teaching.

5 Thus says God, the LORD,
who created the heavens and stretched them out,
who spreads out the earth with its crops,
Who gives breath to its people
and spirit to those who walk on it:
6 I, the LORD, have called you for the victory of justice,
I have grasped you by the hand;
I formed you, and set you
as a covenant of the people,
a light for the nations, [c]
7 To open the eyes of the blind,
to bring out prisoners from confinement,
and from the dungeon, those who live in darkness.
8 I am the LORD, this is my name;
my glory I give to no other,
nor my praise to idols.
9 See, the earlier things have come to pass,
new ones I now foretell;
Before they spring into being,
I announce them to you.

The Salvation of Israel despite Its Sins

10 Sing to the LORD a new song,
his praise from the end of the earth:
Let the sea and what fills it resound,
the coastlands, and those who dwell in them.
11 Let the steppe and its cities cry out,
the villages where Kedar* dwells;
Let the inhabitants of Sela exult,
and shout from the top of the mountains.
12 Let them give glory to the LORD,
and utter his praise in the coastlands.
13 The LORD goes forth like a hero,
like a warrior he stirs up his ardor;
He shouts out his battle cry,
against his enemies he shows his might: [d]
14 I have looked away, and kept silence,
I have said nothing, holding myself in;
But now, I cry out as a woman in labor,
gasping and panting.
15 I will lay waste mountains and hills,
all their herbage I will dry up;
I will turn the rivers into marshes,
and the marshes I will dry up. [e]

41, 25: I summon him: Cyrus.

42, 1–4: Servant: there are three other "Servant-of-the-Lord" oracles, Is 49, 1–7; 50, 4–11; 52, 13—53, 12. Many identifications have been proposed, e.g., historical Israel, ideal Israel, an Old Testament historical character before or during the lifetime of the prophet, the prophet himself. The New Testament and Christian tradition, however, have seen a fulfillment of these prophecies in Jesus Christ.

42, 3: A reference to the mercy of Christ.

42, 4: Coastlands: the lands of the Mediterranean. In the Old Testament the word often refers to the pagan lands of the west.

42, 11: Kedar: cf footnote to Is 21, 16. Sela: Petra, the capital of Edom.

b Is 45, 6; 49, 6. c Is 45, 13. d Ex 14, 3. e Ex 9, 25; 10, 15; 14, 21; Ps 105, 33ff.

16 I will lead the blind on their journey;
by paths unknown I will guide them.
I will turn darkness into light before them,
and make crooked ways straight.
These things I do for them,
and I will not forsake them.[f]
17 They shall be turned back in utter shame
who trust in idols;
Who say to molten images,
"You are our gods."
18 You who are deaf, listen,*
you who are blind, look and see!
19 Who is blind but my servant,
or deaf like the messenger I send?
20 You see many things without taking note;
your ears are open, but without hearing.
21 Though it pleased the LORD in his justice
to make his law great and glorious,
22 This is a people* despoiled and plundered,
all of them trapped in holes,
hidden away in prisons.
They are taken as booty, with no one to rescue them,
as spoil, with no one to demand their return.
23 Who of you gives ear to this?
Who listens and pays heed for the time to come?
24 Who was it that gave Jacob to be plundered,
Israel to the despoilers?*
Was it not the LORD, against whom we have sinned?
In his ways they refused to walk,
his law they disobeyed.
25 So he poured out wrath upon them,
his anger, and the fury of battle;
It blazed round about them, yet they did not realize,
it burned them, but they took it not to heart.

42, 18–20: Because of their unbelief, the Lord rebukes his people, whom he calls his servant, his messenger.
42, 22: A people: Israel in exile.
42, 24: Despoilers: the Assyrians and Babylonians.

CHAPTER 43

Promises of Redemption and Restoration

1 But now, thus says the LORD,
who created you, O Jacob, and formed you, O Israel:
Fear not, for I have redeemed you;
I have called you by name: you are mine.
2 When you pass through the water, I will be with you;
in the rivers you shall not drown.
When you walk through fire, you shall not be burned;
the flames shall not consume you.
3 For I am the LORD, your God,
the Holy One of Israel, your savior.
I give Egypt as your ransom,
Ethiopia and Seba* in return for you.
4 Because you are precious in my eyes
and glorious, and because I love you,
I give men in return for you
and peoples in exchange for your life.[g]
5 Fear not, for I am with you;
from the east I will bring back your descendants,
from the west I will gather you.
6 I will say to the north: Give them up!
and to the south: Hold not back!
Bring back my sons from afar,
and my daughters from the ends of the earth:[h]
7 Everyone who is named as mine,
whom I created for my glory,
whom I formed and made.
8 Lead out the people who are blind though they have eyes,
who are deaf though they have ears.
9 Let all the nations gather together,
let the peoples assemble!
Who among them could have revealed this,
or foretold to us the earlier things?*

43, 3f: Egypt . . . Ethiopia and Seba: countries which God permitted the Persians to conquer in return for having given Israel its freedom.
43, 9: Only God can know and predict future events; cf Is 41, 1–5. 21–29.

f Ex 13, 21. g Dt 4, 37; Hos 11, 1. h Is 49, 22; Ez 16, 20.

Let them produce witnesses to prove
themselves right,
that one may hear and say, "It is true!"
10 You are my witnesses, says the LORD,
my servants whom I have chosen
To know and believe in me
and understand that it is I.
Before me no god was formed,
and after me there shall be none.

11 It is I, I the LORD;
there is no savior but me.
12 It is I who foretold, I who saved;
I made it known, not any strange god
among you;
You are my witnesses, says the LORD.
I am God, 13 yes, from eternity I am He;
There is none who can deliver from my hand:
who can countermand what I do? [i]

14 Thus says the LORD, your redeemer,*
the Holy One of Israel:
For your sakes I send to Babylon;
I will lower all the bars,
and the Chaldeans shall cry out in
lamentation.
15 I am the LORD, your Holy One,
the creator of Israel, your King.
16 Thus says the LORD,
who opens a way in the sea
and a path in the mighty waters, [j]
17 Who leads out chariots and horsemen,
a powerful army,
Till they lie prostrate together, never to rise,
snuffed out and quenched like a wick. [k]
18 Remember not the events of the past,
the things of long ago consider not;*
19 See, I am doing something new!
Now it springs forth, do you not perceive it?
In the desert I make a way,
in the wasteland, rivers.
20 Wild beasts honor me,
jackals and ostriches,
For I put water in the desert
and rivers in the wasteland
for my chosen people to drink,
21 The people whom I formed for myself,
that they might announce my praise.

22 Yet you did not call upon me, O Jacob,*
for you grew weary of me, O Israel.
23 You did not bring me sheep for your
holocausts,
nor honor me with your sacrifices.
I did not exact from you the service of
offerings,
nor weary you for frankincense. [l]
24 You did not buy me sweet cane* for
money,
nor fill me with the fat of your sacrifices;
Instead, you burdened me with your sins,
and wearied me with your crimes.
25 It is I, I, who wipe out,
for my own sake, your offenses;
your sins I remember no more.
26 Would you have me remember, have us come
to trial?
Speak up, prove your innocence!
27 Your first father* sinned;
your spokesmen rebelled against me
28 Till I repudiated the holy gates,
put Jacob under the ban,
and exposed Israel to scorn.

CHAPTER 44

1 Hear then, O Jacob, my servant,
Israel, whom I have chosen.
2 Thus says the LORD who made you,
your help, who formed you from the womb:
Fear not, O Jacob, my servant,
the darling* whom I have chosen.
3 I will pour out water upon the thirsty ground,
and streams upon the dry land;
I will pour out my spirit upon your offspring,
and my blessing upon your descendants.
4 They shall spring up amid the verdure

43, 14–17: The destruction of Babylon.
43, 18: No need to think solely of the past wonders of the exodus from Egypt; equally great is the exodus from Babylon.
43, 22–28: The reason for the liberation of the Israelites is not their fidelity but rather God's mercy.
43, 24: Sweet cane: a fragrant substance used in making incense and the sacred anointing oil; cf Ex 30, 23; Jer 6, 20.
43, 27: First father: Adam or Jacob, or collectively "early ancestors." Spokesmen: leaders, priests, prophets.
44, 2: The darling: see note on Dt 32, 15; cf also Dt 33, 5. 26.

i Is 41, 4. j Is 51, 10f; Ex 14, 21. k Ex 15, 4. l Jer 6, 20.

like poplars beside the flowing waters.[m]
5 One shall say, "I am the LORD's,"
another shall be named after Jacob,
And this one shall write on his hand,* "The
LORD's,"
and Israel shall be his surname.[n]

The True God and False Gods

6 Thus says the LORD, Israel's King
and redeemer, the LORD of hosts:
I am the first and I am the last;
there is no God but me.[o]
7 Who is like me? Let him stand up and speak,
make it evident, and confront me with it.
Who of old announced future events?
Let them foretell to us the things to come.
8 Fear not, be not troubled:
did I not announce and foretell it long ago?
You are my witnesses! Is there a God
or any Rock* besides me?[p]

9 *Idol makers all amount to nothing, and
their precious works are of no avail, as they
themselves give witness. To their shame, they
neither see nor know anything; and they are
more deaf than men are.[q] 10 Indeed, all the
associates of anyone who forms a god, or casts
an idol to no purpose, will be put to shame;
11 they will all assemble and stand forth, to be
reduced to fear and shame.

12 The smith fashions an iron image, works it
over the coals, shapes it with hammers, and
forges it with his strong arm. He is hungry and
weak, drinks no water and becomes exhausted.[r]

13 The carpenter stretches a line and marks
with a stylus the outline of an idol. He shapes it
with a plane and measures it off with a compass,
making it like a man in appearance and dignity,
to occupy a shrine. 14 He cuts down cedars, takes
a holm or an oak, and lays hold of other trees of
the forest, which the Lord had planted and the
rain made grow 15 to serve man for fuel. With a
part of their wood he warms himself, or makes a
fire for baking bread; but with another part he
makes a god which he adores, an idol which he
worships. 16 Half of it he burns in the fire, and on
its embers he roasts his meat; he eats what he
has roasted until he is full, and then warms
himself and says, "Ah! I am warm, I feel the
fire." 17 Of what remains he makes a god, his
idol, and prostrate before it in worship, he
implores it, "Rescue me, for you are my god."

18 The idols have neither knowledge nor rea-
son; their eyes are coated so that they cannot
see, and their hearts so that they cannot under-
stand. 19 Yet he does not reflect, nor have the
intelligence and sense to say, "Half of the wood I
burned in the fire, and on its embers I baked
bread and roasted meat which I ate. Shall I then
make an abomination out of the rest, or worship
a block of wood?" 20 He is chasing ashes*—a
thing that cannot save itself when the flame
consumes it; yet he does not say, "Is not this
thing in my right hand a fraud?"

21 Remember this, O Jacob,
you, O Israel, who are my servant!
I formed you to be a servant to me;
O Israel, by me you shall never be
forgotten:
22 I have brushed away your offenses like a
cloud,
your sins like a mist;
return to me, for I have redeemed you.

23 Raise a glad cry, you heavens: the LORD has
done this;
shout, you depths of the earth.
Break forth, you mountains, into song,
you forest, with all your trees.
For the LORD has redeemed Jacob,
and shows his glory through Israel.

Cyrus, Anointed of the Lord, Liberator of Israel

24 Thus says the LORD, your redeemer,
who formed you from the womb:

44, 5: Write on his hand: an allusion to the Babylonian custom of tatooing the owner's name on the hand of his slave; cf also Rv 13, 16.

44, 8: Rock: place of refuge; said of God in Dt 32, 4. 18; 1 Sm 2, 2; etc.

44, 9–20: Satire on the makers and worshipers of idols.

44, 20: Chasing ashes: exerting efforts in vain; cf Hos 12, 2; Eccl 1, 14; 2, 11. 17.

m Is 54, 1ff. n Is 43, 7; 45, 14. o Is 41, 44; 43, 15; 45, 21; 48, 3. 12; 51, 15; 54, 5. p Is 43, 10. 12; Dt 32, 4. q Is 48, 5. 7. r Wis 13, 11ff.

I am the LORD, who made all things,
who alone stretched out the heavens;
when I spread out the earth, who was with me? [s]
25 It is I who bring to nought the omens of liars,
who make fools of diviners;
I turn wise men back
and make their knowledge foolish.
26 It is I who confirm the words of my servants,
I carry out the plan announced by my messengers;
I say to Jerusalem: Be inhabited;
to the cities of Judah: Be rebuilt;
I will raise up their ruins.
27 It is I who said to the deep: Be dry;
I will dry up your wellsprings. [t]
28 I say of Cyrus:* My shepherd,
who fulfills my every wish;
He shall say of Jerusalem, "Let her be rebuilt,"
and of the temple, "Let its foundations be laid." [u]

CHAPTER 45

1 Thus says the LORD to his anointed,* Cyrus,
whose right hand I grasp,
Subduing nations before him,
and making kings run in his service,
Opening doors before him
and leaving the gates unbarred:
2 I will go before you
and level the mountains;
Bronze doors* I will shatter,
and iron bars I will snap. [v]
3 I will give you treasures out of the darkness,
and riches that have been hidden away,
That you may know that I am the LORD,
the God of Israel, who calls you by your name.
4 For the sake of Jacob, my servant,
of Israel my chosen one,
I have called you by your name,
giving you a title, though you knew me not. [w]
5 I am the LORD and there is no other,
there is no God besides me.
It is I who arm you, though you know me not,
6 so that toward the rising and the setting of the sun
men may know that there is none besides me.*
I am the LORD, there is no other;
7 I form the light, and create the darkness,
I make well-being and create woe;*
I, the LORD, do all these things.
8 Let justice descend, O heavens, like dew from above,
like gentle rain let the skies drop it down.
Let the earth open and salvation bud forth;
let justice also spring up!*
I, the LORD, have created this. [x]
9 Woe to him who contends with his Maker; [y]
a potsherd among potsherds of the earth!*
Dare the clay say to its modeler, "What are you doing?"
or, "What you are making has no hands"?
10 Woe to him who asks a father, "What are you begetting?"
or a woman, "What are you giving birth to?"
11 Thus says the LORD,
the Holy One of Israel, his maker:

44, 28: Cyrus: king of Persia (559–529 B.C.) and conqueror of Babylon (538 B.C.), who liberated the Jews, permitting them to return to their native land and to rebuild Jerusalem and the Temple.

45, 1: Anointed: in Hebrew, meshiah, from which the word "Messiah" is derived; from its Greek translation, Christos, we have the name "Christ." Applied to kings, "anointed" originally referred only to those of Israel, but it is here given to Cyrus because he is the agent of the Lord.

45, 2: Bronze doors: of Babylon.

45, 6: The Gentiles will come to know the true God; cf also vv 20–25.

45, 7: Create woe: God permits evil for the sake of a greater good.

45, 8: The Vulgate rendering gives a more precise Messianic sense to this verse, using "just one" and "savior" in place of justice and salvation. The Advent liturgy uses the Vulgate form, Rorate coeli desuper . . . , to express the world's longing for the coming of Christ.

45, 9: No one may challenge God's freedom of action, exemplified here by the selection of Cyrus as his anointed.

s Is 40, 22; Jb 9, 8. t Is 42, 15; 51, 10. u Jer 3, 15; Ez 34, 23. v Ps 107, 16. w Is 40, 26. x Pss 72, 6; 85, 11. y Jer 18, 6; Rom 9, 20.

You question me about my children,
or prescribe the work of my hands for me!
12 It was I who made the earth
and created mankind upon it;
It was my hands that stretched out the
heavens;
I gave the order to all their host.
13 It was I who stirred up one* for the triumph of
justice;
all his ways I make level.
He shall rebuild my city
and let my exiles go free
Without price or ransom,
says the LORD of hosts.
14 Thus says the LORD:
The earnings of Egypt, the gain of Ethiopia,
and the Sabeans,* tall of stature,
Shall come over to you and belong to you;
they shall follow you, coming in chains.
Before you they shall fall prostrate,
saying in prayer:
"With you only is God, and nowhere else;
the gods are nought.[z]
15 Truly with you God is hidden,*
the God of Israel, the savior![a]
16 Those are put to shame and disgrace
who vent their anger against him;
Those go in disgrace
who carve images.
17 Israel, you are saved by the LORD,
saved forever!
You shall never be put to shame or disgrace
in future ages."
18 For thus says the LORD,
The creator of the heavens,
who is God,
The designer and maker of the earth
who established it,
Not creating it to be a waste,*
but designing it to be lived in:
I am the LORD, and there is no other.
19 I have not spoken from hiding
nor from some dark place of the earth,
And I have not said to the descendants of
Jacob,
"Look for me in an empty waste."
I, the LORD, promise justice,
I foretell what is right.
20 Come and assemble, gather together,
you fugitives from among the gentiles!
They are without knowledge who bear
wooden idols*
and pray to gods that cannot save.
21 Come here and declare
in counsel together:
Who announced this from the beginning
and foretold it from of old?
Was it not I, the LORD,
besides whom there is no other God?
There is no just and saving God but me.
22 Turn to me and be safe,
all you ends of the earth,
for I am God; there is no other!
23 By myself I swear,
uttering my just decree
and my unalterable word:
To me every knee shall bend;
by me every tongue shall swear,[b]
24 Saying, "Only in the LORD
are just deeds and power.
Before him in shame shall come
all who vent their anger against him.
25 In the LORD shall be the vindication and the
glory
of all the descendants of Israel."

CHAPTER 46

The Gods of Babylon

1 Bel bows down, Nebo* stoops,
their idols are upon beasts and cattle;
They must be borne up on shoulders,
carried as burdens by the weary.

45, 13: One: Cyrus, called by God for the deliverance and restoration of Israel.

45, 14: Egypt . . . Ethiopia . . . Sabeans: the Egyptians and their allies who, when conquered by Cyrus, are seen as acknowledging the God of Israel to be the one true God; cf Is 43, 3.

45, 15: God is hidden: he dwells invisibly in the holy of holies.

45, 18: Waste: an allusion to the beginning of creation, when the earth was waste and void (Gn 1, 2), the same Hebrew word, tohu, being used in both passages. The further reference here is to Palestine, which God wishes again to be inhabited by the returning exiles.

45, 20: Who bear wooden idols: in their religious processions. The gods of the pagans have feet but cannot walk; cf Ps 115, 7; Bar 6, 25.

46, 1: Bel . . . Nebo: gods of Babylon; their complete helplessness is here contrasted with God's omnipotence.

z Is 43, 3. a Is 55, 8; Prv 25, 2. b Rom 14, 11; Phil 2, 10.

2 They stoop and bow down together;
unable to save those who bear them,
they too go into captivity.

3 Hear me, O house of Jacob,
all who remain of the house of Israel,
My burden since your birth,
whom I have carried from your infancy. [c]
4 Even to your old age I am the same,
even when your hair is gray I will bear you;
It is I who have done this, I who will continue,
and I who will carry you to safety.

5 Whom would you compare me with, as an equal,
or match me against, as though we were alike?
6 There are those who pour out gold from a purse
and weigh out silver on the scales;
Then they hire a goldsmith to make it into a god
before which they fall down in worship.
7 They lift it to their shoulders to carry;
when they set it in place again, it stays,
and does not move from the spot.
Although they cry out to it, it cannot answer;
it delivers no one from distress.

8 Remember this and be firm,
bear it well in mind, you rebels;
remember the former things, those long ago:
9 I am God, there is no other;
I am God, there is none like me.
10 At the beginning I foretell the outcome;
in advance, things not yet done.
I say that my plan shall stand,
I accomplish my every purpose.

11 I call from the east a bird of prey,*
from a distant land, one to carry out my plan.
Yes, I have spoken, I will accomplish it;
I have planned it, and I will do it.
12 Listen to me, you fainthearted,
you who seem far from the victory of justice:
13 I am bringing on my justice, it is not far off,
my salvation shall not tarry;
I will put salvation within Zion,
and give to Israel my glory.

CHAPTER 47

The Fall of Babylon*

1 Come down, sit in the dust,
O virgin daughter Babylon;
Sit on the ground, dethroned,
O daughter of the Chaldeans.
No longer shall you be called
dainty and delicate.
2 Take the millstone and grind flour,
remove your veil;
Strip off your train, bare your legs,
pass through the streams.
3 Your nakedness shall be uncovered
and your shame be seen;
I will take vengeance,
I will yield to no entreaty,
says our redeemer.
4 Whose name is the LORD of hosts,
the Holy One of Israel.

5 Go into darkness and sit in silence,
O daughter of the Chaldeans,
No longer shall you be called
sovereign mistress of kingdoms.
6 Angry at my people,
I profaned my inheritance,
And I gave them into your hand;
but you showed them no mercy,
And upon old men
you laid a very heavy yoke.
7 You said, "I shall remain always,
a sovereign mistress forever!"
But you did not lay these things to heart,
you disregarded their outcome. [d]
8 Now hear this, voluptuous one,
enthroned securely,
Saying to yourself,

46, 11: From the east a bird of prey: Cyrus; cf Is 41, 2–4.
47, 1–15: A taunt-song, mocking Babylon, once queen of the nations, now made a slave girl.

c Is 44, 2. d Is 14, 13f.

"I, and no one else!
I shall never be a widow,
or suffer the loss of my children"—[e]
9 Both these things shall come to you
suddenly, in a single day:
Complete bereavement and widowhood
shall come upon you
For your many sorceries
and the great number of your
spells;*
10 Because you felt secure in your
wickedness,
and said, "No one sees me."
Your wisdom and your knowledge
led you astray,
And you said to yourself,
"I, and no one else!"
11 But upon you shall come evil
you will not know how to predict;
Disaster shall befall you
which you cannot allay.
Suddenly there shall come upon you
ruin which you will not expect.
12 Keep up, now, your spells
and your many sorceries;
Perhaps you can make them avail,
perhaps you can strike terror!
13 You wearied yourself with many consultations,
at which you toiled from your youth;
Let the astrologers stand forth to save
you,
the stargazers who forecast at each new
moon
what would happen to you.
14 Lo, they are like stubble,
fire consumes them;
They cannot save themselves
from the spreading flames.
This is no warming ember,
no fire to sit before.
15 Thus do your wizards serve you
with whom you have toiled from your
youth;
Each wanders his own way,
with none to save you.

47, 9. 13. 15: Babylon was known for its sorcery and astrology.

CHAPTER 48

Exhortations to the Exiles

1 Hear this, O house of Jacob
called by the name Israel,
sprung from the stock of Judah,
You who swear by the name of the LORD
and invoke the God of Israel
without sincerity or justice,
2 Though you are named after the holy city
and rely on the God of Israel,
whose name is the LORD of hosts.
3 Things of the past I foretold long ago,
they went forth from my mouth, I let you
hear of them;
then suddenly I took action and they came
to be.
4 Because I know that you are stubborn
and that your neck is an iron sinew
and your forehead bronze,
5 I foretold them to you of old;
before they took place I let you hear of
them,
That you might not say, "My idol did them,
my statue, my molten image commanded
them."
6 Now that you have heard, look at all this;
must you not admit it?[f]

From now on I announce new things to you,
hidden events of which you knew not.
7 Now, not long ago, they are brought into
being,
and beforetime you did not hear of them,
so that you cannot claim to have known
them;
8 You neither heard nor knew,
they did not reach your ears beforehand.
Yes, I know you are utterly treacherous,
a rebel you were called from birth.[g]
9 For the sake of my name I restrain my anger,
for the sake of my renown I hold it back
from you,
lest I should destroy you.
10 See, I have refined you like silver,
tested you in the furnace of affliction.[h]

e Zep 2, 15; Rv 18, 7. f Is 42, 9. g Is 43, 22ff. h Is 1, 25; Jer 6, 29f; Zec 13, 9; Mal 3, 2.

11 For my sake, for my own sake, I do this;
why should I suffer profanation?
My glory I will not give to another.

12 Listen to me, Jacob,
Israel, whom I named!
I, it is I who am the first,
and also the last am I. [i]
13 Yes, my hand laid the foundations of the earth;
my right hand spread out the heavens.
When I call them,
they stand forth at once. [j]

14 All of you assemble and listen:
Who among you foretold these things?
The LORD's friend* shall do his will
against Babylon and the progeny of Chaldea.
15 I myself have spoken, I have called him,
I have brought him, and his way succeeds!
16 Come near to me and hear this!
Not from the beginning did I speak it in secret;
At the time it comes to pass, I am present:
"Now the Lord* GOD has sent me,
and his spirit."
17 Thus says the LORD, your redeemer,
the Holy One of Israel:
I, the LORD, your God,
teach you what is for your good,
and lead you on the way you should go.
18 If you would hearken to my commandments,
your prosperity would be like a river,
and your vindication like the waves of the sea;
19 Your descendants would be like the sand,
and those born of your stock like its grains,
Their name never cut off
or blotted out from my presence.
20 Go forth from Babylon, flee from Chaldea!
With shouts of joy proclaim this, make it known;
Publish it to the ends of the earth, and say,
"The LORD has redeemed his servant Jacob.
21 They did not thirst
when he led them through dry lands;
Water from the rock he set flowing for them;
he cleft the rock, and waters welled forth." [k]
22 [There is no peace for the wicked,
says the LORD.]

II: Expiation of Sin, Spiritual Liberation of Israel

CHAPTER 49

The Servant of the Lord*

1 Hear me, O coastlands,
listen, O distant peoples. [l]
The LORD called me from birth,
from my mother's womb he gave me my name.*
2 He made of me a sharp-edged sword
and concealed me in the shadow of his arm.
He made me a polished arrow,
in his quiver he hid me.*
3 You are my servant, he said to me,
Israel,* through whom I show my glory.

4 Though I thought I had toiled in vain,
and for nothing, uselessly, spent my strength,
Yet my reward is with the LORD,
my recompense is with my God. [m]
5 For now the LORD has spoken
who formed me as his servant from the womb,
That Jacob may be brought back to him
and Israel gathered to him;
And I am made glorious in the sight of the LORD,
and my God is now my strength!
6 It is too little, he says, for you to be my servant,

48, 14: The Lord's friend: Cyrus, who carries out God's plans.
48, 16: "Now the Lord . . . spirit": said by Cyrus; cf v 14.
49, 1–7: The second of the four "Servant-of-the-Lord" oracles.
49, 1: Gave me my name: designated me for a special office (cf Jer 1, 5), or perhaps, made me renowned (cf Ps 45, 18).
49, 2: The servant was made ready and fit for the preaching of God's word.
49, 3: Israel: the Servant is identified with the people of Israel as their ideal representative; however, since vv 5f seem to distinguish the Servant from Israel, some regard the word Israel here as a gloss.

i Is 41, 4; 44, 6; 48, 12; Rv 1, 8. 17. j Is 40, 22. 26; 45, 12. 18. k Ex 17, 6; Nm 20, 11. l Is 41, 9; 43, 1; 44, 2. 24; 46, 3. m Is 40, 27.

to raise up the tribes of Jacob,
and restore the survivors of Israel; [n]
I will make you a light to the nations,
that my salvation may reach to the ends of the earth.*

7 Thus says the LORD,
the redeemer and the Holy One of Israel,
To the one despised, whom the nations abhor,
the slave of rulers:
When kings see you, they shall stand up,
and princes shall prostrate themselves
Because of the LORD who is faithful,
the Holy One of Israel who has chosen you. [o]

The Liberation and Restoration of Zion

8 Thus says the LORD:
In a time of favor I answer you,
on the day of salvation I help you,
To restore the land
and allot the desolate heritages, [p]
9 Saying to the prisoners: Come out!
To those in darkness: Show yourselves!
Along the ways they shall find pasture,
on every bare height shall their pastures be. [q]
10 They shall not hunger or thirst,
nor shall the scorching wind or the sun strike them;
For he who pities them leads them
and guides them beside springs of water. [r]
11 I will cut a road through all my mountains,
and make my highways level. [s]
12 See, some shall come from afar,
others from the north and the west,
and some from the land of Syene.*

13 Sing out, O heavens, and rejoice, O earth,
break forth into song, you mountains.
For the LORD comforts his people
and shows mercy to his afflicted.

14 But Zion said, "The LORD has forsaken me;
my Lord has forgotten me." [t]
15 Can a mother forget her infant,
be without tenderness for the child of her womb?
Even should she forget,
I will never forget you. [u]
16 See, upon the palms of my hands I have written your name;*
your walls are ever before me.
17 Your rebuilders make haste,
as those who tore you down and laid you waste
go forth from you;
18 Look about and see,
they are all gathering and coming to you.
As I live, says the LORD,
you shall be arrayed with them all as with adornments,
like a bride you shall fasten them on you.

19 Though you were waste and desolate,
a land of ruins,
Now you shall be too small for your inhabitants,
while those who swallowed you up will be far away.
20 The children whom you had lost
shall yet say to you,
"This place is too small for me,
make room for me to live in."
21 You shall ask yourself:
"Who has borne me these?
I was bereft and barren
[exiled and repudiated];
who has reared them?
I was left all alone;
where then do these come from?" [v]

22 Thus says the Lord GOD:
See, I will lift up my hand to the nations,
and raise my signal to the peoples;
They shall bring your sons in their arms,
and your daughters shall be carried on their shoulders. [w]
23 Kings shall be your foster fathers,

49, 6: The Servant's vocation will be not only the restoration of Israel but the conversion of the world; cf Lk 2, 32.

49, 12: Syene: now called Aswan, at the first cataract of the Nile in southern Egypt.

49, 16: Upon the palms . . . name: for continual remembrance; cf Ex 13, 9. 16; Dt 6, 6–9.

n Is 42, 1–6; 44, 5; 45, 14; Lk 2, 32; Acts 13, 46f. o Is 49, 23; 55, 5. p 2 Cor 6, 2. q Is 42, 7. 18ff. r Is 51, 14; Rv 7, 16. s Is 40, 3f. t Is 40, 27. u Is 43, 4; 44, 21; 46, 3f. v Is 54, 1ff. w Is 5, 26; 13, 2.

their princesses your nurses;
Bowing to the ground, they shall worship you
and lick the dust at your feet.
Then you shall know that I am the LORD,
and those who hope in me shall never be
disappointed.

24 Thus says the LORD:
Can booty be taken from a warrior?
or captives be rescued from a tyrant?
25 Yes, captives can be taken from a warrior,
and booty be rescued from a tyrant;
Those who oppose you I will oppose,
and your sons I will save.
26 I will make your oppressors eat their own
flesh,
and they shall be drunk with their own
blood
as with the juice of the grape.
All mankind shall know
that I, the LORD, am your savior,
your redeemer, the mighty one of Jacob. [x]

CHAPTER 50

Salvation Only through the Lord's Servant

1 Thus says the LORD:
Where is the bill of divorce
with which I dismissed your mother?*
Or to which of my creditors
have I sold you?
It was for your sins that you were sold,
for your crimes that your mother was
dismissed. [y]

2 Why was no one there when I came?
Why did no one answer when I called?*
Is my hand too short to ransom?
Have I not the strength to deliver?
Lo, with my rebuke I dry up the sea,
I turn rivers into a desert;
Their fish rot for lack of water,
and die of thirst. [z]
3 I clothe the heavens in mourning,
and make sackcloth their vesture.

4 The Lord GOD has given me*
a well-trained tongue,
That I might know how to speak to the weary
a word that will rouse them.
Morning after morning
he opens my ear that I may hear;
5 And I have not rebelled,
have not turned back.*
6 I gave my back to those who beat me,
my cheeks to those who plucked my
beard;*
My face I did not shield
from buffets and spitting. [a]

7 The Lord GOD is my help,
therefore I am not disgraced;
I have set my face like flint,
knowing that I shall not be put to shame. [b]
8 He is near who upholds my right;
if anyone wishes to oppose me,
let us appear together.
Who disputes my right?
Let him confront me.
9 See, the Lord GOD is my help;
who will prove me wrong?
Lo, they will all wear out like cloth,
the moth will eat them up. [c]

10 Who among you fears the LORD,*
heeds his servant's voice,
And walks in darkness
without any light,
Trusting in the name of the LORD
and relying on his God? [d]
11 All of you kindle flames
and carry about you fiery darts;
Walk by the light of your own fire
and by the flares you have burnt!

50, 1: Responding to the people's complaint of utter abandonment by God, the prophet shows that their sins were responsible for their banishment. Since there was no bill of divorce, the bond between the Lord and his people still exists and he will ultimately save them.

50, 2: Israel's faith in God is weak; she does not answer his call, nor believe in his promises of deliverance.

50, 4–11: The third of the four "Servant-of-the-Lord" oracles; in vv 4–9 the Servant speaks; in vv 10f God reproves the people for not following the Servant.

50, 5: The Servant does not refuse the divine vocation.

50, 6: He willingly submits to insults and beatings. Plucked my beard: a grave insult.

50, 10f: Instead of trusting in the Lord and his Servant, the people rely on their own devices, to their own destruction.

x Is 19, 2; Ez 38, 21; Zec 14, 13. y Dt 24, 1–4; Mt 19, 3; Mk 10, 2ff; Is 54, 6ff. z Ex 7, 18; Ps 105, 29. a 2 Sm 10, 4ff; Mt 26, 67; 27, 30. b Ez 3, 9. c Is 51, 6–8; Ps 102, 27. d Is 43, 1f; 44, 1f.

This is your fate from my hand:
you shall lie down in a place of pain.

CHAPTER 51

Exhortation To Trust in the Lord

1 Listen to me, you who pursue justice,
who seek the LORD;
Look to the rock from which you were hewn,
to the pit* from which you were quarried; [e]
2 Look to Abraham, your father,
and to Sarah, who gave you birth;
When he was but one I called him,
I blessed him and made him many.[f]
3 Yes, the LORD shall comfort Zion
and have pity on all her ruins;
Her deserts he shall make like Eden,
her wasteland like the garden of the LORD;
Joy and gladness shall be found in her,
thanksgiving and the sound of song.

4 Be attentive to me, my people;*
my folk, give ear to me.
For law shall go forth from my presence,
and my judgment, as the light of the peoples.[g]
5 I will make my justice come speedily;
my salvation shall go forth
[and my arm shall judge the nations];
In me shall the coastlands hope,
and my arm they shall await.

6 Raise your eyes to the heavens,
and look at the earth below;
Though the heavens grow thin like smoke,
the earth wears out like a garment
and its inhabitants die like flies,
My salvation shall remain forever
and my justice shall never be dismayed.*
7 Hear me, you who know justice,
you people who have my teaching at heart:
Fear not the reproach of men,
be not dismayed at their revilings.
8 They shall be like a garment eaten by moths,
like wool consumed by grubs;
But my justice shall remain forever
and my salvation, for all generations.[h]

9 Awake, awake, put on strength,
O arm of the LORD!
Awake as in the days of old,
in ages long ago!
Was it not you who crushed Rahab,*
you who pierced the dragon?[i]
10 Was it not you who dried up the sea,
the waters of the great deep,*
Who made the depths of the sea into a way
for the redeemed to pass over?
11 Those whom the LORD has ransomed will return
and enter Zion singing,
crowned with everlasting joy;
They will meet with joy and gladness,
sorrow and mourning will flee.
12 I, it is I who comfort you.
Can you then fear mortal man,
who is human only, to be looked upon as grass,
13 And forget the LORD, your maker,
who stretched out the heavens
and laid the foundations of the earth?
All the day you are in constant dread
of the fury of the oppressor;
But when he sets himself to destroy,
what is there of the oppressor's fury?

14 The oppressed shall soon be released;
they shall not die and go down into the pit,
nor shall they want for bread.
15 For I am the LORD, your God,
who stirs up the sea so that its waves roar;
the LORD of hosts by name.[j]
16 I have put my words into your mouth
and shielded you in the shadow of my hand,
I, who stretched out the heavens,
who laid the foundations of the earth,
who say to Zion: You are my people.

51, 1: Rock . . . pit: your glorious ancestry.
51, 4f: The conversion of the Gentiles.
51, 6: God's salvation and justice are eternal, in contrast to the impermanence of the heavens and the earth: cf Mt 24, 35.
51, 9: Rahab: see note on Is 30, 7. The dragon: see notes on Is 27, 1; Ps 74, 13.
51, 10: Great deep: another reference to the primeval chaos of Gn 1, 2.

e Rom 9, 30f. f Ez 33, 24; Gn 12, 2ff; 22, 17. g Is 2, 3. h Is 50, 9. i Ex 15, 16; Jb 9, 13; 26, 12; Pss 74, 13; 89, 11. j Jer 31, 35.

The Cup of the Lord

17 Awake, awake!
Arise, O Jerusalem,
You who drank at the LORD's hand
the cup of his wrath;
Who drained to the dregs
the bowl of staggering! [k]
18 She has no one to guide her
of all the sons she bore;
She has no one to grasp her by the hand,
of all the sons she reared!—
19 Your misfortunes are double;
who is there to condole with you?
Desolation and destruction, famine and
sword!
Who is there to comfort you?
20 Your sons lie helpless
at every street corner
like antelopes in a net.
They are filled with the wrath of the LORD,
the rebuke of your God.

21 But now, hear this, O afflicted one,
drunk, but not with wine, [l]
22 Thus says the LORD, your Master,
your God, who defends his people:
See, I am taking from your hand
the cup of staggering;
The bowl of my wrath
you shall no longer drink.
23 I will put it into the hands of your tormentors,
those who ordered you
to bow down, that they might walk over
you,
While you offered your back like the ground,
like the street for them to walk on.

CHAPTER 52

Let Zion Rejoice

1 Awake, awake!
Put on your strength, O Zion;
Put on your glorious garments,
O Jerusalem, holy city.
No longer shall the uncircumcised
or the unclean enter you.
2 Shake off the dust,
ascend to the throne, Jerusalem;
Loose the bonds from your neck,
O captive daughter Zion!
3 For thus says the LORD:
You were sold for nothing,
and without money you shall be redeemed.
4 Thus says the Lord GOD:
To Egypt in the beginning my people went
down,
to sojourn there;
Assyria, too, oppressed them for nought.
5 But now, what am I to do here?
says the LORD.
My people have been taken away without
redress;
their rulers make a boast of it, says the
LORD;
all the day my name is constantly reviled.
6 Therefore on that day my people shall know
my renown,
that it is I who have foretold it. Here I am!
7 How beautiful upon the mountains*
are the feet of him who brings glad tidings,
Announcing peace, bearing good news,
announcing salvation, and saying to Zion,
"Your God is King!" [m]
8 Hark! Your watchmen raise a cry,
together they shout for joy,
For they see directly, before their eyes,
the LORD restoring Zion. [n]
9 Break out together in song,
O ruins of Jerusalem!
For the LORD comforts his people,
he redeems Jerusalem.
10 The LORD has bared his holy arm
in the sight of all the nations;
All the ends of the earth will behold
the salvation of our God.

11 Depart, depart, come forth from there,
touch nothing unclean!

52, 7–10: God leads his people back from Babylon to Zion, from whose ruined walls watchmen . . . shout for joy; cf Rom 10, 15.

k Jer 25, 15ff; Ez 23, 32ff. **l** Is 29, 9. **m** Is 40, 9; Rom 10, 15. **n** 1 Is 62, 6.

Out from there!* Purify yourselves,
you who carry the vessels of the LORD.
12 Yet not in fearful haste will you come out,
nor leave in headlong flight,
For the LORD comes before you,
and your rear guard is the God of Israel. [o]

Suffering and Triumph of the Servant of the Lord*

13 See, my servant shall prosper,
he shall be raised high and greatly exalted.
14 Even as many were amazed at him—
so marred was his look beyond that of man,
and his appearance beyond that of mortals—[p]
15 So shall he startle many nations,
because of him kings shall stand speechless;
For those who have not been told shall see,
those who have not heard shall ponder it. [q]

CHAPTER 53

1 Who would believe what we have heard?
To whom has the arm of the LORD been revealed? [r]
2 He grew up like a sapling before him, [s]
like a shoot from the parched earth;
There was in him no stately bearing to make us look at him,
nor appearance that would attract us to him.*
3 He was spurned* and avoided by men,
a man of suffering, accustomed to infirmity,
One of those from whom men hide their faces,
spurned, and we held him in no esteem. [t]

4 Yet it was our infirmities that he bore,*
our sufferings that he endured,
While we thought of him as stricken,
as one smitten by God and afflicted. [u]
5 But he was pierced for our offenses,
crushed for our sins,
Upon him was the chastisement that makes us whole,
by his stripes we were healed. [v]
6 We had all gone astray like sheep,
each following his own way;
But the LORD laid upon him
the guilt of us all. [w]
7 Though he was harshly treated, he submitted
and opened not his mouth;
Like a lamb led to the slaughter
or a sheep before the shearers,
he was silent and opened not his mouth. [x]
8 Oppressed and condemned, he was taken away,
and who would have thought any more of his destiny?
When he was cut off from the land of the living,
and smitten for the sin of his people,
9 A grave was assigned him among the wicked
and a burial place with evildoers,
Though he had done no wrong
nor spoken any falsehood. [y]
10 [But the LORD was pleased*
to crush him in infirmity.]

If he gives his life as an offering for sin,
he shall see his descendants in a long life,
and the will of the LORD shall be accomplished through him.
11 Because of his affliction
he shall see the light in fullness of days;
Through his suffering, my servant shall justify many,
and their guilt he shall bear.
12 Therefore I will give him his portion among the great,

52, 11: From there: from Babylon. Vessels of the Lord: taken to Babylon by Nebuchadnezzar, now carried back by the exiled priests returning in procession to Zion; cf Ezr 1, 7.

52, 13—53, 12: The last of the four "Servant-of-the-Lord" oracles. An extraordinary description of the sinless Servant, who by his voluntary suffering atones for the sins of his people, and saves them from just punishment at the hands of God. Only in Jesus Christ is the prophecy perfectly fulfilled.

53, 2: Only God appreciated his Servant's true greatness.

53, 3: Because he suffered, he was regarded as a sinner and therefore as one to be spurned.

53, 4ff: He did indeed suffer but it was for the sins of mankind, and through his sufferings men are healed.

53, 10ff: Because he fulfilled the divine will by suffering for the sins of others, the Servant will be rewarded by the Lord. See the light: enjoy happiness. This line may originally have read, "he shall drink and eat to the full"—at the thanksgiving sacrifice at which he shall divide the spoils (v 12).

o Ex 12, 11. p Ps 69, 8. q Mi 7, 16. r Is 52, 10; Jn 12, 38; Rom 10, 16. s Is 11, 1. t Jb 19, 18; Ps 31, 11ff; Mk 9, 11. u Jer 10, 19; Mt 8, 17. v 1 Cor 15, 3; 1 Pt 2, 24. w Lv 16, 21ff. x Mt 26, 63; Acts 8, 32. y 1 Pt 2, 22f; 1 Jn 3, 5.

and he shall divide the spoils with the
mighty,
Because he surrendered himself to death
and was counted among the wicked;
And he shall take away the sins of many,
and win pardon for their offenses. [z]

CHAPTER 54

The New Zion

1 Raise a glad cry, you barren one* who did not
bear,
break forth in jubilant song, you who were
not in labor,
For more numerous are the children of the
deserted wife
than the children of her who has a husband,
says the LORD. [a]
2 Enlarge the space for your tent,
spread out your tent cloths unsparingly;
lengthen your ropes and make firm your
stakes. [b]
3 For you shall spread abroad to the right and to
the left;
your descendants shall dispossess the
nations
and shall people the desolate cities.
4 Fear not, you shall not be put to shame;
you need not blush, for you shall not be
disgraced.
The shame of your youth you shall forget,
the reproach of your widowhood no longer
remember.
5 For he who has become your husband is your
Maker;
his name is the LORD of hosts;
Your redeemer* is the Holy One of Israel,
called God of all the earth.
6 The LORD calls you back,
like a wife forsaken and grieved in spirit,
A wife married in youth and then cast off,
says your God. [c]
7 For a brief moment I abandoned you,
but with great tenderness I will take you
back.
8 In an outburst of wrath, for a moment
I hid my face from you;
But with enduring love I take pity on you,
says the LORD, your redeemer.

9 This is for me like the days of Noah,
when I swore that the waters of Noah
should never again deluge the earth;
So I have sworn not to be angry with you,
or to rebuke you. [d]
10 Though the mountains leave their place
and the hills be shaken,
My love shall never leave you
nor my covenant of peace be shaken,
says the LORD, who has mercy on you. [e]

11 O afflicted one, storm-battered and
unconsoled,*
I lay your pavements in carnelians,
and your foundations in sapphires;[f]
12 I will make your battlements of rubies,
your gates of carbuncles,
and all your walls of precious stones.
13 All your sons shall be taught by the LORD,
and great shall be the peace of your
children.
14 In justice shall you be established,
far from the fear of oppression,
where destruction cannot come near you.
15 Should there be any attack, it shall not be of
my making;
whoever attacks you shall fall before you.
16 Lo, I have created the craftsman
who blows on the burning coals
and forges weapons as his work;
It is I also who have created
the destroyer to work havoc.
17 No weapon fashioned against you shall
prevail;
every tongue you shall prove false
that launches an accusation against you.

54, 1: Jerusalem, pictured as a wife who had been barren and deserted, now suddenly finds herself with innumerable children (the returning exiles); cf Gal 4, 27 for the application of this text to the church, the New Zion.

54, 5: Redeemer: cf note on Is 41, 14.

54, 11f: Cf Rv 21. Afflicted one: Jerusalem; carnelians: reddish quartz, hard and durable; carbuncles: another precious stone of red color.

z Mk 15, 28; Lk 22, 37. a Gal 4, 27. b Is 49, 20. c Mal 2, 14f. d Gn 9, 15. e Pss 76, 5; 46, 3. f Rv 21, 18–21.

This is the lot of the servants of the LORD,
their vindication from me, says the LORD.

CHAPTER 55

An Invitation to Grace

1 All you who are thirsty,*
come to the water!
You who have no money,
come, receive grain and eat;
Come, without paying and without cost,
drink wine and milk! [g]
2 Why spend your money for what is not bread;
your wages for what fails to satisfy?
Heed me, and you shall eat well,
you shall delight in rich fare.
3 Come to me heedfully,
listen, that you may have life.
I will renew with you the everlasting
covenant,
the benefits assured to David. [h]
4 As I made him a witness to the peoples,
a leader and commander of nations,
5 So shall you summon a nation you knew not,
and nations that knew you not shall run to
you,
Because of the LORD, your God,
the Holy One of Israel, who has glorified
you. [i]
6 Seek the LORD while he may be found,
call him while he is near.
7 Let the scoundrel forsake his way,
and the wicked man his thoughts;
Let him turn to the LORD for mercy;
to our God, who is generous in forgiving.
8 For my thoughts are not your thoughts,
nor are your ways my ways, says the LORD.
9 As high as the heavens are above the earth,
so high are my ways above your ways
and my thoughts above your thoughts.
10 For just as from the heavens
the rain and snow come down
And do not return there
till they have watered the earth,
making it fertile and fruitful,
Giving seed to him who sows
and bread to him who eats,
11 So shall my word be
that goes forth from my mouth;
It shall not return to me void,
but shall do my will,
achieving the end for which I sent it.

12 Yes, in joy you shall depart,
in peace you shall be brought back;
Mountains and hills shall break out in song
before you,
and all the trees of the countryside shall clap
their hands.
13 In place of the thornbush, the cypress shall
grow,
instead of nettles,* the myrtle.
This shall be to the LORD's renown,
an everlasting imperishable sign.

III: Return of the First Captives

CHAPTER 56

The Lord's House Open to All*

1 Thus says the LORD:
Observe what is right, do what is just;
for my salvation is about to come,
my justice, about to be revealed.
2 Happy is the man who does this,
the son of man who holds to it;
Who keeps the sabbath free from profanation,
and his hand from any evildoing.
3 Let not the foreigner say,
when he would join himself to the LORD,
"The LORD will surely exclude me from his
people";
Nor let the eunuch say,

55, 1ff: God's salvation is freely extended to his people and to all nations; through him will the benefits assured to David be renewed; cf Is 12, 3; Jn 7, 37.

55, 13: Thornbush . . . nettles: suggestive of the desert and therefore symbolic of suffering and hardship; cypress, myrtle: suggestive of fertile land and therefore symbolic of joy and strength.

56, 1–8: Participation in the future messianic salvation is offered to all who believe in the Lord and keep his commandments, regardless of origin or social condition.

g Jn 4, 10ff; 6, 35; 7, 37ff; Rv 21, 6; 22, 17. h 2 Sm 7, 12–16. i Acts 13, 34.

"See, I am a dry tree."*
4 For thus says the LORD:
To the eunuchs who observe my sabbaths
and choose what pleases me
and hold fast to my covenant,[j]
5 I will give, in my house
and within my walls, a monument and a name*
Better than sons and daughters;
an eternal, imperishable name will I give them.

6 And the foreigners who join themselves to the LORD,
ministering to him,
Loving the name of the LORD,
and becoming his servants—
All who keep the sabbath free from profanation
and hold to my covenant,
7 Them I will bring to my holy mountain
and make joyful in my house of prayer;
Their holocausts and sacrifices
will be acceptable on my altar,
For my house shall be called
a house of prayer for all peoples.[k]
8 Thus says the Lord GOD,
who gathers the dispersed of Israel:
Others will I gather to him
besides those already gathered.

Blind Leaders

9 *All you wild beasts* of the field,
come and eat,
all you beasts in the forest![l]
10 My watchmen are blind,
all of them unaware;
They are all dumb dogs,
they cannot bark;
Dreaming as they lie there,
loving their sleep.
11 They are relentless dogs,
they know not when they have enough.
These are the shepherds
who know no discretion;
Each of them goes his own way,
every one of them to his own gain:
12 "Come, I will fetch some wine;
let us carouse with strong drink,
And tomorrow will be like today,
or even greater."[m]

CHAPTER 57

1 The just man perishes,
but no one takes it to heart;
Devout men are swept away,
with no one giving it a thought.
Though he is taken away from the presence of evil,
the just man 2 enters into peace;
There is rest on his couch
for the sincere, straightforward man.

Faithless People

3 But you, draw near,
you sons of a sorceress,
adulterous, wanton race!
4 Of whom do you make sport,
at whom do you open wide your mouth,
and put out your tongue?
Are you not rebellious children,
a worthless race;
5 You who are in heat among the terebinths,
under every green tree;
You who immolate children in the wadies,
behind the crevices in the cliffs?[n]
6 Among the smooth stones* of the wadi is your portion,
these are your lot;

56, 3: Eunuchs had originally been excluded from the community of the Lord; cf Dt 23, 2; Wis 3, 14. Dry tree: unable to produce the fruit of offspring.

56, 5: A monument and a name: a memorial inscription to prevent oblivion for one who had no children; cf 2 Sm 18, 18; Neh 7, 15; 13, 14.

56, 9—57, 13: This section is apparently preexilic, written in the manner of the older prophets who condemned the pagan rites of Baal worship.

56, 9: Wild beasts: foreign nations, which are invited to come and ravage Israel.

57, 6: Smooth stones: the Hebrew word for this expression has the same consonants as the word for "portion"; instead of making the Lord their portion (cf Ps 16, 5), the people adored slabs of stone which they took from the streambeds in valleys and set up as idols; cf Jer 3, 9. Therefore, it is implied, they will be swept away as by a sudden torrent of waters carrying them down the rocky-bottomed gorge to destruction and death without burial.

j Wis 3, 14f. k 1 Kgs 8, 29f; Mt 21, 13. l Ez 34, 5. m Is 28, 7ff; Wis 2, 7. n Jer 7, 31; 19, 5; Ez 20, 28. 31.

To these you poured out libations,
and brought offerings.
Should I decide not to punish these things?
7 Upon a high and lofty mountain
you made your bed,
and there you went up to offer sacrifice. [o]
8 Behind the door and the doorpost
you placed your indecent symbol.
Deserting me, you spread out
your high, wide bed;
And of those whose embraces you love
you carved the symbol and gazed upon it
9 While you approached the king* with scented oil,
and multiplied your perfumes;
While you sent your ambassadors far away,
down even to the nether world.
10 Though worn out by your many misdeeds,
you never said, "It is hopeless";
New strength you found,
and so you did not weaken.

11 Of whom were you afraid? Whom did you fear,
that you became false
And did not remember me
or give me any thought?
Was I to remain silent and unseeing,
so that you would not have me to fear?
12 I will expose your justice*
and your works;
13 They shall not help you when you cry out,
nor save you in your distress.
All these* the wind shall carry off,
the breeze shall bear away;
But he who takes refuge in me shall inherit the land,
and possess my holy mountain.

Comfort for the Afflicted

14 Build up, build up, prepare the way,
remove the stumbling blocks from my people's path. [p]
15 For thus says he who is high and exalted,
living eternally, whose name is the Holy One:
On high I dwell, and in holiness,
and with the crushed and dejected in spirit,
To revive the spirits of the dejected,
to revive the hearts of the crushed. [q]
16 I will not accuse forever,
nor always be angry;
For their spirits would faint before me,
the souls that I have made.
17 Because of their wicked avarice I was angry,
and struck them, hiding myself in wrath,
as they went their own rebellious way. [r]
18 I saw their ways,
but I will heal them and lead them;
I will give full comfort
to them and to those who mourn for them,
19 I, the Creator, who gave them life.

Peace, peace to the far and the near,
says the LORD; and I will heal them.
20 But the wicked are like the tossing sea
which cannot be calmed,
And its waters cast up mud and filth.
21 No peace for the wicked! says my God. [s]

CHAPTER 58

True Fasting

1 Cry out full-throated and unsparingly,
lift up your voice like a trumpet blast;
Tell my people their wickedness,
and the house of Jacob their sins.*
2 They seek me day after day,*
and desire to know my ways,
Like a nation that has done what is just
and not abandoned the law of their God;
They ask me to declare what is due them,
pleased to gain access to God.
3 "Why do we fast, and you do not see it?
afflict ourselves, and you take no note of it?"
Lo, on your fast day you carry out your own pursuits,

57, 9: The king: the pagan god Moloch. Ambassadors: children sent to him through a sacrificial death.
57, 12: Justice: here used ironically.
57, 13: All these: the wicked mentioned in Is 57, 3–10.
58, 1: This command is directed to the prophet.

58, 2–14: Merely external worship does not avail with God; it must be joined to internal sincerity.

o Hos 4, 13; Jer 2, 20; Ez 6, 13. p Is 40, 3f. q Is 61, 2f. r Is 56, 11. s Is 48, 21.

and drive all your laborers.
4 Yes, your fast ends in quarreling and fighting,
striking with wicked claw.
Would that today you might fast
so as to make your voice heard on high!
5 Is this the manner of fasting I wish,
of keeping a day of penance:
That a man bow his head like a reed,
and lie in sackcloth and ashes?
Do you call this a fast,
a day acceptable to the LORD? [t]
6 This, rather, is the fasting that I wish:
releasing those bound unjustly,
untying the thongs of the yoke;
Setting free the oppressed,
breaking every yoke;
7 Sharing your bread with the hungry,
sheltering the oppressed and the homeless;
Clothing the naked when you see them,
and not turning your back on your own. [u]
8 Then your light shall break forth like the dawn,
and your wound shall quickly be healed;
Your vindication shall go before you,
and the glory of the LORD shall be your rear guard.
9 Then you shall call, and the LORD will answer,
you shall cry for help, and he will say: Here I am!
If you remove from your midst oppression,
false accusation and malicious speech;
10 If you bestow your bread on the hungry
and satisfy the afflicted;
Then light shall rise for you in the darkness,
and the gloom shall become for you like midday;
11 Then the LORD will guide you always
and give you plenty even on the parched land.
He will renew your strength,
and you shall be like a watered garden,
like a spring whose water never fails. [v]
12 The ancient ruins shall be rebuilt for your sake,
and the foundations from ages past you shall raise up;
"Repairer of the breach," they shall call you,
"Restorer of ruined homesteads." [w]

13 If you hold back your foot on the sabbath
from following your own pursuits on my holy day;
If you call the sabbath a delight,
and the LORD's holy day honorable;
If you honor it by not following your ways,
seeking your own interests, or speaking with malice—
14 Then you shall delight in the LORD,
and I will make you ride on the heights of the earth;
I will nourish you with the heritage of Jacob, your father,
for the mouth of the LORD has spoken.

CHAPTER 59

Sin and Confession

1 Lo, the hand of the LORD is not too short to save,
nor his ear too dull to hear. [x]
2 Rather, it is your crimes
that separate you from your God,
It is your sins that make him hide his face
so that he will not hear you.
3 For your hands are stained with blood,
your fingers with guilt;
Your lips speak falsehood,
and your tongue utters deceit. [y]
4 No one brings suit justly,
no one pleads truthfully;
They trust in emptiness* and tell lies;
they conceive mischief and bring forth malice.
5 They hatch adders' eggs,*
and weave spiders' webs:
Whoever eats their eggs will die,
if one of them is pressed, it will hatch as a viper; [z]
6 Their webs cannot serve as clothing,

59, 4: Emptiness: things having no value.
59, 5f: A proverb signifying evil works—adders' eggs—and useless devices—spiders' webs; the former do positive harm to oneself and others, the latter serve no useful purpose.

t Zec 7, 5. u Ez 18, 7. 16; Mt 25, 35. v Is 51, 3; Ps 24. w Is 61, 4. x Is 50, 2; Nm 11, 23. y Is 1, 15. z Jb 20, 12–16.

nor can they cover themselves with their
works.
Their works are evil works,
and deeds of violence come from their
hands.
7 Their feet run to evil,
and they are quick to shed innocent blood;
Their thoughts are destructive thoughts,
plunder and ruin are on their highways. [a]
8 The way of peace they know not,
and there is nothing that is right in their
paths;
Their ways they have made crooked,
whoever treads them knows no peace.

9 That is why right is far from us*
and justice does not reach us.
We look for light, and lo, darkness;
for brightness, but we walk in gloom!
10 Like blind men we grope along the wall,
like people without eyes we feel our way.
We stumble at midday as at dusk,
in Stygian darkness, like the dead.
11 We all growl like bears,
like doves we moan without ceasing.
We look for right, but it is not there;
for salvation, and it is far from us. [b]
12 For our offenses before you are many,
our sins bear witness against us.
Yes, our offenses are present to us,
and our crimes we know:
13 Transgressing, and denying the LORD,
turning back from following our God,
Threatening outrage, and apostasy,
uttering words of falsehood the heart has
conceived.
14 Right is repelled,
and justice stands far off;
For truth stumbles in the public square,
uprightness cannot enter.
15 Honesty is lacking,
and the man who turns from evil is
despoiled.

The Redeemer in Zion

The LORD saw this, and was aggrieved
that right did not exist.
16 He saw that there was no one,
and was appalled that there was none to
intervene;
So his own arm brought about the victory,
and his justice lent him its support.
17 He put on justice as his breastplate,
salvation, as the helmet on his head;
He clothed himself with garments of
vengeance,
wrapped himself in a mantle of zeal. [c]
18 He repays his enemies their deserts,
and requites his foes with wrath.
19 Those in the west shall fear the name of the
LORD,
and those in the east, his glory;
For it shall come like a pent-up river
which the breath of the LORD drives on.
20 He shall come to Zion a redeemer
to those of Jacob who turn from sin, says the
LORD. [d]
21 This is the covenant with them
which I myself have made, says the LORD:
My spirit which is upon you
and my words that I have put into your
mouth
Shall never leave your mouth,
nor the mouths of your children
Nor the mouths of your children's children
from now on and forever, says the LORD.

CHAPTER 60

Glory of the New Zion

1 Rise up in splendor! Your light has come,*
the glory of the Lord shines upon you.
2 See, darkness covers the earth,
and thick clouds cover the peoples;
But upon you the LORD shines,
and over you appears his glory.
3 Nations shall walk by your light,

59, 9–15: Spoken by the people through the mouth of the prophet.

60, 1–6: The Church makes use of these verses for the first reading of the Mass on the feast of Epiphany, for she sees in them symbols of her universality.

a Rom 3, 15. b Is 38, 14. c Wis 5, 17ff; Eph 6, 14; 1 Thes 5, 8. d Rom 11, 26f.

and kings by your shining radiance. [e]
4 Raise your eyes and look about;
they all gather and come to you:
Your sons come from afar,
and your daughters in the arms of their nurses. [f]

5 Then you shall be radiant at what you see,
your heart shall throb and overflow,
For the riches of the sea shall be emptied out before you,
the wealth of nations shall be brought to you.
6 Caravans of camels shall fill you,
dromedaries from Midian and Ephah;
All from Sheba shall come
bearing gold and frankincense,
and proclaiming the praises of the LORD.
7 All the flocks of Kedar shall be gathered for you,
the rams of Nebaioth shall be your sacrifices;
They will be acceptable offerings on my altar,
and I will enhance the splendor of my house.

8 What are these that fly along like clouds,
like doves* to their cotes?
9 All the vessels of the sea are assembled,
with the ships of Tarshish in the lead,
To bring your children from afar
with their silver and gold,
In the name of the LORD, your God,
the Holy One of Israel, who has glorified you.

10 Foreigners shall rebuild your walls,
and their kings shall be your attendants;
Though I struck you in my wrath,
yet in my good will I have shown you mercy.
11 Your gates shall stand open constantly;
day and night they shall not be closed
But shall admit to you the wealth of nations,
and their kings, in the vanguard. [g]
12 For the people or kingdom shall perish
that does not serve you;
those nations shall be utterly destroyed.
13 The glory of Lebanon* shall come to you:
the cypress, the plane and the pine,
To bring beauty to my sanctuary,
and glory to the place where I set my feet. [h]
14 The children of your oppressors shall come,
bowing low before you;
All those who despised you
shall fall prostrate at your feet.
They shall call you "City of the LORD,"
"Zion of the Holy One of Israel."

15 Once you were forsaken,
hated and unvisited,
Now I will make you the pride of the ages,
a joy to generation after generation. [i]
16 You shall suck the milk of nations,
and be nursed at royal breasts;
You shall know that I, the LORD, am your savior,
your redeemer, the mighty one of Jacob.
17 In place of bronze I will bring gold,
instead of iron, silver;
In place of wood, bronze,
instead of stones, iron;
I will appoint peace your governor,
and justice your ruler.
18 No longer shall violence be heard of in your land,
or plunder and ruin within your boundaries.
You shall call your walls "Salvation"
and your gates "Praise."
19 No longer shall the sun
be your light by day,
Nor the brightness of the moon
shine upon you at night;
The LORD shall be your light forever,
your God shall be your glory. [j]
20 No longer shall your sun go down,
or your moon withdraw,
For the LORD will be your light forever,

60, 8f: Like clouds, like doves: the white sails of the ships of Tarshish; cf note on Ps 48, 8.

60, 13: Glory of Lebanon: the cedars, together with the cypress, the plane and the pine, all precious, durable wood.

e Is 42. 6; 45, 14; 49, 6. f Is 49, 18. g Rv 21, 25. h Is 35, 2. i Ez 16. j Rv 21,23; 22, 5.

and the days of your mourning shall be at an
end.
21 Your people shall all be just,
they shall always possess the land,
They, the bud of my planting,
my handiwork to show my glory.
22 The smallest shall become a thousand,
the youngest, a mighty nation;
I, the LORD, will swiftly accomplish these
things
when their time comes. [k]

CHAPTER 61

The Mission to the Afflicted

1 The spirit of the Lord GOD is upon me,*
because the LORD has anointed me;
He has sent me to bring glad tidings to the
lowly,
to heal the brokenhearted,
To proclaim liberty to the captives
and release to the prisoners, [l]
2 To announce a year of favor from the LORD
and a day of vindication by our God,
to comfort all who mourn; [m]
3 To place on those who mourn in Zion
a diadem instead of ashes,
To give them oil of gladness in place of
mourning,
a glorious mantle instead of a listless spirit.
They will be called oaks of justice,
planted by the LORD to show his glory.

The Reward of Israel

4 They shall rebuild the ancient ruins,
the former wastes they shall raise up
And restore the ruined cities,
desolate now for generations. [n]
5 Strangers shall stand ready to pasture your
flocks,
foreigners shall be your farmers and
vinedressers.
6 You yourselves shall be named priests of the
LORD,
ministers of our God you shall be called.
You shall eat the wealth of the nations
and boast of riches from them.
7 Since their shame was double
and disgrace and spittle were their portion,
They shall have a double inheritance in their
land,
everlasting joy shall be theirs. [o]
8 For I, the LORD, love what is right,
I hate robbery and injustice;
I will give them their recompense faithfully,
a lasting covenant I will make with them. [p]
9 Their descendants shall be renowned among
the nations,
and their offspring among the peoples;
All who see them shall acknowledge them
as a race the LORD has blessed.

10 I rejoice heartily in the LORD,
in my God is the joy of my soul;
For he has clothed me with a robe of salvation,
and wrapped me in a mantle of justice,
Like a bridegroom adorned with a diadem,
like a bride bedecked with her jewels.
11 As the earth brings forth its plants,
and a garden makes its growth spring up,
So will the Lord GOD make justice and praise
spring up before all the nations.

CHAPTER 62

Jerusalem the Lord's Bride

1 For Zion's sake I will not be silent,
for Jerusalem's sake I will not be quiet,
Until her vindication shines forth like the
dawn
and her victory like a burning torch.

2 Nations shall behold your vindication,
and all kings your glory;
You shall be called by a new name*
pronounced by the mouth of the LORD. [q]
3 You shall be a glorious crown in the hand of
the LORD,
a royal diadem held by your God.
4 No more shall men call you "Forsaken,"

61, 1f: This was spoken by the prophet in regard to the restoration of Zion, but quoted by Christ as referring to his mission; cf Lk 4, 18f. Year of favor . . . day of vindication: the time of God's salvation.

62, 2: New name: figurative expression for a new state of happiness; cf Rv 2, 17; 3, 12.

k Gn 12, 2; 17, 6. **l** Is 42, 1; 48, 16; Lk 4, 18f. **m** Mt 5, 5. **n** Is 58, 12. **o** Is 40, 2. **p** Is 55, 3; 59, 21. **q** Rv 2, 17; 3, 12.

or your land "Desolate,"
But you shall be called "My Delight,"
and your land "Espoused."
For the LORD delights in you,
and makes your land his spouse. [r]
5 As a young man marries a virgin,
your Builder shall marry you;
And as a bridegroom rejoices in his bride
so shall your God rejoice in you.

Restoration of Zion

6 Upon your walls, O Jerusalem,
I have stationed watchmen;
Never, by day or by night,
shall they be silent.
O you who are to remind the LORD,*
take no rest
7 And give no rest to him,
until he re-establishes Jerusalem
And makes of it
the pride of the earth.
8 The LORD has sworn by his right hand
and by his mighty arm:
No more will I give your grain
as food to your enemies;
Nor shall foreigners drink your wine,
for which you toiled. [s]
9 But you who harvest the grain shall eat it,
and you shall praise the LORD;
You who gather the grapes shall drink the wine
in the courts of my sanctuary. [t]
10 Pass through, pass through the gates,
prepare the way for the people; [u]
Build up, build up the highway,
clear it of stones,
raise up a standard over the nations.*
11 See, the LORD proclaims
to the ends of the earth:
Say to daughter Zion,
your savior comes!
Here is his reward with him,
his recompense before him. [v]
12 They shall be called the holy people,
the redeemed of the LORD,
And you shall be called "Frequented,"
a city that is not forsaken. [w]

CHAPTER 63

Punishment of Edom*

1 Who is this that comes from Edom,
in crimsoned garments, from Bozrah—
This one arrayed in majesty,
marching in the greatness of his strength?
"It is I, I who announce vindication,
I who am mighty to save."
2 Why is your apparel red,
and your garments like those of the wine presser? [x]

3 "The wine press I have trodden alone,
and of my people there was no one with me.
I trod them in my anger,
and trampled them down in my wrath;
Their blood spurted on my garments;
all my apparel I stained.
4 For the day of vengeance was in my heart,
my year for redeeming was at hand. [y]
5 I looked about, but there was no one to help,
I was appalled that there was no one to lend support;
So my own arm brought about the victory
and my own wrath lent me its support. [z]
6 I trampled down the peoples in my anger,
I crushed them in my wrath,
and I let their blood run out upon the ground."

Prayer for the Return of God's Favor*

7 The favors of the LORD I will recall,
the glorious deeds of the LORD,

62, 6f: Remind the Lord . . . give no rest to him: figuratively, as though to make certain that the Lord will remember his pledge to Jerusalem. Cf Lk 11, 7f.

62, 10: The command is given to the workmen to begin the reconstruction of the city.

63, 1–6: In a dramatic dialogue between God and the prophet, the Lord is portrayed as the sole avenger of justice against his enemies.

63, 7—64, 11: A prayer probably composed toward the end of the exile, in which the prophet, after recalling God's blessings on Israel in its past history (63, 7–10), especially at the Exodus (11–14), begs the Lord to come once more to the aid of his people (63, 15—64, 3), who now humbly confess their sins (4–11).

r Is 49, 15f; 54, 1ff. s Is 52, 10. t Dt 12, 17f; 14, 23. u Is 58, 14. v Is 40, 10. w Is 62, 4. x Rv 19, 13. y Is 34, 8; 61, 2. z Is 59, 16.

Because of all he has done for us;
for he is good to the house of Israel,
He has favored us according to his mercy
and his great kindness. [a]
8 He said: They are indeed my people,
children who are not disloyal;
So he became their savior
9 in their every affliction.
It was not a messenger or an angel,
but he himself who saved them.
Because of his love and pity
he redeemed them himself,
Lifting them and carrying them
all the days of old. [b]
10 But they rebelled, and grieved
his holy spirit;
So he turned on them like an enemy,
and fought against them.

11 Then they remembered the days of old
and Moses, his servant;
Where is he who brought up out of the sea
the shepherd of his flock?
Where is he who put his holy spirit
in their midst;
12 Whose glorious arm
was the guide at Moses' right;
Who divided the waters before them,
winning for himself eternal renown;
13 Who led them without stumbling through the depths
like horses in the open country,
14 Like cattle going down into the plain,
the spirit of the LORD guiding them?
Thus you led your people,
bringing glory to your name.

15 Look down from heaven and regard us
from your holy and glorious palace!
Where is your zealous care and your might,
your surge of pity and your mercy? [c]
O Lord, hold not back,
16 for you are our father.
Were Abraham not to know us,
nor Israel to acknowledge us,
You, LORD, are our father,
our redeemer you are named forever.
17 Why do you let us wander, O LORD, from your ways,
and harden our hearts so that we fear you not?
Return for the sake of your servants,
the tribes of your heritage.
18 Why have the wicked invaded your holy place,
why have our enemies trampled your sanctuary?
19 Too long have we been like those you do not rule,
who do not bear your name.

Oh, that you would rend the heavens and come down,
with the mountains quaking before you,

CHAPTER 64

1 As when brushwood is set ablaze,
or fire makes the water boil!
Thus your name would be made known to your enemies
and the nations would tremble before you,
2 While you wrought awesome deeds we could not hope for,
3 such as they had not heard of from of old.
No ear has ever heard, no eye ever seen,
any God but you
doing such deeds for those who wait for him. [d]
4 Would that you might meet us doing right,
that we were mindful of you in our ways!
Behold, you are angry, and we are sinful;
5 all of us have become like unclean men,
all our good deeds are like polluted rags;
We have all withered like leaves,
and our guilt carries us away like the wind.
6 There is none who calls upon your name,
who rouses himself to cling to you;
For you have hidden your face from us
and have delivered us up to our guilt.
7 Yet, O LORD, you are our father;
we are the clay and you the potter:
we are all the work of your hands.

a Is 26, 15. b Dt 4, 37f. c Dt 26, 15; Bar 2, 16. d 1 Cor 2, 9.

8 Be not so very angry, LORD,
keep not our guilt forever in mind;
look upon us, who are all your people.
9 Your holy cities have become a desert,
Zion is a desert, Jerusalem a waste. [e]
10 Our holy and glorious temple
in which our fathers praised you
Has been burned with fire;
all that was dear to us is laid waste.
11 Can you hold back, O LORD, after all this?
Can you remain silent, and afflict us so severely?

CHAPTER 65

Necessity of Punishment

1 I was ready to respond to those who asked me not,
to be found by those who sought me not.
I said: Here I am! Here I am!
To a nation that did not call upon my name.[f]
2 I have stretched out my hands all the day
to a rebellious people,
Who walk in evil paths
and follow their own thoughts,[g]
3 People who provoke me
continually, to my face,
Offering sacrifices in the groves
and burning incense on bricks,
4 Living among the graves
and spending the night in caverns,
Eating swine's flesh,
with carrion broth in their dishes,
5 Crying out, "Hold back,
do not touch me; I am too sacred for you!"*

These things enkindle my wrath,
a fire that burns all the day.
6 Lo, before me it stands written;
I will not be quiet until I have paid in full
7 Your crimes and the crimes of your fathers as well,
says the LORD.
Since they burned incense on the mountains,
and disgraced me on the hills,
I will at once pour out in full measure
their recompense into their laps.

Fate of the Good and the Bad in Israel

8 Thus says the LORD:
When the juice is pressed from grapes,
men say, "Do not discard them,
for there is still good in them";
Thus will I do with my servants:
I will not discard them all;
9 From Jacob I will save offspring,
from Judah, those who are to inherit my mountains;
My chosen ones shall inherit the land,
my servants shall dwell there.
10 Sharon shall be a pasture for the flocks
and the valley of Achor a resting place for the cattle
of my people who have sought me.

11 But you who forsake the LORD,
forgetting my holy mountain,
You who spread a table for Fortune
and fill cups of blended wine for Destiny,*
12 You I will destine for the sword;
you shall all go down in slaughter.
Since I called and you did not answer,
I spoke and you did not listen,
But did what was evil in my sight
and preferred things which displease me,[h]
13 therefore thus says the Lord GOD:
Lo, my servants shall eat,
but you shall go hungry;
My servants shall drink,
but you shall be thirsty;
My servants shall rejoice,
but you shall be put to shame;
14 My servants shall shout
for joy of heart,
But you shall cry out for grief of heart
and howl for anguish of spirit.
15 The Lord GOD shall slay you,
and the name you leave

65, 5: I am too sacred for you: the uncleanness of pork, obvious to a Semite, is what these people claim has made them sacred! The prophet ridicules them. Some translate: "I will render you sacred," and understand this as referring to the concept of sacredness as something contagious.

65, 11f: Destiny: the Hebrew also has a play on the words: Destiny and destine; meni and manithi.

e Ps 79, 1. f Rom 10, 20. g Rom 10, 21. h Is 66, 4; Prv 1, 24; Jer 7, 13.

Shall be used by my chosen ones for cursing;
but my servants shall be called by another name
16 By which he will be blessed
on whom a blessing is invoked in the land;
He who takes an oath in the land
shall swear by the God of truth;
For the hardships of the past shall be forgotten,
and hidden from my eyes.

The World Renewed

17 Lo, I am about to create new heavens
and a new earth;
The things of the past shall not be remembered
or come to mind. [i]
18 Instead, there shall always be rejoicing and happiness
in what I create;
For I create Jerusalem to be a joy
and its people to be a delight;
19 I will rejoice in Jerusalem
and exult in my people.
No longer shall the sound of weeping be heard there,
or the sound of crying;
20 No longer shall there be in it
an infant who lives but a few days,
or an old man who does not round out his full lifetime;
He dies a mere youth who reaches but a hundred years,
and he who fails of a hundred shall be thought accursed.
21 They shall live in the houses they build,
and eat the fruit of the vineyards they plant;
22 They shall not build houses for others to live in,
or plant for others to eat.
As the years of a tree, so the years of my people;
and my chosen ones shall long enjoy
the produce of their hands.
23 They shall not toil in vain,
nor beget children for sudden destruction;
For a race blessed by the LORD
are they and their offspring.
24 Before they call, I will answer;
while they are yet speaking, I will hearken to them.
25 The wolf and the lamb shall graze alike,
and the lion shall eat hay like the ox
[but the serpent's food shall be dust]. [j]
None shall hurt or destroy
on all my holy mountain, says the LORD.*

CHAPTER 66

True and False Worship

1 Thus says the LORD:
The heavens are my throne,
the earth is my footstool.
What kind of house can you build for me;
what is to be my resting place? [k]
2 My hand made all these things
when all of them came to be, says the LORD.
This is the one whom I approve:
the lowly and afflicted man who trembles at my word.

3 Merely slaughtering an ox is like slaying a man;
sacrificing a lamb, like breaking a dog's neck;
Bringing a cereal offering, like offering swine's blood;
burning incense, like paying homage to an idol.
Since these have chosen their own ways
and taken pleasure in their own abominations, [l]
4 I in turn will choose ruthless treatment for them*
and bring upon them what they fear.

Because, when I called, no one answered,
when I spoke, no one listened;
Because they did what was evil in my sight,
and chose what gave me displeasure, [m]
5 Hear the word of the LORD,

65, 25: See note on Is 11, 6–9.
66, 4f: Worship which is merely external is as evil as though it were idolatry.

i Is 66, 22; Rv 21, 1. j Is 11, 6–9. k 2 Sm 7, 4ff; 1 Kgs 8, 27; Acts 7, 49; 17, 24. l Lv 11, 7. m Is 65, 12; Prv 1, 24; Jer 7, 13.

you who tremble at his word:
Your brethren who, because of my name,
hate and reject you, say,
"Let the LORD show his glory
that we may see your joy";
but they shall be put to shame.
6 A sound of roaring from the city,
a sound from the temple,
The sound of the LORD
repaying his enemies their deserts! [n]

Mother Zion

7 Before she comes to labor,*
she gives birth; [o]
Before the pains come upon her,
she safely delivers a male child.
8 Who ever heard of such a thing,
or saw the like?
Can a country be brought forth in one day,
or a nation be born in a single moment?
Yet Zion is scarcely in labor
when she gives birth to her children.
9 Shall I bring a mother to the point of birth,
and yet not let her child be born? says the LORD;
Or shall I who allow her to conceive,
yet close her womb? says your God.

10 Rejoice with Jerusalem and be glad because of her,
all you who love her;
Exult, exult with her,
all you who were mourning over her!
11 Oh, that you may suck fully
of the milk of her comfort,
That you may nurse with delight
at her abundant breasts!
12 For thus says the LORD:
Lo, I will spread prosperity over her like a river,
and the wealth of the nations like
an overflowing torrent.
As nurslings, you shall be carried in her arms,
and fondled in her lap;
13 As a mother comforts her son,
so will I comfort you;
in Jerusalem you shall find your comfort.

14 When you see this, your heart shall rejoice,
and your bodies flourish like the grass;
The LORD's power shall be known to his servants,
but to his enemies, his wrath.

15 Lo, the LORD shall come in fire,
his chariots like the whirlwind,
To wreak his wrath with burning heat
and his punishment with fiery flames.
16 For the LORD shall judge all mankind
by fire and sword,
and many shall be slain by the LORD.

17 They who sanctify and purify themselves to
go to the groves, as followers of one who stands
within, they who eat swine's flesh, loathsome
things and mice, shall all perish with their deeds
and their thoughts, says the LORD. [p]
Gathering of the Nations 18 I come to gather
nations of every language; they shall come and
see my glory.* 19 I will set a sign among them;
from them I will send fugitives to the nations: to
Tarshish, Put and Lud, Mosoch, Tubal and Javan,
to the distant coastlands that have never heard
of my fame, or seen my glory; and they shall
proclaim my glory among the nations. 20 They
shall bring all your brethren from all the nations
as an offering to the LORD, on horses and in
chariots, in carts, upon mules and dromedaries,
to Jerusalem, my holy mountain, says the LORD,
just as the Israelites bring their offering to the
house of the LORD in clean vessels. 21 Some of
these I will take as priests and Levites, says the
LORD.

Lasting Reward and Punishment

22 As the new heavens and the new earth
which I will make
Shall endure before me, says the LORD,
so shall your race and your name endure. [q]

66, 7–9: The absence of labor in Zion's childbearing is a symbol of the joyful begetting of the new people of God.
66, 18–21: God summons the neighboring nations to Zion and from among them will send some to far distant lands to proclaim his glory. All your brethren: Jews in exile.

n Jl 4, 16; Am 1, 2. o 7–9: Is 49, 18–21; 54, 1. p Lv 11, 29. q Is 65, 17; Rv 21, 1.

23 From one new moon to another,
and from one sabbath to another,
All mankind shall come to worship
before me, says the LORD.
24 They shall go out and see the corpses[r]
of the men who rebelled against me;
Their worm shall not die,
nor their fire be extinguished;
and they shall be abhorrent to all mankind.*

66, 24: God's enemies lie dead outside the walls of the New Jerusalem; just as in the past, corpses, filth and refuse lay in the Valley of Hinnom outside the city, where huge fires were constantly burning; cf Jos 15, 8; 2 Chr 28, 3; Mk 9, 45–48.

r Mk 9, 45.

THE BOOK OF JEREMIAH

The Book of Jeremiah combines history, biography, and prophecy. It portrays a nation in crisis and introduces the reader to an extraordinary leader upon whom the Lord placed the heavy burden of the prophetic office. Jeremiah was born about 650 B.C. of a priestly family from the little village of Anathoth, near Jerusalem. While still very young he was called to his task in the thirteenth year of King Josiah (628), whose reform, begun with enthusiasm and hope, ended with his death on the battlefield of Megiddo (609) as he attempted to stop the northward march of the Egyptian Pharaoh Neco.

The prophet heartily supported the reform of the pious King Josiah, which began in 629 B.C. Nineveh, the capital of Assyria, fell in 612, preparing the way for the new colossus, Babylon, which was soon to put an end to Judean independence.

After the death of Josiah the old idolatry returned. Jeremiah opposed it with all his strength. Arrest, imprisonment, and public disgrace were his lot. Jeremiah saw in the nation's impenitence the sealing of its doom. Nebuchadnezzar captured Jerusalem and carried King Jehoiachin into exile (22, 24).

During the years 598–587, Jeremiah attempted to counsel Zedekiah in the face of bitter opposition. The false prophet Hananiah proclaimed that the yoke of Babylon was broken and a strong pro-Egyptian party in Jerusalem induced Zedekiah to revolt. Nebuchadnezzar took swift and terrible vengeance; Jerusalem was destroyed in 587 and its leading citizens sent into exile. About this time Jeremiah uttered the great oracle of the "New Covenant" (31, 31-34) sometimes called "The Gospel before the Gospel." This passage contains his most sublime teaching and is a landmark in Old Testament theology.

The prophet remained amidst the ruins of Jerusalem, but was later forced into Egyptian exile by a band of conspirators. There, according to an old tradition, he was murdered by his own countrymen. The influence of Jeremiah was greater after his death than before. The exiled community read and meditated the lessons of the prophet, and his influence can be seen in Ezekiel, certain of the psalms, and the second part of Isaiah. Shortly after the exile, the Book of Jeremiah as we have it today was published in a final edition.

It is divided as follows:

I: Oracles in the Days of Josiah

CHAPTER 1

1 The words of Jeremiah, son of Hilkiah, of a
priestly family in Anathoth,* in the land of
Benjamin. 2 The word of the LORD first came to
him in the days of Josiah, son of Amon, king of
Judah, in the thirteenth year of his reign,[a] 3 and
continued through the reign of Jehoiakim, son of
Josiah, king of Judah, and until the downfall*
and exile of Jerusalem in the fifth month of the
eleventh year of Zedekiah, son of Josiah, king of
Judah.[b]

Call of Jeremiah

4 The word of the LORD came to me thus:

5 Before I formed you in the womb I knew
you,*
before you were born I dedicated you,
a prophet to the nations I appointed you.[c]
6 "Ah, Lord GOD!" I said,
"I know not how to speak; I am too
young."*

7 But the LORD answered me,

Say not, "I am too young."
To whomever I send you, you shall go;
whatever I command you, you shall speak.
8 Have no fear before them,
because I am with you to deliver you, says
the LORD.

9 Then the LORD extended his hand and tou-
ched my mouth, saying,

See, I place my words in your mouth![d]
10 This day I set you
over nations and over kingdoms,
To root up and to tear down,
to destroy and to demolish,
to build and to plant.

11 The word of the LORD came to me with the
question: What do you see, Jeremiah? "I see a
branch of the watching-tree,"* I replied. 12 Then
the LORD said to me: Well have you seen, for I
am watching to fulfill my word. 13 [e]A second
time the word of the LORD came to me with the
question: What do you see? "I see a boiling
cauldron," I replied, "that appears from the
north."*
14 And from the north, said the LORD to me,
evil will boil over upon all who dwell in the
land.[f]

15 Lo, I am summoning
all the kingdoms of the north, says the
LORD;
Each king shall come and set up his throne

1, 1: Anathoth: a village about three miles northeast of Jerusalem, where Solomon exiled Abiathar (1 Kgs 2, 26f); it is probable that Jeremiah belonged to the priestly family of Abiathar.

1, 3: Until the downfall: these words were originally prefixed as a title to a collection of Jeremiah's prophecies which lacked chapters 40–44. The new title in Jer 40, 1 and the oracles that follow clearly show that Jeremiah continued to prophesy after the destruction of Jerusalem in 587 B.C.

1, 5: Jeremiah was destined to the office of prophet before his birth; cf Is 49, 1. 5; Lk 1, 15; Gal 1, 15f. I knew you: I loved you and chose you. I dedicated you: I set you apart to be a prophet. Some Fathers and later theologians understand this to mean that Jeremiah was freed from original sin before his birth. The context does not justify this conclusion. The nations: the pagan neighbors of Judah, besides the great world powers—Assyria, Babylonia, Egypt—intimately associated with Judah's destiny.

1, 6: I am too young: Jeremiah's youth (he was less than thirty years old) must not be an obstacle to the responsibilities of the prophetic office; God will supply for his human defects (cf vv 7f).

1, 11: The watching-tree: the almond tree, which is the first to blossom in the springtime as though it had not slept. The Hebrew name contains a play on words with "I am watching."

1, 13: Boiling cauldron . . . the north: symbol of an invasion from the north; cf vv 14f.

a Jer 25, 3. b Jer 25, 1. c Jer 49, 1; Gal 1, 15f. d Is 6, 7. e Ez 11, 3. 7; 24, 3. f Jer 4, 6; 6, 1.

at the gateways of Jerusalem,
Opposite her walls all around
and opposite all the cities of Judah. [g]
16 I will pronounce my sentence against them
for all their wickedness in forsaking me,
And in burning incense to strange gods
and adoring their own handiwork. [h]

17 But do you gird your loins;
stand up and tell them
all that I command you.
Be not crushed on their account,
as though I would leave you crushed before them;
18 For it is I this day
who have made you a fortified city,
A pillar of iron, a wall of brass,
against the whole land:
Against Judah's kings and princes,
against its priests and people. [i]
19 They will fight against you, but not prevail over you,
for I am with you to deliver you, says the LORD.

CHAPTER 2

Infidelity of Israel* 1 This word of the LORD came to me: 2 Go, cry out this message for Jerusalem to hear!

I remember the devotion* of your youth,
how you loved me as a bride,
Following me in the desert,
in a land unsown. [j]
3 Sacred to the LORD was Israel,
the first fruits* of his harvest;
Should anyone presume to partake of them,
evil would befall him, says the LORD. [k]

4 Listen to the word of the LORD, O house of Jacob!
All you clans of the house of Israel,
5 thus says the LORD:
What fault did your fathers find in me
that they withdrew from me,
Went after empty idols,
and became empty themselves? [l]
6 They did not ask, "Where is the LORD
who brought us up from the land of Egypt,
Who led us through the desert,
through a land of wastes and gullies,
Through a land of drought and darkness,
through a land which no one crosses,
where no man dwells?" [m]

7 When I brought you into the garden land
to eat its goodly fruits,
You entered and defiled my land,
you made my heritage loathsome. [n]
8 The priests asked not,
"Where is the LORD?"
Those who dealt with the law* knew me not:
the shepherds rebelled against me.
The prophets prophesied by Baal,
and went after useless idols. [o]
9 Therefore will I yet accuse you, says the LORD,
and even your children's children I will accuse. [p]
10 Pass over to the coast of the Kittim* and see,
send to Kedar and carefully inquire:
Where has the like of this been done?
11 Does any other nation change its gods?—
yet they are not gods at all!
But my people have changed their glory
for useless things. [q]
12 Be amazed at this, O heavens,
and shudder with sheer horror, says the LORD.
13 Two evils have my people done:
they have forsaken me, the source of living waters;
They have dug themselves cisterns,

2, 1—3, 5: These verses probably contain the earliest of Jeremiah's preachings. The covenant relationship, symbolized by the figure of a marriage, was frequently broken by Israel, seen here as an unfaithful wife unworthy of reconciliation with God (Jer 3, 1–5).

2, 2: Devotion: Israel's gratitude, fidelity, and love for God.

2, 3: First fruits: an offering to God which became his exclusive property, and could therefore not be put to profane use; cf Lv 22, 1.

2, 8: Those who dealt with the law: the priests. The shepherds: the kings and nobles.

2, 10: Kittim: a Phoenician colony in Cyprus. Kedar: a nomad tribe of the Syrian desert. These two names represent West and East.

g Jer 6, 22. h Is 2, 8. i Jer 6, 27; 15, 20; Ex 3, 8. j Dt 2, 7; 32, 9–12; Mi 6, 4. k Jer 12, 14; Ex 4, 22; Dt 7, 6; 14, 2. l Is 5, 4; Mi 6, 3. m Ex 20, 2f; Dt 8, 14; Is 63, 11ff. n Lv 18, 24f; Dt 8, 7–10; 32, 13f. o Jer 8, 8ff; 23, 1. 13. p Ex 20, 5. q Jer 16, 20; Ps 106, 20.

broken cisterns, that hold no water. [r]

14 Is Israel a slave, a bondman by birth?*
Why then has he become booty?
15 Against him lions roar
full-throated cries.
They have made his land a waste;
his cities are charred ruins, without inhabitant. [s]
16 Yes, the people of Memphis* and Tahpanhes
shave the crown of your head.
17 Has not the forsaking of the LORD, your God,
done this to you? [t]
18 And now, why go to Egypt,*
to drink the waters of the Nile?
Why go to Assyria,
to drink the waters of the Euphrates?
19 Your own wickedness chastises you,
your own infidelities punish you.
Know then, and see, how evil and bitter
is your forsaking the LORD, your God,
And showing no fear of me,
says the Lord, the GOD of hosts. [u]

20 Long ago you broke your yoke, [v]
you tore off your bonds.
"I will not serve," you said.
On every high hill, under every green tree,
you gave yourself to harlotry.*
21 I had planted you, a choice vine
of fully tested stock;
How could you turn out obnoxious to me,
a spurious vine? [w]
22 Though you scour it with soap,
and use much lye,
The stain of your guilt is still before me,
says the Lord GOD. [x]
23 How can you say, "I am not defiled,
I have not gone after the Baals"?
Consider your conduct in the Valley,*
recall what you have done:
A frenzied she-camel, coursing near and far,
24 breaking away toward the desert,
Snuffing the wind in her ardor—
who can restrain her lust?
No beasts need tire themselves seeking her;
in her month they will meet her.

25 Stop wearing out your shoes
and parching your throat!
But you say, "No use! no!
I love these strangers,
and after them I must go." [y]
26 As the thief is shamed when caught,
so shall the house of Israel be shamed:
They, their kings and their princes,
their priests and their prophets; [z]
27 They who say to a piece of wood, "You are my father,"
and to a stone, "You gave me birth."
They turn to me their backs, not their faces;
yet, in their time of trouble they cry out,
"Rise up and save us!"
28 Where are the gods you made for yourselves?
Let them rise up!
Will they save you in your time of trouble?
For as numerous as your cities
are your gods, O Judah!
And as many as the streets of Jerusalem
are the altars you have set up for Baal. [a]

29 How dare you still plead with me?
You have all rebelled against me, says the LORD.
30 In vain I struck your children;
the correction they did not take.
Your sword devoured your prophets
like a ravening lion. [b]
31 You, of this generation,
take note of the word of the Lord:
Have I been a desert to Israel,
a land of darkness?

2, 14: Bondman by birth: a perpetual slave, different from the debt-slave, who was to be freed after six years; cf Ex 21, 2.
2, 16: Memphis: the capital of Lower Egypt. Tahpanhes: a frontier city of Egypt, east of the Delta. Shave the crown of your head: the spoliation of Judah at the hands of the Egyptians.
2, 18: Egypt and Assyria were the protecting foreign powers favored by rival parties within Judah. The desire for such foreign alliances is a further desertion of the Lord, the source of living waters (v 13), in favor of the above-named powers, symbolized by the Nile and the Euphrates rivers.
2, 20: Harlotry: idolatry (because Israel is the bride of God).
2, 23: The Valley: of Ben-hinnom, south of Jerusalem, site of the infamous sanctuary of Topheth where children were sacrificed to Molech; cf Jer 7, 31.

r Jer 17, 13; Ps 36, 9; Is 1, 4. s Jer 9, 11. t Jer 4, 18; 30, 15. u Prv 5, 22; Hos 5, 5. v Jer 3, 6. 13; Jgs 10, 6. w Ex 15, 17; Ps 80, 9; Is 5, 4. x Jb 9, 30. y Jer 18, 12. z Jer 48, 27; Rom 6, 21. a Jer 11, 13; Dt 32, 38; Jgs 10, 14. b Jer 5, 3; Neh 9, 26.

Why do my people say, "We have moved on,
we will come to you no more"?
32 Does a virgin forget her jewelry,
a bride her sash?
Yet my people have forgotten me
days without number. [c]

33 How well you pick your way
when seeking love!
You who, in your wickedness,
have gone by ways unclean!
34 You, on whose clothing there is
the life-blood of the innocent,
whom you found committing no burglary;
35 Yet withal you say, "I am innocent;
at least, his anger is turned away from me."
Behold, I will judge you
on that word of yours, "I have not sinned."
36 How very base you have become
in changing your course!
By Egypt will you be shamed,
as you were shamed by Assyria. [d]
37 From there also shall you go away
with hands upon your head;
For the LORD has rejected those in whom you trust,
with them you will have no success. [e]

CHAPTER 3

1 If a man sends away his wife[f]
and, after leaving him,
she marries another man,
Does the first husband come back to her?
Would not the land be wholly defiled?
But you have sinned with many lovers,
and yet you would return to me! says the LORD.*

2 Lift your eyes to the heights, and see,
where have men not lain with you?
By the waysides you waited for them
like an Arab* in the desert.
You defiled the land
by your wicked harlotry. [g]

3 Therefore the showers were withheld,
the spring rain failed.
But because you have a harlot's brow,
you refused to blush. [h]

4 Even now do you not call me, "My father,
you who are the bridegroom of my youth"?
5 "Will he keep his wrath forever,
will he hold his grudge to the end?"
This is what you say; yet you do
all the evil you can.

Judah and Israel 6 The LORD said to me in the
days of King Josiah: See now what rebellious
Israel has done! She has gone up every high
mountain, and under every green tree she has
played the harlot. [i] 7 And I thought, after she has
done all this she will return to me. But she did
not return. Then, even though her traitor sister
Judah saw 8 that for all the adulteries rebellious
Israel had committed, I put her away and gave
her a bill of divorce, nevertheless her traitor
sister Judah was not frightened; she too went off
and played the harlot. [j] 9 Eager to sin, she pol-
luted the land, committing adultery with stone
and wood. [k] 10 With all this, the traitor sister
Judah did not return to me wholeheartedly, but
insincerely, says the LORD.

Restoration of Israel 11 Then the LORD said to
me: Rebel Israel is inwardly more just than
traitorous Judah. [l] 12 Go, proclaim these words
toward the north, and say:

Return, rebel Israel, says the LORD,
I will not remain angry with you;
For I am merciful, says the LORD,
I will not continue my wrath forever. [m]
13 Only know your guilt:
how you rebelled against the LORD, your God,
How you ran hither and yon to strangers
[under every green tree]
and would not listen to my voice, says the LORD. [n]

3, 1: Such remarriage of divorced spouses was forbidden by Dt 24, 1–4. Under this figure the prophet sees the presumption of Judah, the unfaithful spouse, who thinks she can return to the Lord after uniting herself to other gods.

3, 2: An Arab: a marauding nomad who lay in wait for caravans.

c Jer 13, 25; Dt 32, 18. d 2 Chr 28, 16–21. e 2 Sm 13, 19. f Dt 24, 1–4. g Ex 16, 24f. h Jer 6, 15; 8, 12. i Jer 2, 20; Dt 12, 2. j 2 Kgs 17, 6. 18–23; Ez 23, 11. k Jer 2, 27. l Ez 16, 51; 23, 11. m Dt 4, 29ff. n Jer 2, 20. 25; Lv 26, 40.

14 Return, rebellious children, says the LORD,*
for I am your Master;
I will take you, one from a city, two from a clan,
and bring you to Zion. [o]
15 I will appoint over you shepherds after my own heart,
who will shepherd you wisely and prudently. [p]
16 When you multiply and become fruitful in the land,
says the LORD,
They will in those days no longer say,
"The ark of the covenant of the LORD!"
They will no longer think of it, or remember it,
or miss it, or make another.

17 At that time they will call Jerusalem the
LORD's throne; there all nations will be gathered
together to honor the name of the LORD at
Jerusalem, and they will walk no longer in their
hardhearted wickedness. [q] 18 In those days the
house of Judah will join the house of Israel;
together they will come from the land of the
north to the land which I gave to your fathers as
a heritage. [r]

Conditions for Forgiveness

19 I had thought:
How I should like to treat you as sons,
And give you a pleasant land,
a heritage most beautiful among the nations!
You would call me, "My Father," I thought,
and never cease following me. [s]
20 But like a woman faithless to her lover,
even so have you been faithless to me,
O house of Israel, says the LORD. [t]
21 A cry is heard on the heights!
the plaintive weeping of Israel's children,
Because they have perverted their ways
and forgotten the LORD, their God.
22 Return, rebellious children,
and I will cure you of your rebelling.
"Here we are, we now come to you
because you are the LORD, our God. [u]
23 Deceptive indeed are the hills,
the thronging mountains;
In the LORD, our God, alone
is the salvation of Israel. [v]
24 The shame-god* has devoured
our fathers' toil from our youth,
Their sheep and their cattle,
their sons and their daughters.
25 Let us lie down in our shame,
let our disgrace cover us,
for we have sinned against the LORD, our God,
From our youth to this day, we and our fathers also;
we listened not to the voice of the LORD, our God." [w]

CHAPTER 4

1 If you wish to return, O Israel, says the LORD,
return to me.
If you put your detestable things out of my sight,
and do not stray, [x]
2 Then you can swear, "As the LORD lives,"*
in truth, in judgment, and in justice;
Then shall the nations use his name in blessing,
and glory in him. [y]

3 For to the men of Judah and to Jerusalem,
thus says the LORD:

Till your untilled ground,
sow not among thorns. [z]

3, 14–18: A remnant of Israel (14) will reunite with Judah (18). The elementary cult of the Lord represented by the ark of the covenant will now be replaced by a more deeply spiritual and universal alliance, symbolized by his throne in the ideal Jerusalem around which all nations will be gathered together (17).

3, 24: Shame-god: literally, shame, a term commonly substituted for Baal, the Canaanite god with many local shrines.

4, 2: As the Lord lives: this oath, made sincerely, implies Israel's return to God and loyal adherence to him. Thus the ancient promises are fulfilled; cf Gn 12, 3; 18, 18; 22, 18; 26, 4; Ps 72, 17.

o Jer 23, 3; Is 10, 21f. p Ez 34, 23; Jn 21, 15. q Is 2, 2. r Jer 30, 3; 31, 8. s Jer 31, 9. 20; Is 63, 16. t Jer 5, 11. u Hos 3, 5. v Jer 14, 8. w Jer 16, 11f; 22, 21. x Jer 25, 5. y Jer 12, 16; Dt 10, 20; Is 65, 16. z Hos 10, 12; Mt 13, 7. 22.

4 For the sake of the LORD, be circumcised,*
remove the foreskins of your hearts,
O men of Judah and citizens of Jerusalem;
Lest my anger break out like fire,
and burn till none can quench it,
because of your evil deeds.[a]

The Invasion from the North

5 Proclaim it in Judah,
make it heard in Jerusalem;
Blow the trumpet through the land,
summon the recruits!
Say, "Fall in, let us march
to the fortified cities."
6 Bear the standard to Zion,
seek refuge without delay!
Evil I bring from the north,
and great destruction.
7 Up comes the lion from his lair,
the destroyer of nations has set out,
has left his place,
To turn your land into desolation,
till your cities lie waste and empty.[b]
8 So gird yourselves with sackcloth,
mourn and wail:
"The blazing wrath of the LORD
is not turned away from us."[c]

9 In that day, says the LORD,
The king will lose heart, and the princes;
the priests will be amazed,
and the prophets stunned.
10 "Alas! Lord GOD," they will say,
"You only deceived us*
When you said: Peace shall be yours;
for the sword touches our very soul."[d]
11 At that time it will be said
of this people and of Jerusalem,
"From the glaring heights through the desert
a wind comes toward the daughter of my people."
Not to winnow, not to cleanse,
12 does this wind from the heights come at my bidding;
And I myself now pronounce
sentence upon them.[e]
13 See! like storm clouds he advances,
like a hurricane his chariots;
Swifter than eagles are his steeds:
"Woe to us! we are ruined."
14 Cleanse your heart of evil, O Jerusalem,
that you may be saved.
How long must your pernicious thoughts
lodge within you?
15 Listen! They proclaim it from Dan,
from Mount Ephraim they announce
destruction:
16 "Make this known to the nations,
announce it to Jerusalem:
The besiegers are coming from the distant land,
shouting their war cry against the cities of Judah."[f]
17 Like watchmen of the fields they surround her,
for she has rebelled against me, says the LORD.[g]
18 Your conduct, your misdeeds, have done this
to you;
how bitter is this disaster of yours,
how it reaches to your very heart![h]

19 My breast! my breast! how I suffer!*
The walls of my heart!
My heart beats wildly,
I cannot be still;
For I have heard the sound of the trumpet,
the alarm of war.
20 Ruin after ruin is reported;
the whole earth is laid waste.
In an instant my tents are ravaged;
in a flash, my shelters.[i]
21 How long must I see that signal,
hear that trumpet sound!
22 Fools my people are,
they know me not;
Senseless children they are,

4, 4: The mere external rite of circumcision avails nothing unless accompanied by the removal of blindness and obstinacy of heart; cf Rm 2, 25. 29; 1 Cor 7, 19; Gal 5, 6; 6, 13. 15.

4, 10: You only deceived us: the false prophets blame their deception on God; cf Jer 14, 13–16.

4, 19ff: Probably the prophet's own anguish at the coming destruction of Judah.

a Jer 9, 24. b Jer 2, 15; 5, 6. c Jer 6, 26; Is 5, 25. d Jer 6, 14. e Jer 1, 16. f Jer 5, 15. g Jer 6, 3. h Jer 2, 17. 19. i Jer 10, 20.

having no understanding;
They are wise in evil,
but know not how to do good.[j]
23 I looked at the earth, and it was waste and void;
at the heavens, and their light had gone out![k]
24 I looked at the mountains, and they were trembling,
and all the hills were crumbling!
25 I looked and behold, there was no man;
even the birds of the air had flown away!
26 I looked and behold, the garden land was a desert,
with all its cities destroyed
before the LORD, before his blazing wrath.[l]

27 For thus says the LORD:
Waste shall the whole land be;
I will [not] wholly destroy it.[m]
28 Because of this the earth shall mourn,
the heavens above shall darken;
I have spoken, I will not repent,
I have resolved, I will not turn back.[n]
29 At the shout of horseman and bowman
each city takes to flight;
They shrink into the thickets,
they scale the rocks:
All the cities are abandoned,
and no one dwells in them.
30 You now who are doomed, what do you mean
by putting on purple,
bedecking yourself with gold,
Shading your eyes with cosmetics,
beautifying yourself in vain?
Your lovers spurn you,
they seek your life.
31 Yes, I hear the moaning, as of a woman in travail,
like the anguish of a mother with her first child—
The cry of daughter Zion gasping,
as she stretches forth her hands:
"Ah, woe is me! I sink exhausted
before the slayers!"[o]

CHAPTER 5

Universal Corruption

1 Roam the streets of Jerusalem,
look about and observe,
Search through her public places,
to find even one
Who lives uprightly
and seeks to be faithful,
and I will pardon her!
2 Though they say, "As the LORD lives,"
they swear falsely.
3 O LORD, do your eyes not look for honesty?
You struck them, but they did not cringe;
you laid them low, but they refused correction;
They set their faces harder than stone,
and refused to return to you.[p]
4 It is only the lowly, I thought,
who are foolish;
For they know not the way of the LORD,
their duty to their God.[q]
5 I will go to the great ones
and speak with them;
For they know the way of the LORD,
their duty to their God.
But, one and all, they had broken the yoke,
torn off the harness.[r]
6 Therefore lions from the forest slay them,
wolves of the desert ravage them,
Leopards keep watch round their cities:
all who come out are torn to pieces
For their many crimes
and their numerous rebellions.

7 Why should I pardon you these things?
Your sons have forsaken me,
they swear by gods that are not.
I fed them, but they committed adultery;
to the harlot's house they throng.
8 Lustful stallions they are,
each neighs after another's wife.[s]
9 Shall I not punish them for these things?
says the LORD;
On a nation such as this shall I not take
vengeance?

j Dt 32, 5f. 28. k Is 24, 1. 3. l Lv 26, 31. m Jer 5, 18. n Is 24, 4. o Jer 6, 24. p Jer 2, 30. q Jer 8, 7. r Jer 6, 13. s Jer 13, 27.

10 Climb to her terraces, and ravage them,
destroy them [not] wholly.
Tear away her tendrils,
they do not belong to the LORD. [t]
11 For they have openly rebelled against me,
both the house of Israel and the house of
Judah,
says the LORD, [u]
12 They denied the LORD,*
saying, "Not he—
No evil shall befall us,
neither sword nor famine shall we see. [v]
13 The prophets have become wind,
and the word is not in them.
May their threats be carried out against
themselves!"

14 Now, for this that you have said,
says the LORD, the God of hosts—
Behold, I make my words
in your mouth, a fire,
And this people is the wood
that it shall devour!—
15 Beware, I will bring against you
a nation from afar,
O house of Israel, says the LORD;
A long-lived nation, an ancient nation,
a people whose language you know not,
whose speech you cannot understand. [w]
16 Their quivers are like open graves;
all of them are warriors.
17 They will devour your harvest and your bread,
devour your sons and your daughters,
Devour your sheep and cattle,
devour your vines and fig trees;
They will beat flat with the sword
the fortified city in which you trust. [x]

18 Yet even in those days, says the LORD, I will
not wholly destroy you. [y] 19 And when they ask,
"Why has the LORD done all these things to us?"
say to them, "As you have forsaken me to serve
strange gods in your own land, so shall you serve
strangers in a land not your own."

20 Announce this to the house of Jacob,
proclaim it in Judah:
21 Pay attention to this,
foolish and senseless people
Who have eyes and see not,
who have ears and hear not. [z]
22 Should you not fear me, says the LORD,
should you not tremble before me?
I made the sandy shore the sea's limit,
which by eternal decree it may not
overstep.
Toss though it may, it is to no avail;
though its billows roar, they cannot pass. [a]
23 But this people's heart is stubborn and
rebellious;
they turn and go away,
24 And say not in their hearts,
"Let us fear the LORD, our God,
Who gives us rain
early and late,* in its time;
Who watches for us
over the appointed weeks of harvest." [b]
25 Your crimes have prevented these things,
your sins have turned back these blessings
from you. [c]
26 For there are among my people criminals;
like fowlers they set traps,
but it is men they catch. [d]
27 Their houses are as full of treachery
as a bird-cage is of birds;
Therefore they grow powerful and rich,
28 fat and sleek.
They go their wicked way;
justice they do not defend
By advancing the claim of the fatherless
or judging the cause of the poor. [e]
29 Shall I not punish these things? says the LORD;
on a nation such as this shall I not take
vengeance?
30 A shocking, horrible thing
has happened in the land:
31 The prophets prophesy falsely,
and the priests teach as they wish;

5, 12: They denied the Lord: the people act as though God does not exist and will not interfere.

5, 24: Rain early and late: autumn and spring rains respectively. Appointed weeks of harvest: the seven weeks between the Passover (Dt 16, 9f) and Pentecost, during which it ordinarily did not rain.

t Jer 2, 21. u Jer 3, 20. v Jer 14, 13; Is 28, 15. w Dt 28, 49. x Dt 28, 31. y Jer 4, 27. z Is 6, 9. a Jb 38, 10f. b Gn 8, 22; Dt 11, 14. c Jer 2, 17. 19. d Prv 1, 11. e Jer 12, 1; Is 1, 23.

Yet my people will have it so;
what will you do when the end comes?[f]

CHAPTER 6

The Enemy at the Gates

1 Flee, sons of Benjamin,
out of Jerusalem!
Blow the trumpet in Tekoa,
raise a signal over Beth-haccherem;
For evil threatens from the north,
and mighty destruction.[g]
2 O lovely and delicate
daughter Zion, you are ruined!
3 Against her, shepherds come with their
flocks;*
all around, they pitch their tents,
each one grazes his portion.[h]
4 "Prepare for war against her,
Up! let us rush upon her at midday!
Alas! the day is waning,
evening shadows lengthen;
5 Up! let us rush upon her by night,
destroy her palaces!"[i]
6 For thus says the LORD of hosts:
Hew down her trees,
throw up a siege mound against Jerusalem.
Woe to the city marked for punishment;
nought but oppression within her![j]
7 As the well gushes out its waters,
so she gushes out her wickedness.
Violence and destruction resound in her;
ever before me are wounds and blows.[k]
8 Be warned, O Jerusalem,
lest I be estranged from you;
Lest I turn you into a desert,
a land where no man dwells.

9 Thus says the LORD of hosts:
Glean, glean like a vine
the remnant of Israel;
Pass your hand, like a vintager,
repeatedly over the tendrils.
10 To whom shall I speak?
whom shall I warn, and be heard?
See! their ears are uncircumcised,
they cannot give heed;
See, the word of the LORD has become for
them
an object of scorn, which they will not
have.[l]
11 Therefore my wrath brims up within me,
I am weary of holding it in;
I will pour it out upon the child in the street,
upon the young men gathered together.
Yes, all will be taken, husband and wife,
graybeard with ancient.[m]
12 Their houses will fall to strangers,
their fields and their wives as well;
For I will stretch forth my hand
against those who dwell in this land, says
the LORD.[n]
13 Small and great alike, all are greedy for gain;
prophet and priest, all practice fraud.[o]
14 They would repair, as though it were nought,*
the injury to my people:
"Peace, peace!" they say,
though there is no peace.[p]
15 They are odious; they have done abominable
things,
yet they are not at all ashamed,
they know not how to blush.
Hence they shall be among those who fall;
in their time of punishment they shall go
down,
says the LORD.[q]

16 Thus says the LORD:
Stand beside the earliest roads,
ask the pathways of old*
Which is the way to good, and walk it;
thus you will find rest for your souls.
But they said, "We will not walk it."[r]
17 When I raised up watchmen* for them:

6, 3: Shepherds . . . with their flocks: foreign invaders with their armies.

6, 14: As though it were nought: the false assurance of well-being given by priest and prophet cannot reduce the harm which universal materialism and corruption have done to the people.

6, 16: Earliest roads . . . pathways of old: history and the lessons to be learned from it.

6, 17: Watchmen: the prophets who, like Jeremiah, had upheld God's moral law.

f Jer 14, 14; Mi 2, 11. g Jer 1, 14f. h Jer 4, 17. i 2 Chr 36, 19. j Jer 32, 24; Zep 3, 1-4. k Is 57, 20. l Jer 7, 26; 20, 8. m Ez 9, 6. n Jer 8, 10; Dt 28, 30ff. o Jer 8, 10; 23, 11. p Jer 8, 11. q Jer 3, 3; 8, 12. r Jer 7, 23f; 18, 15.

"Hearken to the sound of the trumpet!"
they said, "We will not hearken."
18 Therefore hear, O nations,
and know, O earth,
what I will do with them:
19 See, I bring evil upon this people,
the fruit of their own schemes,
Because they heeded not my words,
because they despised my law. [s]
20 Of what use to me incense that comes from
Sheba,
or sweet cane from far-off lands?
Your holocausts find no favor with me,
your sacrifices please me not. [t]
21 Therefore, thus says the LORD:
See, I will place before this people
obstacles to bring them down;
Fathers and sons alike,
neighbors and friends shall perish. [u]

22 Thus says the LORD:
See, a people comes from the land of the
north,
a great nation, roused from the ends of the
earth. [v]
23 Bow and javelin they wield;
cruel and pitiless are they.
They sound like the roaring sea
as they ride forth on steeds,
Each in his place, for battle
against you, daughter Zion.
24 We hear the report of them;
helpless fall our hands,
Anguish takes hold of us,
throes like a mother's in childbirth. [w]
25 Go not forth into the field,
step not into the street,
Beware of the enemy's sword;
terror on every side!
26 O daughter of my people, gird on sackcloth,
roll in the ashes.
Mourn as for an only child
with bitter wailing,
For sudden upon us
comes the destroyer. [x]
27 A tester among my people I have appointed
you,
to search and test their way. [y]
28 Arch-rebels are they all,
dealers in slander,
all of them corrupt.
29 The bellows roars,
the lead is consumed by the fire;
In vain has the smelter refined,
the wicked are not drawn off.
30 "Silver rejected" they shall be called,
for the LORD has rejected them.

II: Oracles Mostly in the Days of Jehoiakim

CHAPTER 7

The Temple Sermon* 1 The following mes-
sage came to Jeremiah from the LORD: 2 Stand at
the gate of the house of the LORD, and there
proclaim this message: Hear the word of the
LORD, all you of Judah who enter these gates to
worship the LORD! 3 Thus says the LORD of hosts,
the God of Israel: Reform your ways and your
deeds, so that I may remain with you in this
place. [z] 4 Put not your trust in the deceitful
words: "This is the temple of the LORD! The
temple of the LORD! The temple of the LORD!" [a]
5 Only if you thoroughly reform your ways and
your deeds; if each of you deals justly with his
neighbor; 6 if you no longer oppress the resident
alien,* the orphan, and the widow; if you no
longer shed innocent blood in this place, or
follow strange gods to your own harm, [b] 7 will I
remain with you in this place, in the land which
I gave your fathers long ago and forever. [c]
8 But here you are, putting your trust in
deceitful words to your own loss! 9 Are you to
steal and murder, commit adultery and perjury,
burn incense to Baal, go after strange gods that

7, 1–15: The temple of the Lord will not serve as a place of refuge for the Jews against their enemies if they fail to reform their evil ways.

7, 6: The resident alien: specially protected by law; cf Ex 20, 10; Nm 9, 14; 15, 14; Dt 5, 14; 28, 43.

s Prv 1, 31. t Is 1, 11; 43, 24. u Is 8, 14f. v Jer 1, 15; 5, 15. w Jer 4, 31. x Jer 25, 34; Am 8, 10. y Jer 1, 18. z Jer 18, 11; 26, 13. a Mi 3, 11. b Ex 22, 21–24. c Dt 4, 40.

you know not,[d] 10 and yet come to stand before me in this house which bears my name, and say: "We are safe; we can commit all these abominations again"?[e] 11 Has this house which bears my name become in your eyes a den of thieves? I too see what is being done, says the LORD.[f] 12 You may go to Shiloh,* which I made the dwelling place of my name in the beginning. See what I did to it because of the wickedness of my people Israel.[g] 13 And now, because you have committed all these misdeeds, says the LORD, because you did not listen, though I spoke to you untiringly; because you did not answer, though I called you, 14 I will do to this house named after me, in which you trust, and to this place which I gave to you and your fathers, just as I did to Shiloh.[h] 15 I will cast you away from me, as I cast away all your brethren, all the offspring of Ephraim.[i]

Abuses in Worship 16 You, now, do not intercede for this people; raise not in their behalf a pleading prayer![j] Do not urge me, for I will not listen to you. 17 Do you not see what they are doing in the cities of Judah, in the streets of Jerusalem? 18 The children gather wood, their fathers light the fire, and the women knead dough to make cakes for the queen of heaven,* while libations are poured out to strange gods in order to hurt me.[k] 19 Is it I whom they hurt, says the LORD; is it not rather themselves, to their own confusion?[l] 20 See now, says the Lord GOD, my anger and my wrath will pour out upon this place, upon man and beast, upon the trees of the field and the fruits of the earth; it will burn without being quenched.[m]

21 Thus says the LORD of hosts, the God of Israel: Heap your holocausts upon your sacrifices; eat up the flesh! 22 In speaking to your fathers on the day I brought them out of the land of Egypt, I gave them no command* concerning holocaust or sacrifice. 23 This rather is what I commanded them: Listen to my voice; then I will be your God and you shall be my people. Walk in all the ways that I command you, so that you may prosper.[n]

24 But they obeyed not, nor did they pay heed. They walked in the hardness of their evil hearts and turned their backs, not their faces, to me.[o] 25 From the day that your fathers left the land of Egypt even to this day, I have sent you untiringly all my servants the prophets.[p] 26 Yet they have not obeyed me nor paid heed; they have stiffened their necks and done worse than their fathers.[q] 27 When you speak all these words to them, they will not listen to you either; when you call to them, they will not answer you. 28 Say to them: This is the nation which does not listen to the voice of the LORD, its God, or take correction. Faithfulness has disappeared; the word itself is banished from their speech.

29 Cut off your dedicated hair* and throw it
away!
on the heights intone an elegy;
For the LORD has rejected and cast off
the generation that draws down his wrath.[r]

30 The people of Judah have done what is evil in my eyes, says the LORD. They have defiled the house which bears my name by setting up in it their abominable idols.[s] 31 In the Valley of Ben-hinnom they have built the high place of Topheth to immolate in fire their sons and their daughters, such a thing as I never commanded or had in mind. 32 Therefore, beware! days will come, says the LORD, when Topheth and the Valley of Ben-hinnom will no longer be called such, but rather the Valley of Slaughter. For lack of space, Topheth will be a burial place.[t] 33 The

7, 12: Shiloh: original place of worship from the time of Joshua to that of Samuel. The sanctuary was later rejected by God and destroyed by the Philistines; cf 1 Sm 1, 9; 4, 3f; Ps 78, 60. 68f.

7, 18: Queen of heaven: the Assyro-Babylonian Ishtar, goddess of fertility, whose worship was introduced under King Manasseh and was revived after Josiah's death. Cakes shaped like stars (Ishtar was identified with the planet Venus) were offered in her honor.

7, 22: I gave them no command: right conduct rather than mere external cult was God's will concerning his people (v 23).

7, 29: Dedicated hair: the unshorn hair of the nazirite, regarded as sacred because of a vow, temporary or permanent, to abstain from cutting or shaving the hair, from contact with a corpse, and from all products of the vine; cf Nm 6, 4–8. The cutting of this hair was a sign of extreme mourning.

d Jer 44, 17. e Jer 32, 34. f Mt 21, 13. g Jos 18, 1. h Jer 26, 9. i 1 Kgs 9, 7; 2 Kgs 17, 23. j Jer 11, 14; 14, 11. k Jer 44, 17. 19. l Jb 35, 6. m Jer 36, 29; 2 Kgs 22, 17. n Jer 11, 4; Lv 26, 3. 12. o Jer 17, 23. p 2 Chr 36, 15f; Bar 1, 19. q Jer 19, 15; 2 Chr 30, 8. r Jer 9, 17–21. s Jer 32, 34. t Jer 19, 6; 32, 35.

corpses of this people will be food for the birds of
the sky and for the beasts of the field, which no
one will drive away. [u] 34 In the cities of Judah and
in the streets of Jerusalem I will silence the cry of
joy, the cry of gladness, the voice of the bride-
groom and the voice of the bride; for the land
will be turned to rubble. [v]

CHAPTER 8

1 At that time, says the LORD, the bones of the
kings and princes of Judah, the bones of the
priests and the prophets, and the bones of the
citizens of Jerusalem will be emptied out of their
graves [w] 2 and spread out before the sun and the
moon and the whole army of heaven,* which
they loved and served, which they followed,
consulted, and worshiped. They will not be
gathered up for burial, but will lie like dung
upon the ground. [x] 3 Death will be preferred to
life by all the survivors of this wicked race who
remain in any of the places to which I banish
them, says the LORD of hosts.

Israel's Conduct Incomprehensible

4 Tell them: Thus says the LORD:
When someone falls, does he not rise again?
if he goes astray, does he not turn back?
5 Why do these people rebel
with obstinate resistance?
Why do they cling to deceptive idols,
refuse to turn back? [y]
6 I listen closely:
they speak what is not true;
No one repents of his wickedness,
saying "What have I done!"
Everyone keeps on running his course,
like a steed dashing into battle. [z]
7 Even the stork in the air
knows its seasons;
Turtledove, swallow and thrush
observe their time of return,
But my people do not know
the ordinance of the LORD. [a]
8 How can you say, "We are wise, [b]
we have the law of the LORD"?
Why, that has been changed into falsehood
by the lying pen of the scribes!*
9 The wise are confounded,
dismayed and ensnared;
Since they have rejected the word of the LORD,
of what avail is their wisdom? [c]

Shameless in Their Crimes

10 Therefore, I will give their wives to strangers,
their fields to spoilers.
Small and great alike, all are greedy for gain,
prophet and priest, all practice fraud. [d]
11 They would repair, as though it were nought,
the injury to the daughter of my people:*
"Peace, peace!" they say,
though there is no peace. [e]
12 They are odious; they have done abominable
things,
yet they are not at all ashamed,
they know not how to blush.
Hence they shall be among those who fall;
in their time of punishment they shall go
down,
says the LORD. [f]

Threats of Punishment

13 I will gather them all in, says the LORD:
no grapes on the vine,
No figs on the fig trees,
foliage withered!
14 Why do we remain here?
Let us form ranks and enter the walled
cities,
to perish there;
For the LORD has wrought our destruction,
he has given us poison to drink,
because we have sinned against the LORD. [g]
15 We wait for peace to no avail;
for a time of healing, but terror comes
instead. [h]
16 From Dan is heard

8, 2: Army of heaven: the stars, worshiped by the pagan nations and even by the inhabitants of Jerusalem during the reigns of Manasseh and Amon.

8, 8f: Lying pen of the scribes: because the interpretations and ordinances of the scribes ran counter to the word of the Lord.

8, 11: Daughter of my people: the people itself personified as a woman.

u Jer 16, 4; 34, 20. v Jer 16, 9. w Bar 2, 24. x Dt 4, 19. y Jer 5, 3; 7, 24. 26. z Jb 34, 31f. a Is 1, 3. b Mal 2, 8; Rom 2, 17–23. c 1 Cor 3, 20. d Jer 6, 13; Dt 28, 30. e Jer 6, 14. f Jer 6, 15. g Jer 9, 14; 23, 15. h Jer 14, 19.

the snorting of his steeds;
The neighing of his stallions
shakes the whole land.
They come devouring the land and all it
contains,
the city and those who dwell in it.
17 Yes, I will send against you
poisonous snakes,
Against which no charm will work
when they bite you, says the LORD. [i]

The Prophet's Grief over the People's Suffering

18 My grief is incurable,
my heart within me is faint.
19 Listen! the cry of the daughter of my people,
far and wide in the land!
Is the LORD no longer in Zion,
is her King no longer in her midst?
[Why do they provoke me with their idols,
with their foreign nonentities?] [j]
20 "The harvest has passed, the summer is at an
end,
and yet we are not safe!"
21 I am broken by the ruin of the daughter of my
people.
I am disconsolate; horror has seized me. [k]
22 Is there no balm in Gilead,*
no physician there?
Why grows not new flesh
over the wound of the daughter of my
people? [l]
23 Oh, that my head were a spring of water,
my eyes a fountain of tears,
That I might weep day and night
over the slain of the daughter of my people!

CHAPTER 9

The Corruption of the People

1 Would that I had in the desert
a travelers' lodge!
That I might leave my people
and depart from them.
They are all adulterers,
a faithless band.
2 They ready their tongues like a drawn bow;
with lying, and not with truth,
they hold forth in the land.
They go from evil to evil,
but me they know not, says the LORD.
3 Be on your guard, everyone against his
neighbor;
put no trust in any brother.
Every brother apes Jacob, the supplanter,*
every friend is guilty of slander.
4 Each one deceives the other,
no one speaks the truth.
They have accustomed their tongues to lying,
and are perverse, and cannot repent. [m]
5 Violence upon violence,
deceit upon deceit:
They refuse to recognize me,
says the LORD.

6 Therefore, thus says the LORD of hosts:
I will smelt them and test them;
how else should I deal with their
wickedness?
7 A murderous arrow is his tongue,
his mouth utters deceit;
He speaks cordially with his friends,
but in his heart he lays an ambush! [n]
8 For these things, says the LORD,
shall I not punish them?
On a nation such as this
shall I not take vengeance? [o]

Dirge over the Ravaged Land

9 Over the mountains, break out in cries of
lamentation,
over the pasture lands, intone a dirge:
They are scorched, and no man crosses them,
unheard is the bleat of the flock;
Birds of the air as well as beasts,
all have fled, and are gone. [p]
10 I will turn Jerusalem into a heap of ruins,
a haunt of jackals;

8, 22: Gilead: noted for its healing balm but unable to heal the moral wound of the people.

9, 3: Jacob, the supplanter: in Hebrew, a play on words. Jacob, as his name indicates ("he supplants"), deprived his brother Esau of his birthright; cf Gn 25, 26. 33.

i Dt 32, 24. j Dt 32, 21; Mi 4, 9. k Jer 14, 17. l Jer 46, 11. m Jer 12, 6. n Pss 28, 3; 62, 4. o Jer 5, 9. 29. p Jer 4, 25; 12, 4.

The cities of Judah I will make into a waste,
where no one dwells. [q]

11 Who is so wise that he can understand this?
Let him to whom the mouth of the LORD has
spoken make it known:

Why is the land ravaged,
scorched like a wasteland untraversed? [r]

12 The LORD answered: Because they have
abandoned my law, which I set before them, and
have not followed it or listened to my voice,
13 but followed rather the hardness of their hearts
and the Baals, as their fathers had taught them; [s]
14 therefore, thus says the LORD of hosts, the God
of Israel: See now, I will give them wormwood
to eat and poison to drink. [t] 15 I will scatter them
among nations whom neither they nor their
fathers have known; I will send the sword to
pursue them until I have completely destroyed
them. [u]

16 Thus says the LORD of hosts:
Attention! tell the wailing women to come,
summon the best of them;
17 Let them come quickly
and intone a dirge for us,
That our eyes may be wet with weeping,
our cheeks run with tears. [v]
18 The dirge is heard from Zion:
Ruined we are, and greatly ashamed;
We must leave the land,
give up our homes!
19 Hear, you women, the word of the LORD,
let your ears receive his message.
Teach your daughters this dirge,
and each other this lament.
20 Death has come up through our windows,
has entered our palaces;
It cuts down the children in the street,
young people in the squares. [w]
21 The corpses of the slain
lie like dung on a field,
Like sheaves behind the harvester,
with no one to gather them.

True Glory

22 Thus says the LORD:
Let not the wise man glory in his wisdom,
nor the strong man glory in his strength,
nor the rich man glory in his riches; [x]
23 But rather, let him who glories, glory in this,
that in his prudence he knows me,
Knows that I, the LORD, bring about kindness,
justice and uprightness on the earth;
For with such am I pleased, says the LORD.

Circumcision Worthless 24 See, days are com-
ing, says the LORD, when I will demand an
account of all those circumcised in their flesh: [y]
25 Egypt and Judah, Edom and the Ammonites,
Moab and the desert dwellers who shave their
temples.* For all these nations, like the whole
house of Israel, are uncircumcised in heart.

CHAPTER 10

The Folly of Idolatry 1 Hear the word which
the LORD speaks to you, O house of Israel. 2 Thus
says the LORD:

Learn not the customs of the nations,
and have no fear of the signs of the
heavens,*
though the nations fear them. [z]
3 For the cult idols of the nations are nothing,
wood cut from the forest,
Wrought by craftsmen with the adze, [a]
4 adorned with silver and gold.
With nails and hammers they are fastened,
that they may not totter. [b]
5 Like a scarecrow in a cucumber field are they,
they cannot speak;
They must be carried about,
for they cannot walk.
Fear them not, they can do no harm,
neither is it in their power to do good. [c]
6 No one is like you, O LORD,
great are you,
great and mighty is your name. [d]
7 Who would not fear you,

9, 25: Desert dwellers . . . temples: Arab tribesmen who cut off their hair and shaved their temples in honor of the pagan god of Dushara. This was forbidden the Israelites (Lv 19, 27).

10, 2: Signs of the heavens: phenomena in the sky superstitiously regarded by the pagans as dire omens.

q Is 13, 22. r Ps 107, 43; Hos 14, 10. s Jer 7, 24; 19, 4f. t Jer 23, 15. u Lv 26, 33; Dt 28, 36. 64. v Jer 14, 17. w Jer 14, 16. x Prv 21, 30. y Jer 4, 4. z Bar 6, 6. a Wis 13, 11; Is 44, 9. b Is 40, 19; 41, 7. c Ps 115, 4–8; Bar 6, 15. d Ps 86, 8ff.

King of the nations,
for it is your due!

Among all the wisest of the nations,
and in all their domain,
there is none like you. [e]

8 One and all they are dumb and senseless,
these idols they teach about are wooden:
9 Silver strips brought from Tarshish,
and gold from Ophir,
The work of the craftsman
and the handiwork of the smelter,
Clothed with violet and purple—
all of them the work of artisans.

11 Thus shall you say of them: Let the gods that did not make heaven and earth perish from the earth, and from beneath these heavens![f]

10 The LORD is true God,
he is the living God, the eternal King,
Before whose anger the earth quakes,
whose wrath the nations cannot endure: [g]
12 He who made the earth by his power,
established the world by his wisdom,
and stretched out the heavens by his skill. [h]
13 When he thunders, the waters in the heavens roar,
and he brings up clouds from the end of the earth;
He makes the lightning flash in the rain,
and releases stormwinds from their chambers.
14 Every man is stupid, ignorant;
every artisan is put to shame by his idol:
He has molded a fraud,
without breath of life. [i]
15 Nothingness are they, a ridiculous work;
they will perish in their time of punishment.
16 Not like these is the portion of Jacob:
he is the creator of all things;
Israel is his very own tribe,
LORD of hosts is his name. [j]

Abandonment of Judah

17 Lift your bundle and leave the land,
O city living in a state of siege!
18 For thus says the LORD:
Behold, this time
I will sling away the inhabitants of the land;
I will hem them in,
that they may be taken.
19 Woe is me! I am undone,
my wound is incurable;
Yet I had thought:
if I make light of my wound, I can bear it.
20 My tent is ruined,
all its cords are severed.
My sons have left me, they are no more:
no one to pitch my tent,
no one to raise its curtains. [k]
21 Yes, the shepherds were stupid as cattle,
the LORD they sought not;
Therefore they had no success,
and all their flocks were scattered. [l]
22 Listen! a noise! it comes closer,
a great uproar from the northern land:
To turn the cities of Judah
into a desert haunt of jackals.

Prayer of Jeremiah

23 You know, O LORD,
that man is not master of his way;
Man's course is not within his choice,
nor is it for him to direct his step.
24 Punish us, O LORD, but with equity,
not in anger, lest you have us dwindle away.
25 Pour out your wrath on the nations that know you not,
on the tribes that call not upon your name;
For they have devoured Jacob utterly,
and laid waste his dwelling. [m]

CHAPTER 11

Plea for Fidelity to the Covenant 1 The following message came to Jeremiah from the
LORD: 2 Speak to the men of Judah and to the
citizens of Jerusalem, 3 saying to them: Thus says
the LORD, the God of Israel: Cursed be the man
who does not observe the terms of this covenant, [n] 4 which I enjoined upon your fathers the
day I brought them up out of the land of Egypt,
that iron foundry, saying: Listen to my voice and

e Jer 5, 22; Ps 47, 2. 8. f Ps 96, 5. g Ps 10, 16. h Ps 104, 5. i Rom 1, 22f. j Jer 31, 35. k Jer 4, 20. l Jer 23, 1; Ez 34, 5f.

m Ps 79, 6f. n Dt 27, 26.

do all that I command you. Then you shall be my people, and I will be your God.[o] 5 Thus I will fulfill the oath which I swore to your fathers, to give them a land flowing with milk and honey: the one you have today. "Amen, LORD," I answered.

6 Then the LORD said to me: Proclaim all these words in the cities of Judah and in the streets of Jerusalem: Hear the words of this covenant and obey them. 7 Urgently and constantly I warned your fathers to obey my voice, from the day I brought them up out of the land of Egypt even to this day. 8 But they did not listen or give ear. Each one followed the hardness of his evil heart, till I brought upon them all the threats of this covenant which they had failed to observe as I commanded them.[p]

9 A conspiracy has been found, the LORD said to me, among the men of Judah and the citizens of Jerusalem. 10 They have returned to the crimes of their forefathers who refused to obey my words. They also have followed and served strange gods; the covenant which I had made with their fathers, the house of Israel and the house of Judah have broken.[q] 11 Therefore, thus says the LORD: See, I bring upon them misfortune which they cannot escape. Though they cry out to me, I will not listen to them.[r] 12 Then the cities of Judah and the citizens of Jerusalem will go and cry out to the gods to which they have been offering incense. But these gods will give them no help whatever when misfortune strikes.[s]

13 For as numerous as your cities
are your gods, O Judah!
And as many as the streets of Jerusalem
are the altars for offering sacrifice to Baal.[t]

14 Do not intercede on behalf of this people, nor utter a plea for them. I will not listen when they call to me at the time of their misfortune.[u]

Sacrifices of No Avail

15 What right has my beloved in my house,
while she prepares her plots?
Can vows and sacred meat turn away
your misfortune from you?
Will you still be jubilant
16 when you hear the great invasion?
A spreading olive tree, goodly to behold,
the LORD has named you;
Now he sets fire to it,
its branches burn.

17 The LORD of hosts who planted you has decreed misfortune for you because of the evil done by the house of Israel and by the house of Judah, who provoked me by sacrificing to Baal.[v]

The Plot against Jeremiah 18 I knew it because the LORD informed me; at that time you, O LORD, showed me their doings.

CHAPTER 12

1 You would be in the right, O LORD,
if I should dispute with you;
even so, I must discuss the case with you.
Why does the way of the godless prosper,
why live all the treacherous in
contentment?[w]
2 You planted them; they have taken root,
they keep on growing and bearing fruit.
You are upon their lips,
but far from their inmost thoughts.[x]
3 You, O Lord, know me, you see me,
you have found that at heart I am with
you.[y]
Pick them out like sheep for the slaughter,
set them apart for the day of carnage.*
4 How long must the earth mourn,
the green of the whole countryside wither?
For the wickedness of those who dwell in it
beasts and birds disappear,
because they say, "God does not see our
ways."

5 If running against men has wearied you,
how will you race against horses?
And if in a land of peace you fall headlong,

12, 3: Jeremiah does not seek private vengeance but the punishment of the wicked by the Lord; cf Jer 20, 12. Nevertheless, the prophet's reaction to persecution shows the difference between the spirit of the Old Testament and the New.

o Dt 4, 20; 1 Kgs 8, 51. p 2 Kgs 17, 14. q Dt 31, 16; Ez 20, 21–30. r Jer 14, 12; Mi 3, 4. s Dt 32, 37f. t Jer 2, 28; Hos 10, 1. u Jer 7, 16; 14, 11. v Is 5, 2. w Jb 21, 7; Mal 3, 15. x Is 29, 13. y Jer 17, 18; Jb 23, 10.

what will you do in the thickets of the
Jordan?

[6]For even your own brothers, the members of your father's house, betray you; they have recruited a force against you. Do not believe them, even if they are friendly to you in their words.[z]

[19]*Yet I, like a trusting lamb led to slaughter, had not realized that they were hatching plots against me: "Let us destroy the tree in its vigor; let us cut him off from the land of the living, so that his name will be spoken no more."[a]

[20]But, you, O LORD of hosts, O just Judge,
searcher of mind and heart,
Let me witness the vengeance you take on
them,
for to you I have entrusted my cause![b]

[21]Therefore, thus says the LORD concerning the men of Anathoth who seek your life, saying, "Do not prophesy in the name of the LORD; else you shall die by our hand."[c] [22]Therefore, thus says the LORD of hosts: I am going to punish them. The young men shall die by the sword; their sons and daughters shall die by famine.[d]
[23]None shall be spared among them, for I will bring misfortune upon the men of Anathoth, the year of their punishment.[e]

The Lord's Complaint

[7]I abandon my house,
cast off my heritage;
The beloved of my soul I deliver
into the hand of her foes.[f]
[8]My heritage has turned on me
like a lion in the jungle;
Because she has roared against me,
I treat her as an enemy.[g]
[9]My heritage is a prey for hyenas,
is surrounded by vultures;
Come, gather together, all you beasts of the
field,
come and eat![h]
[10]Many shepherds have ravaged my vineyard,
have trodden my heritage underfoot;
The portion that delighted me they have
turned
into a desert waste.[i]
[11]They have made it a mournful waste,
desolate it lies before me,
Desolate, all the land,
because no one takes it to heart.
[12]Upon every desert height
brigands have come up.
The LORD has a sword which consumes
the land, from end to end:
no peace for all mankind.[j]
[13]They have sown wheat and reaped thorns,
they have tired themselves out to no
purpose;
They recoil before their harvest,
the flaming anger of the LORD.

Judah's Neighbors [14]Thus says the LORD
against all my evil neighbors* who plunder the
heritage which I gave my people Israel as their
own: See, I will pluck them up from their land;
the house of Judah I will pluck up in their
midst.[k] [15]But after plucking them up, I will pity
them again and bring them back, each to his
heritage, each to his land.[l] [16]And if they care-
fully learn my people's custom of swearing by
my name, "As the LORD lives," they who for-
merly taught my people to swear by Baal shall be
built up in the midst of my people.[m] [17]But if they
do not obey, I will uproot and destroy that nation
entirely, says the LORD.[n]

CHAPTER 13

Judah's Corruption* [1]The LORD said to me:
Go buy yourself a linen loincloth; wear it on your

12, 19–23: These verses have been transposed from ch 11.
12, 14: My evil neighbors: nations surrounding Israel, the land belonging to the Lord; cf Is 8, 8.
13, 1–11: This is probably a vision of the prophet symbolizing the religious corruption of Judah at the hands of the Babylonians, represented here by the river Parath, the Euphrates; though a spring of the same name, northeast of Anathoth, may be directly meant.

z Jer 9, 4. a Jer 18, 18; 20, 10; Wis 2, 20. b Jer 15, 15. c Am 7, 13. 16. d Jer 18, 21f. e Jer 23, 12. f Ps 78, 62; Lam 2, 1f. g Ps 106, 40. h 2 Kgs 24, 2; Is 56, 9. i Jer 6, 3; Is 63, 18. j Is 42, 25; 57, 21. k 2 Kgs 24, 2. l Am 9, 14. m Dt 6, 13. n Is 60, 12.

loins, but do not put it in water. 2I bought the
loincloth, as the LORD commanded, and put it
on. 3A second time the word of the LORD came
to me thus: 4Take the loincloth which you
bought and are wearing, and go now to the
Parath; there hide it in a cleft of the rock. 5Obedi-
ent to the LORD's command, I went to the Parath
and buried the loincloth. 6After a long interval,
he said to me: Go now to the Parath and fetch
the loincloth which I told you to hide there.
7Again I went to the Parath, sought out and took
the loincloth from the place where I had hid it.
But it was rotted, good for nothing! 8Then the
message came to me from the LORD: 9Thus says
the LORD: So also I will allow the pride of Judah
to rot, the great pride of Jerusalem.[o] 10This
wicked people who refuse to obey my words,
who walk in the stubbornness of their hearts,
and follow strange gods to serve and adore them,
shall be like this loincloth which is good for noth-
ing.[p] 11For, as close as the loincloth clings to a
man's loins, so had I made the whole house of
Israel and the whole house of Judah cling to me,
says the LORD; to be my people, my renown, my
praise, my beauty. But they did not listen.[q]

The Broken Wineflask 12Now speak to them
this word: Thus says the LORD, the God of Israel:
Every wineflask is meant to be filled with wine.
If they reply, "Do we not know that every
wineflask is meant to be filled with wine?" 13say
to them: Thus says the LORD: Beware! I am
filling with drunkenness all the inhabitants of
this land, the kings who succeed to David's
throne, the priests and prophets, and all the
citizens of Jerusalem.[r] 14I will dash them against
each other, fathers and sons together, says the
LORD; I will show no compassion, I will not
spare or pity, but will destroy them.[s]

A Last Warning

15 Give ear, listen humbly,
for the LORD speaks.
16 Give glory to the LORD, your God,
before it grows dark;
Before your feet stumble
on darkening mountains;
Before the light you look for turns to darkness,
changes into black clouds.[t]
17 If you do not listen to this in your pride,
I will weep in secret many tears;
My eyes will run with tears
for the LORD's flock, led away to exile.[u]

Exile

18 Say to the king and to the queen mother:
come down from your throne;
From your heads fall
your magnificent crowns.[v]
19 The cities of the Negeb are besieged,
with no one to relieve them;
All Judah is banished
in universal exile.

Jerusalem's Disgrace

20 Lift up your eyes and see
men coming from the north.
Where is the flock entrusted to you,
the sheep that were your glory?[w]
21 What will you say when they place as rulers
over you
those whom you taught to be your lovers?
Will not pangs seize you
like those of a woman giving birth?[x]
22 If you ask in your heart
why these things befall you:
For your great guilt your skirts are stripped
away
and you are violated.[y]
23 Can the Ethiopian change his skin?
the leopard his spots?
As easily would you be able to do good,
accustomed to evil as you are.[z]
24 I will scatter them like chaff that flies
when the desert wind blows.[a]
25 This is your lot, the portion measured out to
you
from me, says the LORD.
Because you have forgotten me,
and trusted in the lying idol,[b]
26 I now will strip off your skirts from you,
so that your shame will appear.[c]

o Prv 16, 18. p Jer 2, 20; 7, 24; 16, 11. q Ex 19, 5; Dt 26, 18f. r Jer 25, 15–18; Is 51, 17. s Jer 19, 10f. t Prv 4, 18f; Is 5, 30; Am 8, 9. u Jer 14, 17; Ps 119, 136. v Jer 22, 26; 2 Kgs 24, 12. 15. w Jer 6, 22f. x 2 Kgs 16, 7. y Is 47, 2f. z Ps 55, 20. a Pss 1, 4; 83, 14. b Jb 20, 29. c Ez 16, 32.

[27]Your adulteries, your neighings,
your shameless prostitutions:
On the hills in the highlands
I see these horrible crimes of yours.
Woe to you, Jerusalem, how long will it yet be
before you become clean! [d]

CHAPTER 14

The Great Drought [1]The word of the LORD that came to Jeremiah concerning the drought: [e]

[2]Judah mourns,
her gates are lifeless;
Her people sink down in mourning:
from Jerusalem ascends a cry of anguish.[f]
[3]The nobles send their servants for water,
but when they come to the cisterns
They find no water
and return with empty jars. [g]
Ashamed, despairing, they cover their heads
[4] because of the stricken soil;
Because there is no rain in the land
the farmers are ashamed, they cover their
heads. [h]
[5]Even the hind in the field deserts her offspring
because there is no grass.
[6]The wild asses stand on the bare heights,
gasping for breath like jackals;
Their eyes grow dim,
because there is no vegetation to be seen.
[7]Even though our crimes bear witness against
us,
take action, O LORD, for the honor of your
name—
Even though our rebellions are many,
though we have sinned against you. [i]
[8]O Hope of Israel, O LORD,
our savior in time of need!
Why should you be a stranger in this land,
like a traveler who has stopped but for a
night?
[9]Why are you like a man dumbfounded,
a champion who cannot save?
You are in our midst, O LORD,
your name we bear:
do not forsake us! [j]

[10] Thus says the LORD of this people:
They so love to wander
that they do not spare their feet.
The LORD has no pleasure in them;
now he remembers their guilt,
and will punish their sins. [k]

[11]Then the LORD said to me: Do not intercede
for this people. [l] [12]If they fast, I will not listen to
their supplication. If they offer holocausts or
cereal offerings, I will not accept them. Rather, I
will destroy them with the sword, famine, and
pestilence. [m]
[13]Ah! Lord GOD, I replied, it is the prophets
who say to them, "You shall not see the sword;
famine shall not befall you. Indeed, I will give
you lasting peace in this place." [n]
[14]Lies these prophets utter in my name, the
LORD said to me. I did not send them; I gave
them no command nor did I speak to them.
Lying visions, foolish divination, dreams of their
own imagination, they prophesy to you. [o]
[15]Therefore, thus says the LORD: Concerning the
prophets who prophesy in my name, though I
did not send them; who say, "Sword and famine
shall not befall this land": by the sword and
famine shall these prophets meet their end. [p]
[16]The people to whom they prophesy shall be
cast out into the streets of Jerusalem by famine
and the sword. No one shall bury them, their
wives, their sons, or their daughters, for I will
pour out upon them their own wickedness. [q]
[17]Speak to them this word:

Let my eyes stream with tears
day and night, without rest,
Over the great destruction which overwhelms
the virgin daughter of my people,
over her incurable wound. [r]
[18]If I walk out into the field,
look! those slain by the sword;
If I enter the city,
look! those consumed by hunger.
Even the prophet and the priest
forage in a land they know not.

[19]Have you cast Judah off completely?

d Jer 2, 20. e Lv 26, 19f. f Is 3, 26. g Am 4, 8. h Dt 28, 23. i Dn 9, 4–14. j Is 59, 1f; 63, 19. k Jer 2, 25. l Jer 11, 14; Ex 32, 10. m Jer 6, 20; Is 1, 11. 13. n Jer 4, 10; 5, 12. o Jer 5, 31; 23, 16. p Jer 5, 12f. q Jer 7, 33; 19, 7. r Jer 9, 17.

Is Zion loathsome to you?
Why have you struck us a blow
that cannot be healed?
We wait for peace, to no avail;
for a time of healing, but terror comes
instead.[s]
20 We recognize, O LORD, our wickedness,
the guilt of our fathers;
that we have sinned against you.[t]
21 For your name's sake spurn us not,
disgrace not the throne of your glory;
remember your covenant with us, and
break it not.[u]
22 Among the nations' idols is there any that
gives rain?
Or can the mere heavens send showers?
Is it not you alone, O LORD,
our God, to whom we look?
You alone have done all these things.[v]

CHAPTER 15

1 The LORD said to me: Even if Moses and Samuel stood before me, my heart would not turn toward this people. Send them away from me.[w] 2 If they ask you where they should go, tell them, Thus says the LORD: Whoever is marked for death, to death; whoever is marked for the sword, to the sword; whoever is marked for famine, to famine; whoever is marked for captivity, to captivity.[x] 3 Four kinds of scourge I have decreed against them, says the LORD: the sword to slay them; dogs to drag them about; the birds of the sky and the beasts of the earth to devour and destroy them.[y] 4 And I will make them an object of horror to all the kingdoms of the earth because of what Manasseh, son of Hezekiah, king of Judah, did in Jerusalem.[z]

Scene of Tragedy

5 Who will pity you, Jerusalem,
who will console you?
Who will stop to ask
about your welfare?[a]
6 You have disowned me, says the LORD,
turned your back upon me;
And so I stretched out my hand to destroy you,
I was weary of sparing you.[b]
7 I winnowed them with the fan
in every city gate.
I destroyed my people through bereavement;
they returned not from their evil ways.[c]
8 Their widows were more numerous before me
than the sands of the sea.
I brought against the mother of youths
the spoiler at midday;
Suddenly I struck her
with anguish and terror.
9 The mother of seven swoons away,
gasping out her life;
Her sun sets in full day,
she is disgraced, despairing.
Their survivors I will give to the sword
before their enemies, says the LORD.[d]

Jeremiah's Complaint

10 Woe to me, mother, that you gave me birth!
a man of strife and contention to all the
land!
I neither borrow nor lend,
yet all curse me.[e]
11 Tell me, LORD, have I not served you for their
good?
Have I not interceded with you
in the time of misfortune and anguish?[f] *
15 You know I have.
Remember me, LORD, visit me,
and avenge me on my persecutors.
Because of your long-suffering banish me not;
know that for you I have borne insult.[g]
16 When I found your words, I devoured them;
they became my joy and the happiness of
my heart,
Because I bore your name,
O LORD, God of hosts.
17 I did not sit celebrating
in the circle of merrymakers;
Under the weight of your hand I sat alone
because you filled me with indignation.[h]

15, 12–14: These verses are omitted because v 12 is a dittography of 17, 1. Verses 13–14 are a dittography of 17, 3f.

s Jer 8, 15; 2 Chr 36, 16. t Ps 106, 6; Dn 9, 5. 8. u Jer 14, 7; Lv 26, 44; Ps 25, 11. v Jer 5, 24; Zec 10, 1. w Ps 99, 6; Ez 14, 14. 16. x Jer 14, 12; Ez 5, 12. y Ez 14, 21. z Jer 24, 9; 2 Kgs 21, 11–16; 23, 26; 24, 3f. a Is 51, 19. b Am 7, 8. c Is 41, 16. d 1 Sm 2, 5. e Jer 20, 14. f Jer 39, 11–14. g Jer 11, 20; 12, 3; Ps 69, 8. h Ps 25, 4.

18 Why is my pain continuous,
my wound incurable, refusing to be healed?
You have indeed become for me a treacherous brook,*
whose waters do not abide![i]
19 Thus the LORD answered me:
If you repent, so that I restore you,
in my presence you shall stand;
If you bring forth the precious without the vile,
you shall be my mouthpiece.
Then it shall be they who turn to you,
and you shall not turn to them;
20 And I will make you toward this people
a solid wall of brass.
Though they fight against you,
they shall not prevail,
For I am with you,
to deliver and rescue you, says the LORD.[j]
21 I will free you from the hand of the wicked,
and rescue you from the grasp of the violent.

CHAPTER 16

Jeremiah's Life a Warning 1 This message
came to me from the LORD: 2 Do not marry any
woman; you shall not have sons or daughters in
this place, 3 for thus says the LORD concerning
the sons and daughters who will be born in this
place, the mothers who will give them birth, the
fathers who will beget them in this land: 4 Of
deadly disease they shall die. Unlamented and
unburied they will lie like dung on the ground.
Sword and famine will make an end of them,
and their corpses will become food for the birds
of the sky and the beasts of the field.[k]
5 Go not into a house of mourning, the LORD
continued: go not there to lament or offer sympa-
thy. For I have withdrawn my friendship from this
people, says the LORD, my kindness and my pity.[l]
6 They shall die, the great and the lowly, in this
land, and shall go unburied and unlamented.* No
one will gash himself or shave his head for
them.[m] 7 They will not break bread with the be-
reaved to console them in their bereavement;
they will not give them the cup of consolation to
drink over the death of father or mother.[n]
8 Enter not a house where people are celebrat-
ing, to sit with them eating and drinking. 9 For
thus says the LORD of hosts, the God of Israel:
Before your very eyes and during your lifetime I
will silence from this place the cry of joy and the
cry of gladness, the voice of the bridegroom and
the voice of the bride.[o]
10 When you proclaim all these words to this
people and they ask you: "Why has the LORD
pronounced all these great evils against us? What
is our crime? What sin have we committed
against the LORD, our God?"[p] — 11 [q]you shall
answer them: It is because your fathers have for-
saken me, says the LORD, and followed strange
gods, which they served and worshiped; but me
they have forsaken, and my law they have not
observed. 12 And you have done worse than your
fathers. Here you are, every one of you, walking
in the hardness of his evil heart instead of listen-
ing to me.[r] 13 I will cast you out of this land into a
land that neither you nor your fathers have
known; there you can serve strange gods day and
night, because I will not grant you my mercy.
Return from Exile 14 However, days will surely
come, says the LORD, when it will no longer be
said, "As the LORD lives, who brought the
Israelites out of Egypt";[s] 15 but rather, "As the
LORD lives, who brought the Israelites out of the
land of the north and out of all the countries to
which he had banished them." I will bring them
back to the land which I gave their fathers.[t]
Double Punishment 16 Look! I will send many
fishermen, says the LORD, to catch them. After
that, I will send many hunters to hunt them out
from every mountain and hill and from the clefts
of the rocks.[u] 17 For my eyes are upon all their
ways; they are not hidden from me, nor does
their guilt escape my view.[v] 18 I will at once

15, 18: A treacherous brook: that dries up when its waters are needed. The prophet complains that he cannot rely on God with unfailing assurance of his assistance.

16, 6f: These verses refer to popular mourning practices, sometimes connected with pagan superstition; cf Dt 14, 1f.

i Jer 14, 19; 30, 15. j Jer 1, 18; 6, 27. k Jer 7, 33; 22, 18. l Ez 24, 16f. m Lv 19, 28; Dt 14, 1. n Ez 24, 17. o Jer 7, 34; 25, 10. p Jer 2, 35; 5, 19; 13, 22. q Jer 22, 9; Dt 29, 25. r Jer 7, 24ff. s Jer 23, 7f. t Jer 24, 6. u 2 Kgs 24, 2; Lam 4, 19. v Jer 32, 19; Jb 34, 21.

repay them double for their crime and their sin of profaning my land with their detestable corpses of idols, and filling my heritage with their abominations. [w]

Conversion of the Heathen

19 O LORD, my strength, my fortress,
my refuge in the day of distress!
To you will the nations come
from the ends of the earth, and say,
"Mere frauds are the heritage of our fathers,
empty idols of no use." [x]
20 Can man make for himself gods?
These are not gods. [y]
21 Look, then: I will give them knowledge;
this time I will leave them in no doubt
Of my strength and my power:
they shall know that my name is LORD. [z]

CHAPTER 17

The Sin of Judah and Its Punishment

1 The sin of Judah is written
with an iron stylus,
Engraved with a diamond point
upon the tablets of their hearts. [a]

[And the horns of their altars, 2 when their sons
remember their altars and their sacred poles,
beside the green trees, on the high hills, 3 the
peaks in the highland.]

Your wealth and all your treasures
I will give as spoil.
In recompense for all your sins
throughout your borders,
4 You will relinquish your hold on your heritage
which I have given you.
I will enslave you to your enemies
in a land that you know not:
For a fire has been kindled by my wrath
that will burn forever. [b]

True Wisdom

5 Thus says the LORD:
Cursed is the man who trusts in human beings,
who seeks his strength in flesh,
whose heart turns away from the LORD. [c]
6 He is like a barren bush in the desert
that enjoys no change of season,
But stands in a lava waste,
a salt and empty earth.
7 Blessed is the man who trusts in the LORD,
whose hope is the LORD. [d]
8 He is like a tree planted beside the waters
that stretches out its roots to the stream:
It fears not the heat when it comes,
its leaves stay green;
In the year of drought it shows no distress,
but still bears fruit. [e]
9 More tortuous than all else is the human heart,
beyond remedy; who can understand it?
10 I, the LORD, alone probe the mind
and test the heart,
To reward everyone according to his ways,
according to the merit of his deeds. [f]
11 A partridge that mothers a brood not her own
is the man who acquires wealth unjustly:
In midlife it will desert him;
in the end he is only a fool. [g]

The Source of Life

12 A throne of glory, exalted from the beginning,
such is our holy place. [h]
13 O hope of Israel, O LORD!
all who forsake you shall be in disgrace;
The rebels in the land shall be put to shame;
they have forsaken the source of living waters
[the LORD]. [i]

Prayer for Vengeance

14 Heal me, LORD, that I may be healed;
save me, that I may be saved,
for it is you whom I praise.
15 See how they say to me,
"Where is the word of the LORD?
Let it come to pass!" [j]
16 Yet I did not press you to send calamity;
the day without remedy I have not desired.
You know what passed my lips;
it is present before you.

w Is 40, 2. x Jer 2, 11; Is 2, 2f. y Jer 2, 11; Gal 4, 8. z Am 5, 8. a Jb 19, 24. b Jer 5, 19; Dt 32, 22. c Ps 146, 2f. d Ps 1, 3. e Is 58, 11. f Jer 32, 19; 1 Sm 16, 7; Eccl 12, 14. g Prv 13, 11; Lk 12, 20. h Jer 14, 21. i Jer 2, 13. j Is 5, 19; 2 Pt 3, 4.

17 Do not be my ruin,
you, my refuge in the day of misfortune.[k]
18 Let my persecutors, not me, be confounded;
let them, not me, be broken.
Bring upon them the day of misfortune,
crush them with repeated destruction.[l]

Observance of the Sabbath 19 Thus said the
LORD to me: Go, stand at the Gate of Benjamin,*
where the kings of Judah enter and leave, and at
the other gates of Jerusalem.[m] 20 There say to
them: Hear the word of the LORD, you kings of
Judah, and all Judah, and all you citizens of
Jerusalem who enter these gates! 21 Thus says the
LORD: As you love your lives, take care not to
carry burdens on the sabbath day, to bring them
in through the gates of Jerusalem.[n] 22 Bring no
burden from your homes on the sabbath. Do no
work whatever, but keep holy the sabbath, as I
commanded your fathers,[o] 23 though they did
not listen or give ear, but stiffened their necks so
as not to hear or take correction.[p] 24 If you obey
me wholeheartedly, says the LORD, and carry no
burden through the gates of this city on the
sabbath, keeping the sabbath holy and abstaining
from all work on it,[q] 25 then, through the gates of
this city, kings who sit upon the throne of David
will continue to enter, riding in their chariots or
upon their horses, along with their princes, and
the men of Judah, and the citizens of Jerusalem.
This city will remain inhabited forever.[r] 26 To it
people will come from the cities of Judah and the
neighborhood of Jerusalem, from the land of
Benjamin and from the foothills, from the hill
country and the Negeb, to bring holocausts and
sacrifices, cereal offerings and incense and thank
offerings to the house of the LORD.[s] 27 But if you
do not obey me and keep holy the sabbath, if you
carry burdens and come through the gates of
Jerusalem on the sabbath, I will set unquench-
able fire to its gates, which will consume the
palaces of Jerusalem.[t]

CHAPTER 18

The Potter's Vessel* 1 This word came to
Jeremiah from the LORD: 2 Rise up, be off to the
potter's house; there I will give you my message.
3 I went down to the potter's house and there he
was, working at the wheel. 4 Whenever the
object of clay which he was making turned out
badly in his hand, he tried again, making of the
clay another object of whatever sort he pleased.[u]
5 Then the word of the Lord came to me: 6 Can I
not do to you, house of Israel, as this potter has
done? says the LORD. Indeed, like clay in the
hand of the potter, so are you in my hand, house
of Israel.[v] 7 [w]Sometimes I threaten to uproot and
tear down and destroy a nation or a kingdom.
8 But if that nation which I have threatened turns
from its evil, I also repent of the evil which I
threatened to do.[x] 9 Sometimes, again, I promise
to build up and plant a nation or a kingdom.
10 But if that nation does what is evil in my eyes,
refusing to obey my voice, I repent of the good
with which I promised to bless it.[y]

11 And now, tell this to the men of Judah and
the citizens of Jerusalem: Thus says the LORD:
Take care! I am fashioning evil against you and
making a plan. Return, each of you, from his evil
way; reform your ways and your deeds.[z] 12 But
they will say, "No use! We will follow our own
devices; each one of us will behave according to
the stubbornness of his evil heart!"[a]

Judah's Apostasy Unnatural

13 Therefore thus says the LORD:
Ask among the nations—
who has ever heard the like?
Truly horrible things
has virgin Israel done![b]
14 Does the snow of Lebanon*
desert the rocky heights?
Do the gushing waters dry up
that flow fresh down the mountains?

17, 19: The Gate of Benjamin: probably the northern gate of the temple area and city wall of Jerusalem; cf Jer 20, 2; 37, 12; 38, 7.

18, 1–12: The lesson of the potter is not that God deals arbitrarily with his people, but that he is almighty to destroy or restore, accordingly as they disobey him or fulfill his plans.

18, 14: Lebanon: here apparently including Mount Hermon, whose snow-capped peak can be seen from parts of Palestine all year round. The prophet contrasts the certainties of nature with Israel's unnatural desertion of the Lord for idols (v 15).

k Jer 16, 19. l Jer 15, 15; 18, 20–23; Ps 35, 5f. m Jer 7, 2. n Neh 13, 15–19. o Ex 20, 8; 23, 12. p Jer 5, 3; 7, 24. q Is 58, 14. r Jer 22, 4. s Jer 32, 44. t Ez 22, 8. u Rom 9, 20f. v Wis 15, 7; Is 45, 9. w Jer 1, 10. x Jer 26, 3; Is 55, 7; Ez 18, 21. 27. y Nm 14, 22f. z Jer 7, 3; 25, 5; 35, 15. a Jer 2, 25; 7, 24. b Jer 2, 10f; 5, 30.

15 Yet my people have forgotten me:
they burn incense to a thing that does not exist.
They stumble out of their ways,
the paths of old,
To travel on bypaths,
not the beaten track.[c]
16 Their land shall be turned into a desert,
an object of lasting ridicule:
All passers-by will be amazed,
will shake their heads.[d]
17 Like the east wind, I will scatter them
before their enemies;
I will show them my back, not my face,
in their day of disaster.[e]

Another Prayer for Vengeance 18 "Come,"
they said, "let us contrive a plot against Jere-
miah. It will not mean the loss of instruction
from the priests, nor of counsel from the wise,
nor of messages from the prophets. And so, let us
destroy him by his own tongue; let us carefully
note his every word."[f]

19 Heed me, O LORD,
and listen to what my adversaries say.
20 Must good be repaid with evil
that they should dig a pit to take my life?
Remember that I stood before you
to speak in their behalf,
to turn away your wrath from them.[g]
21 So now, deliver their children to famine,[h]
do away with them by the sword.
Let their wives be made childless and widows;
let their men die of pestilence,
their young men be slain by the sword in battle.*
22 May cries be heard from their homes,
when suddenly you send plunderers against them.
For they have dug a pit to capture me,
they have hid snares for my feet;
23 But you, O LORD, know
all their plans to slay me.
Forgive not their crime,
blot not out their sin in your sight!
Let them go down before you,
proceed against them in the time of your anger.[i]

CHAPTER 19

Symbol of the Potter's Flask 1 Thus said the
LORD: Go, buy a potter's earthen flask. Take
along some of the elders of the people and of the
priests, 2 and go out toward the Valley of Ben-
hinnom, at the entrance of the Potsherd Gate;*
there proclaim the words which I will speak to
you: 3 Listen to the word of the LORD, kings of
Judah and citizens of Jerusalem: Thus says the
LORD of hosts, the God of Israel: I am going to
bring such evil upon this place that all who hear
of it will feel their ears tingle. 4 This is because
they have forsaken me and alienated this place
by burning in it incense to strange gods which
neither they nor their fathers knew; and the
kings of Judah have filled this place with the
blood of the innocent.[j] 5 They have built high
places for Baal to immolate their sons in fire as
holocausts to Baal: such a thing as I neither
commanded nor spoke of, nor did it ever enter
my mind.[k] 6 Therefore, days will come, says the
LORD, when this place will no longer be called
Topheth, or the Valley of Ben-hinnom, but
rather, the Valley of Slaughter.[l] 7 In this place I
will foil the plan of Judah and Jerusalem; I will
make them fall by the sword before their ene-
mies, by the hand of those that seek their lives.
Their corpses I will give as food to the birds of
the sky and the beasts of the field.[m] 8 I will make
this city an object of amazement and derision.
Because of all its wounds, every passer-by will be
amazed and will catch his breath. 9 I will have
them eat the flesh of their sons and daughters;
they shall eat one another's flesh during the
strict siege by which their enemies and those
who seek their lives will confine them.[n]

10 And you shall break the flask in the sight of

18, 21: In the Old Testament a man's family was regarded as part of his personality, to be rewarded or punished along with him; cf Jos 7, 24ff.

19, 2: Potsherd Gate: in the south wall of Jerusalem, through which potsherds and other refuse were carried to the Valley of Ben-hinnom.

c Jer 2, 13. 32. d Jer 19, 8; Lv 26, 32; 1 Kgs 9, 8. e Prv 1, 24–31. f Jer 11, 19; Ps 35, 15f. g Ps 35, 12. h Ps 109, 9f. i Neh 4, 5; Pss 35, 4; 37, 32f. j Jer 1, 16; 2 Kgs 21, 16; 24, 4. k Jer 7, 31f; 32, 35. l Jer 7, 32. m Jer 7, 33. n Lv 26, 29.

the men who went with you, 11and say to them:
Thus says the LORD of hosts: Thus will I smash
this people and this city, as one smashes a clay
pot so that it cannot be repaired. And Topheth
shall be a burial place, for lack of place to bury
elsewhere.[o] 12Thus I will do to this place and to
its inhabitants, says the LORD; I will make this
city like Topheth.[p] 13And the houses of Jerusa-
lem and the palaces of the kings of Judah shall be
defiled like the place of Topheth, all the houses
upon whose roofs they burnt incense to the
whole host of heaven and poured out libations to
strange gods.[q]
14When Jeremiah returned from Topheth,
where the LORD had sent him to prophesy, he
stood in the court of the house of God and said
to all the people:[r] 15Thus says the LORD of hosts,
the God of Israel: I will surely bring upon this
city all the evil with which I threatened it,
because they have stiffened their necks and have
not obeyed my words.[s]

CHAPTER 20

1Jeremiah was heard prophesying these things
by the priest Pashhur,[t] son of Immer, chief
officer in the house of the LORD.* 2So he had the
prophet scourged and placed in the stocks at the
upper Gate of Benjamin in the house of the
LORD.[u] 3The next morning, after Pashhur had
released Jeremiah from the stocks, the prophet
said to him:[v] Instead of Pashhur, the LORD will
name you "Terror on every side."* 4For thus
says the LORD: Indeed, I will deliver you to
terror, you and all your friends. Your own eyes
shall see them fall by the sword of their enemies.
All Judah I will deliver to the king of Babylon,*
who shall take them captive to Babylon or slay
them with the sword. 5All the wealth of this city,
all it has toiled for and holds dear, all the
treasures of the kings of Judah, I will give as
plunder into the hands of their foes, who shall
seize it and carry it away to Babylon.[w] 6You,
Pashhur, and all the members of your household
shall go into exile. To Babylon you shall go, you
and all your friends; there you shall die and be
buried, because you have prophesied lies to
them.[x]

Jeremiah's Interior Crisis

7You duped me,* O LORD, and I let myself be
duped;
you were too strong for me, and you
triumphed.
All the day I am an object of laughter;
everyone mocks me.
8Whenever I speak, I must cry out,
violence and outrage is my message;
The word of the LORD has brought me
derision and reproach all the day.
9I say to myself, I will not mention him,
I will speak in his name no more.
But then it becomes like fire burning in my
heart,
imprisoned in my bones;
I grow weary holding it in,
I cannot endure it.[y]
10Yes, I hear the whisperings of many:
"Terror on every side!
Denounce! let us denounce him!"
All those who were my friends
are on the watch for any misstep of mine.
"Perhaps he will be trapped; then we can
prevail,
and take our vengeance on him."[z]
11But the LORD is with me, like a mighty
champion:
my persecutors will stumble, they will not
triumph.
In their failure they will be put to utter shame,
to lasting, unforgettable confusion.[a]
12O LORD of hosts, you who test the just,
who probe mind and heart,

20, 1: Chief officer in the house of the Lord: head of the temple police; cf Jer 29, 26. By entering the temple court (Jer 19, 14), Jeremiah had put himself under Pashhur's jurisdiction.

20, 3: Terror on every side: Pashhur will share the fate of doomed Jerusalem and will experience personally all that the people as a whole have had to endure.

20, 4: Babylon: mentioned here for the first time as the land of exile. The prophecy probably dates from after 605 B.C., when Nebuchadnezzar defeated Egypt and made the Chaldean empire dominant in Syria and Palestine.

20, 7: You duped me: to be understood in the light of Jeremiah's intimate dealings with God; cf Jer 15, 18.

o Jer 7, 32. p 2 Kgs 23, 10. q Jer 32, 29. r Jer 26, 2. s Jer 7, 26; Prv 29, 1. t Jer 21, 1. u Jer 29, 26. v Jer 6, 25. w 2 Kgs 20, 17; 24, 12–16. x Jer 14, 13f; 28, 15. y Jer 6, 11; Jb 32, 18. z Jb 19, 19; Ps 31, 13; Lk 20, 20. a Jer 1, 8; 15, 20.

Let me witness the vengeance you take on
them,
for to you I have entrusted my cause. [b]
13 Sing to the LORD,
praise the LORD,
For he has rescued the life of the poor
from the power of the wicked! [c]

14 Cursed be the day*
on which I was born!
May the day my mother gave me birth
never be blessed! [d]
15 Cursed be the man who brought the news
to my father, saying,
"A child, a son, has been born to you!"
filling him with great joy.
16 Let that man be like the cities
which the LORD relentlessly overthrew;
Let him hear war cries in the morning,
battle alarms at noonday, [e]
17 because he did not dispatch me in the
womb!
Then my mother would have been my grave,
her womb confining me forever. [f]
18 Why did I come forth from the womb,
to see sorrow and pain,
to end my days in shame? [g]

III: Oracles in the Last Years of Jerusalem

CHAPTER 21

Fate of Zedekiah and Jerusalem 1 The mes-
sage which came to Jeremiah from the LORD
when King Zedekiah* sent him Pashhur, son of
Malchiah, and the priest Zephaniah, son of
Maaseiah, with this request: 2 Inquire for us of
the LORD, because Nebuchadnezzar, king of
Babylon, is attacking us. Perhaps the LORD will
deal with us according to all his wonderful
works, so that he will withdraw from us. 3 But
Jeremiah answered them: This is what you shall
report to Zedekiah: 4 Thus says the LORD, the
God of Israel: I will turn back in your hands the
weapons with which you intend to fight the king
of Babylon and the Chaldeans who besiege you
outside the walls. These weapons I will pile up
in the midst of this city, [h] 5 and I myself will fight
against you with outstretched hand and mighty
arm, in anger, and wrath, and great rage! [i] 6 I will
strike the inhabitants of this city, both man and
beast; they shall die in a great pestilence. [j] 7 After
that, says the LORD, I will hand over Zedekiah,
king of Judah, and his ministers and the people
in this city who survive pestilence, sword, and
famine, into the hand of Nebuchadnezzar, king
of Babylon, into the hands of their enemies and
those who seek their lives. He shall strike them
with the edge of the sword, without quarter,
without pity or mercy. [k] 8 And to this people you
shall say: Thus says the LORD: See, I am giving
you a choice between life and death. [l] 9 Whoever
remains in this city shall die by the sword or
famine or pestilence. But whoever leaves and
surrenders to the besieging Chaldeans shall live
and have his life as booty. 10 For I have turned
against this city, for its woe and not for its good,
says the LORD. It shall be given into the power of
the king of Babylon who shall burn it with fire.*

Oracles regarding the Kings

11 To the royal house of Judah:*
Hear the word of the LORD, 12 O house of
David!
Thus says the LORD:
Each morning dispense justice,
rescue the oppressed from the hand of the
oppressor,
Lest my fury break out like fire
which burns without being quenched,

20, 14–18: Deception, sorrow and terror have brought the prophet close to the point of despair; nevertheless he has expressed his utmost confidence in the triumph of God's will (vv 11ff); cf Jb 3, 3–12.

21, 1: Zedekiah: brother of Jehoiakim, appointed king by Nebuchadnezzar after he had carried Jehoiachin away to captivity (2 Kgs 24, 17). Passhur: different from the one in Jer 20, 1ff but also one of Jeremiah's enemies; cf Jer 38, 1. 4.

21, 10: Jeremiah consistently pointed out the uselessness of resistance to Babylon, since the Lord had delivered Judah to Nebuchadnezzar (Jer 27, 6). Because of this the prophet was denounced and imprisoned as a traitor (Jer 37, 13f).

21, 11—23, 8: This section contains an editor's collection of Jeremiah's oracles against the kings of Judah. They are placed in the chronological order of the kings, and are prefaced by the oracles against the kings of Judah in general (Jer 21, 11—22, 9).

b Jer 11, 20. c Pss 35, 9f; 109, 30f. d Jer 15, 10; Jb 3, 1–10; 10, 18. e Gn 19, 25; Is 13, 19. f Jb 3, 10f; 10, 19. g Jb 14, 1. h Jer 37, 8ff. i Is 63, 10; Lam 2, 4f. j Jer 16, 4. k Jer 24, 8ff; Dt 28, 49f. l Jer 21, 9; Dt 30, 15. 19.

because of the evil of your deeds. [m]
13 Beware! I am against you, Valley-site,
Rock of the Plain,* says the LORD.
You who say, "Who will attack us,
who can penetrate our retreats?"
14 I will punish you, says the LORD,
as your deeds deserve!
I will kindle a fire in its forest*
that shall devour all its surroundings. [n]

CHAPTER 22

1 The LORD told me this: Go down to the
palace of the king of Judah and there deliver this
message: 2 You shall say: Listen to the word of
the LORD, king of Judah, who sit on the throne of
David, you, your ministers, and your people that
enter by these gates! [o] 3 Thus says the LORD: Do
what is right and just. Rescue the victim from
the hand of his oppressor. Do not wrong or
oppress the resident alien, the orphan, or the
widow, and do not shed innocent blood in this
place. [p] 4 If you carry out these commands, kings
who succeed to the throne of David will con-
tinue to enter the gates of this palace, riding in
chariots or mounted on horses, with their minis-
ters, and their people. 5 But if you do not obey
these commands, I swear by myself, says the
LORD: this palace shall become rubble. 6 For thus
says the LORD concerning the palace of the king
of Judah:

Though you be to me like Gilead,
like the peak of Lebanon,*
I will turn you into a waste,
a city uninhabited.
7 Against you I will send destroyers,
each with his axe:
They shall cut down your choice cedars,
and cast them into the fire. [q]

8 Many people will pass by this city and ask
one another: "Why has the LORD done this to so
great a city?" [r] 9 And the answer will be given:
"Because they have deserted their covenant
with the LORD, their God, by worshiping and
serving strange gods." [s]

Jehoahaz

10 Weep not for him who is dead,*
mourn not for him!
Weep rather for him who is going away;
never again will he see
the land of his birth. [t]

11 Thus says the LORD concerning Shallum,*
son of Josiah, king of Judah, who succeeded his
father as king. He has left this place never to
return. 12 Rather, he shall die in the place where
they exiled him; this land he shall not see again.

Jehoiakim

13 Woe to him who builds his house on wrong,
his terraces on injustice;
Who works his neighbor without pay,*
and gives him no wages. [u]
14 Who says, "I will build myself a spacious
house,
with airy rooms,"
Who cuts out windows for it,
panels it with cedar,
and paints it with vermillion.
15 Must you prove your rank among kings*
by competing with them in cedar?
Did not your father eat and drink?
He did what was right and just,
and it went well with him. [v]

21, 13: Valley-site, Rock of the Plain: Mount Zion, surrounded by valleys, was regarded by the royal house as impregnable. Despite this natural fortification, God shows derisively that it is no more than a rock rising from the plain, undefendable against the attack of his fury.

21, 14: Its forest: probably the royal palace, built of cedar wood; cf Jer 22, 14; in 1 Kgs 7, 2 the armory of Solomon's palace is called "the house of the forest of Lebanon."

22, 6: Gilead . . . Lebanon: both were known for their trees; cf v 7.

22, 10: Him who is dead: Josiah. His successor, Jehoahaz, who is going away, was deported by Pharaoh Neco to Egypt, where he died (2 Kgs 23, 33f).

22, 11: Shallum: Jehoahaz is called this only here. Presumably it was his name at birth, while Jehoahaz was his royal name.

22, 13: Without pay: either by forced labor in public works, or in as much as workers were defrauded of their hire. Despite the impoverishment caused in Judah by the payment of foreign tribute, Jehoiakim embarked on a program of lavish building in Jerusalem (v 14). Social injustice is the cause of much of the prophetic condemnation of the kings (v 17).

22, 15f: Josiah, the reforming king, prospered materially without oppressing his people; he embodied all the ideals of kingship.

m Jer 4, 4; 22, 3; Zec 7, 9. n 2 Kgs 25, 9; 2 Chr 36, 19. o Jer 17, 20. p Jer 21, 12; Ex 22, 21–24; Dt 24, 17. q Jer 21, 14. r Dt 29, 24ff. s Jer 19, 4; 40, 2f. t 2 Chr 35, 23ff. u Lv 19, 13; Dt 24, 14; Hb 2, 9. 12. v 2 Kgs 23, 25.

16 Because he dispensed justice to the weak and
the poor,
it went well with him.
Is this not true knowledge of me?
says the LORD.[w]
17 But your eyes and heart are set on nothing
except on your own gain,
On shedding innocent blood,
on practicing oppression and extortion.[x]

18 Therefore, thus says the LORD concerning
Jehoiakim, son of Josiah, king of Judah:

They shall not lament him,
"Alas! my brother"; "Alas! sister."*
They shall not lament him,
"Alas, Lord! alas, Majesty!"[y]
19 The burial of an ass* shall he be given,
dragged forth and cast out
beyond the gates of Jerusalem.[z]

Jeconiah

20 Scale Lebanon and cry out,*
in Bashan lift up your voice;
Cry out from Abarim,
for all your lovers are crushed.[a]
21 I spoke to you when you were secure,
but you answered, "I will not listen."
This has been your way from your youth,
not to listen to my voice.
22 The wind shall shepherd all your shepherds,
your lovers shall go into exile.
Surely then you shall be ashamed and
confounded
because of all your wickedness.
23 You who dwell on Lebanon,
who nest in the cedars,
How you shall groan when pains come upon
you,
like the pangs of a woman in travail!

24 As I live, says the LORD, if you, Coniah,*
son of Jehoiakim, king of Judah, are a signet ring
on my right hand, I will snatch you from it. 25 I
will deliver you into the hands of those who seek
your life; the hands of those whom you fear; the
hands of Nebuchadnezzar, king of Babylon, and
the Chaldeans.[b] 26 I will cast you out, you and
the mother who bore you,* into a different land
from the one you were born in; and there you
shall die.[c] 27 Neither of them shall come back to
the land for which they yearn.[d]

28 Is this man Coniah a vessel despised, to be
broken up,
an instrument that no one wants?
Why are he and his descendants cast out?
why thrown into a land they know not?
29 O land, land, land,
hear the word of the LORD—
30 Thus says the LORD:
[e]Write this man down as one
childless,*
who will never thrive in his lifetime!
No descendant of his shall achieve
a seat on the throne of David
as ruler again over Judah.

22, 18: "Alas! my brother"; "Alas! sister": customary cries of mourning.

22, 19: The burial of an ass: no burial at all, except to be cast outside the city as refuse. This prophecy regards the popular feeling toward Jehoiakim rather than the actual circumstances of his burial. According to 2 Kgs 24, 5 he was buried with his fathers in Jerusalem. However, his grave may have been profaned by Nebuchadnezzar.

22, 20–23: The prophet first apostrophizes Jerusalem, which is bidden to scale Lebanon, Bashan, and Abarim, i.e., the highest surrounding mountains to the north, northeast, and southeast, to gaze on the ruin of its lovers, i.e., the false leaders of Judah, called its shepherds (22); cf Jer 2, 8. The year is 597 B.C., after Nebuchadnezzar's deportation of Jehoiachin. Jerusalem still stands (23), apparently as secure as the heights of Lebanon, but destruction is to follow (cf v 6).

22, 24: Coniah: a shortened form of Jeconiah, the name which Jeremiah gives the king called elsewhere in the Bible Jehoiachin. A signet ring: the seal used by important men—in a sense, their most valuable possession—mounted in a ring worn constantly on the hand. The Lord says that even were Jehoiachin such a precious possession, he would reject him. The words in vv 24–30 date from the short three-month reign of Jehoiachin, before he was carried away by Nebuchadnezzar.

22, 26: You and the mother who bore you: the queen mother held a special position in the monarchy of Judah, and in the Books of Kings she is invariably mentioned by name along with the king (1 Kgs 15, 2; 2 Kgs 18, 2). Jehoiachin did indeed die in Babylon.

22, 30: Childless: Jehoiachin is so considered because none of his descendants will be king. From the Book of Ezekiel, who dates his oracles according to Jehoiachin's fictitious regnal years, it is evident that the people expected Jehoiachin to return. The above prophecy of Jeremiah was uttered to dispel this hope (Jer 28, 4). Of the seven sons born to Jehoiachin in exile, none became king. His grandson Zerubbabel presided for a time over the Jewish community after the return from exile, but not as king.

w Prv 31, 9. x Ez 22, 13. 27. y Jer 16, 4ff; 1 Kgs 13, 30. z Jer 36, 30. a Jer 30, 14f; Dt 32, 49. b Jer 21, 7; 34, 20. c 2 Kgs 24, 15. d Jer 44, 14. e Jer 36, 30; 1 Chr 3, 16f; Mt 1, 12.

CHAPTER 23

Messianic Reign* 1 [f]Woe to the shepherds
who mislead and scatter the flock of my pasture,
says the LORD. 2 Therefore, thus says the LORD,
the God of Israel, against the shepherds who
shepherd my people: You have scattered my
sheep and driven them away. You have not cared
for them, but I will take care to punish your evil
deeds.[g] 3 I myself will gather the remnant of my
flock from all the lands to which I have driven
them and bring them back to their meadow;
there they shall increase and multiply.[h] 4 I will
appoint shepherds for them who will shepherd
them so that they need no longer fear and
tremble; and none shall be missing, says the
LORD.[i]

5 Behold, the days are coming, says the LORD,
when I will raise up a righteous shoot to
David;
As king he shall reign and govern wisely,
he shall do what is just and right in the
land.[j]
6 In his days Judah shall be saved,
Israel shall dwell in security.
This is the name they give him:
"The LORD our justice."[k]

7 [l]Therefore, the days will come, says the
LORD, when they shall no longer say, "As the
LORD lives, who brought the Israelites out of the
land of Egypt"; 8 but rather, "As the LORD lives,
who brought the descendants of the house of
Israel up from the land of the north"—and from
all the lands to which I banished them; they
shall again live on their own land.

The False Prophets*

9 Concerning the prophets:
My heart within me is broken,
my bones all tremble;
I am like a man who is drunk,
overcome by wine,
Because of the LORD,
because of his holy words.
10 With adulterers the land is filled;
on their account the land mourns,
the pasture ranges are seared.[m]
Theirs is an evil course,
theirs is unjust power.
11 Both prophet and priest are godless!
In my very house I find their wickedness,
says the LORD.[n]
12 Hence their way shall become for them
slippery ground.
In the darkness they shall lose their footing,
and fall headlong;
Evil I will bring upon them:
the year of their punishment, says the
LORD.[o]
13 Among Samaria's prophets
I saw unseemly deeds:
They prophesied by Baal
and led my people Israel astray.[p]
14 But among Jerusalem's prophets
I saw deeds still more shocking:
Adultery, living in lies,
siding with the wicked,
so that no one turns from evil;
To me they are all like Sodom,
its citizens like Gomorrah.[q]

15 Therefore, thus says the LORD of hosts
against the prophets:

Behold, I will give them wormwood to eat,
and poison to drink;
For from Jerusalem's prophets
ungodliness has gone forth into the whole
land.[r]
16 Thus says the LORD of hosts:

23, 1–8: With the false rulers who have governed his people the Lord contrasts himself, the good shepherd, who will in the times of restoration appoint worthy rulers (1–4). A messianic King will arise from the line of David who will rule over Judah and Israel with the justice of the Lord, fulfilling all the kingly ideals (5f). "The Lord our justice" is probably an ironic wordplay on the name of the weak King Zedekiah ("The Lord is justice"); the messianic King will be in reality what Zedekiah's name falsely proclaims him. The final verses, 7–8, were probably added during the exile.

23, 9–40: After the collection of oracles against the kings, the editor of the book placed this collection of oracles against the false prophets. With them are associated the priests, for both have betrayed their trust as instructors in the religion of the Lord; cf Jer 2, 8; 4, 9; 6, 13f.

f Jer 22, 22. g Ez 34, 4ff; Zec 11, 16f. h Jer 29, 14; 32, 37. i Jer 3, 15; Ez 34, 11f. j Jer 33, 14ff; Is 4, 2; 9, 5f; 11, 1–5. k Dn 9, 24. l 7f: Jer 16, 14f. m Jer 4, 22; 5, 7f; 9, 2. 10. n Jer 6, 13. o Ps 35, 6. p 1 Kgs 18, 19. q Jer 29, 21ff; Is 1, 9f. r Jer 8, 14; 9, 14.

bring them against this land, against its inhabitants, and against all these neighboring nations. I will doom them, making them an object of horror, of ridicule, of everlasting reproach.[q] 10 Among them I will bring to an end the song of joy and the song of gladness, the voice of the bridegroom and the voice of the bride, the sound of the millstone and the light of the lamp. 11 This whole land shall be a ruin and a desert. Seventy years these nations shall be enslaved to the king of Babylon;[r] 12 but when the seventy years have elapsed, I will punish the king of Babylon and the nation and the land of the Chaldeans for their guilt, says the LORD. Their land I will turn into everlasting desert.[s] 13 Against that land I will fulfill all the words I have spoken against it [all that is written in this book, which Jeremiah prophesied against all the nations]. 14 They also shall be enslaved to great nations and mighty kings, and thus I will repay them according to their own deeds and according to their own handiwork.[t]

The Cup of Judgment on the Nations 15 For thus said the LORD, the God of Israel, to me:* Take this cup of foaming wine from my hand, and have all the nations to whom I will send you drink it.[u] 16 They shall drink, and be convulsed, and go mad, because of the sword I will send among them.[v] 17 I took the cup from the hand of the LORD and gave drink to all the nations to which the LORD sent me: 18 [Jerusalem, the cities of Judah, her kings and her princes, to make them a ruin and a desert, an object of ridicule and cursing, as they are today;] 19 Pharaoh, king of Egypt, and his servants, his princes, all the people under him, native 20 and foreign; all the kings of the land of Uz;* all the kings of the land of the Philistines: Ashkelon, Gaza, Ekron, and the remnant of Ashdod; 21 Edom, Moab, and the Ammonites; 22 all the kings of Tyre, of Sidon, and of the shores beyond the sea;* 23 Dedan and Tema and Buz,* all the desert dwellers who shave their temples; 24 [all the kings of Arabia;] 25 all the kings of Zimri, of Elam, of the Medes; 26 all the kings of the north, near and far, one after the other; all the kingdoms upon the face of the earth [and after them the king of Sheshach* shall drink].

27 Tell them: Thus says the LORD of hosts, the God of Israel: Drink! become drunk and vomit; fall, never to rise, before the sword that I will send among you![w] 28 If they refuse to take the cup from your hand and drink, say to them: Thus says the LORD of hosts: You must drink![x] 29 For since with this city, which is called by my name, I begin to inflict evil, how can you possibly be spared? You shall not be spared! I will call down the sword upon all who inhabit the earth, says the LORD of hosts.

30 Prophesy against them all these things and say to them:

The LORD roars from on high,
from his holy dwelling he raises his voice;
Mightily he roars over the range,
a shout like that of vintagers over the grapes.[y]
31 To all who inhabit the earth to its very ends
the uproar spreads;
For the LORD has an indictment against the nations,
he is to pass judgment upon all mankind:
The godless shall be given to the sword,
says the LORD.
32 Thus says the LORD of hosts:
Lo! calamity stalks
from nation to nation;
A great storm is unleashed
from the ends of the earth.

33 On that day, those whom the LORD has slain will be strewn from one end of the earth to the other. None will mourn them, none will gather

25, 15ff: Jeremiah is a prophet to the nations (cf 1, 5) as well as to his own people. All the nations mentioned here appear again in the more extensive collection of Jeremiah's oracles against the nations in chapters 46–51.

25, 20: Uz: the homeland of Job, in Edomite or Arabian territory.

25, 22: The shores beyond the sea: Phoenician commercial colonies planted throughout the Mediterranean world.

25, 23: Dedan and Tema and Buz: North Arabian tribes.

25, 26: Sheshach: Babylon. The word is formed from babel by substituting letters of the Hebrew alphabet in inverse order.

q Jer 1, 15; 43, 10. r Lv 26, 32–35. s Is 13, 20ff. t Jer 27, 7; 50, 9. 41f; 51, 6. 24. u Rv 14, 10. v Jer 51, 7. w Ob 1, 16. x Jer 49, 12. y Jer 51, 14.

them for burial; they shall lie like dung on the
field.[z]

34 Howl, you shepherds, and wail!
roll in the dust, leaders of the flock!
The time for your slaughter has come;
like choice rams you shall fall.
35 There is no flight for the shepherds,
no escape for the leaders of the flock.[a]
36 Listen! Wailing from the shepherds,
howling by the leaders of the flock!
For the LORD lays waste their grazing place,
37 desolate lie the peaceful pastures;
38 The lion leaves his lair,
and their land is made desolate
By the sweeping sword,
by the burning wrath of the LORD.[b]

CHAPTER 26

Jeremiah Threatened with Death 1In the
beginning of the reign* of Jehoiakim, son of
Josiah, king of Judah, this message came from
the LORD: 2Thus says the LORD: Stand in the
court of the house of the LORD and speak to the
people of all the cities of Judah who come to
worship in the house of the LORD; whatever I
command you, tell them, and omit nothing.[c]
3Perhaps they will listen and turn back, each
from his evil way, so that I may repent of the evil
I have planned to inflict upon them for their evil
deeds.[d] 4Say to them: Thus says the LORD: If
you disobey me, not living according to the law I
placed before you 5and not listening to the
words of my servants the prophets, whom I send
you constantly though you do not obey them,[e]
6I will treat this house like Shiloh, and make this
the city which all the nations of the earth shall
refer to when cursing another.[f]

7Now the priests, the prophets, and all the
people heard Jeremiah speak these words in the
house of the LORD. 8When Jeremiah finished
speaking all that the LORD bade him speak to all
the people, the priests and prophets laid hold of
him, crying, "You must be put to death! 9Why
do you prophesy in the name of the LORD: 'This
house shall be like Shiloh,' and 'This city shall be
desolate and deserted'?" And all the people
gathered about Jeremiah in the house of the
LORD.

10When the princes of Judah were informed
of these things, they came up from the king's
palace to the house of the LORD and held court
at the New Gate of the house of the LORD. 11The
priests and prophets said to the princes and to all
the people, "This man deserves death; he has
prophesied against this city, as you have heard
with your own ears."[g] 12Jeremiah gave this
answer to the princes and all the people: "It was
the LORD who sent me to prophesy against this
house and city all that you have heard. 13Now,
therefore, reform your ways and your deeds;
listen to the voice of the LORD your God, so that
the LORD will repent of the evil with which he
threatens you.[h] 14As for me, I am in your hands;
do with me what you think good and right.
15But mark well: if you put me to death, it is
innocent blood you bring on yourselves, on this
city and its citizens. For in truth it was the LORD
who sent me to you, to speak all these things for
you to hear."

16Thereupon the princes and all the people
said to the priests and the prophets, "This man
does not deserve death; it is in the name of the
LORD, our God, that he speaks to us." 17At this,
some of the elders of the land came forward and
said to all the people assembled, 18"Micah of
Moresheth* used to prophesy in the days of
Hezekiah, king of Judah, and he told all the
people of Judah: Thus says the LORD of hosts:

Zion shall become a plowed field,
Jerusalem a heap of ruins,
and the temple mount a forest ridge.[i]

19Did Hezekiah, king of Judah, and all Judah
condemn him to death? Did they not rather fear

26, 1: The beginning of the reign: a technical expression for the time between a king's accession to the throne and the beginning of his first official (calendar) year as king. Jehoiakim's first regnal year was 608 B.C.

26, 18: Micah of Moresheth: the prophet Micah, who appears among the canonical minor prophets (cf Mi 1, 1).

z Jer 8, 2; 16, 4. 6. a Jer 32, 4. b Jer 4, 7. c Jer 7, 2. d Jer 18, 3. e Jer 25, 4. f Jer 7, 12. 14. g Jer 38, 4. h Jer 7, 3. i Mi 1, 1; 3, 12.

the LORD and entreat the favor of the LORD, so that he repented of the evil with which he had threatened them? But we are on the point of committing this great evil to our own undoing."[j]

The Fate of Uriah [20]There was another man who prophesied in the name of the LORD, Uriah, son of Shemaiah, from Kiriath-jearim; he prophesied the same things against this city and land as Jeremiah did. [21]When King Jehoiakim and all his officers and princes were informed of his words, the king sought to kill him. But Uriah heard of it and fled in fear to Egypt. [22]Thereupon King Jehoiakim sent Elnathan, son of Achbor, and others with him into Egypt [23]to bring Uriah back to the king, who had him slain by the sword and his corpse cast into the common grave. [24]But Ahikam, son of Shaphan,* protected Jeremiah, so that he was not handed over to the people to be put to death.

CHAPTER 27

Serve Babylon or Perish* [1][In the beginning of the reign of Jehoiakim, son of Josiah, king of Judah,]* . . . this message came to Jeremiah from the LORD: [2]Thus said the LORD to me: Make for yourself bands and yoke bars and put them over your shoulders. [3]Send to the kings of Edom, of Moab, of the Ammonites, of Tyre, and of Sidon, through the ambassadors who have come to Jerusalem to Zedekiah, king of Judah, [4]and charge them thus: Tell your masters: Thus says the LORD of hosts, the God of Israel: [5]It was I who made the earth, and man and beast on the face of the earth, by my great power, with my outstretched arm; and I can give them to whomever I think fit.[k] [6]Now I have given all these lands into the hand of Nebuchadnezzar, king of Babylon, my servant; even the beasts of the field I have given him for his use.[l] [7]All nations shall serve him and his son and his grandson, until the time of his land, too, shall come. Then it in turn shall serve great nations and mighty kings.[m] [8]Meanwhile, if any nation or kingdom will not serve Nebuchadnezzar, king of Babylon, or will not bend its neck under the yoke of the king of Babylon, I will punish that nation with sword, famine, and pestilence, says the LORD, until I give them into his hand.[n]

[9]You, however, must not listen to your prophets,* to your diviners and dreamers, to your soothsayers and sorcerers, who say to you, "You need not serve the king of Babylon."[o] [10]For they prophesy lies to you, in order to drive you far from your land, to make me banish you so that you will perish.[p] [11]The people that submits its neck to the yoke of the king of Babylon to serve him I will leave in peace on its own land, says the LORD, to till it and dwell in it.[q]

[12]To Zedekiah, king of Judah, I spoke the same words: Submit your necks to the yoke of the king of Babylon; serve him and his people, so that you may live.[r] [13]Why should you and your people die by sword, famine, and pestilence, with which the LORD has threatened the nation that will not serve the king of Babylon?[s] [14]Do not listen to the words of those prophets who say, "You need not serve the king of Babylon," for they prophesy lies to you.[t] [15]I did not send them, says the LORD, but they prophesy falsely in my name, with the result that I must banish you, and you will perish, you and the prophets who are prophesying to you.[u]

[16][v]To the priests and to all the people I spoke as follows: Thus says the LORD: Do not listen to the words of your prophets who prophesy to you: "The vessels of the house of the LORD will be brought back from Babylon soon now," for they prophesy lies to you. [17]Do not listen to them! Serve the king of Babylon that you may live; else this city will become a heap of ruins.

26, 24: Ahikam, son of Shaphan: one of Josiah's officials (2 Kgs 22, 12) and father of Gedaliah, Jeremiah's friend, who was governor of Judah after Zedekiah's deportation (cf Jer 39, 14; 40, 5ff).

27, 1—29, 32: A special collection of Jeremiah's prophecies dealing with false prophets. From stylistic peculiarities, quite evident in the Hebrew, it is plain that these three chapters once existed independently of the other prophecies of Jeremiah.

27, 1: [In the beginning of the reign of Jehoiakim . . . Judah]: this gloss cannot be correct because according to Jer 28, 1 the time is the fourth year of Zedekiah, 594 B.C., the occasion of an embassy of the neighboring states (v 3), doubtless for the purpose of laying plans against Nebuchadnezzar.

27, 9: Your prophets: seers and diviners served the Gentile kings as the professional prophets served the kings of Judah.

j 2 Chr 32, 26. k Jer 32, 17. l Jer 25, 9; 43, 10; Ez 30, 21. 25. m Jer 25, 11; 2 Chr 36, 20. n Jer 25, 9; Bar 2, 22. o Jer 29, 8. p Jer 14, 13-16. q Bar 2, 21. r Jer 38, 17. s Jer 24, 8ff. t Jer 14, 14; 23, 21. u Jer 20, 6. v Jer 28, 3; 2 Chr 36, 7. 10. 18.

18 If they were prophets, if the word of the LORD
were with them, they would intercede with the
LORD of hosts, that the vessels which remain in
the house of the LORD and in the palace of the
king of Judah and in Jerusalem might not be
taken to Babylon. 19 *For thus says the LORD of
hosts concerning the pillars, the bronze sea, the
stands, and the rest of the vessels that remain in
this city, 20 which Nebuchadnezzar, king of Baby-
lon, did not take when he exiled Jeconiah, son of
Jehoiakim, king of Judah, from Jerusalem to
Babylon, along with all the nobles of Judah and
Jerusalem— 21 yes, thus says the LORD of hosts,
the God of Israel, concerning the vessels that
remain in the house of the LORD, in the palace of
the king of Judah, and in Jerusalem:[w] 22 To
Babylon they shall be brought, and there they
shall remain, until the day I look for them, says
the LORD; then I will bring them back and
restore them to this place.

CHAPTER 28

The Two Yokes 1 That same year, in [the
beginning of] the reign of Zedekiah, king of
Judah, in the fifth month of the fourth year, the
prophet Hananiah, son of Azzur, from Gibeon,
said to me in the house of the LORD in the
presence of the priests and all the people:
2 "Thus says the LORD of hosts, the God of Israel:
'I will break the yoke of the king of Babylon.
3 Within two years I will restore to this place all
the vessels of the temple of the LORD which
Nebuchadnezzar, king of Babylon, took away
from this place to Babylon. 4 And I will bring
back to this place Jeconiah, son of Jehoiakim,
king of Judah, and all the exiles of Judah who
went to Babylon,' says the LORD, 'for I will break
the yoke of the king of Babylon.' "

5 The prophet Jeremiah answered the prophet
Hananiah in the presence of the priests and all
the people assembled in the house of the LORD,
6 and said: Amen! thus may the LORD do! May he
fulfill the things you have prophesied by bringing
the vessels of the house of the LORD and all the
exiles back from Babylon to this place! 7 But
now, listen to what I am about to state in your
hearing and the hearing of all the people. 8 From
of old, the prophets who were before you and
me prophesied war, woe, and pestilence against
many lands and mighty kingdoms. 9 But the
prophet who prophesies peace is recognized as
truly sent by the LORD only when his prophetic
prediction is fulfilled.[x]

10 Thereupon the prophet Hananiah took the
yoke from the neck of the prophet Jeremiah,
broke it, 11 and said in the presence of all the
people: "Thus says the LORD: 'Even so, within
two years I will break the yoke of Nebuchadnez-
zar, king of Babylon, from off the neck of all the
nations.' " At that, the prophet Jeremiah went
away.

12 Some time after the prophet Hananiah had
broken the yoke from off the neck of the prophet
Jeremiah, the word of the LORD came to Jere-
miah: 13 Go tell Hananiah this: Thus says the
LORD: By breaking a wooden yoke, you forge an
iron yoke! 14 For thus says the LORD of hosts, the
God of Israel: A yoke of iron I will place on the
necks of all these nations serving Nebuchadnez-
zar, king of Babylon, and they shall serve him;
even the beasts of the field I give him.[y]

15 To the prophet Hananiah the prophet Jere-
miah said: Hear this, Hananiah! The LORD has
not sent you, and you have raised false confi-
dence in this people. 16 For this, says the LORD, I
will dispatch you from the face of the earth; this
very year you shall die, because you have
preached rebellion against the LORD.[z] 17 That
same year, in the seventh month, Hananiah the
prophet died.

CHAPTER 29

Letter to the Exiles in Babylon 1 This is the
contents of the letter which the prophet Jere-
miah sent from Jerusalem to the remaining
elders among the exiles, to the priests, the
prophets, and all the people who were exiled by
Nebuchadnezzar from Jerusalem to Babylon.
2 This was after King Jeconiah and the queen
mother, the courtiers, the princes of Judah and
Jerusalem, the artisans and the skilled workmen
had left Jerusalem.[a] 3 Delivered in Babylon by

27, 19–22: This prophecy was fulfilled after Zedekiah's disastrous defeat; cf 2 Kgs 25, 13ff.

w 21f: 2 Kgs 25, 13–17; 2 Chr 36, 18. 22. x Dt 18, 22. y Jer 27, 6f; Dt 28, 48. z Dt 13, 6. a 2 Kgs 24, 15.

Elasah,* son of Shaphan, and by Gemariah, son of Hilkiah, whom Zedekiah, king of Judah, sent to the king of Babylon, the letter read:

4 Thus says the LORD of hosts, the God of Israel, to all the exiles whom I exiled from Jerusalem to Babylon: 5 Build houses to dwell in; plant gardens, and eat their fruits. 6 Take wives and beget sons and daughters; find wives for your sons and give your daughters husbands, so that they may bear sons and daughters. There you must increase in number, not decrease. 7 Promote the welfare of the city to which I have exiled you; pray for it to the LORD, for upon its welfare depends your own.[b]

10 Thus says the LORD: Only after seventy years have elapsed for Babylon will I visit you and fulfill for you my promise to bring you back to this place.[c] 11 For I know well the plans I have in mind for you, says the LORD, plans for your welfare, not for woe! plans to give you a future full of hope. 12 When you call me, when you go to pray to me, I will listen to you.[d] 13 When you look for me, you will find me. Yes, when you seek me with all your heart, 14 you will find me with you, says the LORD, and I will change your lot; I will gather you together from all the nations and all the places to which I have banished you, says the LORD, and bring you back to the place from which I have exiled you.[e]

16 Thus says the LORD concerning the king who sits on David's throne, and all the people who remain in this city, your brethren who did not go with you into exile; 17 thus says the LORD of hosts: I am sending against them sword, famine and pestilence. I will make them like rotten figs, too bad to be eaten. 18 I will pursue them with sword, famine, and pestilence, and make them an object of horror to all the kingdoms of the earth, of malediction, astonishment, ridicule, and reproach to all the nations among which I will banish them.[f] 19 For they did not listen to my words, says the LORD, though I kept sending them my servants the prophets, only to have them go unheeded, says the LORD.[g]

20 You, now, listen to the word of the LORD, all you exiles whom I sent away from Jerusalem to Babylon. 15 As for your saying, "The LORD has raised up for us prophets here in Babylon"— 8 thus says the LORD of hosts, the God of Israel: Do not let yourselves be deceived by the prophets and diviners who are among you; do not listen to those among you who dream dreams.[h] 9 For they prophesy lies to you in my name; I did not send them, says the LORD.[i] 21 This is what the LORD of hosts, the God of Israel, has to say about those who prophesy lies to you in my name, Ahab, son of Kolaiah, and Zedekiah, son of Maaseiah: I am handing them over to Nebuchadnezzar, king of Babylon, who will slay them before your eyes.[j] 22 All the exiles of Judah in Babylon will pattern a curse after them: "May the LORD make you like Zedekiah and Ahab, whom the king of Babylon roasted in the flames." 23 For they are criminals in Israel, committing adultery with their neighbors' wives, and alleging in my name things I did not command. I know, I am witness, says the LORD.[k]

The False Prophet Shemaiah 24 Say this to Shemaiah, the Nehelamite: 25 Thus says the LORD of hosts, the God of Israel: Because you sent letters on your own authority to all the people of Jerusalem, to all the priests and to Zephaniah, the priest, son of Maaseiah, with this message: 26 *"The LORD has appointed you priest in place of the priest Jehoiada, so that there may be police officers in the house of the LORD, to take action against all madmen and those who pose as prophets, by putting them into the stocks or the pillory. 27 Why, then, do you not rebuke Jeremiah of Anathoth who poses as a prophet among you? 28 For he sent us in Babylon this message: It will be a long time;

29, 3: Elasah: possibly the brother of Ahikam (cf Jer 26, 24). Gemariah; perhaps the son of the high priest Hilkiah; cf 2 Kgs 22, 4. Zedekiah had dispatched these men to Nebuchadnezzar for some other purpose, possibly the payment of tribute, but Jeremiah took advantage of their mission to send his letter by them.

29, 26–29: The words of Jeremiah to the false prophet Shemaiah are not fully preserved in the current Hebrew text, as is seen in the incomplete sentence of this translation (vv 25–28). In his letter to Zephaniah Shemaiah reminds him of his authority, as Pashhur's successor, to imprison Jeremiah. Zephaniah, however, merely reads the letter to Jeremiah but does not imprison him.

b 1 Tm 2, 1f. c Jer 25, 11; 2 Chr 36, 21f; Ezr 1, 1; Dn 9, 2; Zec 1, 12; 7, 5. d Jer 33, 3. e Jer 23, 3. 8. f Jer 15, 4; 24, 9; 34, 17f. g Jer 25, 4. h Jer 27, 9. 14. i Jer 5, 31. j Jer 14, 14. k Jer 23, 14.

build houses to live in; plant gardens and eat
their fruits. . . ."

29 When the priest Zephaniah read this letter
to the prophet, 30 the word of the LORD came to
Jeremiah: 31 Send the message to all the exiles:
Thus says the LORD concerning Shemaiah, the
Nehelamite: Because Shemaiah prophesies to
you without a mission from me, and raises false
confidence, 32 says the LORD, I will therefore
punish Shemaiah, the Nehelamite, and his off-
spring. None of them shall survive among this
people to see the good I will do to this people,
says the LORD, because he preached rebellion
against the LORD.

CHAPTER 30

The Restoration* 1 The following message
came to Jeremiah from the LORD: 2 Thus says the
LORD, the God of Israel: Write all the words I
have spoken to you in a book.[l] 3 For behold, the
days will come, says the LORD, when I will
change the lot of my people (of Israel and Judah,
says the LORD), and bring them back to the land
which I gave to their fathers; they shall have it as
their possession.[m]

4 These are the words which the LORD spoke
to Israel and to Judah: 5 thus says the LORD:

A cry of dismay we hear;
fear reigns, not peace.
6 Inquire, and see:
since when do men bear children?
Why, then, do I see all these men,
with their hands on their loins
like women in childbirth?
Why have all their faces turned
deathly pale?[n]
7 How mighty is that day—
none like it!
A time of distress for Jacob,
though he shall be saved from it.[o]

8 On that day, says the LORD of hosts, "I will
break his yoke from off your necks and snap your
bonds." Strangers shall no longer enslave them;[p]
9 instead, they shall serve the LORD, their God,
and David, their king,* whom I will raise up for
them.[q]

10 But you, my servant Jacob, fear not, says the
LORD,
be not dismayed, O Israel!
Behold, I will deliver you from the far-off land,
your descendants, from their land of exile;
Jacob shall again find rest,
shall be tranquil and undisturbed,[r]
11 for I am with you, says the LORD, to deliver
you.
I will make an end of all the nations
among which I have scattered you;
but of you I will not make an end.
I will chastise you as you deserve,
I will not let you go unpunished.[s]

12 For thus says the LORD:
Incurable is your wound,
grievous your bruise;[t]
13 There is none to plead your cause,
no remedy for your running sore,
no healing for you.
14 All your lovers have forgotten you,
they do not seek you.
I struck you as an enemy would strike,
punished you cruelly;[u]
15 Why cry out over your wound?
your pain is without relief.
Because of your great guilt,
your numerous sins,
I have done this to you.[v]
16 Yet all who devour you shall be devoured,
all your enemies shall go into exile.
All who plunder you shall be plundered,

30, 1—31, 40: These two chapters do not belong chronologically to those that precede or follow. They contain mainly oracles of salvation which Jeremiah originally uttered on behalf of the conquered remnants of the northern kingdom; then, after Judah began to share Samaria's fate, the oracles were extended to include Judah. Their composition is to be placed early in Jeremiah's ministry, probably after the fall of Nineveh (612 B.C.), when Josiah assumed power over the North; cf 2 Kgs 23, 15ff.

30, 9: David, their king: the messianic King of the Davidic line, often called David by the prophets; cf Ez 34, 23f; 37, 24f; Hos 3, 5.

l Jer 36, 2; Hb 2, 2; Rv 1, 11. m Jer 29, 14; 31, 8. 10. 23; 32, 37. 44; Ez 39, 25; Am 9, 14. n Jer 6, 24; 50, 43. o Am 5, 18; Zep 1, 14f. p Is 14, 5f; Ez 34, 27. q Ez 34, 23; 37, 24; Hos 3, 5; Lk 1, 69. r Jer 46, 27; Is 43, 5. s Jer 46, 28; Ez 11, 16f; Am 9, 8f. t Jer 10, 19; 14, 17; 15, 18. u Jer 22, 22; Lam 1, 19. v Jer 15, 18.

all who pillage you I will hand over to
pillage. [w]
17 For I will restore you to health;
of your wounds I will heal you, says the
LORD.
"The outcast" they have called you,
"with no avenger." [x]
18 Thus says the LORD:
See! I will restore the tents of Jacob,
his dwellings I will pity;
City shall be rebuilt upon hill,
and palace restored as it was. [y]
19 From them will resound songs of praise,
the laughter of happy men.
I will make them not few, but many;
they will not be tiny, for I will glorify them. [z]
20 His sons shall be as of old,
his assembly before me shall stand firm;
I will punish all his oppressors. [a]
21 His leader* shall be one of his own,
and his rulers shall come from his kin.
When I summon him, he shall approach me;
how else should one take the deadly risk
of approaching me? says the LORD.
22 You shall be my people,
and I will be your God. [b]

23 See, the storm of the LORD!
His wrath breaks forth
In a whirling storm
that bursts upon the heads of the wicked. [c]
24 The anger of the LORD will not abate
until he has done and fulfilled
what he has determined in his heart.
When the time comes,
you will fully understand. [d]

CHAPTER 31

Good News of the Return

1 At that time, says the LORD,
I will be the God of all the tribes of Israel,
and they shall be my people. [e]
2 Thus says the LORD:
The people that escaped the sword*
have found favor in the desert.
As Israel comes forward to be given his rest,
3 the LORD appears to him from afar:
With age-old love I have loved you;
so I have kept my mercy toward you. [f]
4 Again I will restore you, and you shall be
rebuilt,
O virgin Israel;
Carrying your festive tambourines,
you shall go forth dancing with the
merrymakers.
5 Again you shall plant vineyards
on the mountains of Samaria;
those who plant them shall enjoy the
fruits. [g]
6 Yes, a day will come when the watchmen
will call out on Mount Ephraim:
"Rise up, let us go to Zion,
to the LORD, our God." [h]

The Road of Return

7 For thus says the LORD:
Shout with joy for Jacob,
exult at the head of the nations;
proclaim your praise and say:
The LORD has delivered his people,
the remnant of Israel. [i]
8 Behold, I will bring them back
from the land of the north;
I will gather them from the ends of the world,
with the blind and the lame in their midst,
The mothers and those with child;
they shall return as an immense throng. [j]
9 They departed in tears,
but I will console them and guide them;
I will lead them to brooks of water,
on a level road, so that none shall
stumble.

30, 21: His leader: probably not the messianic King, but simply any one of the rulers of the restored Israel, who will no longer be foreigners, and with whom the Lord will be on terms of intimacy, as with the whole people. The deadly risk of approaching me: to approach God unsummoned brings death; cf Lv 16, 1f.

31, 2: The people that escaped the sword: the exiles who were not killed but deported; they have found favor in the desert, across which they were driven into captivity. The prophet alludes to the first desert wandering of Israel (Ex 16ff), in which the people found the Lord. His rest: the land of promise. The perfect fulfillment of this promised rest is found only in the New Testament (Heb chapters 3 and 4).

w Jer 2, 3. x Jer 33, 6. y Jer 33, 7. 11; Ezr 6, 3–15; Ez 36, 10. z Is 35, 10; 51, 11. a Is 49, 26. b Jer 24, 7; 31, 1. 33; 32, 38; Lv 26, 12; Ez 11, 20; 36, 28. c Jer 23, 19. d Jer 23, 20. e Jer 30, 22. f Dt 7, 8; 10, 15; Is 43, 4; 63, 9; Hos 11, 1. 4. g Is 65, 21; Am 9, 14. h Is 2, 3; 27, 13; Mi 4, 2. i Is 12, 6. j Jer 3, 18; 23, 3. 8; Is 35, 5f.

For I am a father to Israel,
Ephraim is my first-born. [k]
10 Hear the word of the LORD, O nations,
proclaim it on distant coasts, and say:
He who scattered Israel, now gathers them together,
he guards them as a shepherd his flock.
11 The LORD shall ransom Jacob,
he shall redeem him from the hand of his conqueror. [l]
12 Shouting, they shall mount the heights of Zion,
they shall come streaming to the LORD's blessings:
The grain, the wine, and the oil,
the sheep and the oxen;
They themselves shall be like watered gardens,
never again shall they languish. [m]
13 Then the virgins shall make merry and dance,
and young men and old as well.
I will turn their mourning into joy,
I will console and gladden them after their sorrows.
14 I will lavish choice portions upon the priests,
and my people shall be filled with my blessings,
says the LORD.

End of Rachel's Mourning

15 Thus says the LORD:
In Ramah* is heard the sound of moaning,
of bitter weeping!
Rachel mourns her children,
she refuses to be consoled
because her children are no more. [n]
16 Thus says the LORD:
Cease your cries of mourning,
wipe the tears from your eyes.
The sorrow you have shown shall have its reward,
says the LORD,
they shall return from the enemy's land.
17 There is hope for your future, says the LORD;
your sons shall return to their own borders. [o]

18 I hear, I hear Ephraim pleading:
You chastised me, and I am chastened;
I was an untamed calf.
If you allow me, I will return,
for you are the LORD, my God. [p]
19 I turn in repentance;
I have come to myself, I strike my breast;
I blush with shame,
I bear the disgrace of my youth. [q]
20 Is Ephraim not my favored son,
the child in whom I delight?
Often as I threaten him,
I still remember him with favor;
My heart stirs for him,
I must show him mercy, says the LORD. [r]

Summons To Return Home

21 Set up road markers,
put up guideposts;
Turn your attention to the highway,
the road by which you went.
Turn back, O virgin Israel,
turn back to these your cities.
22 How long will you continue to stray,
rebellious daughter?
The LORD has created a new thing upon the earth:
the woman must encompass the man* with devotion.

31, 15: Ramah: a village about five miles north of Jerusalem, where Rachel was buried (1 Sm 10, 2). Rachel: said to mourn for her children since she was the ancestress of Ephraim, the chief of the northern tribes. Mt 2, 18 applies this verse to the slaughter of the innocents by Herod.

31, 22: The woman must encompass the man: the words "with devotion," not in the Hebrew, are added for the sense. No fully satisfactory explanation has been given this text. Among the more probable are these: (a) Formerly the man (the Lord) encompassed the woman (Israel) with mercy and devotion; now in the spiritual religion of Israel which will follow on the restoration, this order will be reversed. (b) So secure will Israel be after the restoration that women will no longer need the natural protection of their husbands, but even weak women can protect men. (c) St. Jerome in his commentary on this verse understood it of Mary's virginal conception of Christ. "The Lord has created a new thing on earth; without seed of man, without carnal union and conception, 'a woman will encompass a man' within her womb—One who, though He will later appear to advance in wisdom and age through the stages of infancy and childhood, yet, while confined for the usual number of months in his mother's womb, will already be perfect man."

k Ex 4, 22. l Is 44, 23; 48, 20. m Is 58, 11. n Mt 2, 18. o Jer 29, 10-14. p Lv 26, 40ff. q Dt 30, 1ff. r Hos 11, 8.

23 Thus says the LORD of hosts, the God of
Israel: When I change their lot in the land of
Judah and her cities, they shall again repeat this
greeting: "May the LORD bless you, holy moun-
tain, abode of justice!"[s] 24 Judah and all her
cities, the farmers and those who lead the flock,
shall dwell there together. 25 For I will refresh
the weary soul; every soul that languishes I will
replenish. 26 Upon this I awoke and opened my
eyes; but my sleep was sweet to me.*

27 The days are coming, says the LORD, when I
will seed the house of Israel and the house of
Judah with the seed of man and the seed of
beast. 28 As I once watched over them to uproot
and pull down, to destroy, to ruin, and to harm,
so I will watch over them to build and to plant,
says the LORD.[t] 29 In those days they shall no
longer say,

"The fathers ate unripe grapes,[u]
and the children's teeth are set on edge,"*

30 but through his own fault only shall anyone
die: the teeth of him who eats the unripe grapes
shall be set on edge.

The New Covenant* 31 The days are coming,
says the LORD, when I will make a new covenant
with the house of Israel and the house of Judah.[v]
32 It will not be like the covenant I made with
their fathers the day I took them by the hand to
lead them forth from the land of Egypt; for they
broke my covenant and I had to show myself
their master, says the LORD.[w] 33 But this is the
covenant which I will make with the house of
Israel after those days, says the LORD. I will place
my law within them, and write it upon their
hearts; I will be their God, and they shall be my
people.[x] 34 No longer will they have need to
teach their friends and kinsmen how to know
the LORD. All, from least to greatest, shall know
me, says the LORD, for I will forgive their
evildoing and remember their sin no more.[y]

Certainty of God's Promise

35 Thus says the LORD,
He who gives the sun to light the day,
moon and stars to light the night;
Who stirs up the sea till its waves roar,
whose name is LORD of hosts:[z]
36 If ever these natural laws give way
in spite of me, says the LORD,
Then shall the race of Israel cease
as a nation before me forever.[a]
37 Thus says the LORD:
If the heavens on high can be measured,
or the foundations below the earth be
sounded,
Then will I cast off the whole race of Israel
because of all they have done, says the
LORD.

Rebuilding of Jerusalem 38 The days are com-
ing, says the LORD, when the city shall be rebuilt
as the LORD's,[b] from the Tower of Hananel to the
Corner Gate.* 39 The measuring line shall be
stretched from there straight to the hill Gareb and
then turn to Goah. 40 The whole valley of corpses
and ashes,* all the slopes toward the Kidron Val-
ley, as far as the corner of the Horse Gate at the
east, shall be holy to the LORD. Never again shall
the city be rooted up or thrown down.

CHAPTER 32

Pledge of Restoration* 1 This message came
to Jeremiah from the LORD in the tenth year of

31, 26: I awoke . . . sweet to me: probably said by the prophet himself.

31, 29: "The fathers . . . on edge": a proverb used in Israel, expressing the idea that children suffer for the sins of their parents (cf Ez 18, 2). The Israel of the restoration will be characterized instead by personal responsibility and retribution for one's acts (v 30; cf vv 31–34).

31, 31–34: The new covenant to be made with Israel is a common theme of the prophets, beginning with Hosea. According to Jeremiah, the qualities of the new covenant that make it different from the old are: (a) It will not be broken, but will last forever; (b) Its law will be written in the heart, not merely on tablets of stone; (c) The knowledge of God will be so generally shown forth in the life of the people that it will no longer be necessary to put it into words of instruction. In the fullest sense, this prophecy was fulfilled only through the work of Jesus Christ; cf Lk 22, 20; 1 Cor 11, 25.

31, 38: From the Tower of Hananel to the Corner Gate: from the northeast to the northwest.

31, 40: Valley of corpses and ashes: the Valley of Ben-hinnom, which joins the Kidron at the southeast of ancient Jerusalem. The Horse Gate: in the eastern city wall, at the southeast corner of the temple area.

32, 1–44: This chapter recounts a prophecy "in action." At the Lord's command, Jeremiah fulfills his family duty to purchase the land of his cousin, carrying out all the legal forms, including records, to testify that Judah will be restored and that the life of the past will be resumed.

s Jer 30, 3; Ps 122, 8. t Jer 1, 10; 18, 7. u Dt 24, 16; Ez 18, 2. v Jer 32, 40; Heb 9, 15. w Ex 24, 7f; Dt 5, 2. x Jer 32, 40; Ez 37, 26; Heb 10, 16. y Is 54, 13. z Gn 1, 14–18. a Jer 33, 20f. b Neh 12, 38; Zec 14, 10f.

Zedekiah,* king of Judah, the eighteenth year of Nebuchadnezzar. 2 At that time the army of the king of Babylon was besieging Jerusalem, and the prophet Jeremiah was imprisoned in the quarters of the guard, at the king's palace.[c] 3 Zedekiah, king of Judah, had imprisoned him there, remonstrating: "How dare you prophesy: Thus says the LORD: I am handing over this city to the king of Babylon, who will capture it.[d] 4 Neither shall Zedekiah, king of Judah, escape the hands of the Chaldeans; rather shall he be handed over to the king of Babylon. They shall meet and speak face to face,[e] 5 and Zedekiah shall be taken to Babylon. There he shall remain, until I attend to him, says the LORD; in fighting the Chaldeans, you cannot win!"[f]

6 *This message came to me from the LORD, said Jeremiah: 7 Hanamel, son of your uncle Shallum, will come to you with the offer:[g] "Buy for yourself my field in Anathoth, since you, as nearest relative, have the first right of purchase."* 8 Then, as the LORD foretold, Hanamel, my uncle's son, came to me to the quarters of the guard and said, "Please buy my field in Anathoth, in the district of Benjamin; as nearest relative, you have the first claim to possess it; make it yours." I knew this was what the LORD meant, 9 so I bought the field in Anathoth from my cousin Hanamel, paying him the money, seventeen silver shekels.

10 When I had written and sealed the deed, called witnesses and weighed out the silver on the scales, 11 I accepted the deed of purchase, both the sealed copy, containing title and conditions, and the open one.* 12 This deed of purchase I gave to Baruch, son of Neriah, son of Mahseiah, in the presence of my cousin Hanamel and of the witnesses who had signed the deed, and before all the men of Judah who happened to be in the quarters of the guard.[h]

13 In their presence I gave Baruch this charge: 14 Thus says the LORD of hosts, the God of Israel: Take these deeds, both the sealed and the open deed of purchase, and put them in an earthen jar,* so that they can be kept there a long time. 15 For thus says the LORD of hosts, the God of Israel: Houses and fields and vineyards shall again be bought in this land.

16 After giving the deed of purchase to Baruch, son of Neriah, I prayed thus to the LORD: 17 Ah, Lord GOD, you have made heaven and earth by your great might, with your outstretched arm; nothing is impossible to you.[i] 18 You continue your kindness through a thousand generations; and you repay the fathers' guilt, even into the lap of their sons who follow them. O God, great and mighty, whose name is LORD of hosts,[j] 19 great in counsel, mighty in deed, whose eyes are open to all the ways of men, giving to each according to his ways, according to the fruit of his deeds:[k] 20 you have wrought signs and wonders in the land of Egypt and to this day, both in Israel and among all other men, until now you have gained renown.[l] 21 With strong hand and outstretched arm you brought your people Israel out of the land of Egypt amid signs and wonders and great terror. 22 This land you gave them, as you had promised their fathers under oath, a land flowing with milk and honey.[m] 23 They entered and took possession of it, but they did not listen to your voice; by your law they did not live, and what you commanded they failed to do. Hence you let all these evils befall them.[n] 24 See, the siegeworks have arrived at this city to breach

32, 1: The tenth year of Zedekiah: 588 B.C. The eighteenth year of Nebuchadnezzar: dating his reign from his victory at Carchemish; see note on Jer 25, 1–14.

32, 6–9: Jeremiah's imprisonment by the weak-willed Zedekiah was a technical custody that did not deprive him of all freedom of action. The siege maintained by the Chaldeans (v 2) was only now beginning (v 24), and could be bypassed by individual persons going to and fro between Jerusalem and nearby Anathoth.

32, 7: The first right of purchase: the obligation of the closest relative to redeem the property of one in economic distress, so that the ancestral land might remain within the family (Lv 25, 25–28); see note on Ru 2, 20.

32, 11: The sealed copy . . . and the open one: the legal deed of sale was written on a scroll, which was then rolled up and sealed; about it was rolled another scroll, left unsealed, containing a copy or a summary of the first.

32, 14: In an earthen jar: the first of the Dead Sea Scrolls were found in such a jar.

c Jer 33, 1; 37, 20; 38, 6; 39, 14. d Jer 26, 9; 34, 2; 37, 6–10. e Jer 34, 3; 38, 18. 23; 39, 4–7. f Jer 39, 7; 52, 11. g Lv 25, 24–34; Ru 4, 4. h Jer 36, 4. i 2 Kgs 19, 15; Jb 42, 2. j Ex 20, 5f; Dt 5, 9. k Jb 34, 21; Ps 33, 13ff. l Ex 6, 6; Dt 4, 34; Ps 135, 9. m Jer 11, 5; Gn 15, 18; 17, 8; 26, 3. n Jer 7, 24ff; Dn 9, 10–14.

it; the city will be handed over to the Chaldeans who are attacking it, amid sword, famine, and pestilence. What you threatened has happened, you see it yourself;[o] 25and yet you tell me, O Lord GOD: Buy the field with money, call in witnesses. But the city has already been handed over to the Chaldeans!

26Then this word of the LORD came to Jeremiah: 27I am the LORD, the God of all mankind! Is anything impossible to me? 28This now is what the LORD says: I will hand over this city to the Chaldeans, for Nebuchadnezzar, king of Babylon, to take. 29The Chaldeans who are attacking it shall enter this city and set fire to it, burning it and its houses, on the roofs of which incense was burned to Baal and libations were poured out to strange gods as a provocation to me.[p] 30The Israelites and the Judeans from their youth have done only what is evil in my eyes; the Israelites did nothing but provoke me with the works of their hands, says the LORD.[q] 31From the day it was built to this day, this city has excited my anger and wrath, 32so that I must put it out of my sight for all the wickedness the Israelites and Judeans, with their kings and their princes, their priests and their prophets, the men of Judah and the citizens of Jerusalem, have done to provoke me.[r] 33They turned their backs to me, not their faces; though I kept teaching them, they would not listen to my correction.[s] 34They defiled the house named after me by the horrid idols they set up in it.[t] 35They built high places to Baal in the Valley of Ben-hinnom, and immolated their sons and daughters to Molech,* bringing sin upon Judah; this I never commanded them, nor did it even enter my mind that they should practice such abominations.[u]

36Now, therefore, thus says the LORD, the God of Israel, concerning this city, which as you say is handed over to the king of Babylon amid sword, famine, and pestilence: 37Behold, I will gather them together from all the lands to which in anger, wrath, and great rage I banish them; I will bring them back to this place and settle them here in safety.[v] 38They shall be my people, and I will be their God.[w] 39One heart and one way I will give them, that they may fear me always, to their own good and that of their children after them. 40I will make with them an eternal covenant, never to cease doing good to them; into their hearts I will put the fear of me, that they may never depart from me.[x] 41I will take delight in doing good to them: I will replant them firmly in this land, with all my heart and soul.[y]

42For thus says the LORD: Just as I brought upon this people all this great evil, so I will bring upon them all the good I promise them.[z] 43Fields shall again be bought in this land, which you call a desert, without man or beast, handed over to the Chaldeans.[a] 44Fields shall be bought with money, deeds written and sealed, and witnesses shall be used in the land of Benjamin, in the suburbs of Jerusalem, in the cities of Judah and of the hill country, in the cities of the foothills and of the Negeb, when I change their lot, says the LORD.[b]

CHAPTER 33

Restoration of Jerusalem 1The word of the LORD came to Jeremiah a second time while he was still imprisoned in the quarters of the guard: 2Thus says the LORD who made the earth and gave it form and firmness, whose name is LORD: 3Call to me, and I will answer you; I will tell to you things great beyond reach of your knowledge.[c] 4Thus says the LORD, the God of Israel, concerning the houses of this city and the palaces of Judah's kings, which are being destroyed in the face of siegeworks and the sword:[d] 5men come to battle the Chaldeans, and these houses will be filled with the corpses of those whom I slay in my anger and wrath,

32, 35: Molech: the god to whom human sacrifice was offered in the Valley of Ben-hinnom. Here, as in Jer 19, 5, he is given the name Baal; see note on Lv 18, 21.

o Jer 21, 5; 33, 4. p Jer 21, 10; 37, 8ff. q Jer 3, 25; 44, 8. r Jer 2, 26; Is 3, 8. s Jer 7, 24. t Jer 7, 30; 2 Kgs 21, 4f. u Jer 7, 31; 19, 5; Ps 106, 37f. v Jer 23, 3; 29, 14; Is 11, 12; Ez 11, 17. w Jer 24, 7; 31, 33. x Jer 31, 31ff. y Dt 30, 9. z Jer 33, 10–14; Zec 8, 13. a Jer 33, 10. b Jer 17, 26; 33, 7. c Is 48, 6. d Jer 32, 24.

when I hide my face from this city for all their wickedness.[e]

[6]Behold, I will treat and assuage the city's wounds; I will heal them, and reveal to them an abundance of lasting peace.[f] [7]I will change the lot of Judah and the lot of Israel, and rebuild them as of old.[g] [8]I will cleanse them of all the guilt they incurred by sinning against me; all their offenses by which they sinned and rebelled against me, I will forgive.[h] [9]Then Jerusalem shall be my joy, my praise, my glory, before all the nations of the earth, as they hear of all the good I will do among them. They shall be in fear and trembling over all the peaceful benefits I will give her.

[10]Thus says the LORD: In this place of which you say, "How desolate it is, without man, without beast!" and in the cities of Judah, in the streets of Jerusalem that are now deserted, without man, without citizen, without beast, there shall yet be heard[i] [11]the cry of joy, the cry of gladness, the voice of the bridegroom, the voice of the bride, the sound of those who bring thank offerings to the house of the LORD, singing, "Give thanks to the LORD of hosts, for the LORD is good; his mercy endures forever." For I will restore this country as of old, says the LORD.[j]

[12]Thus says the LORD of hosts: In this place, now desolate, without man or beast, and in all its cities there shall again be sheepfolds for the shepherds to couch their flocks. [13]In the cities of the hill country, of the foothills, and of the Negeb, in the land of Benjamin and the suburbs of Jerusalem, and in the cities of Judah, flocks will again pass under the hands of the one who counts them, says the LORD.

[14]*The days are coming, says the LORD, when I will fulfill the promise I made to the house of Israel and Judah. [15]In those days, in that time, I will raise up for David a just shoot; he shall do what is right and just in the land.[k] [16]In those days Judah shall be safe and Jerusalem shall dwell secure; this is what they shall call her: "The LORD our justice." [17]For thus says the LORD: Never shall David lack a successor on the throne of the house of Israel,[l] [18]nor shall priests of Levi ever be lacking, to offer holocausts before me, to burn cereal offerings, and to sacrifice victims.[m]

This word of the LORD also came to Jeremiah: [19]Thus says the LORD: [20]If you can break my covenant with day,[n] and my covenant with night, so that day and night no longer alternate in sequence, [21]then can my covenant with my servant David also be broken, so that he will not have a son to be king upon his throne, and my covenant with the priests of Levi who minister to me. [22]Like the host of heaven which cannot be numbered, and the sands of the sea which cannot be counted, I will multiply the descendants of my servant David and the Levites who minister to me.

[23]This word of the LORD came to Jeremiah: [24]Have you not noticed what these people are saying: "The LORD has rejected the two tribes which he had chosen"? They spurn my people as if it were no longer a nation in their eyes.[o] [25][p]Thus says the LORD: When I have no covenant with day and night, and have given no laws to heaven and earth, [26]then too will I reject the descendants of Jacob and of my servant David, so as not to take from his descendants rulers for the race of Abraham, Isaac, and Jacob. For I will change their lot and show them mercy.

IV: Fall of Jerusalem

CHAPTER 34

Fate of Zedekiah [1]This word came to Jeremiah from the LORD while Nebuchadnezzar, king of Babylon, and his armies and the earth's kingdoms

33, 14–26: This is the longest continuous passage in the Book of Jeremiah that is lacking in the Greek. It appears to be the postexilic composition of an inspired writer who used parts of the prophecies of Jeremiah—often, however, in a sense different from the prophet's. The prediction of an eternal Davidic dynasty (14–17) to fulfill the prophecy of Nathan (2 Sm 7, 11–16), and of a perpetual priesthood and sacrifice (18), was not to be realized in the restoration of the Jewish nation. It finds its fulfillment only in Jesus of Nazareth, who combined with his messianic Davidic kingship an eternal priesthood; cf Heb 6, 20; 7, 24f.

e Jer 21, 4ff. f Is 57, 18. g Jer 30, 3; 32, 44. h Ez 36, 25. i Jer 32, 43. j 1 Chr 16, 34; Ezr 3, 11; Ps 136, 1. k Jer 23, 5; Ps 72, 1–4. 12ff; Is 11.1. l 2 Sm 7, 16; 1 Kgs 2, 4; Ps 89, 4f. 29. 36f. m Ez 44, 15f. n 20f: Jer 31, 36f; Ps 89, 37f. o Rom 11, 1f. p 25f: Jer 31, 36f; 32, 44.

subject to him, as well as the other peoples, were all attacking Jerusalem and all her cities: [q] 2Thus says the LORD, the God of Israel: Go to Zedekiah, king of Judah, and tell him: Thus says the LORD: I am handing this city over to the king of Babylon; he will destroy it with fire. [r] 3Neither shall you escape his hand; rather you will be captured and fall into his hands. You shall see the king of Babylon and speak to him face to face. Then you shall be taken to Babylon. [s]

4But if you obey the word of the LORD, Zedekiah, king of Judah, then, says the LORD to you, you shall not die by the sword. 5You shall die in peace, and they will lament you as their lord, and burn spices for your burial as they did for your fathers, the kings who preceded you from the first; it is I who make this promise, says the LORD.

6The prophet Jeremiah told all these things to Zedekiah, king of Judah, in Jerusalem, 7while the armies of the king of Babylon were attacking Jerusalem and the remaining cities of Judah, Lachish, and Azekah,* since these alone were left of the fortified cities of Judah.

The Pact Broken* 8This is the word that came to Jeremiah from the LORD after King Zedekiah had made an agreement with all the people in Jerusalem to issue an edict of emancipation. 9Everyone was to free his Hebrew slaves, male and female, so that no one should hold a man of Judah, his brother, in slavery. [t] 10All the princes and the others who entered the agreement consented to set free their male and female servants, so that they should be slaves no longer. But though they agreed and freed them, 11afterward they took back their male and female slaves whom they had set free and again forced them into service.

12Then this word of the LORD came to Jeremiah: 13Thus says the LORD, the God of Israel: The day I brought your fathers out of the land of Egypt, out of the place where they were slaves, I made this covenant with them: 14Every seventh year each of you shall set free his Hebrew brother who has sold himself to you; six years he shall serve you, but then you shall let him go free. Your fathers, however, did not heed me or obey me. 15Today you indeed repented and did what is right in my eyes by proclaiming the emancipation of your brethren and making an agreement before me in the house that is named after me. 16But then you changed your mind and profaned my name by taking back your male and female slaves to whom you had given their freedom; you forced them once more into slavery. [u] 17Therefore, thus says the LORD: You did not obey me by proclaiming your neighbors and kinsmen free. I now proclaim you free, says the LORD, for the sword, famine, and pestilence. I will make you an object of horror to all the kingdoms of the earth. 18*The men who violated my covenant and did not observe the terms of the agreement which they made before me, I will make like the calf which they cut in two, between whose two parts they passed. 19The princes of Judah and of Jerusalem, the courtiers, the priests, and the common people, who passed between the parts of the calf, 20I will hand over, all of them, to their enemies, to those who seek their lives: their corpses shall be food for the birds of the air and the beasts of the field. [v]

21Zedekiah, too, king of Judah, and his princes, I will hand over to their enemies, to those who seek their lives, to the soldiers of the king of Babylon who have at present withdrawn from you. [w] 22I will give the command, says the

34, 7: Lachish and Azekah: fortress towns to the southwest of Jerusalem which Nebuchadnezzar besieged to prevent help coming to Jerusalem from Egypt. Between 1935 and 1938, archaeologists found at Lachish several letters written on pottery fragments which date from 598 or 588 B.C., and which mention both Lachish and Azekah.

34, 8–22: While the Chaldean siege of Jerusalem was in progress, the citizens of Jerusalem made a covenant at Zedekiah's instigation to free their brother Judeans who were in slavery. Doubtless this was both to provide additional free defenders for the city and to offer reparation for past violations of the law, according to which Hebrew slaves were to serve no longer than six years (Dt 15, 12–15). But when the siege was temporarily lifted, probably because of the help promised by Pharaoh Hophra (cf Jer 37, 5), the inhabitants of Jerusalem broke the covenant and once more pressed their brethren into slavery (v 11).

34, 18f: As the Bible (Gn 15, 10–17) and also contemporary inscriptions make clear, agreements were sometimes ratified by walking between the divided pieces of animals while the contracting parties invoked on themselves a fate similar to that of the slaughtered beast if they should fail to keep their word. The agreement: that mentioned in vv 10. 15.

q Jer 52, 4; 2 Kgs 25, 1. r Jer 21, 10; 32, 3. 28. s Jer 32, 4; 52, 11. t Ex 21, 2ff; Lv 25, 39. 46; Dt 15, 12–15. u Lv 19, 12. v Jer 7, 33; 16, 4; 19, 7. w Jer 37, 5. 11.

LORD, and bring them back to this city. They shall attack and capture it, and destroy it with fire; the cities of Judah I will turn into a desert where no man dwells.[x]

CHAPTER 35

The Faithful Rechabites 1This word came to Jeremiah from the LORD in the days of Jehoiakim, son of Josiah, king of Judah: 2Approach the Rechabites* and speak to them; bring them into the house of the LORD, to one of the rooms, and give them wine to drink. 3So I went and brought Jaazaniah, son of Jeremiah, son of Habazziniah, his brothers and all his sons, the whole company of the Rechabites, 4into the house of the LORD, to the room of the sons of Hanan,* son of Igdaliah, the man of God, next to the princes' room, above the room of Maaseiah, son of Shallum, keeper of the doorway. 5I set before these Rechabite men bowls full of wine and offered them cups to drink the wine.

6"We do not drink wine," they said to me: "Jonadab,* Rechab's son, our father, forbade us in these words: 'Neither you nor your children shall ever drink wine. 7Build no house and sow no seed; neither plant nor own a vineyard. You shall dwell in tents all your life, so that you may live long on the earth where you are wayfarers.' 8Now we have heeded Jonadab, Rechab's son, our father, in all his prohibitions. All our lives we have not drunk wine, neither we, nor our wives, nor our sons, nor our daughters. 9We build no houses to live in; we own no vineyards or fields or crops, 10and we live in tents; we obediently do everything our father Jonadab commanded us. 11But when Nebuchadnezzar, king of Babylon, invaded this land, we decided to come into Jerusalem to escape the army of the Chaldeans and the army of Aram;* that is why we are now living in Jerusalem."

12Then this word of the LORD came to Jeremiah: 13Thus says the LORD of hosts, the God of Israel: Go, say to the men of Judah and to the citizens of Jerusalem: Will you not take correction and obey my words? says the LORD.[y] 14The advice of Jonadab, Rechab's son, by which he forbade his children to drink wine, has been followed: to this day they have not drunk it; they obeyed their father's command. Me, however, you have not obeyed, although I spoke to you untiringly and insistently.[z] 15I kept sending you all my servants the prophets, telling you to turn back, all of you, from your evil way; to reform your conduct, and not follow strange gods or serve them, if you would remain on the land which I gave you and your fathers; but you did not heed me or obey me.[a] 16Yes, the children of Jonadab, Rechab's son, observed the command which their father laid on them; but this people does not obey me! 17Now, therefore, says the LORD God of hosts, the God of Israel: I will bring upon Judah and all the citizens of Jerusalem every evil that I threatened; because when I spoke they did not obey, when I called they did not answer.[b]

18But to the company of the Rechabites Jeremiah said: Thus says the LORD of hosts, the God of Israel: Since you have obeyed the command of Jonadab, your father, kept all his commands and done everything he commanded you, 19thus therefore says the LORD of hosts, the God of Israel: Never shall there fail to be a descendant of Jonadab, Rechab's son, standing in my service.

CHAPTER 36

Baruch Writes the Prophecies of Jeremiah

1In the fourth year of Jehoiakim, son of Josiah, king of Judah, this word came to Jeremiah from the LORD: 2Take a scroll and write on it all the words I have spoken to you against Israel, Judah, and all the nations, from the day I first spoke to you, in the days of Josiah, until today. 3Perhaps, when the house of Judah hears all the evil I have in mind to do to them, they will turn back each

35, 2: The Rechabites: reactionaries who believed that the Lord could not be well served except by maintaining the original nomadic conditions of Israel's life. Without sharing their convictions, the prophet holds up their fidelity to their ideals as an example to put to shame his faithless countrymen. In the days of Jehoiakim: probably in 599 or 598 B.C.

35, 4: The sons of Hanan: probably the disciples of this man of God or prophet. Maaseiah: possibly the father of the priest Zephaniah (Jer 29, 25; 37, 3). Keeper of the doorway: a priestly function of responsibility; cf Jer 52, 24.

35, 6: Jonadab: a contemporary of King Jehu; cf 2 Kgs 10, 15ff.

35, 11: The army of Aram; Nebuchadnezzar enlisted the help of Judah's foreign neighbors in his assault on Jerusalem.

x Jer 37, 8; 52, 7-13; 2 Chr 36, 17. 19. y Jer 32, 33. z Jer 7, 13; 25, 3; 2 Chr 36, 15f. a Jer 25, 4f. 7. b Jer 11, 8f.

from his evil way, so that I may forgive their wickedness and their sin.[c] 4So Jeremiah called Baruch, son of Neriah, who wrote down on a scroll, as Jeremiah dictated, all the words which the LORD had spoken to him.

9In the ninth month, in the fifth year of Jehoiakim, son of Josiah, king of Judah, a fast to placate the LORD was proclaimed for all the people of Jerusalem and all who came from Judah's cities to Jerusalem. 5Then Jeremiah charged Baruch: I cannot go to the house of the LORD; I am prevented* from doing so. 6Do you go on the fast day and read publicly in the LORD's house the LORD's words from the scroll you wrote at my dictation; read them also to all the men of Judah who come up from their cities. 7Perhaps they will lay their supplication before the LORD and will all turn back from their evil way; for great is the fury of anger with which the LORD has threatened this people.[d]

8Baruch, son of Neriah, did everything the prophet Jeremiah commanded; from the book-scroll he read the LORD's words in the LORD's house. 10It was in the room of Gemariah,* son of the scribe Shaphan, in the upper court of the LORD's house, at the entrance of the New Temple-Gate, that Baruch publicly read the words of Jeremiah from his book.

11Now Micaiah, son of Gemariah, son of Shaphan, heard all the words of the LORD read from the book. 12So he went down to the king's palace, into the scribe's chamber,* where the princes were just then in session: Elishama, the scribe, Delaiah, son of Shemaiah, Elnathan, son of Achbor, Gemariah, son of Shaphan, Zedekiah, son of Hananiah, and the other princes. 13To them Micaiah reported all that he had heard Baruch read publicly from his book. 14Thereupon the princes sent Jehudi, son of Nethaniah, son of Shelemiah, son of Cushi, to Baruch with the order: "Come, and bring with you the scroll you read publicly to the people." Scroll in hand, Baruch, son of Neriah, went to them. 15"Sit down," they said to him, "and read it to us." Baruch read it to them, 16and when they heard all its words, they were frightened and said to one another, "We must certainly tell the king all these things." 17Then they asked Baruch: "Tell us, please, how you came to write down all these words." 18"Jeremiah dictated all these words to me," Baruch answered them, "and I wrote them down with ink in the book." 19At this the princes said to Baruch, "Go into hiding, you and Jeremiah; let no one know where you are."

20Leaving the scroll in safekeeping in the room of Elishama the scribe, they entered the room where the king was. When they told him everything that had happened, 21he sent Jehudi to fetch the scroll. Jehudi brought it from the room of Elishama the scribe, and read it to the king and to all the princes who were in attendance on the king. 22Now the king was sitting in his winter house, since it was the ninth month, and fire was burning in a brazier before him. 23Each time Jehudi finished reading three or four columns, the king would cut off the piece with a scribe's knife* and cast it into the fire in the brazier, until the entire roll was consumed in the fire. 24Hearing all these words did not frighten the king and his ministers or cause them to rend their garments. 25And though Elnathan, Delaiah, and Gemariah urged the king not to burn the scroll, he would not listen to them, 26but commanded Jerahmeel, a royal prince, and Seraiah, son of Azriel, and Shelemiah, son of Abdeel, to arrest Baruch, the secretary, and the prophet Jeremiah. But the LORD kept them concealed.

27This word of the LORD came to Jeremiah, after the king burned the scroll with the text Jeremiah had dictated to Baruch: 28Take another scroll, and write on it everything that the first scroll contained, which Jehoiakim, king of Judah, burned up. 29And against Jehoiakim, king of

36, 5: I am prevented: probably because of his temple sermon (Jer 7, 1–15), or because of temporary ritual uncleanness.

36, 10: Gemariah: member of a family friendly to Jeremiah, which had rights to a room in the fortress of the temple gateway overlooking the court of the temple; from a window in this room Baruch read Jeremiah's prophetic sermon to the people.

36, 12: The scribe's chamber: the office of the royal secretary.

36, 23: A scribe's knife: used to sharpen the reeds which were employed as pens.

c Jer 26, 3; Is 55, 6f. d 2 Kgs 22, 13.

Judah, say this: Thus says the LORD: You burned that scroll, saying, "Why did you write on it: Babylon's king shall surely come and lay waste this land and empty it of man and beast?" 30 The LORD now says of Jehoiakim, king of Judah: [e] No descendant of his shall succeed to David's throne; his corpse shall be cast out, exposed to the heat of day, to the cold of night.* 31 I will punish him and his descendants and his ministers for their wickedness; against them and the citizens of Jerusalem and the men of Judah I will fulfill all the threats of evil which went unheeded.

32 Jeremiah took another scroll, and gave it to his secretary, Baruch, son of Neriah; he wrote on it at Jeremiah's dictation all the words contained in the book which Jehoiakim, king of Judah, had burned in the fire, and many others of the same kind in addition.

CHAPTER 37

Jeremiah in the Dungeon 1 Coniah, son of Jehoiakim, was succeeded by King Zedekiah, son of Josiah; he was made king over the land of Judah by Nebuchadnezzar, king of Babylon.[f] 2 Neither he, nor his ministers, nor the people of the land would listen to the words of the LORD spoken by Jeremiah the prophet. 3 Yet King Zedekiah sent Jehucal, son of Shelemiah, and Zephaniah, son of Maaseiah the priest, to the prophet Jeremiah with this request: "Pray to the LORD, our God, for us."[g] 4 At this time Jeremiah had not yet been put into prison;* he still came and went freely among the people. 5 Also, Pharaoh's army* had set out from Egypt, and when the Chaldeans who were besieging Jerusalem heard this report they marched away from the city.[h]

6 This word of the LORD then came to the prophet Jeremiah: 7 Thus says the LORD, the God of Israel: Give this answer to the king of Judah who sent you to me to consult me: Pharaoh's army which has set out to help you will return to its own land, Egypt.[i] 8 The Chaldeans shall return to the fight against this city; they shall capture it and destroy it with fire.[j]

9 Thus says the LORD: Do not deceive yourselves with the thought that the Chaldeans will leave you for good, because they shall not leave! 10 Even if you were to defeat the whole Chaldean army now attacking you, and only the wounded remained, each in his tent, these would rise up and destroy the city with fire.[k]

11 When the Chaldean army lifted the siege of Jerusalem at the threat of the army of Pharaoh,[l] 12 Jeremiah set out from Jerusalem for the district of Benjamin, to take part with his family in the division of an inheritance. 13 But when he reached the Gate of Benjamin, he met the captain of the guard, a man named Irijah, son of Shelemiah, son of Hananiah; he seized the prophet Jeremiah, saying, "You are deserting to the Chaldeans!" 14 "That is a lie!" Jeremiah answered, "I am not deserting to the Chaldeans." Without listening, Irijah kept Jeremiah in custody and brought him to the princes.

15 The princes were enraged, and had Jeremiah beaten and thrown into prison in the house of Jonathan the scribe, which they were using as a jail.[m] 16 And so Jeremiah entered the vaulted dungeon, where he remained a long time.

17 Once King Zedekiah had him brought to his palace and he asked him secretly whether there was any message from the LORD. Yes! Jeremiah answered: you shall be handed over to the king of Babylon.[n] 18 Jeremiah then asked King Zedekiah: In what have I wronged you, or your ministers, or this people, that you should put me in prison?[o] 19 And where are your own prophets now, 20 who prophesied to you that the king of Babylon would not attack you or this land? Hear now, my lord king, and grant my petition: do not

36, 30: Jehoiakim's son Jehoiachin was named king, but reigned only three months; he was known better for his thirty-seven-year exile in Babylon. His corpse shall be cast out: see note on Jer 22, 19.

37, 4: Put into prison: as described in Jer 32, 1ff. Chronologically, the present episode follows Jer 34, 1–7.

37, 5: Pharaoh's army: the force sent by Pharaoh Hophra which caused the Chaldeans momentarily to lift the siege of Jerusalem (cf Jer 34, 21).

e Jer 22, 19. f Jer 52, 1; 2 Kgs 24, 17; 2 Chr 36, 10. g Jer 21, 1. h Ez 17, 15; 29, 6f. i Ez 17, 17. j Jer 34, 22. k Jer 21, 4. l Zec 14, 10. m Jer 38, 6–13. n Jer 21, 7; 32, 3; 34, 21. o Jer 26, 19.

send me back into the house of Jonathan the scribe, or I shall die there.

21King Zedekiah ordered that Jeremiah be confined in the quarters of the guard, and given a loaf of bread each day from the bakers' shop until all the bread in the city was eaten up. Thus Jeremiah remained in the quarters of the guard.[p]

CHAPTER 38

Jeremiah in the Miry Cistern 1Shephatiah, son of Mattan, Gedaliah, son of Pashhur, Jucal, son of Shelemiah, and Pashhur, son of Malchiah, heard Jeremiah speaking these words to all the people:* 2Thus says the LORD: He who remains in this city shall die by sword, or famine, or pestilence; but he who goes out to the Chaldeans shall live; his life shall be spared him as booty, and he shall live.[q] 3Thus says the LORD: This city shall certainly be handed over to the army of the king of Babylon; he shall capture it.

4"This man ought to be put to death," the princes said to the king; "he demoralizes the soldiers* who are left in this city, and all the people, by speaking such things to them; he is not interested in the welfare of our people, but in their ruin."[r] 5King Zedekiah answered: "He is in your power"; for the king could do nothing with them. 6And so they took Jeremiah and threw him into the cistern of Prince Malchiah, which was in the quarters of the guard, letting him down with ropes. There was no water in the cistern, only mud, and Jeremiah sank into the mud.[s]

7Now Ebed-melech, a Cushite,* a courtier in the king's palace, heard that they had put Jeremiah into the cistern. The king happened just then to be at the Gate of Benjamin, 8and Ebed-melech went there from the palace and said to him, 9"My lord king, these men have been at fault in all they have done to the prophet Jeremiah, casting him into the cistern. He will die of famine on the spot, for there is no more food in the city."[t] 10Then the king ordered Ebed-melech the Cushite to take three men along with him, and draw the prophet Jeremiah out of the cistern before he should die. 11Ebed-melech took the men along with him, and went first to the linen closet in the palace, from which he took some old, tattered rags; these he sent down to Jeremiah in the cistern, with ropes. 12Then he said to Jeremiah, "Put the old, tattered rags between your armpits and the ropes." Jeremiah did so, 13and they drew him up with the ropes out of the cistern. But Jeremiah remained in the quarters of the guard.

14Once King Zedekiah summoned the prophet Jeremiah to come to him at the third entrance to the house of the LORD. "I have a question to ask you," the king said to Jeremiah; "hide nothing from me."[u] Jeremiah answered Zedekiah: 15If I tell you anything, you will have me killed, will you not? If I counsel you, you will not listen to me![v] 16But King Zedekiah swore to Jeremiah secretly: "As the LORD lives who gave us the breath of life, I will not kill you; nor will I hand you over to these men who seek your life."

17Thereupon Jeremiah said to Zedekiah: Thus says the LORD God of hosts, the God of Israel: If you surrender to the princes of Babylon's king, you shall save your life; this city shall not be destroyed with fire, and you and your family shall live.[w] 18But if you do not surrender to the princes of Babylon's king, this city shall fall into the hands of the Chaldeans, who shall destroy it with fire, and you shall not escape their hands.[x]

19King Zedekiah, however, said to Jeremiah, "I am afraid of the men of Judah who have deserted to the Chaldeans; I may be handed over to them, and they will mistreat me."[y] 20You will not be handed over, Jeremiah answered. Please obey the voice of the LORD and do as I tell you; then it shall go well with you, and your life will be spared.[z] 21But if you refuse to surrender, this is what the LORD shows me: 22All the

38, 1: Jeremiah enjoyed sufficient liberty in the quarters of the guard (Jer 37, 21) to speak to the people; cf Jer 32, 6–9. Gedaliah, son of Pashhur: the latter is possibly the Pashhur of Jer 20, 1. Pashhur, son of Malchiah: mentioned in Jer 21, 1.

38, 4: He demoralizes the soldiers: literally, "he weakens their hands." One of the Lachish ostraca (see note on Jer 34, 7) uses the same expression of the princes in Jerusalem.

38, 7: A Cushite: an Ethiopian. Ebed-melech evidently held a position of some authority at court.

p Jer 32, 2; 38, 28. q Jer 21, 9f; 39, 18; 45, 5. r Jer 26, 11. s Jer 37, 14f. t Jer 52, 6. u Jer 37, 16. v Lk 22, 67f. w Jer 27, 12f; 2 Kgs 24, 12. x Jer 32, 4. y 1 Sm 31, 4. z 2 Chr 20, 20.

women left in the house of Judah's king shall be brought out to the princes of Babylon's king, and they shall taunt you thus:

"They betrayed you, outdid you,
your good friends!
Now that your feet are stuck in the mud,
they slink away." [a]

[23]All your wives and sons shall be led forth to the Chaldeans, and you shall not escape their hands; you shall be handed over to the king of Babylon, and this city shall be destroyed with fire. [b]

[24]Then Zedekiah said to Jeremiah, "Let no one know about this conversation, or you shall die. [25]If the princes hear I spoke to you, if they come and ask you, 'Tell us what you said to the king; do not hide it from us, or we will kill you,' or, 'What did the king say to you?' [26]give them this answer: 'I petitioned the king not to send me back to Jonathan's house to die there.' " [27]When all the princes came to Jeremiah, they questioned him, and he answered them in the very words the king had commanded. They said no more to him, for nothing had been heard of the earlier conversation. [28]Thus Jeremiah stayed in the quarters of the guard till the day Jerusalem was taken. [c]

CHAPTER 39

Jeremiah and Gedaliah When Jerusalem was taken . . . . [1]In the tenth month of the ninth year* of Zedekiah, [d] king of Judah, Nebuchadnezzar, king of Babylon, and all his army marched against Jerusalem and besieged it. [2]On the ninth day of the fourth month, in the eleventh year* of Zedekiah, a breach was made in the city's defenses. [3]All the princes of the king of Babylon came and occupied the middle gate: Nergal-sharezer, of Simmagir, the chief officer, Nebushazban, the high dignitary, and all the other princes of the king of Babylon . . . . [4]When Zedekiah, king of Judah, saw them, he and all his warriors fled by night, leaving the city on the Royal Garden Road* through the gate between the two walls. He went in the direction of the Arabah, [e] [5]but the Chaldean army pursued them, and overtook and captured Zedekiah in the desert near Jericho. He was brought to Riblah,* in the land of Hamath, where Nebuchadnezzar, king of Babylon, pronounced sentence upon him. [f] [6]As Zedekiah looked on, his sons were slain at Riblah by order of the king of Babylon, who slew also all the nobles of Judah. [g] [7]He then blinded Zedekiah and bound him in chains to bring him to Babylon. [h]

[8]The Chaldeans set fire to the king's palace and the houses of the people, and demolished the walls of Jerusalem. [i] [9]Nebuzaradan, chief of the bodyguard, deported to Babylon the rest of the people left in the city, those who had deserted to him, and the rest of the workmen. [j] [10]But some of the poor who had no property were left in the land of Judah by Nebuzaradan, chief of the bodyguard, and were given at the same time vineyards and farms. [k]

[11]Concerning Jeremiah, Nebuchadnezzar, king of Babylon, gave the following orders through Nebuzaradan, chief of the bodyguard: [12]"Take him and look after him; let no harm befall him, but treat him as he himself requests." [l] [13]Thereupon Nebuzaradan, chief of the bodyguard, and Nebushazban, the high dignitary, and Nergal-sharezer, the chief officer, and all the nobles of the king of Babylon, [14]had Jeremiah taken out of the quarters of the guard, and entrusted to Gedaliah, son of Ahikam, son of Shaphan, to be brought home. And so he remained among the people. [m]

39, 1: The tenth month of the ninth year: the month Tebet (mid-December to mid-January) of the year 589/8 B.C.

39, 2: The ninth day of the fourth month, in the eleventh year: in July of 587 B.C.

39, 4: The Royal Garden Road: along the southeast side of the city; the royal garden was in the Kidron Valley. The gate between the two walls: the southernmost city gate, at the end of the Tyropoean Valley. The Arabah: the Jordan Valley. Zedekiah was attempting to escape across the Jordan when he was captured near Jericho.

39, 5: Riblah: Nebuchadnezzar's headquarters in Syria, which had also been used by Pharaoh Neco (2 Kgs 23, 33).

a Jb 6, 15; 19, 13f. 19. b Jer 41, 10. c Jer 39, 14. d 1f: Jer 52, 4–16; 2 Kgs 25, 1–12; Ez 24, 1. e Jer 52, 7. f Jer 32, 4f; 38, 18. g Jer 34, 21. h Jer 32, 4f; Ez 12, 13. i Jer 21, 10; 34, 2; 52, 13. j 2 Kgs 25, 11. k 2 Kgs 25, 12. 22. l Jer 40, 4. m Jer 26, 24; 38, 28.

A Word of Comfort for Ebed-melech [15]While Jeremiah was still imprisoned in the quarters of the guard, the word of the LORD came to him: [16]Go, tell this to Ebed-melech the Cushite: Thus says the LORD of hosts, the God of Israel: Behold, I am now fulfilling the words I spoke against this city, for evil and not for good; and this before your very eyes.[n] [17]But on that day I will rescue you, says the LORD; you shall not be handed over to the men of whom you are afraid. [18]I will make certain that you escape and do not fall by the sword. Your life shall be spared as booty, because you trusted in me, says the LORD.[o]

CHAPTER 40

Jeremiah Still in Judah [1]This word* came to Jeremiah from the LORD, after Nebuzaradan, captain of the bodyguard, had released him in Ramah, where he had found him a prisoner in chains, among the captives of Jerusalem and Judah who were being exiled to Babylon.[p] [2]When the captain of the bodyguard took charge of Jeremiah, he said to him, "The LORD, your God, foretold the ruin of this place. [3]Now he has brought about in deed what he threatened; because you sinned against the LORD and did not obey his voice, this fate has befallen you. [4]And now, I am freeing you today from the fetters that bind your hands; if it seems good to you to come with me to Babylon, you may come: I will look after you well. But if it does not please you to come to Babylon, you need not come. See, the whole land is before you; go wherever you think good and proper";[q] [5]and then, before he left—"or go to Gedaliah, son of Ahikam, son of Shaphan, whom the king of Babylon has appointed ruler over the cities of Judah; stay with him among the people, or go wherever you please." The captain of the bodyguard gave him food and gifts and let him go.[r] [6]Jeremiah went to Gedaliah, son of Ahikam, in Mizpah,* and stayed with him among the people left in the land.[s]

[7]When the army leaders who were still in the field with all their men heard that the king of Babylon had given Gedaliah, son of Ahikam, charge of the land, of men, women, and children, and of those poor who had not been led captive to Babylon, [8]they came with their men to Gedaliah in Mizpah: Ishmael, son of Nethaniah; Johanan, son of Kareah; Seraiah, son of Tanhumeth; the sons of Ephai of Netophah; and Jezaniah* of Beth-maacah. [9]Gedaliah, son of Ahikam, son of Shaphan, adjured them and their men not to be afraid to serve the Chaldeans: to stay in the land and submit to the king of Babylon, for their own welfare,[t] [10]saying that he himself would remain in Mizpah, as their intermediary with the Chaldeans who should come to them. They were to collect the wine, the fruit, and the oil, to store them in jars, and to settle in the cities they occupied. [11]When the people of Judah in Moab, those among the Ammonites, those in Edom, and those in all other lands heard that the king of Babylon had left a remnant in Judah, and had appointed over them Gedaliah, son of Ahikam, son of Shaphan, [12]they all returned to the land of Judah from the places to which they had scattered. They went to Gedaliah at Mizpah and had a rich harvest of wine and fruit.

Assassination of Gedaliah [13]Now Johanan, son of Kareah, and all the leaders of the armies in the field came to Gedaliah in Mizpah [14]and asked him whether he did not know that Baalis, the king of the Ammonites,* had sent Ishmael, son of Nethaniah, to assassinate him.[u] [15]But Gedaliah, son of Ahikam, would not believe them. Then Johanan, son of Kareah, said secretly

40, 1: This word: actually, no further word of the Lord is recorded until Jer 42, 7ff. This is a title affixed to the following chapters after they were attached to an earlier form of the book ending with chapter 39.

40, 6: Mizpah: some five miles northwest of Jerusalem, where Israel chose its first king (1 Sm 10, 17–24). Presumably Jerusalem had been damaged too much by the Chaldean conquest to remain a seat of government.

40, 8: Jezaniah: the seal ring of a high official of this name was discovered in 1932 at the site usually identified with Mizpah, Tell en-Nasbe.

40, 14: The Ammonites: they resented the survival of their ancient enemy, Judah. Ishmael: their willing tool, who doubtless aspired to rule over Judah himself, as he was of the house of David; cf Jer 41, 1.

n Jer 21, 10; Dn 9, 12. o Jer 45, 5; Pss 25, 3; 36, 40. p Jer 39, 14. q Jer 39, 12. r Jer 39, 14; 2 Kgs 25, 22. s Jer 39, 14. t Jer 27, 12f; 2 Kgs 25, 24. u Jer 41, 1ff. 10.

to Gedaliah in Mizpah: "Let me go and kill Ishmael, son of Nethaniah; no one will know it. Why should he be allowed to kill you? All the Jews who have now rallied to you will be dispersed and the remnant of Judah will perish."
16Nevertheless, Gedaliah, son of Ahikam, answered Johanan, son of Kareah, "You shall do nothing of the kind; you have lied about Ishmael."

CHAPTER 41

1In the seventh month Ishmael, son of Nethaniah, son of Elishama, of royal descent, one of the king's nobles, came with ten men to Gedaliah, son of Ahikam, at Mizpah.[v] And while they
were together at table in Mizpah, 2Ishmael, son of Nethaniah, and the ten who were with him, rose up and attacked with swords Gedaliah, son of Ahikam, son of Shaphan, whom the king of Babylon had made ruler over the land; and they
killed him. 3Ishmael also slew all the men of Judah of military age who were with Gedaliah and the Chaldean soldiers who were there.

4The second day after the murder of Gedaliah,
before anyone knew of it, 5eighty men with beards shaved off, clothes in rags, and with gashes on their bodies came from Shechem, Shiloh, and Samaria, bringing food offerings and
incense for the house of the LORD. 6Ishmael, son of Nethaniah, went out from Mizpah to meet
them, weeping as he went. 7"Come to Gedaliah,
son of Ahikam," he said as he met them. When they were once inside the city, Ishmael, son of Nethaniah, and his men slew them and threw
them into the cistern. 8But there were ten among them who pleaded with Ishmael: "Do not kill us; we have stores buried in the field: wheat and barley, oil and honey." And so he spared them and did not kill them, as he had
killed their companions. 9The cistern into which
Ishmael threw all the corpses of the men he had killed was the large one made by King Asa to defend himself against Baasha, king of Israel; this cistern Ishmael, son of Nethaniah, filled with the slain.[w]

10Ishmael, son of Nethaniah, led away the remnant of the people left in Mizpah and the princesses,* whom Nebuzaradan, captain of the bodyguard, had confided to Gedaliah, son of Ahikam. With these captives, Ishmael, son of Nethaniah, set out to make his way to the Ammonites.

Flight to Egypt 11But when Johanan, son of
Kareah, and the other army leaders with him heard of the crimes Ishmael, son of Nethaniah,
had committed, 12they took all their men and set
out to attack Ishmael, son of Nethaniah. They overtook him at the Great Waters in Gibeon.*
13At the sight of Johanan, son of Kareah, and the other army leaders, the people who were Ishmael's captives rejoiced. 14All of those whom
Ishmael had brought away from Mizpah went over to Johanan, son of Kareah. 15But Ishmael,
son of Nethaniah, escaped from Johanan and fled to the Ammonites with eight men. 16Then
Johanan, son of Kareah, and all his army leaders took charge of the remnant of the people, both the soldiers and the women and children with their guardians, whom Ishmael, son of Nethaniah, had brought away from Mizpah after he killed Gedaliah, son of Ahikim. From Gibeon,
17they retreated to the lodging place of Chimham near Bethlehem, where they stopped, intending to flee into Egypt. 18They were afraid of
the Chaldeans, because Ishmael, son of Nethaniah, had slain Gedaliah, son of Ahikam, whom the king of Babylon had made ruler in the land of Judah.

CHAPTER 42

1Then all the army leaders, Johanan, son of Kareah, Azariah, son of Hoshaiah, and all the people, high and low, approached the prophet
Jeremiah 2and said, "Grant our petition; pray for us to the LORD, your God, for all this remnant. We are now few who once were many, as you

41, 10: The princesses: of the royal house of Judah. They had not been deported to Babylon with the men of this house.

41, 12: Gibeon: today called El-Jib; it is northwest of Jerusalem. The most recent excavations have revealed the extensive dimensions of the city spring and well, called here the Great Waters; cf 2 Sm 2, 12ff.

v Jer 40, 14ff; 2 Kgs 25, 25. w 1 Kgs 15, 16; 2 Chr 16, 6.

well see. 3Let the LORD, your God, show us what way we should take and what we should do." 4Very well! the prophet Jeremiah answered them: I will pray to the LORD, your God, as you desire; whatever the LORD answers you, I will tell you; I will withhold nothing from you.[x] 5And they said to Jeremiah, "May the LORD be our witness: we will truly and faithfully follow all the instructions the LORD, your God, will send us.[y] 6Whether it is pleasant or difficult, we will obey the command of the LORD, our God, to whom we are sending you, so that it will go well with us for obeying the command of the LORD, our God."[z]

7Ten days passed before the word of the LORD came to Jeremiah. 8Then he called Johanan, son of Kareah, his army leaders, and all the people, high and low, 9and said to them: Thus says the LORD, the God of Israel, to whom you sent me to offer your prayer: 10If you remain quietly in this land I will build you up, and not tear you down; I will plant you, not uproot you; for I regret the evil I have done you.[a] 11Do not fear the king of Babylon, before whom you are now afraid; do not fear him, says the LORD, for I am with you to save you, to rescue you from his power.[b] 12I will grant you mercy, so that he will be sorry for you and let you return to your land.[c] 13But if you disobey the voice of the LORD, your God, and decide not to remain in this land, 14saying, "No, we will go to Egypt, where we will see no more of war, hear the trumpet alarm no longer, nor hunger for bread; there we will live";[d] 15then listen to the word of the LORD, remnant of Judah: Thus says the LORD of hosts, the God of Israel: If you are determined to go to Egypt, when you arrive there to stay, 16the sword you fear shall reach you in the land of Egypt; the hunger you dread shall cling to you no less in Egypt, and there you shall die.[e] 17All those men who determine to go to Egypt to stay, shall die by the sword, famine, and pestilence; not one shall survive or escape the evil that I will bring upon them.[f] 18For thus says the LORD of hosts, the God of Israel: Just as my furious anger was poured out upon the citizens of Jerusalem, so shall my anger be poured out on you when you reach Egypt. You shall become an example of malediction and horror, a curse and a reproach, and you shall never see this place again.[g]

19It is the LORD who has spoken to you, remnant of Judah; do not go to Egypt! You can never say that I did not warn you this day. 20At the cost of your lives you have deceived me, sending me to the LORD, your God, saying, "Pray for us to the LORD, our God; make known to us all that the LORD, our God, shall say, and we will do it." 21Today I proclaim his message, but you obey the voice of the LORD, your God, in nothing that he has commissioned me to make known to you.[h] 22Have no doubt of this, you shall die by the sword, famine, and pestilence in the place where you wish to go and settle.[i]

CHAPTER 43

1When Jeremiah finished speaking to the people all these words of the LORD, their God, with which the LORD had sent him to them, 2Azariah, son of Hoshaiah, Johanan, son of Kareah, and all the insolent men shouted to Jeremiah: "You lie; it was not the LORD, our God, who sent you to tell us not to go to Egypt to settle. 3It is Baruch, son of Neriah, who stirs you up against us, to hand us over to the Chaldeans to be killed or exiled to Babylon."[j]

4Johanan, son of Kareah, and the rest of the leaders and the people did not obey the LORD's command to stay in the land of Judah.[k] 5Instead, Johanan, son of Kareah, and all the army leaders took along the whole remnant of Judah that had been dispersed among the nations and had returned thence to dwell again in the land of Judah: 6men, women, and children, the princesses and everyone whom Nebuzaradan, captain of the bodyguard, had entrusted to Gedaliah, son of Ahikam, son of Shaphan; also

x 1 Sm 3, 18. y Jgs 11, 10. z Jer 7, 23; Dt 5, 33; 6, 3. a Jer 31, 28; 32, 41. b Jer 30, 10f. c Ps 106, 45f; Prv 16, 7. d Dt 28, 68. e Jer 44, 13f. 27. f Jer 29, 17f; 44, 14. 28. g Jer 44, 12. h Zec 7, 11f. i Jer 44, 12; Hos 9, 6. j Jer 38, 4. k Jer 41, 16.

Jeremiah, the prophet, and Baruch, son of Neriah.[l] 7 Against the LORD's command they went to Egypt, and arrived at Tahpanhes . . . .[m]

Jeremiah in Egypt 8 This word of the LORD came to Jeremiah in Tahpanhes: 9 Take with you large stones and sink them in mortar in the brickyard at the entrance to the royal building* in Tahpanhes, while the men of Judah look on, 10 and then say to them: Thus says the LORD of hosts, the God of Israel: I will send for my servant Nebuchadnezzar, king of Babylon, and bring him here. He will set his throne upon these stones which I, Jeremiah, have sunk, and stretch his canopy over them.[n] 11 He shall come and strike the land of Egypt: with death, whoever is marked for death; with exile, everyone destined for exile; with the sword, all who are intended for the sword.[o] 12 He shall set fire to the temples of Egypt's gods, and burn the gods or carry them off. As a shepherd delouses his cloak, he shall delouse the land of Egypt and depart victorious.[p] 13 He shall smash the obelisks of the temple of the sun in the land of Egypt and destroy with fire the temples of the Egyptian gods.

CHAPTER 44

1 This word came to Jeremiah for all the people of Judah who were living in Egypt, at Migdol, Tahpanhes, and Memphis, and in Upper Egypt: 2 *Thus says the LORD of hosts, the God of Israel: You have seen all the evil I brought on Jerusalem and the other cities of Judah. Today they are ruins and uninhabited,[q] 3 because of the evil they did to provoke me, going after strange gods, serving them and sacrificing to them, gods which neither they, nor you, nor your fathers knew.[r] 4 Though I kept sending to you all my servants the prophets, with the plea not to commit this horrible deed which I hate, 5 they would not listen or accept the warning to turn away from the evil of sacrificing to strange gods.[s] 6 Therefore the fury of my anger poured forth in flame over the cities of Judah and the streets of Jerusalem, so that they became the ruinous waste they are today.

7 Now thus says the LORD God of hosts, the God of Israel: Why do you inflict so great an evil upon yourselves? Will you root out from Judah man and wife, child and nursling, and not leave yourselves even a remnant? 8 Will you go on provoking me by the works of your hands, by sacrificing to strange gods here in the land of Egypt where you have come to live? Will you be rooted out and become a curse and a disgrace among all the nations of the earth?[t] 9 Have you forgotten the evil deeds which your fathers, and the kings of Judah and their wives, and you yourselves and your wives have done in the land of Judah and the streets of Jerusalem?[u] 10 To this day they have not been crushed; they do not fear or follow the law and the statutes which I set before you and your fathers.[v]

11 Hence, thus says the LORD of hosts, the God of Israel: I have determined evil against you; and I will uproot all Judah. 12 I will take away the remnant of Judah who insisted on coming to dwell in Egypt, so that they shall be wholly destroyed. In the land of Egypt they shall fall by the sword or be consumed by hunger. High and low, they shall die by the sword, or by hunger, and become an example of malediction, a horror, a curse and a reproach.[w] 13 Thus will I punish those who live in Egypt, just as I punished Jerusalem with sword, hunger, and pestilence. None of the remnant of Judah that have come to settle in the land of Egypt shall escape or survive.[x] 14 None shall return to the land of Judah, though they yearn to return and live there. Only scattered refugees shall return.

15 From all the men who knew that their wives were burning incense to strange gods, from all the women who were present in the immense crowd, and from all the people who lived in Lower and Upper Egypt, Jeremiah re-

43, 9: The royal building: residence of the Egyptian governor.
44, 2–30: Chronologically, this is the last of Jeremiah's prophecies to his countrymen. The narrative leaves him an old man nearing seventy, rejected by his people. According to tradition, he was murdered in Egypt by fellow Judeans.

l Jer 41, 10. m Jer 42, 13f; 44, 1. n Jer 27, 6; Ez 29, 19. o Jer 46, 13; Ez 30, 10. p Jer 46, 25; Ez 30, 13f. q Jer 34, 22; Lv 26, 32f. r Jer 11, 17; Dt 32, 17. s Jer 7, 24. 26; 19, 4. t Jer 25, 6f. u 1 Kgs 11, 1. 8; Ezr 9, 7. 14. v Jer 7, 24. w Jer 42, 15. 18. 22. x Jer 43, 11.

ceived this answer: 16“We will not listen to what you say in the name of the LORD.[y] 17Rather will we continue doing what we had proposed; we will burn incense to the queen of heaven and pour out libations to her, as we and our fathers, our kings and princes have done in the cities of Judah and the streets of Jerusalem. Then we had enough food to eat and we were well off; we suffered no misfortune.[z] 18But since we stopped burning incense to the queen of heaven and pouring out libations to her, we are in need of everything and are being destroyed by the sword and by hunger. 19And when we burned incense to the queen of heaven and poured out libations to her, was it without our husbands' consent that we baked for her cakes in her image and poured out libations to her?”[a]

20To all the people, men and women, who gave him this answer, Jeremiah said: 21Was it not this that the LORD remembered and brought to mind, that you burned incense in the cities of Judah and the streets of Jerusalem: you, your fathers, your kings and princes, and the people generally?[b] 22The LORD could no longer bear your evil deeds, the horrible things which you were doing; and so your land became a waste, a desert, a thing accursed and without inhabitants, as it is today.[c] 23Because you burned incense and sinned against the LORD, not obeying the voice of the LORD, not living by his law, his statutes, and his decrees, this evil has befallen you at the present day.[d]

24Jeremiah said further to all the people, including the women: Hear the word of the LORD, all you Judeans in the land of Egypt: 25Thus says the LORD of hosts, the God of Israel: You and your wives have stated your intentions, and kept them in fact: “We will continue to fulfill the vows we have made to burn incense to the queen of heaven and to pour out libations to her.” Very well! keep your vows, carry out your resolutions! 26But listen then to the word of the LORD, all you people of Judah who live in Egypt; I swear by my own great name, says the LORD, in the whole land of Egypt no man of Judah shall henceforth pronounce my name, saying, “As the Lord GOD lives.” 27I am watching over them to do evil, not good. All the men of Judah in Egypt shall perish by the sword or famine until they are utterly destroyed.[e] 28Those who escape the sword to return from the land of Egypt to the land of Judah shall be few in number. The whole remnant of Judah who came to settle in Egypt shall know whose word stands, mine or theirs.[f]

29That you may know how surely my threats of punishment for you shall be fulfilled, this shall be a sign to you, says the LORD, that I will punish you in this place. 30Thus says the LORD: See! I will hand over Pharaoh Hophra,* king of Egypt, to his enemies, to those who seek his life, just as I handed over Zedekiah, king of Judah, to his enemy and mortal foe, Nebuchadnezzar, king of Babylon.[g]

CHAPTER 45

A Message to Baruch* 1This is the message that the prophet Jeremiah gave to Baruch, son of Neriah, when he wrote in a book the prophecies that Jeremiah dictated in the fourth year of Jehoiakim, son of Josiah, king of Judah:[h] 2Thus says the LORD, God of Israel, to you, Baruch, 3because you said, “Alas! the LORD adds grief to my pain;[i] I am weary from groaning, and can find no rest”: 4say this to him, says the LORD: What I have built, I am tearing down; what I have planted, I am uprooting: even the whole land.[j] 5And do you seek great things for yourself? Seek them not! I am bringing evil on all mankind, says the LORD, but your life I will leave you as booty, wherever you may go.[k]

44, 30: Hophra: killed by his own people. The ruler of Egypt at the time of its conquest by Nebuchadnezzar was Hophra's successor Amasis, who was also slain by his enemies.

45, 1–5: At the conclusion of his narrative, Baruch appends a prophecy given him personally by Jeremiah when he first wrote down Jeremiah's words (cf chap. 36). The future revealed by the prophet had depressed Baruch; this prophecy was to assure him of his personal safety, while repeating the Lord's determination to destroy Judah.

y Jer 6, 16f. z Jer 5, 3; 7, 18. a Jer 7, 18. b Jer 11, 13. c Jer 15, 6. d 2 Kgs 17, 15; Dn 9, 11f. e Ez 7, 3–7. f Dt 28, 62; Is 10, 22. g Jer 39, 5ff; 46, 25f; Ez 29, 3f; 30, 21. h Jer 36, 4. 18. 32. i Lam 1, 3; 5, 5. j Jer 18, 7; Is 5, 5f. k Jer 25, 26–29.

V: Oracles against the Nations*

CHAPTER 46

[1]This is the word of the LORD that came to the prophet Jeremiah against the nations.

Against Egypt [2]Concerning Egypt. Against the army of Pharaoh Neco, king of Egypt, which was defeated at Carchemish on the Euphrates* by Nebuchadnezzar, king of Babylon, in the fourth year of Jehoiakim, son of Josiah, king of Judah:

3 Prepare shield and buckler!
march to battle!
4 Harness the horses,
mount, charioteers
Fall in with your helmets;
polish your spears, put on your breastplates.
5 What do I see?
With broken ranks
They fall back;
their heroes are routed,
They flee headlong
without making a stand.
Terror on every side,
says the LORD! [l]
6 The swift cannot flee,
nor the hero escape:
There in the north, on the Euphrates' bank,
they stumble and fall.
7 Who is this that surges forward like the Nile,
like rivers of billowing waters?
8 Egypt surges like the Nile,
like rivers of billowing waters.
"I will surge forward," he says, "and cover the earth,
destroying the city and its people. [m]
9 Forward, horses!
drive madly, chariots!
Set out, warriors,
Cush and Put, bearing your shields,
Men of Lud, stretching your bows!"
10 But this is the day of the Lord GOD of hosts,
a day of vengeance, vengeance on his foes!
The sword devours, is sated, drunk with their blood:
for the Lord GOD of hosts holds a slaughter feast
in the northland, on the Euphrates. [n]

11 Go up to Gilead, and take balm,
O virgin daughter Egypt!
No use to multiply remedies;
for you there is no cure. [o]
12 The nations hear of your shame,
your cries fill the earth.
Warrior trips over warrior,
both fall together. [p]

13 [q]The message which the LORD gave to the
prophet Jeremiah concerning the advance of
Nebuchadnezzar, king of Babylon, to attack the
land of Egypt:*

14 Announce it in Egypt, publish it in Migdol,
proclaim it in Memphis and Tahpanhes!
Say: Take your stand, prepare yourselves,
the sword has already devoured your neighbors. [r]
15 Why has Apis* fled,
your mighty one failed to stand?
The LORD thrust him down;
16 he stumbled repeatedly, and fell.
They said one to another,
"Up! let us return to our own people,
To the land of our birth,
away from the destroying sword." [s]
17 Call Pharaoh, king of Egypt, by the name
"The noise that let its time go by."*
18 As I live, says the King

46—51: In these chapters most of Jeremiah's oracles against the foreign nations have been gathered together and placed at the end of his book; in the Greek text they appear with the other oracles against the nations, in chap. 25. In general, they are in chronological order: 46, 1—49, 33, from the fourth year of Jehoiakim; 49, 34–39, at the beginning of Zedekiah's reign; 50, 1—51, 64, from the fourth year of Zedekiah.

46, 2: Carchemish on the Euphrates: the western terminus of the Mesopotamian trade route, where Nebuchadnezzar defeated Neco in 605 B.C., thus gaining undisputed control of Syria and Palestine.

46, 13: In 601 B.C. Nebuchadnezzar advanced against Egypt and even entered the country, but finally had to withdraw to Syria.

46, 15: Apis: the chief god of Memphis, venerated in the form of a black bull.

46, 17: "The noise . . . go by": in Hebrew there is wordplay here on the name Hophra, who still made a pretense of power though his career was at an end.

l Jer 6, 25; 49, 29. m Ez 29, 3; 32, 2. n Dt 32, 42; Is 13, 9; Ez 39, 17–20. o Jer 8, 22; 51, 8; Ez 30, 21f. p Ez 32, 9–12. q Jer 43, 10f; 44, 30; Is 19, 1. r Jer 44, 1. s Lv 26, 37.

whose name is LORD of hosts,
Like Tabor among the mountains he shall come,
like Carmel* above the sea.
19 Pack your baggage for exile,
capital city of daughter Egypt;
Memphis shall become a desert,
an empty ruin.
20 Egypt is a pretty heifer,
from the north a horsefly lights upon her.
21 The mercenaries in her ranks
are like fatted calves;
They too turn and flee together,
stand not their ground,
When the day of their ruin comes upon them,
the time of their punishment.
22 She sounds like a retreating reptile!
Yes, they come in force;
like woodchoppers, they attack her with axes.
23 They cut down her forest, says the LORD,
impenetrable though it be;
More numerous than locusts,
they cannot be counted.
24 Disgraced is daughter Egypt,
handed over to the people of the north.

25 The LORD of hosts, the God of Israel, has
said: See! I will punish Amon* of Thebes, and
Egypt, her gods and her kings, Pharaoh, and
those who trust in him. [t] 26 I will hand them over
to those who seek their lives, to Nebuchadnez-
zar, king of Babylon, and his ministers. But later
on Egypt shall be inhabited again, as in times
past, says the LORD. [u]

27 But you, my servant Jacob, fear not;
be not dismayed, O Israel.
Behold, I will deliver you from the far-off land,
your descendants, from their land of exile.
Jacob shall again find rest,
shall be tranquil and undisturbed. [v]
28 You, my servant Jacob, never fear, says the LORD,
for I am with you;
I will make an end of all the nations
to which I have driven you,
But of you I will not make an end:
I will chastise you as you deserve,
I will not let you go unpunished. [w]

CHAPTER 47

Against the Philistines 1 This is the word that
came from the LORD to the prophet Jeremiah
concerning the Philistines, before Pharaoh at-
tacked Gaza: [x] 2 Thus says the LORD:

*Behold: waters are rising from the north,
a torrent in flood;
It shall flood the land and all that is in it,
the cities and their people.
All the people of the land
set up a wailing cry.
3 They hear the stamping hooves of his steeds,
the rattling chariots, the rumbling wheels.
Fathers turn not to save their children;
their hands fall helpless
4 Because of the day which has come
to ruin all the Philistines,
And cut off from Tyre and Sidon*
the last of their allies.
Yes, the LORD is destroying the Philistines,
the remnant from the coasts of Caphtor. [y]
5 Gaza is shaved bald, [z]
Ashkelon is reduced to silence;
Ashdod, the remnant of their strength,
how long will you gash yourself?*
6 Alas, sword of the LORD!
how long till you find rest?
Return into your scabbard;
stop, be still!*
7 How can it find rest

46, 18: Tabor . . . Carmel: outstanding mountains of Palestine, symbols of strength, to which Nebuchadnezzar is compared.

46, 25: Amon: the sun-god worshiped at Thebes, in Upper Egypt.

47, 2–7: This prophecy was fulfilled in 605/4 B.C.

47, 4: Tyre and Sidon: Phoenician cities associated commercially with the Philistines, and enemies of Nebuchadnezzar; cf Jer 27, 1–4. Nebuchadnezzar carried out a thirteen-year siege of Tyre which was only partially successful. Caphtor: probably the island of Crete, the traditional place of origin of the Philistines; cf Am 9, 7.

47, 5: Of the ancient Philistine cities, neither Gath nor Ekron (Jer 25, 20) is mentioned in this period of waning independence of the seacoast.

47, 6: Words of the Philistines.

t Ez 30, 15f. u Jer 44, 30; Ez 30, 4; 32, 11f. v Jer 30, 10; 43, 5. w Jer 30, 11. x Ez 25, 15f; Zep 2, 4. y Jer 25, 22; Ez 25, 16f; Am 1, 8; 9, 7. z Am 1, 7.

when the LORD has commanded it?
Against Ashkelon and the seashore
he has appointed it. [a]

CHAPTER 48

Against Moab* [1]Concerning Moab, thus says the LORD of hosts, the God of Israel:

Woe to Nebo, it is laid waste;
Kiriathaim is disgraced and captured,
Disgraced and overthrown is the stronghold:
2 Moab's glory is no more.
Evil they plan against Heshbon:
"Come, let us put an end to her as a people."
You, too, Madmen, shall be reduced to silence;
behind you stalks the sword.
3 Listen! a cry from Horonaim [b]
of ruin and great destruction!
4 Moab is crushed,
their outcry is heard in Zoar.
5 The ascent of Luhith
they climb weeping;
On the descent to Horonaim
the cry of destruction is heard.
6 "Flee, save your lives,
to survive like the wild ass in the desert!"
7 Because you trusted in your works and your treasures,
you also shall be captured.
Chemosh* shall go into exile,
his priests and princes with him. [c]
8 The destroyer comes upon every city,
not a city escapes;
Ruined is the valley,
wasted the plain, as the LORD has said.
9 Set up a memorial for Moab,
for it is an utter wasteland;
Its cities are turned into ruins
where no one dwells.
10 [Cursed be he who does the LORD's work remissly,
cursed he who holds back his sword from blood.]
11 Moab has been tranquil from his youth,
has rested upon his lees;
He was not poured from one flask to another,
he went not into exile.
Thus he kept his taste,
and his scent was not lost. [d]

12 Hence, the days shall come, says the LORD,
when I will send him coopers to turn him over;
they shall empty his flasks and break his jars.
13 Chemosh shall disappoint Moab, as Israel was
disappointed by Bethel in which they trusted. [e]

14 How can you say, "We are heroes,
men valiant in war"?
15 The ravager of Moab and his cities advances,
the flower of his youth goes down to be slaughtered,
says the King, the LORD of hosts by name.
16 Near at hand is Moab's ruin,
his disaster hastens apace.
17 Mourn for him, all you his neighbors,
all you who knew him well!
Say: How the strong staff is broken,
the glorious rod!
18 Come down from glory, sit on the ground,
you that dwell in Dibon;
Moab's ravager has come up against you,
he has ruined your strongholds. [f]
19 Stand by the wayside, watch closely,
you that dwell in Aroer;
Ask the man who flees, the woman who tries to escape:
say to them, "What has happened?" [g]
20 Moab is disgraced, yes, destroyed,
howl and cry out;
Publish it at the Arnon,
Moab is ruined! [h]

21 For judgment has come on the land of the
plateau: on Holon, Jahzah, and Mephaath, [i] 22 on
Dibon, Nebo, and Beth-diblathaim, 23 on Kiria-
thaim, Beth-gamul, and Beth-meon, 24 on Kerioth
and on Bozrah: on all the cities of Moab, far and
near.

48, 1–47: Moab was one of the Israelites' bitterest enemies. According to Flavius Josephus, Moab and Ammon were conquered by Nebuchadnezzar in his twenty-third year, 582 B.C., five years after the destruction of Jerusalem.

48, 7: Chemosh: chief god of the Moabites.

a Zep 2, 5f. b 3ff: Is 15, 5. c Nm 21, 29. d Zep 1, 12. e Is 16, 12. f Nm 21, 30. g Dt 2, 36. h Is 16, 7. i Is 15, 4.

25 Moab's strength is broken,
his might is shattered, says the LORD.

26 Because he boasted against the LORD, make
Moab drunk so that he retches and vomits, and
he too becomes a laughingstock. 27 Is Israel a
laughingstock to you? Was she caught among
thieves, that you shake your head whenever you
speak of her?[j]

28 Leave the cities, dwell in the crags,
you that dwell in Moab.
Be like a dove that nests
out of reach on the edge of a chasm.
29 We have heard of the pride of Moab,[k]
pride beyond bounds:
His loftiness, his pride, his scorn,
his insolence of heart.
30 I know, says the LORD, his arrogance;
liar in boast, liar in deed.
31 And so I wail over Moab,
over all Moab I cry,
over the men of Kir-heres I moan.[l]
32 More than for Jazer I weep over you,
vineyard of Sibmah.
Your tendrils trailed down to the sea,
as far as Jazer they stretched.
Upon your harvest, upon your vintage,
the ravager has fallen.[m]
33 Joy and jubilation are at an end
in the fruit gardens of the land of Moab.
I drain the wine from the wine vats,
the treader treads no more,
the vintage shout is stilled.

34 The cry of Heshbon and Elealeh is heard as
far as Jahaz; they call from Zoar to Horonaim,
and to Eglath-shelishiyah, for even the waters of
Nimrim turn into a desert.[n] 35 I will leave no one
in Moab, says the LORD, to offer a holocaust on
the high place, or to burn incense to his gods.
36 Hence the wail of flutes for Moab is in my
heart; for the men of Kir-heres the wail of flutes
is in my heart: the wealth they acquired has
perished.[o] 37 Every head has been made bald,
every beard shaved; every hand is gashed, and
the loins of all are clothed in sackcloth.[p] 38 On
every roof of Moab and in all his squares there is
mourning; I have shattered Moab like a pot that
no one wants, says the LORD. 39 How terror
seizes Moab, and wailing! How he turns his back
in shame! Moab has become a laughingstock and
a horror to all his neighbors! 40 For thus says the
LORD:

Behold, like an eagle he soars,
spreads his wings over Moab.[q]
41 Cities are taken,
strongholds seized:
On that day the hearts of Moab's heroes
are like the heart of a woman in travail.[r]
42 Moab shall be destroyed, no more a people,
because he boasted against the LORD.[s]
43 Terror, pit, and trap be upon you,
people of Moab, says the LORD.[t]
44 He who flees from the terror
falls into the pit;
He who climbs from the pit
is caught in the trap;
For I will bring these things upon Moab
in the year of their punishment, says the
LORD.
45 In Heshbon's shadow stop short
the exhausted refugees;
For fire breaks forth from Heshbon,
and a blaze from the house of Sihon:
It consumes the brow of Moab,
the skull of the noisemakers.[u]
46 Woe to you, O Moab,
you are ruined, O people of Chemosh!
Your sons are taken into exile,
your daughters into captivity.
47 But I will change the lot of Moab
in the days to come, says the LORD.[v]
Thus far the judgment of Moab.

CHAPTER 49

Against the Ammonites 1 Concerning the Am-
monites, thus says the LORD:

Has Israel no sons?
has he no heir?

j Zep 2, 8ff. k 29f: Is 16, 6. l Is 16, 7. m Is 16, 8f. n Is 15, 4f. o Is 16, 11. p Jer 47, 5; Is 15, 2f; Ez 7, 18. q Jer 49, 22. r Jer 6, 24; 30, 6. s Zep 2, 9f. t Is 24, 17f. u Nm 21, 28f. v Jer 49, 39.

Why then has Milcom* disinherited Gad,
why have his people settled in Gad's cities?
2 But the days are coming, says the LORD,
when against Rabbah of the Ammonites*
I will sound the battle alarm;
She shall become a mound of ruins,
and her daughter cities shall be destroyed by fire.
Israel shall inherit those who disinherited her,
says the LORD. [w]
3 Howl, Heshbon, for the ravager approaches,
shriek, daughters of Rabbah!
Put on sackcloth and mourn,
run to and fro, gashing yourselves;
For Milcom goes into exile
along with his priests and captains. [x]
4 Why do you glory in your strength,
your ebbing strength, rebellious daughter?
You who trust in your treasures, saying,
"Who can come against me?"
5 I am bringing terror upon you,
says the Lord GOD of hosts,
from all round about you;
You shall be scattered, each man in headlong flight,
with no one to rally the fugitives. [y]
6 But afterward I will change the lot
of the Ammonites, says the LORD.

Against Edom* 7 Concerning Edom, thus says the LORD of hosts:

Is there no more wisdom in Teman,*
has counsel perished from the prudent,
has their wisdom become corrupt?
8 Flee, retreat, hide in deep holes,
you who live in Dedan:
For I will bring destruction upon Esau*
when I come to punish him. [z]
9 If vintagers came upon you,
they would leave no gleanings;
If thieves by night,
they would destroy as they pleased. [a]
10 So I myself will strip Esau;
I will uncover his retreats so that he cannot hide.
He is ruined: sons, and brothers,
and neighbors, so that he is no more. [b]
11 Leave your orphans behind, I will keep them alive;
your widows, let them trust in me. [c]

12 For thus says the LORD: Even those not sentenced to drink the cup must drink it! Shall you then go unpunished? You shall not go unpunished; you shall surely drink it. [d] 13 By my own self I have sworn, says the LORD: Bozrah* shall become an object of horror and a disgrace, a desolation and a curse; she and all her cities shall become ruins forever. [e]

14 I have heard a report from the LORD,
a herald has been sent among the nations:
Gather together, move against her,
rise up for battle.
15 Small will I make you among the nations,
despised among men! [f]
16 The terror you spread beguiled you,
and your presumption of heart;
You that live in rocky crags,
that hold the heights of the hill:
Though you build your nest high as the eagle,
from there I will drag you down, says the LORD. [g]

17 Edom shall become an object of horror. Every passer-by shall be appalled and catch his breath at all her wounds. 18 As when Sodom, Gomorrah, and their neighbors were overthrown, says the LORD, not a man shall dwell there: no one shall visit there. [h]

49, 1: Milcom: chief god of the Ammonites. The Transjordan tribe of Gad bordered on Ammon, and after the collapse of the northern kingdom the Ammonites occupied its territory.

49, 2: Rabbah of the Ammonites: or Rabbath-Ammon, capital of the Ammonite kingdom. The modern Amman is the capital of the kingdom of Jordan.

49, 7–22: Edom: this implacable enemy from ancient times profited from Judah's downfall; cf Ob 11f.

49, 7: Teman: a district of Edom, used here for the whole country; it was famous for its wise men; cf Jb 2, 11.

49, 8: Esau: Jacob's brother, the traditional ancestor of the Edomites; cf Gn 36.

49, 13: Bozrah: capital of Edom, southeast of the Dead Sea.

w Am 1, 14. x Is 15, 2ff. y Jer 48, 47. z Ez 25, 13. a Ob 5. b Mal 1, 3. c Dt 10, 18; Ps 68, 6. d Jer 25, 15. 28; Lam 4, 21f. e Is 34, 6; Ez 35, 3–9; Ob 16. f Ob 2. g Jer 48, 29f. h Jer 50, 40; Dt 29, 23.

[19] As when a lion comes up from the thicket of
Jordan
to the permanent feeding grounds,
So I, in an instant, will drive men off;
and whom I choose I will establish there!
For who is like me? who can call me to
account?
What shepherd can stand against me? [i]
[20] Therefore, hear the counsel of the LORD,
which he has taken against Edom;
Hear the plans he has made
against those that live in Teman:
They shall be dragged away, even the smallest
sheep,
their own pasture shall be aghast because of
them.
[21] At the noise of their fall the earth quakes,
to the Red Sea the outcry is heard!
[22] See! like an eagle he soars aloft,
and spreads his wings over Bozrah;
On that day the hearts of Edom's heroes shall
be
like the heart of a woman in travail. [j]

Against Damascus Concerning Damascus:

[23] Hamath and Arpad* are covered with shame,
they have heard bad news;
Worried, they toss like the sea
which cannot rest. [k]
[24] Damascus is weakened, she turns to flee,
panic has seized her.
Distress and pangs take hold of her,
like those of a woman in travail.
[25] How can the city of glory be forsaken,
the town of delight!
[26] But now her young men shall fall in her
streets,
and all her warriors shall be stilled.
On that day, says the LORD of hosts,
[27] I will set fire to the wall of Damascus,
and it shall devour the palaces of
Ben-hadad.*

Against Arabia [28] Of Kedar and the kingdoms
of Hazor, defeated by Nebuchadnezzar, king of
Babylon, thus says the LORD:

Rise up, attack Kedar,
ravage the Easterners. [l]
[29] Their tents and herds shall be taken away,
their tent curtains and all their goods;
Their camels they shall carry off for
themselves,
and shout from upon them, "Terror on
every side!" [m]
[30] Flee! leave your homes, hide in deep holes,
you that live in Hazor, says the LORD;
For counsel has been taken against you,
a plan has been formed against you
[Nebuchadnezzar, king of Babylon].
[31] Rise up! set out against a nation that is at
peace,
that lives secure, says the LORD,
That has no gates or bars,
and dwells alone.
[32] Their camels shall be your booty,
their many herds your spoil;
I will scatter to the winds those who shave
their temples,
from all sides I will bring ruin upon them,
says the LORD. [n]
[33] Hazor shall become a haunt of jackals,
a desert forever,
Where no man lives,
no human being stays.

Against Elam [34] The following word of the
LORD against Elam* came to the prophet Jere-
miah at the beginning of the reign of Zedekiah,
king of Judah: [35] Thus says the LORD of hosts:

Behold, I will break the bow of Elam,
the mainstay of their might.
[36] I will bring upon Elam the four winds
from the four ends of the heavens:
I will scatter them to all these winds, till there
is no nation

49, 23: Hamath and Arpad: independent Aramean states to the north of Damascus; the invasion is conceived as coming from the north. The situation is of the eighth century B.C. Cf Is 10, 9ff.

49, 27: The palaces of Ben-hadad: the royal palaces in Damascus where at least three kings bore this name; cf 1 Kgs 15, 18; 20.

49, 34: Elam: the ancient kingdom to the east of Babylonia.

i Jer 12, 5; 25, 9; 50, 44f. j Jer 4, 13. k Is 36, 19; 37, 13. l Is 21, 16. m Jer 4, 20. n Jer 9, 25.

to which the outcasts of Elam shall not
come.
37 I will break Elam before their foes,
before those who seek their life;
I will bring evil upon them,
my burning wrath, says the LORD.
I will send the sword to pursue them
until I have completely made an end of
them;
38 My throne I will set up in Elam
and destroy from there king and princes,
says the LORD.
39 But in the days to come I will change
the lot of Elam, says the LORD.

CHAPTER 50

The First Prophecy against Babylon 1 The
word which the LORD spoke against Babylon,*
against the land of the Chaldeans, through the
prophet Jeremiah: [o]

2 Announce and publish it among the nations;
publish it, hide it not, but say:
Babylon is taken, Bel* confounded, Merodach
shattered;
her images are put to shame, her idols
shattered.
3 A people from the north advances against her
to turn her land into a desert,
So that no one shall live there,
because man and beast have fled away. [p]
4 In those days, at that time, says the LORD,
the men of Israel and of Judah shall come,
Weeping as they come, to seek the
LORD, their God; [q]
5 to their goal in Zion they shall ask the way.
"Come, let us join ourselves to the LORD
with covenant everlasting, never to be
forgotten." [r]
6 Lost sheep were my people,
their shepherds misled them,
straggling on the mountains;
From mountain to hill they wandered,
losing the way to their fold. [s]
7 Whoever came upon them devoured them,
and their enemies said, "We incur no guilt,
Because they sinned against the LORD,
the hope of their fathers, their abode of
justice." [t]
8 Flee from Babylon, leave the land of the
Chaldeans,
be like the rams at the head of the flock. [u]
9 See, I am stirring up against Babylon
a band of great nations from the north;
from there they advance, and she shall be
taken.
Their arrows are arrows of the skilled
warrior;
none shall return without effect. [v]
10 Chaldea shall be their plunder,
and all her plunderers shall be enriched,
says the LORD.
11 Yes, rejoice and exult,
you that plunder my portion;
Frisk like calves on the green,
snort like stallions!
12 Your mother shall be sorely put to shame,
she that bore you shall be abashed;
See, the last of the nations,
a desert, dry and waste. [w]
13 Because of the LORD's wrath she shall be
empty,
and become a total desert;
Everyone who passes by Babylon will be
appalled
and catch his breath, at all her wounds. [x]
14 Take your posts encircling Babylon,
you who bend the bow;
Shoot at her, spare not your arrows, [y]
15 raise the war cry against her on all sides.
She surrenders, her bastions fall,

50, 1—51, 58: A collection of miscellaneous prophecies against Babylon which now stands as the introduction to the story in Jer 51, 59–64. The Greek text of Jer 50, 1 omits through the prophet Jeremiah, and it is in fact likely that these oracles are not Jeremiah's, but were composed by other inspired writers after the fall of Jerusalem, who may have used some of Jeremiah's texts. Babylon fell to the Persians in 538 B.C.

50, 2: Bel: originally the name of the god of Nippur in Mesopotamia, then identified with Merodach (Marduk), chief god of Babylon.

o Jer 51, 1; Is 13, 1–14; 21, 1–10. p Jer 51, 48; Is 13, 17. q Jer 3, 18; Ps 126, 6. r Jer 31, 31; 32, 40. s Is 53, 6; I Pt 2, 25. t Jer 31, 23. u Jer 51, 6. 45; Is 48, 20. v Jer 51, 27. w Jer 51, 43; Is 13, 20ff. x Jer 25, 12. y Jer 51, 11; Is 21, 2.

her walls are torn down:*
Vengeance of the LORD is this! Take revenge
on her,
as she has done, do to her;
for she sinned against the LORD.[z]
16 Cut off from Babylon the sower
and him who wields the sickle in harvest
time!
Before the destroying sword,
each of them turns to his own people,
everyone flees to his own land.[a]
17 A stray sheep was Israel
that lions pursued;
Formerly the king of Assyria devoured her,
now Nebuchadnezzar of Babylon gnaws her
bones.[b]

18 Therefore, thus says the LORD of hosts, the God of Israel:

I will punish the king of Babylon and his land,
as once I punished the king of Assyria;[c]
19 But I will bring back Israel to her fold,
to feed on Carmel and Bashan,
And on Mount Ephraim and Gilead,
till she has her fill.[d]

20 In those days, at that time, says the LORD:

They shall seek Israel's guilt, but it shall be no
more,
and Judah's sins, but these shall no longer
be found;
for I will forgive the remnant I preserve.[e]

21 Attack the land of Merathaim,*
and those who live in Pekod;
Slaughter and doom them, says the LORD,
do all I have commanded you.
22 Battle alarm in the land,
dire destruction!
23 How has the hammer of the whole earth
been broken and shattered!
What an object of horror
Babylon has become among the nations.[f]
24 You ensnared yourself, and were caught,
O Babylon, before you knew it!
You were discovered and seized,
because you challenged the LORD.[g]
25 The LORD opens his armory
and brings forth the weapons of his wrath;
For the Lord GOD of hosts has work to do
in the land of the Chaldeans.[h]

26 Come upon her from every side,
open her granaries,
Pile up her goods in heaps and doom it,
leave not a remnant.
27 Slay all her oxen,
let them go down to the slaughter;
Woe to them! their day has come,
the time of their punishment.
28 Listen! the fugitives, the escaped
from the land of Babylon:
They announce in Zion
the vengeance of the LORD, our God.[i]
29 Call up against Babylon archers,
all who bend the bow;
Encamp around her,
let no one escape.
Repay her for her deeds;
as she has done, do to her,
For she insulted the LORD,
the Holy One of Israel.[j]
30 Therefore her young men shall fall in her
streets,
all her warriors shall perish on that day,
says the LORD.[k]

31 I am against you, man of insolence,
says the Lord GOD of hosts;
For your day has come,
the time for me to punish you.
32 Insolence stumbles and falls;
there is no one to raise him up.
I will kindle in his cities a fire
that shall devour everything around him.

33 Thus says the LORD of hosts:

50, 15: Her walls are torn down: the prophet is not predicting the details of Babylon's downfall, but describing such a downfall in conventional language. Actually, Babylon was surrendered peaceably, without destruction.

50, 21: Merathaim, "twice bitter," and Pekod, "punishment," are here symbolic terms for Babylonia, though probably they suggest also the names of regions in that country.

z Jer 51, 11. 44, 58; Ps 137, 8. a Is 13, 14. b 2 Kgs 17, 24; 18, 14. c Is 10, 12; 14, 24f. d Jer 23, 3; Ez 34, 13f. e Jer 31, 34; Is 43, 25; Mi 7, 19. f Jer 51, 20; Is 14, 6. g Jer 51, 57. h Jer 51, 11; Is 13, 5. i Jer 51, 10f. j Jer 51, 56. k Jer 49, 26; 51, 4.

Oppressed are the men of Israel,
and with them the men of Judah;
All their captors hold them fast
and refuse to let them go.
34 Strong is their avenger,
whose name is LORD of hosts;
He will defend their cause with success,
and give rest to the earth,
but unrest to those who live in Babylon. [l]

35 A sword upon the Chaldeans, says the LORD,
upon Babylon's people, her princes and wise men!
36 A sword upon the soothsayers,
that they may become fools!
A sword upon her warriors,
that they may tremble;
37 A sword upon her motley throng,
that they may become women!
A sword upon her treasures,
that they may be plundered; [m]
38 A sword upon her waters,
that they may dry up!
For it is a land of idols,
and they shall be made frantic by fearful things. [n]
39 Hence, wildcats and desert beasts shall dwell there,
and ostriches shall occupy it;
Never again shall it be peopled, or lived in,
from age to age. [o]
40 As when God overturned Sodom
and Gomorrah, with their neighbors, says the LORD,
Not a man shall dwell there,
no human being shall tarry there. [p]
41 See! a people comes from the north,
a great nation, and mighty kings
roused from the ends of the earth. [q]
42 Bow and javelin they wield,
cruel and pitiless are they;
They sound like the roaring sea,
as they ride forth on steeds,
Each in his place for battle
against you, daughter Babylon.
43 The king of Babylon hears news of them,
and helpless fall his hands;
Anguish seizes him,
throes like a mother's in childbirth. [r]
44 As when a lion comes up from the Jordan's thicket
to the permanent feeding grounds,
So I, in one instant, will drive them off,
and whom I choose I will establish there;
For who is like me? who calls me to account?
what shepherd can stand against me? [s]
45 Therefore hear the counsel of the LORD
which he has taken against Babylon;
Hear the plans he has made
against the land of the Chaldeans:
They shall be dragged away, even the smallest sheep;
their own pasture shall be aghast because of them. [t]
46 At the cry "Babylon is captured!" the earth quakes;
the outcry is heard among the nations. [u]

CHAPTER 51

The Second Prophecy against Babylon

1 Thus says the LORD:
See! I rouse against Babylon,
and against those who live in Chaldea,
a destroying wind.
2 Against Babylon I will send winnowers
to winnow her and lay waste her land;
They shall besiege her from all sides
on the day of affliction. [v]
3 Let the bowman draw his bow,
and flaunt his coat of mail;
Spare not her young men,
doom her entire army. [w]
4 The slain shall fall in the land of Chaldea,
the transfixed, in her streets; [x]
5 For Israel and Judah are not widowed
of their God, the LORD of hosts,
And the Chaldean land is full of guilt
to be punished by the Holy One of Israel.

l Jer 51, 36. m Jer 51, 30; Na 3, 13. n Jer 51, 32. 36. o Jer 51, 37; Is 13, 21f. p Jer 51, 43. q Jer 51, 27f. r Is 13, 7. s Jer 49, 19. t Jer 51, 12. 29. u Jer 51, 29. v Jer 15, 7; Is 41, 16. w Jer 50, 14. 29. x Jer 50, 30.

6 Flee out of Babylon;
let each one save his life,
perish not for her guilt;
This is a time of vengeance for the LORD,
he pays her her due.[y]
7 Babylon was a golden cup in the hand of the LORD
which made the whole earth drunk;
The nations drank its wine,
with this they have become mad.[z]
8 Babylon suddenly falls and is crushed:
howl over her!
Bring balm for her wounds,
in case she can be healed.[a]
9 "We have tried to heal Babylon,
but she cannot be healed.
Leave her, let us go, each to his own land."
Her judgment reaches heaven,
it touches the clouds.[b]
10 The LORD has brought to light our just cause;
come, let us tell in Zion
what the LORD, our God, has done.[c]

11 Sharpen the arrows,
fill the quivers;
The LORD has stirred up the spirit of Media's kings;*
Babylon he is resolved to destroy.
Yes, it is the vengeance of the LORD,
vengeance for his temple.[d]
12 Against the walls of Babylon raise a signal,
make strong the watch;
Post sentries,
arrange ambushes!
For the LORD has planned and he will carry out
his threat against the inhabitants of Babylon.
13 You who dwell by mighty waters,
rich in treasure,
Your end has come,
the term at which you shall be cut off![e]
14 The LORD of hosts has sworn by himself:
I will fill you with men as numerous as locusts,
who shall raise over you the vintage shout!
15 He has sworn who made the earth by his power,
and established the world by his wisdom,
and stretched out the heavens by his skill.[f]
16 When he thunders, the waters in the heavens roar,
and he brings up clouds from the end of the earth;
He makes the lightning flash in the rain,
and releases stormwinds from their chambers.
17 Every man is stupid, ignorant;
every artisan is put to shame by his idol:
He molded a fraud,
without breath of life.
18 Nothingness are they, a ridiculous work,
that will perish in their time of punishment.
19 Not like these is the portion of Jacob,
he is the creator of all things;
Israel is his very own tribe,
LORD of hosts is his name.

20 You are my hammer,
my weapon for war;
With you I shatter nations,
with you I destroy kingdoms.
21 With you I shatter horse and rider,
with you I shatter chariot and driver.[g]
22 With you I shatter man and wife,
with you I shatter old and young,
with you I shatter youth and maiden.[h]
23 With you I shatter the shepherd and his flock,
with you I shatter the farmer and his team,
with you I shatter satraps and prefects.
24 Thus will I repay Babylon,
and all who live in Chaldea
All the evil they did to Zion,
as you shall see with your own eyes, says the LORD.[i]
25 Beware! I am against you,
destroying mountain,
destroyer of the entire earth, says the LORD;
I will stretch forth my hand against you,

51, 11: Media's kings: the Medes dwelt with the Persians in the land now known as Iran. At the time these words were written the Medes were the dominant people of the two, but within a short time the Persians had gained the ascendancy.

y Jer 50, 8. 15. 29; Is 48, 20. z Rv 14, 8; 17, 4. a Rv 18, 9–18. b Is 13, 14; Rv 18, 5. c Jer 50, 28. d 2 Kgs 17, 6; Is 13, 17. e Na 2, 1. f Jer 10, 12. g Dn 7, 7. 19. 23. h Is 13, 16. 18. i Jer 25, 14; 50, 29; Ps 137, 8.

roll you down over the cliffs,
and make you a burnt mountain:[j]
26 They will not take from you a cornerstone,
or a foundation stone;
Ruins forever shall you be,
says the LORD.[k]

27 Raise a signal on the earth,
blow the trumpet among the nations;
Dedicate peoples to war against her,
summon against her the kingdoms,
Ararat, Minni, and Ashkenaz;*
Appoint recruiting officers against her,
send up horses like bristling locusts.[l]
28 Dedicate peoples to war against her:
the king of Media,
Its governors and all its prefects,
every land in his domain.
29 The earth quakes and writhes,
the LORD's plan against Babylon is carried out,
Turning the land of Babylon
into a desert where no one lives.
30 Babylon's warriors have ceased to fight,
they remain in their strongholds;
Dried up is their strength,
they have become women.
Burned are their homes,
and broken their bars.
31 One runner meets another,
herald meets herald,
Telling the king of Babylon
that all his city is taken.[m]
32 The fords have been seized,
and the fortresses set on fire,
while warriors are in panic.
33 For thus says the LORD of hosts, the God of
Israel:

Daughter Babylon is like a threshing floor
at the time it is trodden;
Yet a little while,
and the harvest time will come for her.[n]
34 He has consumed me,* routed me,
[Nebuchadnezzar, king of Babylon,]
he has left me as an empty vessel;
He has swallowed me like a dragon:
filled his belly with my delights, and cast me out.
35 My torn flesh be upon Babylon,
says the city on Zion;
My blood upon the people of Chaldea,
says Jerusalem.
36 But now, thus says the LORD:
Surely I will defend your cause,
I will avenge you;
I will dry up her sea,
and drain her fountain.
37 Babylon shall become a heap of ruins,
a haunt of jackals;
A place of horror and ridicule,
where no one lives.[o]
38 They all roar like lions,
growl like lion cubs.[p]
39 When they are parched, I will set a drink before them
to make them drunk, that they may be overcome
with perpetual sleep, never to awaken,
says the LORD.

40 I will bring them down like lambs to the slaughter,
like rams and goats.
41 How has she been seized, made captive,
the glory of the whole world!
What a horror has Babylon become among nations:[q]
42 against Babylon the sea rises,
she is overwhelmed by the roaring waves!
43 Her cities have become a desert,
parched and arid land
Where no man lives,
and no one passes through.
44 I will punish Bel in Babylon,
and make him disgorge what he swallowed;
peoples shall stream to him no more.
The wall of Babylon falls!

51, 27: Ararat, Minni, and Ashkenaz: regions or people in what is now Armenia, subject at this time to Media.
51, 34: Me, my: refers to Jerusalem.

j Rv 8, 7; 18, 8f. k Jer 25, 12; Ps 118, 22. l Na 3, 17. m 2 Chr 30, 6; Jb 1, 14–18. n Rv 14, 15. o Is 25, 2. p Na 2, 11f. q Is 13, 19.

45 Leave her, my people, let each one save himself
from the burning wrath of the LORD.

46 Be not discouraged for fear of rumors spread
in the land; this year the rumor comes, then
violence in the land, tyrant against tyrant. [r] 47 But
behold, the days are coming when I will punish
the idols of Babylon; her whole land shall be put
to shame, and all her slain shall lie fallen within
her. 48 Then heaven, and earth, and everything
in them shall shout over Babylon with joy, when
the destroyers come against her from the north,
says the LORD. [s] 49 Babylon, too, must fall, O slain
of Israel, as at the hands of Babylon have fallen
the slain of all the earth.

50 You who have escaped the sword,
go on, stand not still;
Remember the LORD from afar,
let Jerusalem come to your minds.
51 We are ashamed because we have heard taunts,
confusion covers our faces; strangers have entered
the holy places of the house of the LORD. [t]
52 But behold, the days are coming, says the LORD,
when I will punish her idols,
and in her whole land the wounded will groan.
53 Though Babylon scale the heavens,
and make her strong heights inaccessible,
destroyers from me shall reach her, says the LORD. [u]
54 Hear! loud cries from Babylon,
dire destruction from the land of the Chaldeans;
55 For the LORD lays Babylon waste,
stills her loud cry,
Though her waves were roaring like mighty waters,
and their clamor was heard afar.
56 For the destroyer comes upon her, [Babylon,]
her heroes are captured, their bows broken;
The LORD is a God who requites,
he will surely repay. [v]

57 I will make her princes and her wise men
drunk, her governors, her prefects, and her
warriors, so that they sleep an eternal sleep,
never to awaken, says the King, whose name is
the LORD of hosts. 58 Thus says the LORD of
hosts:

The walls of spacious Babylon shall be leveled utterly;
her lofty gates shall be destroyed by fire.
The toil of the nations is for nothing;
for the flames the peoples weary themselves. [w]

The Prophecy Sent to Babylon 59 This was
the errand given by the prophet Jeremiah to
Seraiah,* son of Neriah, son of Mahseiah, when
he went to Babylon for the king in the fourth
year of the reign of Zedekiah; Seraiah was chief
quartermaster. 60 Jeremiah had written all the
misfortune that was to befall Babylon in a single
book:* all these words that were written
against Babylon. 61 And Jeremiah said to Sera-
iah: When you reach Babylon, see that you
read aloud all these words, [x] 62 and then say: O
LORD, you yourself threatened to destroy this
place, so that neither man nor beast should
dwell in it, since it would remain an everlasting
desert. 63 When you have finished reading this
book, tie a stone to it and throw it in the
Euphrates, [y] 64 and say: Thus shall Babylon sink.
Never shall she rise, because of the evil I am
bringing upon her. [To "weary themselves" are
the words of Jeremiah.]*

51, 59: Seraiah: the brother of Baruch; cf Jer 32, 12. The king: Zedekiah. Perhaps Seraiah went to Babylon to explain away the presence of foreign ambassadors in Jerusalem that same year; cf Jer 27, 3.

51, 60: Jeremiah prophesied against Babylon, even as he foretold Judah's release from Babylon's power (Jer 3, 14–18; 32, 15; 33, 6–9. 12f); but his book against Babylon was thrown in the Euphrates (v 63). The preceding oracles were composed by later writers; see note on Jer 50, 1—51, 58.

51, 64: To "weary themselves" are the words of Jeremiah: an editorial remark concerning the end of v 58.

r Mt 24, 6f. s Rv 18, 20. t Pss 44, 16f; 78, 1–4. u Is 14, 13. v Na 1, 2. w Hb 2, 13. x Jer 50, 1–51. y Rv 18, 21.

VI: Historical Appendix*

CHAPTER 52

Capture of Jerusalem 1 Zedekiah was twenty-
one years old when he became king, and he
reigned eleven years in Jerusalem.[z] His mother's
name was Hamutal, daughter of Jeremiah of
Libnah. 2 He did what was evil in the eyes of the
LORD, just as Jehoiakim had done. 3 Indeed, what
was done in Jerusalem and in Judah so angered
the LORD that he cast them out from his pres-
ence.

Zedekiah rebelled against the king of Babylon.
4 [a]In the tenth month of the ninth year of his
reign, on the tenth day of the month,* Nebu-
chadnezzar, king of Babylon, and his whole
army advanced against Jerusalem, encamped
around it, and built siege walls on every side.
5 The siege of the city continued until the elev-
enth year of King Zedekiah.

6 On the ninth day of the fourth month, when
famine had gripped the city and the people had
no more bread, 7 the city walls were breached.
Then all the soldiers took to flight and left the
city by night through the gate between the two
walls which was near the king's garden. With
the Chaldeans surrounding the city, they went in
the direction of the Arabah. 8 But the Chaldean
army pursued the king and overtook Zedekiah in
the desert near Jericho, while his whole army
fled from him.

9 The king, therefore, was arrested and
brought to Riblah, in the land of Hamath, to the
king of Babylon, who pronounced sentence on
him. 10 As Zedekiah looked on, the king of
Babylon slew his sons as well as all the princes of
Judah at Riblah. 11 Then he blinded Zedekiah,
bound him with fetters, and had him brought to
Babylon and kept in prison until the day of his
death.

Destruction of Jerusalem 12 On the tenth day
of the fifth month (this was in the nineteenth
year* of Nebuchadnezzar, king of Babylon),
Nebuzaradan, captain of the bodyguard, came to
Jerusalem as the representative of the king of
Babylon. 13 He burned the house of the LORD,
the palace of the king, and all the houses of
Jerusalem; every large building he destroyed
with fire. 14 And the Chaldean troops who were
with the captain of the guard tore down all the
walls that surrounded Jerusalem.

15 Then Nebuzaradan, captain of the guard,
led into exile the rest of the people left in the
city, and those who had deserted to the king of
Babylon, and the rest of the artisans. 16 But some
of the country's poor, Nebuzaradan, captain of
the guard, left behind as vinedressers and farm-
ers.

17 The bronze pillars that belonged to the
house of the LORD, and the wheeled carts and
the bronze sea in the house of the LORD, the
Chaldeans broke into pieces; they carried away
all the bronze to Babylon. 18 They took also the
pots, the shovels, the snuffers, the bowls, the
pans, and all the bronze vessels used for service.
19 The basins also, the fire holders, the bowls, the
pots, the lampstands, the pans, the sacrificial
bowls which were of gold or silver, these too the
captain of the guard carried off, 20 as well as the
two pillars, the one sea, and the twelve oxen of
bronze under the sea, and the wheeled carts
which King Solomon had made for the house of
the LORD. The bronze of all these furnishings
could not be weighed.

21 Each of the pillars was eighteen cubits high
and twelve cubits in diameter; each was four
fingers thick, and hollow inside. 22 A bronze
capital five cubits high surmounted the one
pillar, and a network with pomegranates encir-
cled the capital, all of brass; and so for the other
pillar. The pomegranates . . . 23 there were
ninety-six pomegranates. There were a hundred
pomegranates, all around the network.

24 The captain of the guard also took Seraiah,
the high priest, Zephaniah, the second priest,

52, 1–34: This supplement to the Book of Jeremiah was taken by the final editor from 2 Kgs 24, 18—25, 30 and placed here in order to show the fulfillment of Jeremiah's prophecies. In part this repeats the history given in Jer 39—41; the history of Gedaliah in 2 Kgs 25, 22–26, however, has not been reproduced here.

52, 4: In the tenth month of the ninth year of his reign, on the tenth day of the month: January 15, 588 B.C. Cf Jer 39, 1.

52, 12: On the tenth day of the fifth month . . . nineteenth year: the tenth of Ab—July/August in 587 B.C.

z 1–27: 2 Kgs 24, 18—25, 21. a 4–16: Jer 39, 1–10.

and the three keepers of the entry. 25And from the city he took one courtier, a commander of soldiers, and seven men in the personal service of the king who were present in the city, and the scribe of the army commander who mustered the people of the land, and sixty of the common people who were in the city. 26The captain of the guard, Nebuzaradan, arrested these and brought them to the king of Babylon at Riblah, 27who had them struck down and put to death in Riblah, in the land of Hamath.

Thus was Judah exiled from her land. 28*This is the number of the people whom Nebuchadnezzar led away captive: in his seventh year, three thousand and twenty-three people of Judah; 29in the eighteenth year of Nebuchadnezzar, eight hundred and thirty-two persons from Jerusalem; 30in the twenty-third year of Nebuchadnezzar, Nebuzaradan, captain of the guard, exiled seven hundred and forty-five people of Judah: four thousand six hundred persons in all.

Favor Shown to Jehoiachin* 31 [b]In the thirty-seventh year of the exile of Jehoiachin, king of Judah, on the twenty-fifth day of the twelfth month, Evil-merodach, king of Babylon, in the inaugural year of his reign, took up the case of Jehoiachin, king of Judah, and released him from prison. 32He spoke kindly to him and gave him a throne higher than that of the other kings* who were with him in Babylon. 33Jehoiachin took off his prison garb and ate at the king's table as long as he lived. 34The allowance given him by the king of Babylon was a perpetual allowance, in fixed daily amounts, all the days of his life until the day of his death.

52, 28–30: These verses are missing in the Greek text and have not been taken from 2 Kgs 25, but from some other source using a different system of chronology. Besides the deportations of 598 and 587 B.C., mention is made here of a final one that took place in the year 582/1, possibly as a sequel to the murder of Gedaliah; cf Jer 41, 2.

52, 31–34: In the year 561/0 B.C., Jehoiachin was released from prison by Nebuchadnezzar's successor Awel-Marduk (Evil-merodach), who reigned only two years. Babylonian records confirm the fact that Jehoiachin and his family were supported at public expense.

52, 32: The other kings: who had also been brought as captives to Babylon.

b 31–34: 2 Kgs 25, 27–30.

THE BOOK OF LAMENTATIONS

The sixth century B.C. was an age of crisis, a turning point in the history of Israel. With the destruction of the temple and the interruption of its ritual, the exile of the leaders and loss of national sovereignty, an era came to an end. Not long after the fall of Jerusalem (587) an eyewitness of the national humiliation composed these five laments. They combine confession of sin, grief over the suffering and humiliation of Zion, submission to merited chastisement, and strong faith in the constancy of Yahweh's love and power to restore. The union of poignant grief and unquenchable hope reflects the constant prophetic vision of the weakness of man and the strength of God's love; it also shows how Israel's faith in Yahweh could survive the shattering experience of national ruin.

As a literary work, the Book of Lamentations is carefully constructed according to a familiar structural device. The first four poems are acrostics in which the separate stanzas begin with successive letters of the Hebrew alphabet from the first to the last. Far from destroying the spontaneous pathos of the songs, this literary feature permits a symbolic and disciplined expression of the profound grief, the sinful responsibility, and the enduring hope of the suffering community. The figure of Israel as the bride of Yahweh, familiar from the prophets, appears here again; but now Zion is a desolate widow, the *Judaea Capta* of Titus' memorial coins, sustained only by the faith that God's chastisement will eventually give place to his infinite compassion.

CHAPTER 1

Jerusalem Abandoned and Disgraced*

1 How lonely she is now,
the once crowded city!
Widowed is she
who was mistress over nations;
The princess among the provinces
has been made a toiling slave.

2 Bitterly she weeps at night,
tears upon her cheeks,
With not one to console her
of all her dear ones;
Her friends have all betrayed her
and become her enemies. [a]

3 Judah has fled into exile
from oppression and cruel slavery;
Yet where she lives among the nations
she finds no place to rest:
All her persecutors come upon her
where she is narrowly confined. [b]

4 The roads to Zion mourn
for lack of pilgrims going to her feasts;
All her gateways are deserted,
her priests groan,
Her virgins sigh;
she is in bitter grief. [c]

5 Her foes are uppermost,
her enemies are at ease;
The LORD has punished her
for her many sins.
Her little ones have gone away,
captive before the foe.

6 Gone from daughter Zion
is all her glory:
Her princes, like rams
that find no pasture,
Have gone off without strength
before their captors.

7 Jerusalem is mindful of the days
of her wretched homelessness,
When her people fell into enemy hands,
and she had no one to help her;
When her foes gloated over her,
laughed at her ruin.

8 Through the sin of which she is guilty,
Jerusalem is defiled;
All who esteemed her think her vile
now that they see her nakedness;
She herself groans
and turns away. [d]

9 Her filth is on her skirt;
she gave no thought how she would end.
Astounding is her downfall,
with no one to console her.
Look, O LORD, upon her misery,
for the enemy has triumphed!

10 The foe stretched out his hand
to all her treasures;
She has seen those nations
enter her sanctuary
Whom you forbade to come
into your assembly. [e]

11 All her people groan,
searching for bread;
They give their treasures for food,
to retain the breath of life.
"Look, O LORD, and see
how worthless I have become![f]

12 "Come, all you who pass by the way,
look and see
Whether there is any suffering like my
suffering,
which has been dealt me
When the LORD afflicted me
on the day of his blazing wrath.

13 "From on high he sent fire
down into my very frame;
He spread a net for my feet,
and overthrew me.

1, 1–22: In this poem the poet first describes Jerusalem's miserable state after the destruction wrought by the Chaldeans (vv 1–11a); in v 11b the city itself takes up the lament.

a Jer 30, 14; Ez 16, 37. b Dt 28, 65; Jer 45, 3. c Jer 14, 2. d Is 47, 2; Jer 13, 22. 26. e Jer 51, 51. f Jer 52, 6.

He left me desolate,
in pain all the day.[g]

14 "He has kept watch over my sins;
by his hand they have been plaited:
They have settled about my neck,*
he has brought my strength to its knees;
The Lord has delivered me into their grip,
I am unable to rise.

15 "All the mighty ones in my midst
the Lord has cast away;
He summoned an army against me
to crush my young men;
The LORD has trodden in the wine press
virgin daughter Judah.[h]

16 "At this I weep,
my eyes run with tears:
Far from me are all who could console me,
any who might revive me;
My sons were reduced to silence
when the enemy prevailed."[i]

17 Zion stretched out her hands,
but there was no one to console her;
The LORD gave orders against Jacob
for his neighbors to be his foes;
Jerusalem has become in their midst
a thing unclean.[j]

18 "The LORD is just;
I had defied his command.
Listen, all you peoples,
and behold my suffering:
My maidens and my youths
have gone into captivity.[k]

19 "I cried out to my lovers,*
but they failed me.
My priests and my elders
perished in the city;
Where they sought food for themselves,
they found it not.[l]

20 "Look, O LORD, upon my distress:
all within me is in ferment,
My heart recoils within me
from my monstrous rebellion.
In the streets the sword bereaves,
at home death stalks.[m]

21 "Give heed to my groaning;
there is no one to console me.
All my enemies rejoice at my misfortune:
it is you who have wrought it.
Bring on the day you have proclaimed,
that they may be even as I.

22 "Let all their evil come before you;*
deal with them
As you have dealt with me
for all my sins;
My groans are many,
and I am sick at heart."[n]

CHAPTER 2

The Lord's Wrath against Zion

1 How the Lord in his wrath
has detested daughter Zion!
He has cast down from heaven to earth
the glory of Israel,*
Unmindful of his footstool
on the day of his wrath.

2 The Lord has consumed without pity
all the dwellings of Jacob;
He has torn down in his anger
the fortresses of daughter Judah;
He has brought to the ground in dishonor
her king and her princes.

3 He broke off, in fiery wrath,
the horn* that was Israel's whole strength;
He withheld the support of his right hand
when the enemy approached;
He blazed up in Jacob like a flaming fire
devouring all about it.[o]

1, 14: They have been plaited . . . my neck: the sins of the people have been bound together and laid as a yoke on their back; cf Mt 23, 4.

1, 19: My lovers: Zion's foreign allies, who failed to help her, as the prophets had warned.

1, 22: Zion fully acknowledges her guilt and the justness of divine punishment; nevertheless, she pleads that her enemies also be punished for their guilt.

2, 1: The glory of Israel: the temple. His footstool: the ark of the covenant (1 Chr 28, 2; Pss 99, 5; 132, 7); or again, the temple (Ez 43, 7).

2, 3: Horn: symbol of power and strength; cf Lam 2, 17; 1 Sm 2, 10; Lk 1, 69; etc.

g Ez 12, 13. h Jer 8, 16. i Jer 13, 17; 14, 17. j Ps 74, 7. k Dt 28, 41. l Jer 30, 14. m Lam 2, 11. n Lam 3, 64. o Lam 1, 12.

4 Like an enemy he made taut his bow;
with his arrows in his right hand
He took his stand as a foe, and slew
all on whom the eye doted;
Over the tent of daughter Zion
he poured out his wrath like fire. [p]

5 The Lord has become an enemy,
he has consumed Israel:
Consumed all her castles
and destroyed her fortresses;
For daughter Judah he has multiplied
moaning and groaning.

6 He has demolished his shelter like a garden booth,
he has destroyed his dwelling;
In Zion the LORD has made
feast and sabbath to be forgotten;
He has scorned in fierce wrath
both king and priest. [q]

7 The Lord has disowned his altar,
rejected his sanctuary;
The walls of her towers
he has handed over to the enemy,
Who shout in the house of the LORD
as on a feast day. [r]

8 The LORD marked for destruction
the wall of daughter Zion:
He stretched out the measuring line;*
his hand brought ruin, yet he did not relent—
He brought grief on wall and rampart
till both succumbed. [s]

9 Sunk into the ground are her gates;
he has removed and broken her bars.
Her king and her princes are among the pagans;
priestly instruction is wanting,
And her prophets have not received
any vision from the LORD. [t]

10 On the ground in silence sit
the old men of daughter Zion;
They strew dust* on their heads
and gird themselves with sackcloth;
The maidens of Jerusalem
bow their heads to the ground. [u]

11 Worn out from weeping are my eyes,
within me all is in ferment;
My gall is poured out on the ground*
because of the downfall of the daughter of my people,
As child and infant faint away
in the open spaces of the town. [v]

12 They ask their mothers,
"Where is the cereal?"—in vain,
As they faint away like the wounded
in the streets of the city,
And breathe their last
in their mothers' arms. [w]

13 To what can I liken or compare you,
O daughter Jerusalem?
What example can I show you for your comfort,
virgin daughter Zion?
For great as the sea is your downfall;
who can heal you? [x]

14 Your prophets had for you
false and specious visions;
They did not lay bare your guilt,
to avert your fate;
They beheld for you in vision
false and misleading portents. [y]

15 All who pass by
clap their hands at you;
They hiss and wag their heads
over daughter Jerusalem:
"Is this the all-beautiful city,
the joy of the whole earth?" [z]

16 All your enemies
open their mouths against you;
They hiss and gnash their teeth.

2, 8: The measuring line: used not only in building, but in deciding what must be destroyed; cf Is 34, 11; 2 Kgs 21, 13.
2, 10: They strew dust: as a sign of penance; cf Jb 2, 12.
2, 11: My gall is poured out on the ground: I am afflicted with bitter sorrow; cf Jb 16, 13.

p Jer 30, 14. q Lam 1, 4; Is 1, 13; 5, 5. r Ez 24, 21. s Jer 52, 13. t Dt 28, 36. u Is 3, 26. v Lam 3, 48. w Lam 1, 11. x Lam 1, 12. y Is 58, 1; Jer 2, 8; 23, 16. z Jer 18, 16.

They say, "We have devoured her.
This at last is the day we hoped for;
we have lived to see it!" [a]

17 The LORD has done as he decreed:
he has fulfilled the threat
He set forth from days of old;
he has destroyed and had no pity,
Letting the enemy gloat over you
and exalting the horn of your foes. [b]

18 Cry out to the Lord;
moan, O daughter Zion!
Let your tears flow like a torrent
day and night;
Let there be no respite for you,
no repose for your eyes.

19 Rise up, shrill in the night,
at the beginning of every watch;
Pour out your heart like water
in the presence of the Lord;
Lift up your hands to him
for the lives of your little ones
[Who faint from hunger
at the corner of every street].

20 "Look, O LORD, and consider:
whom have you ever treated thus?
Must women eat their offspring,*
their well-formed children?
Are priest and prophet to be slain
in the sanctuary of the LORD? [c]

21 "Dead in the dust of the streets
lie young and old;
My maidens and young men
have fallen by the sword;
You have slain on the day of your
wrath,
slaughtered without pity. [d]

22 "You summoned as for a feast day
terrors against me from all sides;
There was not, on the day of your wrath,
either fugitive or survivor;
Those whom I bore and reared
my enemy has utterly destroyed." [e]

CHAPTER 3

Sufferings of the Prophet and His People

1 I am a man who knows affliction*
from the rod of his anger, [f]
2 One whom he has led and forced to walk
in darkness, not in the light;
3 Against me alone he brings back his hand
again and again all the day.
4 He has worn away my flesh and my skin,
he has broken my bones; [g]
5 He has beset me round about
with poverty and weariness;
6 He has left me to dwell in the dark
like those long dead. [h]

7 He has hemmed me in with no escape
and weighed me down with chains;
8 Even when I cry out for help,
he stops my prayer; [i]
9 He has blocked my ways with fitted stones,
and turned my paths aside.

10 A lurking bear he has been to me,
a lion in ambush! [j]
11 He deranged my ways, set me astray,
left me desolate. [k]
12 He bent his bow, and set me up
as the target for his arrow. [l]

13 He pierces my sides
with shafts from his quiver. [m]
14 I have become a laughingstock for all nations,
their taunt all the day long; [n]
15 He has sated me with bitter food,
made me drink my fill of wormwood. [o]

16 He has broken my teeth with gravel,
pressed my face in the dust;
17 My soul is deprived of peace,
I have forgotten what happiness is;
18 I tell myself my future is lost,
all that I hoped for from the LORD.

2, 20: Must women eat their offspring: extreme famine in a besieged city sometimes led to this form of cannibalism; cf Lam 4, 10; 2 Kgs 6, 28f; Bar 2, 3; Ez 5, 10.
3, 1–21: The author identifies Zion's sufferings with his own.

a Lam 3, 46. b Dt 28, 15. c Lam 4, 10. d Lam 3, 43; 2 Chr 36, 17; Jer 6, 11. e Jer 42, 17. f Jer 20, 18. g Jb 30, 30; Is 38, 13. h Ps 143, 3. i Ps 22, 2. j Jb 10, 16; Hos 13, 8. k Lam 1, 13. l Lam 2, 4; Jb 16, 12. m Jb 6, 4; Ps 38, 3. n Jb 30, 9; Ps 69, 13. o Jer 9, 14; 23, 15.

19 The thought of my homeless poverty
is wormwood and gall;
20 Remembering it over and over
leaves my soul downcast within me.
21 But I will call this to mind,
as my reason to have hope:

22 The favors of the LORD are not exhausted,
his mercies are not spent; [p]
23 They are renewed each morning,
so great is his faithfulness.
24 My portion is the LORD, says my soul;
therefore will I hope in him. [q]

25 Good is the LORD to one who waits for him,
to the soul that seeks him; [r]
26 It is good to hope in silence
for the saving help of the LORD.
27 It is good for a man to bear
the yoke* from his youth.

28 Let him sit alone and in silence,
when it is laid upon him.
29 Let him put his mouth to the dust;*
there may yet be hope. [s]
30 Let him offer his cheek to be struck,
let him be filled with disgrace. [t]

31 For the Lord's rejection
does not last forever; [u]
32 Though he punishes, he takes pity,
in the abundance of his mercies; [v]
33 He has no joy in afflicting
or grieving the sons of men. [w]

34 When anyone tramples underfoot
all the prisoners in the land,
35 When he distorts men's rights
in the very sight of the Most High,
36 When he presses a crooked claim,
the Lord does not look on unconcerned.

37 Who commands, so that it comes to pass,
except the Lord ordains it;
38 Except it proceeds from the mouth of the Most
High,
whether the thing be good or bad! [x]
39 Why should any living man complain,
any mortal, in the face of his sins? [y]

40 Let us search and examine our ways
that we may return to the LORD! [z]
41 Let us reach out our hearts
toward God in heaven!
42 We have sinned and rebelled;
you have not forgiven us.

43 You veiled yourself in wrath and pursued us,
you slew us and took no pity; [a]
44 You wrapped yourself in a cloud
which prayer could not pierce.
45 You have made us offscourings and refuse
among the nations. [b]

46 All our enemies
have opened their mouths against us;
47 Terror and the pit have been our lot,
desolation and destruction; [c]
48 My eyes run with streams of water
over the downfall of the daughter of my
people. [d]

49 My eyes flow without ceasing,
there is no respite,
50 Till the LORD from heaven
looks down and sees.
51 My eyes torment my soul
at the sight of all the daughters of my city.

52 Those who were my enemies without cause
hunted me down like a bird;
53 They struck me down alive in the pit,
and sealed me in with a stone. [e]
54 The waters flowed over my head,
and I said, "I am lost!"

55 I called upon your name, O LORD, [f]
from the bottom of the pit;
56 You heard me call, "Let not your ear
be deaf to my cry for help!"
57 You came to my aid when I called to you;
you said, "Have no fear!"

3, 27: To bear the yoke: to do God's will; cf Jer 2, 20.
3, 29: Let him put his mouth to the dust: in humble submission; cf Ps 72, 9.

p Neh 9, 31. q Pss 16, 5; 73, 26. r Ps 130, 6; Is 30, 18. s Jb 42, 6. t Is 50, 6; Mt 5, 39. u Ps 103, 9. v Is 54, 8f. w Heb 12, 10f. x Is 45, 7. y Prv 19, 3. z Jl 2, 12f. a Lam 2, 21. b 1 Cor 4, 13. c Is 24, 17; Jer 48, 43. d Ps 119, 136. e Jer 37, 16; 38, 6–9. f 55f: Ps 130, 1f.

58 You defended me in mortal danger,
you redeemed my life.
59 You see, O LORD, how I am wronged;
do me justice! [g]
60 You see all their vindictiveness,
all their plots against me.

61 You hear their insults, O LORD,
[all their plots against me],
62 The whispered murmurings of my foes,
against me all the day;
63 Whether they sit or stand,
see, I am their taunt song.

64 Requite them as they deserve, O LORD,
according to their deeds;
65 Give them hardness of heart,
as your curse upon them; [h]
66 Pursue them in wrath and destroy them
from under your heavens!

CHAPTER 4

Miseries of the Besieged City

1 How tarnished is the gold,
how changed the noble metal;
How the sacred stones lie strewn
at every street corner!

2 Zion's precious sons,
fine gold their counterpart,
Now worth no more than earthen jars
made by the hands of a potter! [i]

3 Even the jackals bare their breasts
and suckle their young;
The daughter of my people has become as cruel
as the ostrich* in the desert. [j]

4 The tongue of the suckling cleaves
to the roof of its mouth in thirst;
The babes cry for food,
but there is no one to give it to them.

5 Those accustomed to dainty food
perish in the streets;
Those brought up in purple
now cling to the ash heaps. [k]

6 The punishment of the daughter of my people
is greater than the penalty of Sodom,
Which was overthrown in an instant
without the turning of a hand. [l]

7 Brighter than snow were her princes,
whiter than milk,
More ruddy than coral,
more precious than sapphire.

8 Now their appearance is blacker than soot,
they are unrecognized on the streets;
Their skin shrinks on their bones,
as dry as wood. [m]

9 Better for those who perish by the sword
than for those who die of hunger,
Who waste away, as though pierced through,
lacking the fruits of the field!

10 The hands of compassionate women
boiled their own children,
To serve them as mourners' food
in the downfall of the daughter of my people. [n]

11 The LORD has spent his anger,
poured out his blazing wrath;
He has kindled a fire in Zion
that has consumed her foundations. [o]

12 The kings of the earth did not believe,
nor any of the world's inhabitants,
That enemy or foe could enter
the gates of Jerusalem.

13 Because of the sins of her prophets*
and the crimes of her priests,
Who shed in her midst
the blood of the just!— [p]

14 They staggered blindly in the streets,
soiled with blood,

4, 3: Cruel as the ostrich: see note on Jb 39, 14ff. Jerusalem, in her distress, had abandoned her children.

4, 13ff: The priests and the false prophets lulled the people into an illusory security (Jer 2, 8; 5, 31; 6, 13; etc.), condoning and entering into their crimes so that they themselves became unclean.

g Ps 35, 23. h Jer 11, 20; 2 Tm 4, 14. i Jer 19, 11. j Jb 39, 16. k Dt 28, 56. l Gn 19, 23–29; 2 Pt 2, 6; Jude 1, 7. m Lam 3, 4. n Lam 2, 20; Dt 28, 56f; 2 Kgs 6, 29. o Jer 7, 20; Ez 5, 13. p Jer 6, 13.

So that people could not touch
even their garments: [q]

15 "Away, you unclean!" they cried to them,
"Away, away, do not draw near!"
If they left and wandered among the nations,
nowhere could they remain.

16 The LORD himself has dispersed them,
he regards them no more;
He does not receive the priests with favor,
nor show kindness to the elders.

17 Our eyes ever wasted away,
looking in vain for aid;
From our watchtower we watched
for a nation* that could not save us.

18 Men dogged our steps
so that we could not walk in our streets;
Our end drew near, and came;
our time had expired.

19 Our pursuers were swifter
than eagles in the air,
They harassed us on the mountains
and waylaid us in the desert. [r]

20 The anointed one of the LORD, our breath of life,*
was caught in their snares,
He in whose shadow we thought
we could live on among the nations. [s]

21 Though you rejoice and are glad, O daughter Edom,
you who dwell in the land of Uz,*
To you also shall the cup be passed;
you shall become drunk and naked. [t]

22 Your chastisement is completed, O daughter Zion,
he will not prolong your exile;
But your wickedness, O daughter Edom, he will punish,
he will lay bare your sins. [u]

CHAPTER 5

The Prophet's Lament and Supplication

1 Remember, O LORD, what has befallen us,
look, and see our disgrace:
2 Our inherited lands have been turned over to strangers,
our homes to foreigners. [v]
3 We have become orphans, fatherless;
widowed are our mothers.
4 The water we drink we must buy,
for our own wood we must pay.
5 On our necks is the yoke of those who drive us;
we are worn out, but allowed no rest.

6 To Egypt we submitted,
and to Assyria, to fill our need of bread.*
7 Our fathers,* who sinned, are no more;
but we bear their guilt.
8 Slaves rule over us;
there is no one to rescue us from their hands.*
9 At the peril of our lives we bring in our sustenance,
in the face of the desert heat; [w]
10 Our skin is shriveled up, as though by a furnace,
with the searing blasts of famine. [x]

11 The wives in Zion were ravished by the enemy,
the maidens in the cities of Judah; [y]
12 Princes were gibbeted by them,
elders shown no respect. [z]

4, 17: A nation: Egypt, which failed to give effective aid against Babylon.

4, 20: Our breath of life: the king. This is a royal epithet borrowed from Egyptian usage, while the anointed one of the Lord is Israelite. After the disaster of 598 B.C. (2 Kgs 24, 1–17), Jerusalem could have hoped to live in peace amidst her neighbors; but they (vv 21f) as well as Babylon turned against her to ensure her total devastation in 587 B.C.

4, 21: Uz: see note on Jer 25, 20.

5, 6: In its state of abjection, Judah was forced to depend on its traditional enemies to the west and the east for subsistence. Mesopotamia is here called by the name it had long borne, Assyria, though in these times the power of the Assyrians had been superseded by that of the Chaldeans.

5, 7: Our fathers: collective responsibility, for good and for evil, was recognized in the Old Testament; cf Jer 31, 29. But the present generation is also personally guilty of sin (v 16).

5, 8: Administrations imposed by foreign powers were notoriously corrupt and inept. The Hebrew word for "slave" is the same as that used for an official (servant of the ruler); the author doubtless intends the double meaning here.

q Is 59, 10. r Jer 4, 13; Hb 1, 8. s Lam 2, 9; Ez 19, 4. 8. t Lam 1, 21; Jer 25, 15. u Is 40, 2. v Ps 79, 1. w Jer 6, 25. x Lam 4, 8. y Zec 14, 2. z Lam 4, 16.

13 The youths carry the millstones,
boys stagger under their loads of wood;
14 The old men have abandoned the gate,*
the young men their music.
15 The joy of our hearts has ceased,
our dance has turned into mourning; [a]
16 The garlands have fallen from our heads:
woe to us, for we have sinned!
17 Over this our hearts are sick,
at this our eyes grow dim:
18 That Mount Zion should be desolate,
with jackals roaming there!
19 You, O LORD, are enthroned forever;
your throne stands from age to age. [b]
20 Why, then, should you forget us,
abandon us so long a time? [c]
21 Lead us back to you, O LORD, that we may be restored:
give us anew such days as we had of old. [d]
22 For now you have indeed rejected us,
and in full measure turned your wrath against us. [e]

5, 14: The gate: the place of assembly, where city decisions were made and judgment given by the elders and other notables; see note on Ru 4, 1.

a Jer 16, 9; 25, 10; Am 8, 10. b Pss 9, 8; 45, 7; 102, 13. 27. c Pss 13, 1; 42, 10. d Ps 80, 19f. e Jer 14, 19.

THE BOOK OF BARUCH

The opening verses of this book ascribe it, or at least its first part, to Baruch, the well-known secretary of the prophet Jeremiah. It contains five very different compositions, the first and the last in prose, the others in poetic form. The prose sections were certainly composed in Hebrew, though the earliest known form of the book is in Greek.

An observance of the feast of Booths with a public prayer of penitence and petition (1, 15—3, 8), such as is supposed by the introduction (1, 1-14), would not have been possible during the lifetime of Baruch after the fall of Jerusalem; this indeed is suggested in the prayer itself (2, 26). The prayer is therefore to be understood as the pious reflection of a later Jewish writer upon the circumstances of the exiles in Babylon as he knew them from the Book of Jeremiah. He expresses in their name sentiments called for by the prophet, and ascribes the wording of these sentiments to the person most intimately acquainted with Jeremiah's teaching, namely, Baruch. The purpose of this literary device is to portray for his own and later generations the spirit of repentance which prompted God to bring the Exile to an end.

The lesson thus gained is followed by a hymn in praise of Wisdom (3, 9—4, 4), exalting the law of Moses as the unique gift of God to Israel, the observance of which is the way to life and peace. The ideal city of Jerusalem is then represented (4, 5-29) as the solicitous mother of all exiles, who is assured in the name of God that all her children will be restored to her (4, 30—5, 9).

The final chapter is really a separate work, with a title of its own (6, 1). It is patterned after the earlier letter of Jeremiah (Jer 29), in the spirit of the warnings against idolatry contained in Jer 10 and Is 44. Its earnestness is impressive, but in restating previous inspired teachings at a later day, it does so with no special literary grace.

Thus the principal divisions of the book are seen to be:

I. Prayer of the Exiles (1, 1—3, 8).
II. Praise of Wisdom in the Law of Moses (3, 9—4, 4).
III. Jerusalem Bewails and Consoles Her Captive Children (4, 5-29).
IV. Jerusalem Consoled: The Captivity about To End (4, 30—5, 9).
V. The Letter of Jeremiah against Idolatry (6, 1-72).

I: Prayer of the Exiles

CHAPTER 1

Meeting in Babylon [1]Now these are the words of the scroll which Baruch, son of Neriah, son of Mahseiah, son of Zedekiah, son of Hasadiah, son of Hilkiah, wrote in Babylon,[a] [2]in the fifth year [on the seventh day of the month,* at the time when the Chaldeans took Jerusalem and burnt it with fire].[b] [3] [c]And Baruch read the words of this scroll for Jeconiah, son of Jehoiakim, king of Judah, to hear it, as well as all the people who came to the reading:[d] [4]the nobles, the kings' sons, the elders, and the whole people, small and great alike—all who lived in Babylon by the river Sud.*

[5]They wept and fasted and prayed before the LORD, [6]and collected such funds as each could furnish.[e] [7]These they sent to Jerusalem, to Jehoiakim, son of Hilkiah, son of Shallum, the priest, and to the priests and the whole people who were with him in Jerusalem. [8][This was when he* received the vessels of the house of the LORD that had been removed from the temple, to restore them to the land of Judah, on the tenth of Sivan. These silver vessels Zedekiah, son of Josiah, king of Judah, had had made [9]after Nebuchadnezzar, king of Babylon, carried off Jeconiah, and the princes, and the skilled workers, and the nobles, and the people of the land from Jerusalem, as captives, and brought them to Babylon.]

[10]Their message was: "We send you funds, with which you are to procure holocausts, sin offerings, and frankincense, and to prepare cereal offerings; offer these on the altar of the LORD our God,[f] [11]and pray for the life of Nebuchadnezzar, king of Babylon, and that of Belshazzar, his son,* that their lifetimes may equal the duration of the heavens above the earth;[g] [12]and that the LORD may give us strength, and light to our eyes, that we may live under the protective shadow of Nebuchadnezzar, king of Babylon, and that of Belshazzar, his son, and serve them long, finding favor in their sight.

Confession of Guilt [13]"Pray for us also to the LORD, our God; for we have sinned against the LORD, our God, and the wrath and anger of the LORD have not yet been withdrawn from us at the present day. [14]And read out publicly this scroll which we send you, in the house of the LORD, on the feast day and during the days of assembly:[h]

[15]"Justice is with the LORD, our God; and we today are flushed with shame, we men of Judah and citizens of Jerusalem,[i] [16]that we, with our kings and rulers and priests and prophets, and with our fathers, [17]have sinned in the LORD's sight [18]and disobeyed him. We have neither heeded the voice of the LORD, our God, nor

1, 2: In the fifth year on the seventh day of the month: Jerusalem fell on the seventh day of the fifth month; cf 2 Kgs 25, 8; Jer 52, 12. Either the text read originally "the fifth month," or it refers to the observance of an anniversary of the fall of Jerusalem in 587 B.C.

1, 4: The river Sud: one of the Babylonian canals, not otherwise identified. In ancient non-Biblical Hebrew fragments discovered in 1952, there is reference to a river "Sur" in a similar context.

1, 8f: He: possibly Baruch; less likely Jehoiakim . . . the priest (v 7), a member of the high-priestly family not mentioned elsewhere. The silver vessels here described are distinct from the vessels referred to in 2 Kgs 25, 14 and Ezr 1, 7ff. The author of this note may have thought of the fifth year (v 1) of Zedekiah, in view of Jer 28, 1; 29, 1ff. A "fifth year," again with no month mentioned, is given in Ez 1, 2 for the inaugural vision of Ezekiel's prophetic career.

1, 11: Nebuchadnezzar . . . Belshazzar, his son: as in Dn 5, 1f. Later Jewish tradition seems to have simplified the history of the past by making the last Chaldean ruler of Babylon the son of the conqueror of Jerusalem.

a Jer 32, 12; 36, 4; 45, 1-5. b 2 Kgs 25, 8ff. c 2 Kgs 24, 8-17; Jer 22, 24-30; 51, 59-64. d 3-4; 2 Kgs 23, 1-2. e Dt 16, 17. f Jer 17, 26. g Dt 11, 21; Jer 29, 7; Dn 5, 1-2; 1 Tm 2, 1f. h Ex 23, 14ff; Lv 23, 35f; Hos 9, 5; Sir 50, 6. i Bar 2, 6; 3, 8; Neh 9, 6-37; Ezr 9, 6-15; Dn 9, 4-19.

followed the precepts which the LORD set before
us. 19 From the time the LORD led our fathers out
of the land of Egypt until the present day, we
have been disobedient to the LORD, our God,
and only too ready to disregard his voice. 20 And
the evils and the curse which the LORD enjoined
upon Moses, his servant, at the time he led our
fathers forth from the land of Egypt to give us the
land flowing with milk and honey, cling to us
even today.[j] 21 For we did not heed the voice of
the LORD, our God, in all the words of the
prophets whom he sent us, 22 but each one of us
went off after the devices of our own wicked
hearts, served other gods, and did evil in the
sight of the LORD, our God.

CHAPTER 2

1 "And the LORD fulfilled the warning he had
uttered against us: against our judges, who
governed Israel, against our kings and princes,
and against the men of Israel and Judah. 2 He
brought down upon us evils so great that there
has not been done anywhere under heaven what
has been done in Jerusalem, as was written in
the law of Moses:[k] 3 that one after another of us
should eat* the flesh of his son or of his
daughter. 4 He has made us subject to all the
kingdoms round about us, a reproach and a
horror among all the nations round about to
which the LORD has scattered us.[l] 5 We are
brought low, not raised up, because we sinned
against the LORD, our God, not heeding his
voice.

6 "Justice is with the LORD, our God; and we,
like our fathers, are flushed with shame even
today.[m] 7 All the evils of which the LORD had
warned us have come upon us; 8 and we did not
plead before the LORD, or turn, each from the
figments of his evil heart. 9 And the LORD kept
watch over the evils, and brought them home to
us; for the LORD is just in all the works he
commanded us to do,[n] 10 but we did not heed
his voice, or follow the precepts of the LORD
which he set before us.

Prayer for Deliverance 11 "And now, LORD,
God of Israel, you who led your people out of the
land of Egypt with your mighty hand, with signs
and wonders and great might, and with your
upraised arm, so that you have made for yourself
a name till the present day:[o] 12 we have sinned,
been impious, and violated, O LORD, our God,
all your statutes.[p] 13 Let your anger be with-
drawn from us, for we are left few in number
among the nations to which you scattered us.
14 Hear, O LORD, our prayer of supplication, and
deliver us for your own sake: grant us favor in
the presence of our captors, 15 that the whole
earth may know that you are the LORD, our God,
and that Israel and his descendants bear your
name.[q] 16 O LORD, look down from your holy
dwelling and take thought of us; turn, O LORD,
your ear to hear us.[r] 17 Look directly at us, and
behold: it is not the dead in the nether world,
whose spirits have been taken from within them,
who will give glory and vindication to the
LORD.[s] 18 He whose soul is deeply grieved, who
walks bowed and feeble, with failing eyes and
famished soul, will declare your glory and jus-
tice, LORD![t]

19 "Not on the just deeds of our fathers and
our kings do we base our plea for mercy in your
sight, O LORD, our God. 20 You have brought
your wrath and anger down upon us, as you had
warned us through your servants the prophets:
21 'Thus says the LORD: Bend your shoulders to
the service of the king of Babylon, that you may
continue in the land I gave your fathers:[u] 22 for if
you do not hear the LORD's voice so as to serve
the king of Babylon,

23 I will make to cease from the cities of Judah
    and from the streets of Jerusalem
The sounds of joy and the sounds of gladness,
    the voice of the bridegroom
    and the voice of the bride;
And all the land shall be deserted,
    without inhabitants.'[v]

24 But we did not heed your voice, or serve the

2, 3: One after another of us should eat: see note on Lam 2, 20.

j Lv 26, 14–39; Dt 28, 15–68. k 2f: 2 Kgs 6, 28f; Jer 19, 9; Lam 2, 20; 4, 10; Ez 5, 10. l Jer 29, 18. m Bar 1, 15. n Jer 1, 12; 31, 28; 44, 27. o Dt 6, 21–22. p Ps 106, 6. q Sir 36, 11; Jer 14, 9. r Dt 26, 15. s Ps 6, 6; Is 38, 18. t Zep 2, 3. u Jer 27, 12. v Jer 7, 34.

king of Babylon, and you fulfilled the threats you
had made through your servants the prophets, to
have the bones of our kings and the bones of our
fathers brought out from their burial places.[w]
25 And indeed, they lie exposed* to the heat of
day and the frost of night. They died in dire an-
guish, by hunger and the sword and plague.[x]
26 And you reduced the house which bears your
name* to what it is today, for the wickedness of
the kingdom of Israel and the kingdom of Judah.[y]
God's Promises Recalled 27 "But with us, O
Lord, our God, you have dealt in all your clem-
ency and in all your great mercy. 28 This was your
warning through your servant Moses, the day
you ordered him to write down your law in the
presence of the Israelites: 29 If you do not heed
my voice, surely this great and numerous throng
will dwindle away among the nations to which I
will scatter them. 30 For I know they will not
heed me, because they are a stiff-necked people.
But in the land of their captivity they shall have a
change of heart;[z] 31 they shall know that I, the
LORD, am their God. I will give them hearts, and
heedful ears;[a] 32 and they shall praise me in the
land of their captivity, and shall invoke my
name.[b] 33 Then they shall turn back from their
stiff-necked stubbornness, and from their evil
deeds, because they shall remember the fate of
their fathers who sinned against the LORD.[c]
34 And I will bring them back to the land which
with my oath I promised to their fathers, to Abra-
ham, Isaac and Jacob; and they shall rule it. I will
make them increase; they shall not then dimin-
ish. 35 And I will establish for them, as an eternal
covenant, that I will be their God, and they shall
be my people; and I will not again remove my
people Israel from the land I gave them.[d]

CHAPTER 3

1 "LORD Almighty, God of Israel, afflicted souls
and dismayed spirits call to you. 2 Hear, O LORD,
for you are a God of mercy; and have mercy on
us, who have sinned against you: 3 for you are
enthroned forever, while we are perishing for-
ever.[e] 4 LORD Almighty, God of Israel, hear the
prayer of Israel's few, the sons of those who
sinned against you; they did not heed the voice
of the LORD, their God, and the evils cling to us.
5 Remember at this time not the misdeeds of our
fathers, but your own hand and name: 6 for you
are the LORD our God; and you, O LORD, we will
praise! 7 For this, you put into our hearts the fear
of you: that we may call upon your name, and
praise you in our captivity, when we have
removed from our hearts all the wickedness of
our fathers who sinned against you.[f] 8 Behold us
today in our captivity, where you scattered us, a
reproach, a curse, and a requital for all the
misdeeds of our fathers, who withdrew from the
LORD, our God."

II: Praise of Wisdom in the Law of Moses

9 Hear, O Israel, the commandments of life:
listen, and know prudence![g]
10 How is it, Israel,
that you are in the land of your foes,
grown old in a foreign land,
Defiled with the dead,
11 accounted with those destined for the
nether world?[h]
12 You have forsaken the fountain of wisdom![i]
13 Had you walked in the way of God,
you would have dwelt in enduring peace.[j]
14 Learn where prudence is,
where strength, where understanding;
That you may know also
where are length of days, and life,
where light of the eyes, and peace.[k]
15 Who has found the place of wisdom,[l]
who has entered into her treasuries?
16 Where are the rulers of the nations,
they who lorded it over the wild beasts of
the earth,[m]

2, 25: They lie exposed: probably an allusion to Jer 36, 30; see note on Jer 22, 19.

2, 26: The house which bears your name: the temple of Jerusalem. What it is today: during the exile it lay in ruins.

w Jer 8, 1f. x Jer 7, 34; 14,12; 31, 30. y Jer 7, 10–15. z Dt 30, 1f; 31, 27. a Jer 24, 7; Ez 36, 26; Ps 40, 7. b Tb 13, 7. c 33ff: Dt 30, 1–10. d Jer 31, 31; Lam 4, 22. e Pss 29, 10; 102, 12f. f Jer 31, 33. g Prv 4, 20ff. h Ps 88, 5. i Jer 2, 13; Jn 4, 10. 14. j Is 48, 18. k Prv 3, 2; 8, 14. l 15ff: Jb 28, 1–28. m Jer 27, 6.

17 and made sport of the birds of the heavens:
They who heaped up the silver
and the gold in which men trust;
of whose possessions there was no end?
18 They schemed anxiously for money,
but there is no trace of their work:
19 They have vanished down into the nether world,
and others have risen up in their stead.

20 Later generations have seen the light,
have dwelt in the land,
But the way to understanding they have not known,
21 they have not perceived her paths, or reached her;
their offspring were far from the way to her.
22 She has not been heard of in Canaan,*
nor seen in Teman. [n]
23 The sons of Hagar who seek knowledge on earth,
the merchants of Midian and Teman,
the phrasemakers seeking knowledge,
These have not known the way to wisdom,
nor have they her paths in mind.

24 O Israel, how vast is the house of God,*
how broad the scope of his dominion:
25 Vast and endless,
high and immeasurable!
26 In it were born the giants,
renowned at the first,
stalwarts, skilled in war. [o]
27 Not these did God choose,
nor did he give them the way of understanding; [p]
28 They perished for lack of prudence,
perished through their folly. [q]
29 Who has gone up to the heavens and taken her,
or brought her down from the clouds? [r]
30 Who has crossed the sea and found her,
bearing her away rather than choice gold?
31 None knows the way to her,
nor has any understood her paths.

32 Yet he who knows all things knows her;
he has probed her by his knowledge—
He who established the earth for all time,
and filled it with four-footed beasts;
33 He who dismisses the light, and it departs,
calls it, and it obeys him trembling;
34 Before whom the stars at their posts
shine and rejoice;
35 When he calls them, they answer, "Here we are!"
shining with joy for their Maker. [s]
36 Such is our God;
no other is to be compared to him:
37 He has traced out all the way of understanding,
and has given her to Jacob, his servant,
to Israel, his beloved son. [t]

38 Since then she has appeared on earth,
and moved among men. [u]

CHAPTER 4

1 She is the book of the precepts of God,
the law that endures forever;
All who cling to her will live,
but those will die who forsake her. [v]
2 Turn, O Jacob, and receive her:
walk by her light toward splendor. [w]
3 Give not your glory to another,
your privileges to an alien race.
4 Blessed are we, O Israel;
for what pleases God is known to us! [x]

III: Jerusalem Bewails and Consoles Her Captive Children

5 Fear not, my people!
Remember, Israel,
6 You were sold to the nations
not for your destruction;

3, 22f: Despite the renown for wisdom of the peoples of Canaan or Phoenicia (Ez 28, 3f), of Teman (Jer 49, 7), of the sons of Hagar or the Arabians, they did not possess true wisdom, which is found only in the law of God.

3, 24: The house of God: here, the created universe.

n Jer 49, 7; Ez 28, 4–5; Zec 9, 2; Jb 2, 11. o Gn 6, 4; Wis 14, 6. p 1 Sm 16, 7–10. q Sir 10, 8. r Dt 30, 12f; Sir 24, 4; Rom 10, 6f. s Jb 38, 7; Ps 147, 4; Is 40, 26. t Ps 147, 19; Sir 24, 8–12. u Wis 9, 18; Jn 1, 14. v Dt 4, 6–8; Prv 8, 35f; Sir 24, 22. w Prv 4, 13. 19. x Dt 4, 32–37; 33, 29.

It was because you angered God
that you were handed over to your foes.[y]
7 For you provoked your Maker[z]
with sacrifices to demons, to no-gods;
8 You forsook the Eternal God who nourished you,
and you grieved Jerusalem who fostered you.
9 She indeed saw coming upon you
the anger of God; and she said:

"Hear, you neighbors of Zion!
God has brought great mourning upon me,
10 For I have seen the captivity
that the Eternal God has brought
upon my sons and daughters.
11 With joy I fostered them;
but with mourning and lament I let them go.
12 Let no one gloat over me, a widow,
bereft of many:
For the sins of my children I am left desolate,
because they turned from the law of God,[a]
13 and did not acknowledge his statutes;
In the ways of God's commandments they did not walk,
nor did they tread the disciplined paths of his justice.
14 "Let Zion's neighbors come,
to take note of the captivity of my sons and daughters,
brought upon them by the Eternal God.
15 He has brought against them a nation from afar,
a nation ruthless and of alien speech,
That has neither reverence for age
nor tenderness for childhood;[b]
16 They have led away this widow's cherished sons,
have left me solitary, without daughters.
17 What can I do to help you?
18 He who has brought this evil upon you
must himself deliver you from your enemies' hands.[c]
19 Farewell, my children, farewell:
I am left desolate.
20 I have taken off the garment of peace,
have put on sackcloth for my prayer of supplication,
and while I live I will cry out to the Eternal God.[d]

21 "Fear not, my children; call upon God,
who will deliver you from oppression at enemy hands.[e]
22 I have trusted in the Eternal God for your welfare,
and joy has come to me from the Holy One
Because of the mercy that will swiftly reach you
from your eternal savior.
23 With mourning and lament I sent you forth,
but God will give you back to me
with enduring gladness and joy.[f]
24 As Zion's neighbors lately saw you taken captive,
so shall they soon see God's salvation come to you,
with great glory and the splendor of the Eternal God.[g]

25 "My children, bear patiently the anger[h]
that has come from God upon you;
Your enemies have persecuted you,
and you will soon see their destruction
and trample upon their necks.*
26 My pampered children have trodden rough roads,
carried off by their enemies like sheep in a raid.[i]
27 Fear not, my children; call out to God!
He who brought this upon you will remember you.[j]
28 As your hearts have been disposed to stray from God,
turn now ten times the more to seek him;
29 For he who has brought disaster upon you

4, 25: Trample upon their necks: love of enemies was not an Old Testament ideal. The Babylonians are considered here, however, to be God's enemies as well as Israel's.

y Jgs 2, 14; Is 50, 1; 52, 3. z 7–8: Dt 32, 13–18; 1 Cor 10, 20. a Lam 1, 1. 2. 7. b Dt 28, 49f; Jer 5, 15; 6, 22f. c Jer 32, 42. d Jdt 9, 1; Est 4, 16. e Jer 51, 5. f Jer 31, 12f. g Is 60, 1ff. h Is 51, 23. i Lam 2, 22. j Is 40, 1.

will, in saving you, bring you back enduring
joy." [k]

IV: Jerusalem Consoled: The Captivity About to End

30 Fear not, Jerusalem!
He who gave you your name is your
encouragement. [l]
31 Fearful are those who harmed you,
who rejoiced at your downfall;
32 Fearful are the cities where your children were
enslaved,
fearful the city that took your sons. [m]
33 As that city rejoiced at your collapse, [n]
and made merry at your downfall,
so shall she grieve over her own desolation.
34 I will take from her the joyous throngs,
and her exultation shall be turned to
mourning:
35 For fire shall come upon her [o]
from the Eternal God, for a long time,
and demons shall dwell in her from that
time on.*

36 Look to the east, Jerusalem!
behold the joy that comes to you from
God. [p]
37 Here come your sons whom you once let go,
gathered in from the east and from the west
By the word of the Holy One,
rejoicing in the glory of God.

CHAPTER 5

1 Jerusalem, take off your robe of mourning and
misery;
put on the splendor of glory from God
forever: [q]
2 Wrapped in the cloak of justice from God,
bear on your head the mitre
that displays the glory of the eternal name. [r]
3 For God will show all the earth your splendor:
4 you will be named by God forever
the peace of justice, the glory of God's
worship. [s]

5 Up, Jerusalem! stand upon the heights;
look to the east and see your children
Gathered from the east and the west
at the word of the Holy One,
rejoicing that they are remembered by God.
6 Led away on foot by their enemies they left
you:
but God will bring them back to you
borne aloft in glory as on royal thrones. [t]
7 For God has commanded
that every lofty mountain be made low,
And that the age-old depths and gorges
be filled to level ground,
that Israel may advance secure in the glory
of God. [u]
8 The forests and every fragrant kind of tree
have overshadowed Israel at God's
command; [v]
9 For God is leading Israel in joy
by the light of his glory,
with his mercy and justice for company.

V: The Letter of Jeremiah Against Idolatry

CHAPTER 6

1 A copy of the letter which Jeremiah sent to
those who were being led captive to Babylon by
the king of the Babylonians, to convey to them
what God had commanded him: [w]
For the sins you committed before God, you
are being led captive to Babylon by Nebuchad-
nezzar, king of the Babylonians. 2 When you
reach Babylon you will be there many years, a
period seven generations* long; after which I
will bring you back from there in peace. 3 And
now in Babylon you will see borne upon men's
shoulders gods of silver and gold and wood,
which cast fear upon the pagans. [x] 4 Take care

4, 35: Deserts and desolate places were looked upon as the special habitations of demons; Tb 8, 3; Lk 11, 24.

6, 2: Seven generations: possibly an indication of the date of this composition by an author writing for his contemporaries for whom the conditions of the exile were still realities. He has multiplied the seventy years of Jer 29, 10 by three or four.

k Is 35, 10. l Ps 46, 5; Is 60, 14. m Jer 51, 43. n 33f: Is 13, 20ff; 47, 1–11; Jer 50, 13. o Is 34, 9–14. p Is 60, 4f. q Is 52, 1. r Ex 39, 30; Wis 18, 24; Is 61. 10; 62, 3. s Is 1, 26; 32, 17; Jer 33, 16. t Is 49, 22. u Is 40, 3f. v Is 41, 19. w Jer 29, 1. x Is 46, 7; Jer 10, 1–16.

that you yourselves do not imitate their alien example and stand in fear of them, 5when you see the crowd before them and behind worshiping them. Rather, say in your hearts, "You, O LORD, are to be worshiped!"; 6for my angel is with you, and he is the custodian of your lives.[y]

7Their tongues are smoothed by woodworkers; they are covered with gold and silver—but they are a fraud, and cannot speak.[z] 8People bring gold, as to a maiden in love with ornament, 9and furnish crowns for the heads of their gods. Then sometimes the priests take the silver and gold from their gods and spend it on themselves, 10or give part of it to the harlots on the terrace.* They trick them out in garments like men, these gods of silver and gold and wood; 11but though they are wrapped in purple clothing, they are not safe from corrosion or insects. 12They wipe their faces clean of the house dust which is thick upon them. 13Each has a scepter, like the human ruler of a district; but none does away with those that offend against it. 14Each has in its right hand an axe or dagger, but it cannot save itself from war or pillage. Thus it is known they are not gods; do not fear them.

15As useless as one's broken tools 16are their gods, set up in their houses; their eyes are full of dust from the feet of those who enter. 17Their courtyards are walled in like those of a man brought to execution for a crime against the king; the priests reinforce their houses with gates and bars and bolts, lest they be carried off by robbers. 18They light more lamps for them than for themselves, yet not one of these can they see. 19They are like any beam in the house; it is said their hearts are eaten away. Though the insects out of the ground consume them and their garments, they do not feel it. 20Their faces are blackened by the smoke of the house. 21Bats and swallows alight on their bodies and on their heads; and cats as well as birds. 22Know, therefore, that they are not gods, and do not fear them.

23Despite the gold that covers them for adornment, unless someone wipes away the corrosion, they do not shine; nor did they feel anything when they were molded. 24They are bought at any price, and there is no spirit in them. 25Having no feet, they are carried on men's shoulders, displaying their shame to all; and those who worship them are put to confusion[a] 26because, if they fall to the ground, the worshipers must raise them up. They neither move of themselves if one sets them upright, nor come upright if they fall; but one puts gifts beside them as beside the dead. 27*Their priests resell their sacrifices for their own advantage. Even their wives cure parts of the meat, but do not share it with the poor and the weak;[b] 28the menstruous and women in childbed handle their sacrifices. Knowing from this that they are not gods, do not fear them.

29How can they be called gods? For women bring the offerings to these gods of silver and gold and wood; 30and in their temples the priests squat with torn tunic and with shaven hair and beard, and with their heads uncovered.[c] 31They shout and wail before their gods as others do at a funeral banquet. 32The priests take some of their clothing and put it on their wives and children. 33*Whether they are treated well or ill by anyone, they cannot requite it; they can neither set up a king nor remove him.[d] 34Similarly, they cannot give anyone riches or coppers; if one fails to fulfill a vow to them, they cannot exact it of him. 35They neither save a man from death, nor deliver the weak from the strong.[e] 36To no blind man do they restore his sight, nor do they save any man in an emergency. 37They neither pity the widow nor benefit the orphan. 38These gilded and silvered wooden statues are like stones from the mountains; and their worshipers will be put to shame. 39How then can it be thought or claimed that they are gods?

6, 10: Harlots on the terrace: cult prostitutes, common in the idolatrous religions of the Gentiles.

6, 27–31: From the point of view of Jewish ritual law, the practices named here were grotesque and depraved; cf Lv 12, 2ff; 15, 19–23.

6, 33–39: All that the gods cannot do, the true God does; cf 1 Sm 2, 7; Dt 23, 22; Pss 68, 6; 146, 7–9; Is 35, 4f.

y Ex 23, 20. z Ps 135, 16. a Wis 13, 16. b Lv 12. 4; 15, 19f; Dt 14, 28f. c Lv 10, 6; 21, 5. 10. d Dn 2, 21. e Pss 68, 6; 146, 7ff.

40Even the Chaldeans themselves have no
respect for them; for when they see a deaf mute,
incapable of speech, they bring forward Bel* and
ask the god to make noise, as though the man
could understand; 41and they are themselves
unable to reflect and abandon these gods, for
they have no sense. 42*And their women, girt
with cords, sit by the roads, burning chaff for
incense;[f] 43and whenever one of them is drawn
aside by some passerby who lies with her, she
mocks her neighbor who has not been dignified
as she has, and has not had her cord broken.
44All that takes place around these gods is a
fraud: how then can it be thought or claimed
that they are gods?

45They are produced by woodworkers and
goldsmiths, and they are nothing else than what
these craftsmen wish them to be. 46Even those
who produce them are not long-lived; 47how
then can what they have produced be gods?
They have left frauds and opprobrium to their
successors. 48For when war or disaster comes
upon them, the priests deliberate among them-
selves where they can hide with them. 49How
then can one not know that these are no-gods,
which do not save themselves either from war or
from disaster? 50They are wooden, gilded and
silvered; they will later be known for frauds. To
all peoples and kings it will be clear that they are
not gods, but human handiwork; and that God's
work is not in them.

51Who does not know that they are not gods?
52They set no king over the land, nor do they
give men rain. 53They neither vindicate their
own rights, nor do they recover what is unjustly
taken, for they are unable; 54they are like crows
between heaven and earth. For when fire breaks
out in the temple of these wooden or gilded or
silvered gods, though the priests flee and are
safe, they themselves are burnt up in the fire like
beams. 55They cannot resist a king, or enemy
forces. 56How then can it be admitted or thought
that they are gods?

They are safe from neither thieves nor ban-
dits, these wooden and silvered and gilded gods;
57those who seize them strip off the gold and the
silver, and go away with the clothing that was on
them, and they cannot help themselves. 58How
much better to be a king displaying his valor, or a
handy tool in a house, the joy of its owner, than
these false gods; or the door of a house, that
keeps safe those who are within, rather than
these false gods; or a wooden post in a palace,
rather than these false gods![g] 59The sun and
moon and stars are bright, and obedient in the
service for which they are sent. 60Likewise the
lightning, when it flashes, is a goodly sight; and
the same wind blows over all the land. 61The
clouds, too, when commanded by God to pro-
ceed across the whole world, fulfill the order;
62and fire, sent from on high to burn up the
mountains and the forests, does what has been
commanded. But these false gods are not their
equal, whether in beauty or in power; 63so that
it is unthinkable, and cannot be claimed, that
they are gods. They can neither execute judg-
ment, nor benefit man. 64Know, therefore, that
they are not gods, and do not fear them.

65Kings they neither curse nor bless. 66They
show the nations no signs in the heavens, nor
are they brilliant like the sun, nor shining like
the moon. 67The beasts which can help them-
selves by fleeing to shelter are better than they
are. 68Thus in no way is it clear to us that they
are gods; so do not fear them. 69For like a
scarecrow in a cucumber patch, that is no
protection, are their wooden, gilded, silvered
gods. 70Just like a thornbush in a garden on
which perches every kind of bird, or like a
corpse hurled into darkness, are their silvered
and gilded wooden gods. 71From the rotting of
the purple and the linen upon them, it can be
known that they are not gods; they themselves
will in the end be consumed, and be a disgrace
in the land. 72The better for the just man who
has no idols: he shall be far from disgrace!

6, 40: Bel: cf note on Jer 50, 2.
6, 42f: This seems to refer to the obligation of Babylonian women to serve once in their lives as cult prostitutes. The unbroken cord was a sign that this duty had not yet been fulfilled. Chaff: burnt as an aphrodisiac or for use in erotic rites.

f 42–43: Jer 3, 2. g Wis 13, 10–15; 15, 7ff.

THE BOOK OF EZEKIEL

Ezekiel's complex character makes him one of the most interesting figures in Israelite prophecy. In many ways he resembles the more primitive type of prophet represented by Elijah and Elisha; yet he clearly depends on all his predecessors in prophecy, and his teaching is a development of theirs. His unique contribution to the history of prophetism lies in his manifest interest in the temple and the liturgy, an interest paralleled in no other prophet—not even Jeremiah who, like Ezekiel, was also a priest. Particularly because of this interest, Ezekiel's influence on postexilic religion was enormous, and not without reason has he been called "the father of Judaism." This has resulted in his prophecies reaching us with the evident marks of editing and addition by the postexilic circles that shared his intense interest. However, we may be sure that in this book we have throughout what is in substance the prophet's own work.

Ezekiel became a prophet in Babylon—the first prophet to receive the call to prophesy outside the Holy Land. As one of the exiles deported by Nebuchadnezzar in 597, his first task was to prepare his fellow countrymen in Babylon for the final destruction of Jerusalem, which they believed to be inviolable. Accordingly, the first part of his book consists of reproaches for Israel's past and present sins and the confident prediction of yet a further devastation of the land of promise and a more general exile. In 587, when Nebuchadnezzar destroyed Jerusalem, Ezekiel was vindicated before his unbelieving compatriots.

After this time, Ezekiel's message changes. From now on his prophecy is characterized by the promise of salvation in a new covenant, and he is anxious to lay down the conditions necessary to obtain it. Even as Jeremiah had believed, Ezekiel thought that the exiles were the hope of Israel's restoration, once God's allotted time for the exile had been accomplished. His final eight chapters are an utopian vision of the Israel of the future, rid of its past evils and re-established firmly under the rule of the Lord. The famous vision of the dry bones in chapter 37 expresses his firm belief in a forthcoming restoration, Israel rising to new life from the graveyard of Babylon. But Ezekiel's new covenant, like Jeremiah's, was to see its true fulfillment only in the New Testament.

Perhaps no other prophet has stressed the absolute majesty of God as Ezekiel does. This appears not only in the tremendous vision by the river Chebar with which his prophecy opens, but throughout the book. Ultimately, says Ezekiel, whatever God does to or for man is motivated by zeal for his own holy name. The new heart and the new spirit which must exist under the new covenant cannot be the work of man; they too must be the work of God. By such teachings he helped prepare for the New Testament doctrine of salvation through grace.

The Book of Ezekiel is divided as follows:

I. Call of the Prophet (1, 1—3, 27).
II. Before the Siege of Jerusalem (4, 1—24, 27).
III. Prophecies against Foreign Nations (25, 1—32, 32).
IV. Salvation for Israel (33, 1—39, 29).
V. The New Israel (40, 1—48, 35).

I: Call of the Prophet

CHAPTER 1

The Vision: God on the Cherubim [1]In the
thirtieth year,* on the fifth day of the fourth
month, while I was among the exiles by the river
Chebar, the heavens opened, and I saw divine
visions.[a] — [2]On the fifth day of the month, the
fifth year,* that is, of King Jehoiachin's exile,
[3]the word of the LORD came to the priest
Ezekiel, the son of Buzi, in the land of the
Chaldeans by the river Chebar.—There the hand
of the LORD came upon me.

[4]As I looked, a stormwind came from the
North,* a huge cloud with flashing fire [envel-
oped in brightness], from the midst of which [the
midst of the fire] something gleamed like elec-
trum. [5]Within it were figures resembling four
living creatures* that looked like this: their form
was human, [6]but each had four faces and four
wings, [7]and their legs went straight down; the
soles of their feet were round. They sparkled
with a gleam like burnished bronze.

[10]*Their faces were like this:[b] each of the
four had the face of a man, but on the right side
was the face of a lion, and on the left side the
face of an ox, and finally each had the face of an
eagle. [9]Their faces [and their wings] looked out
on all their four sides; they did not turn when
they moved, but each went straight forward.
[12][Each went straight forward; wherever the
spirit wished to go, there they went; they did
not turn when they moved.]

[8]Human hands were under their wings, and
the wings of one touched those of another.
[11]Each had two wings spread out above so that
they touched one another's, while the other two
wings of each covered his body. [13]In among the
living creatures something like burning coals of
fire could be seen; they seemed like torches,
moving to and fro among the living creatures.
The fire gleamed, and from it came forth flashes
of lightning.

[15]As I looked at the living creatures, I saw
wheels on the ground, one beside each of the
four living creatures. [16]The wheels had the
sparkling appearance of chrysolite, and all four of
them looked the same: they were constructed as
though one wheel were within another. [17]They
could move in any of the four directions they
faced, without veering as they moved. [18][c]The
four of them had rims, and I saw that their rims
were full of eyes all around. [19]When the living
creatures moved, the wheels moved with them;
and when the living creatures were raised from
the ground, the wheels also were raised. [20]Wher-
ever the spirit wished to go, there the wheels
went, and they were raised together with the
living creatures; for the spirit of the living
creatures was in the wheels.

[22]*Over the heads of the living creatures,
something like a firmament could be seen,
seeming like glittering crystal, stretched straight
out above their heads. [23]Beneath the firmament
their wings were stretched out, one toward the
other. [Each of them had two covering his body.]
[24]Then I heard the sound of their wings, like the
roaring of mighty waters, like the voice of the
Almighty. When they moved, the sound of the
tumult was like the din of an army. [And when
they stood still, they lowered their wings.]

[26]Above the firmament over their heads some-
thing like a throne could be seen, looking like
sapphire. Upon it was seated, up above, one who
had the appearance of a man.* [27]Upward from
what resembled his waist I saw what gleamed
like electrum; downward from what resembled
his waist I saw what looked like fire; he was
surrounded with splendor. [28]Like the bow

1, 1: The thirtieth year, which corresponds to the fifth year of exile (v 2), has never been satisfactorily explained; possibly it refers to the prophet's age. The river Chebar: probably a canal near Nippur, southeast of Babylon, one of the sites on which the Jewish exiles were settled.

1, 2: The fifth day of the fourth month, the fifth year: July 31, 593 B.C.; cf v 1.

1, 4: The North: the abode of God; see notes on Jb 37, 22; Ps 48, 3. Electrum: an alloy of gold and silver, used here for some undetermined bright metal.

1, 5: Four living creatures: identified as cherubim in Ez 10, 20f.

1, 10–22: Note the changed order of the verses and the omission of the textually uncertain verses 14 and 21. Such changes also occur elsewhere in this book.

1, 22f. 26: This symbolic description of God's throne is similar to that in Ex 24, 9f.

1, 26: One who had the appearance of a man: God appearing in human form (v 28); cf Ex 33, 18–23.

a Ez 3, 23; 10, 20; 43, 3. b Rv 4, 6f. c Ez 10, 12; Rv 4, 6. 8.

which appears in the clouds on a rainy day was
the splendor that surrounded him. Such was the
vision of the likeness of the glory of the LORD.

CHAPTER 2

Eating of the Scroll When I had seen it, I fell
upon my face and heard a voice that said to me:
[1]Son of man,* stand up! I wish to speak with
you. [2]As he spoke to me, spirit* entered into me
and set me on my feet, and I heard the one who
was speaking [3]say to me: Son of man, I am
sending you to the Israelites, rebels who have
rebelled against me; they and their fathers have
revolted against me to this very day. [4]Hard of
face and obstinate of heart are they to whom I
am sending you. But you shall say to them: Thus
says the Lord GOD! [5]And whether they heed or
resist—for they are a rebellious house—they
shall know that a prophet has been among them.
[6]But as for you, son of man, fear neither them
nor their words when they contradict you and
reject you, and when you sit on scorpions.*
Neither fear their words nor be dismayed at their
looks, for they are a rebellious house. [7][But
speak my words to them, whether they heed or
resist, for they are rebellious.] [8]As for you, son of
man, obey me when I speak to you: be not
rebellious like this house of rebellion, but open
your mouth and eat what I shall give you.

[9] [d]It was then I saw a hand stretched out to
me, in which was a written scroll [10]which he
unrolled before me. It was covered with writing
front and back, and written on it was: Lamenta-
tion and wailing and woe!

CHAPTER 3

[1]He said to me: Son of man, eat what is before
you; eat this scroll, then go, speak to the house
of Israel. [2]So I opened my mouth and he gave
me the scroll to eat. [3] [e]Son of man, he then said
to me, feed your belly and fill your stomach with
this scroll I am giving you. I ate it, and it was as
sweet as honey* in my mouth. He said: [4]Son of
man, go now to the house of Israel, and speak
my words to them.

[5]Not to a people with difficult speech and
barbarous language am I sending you, [6]nor to
the many peoples [with difficult speech and
barbarous language] whose words you cannot
understand. If I were to send you to these, they
would listen to you; [7]but the house of Israel will
refuse to listen to you, since they will not listen
to me. For the whole house of Israel is stubborn
of brow and obstinate in heart. [8]But I will make
your face as hard as theirs, and your brow as
stubborn as theirs, [9]like diamond, harder than
flint. Fear them not, nor be dismayed at their
looks, for they are a rebellious house.

[10]Son of man, he said to me, take into your
heart all my words that I speak to you; hear
them well. [11]Now go to the exiles, to your
countrymen, and say to them: Thus says the
Lord GOD!—whether they heed or resist!

[12]Then spirit lifted me up, and I heard behind
me the noise of a loud rumbling as the glory of
the LORD* rose from its place: [13]the noise made
by the wings of the living creatures striking one
another, and by the wheels alongside them, a
loud rumbling. [14]The spirit which had lifted me
up seized me, and I went off spiritually stirred,
while the hand of the LORD rested heavily upon
me. [15]Thus I came to the exiles who lived at Tel-
abib* by the river Chebar, and for seven days I
sat among them distraught.

The Prophet as Watchman* [17]Thus the word
of the LORD came to me: Son of man, I have
appointed you a watchman for the house of
Israel.[f] When you hear a word from my mouth,
you shall warn them for me.

[18]If I say to the wicked man, You shall surely
die; and you do not warn him or speak out to

2, 1: Son of man: a formal way of saying simply "man"; God's habitual way of addressing the prophet throughout this book. Probably the title is used to emphasize the separation of the divine and the human.

2, 2: Spirit: vital power, coming from God, which enables the prophet to hear the word of God; cf Ez 8, 3; 9, 24; 11, 1.

2, 6: When you sit on scorpions: the prophet must be prepared for the bitterest opposition.

3, 3: As sweet as honey: though the prophet must foretell terrible things, the word of God is sweet to him who receives it.

3, 12: The glory of the Lord: the divine presence, manifested here in visible form.

3, 15: Tel-abib: one of the sites where the exiles were settled, probably near Nippur.

3, 17–21: This passage refers to one of the prophet's most characteristic qualities. It was placed here by an editor, though it properly belongs to a later stage in Ezekiel's ministry; cf chapter 33.

d Rv 5, 1. e Rv 10, 9f. f Ez 33, 7.

dissuade him from his wicked conduct so that he may live: that wicked man shall die for his sin, but I will hold you responsible for his death. 19 If, on the other hand, you have warned the wicked man, yet he has not turned away from his evil nor from his wicked conduct, then he shall die for his sin, but you shall save your life.

20 If a virtuous man turns away from virtue and does wrong when I place a stumbling block before him, he shall die. He shall die for his sin, and his virtuous deeds shall not be remembered; but I will hold you responsible for his death if you did not warn him. 21 When, on the other hand, you have warned a virtuous man not to sin, and he has in fact not sinned, he shall surely live because of the warning, and you shall save your own life.

Ezekiel's Dumbness* 22 The hand of the Lord came upon me, and he said to me: Get up and go out into the plain, where I will speak with you. 23 [g]So I got up and went out into the plain, and I saw that the glory of the LORD was in that place, like the glory I had seen by the river Chebar. I fell prone, 24 but then spirit entered into me and set me on my feet, and he spoke with me.

He said to me: Go shut yourself up in your house. 25 [As for you, son of man, they will put cords upon you and bind you with them, so that you cannot go out among them.] 26 I will make your tongue stick to your palate so that you will be dumb* and unable to rebuke them for being a rebellious house. 27 Only when I speak with you and open your mouth, shall you say to them: Thus says the Lord GOD! Let him heed who will, and let him resist who will, for they are a rebellious house.

II: Before the Siege of Jerusalem

CHAPTER 4

Acts Symbolic of Siege and Exile 16 At the end of seven days . . . :* 1 As for you, son of man, take a clay tablet; lay it in front of you, and draw on it a city [Jerusalem]. 2 Raise a siege against it: build a tower, lay out a ramp, pitch camps, and set up battering rams all around. 3 Then take an iron griddle and set it up as an iron wall between you and the city. Fix your gaze on it: it shall be in the state of siege, and you shall besiege it. This shall be a sign for the house of Israel. 4 Then you shall lie on your left side, while I place the sins of the house of Israel upon you. As many days as you lie thus, you shall bear their sins. 5 For the years of their sins I allot you the same number of days, three hundred and ninety, during which you will bear the sins of the house of Israel. 6 When you finish this, you are to lie down again, but on your right side, and bear the sins of the house of Judah forty days;* one day for each year I have allotted you. 7 Fixing your gaze on the siege of Jerusalem, with bared arm* you shall prophesy against it. 8 See, I will bind you with cords so that you cannot turn from one side to the other until you have completed the days of your siege.

9 *Again, take wheat and barley, and beans and lentils, and millet and spelt; put them in a single vessel and make bread out of them. Eat it for as many days as you lie upon your side, three hundred and ninety. 10 The food you eat shall be twenty shekels a day by weight; each day the same. 11 And the water you drink shall be the sixth of a hin by measure; each day the same. 16 [h]Then he said to me: Son of man, I am breaking the staff of bread* in Jerusalem. They

3, 22–27: This passage also belongs to a later period, with Ez 24, 25ff and 33, 21f, during the time of the final siege of Jerusalem, when Ezekiel's prophecies consisted mainly of symbolic actions rather than words.

3, 26: Dumb: unwilling to speak to the people in exile while Jerusalem was being besieged; cf Ez 24, 27.

3, 16: At the end of seven days . . . : the incomplete sentence probably contained some such words as "the word of the Lord came to me." For seven days, see v 15. (This verse has been transposed from ch 3.)

4, 5f: Three hundred and ninety days . . . forty days: symbolically representing the respective lengths of the periods of exile of northern Israelites and Judahites. Northern Israel had already fallen to Assyria in 722 B.C. The letters in the Hebrew phrase for the days of your siege (v 8), each of which has its own numerical value, add up to three hundred and ninety. Forty years represent one generation.

4, 7: Bared arm: a symbol of unrestrained power.

4, 9–17: This action represents the scarcity of food during the siege of Jerusalem, and the consequent need to eat whatever is at hand. Twenty shekels: about nine ounces. The sixth of a hin: about one quart.

4, 16: Breaking the staff of bread: reducing the supply of bread which sustains the life of man as the walking staff sustains the traveler on his journey; cf Ez 5, 16; 14, 13; Lv 26, 26; Ps 105, 16; Is 3, 1.

g Ez 1, 3; 10, 15. 20. 22; 43, 3. h Ez 5, 16; 14, 13.

shall eat bread which they have weighed out anxiously, and they shall drink water which they have measured out fearfully, 17so that, owing to the scarcity of bread and water, everyone shall be filled with terror and waste away because of his sins.

12For your food you must bake barley loaves over human excrement in their sight, said the LORD. 13Thus the Israelites shall eat their food unclean among the nations where I scatter them.[i] 14"Oh no, Lord GOD!" I protested. "Never have I been made unclean, and from my youth till now, never have I eaten carrion flesh or that torn by wild beasts: never has any unclean meat entered my mouth." 15Very well, he replied, I allow you cow's dung in place of human excrement; bake your bread on that.

CHAPTER 5

1As for you, son of man, take a sharp sword and use it like a barber's razor, passing it over your head and beard. Then take a set of scales and divide the hair you have cut. 2Burn a third in the fire, within the city,* when the days of your siege are completed; place another third around the city and strike it with the sword; the final third strew in the wind, and pursue it with the sword. 3[But of the last take a small number and tie them in the hem of your garment. 4Then take some of these and throw them in the midst of the fire and burn them.]

Say to the whole house of Israel: 5Thus says the Lord GOD: This is Jerusalem! In the midst of the nations I placed her, surrounded by foreign countries. 6But she rebelled against my ordinances more wickedly than the nations, and against my statutes more than the foreign countries surrounding her; she has spurned my ordinances and has not lived by my statutes. 7Therefore thus says the Lord GOD: Because you have been more rebellious than the nations surrounding you, not living by my statutes nor fulfilling my ordinances, but acting according to the ordinances of the surrounding nations; 8therefore thus says the Lord GOD: See, I am coming at you!* I will inflict punishments in your midst while the nations look on. 9Because of all your abominations I will do with you what I have never done before, the like of which I will never do again. 10This means that fathers within you shall eat sons, and sons shall eat fathers.* I will inflict punishments upon you and scatter all that remain of your people in every direction.

11Therefore, as I live, says the Lord GOD, because you have defiled my sanctuary with all your detestable abominations, I swear to cut you down. I will not look upon you with pity nor have mercy. 12A third of your people shall die of pestilence and perish of hunger within you; another third shall fall by the sword all around you; and a third I will scatter in every direction, and I will pursue them with the sword. 16[j]When I loose against you the cruel, destructive arrows of hunger, I will break your staff of bread; 17I will send famine against you, and wild beasts that shall rob you of your children. Pestilence and bloodshed shall stalk through you, and I will bring the sword upon you. I, the LORD, have spoken!

13Thus shall my anger spend itself, and I will wreak my fury upon them till I am appeased; they shall know that I, the LORD, have spoken in my jealousy when I spend my fury upon them. 14I will make you a waste and a reproach among the nations that surround you, which every passer-by may see. 15When I execute judgment upon you in anger and fury and with furious chastisements, you shall be a reproach and an object of scorn, a terrible warning to the nations that surround you. I, the LORD, have spoken!

CHAPTER 6

Against the Mountains of Israel 1Thus the word of the LORD came to me: 2Son of man, turn toward the mountains of Israel, and prophesy against them: 3Mountains of Israel, hear the word of the Lord GOD. Thus says the Lord GOD [to the mountains and hills, the ravines and

5, 2: The city: the one drawn on the tablet.

5, 8: I am coming at you: an expression borrowed from the language of warfare in which enemies attacked one another with the sword. You in vv 8–17 is Jerusalem.

5, 10: Fathers . . . shall eat sons, and sons . . . fathers: see note on Lam 2, 20.

i Hos 9, 4. j Ez 4, 16; 14, 13.

valleys]: [k] See, I am bringing a sword against you,
and I will destroy your high places.* [4]Your altars
shall be laid waste, your incense stands shall be
broken, and I will cast down your slain ones
before your idols; [5]I will scatter their bones all
around your altars.* [6]In all your dwelling places
cities shall be made desolate and high places laid
waste, so that your altars will be made desolate
and laid waste, your idols broken and removed,
and your incense stands smashed to bits. [7][The
slain shall fall in your midst, and you shall know
that I am the LORD. [8]I have warned you.]

When some of your people have escaped to
other nations from the sword, and have been
scattered over the foreign lands, [9]then those
who have escaped will remember me among the
nations to which they have been exiled, after I
have broken their adulterous hearts that turned
away from me [and their eyes which lusted after
idols]. They shall loathe themselves because of
their evil deeds, all their abominations. [10]Then
they shall know that it was not in vain that I, the
LORD, threatened to inflict this calamity upon
them.

[11]Thus says the Lord GOD: Clap your hands,
stamp your feet,* and cry "Alas!" because of all
the abominations of the house of Israel, for
which they shall fall by the sword, by famine,
and by pestilence. [12]He that is far off shall die of
pestilence, he that is near shall fall by the sword,
and he that is besieged shall perish by famine; so
will I spend my fury upon them. [13]Then shall
they know that I am the LORD, when their slain
shall lie amid their idols, all about their altars, on
every high hill and mountaintop, beneath every
green tree and leafy oak,* wherever they offered
appeasing odors to any of their gods. [14]I will
stretch out my hand against them, and wherever
they live I will make the land a desolate waste,
from the desert to Riblah;* thus shall they know
that I am the LORD.

CHAPTER 7

The End Has Come [1]Thus the word of the
LORD came to me: [2]Son of man, now say: Thus
says the Lord GOD to the land of Israel: An end!
The end has come upon the four corners of the
land! [3]Now the end is upon you; I will unleash
my anger against you and judge you according to
your conduct and lay upon you the conse-
quences of all your abominations. [4]I will not
look upon you with pity nor have mercy; I will
bring your conduct down upon you, and the
consequences of your abominations shall be in
your midst; then shall you know that I am the
LORD.

[5]Thus says the Lord GOD: Disaster upon
disaster! See it coming! [6]An end is coming, the
end is coming upon you! See it coming! [7]The
climax has come for you who dwell in the land!
The time has come, near is the day: a time of
consternation, not of rejoicing. [8]Soon now I will
pour out my fury upon you and spend my anger
upon you; I will judge you according to your
conduct and lay upon you the consequences of
all your abominations. [9]I will not look upon you
with pity nor have mercy; I will deal with you
according to your conduct, and the conse-
quences of your abominations shall be in your
midst; then shall you know that it is I, the LORD,
who strike.

[10]See, the day of the LORD! See, the end is
coming! Lawlessness is in full bloom, insolence
flourishes, [11]violence has risen to support wick-
edness. It shall not be long in coming, nor shall it
delay. [12]*The time has come, the day dawns. Let
not the buyer rejoice nor the seller mourn, for
wrath shall be upon all the throng. [13]The seller
shall not regain what he sold as long as he lives,
for wrath shall be upon all the throng. Because
of his sins, no one shall preserve his life. [14]They
shall sound the trumpet and make everything

6, 3: High places: the sanctuaries on the mountaintops where illegal worship, whether of the Lord or of Canaanite deities, was performed.

6, 5: Scatter their bones . . . altars: dead men's bones defiled a place; cf 2 Kgs 23, 14.

6, 11: Clap your hands, stamp your feet: here evidently signs of mourning; in Ez 25, 6, signs of joy.

6, 13: Every green tree and leafy oak: sacred groves had a long history in Palestine as places of worship; cf Dt 12, 2; note on Gn 12, 6.

6, 14: From the desert to Riblah: the whole land, from the far south to the far north.

7, 12f: Mundane affairs will cease to have any meaning in view of the disaster that is to come.

k Ez 36, 1.

ready, yet no one shall go to war, for my wrath is upon all the throng.

15The sword is outside; pestilence and hunger are within. He that is in the country shall die by the sword; pestilence and famine shall devour those in the city. 16Even those who escape and flee to the mountains like the doves of the valleys—I will put them all to death, each one for his own sins. 17All their hands shall be limp, and all their knees shall run with water. 18 [l]They shall put on sackcloth, and horror shall cover them; shame shall be on all their faces and baldness* on all their heads. 19They shall fling their silver into the streets, and their gold shall be considered refuse.[m] Their silver and gold cannot save them on the day of the LORD's wrath. They shall not be allowed to satisfy their craving or fill their bellies, for this has been the occasion of their sin. 20In the beauty of their ornaments they put their pride: they made of them their abominable images [their idols]. For this reason I make them refuse. 21I will hand them over as booty to foreigners, to be spoiled and defiled by the wicked of the earth. 22I will turn away my face from them, and my treasure* shall be profaned: robbers shall enter and profane it.

23They shall wreak slaughter, for the land is filled with bloodshed and the city full of violence. 24I will bring in the worst of the nations, who shall take possession of their houses. I will put an end to their proud strength, and their sanctuaries shall be profaned. 25When anguish comes they shall seek peace, but there will be none. 26There shall be disaster after disaster, rumor after rumor. Prophetic vision shall fade; instruction shall be lacking to the priest, and counsel to the elders, 27while the prince shall be enveloped in terror, and the hands of the common people shall tremble. I will deal with them according to their conduct, and according to their judgments I will judge them; thus they shall know that I am the LORD.

CHAPTER 8

Vision of Abominations in the Temple

3Spirit lifted me up in the air and brought me in divine visions to Jerusalem,[n] to the entrance of the north gate, where stood the statue of jealousy which stirs up jealousy.* 5He* said to me: Son of man, look toward the north! I looked toward the north and saw northward of the gate the altar of the statue of jealousy. 6Son of man, he asked me, do you see what they are doing? Do you see the great abominations that the house of Israel is practicing here, so that I must depart from my sanctuary? But you shall see still greater abominations!

7Then he brought me to the entrance of the court, where I saw there was a hole in the wall. 8Son of man, he ordered, dig through the wall. I dug through the wall and saw a door. 9Enter, he said to me, and see the abominable evils which they are doing here. 10I entered and saw that all around upon the wall were pictured the figures of all kinds of creeping things and loathsome beasts* [all the idols of the house of Israel]. 11Before these stood seventy of the elders of the house of Israel, among whom stood Jaazaniah, son of Shaphan, each of them with his censer in his hand, and the fragrance of the incense was rising upward. 12Then he said to me: Do you see, son of man, what each of these elders of the house of Israel is doing in his idol room? They think: "The LORD cannot see us; the LORD has forsaken the land." 13He continued: You shall see still greater abominations that they are practicing.

14Then he brought me to the entrance of the north gate of the temple, and I saw sitting there

7, 18: Baldness: shaving the head was a sign of mourning.

7, 22: My treasure: the temple of Jerusalem.

8, 3: The statue of jealousy which stirs up jealousy: the statue which provokes the Lord's jealousy for his honor. This was probably the statue of the goddess Asherah erected by the wicked King Manasseh (cf 2 Kgs 21, 7; 2 Chr 33, 7. 15). Though it had been removed by King Josiah (2 Kgs 23, 6), it had no doubt been set up again in the repaganizing of Jerusalem that followed on Josiah's death.

8, 5: He: an angel accompanies Ezekiel in these visions and represents the voice of the Lord; cf Ez 40, 3f.

8, 10: Creeping things and loathsome beasts: probably Egyptian deities, which were represented in animal form. During the last days of Jerusalem King Zedekiah was allied with Egypt, trusting in it for protection against the Chaldeans.

l Is 15, 2; Jer 48, 37. m Prv 11, 4; Sir 5, 10; Zep 1, 18. n Dn 14, 6.

the women who were weeping for Tammuz.* 15 Then he said to me: Do you see this, son of man? You shall see other abominations, greater than these!

16 Then he brought me into the inner court of the LORD's house, and there at the door of the LORD's temple, between the vestibule and the altar, were about twenty-five men with their backs to the LORD's temple and their faces toward the east; they were bowing down to the sun.* 17 Do you see, son of man? he asked me. Is it such a trivial matter for the house of Judah to do the abominable things they have done here—for they have filled the land with violence, and again and again they have provoked me—that now they must also put the branch to my nose?* 18 Therefore I in turn will act furiously: I will not look upon them with pity nor will I show mercy.

CHAPTER 9

Slaughter of the Idolaters 1 Then he cried loud for me to hear: Come, you scourges of the city! 2 With that I saw six men coming from the direction of the upper gate which faces the north, each with a destroying weapon in his hand. In their midst was a man dressed in linen, with a writer's case at his waist. They entered and stood beside the bronze altar. 3 Then he called to the man dressed in linen with the writer's case at his waist, 4 [o]saying to him:* Pass through the city [through Jerusalem] and mark an X on the foreheads of those who moan and groan over all the abominations that are practiced within it. 5 To the others I heard him say: Pass through the city after him and strike! Do not look on them with pity nor show any mercy! 6 Old men, youths and maidens, women and children—wipe them out! But do not touch any marked with the X; begin at my sanctuary. So they began with the men [the elders] who were in front of the temple. 7 Defile the temple, he said to them, and fill the courts with the slain; then go out and strike in the city.

8 As they began to strike, I was left alone. I fell prone, crying out, "Alas, Lord GOD! Will you destroy all that is left of Israel when you pour out your fury on Jerusalem?" 9 He answered me: The sins of the house of Israel are great beyond measure; the land is filled with bloodshed, the city with lawlessness. They think that the LORD has forsaken the land, that he does not see them. 10 I, however, will not look upon them with pity, nor show any mercy. I will bring down their conduct upon their heads.

11 Then I saw the man dressed in linen with the writing case at his waist make his report: "I have done as you ordered."

24 *Spirit lifted me up and brought me back to the exiles in Chaldea [in a vision, by God's spirit]. Then the vision I had seen left me, 25 and I told the exiles everything the LORD had shown me.

CHAPTER 10

God's Glory Leaves Jerusalem 1 *On the fifth day of the sixth month, in the sixth year,* as I was sitting in my house, and the elders of Judah sat before me, the hand of the Lord GOD fell upon me there. 2 I looked up and saw a form that looked like a man. Downward from what seemed to be his waist, there was fire; from his waist upward there seemed to be a brightness like the sheen of electrum. He stretched out what appeared to be a hand and seized me by the hair of my head . . . . *

8, 14: Weeping for Tammuz: the withering of trees and plants in autumn was thought to be due to the descent of Tammuz, the Babylonian god of fertility, to the nether world of the dead; this descent was bewailed by the women.

8, 16: Bowing down to the sun: sun worship had been made an important part of Judahite idolatry by the impious kings; cf 2 Kgs 23, 11.

8, 17: Put the branch to my nose: the meaning is uncertain. Perhaps it refers to an Egyptian practice imported into Judah; the Egyptian sun god Re is pictured with a vine branch at his nose, signifying the transfer of creative power (divine breath) to living things. Such rites were abominable to the Lord.

9, 4: Ezekiel is preeminently the prophet of personal retribution; the innocent inhabitants of Jerusalem are to be spared when the idolatrous are punished. An X: literally, the Hebrew letter taw, which had the form of a cross.

9, 24f: These verses have been transposed from ch 11.

10, 1: In chapters 8, 1—11, 25 of the current Hebrew text, several visions involving the temple of Jerusalem were combined to form a single continuous vision. The redistribution of verses in this translation is an attempt to separate the original visions. (10, 1. 2. 4. have been transposed from ch 8.)

10, 1: The fifth day of the sixth month, in the sixth year: September 17, 592 B.C.

10, 2: The dots suppose the omission of some words describing the prophet's being transported in his visions to the court of the temple.

o Ex 12, 7; Rv 7, 3.

4 I saw there the glory of the God of Israel, like
the vision I had seen in the plain. The cherubim
were stationed to the right of the temple; 20 these
were the living creatures I had seen beneath the
God of Israel by the river Chebar,[p] whom I now
recognized to be cherubim. 21 Each had four faces
and four wings; something like human hands
were under their wings. 22 Their faces looked just
like those I had seen by the river Chebar; each
one went straight forward. 14 [q]Each had four
faces: the first face was that of an ox, the second
that of a man, the third that of a lion, and the
fourth that of an eagle. 15 Such were the living
creatures I had seen by the river Chebar.

9 [r]I also saw four wheels beside them, one
wheel beside each cherub; the wheels appeared
to have the luster of chrysolite stone. 10 All four
of them seemed to be made the same, as though
there were a wheel within a wheel. 11 When
they moved, they went in any one of their four
directions without veering as they moved; for in
whichever direction they were faced, they went
straight towards it without veering as they
moved. 12 [s]The rims of the four wheels were full
of eyes all around. 13 I heard the wheels given
the name "wheelwork." 16 [t]When the cherubim
moved, the wheels went beside them; when the
cherubim lifted their wings to rise from the
earth, even then the wheels did not leave their
sides. 17 When they stood still, the wheels stood
still; when they rose, the wheels rose with
them; for the living creatures' spirit was in them.

1 I looked and saw in the firmament above the
cherubim what appeared to be sapphire stone;
something like a throne could be seen upon it.
2 He said to the man dressed in linen: Go within
the wheelwork under the cherubim; fill both
your hands with burning coals* from among the
cherubim, then scatter them over the city. As I
looked on, he entered.

The glory of the God of Israel had gone up
from the cherubim, upon which it had been, to
the threshold of the temple. 3 As the man en-
tered, the cloud filled the inner court, 4 and the
glory of the LORD rose from over the cherubim to
the threshold of the temple; the temple was
filled with the cloud, and all the court was bright
with the glory of the LORD. 5 The noise of the
wings of the cherubim could be heard as far as
the outer court; it was like the voice of God the
Almighty when he speaks.

6 When he had commanded the man dressed
in linen to take fire from within the wheelwork,
among the cherubim, the man entered and stood
by one of the wheels. 7 Thereupon its cherub
stretched out his hand toward the fire that was
among the cherubim. He took up some of it and
put it in the hands of the one dressed in linen,
who took it and came out. 8 [Something like
human hands could be seen under the wings of
the cherubim.]

18 Then the glory of the LORD left the thresh-
old of the temple and rested upon the cherubim.
19 These lifted their wings, and I saw them rise
from the earth, the wheels rising along with
them. They stood at the entrance of the eastern
gate of the LORD's house, and the glory of the God
of Israel was up above them. 22 *Then the
cherubim lifted their wings, and the wheels went
along with them, while up above them was the
glory of the God of Israel. 23 And the glory of the
LORD rose from the city and took a stand on the
mountain which is to the east of the city.

CHAPTER 11

Judgment of the Princes 1 Spirit lifted me up
and brought me to the east gate of the temple. At
the entrance of the gate I saw twenty-five men,
among whom were Jaazaniah, son of Azzur, and
Pelatiah, son of Benaiah, princes of the people.
2 The LORD said to me: Son of man, these are the
men who are planning evil and giving wicked
counsel in this city. 3 "Shall we not," they say,
"be building houses soon? The city is the kettle,
and we are the meat."* 4 Therefore prophesy
against them, son of man, prophesy! 5 Then the

10, 2: The burning coals within the wheelwork under God's throne, a sign of the divine presence (cf Ez 28, 14; Ps 18, 13), symbolize the judgment to be visited on the city.

10, 22f: These verses have been transposed from ch 11.

11, 3: These words reflect the false confidence of the inhabitants of Jerusalem in the face of the Chaldean invasion. Jerusalem, they think, is like an iron kettle protecting the meat within it from harm; but cf Ez 24, 3–6.

p Ez 1, 1. 3. q Ez 1, 10. r Ez 1, 15f. s Ez 1, 18. t Ez 1, 19.

spirit of the LORD fell upon me, and he told me to say: Thus says the LORD: This is the way you talk, house of Israel, and what you are plotting I well know. [6]You have slain many in this city and have filled its streets with your slain. [7]Therefore thus says the Lord GOD: Your slain whom you have placed within it, they are the meat, and the city is the kettle; but you I will take out of it. [8]You fear the sword, but the sword I will bring upon you, says the Lord GOD. [9]I will bring you out of the city, and hand you over to foreigners, and inflict punishments upon you. [10]By the sword you shall fall; at the boundaries of Israel I will judge you; thus you shall know that I am the LORD. [11]The city shall not be a kettle for you, nor shall you be the meat within it. At the boundaries of Israel I will judge you, [12]and you shall know that I am the LORD, by whose statutes you have not lived, and whose ordinances you have not kept; rather, you have acted according to the ordinances of the nations around you.

[13]While I was prophesying, Pelatiah, the son of Benaiah, died. I fell prone and cried out in a loud voice: "Alas, Lord GOD! will you utterly wipe out what remains of Israel?"

Restoration of the Exiles [14]Thus the word of the LORD came to me: [15]*Son of man, it is about your kinsmen, your fellow exiles, and the whole house of Israel that the inhabitants of Jerusalem say, "They are far away from the LORD; to us the land of Israel has been given as our possession." [16]Therefore say: Thus says the Lord GOD: Though I have removed them far among the nations and scattered them over foreign countries—and was for a while their only sanctuary in the countries to which they had gone— [17]I will gather you from the nations and assemble you from the countries over which you have been scattered, and I will restore to you the land of Israel. [18]They shall return to it and remove from it all its detestable abominations. [19][u]I will give them a new heart and put a new spirit within them; I will remove the stony heart from their bodies, and replace it with a natural heart, [20]so that they will live according to my statutes, and observe and carry out my ordinances; thus they shall be my people and I will be their God. [21]But as for those whose hearts are devoted to their detestable abominations, I will bring down their conduct upon their heads, says the Lord GOD.

CHAPTER 12

Acts Symbolic of the Exile [1]Thus the word of the LORD came to me: [2]Son of man, you live in the midst of a rebellious house; they have eyes to see but do not see, and ears to hear but do not hear, for they are a rebellious house. [3]Now, son of man, during the day while they are looking on, prepare your baggage as though for exile, and again while they are looking on, migrate from where you live to another place; perhaps they will see that they are a rebellious house. [4]You shall bring out your baggage like an exile in the daytime while they are looking on; in the evening, again while they are looking on, you shall go out like one of those driven into exile; [5]while they look on, dig a hole in the wall* and pass through it; [6]while they look on, shoulder the burden and set out in the darkness; cover your face that you may not see the land, for I have made you a sign for the house of Israel.

[7]I did as I was told. During the day I brought out my baggage as though it were that of an exile, and at evening I dug a hole through the wall with my hand and, while they looked on, set out in the darkness, shouldering my burden.

[8]Then, in the morning, the word of the LORD came to me: [9]Son of man, did not the house of Israel, that rebellious house, ask you what you were doing? [10]Tell them: Thus says the Lord GOD: This oracle concerns Jerusalem and the whole house of Israel within it. [11]I am a sign for you: as I have done, so shall it be done to them; as captives they shall go into exile. [12]The prince who is among them shall shoulder his burden

11, 15–21: Like Jeremiah (cf chapter 29), Ezekiel knows that no reform is to be expected from the men of Judah who remained in Palestine; but the exiles will be the ones to form the new Israel. The new, spiritual covenant will replace the former covenant; cf Jer 24, 7.

12, 5: Dig a hole in the wall: the exiles are to leave Jerusalem through the broken walls of the ruined city.

u Ez 36, 26; Jer 31, 33.

and set out in darkness, going through a hole
that he has dug in the wall, and covering his face
lest he be seen by anyone. 13 [v]But I will spread
my net over him, and he shall be taken in my
snare. I will bring him to Babylon, into the land
of the Chaldeans—but he shall not see it*—and
there he shall die. 14 All his retinue, his aides,
and his troops I will scatter in every direction,
and pursue them with the sword. 15 Then shall
they know that I am the LORD, when I disperse
them among the nations and scatter them over
foreign lands. 16 Yet I will leave a few of them to
escape the sword, famine and pestilence, so that
they may tell of all their abominations among the
nations to which they will come; thus they shall
know that I am the LORD.

17 Thus the word of the LORD came to me:
18 Son of man, eat your bread trembling, and
drink your water shaking with anxiety. 19 Then
say to the people of the land: Thus says the Lord
GOD of the inhabitants of Jerusalem [to the land
of Israel]: They shall eat their bread in anxiety
and drink their water in horror, that their land
may be emptied of the violence of all its inhabit-
ants that now fills it. 20 Inhabited cities shall be in
ruins, and the land shall be a waste; thus you
shall know that I am the LORD.

Prophecy Ridiculed 21 Thus the word of the
LORD came to me: 22 Son of man, what is this
proverb that you have in the land of Israel: "The
days drag on, and no vision ever comes to
anything"?* 23 Say to them therefore: Thus says
the Lord GOD: I will put an end to this proverb;
they shall never quote it again in Israel. Rather,
say to them: The days are at hand, and also the
fulfillment of every vision. 25 Whatever I speak is
final, and it shall be done without further delay.
In your days, rebellious house, whatever I speak
I will bring about, says the Lord GOD.

24 There shall no longer be any false visions or
deceitful divinations within the house of Israel,
because it is I, the LORD, who will speak.

26 Thus the word of the LORD came to me:
27 Son of man, listen to the house of Israel saying,
"The vision he sees is a long way off; he
prophesies of the distant future!" 28 Say to them
therefore: Thus says the Lord GOD: None of my
words shall be delayed any longer; whatever I
speak is final, and it shall be done, says the Lord
GOD.

CHAPTER 13

Against the Prophets of Peace 1 Thus the
word of the LORD came to me: 2 Son of man,
prophesy against the prophets of Israel, proph-
esy! Say to those who prophesy their own
thought: Hear the word of the LORD:* 5 You did
not step into the breach, nor did you build a wall
about the house of Israel that would stand firm
against attack on the day of the LORD. 7 Was not
the vision you saw false, and your divination
lying? 8 Therefore thus says the Lord GOD:
Because you have spoken falsehood and have
seen lying visions, therefore see! I am coming at
you, says the Lord GOD.

10 For the very reason that they led my people
astray, saying, "Peace!" when there was no
peace, and that, as one built a wall, they would
cover it with whitewash,* 11 say then to the
whitewashers: I will bring down a flooding rain;
hailstones shall fall, and a stormwind shall break
out. 12 And when the wall has fallen, will you not
be asked: Where is the whitewash you spread
on?

13 Therefore thus says the Lord GOD: In my
fury I will let loose stormwinds; because of my
anger there shall be a flooding rain, and hail-
stones shall fall with destructive wrath. 14 I will
tear down the wall that you have whitewashed
and level it to the ground, laying bare its
foundations. When it falls, you shall be crushed
beneath it; thus you shall know that I am the
LORD. 15 When I have spent my fury on the wall
and its whitewashers, I tell you there shall be no

12, 13: But he shall not see it: Zedekiah was blinded by Nebuchadnezzar before being deported to Babylonia; cf 2 Kgs 25, 7.

12, 22. 27: These words were used against Ezekiel because of the apparent failure of his prophecies; cf Jer 20, 7ff.

13, 3–23: These verses have been transposed according to the following order: 7–8. 10–16. 3–4. 6.9.17. 22–23. 18–21.

13, 10: To the confidence which the people had in their defenses against the Chaldeans, the false prophets contributed the illusion of security by predictions of peace, like men who whitewash a wall rather than allow its defects to be seen.

v Ez 17, 20; 32, 3.

wall, nor shall there be whitewashers— 16those
prophets of Israel who prophesied to Jerusalem
and saw for it visions of peace when there was
no peace, says the Lord GOD.

Against False Prophets in Chaldea 3 [w]Thus
says the Lord GOD: Woe to those prophets who
are fools, who follow their own spirit and have
seen no vision. 4Like foxes among ruins are your
prophets, O Israel! 6Their visions are false and
their divination lying. They say, "Thus says the
LORD!" though the LORD did not send them;
then they wait for him to fulfill their word! 9But
I will stretch out my hand against the prophets
who have false visions and who foretell lies.
They shall not belong to the community of my
people, nor be recorded in the register of the
house of Israel, nor enter the land of Israel; thus
you shall know that I am the LORD.

Against False Prophetesses 17Now, son of
man, turn toward the daughters of your people
who prophesy their own thoughts; against these,
prophesy: Thus says the Lord GOD: 22Because
you have disheartened the upright man with lies
when I did not wish him grieved, and have
encouraged the wicked man not to turn from his
evil conduct and save his life; 23therefore you
shall no longer see false visions and practice
divination, but I will rescue my people from your
power. Thus you shall know that I am the LORD.

Against Sorceresses 18Woe to those who sew
bands for everyone's wrists and make veils* for
every size of head so as to entrap their owners.
Do you think to entrap the lives of my people,
yet keep yourselves alive? 19You dishonor me
before my people with handfuls of barley and
crumbs of bread,* killing those who should not
die and keeping alive those who should not live,
lying to my people who willingly hear lies.
20Therefore thus says the Lord GOD: See! I am
coming at those bands of yours in which you
entrap men's lives: I will tear them from their
arms and set free those you have caught. 21I will
tear off your veils and rescue my people from
your power, so that they shall no longer be prey
to your hands. Thus you shall know that I am
the LORD.

CHAPTER 14

Prophecy Useless for Idolaters 1When cer-
tain elders of Israel came and sat down before
me, 2the word of the LORD came to me: 3Son of
man, these men have the memory of their idols
fresh in their hearts, and they keep the occasion
of their sin before them. Why should I allow
myself to be consulted by them? 4Therefore
speak with them, and say to them: Thus says the
Lord GOD: If anyone of the house of Israel,
holding the memory of his idols in his heart and
keeping the occasion of his sin before him, has
recourse to a prophet, I, the LORD, will be his
answer in person because of his many idols.
5Thus would I bring back to their senses the
house of Israel, who have become estranged
from me through all their idols.

6Therefore say to the house of Israel: Thus
says the Lord GOD: Return and be converted
from your idols; turn yourselves away from all
your abominations. 7For if anyone of the house
of Israel or any alien resident in Israel is es-
tranged from me, and holds the memory of his
idols in his heart and keeps the occasion of his
sin before him, yet asks a prophet to consult me
for him, I, the LORD, will be his answer in
person. 8I will turn against that man, and make
of him an example and a byword. I will cut him
off from the midst of my people. Thus you shall
know that I am the LORD.

9 [x]As for the prophet, if he is beguiled into
speaking a word, I, the LORD, shall have beguiled
that prophet;* I will stretch out my hand against
him and root him out of my people Israel. 10Each
shall receive punishment for his sin, the inquirer
and the prophet shall be punished alike, 11so
that the house of Israel may no longer stray from

13, 18: Sew bands . . . make veils: magical practices believed to give to the sorceresses power over those on whom they placed these objects.

13, 19: Handfuls of barley and crumbs of bread: used in divination and forecasting the future.

14, 9: I, the Lord, shall have beguiled that prophet: the ancient Israelites attributed to God every action, good or evil; cf 1 Sm 18, 10; 2 Sm 24, 1ff. We would say, rather, that God permitted this deceit.

w Ez 14, 9; 34, 2; Jer 23, 1. x 1 Kgs 22, 23.

me and may no longer be defiled by all their sins. Thus they shall be my people, and I will be their God, says the Lord GOD.

Personal Responsibility* 12 Thus the word of the LORD came to me: 13 [y]Son of man, when a land sins against me by breaking faith, I stretch out my hand against it and break its staff of bread, I let famine loose upon it and cut off from it both man and beast; 14 and even if these three men were in it, Noah, Daniel, and Job,* they could save only themselves by their virtue, says the Lord GOD. 15 If I were to cause wild beasts to prowl the land, depopulating it so that it became a waste, traversed by none because of the wild beasts, 16 and these three men were in it, as I live, says the Lord GOD, I swear they could save neither sons nor daughters; they alone would be saved, and the land would be a waste. 17 Or if I brought the sword upon this country, commanding the sword to pass through the land cutting off from it man and beast, 18 and these three men were in it, as I live, says the Lord GOD, they would be unable to save either sons or daughters; they alone would be saved. 19 Or if I were to send pestilence into this land, pouring out upon it my bloodthirsty fury, cutting off from it man and beast, 20 even if Noah, Daniel, and Job were in it, as I live, says the Lord GOD, I swear that they could save neither son nor daughter; they would save only themselves by their virtue.

21 Thus says the Lord GOD: Even though I send Jerusalem my four cruel punishments, the sword, famine, wild beasts, and pestilence, to cut off from it man and beast, 22 still some survivors shall be left in it who will bring out sons and daughters; when they come out to you, you shall see their conduct and their actions and be consoled regarding the evil I have brought on Jerusalem [all that I have brought upon it]. 23 They shall console you when you see their conduct and actions, for you shall then know that it was not without reason that I did to it what I did, says the Lord GOD.

CHAPTER 15

Parable of the Vine 1 Thus the word of the LORD came to me: 2 Son of man, what makes the wood of the vine better than any other wood? That branch among the trees of the forest! 3 Can you use its wood to make anything worthwhile? Can you make even a peg from it, to hang on it any kind of vessel? 4 If you throw it on the fire as fuel and the fire devours both ends and even the middle is scorched, is it still good for anything? 5 Why, even when it was whole it was good for nothing; how much less, when the fire has devoured and scorched it, can it be used for anything! 6 Therefore, thus says the Lord GOD: Like the wood of the vine among the trees of the forest, which I have destined as fuel for the fire, do I make the inhabitants of Jerusalem. 7 I will set my face against them; they have escaped from the fire, but the fire shall devour them. Thus you shall know that I am the LORD, when I turn my face against them. 8 I will make the land a waste, because they have broken faith, says the Lord God.

CHAPTER 16

The Faithless Spouse 1 Thus the word of the LORD came to me: 2 Son of man, make known to Jerusalem her abominations. 3 Thus says the Lord GOD to Jerusalem: By origin and birth you are of the land of Canaan; your father was an Amorite and your mother a Hittite.* 4 As for your birth, the day you were born your navel cord was not cut; you were neither washed with water nor anointed, nor were you rubbed with salt, nor swathed in swaddling clothes. 5 No one looked on you with pity or compassion to do any of these things for you. Rather, you were thrown out on the ground as something loathsome, the day you were born.

14, 12–23: The doctrine of personal responsibility before God was not new (cf Ez 3, 16–21; 18; 33, 1–20); but it had not been emphasized by the prophets before the Exile, who mostly predicted national retribution and called for national repentance.

14, 14: Noah, Daniel, and Job: proverbially virtuous men. The Daniel named here may be the traditional just judge of the ancient past, celebrated in Canaanite literature, who is possibly reflected in Dn 13, but is not the hero of Dn 1–12.

16, 3f: By origin and birth . . . Canaan . . . Amorite . . . Hittite: the inhabitants of Jerusalem and Judah absorbed not only pre-Israelite racial strains, but also many elements of the country's pagan cult and customs.

y Ez 4, 16.

6 Then I passed by and saw you weltering in your blood. I said to you: Live in your blood 7 and grow like a plant in the field. You grew and developed, you came to the age of puberty; your breasts were formed, your hair had grown, but you were still stark naked. 8 Again I passed by you and saw that you were now old enough for love. So I spread the corner of my cloak over you to cover your nakedness;* I swore an oath to you and entered into a covenant with you; you became mine, says the Lord GOD. 9 Then I bathed you with water, washed away your blood, and anointed you with oil. 10 I clothed you with an embroidered gown, put sandals of fine leather on your feet; I gave you a fine linen sash and silk robes to wear. 11 I adorned you with jewelry: I put bracelets on your arms, a necklace about your neck, 12 a ring in your nose, pendants in your ears, and a glorious diadem upon your head. 13 Thus you were adorned with gold and silver; your garments were of fine linen, silk, and embroidered cloth. Fine flour, honey, and oil were your food. You were exceedingly beautiful, with the dignity of a queen. 14 You were renowned among the nations for your beauty, perfect as it was, because of my splendor which I had bestowed on you, says the Lord God.

15 But you were captivated by your own beauty, you used your renown to make yourself a harlot, and you lavished your harlotry on every passer-by, whose own you became. 16 *You took some of your gowns and made for yourself gaudy high places, where you played the harlot . . . . 17 You took the splendid gold and silver ornaments that I had given you and made for yourself male images, with which also you played the harlot. 18 You took your embroidered gowns to cover them; my oil and my incense you set before them; 19 the food that I had given you, the fine flour, the oil, and the honey with which I fed you, you set before them as an appeasing odor, says the Lord GOD. 20 [z]The sons and daughters you had borne me you took and offered as sacrifices* to be devoured by them! Was it not enough that you had become a harlot? 21 [a]You slaughtered and immolated my children to them, making them pass through fire. 22 And through all your abominations and harlotries you remembered nothing of when you were a girl, stark naked and weltering in your blood.

23 Then after all your evildoing—woe, woe to you! says the Lord GOD— 24 you raised for yourself a platform and a dais* in every public place. 25 [b]At every street corner you built a dais for yourself to use your beauty obscenely, spreading your legs for every passer-by, playing the harlot countless times. 26 You played the harlot with the Egyptians, your lustful neighbors, so many times that I was provoked to anger. 27 Therefore I stretched out my hand against you, I diminished your allowance and delivered you over to the will of your enemies, the Philistines, who revolted at your lewd conduct. 28 You also played the harlot with the Assyrians, because you were not satisfied; and after playing the harlot with them, you were still not satisfied. 29 Again and again you played the harlot, now going to Chaldea, the land of the traders; but despite this, you were still not satisfied.

30 How wild your lust! says the Lord GOD, that you did all these things, acting like a shameless prostitute, 31 building your platform at every street corner and erecting your dais in every public place! Yet you were unlike a prostitute, since you disdained payment. 32 The adulterous wife receives, instead of her husband, payment. 33 All harlots receive gifts. But you rather bestowed your gifts on all your lovers, bribing them to come to you from all sides for your harlotry. 34 Thus in your harlotry you were different from all other women. No one sought you out for prostitution. Since you gave payment instead of receiving it, how different you were!

16, 8: I spread the corner of my cloak over you to cover your nakedness: and also to signify the intention of marriage; cf Ru 3, 9.

16, 16: Fine robes were used to cover a couch for harlotry; cf Prv 7, 16f. In the allegory of this chapter the viewpoint often shifts from the figure (harlotry) to the reality (idolatry).

16, 20f: Human sacrifice was introduced under Judah's impious kings; cf 2 Kgs 16, 3; 17, 17; Jer 7, 31.

16, 24: A platform and a dais: associated with ritual prostitution, which the Israelites borrowed from Canaanite practice.

z Ez 20, 26. 31; 23, 37ff; Lv 18, 21; 20, 2; Dt 12, 31; 18, 10; 2 Kgs 21, 6; 23, 10; 24. 4; Jer 7, 31; 19, 5; 32, 34; Mi 6, 7. a 2 Kgs 16, 3; 17, 17; 21, 6; 23, 10. b Ez 23, 8; Is 57, 7; Jer 2, 20; 3, 2; 5, 7; 13, 27; Hos 2, 4; 4, 13.

35 Therefore, harlot, hear the word of the LORD! 36 Thus says the Lord GOD: Because you poured out your lust and revealed your nakedness in your harlotry with your lovers and abominable idols, and because you sacrificed the life-blood of your children to them, 37 [c]I will now gather together all your lovers whom you tried to please, whether you loved them or loved them not; I will gather them against you from all sides and expose you naked for them to see. 38 I will inflict on you the sentence of adulteresses and murderesses; I will wreak fury and jealousy upon you. 39 I will hand you over to them to tear down your platform and demolish your dais; they shall strip you of your garments and take away your splendid ornaments, leaving you stark naked. 40 They shall lead an assembly against you to stone you and hack you with their swords. 41 [d]They shall burn your apartments with fire and inflict punishments on you while many women look on. Thus I will put an end to your harlotry, and you shall never again give payment. 42 When I have wreaked my fury upon you I will cease to be jealous of you, I will be quiet and no longer vexed. 43 Because you did not remember what happened when you were a girl, but enraged me with all these things, therefore in return I am bringing down your conduct upon your head, says the Lord GOD. For did you not add lewdness to the rest of your abominable deeds?

44 See, everyone who is fond of proverbs will say of you, 'Like mother, like daughter.' 45 Yes, you are the true daughter of the mother* who spurned her husband and children, and you are a true sister to those who spurned their husbands and children—your mother was a Hittite and your father an Amorite. 46 Your elder sister was Samaria* with her daughters, living to the north of you; and your younger sister, living to the south of you, was Sodom with her daughters. 47 Yet not only in their ways did you walk, and act as abominably as they did; in a very short time you became more corrupt in all your ways than they. 48 As I live, says the Lord GOD, I swear that your sister Sodom, with her daughters, has not done as you and your daughters have done! 49 [e]And look at the guilt of your sister Sodom: she and her daughters were proud, sated with food, complacent in their prosperity, and they gave no help to the poor and needy. 50 Rather, they became haughty and committed abominable crimes in my presence; then, as you have seen, I removed them. 51 Samaria did not commit half your sins! You have done more abominable things than they, and have even made your sisters appear just, with all the abominable deeds you have done. 52 You, then, bear your shame; you are an argument in favor of your sisters! In view of your sinful deeds, more abominable than theirs, they appear just in comparison with you. Blush for shame, and bear the shame of having made your sisters appear just.

53 I will restore their fortunes, the fortune of Sodom and her daughters and of Samaria and her daughters [and I will restore your fortune along with them], 54 that you may bear your shame and be disgraced for all the comfort you brought them. 55 Yes, your sisters, Sodom and her daughters, Samaria and her daughters, shall return to their former state [you and your daughters shall return to your former state]. 56 Was not your sister Sodom kept in bad repute by you while you felt proud of yourself, 57 before your wickedness became evident? Now you are like her, reproached by the Edomites and all your neighbors, despised on all sides by the Philistines. 58 The penalty of your lewdness and your abominations—you must bear it all, says the LORD.

59 For thus speaks the Lord GOD: I will deal with you according to what you have done, you who despised your oath, breaking a covenant. 60 Yet I will remember the covenant I made with you when you were a girl, and I will set up an everlasting covenant with you. 61 Then you shall

16, 45: True daughter of the mother: Jerusalem has followed in the footsteps of its heathen forebears; cf v 3.

16, 46: Your elder sister was Samaria: Samaria can be called an elder sister in view of the relatively greater importance of the northern kingdom, Israel, during most of Old Testament history. Also, the relatively insignificant Sodom of ancient history can be called your younger sister.

c Ez 23, 10. d 2 Kgs 25, 9. e Gn 19, 24.

remember your conduct and be ashamed when I
take your sisters, those older and younger than
you, and give them to you as daughters, even
though I am not bound by my covenant with
you. 62For I will re-establish my covenant with
you, that you may know that I am the LORD,
63that you may remember and be covered with
confusion, and that you may be utterly silenced
for shame when I pardon you for all you have
done, says the Lord GOD.

CHAPTER 17

The Eagles and the Vine 1Thus the word of
the LORD came to me: 2Son of man, propose a
riddle, and speak this proverb to the house of
Israel: 3Thus speaks the Lord GOD:

The great eagle, with great wings, with long
pinions,
with thick plumage, many-hued, came to
Lebanon.
He took the crest of the cedar,
4 tearing off its topmost branch,
And brought it to a land of tradesmen,
set it in a city of merchants.
5Then he took some seed of the land,
and planted it in a seedbed;
A shoot by plentiful waters,
like a willow he placed it,
6To sprout and grow up a vine,
dense and low-lying,
Its branches turned toward him,
its roots lying under him.
Thus it became a vine, produced branches
and put forth shoots.
7But there was another great eagle,
great of wing, rich in plumage;
To him this vine bent its roots,
sent out its branches,
That he might water it more freely
than the bed where it was planted.
8In a fertile field by plentiful waters it was
planted,
to grow branches, bear fruit,
and become a majestic vine.

9Say: Thus says the Lord GOD: Can it pros-
per? Will he not rather tear it out by the roots
and strip off its fruit, so that all its green growth
will wither when he pulls it up by the roots? [No
need of a mighty arm or many people to do this.]
10True, it is planted, but will it prosper? Will it
not rather wither, when touched by the east
wind, in the bed where it grew?

11*Thus the word of the LORD came to me:
12Son of man, say now to the rebellious house:
Do you not understand what this means? It is
this: The king of Babylon came to Jerusalem and
took away its king and princes with him to
Babylon. 13Then he selected a man of the royal
line with whom he made a covenant, binding him
under oath, while removing the nobles of the
land, 14so that the kingdom would remain a
modest one, without aspirations, and would keep
his covenant and obey him. 15But this man
rebelled against him, sending envoys to Egypt to
obtain horses and a great army. Can he prosper?
Can he who does such things escape? Can he
break a covenant and still go free? 16As I live, says
the Lord GOD, in the home of the king who set
him up to rule, whose oath he spurned, whose
covenant with him he broke, there in Babylon I
swear he shall die! 17When ramps are cast up and
siege towers are built for the destruction of many
lives, he shall not be saved in the conflict by
Pharaoh with a great army and numerous troops.
18He spurned his oath, breaking his covenant.
Though he gave his hand in pledge, he did all
these things. He shall not escape!

19Therefore say: Thus says the Lord GOD: As I
live, my oath which he spurned, my covenant
which he broke, I swear to bring down upon his
head. 20[f]I will spread my net over him, and he
shall be taken in my snare. I will bring him to
Babylon and enter into judgment with him there
over his breaking faith with me. 21All the crack
troops among his forces shall fall by the sword,
and the survivors shall be scattered in every
direction. Thus you shall know that I, the LORD,
have spoken.

17, 11–21: These verses explain the foregoing allegory. In 597 B.C. Nebuchadnezzar removed King Jehoiachin and took him into exile; in his place he set Zedekiah, Jehoiachin's uncle, on the throne and received from him the oath of loyalty. But Zedekiah was beguiled into rebellion by Pharaoh Hophra of Egypt, and thereby merited punishment; cf 2 Kgs 24, 10—25, 7.

f Ez 12, 13; 32, 3.

22 Therefore say: Thus says the Lord GOD:

I, too, will take from the crest of the cedar,
 from its topmost branches tear off a tender shoot,
And plant it on a high and lofty mountain;
23 on the mountain heights of Israel I will plant it.*
It shall put forth branches and bear fruit,
 and become a majestic cedar.
Birds of every kind shall dwell beneath it,
 every winged thing in the shade of its boughs.
24 And all the trees of the field shall know
 that I, the LORD,
Bring low the high tree,
 lift high the lowly tree,
Wither up the green tree,
 and make the withered tree bloom.

As I, the LORD, have spoken, so will I do.

CHAPTER 18

Personal Responsibility 1 Thus the word of
the LORD came to me: Son of man, 2 what is the
meaning of this proverb that you recite in the
land of Israel:

"Fathers have eaten green grapes,[g]
 thus their children's teeth are on edge"?*

3 As I live, says the Lord GOD: I swear that there
shall no longer be anyone among you who will
repeat this proverb in Israel. 4 For all lives are
mine; the life of the father is like the life of the
son, both are mine; only the one who sins shall
die.

5 If a man is virtuous—if he does what is right
and just, 6 if he does not eat on the mountains,*
nor raise his eyes to the idols of the house of
Israel; if he does not defile his neighbor's wife,
nor have relations with a woman in her men-
strual period; 7 [h]if he oppresses no one, gives
back the pledge received for a debt, commits no
robbery; if he gives food to the hungry and
clothes the naked; 8 if he does not lend at
interest nor exact usury; if he holds off from
evildoing, judges fairly between a man and his
opponent; 9 if he lives by my statutes and is
careful to observe my ordinances, that man is
virtuous—he shall surely live, says the Lord
GOD.

10 But if he begets a son who is a thief, a
murderer, or who does any of these things
11 (though the father does none of them), a son
who eats on the mountains, defiles the wife of
his neighbor, 12 oppresses the poor and needy,
commits robbery, does not give back a pledge,
raises his eyes to idols, does abominable things,
13 lends at interest and exacts usury—this son
certainly shall not live. Because he practiced all
these abominations, he shall surely die; his death
shall be his own fault.

14 On the other hand, if a man begets a son
who, seeing all the sins his father commits, yet
fears and does not imitate him; 15 a son who does
not eat on the mountains, or raise his eyes to the
idols of the house of Israel, or defile his neigh-
bor's wife; 16 who does not oppress anyone, or
exact a pledge, or commit robbery; who gives
his food to the hungry and clothes the naked;
17 who holds off from evildoing, accepts no
interest or usury, but keeps my ordinances and
lives by my statutes—this one shall not die for
the sins of his father, but shall surely live. 18 Only
the father, since he violated rights, and robbed,
and did what was not good among his people,
shall in truth die for his sins. 19 You ask: "Why is
not the son charged with the guilt of his father?"
Because the son has done what is right and just,
and has been careful to observe all my statutes,
he shall surely live. 20 [i]Only the one who sins
shall die. The son shall not be charged with the
guilt of his father, nor shall the father be charged
with the guilt of his son. The virtuous man's
virtue shall be his own, as the wicked man's
wickedness shall be his.

17, 22f: I, too, will take from the crest of the cedar . . . plant it: the Lord will restore Israel under a messianic King from the same Davidic dynasty.

18, 2: Fathers . . . on edge: a proverb by which the people claimed that they were being punished for their ancestors' sins rather than for their own; cf Jer 31, 29.

18, 6: Eat on the mountains: partake of ritual meals at the heathen high places.

g Jer 13, 29. h Is 58, 7; Mt 25, 35. i Dt 24, 16; 2 Kgs 14, 6; 2 Chr 25, 4.

21 But if the wicked man turns away from all
the sins he committed, if he keeps all my statutes
and does what is right and just, he shall surely
live, he shall not die. 22 None of the crimes he
committed shall be remembered against him; he
shall live because of the virtue he has practiced.
23 [j]Do I indeed derive any pleasure from the
death of the wicked? says the Lord GOD. Do I
not rather rejoice when he turns from his evil
way that he may live?
24 And if the virtuous man turns from the path
of virtue to do evil, the same kind of abominable
things that the wicked man does, can he do this
and still live? None of his virtuous deeds shall be
remembered, because he has broken faith and
committed sin; because of this, he shall die.
25 [k]You say, "The LORD's way is not fair!" Hear
now, house of Israel: Is it my way that is unfair,
or rather, are not your ways unfair? 26 When a
virtuous man turns away from virtue to commit
iniquity, and dies, it is because of the iniquity he
committed that he must die. 27 But if a wicked
man, turning from the wickedness he has com-
mitted, does what is right and just, he shall
preserve his life; 28 since he has turned away
from all the sins which he committed, he shall
surely live, he shall not die. 29 And yet the house
of Israel says, "The LORD's way is not fair!" Is it
my way that is not fair, house of Israel, or rather,
is it not that your ways are not fair?
30 [l]Therefore I will judge you, house of Israel,
each one according to his ways, says the Lord
GOD. Turn and be converted from all your
crimes, that they may be no cause of guilt for
you. 31 Cast away from you all the crimes you
have committed, and make for yourselves a new
heart and a new spirit. Why should you die, O
house of Israel? 32 [m]For I have no pleasure in the
death of anyone who dies, says the Lord GOD.
Return and live!

CHAPTER 19

1 As for you, son of man, raise a lamentation
over the prince of Israel:

Allegory of the Lions*

2 What a lioness was your mother,
a lion of lions!
Among young lions she couched
to rear her whelps.
3 One whelp she raised up,
a young lion he became;
He learned to seize prey,
men he devoured.
4 Then nations raised cries against him,
in their pit he was caught;
They took him away with hooks
to the land of Egypt.
5 Then she saw that in vain she had waited,
her hope was destroyed.
She took another of her whelps,
him she made a young lion.
6 He prowled among the lions,
a young lion he became;
He learned to seize prey,
men he devoured;
7 He ravaged their strongholds,
their cities he wasted.
The land and all in it were appalled
at the noise of his roar.
8 Nations laid out against him
snares all about him;
They spread their net to take him,
in their pit he was caught.
9 They put him in a cage and took him away
to the king of Babylon,
So that his voice would not be heard
on the mountains of Israel.

Allegory of the Vine Branch

10 Your mother was like a vine*
planted by the water;
Fruitful and branchy was she
because of the abundant water.
11 One strong branch she put out
as a royal scepter.
Stately was her height
amid the dense foliage;
Notably tall was she

19, 2–9: The meaning of this allegory is uncertain. Probably the two young lions are Jehoahaz and Zedekiah, sons of the same mother, who were deported to Egypt and Babylonia respectively. Cf 2 Kgs 23, 31–34; 24, 18ff.

19, 10–14: A vine: Judah. One strong branch: the Davidic king.

j Ez 33, 11; 2 Pt 3, 9. k Ez 33, 20. l Mt 3, 2; Lk 3, 3. m Ez 18, 23; 33, 11; 2 Pt 3, 9.

with her many clusters.
12 But she was torn up in fury
and flung to the ground;
The east wind withered her up,
her fruit was torn off;
Then her strong branch withered up,
fire devoured it.[n]
13 So now she is planted in the desert,
in a land dry and parched,
14 For fire came out of the branch
and devoured her shoots;
She is now without a strong branch,
a ruler's scepter.

This is a lamentation and serves as a lamenta-
tion.

CHAPTER 20

Israel's History of Infidelity 1 In the seventh
year, on the tenth day of the fifth month,* some
of the elders of Israel came to consult the LORD
and sat down before me. 2 Then the word of the
LORD came to me: 3 Son of man, speak with the
elders of Israel and say to them: Thus says the
Lord GOD: Have you come to consult me? As I
live! I swear I will not allow myself to be
consulted by you, says the Lord GOD.

4 Will you judge them? Will you judge, son of
man? Make known to them the abominations of
their ancestors 5 in these words: Thus speaks the
Lord GOD: The day I chose Israel, I swore to the
descendants of the house of Jacob; in the land of
Egypt I revealed myself to them and swore: I am
the LORD, your God. 6 That day I swore to bring
them out of the land of Egypt to the land I had
scouted for them, a land flowing with milk and
honey, a jewel among all lands. 7 Then I said to
them: Throw away, each of you, the detestable
things that have held your eyes; do not defile
yourselves with the idols of Egypt: I am the
LORD, your God.

8 But they rebelled against me and refused to
listen to me; none of them threw away the
detestable things that had held their eyes, they
did not abandon the idols of Egypt. Then I
thought of pouring out my fury on them and
spending my anger on them there in the land of
Egypt; 9 but I acted for my name's sake, that it
should not be profaned in the sight of the nations
among whom they were, in whose presence I
had made myself known to them, revealing that
I would bring them out of the land of Egypt.
10 Therefore I led them out of the land of Egypt
and brought them into the desert. 11 [o]Then I
gave them my statutes and made known to them
my ordinances, which everyone must keep, to
have life through them. 12 [p]I also gave them my
sabbaths to be a sign between me and them, to
show that it was I, the LORD, who made them
holy.

13 But the house of Israel rebelled against me
in the desert. They did not observe my statutes,
and they despised my ordinances that bring life
to those who keep them. My sabbaths, too, they
desecrated grievously. Then I thought of pouring
out my fury on them in the desert to put an end
to them, 14 but I acted for my name's sake, that it
should not be profaned in the sight of the nations
in whose presence I had brought them out.
15 Nevertheless I swore to them in the desert not
to bring them to the land I had given them, a
land flowing with milk and honey, a jewel
among all lands. 16 So much were their hearts
devoted to their idols, they had not lived by my
statutes, but despised my ordinances and dese-
crated my sabbaths. 17 But I looked on them with
pity, not wanting to destroy them, so I did not
put an end to them in the desert.

18 Then I said to their children in the desert:
Do not observe the statutes of your parents or
keep their ordinances; do not defile yourselves
with their idols. 19 I am the LORD, your God:
observe my statutes and be careful to keep my
ordinances; 20 keep holy my sabbaths, as a sign
between me and you to show that I am the
LORD, your God. 21 But their children rebelled
against me: they did not observe my statutes or
keep my ordinances that bring life to those who
observe them, and my sabbaths they desecrated.
Then I thought of pouring out my fury on them,
of spending my anger on them in the desert;

20, 1: The seventh year, on the tenth day of the fifth month: August 14, 591 B.C.

n Hos 13, 15. o Lv 18, 5; Rom 10, 5. p Ex 20, 8; 31, 13; Dt 5, 12.

[22]but I stayed my hand, acting for my name's sake, lest it be profaned in the sight of the nations in whose presence I brought them out. [23]Nevertheless I swore to them in the desert that I would disperse them among the nations and scatter them over foreign lands; [24]for they did not keep my ordinances, but despised my statutes and desecrated my sabbaths, with eyes only for the idols of their fathers. [25]Therefore I gave them statutes that were not good,* and ordinances through which they could not live. [26]I let them become defiled by their gifts, by their immolation of every first-born, so as to make them an object of horror.

[27]Therefore speak to the house of Israel, son of man, and tell them: Thus says the Lord GOD: In this way also your fathers blasphemed me, breaking faith with me: [28]when I had brought them to the land I had sworn to give them, and they saw all its high hills and leafy trees, there they offered their sacrifices [there they brought their offensive offerings], there they sent up appeasing odors, and there they poured out their libations. [29]I asked them: To what sort of high place do you betake yourselves?—and so they call it a high place even to the present day. [30]Therefore say to the house of Israel: Thus says the Lord GOD: Will you defile yourselves like your fathers? Will you lust after their detestable idols? [31]By offering your gifts, by making your children pass through the fire, you defile yourselves with all your idols even to this day. Shall I let myself be consulted by you, house of Israel? As I live! says the Lord GOD: I swear I will not let myself be consulted by you.

[32]What you are thinking of shall never happen: "We shall be like the nations, like the peoples of foreign lands, serving wood and stone." [33]As I live, says the Lord GOD, with a mighty hand and outstretched arm, with poured-out wrath, I swear I will be king over you! [34]With a mighty hand and outstretched arm, with poured-out wrath, I will bring you out from the nations and gather you from the countries over which you are scattered; [35]*then I will lead you to the desert of the peoples, where I will enter into judgment with you face to face. [36]Just as I entered into judgment with your fathers in the desert of the land of Egypt, so will I enter into judgment with you, says the Lord GOD. [37]I will count you with the staff and bring back but a small number. [38]I will separate from you those who have rebelled and transgressed against me; from the land where they sojourned as aliens I will bring them out, but they shall not return to the land of Israel. Thus you shall know that I am the LORD.

[39]As for you, house of Israel, thus says the Lord GOD: Come, each one of you, destroy your idols! Then listen to me, and never again profane my holy name with your gifts and your idols. [40]For on my holy mountain, on the mountain height of Israel, says the Lord GOD, there the whole house of Israel without exception shall worship me; there I will accept them, and there I will claim your tributes and the first fruits of your offerings, and all that you dedicate. [41]As a pleasing odor I will accept you, when I have brought you from among the nations and gathered you out of the countries over which you were scattered; and by means of you I will manifest my holiness in the sight of the nations. [42]Thus you shall know that I am the LORD, when I bring you back to the land of Israel, the land which I swore to give to your fathers. [43]There you shall recall your conduct and all the deeds by which you defiled yourselves; and you shall loathe yourselves because of all the evil things you did. [44]And you shall know that I am the LORD when I deal with you thus, for my name's sake, and not according to your evil conduct and corrupt actions, O house of Israel, says the Lord GOD.

CHAPTER 21

The Sword of the Lord [1]Thus the word of the LORD came to me: [2]*Son of man, look south-

20, 25f: I gave them statutes that were not good: the Lord permitted them to adopt pagan practices, including the abominable sacrifice of their newborn infants, which could only merit their destruction. See note on Ez 14, 9.

20, 35–38: Exile in the pagan lands will serve the same purpose as the desert journey after the Exodus from Egypt: the rebellious will be eliminated, and only a remnant will survive.

21, 2ff: The southern kingdom, Judah, is likened to a forest

ward, preach toward the south, and prophesy
against the forest of the southern land. 3 Hear the
word of the LORD! you shall say to the southern
forest. Thus says the Lord GOD: See! I am
kindling a fire in you that shall devour all trees,
the green as well as the dry. The blazing flame
shall not be quenched, but from south to north
every face shall be scorched by it. 4 Everyone
shall see that I, the LORD, have kindled it, and it
shall not be quenched.

5 But I said, "Alas! Lord GOD, they say to me,
'Is not this the one who is forever spinning
parables?' " 6 Then the word of the LORD came
to me: 7 Son of man, look toward Jerusalem,
preach against their sanctuary, and prophesy
against the land of Israel, 8 saying to the land of
Israel: Thus says the LORD: See! I am coming at
you; I will draw my sword from its sheath and
cut off from you the virtuous and the wicked.*
9 Thus my sword shall leave its sheath against
everyone from south to north, 10 and everyone
shall know that I, the LORD, have drawn my
sword from its sheath, and it shall not be
sheathed again.

Act Symbolic of the City's Fall 11 As for you,
son of man, groan! with shattered strength groan
bitterly while they look on. 12 And when they ask
you, "Why are you groaning?", you shall say:
Because of a report;* when it comes every heart
shall fail, every hand shall fall helpless, every
spirit shall be daunted, and every knee shall run
with water. See, it is coming, it is here! says the
Lord GOD.

Song of the Sword 13 Thus the word of the
LORD came to me: 14 Son of man, prophesy! say:
Thus says the LORD:

A sword, a sword has been sharpened,
  a sword, a sword has been burnished:
15 To work slaughter has it been sharpened,
  to flash lightning has it been burnished.
Why should I now withdraw it?
  You have spurned the rod and every
    judgment!
16 I have given it over to the burnisher
  that he might hold it in his hand,
A sword sharpened and burnished
  to be put in the hand of a slayer.
17 Cry out and wail, son of man,
  for it is destined for my people;
It is for all the princes of Israel,
  victims of the sword with my people.

Therefore, slap your thigh,* 18 for the sword has
been tested; and why should it not be so? says
the Lord GOD, since you have spurned the rod.

19 As for you, son of man, prophesy,
  brushing one hand against the other:
While the sword is doubled and tripled,
  this sword of slaughter,
This great sword of slaughter
  which threatens all around,
20 That every heart may tremble;
  for many will be the fallen.
At all their gates
  I have appointed the sword for slaughter,
Fashioned to flash lightning,
  burnished for slaughter.
21 Cleave to the right! destroy!
  to the left! wherever your edge is turned.

22 Then I, too, shall brush one hand against the
other* and wreak my fury. I, the LORD, have
spoken.

Nebuchadnezzar at the Crossroads 23 Thus
the word of the LORD came to me: 24 Son of man,
make for yourself two roads over which the
sword of the king of Babylon can come. Both
roads shall lead out from the same land. Then
put a signpost at the head of each road, 25 so that
the sword can come to Rabbah of the Ammon-
ites or to Judah's capital, Jerusalem. 26 For at the
fork where the two roads divide stands the king
of Babylon, divining;* he has shaken the arrows,

---

about to be burned; cf Jer 21, 14.

21, 8: Cut off from you the virtuous and the wicked: a more complete devastation of Jerusalem than that described in Ez 9, 6.

21, 12: A report: the news of the fall of Jerusalem; cf Ez 33, 21f.

21, 17: Slap your thigh: a gesture signifying grief and dread.

21, 22: Brush one hand against the other: a gesture signifying the rejection of responsibility; cf Ez 22, 13; Nm 24, 10.

21, 26: Three forms of divination are mentioned: arrow divination, consisting in the use of differently marked arrows extracted or shaken from a case at random; the consultation of the teraphim or household idols; and liver divination, scrutiny of the configurations of the livers of newly slaughtered animals, a common form of divination in Mesopotamia.

inquired of the teraphim, inspected the liver.
27In his right hand is the divining arrow marked
"Jerusalem,"* bidding him to give the order for
slaying, to raise his voice in the battle cry, to post
battering rams at the gates, to cast up a ramp, to
build a siege tower. 28In their eyes this is but a
lying oracle; yet they are bound by the oaths
they have sworn, and the arrow taken in hand
marks their guilt.

29Therefore thus says the Lord GOD: Because
you have drawn attention to your guilt, with
your crimes laid bare and your sinfulness in all
your wicked deeds revealed (because attention
has been drawn to you), you shall be taken in
hand. 30And as for you, depraved and wicked
prince of Israel, whose day is coming when your
life of crime will be ended, 31thus says the Lord
GOD: Off with the turban and away with the
crown! Nothing shall be as it was! Up with the
low and down with the high! 32Twisted, twisted,
twisted will I leave it; it shall not be the same
until he comes who has the claim against the
city; and to him I will hand it over.

Against the Ammonites* 33As for you, son of
man, prophesy: Thus says the Lord GOD against
the Ammonities and their insults: A sword, a
sword is drawn for slaughter, burnished to
consume and to flash lightning, 34because you
planned with false visions and lying divinations
to lay it on the necks of depraved and wicked
men whose day has come when their crimes are
at an end. 35Return it to its sheath! In the place
where you were created, in the land of your
origin, I will judge you. 36I will pour out my
indignation upon you, breathing my fiery wrath
upon you; I will hand you over to ravaging men,
artisans of destruction. 37You shall be fuel for the
fire, your blood shall flow throughout the land.
You shall not be remembered, for I, the LORD,
have spoken.

CHAPTER 22

Crimes of Jerusalem 1Thus the word of the
LORD came to me: 2You, son of man, would you
judge, would you judge the bloody city? Then
make known all her abominations, 3and say:
Thus says the Lord GOD: Woe to the city which
sheds blood within herself so that her time has
come, and which has made idols for her own
defilement. 4By the blood which you shed you
have been made guilty, and with the idols you
made you have become defiled; you have
brought on your day, so that the end of your
years has come. Therefore I make you an object
of scorn to the nations and a laughingstock to all
foreign lands. 5Those near you and those far off
shall deride you because of your foul reputation
and your great perversity. 6See! the princes of
Israel, family by family, are in you only for
bloodshed. 7Within you, father and mother are
despised; in your midst, they extort from the
resident alien; within you, they oppress orphans
and widows. 8What is holy to me you have
spurned, and my sabbaths you have desecrated.
9There are those in you who slander to cause
bloodshed; within you are those who feast on
the mountains; in your midst are those who do
lewd things. 10In you are those who uncover the
nakedness of their fathers, and in you those who
coerce women in their menstrual period.
11 qThere are those in you who do abominable
things with the wives of their neighbors, men
who defile their daughters-in-law by incest, men
who coerce their sisters, the daughters of their
own fathers. 12There are those in you who take
bribes to shed blood. You exact interest and
usury; you despoil your neighbors violently; and
me you have forgotten, says the Lord GOD.

13See, I am brushing one hand against the
other because of the unjust profits you have
made and because of the bloodshed in your
midst. 14Can your heart remain firm, will your
hands be strong, in the days when I deal with

21, 27f: An arrow marked "Jerusalem" is picked out, which marks the guilt of the city's inhabitants for having broken their oath of allegiance to Nebuchadnezzar.

21, 33–37: In the preceding section Nebuchadnezzar is represented as deciding whether to attack Jerusalem or Rabbath-Ammon. As it happened, Jerusalem was chosen for attack; later, however, the Chaldeans also invaded Ammon. The present oracle against Ammon is inserted here, rather than in chapters 25–32, in order to complement the oracle against Jerusalem.

q Jer 5, 7f.

you? I, the LORD, have spoken, and I will act. 15 I
will disperse you among the nations and scatter
you over foreign lands, so that I may purge your
uncleanness. 16 In you I will allow myself to be
profaned in the eyes of the nations; thus you
shall know that I am the LORD.

17 Thus the word of the LORD came to me:
18 Son of man, the house of Israel has become
dross for me. All of them are bronze and tin, iron
and lead [in the midst of a furnace]: dross from
silver have they become. 19 Therefore thus says
the Lord GOD: Because all of you have become
dross, therefore I must gather you together
within Jerusalem. 20 Just as silver, bronze, iron,
lead, and tin are gathered into a furnace and
smelted in the roaring flames, so I will gather
you together in my furious wrath, put you in,
and smelt you. 21 When I have assembled you, I
will blast you with the fire of my anger and smelt
you with it. 22 You shall be smelted by it just as
silver is smelted in a furnace. Thus you shall
know that I, the Lord, have poured out my fury
on you.

23 Thus the word of the LORD came to me:
24 Son of man, say to her: You are a land
unrained on [that is, not rained on] at the time of
my fury. 25 Her princes are like roaring lions that
tear prey; they devour people, seizing their
wealth and precious things, and make widows of
many within her. 26 Her priests violate my law
and profane what is holy to me; they do not
distinguish between the sacred and the profane,
nor teach the difference between the unclean
and the clean; they pay no attention to my
sabbaths, so that I have been profaned in their
midst. 27 [r]Her nobles within her are like wolves
that tear prey, shedding blood and destroying
lives to get unjust gain. 28 Her prophets cover
them with whitewash, pretending to visions that
are false and performing lying divinations, say-
ing, "Thus says the Lord GOD," although the
LORD has not spoken. 29 The people of the land
practice extortion and commit robbery; they
afflict the poor and the needy, and oppress the
resident alien without justice. 30 Thus I have
searched among them for someone who could
build a wall or stand in the breach before me to
keep me from destroying the land; but I found
no one. 31 Therefore I have poured out my fury
upon them; with my fiery wrath I have con-
sumed them; I have brought down their conduct
upon their heads, says the Lord GOD.

CHAPTER 23

The Two Sisters 1 Thus the word of the LORD
came to me: 2 Son of man, there were two
women, daughters of the same mother, 3 who
even as young girls played the harlot in Egypt.
There the Egyptians caressed their bosoms and
fondled their virginal breasts. 4 Oholah was the
name of the elder, and the name of her sister
was Oholibah.* They became mine and bore
sons and daughters. [As for their names: Samaria
is Oholah, and Jerusalem is Oholibah.] 5 Oholah
became a harlot faithless to me; she lusted after
her lovers, the Assyrians, warriors 6 dressed in
purple, governors and officers, all of them attrac-
tive young men, knights mounted on horses.
7 Thus she gave herself as a harlot to them, to all
the elite of the Assyrians, and she defiled herself
with all those for whom she lusted [with all their
idols]. 8 She did not give up the harlotry which
she had begun in Egypt, when they had lain
with her as a young girl, fondling her virginal
breasts and pouring out their impurities on her.
9 Therefore I handed her over to her lovers, the
Assyrians for whom she had lusted. 10 [s]They
exposed her nakedness, her sons and daughters
they took away, and herself they slew with the
sword. Thus she became a byword for women,
for they punished her grievously.

11 Though her sister Oholibah saw all this, her
lust was more depraved than her sister's, and
she outdid her in harlotry. 12 She too lusted after
the Assyrians, governors and officers, warriors
impeccably clothed, knights mounted on horses,
all of them attractive young men. 13 I saw that
she had defiled herself. Both had gone down the

23, 4: Oholah . . . Oholibah: symbolic names. The first, standing for Samaria, may be read to mean "her own tent"; the latter, standing for Jerusalem, means "my tent is in her." The references seem to be to the schismatic temple and cult of the Lord in Samaria, as opposed to their authentic counterpart in Jerusalem.

r Mi 3, 11; Zep 3, 3. s Ez 16, 37.

same path, 14yet she went further in her harlotry. When she saw men drawn on the wall, the images of Chaldeans drawn with vermillion, 15with sashes girded about their waists, flowing turbans on their heads, all looking like chariot warriors, the portraits of Babylonians, natives of Chaldea, 16she lusted for them; no sooner had she set eyes on them than she sent messengers to them in Chaldea. 17Then the Babylonians came to her, to the love couch, and defiled her with their intercourse. As soon as she was defiled by them, she became disgusted with them. 18Her harlotry was discovered and her shame was revealed, and I became disgusted with her as I had become disgusted with her sister. 19But she played the harlot all the more, recalling the days of her girlhood, when she had been a harlot in the land of Egypt. 20She lusted for the lechers of Egypt, whose members are like that of an ass, and whose heat is like those of stallions.

21You yearned for the lewdness of your girlhood, when the Egyptians fondled your breasts, caressing your bosom. 22Therefore, Oholibah, thus says the Lord GOD: I will now stir up your lovers against you, those with whom you are disgusted, and I will bring them against you from every side: 23the men of Babylon and all of Chaldea, Pekod, Shoa and Koa,* along with all those of Assyria, attractive young men, all of them governors and officers, charioteers and warriors, all of them horsemen. 24They shall come against you from the north with chariots and wagons and many peoples. Shields, bucklers, and helmets they shall array against you everywhere. 25I will leave it to them to judge, and they will judge you by their own ordinances. I will let loose my jealousy against you, so that they shall deal with you in fury, cutting off your nose and ears; and what is left of you shall fall by the sword. They shall take away your sons and daughters, and what is left of you shall be devoured by fire. 26They shall strip off your clothes and seize your splendid ornaments. 27I will put an end to your lewdness and to the harlotry you began in Egypt; you shall no longer look toward it, nor shall you remember Egypt again.

28For thus says the Lord GOD: I am now handing you over to those whom you hate, to those who fill you with disgust. 29They shall deal with you in hatred, seizing all that you have worked for and leaving you stark naked, so that your indecent nakedness is exposed. Your lewdness and harlotry 30have brought these things upon you, because you played the harlot with the nations by defiling yourself with their idols.

31Because you followed in the path of your sister, I will hand you her cup. 32Thus says the Lord GOD:

The cup of your sister you shall drink,
  so wide and deep, which holds so much,
33 Filled with destruction and grief,
  a cup of dismay, the cup of your sister.

34You shall drain it dry, and gnaw at the very sherds of the cup, and you shall tear out your breasts; for I have spoken, says the Lord GOD. 35Therefore thus says the Lord GOD: Because you have forgotten me and cast me behind your back, it is for you to bear the penalty of your lewdness and harlotry.

36Then the LORD said to me: Son of man, would you judge Oholah and Oholibah? Then make known to them their abominations. 37For they committed adultery, and blood is on their hands. They committed adultery with their idols; to feed them they immolated the children they had borne me. 38[This, too, they did to me: they defiled my sanctuary and desecrated my sabbaths. 39On the very day they slew their children for their idols, they entered my sanctuary to desecrate it. Thus they acted within my house.] 40Moreover, they sent for men who had to come from afar,* to whom messengers were sent. And so they came—and for them you bathed yourself, painted your eyes, and put on ornaments. 41You sat on a couch prepared for

23, 23: Pekod, Shoa and Koa: peoples living about the Tigris, part of "greater Babylonia."

23, 40: Men who had to come from afar: ambassadors from Assyria and Babylon. Alliances with these countries aided in the corruption of both Israel and Judah.

them, with a table spread before it, on which
you had set my incense and oil. 42Then was
heard the shout of a carefree mob in the city, and
these were men brought in from the desert, who
put bracelets on the women's arms and splendid
diadems on their heads. 43So I said: "Oh, this
woman jaded with adulteries! Now they will
commit whoredom with her, and as for her
. . . ." 44And indeed they did come to her as
men come to a harlot. Thus they came to
Oholah and Oholibah, the lewd women. 45But
just men shall punish them with the sentence
meted out to adulteresses and murderesses, for
they have committed adultery, and blood is on
their hands.

46Thus says the Lord GOD: Summon an assem-
bly against them, and deliver them over to terror
and plunder. 47The assembly shall stone them
and hack them to pieces with their swords. They
shall slay their sons and daughters, and burn their
houses with fire. 48Thus I will put an end to lewd-
ness in the land, and all the women will be
warned not to imitate your lewdness. 49They
shall inflict on you the penalty of your lewdness,
and you shall pay for your sins of idolatry. Thus
you shall know that I am the LORD.

CHAPTER 24

Allegory of the Pot 1On the tenth day of the
tenth month, in the ninth year,* the word of the
LORD came to me: 2Son of man, write down this
date today, for this very day the king of Babylon
has invested Jerusalem. 3Propose this parable to
the rebellious house: Thus says the Lord GOD:

*Set up the pot, set it up,
then pour in some water.
4Put in it pieces of meat,
all good pieces: thigh and shoulder;
Fill it with the choicest joints
5 taken from the pick of the flock.
Then pile the wood beneath it;
bring to a boil these pieces
and the joints that are in it.
6Take out its pieces, one by one,
without casting lots for it.

Therefore, thus says the Lord GOD: Woe to the
bloody city,[t] a pot containing rust, whose rust
has not been removed. 7For the blood she shed
is in her midst; she poured it on the bare rock;
she did not pour it out on the earth, to be
covered with dust.* 8To work up my wrath, to
excite my vengeance, she put her blood on the
bare rock, not to be covered. 9Therefore, thus
says the Lord GOD:

I, too, will heap up a great bonfire,
10 piling on wood and kindling the fire,
Till the meat has been cooked,
till the broth has boiled.

11Then I will set the pot empty on the coals till
its metal glows red hot, till the impurities in it
melt, and its rust disappears. 12Yet not even with
fire will its great rust be removed. 13Because you
have sullied yourself with lewdness when I
would have purified you, and you refused to be
purified of your uncleanness, therefore you shall
not be purified until I wreak my fury on you. 14I,
the LORD, have spoken; it is coming, for I will
bring it about without fail. I will not have pity
nor repent. By your conduct and your deeds you
shall be judged, says the Lord GOD.

Symbol of the Destruction of the Temple
15Thus the word of the LORD came to me: 16Son
of man, by a sudden blow I am taking away from
you the delight of your eyes, but do not mourn
or weep or shed any tears. 17Groan in silence,
make no lament for the dead, bind on your
turban, put your sandals on your feet, do not
cover your beard, and do not eat the customary
bread.* 18That evening my wife died, and the
next morning I did as I had been commanded.
19Then the people asked me, "Will you not tell
us what all these things that you are doing mean

24, 1: The tenth day of the tenth month, in the ninth year: January 15, 588 B.C. The same date is given in Jer 52, 4.

24, 3ff: This present comparison of the inhabitants of Jerusalem to meat boiled in a pot symbolizes their punishment rather than their supposed protection as in Ez 11, 3.

24, 7: Blood . . . to be covered with dust: since blood was sacred to God, it had to be covered with earth (Lv 17, 13); the blood of a murdered man that was left uncovered cried to heaven for vengeance; cf Jb 16, 18; Gn 4, 10.

24, 17: The customary bread: eaten as a mourning observance; cf Jer 16, 7. The other gestures here forbidden were also popular mourning customs.

t Na 3, 1; Hb 2, 12.

for us?" I therefore spoke to the people that morning, [20]saying to them: Thus the word of the LORD came to me: [21]Say to the house of Israel: Thus says the Lord GOD: I will now desecrate my sanctuary, the stronghold of your pride, the delight of your eyes, the desire of your soul. The sons and daughters you left behind shall fall by the sword. [24]Ezekiel shall be a sign for you: all that he did you shall do when it happens. Thus you shall know that I am the LORD. [22]*You shall do as I have done, not covering your beards nor eating the customary bread. [23]Your turbans shall remain on your heads, your sandals on your feet. You shall not mourn or weep, but you shall rot away because of your sins and groan one to another.

End of Ezekiel's Dumbness [25] [u]As for you, son of man, truly, on the day I take away from them their bulwark, their glorious joy, the delight of their eyes, the desire of their soul, and the pride of their hearts, their sons and daughters, [26]that day the fugitive will come to you, that you may hear it for yourself; [27]that day your mouth shall be opened and you shall be dumb no longer. Thus you shall be a sign to them, and they shall know that I am the LORD.

III: Prophecies Against Foreign Nations

CHAPTER 25

Against Ammon [1]Thus the word of the LORD came to me: [2]Son of man, turn toward the Ammonites and prophesy against them. [3] [v]Say to the Ammonites: Hear the word of the LORD! Thus says the Lord GOD: Because you cried out your joy over the desecration of my sanctuary, the devastation of the land of Israel, and the exile of the house of Judah, [4]therefore I will deliver you into the possession of the Easterners.* They shall set up their encampments among you and pitch their tents; they shall eat your fruits and drink your milk. [5]I will make Rabbah a pasture for camels, and the villages of the Ammonites a resting place for flocks. Thus you shall know that I am the LORD.

[6]For thus says the Lord GOD: Because you clapped your hands and stamped your feet, rejoicing most maliciously in your heart over the land of Israel, [7]therefore I will stretch out my hand against you. I will make you plunder for the nations, I will cut you off from the peoples, and remove you from the lands. I will destroy you, and thus you shall know that I am the LORD.

Against Moab [8] [w]Thus says the Lord GOD: Because Moab said, "See! the house of Judah is like all other nations," [9]therefore I will clear the shoulder of Moab* totally of its cities, the jewels of the land: Beth-jesimoth, Baal-meon, and Kiriathaim. [10]I will hand her over, along with the Ammonites, into the possession of the Easterners, that she may not be remembered among the peoples. [11]Thus I will execute judgment upon Moab, that they may know that I am the LORD.

Against Edom [12] [x]Thus says the Lord GOD: Because Edom has taken vengeance on the house of Judah and has made itself grievously guilty by taking vengeance on them, [13]therefore thus says the Lord GOD: I will stretch out my hand against Edom and cut off from it man and beast. I will make it a waste from Teman to Dedan; they shall fall by the sword. [14]My vengeance upon Edom I will entrust to my people Israel, who will deal with Edom in accordance with my anger and my fury; thus they shall know my vengeance, says the Lord GOD.

Against the Philistines [15]Thus says the Lord GOD: Because the Philistines have acted revengefully, and have taken vengeance with destructive malice in their hearts, with an undying enmity, [16]therefore thus says the Lord GOD: See! I am stretching out my hand against the Philistines; I will cut off the Cherethites* and wipe out the

24, 22f: The fall of the city will be so sudden and final that the exiles will have no time to go into mourning.

25, 4: The Easterners: nomadic tribes to the east of Ammon and Moab.

25, 9: The shoulder of Moab: the edge of the Moabite plateau.

25, 16: Cherethites: a people forming part of the Philistine nation; cf Zep 2, 5.

u 25ff: Ez 3, 22–27. v Jer 40, 14; 41, 10: 49, 2; Am 1, 13ff: Zep 2, 8ff. w Sir 50, 26; Is 15, 1–9; 16, 1–14; Jer 48, 1–47; Am 2, 1ff; Zep 2, 8f. x 12ff: Ez 35, 1ff; Is 34, 5; Jer 49, 7–22; Jl 4, 19; Am 1, 11f; Ob 1, 1–21.

remnant on the seacoast. 17 I will execute great acts of vengeance on them, punishing them furiously. Thus they shall know that I am the LORD, when I wreak my vengeance on them.

CHAPTER 26

Against the City of Tyre 1 On the first day of the . . . month in the eleventh year, the word of the LORD came to me: 2 Son of man, because of what Tyre said of Jerusalem:

"Aha! it is broken, the gateway to the peoples;
now that it is ruined, its wealth reverts to me!"
3 therefore thus says the Lord GOD:
See! I am coming at you, Tyre;
I will churn up against you many nations,
even as the sea churns up its waves;[y]
4 They shall destroy the walls of Tyre
and raze her towers.
I will scrape the ground from her
and leave her a bare rock;*
5 She shall be a drying place for nets
in the midst of the sea.

I have spoken, says the Lord GOD: and she shall be booty for the nations. 6 And her daughters* on the mainland shall be slaughtered by the sword; thus they shall know that I am the LORD.

7 For thus says the Lord GOD: I am now bringing up against Tyre from the north Nebuchadnezzar the king of Babylon, the king of kings, with horses and chariots, with cavalry and a great and mighty army.

8 Your daughters on the mainland
he shall slay with the sword;
He shall place a siege tower against you,
cast up a ramp about you,
and raise his shields against you.
9 He shall pound your walls with battering-rams
and break down your towers with his weapons.
10 The surge of his horses shall cover you with dust,
amid the noise of steeds, of wheels and of chariots.
Your walls shall shake as he enters your gates,
even as one enters a city that is breached.
11 With the hoofs of his horses
he shall trample all your streets;
Your people he shall slay by the sword;
your mighty pillars he shall pull to the ground.
12 Your wealth shall be plundered,
your merchandise pillaged;
Your walls shall be torn down,
your precious houses demolished;
Your stones, your timber, and your clay
shall be cast into the sea.
13 I will put an end to the noise of your songs,
and the sound of your lyres shall be heard no more.
14 I will make you a bare rock;
a drying place for nets shall you be.

Never shall you be rebuilt, for I have spoken, says the Lord GOD.

15 Thus says the Lord GOD to Tyre: At the noise of your fall, at the groaning of the wounded, when the sword slays in your midst, shall not the isles quake? 16 All the princes of the sea* shall step down from their thrones, lay aside their robes, and strip off their embroidered garments. They shall be clothed in mourning and, sitting on the ground, they shall tremble at every moment and be horrified at you. 17 Then they shall utter a lament over you:

How have you perished, gone from the seas,
city most prized!
Once she was mighty on the sea,
she and her dwellers,
Who spread terror into all
that dwelt by the sea.

26, 4f: A bare rock: the Tyre of Ezekiel's time was situated on a rocky island just off the Phoenician coast; it was not until the time of Alexander the Great that it was connected by a causeway to the mainland.

26, 6: Her daughters: tributary towns and villages on the mainland.

26, 16: The princes of the sea: the rulers of the islands and coastal cities leagued commercially with Tyre.

y Is 26, 1-21: 47, 4; Jl 4, 4f; Zec 9, 2ff.

18 On this, the day of your fall,
the islands quake!

The isles in the sea are terrified at your passing.
19 For thus says the Lord God: When I make
you a city desolate like cities that are no longer
inhabited, when I churn up the abyss against
you, and its mighty waters cover you, 20 then I
will thrust you down with those who descend
into the pit,* those of the bygone age; and I will
make you dwell in the nether lands, in the
everlasting ruins, with those who go down to
the pit, so that you may never return to take
your place in the land of the living. 21 I will make
you a devastation, and you shall be no more; you
shall be sought, but never again found, says the
Lord God.

CHAPTER 27

The Ship Tyre 1 Thus the word of the Lord
came to me: 2 As for you, son of man, utter a
lament over Tyre, 3 and say to Tyre that is
situated at the approaches of the sea, that
brought the trade of the peoples to many a
coastland: Thus says the Lord God:

Tyre, you said, "I am a ship,
perfect in beauty."
4 In the midst of the sea your builders placed
you,
perfected your beauty.
5 With cypress from Senir* they built for you
all of your decks;
Cedar from Lebanon they took
to make you a mast;
6 From the highest oaks of Bashan*
they made your oars;
Your bridge they made of cypress wood
from the coasts of Kittim.
7 Fine embroidered linen from Egypt
became your sail [to serve you as a banner].
Purple and scarlet from the coasts of Elishah*
covered your cabin.
8 Citizens of Sidon and Arvad
served as your oarsmen;
Skilled men of Zemer were in you
to be your mariners;
9 The elders and experts of Gebal* were in you
to caulk your seams.

Every ship and sailor on the sea came to you to
carry trade. 10 Persia and Lud and Put were in
your army as warriors; shield and helmet they
hung upon you, increasing your splendor. 11 The
men of Arvad were all about your walls, and the
Gamadites were in your towers; they hung their
bucklers all around on your walls, and made
perfect your beauty. 12 Tarshish traded with you,
so great was your wealth, exchanging silver,
iron, tin, and lead for your wares. 13 Javan, Tubal,
and Meshech were also traders with you, ex-
changing slaves and articles of bronze for your
goods. 14 From Beth-togarmah horses, steeds,
and mules were exchanged for your wares.
15 The Rhodanites trafficked with you; many
coastlands traded with you; ivory tusks and
ebony wood they gave you for payment. 16 Edom
traded with you, so many were your products,
exchanging garnets, purple, embroidered cloth,
fine linen, coral, and rubies for your wares.
17 Judah and the land of Israel trafficked with
you, exchanging Minnith wheat, figs, honey, oil,
and balm for your goods. 18 Damascus traded
with you, so great was your wealth, exchanging
Helbon wine and Zahar wool. 19 Javan ex-
changed wrought iron, cassia, and aromatic cane
from Uzal for your wares. 20 Dedan traded with
you for riding gear. 21 The trade of Arabia and of
all the sheikhs of Kedar belonged to you; they
dealt in lambs, rams, and goats. 22 The merchants
of Sheba and Raamah also traded with you,
exchanging for your wares the very choicest
spices, all kinds of precious stones, and gold.
23 Haran, Canneh, and Eden, the merchants of
Sheba, Asshur, and Chilmad 24 traded with you,
marketing with you rich garments, violet man-
tles, embroidered cloth, varicolored carpets, and
firmly woven cords. 25 Ships of Tarshish jour-
neyed for you in your merchandising.

26, 20: Those who descend into the pit: the dead, pictured as dwelling in a place or cave of darkness.

27, 5: Senir: another name for Mount Hermon; cf Dt 3, 9.

27, 6: Bashan: northern Transjordan, which, like Lebanon, was noted for its great forests. Kittim: probably Cyprus.

27, 7: Elishah: probably another term for Cyprus.

27, 8f: Sidon . . . Arvad . . . Zemer . . . Gebal: Phoenician cities in Tyre's orbit of influence; the last-named is the classical Byblos.

You were full and heavily laden
in the heart of the sea.
26 Through the deep waters your oarsmen
brought you home,
But the east wind smashed you
in the heart of the sea.
27 Your wealth, your goods, your wares,
your sailors, and your crew,

[the caulkers of your seams, those who traded for your goods, all your warriors who were in you, and all the great crowd within you]

Sank into the heart of the sea
on the day of your shipwreck.
28 Hearing the shouts of your mariners,
the shores begin to quake.
29 Down from their ships
come all who ply the oar;
The sailors, all the mariners of the sea,
stand on the shore,
30 Making their voice heard on your behalf,
shouting bitter cries,
Strewing dust on their heads,
rolling in the ashes.
31 For you they shave their heads
and put on sackcloth,
For you they weep in anguish,
with bitter lament.
32 In their mourning they utter a lament over
you;
thus they wail over you:
Who was ever destroyed like Tyre
in the midst of the sea?
33 With your goods which you drew from the
seas
you filled many peoples;
With your great wealth and merchandise
you enriched the kings of the earth.
34 Now you are wrecked in the sea,
in the watery depths;
Your wares and all your crew
have gone down with you.
35 All who dwell on the coastlands
are aghast over you,
Their kings are terrified,
their faces convulsed.
36 The traders among the peoples
now hiss at you;
You have become a horror,
and you shall be no more.

CHAPTER 28

The Prince of Tyre 1 Thus the word of the LORD came to me: 2 Son of man, say to the prince of Tyre: Thus says the Lord GOD:

Because you are haughty of heart,
you say, "A god am I!
I occupy a godly throne
in the heart of the sea!"—
And yet you are a man, and not a god,
however you may think yourself like a god.
3 Oh yes, you are wiser than Daniel,*
there is no secret that is beyond you.
4 By your wisdom and your intelligence
you have made riches for yourself;
You have put gold and silver
into your treasuries.
5 By your great wisdom applied to your trading
you have heaped up your riches;
your heart has grown haughty from your
riches—
6 therefore thus says the Lord GOD:
Because you have thought yourself
to have the mind of a god,
7 Therefore I will bring against you
foreigners, the most barbarous of nations.
They shall draw their swords
against your beauteous wisdom,
they shall run them through your splendid
apparel.
8 They shall thrust you down to the pit, there to
die
a bloodied corpse, in the heart of the sea.
9 Will you then say, "I am a god!"
when you face your murderers?
No, you are a man, not a god,
handed over to those who will slay you.
10 You shall die the death of the uncircumcised
at the hands of foreigners,
for I have spoken,
says the Lord GOD.

28, 3: Wiser than Daniel: see note on Ez 14, 14.

[11]Thus the word of the LORD came to me:
[12]Son of man, utter a lament over the king of
Tyre, saying to him: Thus says the Lord GOD:

*You were stamped with the seal of
perfection,
of complete wisdom and perfect beauty.
[13] In Eden, the garden of God, you were,
and every precious stone was your covering
[carnelian, topaz, and beryl, chrysolite, onyx,
and jasper, sapphire, garnet, and emerald];

Of gold your pendants and jewels
were made, on the day you were created.
[14] With the Cherub I placed you;
you were on the holy mountain of God,*
walking among the fiery stones.
[15] Blameless you were in your conduct
from the day you were created,
Until evil was found in you,
[16] the result of your far-flung trade;
violence was your business, and you sinned.
Then I banned you from the mountain of
God;*
the Cherub drove you from among the fiery
stones.
[17] You became haughty of heart because of your
beauty;
for the sake of splendor you debased your
wisdom.
I cast you to the earth, so great was your guilt;
I made you a spectacle in the sight of kings.
[18] Because of your guilt, your sinful trade,
I have profaned your sanctuaries,
And I have brought out fire from your midst
which will devour you.
I have reduced you to dust on the earth
in the sight of all who should see you.
[19] Among the peoples, all who knew you
stand aghast at you;
You have become a horror,
you shall be no more.

Against Sidon [20] [z]Thus the word of the LORD
came to me: Son of man, look toward Sidon,
[21] [a]and prophesy against it: [22]Thus says the Lord
GOD: [b] See! I am coming at you, Sidon; I will be
glorified in your midst. Then they shall know
that I am the LORD, when I inflict punishments
upon it and use it to manifest my holiness.

[23] Into it I will send pestilence,
and blood shall flow in its streets.
Within it shall fall those slain
by the sword that comes against it from
every side.

Thus they shall know that I am the LORD.
[24]Sidon shall no longer be a tearing thorn for the
house of Israel, a brier that scratches them more
than all the others about them who despise
them; thus they shall know that I am the LORD.

[25]Thus says the Lord GOD: When I gather the
house of Israel from the peoples among whom
they are scattered, then I will manifest my
holiness through them in the sight of the na-
tions. Then they shall live on their land which I
gave to my servant Jacob; [26]they shall live on it
in security, building houses and planting vine-
yards. They shall dwell secure while I inflict
punishments on all their neighbors who despised
them; thus they shall know that I, the LORD, am
their God.

CHAPTER 29

Egypt the Crocodile [1]On the twelfth day of
the tenth month in the tenth year,* the word of
the LORD came to me: [2]Son of man, set your face
against Pharaoh, king of Egypt, and prophesy
against him and against all Egypt.* [3]Say this to
him: Thus says the Lord GOD:

See! I am coming at you, Pharaoh,
king of Egypt,
Great crouching monster
amidst your Niles:*

28, 12–19: This picture of Tyre and its fall recalls images of the earthly paradise portraying the creation of man in perfection and his fall (Gn, chapters 2–3).

28, 14: The holy mountain of God: the residence of God was sometimes designated as a mountain; cf Is 14, 13. The fiery stones: associated with the divine presence; cf Ez 1, 13; Ps 18, 13.

29, 1: The twelfth day of the tenth month in the tenth year: January 7, 587 B.C. The siege of Jerusalem had begun a year earlier; cf Ez 24, 1.

29, 2: Egypt was allied with Judah against the Chaldeans.

29, 3: Niles: the many rivulets of the Nile as it branches out into the Delta.

z Is 23, 1–18. a Jer 47, 4. b Jl 4, 4; Zec 9, 2ff.

Who say, "The Niles are mine;
it is I who made them!"

[4]I will put hooks in your jaws and make the fish
of your Niles stick to your scales, then draw you
up from the midst of your Niles along with all
the fish of your Niles sticking to your scales.

[5]I will cast you into the desert,
you and all the fish of your Niles;
You shall fall upon the open field,
you shall not be taken up or buried;
To the beasts of the earth and the birds of the
air
I give you as food,
[6]That all who dwell in Egypt may know
that I am the LORD.
Because you have been a reed staff
for the house of Israel: [c]
[7]When they held you in hand, you splintered,
throwing every shoulder out of joint;
When they leaned on you, you broke,
bringing each one of them down headlong;

[8]therefore thus says the Lord GOD: See! I will
bring the sword against you, and cut off from
you both man and beast. [9]The land of Egypt
shall become a desolate waste; thus they shall
know that I am the LORD.
Because you said, "The Niles are mine; it is I
who made them," [10]therefore see! I am coming
at you and against your Niles; I will make the
land of Egypt a waste and a desolation from
Migdol to Syene,* and even to the frontier of
Ethiopia. [11]No foot of man or beast shall pass
through it; they shall not pass through it, and it
will be uninhabited for forty years. [12]I will make
the land of Egypt the most desolate of lands, and
its cities shall be the most deserted of cities for
forty years; and I will scatter the Egyptians
among the nations and strew them over foreign
lands. [13]Yet thus says the Lord GOD: At the end
of forty years I will gather the Egyptians from the
peoples among whom they are scattered, [14]and I
will restore Egypt's fortune, bringing them back
to the land of Pathros, the land of their origin,*
where it will be the lowliest [15]of kingdoms,
never more to set itself above the nations. I will
make them few, that they may not dominate the
nations. [16]No longer shall they be for the house
of Israel to trust in, but the living reminder of its
guilt for having turned to follow after them.
Thus they shall know that I am the LORD.

The Wages of Nebuchadnezzar [17]On the
first day of the first month in the twenty-seventh
year,* the word of the LORD came to me: [18]Son
of man, Nebuchadnezzar, the king of Babylon,
has led his army in an exhausting campaign
against Tyre.* Their heads became bald and
their shoulders were galled; but neither he nor
his army received any wages from Tyre for the
campaign he led against it. [19]Therefore thus says
the Lord GOD: [d] I am now giving the land of
Egypt to Nebuchadnezzar, king of Babylon. He
shall carry off its riches, plundering and pillaging
it for the wages of his soldiers, who did it for me;
[20]as payment for his toil I have given him the
land of Egypt, says the Lord GOD.
[21]On that day I will make a horn sprout for
the house of Israel, and I will cause you to speak
out in their midst; thus they shall know that I
am the LORD.

CHAPTER 30

The Day of the Lord against Egypt [1]Thus the
word of the LORD came to me: [2]Son of man,
speak this prophecy: Thus says the Lord GOD:
Cry, Oh, the day! [3]for near is the day, near is the
day of the Lord; a day of clouds, doomsday for
the nations shall it be. [4]Then a sword shall come
upon Egypt, and anguish shall be in Ethiopia,
when the slain fall in Egypt, when her riches are
seized and her foundations are overthrown.

29, 10: From Migdol to Syene: from the northern to the southern extremity of Egypt. Syene is the modern Assuan.

29, 14: Pathros, the land of their origin: upper Egypt, that is, southern Egypt, where the Egyptians were thought to have originated; Is 11, 11; Jer 44, 1. 15.

29, 17: The first day of the first month in the twenty-seventh year: April 26, 571 B.C. This is the latest date attached to any prophecy in Ezekiel.

29, 18f: The fulfillment of Ezekiel's prophecy against Tyre (chapters 26–28) was a thirteen-year siege of the city by Nebuchadnezzar (587–574 B.C.). Tyre seems to have been taken, but its resources were exhausted and the booty was small. Therefore Ezekiel now prophesies that Nebuchadnezzar will collect his wages as God's instrument in the punishment of Tyre, by plundering Egypt.

c Is 36, 6. d Jer 46, 2.

5 Ethiopia, Put, Lud, all Arabia, Libya, and people
of the allied territory shall fall by the sword with
them. 6 Those who support Egypt shall fall, and
down shall come her proud strength; from
Migdol to Syene they shall fall there by the
sword, says the Lord GOD. 7 She shall be the
most devastated of lands, and her cities shall be
the most desolate of all. 8 Then they shall know
that I am the LORD, when I set fire to Egypt and
when all who help her are broken. 9 On that day
messengers shall hasten forth at my command to
terrify unsuspecting Ethiopia; they shall be in
anguish on the day of Egypt, which is surely
coming.

10 Thus says the Lord GOD: I will put an end to
the throngs of Egypt by the hand of Nebuchad-
nezzar, king of Babylon. 11 He and his people
with him, the most ruthless of nations, shall be
brought in to devastate the land. They shall draw
their swords against Egypt, and fill the land with
the slain. 12 I will turn the Niles into dry land and
sell the land over to the power of the wicked.
The land and everything in it I will hand over to
foreigners to devastate. I, the LORD, have
spoken.

13 [e]Thus says the Lord GOD: I will put an end
to the great ones of Memphis and the princes of
the land of Egypt, that they may be no more. I
will cast fear into the land of Egypt, and devas-
tate Pathros. 14 I will set fire to Zoan, and inflict
punishments on Thebes. 15 I will pour out my
wrath on Pelusium, Egypt's stronghold, and cut
down the crowds in Memphis. 16 I will set fire to
Egypt; Syene shall writhe in anguish; Thebes
shall be breached and its walls shall be demol-
ished. 17 The young men of On and of Pibeseth
shall fall by the sword, and the cities themselves
shall go into captivity. 18 In Tehaphnehes the day
shall be darkened when I break the scepter of
Egypt. Her haughty pride shall cease from her,
clouds shall cover her, and her daughters shall
go into captivity. 19 Thus will I inflict punish-
ments on Egypt, that they may know that I am
the LORD.

Pharaoh's Broken Arm 20 On the seventh day
of the first month in the eleventh year,* the
word of the LORD came to me: 21 *Son of man, I
have broken the arm of Pharaoh, the king of
Egypt, and see, it has not been bound up with
bandages and healing remedies that it may be
strong enough to hold the sword. 22 Therefore
thus says the Lord GOD: See! I am coming at
Pharaoh, the king of Egypt. I will break his
strong arm, so that the sword drops from his
hand. 23 I will scatter the Egyptians among the
nations and strew them over foreign lands. 24 But
I will strengthen the arms of the king of Babylon,
and put my sword in his hand, which he will
bring against Egypt so as to plunder and pillage
it. 25 [I will make the arms of the king of Babylon
strong, but the arms of Pharaoh shall drop.] Then
they shall know that I am the LORD, when I put
my sword in the hand of the king of Babylon for
him to wield against the land of Egypt. 26 [I will
scatter the Egyptians among the nations and
strew them over foreign lands.] Thus they shall
know that I am the LORD.

CHAPTER 31

Allegory of the Cypress 1 On the first day of
the third month in the eleventh year,* the word
of the LORD came to me: 2 Son of man, say to
Pharaoh, the king of Egypt, and to his hordes:
What are you like in your greatness?

3 Behold, a cypress [cedar] in Lebanon,
beautiful of branch, lofty of stature,
amid the very clouds lifted its crest.
4 Waters made it grow, the abyss made it
flourish,
sending its rivers round where it was
planted,
turning its streams to all the trees of the
field.

30, 20: The seventh day of the first month in the eleventh year: April 29, 587 B.C.

30, 21–26: This oracle was uttered during the siege of Jerusalem, which had now lasted more than a year (Ez 24, 1). Pharaoh Hophra went to the aid of Jerusalem, causing the Chaldeans to lift the siege temporarily; cf Jer 34, 21; 37, 6f. In the prophet's eyes, this was interfering with the divine punishment of Judah that was to be inflicted by the Chaldeans. The Egyptians were routed by the Chaldeans, and were able to offer no more help to Jerusalem; cf chapter 31.

31, 1: The first day of the third month in the eleventh year: June 21, 587 B.C.

e Zec 13, 2.

5 Thus it grew taller than every other tree of the field,
and longer of branch because of the abundant water.
6 In its boughs nested all the birds of the air,
under its branches all beasts of the field gave birth,
in its shade dwelt numerous peoples of every race.
7 It became beautiful and stately in its spread of foliage,
for its roots were turned toward abundant water.
8 The cedars in the garden of God were not its equal,
nor could the fir trees match its boughs,
Neither were the plane trees like it for branches;
no tree in the garden of God matched its beauty.
9 I made it beautiful, with much foliage,
the envy of all Eden's trees in the garden of God.

10 Therefore thus says the Lord GOD: Because it
became lofty in stature, raising its crest among
the clouds, and because it became proud in heart
at its height, 11 I have handed it over to the
mightiest of the nations, which has dealt with it
in keeping with its wickedness. I humiliated it.
12 Foreigners, the most ruthless of the nations,
cut it down and left it on the mountains. Its
foliage was brought low in all the valleys, its
branches lay broken in all the ravines of the land,
and all the peoples of the land withdrew from its
shade, abandoning it.

13 On its fallen trunk rested all the birds of the air,
and by its branches were all the beasts of the field.

14 Thus no tree may grow lofty in stature or raise
its crest among the clouds; no tree fed by water
may stand by itself in its loftiness.

For all of them are destined for death,
for the land below,
For the company of mortals,
those who go down into the pit.

15 Thus says the Lord GOD: On the day he
went down to the nether world I made the abyss
close up over him; I stopped its streams so that
the deep waters were held back. I cast gloom
over Lebanon because of him, so that all the
trees in the land drooped on his account. 16 At
the crash of his fall I made the nations rock,
when I cast him down to the nether world with
those who go down into the pit. In the land
below, all Eden's trees were consoled, Lebanon's
choice and best, all that were fed by water.
17 They too have come down with him to the
nether world, to those slain by the sword; those
who dwelt in his shade are dispersed among the
nations. 18 Which was your equal in glory or size
among the trees of Eden? Yet you have been
brought down with the trees of Eden to the land
below. You shall lie with the uncircumcised,
with those slain by the sword. Such are Pharaoh
and all his hordes, says the Lord GOD.

CHAPTER 32

Dirge over Pharaoh 1 On the first day of the
twelfth month in the twelfth year,* the word of
the LORD came to me: 2 Son of man, utter a
lament over Pharaoh, the king of Egypt, saying
to him: Lion of the nations, you are destroyed.

You were like a monster in the sea,
spouting in your streams,
Stirring the water with your feet
and churning its streams.
3 Thus says the Lord GOD:
I will spread my net over you
[with a host of many nations],
and draw you up in my seine.[f]
4 I will leave you on the land;
on the open field I will cast you.
I will have all the birds of the air alight on you,
and all the beasts of the earth eat their fill of you.
5 I will leave your flesh on the mountains,
and fill the valleys with your carcass.

32, 1: The first day of the twelfth month in the twelfth year: March 3, 585 B.C.

f Ez 12, 13; 17, 20.

6 I will water the land with what flows from
you,
and the river beds shall be filled with your
blood.
7 When I snuff you out I will cover the heavens,
and all their stars I will darken;
The sun I will cover with clouds,
and the moon shall not give its light.[g]
8 All the shining lights in the heavens
I will darken on your account,
And I will spread darkness over your land,
says the Lord GOD.

9 I will grieve the hearts of many peoples
when I lead you captive among the nations, to
lands which you do not know. 10 Many peoples
shall be appalled at you, and their kings shall
shudder over you in horror when they see me
brandish my sword, and on the day of your
downfall every one of them shall continuously
tremble for his own life. 11 For thus says the Lord
GOD: The sword of the king of Babylon shall
come upon you.

12 I will cut down your horde with the blades of
warriors,
all of them the most ruthless of the nations;
They shall lay waste the glory of Egypt,
and all her hordes shall be destroyed.
13 I will have all of her animals perish
beside her abundant waters;
The foot of man shall stir them no longer,
nor shall the hoof of beast disturb them.
14 Then will I make their waters clear,
and their streams flow like oil,
says the Lord GOD.

15 When I turn Egypt into a waste, the land
shall be devastated of all that is in it; when I
strike all who live there, they shall know that I
am the LORD. 16 This is a dirge, and it shall be
sung: the daughters of the nations shall chant it;
over Egypt and all its hordes shall they chant it,
says the Lord GOD.

Dirge over Egypt 17 On the fifteenth day of the
first month in the twelfth year, the word of the
LORD came to me: 18 Son of man, lament over
the throngs of Egypt, for the mighty nations have
thrust them down to the bottom of the earth,
with those who go down into the pit. 20 In the
midst of those slain by the sword shall they fall,
and place shall be made with them for all their
hordes. Then from the midst of the nether
world, the mighty warriors shall speak to Egypt:
19 "Whom do you excel in beauty? 21 Come
down, you and your allies, lie with the uncircum-
cised, with those slain by the sword."

22 There is Assyria with all her company, all of
them slain, 23 whose graves have been made in
the recesses of the pit; her company is around
Egypt's grave, all of them slain, fallen by the
sword, who spread terror in the land of the
living. 24 There is Elam with all her throng about
Egypt's grave, all of them slain, fallen by the
sword: they have gone down uncircumcised to
the bottom of the earth, who spread their terror
in the land of the living, and they bear their
disgrace with those who go down into the pit;
25 in the midst of the slain they are placed.
26 There are Meshech and Tubal and all their
throng about her grave, all of them uncircum-
cised, slain by the sword, for they spread their
terror in the land of the living.

27 They do not lie with the mighty men fallen
of old,* who went down to the nether world
with their weapons of war, whose swords were
placed under their heads and whose shields
were laid over their bones, though the mighty
men caused terror in the land of the living. 28 But
in the midst of the uncircumcised shall you lie,
with those slain by the sword.

29 There are Edom, her kings, and all her
princes, who despite their might have been
placed with those slain by the sword; with the
uncircumcised they lie, and with those who go
down into the pit. 30 There are all the princes of
the north and all the Sidonians, who have gone
down with the slain, because of the terror their
might inspired; they lie uncircumcised with
those slain by the sword and bear their disgrace

32, 27: The mighty men fallen of old: the semilegendary heroes of the prehistoric past, who were thought to have once dominated the world; cf Is 14, 9.

g Is 13, 10; Jl 2, 10; 4, 15; Mt 24, 29.

with those who go down to the pit. [31]When Pharaoh sees these, he shall be comforted for all his hordes slain by the sword—Pharaoh and all his army, says the Lord GOD. [32]Since he spread his terror in the land of the living, therefore is he laid to rest among the uncircumcised, with those slain by the sword—Pharaoh and all his hordes, says the Lord GOD.

IV: Salvation for Israel

CHAPTER 33

The Prophet a Watchman [1]Thus the word of the LORD came to me: [2]Son of man, speak thus to your countrymen: When I bring the sword against a country, and the people of this country select one of their number to be their watchman, [3]and the watchman, seeing the sword coming against the country, blows the trumpet to warn the people, [4]anyone hearing but not heeding the warning of the trumpet and therefore slain by the sword that comes against him, shall be responsible for his own death. [5]He heard the trumpet blast yet refused to take warning; he is responsible for his own death, for had he taken warning he would have escaped with his life. [6]But if the watchman sees the sword coming and fails to blow the warning trumpet, so that the sword comes and takes anyone, I will hold the watchman responsible for that person's death, even though that person is taken because of his own sin.

[7] [h]You, son of man, I have appointed watchman for the house of Israel; when you hear me say anything, you shall warn them for me. [8]If I tell the wicked man that he shall surely die, and you do not speak out to dissuade the wicked man from his way, he [the wicked man] shall die for his guilt, but I will hold you responsible for his death. [9]But if you warn the wicked man, trying to turn him from his way, and he refuses to turn from his way, he shall die for his guilt, but you shall save yourself.

Individual Retribution [10]As for you, son of man, speak to the house of Israel: You people say, "Our crimes and our sins weigh us down; we are rotting away because of them. How can we survive?" [11] [i]Answer them: As I live, says the Lord GOD, I swear I take no pleasure in the death of the wicked man, but rather in the wicked man's conversion, that he may live. Turn, turn from your evil ways! Why should you die, O house of Israel?

[12]As for you, son of man, tell your countrymen: The virtue which a man has practiced will not save him on the day that he sins; neither will the wickedness that a man has done bring about his downfall on the day that he turns from his wickedness [nor can the virtuous man, when he sins, remain alive]. [13]Though I say to the virtuous man that he shall surely live, if he then presumes on his virtue and does wrong, none of his virtuous deeds shall be remembered; because of the wrong he has done, he shall die. [14]And though I say to the wicked man that he shall surely die, if he turns away from his sin and does what is right and just, [15]giving back pledges, restoring stolen goods, living by the statutes that bring life, and doing no wrong, he shall surely live, he shall not die. [16]None of the sins he committed shall be held against him; he has done what is right and just, he shall surely live.

[17]Yet your countrymen say, "The way of the LORD is not fair!"; but it is their way that is not fair. [18]When a virtuous man turns away from what is right and does wrong, he shall die for it. [19]But when a wicked man turns away from wickedness and does what is right and just, because of this he shall live. [20] [j]And still you say, "The way of the LORD is not fair!"? I will judge every one of you according to his ways, O house of Israel.

The Fugitive from Jerusalem* [21]On the fifth day of the tenth month, in the twelfth year of our exile, the fugitive came to me from Jerusalem and said, "The city is taken!" [22]The hand of

33, 21f: January 8, 585 B.C. According to Jeremiah (39, 2), Jerusalem was taken in July, 587. Some MSS read "eleventh" for twelfth year (January, 586); even so, there was ample time between the fall of Jerusalem and the arrival of the fugitive from that city to journey to Babylon. However, this is the fugitive sent to fulfill the promise of Ez 24, 25. 27, the eyewitness who would release Ezekiel from his dumbness; cf Ez, 2, 26f.

h Ez 3, 17. i Ez 18, 23–32. j Ez 18, 25.

the LORD had come upon me the evening before the fugitive arrived, and he opened my mouth when the fugitive reached me in the morning. My mouth was opened, and I was dumb no longer.

The Survivors in Judah* 23 Thus the word of the Lord came to me: 24 Son of man, they who live in the ruins on the land of Israel reason thus: "Abraham, though but a single individual, received possession of the land; we, therefore, being many, have as permanent possession the land that has been given to us." 25 Give them this answer: Thus says the Lord GOD: You eat on the mountains, you raise your eyes to your idols, you shed blood—yet you would keep possession of the land? 26 You rely on your sword, you do abominable things, each one of you defiles his neighbor's wife—yet you would keep possession of the land? 27 Tell them this: Thus says the Lord GOD: As I live, those who are in the ruins I swear shall fall by the sword; those who are in the open field I have given to the wild beasts for food; and those who are in fastnesses and in caves shall die by the plague. 28 I will make the land a desolate waste, so that its proud strength will come to an end, and the mountains of Israel shall be so desolate that no one will cross them. 29 Thus they shall know that I am the LORD, when I make the land a desolate waste because of all the abominable things they have done.

The Prophet's False Popularity 30 As for you, son of man, your countrymen are talking about you along the walls and in the doorways of houses. They say to one another, "Come and hear the latest word that comes from the LORD."* 31 My people come to you as people always do; they sit down before you and hear your words, but they will not obey them, for lies are on their lips and their desires are fixed on dishonest gain. 32 For them you are only a ballad singer, with a pleasant voice and a clever touch. They listen to your words, but they will not obey them. 33 But when it comes—and it is surely coming!—they shall know that there was a prophet among them.

CHAPTER 34

Parable of the Shepherds 1 Thus the word of the LORD came to me: 2 Son of man, prophesy against the shepherds of Israel,* in these words prophesy to them [to the shepherds]: Thus says the Lord GOD: Woe to the shepherds of Israel who have been pasturing themselves![k] Should not shepherds, rather, pasture sheep? 3 You have fed off their milk, worn their wool, and slaughtered the fatlings, but the sheep you have not pastured. 4 You did not strengthen the weak nor heal the sick nor bind up the injured. You did not bring back the strayed nor seek the lost, but you lorded it over them harshly and brutally. 5 So they were scattered for lack of a shepherd, and became food for all the wild beasts. My sheep were scattered 6 and wandered over all the mountains and high hills; my sheep were scattered over the whole earth, with no one to look after them or to search for them.

7 Therefore, shepherds, hear the word of the LORD: 8 As I live, says the Lord GOD, because my sheep have been given over to pillage, and because my sheep have become food for every wild beast, for lack of a shepherd; because my shepherds did not look after my sheep, but pastured themselves and did not pasture my sheep; 9 because of this, shepherds, hear the word of the LORD: 10 Thus says the Lord GOD: I swear I am coming against these shepherds. I will claim my sheep from them and put a stop to their shepherding my sheep so that they may no longer pasture themselves. I will save my sheep, that they may no longer be food for their mouths.

11 For thus says the Lord GOD: I myself will look after and tend my sheep. 12 As a shepherd tends his flock when he finds himself among his

33, 23–29: News brought by the fugitive furnished the occasion of this prophecy. Like Jeremiah, Ezekiel rejects the idea that the survivors in Judah have any claim to the land. The new Israel is to be formed from the exiles.

33, 30: The fulfillment of Ezekiel's prophecies about Jerusalem was responsible for this temporary enthusiasm among the unstable people.

34, 2: The shepherds of Israel: the leaders of the people.

k Ez 13, 3; Jer 23, 1.

scattered sheep, so will I tend my sheep. I will rescue them from every place where they were scattered when it was cloudy and dark. 13 I will lead them out from among the peoples and gather them from the foreign lands; I will bring them back to their own country and pasture them upon the mountains of Israel [in the land's ravines and all its inhabited places]. 14 In good pastures will I pasture them, and on the mountain heights of Israel shall be their grazing ground. There they shall lie down on good grazing ground, and in rich pastures shall they be pastured on the mountains of Israel. 15 I myself will pasture my sheep; I myself will give them rest, says the Lord GOD. 16 The lost I will seek out, the strayed I will bring back, the injured I will bind up, the sick I will heal [but the sleek and the strong I will destroy], shepherding them rightly.

Separation of the Sheep 17 As for you, my sheep, says the Lord GOD, I will judge between one sheep and another, between rams and goats. 18 Was it not enough for you to graze on the best pasture, that you had to trample the rest of your pastures with your feet? Was it not enough for you to drink the clearest water, that you had to foul the remainder with your feet? 19 Thus my sheep had to graze on what your feet had trampled and drink what your feet had fouled. 20 Therefore thus says the Lord GOD: Now will I judge between the fat and the lean sheep. 21 Because you push with side and shoulder, and butt all the weak sheep with your horns until you have driven them out, 22 I will save my sheep so that they may no longer be despoiled, and I will judge between one sheep and another. 23 [l] I will appoint one shepherd over them to pasture them, my servant David;* he shall pasture them and be their shepherd. 24 I, the Lord, will be their God, and my servant David shall be prince among them. I, the LORD, have spoken.

25 I will make a covenant of peace with them, and rid the country of ravenous beasts, that they may dwell securely in the desert and sleep in the forests. 26 I will place them about my hill, sending rain in due season, rains that shall be a blessing to them. 27 The trees of the field shall bear their fruits, and the land its crops, and they shall dwell securely on their own soil. Thus they shall know that I am the LORD when I break the bonds of their yoke and free them from the power of those who enslaved them. 28 They shall no longer be despoiled by the nations or devoured by beasts of the earth, but shall dwell secure, with no one to frighten them. 29 I will prepare for them peaceful fields for planting; they shall no longer be carried off by famine in the land, or bear the reproaches of the nations. 30 Thus they shall know that I, the LORD, am their God, and they are my people, the house of Israel, says the Lord GOD. 31 [You, my sheep, you are the sheep of my pasture, and I am your God, says the Lord GOD.]

CHAPTER 35

Against Edom* 1 Thus the word of the LORD came to me: [m] 2 Son of man, set your face against Mount Seir, and prophesy against it. 3 Say to it: Thus says the Lord GOD: See! I am coming at you, Mount Seir. I will stretch out my hand against you and make you a desolate waste. 4 Your cities I will turn into ruins, and you shall be a waste; thus you shall know that I am the LORD.

5 Because you never let die your hatred for the Israelites, whom you delivered over to the power of the sword at the time of their trouble, when their crimes came to an end, 6 therefore, as I live, says the Lord GOD, you have been guilty of blood, and blood, I swear, shall pursue you. 7 I will make Mount Seir a desolate waste, and cut off from it any traveler. 8 With the slain I will fill your hills, your valleys, and all your ravines [in them the slain shall fall by the sword]: 9 desolate will I make you forever, and leave your cities

34, 23: One shepherd . . . my servant David: a messianic Davidic King who will rule over the restored Israel (vv 25–31) in the name of the Lord.

35, 1–15: After the fall of Jerusalem, Edom assisted the Chaldeans in devastating the land and subduing the population, and ended by occupying part of Judah's former territory. For this reason these oracles against Edom are found in the context of the city's fall.

l Is 40, 21; Hos 3, 5; Jn 10, 11. 14. m 1ff: Ez 25, 12ff.

without inhabitants; thus you shall know that I am the LORD.

[10]Because you said: The two nations and the two lands* have become mine; we shall possess them—although the LORD was there— [11]therefore, as I live, says the Lord GOD, I will deal with you according to your anger and your envy which you have exercised [in your hatred] against them. I will make myself known among you when I judge you, [12]and you shall know that I am the LORD.

I have heard all the contemptuous things you have uttered against the mountains of Israel: "They are desolate, they have been given us to devour." [13]I have heard the insolent and wild words you have spoken against me. [14]Thus says the Lord GOD: Just as you rejoiced over my land because it was desolate, so will I do to you. [15]In keeping with your glee over the devastation of the inheritance of the house of Israel, so will I treat you. A waste shall you be, Mount Seir, you and the whole of Edom. Thus they shall know that I am the LORD.

CHAPTER 36

Regeneration of the Land [1]As for you, son of man, prophesy to the mountains of Israel: Mountains of Israel,[n] hear the word of the LORD! [2]Thus says the Lord GOD: Because the enemy has said of you, "Ha! the everlasting heights have become our possession" [3][therefore prophesy in these words: Thus says the Lord GOD:]; because you have been ridiculed and despised on all sides for having become a possession for the rest of the nations, and have become a byword and a popular jeer; [4]therefore, mountains of Israel, hear the word of the LORD: [Thus says the Lord GOD to the mountains and hills, the ravines and valleys, the desolate ruins and abandoned cities, which have been given over to the pillage and mockery of the remaining nations round about; [5]therefore thus says the Lord GOD:] Truly, with burning jealousy I speak against the rest of the nations [and against all of Edom] who with wholehearted joy and utter contempt have considered my land their possession to be delivered over to plunder. [6][Therefore, prophesy concerning the land of Israel, and say to the mountains and hills, the ravines and valleys: Thus says the Lord GOD:] With jealous fury I speak, because you have borne the reproach of the nations. [7]Therefore do I solemnly swear that your neighboring nations shall bear their own reproach.

[8]As for you, mountains of Israel, you shall grow branches and bear fruit for my people Israel, for they shall soon return. [9]See, I come to you, it is to you that I turn; you will be tilled and sown, [10]and I will settle crowds of men upon you, the whole house of Israel; cities shall be repeopled, and ruins rebuilt. [11]I will settle crowds of men and beasts upon you, to multiply and be fruitful. I will repeople you as in the past, and be more generous to you than in the beginning; thus you shall know that I am the LORD.

[12][My people Israel are the ones whom I will have walk upon you; they shall take possession of you, and you shall be their heritage. Never again shall you rob them of their children.]

[13]Thus says the Lord GOD: Because they have said of you, "You are a land that devours men,* and you rob your people of their children"; [14]therefore, never again shall you devour men or rob your people of their children, says the Lord GOD. [15]No more will I permit you to hear the reproach of nations, or bear insults from peoples, or rob your people of their children, says the Lord GOD.

Regeneration of the People [16]Thus the word of the LORD came to me: [17]Son of man, when the house of Israel lived in their land, they defiled it by their conduct and deeds. In my sight their conduct was like the defilement of a menstruous woman. [18]Therefore I poured out my fury upon them [because of the blood which they poured out on the ground, and because they defiled it with idols]. [19]I scattered them among the nations, dispersing them over foreign

35, 10: The two nations and the two lands: the superseded kingdoms of Israel and Judah and their territories.

36, 13: A land that devours men: destroys its own population, as could be seen in its disastrous political history.

n Ez 6, 3.

lands; according to their conduct and deeds I judged them. [20] [o]But when they came among the nations [wherever they came], they served to profane my holy name, because it was said of them: "These are the people of the LORD, yet they had to leave their land." [21]So I have relented because of my holy name which the house of Israel profaned among the nations where they came. [22]Therefore say to the house of Israel: Thus says the Lord GOD: Not for your sakes do I act, house of Israel, but for the sake of my holy name, which you profaned among the nations to which you came. [23]I will prove the holiness of my great name, profaned among the nations, in whose midst you have profaned it. Thus the nations shall know that I am the LORD, says the Lord GOD, when in their sight I prove my holiness through you. [24]For I will take you away from among the nations, gather you from all the foreign lands, and bring you back to your own land. [25] [p]I will sprinkle clean water upon you to cleanse you from all your impurities, and from all your idols I will cleanse you. [26] [q]I will give you a new heart and place a new spirit within you, taking from your bodies your stony hearts and giving you natural hearts. [27] [r]I will put my spirit within you and make you live by my statutes, careful to observe my decrees. [28]You shall live in the land I gave your fathers; you shall be my people, and I will be your God. [29]I will save you from all your impurities; I will order the grain to be abundant, and I will not send famine against you. [30]I will increase the fruit on your trees and the crops in your fields; thus you shall no longer bear among the nations the reproach of famine. [31]Then you shall remember your evil conduct, and that your deeds were not good; you shall loathe yourselves for your sins and your abominations. [32]Not for your sakes do I act, says the Lord GOD—let this be known to you! Be ashamed and abashed because of your conduct, O house of Israel.

[33]Thus says the Lord GOD: When I purify you from all your crimes, I will repeople the cities, and the ruins shall be rebuilt; [34]the desolate land shall be tilled, which was formerly a wasteland exposed to the gaze of every passer-by. [35]"This desolate land has been made into a garden of Eden," they shall say. "The cities that were in ruins, laid waste, and destroyed are now repeopled and fortified." [36]Thus the neighboring nations that remain shall know that I, the LORD, have rebuilt what was destroyed and replanted what was desolate. I, the LORD, have promised, and I will do it.

[37]Thus says the Lord GOD: This also I will be persuaded to do for the house of Israel: to multiply them like sheep. [38]As with sacrificial sheep, the sheep of Jerusalem on its feast days, the cities which were in ruins shall be filled with flocks of men; thus they shall know that I am the LORD.

CHAPTER 37

Vision of the Dry Bones* [1]The hand of the LORD came upon me, and he led me out in the spirit of the LORD and set me in the center of the plain, which was now filled with bones. [2]He made me walk among them in every direction so that I saw how many they were on the surface of the plain. How dry they were! [3]He asked me: Son of man, can these bones come to life? "Lord GOD," I answered, "you alone know that." [4]Then he said to me: Prophesy over these bones, and say to them: Dry bones, hear the word of the LORD! [5]Thus says the Lord GOD to these bones: See! I will bring spirit into you, that you may come to life. [6]I will put sinews upon you, make flesh grow over you, cover you with skin, and put spirit in you so that you may come to life and know that I am the LORD. [7]I prophesied as I had been told, and even as I was prophesying I heard a noise; it was a rattling as the bones came together, bone joining bone. [8]I saw the sinews and the flesh come upon them, and the skin cover them, but there was no spirit in them. [9]Then he said to me: Prophesy to the spirit, prophesy, son of man, and say to the spirit: Thus

37, 1–14: This vision is a prediction of the restoration of Israel under the figure of a resurrection from the dead; it is not concerned with the doctrine of resurrection itself.

o Is 52, 5; Rom 2, 24. p Ps 51, 4; Zec 13, 1; Hb 10, 22; Jn 3, 5. q Jer 31, 33. r Ez 37, 14; 39, 29; Is 42, 1; 44, 3; 59, 21; Hg 2, 5; Jl 3, 1f.

says the Lord GOD: From the four winds come,
O spirit, and breathe into these slain that they
may come to life. [10]I prophesied as he told me,
and the spirit came into them; they came alive
and stood upright, a vast army. [11]Then he said to
me: Son of man, these bones are the whole
house of Israel. They have been saying, "Our
bones are dried up, our hope is lost, and we are
cut off." [12]Therefore, prophesy and say to them:
Thus says the Lord GOD: O my people, I will
open your graves and have you rise from them,
and bring you back to the land of Israel. [13]Then
you shall know that I am the LORD, when I open
your graves and have you rise from them, O my
people! [14]I will put my spirit in you that you may
live, and I will settle you upon your land; thus
you shall know that I am the LORD. I have
promised, and I will do it, says the LORD.

The Two Sticks [15]*Thus the word of the LORD
came to me: [16]Now, son of man, take a single
stick, and write on it: Judah and those Israelites
who are associated with him. Then take another
stick and write on it: Joseph [the stick of
Ephraim] and all the house of Israel associated
with him. [17]Then join the two sticks together, so
that they form one stick in your hand. [18]When
your countrymen ask you, "Will you not tell us
what you mean by all this?", [19]answer them:
Thus says the Lord GOD: [I will take the stick of
Joseph, which is in the hand of Ephraim, and of
the tribes of Israel associated with him, and I will
join to it the stick of Judah, making them a single
stick; they shall be one in my hand. [20]The sticks
on which you write you shall hold up before
them to see. [21]Tell them: Thus speaks the Lord
GOD:] I will take the Israelites from among the
nations to which they have come, and gather
them from all sides to bring them back to their
land. [22]I will make them one nation upon the
land, in the mountains of Israel, and there shall
be one prince for them all. Never again shall they
be two nations, and never again shall they be
divided into two kingdoms.
[23]No longer shall they defile themselves with
their idols, their abominations, and all their
transgressions. I will deliver them from all their
sins of apostasy, and cleanse them so that they
may be my people and I may be their God.
[24] [s]My servant David shall be prince over them,
and there shall be one shepherd for them all;
they shall live by my statutes and carefully
observe my decrees. [25]They shall live on the
land which I gave to my servant Jacob, the land
where their fathers lived; they shall live on it
forever, they, and their children, and their chil-
dren's children, with my servant David their
prince forever. [26] [t]I will make with them a
covenant of peace; it shall be an everlasting
covenant with them, and I will multiply them,
and put my sanctuary among them forever. [27]My
dwelling shall be with them; I will be their God,
and they shall be my people. [28]Thus the nations
shall know that it is I, the LORD, who make Israel
holy, when my sanctuary shall be set up among
them forever.

CHAPTER 38

First Prophecy against Gog [1]Thus the word
of the LORD came to me:* [2]Son of man, turn
toward Gog* [the land of Magog], [u] the chief
prince of Meshech and Tubal, and prophesy
against him: [3]Thus says the Lord GOD: See! I am
coming at you, Gog, chief prince of Meshech
and Tubal. [4]I will lead you forth with all your
army, horses and riders all handsomely outfitted,
a great horde with bucklers and shields, all of
them carrying swords: [5]Persia, Cush, and Put
with them [all with shields and helmets], [6]Go-
mer with all its troops, Beth-togarmah from the
recesses of the north with all its troops, many

37, 15–22: The symbolic action of joining two sticks into one signifies the future union of Israel and Judah under one messianic King.

38, 1—39, 20: These three oracles against Gog may refer either to a specific foreign invasion in the future, or to the apocalyptic struggle between good and evil at the end of time. By some they are ascribed to a later author than Ezekiel, who lived after the exile and the return to Palestine.

38, 2: Gog: the name is almost certainly a symbolic one taken from that of Gyges, king of Lydia, whether or not the prophet has a specific person in mind. The gloss Magog may be an Akkadian expression, mat-Gog, "the land of Gog." Meshech and Tubal, as well as Gomer and Beth-togarmah (v 6), were countries around the Black Sea, the northernmost countries known to the Hebrews: the north (cf also v 15) was the traditional direction from which invasion was expected; cf Jer 1, 13ff.

s Ez 34, 23; Jer 23, 5; 33, 15. t Ps 110, 4. u Rv 20, 7f.

peoples with you. 7Prepare yourself, be ready,
you and all your horde assembled about you, and
be at my disposal. 8After many days you will be
mustered [in the last years you will come] against
a nation which has survived the sword, which
has been assembled from many peoples [on the
mountains of Israel which were long a ruin],
which has been brought forth from among the
peoples and all of whom now dwell in security.
9You shall come up like a sudden storm, advanc-
ing like a cloud to cover the earth, you and all
your troops and the many peoples with you.

10Thus says the Lord GOD: At that time
thoughts shall arise in your mind, and you shall
devise an evil scheme: 11"I will go up against a
land of open villages and attack the peaceful
people who are living in security, all of them
living without walls, having neither bars nor
gates, 12to plunder and pillage, turning my hand
against the ruins that were repeopled and against
a people gathered from the nations, a people
concerned with cattle and goods, who dwell at
the navel of the earth."* 13Sheba and Dedan,
the merchants of Tarshish and all her young lions
shall ask you: "Is it for plunder that you have
come? Is it for pillage that you have summoned
your horde, to carry off silver and gold, to take
away cattle and goods, to seize much plunder?"

17Thus says the Lord GOD: It is of you that I
spoke in ancient times through my servants, the
prophets of Israel, who prophesied in those days
that I would bring you against them. 18But on
that day, the day when Gog invades the land of
Israel, says the Lord GOD, my fury shall be
aroused. In my anger 19and in my jealousy, in my
fiery wrath, I swear: On that day there shall be a
great shaking upon the land of Israel. 20Before
me shall tremble the fish of the sea and the birds
of the air, the beasts of the field and all the
reptiles that crawl upon the ground, and all men
who are on the land. Mountains shall be over-
turned, and cliffs shall tumble, and every wall
shall fall to the ground. 21Against him I will
summon every terror, says the Lord GOD, every
man's sword against his brother. I will hold
judgment with him in pestilence and bloodshed;
22flooding rain and hailstones, fire and brim-
stone, I will rain upon him, upon his troops, and
upon the many peoples with him. 23I will prove
my greatness and holiness and make myself
known in the sight of many nations; thus they
shall know that I am the LORD.

Second Prophecy against Gog 14Therefore
prophesy, son of man, and say to Gog: Thus says
the Lord GOD: When my people Israel are
dwelling in security, will you not bestir yourself
15and come from your home in the recesses of
the north, you and many peoples with you, all
mounted on horses, a great horde and a mighty
army? 16You shall come up against my people
Israel like a cloud covering the land. In the last
days I will bring you against my land, that the
nations may know of me, when in their sight I
prove my holiness through you, O Gog.

CHAPTER 39

Third Prophecy against Gog 1Now, son of
man, prophesy against Gog in these words: Thus
says the Lord GOD: See! I am coming at you,
Gog, chief prince of Meshech and Tubal. 2I will
turn you about, I will urge you on, and I will
make you come up from the recesses of the
north; I will lead you against the mountains of
Israel. 3Then I will strike the bow from your left
hand, and make the arrows drop from your
right. 4Upon the mountains of Israel you shall
fall, you and all your troops and the peoples who
are with you. To birds of prey of every kind and
to the wild beasts I am giving you to be eaten.
5On the open field you shall fall, for I have
decreed it, says the Lord GOD.

6I will send fire upon Magog and upon those
who live securely in the coastlands; thus they
shall know that I am the LORD. 7I will make my
holy name known among my people Israel; I will
no longer allow my holy name to be profaned.
Thus the nations shall know that I am the LORD,
the Holy One in Israel. 8Yes, it is coming and
shall be fulfilled, says the Lord GOD. This is the
day I have decreed.

38, 12: Who dwell at the navel of the earth: the people of Israel (cf v 18; also Ez 5, 5). Many ancient peoples spoke of their own homelands as "the navel," that is, the center of the earth.

9Then shall those who live in the cities of Israel go out and burn weapons: [shields and bucklers,] bows and arrows, clubs and lances; for seven years they shall make fires with them. 10They shall not have to bring in wood from the fields or cut it down in the forests, for they shall make fires with the weapons. Thus they shall plunder those who plundered them and pillage those who pillaged them, says the Lord GOD.

11On that day I will give Gog for his tomb a well-known place in Israel, the Valley of Abarim* east of the sea [it is blocked to travelers]. Gog shall be buried there with all his horde, and it shall be named "Valley of Hamon-gog." 12To purify the land, the house of Israel shall need seven months to bury them. 13All the people of the land shall bury them and gain renown for it, when I reveal my glory, says the Lord GOD. 14Men shall be permanently employed to pass through the land burying those who lie unburied, so as to purify the land. For seven months they shall keep searching. 15When they pass through, should they see a human bone, let them put up a marker beside it, until others have buried it in the Valley of Hamon-gog. 16[Also the name of the city shall be Hamonah.] Thus the land shall be purified.

17As for you, son of man, says the Lord GOD, say to birds of every kind and to all the wild beasts: Come together, from all sides gather for the slaughter I am about to provide for you, a great slaughter on the mountains of Israel: you shall have flesh to eat and blood to drink. 18You shall eat the flesh of warriors and drink the blood of the princes of the land [rams, lambs, and goats, bullocks, fatlings of Bashan, all of them]. 19From the slaughter which I will provide for you, you shall eat fat until you are filled and drink blood until you are drunk. 20You shall be filled at my table with horses and riders, with warriors and soldiers of every kind, says the Lord GOD.

Israel's Return 21Thus I will display my glory among the nations, and all the nations shall see the judgment I have executed and the hand I have laid upon them. 22From that day forward the house of Israel shall know that I am the LORD, their God. 23The nations shall know that because of its sins the house of Israel went into exile; for they transgressed against me, and I hid my face from them and handed them over to their foes, so that all of them fell by the sword. 24According to their uncleanness and their transgressions I dealt with them, hiding my face from them.

25Therefore, thus says the Lord GOD: Now I will restore the fortunes of Jacob and have pity on the whole house of Israel, and I will be jealous for my holy name. 26They shall forget their disgrace and all the times they broke faith with me, when they live in security on their land with no one to frighten them. 27When I bring them back from among the peoples, I will gather them from the lands of their enemies, and will prove my holiness through them in the sight of many nations. 28 [v]Thus they shall know that I, the LORD, am their God, since I who exiled them among the nations, will gather them back on their land, not leaving any of them behind. 29No longer will I hide my face from them, for I have poured out my spirit upon the house of Israel, says the Lord GOD.

V: The New Israel*

The New Temple

CHAPTER 40

The Man with a Measure 1On the tenth day of the month beginning the twenty-fifth year of our exile, fourteen years after the city was taken, that very day the hand of the LORD came upon me and brought me 2in divine visions to the land of Israel, where he set me down on a very high mountain. On it there seemed to be a city being

39, 11: The Valley of Abarim: in the Abarim mountains, east of the Jordan. Hamon-gog: means "the horde of Gog."

40, 1—48, 35: This lengthy vision of the new Israel is dated (Ez 40, 1) April 28, 573 B.C. It is largely concerned with the new temple and the prescriptions to govern it, but other details of the restored commonwealth are included, forming a kind of program for the future. The literary form of the vision has been aptly termed "utopian": it is plain that the prophet did not expect a literal fulfillment of much of what he described. The passage doubtless underwent successive additions, both from the prophet and from later inspired writers.

v Ez 36, 23.

built before me. 3When he had brought me there, all at once I saw a man whose appearance was that of bronze; he was standing in the gate, holding a linen cord and a measuring rod. 4The man said to me, "Son of man, look carefully and listen intently, and pay strict attention to all that I will show you, for you have been brought here so that I might show it to you. Tell the house of Israel all that you see." 5[Then I saw an outer wall that completely surrounded the temple. The man was holding a measuring rod six cubits long, each cubit being a cubit and a handbreadth;* he measured the width and the height of the structure, each of which was found to be one rod.]

The East Gate* 6Then he went to the gate which faced the east, climbed its steps, and measured the gate's threshold, which was found to be a rod wide. 7The cells were a rod long and a rod wide, and the pilasters between the cells measured five cubits. The threshold of the gate adjoining the vestibule of the gate toward the inside measured one rod. 8He measured the vestibule of the gate, 9which was eight cubits, and its pilasters, which were two cubits. The vestibule of the gate was toward the inside. 10The cells of the east gate were three on either side, of equal size, and the pilasters on either side were also of equal size. 11He measured the gate's entrance, which was ten cubits wide, while the width of the gate's passage itself was thirteen cubits. 12The border before each of the cells on both sides was one cubit; the cells themselves were six cubits on either side, from opening to opening. 13He measured the gate from the back wall of one cell to the back wall of the cell on the opposite side: the width was twenty-five cubits. 14He measured the vestibule, which was twenty-five cubits. The pilasters adjoining the court on either side were six cubits. 15The length of the gate from the front entrance to the front of the vestibule on the inside was fifty cubits. 16Within the gateway on both sides there were splayed windows let into the cells [and into their pilasters]; likewise, within the vestibule on both sides there were windows. The pilasters were decorated with palms.

The Outer Court 17Then he brought me to the outer court,* where there were chambers and a pavement. The pavement was laid all around the court, and the chambers, which were on the pavement, were thirty in number. 18The pavement lay alongside the gates, as wide as the gates were long; this was the lower pavement. 19He measured the width of the court from the front of the lower gate to the front of the inner gate; it was one hundred cubits between them.

The North Gate Then he proceeded north, 20where, on the outer court, there was a gate facing north, whose length and width he measured. 21Its cells, three on either side, its pilasters, and its vestibule had the same measurements as those of the first gate; it was fifty cubits long and twenty-five cubits wide. 22Its windows, the windows of its vestibule, and its palm decorations were of the same proportions as those of the gate facing the east. Seven steps led up to it, and its vestibule was toward the inside. 23The inner court had a gate opposite the north gate, just as at the east gate; he measured one hundred cubits from one gate to the other.

The South Gate 24Then he led me south, to where there was a southern gate, whose cells, pilasters, and vestibule he measured; they were the same size as the others. 25The gate and its vestibule had windows on both sides, like the other windows. It was fifty cubits long and twenty-five cubits wide. 26It was ascended by seven steps; its vestibule was toward the inside; and it was decorated with palms here and there on its pilasters. 27The inner court also had a southern gate; from gate to gate he measured one hundred cubits.

40, 5: A cubit and a handbreadth: the ordinary cubit consisted of six handbreadths; the great cubit, of seven. In measuring the temple, a rod six great cubits long was used. The ordinary cubit was about one and a half feet, or, more exactly, 17.5 inches; the large cubit, 20.4 inches.

40, 6–16: The east gate, leading into the outer court of the temple, is described more fully than the north and south gates, which, however, were of the same dimensions. On the west side of the outer court there was a large building instead of a gate (Ez 41, 12).

40, 17: The outer court: the court outside the temple area proper, which had its own inner court (vv 28–37).

Gates of the Inner Court* 28 Then he brought me to the inner court by the south gate, where he measured the south gate. Its dimensions were the same as the others; 29 its cells, its pilasters, and its vestibule were the same size as the others. The gate and its vestibule had windows on both sides; and it was fifty cubits long and twenty-five cubits wide. 31 But its vestibule was toward the outer court; palms were on its pilasters, and it had a stairway of eight steps. 32 Then he brought me to the gate facing the east, where he measured the gate, whose dimensions were found to be the same. 33 Its cells, its pilasters, and its vestibule were the same size as the others; the gate and its vestibule had windows on both sides; it was fifty cubits long and twenty-five cubits wide. 34 But its vestibule was toward the outer court; palms were on its pilasters here and there, and it had a stairway of eight steps. 35 Then he brought me to the north gate, where he measured the dimensions 36 of its cells, its pilasters, and its vestibule, and found them the same. The gate and its vestibule had windows on both sides; it was fifty cubits long and twenty-five cubits wide. 37 Its vestibule was toward the outer court; palms were on its pilasters here and there, and it had a stairway of eight steps.

Side Rooms 38 There was a chamber opening off the vestibule of the gate, where the holocausts were rinsed. 39 In the vestibule of the gate there were two tables on either side, on which were slaughtered the sin offerings and guilt offerings. 40 Along the wall of the vestibule, but outside, near the entrance of the north gate, were two tables, and on the other side of the vestibule of the gate there were two tables. 41 There were four tables on either side of the gate [eight tables], on which the sacrifices were slaughtered. 42 There were four tables for holocausts, made of cut stone, one and a half cubits long, one and a half cubits wide, and one cubit high. 43 The ledges, a handbreadth wide, were set on the inside all around, and on them were laid the instruments with which the holocausts were slaughtered. On the tables themselves the flesh was laid. 44 He then led me to the inner court where there were two chambers, one beside the north gate, facing south, and the other beside the south gate, facing north. 45 He said to me, "This chamber which faces south is for the priests who have charge of the temple, 46 and the chamber which faces north is for the priests who have charge of the altar. These are the Zadokites,* the only Levites who may come near to minister to the LORD." 47 Then he measured the court, which was a hundred cubits long and a hundred cubits wide, a perfect square. The altar stood in front of the temple.

The Temple Building* 48 Then he brought me into the vestibule of the temple and measured the pilasters on each side, which were five cubits. The width of the doorway was fourteen cubits, and the side walls on either side of the door measured three cubits. 49 The vestibule was twenty cubits wide and twelve cubits deep; ten steps led up to it, and there were columns by the pilasters, one on either side.

CHAPTER 41

1 Then he brought me to the nave and measured the pilasters, which were six cubits thick on either side. 2 The width of the entrance was ten cubits, and the walls at either side of it measured five cubits each. He measured the length of the nave, which was found to be forty cubits, while its width was twenty.

3 Then he went in beyond and measured the pilasters flanking that entrance, which were two cubits; the width of the entrance was six cubits, and the walls at either side of it extended seven cubits each. 4 He measured the space beyond the nave, twenty cubits long and twenty cubits wide, and said to me, "This is the holy of holies."*

40, 28–37: The gates leading into the inner court of the temple area correspond to the gates leading into the outer court, with the exception that their vestibules are on the outer rather than the inner side. (Verse 30, a dittography of v 29, is omitted.)

40, 46: The Zadokites: descendants of the priestly line of Zadok; cf 2 Sm 15, 24–29; 1 Kgs 1, 32ff; 2, 35.

40, 48—41, 15: The description of Ezekiel's visionary temple closely follows the description of the temple of Solomon (1 Kgs 6).

40, 49—41, 4: Vestibule . . . nave . . . holy of holies: the three divisions of the temple building in progressing order of sanctity. The last is called "the inner sanctuary" in 1 Kgs 6.

[5]Then he measured the wall of the temple, which was six cubits thick; the side chambers, which extended all the way around the temple, had a width of four cubits. [6]There were thirty side chambers built one above the other in three stories, and there were offsets in the outside wall of the temple that enclosed the side chambers; these served as supports, so that there were no supports in the temple wall proper. [7]There was a broad circular passageway that led upward to the side chambers, for the temple was enclosed all the way around and all the way upward; therefore the temple had a broad way running upward so that one could pass from the lowest to the middle and the highest story. [8]About the temple was a raised pavement completely enclosing it—the foundations of the side chambers—a full rod of six cubits in extent. [9]The width of the outside wall which enclosed the side chambers was five cubits. Between the side chambers of the temple [10]and the chambers of the court was an open space twenty cubits wide going all around the temple. [11]The side chambers had entrances to the open space, one entrance on the north and another on the south. The width of the wall surrounding the open space was five cubits. [12]The building* fronting the free area on the west side was seventy cubits front to back; the wall of the building was five cubits thick all around, and it measured ninety cubits from side to side. [13]He measured the temple, which was one hundred cubits long. The free area, together with the building and its walls, was a hundred cubits in length. [14]The façade of the temple, along with the free area, on the east side, was one hundred cubits wide. [15]He measured the building which lay the length of the free area and behind it, and together with its walls on both sides it was one hundred cubits.

Interior of the Temple The inner nave and the outer vestibule [16]were paneled with precious wood all around, covered from the ground to the windows. There were splayed windows with trellises about them [facing the threshold]. [17]As high as the lintel of the door, even into the interior part of the temple as well as outside, on every wall on every side in both the inner and outer rooms were carved [18]the figures of cherubim and palmtrees: a palmtree between every two cherubim. Each cherub had two faces: [19]a man's face looking at a palmtree on one side, and a lion's face looking at a palmtree on the other; thus they were figured on every side throughout the whole temple. [20]From the ground to the lintel of the door the cherubim and palmtrees were carved on the walls. [21]The way into the nave was a square doorframe. In front of the holy place was something that looked like [22]a wooden altar,* three cubits in height, two cubits long, and two cubits wide. It had corners, and its base and sides were of wood. He said to me, "This is the table which is before the LORD." [23]The nave had a double door, and also the holy place had [24]a double door. Each door had two movable leaves; two leaves were on one doorjamb and two on the other. [25]Carved upon them [on the doors of the nave] were cherubim and palmtrees, like those carved on the walls. Before the vestibule outside was a wooden lattice. [26]There were splayed windows [and palmtrees] on both side walls of the vestibule, and the side chambers of the temple . . . .

CHAPTER 42

Other Structures [1]Then he led me north to the outer court, bringing me to some chambers on the north that lay across the free area and which were also across from the building. [2]Their length was a hundred cubits on the north side, and they were fifty cubits wide. [3]Across the twenty cubits of the inner court and the pavement of the outer court, there were three parallel rows of them on different levels. [4]In front of the chambers, to the inside, was a walk ten cubits broad and a wall of one cubit; but the entrances of the chambers were on the north. [5]The outermost chambers were the lowest, for the system of levels set them at a level lower than the closest chambers and those in be-

41, 12: The building: the function of this structure lying behind the temple is never specified.

41, 22: A wooden altar: the altar of incense, standing in the nave at the entrance to the holy of holies.

tween;* [6]for they were in three rows and had no foundations to conform with the foundations of the courts, therefore they were on a lower terrace of the ground than the closest and the middle chambers. [7]On the far side there was a wall running parallel to the chambers along the outer court; its length before these chambers was fifty cubits, [8]for the length of the chambers belonging to the outer court was fifty cubits, but along its entire length the wall measured one hundred cubits. [9]Below these chambers there was the way in from the east, so that one could enter from the outer court [10]where the wall of the court began.

To the south along the side of the free area and the building there were also chambers, [11]before which was a passage. These looked like the chambers to the north, just as long and just as wide, with the same exits and plan and entrances. [12]Below the chambers to the south there was an entrance at the beginning of the way which led to the back wall, by which one could enter from the east. [13]He said to me, "The north and south chambers which border on the free area are the sanctuary chambers; here the priests who draw near to the LORD shall eat the most sacred meals, and here they shall keep the most sacred offerings: cereal offerings, sin offerings, and guilt offerings; for it is a holy place.* [14]When the priests have once entered, they shall not leave the holy place for the outer court until they have left here the clothing in which they ministered, for it is holy. They shall put on other garments, and then approach the place destined for the people."

Measuring the Outer Court [15]When he had finished measuring the inner temple area, he brought me out by way of the gate which faces east and measured all the limits of the court. [16]He measured the east side: five hundred cubits by his measuring rod. Then he turned [17]and measured the north side: five hundred cubits by the measuring rod. He turned [18]to the south and measured five hundred cubits by the measuring rod. [19]Then he turned to the west and measured five hundred cubits by the measuring rod. [20]Thus he measured it in the four directions, five hundred cubits long and five hundred cubits wide. It was surrounded by a wall, to separate the sacred from the profane.

Restoration of the Temple

CHAPTER 43

The Return of the Lord [1]Then he led me to the gate which faces the east, [2]and there I saw the glory of the God of Israel coming from the east. I heard a sound like the roaring of many waters, and the earth shone with his glory. [3] [w]The vision was like that which I had seen when he came to destroy the city, and like that which I had seen by the river Chebar. I fell prone [4]as the glory of the LORD entered the temple by way of the gate which faces the east, [5]but spirit lifted me up and brought me to the inner court. And I saw that the temple was filled with the glory of the LORD. [6]Then I heard someone speaking to me from the temple, while the man stood beside me. [7]The voice said to me: Son of man, this is where my throne shall be, this is where I will set the soles of my feet; here I will dwell among the Israelites forever. Never again shall they and their kings profane my holy name with their harlotries and with the corpses of their kings [their high places]. [8]When they placed their threshold against my threshold* and their doorpost next to mine, so that only a wall was between us, they profaned my holy name by their abominable deeds; therefore I consumed them in my wrath. [9]From now on they shall put far from me their harlotry and the corpses of their kings, and I will dwell in their midst forever.

The Law of the Temple [10]As for you, son of man, describe the temple to the house of Israel

42, 5f: The three rows of identical chambers, since they rested on different ground levels, necessarily had roofs on correspondingly different levels.

42, 13: The function of these chambers is explained again in Ez 46, 19f.

43, 8: They placed their threshold against my threshold: the preexilic temple and the royal palace belonged to the same complex of buildings, and this physical proximity was reflected in the use made of the temple by kings like Ahaz and Manasseh, who treated it as their private chapel for pagan rites. In the new Israel the temple is free, even physically, from civil jurisdiction; cf Ez 45, 7f.

w Ez 1, 1.

[that they may be ashamed of their sins], both its measurements and its design; [11][and if they are ashamed of all that they have done,] make known to them the form and design of the temple, its exits and entrances, all its statutes and laws; write these down for them to see, that they may carefully observe all its laws and statutes. [12]This is the law of the temple: its whole surrounding area on the mountain top shall be most sacred.

The Altar [13]These were the measurements of the altar* in cubits of one cubit plus a handbreadth. Its base was one cubit high and one cubit deep, with a rim around its edge of one span. The height of the altar itself was as follows: [14]from its base at the bottom up to the lower ledge it was two cubits high, and this ledge was one cubit deep; from the lower to the upper ledge it was four cubits high, and this ledge also was one cubit deep; [15]the hearth of the altar was four cubits high, and extending from the top of the hearth were the four horns of the altar. [16]The hearth was a square: twelve cubits long and twelve cubits wide. [17]The upper ledge was also a square: fourteen cubits long and fourteen cubits wide. The lower ledge, likewise a square, was sixteen cubits long and sixteen cubits wide, with a half-cubit rim surrounding it. And there was a base of one cubit all around. The steps of the altar face the east.

[18]Then he said to me: Son of man, thus says the Lord GOD: These are the statutes for the altar when it is set up for the offering of holocausts upon it and for the sprinkling of blood against it. [19]Give a young bull as a sin offering to the priests, the Levites who are of the line of Zadok, who draw near me to minister to me, says the Lord GOD. [20]Take some of its blood and put it on the four horns of the altar, and on the four corners of the ledge, and on the rim all around. Thus you shall purify it and make atonement for it. [21]Then take the bull of the sin offering, which is to be burnt in a designated part of the temple, outside the sanctuary. [22]On the second day present an unblemished he-goat as a sin offering, to purify the altar as was done with the bull. [23]When you have finished the purification, bring an unblemished young bull and an unblemished ram from the flock, [24]and present them before the LORD; the priests shall strew salt on them and offer them to the LORD as holocausts. [25]Daily for seven days you shall offer a he-goat as a sin offering, and a young bull and a ram from the flock, all unblemished, shall be offered [26]for seven days. Thus atonement shall be made for the altar, and it shall be purified and dedicated. [27]And when these days are over, from the eighth day on, the priests shall offer your holocausts and peace offerings on the altar. Then I will accept you, says the Lord GOD.

CHAPTER 44

The Closed Gate [1]Then he brought me back to the outer gate of the sanctuary, facing the east; but it was closed. [2]He said to me: This gate is to remain closed; it is not to be opened for anyone to enter by it; since the LORD, the God of Israel, has entered by it, it shall remain closed. [3]Only the prince may sit down in it to eat his meal in the presence of the LORD. He must enter by way of the vestibule of the gate, and leave by the same way.*

The New Law

Admission to the Temple [4]Then he brought me by way of the north gate to the façade of the temple, and when I looked I saw the glory of the LORD filling the LORD's temple, and I fell prone. [5]Then he said to me: Son of man, pay strict attention, look carefully, and listen intently to all that I will tell you about the statutes and laws of the LORD's temple; be attentive in regard to those who are to be admitted to the temple and all those who are to be excluded from the sanctuary. [6]Say to that rebellious house, the house of Israel: Thus says the Lord GOD: Enough of all these abominations of yours, O house of Israel! [7]You have admitted foreigners, uncircumcised both in heart and flesh, to my

43, 13: The altar: of holocausts, standing in the inner court of the temple area; cf Ez 40, 47.

44, 3: The prince stands at the eastern gate of the inner court while his sacrifice is offered up (Ez 46, 2); he then goes to the vestibule of the outer court, there to partake of his sacrificial meal. The closed outer gate on the eastern side signifies that the Lord has entered the temple permanently, not to depart again.

sanctuary to profane it when you offered me food, fat, and blood;* thus you have broken my covenant by all your abominations. 8 Instead of caring for the service of my temple, you have appointed such as these to serve me in my sanctuary in your stead. 9 Thus says the Lord GOD: No foreigners, uncircumcised in heart and in flesh, shall ever enter my sanctuary; none of the foreigners who live among the Israelites.

Levites* 10 But as for the Levites who departed from me when Israel strayed from me to pursue their idols, they shall bear the consequences of their sin. 11 They shall serve in my sanctuary as gatekeepers and temple servants; they shall slaughter the holocausts and the sacrifices for the people, and they shall stand before the people to minister for them. 12 Because they used to minister for them before their idols, and became an occasion of sin to the house of Israel, therefore I have sworn an oath against them, says the Lord GOD: they shall bear the consequences of their sin. 13 They shall no longer draw near me to serve as my priests, nor shall they touch any of my sacred things, or the most sacred things. Thus they shall bear their disgrace because of all their abominable deeds. 14 But I will set them to the service of the temple, for all its work and for everything that is to be done in it.

Priests 15 As for the levitical priests, however, the Zadokites who cared for my sanctuary when the Israelites strayed from me, they shall draw near me to minister to me, and they shall stand before me to offer me fat and blood, says the Lord GOD. 16 It is they who shall enter my sanctuary, they who shall approach my table to minister to me, and they who shall carry out my service. 17 Whenever they enter the gates of the inner court, they shall wear linen garments; they shall not put on anything woolen when they minister at the gates of the inner court or within the temple. 18 [x]They shall have linen turbans on their heads and linen drawers on their loins; they shall not gird themselves with anything that causes sweat. 19 [y]When they are to go out to the people in the outer court, they shall take off the garments in which they ministered and leave them in the chambers of the sanctuary, putting on other garments; thus they will not transmit holiness to the people* with their garments.

20 [z]They shall not shave their heads nor let their hair hang loose, but they shall keep their hair carefully trimmed. 21 [a]No priest shall drink wine when he is to enter the inner court. 22 [b]They shall not take for their wives either widows or divorced women, but only virgins of the race of Israel; however, they may marry women who are the widows of priests. 23 They shall teach my people to distinguish between the sacred and the profane, and make known to them the difference between the clean and the unclean. 24 [c]In capital cases they shall stand as judges, judging them according to my decrees. They shall observe my laws and statutes on all my festivals, and keep my sabbaths holy.

25 [d]They shall not make themselves unclean by coming near any dead person, unless it be their father, mother, son, daughter, brother, or maiden sister; for these they may make themselves unclean. 26 After a priest has been cleansed, he must wait an additional seven days, 27 and on the day he enters the inner court to minister in the sanctuary, he shall present his sin offering, says the Lord GOD. 28 [e]They shall have no inheritance, for I am their inheritance; you shall give them no property in Israel, for I am their property. 29 [f]They shall eat the cereal offering, the sin offering, and the guilt offering; whatever is under the ban* in Israel shall be

44, 7ff: In the preexilic temple various menial services had been performed by foreigners; cf Jos 9, 22–27. In the new temple the Levites will perform these services (vv 10–14).

44, 10–14: Levites other than the Zadokite priesthood of Jerusalem had performed priestly functions at the various sanctuaries and high places in Israel and Judah, where the worship of the Lord had often been corrupted with pagan elements. The demotion of the Levites to menial service in the temple was enforced in the actual restoration after the exile, and explains why relatively few Levites were willing to return; cf 1 Ezr 8, 15ff.

44, 19: Thus they will not transmit holiness to the people: holiness was thought of as something physical, as though it were communicable, and therefore not to be brought in contact with unconsecrated persons.

44, 29: Under the ban: dedicated to the Lord, withdrawn from profane use.

x Ex 28, 40. 42; 29, 9; 38, 28; Lv 6, 3. **y** Ez 42, 13. 14. **z** Lv 21, 5. **a** Lv 10, 9. **b** Lv 21, 7. 14. **c** Dt 17, 9; 19, 17. **d** Lv 21, 1ff. 11. **e** Nm 18, 20; Dt 18, 1. **f** Lv 2, 3. 10; 6, 9. 22; 7, 9; 10, 12; Nm 18, 9; 18, 14.

theirs. 30 [g]All the choicest first fruits of every kind, and all the best of your offerings of every kind, shall belong to the priests; likewise the best of your dough you shall give to the priests to bring a blessing down upon your house. 31 [h]The priests shall not eat anything, whether flesh or fowl, that has died of itself or has been killed by wild beasts.

CHAPTER 45

The Sacred Tract 1 When you apportion the land into inheritances, you shall set apart a sacred tract of land for the LORD, twenty-five thousand cubits long and twenty thousand wide; its whole area shall be sacred. 2 Of this land a square plot, five hundred by five hundred cubits, surrounded by a free space of fifty cubits, shall be assigned to the sanctuary. 3 Also from this sector measure off a strip, twenty-five thousand cubits long and ten thousand wide, within which shall be the sanctuary, the holy of holies. 4 This shall be the sacred part of the land belonging to the priests, the ministers of the sanctuary, who draw near to minister to the LORD; it shall be a place for their homes and pasture land for their cattle. 5 Also there shall be a strip twenty-five thousand cubits long and ten thousand wide as property for the Levites, the ministers of the temple, that they may have cities to live in. 6 As property of the City you shall designate a strip five thousand cubits wide and twenty-five thousand long, parallel to the sacred tract; this shall belong to the whole house of Israel. 7 The prince shall have a section bordering on both sides of the combined sacred tract and City property, extending westward on the western side and eastward on the eastern side, corresponding in length to one of the tribal portions from the western boundary to the eastern boundary 8 of the land. This shall be his property in Israel, so that the princes of Israel will no longer oppress my people, but will leave the land to the house of Israel according to their tribes.

Weights and Measures* 9 Thus says the Lord GOD: Enough, you princes of Israel! Put away violence and oppression, and do what is right and just! Stop evicting my people! says the Lord GOD. 10 [i]You shall have honest scales, an honest ephah, and an honest liquid measure. 11 The ephah and the liquid measure shall be of the same size: the liquid measure equal to a tenth of a homer, and the ephah equal to a tenth of a homer; by the homer they shall be determined. 12 [j]The shekel shall be twenty gerahs. Twenty shekels, twenty-five shekels, plus fifteen shekels shall be your mina.

Offerings 13 These are the offerings you shall make: one sixth of an ephah from each homer of wheat, and one sixth of an ephah from each homer of barley. 14 The regulation for oil: for every measure of oil, a tenth of a measure, computed by the kor* of ten liquid measures [or a homer, for ten liquid measures make a homer]. 15 One sheep from the flock for every two hundred from the pasturage of Israel, for sacrifice—holocausts and peace offerings and atonement sacrifices, says the Lord GOD. 16 All the people of the land shall be bound to this offering [for the prince in Israel]. 17 It shall be the duty of the prince to provide the holocausts, cereal offerings, and libations on the feasts, new moons, and sabbaths, on all the festivals of the house of Israel. He shall offer the sin offerings, cereal offerings, holocausts, and peace offerings, to make atonement on behalf of the house of Israel.

The Passover 18 Thus says the Lord GOD: On the first day of the first month you shall use an unblemished young bull as a sacrifice to purify the sanctuary. 19 Then the priest shall take some

45, 9–12: Besides the land monopoly fostered by royal greed and collusion with the wealthy (Mi 2, 2; Is 3, 12–15; 5, 8–10), one grave social evil of preexilic Israel was dishonesty in business; cf Hos 12, 8; Am 8, 5. Ephah: a dry measure; liquid measure: in Hebrew, a "bath," standardized according to the homer (a dry measure of about 10 bushels, or 80 gallons). In v 12 reference is made to the change in value of the mina: before the exile it was valued at 50 shekels, but afterward, in imitation of Babylonian practice, the 60-shekel mina was adopted. The shekel was a unit of weight slightly less than half an ounce. As a monetary unit, the value obviously differed greatly, depending on whether it was a gold or a silver shekel.

45, 14: Kor: both a liquid and a dry measure, corresponding to the homer.

g Ex 34, 26; Dt 18, 4. h Lv 22, 8. i Lv 19, 35; Dt 25, 13–16; Hos 12, 8; Am 8, 5; Mi 6, 10f. j Ex 30, 13; Lv 27, 25; Nm 3, 47; 18, 16.

of the blood from the sin offering and put it on the doorposts of the temple, on the four corners of the ledge of the altar, and on the doorposts of the gates of the inner court. [20]You shall repeat this on the first day of the seventh month for those who have sinned through inadvertence or ignorance; thus you shall make atonement for the temple. [21] [k]On the fourteenth day of the first month you shall observe the feast of the Passover; for seven days unleavened bread is to be eaten. [22]On that day the prince shall offer on his own behalf, and on behalf of all the people of the land, a bull as a sin offering. [23]On each of the seven days of the feast he shall offer as a holocaust to the Lord seven bulls and seven rams without blemish, and as a sin offering he shall offer one male goat each day. [24]As a cereal offering he shall offer one ephah for each bull and one ephah for each ram; and he shall offer one hin* of oil for each ephah.

The Feast of Booths [25]On the fifteenth day of the seventh month, the feast day, and for seven days, he shall perform the same rites, making the same sin offerings, the same holocausts, the same cereal offerings and offerings of oil.

CHAPTER 46

Sabbaths [1]Thus says the Lord GOD: The gate toward the east of the inner court shall remain closed throughout the six working days, but on the sabbath and on the day of the new moon it shall be open. [2]The prince shall enter from outside by way of the vestibule of the gate and remain standing at the doorpost of the gate; then while the priests offer his holocausts and peace offerings, he shall worship at the threshold of the gate and then leave; the gate shall not be closed until evening. [3]The people of the land shall worship before the LORD at the door of this gate on the sabbaths and new moons. [4] [l]The holocausts which the prince presents to the LORD on the sabbath shall consist of six unblemished lambs and an unblemished ram, [5]together with a cereal offering of one ephah for the ram, whatever he pleases for the lambs, and a hin of oil for each ephah. [6] [m]On the day of the new moon he shall provide an unblemished young bull, also six lambs and a ram without blemish, [7]with a cereal offering of one ephah for the bull and one for the ram, for the lambs as much as he has at hand, and for each ephah a hin of oil.

Ritual Laws [8]The prince shall always enter and depart by the vestibule of the gate. [9] [n]When the people of the land enter the presence of the LORD to worship on the festivals, if they enter by the north gate they shall leave by the south gate, and if they enter by the south gate they shall leave by the north gate; no one shall return by the gate through which he has entered, but he shall leave by the opposite gate. [10]The prince shall be in their midst when they enter, and he shall also leave with them. [11]On the feasts and festivals the cereal offering shall be an ephah for a bull, an ephah for a ram, but for the lambs as much as one pleases, and a hin of oil with each ephah. [12]When the prince makes a freewill offering to the LORD, whether holocausts or peace offerings, the eastern gate shall be opened for him, and he shall offer his holocausts or his peace offerings as on the sabbath; then he shall leave, and the gate shall be closed after his departure. [13] [o]He shall offer as a daily holocaust to the LORD an unblemished yearling lamb; this he shall offer every morning. [14]With it every morning he shall provide as a cereal offering one sixth of an ephah, with a third of a hin of oil to moisten the fine flour. This cereal offering to the LORD is mandatory with the established holocaust. [15] [p]The lamb, the cereal offering, and the oil are to be offered every morning as an established holocaust.

The Prince and the Land [16]Thus says the Lord GOD: If the prince makes a gift of part of his inheritance to any of his sons, it shall belong to his sons; that property is theirs by inheritance. [17]But if he makes a gift of part of his inheritance to one of his servants, it shall belong to the latter only until the year of release,* when it shall revert to the prince. Only the inheritance given

45, 24: Hin: a sixth part of the liquid measure called a bath.
46, 17: The year of release: the jubilee year; cf Lv 25, 23–55.

k Ex 12, 6; Lv 23, 5; Nm 28, 16. l Nm 28, 9f. m Nm 28, 11–15. n Ex 23, 17; 34, 23; Dt 16, 16. o Ex 29, 38–42; Nm 28, 3–8. p Ex 29, 42.

to his sons is permanent. [18]The prince shall not seize any part of the inheritance of the people by evicting them from their property. He shall provide an inheritance for his sons from his own property, so that none of my people will be driven from their property.

The Temple Kitchens [19]Then he brought me by the entrance which is on the side of the gate to the chambers [of the sanctuary, reserved to the priests] which face the north. There, at their west end, I saw a place, [20]concerning which he said to me, "Here the priests cook the guilt offerings and the sin offerings, and bake the cereal offerings, so that they do not have to take them into the outer court at the risk of transmitting holiness to the people." [21]Then he led me into the outer court and had me pass around the four corners of the court, and I saw that in each corner there was another court: [22]in the four corners of the court, minor courts, forty cubits long and thirty wide, all four of them the same size. [23]A wall of stones surrounded each of the four, and hearths were built beneath the stones all the way around. [24]He said to me, "These are the kitchens where the temple ministers cook the sacrifices of the people."

CHAPTER 47

The Wonderful Stream* [1]Then he brought me back to the entrance of the temple, and I saw water flowing out from beneath the threshold of the temple toward the east, for the façade of the temple was toward the east; the water flowed down from the southern side of the temple, south of the altar.[q] [2]He led me outside by the north gate, and around to the outer gate facing the east, where I saw water trickling from the southern side. [3]Then when he had walked off to the east with a measuring cord in his hand, he measured off a thousand cubits and had me wade through the water, which was ankle-deep. [4]He measured off another thousand and once more had me wade through the water, which was now knee-deep. Again he measured off a thousand and had me wade; the water was up to my waist. [5]Once more he measured off a thousand, but there was now a river through which I could not wade; for the water had risen so high it had become a river that could not be crossed except by swimming. [6]He asked me, "Have you seen this, son of man?" Then he brought me to the bank of the river, where he had me sit. [7]Along the bank of the river I saw very many trees on both sides. [8]He said to me, "This water flows into the eastern district down upon the Arabah, and empties into the sea, the salt waters, which it makes fresh. [9]Wherever the river flows, every sort of living creature that can multiply shall live, and there shall be abundant fish, for wherever this water comes the sea shall be made fresh. [10]Fishermen shall be standing along it from En-gedi to En-eglaim,* spreading their nets there. Its kinds of fish shall be like those of the Great Sea, very numerous. [11]Only its marshes and swamps shall not be made fresh; they shall be left for salt. [12]Along both banks of the river, fruit trees of every kind shall grow; their leaves shall not fade, nor their fruit fail. Every month they shall bear fresh fruit, for they shall be watered by the flow from the sanctuary. Their fruit shall serve for food, and their leaves for medicine."

The New Israel

Boundaries of the Land* [13]Thus says the Lord GOD: These are the boundaries within which you shall apportion the land among the twelve tribes of Israel [Joseph having two portions]. [14]All of you shall have a like portion in this land which I swore to give to your fathers, that it might fall to you as your inheritance. [15][r]This is the boundary of the land on the north side: from the Great Sea in the direction of Hethlon, past Labo of Hamath, to Zedad, [16]Bero-

47, 1–12: The wonderful and superabundant stream flowing from the temple, restoring to fertility traditionally arid ground, is symbolic of the return of the conditions of primeval paradise; cf Gn 2, 10–14. Water signifies great blessings, just as dryness signifies a curse; cf Ez 26, 5. 14.

47, 10: From En-gedi to En-eglaim: the former was about halfway down the western shore of the Dead Sea, the latter may have been at its northern extremity.

47, 13–20: These boundaries of the restored Israel correspond to those of the Davidic kingdom at its fullest extent, the so-called "ideal boundaries" of the promised land; cf Nm 34, 3–12.

q Sir 24, 28f; Jl 4, 18; Zec 13, 1; Rv 22, 1f. r Nm 34, 7ff.

thah, and Sibraim, along the frontiers of Hamath and Damascus, to Hazar-enon which is on the border of the Hauran. [17]Thus the border shall extend from the sea to Hazar-enon, with the frontier of Hamath and Damascus to the north. This is the northern boundary. [18]The eastern boundary: between the Hauran—toward Damascus—and Gilead on the one side, and the land of Israel on the other side, the Jordan shall form the boundary down to the eastern sea as far as Tamar. This is the eastern boundary. [19]The southern boundary: from Tamar to the waters of Meribath-kadesh, thence to the Wadi of Egypt, and on to the Great Sea. This is the southern boundary. [20]The western boundary: the Great Sea forms the boundary up to a point parallel to Labo of Hamath. This is the western boundary.

The Northern Portions [21]You shall distribute this land among yourselves according to the tribes of Israel. [22] [s]You shall allot it as inheritances for yourselves and for the aliens resident in your midst who have bred children among you. The latter shall be to you like native Israelites; along with you they shall receive inheritances among the tribes of Israel. [23]In whatever tribe the alien may be resident, there you shall assign him his inheritance, says the Lord GOD.

CHAPTER 48

[1]This is the list* of the tribes.[t] Dan: at the northern extremity, adjoining Hamath, all along from the approaches to Hethlon through Labo of Hamath to Hazar-enon, on the northerly border with Damascus, with his possession reaching from the eastern to the western boundary. [2]Asher: on the frontier of Dan, from the eastern to the western boundary. [3]Naphtali: on the frontier of Asher, from the eastern to the western boundary. [4]Manasseh: on the frontier of Naphtali, from the eastern to the western boundary. [5]Ephraim: on the frontier of Manasseh, from the eastern to the western boundary. [6]Reuben: on the frontier of Ephraim, from the eastern to the western boundary. [7]Judah: on the frontier of Reuben, from the eastern to the western boundary.

The Sacred Tract [8]On the frontier of Judah, from the eastern to the western boundary there shall be the tract which you shall set apart, twenty-five thousand cubits from north to south, and as wide as one of the tribal portions from the eastern to the western boundary. In the center of the tract shall be the sanctuary. [9]The tract that you set aside for the LORD shall be twenty-five thousand cubits across by twenty thousand north and south. [10]In this sacred tract the priests shall have twenty-five thousand cubits on the north, ten thousand on the west, ten thousand on the east, and twenty-five thousand on the south; and the sanctuary of the LORD shall be in its center. [11]The consecrated priests, the Zadokites, who fulfilled my service and did not stray along with the Israelites as the Levites did, [12]shall have within this tract of land their own most sacred domain, next to the territory of the Levites. [13]The Levites shall have a territory corresponding to that of the priests, twenty-five thousand cubits by ten thousand. The whole tract shall be twenty-five thousand cubits across and twenty thousand north and south. [14]They may not sell or exchange or alienate this, the best part of the land, for it is sacred to the LORD. [15]The remaining five thousand cubits along the twenty-five-thousand-cubit line are profane land, assigned to the City for dwellings and pasture; the City shall be at their center. [16]These are the dimensions of the City: the north side, forty-five hundred cubits; the south side, forty-five hundred cubits; the east side, forty-five hundred cubits; and the west side, forty-five hundred cubits. [17]The pasture lands of the City shall extend north two hundred and fifty cubits, south two hundred and fifty cubits, east two hundred and fifty cubits, and west two hundred and fifty cubits. [18]There shall remain an area along the sacred tract, ten thousand cubits to the east and ten thousand to the west, whose produce shall provide food for the workers of the City. [19]The

48, 1–29: This distribution of the land among the tribes does not correspond to the geographical realities of Palestine. It is a description of the ideal order, like that in Ez 47, 1–12.

s Ex 12, 48; Lv 19, 34; 24, 22; Nm 9, 14; Jos 8, 33. t Ez 47, 15ff.

workers in the City shall be taken from all the tribes of Israel. 20The entire tract shall be twenty-five thousand by twenty-five thousand cubits; as a perfect square you shall set apart the sacred tract together with the City property.

21The remainder shall belong to the prince: the land on both sides of the sacred tract and the City property, extending along the twenty-five-thousand-cubit line eastward to the eastern boundary, and westward along the twenty-five-thousand-cubit line to the western boundary, a territory parallel with the tribal portions for the prince. The sacred tract and the sanctuary of the temple shall be in the middle. 22Thus, except for the property of the Levites and the City property, which lie in the midst of the prince's property, the territory between the portions of Judah and of Benjamin shall belong to the prince.

The Southern Portions 23These are the remaining tribes. Benjamin: from the eastern to the western boundary. 24Simeon: on the frontier of Benjamin, from the eastern to the western boundary. 25Issachar: on the frontier of Simeon, from the eastern to the western boundary. 26Zebulun: on the frontier of Issachar, from the eastern to the western boundary. 27Gad: on the frontier of Zebulun, from the eastern to the western boundary. 28Along the frontier of Gad shall be the southern boundary, which shall extend from Tamar to the waters of Meribath-kadesh, and from there to the Wadi of Egypt, and on to the Great Sea. 29Such is the land which you shall apportion as inheritances among the tribes of Israel, and these are their portions, says the Lord GOD.

The Gates of the City 30These are the exits of the City, the gates of which are named after the tribes of Israel. On the north side, measuring forty-five hundred cubits, 31there shall be three gates: the gate of Reuben, the gate of Judah, and the gate of Levi. 32On the east side, measuring forty-five hundred cubits, there shall be three gates: the gate of Joseph, the gate of Benjamin, and the gate of Dan. 33On the south side, measuring forty-five hundred cubits, there shall be three gates: the gate of Simeon, the gate of Issachar, and the gate of Zebulun. 34On the west side, measuring forty-five hundred cubits, there shall be three gates: the gate of Gad, the gate of Asher, and the gate of Naphtali. 35The perimeter of the City is eighteen thousand cubits. The name of the City shall henceforth be "The LORD is here."

THE BOOK OF DANIEL

This Book takes its name, not from the author, who is actually unknown, but from its hero, a young Jew taken early to Babylon, where he lived at least until 538 B.C. Strictly speaking, the book does not belong to the prophetic writings but rather to a distinctive type of literature known as "apocalyptic," of which it is an early specimen. Apocalyptic writing enjoyed its greatest popularity from 200 B.C. to 100 A.D., a time of distress and persecution for Jews, and later, for Christians. Though subsequent in time to the prophetic, apocalyptic literature has its roots in the teaching of the prophets, who often pointed ahead to the day of the Lord, the consummation of history. For both prophet and apocalyptist Yahweh was the Lord of history, and he would ultimately vindicate his people.

This work was composed during the bitter persecution carried on by Antiochus IV Epiphanes (167–164) and was written to strengthen and comfort the Jewish people in their ordeal.

The Book contains stories originating in and transmitted by popular traditions which tell of the trials and triumphs of the wise Daniel and his three companions. The moral is that men of faith can resist temptation and conquer adversity. The characters are not purely legendary but rest on older historical tradition. What is more important than the question of historicity, and closer to the intention of the author, is the fact that a persecuted Jew of the second century B.C. would quickly see the application of these stories to his own plight.

There follows a series of visions promising deliverance and glory to the Jews in the days to come. The great nations of the ancient world have risen in vain against Yahweh; his kingdom shall overthrow existing powers and last forever. Under this apocalyptic imagery are contained some of the best elements of prophetic teaching: the insistence on right conduct, the divine control over events, the certainty that the kingdom of God will ultimately triumph. The arrival of the kingdom is a central theme of the synoptic gospels, and Jesus, in calling himself the "Son of Man," reminds us that he fulfills the destiny of this mysterious figure in the seventh chapter of Daniel.

The added episodes of Susanna, Bel, and the Dragon, found only in the Greek version, are edifying short stories with a didactic purpose.

These three sections constitute the divisions of the Book of Daniel:

I. Daniel and the Kings of Babylon (1, 1—6, 29).
II. Daniel's Visions (7, 1—12, 13).
III. Appendix (13, 1—14, 42).

I: Daniel and the Kings of Babylon

CHAPTER 1

The Food Test 1 In the third year of the reign of Jehoiakim, king of Judah, King Nebuchadnezzar of Babylon came and laid siege to Jerusalem.[a] 2 [b]The Lord handed over to him Jehoiakim, king of Judah, and some of the vessels of the temple of God, which he carried off to the land of Shinar,* and placed in the temple treasury of his god.

3 The king told Ashpenaz, his chief chamberlain, to bring in some of the Israelites of royal blood and of the nobility, 4 young men without any defect, handsome, intelligent and wise, quick to learn, and prudent in judgment, such as could take their place in the king's palace; they were to be taught the language and literature of the Chaldeans; 5 after three years' training they were to enter the king's service. The king allotted them a daily portion of food and wine from the royal table. 6 Among these were men of Judah: Daniel, Hananiah, Mishael, and Azariah. 7 The chief chamberlain changed their names: Daniel to Belteshazzar, Hananiah to Shadrach, Mishael to Meshach, and Azariah to Abednego.*

8 But Daniel was resolved not to defile himself with the king's food or wine; so he begged the chief chamberlain to spare him this defilement.* 9 Though God had given Daniel the favor and sympathy of the chief chamberlain, 10 he nevertheless said to Daniel, "I am afraid of my lord the king; it is he who allotted your food and drink. If he sees that you look wretched by comparison with the other young men of your age, you will endanger my life with the king." 11 Then Daniel said to the steward whom the chief chamberlain had put in charge of Daniel, Hananiah, Mishael, and Azariah, 12 "Please test your servants for ten days. Give us vegetables to eat and water to drink. 13 Then see how we look in comparison with the other young men who eat from the royal table, and treat your servants according to

1, 2: Shinar: ancient name for Babylonia, a deliberate archaism in this text: cf Gn 10, 10; 11, 2.

1, 7: The young men are given Babylonian names as a sign of their adoption by the king.

1, 8: This defilement: the bread, meat, and wine of the Gentiles, which were unclean (Hos 9, 3; Tb 1, 12; Jdt 10, 5; 12, 1f) because they might have been offered to idols or prepared over firewood taken from a sacred grove. Only raw vegetables and water were safe from this danger (v 12).

a 2 Kgs 24, 1; 2 Chr 36, 6; Jer 25, 1. b Dn 5, 2; Gn 10, 10; 2 Kgs 24, 2; 2 Chr 36, 7.

what you see." [14]He acceded to this request, and tested them for ten days; [15]after ten days they looked healthier and better fed than any of the young men who ate from the royal table. [16]So the steward continued to take away the food and wine they were to receive, and gave them vegetables.

[17]To these four young men God gave knowledge and proficiency in all literature and science, and to Daniel the understanding of all visions and dreams. [18]At the end of the time the king had specified for their preparation, the chief chamberlain brought them before Nebuchadnezzar. [19]When the king had spoken with all of them, none was found equal to Daniel, Hananiah, Mishael, and Azariah; and so they entered the king's service. [20]In any question of wisdom or prudence which the king put to them, he found them ten times better than all the magicians and enchanters in his kingdom. [21] [c]Daniel remained there until the first year of King Cyrus.*

CHAPTER 2

The King's Dream* [1]In the second year of his reign, King Nebuchadnezzar had a dream which left his spirit no rest and robbed him of his sleep. [2]So he ordered that the magicians, enchanters, sorcerers, and Chaldeans* be summoned to interpret the dream for him. When they came and presented themselves to the king, [3]he said to them, "I had a dream which will allow my spirit no rest until I know what it means." [4]The Chaldeans answered the king [Aramaic]:* "O king, live forever! Tell your servants the dream and we will give its meaning." [5]The king answered the Chaldeans, "This is what I have decided: unless you tell me the dream and its meaning, you shall be cut to pieces and your houses destroyed. [6]But if you tell me the dream and its meaning, you shall receive from me gifts and presents and great honors. Now tell me the dream and its meaning."

[7]Again they answered, "Let the king tell his servants the dream and we will give its meaning." [8]But the king replied: "I know for certain that you are bargaining for time, since you know what I have decided. [9]If you do not tell me the dream, there can be but one decree for you. You have framed a false and deceitful interpretation to present me with till the crisis is past. Tell me the dream, therefore, that I may be sure that you can also give its correct interpretation."

[10]The Chaldeans answered the king: "There is not a man on earth who can do what you ask, O king; never has any king, however great and mighty, asked such a thing of any magician, enchanter, or Chaldean. [11]What you demand, O king, is too difficult; there is no one who can tell it to the king except the gods who do not dwell among men." [12]At this the king became violently angry and ordered all the wise men of Babylon to be put to death. [13]When the decree was issued that the wise men should be slain, Daniel and his companions were also sought out.

[14]Then Daniel prudently took counsel with Arioch, the captain of the king's guard, who had set out to kill the wise men of Babylon: [15]"O officer of the king," he asked, "what is the reason for this harsh order from the king?" When Arioch told him, [16]Daniel went and asked for time from the king, that he might give him the interpretation.

[17]Daniel went home and informed his companions Hananiah, Mishael, and Azariah, [18]that they might implore the mercy of the God of heaven in regard to this mystery, so that Daniel and his companions might not perish with the rest of the wise men of Babylon. [19]During the night the mystery was revealed to Daniel in a vision, and he blessed the God of heaven:

1, 21: The first year of King Cyrus: the year of this Persian king's conquest of Babylon, 539/8 B.C.

2, 1–49: The chronology of v 1 is in conflict with that of Dn 1, 5. 18, and in v 25 Daniel appears to be introduced to the king for the first time. It seems that the story of this chapter was originally entirely independent of chapter 1, and later retouched slightly to fit its present setting.

2, 2: Chaldeans: here probably astrologers, who were so associated with the Chaldeans in the Hebrew mind that in the later language they are sometimes simply called by the name of that people.

2, 4: Aramaic: from Dn 2, 4 to 7, 28 the text of Daniel is in Aramaic, not Hebrew, as indicated by this gloss.

c Dn 6, 28.

20 “Blessed be the name of God forever and ever,
for wisdom and power are his.
21 He causes the changes of the times and
seasons,
makes kings and unmakes them.
He gives wisdom to the wise
and knowledge to those who understand.
22 He reveals deep and hidden things
and knows what is in the darkness,
for the light dwells with him.[d]
23 To you, O God of my fathers,
I give thanks and praise,
because you have given me wisdom and
power.
Now you have shown me what we asked of
you,
you have made known to us the king’s
dream.”

24 So Daniel went to Arioch, whom the king
had appointed to destroy the wise men of
Babylon, and said to him, “Do not put the wise
men of Babylon to death. Bring me before the
king, and I will tell him the interpretation of the
dream.” Arioch quickly brought Daniel to the
king and said, 25 “I have found a man among the
Judean captives who can give the interpretation
to the king.” 26 The king asked Daniel, whose
name was Belteshazzar, “Can you tell me the
dream that I had, and its meaning?” 27 In the
king’s presence Daniel made this reply:

“The mystery about which the king has in-
quired, the wise men, enchanters, magicians,
and astrologers could not explain to the king.
28 But there is a God in heaven who reveals
mysteries, and he has shown King Nebuchadnez-
zar what is to happen in days to come; this was
the dream you saw as you lay in bed. 29 To you in
your bed there came thoughts about what
should happen in the future, and he who reveals
mysteries showed you what is to be. 30 To me
also this mystery has been revealed; not that I
am wiser than any other living person, but in
order that its meaning may be made known to
the king, that you may understand the thoughts
in your own mind.

31 “In your vision, O king, you saw a statue,
very large and exceedingly bright, terrifying in
appearance as it stood before you. 32 The head of
the statue was pure gold, its chest and arms
were silver, its belly and thighs bronze, 33 the
legs iron, its feet partly iron and partly tile.*
34 While you looked at the statue, a stone which
was hewn from a mountain without a hand
being put to it, struck its iron and tile feet,
breaking them in pieces. 35 The iron, tile, bronze,
silver, and gold all crumbled at once, fine as the
chaff on the threshing floor in summer, and the
wind blew them away without leaving a trace.
But the stone that struck the statue became a
great mountain and filled the whole earth.

36 * “This was the dream; the interpretation
we shall also give in the king’s presence. 37 You,
O king, are the king of kings; to you the God of
heaven has given dominion and strength, power
and glory; 38 men, wild beasts, and birds of the
air, wherever they may dwell, he has handed
over to you, making you ruler over them all; you
are the head of gold. 39 Another kingdom shall
take your place, inferior to yours, then a third
kingdom, of bronze, which shall rule over the
whole earth. 40 There shall be a fourth kingdom,
strong as iron; it shall break in pieces and subdue
all these others, just as iron breaks in pieces and
crushes everything else. 41 The feet and toes you
saw, partly of potter’s tile and partly of iron,
mean that it shall be a divided kingdom, but yet
have some of the hardness of iron. As you saw
the iron mixed with clay tile, 42 and the toes
partly iron and partly tile, the kingdom shall be
partly strong and partly fragile. 43 The iron mixed
with clay tile means that they shall seal their
alliances by intermarriage, but they shall not stay

2, 33: Partly tile: terra cotta tile was much in use among the Babylonians for decoration and for actual construction.

2, 36–45: The four successive kingdoms in this apocalyptic perspective are the Babylonian (gold), the Median (silver), the Persian (bronze), and the Hellenistic (iron). The last, after Alexander’s death, was divided among his generals (vv 41f). The two resulting kingdoms, which most affected the Jews, were the dynasty of the Ptolemies in Egypt and that of the Seleucids in Syria, who tried in vain, by war and through intermarriage, to restore the unity of Alexander’s empire (v 43). The stone hewn from the mountain is the messianic kingdom awaited by the Jews (vv 44f). Our Lord made this image personal to himself; cf Lk 20, 17f.

d Jn 1, 9; 8, 12; 1 Cor 4, 5; 1 Jn 1, 6.

united, any more than iron mixes with clay. 44 [e]In the lifetime of those kings the God of heaven will set up a kingdom that shall never be destroyed or delivered up to another people; rather, it shall break in pieces all these kingdoms and put an end to them, and it shall stand forever. 45 That is the meaning of the stone you saw hewn from the mountain without a hand being put to it, which broke in pieces the tile, iron, bronze, silver, and gold. The great God has revealed to the king what shall be in the future; this is exactly what you dreamed, and its meaning is sure."

46 Then King Nebuchadnezzar fell down and worshiped Daniel and ordered sacrifice and incense offered to him. 47 To Daniel the king said, "Truly your God is the God of gods and Lord of kings and a revealer of mysteries; that is why you were able to reveal this mystery." 48 He advanced Daniel to a high post, gave him many generous presents, made him ruler of the whole province of Babylon and chief prefect over all the wise men of Babylon. 49 At Daniel's request the king made Shadrach, Meshach, and Abednego administrators of the province of Babylon, while Daniel himself remained at the king's court.

CHAPTER 3

The Fiery Furnace 1 King Nebuchadnezzar had a golden statue made, sixty cubits high and six cubits wide, which he set up in the plain of Dura* in the province of Babylon. 2 He then ordered the satraps,* prefects, and governors, the counselors, treasurers, judges, magistrates and all the officials of the provinces to be summoned to the dedication of the statue which he had set up. 3 The satraps, prefects, and governors, the counselors, treasurers, judges, and magistrates and all the officials of the provinces, all these came together for the dedication and stood before the statue which King Nebuchadnezzar had set up. 4 A herald cried out: "Nations and peoples of every language, when you hear the sound of the trumpet, flute, lyre, harp, psaltery,* bagpipe, and all the other musical instruments, 5 you are ordered to fall down and worship the golden statue which King Nebuchadnezzar has set up. 6 Whoever does not fall down and worship shall be instantly cast into a white-hot furnace."* 7 Therefore, as soon as they heard the sound of the trumpet, flute, lyre, harp, psaltery, bagpipe, and all the other musical instruments, the nations and peoples of every language all fell down and worshiped the golden statue which King Nebuchadnezzar had set up.

8 At that point, some of the Chaldeans came and accused the Jews 9 to King Nebuchadnezzar: "O king, live forever! 10 O king, you issued a decree that everyone who heard the sound of the trumpet, flute, lyre, harp, psaltery, bagpipe, and all the other musical instruments should fall down and worship the golden statue; 11 whoever did not was to be cast into a white-hot furnace. 12 There are certain Jews whom you have made administrators of the province of Babylon: Shadrach, Meshach, Abednego; these men, O king, have paid no attention to you; they will not serve your god or worship the golden statue which you set up."

13 Nebuchadnezzar flew into a rage and sent for Shadrach, Meshach, and Abednego, who were promptly brought before the king. 14 King Nebuchadnezzar questioned them: "Is it true, Shadrach, Meshach, and Abednego, that you will not serve my god, or worship the golden statue that I set up? 15 Be ready now to fall down and worship the statue I had made, whenever you hear the sound of the trumpet, flute, lyre, harp, psaltery, bagpipe, and all the other musical instruments; otherwise, you shall be instantly cast into the white-hot furnace; and who is the God that can deliver you out of my hands?" 16 Shadrach, Meshach, and Abednego answered King Nebuchadnezzar, "There is no need for us to defend ourselves before you in this matter.

3, 1: Dura: several places in Babylonia bore this name. Probably the present reference is to one a few miles south of Babylon. Colossi of the type mentioned here were not uncommon in antiquity; a cubit was seventeen and a half inches.

3, 2: Satraps: the Persian major governors.

3, 4: Psaltery: a harplike instrument.

3, 6: Death by fire was not unknown as a punishment in Babylonia; cf Jer 29, 22.

e Mt 21, 44; Lk 20, 18.

17 If our God, whom we serve, can save us* from
the white-hot furnace and from your hands, O
king, may he save us! 18 But even if he will not,
know, O king, that we will not serve your god or
worship the golden statue which you set up."

19 Nebuchadnezzar's face became livid with
utter rage against Shadrach, Meshach, and Abed-
nego. He ordered the furnace to be heated seven
times more than usual 20 and had some of the
strongest men in his army bind Shadrach, Me-
shach, and Abednego and cast them into the
white-hot furnace. 21 They were bound and cast
into the white-hot furnace with their coats, hats,
shoes and other garments, 22 for the king's order
was urgent. So huge a fire was kindled in the
furnace that the flames devoured the men who
threw Shadrach, Meshach, and Abednego into
it. 23 But these three fell, bound, into the midst of
the white-hot furnace.

24 *They walked about in the flames, singing
to God and blessing the Lord. 25 In the fire
Azariah stood up and prayed aloud:

26 "Blessed are you, and praiseworthy,
O Lord, the God of our fathers,
and glorious forever is your name.
27 For you are just in all you have done;
all your deeds are faultless, all your ways
right,
and all your judgments proper.
28 You have executed proper judgments
in all that you have brought upon us
and upon Jerusalem, the holy city of our
fathers.
By a proper judgment you have done all this
because of our sins;
29 For we have sinned and transgressed
by departing from you,
and we have done every kind of evil.
30 Your commandments we have not heeded or
observed,
nor have we done as you ordered us for our
good.
31 Therefore all you have brought upon us,
all you have done to us,
you have done by a proper judgment.
32 You have handed us over to our enemies,
lawless and hateful rebels;
to an unjust king, the worst in all the world.
33 Now we cannot open our mouths;
we, your servants, who revere you,
have become a shame and a reproach.
34 For your name's sake, do not deliver us up
forever,
or make void your covenant.
35 Do not take away your mercy from us,
for the sake of Abraham, your beloved,
Isaac your servant, and Israel your holy one,
36 To whom you promised to multiply their
offspring
like the stars of heaven,
or the sand on the shore of the sea.
37 For we are reduced, O Lord, beyond any other
nation,
brought low everywhere in the world this
day
because of our sins.
38 We have in our day no prince, prophet, or
leader,
no holocaust, sacrifice, oblation, or incense,
no place to offer first fruits, to find favor
with you.
39 But with contrite heart and humble spirit
let us be received;
40 As though it were holocausts of rams and
bullocks,
or thousands of fat lambs,
So let our sacrifice be in your presence today
as we follow you unreservedly;
for those who trust in you cannot be put to
shame.
41 And now we follow you with our whole heart,
we fear you and we pray to you.
42 Do not let us be put to shame,
but deal with us in your kindness and great
mercy.
43 Deliver us by your wonders,
and bring glory to your name, O Lord:

3, 17: If our God . . . can save us: the youths do not question the efficacy of the divine power, but whether it will be exercised (v 18).

3, 24–90: These verses are inspired additions to the Aramaic text of Daniel, translated from the Greek form of the book. They were originally composed in Hebrew or Aramaic, which has not been preserved. The church has always regarded them as part of the canonical Scriptures.

44 Let all those be routed
who inflict evils on your servants;
Let them be shamed and powerless,
and their strength broken;
45 Let them know that you alone are the Lord God,
glorious over the whole world."

46 Now the king's men who had thrown them
in continued to stoke the furnace with brim-
stone, pitch, tow, and faggots. 47 The flames rose
forty-nine cubits above the furnace, 48 and spread
out, burning the Chaldeans nearby. 49 But the
angel of the Lord went down into the furnace
with Azariah and his companions, drove the
fiery flames out of the furnace, 50 and made the
inside of the furnace as though a dew-laden
breeze were blowing through it. The fire in no
way touched them or caused them pain or harm.
51 Then these three in the furnace with one voice
sang, glorifying and blessing God:

52 "Blessed are you, O Lord, the God of our fathers,
praiseworthy and exalted above all forever;
And blessed is your holy and glorious name,
praiseworthy and exalted above all for all ages.
53 Blessed are you in the temple of your holy glory,
praiseworthy and glorious above all forever.
54 Blessed are you on the throne of your kingdom,
praiseworthy and exalted above all forever.
55 Blessed are you who look into the depths
from your throne upon the cherubim,
praiseworthy and exalted above all forever.
56 Blessed are you in the firmament of heaven,
praiseworthy and glorious forever.
57 Bless the Lord, all you works of the Lord,
praise and exalt him above all forever.
58 Angels of the Lord, bless the Lord,
praise and exalt him above all forever.
59 You heavens, bless the Lord,
praise and exalt him above all forever.[f]
60 All you waters above the heavens, bless the Lord,
praise and exalt him above all forever.
61 All you hosts of the Lord, bless the Lord;
praise and exalt him above all forever.
62 Sun and moon, bless the Lord;
praise and exalt him above all forever.
63 Stars of heaven, bless the Lord;
praise and exalt him above all forever.
64 Every shower and dew, bless the Lord;
praise and exalt him above all forever.
65 All you winds, bless the Lord;
praise and exalt him above all forever.
66 Fire and heat, bless the Lord;
praise and exalt him above all forever.
67 [Cold and chill, bless the Lord;
praise and exalt him above all forever.
68 Dew and rain, bless the Lord;
praise and exalt him above all forever.]
69 Frost and chill, bless the Lord;
praise and exalt him above all forever.
70 Ice and snow, bless the Lord;
praise and exalt him above all forever.
71 Nights and days, bless the Lord;
praise and exalt him above all forever.
72 Light and darkness, bless the Lord;
praise and exalt him above all forever.
73 Lightnings and clouds, bless the Lord;
praise and exalt him above all forever.
74 Let the earth bless the Lord,
praise and exalt him above all forever.
75 Mountains and hills, bless the Lord;
praise and exalt him above all forever.
76 Everything growing from the earth, bless the Lord;
praise and exalt him above all forever.
77 You springs, bless the Lord;
praise and exalt him above all forever.
78 Seas and rivers, bless the Lord;
praise and exalt him above all forever.
79 You dolphins and all water creatures, bless the Lord;
praise and exalt him above all forever.
80 All you birds of the air, bless the Lord;
praise and exalt him above all forever.
81 All you beasts, wild and tame, bless the Lord;
praise and exalt him above all forever.
82 You sons of men, bless the Lord;

f 59f: Ps 148, 4.

praise and exalt him above all forever.
83 O Israel, bless the Lord;
praise and exalt him above all forever.
84 Priests of the Lord, bless the Lord;
praise and exalt him above all forever.
85 Servants of the Lord, bless the Lord;
praise and exalt him above all forever.
86 Spirits and souls of the just, bless the Lord;
praise and exalt him above all forever.
87 Holy men of humble heart, bless the Lord;
praise and exalt him above all forever.
88 Hananiah, Azariah, Mishael, bless the Lord;
praise and exalt him above all forever.
For he has delivered us from the nether world,
and saved us from the power of death;
He has freed us from the raging flame
and delivered us from the fire.
89 Give thanks to the Lord, for he is good,
for his mercy endures forever.
90 Bless the God of gods, all you who fear the
Lord;
praise him and give him thanks,
because his mercy endures forever."

Hearing them sing, and astonished at seeing
them alive, 91 King Nebuchadnezzar rose in
haste and asked his nobles, "Did we not cast
three men bound into the fire?" "Assuredly, O
king," they answered. 92 "But," he replied, "I see
four men unfettered and unhurt, walking in the
fire, and the fourth looks like a son of God."*
93 Then Nebuchadnezzar came to the opening of
the white-hot furnace and called to Shadrach,
Meshach, and Abednego: "Servants of the most
high God, come out." Thereupon Shadrach,
Meshach, and Abednego came out of the fire.
94 When the satraps, prefects, governors, and
nobles of the king came together, they saw that
the fire had had no power over the bodies of
these men; not a hair of their heads had been
singed, nor were their garments altered; there
was not even a smell of fire about them.
95 Nebuchadnezzar exclaimed, "Blessed be the
God of Shadrach, Meshach, and Abednego, who
sent his angel to deliver the servants that trusted
in him; they disobeyed the royal command and
yielded their bodies rather than serve or worship
any god except their own God. 96 Therefore I
decree for nations and peoples of every language
that whoever blasphemes the God of Shadrach,
Meshach, and Abednego shall be cut to pieces
and his house destroyed. For there is no other
God who can rescue like this." 97 Then the king
promoted Shadrach, Meshach, and Abednego in
the province of Babylon.

Vision of the Great Tree* 98 King Nebuchad-
nezzar to the nations and peoples of every
language, wherever they dwell on earth: abun-
dant peace! 99 It has seemed good to me to
publish the signs and wonders which the most
high God* has accomplished in my regard.

100 How great are his signs, how mighty his
wonders;
his kingdom is an everlasting kingdom,
and his dominion endures through all
generations.[g]

CHAPTER 4

1 I, Nebuchadnezzar, was at home in my
palace, content and prosperous. 2 I had a terrify-
ing dream as I lay in bed, and the images and the
visions of my mind frightened me. 3 So I issued a
decree that all the wise men of Babylon should
be brought before me to give the interpretation
of the dream. 4 When the magicians, enchanters,
Chaldeans, and astrologers had come in, I re-
lated the dream before them; but none of them
could tell me its meaning. 5 [h]Finally there came
before me Daniel, whose name is Belteshazzar
after the name of my god,* and in whom is the
spirit of the holy God. I repeated the dream to

3, 92: A son of God: an angel; cf Jb 1, 6.

3, 98—4, 34: This section has the form of a letter written by Nebuchadnezzar to his subjects.

3, 99: The most high God: the Jews, especially in the diaspora, used this title to distinguish their God from those of the pagans. On the lips of a polytheist (so also in v 93) it was merely the title of another god. It was an ancient divine name used in Canaan; cf Gn 14, 18.

4, 5: After the name of my god: Belteshazzar, the Babylonian name given to Daniel at the king's orders (Dn 1, 7), is Balatsu-ussur, "protect his life." In the king's intention, this would be an abbreviation for Bel-balatsu-ussur. It would thus include an appeal to the god Bel, originally the name of the city god of Nippur, and later identified with Marduk, the chief god of Babylon. Daniel's use of the name would refer the prayer rather to the true God.

g Dn 4, 31; 7, 14. h Gn 41, 38.

him: 6“Belteshazzar, chief of the magicians, I
know that the spirit of the holy God is in you and
no mystery is too difficult for you; tell me the
meaning of the visions that I saw in my dream.
7“These were the visions I saw while in bed: I
saw a tree of great height at the center of the
world. 8It was large and strong, with its top
touching the heavens, and it could be seen to the
ends of the earth. 9Its leaves were beautiful and
its fruit abundant, providing food for all. Under it
the wild beasts found shade, in its branches the
birds of the air nested; all men ate of it. 10In the
vision I saw while in bed, a holy sentinel* came
down from heaven, 11and cried out:

*“ ‘Cut down the tree and lop off its branches,
strip off its leaves and scatter its fruit;
let the beasts flee its shade, and the birds its
branches.
12 But leave in the earth its stump and roots,
fettered with iron and bronze, in the grass
of the field.
Let him be bathed with the dew of heaven;
his lot be to eat, among beasts, the grass of
the earth.
13 Let his mind be changed from the human;
let him be given the sense of a beast,
till seven years pass over him.
14 By decree of the sentinels is this decided,
by order of the holy ones, this sentence;
That all who live may know
that the Most High rules over the kingdom
of men:
He can give it to whom he will,
or set over it the lowliest of men.’ [i]

15“This is the dream that I, King Nebuchad-
nezzar, had. Now, Belteshazzar, tell me its
meaning. Although none of the wise men in my
kingdom can tell me the meaning, you can,
because the spirit of the holy God is in you.”
16Then Daniel, whose name was Belteshaz-
zar, was appalled for a while, terrified by his
thoughts. “Belteshazzar,” the king said to him,
“let not the dream or its meaning terrify you.”
17“My lord,” Belteshazzar replied, “this dream
should be for your enemies, and its meaning for
your foes.* The large, strong tree that you saw,
with its top touching the heavens, that could be
seen by the whole earth, 18which had beautiful
foliage and abundant fruit, providing food for all,
under which the wild beasts lived, and in whose
branches the birds of the air dwelt— 19you are
that tree, O king, large and strong! Your majesty
has become so great as to touch the heavens,
and your rule extends over the whole earth.
20As for the king’s vision of a holy sentinel that
came down from heaven and proclaimed: ‘Cut
down the tree and destroy it, but leave in the
earth its stump and roots, fettered with iron and
bronze in the grass of the field; let him be bathed
with the dew of heaven, and let his lot be among
wild beasts till seven years pass over him’—
21this is its meaning, O king; this is the sentence
which the Most High has passed upon my lord
king: 22 [j]You shall be cast out from among men
and dwell with wild beasts; you shall be given
grass to eat like an ox and be bathed with the
dew of heaven;* seven years shall pass over you,
until you know that the Most High rules over
the kingdom of men and gives it to whom he
will. 23The command that the stump and roots
of the tree are to be left means that your
kingdom shall be preserved for you, once you
have learned it is heaven that rules.
24 [k]Therefore, O king, take my advice; atone for
your sins by good deeds, and for your misdeeds
by kindness to the poor; then your prosperity
will be long.”*
25All this happened to King Nebuchadnezzar.
26Twelve months later, as he was walking on the
roof of the royal palace in Babylon, 27the king
said, “Babylon the great! Was it not I, with my
great strength, who built it as a royal residence
for my splendor and majesty?”* 28While these

4, 10: A holy sentinel: an angel. This term is found in the Bible only in this chapter of Daniel, but it is common in later Jewish literature.

4, 11ff: As the tree is Nebuchadnezzar (v 19), the description passes from metaphor to the reality.

4, 17: “This dream . . . for your foes”: Daniel speaks as a courtier.

4, 22: The description is of a form of insanity called lycanthropy, in which the patient acts like a wolf.

4, 24: A classic Scriptural text for the efficacy of good works.

4, 27: The words attributed to the king are similar to the boastings in the royal inscriptions by which the Mesopotamian

i 1 Sm 2, 8; 16, 11; Is 62, 6. j Dn 5, 21. k Sir 3, 30; 4, 8.

words were still on the king's lips, a voice spoke from heaven, "It has been decreed for you, King Nebuchadnezzar, that your kingdom is taken from you! 29 You shall be cast out from among men, and shall dwell with wild beasts; you shall be given grass to eat like an ox, and seven years shall pass over you, until you learn that the Most High rules over the kingdom of men and gives it to whom he will." 30 *At once this was fulfilled. Nebuchadnezzar was cast out from among men, he ate grass like an ox, and his body was bathed with the dew of heaven, until his hair grew like the feathers of an eagle, and his nails like the claws of a bird.

31 [l]When this period was over, I, Nebuchadnezzar, raised my eyes to heaven; my reason was restored to me, and I blessed the Most High, I praised and glorified him who lives forever:

His dominion is an everlasting dominion,
and his kingdom endures through all generations.
32 All who live on the earth are counted as nothing;
he does as he pleases with the powers of heaven
as well as with those who live on the earth.
There is no one who can stay his hand
or say to him, "What have you done?"

33 At the same time my reason returned to me, and for the glory of my kingdom, my majesty and my splendor returned to me. My nobles and lords sought me out; I was restored to my kingdom, and became much greater than before. 34 Therefore, I, Nebuchadnezzar, now praise and exalt and glorify the King of heaven, because all his works are right and his ways just; and those who walk in pride he is able to humble.

CHAPTER 5

The Writing on the Wall 1 King Belshazzar* gave a great banquet for a thousand of his lords, with whom he drank. 2 Under the influence of the wine, he ordered the gold and silver vessels which Nebuchadnezzar, his father,* had taken from the temple in Jerusalem, to be brought in so that the king, his lords, his wives and his entertainers might drink from them. 3 When the gold and silver vessels taken from the house of God in Jerusalem had been brought in, and while the king, his lords, his wives and his entertainers were drinking 4 wine from them, they praised their gods of gold and silver, bronze and iron, wood and stone.

5 Suddenly, opposite the lampstand, the fingers of a human hand appeared, writing on the plaster of the wall in the king's palace. When the king saw the wrist and hand that wrote, 6 his face blanched; his thoughts terrified him, his hip joints shook, and his knees knocked. 7 The king shouted for the enchanters, Chaldeans, and astrologers to be brought in. "Whoever reads this writing and tells me what it means," he said to the wise men of Babylon, "shall be clothed in purple, wear a golden collar about his neck, and be third in the government of the kingdom." 8 But though all the king's wise men came in, none of them could either read the writing or tell the king what it meant. 9 Then King Belshazzar was greatly terrified; his face went ashen, and his lords were thrown into confusion.

10 When the queen heard of the discussion between the king and his lords, she entered the banquet hall and said, "O king, live forever! Be not troubled in mind, nor look so pale! 11 There is a man in your kingdom in whom is the spirit of the holy God; during the lifetime of your father he was seen to have brilliant knowledge and god-like wisdom. In fact, King Nebuchadnezzar,

---

kings testified to their mighty works.

4, 30ff: There is no certainty of any such thing happening to Nebuchadnezzar as is described here. Some scholars think that the Nebuchadnezzar of this chapter is actually Nabonidus, the father of Belshazzar, who was mysteriously absent from Babylon for a number of years. The Biblical author's chief interest was not in the historicity of this popular tale, but in the object lesson it contained for the proud "divine" kings of the Seleucid dynasty.

5, 1: King Belshazzar: Belshazzar was actually the crown prince, but he had been given royal authority in Babylon by his father Nabonidus.

5, 2: Nebuchadnezzar, his father: several kings of Babylon intervened between Nebuchadnezzar and Belshazzar. Either the term father is used here in the broad sense of "remote predecessor," or the name Nebuchadnezzar is used for "Nabonidus."

l Dn 3, 100; 7, 14.

your father, made him chief of the magicians, enchanters, Chaldeans, and astrologers, 12because of the extraordinary mind possessed by this Daniel, whom the king named Belteshazzar. He knew and understood how to interpret dreams, explain enigmas, and solve difficulties. Now therefore, summon Daniel to tell you what this means."

13Then Daniel was brought into the presence of the king. The king asked him, "Are you the Daniel, the Jewish exile, whom my father, the king, brought from Judah? 14I have heard that the spirit of God is in you, that you possess brilliant knowledge and extraordinary wisdom. 15Now, the wise men and enchanters were brought in to me to read this writing and tell me its meaning, but they could not say what the words meant. 16But I have heard that you can interpret dreams and solve difficulties; if you are able to read the writing and tell me what it means, you shall be clothed in purple, wear a gold collar about your neck, and be third in the government of the kingdom."

17Daniel answered the king: "You may keep your gifts, or give your presents to someone else; but the writing I will read for you, O king, and tell you what it means. 18The Most High God gave your father Nebuchadnezzar a great kingdom and glorious majesty. 19Because he made him so great, the nations and peoples of every language dreaded and feared him. Whomever he wished, he killed or let live; whomever he wished, he exalted or humbled. 20But when his heart became proud and his spirit hardened by insolence, he was put down from his royal throne and deprived of his glory; 21 [m]he was cast out from among men and was made insensate as a beast; he lived with wild asses, and ate grass like an ox; his body was bathed with the dew of heaven, until he learned that the Most High God rules over the kingdom of men and appoints over it whom he will. 22You, his son, Belshazzar, have not humbled your heart, though you knew all this; 23you have rebelled against the Lord of heaven. You had the vessels of his temple brought before you, so that you and your nobles, your wives and your entertainers, might drink wine from them; and you praised the gods of silver and gold, bronze and iron, wood and stone, that neither see nor hear nor have intelligence. But the God in whose hand is your life breath and the whole course of your life, you did not glorify. 24By him were the wrist and hand sent, and the writing set down.

25"This is the writing that was inscribed: MENE, TEKEL, and PERES.* These words mean: 26*MENE, God has numbered your kingdom and put an end to it; 27TEKEL, you have been weighed on the scales and found wanting; 28PERES, your kingdom has been divided and given to the Medes and Persians."

29Then by order of Belshazzar they clothed Daniel in purple, with a gold collar about his neck, and proclaimed him third in the government of the kingdom. 30The same night Belshazzar, the Chaldean king, was slain:

CHAPTER 6

1And Darius the Mede* succeeded to the kingdom at the age of sixty-two.

In the Lions' Den 2Darius decided to appoint over his entire kingdom one hundred and twenty satraps, to safeguard his interests; 3these were accountable to three supervisors, one of whom was Daniel. 4Daniel outshone all the supervisors and satraps because an extraordinary spirit was in him, and the king thought of giving him authority over the entire kingdom. 5Therefore the supervisors and satraps tried to find grounds for accusation against Daniel as regards

5, 25: Mene, Tekel, and Peres: these seem to be the Aramaic names of weights and monetary values: the mina, the shekel (the sixtieth part of a mina), and the parsu (a half-mina).

5, 26ff: Daniel interprets these three terms by a play on the words: Mene, connected with the verb meaning to number; Tekel, with the verb meaning to weigh; Peres, with the verb meaning to divide. There is also a play on the last term with the word for Persians.

6, 1: Darius the Mede: unknown in profane history. The Median kingdom had already been conquered by Cyrus the Persian, and it was Cyrus who captured Babylon. Evidently the author of Daniel has deliberately adopted an apocalyptic view of history, derived from prophecy (cf Is 13, 17ff; Jer 51, 11. 28ff), according to which the Medes formed the second of four world kingdoms preceding the messianic times; see note on Dn 2, 36–45. The character of Darius the Mede has probably been modeled on that of the Persian King Darius the Great (522–486 B.C.), the second successor of Cyrus.

m Dn 4, 22.

the administration. But they could accuse him of no wrongdoing; because he was trustworthy, no fault of neglect or misconduct was to be found in him. [6]Then these men said to themselves, "We shall find no grounds for accusation against this Daniel unless by way of the law of his God." [7]So these supervisors and satraps went thronging to the king and said to him, "King Darius, live forever! [8] [n]All the supervisors of the kingdom, the prefects, satraps, nobles, and governors are agreed that the following prohibition ought to be put in force by royal decree: no one is to address any petition to god or man for thirty days, except to you, O king; otherwise he shall be cast into a den of lions. [9]Now, O king, issue the prohibition over your signature, immutable and irrevocable* under Mede and Persian law." [10]So King Darius signed the prohibition and made it law.

[11]Even after Daniel heard that this law had been signed, he continued his custom of going home to kneel in prayer and give thanks to his God in the upper chamber three times a day, with the windows open toward Jerusalem. [12]So these men rushed in and found Daniel praying and pleading before his God. [13]Then they went to remind the king about the prohibition: "Did you not decree, O king, that no one is to address a petition to god or man for thirty days, except to you, O king; otherwise he shall be cast into a den of lions?" The king answered them, "The decree is absolute, irrevocable under the Mede and Persian law." [14]To this they replied, "Daniel, the Jewish exile, has paid no attention to you, O king, or to the decree you issued; three times a day he offers his prayer." [15]The king was deeply grieved at this news and he made up his mind to save Daniel; he worked till sunset to rescue him. [16]But these men insisted. "Keep in mind, O king," they said, "that under the Mede and Persian law every royal prohibition or decree is irrevocable." [17]So the king ordered Daniel to be brought and cast into the lions' den.* To Daniel he said, "May your God, whom you serve so constantly, save you." [18]To forestall any tampering, the king sealed with his own ring and the rings of the lords the stone that had been brought to block the opening of the den.

[19]Then the king returned to his palace for the night; he refused to eat and he dismissed the entertainers. Since sleep was impossible for him, [20]the king rose very early the next morning and hastened to the lions' den. [21]As he drew near, he cried out to Daniel sorrowfully, "O Daniel, servant of the living God, has the God whom you serve so constantly been able to save you from the lions?" [22] [o]Daniel answered the king: "O king, live forever! [23]My God has sent his angel and closed the lions' mouths so that they have not hurt me. For I have been found innocent before him; neither to you have I done any harm, O king!" [24]This gave the king great joy. At his order Daniel was removed from the den, unhurt because he trusted in his God. [25]The king then ordered the men who had accused Daniel, along with their children and their wives, to be cast into the lions' den. Before they reached the bottom of the den, the lions overpowered them and crushed all their bones.

[26]Then King Darius wrote to the nations and peoples of every language, wherever they dwell on the earth: "All peace to you! [27]I decree that throughout my royal domain the God of Daniel is to be reverenced and feared:

"For he is the living God, enduring forever;
  his kingdom shall not be destroyed,
  and his dominion shall be without end.
[28]He is a deliverer and savior,
  working signs and wonders in heaven and
    on earth,
  and he delivered Daniel from the lions'
    power." [p]

[29]So Daniel fared well during the reign of Darius and the reign of Cyrus the Persian.

6, 9: Immutable and irrevocable: the passages in Est 1, 19 and 8, 8 also refer to the immutability of Medo-Persian laws. The historian Diodorus Siculus indicates that such a concept existed in the time of Darius III (335–331 B.C.), the last of the Persian kings. Cf vv 13. 16.

6, 17: The lions' den: a pit too deep to be easily scaled; its opening was blocked with a stone (v 18).

n Est 1, 19. o 1 Mc 2, 60. p Dn 1, 21.

II: Daniel's Visions

CHAPTER 7

Vision of the Four Beasts* 1 In the first year of
King Belshazzar of Babylon, Daniel had a dream
as he lay in bed, and was terrified by the visions
of his mind. Then he wrote down the dream;
the account began: 2 In the vision I saw during
the night, suddenly the four winds of heaven
stirred up the great sea,* 3 from which emerged
four immense beasts, each different from the
others. 4 The first was like a lion, but with eagle's
wings.* While I watched, the wings were
plucked; it was raised from the ground to stand
on two feet like a man, and given a human
mind. 5 The second was like a bear;* it was
raised up on one side, and among the teeth in its
mouth were three tusks. It was given the order,
"Up, devour much flesh." 6 After this I looked
and saw another beast, like a leopard;* on its
back were four wings like those of a bird, and it
had four heads. To this beast dominion was
given. 7 After this, in the visions of the night I
saw the fourth beast,* different from all the
others, terrifying, horrible, and of extraordinary
strength; it had great iron teeth with which it
devoured and crushed, and what was left it
trampled with its feet. 8 I was considering the ten
horns it had, when suddenly another, a little
horn, sprang out of their midst, and three of the
previous horns were torn away to make room for
it. This horn had eyes like a man, and a mouth
that spoke arrogantly. 9 *As I watched,

Thrones were set up
  and the Ancient One took his throne.
His clothing was snow bright,
  and the hair on his head as white as wool;
His throne was flames of fire,
  with wheels of burning fire.
10 A surging stream of fire
  flowed out from where he sat;
Thousands upon thousands were ministering
  to him,
  and myriads upon myriads attended him. [q]

The court was convened, and the books were
opened. 11 I watched, then, from the first of the
arrogant words which the horn spoke, until the
beast was slain and its body thrown into the fire
to be burnt up. 12 The other beasts, which also
lost their dominion, were granted a prolongation
of life for a time and a season. 13 As the visions
during the night continued, I saw

One like a son of man* coming,
  on the clouds of heaven;
When he reached the Ancient One
  and was presented before him,
14 He received dominion, glory, and kingship;
  nations and peoples of every language serve
  him.
His dominion is an everlasting dominion
  that shall not be taken away,
  his kingship shall not be destroyed. [r]

7, 1–27: The significance of this vision is the same as that of Nebuchadnezzar's dream in chapter 2; see note on Dn 2, 36–45. To the four succeeding world kingdoms, Babylonian, Median, Persian, and Greek, is opposed and messianic kingdom of the people of God. The imagery of this chapter has been used extensively in the Revelation of St. John, where it is applied to the Roman empire, the persecutor of the church.

7, 2: The great sea: the primordial ocean beneath the earth, according to primitive cosmology (Gn 7, 11; 49, 25). This was thought to contain various monsters (Is 27, 1; Jb 7, 12), and in particular mythological monsters symbolizing the chaos which God had vanquished in ancient times (Jb 9, 13; 26, 13; etc.).

7, 4: The representation of the Babylonian empire as a winged lion, a common motif in Babylonian art, symbolizes the bestial power hostile to God. The two wings that were plucked represent Nebuchadnezzar and Belshazzar. On two feet like a man . . . a human mind: contrasts with what is said in Dn 4, 13. 30.

7, 5: A bear: represents the Median empire, its three tusks symbolizing its destructive nature; hence, the command: "Up, devour much flesh."

7, 6: A leopard: used to symbolize the swiftness with which Cyrus the Persian established his kingdom. Four heads: corresponding to the four Persian kings of Dn 11, 2.

7, 7f: Alexander's empire was different from all the others in that it was Western rather than Oriental in inspiration. The ten horns represent the kings of the Seleucid dynasty, the only part of the Hellenistic empire that concerned the author. The little horn is Antiochus IV Epiphanes (175–163 B.C.), the worst of the Seleucid kings, who usurped the throne.

7, 9f: A vision of the heavenly throne of God (the Ancient One), who sits in judgment (symbolized by fire) over the nations. Some of the details of the vision, depicting the divine majesty and omnipotence, are to be found in Ez 1.

7, 13f: One like a son of man: in contrast to the wordly kingdoms opposed to God, which appear as beasts, the glorified people of God that will form his kingdom on earth is represented in human form (v 18). Just as our Lord applied the figure of the stone hewn from the mountain to himself (Dn 2, 36–45), he also made the title, "Son of Man" his most characteristic way of referring to himself, as the One in whom and through whom the salvation of God's people came to be realized.

q Rv 5, 11. r Dn 3, 100; 4, 31; Mi 4, 7; Lk 1, 32.

15 I, Daniel, found my spirit anguished within
its sheath of flesh, and I was terrified by the
visions of my mind. 16 I approached one of those
present and asked him what all this meant in
truth; in answer, he made known to me the
meaning of the things: 17 "These four great
beasts stand for four kingdoms which shall arise
on the earth. 18 But the holy ones of the Most
High shall receive the kingship, to possess it
forever and ever."

19 But I wished to make certain about the
fourth beast, so very terrible and different from
the others, devouring and crushing with its iron
teeth and bronze claws, and trampling with its
feet what was left; 20 about the ten horns on its
head, and the other one that sprang up, before
which three horns fell; about the horn with the
eyes and the mouth that spoke arrogantly, which
appeared greater than its fellows. 21 For, as I
watched, that horn made war against the holy
ones and was victorious 22 until the Ancient One
arrived; judgment was pronounced in favor of
the holy ones of the Most High, and the time
came when the holy ones possessed the king-
dom. 23 He answered me thus:

"The fourth beast shall be a fourth kingdom on
earth,
different from all the others;
It shall devour the whole earth,
beat it down, and crush it.
24 The ten horns shall be ten kings
rising out of that kingdom;
another shall rise up after them,
Different from those before him,
who shall lay low three kings.
25 He shall speak against the Most High
and oppress the holy ones of the Most High,
thinking to change the feast days and the
law.*
They shall be handed over to him
for a year, two years, and a half-year.
26 But when the court is convened,
and his power is taken away
by final and absolute destruction,
27 Then the kingship and dominion and majesty
of all the kingdoms under the heavens
shall be given to the holy people of the Most
High,
Whose kingdom shall be everlasting:
all dominions shall serve and obey him."

28 The report concluded: I, Daniel, was greatly
terrified by my thoughts, and my face blanched,
but I kept the matter to myself.*

CHAPTER 8

Vision of the Ram and He-goat* 1 After this
first vision, I, Daniel, had another, in the third
year of the reign of King Belshazzar. 2 In my
vision I saw myself in the fortress of Susa* in the
province of Elam; I was beside the river Ulai. 3 I
looked up and saw standing by the river a ram
with two great horns, the one larger and newer
than the other. 4 I saw the ram butting toward
the west, north, and south. No beast could
withstand it or be rescued from its power; it did
what it pleased and became very powerful.

5 As I was reflecting, a he-goat with a promi-
nent horn on its forehead suddenly came from
the west across the whole earth without touch-
ing the ground. 6 It approached the two-horned
ram I had seen standing by the river, and rushed
toward it with savage force. 7 I saw it attack the
ram with furious blows when they met, and
break both its horns. It threw the ram, which
had not the force to withstand it, to the ground,
and trampled upon it; and no one could rescue it
from its power.

8 The he-goat became very powerful, but at
the height of its power the great horn was
shattered, and in its place came up four others,

7, 25: The reference is to the persecutions of Antiochus IV and his attempt to force the Jews to give up their customs and to adopt Hellenistic ways (1 Mc 1, 33f). A year, two years, and a half-year: an indefinite, evil period of time. As seven is the Jewish "perfect" number, half of it signifies great imperfection. Actually, this corresponds fairly accurately to the duration of Antiochus' persecution.

7, 28: This verse ends the Aramaic part of the Book of Daniel.

8, 1–27: This vision repeats the major part of the preceding one, though in a more explicit fashion. As explained in vv 20ff, the two-horned ram represents the combined kingdom of the Medes and Persians, destroyed by Alexander's Hellenistic empire originating in the west. Once again the author is interested only in the Seleucid dynasty, which emerged from the dissolution of Alexander's empire after his death in 323 B.C.

8, 2: The fortress of Susa: the royal palace of the Persian kings in the ancient territory of Elam, east of Babylonia. The river Ulai: a canal along the northern side of Susa.

facing the four winds of heaven. 9 Out of one of
them came a little horn* which kept growing
toward the south, the east, and the glorious
country. 10 Its power extended to the host of
heaven,* so that it cast down to earth some of
the host and some of the stars and trampled on
them. 11 It boasted even against the prince of the
host, from whom it removed the daily sacrifice,
and whose sanctuary it cast down, 12 as well as
the host, while sin replaced the daily sacrifice. It
cast truth to the ground, and was succeeding in
its undertaking.

13 I heard a holy one speaking, and another
said to whichever one it was that spoke, "How
long shall the events of this vision last concern-
ing the daily sacrifice, the desolating sin* which
is placed there, the sanctuary, and the trampled
host?" 14 He answered him, "For two thousand
three hundred evenings and mornings; then the
sanctuary shall be purified."

15 While I, Daniel, sought the meaning of the
vision I had seen, a manlike figure stood before
me, 16 and on the Ulai I heard a human voice
that cried out, "Gabriel,* explain the vision to
this man." 17 When he came near where I was
standing, I fell prostrate in terror. But he said to
me, "Understand, son of man, that the vision
refers to the end time."* 18 As he spoke to me, I
fell forward in a faint; he touched me and made
me stand up. 19 "I will show you," he said, "what
is to happen later in the period of wrath; for at
the appointed time, there will be an end.

20 "The two-horned ram you saw represents
the kings of the Medes and Persians. 21 The he-
goat is the king of the Greeks, and the great horn
on its forehead is the first king. 22 The four that
rose in its place when it was broken are four
kingdoms that will issue from his nation, but
without his strength.

23 "After their reign,
when sinners have reached their measure,
There shall arise a king, impudent
and skilled in intrigue.
24 He shall be strong and powerful,
bring about fearful ruin,
and succeed in his undertaking.
He shall destroy powerful peoples;
25 his cunning shall be against the holy ones,
his treacherous conduct shall succeed.
He shall be proud of heart
and destroy many by stealth.
But when he rises against the prince of
princes,
he shall be broken without a hand being
raised.
26 The vision of the evenings and the mornings
is true, as spoken;
Do you, however, keep this vision
undisclosed,
because the days are to be many."

27 I, Daniel, was weak and ill for some days;
then I arose and took care of the king's affairs.
But I was appalled at the vision, which I could
not understand.

CHAPTER 9

Gabriel and the Seventy Weeks 1 It was the
first year that Darius,* son of Ahasuerus, of the
race of the Medes, reigned over the kingdom of
the Chaldeans; 2 [s]in the first year of his reign I,
Daniel, tried to understand in the Scriptures the
counting of the years of which the LORD spoke to
the prophet Jeremiah: that for the ruins of
Jerusalem seventy years* must be fulfilled.

3 I turned to the Lord God, pleading in earnest
prayer, with fasting, sackcloth, and ashes. 4 [t]I
prayed to the LORD, my God, and confessed,

8, 9: The little horn, as in chapter 7, is Antiochus IV. The glorious country: Palestine.

8, 10ff: The host of heaven: ordinarily meaning the stars, here refers to the people of God; cf Dn 12, 3. The prince of the host: God himself, with whose holy religion Antiochus interfered (1 Mc 1, 45).

8, 13: The desolating sin: the Hebrew contains a wordplay (shomem) on the name Baal Shamem ("lord of the heavens," the Greek Zeus Olympios), referring to the statue with which Antiochus profaned the temple of Jerusalem (2 Mc 6, 2).

8, 16: The angel Gabriel is mentioned here for the first time in the Bible. There is wordplay in the preceding verse on geber—manlike figure.

8, 17: The end time: the day of the Lord, when God sits in judgment on his enemies (v 19).

9, 1: Darius: see the note on Dn 6, 1.

9, 2: Seventy years: the prophet Jeremiah (25, 11; 29, 10) prophesied a Babylonian captivity of seventy years, a round number signifying the complete passing away of the existing generation. Jeremiah's prophecy was fulfilled in the capture of Babylon by Cyrus and the subsequent return of the Jews to Palestine.

s 2f: Jer 25, 11; 29, 10. t Neh 1, 5.

"Ah, Lord, great and awesome God, you who
keep your merciful covenant toward those who
love you and observe your commandments!
5 [u]We have sinned, been wicked and done evil;
we have rebelled and departed from your com-
mandments and your laws. 6 We have not
obeyed your servants the prophets, who spoke
in your name to our kings, our princes, our
fathers, and all the people of the land. 7 Justice,
O Lord, is on your side; we are shamefaced
even to this day: the men of Judah, the resi-
dents of Jerusalem, and all Israel, near and far,
in all the countries to which you have scattered
them because of their treachery toward you. 8 O
LORD, we are shamefaced, like our kings, our
princes, and our fathers, for having sinned
against you. 9 But yours, O Lord, our God, are
compassion and forgiveness! Yet we rebelled
against you 10 and paid no heed to your com-
mand, O LORD, our God, to live by the law you
gave us through your servants the prophets.
11 [v]Because all Israel transgressed your law and
went astray, not heeding your voice, the sworn
malediction, recorded in the law of Moses, the
servant of God, was poured out over us for our
sins. 12 You carried out the threats you spoke
against us and against those who governed us,
by bringing upon us in Jerusalem the greatest
calamity that has ever occurred under heaven.
13 As it is written* in the law of Moses, this
calamity came full upon us. As we did not
appease the LORD, our God, by turning back
from our wickedness and recognizing his con-
stancy, 14 so the Lord kept watch over the
calamity and brought it upon us. You, O LORD,
our God, are just in all that you have done, for
we did not listen to your voice.

15 [w]"Now, O Lord, our God, who led your
people out of the land of Egypt with a strong
hand, and made a name for yourself even to this
day, we have sinned, we are guilty. 16 O Lord, in
keeping with all your just deeds, let your anger
and your wrath be turned away from your city
Jerusalem, your holy mountain. On account of
our sins and the crimes of our fathers, Jerusalem
and your people have become the reproach of all
our neighbors. 17 Hear, therefore, O God, the
prayer and petition of your servant; and for your
own sake, O Lord, let your face shine upon your
desolate sanctuary. 18 [x]Give ear, O my God, and
listen; open your eyes and see our ruins and the
city which bears your name. When we present
our petition before you, we rely not on our just
deeds, but on your great mercy. 19 O Lord, hear!
O Lord, pardon! O Lord, be attentive and act
without delay, for your own sake, O my God,
because this city and your people bear your
name!"

20 I was still occupied with my prayer, confess-
ing my sin and the sin of my people Israel,
presenting my petition to the LORD, my God, on
behalf of his holy mountain— 21 [y]I was still
occupied with this prayer, when Gabriel, the one
whom I had seen before in vision, came to me in
rapid flight at the time of the evening sacrifice.*
22 He instructed me in these words: "Daniel, I
have now come to give you understanding.
23 When you began your petition, an answer was
given which I have come to announce, because
you are beloved. Therefore, mark the answer
and understand the vision.

24 "Seventy weeks* are decreed
for your people and for your holy city:

However, the author of Daniel, living during the persecution of Antiochus, sees the conditions of the exile still existing; therefore in his mediation he extends Jeremiah's number to seventy weeks of years (v 24), i.e., seven times seventy years, to characterize the Jewish victory over the Seleucids as the ultimate fulfillment of the prophecy.

9, 13: As it is written: the first time that this formula of Scriptural citation is used in the Bible. The reference (v 11) is to the sanctions of Lv 26, 14ff; Dt 28, 15ff.

9, 21: At the time of the evening sacrifice: between three and four in the afternoon.

9, 24: Seventy weeks: i. e., of years. Just as Jeremiah's seventy years was an approximation (see note on v 2), the four hundred and ninety years here is not to be taken literally. Similarly, the distribution of the "weeks" in the following verses indicates only relative proportions of the total figure. A most holy: an expression used almost always of an object, the altar or the temple, but once (1 Chr 23, 13) of Aaron the high priest. The author sees the definitive establishment of the kingdom of God, realized in the reconsecration of the temple after Antiochus' desecration, or personified in the holy community (like the Son of Man of chapter 7). The Fathers of the church almost unanimously understood the reference to be to Christ, the final realization of the prophecy.

u Bar 1, 17. v Dt 27, 15. w Bar 2, 11; Ex 14, 22. x Jer 25, 29. y Dn 8, 16.

Then transgression will stop and sin will end,
guilt will be expiated,
Everlasting justice will be introduced,
vision and prophecy ratified,
and a most holy will be anointed.
25 Know and understand this:
From the utterance of the word
that Jerusalem was to be rebuilt*
Until one who is anointed and a leader,
there shall be seven weeks.
During sixty-two weeks
it shall be rebuilt,
With streets and trenches,
in time of affliction.
26 After the sixty-two weeks
an anointed* shall be cut down
when he does not possess the city;
And the people of a leader who will come
shall destroy the sanctuary.
Then the end shall come like a torrent;
until the end there shall be war,
the desolation that is decreed.
27 For one week* he shall make
a firm compact with the many;
Half the week
he shall abolish sacrifice and oblation;
On the temple wing shall be the horrible
abomination
until the ruin that is decreed
is poured out upon the horror."[z]

CHAPTER 10

Vision of the Hellenistic Wars* 1 In the third
year of Cyrus, king of Persia, a revelation was
given to Daniel, who had been named Belteshaz-
zar. The revelation was certain: a great war; he
understood it from the vision. 2 In those days, I,
Daniel, mourned* three full weeks. 3 I ate no
savory food, I took no meat or wine, and I did
not anoint myself at all until the end of the three
weeks.

4 On the twenty-fourth day of the first month*
I was on the bank of the great river, the Tigris.
5 As I looked up, I saw a man* dressed in linen
with a belt of fine gold around his waist. 6 His
body was like chrysolite, his face shone like
lightning, his eyes were like fiery torches, his
arms and feet looked like burnished bronze, and
his voice sounded like the roar of a multitude. 7 I
alone, Daniel, saw the vision; but great fear
seized the men who were with me; they fled
and hid themselves, although they did not see
the vision. 8 So I was left alone, seeing this great
vision. No strength remained in me; I turned the
color of death and was powerless. 9 When I
heard the sound of his voice, I fell face forward
in a faint.

10 But then a hand touched me, raising me to
my hands and knees. 11 "Daniel, beloved," he
said to me, "understand the words which I am
speaking to you; stand up, for my mission now is
to you." When he said this to me, I stood up
trembling. 12 "Fear not, Daniel," he continued;
"from the first day you made up your mind to
acquire understanding and humble yourself be-
fore God, your prayer was heard. Because of it I
started out, 13 but the prince of the kingdom of
Persia* stood in my way for twenty-one days,

9, 25: From the utterance . . . to be rebuilt: from the time of Jeremiah's prophecy. One . . . anointed and a leader: either Cyrus, who was called the anointed of the Lord to end the exile (Is 45, 1), or the high priest Joshua, who presided over the rebuilding of the altar of sacrifice after the exile (Ezr 3, 2). Seven weeks: forty-nine years, an approximation of the time of the exile. During sixty-two weeks . . . rebuilt: a period of 434 years, roughly approximating the interval between the rebuilding of Jerusalem after the exile and the beginning of the Seleucid persecution.

9, 26: An anointed: doubtless the high priest Onias III, murdered in 171 B.C., from which the author dates the beginning of the persecution. Onias was in exile when he was killed. A leader: Antiochus IV.

9, 27: One week: the final phase of the period in view, the time of Antiochus' persecution; he is Antiochus himself. The many: the faithless Jews who allied themselves with the heathen; cf 1 Mc 1, 11ff. Half the week: three and a half years; see note on Dn 7, 25. The temple was desecrated by Antiochus from 167 to 165 B.C. The temple wing: probably the main portal. The horrible abomination: see note on Dn 8, 13. Perhaps an inscription was placed on the portal of the temple dedicating it to the Olympian Zeus. Our Lord referred to this passage in his own prediction of the destruction of Jerusalem (Mt 24, 15).

10, 1—12, 13: This final vision repeats some of the material contained in the others. It is concerned with history of the worldly kingdoms from the time of Cyrus to the defeat of the tyrant Antiochus.

10, 2: Mourned: perhaps the author intends to recall the interruption in the rebuilding of the temple, which occurred during this time (Ezr 4, 1-4).

10, 4: The first month: the month Nisan (mid-March to mid-April).

10, 5f: The heavenly person of the vision is probably the angel Gabriel, as in Dn 9, 21. Chrysolite: or topaz, a yellowish precious stone.

10, 13: The prince of the kingdom of Persia: the guardian angel

z Mt 24, 15; 2 Mc 6, 2.

until finally Michael, one of the chief princes, came to help me. I left him there with the prince of the kings of Persia, 14and came to make you understand what shall happen to your people in the days to come; for there is yet a vision concerning those days."

15While he was speaking thus to me, I fell forward and kept silent. 16Then something like a man's hand touched my lips; I opened my mouth and said to the one facing me, "My lord, I was seized with pangs at the vision and I was powerless. 17How can my lord's servant speak with you, my lord? For now no strength or even breath is left in me." 18The one who looked like a man touched me again and strengthened me, saying, 19"Fear not, beloved, you are safe; take courage and be strong." 20When he spoke to me, I grew strong and said, "Speak, my lord, for you have strengthened me." "Do you know," he asked, "why I have come to you? Soon I must fight the prince of Persia again. When I leave, the prince of Greece will come; 21 [a]but I shall tell you what is written in the truthful book. No one supports me against all these except Michael, your prince, 1standing* as a reinforcement and a bulwark for me. 2Now I shall tell you the truth.

CHAPTER 11

"Three kings of Persia* are yet to come; and a fourth shall acquire the greatest riches of all. Strengthened by his riches, he shall rouse all the kingdom of Greece. 3But a powerful king shall appear and rule with great might, doing as he pleases. 4No sooner shall he appear than his kingdom shall be broken and divided in the four directions under heaven; but not among his descendants or in keeping with his mighty rule, for his kingdom shall be torn to pieces and belong to others than they.

5*"The king of the south shall grow strong, but one of his princes shall grow stronger still and govern a domain greater than his. 6After some years they shall become allies: the daughter of the king of the south shall come to the king of the north in the interest of peace. But her bid for power shall fail: and her line shall not be recognized, and she shall be given up, together with those who brought her, her son and her husband. But later 7a descendant of her line shall succeed to his rank, and shall come against the rampart and enter the stronghold of the king of the north, and conquer them. 8Even their gods, with their molten images and their precious vessels of silver and gold, he shall carry away as booty into Egypt. For years he shall have nothing to do with the king of the north. 9Then the latter shall invade the land of the king of the south, and return to his own country.

10"But his sons shall prepare and assemble a great armed host, which shall advance like a flood, then withdraw. When it returns and surges around the stronghold, 11the king of the south, provoked, shall go out to fight against the king of the north, whose great host shall make a stand but shall be given into his hand 12and be carried off. In the pride of his heart, he shall lay low tens of thousands, but he shall not triumph. 13For the king of the north shall raise another army, greater than before; after some years he shall attack with this large army and great resources. 14 [b]In those times many shall resist the king of the south, and outlaws of your people shall rise up in fulfillment of vision, but they shall fail. 15When the king of the north comes, he shall set up siegeworks and take the fortified city by storm. The power of the south shall not withstand him, and not even his picked troops shall have the strength to resist. 16He shall attack

of Persia. The later Judaism ascribed protecting angels to various groups of human society, often as little more than personifications. Michael: the angel who is the protector of God's people (v 21).

10, 1f: Standing . . . truth: these are the first two verses of ch 11.

11, 2–4: The three kings of Persia who follow Cyrus are uncertain, since there were more than three Persian kings between Cyrus and the dissolution of the kingdom. The fourth is doubtless Xerxes I (486–465 B.C.), the great campaigner against Greece. The powerful king is Alexander the Great, who ended the Persian empire by his victory at Issus in 333 B.C.

11, 5–45: These verses describe the dynastic histories of the Ptolemies in Egypt (the king of the south) and the Seleucids in Syria (the king of the north), the two divisions of the Hellenistic empire that were of interest to the author (v 6). In vv 10–20 is described the struggle between the two kingdoms for the control of Palestine, in which the Seleucids were eventually victorious. The reference in v 20 is to Seleucus IV, who sent Heliodorus to plunder the temple treasure in Jerusalem (2 Mc 3). Finally, vv 21–45 describe the career of Antiochus IV and his persecution, in details that have been seen above.

a Rv 12, 7. b Is 19, 1.

him and do as he pleases, with no one to withstand him. He shall stop in the glorious land, dealing destruction. 17 He shall set himself to penetrate the entire strength of his kingdom. He shall conclude an agreement with him and give him a daughter in marriage in order to destroy the kingdom, but this shall not succeed in his favor. 18 He shall turn to the coastland and take many, but a leader shall put an end to his shameful conduct, so that he cannot renew it against him. 19 He shall turn to the strongholds of his own land, but shall stumble and fall, to be found no more. 20 In his stead one shall arise who will send a tax collector through the glorious kingdom, but he shall soon be destroyed, though not in conflict or in battle.

21 "There shall rise in his place a despicable person, to whom the royal insignia shall not be given. By stealth and fraud he shall seize the kingdom. 22 Armed might shall be completely overwhelmed by him and crushed, and even the prince of the covenant. 23 After allying with him, he shall treacherously rise to power with a small party. 24 By stealth he shall enter prosperous provinces and do that which his fathers or grandfathers never did; he shall distribute spoil, booty, and riches among them and devise plots against their strongholds; but only for a time. 25 He shall call on his strength and cleverness to meet the king of the south with a great army; the king of the south shall prepare for battle with a very large and strong army, but he shall not succeed because of the plots devised against him. 26 Even his table companions shall seek to destroy him, his army shall be overwhelmed, and many shall fall slain. 27 The two kings, resolved on evil, shall sit at table together and exchange lies, but they shall have no success, because the appointed end is not yet.

28 "He shall turn back toward his land with great riches, his mind set against the holy covenant; he shall arrange matters and return to his land. 29 At the time appointed he shall come again to the south, but this time it shall not be as before. 30 When ships of the Kittim* confront him, he shall lose heart and retreat. Then he shall direct his rage and energy against the holy covenant; those who forsake it he shall once more single out. 31 Armed forces shall move at his command and defile the sanctuary stronghold, abolishing the daily sacrifice and setting up the horrible abomination. 32 By his deceit he shall make some who were disloyal to the covenant apostatize; but those who remain loyal to their God shall take strong action. 33 The nation's wise men shall instruct the many; though for a time they will become victims of the sword, of flames, exile, and plunder. 34 When they fall, few people shall help them, but many shall join them out of treachery. 35 Of the wise men, some shall fall, so that the rest may be tested, refined, and purified, until the end time which is still appointed to come.

36 *"The king shall do as he pleases, exalting himself and making himself greater than any god; he shall utter dreadful blasphemies against the God of gods. He shall prosper only till divine wrath is ready, for what is determined must take place. 37 He shall have no regard for the gods of his ancestors or for the one in whom women delight; for no god shall he have regard, because he shall make himself greater than all. 38 Instead, he shall give glory to the god of strongholds; a god unknown to his fathers he shall glorify with gold, silver, precious stones, and other treasures. 39 To defend the strongholds he shall station a people of a foreign god. Whoever acknowledges him he shall provide with abundant honor; he shall make them rule over the many and distribute the land as a reward.

40 "At the appointed time the king of the south shall come to grips with him, but the king of the north shall overwhelm him with chariots and horsemen and a great fleet, passing through the countries like a flood. 41 He shall enter the glorious land and many shall fall, except Edom, Moab, and the chief part of Ammon, which shall escape from his power. 42 He shall extend his

11, 30: Kittim: originally this word meant Cypriots or other island dwellers. Here it means the Romans, who forced Antiochus to withdraw from Egypt during his second campaign there.

11, 36–39: Instead of venerating Apollo, one of the gods of his ancestors, Antiochus venerated, and even identified himself with, Zeus Olympios, whom the Romans equated with the god of their fortress in Rome, Jupiter Capitolinus, the god of strongholds.

power over the countries, and not even the land of Egypt shall escape. [43]He shall control the riches of gold and silver and all the treasures of Egypt; Libya and Ethiopia shall be in his train. [44]When news from the east and the north terrifies him, he shall set out with great fury to slay and to doom many. [45]He shall pitch the tents of his royal pavilion between the sea and the glorious holy mountain, but he shall come to his end with none to help him.

CHAPTER 12

[1] "At that time there shall arise
Michael, the great prince,
guardian of your people; [c]
It shall be a time unsurpassed in distress
since nations began until that time.
At that time your people shall escape,
everyone who is found written in the book.*
[2] Many of those who sleep
in the dust of the earth shall awake;*
Some shall live forever,
others shall be an everlasting horror and disgrace. [d]
[3] But the wise shall shine brightly
like the splendor of the firmament,
And those who lead the many to justice
shall be like the stars forever. [e]

[4]"As for you, Daniel, keep secret the message and seal the book until the end time; many shall fall away and evil shall increase."

[5]I, Daniel, looked and saw two others, one standing on either bank of the river. [6]One of them said to the man clothed in linen, who was upstream, "How long shall it be to the end of these appalling things?" [7][f]The man clothed in linen, who was upstream, lifted his right and left hands to heaven; and I heard him swear by him who lives forever that it should be for a year, two years, a half-year;* and that, when the power of the destroyer of the holy people was brought to an end, all these things should end. [8]I heard, but I did not understand; so I asked, "My lord, what follows this?" [9]"Go, Daniel," he said, "because the words are to be kept secret and sealed until the end time. [10]Many shall be refined, purified, and tested, but the wicked shall prove wicked; none of them shall have understanding, but the wise shall have it. [11]From the time that the daily sacrifice is abolished and the horrible abomination is set up, there shall be one thousand two hundred and ninety days. [12]Blessed is the man who has patience and perseveres until the one thousand three hundred and thirty-five days. [13]Go, take your rest, you shall rise for your reward at the end of days."

III: Appendix*

CHAPTER 13

Susanna's Virtue [1]In Babylon there lived a man named Joakim, [2]who married a very beautiful and God-fearing woman, Susanna, the daughter of Hilkiah; [3]her pious parents had trained their daughter according to the law of Moses. [4]Joakim was very rich; he had a garden near his house, and the Jews had recourse to him often because he was the most respected of them all.

[5]That year, two elders of the people were appointed judges, of whom the Lord said, "Wickedness has come out of Babylon: from the elders who were to govern the people as judges." [6]These men, to whom all brought their cases, frequented the house of Joakim. [7]When the people left at noon, Susanna used to enter her husband's garden for a walk. [8]When the old men saw her enter every day for her walk, they began to lust for her. [9]They suppressed their consciences; they would not allow their eyes to look to heaven, and did not keep in mind just judgments. [10]Though both were enamored of her, they did not tell each other their trouble,

12, 1: Written in the book: the book of God's predestination.

12, 2: The first Israelites who have fallen (Dn 11, 33ff) shall awake, that is, rise to live forever. A resurrection of the wicked as in later, Christian teaching (Jn 5, 28f) is implied here if the others are included in the many; but cf Is 66, 24.

12, 7: A year, two years, a half-year: see note on Dn 7, 25. The author's perspective is the end of Antiochus, and beyond, the final consummation of all things.

13, 1—14, 42: The short stories in these two chapters may have originally been about some other Daniel or Daniels than the hero of the main part of the book. They exist now only in Greek, but probably were first composed in Hebrew or Aramaic. They are excluded from the Jewish canon of Scripture, but the church has always included them among the inspired writings.

c Rv 12, 7. d Mt 25, 46; Jn 5, 29. e Wis 3, 7. f Rv 10, 5f.

11for they were ashamed to reveal their lustful desire to have her. 12Day by day they watched eagerly for her. 13One day they said to each other, "Let us be off for home, it is time for lunch." So they went out and parted; 14but both turned back, and when they met again, they asked each other the reason. They admitted their lust, and then they agreed to look for an occasion when they could meet her alone.

15One day, while they were waiting for the right moment, she entered the garden as usual, with two maids only. She decided to bathe, for the weather was warm. 16Nobody else was there except the two elders, who had hidden themselves and were watching her. 17"Bring me oil and soap," she said to the maids, "and shut the garden doors while I bathe." 18They did as she said; they shut the garden doors and left by the side gate to fetch what she had ordered, unaware that the elders were hidden inside.

19As soon as the maids had left, the two old men got up and hurried to her. 20"Look," they said, "the garden doors are shut, and no one can see us; give in to our desire, and lie with us. 21If you refuse, we will testify against you that you dismissed your maids because a young man was here with you."

22"I am completely trapped," Susanna groaned. "If I yield, it will be my death; if I refuse, I cannot escape your power. 23Yet it is better for me to fall into your power without guilt than to sin before the Lord." 24Then Susanna shrieked, and the old men also shouted at her, 25as one of them ran to open the garden doors. 26When the people in the house heard the cries from the garden, they rushed in by the side gate to see what had happened to her. 27At the accusations by the old men, the servants felt very much ashamed, for never had any such thing been said about Susanna.

28When the people came to her husband Joakim the next day, the two wicked elders also came, fully determined to put Susanna to death. Before all the people they ordered: 29"Send for Susanna, the daughter of Hilkiah, the wife of Joakim." When she was sent for, 30she came with her parents, children and all her relatives. 31Susanna, very delicate and beautiful, 32was veiled; but those wicked men ordered her to uncover her face so as to sate themselves with her beauty. 33All her relatives and the onlookers were weeping.

34In the midst of the people the two elders rose up and laid their hands on her head. 35Through her tears she looked up to heaven, for she trusted in the Lord wholeheartedly. 36The elders made this accusation: "As we were walking in the garden alone, this woman entered with two girls and shut the doors of the garden, dismissing the girls. 37A young man, who was hidden there, came and lay with her. 38When we, in a corner of the garden, saw this crime, we ran toward them. 39We saw them lying together, but the man we could not hold, because he was stronger than we; he opened the doors and ran off. 40Then we seized this one and asked who the young man was, 41but she refused to tell us. We testify to this." The assembly believed them, since they were elders and judges of the people, and they condemned her to death.

42But Susanna cried aloud: "O eternal God, you know what is hidden and are aware of all things before they come to be: 43you know that they have testified falsely against me. Here I am about to die, though I have done none of the things with which these wicked men have charged me."

44The Lord heard her prayer. 45As she was being led to execution, God stirred up the holy spirit of a young boy named Daniel, 46and he cried aloud: "I will have no part in the death of this woman." 47All the people turned and asked him, "What is this you are saying?" 48He stood in their midst and continued, "Are you such fools, O Israelites! To condemn a woman of Israel without examination and without clear evidence? 49Return to court, for they have testified falsely against her."

50Then all the people returned in haste. To Daniel the elders said, "Come, sit with us and inform us, since God has given you the prestige of old age." 51But he replied, "Separate these two far from one another that I may examine them."

52 After they were separated one from the other, he called one of them and said: “How you have grown evil with age! Now have your past sins come to term: 53 [g]passing unjust sentences, condemning the innocent, and freeing the guilty, although the Lord says, ‘The innocent and the just you shall not put to death.’ 54 Now, then, if you were a witness, tell me under what tree you saw them together.” 55 “Under a mastic tree,”* he answered. “Your fine lie has cost you your head,” said Daniel; “for the angel of God shall receive the sentence from him and split you in two.” 56 Putting him to one side, he ordered the other one to be brought. “Offspring of Canaan, not of Judah,” Daniel said to him, “beauty has seduced you, lust has subverted your conscience. 57 This is how you acted with the daughters of Israel, and in their fear they yielded to you; but a daughter of Judah did not tolerate your wickedness.* 58 Now then, tell me under what tree you surprised them together.” 59 “Under an oak,” he said. “Your fine lie has cost you also your head,” said Daniel; “for the angel of God waits with a sword to cut you in two so as to make an end of you both.”

60 The whole assembly cried aloud, blessing God who saves those that hope in him. 61 [h]They rose up against the two elders, for by their own words Daniel had convicted them of perjury. According to the law of Moses, they inflicted on them the penalty they had plotted to impose on their neighbor: 62 they put them to death. Thus was innocent blood spared that day.

63 Hilkiah and his wife praised God for their daughter Susanna, as did Joakim her husband and all her relatives, because she was found innocent of any shameful deed. 64 And from that day onward Daniel was greatly esteemed by the people.

CHAPTER 14

Bel and the Dragon 1 After King Astyages* was laid with his fathers, Cyrus the Persian succeeded to his kingdom. 2 Daniel was the king’s favorite and was held in higher esteem than any of the friends of the king.* 3 The Babylonians had an idol called Bel,* and every day they provided for it six barrels of fine flour, forty sheep, and six measures of wine. 4 The king worshiped it and went every day to adore it; but Daniel adored only his God. 5 When the king asked him, “Why do you not adore Bel?” Daniel replied, “Because I worship not idols made with hands, but only the living God who made heaven and earth and has dominion over all mankind.” 6 Then the king continued, “You do not think Bel is a living god? Do you not see how much he eats and drinks every day?” 7 Daniel began to laugh. “Do not be deceived, O king,” he said; “it is only clay inside and bronze outside; it has never taken any food or drink.” 8 Enraged, the king called his priests and said to them, “Unless you tell me who it is that consumes these provisions, you shall die. 9 But if you can show that Bel consumes them, Daniel shall die for blaspheming Bel.” Daniel said to the king, “Let it be as you say!” 10 There were seventy priests of Bel, besides their wives and children.

When the king went with Daniel into the temple of Bel, 11 the priests of Bel said, “See, we are going to leave. Do you, O king, set out the food and prepare the wine; then shut the door and seal it with your ring. 12 If you do not find that Bel has eaten it all when you return in the morning, we are to die; otherwise Daniel shall die for his lies against us.” 13 They were not perturbed, because under the table they had made a secret entrance through which they always came in to consume the food. 14 After they departed the king set the food before Bel,

13, 55–59: The contrast between the mastic tree, which is small, and the majestic oak emphasizes the contradiction between the statements of the two elders. In the Greek text there is a play on words between the names of these two trees and the mortal punishment decreed by Daniel for the elders.

13, 57: Besides the evident moral intent of this story, it appears to have served the purpose of contrasting the northern and the southern kingdom, Israel and Judah, in favor of the latter.

14, 1: King Astyages: the last of the Median kings, defeated by Cyrus in 550 B.C. This story preserves the fiction of a successive Median and Persian rule of Babylon.

14, 2: This verse in the Septuagint Greek text reads: “There was once a priest, Daniel by name, the son of Abal, a favorite of the king of Babylon.” This may represent an earlier form of the story, before it was attached to the Book of Daniel.

14, 3: Bel: see the note on Dn 4, 5.

g Ex 23, 7. h 61f: Dt 19, 18. 19.

while Daniel ordered his servants to bring some ashes, which they scattered through the whole temple; the king alone was present. Then they went outside, sealed the closed door with the king's ring, and departed. 15 The priests entered that night as usual, with their wives and children, and they ate and drank everything.

16 Early the next morning, the king came with Daniel. 17 "Are the seals unbroken, Daniel?" he asked. And Daniel answered, "They are unbroken, O king." 18 As soon as he had opened the door, the king looked at the table and cried aloud, "Great you are, O Bel; there is no trickery in you." 19 But Daniel laughed and kept the king from entering. "Look at the floor," he said; "whose footprints are these?" 20 "I see the footprints of men, women, and children!" said the king. 21 The angry king arrested the priests, their wives, and their children. They showed him the secret door by which they used to enter to consume what was on the table. 22 He put them to death, and handed Bel over to Daniel, who destroyed it and its temple.

23 There was a great dragon which the Babylonians worshiped. 24 "Look!" said the king to Daniel, "you cannot deny that this is a living god, so adore it." 25 But Daniel answered, "I adore the Lord, my God, for he is the living God. 26 Give me permission, O king, and I will kill this dragon without sword or club." "I give you permission," the king said. 27 Then Daniel took some pitch, fat, and hair; these he boiled together and made into cakes. He put them into the mouth of the dragon, and when the dragon ate them, he burst asunder. "This," he said, "is what you worshiped."

28 When the Babylonians heard this, they were angry and turned against the king. "The king has become a Jew," they said; "he has destroyed Bel, killed the dragon, and put the priests to death." 29 They went to the king and demanded: "Hand Daniel over to us, or we will kill you and your family." 30 When he saw himself threatened with violence, the king was forced to hand Daniel over to them. 31 They threw Daniel into a lions' den, where he remained six days. 32 In the den were seven lions, and two carcasses and two sheep had been given to them daily. But now they were given nothing, so that they would devour Daniel.

33 In Judea there was a prophet, Habakkuk; he mixed some bread in a bowl with the stew he had boiled, and was going to bring it to the reapers in the field, 34 when an angel of the Lord told him, "Take the lunch you have to Daniel in the lions' den at Babylon." 35 But Habakkuk answered, "Babylon, sir, I have never seen, and I do not know the den!" 36 [i]The angel of the Lord seized him by the crown of his head and carried him by the hair; with the speed of the wind, he set him down in Babylon above the den. 37 "Daniel, Daniel," cried Habakkuk, "take the lunch God has sent you." 38 "You have remembered me, O God," said Daniel; "you have not forsaken those who love you." 39 While Daniel began to eat, the angel of the Lord at once brought Habakkuk back to his own place.

40 On the seventh day the king came to mourn for Daniel. As he came to the den and looked in, there was Daniel, sitting there! 41 The king cried aloud, "You are great, O Lord, the God of Daniel, and there is no other besides you!" 42 Daniel he took out, but those who had tried to destroy him he threw into the den, and they were devoured in a moment before his eyes.

i Ez 8, 3.

THE BOOK OF HOSEA

Hosea belonged to the northern kingdom and began his prophetic career in the last years of Jeroboam II (786–746 B.C.). Some believe that he was a priest, others that he was a cult prophet; the prophecy, our only source of information concerning his life, gives us no certain answer in the matter. The collected oracles reveal a very sensitive, emotional man who could pass quickly from violent anger to the deepest tenderness. The prophecy pivots around his own unfortunate marriage to Gomer, a personal tragedy which profoundly influenced his teaching. In fact, his own prophetic vocation and message were immeasurably deepened by the painful experience he underwent in his married life.

Gomer, the adulteress, symbolized faithless Israel. And just as Hosea could not give up his wife forever even when she played the harlot, so Yahweh could not renounce Israel, who had been betrothed to him. God would chastise, but it would be the chastisement of the jealous lover, longing to bring back the beloved to the fresh and pure joy of their first love.

Israel's infidelity took the form of idolatry and ruthless oppression of the poor. No amount of mechanically offered sacrifices could atone for her serious sins. Chastisement alone remained; God would have to strip her of the rich ornaments bestowed by her false lovers and thus bring her back to the true lover. A humiliated Israel would again seek Yahweh. The eleventh chapter of Hosea is one of the summits of Old Testament theology; God's love for his people has never been expressed more tenderly. Hosea began the tradition of describing the relation between Yahweh and Israel in terms of marriage. This symbolism appears later on in the Old Testament; and, in the New, both St. John and St. Paul express in the same imagery the union between Christ and his church.

The Book of Hosea is divided as follows:

I. The Prophet's Marriage and Its Lesson (1, 1—3, 5).
II. Israel's Guilt and Punishment (4, 1—14, 10).

I: The Prophet's Marriage and Its Lesson*

CHAPTER 1

Marriage with an Unfaithful Wife 1 The word
of the LORD that came to Hosea, the son of Beeri,
in the days of Uzziah, Jotham, Ahaz, Hezekiah,
kings of Judah, and in the days of Jeroboam, son
of Joash, king of Israel. 2 In the beginning of the
LORD's speaking to Hosea, the LORD said to
Hosea:

Go, take a harlot wife* and harlot's children,
for the land gives itself to harlotry,
turning away from the LORD.

3 So he went and took Gomer, the daughter of
Diblaim; and she conceived and bore him a son.
4 Then the LORD said to him:

1—3: This section is ordinarily thought to be biographical, the prophet's personal tragedy figuring as the relation of God to his people Israel. Hosea's marriage to a harlot wife represents Israel's infidelity to her Lord; hence the symbolic names of the children (Hos 1, 4–9). In Hos 2, 4–25 the Lord protests this infidelity and decrees its consequences, but promises restoration in return for amendment; his punishments are medicinal. In chapter 3 Hosea once more takes back his wife, but only conditionally, signifying God's long-suffering love for Israel and hope for her return.

1, 2: A harlot wife: this does not necessarily mean that Gomer was a harlot when Hosea married her; the verse describes the event in its final consequences.

Give him the name Jezreel,*
for in a little while
I will punish the house of Jehu
for the bloodshed at Jezreel
And bring to an end the kingdom
of the house of Israel;
5 On that day I will break the bow of Israel
in the valley of Jezreel.

6 When she conceived again and bore a daughter, the LORD said to him:

Give her the name Lo-ruhama;*
I no longer feel pity for the house of Israel:
rather, I abhor them utterly.
7 Yet for the house of Judah I feel pity;
I will save them by the LORD, their God;
But I will not save them by war,
by sword or bow, by horses or horsemen.*

8 After she weaned Lo-ruhama, she conceived and bore a son. 9 Then the LORD said:

Give him the name Lo-ammi,*
for you are not my people,
and I will not be your God.

CHAPTER 2

Israel's Punishment and Restoration

4 Protest against your mother, protest!*
for she is not my wife,
and I am not her husband.
Let her remove her harlotry from before her,
her adultery from between her breasts,
5 Or I will strip her naked,*
leaving her as on the day of her birth;
I will make her like the desert,
reduce her to an arid land,
and slay her with thirst.
6 I will have no pity on her children,
for they are the children of harlotry.
7 Yes, their mother has played the harlot;
she that conceived them has acted
shamefully.
"I will go after my lovers,"* she said,
"who give me my bread and my water,
my wool and my flax, my oil and my drink."
10 Since she has not known
that it was I who gave her
the grain, the wine, and the oil,
And her abundance of silver,
and of gold, which they used for Baal,
11 Therefore I will take back my grain in its time,
and my wine in its season;
I will snatch away my wool and my flax,
with which she covers her nakedness.
12 So now I will lay bare her shame
before the eyes of her lovers,
and no one can deliver her out of my hand.
13 I will bring an end to all her joy,
her feasts, her new moons, her sabbaths,
and all her solemnities.
14 I will lay waste her vines and fig trees,
of which she said, "These are the hire
my lovers have given me";
I will turn them into rank growth
and wild beasts shall devour them.
15 I will punish her for the days of the Baals,*
for whom she burnt incense
While she decked herself out with her rings
and her jewels,
and, in going after her lovers,
forgot me, says the LORD.

1, 4: Jezreel: the strategic valley in northern Israel where Jehu brought the dynasty of Omri to an end through bloodshed (2 Kgs 9–10). Jeroboam II was the last king but one of the house of Jehu; the prophecy in this verse was fulfilled by the murder of his son, who reigned only six months (2 Kgs 15, 8–10).

1, 6: Lo-ruhama: "she is not pitied." The "pity" that is here withheld from Israel is God's gratuitous love which inspires his beneficent acts.

1, 7: The terrible punishments announced by the prophets were so fully realized that later generations made a point of recalling the same prophets' messages of consolation also, even though it meant taking these from another context. Thus, an editor placed the words of Hos 2, 1ff after the repudiation of Israel in Hos 1, 9; here the more natural order has been restored. The present verse is another example of the same thing. In addition, it may be the work of a later hand, dating from a time when the prophecies of Hosea were circulated in the south, after the dissolution of the northern kingdom that he had prophesied. The second part of the verse emphasizes the power of the Lord, who needs no human agents to fulfill his will. It may refer to the deliverance of Jerusalem from the siege of Sennacherib (2 Kgs 19, 35ff).

1, 9: Lo-ammi: "not my people."

2, 4: The Lord speaks of Israel, still using the example of Hosea's wife.

2, 5: I will strip her naked: contemporary documents indicate that this was a conventional punishment for adultery.

2, 7: My lovers: the local fertility deities to whom, rather than to the Lord (v 10), the unfaithful Israelites attributed the produce of the land.

2, 15: The days of the Baals: ritual observances held in various local shrines in honor of Baal.

[8] Therefore, I will hedge in her way with
thorns*
and erect a wall against her,
so that she cannot find her paths.
[9] If she runs after her lovers, she shall not
overtake them;
if she looks for them she shall not find them.
Then she shall say,
"I will go back to my first husband,
for it was better with me then than now."

[16] So I will allure her;*
I will lead her into the desert
and speak to her heart.
[17] From there I will give her the vineyards she
had,
and the valley of Achor as a door of hope.
She shall respond there as in the days of her
youth,
when she came up from the land of Egypt.

[18] On that day, says the LORD,
She shall call me "My husband,"
and never again "My baal."*
[19] Then will I remove from her mouth the names
of the Baals,
so that they shall no longer be invoked.
[20] I will make a covenant for them on that day,
with the beasts of the field,
With the birds of the air,
and with the things that crawl on the
ground.
Bow and sword and war
I will destroy from the land,
and I will let them take their rest in security.
[21] I will espouse you to me forever:*
I will espouse you in right and in justice,
in love and in mercy;
[22] I will espouse you in fidelity,
and you shall know the LORD.
[23] On that day I will respond, says the LORD;
I will respond to the heavens,
and they shall respond to the earth;
[24] The earth shall respond to the grain, and wine,
and oil,
and these shall respond to Jezreel.
[25] I will sow him for myself in the land,
and I will have pity on Lo-ruhama.
I will say to Lo-ammi, "You are my people,"
and he shall say, "My God!"[a]

CHAPTER 3

Triumph of Love

[1] *Again the LORD said to me:
Give your love to a woman
beloved of a paramour, an adulteress;
Even as the LORD loves the people of Israel,
though they turn to other gods
and are fond of raisin cakes.*

[2] So I bought her for fifteen pieces of silver and
a homer* and a lethech of barley. [3] Then I said to
her:

"Many days you shall wait for me;
you shall not play the harlot
Or belong to any man;

2, 8f: The crop failures, blight, etc., sent by the Lord (vv 11–14) have as their purpose to make Israel see the folly of her ways.

2, 16f: Israel's journey in the desert represents for Hosea the time of Israel's fidelity, before it was corrupted by the ways of Canaan; cf Jer 2, 2–7; Am 5, 25. Thus, he pictures a restoration in terms of a new entry into the promised land.

2, 18: My baal: the word means "lord, master." It was commonly used by women of their husbands, but it is to be shunned as a title for the Lord because of its association with the pagan god Baal. Probably it had been so used by many Israelites, who saw little if any difference between the worship of the Lord and the worship of Baal.

2, 21f: The Lord will once more espouse Israel; the qualities ascribed to the renewed people are the bridal gift (cf Gn 24, 53) with which he will endow it. In right and in justice: two terms dear to Hosea, used by him especially to condemn the popular social injustice and corruption of the legal processes. Here they mean right conduct in general. Love: one of the most characteristic words of Hosea's prophecy. It means a dutiful love, based on a social relation; here it refers to the covenant between God and his people. It is a love fulfilled by the performance of mutual obligations. Mercy: from the same root as the word translated pity in Hos 1, 6; cf v 25. And you shall know the Lord: another characteristic expression of Hosea; cf Hos 4, 1; 5, 4; 6, 3. 6. It means not an abstract but a practical knowledge, i.e., acknowledgment of his will, obedience to his law.

3, 1–5: Hosea is instructed to take Gomer back, redeeming her from her paramours. On condition of her amendment, she will be restored to her former position of wife. This in turn signifies God's enduring love for his people. He will put the people through a period of trial—the dissolution of the kingdom—in order that they may return to him wholeheartedly.

3, 1: Raisin cakes: offerings to the fertility goddess Ashera, the female counterpart of Baal; cf Jer 7, 18; 44, 19.

3, 2: Homer: about ten bushels. Lethech: a half-homer.

a Rom 9, 25; 1 Pt 2, 10.

I in turn will wait for you."
4 For the people of Israel shall remain many days
without king or prince,
Without sacrifice or sacred pillar,*
without ephod or household idols.
5 Then the people of Israel shall turn back
and seek the LORD, their God,
and David, their king;*
They shall come trembling to the LORD
and to his bounty, in the last days. [b]
1 *The number of the Israelites
shall be like the sand of the sea,
which can be neither measured nor
counted.
Whereas they were called,
"Lo-ammi,"
They shall be called,
"Children of the living God." [c]
2 Then the people of Judah and of Israel
shall be gathered together;
They shall appoint for themselves one head
and come up from other lands,
for great shall be the day of Jezreel.
3 Say to your brothers, "Ammi,"
and to your sisters, "Ruhama."

II: Israel's Guilt and Punishment

CHAPTER 4

Crimes of Israel

1 Hear the word of the LORD, O people of Israel,
for the LORD has a grievance
against the inhabitants of the land:
There is no fidelity, no mercy,
no knowledge of God in the land.
2 False swearing, lying, murder, stealing and
adultery!
in their lawlessness, bloodshed follows
bloodshed. [d]
3 Therefore the land mourns,
and everything that dwells in it languishes:
The beasts of the field,
the birds of the air,
and even the fish of the sea perish.

Guilt of the Priests

4 But let no one protest, let no one complain;
with you is my grievance, O priests!*
5 You shall stumble in the day,
and the prophets shall stumble with you at
night;
I will destroy your mother.
6 My people perish for want of knowledge!
Since you have rejected knowledge,
I will reject you from my priesthood;
Since you have ignored the law of your God,
I will also ignore your sons.
7 One and all they sin against me,
exchanging their glory for shame.
8 They feed on the sin of my people,
and are greedy for their guilt.
9 The priests shall fare no better than the
people:
I will punish them for their ways,
and repay them for their deeds. [e]
10 They shall eat but not be satisfied,
they shall play the harlot but not increase,
Because they have abandoned the LORD
11 to practice harlotry.
Old wine and new
deprive my people of understanding.
12 They consult their piece of wood,
and their wand* makes pronouncements
for them,
For the spirit of harlotry has led them astray;
they commit harlotry, forsaking their God.
13 On the mountaintops they offer sacrifice
and on the hills they burn incense,

3, 4: Sacred pillar: the stone massebah, originally perhaps a phallic symbol, representing Baal. These were also used, with another signification, in Israelite worship; see notes on Gn 28, 18; Ex 34, 13. Ephod: an instrument used in consulting the deity; cf 1 Sm 23, 6–12; 30, 7; see notes on Ex 28, 6. 15–30. Household idols: images regarded as the tutelary deities of the household; cf Gn 31, 19; Jgs 17, 5; 18, 14. 17f.

3, 5: David, their king: the messianic King of the Davidic line who will restore the kingdom of God's people; cf Jer 23, 5; Ez 34, 23f. The last days: the messianic age.

3, 1–3: These verses (The number . . . Ruhama) (transposed from ch 2) continue the conditional promise of restoration made in Hos 3, 1–5, reversing the dire predictions of chapter 1; the symbolic names now become names of honor: Jezreel, "God sows"; Ammi, "my people"; Ruhama, "she is pitied."

4, 4ff: Hosea is particularly severe with the priests in the northern kingdom, who had led the way in the general apostasy from God's law. The prophets here associated with the priests (v 5) were doubtless cult prophets, who were often unworthy of their pretended calling; cf Jer 2, 8; 4, 9f; 6, 13f; 23, 9–40.

4, 12: Wood . . . wand: an idol used in divination.

b Ez 34, 23. c Rom 9, 26. d Ex 20, 13–17. e Is 24, 2.

Beneath oak and poplar and terebinth,
because of their pleasant shade.
That is why your daughters play the harlot,
and your daughters-in-law are adulteresses.
14 Am I then to punish your daughters for their harlotry,
your daughters-in-law for their adultery?
You yourselves consort with harlots,
and with prostitutes you offer sacrifice!*
So must a people without understanding come to ruin.
15 Though you play the harlot, O Israel,
let not Judah become guilty!
Come not to Gilgal,*
nor up to Beth-aven,
to swear, "As the Lord lives!"
16 For Israel is as stubborn as a heifer;
will the LORD now give them broad pastures
as though they were lambs?
17 Ephraim* is an associate of idols,
let him alone!
18 When their carousing is over,
they give themselves to harlotry;
in their arrogance they love shame.
19 The wind has bound them up in its pinions;*
they shall have only shame from their altars.

CHAPTER 5

Guilt of the Leaders

1 Hear this, O priests,
Pay attention, O house of Israel,
O household of the king, give ear!
It is you who are called to judgment.[f]
For you have become a snare at Mizpah,*
and a net spread upon Tabor.
2 In their perversity they have sunk into wickedness,
and I am rejected by them all.
3 I know Ephraim,
and Israel is not hidden from me;
Now Ephraim has played the harlot,
Israel is defiled.
4 Their deeds do not allow them
to return to their God;
For the spirit of harlotry is in them,
and they do not recognize the LORD.
5 The arrogance of Israel bears witness against him;
Ephraim stumbles in his guilt,
and Judah stumbles with them.
6 With their flocks and their herds they shall go
to seek the LORD, but they shall not find him:
he has withdrawn himself from them.
7 They have been untrue to the LORD,
for they have begotten illegitimate children;
Now shall the new moon devour them
together with their fields.

Political Upheavals*

8 Blow the horn in Gibeah,
the trumpet in Ramah!
Sound the alarm in Beth-aven:
"Look behind you, O Benjamin!"*
9 Ephraim shall become a waste
on the day of chastisement:
Against the tribes of Israel
I announce what is sure to be.
10 The princes of Judah have become

4, 14: With prostitutes you offer sacrifice: the ritual prostitution practiced at the Canaanite shrines was introduced even into sanctuaries dedicated to the Lord. In comparison, the adultery that had become common in Israel was a far less reprehensible crime.

4, 15: Gilgal: not the Gilgal of the south (Jos 4, 19f), but a sanctuary north of Bethel where there was an association of cult prophets (2 Kgs 2, 1ff; 4, 38). Beth-aven: literally, "house of iniquity," Hosea's nickname for Bethel, or a scribal substitute for Bethel, "house of god," in this context. Bethel was one of the royal shrines of Israel, where there was a schismatic public worsihp of the Lord; cf 1 Kgs 12, 26–30.

4, 17: Ephraim: the heartland of the northern kingdom. During the latter part of Hosea's prophetic career, Ephraim was all that remained of Israel after the Assyrians had overrun Transjordan and Galilee.

4, 19: The Israelites shall be carried from their country as by a whirlwind. To this their idolatry has brought them.

5, 1: Mizpah: probably the Mizpah in Transjordan is meant; cf Jos 11, 8. Tabor: the mountain that dominates the valley of Jezreel.

5, 8–14: This passage refers to the Syro-Ephraimite war of 735–734 B.C., when a coalition of Arameans and Israelites attempted to dethrone the king of Judah. Judah repulsed the attempt with the aid of Assyria, and the latter devastated both Aram and Israel; cf 2 Kgs 16, 5–9. Hosea condemns both Israel and Judah for the war.

5, 8: A vision of invasion, from Gibeah and Ramah in northern Judah, into Israel.

f Mi 3, 1.

like those that move a boundary line;*
Upon them I will pour out
my wrath like water.[g]

11 Is Ephraim maltreated, his rights violated?
No, he has willingly gone after filth!*
12 I am like a moth for Ephraim,
like maggots* for the house of Judah.
13 When Ephraim saw his infirmity,
and Judah his sore,
Ephraim went to Assyria,
and Judah sent to the great king.*
But he cannot heal you
nor take away your sore.
14 For I am like a lion to Ephraim,
like a young lion to the house of Judah;
It is I who rend the prey and depart,
I carry it away and no one can save it from me.

Insincere Conversion

15 I will go back to my place
until they pay for their guilt
and seek my presence.*

CHAPTER 6

*In their affliction, they shall look for me:
1 "Come, let us return to the LORD,
For it is he who has rent, but he will heal us;
he has struck us, but he will bind our wounds.
2 He will revive us after two days;*
on the third day he will raise us up,
to live in his presence.[h]
3 Let us know, let us strive to know the LORD;
as certain as the dawn is his coming,
and his judgment shines forth like the light of day!
He will come to us like the rain,
like spring rain that waters the earth."
4 What can I do with you, Ephraim?
What can I do with you, Judah?
Your piety* is like a morning cloud,
like the dew that early passes away.
5 For this reason I smote them through the prophets,
I slew them by the words of my mouth;
6 For it is love that I desire, not sacrifice,
and knowledge of God rather than holocausts.[i]
7 But they, in their land, violated the covenant;
there they were untrue to me.
8 Gilead is a city of evildoers,
tracked with blood.
9 As brigands ambush a man,
a band of priests slay on the way to Shechem,
committing monstrous crime.
10 In the house of Israel I have seen a horrible thing:
there harlotry is found in Ephraim,
Israel is defiled.
11 For you also, O Judah,
a harvest* has been appointed.

CHAPTER 7

1 When I would bring about the restoration of my people,
when I would heal Israel,
The guilt of Ephraim stands out,
the wickedness of Samaria;
They practice falsehood,
thieves break in, bandits plunder abroad.
2 Yet they do not remind themselves
that I remember all their wickedness.
Even now their crimes surround them,
present to my sight.

5, 10: Like those that move a boundary line: comparison of the invaders to a classic case of social injustice; cf Dt 19, 14; 27, 17; Prv 23, 10f.

5, 11: Gone after filth: by allying himself with Aram.

5, 12: Moth . . . maggots: internal corruption will work the Lord's punishment on both Israel and Judah.

5, 13: Ephraim went . . . the great king: in 738 B.C. the Israelite king Manahem had to pay tribute to the Assyrian king Tiglath-pileser III, whose vassal he became (2 Kgs 15, 19f). Under the threat of the Syro-Ephraimite invasion King Ahaz of Judah also submitted himself and his country to Tiglath-pileser (2 Kgs 16, 7–9). "The great king" was the title used by the Assyrian kings.

5, 15: The Lord withdraws himself from Israel, hoping for its repentance.

6, 1: In . . . me: this is the last line of ch 5.

6, 2: After two days; on the third day: after a short lapse of time.

6, 4: Piety: the word is translated "love" in Hos 2, 21 and in v 6 below.

6, 11: Harvest: when the land will reap the consequences of its sins.

g Dt 19, 14; 27, 17. h 1 Cor 15, 4. i 1 Sm 15, 22; Eccl 4, 17; Mt 9, 13; 12, 7.

Failure of the Monarchy*

3 In their wickedness they regale the king,
the princes too, with their deceits.
4 They are all kindled to wrath
like a blazing oven,
Whose fire the baker desists from stirring
once the dough is kneaded until it has risen.
5 On the day of our king,
the princes are overcome with the heat of wine.
He extends his hand among dissemblers;
6 the plotters approach with hearts like ovens.
All the night their anger sleeps;
in the morning it flares like a blazing fire.
7 They are all heated like ovens,
and consume their rulers.
All their kings have fallen;
none of them calls upon me.

Foreign Alliances

8 Ephraim mingles with the nations,
Ephraim is a hearth cake unturned.*
9 Strangers have sapped his strength,
but he takes no notice of it;
Of gray hairs, too, there is a sprinkling,
but he takes no notice of it.
10 The arrogance of Israel bears witness against him;
yet they do not return to the LORD, their God,
nor seek him, for all that.
11 Ephraim is like a dove,
silly and senseless;
They call upon Egypt,
they go to Assyria.
12 Even as they go I will spread my net around them,
like birds in the air I will bring them down.
In an instant I will send them captive from their land.

Perversity of Israel

13 Woe to them, they have strayed from me!
Ruin to them, they have sinned against me!
Though I wished to redeem them,
they spoke lies against me.
14 They have not cried to me from their hearts
when they wailed upon their beds;
For wheat and wine they lacerated themselves,*
while they rebelled against me.
15 Though I trained and strengthened their arms,
yet they devised evil against me.
16 They have again become useless,
like a treacherous bow.
Their princes shall fall by the sword
because of the insolence of their tongues;
thus they shall be mocked in the land of Egypt.

CHAPTER 8

1 A trumpet to your lips,
You who watch over the house of the LORD!
Since they have violated my covenant,
and sinned against my law,
2 While to me they cry out,
"O God of Israel, we know you!"
3 The men of Israel have thrown away what is good;
the enemy shall pursue them.
4 *They made kings, but not by my authority;
they established princes, but without my approval.
With their silver and gold they made
idols for themselves, to their own destruction.

7, 3–7: This passage refers to the dynastic upheavals of Israel's declining days. Between the death of Jeroboam II and the fall of Samaria to the Assyrians, a matter of some twenty-five years, there were four separate dynasties on the throne and as many murdered kings. The prophet compares the Israelite nobles who were inflamed with passion to an overheated oven that consumes what it is supposed to bake; thus the land consumes its kings. Regale: with wine (v 3). Like fire smoldering through the night and blazing up in the morning, the sleeping anger of plotters soon breaks out in open rebellion; the succession of night and morning suggests the short reigns of the various kings of this troubled period.

7, 8: A hearth cake unturned: burnt on one side, half baked on the other, and therefore useless. Israel's decline in power is ascribed to its disastrous meddling in the power politics of the neighboring nations.

7, 14: They lacerated themselves: a common oriental practice in prayers of earnest impetration (1 Kgs 18, 28); the practice was forbidden in Israelite religion (Lv 19, 28; Dt 14, 1).

8, 4–6: Israel's monarchy and separate sanctuary are here associated, as in 1 Kgs 12, 20–33; both were the result of rebellion against the divinely approved Davidic dynasty and the Jerusalem temple with the ark of the covenant. The calf image set up by Jeroboam I in the royal shrines prevented Israel from attaining innocence (vv 5f).

5 Cast away your calf, O Samaria!
my wrath is kindled against them;
How long will they be unable to attain
innocence in Israel?
6 The work of an artisan,
no god at all,
Destined for the flames—
such is the calf of Samaria!

7 When they sow the wind,
they shall reap the whirlwind;
The stalk of grain that forms no ear
can yield no flour;
Even if it could,
strangers would swallow it.
8 Israel is swallowed up;
he is now among the nations
a thing of no value.
9 They went up to Assyria—
a wild ass off on its own—
Ephraim bargained for lovers.
10 Even though they bargain with the nations,
I will now gather an army;
King and princes shall shortly
succumb under the burden.

11 When Ephraim made many altars to expiate
sin,
his altars became occasions of sin.*
12 Though I write for him my many ordinances,
they are considered as a stranger's.
13 Though they offer sacrifice,
immolate flesh and eat it,
the LORD is not pleased with them.
He shall still remember their guilt
and punish their sins;
they shall return to Egypt.
14 Israel has forgotten his maker
and built palaces.
Judah, too, has fortified many cities;
but I will send fire upon his cities,
to devour their castles.[j]

CHAPTER 9

Exile without Worship

1 Rejoice not, O Israel,
exult not like the nations!
For you have been unfaithful to your God,
loving a harlot's hire
upon every threshing floor.*
2 Threshing floor and wine press shall not
nourish them,
the new wine shall fail them.

3 They shall not dwell in the LORD's land;
Ephraim shall return to Egypt,
and in Assyria they shall eat unclean food.
4 They shall not pour libations of wine to the
LORD,
or proffer their sacrifices before him.
Theirs will be like mourners' bread,*
that makes unclean all who eat of it;
Such food as they have shall be for
themselves;
it cannot enter the house of the LORD.

5 What will you do on the festival day,
the day of the LORD's feast?*
6 When they go from the ruins,
Egypt shall gather them in, Memphis shall
bury them.
Weeds shall overgrow their silver treasures,
and thorns invade their tents.

The Prophet Ridiculed

7 They have come, the days of punishment!
they have come, the days of recompense!
Let Israel know it!
"The prophet is a fool,
the man of the spirit is mad!"
Because your iniquity is great,
great, too, is your hostility.
8 A prophet is Ephraim's watchman with God,
yet a fowler's snare is on all his ways,

8, 11: The very multiplicity of sanctuaries throughout the land was a danger to the purity of worship. The local shrines were speedily assimilated to the cult places used by the Canaanites, and the Lord was identified with the god Baal worshiped there. Thus the Deuteronomic writers, influenced by prophetic ideas, ended by restricting sacrificial worship to the one temple in Jerusalem.

9, 1f: Upon every threshing floor: an allusion to harvest festivals in honor of Baal, to whom the Israelites had attributed the fertility of the land; cf Hos 2, 7.

9, 4: Mourners' bread: bread eaten at funeral rites; cf Dt 26, 13f. Contact with a corpse made a person ritually unclean, together with everything he touched. Such bread could not be offered to the Lord.

9, 5: The Lord's feast: doubtless the autumn feast of Booths, the most important of the Israelite public celebrations; cf Lv 23, 34.

j Am 2, 5.

hostility in the house of his God.
9 They have sunk to the depths of corruption,
as in the days of Gibeah;*
He shall remember their iniquity
and punish their sins.

Crime of Baal-peor

10 Like grapes in the desert,
I found Israel;
Like the first fruits of the fig tree in its prime,
I considered your fathers.
When they came to Baal-peor*
and consecrated themselves to the Shame,
they became as abhorrent as the thing they loved.
11 The glory of Ephraim flies away like a bird:
no birth, no carrying in the womb, no conception.
Were they to bear children,
I would slay the darlings of their womb.
12 Even though they bring up their children,
I will make them childless, till not one is left.
Woe to them
when I turn away from them!
13 Ephraim, as I saw, was like Tyre,
planted in a beauteous spot;
But Ephraim shall bring out
his children to the slayer.
14 Give them, O LORD!
give them what?
Give them an unfruitful womb,*
and dry breasts!

Crime of Gilgal

15 All their wickedness is in Gilgal;*
yes, there they incurred my hatred.
Because of their wicked deeds
I will drive them out of my house.
I will love them no longer;
all their princes are rebels. [k]
16 Ephraim is stricken,
their root is dried up;
they shall bear no fruit.
17 My God will disown them
because they have not listened to him;
they shall be wanderers among the nations.

CHAPTER 10

Punishment of Idolatry

1 Israel is a luxuriant vine
whose fruit matches its growth.
The more abundant his fruit,
the more altars he built;
The more productive his land,
the more sacred pillars* he set up.
2 Their heart is false,
now they pay for their guilt;
God shall break down their altars
and destroy their sacred pillars.
3 If they would say,
"We have no king"—
Since they do not fear the LORD,
what can the king do for them?
4 Nothing but make promises,
swear false oaths, and make alliances,
While justice grows wild
like wormwood* in a plowed field!
5 The inhabitants of Samaria fear
for the calf of Beth-aven;*
The people mourn for it
and its priests wail over it,
because the glory has departed from it.
6 It too shall be carried to Assyria,
as an offering to the great king.
Ephraim shall be taken into captivity,
Israel be shamed by his schemes.
7 The king of Samaria shall disappear,
like foam upon the waters.
8 The high places of Aven shall be destroyed,

9, 9: The days of Gibeah: a reference to the outrage committed at Gibeah in the days of the Judges (Jgs 19, 22–30).

9, 10: At Baal-peor (Nm 25, 1–5) the Israelites consecrated themselves to Baal, here called the Shame.

9, 14: An unfruitful womb: this appears to be a reversal of the ancient blessing of Joseph contained in Gn 49, 25f, in which the increase, hence fruitfulness, promised to the patriarch is even signified by the name of his son Ephraim, on whose descendants the prophet now invokes the curse of extinction.

9, 15: Gilgal: see note on Hos 4, 15.

10, 1: Sacred pillars: see note on Hos 3, 4.

10, 4: Justice . . . like wormwood: the administration of justice, which should have been the mainstay of the people, has in corrupt hands become another instrument of oppression; cf Am 6, 13.

10, 5: The calf of Beth-aven: see notes on Hos 4, 15; 8, 4ff.

k 1 Sm 8, 5.

the sin of Israel;
thorns and thistles shall overgrow their altars.
Then they shall cry out to the mountains,
"Cover us!"
and to the hills, "Fall upon us!" [l]

9 Since the days of Gibeah
you have sinned, O Israel.
There they took their stand;
war was not to reach them in Gibeah. [m]
10 Against the wanton people I came
and I chastised them; [n]
I gathered troops against them
when I chastised them for their two crimes.*

Time To Seek the Lord

11 Ephraim was a trained heifer,
willing to thresh;
I myself laid a yoke
upon her fair neck;
Ephraim was to be harnessed, Judah was to plow,
Jacob was to break his furrows:
12 "Sow for yourselves justice,
reap the fruit of piety;
Break up for yourselves a new field,
for it is time to seek the LORD,
till he come and rain down justice upon you." [o]
13 But you have cultivated wickedness,
reaped perversity,
and eaten the fruit of falsehood.

Because you have trusted in your chariots,
and in your many warriors,
14 Turmoil shall break out among your tribes
and all your fortresses shall be ravaged
As Salman ravaged Beth-arbel* in time of war,
smashing mothers and their children. [p]
15 So shall it be done to you, Bethel,
because of your utter wickedness:
At dawn the king of Israel
shall perish utterly.

CHAPTER 11

When Israel Was a Child

1 When Israel was a child I loved him,
out of Egypt* I called my son. [q]
2 The more I called them,
the farther they went from me,
Sacrificing to the Baals
and burning incense to idols.
3 Yet it was I who taught Ephraim to walk,
who took them in my arms;
4 I drew them with human cords,
with bands of love;*
I fostered them like one
who raises an infant to his cheeks;
Yet, though I stooped to feed my child,
they did not know that I was their healer.

5 He shall return to the land of Egypt,
and Assyria shall be his king;
6 The sword shall begin with his cities
and end by consuming his solitudes.
Because they refused to repent,
their own counsels shall devour them.
7 His people are in suspense about returning to him;
and God, though in unison they cry out to him,
shall not raise them up.

End of the Exile

8 How could I give you up, O Ephraim,
or deliver you up, O Israel?
How could I treat you as Admah,
or make you like Zeboiim?*
My heart is overwhelmed,

10, 10: Their two crimes: possibly the outrage described in Jgs 19 is conceived as a double crime, of adultery and murder. Or the prophet regards the proclamation of the monarchy (cf 1 Sm 10, 23f) as a crime.

10, 14: As Salman ravaged Beth-arbel: allusion to an invasion not otherwise mentioned in the Bible. Salman may have been the Moabite king of this name mentioned in an inscription of Tiglath-pileser III. There were several Beth-arbels in Palestine; this one was probably in Transjordan.

11, 1: Out of Egypt: Hosea, like most of the prophets, dates the real beginning of Israel from the time of Moses and the Exodus. Mt 2, 15 applies this text to the return of the Christ Child from Egypt.

11, 4: I drew them . . . with bands of love: not forcing them like draft animals, but drawing them with kindness and affection.

11, 8: Admah . . . Zeboiim: cities destroyed with Sodom and Gomorrah (Dt 29, 22).

l Is 2, 19; Lk 23, 30; Rv 6, 16. m Jgs 20, 1. n Jer 4, 3. o Is 45, 8. p Jgs 8, 10ff. q Mt 2, 15.

my pity is stirred.[r]
9 I will not give vent to my blazing anger,
I will not destroy Ephraim again;
For I am God and not man,
the Holy One present among you;
I will not let the flames consume you.

10 They shall follow the LORD,
who roars like a lion;
When he roars,
his sons shall come frightened from the west,
11 Out of Egypt they shall come trembling, like sparrows,
from the land of Assyria, like doves;
And I will resettle them in their homes,
says the LORD.

CHAPTER 12

Infidelity of Israel

1 Ephraim has surrounded me with lies,
the house of Israel, with deceit;
Judah is still rebellious against God,
against the Holy One, who is faithful.
2 Ephraim chases the wind,
ever pursuing the gale.
His lies and falsehoods are many:
he comes to terms with Assyria,
and carries oil to Egypt.*
3 *The LORD has a grievance against Israel:
he shall punish Jacob for his conduct,
for his deeds he shall repay him.
4 In the womb he supplanted his brother,
and as a man he contended with God;[s]
5 He contended with the angel and triumphed,
entreating him with tears.
At Bethel he met God
and there he spoke with him:
6 The LORD, the God of hosts,
the LORD is his name!
7 You shall return by the help of your God,
if you remain loyal and do right
and always hope in your God.
8 A merchant who holds a false balance,
who loves to defraud!
9 Though Ephraim says,
"How rich I have become;
I have made a fortune!"
All his gain shall not suffice him
for the guilt of his sin.
10 I am the LORD, your God,
since the land of Egypt;
I will again have you live in tents,
as in that appointed time.
11 I granted many visions
and spoke to the prophets,
through whom I set forth examples.
12 In Gilead is falsehood, they have come to nought,
in Gilgal they sacrifice to bullocks;
Their altars are like heaps of stones
in the furrows of the field.

13 When Jacob fled to the land of Aram,
he served for a wife;
for a wife Israel tended sheep.[t]
14 By a prophet* the LORD brought Israel out of Egypt,
and by a prophet they were protected.[u]
15 Ephraim has exasperated his lord;
therefore he shall cast his bloodguilt upon him
and repay him for his outrage.

CHAPTER 13

Furrows of the Field

1 Ephraim's word caused fear,
for he was exalted in Israel;
but he sinned through Baal and died.

Punishment for Ingratitude

2 Now they continue to sin,
making for themselves molten images,
Silver idols according to their fancy,

12, 2: He comes . . . Egypt: allusion to the commercial and military pacts with the great powers, consistently condemned by the prophets as derogatory of the Lord's claim on his people.

12, 3–7: Contemporary Israel and the Israel represented by its ancestor Jacob (Israel) are here alternated, a splendid example of the Hebrew concept of "corporate personality" or easy transition from the individual to the community of which he is part. Hosea recalls the history of Jacob as it now appears in Genesis, but with some differences of detail and order.

12, 14: A prophet: Moses.

r Gn 19, 24f. s Gn 25, 26; 32, 25. t Gn 28, 5; 29, 20. u Ex 14, 21f.

all of them the work of artisans.
"To these," they say, "offer sacrifice."
Men kiss calves!
3 Therefore, they shall be like a morning cloud
or like the dew that early passes away,
Like chaff storm-driven from the threshing floor
or like smoke out of the window.

4 I am the LORD, your God,
since the land of Egypt;
You know no God besides me,
and there is no savior but me. [v]
5 I fed you in the desert,
in the torrid land.
6 They ate their fill;
when filled, they became proud of heart
and forgot me.

7 Therefore, I will be like a lion to them,
like a panther by the road I will keep watch.
8 I will attack them like a bear robbed of its young,
and tear their hearts from their breasts;
I will devour them on the spot like a lion,
as though a wild beast were to rend them.

9 Your destruction, O Israel!
who is there to help you?
10 Where now is your king,
that he may rescue you in all your cities?
And your rulers, of whom you said,
"Give me a king and princes"? [w]
11 I give you a king in my anger,
and I take him away in my wrath.*

12 The guilt of Israel is wrapped up,
his sin is stored away.

13 The birth pangs shall come for him,
but he shall be an unwise child;
For when it is time he shall not present himself
where children break forth.*

14 Shall I deliver them from the power of the nether world?*
shall I redeem them from death? [x]
Where are your plagues, O death!
where is your sting, O nether world!
My eyes are closed to compassion.

15 Though he be fruitful among his fellows,
an east wind shall come, a wind from the LORD,
rising from the desert,
That shall dry up his spring,
and leave his fountain dry.
It shall loot his land
of every precious thing. [y]

CHAPTER 14

1 Samaria shall expiate her guilt,
for she has rebelled against her God.
They shall fall by the sword,
their little ones shall be dashed to pieces,
their expectant mothers shall be ripped open.

Sincere Conversion

2 Return, O Israel, to the LORD, your God;
you have collapsed through your guilt.
3 Take with you words,
and return to the LORD;
Say to him, "Forgive all iniquity,
and receive what is good, that we may render
as offerings the bullocks from our stalls.
4 Assyria will not save us,
nor shall we have horses to mount;
We shall say no more, 'Our god,'
to the work of our hands;
for in you the orphan finds compassion."

5 I will heal their defection,
I will love them freely;
for my wrath is turned away from them.

13, 11: I give you a king . . . in my wrath: the Lord punishes the people of the northern kingdom by giving them incompetent kings who are soon deposed.

13, 13: Israel's sin is such as to warrant its destruction (v 12), because it refuses to do penance. It will therefore perish as surely as the unborn child which dies in its mother's body because it does not properly employ the only way to safety.

13, 14: Shall . . . nether world: a vigorous affirmation of the Lord's determination to destroy Israel. St. Paul cites these words in a different sense (1 Cor 15, 54f), that of the ultimate victory of life over death in the resurrection of the body on the last day, wrought through the merits of Christ's passion and resurrection.

v Is 43, 11. w 1 Sm 8, 5. x 1 Cor 15, 54. y Ex 19, 12.

6 I will be like the dew for Israel:
he shall blossom like the lily;
He shall strike root like the Lebanon cedar,
7 and put forth his shoots.
His splendor shall be like the olive tree
and his fragrance like the Lebanon cedar.
8 Again they shall dwell in his shade
and raise grain;
They shall blossom like the vine,
and his fame shall be like the wine of
Lebanon.
9 Ephraim! What more has he to do with idols?
I have humbled him, but I will prosper him.
"I am like a verdant cypress tree"—
Because of me you bear fruit!

* * *

10 Let him who is wise understand these things;
let him who is prudent know them.
Straight are the paths of the LORD,
in them the just walk,
but sinners stumble in them.*

14, 10: A later addition in the style of the wisdom literature.

THE BOOK OF JOEL

This prophecy is rich in apocalyptic imagery and strongly eschatological in tone. It was composed about 400 B.C. Its prevailing theme is the day of the Lord.

A terrible invasion of locusts ravaged Judah. So frightful was the scourge that the prophet visualized it as a symbol of the coming day of the Lord. In the face of this threatening catastrophe, the prophet summoned the people to repent, to turn to the Lord with fasting and weeping. They were ordered to convoke a solemn assembly in which the priests would pray for deliverance. The Lord answered their prayer and promised to drive away the locusts and bless the land with peace and prosperity. To these material blessings would be added an outpouring of the spirit on all flesh. St. Peter, in his first discourse before the people at Pentecost (Acts 2, 16-21), sees in the coming of the Holy Spirit the fulfillment of this promise (1, 1—3, 5).

The concluding poem pictures the nations gathered in the Valley of Jehoshaphat, where the Lord is about to pass judgment. Israel's enemies are summoned to hear the solemn indictment; their evil deeds are at last requited. The tumultuous throng assembled in the valley of decision is made up of the enemies of God and they face inevitable destruction. The oracle changes abruptly from the terrifying image of judgment to a vision of Israel restored and forever secure from her enemies. God is both the vindicator of his people and the source of their blessing (4, 1-21).

CHAPTER 1

The Land Invaded 1 The word of the LORD which came to Joel, the son of Pethuel.

2 Hear this, you elders!
Pay attention, all you who dwell in the
land!
Has the like of this happened in your days,
or in the days of your fathers?
3 Tell it to your children,
and your children to their children,
and their children to the next generation.
4 What the cutter left,
the locust swarm has eaten;
What the locust swarm left,
the grasshopper has eaten;
And what the grasshopper left,
the devourer* has eaten.

1, 4: Cutter . . . locust . . . grasshopper . . . devourer: these names refer to various species of locusts: they can only be approximate.

5 Wake up, you drunkards, and weep;
wail, all you drinkers of wine,
Because the juice of the grape
will be withheld from your mouths.
6 For a people* has invaded my land,
mighty and without number;
His teeth are the teeth of a lion,
and his molars those of a lioness.
7 He has laid waste my vine,
and blighted my fig tree;
He has stripped it, sheared off its bark;
its branches are made white.
8 Lament like a virgin girt with sackcloth
for the spouse of her youth.
9 Abolished are offering and libation
from the house of the LORD;
In mourning are the priests,
the ministers of the LORD.
10 The field is ravaged,
the earth mourns,
Because the grain is ravaged,
the must has failed,
the oil languishes.
11 Be appalled, you husbandmen!
wail, you vinedressers!
Over the wheat and the barley,
because the harvest of the field has perished.
12 The vine has dried up,
the fig tree is withered;
The pomegranate, the date palm also, and the apple,
all the trees of the field are dried up;
Yes, joy has withered away
from among mankind.

Call to Penance

13 Gird yourselves and weep, O priests!
wail, O ministers of the altar!
Come, spend the night in sackcloth,
O ministers of my God!
The house of your God is deprived
of offering and libation.
14 Proclaim a fast,
call an assembly;
Gather the elders,
all who dwell in the land,
Into the house of the LORD, your God,
and cry to the LORD! [a]

15 Alas, the day!
for near is the day of the LORD,
and it comes as ruin from the Almighty.
16 From before our very eyes
has not the food been cut off;
And from the house of our God,
joy and gladness?
17 The seed lies shriveled under its clods;
the stores are destroyed,
The barns are broken down,
for the grain has failed.
18 How the beasts groan!
The herds of cattle are bewildered!
Because they have no pasturage,
even the flocks of sheep have perished.

19 To you, O LORD, I cry!
for fire has devoured the pastures of the plain,
and flame has enkindled all the trees of the field.
20 Even the beasts of the field
cry out to you;
For the streams of water are dried up,
and fire has devoured the pastures of the plain.

CHAPTER 2

The Day of the Lord

1 Blow the trumpet in Zion,
sound the alarm on my holy mountain!
Let all who dwell in the land tremble,
for the day of the LORD is coming;
2 Yes, it is near, a day of darkness and of gloom,
a day of clouds and somberness!
Like dawn spreading over the mountains,
a people numerous and mighty!
Their like has not been from of old,
nor will it be after them,
even to the years of distant generations.
3 Before them a fire devours,
and after them a flame enkindles;

1, 6: A people: the locusts compared to an invading army.

a Jl 2, 15.

Like the garden of Eden is the land before
them,
and after them a desert waste;
from them there is no escape.

4 Their appearance is that of horses;
like steeds they run.
5 As with the rumble of chariots
they leap on the mountaintops;
As with the crackling of a fiery flame
devouring stubble;
Like a mighty people
arrayed for battle.
6 Before them peoples are in torment,
every face blanches.

7 Like warriors they run,
like soldiers they scale the wall;
They advance, each in his own lane,
without swerving from their paths.
8 No one crowds another,
each advances in his own track;
Though they fall into the ditches,
they are not checked.

9 They assault the city,
they run upon the wall,
they climb into the houses;
In at the windows
they come like thieves.
10 Before them the earth trembles,
the heavens shake;
The sun and the moon are darkened,
and the stars withhold their brightness. [b]

11 The LORD raises his voice
at the head of his army;
For immense indeed is his camp,
yes, mighty, and it does his bidding.
For great is the day of the LORD,
and exceedingly terrible; who can bear it? [c]
12 Yet even now, says the LORD,
return to me with your whole heart,
with fasting, and weeping, and mourning;
13 Rend your hearts, not your garments,
and return to the LORD, your God.
For gracious and merciful is he,
slow to anger, rich in kindness,
and relenting in punishment. [d]
14 Perhaps he will again relent
and leave behind him a blessing,
Offerings and libations
for the LORD, your God. [e]
15 Blow the trumpet in Zion!
proclaim a fast,
call an assembly; [f]
16 Gather the people,
notify the congregation;
Assemble the elders,
gather the children
and the infants at the breast;
Let the bridegroom quit his room,
and the bride her chamber.
17 Between the porch and the altar*
let the priests, the ministers of the LORD,
weep,
And say, "Spare, O LORD, your people,
and make not your heritage a reproach,
with the nations ruling over them!
Why should they say among the peoples,
'Where is their God?' "

Blessings for God's People 18 Then the LORD
was stirred to concern for his land and took pity
on his people. 19 The LORD answered and said to
his people:

See, I will send you
grain, and wine, and oil,
and you shall be filled with them;
No more will I make you
a reproach among the nations.
20 No, the northerner* I will remove far from
you,
and drive him out into a land arid and
waste,
With his van toward the eastern sea,
and his rear toward the western sea;

2, 17: The priests stood in the open space between the outdoor altar of holocausts and the temple building, facing the latter in order thereby to look toward God present in the holy of holies.

2, 20: The northerner: the locusts, that are compared to an invading army, which in Palestine came from the north; cf Jer 1, 14f; 4, 6; Ez 26, 7; 38, 6. 15.

b Jl 4, 15; Is 13, 10; Ez 32, 7f; Mt 24, 29; Mk 13, 24; Lk 21, 25f. c Jer 30, 7; Am 5, 18; Zep 1, 15. d Ps 86, 5; Jon 4, 2. e Jon 3, 9. f Jl 1, 14.

And his foulness shall go up,
and his stench shall go up.

21 Fear not, O land!
exult and rejoice!
for the LORD has done great things.
22 Fear not, beasts of the field!
for the pastures of the plain are green;
The tree bears its fruit,
the fig tree and the vine give their yield.
23 And do you, O children of Zion, exult
and rejoice in the LORD, your God!
He has given you the teacher of justice:*
he has made the rain come down for you,
the early and the late rain as before.[g]
24 The threshing floors shall be full of grain
and the vats shall overflow with wine and oil.
25 And I will repay you for the years
which the locust has eaten,
The grasshopper, the devourer, and the cutter,
my great army which I sent among you.
26 You shall eat and be filled,
and shall praise the name of the LORD, your God,
Because he has dealt wondrously with you;
my people shall nevermore be put to shame.
27 And you shall know that I am in the midst of Israel;
I am the LORD, your God, and there is no other;
my people shall nevermore be put to shame.

CHAPTER 3

1 Then afterward I will pour out[h]
my spirit* upon all mankind.
Your sons and daughters shall prophesy,
your old men shall dream dreams,
your young men shall see visions;
2 Even upon the servants and the handmaids,
in those days, I will pour out my spirit.
3 And I will work wonders in the heavens and on the earth,
blood, fire, and columns of smoke;
4 The sun will be turned to darkness,
and the moon to blood,
At the coming of the day of the LORD,
the great and terrible day.[i]
5 Then everyone shall be rescued
who calls on the name of the LORD;
For on Mount Zion there shall be a remnant,
as the LORD has said,
And in Jerusalem survivors
whom the LORD shall call.[j]

CHAPTER 4

Judgment upon the Nations

1 Yes, in those days, and at that time,
when I would restore the fortunes
of Judah and Jerusalem,
2 I will assemble all the nations
and bring them down to the Valley of Jehoshaphat,*
And I will enter into judgment with them there
on behalf of my people and my inheritance, Israel;
Because they have scattered them among the nations,
and divided my land.
3 Over my people they have cast lots;
they gave a boy for a harlot,
and sold a girl for the wine they drank.

4 Moreover, what are you to me, Tyre and
Sidon, and all the regions of Philistia? Would you
take vengeance upon me by some action? But if
you do take action against me, swiftly, speedily, I
will return your deed upon your own head. 5 You
took my silver and my gold, and brought my
precious treasures into your temples! 6 You sold

2, 23: The teacher of justice: the rain sent by God to show his fidelity to his promises, and to teach his people to be faithful to his commandments; cf Dt 11, 14. There is also a play on words here between the Hebrew word moreh (teacher) and the Hebrew word yoreh (the early rain). The expression likewise has a messianic connotation; cf Is 30, 20. The founder of the Essene sect of Qumran (second century B.C.) was known as "The Teacher of Justice."

3, 1f: I will pour out my spirit: in the Old Testament the spirit is the gift of God bestowed on those acting as his agents. The promise of the spirit is quoted by St. Peter in Acts 2, 17–21 as fulfilled in an eminent way by the gift of the Holy Spirit, the Third Person of the Blessed Trinity, bestowed on the Apostles.

4, 2: Valley of Jehoshaphat: a symbolic name of the place of final judgment (v 14). The name Jehoshaphat signifies "Yahweh judges." This place has been popularly identified with the Kidron Valley.

g Hos 10, 12. h 1–5: Is 44, 3; Acts 2, 17–21. i Jl 2, 10. j Rom 10, 13.

the people of Judah and Jerusalem to the Greeks,
removing them far from their own country!
7 See, I will rouse them from the place into
which you have sold them, and I will return
your deed upon your own head. 8 I will sell your
sons and your daughters to the people of Judah,
who shall sell them to the Sabeans,* a nation far
off. Indeed, the LORD has spoken.

9 Declare this among the nations:
proclaim a war,
rouse the warriors to arms!
Let all the soldiers
report and march!
10 Beat your plowshares into swords,
and your pruning hooks into spears;
let the weak man say, "I am a warrior!"*
11 Hasten and come, all you neighboring peoples,
assemble there!
[Bring down, O Lord, your warriors!*]
12 Let the nations bestir themselves and come up
to the Valley of Jehoshaphat;
For there will I sit in judgment
upon all the neighboring nations.

13 Apply the sickle,[k]
for the harvest is ripe;
Come and tread,
for the wine press is full;
The vats overflow,
for great is their malice.*
14 Crowd upon crowd
in the valley of decision;
For near is the day of the LORD
in the valley of decision.
15 Sun and moon are darkened,
and the stars withhold their brightness.[l]
16 The LORD roars from Zion,
and from Jerusalem raises his voice;
The heavens and the earth quake,
but the LORD is a refuge to his people,
a stronghold to the men of Israel.[m]

Salvation for God's Elect

17 Then shall you know that I, the LORD, am your God,
dwelling on Zion, my holy mountain;
Jerusalem shall be holy,
and strangers shall pass through her no more.
18 And then, on that day,[n]
the mountains shall drip new wine,
and the hills shall flow with milk;
And the channels of Judah
shall flow with water:
A fountain shall issue from the house of the LORD,
to water the Valley of Shittim.*
19 Egypt shall be a waste,
and Edom a desert waste,
Because of violence done to the people of Judah,
because they shed innocent blood in their land.
20 But Judah shall abide forever,
and Jerusalem for all generations.
21 I will avenge their blood,
and not leave it unpunished.
The LORD dwells in Zion.

4, 8: Sabeans: a south Arabian people known for their commerce.

4, 10: This imagery is used in the reverse sense in Is 2, 4; Mi 4, 3. Here the warlike weapons are made in response to God's summons to armies which he selected to expel forever the unlawful invaders from the land of his chosen people.

4, 11: Warriors: the angels; cf Zec 14, 5.

4, 13: Because of their numerous crimes, the nations are ripe for punishment. The use of warlike weapons against them is likened to the onslaught on the fields and vines at harvest time.

4, 18: The Valley of Shittim, or "the ravine of the acacia trees": perhaps a part of the Kidron Valley southeast of Jerusalem; the prophetic picture of a stream of water flowing from a fountain in the temple of Jerusalem is to be found in Ez 47, 1. The Shittim east of the Jordan (see note on Nm 25, 1) is hardly referred to here.

k Rv 14, 15. l Jl 2, 10; 3, 4. m Jer 25, 30; Am 1, 2. n Am 9, 13; Ez 47, 1-12; Zec 14, 8.

THE BOOK OF AMOS

Amos was a shepherd of Tekoa in Judah, who exercised his ministry during the prosperous reign of Jeroboam II (786–746 B.C.). He prophesied in Israel at the great cult center of Bethel, from which he was finally expelled by the priest in charge of this royal sanctuary. The poetry of Amos, who denounces the hollow prosperity of the northern kingdom, is filled with imagery and language taken from his own pastoral background. The book is an anthology of his oracles and was compiled either by the prophet or by some of his disciples.

The prophecy begins with a sweeping indictment of Damascus, Philistia, Tyre, and Edom; but the forthright herdsman saves his climactic denunciation for Israel, whose injustice and idolatry are sins against the light granted to her. Israel could indeed expect the day of Yahweh, but it would be a day of darkness and not light. When Amos prophesied the overthrow of the sanctuary, the fall of the royal house, and the captivity of the people, it was more than Israelite officialdom could bear. The priest of Bethel drove Amos from the shrine—but not before hearing a terrible sentence pronounced upon himself.

Amos is a prophet of divine judgment, and the sovereignty of Yahweh in nature and history dominates his thought. But he was no innovator; his conservatism was in keeping with the whole prophetic tradition calling the people back to the high moral and religious demands of Yahweh's revelation. In common with the other prophets, Amos knew that divine punishment is never completely destructive; it is part of the hidden plan of God to bring salvation to men. The perversity of the human will may retard, but it cannot totally frustrate, this design of a loving God. The last oracle opens up a perspective of restoration under a Davidic king.

The Book of Amos may be divided as follows:

I. Judgment of the Nations (1, 1—2, 16).
II. Words and Woes for Israel (3, 1—6, 14).
III. Symbolic Visions: Threats and Promises (7, 1—9, 8b);
Epilogue: Messianic Perspective (9, 8c-15).

I: Judgment of the Nations

CHAPTER 1

1 The words of Amos, a shepherd from Tekoa,[a] which he received in vision concerning Israel, in the days of Uzziah, king of Judah, and in the days of Jeroboam, son of Joash, king of Israel, two years before the earthquake:*

2 The LORD will roar from Zion,
and from Jerusalem raise his voice:
The pastures of the shepherds will languish,
and the summit of Carmel wither.[b]

Aram

3 Thus says the LORD:
For three crimes of Damascus, and for four,*
I will not revoke my word;
Because they threshed Gilead
with sledges of iron,

1, 1: The earthquake: which according to Hebrew tradition marked the crime of Uzziah when he attempted to offer incense in the temple (2 Chr 26, 16–21). Zechariah mentions it several centuries later (Zec 14, 5).

1, 3: For three crimes . . . four: crime after crime, an indefinite number; cf Am 1, 6. The series of judgments on the foreign nations shows that the Lord demands the observance of the moral order everywhere; Israel and Judah, despite their privileged position, are no exception. I will not revoke my word: God will not withdraw his threat of punishment against each of these nations. They threshed Gilead: the people of Aram under King Hazael had devastated Gilead; cf 2 Kgs 10, 32f.

a Zec 14, 5. b Jer 25, 30; Jl 3, 16.

4 I will send fire* upon the house of Hazael,
to devour the castles of Ben-hadad.
5 I will break the bar of Damascus;*
I will root out those who live in the Valley of Aven,
And the sceptered ruler of Beth-eden;
the people of Aram shall be exiled to Kir,
says the LORD.

Philistia

6 Thus says the LORD:
For three crimes of Gaza, and for four,
I will not revoke my word;
Because they took captive whole groups
to hand over to Edom,
7 I will send fire upon the wall of Gaza,
to devour her castles;
8 I will root out those who live in Ashdod,
and the sceptered ruler of Ashkelon;
I will turn my hand against Ekron,
and the last of the Philistines shall perish,
says the Lord GOD.

Tyre

9 Thus says the LORD:
For three crimes of Tyre, and for four,
I will not revoke my word;
Because they delivered whole groups captive
to Edom,
and did not remember the pact of
brotherhood,*
10 I will send fire upon the wall of Tyre,
to devour her castles.

Edom

11 Thus says the LORD:
For three crimes of Edom, and for four,
I will not revoke my word;
Because he pursued his brother* with the
sword,
choking up all pity;
Because he persisted in his anger
and kept his wrath to the end,
12 I will send fire upon Teman,
and it will devour the castles of Bozrah.*

Ammon

13 Thus says the LORD:
For three crimes of the Ammonites, and for
four,
I will not revoke my word;
Because they ripped open expectant mothers
in Gilead,
while extending their territory,
14 I will kindle a fire upon the wall of Rabbah,*
and it will devour her castles
Amid clamor on the day of battle
and stormwind in a time of tempest.
15 Their king shall go into captivity,
he and his princes with him, says the LORD.

CHAPTER 2

Moab

1 Thus says the LORD:
For three crimes of Moab, and for four,
I will not revoke my word;
Because he burned to ashes
the bones of Edom's king,*
2 I will send fire upon Moab,
to devour the castles of Kerioth;
Moab shall meet death amid uproar
and shouts and trumpet blasts.
3 I will root out the judge from her midst,
and her princes I will slay with him, says the
LORD.

Judah

4 Thus says the LORD:
For three crimes of Judah, and for four,
I will not revoke my word;
Because they spurned the law of the LORD,

1, 4: Fire: devastation caused by the Assyrians (Am 1, 7. 10. 12. 14; 2, 2. 5); cf 1 Sm 15, 18. Hazael and Ben-hadad: kings of the Arameans whose capital was Damascus (v 5); they fought against Israel (2 Kgs 13, 3), and had long occupied the region of Gilead (v 3) in Transjordan.

1, 5: Bar of Damascus: the beam securing the main gate of the city against invaders, symbol of its defenses. Valley of Aven ("vale of wickedness") and Beth-eden ("house of pleasure"): Aramean territory from southwest to northeast.

1, 9: Pact of brotherhood: Hiram of Tyre had made a pact with Solomon and called him brother (1 Kgs 5, 12; 9, 13).

1, 11: Pursued his brother: the Edomites were descended from Esau, the brother of Jacob (Gn 25—27); nevertheless they constantly nourished enmity against Jacob's descendants, the Israelites.

1, 12: Teman and Bozrah: two of the chief cities of Edom; cf Jer 49, 20.

1, 14: Rabbah: now called Amman, the modern capital of the Hashemite Kingdom of Jordan.

2, 1: Here the prophet stresses the gravity of Moab's violation of the Semitic custom of providing honorable burial for the dead.

and did not keep his statutes;
Because the lies* which their fathers followed
have led them astray,
5 I will send fire upon Judah,
to devour the castles of Jerusalem.

Israel

6 Thus says the LORD:
For three crimes of Israel, and for four,*
I will not revoke my word;
Because they sell the just man for silver,
and the poor man for a pair of sandals.*
7 They trample the heads of the weak
into the dust of the earth,
and force the lowly out of the way.
Son and father go to the same prostitute,
profaning my holy name.
8 Upon garments taken in pledge
they recline beside any altar;*
And the wine of those who have been fined
they drink in the house of their god.

9 Yet it was I who destroyed the Amorites before them,
who were as tall as the cedars,
and as strong as the oak trees.
I destroyed their fruit above,
and their roots beneath. [c]
10 It was I who brought you up from the land of Egypt,
and who led you through the desert for forty years,
to occupy the land of the Amorites: [d]
11 I who raised up prophets among your sons,
and nazirites* among your young men.
Is this not so, O men of Israel?
says the LORD.
12 But you gave the nazirites wine to drink,
and commanded the prophets not to prophesy.
13 Beware, I will crush you into the ground
as a wagon crushes when laden with sheaves.
14 Flight shall perish from the swift,
and the strong man shall not retain his strength;
The warrior shall not save his life,
15 nor the bowman stand his ground;
The swift of foot shall not escape,
nor the horseman save his life.
16 And the most stouthearted of warriors
shall flee naked on that day, says the LORD.

II: Words and Woes for Israel

CHAPTER 3

First Word 1 Hear this word, O men of Israel, that the LORD pronounces over you, over the whole family that I brought up from the land of Egypt:

2 You alone have I favored,
more than all the families of the earth;
Therefore I will punish you
for all your crimes.*

3 Do two walk together
unless they have agreed?
4 Does a lion roar in the forest
when it has no prey?
Does a young lion cry out from its den
unless it has seized something?
5 Is a bird brought to earth by a snare
when there is no lure for it?
Does a snare spring up from the ground
without catching anything?
6 If the trumpet sounds in a city,
will the people not be frightened?
If evil befalls a city,
has not the LORD caused it?*
7 Indeed, the Lord GOD does nothing

2, 4: The lies: false gods, who exist only in the minds of their worshipers. The crimes of Judah are infidelity and idolatry, in contrast to the sins for which the surrounding nations are judged.
2, 6–13: The detailed crimes of Israel are placed in strong contrast with the benefits with which the Lord favored his people.
2, 6: A pair of sandals: indicating how cheaply the rich regarded the poor.
2, 8: Upon garments . . . any altar: usurers kept the garments taken as pledges from the poor; but instead of restoring them to their owners before nightfall (Ex 22, 25; Dt 24, 12), they used them in idolatrous worship. Wine . . . their god: under the guise of a religious ceremony they drink the wine obtained through unjust fines.
2, 11: Nazirites: see note on Nm 6, 1ff.
3, 2: God's choice of Israel brought its own responsibility.
3, 6: The sufferings which sinful man experiences through the permissive will of God are presented here, as elsewhere in the Old Testament, simply as caused by the Lord.

c Nm 21, 24; Dt 2, 24. d Ex 14, 21; Dt 8, 2. 14.

without revealing his plan
to his servants, the prophets.

8 The lion roars—
who will not be afraid!
The Lord GOD speaks—
who will not prophesy!

9 Proclaim this in the castles of Ashdod,
in the castles of the land of Egypt:
"Gather about the mountain of Samaria,
and see the great disorders within her,
the oppression in her midst."*
10 For they know not how to do what is right,
says the LORD,
Storing up in their castles
what they have extorted and robbed.
11 Therefore, thus says the Lord GOD:
An enemy shall surround the land,
and strip you of your strength,
and pillage your castles.

12 Thus says the LORD:
As the shepherd snatches from the mouth of
the lion
a pair of legs or the tip of an ear of his sheep,
So the Israelites who dwell in Samaria shall
escape
with the corner of a couch or a piece of a
cot.

13 Hear and bear witness against the house of
Jacob, says the Lord GOD, the God of hosts:

14 On the day when I punish Israel for his crimes,
I will visit also the altars of Bethel:
The horns of the altar shall be broken off
and fall to the ground.
15 Then will I strike the winter house
and the summer house;
The ivory apartments* shall be ruined,
and their many rooms shall be no more,
says the LORD.

CHAPTER 4

Second Word

1 Hear this word, women of the mountain of
Samaria,
you cows of Bashan,*
You who oppress the weak
and abuse the needy;
Who say to your lords,
"Bring drink for us!"
2 The Lord GOD has sworn by his holiness:
Truly the days are coming upon you
When they shall drag you away with hooks,
the last of you with fishhooks;
3 You shall go out through the breached walls
each by the most direct way,
And you shall be cast into the mire,
says the LORD.

4 Come to Bethel and sin,
to Gilgal, and sin the more;*
Each morning bring your sacrifices,
every third day, your tithes;
5 Burn leavened food as a thanksgiving sacrifice,
proclaim publicly your freewill offerings,
For so you love to do, O men of Israel,
says the Lord GOD.

6 Though I have made your teeth
clean of food in all your cities,
and have made bread scarce in all your
dwellings,
Yet you returned not to me,
says the LORD.

7 Though I also withheld the rain from you
when the harvest was still three months
away;
I sent rain upon one city
but not upon another;
One field was watered by rain,
but another without rain dried up;
8 Though two or three cities staggered to one
city

3, 9: Israel's southern neighbors, beyond Judah, are invited by the prophetic orator to witness the moral disorders of God's people.

3, 15: Ivory apartments: rooms containing furniture inlaid in ivory, similar to the pieces discovered in the excavations at Samaria.

4, 1: Bashan: the region east of the Sea of Galilee, famous for its rich pasture and fattened herds, to which Amos likens the indolent women of Samaria.

4, 4f: This invitation to the sanctuaries of the northern kingdom is ironical. Pilgrimages to the shrines of Bethel and Gilgal were the more displeasing to God because they were contrary to his will and ineffective toward improvement of morals.

for water that did not quench their thirst;
Yet you returned not to me,
says the LORD.

9 I struck you with blight and searing wind;
your many gardens and vineyards,
your fig trees and olive trees the locust
devoured;
Yet you returned not to me,
says the LORD. [e]

10 I sent upon you a pestilence like that of
Egypt,*
and with the sword I slew your young men;
Your horses I let be captured,
to your nostrils I brought the stench of your
camps;
Yet you returned not to me,
says the LORD.

11 I brought upon you such upheaval
as when God overthrew Sodom and
Gomorrah:
you were like a brand plucked from the fire;
Yet you returned not to me,
says the LORD. [f]

12 So now I will deal with you in my own way,
O Israel!
and since I will deal thus with you,
prepare to meet your God, O Israel:
13 Him who formed the mountains, and created
the wind,
and declares to man his thoughts;
Who made the dawn and the darkness,
and strides upon the heights of the earth:
The LORD, the God of hosts by name.

CHAPTER 5

Third Word

1 Hear this word which I utter over you,
a lament, O house of Israel:
2 She is fallen, to rise no more,
the virgin Israel;
She lies abandoned upon her land,
with no one to raise her up.

3 For thus says the Lord GOD:
The city that marched out with a thousand
shall be left with a hundred,
Another that marched out with a hundred
shall be left with ten,
of the house of Israel.

4 For thus says the LORD
to the house of Israel:
Seek me, that you may live,
5 but do not seek Bethel;
Do not come to Gilgal,
and do not cross to Beer-sheba.
For Gilgal shall be led into exile,
and Bethel shall become nought.
6 Seek the LORD, that you may live,
lest he come upon the house of Joseph* like
a fire
That shall consume, with none to quench it
for the house of Israel:
8 He who made the Pleiades and Orion,
who turns darkness into dawn,
and darkens day into night;
Who summons the waters of the sea,
and pours them out upon the surface of the
earth; [g]
9 Who flashes destruction upon the strong,
and brings ruin upon the fortress;
whose name is LORD.

First Woe

7 Woe to those who turn judgment to
wormwood
and cast justice to the ground!
10 They hate him who reproves at the gate*
and abhor him who speaks the truth.
11 Therefore, because you have trampled upon
the weak
and exacted of them levies of grain,
Though you have built houses of hewn stone,
you shall not live in them!

4, 10: Pestilence like that of Egypt: plagues were well known in Egypt; cf Dt 7, 15; 28, 27. 60. Stench of your camps: caused by the unburied bodies.

5, 6: House of Joseph: the kingdom of Israel or northern kingdom, the chief tribes of which were descended from Ephraim and Manasseh, the sons of Joseph; cf Am 5, 15; 6, 6.

5, 10: At the gate: see note on Ps 127, 5.

e Hg 2, 17. f Gn 19, 24. g Am 9, 6.

Though you have planted choice vineyards,
you shall not drink their wine! [h]
12 Yes, I know how many are your crimes,
how grievous your sins:
Oppressing the just, accepting bribes,
repelling the needy at the gate!
13 Therefore the prudent man is silent at this time,
for it is an evil time.
14 Seek good and not evil,
that you may live;
Then truly will the LORD, the God of hosts,
be with you as you claim!
15 Hate evil and love good,
and let justice prevail at the gate;
Then it may be that the LORD, the God of hosts,
will have pity on the remnant of Joseph. [i]

16 Therefore, thus says the LORD,
the God of hosts, the Lord:
In every square there shall be lamentation,
and in every street they shall cry, Alas! Alas!
They shall summon the farmers to wail
and professional mourners to lament,
17 And in every vineyard there shall be lamentation
when I pass through your midst, says the LORD.

Second Woe

18 Woe to those who yearn for the day of the LORD!*
What will this day of the LORD mean for you?
Darkness and not light! [j]
19 As if a man were to flee from a lion,
and a bear should meet him;
Or as if on entering his house
he were to rest his hand against the wall,
and a snake should bite him.
20 Will not the day of the LORD be darkness and not light,
gloom without any brightness?

21 *I hate, I spurn your feasts,
I take no pleasure in your solemnities; [k]
22 Your cereal offerings I will not accept,
nor consider your stall-fed peace offerings.
23 Away with your noisy songs!
I will not listen to the melodies of your harps.
But if you would offer me holocausts,
24 then let justice surge like water,
and goodness like an unfailing stream.
25 Did you bring me sacrifices and offerings [l]
for forty years in the desert, O house of Israel?*
26 You will carry away Sakkuth, your king,
and Kaiwan, your star god,*
the images that you have made for yourselves;
27 For I will exile you beyond Damascus,
say I, the LORD, the God of hosts by name.

CHAPTER 6

Third Woe

1 *Woe to the complacent in Zion,
to the overconfident on the mount of Samaria,*

5, 18: Day of the Lord: a technical expression which in earliest times referred to God's special intervention in human affairs. Through it his power and justice triumphed in his people. The present passage is the first instance in which it means a day of punishment of sinners. During the exile it assumed the meaning of a time when God would avenge Israel against her oppressors and bring about her restoration (Jer 50, 27; Ez 30, 3ff). Still later it came to mean the day of final judgment of the world when the good will be rewarded and the wicked punished (Mal 3, 19ff; Jl 2, 1ff; Zep 1, 14ff).

5, 21–27: The Lord condemns, not ritual worship in itself, but the cult whose exterior rites and solemnity have no relation to interior morality and justice. The Israelites falsely worshiped him as neighboring nations adored Baal or Chamos, deities which were thought to protect their respective peoples against their enemies in return for ritual observances, without any relation to right conduct.

5, 25: The meaning is not certain; according to some, the idea is that during the forty years' wandering in the desert the simple, rudimentary worship of God was accompanied by the practice of justice, in contrast to the elaborate ritual unaccompanied by works of justice in the prophet's time.

5, 26: Sakkuth . . . star god: although the text is uncertain, it seems quite probable that reference is made to the Assyrian deities, Sakkuth, god of war and light, and Kaiwan, the planet Saturn. The people will go into exile, from which these gods have been unable to save them.

6, 1–7: The luxury of the people in Samaria will be punished by exile. They failed to learn the lesson from Calneh, Hamath and Gath at the approach of the powerful and warlike Assyrians.

6, 1: The complacent in Zion . . . the overconfident . . . of Samaria: the proud and self-interested rulers of Judah and Israel.

h Zep 1, 13. i Ps 97, 10; Rom 12, 9. j Jer 30, 7; Jl 2, 11; Zep 1, 15. k Is 1, 11; Jer 6, 20; Mal 1, 12. l Acts 7, 42.

Leaders of a nation favored from the first,
to whom the people of Israel have
recourse! [m]
2 Pass over to Calneh and see,
go from there to Hamath the great,
and down to Gath of the Philistines!
Are you better than these kingdoms,
or is your territory wider than theirs?
3 You would put off the evil day,
yet you hasten the reign of violence!

4 Lying upon beds of ivory,
stretched comfortably on their couches,
They eat lambs taken from the flock,
and calves from the stall!
5 Improvising to the music of the harp,
like David, they devise their own
accompaniment.
6 They drink wine from bowls
and anoint themselves with the best oils;
yet they are not made ill by the collapse of
Joseph!
7 Therefore, now they shall be the first to go
into exile,
and their wanton revelry shall be done
away with.

8 The Lord GOD has sworn by his very self,
say I, the LORD, the God of hosts:
I abhor the pride of Jacob,
I hate his castles,
and I give over the city with everything in
it; [n]
9 Should there remain ten men
in a single house, these shall die.
10 Only a few shall be left
to carry the dead out of the houses;
If one says to a man inside a house,
"Is anyone with you?" and he answers, "No
one,"
Then he shall say, "Silence!"
for no one must mention the name of the
LORD.

11 Indeed, the LORD has given the command
to shatter the great house to bits,
and reduce the small house to rubble.
12 Can horses run across a cliff?
or can one plow the sea with oxen?*
Yet you have turned judgment into gall,
and the fruit of justice into wormwood.
13 You rejoice in Lodebar,
and say, "Have we not, by our own
strength,
seized for ourselves Karnaim?"*
14 Beware, I am raising up against you, O house
of Israel,
say I, the LORD, the God of hosts,
A nation* that shall oppress you
from Labo of Hamath even to the Wadi
Arabah.

III: Symbolic Visions: Threats and Promises

CHAPTER 7

Vision of Locusts 1 This is what the Lord GOD
showed me: He was forming a locust swarm
when the late growth began to come up (the late
growth after the king's mowing*). 2 While they
were eating all the grass in the land, I said:

Forgive, O Lord GOD!
How can Jacob stand?
He is so small!

3 And the LORD repented of this. "It shall not
be," said the Lord GOD.
Vision of Fire 4 Then the Lord GOD showed
me this: he called for a judgment by fire.* It had
devoured the great abyss, and was consuming
the land, 5 when I said:

Cease, O Lord GOD!
How can Jacob stand?
He is so small!

6, 12: Can horses . . . oxen?: one cannot change the course of nature, as the Israelites attempted to do by their sins of injustice.

6, 13: Lodebar . . . Karnaim: in Transjordan; they had been captured by the Israelites. Perhaps it is in irony that reference is made to these two cities, for the root of the first suggests "nothing" and that of the second, "horns" or "strength."

6, 14: A nation: Assyria.

7, 1: The king's mowing: the first mowing, a portion of which was payable to the king as a tax.

7, 4: Fire: understood by many as a burning drought.

m Lk 6, 24. n Jer 51, 14.

6The LORD repented of this. "This also shall
not be," said the Lord GOD.
Vision of the Plummet 7Then the Lord GOD
showed me this: he was standing by a wall,
plummet in hand.* 8The LORD asked me, "What
do you see, Amos?" And when I answered, "A
plummet," the LORD said:

See, I will lay the plummet
in the midst of my people Israel;
I will forgive them no longer.
9 The high places of Isaac shall be laid waste,
and the sanctuaries of Israel made desolate;
I will attack the house of Jeroboam with the sword.

Amos and Amaziah 10Amaziah, the priest of
Bethel, sent word to Jeroboam, king of Israel:
"Amos has conspired against you here within
Israel; the country cannot endure all his words.
11 For this is what Amos says:

Jeroboam shall die by the sword,
and Israel shall surely be exiled from its land."

12To Amos, Amaziah said: "Off with you,
visionary, flee to the land of Judah! There earn
your bread by prophesying, 13but never again
prophesy in Bethel; for it is the king's sanctuary
and a royal temple." 14Amos answered Amaziah,
"I was no prophet, nor have I belonged to a
company of prophets; I was a shepherd and a
dresser of sycamores.* 15The LORD took me
from following the flock, and said to me, Go,
prophesy to my people Israel. 16Now hear the
word of the LORD!"

You say: prophesy not against Israel,
preach not against the house of Isaac.
17 Now thus says the LORD:
Your wife shall be made a harlot in the city,
and your sons and daughters shall fall by the sword;
Your land shall be divided by measuring line,
and you yourself shall die in an unclean land;
Israel shall be exiled far from its land.

CHAPTER 8

Vision of the Fruit Basket 1This is what the
Lord GOD showed me: a basket of ripe fruit.
2"What do you see, Amos?" he asked. I an-
swered, "A basket of ripe fruit." Then the LORD
said to me:

The time is ripe to have done with my people Israel;
I will forgive them no longer.
3 The temple songs shall become wailings on that day,
says the Lord GOD.
Many shall be the corpses,
strewn everywhere.—Silence!

Against Greed

4 Hear this, you who trample upon the needy
and destroy the poor of the land!
5 "When will the new moon be over," you ask,
"that we may sell our grain,
and the sabbath, that we may display the wheat?
We will diminish the ephah,*
add to the shekel,
and fix our scales for cheating!
6 We will buy the lowly man for silver,
and the poor man for a pair of sandals;
even the refuse of the wheat we will sell!"
7 The LORD has sworn by the pride of Jacob:*
Never will I forget a thing they have done!
8 Shall not the land tremble because of this,
and all who dwell in it mourn,
While it rises up and tosses like the Nile,
and settles back like the river of Egypt?*
9 On that day, says the Lord GOD,
I will make the sun set at midday
and cover the earth with darkness in broad daylight.

7, 7: Plummet in hand: signifying that God is about to withdraw his mercy from his people and that the nation is to be measured for destruction.

7, 14f: Amos denies that he belonged to the class of professional prophets; his vocation is due to the personal intervention of the Lord.

8, 5: Ephah: a standard of measure; a little more than a bushel.

8, 7: The pride of Jacob: the sinful pride detested by God (Am 6, 8), in contrast to God himself, who is the true Pride of Jacob.

8, 8: The figure is based on the annual flooding of the river Nile.

[10] I will turn your feasts into mourning
and all your songs into lamentations.
I will cover the loins of all with sackcloth
and make every head bald.
I will make them mourn as for an only son,
and bring their day to bitter end. [o]

[11] Yes, days are coming, says the Lord GOD,
when I will send famine upon the land:
Not a famine of bread, or thirst for water,
but for hearing the word of the LORD.
[12] Then shall they wander from sea to sea
and rove from the north to the east
In search of the word of the LORD,
but they shall not find it.

[13] On that day, fair virgins and young men
shall faint from thirst;
[14] Those who swear by the shameful idol of
Samaria,
"By the life of your god, O Dan!"
"By the life of your love, O Beer-sheba!"
those shall fall, never to rise again.*

CHAPTER 9

Vision of the Altar* [1] I saw the Lord standing beside the altar, and he said:

Strike the bases, so that the doorjambs totter
till you break them off on the heads of them
all!
Those who are left I will slay with the sword;
not one shall flee,
no survivor shall escape.
[2] Though they break through to the nether
world,
even from there my hand shall bring them
out;
Though they climb to the heavens,
I will bring them down; [p]
[3] Though they hide on the summit of Carmel,
there too I will hunt them out and take
them away;
Though they hide from my gaze
in the bottom of the sea,
I will command the serpent* there to bite
them;
[4] Though they are led into captivity by their
enemies,
there will I command the sword to slay
them.
I will fix my gaze upon them
for evil, and not for good, [q]
[5] I, the Lord GOD of hosts.
I melt the earth with my touch,
so that all who dwell on it mourn,
While it all rises up like the Nile,
and settles back like the river of Egypt;
[6] I have built heaven, my upper chamber,
and established my vault over the earth;
I summon the waters of the sea
and pour them out upon the surface of the
earth,
I, the LORD by name. [r]

[7] Are you not like the Ethiopians to me,
O men of Israel, says the LORD?
Did I not bring the Israelites from the land of
Egypt
As I brought the Philistines from Caphtor
and the Arameans* from Kir? [s]
[8] The eyes of the Lord GOD are on this sinful
kingdom:
I will destroy it from off the face of the
earth.

Epilogue: Messianic Perspective

But I will not destroy the house of Jacob
completely,
says the LORD.
[9] For see, I have given the command
to sift the house of Israel among all the
nations,
As one sifts with a sieve,
letting no pebble fall to the ground.

8, 14: Dan and Beer-sheba, the extreme northern and southern limits of the country, where idolatrous worship was offered.

9, 1–8: There will be no escape from God's punishment, symbolized here by the destruction of a building, probably the schismatic temple at Bethel.

9, 3: Serpent: the sea monster of familiar legend, subdued by God at the time of creation and lurking still in the ocean depths; cf Ps 89, 10f.

9, 7: The Ethiopians . . . the Philistines . . . the Arameans: by nature Israel is not different from any other nation. It was not because of any merit on Israel's part that God delivered them from Egypt. Caphtor: the island of Crete.

o Tb 2, 6; 1 Mc 1, 41. p Ps 139, 8. q Jer 44, 11. r Am 5, 8. s Dt 2, 23; Jer 47, 4.

10 By the sword shall all sinners among my
people die,
those who say, "Evil will not reach or
overtake us."
11 *On that day I will raise up
the fallen hut of David;
I will wall up its breaches,
raise up its ruins,
and rebuild it as in the days of old, [t]
12 That they may conquer what is left of Edom
and all the nations that shall bear my name,
say I, the LORD, who will do this.
13 Yes, days are coming,
says the LORD,
When the plowman shall overtake the reaper,
and the vintager, him who sows the seed;
The juice of grapes shall drip down the
mountains,
and all the hills shall run with it. [u]
14 I will bring about the restoration of my people
Israel;
they shall rebuild and inhabit their ruined
cities,
Plant vineyards and drink the wine,
set out gardens and eat the fruits.
15 I will plant them upon their own ground;
never again shall they be plucked
From the land I have given them,
say I, the LORD, your God.

9, 11f: In Acts 15, 15ff St. James interprets this passage in a messianic sense. Fallen hut: the kingdom. The nations that shall bear my name: the Gentile peoples who shall be converted to the Lord, that is, conquered by him, and therefore shall bear his name.

t Acts 15, 16. u Jl 3, 18.

THE BOOK OF OBADIAH

The twenty-one verses of this book contain the shortest and sternest prophecy in the Old Testament. Nothing is known of the author, although his oracle against Edom, a long-standing enemy of Israel, indicates a date of composition sometime in the fifth century B.C. During this period the Edomites had been forced to abandon their ancient home near the Gulf of Aqaba and had settled in southern Judah, where they appear among the adversaries of the Jews returning from exile.

The prophecy is a bitter cry for vengeance against Edom for its heinous crimes. The mountain of Esau will be occupied and ravaged by the enemy but Zion shall remain inviolate. Judah and Israel shall again form one nation; and that triumphant refrain of Israelite eschatology will be heard once more: "The Kingdom is the Lord's!" Many of the verses in this prophecy can be paralleled in Jer 49, 7-22, but it is difficult to determine the precise relationship between these similar passages.

Title and Theme

1 The vision of Obadiah.
[Thus says the LORD God:]
Of Edom we have heard a message from the
LORD,
and a herald has been sent among the
nations:
"Up! let us go to war against him!" [a]

Edom Shall Perish

2 See, I make you small among the nations; [b]
you are held in dire contempt.
3 The pride of your heart has deceived you:
you who dwell in the clefts of the rock,
whose abode is in the heights,
Who say in your heart,
"Who will bring me down to earth?"

a Jer 49, 14. b 2ff: Jer 49, 15f.

4 Though you go as high as the eagle,
and your nest be set among the stars,
From there will I bring you down,
says the LORD.
5 If thieves came to you, if robbers by night, [c]
how could you be thus destroyed:
would they not steal merely till they had enough?
If vintagers came to you,
would they not leave some gleanings?*
6 How they search Esau,
seek out his hiding places!
7 To the border they drive you—
all your allies;
They deceive you, they overpower you—
those at peace with you;
Those who eat your bread
lay snares beneath you:
There is no understanding in him!*
8 Shall I not, says the LORD, on that day
make the wise men* disappear from Edom,
and understanding from the mount of Esau? [d]
9 Your warriors, O Teman,* shall be crushed,
till all on Mount Esau are destroyed.

The Cause

10 Because of violence to your brother Jacob,*
disgrace shall cover you
and you shall be destroyed forever. [e]
11 On the day when you stood by,
on the day when aliens carried off his possessions,
And strangers entered his gates
and cast lots over Jerusalem,
you too were one of them.*
12 Gaze not upon the day of your brother,
the day of his disaster;
Exult not over the children of Judah
on the day of their ruin;
Speak not haughtily
on the day of distress!
13 Enter not the gate of my people
on the day of their calamity;
Gaze not, you at least, upon his misfortune
on the day of his calamity;
Lay not hands upon his possessions
on the day of his calamity!
14 Stand not at the crossroads
to slay his refugees;
Betray not his fugitives
on the day of distress!

Judgment upon the Nations

15 For near is the day of the LORD[f]
for all the nations!
As you have done, so shall it be done to you,
your deed shall come back upon your own head;
16 As you have drunk* upon my holy mountain,
so shall all the nations drink continually.
Yes, they shall drink and swallow,
and shall become as though they had not been.

Judah Shall Be Restored

17 But on Mount Zion there shall be a portion saved;*
the mountain shall be holy,
And the house of Jacob shall take possession
of those that dispossessed them.
18 The house of Jacob shall be a fire,
and the house of Joseph a flame;
The house of Esau shall be stubble,
and they shall set them ablaze and devour them;

5: Something of value may escape the robber, and the vintager always leaves something for the gleaners, but God's devastation of Edom will be complete.

7: There is no understanding in him: Edom's faithless allies assure one another that he does not have sense enough to be able to defend himself.

8: The wise men: Edom was proverbial for its wise men; cf Jer 49, 7.

9: Teman: one of the names used for the land southeast of Palestine, here synonymous with Edom. Esau: here used as the name of the land.

10: Your brother Jacob: Esau, also called Edom, and Jacob, the father of Judah, were the sons of Isaac (Gn 25, 24ff).

11: After the devastation of Judah, Edom occupied the southern part of its territory. Edomites also joined the invading Chaldean forces (13) and assisted them in capturing the people of Judah (14).

16: As you have drunk: the Lord addresses the people of Judah. As the people of Jerusalem have drunk the cup of retribution, so shall the nations, and especially Edom (18), suffer punishment. This metaphorical use of drinking the cup of God's wrath is common in the Bible; cf Jb 21, 20; Is 19, 14; Jer 25, 15f.

17ff: The Israelites shall be restored and shall occupy the lands of those who oppressed them. The survivors of Judah shall be rejoined by the returned exiles from northern Israel.

c Jer 49, 9. d Is 29, 14; 1 Cor 1, 19. e Gn 27, 41f. f 15f: Ps 137, 7ff.

Then none shall survive of the house of Esau,
for the LORD has spoken.
19 They shall occupy the Negeb, the mount of Esau,
and the foothills of the Philistines;
And they shall occupy the lands of Ephraim
and the lands of Samaria,
and Benjamin shall occupy Gilead.
20 The captives of this host of the children of Israel
shall occupy the Canaanite land as far as Zarephath,*
And the captives of Jerusalem who are in Sepharad
shall occupy the cities of the Negeb.
21 And saviors* shall ascend Mount Zion
to rule the mount of Esau,
and the kingship shall be the LORD's.

20: Zarephath: a town in Phoenicia, north of Tyre; cf 1 Kgs 17, 10. Ezekiel's ideal boundaries of the new Israel (Ez 47, 13ff) extend farther north. Sepharad: probably Sardis in western Asia Minor. The later rabbis thought it to be Spain.

21: Saviors: the victorious Israelites who will rule over their enemies after the fashion of the ancient Judges; cf Jgs 3, 9. 15. 31; 10, 1.

THE BOOK OF JONAH

Written in the postexilic era, probably in the fifth century B.C., this book is a didactic story with an important theological message. It concerns a disobedient prophet who attempted to run away from his divine commission, was cast overboard and swallowed by a great fish, rescued in a marvelous manner, and sent on his way to Nineveh, the traditional enemy of Israel. To the surprise of Jonah, the wicked city listened to his message of doom and repented immediately. All, from king to lowliest subject, humbled themselves in sackcloth and ashes. Seeing their repentance, God did not carry out the punishment he had planned for them. Whereupon Jonah complained to God about the unexpected success of his mission; he was bitter because Yahweh, instead of destroying had led the people to repentance and then spared them.

From this partly humorous story, a very sublime lesson may be drawn. Jonah stands for a narrow and vindictive mentality, all too common among the Jews of that period. Because they were the chosen people, a good many of them cultivated an intolerant nationalism which limited the mercy of God to their nation. It was abhorrent to their way of thinking that nations as wicked as Assyria should escape his wrath.

The prophecy, which is both instructive and entertaining, strikes directly at this viewpoint. It is a parable of mercy, showing that God's threatened punishments are but the expression of a merciful will which moves all men to repent and seek forgiveness. The universality of the story contrasts sharply with the particularistic spirit of many in the postexilic community. The book has also prepared the way for the gospel with its message of redemption for all, both Jew and Gentile.

CHAPTER 1

The First Mission 1 This is the word of the
LORD that came to Jonah,[a] son of Amittai:*
2 "Set out for the great city of Nineveh, and
preach against it; their wickedness has come up
before me."[b] 3 But Jonah made ready to flee to
Tarshish* away from the LORD. He went down
to Joppa, found a ship going to Tarshish, paid the
fare, and went aboard to journey with them to
Tarshish, away from the LORD.

1, 1: Jonah, son of Amittai: a prophet of this name lived at the time of Jeroboam II (786–746 B.C.).

1, 3: Tarshish: identified by many with Tartessus, an ancient Phoenician colony in southwest Spain; precise identification with any particular Phoenician center in the western Mediterranean is uncertain. To the Hebrews it stood for the far west.

a 2 Kgs 14, 25. b Jon 3, 3; 4, 11.

4The LORD, however, hurled a violent wind
upon the sea, and in the furious tempest that
arose the ship was on the point of breaking up.
5Then the mariners became frightened and each
one cried to his god. To lighten the ship for
themselves, they threw its cargo into the sea.
Meanwhile, Jonah had gone down into the hold
of the ship, and lay there fast asleep. 6The
captain came to him and said, "What are you
doing asleep? Rise up, call upon your God!
Perhaps God will be mindful of us so that we
may not perish."

7Then they said to one another, "Come, let us
cast lots to find out on whose account we have
met with this misfortune." So they cast lots, and
thus singled out Jonah. 8"Tell us," they said,
"what is your business? Where do you come
from? What is your country, and to what people
do you belong?" 9"I am a Hebrew," Jonah
answered them; "I worship the LORD, the God
of heaven, who made the sea and the dry land."

10Now the men were seized with great fear
and said to him, "How could you do such a
thing!"—They knew that he was fleeing from
the LORD, because he had told them.— 11"What
shall we do with you," they asked, "that the sea
may quiet down for us?" For the sea was
growing more and more turbulent. 12Jonah said
to them, "Pick me up and throw me into the sea,
that it may quiet down for you; since I know it is
because of me that this violent storm has come
upon you."

13Still the men rowed hard to regain the land,
but they could not, for the sea grew ever more
turbulent. 14Then they cried to the LORD: "We
beseech you, O LORD, let us not perish for taking
this man's life; do not charge us with shedding
innocent blood, for you, LORD, have done as you
saw fit."* 15Then they took Jonah and threw
him into the sea, and the sea's raging abated.
16Struck with great fear of the LORD, the men
offered sacrifice and made vows to him.

1, 14: Since it has pleased the Lord to punish Jonah, the mariners ask that in ridding themselves of him they be not charged with the crime of murder.

CHAPTER 2

1But the LORD sent a large fish, that swal-
lowed Jonah; and he remained in the belly of the
fish three days and three nights.[c] 2From the
belly of the fish Jonah said this prayer to the
LORD, his God:

Psalm of Thanksgiving

3 Out of my distress I called to the LORD,
and he answered me;
From the midst of the nether world I cried for help,
and you heard my voice.[d]
4 For you cast me into the deep, into the heart of the sea,
and the flood enveloped me;
All your breakers and your billows
passed over me.[e]
5 Then I said, "I am banished from your sight!
yet would I again look upon your holy temple."[f]
6 The waters swirled about me, threatening my life;
the abyss enveloped me;
seaweed clung about my head.[g]
7 Down I went to the roots of the mountains;
the bars of the nether world
were closing behind me forever,
But you brought up my life from the pit,
O LORD, my God.[h]
8 When my soul fainted within me,
I remembered the LORD;
My prayer reached you
in your holy temple.[i]
9 Those who worship vain idols
forsake their source of mercy.[j]
10 But I, with resounding praise,
will sacrifice to you;
What I have vowed I will pay:
deliverance is from the LORD.[k]

11Then the LORD commanded the fish to spew
Jonah upon the shore.

c Mt 12, 40; 16, 4; Lk 11, 30; 1 Cor 15, 4. d Pss 18, 7; 120, 1. e Ps 42, 8. f Ps 31, 23; Is 38, 11. g Pss 18, 5; 69, 2. h Pss 16, 10; 30, 4. i Pss 5, 8; 18, 7; 88, 3. j Ps 31, 7. k Ps 50, 14.

CHAPTER 3

Conversion of Nineveh [1]The word of the LORD came to Jonah a second time: [2]"Set out for the great city of Nineveh, and announce to it the message that I will tell you." [3]So Jonah made ready and went to Nineveh, according to the LORD's bidding. Now Nineveh was an enormously large city; it took three days to go through it. [4]Jonah began his journey through the city, and had gone but a single day's walk announcing, "Forty days more and Nineveh shall be destroyed,"* [5]when the people of Nineveh believed God; they proclaimed a fast and all of them, great and small, put on sackcloth.[l]

[6]When the news reached the king of Nineveh, he rose from his throne, laid aside his robe, covered himself with sackcloth, and sat in the ashes. [7]Then he had this proclaimed throughout Nineveh, by decree of the king and his nobles: "Neither man nor beast, neither cattle nor sheep, shall taste anything; they shall not eat, nor shall they drink water. [8]Man and beast shall be covered with sackcloth* and call loudly to God; every man shall turn from his evil way and from the violence he has in hand. [9]Who knows, God may relent and forgive, and withold his blazing wrath, so that we shall not perish."[m] [10]When God saw by their actions how they turned from their evil way, he repented of the evil that he had threatened to do to them; he did not carry it out.

CHAPTER 4

Jonah's Anger: God's Reproof [1]But this was greatly displeasing to Jonah, and he became angry.* [2]"I beseech you, LORD," he prayed, "is not this what I said while I was still in my own country? This is why I fled at first to Tarshish. I knew that you are a gracious and merciful God, slow to anger, rich in clemency, loathe to punish.[n] [3]And now, LORD, please take my life from me; for it is better for me to die than to live."[o] [4]But the LORD asked, "Have you reason to be angry?"

[5]Jonah then left the city for a place to the east of it, where he built himself a hut and waited under it in the shade, to see what would happen to the city. [6]And when the LORD God provided a gourd plant,* that grew up over Jonah's head, giving shade that relieved him of any discomfort, Jonah was very happy over the plant. [7]But the next morning at dawn God sent a worm which attacked the plant, so that it withered. [8]And when the sun arose, God sent a burning east wind; and the sun beat upon Jonah's head till he became faint. Then he asked for death, saying, "I would be better off dead than alive."

[9]But God said to Jonah, "Have you reason to be angry over the plant?" "I have reason to be angry," Jonah answered, "angry enough to die." [10]Then the LORD said, "You are concerned over the plant which cost you no labor and which you did not raise; it came up in one night and in one night it perished.* [11]And should I not be concerned over Nineveh, the great city, in which there are more than a hundred and twenty thousand persons who cannot distinguish their right hand from their left, not to mention the many cattle?"

3, 4: Shall be destroyed: the Hebrew expression reminds the reader of the "overthrowing" of the wicked cities, Sodom and Gomorrah, by a special act of God.

3, 8: Beast . . . sackcloth: the animals carried the signs of this repentance, as on occasions of joy they bore garlands.

4, 1: He became angry: because of his narrowly nationalistic vindictiveness, Jonah did not wish the Lord to forgive the Ninevites.

4, 6: Gourd plant: the Hebrew word, kikayon, means here a wide-leafed plant of the cucumber or castor-bean variety.

4, 10f: Jonah is selfish in bemoaning his personal loss of a shady gourd plant without any concern over the threat of loss of life to the Ninevites through the destruction of their city. If God in his kindness provided the plant for his prophet without the latter's effort or merit, how much more is he disposed to show love and mercy toward all men, Jew and Gentile, when they repent of their sins and implore his pardon! God's providence is also shown here to extend even to animals.

l Mt 12, 41; Lk 11, 32. m Jl 2, 14. n Ps 86, 5; Jl 2, 13. o 1 Kgs 19, 4.

THE BOOK OF MICAH

Micah was a contemporary of Isaiah. Of his personal life and call we know nothing except that he came from the obscure village of Moresheth in the foothills. His were the broad vistas of the Judean lowland and the distant sea on the western horizon. With burning eloquence he attacked the rich exploiters of the poor, fraudulent merchants, venal judges, corrupt priests and prophets. To the man of the countryside the vices of the nation seemed centered in its capitals, for both Samaria and Jerusalem are singled out for judgment. An interesting notice in Jer 26, 17f informs us that the reform of Hezekiah was influenced by the preaching of Micah.

The prophecy may be divided into three parts: I. The impending judgment of the Lord, followed by an exposition of its causes, Israel's sins. Censure of Judah's leaders for betrayal of their responsibility (1, 1—3, 12). II. The glory of the restored Zion. A prince of David's house will rule over a reunited Israel. (St. Matthew's Nativity narrative points to Christ's birth in Bethlehem as the fulfillment of this prophecy.) A remnant shall survive the chastisement of Judah and her adversaries shall be destroyed (4, 1—5, 14). III. The case against Israel, in which the Lord is portrayed as the plaintiff who has maintained fidelity to the covenant. The somber picture closes with a prayer for national restoration and a beautiful expression of trust in God's pardoning mercy (6, 1—7, 20).

It should be noted that each of these three divisions begins with reproach and the threat of punishment, and ends on a note of hope and promise.

I: Punishment of Israel's Sins

CHAPTER 1

Divine Judgment 1 The word of the LORD which came to Micah of Moresheth in the days of Jotham, Ahaz, and Hezekiah, kings of Judah: that is, the vision he received concerning Samaria and Jerusalem.

2 Hear, O peoples, all of you,
give heed, O earth, and all that fills you! [a]
Let the Lord GOD be witness against you,
the Lord from his holy temple!*
3 For see, the LORD comes forth from his place, [b]
he descends and treads upon the heights of the earth.
4 The mountains melt under him
and the valleys split open,
Like wax before the fire,
like water poured down a slope.

5 For the crime of Jacob all this comes to pass,
and for the sins of the house of Israel.
What is the crime of Jacob?
Is it not Samaria?
And what is the sin of the house of Judah?
Is it not Jerusalem?
6 I will make Samaria a stone heap in the field,
a place to plant for vineyards;
I will throw down into the valley her stones,
and lay bare her foundations.
7 All her idols shall be broken to pieces, [c]
all her wages shall be burned in the fire,
and all her statues I will destroy.
As the wages of a harlot they were gathered,
and to the wages of a harlot shall they return.*

8 For this reason I lament and wail,
I go barefoot and naked;
I utter lamentation like the jackals,
and mourning like the ostriches. [d]
9 There is no remedy for the blow she has been struck;
rather, it has come even to Judah,

1, 2: His holy temple: God's heavenly temple; the prophet pictures a theophany (3f).

1, 7: The comparison of the unfaithful people with a prostitute, first found in Hosea, is frequent with the prophets; probably ritual prostitution is meant; cf Am 2, 7f; Hos 4, 14.

a Dt 32, 1; Is 1, 2. b 3f: Is 26, 21; Na 1, 5; Hb 3, 10. c Hos 9, 1. d Jb 30, 29.

It reaches to the gate of my people,
even to Jerusalem.
10 Publish it not in Gath,*
weep not at all;
In Beth-leaphrah
roll in the dust.[e]
11 Pass by,
you who dwell in Shaphir!
The inhabitants of Zaanan
come not forth from their city.
The lamentation of Beth-ezel
finds in you its grounds.
12 How can the inhabitants of Maroth
hope for good?
For evil has come down from the LORD
to the gate of Jerusalem.
13 Harness steeds to the chariots,
O inhabitants of Lachish;
Lachish, the beginning of sin
for daughter Zion,
Because there were in you
the crimes of Israel.
14 Therefore you shall give parting gifts
to Moresheth-gath;
Beth-achzib is a deception
to the kings of Israel.
15 Yet must I bring to you the conqueror,
O inhabitants of Mareshah;
Even to Adullam shall go
the glory of Israel.

16 Make yourself bald, pluck out your hair,
for the children whom you cherish;
Let your baldness be as the eagle's,
because they are exiled from you.*

CHAPTER 2

Social Evils

1 Woe to those who plan iniquity,
and work out evil on their couches;
In the morning light they accomplish it
when it lies within their power.
2 They covet fields, and seize them;
houses, and they take them;
They cheat an owner of his house,
a man of his inheritance.*
3 Therefore thus says the LORD:
Behold, I am planning against this race an evil
from which you shall not withdraw your
necks;
Nor shall you walk with head high,
for it will be a time of evil.

4 On that day a satire shall be sung over you,
and there shall be a plaintive chant:
"Our ruin is complete,
our fields are portioned out among our
captors,
The fields of my people are measured out,
and no one can get them back!"
5 Thus you shall have no one
to mark out boundaries by lot*
in the assembly of the LORD.

6 "Preach not," they preach,
"let them not preach of these things!"*
The shame will not withdraw.
7 How can it be said, O house of Jacob,
"Is the LORD short of patience,
or are such his deeds?"
Do not my words promise good
to him who walks uprightly?

8 But of late my people has risen up as an
enemy:
you have stripped off the mantle covering
the tunic
Of those who go their way in confidence,
as though it were spoils of war.
9 The women of my people you drive out
from their pleasant houses;

1, 10–15: The Judean cities here named were in the vicinity of Moresheth, the region with which Micah was most familiar. They were to experience divine chastisement. In the Hebrew, wordplays on the names of these cities abound. The text is partly obscure.

1, 16: Shaving the head was a sign of mourning; cf Is 3, 24; Am 8, 10.

2, 2: Land monopoly, also denounced by Isaiah, was a chronic vice in Judah. To protect the poor against it, a man's inheritance, his ancestral property, was supposed to be inviolate; cf 1 Kgs 21, 1–4; but the wealthy in their greed were enslaving men for their debts and depriving them of their land.

2, 5: To mark out boundaries by lot: an allusion to the initial distribution of the land of Palestine among the Israelites; cf Jos 13–21. The appropriate punishment of those greedy for land will be the loss of their land to their enemies (v 4), a loss that will be irrevocable.

2, 6f: The words in quotation marks are the protestations of the people against the prophet's predictions of doom.

e 2 Sm 1, 20.

From their children you take away
forever the honor I gave them.*
10 "Up! Be off,
this is no place to rest";
For any trifle you exact
a crippling pledge.*
11 If one, acting on impulse, should make the futile claim:
"I pour you wine and strong drink as my prophecy,"
then he would be the prophet of this people.
12 I will gather you, O Jacob, each and every one,*
I will assemble all the remnant of Israel;
I will group them like a flock in the fold,
like a herd in the midst of its corral;
they shall not be thrown into panic by men.
13 With a leader to break the path
they shall burst open the gate and go out through it;
Their king shall go through before them,
and the LORD at their head.

CHAPTER 3

Downfall of Present Leaders

1 And I said:
Hear, you leaders of Jacob,
rulers of the house of Israel!
Is it not your duty to know what is right,
2 you who hate what is good, and love evil?
You who tear their skin from them,
and their flesh from their bones![f]
3 They eat the flesh of my people,
and flay their skin from them,
and break their bones.
They chop them in pieces like flesh in a kettle,
and like meat in a caldron.
4 When they cry to the LORD,
he shall not answer them;
Rather shall he hide his face from them at that time,
because of the evil they have done.

5 Thus says the LORD regarding the prophets*
who lead my people astray;
Who, when their teeth have something to bite,
announce peace,
But when one fails to put something in their mouth,
proclaim war against him.[g]
6 Therefore you shall have night, not vision,
darkness, not divination;
The sun shall go down upon the prophets,
and the day shall be dark for them.[h]
7 Then shall the seers be put to shame,
and the diviners confounded;
They shall cover their lips, all of them,
because there is no answer from God.
8 But as for me, I am filled with power,
with the spirit of the LORD,
with authority and with might;
To declare to Jacob his crimes
and to Israel his sins.
9 Hear this, you leaders of the house of Jacob,
you rulers of the house of Israel!
You who abhor what is just,
and pervert all that is right;
10 Who build up Zion with bloodshed,
and Jerusalem with wickedness!
11 Her leaders render judgment for a bribe,
her priests give decisions for a salary,
her prophets divine for money,
While they rely on the LORD, saying,
"Is not the LORD in the midst of us?
No evil can come upon us!"[i]
12 Therefore, because of you,
Zion shall be plowed like a field,
and Jerusalem reduced to rubble,
And the mount of the temple
to a forest ridge.[j]

2, 9: The honor I gave them: their dignity as free Israelites.

2, 10: A crippling pledge: Israelite law forbade exacting pledges for loans that would work hardship on the borrower (Ex 22, 25f; Dt 24, 6. 10–13. 17); but the law was habitually violated.

2, 12f: This messianic passage concerning the restoration after the Babylonian exile seems out of place here and is probably a later addition.

3, 5–8: Almost all the prophetic books contain oracles against the false prophets. Here Micah accuses them of prophesying for venal motives and determining the prophecy by the price that is paid them; he contrasts his own disinterested preaching of the word of God.

f Am 2, 7. g Ez 13, 10. h Jer 15, 9; Am 8, 9; Zec 13, 3. i Ez 22, 27; Zep 3, 3. j Jer 26, 18.

II: The New Israel

CHAPTER 4

The People To Be Restored

1 In days to come*
the mount of the LORD's house
Shall be established higher than the mountains;
it shall rise high above the hills,
And peoples shall stream to it: [k]
2 Many nations shall come, and say,
"Come, let us climb the mount of the LORD,
to the house of the God of Jacob,
That he may instruct us in his ways,
that we may walk in his paths."
For from Zion shall go forth instruction,
and the word of the LORD from Jerusalem.
3 He shall judge between many peoples
and impose terms on strong and distant nations;
They shall beat their swords into plowshares,
and their spears into pruning hooks;
One nation shall not raise the sword against another,
nor shall they train for war again.
4 Every man shall sit under his own vine
or under his own fig tree, undisturbed;
for the mouth of the LORD of hosts has spoken. [l]
5 For all the peoples walk
each in the name of its god,
But we will walk in the name of the LORD,
our God, forever and ever.
6 On that day, says the LORD,
I will gather the lame,
And I will assemble the outcasts,
and those whom I have afflicted.
7 I will make of the lame a remnant,
and of those driven far off a strong nation;
And the LORD shall be king over them on Mount Zion,
from now on forever. [m]
8 And you, O Magdal-eder,*
hillock of daughter Zion!
Unto you shall it come:
the former dominion shall be restored,
the kingdom of daughter Jerusalem.

9 Now why do you cry out so?
Are you without a king?
Or has your counselor perished,
That you are seized with pains
like a woman in travail?
10 Writhe in pain, grow faint,
O daughter Zion,
like a woman in travail;
For now shall you go forth from the city
and dwell in the fields;
To Babylon shall you go,
there shall you be rescued.
There shall the LORD redeem you
from the hand of your enemies.*

11 How many nations are gathered against you!
They say, "Let her be profaned,
let our eyes see Zion's downfall!"
12 But they know not the thoughts of the LORD,
nor understand his counsel,
When he has gathered them
like sheaves on the threshing floor.
13 Arise and thresh, O daughter Zion;
your horn I will make iron
And your hoofs bronze,
that you may crush many peoples;
You shall devote their spoils to the LORD,
and their riches to the Lord of the whole earth. [n]

Restoration through the Messiah

14 Now fence yourself in, Bat-gader!*
"They have laid siege against us!"
With the rod they strike on the cheek
the ruler of Israel.

4, 1ff: See note on Is 2, 2ff.
4, 8: Magdal-eder: "tower of the flock," an ancient place name (cf Gn 35, 21), here used symbolically of Jerusalem.
4, 10: For now . . . your enemies: probably a later addition to the text, when the prediction of exile had been fulfilled in the Babylonian captivity. The prophet sees the exile as the means whereby God will purify and restore his people.
4, 14: Bat-gader: "fenced-in maiden," another symbolic name for Jerusalem, then under siege from the Assyrians.

k 1ff: Is 2, 2ff. l Hos 14, 8; Am 9, 14. m Is 6, 13; Dn 7, 14; Zep 3, 19; Lk 1, 32. n Is 41, 15; Hos 10, 11.

CHAPTER 5

[1] But you, Bethlehem-Ephrathah, [o]
too small to be among the clans of Judah,
From you shall come forth for me
one who is to be ruler in Israel;
Whose origin is from of old,
from ancient times.*
[2] (Therefore the Lord will give them up, until
the time
when she who is to give birth* has borne,
And the rest of his brethren shall return
to the children of Israel.) [p]
[3] He shall stand firm and shepherd his flock
by the strength of the LORD,
in the majestic name of the LORD, his God;
And they shall remain, for now his greatness
shall reach to the ends of the earth;
[4] he shall be peace.

If Assyria invades our country*
and treads upon our land,
We shall raise against it seven shepherds,
eight men of royal rank;
[5] And they shall tend the land of Assyria with
the sword,
and the land of Nimrod* with the drawn
sword;
And we shall be delivered from Assyria,
if it invades our land
and treads upon our borders.

[6] The remnant of Jacob shall be
in the midst of many peoples,
Like dew coming from the LORD,
like raindrops on the grass,
Which wait for no man,
nor tarry for the sons of men.
[7] And the remnant of Jacob shall be among the
nations,
in the midst of many peoples,
Like a lion among beasts of the forest,
like a young lion among flocks of sheep;
When it passes through, it tramples
and tears, and there is none to deliver.
[8] Your hand shall be lifted above your foes,
and all your enemies shall be destroyed.

[9] On that day, says the LORD,*
I will destroy the horses from your midst
and ruin your chariots;
[10] I will demolish the cities of your land
and tear down all your fortresses.
[11] I will abolish the means of divination from
your use,
and there shall no longer be soothsayers
among you.
[12] I will abolish your carved images
and the sacred pillars from your midst;
And you shall no longer adore
the works of your hands. [q]
[13] I will tear out the sacred poles* from your
midst,
and destroy your cities.
[14] I will wreak vengeance in anger and wrath
upon the nations that have not hearkened.

III: Admonition

CHAPTER 6

Accusation and Answer

[1] Hear, then, what the LORD says:
Arise, present your plea before the mountains,
and let the hills hear your voice! [r]
[2] Hear, O mountains, the plea of the LORD,
pay attention, O foundations of the earth!
For the LORD has a plea against his people,
and he enters into trial with Israel.

5, 1: In contrast to Bat-gader (Mi 4, 14), where the ruler of Israel, the reigning king, is in peril of his life from the Assyrians, is the tiny city and clan of Bethlehem-Ephrathah, from which comes the ancient Davidic dynasty (whose origin is from of old, from ancient times) with its messianic King, one who is to be ruler in Israel.

5, 2: She who is to give birth: the mother of the Messiah: cf Is 7, 14.

5, 4f: This passage, expressing confidence in Judah's ability to deliver itself from Assyria, is in contrast with the preceding messianic oracle, which ascribes deliverance to the Lord and his agent. Some believe that here the prophet is quoting the words of the defiant men of Judah. The shepherds and men of royal rank are one and the same: warriors capable of routing Assyria. The same kind of numerical progression is used by Amos (1, 3), and elsewhere in the Bible.

5, 5: Nimrod: the legendary ancestor of the Mesopotamians; cf Gn 10, 10ff.

5, 9–13: Part of the messianic restoration will consist in the removal of everything that has drawn Israel away from the Lord; this includes not only the objects of false worship, but also the armaments in which the idolators had trusted.

5, 12f: Sacred pillars . . . sacred poles: see note on Ex 34, 13.

o Ru 1, 2; 1 Sm 17, 12; Mt 2, 6; Jn 7, 42. p 2f: Is 7, 14; 11, 1f. q Hos 3, 4; 10, 1f. r Is 6, 2; Ob 1.

3 O my people, what have I done to you,
or how have I wearied you? Answer me! [s]
4 For I brought you up from the land of Egypt,
from the place of slavery I released you;
And I sent before you Moses,
Aaron, and Miriam. [t]
5 My people, remember what Moab's King
Balak planned,
and how Balaam, the son of Beor, answered
him
. . . from Shittim to Gilgal,*
that you may know the just deeds of the
LORD. [u]
6 With what shall I come before the LORD,*
and bow before God most high?
Shall I come before him with holocausts,
with calves a year old? [v]
7 Will the LORD be pleased with thousands of
rams,
with myriad streams of oil?
Shall I give my first-born* for my crime,
the fruit of my body for the sin of my soul?
8 You have been told, O man, what is good,
and what the LORD requires of you:
Only to do the right and to love goodness,
and to walk humbly with your God. [w]

9 Hark! the LORD cries to the city.*
[It is wisdom to fear your name!]
Hear, O tribe and city council,
12 You whose rich men are full of violence,
whose inhabitants speak falsehood
with deceitful tongues in their heads!
10 Am I to bear any longer criminal hoarding
and the meager ephah that is accursed?
11 Shall I acquit criminal balances,
bags of false weights?
13 Rather I will begin to strike you
with devastation because of your sins.
15 You shall sow, yet not reap,
tread out the olive, yet pour no oil,
and the grapes, yet drink no wine. [x]
14 You shall eat, without being satisfied,
food that will leave you empty;
What you acquire, you cannot save;
what you do save, I will deliver up to the
sword. [y]
16 You have kept the decrees of Omri,
and all the works of the house of Ahab,
and you have walked in their counsels;
Therefore I will deliver you up to ruin,
and your citizens to derision;
and you shall bear the reproach of the
nations.*

CHAPTER 7

Condemnation and Prayer

1 Alas! I am as when the fruit is gathered,
as when the vines have been gleaned;
There is no cluster to eat,
no early fig that I crave.
2 The faithful are gone from the earth,
among men the upright are no more!
They all lie in wait to shed blood,
each one ensnares the other. [z]
3 Their hands succeed at evil;
the prince makes demands,
The judge is had for a price,
the great man speaks as he pleases, [a]
4 The best of them is like a brier,
the most upright like a thorn hedge.
The day announced by your watchmen!
your punishment has come;
now is the time of your confusion.

6, 5: From Shittim to Gilgal: from the east to the west side of the Jordan; the events described in Jos 3—5 are meant. The text is defective; however, it is evident that this verse continues the remembrance of God's deeds of mercy to Israel, beginning with the Exodus (v 4) and extending to the conquest, deeds which have provoked so little response from his people.

6, 6ff: The people ask how they shall worship the Lord, proposing the various forms of sacrifice. The prophet replies that sacrifice avails nothing without the true spirit of religion. This is one of the best expressions of the prophetic teaching on religion, the preparation for such New Testament passages as Jas 1, 27.

6, 7: Shall I give my first-born: through Canaanite influence the abominable practice of human sacrifice had been introduced under impious kings (cf 2 Kgs 16, 3; 21, 6).

6, 9: The city: Jerusalem as the embodiment of the crimes of the entire land.

6, 16: Judah has followed the example of the northern kingdom epitomized in the semipaganism of Omri and his son Ahab (1 Kgs 16, 25–34), copying both the corrupted worship and the social injustice of their reigns.

s Jer 2, 5. t Ex 15, 20. u Nm 22, 23. v 6f: Hos 6, 6; 8, 13; Am 5, 21. w Dt 26, 16; Zec 7, 9; Mt 23, 23. x Dt 28, 38; Am 5, 11; Hg 1, 6. y Hos 4, 10. z Is 1, 21; Hos 4, 2. a Is 1, 23.

5 Put no trust in a friend,*
have no confidence in a companion;
Against her who lies in your bosom
guard the portals of your mouth.[b]
6 For the son dishonors his father,
the daughter rises up against her mother,
The daughter-in-law against her
mother-in-law,
and a man's enemies are those of his
household.[c]
7 But as for me, I will look to the LORD,
I will put my trust in God my savior;
my God will hear me![d]

8 Rejoice not over me, O my enemy!*
though I have fallen, I will arise;
though I sit in darkness, the LORD is my
light.
9 The wrath of the LORD I will endure
because I have sinned against him,
Until he takes up my cause,
and establishes my right.
He will bring me forth to the light;
I will see his justice.
10 When my enemy sees this,
shame shall cover her:
She who said to me,
"Where is the LORD, thy God?"
My eyes shall see her downfall;
now shall she be trampled underfoot,
like the mire in the streets.

11 It is the day for building your walls;*
on that day the boundary shall be taken
away.
12 It is the day; and they shall come to you
from Assyria and from Egypt,
From Tyre even to the River,
from sea to sea, and from mountain to
mountain;[e]
13 And the land shall be a waste
because of its citizens,
as a result of their deeds.

14 Shepherd your people with your staff,*
the flock of your inheritance,
That dwells apart in a woodland,
in the midst of Carmel.
Let them feed in Bashan and Gilead,
as in the days of old;
15 As in the days when you came from the land
of Egypt,
show us wonderful signs.

16 The nations shall behold and be put to shame,
in spite of all their strength;
They shall put their hands over their mouths;
their ears shall become deaf.
17 They shall lick the dust like the serpent,
like reptiles on the ground;
They shall come quaking from their fastnesses,
trembling in fear of you [the LORD, our
God].

18 Who is there like you, the God who removes
guilt
and pardons sin for the remnant of his
inheritance;
Who does not persist in anger forever,
but delights rather in clemency,[f]
19 And will again have compassion on us,
treading underfoot our guilt?
You will cast into the depths of the sea
all our sins;
20 You will show faithfulness to Jacob,
and grace to Abraham,
As you have sworn to our fathers
from days of old.[g]

7, 5f: Corresponding to the widespread civil corruption and apostasy from religion is the breakdown of normal human and family relations.

7, 8ff: The unnamed enemy of Judah mentioned in these verses may be Assyria or one of the neighboring countries, such as Edom, which stood by to profit at Judah's downfall.

7, 11ff: This prophecy of restoration and repopulation of the promised land by the Jews now in exile appears to be from the period after the destruction of Jerusalem by the Chaldeans (587 B.C.).

7, 14–17: This prayer appears to be from the time after the return from exile (537 B.C.), when the people, few in number, possessed only a fragment of their former land, and were surrounded by hostile nations.

b Jer 9, 3. c Mt 10, 35f. d Is 8, 17. e Zec 14, 16. f Jer 10, 6; Acts 10, 43. g Ps 105, 6; Is 41, 8; 63, 16.

THE BOOK OF NAHUM

Shortly before the fall of Nineveh in 612 B.C., Nahum uttered his prophecy against the hated city. To understand the prophet's exultant outburst of joy over the impending destruction it is necessary to recall the savage cruelty of Assyria, which had made it the scourge of the ancient Near East for almost three centuries. The royal inscriptions of Assyria afford the best commentary on the burning denunciation of "the bloody city." In the wake of their conquests, mounds of heads, impaled bodies, enslaved citizens, and avaricious looters testified to the ruthlessness of the Assyrians. Little wonder that Judah joined in the general outburst of joy over the destruction of Nineveh!

But Nahum is not a prophet of unrestrained revenge. God's moral government of the world is asserted. Yahweh is the avenger but he is also merciful, a citadel in the day of distress. Nineveh's doom was a judgment on the wicked city. Before many years passed, Jerusalem too was to learn the meaning of such a judgment.

The book is divided as follows: The Lord's Coming in Judgment (1, 2—2, 1.3). The Fall of Nineveh (2, 2—3, 19).

CHAPTER 1

1 Oracle about Nineveh. The book of the vision of Nahum of Elkosh.

The Lord's Coming in Judgment

2 *A jealous and avenging God* is the LORD,
an avenger is the LORD, and angry;
The LORD brings vengeance on his adversaries,
and lays up wrath for his enemies;
3 The LORD is slow to anger, yet great in power,
and the LORD never leaves the guilty unpunished.
In hurricane and tempest is his path,
and clouds are the dust at his feet; [a]
4 He rebukes the sea and leaves it dry,
and all the rivers he dries up. [b]
Withered are Bashan and Carmel,
and the bloom of Lebanon fades;*
5 The mountains quake before him,
and the hills dissolve;
The earth is laid waste before him,
the world and all who dwell in it.
6 Before his wrath, who can stand firm, [c]
and who can face his blazing anger?
His fury is poured out like fire,
and the rocks are rent asunder before him.*
7 The LORD is good,
a refuge on the day of distress;
He takes care of those who have recourse to him,
8 when the flood rages;
He makes an end of his opponents,
and his enemies he pursues with darkness.
9 What are you imputing to the LORD?*
It is he who will make an end!
The enemy shall not rise a second time;
10 As when a tangle of thornbushes is set aflame,
like dry stubble, they shall be utterly consumed.
12 For, says the LORD,
be they* ever so many and so vigorous,
still they shall be mown down and disappear.

1, 2–8: A poem written in the style of the alphabetic psalms; cf Pss 9A; 25; 111; 119. Here, however, most of the verses beginning with the letters of the second half of the alphabet are not preserved.

1, 2: A jealous . . . God: see note on Ex 20, 5.

1, 4: Bashan, Carmel and Lebanon were famous for their forests.

1, 6f: The coming of God in judgment has two aspects: to those who oppose him it will be unbearable; to those who have recourse to him it will bring strength and consolation.

1, 9: What are you imputing to the Lord?: the people of Judah are asked what they think God has in mind.

1, 12f: They: the enemies of Judah. You: Judah. His yoke: the dominion of the Assyrian king over Judah.

a Ex 19, 16ff. b Is 33, 9; Hb 3, 6ff. c Zep 1, 15; 2, 3.

Though I have humbled you,
I will humble you no more.
13 Now will I break his yoke from off you,
and burst asunder your bonds. [d]
11 From you he came
who devised evil against the LORD,
the scoundrel planner.*
14 The LORD has commanded regarding you:*
no descendant shall come to bear your name;
From your temple I will abolish
the carved and the molten image;
I will make your grave a mockery.

CHAPTER 2

1 See, upon the mountains there advances
the bearer of good news, announcing peace!
Celebrate your feasts, O Judah,
fulfill your vows!
For nevermore shall you be invaded
by the scoundrel; he is completely destroyed. [e]
3 The LORD will restore the vine of Jacob,
the pride of Israel,
Though ravagers have ravaged them
and ruined the tendrils.

The Fall of Nineveh

2 The hammer comes up against you;*
guard the rampart,
Keep watch on the road, gird your loins,
marshal all your strength!
4 The shields of his warriors are crimsoned,
the soldiers colored in scarlet;
Fiery steel are the chariots
on the day of his mustering.
The horses are frenzied;
5 the chariots dash madly through the streets
And wheel in the squares,
looking like firebrands,
flashing like lightning bolts.
6 His picked troops are called,
ranks break at their charge;
To the wall they rush,
the mantelet* is set up.
7 The river gates are opened,
the palace shudders,
8 Its mistress is led forth captive,
and her handmaids,* under guard,
Moaning like doves,
beating their breasts.
9 Nineveh is like a pool
whose waters escape;
"Stop! Stop!"
but none turns back.
10 "Plunder the silver, plunder the gold!"
There is no end to the treasure,
to their wealth in precious things of every kind!
11 Emptiness, desolation, waste;
melting hearts and trembling knees,
Writhing in every frame,
every face blanched! [f]
12 Where is the lions' cave,
the young lions' den,
Where the lion* went in and out,
and the cub, with no one to disturb them?
13 The lion snatched enough for his cubs,
and strangled for his lionesses;
He filled his dens with prey,
and his caves with plunder.
14 I come against you,
says the LORD of hosts;
I will consume in smoke your chariots,
and the sword shall devour your young lions;
Your preying on the land I will bring to an end,
the cry of your lionesses shall be heard no more.

CHAPTER 3

Ruin Imminent and Inevitable

1 Woe to the bloody city, all lies,
full of plunder, whose looting never stops! [g]

1, 11: From you . . . the scoundrel planner: addressed to Nineveh, the capital city of Sennacherib, king of Assyria, who besieged Jerusalem c. 700 B.C.
1, 14: You: the king of Assyria.
2, 2: The hammer comes up against you: the enemy is about to crush Nineveh.
2, 6: Mantelet: a movable shelter protecting the besiegers.
2, 8: Mistress . . . and her handmaids: either the queen of Nineveh with the ladies of her court, or the statute of Ishtar, Nineveh's chief goddess, with her temple prostitutes.
2, 12: The lion: the king of Assyria.

d Is 9, 4; 10, 27. e Is 52, 7; Rom 10, 15. f Jl 2, 6. g Hb 2, 12.

2 The crack of the whip, the rumbling sounds of
wheels;
horses a-gallop, chariots bounding,
3 Cavalry charging,
The flame of the sword, the flash of the spear,
the many slain, the heaping corpses,
the endless bodies to stumble upon!
4 For the many debaucheries of the harlot,
fair and charming, a mistress of witchcraft,
Who enslaved nations with her harlotries,
and peoples by her witchcraft: [h]
5 I am come against you, [i]
and I will strip your skirt from you;
I will show your nakedness to the nations,
to the kingdoms your shame!*
6 I will cast filth upon you,
disgrace you and put you to shame;
7 Till everyone who sees you runs from you,
saying,
"Nineveh is destroyed; who can pity her?
Where can one find any to console her?"

8 Are you better than No-amon*
that was set among the streams,
Surrounded by waters,
with the flood for her rampart
and water her wall? [j]
9 Ethiopia was her strength, and Egypt,
and others without end;
Put and the Libyans were her auxiliaries.
10 Yet even she went captive into exile,
even her little ones were dashed to pieces
at the corner of every street;
For her nobles they cast lots,
and all her great men were put into chains.
11 You, too, shall drink of this till you faint away;
you, too, shall seek a refuge from the foe. [k]
12 All your fortresses are but fig trees,
bearing early figs
That fall, when shaken,
into the hungry mouth.
13 See, the troops are women in your midst;
to your foes the gates of your land are open
wide,
fire has consumed their bars. [l]
14 Draw water for the siege,*
strengthen your fortresses;
Go down into the mud and tread the clay,
take hold of the brick mold!
15 There the fire shall consume you,
the sword shall cut you down.
Multiply like the grasshoppers,
multiply like the locusts!
16 Make your couriers more numerous than the
stars,
17 your garrisons as many as grasshoppers,
And your scribes as locust swarms
gathered on the rubble fences on a cold day!
Yet when the sun warms them,
the grasshoppers will spread their wings and
fly,
and vanish, no one knows where.
18 Alas! how your shepherds slumber, O king of
Assyria,
your nobles have gone to rest;
Your people are scattered upon the mountains,
with none to gather them.
19 There is no healing for your hurt,
your wound is mortal.
All who hear this news of you
clap their hands over you;
For who has not been overwhelmed,
steadily, by your malice?

3, 5f: The punishment of adulteresses.

3, 8: No-amon: No was the Egyptian name of the capital of Upper Egypt, called Thebes by the Greeks; its tutelary deity was Amon. This great city was destroyed by the Assyrians in 663 B.C.

3, 14: An ironic exhortation to prepare the city for a futile defense. Go down . . . brick mold: make bricks for the city walls.

h Mi 1, 7; Rv 17, 1f. i Is 47, 3; Jer 13, 26; Hos 2, 12. j Jer 46, 25. k Mi 2, 11. l Jer 51, 30.

THE BOOK OF HABAKKUK

This prophecy dates from the years 605–597 B.C., or between the great Babylonian victory at Carchemish and Nebuchadnezzar's invasion of Judah which culminated in the capture of Jerusalem. The situation of Judah was desperate at this time, with political intrigue and idolatry widespread in the small kingdom. The first two chapters consist of a dialogue between the prophet and the Lord. For what may be the first time in Israelite literature, a man questions the ways of God, as Habukkuk calls him to account for his government of the world. To this question God replies that he has prepared a chastising rod, Babylon, which will be the avenging instrument in his hand. There is added the divine assurance that the just Israelite will not perish in the calamities about to be visited on the nation.

The third chapter is a magnificent religious lyric, filled with reminiscences of Israel's past and rich in literary borrowings from the poetry of ancient Canaan, though still expressing authentic Israelite faith. God appears in all his majestic splendor and executes vengeance on Judah's enemies. The prophecy ends with a joyous profession of confidence in the Lord, the Savior.

CHAPTER 1

1 The oracle which Habakkuk the prophet received in vision.

The Prophet's Complaint and Its Answer

2 How long, O LORD? I cry for help*
but you do not listen!
I cry out to you, "Violence!"
but you do not intervene.
3 Why do you let me see ruin;
why must I look at misery?
Destruction and violence are before me;
there is strife, and clamorous discord.
4 This is why the law is benumbed,
and judgment is never rendered:
Because the wicked circumvent the just;
this is why judgment comes forth perverted.

5 Look over the nations and see,*
and be utterly amazed!
For a work is being done in your days
that you would not have believed, were it
told. [a]
6 For see, I am raising up Chaldea,
that bitter and unruly people,
That marches the breadth of the land
to take dwellings not his own.
7 Terrible and dreadful is he,
from himself derive his law and his majesty.
8 Swifter than leopards are his horses,
and keener than wolves at evening.*
His horses prance,
his horsemen come from afar:
They fly like the eagle hastening to devour;
9 each comes for the rapine,
Their combined onset is that of a stormwind
that heaps up captives like sand.
10 He scoffs at kings,
and princes are his laughingstock;
He laughs at any fortress,
heaps up a ramp, and conquers it.

1, 2–4: Traditionally, these verses have been taken as the prophet's complaint against the internal evils of Judah; the language used is that employed by Amos, Isaiah, and Jeremiah to condemn the social abuses of their day. In vv 5ff the Lord answers this complaint by indicating the Chaldean empire as his instrument for punishing his people for these sins.

1, 5: Look over the nations and see: after Nebuchadnezzar's defeat of Egypt in 605 B.C., there could be little doubt that it was the Chaldean ambition to dominate the entire Near East.

1, 8: Wolves at evening: the wolf is apparently thought of as more rabid and vicious in the evening when setting out for prey (Jer 5, 6; Zep 3, 3).

a Acts 13, 41.

11 Then he veers like the wind* and is gone—
this culprit who makes his own strength his god!
12 Are you not from eternity, O LORD,*
my holy God, immortal?
O LORD, you have marked him for judgment,
O Rock,* you have readied him for punishment!
13 Too pure are your eyes to look upon evil,
and the sight of misery you cannot endure.
Why, then, do you gaze on the faithless in silence
while the wicked man devours
one more just than himself?
14 You have made man like the fish of the sea,
like creeping things without a ruler.
15 He* brings them all up with his hook,
he hauls them away with his net,
He gathers them in his seine;
and so he rejoices and exults.
16 Therefore he sacrifices to his net,*
and burns incense to his seine;
For thanks to them his portion is generous,
and his repast sumptuous.
17 Shall he, then, keep on brandishing his sword
to slay peoples without mercy?

CHAPTER 2

1 I will stand at my guard post,
and station myself upon the rampart,
And keep watch to see what he will say to me,
and what answer he will give to my complaint. [b]
2 Then the LORD answered me and said:
Write down the vision
Clearly upon the tablets,
so that one can read it readily.
3 For the vision still has its time,
presses on to fulfillment, and will not disappoint;
If it delays, wait for it,
it will surely come, it will not be late.
4 The rash man has no integrity; [c]
but the just man, because of his faith, shall live.*
Wealth, too, is treacherous:
the proud, unstable man—
5 He who opens wide his throat like the nether world,
and is insatiable as death,
Who gathers to himself all the nations,
and rallies to himself all the peoples—
6 Shall not all these take up a taunt against him,
satire and epigrams about him, to say:

Woe to him who stores up what is not his:
how long can it last!
he loads himself down with debts.
7 Shall not your creditors rise suddenly?
Shall not they who make you tremble awake?
You shall become their spoil!
8 Because you despoiled many peoples
all the rest of the nations shall despoil you;
Because of men's blood shed,
and violence done to the land,
to the city and to all who dwell in it.

9 Woe to him who pursues evil gain for his household,
setting his nest on high
to escape the reach of misfortune!
10 You have devised shame for your household,

1, 11: Veers like the wind: the conquests of the ancient Near East were mainly raiding expeditions to collect tribute. As far as administration of conquered territories was concerned, both the Assyrians and Chaldeans were usually content to install friendly rulers and then depart. This culprit: though the Chaldeans were used by God as the agents of his punishment, this did not diminish their own guilt as ruthless marauders.

1, 12—2, 1: It is generally thought that this complaint is directed against the Chaldeans and their terrible destruction. But it may well be a continuation of Hb 1, 2–4, against the wicked Judahites who have merited God's punishment.

1, 12: O Rock: an ancient title celebrating the Lord's power; cf Ps 18, 32.

1, 15: The he of this and the following verses, to whom is attributed such extensive evil and the destruction of many peoples, may be the wicked of Judah embodied in King Jehoiakim, ally of the powerful Pharaoh Neco of Egypt; the devastation wrought by Jehoiakim and Neco together is condemned.

1, 16: He sacrifices to his net: in v 15 the wicked ruler in question is represented as catching men in a net. This verse alludes to some rite involving the sacrificial veneration of the weapons of war.

2, 4: The just man, because of his faith, shall live: the faith which here enables the virtuous man to survive the impending doom is both a confident belief in God's justice, and patience in awaiting its execution. St. Paul quotes these words (Rom 1, 17; Gal 3, 11; Heb 10, 38) to confirm his teaching that man receives justification and supernatural life through faith in Christ.

b Ps 85, 9. c Rom 1, 17; Gal 3, 11; Heb 10, 38.

cutting off many peoples, forfeiting your
own life:
11 For the stone in the wall shall cry out,*
and the beam in the woodwork shall
answer it!

12 Woe to him who builds a city by bloodshed,
and establishes a town by wickedness! [d]

13 Is not this from the LORD of hosts:
peoples toil for the flames,*
and nations grow weary for nought! [e]
14 But the earth shall be filled
with the knowledge of the LORD's glory
as water covers the sea.[f]
15 Woe to you who give your neighbors
a flood of your wrath to drink,
and make them drunk, till their nakedness
is seen!
16 You are filled with shame instead of glory;
drink, you too, and stagger!
On you shall revert the cup from the LORD's
right hand,
and utter shame on your glory.
17 For the violence done to Lebanon* shall cover
you,
and the destruction of the beasts shall terrify
you;
Because of men's blood shed,
and violence done to the land,
to the city and to all who dwell in it.
19 Woe to him who says to wood, "Awake!"
to dumb stone, "Arise!"
Can such a thing give oracles?
See, it is overlaid with gold and silver,
but there is no life breath in it.
18 Of what avail is the carved image,*
that its maker should carve it?
Or the molten image and lying oracle,
that its very maker should trust in it,
and make dumb idols?
20 But the LORD is in his holy temple;
silence before him, all the earth! [g]

CHAPTER 3

Canticle

1 **Prayer of Habakkuk, the prophet. To a plaintive tune.***

2 O LORD, I have heard your renown,
and feared, O LORD, your work.
In the course of the years revive it,*
in the course of the years make it known;
in your wrath remember compassion!

3 *God comes from Teman,*
the Holy One from Mount Paran.
Covered are the heavens with his glory,
and with his praise the earth is filled.
4 His splendor spreads like the light;
rays shine forth from beside him,
where his power is concealed.
5 Before him goes pestilence,
and the plague follows in his steps.
6 He pauses to survey the earth;
his look makes the nations tremble.
The eternal mountains are shattered,
the age-old hills bow low
along his ancient ways.
7 I see the tents of Cushan collapse;
trembling are the pavilions of the land of
Midian.
8 Is your anger against the streams, O LORD?
Is your wrath against the streams,
your rage against the sea,
That you drive the steeds
of your victorious chariot?
9 Bared and ready is your bow,

2, 11f: The palaces, built at the expense of gross injustice (vv 6–10), call down vengeance on their builders. This is typical prophetic language for the condemnation of social crimes within Israel and Judah.

2, 13: Peoples toil for the flames: they build only to have fire consume their work, when they build contrary to God's will.

2, 17: The violence done to Lebanon: the spoliation of the cedar forests of Lebanon, used in lavish building projects by the great conquerors; cf Is 14, 8; 37, 24. The destruction of the beasts: the killing-off of the wild animals through excessive hunting by the same conquerors; cf Bar 3, 16.

2, 18–20: Idolatrous worship is here shown to be folly by contrasting man-made idols with the majesty of the one true God.

3, 1: A later liturgical rubric. So also the end of v 19.

3, 2: In the course of the years revive it: renew today your wondrous deeds of the past.

3, 3–15: Cf the theophanies in Dt 33, 2f; Jgs 5, 4f; Pss 18, 8–16; 68, 8f; 77, 17–21; 97, 1–5; Na 1, 3–6, etc. Conventional language is employed to describe the appearance of the Lord, as in Ex 19, 16–19.

3, 3: Teman: a region in Edom. Mount Paran: in the territory of Edom, or the northern part of the Sinaitic peninsula. The Lord is represented as coming from Sinai, where he had appeared to Moses and given Israel the covenant and the law.

d Ez 24, 9; Na 3, 1. e Jer 51, 58. f Is 11, 9. g Ps 11, 4.

filled with arrows is your quiver.
Into streams you split the earth;
10 at sight of you the mountains tremble.
A torrent of rain descends;
the ocean gives forth its roar.
The sun forgets to rise,
11 the moon remains in its shelter,
At the light of your flying arrows,
at the gleam of your flashing spear.[h]

12 In wrath you bestride the earth,
in fury you trample the nations.
13 You come forth to save your people,
to save your anointed one.*
You crush the heads of the wicked,
you lay bare their bases at the neck.[i]
14 You pierce with your shafts the heads of their princes
whose boast would be of devouring
the wretched in their lair.
15 You tread the sea with your steeds
amid the churning of the deep waters.

3, 13: Your anointed one: the theocratic king, the head of God's people.

16 I hear, and my body trembles;
at the sound, my lips quiver.
Decay invades my bones,
my legs tremble beneath me.
I await the day of distress
that will come upon the people who attack us.
17 For though the fig tree blossom not
nor fruit be on the vines,
Though the yield of the olive fail
and the terraces produce no nourishment,
Though the flocks disappear from the fold
and there be no herd in the stalls,
18 Yet will I rejoice in the LORD[j]
and exult in my saving God.
19 GOD, my Lord, is my strength;
he makes my feet swift as those of hinds
and enables me to go upon the heights.

For the leader; with stringed instruments.

h Jos 10, 12. i Is 51, 9ff. j 18f: Ps 18, 32f; Mi 7, 7.

THE BOOK OF ZEPHANIAH

The title of the prophecy informs us that the ministry of Zephaniah took place during the reign of Josiah (640–609 B.C.). The protest against the worship of false gods, and the condemnation of the pro-Assyrian court ministers who served as regents during Josiah's minority, allow us to place the work in the first decade of the reign. Accordingly, the prophecy of Zephaniah comes rightly before that of Jeremiah, who was probably influenced by it in both language and ideas.

The age of Zephaniah was a time of religious degradation, when the old idolatries reappeared and men worshiped sun, moon, and stars. Rites completely alien to the pure monotheism taught by Moses flourished in Jerusalem. To the corrupt city Zephaniah announced the impending judgment, the day of the Lord. The prophecy may be divided into three sections, corresponding to the three chapters of the book:

The Day of the Lord: A day of doom. The last few verses of this oracle give the classic description of the Day of the Lord as an overwhelming disaster. The Christian hymn *Dies Irae* is based on this passage (1, 2-18).

The Day of the Lord: A day of judgment of the nations, traditional enemies of God's people (2, 1-15).

Reproach and Promise for Jerusalem: Despite Judah's infidelities, the Lord in his mercy will spare a holy remnant, which will finally enjoy peace. The prophecy closes with a hymn of joy sung by the remnant restored to Zion (3, 1-20).

CHAPTER 1

1 The word of the LORD which came to
Zephaniah, the son of Cushi, the son of Geda-
liah, the son of Amariah, the son of Hezekiah, in
the days of Josiah, the son of Amon, king of
Judah.

The Day of the Lord: A Day of Doom

2 I will completely sweep away all things
from the face of the earth, says the LORD.
3 I will sweep away man and beast,
I will sweep away the birds of the sky,
and the fishes of the sea.
I will overthrow the wicked;
I will destroy mankind
from the face of the earth, says the LORD. [a]
4 I will stretch out my hand against Judah,
and against all the inhabitants of Jerusalem;
I will destroy from this place the last vestige of
Baal,
the very names of his priests,
5 And those who adore the host of heaven* on
the roofs,
with those who adore the LORD
but swear by Milcom; [b]
6 And those who have fallen away from the
LORD,
and those who do not seek the LORD.
7 Silence in the presence of the Lord GOD!
for near is the day of the LORD,
Yes, the LORD has prepared a slaughter feast,
he has consecrated his guests.*
8 On the day of the LORD's slaughter feast
I will punish the princes, and the king's sons,
and all that dress in foreign apparel.
9 I will punish, on that day,
all who leap over the threshold,*
Who fill the house of their master
with violence and deceit.
10 On that day, says the LORD,
A cry will be heard from the Fish Gate,
a wail from the New Quarter,
loud crashing from the hills.
11 Wail, O inhabitants of the Mortar!*
for all the merchants will be destroyed,
all who weigh out silver, done away with.
12 At that time I will explore Jerusalem with
lamps;
I will punish the men who thicken on their
lees,*
Who say in their hearts,
"Neither good nor evil can the LORD do."
13 Their wealth shall be given to pillage
and their houses to devastation;
They will build houses, but shall not dwell in
them,
plant vineyards, but not drink their wine. [c]
14 Near is the great day of the LORD,
near and very swiftly coming;
Hark, the day of the LORD!
bitter, then, the warrior's cry.
15 A day of wrath is that day, [d]
a day of anguish and distress,
A day of destruction and desolation,
a day of darkness and gloom,
A day of thick black clouds,
16 a day of trumpet blasts and battle alarm
Against fortified cities,
against battlements on high. [e]
17 I will hem men in
till they walk like the blind,
because they have sinned against the LORD;
And their blood shall be poured out like dust,
and their brains like dung.
18 Neither their silver nor their gold
shall be able to save them
on the day of the LORD's wrath,
When in the fire of his jealousy
all the earth shall be consumed.

1, 5: The host of heaven: the stars, the worship of which was introduced into Judah by the Assyrians. Milcom: the god of the Ammonites; cf 1 Kgs 11, 5. 7. 33; 2 Kgs 23, 13.

1, 7: He has consecrated his guests: God has prepared those whom he has invited to share as soldiers in the booty, or as beast and bird scavengers of carrion, on the day of slaughter. Cf Jer 46, 10; Ez 39, 17.

1, 9: Leap over the threshold: the reference is to a superstitious custom of the pagans, witnessed to at least in regard to the worship of Dagon (1 Sm 5, 5).

1, 10f: The New Quarter . . . the Mortar: sections of Jerusalem (cf 2 Kgs 22, 14).

1, 12: The men who thicken on their lees: those who are overconfident because, like bottles of wine in which the sediment has settled to the bottom, they have remained at peace and undisturbed for a long time.

a Hos 4, 3. b Jer 8, 2; 19, 13. c Am 5, 11. d Jer 30, 7; Jl 2, 11; Am 5, 18. e Am 2, 2.

For he shall make an end, yes, a sudden end,
of all who live on the earth.[f]

CHAPTER 2

The Day of the Lord: A Day of Judgment

1 Gather, gather yourselves together,
O nation without shame!*
2 Before you are driven away,
like chaff that passes on;
Before there comes upon you
the blazing anger of the LORD;
Before there comes upon you
the day of the LORD's anger.
3 Seek the LORD, all you humble of the earth,
who have observed his law;
Seek justice, seek humility;
perhaps you may be sheltered
on the day of the LORD's anger.
4 For Gaza shall be forsaken,
and Ashkelon shall be a waste,
Ashdod they shall drive out at midday,
and Ekron* shall be uprooted.[g]
5 Woe to you who dwell by the seacoast,
to the Cretan folk!*
The word of the LORD is against you,
I will humble you, land of the Philistines,
and leave you to perish without an
inhabitant!
6 The coastland of the Cretans shall become
fields for shepherds, and folds for flocks.
7 The coast shall belong
to the remnant of the house of Judah;
by the sea they shall pasture.
In the houses of Ashkelon at evening
they shall couch their flocks,
For the LORD their God shall visit them,
and bring about their restoration.

8 I have heard the revilings uttered by Moab,
and the insults of the Ammonites,
When they reviled my people
and made boasts against their territory.
9 Therefore, as I live, says the LORD of hosts,
the God of Israel,
Moab shall become like Sodom,
the land of Ammon like Gomorrah:
A field of nettles and a salt pit
and a waste forever.
The remnant of my people shall plunder them,
the survivors of my nation dispossess them.
10 Such shall be the requital of their pride,
because they reviled and boasted against
the people of the LORD of hosts.
11 The LORD shall inspire them with fear
when he makes all the gods of earth to
waste away;
Then, each from its own place,
all the coastlands of the nations shall adore
him.

12 You too, O Cushites,*
shall be slain by the sword of the LORD.
13 He will stretch out his hand against the north,
to destroy Assyria;
He will make Nineveh a waste,
dry as the desert.
14 In her midst shall settle in droves
all the wild life of the hollows;
The screech owl and the desert owl
shall roost in her columns;
Their call shall resound from the window,
the raven's croak from the doorway.[h]
15 Is this the exultant city*
that dwelt secure;
That told herself,
"There is no other than I!"
How has she become a waste,
a lair for wild beasts?
Whoever passes by her
hisses, and shakes his fist!

CHAPTER 3

Reproach and Promise for Jerusalem

1 Woe to the city, rebellious and polluted,
to the tyrannical city!

2, 1: Nation without shame: Judah.
2, 4: Gaza . . . Ashkelon . . . Ashdod . . . Ekron: four of the five cities of the Philistine confederation. The fifth city, Gath, is not mentioned, perhaps because it was already destroyed.
2, 5: Cretan folk: the Philistines, who came from Crete; see note on Dt 2, 23.
2, 12: Cushites: the Egyptians, at this time under a Cushite or Ethiopian dynasty.
2, 15: The exultant city: Nineveh.

f Zep 3, 8; Ez 7, 19. g Am 1, 6ff, Zec 9, 5. h Is 34, 11.

2 She hears no voice,
accepts no correction;
In the LORD she has not trusted,
to her God she has not drawn near. [i]
3 Her princes in her midst
are roaring lions;
Her judges are wolves of the night
that have had no bones to gnaw by
morning. [j]
4 Her prophets are insolent,
treacherous men;
Her priests profane what is holy,
and do violence to the law. [k]
5 The LORD within her is just,
who does no wrong;
Morning after morning he renders judgment
unfailingly, at dawn.

6 I have destroyed nations,
their battlements are laid waste;
I have made their streets deserted,
with no one passing through;
Their cities are devastated,
with no man dwelling in them. [l]
7 I said, "Surely now you will fear me,
you will accept correction";
She should not fail to see
all I have visited upon her.
Yet all the more eagerly have they done
all their corrupt deeds.
8 Therefore, wait for me, says the LORD,
against the day when I arise as accuser;
For it is my decision to gather together the
nations,
to assemble the kingdoms,
In order to pour out upon them my wrath,
all my blazing anger;
For in the fire of my jealousy
shall all the earth be consumed. [m]
9 For then I will change and purify
the lips of the peoples,
That they all may call upon the name of the
LORD,
to serve him with one accord;
10 From beyond the rivers of Ethiopia
and as far as the recesses of the North,
they shall bring me offerings.

11 On that day
You need not be ashamed
of all your deeds,
your rebellious actions against me;
For then will I remove from your midst
the proud braggarts,
And you shall no longer exalt yourself
on my holy mountain.
12 But I will leave as a remnant in your midst
a people humble and lowly,
Who shall take refuge in the name of the
LORD: [n]
13 the remnant of Israel.
They shall do no wrong
and speak no lies;
Nor shall there be found in their mouths
a deceitful tongue;
They shall pasture and couch their flocks
with none to disturb them. [o]

14 Shout for joy, O daughter Zion!
sing joyfully, O Israel!
Be glad and exult with all your heart,
O daughter Jerusalem! [p]
15 The LORD has removed the judgment against
you,
he has turned away your enemies;
The King of Israel, the LORD, is in your midst,
you have no further misfortune to fear.
16 On that day, it shall be said to Jerusalem:
Fear not, O Zion, be not discouraged! [q]
17 The LORD, your God, is in your midst,
a mighty savior;
He will rejoice over you with gladness,
and renew you in his love,
He will sing joyfully because of you,
18 as one sings at festivals.
I will remove disaster from among you,
so that none may recount your disgrace.
19 Yes, at that time I will deal
with all who oppress you:
I will save the lame,
and assemble the outcasts;

i Jer 2, 30; 7, 28. j Ez 22, 27; Mi 3, 11. k Jer 23, 32. l Jer 2, 15. m Zep 1, 18. n Hos 14, 4. o Ml 4, 4. p Zec 9, 9. q Mt 14, 27.

I will give them praise and renown
in all the earth, when I bring about their
restoration.[r]
20 At that time I will bring you home,
and at that time I will gather you;
For I will give you renown and praise,
among all the peoples of the earth,
When I bring about your restoration
before your very eyes, says the LORD.

r Mi 4, 6.

THE BOOK OF HAGGAI

Postexilic prophecy begins with Haggai, who received the word of the Lord in the second year of Darius (520 B.C.). The Jews who returned from the Exile in Babylonia had encountered formidable obstacles in their efforts to re-establish Jewish life in Judah. The Samaritans had succeeded in blocking the rebuilding of the temple; but after Darius acceded to the throne (522), permission was given to resume the work. At this critical moment, when defeatism and a certain lethargy had overtaken his repatriated countrymen, Haggai came forward with his exhortations to them to complete the great task. The first oracle, an appeal to the Jews, is contained in chapter 1. To this appeal Haggai added a short oracle of encouragement (2, 1-9) for the sake of those who gloomily contrasted the former magnificence of Solomon's temple with the second temple: the Lord would be present in this new abode, and its glory, enhanced by the offerings of the Gentiles, would surpass the ancient splendor.

The prophecy may be divided into five oracles:

The call to rebuild the temple. The economic distress so apparent in Judah is due to the Jews' neglect of the Lord while they provide for their own needs (1, 1-15).

The future glory of the new temple, surpassing that of the old (2, 1-9).

Unworthiness of a people, who may be the Samaritans, to offer sacrifice at the newly restored altar. This oracle is cast in the literary form of a *torah,* an instruction given the people by a priest (2, 10-14).

A promise of immediate blessings, which follows upon the undertaking (chapter 1) to rebuild the temple (2, 15-19).

A pledge to Zerubbabel, descendant of David, repository of the Messianic hopes (2, 20-23).

CHAPTER 1

Exhortation To Rebuild the Temple of the Lord 1 On the first day of the sixth month in the second year* of King Darius, the word of the LORD came through the prophet Haggai to the governor of Judah, Zerubbabel, son of Shealtiel, and to the high priest Joshua, son of Jehozadak: [a]
2 Thus says the LORD of hosts: This people says: "Not now has the time come to rebuild the house of the LORD." 3 (Then this word of the LORD came through Haggai, the prophet:) 4 Is it time for you to dwell in your own paneled houses, [b] while this house lies in ruins?*

5 Now thus says the LORD of hosts:
Consider your ways!
6 You have sown much, but have brought in
little;

1, 1: The sixth month in the second year: August/September in 520 B.C.
1, 4: The luxury of the homes of the wealthy with their paneled houses contrasts sadly with the ruined state of the Lord's house.

a Ezr 4, 24; 5, 1; 6, 14. b 2 Sm 7, 2.

you have eaten, but have not been satisfied;
You have drunk, but have not been
exhilarated;
have clothed yourselves, but not been
warmed;
And he who earned wages
earned them for a bag with holes in it.[c]

7 Thus says the LORD of hosts:
Consider your ways!
8 Go up into the hill country;
bring timber, and build the house
That I may take pleasure in it
and receive my glory, says the LORD.
9 You expected much, but it came to little;
and what you brought home, I blew away.
For what cause? says the LORD of hosts.
Because my house lies in ruins,
while each of you hurries to his own
house.[d]
10 Therefore the heavens withheld from you
their dew,
and the earth her crops.[e]
11 And I called for a drought
upon the land and upon the mountains;
Upon the grain, and upon the wine, and upon
the oil,
and upon all that the ground brings forth;
Upon men and upon beasts,
and upon all that is produced by hand.

12 Then Zerubbabel, son of Shealtiel, and the
high priest Joshua, son of Jehozadak, and all the
remnant of the people* listened to the voice of
the LORD, their God, and to the words of the
prophet Haggai, because the LORD, their God,
had sent him, and the people feared because of
the LORD. 13 And the LORD's messenger, Haggai,
proclaimed to the people as the message of the
LORD: I am with you, says the LORD.

14 Then the LORD stirred up the spirit of the
governor of Judah, Zerubbabel, son of Shealtiel,
and the spirit of the high priest Joshua, son of
Jehozadak, and the spirit of all the remnant of
the people, so that they came and set to work on
the house of the LORD of hosts, their God, 15 on
the twenty-fourth day of the sixth month.

CHAPTER 2

Future Glory of the New Temple In the
second year of King Darius,[1] on the twenty-first
day of the seventh month, the word of the LORD
came through the prophet Haggai: 2 Tell this to
the governor of Judah, Zerubbabel, son of Sheal-
tiel, and to the high priest Joshua, son of
Jehozadak, and to the remnant of the people:

3 Who is left among you
that saw this house in its former glory?
And how do you see it now?
Does it not seem like nothing in your eyes?
4 But now take courage, Zerubbabel, says the
LORD,
and take courage, Joshua, high priest, son of
Jehozadak,
And take courage, all you people of the land,
says the LORD, and work!
For I am with you, says the LORD of hosts.[f]
5 This is the pact that I made with you
when you came out of Egypt,
And my spirit continues in your midst;
do not fear![g]

6 For thus says the LORD of hosts:*
One moment yet, a little while,
and I will shake the heavens and the earth,
the sea and the dry land.[h]
7 I will shake all the nations,
and the treasures of all the nations will
come in,
And I will fill this house with glory,
says the LORD of hosts.[i]
8 Mine is the silver and mine the gold,
says the LORD of hosts.
9 Greater will be the future glory of this house
than the former, says the LORD of hosts;

1, 12: The remnant of the people: a technical term in Haggai and Zechariah for the returned exiles.

2, 6–9: From the later period of Ezekiel's preaching onward, the temple became, as here, one of the dominant messianic themes. Greater will be the future glory of this house than the former: because Christ will enter it.

c Dt 28, 38ff; Mi 6, 15. d 2 Kgs 25, 9. e Gn 27, 28; Am 4, 6–9. f Zec 8, 9. g Ex 29, 45; Lv 26, 45. h Heb 12, 26. i Gn 49, 10; Is 60, 5. 9. 11; Mal 3, 1; Rv 21, 26.

And in this place I will give peace,
says the LORD of hosts![j]

Offerings of the Unclean Rejected 10On the
twenty-fourth day of the ninth month, in the
second year of King Darius, the word of the
LORD came to the prophet Haggai: 11Thus says
the LORD of hosts: Ask the priests for a deci-
sion:[k] 12If a man carries sanctified flesh in the
fold of his garment and the fold touches bread,
or pottage, or wine, or oil, or any other food, do
they become sanctified? "No," the priests an-
swered.* 13Then Haggai said: If a person un-
clean from contact with a corpse touches any of
these, do they become unclean? The priests
answered, "They become unclean."[l] 14Then
Haggai continued:

So is this people, and so is this nation
in my sight, says the LORD:
And so are all the works of their hands;
and what they offer there is unclean.

Promise of Immediate Blessings* 15But
now, consider from this day forward. Before
there was a stone laid upon a stone in the temple
of the LORD, 16how did you fare?

When one went to a heap of grain for twenty
measures,
it would yield but ten;
When another went to the vat to draw fifty
measures,
there would be but twenty.[m]
17I struck you in all the works of your hands
with blight, searing wind, and hail,
yet you did not return to me, says the LORD.

18[Consider from this day forward: from the
twenty-fourth day of the ninth month.* From
the day on which the temple of the LORD was
founded, consider!]

19Indeed, the seed has not sprouted,
nor have the vine, the fig, the pomegranate
and the olive tree yet borne.
From this day, I will bless!

Pledge to Zerubbabel 20The message of the
LORD came a second time to Haggai on the
twenty-fourth day of the month:* 21Tell this to
Zerubbabel, the governor of Judah:

I will shake the heavens and the earth;
22 I will overthrow the thrones of kingdoms,
destroy the power of the kingdoms of the
nations.
I will overthrow the chariots and their riders,
and the riders with their horses
shall go down by one another's sword.[n]
23 On that day, says the LORD of hosts,[o]
I will take you, Zerubbabel,
son of Shealtiel, my servant, says the LORD,
And I will set you as a signet ring;
for I have chosen you, says the LORD of
hosts.*

2, 12ff: According to the ritual concepts of the Jews, uncleanness was more contagious than sacredness. Inasmuch as the people were unclean, their offerings became unclean (Nm 19, 22).

2, 15–19: This prophecy is intimately linked with chapter 1, and should be read with it.

2, 18: The ninth month: the ordinal ninth has been copied incorrectly from Hg 2, 10. This note clearly concerns the twenty-fourth day of the sixth month, on which the temple of the Lord was founded (Hg 1, 15).

2, 20: The month: probably again the sixth month, as in Hg 1, 15 and 2, 18; see note on the latter.

2, 23: This promise to Zerubbabel, reversing the punishment of his grandfather (Jer 22, 24), is a continuation of the messianic hope; cf Zec 6, 11f.

j Is 2, 2ff; Zec 6, 13. k Dt 17, 8–13; Zec 7, 3. l Nm 19, 11. 13, 22. m Is 5, 10. n Ez 38, 21; Dn 2, 44; Zec 14, 13; Lk 1, 52. o Song 8, 6; Sir 49, 11; Is 42, 1; 44, 1f.

THE BOOK OF ZECHARIAH

Zechariah's initial prophecy is dated to 520 B.C., the same year as that in which Haggai received the prophetic call. The first eight chapters of the Book of Zechariah contain oracles which certainly belong to him while the last six (sometimes called "Deutero-Zechariah") represent the work of one or more unknown authors. In the prophecies proper to Zechariah eight symbolic visions are recorded, all meant to promote the work of rebuilding the temple and to encourage the returned exiles, especially their leaders, Joshua and Zerubbabel. In the final chapter of this first division Zechariah portrays the messianic future under the figure of a prosperous land to which the nations come in pilgrimage, eager to follow the God of Israel.

The second part of Zechariah is divided into two sections, each with its own introductory title. The first (9—11) consists of oracles whose historical background, date and authorship are extremely difficult to determine. With 9, 9 begins the messianic vision of the coming of the Prince of Peace. The verses describing the triumphant appearance of the humble king are taken up by the four Evangelists to describe the entry of Christ into Jerusalem on Palm Sunday. Chapter 12 is introduced by an oracle proclaiming the victory of God's people over the heathen. The prophecy closes by describing, in apocalyptic imagery, the final assault of the enemy on Jerusalem, after which the messianic age begins.

CHAPTER 1

Necessity of Conversion 1 In the second year of Darius, in the eighth month,* the word of the LORD came to the prophet Zechariah, son of Berechiah, son of Iddo: [a] 2 The LORD was indeed angry with your fathers . . . . 3 and say to them: Thus says the LORD of hosts: Return to me, says the LORD of hosts, and I will return to you, says the LORD of hosts. 4 Be not like your fathers whom the former prophets warned: Thus says the LORD of hosts: Turn from your evil ways and from your wicked deeds. But they would not listen or pay attention to me, says the LORD. [b] 5 Your fathers, where are they? And the prophets, can they live forever? 6 But my words and my decrees, which I entrusted to my servants the prophets, did not these overtake your fathers? Then they repented and admitted: "The LORD of hosts has treated us according to our ways and deeds, just as he had determined he would." [c]

The Four Horsemen 7 In the second year of Darius, on the twenty-fourth day of Shebat, the eleventh month,* the word of the LORD came to the prophet Zechariah, son of Berechiah, son of Iddo, in the following way: 8 I had a vision during the night. There appeared the driver of a red horse,* standing among myrtle trees in a shady place, and behind him were red, sorrel, and white horses. [d] 9 Then I asked, "What are these, my lord?"; and the angel who spoke with me answered me, "I will show you what these are." 10 The man who was standing among the myrtle trees spoke up and said, "These are they whom the LORD has sent to patrol the earth." [e] 11 And they answered the angel of the LORD who was standing among the myrtle trees and said, "We have patrolled the earth; see, the whole earth is tranquil and at rest!"

12 [f] Then the angel of the Lord spoke out and said, "O LORD of hosts, how long will you be without mercy for Jerusalem and the cities of Judah that have felt your anger these seventy years?"* 13 To the angel who spoke with me, the LORD replied with comforting words. [g]

14 And the angel who spoke with me said to me, Proclaim: Thus says the LORD of hosts: I am deeply moved for the sake of Jerusalem and Zion, [h] 15 and I am exceedingly angry with the complacent nations;* whereas I was but a little angry, they added to the harm. [i] 16 Therefore, says the LORD: I will turn to Jerusalem in mercy; my house shall be built in it, says the LORD of

1, 1: The second year . . . eighth month: October/November, 520 B.C.

1, 7: The second year . . . eleventh month: January/February, 519 B.C.

1, 8–11: The driver of a red horse: apparently distinct from the man, or angel of the Lord . . . standing among the myrtle trees, who spoke with the prophet. The four horsemen are sent by God to the four corners of the earth (Zec 2, 10), to see if the whole earth is at peace.

1, 12: These seventy years: see note on Jer 25, 1–14.

1, 15: The complacent nations: the neighbors of Judah, especially Edom, which enjoyed their present prosperity and security at Judah's expense.

a Ezr 4, 24; 5, 1; 6, 14. b Jer 25, 5; 35, 15; Mal 3, 7. c Lam 2, 17; Lv 26, 14ff; Dt 28, 15. d Rv 6, 4. e Zec 6, 7. f Zec 7, 5; Jer 25, 11; Dn 9, 2. g Jer 29, 10. h Zec 8, 2; Jl 2, 18. i Is 47, 6; Ob 10–14.

hosts, and a measuring line* shall be stretched over Jerusalem.[j] 17 Proclaim further: Thus says the LORD of hosts: My cities shall again overflow with prosperity; the LORD will again comfort Zion, and again choose Jerusalem.[k]

CHAPTER 2

Four Horns and Four Blacksmiths 1 I raised my eyes and looked: there were four horns.* 2 Then I asked the angel who spoke with me what these were. He answered me, "These are the horns that scattered Judah and Israel and Jerusalem."

3 Then the LORD showed me four blacksmiths. And I asked, "What are these coming to do?" 4 And he said, "Here are the horns that scattered Judah, so that no man raised his head any more; but these have come to terrify them: to cast down the horns of the nations that raised their horns to scatter the land of Judah."

The New Jerusalem 5 Again I raised my eyes and looked: there was a man with a measuring line in his hand.[l] 6 "Where are you going?" I asked. "To measure Jerusalem," he answered; "to see how great is its width and how great its length."[m]

7 Then the angel who spoke with me advanced, and another angel came out to meet him 8 and said to him, "Run, tell this to that young man:* People will live in Jerusalem as though in open country, because of the multitude of men and beasts in her midst.[n] 9 But I will be for her an encircling wall of fire, says the LORD, and I will be the glory in her midst."

10 Up, up! Flee from the land of the north,* says the LORD; for I scatter you to the four winds of heaven, says the LORD. 11 Up, escape to Zion! you who dwell in daughter Babylon. 12 For thus said the LORD of hosts (after he had already sent me) concerning the nations that have plundered you: Whoever touches you touches the apple of my eye.[o] 13 See, I wave my hand over them; they become plunder for their slaves. Thus you shall know that the LORD of hosts has sent me.

14 Sing and rejoice, O daughter Zion! See, I am coming to dwell among you, says the LORD.[p] 15 Many nations shall join themselves to the LORD on that day, and they shall be his people, and he will dwell among you, and you shall know that the LORD of hosts has sent me to you. 16 The LORD will possess Judah as his portion in the holy land, and he will again choose Jerusalem. 17 Silence, all mankind, in the presence of the LORD! for he stirs forth from his holy dwelling.

CHAPTER 3

Joshua the High Priest 1 Then he showed me Joshua the high priest standing before the angel of the LORD, while Satan stood at his right hand to accuse him.[q] 2 And the angel of the LORD said to Satan, "May the LORD rebuke you, Satan; may the LORD who has chosen Jerusalem rebuke you! Is not this man a brand snatched from the fire?"[r]

3 Now Joshua was standing before the angel, clad in filthy garments.* 4 He spoke and said to those who were standing before him, "Take off his filthy garments, and clothe him in festal garments."[s] 5 He also said, "Put a clean miter on his head." And they put a clean miter on his head and clothed him with the garments. Then the angel of the LORD, standing, said, "See, I have taken away your guilt."

6 The angel of the LORD then gave Joshua this assurance: 7 "Thus says the LORD of hosts: If you walk in my ways and heed my charge, you shall judge my house and keep my courts, and I will give you access among these standing here. 8 Listen, O Joshua, high priest! You and your associates who sit before you are men of good omen.* Yes, I will bring my servant the Shoot.[t]

1, 16: Measuring line: not for devastation, as in Is 34, 11, but for reconstruction.

2, 1–4: Four horns: symbolic of the hostile forces which, from the four corners of the earth, invaded and devastated the land of Judah. Four blacksmiths: the powers used by God to destroy these enemies of his people.

2, 8: That young man: the angel or man with a measuring line of v 5.

2, 10: The land of the north: Babylonia (v 11).

3, 3: Filthy garments: symbolic of mourning for the dead, or of national catastrophe, and implying acknowledgment of guilt (v 5).

3, 8: Men of good omen: the restoration of the priesthood is a

j Zec 8, 3; Ezr 6, 14. k Is 51, 3. l Rv 11, 1. m Dt 28, 64. n Ez 36, 11. o Dt 32, 10; Ps 17, 8. p Ez 37, 26. q Hg 1, 1; 1 Chr 21, 1. r Rom 8, 33; Jude 9. s Lk 15, 22. t Is 4, 2; 11, 1; Jer 23, 5; 33, 15.

9Look at the stone that I have placed before Joshua, one stone with seven facets.* I will engrave its inscription, says the LORD of hosts, and I will take away the guilt of the land in one day.[u] 10On that day, says the LORD of hosts, you will invite one another under your vines and fig trees."[v]

CHAPTER 4

4Then I said to the angel who spoke with me, "What are these things, my lord?" 5And the angel who spoke with me replied, "Do you not know what these things are?" "No, my lord," I answered. 6Then he said to me, "This is the LORD's message to Zerubbabel: Not by an army, nor by might, but by my spirit, says the LORD of hosts. 7What are you, O great mountain?* Before Zerubbabel you are but a plain. He shall bring out the capstone amid exclamations of 'Hail, Hail' to it."[w]

8This word of the LORD then came to me: 9The hands of Zerubbabel have laid the foundations of this house,[x] and his hands shall finish it; then you shall know that the LORD of hosts has sent me to you. 10[y]For even they who were scornful on that day of small beginnings shall rejoice to see the select stone in the hands of Zerubbabel. These seven facets are the eyes of the LORD that range over the whole earth.

The Lampstand 1Then the angel who spoke with me returned and awakened me, like a man awakened from his sleep. 2"What do you see?" he asked me. "I see a lampstand all of gold, with a bowl at the top," I replied; "on it are seven lamps with their tubes,[z] 3and beside it are two olive trees, one on the right and the other on the left."[a] 11I then asked him, "What are these two olive trees at each side of the lampstand?" 12And again I asked, "What are the two olive tufts which freely pour out fresh oil through the two golden channels?" 13"Do you not know what these are?" he said to me. "No, my lord," I answered him. 14He said, "These are the two anointed* who stand by the LORD of the whole earth."

CHAPTER 5

The Flying Scroll* 1Then I raised my eyes again and saw a scroll flying.[b] 2"What do you see?" he asked me. I answered, "I see a scroll flying; it is twenty cubits long and ten cubits wide." 3Then he said to me: "This is the curse which is to go forth over the whole earth; in accordance with it shall every thief be swept away, and in accordance with it shall every perjurer be expelled from here. 4I will send it forth, says the LORD of hosts, and it shall come into the house of the thief, or into the house of him who perjures himself with my name; it shall lodge within his house, consuming it, timber and stones."[c]

The Flying Bushel* 5Then the angel who spoke with me came forward and said to me, "Raise your eyes and see what this is that comes forth." 6"What is it?" I asked. And he answered, "This is a bushel container coming. This is their guilt in all the land." 7Then a leaden cover was lifted, and there was a woman sitting inside the bushel. 8"This is Wickedness," he said; and he thrust her inside the bushel, pushing the leaden

---

sign of the coming of the messianic times. My servant the Shoot: identified, in the earliest form of Zec 6, 11f as the prophet composed it, with Zerubbabel, direct descendant of King David and rebuilder of the temple; and, as such, a type of the Messiah; cf Jer 23, 5.

3, 9: One stone with seven facets: apparently the same as the select stone of Zec 4, 10, which seems to be a precious gem. The seven facets are explained in Zec 4, 10 as signifying the Lord's vigilance over the world. I will engrave its inscription: the same Hebrew verb for engrave is used in Ex 28, 9. 11 in regard to the inscriptions on the twelve precious stones of the priestly breastpiece.

4, 7: Great mountain: figure of the obstacles confronting Zerubbabel in building the temple. A plain: figure of the ease with which he will overcome these obstacles.

4, 1ff. 11–14: The two anointed: literally, "the two sons of oil," Joshua, the anointed high priest, and Zerubbabel, the anointed prince. Just as the two olive trees in this imagery supply the sacred seven-branched lampstand (Ex 25, 31–40) with oil (v 12), so these two men, in ministering to the community, stand by (serve) the Lord.

5, 1–4: The enormous scroll, thirty feet by fifteen (the dimensions in length and breadth of the portico of Solomon's temple, 1 Kgs 6, 3), contains a list of maledictions on sinners, similar to that in Dt 27, 15–26. The thief and the perjurer represent all sinners, who are expelled from the holy community.

5, 5–11: The woman sealed in the bushel container is a figure of the general corruption of the people of Judah. She is removed from the Holy Land and transported to Shinar, that is, Babylonia, where a dwelling is being prepared for her; that is a symbol of the reign of Wickedness in pagan lands, contrasted with the reign of holiness in the Lord's dwelling on Mount Zion.

u Zec 4, 10. v 1 Kgs 4, 25. w Ezr 3, 11f; Ps 118, 22. x Ezr 6, 14ff. y Zec 3, 9. z Rv 1, 12. a Rv 11, 4. b Ez 2, 9. c Lv 19, 12.

cover into the opening. [9]Then I raised my eyes and saw two women coming forth with a wind ruffling their wings, for they had wings like the wings of a stork. As they lifted up the bushel into the air, [10]I said to the angel who spoke with me, "Where are they taking the bushel?" [11]He replied, "To build a temple for it in the land of Shinar; when the temple is ready, they will deposit it there in its place." [d]

CHAPTER 6

Four Chariots* [1]Again I raised my eyes and saw four chariots coming out from between two mountains; and the mountains were of bronze. [2]The first chariot had red horses, the second chariot black horses, [e] [3]the third chariot white horses, and the fourth chariot spotted horses—all of them strong horses. [4]I asked the angel who spoke with me, "What are these, my lord?" [5]The angel said to me in reply, "These are the four winds of the heavens, which are coming forth after being reviewed by the LORD of all the earth."[f] [6]The chariot with the black horses was turning toward the land of the north, the red and the white horses went after them, and the spotted ones went toward the land of the south. [7]As these strong horses emerged, eager to set about patrolling the earth, he said, "Go, patrol the earth!" Then, as they patrolled the earth, [8]he called out to me and said, "See, they that go forth to the land of the north will make my spirit rest in the land of the north."

The Coronation [9]This word of the LORD then came to me: [10]Take from the returned captives Heldai, Tobijah, Jedaiah; and go the same day to the house of Josiah, son of Zephaniah (these had come from Babylon). [11]Silver and gold you shall take, and make a crown; place it on the head of [Joshua, son of Jehozadak, the high priest] Zerubbabel.* [12]And say to him: Thus says the LORD of hosts: Here is a man whose name is Shoot, and where he is he shall sprout, and he shall build the temple of the LORD.[g] [13]Yes, he shall build the temple of the LORD, and taking up the royal insignia, he shall sit as ruler upon his throne. The priest shall be at his right hand, and between the two of them there shall be friendly understanding.[h] [14]The crown itself shall be a memorial offering in the temple of the LORD in favor of Heldai, Tobijah, Jedaiah, and the son of Zephaniah. [15]And they who are from afar shall come and build the temple of the LORD, and you shall know that the LORD of hosts has sent me to you.[i] And if you heed carefully the voice of the LORD your God. . . .

CHAPTER 7

True Fasting [1]In the fourth year of Darius the king [the word of the LORD came to Zechariah], on the fourth day of Chislev, the ninth month,* [2]Bethel-sarezer sent Regemmelech and his men to implore favor of the LORD [3]and to ask the priests of the house of the LORD of hosts, and the prophets, "Must I mourn and abstain in the fifth month as I have been doing these many years?"[j] [4]Thereupon this word of the LORD of hosts came to me: [5]Say to all the people of the land and to the priests: When you fasted and mourned in the fifth and in the seventh month these seventy years, was it really for me that you fasted?[k] [6]And when you were eating and drinking, was it not for yourselves that you ate, and for yourselves that you drank? [7]Were not these the words which the LORD spoke through the former prophets, when Jerusalem and the surrounding cities were inhabited and at peace, when the Negeb and the foothills were inhabited?[l] [8][This word of the LORD came to Zechariah: [9]Thus says the LORD of hosts:] Render true judgment, and show kindness and compassion toward each other.[m] [10]Do not oppress the widow or the orphan, the alien or the poor; do not plot evil

6, 1–8: The four chariots represent the angelic hosts sent by the Lord to the four ends of the earth. The chariot with the black horses brings the spirit, i.e., anger of the Lord against the land of the north, Babylonia.

6, 11: Make a crown; place it on the head of [Joshua, son of Jehozadak, the high priest] Zerubbabel: according to the current Hebrew text, Joshua the high priest is to be crowned. However, since the crown is a sign of royalty, the original text must have had the name of Zerubbabel here, not that of Joshua. In Zec 3, 8 Joshua is a different man from the one called the Shoot, and in v 12 it is upon the Shoot that the crown is to be placed.

7, 1: The fourth year of Darius . . . the fourth day of Chislev, the ninth month: November, 518 B.C.

d Gn 11, 2ff. e Zec 1, 8; Rv 6, 4. f Ps 104, 4. g Zec 3, 8; Eph 2, 20; Heb 3, 3. h Ps 110, 4; Heb 3, 1. i Eph 2, 19f. j Zec 8, 19. k Is 58, 5; Rom 14, 6. l Jer 17, 26. m Is 58, 6.

against one another in your hearts.[n] 11But they refused to listen; they stubbornly turned their backs and stopped their ears so as not to hear.[o] 12And they made their hearts diamond-hard so as not to hear the teaching and the message that the LORD of hosts had sent by his spirit through the former prophets.[p] 13Then the LORD of hosts in his great anger said that, as they had not listened when he called, so he would not listen when they called,[q] 14but would scatter them with a whirlwind among all the nations that they did not know. Thus the land was left desolate after them with no one traveling to and fro; they made the pleasant land into a desert.[r]

CHAPTER 8

In the Days of the Messiah 1This word of the LORD of hosts came: Thus says the LORD of hosts:

2I am intensely jealous for Zion,
  stirred to jealous wrath for her.[s]
3 Thus says the LORD:
I will return to Zion,
  and I will dwell within Jerusalem;
Jerusalem shall be called the faithful city,
  and the mountain of the LORD of hosts,
  the holy mountain.[t]

4Thus says the LORD of hosts: Old men and old women, each with staff in hand because of old age, shall again sit in the streets of Jerusalem. 5The city shall be filled with boys and girls playing in her streets. 6Thus says the LORD of hosts: Even if this should seem impossible in the eyes of the remnant of this people, shall it in those days be impossible in my eyes also, says the LORD of hosts? 7Thus says the LORD of hosts: Lo, I will rescue my people from the land of the rising sun, and from the land of the setting sun.[u] 8I will bring them back to dwell within Jerusalem. They shall be my people, and I will be their God, with faithfulness and justice.[v]

9Thus says the LORD of hosts: Let your hands be strong, you who in these days hear these words spoken by the prophets on the day when the foundation of the house of the LORD of hosts was laid for the building of the temple.[w] 10For before those days there were no wages for men, or hire for beasts; those who came and went had no security from the enemy, for I set every man against his neighbor. 11But now I will not deal with the remnant of this people as in former days, says the LORD of hosts, 12for it is the seedtime of peace: the vine shall yield its fruit, the land shall bear its crops, and the heavens shall give their dew; all these things I will have the remnant of the people possess. 13Just as you were a curse among the nations, O house of Judah and house of Israel, so will I save you that you may be a blessing; do not fear, but let your hands be strong.[x]

14Thus says the LORD of hosts: As I determined to harm you when your fathers provoked me to wrath, says the LORD of hosts, and I did not relent,[y] 15so again in these days I have determined to favor Jerusalem and the house of Judah; do not fear! 16These then are the things you should do: Speak the truth to one another; let there be honesty and peace in the judgments at your gates,[z] 17and let none of you plot evil against another in his heart, nor love a false oath. For all these things I hate, says the LORD.[a]

18This word of the LORD of hosts came to me: 19Thus says the LORD of hosts: The fast days of the fourth, the fifth, the seventh, and the tenth months shall become occasions of joy and gladness, cheerful festivals for the house of Judah; only love faithfulness and peace.* 20Thus says the LORD of hosts: There shall yet come peoples, the inhabitants of many cities; 21and the inhabitants of one city shall approach those of another, and say, "Come! let us go to implore the favor of the LORD"; and, "I too will go to seek the LORD."[b] 22Many peoples and strong nations

8, 19: The fast day of the fourth month recalled the fall of Jerusalem in June. 587 B.C. (2 Kgs 25, 3f); that of the fifth month, the burning of the temple by Nebuzaradan in July of the same year (2 Kgs 25, 8f); that of the seventh month, the murder of Gedaliah in September of the same year (Jer 41, 1f); that of the tenth month, the beginning of the final siege of Jerusalem in January, 588 B.C. (2 Kgs 25, 1).

n Ex 22, 21–24; Dt 24, 17; Is 1, 17; Jer 5, 28. o Neh 9, 29; Hos 4, 16. p Ez 11, 19; 36, 26; Neh 9, 29. q Is 1, 15; Mi 3, 4. r Dt 4, 27. s Na 1, 2. t Is 2, 2; Jer 31, 23. u Is 11, 11; Jer 30, 18. v Jer 4, 2. w Ezr 5, 1; Hg 2, 18. x Is 19, 24; Jer 42, 18; Hg 2, 19; Zep 3, 20. y Jer 31, 28. z Zec 7, 9. a Zec 7, 10. b Is 2, 3.

shall come to seek the LORD of hosts in Jerusalem and to implore the favor of the LORD.[c]
23 Thus says the LORD of hosts: In those days ten men of every nationality, speaking different tongues, shall take hold, yes, take hold of every Jew by the edge of his garment and say, "Let us go with you, for we have heard that God is with you."[d]

CHAPTER 9

Invasion by the Lord*

1 An oracle:
The word of the LORD is upon the land of
Hadrach,
and Damascus is its resting place,
For the cities of Aram are the LORD's,
as are all the tribes of Israel,
2 Hamath also, on its border,
Tyre, too, and Sidon, however wise they
be.[e]
3 Tyre built herself a stronghold,
and heaped up silver like dust,
and gold like the mire of the streets.
4 Lo, the LORD will strip her of her possessions,
and smite her power on the sea,
and she shall be devoured by fire.[f]
5 Ashkelon shall see it and be afraid;
Gaza also: she shall be in great anguish;
Ekron, too, for her hope shall come to
nought.
The king shall disappear from Gaza,
and Ashkelon shall not be inhabited,
6 and the baseborn* shall occupy Ashdod.
I will destroy the pride of the Philistine[g]
7 and take from his mouth his bloody meat,
and his abominations from between his
teeth:
He also shall become a remnant* for our God,
and shall be like a family in Judah,
and Ekron shall be like the Jebusites.
8 I will encamp by my house* as a guard
that none may pass to and fro;
No oppressor shall pass over them again,
for now I have regard for their affliction.

Restoration under the Messiah

9 Rejoice heartily, O daughter Zion,[h]
shout for joy, O daughter Jerusalem!
See, your king shall come to you;
a just savior is he,
Meek, and riding on an ass,
on a colt, the foal of an ass.*
10 He shall banish the chariot from Ephraim,
and the horse from Jerusalem;
The warrior's bow shall be banished,
and he shall proclaim peace to the nations.
His dominion shall be from sea to sea,
and from the River* to the ends of the
earth.[i]
11 As for you, for the blood of your covenant with
me,*
I will bring forth your prisoners from the
dungeon.[j]
12 In the return to the fortress
of the waiting prisoners,*
This very day, I will return you
double for your exile.[k]
13 For I will bend Judah as my bow,
I will arm myself with Ephraim;
I will arouse your sons, O Zion,
[against your sons, O Yavan,]
and I will use you as a warrior's sword.
14 The LORD shall appear over them,
and his arrow shall shoot forth as lightning;
The LORD God shall sound the trumpet,
and come in a storm from the south.

9, 1–8: Divine judgment is about to fall on the surrounding hostile peoples: Aram (Syria), including the cities of Hadrach and Damascus; Phoenicia, with its cities of Tyre and Sidon; Philistia, with its cities of Ashkelon, Gaza, Ekron, and Ashdod.

9, 6: The baseborn: people of mixed ancestry.

9, 7: Remnant: see note on Hg 1, 12. The Jebusites: the pre-Israelite inhabitants of Jerusalem, conquered by David and incorporated into Israel.

9, 8: My house: the Holy Land; cf Hos 8, 1; 9, 15; Jer 12, 7.

9, 9: The Messiah will come, not as a conquering warrior, but in lowliness and peace. Not like the last kings of Judah, who rode in chariots and on horses (Jer 17, 25; 22, 4), but like the princes of old (Gn 49, 11; Jgs 5, 10; 10, 4), the Messiah will ride on an ass. The Evangelists see a literal fulfillment of this prophecy in the Savior's triumphant entry into Jerusalem (Mt 21, 4f; Jn 12, 14f).

9, 10: The River: the Euphrates; see note on Ps 72, 8.

9, 11: The blood of your covenant with me: the covenant between the Lord and Israel sealed with sacrificial blood (Ex 24, 8).

9, 12: The waiting prisoners: the exiles awaiting the return to their country, where they will receive a double compensation for the double punishment they had suffered; cf Is 40, 2; 61, 7.

c Is 60, 3. d Is 66, 23. e Jer 49, 23. f Is 23, 1–18; Ez 26, 1—28, 26. g Am 1, 8. h Is 62, 11; Jer 23, 5; Mt 21, 5; Jn 12, 15. i Hos 1, 7. j Is 42, 7; Ez 24, 8. k Is 61, 7.

15 The LORD of hosts shall be a shield over them,
they shall overcome sling stones
and trample them underfoot;
They shall drink blood like wine,
till they are filled with it like libation bowls,
like the corners of the altar.
16 And the LORD, their God, shall save them on
that day,
his people, like a flock.
For they are the jewels in a crown
raised aloft over his land. [l]
17 For what wealth is theirs, and what beauty!
grain that makes the youths flourish,
and new wine, the maidens!

CHAPTER 10

The New Order of Things

1 Ask of the LORD rain in the spring season!
It is the LORD who makes the storm clouds,
And sends men the pouring rain;
for everyone, grassy fields. [m]
2 For the teraphim* speak nonsense,
the diviners have false visions:
Deceitful dreams they tell,
empty comfort they offer.
This is why they wander like sheep,
wretched: they have no shepherd. [n]
3 My wrath is kindled against the shepherds,
and I will punish the leaders;
For the LORD of hosts will visit his flock,
the house of Judah,
and make them his stately war horse.

4 From him shall come leader and chief,
from him warrior's bow and every officer.
5 They shall all be warriors,
trampling the mire of the streets in battle;
They shall wage war because the LORD is with
them,
and shall put the horsemen to rout.
6 I will strengthen the house of Judah,
the house of Joseph I will save;
I will bring them back, because I have mercy
on them,
they shall be as though I had never cast
them off,
for I am the LORD, their God, and I will hear
them.
7 Then Ephraim shall be valiant men,
and their hearts shall be cheered as by wine.
Their children shall see it and be glad,
their hearts shall rejoice in the LORD.

8 I will whistle for them to come together,
and when I redeem them
they will be as numerous as before. [o]
9 I sowed them among the nations,
yet in distant lands they remember me;
they shall rear their children and return.
10 I will bring them back from the land of Egypt,
and gather them from Assyria.
I will bring them into Gilead and into
Lebanon,
but these shall not suffice them; [p]
11 I will cross over to Egypt
and smite the waves of the sea
and all the depths of the Nile shall be dried
up.
The pride of Assyria shall be cast down,
and the scepter of Egypt taken away. [q]
12 I will strengthen them in the LORD,
and they shall walk in his name, says the
LORD. [r]

CHAPTER 11

1 Open your doors, O Lebanon,
that the fire may devour your cedars!
2 Wail, you cypress trees,
for the cedars are fallen,
the mighty have been despoiled.
Wail, you oaks of Bashan,
for the impenetrable forest is cut down!
3 Hark! the wailing of the shepherds,
their glory has been ruined.
Hark! the roaring of the young lions,
the jungle of the Jordan is laid waste.

Allegory of the Shepherds* 4 Thus said the

10, 2: Teraphim: household idols, used for divination; cf Gn 31, 19. 34f; Jgs 17, 5; 18, 17f. 20; Ez 21, 26; Hos 3, 4.

11, 4–17: In this allegory the prophet becomes the good shepherd of God's flock, which is being slaughtered; he is the defender of the people exploited by bad rulers. The three shep-

l Is 62, 3. m Dt 11, 14; Jer 14, 22. n Jer 10, 8; Ez 34, 5. o Ez 36, 37. p Is 11, 11; 49, 20; Hos 11, 11. q Is 11, 15; Ez 30, 13. r Mi 4, 5.

LORD, my God: Shepherd the flock to be slaughtered. 5For they who buy them slay them with impunity; while those who sell them say, "Blessed be the LORD, I have become rich!" Even their own shepherds do not feel for them.[s] 6(Nor shall I spare the inhabitants of the earth any more, says the LORD. Yes, I will deliver each of them into the power of his neighbor, or into the power of his king; they shall crush the earth, and I will not deliver it out of their power.)

7So I became the shepherd of the flock to be slaughtered for the sheep merchants. I took two staffs, one of which I called "Favor," and the other, "Bonds," and I fed the flock.[t] 8In a single month I did away with the three shepherds. I wearied of them, and they behaved badly toward me. 9"I will not feed you," I said. "What is to die, let it die; what is to perish, let it perish, and let those that are left devour one another's flesh."[u]

10Then I took my staff "Favor" and snapped it asunder, breaking off the covenant which I had made with all peoples; 11that day it was broken off. The sheep merchants who were watching me understood that this was the word of the LORD. 12I said to them, "If it seems good to you, give me my wages; but if not, let it go." And they counted out my wages, thirty pieces of silver.[v] 13But the LORD said to me, "Throw it in the treasury, the handsome price at which they valued me." So I took the thirty pieces of silver and threw them into the treasury in the house of the LORD.[w]

14Then I snapped asunder my other staff, "Bonds," breaking off the brotherhood between Judah and Israel. 15The LORD said to me: This time take the gear of a foolish shepherd. 16For I will raise up a shepherd in the land who will take no note of those that perish, nor seek the strays, nor heal the injured, nor feed what survives—he will eat the flesh of the fat ones and tear off their hoofs![x]

17Woe to my foolish shepherd
who forsakes the flock!
May the sword fall upon his arm
and upon his right eye;
Let his arm wither away entirely,
and his right eye be blind forever![y]

CHAPTER 12

Jerusalem God's Instrument* 1An oracle: the word of the LORD concerning Israel. Thus says the LORD, who spreads out the heavens, lays the foundations of the earth, and forms the spirit of man within him:[z] 2See, I will make Jerusalem a bowl to stupefy all peoples round about. [Judah will be besieged, even Jerusalem.][a] 3On that day I will make Jerusalem a weighty stone for all peoples. All who attempt to lift it shall injure themselves badly, and all the nations of the earth shall be gathered against her.[b] 4On that day, says the LORD, I will strike every horse with fright, and its rider with madness. I will strike blind all the horses of the peoples, but upon the house of Judah I will open my eyes, 5and the princes of Judah shall say to themselves, "The inhabitants of Jerusalem have their strength in the LORD of hosts, their God." 6On that day I will make the princes of Judah like a brazier of fire in the woodland, and like a burning torch among sheaves, and they shall devour right and left all the surrounding peoples; but Jerusalem shall still abide on its own site.[c] 7The LORD shall save the tents of Judah first, that the glory of the house of David and the glory of the inhabitants of Jerusalem may not be exalted over Judah. 8On that day, the LORD will shield the inhabitants of Jerusalem, and the weakling among them shall be like David on that day, and the house of David godlike, like an angel of the

---

herds, rulers in general, are to destroy one another in a short time (a single month). The service of the good shepherd is contemptuously valued at thirty pieces of silver, the legal indemnity (Ex 21, 32) for a gored slave. The prophet is thus a type of Christ whose mission of salvation to his people was appraised by the Sanhedrists, the false shepherds, at the same base price (Mt 26, 14ff). In the case of the prophet as well as of Christ (Mt 27, 5), the money is thrown into the temple treasury, i.e., paid to God, showing thereby how shamefully his divine love and care are requited.

12, 1–9: Under the image of the deliverance of Judah and Jerusalem from invading enemies, the prophet foretells the ultimate victory of God's people in the messianic age.

s Jer 50, 7. t Hos 5, 6. u Jer 15, 2. v Ex 21, 32; Mt 26, 15. w Mt 27, 9f. x Ez 34, 2ff. y Jn 10, 12. z Is 42, 5. a Is 51, 17; Jer 51, 7. b Mt 21, 44. c Ob 18.

LORD before them.[d] 9On that day I will seek the destruction of all nations that come against Jerusalem.

Messianic Jerusalem 10I will pour out on the house of David and on the inhabitants of Jerusalem a spirit of grace and petition;[e] and they shall look on him whom they have thrust through, and they shall mourn for him as one mourns for an only son, and they shall grieve over him as one grieves over a first-born.*

11*On that day the mourning in Jerusalem shall be as great as the mourning of Hadadrimmon in the plain of Megiddo.[f] 12And the land shall mourn, each family apart: the family of the house of David, and their wives; the family of the house of Nathan, and their wives; 13the family of the house of Levi, and their wives; the family of Shemei, and their wives; 14and all the rest of the families, each family apart, and the wives apart.

CHAPTER 13

The End of Falsehood 1On that day there shall be open to the house of David and to the inhabitants of Jerusalem, a fountain to purify from sin* and uncleanness.[g] 2On that day, says the LORD of hosts, I will destroy the names of the idols from the land, so that they shall be mentioned no more; I will also take away the prophets and the spirit of uncleanness from the land.[h] 3If a man still prophesies, his parents, father and mother, shall say to him, "You shall not live, because you have spoken a lie in the name of the LORD." When he prophesies, his parents, father and mother, shall thrust him through.[i]

4On that day, every prophet shall be ashamed to prophesy his vision, neither shall he assume the hairy mantle* to mislead, 5but he shall say, "I am no prophet, I am a tiller of the soil, for I have owned land since my youth."[j] 6And if anyone asks him, "What are these wounds on your chest?"* he shall answer, "With these I was wounded in the house of my dear ones."

The Song of the Sword

7Awake, O sword, against my shepherd,
against the man who is my associate,
says the LORD of hosts.
Strike the shepherd
that the sheep may be dispersed,*
and I will turn my hand against the little ones.[k]
8In all the land, says the LORD,
two thirds of them shall be cut off and perish,
and one third shall be left.
9I will bring the one third through fire,
and I will refine them as silver is refined,
and I will test them as gold is tested.[l]
They shall call upon my name, and I will hear them.
I will say, "They are my people,"
and they shall say, "The LORD is my God."

CHAPTER 14

The Fight for Jerusalem* 1Lo, a day shall come for the LORD when the spoils shall be

12, 10: The divine blessings (a spirit of grace and petition) will be poured out on God's people through the intervention of an unnamed sufferer (him whom they have thrust through), similar to the Servant of the Lord in Is 52, 13—53, 12. In Jn 19, 37 the Evangelist sees in this passage a prophecy fulfilled in the piercing of Christ's side.

12, 11: The mourning for the pierced victim in Jerusalem is compared to a lamentation in the plain of Megiddo apparently over a certain personage called Hadadrimmon. The reference is no longer clear. Both Hadad and Rimmon were names of the Semitic storm god, often identified with the god Baal. Some see here a reference to the annual mourning by the pagans over the death of the fertility god. According to others, Hadadrimmon is the name of a place near Megiddo, and the reference would then be to the mourning over the death of King Josiah, who was killed in battle there; cf 2 Chr 35, 22–25.

13, 1: A fountain to purify from sin: in contrast to the lustral water used in ritual purification; cf Nm 19, 9. 13. 20; 31, 23. The Lord himself is the fountain of living water (Jer 2, 13); cf Is 12, 2ff.

13, 4: Hairy mantle: worn by prophets as a mark of their calling; cf 2 Kgs 1, 8; Mt 3, 4.

13, 6: Wounds on your chest: literally, "wounds between your hands." The false prophets, like the prophet of Baal (1 Kgs 13, 28), apparently inflicted wounds on themselves; to defend himself against the accusation of being a false prophet, a man will deny having inflicted wounds on himself and say instead that he received them at home, "in the house of my dear ones." In the liturgy this text is applied to Christ in an accommodated sense.

13, 7: When the shepherd is killed, the sheep are scattered. In Mt 26, 31 the Evangelist quotes from this verse, in somewhat different form, the words, I will smite the shepherd, and the sheep of the flock will be scattered, as said by Christ shortly before his arrest in the Garden of Olives and the flight of the Apostles.

14, 1–21: An apocalyptic description of the day of the Lord, in which Jerusalem, the figure of God's elect, after much suffering (siege: vv 1ff; riot: v 13; plague: vv 12, 15), is rescued by the Lord (vv 4f) and given great blessings (vv 6–11. 14. 16–21).

d Ex 32, 34. e Jer 6, 26; Jn 19, 34; Rv 1, 7. f 2 Chr 35, 22–25. g Heb 9, 14; 1 Pt 1, 18f; Rv 1, 5. h Mi 5, 12; 2 Pt 2, 1. i Dt 18, 20; Mi 3, 5ff. j Am 7, 14. k Mt 26, 31. l Jer 30, 22; Ps 66, 10.

divided in your midst. 2And I will gather all the nations against Jerusalem for battle: the city shall be taken, houses plundered, women ravished; half of the city shall go into exile, but the rest of the people shall not be removed from the city. 3Then the LORD shall go forth and fight against those nations, fighting as on a day of battle. 4That day his feet shall rest upon the Mount of Olives, which is opposite Jerusalem to the east. The Mount of Olives shall be cleft in two from east to west by a very deep valley, and half of the mountain shall move to the north and half of it to the south. 5And the valley of the LORD's mountain shall be filled up when the valley of those two mountains reaches its edge; it shall be filled up as it was filled up by the earthquake in the days of King Uzziah of Judah. Then the LORD, my God, shall come, and all his holy ones with him.

6On that day there shall no longer be cold or frost. 7There shall be one continuous day, known to the LORD, not day and night, for in the evening time there shall be light.[m]

8On that day, living waters shall flow from Jerusalem, half to the eastern sea, and half to the western sea, and it shall be so in summer and in winter.[n] 9The LORD shall become king over the whole earth; on that day the LORD shall be the only one, and his name the only one.[o]

10And from Geba to Rimmon in the Negeb, all the land shall turn into a plain; but Jerusalem shall remain exalted in its place. From the Gate of Benjamin to the place of the First Gate, to the Corner Gate; and from the Tower of Hananel to the king's wine presses,[p] 11they shall occupy her. Never again shall she be doomed; Jerusalem shall abide in security.[q]

12And this shall be the plague with which the LORD shall strike all the nations that have fought against Jerusalem: their flesh shall rot while they stand upon their feet, and their eyes shall rot in their sockets, and their tongues shall rot in their mouths.

13On that day there shall be among them a great tumult from the LORD: every man shall seize the hand of his neighbor, and the hand of each shall be raised against that of his neighbor. 14Judah also shall fight against Jerusalem. The riches of all the surrounding nations shall be gathered together, gold, silver, and garments, in great abundance.

15Similar to this plague shall be the plague upon the horses, mules, camels, asses, and upon all the beasts that are in those camps.

16All who are left of all the nations that came against Jerusalem shall come up year after year to worship the King, the LORD of hosts, and to celebrate the feast of Booths.[r] 17If any of the families of the earth does not come up to Jerusalem to worship the King, the LORD of hosts, no rain shall fall upon them. 18And if the family of Egypt does not come up, or enter, upon them shall fall the plague which the LORD will inflict upon all the nations that do not come up to celebrate the feast of Booths. 19This shall be the punishment of Egypt, and the punishment of all the nations that do not come up to celebrate the feast of Booths.

20On that day there shall be upon the bells of the horses, "Holy to the LORD." The pots in the house of the LORD shall be as the libation bowls before the altar. 21And every pot in Jerusalem and in Judah shall be holy to the LORD of hosts; and all who come to sacrifice shall take them and cook in them. On that day there shall no longer be any merchant in the house of the LORD of hosts.[s]

m Rv 21, 23. n Zec 13, 1; Ez 47, 1–8; Jl 3, 18. o Dt 6, 4; Eph 4, 5f; Rv 11, 15. p Zec 12, 6; Neh 3, 6; 12, 38. q Jer 31, 40; Rv 22, 3. r Lv 23, 34. 43; Neh 8, 14; Is 60, 6. 9. s Mt 21, 12; Jn 2, 13–16.

THE BOOK OF MALACHI

This work was composed by an anonymous writer shortly before Nehemiah's arrival in Jerusalem (455 B.C.). Because of the sharp reproaches he was leveling against the priests and rulers of the people, the author probably wished to conceal his identity. To do this he made a proper name out of the Hebrew expression for "My Messenger" (Malachi), which occurs in 1, 1 and 3, 1. The historical value of the prophecy is considerable in that it gives us a picture of life in the Jewish community returned from Babylon, between the period of Haggai and the reform measures of Ezra and Nehemiah. It is likely that the author's trenchant criticism of abuses and religious indifference in the community prepared the way for these necessary reforms.

The chosen people had made a sorry return for divine love. The priests, who should have been leaders, had dishonored God by their blemished sacrifices. In his first chapter, the writer foresees the time when all nations will offer a pure oblation (1, 11)—a prophecy whose fulfillment the church sees in the Sacrifice of the Mass. The author then turns from priests to people, denouncing their marriages with pagans and their callous repudiation of Israelite wives. Imbued with the rationalist and critical spirit of the times, many had wearied God with the question, "Where is the God of justice?" To this question the prophet replies that the day of the Lord is coming. But first the forerunner must come, who will prepare the soil for repentance and true worship. The gospel writers point to John the Baptizer as the forerunner ushering in the messianic age, the true day of the Lord. When the ground is prepared God will appear, measuring out rewards and punishments and purifying the nation in the furnace of judgment. He will create a new order in which the ultimate triumph of good is inevitable.

CHAPTER 1

1 An oracle. The word of the LORD to Israel through Malachi.

Israel Preferred to Edom

2 I have loved you, says the LORD;
but you say, "How have you loved us?" [a]
3 Was not Esau Jacob's brother? says the LORD:*
yet I loved Jacob, but hated Esau;
I made his mountains a waste,
his heritage a desert for jackals. [b]
4 If Edom says, "We have been crushed
but we will rebuild the ruins,"
Thus says the LORD of hosts:
They indeed may build, but I will tear down,
And they shall be called the land of guilt, [c]
the people with whom the LORD is angry forever.
5 Your own eyes shall see it, and you will say,
"Great is the LORD, even beyond the land of Israel." [d]

Sins of the Priests and Levites

6 A son honors his father,
and a servant fears his master;
If then I am a father,
where is the honor due to me?
And if I am a master,
where is the reverence due to me?—
So says the LORD of hosts to you, O priests,
who despise his name.
But you ask, "How have we despised your name?"
7 By offering polluted food on my altar!

1, 3ff: The thought passes from the person Esau to his descendants, Edom, and from the person Jacob to his descendants, Israel. Loved: preferred; hated: rejected; cf Gn 25, 21ff. St. Paul uses this passage as an example of God's freedom of choice in calling the Gentiles to the faith (Rom 9, 13).

a Dt 7, 6ff; Ez 16; Am 1, 11. b Gn 25, 23; Rom 9, 13. c Is 34, 5f; 63, 1–6; Jer 49, 7–22; Ob 21. d Is 60.

Then you ask, "How have we polluted it?"
By saying the table of the LORD may be slighted!
8 When you offer a blind animal for sacrifice, [e]
is this not evil?
When you offer the lame or the sick,
is it not evil?
Present it to your governor; see if he will accept it,
or welcome you, says the LORD of hosts.*
9 So now if you implore God for mercy on us,
when you have done the like
Will he welcome any of you?
says the LORD of hosts.

10 Oh, that one among you would shut the temple gates*
to keep you from kindling fire on my altar in vain!
I have no pleasure in you, says the LORD of hosts;
neither will I accept any sacrifice from your hands,
11 For from the rising of the sun, even to its setting,
my name is great among the nations;
And everywhere they bring sacrifice to my name,
and a pure offering;
For great is my name among the nations,
says the LORD of hosts.[f]
12 But you behave profanely toward me by thinking
the LORD's table and its offering may be polluted,
and its food slighted.
13 You also say, "What a burden!"
and you scorn it, says the LORD of hosts;
You bring in what you seize, or the lame, or the sick;
yes, you bring it as a sacrifice.
Shall I accept it from your hands?
says the LORD.
14 Cursed is the deceiver, who has in his flock a male,
but under his vow sacrifices to the LORD a gelding;
For a great King am I, says the LORD of hosts,
and my name will be feared among the nations.

CHAPTER 2

1 And now, O priests, this commandment is for you:
If you do not listen,
2 And if you do not lay it to heart,
to give glory to my name, says the LORD of hosts,
I will send a curse upon you
and of your blessing I will make a curse.
Yes, I have already cursed it,
because you do not lay it to heart.[g]
3 Lo, I will deprive you of the shoulder*
and I will strew dung in your faces,
The dung of your feasts,
and you will be carried off with it.
4 Then you will know that I sent you this commandment
because I have a covenant with Levi,
says the LORD of hosts.[h]
5 My covenant with him was one of life and peace;
fear I put in him, and he feared me,
and stood in awe of my name.[i]
6 True doctrine was in his mouth,
and no dishonesty was found upon his lips;
He walked with me in integrity and uprightness,
and turned many away from evil.[j]
7 For the lips of the priest are to keep knowledge,

1, 8: The offering in sacrifice of a lame, sick or blind animal was forbidden in the law (Lv 22, 17–25; Dt 17, 1).

1, 10f: The imperfect sacrifices offered without sincerity by the people of Judah are displeasing to the Lord. He will rather be pleased with the offerings of the Gentile nations throughout the world (from the rising of the sun, even to its setting), which anticipate the pure offering to be sacrificed in messianic times, the universal Sacrifice of the Mass, as we are told by the Council of Trent.

2, 3: I will deprive you of the shoulder: this part of a sacrificial animal, allotted by the law (Dt 18, 3) to the priests, will be withheld from them.

e Lv 22, 19–25; Dt 15, 21. f Ps 113, 3; Is 59, 19. g Lv 26, 14–45; Dt 28, 15–68. h Nm 25, 12f. i Nm 25, 12; Ez 37, 26ff. j Dt 33, 8–11.

and instruction is to be sought from his
mouth,
because he is the messenger of the LORD of
hosts. [k]
8 But you have turned aside from the way,
and have caused many to falter by your
instruction;
You have made void the covenant of Levi,
says the LORD of hosts.
9 I, therefore, have made you contemptible
and base before all the people,
Since you do not keep my ways,
but show partiality in your decisions.

Sins of the People

10 Have we not all the one Father?*
Has not the one God created us?
Why then do we break faith with each other,
violating the covenant of our fathers? [l]
11 Judah has broken faith; an abominable thing
has been done in Israel and in Jerusalem.
Judah has profaned the temple which the
LORD loves,
and has married an idolatrous woman. [m]
12 May the LORD cut off from the man who does
this
both witness and advocate out of the tents
of Jacob,
and anyone to offer sacrifice to the LORD of
hosts!

13 This also you do: the altar of the LORD you
cover
with tears, weeping and groaning,
Because he no longer regards your sacrifice
nor accepts it favorably from your hand;
14 And you say, "Why is it?"—
Because the LORD is witness
between you and the wife of your youth,
With whom you have broken faith
though she is your companion, your
betrothed wife. [n]
15 Did he not make one being, with flesh and
spirit:
and what does that one require but godly
offspring?
You must then safeguard life that is your own,
and not break faith with the wife of your
youth. [o]
16 For I hate divorce,
says the LORD, the God of Israel,
And covering one's garment with injustice,
says the LORD of hosts;
You must then safeguard life that is your own,
and not break faith.

17 You have wearied the LORD with your words,
yet you say, "How have we wearied him?"
By your saying, "Every evildoer
is good in the sight of the LORD,
And he is pleased with him";
or else, "Where is the just God?"

CHAPTER 3

The Messenger of the Covenant

1 Lo, I am sending my messenger
to prepare the way before me;*
And suddenly there will come to the temple
the LORD whom you seek,
And the messenger of the covenant whom you
desire.
Yes, he is coming, says the LORD of hosts. [p]
2 But who will endure the day of his coming?
And who can stand when he appears?
For he is like the refiner's fire,
or like the fuller's lye.
3 He will sit refining and purifying [silver],
and he will purify the sons of Levi,
Refining them like gold or like silver

2, 10–16: Intermarriage of Israelites with foreigners was forbidden according to Dt 7, 1–4. After the exile this law was strictly enforced (Ezr 9—10). Foreign marriages are here portrayed as a violation of the covenant (v 10), which made the sacrifices offered by the offenders unacceptable to God (v 13). They were all the more reprehensible when accompanied by the divorce of Israelite wives (vv 14ff). This gradual return to the primitive ideal of the indissolubility of marriage was fully realized in New Testament times through the teaching of Christ; cf Mt 19, 3–12.

3, 1: My messenger . . . before me: in v 23 this messenger is called Elijah. In Mt 11, 10 these words are quoted by Christ as referring to John the Baptizer, who prepared the way for the coming of the Savior; cf Mt 3, 1ff. 11f; 17, 11ff; Mk 1, 2–8; Lk 3, 2–18; Jn 1, 31–34.

k Lv 10, 10f; Dt 17, 9f; Jer 18, 18; Hg 2, 12. **l** Mt 23, 9; Jb 31, 15; Eph 4, 6. **m** Ezr 9, 2; Neh 13, 25. **n** Gn 31, 49f; Prv 5, 18ff. **o** Gn 2, 7. 22ff. **p** Is 40, 3; Mt 11, 10; Mk 1, 2; Lk 1, 17; 7, 27.

that they may offer due sacrifice to the
LORD.[q]
4 Then the sacrifice of Judah and Jerusalem
will please the LORD,
as in the days of old, as in years gone by.
5 I will draw near to you for judgment,
and I will be swift to bear witness
Against the sorcerers, adulterers, and
perjurers,
those who defraud the hired man of his
wages,
Against those who defraud widows and
orphans;
those who turn aside the stranger,
and those who do not fear me, says the
LORD of hosts.

6 Surely I, the LORD, do not change,*
nor do you cease to be sons of Jacob.
7 Since the days of your fathers you have turned
aside
from my statutes, and have not kept them.
Return to me, and I will return to you,
says the LORD of hosts.
Yet you say, "How must we return?"[r]
8 Dare a man rob God? Yet you are robbing
me!
And you say, "How do we rob you?"
In tithes and in offerings![s]
9 You are indeed accursed,
for you, the whole nation, rob me.
10 Bring the whole tithe
into the storehouse,*
That there may be food in my house,
and try me in this, says the LORD of hosts:
Shall I not open for you the floodgates of
heaven,
to pour down blessing upon you without
measure?[t]
11 For your sake I will forbid the locust
to destroy your crops;
And the vine in the field will not be barren,
says the LORD of hosts.
12 Then all nations will call you blessed,
for you will be a delightful land,
says the LORD of hosts.

13 You have defied me in word, says the LORD,
yet you ask, "What have we spoken against
you?"
14 You have said, "It is vain to serve God,
and what do we profit by keeping his
command,
And going about in penitential dress
in awe of the LORD of hosts?[u]
15 Rather must we call the proud blessed;
for indeed evildoers prosper,
and even tempt God with impunity."
16 Then they who fear the LORD spoke with one
another,
and the LORD listened attentively;
And a record book* was written before him
of those who fear the LORD and trust in his
name.[v]
17 And they shall be mine, says the LORD of hosts,
my own special possession, on the day I
take action.
And I will have compassion on them,
as a man has compassion on his son who
serves him.[w]
18 Then you will again see the distinction
between the just and the wicked;
Between him who serves God,
and him who does not serve him.
19 For lo, the day is coming, blazing like an oven,
when all the proud and all evildoers will be
stubble,
And the day that is coming will set them on
fire,
leaving them neither root nor branch,
says the LORD of hosts.[x]
20 But for you who fear my name, there will arise
the sun of justice with its healing rays;
And you will gambol like calves out of the stall
21 and tread down the wicked;[y]
They will become ashes under the soles of
your feet,

3, 6f: God is faithful to his promises. He will not abandon the Israelites, who are still his people.
3, 10: Storehouse: the temple treasury.
3, 16: Record book: see note on Ex 32, 32.

q Is 1, 25; Zec 13, 9. **r** Zec 1, 3f; Acts 7, 51. **s** Neh 13, 10–14. **t** 2 Chr 31, 10f; Neh 10, 38; 13, 12; Prv 3, 9f. **u** Jb 21, 14f; 22, 17; Ps 73, 11f. **v** Rv 20, 12. **w** Ex 19, 5; Dt 7, 6; Pss 103, 13; 135, 4. **x** Is 13, 9; 34, 8; Jl 3, 3; Zep 1, 18; 2 Pt 3, 7. **y** Lk 1, 78f.

on the day I take action, says the LORD of
hosts.

22 Remember the law of Moses my servant,
which I enjoined upon him on Horeb,
The statutes and ordinances
for all Israel. [z]
23 Lo, I will send you
Elijah,* the prophet,
Before the day of the LORD comes,
the great and terrible day,
24 To turn the hearts of the fathers to their
children,
and the hearts of the children to their
fathers, [a]
Lest I come and strike
the land with doom.

Lo, I will send you
Elijah, the prophet,
Before the day of the LORD comes,
the great and terrible day.*

3, 23: Elijah: described in 2 Kgs 2, 11 as taken heavenward in a fiery chariot. Here his return to earth seems to be foretold. Jewish tradition has interpreted this literally; Christ declares it to be fulfilled in the coming of John the Baptizer (Mt 17, 10–13).

3, 24: The words in fine print, a repetition of v 23a-d, have been added by the scribes so that the collection of the twelve minor prophets will not end with the threat of doom.

z Ex 20; Lv 26; Dt 4, 1. 5f. a Mt 11, 14; 17, 10; Mk 9, 10ff; Lk 1, 17.

THE NEW TESTAMENT

PREFACE TO THE NEW AMERICAN BIBLE

FIRST EDITION OF THE NEW TESTAMENT

The New Testament translation has been approached with essentially the same fidelity to the thought and individual style of the biblical writers as was applied in the Old Testament. In some cases, however, the problem of marked literary peculiarities had to be met. What by any Western standard are the limited vocabularies and stylistic infelicities of the evangelists cannot be retained in the exact form in which they appear in the originals without displeasing the modern ear. A compromise is here attempted whereby some measure of the poverty of the evangelists' expression is kept and placed at the service of their message in its richness. Similarly, the syntactical shortcomings of Paul, his frequent lapses into anacoluthon, and the like, are rendered as they occur in his epistles rather than "smoothed out." Only thus, the translators suppose, will contemporary readers have some adequate idea of the kind of writing they have before them. When the prose of the original flows more smoothly, as in Luke, Acts, and Hebrews, it is reflected in the translation.

The Gospel according to John comprises a special case. Absolute fidelity to his technique of reiterated phrasing would result in an assault on the English ear, yet the softening of the vocal effect by substitution of other words and phrases would destroy the effectiveness of his poetry. Again, resort is had to compromise. This is not an easy matter when the very repetitiousness which the author deliberately employed is at the same time regarded by those who read and speak English to be a serious stylistic defect. Only those familiar with the Greek originals can know what a relentless tattoo Johannine poetry can produce. A similar observation could be made regarding other New Testament books as well. Matthew and Mark are given to identical phrasing twice and three times in the same sentence. As for the rhetorical overgrowth and mixed figures of speech in the letters of Peter, James, and Jude, the translator must resist a powerful compulsion to tidy them up if only to render these letters intelligibly.

Without seeking refuge in complaints against the inspired authors, however, the translators of *The New American Bible* here state that what they have attempted is a translation rather than a paraphrase. To be sure, all translation can be called paraphrase by definition. Any striving for complete fidelity will shortly end in infidelity. Nonetheless, it must be pointed out that the temptation to improve overladen sentences by the consolidation or elimination of multiplied adjectives, or the simplification of clumsy hendiadys, has been resisted here. For the most part, rhetorically ineffective words and phrases are retained in this translation in some form, even when it is clear that a Western contemporary writer would never have employed them.

The spelling of proper names in *The New American Bible* follows the customary forms found in most English Bibles since the Authorized Version.

Despite the arbitrary character of the divisions into numbered verses (a scheme which in its present form is only four centuries old), the translators have made a constant effort to keep within an English verse the whole verbal content of the Greek verse. At times the effort has not seemed worth the result since it often does violence to the original author's flow of expression, which preceded it by so many centuries. If this translation had been prepared for purposes of public reading only, the editors would have foregone the effort at an early stage. But since they never departed from the threefold objective of preparing a translation suitable for liturgical use, private reading, and the purposes of students, the last-named consideration prevailed. Those familiar with Greek should be able to discover how the translators of the New Testament have rendered any given original verse of scripture, if their exegetical or theological tasks require them to know this. At the same time, the fact should be set down here that the editors did not commit themselves in the synoptic gospels to rendering repeated words or phrases identically.

This leads to a final consideration: the Greek text used for the New Testament. Here, punctuation and verse division are at least as important as variant reading. In general, Nestle-Aland's *Novum Testamentum Graece* (25th edition, 1963) was followed. Additional help was derived from *The Greek New Testament* (Aland, Black, Metzger, Wikgren), produced for the use of translators by the United Bible Societies in 1966. However, the editors did not confine themselves strictly to these texts; at times, they inclined toward readings otherwise attested. The omission of alternative translations does not mean that the translators think them without merit, but only that in every case they had to make a choice.

Poorly attested readings do not occur in this translation. Doubtful readings of some merit appear within brackets; public readers may include such words or phrases, or omit them entirely without any damage to sense. Parentheses are used, as ordinarily in English, as a punctuation device. Material they enclose is in no sense textually doubtful. It is simply thought to be parenthetical in the intention of the biblical author, even though there is no such punctuation mark in Greek. The difficulty in dealing with quotation marks is well known. Since they do not appear in any form in the original text, wherever they occur here they constitute an editorial decision.

PREFACE TO THE REVISED EDITION

The New Testament of *The New American Bible,* a fresh translation from the Greek text, was first published in complete form in 1970, together with the Old Testament translation that had been completed the previous year. Portions of the New Testament had appeared earlier, in somewhat different form, in the provisional Mass lectionary of 1964 and in the *Lectionary for Mass* of 1970.

Since 1970 many different printings of the New Testament have been issued by a number of publishers, both separately and in complete Bibles, and the text has become widely known both in the United States and in other English-speaking countries. Most American Catholics have been influenced by it because of its widespread use in the liturgy, and it has received a generally favorable reception from many other Christians as well. It has taken its place among the standard contemporary translations of the New Testament, respected for its fidelity to the original and its attempt to render this into current American English.

Although the scriptures themselves are timeless, translations and explanations of them quickly become dated in an era marked by rapid cultural change to a degree never previously experienced. The explosion of biblical studies that has taken place in our century and the changing nature of our language itself require periodic adjustment both in translations and in the accompanying explanatory materials. The experience of actual use of the New Testament of *The New American Bible,* especially in oral proclamation, has provided a basis for further improvement. Accordingly, it was decided in 1978 to proceed with a thorough revision of the New Testament to reflect advances in scholarship and to satisfy needs identified through pastoral experience.

For this purpose a steering committee was formed to plan, organize, and direct the work of revision, to engage collaborators, and to serve as an editorial board to coordinate the work of the various revisers and to determine the final form of the text and the explanatory materials. Guidelines were drawn up and collaborators selected in 1978 and early 1979, and November of 1980 was established as the deadline for manuscripts. From December 1980 through September 1986 the editorial board met a total of fifty times and carefully reviewed and revised all the material in order to ensure accuracy and consistency of approach. The editors also worked together with the bishops' ad hoc committee that was appointed by the National Conference of Catholic Bishops in 1982 to oversee the revision.

The threefold purpose of the translation that was expressed in the preface to the first edition has been maintained in the revision: to provide a version suitable for liturgical proclamation, for private reading, and for purposes of study. Special attention has been given to the first of these purposes, since oral proclamation demands special qualities in a translation, and experience had provided insights and suggestions that could lead to improvement in this area. Efforts have also been made, however, to facilitate devotional reading by providing suitable notes and introductory materials, and to assist the student by achieving greater accuracy and consistency in the translation and supplying more abundant information in the introductions and notes.

The primary aim of the revision is to produce a version as accurate and faithful to the meaning of the Greek original as is possible for a translation. The editors have consequently moved in the direction of a formal-equivalence approach to translation, matching the vocabulary, structure, and even word order of the original as closely as possible in the receptor language. Some other contemporary biblical versions have adopted, in varying degrees, a dynamic-equivalence approach, which attempts to respect the individuality of each language by expressing the meaning of the original in a linguistic structure suited to English, even though this may be very different from the corresponding Greek structure. While this approach often results in fresh and brilliant renderings, it has the disadvantages of more or less radically abandoning traditional biblical and liturgical terminology and phraseology, of expanding the text to include what more properly belongs in notes, commentaries, or preaching, and of tending toward paraphrase. A more formal approach seems better suited to the specific purposes intended for this translation.

At the same time, the editors have wished to produce a version in English that reflects contemporary American usage and is readily understandable to ordinary educated people, but one that will be recognized as dignified speech, on the level of formal rather than colloquial usage. These aims are not in fact contradictory, for there are different levels of language in current use: the language of formal situations is not that of colloquial conversation, though people understand both and may pass from one to the other without adverting to the transition. The liturgy is a formal situation that requires a level of discourse more dignified, formal, and hieratic than the world of business, sport, or informal communication. People readily understand this more formal level even though they may not often use it; our passive vocabulary is much larger than our active vocabulary. Hence this revision, while avoiding archaisms, does not shrink from traditional biblical terms that are easily understood even though not in common use in everyday speech. The level of language consciously aimed at is one appropriate for liturgical proclamation; this may also permit the translation to serve the purposes of devotional reading and serious study.

A particular effort has been made to insure consistency of vocabulary. Always to translate a give Greek word by the same English equivalent would lead to ludicrous results and to infidelity to the meaning of the text. But in passages where a particular Greek term retains the same meaning, it has been rendered in the same way insofar as this has been feasible; this is particularly significant in the case of terms that have a specific theological meaning. The synoptic gospels have been carefully translated so as to reveal both the similarities and the differences of the Greek.

An especially sensitive problem today is the question of discrimination in language. In recent years there has been much discussion about allegations of anti-Jewish expressions in the New Testament and of language that discriminates against various minorities. Above all, however, the question of discrimination against women affects the largest number of people and arouses the greatest degree of interest and concern. At present there is little agreement about these problems or about the best way to deal with them. In all these areas the present translation attempts to display a sensitivity appropriate to the present state of the questions under discussion, which are not yet resolved and in regard to which it is impossible to please everyone, since intelligent and sincere participants in the debate hold mutually contradictory views.

The primary concern in this revision is fidelity to what the text says. When the meaning of the Greek is inclusive of both sexes, the translation seeks to reproduce such inclusivity insofar as this is possible in normal English usage, without resort to inelegant circumlocutions or neologisms that would offend against the dignity of the language. Although the generic sense of *man* is traditional in English, many today reject it; its use has therefore generally been avoided, though it is retained in cases where no fully satisfactory equivalent could be found. English does not possess a gender-inclusive third personal pronoun in the singular, and this translation continues to use the masculine resumptive pronoun after *everyone* or *anyone,* in the traditional way, where this cannot be avoided without infidelity to the meaning.

The translation of the Greek word *adelphos,* particularly in the plural form *adelphoi,* poses an especially delicate problem. While the term literally means *brothers* or other male blood relatives, even in profane Greek the plural can designate two persons, one of either sex, who were born of the same parents. It was adopted by the early Christians to designate, in a figurative sense, the members of the Christian community, who were conscious of a new familial relationship to one another by reason of their adoption as children of God. They are consequently addressed as *adelphoi.* This has traditionally been rendered into English by *brothers* or, more archaically, *brethren.* There has never been any doubt that this designation includes *all* the members of the Christian community, both male and female. Given the absence in English of a corresponding term that explicitly includes both sexes, this translation retains the usage of *brothers,* with the inclusive meaning that has been traditionally attached to it in this biblical context.

Since the New Testament is the product of a particular time and culture, the views expressed in it and the language in which they are expressed reflect a particular cultural conditioning, which sometimes makes them quite different from contemporary ideas and concerns. Discriminatory language should be eliminated insofar as possible whenever it is unfaithful to the meaning of the New Testament, but the text should not be altered in order to adjust it to contemporary concerns. This translation does not introduce any changes, expansions, additions to, or subtractions from the text of scripture. It further retains the traditional biblical ways of speaking about God and about Christ, including the use of masculine nouns and pronouns.

The Greek text followed in this translation is that of the third edition of *The Greek New Testament,* edited by Kurt Aland, Matthew Black, Carlo Martini, Bruce Metzger, and Allen Wikgren, and published by the United Bible Societies in 1975. The same text, with a different critical apparatus and variations in punctuation and typography, was published as the twenty-sixth edition of the Nestle-Aland *Novum Testamentum Graece* in 1979 by the Deutsche Bibelstiftung, Stuttgart. This edition has also been consulted. When variant readings occur, the translation, with few exceptions, follows the reading that was placed in the text of these Greek editions, though the occurrence of the principal variants is pointed out in the notes.

The editors of the Greek text placed square brackets around words or portions of words of which the authenticity is questionable because the evidence of textual witnesses is inconclusive. The same has been done in the translation insofar as it is possible to reproduce this convention in English. It should be possible to read the text either with or without the disputed words, but in English it is not always feasible to provide this alternative, and in some passages the bracketed words must be included to make sense. As in the first edition, parentheses do not indicate textual uncertainty, but are simply a punctuation device to indicate a passage that in the editors' judgment appears parenthetical to the thought of the author.

Citations from the Old Testament are placed within quotation marks; longer citations are set off as block quotations in a separate indented paragraph. The sources of such citations, as well as those of many more or less subtle allusions to the Old Testament, are identified in the biblical cross-reference section at the bottom of each page. Insofar as possible, the translation of such Old Testament citations agrees with that of *The New American Bible* Old Testament whenever the underlying Greek agrees with the Hebrew (or, in some cases, the Aramaic or Greek) text from which the Old Testament translation was made. But citations in the New Testament frequently follow the Septuagint or some other version, or were made from memory; hence, in many cases the translation in the New Testament passage will not agree with what appears in the Old Testament. Some of these cases are explained in the notes.

It is a further aim of the revised edition to supply explanatory materials more abundantly than in the first edition. In most cases the introductions and notes have been entirely rewritten and expanded, and the cross-references checked and revised. It is intended that these materials should reflect the present state of sound biblical scholarship and should be presented in such a form that they can be assimilated by the ordinary intelligent reader without specialized biblical training. While they have been written with the ordinary educated Christian in mind, not all technical vocabulary can be entirely dispensed with in approaching the Bible, any more than in any other field. It is the hope of the editors that these materials, even if they sometimes demand an effort, will help the reader to a fuller and more intelligent understanding of the New Testament and a fruitful appropriation of its meaning for personal spiritual growth.

The New American Bible is a Roman Catholic translation. This revision, however, like the first edition, has been accomplished with the collaboration of scholars from other Christian churches, both among the revisers and on the editorial board, in response to the encouragement of Vatican Council II (*Dei Verbum,* 22). The editorial board expresses gratitude to all who have collaborated in the revision: to all the revisers, consultants, and bishops who contributed to it, to reviewers of the first edition, and to those who voluntarily submitted suggestions. May this translation fulfill its threefold purpose, "so that the word of the Lord may speed forward and be glorified" (2 Thes 3, 1).

September 30, 1986 *The Feast of St. Jerome*

THE GOSPELS

The collection of writings that constitutes the New Testament begins with four gospels. Next comes the Acts of the Apostles, followed by twenty-one letters that are attributed to Paul, James, Peter, John, and Jude. Finally, at the end of the early church's scriptures stands the Revelation to John. Virtually all Christians agree that these twenty-seven books constitute the "canon," a term that means "rule" and designates the list of writings that are regarded as authoritative for Christian faith and life.

It is the purpose of this Introduction to describe those features that are common to the four gospels. A similar treatment of the letters of the New Testament is provided in the two Introductions that appear before the Letter to the Romans and before the Letter of James, respectively. The Acts of the Apostles, a work that is both historical and theological, and Revelation, an apocalyptic work, have no counterparts in the New Testament; the special Introductions prefixed to these books treat of the literary characteristics proper to each of them.

While the New Testament contains four writings called "gospels," there is in reality only one gospel running through all of the Christian scriptures, the gospel of and about Jesus Christ. Our English word "gospel" translates the Greek term *euangelion,* meaning "good news." This noun was used in the plural by the Greek translators of the Old Testament to render the Hebrew term for "good news" (2 Sm 4, 10; possibly also 18, 20.25). But it is the corresponding verb *euangelizomai,* "to proclaim good news," that was especially significant in preparing for the New Testament idea of "gospel," since this term is used by Deutero-Isaiah of announcing the great victory of God that was to establish his universal kingship and inaugurate the new age (Is 40, 9; 52, 7; 61, 1).

Paul used the word *euangelion* to designate the message that he and the other apostles proclaimed, the "gospel of God" (Rom 1, 1; 15, 16; 2 Cor 11, 7; 1 Thes 2, 2.8.9). He often referred to it simply as "the gospel" (Rom 1, 16; 10, 16; 11, 28; etc.) or, because of its content and origin, as "the gospel of Christ" (Rom 15, 19; 1 Cor 9, 12; 1 Thes 3, 2; etc.). Because of its personal meaning for him and his own particular manner of telling the story about Jesus Christ and of explaining the significance of his cross and resurrection, Paul also referred to this message as "my gospel" (Rom 2, 16; cf Gal 1, 11; 2, 2) or "our gospel" (2 Cor 4, 3; 1 Thes 1, 5; 2 Thes 2, 14).

It was Mark, as far as we know, who first applied the term "gospel" to a book telling the story of Jesus; see Mk 1, 1 and the note there. This form of presenting Jesus' life, works, teachings, passion, and resurrection was developed further by the other evangelists; see the Introduction to each gospel. The first three of the canonical gospels, Matthew, Mark, and Luke, are so similar at many points when viewed together, particularly when arranged in parallel columns or lines, that they are called "synoptic" gospels, from the Greek word for such a general view. The fourth gospel, John, often differs significantly from the synoptics in outline and approach. This work never uses the word "gospel" or its corresponding verb; nevertheless, its message concerns the same Jesus, and the reader is urged to believe in him as the Messiah, "that through this belief you may have life in his name" (20, 31).

From the second century onward, the practice arose of designating each of these four books as a "gospel," understood as a title, and of adding a phrase with a name that identified the traditional author, e.g., "The Gospel according to Matthew." The arrangement of the canon that was adopted, with the four gospels grouped together at the beginning followed by Acts, provides a massive focus upon Jesus and allows Acts to serve as a framework for the letters of the New Testament. This order, however, conceals the fact that Luke's two volumes, a gospel and Acts, were intended by their author to go together. It further obscures the point that Paul's letters were written before any of our gospels, though the sayings and deeds of Jesus stand behind all the New Testament writings.

THE GOSPEL ACCORDING TO MATTHEW

The position of the Gospel according to Matthew as the first of the four gospels in the New Testament reflects both the view that it was the first to be written, a view that goes back to the late second century A.D., and the esteem in which it was held by the church; no other was so frequently quoted in the noncanonical literature of earliest Christianity. Although the majority of scholars now reject the opinion about the time of its composition, the high estimation of this work remains. The reason for that becomes clear upon study of the way in which Matthew presents his story of Jesus, the demands of Christian discipleship, and the breaking-in of the new and final age through the ministry but particularly through the death and resurrection of Jesus.

The gospel begins with a narrative prologue (1, 1—2, 23), the first part of which is a genealogy of Jesus starting with Abraham, the father of Israel (1, 1-17). Yet at the beginning of that genealogy Jesus is designated as "the son of David, the son of Abraham" (1, 1). The kingly ancestor who lived about a thousand years after Abraham is named first, for this is the genealogy of Jesus Christ, the Messiah, the royal anointed one (1, 16). In the first of the episodes of the infancy narrative that follow the genealogy, the mystery of Jesus' person is declared. He is conceived of a virgin by the power of the Spirit of God (1, 18-25). The first of the gospel's fulfillment citations, whose purpose it is to show that he was the one to whom the prophecies of Israel were pointing, occurs here (1, 23): he shall be named Emmanuel, for in him God is with us.

The announcement of the birth of this newborn king of the Jews greatly troubles not only King Herod but all Jerusalem (2, 1-3), yet the Gentile magi are overjoyed to find him and offer him their homage and their gifts (2, 10-11). Thus his ultimate rejection by the mass of his own people and his acceptance by the Gentile nations is foreshadowed. He must be taken to Egypt to escape the murderous plan of Herod. By his sojourn there and his subsequent return after the king's death he relives the Exodus experience of Israel. The words of the Lord spoken through the prophet Hosea, "Out of Egypt I called my son," are fulfilled in him (2, 15); if Israel was God's son, Jesus is so in a way far surpassing the dignity of that nation, as his marvelous birth and the unfolding of his story show (see 3, 17; 4, 1-11; 11, 27; 14, 33; 16, 16; 27, 54). Back in the land of Israel, he must be taken to Nazareth in Galilee because of the danger to his life in Judea, where Herod's son Archelaus is now ruling (2, 22-23). The sufferings of Jesus in the infancy narrative anticipate those of his passion, and if his life is spared in spite of the dangers, it is because his destiny is finally to give it on the cross as "a ransom for many" (20, 28). Thus the word of the angel will be fulfilled, ". . . he will save his people from their sins" (1, 21; cf 26, 28).

In 4, 12 Matthew begins his account of the ministry of Jesus, introducing it by the preparatory preaching of John the Baptist (3, 1-12), the baptism of Jesus that culminates in God's proclaiming him his "beloved Son" (3, 13-17), and the temptation in which he proves his true sonship by his victory over the devil's attempt to deflect him from the way of obedience to the Father (4, 1-11). The central message of Jesus' preaching is the coming of the kingdom of heaven and the need for repentance, a complete change of heart and conduct, on the part of those who are to receive this great gift of God (4, 17). Galilee is the setting for most of his ministry; he leaves there for Judea only in 19, 1, and his ministry in Jerusalem, the goal of his journey, is limited to a few days (21, 1—25, 46).

In this extensive material there are five great discourses of Jesus, each concluding with the formula "When Jesus finished these words" or one closely similar (7, 28; 11, 1; 13, 53; 19, 1; 26, 1). These are an important structure of the gospel. In every case the discourse is preceded by a narrative section, each narrative and discourse together constituting a "book" of the gospel. The discourses are, respectively, the "Sermon on the Mount" (5, 3—7, 27), the missionary discourse (10, 5-42), the parable discourse (13, 3-52), the "church order" discourse (18, 3-35), and the eschatological discourse (24, 4—25, 46). In large measure the material of these discourses came to Matthew from his tradition, but his work in modifying and adding to what he had received is abundantly evident. No other evangelist gives the teaching of Jesus with such elegance and order as he.

In the "Sermon on the Mount" the theme of righteousness is prominent, and even at this early stage of the ministry the note of opposition is struck between Jesus and the Pharisees, who are designated as "the hypocrites" (6, 2.5.16). The righteousness of his disciples must surpass that of the scribes and Pharisees; otherwise, in spite of their alleged following of Jesus, they will not enter into the kingdom of heaven (5, 20). Righteousness means doing the will of the heavenly Father (7, 21), and his will is proclaimed in a manner that is startling to all who have identified it with the law of Moses. The antitheses of the Sermon (5, 21-48) both accept (5, 21-30.43-48) and reject (5, 31-42) elements of that law, and in the former case the understanding of the law's demands is deepened and extended. The antitheses are the best commentary on the meaning of Jesus' claim that he has come not to abolish but to fulfill the law (5, 17). What is meant by fulfillment of the law is not the demand to keep it exactly as it stood before the coming of Jesus, but rather his bringing the law to be a lasting expression of the will of God, and in that fulfillment there is much that will pass away. Should this appear contradictory to his saying that "until heaven and earth pass away" not even the smallest part of the law will pass (5, 18), that time of fulfillment is not the dissolution of the universe but the coming of the new age, which will occur with Jesus' death and resurrection. While righteousness in the new age will continue to mean conduct that is in accordance with the law, it will be conduct in accordance with the law as expounded and interpreted by Jesus (cf 28, 20, ". . . all that I have commanded you").

Though Jesus speaks harshly about the Pharisees in the Sermon, his judgment is not solely a condemnation of them. The Pharisees are portrayed as a negative example for his disciples, and his condemnation of those who claim to belong to him while disobeying his word is no less severe (7, 21-23.26-27).

In 4, 23 a summary statement of Jesus' activity speaks not only of his teaching and proclaiming the gospel but of his "curing every disease and illness among the people"; this is repeated almost verbatim in 9, 35. The narrative section that follows the Sermon on the Mount (8, 1—9,

38) is composed principally of accounts of those merciful deeds of Jesus, but it is far from being simply a collection of stories about miraculous cures. The nature of the community that Jesus will establish is shown; it will always be under the protection of him whose power can deal with all dangers (8, 23-27), but it is only for those who are prepared to follow him at whatever cost (8, 16-22), not only believing Israelites but Gentiles who have come to faith in him (8, 10-12). The disciples begin to have some insight, however imperfect, into the mystery of Jesus' person. They wonder about him whom "the winds and the sea obey" (8, 27), and they witness his bold declaration of the forgiveness of the paralytic's sins (9, 2). That episode of the narrative moves on two levels. When the crowd sees the cure that testifies to the authority of Jesus, the Son of Man, to forgive sins (9, 6), they glorify God "who had given such authority to human beings" (9, 8). The forgiveness of sins is now not the prerogative of Jesus alone but of "human beings," that is, of the disciples who constitute the community of Jesus, the church. The ecclesial character of this narrative section could hardly be more plainly indicated.

The end of the section prepares for the discourse on the church's mission (10, 5-42). Jesus is moved to pity at the sight of the crowds who are like sheep without a shepherd (9, 36), and he sends out the twelve disciples to make the proclamation with which his own ministry began, "The kingdom of heaven is at hand" (10, 7; cf 4, 17), and to drive out demons and cure the sick as he has done (10, 1). Their mission is limited to Israel (10, 5-6) as Jesus' own was (15, 24), yet in v 16 that perspective broadens and the discourse begins to speak of the mission that the disciples will have after the resurrection and of the severe persecution that will attend it (10, 18). Again, the discourse moves on two levels: that of the time of Jesus and that of the time of the church.

The narrative section of the third book (11, 2—12, 50) deals with the growing opposition to Jesus. Hostility toward him has already been manifested (8, 10; 9, 3.10-13.34), but here it becomes more intense. The rejection of Jesus comes, as before, from Pharisees, who take "counsel against him to put him to death" (12, 14) and repeat their earlier accusation that he drives out demons because he is in league with demonic power (12, 22-24). But they are not alone in their rejection. Jesus complains of the lack of faith of "this generation" of Israelites (11, 16-19) and reproaches the towns "where most of his mighty deeds had been done" for not heeding his call to repentance (11, 20-24). This dark picture is relieved by Jesus' praise of the Father who has enabled "the childlike" to accept him (11, 25-27), but on the whole the story is one of opposition to his word and blindness to the meaning of his deeds. The whole section ends with his declaring that not even the most intimate blood relationship with him counts for anything; his only true relatives are those who do the will of his heavenly Father (12, 48-50).

The narrative of rejection leads up to the parable discourse (13, 3-52). The reason given for Jesus' speaking to the crowds in parables is that they have hardened themselves against his clear teaching, unlike the disciples to whom knowledge of "the mysteries of the kingdom has been granted" (13, 10-16). In 13, 36 he dismisses the crowds and continues the discourse to his disciples alone, who claim, at the end, to have understood all that he has said (13, 51). But, lest the impression be given that the church of Jesus is made up only of true disciples, the explanation of the parable of the weeds among the wheat (13, 37-43), as well as the parable of the net thrown into the sea "which collects fish of every kind" (13, 47-49), shows that it is composed of both the righteous and the wicked, and that separation between the two will be made only at the time of the final judgment.

In the narrative that constitutes the first part of the fourth book of the gospel (13, 54—17, 27), Jesus is shown preparing for the establishment of his church with its teaching authority that will supplant the blind guidance of the Pharisees (15, 13-14), whose teaching, curiously said to be that of the Sadducees also, is repudiated by Jesus as the norm for his disciples (16, 6.11-12). The church of Jesus will be built on Peter (16, 18), who will be given authority to bind and loose on earth, an authority whose exercise will be confirmed in heaven (16, 19). The metaphor of binding and loosing has a variety of meanings, among them that of giving authoritative teaching. This promise is made to Peter directly after he has confessed Jesus to be the Messiah, the Son of the living God (16, 16), a confession that he has made as the result of revelation given to him by the heavenly Father (16, 17); Matthew's ecclesiology is based on his high christology.

Directly after that confession Jesus begins to instruct his disciples about how he must go the way of suffering and death (16, 21). Peter, who has been praised for his confession, protests against this and receives from Jesus the sharpest of rebukes for attempting to deflect Jesus from his God-appointed destiny. The future rock upon whom the church will be built is still a man of "little faith" (see 14, 31). Both he and the other disciples must know not only that Jesus will have to suffer and die but that they too will have to follow him on the way of the cross if they are truly to be his disciples (16, 24-25).

The discourse following this narrative (18, 1-35) is often called the "church order" discourse, although that title is perhaps misleading since the emphasis is not on the structure of the church but on the care that the disciples must have for one another in respect to guarding each other's faith in Jesus (18, 6-7), to seeking out those who have wandered from the fold (18, 10-14), and to repeated forgiving of their fellow disciples who have offended them (18, 21-35). But there is also the obligation to correct the sinful fellow Christian and, should one refuse to be corrected, separation from the community is demanded (18, 15-18).

The narrative of the fifth book (19, 1—23, 39) begins with the departure of Jesus and his disciples from Galilee for Jerusalem. In the course of their journey Jesus for the third time predicts the passion that awaits him at Jerusalem and also his resurrection (20, 17-19). At his entrance into the city he is hailed as the Son of David by the crowds accompanying him (21, 9). He cleanses the temple (21, 12-17), and in the few days of his Jerusalem ministry he engages in a series of controversies with the Jewish religious leaders (21, 23-27; 22, 15-22.23-33.34-40.41-46), meanwhile speaking parables against them (21, 28-32.33-46), against all those Israelites who have rejected God's invitation to the messianic banquet (22, 1-10), and against all, Jew and Gentile, who have accepted but have shown themselves unworthy of it (22, 11-14). Once again, the perspective of the evangelist includes not only the time of Jesus' ministry but that of the preaching of the gospel after his resurrection. The narrative culminates in Jesus' denunciation of the scribes and Pharisees, reflecting not only his own opposition to them but that of Matthew's church (23, 1-36), and in Jesus' lament over Jerusalem (23, 37-39).

In the discourse of the fifth book (24, 1—25, 46), the last of the great structural discourses of the gospel, Jesus predicts the destruction of the temple and his own final coming. The time of the latter is unknown (24, 36.44), and the disciples are exhorted in various parables to live in readiness for it, a readiness that entails faithful attention to the duties of the interim period (24, 45—25, 30). The coming of Jesus will bring with it the great judgment by which the everlasting destiny of all will be determined (25, 31-46).

The story of Jesus' passion and resurrection (26, 1—28, 20), the climax of the gospel, throws light on all that has preceded. In Mt "righteousness" means both the faithful response to the will of God demanded of all to whom that will is announced and also the saving activity of God for his people (see 3, 15; 5, 6; 6, 33). The passion supremely exemplifies both meanings of that central Matthean word. In Jesus' absolute faithfulness to the Father's will that he drink the cup of suffering (26, 39), the incomparable model for Christian obedience is given; in his death "for the forgiveness of sins" (26, 28), the saving power of God is manifested as never before.

Matthew's portrayal of Jesus in his passion combines both the majestic serenity of the obedient Son who goes his destined way in fulfillment of the scriptures (26, 52-54), confident of his ultimate vindication by God, and the depths of fear and abandonment that he feels in face of death (26, 38-39; 27, 46). These two aspects are expressed by an Old Testament theme that occurs often in the narrative, i.e., the portrait of the suffering Righteous One who complains to God in his misery, but is certain of eventual deliverance from his terrible ordeal.

The passion-resurrection of God's Son means nothing less than the turn of the ages, a new stage of history, the coming of the Son of Man in his kingdom (28, 18; cf 16, 28). That is the sense of the apocalyptic signs that accompany Jesus' death (27, 51-53) and resurrection (28, 2). Although the old age continues, as it will until the manifestation of Jesus' triumph at his parousia, the final age has now begun. This is known only to those who have seen the Risen One and to those, both Jews and Gentiles, who have believed in their announcement of Jesus' triumph and have themselves become his disciples (cf 28, 19). To them he is constantly, though invisibly, present (28, 20), verifying the name Emmanuel, "God is with us" (cf 1, 23).

The questions of authorship, sources, and the time of composition of this gospel have received many answers, none of which can claim more than a greater or less degree of probability. The one now favored by the majority of scholars is the following.

The ancient tradition that the author was the disciple and apostle of Jesus named Matthew (see 10, 3) is untenable because the gospel is based, in large part, on the Gospel according to Mark (almost all the verses of that gospel have been utilized in this), and it is hardly likely that a companion of Jesus would have followed so extensively an account that came from one who admittedly never had such an association rather than rely on his own memories. The attribution of the gospel to the disciple Matthew may have been due to his having been responsible for some of the traditions found in it, but that is far from certain.

The unknown author, whom we shall continue to call Matthew for the sake of convenience, drew not only upon the Gospel according to Mark but upon a large body of material (principally, sayings of Jesus) not found in Mk that corresponds, sometimes exactly, to material found also in the Gospel according to Luke. This material, called "Q" (probably from the first letter of the German word *Quelle,* meaning ("source"), represents traditions, written and oral, used by both Matthew and Luke. Mark and Q are sources common to the two other synoptic gospels; hence the name the "Two-Source Theory" given to this explanation of the relation among the synoptics.

In addition to what Matthew drew from Mk and Q, his gospel contains material that is found only there. This is often designated "M," written or oral tradition that was available to the author. Since Mk was written shortly before or shortly after A.D. 70 (see Introduction to Mk), Mt was composed certainly after that date, which marks the fall of Jerusalem to the Romans at the time of the First Jewish Revolt (A.D. 66–70), and probably at least a decade later since Matthew's use of Mk presupposes a wide diffusion of that gospel. The post-A.D. 70 date is confirmed within the text by 22, 7, which refers to the destruction of Jerusalem.

As for the place where the gospel was composed, a plausible suggestion is that it was Antioch, the capital of the Roman province of Syria. That large and important city had a mixed population of Greek-speaking Gentiles and Jews. The tensions between Jewish and Gentile Christians there in the time of Paul (see Gal 2, 1-14) in respect to Christian obligation to observe Mosaic law are partially similar to tensions that can be seen between the two groups in Matthew's gospel. The church of Matthew, originally strongly Jewish Christian, had become one in which Gentile Christians were predominant. His gospel answers the question how obedience to the will of God is to be expressed by those who live after the "turn of the ages," the death and resurrection of Jesus.

The principal divisions of the Gospel according to Matthew are the following:

I. The Infancy Narrative (1, 1—2, 23)
II. The Proclamation of the Kingdom (3, 1—7, 29)
III. Ministry and Mission in Galilee (8, 1—11, 1)
IV. Opposition from Israel (11, 2—13, 53)
V. Jesus, the Kingdom, and the Church (13, 54—18, 35)
VI. Ministry in Judea and Jerusalem (19, 1—25, 46)
VII. The Passion and Resurrection (26, 1—28, 20)

I: The Infancy Narrative

CHAPTER 1

The Genealogy of Jesus 1 [a]*The book of the
genealogy of Jesus Christ, the son of David, the
son of Abraham.
2 [b] [c]Abraham became the father of Isaac, Isaac
the father of Jacob, Jacob the father of Judah and
his brothers. 3 [d]Judah became the father of Perez
and Zerah, whose mother was Tamar. Perez
became the father of Hezron, Hezron the father
of Ram, 4 [e]Ram the father of Amminadab. Am-
minadab became the father of Nahshon, Nah-
shon the father of Salmon, 5 [f]Salmon the father
of Boaz, whose mother was Rahab. Boaz became
the father of Obed, whose mother was Ruth.
Obed became the father of Jesse, 6 [g]Jesse the
father of David the king.
David became the father of Solomon, whose
mother had been the wife of Uriah. 7 [h]*Solomon

1, 1—2, 23: The infancy narrative forms the prologue of the gospel. Consisting of a genealogy and five stories, it presents the coming of Jesus as the climax of Israel's history, and the events of his conception, birth, and early childhood as the fulfillment of Old Testament prophecy. The genealogy is probably traditional material that Matthew edited. In its first two sections (1, 2–11) it was drawn from Ru 4, 18–22 and 1 Chr 1—3. Except for Jechoniah, Shealtiel, and Zerubbabel, none of the names in the third section (1, 12–16) is found in any Old Testament genealogy. While the genealogy shows the continuity of God's providential plan from Abraham on, discontinuity is also present. The women Tamar (1, 3), Rahab and Ruth (1, 5), and the wife of Uriah, Bathsheba (1, 6), bore their sons through unions that were in varying degrees strange and unexpected. These "irregularities" culminate in the supreme "irregularity" of the Messiah's birth of a virgin mother; the age of fulfillment is inaugurated by a creative act of God.

Drawing upon both biblical tradition and Jewish stories, Matthew portrays Jesus as reliving the Exodus experience of Israel and the persecutions of Moses. His rejection by his own people and his passion are foreshadowed by the troubled reaction of "all Jerusalem" to the question of the magi who are seeking the "newborn king of the Jews" (2, 2–3), and by Herod's attempt to have him killed. The magi who do him homage prefigure the Gentiles who will accept the preaching of the gospel. The infancy narrative proclaims who Jesus is, the savior of his people from their sins (1, 21), Emmanuel in whom "God is with us" (1, 23), and the Son of God (2, 15).

1, 1: The Son of David, the son of Abraham: two links of the genealogical chain are singled out. Although the later, David is placed first in order to emphasize that Jesus is the royal Messiah. The mention of Abraham may be due not only to his being the father of the nation Israel but to Matthew's interest in the universal scope of Jesus' mission; cf Gn 22, 18, ". . . in your descendants all the nations of the earth shall find blessing."

1, 7: The successor of Abijah was not Asaph but Asa (see 1 Chr 3, 10). Some textual witnesses read the latter name; however, **Asaph** is better attested. Matthew may have deliberately introduced the psalmist Asaph into the genealogy (and in v 10 the prophet Amos) in order to show that Jesus is the fulfillment not only of the promises made to David (see 2 Sm 7) but of all the Old Testament.

a Gn 5, 1 / 1 Chr 17, 11 / Gn 22, 18. b Lk 3, 23–38. c Gn 21, 3; 25, 26; 29, 35; 1 Chr 2, 1. d Gn 38, 29–30; Ru 4, 18; 1 Chr 2, 4–9. e Ru 4, 19–20; 1 Chr 2, 10–11. f Ru 4, 21–22; 1 Chr 2, 11–12. g 2 Sm 12, 24; 1 Chr 2, 15; 3, 5. h 2 Kgs 25, 1–21; 1 Chr 3, 10–15.

became the father of Rehoboam, Rehoboam the father of Abijah, Abijah the father of Asaph. [8]Asaph became the father of Jehoshaphat, Jehoshaphat the father of Joram, Joram the father of Uzziah. [9]Uzziah became the father of Jotham, Jotham the father of Ahaz, Ahaz the father of Hezekiah. [10]*Hezekiah became the father of Manasseh, Manasseh the father of Amos, Amos the father of Josiah. [11]Josiah became the father of Jechoniah and his brothers at the time of the Babylonian exile.

[12] [i]After the Babylonian exile, Jechoniah became the father of Shealtiel, Shealtiel the father of Zerubbabel, [13]Zerubbabel the father of Abiud. Abiud became the father of Eliakim, Eliakim the father of Azor, [14]Azor the father of Zadok. Zadok became the father of Achim, Achim the father of Eliud, [15]Eliud the father of Eleazar. Eleazar became the father of Matthan, Matthan the father of Jacob, [16]Jacob the father of Joseph, the husband of Mary. Of her was born Jesus who is called the Messiah.

[17]*Thus the total number of generations from Abraham to David is fourteen generations; from David to the Babylonian exile, fourteen generations; from the Babylonian exile to the Messiah, fourteen generations.

The Birth of Jesus [18]*Now this is how the birth of Jesus Christ came about. When his mother Mary was betrothed to Joseph, but before they lived together, she was found with child through the holy Spirit. [19]*Joseph her husband, since he was a righteous man, yet unwilling to expose her to shame, decided to divorce her quietly. [20] [j]*Such was his intention when, behold, the angel of the Lord appeared to him in a dream and said, "Joseph, son of David, do not be afraid to take Mary your wife into your home. For it is through the holy Spirit that this child has been conceived in her. [21]*She will bear a son and you are to name him Jesus, because he will save his people from their sins." [22]All this took place to fulfill what the Lord had said through the prophet:

[23] [k]*"Behold, the virgin shall be with child and
bear a son,
and they shall name him Emmanuel,"

which means "God is with us." [24]When Joseph awoke, he did as the angel of the Lord had commanded him and took his wife into his home. [25] [l]*He had no relations with her until she bore a son, and he named him Jesus.

1, 10: **Amos:** some textual witnesses read **Amon,** who was the actual successor of Manasseh (see 1 Chr 3, 14).

1, 17: Matthew is concerned with fourteen generations, probably because fourteen is the numerical value of the Hebrew letters forming the name of David. In the second section of the genealogy (6b-11), three kings of Judah, Ahaziah, Joash, and Amaziah, have been omitted (see 1 Chr 3, 11–12), so that there are fourteen generations in that section. Yet the third (12–16) apparently has only thirteen. Since Matthew here emphasizes that each section has fourteen, it is unlikely that the thirteen of the last was due to his oversight. Some scholars suggest that **Jesus who is called the Messiah** (16b) doubles the final member of the chain: **Jesus,** born within the family of David, opens up the new age as **Messiah,** so that in fact there are fourteen generations in the third section. This is perhaps too subtle, and the hypothesis of a slip not on the part of Matthew but of a later scribe seems likely. On **Messiah,** see the note on Lk 2, 11.

1, 18–25: This first story of the infancy narrative spells out what is summarily indicated in v 16. The virginal conception of Jesus is the work of the Spirit of God. Joseph's decision to divorce Mary is overcome by the heavenly command that he take her into his home and accept the child as his own. The natural genealogical line is broken but the promises to David are fulfilled; through Joseph's adoption the child belongs to the family of David. Matthew sees the virginal conception as the fulfillment of Is 7, 14.

1, 18: **Betrothed to Joseph:** betrothal was the first part of the marriage, constituting a man and woman as husband and wife. Subsequent infidelity was considered adultery. The betrothal was followed some months later by the husband's taking his wife into his home, at which time normal married life began.

1, 19: **A righteous man:** as a devout observer of the Mosaic law, Joseph wished to break his union with someone whom he suspected of gross violation of the law. It is commonly said that the law required him to do so, but the texts usually given in support of that view, e.g., Dt 22, 20–21, do not clearly pertain to Joseph's situation. **Unwilling to expose her to shame:** the penalty for proved adultery was death by stoning; cf Dt 22, 21–23.

1, 20: **The angel of the Lord:** in the Old Testament a common designation of God in communication with a human being. **In a dream:** see 2, 13.19.22. These dreams may be meant to recall the dreams of Joseph, son of Jacob the patriarch (Gn 37, 5–11.19). A closer parallel is the dream of Amram, father of Moses, related by Josephus (**Antiquities** 2, 9, 3 §§212, 215–16).

1, 21: **Jesus:** in first-century Judaism the Hebrew name Joshua (Greek Iēsous) meaning "Yahweh helps" was interpreted as "Yahweh saves."

1, 23: **God is with us:** God's promise of deliverance to Judah in Isaiah's time is seen by Matthew as fulfilled in the birth of Jesus, in whom God is with his people. The name Emmanuel is alluded to at the end of the gospel where the risen Jesus assures his disciples of his continued presence, ". . . I am with you always, until the end of the age" (28, 20).

1, 25: **Until she bore a son:** the evangelist is concerned to emphasize that Joseph was not responsible for the conception of Jesus. The Greek word translated "until" does not imply normal marital conduct after Jesus' birth, nor does it exclude it.

i 1 Chr 3, 16–19. j 2, 13.19; Lk 1, 35. k Is 7, 14 LXX. l Lk 2, 7.

CHAPTER 2

The Visit of the Magi [1]*When Jesus was born
in Bethlehem of Judea, in the days of King
Herod, behold, magi from the east arrived in
Jerusalem, [2] [m]*saying, "Where is the newborn
king of the Jews? We saw his star at its rising and
have come to do him homage." [3]When King
Herod heard this, he was greatly troubled, and
all Jerusalem with him. [4]*Assembling all the
chief priests and the scribes of the people, he
inquired of them where the Messiah was to be
born. [5] [n]They said to him, "In Bethlehem of
Judea, for thus it has been written through the
prophet:

[6]'And you, Bethlehem, land of Judah,
are by no means least among the rulers of
Judah;
since from you shall come a ruler,
who is to shepherd my people Israel.' "

[7]Then Herod called the magi secretly and ascer-
tained from them the time of the star's appear-
ance. [8]He sent them to Bethlehem and said, "Go
and search diligently for the child. When you
have found him, bring me word, that I too may
go and do him homage." [9]After their audience
with the king they set out. And behold, the star
that they had seen at its rising preceded them,
until it came and stopped over the place where
the child was. [10]They were overjoyed at seeing
the star, [11] [o]*and on entering the house they saw
the child with Mary his mother. They prostrated
themselves and did him homage. Then they
opened their treasures and offered him gifts of
gold, frankincense, and myrrh. [12]And having
been warned in a dream not to return to Herod,
they departed for their country by another way.

The Flight to Egypt [13]*When they had de-
parted, behold, the angel of the Lord appeared to
Joseph in a dream and said, "Rise, take the child
and his mother, flee to Egypt, and stay there
until I tell you. Herod is going to search for the
child to destroy him." [14]Joseph rose and took the
child and his mother by night and departed for
Egypt. [15] [p]*He stayed there until the death of
Herod, that what the Lord had said through the
prophet might be fulfilled, "Out of Egypt I called
my son."

The Massacre of the Infants [16]When Herod
realized that he had been deceived by the magi,
he became furious. He ordered the massacre of
all the boys in Bethlehem and its vicinity two
years old and under, in accordance with the time
he had ascertained from the magi. [17]Then was
fulfilled what had been said through Jeremiah
the prophet:

[18] [q]*"A voice was heard in Ramah,
sobbing and loud lamentation;
Rachel weeping for her children,
and she would not be consoled,
since they were no more."

2, 1–12: The future rejection of Jesus by Israel and his acceptance by the Gentiles are retrojected into this scene of the narrative.

2, 1: In the days of King Herod: Herod reigned from 37 to 4 B.C. **Magi:** originally a designation of the Persian priestly caste, the word became used of those who were regarded as having more than human knowledge. Matthew's magi are astrologers.

2, 2: We saw his star: it was a common ancient belief that a new star appeared at the time of a ruler's birth. Matthew also draws upon the Old Testament story of Balaam, who had prophesied that "A star shall advance from Jacob" (Nm 24, 17), though there the star means not an astral phenomenon but the king himself.

2, 4: Herod's consultation with the chief priests and scribes has some similarity to a Jewish legend about the child Moses in which the "sacred scribes" warn Pharaoh about the imminent birth of one who will deliver Israel from Egypt and the king makes plans to destroy him.

2, 11: Cf Ps 72, 10.15; Is 60, 6. These Old Testament texts led to the interpretation of the magi as kings.

2, 13–23: Biblical and nonbiblical traditions about Moses are here applied to the child Jesus, though the dominant Old Testament type is not Moses but Israel (see v 15).

2, 13: Flee to Egypt: Egypt was a traditional place of refuge for those fleeing from danger in Palestine (see 1 Kgs 11, 40; Jer 26, 21), but the main reason why the child is to be taken to Egypt is that he may relive the Exodus experience of Israel.

2, 15: The fulfillment citation is taken from Hos 11, 1. Israel, God's son, was called out of Egypt at the time of the Exodus; Jesus, the Son of God, will similarly be called out of that land in a new exodus. The father-son relationship between God and the nation is set in a higher key. Here the son is not a group adopted as "son of God," but the child who, as conceived by the holy Spirit, stands in unique relation to God. He is son of David and of Abraham, of Mary and of Joseph, but, above all, of God.

2, 18: Jer 31, 15 portrays Rachel, wife of the patriarch Jacob, weeping for her children taken into exile at the time of the Assyrian invasion of the northern kingdom (722–21 B.C.). Bethlehem was traditionally identified with Ephrath, the place near which Rachel was buried (see Gn 35, 19; 48, 7), and the mourning of Rachel is here applied to her lost children of a later age. **Ramah:** about six miles north of Jerusalem. The lamentation of Rachel is so great as to be heard at a far distance.

m Nm 24, 17. n Mi 5, 1 / 2 Sm 5, 2. o Ps 72, 10–11.15; Is 60, 6. p Hos 11, 1. q Jer 31, 15.

The Return from Egypt [19]When Herod had
died, behold, the angel of the Lord appeared in a
dream to Joseph in Egypt [20 r*]and said, "Rise,
take the child and his mother and go to the land
of Israel, for those who sought the child's life are
dead." [21]He rose, took the child and his mother,
and went to the land of Israel. [22*]But when he
heard that Archelaus was ruling over Judea in
place of his father Herod, he was afraid to go
back there. And because he had been warned in
a dream, he departed for the region of Galilee.
[23 s*]He went and dwelt in a town called Naza-
reth, so that what had been spoken through the
prophets might be fulfilled, "He shall be called a
Nazorean."

II: The Proclamation of the Kingdom

CHAPTER 3

The Preaching of John the Baptist [1 t*]In
those days John the Baptist appeared, preaching
in the desert of Judea [2 u*][and] saying, "Repent,
for the kingdom of heaven is at hand!" [3 v*]It was
of him that the prophet Isaiah had spoken when
he said:

"A voice of one crying out in the desert,
'Prepare the way of the Lord,
make straight his paths.' "

[4 w*]John wore clothing made of camel's hair and
had a leather belt around his waist. His food was
locusts and wild honey. [5]At that time Jerusalem,
all Judea, and the whole region around the
Jordan were going out to him [6*]and were being
baptized by him in the Jordan River as they
acknowledged their sins.

[7 x*]When he saw many of the Pharisees and
Sadducees coming to his baptism, he said to
them, "You brood of vipers! Who warned you to
flee from the coming wrath? [8]Produce good fruit
as evidence of your repentance. [9 y]And do not
presume to say to yourselves, 'We have Abraham
as our father.' For I tell you, God can raise up

2, 20: For those who sought the child's life are dead: Moses, who had fled from Egypt because the Pharaoh sought to kill him (see Ex 2, 15), was told to return there, "for all the men who sought your life are dead" (Ex 4, 19).

2, 22: With the agreement of the emperor Augustus, Archelaus received half of his father's kingdom, including Judea, after Herod's death. He had the title "ethnarch" (i.e., "ruler of a nation") and reigned from 4 B.C. to A.D. 6.

2, 23: Nazareth . . . he shall be called a Nazorean: the tradition of Jesus' residence in Nazareth was firmly established, and Matthew sees it as being in accordance with the foreannounced plan of God. The town of Nazareth is not mentioned in the Old Testament, and no such prophecy can be found there. The vague expression "through the prophets" may be due to Matthew's seeing a connection between Nazareth and certain texts in which there are words with a remote similarity to the name of that town. Some such Old Testament texts are Is 11, 1 where the Davidic king of the future is called "a bud" **(nēser)** that shall blossom from the roots of Jesse, and Jgs 13, 5.7 where Samson, the future deliverer of Israel from the Philistines, is called one who shall be consecrated (a **nāzîr**) to God.

3, 1–12: Here Matthew takes up the order of Jesus' ministry found in the gospel of Mark, beginning with the preparatory preaching of John the Baptist.

3, 1: Unlike Luke, Matthew says nothing of the Baptist's origins and does not make him a relative of Jesus. **The desert of Judea:** the barren region west of the Dead Sea extending up the Jordan valley.

3, 2: Repent: the Baptist calls for a change of heart and conduct, a turning of one's life from rebellion to obedience towards God. **The kingdom of heaven is at hand:** "heaven" (literally, "the heavens") is a substitute for the name "God" that was avoided by devout Jews of the time out of reverence. The expression "the kingdom of heaven" occurs only in the gospel of Matthew. It means the effective rule of God over his people. In its fullness it includes not only human obedience to God's word, but the triumph of God over physical evils, supremely over death. In the expectation found in Jewish apocalyptic, the kingdom was to be ushered in by a judgment in which sinners would be condemned and perish, an expectation shared by the Baptist. This was modified in Christian understanding where the kingdom was seen as being established in stages, culminating with the parousia of Jesus.

3, 3: See the note on Jn 1, 23.

3, 4: The clothing of John recalls the austere dress of the prophet Elijah (2 Kgs 1, 8). The expectation of the return of Elijah from heaven to prepare Israel for the final manifestation of God's kingdom was widespread, and according to Matthew this expectation was fulfilled in the Baptist's ministry (11, 14; 17, 11–13).

3, 6: Ritual washing was practiced by various groups in Palestine between 150 B.C. and A.D. 250. John's baptism may have been related to the purificatory washings of the Essenes at Qumran.

3, 7: Pharisees and Sadducees: the former were marked by devotion to the law, written and oral, and the scribes, experts in the law, belonged predominantly to this group. The Sadducees were the priestly aristocratic party, centered in Jerusalem. They accepted as scripture only the first five books of the Old Testament, followed only the letter of the law, rejected the oral legal traditions, and were opposed to teachings not found in the Pentateuch, such as the resurrection of the dead. Matthew links both of these groups together as enemies of Jesus (16, 1.6.11.12; cf Mk 8, 11–13.15). The threatening words that follow are addressed to them rather than to "the crowds" as in Lk 3, 7. **The coming wrath:** the judgment that will bring about the destruction of unrepentant sinners.

r Ex 4, 19. s 13, 54; Mk 1, 9; Lk 2, 39; 4, 34; Jn 19, 19.
t Mk 1, 2–8; Lk 3, 2–17. u 4, 17; 10, 7. v Is 40, 3. w 11,7–8; 2 Kgs 1, 8; Zec 13, 4. x 12, 34; 23, 33; Is 59, 5. y Jn 8, 33.39; Rom 9, 7–8; Gal 4, 21–31.

children to Abraham from these stones. 10 Even
now the ax lies at the root of the trees. Therefore
every tree that does not bear good fruit will be
cut down and thrown into the fire. 11 z*I am
baptizing you with water, for repentance, but
the one who is coming after me is mightier than
I. I am not worthy to carry his sandals. He will
baptize you with the holy Spirit and fire. 12 a*His
winnowing fan is in his hand. He will clear his
threshing floor and gather his wheat into his
barn, but the chaff he will burn with unquench-
able fire."
The Baptism of Jesus 13 b*Then Jesus came
from Galilee to John at the Jordan to be baptized
by him. 14*John tried to prevent him, saying, "I
need to be baptized by you, and yet you are
coming to me?" 15 Jesus said to him in reply,
"Allow it now, for thus it is fitting for us to fulfill
all righteousness." Then he allowed him.
16 c*After Jesus was baptized, he came up from
the water and behold, the heavens were opened
[for him], and he saw the Spirit of God descend-
ing like a dove [and] coming upon him. 17 d*And
a voice came from the heavens, saying, "This is
my beloved Son, with whom I am well pleased."

CHAPTER 4

The Temptation of Jesus 1 e*Then Jesus was
led by the Spirit into the desert to be tempted by
the devil. 2 f*He fasted for forty days and forty
nights, and afterwards he was hungry. 3 The
tempter approached and said to him, "If you are
the Son of God, command that these stones
become loaves of bread." 4 g*He said in reply, "It
is written:

'One does not live by bread alone,
but by every word that comes forth
from the mouth of God.' "

5*Then the devil took him to the holy city, and
made him stand on the parapet of the temple,
6 h and said to him, "If you are the Son of God,
throw yourself down. For it is written:

'He will command his angels concerning you'
and 'with their hands they will support you,
lest you dash your foot against a stone.' "

7 i Jesus answered him, "Again it is written, 'You
shall not put the Lord, your God, to the test.' "
8 Then the devil took him up to a very high
mountain, and showed him all the kingdoms of
the world in their magnificence, 9*and he said to

3, 11: Baptize you with the holy Spirit and fire: the water baptism of John will be followed by an "immersion" of the repentant in the cleansing power of the Spirit of God, and of the unrepentant in the destroying power of God's judgment. However, some see **the holy Spirit** and **fire** as synonymous, and the effect of this "baptism" as either purification or destruction. See the note on Lk 3, 16.

3, 12: The discrimination between the good and the bad is compared to the procedure by which a farmer separates wheat and chaff. The **winnowing fan** was a forklike shovel with which the threshed wheat was thrown into the air. The kernels fell to the ground; the light chaff, blown off by the wind, was gathered and burned up.

3, 13–17: The baptism of Jesus is the occasion on which he is equipped for his ministry by the holy Spirit and proclaimed to be the Son of God.

3, 14–15: This dialogue, peculiar to Matthew, reveals John's awareness of Jesus' superiority to him as the mightier one who is coming and who will baptize with the holy Spirit (11). His reluctance to admit Jesus among the sinners whom he is baptizing with water is overcome by Jesus' response. **To fulfill all righteousness:** in this gospel to **fulfill** usually refers to fulfillment of prophecy, and **righteousness** to moral conduct in conformity with God's will. Here, however, as in 5, 6 and 6, 33, **righteousness** seems to mean the saving activity of God. **To fulfill all righteousness** is to submit to the plan of God for the salvation of the human race. This involves Jesus' identification with sinners; hence the propriety of his accepting John's baptism.

3, 16: The Spirit . . . coming upon him: cf Is 42, 1.

3, 17: This is my beloved Son: the Marcan address to Jesus (Mk 1, 11) is changed into a proclamation. The Father's voice speaks in terms that reflect Is 42, 1, Ps 2, 7, and Gn 22, 2.

4, 1–11: Jesus, proclaimed Son of God at his baptism, is subjected to a triple temptation. Obedience to the Father is a characteristic of true sonship, and Jesus is tempted by the devil to rebel against God, overtly in the third case, more subtly in the first two. Each refusal of Jesus is expressed in language taken from the Book of Deuteronomy (Dt 8, 3; 6, 13.16). The testings of Jesus resemble those of Israel during the wandering in the desert and later in Canaan, and the victory of Jesus, the true Israel and the true Son, contrasts with the failure of the ancient and disobedient "son," the old Israel. In the temptation account Matthew is almost identical with Luke; both seem to have drawn upon the same source.

4, 2: Forty days and forty nights: the same time as that during which Moses remained on Sinai (Ex 24, 18). The time reference, however, seems primarily intended to recall the forty years during which Israel was tempted in the desert (Dt 8, 2).

4, 4: Cf Dt 8, 3. Jesus refuses to use his power for his own benefit and accepts whatever God wills.

4, 5–7: The devil supports his proposal by an appeal to the scriptures, Ps 91, 11a.12. Unlike Israel (Dt 6, 16), Jesus refuses to "test" God by demanding from him an extraordinary show of power.

4, 9: The worship of Satan to which Jesus is tempted is probably intended to recall Israel's worship of false gods. His refusal is expressed in the words of Dt 6, 13.

z Jn 1, 26–27.33; Acts 1, 5. a 13, 30; Is 41, 16; Jer 15, 7. b Mk 1, 9–11; Lk 3, 21–22; Jn 1, 31–34. c Is 42, 1. d 12, 18; 17, 5; Gn 22, 2; Ps 2, 7; Is 42, 1. e Mk 1, 12–13; Lk 4, 1–13. f Ex 24, 18; Dt 8, 2. g Dt 8, 3. h Ps 91, 11–12. i Dt 6, 16.

him, "All these I shall give to you, if you will
prostrate yourself and worship me." 10 jAt this,
Jesus said to him, "Get away, Satan! It is written:

'The Lord, your God, shall you worship
and him alone shall you serve.' "

11 Then the devil left him and, behold, angels
came and ministered to him.

The Beginning of the Galilean Ministry
12 k*When he heard that John had been arrested,
he withdrew to Galilee. 13 lHe left Nazareth and
went to live in Capernaum by the sea, in the
region of Zebulun and Naphtali, 14 that what had
been said through Isaiah the prophet might be
fulfilled:

15 m"Land of Zebulun and land of Naphtali,
the way to the sea, beyond the Jordan,
Galilee of the Gentiles,
16 nthe people who sit in darkness
have seen a great light,
on those dwelling in a land overshadowed by
death
light has arisen."

17 o*From that time on, Jesus began to preach
and say, "Repent, for the kingdom of heaven is at
hand."

The Call of the First Disciples 18 p*As he was
walking by the Sea of Galilee, he saw two
brothers, Simon who is called Peter, and his
brother Andrew, casting a net into the sea; they
were fishermen. 19 He said to them, "Come after
me, and I will make you fishers of men." 20 *At
once they left their nets and followed him. 21 He
walked along from there and saw two other
brothers, James, the son of Zebedee, and his
brother John. They were in a boat, with their
father Zebedee, mending their nets. He called
them, 22 and immediately they left their boat and
their father and followed him.

Ministering to a Great Multitude 23 q*He
went around all of Galilee, teaching in their
synagogues, proclaiming the gospel of the king-
dom, and curing every disease and illness among
the people. 24 *His fame spread to all of Syria,
and they brought to him all who were sick with
various diseases and racked with pain, those
who were possessed, lunatics, and paralytics,
and he cured them. 25 r*And great crowds from
Galilee, the Decapolis, Jerusalem, and Judea, and
from beyond the Jordan followed him.

CHAPTER 5

The Sermon on the Mount 1 *When he saw
the crowds, he went up the mountain, and after
he had sat down, his disciples came to him. 2 He
began to teach them, saying:

4, 12–17: Isaiah's prophecy of the light rising upon Zebulun and Naphtali (Is 8, 23—9, 1) is fulfilled in Jesus' residence at Capernaum. The territory of these two tribes was the first to be devastated (733–32 B.C.) at the time of the Assyrian invasion. In order to accommodate Jesus' move to Capernaum to the prophecy, Matthew speaks of that town as being "in the region of Zebulun and Naphtali" (13), whereas it was only in the territory of the latter, and he understands the sea of the prophecy, the Mediterranean, as the sea of Galilee.

4, 17: At the beginning of his preaching Jesus takes up the words of John the Baptist (3, 2) although with a different meaning; in his ministry the kingdom of heaven has already begun to be present (12, 28).

4, 18–22: The call of the first disciples promises them a share in Jesus' work and entails abandonment of family and former way of life. Three of the four, Simon, James, and John, are distinguished among the disciples by a closer relation with Jesus (17, 1; 26, 37).

4, 20: Here and in v 22, as in Mark (1, 16–20) and unlike the Lucan account (5, 1–11), the disciples' response is motivated only by Jesus' invitation, an element that emphasizes his mysterious power.

4, 23–25: This summary of Jesus' ministry concludes the narrative part of the first book of Matthew's gospel (chs 3–4). The activities of his ministry are teaching, proclaiming the gospel, and healing; cf 9, 35.

4, 23: Their synagogues: Matthew usually designates the Jewish synagogues as **their synagogue(s)** (9, 35; 10, 17; 12, 9; 13, 54) or, in address to Jews, **your synagogues** (23, 34), an indication that he wrote after the break between church and synagogue.

4, 24: Syria: the Roman province to which Palestine belonged.

4, 25: The Decapolis: a federation of Greek cities in Palestine, originally ten in number, all but one east of the Jordan.

5, 1—7, 29: The first of the five discourses that are a central part of the structure of this gospel. It is the discourse section of the first book and contains sayings of Jesus derived from Q and from M. The Lucan parallel is in that gospel's "Sermon on the Plain" (Lk 6, 20–49), although some of the sayings in Matthew's "Sermon on the Mount" have their parallels in other parts of Luke. The careful topical arrangement of the sermon is probably not due only to Matthew's editing; he seems to have had a structured discourse of Jesus as one of his sources. The form of that source may have been as follows: four beatitudes (5, 3–4.6.11–12), a section on the new righteousness with illustrations (5, 17.20–24.27–28.33–48), a section on good works (6, 1–6.16–18), and three warnings (7, 1–2.15–21.24–27).

5, 1–2: Unlike Luke's sermon, this is addressed not only to the disciples but to the crowds (see 7, 28).

j 16, 23; Dt 6, 13. k Mk 1, 14–15; Lk 4, 14.31. l Jn 2, 12. m Is 8, 23 LXX; 9, 1. n Lk 1, 79. o 3, 2. p Mk 1, 16–20; Lk 5, 1–11. q 9, 35; Mk 1, 39; Lk 4, 15.44. r Mk 3, 7–8; Lk 6, 17–19.

The Beatitudes

3 s*“Blessed are the poor in spirit,
for theirs is the kingdom of heaven.
4 t*Blessed are they who mourn,
for they will be comforted.
5 u*Blessed are the meek,
for they will inherit the land.
6 *Blessed are they who hunger and thirst for
righteousness,
for they will be satisfied.
7 vBlessed are the merciful,
for they will be shown mercy.
8 w*Blessed are the clean of heart,
for they will see God.
9 Blessed are the peacemakers,
for they will be called children of God.
10 x*Blessed are they who are persecuted for the
sake of righteousness,
for theirs is the kingdom of heaven.
11 yBlessed are you when they insult you and
persecute you and utter every kind of evil against
you [falsely] because of me. 12 z*Rejoice and be
glad, for your reward will be great in heaven.
Thus they persecuted the prophets who were
before you.

The Similes of Salt and Light 13 a*“You are
the salt of the earth. But if salt loses its taste,
with what can it be seasoned? It is no longer
good for anything but to be thrown out and
trampled underfoot. 14 bYou are the light of the
world. A city set on a mountain cannot be
hidden. 15 cNor do they light a lamp and then put
it under a bushel basket; it is set on a lampstand,
where it gives light to all in the house. 16 dJust so,
your light must shine before others, that they
may see your good deeds and glorify your
heavenly Father.

Teaching about the Law 17*“Do not think
that I have come to abolish the law or the
prophets. I have come not to abolish but to
fulfill. 18 eAmen, I say to you, until heaven and
earth pass away, not the smallest letter or the
smallest part of a letter will pass from the law,

5, 3–12: The form **Blessed are (is)** occurs frequently in the Old Testament in the Wisdom literature and in the psalms. Although modified by Matthew, the first, second, fourth, and ninth beatitudes have Lucan parallels (5, 3 // Lk 6, 20; 5, 4 // Lk 6, 21b; 5, 6 // Lk 6, 21a; 5, 11–12 // Lk 5, 22–23). The others were added by the evangelist and are probably his own composition. A few manuscripts, Western and Alexandrian, and many versions and patristic quotations give the second and third beatitudes in inverted order.

5, 3: The poor in spirit: in the Old Testament, the **poor** (**ănāwîm**) are those who are without material possessions and whose confidence is in God (see Is 61, 1; Zep 2, 3; in the NAB the word is translated **lowly** and **humble,** respectively, in those texts). Matthew added **in spirit** in order either to indicate that only the devout poor were meant or to extend the beatitude to all, of whatever social rank, who recognized their complete dependence on God. The same phrase **poor in spirit** is found in the Qumran literature (1QM 14, 7).

5, 4: Cf Is 61, 2, “(The Lord has sent me) . . . to comfort all who mourn.” **They will be comforted:** here the passive is a “theological passive” equivalent to the active “God will comfort them”; so also in vv 6 and 7.

5, 5: Cf Ps 37, 11, “. . . the meek shall possess the land.” In the psalm “the land” means the land of Palestine; here it means the kingdom.

5, 6: For righteousness: a Matthean addition. For the meaning of **righteousness** here, see the note on 3, 14–15.

5, 8: Cf Ps 24, 4. Only one “whose heart is clean” can take part in the temple worship. To be with God in the temple is described in Ps 42, 3 as “beholding his face,” but here the promise to **the clean of heart** is that they will **see God** not in the temple but in the coming kingdom.

5, 10: Righteousness here, as usually in Matthew, means conduct in conformity with God’s will.

5, 12: The prophets who were before you: the disciples of Jesus stand in the line of the persecuted prophets of Israel. Some would see the expression as indicating also that Matthew considered all Christian disciples as prophets.

5, 13–16: By their deeds the disciples are to influence the world for good. They can no more escape notice than **a city set on a mountain.** If they fail in good works, they are as useless as flavorless salt or as a lamp whose light is concealed.

5, 13: The unusual supposition of salt losing its flavor has led some to suppose that the saying refers to the salt of the Dead Sea that, because chemically impure, could lose its taste.

5, 17–20: This statement of Jesus’ position concerning the Mosaic law is composed of traditional material from Matthew’s sermon documentation (see the note on 5, 1—7, 29), other Q material (cf 18 and Lk 16, 17), and the evangelist’s own editorial touches. **To fulfill** the law appears at first to mean a literal enforcement of the law in the least detail: **until heaven and earth pass away** nothing of the law **will pass** (18). Yet the “passing away” of heaven and earth is not necessarily the end of the world understood, as in much apocalyptic literature, as the dissolution of the existing universe. The “turning of the ages” comes with the apocalyptic event of Jesus’ death and resurrection, and those to whom this gospel is addressed are living in the new and final age, prophesied by Isaiah as the time of “new heavens and a new earth” (Is 65, 17; 66, 22). Meanwhile, during Jesus’ ministry when the kingdom is already breaking in, his mission remains within the framework of the law, though with significant anticipation of the age to come, as the following antitheses (vv 21–48) show.

s Lk 6, 20–23. t Is 61, 2–3; Rv 21, 4. u Gn 13, 15; Ps 37, 11. v 18, 33; Jas 2, 13. w Pss 24, 4–5; 73, 1. x 1 Pt 2, 20; 3, 14; 4, 14. y 10, 22; Acts 5, 41. z 2 Chr 36, 16; Heb 11, 32–38; Jas 5, 10. a Mk 9, 50; Lk 14, 34–35. b Jn 8, 12. c Mk 4, 21; Lk 8, 16; 11, 33. d Jn 3, 21. e Lk 16, 17.

until all things have taken place. [19]*Therefore, whoever breaks one of the least of these commandments and teaches others to do so will be called least in the kingdom of heaven. But whoever obeys and teaches these commandments will be called greatest in the kingdom of heaven. [20]I tell you, unless your righteousness surpasses that of the scribes and Pharisees, you will not enter into the kingdom of heaven.

Teaching about Anger [21 f]*"You have heard that it was said to your ancestors, 'You shall not kill; and whoever kills will be liable to judgment.' [22 g]*But I say to you, whoever is angry with his brother will be liable to judgment, and whoever says to his brother, 'Raqa,' will be answerable to the Sanhedrin, and whoever says, 'You fool,' will be liable to fiery Gehenna. [23 h]Therefore, if you bring your gift to the altar, and there recall that your brother has anything against you, [24]leave your gift there at the altar, go first and be reconciled with your brother, and then come and offer your gift. [25 i]Settle with your opponent quickly while on the way to court with him. Otherwise your opponent will hand you over to the judge, and the judge will hand you over to the guard, and you will be thrown into prison. [26]Amen, I say to you, you will not be released until you have paid the last penny.

Teaching about Adultery [27 j]*"You have heard that it was said, 'You shall not commit adultery.' [28]But I say to you, everyone who looks at a woman with lust has already committed adultery with her in his heart. [29 k]*If your right eye causes you to sin, tear it out and throw it away. It is better for you to lose one of your members than to have your whole body thrown into Gehenna. [30]And if your right hand causes you to sin, cut it off and throw it away. It is better for you to lose one of your members than to have your whole body go into Gehenna.

Teaching about Divorce [31 l]*"It was also said, 'Whoever divorces his wife must give her a bill of divorce.' [32 m]But I say to you, whoever divorces his wife (unless the marriage is unlawful) causes her to commit adultery, and whoever marries a divorced woman commits adultery.

Teaching about Oaths [33 n]*"Again you have heard that it was said to your ancestors, 'Do not

5, 19: Probably **these commandments** means those of the Mosaic law. But this is an interim ethic "until heaven and earth pass away."

5, 21–48: Six examples of the conduct demanded of the Christian disciple. Each deals with a commandment of the law, introduced by **You have heard that it was said to your ancestors** or an equivalent formula, followed by Jesus' teaching in respect to that commandment, **But I say to you;** thus their designation as "antitheses." Three of them accept the Mosaic law but extend or deepen it (21–22; 27–28; 43–44); three reject it as a standard of conduct for the disciples (31–32; 33–37; 38–39).

5, 21: Cf Ex 20, 13; Dt 5, 17. The second part of the verse is not an exact quotation from the Old Testament, but cf Ex 21, 12.

5, 22: Anger is the motive behind murder, as the insulting epithets are steps that may lead to it. They, as well as the deed, are all forbidden. **Raqa:** an Aramaic word **rēqā'** or **rēqâ** probably meaning "imbecile," "blockhead," a term of abuse. The ascending order of punishment, **judgment** (by a local council?), trial before **the Sanhedrin,** condemnation to **Gehenna,** points to a higher degree of seriousness in each of the offenses. **Sanhedrin:** the highest judicial body of Judaism. **Gehenna:** in Hebrew **gê-hinnōm,** "Valley of Hinnom," or **gê ben-hinnōm,** "Valley of the son of Hinnom," southwest of Jerusalem, the center of an idolatrous cult during the monarchy in which children were offered in sacrifice (see 2 Kgs 23, 10; Jer 7, 31). In Jos 18, 16 (Septuagint, Codex Vaticanus) the Hebrew is transliterated into Greek as **gaienna,** which appears in the New Testament as **geenna.** The concept of punishment of sinners by fire either after death or after the final judgment is found in Jewish apocalyptic literature (e.g., Enoch 90, 26) but the name **geenna** is first given to the place of punishment in the New Testament.

5, 22–26: Reconciliation with an offended brother is urged in the admonition of vv 23–24 and the parable of vv 25–26 (// Lk 12, 58–59). The severity of the judge in the parable is a warning of the fate of unrepentant sinners in the coming judgment by God.

5, 27: See Ex 20, 14; Dt 5, 18.

5, 29–30: No sacrifice is too great to avoid total destruction in **Gehenna.**

5, 31–32: See Dt 24, 1–5. The Old Testament commandment that a bill of divorce be given to the woman assumes the legitimacy of divorce itself. It is this that Jesus denies. (**Unless the marriage is unlawful**): this "exceptive clause," as it is often called, occurs also in 19, 9, where the Greek is slightly different. There are other sayings of Jesus about divorce that prohibit it absolutely (see Mk 10, 11–12; Lk 16, 18; cf 1 Cor 7, 10.11b), and most scholars agree that they represent the stand of Jesus. Matthew's "exceptive clauses" are understood by some as a modification of the absolute prohibition. It seems, however, that the unlawfulness that Matthew gives as a reason why a marriage must be broken refers to a situation peculiar to his community: the violation of Mosaic law forbidding marriage between persons of certain blood and/or legal relationship (Lv 18, 6–18). Marriages of that sort were regarded as incest (**porneia**), but some rabbis allowed Gentile converts to Judaism who had contracted such marriages to remain in them. Matthew's "exceptive clause" is against such permissiveness for Gentile converts to Christianity; cf the similar prohibition of **porneia** in Acts 15, 20.29. In this interpretation, the clause constitutes no exception to the absolute prohibition of divorce when the marriage is lawful.

5, 33: This is not an exact quotation of any Old Testament text, but see Ex 20, 7, Dt 5, 11, and Lv 19, 12. The purpose of an oath was to guarantee truthfulness by one's calling on God as witness.

f Ex 20, 13; Dt 5, 17. g Jas 1, 19–20. h Mk 11, 25. i 18, 34–35; Lk 12, 58–59. j Ex 20, 14; Dt 5, 18. k 18, 8–9; Mk 9, 43–47. l 19, 3–9; Dt 24, 1. m Lk 16, 18; 1 Cor 7, 10–11. n Lv 19, 12; Nm 30, 3.

take a false oath, but make good to the Lord all
that you vow.' [34 o]*But I say to you, do not
swear at all; not by heaven, for it is God's
throne; [35]nor by the earth, for it is his footstool;
nor by Jerusalem, for it is the city of the great
King. [36]Do not swear by your head, for you
cannot make a single hair white or black. [37]*Let
your 'Yes' mean 'Yes,' and your 'No' mean 'No.'
Anything more is from the evil one.
Teaching about Retaliation [38 p]*"You have
heard that it was said, 'An eye for an eye and a
tooth for a tooth.' [39 q]But I say to you, offer no
resistance to one who is evil. When someone
strikes you on [your] right cheek, turn the other
one to him as well. [40]If anyone wants to go to
law with you over your tunic, hand him your
cloak as well. [41 r]*Should anyone press you into
service for one mile, go with him for two miles.
[42 s]Give to the one who asks of you, and do not
turn your back on one who wants to borrow.
Love of Enemies [43 t u]*"You have heard that it
was said, 'You shall love your neighbor and hate
your enemy.' [44]But I say to you, love your
enemies, and pray for those who persecute you,
[45]that you may be children of your heavenly
Father, for he makes his sun rise on the bad and
the good, and causes rain to fall on the just and
the unjust. [46]*For if you love those who love
you, what recompense will you have? Do not
the tax collectors do the same? [47]*And if you
greet your brothers only, what is unusual about
that? Do not the pagans do the same? [48 v]*So be
perfect, just as your heavenly Father is perfect.

CHAPTER 6

Teaching about Almsgiving [1 w]*"[But] take
care not to perform righteous deeds in order that
people may see them; otherwise, you will have
no recompense from your heavenly Father.
[2 x]*When you give alms, do not blow a trumpet
before you, as the hypocrites do in the syna-
gogues and in the streets to win the praise of
others. Amen, I say to you, they have received
their reward. [3]But when you give alms, do not
let your left hand know what your right is doing,
[4]so that your almsgiving may be secret. And
your Father who sees in secret will repay you.
Teaching about Prayer [5]"When you pray, do
not be like the hypocrites, who love to stand and
pray in the synagogues and on street corners so
that others may see them. Amen, I say to you,
they have received their reward. [6]But when you
pray, go to your inner room, close the door, and
pray to your Father in secret. And your Father

5, 34–36: The use of these oath formularies that avoid the divine name is in fact equivalent to swearing by it, for all the things sworn by are related to God.

5, 37: Let your 'Yes' mean 'Yes,' and your 'No' mean 'No': literally, "let your speech be 'Yes, yes,' 'No, no.' " Some have understood this as a milder form of oath, permitted by Jesus. In view of v 34, "Do not swear at all," that is unlikely. **From the evil one:** i.e., from the devil. Oath-taking presupposes a sinful weakness of the human race, namely, the tendency to lie. Jesus demands of his disciples a truthfulness that makes oaths unnecessary.

5, 38–42: See Lv 24, 20. The Old Testament commandment was meant to moderate vengeance; the punishment should not exceed the injury done. Jesus forbids even this proportionate retaliation. Of the five examples that follow, only the first deals directly with retaliation for evil; the others speak of liberality.

5, 41: Roman garrisons in Palestine had the right to requisition the property and services of the native population.

5, 43–48: See Lv 19, 18. There is no Old Testament commandment demanding hatred of one's enemy, but the "neighbor" of the love commandment was understood as one's fellow countryman. Both in the Old Testament (Ps 139, 19–22) and at Qumran (1QS 9, 21) hatred of evil persons is assumed to be right. Jesus extends the love commandment to the enemy and the persecutor. His disciples, as children of God, must imitate the example of their Father, who grants his gifts of sun and rain to both the good and the bad.

5, 46: Tax collectors: Jews who were engaged in the collection of indirect taxes such as tolls and customs. See the note on Mk 2, 14.

5, 47: Jesus' disciples must not be content with merely usual standards of conduct; see v 20 where the verb "surpass" (Greek **perisseuō**) is cognate with the **unusual** (**perisson**) of this verse.

5, 48: Perfect: in the gospels this word occurs only in Matthew, here and in 19, 21. The Lucan parallel (6, 36) demands that the disciples be **merciful**.

6, 1–18: The sermon continues with a warning against doing good in order to be seen and gives three examples, almsgiving (2–4), prayer (5, 15), and fasting (16–18). In each, the conduct of **the hypocrites** (2) is contrasted with that demanded of the disciples. The sayings about **reward** found here and elsewhere (5, 12.46; 10, 41–42) show that this is a genuine element of Christian moral exhortation. Possibly to underline the difference between the Christian idea of **reward** and that of **the hypocrites,** the evangelist uses two different Greek verbs to express the rewarding of the disciples and that of **the hypocrites;** in the latter case it is the verb **apechō**, a commercial term for giving a receipt for what has been paid in full (2.5.16).

6, 2: The hypocrites: the scribes and Pharisees, see 23, 13.15. 23.25.27.29. The designation reflects an attitude resulting not only from the controversies at the time of Jesus' ministry but from the opposition between Pharisaic Judaism and the church of Matthew. **They have received their reward:** they desire praise and have received what they were looking for.

o Ps 48, 3; Sir 23, 9; Is 66, 1; Jas 5, 12. p Ex 21, 24; Lv 24, 19–20. q Lk 6, 29–30. r Lam 3, 30. s Dt 15, 7–8. t Lk 6, 27.32–36. u Lv 19, 18. v Lv 11, 44; 19, 2; Dt 18, 13; Jas 1, 4; 1 Pt 1, 16; 1 Jn 3, 3. w 23, 5. x Jn 12, 43.

who sees in secret will repay you. 7*In praying,
do not babble like the pagans, who think that
they will be heard because of their many words.
8Do not be like them. Your Father knows what
you need before you ask him.

The Lord's Prayer 9 y*“This is how you are to
pray:

Our Father in heaven,
hallowed be your name,
10 z*your kingdom come,
your will be done,
on earth as in heaven.
11 a*Give us today our daily bread;
12 b*and forgive us our debts,
as we forgive our debtors;
13 c*and do not subject us to the final test,
but deliver us from the evil one.

14 d*If you forgive others their transgressions,
your heavenly Father will forgive you. 15 eBut if
you do not forgive others, neither will your
Father forgive your transgressions.

Teaching about Fasting 16*“When you fast,
do not look gloomy like the hypocrites. They
neglect their appearance, so that they may
appear to others to be fasting. Amen, I say to
you, they have received their reward. 17But
when you fast, anoint your head and wash your
face, 18so that you may not appear to be fasting,
except to your Father who is hidden. And your
Father who sees what is hidden will repay you.

Treasure in Heaven 19f*“Do not store up for
yourselves treasures on earth, where moth and
decay destroy, and thieves break in and steal.
20 gBut store up treasures in heaven, where
neither moth nor decay destroy, nor thieves
break in and steal. 21For where your treasure is,
there also will your heart be.

The Light of the Body 22 h*“The lamp of the
body is the eye. If your eye is sound, your whole
body will be filled with light; 23but if your eye is
bad, your whole body will be in darkness. And if
the light in you is darkness, how great will the
darkness be.

God and Money 24 i*“No one can serve two
masters. He will either hate one and love the
other, or be devoted to one and despise the
other. You cannot serve God and mammon.

6, 7–15: Matthew inserts into his basic traditional material an expansion of the material on prayer that includes the model prayer, the “Our Father.” That prayer is found in Lk 11, 2–4 in a different context and in a different form.

6, 7: The example of what Christian prayer should be like contrasts it now not with the prayer of the hypocrites but with that of **the pagans.** Their babbling probably means their reciting a long list of divine names, hoping that one of them will force a response from the deity.

6, 9–13: Matthew's form of the “Our Father” follows the liturgical tradition of his church. Luke's less developed form also represents the liturgical tradition known to him, but it is probably closer than Matthew's to the original words of Jesus.

6, 9: **Our Father in heaven:** this invocation is found in many rabbinic prayers of the post-New Testament period. **Hallowed be your name:** though the “hallowing” of the divine name could be understood as reverence done to God by human praise and by obedience to his will, this is more probably a petition that God hallow his own name, i.e., that he manifest his glory by an act of power (cf Ez 36, 23), in this case, by the establishment of his kingdom in its fullness.

6, 10: **Your kingdom come:** this petition sets the tone of the prayer, and inclines the balance toward divine rather than human action in the petitions that immediately precede and follow it. **Your will be done, on earth as in heaven:** a petition that the divine purpose to establish the kingdom, a purpose present now **in heaven,** be executed **on earth.**

6, 11: **Give us today our daily bread:** the rare Greek word **epiousios, here daily,** occurs in the New Testament only here and in Lk 11, 3. A single occurrence of the word outside of these texts and of literature dependent on them has been claimed, but the claim is highly doubtful. The word may mean **daily** or “future” (other meanings have also been proposed). The latter would conform better to the eschatological tone of the whole prayer. So understood, the petition would be for a speedy coming of the kingdom (**today**), which is often portrayed in both the Old Testament and the New under the image of a feast (Is 25, 6; Mt 8, 11; 22, 1–10; Lk 13, 29; 14, 15–24).

6, 12: **Forgive us our debts:** the word **debts** is used metaphorically of sins, “debts” owed to God (see Lk 11, 4). The request is probably for forgiveness at the final judgment.

6, 13: Jewish apocalyptic writings speak of a period of severe trial before the end of the age, sometimes called the “messianic woes.” This petition asks that the disciples be spared that **final test.**

6, 14–15: These verses reflect a set pattern called “Principles of Holy Law.” Human action now will be met by a corresponding action of God at the final judgment.

6, 16: The only fast prescribed in the Mosaic law was that of the Day of Atonement (Lv 16, 31), but the practice of regular fasting was common in later Judaism; cf **Didache** 9, 1.

6, 19–34: The remaining material of this chapter is taken almost entirely from Q. It deals principally with worldly possessions, and the controlling thought is summed up in v 24: the disciple can serve only one master and must choose between God and wealth (**mammon**). See further the note on Lk 16, 9.

6, 22–23: In this context the parable probably points to the need for the disciple to be enlightened by Jesus' teaching on the transitory nature of earthly riches.

6, 24: **Mammon:** an Aramaic word meaning wealth or property.

y Lk 11, 2–4. z 26, 42. a Prv 30, 8–9. b 18, 21–22; Sir 28, 2. c Jn 17, 15; 2 Thes 3, 3. d 18, 35; Sir 28, 1–5; Mk 11, 25. e Jas 2, 13. f Jas 5, 2–3. g Lk 12, 33–34. h Lk 11, 34–36. i Lk 16, 13.

Dependence on God [25][j]*"Therefore I tell you, do not worry about your life, what you will eat [or drink], or about your body, what you will wear. Is not life more than food and the body more than clothing? [26][k]Look at the birds in the sky; they do not sow or reap, they gather nothing into barns, yet your heavenly Father feeds them. Are not you more important than they? [27]*Can any of you by worrying add a single moment to your life-span? [28]Why are you anxious about clothes? Learn from the way the wild flowers grow. They do not work or spin. [29]But I tell you that not even Solomon in all his splendor was clothed like one of them. [30]*If God so clothes the grass of the field, which grows today and is thrown into the oven tomorrow, will he not much more provide for you, O you of little faith? [31]So do not worry and say, 'What are we to eat?' or 'What are we to drink?' or 'What are we to wear?' [32]All these things the pagans seek. Your heavenly Father knows that you need them all. [33]*But seek first the kingdom [of God] and his righteousness, and all these things will be given you besides. [34]Do not worry about tomorrow; tomorrow will take care of itself. Sufficient for a day is its own evil.

CHAPTER 7

Judging Others [1][l m]*"Stop judging, that you may not be judged. [2][n]For as you judge, so will you be judged, and the measure with which you measure will be measured out to you. [3]Why do you notice the splinter in your brother's eye, but do not perceive the wooden beam in your own eye? [4]How can you say to your brother, 'Let me remove that splinter from your eye,' while the wooden beam is in your eye? [5]*You hypocrite, remove the wooden beam from your eye first; then you will see clearly to remove the splinter from your brother's eye.

Pearls before Swine [6][o]*"Do not give what is holy to dogs, or throw your pearls before swine, lest they trample them underfoot, and turn and tear you to pieces.

The Answer to Prayers [7][p q]"Ask and it will be given to you; seek and you will find; knock and the door will be opened to you. [8][r]For everyone who asks, receives; and the one who seeks, finds; and to the one who knocks, the door will be opened. [9]*Which one of you would hand his son a stone when he asks for a loaf of bread, [10]or a snake when he asks for a fish? [11][s]If you then, who are wicked, know how to give good gifts to your children, how much more will your heavenly Father give good things to those who ask him.

The Golden Rule [12][t]*"Do to others whatever you would have them do to you. This is the law and the prophets.

6, 25–34: Jesus does not deny the reality of human needs (32), but forbids making them the object of anxious care and, in effect, becoming their slave.

6, 27: Life-span: the Greek word can also mean "stature." If it is taken in that sense, the word here translated **moment** (literally, "cubit") must be translated literally as a unit not of time but of spatial measure. The cubit is about eighteen inches.

6, 30: Of little faith: except for the parallel in Lk 12, 28, the word translated of **little faith** is found in the New Testament only in Matthew. It is used by him of those who are disciples of Jesus but whose faith in him is not as deep as it should be (see Mt 8, 26; 14, 31; 16, 8 and the cognate noun in 17, 20).

6, 33: Righteousness: see the note on 3, 14–15.

7, 1–12: In v 1 Matthew returns to the basic traditional material of the sermon (Lk 6, 37–38.41–42). The governing thought is the correspondence between conduct toward one's fellows and God's conduct toward the one so acting.

7, 1: This is not a prohibition against recognizing the faults of others, which would be hardly compatible with vv 5 and 6, but against passing judgment in a spirit of arrogance, forgetful of one's own faults.

7, 5: Hypocrite: the designation previously given to the scribes and Pharisees is here given to the Christian disciple who is concerned with the faults of another and ignores his own more serious offenses.

7, 6: Dogs and **swine** were Jewish terms of contempt for Gentiles. This saying may originally have derived from a Jewish Christian community opposed to preaching the gospel (**what is holy, pearls**) to Gentiles. In the light of 28, 19 that can hardly be Matthew's meaning. He may have taken the saying as applying to a Christian dealing with an obstinately impenitent fellow Christian (18, 17).

7, 9–10: There is a resemblance between a stone and a round loaf of bread and between a serpent and the scaleless fish called **barbut**.

7, 12: See Lk 6, 31. This saying, known since the eighteenth century as the "Golden Rule," is found in both positive and negative form in pagan and Jewish sources, both earlier and later than the gospel. **This is the law and the prophets** is an addition probably due to the evangelist.

j Lk 12, 22–31. k Pss 145, 15–16; 147, 9. l Lk 6, 37–38.41–42. m Rom 2, 1–2; 1 Cor 4, 5. n Wis 12, 22; Mk 4, 24. o Prv 23, 9. p Mk 11, 24; Lk 11, 9–13. q 18, 19. r Lk 18, 1–8; Jn 14, 13. s 1 Jn 5, 14–15. t Lk 6, 31.

The Narrow Gate [13][u]*"Enter through the narrow gate; for the gate is wide and the road broad that leads to destruction, and those who enter through it are many. [14]How narrow the gate and constricted the road that leads to life. And those who find it are few.

False Prophets [15][v]*"Beware of false prophets, who come to you in sheep's clothing, but underneath are ravenous wolves. [16][w]By their fruits you will know them. Do people pick grapes from thornbushes, or figs from thistles? [17]Just so, every good tree bears good fruit, and a rotten tree bears bad fruit. [18]A good tree cannot bear bad fruit, nor can a rotten tree bear good fruit. [19][x]Every tree that does not bear good fruit will be cut down and thrown into the fire. [20]So by their fruits you will know them.

The True Disciple [21][y]*"Not everyone who says to me, 'Lord, Lord,' will enter the kingdom of heaven, but only the one who does the will of my Father in heaven. [22][z][a]Many will say to me on that day, 'Lord, Lord, did we not prophesy in your name? Did we not drive out demons in your name? Did we not do mighty deeds in your name?' [23][b]*Then I will declare to them solemnly, 'I never knew you. Depart from me, you evildoers.'

The Two Foundations [24][c]*"Everyone who listens to these words of mine and acts on them will be like a wise man who built his house on rock. [25][d]The rain fell, the floods came, and the winds blew and buffeted the house. But it did not collapse; it had been set solidly on rock. [26]And everyone who listens to these words of mine but does not act on them will be like a fool who built his house on sand. [27]The rain fell, the floods came, and the winds blew and buffeted the house. And it collapsed and was completely ruined."

[28]*When Jesus finished these words, the crowds were astonished at his teaching, [29][e]*for he taught them as one having authority, and not as their scribes.

III: Ministry and Mission in Galilee

CHAPTER 8

The Cleansing of a Leper [1][f]*When Jesus came down from the mountain, great crowds followed him. [2]*And then a leper approached, did him homage, and said, "Lord, if you wish, you can make me clean." [3]He stretched out his hand, touched him, and said, "I will do it. Be

7, 13–28: The final section of the discourse is composed of a series of antitheses, contrasting two kinds of life within the Christian community, that of those who obey the words of Jesus and that of those who do not. Most of the sayings are from Q and are found also in Luke.

7, 13–14: The metaphor of the "two ways" was common in pagan philosophy and in the Old Testament. In Christian literature it is found also in the **Didache** (1–6) and the **Epistle of Barnabas** (18–20).

7, 15–20: Christian disciples who claimed to speak in the name of God are called **prophets** (15) in 10, 41 and in 23, 34. They were presumably an important group within the church of Matthew. As in the case of the Old Testament prophets, there were both true and false ones, and for Matthew the difference could be recognized by the quality of their deeds, the **fruits** (16). The mention of **fruits** leads to the comparison with trees, some producing good fruit, others bad.

7, 21–23: The attack on the false prophets is continued, but is broadened to include those disciples who perform works of healing and exorcism in the name of Jesus (**Lord**) but live evil lives. Entrance into the kingdom is only for those who do the will of the Father. On the day of judgment (**on that day**) the morally corrupt prophets and miracle workers will be rejected by Jesus.

7, 23: I never knew you: cf 10, 33. **Depart from me, you evildoers:** cf Ps 6, 9.

7, 24–27: The conclusion of the discourse (cf Lk 6, 47–49). Here the relation is not between saying and doing as in vv 15–23 but between hearing and doing, and the words of Jesus are applied to every Christian (**everyone who listens**).

7, 28–29: When Jesus finished these words: this or a similar formula is used by Matthew to conclude each of the five great discourses of Jesus (cf 11, 1; 13, 53; 19, 1; 26, 1).

7, 29: Not as their scribes: scribal instruction was a faithful handing down of the traditions of earlier teachers; Jesus' teaching is based on his own authority. **Their scribes:** for the implications of **their,** see the note on 4, 23.

8, 1—9, 38: This narrative section of the second book of the gospel is composed of nine miracle stories, most of which are found in Mark, although Matthew does not follow the Marcan order and abbreviates the stories radically. The stories are arranged in three groups of three, each group followed by a section composed principally of sayings of Jesus about discipleship. Verse 9, 35 is an almost verbatim repetition of 4, 23. Each speaks of Jesus' teaching, preaching, and healing. The teaching and preaching form the content of chs 5–7; the healing, that of chs 8–9. Some scholars speak of a portrayal of Jesus as "Messiah of the Word" in 5–7 and "Messiah of the Deed" in 8–9. That is accurate so far as it goes, but there is also a strong emphasis on discipleship in 8–9; these chapters have not only christological but ecclesiological import.

8, 2: A leper: see the note on Mk 1, 40.

u Lk 13, 24. v 2 Pt 2, 1. w 12, 33; Lk 6, 43–44. x 3, 10. y Is 29, 13; Lk 6, 46. z Lk 13, 26–27. a 25, 11–12. b Pss 5, 5; 6, 9. c Lk 6, 47–49. d Prv 10, 25. e Mk 1, 22; Lk 4, 32. f Mk 1, 40–44; Lk 5, 12–14.

made clean." His leprosy was cleansed immediately. 4 g*Then Jesus said to him, "See that you tell no one, but go show yourself to the priest, and offer the gift that Moses prescribed; that will be proof for them."

The Healing of a Centurion's Servant

5 h*When he entered Capernaum, a centurion approached him and appealed to him, 6saying, "Lord, my servant is lying at home paralyzed, suffering dreadfully." 7He said to him, "I will come and cure him." 8*The centurion said in reply, "Lord, I am not worthy to have you enter under my roof; only say the word and my servant will be healed. 9For I too am a person subject to authority, with soldiers subject to me. And I say to one, 'Go,' and he goes; and to another, 'Come here,' and he comes; and to my slave, 'Do this,' and he does it." 10*When Jesus heard this, he was amazed and said to those following him, "Amen, I say to you, in no one in Israel have I found such faith. 11 i*I say to you, many will come from the east and the west, and will recline with Abraham, Isaac, and Jacob at the banquet in the kingdom of heaven, 12but the children of the kingdom will be driven out into the outer darkness, where there will be wailing and grinding of teeth." 13And Jesus said to the centurion, "You may go; as you have believed, let it be done for you." And at that very hour [his] servant was healed.

The Cure of Peter's Mother-in-Law

14 j*Jesus entered the house of Peter, and saw his mother-in-law lying in bed with a fever. 15 kHe touched her hand, the fever left her, and she rose and waited on him.

Other Healings 16*When it was evening, they brought him many who were possessed by demons, and he drove out the spirits by a word and cured all the sick, 17 l*to fulfill what had been said by Isaiah the prophet:

"He took away our infirmities
and bore our diseases."

The Would-be Followers of Jesus 18 m*When Jesus saw a crowd around him, he gave orders to cross to the other side. 19 n*A scribe approached and said to him, "Teacher, I will follow you wherever you go." 20*Jesus answered him, "Foxes have dens and birds of the sky have nests, but the Son of Man has nowhere to rest his head." 21Another of [his] disciples said to him, "Lord, let me go first and bury my father."

8, 4: Cf Lv 14, 2–9. **That will be proof for them:** the Greek can also mean "that will be proof against them." It is not clear whether **them** refers to the priests or the people.

8, 5–13: This story comes from Q (see Lk 7, 1–10) and is also reflected in Jn 4, 46–54. The similarity between the Q story and the Johannine is due to a common oral tradition, not to a common literary source. As in the later story of the daughter of the Canaanite woman (15, 21–28) Jesus here breaks with his usual procedure of ministering only to Israelites and anticipates the mission to the Gentiles.

8, 5: **A centurion:** a military officer commanding a hundred men. He was probably in the service of Herod Antipas, tetrarch of Galilee; see the note on 14, 1.

8, 8–9: Acquainted by his position with the force of a command, the centurion expresses faith in the power of Jesus' mere word.

8, 10: **In no one in Israel:** there is good textual attestation (e.g., Codex Sinaiticus) for a reading identical with that of Lk 7, 9, "not even in Israel." But that seems to be due to a harmonization of Matthew with Luke.

8, 11–12: Matthew inserts into the story a Q saying (see Lk 13, 28–29) about the entrance of Gentiles into the kingdom and the exclusion of those Israelites who, though descended from the patriarchs and members of the chosen nation (**the children of the kingdom**), refused to believe in Jesus. **There will be wailing and grinding of teeth:** the first occurrence of a phrase used frequently in this gospel to describe final condemnation (13, 42.50; 22, 13; 24, 51; 25, 30). It is found elsewhere in the New Testament only in Lk 13, 28.

8, 14–15: Cf Mk 1, 29–31. Unlike Mark, Matthew has no implied request by others for the woman's cure. Jesus acts on his own initiative, and the cured woman rises and waits not on "them" (Mk 1, 31) but on **him.**

8, 16: **By a word:** a Matthean addition to Mk 1, 34; cf 8, 8.

8, 17: This fulfillment citation from Is 53, 4 follows the MT, not the LXX. The prophet speaks of the Servant of the Lord who suffers vicariously for the sins ("infirmities") of others; Matthew takes the **infirmities** as physical afflictions.

8, 18–22: This passage between the first and second series of miracles about following Jesus is taken from Q (see Lk 9, 57–62). The third of the three sayings found in the source is absent from Matthew.

8, 18: **The other side:** i.e., of the Sea of Galilee.

8, 19: **Teacher:** for Matthew, this designation of Jesus is true, for he has Jesus using it of himself (10, 24.25; 23, 8; 26, 18), yet when it is used of him by others they are either his opponents (9, 11; 12, 38; 17, 24; 22, 16.24.36) or, as here and in 19, 16, well-disposed persons who cannot see more deeply. Thus it reveals an inadequate recognition of who Jesus is.

8, 20: **Son of Man:** see the note on Mk 8, 31. This is the first occurrence in Mt of a term that appears in the New Testament only in sayings of Jesus, except for Acts 7, 56 and possibly 9, 6 (// Mk 2, 10; Lk 5, 24). In Mt it refers to Jesus in his ministry (seven times, as here), in his passion and resurrection (nine times, e.g., 17, 22), and in his glorious coming at the end of the age (thirteen times, e.g., 24, 30).

g Lv 14, 2–32; Lk 17, 14. h Lk 7, 1–10; Jn 4, 46–53. i 13, 42.50; 22, 13; 24, 51; 25, 30; Lk 13, 28–29. j Mk 1, 29–34; Lk 4, 38–41. k 9, 25. l Is 53, 4. m Mk 4, 35. n Lk 9, 57–60.

22*But Jesus answered him, "Follow me, and let
the dead bury their dead."
The Calming of the Storm at Sea 23 o*He got
into a boat and his disciples followed him.
24*Suddenly a violent storm came up on the sea,
so that the boat was being swamped by waves;
but he was asleep. 25 p*They came and woke
him, saying, "Lord, save us! We are perishing!"
26*He said to them, "Why are you terrified, O
you of little faith?" Then he got up, rebuked the
winds and the sea, and there was great calm.
27The men were amazed and said, "What sort of
man is this, whom even the winds and the sea
obey?"
The Healing of the Gadarene Demoniacs
28 q*When he came to the other side, to the
territory of the Gadarenes, two demoniacs who
were coming from the tombs met him. They
were so savage that no one could travel by that
road. 29*They cried out, "What have you to do
with us, Son of God? Have you come here to
torment us before the appointed time?" 30*Some
distance away a herd of many swine was feed-
ing. 31 rThe demons pleaded with him, "If you
drive us out, send us into the herd of swine."
32And he said to them, "Go then!" They came
out and entered the swine, and the whole herd
rushed down the steep bank into the sea where
they drowned. 33The swineherds ran away, and
when they came to the town they reported
everything, including what had happened to the
demoniacs. 34Thereupon the whole town came
out to meet Jesus, and when they saw him they
begged him to leave their district.

CHAPTER 9

The Healing of a Paralytic 1 s*He entered a
boat, made the crossing, and came into his own
town. 2 tAnd there people brought to him a
paralytic lying on a stretcher. When Jesus saw
their faith, he said to the paralytic, "Courage,
child, your sins are forgiven." 3*At that, some of
the scribes said to themselves, "This man is
blaspheming." 4Jesus knew what they were
thinking, and said, "Why do you harbor evil
thoughts? 5Which is easier, to say, 'Your sins are
forgiven,' or to say, 'Rise and walk'? 6 u*But that
you may know that the Son of Man has authority
on earth to forgive sins"—he then said to the
paralytic, "Rise, pick up your stretcher, and go
home." 7He rose and went home. 8*When the
crowds saw this they were struck with awe and
glorified God who had given such authority to
human beings.

8, 22: Let the dead bury their dead: the demand of Jesus overrides what both the Jewish and the Hellenistic world regarded as a filial obligation of the highest importance. See the note on Lk 9, 60.

8, 23: His disciples followed him: the first miracle in the second group (8, 23—9, 8) is introduced by a verse that links it with the preceding sayings by the catchword "follow." In Mk the initiative in entering the boat is taken by the disciples (Mk 4, 35–41); here, Jesus enters first and the disciples follow.

8, 24: Storm: literally, "earthquake," a word commonly used in apocalyptic literature for the shaking of the old world when God brings in his kingdom. All the synoptics use it in depicting the events preceding the parousia of the Son of Man (24, 7; Mk 13, 8; Lk 21, 11). Matthew has introduced it here and in his account of the death and resurrection of Jesus (27, 51–54; 28, 2).

8, 25: The reverent plea of the disciples contrasts sharply with their reproach of Jesus in Mk 4, 38.

8, 26: You of little faith: see the note on 6, 30. **Great calm:** Jesus' calming the sea may be meant to recall the Old Testament theme of God's control over the chaotic waters (Pss 65, 8; 89, 10; 93, 3–4; 107, 29).

8, 28: Gadarenes: this is the reading of Codex Vaticanus, supported by other important textual witnesses. The original reading of Codex Sinaiticus was Gazarenes, later changed to Gergesenes, and a few versions have Gerasenes. Each of these readings points to a different territory connected, respectively, with the cities Gadara, Gergesa, and Gerasa (modern Jerash). There is the same confusion of readings in the parallel texts, Mk 5, 1 and Lk 8, 26; there the best reading seems to be "Gerasenes," whereas "Gadarenes" is probably the original reading in Mt. The town of Gadara was about five miles southeast of the Sea of Galilee, and Josephus (**Life** 9 §42) refers to it as possessing territory that lay on that sea. **Two demoniacs:** Mark (5, 1–20) has one.

8, 29: What have you to do with us?: see the note on Jn 2, 4. **Before the appointed time:** the notion that evil spirits were allowed by God to afflict human beings until the time of the final judgment is found in Enoch 16, 1 and Jubilees 10, 7–10.

8, 30: The tending of pigs, animals considered unclean by Mosaic law (Lv 11, 6–7), indicates that the population was Gentile.

9, 1: His own town: Capernaum; see 4, 13.

9, 3: Scribes: see the note on Mk 2, 6. Matthew omits the reason given in the Marcan story for the charge of blasphemy: "Who but God alone can forgive sins?" (Mk 2, 7).

9, 6: It is not clear whether "But that you may know . . . to forgive sins" is intended to be a continuation of the words of Jesus or a parenthetical comment of the evangelist to those who would hear or read this gospel. In any case, Matthew here follows the Marcan text.

9, 8: Who had given such authority to human beings: a significant difference from Mk 2, 12 ("They . . . glorified God saying, 'We have never seen anything like this' "). Matthew's extension to **human beings** of the authority to forgive sins points to the belief that such authority was being claimed by Matthew's church.

o Mk 4, 35–40; Lk 8, 22–25. p Ps 107, 28–29. q Mk 5, 1–17; Lk 8, 26–37. r Lk 4, 34.41. s Mk 2, 3–12; Lk 5, 18–26. t Lk 7, 48. u Jn 5, 27.

The Call of Matthew 9 [v]*As Jesus passed on from there, he saw a man named Matthew sitting at the customs post. He said to him, "Follow me." And he got up and followed him. 10 [w]*While he was at table in his house, many tax collectors and sinners came and sat with Jesus and his disciples. 11 *The Pharisees saw this and said to his disciples, "Why does your teacher eat with tax collectors and sinners?" 12 *He heard this and said, "Those who are well do not need a physician, but the sick do. 13 [x]*Go and learn the meaning of the words, 'I desire mercy, not sacrifice.' I did not come to call the righteous but sinners."

The Question about Fasting 14 [y]Then the disciples of John approached him and said, "Why do we and the Pharisees fast [much], but your disciples do not fast?" 15 *Jesus answered them, "Can the wedding guests mourn as long as the bridegroom is with them? The days will come when the bridegroom is taken away from them, and then they will fast. 16 *No one patches an old cloak with a piece of unshrunken cloth, for its fullness pulls away from the cloak and the tear gets worse. 17 People do not put new wine into old wineskins. Otherwise the skins burst, the wine spills out, and the skins are ruined. Rather, they pour new wine into fresh wineskins, and both are preserved."

The Official's Daughter and the Woman with a Hemorrhage 18 [z]*While he was saying these things to them, an official came forward, knelt down before him, and said, "My daughter has just died. But come, lay your hand on her, and she will live." 19 Jesus rose and followed him, and so did his disciples. 20 *A woman suffering hemorrhages for twelve years came up behind him and touched the tassel on his cloak. 21 [a]She said to herself, "If only I can touch his cloak, I shall be cured." 22 Jesus turned around and saw her, and said, "Courage, daughter! Your faith has saved you." And from that hour the woman was cured.

23 When Jesus arrived at the official's house and saw the flute players and the crowd who were making a commotion, 24 *he said, "Go away! The girl is not dead but sleeping." And they ridiculed him. 25 When the crowd was put out, he came and took her by the hand, and the little girl arose. 26 And news of this spread throughout all that land.

9, 9–17: In this section the order is the same as that of Mk 2, 13–22.

9, 9: **A man named Matthew:** Mark names this tax collector Levi (2, 14). No such name appears in the four lists of the twelve who were the closest companions of Jesus (10, 2–4; Mk 3, 16–19; Lk 6, 14–16; Acts 1, 13 [eleven, because of the defection of Judas Iscariot]), whereas all four list a Matthew, designated in 10, 3 as "the tax collector." The evangelist may have changed the "Levi" of his source to **Matthew** so that this man, whose call is given special notice, like that of the first four disciples (4, 18–22), might be included among the twelve. Another reason for the change may be that the disciple Matthew was the source of traditions peculiar to the church for which the evangelist was writing.

9, 10: **His house:** it is not clear whether **his** refers to Jesus or Matthew. **Tax collectors:** see the note on 5, 46. Table association with such persons would cause ritual impurity.

9, 11: **Teacher:** see the note on 8, 19.

9, 12: See the note on Mk 2, 17.

9, 13: **Go and learn . . . not sacrifice:** Matthew adds the prophetic statement of Hos 6, 6 to the Marcan account (see also 12, 7). If mercy is superior to the temple sacrifices, how much more to the laws of ritual impurity.

9, 15: Fasting is a sign of mourning and would be as inappropriate at this time of joy, when Jesus is proclaiming the kingdom, as it would be at a marriage feast. Yet the saying looks forward to the time when Jesus will no longer be with the disciples visibly, the time of Matthew's church. **Then they will fast:** see **Didache** 8, 1.

9, 16–17: Each of these parables speaks of the unsuitability of attempting to combine the old and the new. Jesus' teaching is not a patching up of Judaism, nor can the gospel be contained within the limits of Mosaic law.

9, 18–34: In this third group of miracles, the first (18–26) is clearly dependent on Mark (Mk 5, 21–43). Though it tells of two miracles, the cure of the woman had already been included within the story of the raising of the official's daughter, so that the two were probably regarded as a single unit. The other miracles seem to have been derived from Mark and Q respectively, though there Matthew's own editing is much more evident.

9, 18: **Official:** literally, "ruler." Mark calls him "one of the synagogue officials" (Mk 5, 22). **My daughter has just died:** Matthew heightens the Marcan "my daughter is at the point of death" (Mk 5, 23).

9, 20: **Tassel:** possibly "fringe." The Mosaic law prescribed that tassels be worn on the corners of one's garment as a reminder to keep the commandments (see Nm 15, 37–39; Dt 22, 12).

9, 24: **Sleeping:** sleep is a biblical metaphor for death (see Ps 87, 6 LXX; Dn 12, 2; 1 Thes 5, 10). Jesus' statement is not a denial of the child's real death, but an assurance that she will be roused from her sleep of death.

v Mk 2, 14–17; Lk 5, 27–32. w 11, 19; Lk 15, 1–2. x 12, 7; Hos 6, 6. y Mk 2, 18–22; Lk 5, 33–39. z Mk 5, 22–43; Lk 8, 41–56. a 14, 36; Nm 15, 37.

The Healing of Two Blind Men 27 [b] [c]*And as Jesus passed on from there, two blind men followed [him], crying out, "Son of David, have pity on us!" 28When he entered the house, the blind men approached him and Jesus said to them, "Do you believe that I can do this?" "Yes, Lord," they said to him. 29Then he touched their eyes and said, "Let it be done for you according to your faith." 30And their eyes were opened. Jesus warned them sternly, "See that no one knows about this." 31But they went out and spread word of him through all that land.

The Healing of a Mute Person 32 [d]*As they were going out, a demoniac who could not speak was brought to him, 33 [e]and when the demon was driven out the mute person spoke. The crowds were amazed and said, "Nothing like this has ever been seen in Israel." 34[f]*But the Pharisees said, "He drives out demons by the prince of demons."

The Compassion of Jesus 35 [g]*Jesus went around to all the towns and villages, teaching in their synagogues, proclaiming the gospel of the kingdom, and curing every disease and illness. 36 [h]*At the sight of the crowds, his heart was moved with pity for them because they were troubled and abandoned, like sheep without a shepherd. 37 [i]*Then he said to his disciples, "The harvest is abundant but the laborers are few; 38so ask the master of the harvest to send out laborers for his harvest."

CHAPTER 10

The Mission of the Twelve 1 [j]*Then he summoned his twelve disciples and gave them authority over unclean spirits to drive them out and to cure every disease and every illness. 2*The names of the twelve apostles are these: first, Simon called Peter, and his brother Andrew; James, the son of Zebedee, and his brother John; 3Philip and Bartholomew, Thomas and Matthew the tax collector; James, the son of Alphaeus, and Thaddeus; 4Simon the Cananean, and Judas Iscariot who betrayed him.

The Commissioning of the Twelve 5 [k]*Jesus sent out these twelve after instructing them thus, "Do not go into pagan territory or enter a

9, 27–31: This story was probably composed by Matthew out of Mark's story of the healing of a blind man named Bartimaeus (Mk 10, 46–52). Mark places the event late in Jesus' ministry, just before his entrance into Jerusalem, and Matthew has followed his Marcan source at that point in his gospel also (see 20, 29–34). In each of the Matthean stories the single blind man of Mark becomes two. The reason why Matthew would have given a double version of the Marcan story and placed the earlier one here may be that he wished to add a story of Jesus' curing the blind at this point in order to prepare for Jesus' answer to the emissaries of the Baptist (11, 4–6) in which Jesus, recounting his works, begins with his giving sight to the blind.

9, 27: Son of David: this messianic title is connected once with the healing power of Jesus in Mark (10, 47–48) and Luke (18, 38–39) but more frequently in Matthew (see also 12, 23; 15, 22; 20, 30–31).

9, 32–34: The source of this story seems to be Q (see Lk 11, 14–15). As in the preceding healing of the blind, Matthew has two versions of this healing, the later in 12, 22–24 and the earlier here.

9, 34: This spiteful accusation foreshadows the growing opposition to Jesus in chs 11 and 12.

9, 35: See the notes on 4, 23–25 and 8, 1—9, 38.

9, 36: See Mk 6, 34; Nm 27, 17; 1 Kgs 22, 17.

9, 37–38: This Q saying (see Lk 10, 2) is only imperfectly related to this context. It presupposes that only God (**the master of the harvest**) can take the initiative in sending out preachers of the gospel, whereas in Matthew's setting it leads into ch 10, where Jesus does so.

10, 1—11, 1: After an introductory narrative (10, 1–4), the second of the discourses of the gospel. It deals with the mission now to be undertaken by the disciples (5–15), but the perspective broadens and includes the missionary activity of the church between the time of the resurrection and the parousia.

10, 1: His twelve disciples: although, unlike Mark (3, 13–14) and Luke (6, 12–16), Matthew has no story of Jesus' choosing the Twelve, he assumes that the group is known to the reader. The earliest New Testament text to speak of it is 1 Cor 15, 5. The number probably is meant to recall the twelve tribes of Israel and implies Jesus' authority to call all Israel into the kingdom. While Luke (6, 13) and probably Mark (4, 10.34) distinguish between the Twelve and a larger group also termed disciples, Matthew tends to identify the disciples and the Twelve. **Authority . . . every illness:** activities the same as those of Jesus; see 4, 23; 9, 35; 10, 8. The Twelve also share in his proclamation of the kingdom (10, 7). But although he teaches (4, 23; 7, 28; 9, 35), they do not. Their commission to teach comes only after Jesus' resurrection, after they have been fully instructed by him (28, 20).

10, 2–4: Here, for the only time in Matthew, the Twelve are designated **apostles.** The word "apostle" means "one who is sent," and therefore fits the situation here described. In the Pauline letters, the place where the term occurs most frequently in the New Testament, it means primarily one who has seen the risen Lord and has been commissioned to proclaim the resurrection. With slight variants in Luke and Acts, the names of those who belong to this group are the same in the four lists given in the New Testament (see the note on 9, 9). **Cananean:** this represents an Aramaic word meaning "zealot." The meaning of that designation is unclear (see the note on Lk 6, 15).

10, 5–6: Like Jesus (15, 24), the Twelve are sent only to Israel. This saying may reflect an original Jewish Christian refusal of the mission to the Gentiles, but for Matthew it expresses rather the limitation that Jesus himself observed during his ministry.

b 20, 29–34. c 15, 22. d 12, 22–24; Lk 11, 14–15. e Mk 2, 12; 7, 37. f 10, 25; Mk 3, 22. g 4, 23; Lk 8, 1. h Nm 27, 17; 1 Kgs 22, 17; Jer 50, 6; Ez 34, 5; Mk 6, 34. i Lk 10, 2; Jn 4, 35. j Mk 3, 14–19; Lk 6, 13–16; Acts 1, 13. k Mk 6, 7–13; Lk 9, 1–6.

Samaritan town. [6 l]Go rather to the lost sheep of
the house of Israel. [7 m]As you go, make this
proclamation: ‘The kingdom of heaven is at
hand.’ [8*]Cure the sick, raise the dead, cleanse
lepers, drive out demons. Without cost you have
received; without cost you are to give. [9 n]Do not
take gold or silver or copper for your belts; [10 o]no
sack for the journey, or a second tunic, or
sandals, or walking stick. The laborer deserves
his keep. [11 p]Whatever town or village you enter,
look for a worthy person in it, and stay there
until you leave. [12]As you enter a house, wish it
peace. [13*]If the house is worthy, let your peace
come upon it; if not, let your peace return to
you. [14 q*]Whoever will not receive you or listen
to your words—go outside that house or town
and shake the dust from your feet. [15 r]Amen, I
say to you, it will be more tolerable for the land
of Sodom and Gomorrah on the day of judgment
than for that town.

Coming Persecutions [16 s]“Behold, I am send-
ing you like sheep in the midst of wolves; so be
shrewd as serpents and simple as doves. [17 tu*]But
beware of people, for they will hand you over to
courts and scourge you in their synagogues,
[18]and you will be led before governors and kings
for my sake as a witness before them and the
pagans. [19 v]When they hand you over, do not
worry about how you are to speak or what you
are to say. You will be given at that moment what
you are to say. [20]For it will not be you who speak
but the Spirit of your Father speaking through
you. [21 w*]Brother will hand over brother to
death, and the father his child; children will rise
up against parents and have them put to death.
[22*]You will be hated by all because of my name,
but whoever endures to the end will be saved.
[23*]When they persecute you in one town, flee to
another. Amen, I say to you, you will not finish
the towns of Israel before the Son of Man comes.
[24 x]No disciple is above his teacher, no slave
above his master. [25*]It is enough for the disciple
that he become like his teacher, for the slave that
he become like his master. If they have called the
master of the house Beelzebul, how much more
those of his household!

Courage under Persecution [26 yz*]“Therefore
do not be afraid of them. Nothing is concealed
that will not be revealed, nor secret that will not
be known. [27]What I say to you in the darkness,
speak in the light; what you hear whispered,
proclaim on the housetops. [28 a]And do not be
afraid of those who kill the body but cannot kill
the soul; rather, be afraid of the one who can
destroy both soul and body in Gehenna. [29]Are
not two sparrows sold for a small coin? Yet not
one of them falls to the ground without your
Father’s knowledge. [30]Even all the hairs of your
head are counted. [31]So do not be afraid; you are
worth more than many sparrows. [32*]Everyone

10, 8–11: The Twelve have received their own call and mission through God’s gift, and the benefits they confer are likewise to be given freely. They are not to take with them money, provisions, or unnecessary clothing; their lodging and food will be provided by those who receive them.

10, 13: The greeting of peace is conceived of not merely as a salutation but as an effective word. If it finds no worthy recipient, it will return to the speaker.

10, 14: Shake the dust from your feet: this gesture indicates a complete disassociation from such unbelievers.

10, 17: The persecutions attendant upon the post-resurrection mission now begin to be spoken of. Here Matthew brings into the discourse sayings found in Mk 13, which deals with events preceding the parousia.

10, 21: See Mi 7, 6, which is cited in vv 35.36.

10, 22: To the end: the original meaning was probably “until the parousia.” But it is not likely that Matthew expected no missionary disciples to suffer death before then, since he envisages the martyrdom of other Christians (21). For him, **the end** is probably that of the individual’s life (see 28).

10, 23: Before the Son of Man comes: since the coming of the Son of Man at the end of the age had not taken place when this gospel was written, much less during the mission of the Twelve during Jesus’ ministry, Matthew cannot have meant the coming to refer to the parousia. It is difficult to know what he understood it to be: perhaps the “proleptic parousia” of 28, 16–20, or the destruction of the temple in A.D. 70, viewed as a coming of Jesus in judgment on unbelieving Israel.

10, 25: Beelzebul: see 9, 34 for the charge linking Jesus with “the prince of demons,” who is named **Beelzebul** in 12, 24. The meaning of the name is uncertain; possibly, “lord of the house.”

10, 26: The **concealed** and **secret** coming of the kingdom is to be proclaimed by them, and no fear must be allowed to deter them from that proclamation.

10, 32–33: In the Q parallel (Lk 12, 8–9), the Son of Man will acknowledge those who have acknowledged Jesus, and those who deny him will be denied (by the Son of Man) before the angels of God at the judgment. Here Jesus and the Son of Man are identified, and the acknowledgment or denial will be before his heavenly Father.

l 15, 24. m 3, 2; 4, 17. n Mk 6, 8–9; Lk 9, 3; 10, 4. o Lk 10, 7; 1 Cor 9, 14; 2 Tm 5, 18. p Mk 6, 10–11; Lk 9, 4–5; 10, 5–12. q Acts 13, 51; 18, 6. r 11, 24; Gn 19, 1–29; Jude 7. s Lk 10, 3. t Mk 13, 9–13; Lk 21, 12–19. u Acts 5, 40. v Ex 4, 11–12; Jer 1, 6–10; Lk 12, 11–12. w 24, 9.13. x Lk 6, 40; Jn 13, 16; 15, 20. y Lk 12, 2–9. z Mk 4, 22; Lk 8, 17; 1 Tm 5, 25. a Jas 4, 12.

who acknowledges me before others I will
acknowledge before my heavenly Father. 33 [b]But
whoever denies me before others, I will deny
before my heavenly Father.

Jesus: A Cause of Division 34 [c]"Do not think
that I have come to bring peace upon the earth. I
have come to bring not peace but the sword.
35 For I have come to set

a man 'against his father,
    a daughter against her mother,
and a daughter-in-law against her
        mother-in-law;
36 and one's enemies will be those of his
        household.'

The Conditions of Discipleship 37 [d]"Who-
ever loves father or mother more than me is not
worthy of me, and whoever loves son or daugh-
ter more than me is not worthy of me; 38 *and
whoever does not take up his cross and follow
after me is not worthy of me. 39 [e]*Whoever finds
his life will lose it, and whoever loses his life for
my sake will find it.

Rewards 40 [f]*"Whoever receives you receives
me, and whoever receives me receives the one
who sent me. 41 *Whoever receives a prophet
because he is a prophet will receive a prophet's
reward, and whoever receives a righteous man
because he is righteous will receive a righteous
man's reward. 42 [g]And whoever gives only a cup
of cold water to one of these little ones to drink
because he is a disciple—amen, I say to you, he
will surely not lose his reward."

CHAPTER 11

1 *When Jesus finished giving these commands
to his twelve disciples, he went away from that
place to teach and to preach in their towns.

IV: Opposition from Israel

The Messengers from John the Baptist
2 [h]*When John heard in prison of the works of
the Messiah, he sent his disciples to him 3 *with
this question, "Are you the one who is to come,
or should we look for another?" 4 Jesus said to
them in reply, "Go and tell John what you hear
and see: 5 [i]*the blind regain their sight, the lame
walk, lepers are cleansed, the deaf hear, the
dead are raised, and the poor have the good
news proclaimed to them. 6 And blessed is the
one who takes no offense at me."

Jesus' Testimony to John 7 [j]*As they were
going off, Jesus began to speak to the crowds
about John, "What did you go out to the desert
to see? A reed swayed by the wind? 8 Then what
did you go out to see? Someone dressed in fine
clothing? Those who wear fine clothing are in
royal palaces. 9 *Then why did you go out? To
see a prophet? Yes, I tell you, and more than a

10, 38: The first mention of the cross in Matthew, explicitly that of the disciple, but implicitly that of Jesus (**and follow after me**). Crucifixion was a form of capital punishment used by the Romans for offenders who were not Roman citizens.

10, 39: One who denies Jesus in order to save one's earthly life will be condemned to everlasting destruction; loss of earthly life for Jesus' sake will be rewarded by everlasting life in the kingdom.

10, 40–42: All who receive the disciples of Jesus receive him, and God who sent him, and will be rewarded accordingly.

10, 41: **A prophet:** one who speaks in the name of God; here, the Christian prophets who proclaim the gospel. **Righteous man:** since righteousness is demanded of all the disciples, it is difficult to take the **righteous man** of this verse and **one of these little ones** (42) as indicating different groups within the followers of Jesus. Probably all three designations are used here of Christian missionaries as such.

11, 1: The closing formula of the discourse refers back to the original addressees, the Twelve.

11, 2—12, 50: The narrative section of the third book deals with the growing opposition to Jesus. It is largely devoted to disputes and attacks relating to faith and discipleship and thus contains much sayings-material, drawn in large part from Q.

11, 2: **In prison:** see 4, 12; 14, 1–12. **The works of the Messiah:** the deeds of chs 8–9.

11, 3: The question probably expresses a doubt of the Baptist that Jesus is **the one who is to come** (cf Mal 3, 1) because his mission has not been one of fiery judgment as John had expected (3, 2).

11, 5–6: Jesus' response is taken from passages of Isaiah (26, 19; 29, 18–19; 35, 5–6; 61, 1) that picture the time of salvation as marked by deeds such as those that Jesus is doing. The beatitude is a warning to the Baptist not to disbelieve because his expectations have not been met.

11, 7–19: Jesus' rebuke of John is counterbalanced by a reminder of the greatness of the Baptist's function (7–15) that is followed by a complaint about those who have heeded neither John nor Jesus (16–19).

11, 9–10: In common Jewish belief there had been no prophecy in Israel since the last of the Old Testament prophets, Malachi. The coming of a new prophet was eagerly awaited, and Jesus agrees that John was such. Yet he was **more than a prophet,** for he was the precursor of the one who would bring in the new and final age. The Old Testament quotation is a combination of Mal 3, 1 and Ex 23, 20, with the significant change that the **before me** of Malachi becomes **before you.** The messenger now precedes not God, as in the original, but Jesus.

b Mk 8, 38; Lk 9, 26; 2 Tm 2, 12; Rv 3, 5. c Lk 12, 51–53. d 16, 24–25; Lk 14, 26–27. e Mk 8, 35; Lk 9, 24; Jn 12, 25. f Lk 10, 16; Jn 12, 44; 13, 20. g 25, 40; Mk 9, 41. h Lk 7, 18–28. i Is 26, 19; 29, 18–19; 35, 5–6; 61, 1. j 3,3.5.

prophet. 10 [k]This is the one about whom it is written:

> 'Behold, I am sending my messenger ahead of you;
> he will prepare your way before you.'

11 *Amen, I say to you, among those born of women there has been none greater than John the Baptist; yet the least in the kingdom of heaven is greater than he. 12 [l]*From the days of John the Baptist until now, the kingdom of heaven suffers violence, and the violent are taking it by force. 13 *All the prophets and the law prophesied up to the time of John. 14 [m]And if you are willing to accept it, he is Elijah, the one who is to come. 15 Whoever has ears ought to hear.

16 [n]*"To what shall I compare this generation? It is like children who sit in marketplaces and call to one another, 17 'We played the flute for you, but you did not dance, we sang a dirge but you did not mourn.' 18 [o]For John came neither eating nor drinking, and they said, 'He is possessed by a demon.' 19 [p]The Son of Man came eating and drinking and they said, 'Look, he is a glutton and a drunkard, a friend of tax collectors and sinners.' But wisdom is vindicated by her works."

Reproaches to Unrepentant Towns 20 [q]Then he began to reproach the towns where most of his mighty deeds had been done, since they had not repented. 21 [r]*"Woe to you, Chorazin! Woe to you, Bethsaida! For if the mighty deeds done in your midst had been done in Tyre and Sidon, they would long ago have repented in sackcloth and ashes. 22 But I tell you, it will be more tolerable for Tyre and Sidon on the day of judgment than for you. 23 [s]*And as for you, Capernaum:

> 'Will you be exalted to heaven?
> You will go down to the netherworld.'

For if the mighty deeds done in your midst had been done in Sodom, it would have remained until this day. 24 [t]But I tell you, it will be more tolerable for the land of Sodom on the day of judgment than for you."

The Praise of the Father 25 [u]*At that time Jesus said in reply, "I give praise to you, Father, Lord of heaven and earth, for although you have hidden these things from the wise and the learned you have revealed them to the childlike. 26 Yes, Father, such has been your gracious will. 27 [v]All things have been handed over to me by my Father. No one knows the Son except the Father, and no one knows the Father except the Son and anyone to whom the Son wishes to reveal him.

11, 11: John's preeminent greatness lies in his function of announcing the imminence of the kingdom (3, 1). But to be in the kingdom is so great a privilege that the least who has it is greater than the Baptist.

11, 12: The meaning of this difficult saying is probably that the opponents of Jesus are trying to prevent people from accepting the kingdom and to snatch it away from those who have received it.

11, 13: All the prophets and the law: Matthew inverts the usual order, "law and prophets," and says that both have **prophesied.** This emphasis on the prophetic character of the law points to its fulfillment in the teaching of Jesus and to the transitory nature of some of its commandments (see the note on 5, 17–20).

11, 16–19: See Lk 7, 31–35. The meaning of the parable (16–17) and its explanation (18–19b) is much disputed. A plausible view is that the **children** of the parable are two groups, one of which proposes different entertainments to the other that will not agree with either proposal. The first represents John, Jesus, and their disciples; the second those who reject John for his asceticism and Jesus for his table association with those despised by the religiously observant. Verse 19c (**her works**) forms an inclusion with v 2 ("the works of the Messiah"). The original form of the saying is better preserved in Lk 7, 35, "... wisdom is vindicated by all her children." There John and Jesus are the children of Wisdom; here the works of Jesus the Messiah are those of divine Wisdom, of which he is the embodiment. Some important textual witnesses, however, have essentially the same reading as in Luke.

11, 21: Tyre and Sidon were pagan cities denounced for their wickedness in the Old Testament; cf Jl 4, 4–7.

11, 23: Capernaum's pride and punishment are described in language taken from the taunt song against the king of Babylon (Is 14, 13–15).

11, 25–27: This Q saying, identical with Lk 10, 21–22 except for minor variations, introduces a joyous note into this section, so dominated by the theme of unbelief. While **the wise and the learned,** the scribes and Pharisees, have rejected Jesus' preaching and the significance of his mighty deeds, **the childlike** have accepted them. Acceptance depends upon the Father's revelation, but this is granted to those who are open to receive it and refused to the arrogant. Jesus can speak of all mysteries because he is the **Son** and there is perfect reciprocity of knowledge between him and the Father; what has been **handed over** to him is revealed only to those whom he wishes.

k Ex 23, 20; Mal 3, 1; Mk 1, 2; Lk 1, 76. l Lk 16, 16. m 17, 10–13; Mal 3, 23; Lk 1, 17. n Lk 7, 31–35. o Lk 1, 15. p 9, 10–11. q Lk 10, 12–15. r Jl 4, 4–7. s Is 14, 13–15. t 10, 15. u Lk 10, 21–22. v Jn 3, 35; 6, 46; 7, 28; 10, 15.

The Gentle Mastery of Christ 28*"Come to
me, all you who labor and are burdened, and I
will give you rest. 29 w*Take my yoke upon you
and learn from me, for I am meek and humble of
heart; and you will find rest for yourselves. 30For
my yoke is easy, and my burden light."

CHAPTER 12

Picking Grain on the Sabbath 1 xy*At that
time Jesus was going through a field of grain on
the sabbath. His disciples were hungry and
began to pick the heads of grain and eat them.
2When the Pharisees saw this, they said to him,
"See, your disciples are doing what is unlawful
to do on the sabbath." 3 z*He said to them,
"Have you not read what David did when he
and his companions were hungry, 4 ahow he
went into the house of God and ate the bread of
offering, which neither he nor his companions
but only the priests could lawfully eat? 5 b*Or
have you not read in the law that on the sabbath
the priests serving in the temple violate the
sabbath and are innocent? 6I say to you, some-
thing greater than the temple is here. 7 c*If you
knew what this meant, 'I desire mercy, not
sacrifice,' you would not have condemned these
innocent men. 8 d*For the Son of Man is Lord of
the sabbath."

The Man with a Withered Hand 9 eMoving
on from there, he went into their synagogue.
10*And behold, there was a man there who had
a withered hand. They questioned him, "Is it
lawful to cure on the sabbath?" so that they
might accuse him. 11*He said to them, "Which
one of you who has a sheep that falls into a pit
on the sabbath will not take hold of it and lift it
out? 12How much more valuable a person is
than a sheep. So it is lawful to do good on the
sabbath." 13Then he said to the man, "Stretch
out your hand." He stretched it out, and it was
restored as sound as the other. 14f*But the
Pharisees went out and took counsel against him
to put him to death.

The Chosen Servant 15*When Jesus realized
this, he withdrew from that place. Many [people]
followed him, and he cured them all, 16but he
warned them not to make him known. 17This
was to fulfill what had been spoken through
Isaiah the prophet:

18 g"Behold, my servant whom I have chosen,
my beloved in whom I delight;
I shall place my spirit upon him,

11, 28–29: These verses are peculiar to Matthew and are similar to Ben Sirach's invitation to learn wisdom and submit to her yoke (Sir 51, 23.26).

11, 28: Who labor and are burdened: burdened by the law as expounded by the scribes and Pharisees (23, 4).

11, 29: In place of the yoke of the law, complicated by scribal interpretation, Jesus invites the burdened to take the yoke of obedience to his word, under which they **will find rest;** cf Jer 6, 16.

12, 1–14: Matthew here returns to the Marcan order that he left in 9, 18. The two stories depend on Mk 2, 23–28 and 3, 1–6, respectively, and are the only places in either gospel that deal explicitly with Jesus' attitude toward sabbath observance.

12, 1–2: The picking of the heads of grain is here equated with reaping, which was forbidden on the sabbath (Ex 34, 21).

12, 3–4: See 1 Sm 21, 2–7. In the Marcan parallel (2, 25–26) the high priest is mistakenly called Abiathar, although in 1 Sm this action is attributed to Ahimelech. The Old Testament story is not about a violation of the sabbath rest; its pertinence to this dispute is that a violation of the law was permissible because of David's men being without food.

12, 5–6: This and the following argument (7) are peculiar to Matthew. The temple service seems to be the changing of the showbread on the sabbath (Lv 24, 8) and the doubling on the sabbath of the usual daily holocausts (Nm 28, 9–10). The argument is that the law itself requires work that breaks the sabbath rest, because of the higher duty of temple service. If temple duties outweigh the sabbath law, how much more does the presence of Jesus, with his proclamation of the kingdom (**something greater than the temple**), justify the conduct of his disciples.

12, 7: See the note on 9, 13.

12, 8: The ultimate justification for the disciples' violation of the sabbath rest is that Jesus, the Son of Man, has supreme authority over the law.

12, 10: Rabbinic tradition later than the gospels allowed relief to be given to a sufferer on the sabbath if life was in danger. This may also have been the view of Jesus' Pharisaic contemporaries. But the case here is not about one in danger of death.

12, 11: Matthew omits the question posed by Jesus in Mk 3, 4 and substitutes one about rescuing a sheep on the sabbath, similar to that in Lk 14, 5.

12, 14: See Mk 3, 6. Here the plan to bring about Jesus' death is attributed to the Pharisees only. This is probably due to the situation of Matthew's church, when the sole opponents were the Pharisees.

12, 15–21: Matthew follows Mk 3, 7–12 but summarizes his source in two verses (15.16) that pick up the withdrawal, the healings, and the command for silence. To this he adds a fulfillment citation from the first Servant Song (Is 42, 1–4) that does not correspond exactly to either the Hebrew or the LXX of that passage. It is the longest Old Testament citation in this gospel, emphasizing the meekness of Jesus, the Servant of the Lord, and foretelling the extension of his mission to the Gentiles.

12, 15: Jesus' knowledge of the Pharisees' plot and his healing **all** are peculiar to Matthew.

w Sir 51, 26; Jer 6, 16. x Mk 2, 23–28; Lk 6, 1–5. y Dt 23, 26. z 1 Sm 21, 2–7. a Lv 24, 5–9. b Lv 24, 8; Nm 28, 9–10. c Hos 6, 6. d Jn 5, 16–17. e Mk 3, 1–6; Lk 6, 6–11. f Jn 5, 18. g Is 42, 1–4.

and he will proclaim justice to the Gentiles.
19 *He will not contend or cry out,
nor will anyone hear his voice in the streets.
20 A bruised reed he will not break,
a smoldering wick he will not quench,
until he brings justice to victory.
21 *And in his name the Gentiles will hope."

Jesus and Beelzebul 22 h*Then they brought
to him a demoniac who was blind and mute.
He cured the mute person so that he could
speak and see. 23 i*All the crowd was as-
tounded, and said, "Could this perhaps be the
Son of David?" 24 j*But when the Pharisees
heard this, they said, "This man drives out
demons only by the power of Beelzebul, the
prince of demons." 25 k*But he knew what they
were thinking and said to them, "Every king-
dom divided against itself will be laid waste,
and no town or house divided against itself will
stand. 26 And if Satan drives out Satan, he is
divided against himself; how, then, will his
kingdom stand? 27 *And if I drive out demons
by Beelzebul, by whom do your own people
drive them out? Therefore they will be your
judges. 28 l*But if it is by the Spirit of God that I
drive out demons, then the kingdom of God
has come upon you. 29 *How can anyone enter
a strong man's house and steal his property,
unless he first ties up the strong man? Then he
can plunder his house. 30 m*Whoever is not
with me is against me, and whoever does not
gather with me scatters. 31 n*Therefore, I say to
you, every sin and blasphemy will be forgiven
people, but blasphemy against the Spirit will
not be forgiven. 32 And whoever speaks a word
against the Son of Man will be forgiven; but
whoever speaks against the holy Spirit will not
be forgiven, either in this age or in the age to
come.

A Tree and Its Fruits 33 o*"Either declare the
tree good and its fruit is good, or declare the tree
rotten and its fruit is rotten, for a tree is known
by its fruit. 34 p*You brood of vipers, how can
you say good things when you are evil? For from
the fullness of the heart the mouth speaks. 35 A
good person brings forth good out of a store of
goodness, but an evil person brings forth evil out
of a store of evil. 36 q*I tell you, on the day of
judgment people will render an account for
every careless word they speak. 37 By your words
you will be acquitted, and by your words you
will be condemned."

12, 19: The servant's not contending is seen as fulfilled in Jesus' withdrawal from the disputes narrated in 1–14.

12, 21: Except for a minor detail, Matthew here follows the LXX, although the meaning of the Hebrew ("the coastlands will wait for his teaching") is similar.

12, 22–32: For the exorcism, see the note on 9, 32–34. The long discussion combines Marcan and Q material (Mk 3, 22–30; Lk 11, 19–20.23; 12, 10). Mk 3, 20–21 is omitted, with a consequent lessening of the sharpness of 12, 48.

12, 23: See the note on 9, 27.

12, 24: See the note on 10, 25.

12, 25–26: Jesus' first response to the Pharisees' charge is that if it were true, Satan would be destroying his own kingdom.

12, 27: Besides pointing out the absurdity of the charge, Jesus asks how the work of Jewish exorcists (**your own people**) is to be interpreted. Are they, too, to be charged with collusion with Beelzebul? For an example of Jewish exorcism see Josephus, **Antiquities** 8, 2, 5 §§42–49.

12, 28: The Q parallel (Lk 11, 20) speaks of the "finger" rather than of the "spirit" of God. While the difference is probably due to Matthew's editing, he retains **the kingdom of God** rather than changing it to his usual "kingdom of heaven." **Has come upon you:** see 4, 17.

12, 29: A short parable illustrates what Jesus is doing. The **strong man** is Satan, whom Jesus has tied up and whose **house** he is plundering. Jewish expectation was that Satan would be chained up in the last days (Rv 20, 2); Jesus' exorcisms indicate that those days have begun.

12, 30: This saying, already attached to the preceding verses in Q (see Lk 11, 23), warns that there can be no neutrality where Jesus is concerned. Its pertinence in a context where Jesus is addressing not the neutral but the bitterly opposed is not clear. The accusation of scattering, however, does fit the situation. Jesus is the shepherd of God's people (2, 6), his mission is to the lost sheep of Israel (15, 24); the Pharisees, who oppose him, are guilty of scattering the sheep.

12, 31: Blasphemy against the Spirit: the sin of attributing to Satan (24) what is the work of the Spirit of God (28).

12, 33: Declare: literally, "make." The meaning of this verse is obscure. Possibly it is a challenge to the Pharisees either to declare Jesus and his exorcisms good or both of them bad. A tree is known by its fruit; if the fruit is good, so must the tree be. If the driving out of demons is good, so must its source be.

12, 34: The admission of Jesus' goodness cannot be made by the Pharisees, for they are evil, and the words that proceed from their evil hearts cannot be good.

12, 36–37: If on the day of judgment people will be held accountable for even their **careless** words, the vicious accusations of the Pharisees will surely lead to their condemnation.

h 9, 32–34; Lk 11, 14–15. i 9, 27. j 10, 25; Mk 3, 22. k Mk 3, 23–27; Lk 11, 17–22. l Lk 11, 20. m Lk 11, 23. n Mk 3, 28–30; Lk 12, 10. o Lk 6, 43–45. p 3, 7; 23, 33; 15, 11–12; Lk 3, 7. q Jas 3, 1–2.

The Demand for a Sign [38][r]*Then some of the scribes and Pharisees said to him, "Teacher, we wish to see a sign from you." [39]*He said to them in reply, "An evil and unfaithful generation seeks a sign, but no sign will be given it except the sign of Jonah the prophet. [40]*Just as Jonah was in the belly of the whale three days and three nights, so will the Son of Man be in the heart of the earth three days and three nights. [41]*At the judgment, the men of Nineveh will arise with this generation and condemn it, because they repented at the preaching of Jonah; and there is something greater than Jonah here. [42][s]At the judgment the queen of the south will arise with this generation and condemn it, because she came from the ends of the earth to hear the wisdom of Solomon; and there is something greater than Solomon here.

The Return of the Unclean Spirit [43][t]*"When an unclean spirit goes out of a person it roams through arid regions searching for rest but finds none. [44]Then it says, 'I will return to my home from which I came.' But upon returning, it finds it empty, swept clean, and put in order. [45]Then it goes and brings back with itself seven other spirits more evil than itself, and they move in and dwell there; and the last condition of that person is worse than the first. Thus it will be with this evil generation."

The True Family of Jesus [46][u]*While he was still speaking to the crowds, his mother and his brothers appeared outside, wishing to speak with him. [[47]*Someone told him, "Your mother and your brothers are standing outside, asking to speak with you."] [48]But he said in reply to the one who told him, "Who is my mother? Who are my brothers?" [49]And stretching out his hand toward his disciples, he said, "Here are my mother and my brothers. [50]For whoever does the will of my heavenly Father is my brother, and sister, and mother."

CHAPTER 13

The Parable of the Sower [1][v]*On that day, Jesus went out of the house and sat down by the sea. [2]Such large crowds gathered around him that he got into a boat and sat down, and the whole crowd stood along the shore. [3]*And he

12, 38–42: This section is mainly from Q (see Lk 11, 29–32). Mk 8, 11–12, which Matthew has followed in 16, 1–4, has a similar demand for a sign. The scribes and Pharisees refuse to accept the exorcisms of Jesus as authentication of his claims and demand a sign that will end all possibility of doubt. Jesus' response is that no such sign will be given. Because his opponents are evil and see him as an agent of Satan, nothing will convince them.

12, 38: **Teacher:** see the note on 8, 19. In 16, 1 the request is for a sign "from heaven" (Mk 8, 11).

12, 39: **Unfaithful:** literally, "adulterous." The covenant between God and Israel was portrayed as a marriage bond, and unfaithfulness to the covenant as adultery; cf Hos 2, 4–15; Jer 3, 6–10.

12, 40: See Jon 2, 1. While in Q the sign was simply Jonah's preaching to the Ninevites (Lk 11, 30.32), Matthew here adds Jonah's sojourn **in the belly of the whale** for **three days and three nights,** a prefigurement of Jesus' sojourn in the abode of the dead and, implicitly, of his resurrection.

12, 41–42: The Ninevites who **repented** (see Jon 3, 1–10) and **the queen of the south** (i.e., of Sheba; see 1 Kgs 10, 1–13) were pagans who responded to lesser opportunities than have been offered to Israel in the ministry of Jesus, **something greater than Jonah** or **Solomon.** At the final judgment they will condemn the faithless **generation** that has rejected him.

12, 43–45: Another Q passage; cf 11, 24–26. Jesus' ministry has broken Satan's hold over Israel, but the refusal of **this evil generation** to accept him will lead to a worse situation than what preceded his coming.

12, 46–50: See Mk 3, 31–35. Matthew has omitted Mk 3, 20–21, which is taken up in Mk 3, 31 (see the note on 12, 22–32), yet the point of the story is the same in both gospels: natural kinship with Jesus counts for nothing; only one who **does the will of his heavenly Father** belongs to his true family.

12, 47: This verse is omitted in some important textual witnesses, including Codex Sinaiticus (original reading) and Codex Vaticanus.

13, 1–53: The discourse in parables is the third great discourse of Jesus in Mt and constitutes the second part of the third book of the gospel. Matthew follows the Marcan outline (Mk 4, 1–35) but has only two of Mark's parables, the five others being from Q and M. In addition to the seven parables, the discourse gives the reason why Jesus uses this type of speech (10–15), declares the blessedness of those who understand his teaching (16–17), explains the parable of the sower (18–23) and of the weeds (36–43), and ends with a concluding statement to the disciples (51–52).

13, 3: **In parables:** the word "parable" (Greek **parabolē**) is used in the LXX to translate the Hebrew **māshāl,** a designation covering a wide variety of literary forms such as axioms, proverbs, similitudes, and allegories. In the New Testament the same breadth of meaning of the word is found, but there it primarily designates stories that are illustrative comparisons between Christian truths and events of everyday life. Sometimes the event has a strange element that is quite different from usual experience (e.g., in v 33, the enormous amount of dough in the parable of the yeast); this is meant to sharpen the curiosity of the hearer. If each detail of such a story is given a figurative meaning, the story is an allegory. Those who maintain a sharp distinction between parable and allegory insist that a parable has only one point of comparison, and that while parables were characteristic of Jesus' teaching, to see allegorical details in them is to introduce meanings that go beyond their original intention and even falsify it. However, to exclude any allegorical elements from a parable is an excessively rigid mode of interpretation, now abandoned by many scholars.

13, 3–8: Since in Palestine sowing often preceded plowing, much of the seed is scattered on ground that is unsuitable. Yet while much is wasted, the seed that falls on good ground bears

r 16, 1–4; Jon 2, 1; 3, 1–10; Mk 8, 11–12; Lk 11, 29–32. s 1 Kgs 10, 1–10. t Lk 11, 24–26. u Mk 3, 31–35; Lk 8, 19–21. v Mk 4, 1–12; Lk 8, 4–10.

spoke to them at length in parables, saying: "A sower went out to sow. [4]And as he sowed, some seed fell on the path, and birds came and ate it up. [5]Some fell on rocky ground, where it had little soil. It sprang up at once because the soil was not deep, [6]and when the sun rose it was scorched, and it withered for lack of roots. [7]Some seed fell among thorns, and the thorns grew up and choked it. [8]But some seed fell on rich soil, and produced fruit, a hundred or sixty or thirtyfold. [9]Whoever has ears ought to hear."

The Purpose of Parables [10]The disciples approached him and said, "Why do you speak to them in parables?" [11]*He said to them in reply, "Because knowledge of the mysteries of the kingdom of heaven has been granted to you, but to them it has not been granted. [12 w]*To anyone who has, more will be given and he will grow rich; from anyone who has not, even what he has will be taken away. [13 x]*This is why I speak to them in parables, because 'they look but do not see and hear but do not listen or understand.' [14 y]Isaiah's prophecy is fulfilled in them, which says:

'You shall indeed hear but not understand,
you shall indeed look but never see.
[15]Gross is the heart of this people,
they will hardly hear with their ears,
they have closed their eyes,
lest they see with their eyes
and hear with their ears
and understand with their heart and be converted
and I heal them.'

The Privilege of Discipleship [16 z]*"But blessed are your eyes, because they see, and your ears, because they hear. [17]Amen, I say to you, many prophets and righteous people longed to see what you see but did not see it, and to hear what you hear but did not hear it.

The Explanation of the Parable of the Sower [18 a]*"Hear then the parable of the sower. [19]The seed sown on the path is the one who hears the word of the kingdom without understanding it, and the evil one comes and steals away what was sown in his heart. [20]The seed sown on rocky ground is the one who hears the word and receives it at once with joy. [21]But he has no root and lasts only for a time. When some tribulation or persecution comes because of the word, he immediately falls away. [22]The seed sown among thorns is the one who hears the word, but then worldly anxiety and the lure of riches choke the word and it bears no fruit. [23]But the seed sown on rich soil is the one who

---

fruit in extraordinarily large measure. The point of the parable is that, in spite of some failure because of opposition and indifference, the message of Jesus about the coming of the kingdom will have enormous success.

13, 11: Since a parable is figurative speech that demands reflection for understanding, only those who are prepared to explore its meaning can come to know it. To understand is a gift of God, granted to the disciples but not to the crowds. In Semitic fashion, both the disciples' understanding and the crowd's obtuseness are attributed to God. The question of human responsibility for the obtuseness is not dealt with, although it is asserted in v 13. **The mysteries:** as in Lk 8, 10; Mk 4, 11 has "the mystery." The word is used in Dn 2, 18.19.27 and in the Qumran literature (1QpHab 7, 8; 1QS 3, 23; 1QM 3, 9) to designate a divine plan or decree affecting the course of history that can be known only when revealed. **Knowledge of the mysteries of the kingdom of heaven** means recognition that the kingdom has become present in the ministry of Jesus.

13, 12: In the New Testament use of this axiom of practical "wisdom" (see 25, 29; Mk 4, 25; Lk 8, 18; 19, 26), the reference transcends the original level. God gives further understanding to one who accepts the revealed mystery; from the one who does not, he will take it away (note the "theological passive," **more will be given, what he has will be taken away**).

13, 13: Because 'they look . . . or understand': Matthew softens his Marcan source, which states that Jesus speaks in parables so that the crowds may not understand (Mk 4, 12), and makes such speaking a punishment given **because** they have not accepted his previous clear teaching. However, his citation of Is 6, 9–10 in v 14 supports the harsher Marcan view.

13, 16–17: Unlike the unbelieving crowds, the disciples have seen that which the **prophets** and the **righteous** of the Old Testament **longed to see** without having their longing fulfilled.

13, 18–23: See Mk 4, 14–20; Lk 8, 11–15. In this explanation of the parable the emphasis is on the various types of soil on which the seed falls, i.e., on the dispositions with which the preaching of Jesus is received. The second and third types particularly are explained in such a way as to support the view held by many scholars that the explanation derives not from Jesus but from early Christian reflection upon apostasy from the faith that was the consequence of persecution and worldliness respectively. Others, however, hold that the explanation may come basically from Jesus even though it was developed in the light of later Christian experience. The four types of persons envisaged are (1) those who never accept **the word of the kingdom** (19); (2) those who believe for a while but fall away because of **persecution** (20–21); (3) those who believe, but in whom **the word** is choked by **worldly anxiety** and the seduction of **riches** (22); (4) those who respond to **the word** and produce **fruit** abundantly (23).

w 25, 29; Mk 4, 25; Lk 8, 18; 19, 26. x Jn 9, 39. y Is 6, 9–10; Jn 12, 40; Acts 28, 26–27; Rom 11, 8. z Lk 10, 23–24; 1 Pt 1, 10–12. a Mk 4, 13–20; Lk 8, 11–15.

hears the word and understands it, who indeed bears fruit and yields a hundred or sixty or thirtyfold."

The Parable of the Weeds among the Wheat 24*He proposed another parable to them. "The kingdom of heaven may be likened to a man who sowed good seed in his field. 25*While everyone was asleep his enemy came and sowed weeds all through the wheat, and then went off. 26When the crop grew and bore fruit, the weeds appeared as well. 27The slaves of the householder came to him and said, 'Master, did you not sow good seed in your field? Where have the weeds come from?' 28He answered, 'An enemy has done this.' His slaves said to him, 'Do you want us to go and pull them up?' 29He replied, 'No, if you pull up the weeds you might uproot the wheat along with them. 30 b*Let them grow together until harvest; then at harvest time I will say to the harvesters, "First collect the weeds and tie them in bundles for burning; but gather the wheat into my barn." ' "

The Parable of the Mustard Seed 31 c*He proposed another parable to them. "The kingdom of heaven is like a mustard seed that a person took and sowed in a field. 32 d*It is the smallest of all the seeds, yet when full-grown it is the largest of plants. It becomes a large bush, and the 'birds of the sky come and dwell in its branches.' "

The Parable of the Yeast 33 e*He spoke to them another parable. "The kingdom of heaven is like yeast that a woman took and mixed with three measures of wheat flour until the whole batch was leavened."

The Use of Parables 34 f*All these things Jesus spoke to the crowds in parables. He spoke to them only in parables, 35 g*to fulfill what had been said through the prophet:

"I will open my mouth in parables,
I will announce what has lain hidden from
the foundation [of the world]."

The Explanation of the Parable of the Weeds 36*Then, dismissing the crowds, he went into the house. His disciples approached him and said, "Explain to us the parable of the weeds in the field." 37*He said in reply, "He who sows good seed is the Son of Man, 38*the field is the world, the good seed the children of the kingdom. The weeds are the children of the evil one, 39*and the enemy who sows them is the devil. The harvest is the end of the age, and the harvesters are angels. 40Just as weeds are collected and burned [up] with fire, so will it be at the end of the age. 41*The Son of Man will

13, 24–30: This parable is peculiar to Matthew. The comparison in v 24 does not mean that **the kingdom of heaven may be likened** simply to the person in question but to the situation narrated in the whole story. The refusal of **the householder** to allow his **slaves** to separate **the wheat** from **the weeds** while they are still growing is a warning to the disciples not to attempt to anticipate the final judgment of God by a definitive exclusion of sinners from the kingdom. In its present stage it is composed of the good and the bad. The judgment of God alone will eliminate the sinful. Until then there must be patience and the preaching of repentance.

13, 25: **Weeds:** darnel, a poisonous weed that in its first stage of growth resembles wheat.

13, 30: **Harvest:** a common biblical metaphor for the time of God's judgment; cf Jer 51, 33; Jl 4, 13; Hos 6, 11.

13, 31–33: See Mk 4, 30–32; Lk 13, 18–21. The parables of the mustard seed and the yeast illustrate the same point: the amazing contrast between the small beginnings of the kingdom and its marvelous expansion.

13, 32: See Dn 4, 7–9.17–19, where the birds nesting in the tree represent the people of Nebuchadnezzar's kingdom. See also Ez 17, 23 and 31, 6.

13, 33: Except in this Q parable and in 16, 12, **yeast** (or "leaven") is, in New Testament usage, a symbol of corruption (see 16, 6.11–12; Mk 8, 15; Lk 12, 1; 1 Cor 5, 6–8; Gal 5, 9). **Three measures:** an enormous amount, enough to feed a hundred people. The exaggeration of this element of the parable points to the greatness of the kingdom's effect.

13, 34: **Only in parables:** see vv 10–15.

13, 35: **The prophet:** some textual witnesses read "Isaiah the prophet." The quotation is actually from Ps 78, 2; the first line corresponds to the LXX text of the psalm. The psalm's title ascribes it to Asaph, the founder of one of the guilds of temple musicians. He is called "the prophet" (NAB "the seer") in 2 Chr 29, 30, but it is doubtful that Matthew averted to that; for him, any Old Testament text that could be seen as fulfilled in Jesus was prophetic.

13, 36: **Dismissing the crowds:** the return of Jesus to the house marks a break with the crowds, who represent unbelieving Israel. From now on his attention is directed more and more to his disciples and to their instruction. The rest of the discourse is addressed to them alone.

13, 37–43: In the explanation of the parable of the weeds emphasis lies on the fearful end of the wicked, whereas the parable itself concentrates on patience with them until judgment time.

13, 38: **The field is the world:** this presupposes the resurrection of Jesus and the granting to him of "all power in heaven and on earth" (28, 18).

13, 39: **The end of the age:** this phrase is found only in Mt (13, 40.49; 24, 3; 28, 20).

13, 41: **His kingdom:** the **kingdom** of the Son of Man is distin-

b 3, 12. c Mk 4, 30–32; Lk 13, 18–19. d Ez 17, 23; 31, 6; Dn 4, 7–9.17–19. e Lk 13, 20–21. f Mk 4, 33–34. g Ps 78, 2.

send his angels, and they will collect out of his kingdom all who cause others to sin and all evildoers. 42 [h]They will throw them into the fiery furnace, where there will be wailing and grinding of teeth. 43 [i]*Then the righteous will shine like the sun in the kingdom of their Father. Whoever has ears ought to hear.

More Parables 44 [j]*"The kingdom of heaven is like a treasure buried in a field, which a person finds and hides again, and out of joy goes and sells all that he has and buys that field. 45 Again, the kingdom of heaven is like a merchant searching for fine pearls. 46 When he finds a pearl of great price, he goes and sells all that he has and buys it. 47 Again, the kingdom of heaven is like a net thrown into the sea, which collects fish of every kind. 48 When it is full they haul it ashore and sit down to put what is good into buckets. What is bad they throw away. 49 Thus it will be at the end of the age. The angels will go out and separate the wicked from the righteous 50 and throw them into the fiery furnace, where there will be wailing and grinding of teeth.

Treasures New and Old 51 *"Do you understand all these things?" They answered, "Yes." 52 *And he replied, "Then every scribe who has been instructed in the kingdom of heaven is like the head of a household who brings from his storeroom both the new and the old." 53 When Jesus finished these parables, he went away from there.

V: Jesus, the Kingdom, and the Church

The Rejection at Nazareth 54 [k l]*He came to his native place and taught the people in their synagogue. They were astonished and said, "Where did this man get such wisdom and mighty deeds? 55 [m]Is he not the carpenter's son? Is not his mother named Mary and his brothers James, Joseph, Simon, and Judas? 56 Are not his sisters all with us? Where did this man get all this?" 57 [n]And they took offense at him. But Jesus said to them, "A prophet is not without honor except in his native place and in his own house." 58 And he did not work many mighty deeds there because of their lack of faith.

CHAPTER 14

Herod's Opinion of Jesus 1 [o p q]*At that time Herod the tetrarch heard of the reputation of

guished from that of the Father (43); see 1 Cor 15, 24–25. The church is the place where Jesus' kingdom is manifested, but his royal authority embraces the entire world; see the note on 13, 38.

13, 43: See Dn 12, 3.

13, 44–50: The first two of the last three parables of the discourse have the same point. The **person** who **finds** a buried **treasure** and the **merchant** who finds a **pearl of great price** sell **all** that they have to acquire these finds; similarly, the one who understands the supreme value of the kingdom gives up whatever he must to obtain it. The **joy** with which this is done is made explicit in the first parable, but it may be presumed in the second also. The concluding parable of the fishnet resembles the explanation of the parable of the weeds with its stress upon the final exclusion of evil persons from the kingdom.

13, 44: In the unsettled conditions of Palestine in Jesus' time, it was not unusual to guard valuables by burying them in the ground.

13, 51: Matthew typically speaks of the understanding of the disciples.

13, 52: Since Matthew tends to identify the disciples and the Twelve (see the note on 10, 1), this saying about the Christian **scribe** cannot be taken as applicable to all who accept the message of Jesus. While the Twelve are in many ways representative of all who believe in him, they are also distinguished from them in certain respects. The church of Matthew has leaders among whom are a group designated as "scribes" (23, 34). Like the scribes of Israel, they are teachers. It is the Twelve and these their later counterparts to whom this verse applies. The **scribe . . . instructed in the kingdom of heaven** knows both the teaching of Jesus (**the new**) and the law and prophets (**the old**) and provides in his own teaching **both the new and the old** as interpreted and fulfilled by **the new.** On the translation **head of a household** (for the same Greek word translated **householder** in v 27), see the note on 24, 45–51.

13, 54—17, 27: This section is the narrative part of the fourth book of the gospel.

13, 54–58: After the Sermon on the Mount the crowds are in admiring astonishment at Jesus' teaching (7, 28); here the astonishment is of those who take **offense at him.** Familiarity with his background and family leads them to regard him as pretentious. Matthew modifies his Marcan source (6, 1–6). Jesus is not the carpenter but **the carpenter's son** (55), "and among his own kin" is omitted (57), **he did not work many mighty deeds** in face of such unbelief (58) rather than the Marcan " . . . he was not able to perform any mighty deed there" (6, 5), and there is no mention of his amazement at his townspeople's lack of faith.

14, 1–12: The murder of the Baptist by Herod Antipas prefigures the death of Jesus (see 17, 12). The Marcan source (6, 14–29) is much reduced and in some points changed. In Mk Herod reveres John as a holy man and the desire to kill him is attributed to Herodias (6, 19.20), whereas here that desire is Herod's from the beginning (5).

14, 1: Herod the tetrarch: Herod Antipas, son of Herod the Great. When the latter died, his territory was divided among three of his surviving sons, Archelaus who received half of it (2, 23), Herod Antipas who became ruler of Galilee and Perea, and Philip who became ruler of northern Transjordan. Since he received a quarter of his father's domain, Antipas is accurately designated **tetrarch** ("ruler of a fourth [part]"), although in v 9 Matthew repeats the "king" of his Marcan source (6, 26).

h 8, 12; Rv 21, 8. i Dn 12, 3. j Prv 2, 4; 4, 7. k Mk 6, 1–6; Lk 4, 16–30. l 2, 23; Jn 1, 46; 7, 15. m 12, 46; 27, 56; Jn 6, 42. n Jn 4, 44. o Mk 6, 14–29. p Lk 3, 1. q Lk 9, 7–9.

Jesus [2]and said to his servants, "This man is John the Baptist. He has been raised from the dead; that is why mighty powers are at work in him."

The Death of John the Baptist [3] [r]*Now Herod had arrested John, bound [him], and put him in prison on account of Herodias, the wife of his brother Philip, [4] [s]for John had said to him, "It is not lawful for you to have her." [5] [t]Although he wanted to kill him, he feared the people, for they regarded him as a prophet. [6]But at a birthday celebration for Herod, the daughter of Herodias performed a dance before the guests and delighted Herod [7]so much that he swore to give her whatever she might ask for. [8]Prompted by her mother, she said, "Give me here on a platter the head of John the Baptist." [9]The king was distressed, but because of his oaths and the guests who were present, he ordered that it be given, [10]and he had John beheaded in the prison. [11]His head was brought in on a platter and given to the girl, who took it to her mother. [12]His disciples came and took away the corpse and buried him; and they went and told Jesus.

The Return of the Twelve and the Feeding of the Five Thousand [13] [u]*When Jesus heard of it, he withdrew in a boat to a deserted place by himself. The crowds heard of this and followed him on foot from their towns. [14]When he disembarked and saw the vast crowd, his heart was moved with pity for them, and he cured their sick. [15]When it was evening, the disciples approached him and said, "This is a deserted place and it is already late; dismiss the crowds so that they can go to the villages and buy food for themselves." [16][Jesus] said to them, "There is no need for them to go away; give them some food yourselves." [17]But they said to him, "Five loaves and two fish are all we have here." [18]Then he said, "Bring them here to me," [19]*and he ordered the crowds to sit down on the grass. Taking the five loaves and the two fish, and looking up to heaven, he said the blessing, broke the loaves, and gave them to the disciples, who in turn gave them to the crowds. [20]*They all ate and were satisfied, and they picked up the fragments left over—twelve wicker baskets full. [21]Those who ate were about five thousand men, not counting women and children.

The Walking on the Water [22] [v]*Then he made the disciples get into the boat and precede him to the other side, while he dismissed the crowds. [23] [w]After doing so, he went up on the mountain by himself to pray. When it was evening he was there alone. [24]Meanwhile the boat, already a few miles offshore, was being tossed about by the waves, for the wind was against it. [25]*During the fourth watch of the night, he came toward them, walking on the sea. [26]When the disciples saw him walking on the sea they were terrified. "It is a ghost," they said, and they cried out in fear. [27]*At once [Jesus] spoke to them, "Take courage, it is I; do not be afraid." [28]Peter said to him in reply, "Lord, if it is you, command me to come to you

14, 3: Herodias was not the wife of Herod's half-brother Philip but of another half-brother, Herod Boethus. The union was prohibited by Lv 18, 16; 20, 21. According to Josephus (**Antiquities** 18, 5, 2 §§116–19), Herod imprisoned and then executed John because he feared that the Baptist's influence over the people might enable him to lead a rebellion.

14, 13–21: The feeding of the five thousand is the only miracle of Jesus that is recounted in all four gospels. The principal reason for that may be that it was seen as anticipating the Eucharist and the final banquet in the kingdom (8, 11; 26, 29), but it looks not only forward but backward, to the feeding of Israel with manna in the desert at the time of the Exodus (Ex 16), a miracle that in some contemporary Jewish expectation would be repeated in the messianic age (2 Baruch 29, 8). It may also be meant to recall Elisha's feeding a hundred men with small provisions (2 Kgs 4, 42–44).

14, 19: The **taking,** saying the blessing, breaking, and giving to the disciples correspond to the actions of Jesus over the bread at the Last Supper (26, 26). Since they were usual at any Jewish meal, that correspondence does not necessarily indicate a eucharistic reference here. Matthew's silence about Jesus' dividing the fish among the people (Mk 6, 41) is perhaps more significant in that regard.

14, 20: The fragments left over: as in Elisha's miracle, food was **left over** after all had been fed. The word **fragments** (Greek **klasmata**) is used, in the singular, of the broken bread of the Eucharist in **Didache** 9, 3–4.

14, 22–33: The disciples, laboring against the turbulent sea, are saved by Jesus. For his power over the waters, see the note on 8, 26. Here that power is expressed also by his **walking on the sea** (25; cf Ps 77, 20; Jb 9, 8). Matthew has inserted into the Marcan story (Mk 6, 45–52) material that belongs to his special traditions on Peter (28–31).

14, 25: The fourth watch of the night: between 3 a.m. and 6 a.m. The Romans divided the twelve hours between 6 p.m. and 6 a.m. into four equal parts called "watches."

14, 27: It is I: see the note on Mk 6, 50.

r Lk 3, 19–20. s Lv 18, 16; 20, 21. t 21, 26. u 15, 32–38; Mk 6, 32–44; Lk 9, 10–17; Jn 6, 1–13. v Mk 6, 45–52; Jn 6, 16–21. w Mk 1, 35; Lk 5, 16; 6, 12.

on the water." [29]He said, "Come." Peter got out
of the boat and began to walk on the water
toward Jesus. [30][x]*But when he saw how [strong]
the wind was he became frightened; and, begin-
ning to sink, he cried out, "Lord, save me!"
[31]*Immediately Jesus stretched out his hand and
caught him, and said to him, "O you of little
faith, why did you doubt?" [32]After they got into
the boat, the wind died down. [33][y]*Those who
were in the boat did him homage, saying, "Truly,
you are the Son of God."

The Healings at Gennesaret [34][z]After making
the crossing, they came to land at Gennesaret.
[35]When the men of that place recognized him,
they sent word to all the surrounding country.
People brought to him all those who were sick
[36][a]and begged him that they might touch only
the tassel on his cloak, and as many as touched it
were healed.

CHAPTER 15

The Tradition of the Elders [1][b]*Then Phari-
sees and scribes came to Jesus from Jerusalem
and said, [2][c]*"Why do your disciples break the
tradition of the elders? They do not wash [their]
hands when they eat a meal." [3]*He said to them
in reply, "And why do you break the command-
ment of God for the sake of your tradition? [4][d]For
God said, 'Honor your father and your mother,'
and 'Whoever curses father or mother shall die.'
[5]*But you say, 'Whoever says to father or
mother, "Any support you might have had from
me is dedicated to God," [6]need not honor his
father.' You have nullified the word of God for
the sake of your tradition. [7]Hypocrites, well did
Isaiah prophesy about you when he said:

[8][e]*'This people honors me with their lips,
but their hearts are far from me;
[9][f]in vain do they worship me,
teaching as doctrines human precepts.' "

[10][g]He summoned the crowd and said to them,
"Hear and understand. [11]It is not what enters
one's mouth that defiles that person; but what
comes out of the mouth is what defiles one."
[12]Then his disciples approached and said to him,
"Do you know that the Pharisees took offense
when they heard what you said?" [13]*He said in
reply, "Every plant that my heavenly Father has
not planted will be uprooted. [14][h]Let them alone;
they are blind guides [of the blind]. If a blind
person leads a blind person, both will fall into a
pit." [15]*Then Peter said to him in reply, "Ex-
plain [this] parable to us." [16]He said to them,
"Are even you still without understanding? [17]Do
you not realize that everything that enters the
mouth passes into the stomach and is expelled
into the latrine? [18][i]But the things that come out
of the mouth come from the heart, and they

14, 31: You of little faith: see the note on 6, 30. **Why did you doubt?:** the verb is peculiar to Matthew and occurs elsewhere only in 28, 17.

14, 33: This confession is in striking contrast to the Marcan parallel (6, 51) where the disciples are "completely astounded."

15, 1–20: This dispute begins with the question of the Pharisees and scribes why Jesus' disciples are breaking **the tradition of the elders** about washing one's hands before eating (2). Jesus' counterquestion accuses his opponents of breaking **the commandment of God for the sake of** their **tradition** (3) and illustrates this by their interpretation of the commandment of the Decalogue concerning parents (4–6). Denouncing them as hypocrites, he applies to them a derogatory prophecy of Isaiah (7–8). Then with a wider audience (**the crowd,** 10) he goes beyond the violation of tradition with which the dispute has started. The parable (11) is an attack on the Mosaic law concerning clean and unclean foods, similar to those antitheses that abrogate the law (5, 31–32.33–34.38–39). After a warning to his disciples not to follow the moral guidance of the Pharisees (13–14), he explains the **parable** (**15**) to them, saying that defilement comes not from what **enters the mouth** (17) but from the evil thoughts and deeds that rise from within, **from the heart** (18–20). The last verse returns to the starting point of the dispute (eating **with unwashed hands**). Because of Matthew's omission of Mk 7, 19b, some scholars think that Matthew has weakened the Marcan repudiation of the Mosaic food laws. But that half verse is ambiguous in the Greek, which may be the reason for its omission here.

15, 2: The tradition of the elders: see the note on Mk 7, 5. The purpose of the handwashing was to remove defilement caused by contact with what was ritually unclean.

15, 3–4: For the commandment see Ex 20, 12 (// Dt 5, 16); 21, 17. The honoring of one's parents had to do with supporting them in their needs.

15, 5: See the note on Mk 7, 11.

15, 8: The text of Is 29, 13 is quoted approximately according to the Septuagint.

15, 13–14: Jesus leads his disciples away from the teaching authority of the Pharisees.

15, 15: Matthew specifies **Peter** as the questioner, unlike Mk 7, 17. Given his tendency to present the disciples as more understanding than in his Marcan source, it is noteworthy that here he retains the Marcan rebuke, although in a slightly milder form. This may be due to his wish to correct the Jewish Christians within his church who still held to the food laws and thus separated themselves from Gentile Christians who did not observe them.

x 8, 25–26. y 16, 16. z Mk 6, 53–56. a 9, 20–22. b Mk 7, 1–23. c Lk 11, 38. d Ex 20, 12; 21, 17; Lv 20, 9; Dt 5, 16; Prv 20, 20. e Is 29, 13 LXX. f Col 2, 23. g Mk 7, 14. h 23, 16.19.24; Lk 6, 39; Jn 9, 40. i 12, 34.

defile. 19*For from the heart come evil thoughts,
murder, adultery, unchastity, theft, false witness,
blasphemy. 20These are what defile a person, but
to eat with unwashed hands does not defile."

The Canaanite Woman's Faith 21 j*Then Je-
sus went from that place and withdrew to the
region of Tyre and Sidon. 22And behold, a
Canaanite woman of that district came and
called out, "Have pity on me, Lord, Son of
David! My daughter is tormented by a demon."
23But he did not say a word in answer to her. His
disciples came and asked him, "Send her away,
for she keeps calling out after us." 24*He said in
reply, "I was sent only to the lost sheep of the
house of Israel." 25 kBut the woman came and
did him homage, saying, "Lord, help me." 26*He
said in reply, "It is not right to take the food of
the children and throw it to the dogs." 27She
said, "Please, Lord, for even the dogs eat the
scraps that fall from the table of their masters."
28 l*Then Jesus said to her in reply, "O woman,
great is your faith! Let it be done for you as you
wish." And her daughter was healed from that
hour.

The Healing of Many People 29Moving on
from there Jesus walked by the Sea of Galilee,
went up on the mountain, and sat down there.
30 mGreat crowds came to him, having with
them the lame, the blind, the deformed, the
mute, and many others. They placed them at his
feet, and he cured them. 31The crowds were
amazed when they saw the mute speaking, the
deformed made whole, the lame walking, and
the blind able to see, and they glorified the God
of Israel.

The Feeding of the Four Thousand
32 n*Jesus summoned his disciples and said, "My
heart is moved with pity for the crowd, for they
have been with me now for three days and have
nothing to eat. I do not want to send them away
hungry, for fear they may collapse on the way."
33The disciples said to him, "Where could we
ever get enough bread in this deserted place to
satisfy such a crowd?" 34Jesus said to them,
"How many loaves do you have?" "Seven," they
replied, "and a few fish." 35He ordered the
crowd to sit down on the ground. 36*Then he
took the seven loaves and the fish, gave thanks,
broke the loaves, and gave them to the disciples,
who in turn gave them to the crowds. 37 oThey
all ate and were satisfied. They picked up the
fragments left over—seven baskets full. 38Those
who ate were four thousand men, not counting
women and children. 39And when he had dis-
missed the crowds, he got into the boat and
came to the district of Magadan.

CHAPTER 16

The Demand for a Sign 1 p*The Pharisees and
Sadducees came and, to test him, asked him to
show them a sign from heaven. 2*He said to
them in reply, "[In the evening you say, 'Tomor-
row will be fair, for the sky is red'; 3 qand, in the
morning, 'Today will be stormy, for the sky is red
and threatening.' You know how to judge the
appearance of the sky, but you cannot judge the
signs of the times.] 4 r*An evil and unfaithful
generation seeks a sign, but no sign will be given
it except the sign of Jonah." Then he left them
and went away.

15, 19: The Marcan list of thirteen things that defile (7, 21–22) is here reduced to seven that partially cover the content of the Decalogue.

15, 21–28: See the note on 8, 5–13.

15, 24: See the note on 10, 5–6.

15, 26: **The children:** the people of Israel. **Dogs:** see the note on 7, 6.

15, 28: As in the case of the cure of the centurion's servant (8, 10), Matthew ascribes Jesus' granting the request to the woman's **great faith,** a point not made equally explicit in the Marcan parallel (7, 24–30).

15, 32–39: Most probably this story is a doublet of that of the feeding of the five thousand (14, 13–21). It differs from it notably only in that Jesus takes the initiative, not the disciples (32), and in the numbers: the crowd has been with Jesus **three days** (32), **seven loaves** are multiplied (36), **seven baskets** of **fragments** remain after the feeding (37), and **four thousand** men are fed (38).

15, 36: **Gave thanks:** see 14, 19, "said the blessing." There is no difference in meaning. The thanksgiving was a blessing of God for his benefits.

16, 1: **A sign from heaven:** see the note on 12, 38–42.

16, 2–3: The answer of Jesus in these verses is omitted in many important textual witnesses, and it is very uncertain that it is an original part of this gospel. It resembles Lk 12, 54–56 and may have been inserted from there. It rebukes the Pharisees and Sadducees who are able to read indications of coming weather but not the indications of the coming kingdom in the signs that Jesus does offer, his mighty deeds and teaching.

16, 4: See the notes on 12, 39.40.

j Mk 7, 24–30. k 10, 6. 18, 10. m Is 35, 5–6. n Mk 8, 1–10. o 16, 10. p Mk 8, 11–21. q Lk 12, 54–56. r 12, 39; Jon 2, 1.

**The Leaven of the Pharisees and
Sadducees** 5 s*In coming to the other side of
the sea, the disciples had forgotten to bring
bread. 6 t*Jesus said to them, "Look out, and
beware of the leaven of the Pharisees and
Sadducees." 7*They concluded among them-
selves, saying, "It is because we have brought no
bread." 8When Jesus became aware of this he
said, "You of little faith, why do you conclude
among yourselves that it is because you have no
bread? 9 uDo you not yet understand, and do you
not remember the five loaves for the five thou-
sand, and how many wicker baskets you took
up? 10 vOr the seven loaves for the four thou-
sand, and how many baskets you took up?
11How do you not comprehend that I was not
speaking to you about bread? Beware of the
leaven of the Pharisees and Sadducees."
12*Then they understood that he was not telling
them to beware of the leaven of bread, but of the
teaching of the Pharisees and Sadducees.
Peter's Confession about Jesus 13 w*When
Jesus went into the region of Caesarea Philippi
he asked his disciples, "Who do people say that
the Son of Man is?" 14 x*They replied, "Some say
John the Baptist, others Elijah, still others Jere-
miah or one of the prophets." 15He said to them,
"But who do you say that I am?" 16 y*Simon
Peter said in reply, "You are the Messiah, the
Son of the living God." 17*Jesus said to him in
reply, "Blessed are you, Simon son of Jonah. For
flesh and blood has not revealed this to you, but
my heavenly Father. 18 z*And so I say to you,
you are Peter, and upon this rock I will build my
church, and the gates of the netherworld shall
not prevail against it. 19 a*I will give you the keys

16, 5–12: Jesus' warning his disciples against **the teaching of the Pharisees and Sadducees** comes immediately before his promise to confer on Peter the authority to bind and to loose on earth (19), an authority that will be confirmed in heaven. Such authority most probably has to do, at least in part, with teaching. The rejection of the teaching authority of the Pharisees (see also 12, 12–14) prepares for a new one derived from Jesus.

16, 6: **Leaven:** see the note on 13, 33. **Sadducees:** Matthew's Marcan source speaks rather of "the leaven of Herod" (8, 15).

16, 7–11: The disciples, men **of little faith,** misunderstand Jesus' metaphorical use of **leaven,** forgetting that, as the feeding of the crowds shows, he is not at a loss to provide them with bread.

16, 12: After his rebuke, the disciples understand that by **leaven** he meant the corrupting influence of **the teaching of the Pharisees and Sadducees.** The evangelist probably understands this **teaching** as common to both groups. Since at the time of Jesus' ministry the two differed widely on points of teaching, e.g., the resurrection of the dead, and at the time of the evangelist the Sadducee party was no longer a force in Judaism, the supposed common **teaching** fits neither period. The disciples' eventual understanding of Jesus' warning contrasts with their continuing obtuseness in the Marcan parallel (8, 14–21).

16, 13–20: The Marcan confession of Jesus as Messiah, made by Peter as spokesman for the other disciples (8, 27–29; cf also Lk 9, 18–20), is modified significantly here. The confession is of Jesus both as **Messiah** and as **Son of the living God** (16). Jesus' response, drawn principally from material peculiar to Matthew, attributes the confession to a divine revelation granted to Peter alone (17) and makes him the **rock** on which Jesus **will build** his **church** (18) and the disciple whose authority in the church **on earth** will be confirmed **in heaven,** i.e., by God (19).

16, 13: **Caesarea Philippi:** situated about twenty miles north of the Sea of Galilee in the territory ruled by Philip, a son of Herod the Great, tetrarch from 4 B.C. until his death in A.D. 34 (see the note on 14, 1). He rebuilt the town of Paneas, naming it **Caesarea** in honor of the emperor, and **Philippi** ("of Philip") to distinguish it from the seaport in Samaria that was also called Caesarea. **Who do people say that the Son of Man is?:** although the question differs from the Marcan parallel (8, 27: "Who . . . that I am?"), the meaning is the same, for Jesus here refers to himself as **the Son of Man** (cf 15).

16, 14: **John the Baptist:** see 14, 2. **Elijah:** cf Mal 3, 23–24; Sir 48, 10; and see the note on 3, 4. **Jeremiah:** an addition of Matthew to the Marcan source.

16, 16: **The Son of the living God:** see 2, 15; 3, 17. The addition of this exalted title to the Marcan confession eliminates whatever ambiguity was attached to the title Messiah. This, among other things, supports the view proposed by many scholars that Matthew has here combined his source's confession with a post-resurrectional confession of faith in Jesus as **Son of the living God** that belonged to the appearance of the risen Jesus to Peter; cf 1 Cor 15, 5; Lk 24, 34.

16, 17: **Flesh and blood:** a Semitic expression for human beings, especially in their weakness. **Has not revealed this . . . but my heavenly Father:** that Peter's faith is spoken of as coming not through human means but through a revelation from God is similar to Paul's description of his recognition of who Jesus was; see Gal 1, 15–16, " . . . when he [God] . . . was pleased to reveal his Son to me . . . ."

16, 18: **You are Peter, and upon this rock I will build my church:** the Aramaic word kēpā' meaning **rock** and transliterated into Greek as **Kēphas** is the name by which Peter is called in the Pauline letters (1 Cor 1, 12; 3, 22; 9, 5; 15, 4; Gal 1, 18; 2, 9.11.14) except in Gal 2, 7–8 ("Peter"). It is translated as **Petros** ("Peter") in Jn 1, 42. The presumed original Aramaic of Jesus' statement would have been, in English, "You are the Rock (**Kēpā'**) and upon this rock (**kēpā'**) I will build my church." The Greek text probably means the same, for the difference in gender between the masculine noun **petros,** the disciple's new name, and the feminine noun **petra** (rock) may be due simply to the unsuitability of using a feminine noun as the proper name of a male. Although the two words were generally used with slightly different nuances, they were also used interchangeably with the same meaning, "rock." **Church:** this word (Greek **ekklēsia**) occurs in the gospels only here and in 18, 17 (twice). There are several possibilities for an Aramaic original. Jesus' **church** means the community that he **will** gather and that, like a building, will have Peter as its solid foundation. That function of Peter consists in his being witness to Jesus as **the Messiah, the Son of the living God. The gates of the netherworld shall not prevail against it:** the netherworld (Greek **Hadēs,** the abode of the dead) is conceived of as a walled city whose **gates** will not close in upon the church of Jesus, i.e., it will not be overcome by the power of death.

16, 19: **The keys to the kingdom of heaven:** the image of the

s Mk 8, 14–21. t Lk 12, 1. u 14, 17–21; Jn 6, 9. v 15,34–38. w Mk 8, 27–29; Lk 9, 18–20. x 14, 2. y Jn 6, 69. z Jn 1, 42. a Is 22, 22; Rv 3, 7.

to the kingdom of heaven. Whatever you bind
on earth shall be bound in heaven; and what-
ever you loose on earth shall be loosed in
heaven." 20 b*Then he strictly ordered his disci-
ples to tell no one that he was the Messiah.

The First Prediction of the Passion

21 c d*From that time on, Jesus began to show his
disciples that he must go to Jerusalem and suffer
greatly from the elders, the chief priests, and the
scribes, and be killed and on the third day be
raised. 22*Then Peter took him aside and began
to rebuke him, "God forbid, Lord! No such thing
shall ever happen to you." 23 eHe turned and said
to Peter, "Get behind me, Satan! You are an
obstacle to me. You are thinking not as God
does, but as human beings do."

The Conditions of Discipleship 24 f*Then Je-
sus said to his disciples, "Whoever wishes to
come after me must deny himself, take up his
cross, and follow me. 25 g*For whoever wishes
to save his life will lose it, but whoever loses his
life for my sake will find it. 26What profit would
there be for one to gain the whole world and
forfeit his life? Or what can one give in exchange
for his life? 27 h*For the Son of Man will come
with his angels in his Father's glory, and then he
will repay everyone according to his conduct.
28*Amen, I say to you, there are some standing
here who will not taste death until they see the
Son of Man coming in his kingdom."

CHAPTER 17

The Transfiguration of Jesus 1 i*After six
days Jesus took Peter, James, and John his
brother, and led them up a high mountain by

---

keys is probably drawn from Is 22, 15–25, where Eliakim, who succeeds Shebnah as master of the palace, is given "the key of the house of David," which he authoritatively "opens" and "shuts" (22, 22). **Whatever you bind . . . loosed in heaven:** there are many instances in rabbinic literature of the binding-loosing imagery. Of the several meanings given there to the metaphor, two are of special importance here: the giving of authoritative teaching, and the lifting or imposing of the ban of excommunication. It is disputed whether the image of **the keys** and that of binding and loosing are different metaphors meaning the same thing. In any case, the promise of the keys is given to Peter alone. In 18, 18 all the disciples are given the power of binding and loosing, but the context of that verse suggests that there the power of excommunication alone is intended. That **the keys** are those to **the kingdom of heaven** and that Peter's exercise of authority in the church **on earth** will be confirmed **in heaven** show an intimate connection between, but not an identification of, the church and **the kingdom of heaven.**

16, 20: Cf Mk 8, 30. Matthew makes explicit that the prohibition has to do with speaking of Jesus as **the Messiah;** see the note on Mk 8, 27–30.

16, 21–23: This first prediction of the passion follows Mk 8, 31–33 in the main and serves as a corrective to an understanding of Jesus' messiahship as solely one of glory and triumph. By his addition of **from that time on** (21) Matthew has emphasized that Jesus' revelation of his coming suffering and death marks a new phase of the gospel. Neither this nor the two later passion predictions (17, 22–23; 20, 17–19) can be taken as sayings that, as they stand, go back to Jesus himself. However, it is probable that he foresaw that his mission would entail suffering and perhaps death, but was confident that he would ultimately be vindicated by God (see 26, 29).

16, 21: He: the Marcan parallel (8, 31) has "the Son of Man." Since Matthew has already designated Jesus by that title (13), its omission here is not significant. The Matthean prediction is equally about the sufferings of the Son of Man. **Must:** this necessity is part of the tradition of all the synoptics; cf Mk 8, 31; Lk 9, 21. **The elders, the chief priests, and the scribes:** see the note on Mk 8, 31. **On the third day:** so also Lk 9, 22, against the Marcan "after three days" (8, 31). Matthew's formulation is, in the Greek, almost identical with the pre-Pauline fragment of the kerygma in 1 Cor 15, 4, and also with Hos 6, 2, which many take to be the Old Testament background to the confession that Jesus was raised **on the third day.** Josephus uses "after three days" and "on the third day" interchangeably (**Antiquities** 7, 11, 6 §§280–81; 8, 8, 1–2 §§214, 218) and there is probably no difference in meaning between the two phrases.

16, 22–23: Peter's refusal to accept Jesus' predicted suffering and death is seen as a satanic attempt to deflect Jesus from his God-appointed course, and the disciple is addressed in terms that recall Jesus' dismissal of the devil in the temptation account (4, 10: "Get away, Satan!"). Peter's satanic purpose is emphasized by Matthew's addition to the Marcan source of the words **You are an obstacle to me.**

16, 24–28: A readiness to follow Jesus even to giving up one's life for him is the condition for true discipleship; this will be repaid by him at the final judgment.

16, 24: Deny himself: to deny someone is to disown him (see 10, 33; 26, 34–35) and to deny oneself is to disown oneself as the center of one's existence.

16, 25: See the notes on 10, 38.39.

16, 27: The parousia and final judgment are described in 25, 31 in terms almost identical with these.

16, 28: Coming in his kingdom: since the **kingdom** of the **Son of Man** has been described as "the world" and Jesus' sovereignty precedes his final coming in glory (13, 38.41), the **coming** in this verse is not the parousia as in the preceding but the manifestation of Jesus' rule after his resurrection; see the notes on 13, 38.41.

17, 1–8: The account of the transfiguration confirms that Jesus is the **Son** of God (5) and points to fulfillment of the prediction that he will come **in his Father's glory** at the end of the age (16, 27). It has been explained by some as a resurrection appearance retrojected into the time of Jesus' ministry, but that is not probable since the account lacks many of the usual elements of the resurrection-appearance narratives. It draws upon motifs from the Old Testament and noncanonical Jewish apocalyptic literature that express the presence of the heavenly and the divine, e.g., brilliant light, white garments, and the overshadowing cloud.

17, 1: These three disciples are also taken apart from the others by Jesus in Gethsemane (26, 37). **A high mountain:** this has been

b Mk 8, 30; Lk 9, 21. c Mk 8, 31—9, 1; Lk 9, 22–27. d 17, 22–23; 20, 17–19. e 4, 10. f Lk 14, 27. g Lk 17, 33; Jn 12, 25. h 25, 31–33; Jb 34, 11; Ps 62, 13; Jer 17, 10; 2 Thes 1, 7–8. i Mk 9, 2–8; Lk 9, 28–36.

themselves. [2][j]*And he was transfigured before them; his face shone like the sun and his clothes became white as light. [3]*And behold, Moses and Elijah appeared to them, conversing with him. [4]*Then Peter said to Jesus in reply, "Lord, it is good that we are here. If you wish, I will make three tents here, one for you, one for Moses, and one for Elijah." [5][k]*While he was still speaking, behold, a bright cloud cast a shadow over them, then from the cloud came a voice that said, "This is my beloved Son, with whom I am well pleased; listen to him." [6]*When the disciples heard this, they fell prostrate and were very much afraid. [7]But Jesus came and touched them, saying, "Rise, and do not be afraid." [8]And when the disciples raised their eyes, they saw no one else but Jesus alone.

The Coming of Elijah [9][l]*As they were coming down from the mountain, Jesus charged them, "Do not tell the vision to anyone until the Son of Man has been raised from the dead." [10][m]*Then the disciples asked him, "Why do the scribes say that Elijah must come first?" [11][n]*He said in reply, "Elijah will indeed come and restore all things; [12][o]but I tell you that Elijah has already come, and they did not recognize him but did to him whatever they pleased. So also will the Son of Man suffer at their hands." [13]*Then the disciples understood that he was speaking to them of John the Baptist.

The Healing of a Boy with a Demon

[14][p]*When they came to the crowd a man approached, knelt down before him, [15]*and said, "Lord, have pity on my son, for he is a lunatic and suffers severely; often he falls into fire, and often into water. [16]I brought him to your disciples, but they could not cure him." [17][q]*Jesus said in reply, "O faithless and perverse generation, how long will I be with you? How long will I endure you? Bring him here to me." [18]*Jesus rebuked him and the demon came out of him, and from that hour the boy was cured.

identified with Tabor or Hermon, but probably no specific mountain was intended by the evangelist or by his Marcan source (9, 2). Its meaning is theological rather than geographical, possibly recalling the revelation to Moses on Mount Sinai (Ex 24, 12–18) and to Elijah at the same place (1 Kgs 19, 8–18; Horeb=Sinai).

17, 2: His face shone like the sun: this is a Matthean addition; cf Dn 10, 6. **His clothes became white as light:** cf Dn 7, 9, where the clothing of God appears "snow bright." For the **white** garments of other heavenly beings, see Rv 4, 4; 7, 9; 19, 14.

17, 3: See the note on Mk 9, 5.

17, 4: Three tents: the booths in which the Israelites lived during the feast of Tabernacles (cf Jn 7, 2) were meant to recall their ancestors' dwelling in booths during the journey from Egypt to the promised land (Lv 23, 39–42). The same Greek word, **skēnē,** here translated **tents,** is used in the LXX for the booths of that feast, and some scholars have suggested that there is an allusion here to that liturgical custom.

17, 5: Cloud cast a shadow over them: see the note on Mk 9, 7. **This is my beloved Son . . . listen to him:** cf 3, 17. The voice repeats the baptismal proclamation about Jesus, with the addition of the command **listen to him.** The latter is a reference to Dt 18, 15 in which the Israelites are commanded to **listen to** the prophet like Moses whom God will raise up for them. The command to **listen to** Jesus is general, but in this context it probably applies particularly to the preceding predictions of his passion and resurrection (16, 21) and of his coming (16, 27.28).

17, 6–7: A Matthean addition; cf Dn 10, 9–10.18–19.

17, 9–13: In response to the disciples' question about the expected return of Elijah, Jesus interprets the mission of the Baptist as the fulfillment of that expectation. But that was not suspected by those who opposed and finally killed him, and Jesus predicts a similar fate for himself.

17, 9: The vision: Matthew alone uses this word to describe the transfiguration. **Until the Son of Man has been raised from the dead:** only in the light of Jesus' resurrection can the meaning of his life and mission be truly understood; until then no testimony to **the vision** will lead people to faith.

17, 10: See the notes on 3, 4; 16, 14.

17, 11–12: The preceding question and this answer may reflect later controversy with Jews who objected to the Christian claims for Jesus that Elijah had not yet come.

17, 13: See 11, 14.

17, 14–20: Matthew has greatly shortened the Marcan story (9, 14–29). Leaving aside several details of the boy's illness, he concentrates on the need for faith, not so much on the part of the boy's father (as does Mark, for Matthew omits Mk 9, 22b-24) but on that of his own disciples whose inability to drive out the demon is ascribed to their **little faith** (20).

17, 15: A lunatic: this description of the boy is peculiar to Matthew. The word occurs in the New Testament only here and in 4, 24 and means one affected or struck by the moon. The symptoms of the boy's illness point to epilepsy, and attacks of this were thought to be caused by phases of the moon.

17, 17: Faithless and perverse: so Matthew and Luke (9, 41) against Mark's **faithless** (9, 19). The Greek word here translated **perverse** is the same as that in Dt 32, 5 LXX, where Moses speaks to his people. There is a problem in knowing to whom the reproach is addressed. Since the Matthean Jesus normally chides his disciples for their **little faith** (as in 20), it would appear that the charge of lack of faith could not be made against them and that the reproach is addressed to unbelievers among the Jews. However in v 20b (**if you have faith the size of a mustard seed**), which is certainly addressed to the disciples, they appear to have not even the smallest faith; if they had, they would have been able to cure the boy. In the light of v 20b the reproach of v 17 could have applied to the disciples. There seems to be an inconsistency between the charge of **little faith** in v 20a and that of not even a little in v 20b.

17, 18: The demon came out of him: not until this verse does Matthew indicate that the boy's illness is a case of demoniacal possession.

j 28, 3; Dn 7, 9; 10, 6; Rv 4, 4; 7, 9; 19, 14. k 3, 17; Dt 18, 15; 2 Pt 1, 17. l Mk 9, 9–13. m Mal 3, 23–24. n Lk 1, 17. o 11, 14. p Mk 9, 14–29; Lk 9, 37–43. q Dt 32, 5 LXX.

19 Then the disciples approached Jesus in private
and said, "Why could we not drive it out?"
20 r *He said to them, "Because of your little
faith. Amen, I say to you, if you have faith the
size of a mustard seed, you will say to this
mountain, 'Move from here to there,' and it will
move. Nothing will be impossible for you." [21]*
The Second Prediction of the Passion 22 s *As they were gathering in Galilee,
Jesus said to them, "The Son of Man is to be
handed over to men, 23 and they will kill him,
and he will be raised on the third day." And they
were overwhelmed with grief.
Payment of the Temple Tax 24 t *When they
came to Capernaum, the collectors of the temple tax approached Peter and said, "Doesn't
your teacher pay the temple tax?" 25 *"Yes," he
said. When he came into the house, before he
had time to speak, Jesus asked him, "What is
your opinion, Simon? From whom do the kings
of the earth take tolls or census tax? From their
subjects or from foreigners?" 26 *When he said,
"From foreigners," Jesus said to him, "Then the
subjects are exempt. 27 *But that we may not
offend them, go to the sea, drop in a hook, and
take the first fish that comes up. Open its
mouth and you will find a coin worth twice the
temple tax. Give that to them for me and for
you."

CHAPTER 18

The Greatest in the Kingdom 1 u *At that
time the disciples approached Jesus and said,
"Who is the greatest in the kingdom of heaven?"
2 He called a child over, placed it in their midst,
3 v *and said, "Amen, I say to you, unless you
turn and become like children, you will not

17, 20: The entire verse is an addition of Matthew who (according to the better attested text) omits the reason given for the disciples' inability in Mk 9, 29. **Little faith:** see the note on 6, 30. **Faith the size of a mustard seed . . . and it will move:** a combination of a Q saying (cf Lk 17, 6) with a Marcan saying (cf Mk 11, 23).

17, 21: Some manuscripts add, "But this kind does not come out except by prayer and fasting"; this is a variant of the better reading of Mk 9, 29.

17, 22–23: The second passion prediction (cf 16, 21–23) is the least detailed of the three and may be the earliest. In the Marcan parallel the disciples do not understand (9, 32); here they understand and are **overwhelmed with grief** at the prospect of Jesus' death (23).

17, 24–27: Like 14, 28–31 and 16, 16b-19, this episode comes from Matthew's special material on Peter. Although the question of **the collectors** concerns Jesus' payment of **the temple tax,** it is put to **Peter.** It is he who receives instruction from Jesus about freedom from the obligation of payment and yet why it should be made. The means of doing so is provided miraculously. The pericope deals with a problem of Matthew's church, whether its members should pay the temple tax, and the answer is given through a word of Jesus conveyed to Peter. Some scholars see here an example of the teaching authority of Peter exercised in the name of Jesus (see 16, 19). The specific problem was a Jewish Christian one and may have arisen when the Matthean church was composed largely of that group.

17, 24: The temple tax: before the destruction of the Jerusalem temple in A.D. 70 every male Jew above nineteen years of age was obliged to make an annual contribution to its upkeep (cf Ex 30, 11–16; Neh 10, 33). After the destruction the Romans imposed upon Jews the obligation of paying that tax for the temple of Jupiter Capitolinus. There is disagreement about which period the story deals with.

17, 25: From their subjects or from foreigners?: the Greek word here translated **subjects** literally means "sons."

17, 26: Then the subjects are exempt: just as **subjects** are not bound by laws applying to **foreigners,** neither are Jesus and his disciples, who belong to the kingdom of heaven, bound by the duty of paying the temple tax imposed on those who are not of the kingdom. If the Greek is translated "sons," the freedom of Jesus, the Son of God, and of his disciples, children ("sons") of the kingdom (cf 13, 38), is even more clear.

17, 27: That we may not offend them: though they are **exempt** (26), Jesus and his disciples are to avoid giving offense; therefore the tax is to be paid. **A coin worth twice the temple tax:** literally, "a stater," a Greek coin worth two double drachmas. Two double drachmas were equal to the Jewish shekel and the tax was a half-shekel. **For me and for you:** not only Jesus but Peter pays the tax, and this example serves as a standard for the conduct of all the disciples.

18, 1–35: This discourse of the fourth book of the gospel is often called the "church order" discourse, but it lacks most of the considerations usually connected with church order, such as various offices in the church and the duties of each, and deals principally with the relations that must obtain among the members of the church. Beginning with the warning that greatness in **the kingdom of heaven** is measured not by rank or power but by childlikeness (1–5), it deals with the care that the disciples must take not to cause the **little ones to sin** or to neglect them if they stray from the community (6–14), the correction of members who sin (15–18), the efficacy of the prayer of the disciples because of the presence of Jesus (19–20), and the forgiveness that must be repeatedly extended to sinful members who repent (21–35).

18, 1: The initiative is taken not by Jesus as in the Marcan parallel (9, 33–34) but by the disciples. **Kingdom of heaven:** this may mean **the kingdom** in its fullness, i.e., after the parousia and the final judgment. But what follows about causes of sin, church discipline, and forgiveness, all dealing with the present age, suggests that the question has to do with rank also in the church, where **the kingdom** is manifested here and now, although only partially and by anticipation; see the notes on 3, 2; 4, 17.

18, 3: Become like children: the child is held up as a model for the disciples not because of any supposed innocence of children but because of their complete dependence on, and trust in, their parents. So must the disciples be, in respect to God.

r 21, 21; Lk 17, 6; 1 Cor 13, 2. s 16, 21; 20, 18–19. t Ex 30, 11–16; Neh 10, 33. u Mk 9, 36–37; Lk 9, 46–48. v 19, 14; Mk 10, 15; Lk 18, 17.

enter the kingdom of heaven. [4][w]Whoever hum-
bles himself like this child is the greatest in the
kingdom of heaven. [5]*And whoever receives
one child such as this in my name receives me.
Temptations to Sin [6][x]*"Whoever causes one
of these little ones who believe in me to sin, it
would be better for him to have a great millstone
hung around his neck and to be drowned in the
depths of the sea. [7]*Woe to the world because of
things that cause sin! Such things must come,
but woe to the one through whom they come!
[8][y]*If your hand or foot causes you to sin, cut it
off and throw it away. It is better for you to enter
into life maimed or crippled than with two
hands or two feet to be thrown into eternal fire.
[9]And if your eye causes you to sin, tear it out and
throw it away. It is better for you to enter into
life with one eye than with two eyes to be
thrown into fiery Gehenna.

The Parable of the Lost Sheep [10][z]*"See that
you do not despise one of these little ones, for I
say to you that their angels in heaven always
look upon the face of my heavenly Father.* [[11]]* [a]
[12]What is your opinion? If a man has a hundred
sheep and one of them goes astray, will he not
leave the ninety-nine in the hills and go in search
of the stray? [13]And if he finds it, amen, I say to
you, he rejoices more over it than over the
ninety-nine that did not stray. [14]In just the same
way, it is not the will of your heavenly Father
that one of these little ones be lost.
A Brother Who Sins [15][b]*"If your brother sins
[against you], go and tell him his fault between
you and him alone. If he listens to you, you have
won over your brother. [16][c]*If he does not listen,
take one or two others along with you, so that
'every fact may be established on the testimony
of two or three witnesses.' [17][d]*If he refuses to

18, 5: Cf 10, 40.

18, 6: One of these little ones: the thought passes from the child of vv 2–4 to the disciples, **little ones** because of their becoming **like children.** It is difficult to know whether this is a designation of all who are disciples or of those who are insignificant in contrast to others, e.g., the leaders of the community. Since apart from this chapter the designation **little ones** occurs in Mt only in 10, 42 where it means disciples as such, that is its more likely meaning here. **Who believe in me:** since discipleship is impossible without at least some degree of faith, this further specification seems superfluous. However, it serves to indicate that the warning against causing a **little one** to sin is principally directed against whatever would lead such a one to a weakening or loss of faith. The Greek verb **skandalizein,** here translated **causes . . . to sin,** means literally "causes to stumble"; what the stumbling is depends on the context. It is used of falling away from faith in 13, 21. According to the better reading of Mk 9, 42, **in me** is a Matthean addition to the Marcan source. **It would be better . . . depths of the sea:** cf Mk 9, 42.

18, 7: This is a Q saying; cf Lk 17, 1. The inevitability of **things that cause sin** (literally, "scandals") does not take away the responsibility of **the one through whom they come.**

18, 8–9: These verses are a doublet of 5, 29–30. In that context they have to do with causes of sexual sin. As in the Marcan source from which they have been drawn (Mk 9, 42–48), they differ from the first warning about scandal, which deals with causing another person to sin, for they concern what **causes** oneself **to sin** and they do not seem to be related to another's loss of faith, as the first warning is. It is difficult to know how Matthew understood the logical connection between these verses and vv 6–7.

18, 10–14: The first and last verses are peculiar to Mt. The parable itself comes from Q; see Lk 15, 3–7. In Lk it serves as justification for Jesus' table-companionship with sinners; here, it is an exhortation for the disciples to seek out fellow disciples who have gone **astray.** Not only must no one cause a fellow disciple to sin, but those who have strayed must be sought out and, if possible, brought back to the community. The joy of the shepherd on finding the sheep, though not absent in Mt (13), is more emphasized in Lk. By his addition of vv 10 and 14, Matthew has drawn out explicitly the application of the parable to the care of the **little ones.**

18, 10: Their angels in heaven . . . my heavenly Father: for the Jewish belief in angels as guardians of nations and individuals, see Dn 10, 13.20–21; Tb 5, 4–7; 1QH 5, 20–22; as intercessors who present the prayers of human beings to God, see Tb 13, 12.15. The high worth of the **little ones** is indicated by their being represented before God by these heavenly beings.

18, 11: Some manuscripts add, "For the Son of Man has come to save what was lost"; cf 9, 13. This is practically identical with Lk 19, 10 and is probably a copyist's addition from that source.

18, 15–20: Passing from the duty of Christian disciples, toward those who have strayed from their number, the discourse now turns to how they are to deal with one who sins and yet remains within the community. First there is to be private correction (15); if this is unsuccessful, further correction before **two or three witnesses** (16); if this fails, the matter is to be brought before the assembled community (**the church**), and if the sinner refuses to attend to the correction of **the church,** he is to be expelled (17). The church's judgment will be ratified **in heaven,** i.e., by God (18). This three-step process of correction corresponds, though not exactly, to the procedure of the Qumran community; see 1QS 5, 25—6, 1; 6, 24—7, 25; CD 9, 2–8. The section ends with a saying about the favorable response of God to prayer, even to that of a very small number, for Jesus is in the midst of any gathering of his disciples, however small (19–20). Whether this prayer has anything to do with the preceding judgment is uncertain.

18, 15: Your brother: a fellow disciple; see 23, 8. The bracketed words, **against you,** are widely attested but they are not in the important codices Sinaiticus and Vaticanus or in some other textual witnesses. Their omission broadens the type of sin in question. **Won over:** literally, "gained."

18, 16: Cf Dt 19, 15.

18, 17: The church: the second of the only two instances of this word in the gospels; see the note on 16, 18. Here it refers not to the entire **church** of Jesus, as in 16, 18, but to the local congregation. **Treat him . . . a Gentile or a tax collector:** just as the observant Jew avoided the company of Gentiles and tax collectors, so must the congregation of Christian disciples separate

w 23, 12. x Mk 9, 42; Lk 17, 1–2. y 5, 29–30; Mk 9, 43–47. z Ez 34, 1–3.16; Lk 15, 3–7. a Lk 19, 10. b Lv 19, 17; Sir 19, 13; Gal 6, 1. c Dt 19, 15; Jn 8, 17; 1 Tm 5, 19. d 1 Cor 5, 1–13.

listen to them, tell the church. If he refuses to
listen even to the church, then treat him as you
would a Gentile or a tax collector. 18 e*Amen, I
say to you, whatever you bind on earth shall be
bound in heaven, and whatever you loose on
earth shall be loosed in heaven. 19 f*Again,
[amen,] I say to you, if two of you agree on earth
about anything for which they are to pray, it shall
be granted to them by my heavenly Father.
20 g*For where two or three are gathered to-
gether in my name, there am I in the midst of
them."

The Parable of the Unforgiving Servant

21 h*Then Peter approaching asked him, "Lord, if
my brother sins against me, how often must I
forgive him? As many as seven times?" 22*Jesus
answered, "I say to you, not seven times but
seventy-seven times. 23 iThat is why the king-
dom of heaven may be likened to a king who
decided to settle accounts with his servants.
24*When he began the accounting, a debtor was
brought before him who owed him a huge
amount. 25Since he had no way of paying it
back, his master ordered him to be sold, along
with his wife, his children, and all his property,
in payment of the debt. 26*At that, the servant
fell down, did him homage, and said, 'Be patient
with me, and I will pay you back in full.'
27Moved with compassion the master of that
servant let him go and forgave him the loan.
28*When that servant had left, he found one of
his fellow servants who owed him a much
smaller amount. He seized him and started to
choke him, demanding, 'Pay back what you
owe.' 29Falling to his knees, his fellow servant
begged him, 'Be patient with me, and I will pay
you back.' 30But he refused. Instead, he had him
put in prison until he paid back the debt. 31Now
when his fellow servants saw what had hap-
pened, they were deeply disturbed, and went to
their master and reported the whole affair. 32His
master summoned him and said to him, 'You
wicked servant! I forgave you your entire debt
because you begged me to. 33 jShould you not
have had pity on your fellow servant, as I had
pity on you?' 34*Then in anger his master
handed him over to the torturers until he should
pay back the whole debt. 35 k*So will my heav-
enly Father do to you, unless each of you
forgives his brother from his heart."

---

itself from the arrogantly sinful member who refuses to repent even when convicted of his sin by the whole **church**. Such a one is to be set outside the fellowship of the community. The harsh language about **Gentile** and **tax collector** probably reflects a stage of the Matthean **church** when it was principally composed of Jewish Christians. That time had long since passed, but the principle of exclusion for such a sinner remained. Paul makes a similar demand for excommunication in 1 Cor 5, 1–13.

18, 18: Except for the plural of the verbs **bind** and **loose**, this verse is practically identical with 16, 19b, and many scholars understand it as granting to all the disciples what was previously given to Peter alone. For a different view, based on the different contexts of the two verses, see the note on 16, 19.

18, 19–20: Some take these verses as applying to prayer on the occasion of the church's gathering to deal with the sinner of v 17. Unless an **a fortiori** argument is supposed, this seems unlikely. God's answer to the prayer of **two or three** envisages a different situation from one that involves the entire congregation. In addition, the object of this prayer is expressed in most general terms as **anything for which they are to pray.**

18, 20: For where two or three . . . midst of them: the presence of Jesus guarantees the efficacy of the prayer. This saying is similar to one attributed to a rabbi executed in A.D. 135 at the time of the second Jewish revolt: ". . . When two sit and there are between them the words of the Torah, the divine presence (Shekinah) rests upon them" (**Pirqê 'Abôt** 3, 3).

18, 21–35: The final section of the discourse deals with the forgiveness that the disciples are to give to their fellow disciples who sin against them. To the question of Peter how often forgiveness is to be granted (21), Jesus answers that it is to be given without limit (22) and illustrates this with the parable of the unmerciful servant (23–34), warning that his **heavenly Father** will give those who do not forgive the same treatment as that given to the unmerciful servant (35). Verses 21–22 correspond to Lk 17, 4; the parable and the final warning are peculiar to Mt. That the parable did not originally belong to this context is suggested by the fact that it really does not deal with repeated forgiveness, which is the point of Peter's question and Jesus' reply.

18, 22: Seventy-seven times: the Greek corresponds exactly to the LXX of Gn 4, 24. There is probably an allusion, by contrast, to the limitless vengeance of Lamech in the Gn text. In any case, what is demanded of the disciples is limitless forgiveness.

18, 24: A huge amount: literally, "ten thousand talents." The talent was a unit of coinage of high but varying value depending on its metal (gold, silver, copper) and its place of origin. It is mentioned in the New Testament only here and in 25, 14–30.

18, 26: Pay you back in full: an empty promise, given the size of the debt.

18, 28: A much smaller amount: literally, "a hundred denarii." A denarius was the normal daily wage of a laborer. The difference between the two debts is enormous and brings out the absurdity of the conduct of the Christian who has received the great forgiveness of God and yet refuses to forgive the relatively minor offenses done to him.

18, 34: Since the debt is so great as to be unpayable, the punishment will be endless.

18, 35: The Father's forgiveness, already given, will be withdrawn at the final judgment for those who have not imitated his forgiveness by their own.

e 16, 19; Jn 20, 23. f 7, 7–8; Jn 15, 7. g 1 Cor 5, 4. h 6, 12; Lk 17, 4. i 25, 19. j Sir 28, 4. k 6, 15; Jas 2, 13.

VI: Ministry in Judea and Jerusalem

CHAPTER 19

Marriage and Divorce 1*When Jesus finished these words, he left Galilee and went to the district of Judea across the Jordan. 2Great crowds followed him, and he cured them there. 3[l]*Some Pharisees approached him, and tested him, saying, "Is it lawful for a man to divorce his wife for any cause whatever?" 4[m]*He said in reply, "Have you not read that from the beginning the Creator 'made them male and female' 5[n]and said, 'For this reason a man shall leave his father and mother and be joined to his wife, and the two shall become one flesh'? 6So they are no longer two, but one flesh. Therefore, what God has joined together, no human being must separate." 7[o]*They said to him, "Then why did Moses command that the man give the woman a bill of divorce and dismiss [her]?" 8He said to them, "Because of the hardness of your hearts Moses allowed you to divorce your wives, but from the beginning it was not so. 9[p]*I say to you, whoever divorces his wife (unless the marriage is unlawful) and marries another commits adultery." 10[His] disciples said to him, "If that is the case of a man with his wife, it is better not to marry." 11*He answered, "Not all can accept [this] word, but only those to whom that is granted. 12*Some are incapable of marriage because they were born so; some, because they were made so by others; some, because they have renounced marriage for the sake of the kingdom of heaven. Whoever can accept this ought to accept it."

19, 1—23, 39: The narrative section of the fifth book of the gospel. The first part (19, 1—20, 34) has for its setting the journey of Jesus from Galilee to Jerusalem; the second (21, 1—23, 39) deals with Jesus' ministry in Jerusalem up to the final great discourse of the gospel (chs 24–25). Matthew follows the Marcan sequence of events, though adding material both special to this gospel and drawn from Q. The second part ends with the denunciation of the scribes and Pharisees (23, 1–36) followed by Jesus' lament over Jerusalem (37–39). This long and important speech raises a problem for the view that Mt is structured around five other discourses of Jesus (see Introduction) and that this one has no such function in the gospel. However, it is to be noted that this speech lacks the customary concluding formula that follows the five discourses (see the note on 7, 28), and that those discourses are all addressed either exclusively (chs 10, 18, 24–25) or primarily (chs 5–7, 13) to the disciples, whereas this is addressed primarily to the scribes and Pharisees (13–36). Consequently, it seems plausible to maintain that the evangelist did not intend to give it the structural importance of the five other discourses, and that, in spite of its being composed of sayings-material, it belongs to the narrative section of this book. In that regard, it is similar to the sayings-material of 11, 7–30. Some have proposed that Matthew wished to regard it as part of the final discourse of chs 24–25, but the intervening material (24, 1–4) and the change in matter and style of those chapters do not support that view.

19, 1–12: In giving Jesus' teaching on divorce (3–9), Matthew here follows his Marcan source (10, 2–12) as he does Q in 5, 31–32 (cf Lk 16, 18). Verses 10–12 are peculiar to Mt.

19, 1: When Jesus finished these words: see the note on 7, 28–29. **The district of Judea across the Jordan:** an inexact designation of the territory. Judea did not extend **across the Jordan;** the territory east of the river was Perea. The route to Jerusalem by way of Perea avoided passage through Samaria.

19, 3: Tested him: the verb is used of attempts of Jesus' opponents to embarrass him by challenging him to do something they think impossible (16, 1; Mk 8, 11; Lk 11, 16) or by having him say something that they can use against him (22, 18.35; Mk 10, 2; 12, 15). **For any cause whatever:** this is peculiar to Mt and has been interpreted by some as meaning that Jesus was being asked to take sides in the dispute between the schools of Hillel and Shammai on the reasons for divorce, the latter holding a stricter position than the former. It is unlikely, however, that to ask Jesus' opinion about the differing views of two Jewish schools, both highly respected, could be described as "testing" him, for the reason indicated above.

19, 4–6: Matthew recasts his Marcan source, omitting Jesus' question about Moses' command (Mk 10, 3) and having him recall at once two Genesis texts that show the will and purpose of **the Creator** in making human beings **male and female** (Gn 1, 27), namely, that **a man** may **be joined to his wife** in marriage in the intimacy of **one flesh** (Gn 2, 24). **What God has** thus **joined** must not be separated by any **human being.** (The NAB translation of the Hebrew **bāśār** of Gn 2, 24 as "body" rather than "flesh" obscures the reference of Mt to that text.)

19, 7: See Dt 24, 1–4.

19, 9: Moses' concession to human sinfulness (**the hardness of your hearts,** 8) is repudiated by Jesus, and the original will of the Creator is reaffirmed against that concession. (**Unless the marriage is unlawful**): see the note on 5, 31–32. There is some evidence suggesting that Jesus' absolute prohibition of divorce was paralleled in the Qumran community (see 11QTemple 57, 17–19; CD 4, 12b—5, 14). Matthew removes Mark's setting of this verse as spoken to the disciples alone "in the house" (Mk 10, 10) and also his extension of the divorce prohibition to the case of a woman's divorcing her husband (10, 12), probably because in Palestine, unlike the places where Roman and Greek law prevailed, the woman was not allowed to initiate the divorce.

19, 11: [This] word: probably the disciples' **it is better not to marry** (10). Jesus agrees but says that celibacy is not for all but only for those **to whom that is granted** by God.

19, 12: Incapable of marriage: literally, "eunuchs." Three classes are mentioned, eunuchs from birth, eunuchs by castration, and those who have voluntarily **renounced marriage** (literally, "have made themselves eunuchs") **for the sake of the kingdom,** i.e., to devote themselves entirely to its service. Some scholars take the last class to be those who have been divorced by their spouses and have refused to enter another marriage. But it is more likely that it is rather those who have chosen never to marry, since that suits better the optional nature of the decision: **whoever can . . . ought to accept it.**

l Mk 10, 2–12. m Gn 1, 27. n Gn 2, 24; 1 Cor 6, 16; Eph 5, 31. o Dt 24, 1–4. p 5, 32; Lk 16, 18; 1 Cor 7, 10–11.

Blessing of the Children [13] [q]*Then children
were brought to him that he might lay his hands
on them and pray. The disciples rebuked them,
[14] [r]but Jesus said, "Let the children come to me,
and do not prevent them; for the kingdom of
heaven belongs to such as these." [15]After he
placed his hands on them, he went away.

The Rich Young Man [16] [s]*Now someone ap-
proached him and said, "Teacher, what good
must I do to gain eternal life?" [17]*He answered
him, "Why do you ask me about the good? There
is only One who is good. If you wish to enter into
life, keep the commandments." [18] [t]*He asked
him, "Which ones?" And Jesus replied, " 'You
shall not kill; you shall not commit adultery; you
shall not steal; you shall not bear false witness;
[19]honor your father and your mother'; and 'you
shall love your neighbor as yourself.' " [20]*The
young man said to him, "All of these I have ob-
served. What do I still lack?" [21] [u]*Jesus said to
him, "If you wish to be perfect, go, sell what you
have and give to [the] poor, and you will have
treasure in heaven. Then come, follow me."
[22]When the young man heard this statement, he
went away sad, for he had many possessions.
[23]*Then Jesus said to his disciples, "Amen, I say
to you, it will be hard for one who is rich to enter
the kingdom of heaven. [24] [v]Again I say to you, it is
easier for a camel to pass through the eye of a
needle than for one who is rich to enter the king-
dom of God." [25]*When the disciples heard this,
they were greatly astonished and said, "Who then
can be saved?" [26] [w]Jesus looked at them and said,
"For human beings this is impossible, but for God
all things are possible." [27] [x]Then Peter said to him
in reply, "We have given up everything and fol-
lowed you. What will there be for us?" [28] [y]*Jesus
said to them, "Amen, I say to you that you who
have followed me, in the new age, when the Son
of Man is seated on his throne of glory, will your-
selves sit on twelve thrones, judging the twelve
tribes of Israel. [29]And everyone who has given up
houses or brothers or sisters or father or mother or
children or lands for the sake of my name will
receive a hundred times more, and will inherit

19, 13–15: This account is understood by some as intended to justify the practice of infant baptism. That interpretation is based principally on the command not to **prevent** the children from coming, since that word sometimes has a baptismal connotation in the New Testament; see Acts 8, 36.

19, 16–30: Cf Mk 10, 17–31. This story does not set up a "two-tier" morality, that of those who seek (only) **eternal life** (16) and that of those who **wish to be perfect** (21). It speaks rather of the obstacle that riches constitute for the following of Jesus and of the impossibility, humanly speaking, for one who has **many possessions** (22) **to enter the kingdom** (24). Actual renunciation of riches is not demanded of all; Matthew counts the rich Joseph of Arimathea as a disciple of Jesus (27, 57). But only the poor in spirit (5, 3) can **enter the kingdom** and, as here, such poverty may entail the sacrifice of one's **possessions.** The Twelve, who **have given up everything** (27) to follow Jesus, will have as their reward a share in Jesus' (the Son of Man's) **judging the twelve tribes of Israel** (28), and all who have similarly sacrificed family or property for his sake **will inherit eternal life** (29).

19, 16: Gain eternal life: this is equivalent to "entering into life" (17) and "being saved" (25); the **life** is that of the new age after the final judgment (see 25, 46). It probably is also equivalent here to "entering the kingdom of heaven" (23) or "the kingdom of God" (24), but see the notes on 3, 2; 4, 17; 18, 1 for the wider reference of **the kingdom** in Mt.

19, 17: By Matthew's reformulation of the Marcan question and reply (Mk 10, 17–18) Jesus' repudiation of the term "good" for himself has been softened. Yet the Marcan assertion that "no one is good but God alone" stands, with only unimportant verbal modification.

19, 18–19: The first five commandments cited are from the Decalogue (see Ex 20, 12–16; Dt 5, 16–20). Matthew omits Mark's "you shall not defraud" (10, 19; see Dt 24, 14) and adds Lv 19, 18. This combination of commandments of the Decalogue with Lv 19, 18 is partially the same as Paul's enumeration of the demands of Christian morality in Rom 13, 9.

19, 20: Young man: in Mt alone of the synoptics the questioner is said to be a **young man;** thus the Marcan "from my youth" (10, 20) is omitted.

19, 21: If you wish to be perfect: to be perfect is demanded of all Christians; see 5, 48. In the case of this man, it involves selling his possessions and giving to the poor; only so can he **follow** Jesus.

19, 23–24: Riches are an obstacle to entering **the kingdom** that cannot be overcome by human power. The comparison with the impossibility of a camel's passing **through the eye of a needle** should not be mitigated by such suppositions as that **the eye of a needle** means a low or narrow gate. **The kingdom of God:** as in 12, 28; 21, 31.43, instead of Mt's usual **kingdom of heaven.**

19, 25–26: See the note on Mk 10, 23–27.

19, 28: This saying, directed to the Twelve, is from Q; see Lk 22, 29–30. **The new age:** the Greek word here translated "new age" occurs in the New Testament only here and in Ti 3, 5. Literally, it means "rebirth" or "regeneration," and is used in Ti of spiritual rebirth through baptism. Here it means the "rebirth" effected by the coming of the kingdom. Since that coming has various stages (see the notes on 3, 2; 4, 17), **the new age** could be taken as referring to the time after the resurrection when the Twelve will govern the true Israel, i.e., the church of Jesus. (For "judge" in the sense of "govern," cf Jgs 12, 8.9.11; 15, 20; 16, 31; Ps 2, 10). But since it is connected here with the time when **the Son of Man will be seated on his throne of glory,** language that Matthew uses in 25, 31 for the time of final judgment, it is more likely that what the Twelve are promised is that they will be joined with Jesus then in judging the people of Israel.

q Mk 10, 13–16; Lk 18, 15–17. r 18, 3; Acts 8, 36. s Mk 10, 17–31; Lk 18, 18–30. t Ex 20, 12–16; Dt 5, 16–20 / Lv 19, 18; Rom 13, 9. u 5, 48; 6, 20. v 7, 14. w Gn 18, 14; Jb 42, 2; Lk 1, 37. x 4, 20.22. y 25, 31; Dn 7, 9.22; Lk 22, 30; Rv 3, 21; 20, 4.

eternal life. [30] [z]*But many who are first will be last, and the last will be first.

CHAPTER 20

The Workers in the Vineyard [1]*"The kingdom of heaven is like a landowner who went out at dawn to hire laborers for his vineyard. [2]After agreeing with them for the usual daily wage, he sent them into his vineyard. [3]Going out about nine o'clock, he saw others standing idle in the marketplace, [4]*and he said to them, 'You too go into my vineyard, and I will give you what is just.' [5]So they went off. [And] he went out again around noon, and around three o'clock, and did likewise. [6]Going out about five o'clock, he found others standing around, and said to them, 'Why do you stand here idle all day?' [7]They answered, 'Because no one has hired us.' He said to them, 'You too go into my vineyard.' [8] [a]*When it was evening the owner of the vineyard said to his foreman, 'Summon the laborers and give them their pay, beginning with the last and ending with the first.' [9]When those who had started about five o'clock came, each received the usual daily wage. [10]So when the first came, they thought that they would receive more, but each of them also got the usual wage. [11]And on receiving it they grumbled against the landowner, [12]saying, 'These last ones worked only one hour, and you have made them equal to us, who bore the day's burden and the heat.' [13]*He said to one of them in reply, 'My friend, I am not cheating you. Did you not agree with me for the usual daily wage? [14]*Take what is yours and go. What if I wish to give this last one the same as you? [15][Or] am I not free to do as I wish with my own money? Are you envious because I am generous?' [16]*Thus, the last will be first, and the first will be last."

The Third Prediction of the Passion [17] [b]*As Jesus was going up to Jerusalem, he took the twelve [disciples] aside by themselves, and said to them on the way, [18]"Behold, we are going up to Jerusalem, and the Son of Man will be handed over to the chief priests and the scribes, and they will condemn him to death, [19]and hand him over to the Gentiles to be mocked and scourged and crucified, and he will be raised on the third day."

The Request of James and John [20] [c]*Then the mother of the sons of Zebedee approached him with her sons and did him homage, wishing to ask him for something. [21]He said to her, "What do you wish?" She answered him, "Command that these two sons of mine sit, one at your right and the other at your left, in your kingdom." [22]*Jesus said in reply, "You do not know what you are asking. Can you drink the cup that I am going to drink?" They said to him, "We can." [23]He replied, "My cup you will

19, 30: Different interpretations have been given to this saying, which comes from Mk 10, 31. In view of Matthew's associating it with the following parable (20, 1–15) and substantially repeating it (in reverse order) at the end of that parable (20, 16), it may be that his meaning is that all who respond to the call of Jesus, at whatever time (**first** or **last**), will be the same in respect to inheriting the benefits of the kingdom, which is the gift of God.

20, 1–16: This parable is peculiar to Mt. It is difficult to know whether the evangelist composed it or received it as part of his traditional material and, if the latter is the case, what its original reference was. In its present context its close association with 19, 30 suggests that its teaching is the equality of all the disciples in the reward of inheriting eternal life.

20, 4: What is just: although the wage is not stipulated as in the case of those first hired, it will be fair.

20, 8: Beginning with the last . . . the first: this element of the parable has no other purpose than to show how **the first** knew what **the last** were given (12).

20, 13: I am not cheating you: literally, "I am not treating you unjustly."

20, 14–15: The owner's conduct involves no violation of justice (4.13), and that all the workers receive the same wage is due only to his generosity to the latest arrivals; the resentment of the first comes from envy.

20, 16: See the note on 19, 30.

20, 17–19: Cf Mk 10, 32–34. This is the third and the most detailed of the passion predictions (16, 21–23; 17, 22–23). It speaks of Jesus' being **handed over to the Gentiles** (27, 2), his being **mocked** (27, 27–30), **scourged** (27, 26), and **crucified** (27, 31.35). In all but the last of these points Matthew agrees with his Marcan source, but whereas Mk speaks of Jesus' being killed (10, 34), Mt has the specific **to be . . . crucified.**

20, 20–28: Cf Mk 10, 35–45. The request of the sons of Zebedee, made through their mother, for the highest places of honor in the **kingdom,** and the indignation of the other **ten** disciples at this request, show that neither **the two brothers** nor the others have understood that what makes for greatness in the kingdom is not lordly power but humble service. Jesus gives the example, and his ministry of service will reach its highest point when he gives his life for the deliverance of the human race from sin.

20, 20–21: The reason for Matthew's making **the mother** the petitioner (cf Mk 10, 35) is not clear. Possibly he intends an allusion to Bathsheba's seeking the kingdom for Solomon; see 1 Kgs 1, 11–21. **Your kingdom:** see the note on 16, 28.

20, 22: You do not know what you are asking: the Greek verbs are plural and, with the rest of the verse, indicate that the answer is addressed not to the woman but to her sons. **Drink the cup:** see the note on Mk 10, 38–40. Matthew omits the Marcan "or be baptized with the baptism with which I am baptized" (10, 38).

z 20, 16. a Lv 19, 13; Dt 24, 15. b 16, 21; 17, 22–23; Mk 10, 32–34; Lk 18, 31–33. c Mk 10, 35–45.

indeed drink, but to sit at my right and at my left
[, this] is not mine to give but is for those for
whom it has been prepared by my Father."
24 dWhen the ten heard this, they became indig-
nant at the two brothers. 25 But Jesus summoned
them and said, "You know that the rulers of the
Gentiles lord it over them, and the great ones
make their authority over them felt. 26 But it
shall not be so among you. Rather, whoever
wishes to be great among you shall be your
servant; 27 ewhoever wishes to be first among
you shall be your slave. 28 f*Just so, the Son of
Man did not come to be served but to serve and
to give his life as a ransom for many."
The Healing of Two Blind Men 29 g*As they
left Jericho, a great crowd followed him.
30 h*Two blind men were sitting by the roadside,
and when they heard that Jesus was passing by,
they cried out, "[Lord,] Son of David, have pity
on us!" 31 The crowd warned them to be silent,
but they called out all the more, "Lord, Son of
David, have pity on us!" 32 Jesus stopped and
called them and said, "What do you want me to
do for you?" 33 They answered him, "Lord, let
our eyes be opened." 34 Moved with pity, Jesus
touched their eyes. Immediately they received
their sight, and followed him.

CHAPTER 21

The Entry into Jerusalem 1 i*When they
drew near Jerusalem and came to Bethphage on
the Mount of Olives, Jesus sent two disciples,
2*saying to them, "Go into the village opposite
you, and immediately you will find an ass
tethered, and a colt with her. Untie them and
bring them here to me. 3 And if anyone should
say anything to you, reply, 'The master has need
of them.' Then he will send them at once."
4*This happened so that what had been spoken
through the prophet might be fulfilled:

5 j"Say to daughter Zion,
'Behold, your king comes to you,
meek and riding on an ass,
and on a colt, the foal of a beast of
burden.' "

6 The disciples went and did as Jesus had ordered
them. 7*They brought the ass and the colt and
laid their cloaks over them, and he sat upon
them. 8 k*The very large crowd spread their

20, 28: Ransom: this noun, which occurs in the New Testament only here and in the Marcan parallel (Mk 10, 45), does not necessarily express the idea of liberation by payment of some price. The cognate verb is used frequently in the LXX of God's liberating Israel from Egypt or from Babylonia after the Exile; see Ex 6, 6; 15, 13; Ps 77 (76 LXX), 16; Is 43, 1; 44, 22. The liberation brought by Jesus' death will be **for many;** cf Is 53, 12. **Many** does not mean that some are excluded, but is a Semitism designating the collectivity who benefit from the service of the one, and is equivalent to "all." While there are few verbal contacts between this saying and the fourth Servant Song (Is 52, 13—53, 12), the ideas of that passage are reflected here.

20, 29–34: The cure of the blind men is probably symbolic of what will happen to the disciples, now blind to the meaning of Jesus' passion and to the necessity of their sharing his suffering. As the men are given sight, so, after the resurrection, will the disciples come to see that to which they are now blind. Matthew has abbreviated his Marcan source (10, 46–52) and has made Mk's one man two. Such doubling is characteristic of this gospel; see 8, 28–34 (// Mk 5, 1–20) and the note on 9, 27–31.

20, 30: [Lord]: some important textual witnesses omit this, but that may be because copyists assimilated this verse to 9, 27. **Son of David:** see the note on 9, 27.

21, 1–11: Jesus' coming to Jerusalem is in accordance with the divine will that he must go there (cf 16, 21) to suffer, die, and be raised. He prepares for his entry into the city in such a way as to make it a fulfillment of the prophecy of Zec 9, 9 (2) that emphasizes the humility of the **king** who **comes** (5). That prophecy, absent from the Marcan parallel account (11, 1–11) although found also in the Johannine account of the entry (12, 15), is the center of the Matthean story. During the procession from Bethphage to Jerusalem, Jesus is acclaimed as the Davidic messianic king by the crowds who accompany him (9). On his arrival **the whole city was shaken,** and to the inquiry of the amazed populace about Jesus' identity the crowds with him reply that he is **the prophet, from Nazareth in Galilee** (10.11).

21, 1: Bethphage: a village that can no longer be certainly identified. Mk mentions it before Bethany (11, 1), which suggests that it lay to the east of the latter. **The Mount of Olives:** the hill east of Jerusalem that is spoken of in Zec 14, 4 as the place where the Lord will come to rescue Jerusalem from the enemy nations.

21, 2: An ass tethered, and a colt with her: instead of the one animal of Mk 11, 2, Mt has two, as demanded by his understanding of Zec 9, 9.

21, 4–5: The prophet: this fulfillment citation is actually composed of two distinct Old Testament texts, Is 62, 11 **(Say to daughter Zion)** and Zec 9, 9. The **ass** and the **colt** are the same animal in the prophecy, mentioned twice in different ways, the common Hebrew literary device of poetic parallelism. That Matthew takes them as two is one of the reasons why some scholars think that he was a Gentile rather than a Jewish Christian who would presumably not make that mistake (see Introduction).

21, 7: Upon them: upon the two animals; an awkward picture resulting from Matthew's misunderstanding of the prophecy.

21, 8: Spread . . . on the road: cf 2 Kgs 9, 13. There is a similarity between the cutting and strewing of the **branches** and the festivities of Tabernacles (Lv 23, 39–40); see also 2 Mc 10, 5–8 where the celebration of the rededication of the temple is compared to that of Tabernacles.

d Lk 22, 25–27. e Mk 9, 35. f 26, 28; Is 53, 12; Rom 5, 6; 1 Tm 2, 6. g Mk 10, 46–52; Lk 18, 35–43. h 9, 27. i Mk 11, 1–11; Lk 19, 28–38; Jn 12, 12–15. j Is 62, 11; Zec 9, 9. k 2 Kgs 9, 13.

cloaks on the road, while others cut branches
from the trees and strewed them on the road.
[9] [l]*The crowds preceding him and those following kept crying out and saying:

"Hosanna to the Son of David;
blessed is he who comes in the name of the Lord;
hosanna in the highest."

[10]*And when he entered Jerusalem the whole
city was shaken and asked, "Who is this?"
[11]*And the crowds replied, "This is Jesus the
prophet, from Nazareth in Galilee."

The Cleansing of the Temple [12] [m] [n]*Jesus
entered the temple area and drove out all those
engaged in selling and buying there. He overturned the tables of the money changers and the
seats of those who were selling doves. [13] [o]*And
he said to them, "It is written:

'My house shall be a house of prayer,'
but you are making it a den of thieves."

[14] [p]*The blind and the lame approached him in
the temple area, and he cured them. [15]*When
the chief priests and the scribes saw the wondrous things he was doing, and the children
crying out in the temple area, "Hosanna to the
Son of David," they were indignant [16] [q]*and said
to him, "Do you hear what they are saying?"
Jesus said to them, "Yes; and have you never
read the text, 'Out of the mouths of infants and
nurslings you have brought forth praise'?" [17]And
leaving them, he went out of the city to Bethany,
and there he spent the night.

The Cursing of the Fig Tree [18] [r]*When he
was going back to the city in the morning, he
was hungry. [19] [s]Seeing a fig tree by the road, he
went over to it, but found nothing on it except
leaves. And he said to it, "May no fruit ever
come from you again." And immediately the fig
tree withered. [20]When the disciples saw this,
they were amazed and said, "How was it that
the fig tree withered immediately?" [21] [t]*Jesus
said to them in reply, "Amen, I say to you, if you
have faith and do not waver, not only will you
do what has been done to the fig tree, but even if
you say to this mountain, 'Be lifted up and
thrown into the sea,' it will be done.
[22] [u]Whatever you ask for in prayer with faith,
you will receive."

21, 9: **Hosanna:** the Hebrew means "(O LORD) grant salvation"; see Ps 118, 25, but that invocation had become an acclamation of jubilation and welcome. **Blessed is he . . . in the name of the Lord:** see Ps 118, 26 and the note on Jn 12, 13. **In the highest:** probably only an intensification of the acclamation, although **Hosanna in the highest** could be taken as a prayer, "May God save (him)."

21, 10: Was shaken: in the gospels this verb is peculiar to Mt where it is used also of the earthquake at the time of the crucifixion (27, 51) and of the terror of the guards of Jesus' tomb at the appearance of the angel (28, 4). For Matthew's use of the cognate noun, see the note on 8, 24.

21, 11: The prophet: see 16, 14 ("one of the prophets") and 21, 46.

21, 12–17: Matthew changes the order of Mk (11, 11.12.15) and places the cleansing of the temple on the same day as the entry into Jerusalem, immediately after it. The activities going on in **the temple area** were not secular but connected with the temple worship. Thus Jesus' attack on those so engaged and his charge that they were **making** God's **house of prayer a den of thieves** (12–13) constituted a claim to authority over the religious practices of Israel and were a challenge to the priestly authorities. Verses 14–17 are peculiar to Mt. Jesus' healings and his countenancing the children's cries of praise rouse the indignation of **the chief priests and the scribes** (15). These two groups appear in the infancy narrative (2, 4) and have been mentioned in the first and third passion predictions (16, 21; 20, 18). Now, as the passion approaches, they come on the scene again, exhibiting their hostility to Jesus.

21, 12: These activities were carried on in the court of the Gentiles, the outermost court of **the temple area.** Animals for sacrifice were sold; the **doves** were for those who could not afford a more expensive offering; see Lv 5, 7. **Tables of the money changers:** only the coinage of Tyre could be used for the purchases; other money had to be exchanged for that.

21, 13: 'My house . . . prayer': cf Is 56, 7. Matthew omits the final words of the quotation, "for all peoples" ("all nations"), possibly because for him the worship of the God of Israel by all nations belongs to the time after the resurrection; see 28, 19. **A den of thieves:** the phrase is taken from Jer 7, 11.

21, 14: The blind and the lame: according to 2 Sm 5, 8 (LXX) **the blind and the lame** were forbidden to enter "the house of the Lord," the temple. These are the last of Jesus' healings in Mt.

21, 15: The wondrous things: the healings.

21, 16: 'Out of the mouths . . . praise': cf Ps 8, 3 (LXX).

21, 18–22: In Mk the effect of Jesus' cursing the fig tree is not immediate; see 11, 14.20. By making it so, Matthew has heightened the miracle. Jesus' act seems arbitrary and ill-tempered, but it is a prophetic action similar to those of Old Testament prophets that vividly symbolize some part of their preaching; see, e.g., Ez 12, 1–20. It is a sign of the judgment that is to come upon the Israel that with all its apparent piety lacks the fruit of good deeds (3, 10) and will soon bear the punishment of its fruitlessness (43). Some scholars propose that this story is the development in tradition of a parable of Jesus about the destiny of a fruitless tree, such as Lk 13, 6–9. Jesus' answer to the question of the amazed disciples (20) makes the miracle an example of the power of prayer made with unwavering **faith** (21–22).

21, 21: See 17, 20.

l Ps 118, 25–26. m Mk 11, 15–19; Lk 19, 45–48; Jn 2, 14–22. n Lv 5, 7. o Is 56, 7; Jer 7, 11. p 2 Sm 5, 8 LXX. q Ps 8, 2 LXX; Wis 10, 21. r Mk 11, 12–14.20–24. s Jer 8, 13; Lk 13, 6–9. t 17, 20; Lk 17, 6. u 7, 7; 1 Jn 3, 22.

The Authority of Jesus Questioned
23vw*When he had come into the temple area,
the chief priests and the elders of the people
approached him as he was teaching and said,
"By what authority are you doing these things?
And who gave you this authority?" 24*Jesus said
to them in reply, "I shall ask you one question,
and if you answer it for me, then I shall tell you
by what authority I do these things. 25Where
was John's baptism from? Was it of heavenly or
of human origin?" They discussed this among
themselves and said, "If we say 'Of heavenly
origin,' he will say to us, 'Then why did you not
believe him?' 26x*But if we say, 'Of human
origin,' we fear the crowd, for they all regard
John as a prophet." 27*So they said to Jesus in
reply, "We do not know." He himself said to
them, "Neither shall I tell you by what authority
I do these things.
The Parable of the Two Sons 28*"What is
your opinion? A man had two sons. He came to
the first and said, 'Son, go out and work in the
vineyard today.' 29He said in reply, 'I will not,'
but afterwards he changed his mind and went.
30The man came to the other son and gave the
same order. He said in reply, 'Yes, sir,' but did
not go. 31*Which of the two did his father's
will?" They answered, "The first." Jesus said to
them, "Amen, I say to you, tax collectors and
prostitutes are entering the kingdom of God
before you. 32y*When John came to you in the
way of righteousness, you did not believe him;
but tax collectors and prostitutes did. Yet even
when you saw that, you did not later change
your minds and believe him.
The Parable of the Tenants 33za*"Hear an-
other parable. There was a landowner who
planted a vineyard, put a hedge around it, dug a
wine press in it, and built a tower. Then he
leased it to tenants and went on a journey.
34*When vintage time drew near, he sent his
servants to the tenants to obtain his produce.
35But the tenants seized the servants and one
they beat, another they killed, and a third they
stoned. 36Again he sent other servants, more
numerous than the first ones, but they treated

21, 23–27: Cf Mk 11, 27–33. This is the first of five controversies between Jesus and the religious authorities of Judaism in 21, 23—22, 46, presented in the form of questions and answers.

21, 23: These things: probably his entry into the city, his cleansing of the temple, and his healings there.

21, 24: To reply by counterquestion was common in rabbinical debate.

21, 26: We fear . . . as a prophet: cf 14, 5.

21, 27: Since through embarrassment on the one hand and fear on the other the religious authorities claim ignorance of the origin of John's baptism, they show themselves incapable of speaking with authority; hence Jesus refuses to discuss with them the grounds of his authority.

21, 28–32: The series of controversies is interrupted by three parables on the judgment of Israel (21, 28—22, 14) of which this, peculiar to Mt, is the first. The second (21, 33–46) comes from Mk (12, 1–12), and the third (22, 1–14) from Q; see Lk 14, 15–24. This interruption of the controversies is similar to that in Mk, although Mk has only one parable between the first and second controversy. As regards Mt's first parable, vv 28–30 if taken by themselves could point simply to the difference between saying and doing, a theme of much importance in this gospel (cf 7, 21; 12, 50); that may have been the parable's original reference. However, it is given a more specific application by the addition of vv 31–32. The two sons represent, respectively, the religious leaders and the religious outcasts who followed John's call to repentance. By the answer they give to Jesus' question (31) the leaders condemn themselves. There is much confusion in the textual tradition of the parable. Of the three different forms of the text given by important textual witnesses, one has the leaders answer that the son who agreed to go but did not was the one who did the father's will. Although some scholars accept that as the original reading, their arguments in favor of it seem unconvincing. The choice probably lies only between a reading that puts the son who agrees and then disobeys before the son who at first refuses and then obeys, and the reading followed in the present translation. The witnesses to the latter reading are slightly better than those that support the other.

21, 31: Entering . . . before you: this probably means "they enter; you do not."

21, 32: Cf Lk 7, 29–30. Although the thought is similar to that of the Lucan text, the formulation is so different that it is improbable that the saying comes from Q. **Came to you . . . way of righteousness:** several meanings are possible: that John himself was righteous, that he taught righteousness to others, or that he had an important place in God's plan of salvation. For the last, see the note on 3, 14–15.

21, 33–46: Cf Mk 12, 1–12. In this parable there is a close correspondence between most of the details of the story and the situation that it illustrates, the dealings of God with his people. Because of that heavy allegorizing, some scholars think that it does not in any way go back to Jesus, but represents the theology of the later church. That judgment applies to the Marcan parallel as well, although the allegorizing has gone farther in Mt. There are others who believe that while many of the allegorical elements are due to church sources, they have been added to a basic parable spoken by Jesus. This view is now supported by the Gospel of Thomas, #65, where a less allegorized and probably more primitive form of the parable is found.

21, 33: Planted a vineyard . . . a tower: cf Is 5, 1–2. The **vineyard** is defined in Is 5, 7 as "the house of Israel."

21, 34–35: His servants: Mt has two sendings of **servants** as against Mk's three sendings of a single servant (11, 2–5a) followed by a statement about the sending of "many others" (11, 2.5b). That these **servants** stand for the prophets sent by God to Israel is clearly implied but not made explicit here, but see 23, 37. **His produce:** cf Mk 12, 2, "some of the produce." The **produce** is the good works demanded by God, and his claim to them is total.

v Mk 11, 27–33; Lk 20, 1–8. w Jn 2, 18. x 14, 5. y Lk 7, 29–30. z Mk 12, 1–12; Lk 20, 9–19. a Is 5, 1–2.7.

them in the same way. 37 Finally, he sent his son
to them, thinking, 'They will respect my son.'
38 *But when the tenants saw the son, they said
to one another, 'This is the heir. Come, let us kill
him and acquire his inheritance.' 39 [b]*They
seized him, threw him out of the vineyard, and
killed him. 40 What will the owner of the vine-
yard do to those tenants when he comes?"
41 *They answered him, "He will put those
wretched men to a wretched death and lease his
vineyard to other tenants who will give him the
produce at the proper times." 42 [c]*Jesus said to
them, "Did you never read in the scriptures:

'The stone that the builders rejected
has become the cornerstone;
by the Lord has this been done,
and it is wonderful in our eyes'?

43 *Therefore, I say to you, the kingdom of God
will be taken away from you and given to a
people that will produce its fruit.[44 *The one
who falls on this stone will be dashed to pieces;
and it will crush anyone on whom it falls.]"
45 *When the chief priests and the Pharisees
heard his parables, they knew that he was
speaking about them. 46 And although they were
attempting to arrest him, they feared the crowds,
for they regarded him as a prophet.

CHAPTER 22

The Parable of the Wedding Feast 1 [d]*Jesus
again in reply spoke to them in parables, saying,
2 *"The kingdom of heaven may be likened to a
king who gave a wedding feast for his son. 3 *He
dispatched his servants to summon the invited
guests to the feast, but they refused to come. 4 A
second time he sent other servants, saying, 'Tell
those invited: "Behold, I have prepared my
banquet, my calves and fattened cattle are killed,
and everything is ready; come to the feast." '
5 Some ignored the invitation and went away,
one to his farm, another to his business. 6 [e]The
rest laid hold of his servants, mistreated them,
and killed them. 7 *The king was enraged and
sent his troops, destroyed those murderers, and
burned their city. 8 Then he said to his servants,
'The feast is ready, but those who were invited
were not worthy to come. 9 Go out, therefore,
into the main roads and invite to the feast
whomever you find.' 10 *The servants went out
into the streets and gathered all they found, bad
and good alike, and the hall was filled with
guests. 11 *But when the king came in to meet
the guests he saw a man there not dressed in a
wedding garment. 12 He said to him, 'My friend,
how is it that you came in here without a
wedding garment?' But he was reduced to

21, 38: Acquire his inheritance: if a Jewish proselyte died without heir, the tenants of his land would have final claim on it.

21, 39: Threw him out . . . and killed him: the change in the Marcan order where the son is killed and his corpse then thrown out (12, 8) was probably made because of the tradition that Jesus died outside the city of Jerusalem; see Jn 19, 17; Heb 13, 12.

21, 41: They answered: in Mk 12, 9 the question is answered by Jesus himself; here the leaders answer and so condemn themselves; cf v 31. Matthew adds that the new **tenants** to whom the vineyard will be transferred **will give** the owner **the produce at the proper times.**

21, 42: Cf Ps 118, 22–23. The psalm was used in the early church as a prophecy of Jesus' resurrection; see Acts 4, 11; 1 Pt 2, 7. If, as some think, the original parable ended at v 39, it was thought necessary to complete it by a reference to Jesus' vindication by God.

21, 43: Peculiar to Mt. **Kingdom of God:** see the note on 19, 23–24. Its presence here instead of Mt's usual "kingdom of heaven" may indicate that the saying came from Matthew's own traditional material. **A people that will produce its fruit:** believing Israelites and Gentiles, the church of Jesus.

21, 44: The majority of textual witnesses omit this verse. It is probably an early addition to Mt from Lk 20, 18 with which it is practically identical.

21, 45: The Pharisees: Matthew inserts into the group of Jewish leaders (23) those who represented the Judaism of his own time.

22, 1–14: This parable is from Q; see Lk 14, 15–24. It has been given many allegorical traits by Matthew, e.g., the burning of the **city** of the guests who refused the invitation (7), which corresponds to the destruction of Jerusalem by the Romans in A.D. 70. It has similarities with the preceding parable of the tenants: the sending of two groups of **servants** (3.4), the murder of the **servants** (6), the punishment of the **murderers** (7), and the entrance of a new group into a privileged situation of which the others had proved themselves unworthy (8–10). The parable ends with a section that is peculiar to Mt (11–14), which some take as a distinct parable. Mt presents the **kingdom** in its double aspect, already present and something that can be entered here and now (1–10), and something that will be possessed only by those present members who can stand the scrutiny of the final judgment (11–14). The parable is not only a statement of God's judgment on Israel but a warning to Matthew's church.

22, 2: Wedding feast: the Old Testament's portrayal of final salvation under the image of a banquet (Is 25, 6) is taken up also in 8, 11; cf Lk 13, 15.

22, 3–4: Servants . . . other servants: probably Christian missionaries in both instances; cf 23, 34.

22, 7: See the note on vv 1–14.

22, 10: Bad and good alike: cf 13, 47.

22, 11: A wedding garment: the repentance, change of heart and mind, that is the condition for entrance into the kingdom (3, 2; 4, 17) must be continued in a life of good deeds (7, 21–23).

b Heb 13, 12. c Ps 118, 22–23; Is 28, 16; Acts 4, 11; 1 Pt 2, 7. d Lk 14, 15–24. e 21, 35.

silence. 13f*Then the king said to his attendants,
'Bind his hands and feet, and cast him into the
darkness outside, where there will be wailing
and grinding of teeth.' 14Many are invited, but
few are chosen."

Paying Taxes to the Emperor 15g*Then the
Pharisees went off and plotted how they might
entrap him in speech. 16*They sent their disci-
ples to him, with the Herodians, saying,
"Teacher, we know that you are a truthful man
and that you teach the way of God in accordance
with the truth. And you are not concerned with
anyone's opinion, for you do not regard a
person's status. 17*Tell us, then, what is your
opinion: Is it lawful to pay the census tax to
Caesar or not?" 18Knowing their malice, Jesus
said, "Why are you testing me, you hypocrites?
19*Show me the coin that pays the census tax."
Then they handed him the Roman coin. 20He
said to them, "Whose image is this and whose
inscription?" 21h*They replied, "Caesar's." At
that he said to them, "Then repay to Caesar
what belongs to Caesar and to God what belongs
to God." 22When they heard this they were
amazed, and leaving him they went away.

The Question about the Resurrection
23i*On that day Sadducees approached him,
saying that there is no resurrection. They put
this question to him, 24j*saying, "Teacher, Mo-
ses said, 'If a man dies without children, his
brother shall marry his wife and raise up descen-
dants for his brother.' 25Now there were seven
brothers among us. The first married and died
and, having no descendants, left his wife to his
brother. 26The same happened with the second
and the third, through all seven. 27Finally the
woman died. 28Now at the resurrection, of the
seven, whose wife will she be? For they all had
been married to her." 29*Jesus said to them in
reply, "You are misled because you do not know
the scriptures or the power of God. 30At the
resurrection they neither marry nor are given in
marriage but are like the angels in heaven.
31*And concerning the resurrection of the dead,

22, 13: Wailing and grinding of teeth: the Christian who lacks the wedding garment of good deeds will suffer the same fate as those Jews who have rejected Jesus; see the note on 8, 11–12.

22, 15–22: The series of controversies between Jesus and the representatives of Judaism (see the note on 21, 23–27) is resumed. As in the first (21, 23–27), here and in the following disputes Matthew follows his Marcan source with few modifications.

22, 15: The Pharisees: while Matthew retains the Marcan union of Pharisees and Herodians in this account, he clearly emphasizes the Pharisees' part. They alone are mentioned here, and the Herodians are joined with them only in a prepositional phrase of v 16. **Entrap him in speech:** the question that they will pose is intended to force Jesus to take either a position contrary to that held by the majority of the people or one that will bring him into conflict with the Roman authorities.

22, 16: Herodians: see the note on Mk 3, 6. They would favor payment of the tax; the Pharisees did not.

22, 17: Is it lawful: the law to which they refer is the law of God.

22, 19: They handed him the Roman coin: their readiness in producing the money implies their use of it and their acceptance of the financial advantages of the Roman administration in Palestine.

22, 21: Caesar's: the emperor Tiberius (A.D. 14–37). **Repay to Caesar what belongs to Caesar:** those who willingly use the coin that is Caesar's should **repay** him in kind. The answer avoids taking sides in the question of the lawfulness of the tax. **To God what belongs to God:** Jesus raises the debate to a new level. Those who have hypocritically asked about tax in respect to its relation to the law of God should be concerned rather with repaying **God** with the good deeds that are his due; cf 21, 41.43.

22, 23–33: Here Jesus' opponents are the **Sadducees,** members of the powerful priestly party of his time; see the note on 3, 7. Denying the resurrection of the dead, a teaching of relatively late origin in Judaism (cf Dn 12, 2), they appeal to a law of the Pentateuch (Dt 25, 5–10) and present a case based on it that would make resurrection from the dead ridiculous (24–28). Jesus chides them for knowing neither **the scriptures** nor **the power of God** (29). His argument in respect to God's **power** contradicts the notion, held even by many proponents as well as by opponents of the teaching, that the life of those raised from the dead would be essentially a continuation of the type of life they had had before death (30). His argument based on the scriptures (31–32) is of a sort that was accepted as valid among Jews of the time.

22, 23: Saying that there is no resurrection: in the Marcan parallel (12, 18) the Sadducees are correctly defined as those "who say there is no resurrection"; see also Lk 20, 27. Matthew's rewording of Mk can mean that these particular Sadducees deny the resurrection, which would imply that he was not aware that the denial was characteristic of the party. For some scholars this is an indication of his being a Gentile Christian; see the note on 21, 4–5.

22, 24: 'If a man dies . . . his brother': this is known as the "law of the levirate," from the Latin **levir,** "brother-in-law." Its purpose was to continue the family line of the deceased **brother** (Dt 25, 6).

22, 29: The sexual relationships of this world will be transcended; the risen body will be the work of the creative **power of God.**

22, 31–32: Cf Ex 3, 6. In the Pentateuch, which the Sadducees accepted as normative for Jewish belief and practice, God speaks even now (**to you**) of himself as the God of the patriarchs who died centuries ago. He identifies himself in relation to them, and because of their relation to him, the living God, they too are alive. This might appear no argument for the resurrection, but simply for life after death as conceived in Wis 3, 1–3. But the general thought of early first-century Judaism was not influenced by that conception; for it human immortality was connected with the existence of the body.

f 8, 12; 25, 30. g Mk 12, 13–17; Lk 20, 20–26. h Rom 13, 7. i Mk 12, 18–27; Lk 20, 27–40. j Gn 38, 8; Dt 25, 5–6.

have you not read what was said to you by God,
[32] [k]'I am the God of Abraham, the God of Isaac,
and the God of Jacob'? He is not the God of the
dead but of the living." [33]When the crowds
heard this, they were astonished at his teaching.

The Greatest Commandment [34] [l]*When the
Pharisees heard that he had silenced the Saddu-
cees, they gathered together, [35]*and one of
them [a scholar of the law] tested him by asking,
[36]*"Teacher, which commandment in the law is
the greatest?" [37] [m]*He said to him, "You shall
love the Lord, your God, with all your heart,
with all your soul, and with all your mind. [38]This
is the greatest and the first commandment.
[39] [n]*The second is like it: You shall love your
neighbor as yourself. [40] [o]*The whole law and the
prophets depend on these two commandments."

The Question about David's Son [41] [p]*While
the Pharisees were gathered together, Jesus ques-
tioned them, [42]*saying, "What is your opinion
about the Messiah? Whose son is he?" They
replied, "David's." [43]He said to them, "How,
then, does David, inspired by the Spirit, call him
'lord,' saying:

[44] [q]'The Lord said to my lord,
"Sit at my right hand
until I place your enemies under your
feet" '?

[45]*If David calls him 'lord,' how can he be his
son?" [46] [r]No one was able to answer him a word,
nor from that day on did anyone dare to ask him
any more questions.

CHAPTER 23

Denunciation of the Scribes and Pharisees

[1] [s]*Then Jesus spoke to the crowds and to his
disciples, [2]*saying, "The scribes and the Phari-

22, 34–40: The Marcan parallel (12, 28–34) is an exchange between Jesus and a scribe who is impressed by the way in which Jesus has conducted himself in the previous controversy (12, 28), who compliments him for the answer he gives him (12, 32), and who is said by Jesus to be "not far from the kingdom of God" (12, 34). Matthew has sharpened that scene. The questioner, as the representative of other Pharisees, tests Jesus by his question (34–35), and both his reaction to Jesus' reply and Jesus' commendation of him are lacking.

22, 35: [A scholar of the law]: meaning "scribe." Although this reading is supported by the vast majority of textual witnesses, it is the only time that the Greek word so translated occurs in Mt. It is relatively frequent in Lk, and there is reason to think that it may have been added here by a copyist since it occurs in the Lucan parallel (10, 25–28). **Tested:** see the note on 19, 3.

22, 36: For the devout Jew all the commandments were to be kept with equal care, but there is evidence of preoccupation in Jewish sources with the question put to Jesus.

22, 37–38: Cf Dt 6, 5. Matthew omits the first part of Mk's fuller quotation (12, 29; Dt 6, 4–5), probably because he considered its monotheistic emphasis needless for his church. The love of God must engage the total person (**heart, soul, mind**).

22, 39: Jesus goes beyond the extent of the question put to him and joins to **the greatest and the first commandment a second,** that of **love of neighbor,** Lv 19, 18; see the note on 19, 18–19. This combination of the two commandments may already have been made in Judaism.

22, 40: The double commandment is the source from which **the whole law and the prophets** are derived.

22, 41–46: Having answered the questions of his opponents in the preceding three controversies, Jesus now puts a question to them about the sonship of the Messiah. Their easy response (43a) is countered by his quoting a verse of Ps 110 that raises a problem for their response (43b-45). They are unable to solve it and **from that day** on their questioning of him is ended.

22, 41: The Pharisees . . . questioned them: Mk is not specific about who are questioned (12, 35).

22, 42–44: David's: this view of the Pharisees was based on such Old Testament texts as Is 11, 1–9; Jer 23, 5; and Ez 34, 23; see also the extrabiblical Psalms of Solomon 17, 21. **How, then . . . saying:** Jesus cites Ps 110, 1, accepting the Davidic authorship of the psalm, a common view of his time. The psalm was probably composed for the enthronement of a Davidic king of Judah. Matthew assumes that the Pharisees interpret it as referring to the Messiah, although there is no clear evidence that it was so interpreted in the Judaism of Jesus' time. It was widely used in the early church as referring to the exaltation of the risen Jesus. **My lord:** understood as the Messiah.

22, 45: Since Matthew presents Jesus both as Messiah (16, 16) and as Son of David (1, 1; see also the note on 9, 27), the question is not meant to imply Jesus' denial of Davidic sonship. It probably means that although he is the Son of David, he is someone greater, Son of Man and Son of God, and recognized as greater by David who calls him my **'lord.'**

23, 1–39: The final section of the narrative part of the fifth book of the gospel is a denunciation by Jesus of the scribes and the Pharisees (see the note on 3, 7). It depends in part on Mk and Q (cf Mk 12, 38–39; Lk 11, 37–52; 13, 34–35), but in the main it is peculiar to Mt. (For the reasons against considering this extensive body of sayings-material either as one of the structural discourses of this gospel or as part of the one that follows in chs 24–25, see the note on 19, 1—23, 39.) While the tradition of a deep opposition between Jesus and the Pharisees is well founded, this speech reflects an opposition that goes beyond that of Jesus' ministry and must be seen as expressing the bitter conflict between Pharisaic Judaism and the church of Matthew at the time when the gospel was composed. The complaint often made that the speech ignores the positive qualities of Pharisaism and of its better representatives is true, but the complaint overlooks the circumstances that gave rise to the invective. Nor is the speech purely anti-Pharisaic. The evangelist discerns in his church many of the same faults that he finds in its opponents and warns his fellow Christians to look to their own conduct and attitudes.

23, 2–3: Have taken their seat . . . Moses: it is uncertain whether this is simply a metaphor for Mosaic teaching authority or refers to an actual **chair** on which the teacher sat. It has been proved that there was a seat so designated in synagogues of a later period than that of this gospel. **Do and observe . . . they tell you:** since the Matthean Jesus abrogates Mosaic law (5, 31–42), warns

k Ex 3, 6. l Mk 12, 28–34; Lk 10, 25–28. m Dt 6, 5. n Lv 19, 18; Jas 2, 8. o Rom 13, 8–10; Gal 5, 14. p Mk 12, 35–37; Lk 20, 41–44. q Ps 110, 1; Acts 2, 35; Heb 1, 13. r Lk 20, 40. s Mk 12, 38–39; Lk 11, 37–52; 13, 34–35.

sees have taken their seat on the chair of
Moses. 3 Therefore, do and observe all things
whatsoever they tell you, but do not follow
their example. For they preach but they do not
practice. 4 t*They tie up heavy burdens [hard to
carry] and lay them on people's shoulders, but
they will not lift a finger to move them. 5 u*All
their works are performed to be seen. They
widen their phylacteries and lengthen their tas-
sels. 6 v*They love places of honor at banquets,
seats of honor in synagogues, 7 greetings in
marketplaces, and the salutation 'Rabbi.' 8 *As
for you, do not be called 'Rabbi.' You have but
one teacher, and you are all brothers. 9 Call no
one on earth your father; you have but one
Father in heaven. 10 Do not be called 'Master';
you have but one master, the Messiah. 11 wThe
greatest among you must be your servant.
12 xWhoever exalts himself will be humbled;
but whoever humbles himself will be exalted.

13 y*"Woe to you, scribes and Pharisees, you
hypocrites. You lock the kingdom of heaven
before human beings. You do not enter your-
selves, nor do you allow entrance to those trying
to enter. [14] *

15 *"Woe to you, scribes and Pharisees, you
hypocrites. You traverse sea and land to make
one convert, and when that happens you make
him a child of Gehenna twice as much as
yourselves.

16 z*"Woe to you, blind guides, who say, 'If
one swears by the temple, it means nothing, but
if one swears by the gold of the temple, one is
obligated.' 17 Blind fools, which is greater, the
gold, or the temple that made the gold sacred?
18 And you say, 'If one swears by the altar, it
means nothing, but if one swears by the gift on

---

his disciples against the teaching of the Pharisees (14, 1–12), and, in this speech, denounces the Pharisees as blind guides in respect to their teaching on oaths (16–22), this commandment to **observe all things whatsoever they** (the scribes and Pharisees) **tell you** cannot be taken as the evangelist's understanding of the proper standard of conduct for his church. The saying may reflect a period when the Matthean community was largely Jewish Christian and was still seeking to avoid a complete break with the synagogue. Matthew has incorporated this traditional material into the speech in accordance with his view of the course of salvation history, in which he portrays the time of Jesus' ministry as marked by the fidelity to the law, although with significant pointers to the new situation that would exist after his death and resurrection (see the note on 5, 17–20). The crowds and the disciples (1) are exhorted not to **follow** the **example** of the Jewish leaders, whose deeds do not conform to their teaching (3).

23, 4: Tie up heavy burdens: see the note on 11, 28.

23, 5: To the charge of preaching but not practicing (3), Jesus adds that of acting in order to earn praise. The disciples have already been warned against this same fault (see the note on 6, 1–18). **Phylacteries:** the Mosaic law required that during prayer small boxes containing parchments on which verses of scripture were written be worn on the left forearm and the forehead (see Ex 13, 9.16; Dt 6, 8; 11, 18). **Tassels:** see the note on 9, 20. The widening of **phylacteries** and the lengthening of **tassels** were for the purpose of making these evidences of piety more noticeable.

23, 6–7: Cf Mk 12, 38–39. **'Rabbi':** literally, "my great one," a title of respect for teachers and leaders.

23, 8–12: These verses, warning against the use of various titles, are addressed to the disciples alone. While only the title **'Rabbi'** has been said to be used in addressing the scribes and Pharisees (7), the implication is that **Father** and **'Master'** also were. The prohibition of these titles to the disciples suggests that their use was present in Matthew's church. The Matthean Jesus forbids not only the titles but the spirit of superiority and pride that is shown by their acceptance. **Whoever exalts . . . will be exalted:** cf Lk 14, 11.

23, 13–36: This series of seven "woes," directed against the **scribes and Pharisees** and addressed to them, is the heart of the speech. The phrase **woe to** occurs often in the prophetic and apocalyptic literature, expressing horror of a sin and punishment for those who commit it. **Hypocrites:** see the note on 6, 2. The hypocrisy of the **scribes and Pharisees** consists in the difference between their speech and action (3) and in demonstrations of piety that have no other purpose than to enhance their reputation as religious persons (5).

23, 13: You lock the kingdom of heaven: cf 16, 19 where Jesus tells Peter that he will give him the keys to **the kingdom of heaven.** The purpose of the authority expressed by that metaphor is to give entrance into the kingdom (the kingdom is closed only to those who reject the authority); here the charge is made that the authority of the **scribes and Pharisees** is exercised in such a way as to be an obstacle to entrance. Cf Lk 11, 52 where the accusation against the "scholars of the law" (Mt's **scribes**) is that they "have taken away the key of knowledge."

23, 14: Some manuscripts add a verse here or after v 12, "Woe to you, scribes and Pharisees, you hypocrites. You devour the houses of widows and, as a pretext, recite lengthy prayers. Because of this, you will receive a very severe condemnation." Cf Mk 12, 40; Lk 20, 47. This "woe" is almost identical with Mk 12, 40 and seems to be an interpolation derived from that text.

23, 15: In the first century A.D. until the First Jewish Revolt against Rome (A.D. 66–70), many Pharisees conducted a vigorous missionary campaign among Gentiles. **Convert:** literally, "proselyte," a Gentile who accepted Judaism fully by submitting to circumcision and all other requirements of Mosaic law. **Child of Gehenna:** worthy of everlasting punishment; for **Gehenna,** see the note on 5, 22. **Twice as much as yourselves:** possibly this refers simply to the zeal of the **convert,** surpassing that of the one who converted him.

23, 16–22: An attack on the casuistry that declared some oaths binding (**one is obligated**) and others not (**it means nothing**) and held the binding oath to be the one made by something of lesser value (**the gold; the gift on the altar**). Such teaching, which inverts the order of values, reveals the teachers to be **blind guides;** cf 15, 14. Since the Matthean Jesus forbids all oaths to his disciples (5, 33–37), this **woe** does not set up a standard for Christian moral conduct, but ridicules the Pharisees on their own terms.

t Lk 11, 46. u 6, 1–6; Ex 13, 9.16; Nm 15, 38–39; Dt 6, 8; 11, 18. v Mk 12, 38–39; Lk 11, 43; 20, 46. w 20, 26. x Lk 14, 11; 18, 14. y Lk 11, 52. z 15, 14.

the altar, one is obligated.' [19]You blind ones, which is greater, the gift, or the altar that makes the gift sacred? [20] [a]One who swears by the altar swears by it and all that is upon it; [21]one who swears by the temple swears by it and by him who dwells in it; [22]one who swears by heaven swears by the throne of God and by him who is seated on it.

[23] [b]*"Woe to you, scribes and Pharisees, you hypocrites. You pay tithes of mint and dill and cummin, and have neglected the weightier things of the law: judgment and mercy and fidelity. [But] these you should have done, without neglecting the others. [24] [c]*Blind guides, who strain out the gnat and swallow the camel!

[25] [d]*"Woe to you, scribes and Pharisees, you hypocrites. You cleanse the outside of cup and dish, but inside they are full of plunder and self-indulgence. [26]Blind Pharisee, cleanse first the inside of the cup, so that the outside also may be clean.

[27]*"Woe to you, scribes and Pharisees, you hypocrites. You are like whitewashed tombs, which appear beautiful on the outside, but inside are full of dead men's bones and every kind of filth. [28] [e]Even so, on the outside you appear righteous, but inside you are filled with hypocrisy and evildoing.

[29]*"Woe to you, scribes and Pharisees, you hypocrites. You build the tombs of the prophets and adorn the memorials of the righteous, [30] [f]and you say, 'If we had lived in the days of our ancestors, we would not have joined them in shedding the prophets' blood.' [31] [g]Thus you bear witness against yourselves that you are the children of those who murdered the prophets; [32]now fill up what your ancestors measured out! [33] [h]You serpents, you brood of vipers, how can you flee from the judgment of Gehenna? [34] [i]*Therefore, behold, I send to you prophets and wise men and scribes; some of them you will kill and crucify, some of them you will scourge in your synagogues and pursue from town to town, [35]so that there may come upon you all the righteous blood shed upon earth, from the righteous blood of Abel to the blood of Zechariah, the son of Barachiah, whom you murdered between the sanctuary and the altar. [36]Amen, I say to you, all these things will come upon this generation.

23, 23: The Mosaic law ordered tithing of the produce of the land (Lv 27, 30; Dt 14, 22–23), and the scribal tradition is said here to have extended this law to even the smallest herbs. The practice is criticized not in itself but because it shows the Pharisees' preoccupation with matters of less importance while they neglect **the weightier things of the law.**

23, 24: Cf Lv 11, 41–45 that forbids the eating of any "swarming creature." The Pharisees' scrupulosity about minor matters and neglect of greater ones (23) is further brought out by this contrast between straining liquids that might contain a tiny "swarming creature" and yet swallowing **the camel.** The latter was one of the unclean animals forbidden by the law (Lv 11, 4), but it is hardly possible that the scribes and Pharisees are being denounced as guilty of so gross a violation of the food laws. To **swallow the camel** is only a hyperbolic way of speaking of their neglect of what is important.

23, 25–26: The ritual washing of utensils for dining (cf Mk 7, 4) is turned into a metaphor illustrating a concern for appearances while inner purity is ignored. The **scribes and Pharisees** are compared to cups carefully washed on the outside but filthy within. **Self-indulgence:** the Greek word here translated means lack of self-control, whether in drinking or in sexual conduct.

23, 27–28: The sixth **woe,** like the preceding one, deals with concern for externals and neglect of what is **inside.** Since contact with dead bodies, even when one was unaware of it, caused ritual impurity (Nm 19, 11–22), tombs were whitewashed so that no one would contract such impurity inadvertently.

23, 29–36: The final **woe** is the most serious indictment of all. It portrays the **scribes and Pharisees** as standing in the same line as their **ancestors** who murdered **the prophets** and **the righteous.**

23, 29–32: In spite of honoring the slain dead by building their **tombs** and adorning their **memorials,** and claiming that they would not have joined in their ancestors' crimes if they **had lived in their days,** the **scribes and Pharisees** are true **children** of their ancestors and are defiantly ordered by Jesus to **fill up** what those **ancestors measured out.** This order reflects the Jewish notion that there was an allotted measure of suffering that had to be completed before God's final judgment would take place.

23, 34–36: There are important differences between the Matthean and the Lucan form of this Q material; cf Lk 11, 49–51. In Lk the one who sends the emissaries is the "wisdom of God." If, as many scholars think, that is the original wording of Q, Matthew, by making Jesus the sender, has presented him as the personified divine wisdom. In Lk, wisdom's emissaries are the Old Testament "prophets" and the Christian "apostles." Mt's **prophets and wise men and scribes** are probably Christian disciples alone; cf 10, 41 and see the note on 13, 52. **You will kill:** see 24, 9. **Scourge in your synagogues . . . town to town:** see 10, 17.23 and the note on 10, 17. **All the righteous blood shed upon the earth:** the slaying of the disciples is in continuity with all the shedding of **righteous blood** beginning with that of **Abel.** The persecution of Jesus' disciples by **this generation** involves the persecutors in the guilt of their murderous ancestors. **The blood of Zechariah:** see the note on Lk 11, 51. By identifying him as **the son of Barachiah** Matthew understands him to be Zechariah the Old Testament minor prophet; see Zec 1, 1.

a 5, 34–35. b Lv 27, 30; Dt 14, 22; Lk 11, 42. c Lv 11, 41–45. d Mk 7, 4; Lk 11, 39. e Lk 16, 15; 18, 9. f Lk 11, 47. g Acts 7, 52. h 3, 7; 12, 34. i 5, 12; Gn 4, 8; 2 Chr 24, 20–22; Zec 1, 1; Lk 11, 49–51; Rv 18, 24.

The Lament over Jerusalem 37 [j,k]*“Jeru-
salem, Jerusalem, you who kill the prophets and
stone those sent to you, how many times I
yearned to gather your children together, as a
hen gathers her young under her wings, but you
were unwilling! 38 [l]Behold, your house will be
abandoned, desolate. 39 [m]I tell you, you will not
see me again until you say, ‘Blessed is he who
comes in the name of the Lord.’ ”

CHAPTER 24

The Destruction of the Temple Foretold

1 [n]*Jesus left the temple area and was going
away, when his disciples approached him to
point out the temple buildings. 2 *He said to
them in reply, “You see all these things, do you
not? Amen, I say to you, there will not be left
here a stone upon another stone that will not be
thrown down.”
The Beginning of Calamities 3 *As he was
sitting on the Mount of Olives, the disciples
approached him privately and said, “Tell us,
when will this happen, and what sign will there
be of your coming, and of the end of the age?”
4 *Jesus said to them in reply, “See that no one
deceives you. 5 For many will come in my name,
saying, ‘I am the Messiah,’ and they will deceive
many. 6 [o]*You will hear of wars and reports of
wars; see that you are not alarmed, for these
things must happen, but it will not yet be the
end. 7 [p]Nation will rise against nation, and king-
dom against kingdom; there will be famines and
earthquakes from place to place. 8 *All these are
the beginning of the labor pains. 9 [q]*Then they

23, 37–39: Cf Lk 13, 34–35. The denunciation of Pharisaic Judaism ends with this lament over **Jerusalem,** which has repeatedly rejected and murdered those whom God has **sent to** her. **How many times:** this may refer to various visits of Jesus to the city, an aspect of his ministry found in Jn but otherwise not in the synoptics. **As a hen . . . under her wings:** for imagery similar to this, see Pss 17, 8; 91, 4. **Your house . . . desolate:** probably an allusion to the destruction of the temple in A.D. 70. **You will not see me . . . in the name of the Lord:** Israel will not see Jesus again until he comes in glory for the final judgment. The acclamation has been interpreted in contrasting ways, as an indication that Israel will at last accept Jesus at that time, and as its troubled recognition of him as its dreaded judge who will pronounce its condemnation; in support of the latter view see 24, 30.

24, 1—25, 46: The discourse of the fifth book, the last of the five around which the gospel is structured. It is called the “eschatological” discourse since it deals with the coming of the new age (the **eschaton**) in its fullness, with events that will precede it, and with how the disciples are to conduct themselves while awaiting an event that is as certain as its exact time is unknown to all but the Father (24, 36). The discourse may be divided into two parts, 24, 1–44 and 24, 45—25, 46. In the first, Matthew follows his Marcan source (13, 1–37) closely. The second is drawn from Q and from the evangelist’s own traditional material. Both parts show Matthew’s editing of his sources by deletions, additions, and modifications. The vigilant waiting that is emphasized in the second part does not mean a cessation of ordinary activity and concentration only on what is to come, but a faithful accomplishment of duties at hand, with awareness that the end, for which the disciples must always be ready, will entail the great judgment by which the everlasting destiny of all will be determined.

24, 2: As in Mk, Jesus predicts the destruction of the temple. By omitting the Marcan story of the widow’s contribution (12, 41–44) that immediately precedes the prediction in that gospel, Matthew has established a close connection between it and 23, 38, “ . . . your house will be abandoned, desolate.”

24, 3: The Mount of Olives: see the note on 21, 1. **The disciples:** cf Mk 13, 3–4 where only Peter, James, John, and Andrew put the question that is answered by the discourse. In both gospels, however, the question is put **privately:** the ensuing discourse is only for those who are **disciples** of Jesus. **When will this happen . . . end of the age?:** Matthew distinguishes carefully between the destruction of the temple (**this**) and the **coming** of Jesus that will bring **the end of the age.** In Mk the two events are more closely connected, a fact that may be explained by Mark’s believing that the one would immediately succeed the other. **Coming:** this translates the Greek word **parousia,** which is used in the gospels only here and in vv 27, 37, and 39. It designated the official visit of a ruler to a city or the manifestation of a saving deity, and it was used by Christians to refer to the final coming of Jesus in glory, a term first found in the New Testament with that meaning in 1 Thes 2, 19. **The end of the age:** see the note on 13, 39.

24, 4–14: This section of the discourse deals with calamities in the world (6–7) and in the church (9–12). The former **must happen** before **the end** comes (6), but they are only **the beginning of the labor pains** (8). (It may be noted that the Greek word translated **the end** in v 6 and in vv 13–14 is not the same as the phrase “the end of the age” in v 3, although the meaning is the same.) The latter are sufferings of the church, both from within and without, that will last until the **gospel is preached . . . to all nations. Then the end will come** and those who have endured the sufferings with fidelity **will be saved** (13–14).

24, 6–7: The disturbances mentioned here are a commonplace of apocalyptic language, as is the assurance that they **must happen** (see Dn 2, 28 LXX), for that is the plan of God. **Kingdom against kingdom:** see Is 19, 2.

24, 8: The labor pains: the tribulations leading up to the end of the age are compared to the pains of a woman about to give birth. There is much attestation for rabbinic use of the phrase “the woes (or birth pains) of the Messiah” after the New Testament period, but in at least one instance it is attributed to a rabbi who lived in the late first century A.D. In this Jewish usage it meant the distress of the time preceding the coming of the Messiah; here, the **labor pains** precede the coming of the Son of Man in glory.

24, 9–12: Matthew has used Mk 13, 9–12 in his missionary discourse (10, 17–21) and omits it here. Besides the sufferings, including death, and the hatred of **all nations** that the disciples will have to endure, there will be worse affliction within the church itself. This is described in vv 10–12, which are peculiar to Mt. **Will be led into sin:** literally, “will be scandalized,” probably meaning that they will become apostates; see 13, 21 where “fall away” translates the same Greek word as here. **Betray:** in the Greek this is the same word as the **hand over** of v 9. The handing over to persecution and hatred from outside will have their counterpart within the church. **False prophets:** these are Chris-

j Lk 13, 34–35; 19, 41–44. k 21, 35. l Jer 12, 7. m Ps 118, 26. n Mk 13, 1–37; Lk 21, 5–36. o Dn 2, 28 LXX. p Is 19, 2. q 10, 17.

will hand you over to persecution, and they will
kill you. You will be hated by all nations because
of my name. 10 And then many will be led into
sin; they will betray and hate one another.
11 Many false prophets will arise and deceive
many; 12 and because of the increase of
evildoing, the love of many will grow cold.
13 r But the one who perseveres to the end will be
saved. 14 s *And this gospel of the kingdom will
be preached throughout the world as a witness
to all nations, and then the end will come.

The Great Tribulation 15 t *"When you see
the desolating abomination spoken of through
Daniel the prophet standing in the holy place (let
the reader understand), 16 *then those in Judea
must flee to the mountains, 17 u *a person on the
housetop must not go down to get things out of
his house, 18 a person in the field must not return
to get his cloak. 19 Woe to pregnant women and
nursing mothers in those days. 20 *Pray that your
flight not be in winter or on the sabbath, 21 v *for
at that time there will be great tribulation, such
as has not been since the beginning of the world
until now, nor ever will be. 22 And if those days
had not been shortened, no one would be saved;
but for the sake of the elect they will be
shortened. 23 w If anyone says to you then, 'Look,
here is the Messiah!' or, 'There he is!' do not
believe it. 24 False messiahs and false prophets
will arise, and they will perform signs and
wonders so great as to deceive, if that were
possible, even the elect. 25 Behold, I have told it
to you beforehand. 26 *So if they say to you, 'He
is in the desert,' do not go out there; if they say,
'He is in the inner rooms,' do not believe it.
27 x For just as lightning comes from the east and
is seen as far as the west, so will the coming of
the Son of Man be. 28 Wherever the corpse is,
there the vultures will gather.

The Coming of the Son of Man 29 y *"Immedi-
ately after the tribulation of those days,

the sun will be darkened,
  and the moon will not give its light,
and the stars will fall from the sky,

---

tians; see the note on 7, 15–20. **Evildoing:** see 7, 23. Because of the apocalyptic nature of much of this discourse, the literal meaning of this description of the church should not be pressed too hard. However, there is reason to think that Mt's addition of these verses reflects in some measure the condition of his community.

24, 14: Except for the last part (**and then the end will come**), this verse substantially repeats Mk 13, 10. The Matthean addition raises a problem since what follows in vv 15–23 refers to the horrors of the First Jewish Revolt including the destruction of the temple, and Matthew, writing after that time, knew that the parousia of Jesus was still in the future. A solution may be that the evangelist saw the events of those verses as foreshadowing the cosmic disturbances that he associates with the parousia (29) so that the period in which the former took place could be understood as belonging to **the end.**

24, 15–28: Cf Mk 13, 14–23; Lk 17, 23–24.37. A further stage in the tribulations that will precede the coming of the Son of Man, and an answer to the question of v 3a, "when will this (the destruction of the temple) happen?"

24, 15: The desolating abomination: in 167 B.C. the Syrian king Antiochus IV Epiphanes desecrated the temple by setting up in it a statue of Zeus Olympios (see 1 Mc 1, 54). That event is referred to in Dn 12, 11 LXX as the "desolating abomination" (NAB "horrible abomination") and the same Greek term is used here; cf also Dn 9, 27; 11, 31. Although the desecration had taken place before Dn was written, it is presented there as a future event, and Matthew sees that "prophecy" fulfilled in the desecration of the temple by the Romans. **In the holy place:** the temple; more precise than Mk's **where he should not** (13, 14). **Let the reader understand:** this parenthetical remark, taken from Mk 13, 14, invites **the reader** to realize the meaning of Dn's "prophecy."

24, 16: The tradition that the Christians of Jerusalem fled from that city to Pella, a city of Transjordan, at the time of the First Jewish Revolt is found in Eusebius (**Ecclesiastical History,** 3, 5, 3), who attributes the flight to "a certain oracle given by revelation before the war." The tradition is not improbable but the Matthean command, derived from its Marcan source, is vague in respect to the place of flight (**to the mountains**), although some scholars see it as applicable to the flight to Pella.

24, 17–19: Haste is essential, and the journey will be particularly difficult for women who are burdened with unborn or infant children.

24, 20: On the sabbath: this addition to **in winter** (cf Mk 13, 18) has been understood as an indication that Mt was addressed to a church still observing the Mosaic law of sabbath rest and the scribal limitations upon the length of journeys that might lawfully be made on that day. That interpretation conflicts with Mt's view on sabbath observance (cf 12, 1–14). The meaning of the addition may be that those undertaking on the sabbath a journey such as the one here ordered would be offending the sensibilities of law-observant Jews and would incur their hostility.

24, 21: For the unparalleled distress of that time, see Dn 12, 1.

24, 26–28: Claims that the Messiah is to be found in some distant or secret place must be ignored. **The coming of the Son of Man** will be as clear as **lightning** is to all and as **the corpse** of an animal is to **vultures;** cf Lk 17, 24.37. Here there is clear identification of **the Son of Man** and the Messiah; cf v 23.

24, 29: The answer to the question of v 3b, "What will be the sign of your coming?" **Immediately after . . . those days:** the shortening of time between the preceding **tribulation** and the parousia has been explained as Matthew's use of a supposed device of Old Testament prophecy whereby certainty that a predicted event will occur is expressed by depicting it as imminent. While it is questionable that that is an acceptable understanding of the Old Testament predictions, it may be applicable here, for Matthew knew that the parousia had not come **immediately after** the fall of Jerusalem, and it is unlikely that he is attributing a mistaken calculation of time to Jesus. **The sun . . . be shaken:** cf Is 13, 10.13.

r 10, 22. s 28, 19; Rom 10, 18. t Dn 9, 27; 11, 31; 12, 11; Mk 13, 14. u Lk 17, 31. v Dn 12, 1. w Lk 17, 23. x Lk 17, 24.37. y Is 13, 10.13; Ez 32, 7; Am 8, 9.

and the powers of the heavens will be
shaken.

[30][z]*And then the sign of the Son of Man will appear in heaven, and all the tribes of the earth will mourn, and they will see the Son of Man coming upon the clouds of heaven with power and great glory. [31][a]*And he will send out his angels with a trumpet blast, and they will gather his elect from the four winds, from one end of the heavens to the other.

The Lesson of the Fig Tree [32]*"Learn a lesson from the fig tree. When its branch becomes tender and sprouts leaves, you know that summer is near. [33]In the same way, when you see all these things, know that he is near, at the gates. [34]*Amen, I say to you, this generation will not pass away until all these things have taken place. [35][b]Heaven and earth will pass away, but my words will not pass away.

The Unknown Day and Hour [36][c]*"But of that day and hour no one knows, neither the angels of heaven, nor the Son, but the Father alone. [37][d]*For as it was in the days of Noah, so it will be at the coming of the Son of Man. [38]In [those] days before the flood, they were eating and drinking, marrying and giving in marriage, up to the day that Noah entered the ark. [39]They did not know until the flood came and carried them all away. So will it be [also] at the coming of the Son of Man. [40][e]*Two men will be out in the field; one will be taken, and one will be left. [41]Two women will be grinding at the mill; one will be taken, and one will be left. [42][f]*Therefore, stay awake! For you do not know on which day your Lord will come. [43][g]Be sure of this: if the master of the house had known the hour of night when the thief was coming, he would have stayed awake and not let his house be broken into. [44]So too, you also must be prepared, for at an hour you do not expect, the Son of Man will come.

The Faithful or the Unfaithful Servant [45][h]*"Who, then, is the faithful and prudent servant, whom the master has put in charge of his household to distribute to them their food at the proper time? [46]Blessed is that servant whom his master on his arrival finds doing so. [47]Amen, I say to you, he will put him in charge of all his property. [48]*But if that wicked servant says to himself, 'My master is long delayed,' [49]and begins to beat his fellow servants, and eat and drink with drunkards, [50]the servant's master will come on an unexpected day and at an unknown hour [51][i]*and will punish him severely and

24, 30: The sign of the Son of Man: perhaps this means **the sign** that is the glorious appearance **of the Son of Man;** cf 12, 39–40 where "the sign of Jonah" is Jonah's being in the "belly of the whale." **Tribes of the earth will mourn:** peculiar to Mt; cf Zec 12, 12–14. **Coming upon the clouds . . . glory:** cf Dn 7, 13, although there the "one like a son of man" comes to God to receive kingship; here **the Son of Man** comes from heaven for judgment.

24, 31: Send out his angels: cf 13, 41 where they are sent out to collect the wicked for punishment. **Trumpet blast:** cf Is 27, 13; 1 Thes 4, 16.

24, 32–35: Cf Mk 13, 28–31.

24, 34: The difficulty raised by this verse cannot be satisfactorily removed by the supposition that **this generation** means the Jewish people throughout the course of their history, much less the entire human race. Perhaps for Matthew it means the **generation** to which he and his community belonged.

24, 36–44: The statement of v 34 is now counterbalanced by one that declares that the exact time of the parousia is known only to **the Father** (36), and the disciples are warned to be always ready for it. This section is drawn from Mk and Q (cf Lk 17, 26–27.34–35; 12, 39–40).

24, 36: Many textual witnesses omit **nor the Son,** which follows Mk 13, 32. Since its omission can be explained by reluctance to attribute this ignorance to **the Son,** the reading that includes it is probably original.

24, 37–39: Cf Lk 17, 26–27. **In the days of Noah:** the Old Testament account of the flood lays no emphasis upon what is central for Matthew, i.e., the unexpected coming of the flood upon those who were unprepared for it.

24, 40–41: Cf Lk 17, 34–35. **Taken . . . left:** the former probably means **taken** into the kingdom; the latter, **left** for destruction. People in the same situation will be dealt with in opposite ways. In this context, the discrimination between them will be based on their readiness for the coming of the Son of Man.

24, 42–44: Cf Lk 12, 39–40. The theme of vigilance and readiness is continued with the bold comparison of the Son of Man to a thief who comes to break into a house.

24, 45–51: The second part of the discourse (see the note on 24, 1—25, 46) begins with this parable of **the faithful** or unfaithful **servant;** cf Lk 12, 41–46. It is addressed to the leaders of Matthew's church; **the servant has** been **put in charge** of his master's **household** (45) even though that **household** is composed of those who are his **fellow servants** (49).

24, 45: To distribute . . . proper time: readiness for the master's return means a vigilance that is accompanied by faithful performance of the duty assigned.

24, 48: My master . . . delayed: the note of delay is found also in the other parables of this section; cf 25, 5.19.

24, 51: Punish him severely: the Greek verb, found in the New Testament only here and in the Lucan parallel (12, 46),

z Dn 7, 13; Zec 12, 12–14; Rv 1, 7. a Is 27, 13; 1 Cor 15, 52; 1 Thes 4, 16. b Is 40, 8. c Acts 1, 7. d Gn 6, 5—7, 23; Lk 17, 26–27; 2 Pt 3, 6. e Lk 17, 34–35. f 25, 13; Lk 12, 39–40. g 1 Thes 5, 2. h Lk 12, 41–46. i 13, 42; 25, 30.

assign him a place with the hypocrites, where there will be wailing and grinding of teeth.

CHAPTER 25

The Parable of the Ten Virgins 1 *“Then the kingdom of heaven will be like ten virgins who took their lamps and went out to meet the bridegroom. 2 *Five of them were foolish and five were wise. 3 The foolish ones, when taking their lamps, brought no oil with them, 4 but the wise brought flasks of oil with their lamps. 5 Since the bridegroom was long delayed, they all became drowsy and fell asleep. 6 At midnight, there was a cry, ‘Behold, the bridegroom! Come out to meet him!’ 7 Then all those virgins got up and trimmed their lamps. 8 The foolish ones said to the wise, ‘Give us some of your oil, for our lamps are going out.’ 9 But the wise ones replied, ‘No, for there may not be enough for us and you. Go instead to the merchants and buy some for yourselves.’ 10 While they went off to buy it, the bridegroom came and those who were ready went into the wedding feast with him. Then the door was locked. 11 *j* *Afterwards the other virgins came and said, ‘Lord, Lord, open the door for us!’ 12 But he said in reply, ‘Amen, I say to you, I do not know you.’ 13 *k* *Therefore, stay awake, for you know neither the day nor the hour.

The Parable of the Talents 14 *l* *“It will be as when a man who was going on a journey called in his servants and entrusted his possessions to them. 15 *To one he gave five talents; to another, two; to a third, one—to each according to his ability. Then he went away. Immediately 16 the one who received five talents went and traded with them, and made another five. 17 Likewise, the one who received two made another two. 18 *But the man who received one went off and dug a hole in the ground and buried his master’s money. 19 After a long time the master of those servants came back and settled accounts with them. 20 *The one who had received five talents came forward bringing the additional five. He said, ‘Master, you gave me five talents. See, I have made five more.’ 21 *m* His master said to him, ‘Well done, my good and faithful servant. Since you were faithful in small matters, I will give you great responsibilities. Come, share your master’s joy.’ 22 [Then] the one who had received two talents also came forward and said, ‘Master, you gave me two talents. See, I have made two more.’ 23 His master said to him, ‘Well done, my good and faithful servant. Since you were faithful in small matters, I will give you great responsibilities. Come, share your master’s joy.’ 24 Then the one who had received the one talent came forward and said, ‘Master, I knew you were a demanding person, harvesting where you did not plant and gathering where you did not scatter; 25 so out of fear I went off and buried your talent in the ground. Here it is back.’ 26 *His master said to him in reply, ‘You wicked, lazy servant! So you knew that I harvest where I did not plant and gather where I did not scatter? 27 Should you not then have put my money in

---

means, literally, “cut in two.” **With the hypocrites:** see the note on 6, 2. Matthew classes the unfaithful Christian leader with the unbelieving leaders of Judaism. **Wailing and grinding of teeth:** see the note on 8, 11–12.

25, 1–13: Peculiar to Mt.

25, 1: Then: at the time of the parousia. **Kingdom . . . will be like:** see the note on 13, 24–30.

25, 2–4: Foolish . . . wise: cf the contrasted “wise man” and “fool” of 7, 24.26, where the two are distinguished by good deeds and lack of them, and such deeds may be signified by the **oil** of this parable.

25, 11–12: Lord, Lord: cf 7, 21. **I do not know you:** cf 7, 23, where the Greek verb is different but synonymous.

25, 13: Stay awake: some scholars see this command as an addition to the original parable of Matthew’s traditional material, since in v 5 all the virgins, wise and foolish, fall asleep. But the wise virgins are adequately equipped for their task, and **stay awake** may mean no more than to be prepared; cf 24, 42.44.

25, 14–30: Cf Lk 19, 12–27.

25, 14: It will be as when . . . journey: literally, “For just as a man who was going on a journey.” Although the comparison is not completed, the sense is clear; the kingdom of heaven is like the situation here described. Faithful use of one’s gifts will lead to participation in the fullness of the kingdom, lazy inactivity to exclusion from it.

25, 15: Talents: see the note on 18, 24.

25, 18: Buried his master’s money: see the note on 13, 44.

25, 20–23: Although the first two servants have received and doubled large sums, their faithful trading is regarded by the master as fidelity **in small matters** only, compared with the **great responsibilities** now to be given to them. The latter are unspecified. **Share your master’s joy:** probably the joy of the banquet of the kingdom; cf 8, 11.

25, 26–28: Wicked, lazy servant: this man’s inactivity is not negligible but seriously culpable. As punishment, he loses the gift he had received, that is now given to the first servant, whose possessions are already great.

j 7, 21.23; Lk 13, 25.27. k 24, 42; Mk 13, 33. l Lk 19, 12–27. m Lk 16, 10.

the bank so that I could have got it back with interest on my return?' 28 Now then! Take the talent from him and give it to the one with ten. 29 n*For to everyone who has, more will be given and he will grow rich; but from the one who has not, even what he has will be taken away. 30 *And throw this useless servant into the darkness outside, where there will be wailing and grinding of teeth.'

The Judgment of the Nations 31 o*"When the Son of Man comes in his glory, and all the angels with him, he will sit upon his glorious throne, 32 p*and all the nations will be assembled before him. And he will separate them one from another, as a shepherd separates the sheep from the goats. 33 He will place the sheep on his right and the goats on his left. 34 Then the king will say to those on his right, 'Come, you who are blessed by my Father. Inherit the kingdom prepared for you from the foundation of the world. 35 qFor I was hungry and you gave me food, I was thirsty and you gave me drink, a stranger and you welcomed me, 36 naked and you clothed me, ill and you cared for me, in prison and you visited me.' 37 *Then the righteous will answer him and say, 'Lord, when did we see you hungry and feed you, or thirsty and give you drink? 38 When did we see you a stranger and welcome you, or naked and clothe you? 39 When did we see you ill or in prison, and visit you?' 40 rAnd the king will say to them in reply, 'Amen, I say to you, whatever you did for one of these least brothers of mine, you did for me.' 41 s*Then he will say to those on his left, 'Depart from me, you accursed, into the eternal fire prepared for the devil and his angels. 42 tFor I was hungry and you gave me no food, I was thirsty and you gave me no drink, 43 a stranger and you gave me no welcome, naked and you gave me no clothing, ill and in prison, and you did not care for me.' 44 *Then they will answer and say, 'Lord, when did we see you hungry or thirsty or a stranger or naked or ill or in prison, and not minister to your needs?' 45 He will answer them, 'Amen, I say to you, what you did not do for one of these least ones, you did not do for me.' 46 uAnd these will go off to eternal punishment, but the righteous to eternal life."

VII: The Passion and Resurrection

CHAPTER 26

The Conspiracy against Jesus 1 *When Jesus finished all these words, he said to his disciples,

25, 29: See the note on 13, 12 where there is a similar application of this maxim.

25, 30: See the note on 8, 11–12.

25, 31–46: The conclusion of the discourse, which is peculiar to Mt, portrays the final judgment that will accompany the parousia. Although often called a "parable," it is not really such, for the only parabolic elements are the depiction of **the Son of Man** as **a shepherd** and of **the righteous** and the wicked as **sheep** and **goats** respectively (32–33). The criterion of judgment will be the deeds of mercy that have been done for the **least** of Jesus' **brothers** (40). A difficult and important question is the identification of these **least brothers.** Are they all people who have suffered hunger, thirst, etc. (35.36) or a particular group of such sufferers? Scholars are divided in their response and arguments can be made for either side. But leaving aside the problem of what the traditional material that Matthew edited may have meant, it seems that a stronger case can be made for the view that in the evangelist's sense the sufferers are Christians, probably Christian missionaries whose sufferings were brought upon them by their preaching of the gospel. The criterion of judgment for **all the nations** is their treatment of those who have borne to the world the message of Jesus, and this means ultimately their acceptance or rejection of Jesus himself; cf 10, 40, "Whoever receives you, receives me."

25, 31: See the note on 16, 27.

25, 32: All the nations: before the end the gospel will have been preached throughout the world (24, 14); thus the Gentiles will be judged on their response to it. But the phrase **all the nations** includes the Jews also, for at the judgment "the Son of Man . . . will repay everyone according to his conduct" (16, 27).

25, 37–40: The righteous will be astonished that in caring for the needs of the sufferers they were ministering to the **Lord** himself. **One of these least brothers of mine:** cf 10, 42.

25, 41: Fire prepared . . . his angels: cf 1 Enoch 10, 13 where it is said of the evil angels and Semyaza, their leader, "In those days they will lead them into the bottom of the fire—and in torment—in the prison (where) they will be locked up forever."

25, 44–45: The **accursed** (41) will be likewise astonished that their neglect of the sufferers was neglect of the **Lord** and will receive from him a similar answer.

26, 1—28, 20: The five books with alternating narrative and discourse (3, 1—25, 46) that give this gospel its distinctive structure lead up to the climactic events that are the center of Christian belief and the origin of the Christian church, the passion and resurrection of Jesus. In his passion narrative (chs 26–27) Matthew follows his Marcan source closely but with omissions (e.g., Mk 14, 51–52) and additions (e.g., 27, 3–10.19). Some of the additions indicate that he utilized traditions that he had received from elsewhere; others are due to his own theological insight (e.g., 26, 28, " . . . for the forgiveness of sins"; 27, 52). In his editing Matthew also altered Mk in some minor details. But there is no need to suppose that he knew any passion narrative other than Mark's.

26, 1–2: When Jesus finished all these words: see the note on 7, 28–29. **"You know . . . crucified":** Matthew turns Mk's statement of the time (14, 1) into Jesus' final prediction of his passion. **Passover:** see the note on Mk 14, 1.

n 13, 12; Mk 4, 25; Lk 8, 18; 19, 26. o 16, 27; Dt 33, 2 LXX. p Ez 34, 17. q Is 58, 7; Ez 18, 7. r 10, 40.42. s 7, 23; Lk 13, 27. t Jb 22, 7; Jas 2, 15–16. u Dn 12, 2.

[2][v]“You know that in two days’ time it will be
Passover, and the Son of Man will be handed
over to be crucified.” [3]*Then the chief priests
and the elders of the people assembled in the
palace of the high priest, who was called Caia-
phas, [4][w]and they consulted together to arrest
Jesus by treachery and put him to death. [5]*But
they said, “Not during the festival, that there
may not be a riot among the people.”

The Anointing at Bethany [6][x]*Now when
Jesus was in Bethany in the house of Simon the
leper, [7]a woman came up to him with an
alabaster jar of costly perfumed oil, and poured it
on his head while he was reclining at table.
[8]When the disciples saw this, they were indig-
nant and said, “Why this waste? [9]It could have
been sold for much, and the money given to the
poor.” [10]Since Jesus knew this, he said to them,
“Why do you make trouble for the woman? She
has done a good thing for me. [11][y]The poor you
will always have with you; but you will not
always have me. [12]*In pouring this perfumed oil
upon my body, she did it to prepare me for
burial. [13]Amen, I say to you, wherever this
gospel is proclaimed in the whole world, what
she has done will be spoken of, in memory of
her.”

The Betrayal by Judas [14][z]*Then one of the
Twelve, who was called Judas Iscariot, went to
the chief priests [15][a]*and said, “What are you
willing to give me if I hand him over to you?”
They paid him thirty pieces of silver, [16]and from
that time on he looked for an opportunity to
hand him over.

Preparations for the Passover [17][b c]*On the
first day of the Feast of Unleavened Bread, the
disciples approached Jesus and said, “Where do
you want us to prepare for you to eat the
Passover?” [18]*He said, “Go into the city to a
certain man and tell him, ‘The teacher says, “My
appointed time draws near; in your house I shall
celebrate the Passover with my disciples.” ’ ”
[19]The disciples then did as Jesus had ordered,
and prepared the Passover.

The Betrayer [20]When it was evening, he re-
clined at table with the Twelve. [21]*And while
they were eating, he said, “Amen, I say to you,
one of you will betray me.” [22]Deeply distressed
at this, they began to say to him one after
another, “Surely it is not I, Lord?” [23]He said in
reply, “He who has dipped his hand into the dish
with me is the one who will betray me. [24][d]*The
Son of Man indeed goes, as it is written of him,
but woe to that man by whom the Son of Man is
betrayed. It would be better for that man if he
had never been born.” [25]*Then Judas, his be-
trayer, said in reply, “Surely it is not I, Rabbi?”
He answered, “You have said so.”

26, 3: Caiaphas was high priest from A.D. 18 to 36.

26, 5: Not during the festival: the plan to delay Jesus’ arrest and execution until after the **festival** was not carried out, for according to the synoptics he was arrested on the night of Nisan 14 and put to death the following day. No reason is given why the plan was changed.

26, 6–13: See the notes on Mk 14, 3–9 and Jn 12, 1–8.

26, 12: To prepare me for burial: cf Mk 14, 8. In accordance with the interpretation of this act as Jesus’ **burial** anointing, Matthew, more consistent than Mark, changes the purpose of the visit of the women to Jesus’ tomb; they do not go to anoint him (Mk 16, 1) but “to see the tomb” (28, 1).

26, 14: Iscariot: see the note on Lk 6, 16.

26, 15: The motive of avarice is introduced by Judas’s question about the price for betrayal, which is absent in the Marcan source (14, 10–11). **Hand him over:** the same Greek verb is used to express the saving purpose of God by which Jesus is handed over to death (cf 17, 22; 20, 18; 26, 2) and the human malice that hands him over. **Thirty pieces of silver:** the price of the betrayal is found only in Mt. It is derived from Zec 11, 12 where it is the wages paid to the rejected shepherd, a cheap price (Zec 11, 13). That amount is also the compensation paid to one whose slave has been gored by an ox (Ex 21, 32).

26, 17: The first day of the Feast of Unleavened Bread: see the note on Mk 14, 1. Matthew omits Mk’s “when they sacrificed the Passover lamb.”

26, 18: By omitting much of Mk 14, 13–15, adding **My appointed time draws near,** and turning the question into a statement, **in your house I shall celebrate the Passover,** Matthew has given this passage a solemnity and majesty greater than that of his source.

26, 21: Given Matthew’s interest in the fulfillment of the Old Testament, it is curious that he omits the Marcan designation of Jesus’ betrayer as “one who is eating with me” (14, 18), since that is probably an allusion to Ps 41, 10. However, the shocking fact that the betrayer is one who shares table fellowship with Jesus is emphasized in v 23.

26, 24: It would be better . . . born: the enormity of the deed is such that it would be better not to exist than to do it.

26, 25: Peculiar to Mt. **You have said so:** cf 26, 64; 27, 11. This is a half-affirmative. Emphasis is laid on the pronoun and the answer implies that the statement would not have been made if the question had not been asked.

v Mk 14, 1–2; Lk 22, 1–2. w Jn 11, 47–53. x Mk 14, 3–9; Jn 12, 1–8. y Dt 15, 11. z Mk 14, 10–11; Lk 22, 3–6. a Zec 11, 12. b Mk 14, 12–21; Lk 22, 7–23. c Ex 12, 14–20. d Is 53, 8–10.

The Lord's Supper 26[e,f]*While they were eating, Jesus took bread, said the blessing, broke it, and giving it to his disciples said, "Take and eat; this is my body." 27*Then he took a cup, gave thanks, and gave it to them, saying, "Drink from it, all of you, 28[g]for this is my blood of the covenant, which will be shed on behalf of many for the forgiveness of sins. 29*I tell you, from now on I shall not drink this fruit of the vine until the day when I drink it with you new in the kingdom of my Father." 30*Then, after singing a hymn, they went out to the Mount of Olives.

Peter's Denial Foretold 31[h,i]*Then Jesus said to them, "This night all of you will have your faith in me shaken, for it is written:

'I will strike the shepherd,
    and the sheep of the flock will be
        dispersed';

32but after I have been raised up, I shall go before you to Galilee." 33Peter said to him in reply, "Though all may have their faith in you shaken, mine will never be." 34[j,k]*Jesus said to him, "Amen, I say to you, this very night before the cock crows, you will deny me three times." 35Peter said to him, "Even though I should have to die with you, I will not deny you." And all the disciples spoke likewise.

The Agony in the Garden 36[l,m]*Then Jesus came with them to a place called Gethsemane, and he said to his disciples, "Sit here while I go over there and pray." 37[n]*He took along Peter and the two sons of Zebedee, and began to feel sorrow and distress. 38[o]*Then he said to them, "My soul is sorrowful even to death. Remain here and keep watch with me." 39[p]*He advanced a little and fell prostrate in prayer, saying, "My Father, if it is possible, let this cup pass from me; yet, not as I will, but as you will." 40When he returned to his disciples he found them asleep. He said to Peter, "So you could not keep

26, 26–29: See the note on Mk 14, 22–24. The Marcan-Matthean is one of the two major New Testament traditions of the words of Jesus when instituting the Eucharist. The other (and earlier) is the Pauline-Lucan (1 Cor 11, 23–25; Lk 22, 19–20). Each shows the influence of Christian liturgical usage, but the Marcan-Matthean is more developed in that regard than the Pauline-Lucan. The words over the bread and cup succeed each other without the intervening meal mentioned in 1 Cor 11, 25; Lk 22, 20; and there is parallelism between the consecratory words (**this is my body . . . this is my blood**). Matthew follows Mk closely but with some changes.

26, 26: See the note on 14, 19. **Said the blessing:** a prayer blessing God. **Take and eat:** literally, **Take, eat. Eat** is an addition to Mk's "take it" (literally, "take"; 14, 22). **This is my body:** the bread is identified with Jesus himself.

26, 27–28: Gave thanks: see the note on 15, 36. **Gave it to them . . . all of you:** cf Mk 14, 23–24. In the Marcan sequence the disciples drink and then Jesus says the interpretative words. Matthew has changed this into a command to **drink** followed by those words. **My blood:** see Lv 17, 11 for the concept that the **blood** is "the seat of life" and that when placed on the altar it "makes atonement." **Which will be shed:** the present participle, "being shed" or "going to be shed," is future in relation to the Last Supper. **On behalf of:** Greek **peri**; see the note on Mk 14, 24. **Many:** see the note on 20, 28. **For the forgiveness of sins:** a Matthean addition. The same phrase occurs in Mk 1, 4 in connection with John's baptism but Matthew avoids it there (3, 11). He places it here probably because he wishes to emphasize that it is the sacrificial death of Jesus that brings **forgiveness of sins.**

26, 29: Although his death will interrupt the table fellowship he has had with the disciples, Jesus confidently predicts his vindication by God and a new table fellowship with them at the banquet of the kingdom.

26, 30: See the note on Mk 14, 26.

26, 31: Will have . . . shaken: literally, "will be scandalized in me"; see the note on 24, 9–12. **I will strike . . . dispersed:** cf Zec 13, 7.

26, 34: Before the cock crows: see the note on 14, 25. The third watch of the night was called "cockcrow." **Deny me:** see the note on 16, 24.

26, 36–56: Cf Mk 14, 32–52. The account of Jesus in Gethsemane is divided between that of his agony (36–46) and that of his betrayal and arrest (47–56). Jesus' **sorrow and distress** (37) in face of death is unrelieved by the presence of his three disciples who, though urged to **watch with** him (38.41), fall asleep (40.43). He prays that **if . . . possible** his death may be avoided (39) but that his Father's will be done (39.42.44). Knowing then that his death must take place, he announces to his companions that **the hour** for his being **handed over** has come (45). Judas arrives with an armed band provided by the Sanhedrin and greets Jesus with a kiss, the prearranged sign for his identification (47–49). After his arrest, he rebukes a disciple who has attacked **the high priest's servant** with **a sword** (51–54), and chides those who have come out to seize him with **swords and clubs** as if he were **a robber** (55–56). In both rebukes Jesus declares that the treatment he is now receiving is the fulfillment of the scriptures (55.56). The subsequent flight of **all the disciples** is itself the fulfillment of his own prediction (cf 31). In this episode, Matthew follows Mk with a few alterations.

26, 36: Gethsemane: the Hebrew name means "oil press" and designates an olive orchard on the western slope of the Mount of Olives; see the note on 21, 1. The name appears only in Mt and Mk. The place is called a "garden" in Jn 18, 1.

26, 37: Peter and the two sons of Zebedee: cf 17, 1.

26, 38: Cf Ps 42, 6.12. In the Septuagint (Ps 41, 5.12) the same Greek word for **sorrowful** is used as here. **To death:** i.e., "enough to die"; cf Jon 4, 9.

26, 39: My Father: see the note on Mk 14, 36. Matthew omits the Aramaic **'abbā'** and adds the qualifier **my. This cup:** see the note on Mk 10, 38–40.

e Mk 14, 22–26; Lk 22, 14–23; 1 Cor 11, 23–25. f 1 Cor 10, 16. g Ex 24, 8; Is 53, 12. h Mk 14, 7–31. i Zec 13, 7; Jn 16, 32. j Lk 22, 33–34; Jn 13, 37–38. k 26, 69–75. l Mk 14, 32–42; Lk 22, 39–46. m Jn 18, 1. n Heb 5, 7. o Ps 42, 6.12; Jon 4, 9. p Jn 4, 34; 6, 38; Phil 2, 8.

watch with me for one hour? [41] *Watch and pray that you may not undergo the test. The spirit is willing, but the flesh is weak." [42 q] *Withdrawing a second time, he prayed again, "My Father, if it is not possible that this cup pass without my drinking it, your will be done!" [43] Then he returned once more and found them asleep, for they could not keep their eyes open. [44] He left them and withdrew again and prayed a third time, saying the same thing again. [45 r] Then he returned to his disciples and said to them, "Are you still sleeping and taking your rest? Behold, the hour is at hand when the Son of Man is to be handed over to sinners. [46] Get up, let us go. Look, my betrayer is at hand."

The Betrayal and Arrest of Jesus [47 s] While he was still speaking, Judas, one of the Twelve, arrived, accompanied by a large crowd, with swords and clubs, who had come from the chief priests and the elders of the people. [48] His betrayer had arranged a sign with them, saying, "The man I shall kiss is the one; arrest him." [49] *Immediately he went over to Jesus and said, "Hail, Rabbi!" and he kissed him. [50] Jesus answered him, "Friend, do what you have come for." Then stepping forward they laid hands on Jesus and arrested him. [51] And behold, one of those who accompanied Jesus put his hand to his sword, drew it, and struck the high priest's servant, cutting off his ear. [52] Then Jesus said to him, "Put your sword back into its sheath, for all who take the sword will perish by the sword. [53] Do you think that I cannot call upon my Father and he will not provide me at this moment with more than twelve legions of angels? [54] But then how would the scriptures be fulfilled which say that it must come to pass in this way?" [55] *At that hour Jesus said to the crowds, "Have you come out as against a robber, with swords and clubs to seize me? Day after day I sat teaching in the temple area, yet you did not arrest me. [56 t] But all this has come to pass that the writings of the prophets may be fulfilled." Then all the disciples left him and fled.

Jesus before the Sanhedrin [57 u] *Those who had arrested Jesus led him away to Caiaphas the high priest, where the scribes and the elders were assembled. [58] Peter was following him at a distance as far as the high priest's courtyard, and going inside he sat down with the servants to see the outcome. [59] *The chief priests and the entire Sanhedrin kept trying to obtain false testimony against Jesus in order to put him to death, [60 v] *but they found none, though many false

26, 41: Undergo the test: see the note on 6, 13. In that verse "the final test" translates the same Greek word as is here translated **the test,** and these are the only instances of the use of that word in Mt. It is possible that the passion of Jesus is seen here as an anticipation of the great tribulation that will precede the parousia (see the notes on 24, 8; 24, 21) to which 6, 13 refers, and that just as Jesus prays to be delivered from death (39), so he exhorts the disciples to pray that they will not have to **undergo** the great **test** that his passion would be for them. Some scholars, however, understand **not undergo** (literally, "not enter") **the test** as meaning not that the disciples may be spared **the test** but that they may not yield to the temptation of falling away from Jesus because of his passion even though they will have to endure it.

26, 42: Your will be done: cf 6, 10.

26, 49: Rabbi: see the note on 23, 6–7. Jesus is so addressed twice in Mt (cf 25), both times by Judas. For the significance of the closely related address "teacher" in Mt, see the note on 8, 19.

26, 55: Day after day . . . arrest me: cf Mk 14, 49. This suggests that Jesus had taught for a relatively long period in Jerusalem, whereas 21, 1–11 puts his coming to the city for the first time only a few days before.

26, 57–68: Following Mk 14, 53–65, Matthew presents the nighttime appearance of Jesus before **the Sanhedrin** as a real trial. After **many false witnesses** bring charges against him that do not suffice for the death sentence (60), **two came forward** who charge him with claiming to be able to **destroy the temple . . . and within three days** to **rebuild it** (60–61). Jesus makes no answer even when challenged to do so by **the high priest,** who then orders him to declare **under oath . . . whether** he is **the Messiah, the Son of God** (62–63). Matthew changes Mk's clear affirmative response (14, 62) to the same one as that given to Judas (cf 25), but follows Mk almost verbatim in Jesus' predicting that his judges will see him (**the Son of Man**) **seated at the right hand of God and coming on the clouds of heaven** (64). **The high priest** then charges him with blasphemy (65), a charge with which the other members of **the Sanhedrin** agree by declaring that **he deserves to die** (66). They then attack him (67) and mockingly demand that he **prophesy** (68). This account contains elements that are contrary to the judicial procedures prescribed in the Mishnah, the Jewish code of law that dates in written form from ca. A.D. 200, e.g., trial on a feast day, a night session of the court, pronouncement of a verdict of condemnation at the same session at which testimony was received. Consequently, some scholars regard the account entirely as a creation of the early Christians without historical value. However, it is disputable whether the norms found in the Mishnah were in force at the time of Jesus. More to the point is the question whether the Matthean-Marcan night trial derives from a combination of two separate incidents, a nighttime preliminary investigation (cf Jn 18, 13.19–24) and a formal trial on the following morning (cf Lk 22, 66–71).

26, 57: Caiaphas: see the note on 26, 3.

26, 59: Sanhedrin: see the note on Lk 22, 66.

26, 60–61: Two: cf Dt 19, 15. **I can destroy . . . rebuild it:** there are significant differences from the Marcan parallel (14, 58).

q 6, 10; Heb 10, 9. r Jn 12, 23; 13, 1; 17, 1. s Mk 14, 43–50; Lk 22, 47–53; Jn 18, 3–11. t 26, 31. u Mk 14, 53–65; Lk 22, 54–55.63–71; Jn 18, 12–14.19–24. v Dt 19, 15; Jn 2, 19; Acts 6, 14.

witnesses came forward. Finally two came forward [61]who stated, "This man said, 'I can destroy the temple of God and within three days rebuild it.' " [62]The high priest rose and addressed him, "Have you no answer? What are these men testifying against you?" [63 w]*But Jesus was silent. Then the high priest said to him, "I order you to tell us under oath before the living God whether you are the Messiah, the Son of God." [64 x]*Jesus said to him in reply, "You have said so. But I tell you:

From now on you will see 'the Son of Man
seated at the right hand of the Power'
and 'coming on the clouds of heaven.' "

[65]*Then the high priest tore his robes and said, "He has blasphemed! What further need have we of witnesses? You have now heard the blasphemy; [66]what is your opinion?" They said in reply, "He deserves to die!" [67 y]*Then they spat in his face and struck him, while some slapped him, [68]saying, "Prophesy for us, Messiah: who is it that struck you?"

Peter's Denial of Jesus [69 z]Now Peter was sitting outside in the courtyard. One of the maids came over to him and said, "You too were with Jesus the Galilean." [70]*But he denied it in front of everyone, saying, "I do not know what you are talking about!" [71]As he went out to the gate, another girl saw him and said to those who were there, "This man was with Jesus the Nazorean." [72]Again he denied it with an oath, "I do not know the man!" [73]*A little later the bystanders came over and said to Peter, "Surely you too are one of them; even your speech gives you away." [74]At that he began to curse and to swear, "I do not know the man." And immediately a cock crowed. [75 a]Then Peter remembered the word that Jesus had spoken: "Before the cock crows you will deny me three times." He went out and began to weep bitterly.

CHAPTER 27

Jesus before Pilate [1 b]*When it was morning, all the chief priests and the elders of the people took counsel against Jesus to put him to death. [2]They bound him, led him away, and handed him over to Pilate, the governor.

The Death of Judas [3 c d]*Then Judas, his betrayer, seeing that Jesus had been condemned, deeply regretted what he had done. He returned the thirty pieces of silver to the chief priests and elders, [4]saying, "I have sinned in betraying innocent blood." They said, "What is that to us?

Matthew omits "made with hands" and "not made with hands" and changes Mk's "will destroy" and "will build another" to **can destroy** and (can) **rebuild.** The charge is probably based on Jesus' prediction of the temple's destruction; see the notes on 23, 37–39; 24, 2; and Jn 2, 19. A similar prediction by Jeremiah was considered as deserving death; cf Jer 7, 1–15; 26, 1–8.

26, 63: Silent: possibly an allusion to Is 53, 7. **I order you . . . living God:** peculiar to Mt; cf Mk 14, 61.

26, 64: You have said so: see the note on 26, 25. **From now on . . . heaven:** the Son of Man who is to be crucified (cf 20, 19) will be seen in glorious majesty (cf Ps 110, 1) and **coming on the clouds of heaven** (cf Dn 7, 13). **The Power:** see the note on Mk 14, 61–62.

26, 65: Blasphemed: the punishment for **blasphemy** was death by stoning (see Lv 24, 10–16). According to the Mishnah, to be guilty of **blasphemy** one had to pronounce "the Name itself," i.e., Yahweh; cf **Sanhedrin** 7, 4.5. Those who judge the gospel accounts of Jesus' trial by the later Mishnah standards point out that Jesus uses the surrogate "the Power," and hence no Jewish court would have regarded him as guilty of **blasphemy;** others hold that the Mishnah's narrow understanding of **blasphemy** was a later development.

26, 67–68: The physical abuse, apparently done to Jesus by the members of the Sanhedrin themselves, recalls the sufferings of the Isaian Servant of the Lord; cf Is 50, 6. The mocking challenge to **prophesy** is probably motivated by Jesus' prediction of his future glory (64).

26, 70: Denied it in front of everyone: see 10, 33. Peter's repentance (75) saves him from the fearful destiny of which Jesus speaks there.

26, 73: Your speech . . . away: Matthew explicates Mk's "you too are a Galilean" (14, 70).

27, 1–31: Cf Mk 15, 1–20. Matthew's account of the Roman trial before **Pilate** is introduced by a consultation of the Sanhedrin after which Jesus is **handed over to . . . the governor** (1–2). Matthew follows his Marcan source closely but adds some material that is peculiar to him, the death of **Judas** (3–10), possibly the name **Jesus** as the name of **Barabbas** also (16–17), the intervention of Pilate's **wife** (19), Pilate's washing **his hands** in token of his disclaiming responsibility for Jesus' death (24), and the assuming of that responsibility by **the whole people** (25).

27, 1–2: There is scholarly disagreement about the meaning of the Sanhedrin's taking **counsel** (**symboulion elabon;** cf 12, 14; 22, 15; 27, 7; 28, 12); see the note on Mk 15, 1. Some understand it as a discussion about the strategy for putting their death sentence against **Jesus** into effect since they lacked the right to do so themselves. Others see it as the occasion for their passing that sentence, holding that Matthew, unlike Mark (14, 64), does not consider that it had been passed in the night session (26, 66). Even in the latter interpretation, their handing **him over to Pilate** is best explained on the hypothesis that they did not have competence to put their sentence into effect, as is stated in Jn 18, 31.

27, 3: The thirty pieces of silver: see 26, 15.

w Is 53, 7. x Ps 110, 1; Dn 7, 13. y Wis 2, 19; Is 50, 6. z Mk 14, 66–72; Lk 22, 56–62; Jn 18, 17–18.25–27. a 26, 34. b Mk 15, 1; Lk 23, 1; Jn 18, 28. c Acts 1, 18–19. d 26, 15.

Look to it yourself." 5*Flinging the money into
the temple, he departed and went off and
hanged himself. 6The chief priests gathered up
the money, but said, "It is not lawful to deposit
this in the temple treasury, for it is the price of
blood." 7After consultation, they used it to buy
the potter's field as a burial place for foreigners.
8That is why that field even today is called the
Field of Blood. 9*Then was fulfilled what had
been said through Jeremiah the prophet, "And
they took the thirty pieces of silver, the value of a
man with a price on his head, a price set by some
of the Israelites, 10 [e]and they paid it out for the
potter's field just as the Lord had commanded
me."

Jesus Questioned by Pilate 11 [f]*Now Jesus
stood before the governor, and he questioned
him, "Are you the king of the Jews?" Jesus said,
"You say so." 12 [g]*And when he was accused by
the chief priests and elders, he made no answer.
13Then Pilate said to him, "Do you not hear how
many things they are testifying against you?"
14But he did not answer him one word, so that
the governor was greatly amazed.

The Sentence of Death 15 [h]*Now on the occa-
sion of the feast the governor was accustomed to
release to the crowd one prisoner whom they
wished. 16*And at that time they had a notori-
ous prisoner called [Jesus] Barabbas. 17So when
they had assembled, Pilate said to them, "Which
one do you want me to release to you, [Jesus]
Barabbas, or Jesus called Messiah?" 18*For he
knew that it was out of envy that they had
handed him over. 19*While he was still seated
on the bench, his wife sent him a message,
"Have nothing to do with that righteous man. I
suffered much in a dream today because of
him." 20 [i]The chief priests and the elders per-
suaded the crowds to ask for Barabbas but to
destroy Jesus. 21The governor said to them in
reply, "Which of the two do you want me to
release to you?" They answered, "Barabbas!"
22*Pilate said to them, "Then what shall I do
with Jesus called Messiah?" They all said, "Let
him be crucified!" 23But he said, "Why? What
evil has he done?" They only shouted the louder,
"Let him be crucified!" 24 [j]*When Pilate saw
that he was not succeeding at all, but that a riot

27, 5–8: For another tradition about the death of Judas, cf Acts 1, 18–19. The two traditions agree only in the purchase of a **field** with **the money** paid to Judas for his betrayal of Jesus and the name given to the **field, the Field of Blood.** In Acts Judas himself buys the field and its name comes from his own blood shed in his fatal accident on it. **The potter's field:** this designation of the field is based on the fulfillment citation in v 10.

27, 9–10: Cf 26, 15. Matthew's attributing this text to Jeremiah is puzzling, for there is no such text in that book, and **the thirty pieces of silver** thrown by Judas "into the temple" (5) recall rather Zec 11, 12–13. It is usually said that the attribution of the text to Jeremiah is due to Matthew's combining the Zechariah text with texts from Jeremiah that speak of a **potter** (18, 2–3), the buying of a **field** (32, 6–9), or the breaking of a potter's flask at Topheth in the valley of Ben-Hinnom with the prediction that it will become a burial place (19, 1–13).

27, 11: King of the Jews: this title is used of Jesus only by pagans. The Matthean instances are, besides this verse, 2, 2; 27, 29.37. Matthew equates it with "Messiah"; cf 2, 2.4 and 27, 17.22 where he has changed "the king of the Jews" of his Marcan source (15, 9.12) to "(Jesus) called Messiah." The normal political connotation of both titles would be of concern to the Roman **governor. You say so:** see the note on 26, 25. An unqualified affirmative response is not made because Jesus' kingship is not what Pilate would understand it to be.

27, 12–14: Cf 26, 62–63. As in the trial before the Sanhedrin, Jesus' silence may be meant to recall Is 53, 7. **Greatly amazed:** possibly an allusion to Is 52, 14–15.

27, 15–26: The choice that Pilate offers **the crowd** between **Barabbas** and **Jesus** is said to be in accordance with a custom of releasing at the Passover feast **one prisoner** chosen by **the crowd** (15). This custom is mentioned also in Mk 15, 6 and Jn 18, 39 but not in Lk; see the note on Lk 23, 17. Outside of the gospels there is no direct attestation of it, and scholars are divided in their judgment of the historical reliability of the claim that there was such a practice.

27, 16–17: [Jesus] Barabbas: it is possible that the double name is the original reading; **Jesus** was a common Jewish name; see the note on 1, 21. This reading is found in only a few textual witnesses, although its absence in the majority can be explained as an omission of **Jesus** made for reverential reasons. That name is bracketed because of its uncertain textual attestation. The Aramaic name **Barabbas** means "son of the father"; the irony of the choice offered between him and Jesus, the true son of the Father, would be evident to those addressees of Mt who knew that.

27, 18: Cf Mk 14, 10. This is an example of the tendency, found in varying degree in all the gospels, to present Pilate in a relatively favorable light and emphasize the hostility of the Jewish authorities and eventually of the people.

27, 19: Jesus' innocence is declared by a Gentile woman. **In a dream:** in Mt's infancy narrative, dreams are the means of divine communication; cf 1, 20; 2, 12.13.19.22.

27, 22: Let him be crucified: incited by the chief priests and elders (20), the crowds demand that Jesus be executed by crucifixion, a peculiarly horrible form of Roman capital punishment. The Marcan parallel, "Crucify him" (15, 3), addressed to Pilate, is changed by Matthew to the passive, probably to emphasize the responsibility of the crowds.

27, 24–25: Peculiar to Mt. **Took water . . . blood:** cf Dt 21, 1–8, the handwashing prescribed in the case of a murder when the killer is unknown. The elders of the city nearest to where the corpse is found must wash their hands, declaring, "Our hands did not shed this blood." **Look to it yourselves:** cf v 4. **The whole people:** Matthew sees in those who speak these words **the** entire

e Zec 11, 12–13. f Mk 15, 2–5; Lk 23, 2–3; Jn 18, 29–38. g Is 53, 7. h Mk 15, 6–15; Lk 23, 17–25; Jn 18, 39—19, 16. i Acts 3, 14. j Dt 21, 1–8.

was breaking out instead, he took water and washed his hands in the sight of the crowd, saying, "I am innocent of this man's blood. Look to it yourselves." 25And the whole people said in reply, "His blood be upon us and upon our children." 26*Then he released Barabbas to them, but after he had Jesus scourged, he handed him over to be crucified.

Mockery by the Soldiers 27 k*Then the soldiers of the governor took Jesus inside the praetorium and gathered the whole cohort around him. 28*They stripped off his clothes and threw a scarlet military cloak about him. 29 l*Weaving a crown out of thorns, they placed it on his head, and a reed in his right hand. And kneeling before him, they mocked him, saying, "Hail, King of the Jews!" 30 m*They spat upon him and took the reed and kept striking him on the head. 31And when they had mocked him, they stripped him of the cloak, dressed him in his own clothes, and led him off to crucify him.

The Way of the Cross 32 n*As they were going out, they met a Cyrenian named Simon; this man they pressed into service to carry his cross.

The Crucifixion 33 oAnd when they came to a place called Golgotha (which means Place of the Skull), 34 p*they gave Jesus wine to drink mixed with gall. But when he had tasted it, he refused to drink. 35 q*After they had crucified him, they divided his garments by casting lots; 36then they sat down and kept watch over him there. 37*And they placed over his head the written charge against him: This is Jesus, the King of the Jews. 38*Two revolutionaries were crucified with him, one on his right and the other on his left. 39 r*Those passing by reviled him, shaking their heads 40 sand saying, "You who would destroy the temple and rebuild it in three days, save yourself, if you are the Son of God, [and] come down from the cross!" 41Likewise the chief priests with the scribes and elders mocked him and said, 42*"He saved others; he cannot save himself. So he is the king of Israel! Let him come down from the cross now, and we will believe in him. 43 t*He trusted in God; let him

---

people: (Greek **laos**) of Israel. **His blood . . . and upon our children:** cf Jer 26, 15. The responsibility for Jesus' death is accepted by the nation that was God's special possession (Ex 19, 5), his own **people** (Hos 2, 25), and they thereby lose that high privilege; see 21, 43 and the note on that verse. The controversy between Matthew's church and Pharisaic Judaism about which was the true people of God is reflected here. As the Second Vatican Council has pointed out, guilt for Jesus' death is not attributable to all the Jews of his time or to any Jews of later times.

27, 26: **He had Jesus scourged:** the usual preliminary to crucifixion.

27, 27: **The praetorium:** the residence of the Roman **governor.** His usual place of residence was at Caesarea Maritima on the Mediterranean coast, but he went to Jerusalem during the great feasts, when the influx of pilgrims posed the danger of a nationalistic riot. It is disputed whether **the praetorium** in Jerusalem was the old palace of Herod in the west of the city or the fortress of Antonia northwest of the temple area. **The whole cohort:** normally six hundred soldiers.

27, 28: **Scarlet military cloak:** so Mt as against the royal purple of Mk 15, 17 and Jn 19, 2.

27, 29: **Crown out of thorns:** probably of long **thorns** that stood upright so that it resembled the "radiant" **crown,** a diadem with spikes worn by Hellenistic kings. The soldiers' purpose was mockery, not torture. **A reed:** peculiar to Mt; a mock scepter.

27, 30: **Spat upon him:** cf 26, 67 where there also is a possible allusion to Is 50, 6.

27, 32: See the note on Mk 15, 21. **Cyrenian named Simon:** Cyrenaica was a Roman province on the north coast of Africa and Cyrene was its capital city. The city had a large population of Greek-speaking Jews. **Simon** may have been living in Palestine or have come there for the Passover as a pilgrim. **Pressed into service:** see the note on 5, 41.

27, 34: **Wine . . . mixed with gall:** cf Mk 15, 23 where the drink is "wine drugged with myrrh," a narcotic. Mt's text is probably an inexact allusion to Ps 69, 22. That psalm belongs to the class called the individual lament, in which a persecuted just man prays for deliverance in the midst of great suffering and also expresses confidence that his prayer will be heard. That theme of the suffering Just One is frequently applied to the sufferings of Jesus in the passion narratives.

27, 35: The clothing of an executed criminal went to his executioner(s), but the description of that procedure in the case of Jesus, found in all the gospels, is plainly inspired by Ps 22, 19. However, that psalm verse is quoted only in Jn 19, 24.

27, 37: The offense of a person condemned to death by crucifixion was written on a tablet that was displayed on his cross. The **charge against Jesus** was that he had claimed to be **the King of the Jews** (cf 11), i.e., the Messiah (cf 17.22).

27, 38: **Revolutionaries:** see the note on Jn 18, 40 where the same Greek word as that found here is used for Barabbas.

27, 39–40: **Reviled him . . . heads:** cf Ps 22, 8. **You who would destroy . . . three days:** cf 26, 61. **If you are the Son of God:** the same words as those of the devil in the temptation of Jesus; cf 4, 3.6.

27, 42: **King of Israel:** in their mocking of Jesus the members of the Sanhedrin call themselves and their people not "the Jews" but **Israel.**

27, 43: Peculiar to Mt. **He trusted in God . . . wants him:** cf Ps 22, 9. **He said . . . of God:** probably an allusion to Wis 2, 12–20 where the theme of the suffering Just One appears.

k Mk 15, 16–20; Jn 19, 2–3. l 27, 11. m Is 50, 6. n Mk 15, 21; Lk 23, 26. o Mk 15, 22–32; Lk 23, 32–38; Jn 19, 17–19.23–24. p Ps 69, 21. q Ps 22, 19. r Ps 22, 8. s 4, 3.6; 26, 61. t Ps 22, 9; Wis 2, 12–20.

deliver him now if he wants him. For he said, 'I
am the Son of God.' " [44]The revolutionaries who
were crucified with him also kept abusing him in
the same way.
The Death of Jesus [45 u v]*From noon onward,
darkness came over the whole land until three in
the afternoon. [46 w]*And about three o'clock
Jesus cried out in a loud voice, *"Eli, Eli, lema
sabachthani?"* which means, "My God, my God,
why have you forsaken me?" [47]*Some of the
bystanders who heard it said, "This one is calling
for Elijah." [48 x]Immediately one of them ran to
get a sponge; he soaked it in wine, and putting it
on a reed, gave it to him to drink. [49]But the rest
said, "Wait, let us see if Elijah comes to save
him." [50]*But Jesus cried out again in a loud
voice, and gave up his spirit. [51 y]*And behold,
the veil of the sanctuary was torn in two from
top to bottom. The earth quaked, rocks were
split, [52 z]tombs were opened, and the bodies of
many saints who had fallen asleep were raised.
[53]And coming forth from their tombs after his
resurrection, they entered the holy city and
appeared to many. [54]*The centurion and the
men with him who were keeping watch over
Jesus feared greatly when they saw the earth-
quake and all that was happening, and they said,
"Truly, this was the Son of God!" [55]*There were
many women there, looking on from a distance,
who had followed Jesus from Galilee, minister-
ing to him. [56 a]Among them were Mary Magda-
lene and Mary the mother of James and Joseph,
and the mother of the sons of Zebedee.
The Burial of Jesus [57 b c]*When it was eve-
ning, there came a rich man from Arimathea
named Joseph, who was himself a disciple of
Jesus. [58]He went to Pilate and asked for the body
of Jesus; then Pilate ordered it to be handed
over. [59]Taking the body, Joseph wrapped it [in]
clean linen [60]and laid it in his new tomb that he
had hewn in the rock. Then he rolled a huge
stone across the entrance to the tomb and
departed. [61]But Mary Magdalene and the other
Mary remained sitting there, facing the tomb.
The Guard at the Tomb [62]*The next day, the
one following the day of preparation, the chief

27, 45: Cf Amos 8, 9 where on the day of the Lord "the sun will set at midday."

27, 46: Eli, Eli, lema sabachthani?: Jesus cries out in the words of Ps 22, 2a, a psalm of lament that is the Old Testament passage most frequently drawn upon in this narrative. In Mk the verse is cited entirely in Aramaic, which Matthew partially retains but changes the invocation of God to the Hebrew **Eli,** possibly because that is more easily related to the statement of the following verse about Jesus' calling for Elijah.

27, 47: Elijah: see the note on 3, 4. This prophet, taken up into heaven (2 Kgs 2, 11), was believed to come to the help of those in distress, but the evidences of that belief are all later than the gospels.

27, 50: Gave up his spirit: cf the Marcan parallel (15, 37), "breathed his last." Matthew's alteration expresses both Jesus' control over his destiny and his obedient giving up of his life to God.

27, 51–53: Veil of the sanctuary . . . bottom: cf Mk 15, 38; Lk 23, 45. Lk puts this event immediately before the death of Jesus. There were two veils in the Mosaic tabernacle on the model of which the temple was constructed, the outer one before the entrance of the Holy Place and the inner one before the Holy of Holies (see Ex 26, 31–36). Only the high priest could pass through the latter and that only on the Day of Atonement (see Lv 16, 1–18). Probably the **torn veil** of the gospels is the inner one. The meaning of the scene may be that now, because of Jesus' death, all people have access to the presence of God, or that the temple, its holiest part standing exposed, is now profaned and will soon be destroyed. **The earth quaked . . . appeared to many:** peculiar to Mt. The earthquake, the splitting of the **rocks,** and especially the resurrection of the dead **saints** indicate the coming of the final age. In the Old Testament the coming of God is frequently portrayed with the imagery of an earthquake (see Pss 68, 9; 77, 19), and Jesus speaks of the earthquakes that will accompany the "labor pains" that signify the beginning of the dissolution of the old world (24, 7–8). For the expectation of the resurrection of the dead at the coming of the new and final age, see Dn 12, 1–3. Matthew knows that the end of the old age has not yet come (28, 20), but the new age has broken in with the death (and resurrection; cf the earthquake in 28, 2) of Jesus; see the note on 16, 28. **After his resurrection:** this qualification seems to be due to Matthew's wish to assert the primacy of Jesus' **resurrection** even though he has placed the resurrection of the dead **saints** immediately after Jesus' death.

27, 54: Cf Mk 15, 39. The Christian confession of faith is made by Gentiles, not only **the centurion,** as in Mk, but the other soldiers **who were keeping watch over Jesus** (cf 36).

27, 55–56: Looking on from a distance: cf Ps 38, 12. **Mary Magdalene . . . Joseph:** these two women are mentioned again in v 61 and 28, 1 and are important as witnesses of the reality of the empty tomb. A **James** and **Joseph** are referred to in 13, 55 as brothers of Jesus.

27, 57–61: Cf Mk 15, 42–47. Matthew drops Mk's designation of **Joseph** of **Arimathea** as "a distinguished member of the council" (the Sanhedrin), and makes him **a rich man** and **a disciple of Jesus.** The former may be an allusion to Is 53, 9 (the Hebrew reading of that text is disputed and the one followed in the NAB OT has nothing about the rich, but they are mentioned in the LXX version). That the tomb was the **new tomb of a rich man** and that it was seen by the women are indications of an apologetic intent of Matthew; there could be no question about the identity of Jesus' burial place. **The other Mary:** the mother of James and Joseph (56).

27, 62–66: Peculiar to Mt. The story prepares for 28, 11–15 and the Jewish charge that the tomb was empty because the **disciples** had stolen the body of Jesus (28, 13.15).

27, 62: The next day . . . preparation: the sabbath. According

u Mk 15, 33–41; Lk 23, 44–49; Jn 19, 28–30. v Am 8, 9. w Ps 22, 2. x Ps 69, 21. y Ex 26, 31–36; Ps 68, 9; 77, 19. z Dn 12, 1–3. a 13, 55. b Mk 15, 42–47; Lk 23, 50–56; Jn 19, 38–42. c Is 53, 9.

priests and the Pharisees gathered before Pilate
63 [d]and said, "Sir, we remember that this impos-
tor while still alive said, 'After three days I will
be raised up.' 64 *Give orders, then, that the
grave be secured until the third day, lest his
disciples come and steal him and say to the
people, 'He has been raised from the dead.' This
last imposture would be worse than the first."
65 *Pilate said to them, "The guard is yours; go
secure it as best you can." 66 So they went and
secured the tomb by fixing a seal to the stone
and setting the guard.

CHAPTER 28

The Resurrection of Jesus 1 [e]*After the sab-
bath, as the first day of the week was dawning,
Mary Magdalene and the other Mary came to
see the tomb. 2 [f]*And behold, there was a great
earthquake; for an angel of the Lord descended
from heaven, approached, rolled back the stone,
and sat upon it. 3 [g]His appearance was like
lightning and his clothing was white as snow.
4 The guards were shaken with fear of him and
became like dead men. 5 Then the angel said to
the women in reply, "Do not be afraid! I know
that you are seeking Jesus the crucified. 6 *He is
not here, for he has been raised just as he said.
Come and see the place where he lay. 7 [h]Then go
quickly and tell his disciples, 'He has been raised
from the dead, and he is going before you to
Galilee; there you will see him.' Behold, I have
told you." 8 *Then they went away quickly from
the tomb, fearful yet overjoyed, and ran to
announce this to his disciples. 9 [i]*And behold,
Jesus met them on their way and greeted them.
They approached, embraced his feet, and did
him homage. 10 Then Jesus said to them, "Do not

---

to the synoptic chronology, in that year **the day of preparation** (for the sabbath) was the Passover; cf Mk 15, 42. **The Pharisees:** the principal opponents of Jesus during his ministry and, in Matthew's time, of the Christian church, join with **the chief priests** to guarantee against a possible attempt of Jesus' **disciples** to steal his body.

27, 64: This last imposture . . . the first: the claim that Jesus **has been raised from the dead** is clearly the **last imposture; the first** may be either his claim that he would **be raised up** (63) or his claim that he was the one with whose ministry the kingdom of God had come (see 12, 28).

27, 65: The guard is yours: literally, "have a guard" or "you have a guard." Either the imperative or the indicative could mean that Pilate granted the petitioners some Roman soldiers as guards, which is the sense of the present translation. However, if the verb is taken as an indicative it could also mean that Pilate told them to use their own Jewish guards.

28, 1–20: Except for vv 1–8, based on Mk 16, 1–8, the material of this final chapter is peculiar to Mt. Even where he follows Mk, Matthew has altered his source so greatly that a very different impression is given from that of the Marcan account. The two points that are common to the resurrection testimony of all the gospels are that the tomb of Jesus had been found empty and that the risen Jesus had appeared to certain persons, or, in the original form of Mk, that such an appearance was promised as soon to take place (see Mk 16, 7). On this central and all-important basis, Matthew has constructed an account that interprets the resurrection as the turning of the ages (2–4), shows the Jewish opposition to Jesus as continuing **to the present** in the claim that the resurrection is a deception perpetrated by the **disciples** who stole his body from the tomb (11–15), and marks a new stage in the mission of **the disciples** once limited to Israel (10, 5–6); now they are to **make disciples of all nations.** In this work they will be strengthened by the presence of the exalted Son of Man, who will be with them **until** the kingdom comes in fullness at **the end of the age** (16–20).

28, 1: After the sabbath . . . dawning: since the sabbath ended at sunset, this could mean in the early evening, for **dawning** can refer to the appearance of the evening star; cf Lk 23, 54. However, it is probable that Matthew means the morning dawn of the day after the sabbath, as in the similar though slightly different text of Mk, "when the sun had risen" (16, 2). **Mary Magdalene and the other Mary:** see the notes on 27, 55–56; 57–61. **To see the tomb:** cf Mk 16, 1–2 where the purpose of the women's visit is to anoint Jesus' body.

28, 2–4: Peculiar to Mt. **A great earthquake:** see the note on 27, 51–53. **Descended from heaven:** this trait is peculiar to Mt, although his interpretation of the "young man" of his Marcan source (16, 5) as an **angel** is probably true to Mk's intention; cf Lk 24, 23 where the "two men" of 24, 4 are said to be "angels." **Rolled back the stone . . . upon it:** not to allow the risen Jesus to leave the tomb but to make evident that the tomb is empty (see 6). Unlike the apocryphal Gospel of Peter (9, 35—11, 44), the New Testament does not describe the resurrection of Jesus, nor is there anyone who sees it. **His appearance was like lightning . . . snow:** see the note on 17, 2.

28, 6–7: Cf Mk 16, 6–7. **Just as he said:** a Matthean addition referring to Jesus' predictions of his resurrection, e.g., 16, 21; 17, 23; 20, 19. **Tell his disciples:** like the angel of the Lord of the infancy narrative, the angel interprets a fact and gives a commandment about what is to be done; cf 1, 20–21. Matthew omits Mk's "and Peter" (16, 7); considering his interest in Peter, this omission is curious. Perhaps the reason is that the Marcan text may allude to a first appearance of Jesus to Peter alone (cf 1 Cor 15, 5; Lk 24, 34) which Matthew has already incorporated into his account of Peter's confession at Caesarea Philippi; see the note on 16, 16. **He is going . . . Galilee:** like Mk 16, 7, a reference to Jesus' prediction at the Last Supper (26, 32; Mk 14, 28). Matthew changes Mk's "as he told you" to a declaration of the angel.

28, 8: Contrast Mk 16, 8 where the women in their fear "said nothing to anyone."

28, 9–10: Although these verses are peculiar to Mt, there are similarities between them and Jn's account of the appearance of Jesus to Mary Magdalene (20, 17). In both there is a touching of Jesus' body, and a command of Jesus to bear a message to his disciples, designated as his **brothers.** Matthew may have drawn upon a tradition that appears in a different form in Jn. Jesus' words to the women are mainly a repetition of those of the angel (5a; 7b).

d 12, 40; 16, 21; 17, 23; 20, 19. e Mk 16, 1–8; Lk 24, 1–12; Jn 20, 1–10. f 25, 51. g 17, 2. h 26, 32. i Jn 20, 17.

be afraid. Go tell my brothers to go to Galilee, and there they will see me."

The Report of the Guard [11]*While they were going, some of the guard went into the city and told the chief priests all that had happened. [12]They assembled with the elders and took counsel; then they gave a large sum of money to the soldiers, [13]telling them, "You are to say, 'His disciples came by night and stole him while we were asleep.' [14]And if this gets to the ears of the governor, we will satisfy [him] and keep you out of trouble." [15]The soldiers took the money and did as they were instructed. And this story has circulated among the Jews to the present [day].

The Commissioning of the Disciples [16 j]*The eleven disciples went to Galilee, to the mountain to which Jesus had ordered them. [17]*When they saw him, they worshiped, but they doubted. [18 k]*Then Jesus approached and said to them, "All power in heaven and on earth has been given to me. [19 l]*Go, therefore, and make disciples of all nations, baptizing them in the name of the Father, and of the Son, and of the holy Spirit, [20 m]*teaching them to observe all that I have commanded you. And behold, I am with you always, until the end of the age."

28, 11–15: This account indicates that the dispute between Christians and Jews about the empty tomb was not whether the tomb was empty but why.

28, 16–20: This climactic scene has been called a "proleptic parousia," for it gives a foretaste of the final glorious coming of the Son of Man (26, 64). Then his triumph will be manifest to all; now it is revealed only to **the disciples,** who are commissioned to announce it to **all nations** and bring them to belief in Jesus and obedience to his commandments.

28, 16: The eleven: the number recalls the tragic defection of Judas Iscariot. **To the mountain . . . ordered them:** since the message to **the disciples** was simply that they were to go to Galilee (10), some think that **the mountain** comes from a tradition of the message known to Matthew and alluded to here. For the significance of **the mountain,** see the note on 17, 1.

28, 17: But they doubted: the Greek can also be translated, "but some doubted." The verb occurs elsewhere in the New Testament only in 14, 31 where it is associated with Peter's being of "little faith." For the meaning of that designation, see the note on 6, 30.

28, 18: All power . . . me: the Greek word here translated **power** is the same as that found in the LXX translation of Dn 7, 13–14 where one "like a son of man" is given **power** and an everlasting kingdom by God. The risen Jesus here claims universal power, i.e., **in heaven and on earth.**

28, 19: Therefore: since universal power belongs to the risen Jesus (18), he gives the eleven a mission that is universal. They are to **make disciples of all nations.** While **all nations** is understood by some scholars as referring only to **all** Gentiles, it is probable that it included the Jews as well. **Baptizing them:** baptism is the means of entrance into the community of the risen One, the Church. **In the name of the Father . . . holy Spirit:** this is perhaps the clearest expression in the New Testament of trinitarian belief. It may have been the baptismal formula of Matthew's church, but primarily it designates the effect of baptism, the union of the one baptized with the Father, Son, and holy Spirit.

28, 20: All that I have commanded you: the moral teaching found in this gospel, preeminently that of the Sermon on the Mount (chs 5–7). The commandments of Jesus are the standard of Christian conduct, not the Mosaic law as such, even though some of the Mosaic commandments have now been invested with the authority of Jesus. **Behold, I am with you always:** the promise of Jesus' real though invisible presence echoes the name Emmanuel given to him in the infancy narrative; see the note on 1, 23. **End of the age:** see the notes on 13, 39 and 24, 3.

j Mk 16, 14–16; Lk 24, 36–49; Jn 20, 19–23. k Dn 7, 14 LXX. l Acts 1, 8. m 1, 23; 13, 39; 24, 3.

THE GOSPEL ACCORDING TO MARK

This shortest of all New Testament gospels is likely the first to have been written, yet it often tells of Jesus' ministry in more detail than either Matthew or Luke (for example, the miracle stories at 5, 1-20 or 9, 14-29). It recounts what Jesus did in a vivid style, where one incident follows directly upon another. In this almost breathless narrative, Mark stresses Jesus' message about the kingdom of God now breaking into human life as good news (1, 14-15) and Jesus himself as the gospel of God (1, 1; 8, 35; 10, 29). Jesus is the Son whom God has sent to rescue humanity by serving and by sacrificing his life (10, 45).

The opening verse about good news in Mark (1, 1) serves as a title for the entire book. The action begins with the appearance of John the Baptist, a messenger of God attested by scripture.

But John points to a mightier one, Jesus, at whose baptism God speaks from heaven, declaring Jesus his Son. The Spirit descends upon Jesus, who eventually, it is promised, will baptize "with the holy Spirit." This presentation of who Jesus really is (1, 1-13) is rounded out with a brief reference to the temptation of Jesus and how Satan's attack fails. Jesus as Son of God will be victorious, a point to be remembered as one reads of Jesus' death and the enigmatic ending to Mark's Gospel.

The key verses at 1, 14-15, which are programmatic, summarize what Jesus proclaims as gospel: fulfillment, the nearness of the kingdom, and therefore the need for repentance and for faith. After the call of the first four disciples, all fishermen (1, 16-20), we see Jesus engaged in teaching (1, 21.22.27), preaching (1, 38.39), and healing (1, 29-31.34.40-45), and exorcising demons (1, 22-27.34.39). The content of Jesus' teaching is only rarely stated, and then chiefly in parables (ch 4) about the kingdom. His cures, especially on the sabbath (3, 1-5); his claim, like God, to forgive sins (2, 3-12); his table fellowship with tax collectors and sinners (2, 14-17); and the statement that his followers need not now fast but should rejoice while Jesus is present (2, 18-22), all stir up opposition that will lead to Jesus' death (3, 6).

In Mark, Jesus is portrayed as immensely popular with the people in Galilee during his ministry (2, 2; 3, 7; 4, 1). He appoints twelve disciples to help preach and drive out demons, just as he does (3, 13-19). He continues to work many miracles; the blocks 4, 35—6, 44 and 6, 45—7, 10 are cycles of stories about healings, miracles at the Sea of Galilee, and marvelous feedings of the crowds. Jesus' teaching in ch 7 exalts the word of God over "the tradition of the elders" and sees defilement as a matter of the heart, not of unclean foods. Yet opposition mounts. Scribes charge that Jesus is possessed by Beelzebul (3, 22). His relatives think him "out of his mind" (3, 21). Jesus' kinship is with those who do the will of God, in a new eschatological family, not even with mother, brothers, or sisters by blood ties (3, 31-35; cf 6, 1-6). But all too often his own disciples do not understand Jesus (4, 13.40; 6, 52; 8, 17-21). The fate of John the Baptist (6, 17-29) hints ominously at Jesus' own passion (9, 13; cf 8, 31).

A breakthrough seemingly comes with Peter's confession that Jesus is the Christ (Messiah; 8, 27-30). But Jesus himself emphasizes his passion (8, 31; 9, 31; 10, 33-34), not glory in the kingdom (10, 35-45). Momentarily he is glimpsed in his true identity when he is transfigured before three of the disciples (9, 2-8), but by and large Jesus is depicted in Mark as moving obediently along the way to his cross in Jerusalem. Occasionally there are miracles (9, 17-27; 10, 46-52; 11, 12-14.20-21, the only such account in Jerusalem), sometimes teachings (10, 2-11.23-31), but the greatest concern is with discipleship (8, 34—9, 1; 9, 33-50). For the disciples do not grasp the mystery being revealed (9, 32; 10, 32.38). One of them will betray him, Judas (14, 10-11.43-45); one will deny him, Peter (14, 27.31.54.66-72); all eleven men will desert Jesus (14, 27.50).

The passion account, with its condemnation of Jesus by the Sanhedrin (14, 53.55-65; 15, 1a) and sentencing by Pilate (15, 1b-15), is prefaced with the entry into Jerusalem (11, 1-11), ministry and controversies there (11, 15—12, 44), Jesus' Last Supper with the disciples (14, 1-26), and his arrest at Gethsemane (14, 32-52). A chapter of apocalyptic tone about the destruction of the temple (13, 1-2.14-23) and the coming of the Son of Man (13, 24-27), a discourse filled with promises (13, 11.31) and admonitions to be watchful (13, 2.23.37), is significant for Mark's Gospel, for it helps one see that God, in Jesus, will be victorious after the cross and at the end of history.

The Gospel of Mark ends in the most ancient manuscripts with an abrupt scene at Jesus' tomb, which the women find empty (16, 1-8). His own prophecy of 14, 28 is reiterated, that Jesus goes before the disciples into Galilee; "there you will see him." These words may imply resurrection appearances there, or Jesus' parousia there, or the start of Christian mission, or a return to the roots depicted in 1, 9.14-15 in Galilee. Other hands have attached additional endings after 16, 8; see the note on 16, 9-20.

The framework of Mark's Gospel is partly geographical: Galilee (1, 14—9, 49), through the area "across the Jordan" (10, 1) and through Jericho (10, 46-52), to Jerusalem (11, 1—16, 8). Only rarely does Jesus go into Gentile territory (5, 1-20; 7, 24-37), but those who acknowledge him there and the centurion who confesses Jesus at the cross (15, 39) presage the gospel's expansion into the world beyond Palestine.

Mark's Gospel is even more oriented to christology. Jesus is the Son of God (1, 11; 9, 7; 15, 39; cf 1, 1; 14, 61). He is the Messiah, the anointed king of Davidic descent (12, 35; 15, 32), the Greek for which, *Christos,* has, by the time Mark wrote, become in effect a proper name (1, 1; 9, 41). Jesus is also seen as Son of Man, a term used in Mark not simply as a substitute for "I" or for humanity in general (cf 2, 10.27-28; 14, 21) or with reference to a mighty figure who is to come (13, 26; 14, 62), but also in connection with Jesus' predestined, necessary path of suffering and vindication (8, 31; 10, 45).

The unfolding of Mark's story about Jesus is sometimes viewed by interpreters as centered around the term "mystery." The word is employed just once, at 4, 11, in the singular, and its content there is the kingdom, the open secret that God's reign is now breaking into human life with its reversal of human values. There is a related sense in which Jesus' real identity remained a secret during his lifetime, according to Mark, although demons and demoniacs knew it (1, 24; 3, 11; 5, 7); Jesus warned against telling of his mighty deeds and revealing his identity (1, 44; 3, 12; 5, 43; 7, 36; 8, 26.30), an injunction sometimes broken (1, 45; cf 5, 19-20). Further, Jesus teaches by parables, according to Mark, in such a way that those "outside" the kingdom do not understand, but only those to whom the mystery has been granted by God.

Mark thus shares with Paul, as well as with other parts of the New Testament, an emphasis on election (13, 20.22) and upon the gospel as Christ and his cross (cf 1 Cor 1, 23). Yet in Mark the person of Jesus is also depicted with an unaffected naturalness. He reacts to events with authentic human emotion: pity (1, 44), anger (3, 5), triumph (4, 40), sympathy (5, 36; 6, 34), surprise (6, 9), admiration (7, 29; 10, 21), sadness (14, 33-34), and indignation (14, 48-49).

Although the book is anonymous, apart from the ancient heading "According to Mark" in manuscripts, it has traditionally been assigned to John Mark, in whose mother's house (at Jerusalem) Christians assembled (Acts 12, 12). This Mark was a cousin of Barnabas (Col 4, 10) and accompanied Barnabas and Paul on a missionary journey (Acts 12, 25; 13, 3; 15, 36-39). He appears in Pauline letters (Phlm 24; 2 Tm 4, 11) and with Peter (1 Pt 5, 13). Papias (ca. A.D. 135) described Mark as Peter's "interpreter," a view found in other patristic writers. Petrine influence should not, however, be exaggerated. The evangelist has put together various oral and possibly written sources—miracle stories, parables, sayings, stories of controversies, and the passion—so as to speak of the crucified Messiah for Mark's own day.

Traditionally, the gospel is said to have been written shortly before A.D. 70 in Rome, at a time of impending persecution and when destruction loomed over Jerusalem. Its audience seems to have been Gentile, unfamiliar with Jewish customs (hence 7, 3-4.11). The book aimed to equip such Christians to stand faithful in the face of persecution (13, 9-13), while going on with the proclamation of the gospel begun in Galilee (13, 10; 14, 9). Modern research often proposes as the author an unknown Hellenistic Jewish Christian, possibly in Syria, and perhaps shortly after the year 70.

The principal divisions of the Gospel according to Mark are the following:

I. The Preparation for the Public Ministry of Jesus (1, 1-13)
II. The Mystery of Jesus (1, 14—8, 26)
III. The Mystery Begins to Be Revealed (8, 27—9, 32)
IV. The Full Revelation of the Mystery (9, 33—16, 8)
The Longer Ending (16, 9-20)
The Shorter Ending
The Freer Logion (in the note on 16, 9-20)

I: The Preparation for the Public Ministry of Jesus

CHAPTER 1

[1]*The beginning of the gospel of Jesus Christ [the Son of God].

The Preaching of John the Baptist [2][a][b]*As it is written in Isaiah the prophet:

"Behold, I am sending my messenger ahead of you;
he will prepare your way.
[3][c]A voice of one crying out in the desert:
'Prepare the way of the Lord,
make straight his paths.' "

[4]John [the] Baptist appeared in the desert proclaiming a baptism of repentance for the forgiveness of sins. [5]People of the whole Judean countryside and all the inhabitants of Jerusalem were going out to him and were being baptized by him in the Jordan River as they acknowledged their sins. [6]*John was clothed in camel's hair, with a leather belt around his waist. He fed on locusts and wild honey. [7]And this is what he proclaimed: "One mightier than I is coming after me. I am not worthy to stoop and loosen the thongs of his sandals. [8][d]*I have baptized you with water; he will baptize you with the holy Spirit."

The Baptism of Jesus [9][e]It happened in those days that Jesus came from Nazareth of Galilee and was baptized in the Jordan by John. [10]*On coming up out of the water he saw the heavens being torn open and the Spirit, like a dove, descending upon him. [11][f]And a voice came from the heavens, "You are my beloved Son; with you I am well pleased."

The Temptation of Jesus [12][g]*At once the Spirit drove him out into the desert, [13]and he

1, 1–13: The prologue of the Gospel according to Mark begins with the title (1) followed by three events preparatory to Jesus' preaching: (1) the appearance in the Judean wilderness of John, baptizer, preacher of repentance, and precursor of Jesus (2–8); (2) the baptism of Jesus, at which a voice from heaven acknowledges Jesus to be God's Son, and the holy Spirit descends on him (9–11); (3) the temptation of Jesus by Satan (12–13).

1, 1: The gospel of Jesus Christ [the Son of God]: the "good news" of salvation in and through Jesus, crucified and risen, acknowledged by the Christian community as Messiah (8, 29; 14, 61–62) and Son of God (11; 9, 7; 15, 39), although some important manuscripts here omit **the Son of God.**

1, 2–3: Although Mark attributes the prophecy to Isaiah, the text is a combination of Mal 3, 1; Is 40, 3; and Ex 23, 20; cf Mt 11, 10; Lk 7, 27. John's ministry is seen as God's prelude to the saving mission of his Son. **The way of the Lord:** this prophecy of Deutero-Isaiah concerning the end of the Babylonian exile is here applied to the coming of Jesus; John the Baptist is to prepare the way for him.

1, 6: Clothed in camel's hair . . . waist: the Baptist's garb recalls that of Elijah in 2 Kgs 1, 8. Jesus speaks of the Baptist as Elijah who has already come (9, 11–13; Mt 17, 10–12; cf Mal 3, 23–24; Lk 1, 17).

1, 8–9: Through the life-giving baptism with the holy Spirit (8), Jesus will create a new people of God. But first he identifies himself with the people of Israel in submitting to John's baptism of repentance and in bearing on their behalf the burden of God's decisive judgment (9; cf 4). As in the desert of Sinai, so here in the wilderness of Judea, Israel's sonship with God is to be renewed.

1, 10–11: He saw the heavens . . . and the Spirit . . . upon him: indicating divine intervention in fulfillment of promise. Here the descent of the Spirit on Jesus is meant, anointing him for his ministry; cf Is 11, 2; 42, 1; 61, 1; 63, 9. **A voice . . . with you I am well pleased:** God's acknowledgment of Jesus as his unique Son, the object of his love. His approval of Jesus is the assurance that Jesus will fulfill his messianic mission of salvation.

1, 12–13: The same Spirit who descended on Jesus in his baptism now drives him into the desert for forty days. The result is radical confrontation and temptation by Satan who attempts to frustrate the work of God. The presence of wild beasts may indicate the horror and danger of the desert regarded as the abode of demons or may reflect the paradise motif of harmony among all creatures; cf Is 11, 6–9. The presence of ministering angels to sustain Jesus recalls the angel who guided the Israelites in the

a Mt 3, 1–11; Lk 3, 2–16. b Mal 3, 1. c Is 40, 3; Jn 1, 23. d Jn 1, 27; Acts 1, 5; 11, 16. e Mt 3, 13–17; Lk 3, 21–23; Jn 1, 32–33. f Ps 2, 7. g Mt 4, 1–11; Lk 4, 1–13.

remained in the desert for forty days, tempted by Satan. He was among wild beasts, and the angels ministered to him.

II: The Mystery of Jesus

The Beginning of the Galilean Ministry 14 [h]*After John had been arrested, Jesus came to Galilee proclaiming the gospel of God: 15 [i]"This is the time of fulfillment. The kingdom of God is at hand. Repent, and believe in the gospel."

The Call of the First Disciples 16 [j]*As he passed by the Sea of Galilee, he saw Simon and his brother Andrew casting their nets into the sea; they were fishermen. 17 Jesus said to them, "Come after me, and I will make you fishers of men." 18 Then they left their nets and followed him. 19 He walked along a little farther and saw James, the son of Zebedee, and his brother John. They too were in a boat mending their nets. 20 Then he called them. So they left their father Zebedee in the boat along with the hired men and followed him.

The Cure of a Demoniac 21 [k]*Then they came to Capernaum, and on the sabbath he entered the synagogue and taught. 22 [l]The people were astonished at his teaching, for he taught them as one having authority and not as the scribes. 23 *In their synagogue was a man with an unclean spirit; 24 *he cried out, "What have you to do with us, Jesus of Nazareth? Have you come to destroy us? I know who you are—the Holy One of God!" 25 Jesus rebuked him and said, "Quiet! Come out of him!" 26 The unclean spirit convulsed him and with a loud cry came out of him. 27 All were amazed and asked one another, "What is this? A new teaching with authority. He commands even the unclean spirits and they obey him." 28 His fame spread everywhere throughout the whole region of Galilee.

The Cure of Simon's Mother-in-Law 29 [m]On leaving the synagogue he entered the house of Simon and Andrew with James and John. 30 Simon's mother-in-law lay sick with a fever. They immediately told him about her. 31 He approached, grasped her hand, and helped her up. Then the fever left her and she waited on them.

Other Healings 32 When it was evening, after sunset, they brought to him all who were ill or possessed by demons. 33 The whole town was gathered at the door. 34 He cured many who were sick with various diseases, and he drove out many demons, not permitting them to speak because they knew him.

Jesus Leaves Capernaum 35 [n]Rising very early before dawn, he left and went off to a deserted place, where he prayed. 36 Simon and those who were with him pursued him 37 and on finding him said, "Everyone is looking for you." 38 He told them, "Let us go on to the nearby villages that I may preach there also. For this purpose have I come." 39 So he went into their synagogues, preaching and driving out demons throughout the whole of Galilee.

The Cleansing of a Leper 40 [o]*A leper came to him [and kneeling down] begged him and

---

desert in the first Exodus (14, 19; 23, 20) and the angel who supplied nourishment to Elijah in the wilderness (1 Kgs 19, 5–7). The combined forces of good and evil were present to Jesus in the desert. His sustained obedience brings forth the new Israel of God there where Israel's rebellion had brought death and alienation.

1, 14–15: **After John had been arrested:** in the plan of God, Jesus was not to proclaim the good news of salvation prior to the termination of the Baptist's active mission. **Galilee:** in the Marcan account, scene of the major part of Jesus' public ministry before his arrest and condemnation. **The gospel of God:** not only the good news from God but about God at work in Jesus Christ. **This is the time of fulfillment:** i.e., of God's promises. **The kingdom of God . . . repent:** see the note on Mt 3, 2.

1, 16–20: These verses narrate the call of the first disciples. See the notes on Mt 4, 18–22 and 4, 20.

1, 21–45: The account of a single day's ministry of Jesus on a sabbath in and outside the synagogue of Capernaum (21–31) combines teaching and miracles of exorcism and healing. Mention is not made of the content of the teaching but of the effect of astonishment and alarm on the people. Jesus' teaching with authority, making an absolute claim on the hearer, was in the best tradition of the ancient prophets, not of the scribes. The narrative continues with events that evening (32–34; see the notes on Mt 8, 14–17) and the next day (35–39). The cleansing in vv 40–45 stands as an isolated story.

1, 23: **An unclean spirit:** so called because of the spirit's resistance to the holiness of God. The spirit knows and fears the power of Jesus to destroy his influence; cf 32.34; 3, 11; 6, 13.

1, 24: **What have you to do with us?:** see the note on Jn 2, 4.

1, 24–25: **The Holy One of God:** not a confession but an attempt to ward off Jesus' power, reflecting the notion that use of the precise name of an opposing spirit would guarantee mastery over him. Jesus silenced the cry of the unclean spirit and drove him out of the man.

1, 40: **A leper:** for the various forms of skin disease, see Lv 13, 1–50 and the note on Lv 13, 2–4. There are only two instances in

h Mt 4, 12–17; Lk 4, 14–15. i Mt 3, 2. j Mt 4, 18–22; Lk 5, 2–11. k Lk 4, 31–37. l Mt 7, 28–29. m Mt 8, 14–16; Lk 4, 38–41. n Lk 4, 42–44. o Mt 8, 2–4; Lk 5, 12–14.

said, "If you wish, you can make me clean." [41] [p]Moved with pity, he stretched out his hand, touched him, and said to him, "I do will it. Be made clean." [42] [q]The leprosy left him immediately, and he was made clean. [43]Then, warning him sternly, he dismissed him at once. [44] [r]Then he said to him, "See that you tell no one anything, but go, show yourself to the priest and offer for your cleansing what Moses prescribed; that will be proof for them." [45]The man went away and began to publicize the whole matter. He spread the report abroad so that it was impossible for Jesus to enter a town openly. He remained outside in deserted places, and people kept coming to him from everywhere.

CHAPTER 2

The Healing of a Paralytic [1] [s]*When Jesus returned to Capernaum after some days, it became known that he was at home. [2]Many gathered together so that there was no longer room for them, not even around the door, and he preached the word to them. [3]They came bringing to him a paralytic carried by four men. [4]Unable to get near Jesus because of the crowd, they opened up the roof above him. After they had broken through, they let down the mat on which the paralytic was lying. [5]*When Jesus saw their faith, he said to the paralytic, "Child, your sins are forgiven." [6]*Now some of the scribes were sitting there asking themselves, [7] [t]*"Why does this man speak that way? He is blaspheming. Who but God alone can forgive sins?" [8]Jesus immediately knew in his mind what they were thinking to themselves, so he said, "Why are you thinking such things in your hearts? [9]Which is easier, to say to the paralytic, 'Your sins are forgiven,' or to say, 'Rise, pick up your mat and walk'? [10]*But that you may know that the Son of Man has authority to forgive sins on earth"— [11]he said to the paralytic, "I say to you, rise, pick up your mat, and go home." [12]He rose, picked up his mat at once, and went away in the sight of everyone. They were all astounded and glorified God, saying, "We have never seen anything like this."

The Call of Levi [13] [u]*Once again he went out along the sea. All the crowd came to him and he taught them. [14] [v]*As he passed by, he saw Levi, son of Alphaeus, sitting at the customs post. He said to him, "Follow me." And he got up and followed him. [15]*While he was at table in his house, many tax collectors and sinners sat with Jesus and his disciples; for there were many who followed him. [16]*Some scribes who were Pharisees saw that he was eating with sinners and tax collectors and said to his disciples, "Why does he eat with tax collectors and sinners?" [17]*Jesus

---

the Old Testament in which God is shown to have cured a leper (Nm 12, 10–15 and 2 Kgs 5, 1–14). The law of Moses provided for the ritual purification of a leper. In curing the leper, Jesus assumes that the priests will reinstate the cured man into the religious community. See also the note on Lk 5, 14.

2, 1—3, 6: This section relates a series of conflicts between Jesus and the scribes and Pharisees in which the growing opposition of the latter leads to their plot to put Jesus to death (3, 6).

2, 1–2: **He was at home:** to the crowds that gathered in and outside the house Jesus **preached the word,** i.e., the gospel concerning the nearness of the kingdom and the necessity of repentance and faith (1, 14).

2, 5: It was the faith of the paralytic and those who carried him that moved Jesus to heal the sick man. Accounts of other miracles of Jesus reveal more and more his emphasis on faith as the requisite for exercising his healing powers (5, 34; 9, 23–24; 10, 52).

2, 6: **Scribes:** trained in oral interpretation of the written law; in Mark's gospel, adversaries of Jesus, with one exception (12, 28.34).

2, 7: **He is blaspheming:** an accusation made here and repeated during the trial of Jesus (14, 60–64).

2, 10: **But that you may know that the Son of Man . . . on earth:** although vv 8–9 are addressed to the scribes, the sudden interruption of thought and structure in v 10 seems not addressed to them nor to the paralytic. Moreover, the early public use of the designation "Son of Man" to unbelieving scribes is most unlikely. The most probable explanation is that Mark's insertion of v 10 is a commentary addressed to Christians for whom he recalls this miracle and who already accept in faith that Jesus is Messiah and Son of God.

2, 13: **He taught them:** see the note on 1, 21–45.

2, 14: **As he passed by:** see the note on 1, 16–20. **Levi, son of Alphaeus:** see the note on Mt 9, 9. **Customs post:** such tax collectors paid a fixed sum for the right to collect customs duties within their districts. Since whatever they could collect above this amount constituted their profit, the abuse of extortion was widespread among them. Hence, Jewish customs officials were regarded as sinners (16), outcasts of society, and disgraced along with their families. **He got up and followed him:** i.e., became a disciple of Jesus.

2, 15: **In his house:** cf v 1; Mt 9, 10. Lk 5, 29 clearly calls it Levi's house.

2, 16–17: This and the following conflict stories reflect a similar pattern: a statement of fact, a question of protest, and a reply by Jesus.

2, 17: **Do not need a physician:** this maxim of Jesus with its implied irony was uttered to silence his adversaries who objected

p 5, 30. q Lk 17, 14. r Lv 14, 2–32. s Mt 9, 2–8; Lk 5, 18–26. t Is 43, 25. u 4, 1. v Mt 9, 9–13; Lk 5, 27–32.

heard this and said to them [that], "Those who
are well do not need a physician, but the sick do.
I did not come to call the righteous but sinners."

The Question about Fasting 18 w*The disci-
ples of John and of the Pharisees were accus-
tomed to fast. People came to him and objected,
"Why do the disciples of John and the disciples
of the Pharisees fast, but your disciples do not
fast?" 19*Jesus answered them, "Can the wed-
ding guests fast while the bridegroom is with
them? As long as they have the bridegroom with
them they cannot fast. 20But the days will come
when the bridegroom is taken away from them,
and then they will fast on that day. 21No one
sews a piece of unshrunken cloth on an old
cloak. If he does, its fullness pulls away, the new
from the old, and the tear gets worse. 22Like-
wise, no one pours new wine into old wineskins.
Otherwise, the wine will burst the skins, and
both the wine and the skins are ruined. Rather,
new wine is poured into fresh wineskins."

The Disciples and the Sabbath 23 x*As he
was passing through a field of grain on the
sabbath, his disciples began to make a path while
picking the heads of grain. 24 yAt this the Phari-
sees said to him, "Look, why are they doing
what is unlawful on the sabbath?" 25*He said to
them, "Have you never read what David did
when he was in need and he and his compan-
ions were hungry? 26 zHow he went into the
house of God when Abiathar was high priest and
ate the bread of offering that only the priests
could lawfully eat, and shared it with his com-
panions?" 27 a*Then he said to them, "The
sabbath was made for man, not man for the
sabbath. 28*That is why the Son of Man is lord
even of the sabbath."

CHAPTER 3

A Man with a Withered Hand 1 b*Again he
entered the synagogue. There was a man there
who had a withered hand. 2They watched him
closely to see if he would cure him on the
sabbath so that they might accuse him. 3He said
to the man with the withered hand, "Come up
here before us." 4Then he said to them, "Is it
lawful to do good on the sabbath rather than to
do evil, to save life rather than to destroy it?" But
they remained silent. 5 cLooking around at them
with anger and grieved at their hardness of
heart, he said to the man, "Stretch out your
hand." He stretched it out and his hand was
restored. 6*The Pharisees went out and immedi-
ately took counsel with the Herodians against
him to put him to death.

The Mercy of Jesus 7 d*Jesus withdrew to-
ward the sea with his disciples. A large number

---

that he ate with **tax collectors and sinners** (16). Because the scribes and Pharisees were self-righteous, they were not capable of responding to Jesus' call to repentance and faith in the gospel.

2, 18–22: This conflict over the question of fasting has the same pattern as vv 16–17; see the notes on Mt 9, 15 and 9, 16–17.

2, 19: Can the wedding guests fast?: the bridal metaphor expresses a new relationship of love between God and his people in the person and mission of Jesus to his disciples. It is the inauguration of the new and joyful messianic time of fulfillment and the passing of the old. Any attempt at assimilating the Pharisaic practice of fasting, or of extending the preparatory discipline of John's disciples beyond the arrival of the bridegroom, would be as futile as sewing **a piece of unshrunken cloth on an old cloak** or pouring **new wine into old wineskins** with the resulting destruction of both cloth and wine (21–22). Fasting is rendered superfluous during the earthly ministry of Jesus; cf v 20.

2, 23–28: This conflict regarding the sabbath follows the same pattern as in vv 18–22.

2, 25–26: Have you never read what David did?: Jesus defends the action of his disciples on the basis of 1 Sm 21, 2–7 in which an exception is made to the regulation of Lv 24, 9 because of the extreme hunger of David and his men. According to 1 Sm, the priest who gave the bread to David was Ahimelech, father of Abiathar.

2, 27: The sabbath was made for man: a reaffirmation of the divine intent of the sabbath to benefit Israel as contrasted with the restrictive Pharisaic tradition added to the law.

2, 28: The Son of Man is lord even of the sabbath: Mark's comment on the theological meaning of the incident is to benefit his Christian readers; see the note on 2, 10.

3, 1–5: Here Jesus is again depicted in conflict with his adversaries over the question of sabbath-day observance. His opponents were already ill disposed toward him because they regarded Jesus as a violator of the sabbath. Jesus' question **Is it lawful to do good on the sabbath rather than to do evil?** places the matter in the broader theological context outside the casuistry of the scribes. The answer is obvious. Jesus heals the man with the withered hand in the sight of all and reduces his opponents to silence; cf Jn 5, 17–18.

3, 6: In reporting the plot of the Pharisees and Herodians to put Jesus to death after this series of conflicts in Galilee, Mark uses a pattern that recurs in his account of later controversies in Jerusalem (11, 17–18; 12, 13–17). The help of the Herodians, supporters of Herod Antipas, tetrarch of Galilee and Perea, is needed to take action against Jesus. Both series of conflicts point to their gravity and to the impending passion of Jesus.

3, 7–19: This overview of the Galilean ministry manifests the

w Mt 9, 14–17; Lk 5, 33–39. x Mt 12, 1–8; Lk 6, 1–5. y Dt 23, 25. z 1 Sm 21, 2–7 / Lv 24, 5–9. a 2 Mc 5, 19. b Mt 12, 9–14; Lk 6, 6–11. c Lk 14, 4. d Mt 4, 23–25; 12, 15; Lk 6, 17–19.

of people [followed] from Galilee and from Judea. 8 Hearing what he was doing, a large number of people came to him also from Jerusalem, from Idumea, from beyond the Jordan, and from the neighborhood of Tyre and Sidon. 9 He told his disciples to have a boat ready for him because of the crowd, so that they would not crush him. 10 e He had cured many and, as a result, those who had diseases were pressing upon him to touch him. 11 f *And whenever unclean spirits saw him they would fall down before him and shout, "You are the Son of God." 12 He warned them sternly not to make him known.

The Mission of the Twelve 13 g *He went up the mountain and summoned those whom he wanted and they came to him. 14 h *He appointed twelve [whom he also named apostles] that they might be with him and he might send them forth to preach 15 and to have authority to drive out demons: 16 *[he appointed the twelve:] Simon, whom he named Peter; 17 i James, son of Zebedee, and John the brother of James, whom he named Boanerges, that is, sons of thunder; 18 Andrew, Philip, Bartholomew, Matthew, Thomas, James the son of Alphaeus; Thaddeus, Simon the Cananean, 19 and Judas Iscariot who betrayed him.

Blasphemy of the Scribes 20 j *He came home. Again [the] crowd gathered, making it impossible for them even to eat. 21 k When his relatives heard of this they set out to seize him, for they said, "He is out of his mind." 22 l *The scribes who had come from Jerusalem said, "He is possessed by Beelzebul," and "By the prince of demons he drives out demons."

Jesus and Beelzebul 23 Summoning them, he began to speak to them in parables, "How can Satan drive out Satan? 24 If a kingdom is divided against itself, that kingdom cannot stand. 25 And if a house is divided against itself, that house will not be able to stand. 26 And if Satan has risen up against himself and is divided, he cannot stand; that is the end of him. 27 But no one can enter a strong man's house to plunder his property unless he first ties up the strong man. Then he can plunder his house. 28 m Amen, I say to you, all sins and all blasphemies that people utter will be forgiven them. 29 *But whoever blasphemes against the holy Spirit will never have forgiveness, but is guilty of an everlasting sin." 30 For they had said, "He has an unclean spirit."

Jesus and His Family 31 n His mother and his brothers arrived. Standing outside they sent word to him and called him. 32 *A crowd seated around him told him, "Your mother and your brothers [and your sisters] are outside asking for you." 33 But he said to them in reply, "Who are my mother and [my] brothers?" 34 And looking around at those seated in the circle he said, "Here are my mother and my brothers. 35 [For]

---

power of Jesus to draw people to himself through his teaching and deeds of power. The crowds of Jews from many regions surround Jesus (7–12). This phenomenon prepares the way for creating a new people of Israel. The choice and mission of the Twelve is the prelude (13–19).

3, 11–12: See the note on 1, 24–25.

3, 13: He went up the mountain: here and elsewhere the mountain is associated with solemn moments and acts in the mission and self-revelation of Jesus (6, 46; 9, 2–8; 13, 3). Jesus acts with authority as he **summoned those whom he wanted and they came to him.**

3, 14–15: He appointed twelve [whom he also named apostles] that they might be with him: literally "he made," i.e., instituted them as apostles to extend his messianic mission through them (6, 7–13). See the notes on Mt 10, 1 and 10, 2–4.

3, 16: Simon, whom he named Peter: Mark indicates that Simon's name was changed on this occasion. Peter is first in all lists of the apostles (Mt 10, 2; Lk 6, 14; Acts 1, 13; cf 1 Cor 15, 5–8).

3, 20–35: Within the narrative of the coming of Jesus' relatives (20–21) is inserted the account of the unbelieving scribes from Jerusalem who attributed Jesus' power over demons to Beelzebul (22–30); see the note on 5, 21–43. There were those even among the relatives of Jesus who disbelieved and regarded Jesus as **out of his mind** (21). Against this background, Jesus is informed of the arrival of his mother and brothers [and sisters] (32). He responds by showing that not family ties but doing God's will (35) is decisive in the kingdom; cf the note on Mt 12, 46–50.

3, 20: He came home: cf 2, 1–2 and see the note on 2, 15.

3, 22: By Beelzebul: see the note on Mt 10, 25. Two accusations are leveled against Jesus: (1) that **he is possessed** by an unclean spirit, and (2) **by the prince of demons he drives out demons.** Jesus answers the second charge by a parable (24–27) and responds to the first charge in vv 28–29.

3, 29: Whoever blasphemes against the holy Spirit: this sin is called **an everlasting sin** because it attributes to Satan, who is the power of evil, what is actually the work of the holy Spirit, namely, victory over the demons.

3, 32: Your brothers: see the note on 6, 3.

e 5, 30. f 1, 34; Lk 4, 41. g Mt 10, 1–4; Lk 6, 12–16. h 6, 7. i Mt 16, 18; Jn 1, 42. j 2, 2. k Jn 10, 20. l Mt 12, 24–32; Lk 11, 15–22; 12, 10. m Lk 12, 10. n Mt 12, 46–50; Lk 8, 19–21.

whoever does the will of God is my brother and
sister and mother."

CHAPTER 4

The Parable of the Sower 1 [o p]*On another
occasion he began to teach by the sea. A very
large crowd gathered around him so that he got
into a boat on the sea and sat down. And the
whole crowd was beside the sea on land. 2 And
he taught them at length in parables, and in the
course of his instruction he said to them,
3 *"Hear this! A sower went out to sow. 4 And as
he sowed, some seed fell on the path, and the
birds came and ate it up. 5 Other seed fell on
rocky ground where it had little soil. It sprang up
at once because the soil was not deep. 6 And
when the sun rose, it was scorched and it
withered for lack of roots. 7 Some seed fell
among thorns, and the thorns grew up and
choked it and it produced no grain. 8 And some
seed fell on rich soil and produced fruit. It came
up and grew and yielded thirty, sixty, and a
hundredfold." 9 He added, "Whoever has ears to
hear ought to hear."

The Purpose of the Parables 10 And when he
was alone, those present along with the Twelve
questioned him about the parables. 11 *He an-
swered them, "The mystery of the kingdom of
God has been granted to you. But to those
outside everything comes in parables, 12 [q]so that

'they may look and see but not perceive,
and hear and listen but not understand,
in order that they may not be converted and
be forgiven.' "

13 [r]*Jesus said to them, "Do you not understand
this parable? Then how will you understand any
of the parables? 14 The sower sows the word.
15 These are the ones on the path where the
word is sown. As soon as they hear, Satan comes
at once and takes away the word sown in them.
16 And these are the ones sown on rocky ground
who, when they hear the word, receive it at
once with joy. 17 But they have no root; they last
only for a time. Then when tribulation or
persecution comes because of the word, they
quickly fall away. 18 Those sown among thorns
are another sort. They are the people who hear
the word, 19 but worldly anxiety, the lure of
riches, and the craving for other things intrude
and choke the word, and it bears no fruit. 20 But
those sown on rich soil are the ones who hear
the word and accept it and bear fruit thirty and
sixty and a hundredfold."

Parable of the Lamp 21 [s t]He said to them, "Is
a lamp brought in to be placed under a bushel
basket or under a bed, and not to be placed on a
lampstand? 22 [u]For there is nothing hidden ex-
cept to be made visible; nothing is secret except
to come to light. 23 Anyone who has ears to hear
ought to hear." 24 [v]He also told them, "Take care
what you hear. The measure with which you
measure will be measured out to you, and still
more will be given to you. 25 [w]To the one who
has, more will be given; from the one who has
not, even what he has will be taken away."

Seed Grows of Itself 26 [x]*He said, "This is
how it is with the kingdom of God; it is as if a
man were to scatter seed on the land 27 and

4, 1–34: In parables (2): see the note on Mt 13, 3. The use of parables is typical of Jesus' enigmatic method of teaching the crowds (2–9.12) as compared with the interpretation of the parables he gives to his disciples (10–25.33–34), to each group according to its capacity to understand (9–11). The key feature of the parable at hand is the sowing of the seed (3), representing the breakthrough of the kingdom of God into the world. The various types of soil refer to the diversity of response accorded the word of God (4–7). The climax of the parable is the harvest of thirty, sixty, and a hundredfold, indicating the consummation of the kingdom (8). Thus both the present and the future action of God, from the initiation to the fulfillment of the kingdom, is presented through this and other parables (26–29.30–32).

4, 1: By the sea: the shore of the Sea of Galilee or a boat near the shore (2, 13; 3, 7–8) is the place where Mark depicts Jesus teaching the crowds. By contrast the mountain is the scene of Jesus at prayer (6, 46) or in the process of forming his disciples (3, 13; 9, 2).

4, 3–8: See the note on Mt 13, 3–8.

4, 11–12: These verses are to be viewed against their background in 3, 6.22 concerning the unbelief and opposition Jesus encountered in his ministry. It is against this background that the distinction in Jesus' method becomes clear of presenting the kingdom to the disbelieving crowd in one manner and to the disciples in another. To the former it is presented in parables and the truth remains hidden; for the latter the parable is interpreted and the mystery is partially revealed because of their faith; see the notes on Mt 13, 11 and 13, 13.

4, 13–20: See the note on Mt 13, 18–23.

4, 26–29: Only Mark records the parable of the seed's growth.

o Mt 13, 1–13; Lk 8, 4–10. p 2, 13; Lk 5, 1. q Is 6, 9; Jn 12, 40; Acts 28, 26; Rom 11, 8. r Mt 13, 18–23; Lk 8, 11–15. s Lk 8, 16–18. t Mt 5, 15; Lk 11, 33. u Mt 10, 26; Lk 12, 2. v Mt 7, 2; Lk 6, 38. w Mt 13, 12; Lk 19, 26. x Jas 5, 7.

would sleep and rise night and day and the seed
would sprout and grow, he knows not how. 28 Of
its own accord the land yields fruit, first the
blade, then the ear, then the full grain in the ear.
29 And when the grain is ripe, he wields the
sickle at once, for the harvest has come."
The Mustard Seed 30 y He said, "To what shall
we compare the kingdom of God, or what
parable can we use for it? 31 It is like a mustard
seed that, when it is sown in the ground, is the
smallest of all the seeds on the earth. 32 *But
once it is sown, it springs up and becomes the
largest of plants and puts forth large branches, so
that the birds of the sky can dwell in its shade."
33 z With many such parables he spoke the word
to them as they were able to understand it.
34 Without parables he did not speak to them,
but to his own disciples he explained everything
in private.
The Calming of a Storm at Sea 35 a *On that
day, as evening drew on, he said to them, "Let
us cross to the other side." 36 Leaving the crowd,
they took him with them in the boat just as he
was. And other boats were with him. 37 A violent
squall came up and waves were breaking over
the boat, so that it was already filling up. 38 Jesus
was in the stern, asleep on a cushion. They woke
him and said to him, "Teacher, do you not care
that we are perishing?" 39 *He woke up, rebuked
the wind, and said to the sea, "Quiet! Be still!"
The wind ceased and there was great calm.
40 Then he asked them, "Why are you terrified?
Do you not yet have faith?" 41 b *They were filled
with great awe and said to one another, "Who
then is this whom even wind and sea obey?"

CHAPTER 5

The Healing of the Gerasene Demoniac

1 c *They came to the other side of the sea, to the
territory of the Gerasenes. 2 *When he got out of
the boat, at once a man from the tombs who had
an unclean spirit met him. 3 The man had been
dwelling among the tombs, and no one could
restrain him any longer, even with a chain. 4 In
fact, he had frequently been bound with shack-
les and chains, but the chains had been pulled
apart by him and the shackles smashed, and no
one was strong enough to subdue him. 5 Night
and day among the tombs and on the hillsides he
was always crying out and bruising himself with
stones. 6 Catching sight of Jesus from a distance,
he ran up and prostrated himself before him,
7 *crying out in a loud voice, "What have you to
do with me, Jesus, Son of the Most High God? I
adjure you by God, do not torment me!" 8 (He
had been saying to him, "Unclean spirit, come
out of the man!") 9 d *He asked him, "What is
your name?" He replied, "Legion is my name.
There are many of us." 10 And he pleaded
earnestly with him not to drive them away from
that territory.

11 *Now a large herd of swine was feeding
there on the hillside. 12 And they pleaded with
him, "Send us into the swine. Let us enter
them." 13 And he let them, and the unclean
spirits came out and entered the swine. The herd
of about two thousand rushed down a steep
bank into the sea, where they were drowned.
14 The swineherds ran away and reported the
incident in the town and throughout the country-
side. And people came out to see what had

Sower and harvester are the same. The emphasis is on the power of the seed to grow of itself without human intervention (27). Mysteriously it produces **blade** and **ear** and **full grain** (28). Thus the kingdom of God initiated by Jesus in proclaiming the word develops quietly yet powerfully until it is fully established by him at the final judgment (29); cf Rv 14, 15.

4, 32: The universality of the kingdom of God is indicated here; cf Ez 17, 23; 31, 6; Dn 4, 17–19.

4, 35—5, 43: After the chapter on parables, Mark narrates four miracle stories: 4, 35–41; 5, 1–20; and two joined together in 5, 21–43. See also the notes on Mt 8, 23–34 and 9, 8–26.

4, 39: Quiet! Be still!: as in the case of silencing a demon (1, 25), Jesus rebukes the wind and subdues the turbulence of the sea by a mere word; see the note on Mt 8, 26.

4, 41: Jesus is here depicted as exercising power over wind and sea. In the Christian community this event was seen as a sign of Jesus' saving presence amid persecutions that threatened its existence.

5, 1: The territory of the Gerasenes: the reference is to pagan territory; cf Is 65, 1. Another reading is "Gadarenes"; see the note on Mt 8, 28.

5, 2–6: The man was an outcast from society, dominated by unclean spirits (8.13), living among the tombs. The prostration before Jesus (6) indicates Jesus' power over evil spirits.

5, 7: What have you to do with me?: cf 1, 24 and see the note on Jn 2, 4.

5, 9: Legion is my name: the demons were numerous and the condition of the possessed man was extremely serious; cf Mt 12, 45.

5, 11: Herd of swine: see the note on Mt 8, 30.

y Mt 13, 31–32; Lk 13, 18–19. z Mt 13, 34. a Mt 8, 18.23–37; Lk 8, 22–25. b 1, 27. c Mt 8, 28–34; Lk 8, 26–39. d Mt 12, 45; Lk 8, 2; 11, 26.

happened. [15]As they approached Jesus, they caught sight of the man who had been possessed by Legion, sitting there clothed and in his right mind. And they were seized with fear. [16]Those who witnessed the incident explained to them what had happened to the possessed man and to the swine. [17]Then they began to beg him to leave their district. [18]As he was getting into the boat, the man who had been possessed pleaded to remain with him. [19]*But he would not permit him but told him instead, "Go home to your family and announce to them all that the Lord in his pity has done for you." [20]Then the man went off and began to proclaim in the Decapolis what Jesus had done for him; and all were amazed.

Jairus's Daughter and the Woman with a Hemorrhage [21 e]*When Jesus had crossed again [in the boat] to the other side, a large crowd gathered around him, and he stayed close to the sea. [22 f]One of the synagogue officials, named Jairus, came forward. Seeing him he fell at his feet [23]*and pleaded earnestly with him, saying, "My daughter is at the point of death. Please, come lay your hands on her that she may get well and live." [24]He went off with him, and a large crowd followed him and pressed upon him.

[25]There was a woman afflicted with hemorrhages for twelve years. [26]She had suffered greatly at the hands of many doctors and had spent all that she had. Yet she was not helped but only grew worse. [27]She had heard about Jesus and came up behind him in the crowd and touched his cloak. [28]*She said, "If I but touch his clothes, I shall be cured." [29]Immediately her flow of blood dried up. She felt in her body that she was healed of her affliction. [30]Jesus, aware at once that power had gone out from him, turned around in the crowd and asked, "Who has touched my clothes?" [31]But his disciples said to him, "You see how the crowd is pressing upon you, and yet you ask, 'Who touched me?' " [32]And he looked around to see who had done it. [33]The woman, realizing what had happened to her, approached in fear and trembling. She fell down before Jesus and told him the whole truth. [34 g]He said to her, "Daughter, your faith has saved you. Go in peace and be cured of your affliction."

[35]*While he was still speaking, people from the synagogue official's house arrived and said, "Your daughter has died; why trouble the teacher any longer?" [36]Disregarding the message that was reported, Jesus said to the synagogue official, "Do not be afraid; just have faith." [37]He did not allow anyone to accompany him inside except Peter, James, and John, the brother of James. [38]When they arrived at the house of the synagogue official, he caught sight of a commotion, people weeping and wailing loudly. [39 h]*So he went in and said to them, "Why this commotion and weeping? The child is not dead but asleep." [40]And they ridiculed him. Then he put them all out. He took along the child's father and mother and those who were with him and entered the room where the child was. [41]*He took the child by the hand and said to her, "*Talitha koum,*" which means, "Little girl, I say to you, arise!" [42]The girl, a child of twelve, arose immediately and walked around. [At that] they

5, 19: Go home: Jesus did not accept the man's request to **remain with him** as a disciple (18), yet invited him to announce to his own people what the Lord had done for him, i.e., proclaim the gospel message to his pagan family; cf 1, 14.39; 3, 14; 13, 10.

5, 21–43: The story of the raising to life of Jairus's daughter is divided into two parts: vv 21–24 and 35–43. Between these two separated parts the account of the cure of the hemorrhage victim (25–34) is interposed. This technique of intercalating or sandwiching one story within another occurs several times in Mk: 3, 19b-21 (22–30) 31–35; 6, 6b-13 (14–29) 30; 11, 12–14 (15–19) 20–25; 14, 53 (54) 55–65 (66–73).

5, 23: Lay your hands on her: this act for the purpose of healing is frequent in Mk (6, 5; 7, 32–35; 8, 23–25; 16, 18) and is also found in Mt 9, 18; Lk 4, 40; 13, 13; Acts 9, 17; 28, 8.

5, 28: Both in the case of Jairus and his daughter (23) and in the case of the hemorrhage victim, the inner conviction that physical contact (30) accompanied by faith in Jesus' saving power could effect a cure was rewarded.

5, 35: The faith of Jairus was put to a twofold test: (1) that his daughter might be cured and, now that she had died, (2) that she might be restored to life. His faith contrasts with the lack of faith of the crowd.

5, 39: Not dead but asleep: the New Testament often refers to death as sleep (Mt 27, 52; Jn 11, 11; 1 Cor 15, 6; 1 Thes 4, 13–15); see the note on Mt 9, 24.

5, 41: Arise: the Greek verb **egeirein** is the verb generally used to express resurrection from death (6, 14.16; Mt 11, 5; Lk 7, 14) and Jesus' own resurrection (16, 6; Mt 28, 6; Lk 24, 6).

e 2, 13. f Mt 9, 18–26; Lk 8, 41–56. g Lk 7, 30. h Acts 9, 40.

were utterly astounded. [43]He gave strict orders that no one should know this and said that she should be given something to eat.

CHAPTER 6

The Rejection at Nazareth [1 i*]He departed from there and came to his native place, accompanied by his disciples. [2*]When the sabbath came he began to teach in the synagogue, and many who heard him were astonished. They said, "Where did this man get all this? What kind of wisdom has been given him? What mighty deeds are wrought by his hands! [3 j*]Is he not the carpenter, the son of Mary, and the brother of James and Joses and Judas and Simon? And are not his sisters here with us?" And they took offense at him. [4 k*]Jesus said to them, "A prophet is not without honor except in his native place and among his own kin and in his own house." [5*]So he was not able to perform any mighty deed there, apart from curing a few sick people by laying his hands on them. [6]He was amazed at their lack of faith.

The Mission of the Twelve He went around to the villages in the vicinity teaching. [7 l*]He summoned the Twelve and began to send them out two by two and gave them authority over unclean spirits. [8*]He instructed them to take nothing for the journey but a walking stick—no food, no sack, no money in their belts. [9]They were, however, to wear sandals but not a second tunic. [10*]He said to them, "Wherever you enter a house, stay there until you leave from there. [11]Whatever place does not welcome you or listen to you, leave there and shake the dust off your feet in testimony against them." [12]So they went off and preached repentance. [13 m*]They drove out many demons, and they anointed with oil many who were sick and cured them.

Herod's Opinion of Jesus [14 n o*]King Herod heard about it, for his fame had become widespread, and people were saying, "John the Baptist has been raised from the dead; that is why mighty powers are at work in him." [15 p]Others were saying, "He is Elijah"; still others, "He is a prophet like any of the prophets." [16]But when Herod learned of it, he said, "It is John whom I beheaded. He has been raised up."

The Death of John the Baptist [17 q*]Herod was the one who had John arrested and bound

6, 1: **His native place:** the Greek word **patris** here refers to Nazareth (cf 1, 9; Lk 4, 16.23–24), though it can also mean native land.

6, 2–6: See the note on Mt 13, 54–58.

6, 3: **Is he not the carpenter?:** no other gospel calls Jesus a carpenter. Some witnesses have "the carpenter's son," as in Mt 13, 55. **Son of Mary:** contrary to Jewish custom, which calls a man the son of his father, this expression may reflect Mark's own faith that God is the Father of Jesus (1, 1.11; 8, 38; 13, 32; 14, 36). **The brother of James . . . Simon:** in Semitic usage, the terms 'brother,' 'sister' are applied not only to children of the same parents, but to nephews, nieces, cousins, half-brothers, and half-sisters; cf Gn 14, 16; 29, 15; Lv 10, 4. While one cannot suppose that the meaning of a Greek word should be sought in the first place from Semitic usage, the Septuagint often translates the Hebrew **'āh** by the Greek word **adelphos,** "brother," as in the cited passages, a fact that may argue for a similar breadth of meaning in some New Testament passages. For instance, there is no doubt that in v 17, "brother" is used of Philip, who was actually the half-brother of Herod Antipas. On the other hand, Mark may have understood the terms literally; see also Mt 3, 31–32; 12, 46; 13, 55–56; Lk 8, 19; Jn 7, 3.5. The question of meaning here would not have arisen but for the faith of the church in Mary's perpetual virginity.

6, 4: **A prophet is not without honor except . . . in his own house:** a saying that finds parallels in other literatures, especially Jewish and Greek, but without reference to a prophet. Comparing himself to previous Hebrew prophets whom the people rejected, Jesus intimates his own eventual rejection by the nation especially in view of the dishonor his own relatives had shown him (3, 21) and now his townspeople as well.

6, 5: **He was not able to perform any mighty deed there:** according to Mark, Jesus' power could not take effect because of a person's lack of faith.

6, 7–13: The preparation for the mission of the Twelve is seen in the call (1) of the first disciples to be fishers of men (1, 16–20), (2) then of the Twelve set apart to be with Jesus and to receive authority to preach and expel demons (3, 13–19). Now they are given the specific mission to exercise that authority in word and power as representatives of Jesus during the time of their formation.

6, 8–9: In Mk the use of a **walking stick** (8) and **sandals** (9) is permitted, but not in Mt 10, 10 nor in Lk 10, 4. Mark does not mention any prohibition to visit pagan territory and to enter Samaritan towns. These differences indicate a certain adaptation to conditions in and outside of Palestine and suggest in Mark's account a later activity in the church. For the rest, Jesus required of his apostles a total dependence on God for food and shelter; cf vv 35–44; 8, 1–9.

6, 10–11: Remaining in the same house as a guest (10) rather than moving to another offering greater comfort avoided any impression of seeking advantage for oneself and prevented dishonor to one's host. Shaking the dust off one's feet served as testimony against those who rejected the call to repentance.

6, 13: **Anointed with oil . . . cured them:** a common medicinal remedy, but seen here as a vehicle of divine power for healing.

6, 14–16: The various opinions about Jesus anticipate the theme of his identity that reaches its climax in 8, 27–30.

6, 14: **King Herod:** see the note on Mt 14, 1.

6, 17–29: Similarities are to be noted between Mark's account of the imprisonment and death of John the Baptist in this pericope, and

i Mt 13, 54–58; Lk 4, 16–30. j 15, 40; Mt 12, 46; Jn 6, 42. k Jn 4, 44. l Mt 10, 1.9–14; Lk 9, 15; 10, 4–11. m Jas 5, 14. n Lk 9, 7–8. o Mt 14, 1–12. p Mt 16, 14. q Lk 3, 19–20.

in prison on account of Herodias, the wife of his brother Philip, whom he had married. 18 [r]John had said to Herod, "It is not lawful for you to have your brother's wife." 19 *Herodias harbored a grudge against him and wanted to kill him but was unable to do so. 20 Herod feared John, knowing him to be a righteous and holy man, and kept him in custody. When he heard him speak he was very much perplexed, yet he liked to listen to him. 21 She had an opportunity one day when Herod, on his birthday, gave a banquet for his courtiers, his military officers, and the leading men of Galilee. 22 Herodias's own daughter came in and performed a dance that delighted Herod and his guests. The king said to the girl, "Ask of me whatever you wish and I will grant it to you." 23 [s]He even swore [many things] to her, "I will grant you whatever you ask of me, even to half of my kingdom." 24 She went out and said to her mother, "What shall I ask for?" She replied, "The head of John the Baptist." 25 The girl hurried back to the king's presence and made her request, "I want you to give me at once on a platter the head of John the Baptist." 26 The king was deeply distressed, but because of his oaths and the guests he did not wish to break his word to her. 27 [t]So he promptly dispatched an executioner with orders to bring back his head. He went off and beheaded him in the prison. 28 He brought in the head on a platter and gave it to the girl. The girl in turn gave it to her mother. 29 When his disciples heard about it, they came and took his body and laid it in a tomb.

The Return of the Twelve 30 [u]*The apostles gathered together with Jesus and reported all they had done and taught. 31 [v]*He said to them, "Come away by yourselves to a deserted place and rest a while." People were coming and going in great numbers, and they had no opportunity even to eat. 32 [w]So they went off in the boat by themselves to a deserted place. 33 People saw them leaving and many came to know about it. They hastened there on foot from all the towns and arrived at the place before them.

The Feeding of the Five Thousand 34 When he disembarked and saw the vast crowd, his heart was moved with pity for them, for they were like sheep without a shepherd; and he began to teach them many things. 35 *By now it was already late and his disciples approached him and said, "This is a deserted place and it is already very late. 36 Dismiss them so that they can go to the surrounding farms and villages and buy themselves something to eat." 37 He said to them in reply, "Give them some food yourselves." But they said to him, "Are we to buy two hundred days' wages worth of food and give it to them to eat?" 38 He asked them, "How many loaves do you have? Go and see." And when they had found out they said, "Five loaves and two fish." 39 So he gave orders to have them sit down in groups on the green grass. 40 *The people took their places in rows by hundreds and by fifties. 41 *Then, taking the five loaves and the two fish and looking up to heaven, he said the blessing, broke the loaves, and gave them to [his] disciples to set before the people;

---

that of the passion of Jesus (15, 1–47). Herod and Pilate, each in turn, acknowledges the holiness of life of one over whom he unjustly exercises the power of condemnation and death (26–27; 15, 9–10.14–15). The hatred of Herodias toward John parallels that of the Jewish leaders toward Jesus. After the deaths of John and of Jesus, well-disposed persons request the bodies of the victims of Herod and of Pilate in turn to give them respectful burial (29; 15, 45–46).

6, 19: Herodias: see the note on Mt 14, 3.

6, 30: Apostles: here, and in some manuscripts at 3, 14, Mark calls apostles (i.e., those sent forth) the Twelve whom Jesus sends as his emissaries, empowering them to preach, to expel demons, and to cure the sick (13). Only after Pentecost is the title used in the technical sense.

6, 31–34: The withdrawal of Jesus with his disciples to a desert place to rest attracts a great number of people to follow them. Toward this people of the new exodus Jesus is moved with pity; he satisfies their spiritual hunger by teaching them many things, thus gradually showing himself the faithful shepherd of a new Israel; cf Nm 27, 17; Ez 34, 15.

6, 35–44: See the note on Mt 14, 13–21. Compare this section with 8, 1–9. The various accounts of the multiplication of loaves and fishes, two each in Mark and in Matthew and one each in Luke and in John, indicate the wide interest of the early church in their eucharistic gatherings; see, e.g., v 41; 8, 6; 14, 22; and recall also the sign of bread in Ex 16; Dt 8, 3–16; Pss 78, 24–25; 105, 40; Wis 16, 20–21.

6, 40: The people . . . in rows by hundreds and by fifties: reminiscent of the groupings of Israelites encamped in the desert (Ex 18, 21–25) and of the wilderness tradition of the prophets depicting the transformation of the wasteland into pastures where the true shepherd feeds his flock (Ez 34, 25–26) and makes his people beneficiaries of messianic grace.

6, 41: On the language of this verse as eucharistic (cf 14, 22),

r Lv 18, 16. s Est 5, 3. t Lk 9, 9. u Lk 9, 10. v 3, 20; Mt 14, 13; Lk 9, 10. w Mt 14, 13–21; Lk 9, 10–17; Jn 6, 1–13.

he also divided the two fish among them all. [42]They all ate and were satisfied. [43]And they picked up twelve wicker baskets full of fragments and what was left of the fish. [44]Those who ate [of the loaves] were five thousand men.

The Walking on the Water [45][x]*Then he made his disciples get into the boat and precede him to the other side toward Bethsaida, while he dismissed the crowd. [46]*And when he had taken leave of them, he went off to the mountain to pray. [47]When it was evening, the boat was far out on the sea and he was alone on shore. [48]*Then he saw that they were tossed about while rowing, for the wind was against them. About the fourth watch of the night, he came toward them walking on the sea. He meant to pass by them. [49]But when they saw him walking on the sea, they thought it was a ghost and cried out. [50]*They had all seen him and were terrified. But at once he spoke with them, "Take courage, it is I, do not be afraid!" [51]He got into the boat with them and the wind died down. They were [completely] astounded. [52][y]*They had not understood the incident of the loaves. On the contrary, their hearts were hardened.

The Healings at Gennesaret [53][z]After making the crossing, they came to land at Gennesaret and tied up there. [54]As they were leaving the boat, people immediately recognized him. [55]They scurried about the surrounding country and began to bring in the sick on mats to wherever they heard he was. [56][a]Whatever villages or towns or countryside he entered, they laid the sick in the marketplaces and begged him that they might touch only the tassel on his cloak; and as many as touched it were healed.

CHAPTER 7

The Tradition of the Elders [1][b]*Now when the Pharisees with some scribes who had come from Jerusalem gathered around him, [2]they observed that some of his disciples ate their meals with unclean, that is, unwashed, hands. [3]*(For the Pharisees and, in fact, all Jews, do not eat without carefully washing their hands, keeping the tradition of the elders. [4]And on coming from the marketplace they do not eat without purifying themselves. And there are many other things that they have traditionally observed, the purification of cups and jugs and kettles [and beds].) [5]*So the Pharisees and scribes questioned him, "Why do your disciples not follow the tradition of the elders but instead eat a meal with unclean hands?" [6][c]He responded, "Well did Isaiah prophesy about you hypocrites, as it is written:

'This people honors me with their lips,
but their hearts are far from me;
[7]In vain do they worship me,
teaching as doctrines human precepts.'

[8]You disregard God's commandment but cling to human tradition." [9]He went on to say, "How well you have set aside the commandment of God in order to uphold your tradition! [10][d]For Moses said, 'Honor your father and your

see the notes on Mt 14, 19.20. Jesus observed the Jewish table ritual of blessing God before partaking of food.

6, 45–52: See the note on Mt 14, 22–33.

6, 45: To the other side toward Bethsaida: a village at the northeastern shore of the Sea of Galilee.

6, 46: He went off to the mountain to pray: see 1, 35–38. In Jn 6, 15 Jesus withdrew to evade any involvement in the false messianic hopes of the multitude.

6, 48: Walking on the sea: see the notes on Mt 14, 22–33 and on Jn 6, 19.

6, 50: It is I, do not be afraid!: literally, "I am." This may reflect the divine revelatory formula of Ex 3, 14; Is 41, 4.10.14; 43, 1–3.10.13. Mark implies the hidden identity of Jesus as Son of God.

6, 52: They had not understood . . . the loaves: the revelatory character of this sign and that of the walking on the sea completely escaped the disciples. **Their hearts were hardened:** in 3, 5–6 hardness of heart was attributed to those who did not accept Jesus and plotted his death. Here the same disposition prevents the disciples from comprehending Jesus' self-revelation through signs; cf 8, 17.

7, 1–23: See the note on Mt 15, 1–20. Against the Pharisees' narrow, legalistic, and external practices of piety in matters of purification (2–5), external worship (6–7), and observance of commandments, Jesus sets in opposition the true moral intent of the divine law (8–13). But he goes beyond contrasting the law and Pharisaic interpretation of it. The parable of vv 14–15 in effect sets aside the law itself in respect to clean and unclean food. He thereby opens the way for unity between Jew and Gentile in the kingdom of God, intimated by Jesus' departure for pagan territory beyond Galilee. For similar contrast see 2, 1—3, 6; 3, 20–35; 6, 1–6.

7, 3: Carefully washing their hands: refers to ritual purification.

7, 5: Tradition of the elders: the body of detailed, unwritten, human laws regarded by the scribes and Pharisees to have the same binding force as that of the Mosaic law; cf Gal 1, 14.

x Mt 14, 22–32; Jn 6, 15–21. y 4, 13. z Mt 14, 34–36. a 5, 27–28; Acts 5, 15. b Mt 15, 1–20. c Is 29, 13. d Ex 21, 17; Lv 20, 9; Dt 5, 16; Eph 6, 2.

mother,' and 'Whoever curses father or mother shall die.' 11*Yet you say, 'If a person says to father or mother, "Any support you might have had from me is *qorban*" ' (meaning, dedicated to God), 12you allow him to do nothing more for his father or mother. 13You nullify the word of God in favor of your tradition that you have handed on. And you do many such things." 14 [e]He summoned the crowd again and said to them, "Hear me, all of you, and understand. 15Nothing that enters one from outside can defile that person; but the things that come out from within are what defile." [16]*

17 [f]*When he got home away from the crowd his disciples questioned him about the parable. 18He said to them, "Are even you likewise without understanding? Do you not realize that everything that goes into a person from outside cannot defile, 19 [g]*since it enters not the heart but the stomach and passes out into the latrine?" (Thus he declared all foods clean.) 20"But what comes out of a person, that is what defiles. 21 [h]From within people, from their hearts, come evil thoughts, unchastity, theft, murder, 22adultery, greed, malice, deceit, licentiousness, envy, blasphemy, arrogance, folly. 23All these evils come from within and they defile."

The Syrophoenician Woman's Faith 24 [i]*From that place he went off to the district of Tyre. He entered a house and wanted no one to know about it, but he could not escape notice. 25Soon a woman whose daughter had an unclean spirit heard about him. She came and fell at his feet. 26 [j]The woman was a Greek, a Syrophoenician by birth, and she begged him to drive the demon out of her daughter. 27*He said to her, "Let the children be fed first. For it is not right to take the food of the children and throw it to the dogs." 28She replied and said to him, "Lord, even the dogs under the table eat the children's scraps." 29Then he said to her, "For saying this, you may go. The demon has gone out of your daughter." 30When the woman went home, she found the child lying in bed and the demon gone.

The Healing of a Deaf Man 31 [k]Again he left the district of Tyre and went by way of Sidon to the Sea of Galilee, into the district of the Decapolis. 32And people brought to him a deaf man who had a speech impediment and begged him to lay his hand on him. 33He took him off by himself away from the crowd. He put his finger into the man's ears and, spitting, touched his tongue; 34then he looked up to heaven and groaned, and said to him, "*Ephphatha*!" (that is, "Be opened!") 35And [immediately] the man's ears were opened, his speech impediment was removed, and he spoke plainly. 36*He ordered them not to tell anyone. But the more he ordered them not to, the more they proclaimed it. 37 [l]They were exceedingly astonished and they said, "He has done all things well. He makes the deaf hear and [the] mute speak."

CHAPTER 8

The Feeding of the Four Thousand 1 [m]*In those days when there again was a great crowd

7, 11: Qorban: a formula for a gift to God, dedicating the offering to the temple, so that the giver might continue to use it for himself but not give it to others, even needy parents.

7, 16: Verse 16, "Anyone who has ears to hear ought to hear," is omitted because it is lacking in some of the best Greek manuscripts and was probably transferred here by scribes from 4, (9).23.

7, 17: Away from the crowd . . . the parable: in this context of privacy the term **parable** refers to something hidden, about to be revealed to the disciples; cf 4, 10–11.34. Jesus sets the Mosaic food laws in the context of the kingdom of God where they are abrogated, and he declares moral defilement the only cause of uncleanness.

7, 19: (Thus he declared all foods clean): if this bold declaration goes back to Jesus, its force was not realized among Jewish Christians in the early church; cf Acts 10, 1—11, 18.

7, 24–37: The withdrawal of Jesus to the district of Tyre may have been for a respite (24), but he soon moved onward to Sidon and, by way of the Sea of Galilee, to the Decapolis. These districts provided a Gentile setting for the extension of his ministry of healing because the people there acknowledged his power (29.37). The actions attributed to Jesus (33–35) were also used by healers of the time.

7, 27–28: The figure of a household in which children at table are fed first and then their leftover food is given to the dogs under the table is used effectively to acknowledge the prior claim of the Jews to the ministry of Jesus; however, Jesus accedes to the Gentile woman's plea for the cure of her afflicted daughter because of her faith.

7, 36: The more they proclaimed it: the same verb **proclaim** attributed here to the crowd in relation to the miracles of Jesus is elsewhere used in Mark for the preaching of the gospel on the part of Jesus, of his disciples, and of the Christian community (1, 14; 13, 10; 14, 9). Implied in the action of the crowd is a recognition of the salvific mission of Jesus; see the note on Mt 11, 5–6.

8, 1–10: The two accounts of the multiplication of loaves and fishes (8, 1–10 and 6, 31–44) have eucharistic significance. Their similarity of structure and themes but dissimilarity of detail are

e Mt 15, 10–20. f 4, 10.13. g Acts 10, 15. h Jer 17, 9. i Mt 15, 21–28. j Mt 8, 29. k Mt 15, 29–31. l Mt 15, 31. m 6, 34–44; Mt 15, 32–39.

without anything to eat, he summoned the disciples and said, [2]"My heart is moved with pity for the crowd, because they have been with me now for three days and have nothing to eat. [3]If I send them away hungry to their homes, they will collapse on the way, and some of them have come a great distance." [4]His disciples answered him, "Where can anyone get enough bread to satisfy them here in this deserted place?" [5]Still he asked them, "How many loaves do you have?" "Seven," they replied. [6]*He ordered the crowd to sit down on the ground. Then, taking the seven loaves he gave thanks, broke them, and gave them to his disciples to distribute, and they distributed them to the crowd. [7]They also had a few fish. He said the blessing over them and ordered them distributed also. [8]They ate and were satisfied. They picked up the fragments left over—seven baskets. [9]There were about four thousand people.

He dismissed them [10]and got into the boat with his disciples and came to the region of Dalmanutha.

The Demand for a Sign [11] *n o**The Pharisees came forward and began to argue with him, seeking from him a sign from heaven to test him. [12]He sighed from the depth of his spirit and said, "Why does this generation seek a sign? Amen, I say to you, no sign will be given to this generation." [13]Then he left them, got into the boat again, and went off to the other shore.

The Leaven of the Pharisees [14] *p*They had forgotten to bring bread, and they had only one loaf with them in the boat. [15]*He enjoined them, "Watch out, guard against the leaven of the Pharisees and the leaven of Herod." [16]They concluded among themselves that it was because they had no bread. [17] *q*When he became aware of this he said to them, "Why do you conclude that it is because you have no bread? Do you not yet understand or comprehend? Are your hearts hardened? [18] *r*Do you have eyes and not see, ears and not hear? And do you not remember, [19]when I broke the five loaves for the five thousand, how many wicker baskets full of fragments you picked up?" They answered him, "Twelve." [20]"When I broke the seven loaves for the four thousand, how many full baskets of fragments did you pick up?" They answered [him], "Seven." [21]He said to them, "Do you still not understand?"

The Blind Man of Bethsaida [22]*When they arrived at Bethsaida, they brought to him a blind man and begged him to touch him. [23] *s*He took the blind man by the hand and led him outside the village. Putting spittle on his eyes he laid his hands on him and asked, "Do you see anything?" [24]Looking up he replied, "I see people looking like trees and walking." [25]Then he laid hands on his eyes a second time and he saw clearly; his sight was restored and he could see everything distinctly. [26]Then he sent him home and said, "Do not even go into the village."

III: The Mystery Begins to Be Revealed

Peter's Confession about Jesus [27] *t**Now Jesus and his disciples set out for the villages of Caesarea Philippi. Along the way he asked his disciples, "Who do people say that I am?"

---

considered by many to refer to a single event that, however, developed in two distinct traditions, one Jewish Christian and the other Gentile Christian, since Jesus in Mark's presentation (7, 24–37) has extended his saving mission to the Gentiles.

8, 6: See the note on 6, 41.

8, 11–12: The objection of the Pharisees that Jesus' miracles are unsatisfactory for proving the arrival of God's kingdom is comparable to the request of the crowd for a sign in Jn 6, 30–31. Jesus' response shows that a sign originating in human demand will not be provided; cf Nm 14, 11.22.

8, 15: The leaven of the Pharisees . . . of Herod: the corruptive action of leaven (1 Cor 5, 6–8; Gal 5, 9) was an apt symbol of the evil dispositions both of the Pharisees (11–13; 7, 5–13) and of Herod (6, 14–29) toward Jesus. The disciples of Jesus are warned against sharing such rebellious attitudes toward Jesus; cf vv 17, 21.

8, 22–26: Jesus' actions and the gradual cure of the blind man probably have the same purpose as in the case of the deaf man (7, 31–37). Some commentators regard the cure as an intended symbol of the gradual enlightenment of the disciples concerning Jesus' messiahship.

8, 27–30: This episode is the turning point in Mark's account of Jesus in his public ministry. Popular opinions concur in regard-

n Mt 12, 38–39; 16, 1–4. o Lk 11, 16. p Mt 16, 5–12; Lk 12, 1. q 4, 13. r Jer 5, 21; Ez 12, 2. s 7, 33; Jn 9, 6. t Mt 16, 13–20; Lk 9, 18–21.

[28]They said in reply, "John the Baptist, others Elijah, still others one of the prophets." [29]And he asked them, "But who do you say that I am?" Peter said to him in reply, "You are the Messiah." [30]Then he warned them not to tell anyone about him.

The First Prediction of the Passion [31][u]*He began to teach them that the Son of Man must suffer greatly and be rejected by the elders, the chief priests, and the scribes, and be killed, and rise after three days. [32]He spoke this openly. Then Peter took him aside and began to rebuke him. [33]At this he turned around and, looking at his disciples, rebuked Peter and said, "Get behind me, Satan. You are thinking not as God does, but as human beings do."

The Conditions of Discipleship [34][v]*He summoned the crowd with his disciples and said to them, "Whoever wishes to come after me must deny himself, take up his cross, and follow me. [35][w]*For whoever wishes to save his life will lose it, but whoever loses his life for my sake and that of the gospel will save it. [36]What profit is there for one to gain the whole world and forfeit his life? [37]What could one give in exchange for his life? [38][x]Whoever is ashamed of me and of my words in this faithless and sinful generation, the Son of Man will be ashamed of when he comes in his Father's glory with the holy angels."

CHAPTER 9

[1][y]*He also said to them, "Amen, I say to you, there are some standing here who will not taste death until they see that the kingdom of God has come in power."

The Transfiguration of Jesus [2][z]*After six days Jesus took Peter, James, and John and led them up a high mountain apart by themselves. And he was transfigured before them, [3]and his clothes became dazzling white, such as no fuller on earth could bleach them. [4]Then Elijah appeared to them along with Moses, and they were conversing with Jesus. [5]*Then Peter said to Jesus in reply, "Rabbi, it is good that we are here! Let us make three tents: one for you, one for Moses, and one for Elijah." [6]He hardly knew what to say, they were so terrified. [7]*Then a cloud came, casting a shadow over them; then from the cloud came a voice, "This is my beloved Son. Listen to him." [8]Suddenly, looking around, they

---

ing him as a prophet. The disciples by contrast believe him to be the Messiah. Jesus acknowledges this identification but prohibits them from making his messianic office known to avoid confusing it with ambiguous contemporary ideas on the nature of that office. See further the notes on Mt 16, 13–20.

8, 31: Son of Man: an enigmatic title. It is used in Dn 7, 13–14 as a symbol of "the saints of the Most High," the faithful Israelites who receive the everlasting kingdom from the Ancient One (God). They are represented by a human figure that contrasts with the various beasts who represent the previous kingdoms of the earth. In the Jewish apocryphal books of 1 Enoch and 4 Ezra the "Son of Man" is not, as in Dn, a group, but a unique figure of extraordinary spiritual endowments, who will be revealed as the one through whom the everlasting kingdom decreed by God will be established. It is possible though doubtful that this individualization of the Son of Man figure had been made in Jesus' time, and therefore his use of the title in that sense is questionable. Of itself, this expression means simply a human being, or, indefinitely, someone, and there are evidences of this use in pre-Christian times. Its use in the New Testament is probably due to Jesus' speaking of himself in that way, "a human being," and the later church's taking this in the sense of the Jewish apocrypha and applying it to him with that meaning. **Rejected by the elders, the chief priests, and the scribes:** the supreme council called the Sanhedrin was made up of seventy-one members of these three groups and presided over by the high priest. It exercised authority over the Jews in religious matters. See the note on Mt 8, 20.

8, 34–35: This utterance of Jesus challenges all believers to authentic discipleship and total commitment to himself through self-renunciation and acceptance of the cross of suffering, even to the sacrifice of life itself. **Whoever wishes to save his life will lose it . . . will save it:** an expression of the ambivalence of life and its contrasting destiny. Life seen as mere self-centered earthly existence and lived in denial of Christ ends in destruction, but when lived in loyalty to Christ, despite earthly death, it arrives at fullness of life.

8, 35: For my sake and that of the gospel: Mark here, as at 10, 29, equates Jesus with the gospel.

9, 1: There are some standing . . . come in power: understood by some to refer to the establishment by God's power of his kingdom on earth in and through the church; more likely, as understood by others, a reference to the imminent parousia.

9, 2–8: Mk and Mt 17, 1 place the transfiguration of Jesus six days after the first prediction of his passion and death and his instruction to the disciples on the doctrine of the cross; Lk 9, 28 has "about eight days." Thus the transfiguration counterbalances the prediction of the passion by affording certain of the disciples insight into the divine glory that Jesus possessed. His glory will overcome his death and that of his disciples; cf 2 Cor 3, 18; 2 Pt 1, 16–19. The heavenly voice (7) prepares the disciples to understand that in the divine plan Jesus must die ignominiously before his messianic glory is made manifest; cf Lk 24, 25–27. See further the note on Mt 17, 1–8.

9, 5: Moses and Elijah represent respectively law and prophecy in the Old Testament and are linked to Mt. Sinai; cf Ex 19, 16—20, 17; 1 Kgs 19, 2.8–14. They now appear with Jesus as witnesses to the fulfillment of the law and the prophets taking place in the person of Jesus as he appears in glory.

9, 7: A cloud came, casting a shadow over them: even the disciples enter into the mystery of his glorification. In the Old

u Mt 16, 21–27; Lk 9, 22–26. v Mt 10, 38–39; 16, 24–27; Lk 14, 26–27. w Jn 12, 25. x Mt 10, 33; Lk 12, 8. y Mt 16, 28; Lk 9, 27. z Mt 17, 1–13; Lk 9, 28–36.

no longer saw anyone but Jesus alone with them.

The Coming of Elijah [9][a]*As they were coming down from the mountain, he charged them not to relate what they had seen to anyone, except when the Son of Man had risen from the dead. [10]So they kept the matter to themselves, questioning what rising from the dead meant. [11][b]Then they asked him, "Why do the scribes say that Elijah must come first?" [12]He told them, "Elijah will indeed come first and restore all things, yet how is it written regarding the Son of Man that he must suffer greatly and be treated with contempt? [13][c]But I tell you that Elijah has come and they did to him whatever they pleased, as it is written of him."

The Healing of a Boy with a Demon [14][d]*When they came to the disciples, they saw a large crowd around them and scribes arguing with them. [15]Immediately on seeing him, the whole crowd was utterly amazed. They ran up to him and greeted him. [16]He asked them, "What are you arguing about with them?" [17]Someone from the crowd answered him, "Teacher, I have brought to you my son possessed by a mute spirit. [18]Wherever it seizes him, it throws him down; he foams at the mouth, grinds his teeth, and becomes rigid. I asked your disciples to drive it out, but they were unable to do so." [19]He said to them in reply, "O faithless generation, how long will I be with you? How long will I endure you? Bring him to me." [20]They brought the boy to him. And when he saw him, the spirit immediately threw the boy into convulsions. As he fell to the ground, he began to roll around and foam at the mouth. [21]Then he questioned his father, "How long has this been happening to him?" He replied, "Since childhood. [22]It has often thrown him into fire and into water to kill him. But if you can do anything, have compassion on us and help us." [23]Jesus said to him, " 'If you can!' Everything is possible to one who has faith." [24]Then the boy's father cried out, "I do believe, help my unbelief!" [25]Jesus, on seeing a crowd rapidly gathering, rebuked the unclean spirit and said to it, "Mute and deaf spirit, I command you: come out of him and never enter him again!" [26]Shouting and throwing the boy into convulsions, it came out. He became like a corpse, which caused many to say, "He is dead!" [27]But Jesus took him by the hand, raised him, and he stood up. [28]When he entered the house, his disciples asked him in private, "Why could we not drive it out?" [29]*He said to them, "This kind can only come out through prayer."

The Second Prediction of the Passion [30][ef]They left from there and began a journey through Galilee, but he did not wish anyone to know about it. [31]He was teaching his disciples and telling them, "The Son of Man is to be handed over to men and they will kill him, and three days after his death he will rise." [32]But they did not understand the saying, and they were afraid to question him.

IV: The Full Revelation of the Mystery

The Greatest in the Kingdom [33][g]*They came to Capernaum and, once inside the house, he began to ask them, "What were you arguing about on the way?" [34]But they remained silent. They had been discussing among themselves on the way who was the greatest. [35][h]Then he sat down, called the Twelve, and said to them, "If

---

Testament the cloud covered the meeting tent, indicating the Lord's presence in the midst of his people (Ex 40, 34–35) and came to rest upon the temple in Jerusalem at the time of its dedication (1 Kgs 8, 10).

9, 9–13: At the transfiguration of Jesus his disciples had seen Elijah. They were perplexed because, according to the rabbinical interpretation of Mal 3, 23–24, Elijah was to come first. Jesus' response shows that Elijah has come, in the person of John the Baptist, to prepare for the day of the Lord. Jesus **must suffer greatly and be treated with contempt** (12) like the Baptist (13); cf 6, 17–29.

9, 14–29: The disciples' failure to effect a cure seems to reflect unfavorably on Jesus (14–18.22). In response Jesus exposes their lack of trust in God (19) and scores their lack of prayer (29), i.e., of conscious reliance on God's power when acting in Jesus' name. For Mt, see the note on 17, 14–20. Luke 9, 37–43 centers attention on Jesus' sovereign power.

9, 29: This kind can only come out through prayer: a variant reading adds "and through fasting."

9, 33–37: Mark probably intends this incident and the sayings

a 8, 31. b Is 53, 3; Mal 3, 23. c 1 Kgs 19, 2–10. d Mt 17, 14–21; Lk 9, 37–43. e Jn 7, 1. f 8, 31; Mt 17, 22–23; Lk 9, 43–45. g Mt 18, 1–5; Lk 9, 46–48. h Mt 20, 27.

anyone wishes to be first, he shall be the last of
all and the servant of all.” 36 Taking a child he
placed it in their midst, and putting his arms
around it he said to them, 37 [i]“Whoever receives
one child such as this in my name, receives me;
and whoever receives me, receives not me but
the One who sent me.”
Another Exorcist 38 [j]*John said to him,
“Teacher, we saw someone driving out demons in
your name, and we tried to prevent him because
he does not follow us.” 39 Jesus replied, “Do not
prevent him. There is no one who performs a
mighty deed in my name who can at the same
time speak ill of me. 40 [k]For whoever is not against
us is for us. 41 [l]Anyone who gives you a cup of
water to drink because you belong to Christ,
amen, I say to you, will surely not lose his reward.
Temptations to Sin 42 [m]“Whoever causes one
of these little ones who believe [in me] to sin, it
would be better for him if a great millstone were
put around his neck and he were thrown into
the sea. 43 *If your hand causes you to sin, cut it
off. It is better for you to enter into life maimed
than with two hands to go into Gehenna, into
the unquenchable fire. [44]* 45 And if your foot
causes you to sin, cut if off. It is better for you to
enter into life crippled than with two feet to be
thrown into Gehenna. [46]* 47 And if your eye
causes you to sin, pluck it out. Better for you to
enter into the kingdom of God with one eye
than with two eyes to be thrown into Gehenna,
48 [n]where ‘their worm does not die, and the fire
is not quenched.’
The Simile of Salt 49 *“Everyone will be salted
with fire. 50 [o]Salt is good, but if salt becomes
insipid, with what will you restore its flavor?
Keep salt in yourselves and you will have peace
with one another.”

CHAPTER 10

Marriage and Divorce 1 He set out from there
and went into the district of Judea [and] across
the Jordan. Again crowds gathered around him
and, as was his custom, he again taught them.
2 [p]*The Pharisees approached and asked, “Is it
lawful for a husband to divorce his wife?” They
were testing him. 3 He said to them in reply,
“What did Moses command you?” 4 [q]They re-
plied, “Moses permitted him to write a bill of
divorce and dismiss her.” 5 But Jesus told them,
“Because of the hardness of your hearts he wrote
you this commandment. 6 [r]But from the begin-
ning of creation, ‘God made them male and
female. 7 [s]For this reason a man shall leave his
father and mother [and be joined to his wife],
8 and the two shall become one flesh.’ So they
are no longer two but one flesh. 9 Therefore what
God has joined together, no human being must
separate.” 10 In the house the disciples again
questioned him about this. 11 [t]He said to them,
“Whoever divorces his wife and marries another
commits adultery against her; 12 and if she di-
vorces her husband and marries another, she
commits adultery.”

---

that follow as commentary on the disciples’ lack of understanding (32). Their role in Jesus’ work is one of service, especially to the poor and lowly. Children were the symbol Jesus used for the **anawim,** the poor in spirit, the lowly in the Christian community.

9, 38–41: Jesus warns against jealousy and intolerance toward others, such as exorcists who do **not follow us.** The saying in v 40 is a broad principle of the divine tolerance. Even the smallest courtesies shown to those who teach in Jesus’ name do not go unrewarded.

9, 43.45.47: **Gehenna:** see the note on Mt 5, 22.

9, 44.46: These verses, lacking in some important early manuscripts, are here omitted as scribal additions. They simply repeat v 48, itself a modified citation of Is 66, 24.

9, 49: **Everyone will be salted with fire:** so the better manuscripts. Some add “every sacrifice will be salted with salt.” The purifying and preservative use of salt in food (Lv 2, 13) and the refinement effected through fire refer here to comparable effects in the spiritual life of the disciples of Jesus.

10, 2–9: In the dialogue between Jesus and the Pharisees on the subject of divorce, Jesus declares that the law of Moses permitted divorce (Dt 24, 1) only **because of the hardness of your hearts** (4–5). In citing Gn 1, 27 and 2, 24, Jesus proclaims permanence to be the divine intent from the beginning concerning human marriage (6–8). He reaffirms this with the declaration that **what God has joined together, no human being must separate** (9). See further the notes on Mt 5, 31–32 and 19, 3–9.

i Mt 10, 40; 18, 5; Jn 13, 20. j Nm 11, 28; Lk 9, 49–50; 1 Cor 12, 3. k Mt 12, 30. l Mt 10, 42; 1 Cor 3, 23. m Mt 5, 29–30; 18, 6–9; Lk 17, 1–2. n Is 66, 24. o Lv 2, 13; Mt 5, 13; Lk 14, 34–35; Col 4, 6. p Mt 19, 3–9. q Dt 24, 1–4. r Gn 1, 27. s Gn 2, 24; 1 Cor 6, 16; Eph 5, 31. t Mt 5, 32; Lk 16, 18; 1 Cor 7, 10–11.

Blessing of the Children 13 [u] [v]And people
were bringing children to him that he might
touch them, but the disciples rebuked them.
14 When Jesus saw this he became indignant and
said to them, "Let the children come to me; do
not prevent them, for the kingdom of God
belongs to such as these. 15 [w]*Amen, I say to
you, whoever does not accept the kingdom of
God like a child will not enter it." 16 Then he
embraced them and blessed them, placing his
hands on them.

The Rich Man 17 [x]As he was setting out on a
journey, a man ran up, knelt down before him,
and asked him, "Good teacher, what must I do to
inherit eternal life?" 18 *Jesus answered him,
"Why do you call me good? No one is good but
God alone. 19 [y]You know the commandments:
'You shall not kill; you shall not commit adultery;
you shall not steal; you shall not bear false wit-
ness; you shall not defraud; honor your father
and your mother.' " 20 He replied and said to him,
"Teacher, all of these I have observed from my
youth." 21 Jesus, looking at him, loved him and
said to him, "You are lacking in one thing. Go, sell
what you have, and give to [the] poor and you will
have treasure in heaven; then come, follow me."
22 At that statement his face fell, and he went
away sad, for he had many possessions.

23 [z]*Jesus looked around and said to his disci-
ples, "How hard it is for those who have wealth
to enter the kingdom of God!" 24 The disciples
were amazed at his words. So Jesus again said to
them in reply, "Children, how hard it is to enter
the kingdom of God! 25 It is easier for a camel to
pass through [the] eye of [a] needle than for one
who is rich to enter the kingdom of God."
26 They were exceedingly astonished and said
among themselves, "Then who can be saved?"
27 Jesus looked at them and said, "For human
beings it is impossible, but not for God. All
things are possible for God." 28 Peter began to say
to him, "We have given up everything and
followed you." 29 Jesus said, "Amen, I say to you,
there is no one who has given up house or
brothers or sisters or mother or father or children
or lands for my sake and for the sake of the
gospel 30 who will not receive a hundred times
more now in this present age: houses and
brothers and sisters and mothers and children
and lands, with persecutions, and eternal life in
the age to come. 31 [a]But many that are first will
be last, and [the] last will be first."

The Third Prediction of the Passion
32 [b]They were on the way, going up to Jerusa-
lem, and Jesus went ahead of them. They were
amazed, and those who followed were afraid.
Taking the Twelve aside again, he began to tell
them what was going to happen to him. 33 "Be-
hold, we are going up to Jerusalem, and the
Son of Man will be handed over to the chief
priests and the scribes, and they will condemn
him to death and hand him over to the Gentiles
34 who will mock him, spit upon him, scourge
him, and put him to death, but after three days
he will rise."

Ambition of James and John 35 [c]Then James
and John, the sons of Zebedee, came to him and
said to him, "Teacher, we want you to do for us
whatever we ask of you." 36 He replied, "What
do you wish [me] to do for you?" 37 They
answered him, "Grant that in your glory we may
sit one at your right and the other at your left."
38 [d]*Jesus said to them, "You do not know what
you are asking. Can you drink the cup that I

10, 15: Whoever does not accept the kingdom of God like a child: i.e., in total dependence upon and obedience to the gospel; cf Mt 18, 3–4.

10, 18: Why do you call me good?: Jesus repudiates the term "good" for himself and directs it to God, the source of all goodness who alone can grant the gift of eternal life; cf Mt 19, 16–17.

10, 23–27: In the Old Testament wealth and material goods are considered a sign of God's favor (Jb 1, 10; Ps 128, 1–2; Is 3, 10). The words of Jesus in 23–25 provoke astonishment among the disciples because of their apparent contradiction of the Old Testament concept (24.26). Since wealth, power, and merit generate false security, Jesus rejects them utterly as a claim to enter the kingdom. Achievement of salvation is beyond human capability and depends solely on the goodness of God who offers it as a gift (27).

10, 38–40: Can you drink the cup . . . I am baptized?: the metaphor of drinking the cup is used in the Old Testament to refer to acceptance of the destiny assigned by God; see the note on Ps 11, 6. In Jesus' case, this involves divine judgment on sin that Jesus the innocent one is to expiate on behalf of the guilty (14, 24; Is 53, 5). His baptism is to be his crucifixion and death for the salvation of the human race; cf Lk 12, 50. The request of James and John for a share in the glory (35–37) must of necessity involve a share in Jesus' sufferings, the endurance of tribulation and suffering for the gospel (39). The authority of assigning places of honor in the kingdom is reserved to God (40).

u Mt 19, 13–15; Lk 18, 15–17. v Lk 9, 47. w Mt 18, 3. x Mt 19, 16–30; Lk 18, 18–30. y Ex 20, 12–16; Dt 5, 16–21. z Prv 11, 28. a Mt 19, 30; Lk 13, 30. b 8, 31; Mt 20, 17–19; Lk 18, 31–33. c Mt 20, 20–28. d Lk 12, 50.

drink or be baptized with the baptism with which I am baptized?" [39]They said to him, "We can." Jesus said to them, "The cup that I drink, you will drink, and with the baptism with which I am baptized, you will be baptized; [40]but to sit at my right or at my left is not mine to give but is for those for whom it has been prepared." [41]When the ten heard this, they became indignant at James and John. [42] [e]*Jesus summoned them and said to them, "You know that those who are recognized as rulers over the Gentiles lord it over them, and their great ones make their authority over them felt. [43]But it shall not be so among you. Rather, whoever wishes to be great among you will be your servant; [44]whoever wishes to be first among you will be the slave of all. [45]For the Son of Man did not come to be served but to serve and to give his life as a ransom for many."

The Blind Bartimaeus [46] [f]*They came to Jericho. And as he was leaving Jericho with his disciples and a sizable crowd, Bartimaeus, a blind man, the son of Timaeus, sat by the roadside begging. [47]On hearing that it was Jesus of Nazareth, he began to cry out and say, "Jesus, son of David, have pity on me." [48]And many rebuked him, telling him to be silent. But he kept calling out all the more, "Son of David, have pity on me." [49]Jesus stopped and said, "Call him." So they called the blind man, saying to him, "Take courage; get up, he is calling you." [50]He threw aside his cloak, sprang up, and came to Jesus. [51]Jesus said to him in reply, "What do you want me to do for you?" The blind man replied to him, "Master, I want to see." [52]Jesus told him, "Go your way; your faith has saved you." Immediately he received his sight and followed him on the way.

CHAPTER 11

The Entry into Jerusalem [1] [g]*When they drew near to Jerusalem, to Bethphage and Bethany at the Mount of Olives, he sent two of his disciples [2]and said to them, "Go into the village opposite you, and immediately on entering it, you will find a colt tethered on which no one has ever sat. Untie it and bring it here. [3]If anyone should say to you, 'Why are you doing this?' reply, 'The Master has need of it and will send it back here at once.' " [4]So they went off and found a colt tethered at a gate outside on the street, and they untied it. [5]Some of the bystanders said to them, "What are you doing, untying the colt?" [6]They answered them just as Jesus had told them to, and they permitted them to do it. [7]So they brought the colt to Jesus and put their cloaks over it. And he sat on it. [8]Many people spread their cloaks on the road, and others spread leafy branches that they had cut from the fields. [9] [h]Those preceding him as well as those following kept crying out:

"Hosanna!
Blessed is he who comes in the name of the Lord!
10 Blessed is the kingdom of our father David that is to come!
Hosanna in the highest!"

[11] [i]He entered Jerusalem and went into the temple area. He looked around at everything and, since it was already late, went out to Bethany with the Twelve.

Jesus Curses a Fig Tree [12] [j]*The next day as they were leaving Bethany he was hungry. [13]Seeing from a distance a fig tree in leaf, he went over to see if he could find anything on it. When he reached it he found nothing but

10, 42–45: Whatever authority is to be exercised by the disciples must, like that of Jesus, be rendered as service to others (45) rather than for personal aggrandizement (42–44). The service of Jesus is his passion and death for the sins of the human race (45); cf 14, 24; Is 53, 11–12; Mt 26, 28; Lk 22, 19–20.

10, 46–52: See the notes on Mt 9, 27–31 and 20, 29–34.

11, 1–11: In Mark's account Jesus takes the initiative in ordering the preparation for his entry into Jerusalem (1–6) even as he later orders the preparation of his last Passover supper (14, 12–16). In vv 9–10 the greeting Jesus receives stops short of proclaiming him Messiah. He is greeted rather as the prophet of the coming messianic kingdom. Contrast Mt 21, 9.

11, 12–14: Jesus' search for fruit on the fig tree recalls the prophets' earlier use of this image to designate Israel; cf Jer 8, 13; 29, 17; Jl 1, 7; Hos 9, 10.16. Cursing the fig tree is a parable in action representing Jesus' judgment (20) on barren Israel and the fate of Jerusalem for failing to receive his teaching; cf Is 34, 4; Hos 2, 14; Lk 13, 6–9.

e Lk 22, 25–27. f Mt 20, 29–34; Lk 18, 35–43. g Mt 21, 1–9; Lk 19, 29–38; Jn 12, 12–15. h 2 Sm 7, 16; Ps 118, 26. i Mt 21, 10.17. j Mt 21, 18–20; Lk 13, 6–9.

leaves; it was not the time for figs. [14]And he said to it in reply, "May no one ever eat of your fruit again!" And his disciples heard it.

Cleansing of the Temple [15][k]*They came to Jerusalem, and on entering the temple area he began to drive out those selling and buying there. He overturned the tables of the money changers and the seats of those who were selling doves. [16]He did not permit anyone to carry anything through the temple area. [17][l]Then he taught them saying, "Is it not written:

'My house shall be called a house of prayer for all peoples'?
But you have made it a den of thieves."

[18]The chief priests and the scribes came to hear of it and were seeking a way to put him to death, yet they feared him because the whole crowd was astonished at his teaching. [19][m]When evening came, they went out of the city.

The Withered Fig Tree [20][n]Early in the morning, as they were walking along, they saw the fig tree withered to its roots. [21]Peter remembered and said to him, "Rabbi, look! The fig tree that you cursed has withered." [22]Jesus said to them in reply, "Have faith in God. [23][o]Amen, I say to you, whoever says to this mountain, 'Be lifted up and thrown into the sea,' and does not doubt in his heart but believes that what he says will happen, it shall be done for him. [24][p]Therefore I tell you, all that you ask for in prayer, believe that you will receive it and it shall be yours. [25][q]When you stand to pray, forgive anyone against whom you have a grievance, so that your heavenly Father may in turn forgive you your transgressions. [26]"*

The Authority of Jesus Questioned

[27]*They returned once more to Jerusalem.[r] As he was walking in the temple area, the chief priests, the scribes, and the elders approached him [28]and said to him, "By what authority are you doing these things? Or who gave you this authority to do them?" [29]Jesus said to them, "I shall ask you one question. Answer me, and I will tell you by what authority I do these things. [30]Was John's baptism of heavenly or of human origin? Answer me." [31]They discussed this among themselves and said, "If we say, 'Of heavenly origin,' he will say, '[Then] why did you not believe him?' [32]But shall we say, 'Of human origin'?"—they feared the crowd, for they all thought John really was a prophet. [33]So they said to Jesus in reply, "We do not know." Then Jesus said to them, "Neither shall I tell you by what authority I do these things."

CHAPTER 12

Parable of the Tenants [1][s][t]*He began to speak to them in parables. "A man planted a vineyard, put a hedge around it, dug a wine press, and built a tower. Then he leased it to tenant farmers and left on a journey. [2]At the proper time he sent a servant to the tenants to obtain from them some of the produce of the vineyard. [3]But they seized him, beat him, and sent him away empty-handed. [4]Again he sent them another servant. And that one they beat over the head and treated shamefully. [5]He sent yet another whom they killed. So, too, many others; some they beat, others they killed. [6]He had one other to send, a beloved son. He sent him to them last of all, thinking, 'They will respect my son.' [7]But those tenants said to one another, 'This is the heir. Come, let us kill him, and the inheritance will be ours.' [8]So they seized him and killed him, and threw him out of the vineyard. [9]What [then] will the owner of the vineyard do? He will come,

11, 15–19: See the note on Mt 21, 12–17.

11, 26: This verse, which reads, "But if you do not forgive, neither will your heavenly Father forgive your transgressions," is omitted in the best manuscripts. It was probably added by copyists under the influence of Mt 6, 15.

11, 27–33: The mounting hostility toward Jesus came from the chief priests, the scribes, and the elders (27); the Herodians and the Pharisees (12, 13); and the Sadducees (12, 18). By their rejection of God's messengers, John the Baptist and Jesus, they incurred the divine judgment implied in vv 27–33 and confirmed in the parable of the vineyard tenants (12, 1–12).

12, 1–12: The vineyard denotes Israel (Is 5, 1–7). The tenant farmers are the religious leaders of Israel. God is the owner of the vineyard. His servants are his messengers, the prophets. The beloved son is Jesus (1, 11; 9, 7; Mt 3, 17; 17, 5; Lk 3, 22; 9, 35). The punishment of the tenants refers to the religious leaders, and the transfer of the vineyard to others refers to the people of the new Israel.

k Mt 21, 12–13; Lk 19, 45–46; Jn 2, 14–16. l Is 56, 7; Jer 7, 11. m Lk 21, 37. n Mt 21, 20–22. o Mt 17, 20–21; Lk 17, 6. p Mt 7, 7; Jn 11, 22; 14, 13. q Mt 6, 14; 18, 35. r Mt 21, 23–27; Lk 20, 1–8. s Mt 21, 33–46; Lk 20, 9–19. t Is 5, 1–7; Jer 2, 21.

put the tenants to death, and give the vineyard to others. 10 [u]Have you not read this scripture passage:

'The stone that the builders rejected
has become the cornerstone;
11 by the Lord has this been done,
and it is wonderful in our eyes'?"

12 They were seeking to arrest him, but they feared the crowd, for they realized that he had addressed the parable to them. So they left him and went away.

Paying Taxes to the Emperor 13 [v] [w] *They sent some Pharisees and Herodians to him to ensnare him in his speech. 14 They came and said to him, "Teacher, we know that you are a truthful man and that you are not concerned with anyone's opinion. You do not regard a person's status but teach the way of God in accordance with the truth. Is it lawful to pay the census tax to Caesar or not? Should we pay or should we not pay?" 15 Knowing their hypocrisy he said to them, "Why are you testing me? Bring me a denarius to look at." 16 They brought one to him and he said to them, "Whose image and inscription is this?" They replied to him, "Caesar's." 17 [x]So Jesus said to them, "Repay to Caesar what belongs to Caesar and to God what belongs to God." They were utterly amazed at him.

The Question about the Resurrection 18 *Some Sadducees, who say there is no resurrection, came to him and put this question to him, 19 [y]saying, "Teacher, Moses wrote for us, 'If someone's brother dies, leaving a wife but no child, his brother must take the wife and raise up descendants for his brother.' 20 Now there were seven brothers. The first married a woman and died, leaving no descendants. 21 So the second married her and died, leaving no descendants, and the third likewise. 22 And the seven left no descendants. Last of all the woman also died. 23 At the resurrection [when they arise] whose wife will she be? For all seven had been married to her." 24 Jesus said to them, "Are you not misled because you do not know the scriptures or the power of God? 25 When they rise from the dead, they neither marry nor are given in marriage, but they are like the angels in heaven. 26 [z]As for the dead being raised, have you not read in the Book of Moses, in the passage about the bush, how God told him, 'I am the God of Abraham, [the] God of Isaac, and [the] God of Jacob'? 27 He is not God of the dead but of the living. You are greatly misled."

The Greatest Commandment 28 [a] *One of the scribes, when he came forward and heard them disputing and saw how well he had answered them, asked him, "Which is the first of all the commandments?" 29 Jesus replied, "The first is this: 'Hear, O Israel! The Lord our God is Lord alone! 30 [b]You shall love the Lord your God with all your heart, with all your soul, with all your mind, and with all your strength.' 31 [c]The second is this: 'You shall love your neighbor as yourself.' There is no other commandment greater than these." 32 The scribe said to him, "Well said, teacher. You are right in saying, 'He is One and there is no other than he.' 33 [d]And 'to love him with all your heart, with all your understanding, with all your strength, and to love your neighbor as yourself' is worth more than all burnt offerings and sacrifices." 34 [e]And when Jesus saw that [he] answered with understanding, he said to him, "You are not far from the kingdom of God." And no one dared to ask him any more questions.

The Question about David's Son 35 [f] *As Jesus was teaching in the temple area he said, "How do the scribes claim that the Messiah is

12, 13–34: In the ensuing conflicts (cf also 2, 1—3, 6) Jesus vanquishes his adversaries by his responses to their questions and reduces them to silence (34).

12, 13–17: See the note on Mt 22, 15–22.

12, 18–27: See the note on Mt 22, 23–33.

12, 28–34: See the note on Mt 22, 34–40.

12, 35–37: Jesus questions the claim of the scribes about the Davidic descent of the Messiah, not to deny it (Mt 1, 1; Acts 2, 20.34; Rom 1, 3; 2 Tm 2, 8) but to imply that he is more than this. His superiority derives from his transcendent origin, to which David himself attested when he spoke of the Messiah with the name "Lord" (Ps 110, 1). See also the note on Mt 22, 41–46.

u Ps 118, 22–23; Is 28, 16. v Mt 22, 15–33; Lk 20, 20–39. w 3, 6. x Rom 13, 7. y Dt 25, 5. z Ex 3, 6. a Mt 22, 34–40; Lk 10, 25–28. b Dt 6, 4–5. c Lv 19, 18; Rom 13, 9; Gal 5, 14; Jas 2, 8. d Dt 6, 4; Ps 40, 7–9. e Mt 22, 46; Lk 20, 40. f Mt 22, 41–45; Lk 20, 41–44.

the son of David? 36[g]David himself, inspired by the holy Spirit, said:

'The Lord said to my lord,
"Sit at my right hand
until I place your enemies under your
feet." '

37David himself calls him 'lord'; so how is he his son?" [The] great crowd heard this with delight.

Denunciation of the Scribes 38[h]*In the course of his teaching he said, "Beware of the scribes, who like to go around in long robes and accept greetings in the marketplaces, 39seats of honor in synagogues, and places of honor at banquets. 40They devour the houses of widows and, as a pretext, recite lengthy prayers. They will receive a very severe condemnation."

The Poor Widow's Contribution 41[i]*He sat down opposite the treasury and observed how the crowd put money into the treasury. Many rich people put in large sums. 42A poor widow also came and put in two small coins worth a few cents. 43Calling his disciples to himself, he said to them, "Amen, I say to you, this poor widow put in more than all the other contributors to the treasury. 44For they have all contributed from their surplus wealth, but she, from her poverty, has contributed all she had, her whole livelihood."

CHAPTER 13

The Destruction of the Temple Foretold

1[j]*As he was making his way out of the temple area one of his disciples said to him, "Look, teacher, what stones and what buildings!" 2Jesus said to him, "Do you see these great buildings? There will not be one stone left upon another that will not be thrown down."

The Signs of the End 3[k]*As he was sitting on the Mount of Olives opposite the temple area, Peter, James, John, and Andrew asked him privately, 4"Tell us, when will this happen, and what sign will there be when all these things are about to come to an end?" 5[l]Jesus began to say to them, "See that no one deceives you. 6Many will come in my name saying, 'I am he,' and they will deceive many. 7When you hear of wars and reports of wars do not be alarmed; such things must happen, but it will not yet be the end. 8Nation will rise against nation and kingdom against kingdom. There will be earthquakes from place to place and there will be famines. These are the beginnings of the labor pains.

The Coming Persecution 9[m]"Watch out for yourselves. They will hand you over to the courts. You will be beaten in synagogues. You will be arraigned before governors and kings because of me, as a witness before them. 10*But the gospel must first be preached to all nations. 11[n]When they lead you away and hand you over, do not worry beforehand about what you are to say. But say whatever will be given to you at that hour. For it will not be you who are speaking but the holy Spirit. 12Brother will hand over brother to death, and the father his child; children will rise up against parents and have them put to death. 13You will be hated by all because of my name. But the one who perseveres to the end will be saved.

The Great Tribulation 14[o p]*"When you see the desolating abomination standing where he

12, 38–40: See the notes on 7, 1–23 and Mt 23, 1–39.

12, 41–44: See the note on Lk 21, 1–4.

13, 1–2: The reconstructed temple with its precincts, begun under Herod the Great ca. 20 B.C., was completed only some seven years before it was destroyed by fire in A.D. 70 at the hands of the Romans; cf Jer 26, 18; Mt 24, 1–2. For the dating of the reconstruction of the temple, see further the note on Jn 2, 20.

13, 3–37: Jesus' prediction of the destruction of the temple (2) provoked questions that the four named disciples put to him in private regarding the time and the sign when all **these things are about to come to an end** (3–4). The response to their questions was Jesus' eschatological discourse prior to his imminent death. It contained instruction and consolation exhorting the disciples and the church to faith and obedience through the trials that would confront them (5–13). The sign is the presence of **the desolating abomination** (14; see Dn 9, 27), i.e., of the Roman power profaning the temple. Flight from Jerusalem is urged rather than defense of the city through misguided messianic hope (14–23). Intervention will occur only after destruction (24–27), which will happen before the end of the first Christian generation (28–31). No one but the Father knows the precise time, or that of the parousia (32); hence the necessity of constant vigilance (33–37). Luke sets the parousia at a later date, after "the time of the Gentiles" (Lk 21, 24). See also the notes on Mt 24, 1—25, 46.

13, 10: The gospel . . . to all nations: the period of the Christian mission.

13, 14: The participle **standing** is masculine, in contrast to the neuter at Mt 24, 15.

g Ps 110, 1. h Mt 23, 1–7; Lk 11, 43; 20, 45–47. i Lk 21, 1–4. j Mt 24, 1–2; Lk 21, 5–6. k Mt 24, 3–8; Lk 21, 7–11. l Eph 5, 6; 2 Thes 2, 3. m Mt 24, 9–14; Lk 21, 12–19. n Mt 10, 19–22; Lk 12, 11–12. o Mt 24, 15–22; Lk 21, 20–24. p Dn 9, 27; Mt 24, 15.

should not (let the reader understand), then those in Judea must flee to the mountains, 15 [q][and] a person on a housetop must not go down or enter to get anything out of his house, 16and a person in a field must not return to get his cloak. 17Woe to pregnant women and nursing mothers in those days. 18Pray that this does not happen in winter. 19 [r]For those times will have tribulation such as has not been since the beginning of God's creation until now, nor ever will be. 20If the Lord had not shortened those days, no one would be saved; but for the sake of the elect whom he chose, he did shorten the days. 21If anyone says to you then, 'Look, here is the Messiah! Look, there he is!' do not believe it. 22False messiahs and false prophets will arise and will perform signs and wonders in order to mislead, if that were possible, the elect. 23Be watchful! I have told it all to you beforehand.

The Coming of the Son of Man 24 [s t]"But in those days after that tribulation

the sun will be darkened,
and the moon will not give its light,
25 and the stars will be falling from the sky,
and the powers in the heavens will be shaken.

26 [u]*And then they will see 'the Son of Man coming in the clouds' with great power and glory, 27and then he will send out the angels and gather [his] elect from the four winds, from the end of the earth to the end of the sky.

The Lesson of the Fig Tree 28 [v]"Learn a lesson from the fig tree. When its branch becomes tender and sprouts leaves, you know that summer is near. 29In the same way, when you see these things happening, know that he is near, at the gates. 30Amen, I say to you, this generation will not pass away until all these things have taken place. 31Heaven and earth will pass away, but my words will not pass away.

Need for Watchfulness 32"But of that day or hour, no one knows, neither the angels in heaven, nor the Son, but only the Father. 33 [w]Be watchful! Be alert! You do not know when the time will come. 34 [x]It is like a man traveling abroad. He leaves home and places his servants in charge, each with his work, and orders the gatekeeper to be on the watch. 35Watch, therefore; you do not know when the lord of the house is coming, whether in the evening, or at midnight, or at cockcrow, or in the morning. 36May he not come suddenly and find you sleeping. 37What I say to you, I say to all: 'Watch!' "

CHAPTER 14

The Conspiracy against Jesus 1 [y]*The Passover and the Feast of Unleavened Bread were to take place in two days' time. So the chief priests and the scribes were seeking a way to arrest him by treachery and put him to death. 2They said, "Not during the festival, for fear that there may be a riot among the people."

The Anointing at Bethany 3 [z]*When he was in Bethany reclining at table in the house of Simon the leper, a woman came with an alabaster jar of perfumed oil, costly genuine spikenard. She

13, 26: Son of Man . . . with great power and glory: Jesus cites this text from Dn 7, 13 in his response to the high priest, **Are you the Messiah?** (14, 61). In Ex 34, 5; Lv 16, 2; and Nm 11, 25 the clouds indicate the presence of the divinity. Thus in his role of Son of Man, Jesus is a heavenly being who will come in power and glory.

14, 1—16, 8: In the movement of Mark's gospel the cross is depicted as Jesus' way to glory in accordance with the divine will. Thus the passion narrative is seen as the climax of Jesus' ministry.

14, 1: The Passover and the Feast of Unleavened Bread: the connection between the two festivals is reflected in Ex 12, 3–20; 34, 18; Lv 23, 4–8; Nm 9, 2–14; 28, 16–17; Dt 16, 1–8. The Passover commemorated the redemption from slavery and the departure of the Israelites from Egypt by night. It began at sundown after the Passover lamb was sacrificed in the temple in the afternoon of the fourteenth day of the month of Nisan. With the Passover supper on the same evening was associated the eating of unleavened bread. The latter was continued through Nisan 21, a reminder of the affliction of the Israelites and of the haste surrounding their departure. Praise and thanks to God for his goodness in the past were combined at this dual festival with the hope of future salvation. **The chief priests . . . to death:** the intent to put Jesus to death was plotted for a long time but delayed for fear of the crowd (3, 6; 11, 18; 12, 12).

14, 3–9: At Bethany on the Mount of Olives, a few miles from Jerusalem, **in the house of Simon the leper,** Jesus defends a woman's loving action of anointing his head with perfumed oil in view of his impending death and burial as a criminal, in which case his body would not be anointed. See further the note on Jn 12, 7. He assures the woman of the remembrance of her deed in the worldwide preaching of the good news.

q Lk 17, 31. r Dn 12, 1. s Mt 24, 29–31; Lk 21, 25–27. t Is 13, 10; Ez 32, 7; Jl 2, 10. u 14, 62; Dn 7, 13–14. v Mt 24, 32–36; Lk 21, 29–33. w Mt 24, 42; 25, 13–15. x Mt 25, 14–30; Lk 19, 12–27. y Mt 26, 2–5; Lk 22, 1–2; Jn 11, 45–53. z Mt 26, 6–13; Jn 12, 1–8.

broke the alabaster jar and poured it on his head. 4 There were some who were indignant. "Why has there been this waste of perfumed oil? 5 It could have been sold for more than three hundred days' wages and the money given to the poor." They were infuriated with her. 6 Jesus said, "Let her alone. Why do you make trouble for her? She has done a good thing for me. 7 The poor you will always have with you, and whenever you wish you can do good to them, but you will not always have me. 8 She has done what she could. She has anticipated anointing my body for burial. 9 Amen, I say to you, wherever the gospel is proclaimed to the whole world, what she has done will be told in memory of her."

The Betrayal by Judas 10 a Then Judas Iscariot, one of the Twelve, went off to the chief priests to hand him over to them. 11 When they heard him they were pleased and promised to pay him money. Then he looked for an opportunity to hand him over.

Preparations for the Passover 12 b*On the first day of the Feast of Unleavened Bread, when they sacrificed the Passover lamb, his disciples said to him, "Where do you want us to go and prepare for you to eat the Passover?" 13 *He sent two of his disciples and said to them, "Go into the city and a man will meet you, carrying a jar of water. Follow him. 14 Wherever he enters, say to the master of the house, 'The Teacher says, "Where is my guest room where I may eat the Passover with my disciples?" ' 15 Then he will show you a large upper room furnished and ready. Make the preparations for us there." 16 The disciples then went off, entered the city, and found it just as he had told them; and they prepared the Passover.

The Betrayer 17 c When it was evening, he came with the Twelve. 18 *And as they reclined at table and were eating, Jesus said, "Amen, I say to you, one of you will betray me, one who is eating with me." 19 They began to be distressed and to say to him, one by one, "Surely it is not I?" 20 He said to them, "One of the Twelve, the one who dips with me into the dish. 21 *For the Son of Man indeed goes, as it is written of him, but woe to that man by whom the Son of Man is betrayed. It would be better for that man if he had never been born."

The Lord's Supper 22 d*While they were eating, he took bread, said the blessing, broke it, and gave it to them, and said, "Take it; this is my body." 23 Then he took a cup, gave thanks, and gave it to them, and they all drank from it. 24 *He said to them, "This is my blood of the covenant, which will be shed for many. 25 Amen, I say to you, I shall not drink again the fruit of the vine until the day when I drink it new in the kingdom of God." 26 e*Then, after singing a hymn, they went out to the Mount of Olives.

Peter's Denial Foretold 27 f*Then Jesus said to them, "All of you will have your faith shaken, for it is written:

'I will strike the shepherd,
and the sheep will be dispersed.'

14, 12: The first day of the Feast of Unleavened Bread . . . the Passover lamb: a less precise designation of the day for sacrificing the Passover lamb as evidenced by some rabbinical literature. For a more exact designation, see the note on 14, 1. It was actually Nisan 14.

14, 13: A man . . . carrying a jar of water: perhaps a prearranged signal, for only women ordinarily carried water in jars. The Greek word used here, however, implies simply a person and not necessarily a male.

14, 18: One of you will betray me, one who is eating with me: contrasts the intimacy of table fellowship at the Passover meal with the treachery of the traitor; cf Ps 41, 10.

14, 21: The Son of Man indeed goes, as it is written of him: a reference to Ps 41, 10 cited by Jesus concerning Judas at the Last Supper; cf Jn 13, 18–19.

14, 22–24: The actions and words of Jesus express within the framework of the Passover meal and the transition to a new covenant the sacrifice of himself through the offering of his body and blood in anticipation of his passion and death. His **blood of the covenant** both alludes to the ancient rite of Ex 24, 4–8 and indicates the new community that the sacrifice of Jesus will bring into being (Mt 26, 26–28; Lk 22, 19–20; 1 Cor 11, 23–25).

14, 24: Which will be shed: see the note on Mt 26, 27–28. **For many:** the Greek preposition **hyper** is a different one from that at Mt 26, 28 but the same as that found at Lk 22, 19.20 and 1 Cor 11, 24. The sense of both words is vicarious, and it is difficult in Hellenistic Greek to distinguish between them. For **many** in the sense of "all," see the note on Mt 20, 28.

14, 26: After singing a hymn: Pss 114–118, thanksgiving songs concluding the Passover meal.

14, 27–31: Jesus predicted that the Twelve would waver in their faith, even abandon him, despite their protestations to the contrary. Yet he reassured them that after his resurrection he would regather them in Galilee (16, 7; cf Mt 26, 32; 28, 7.10.16; Jn 21), where he first summoned them to be his followers as he began to preach the good news (1, 14–20).

a Mt 26, 14–16; Lk 22, 3–6. b Mt 26, 17–19; Lk 22, 7–13. c Mt 26, 20–24; Lk 22, 21–23; Jn 13, 21–26. d Mt 26, 26–30; Lk 22, 19–20; 1 Cor 11, 23–25. e Mt 26, 30–35; Lk 22, 34.39; Jn 13, 36–38. f Zec 13, 7; Jn 16, 32.

[28]But after I have been raised up, I shall go before you to Galilee." [29]Peter said to him, "Even though all should have their faith shaken, mine will not be." [30]Then Jesus said to him, "Amen, I say to you, this very night before the cock crows twice you will deny me three times." [31]But he vehemently replied, "Even though I should have to die with you, I will not deny you." And they all spoke similarly.

The Agony in the Garden [32][g h]*Then they came to a place named Gethsemane, and he said to his disciples, "Sit here while I pray." [33]He took with him Peter, James, and John, and began to be troubled and distressed. [34]Then he said to them, "My soul is sorrowful even to death. Remain here and keep watch." [35]He advanced a little and fell to the ground and prayed that if it were possible the hour might pass by him; [36]*he said, "Abba, Father, all things are possible to you. Take this cup away from me, but not what I will but what you will." [37]When he returned he found them asleep. He said to Peter, "Simon, are you asleep? Could you not keep watch for one hour? [38][i]*Watch and pray that you may not undergo the test. The spirit is willing but the flesh is weak." [39]Withdrawing again, he prayed, saying the same thing. [40]Then he returned once more and found them asleep, for they could not keep their eyes open and did not know what to answer him. [41]He returned a third time and said to them, "Are you still sleeping and taking your rest? It is enough. The hour has come. Behold, the Son of Man is to be handed over to sinners. [42]Get up, let us go. See, my betrayer is at hand."

The Betrayal and Arrest of Jesus [43][j]Then, while he was still speaking, Judas, one of the Twelve, arrived, accompanied by a crowd with swords and clubs who had come from the chief priests, the scribes, and the elders. [44]His betrayer had arranged a signal with them, saying, "The man I shall kiss is the one; arrest him and lead him away securely." [45]He came and immediately went over to him and said, "Rabbi." And he kissed him. [46]At this they laid hands on him and arrested him. [47]One of the bystanders drew his sword, struck the high priest's servant, and cut off his ear. [48]Jesus said to them in reply, "Have you come out as against a robber, with swords and clubs, to seize me? [49]Day after day I was with you teaching in the temple area, yet you did not arrest me; but that the scriptures may be fulfilled." [50]And they all left him and fled. [51]Now a young man followed him wearing nothing but a linen cloth about his body. They seized him, [52]but he left the cloth behind and ran off naked.

Jesus before the Sanhedrin [53][k]*They led Jesus away to the high priest, and all the chief priests and the elders and the scribes came together. [54]Peter followed him at a distance into the high priest's courtyard and was seated with the guards, warming himself at the fire. [55]The chief priests and the entire Sanhedrin kept trying to obtain testimony against Jesus in order to put him to death, but they found none. [56]Many gave false witness against him, but their testimony did not agree. [57]*Some took the stand and testified falsely against him, alleging, [58][l]"We heard him say, 'I will destroy this temple made with hands and within three days I will build another not made with hands.' " [59]Even so their testimony did not agree. [60]The high priest rose before the assembly and questioned Jesus, saying, "Have you no answer? What are these men testifying

14, 32–34: The disciples who had witnessed the raising to life of the daughter of Jairus (5, 37) and the transfiguration of their Master (9, 2) were now invited to witness his degradation and agony and to watch and pray with him.

14, 36: Abba, Father: an Aramaic term, here also translated by Mark, Jesus' special way of addressing God with filial intimacy. The word **'abbā'** seems not to have been used in earlier or contemporaneous Jewish sources to address God without some qualifier. Cf Rom 8, 15; Gal 4, 6 for other occurrences of the Aramaic word in the Greek New Testament. **Not what I will but what you will:** note the complete obedient surrender of the human will of Jesus to the divine will of the Father; cf Jn 4, 34; 8, 29; Rom 5, 19; Phil 2, 8; Heb 5, 8.

14, 38: The spirit is willing but the flesh is weak: the spirit is drawn to what is good yet found in conflict with the flesh, inclined to sin; cf Ps 51, 7.12. Everyone is faced with this struggle, the full force of which Jesus accepted on our behalf and, through his bitter passion and death, achieved the victory.

14, 53: They led Jesus away . . . came together: Mark presents a formal assembly of the whole Sanhedrin (chief priests, elders, and scribes) at night, leading to the condemnation of Jesus (64), in contrast to Lk 22, 66.71, where Jesus is condemned in a daytime meeting of the council; see also Jn 18, 13.19–24.

14, 57–58: See the notes on Mt 26, 60–61 and Jn 2, 19.

g Mt 26, 36–46; Lk 22, 40–46. h Jn 18, 1. i Rom 7, 5. j Mt 26, 47–56; Lk 22, 47–53; Jn 18, 3–11. k Mt 26, 57–68; Lk 22, 54–55.63–65.67–71; Jn 18, 12–13. l 15, 29; 2 Cor 5, 1.

against you?" [61] *But he was silent and answered nothing. Again the high priest asked him and said to him, "Are you the Messiah, the son of the Blessed One?" [62] [m]Then Jesus answered, "I am;

and 'you will see the Son of Man
seated at the right hand of the Power
and coming with the clouds of heaven.' "

[63]At that the high priest tore his garments and said, "What further need have we of witnesses? [64]You have heard the blasphemy. What do you think?" They all condemned him as deserving to die. [65] [n]Some began to spit on him. They blindfolded him and struck him and said to him, "Prophesy!" And the guards greeted him with blows.

Peter's Denial of Jesus [66] [o]While Peter was below in the courtyard, one of the high priest's maids came along. [67]Seeing Peter warming himself, she looked intently at him and said, "You too were with the Nazarene, Jesus." [68] *But he denied it saying, "I neither know nor understand what you are talking about." So he went out into the outer court. [Then the cock crowed.] [69]The maid saw him and began again to say to the bystanders, "This man is one of them." [70]Once again he denied it. A little later the bystanders said to Peter once more, "Surely you are one of them; for you too are a Galilean." [71]He began to curse and to swear, "I do not know this man about whom you are talking." [72] [p]And immediately a cock crowed a second time. Then Peter remembered the word that Jesus had said to him, "Before the cock crows twice you will deny me three times." He broke down and wept.

CHAPTER 15

Jesus before Pilate [1] [q r]*As soon as morning came, the chief priests with the elders and the scribes, that is, the whole Sanhedrin, held a council. They bound Jesus, led him away, and handed him over to Pilate. [2] *Pilate questioned him, "Are you the king of the Jews?" He said to him in reply, "You say so." [3]The chief priests accused him of many things. [4]Again Pilate questioned him, "Have you no answer? See how many things they accuse you of." [5]Jesus gave him no further answer, so that Pilate was amazed.

The Sentence of Death [6] [s]*Now on the occasion of the feast he used to release to them one prisoner whom they requested. [7] *A man called Barabbas was then in prison along with the rebels who had committed murder in a rebellion. [8]The crowd came forward and began to ask him to do for them as he was accustomed. [9]Pilate answered, "Do you want me to release to you the king of the Jews?" [10]For he knew that it was out of envy that the chief priests had handed him over. [11]But the chief priests stirred up the crowd to have him release Barabbas for them instead. [12]Pilate again said to them in reply, "Then what [do you want] me to do with [the man you call] the king of the Jews?" [13] *They shouted again, "Crucify him." [14]Pilate said to them, "Why? What evil has he done?" They only shouted the louder, "Crucify him." [15] *So Pilate, wishing to satisfy the crowd, released Barabbas to them and, after he had Jesus scourged, handed him over to be crucified.

14, 61–62: **The Blessed One:** a surrogate for the divine name, which Jews did not pronounce. **I am:** indicates Jesus' acknowledgment that he is the Messiah and Son of God; cf 1, 1. Contrast Mt 26, 64 and Lk 22, 67–70, in which Jesus leaves his interrogators to answer their own question. **You will see the Son of Man . . . with the clouds of heaven:** an allusion to Dn 7, 13 and Ps 110, 1, portending the enthronement of Jesus as judge in the transcendent glory of God's kingdom. **The Power:** another surrogate for the name of God.

14, 68: **[Then the cock crowed]:** found in most manuscripts, perhaps in view of vv 30 and 72, but omitted in others.

15, 1: **Held a council:** the verb here, **poieō**, can mean either "convene a council" or "take counsel." This reading is preferred to a variant "reached a decision" (cf 3, 6), which 14, 64 describes as having happened at the night trial; see the note on Mt 27, 1–2. **Handed him over to Pilate:** lacking authority to execute their sentence of condemnation (14, 64), the Sanhedrin had recourse to Pilate to have Jesus tried and put to death (15); cf Jn 18, 31.

15, 2: **The king of the Jews:** in the accounts of the evangelists a certain irony surrounds the use of this title as an accusation against Jesus (see the note on 15, 26). While Pilate uses this term (2.9.12), he is aware of the evil motivation of the chief priests who handed Jesus over for trial and condemnation (10; Lk 23, 14–16.20; Mt 27, 18.24; Jn 18, 38; 19, 4.6.12).

15, 6–15: See the note on Mt 27, 15–26.

15, 7: **Barabbas:** see the note on Mt 27, 16–17.

15, 13: **Crucify him:** see the note on Mt 27, 22.

15, 15: See the note on Mt 27, 26.

m 13, 26; Ps 110, 1; Dn 7, 13; Mt 24, 30. n Lk 22, 63–65. o Mt 26, 69–75; Lk 22, 56–62; Jn 18, 16–18.25–27. p Jn 13, 38. q Mt 27, 1–2.11–14; Lk 23, 1–3. r Jn 18, 28. s Mt 27, 15–26; Lk 23, 17–25; Jn 18, 39–40.

Mockery by the Soldiers 16 t*The soldiers led him away inside the palace, that is, the praetorium, and assembled the whole cohort. 17They clothed him in purple and, weaving a crown of thorns, placed it on him. 18They began to salute him with, "Hail, King of the Jews!" 19and kept striking his head with a reed and spitting upon him. They knelt before him in homage. 20And when they had mocked him, they stripped him of the purple cloak, dressed him in his own clothes, and led him out to crucify him.

The Way of the Cross 21 u*They pressed into service a passer-by, Simon, a Cyrenian, who was coming in from the country, the father of Alexander and Rufus, to carry his cross.

The Crucifixion 22 vThey brought him to the place of Golgotha (which is translated Place of the Skull). 23They gave him wine drugged with myrrh, but he did not take it. 24 w*Then they crucified him and divided his garments by casting lots for them to see what each should take. 25*It was nine o'clock in the morning when they crucified him. 26*The inscription of the charge against him read, "The King of the Jews." 27 xWith him they crucified two revolutionaries, one on his right and one on his left. [28]* 29 y*Those passing by reviled him, shaking their heads and saying, "Aha! You who would destroy the temple and rebuild it in three days, 30save yourself by coming down from the cross." 31Likewise the chief priests, with the scribes, mocked him among themselves and said, "He saved others; he cannot save himself. 32 zLet the Messiah, the King of Israel, come down now from the cross that we may see and believe." Those who were crucified with him also kept abusing him.

The Death of Jesus 33At noon darkness came over the whole land until three in the afternoon. 34 a*And at three o'clock Jesus cried out in a loud voice, "*Eloi, Eloi, lema sabachthani?*" which is translated, "My God, my God, why have you forsaken me?" 35*Some of the bystanders who heard it said, "Look, he is calling Elijah." 36One of them ran, soaked a sponge with wine, put it on a reed, and gave it to him to drink, saying, "Wait, let us see if Elijah comes to take him down." 37Jesus gave a loud cry and breathed his last. 38*The veil of the sanctuary was torn in two from top to bottom. 39 b*When the centurion who stood facing him saw how he breathed his last he said, "Truly this man was the Son of God!" 40 c*There were also women looking on from a distance. Among them were Mary Magdalene, Mary the mother of the younger James and of Joses, and Salome. 41These women had followed him when he was in Galilee and ministered to him. There were also many other women who had come up with him to Jerusalem.

The Burial of Jesus 42 dWhen it was already evening, since it was the day of preparation, the day before the sabbath, 43*Joseph of Arimathea, a distinguished member of the council, who was himself awaiting the kingdom of God, came and courageously went to Pilate and asked for the

15, 16: Praetorium: see the note on Mt 27, 27.

15, 21: They pressed into service . . . Simon, a Cyrenian: a condemned person was constrained to bear his own instrument of torture, at least the crossbeam. The precise naming of Simon and his sons is probably due to their being known among early Christian believers to whom Mark addressed his gospel. See also the notes on Mt 27, 32 and Lk 23, 26–32.

15, 24: See the notes on Mt 27, 35 and Jn 19, 23–25a.

15, 25: It was nine o'clock in the morning: literally, "the third hour," thus between 9 a.m. and 12 noon. Cf vv 33.34.42 for Mark's chronological sequence, which may reflect liturgical or catechetical considerations rather than the precise historical sequence of events; contrast the different chronologies in the other gospels, especially Jn 19, 14.

15, 26: The inscription . . . the King of the Jews: the political reason for the death penalty falsely charged by the enemies of Jesus. See further the notes on Mt 27, 37 and Jn 19, 19.

15, 28: This verse, "And the scripture was fulfilled that says, 'And he was counted among the wicked,' " is omitted in the earliest and best manuscripts. It contains a citation from Is 53, 12, and was probably introduced from Lk 22, 37.

15, 29: See the note on Mt 27, 39–40.

15, 34: An Aramaic rendering of Ps 22, 2. See also the note on Mt 27, 46.

15, 35: Elijah: a verbal link with **Eloi** (34). See the note on 9, 9–13; cf Mal 3, 23–24. See also the note on Mt 27, 47.

15, 38: See the note on Mt 27, 51–53.

15, 39: The closing portion of Mark's gospel returns to the theme of its beginning in the Gentile centurion's climactic declaration of belief that Jesus **was the Son of God.** It indicates the fulfillment of the good news announced in the prologue (1, 1) and may be regarded as the firstfruit of the passion and death of Jesus.

15, 40–41: See the note on Mt 27, 55–56.

15, 43: Joseph of Arimathea: see the note on Mt 27, 57–61.

t Mt 27, 27–31; Jn 19, 2–3. u Mt 27, 32; Lk 23, 26. v Mt 27, 33–51; Lk 23, 32–46; Jn 19, 17–30. w Ps 22, 18. x Lk 23, 33. y Jn 2, 19. z Lk 23, 39. a Ps 22, 2. b Mt 27, 54–56; Lk 23, 47–49. c 6, 3; Lk 8, 2–3. d Mt 27, 57–61; Lk 23, 50–56; Jn 19, 38–42.

body of Jesus. 44 Pilate was amazed that he was already dead. He summoned the centurion and asked him if Jesus had already died. 45 And when he learned of it from the centurion, he gave the body to Joseph. 46 Having bought a linen cloth, he took him down, wrapped him in the linen cloth and laid him in a tomb that had been hewn out of the rock. Then he rolled a stone against the entrance to the tomb. 47 Mary Magdalene and Mary the mother of Joses watched where he was laid.

CHAPTER 16

The Resurrection of Jesus 1 [e f]*When the sabbath was over, Mary Magdalene, Mary, the mother of James, and Salome bought spices so that they might go and anoint him. 2 Very early when the sun had risen, on the first day of the week, they came to the tomb. 3 They were saying to one another, "Who will roll back the stone for us from the entrance to the tomb?" 4 When they looked up, they saw that the stone had been rolled back; it was very large. 5 [g]On entering the tomb they saw a young man sitting on the right side, clothed in a white robe, and they were utterly amazed. 6 He said to them, "Do not be amazed! You seek Jesus of Nazareth, the crucified. He has been raised; he is not here. Behold, the place where they laid him. 7 [h]But go and tell his disciples and Peter, 'He is going before you to Galilee; there you will see him, as he told you.' " 8 Then they went out and fled from the tomb, seized with trembling and bewilderment. They said nothing to anyone, for they were afraid.

The Longer Ending

The Appearance to Mary Magdalene [9 [i]*When he had risen, early on the first day of the week, he appeared first to Mary Magdalene, out of whom he had driven seven demons. 10 [j]She went and told his companions who were mourning and weeping. 11 When they heard that he was alive and had been seen by her, they did not believe.

The Appearance to Two Disciples 12 [k]After this he appeared in another form to two of them walking along on their way to the country. 13 They returned and told the others; but they did not believe them either.

The Commissioning of the Eleven 14 [l][But] later, as the eleven were at table, he appeared to them and rebuked them for their unbelief and hardness of heart because they had not believed those who saw him after he had been raised. 15 [m]He said to them, "Go into the whole world and proclaim the gospel to every creature. 16 Whoever believes and is baptized will be saved; whoever does not believe will be condemned. 17 These signs will accompany those who believe: in my name they will drive out demons, they will speak new languages. 18 [n]They will pick up serpents [with their hands], and if they drink any deadly thing, it will not

16, 1–8: The purpose of this narrative is to show that the tomb is empty and that Jesus **has been raised** (6) and **is going before you to Galilee** (7) in fulfillment of 14, 28. The women find the tomb empty, and an angel stationed there announces to them what has happened. They are told to proclaim the news to Peter and the disciples in order to prepare them for a reunion with him. Mark's composition of the gospel ends at v 8 with the women telling no one, because they were afraid. This abrupt termination causes some to believe that the original ending of this gospel may have been lost. See the following note.

16, 9–20: This passage, termed the Longer Ending to the Marcan gospel by comparison with a much briefer conclusion found in some less important manuscripts, has traditionally been accepted as a canonical part of the gospel and was defined as such by the Council of Trent. Early citations of it by the Fathers indicate that it was composed by the second century, although vocabulary and style indicate that it was written by someone other than Mark. It is a general resume of the material concerning the appearances of the risen Jesus, reflecting, in particular, traditions found in Luke (24) and John (20).

The Shorter Ending: Found after v 8 before the Longer Ending in four seventh-to-ninth-century Greek manuscripts as well as in one Old Latin version, where it appears alone without the Longer Ending.

The Freer Logion: Found after v 14 in a fourth-fifth century manuscript preserved in the Freer Gallery of Art, Washington, DC, this ending was known to Jerome in the fourth century. It reads: "And they excused themselves, saying, 'This age of lawlessness and unbelief is under Satan, who does not allow the truth and power of God to prevail over the unclean things dominated by the spirits [or, does not allow the unclean things dominated by the spirits to grasp the truth and power of God]. Therefore reveal your righteousness now.' They spoke to Christ. And Christ responded to them, 'The limit of the years of Satan's power is completed, but other terrible things draw near. And for those who sinned I was handed over to death, that they might return to the truth and no longer sin, in order that they might inherit the spiritual and incorruptible heavenly glory of righteousness. But . . . .' "

e Mt 28, 1–8; Lk 24, 1–10; Jn 20, 1–10. f Mt 28, 1; Lk 23, 56. g Jn 20, 12. h 14, 28. i Mt 28, 1–10; Jn 20, 11–18. j Lk 24, 10–11; Jn 20, 18. k Lk 24, 13–35. l Lk 24, 36–49; 1 Cor 15, 5. m 13, 10; Mt 28, 18–20; Lk 24, 47; Jn 20, 21. n Mt 10, 1; Lk 10, 19; Acts 28, 3–6.

harm them. They will lay hands on the sick, and they will recover."

The Ascension of Jesus 19 oSo then the Lord Jesus, after he spoke to them, was taken up into heaven and took his seat at the right hand of God. 20 pBut they went forth and preached everywhere, while the Lord worked with them and confirmed the word through accompanying signs.]

o Lk 24, 50-53. p 1 Tm 3, 16.

The Shorter Ending

[And they reported all the instructions briefly to Peter's companions. Afterwards Jesus himself, through them, sent forth from east to west the sacred and imperishable proclamation of eternal salvation. Amen.]

THE GOSPEL ACCORDING TO LUKE

The Gospel according to Luke is the first part of a two-volume work that continues the biblical history of God's dealings with humanity found in the Old Testament, showing how God's promises to Israel have been fulfilled in Jesus and how the salvation promised to Israel and accomplished by Jesus has been extended to the Gentiles. The stated purpose of the two volumes is to provide Theophilus and others like him with certainty—assurance—about earlier instruction they have received (1, 4). To accomplish his purpose, Luke shows that the preaching and teaching of the representatives of the early church are grounded in the preaching and teaching of Jesus, who during his historical ministry (Acts 1, 21-22) prepared his specially chosen followers and commissioned them to be witnesses to his resurrection and to all else that he did (Acts 10, 37-42). This continuity between the historical ministry of Jesus and the ministry of the apostles is Luke's way of guaranteeing the fidelity of the church's teaching to the teaching of Jesus.

Luke's story of Jesus and the church is dominated by a historical perspective. This history is first of all salvation history. God's divine plan for human salvation was accomplished during the period of Jesus, who through the events of his life (22, 22) fulfilled the Old Testament prophecies (4, 21; 18, 31; 22, 37; 24, 26-27.44), and this salvation is now extended to all humanity in the period of the church (Acts 4, 12). This salvation history, moreover, is a part of human history. Luke relates the story of Jesus and the church to events in contemporary Palestinian (1, 5; 3, 1-2; Acts 4, 6) and Roman (2, 1-2; 3, 1; Acts 11, 28; 18, 2.12) history, for, as Paul says in Acts 26, 26, "this was not done in a corner." Finally, Luke relates the story of Jesus and the church to contemporaneous church history. Luke is concerned with presenting Christianity as a legitimate form of worship in the Roman world, a religion that is capable of meeting the spiritual needs of a world empire like that of Rome. To this end, Luke depicts the Roman governor Pilate declaring Jesus innocent of any wrongdoing three times (Acts 23, 29; 25, 25; 26, 31-32). At the same time Luke argues in Acts that Christianity is the logical development and proper fulfillment of Judaism and is therefore deserving of the same toleration and freedom traditionally accorded Judaism by Rome (Acts 13, 16-41; 23, 6-9; 24, 10-21; 26, 2-23).

The prominence given to the period of the church in the story has important consequences for Luke's interpretation of the teachings of Jesus. By presenting the time of the church as a distinct phase of salvation history, Luke accordingly shifts the early Christian emphasis away from the expectation of an imminent parousia to the day-to-day concerns of the Christian community in the world. He does this in the gospel by regularly emphasizing the words "each day" (9, 23; cf Mk 8, 34; 11, 3; 16, 19; 19, 47) in the sayings of Jesus. Although Luke still believes the parousia to be a reality that will come unexpectedly (12, 38.45-46), he is more concerned with presenting the words and deeds of Jesus as guides for the conduct of Christian disciples in the interim period between the ascension and the parousia and with presenting Jesus himself as the model of Christian life and piety.

Throughout the gospel, Luke calls upon the Christian disciple to identify with the master Jesus, who is caring and tender toward the poor and lowly, the outcast, the sinner, and the afflicted, toward all those who recognize their dependence on God (4, 18; 6, 20-23; 7, 36-50; 14, 12-14; 15, 1-32; 16, 19-31; 18, 9-14; 19, 1-10; 21, 1-4), but who is severe toward the proud and self-righteous, and particularly toward those who place their material wealth before the service of God and his people (6, 24-26; 12, 13-21; 16, 13-15.19-31; 18, 9-14.15-25; cf 1, 50-53). No gospel writer is more concerned than Luke with the mercy and compassion of Jesus (7, 41-43; 10, 29-37; 13, 6-9; 15, 11-32). No gospel writer is more concerned with the role of the Spirit in the life of Jesus and the Christian disciple (1, 35.41; 2, 25-27; 4, 1.14.18; 10, 21; 11, 13; 24, 49), with the importance of prayer (3, 21; 5, 16; 6, 12; 9, 28; 11, 1-13; 18, 1-8), or with Jesus' concern for women (7, 11-17.36-50; 8, 2-3; 10, 38-42). While Jesus calls all humanity to repent (5, 32; 10, 13; 11, 32; 13, 1-5; 15, 7-10; 16, 30; 17, 3-4; 24, 47), he is particularly demanding of those who would be his disciples. Of them he demands absolute and total detachment from family and material possessions (9, 57-62; 12, 32-34; 14, 25-35). To all who respond in faith and repentance to the word Jesus preaches, he brings salvation (2, 30-32; 3, 6; 7, 50; 8, 48.50; 17, 19; 19, 9) and peace (2, 14; 7, 50; 8, 48; 19, 38.42) and life (10, 25-28; 18, 26-30).

Early Christian tradition, from the late second century on, identifies the author of this gospel and of the Acts of the Apostles as Luke, a Syrian from Antioch, who is mentioned in the New Testament in Col 4, 14, Phlm 24, and 2 Tm 4, 11. The prologue of the gospel makes it clear that Luke is not part of the first generation of Christian disciples but is himself dependent upon the traditions he received from those who were eyewitnesses and ministers of the word (1, 2). His two-volume work marks him as someone who was highly literate both in the Old Testament traditions according to the Greek versions and in Hellenistic Greek writings.

Among the likely sources for the composition of this gospel (1, 3) were the Gospel of Mark, a written collection of sayings of Jesus known also to the author of the Gospel of Matthew (Q; see Introduction to Matthew), and other special traditions that were used by Luke alone among the gospel writers. Some hold that Luke used Mark only as a complementary source for rounding out the material he took from other traditions. Because of its dependence on the Gospel of Mark and because details in Luke's Gospel (13, 35a; 19, 43-44; 21, 20; 23, 28-31) imply that the author was acquainted with the destruction of the city of Jerusalem by the Romans in A.D. 70, the Gospel of Luke is dated by most scholars after that date; many propose A.D. 80–90 as the time of composition.

Luke's consistent substitution of Greek names for the Aramaic or Hebrew names occurring in his sources (e.g., 23, 33 // Mk 15, 22; 18, 41 // Mk 10, 51), his omission from the gospel of specifically Jewish Christian concerns found in his sources (e.g., Mk 7, 1-23), his interest in Gentile Christians (2, 30-32; 3, 6.38; 4, 16-30; 13, 28–30; 14, 15-24; 17, 11-19; 24, 47-48), and his incomplete knowledge of Palestinian geography, customs, and practices are among the characteristics of this gospel that suggest that Luke was a non-Palestinian writing to a non-Palestinian audience that was largely made up of Gentile Christians.

The principal divisions of the Gospel according to Luke are the following:

I. The Prologue (1, 1-4)
II. The Infancy Narrative (1, 5—2, 52)
III. The Preparation for the Public Ministry (3, 1—4, 13)
IV. The Ministry in Galilee (4, 14—9, 50)
V. The Journey to Jerusalem: Luke's Travel Narrative (9, 51—19, 27)
VI. The Teaching Ministry in Jerusalem (19, 28—21, 38)
VII. The Passion Narrative (22, 1—23, 56)
VIII. The Resurrection Narrative (24, 1-53)

I: The Prologue

CHAPTER 1

1 [a]*Since many have undertaken to compile a
narrative of the events that have been fulfilled
among us, 2 [b]just as those who were eyewit-
nesses from the beginning and ministers of the
word have handed them down to us, 3 I too have
decided, after investigating everything accu-
rately anew, to write it down in an orderly
sequence for you, most excellent Theophilus,
4 so that you may realize the certainty of the
teachings you have received.

II: The Infancy Narrative

Announcement of the Birth of John 5 [c]*In the
days of Herod, King of Judea, there was a priest
named Zechariah of the priestly division of Abi-
jah; his wife was from the daughters of Aaron,
and her name was Elizabeth. 6 Both were righ-
teous in the eyes of God, observing all the com-
mandments and ordinances of the Lord blame-
lessly. 7 [d]*But they had no child, because Eliza-
beth was barren and both were advanced in
years. 8 Once when he was serving as priest in his
division's turn before God, 9 [e]according to the

1, 1-4: The Gospel according to Luke is the only one of the synoptic gospels to begin with a literary prologue. Making use of a formal, literary construction and vocabulary, the author writes the prologue in imitation of Hellenistic Greek writers and, in so doing, relates his story about Jesus to contemporaneous Greek and Roman literature. Luke is not only interested in the words and deeds of Jesus, but also in the larger context of the birth, ministry, death, and resurrection of Jesus as the fulfillment of the promises of God in the Old Testament. As a second- or third-generation Christian, Luke acknowledges his debt to earlier **eyewitnesses** and **ministers of the word,** but claims that his contribution to this developing tradition is a complete and accurate account, told in an orderly manner, and intended to provide **Theophilus** ("friend of God," literally) and other readers with certainty about earlier teachings they have received.

1, 5—2, 52: Like the Gospel according to Matthew, this gospel opens with an infancy narrative, a collection of stories about the birth and childhood of Jesus. The narrative uses early Christian traditions about the birth of Jesus, traditions about the birth and circumcision of John the Baptist, and canticles such as the Magnificat (1, 46-55) and Benedictus (1, 67-79), composed of phrases drawn from the Greek Old Testament. It is largely, however, the composition of Luke who writes in imitation of Old Testament birth stories, combining historical and legendary details, literary ornamentation and interpretation of scripture, to answer in advance the question, "Who is Jesus Christ?" The focus of the narrative, therefore, is primarily christological. In this section Luke announces many of the themes that will become prominent in the rest of the gospel: the centrality of Jerusalem and the temple, the journey motif, the universality of salvation, joy and peace, concern for the lowly, the importance of women, the presentation of Jesus as savior, Spirit-guided revelation and prophecy, and the fulfillment of Old Testament promises. The account presents parallel scenes (diptychs) of angelic announcements of the birth of John the Baptist and of Jesus, and of the birth, circumcision, and presentation of John and Jesus. In this parallelism, the ascendency of Jesus over John is stressed: John is prophet of the Most High (1, 76); Jesus is Son of the Most High (1, 32). John is great in the sight of the Lord (1, 15); Jesus will be Great (a LXX attribute, used absolutely, of God) (1, 32). John will go before the Lord (1, 16-17); Jesus will be Lord (1, 43; 2, 11).

1, 5: In the days of Herod, King of Judea: Luke relates the story of salvation history to events in contemporary world history. Here and in 3, 1-2, he connects his narrative with events in Palestinian history; in 2, 1-2 and 3, 1, he casts the Jesus story in the light of events of Roman history. Herod the Great, the son of the Idumean Antipater, was declared "King of Judea" by the Roman Senate in 40 B.C., but became the undisputed ruler of Palestine only in 37 B.C. He continued as king until his death in 4 B.C. **Priestly division of Abijah:** a reference to the eighth of the twenty-four divisions of priests who, for a week at a time, twice a year, served in the Jerusalem temple.

1, 7: They had no child: though childlessness was looked upon in contemporaneous Judaism as a curse or punishment for sin, it is intended here to present Elizabeth in a situation similar to that of some of the great mothers of important Old Testament figures: Sarah (Gn 15, 3; 16, 1); Rebekah (Gn 25, 21); Rachel (Gn 29, 31; 30, 1); the mother of Samson and wife of Manoah (Jgs 13, 2-3); Hannah (1 Sm 1, 2).

a Acts 1, 1; 1 Cor 15, 3. b 24, 48; Jn 15, 27; Acts 1, 21-22. c 1 Chr 24, 10. d Gn 18, 11; Jgs 13, 2-5; 1 Sm 1, 5-6. e Ex 30, 7.

practice of the priestly service, he was chosen by lot to enter the sanctuary of the Lord to burn incense. 10 Then, when the whole assembly of the people was praying outside at the hour of the incense offering, 11 the angel of the Lord appeared to him, standing at the right of the altar of incense. 12 Zechariah was troubled by what he saw, and fear came upon him. 13 f *But the angel said to him, "Do not be afraid, Zechariah, because your prayer has been heard. Your wife Elizabeth will bear you a son, and you shall name him John. 14 And you will have joy and gladness, and many will rejoice at his birth, 15 g *for he will be great in the sight of [the] Lord. He will drink neither wine nor strong drink. He will be filled with the holy Spirit even from his mother's womb, 16 and he will turn many of the children of Israel to the Lord their God. 17 h *He will go before him in the spirit and power of Elijah to turn the hearts of fathers toward children and the disobedient to the understanding of the righteous, to prepare a people fit for the Lord." 18 Then Zechariah said to the angel, "How shall I know this? For I am an old man, and my wife is advanced in years." 19 i *And the angel said to him in reply, "I am Gabriel, who stand before God. I was sent to speak to you and to announce to you this good news. 20 j *But now you will be speechless and unable to talk until the day these things take place, because you did not believe my words, which will be fulfilled at their proper time."

21 Meanwhile the people were waiting for Zechariah and were amazed that he stayed so long in the sanctuary. 22 But when he came out, he was unable to speak to them, and they realized that he had seen a vision in the sanctuary. He was gesturing to them but remained mute. 23 Then, when his days of ministry were completed, he went home. 24 After this time his wife Elizabeth conceived, and she went into seclusion for five months, saying, 25 k "So has the Lord done for me at a time when he has seen fit to take away my disgrace before others."

Announcement of the Birth of Jesus 26 *In the sixth month, the angel Gabriel was sent from God to a town of Galilee called Nazareth, 27 l to a virgin betrothed to a man named Joseph, of the house of David, and the virgin's name was Mary. 28 m And coming to her, he said, "Hail, favored one! The Lord is with you." 29 But she was greatly troubled at what was said and pondered what sort of greeting this might be. 30 Then the angel said to her, "Do not be afraid, Mary, for you have found favor with God. 31 n Behold, you will conceive in your womb and bear a son, and you shall name him Jesus. 32 o *He will be great and will be called Son of the Most High, and the Lord God will give him the throne of David his father, 33 p and he will rule over the house of Jacob forever, and of his kingdom there will be

1, 13: Do not be afraid: a stereotyped Old Testament phrase spoken to reassure the recipient of a heavenly vision (Gn 15, 1; Jos 1, 9; Dn 10, 12.19 and elsewhere in 1, 30; 2, 10). **You shall name him John:** the name means "Yahweh has shown favor," an indication of John's role in salvation history.

1, 15: He will drink neither wine nor strong drink: like Samson (Jgs 13, 4–5) and Samuel (1 Sm 1, 11 LXX and 4QSam[a]), John is to be consecrated by Nazirite vow and set apart for the Lord's service.

1, 17: He will go before him in the spirit and power of Elijah: John is to be the messenger sent before Yahweh, as described in Mal 3, 1–2. He is cast, moreover, in the role of the Old Testament fiery reformer, the prophet Elijah, who according to Mal 3, 23 (4, 5) is sent before "the great and terrible day of the Lord comes."

1, 19: I am Gabriel: "the angel of the Lord" is identified as Gabriel, the angel who in Dn 9, 20–25 announces the seventy weeks of years and the coming of an anointed one, a prince. By alluding to Old Testament themes in vv 17 and 19, such as the coming of the day of the Lord and the dawning of the messianic era, Luke is presenting his interpretation of the significance of the births of John and Jesus.

1, 20: You will be speechless and unable to talk: Zechariah's becoming mute is the sign given in response to his question in v 18. When Mary asks a similar question in 1, 34, unlike Zechariah who was punished for his doubt, she, in spite of her doubt, is praised and reassured (35–37).

1, 26–38: The announcement to Mary of the birth of Jesus is parallel to the announcement to Zechariah of the birth of John. In both the angel Gabriel appears to the parent who is troubled by the vision (11–12.26–29) and then told by the angel not to fear (13.30). After the announcement is made (14–17.31–33) the parent objects (18.34) and a sign is given to confirm the announcement (20.36). The particular focus of the announcement of the birth of Jesus is on his identity as Son of David (32–33) and Son of God (32.35).

1, 32: Son of the Most High: cf 1, 76 where John is described as "prophet of the Most High." "Most High" is a title for God commonly used by Luke (35.76; 6, 35; 8, 28; Acts 7, 48; 16, 17).

f 1, 57.60.63; Mt 1, 20–21. g 7, 33; Nm 6, 1–21; Jgs 13, 4; 1 Sm 1, 11 LXX. h Sir 48, 10; Mal 3, 1; 3, 23–24; Mt 11, 14; 17, 11–13. i Dn 8, 16; 9, 21. j 1, 45. k Gn 30, 23. 12, 5; Mt 1, 16.18. m Jgs 6, 12; Ru 2, 4; Jdt 13, 18. n Gn 16, 11; Jgs 13, 3; Is 7, 14; Mt 1, 21–23. o 2 Sm 7, 12.13.16; Is 9, 7. p Dn 2, 44; 7, 14; Mi 4, 7; Mt 28, 18.

no end." 34 *But Mary said to the angel, "How
can this be, since I have no relations with a
man?" 35 [q]And the angel said to her in reply,
"The holy Spirit will come upon you, and the
power of the Most High will overshadow you.
Therefore the child to be born will be called
holy, the Son of God. 36 *And behold, Elizabeth,
your relative, has also conceived a son in her old
age, and this is the sixth month for her who was
called barren; 37 [r]for nothing will be impossible
for God." 38 Mary said, "Behold, I am the hand-
maid of the Lord. May it be done to me
according to your word." Then the angel de-
parted from her.

Mary Visits Elizabeth 39 During those days
Mary set out and traveled to the hill country in
haste to a town of Judah, 40 where she entered
the house of Zechariah and greeted Elizabeth.
41 [s]When Elizabeth heard Mary's greeting, the
infant leaped in her womb, and Elizabeth, filled
with the holy Spirit, 42 [t]cried out in a loud voice
and said, "Most blessed are you among women,
and blessed is the fruit of your womb. 43 *And
how does this happen to me, that the mother of
my Lord should come to me? 44 For at the
moment the sound of your greeting reached my
ears, the infant in my womb leaped for joy.
45 [u]*Blessed are you who believed that what was
spoken to you by the Lord would be fulfilled."

The Canticle of Mary 46 [v w]*And Mary said:

"My soul proclaims the greatness of the Lord;
47 [x]my spirit rejoices in God my savior.
48 [y]For he has looked upon his handmaid's
lowliness;
behold, from now on will all ages call me
blessed.
49 [z]The Mighty One has done great things for
me,
and holy is his name.
50 [a]His mercy is from age to age
to those who fear him.
51 [b]He has shown might with his arm,
dispersed the arrogant of mind and heart.
52 [c]He has thrown down the rulers from their
thrones
but lifted up the lowly.
53 [d]The hungry he has filled with good things;
the rich he has sent away empty.
54 [e]He has helped Israel his servant,
remembering his mercy,
55 [f]according to his promise to our fathers,
to Abraham and to his descendants
forever."

56 Mary remained with her about three months
and then returned to her home.

The Birth of John 57 *When the time arrived
for Elizabeth to have her child she gave birth to a

1, 34: Mary's questioning response is a denial of sexual relations and is used by Luke to lead to the angel's declaration about the Spirit's role in the conception of this child (35). According to Luke, the virginal conception of Jesus takes place through the holy Spirit, the power of God, and therefore Jesus has a unique relationship to Yahweh: he is Son of God.

1, 36–37: The sign given to Mary in confirmation of the angel's announcement to her is the pregnancy of her aged relative Elizabeth. If a woman past the childbearing age could become pregnant, why, the angel implies, should there be doubt about Mary's pregnancy, for **nothing will be impossible for God.**

1, 43: Even before his birth, Jesus is identified in Lk as the **Lord.**

1, 45: Blessed are you who believed: Luke portrays Mary as a believer whose faith stands in contrast to the disbelief of Zechariah (20). Mary's role as believer in the infancy narrative should be seen in connection with the explicit mention of her presence among "those who believed" after the resurrection at the beginning of the Acts of the Apostles (14).

1, 46–55: Although Mary is praised for being the mother of the Lord and because of her belief, she reacts as the servant in a psalm of praise, the Magnificat. Because there is no specific connection of the canticle to the context of Mary's pregnancy and her visit to Elizabeth, the Magnificat (with the possible exception of v 48) may have been a Jewish Christian hymn that Luke found appropriate at this point in his story. Even if not composed by Luke, it fits in well with themes found elsewhere in Lk: joy and exultation in the Lord; the lowly being singled out for God's favor; the reversal of human fortunes; the fulfillment of Old Testament promises. The loose connection between the hymn and the context is further seen in the fact that a few Old Latin manuscripts identify the speaker of the hymn as Elizabeth, even though the overwhelming textual evidence makes Mary the speaker.

1, 57–66: The birth and circumcision of John above all emphasize John's incorporation into the people of Israel by the sign of the covenant (Gn 17, 1–12). The narrative of John's circumcision also prepares the way for the subsequent description of the circumcision of Jesus in 2, 21. At the beginning of his two-volume work Luke shows those who play crucial roles in the inauguration of Christianity to be wholly a part of the people of Israel. At the end of the Acts of the Apostles (21, 20; 22, 3; 23, 6–9; 24, 14–16; 26, 2–8.22–23) he will argue that Christianity is the direct descendant of Pharisaic Judaism.

q Mt 1, 20. r Gn 18, 14; Jer 32, 27; Mt 19, 26. s 1, 15; Gn 25, 22 LXX. t 11, 27–28; Jgs 5, 24; Jdt 13, 18; Dt 28, 4. u 1, 20. v 1 Sm 2, 1–10. w Ps 35, 9; Is 61, 10; Hb 3, 18. x Ti 3, 4; Jude 25. y 11, 27; 1 Sm 1, 11; 2 Sm 16, 12; 2 Kgs 14, 26; Ps 113, 7. z Dt 10, 21; Pss 71, 19; 111, 9; 126, 2–3. a Pss 89, 2; 103, 13.17. b Pss 89, 10; 118, 15; Jer 32, 17 (39, 17 LXX). c 1 Sm 2, 7; 2 Sm 22, 28; Jb 5, 11; 12, 19; Ps 147, 6; Sir 10, 14; Jas 4, 6; 1 Pt 5, 5. d 1 Sm 2, 5; Ps 107, 9. e Ps 98, 3; Is 41, 8–9. f Gn 13, 15; 17, 7; 18, 18; 22, 17–18; Mi 7, 20.

son. 58 [g]Her neighbors and relatives heard that
the Lord had shown his great mercy toward her,
and they rejoiced with her. 59 [h]*When they
came on the eighth day to circumcise the child,
they were going to call him Zechariah after his
father, 60 [i]but his mother said in reply, "No. He
will be called John." 61 But they answered her,
"There is no one among your relatives who has
this name." 62 So they made signs, asking his
father what he wished him to be called. 63 He
asked for a tablet and wrote, "John is his name,"
and all were amazed. 64 [j]Immediately his mouth
was opened, his tongue freed, and he spoke
blessing God. 65 Then fear came upon all their
neighbors, and all these matters were discussed
throughout the hill country of Judea. 66 All who
heard these things took them to heart, saying,
"What, then, will this child be?" For surely the
hand of the Lord was with him.

The Canticle of Zechariah 67 Then Zechariah
his father, filled with the holy Spirit, prophesied,
saying:

68 [k]*"Blessed be the Lord, the God of Israel,
for he has visited and brought redemption
to his people.
69 [l]*He has raised up a horn for our salvation
within the house of David his servant,
70 even as he promised through the mouth of his
holy prophets from of old:
71 [m]salvation from our enemies and from the
hand of all who hate us,
72 [n] [o]to show mercy to our fathers
and to be mindful of his holy covenant
73 [p]and of the oath he swore to Abraham our
father,
and to grant us that, 74 rescued from the
hand of enemies,
without fear we might worship him 75 [q]in
holiness and righteousness
before him all our days.
76 [r]*And you, child, will be called prophet of the
Most High,
for you will go before the Lord to prepare
his ways,
77 to give his people knowledge of salvation
through the forgiveness of their sins,
78 [s] [t]*because of the tender mercy of our God
by which the daybreak from on high will
visit us
79 to shine on those who sit in darkness and
death's shadow,
to guide our feet into the path of peace."

80 [u]The child grew and became strong in spirit,
and he was in the desert until the day of his
manifestation to Israel.

CHAPTER 2

The Birth of Jesus 1 *In those days a decree
went out from Caesar Augustus that the whole
world should be enrolled. 2 This was the first
enrollment, when Quirinius was governor of

1, 59: The practice of Palestinian Judaism at this time was to name the child at birth; moreover, though naming a male child after the father is not completely unknown, the usual practice was to name the child after the grandfather (see 61). The naming of the child John and Zechariah's recovery from his loss of speech should be understood as fulfilling the angel's announcement to Zechariah in 1, 13 and 20.

1, 68–79: Like the canticle of Mary (46–55) the canticle of Zechariah is only loosely connected with its context. Apart from vv 76–77, the hymn in speaking of **a horn for our salvation** (69) and **the daybreak from on high** (78) applies more closely to Jesus and his work than to John. Again like Mary's canticle, it is largely composed of phrases taken from the Greek Old Testament and may have been a Jewish Christian hymn of praise that Luke adapted to fit the present context by inserting vv 76–77 to give Zechariah's reply to the question asked in v 66.

1, 69: **A horn for our salvation:** the horn is a common Old Testament figure for strength (Pss 18, 3; 75, 5–6; 89, 18; 112, 9; 148, 14). This description is applied to God in Ps 18, 3 and is here transferred to Jesus. The connection of the phrase with **the house of David** gives the title messianic overtones and may indicate an allusion to a phrase in Hannah's song of praise (1 Sm 2, 10), "the horn of his anointed."

1, 76: **You will go before the Lord:** here **the Lord** is most likely a reference to Jesus (contrast 15–17 where Yahweh is meant) and John is presented as the precursor of Jesus.

1, 78: **The daybreak from on high:** three times in the LXX (Jer 23, 5; Zec 3, 8; 6, 12), the Greek word used here for **daybreak** translates the Hebrew word for "scion, branch," an Old Testament messianic title.

2, 1–2: Although universal registrations of Roman citizens are attested in 28 B.C., 8 B.C., and A.D. 14 and enrollments in individual provinces of those who are not Roman citizens are also attested, such a universal census of the Roman world under

g 1, 14. h 2, 21; Gn 17, 10.12; Lv 12, 3. i 1, 13. j 1, 20. k 7, 16; Pss 41, 13; 72, 18; 106, 48; 111, 9. l Ps 18, 3. m Ps 106, 10. n Ps 106, 45–46. o Gn 17, 7; Lv 26, 42; Ps 105, 8–9; Mi 7, 20. p Gn 22, 16–17. q Ti 2, 12. r Is 40, 3; Mal 3, 1; Mt 3, 3; 11, 10. s Mal 3, 20. t Is 60, 1–2. u 2, 40; Mt 3, 1.

Syria. 3 So all went to be enrolled, each to his own town. 4 [v]And Joseph too went up from Galilee from the town of Nazareth to Judea, to the city of David that is called Bethlehem, because he was of the house and family of David, 5 [w]to be enrolled with Mary, his betrothed, who was with child. 6 While they were there, the time came for her to have her child, 7 [x]*and she gave birth to her firstborn son. She wrapped him in swaddling clothes and laid him in a manger, because there was no room for them in the inn.

8 *Now there were shepherds in that region living in the fields and keeping the night watch over their flock. 9 [y]The angel of the Lord appeared to them and the glory of the Lord shone around them, and they were struck with great fear. 10 The angel said to them, "Do not be afraid; for behold, I proclaim to you good news of great joy that will be for all the people. 11 [z]*For today in the city of David a savior has been born for you who is Messiah and Lord. 12 And this will be a sign for you: you will find an infant wrapped in swaddling clothes and lying in a manger." 13 And suddenly there was a multitude of the heavenly host with the angel, praising God and saying:

14 [a]*"Glory to God in the highest
and on earth peace to those on whom his favor rests."

The Visit of the Shepherds 15 When the angels went away from them to heaven, the shepherds said to one another, "Let us go, then, to Bethlehem to see this thing that has taken place, which the Lord has made known to us." 16 So they went in haste and found Mary and Joseph, and the infant lying in the manger. 17 When they saw this, they made known the message that had been told them about this

---

Caesar Augustus is unknown outside the New Testament. Moreover, there are notorious historical problems connected with Luke's dating the census **when Quirinius was governor of Syria,** and the various attempts to resolve the difficulties have proved unsuccessful. P. Sulpicius Quirinius became legate of the province of Syria in A.D. 6–7 when Judea was annexed to the province of Syria. At that time, a provincial census of Judea was taken up. If Quirinius had been legate of Syria previously, it would have to have been before 10 B.C. because the various legates of Syria from 10 B.C. to 4 B.C. (the death of Herod) are known, and such a dating for an earlier census under Quirinius would create additional problems for dating the beginning of Jesus' ministry (3, 1.23). A previous legateship after 4 B.C. (and before A.D. 6) would not fit with the dating of Jesus' birth in the days of Herod (1, 5; Mt 2, 1). Luke may simply be combining Jesus' birth in Bethlehem with his vague recollection of a census under Quirinius (see also Acts 5, 37) to underline the significance of this birth for the whole Roman world: through this child born in Bethlehem peace and salvation come to the empire.

2, 1: Caesar Augustus: the reign of the Roman emperor Caesar Augustus is usually dated from 27 B.C. to his death in A.D. 14. According to Greek inscriptions, Augustus was regarded in the Roman Empire as "savior" and "god," and he was credited with establishing a time of peace, the **pax Augusta,** throughout the Roman world during his long reign. It is not by chance that Luke relates the birth of Jesus to the time of Caesar Augustus: the real savior (11) and peace-bearer (14; see also 19, 38) is the child born in Bethlehem. The great emperor is simply God's agent (like the Persian king Cyrus in Is 44, 28—45, 1) who provides the occasion for God's purposes to be accomplished. **The whole world:** that is, the whole Roman world: Rome, Italy, and the Roman provinces.

2, 7: Firstborn son: the description of Jesus as **firstborn son** does not necessarily mean that Mary had other sons. It is a legal description indicating that Jesus possessed the rights and privileges of the firstborn son (Gn 27; Ex 13, 2; Nm 3, 12–13; 18, 15–16; Dt 21, 15–17). See the notes on Mt 1, 25 and Mk 6, 3. **Wrapped him in swaddling clothes:** there may be an allusion here to the birth of another descendant of David, his son Solomon, who though a great king was wrapped in swaddling clothes like any other infant (Wis 7, 4–6). **Laid him in a manger:** a feeding trough for animals. A possible allusion to Is 1, 3 LXX.

2, 8–20: The annoucement of Jesus' birth to the shepherds is in keeping with Luke's theme that the lowly are singled out as the recipients of God's favors and blessings (see also 1, 48.52).

2, 11: The basic message of the infancy narrative is contained in the angel's announcement: this child is **savior, Messiah,** and **Lord.** Luke is the only synoptic gospel writer to use the title **savior** for Jesus (11; Acts 5, 31; 13, 23; see also 1, 69; 19, 9; Acts 4, 12). As savior, Jesus is looked upon by Luke as the one who rescues humanity from sin and delivers humanity from the condition of alienation from God. The title **christos,** "Christ," is the Greek equivalent of the Hebrew **māšîah,** "Messiah," "anointed one." Among certain groups in first-century Palestinian Judaism, the title was applied to an expected royal leader from the line of David who would restore the kingdom to Israel (see Acts 1, 6). The political overtones of the title are played down in Lk and instead the Messiah of the Lord (26) or the Lord's anointed is the one who now brings salvation to all humanity, Jew and Gentile (29–32). **Lord** is the most frequently used title for Jesus in Lk and Acts. In the New Testament it is also applied to Yahweh, as it is in the Old Testament. When used of Jesus it points to his transcendence and dominion over humanity.

2, 14: On earth peace to those on whom his favor rests: the peace that results from the Christ event is for those whom God has favored with his grace. This reading is found in the oldest representatives of the Western and Alexandrian text traditions and is the preferred one; the Byzantine text tradition, on the other hand, reads: "on earth peace, good will toward men." The peace of which Luke's gospel speaks (14; 7, 50; 8, 48; 10, 5–6; 19, 38.42; 24, 36) is more than the absence of war of the **pax Augusta;** it also includes the security and well-being characteristic of peace in the Old Testament.

v Mi 5, 2; Mt 2, 6. w 1, 27; Mt 1, 18. x Mt 1, 25. y 1, 11.26. z Mt 1, 21; 16, 16; Jn 4, 42; Acts 2, 36; 5, 31; Phil 2, 11. a 19, 38.

child. 18All who heard it were amazed by what
had been told them by the shepherds. 19And
Mary kept all these things, reflecting on them in
her heart. 20Then the shepherds returned, glori-
fying and praising God for all they had heard and
seen, just as it had been told to them.

The Circumcision and Naming of Jesus

21 b*When eight days were completed for his
circumcision, he was named Jesus, the name
given him by the angel before he was conceived
in the womb.

The Presentation in the Temple 22 c*When
the days were completed for their purification
according to the law of Moses, they took him up
to Jerusalem to present him to the Lord, 23 djust
as it is written in the law of the Lord, "Every
male that opens the womb shall be consecrated
to the Lord," 24and to offer the sacrifice of "a
pair of turtledoves or two young pigeons," in
accordance with the dictate in the law of the
Lord.

25*Now there was a man in Jerusalem whose
name was Simeon. This man was righteous and
devout, awaiting the consolation of Israel, and
the holy Spirit was upon him. 26It had been
revealed to him by the holy Spirit that he should
not see death before he had seen the Messiah of
the Lord. 27He came in the Spirit into the
temple; and when the parents brought in the
child Jesus to perform the custom of the law in
regard to him, 28he took him into his arms and
blessed God, saying:

29 "Now, Master, you may let your servant go
in peace, according to your word,
30 efor my eyes have seen your salvation,
31 which you prepared in sight of all the
peoples,
32 fa light for revelation to the Gentiles,
and glory for your people Israel."

33The child's father and mother were amazed at
what was said about him; 34 gand Simeon
blessed them and said to Mary his mother,
"Behold, this child is destined for the fall and rise
of many in Israel, and to be a sign that will be
contradicted 35*(and you yourself a sword will
pierce) so that the thoughts of many hearts may
be revealed." 36There was also a prophetess,
Anna, the daughter of Phanuel, of the tribe of
Asher. She was advanced in years, having lived
seven years with her husband after her marriage,
37and then as a widow until she was eighty-four.
She never left the temple, but worshiped night
and day with fasting and prayer. 38 hAnd coming
forward at that very time, she gave thanks to
God and spoke about the child to all who were
awaiting the redemption of Jerusalem.

The Return to Nazareth 39 iWhen they had
fulfilled all the prescriptions of the law of the
Lord, they returned to Galilee, to their own

2, 21: Just as John before him had been incorporated into the people of Israel through his circumcision, so too this child (see the note on 1, 57–66).

2, 22–40: The presentation of Jesus in the temple depicts the parents of Jesus as devout Jews, faithful observers of the law of the Lord (23.24.39), i.e., the law of Moses. In this respect, they are described in a fashion similar to the parents of John (1, 6) and Simeon (25) and Anna (36–37).

2, 22: Their purification: syntactically, **their** must refer to Mary and Joseph, even though the Mosaic law never mentions the purification of the husband. Recognizing the problem, some Western scribes have altered the text to read "his purification," understanding the presentation of Jesus in the temple as a form of purification; the Vulgate version has a Latin form that could be either "his" or "her." According to the Mosaic law (Lv 12, 2–8), the woman who gives birth to a boy is unable for forty days to touch anything sacred or to enter the temple area by reason of her legal impurity. At the end of this period she is required to offer a year-old lamb as a burnt offering and a turtledove or young pigeon as an expiation of sin. The woman who could not afford a lamb offered instead two turtledoves or two young pigeons, as Mary does here. **They took him up to Jerusalem to present him to the Lord:** as the firstborn son (7) Jesus was consecrated to the Lord as the law required (Ex 13, 2.12), but there was no requirement that this be done at the temple. The concept of a presentation at the temple is probably derived from 1 Sm 1, 24–28, where Hannah offers the child Samuel for sanctuary services. The law further stipulated (Nm 3, 47–48) that the firstborn son should be redeemed by the parents through their payment of five shekels to a member of a priestly family. About this legal requirement Luke is silent.

2, 25: Awaiting the consolation of Israel: Simeon here and later Anna who speak about the child to all who were awaiting the redemption of Jerusalem represent the hopes and expectations of faithful and devout Jews who at this time were looking forward to the restoration of God's rule in Israel. The birth of Jesus brings these hopes to fulfillment.

2, 35: (And you yourself a sword will pierce): Mary herself will not be untouched by the various reactions to the role of Jesus (34). Her blessedness as mother of the Lord will be challenged by her son who describes true blessedness as "hearing the word of God and observing it" (11, 27–28 and 8, 20–21).

b 1, 31; Gn 17, 12; Mt 1, 21. c Lv 12, 2–8. d Ex 13, 2.12. e 3, 6; Is 40, 5 LXX; 52, 10. f Is 42, 6; 46, 13; 49, 6; Acts 13, 47; 26, 23. g 12, 51; Is 8, 14; Jn 9, 39; Rom 9, 33; 1 Cor 1, 23; 1 Pt 2, 7–8. h Is 52, 9. i Mt 2, 23.

town of Nazareth. 40 [j]The child grew and be-
came strong, filled with wisdom; and the favor
of God was upon him.

The Boy Jesus in the Temple 41 [k]*Each year
his parents went to Jerusalem for the feast of
Passover, 42and when he was twelve years old,
they went up according to festival custom.
43After they had completed its days, as they
were returning, the boy Jesus remained behind
in Jerusalem, but his parents did not know it.
44Thinking that he was in the caravan, they
journeyed for a day and looked for him among
their relatives and acquaintances, 45but not find-
ing him, they returned to Jerusalem to look for
him. 46After three days they found him in the
temple, sitting in the midst of the teachers,
listening to them and asking them questions,
47and all who heard him were astounded at his
understanding and his answers. 48When his
parents saw him, they were astonished, and his
mother said to him, "Son, why have you done
this to us? Your father and I have been looking
for you with great anxiety." 49*And he said to
them, "Why were you looking for me? Did you
not know that I must be in my Father's house?"
50But they did not understand what he said to
them. 51 [l]He went down with them and came to
Nazareth, and was obedient to them; and his
mother kept all these things in her heart.
52 [m]And Jesus advanced [in] wisdom and age and
favor before God and man.

III: The Preparation for the Public Ministry

CHAPTER 3

The Preaching of John the Baptist 1 [n]*In the
fifteenth year of the reign of Tiberius Caesar,
when Pontius Pilate was governor of Judea, and
Herod was tetrarch of Galilee, and his brother
Philip tetrarch of the region of Ituraea and
Trachonitis, and Lysanias was tetrarch of Abi-
lene, 2 [o]*during the high priesthood of Annas
and Caiaphas, the word of God came to John the
son of Zechariah in the desert. 3 [p]*He went
throughout [the] whole region of the Jordan,
proclaiming a baptism of repentance for the

2, 41–52: This story's concern with an incident from Jesus' youth is unique in the canonical gospel tradition. It presents Jesus in the role of the faithful Jewish boy, raised in the traditions of Israel, and fulfilling all that the law requires. With this episode, the infancy narrative ends just as it began, in the setting of the Jerusalem temple.

2, 49: I must be in my Father's house: this phrase can also be translated, "I must be about my Father's work." In either translation, Jesus refers to God as his Father. His divine sonship, and his obedience to his heavenly Father's will, take precedence over his ties to his family.

3, 1–20: Although Luke is indebted in this section to his sources, the Gospel of Mark and a collection of sayings of John the Baptist, he has clearly marked this introduction to the ministry of Jesus with his own individual style. Just as the gospel began with a long periodic sentence (1, 1–4), so too this section (1–2). He casts the call of John the Baptist in the form of an Old Testament prophetic call (2) and extends the quotation from Isaiah found in Mk 1, 3 (Is 40, 3) by the addition of Is 40, 4–5 in vv 5–6. In doing so, he presents his theme of the universality of salvation, which he has announced earlier in the words of Simeon (2, 30–32). Moreover, in describing the expectation of the people (15), Luke is characterizing the time of John's preaching in the same way as he had earlier described the situation of other devout Israelites in the infancy narrative (2, 25–26.37–38). In vv 7–18 Luke presents the preaching of John the Baptist who urges the crowds to reform in view of **the coming wrath** (7.9: eschatological preaching), and who offers the crowds certain standards for reforming social conduct (10–14: ethical preaching), and who announces to the crowds the coming of **one mightier than** he (15–18: messianic preaching).

3, 1: Tiberius Caesar: Tiberius succeeded Augustus as emperor in A.D. 14 and reigned until A.D. 37. The fifteenth year of his reign, depending on the method of calculating his first regnal year, would have fallen between A.D. 27 and 29. **Pontius Pilate:** prefect of Judea from A.D. 26 to 36. The Jewish historian Josephus describes him as a greedy and ruthless prefect who had little regard for the local Jewish population and their religious practices (see 13, 1). **Herod:** i.e., Herod Antipas, the son of Herod the Great. He ruled over Galilee and Perea from 4 B.C. to A.D. 39. His official title **tetrarch** means literally, "ruler of a quarter," but came to designate any subordinate prince. **Philip:** also a son of Herod the Great, tetrarch of the territory to the north and east of the Sea of Galilee from 4 B.C. to A.D. 34. Only two small areas of this territory are mentioned by Luke. **Lysanias:** nothing is known about this Lysanias who is said here to have been tetrarch of Abilene, a territory northwest of Damascus.

3, 2: During the high priesthood of Annas and Caiaphas: after situating the call of John the Baptist in terms of the civil rulers of the period, Luke now mentions the religious leadership of Palestine (see the note on 1, 5). Annas had been high priest A.D. 6–15. After being deposed by the Romans in A.D. 15 he was succeeded by various members of his family and eventually by his son-in-law, Caiaphas, who was high priest A.D. 18–36. Luke refers to Annas as high priest at this time (but see Jn 18, 13.19), possibly because of the continuing influence of Annas or because the title continued to be used for the ex-high priest. **The word of God came to John:** Luke is alone among the New Testament writers in associating the preaching of John with a call from God. Luke is thereby identifying John with the prophets whose ministries began with similar calls. In 7, 26 John will be described as "more than a prophet"; he is also the precursor of Jesus (7, 27), a transitional figure inaugurating the period of the fulfillment of prophecy and promise.

3, 3: See the note on Mt 3, 2.

j 1, 80; 2, 52. k Ex 12, 24–27; 23, 15; Dt 16, 1–8. l 2, 19. m 1, 80; 2, 40; 1 Sm 2, 26. n Mt 3, 1–12; Mk 1, 1–8; Jn 1, 19–28. o 1, 80. p Acts 13, 24; 19, 4.

forgiveness of sins, [4 q r]*as it is written in the book of the words of the prophet Isaiah:

"A voice of one crying out in the desert:
'Prepare the way of the Lord,
make straight his paths.
[5]Every valley shall be filled
and every mountain and hill shall be made low.
The winding roads shall be made straight,
and the rough ways made smooth,
[6 s]and all flesh shall see the salvation of God.' "

[7 t]He said to the crowds who came out to be baptized by him, "You brood of vipers! Who warned you to flee from the coming wrath? [8 u]Produce good fruits as evidence of your repentance; and do not begin to say to yourselves, 'We have Abraham as our father,' for I tell you, God can raise up children to Abraham from these stones. [9 v]Even now the ax lies at the root of the trees. Therefore every tree that does not produce good fruit will be cut down and thrown into the fire."

[10]And the crowds asked him, "What then should we do?" [11]He said to them in reply, "Whoever has two cloaks should share with the person who has none. And whoever has food should do likewise." [12 w]Even tax collectors came to be baptized and they said to him, "Teacher, what should we do?" [13]He answered them, "Stop collecting more than what is prescribed." [14]Soldiers also asked him, "And what is it that we should do?" He told them, "Do not practice extortion, do not falsely accuse anyone, and be satisfied with your wages."

[15 x]Now the people were filled with expectation, and all were asking in their hearts whether John might be the Messiah. [16 y]*John answered them all, saying, "I am baptizing you with water, but one mightier than I is coming. I am not worthy to loosen the thongs of his sandals. He will baptize you with the holy Spirit and fire. [17 z]*His winnowing fan is in his hand to clear his threshing floor and to gather the wheat into his barn, but the chaff he will burn with unquenchable fire." [18]Exhorting them in many other ways, he preached good news to the people. [19 a]*Now Herod the tetrarch, who had been censured by him because of Herodias, his brother's wife, and because of all the evil deeds Herod had committed, [20]added still another to these by [also] putting John in prison.

The Baptism of Jesus [21 b]*After all the people had been baptized and Jesus also had been baptized and was praying, heaven was opened [22 c]*and the holy Spirit descended upon him in bodily form like a dove. And a voice came from heaven, "You are my beloved Son; with you I am well pleased."

3, 4: The Essenes from Qumran used the same passage to explain why their community was in the desert studying and observing the law and the prophets (1QS 8, 12–15).

3, 16: He will baptize you with the holy Spirit and fire: in contrast to John's baptism with water, Jesus is said to baptize with the holy Spirit and with fire. From the point of view of the early Christian community, the Spirit and fire must have been understood in the light of the fire symbolism of the pouring out of the Spirit at Pentecost (Acts 2, 1–4); but as part of John's preaching, the Spirit and fire should be related to their purifying and refining characteristics (Ez 36, 25–27; Mal 3, 2–3). See the note on Mt 3, 11.

3, 17: Winnowing fan: see the note on Mt 3, 12.

3, 19–20: Luke separates the ministry of John the Baptist from that of Jesus by reporting the imprisonment of John before the baptism of Jesus (21–22). Luke uses this literary device to serve his understanding of the periods of salvation history. With John the Baptist, the time of promise, the period of Israel, comes to an end; with the baptism of Jesus and the descent of the Spirit upon him, the time of fulfillment, the period of Jesus, begins. In his second volume, the Acts of the Apostles, Luke will introduce the third epoch in salvation history, the period of the church.

3, 21–22: This episode in Luke focuses on the heavenly message identifying Jesus as **Son** and, through the allusion to Is 42, 1, as Servant of Yahweh. The relationship of Jesus to the Father has already been announced in the infancy narrative (1, 32.35; 2, 49); it occurs here at the beginning of Jesus' Galilean ministry and will reappear in 9, 35 before another major section of Luke's gospel, the travel narrative (9, 51—19, 27). Elsewhere in Luke's writings (4, 18; Acts 10, 38), this incident will be interpreted as a type of anointing of Jesus.

3, 21: Was praying: Luke regularly presents Jesus at prayer at important points in his ministry: here at his baptism; at the choice of the Twelve (6, 12); before Peter's confession (9, 18); at the transfiguration (9, 28); when he teaches his disciples to pray (11, 1); at the Last Supper (22, 32); on the Mount of Olives (22, 41); on the cross (23, 46).

3, 22: You are my beloved Son; with you I am well pleased: this is the best attested reading in the Greek manuscripts. The Western reading, "You are my Son, this day I have begotten you," is derived from Ps 2, 7.

q Is 40, 3–5. r Jn 1, 23. s 2, 30–31. t Mt 12, 34. u Jn 8, 39. v Mt 7, 19; Jn 15, 6. w 7, 29. x Acts 13, 25. y 7, 19–20; Jn 1, 27; Acts 1, 5; 11, 16. z Mt 3, 12. a Mt 14, 3–4; Mk 6, 17–18. b Mt 3, 13–17; Mk 1, 9–11. c 9, 35; Ps 2, 7; Is 42, 1; Mt 12, 18; 17, 5; Mk 9, 7; Jn 1, 32; 2 Pt 1, 17.

The Genealogy of Jesus 23[d,e]*When Jesus
began his ministry he was about thirty years of
age. He was the son, as was thought, of Joseph,
the son of Heli, 24the son of Matthat, the son of
Levi, the son of Melchi, the son of Jannai, the
son of Joseph, 25the son of Mattathias, the son of
Amos, the son of Nahum, the son of Esli, the son
of Naggai, 26the son of Maath, the son of
Mattathias, the son of Semein, the son of Josech,
the son of Joda, 27[f]the son of Joanan, the son of
Rhesa, the son of Zerubbabel, the son of Sheal-
tiel, the son of Neri, 28the son of Melchi, the son
of Addi, the son of Cosam, the son of Elmadam,
the son of Er, 29the son of Joshua, the son of
Eliezer, the son of Jorim, the son of Matthat, the
son of Levi, 30the son of Simeon, the son of
Judah, the son of Joseph, the son of Jonam, the
son of Eliakim, 31[g,h,i]*the son of Melea, the son
of Menna, the son of Mattatha, the son of
Nathan, the son of David, 32the son of Jesse, the
son of Obed, the son of Boaz, the son of Sala, the
son of Nahshon, 33[j]the son of Amminadab, the
son of Admin, the son of Arni, the son of
Hezron, the son of Perez, the son of Judah,
34[k,l]the son of Jacob, the son of Isaac, the son of
Abraham, the son of Terah, the son of Nahor,
35the son of Serug, the son of Reu, the son of
Peleg, the son of Eber, the son of Shelah, 36[m]the
son of Cainan, the son of Arphaxad, the son of
Shem, the son of Noah, the son of Lamech, 37the
son of Methuselah, the son of Enoch, the son of
Jared, the son of Mahalaleel, the son of Cainan,
38the son of Enos, the son of Seth, the son of
Adam, the son of God.

CHAPTER 4

The Temptation of Jesus 1[n]*Filled with the
holy Spirit, Jesus returned from the Jordan and
was led by the Spirit into the desert 2[o]*for forty
days, to be tempted by the devil. He ate nothing
during those days, and when they were over he
was hungry. 3The devil said to him, "If you are
the Son of God, command this stone to become
bread." 4[p]Jesus answered him, "It is written,
'One does not live by bread alone.' " 5Then he
took him up and showed him all the kingdoms of
the world in a single instant. 6[q]The devil said to
him, "I shall give to you all this power and their
glory; for it has been handed over to me, and I
may give it to whomever I wish. 7All this will be
yours, if you worship me." 8[r]Jesus said to him in
reply, "It is written:

'You shall worship the Lord, your God,
and him alone shall you serve.' "

9*Then he led him to Jerusalem, made him
stand on the parapet of the temple, and said to
him, "If you are the Son of God, throw yourself
down from here, 10[s]for it is written:

'He will command his angels concerning you,
to guard you,'

11[t]and:

'With their hands they will support you,
lest you dash your foot against a stone.' "

12[u]Jesus said to him in reply, "It also says, 'You
shall not put the Lord, your God, to the test.' "
13[v]*When the devil had finished every tempta-
tion, he departed from him for a time.

3, 23–38: Whereas Mt 1, 2 begins the genealogy of Jesus with Abraham to emphasize Jesus' bonds with the people of Israel, Luke's universalism leads him to trace the descent of Jesus beyond Israel to Adam and beyond that to God (38) to stress again Jesus' divine sonship.

3, 31: The son of Nathan, the son of David: in keeping with Jesus' prophetic role in Lk and Acts (e.g., 7, 16.39; 9, 8; 13, 33; 24, 19; Acts 3, 22–23; 7, 37) Luke traces Jesus' Davidic ancestry through the prophet Nathan (see 2 Sm 7, 2) rather than through King Solomon, as Mt 1, 6–7.

4, 1–13: See the note on Mt 4, 1–11.

4, 1: Filled with the holy Spirit: as a result of the descent of the Spirit upon him at his baptism (3, 21–22), Jesus is now equipped to overcome the devil. Just as the Spirit is prominent at this early stage of Jesus' ministry (1.14.18), so too it will be at the beginning of the period of the church in Acts (Acts 1, 4; 2, 4.17).

4, 2: For forty days: the mention of forty days recalls the forty years of the wilderness wanderings of the Israelites during the Exodus (Dt 8, 2).

4, 9: To Jerusalem: the Lucan order of the temptations concludes on the parapet of the temple in Jerusalem, the city of destiny in Luke-Acts. It is in Jerusalem that Jesus will ultimately face his destiny (9, 51; 13, 33).

4, 13: For a time: the devil's opportune time will occur before the passion and death of Jesus (Lk 22, 3.31–32.53).

d Mt 1, 1–17. e 4, 22; Jn 6, 42. f 1 Chr 3, 17; Ez 3, 2. g 2 Sm 5, 14. h 1 Sm 16, 1.18. i Ru 4, 17–22; 1 Chr 2, 1–15. j Gn 29, 35; 38, 29. k Gn 21, 3; 25, 26; 1 Chr 1, 34; 28, 34. l Gn 11, 10–26; 1 Chr 1, 24–27. m Gn 4, 25—5, 32; 1 Chr 1, 1–4. n Mt 4, 1–11; Mk 1, 12–13. o Heb 4, 15. p Dt 8, 3. q Jer 27, 5; Mt 28, 18. r Dt 6, 13. s Ps 91, 11. t Ps 91, 12. u Dt 6, 16; 1 Cor 10, 9. v 22, 3; Jn 13, 2.27; Heb 4, 15.

IV: The Ministry in Galilee

The Beginning of the Galilean Ministry
14 [w][x]*Jesus returned to Galilee in the power of
the Spirit, and news of him spread throughout
the whole region. 15 He taught in their syna-
gogues and was praised by all.
The Rejection at Nazareth 16 [y]*He came to
Nazareth, where he had grown up, and went
according to his custom into the synagogue on
the sabbath day. He stood up to read 17 and was
handed a scroll of the prophet Isaiah. He un-
rolled the scroll and found the passage where it
was written:

18 [z]*"The Spirit of the Lord is upon me,
because he has anointed me
to bring glad tidings to the poor.
He has sent me to proclaim liberty to captives
and recovery of sight to the blind,
to let the oppressed go free,
19 and to proclaim a year acceptable to the Lord."

20 Rolling up the scroll, he handed it back to the
attendant and sat down, and the eyes of all in
the synagogue looked intently at him. 21 *He said
to them, "Today this scripture passage is fulfilled
in your hearing." 22 [a]And all spoke highly of him
and were amazed at the gracious words that
came from his mouth. They also asked, "Isn't
this the son of Joseph?" 23 *He said to them,
"Surely you will quote me this proverb, 'Physi-
cian, cure yourself,' and say, 'Do here in your
native place the things that we heard were done
in Capernaum.' " 24 And he said, "Amen, I say to
you, no prophet is accepted in his own native
place. 25 [b]*Indeed, I tell you, there were many
widows in Israel in the days of Elijah when the
sky was closed for three and a half years and a
severe famine spread over the entire land. 26 [c]*It
was to none of these that Elijah was sent, but
only to a widow in Zarephath in the land of
Sidon. 27 [d]Again, there were many lepers in
Israel during the time of Elisha the prophet; yet
not one of them was cleansed, but only Naaman
the Syrian." 28 When the people in the syna-
gogue heard this, they were all filled with fury.
29 They rose up, drove him out of the town, and
led him to the brow of the hill on which their
town had been built, to hurl him down head-
long. 30 But he passed through the midst of them
and went away.
The Cure of a Demoniac 31 [e][f]*Jesus then
went down to Capernaum, a town of Galilee. He
taught them on the sabbath, 32 [g]and they were
astonished at his teaching because he spoke with

4, 14: **News of him spread:** a Lucan theme; see v 37; 5, 15; 7, 17.

4, 16–30: Luke has transposed to the beginning of Jesus' ministry an incident from his Marcan source, which situated it near the end of the Galilean ministry (Mk 6, 1–6a). In doing so, Luke turns the initial admiration (22) and subsequent rejection of Jesus (28–29) into a foreshadowing of the whole future ministry of Jesus. Moreover, the rejection of Jesus in his own hometown hints at the greater rejection of him by Israel (Acts 13, 46).

4, 16: **According to his custom:** Jesus' practice of regularly attending synagogue is carried on by the early Christians' practice of meeting in the temple (Acts 2, 46; 3, 1; 5, 12).

4, 18: **The Spirit of the Lord is upon me, because he has anointed me:** see the note on 3, 21–22. As this incident develops, Jesus is portrayed as a prophet whose ministry is compared to that of the prophets Elijah and Elisha. Prophetic anointings are known in first-century Palestinian Judaism from the Qumran literature that speaks of prophets as God's anointed ones. **To bring glad tidings to the poor:** more than any other gospel writer Luke is concerned with Jesus' attitude toward the economically and socially poor (see 6, 20.24; 12, 16–21; 14, 12–14; 16, 19–26; 19, 8). At times, the poor in Luke's gospel are associated with the downtrodden, the oppressed and afflicted, the forgotten and the neglected (18; 6, 20–22; 7, 22; 14, 12–14), and it is they who accept Jesus' message of salvation.

4, 21: **Today this scripture passage is fulfilled in your hearing:** this sermon inaugurates the time of fulfillment of Old Testament prophecy. Luke presents the ministry of Jesus as fulfilling Old Testament hopes and expectations (7, 22); for Luke, even Jesus' suffering, death, and resurrection are done in fulfillment of the scriptures (24, 25–27.44–46; Acts 3, 18).

4, 23: **The things that we heard were done in Capernaum:** Luke's source for this incident reveals an awareness of an earlier ministry of Jesus in Capernaum that Luke has not yet made use of because of his transposition of this Nazareth episode to the beginning of Jesus' Galilean ministry. It is possible that by use of the future tense **you will quote me . . .** , Jesus is being portrayed as a prophet.

4, 25–26: The references to Elijah and Elisha serve several purposes in this episode: they emphasize Luke's portrait of Jesus as a prophet like Elijah and Elisha; they help to explain why the initial admiration of the people turns to rejection; and they provide the scriptural justification for the future Christian mission to the Gentiles.

4, 26: **A widow in Zarephath in the land of Sidon:** like Naaman the Syrian in v 27, a non-Israelite becomes the object of the prophet's ministry.

4, 31–44: The next several incidents in Jesus' ministry take place in Capernaum and are based on Luke's source, Mk 1, 21–39. To the previous portrait of Jesus as prophet (16–30) they now add a presentation of him as teacher (31–32), exorcist (32–37.41), healer (38–40), and proclaimer of God's kingdom (43).

w Mt 4, 12–17; Mk 1, 14–15. x 5, 15; Mt 3, 16. y Mt 13, 53–58; Mk 6, 1–6. z Is 61, 1–2; 58, 6. a 3, 23; Jn 6, 42. b 1 Kgs 17, 1–7; 18, 1; Jas 5, 17. c 1 Kgs 17, 9. d 2 Kgs 5, 1–14. e Mk 1, 21–28. f Mt 4, 13; Jn 2, 12. g Mt 7, 28–29.

authority. 33 [h]In the synagogue there was a man with the spirit of an unclean demon, and he cried out in a loud voice, 34 [i]*"Ha! What have you to do with us, Jesus of Nazareth? Have you come to destroy us? I know who you are—the Holy One of God!" 35Jesus rebuked him and said, "Be quiet! Come out of him!" Then the demon threw the man down in front of them and came out of him without doing him any harm. 36They were all amazed and said to one another, "What is there about his word? For with authority and power he commands the unclean spirits, and they come out." 37And news of him spread everywhere in the surrounding region.

The Cure of Simon's Mother-in-Law 38 [j]*After he left the synagogue, he entered the house of Simon. Simon's mother-in-law was afflicted with a severe fever, and they interceded with him about her. 39He stood over her, rebuked the fever, and it left her. She got up immediately and waited on them.

Other Healings 40 [k]At sunset, all who had people sick with various diseases brought them to him. He laid his hands on each of them and cured them. 41 [l]*And demons also came out from many, shouting, "You are the Son of God." But he rebuked them and did not allow them to speak because they knew that he was the Messiah.

Jesus Leaves Capernaum 42 [m]*At daybreak, Jesus left and went to a deserted place. The crowds went looking for him, and when they came to him, they tried to prevent him from leaving them. 43 [n]But he said to them, "To the other towns also I must proclaim the good news of the kingdom of God, because for this purpose I have been sent." 44*And he was preaching in the synagogues of Judea.

CHAPTER 5

The Call of Simon the Fisherman 1 [o p]*While the crowd was pressing in on Jesus and listening to the word of God, he was standing by the Lake of Gennesaret. 2He saw two boats there alongside the lake; the fishermen had disembarked and were washing their nets. 3Getting into one of the boats, the one belonging to Simon, he asked him to put out a short distance from the shore. Then he sat down and taught the crowds from the boat. 4 [q]After he had finished speaking, he said to Simon, "Put out into deep water and lower your nets for a catch." 5Simon said in reply, "Master, we have worked hard all night and have caught nothing, but at your command I will lower the nets." 6When they had done this, they caught a great number of fish and their nets were tearing. 7They signaled to their partners in the other boat to come to help them. They came and filled both boats so that they were in danger

4, 34: What have you to do with us?: see the note on Jn 2, 4. **Have you come to destroy us?:** the question reflects the current belief that before the day of the Lord control over humanity would be wrested from the evil spirits, evil destroyed, and God's authority over humanity reestablished. The synoptic gospel tradition presents Jesus carrying out this task.

4, 38: The house of Simon: because of Luke's arrangement of material, the reader has not yet been introduced to Simon (cf Mk 1, 16–18.29–31). Situated as it is before the call of Simon (5, 1–11), it helps the reader to understand Simon's eagerness to do what Jesus says (5, 5) and to follow him (5, 11).

4, 41: They knew that he was the Messiah: that is, the Christ (see the note on 2, 11).

4, 42: They tried to prevent him from leaving them: the reaction of these strangers in Capernaum is presented in contrast to the reactions of those in his hometown who rejected him (28–30).

4, 44: In the synagogues of Judea: instead of **Judea,** which is the best reading of the manuscript tradition, the Byzantine text tradition and other manuscripts read "Galilee," a reading that harmonizes Lk with Mt 4, 23 and Mk 1, 39. Up to this point Luke has spoken only of a ministry of Jesus in Galilee. Luke may be using **Judea** to refer to the land of Israel, the territory of the Jews, and not to a specific portion of it.

5, 1–11: This incident has been transposed from his source, Mk 1, 16–20, which places it immediately after Jesus makes his appearance in Galilee. By this transposition Luke uses this example of Simon's acceptance of Jesus to counter the earlier rejection of him by his hometown people, and since several incidents dealing with Jesus' power and authority have already been narrated, Luke creates a plausible context for the acceptance of Jesus by Simon and his partners. Many commentators have noted the similarity between the wondrous catch of fish reported here (4–9) and the post-resurrectional appearance of Jesus in Jn 21, 1–11. There are traces in Luke's story that the post-resurrectional context is the original one: in v 8 Simon addresses Jesus as **Lord** (a post-resurrectional title for Jesus—see 24, 34; Acts 2, 36—that has been read back into the historical ministry of Jesus) and recognizes himself as a sinner (an appropriate recognition for one who has denied knowing Jesus—22, 54–62). As used by Luke, the incident looks forward to Peter's leadership in Luke-Acts (6, 14; 9, 20; 22, 31–32; 24, 34; Acts 1, 15; 2, 14–40; 10, 11–18; 15, 7–12) and symbolizes the future success of Peter as fisherman (Acts 2, 41).

h 8, 28; Mt 8, 29; Mk 1, 23–24; 5, 7. i 4, 41; Jn 6, 69. j Mt 8, 14–15; Mk 1, 29–31. k Mt 8, 16; Mk 1, 32–34. l 4, 34; Mt 8, 29; Mk 3, 11–12. m Mk 1, 35–39. n 8, 1; Mk 1, 14–15. o Mt 4, 18–22; Mk 1, 16–20. p Mt 13, 1–2; Mk 2, 13; 3, 9–10; 4, 1–2. q Jn 21, 1–11.

of sinking. [8]When Simon Peter saw this, he fell at the knees of Jesus and said, "Depart from me, Lord, for I am a sinful man." [9]For astonishment at the catch of fish they had made seized him and all those with him, [10] [r]and likewise James and John, the sons of Zebedee, who were partners of Simon. Jesus said to Simon, "Do not be afraid; from now on you will be catching men." [11] [s]*When they brought their boats to the shore, they left everything and followed him.

The Cleansing of a Leper [12] [t]*Now there was a man full of leprosy in one of the towns where he was; and when he saw Jesus, he fell prostrate, pleaded with him, and said, "Lord, if you wish, you can make me clean." [13]Jesus stretched out his hand, touched him, and said, "I do will it. Be made clean." And the leprosy left him immediately. [14] [u]*Then he ordered him not to tell anyone, but "Go, show yourself to the priest and offer for your cleansing what Moses prescribed; that will be proof for them." [15]The report about him spread all the more, and great crowds assembled to listen to him and to be cured of their ailments, [16] [v]but he would withdraw to deserted places to pray.

The Healing of a Paralytic [17] [w]*One day as Jesus was teaching, Pharisees and teachers of the law were sitting there who had come from every village of Galilee and Judea and Jerusalem, and the power of the Lord was with him for healing. [18]And some men brought on a stretcher a man who was paralyzed; they were trying to bring him in and set [him] in his presence. [19]*But not finding a way to bring him in because of the crowd, they went up on the roof and lowered him on the stretcher through the tiles into the middle in front of Jesus. [20]*When he saw their faith, he said, "As for you, your sins are forgiven." [21] [x]*Then the scribes and Pharisees began to ask themselves, "Who is this who speaks blasphemies? Who but God alone can forgive sins?" [22] [y]Jesus knew their thoughts and said to them in reply, "What are you thinking in your hearts? [23]Which is easier, to say, 'Your sins are forgiven,' or to say, 'Rise and walk'? [24] [z]*But that you may know that the Son of Man has authority on earth to forgive sins"—he said to the man who was paralyzed, "I say to you, rise, pick up your stretcher, and go home." [25]He stood up immediately before them, picked up what he had been lying on, and went home, glorifying God. [26]Then astonishment seized them all and they glorified God, and, struck with awe, they said, "We have seen incredible things today."

The Call of Levi [27] [a]After this he went out and saw a tax collector named Levi sitting at the customs post. He said to him, "Follow me." [28]*And leaving everything behind, he got up and followed him. [29] [b]Then Levi gave a great banquet for him in his house, and a large crowd of tax collectors and others were at table with them. [30]The Pharisees and their scribes complained to his disciples, saying, "Why do you eat and drink with tax collectors and sinners?" [31]Jesus said to them in reply, "Those who are healthy do not need a physician, but the sick do. [32]I have not come to call the righteous to repentance but sinners."

5, 11: They left everything: in Mk 1, 16–20 and Mt 4, 18–22 the fishermen who follow Jesus leave their nets and their father; in Luke, they leave **everything** (see also 28; 12, 33; 14, 33; 18, 22), an indication of Luke's theme of complete detachment from material possessions.

5, 12: Full of leprosy: see the note on Mk 1, 40.

5, 14: Show yourself to the priest . . . what Moses prescribed: this is a reference to Lv 14, 2–9 that gives detailed instructions for the purification of one who had been a victim of leprosy and thereby excluded from contact with others (see Lv 13, 45–46.49; Nm 5, 2–3). **That will be proof for them:** see the note on Mt 8, 4.

5, 17—6, 11: From his Marcan source, Luke now introduces a series of controversies with Pharisees: controversy over Jesus' power to forgive sins (17–26); controversy over his eating and drinking with tax collectors and sinners (27–32); controversy over not fasting (33–36); and finally two episodes narrating controversies over observance of the sabbath (1–11).

5, 17: Pharisees: see the note on Mt 3, 7.

5, 19: Through the tiles: Luke has adapted the story found in Mk to his non-Palestinian audience by changing "opened up the roof" (Mk 2, 4, a reference to Palestinian straw and clay roofs) to **through the tiles,** a detail that reflects the Hellenistic Greco-Roman house with tiled roof.

5, 20: As for you, your sins are forgiven: literally, "O man, your sins are forgiven you." The connection between the forgiveness of sins and the cure of the paralytic reflects the belief of first-century Palestine (based on the Old Testament: Ex 20, 5; Dt 5, 9) that sickness and infirmity are the result of sin, one's own or that of one's ancestors (see also 13, 2; Jn 5, 14; 9, 2).

5, 21: The scribes: see the note on Mk 2, 6.

5, 24: See the notes on Mt 9, 6 and Mk 2, 10.

5, 28: Leaving everything behind: see the note on 5, 11.

r Jer 16, 16. s Mt 19, 27. t Mt 8, 2–4; Mk 1, 40–45. u 8, 56; Lv 14, 2–32; Mk 7, 36. v Mk 1, 35. w Mt 9, 1–8; Mk 2, 1–12. x 7, 49; Is 43, 25. y 6, 8; 9, 47. z Jn 5, 8–9.27. a Mt 9, 9–13; Mk 2, 13–17. b 15, 1–2.

The Question about Fasting 33 [c]And they said to him, "The disciples of John fast often and offer prayers, and the disciples of the Pharisees do the same; but yours eat and drink." 34 *Jesus answered them, "Can you make the wedding guests fast while the bridegroom is with them? 35 But the days will come, and when the bridegroom is taken away from them, then they will fast in those days." 36 *And he also told them a parable. "No one tears a piece from a new cloak to patch an old one. Otherwise, he will tear the new and the piece from it will not match the old cloak. 37 Likewise, no one pours new wine into old wineskins. Otherwise, the new wine will burst the skins, and it will be spilled, and the skins will be ruined. 38 Rather, new wine must be poured into fresh wineskins. 39 *[And] no one who has been drinking old wine desires new, for he says, 'The old is good.' "

CHAPTER 6

Debates about the Sabbath 1 [d e]*While he was going through a field of grain on a sabbath, his disciples were picking the heads of grain, rubbing them in their hands, and eating them. 2 Some Pharisees said, "Why are you doing what is unlawful on the sabbath?" 3 [f]Jesus said to them in reply, "Have you not read what David did when he and those [who were] with him were hungry? 4 [g]*[How] he went into the house of God, took the bread of offering, which only the priests could lawfully eat, ate of it, and shared it with his companions." 5 Then he said to them, "The Son of Man is lord of the sabbath."

6 [h]On another sabbath he went into the synagogue and taught, and there was a man there whose right hand was withered. 7 [i]The scribes and the Pharisees watched him closely to see if he would cure on the sabbath so that they might discover a reason to accuse him. 8 [j]But he realized their intentions and said to the man with the withered hand, "Come up and stand before us." And he rose and stood there. 9 Then Jesus said to them, "I ask you, is it lawful to do good on the sabbath rather than to do evil, to save life rather than to destroy it?" 10 Looking around at them all, he then said to him, "Stretch out your hand." He did so and his hand was restored. 11 But they became enraged and discussed together what they might do to Jesus.

The Mission of the Twelve 12 [k]*In those days he departed to the mountain to pray, and he spent the night in prayer to God. 13 *When day came, he called his disciples to himself, and from them he chose Twelve, whom he also named apostles: 14 [l]*Simon, whom he named Peter, and his brother Andrew, James, John, Philip, Bartholomew, 15 *Matthew, Thomas, James the son of Alphaeus, Simon who was called a Zealot,

5, 34–35: See the notes on Mt 9, 15 and Mk 2, 19.

5, 34: **Wedding guests:** literally, "sons of the bridal chamber."

5, 36–39: See the notes on Mt 9, 16–17 and Mk 2, 19.

5, 39: **The old is good:** this saying is meant to be ironic and offers an explanation for the rejection by some of the new wine that Jesus offers: satisfaction with old forms will prevent one from sampling the new.

6, 1–11: The two episodes recounted here deal with gathering grain and healing, both of which were forbidden on the sabbath. In his defense of his disciples' conduct and his own charitable deed, Jesus argues that satisfying human needs such as hunger and performing works of mercy take precedence even over the sacred sabbath rest. See also the notes on Mt 12, 1–14 and Mk 2, 25–26.

6, 4: **The bread of offering:** see the note on Mt 12, 5–6.

6, 12–16: See the notes on Mt 10, 1—11, 1 and Mk 3, 14–15.

6, 12: **Spent the night in prayer:** see the note on 3, 21.

6, 13: **He chose Twelve:** the identification of this group as the **Twelve** is a part of early Christian tradition (see 1 Cor 15, 5), and in Mt and Lk, the Twelve are associated with the twelve tribes of Israel (22, 29–30; Mt 19, 28). After the fall of Judas from his position among the Twelve, the need is felt on the part of the early community to reconstitute this group before the Christian mission begins at Pentecost (Acts 1, 15–26). From Luke's perspective, they are an important group who because of their association with Jesus from the time of his baptism to his ascension (Acts 1, 21–22) provide the continuity between the historical Jesus and the church of Luke's day and who as the original eyewitnesses guarantee the fidelity of the church's beliefs and practices to the teachings of Jesus (1, 1–4). **Whom he also named apostles:** only Luke among the gospel writers attributes to Jesus the bestowal of the name **apostles** upon the Twelve. See the note on Mt 10, 2–4. "Apostle" becomes a technical term in early Christianity for a missionary sent out to preach the word of God. Although Luke seems to want to restrict the title to the Twelve (only in Acts 4, 4.14 are Paul and Barnabas termed apostles), other places in the New Testament show an awareness that the term was more widely applied (1 Cor 15, 5–7; Gal 1, 19; 1 Cor 1, 1; 9, 1; Rom 16, 7).

6, 14: **Simon, whom he named Peter:** see the note on Mk 3, 16.

6, 15: **Simon who was called a Zealot:** the Zealots were the instigators of the First Revolt of Palestinian Jews against Rome in A.D. 66–70. Because the existence of the Zealots as a distinct group during the lifetime of Jesus is the subject of debate, the meaning of the identification of Simon as a Zealot is unclear.

c Mt 9, 14–17; Mk 2, 18–22. d Mt 12, 1–8; Mk 2, 23–28. e Dt 23, 26. f 1 Sm 21, 1–6. g Lv 24, 5–9. h Mt 12, 9–14; Mk 3, 1–6. i 14, 1. j 5, 22; 9, 47. k Mt 10, 1–4; Mk 3, 13–19. l Acts 1, 13.

16*and Judas the son of James, and Judas Iscar-
iot, who became a traitor.

Ministering to a Great Multitude 17 [m]*And
he came down with them and stood on a stretch
of level ground. A great crowd of his disciples
and a large number of the people from all Judea
and Jerusalem and the coastal region of Tyre and
Sidon 18came to hear him and to be healed of
their diseases; and even those who were tor-
mented by unclean spirits were cured. 19Every-
one in the crowd sought to touch him because
power came forth from him and healed them all.

Sermon on the Plain 20 [n]*And raising his eyes
toward his disciples he said:

"Blessed are you who are poor,
  for the kingdom of God is yours.
21 [o]Blessed are you who are now hungry,
  for you will be satisfied.
Blessed are you who are now weeping,
  for you will laugh.
22 [p]Blessed are you when people hate you,
  and when they exclude and insult you,
  and denounce your name as evil
  on account of the Son of Man.

23 [q]Rejoice and leap for joy on that day! Be-
hold, your reward will be great in heaven. For their
ancestors treated the prophets in the same way.

24 [r]But woe to you who are rich,
  for you have received your consolation.
25 [s]But woe to you who are filled now,
  for you will be hungry.
Woe to you who laugh now,
  for you will grieve and weep.
26 [t]Woe to you when all speak well of you,
  for their ancestors treated the false prophets
    in this way.

Love of Enemies 27 [u] [v]*"But to you who hear I
say, love your enemies, do good to those who
hate you, 28 [w]bless those who curse you, pray for
those who mistreat you. 29To the person who
strikes you on one cheek, offer the other one as
well, and from the person who takes your cloak,
do not withhold even your tunic. 30Give to
everyone who asks of you, and from the one
who takes what is yours do not demand it back.
31 [x]Do to others as you would have them do to
you. 32For if you love those who love you, what
credit is that to you? Even sinners love those
who love them. 33And if you do good to those
who do good to you, what credit is that to you?
Even sinners do the same. 34 [y]If you lend money
to those from whom you expect repayment,
what credit [is] that to you? Even sinners lend to
sinners, and get back the same amount. 35 [z]But
rather, love your enemies and do good to them,
and lend expecting nothing back; then your
reward will be great and you will be children of
the Most High, for he himself is kind to the
ungrateful and the wicked. 36Be merciful, just as
[also] your Father is merciful.

6, 16: **Judas Iscariot:** the name **Iscariot** may mean "man from Kerioth."

6, 17: **The coastal region of Tyre and Sidon:** not only Jews from Judea and Jerusalem, but even Gentiles from outside Palestine come to hear Jesus (see 2, 31–32; 3, 6; 4, 24–27).

6, 20–49: Luke's "Sermon on the Plain" is the counterpart to Mt's "Sermon on the Mount" (Mt 5, 1—7, 27). It is addressed to the disciples of Jesus, and, like the sermon in Mt, it begins with beatitudes (20–22) and ends with the parable of the two houses (46–49). Almost all the words of Jesus reported by Lk are found in Mt's version, but because Mt includes sayings that were related to specifically Jewish Christian problems (e.g., Mt 5, 17–20; 6, 1–8.16–18) that Luke did not find appropriate for his predominantly Gentile Christian audience, the "Sermon on the Mount" is considerably longer. Lk's sermon may be outlined as follows: an introduction consisting of blessings and woes (20–26); the love of one's enemies (27–36); the demands of loving one's neighbor (37–42); good deeds as proof of one's goodness (43–45); a parable illustrating the result of listening to and acting on the words of Jesus (46–49). At the core of the sermon is Jesus' teaching on the love of one's enemies (27–36) that has as its source of motivation God's graciousness and compassion for all humanity (35–36) and Jesus' teaching on the love of one's neighbor (37–42) that is characterized by forgiveness and generosity.

6, 20–26: The introductory portion of the sermon consists of blessings and woes that address the real economic and social conditions of humanity (the poor—the rich; the hungry—the satisfied; those grieving—those laughing; the outcast—the socially acceptable). By contrast, Matthew emphasizes the religious and spiritual values of disciples in the kingdom inaugurated by Jesus ("poor in spirit," 5, 5; "hunger and thirst for righteousness," 5, 6). In the sermon, **blessed** extols the fortunate condition of persons who are favored with the blessings of God; the woes, addressed as they are to the disciples of Jesus, threaten God's profound displeasure on those so blinded by their present fortunate situation that they do not recognize and appreciate the real values of God's kingdom. In all the blessings and woes, the present condition of the persons addressed will be reversed in the future.

6, 27–36: See the notes on Mt 5, 43–48 and 5, 48.

m Mt 4, 23–25; Mk 3, 7–10. n Mt 5, 1–12. o Ps 126, 5–6; Is 61, 3; Jer 31, 25; Rv 7, 16–17. p Jn 15, 19; 16, 2; 1 Pt 4, 14. q 11, 47–48; 2 Chr 36, 16; Mt 23, 30–31. r Jas 5, 1. s Is 65, 13–14. t Jas 4, 4. u Mt 5, 38–48. v Prv 25, 21; Rom 12, 20–21. w Rom 12, 14; 1 Pt 3, 9. x Mt 7, 12. y Dt 15, 7–8. z Lv 25, 35–36.

Judging Others 37 [a][b]*“Stop judging and you
will not be judged. Stop condemning and you
will not be condemned. Forgive and you will be
forgiven. 38 [c]Give and gifts will be given to you;
a good measure, packed together, shaken down,
and overflowing, will be poured into your lap.
For the measure with which you measure will in
return be measured out to you.” 39 [d]And he told
them a parable, “Can a blind person guide a
blind person? Will not both fall into a pit? 40 [e]No
disciple is superior to the teacher; but when fully
trained, every disciple will be like his teacher.
41 Why do you notice the splinter in your
brother’s eye, but do not perceive the wooden
beam in your own? 42 How can you say to your
brother, ‘Brother, let me remove that splinter in
your eye,’ when you do not even notice the
wooden beam in your own eye? You hypocrite!
Remove the wooden beam from your eye first;
then you will see clearly to remove the splinter
in your brother’s eye.

A Tree Known by Its Fruit 43 [f]*“A good tree
does not bear rotten fruit, nor does a rotten tree
bear good fruit. 44 For every tree is known by its
own fruit. For people do not pick figs from
thornbushes, nor do they gather grapes from
brambles. 45 A good person out of the store of
goodness in his heart produces good, but an evil
person out of a store of evil produces evil; for
from the fullness of the heart the mouth speaks.

The Two Foundations 46 [g]“Why do you call
me, ‘Lord, Lord,’ but not do what I command?
47 [h]*I will show you what someone is like who
comes to me, listens to my words, and acts on
them. 48 That one is like a person building a
house, who dug deeply and laid the foundation
on rock; when the flood came, the river burst
against that house but could not shake it because
it had been well built. 49 But the one who listens
and does not act is like a person who built a
house on the ground without a foundation.
When the river burst against it, it collapsed at
once and was completely destroyed.”

CHAPTER 7

The Healing of a Centurion’s Slave
1 [i]*When he had finished all his words to the
people, he entered Capernaum. 2 *A centurion
there had a slave who was ill and about to die,
and he was valuable to him. 3 When he heard
about Jesus, he sent elders of the Jews to him,
asking him to come and save the life of his slave.
4 They approached Jesus and strongly urged him
to come, saying, “He deserves to have you do
this for him, 5 for he loves our nation and he built
the synagogue for us.” 6 *And Jesus went with
them, but when he was only a short distance
from the house, the centurion sent friends to tell
him, “Lord, do not trouble yourself, for I am not
worthy to have you enter under my roof. 7 There-
fore, I did not consider myself worthy to come to
you; but say the word and let my servant be
healed. 8 For I too am a person subject to
authority, with soldiers subject to me. And I say
to one, ‘Go,’ and he goes; and to another, ‘Come
here,’ and he comes; and to my slave, ‘Do this,’
and he does it.” 9 When Jesus heard this he was
amazed at him and, turning, said to the crowd
following him, “I tell you, not even in Israel have
I found such faith.” 10 When the messengers
returned to the house, they found the slave in
good health.

6, 37–42: See the notes on Mt 7, 1–12; 7, 1; 7, 5.

6, 43–46: See the notes on Mt 7, 15–20 and 12, 33.

6, 47–49: See the note on Mt 7, 24–27.

7, 1—8, 3: The episodes in this section present a series of reactions to the Galilean ministry of Jesus and reflect some of Luke’s particular interests: the faith of a Gentile (1–10); the prophet Jesus’ concern for a widowed mother (11–17); the ministry of Jesus directed to the afflicted and unfortunate of Is 61, 1 (18–23); the relation between John and Jesus and their role in God’s plan for salvation (24–35); a forgiven sinner’s manifestation of love (36–50); the association of women with the ministry of Jesus (8, 1–3).

7, 1–10: This story about the faith of the centurion, a Gentile who cherishes the Jewish nation (5), prepares for the story in Acts of the conversion by Peter of the Roman centurion Cornelius who is similarly described as one who is generous to the Jewish nation (Acts 10, 2). See also Acts 10, 34–35 in the speech of Peter: “God shows no partiality . . . the person who fears him and acts righteously is acceptable to him.” See also the notes on Mt 8, 5–13 and Jn 4, 43–54.

7, 2: A centurion: see the note on Mt 8, 5.

7, 6: I am not worthy to have you enter under my roof: to enter the house of a Gentile was considered unclean for a Jew; cf Acts 10, 28.

a Mt 7, 1–5. b Mt 6, 14; Jas 2, 13. c Mk 4, 24. d Mt 15, 14; 23, 16–17.24. e Mt 10, 24–25; Jn 13, 16; 15, 20. f Mt 7, 16–20; 12, 33.35. g Mt 7, 21; Rom 2, 13; Jas 1, 22. h Mt 7, 24–27. i Mt 8, 5–13; Jn 4, 43–54.

Raising of the Widow's Son 11 j*Soon afterward he journeyed to a city called Nain, and his disciples and a large crowd accompanied him. 12 kAs he drew near to the gate of the city, a man who had died was being carried out, the only son of his mother, and she was a widow. A large crowd from the city was with her. 13When the Lord saw her, he was moved with pity for her and said to her, "Do not weep." 14He stepped forward and touched the coffin; at this the bearers halted, and he said, "Young man, I tell you, arise!" 15 lThe dead man sat up and began to speak, and Jesus gave him to his mother. 16 mFear seized them all, and they glorified God, exclaiming, "A great prophet has arisen in our midst," and "God has visited his people." 17This report about him spread through the whole of Judea and in all the surrounding region.

The Messengers from John the Baptist 18 n*The disciples of John told him about all these things. John summoned two of his disciples 19 oand sent them to the Lord to ask, "Are you the one who is to come, or should we look for another?" 20When the men came to him, they said, "John the Baptist has sent us to you to ask, 'Are you the one who is to come, or should we look for another?' " 21At that time he cured many of their diseases, sufferings, and evil spirits; he also granted sight to many who were blind. 22 pAnd he said to them in reply, "Go and tell John what you have seen and heard: the blind regain their sight, the lame walk, lepers are cleansed, the deaf hear, the dead are raised, the poor have the good news proclaimed to them. 23*And blessed is the one who takes no offense at me."

Jesus' Testimony to John 24 q*When the messengers of John had left, Jesus began to speak to the crowds about John. "What did you go out to the desert to see—a reed swayed by the wind? 25Then what did you go out to see? Someone dressed in fine garments? Those who dress luxuriously and live sumptuously are found in royal palaces. 26 rThen what did you go out to see? A prophet? Yes, I tell you, and more than a prophet. 27 sThis is the one about whom scripture says:

'Behold, I am sending my messenger ahead of you,
he will prepare your way before you.'

28I tell you, among those born of women, no one is greater than John; yet the least in the kingdom of God is greater than he." 29 t(All the people who listened, including the tax collectors, and who were baptized with the baptism of John, acknowledged the righteousness of God; 30but the Pharisees and scholars of the law, who were not baptized by him, rejected the plan of God for themselves.)

31 u*"Then to what shall I compare the people of this generation? What are they like? 32They are like children who sit in the marketplace and call to one another,

'We played the flute for you, but you did not dance.
We sang a dirge, but you did not weep.'

33For John the Baptist came neither eating food nor drinking wine, and you said, 'He is possessed by a demon.' 34 vThe Son of Man came eating and drinking and you said, 'Look, he is a glutton

7, 11–17: In the previous incident Jesus' power was displayed for a Gentile whose servant was dying; in this episode it is displayed toward a widowed mother whose only son has already died. Jesus' power over death prepares for his reply to John's disciples in v 22: "the dead are raised." This resuscitation in alluding to the prophet Elijah's resurrection of the only son of a widow of Zarephath (1 Kgs 7, 8–24) leads to the reaction of the crowd: "A great prophet has arisen in our midst" (16).

7, 18–23: In answer to John's question, **Are you the one who is to come?**—a probable reference to the return of the fiery prophet of reform, Elijah, "before the day of the Lord comes, the great and terrible day" (Mal 3, 23)—Jesus responds that his role is rather to bring the blessings spoken of in Is 61, 1 to the oppressed and neglected of society (22; cf 4, 18).

7, 23: **Blessed is the one who takes no offense at me**: this beatitude is pronounced on the person who recognizes Jesus' true identity in spite of previous expectations of what "the one who is to come" would be like.

7, 24–30: In his testimony to John, Jesus reveals his understanding of the relationship between them: John is the precursor of Jesus (27); John is the messenger spoken of in Mal 3, 1 who in Mal 3, 23 is identified as Elijah. Taken with the previous episode, it can be seen that Jesus identifies John as precisely the person John envisioned Jesus to be: the Elijah who prepares the way for the coming of the day of the Lord.

7, 31–35: See the note on Mt 11, 16–19.

j 4, 25–26; 1 Kgs 17, 17–24. k 8, 42; 1 Kgs 17, 17. l 1 Kgs 17, 23; 2 Kgs 4, 36. m 1, 68; 19, 44. n Mt 11, 2–6. o Mal 3, 1; Rv 1, 4.8; 4, 8. p 4, 18; Is 35, 5–6; 61, 1. q Mt 11, 7–15. r 1, 76. s Mal 3, 1 / Is 40, 3. t 3, 7.12; Mt 21, 32. u Mt 11, 16–19. v 15, 2.

and a drunkard, a friend of tax collectors and sinners.' 35 But wisdom is vindicated by all her children."

The Pardon of the Sinful Woman 36 [w*]A Pharisee invited him to dine with him, and he entered the Pharisee's house and reclined at table. 37 [xy]Now there was a sinful woman in the city who learned that he was at table in the house of the Pharisee. Bringing an alabaster flask of ointment, 38 she stood behind him at his feet weeping and began to bathe his feet with her tears. Then she wiped them with her hair, kissed them, and anointed them with the ointment. 39 When the Pharisee who had invited him saw this he said to himself, "If this man were a prophet, he would know who and what sort of woman this is who is touching him, that she is a sinner." 40 Jesus said to him in reply, "Simon, I have something to say to you." "Tell me, teacher," he said. 41 [*]"Two people were in debt to a certain creditor; one owed five hundred days' wages and the other owed fifty. 42 Since they were unable to repay the debt, he forgave it for both. Which of them will love him more?" 43 Simon said in reply, "The one, I suppose, whose larger debt was forgiven." He said to him, "You have judged rightly." 44 Then he turned to the woman and said to Simon, "Do you see this woman? When I entered your house, you did not give me water for my feet, but she has bathed them with her tears and wiped them with her hair. 45 You did not give me a kiss, but she has not ceased kissing my feet since the time I entered. 46 You did not anoint my head with oil, but she anointed my feet with ointment. 47 [*]So I tell you, her many sins have been forgiven; hence, she has shown great love. But the one to whom little is forgiven, loves little." 48 [z]He said to her, "Your sins are forgiven." 49 [a]The others at table said to themselves, "Who is this who even forgives sins?" 50 But he said to the woman, "Your faith has saved you; go in peace."

CHAPTER 8

Galilean Women Follow Jesus 1 [b*]Afterward he journeyed from one town and village to another, preaching and proclaiming the good news of the kingdom of God. Accompanying him were the Twelve 2 [c]and some women who had been cured of evil spirits and infirmities, Mary, called Magdalene, from whom seven demons had gone out, 3 Joanna, the wife of Herod's steward Chuza, Susanna, and many others who provided for them out of their resources.

The Parable of the Sower 4 [d*]When a large crowd gathered, with people from one town after another journeying to him, he spoke in a parable. 5 "A sower went out to sow his seed. And as he sowed, some seed fell on the path and was trampled, and the birds of the sky ate it up. 6 Some seed fell on rocky ground, and when it

7, 36–50: In this story of the pardoning of the sinful woman Luke presents two different reactions to the ministry of Jesus. A Pharisee, suspecting Jesus to be a prophet, invites Jesus to a festive banquet in his house, but the Pharisee's self-righteousness leads to little forgiveness by God and consequently little love shown toward Jesus. The sinful woman, on the other hand, manifests a faith in God (50) that has led her to seek forgiveness for her sins, and because so much was forgiven, she now overwhelms Jesus with her display of love; cf the similar contrast in attitudes in 18, 9–14. The whole episode is a powerful lesson on the relation between forgiveness and love.

7, 36: Reclined at table: the normal posture of guests at a banquet. Other oriental banquet customs alluded to in this story include the reception by the host with a kiss (45), washing the feet of the guests (44), and the anointing of the guests' heads (46).

7, 41: Days' wages: one denarius is the normal daily wage of a laborer.

7, 47: Her many sins have been forgiven; hence, she has shown great love: literally, "her many sins have been forgiven, seeing that she has loved much." That the woman's sins have been forgiven is attested by the great love she shows toward Jesus. Her love is the consequence of her forgiveness. This is also the meaning demanded by the parable in vv 41–43.

8, 1–3: Luke presents Jesus as an itinerant preacher traveling in the company of the Twelve and of the Galilean women who are sustaining them out of their means. These Galilean women will later accompany Jesus on his journey to Jerusalem and become witnesses to his death (23, 49) and resurrection (24, 9–11, where Mary Magdalene and Joanna are specifically mentioned; cf also Acts 1, 14). The association of women with the ministry of Jesus is most unusual in the light of the attitude of first-century Palestinian Judaism toward women. The more common attitude is expressed in Jn 4, 27, and early rabbinic documents caution against speaking with women in public.

8, 4–21: The focus in this section is on how one should hear the word of God and act on it. It includes the parable of the sower and its explanation (4–15), a collection of sayings on how one should act on the word that is heard (16–18), and the identification of the mother and brothers of Jesus as the ones who hear the word and act on it (19–21). See also the notes on Mt 13, 1–53 and Mk 4, 1–34.

8, 4–8: See the note on Mt 13, 3–8.

w 11, 37; 14, 1. x Mt 26, 7; Mk 14, 3. y Jn 12, 3. z 5, 20; Mt 9, 20; Mk 2, 5. a 5, 21. b 4,43. c 23, 49; 24, 10; Mt 27, 55–56; Mk 15, 40–41; Jn 19, 5. d Mt 13, 1–9; Mk 4, 1–9.

grew, it withered for lack of moisture. [7]Some seed fell among thorns, and the thorns grew with it and choked it. [8][e]And some seed fell on good soil, and when it grew, it produced fruit a hundredfold." After saying this, he called out, "Whoever has ears to hear ought to hear."

The Purpose of the Parables [9][f]Then his disciples asked him what the meaning of this parable might be. [10][g]He answered, "Knowledge of the mysteries of the kingdom of God has been granted to you; but to the rest, they are made known through parables so that 'they may look but not see, and hear but not understand.'

The Parable of the Sower Explained [11][h][i][*]"This is the meaning of the parable. The seed is the word of God. [12]Those on the path are the ones who have heard, but the devil comes and takes away the word from their hearts that they may not believe and be saved. [13]Those on rocky ground are the ones who, when they hear, receive the word with joy, but they have no root; they believe only for a time and fall away in time of trial. [14]As for the seed that fell among thorns, they are the ones who have heard, but as they go along, they are choked by the anxieties and riches and pleasures of life, and they fail to produce mature fruit. [15]But as for the seed that fell on rich soil, they are the ones who, when they have heard the word, embrace it with a generous and good heart, and bear fruit through perseverance.

The Parable of the Lamp [16][j][k][*]"No one who lights a lamp conceals it with a vessel or sets it under a bed; rather, he places it on a lampstand so that those who enter may see the light. [17][l]For there is nothing hidden that will not become visible, and nothing secret that will not be known and come to light. [18][m]Take care, then, how you hear. To anyone who has, more will be given, and from the one who has not, even what he seems to have will be taken away."

Jesus and His Family [19][n][*]Then his mother and his brothers came to him but were unable to join him because of the crowd. [20][o]He was told, "Your mother and your brothers are standing outside and they wish to see you." [21][*]He said to them in reply, "My mother and my brothers are those who hear the word of God and act on it."

The Calming of a Storm at Sea [22][p][*]One day he got into a boat with his disciples and said to them, "Let us cross to the other side of the lake." So they set sail, [23]and while they were sailing he fell asleep. A squall blew over the lake, and they were taking in water and were in danger. [24]They came and woke him saying, "Master, master, we are perishing!" He awakened, rebuked the wind and the waves, and they subsided and there was a calm. [25]Then he asked them, "Where is your faith?" But they were filled with awe and amazed and said to one another, "Who then is this, who commands even the winds and the sea, and they obey him?"

The Healing of the Gerasene Demoniac [26][q][*]Then they sailed to the territory of the Gerasenes, which is opposite Galilee. [27]When he came ashore a man from the town who was possessed by demons met him. For a long time he had not worn clothes; he did not live in a house, but lived among the tombs. [28][r]When he saw Jesus, he cried out and fell down before

8, 11–15: On the interpretation of the parable of the sower, see the note on Mt 13, 18–23.

8, 16–18: These sayings continue the theme of responding to the word of God. Those who hear the word must become a light to others (16); even the mysteries of the kingdom that have been made known to the disciples (9–10) must come to light (17); a generous and persevering response to the word of God leads to a still more perfect response to the word.

8, 19: His brothers: see the note on Mk 6, 3.

8, 21: The family of Jesus is not constituted by physical relationship with him but by obedience to the word of God. In this, Luke agrees with the Marcan parallel (3, 31–35), although by omitting Mk 3, 33 and especially Mk 3, 20–21 Luke has softened the Marcan picture of Jesus' natural family. Probably he did this because Mary has already been presented in 1, 38 as the obedient handmaid of the Lord who fulfills the requirement for belonging to the eschatological family of Jesus; cf also 11, 27–28.

8, 22–56: This section records four miracles of Jesus that manifest his power and authority: (1) the calming of a storm on the lake (22–25); (2) the exorcism of a demoniac (26–39); (3) the cure of a hemorrhaging woman (40–48); (4) the raising of Jairus's daughter to life (49–56). They parallel the same sequence of stories at Mk 4, 35—5, 43.

8, 26: Gerasenes: other manuscripts read Gadarenes or Gergesenes. See also the note on Mt 8, 28. **Opposite Galilee:** probably Gentile territory (note the presence in the area of pigs—unclean animals to Jews) and an indication that the person who receives salvation (36) is a Gentile.

e 14, 35; Mt 11, 15; 13, 43; Mk 4, 23. f Mt 13, 10–13; Mk 4, 10–12. g Is 6, 9. h Mt 13, 18–23; Mk 4, 13–20. i 1 Pt 1, 23. j Mk 4, 21–25. k 11, 33; Mt 5, 15. l 12, 2; Mt 10, 26. m 19, 26; Mt 13, 12; 25, 29. n Mt 12, 46–50; Mk 3, 31–35. o 11, 27–28. p Mt 8, 18.23–27; Mk 4, 35–41. q Mt 8, 28–34; Mk 5, 1–20. r 4, 33–35; Mt 8, 29; Mk 1, 23–24.

him; in a loud voice he shouted, "What have you to do with me, Jesus, son of the Most High God? I beg you, do not torment me!" 29For he had ordered the unclean spirit to come out of the man. (It had taken hold of him many times, and he used to be bound with chains and shackles as a restraint, but he would break his bonds and be driven by the demon into deserted places.) 30*Then Jesus asked him, "What is your name?" He replied, "Legion," because many demons had entered him. 31*And they pleaded with him not to order them to depart to the abyss.

32A herd of many swine was feeding there on the hillside, and they pleaded with him to allow them to enter those swine; and he let them. 33The demons came out of the man and entered the swine, and the herd rushed down the steep bank into the lake and was drowned. 34When the swineherds saw what had happened, they ran away and reported the incident in the town and throughout the countryside. 35*People came out to see what had happened and, when they approached Jesus, they discovered the man from whom the demons had come out sitting at his feet. He was clothed and in his right mind, and they were seized with fear. 36Those who witnessed it told them how the possessed man had been saved. 37The entire population of the region of the Gerasenes asked Jesus to leave them because they were seized with great fear. So he got into a boat and returned. 38The man from whom the demons had come out begged to remain with him, but he sent him away, saying, 39"Return home and recount what God has done for you." The man went off and proclaimed throughout the whole town what Jesus had done for him.

Jairus's Daughter and the Woman with a Hemorrhage 40 [s]*When Jesus returned, the crowd welcomed him, for they were all waiting for him. 41And a man named Jairus, an official of the synagogue, came forward. He fell at the feet of Jesus and begged him to come to his house, 42*because he had an only daughter, about twelve years old, and she was dying. As he went, the crowds almost crushed him. 43*And a woman afflicted with hemorrhages for twelve years, who [had spent her whole livelihood on doctors and] was unable to be cured by anyone, 44came up behind him and touched the tassel on his cloak. Immediately her bleeding stopped. 45Jesus then asked, "Who touched me?" While all were denying it, Peter said, "Master, the crowds are pushing and pressing in upon you." 46 [t]But Jesus said, "Someone has touched me; for I know that power has gone out from me." 47When the woman realized that she had not escaped notice, she came forward trembling. Falling down before him, she explained in the presence of all the people why she had touched him and how she had been healed immediately. 48 [u]He said to her, "Daughter, your faith has saved you; go in peace."

49While he was still speaking, someone from the synagogue official's house arrived and said, "Your daughter is dead; do not trouble the teacher any longer." 50On hearing this, Jesus answered him, "Do not be afraid; just have faith and she will be saved." 51When he arrived at the house he allowed no one to enter with him except Peter and John and James, and the child's father and mother. 52 [v]*All were weeping and mourning for her, when he said, "Do not weep any longer, for she is not dead, but sleeping." 53And they ridiculed him, because they knew

8, 30: What is your name?: the question reflects the popular belief that knowledge of the spirit's name brought control over the spirit. **Legion:** to Jesus' question the demon replies with a Latin word transliterated into Greek. The Roman legion at this period consisted of 5,000 to 6,000 foot soldiers; hence the name implies a very large number of demons.

8, 31: Abyss: the place of the dead (Rom 10, 7) or the prison of Satan (Rv 20, 3) or the subterranean "watery deep" that symbolizes the chaos before the order imposed by creation (Gn 1, 2).

8, 35: Sitting at his feet: the former demoniac takes the position of a disciple before the master (10, 39; Acts 22, 3).

8, 40–56: Two interwoven miracle stories, one a healing and the other a resuscitation, present Jesus as master over sickness and death. In the Lucan account, faith in Jesus is responsible for the cure (48) and for the raising to life (50).

8, 42: An only daughter: cf the son of the widow of Nain whom Luke describes as an "only" son (7, 12; see also 9, 38).

8, 43: Afflicted with hemorrhages for twelve years: according to the Mosaic law (Lv 15, 25–30) this condition would render the woman unclean and unfit for contact with other people.

8, 52: Sleeping: her death is a temporary condition; cf Jn 11, 11–14.

s Mt 9, 18–26; Mk 5, 21–43. t 6, 19. u 7, 50; 17, 19; 18, 42. v 7, 13.

that she was dead. [54]But he took her by the hand and called to her, "Child, arise!" [55]Her breath returned and she immediately arose. He then directed that she should be given something to eat. [56]Her parents were astounded, and he instructed them to tell no one what had happened.

CHAPTER 9

The Mission of the Twelve [1] [w]*He summoned the Twelve and gave them power and authority over all demons and to cure diseases, [2]and he sent them to proclaim the kingdom of God and to heal [the sick]. [3]*He said to them, "Take nothing for the journey, neither walking stick, nor sack, nor food, nor money, and let no one take a second tunic. [4] [x]Whatever house you enter, stay there and leave from there. [5] [y]*And as for those who do not welcome you, when you leave that town, shake the dust from your feet in testimony against them." [6]Then they set out and went from village to village proclaiming the good news and curing diseases everywhere.

Herod's Opinion of Jesus [7] [z] [a]*Herod the tetrarch heard about all that was happening, and he was greatly perplexed because some were saying, "John has been raised from the dead"; [8]others were saying, "Elijah has appeared"; still others, "One of the ancient prophets has arisen." [9] [b]*But Herod said, "John I beheaded. Who then is this about whom I hear such things?" And he kept trying to see him.

The Return of the Twelve and the Feeding of the Five Thousand [10] [c]When the apostles returned, they explained to him what they had done. He took them and withdrew in private to a town called Bethsaida. [11]The crowds, meanwhile, learned of this and followed him. He received them and spoke to them about the kingdom of God, and he healed those who needed to be cured. [12]As the day was drawing to a close, the Twelve approached him and said, "Dismiss the crowd so that they can go to the surrounding villages and farms and find lodging and provisions; for we are in a deserted place here." [13] [d]He said to them, "Give them some food yourselves." They replied, "Five loaves and two fish are all we have, unless we ourselves go and buy food for all these people." [14]Now the men there numbered about five thousand. Then he said to his disciples, "Have them sit down in groups of [about] fifty." [15]They did so and made them all sit down. [16] [e]*Then taking the five loaves and the two fish, and looking up to heaven, he said the blessing over them, broke them, and gave them to the disciples to set before the crowd. [17]They all ate and were satisfied. And when the leftover fragments were picked up, they filled twelve wicker baskets.

Peter's Confession about Jesus [18] [f]*Once when Jesus was praying in solitude, and the disciples were with him, he asked them, "Who do the crowds say that I am?" [19] [g]They said in reply, "John the Baptist; others, Elijah; still

9, 1–6: Armed with the power and authority that Jesus himself has been displaying in the previous episodes, the Twelve are now sent out to continue the work that Jesus has been performing throughout his Galilean ministry: (1) proclaiming the kingdom (4, 43; 8, 1); (2) exorcising demons (4, 33–37.41; 8, 26–39) and (3) healing the sick (4, 38–40; 5, 12–16.17–26; 6, 6–10; 7, 1–10.17.22; 8, 40–56).

9, 3: **Take nothing for the journey**: the absolute detachment required of the disciple (14, 33) leads to complete reliance on God (12, 22–31).

9, 5: **Shake the dust from your feet**: see the note on Mt 10, 14.

9, 7–56: This section in which Luke gathers together incidents that focus on the identity of Jesus is introduced by a question that Herod is made to ask in this gospel: "Who then is this about whom I hear such things?" (9). In subsequent episodes, Luke reveals to the reader various answers to Herod's question: Jesus is one in whom God's power is present and who provides for the needs of God's people (10–17); Peter declares Jesus to be "the Messiah of God" (18–21); Jesus says he is the suffering Son of Man (22.43–45); Jesus is the Master to be followed, even to death (23–27); Jesus is God's Son, his Chosen One (28–36).

9, 7: **Herod the tetrarch**: see the note on 3, 1.

9, 9: **And he kept trying to see him**: this indication of Herod's interest in Jesus prepares for 13, 31–33 and for 23, 8–12 where Herod's curiosity about Jesus' power to perform miracles remains unsatisfied.

9, 16: **Then taking . . .** : the actions of Jesus recall the institution of the Eucharist in 22, 19; see also the note on Mt 14, 19.

9, 18–22: This incident is based on Mk 8, 27–33, but Luke has eliminated Peter's refusal to accept Jesus as suffering Son of Man (Mk 8, 32) and the rebuke of Peter by Jesus (Mk 8, 33). Elsewhere in the gospel, Luke softens the harsh portrait of Peter and the other apostles found in his Marcan source (cf 22, 39–46, which similarly lacks a rebuke of Peter that occurs in the source, Mk 14, 37–38).

9, 18: **When Jesus was praying in solitude**: see the note on 3, 21.

w Mt 10, 1.5–15; Mk 6, 7–13. x 10, 5–7. y 10, 10–11; Acts 13, 51. z Mt 14, 1–12; Mk 6, 14–29. a 9, 19; Mt 16, 14; Mk 8, 28. b 23, 8. c Mt 14, 13–21; Mk 6, 30–44; Jn 6, 1–14. d 2 Kgs 4, 42–44. e 22, 19; 24, 30–31; Acts 2, 42; 20, 11; 27, 35. f Mt 16, 13–20; Mk 8, 27–30. g 9, 7–8.

others, 'One of the ancient prophets has arisen.' " [20]*Then he said to them, "But who do you say that I am?" Peter said in reply, "The Messiah of God." [21]He rebuked them and directed them not to tell this to anyone.

The First Prediction of the Passion [22][h]He said, "The Son of Man must suffer greatly and be rejected by the elders, the chief priests, and the scribes, and be killed and on the third day be raised."

The Conditions of Discipleship [23][i][j]*Then he said to all, "If anyone wishes to come after me, he must deny himself and take up his cross daily and follow me. [24][k]For whoever wishes to save his life will lose it, but whoever loses his life for my sake will save it. [25]What profit is there for one to gain the whole world yet lose or forfeit himself? [26][l]Whoever is ashamed of me and of my words, the Son of Man will be ashamed of when he comes in his glory and in the glory of the Father and of the holy angels. [27]Truly I say to you, there are some standing here who will not taste death until they see the kingdom of God."

The Transfiguration of Jesus [28][m]*About eight days after he said this, he took Peter, John, and James and went up the mountain to pray. [29]While he was praying his face changed in appearance and his clothing became dazzling white. [30]*And behold, two men were conversing with him, Moses and Elijah, [31][n]*who appeared in glory and spoke of his exodus that he was going to accomplish in Jerusalem. [32][o]*Peter and his companions had been overcome by sleep, but becoming fully awake, they saw his glory and the two men standing with him. [33]*As they were about to part from him, Peter said to Jesus, "Master, it is good that we are here; let us make three tents, one for you, one for Moses, and one for Elijah." But he did not know what he was saying. [34]*While he was still speaking, a cloud came and cast a shadow over them, and they became frightened when they entered the cloud. [35][p]*Then from the cloud came a voice that said, "This is my chosen Son; listen to him." [36]*After the voice had spoken, Jesus was found alone. They fell silent and did not at that time tell anyone what they had seen.

The Healing of a Boy with a Demon [37][q]*On the next day, when they came down from the mountain, a large crowd met him. [38]There was a man in the crowd who cried out, "Teacher, I beg you, look at my son; he is my only child. [39]For a spirit seizes him and he suddenly screams and it convulses him until he foams at the mouth; it releases him only with difficulty, wearing him out. [40]I begged your disciples to cast it out but they could not." [41]Jesus said in reply, "O faithless and perverse generation, how long will I be with you and endure you? Bring your son here." [42]As he was coming forward, the demon threw

9, 20: The Messiah of God: on the meaning of this title in first-century Palestinian Judaism, see the notes on 2, 11 and on Mt 16, 13–20 and Mk 8, 27–30.

9, 23: Daily: this is a Lucan addition to a saying of Jesus, removing the saying from a context that envisioned the imminent suffering and death of the disciple of Jesus (as does the saying in Mk 8, 34–35) to one that focuses on the demands of daily Christian existence.

9, 28–36: Situated shortly after the first announcement of the passion, death, and resurrection, this scene of Jesus' transfiguration provides the heavenly confirmation to Jesus' declaration that his suffering will end in glory (32); see also the notes on Mt 17, 1–8 and Mk 9, 2–8.

9, 28: Up the mountain to pray: the "mountain" is the regular place of prayer in Lk (see 6, 12; 22, 39–41).

9, 30: Moses and Elijah: the two figures represent the Old Testament law and the prophets. At the end of this episode, the heavenly voice will identify Jesus as the one to be listened to now (35). See also the note on Mk 9, 5.

9, 31: His exodus that he was going to accomplish in Jerusalem: Luke identifies the subject of the conversation as the **exodus** of Jesus, a reference to the death, resurrection, and ascension of Jesus that will take place in Jerusalem, the city of destiny (see 9, 51). The mention of **exodus,** however, also calls to mind the Israelite Exodus from Egypt to the promised land.

9, 32: They saw his glory: the **glory** that is proper to God is here attributed to Jesus (see 24, 26).

9, 33: Let us make three tents: in a possible allusion to the feast of Tabernacles, Peter may be likening his joy on the occasion of the transfiguration to the joyful celebration of this harvest festival.

9, 34: Over them: it is not clear whether **them** refers to Jesus, Moses, and Elijah, or to the disciples. For the cloud casting its shadow, see the note on Mk 9, 7.

9, 35: Like the heavenly voice that identified Jesus at his baptism prior to his undertaking the Galilean ministry (3, 22), so too here before the journey to the city of destiny is begun (51) the heavenly voice again identifies Jesus as Son. **Listen to him:** the two representatives of Israel of old depart (33) and Jesus is left alone (36) as the teacher whose words must be heeded (see also Acts 3, 22).

9, 36: At that time: i.e., before the resurrection.

9, 37–43a: See the note on Mk 9, 14–29.

h 24, 7.26; Mt 16, 21; 20, 18–19; Mk 8, 31; 10, 33–34. i Mt 16, 24–28; Mk 8, 34—9, 1. j 14, 27; Mt 10, 38. k 17, 33; Mt 10, 39; Jn 12, 25. l 12, 9; Mt 10, 33; 2 Tm 2, 12. m Mt 17, 1–8; Mk 9, 2–8. n 9, 22; 13, 33. o Jn 1, 14; 2 Pt 1, 16. p 3, 22; Dt 18, 15; Ps 2, 7; Is 42, 1; Mt 3, 17; 12, 18; Mk 1, 11;2 Pt 1, 17–18. q Mt 17, 14–18; Mk 9, 14–27.

him to the ground in a convulsion; but Jesus rebuked the unclean spirit, healed the boy, and returned him to his father. [43] [r]And all were astonished by the majesty of God.

The Second Prediction of the Passion While they were all amazed at his every deed, he said to his disciples, [44]"Pay attention to what I am telling you. The Son of Man is to be handed over to men." [45]But they did not understand this saying; its meaning was hidden from them so that they should not understand it, and they were afraid to ask him about this saying.

The Greatest in the Kingdom [46] [s t]*An argument arose among the disciples about which of them was the greatest. [47]Jesus realized the intention of their hearts and took a child and placed it by his side [48] [u]and said to them, "Whoever receives this child in my name receives me, and whoever receives me receives the one who sent me. For the one who is least among all of you is the one who is the greatest."

Another Exorcist [49] [v]Then John said in reply, "Master, we saw someone casting out demons in your name and we tried to prevent him because he does not follow in our company." [50]Jesus said to him, "Do not prevent him, for whoever is not against you is for you."

V: The Journey to Jerusalem: Luke's Travel Narrative

Departure for Jerusalem; Samaritan Inhospitality [51] [w]*When the days for his being taken up were fulfilled, he resolutely determined to journey to Jerusalem, [52] [x]*and he sent messengers ahead of him. On the way they entered a Samaritan village to prepare for his reception there, [53]but they would not welcome him because the destination of his journey was Jerusalem. [54] [y]When the disciples James and John saw this they asked, "Lord, do you want us to call down fire from heaven to consume them?" [55]Jesus turned and rebuked them, [56]and they journeyed to another village.

The Would-be Followers of Jesus [57] [z]*As they were proceeding on their journey someone said to him, "I will follow you wherever you go." [58]Jesus answered him, "Foxes have dens and birds of the sky have nests, but the Son of Man has nowhere to rest his head." [59]And to another he said, "Follow me." But he replied, "[Lord,] let me go first and bury my father." [60]*But he answered him, "Let the dead bury their dead. But you, go and proclaim the kingdom of God." [61] [a]And another said, "I will follow you, Lord, but first let me say farewell to my family at home." [62][To him] Jesus said, "No one who sets a

9, 46–50: These two incidents focus on attitudes that are opposed to Christian discipleship: rivalry and intolerance of outsiders.

9, 51—18, 14: The Galilean ministry of Jesus finishes with the previous episode and a new section of Luke's gospel begins, the journey to Jerusalem. This journey is based on Mk 10, 1–52, but Luke uses his Marcan source only in 18, 15—19, 27. Before that point he has inserted into his gospel a distinctive collection of sayings of Jesus and stories about him that he has drawn from Q, a collection of sayings of Jesus used also by Matthew, and from his own special traditions. All of the material collected in this section is loosely organized within the framework of a journey of Jesus to Jerusalem, the city of destiny, where his exodus (suffering, death, resurrection, ascension) is to take place (9, 31), where salvation is accomplished, and from where the proclamation of God's saving word is to go forth (24, 47; Acts 1, 8). Much of the material in the Lucan travel narrative is teaching for the disciples. During the course of this journey Jesus is preparing his chosen Galilean witnesses for the role they will play after his exodus (9, 31): they are to be his witnesses to the people (Acts 10, 39; 13, 31) and thereby provide certainty to the readers of Luke's gospel that the teachings they have received are rooted in the teachings of Jesus (1, 1–4).

9, 51–55: Just as the Galilean ministry began with a rejection of Jesus in his hometown, so too the travel narrative begins with the rejection of him by Samaritans. In this episode Jesus disassociates himself from the attitude expressed by his disciples that those who reject him are to be punished severely. The story alludes to 2 Kgs 1, 10.12, where the prophet Elijah takes the course of action Jesus rejects, and Jesus thereby rejects the identification of himself with Elijah.

9, 51: Days for his being taken up: like the reference to his exodus in v 31, this is probably a reference to all the events (suffering, death, resurrection, ascension) of his last days in Jerusalem. **He resolutely determined:** literally, "he set his face."

9, 52: Samaritan: Samaria was the territory between Judea and Galilee west of the Jordan river. For ethnic and religious reasons, the Samaritans and the Jews were bitterly opposed to one another (see Jn 4, 9).

9, 57–62: In these sayings Jesus speaks of the severity and the unconditional nature of Christian discipleship. Even family ties and filial obligations, such as burying one's parents, cannot distract one no matter how briefly from proclaiming the kingdom of God. The first two sayings are paralleled in Mt 8, 19–22; see also the notes there.

9, 60: Let the dead bury their dead: i.e., let the spiritually dead (those who do not follow) bury their physically dead. See also the note on Mt 8, 22.

r 18, 32–34; Mt 17, 22–23; Mk 9, 30–32. s Mt 18, 1–5; Mk 9, 33–37. t 22, 24. u 10, 16; Mt 10, 40; Jn 13, 20. v Mk 9, 38–40. w 9, 53; 13, 22.33; 17, 11; 18, 31; 19, 28; 24, 51; Acts 1, 2.9–11.22. x Mal 3, 1. y 2 Kgs 1, 10.12. z Mt 8, 19–22. a 1 Kgs 19, 20.

hand to the plow and looks to what was left
behind is fit for the kingdom of God."

CHAPTER 10

The Mission of the Seventy-two [1] [b]*After
this the Lord appointed seventy[-two] others
whom he sent ahead of him in pairs to every
town and place he intended to visit. [2] [c]He said to
them, "The harvest is abundant but the laborers
are few; so ask the master of the harvest to send
out laborers for his harvest. [3] [d]Go on your way;
behold, I am sending you like lambs among
wolves. [4] [e f]*Carry no money bag, no sack, no
sandals; and greet no one along the way. [5]*Into
whatever house you enter, first say, 'Peace to
this household.' [6]*If a peaceful person lives
there, your peace will rest on him; but if not, it
will return to you. [7] [g]Stay in the same house and
eat and drink what is offered to you, for the
laborer deserves his payment. Do not move
about from one house to another. [8] [h]Whatever
town you enter and they welcome you, eat what
is set before you, [9] [i]cure the sick in it and say to
them, 'The kingdom of God is at hand for you.'
[10] [j]Whatever town you enter and they do not
receive you, go out into the streets and say,
[11] [k]'The dust of your town that clings to our feet,
even that we shake off against you.' Yet know
this: the kingdom of God is at hand. [12] [l]I tell you,
it will be more tolerable for Sodom on that day
than for that town.

Reproaches to Unrepentant Towns
[13] [m n]*"Woe to you, Chorazin! Woe to you,
Bethsaida! For if the mighty deeds done in your
midst had been done in Tyre and Sidon, they
would long ago have repented, sitting in sack-
cloth and ashes. [14]But it will be more tolerable
for Tyre and Sidon at the judgment than for you.
[15] [o]*And as for you, Capernaum, 'Will you be
exalted to heaven? You will go down to the
netherworld.' " [16] [p]Whoever listens to you lis-
tens to me. Whoever rejects you rejects me. And
whoever rejects me rejects the one who sent
me."
Return of the Seventy-two [17]The seventy
[-two] returned rejoicing, and said, "Lord, even
the demons are subject to us because of your
name." [18] [q]*Jesus said, "I have observed Satan
fall like lightning from the sky. [19] [r]Behold, I have
given you the power 'to tread upon serpents'
and scorpions and upon the full force of the
enemy and nothing will harm you.
[20] [s]Nevertheless, do not rejoice because the
spirits are subject to you, but rejoice because
your names are written in heaven."
Praise of the Father [21] [t u]*At that very mo-
ment he rejoiced [in] the holy Spirit and said, "I
give you praise, Father, Lord of heaven and
earth, for although you have hidden these things
from the wise and the learned you have revealed
them to the childlike. Yes, Father, such has been
your gracious will. [22] [v]All things have been

10, 1–12: Only the Gospel of Luke contains two episodes in which Jesus sends out his followers on a mission: the first (9, 1–6) is based on the mission in Mk 6, 6b-13 and recounts the sending out of the Twelve; here in vv 1–12 a similar report based on Q becomes the sending out of seventy-two in this gospel. The episode continues the theme of Jesus preparing witnesses to himself and his ministry. These witnesses include not only the Twelve but also the seventy-two who may represent the Christian mission in Luke's own day. Note that the instructions given to the Twelve and to the seventy-two are similar and that what is said to the seventy-two in v 4 is directed to the Twelve in 22, 35.

10, 1: Seventy[-two]: important representatives of the Alexandrian and Caesarean text types read "seventy," while other important Alexandrian texts and Western readings have "seventy-two."

10, 4: Carry no money bag . . . greet no one along the way: because of the urgency of the mission and the singlemindedness required of missionaries, attachment to material possessions should be avoided and even customary greetings should not distract from the fulfillment of the task.

10, 5: First say, 'Peace to this household': see the notes on 2, 14 and Mt 10, 13.

10, 6: A peaceful person: literally, "a son of peace."

10, 13–16: The call to repentance that is a part of the proclamation of the kingdom brings with it a severe judgment for those who hear it and reject it.

10, 15: The netherworld: the underworld, the place of the dead (Acts 2, 27.31), here contrasted with heaven; see also the note on Mt 11, 23.

10, 18: I have observed Satan fall like lightning: the effect of the mission of the seventy-two is characterized by the Lucan Jesus as a symbolic fall of Satan. As the kingdom of God is gradually being established, evil in all its forms is being defeated; the dominion of Satan over humanity is at an end.

10, 21: Revealed them to the childlike: a restatement of the theme announced in 8, 10: the mysteries of the kingdom are revealed to the disciples. See also the note on Mt 11, 25–27.

b Mk 6, 7. c Mt 9, 37–38; Jn 4, 35. d Mt 10, 16. e 9, 3; 2 Kgs 4, 29. f Mt 10, 7–14. g 9, 4; Mt 10, 10; 1 Cor 9, 6–14; 1 Tm 5, 18. h 1 Cor 10, 27. i Mt 3, 2; 4, 17; Mk 1, 15. j 9, 5. k Acts 13, 51; 18, 6. l Mt 10, 15; 11, 24. m Mt 11, 20–24. n Is 23; Ez 26–28; Jl 3, 4–8; Am 1, 1–10; Zec 9, 2–4. o Is 14, 13–15. p Mt 10, 40; Jn 5, 23; 13, 20; 15, 23. q Is 14, 12; Jn 12, 31; Rv 12, 7–12. r Ps 19, 13; Mk 16, 18. s Ex 32, 32; Dn 12, 1; Mt 7, 22; Phil 4, 3; Heb 12, 23; Rv 3, 5; 21, 27. t Mt 11, 25–27. u 1 Cor 1, 26–28. v Jn 3, 35; 10, 15.

handed over to me by my Father. No one knows
who the Son is except the Father, and who the
Father is except the Son and anyone to whom
the Son wishes to reveal him."
The Privileges of Discipleship 23[w]Turning to
the disciples in private he said, "Blessed are the
eyes that see what you see. 24For I say to you,
many prophets and kings desired to see what
you see, but did not see it, and to hear what you
hear, but did not hear it."
The Greatest Commandment 25[x][y]*There
was a scholar of the law who stood up to test
him and said, "Teacher, what must I do to
inherit eternal life?" 26Jesus said to him, "What
is written in the law? How do you read it?"
27[z]He said in reply, "You shall love the Lord,
your God, with all your heart, with all your
being, with all your strength, and with all your
mind, and your neighbor as yourself." 28[a]He
replied to him, "You have answered correctly;
do this and you will live."
The Parable of the Good Samaritan 29But
because he wished to justify himself, he said to
Jesus, "And who is my neighbor?" 30Jesus re-
plied, "A man fell victim to robbers as he went
down from Jerusalem to Jericho. They stripped
and beat him and went off leaving him half-dead.
31*A priest happened to be going down that
road, but when he saw him, he passed by on the
opposite side. 32Likewise a Levite came to the
place, and when he saw him, he passed by on
the opposite side. 33But a Samaritan traveler
who came upon him was moved with compas-
sion at the sight. 34He approached the victim,
poured oil and wine over his wounds and
bandaged them. Then he lifted him up on his
own animal, took him to an inn and cared for
him. 35The next day he took out two silver coins
and gave them to the innkeeper with the instruc-
tion, 'Take care of him. If you spend more than
what I have given you, I shall repay you on my
way back.' 36Which of these three, in your
opinion, was neighbor to the robbers' victim?"
37He answered, "The one who treated him with
mercy." Jesus said to him, "Go and do likewise."
Martha and Mary 38[b]*As they continued their
journey he entered a village where a woman
whose name was Martha welcomed him. 39*She
had a sister named Mary [who] sat beside the
Lord at his feet listening to him speak. 40Martha,
burdened with much serving, came to him and
said, "Lord, do you not care that my sister has
left me by myself to do the serving? Tell her to
help me." 41The Lord said to her in reply,
"Martha, Martha, you are anxious and worried
about many things. 42*There is need of only one
thing. Mary has chosen the better part and it will
not be taken from her."

CHAPTER 11

The Lord's Prayer 1[c]*He was praying in a
certain place, and when he had finished, one of

10, 25–37: In response to a question from a Jewish legal expert about inheriting eternal life, Jesus illustrates the superiority of love over legalism through the story of the good Samaritan. The law of love proclaimed in the "Sermon on the Plain" (6, 27–36) is exemplified by one whom the legal expert would have considered ritually impure (see Jn 4, 9). Moreover, the identity of the "neighbor" requested by the legal expert (29) turns out to be a Samaritan, the enemy of the Jew (see the note on 9, 52).

10, 25: Scholar of the law: an expert in the Mosaic law, and probably a member of the group elsewhere identified as the scribes (5, 21).

10, 31–32: Priest . . . Levite: those religious representatives of Judaism who would have been expected to be models of "neighbor" to the victim pass him by.

10, 38–42: The story of Martha and Mary further illustrates the importance of hearing the words of the teacher and the concern with women in Lk.

10, 39: Sat beside the Lord at his feet: it is remarkable for first-century Palestinian Judaism that a woman would assume the posture of a disciple at the master's feet (see also 8, 35; Acts 22, 3), and it reveals a characteristic attitude of Jesus toward women in this gospel (see 8, 2–3).

10, 42: There is need of only one thing: some ancient versions read, "there is need of few things"; another important, although probably inferior, reading found in some manuscripts is, "there is need of few things, or of one."

11, 1–13: Luke presents three episodes concerned with prayer. The first (1–4) recounts Jesus teaching his disciples the Christian communal prayer, the "Our Father"; the second (5–8), the importance of persistence in prayer; the third (9–13), the effectiveness of prayer.

11, 1–4: The Matthean form of the "Our Father" occurs in the "Sermon on the Mount" (Mt 6, 9–15); the shorter Lucan version is presented while Jesus is at prayer (see the note on 3, 21) and his disciples ask him to teach them to pray just as John taught his disciples to pray. In answer to their question, Jesus presents them with an example of a Christian communal prayer that stresses the fatherhood of God and acknowledges him as the one to whom the Christian disciple owes daily sustenance (3), forgiveness (4), and deliverance from the final trial (4). See also the notes on Mt 6, 9–13.

w Mt 13, 16–17. x Mt 22, 34–40; Mk 12, 28–34. y 18, 18; Mt 19, 16; Mk 10, 17. z Lv 19, 18; Dt 6, 5; 10, 12; Jos 22, 5; Mt 19, 19; 22, 37–39; Rom 13, 9; Gal 5, 14; Jas 2, 8. a Lv 18, 5; Prv 19, 16; Rom 10, 5; Gal 3, 12. b Jn 11, 1; 12, 2–3. c Mt 6, 9–15.

his disciples said to him, "Lord, teach us to pray just as John taught his disciples." [2]*He said to them, "When you pray, say:

Father, hallowed be your name,
your kingdom come.
3 *Give us each day our daily bread
4 and forgive us our sins
for we ourselves forgive everyone in debt to us,
and do not subject us to the final test."

Further Teachings on Prayer [5][d]And he said to them, "Suppose one of you has a friend to whom he goes at midnight and says, 'Friend, lend me three loaves of bread, [6]for a friend of mine has arrived at my house from a journey and I have nothing to offer him,' [7]and he says in reply from within, 'Do not bother me; the door has already been locked and my children and I are already in bed. I cannot get up to give you anything.' [8]I tell you, if he does not get up to give him the loaves because of their friendship, he will get up to give him whatever he needs because of his persistence.

The Answer to Prayer [9][ef]"And I tell you, ask and you will receive; seek and you will find; knock and the door will be opened to you. [10]For everyone who asks, receives; and the one who seeks, finds; and to the one who knocks, the door will be opened. [11]What father among you would hand his son a snake when he asks for a fish? [12]Or hand him a scorpion when he asks for an egg? [13]*If you then, who are wicked, know how to give good gifts to your children, how much more will the Father in heaven give the holy Spirit to those who ask him?"

Jesus and Beelzebul [14][g]He was driving out a demon [that was] mute, and when the demon had gone out, the mute person spoke and the crowds were amazed. [15][h]Some of them said, "By the power of Beelzebul, the prince of demons, he drives out demons." [16][i]Others, to test him, asked him for a sign from heaven. [17]But he knew their thoughts and said to them, "Every kingdom divided against itself will be laid waste and house will fall against house. [18]And if Satan is divided against himself, how will his kingdom stand? For you say that it is by Beelzebul that I drive out demons. [19]*If I, then, drive out demons by Beelzebul, by whom do your own people drive them out? Therefore they will be your judges. [20][j]But if it is by the finger of God that [I] drive out demons, then the kingdom of God has come upon you. [21]When a strong man fully armed guards his palace, his possessions are safe. [22]*But when one stronger than he attacks and overcomes him, he takes away the armor on which he relied and distributes the spoils. [23][k]Whoever is not with me is against me, and whoever does not gather with me scatters.

The Return of the Unclean Spirit [24][l]"When an unclean spirit goes out of someone, it roams through arid regions searching for rest but, finding none, it says, 'I shall return to my home from which I came.' [25]But upon returning, it finds it swept clean and put in order. [26][m]Then it goes and brings back seven other spirits more wicked than itself who move in and dwell there, and the last condition of that person is worse than the first."

True Blessedness [27][n]*While he was speaking, a woman from the crowd called out and said to him, "Blessed is the womb that carried you and the breasts at which you nursed." [28]He replied,

11, 2: **Your kingdom come:** in place of this petition, some early church Fathers record: "May your holy Spirit come upon us and cleanse us," a petition that may reflect the use of the "Our Father" in a baptismal liturgy.

11, 3–4: **Daily bread:** see the note on Mt 6, 11. **The final test:** see the note on Mt 6, 13.

11, 13: **The holy Spirit:** this is a Lucan editorial alteration of a traditional saying of Jesus (see Mt 7, 11). Luke presents the gift of the holy Spirit as the response of the Father to the prayer of the Christian disciple.

11, 19: **Your own people:** the Greek reads "your sons." Other Jewish exorcists (see Acts 19, 13–20), who recognize that the power of God is active in the exorcism, would themselves convict the accusers of Jesus. See also the note on Mt 12, 27.

11, 22: **One stronger:** i.e., Jesus. Cf 3, 16 where John the Baptist identifies Jesus as "more powerful than I."

11, 27–28: The beatitude in v 28 should not be interpreted as a rebuke of the mother of Jesus; see the note on 8, 21. Rather, it emphasizes (like 2, 35) that attentiveness to God's word is more important than biological relationship to Jesus.

d 18, 1–5. e Mt 7, 7–11. f Mt 21, 22; Mk 11, 24; Jn 14, 13; 15, 7; 1 Jn 5, 14–15. g Mt 12, 22–30; Mk 3, 20–27. h Mt 9, 34. i Mt 12, 38; 16, 1; Mk 8, 11; 1 Cor 1, 22. j Ex 8, 19. k 9, 50; Mk 9, 40. l Mt 12, 43–45. m Jn 5, 14. n 1, 28.42.48.

"Rather, blessed are those who hear the word of God and observe it."

The Demand for a Sign 29 o p*While still more people gathered in the crowd, he said to them, "This generation is an evil generation; it seeks a sign, but no sign will be given it, except the sign of Jonah. 30Just as Jonah became a sign to the Ninevites, so will the Son of Man be to this generation. 31 qAt the judgment the queen of the south will rise with the men of this generation and she will condemn them, because she came from the ends of the earth to hear the wisdom of Solomon, and there is something greater than Solomon here. 32 rAt the judgment the men of Nineveh will arise with this generation and condemn it, because at the preaching of Jonah they repented, and there is something greater than Jonah here.

The Simile of Light 33 s"No one who lights a lamp hides it away or places it [under a bushel basket], but on a lampstand so that those who enter might see the light. 34 tThe lamp of the body is your eye. When your eye is sound, then your whole body is filled with light, but when it is bad, then your body is in darkness. 35Take care, then, that the light in you not become darkness. 36If your whole body is full of light, and no part of it is in darkness, then it will be as full of light as a lamp illuminating you with its brightness."

Denunciation of the Pharisees and Scholars of the Law 37 u v*After he had spoken, a Pharisee invited him to dine at his home. He entered and reclined at table to eat. 38 wThe Pharisee was amazed to see that he did not observe the prescribed washing before the meal. 39 xThe Lord said to him, "Oh you Pharisees! Although you cleanse the outside of the cup and the dish, inside you are filled with plunder and evil. 40You fools! Did not the maker of the outside also make the inside? 41But as to what is within, give alms, and behold, everything will be clean for you. 42 yWoe to you Pharisees! You pay tithes of mint and of rue and of every garden herb, but you pay no attention to judgment and to love for God. These you should have done, without overlooking the others. 43 zWoe to you Pharisees! You love the seat of honor in synagogues and greetings in marketplaces. 44 a*Woe to you! You are like unseen graves over which people unknowingly walk."

45 b*Then one of the scholars of the law said to him in reply, "Teacher, by saying this you are insulting us too." 46And he said, "Woe also to you scholars of the law! You impose on people burdens hard to carry, but you yourselves do not lift one finger to touch them. 47 cWoe to you! You build the memorials of the prophets whom your ancestors killed. 48Consequently, you bear witness and give consent to the deeds of your ancestors, for they killed them and you do the building. 49 d*Therefore, the wisdom of God said, 'I will send to them prophets and apostles; some of them they will kill and persecute' 50in order that this generation might be charged with the blood of all the prophets shed since the foundation of the world, 51 e*from the blood of Abel to the blood of Zechariah who died between the altar and the temple building. Yes, I tell you, this generation will be charged with

11, 29–32: The "sign of Jonah" in Lk is the preaching of the need for repentance by a prophet who comes from afar. Cf Mt 12, 38–42 (and see the notes there) where the "sign of Jonah" is interpreted by Jesus as his death and resurrection.

11, 37–54: This denunciation of the Pharisees (39–44) and the scholars of the law (45–52) is set by Luke in the context of Jesus' dining at the home of a Pharisee. Controversies with or reprimands of Pharisees are regularly set by Luke within the context of Jesus' eating with Pharisees (see 5, 29–39; 7, 36–50; 14, 1–24). A different compilation of similar sayings is found in Mt 23 (see also the notes there).

11, 44: Unseen graves: contact with the dead or with human bones or graves (see Nm 19, 16) brought ritual impurity. Jesus presents the Pharisees as those who insidiously lead others astray through their seeming attention to the law.

11, 45: Scholars of the law: see the note on 10, 25.

11, 49: I will send to them prophets and apostles: Jesus connects the mission of the church (apostles) with the mission of the Old Testament prophets who often suffered the rebuke of their contemporaries.

11, 51: From the blood of Abel to the blood of Zechariah: the murder of Abel is the first murder recounted in the Old Testament (Gn 4, 8). The Zechariah mentioned here may be the Zechariah whose murder is recounted in 2 Chr 24, 20–22, the last murder presented in the Hebrew canon of the Old Testament.

o Mt 12, 38–42; Mk 8, 12. p Mt 16, 1.4; Jn 6, 30; 1 Cor 1, 22. q 1 Kgs 10, 1–10; 2 Chr 9, 1–12. r Jon 3, 8.10. s 8, 16; Mt 5, 15; Mk 4, 21. t Mt 6, 22–23. u 20, 45–47; Mt 23, 1–36; Mk 12, 38–40. v 7, 36; 14, 1. w Mt 15, 2; Mk 7, 2–5. x Mt 23, 25–26. y Lv 27, 30; Mt 23, 23. z 20, 46; Mt 23, 6; Mk 12, 38–39. a Mt 23, 27. b Mt 23, 4. c Mt 23, 29–32. d Mt 23, 34–36. e Gn 4, 8; 2 Chr 24, 20–22.

their blood! 52 [f]Woe to you, scholars of the law! You have taken away the key of knowledge. You yourselves did not enter and you stopped those trying to enter." 53 [g]When he left, the scribes and Pharisees began to act with hostility toward him and to interrogate him about many things, 54 [h]for they were plotting to catch him at something he might say.

CHAPTER 12

The Leaven of the Pharisees 1 [i]*Meanwhile, so many people were crowding together that they were trampling one another underfoot. He began to speak, first to his disciples, "Beware of the leaven—that is, the hypocrisy—of the Pharisees.

Courage under Persecution 2 [j][k]*"There is nothing concealed that will not be revealed, nor secret that will not be known. 3 Therefore whatever you have said in the darkness will be heard in the light, and what you have whispered behind closed doors will be proclaimed on the housetops. 4 I tell you, my friends, do not be afraid of those who kill the body but after that can do no more. 5 *I shall show you whom to fear. Be afraid of the one who after killing has the power to cast into Gehenna; yes, I tell you, be afraid of that one. 6 *Are not five sparrows sold for two small coins? Yet not one of them has escaped the notice of God. 7 [l]Even the hairs of your head have all been counted. Do not be afraid. You are worth more than many sparrows. 8 I tell you, everyone who acknowledges me before others the Son of Man will acknowledge before the angels of God. 9 [m]But whoever denies me before others will be denied before the angels of God.

Sayings about the holy Spirit 10 [n]*"Everyone who speaks a word against the Son of Man will be forgiven, but the one who blasphemes against the holy Spirit will not be forgiven. 11 [o]When they take you before synagogues and before rulers and authorities, do not worry about how or what your defense will be or about what you are to say. 12 For the holy Spirit will teach you at that moment what you should say."

Saying against Greed 13 *Someone in the crowd said to him, "Teacher, tell my brother to share the inheritance with me." 14 [p]He replied to him, "Friend, who appointed me as your judge and arbitrator?" 15 [q]Then he said to the crowd, "Take care to guard against all greed, for though one may be rich, one's life does not consist of possessions."

Parable of the Rich Fool 16 Then he told them a parable. "There was a rich man whose land produced a bountiful harvest. 17 He asked himself, 'What shall I do, for I do not have space to store my harvest?' 18 And he said, 'This is what I shall do: I shall tear down my barns and build larger ones. There I shall store all my grain and other goods 19 [r][s]and I shall say to myself, "Now as for you, you have so many good things stored up for many years, rest, eat, drink, be merry!" ' 20 But God said to him, 'You fool, this night your life will be demanded of you; and the things you have prepared, to whom will they belong?' 21 *Thus will it be for the one who stores up treasure for himself but is not rich in what matters to God."

Dependence on God 22 [t]He said to [his] disciples, "Therefore I tell you, do not worry about your life and what you will eat, or about your body and what you will wear. 23 For life is more

12, 1: See the notes on Mk 8, 15 and Mt 16, 5–12.

12, 2–9: Luke presents a collection of sayings of Jesus exhorting his followers to acknowledge him and his mission fearlessly and assuring them of God's protection even in times of persecution. They are paralleled in Mt 10, 26–33.

12, 5: Gehenna: see the note on Mt 5, 22.

12, 6: Two small coins: the Roman copper coin, the assarion (Latin **as**), was worth about one-sixteenth of a denarius (see the note on 7, 41).

12, 10–12: The sayings about the holy Spirit are set in the context of fearlessness in the face of persecution (2–9; cf Mt 12, 31–32). The holy Spirit will be presented in Luke's second volume, the Acts of the Apostles, as the power responsible for the guidance of the Christian mission and the source of courage in the face of persecution.

12, 13–34: Luke has joined together sayings contrasting those whose focus and trust in life is on material possessions, symbolized here by the rich fool of the parable (16–21), with those who recognize their complete dependence on God (21), those whose radical detachment from material possessions symbolizes their heavenly treasure (33–34).

12, 21: Rich in what matters to God: literally, "rich for God."

f Mt 23, 13. g 6, 11; Mt 22, 15–22. h 20, 20. i Mt 16, 6; Mk 8, 15. j Mt 10, 26–33. k 8, 17; Mk 4, 22. l 12, 24; 21, 18; Acts 27, 34. m 9, 26; Mk 8, 38; 2 Tm 2, 12. n Mt 12, 31–32; Mk 3, 28–29. o 21, 12–15; Mt 10, 17–20; Mk 13, 11. p Ex 2, 14; Acts 7, 27. q 1 Tm 6, 9–10. r Mt 6, 19–21; 1 Tm 6, 17. s Sir 11, 19. t Mt 6, 25–34.

than food and the body more than clothing. 24 [u]Notice the ravens: they do not sow or reap; they have neither storehouse nor barn, yet God feeds them. How much more important are you than birds! 25 Can any of you by worrying add a moment to your life-span? 26 If even the smallest things are beyond your control, why are you anxious about the rest? 27 [v]Notice how the flowers grow. They do not toil or spin. But I tell you, not even Solomon in all his splendor was dressed like one of them. 28 If God so clothes the grass in the field that grows today and is thrown into the oven tomorrow, will he not much more provide for you, O you of little faith? 29 As for you, do not seek what you are to eat and what you are to drink, and do not worry anymore. 30 All the nations of the world seek for these things, and your Father knows that you need them. 31 Instead, seek his kingdom, and these other things will be given you besides. 32 [w]Do not be afraid any longer, little flock, for your Father is pleased to give you the kingdom. 33 [x]Sell your belongings and give alms. Provide money bags for yourselves that do not wear out, an inexhaustible treasure in heaven that no thief can reach nor moth destroy. 34 For where your treasure is, there also will your heart be.

Vigilant and Faithful Servants 35 [y]*"Gird your loins and light your lamps 36 [z]and be like servants who await their master's return from a wedding, ready to open immediately when he comes and knocks. 37 Blessed are those servants whom the master finds vigilant on his arrival. Amen, I say to you, he will gird himself, have them recline at table, and proceed to wait on them. 38 And should he come in the second or third watch and find them prepared in this way, blessed are those servants. 39 [a]Be sure of this: if the master of the house had known the hour when the thief was coming, he would not have let his house be broken into. 40 You also must be prepared, for at an hour you do not expect, the Son of Man will come."

41 Then Peter said, "Lord, is this parable meant for us or for everyone?" 42 And the Lord replied, "Who, then, is the faithful and prudent steward whom the master will put in charge of his servants to distribute [the] food allowance at the proper time? 43 Blessed is that servant whom his master on arrival finds doing so. 44 Truly, I say to you, he will put him in charge of all his property. 45 *But if that servant says to himself, 'My master is delayed in coming,' and begins to beat the menservants and the maidservants, to eat and drink and get drunk, 46 then that servant's master will come on an unexpected day and at an unknown hour and will punish him severely and assign him a place with the unfaithful. 47 [b]That servant who knew his master's will but did not make preparations nor act in accord with his will shall be beaten severely; 48 and the servant who was ignorant of his master's will but acted in a way deserving of a severe beating shall be beaten only lightly. Much will be required of the person entrusted with much, and still more will be demanded of the person entrusted with more.

Jesus: A Cause of Division 49 *"I have come to set the earth on fire, and how I wish it were already blazing! 50 [c]*There is a baptism with which I must be baptized, and how great is my anguish until it is accomplished! 51 [d] [e]Do you think that I have come to establish peace on the earth? No, I tell you, but rather division. 52 From now on a household of five will be divided, three against two and two against three; 53 [f]a father will be divided against his son and a son against his father, a mother against her daughter and a daughter against her mother, a mother-in-law against her daughter-in-law and a daughter-in-law against her mother-in-law."

12, 35–48: This collection of sayings relates to Luke's understanding of the end time and the return of Jesus. Luke emphasizes for his readers the importance of being faithful to the instructions of Jesus in the period before the parousia.

12, 45: My master is delayed in coming: this statement indicates that early Christian expectations for the imminent return of Jesus had undergone some modification. Luke cautions his readers against counting on such a delay and acting irresponsibly. Cf the similar warning in Mt 24, 48.

12, 49–53: Jesus' proclamation of the kingdom is a refining and purifying fire. His message that meets with acceptance or rejection will be a source of conflict and dissension even within families.

12, 50: Baptism: i.e., his death.

u 12, 7. v 1 Kgs 10, 4–7; 2 Chr 9, 3–6. w 22, 29; Rv 1, 6. x 18, 22; Mt 6, 20–21; Mk 10, 21. y Mt 24, 45–51. z Mt 25, 1–13; Mk 13, 35–37. a Mt 24, 43–44; 1 Thes 5, 2. b Jas 4, 17. c Mk 10, 38–39. d Mt 10, 34–35. e 2, 14. f Mi 7, 6.

Signs of the Times 54[g]He also said to the crowds, "When you see [a] cloud rising in the west you say immediately that it is going to rain—and so it does; 55and when you notice that the wind is blowing from the south you say that it is going to be hot—and so it is. 56You hypocrites! You know how to interpret the appearance of the earth and the sky; why do you not know how to interpret the present time?

Settlement with an Opponent 57[h]"Why do you not judge for yourselves what is right? 58If you are to go with your opponent before a magistrate, make an effort to settle the matter on the way; otherwise your opponent will turn you over to the judge, and the judge hand you over to the constable, and the constable throw you into prison. 59*I say to you, you will not be released until you have paid the last penny."

CHAPTER 13

A Call to Repentance 1*At that time some people who were present there told him about the Galileans whose blood Pilate had mingled with the blood of their sacrifices. 2[i]He said to them in reply, "Do you think that because these Galileans suffered in this way they were greater sinners than all other Galileans? 3[j]By no means! But I tell you, if you do not repent, you will all perish as they did! 4*Or those eighteen people who were killed when the tower at Siloam fell on them—do you think they were more guilty than everyone else who lived in Jerusalem? 5By no means! But I tell you, if you do not repent, you will all perish as they did!"

The Parable of the Barren Fig Tree 6[k]*And he told them this parable: "There once was a person who had a fig tree planted in his orchard, and when he came in search of fruit on it but found none, 7he said to the gardener, 'For three years now I have come in search of fruit on this fig tree but have found none. [So] cut it down. Why should it exhaust the soil?' 8He said to him in reply, 'Sir, leave it for this year also, and I shall cultivate the ground around it and fertilize it; 9it may bear fruit in the future. If not you can cut it down.' "

Cure of a Crippled Woman on the Sabbath 10*He was teaching in a synagogue on the sabbath. 11And a woman was there who for eighteen years had been crippled by a spirit; she was bent over, completely incapable of standing erect. 12When Jesus saw her, he called to her and said, "Woman, you are set free of your infirmity." 13He laid his hands on her, and she at once stood up straight and glorified God. 14[l]But the leader of the synagogue, indignant that Jesus had cured on the sabbath, said to the crowd in reply, "There are six days when work should be done. Come on those days to be cured, not on the sabbath day." 15[m]*The Lord said to him in

12, 59: The last penny: Greek, **lepton,** a very small amount. Mt 5, 26 has for "the last penny" the Greek word **kodrantēs** (Latin **quadrans,** "farthing").

13, 1–5: The death of the Galileans at the hands of Pilate (1) and the accidental death of those on whom the tower fell (4) are presented by the Lucan Jesus as timely reminders of the need for all to repent, for the victims of these tragedies should not be considered outstanding sinners who were singled out for punishment.

13, 1: The slaughter of the Galileans by Pilate is unknown outside Lk; but from what is known about Pilate from the Jewish historian Josephus, such a slaughter would be in keeping with the character of Pilate. Josephus reports that Pilate had disrupted a religious gathering of the Samaritans on Mt. Gerizim with a slaughter of the participants (**Antiquities** 18, 4, 1 §§86–87), and that on another occasion Pilate had killed many Jews who had opposed him when he appropriated money from the temple treasury to build an aqueduct in Jerusalem (**Jewish War** 2, 9, 4 §§175–77; **Antiquities** 18, 3, 2 §§60–62).

13, 4: Like the incident mentioned in v 1, nothing of this accident in Jerusalem is known outside Lk and the New Testament.

13, 6–9: Following on the call to repentance in vv 1–5, the parable of the barren fig tree presents a story about the continuing patience of God with those who have not yet given evidence of their repentance (see 3, 8). The parable may also be alluding to the delay of the end time, when punishment will be meted out, and the importance of preparing for the end of the age because the delay will not be permanent (8–9).

13, 10–17: The cure of the crippled woman on the sabbath and the controversy that results furnishes a parallel to an incident that will be reported by Lk in 14, 1–6, the cure of the man with dropsy on the sabbath. A characteristic of Luke's style is the juxtaposition of an incident that reveals Jesus' concern for a man with an incident that reveals his concern for a woman; cf, e.g., 7, 11–17 and 8, 49–56.

13, 15–16: If the law as interpreted by Jewish tradition allowed for the untying of bound animals on the sabbath, how much more should this woman who has been bound by Satan's power be freed on the sabbath from her affliction.

g Mt 16, 2–3. h Mt 5, 25–26. i Jn 9, 2. j Jn 8, 24. k Jer 8, 13; Hb 3, 17; Mt 21, 19; Mk 11, 13. 16, 7; 14, 3; Ex 20, 8–11; Dt 5, 12–15; Mt 12, 10; Mk 3, 2–4; Jn 5, 16; 7, 23; 9, 14.16. m 14, 5; Dt 22, 4; Mt 12, 11.

reply, "Hypocrites! Does not each one of you on the sabbath untie his ox or his ass from the manger and lead it out for watering? [16] [n]*This daughter of Abraham, whom Satan has bound for eighteen years now, ought she not to have been set free on the sabbath day from this bondage?" [17]When he said this, all his adversaries were humiliated; and the whole crowd rejoiced at all the splendid deeds done by him.

The Parable of the Mustard Seed [18] [o]*Then he said, "What is the kingdom of God like? To what can I compare it? [19] [p]It is like a mustard seed that a person took and planted in the garden. When it was fully grown, it became a large bush and 'the birds of the sky dwelt in its branches.' "

The Parable of the Yeast [20] [q]Again he said, "To what shall I compare the kingdom of God? [21]It is like yeast that a woman took and mixed [in] with three measures of wheat flour until the whole batch of dough was leavened."

The Narrow Door; Salvation and Rejection [22]*He passed through towns and villages, teaching as he went and making his way to Jerusalem. [23]Someone asked him, "Lord, will only a few people be saved?" He answered them, [24] [r s]"Strive to enter through the narrow gate, for many, I tell you, will attempt to enter but will not be strong enough. [25] [t]After the master of the house has arisen and locked the door, then will you stand outside knocking and saying, 'Lord, open the door for us.' He will say to you in reply, 'I do not know where you are from.' [26]And you will say, 'We ate and drank in your company and you taught in our streets.' [27] [u]Then he will say to you, 'I do not know where [you] are from. Depart from me, all you evildoers!' [28] [v]And there will be wailing and grinding of teeth when you see Abraham, Isaac, and Jacob and all the prophets in the kingdom of God and you yourselves cast out. [29] [w]And people will come from the east and the west and from the north and the south and will recline at table in the kingdom of God. [30] [x]For behold, some are last who will be first, and some are first who will be last."

Herod's Desire to Kill Jesus [31]At that time some Pharisees came to him and said, "Go away, leave this area because Herod wants to kill you." [32]*He replied, "Go and tell that fox, 'Behold, I cast out demons and I perform healings today and tomorrow, and on the third day I accomplish my purpose. [33] [y]*Yet I must continue on my way today, tomorrow, and the following day, for it is impossible that a prophet should die outside of Jerusalem.'

The Lament over Jerusalem [34] [z]"Jerusalem, Jerusalem, you who kill the prophets and stone those sent to you, how many times I yearned to gather your children together as a hen gathers her brood under her wings, but you were unwilling! [35] [a]Behold, your house will be abandoned. [But] I tell you, you will not see me until [the time comes when] you say, 'Blessed is he who comes in the name of the Lord.' "

CHAPTER 14

Healing of the Man with Dropsy on the Sabbath [1] [b c]*On a sabbath he went to dine at

13, 16: Whom Satan has bound: affliction and infirmity are taken as evidence of Satan's hold on humanity. The healing ministry of Jesus reveals the gradual wresting from Satan of control over humanity and the establishment of God's kingdom.

13, 18–21: Two parables are used to illustrate the future proportions of the kingdom of God that will result from its deceptively small beginning in the preaching and healing ministry of Jesus. They are paralleled in Mt 13, 31–33 and Mk 4, 30–32.

13, 22–30: These sayings of Jesus follow in Lk upon the parables of the kingdom (18–21) and stress that great effort is required for entrance into the kingdom (24) and that there is an urgency to accept the present opportunity to enter because the narrow door will not remain open indefinitely (25). Lying behind the sayings is the rejection of Jesus and his message by his Jewish contemporaries (26) whose places at table in the kingdom will be taken by Gentiles from the four corners of the world (29). Those called last (the Gentiles) will precede those to whom the invitation to enter was first extended (the Jews). See also 14, 15–24.

13, 32: Nothing, not even Herod's desire to kill Jesus, stands in the way of Jesus' role in fulfilling God's will and in establishing the kingdom through his exorcisms and healings.

13, 33: It is impossible that a prophet should die outside of Jerusalem: Jerusalem is the city of destiny and the goal of the journey of the prophet Jesus. Only when he reaches the holy city will his work be accomplished.

14, 1–6: See the note on 13, 10–17.

n 19, 9. o Mt 13, 31–32; Mk 4, 30–32. p Ez 17, 23–24; 31, 6. q Mt 13, 33. r Mt 7, 13–14.21–23. s Mk 10, 25. t Mt 25, 10–12. u Ps 6, 9; Mt 7, 23; 25, 41. v Mt 8, 11–12. w Ps 107, 2–3. x Mt 19, 20; 20, 16; Mk 10, 31. y 2, 38; Jn 6, 30; 8, 20. z 19, 41–44; Mt 23, 37–39. a 19, 38; 1 Kgs 9, 7–8; Ps 118, 26; Jer 7, 4–7.13–15; 12, 7; 22, 5. b 6, 6–11; 13, 10–17. c 11, 37.

the home of one of the leading Pharisees, and the people there were observing him carefully. 2 *In front of him there was a man suffering from dropsy. 3 [d]Jesus spoke to the scholars of the law and Pharisees in reply, asking, "Is it lawful to cure on the sabbath or not?" 4 But they kept silent; so he took the man and, after he had healed him, dismissed him. 5 [e]*Then he said to them, "Who among you, if your son or ox falls into a cistern, would not immediately pull him out on the sabbath day?" 6 [f]But they were unable to answer his question.

Conduct of Invited Guests and Hosts 7 [g]*He told a parable to those who had been invited, noticing how they were choosing the places of honor at the table. 8 [h]"When you are invited by someone to a wedding banquet, do not recline at table in the place of honor. A more distinguished guest than you may have been invited by him, 9 and the host who invited both of you may approach you and say, 'Give your place to this man," and then you would proceed with embarrassment to take the lowest place. 10 Rather, when you are invited, go and take the lowest place so that when the host comes to you he may say, 'My friend, move up to a higher position.' Then you will enjoy the esteem of your companions at the table. 11 [i]For everyone who exalts himself will be humbled, but the one who humbles himself will be exalted." 12 [j]Then he said to the host who invited him, "When you hold a lunch or a dinner, do not invite your friends or your brothers or your relatives or your wealthy neighbors, in case they may invite you back and you have repayment. 13 Rather, when you hold a banquet, invite the poor, the crippled, the lame, the blind; 14 [k]blessed indeed will you be because of their inability to repay you. For you will be repaid at the resurrection of the righteous."

The Parable of the Great Feast 15 *One of his fellow guests on hearing this said to him, "Blessed is the one who will dine in the kingdom of God." 16 [l]He replied to him, "A man gave a great dinner to which he invited many. 17 When the time for the dinner came, he dispatched his servant to say to those invited, 'Come, everything is now ready.' 18 But one by one, they all began to excuse themselves. The first said to him, 'I have purchased a field and must go to examine it; I ask you, consider me excused.' 19 And another said, 'I have purchased five yoke of oxen and am on my way to evaluate them; I ask you, consider me excused.' 20 And another said, 'I have just married a woman, and therefore I cannot come.' 21 The servant went and reported this to his master. Then the master of the house in a rage commanded his servant, 'Go out quickly into the streets and alleys of the town and bring in here the poor and the crippled, the blind and the lame.' 22 The servant reported, 'Sir, your orders have been carried out and still there is room.' 23 The master then ordered the servant, 'Go out to the highways and hedgerows and make people come in that my home may be filled. 24 For, I tell you, none of those men who were invited will taste my dinner.' "

Sayings on Discipleship 25 *Great crowds were traveling with him, and he turned and addressed them, 26 [m] [n]*"If anyone comes to me without hating his father and mother, wife and

14, 2: Dropsy: an abnormal swelling of the body because of the retention and accumulation of fluid.

14, 5: Your son or ox: this is the reading of many of the oldest and most important New Testament manuscripts. Because of the strange collocation of **son** and **ox,** some copyists have altered it to "your ass or ox," on the model of the saying in 13, 15.

14, 7–14: The banquet scene found only in Luke provides the opportunity for these teachings of Jesus on humility and presents a setting to display Luke's interest in Jesus' attitude toward the rich and the poor (see the notes on 4, 18; 6, 20–26; 12, 13–34).

14, 15–24: The parable of the great dinner is a further illustration of the rejection by Israel, God's chosen people, of Jesus' invitation to share in the banquet in the kingdom and the extension of the invitation to other Jews whose identification as the poor, crippled, blind, and lame (21) classifies them among those who recognize their need for salvation, and to Gentiles (23). A similar parable is found in Mt 22, 1–10.

14, 25–33: This collection of sayings, most of which are peculiar to Lk, focuses on the total dedication necessary for the disciple of Jesus. No attachment to family (26) or possessions (33) can stand in the way of the total commitment demanded of the disciple. Also, acceptance of the call to be a disciple demands readiness to accept persecution and suffering (27) and a realistic assessment of the hardships and costs (28–32).

14, 26: Hating his father . . . : cf the similar saying in Mt 10,

d 6, 9; Mk 3, 4. e 13, 15; Dt 22, 4; Mt 12, 11. f Mt 22, 46. g 11, 43; Mt 23, 6; Mk 12, 38–39. h Prv 25, 6–7. i 18, 14. j 6, 32–35. k Jn 5, 29. l Mt 22, 2–10. m Mt 10, 37–38. n 9, 57–62; 18, 29; Jn 12, 25.

children, brothers and sisters, and even his own life, he cannot be my disciple. [27][o]Whoever does not carry his own cross and come after me cannot be my disciple. [28]Which of you wishing to construct a tower does not first sit down and calculate the cost to see if there is enough for its completion? [29]Otherwise, after laying the foundation and finding himself unable to finish the work the onlookers should laugh at him [30]and say, 'This one began to build but did not have the resources to finish.' [31]Or what king marching into battle would not first sit down and decide whether with ten thousand troops he can successfully oppose another king advancing upon him with twenty thousand troops? [32]But if not, while he is still far away, he will send a delegation to ask for peace terms. [33][p]In the same way, everyone of you who does not renounce all his possessions cannot be my disciple.

The Simile of Salt [34][q]*"Salt is good, but if salt itself loses its taste, with what can its flavor be restored? [35][r]It is fit neither for the soil nor for the manure pile; it is thrown out. Whoever has ears to hear ought to hear."

CHAPTER 15

The Parable of the Lost Sheep [1][s]*The tax collectors and sinners were all drawing near to listen to him, [2][t]but the Pharisees and scribes began to complain, saying, "This man welcomes sinners and eats with them." [3]So to them he addressed this parable. [4][u v w]"What man among you having a hundred sheep and losing one of them would not leave the ninety-nine in the desert and go after the lost one until he finds it? [5]And when he does find it, he sets it on his shoulders with great joy [6]and, upon his arrival home, he calls together his friends and neighbors and says to them, 'Rejoice with me because I have found my lost sheep.' [7][x]I tell you, in just the same way there will be more joy in heaven over one sinner who repents than over ninety-nine righteous people who have no need of repentance.

The Parable of the Lost Coin [8]*"Or what woman having ten coins and losing one would not light a lamp and sweep the house, searching carefully until she finds it? [9]And when she does find it, she calls together her friends and neighbors and says to them, 'Rejoice with me because I have found the coin that I lost.' [10]In just the same way, I tell you, there will be rejoicing among the angels of God over one sinner who repents."

The Parable of the Lost Son [11]Then he said, "A man had two sons, [12]and the younger son said to his father, 'Father, give me the share of your estate that should come to me.' So the father divided the property between them. [13][y]After a few days, the younger son collected all his belongings and set off to a distant country where he squandered his inheritance on a life of dissipation. [14]When he had freely spent everything, a severe famine struck that country, and he found himself in dire need. [15]So he hired himself out to one of the local citizens who sent him to his farm to tend the swine. [16]And he longed to eat his fill of the pods on which the swine fed, but nobody gave him any. [17]Coming to his senses he thought, 'How many of my father's hired workers have more than enough food to eat, but here am I, dying from hunger. [18]I shall get up and go to my father and I shall say to him, "Father, I have sinned against heaven and against you. [19]I no longer deserve to be called your son; treat me as you would treat one of your hired workers."' [20]So he got up and went back to his father. While he was

---

37. The disciple's family must take second place to the absolute dedication involved in following Jesus (see also 9, 59–62).

14, 34–35: The simile of salt follows the sayings of Jesus that demanded of the disciple total dedication and detachment from family and possessions and illustrates the condition of one who does not display this total commitment. The halfhearted disciple is like salt that cannot serve its intended purpose. See the simile of salt in Mt 5, 13 and the note there.

15, 1–32: To the parable of the lost sheep (1–7) that Luke shares with Matthew (Mt 18, 12–14), Luke adds two parables (the lost coin, 8–10; the prodigal son, 11–32) from his own special tradition to illustrate Jesus' particular concern for the lost and God's love for the repentant sinner.

15, 8: Ten coins: literally, "ten drachmas." A drachma was a Greek silver coin.

o 9, 23; Mt 16, 24; Mk 8, 34. p 5, 11. q Mt 5, 13; Mk 9, 50. r 8, 8; Mt 11, 15; 13, 9; Mk 4, 9.23. s Mt 9, 10–13. t 5, 30; 19, 7. u Mt 18, 12–14. v 19, 10. w Ez 34, 11–12.16. x Ez 18, 23. y Prv 29, 3.

still a long way off, his father caught sight of
him, and was filled with compassion. He ran to
his son, embraced him and kissed him. [21]His
son said to him, 'Father, I have sinned against
heaven and against you; I no longer deserve to
be called your son.' [22]But his father ordered his
servants, 'Quickly bring the finest robe and put
it on him; put a ring on his finger and sandals
on his feet. [23]Take the fattened calf and slaugh-
ter it. Then let us celebrate with a feast, [24]be-
cause this son of mine was dead, and has come
to life again; he was lost, and has been found.'
Then the celebration began. [25]Now the older
son had been out in the field and, on his way
back, as he neared the house, he heard the
sound of music and dancing. [26]He called one of
the servants and asked what this might mean.
[27]The servant said to him, 'Your brother has
returned and your father has slaughtered the
fattened calf because he has him back safe and
sound.' [28]He became angry, and when he re-
fused to enter the house, his father came out
and pleaded with him. [29]He said to his father in
reply, 'Look, all these years I served you and
not once did I disobey your orders; yet you
never gave me even a young goat to feast on
with my friends. [30]But when your son returns
who swallowed up your property with prosti-
tutes, for him you slaughter the fattened calf.'
[31]He said to him, 'My son, you are here with
me always; everything I have is yours. [32]But
now we must celebrate and rejoice, because
your brother was dead and has come to life
again; he was lost and has been found.' "

CHAPTER 16

The Parable of the Dishonest Steward

[1]*Then he also said to his disciples, "A rich man
had a steward who was reported to him for squan-
dering his property. [2]He summoned him and said,
'What is this I hear about you? Prepare a full
account of your stewardship, because you can no
longer be my steward.' [3]The steward said to him-
self, 'What shall I do, now that my master is taking
the position of steward away from me? I am not
strong enough to dig and I am ashamed to beg. [4]I
know what I shall do so that, when I am removed
from the stewardship, they may welcome me into
their homes.' [5]He called in his master's debtors
one by one. To the first he said, 'How much do you
owe my master?' [6]*He replied, 'One hundred
measures of olive oil.' He said to him, 'Here is your
promissory note. Sit down and quickly write one
for fifty.' [7]*Then to another he said, 'And you,
how much do you owe?' He replied, 'One hun-
dred kors of wheat.' He said to him, 'Here is your
promissory note; write one for eighty.' [8][z]*And
the master commended that dishonest steward
for acting prudently.

Application of the Parable "For the children
of this world are more prudent in dealing with
their own generation than are the children of
light. [9][a]*I tell you, make friends for yourselves
with dishonest wealth, so that when it fails, you
will be welcomed into eternal dwellings.
[10][b]*The person who is trustworthy in very small
matters is also trustworthy in great ones; and the
person who is dishonest in very small matters is
also dishonest in great ones. [11]If, therefore, you

16, 1–8a: The parable of the dishonest steward has to be understood in the light of Palestinian customs of agents acting on behalf of their masters and the usurious practices common to such agents. The dishonesty of the steward consisted in the squandering of his master's property (1) and not in any subsequent graft. The master commends the dishonest steward who has forgone his own usurious commission on the business transaction by having the debtors write new notes that reflected only the real amount owed the master (i.e., minus the steward's profit). The dishonest steward acts in this way in order to ingratiate himself with the debtors because he knows he is being dismissed from his position (3). The parable, then, teaches the prudent use of one's material goods in light of an imminent crisis.

16, 6: One hundred measures: literally, "one hundred **baths**." A **bath** is a Hebrew unit of liquid measurement equivalent to eight or nine gallons.

16, 7: One hundred kors: a **kor** is a Hebrew unit of dry measure for grain or wheat equivalent to ten or twelve bushels.

16, 8b-13: Several originally independent sayings of Jesus are gathered here by Luke to form the concluding application of the parable of the dishonest steward.

16, 8b-9: The first conclusion recommends the prudent use of one's wealth (in the light of the coming of the end of the age) after the manner of the children of this world, represented in the parable by the dishonest steward.

16, 9: Dishonest wealth: literally, "mammon of iniquity." Mammon is the Greek transliteration of a Hebrew or Aramaic word that is usually explained as meaning "that in which one trusts." The characterization of this wealth as **dishonest** expresses a tendency of wealth to lead one to dishonesty. **Eternal dwellings:** or, "eternal tents," i.e., heaven.

16, 10–12: The second conclusion recommends constant fidelity to those in positions of responsibility.

z Eph 5, 8; 1 Thes 5, 5. a 12, 33. b 19, 17; Mt 25, 20–23.

are not trustworthy with dishonest wealth, who will trust you with true wealth? 12 If you are not trustworthy with what belongs to another, who will give you what is yours? 13 [c]*No servant can serve two masters. He will either hate one and love the other, or be devoted to one and despise the other. You cannot serve God and mammon."

A Saying against the Pharisees 14 *The Pharisees, who loved money, heard all these things and sneered at him. 15 [d]And he said to them, "You justify yourselves in the sight of others, but God knows your hearts; for what is of human esteem is an abomination in the sight of God.

Sayings about the Law 16 [e]*"The law and the prophets lasted until John; but from then on the kingdom of God is proclaimed, and everyone who enters does so with violence. 17 [f]It is easier for heaven and earth to pass away than for the smallest part of a letter of the law to become invalid.

Sayings about Divorce 18 [g]"Everyone who divorces his wife and marries another commits adultery, and the one who marries a woman divorced from her husband commits adultery.

The Parable of the Rich Man and Lazarus

19 *"There was a rich man who dressed in purple garments and fine linen and dined sumptuously each day. 20 And lying at his door was a poor man named Lazarus, covered with sores, 21 [h]who would gladly have eaten his fill of the scraps that fell from the rich man's table. Dogs even used to come and lick his sores. 22 When the poor man died, he was carried away by angels to the bosom of Abraham. The rich man also died and was buried, 23 *and from the netherworld, where he was in torment, he raised his eyes and saw Abraham far off and Lazarus at his side. 24 And he cried out, 'Father Abraham, have pity on me. Send Lazarus to dip the tip of his finger in water and cool my tongue, for I am suffering torment in these flames.' 25 [i]Abraham replied, 'My child, remember that you received what was good during your lifetime while Lazarus likewise received what was bad; but now he is comforted here, whereas you are tormented. 26 Moreover, between us and you a great chasm is established to prevent anyone from crossing who might wish to go from our side to yours or from your side to ours.' 27 He said, 'Then I beg you, father, send him to my father's house, 28 for I have five brothers, so that he may warn them, lest they too come to this place of torment.' 29 But Abraham replied, 'They have Moses and the prophets. Let them listen to them.' 30 *He said, 'Oh no, father Abraham, but if someone from the dead goes to them, they will repent.' 31 [j]Then Abraham said, 'If they will not listen to Moses and the prophets, neither will they be persuaded if someone should rise from the dead.' "

CHAPTER 17

Temptations to Sin 1 [k]He said to his disciples, "Things that cause sin will inevitably occur, but woe to the person through whom they occur. 2 It would be better for him if a millstone were put around his neck and he be thrown into the sea than for him to cause one of these little ones to

16, 13: The third conclusion is a general statement about the incompatibility of serving God and being a slave to riches. To be dependent upon wealth is opposed to the teachings of Jesus who counseled complete dependence on the Father as one of the characteristics of the Christian disciple (12, 22–39). **God and mammon:** see the note on 16, 9. Mammon is used here as if it were itself a god.

16, 14–18: The two parables about the use of riches in ch 16 are separated by several isolated sayings of Jesus on the hypocrisy of the Pharisees (14–15), on the law (16–17), and on divorce (18).

16, 14–15: The Pharisees are here presented as examples of those who are slaves to wealth (see 16, 13) and, consequently, they are unable to serve God.

16, 16: John the Baptist is presented in Luke's gospel as a transitional figure between the period of Israel, the time of promise, and the period of Jesus, the time of fulfillment. With John, the fulfillment of the Old Testament promises has begun.

16, 19–31: The parable of the rich man and Lazarus again illustrates Luke's concern with Jesus' attitude toward the rich and the poor. The reversal of the fates of the rich man and Lazarus (22–23) illustrates the teachings of Jesus in Luke's "Sermon on the Plain" (6, 20–21.24–25).

16, 19: The oldest Greek manuscript of Lk dating from ca. A.D. 175–225 records the name of the rich man as an abbreviated form of "Nineveh," but there is very little textual support in other manuscripts for this reading. "Dives" of popular tradition is the Latin Vulgate's translation for "rich man."

16, 23: **The netherworld:** see the note on 10, 15.

16, 30–31: A foreshadowing in Luke's gospel of the rejection of the call to repentance even after Jesus' resurrection.

c Mt 6, 24. d 18, 9–14. e Mt 11, 12–13. f Mt 5, 18. g Mt 5, 32; 19, 9; Mk 10, 11–12; 1 Cor 7, 10–11. h Mt 15, 27; Mk 7, 28. i 6, 24–25. j Jn 5, 46–47; 11, 44–48. k Mt 18, 6–7.

sin. [3][l]*Be on your guard! If your brother sins, rebuke him; and if he repents, forgive him. [4][m]And if he wrongs you seven times in one day and returns to you seven times saying, 'I am sorry,' you should forgive him."

Saying of Faith [5]And the apostles said to the Lord, "Increase our faith." [6][n]The Lord replied, "If you have faith the size of a mustard seed, you would say to [this] mulberry tree, 'Be uprooted and planted in the sea,' and it would obey you.

Attitude of a Servant [7]*"Who among you would say to your servant who has just come in from plowing or tending sheep in the field, 'Come here immediately and take your place at table'? [8]Would he not rather say to him, 'Prepare something for me to eat. Put on your apron and wait on me while I eat and drink. You may eat and drink when I am finished'? [9]Is he grateful to that servant because he did what was commanded? [10]So should it be with you. When you have done all you have been commanded, say, 'We are unprofitable servants; we have done what we were obliged to do.' "

The Cleansing of Ten Lepers [11][o]*As he continued his journey to Jerusalem, he traveled through Samaria and Galilee. [12]As he was entering a village, ten lepers met [him]. They stood at a distance from him [13][p]and raised their voice, saying, "Jesus, Master! Have pity on us!" [14][q]*And when he saw them, he said, "Go show yourselves to the priests." As they were going they were cleansed. [15]And one of them, realizing he had been healed, returned, glorifying God in a loud voice; [16]and he fell at the feet of Jesus and thanked him. He was a Samaritan. [17]Jesus said in reply, "Ten were cleansed, were they not? Where are the other nine? [18]Has none but this foreigner returned to give thanks to God?" [19][r]Then he said to him, "Stand up and go; your faith has saved you."

The Coming of the Kingdom of God [20][s]*Asked by the Pharisees when the kingdom of God would come, he said in reply, "The coming of the kingdom of God cannot be observed, [21][t]*and no one will announce, 'Look, here it is,' or, 'There it is.' For behold, the kingdom of God is among you."

The Day of the Son of Man [22]Then he said to his disciples, "The days will come when you will long to see one of the days of the Son of Man, but you will not see it. [23][u]There will be those who will say to you, 'Look, there he is,' [or] 'Look, here he is.' Do not go off, do not run in pursuit. [24][v]For just as lightning flashes and lights up the sky from one side to the other, so will the Son of Man be [in his day]. [25][w]But first he must suffer greatly and be rejected by this generation. [26][x]As it was in the days of Noah, so it will be in the days of the Son of Man; [27]they were eating and drinking, marrying and giving in marriage up to the day that Noah entered the ark, and the flood came and destroyed them all. [28][y]Similarly, as it was in the days of Lot: they were eating, drinking, buying, selling, planting, building; [29]on

17, 3a: Be on your guard: the translation takes v 3a as the conclusion to the saying on scandal in vv 1–2. It is not impossible that it should be taken as the beginning of the saying on forgiveness in vv 3b-4.

17, 7–10: These sayings of Jesus, peculiar to Luke, which continue his response to the apostles' request to increase their faith (5–6), remind them that Christian disciples can make no claim on God's graciousness; in fulfilling the exacting demands of discipleship, they are only doing their duty.

17, 11–19: This incident recounting the thankfulness of the cleansed Samaritan leper is narrated only in Luke's gospel and provides an instance of Jesus holding up a non-Jew (18) as an example to his Jewish contemporaries (cf 10, 33 where a similar purpose is achieved in the story of the good Samaritan). Moreover, it is the faith in Jesus manifested by the foreigner that has brought him salvation (19; cf the similar relationship between faith and salvation in 7, 50; 8, 48.50).

17, 11: Through Samaria and Galilee: or, "between Samaria and Galilee."

17, 14: See the note on 5, 14.

17, 20–37: To the question of the Pharisees about the time of the coming of God's kingdom, Jesus replies that the kingdom is **among you** (20–21). The emphasis has thus been shifted from an imminent observable coming of the kingdom to something that is already present in Jesus' preaching and healing ministry. Luke has also appended further traditional sayings of Jesus about the unpredictable suddenness of the day of the Son of Man, and assures his readers that in spite of the delay of that day (12, 45), it will bring judgment unexpectedly on those who do not continue to be vigilant.

17, 21: Among you: the Greek preposition translated as **among** can also be translated as "within." In the light of other statements in Luke's gospel about the presence of the kingdom (see 10, 9.11; 11, 20) "among" is to be preferred.

l Mt 18, 15. m Mt 6, 14; 18, 21–22.35; Mk 11, 25. n Mt 17, 20; 21, 21; Mk 11, 23. o 9, 51–53; 13, 22.33; 18, 31; 19, 28; Jn 4, 4. p 18, 38; Mt 9, 27; 15, 22. q 5, 14; Lv 14, 2–32; Mt 8, 4; Mk 1, 44. r 7, 50; 18, 42. s Jn 3, 3. t 17, 23; Mt 24, 23; Mk 13, 21. u 17, 21; Mt 24, 23.26; Mk 13, 21. v Mt 24, 27. w 9, 22; 18, 32–33; Mt 16, 21; 17, 22–23; 20, 18–19; Mk 8, 31; 9, 31; 10, 33–34. x Gn 6–8; Mt 24, 37–39. y Gn 18, 20–21; 19, 1–29.

the day when Lot left Sodom, fire and brimstone
rained from the sky to destroy them all. 30 So it
will be on the day the Son of Man is revealed.
31 [z] [a]On that day, a person who is on the house-
top and whose belongings are in the house must
not go down to get them, and likewise a person
in the field must not return to what was left
behind. 32 Remember the wife of Lot.
33 [b]Whoever seeks to preserve his life will lose it,
but whoever loses it will save it. 34 I tell you, on
that night there will be two people in one bed;
one will be taken, the other left. 35 [c]And there
will be two women grinding meal together; one
will be taken, the other left." [36]* 37 [d]They said
to him in reply, "Where, Lord?" He said to them,
"Where the body is, there also the vultures will
gather."

CHAPTER 18

The Parable of the Persistent Widow

1 [e]*Then he told them a parable about the
necessity for them to pray always without becom-
ing weary. He said, 2 "There was a judge in a
certain town who neither feared God nor re-
spected any human being. 3 And a widow in that
town used to come to him and say, 'Render a
just decision for me against my adversary.' 4 For a
long time the judge was unwilling, but eventu-
ally he thought, 'While it is true that I neither
fear God nor respect any human being,
5 [f]*because this widow keeps bothering me I
shall deliver a just decision for her lest she finally
come and strike me.' " 6 The Lord said, "Pay
attention to what the dishonest judge says. 7 Will
not God then secure the rights of his chosen
ones who call out to him day and night? Will he
be slow to answer them? 8 I tell you, he will see
to it that justice is done for them speedily. But
when the Son of Man comes, will he find faith
on earth?"

The Parable of the Pharisee and the Tax Collector

9 [g]He then addressed this parable to
those who were convinced of their own righ-
teousness and despised everyone else. 10 "Two
people went up to the temple area to pray; one
was a Pharisee and the other was a tax collector.
11 The Pharisee took up his position and spoke
this prayer to himself, 'O God, I thank you that I
am not like the rest of humanity—greedy, dis-
honest, adulterous—or even like this tax collec-
tor. 12 [h]I fast twice a week, and I pay tithes on
my whole income.' 13 [i]But the tax collector
stood off at a distance and would not even raise
his eyes to heaven but beat his breast and
prayed, 'O God, be merciful to me a sinner.' 14 [j]I
tell you, the latter went home justified, not the
former; for everyone who exalts himself will be
humbled, and the one who humbles himself will
be exalted."

Saying on Children and the Kingdom

15 [k]*People were bringing even infants to him
that he might touch them, and when the disci-
ples saw this, they rebuked them. 16 Jesus, how-
ever, called the children to himself and said, "Let
the children come to me and do not prevent
them; for the kingdom of God belongs to such as
these. 17 [l]Amen, I say to you, whoever does not
accept the kingdom of God like a child will not
enter it."

17, 36: The inclusion of v 36, "There will be two men in the field; one will be taken, the other left behind," in some Western manuscripts appears to be a scribal assimilation to Mt 24, 40.

18, 1-14: The particularly Lucan material in the travel narrative concludes with two parables on prayer. The first (1-8) teaches the disciples the need of persistent prayer so that they not fall victims to apostasy (8). The second (9-14) condemns the self-righteous, critical attitude of the Pharisee and teaches that the fundamental attitude of the Christian disciple must be the recognition of sinfulness and complete dependence on God's graciousness. The second parable recalls the story of the pardoning of the sinful woman (7, 36-50) where a similar contrast is presented between the critical attitude of the Pharisee Simon and the love shown by the pardoned sinner.

18, 5: Strike me: the Greek verb translated as **strike** means "to strike under the eye" and suggests the extreme situation to which the persistence of the widow might lead. It may, however, be used here in the much weaker sense of "to wear one out."

18, 15—19, 27: Luke here includes much of the material about the journey to Jerusalem found in his Marcan source (10, 1-52) and adds to it the story of Zacchaeus (19, 1-10) from his own particular tradition and the parable of the gold coins (minas) (19, 11-27) from Q, the source common to Lk and Mt.

18, 15-17: The sayings on children furnish a contrast to the attitude of the Pharisee in the preceding episode (9-14) and that of the wealthy official in the following one (18-23) who think that they can lay claim to God's favor by their own merit. The attitude of the disciple should be marked by the receptivity and trustful dependence characteristic of the child.

z Mt 24, 17-18; Mk 13, 15-16. a Gn 19, 17.26. b 9, 24; Mt 10, 39; 16, 25; Mk 8, 35; Jn 12, 25. c Mt 24, 40-41. d Jb 39, 30; Mt 24, 28. e Rom 12, 12; Col 4, 2; 1 Thes 5, 17. f 11, 8. g 16, 5; Mt 23, 25-28. h Mt 23, 23. i Ps 51, 3. j 14, 11; Mt 23, 12. k Mt 19, 13-15; Mk 10, 13-16. l Mt 18, 3.

The Rich Official [18][m][n]An official asked him this question, "Good teacher, what must I do to inherit eternal life?" [19]Jesus answered him, "Why do you call me good? No one is good but God alone. [20][o]You know the commandments, 'You shall not commit adultery; you shall not kill; you shall not steal; you shall not bear false witness; honor your father and your mother.' " [21]And he replied, "All of these I have observed from my youth." [22][p]*When Jesus heard this he said to him, "There is still one thing left for you: sell all that you have and distribute it to the poor, and you will have a treasure in heaven. Then come, follow me." [23]But when he heard this he became quite sad, for he was very rich.

On Riches and Renunciation [24]Jesus looked at him [now sad] and said, "How hard it is for those who have wealth to enter the kingdom of God! [25]For it is easier for a camel to pass through the eye of a needle than for a rich person to enter the kingdom of God." [26]Those who heard this said, "Then who can be saved?" [27][q]And he said, "What is impossible for human beings is possible for God." [28]Then Peter said, "We have given up our possessions and followed you." [29][r]He said to them, "Amen, I say to you, there is no one who has given up house or wife or brothers or parents or children for the sake of the kingdom of God [30]who will not receive [back] an overabundant return in this present age and eternal life in the age to come."

The Third Prediction of the Passion [31][s]*Then he took the Twelve aside and said to them, "Behold, we are going up to Jerusalem and everything written by the prophets about the Son of Man will be fulfilled. [32][t]He will be handed over to the Gentiles and he will be mocked and insulted and spat upon; [33]and after they have scourged him they will kill him, but on the third day he will rise." [34][u]But they understood nothing of this; the word remained hidden from them and they failed to comprehend what he said.

The Healing of the Blind Beggar [35][v]Now as he approached Jericho a blind man was sitting by the roadside begging, [36]and hearing a crowd going by, he inquired what was happening. [37]They told him, "Jesus of Nazareth is passing by." [38][w]*He shouted, "Jesus, Son of David, have pity on me!" [39]The people walking in front rebuked him, telling him to be silent, but he kept calling out all the more, "Son of David, have pity on me!" [40]Then Jesus stopped and ordered that he be brought to him; and when he came near, Jesus asked him, [41][x]"What do you want me to do for you?" He replied, "Lord, please let me see." [42][y]Jesus told him, "Have sight; your faith has saved you." [43]He immediately received his sight and followed him, giving glory to God. When they saw this, all the people gave praise to God.

CHAPTER 19

Zacchaeus the Tax Collector [1]*He came to Jericho and intended to pass through the town. [2]Now a man there named Zacchaeus, who was a chief tax collector and also a wealthy man, [3]was seeking to see who Jesus was; but he could not see him because of the crowd, for he was short in stature. [4]So he ran ahead and climbed a

18, 22: Detachment from material possessions results in the total dependence on God demanded of one who would inherit eternal life. **Sell all that you have:** the original saying (cf Mk 10, 21) has characteristically been made more demanding by Luke's addition of "all."

18, 31–33: The details included in this third announcement of Jesus' suffering and death suggest that the literary formulation of the announcement has been directed by the knowledge of the historical passion and death of Jesus.

18, 31: Everything written by the prophets . . . will be fulfilled: this is a Lucan addition to the words of Jesus found in the Marcan source (Mk 10, 32–34). Luke understands the events of Jesus' last days in Jerusalem to be the fulfillment of Old Testament prophecy, but, as is usually the case in Luke-Acts, the author does not specify which Old Testament prophets he has in mind; cf 24, 25.27.44; Acts 3, 8; 13, 27; 26, 22–23.

18, 38: Son of David: the blind beggar identifies Jesus with a title that is related to Jesus' role as Messiah (see the note on 2, 11). Through this Son of David, salvation comes to the blind man. Note the connection between salvation and house of David mentioned earlier in Zechariah's canticle (1, 69). See also the note on Mt 9, 27.

19, 1–10: The story of the tax collector Zacchaeus is unique to this gospel. While a rich man (2), Zacchaeus provides a contrast to the rich man of 18, 18–23 who cannot detach himself from his material possessions to become a follower of Jesus. Zacchaeus, according to Luke, exemplifies the proper attitude toward wealth: he promises to give half of his possessions to the poor (8) and consequently is the recipient of salvation (9–10).

m Mt 19, 16–30; Mk 10, 17–31. n 10, 25. o Ex 20, 12–16; Dt 5, 16–20. p 12, 33; Sir 29, 11; Mt 6, 20. q Mk 14, 36. r 14, 26. s 24, 25–27.44; Mt 20, 17–19; Mk 10, 32–34; Acts 3, 18. t 9, 22.44. u Mk 9, 32. v Mt 20, 29–34; Mk 10, 46–52. w 17, 13; Mt 9, 27; 15, 22. x Mk 10, 36. y 7, 50; 17, 19.

sycamore tree in order to see Jesus, who was about to pass that way. [5]When he reached the place, Jesus looked up and said to him, "Zacchaeus, come down quickly, for today I must stay at your house." [6]And he came down quickly and received him with joy. [7] [z]When they all saw this, they began to grumble, saying, "He has gone to stay at the house of a sinner." [8] [a]But Zacchaeus stood there and said to the Lord, "Behold, half of my possessions, Lord, I shall give to the poor, and if I have extorted anything from anyone I shall repay it four times over." [9] [b]*And Jesus said to him, "Today salvation has come to this house because this man too is a descendant of Abraham. [10] [c]*For the Son of Man has come to seek and to save what was lost."

The Parable of the Ten Gold Coins

[11] [d]*While they were listening to him speak, he proceeded to tell a parable because he was near Jerusalem and they thought that the kingdom of God would appear there immediately. [12] [e]So he said, "A nobleman went off to a distant country to obtain the kingship for himself and then to return. [13]*He called ten of his servants and gave them ten gold coins and told them, 'Engage in trade with these until I return.' [14]His fellow citizens, however, despised him and sent a delegation after him to announce, 'We do not want this man to be our king.' [15]But when he returned after obtaining the kingship, he had the servants called, to whom he had given the money, to learn what they had gained by trading. [16]The first came forward and said, 'Sir, your gold coin has earned ten additional ones.' [17] [f]He replied, 'Well done, good servant! You have been faithful in this very small matter; take charge of ten cities.' [18]Then the second came and reported, 'Your gold coin, sir, has earned five more.' [19]And to this servant too he said, 'You, take charge of five cities.' [20]Then the other servant came and said, 'Sir, here is your gold coin; I kept it stored away in a handkerchief, [21]for I was afraid of you, because you are a demanding person; you take up what you did not lay down and you harvest what you did not plant.' [22]He said to him, 'With your own words I shall condemn you, you wicked servant. You knew I was a demanding person, taking up what I did not lay down and harvesting what I did not plant; [23]why did you not put my money in a bank? Then on my return I would have collected it with interest.' [24]And to those standing by he said, 'Take the gold coin from him and give it to the servant who has ten.' [25]But they said to him, 'Sir, he has ten gold coins.' [26] [g]'I tell you, to everyone who has, more will be given, but from the one who has not, even what he has will be taken away. [27]Now as for those enemies of mine who did not want me as their king, bring them here and slay them before me.' "

VI: The Teaching Ministry in Jerusalem

The Entry into Jerusalem [28] [h]*After he had said this, he proceeded on his journey up to

19, 9: **A descendant of Abraham:** literally, "a son of Abraham." The tax collector Zacchaeus, whose repentance is attested by his determination to amend his former ways, shows himself to be a true descendant of Abraham, the true heir to the promises of God in the Old Testament. Underlying Luke's depiction of Zacchaeus as a descendant of Abraham, the father of the Jews (1, 73; 16, 22–31), is his recognition of the central place occupied by Israel in the plan of salvation.

19, 10: This verse sums up for Luke his depiction of the role of Jesus as savior in this gospel.

19, 11–27: In this parable Luke has combined two originally distinct parables: (1) a parable about the conduct of faithful and productive servants (13.15b-26) and (2) a parable about a rejected king (12.14–15a.27). The story about the conduct of servants occurs in another form in Mt 25, 14–20. The story about the rejected king may have originated with a contemporary historical event. After the death of Herod the Great, his son Archelaus traveled to Rome to receive the title of king. A delegation of Jews appeared in Rome before Caesar Augustus to oppose the request of Archelaus. Although not given the title of king, Archelaus was made ruler over Judea and Samaria. As the story is used by Luke, however, it furnishes a correction to the expectation of the imminent end of the age and of the establishment of the kingdom in Jerusalem (11). Jesus is not on his way to Jerusalem to receive the kingly power; for that, he must go away and only after returning from the distant country (a reference to the parousia) will reward and judgment take place.

19, 13: **Ten gold coins:** literally, "ten minas." A mina was a monetary unit that in ancient Greece was the equivalent of one hundred drachmas.

19, 28—21, 38: With the royal entry of Jesus into Jerusalem, a new section of Luke's gospel begins, the ministry of Jesus in Jerusalem before his death and resurrection. Luke suggests that this was a lengthy ministry in Jerusalem (19, 47; 20, 1; 21, 37–38; 22, 53) and it is characterized by Jesus' daily teaching in the temple (21, 37–38). For the story of the entry of Jesus into Jerusalem, see also Mt 21, 1–11; Mk 11, 1–10; Jn 12, 12–19 and the notes there.

z 5, 30; 15, 2. a Ex 21, 37; Nm 5, 6–7; 2 Sm 12, 6. b 13, 16; Mt 21, 31. c 15, 4–10; Ez 34, 16. d Mt 25, 14–30. e Mk 13, 34. f 16, 10. g 8, 18; Mt 13, 12; Mk 4, 25. h Mt 21, 1–11; Mk 11, 1–11; Jn 12, 12–19.

Jerusalem. 29 [i]As he drew near to Bethphage
and Bethany at the place called the Mount of
Olives, he sent two of his disciples. 30 [j]He said,
"Go into the village opposite you, and as you
enter it you will find a colt tethered on which
no one has ever sat. Untie it and bring it here.
31 And if anyone should ask you, 'Why are you
untying it?' you will answer, 'The Master has
need of it.' " 32 [k]So those who had been sent
went off and found everything just as he had
told them. 33 And as they were untying the colt,
its owners said to them, "Why are you untying
this colt?" 34 They answered, "The Master has
need of it." 35 [l]So they brought it to Jesus,
threw their cloaks over the colt, and helped
Jesus to mount. 36 As he rode along, the people
were spreading their cloaks on the road; 37 and
now as he was approaching the slope of the
Mount of Olives, the whole multitude of his
disciples began to praise God aloud with joy for
all the mighty deeds they had seen. 38 [m]*They
proclaimed:

"Blessed is the king who comes
in the name of the Lord.
Peace in heaven
and glory in the highest."

39 *Some of the Pharisees in the crowd said to
him, "Teacher, rebuke your disciples." 40 He said
in reply, "I tell you, if they keep silent, the stones
will cry out!"

The Lament for Jerusalem 41 [n o]*As he drew
near, he saw the city and wept over it, 42 [p]saying,
"If this day you only knew what makes for
peace—but now it is hidden from your eyes.
43 [q]*For the days are coming upon you when
your enemies will raise a palisade against you;
they will encircle you and hem you in on all
sides. 44 [r]They will smash you to the ground and
your children within you, and they will not leave
one stone upon another within you because you
did not recognize the time of your visitation."

The Cleansing of the Temple 45 [s t]*Then Je-
sus entered the temple area and proceeded to
drive out those who were selling things,
46 [u]saying to them, "It is written, 'My house shall
be a house of prayer, but you have made it a den
of thieves.' " 47 [v w]And every day he was teach-
ing in the temple area. The chief priests, the
scribes, and the leaders of the people, mean-
while, were seeking to put him to death, 48 but
they could find no way to accomplish their
purpose because all the people were hanging on
his words.

CHAPTER 20

The Authority of Jesus Questioned 1 [x]*One
day as he was teaching the people in the temple
area and proclaiming the good news, the chief
priests and scribes, together with the elders,
approached him 2 [y]and said to him, "Tell us, by
what authority are you doing these things? Or

19, 38: Blessed is the king who comes in the name of the Lord: only in Lk is Jesus explicitly given the title **king** when he enters Jerusalem in triumph. Luke has inserted this title into the words of Ps 118, 26 that heralded the arrival of the pilgrims coming to the holy city and to the temple. Jesus is thereby acclaimed as **king** (see 1, 32) and as the one **who comes** (see Mal 3, 1; Lk 7, 19). **Peace in heaven . . .** : the acclamation of the disciples of Jesus in Lk echoes the announcement of the angels at the birth of Jesus (2, 14). The peace Jesus brings is associated with the salvation to be accomplished here in Jerusalem.

19, 39: Rebuke your disciples: this command, found only in Lk, was given so that the Roman authorities would not interpret the acclamation of Jesus as king as an uprising against them; cf 23, 2–3.

19, 41–44: The lament for Jerusalem is found only in Lk. By not accepting Jesus (the one who mediates peace), Jerusalem will not find peace but will become the victim of devastation.

19, 43–44: Luke may be describing the actual disaster that befell Jerusalem in A.D. 70 when it was destroyed by the Romans during the First Revolt.

19, 45–46: Immediately upon entering the holy city, Jesus in a display of his authority enters the temple (see Mal 3, 1–3) and lays claim to it after cleansing it that it might become a proper place for his teaching ministry in Jerusalem (19, 47; 20, 1; 21, 37; 22, 53). See Mt 21, 12–17; Mk 11, 15–19; Jn 2, 13–17 and the notes there.

20, 1–47: The Jerusalem religious leaders or their representatives, in an attempt to incriminate Jesus with the Romans and to discredit him with the people, pose a number of questions to him (about his authority, 2; about payment of taxes, 22; about the resurrection, 28–33).

i Zec 14, 4. j Nm 19, 2; Dt 21, 3, 1 Sm 6, 7; Zec 9, 9. k 22, 13. l 2 Kgs 9, 13. m 2, 14; Ps 118, 26. n 13, 34–35. o 2 Kgs 8, 11–12; Jer 14, 17; 15, 5. p 8, 10; Is 6, 9–10; Mt 13, 14; Mk 4, 12; Acts 28, 26–27; Rom 11, 8.10. q Is 29, 3. r 1, 68; 21, 6; Ps 137, 9; Mt 24, 2; Mk 13, 2. s Mt 21, 12–13; Mk 11, 15–17; Jn 2, 13–17. t 3, 1 / Hos 9, 15. u Is 56, 7; Jer 7, 11. v 20, 19; 22, 2; Mt 21, 46; Mk 11, 18; 12, 12; 14, 1–2; Jn 5, 18; 7, 30. w 21, 37; 22, 53; Jn 18, 20. x Mt 21, 23–27; Mk 11, 27–33. y Acts 4, 7.

who is the one who gave you this authority?" 3 He said to them in reply, "I shall ask you a question. Tell me, 4 [z]was John's baptism of heavenly or of human origin?" 5 [a]They discussed this among themselves, and said, "If we say, 'Of heavenly origin,' he will say, 'Why did you not believe him?' 6 But if we say, 'Of human origin,' then all the people will stone us, for they are convinced that John was a prophet." 7 So they answered that they did not know from where it came. 8 Then Jesus said to them, "Neither shall I tell you by what authority I do these things."

The Parable of the Tenant Farmers

9 [b c]*Then he proceeded to tell the people this parable. "[A] man planted a vineyard, leased it to tenant farmers, and then went on a journey for a long time. 10 [d]At harvest time he sent a servant to the tenant farmers to receive some of the produce of the vineyard. But they beat the servant and sent him away empty-handed. 11 So he proceeded to send another servant, but him also they beat and insulted and sent away empty-handed. 12 Then he proceeded to send a third, but this one too they wounded and threw out. 13 [e]The owner of the vineyard said, 'What shall I do? I shall send my beloved son; maybe they will respect him.' 14 But when the tenant farmers saw him they said to one another, 'This is the heir. Let us kill him that the inheritance may become ours.' 15 *So they threw him out of the vineyard and killed him. What will the owner of the vineyard do to them? 16 He will come and put those tenant farmers to death and turn over the vineyard to others." When the people heard this, they exclaimed, "Let it not be so!" 17 [f]But he looked at them and asked, "What then does this scripture passage mean:

'The stone which the builders rejected
has become the cornerstone'?

18 Everyone who falls on that stone will be dashed to pieces; and it will crush anyone on whom it falls." 19 [g]The scribes and chief priests sought to lay their hands on him at that very hour, but they feared the people, for they knew that he had addressed this parable to them.

Paying Taxes to the Emperor

20 [h i]*They watched him closely and sent agents pretending to be righteous who were to trap him in speech, in order to hand him over to the authority and power of the governor. 21 [j]They posed this question to him, "Teacher, we know that what you say and teach is correct, and you show no partiality, but teach the way of God in accordance with the truth. 22 *Is it lawful for us to pay tribute to Caesar or not?" 23 Recognizing their craftiness he said to them, 24 *"Show me a denarius; whose image and name does it bear?" They replied, "Caesar's." 25 [k]So he said to them, "Then repay to Caesar what belongs to Caesar and to God what belongs to God." 26 They were unable to trap him by something he might say before the people, and so amazed were they at his reply that they fell silent.

The Question about the Resurrection

27 [l m]*Some Sadducees, those who deny that there is a resurrection, came forward and put this question to him, 28 [n]*saying, "Teacher, Mo-

20, 9–19: This parable about an absentee landlord and a tenant farmers' revolt reflects the social and economic conditions of rural Palestine in the first century. The synoptic gospel writers use the parable to describe how the rejection of the landlord's son becomes the occasion for the vineyard to be taken away from those to whom it was entrusted (the religious leadership of Judaism that rejects the teaching and preaching of Jesus; 19).

20, 15: They threw him out of the vineyard and killed him: cf Mk 12, 8. Luke has altered his Marcan source and reports that the murder of the son takes place outside the vineyard to reflect the tradition of Jesus' death outside the walls of the city of Jerusalem (see Heb 13, 12).

20, 20: The governor: i.e., Pontius Pilate, the Roman administrator responsible for the collection of taxes and maintenance of order in Palestine.

20, 22: Through their question the agents of the Jerusalem religious leadership hope to force Jesus to take sides on one of the sensitive political issues of first-century Palestine. The issue of nonpayment of taxes to Rome becomes one of the focal points of the First Jewish Revolt (A.D. 66–70) that resulted in the Roman destruction of Jerusalem and the temple. See also the note on Mt 22, 15–22.

20, 24: Denarius: a Roman silver coin (see the note on 7, 41).

20, 27: Sadducees: see the note on Mt 3, 7.

20, 28–33: The Sadducees' question, based on the law of levirate marriage recorded in Dt 25, 5–10, ridicules the idea of the resurrection. Jesus rejects their naive understanding of the resurrection (35–36) and then argues on behalf of the resurrection of the dead on the basis of the written law (37–38) that the Sadducees accept. See also the notes on Mt 22, 23–33.

z 3, 3.16. a Mt 21, 32. b Mt 21, 33–46; Mk 12, 1–12. c Is 5, 1–7. d 2 Chr 36, 15–16. e 3, 22. f Ps 118, 22; Is 28, 16. g 19, 47–48; 22, 2; Mt 21, 46; Mk 11, 18; 12, 12; 14, 1–2; Jn 5, 18; 7, 30. h Mt 22, 15–22; Mk 12, 13–17. i 11, 54. j Jn 3, 2. k Rom 13, 6–7. l Mt 22, 23–33; Mk 12, 18–27. m Acts 23, 8. n Gn 38, 8; Dt 25, 5.

ses wrote for us, 'If someone's brother dies leaving a wife but no child, his brother must take the wife and raise up descendants for his brother.' 29 Now there were seven brothers; the first married a woman but died childless. 30 Then the second 31 and the third married her, and likewise all the seven died childless. 32 Finally the woman also died. 33 Now at the resurrection whose wife will that woman be? For all seven had been married to her." 34 Jesus said to them, "The children of this age marry and remarry; 35 but those who are deemed worthy to attain to the coming age and to the resurrection of the dead neither marry nor are given in marriage. 36 *They can no longer die, for they are like angels; and they are the children of God because they are the ones who will rise. 37 [o]That the dead will rise even Moses made known in the passage about the bush, when he called 'Lord' the God of Abraham, the God of Isaac, and the God of Jacob; 38 [p]and he is not God of the dead, but of the living, for to him all are alive." 39 Some of the scribes said in reply, "Teacher, you have answered well." 40 [q]And they no longer dared to ask him anything.

The Question about David's Son 41 [r]*Then he said to them, "How do they claim that the Messiah is the Son of David? 42 [s]For David himself in the Book of Psalms says:

'The Lord said to my lord,
"Sit at my right hand
43 till I make your enemies your footstool." '

44 Now if David calls him 'lord,' how can he be his son?"

Denunciation of the Scribes 45 [t]Then, within the hearing of all the people, he said to [his] disciples, 46 [u]"Be on guard against the scribes, who like to go around in long robes and love greetings in marketplaces, seats of honor in synagogues, and places of honor at banquets. 47 They devour the houses of widows and, as a pretext, recite lengthy prayers. They will receive a very severe condemnation."

CHAPTER 21

The Poor Widow's Contribution 1 [v]*When he looked up he saw some wealthy people putting their offerings into the treasury 2 and he noticed a poor widow putting in two small coins. 3 He said, "I tell you truly, this poor widow put in more than all the rest; 4 for those others have all made offerings from their surplus wealth, but she, from her poverty, has offered her whole livelihood."

The Destruction of the Temple Foretold 5 [w]*While some people were speaking about how the temple was adorned with costly stones and votive offerings, he said, 6 [x]"All that you see here—the days will come when there will not be left a stone upon another stone that will not be thrown down."

The Signs of the End 7 [y]Then they asked him, "Teacher, when will this happen? And what sign will there be when all these things are about to happen?" 8 [z]*He answered, "See that you not be

20, 36: Because they are the ones who will rise: literally, "being sons of the resurrection."

20, 41–44: After successfully answering the three questions of his opponents, Jesus now asks them a question. Their inability to respond implies that they have forfeited their position and authority as the religious leaders of the people because they do not understand the scriptures. This series of controversies between the religious leadership of Jerusalem and Jesus reveals Jesus as the authoritative teacher whose words are to be listened to (see 9, 35). See also the notes on Mt 22, 41–46.

21, 1–4: The widow is another example of the poor ones in this gospel whose detachment from material possessions and dependence on God leads to their blessedness (6, 20). Her simple offering provides a striking contrast to the pride and pretentiousness of the scribes denounced in the preceding section (20, 45–47). The story is taken from Mk 12, 41–44.

21, 5–36: Jesus' eschatological discourse in Lk is inspired by Mk 13, but Luke has made some significant alterations to the words of Jesus found there. Luke maintains, though in a modified form, the belief in the early expectation of the end of the age (see 27.28. 31.32.36), but, by focusing attention throughout the gospel on the importance of the day-to-day following of Jesus and by reinterpreting the meaning of some of the signs of the end from Mk 13, he has come to terms with what seemed to the early Christian community to be a delay of the parousia. Mark, for example, described the desecration of the Jerusalem temple by the Romans (Mk 13, 14) as the apocalyptic symbol (see Dn 9, 27; 12, 11) accompanying the end of the age and the coming of the Son of Man. Luke (21, 20–24), however, removes the apocalyptic setting and separates the historical destruction of Jerusalem from the signs of the coming of the Son of Man by a period that he refers to as "the times of the Gentiles" (21, 24). See also the notes on Mt 24, 1–36 and Mk 13, 1–37.

21, 8: The time has come: in Lk, the proclamation of the imminent end of the age has itself become a false teaching.

o Ex 3, 2.6.15–16. p Rom 14, 8–9. q Mt 22, 46; Mk 12, 34. r Mt 22, 41–45; Mk 12, 35–37. s Ps 110, 1. t 11, 37–54; Mt 23, 1–36; Mk 12, 38–40. u 14, 7–11. v Mk 12, 41–44. w Mt 24, 1–2; Mk 13, 1–2. x 19, 44. y Mt 24, 3–14; Mk 13, 3–13. z 17, 23; Mk 13, 5.6.21; 1 Jn 2, 18.

deceived, for many will come in my name, saying, 'I am he,' and 'The time has come.' Do not follow them! 9 When you hear of wars and insurrections, do not be terrified; for such things must happen first, but it will not immediately be the end." 10 [a] Then he said to them, "Nation will rise against nation, and kingdom against kingdom. 11 There will be powerful earthquakes, famines, and plagues from place to place; and awesome sights and mighty signs will come from the sky.

The Coming Persecution 12 [b c] * "Before all this happens, however, they will seize and persecute you, they will hand you over to the synagogues and to prisons, and they will have you led before kings and governors because of my name. 13 It will lead to your giving testimony. 14 Remember, you are not to prepare your defense beforehand, 15 [d] * for I myself shall give you a wisdom in speaking that all your adversaries will be powerless to resist or refute. 16 [e f] You will even be handed over by parents, brothers, relatives, and friends, and they will put some of you to death. 17 You will be hated by all because of my name, 18 [g] but not a hair on your head will be destroyed. 19 [h] By your perseverance you will secure your lives.

The Great Tribulation 20 [i j] * "When you see Jerusalem surrounded by armies, know that its desolation is at hand. 21 [k] Then those in Judea must flee to the mountains. Let those within the city escape from it, and let those in the countryside not enter the city, 22 for these days are the time of punishment when all the scriptures are fulfilled. 23 [l] Woe to pregnant women and nursing mothers in those days, for a terrible calamity will come upon the earth and a wrathful judgment upon this people. 24 [m] * They will fall by the edge of the sword and be taken as captives to all the Gentiles; and Jerusalem will be trampled underfoot by the Gentiles until the times of the Gentiles are fulfilled.

The Coming of the Son of Man 25 [n o] "There will be signs in the sun, the moon, and the stars, and on earth nations will be in dismay, perplexed by the roaring of the sea and the waves. 26 [p] * People will die of fright in anticipation of what is coming upon the world, for the powers of the heavens will be shaken. 27 [q] And then they will see the Son of Man coming in a cloud with power and great glory. 28 [r] But when these signs begin to happen, stand erect and raise your heads because your redemption is at hand."

The Lesson of the Fig Tree 29 [s] He taught them a lesson. "Consider the fig tree and all the other trees. 30 When their buds burst open, you see for yourselves and know that summer is now near; 31 in the same way, when you see these things happening, know that the kingdom of God is near. 32 [t] Amen, I say to you, this generation will not pass away until all these things have taken place. 33 [u] Heaven and earth will pass away, but my words will not pass away.

Exhortation to be Vigilant 34 [v] "Beware that your hearts do not become drowsy from carousing and drunkenness and the anxieties of daily life, and that day catch you by surprise 35 like a trap. For that day will assault everyone who lives on the face of the earth. 36 [w] Be vigilant at all times and pray that you have the strength to escape the tribulations that are imminent and to stand before the Son of Man."

Ministry in Jerusalem 37 [x] During the day, Jesus was teaching in the temple area, but at night

21, 12: Before all this happens . . . : to Luke and his community, some of the signs of the end just described (10–11) still lie in the future. Now in dealing with the persecution of the disciples (12–19) and the destruction of Jerusalem (20–24) Luke is pointing to eschatological signs that have already been fulfilled.

21, 15: A wisdom in speaking: literally, "a mouth and wisdom."

21, 20–24: The actual destruction of Jerusalem by Rome in A.D. 70 upon which Luke and his community look back provides the assurance that, just as Jesus' prediction of Jerusalem's destruction was fulfilled, so too will be his announcement of their final redemption (27–28).

21, 24: The times of the Gentiles: a period of indeterminate length separating the destruction of Jerusalem from the cosmic signs accompanying the coming of the Son of Man.

21, 26: The powers of the heavens: the heavenly bodies mentioned in v 25 and thought of as cosmic armies.

a 2 Chr 15, 6; Is 19, 2. b 12, 11–12; Mt 10, 17–20; Mk 13, 9–11. c Jn 16, 2; Acts 25, 24. d Acts 6, 10. e Mt 10, 21–22. f 12, 52–53. g 12, 7; 1 Sm 14, 45; Mt 10, 30; Acts 27, 34. h 8, 15. i Mt 24, 15–21; Mk 13, 14–19. j 19, 41–44. k 17, 31. l 1 Cor 7, 26. m Tb 14, 5; Ps 79, 1; Is 63, 18; Jer 21, 7; Rom 11, 25; Rv 11, 2. n Mt 24, 29–31; Mk 13, 24–27. o Wis 5, 22; Is 13, 10; Ez 32, 7; Jl 2, 10; 3, 3–4; 4, 15; Rv 6, 12–14. p Hg 2, 6.21. q Dn 7, 13–14; Mt 26, 64; Rv 1, 7. r 2, 38. s Mt 24, 32–35; Mk 13, 28–31. t 9, 27; Mt 16, 28. u 16, 17. v 12, 45–46; Mt 24, 48–50; 1 Thes 5, 3.6–7. w Mk 13, 33. x 19, 47; 22, 39.

he would leave and stay at the place called the Mount of Olives. 38 And all the people would get up early each morning to listen to him in the temple area.

VII: The Passion Narrative

CHAPTER 22

The Conspiracy against Jesus 1 [y]*Now the feast of Unleavened Bread, called the Passover, was drawing near, 2 [z]and the chief priests and the scribes were seeking a way to put him to death, for they were afraid of the people. 3 [a] [b]*Then Satan entered into Judas, the one surnamed Iscariot, who was counted among the Twelve, 4 and he went to the chief priests and temple guards to discuss a plan for handing him over to them. 5 They were pleased and agreed to pay him money. 6 He accepted their offer and sought a favorable opportunity to hand him over to them in the absence of a crowd.

Preparations for the Passover 7 [c] [d]When the day of the Feast of Unleavened Bread arrived, the day for sacrificing the Passover lamb, 8 he sent out Peter and John, instructing them, "Go and make preparations for us to eat the Passover." 9 They asked him, "Where do you want us to make the preparations?" 10 *And he answered them, "When you go into the city, a man will meet you carrying a jar of water. Follow him into the house that he enters 11 and say to the master of the house, 'The teacher says to you, "Where is the guest room where I may eat the Passover with my disciples?" ' 12 He will show you a large upper room that is furnished. Make the preparations there." 13 [e]Then they went off and found everything exactly as he had told them, and there they prepared the Passover.

The Last Supper 14 [f]When the hour came, he took his place at table with the apostles. 15 *He said to them, "I have eagerly desired to eat this Passover with you before I suffer, 16 [g]for, I tell you, I shall not eat it [again] until there is fulfillment in the kingdom of God." 17 *Then he took a cup, gave thanks, and said, "Take this and share it among yourselves; 18 for I tell you [that] from this time on I shall not drink of the fruit of the vine until the kingdom of God comes." 19 [h]*Then he took the bread, said the blessing, broke it, and gave it to them, saying, "This is my body, which will be given for you; do this in memory of me." 20 [i]And likewise the cup after they had eaten, saying, "This cup is the new covenant in my blood, which will be shed for you.

The Betrayal Foretold 21 [j]"And yet behold, the hand of the one who is to betray me is with me on the table; 22 for the Son of Man indeed goes as it has been determined; but woe to that man by whom he is betrayed." 23 And they began

22, 1—23, 56a: The passion narrative. Luke is still dependent upon Mk for the composition of the passion narrative but has incorporated much of his own special tradition into the narrative. Among the distinctive sections in Lk are: (1) the tradition of the institution of the Eucharist (22, 15–20); (2) Jesus' farewell discourse (22, 21–38); (3) the mistreatment and interrogation of Jesus (22, 63–71); (4) Jesus before Herod and his second appearance before Pilate (23, 6–16); (5) words addressed to the women followers on the way to the crucifixion (23, 27–32); (6) words to the penitent thief (23, 39–41); (7) the death of Jesus (23, 46.47b-49). Luke stresses the innocence of Jesus (23, 4.14–15.22) who is the victim of the powers of evil (22, 3.31.53) and who goes to his death in fulfillment of his Father's will (22, 42.46). Throughout the narrative Luke emphasizes the mercy, compassion, and healing power of Jesus (22, 51; 23, 43) who does not go to death lonely and deserted, but is accompanied by others who follow him on the way of the cross (23, 26–31.49).

22, 1: Feast of Unleavened Bread, called the Passover: see the note on Mk 14, 1.

22, 3: Satan entered into Judas: see the note on 4, 13.

22, 10: A man will meet you carrying a jar of water: see the note on Mk 14, 13.

22, 15: This Passover: Luke clearly identifies this last supper of Jesus with the apostles as a Passover meal that commemorated the deliverance of the Israelites from slavery in Egypt. Jesus reinterprets the significance of the Passover by setting it in the context of the kingdom of God (16). The "deliverance" associated with the Passover finds its new meaning in the blood that will be shed (20).

22, 17: Because of a textual problem in vv 19 and 20, some commentators interpret this cup as the eucharistic cup.

22, 19c-20: Which will be given . . . do this in memory of me: these words are omitted in some important Western text manuscripts and a few Syriac manuscripts. Other ancient text types, including the oldest papyrus manuscript of Lk dating from the late second or early third century, contain the longer reading presented here. The Lucan account of the words of institution of the Eucharist bears a close resemblance to the words of institution in the Pauline tradition (see 1 Cor 11, 23–26). See also the notes on Mt 26, 26–29; 26, 27–28; and Mk 14, 22–24.

y Mt 26, 1–5; Mk 14, 1–2; Jn 11, 47–53. z 19, 47–48; 20, 19; Mt 21, 46; Mk 12, 12; Jn 5, 18; 7, 30. a Mt 26, 14–16; Mk 14, 10–11; Jn 13, 2.27. b Acts 1, 17. c Mt 26, 17–19; Mk 14, 12–16. d Ex 12, 6.14–20. e 19, 32. f Mt 26, 20.26–30; Mk 14, 17.22–26; 1 Cor 11, 23–25. g 13, 29. h 24, 30; Acts 27, 35. i Ex 24, 8; Jer 31, 31; 32, 40; Zec 9, 11. j Ps 41, 10; Mt 26, 21–25; Mk 14, 18–21; Jn 13, 21–30.

to debate among themselves who among them would do such a deed.

The Role of the Disciples 24 [k]*Then an argument broke out among them about which of them should be regarded as the greatest. 25 [l]*He said to them, "The kings of the Gentiles lord it over them and those in authority over them are addressed as 'Benefactors'; 26 [m]but among you it shall not be so. Rather, let the greatest among you be as the youngest, and the leader as the servant. 27 For who is greater: the one seated at table or the one who serves? Is it not the one seated at table? I am among you as the one who serves. 28 It is you who have stood by me in my trials; 29 [n]and I confer a kingdom on you, just as my Father has conferred one on me, 30 [o]that you may eat and drink at my table in my kingdom; and you will sit on thrones judging the twelve tribes of Israel.

Peter's Denial Foretold 31 [p] [q]*"Simon, Simon, behold Satan has demanded to sift all of you like wheat, 32 but I have prayed that your own faith may not fail; and once you have turned back, you must strengthen your brothers." 33 [r]He said to him, "Lord, I am prepared to go to prison and to die with you." 34 [s]But he replied, "I tell you, Peter, before the cock crows this day, you will deny three times that you know me."

Instructions for the Time of Crisis 35 [t]He said to them, "When I sent you forth without a money bag or a sack or sandals, were you in need of anything?" "No, nothing," they replied. 36 [u]*He said to them, "But now one who has a money bag should take it, and likewise a sack, and one who does not have a sword should sell his cloak and buy one. 37 [v]For I tell you that this scripture must be fulfilled in me, namely, 'He was counted among the wicked'; and indeed what is written about me is coming to fulfillment." 38 *Then they said, "Lord, look, there are two swords here." But he replied, "It is enough!"

The Agony in the Garden 39 [w]Then going out he went, as was his custom, to the Mount of Olives, and the disciples followed him. 40 [x]When he arrived at the place he said to them, "Pray that you may not undergo the test." 41 [y]After withdrawing about a stone's throw from them and kneeling, he prayed, 42 [z]saying, "Father, if you are willing, take this cup away from me; still, not my will but yours be done." [43 *And to strengthen him an angel from heaven appeared to him. 44 He was in such agony and he prayed so fervently that his sweat became like drops of blood falling on the ground.] 45 When he rose from prayer and returned to his disciples, he found them sleeping from grief. 46 [a]He said to them, "Why are you sleeping? Get up and pray that you may not undergo the test."

The Betrayal and Arrest of Jesus 47 [b]While he was still speaking, a crowd approached and in front was one of the Twelve, a man named Judas. He went up to Jesus to kiss him. 48 Jesus said to him, "Judas, are you betraying the Son of Man with a kiss?" 49 [c]His disciples realized what was about to happen, and they asked, "Lord, shall we strike with a sword?" 50 [d]And one of them struck the high priest's servant and cut off his right ear. 51 *But Jesus said in reply, "Stop, no more of this!" Then he touched the servant's ear

22, 24–38: The Gospel of Luke presents a brief farewell discourse of Jesus; compare the lengthy farewell discourses and prayer in Jn, chs 13–17.

22, 25: 'Benefactors': this word occurs as a title of rulers in the Hellenistic world.

22, 31: All of you: literally, "you." The translation reflects the meaning of the Greek text that uses a second person plural pronoun here.

22, 31–32: Jesus' prayer for Simon's faith and the commission to strengthen his brothers anticipates the post-resurrectional prominence of Peter in the first half of Acts, where he appears as the spokesman for the Christian community and the one who begins the mission to the Gentiles (Acts 10—11).

22, 36: In contrast to the ministry of the Twelve and of the seventy-two during the period of Jesus (9, 3; 10, 4), in the future period of the church the missionaries must be prepared for the opposition they will face in a world hostile to their preaching.

22, 38: It is enough!: the farewell discourse ends abruptly with these words of Jesus spoken to the disciples when they take literally what was intended as figurative language about being prepared to face the world's hostility.

22, 43–44: These verses, though very ancient, were probably not part of the original text of Lk. They are absent from the oldest papyrus manuscripts of Lk and from manuscripts of wide geographical distribution.

22, 51: And healed him: only Luke recounts this healing of the injured servant.

k 9, 46; Mt 18, 1; Mk 9, 34. l Mt 20, 25–27; Mk 10, 42–44; Jn 13, 3–16. m Mt 23, 11; Mk 9, 35. n 12, 32. o Mt 19, 28. p Mt 26, 33–35; Mk 14, 29–31; Jn 13, 37–38. q Jb 1, 6–12; Am 9, 9. r 22, 54. s 22, 54–62. t 9, 3; 10, 4; Mt 10, 9–10; Mk 6, 7–9. u 22, 49. v Is 53, 12. w Mt 26, 30.36–46; Mk 14, 26.32–42; Jn 18, 1–2. x 22, 46. y Heb 5, 7–8. z Mt 6, 10. a 22, 40. b Mt 26, 47–56; Mk 14, 43–50; Jn 18, 3–4. c 22, 36. d Jn 18, 26.

and healed him. 52 [e]And Jesus said to the chief priests and temple guards and elders who had come for him, "Have you come out as against a robber, with swords and clubs? 53 [f]Day after day I was with you in the temple area, and you did not seize me; but this is your hour, the time for the power of darkness."

Peter's Denial of Jesus 54 [g h]After arresting him they led him away and took him into the house of the high priest; Peter was following at a distance. 55 They lit a fire in the middle of the courtyard and sat around it, and Peter sat down with them. 56 When a maid saw him seated in the light, she looked intently at him and said, "This man too was with him." 57 But he denied it saying, "Woman, I do not know him." 58 A short while later someone else saw him and said, "You too are one of them"; but Peter answered, "My friend, I am not." 59 About an hour later, still another insisted, "Assuredly, this man too was with him, for he also is a Galilean." 60 But Peter said, "My friend, I do not know what you are talking about." Just as he was saying this, the cock crowed, 61 [i]*and the Lord turned and looked at Peter; and Peter remembered the word of the Lord, how he had said to him, "Before the cock crows today, you will deny me three times." 62 He went out and began to weep bitterly. 63 [j]The men who held Jesus in custody were ridiculing and beating him. 64 They blindfolded him and questioned him, saying, "Prophesy! Who is it that struck you?" 65 And they reviled him in saying many other things against him.

Jesus before the Sanhedrin 66 [k l]*When day came the council of elders of the people met, both chief priests and scribes, and they brought him before their Sanhedrin. 67 [m]They said, "If you are the Messiah, tell us," but he replied to them, "If I tell you, you will not believe, 68 and if I question, you will not respond. 69 [n]But from this time on the Son of Man will be seated at the right hand of the power of God." 70 They all asked, "Are you then the Son of God?" He replied to them, "You say that I am." 71 Then they said, "What further need have we for testimony? We have heard it from his own mouth."

CHAPTER 23

Jesus before Pilate 1 [o]*Then the whole assembly of them arose and brought him before Pilate. 2 [p]They brought charges against him, saying, "We found this man misleading our people; he opposes the payment of taxes to Caesar and maintains that he is the Messiah, a king." 3 [q]Pilate asked him, "Are you the king of the Jews?" He said to him in reply, "You say so." 4 [r]Pilate then addressed the chief priests and the crowds, "I find this man not guilty." 5 But they were adamant and said, "He is inciting the people with his teaching throughout all Judea, from Galilee where he began even to here."

Jesus before Herod 6 *On hearing this Pilate asked if the man was a Galilean; 7 [s]and upon learning that he was under Herod's jurisdiction, he sent him to Herod who was in Jerusalem at that time. 8 [t]Herod was very glad to see Jesus; he

22, 61: Only Luke recounts that **the Lord turned and looked at Peter.** This look of Jesus leads to Peter's weeping bitterly over his denial (62).

22, 66–71: Luke recounts one daytime trial of Jesus (66–71) and hints at some type of preliminary nighttime investigation (54–65). Mark (and Matthew who follows Mk) has transferred incidents of this day into the nighttime interrogation with the result that there appear to be two Sanhedrin trials of Jesus in Mk (and Mt); see the note on Mk 14, 53.

22, 66: Sanhedrin: the word is a Hebraized form of a Greek word meaning a "council," and refers to the elders, chief priests, and scribes who met under the high priest's leadership to decide religious and legal questions that did not pertain to Rome's interests. Jewish sources are not clear on the competence of the Sanhedrin to sentence and to execute during this period.

23, 1–5.13–25: Twice Jesus is brought before Pilate in Luke's account, and each time Pilate explicitly declares Jesus innocent of any wrongdoing (4.14.22). This stress on the innocence of Jesus before the Roman authorities is also characteristic of John's gospel (Jn 18, 38; 19, 4.6). Luke presents the Jerusalem Jewish leaders as the ones who force the hand of the Roman authorities (1–2.5.10.13.18.21.23–25).

23, 6–12: The appearance of Jesus before Herod is found only in this gospel. Herod has been an important figure in Lk (9, 7–9; 13, 31–33) and has been presented as someone who has been curious about Jesus for a long time. His curiosity goes unrewarded. It is faith in Jesus, not curiosity, that is rewarded (7, 50; 8, 48.50; 17, 19).

e 22, 37. f 19, 47; 21, 37; Jn 7, 30; 8, 20; Col 1, 13. g Mt 26, 57–58.69–75; Mk 14, 53–54.66–72; Jn 18, 12–18.25–27. h 22, 33. i 22, 34. j Mt 26, 67–68; Mk 14, 65. k Mt 26, 59–66; Mk 14, 55–64. l Mt 27, 1; Mk 15, 1. m Jn 3, 12; 8, 45; 10, 24. n Ps 110, 1; Dn 7, 13–14; Acts 7, 56. o Mt 27, 1–2.11–14; Mk 15, 1–5; Jn 18, 28–38. p 20, 22–25; Acts 17, 7; 24, 5. q 22, 70; 1 Tm 6, 13. r 23, 14.22.41; Mt 27, 24; Jn 19, 4.6; Acts 13, 28. s 3, 1; 9, 7. t 9, 9; Acts 4, 27–28.

had been wanting to see him for a long time, for he had heard about him and had been hoping to see him perform some sign. 9 [u]He questioned him at length, but he gave him no answer. 10 [v]The chief priests and scribes, meanwhile, stood by accusing him harshly. 11 [w][Even] Herod and his soldiers treated him contemptuously and mocked him, and after clothing him in resplendent garb, he sent him back to Pilate. 12 Herod and Pilate became friends that very day, even though they had been enemies formerly. 13 Pilate then summoned the chief priests, the rulers, and the people 14 [x]and said to them, "You brought this man to me and accused him of inciting the people to revolt. I have conducted my investigation in your presence and have not found this man guilty of the charges you have brought against him, 15 nor did Herod, for he sent him back to us. So no capital crime has been committed by him. 16 [y]Therefore I shall have him flogged and then release him." [17]*

The Sentence of Death 18 [z]But all together they shouted out, "Away with this man! Release Barabbas to us." 19 (Now Barabbas had been imprisoned for a rebellion that had taken place in the city and for murder.) 20 Again Pilate addressed them, still wishing to release Jesus, 21 but they continued their shouting, "Crucify him! Crucify him!" 22 Pilate addressed them a third time, "What evil has this man done? I found him guilty of no capital crime. Therefore I shall have him flogged and then release him." 23 With loud shouts, however, they persisted in calling for his crucifixion, and their voices prevailed. 24 The verdict of Pilate was that their demand should be granted. 25 So he released the man who had been imprisoned for rebellion and murder, for whom they asked, and he handed Jesus over to them to deal with as they wished.

The Way of the Cross 26 [a]*As they led him away they took hold of a certain Simon, a Cyrenian, who was coming in from the country; and after laying the cross on him, they made him carry it behind Jesus. 27 A large crowd of people followed Jesus, including many women who mourned and lamented him. 28 [b]Jesus turned to them and said, "Daughters of Jerusalem, do not weep for me; weep instead for yourselves and for your children, 29 for indeed, the days are coming when people will say, 'Blessed are the barren, the wombs that never bore and the breasts that never nursed.' 30 [c]At that time people will say to the mountains, 'Fall upon us!' and to the hills, 'Cover us!' 31 for if these things are done when the wood is green what will happen when it is dry?" 32 Now two others, both criminals, were led away with him to be executed.

The Crucifixion 33 [d e]When they came to the place called the Skull, they crucified him and the criminals there, one on his right, the other on his left. 34 [f]*[Then Jesus said, "Father, forgive them, they know not what they do."] They divided his garments by casting lots. 35 [g h]The people stood by and watched; the rulers, meanwhile, sneered at him and said, "He saved others, let him save himself if he is the chosen one, the Messiah of God." 36 [i]Even the soldiers jeered at him. As they approached to offer him wine 37 they called out, "If you are King of the Jews, save yourself." 38 Above him there was an inscription that read, "This is the King of the Jews."

39 *Now one of the criminals hanging there reviled Jesus, saying, "Are you not the Messiah?

23, 17: This verse, "He was obliged to release one prisoner for them at the festival," is not part of the original text of Lk. It is an explanatory gloss from Mk 15, 6 (also Mt 27, 15) and is not found in many early and important Greek manuscripts. On its historical background, see the notes on Mt 27, 15–26.

23, 26–32: An important Lucan theme throughout the gospel has been the need for the Christian disciple to follow in the footsteps of Jesus. Here this theme comes to the fore with the story of Simon of Cyrene who takes up the cross and follows Jesus (see 9, 23; 14, 27) and with the large crowd who likewise follow Jesus on the way of the cross. See also the note on Mk 15, 21.

23, 34a: [Then Jesus said, "Father, forgive them, they know not what they do."]: this portion of v 34 does not occur in the oldest papyrus manuscript of Lk and in other early Greek manuscripts and ancient versions of wide geographical distribution.

23, 39–43: This episode is recounted only in this gospel. The penitent sinner receives salvation through the crucified Jesus. Jesus' words to the penitent thief reveal Luke's understanding that the destiny of the Christian is "to be with Jesus."

u Mk 15, 5. v Mt 27, 12; Mk 15, 3. w Mt 27, 28–30; Mk 15, 17–19; Jn 19, 2–3. x 23, 4.22.41. y 23, 22; Jn 19, 12–14. z Mt 27, 20–26; Mk 15, 6–7.11–15; Jn 18, 38b-40; 19, 14–16; Acts 3, 13–14. a Mt 27, 32.38; Mk 15, 21.27; Jn 19, 17. b 19, 41–44; 21, 23–24. c Hos 10, 8; Rv 6, 16. d Mt 27, 33–44; Mk 15, 22–32; Jn 19, 17–24. e 22, 37; Is 53, 12. f Nm 15, 27–31; Ps 22, 19; Mt 5, 44; Acts 7, 60. g Ps 22, 8–9. h 4, 23. i Ps 69, 22; Mt 27, 48; Mk 15, 36.

Save yourself and us." 40 The other, however,
rebuking him, said in reply, "Have you no fear of
God, for you are subject to the same condemna-
tion? 41 [j]And indeed, we have been condemned
justly, for the sentence we received corresponds
to our crimes, but this man has done nothing
criminal." 42 [k]Then he said, "Jesus, remember
me when you come into your kingdom." 43 [l]He
replied to him, "Amen, I say to you, today you
will be with me in Paradise."

The Death of Jesus 44 [m n]*It was now about
noon and darkness came over the whole land
until three in the afternoon 45 [o]because of an
eclipse of the sun. Then the veil of the temple
was torn down the middle. 46 [p]Jesus cried out in
a loud voice, "Father, into your hands I com-
mend my spirit"; and when he had said this he
breathed his last. 47 *The centurion who wit-
nessed what had happened glorified God and
said, "This man was innocent beyond doubt."
48 [q]When all the people who had gathered for
this spectacle saw what had happened, they
returned home beating their breasts; 49 [r]but all
his acquaintances stood at a distance, including
the women who had followed him from Galilee
and saw these events.

The Burial of Jesus 50 [s]Now there was a virtu-
ous and righteous man named Joseph who,
though he was a member of the council, 51 [t]had
not consented to their plan of action. He came
from the Jewish town of Arimathea and was
awaiting the kingdom of God. 52 He went to
Pilate and asked for the body of Jesus. 53 [u]After
he had taken the body down, he wrapped it in a
linen cloth and laid him in a rock-hewn tomb in
which no one had yet been buried. 54 It was the
day of preparation, and the sabbath was about to
begin. 55 [v]The women who had come from
Galilee with him followed behind, and when
they had seen the tomb and the way in which
his body was laid in it, 56 [w]they returned and
prepared spices and perfumed oils. Then they
rested on the sabbath according to the command-
ment.

VIII: The Resurrection Narrative

CHAPTER 24

The Resurrection of Jesus 1 [x]*But at day-
break on the first day of the week they took the
spices they had prepared and went to the tomb.
2 They found the stone rolled away from the
tomb; 3 but when they entered, they did not find
the body of the Lord Jesus. 4 [y]While they were
puzzling over this, behold, two men in dazzling
garments appeared to them. 5 [z]They were terri-
fied and bowed their faces to the ground. They
said to them, "Why do you seek the living one
among the dead? 6 *He is not here, but he has
been raised. Remember what he said to you
while he was still in Galilee, 7 [a]that the Son of
Man must be handed over to sinners and be
crucified, and rise on the third day." 8 [b]And they
remembered his words. 9 [c]*Then they returned
from the tomb and announced all these things to
the eleven and to all the others. 10 [d]The women
were Mary Magdalene, Joanna, and Mary the
mother of James; the others who accompanied

23, 44: Noon . . . three in the afternoon: literally, the sixth and ninth hours. See the note on Mk 15, 25.

23, 47: This man was innocent: or, "This man was righteous."

24, 1–53: The resurrection narrative in Lk consists of five sections: (1) the women at the empty tomb (23, 56b—24, 12); (2) the appearance to the two disciples on the way to Emmaus (24, 13–35); (3) the appearance to the disciples in Jerusalem (24, 36–43); (4) Jesus' final instructions (24, 44–49); (5) the ascension (24, 50–53). In Lk, all the resurrection appearances take place in and around Jerusalem; moreover, they are all recounted as having taken place on Easter Sunday. A consistent theme throughout the narrative is that the suffering, death, and resurrection of Jesus were accomplished in fulfillment of Old Testament promises and of Jewish hopes (19a.21.26–27.44.46). In his second volume, Acts, Luke will argue that Christianity is the fulfillment of the hopes of Pharisaic Judaism and its logical development (see Acts 24, 10–21).

24, 6a: He is not here, but he has been raised: this part of the verse is omitted in important representatives of the Western text tradition, but its presence in other text types and the slight difference in wording from Mt 28, 6 and Mk 16, 6 argue for its retention.

24, 9: The women in this gospel do not flee from the tomb and tell no one, as in Mk 16, 8, but return and tell the disciples about their experience. The initial reaction to the testimony of the women is disbelief (11).

j 23, 4.14.22. k 9, 27; 23, 2.3.38. l 2 Cor 12, 3; Rv 2, 7. m Mt 27, 45–56; Mk 15, 33–41; Jn 19, 25–30. n Am 8, 9. o Ex 26, 31–33; 36, 35. p Ps 31, 6; Acts 7, 59. q 18, 13; Zec 12, 10. r 8, 1–3; 23, 55–56; 24, 10; Ps 38, 12. s Mt 27, 57–61; Mk 15, 42–47; Jn 19, 38–42; Acts 13, 29. t 2, 25.38. u 19, 30; Acts 13, 29. v 8, 2; 23, 49; 24, 10. w Ex 12, 16; 20, 10; Dt 5, 14. x Mt 28, 1–8; Mk 16, 1–8; Jn 20, 1–17. y 2 Mc 3, 26; Acts 1, 10. z Acts 2, 9. a 9, 22.44; 17, 25; 18, 32–33; Mt 16, 21; 17, 22–23; Mk 9, 31; Acts 17, 3. b Jn 2, 22. c Mk 16, 10–11; Jn 20, 18. d 8, 2–3; Mk 16, 9.

them also told this to the apostles, [11]but their story seemed like nonsense and they did not believe them. [12 e]*But Peter got up and ran to the tomb, bent down, and saw the burial cloths alone; then he went home amazed at what had happened.

The Appearance on the Road to Emmaus [13 f]*Now that very day two of them were going to a village seven miles from Jerusalem called Emmaus, [14]and they were conversing about all the things that had occurred. [15]And it happened that while they were conversing and debating, Jesus himself drew near and walked with them, [16 g]*but their eyes were prevented from recognizing him. [17]He asked them, "What are you discussing as you walk along?" They stopped, looking downcast. [18]One of them, named Cleopas, said to him in reply, "Are you the only visitor to Jerusalem who does not know of the things that have taken place there in these days?" [19 h]And he replied to them, "What sort of things?" They said to him, "The things that happened to Jesus the Nazarene, who was a prophet mighty in deed and word before God and all the people, [20]how our chief priests and rulers both handed him over to a sentence of death and crucified him. [21 i]But we were hoping that he would be the one to redeem Israel; and besides all this, it is now the third day since this took place. [22 j]Some women from our group, however, have astounded us: they were at the tomb early in the morning [23]and did not find his body; they came back and reported that they had indeed seen a vision of angels who announced that he was alive. [24 k]Then some of those with us went to the tomb and found things just as the women had described, but him they did not see." [25 l]And he said to them, "Oh, how foolish you are! How slow of heart to believe all that the prophets spoke! [26]*Was it not necessary that the Messiah should suffer these things and enter into his glory?" [27 m]Then beginning with Moses and all the prophets, he interpreted to them what referred to him in all the scriptures. [28]As they approached the village to which they were going, he gave the impression that he was going on farther. [29]But they urged him, "Stay with us, for it is nearly evening and the day is almost over." So he went in to stay with them. [30]And it happened that, while he was with them at table, he took bread, said the blessing, broke it, and gave it to them. [31]With that their eyes were opened and they recognized him, but he vanished from their sight. [32]Then they said to each other, "Were not our hearts burning [within us] while he spoke to us on the way and opened the scriptures to us?" [33]So they set out at once and returned to Jerusalem where they found gathered together the eleven and those with them [34 n]who were saying, "The Lord has truly been raised and has appeared to Simon!" [35]Then the two recounted what had taken place on the way and how he was made known to them in the breaking of the bread.

The Appearance to the Disciples in Jerusalem [36 o p]*While they were still speaking about this, he stood in their midst and said to them, "Peace be with you." [37 q]But they were startled and terrified and thought that they were seeing a ghost. [38]Then he said to them, "Why are you troubled? And why do

24, 12: This verse is missing from the Western textual tradition but is found in the best and oldest manuscripts of other text types.

24, 13–35: This episode focuses on the interpretation of scripture by the risen Jesus and the recognition of him in the breaking of the bread. The references to the quotations of scripture and explanation of it (25–27), the kerygmatic proclamation (34), and the liturgical gesture (30) suggest that the episode is primarily catechetical and liturgical rather than apologetic.

24, 13: Seven miles: literally, "sixty stades." A stade was 607 feet. Some manuscripts read "160 stades" or more than eighteen miles. The exact location of Emmaus is disputed.

24, 16: A consistent feature of the resurrection stories is that the risen Jesus was different and initially unrecognizable (37; Mk 16, 12; Jn 20, 14; 21, 4).

24, 26: That the Messiah should suffer . . . : Luke is the only New Testament writer to speak explicitly of a suffering Messiah (26.46; Acts 3, 18; 17, 3; 26, 23). The idea of a suffering Messiah is not found in the Old Testament or in other Jewish literature prior to the New Testament period, although the idea is hinted at in Mk 8, 31–33. See the notes on Mt 26, 63 and 26, 67–68.

24, 36–43.44–49: The Gospel of Luke, like each of the other gospels (Mt 28, 16–20; Mk 16, 14–15; Jn 20, 19–23), focuses on an important appearance of Jesus to the Twelve in which they are commissioned for their future ministry. As in vv 6 and 12, so in vv 36 and 40 there are omissions in the Western text.

e Jn 20, 3–7. f Mk 16, 12–13. g Jn 20, 14; 21, 4. h Mt 2, 23; 21, 11; Acts 2, 22. i 1, 54.68; 2, 38. j 24, 1–11; Mt 28, 1–8; Mk 16, 1–8. k Jn 20, 3–10. 19, 22; 18, 31; 24, 44; Acts 3, 24; 17, 3. m 24, 44; Dt 18, 25; Ps 22, 1–18; Is 53; 1 Pt 1, 10–11. n 1 Cor 15, 4–5. o Mk 16, 14–19; Jn 20, 19–20. p 1 Cor 15, 5. q Mt 14, 26.

questions arise in your hearts? 39 *Look at my
hands and my feet, that it is I myself. Touch me
and see, because a ghost does not have flesh
and bones as you can see I have." 40 [r]And as he
said this, he showed them his hands and his
feet. 41 While they were still incredulous for joy
and were amazed, he asked them, "Have you
anything here to eat?" 42 [s]They gave him a
piece of baked fish; 43 he took it and ate it in
front of them.

44 [t]He said to them, "These are my words that
I spoke to you while I was still with you, that
everything written about me in the law of Moses
and in the prophets and psalms must be ful-
filled." 45 [u]Then he opened their minds to under-
stand the scriptures. 46 [v]*And he said to them,
"Thus it is written that the Messiah would suffer
and rise from the dead on the third day 47 [w]and
that repentance, for the forgiveness of sins,
would be preached in his name to all the
nations, beginning from Jerusalem. 48 [x]You are
witnesses of these things. 49 [y]*And [behold] I am
sending the promise of my Father upon you; but
stay in the city until you are clothed with power
from on high."

The Ascension 50 [z]*Then he led them [out] as
far as Bethany, raised his hands, and blessed
them. 51 As he blessed them he parted from them
and was taken up to heaven. 52 [a]They did him
homage and then returned to Jerusalem with
great joy, 53 *and they were continually in the
temple praising God.

24, 39–42: The apologetic purpose of this story is evident in the concern with the physical details and the report that Jesus ate food.

24, 46: See the note on 24, 26.

24, 49: The promise of my Father: i.e., the gift of the holy Spirit.

24, 50–53: Luke brings his story about the time of Jesus to a close with the report of the ascension. He will also begin the story of the time of the church with a recounting of the ascension. In the gospel, Luke recounts the ascension of Jesus on Easter Sunday night, thereby closely associating it with the resurrection. In Acts (1, 3.9–11; 13, 31) he historicizes the ascension by speaking of a forty-day period between the resurrection and the ascension. The Western text omits some phrases in vv 51 and 52, perhaps to avoid any chronological conflict with Acts 1 about the time of the ascension.

24, 53: The Gospel of Luke ends as it began (1, 9), in the Jerusalem temple.

r Jn 21, 5.9–10.13. s Acts 10, 41. t 18, 31; 24, 27; Mt 16, 21; Jn 5, 39.46. u Jn 20, 9. v 9, 22; Is 53; Hos 6, 2. w Mt 3, 2; 28, 19–20; Mk 16, 15–16; Acts 10, 41. x Acts 1, 8. y Jn 14, 26; Acts 1, 4; 2, 3–4. z Mk 16, 19; Acts 1, 9–11. a Acts 1, 12.

THE GOSPEL ACCORDING TO JOHN

The Gospel according to John is quite different in character from the three synoptic gospels. It is highly literary and symbolic. It does not follow the same order or reproduce the same stories as the synoptic gospels. To a much greater degree, it is the product of a developed theological reflection and grows out of a different circle and tradition. It was probably written in the 90's of the first century.

The Gospel of John begins with a magnificent prologue, which states many of the major themes and motifs of the gospel, much as an overture does for a musical work. The prologue proclaims Jesus as the preexistent and incarnate Word of God who has revealed the Father to us. The rest of the first chapter forms the introduction to the gospel proper and consists of the Baptist's testimony about Jesus (there is no baptism of Jesus in this gospel—John simply points him out as the Lamb of God), followed by stories of the call of the first disciples, in which various titles predicated of Jesus in the early church are presented.

The gospel narrative contains a series of "signs"—the gospel's word for the wondrous deeds of Jesus. The author is primarily interested in the significance of these deeds, and so interprets them for the reader by various reflections, narratives, and discourses. The first sign is the transformation of water into wine at Cana (2, 1-11); this represents the replacement of the

Jewish ceremonial washings and symbolizes the entire creative and transforming work of Jesus. The second sign, the cure of the royal official's son (4, 46-54) simply by the word of Jesus at a distance, signifies the power of Jesus' life-giving word. The same theme is further developed by other signs, probably for a total of seven. The third sign, the cure of the paralytic at the pool with five porticoes in ch 5, continues the theme of water offering newness of life. In the preceding chapter, to the woman at the well in Samaria Jesus had offered living water springing up to eternal life, a symbol of the revelation that Jesus brings; here Jesus' life-giving word replaces the water of the pool that failed to bring life. Chapter 6 contains two signs, the multiplication of loaves and the walking on the waters of the Sea of Galilee. These signs are connected much as the manna and the crossing of the Red Sea are in the Passover narrative and symbolize a new exodus. The multiplication of the loaves is interpreted for the reader by the discourse that follows, where the bread of life is used first as a figure for the revelation of God in Jesus and then for the Eucharist. After a series of dialogues reflecting Jesus' debates with the Jewish authorities at the Feast of Tabernacles in chs 7 and 8, the sixth sign is presented in ch 9, the sign of the young man born blind. This is a narrative illustration of the theme of conflict in the preceding two chapters; it proclaims the triumph of light over darkness, as Jesus is presented as the Light of the world. This is interpreted by a narrative of controversy between the Pharisees and the young man who had been given his sight by Jesus, ending with a discussion of spiritual blindness and spelling out the symbolic meaning of the cure. And finally, the seventh sign, the raising of Lazarus in ch 11, is the climax of signs. Lazarus is presented as a token of the real life that Jesus, the Resurrection and the Life, who will now ironically be put to death because of his gift of life to Lazarus, will give to all who believe in him once he has been raised from the dead.

After the account of the seven signs, the "hour" of Jesus arrives, and the author passes from sign to reality, as he moves into the discourses in the upper room that interpret the meaning of the passion, death, and resurrection narratives that follow. The whole gospel of John is a progressive revelation of the glory of God's only Son, who comes to reveal the Father and then returns in glory to the Father. The author's purpose is clearly expressed in what must have been the original ending of the gospel at the end of ch 20: "Now Jesus did many other signs in the presence of [his] disciples that are not written in this book. But these are written that you may [come to] believe that Jesus is the Messiah, the Son of God, and that through this belief you may have life in his name."

Critical analysis makes it difficult to accept the idea that the gospel as it now stands was written by one person. Chapter 21 seems to have been added after the gospel was completed; it exhibits a Greek style somewhat different from that of the rest of the work. The prologue (1, 1-18) apparently contains an independent hymn, subsequently adapted to serve as a preface to the gospel. Within the gospel itself there are also some inconsistencies, e.g., there are two endings of Jesus' discourse in the upper room (14, 31; 18, 1). To solve these problems, scholars have proposed various rearrangements that would produce a smoother order. However, most have come to the conclusion that the inconsistencies were probably produced by subsequent editing in which homogeneous materials were added to a shorter original.

Other difficulties for any theory of eyewitness authorship of the gospel in its present form are presented by its highly developed theology and by certain elements of its literary style. For instance, some of the wondrous deeds of Jesus have been worked into highly effective dramatic scenes (ch 9); there has been a careful attempt to have these followed by discourses that explain them (chs 5 and 6); and the sayings of Jesus have been woven into long discourses of a quasi-poetic form resembling the speeches of personified Wisdom in the Old Testament.

The gospel contains many details about Jesus not found in the synoptic gospels, e.g., that Jesus engaged in a baptizing ministry (3, 22) before he changed to one of preaching and signs; that Jesus' public ministry lasted for several years (see the note on 2, 13); that he traveled to Jerusalem for various festivals and met serious opposition long before his death (2, 14-25; chs 5 and 7—8); and that he was put to death on the day before Passover (18, 28). These events are not always in chronological order because of the development and editing that took place. However, the accuracy of much of the detail of the fourth gospel constitutes a strong argument that the Johannine tradition rests upon the testimony of an eyewitness. Although tradition identified this person as John, the son of Zebedee, most modern scholars find that the evidence does not support this.

The fourth gospel is not simply history; the narrative has been organized and adapted to serve the evangelist's theological purposes as well. Among them are the opposition to the synagogue of the day and to John the Baptist's followers, who tried to exalt their master at Jesus' expense, the desire to show that Jesus was the Messiah, and the desire to convince Christians that their religious belief and practice must be rooted in Jesus. Such theological purposes have impelled the evangelist to emphasize motifs that were not so clear in the synoptic account of Jesus' ministry, e.g., the explicit emphasis on his divinity.

The polemic between synagogue and church produced bitter and harsh invective, especially regarding the hostility toward Jesus of the authorities—Pharisees and Sadducees—who are combined and referred to frequently as "the Jews" (see the note on 1, 19). These opponents are even described in 8, 44 as springing from their father the devil, whose conduct they imitate in opposing God by rejecting Jesus, whom God has sent. On the other hand, the author of this gospel seems to take pains to show that women are not inferior to men in the Christian community: the woman at the well in Samaria (ch 4) is presented as a prototype of a missionary (4, 4-42), and the first witness of the resurrection is a woman (20, 11-18).

The final editing of the gospel and arrangement in its present form probably dates from between A.D. 90 and 100. Traditionally, Ephesus has been favored as the place of composition, though many support a location in Syria, perhaps the city of Antioch, while some have suggested other places, including Alexandria.

The principal divisions of the Gospel according to John are the following:

I. Prologue (1, 1-18)
II. The Book of Signs (1, 19—12, 50)
III. The Book of Glory (13, 1—20, 31)
IV. Epilogue: The Resurrection Appearance in Galilee (21, 1-25)

I: Prologue

CHAPTER 1

1 [a]*In the beginning was the Word,
and the Word was with God,
and the Word was God.
2 He was in the beginning with God.
3 [b]*All things came to be through him,
and without him nothing came to be.
What came to be 4 [c]through him was life,
and this life was the light of the human race;
5 [d]*the light shines in the darkness,
and the darkness has not overcome it.

6 [e]*A man named John was sent from God.
7 [f]*He came for testimony, to testify to the light,
so that all might believe through him. 8 [g]He was
not the light, but came to testify to the light.
9 [h]The true light, which enlightens everyone,
was coming into the world.

10 He was in the world,
and the world came to be through him,
but the world did not know him.
11 *He came to what was his own,
but his own people did not accept him.

12 [i]But to those who did accept him he gave
power to become children of God, to those who
believe in his name, 13 [j]*who were born not by
natural generation nor by human choice nor by a
man's decision but of God.

14 [k]*And the Word became flesh
and made his dwelling among us,
and we saw his glory,
the glory as of the Father's only Son,
full of grace and truth.

15 [l]*John testified to him and cried out, saying,
"This was he of whom I said, 'The one who is
coming after me ranks ahead of me because he
existed before me.' " 16*From his fullness we
have all received, grace in place of grace,
17 [m]because while the law was given through

1, 1–18: The prologue states the main themes of the gospel: life, light, truth, the world, testimony, and the preexistence of Jesus Christ, the incarnate **Logos,** who reveals God the Father. In origin, it was probably an early Christian hymn. Its closest parallel is in other christological hymns, Col 1, 15–20 and Phil 2, 6–11. Its core (1–5.10–11.14) is poetic in structure, with short phrases linked by "staircase parallelism," in which the last word of one phrase becomes the first word of the next. Prose inserts (at least 6–8 and 15) deal with John the Baptist.

1, 1: **In the beginning:** also the first words of the Old Testament (Gn 1, 1). **Was:** this verb is used three times with different meanings in this verse: existence, relationship, and predication. **The Word** (Greek **logos**): this term combines God's dynamic, creative word (Genesis), personified preexistent Wisdom as the instrument of God's creative activity (Proverbs), and the ultimate intelligibility of reality (Hellenistic philosophy). **With God:** the Greek preposition here connotes communication with another. **Was God:** lack of a definite article with "God" in Greek signifies predication rather than identification.

1, 3: **What came to be:** while the oldest manuscripts have no punctuation here, the corrector of Bodmer Papyrus P^{75}, some manuscripts, and the Ante-Nicene Fathers take this phrase with what follows, as staircase parallelism. Connection with v 3 reflects fourth-century anti-Arianism.

1, 5: The ethical dualism of light and darkness is paralleled in intertestamental literature and in the Dead Sea Scrolls. **Overcome:** "comprehend" is another possible translation, but cf 12, 35; Wis 7, 29–30.

1, 6: John was **sent** just as Jesus was "sent" (4, 34) in divine mission. Other references to John the Baptist in this gospel emphasize the differences between them and John's subordinate role.

1, 7: **Testimony:** the testimony theme of Jn is introduced, which portrays Jesus as if on trial throughout his ministry. All testify to Jesus: John the Baptist, the Samaritan woman, scripture, his works, the crowds, the Spirit, and his disciples.

1, 11: **What was his own . . . his own people:** first a neuter, literally, "his own property/possession" (probably = Israel), then a masculine, "his own people" (the Israelites).

1, 13: Believers in Jesus become children of God not through any of the three natural causes mentioned but through God who is the immediate cause of the new spiritual life. **Were born:** the Greek verb can mean "begotten" (by a male) or "born" (from a female or of parents). The variant "he who was begotten," asserting Jesus' virginal conception, is weakly attested in Old Latin and Syriac versions.

1, 14: **Flesh:** the whole person, used probably against docetic tendencies (cf 1 Jn 4, 2; 2 Jn 7). **Made his dwelling:** literally, "pitched his tent/tabernacle." Cf the tabernacle or tent of meeting that was the place of God's presence among his people (Ex 25, 8–9). The incarnate Word is the new mode of God's presence among his people. The Greek verb has the same consonants as the Aramaic word for God's presence (Shekinah). **Glory:** God's visible manifestation of majesty in power, which once filled the tabernacle (Ex 40, 34) and the temple (1 Kgs 8, 10–11.27), is now centered in Jesus. **Only Son:** Greek, **monogenēs,** but see the note on 1, 18. **Grace and truth:** these words may represent two Old Testament terms describing Yahweh in covenant relationship with Israel (cf Ex 34, 6), thus God's "love" and "fidelity." The Word shares Yahweh's covenant qualities.

1, 15: This verse, interrupting vv 14 and 16, seems drawn from v 30.

1, 16: **Grace in place of grace:** replacement of the Old Covenant with the New (cf 17). Other possible translations are "grace upon grace" (accumulation) and "grace for grace" (correspondence).

a 10, 30; Gn 1, 1–5; Jb 28, 12–27; Prv 8, 22–25; Wis 9, 1–2; 1 Jn 1, 1–2; Col 1, 1.15; Rv 3, 14; 19, 13. b Ps 33, 9; Wis 9, 1; Sir 42, 15; 1 Cor 8, 6; Col 1, 16; Heb 1, 2; Rv 3, 14. c 5, 26; 8, 12; 1 Jn 1, 2. d 3, 19; 8, 12; 9, 5; 12, 35.46; Wis 7, 29–30; 1 Thes 5, 4; 1 Jn 2, 8. e Mt 3, 1; Mk 1, 4; Lk 3, 2–3. f 1, 19–34; 5, 33. g 5, 35. h 3, 19; 8, 12; 9, 39; 12, 46. i 3, 11–12; 5, 43–44; 12, 46–50; Gal 3, 26; 4, 6–7; Eph 1, 5; 1 Jn 3, 2. j 3, 5–6. k Ex 16, 10; 24, 17; 25, 8–9; 33, 22; 34, 6; Sir 24, 4.8; Is 60,1; Ez 43, 7; Jl 4, 17; Hb 2, 14; 1 Jn 1, 2; 4, 2; 2 Jn 7. l 1, 30; 3, 27–30. m 7, 19; Ex 31, 18; 34, 28.

Moses, grace and truth came through Jesus Christ. 18 [n]*No one has ever seen God. The only Son, God, who is at the Father's side, has revealed him.

II: The Book of Signs

John the Baptist's Testimony to Himself

19 *And this is the testimony of John. When the Jews from Jerusalem sent priests and Levites [to him] to ask him, "Who are you?" 20 [o]*he admitted and did not deny it, but admitted, "I am not the Messiah." 21 [p]*So they asked him, "What are you then? Are you Elijah?" And he said, "I am not." "Are you the Prophet?" He answered, "No." 22 So they said to him, "Who are you, so we can give an answer to those who sent us? What do you have to say for yourself?" 23 [q]*He said:

"I am 'the voice of one crying out in the
desert,
"Make straight the way of the Lord," '

as Isaiah the prophet said." 24 *Some Pharisees were also sent. 25 [r]They asked him, "Why then do you baptize if you are not the Messiah or Elijah or the Prophet?" 26 [s]*John answered them, "I baptize with water; but there is one among you whom you do not recognize, 27 the one who is coming after me, whose sandal strap I am not worthy to untie." 28 *This happened in Bethany across the Jordan, where John was baptizing.

John the Baptist's Testimony to Jesus

29 [t]*The next day he saw Jesus coming toward him and said, "Behold, the Lamb of God, who takes away the sin of the world. 30 [u]*He is the one of whom I said, 'A man is coming after me who ranks ahead of me because he existed before me.' 31 *I did not know him, but the reason why I came baptizing with water was that he might be made known to Israel." 32 [v]*John testified further, saying, "I saw the Spirit come down like a dove from the sky and remain upon him. 33 [w]I did not know him, but the one who sent me to baptize with water told me, 'On whomever you see the Spirit come down and remain, he is the one who will baptize

1, 18: The only Son, God: while the vast majority of later textual witnesses have another reading, "the Son, the only one" or "the only Son," the translation above follows the best and earliest manuscripts, **monogenēs theos,** but takes the first term to mean not just "Only One" but to include a filial relationship with the Father, as at Lk 9, 38 ("only child") or Heb 11, 17 ("only son") and as translated at Jn 1, 14. The Logos is thus "only Son" and God but not Father/God.

1, 19–51: The testimony of John the Baptist about the Messiah and Jesus' self-revelation to the first disciples. This section constitutes the introduction to the gospel proper and is connected with the prose inserts in the prologue. It develops the major theme of testimony in four scenes: John's negative testimony about himself; his positive testimony about Jesus; the revelation of Jesus to Andrew and Peter; the revelation of Jesus to Philip and Nathanael.

1, 19: The Jews: throughout most of the gospel, the "Jews" does not refer to the Jewish people as such but to the hostile authorities, both Pharisees and Sadducees, particularly in Jerusalem, who refuse to believe in Jesus. The usage reflects the atmosphere, at the end of the first century, of polemics between church and synagogue, or possibly it refers to Jews as representative of a hostile world (10–11).

1, 20: Messiah: the anointed agent of Yahweh, usually considered to be of Davidic descent. See further the note on 1, 41.

1, 21: Elijah: the Baptist did not claim to be Elijah returned to earth (cf Mal 3, 23; Mt 11, 14). **The Prophet:** probably the prophet like Moses (Dt 18, 15; cf Acts 3, 22).

1, 23: This is a repunctuation and reinterpretation (as in the synoptic gospels and Septuagint) of the Hebrew text of Is 40, 3, which reads, "A voice cries out: In the desert prepare the way of the LORD."

1, 24: Some Pharisees: other translations, such as "Now they had been sent from the Pharisees," misunderstand the grammatical construction. This is a different group from that in v 19; the priests and Levites would have been Sadducees, not Pharisees.

1, 26: I baptize with water: the synoptics add "but he will baptize you with the holy Spirit" (Mk 1, 8) or ". . . holy Spirit and fire" (Mt 3, 11; Lk 3, 16). John's emphasis is on purification and preparation for a better baptism.

1, 28: Bethany across the Jordan: site unknown. Another reading is "Bethabara."

1, 29: The Lamb of God: the background for this title may be the victorious apocalyptic lamb who would destroy evil in the world (Rv 5—7; 17, 14); the paschal lamb, whose blood saved Israel (Ex 12); and/or the suffering servant led like a lamb to the slaughter as a sin-offering (Is 53, 7.10).

1, 30: He existed before me: possibly as Elijah (to come, 27); for the evangelist and his audience, Jesus' preexistence would be implied (see the note on 1, 1).

1, 31: I did not know him: this gospel shows no knowledge of the tradition (Lk 1) about the kinship of Jesus and John the Baptist. **The reason why I came baptizing with water:** in this gospel, John's baptism is not connected with forgiveness of sins; its purpose is revelatory, that Jesus may be made known to Israel.

1, 32: Like a dove: a symbol of the new creation (Gn 8, 8) or the community of Israel (Hos 11, 11). **Remain:** the first use of a favorite verb in Jn, emphasizing the permanency of the relationship between Father and Son (as here) and between the Son and the Christian. Jesus is the permanent bearer of the Spirit.

n 5, 37; 6, 46; Ex 33, 20; Jgs 13, 21–22; 1 Tm 6, 16; 1 Jn 4, 12. o 3, 28; Lk 3, 15; Acts 13, 25. p Dt 18, 15.18; 2 Kgs 2, 11; Sir 48, 10; Mal 3, 1.23; Mt 11, 14; 17, 11–13; Mk 9, 13; Acts 3, 22. q Is 40, 3; Mt 3, 3; Mk 1, 2; Lk 3, 4. r Ez 36, 25; Zec 13, 1; Mt 16, 14. s Mt 3, 11; Mk 1, 7–8; Lk 3, 16; Acts 13, 25. t 1, 36; Ex 12; Is 53, 7; Rv 5–7; 17, 14. u 1, 15; Mt 3, 11; Mk 1, 7; Lk 3, 16. v Sg 5, 2; Is 11, 2; Hos 11, 11; Mt 3, 16; Mk 1, 10; Lk 3, 21–22. w Is 42, 1; Mt 3, 11; Mk 1, 8; Lk 3, 16.

with the holy Spirit.' 34 x*Now I have seen and
testified that he is the Son of God."

The First Disciples 35 yThe next day John was
there again with two of his disciples, 36*and as
he watched Jesus walk by, he said, "Behold, the
Lamb of God." 37*The two disciples heard what
he said and followed Jesus. 38Jesus turned and
saw them following him and said to them,
"What are you looking for?" They said to him,
"Rabbi" (which translated means Teacher),
"where are you staying?" 39*He said to them,
"Come, and you will see." So they went and saw
where he was staying, and they stayed with him
that day. It was about four in the afternoon.
40Andrew, the brother of Simon Peter, was one
of the two who heard John and followed Jesus.
41 z*He first found his own brother Simon and
told him, "We have found the Messiah" (which
is translated Anointed). 42 a*Then he brought
him to Jesus. Jesus looked at him and said, "You
are Simon the son of John; you will be called
Kephas" (which is translated Peter).

43*The next day he decided to go to Galilee,
and he found Philip. And Jesus said to him, "Fol-
low me." 44Now Philip was from Bethsaida, the
town of Andrew and Peter. 45 bPhilip found Na-
thanael and told him, "We have found the one
about whom Moses wrote in the law, and also the
prophets, Jesus son of Joseph, from Nazareth."
46But Nathanael said to him, "Can anything good
come from Nazareth?" Philip said to him, "Come
and see." 47*Jesus saw Nathanael coming toward
him and said of him, "Here is a true Israelite.
There is no duplicity in him." 48 c*Nathanael said
to him, "How do you know me?" Jesus answered
and said to him, "Before Philip called you, I saw
you under the fig tree." 49 d*Nathanael answered
him, "Rabbi, you are the Son of God; you are the
King of Israel." 50*Jesus answered and said to
him, "Do you believe because I told you that I saw
you under the fig tree? You will see greater things
than this." 51 e*And he said to him, "Amen,
amen, I say to you, you will see the sky opened
and the angels of God ascending and descending
on the Son of Man."

CHAPTER 2

The Wedding at Cana 1 f*On the third day
there was a wedding in Cana in Galilee, and the
mother of Jesus was there. 2Jesus and his disci-
ples were also invited to the wedding. 3When
the wine ran short, the mother of Jesus said to

1, 34: The Son of God: this reading is supported by good Greek manuscripts, including the Chester Beatty and Bodmer Papyri and the Vatican Codex, but is suspect because it harmonizes this passage with the synoptic version: "This is my beloved Son" (Mt 3, 17; Mk 1, 11; Lk 3, 22). The poorly attested alternate reading, "God's chosen One," is probably a reference to the Servant of Yahweh (Is 42, 1).

1, 36: John the Baptist's testimony makes his disciples' following of Jesus plausible.

1, 37: The two disciples: Andrew (40) and, traditionally, John, son of Zebedee (see the note on 13, 23).

1, 39: Four in the afternoon: literally, the tenth hour, from sunrise, in the Roman calculation of time. Some suggest that the next day, beginning at sunset, was the sabbath; they would have stayed with Jesus to avoid travel on it.

1, 41: Messiah: the Hebrew word **māšîah,** "anointed one" (see the note on Lk 2, 11), appears in Greek as the transliterated **messias** only here and in 4, 25. Elsewhere the Greek translation **christos** is used.

1, 42: Simon, the son of John: in Mt 16, 17, Simon is called **Bariōna,** "son of Jonah," a different tradition for the name of Simon's father. **Kephas:** in Aramaic = the Rock; cf Mt 16, 18. Neither the Greek equivalent **Petros** nor, with one isolated exception, **Kephas** is attested as a personal name before Christian times.

1, 43: He: grammatically, could be Peter, but logically is probably Jesus.

1, 47: A true Israelite. There is no duplicity in him: Jacob was the first to bear the name "Israel" (Gn 32, 29), but Jacob was a man of duplicity (Gn 27, 35–36).

1, 48: Under the fig tree: a symbol of messianic peace (cf Mi 4, 4; Zec 3, 10).

1, 49: Son of God: this title is used in the Old Testament, among other ways, as a title of adoption for the Davidic king (2 Sm 7, 14; Pss 2, 7; 89, 27), and thus here, with **King of Israel,** in a messianic sense. For the evangelist, Son of God also points to Jesus' divinity (cf 20, 28).

1, 50: Possibly a statement: "You [singular] believe because I saw you under the fig tree."

1, 51: The double "Amen" is characteristic of John. **You** is plural in Greek. The allusion is to Jacob's ladder (Gn 28, 12).

2, 1—6, 71: Signs revealing Jesus as the Messiah to all Israel. "Sign" (**sēmeion**) is John's symbolic term for Jesus' wondrous deeds (see Introduction). The Old Testament background lies in the Exodus story (cf Dt 11, 3; 29, 2). John is interested primarily in what the **sēmeia** signify: God's intervention in human history in a new way through Jesus.

2, 1–11: The first sign. This story of replacement of Jewish ceremonial washings (6) presents the initial revelation about Jesus at the outset of his ministry. He manifests his glory; the disciples believe. There is no synoptic parallel.

2, 1: Cana: unknown from the Old Testament. **The mother of Jesus:** she is never named in John.

x Is 42, 1; Mt 3, 17; Mk 1, 11; Lk 9, 35. y Mt 4, 18–22; Mk 1, 16–20; Lk 5, 1–11. z 4, 25. a Mt 16, 18; Mk 3, 16. b 21, 2. c Mi 4, 4; Zec 3, 10. d 12, 13; Ex 4, 22; Dt 14, 1; 2 Sm 7, 14; Jb 1, 6; 2, 1; 38, 7; Pss 2, 7; 29, 1; 89, 27; Wis 2, 18; Sir 4, 10; Dn 3, 25; Hos 11, 1; Mt 14, 33; 16, 16; Mk 13, 32. e Gn 28, 10–17; Dn 7, 13. f 4, 46; Jgs 14, 12; Tb 11, 8.

him, "They have no wine." 4 g*[And] Jesus said to her, "Woman, how does your concern affect me? My hour has not yet come." 5 h His mother said to the servers, "Do whatever he tells you." 6 i*Now there were six stone water jars there for Jewish ceremonial washings, each holding twenty to thirty gallons. 7 Jesus told them, "Fill the jars with water." So they filled them to the brim. 8*Then he told them, "Draw some out now and take it to the headwaiter." So they took it. 9 And when the headwaiter tasted the water that had become wine, without knowing where it came from (although the servers who had drawn the water knew), the headwaiter called the bridegroom 10 and said to him, "Everyone serves good wine first, and then when people have drunk freely, an inferior one; but you have kept the good wine until now." 11 j*Jesus did this as the beginning of his signs in Cana in Galilee and so revealed his glory, and his disciples began to believe in him.

12*After this, he and his mother, [his] brothers, and his disciples went down to Capernaum and stayed there only a few days.

Cleansing of the Temple 13 k*Since the Passover of the Jews was near, Jesus went up to Jerusalem. 14 l*He found in the temple area those who sold oxen, sheep, and doves, as well as the money-changers seated there. 15 He made a whip out of cords and drove them all out of the temple area, with the sheep and oxen, and spilled the coins of the money-changers and overturned their tables, 16 m and to those who sold doves he said, "Take these out of here, and stop making my Father's house a marketplace." 17 n*His disciples recalled the words of scripture, "Zeal for your house will consume me." 18 o At this the Jews answered and said to him, "What sign can you show us for doing this?" 19 p*Jesus answered and said to them, "Destroy this temple and in three days I will raise it up." 20*The Jews said, "This temple has been under construction for forty-six years, and you will raise it up in three days?" 21 But he was speaking about the temple of his body. 22 q Therefore, when he was raised from the dead, his disciples remembered that he had said this, and they came to believe the scripture and the word Jesus had spoken.

2, 4: This verse may seek to show that Jesus did not work miracles to help his family and friends, as in the apocryphal gospels. **Woman:** a normal, polite form of address, but unattested in reference to one's mother. Cf also 19, 26. **How does your concern affect me?:** literally, "What is this to me and to you?"—a Hebrew expression of either hostility (Jgs 11, 12; 2 Chr 35, 21; 1 Kgs 17, 18) or denial of common interest (Hos 14, 9; 2 Kgs 3, 13). Cf Mk 1, 24; 5, 7, used by demons to Jesus. **My hour has not yet come:** the translation as a question ("Has not my hour now come?"), while preferable grammatically and supported by Greek Fathers, seems unlikely from a comparison with 7, 6.30. The "hour" is that of Jesus' passion, death, resurrection, and ascension (13, 1).

2, 6: Twenty to thirty gallons: literally, "two or three measures"; the Attic liquid measure contained 39.39 liters. The vast quantity recalls prophecies of abundance in the last days; cf Am 9, 13–14; Hos 14, 7; Jer 31, 12.

2, 8: Headwaiter: used of the official who managed a banquet, but there is no evidence of such a functionary in Palestine. Perhaps here a friend of the family acted as master of ceremonies; cf Sir 32, 1.

2, 11: The beginning of his signs: the first of seven (see Introduction).

2, 12—3, 21: The next three episodes take place in Jerusalem. Only the first is paralleled in the synoptic gospels.

2, 12: This transitional verse may be a harmonization with the synoptic tradition in Lk 4, 31 and Mt 4, 13. There are many textual variants. John depicts no extended ministry in Capernaum as do the synoptics.

2, 13–22: This episode indicates the post-resurrectional replacement of the temple by the person of Jesus.

2, 13: Passover: this is the first Passover mentioned in John; a second is mentioned in 6, 4, a third in 13, 1. Taken literally, they point to a ministry of at least two years.

2, 14–22: The other gospels place the cleansing of the temple in the last days of Jesus' life (Mt, on the day Jesus entered Jerusalem; Mk, on the next day). The order of events in the gospel narratives is often determined by theological motives rather than by chronological data.

2, 14: Oxen, sheep, and doves: intended for sacrifice. The doves were the offerings of the poor (Lv 5, 7). **Money-changers:** for a temple tax paid by every male Jew more than nineteen years of age, with a half-shekel coin (Ex 30, 11–16), in Tyrian currency. See the note on Mt 17, 24.

2, 17: Ps 69, 10, changed to future tense to apply to Jesus.

2, 19: This saying about the destruction of the temple occurs in various forms (Mt 24, 2; 27, 40; Mk 13, 2; 15, 29; Lk 21, 6; cf Acts 6, 14). Mt 26, 61 has: "I **can** destroy the temple of God . . ."; see the note there. In Mk 14, 58, there is a metaphorical contrast with a new temple: "I will destroy this temple **made with hands** and within three days I will build another **not made with hands.**" Here it is symbolic of Jesus' resurrection and the resulting community (see 21 and Rv 21, 2). **In three days:** an Old Testament expression for a short, indefinite period of time; cf Hos 6, 2.

2, 20: Forty-six years: based on references in Josephus (**Jewish Wars** 1, 21, 1 »»401; **Antiquities** 15, 11, 1 §380), possibly the spring of A.D. 28. Cf the note on Lk 3, 1.

g 7, 30; 8, 20; 12, 23; 13, 1; Jgs 11, 12; 1 Kgs 17, 18; 2 Kgs 3, 13; 2 Chr 35, 21; Hos 14, 9; Mk 1, 24; 5, 7; 7, 30; 8, 20; 12, 23; 13, 1. h Gn 41, 55. i 3, 25; Lv 11, 33; Am 9, 13–14; Mt 15, 2; 23, 25–26; Mk 7, 2–4; Lk 11, 38. j 4, 54. k Mt 21, 12–13; Mk 11, 15–17; Lk 19, 45–46. l Ex 30, 11–16; Lv 5, 7. m Zec 14, 21. n Ps 69, 9. o 6, 30. p Mt 24, 2; 26, 61; 27, 40; Mk 13, 2; 14, 58; 15, 29; Lk 21, 6; Acts 6, 14. q 5, 39; 12, 16; 14, 26; 20, 9; Mt 12, 6; Lk 24, 6–8; Rv 21, 22.

23 [r]While he was in Jerusalem for the feast of
Passover, many began to believe in his name
when they saw the signs he was doing. 24 But
Jesus would not trust himself to them because he
knew them all, 25 [s]and did not need anyone to
testify about human nature. He himself under-
stood it well.

CHAPTER 3

Nicodemus 1 [t]*Now there was a Pharisee
named Nicodemus, a ruler of the Jews. 2 [u]He
came to Jesus at night and said to him, "Rabbi,
we know that you are a teacher who has come
from God, for no one can do these signs that you
are doing unless God is with him." 3 *Jesus
answered and said to him, "Amen, amen, I say
to you, no one can see the kingdom of God
without being born from above." 4 [v]Nicodemus
said to him, "How can a person once grown old
be born again? Surely he cannot reenter his
mother's womb and be born again, can he?"
5 [w]Jesus answered, "Amen, amen, I say to you,
no one can enter the kingdom of God without
being born of water and Spirit. 6 [x]What is born of
flesh is flesh and what is born of spirit is spirit.
7 Do not be amazed that I told you, 'You must be
born from above.' 8 [y]*The wind blows where it
wills, and you can hear the sound it makes, but
you do not know where it comes from or where
it goes; so it is with everyone who is born of the
Spirit." 9 Nicodemus answered and said to him,
"How can this happen?" 10 Jesus answered and
said to him, "You are the teacher of Israel and
you do not understand this? 11 [z]Amen, amen, I
say to you, we speak of what we know and we
testify to what we have seen, but you people do
not accept our testimony. 12 [a]If I tell you about
earthly things and you do not believe, how will
you believe if I tell you about heavenly things?
13 [b]No one has gone up to heaven except the one
who has come down from heaven, the Son of
Man. 14 [c]*And just as Moses lifted up the serpent
in the desert, so must the Son of Man be lifted
up, 15 *so that everyone who believes in him
may have eternal life."

16 [d]*For God so loved the world that he gave
his only Son, so that everyone who believes in
him might not perish but might have eternal life.
17 [e]*For God did not send his Son into the world
to condemn the world, but that the world might
be saved through him. 18 [f]Whoever believes in
him will not be condemned, but whoever does
not believe has already been condemned, be-
cause he has not believed in the name of the
only Son of God. 19 [g]*And this is the verdict, that
the light came into the world, but people pre-
ferred darkness to light, because their works
were evil. 20 [h]For everyone who does wicked
things hates the light and does not come toward
the light, so that his works might not be
exposed. 21 [i]But whoever lives the truth comes

3, 1–21: Jesus instructs Nicodemus on the necessity of a new birth from above. This scene in Jerusalem at Passover exemplifies the faith engendered by signs (2, 23). It continues the self-manifestation of Jesus in Jerusalem begun in ch 2. This is the first of the Johannine discourses, shifting from dialogue to monologue (11–15) to reflection of the evangelist (16–21). The shift from singular through v 10 to plural in v 11 may reflect the early church's controversy with the Jews.

3, 1: **A ruler of the Jews**: most likely a member of the Jewish council, the Sanhedrin; see the note on Mk 8, 31.

3, 3: **Born**: see the note on 1, 13. **From above**: the Greek adverb **anōthen** means both "from above" and "again." Jesus means "from above" (see 31), but Nicodemus misunderstands it as "again." This misunderstanding serves as a springboard for further instruction.

3, 8: **Wind**: the Greek word **pneuma** (as well as the Hebrew **rûah**) means both "wind" and "spirit." In the play on the double meaning, "wind" is primary.

3, 14: **Lifted up**: in Nm 21, 9, Moses simply "mounted" a serpent upon a pole. John here substitutes a verb implying glorification. Jesus, exalted to glory at his cross and resurrection, represents healing for all.

3, 15: **Eternal life**: used here for the first time in John, this term stresses quality of life rather than duration.

3, 16: **Gave**: as a gift in the incarnation, and also "over to death" in the crucifixion; cf Rom 8, 32.

3, 17–19: **Condemn**: the Greek root means both judgment and condemnation. Jesus' purpose is to save, but his coming provokes judgment; some condemn themselves by turning from the light.

3, 19: Judgment is not only future but is partially realized here and now.

r 4, 45. s 1 Kgs 8, 39; Pss 33, 15; 94, 11; Sir 42, 18; Jer 17, 10; 20, 12. t 7, 50–51; 19, 39. u 9, 4.16.33; 10, 21; 11, 10; 13, 30; Mt 22, 16; Mk 12, 14; Lk 20, 21. v 1, 13. w 1, 32; 7, 39; 19, 30.34–35; Is 32, 15; 44, 3; Ez 36, 25–27; Jl 3, 1–2. x 6, 63; 1 Cor 15, 44–50. y Eccl 11, 4–5; Acts 2, 2–4. z 3, 32.34; 8, 14; Mt 11, 27. a 6, 62–65; Wis 9, 16–17; 1 Cor 15, 40; 2 Cor 5, 1; Phil 2, 10; 3, 19–20. b 1, 18; 6, 62; Dn 7, 13; Rom 10, 6; Eph 4, 9. c 8, 28; 12, 32.34; Nm 21, 4–9; Wis 16, 5–7. d 1 Jn 4, 9. e 5, 22.30; 8, 15–18; 12, 47. f 5, 24; Mk 16, 16. g 1, 5.9–11; 8, 12; 9, 5. h Jb 24, 13–17. i Gn 47, 29 LXX; Jos 2, 14 LXX; 2 Sm 2, 6 LXX; 15, 20 LXX; Tb 4, 6 LXX; 13, 6; Is 26, 10 LXX; Mt 5, 14–16.

to the light, so that his works may be clearly seen as done in God.

Final Witness of the Baptist [22][j]*After this, Jesus and his disciples went into the region of Judea, where he spent some time with them baptizing. [23]*John was also baptizing in Aenon near Salim, because there was an abundance of water there, and people came to be baptized, [24][k]*for John had not yet been imprisoned. [25]*Now a dispute arose between the disciples of John and a Jew about ceremonial washings. [26][l]So they came to John and said to him, "Rabbi, the one who was with you across the Jordan, to whom you testified, here he is baptizing and everyone is coming to him." [27][m]John answered and said, "No one can receive anything except what has been given him from heaven. [28][n]You yourselves can testify that I said [that] I am not the Messiah, but that I was sent before him. [29][o]*The one who has the bride is the bridegroom; the best man, who stands and listens for him, rejoices greatly at the bridegroom's voice. So this joy of mine has been made complete. [30][p]He must increase; I must decrease."

The One from Heaven [31][q]*The one who comes from above is above all. The one who is of the earth is earthly and speaks of earthly things. But the one who comes from heaven [is above all]. [32][r]He testifies to what he has seen and heard, but no one accepts his testimony. [33][s]Whoever does accept his testimony certifies that God is trustworthy. [34]*For the one whom God sent speaks the words of God. He does not ration his gift of the Spirit. [35][t]The Father loves the Son and has given everything over to him. [36][u]Whoever believes in the Son has eternal life, but whoever disobeys the Son will not see life, but the wrath of God remains upon him.

CHAPTER 4

[1]*Now when Jesus learned that the Pharisees had heard that Jesus was making and baptizing more disciples than John [2]*(although Jesus himself was not baptizing, just his disciples), [3]he left Judea and returned to Galilee.

The Samaritan Woman [4]*He had to pass through Samaria. [5][v]*So he came to a town of Samaria called Sychar, near the plot of land that Jacob had given to his son Joseph. [6]Jacob's well was there. Jesus, tired from his journey, sat down there at the well. It was about noon.

[7]A woman of Samaria came to draw water. Jesus said to her, "Give me a drink." [8]His disciples had gone into the town to buy food. [9][w]*The Samaritan woman said to him, "How can you, a Jew, ask me, a Samaritan woman, for a drink?" (For Jews use nothing in common with Samaritans.) [10][x]*Jesus answered and said to her, "If you knew the gift of God and who is saying to you, 'Give me a drink,' you would have asked him and he would have given you living water."

3, 22–26: Jesus' ministry in Judea is only loosely connected with 2, 13—3, 21; cf 1, 19–36. Perhaps John the Baptist's further testimony was transposed here to give meaning to "water" in v 5. Jesus is depicted as baptizing (22); contrast 4, 2.

3, 23: Aenon near Salim: site uncertain, either in the upper Jordan valley or in Samaria.

3, 24: A remark probably intended to avoid objections based on a chronology like that of the synoptics (Mt 4, 12; Mk 1, 14).

3, 25: A Jew: some think Jesus is meant. Many manuscripts read "Jews."

3, 29: The best man: literally, "the friend of the groom," the **shoshben** of Jewish tradition, who arranged the wedding. Competition between him and the groom would be unthinkable.

3, 31–36: It is uncertain whether these are words by the Baptist, Jesus, or the evangelist. They are reflections on the two preceding scenes.

3, 34: His gift: of God or to Jesus, perhaps both. This verse echoes vv 5 and 8.

4, 1–42: Jesus in Samaria. The self-revelation of Jesus continues with his second discourse, on his mission to "half-Jews." It continues the theme of replacement, here with regard to cult (21). Water (7–15) serves as a symbol (as at Cana and in the Nicodemus episode).

4, 2: An editorial refinement of 3, 22, perhaps directed against followers of John the Baptist who claimed that Jesus imitated him.

4, 4: He had to: a theological necessity; geographically, Jews often bypassed Samaria by taking a route across the Jordan.

4, 5: Sychar: Jerome identifies this with Shechem, a reading found in Syriac manuscripts.

4, 9: Samaritan women were regarded by Jews as ritually impure, and therefore Jews were forbidden to drink from any vessel they had handled.

4, 10: Living water: the water of life, i.e., the revelation that Jesus brings; the woman thinks of "flowing water," so much more desirable than stagnant cistern water. On John's device of such misunderstanding, cf the note on 3, 3.

j 4, 1–2. k Mt 4, 12; 14, 3; Mk 1, 14; 6, 17; Lk 3, 20. l 1, 26.32–34.36. m 19, 11; 1 Cor 4, 7; 2 Cor 3, 5; Heb 5, 4. n 1, 20–23; Lk 3, 15. o 15, 11; 17, 13; Mt 9, 15. p 2 Sm 3, 1. q 8, 23. r 3, 11. s 8, 26; 12, 44–50; 1 Jn 5, 10. t 13, 3; Mt 11, 27; 28, 18; Lk 10, 22. u 3, 16; 1 Jn 5, 13. v Gn 33, 18–19; 48, 22; Jos 24, 32. w Sir 50, 25–26; Mt 10, 5. x Sir 24, 20–21; Is 55, 1; Jer 2, 13.

11 *[The woman] said to him, "Sir, you do not even have a bucket and the cistern is deep; where then can you get this living water? 12[y] Are you greater than our father Jacob, who gave us this cistern and drank from it himself with his children and his flocks?" 13 Jesus answered and said to her, "Everyone who drinks this water will be thirsty again; 14[z] but whoever drinks the water I shall give will never thirst; the water I shall give will become in him a spring of water welling up to eternal life." 15 The woman said to him, "Sir, give me this water, so that I may not be thirsty or have to keep coming here to draw water."

16 Jesus said to her, "Go call your husband and come back." 17 The woman answered and said to him, "I do not have a husband." Jesus answered her, "You are right in saying, 'I do not have a husband.' 18[a] For you have had five husbands, and the one you have now is not your husband. What you have said is true." 19[b] The woman said to him, "Sir, I can see that you are a prophet. 20[c]*Our ancestors worshiped on this mountain; but you people say that the place to worship is in Jerusalem." 21 Jesus said to her, "Believe me, woman, the hour is coming when you will worship the Father neither on this mountain nor in Jerusalem. 22[d] You people worship what you do not understand; we worship what we understand, because salvation is from the Jews. 23 *But the hour is coming, and is now here, when true worshipers will worship the Father in Spirit and truth; and indeed the Father seeks such people to worship him. 24[e] God is Spirit, and those who worship him must worship in Spirit and truth." 25[f]*The woman said to him, "I know that the Messiah is coming, the one called the Anointed; when he comes, he will tell us everything." 26[g]*Jesus said to her, "I am he, the one who is speaking with you."

27 *At that moment his disciples returned, and were amazed that he was talking with a woman, but still no one said, "What are you looking for?" or "Why are you talking with her?" 28 The woman left her water jar and went into the town and said to the people, 29 "Come see a man who told me everything I have done. Could he possibly be the Messiah?" 30 They went out of the town and came to him. 31 Meanwhile, the disciples urged him, "Rabbi, eat." 32 But he said to them, "I have food to eat of which you do not know." 33 So the disciples said to one another, "Could someone have brought him something to eat?" 34[h] Jesus said to them, "My food is to do the will of the one who sent me and to finish his work. 35[i]*Do you not say, 'In four months the harvest will be here'? I tell you, look up and see the fields ripe for the harvest. 36[j]*The reaper is already receiving his payment and gathering crops for eternal life, so that the sower and reaper can rejoice together. 37[k] For here the saying is verified that 'One sows and another reaps.' 38 I sent you to reap what you have not worked for; others have done the work, and you are sharing the fruits of their work."

39 *Many of the Samaritans of that town began to believe in him because of the word of the woman who testified, "He told me everything I have done." 40 When the Samaritans came to him, they invited him to stay with them; and he

4, 11: Sir: the Greek **kyrios** means "master" or "lord," as a respectful mode of address for a human being or a deity; cf 4, 19. It is also the word used in the Septuagint for the Hebrew **'ădônai**, substituted for the tetragrammaton YHWH.

4, 20: This mountain: Gerizim, on which a temple was erected in the fourth century B.C. by Samaritans to rival Mt. Zion in Jerusalem; cf Dt 27, 4 (Mt. Ebal = the Jews' term for Gerizim).

4, 23: In Spirit and truth: not a reference to an interior worship within one's own spirit. The Spirit is the spirit given by God that reveals truth and enables one to worship God appropriately (14, 16–17). Cf "born of water and Spirit" (3, 5).

4, 25: The expectations of the Samaritans are expressed here in Jewish terminology. They did not expect a messianic king of the house of David but a prophet like Moses (Dt 18, 15).

4, 26: I am he: it could also be translated "I am," an Old Testament self-designation of Yahweh (Is 43, 3, etc.); cf 6, 20; 8, 24.28.58; 13, 19; 18, 5.6.8. See the note on Mk 6, 50.

4, 27: Talking with a woman: a religious and social restriction that Jesus is pictured treating as unimportant.

4, 35: 'In four months . . . ': probably a proverb; cf Mt 9, 37–38.

4, 36: Already: this word may go with the preceding verse rather than with 36.

4, 39: The woman is presented as a missionary, described in virtually the same words as the disciples are in Jesus' prayer (17, 20).

y 8, 53; Mt 12, 41. z 6, 35.58; 7, 37–39; Is 44, 3; 49, 10; Jl 4, 18; Rv 7, 16; 21, 6. a 2 Kgs 17, 24–34. b 9, 17; Hos 1, 3. c Dt 11, 29; 27, 4; Jos 8, 33; Ps 122, 1–5. d 2 Kgs 17, 27; Ps 76, 2–3. e 2 Cor 3, 17. f 1, 41. g 9, 37. h 5, 30.36; 6, 38; 9, 4; 17, 4. i Mt 9, 37–38; Lk 10, 2; Rv 14, 15. j Ps 126, 5–6; Am 9, 13–14. k Dt 20, 6; 28, 30; Jb 31, 8; Mi 6, 15.

stayed there two days. [41]Many more began to believe in him because of his word, [42 l]and they said to the woman, "We no longer believe because of your word; for we have heard for ourselves, and we know that this is truly the savior of the world."

Return to Galilee [43]*After the two days, he left there for Galilee. [44 m]*For Jesus himself testified that a prophet has no honor in his native place. [45]When he came into Galilee, the Galileans welcomed him, since they had seen all he had done in Jerusalem at the feast; for they themselves had gone to the feast.

Second Sign at Cana [46 n]*Then he returned to Cana in Galilee, where he had made the water wine. Now there was a royal official whose son was ill in Capernaum. [47]When he heard that Jesus had arrived in Galilee from Judea, he went to him and asked him to come down and heal his son, who was near death. [48 o]Jesus said to him, "Unless you people see signs and wonders, you will not believe." [49]The royal official said to him, "Sir, come down before my child dies." [50 p]Jesus said to him, "You may go; your son will live." The man believed what Jesus said to him and left. [51]While he was on his way back, his slaves met him and told him that his boy would live. [52]He asked them when he began to recover. They told him, "The fever left him yesterday, about one in the afternoon." [53]The father realized that just at that time Jesus had said to him, "Your son will live," and he and his whole household came to believe. [54 q][Now] this was the second sign Jesus did when he came to Galilee from Judea.

CHAPTER 5

Cure on a Sabbath [1 r]*After this, there was a feast of the Jews, and Jesus went up to Jerusalem. [2 s]*Now there is in Jerusalem at the Sheep [Gate] a pool called in Hebrew Bethesda, with five porticoes. [3]*In these lay a large number of ill, blind, lame, and crippled. [4]* [5]One man was there who had been ill for thirty-eight years. [6]When Jesus saw him lying there and knew that he had been ill for a long time, he said to him, "Do you want to be well?" [7]The sick man answered him, "Sir, I have no one to put me into the pool when the water is stirred up; while I am on my way, someone else gets down there before me." [8 t]Jesus said to him, "Rise, take up your mat, and walk." [9 u]Immediately the man became well, took up his mat, and walked.

Now that day was a sabbath. [10 v]So the Jews said to the man who was cured, "It is the sabbath, and it is not lawful for you to carry your mat." [11]He answered them, "The man who made me well told me, 'Take up your mat and walk.' " [12]They asked him, "Who is the man who told you, 'Take it up and walk'?" [13 w]The

4, 43–54: Jesus' arrival in Cana in Galilee; the second sign. This section introduces another theme, that of the life-giving word of Jesus. It is explicitly linked to the first sign (2, 11). The royal official believes (50). The natural life given his son is a sign of eternal life.

4, 44: Probably a reminiscence of a tradition as in Mk 6, 4. Cf Gospel of Thomas 31: "No prophet is acceptable in his village, no physician heals those who know him."

4, 46–54: The story of the cure of the royal official's son may be a third version of the cure of the centurion's son (Mt 8, 5–13) or servant (Lk 7, 1–10). Cf also Mt 15, 21–28 // Mk 7, 24–30.

5, 1–47: The self-revelation of Jesus continues in Jerusalem at a feast. The third sign (cf 2, 11; 4, 54) is performed, the cure of a paralytic by Jesus' life-giving word. The water of the pool fails to bring life; Jesus' word does.

5, 1: The reference in vv 45–46 to Moses suggests that the feast was Pentecost. The connection of that feast with the giving of the law to Moses on Sinai, attested in later Judaism, may already have been made in the first century. The feast could also be Passover (cf 6, 4). John stresses that the day was a sabbath (9).

5, 2: There is no noun with **Sheep.** "Gate" is supplied on the grounds that there must have been a gate in the NE wall of the temple area where animals for sacrifice were brought in; cf Neh 3, 1.32; 12, 39. **Hebrew:** more precisely, Aramaic. **Bethesda:** preferred to variants "Be(th)zatha" and "Bethsaida"; **bêt-ʾeŝdatayīn** is given as the name of a double pool northeast of the temple area in the Qumran Copper Roll. **Five porticoes:** a pool excavated in Jerusalem actually has five porticoes.

5, 3: The Caesarean and Western recensions, followed by the Vulgate, add "waiting for the movement of the water." Apparently an intermittent spring in the pool bubbled up occasionally (see 7). This turbulence was believed to cure.

5, 4: Toward the end of the second century in the West and among the fourth-century Greek Fathers, an additional verse was known: "For [from time to time] an angel of the Lord used to come down into the pool; and the water was stirred up, so the first one to get in [after the stirring of the water] was healed of whatever disease afflicted him." The angel was a popular explanation of the turbulence and the healing powers attributed to it. This verse is missing from all early Greek manuscripts and the earliest versions, including the original Vulgate. Its vocabulary is markedly non-Johannine.

l 1 Jn 4, 14. m Mt 13, 57; Mk 6, 4; Lk 4, 24. n 2, 1–11; Mt 8, 5–13; 15, 21–28; Mk 7, 24–30; Lk 7, 1–10. o 2, 18.23; Wis 8, 8; Mt 12, 38; 1 Cor 1, 22. p 1 Kgs 17, 23. q 2, 11. r 6, 4. s Neh 3, 1.32; 12, 39. t Mt 9, 6; Mk 2, 11; Lk 5, 24; Acts 3, 6. u Mk 2, 12; Lk 5, 25 / 9, 14. v Ex 20, 8; Jer 17, 21–27; Mk 3, 2; Lk 13, 10; 14, 1. w Mt 8, 18; 13, 36; Mk 4, 36; 7, 17.

man who was healed did not know who it was, for Jesus had slipped away, since there was a crowd there. [14] [x]*After this Jesus found him in the temple area and said to him, “Look, you are well; do not sin any more, so that nothing worse may happen to you.” [15]The man went and told the Jews that Jesus was the one who had made him well. [16] [y]Therefore, the Jews began to persecute Jesus because he did this on a sabbath. [17] [z]*But Jesus answered them, “My Father is at work until now, so I am at work.” [18] [a]For this reason the Jews tried all the more to kill him, because he not only broke the sabbath but he also called God his own father, making himself equal to God.

The Work of the Son [19] [b]*Jesus answered and said to them, “Amen, amen, I say to you, a son cannot do anything on his own, but only what he sees his father doing; for what he does, his son will do also. [20] [c]For the Father loves his Son and shows him everything that he himself does, and he will show him greater works than these, so that you may be amazed. [21] [d]*For just as the Father raises the dead and gives life, so also does the Son give life to whomever he wishes. [22] [e]*Nor does the Father judge anyone, but he has given all judgment to his Son, [23]so that all may honor the Son just as they honor the Father. Whoever does not honor the Son does not honor the Father who sent him. [24] [f]Amen, amen, I say to you, whoever hears my word and believes in the one who sent me has eternal life and will not come to condemnation, but has passed from death to life. [25] [g]Amen, amen, I say to you, the hour is coming and is now here when the dead will hear the voice of the Son of God, and those who hear will live. [26] [h]For just as the Father has life in himself, so also he gave to his Son the possession of life in himself. [27] [i]And he gave him power to exercise judgment, because he is the Son of Man. [28] [j]*Do not be amazed at this, because the hour is coming in which all who are in the tombs will hear his voice [29] [k]and will come out, those who have done good deeds to the resurrection of life, but those who have done wicked deeds to the resurrection of condemnation.

[30] [l]“I cannot do anything on my own; I judge as I hear, and my judgment is just, because I do not seek my own will but the will of the one who sent me.

Witnesses to Jesus [31] [m]“If I testify on my own behalf, my testimony cannot be verified. [32]*But there is another who testifies on my behalf, and I know that the testimony he gives on my behalf is true. [33] [n]You sent emissaries to John, and he testified to the truth. [34] [o]I do not accept testimony from a human being, but I say this so that you may be saved. [35] [p]*He was a burning and shining lamp, and for a while you were content to rejoice in his light. [36] [q]But I have testimony greater than John’s. The works that the Father gave me to accomplish, these works that I perform testify on my behalf that the Father has sent me. [37] [r]Moreover, the Father who sent me

5, 14: While the cure of the paralytic in Mk 2, 1–12 is associated with the forgiveness of sins, Jesus never drew a one-to-one connection between sin and suffering (cf 9, 3; Lk 12, 1–5), as did Ez 18, 20.

5, 17: Sabbath observance (10) was based on God’s resting on the seventh day (cf Gn 2, 2–3; Ex 20, 11). Philo and some rabbis insisted that God’s providence remains active on the sabbath, keeping all things in existence, giving life in birth and taking it away in death. Other rabbis taught that God rested from creating, but not from judging (= ruling, governing). Jesus here claims the same authority to work as the Father, and, in the discourse that follows, the same divine prerogatives: power over life and death (21.24–26) and judgment (22.27).

5, 19: This proverb or parable is taken from apprenticeship in a trade: the activity of a son is modeled on that of his father. Jesus’ dependence on the Father is justification for doing what the Father does.

5, 21: Gives life: in the Old Testament, a divine prerogative (Dt 32, 39; 1 Sm 2, 6; 2 Kgs 5, 7; Tob 13, 2; Is 26, 19; Dan 12, 2).

5, 22: Judgment: another divine prerogative, often expressed as acquittal or condemnation (Dt 32, 36; Ps 43, 1).

5, 28–29: While vv 19–27 present realized eschatology, vv 28–29 are future eschatology; cf Dn 12, 2.

5, 32: Another: likely the Father, who in four different ways gives testimony to Jesus, as indicated in the verse groupings 33–34, 36, 37–38, 39–40.

5, 35: Lamp: cf Ps 132, 17 “I will place a lamp for my anointed (= David),” and possibly the description of Elijah in Sir 48, 1. But only **for a while,** indicating the temporary and subordinate nature of John’s mission.

x 8, 11; 9, 2; Ez 18, 20. y 7, 23; Mt 12, 8. z Ex 20, 11. a 7, 1.25; 8, 37.40; 10, 33.36; 14, 28; Gn 3, 5–6; Wis 2, 16; Mt 26, 4; 2 Thes 2, 4. b 3, 34; 8, 26; 12, 49; 9, 4; 10, 30. c 3, 35. d 11, 25; Dt 32, 39; 1 Sm 2, 6; 2 Kgs 5, 7; Tb 13, 2; Wis 16, 13; Is 26, 19; Dn 7, 10.13; 12, 2; Rom 4, 17; 2 Cor 1, 9. e Acts 10, 42; 17, 31. f 3, 18; 8, 51; 1 Jn 3, 14. g 5, 28; 8, 51; 11, 25–26; Eph 2, 1; 5, 14; Rv 3, 1. h 1, 4; 1 Jn 5, 11. i 5, 22; Dn 7, 13.22; Mt 25, 31; Lk 21, 36. j 11, 43. k Dn 12, 2; Mt 16, 27; 25, 46; Acts 24, 15; 2 Cor 5, 10. l 6, 38. m 8, 13–14.18. n 1, 19–27; Mt 11, 10–11. o 1 Jn 5, 9. p 1, 8; Ps 132, 17; Sir 48, 1. q 10, 25. r 8, 18; Dt 4, 12.15; 1 Jn 5, 9.

has testified on my behalf. But you have never heard his voice nor seen his form, 38 [s]and you do not have his word remaining in you, because you do not believe in the one whom he has sent. 39 [t]*You search the scriptures, because you think you have eternal life through them; even they testify on my behalf. 40 But you do not want to come to me to have life.

Unbelief of Jesus' Hearers 41 *"I do not accept human praise; 42 [u]moreover, I know that you do not have the love of God in you. 43 [v]I came in the name of my Father, but you do not accept me; yet if another comes in his own name, you will accept him. 44 [w]How can you believe, when you accept praise from one another and do not seek the praise that comes from the only God? 45 [x]Do not think that I will accuse you before the Father: the one who will accuse you is Moses, in whom you have placed your hope. 46 [y]For if you had believed Moses, you would have believed me, because he wrote about me. 47 But if you do not believe his writings, how will you believe my words?"

CHAPTER 6

Multiplication of the Loaves 1 [z]*After this, Jesus went across the Sea of Galilee [of Tiberias]. 2 A large crowd followed him, because they saw the signs he was performing on the sick. 3 Jesus went up on the mountain, and there he sat down with his disciples. 4 [a]The Jewish feast of Passover was near. 5 [b]*When Jesus raised his eyes and saw that a large crowd was coming to him, he said to Philip, "Where can we buy enough food for them to eat?" 6 *He said this to test him, because he himself knew what he was going to do. 7 [c]*Philip answered him, "Two hundred days' wages worth of food would not be enough for each of them to have a little [bit]." 8 One of his disciples, Andrew, the brother of Simon Peter, said to him, 9 [d]*"There is a boy here who has five barley loaves and two fish; but what good are these for so many?" 10 [e]*Jesus said, "Have the people recline." Now there was a great deal of grass in that place. So the men reclined, about five thousand in number. 11 [f]Then Jesus took the loaves, gave thanks, and distributed them to those who were reclining, and also as much of the fish as they wanted. 12 When they had had their fill, he said to his disciples, "Gather the fragments left over, so that nothing will be wasted." 13 *So they collected them, and filled twelve wicker baskets with fragments from the five barley loaves that had been more than they could eat. 14 [g]*When the people saw the sign he had done, they said, "This is truly the Prophet, the one who is to come into the world." 15 [h]Since Jesus knew that they were going to come and carry him off to make him king, he withdrew again to the mountain alone.

Walking on the Water 16 [i]*When it was evening, his disciples went down to the sea, 17 em-

5, 39: You search: this may be an imperative: "Search the scriptures, because you think that you have eternal life through them."

5, 41: Praise: the same Greek word means "praise" or "honor" (from others) and "glory" (from God). There is a play on this in v 44.

6, 1–15: This story of the multiplication of the loaves is the fourth sign (cf the note on 5, 1–47). It is the only miracle story found in all four gospels (occurring twice in Mk and Mt). See the notes on Mt 14, 13–21 and 15, 32–39. John differs on the roles of Philip and Andrew, the proximity of Passover (4), and the allusion to Elisha (see 9). The story here symbolizes the food that is really available through Jesus. It connotes a new exodus and has eucharistic overtones.

6, 1: [Of Tiberias]: the awkward apposition represents a later name of the Sea of Galilee. It was probably originally a marginal gloss.

6, 5: Jesus takes the initiative (in the synoptics, the disciples do), possibly pictured as (cf 14) the new Moses (cf Nm 11, 13).

6, 6: Probably the evangelist's comment; in this gospel Jesus is never portrayed as ignorant of anything.

6, 7: Days' wages: literally, "denarii"; a Roman denarius is a day's wage in Mt 20, 2.

6, 9: Barley loaves: the food of the poor. There seems an allusion to the story of Elisha multiplying the barley bread in 2 Kgs 4, 42–44.

6, 10: Grass: implies springtime, and therefore Passover. **Five thousand:** so Mk 6, 39.44 and parallels.

6, 13: Baskets: the word describes the typically Palestinian wicker basket, as in Mk 6, 43 and parallels.

6, 14: The Prophet: probably the prophet like Moses (see the note on 1, 21). **The one who is to come into the world:** probably Elijah; cf Mal 3, 1.23.

6, 16–21: The fifth sign is a nature miracle, portraying Jesus sharing Yahweh's power. Cf the parallel stories following the multiplication of the loaves in Mk 6, 45–52 and Mt 14, 22–33.

s 1 Jn 2, 14. t 12, 16; 19, 28; 20, 9; Lk 24, 27.44; 1 Pt 1, 10. u 1 Jn 2, 15. v Mt 24, 5.24. w 12, 43. x Dt 31, 26. y 5, 39; Dt 18, 15; Lk 16, 31; 24, 44. z Mt 14, 13–21; Mk 6, 32–44; Lk 9, 10–17. a 2, 13; 11, 55. b Nm 11, 13. c Mt 20, 2. d 2 Kgs 4, 42–44. e Mt 14, 21; Mk 6, 44. f 21, 13. g Dt 18, 15.18; Mal 3, 1.23; Acts 3, 22. h 18, 36. i Mt 14, 22–27; Mk 6, 45–52.

barked in a boat, and went across the sea to
Capernaum. It had already grown dark, and
Jesus had not yet come to them. [18]The sea was
stirred up because a strong wind was blowing.
[19][j]*When they had rowed about three or four
miles, they saw Jesus walking on the sea and
coming near the boat, and they began to be
afraid. [20]*But he said to them, "It is I. Do not be
afraid." [21]They wanted to take him into the
boat, but the boat immediately arrived at the
shore to which they were heading.
The Bread of Life Discourse [22]*The next day,
the crowd that remained across the sea saw that
there had been only one boat there, and that
Jesus had not gone along with his disciples in the
boat, but only his disciples had left. [23]*Other
boats came from Tiberias near the place where
they had eaten the bread when the Lord gave
thanks. [24]When the crowd saw that neither
Jesus nor his disciples were there, they them-
selves got into boats and came to Capernaum
looking for Jesus. [25]And when they found him
across the sea they said to him, "Rabbi, when did
you get here?" [26]Jesus answered them and said,
"Amen, amen, I say to you, you are looking for
me not because you saw signs but because you
ate the loaves and were filled. [27][k]*Do not work
for food that perishes but for the food that
endures for eternal life, which the Son of Man
will give you. For on him the Father, God, has
set his seal." [28]So they said to him, "What can
we do to accomplish the works of God?" [29]Jesus
answered and said to them, "This is the work of
God, that you believe in the one he sent." [30][l]So
they said to him, "What sign can you do, that we
may see and believe in you? What can you do?
[31][m]*Our ancestors ate manna in the desert, as it
is written:

'He gave them bread from heaven to eat.' "

[32][n]So Jesus said to them, "Amen, amen, I say to
you, it was not Moses who gave the bread from
heaven; my Father gives you the true bread from
heaven. [33]For the bread of God is that which
comes down from heaven and gives life to the
world."

[34][o]So they said to him, "Sir, give us this bread
always." [35][p]*Jesus said to them, "I am the
bread of life; whoever comes to me will never
hunger, and whoever believes in me will never
thirst. [36][q]But I told you that although you have
seen [me], you do not believe. [37]Everything that
the Father gives me will come to me, and I will
not reject anyone who comes to me, [38][r]because
I came down from heaven not to do my own
will but the will of the one who sent me.
[39][s]And this is the will of the one who sent me,
that I should not lose anything of what he gave
me, but that I should raise it [on] the last day.
[40][t]For this is the will of my Father, that every-
one who sees the Son and believes in him may
have eternal life, and I shall raise him [on] the
last day."

[41]The Jews murmured about him because he
said, "I am the bread that came down from
heaven," [42][u]and they said, "Is this not Jesus, the
son of Joseph? Do we not know his father and
mother? Then how can he say, 'I have come
down from heaven'?" [43][v]*Jesus answered and
said to them, "Stop murmuring among your-
selves. [44]No one can come to me unless the
Father who sent me draw him, and I will raise

6, 19: **Walking on the sea:** although the Greek (cf 16) could mean "on the seashore" or "by the sea" (cf 21, 1), the parallels, especially Mt 14, 25, make clear that Jesus walked upon the water. John may allude to Job 9, 8: God "treads upon the crests of the sea."

6, 20: **It is I:** literally, "I am." See also the notes on 4, 26 and Mk 6, 50.

6, 22–71: Discourse on the bread of life; replacement of the manna. Verses 22–34 serve as an introduction, vv 35–59 constitute the discourse proper, vv 60–71 portray the reaction of the disciples and Peter's confession.

6, 23: Possibly a later interpolation, to explain how the crowd got to Capernaum.

6, 27: **The food that endures for eternal life:** cf 4, 14, on water "springing up to eternal life."

6, 31: **Bread from heaven:** cf Ex 16, 4.15.32–34 and the notes there; Ps 78, 24. The manna, thought to have been hidden by Jeremiah (2 Mc 2, 5–8), was expected to reappear miraculously at Passover, in the last days.

6, 35–59: Up to v 50, "bread of life" is a figure for God's revelation in Jesus; in vv 51–58, the eucharistic theme comes to the fore. There may thus be a break between vv 50 and 51.

6, 43: **Murmuring:** the word may reflect the Greek of Ex 16, 2.7.8.

j Jb 9, 8; Pss 29, 3–4; 77, 20; Is 43, 16. k 6, 50.51.54.58. l Mt 16, 1–4; Lk 11, 29–30. m Ex 16, 4–5; Nm 11, 7–9; Ps 78, 24. n Mt 6, 11. o 4, 15. p Is 55, 1–3; Am 8, 11–13. q 20, 29. r 4, 34; Mt 26, 39; Heb 10, 9. s 10, 28–29; 17, 12; 18, 9. t 1 Jn 2, 25. u Mt 13, 54–57; Mk 6, 1–4; Lk 4, 22. v Ex 16, 2.7.8; Lk 4, 22.

him on the last day. 45 [w]It is written in the prophets:

'They shall all be taught by God.'

Everyone who listens to my Father and learns from him comes to me. 46 [x]Not that anyone has seen the Father except the one who is from God; he has seen the Father. 47 Amen, amen, I say to you, whoever believes has eternal life. 48 I am the bread of life. 49 [y]Your ancestors ate the manna in the desert, but they died; 50 this is the bread that comes down from heaven so that one may eat it and not die. 51 [z]I am the living bread that came down from heaven; whoever eats this bread will live forever; and the bread that I will give is my flesh for the life of the world."

52 The Jews quarreled among themselves, saying, "How can this man give us [his] flesh to eat?" 53 Jesus said to them, "Amen, amen, I say to you, unless you eat the flesh of the Son of Man and drink his blood, you do not have life within you. 54 *Whoever eats my flesh and drinks my blood has eternal life, and I will raise him on the last day. 55 For my flesh is true food, and my blood is true drink. 56 Whoever eats my flesh and drinks my blood remains in me and I in him. 57 [a]Just as the living Father sent me and I have life because of the Father, so also the one who feeds on me will have life because of me. 58 This is the bread that came down from heaven. Unlike your ancestors who ate and still died, whoever eats this bread will live forever." 59 These things he said while teaching in the synagogue in Capernaum.

The Words of Eternal Life 60 *Then many of his disciples who were listening said, "This saying is hard; who can accept it?" 61 Since Jesus knew that his disciples were murmuring about this, he said to them, "Does this shock you? 62 *What if you were to see the Son of Man ascending to where he was before? 63 *It is the spirit that gives life, while the flesh is of no avail. The words I have spoken to you are spirit and life. 64 [b]But there are some of you who do not believe." Jesus knew from the beginning the ones who would not believe and the one who would betray him. 65 And he said, "For this reason I have told you that no one can come to me unless it is granted him by my Father."

66 As a result of this, many [of] his disciples returned to their former way of life and no longer accompanied him. 67 Jesus then said to the Twelve, "Do you also want to leave?" 68 Simon Peter answered him, "Master, to whom shall we go? You have the words of eternal life. 69 [c]We have come to believe and are convinced that you are the Holy One of God." 70 Jesus answered them, "Did I not choose you twelve? Yet is not one of you a devil?" 71 [d]He was referring to Judas, son of Simon the Iscariot; it was he who would betray him, one of the Twelve.

CHAPTER 7*

The Feast of Tabernacles 1 [e]After this, Jesus moved about within Galilee; but he did not wish to travel in Judea, because the Jews were trying to kill him. 2 [f]But the Jewish feast of Tabernacles was near. 3 *So his brothers said to him, "Leave

6, 54–58: Eats: the verb used in these verses is not the classical Greek verb used of human eating, but that of animal eating: "munch," "gnaw." This may be part of John's emphasis on the reality of the flesh and blood of Jesus (cf 55), but the same verb eventually became the ordinary verb in Greek meaning "eat."

6, 60–71: These verses refer more to themes of vv 35–50 than to those of 51–58 and seem to be addressed to members of the Johannine community who found it difficult to accept the high christology reflected in the bread of life discourse.

6, 62: This unfinished conditional sentence is obscure. Probably there is a reference to vv 49–51. Jesus claims to be **the bread that comes down from heaven** (50); this claim provokes incredulity (60); and so Jesus is pictured as asking what his disciples will say when he goes up to heaven.

6, 63: Spirit . . . flesh: probably not a reference to the eucharistic body of Jesus but to the supernatural and the natural, as in 3, 6. **Spirit and life:** all Jesus said about the bread of life is the revelation of the Spirit.

7–8: These chapters contain events about the feast of Tabernacles (Sukkoth, Ingathering: Ex 23, 16; Tents, Booths: Dt 16, 13–16), with its symbols of booths (originally built to shelter harvesters), rain (water from Siloam poured on the temple altar), and lights (illumination of the four torches in the Court of the Women). They continue the theme of the replacement of feasts (Passover, 2, 13; 6, 4; Hanukkah, 10, 22; Pentecost, 5, 1), here accomplished by Jesus as the Living Water. These chapters comprise seven miscellaneous controversies and dialogues. There is a literary inclusion with Jesus in hiding in 7, 4.10 and 8, 59. There are frequent references to attempts on his life: 7, 1.13.19.25.30.32.44; 8, 37.40.59.

7, 3: Brothers: these relatives (cf 2, 12 and see the note on Mk 6, 3) are never portrayed as disciples until after the resurrection

w Is 54, 13; Jer 31, 33–34. x 1, 18; 7, 29; Ex 33, 20. y 1 Cor 10, 3.5. z Mt 26, 26–27; Lk 22, 19. a 5, 26. b 13, 11. c 11, 27; Mt 16, 16; Mk 1, 24; Lk 4, 34. d 12, 4; 13, 2.27. e 5, 18; 8, 37.40. f Ex 23, 16; Lv 23, 34; Nm 29, 12; Dt 16, 13–16; Zec 14, 16–19.

here and go to Judea, so that your disciples also may see the works you are doing. [4] [g]No one works in secret if he wants to be known publicly. If you do these things, manifest yourself to the world." [5]For his brothers did not believe in him. [6]*So Jesus said to them, "My time is not yet here, but the time is always right for you. [7] [h]The world cannot hate you, but it hates me, because I testify to it that its works are evil. [8]*You go up to the feast. I am not going up to this feast, because my time has not yet been fulfilled." [9]After he had said this, he stayed on in Galilee.

[10]But when his brothers had gone up to the feast, he himself also went up, not openly but [as it were] in secret. [11]The Jews were looking for him at the feast and saying, "Where is he?" [12]And there was considerable murmuring about him in the crowds. Some said, "He is a good man," [while] others said, "No; on the contrary, he misleads the crowd." [13] [i]Still, no one spoke openly about him because they were afraid of the Jews.

The First Dialogue [14]*When the feast was already half over, Jesus went up into the temple area and began to teach. [15] [j]*The Jews were amazed and said, "How does he know scripture without having studied?" [16]Jesus answered them and said, "My teaching is not my own but is from the one who sent me. [17] [k]*Whoever chooses to do his will shall know whether my teaching is from God or whether I speak on my own. [18]Whoever speaks on his own seeks his own glory, but whoever seeks the glory of the one who sent him is truthful, and there is no wrong in him. [19] [l]Did not Moses give you the law? Yet none of you keeps the law. Why are you trying to kill me?" [20] [m]*The crowd answered, "You are possessed! Who is trying to kill you?" [21] [n]*Jesus answered and said to them, "I performed one work and all of you are amazed [22] [o]because of it. Moses gave you circumcision—not that it came from Moses but rather from the patriarchs—and you circumcise a man on the sabbath. [23] [p]If a man can receive circumcision on a sabbath so that the law of Moses may not be broken, are you angry with me because I made a whole person well on a sabbath? [24] [q]Stop judging by appearances, but judge justly."

[25]So some of the inhabitants of Jerusalem said, "Is he not the one they are trying to kill? [26]*And look, he is speaking openly and they say nothing to him. Could the authorities have realized that he is the Messiah? [27] [r]But we know where he is from. When the Messiah comes, no one will know where he is from." [28] [s]So Jesus cried out in the temple area as he was teaching and said, "You know me and also know where I am from. Yet I did not come on my own, but the one who sent me, whom you do not know, is true. [29] [t]I know him, because I am from him, and he sent me." [30] [u]So they tried to arrest him, but no one laid a hand upon him, because his hour had not yet come. [31] [v]But many of the crowd began to believe in him, and said, "When the Messiah comes, will he perform more signs than this man has done?"

Officers Sent to Arrest Jesus [32]*The Pharisees heard the crowd murmuring about him to

---

(Acts 1, 14). Mt 13, 55 and Mk 6, 3 give the names of four of them. Jesus has already performed works/signs in Judea; cf 2, 23; 3, 2; 4, 45; 5, 8.

7, 6: Time: the Greek word means "opportune time," here a synonym for Jesus' "hour" (see the note on 2, 4), his death and resurrection. In the wordplay, any time is suitable for Jesus' brothers, because they are not dependent on God's will.

7, 8: I am not going up: an early attested reading "not yet" seems a correction, since Jesus in the story does go up to the feast. "Go up," in a play on words, refers not only to going up to Jerusalem but also to exaltation at the cross, resurrection, and ascension; cf 3, 14; 6, 62; 20, 17.

7, 14–31: Jesus teaches in the temple; debate with the Jews.

7, 15: Without having studied: literally, "How does he know letters without having learned?" Children were taught to read and write by means of the scriptures. But here more than Jesus' literacy is being discussed; the people are wondering how he can teach like a rabbi. Rabbis were trained by other rabbis and traditionally quoted their teachers.

7, 17: To do his will: presumably a reference back to the "work" of 6, 29: belief in the one whom God has sent.

7, 20: You are possessed: literally, "You have a demon." The insane were thought to be possessed by a demoniacal spirit.

7, 21: One work: the cure of the paralytic (5, 1–9) because of the reference to the sabbath (22; 5, 9–10).

7, 26: The authorities: the members of the Sanhedrin (same term as 3, 1).

7, 32–36: Jesus announces his approaching departure (cf also 8, 21; 12, 36; 13, 33) and complete control over his destiny.

g 14, 22. h 15, 18. i 9, 22; 19, 38; 20, 19. j Lk 2, 47. k 6, 29. l Acts 7, 53. m 8, 48–49; 10, 20. n 5, 1–9. o Gn 17, 10; Lv 12, 3. p 5, 2–9.16; Mt 12, 11–12; Lk 14, 5. q 8, 15; Lv 19, 15; Is 11, 3–4. r Heb 7, 3. s 8, 19. t 6, 46; 8, 55. u 7, 44; 8, 20; Lk 4, 29–30. v 2, 11; 10, 42; 11, 45.

this effect, and the chief priests and the Pharisees sent guards to arrest him. [33] [w]So Jesus said, "I will be with you only a little while longer, and then I will go to the one who sent me. [34] [x]You will look for me but not find [me], and where I am you cannot come." [35] *So the Jews said to one another, "Where is he going that we will not find him? Surely he is not going to the dispersion among the Greeks to teach the Greeks, is he? [36]What is the meaning of his saying, 'You will look for me and not find [me], and where I am you cannot come'?"

Rivers of Living Water [37] [y]*On the last and greatest day of the feast, Jesus stood up and exclaimed, "Let anyone who thirsts come to me and drink. [38] [z]*Whoever believes in me, as scripture says:

'Rivers of living water will flow from within him.' "

[39] [a]*He said this in reference to the Spirit that those who came to believe in him were to receive. There was, of course, no Spirit yet, because Jesus had not yet been glorified.

Discussion about the Origins of the Messiah [40] [b]*Some in the crowd who heard these words said, "This is truly the Prophet." [41]Others said, "This is the Messiah." But others said, "The Messiah will not come from Galilee, will he? [42] [c]Does not scripture say that the Messiah will be of David's family and come from Bethlehem, the village where David lived?" [43]So a division occurred in the crowd because of him. [44]Some of them even wanted to arrest him, but no one laid hands on him.

[45]So the guards went to the chief priests and Pharisees, who asked them, "Why did you not bring him?" [46]The guards answered, "Never before has anyone spoken like this one." [47]So the Pharisees answered them, "Have you also been deceived? [48] [d]Have any of the authorities or the Pharisees believed in him? [49]But this crowd, which does not know the law, is accursed." [50] [e]Nicodemus, one of their members who had come to him earlier, said to them, [51] [f]"Does our law condemn a person before it first hears him and finds out what he is doing?" [52]They answered and said to him, "You are not from Galilee also, are you? Look and see that no prophet arises from Galilee."

CHAPTER 8

A Woman Caught in Adultery [[53]*Then each went to his own house, [1] [g]*while Jesus went to the Mount of Olives. [2]But early in the morning he arrived again in the temple area, and all the people started coming to him, and he sat down and taught them. [3]Then the scribes and the Pharisees brought a woman who had been caught in adultery and made her stand in the middle. [4]They said to him, "Teacher, this woman was caught in the very act of committing adultery. [5] [h]*Now in the law, Moses commanded us to stone such women. So what do you say?" [6]*They said this to test him, so that they could have some charge to bring against

7, 35: Dispersion: or "diaspora": Jews living outside Palestine. **Greeks:** probably refers to the Gentiles in the Mediterranean area; cf 12, 20.

7, 37–39: Promise of living water through the Spirit.

7, 38: Living water: not an exact quotation from any Old Testament passage; in the gospel context the gift of the Spirit is meant; cf 3, 5. **From within him:** either Jesus or the believer; if Jesus, it continues the Jesus-Moses motif (water from the rock, Ex 17, 6; Nm 20, 11) as well as Jesus as the new temple (cf Ez 47, 1). Grammatically, it goes better with the believer.

7, 39: No Spirit yet: Codex Vaticanus and early Latin, Syriac, and Coptic versions add "given." In this gospel, the sending of the Spirit cannot take place until Jesus' glorification through his death, resurrection, and ascension; cf 20, 22.

7, 40–53: Discussion of the Davidic lineage of the Messiah.

7, 53—8, 11: The story of the woman caught in adultery is a later insertion here, missing from all early Greek manuscripts. A Western text-type insertion, attested mainly in Old Latin translations, it is found in different places in different manuscripts: here, or after 7, 36, or at the end of this gospel, or after Lk 21, 38, or at the end of that gospel. There are many non-Johannine features in the language, and there are also many doubtful readings within the passage. The style and motifs are similar to those of Luke, and it fits better with the general situation at the end of Lk 21, but it was probably inserted here because of the allusion to Jer 17, 13 (cf the note on 8, 6) and the statement, "I do not judge anyone," in 8, 15. The Catholic Church accepts this passage as canonical scripture.

8, 1: Mount of Olives: not mentioned elsewhere in the gospel tradition outside of passion week.

8, 5: Lv 20, 10 and Dt 22, 22 mention only death, but Dt 22, 23–24 prescribes stoning for a betrothed virgin.

8, 6: Cf Jer 17, 13 (RSV): "Those who turn away from thee shall be written in the earth, for they have forsaken the LORD, the fountain of living water"; cf 7, 38.

w 13, 33; 16, 16. x 8, 21; 12, 36; 13, 33.36; 16, 5; Dt 4, 29; Prv 1, 28; Is 55, 6; Hos 5, 6. y Rv 21, 6. z 4, 10.14; 19, 34; Is 12, 3; Ez 47, 1. a 16, 7. b Dt 18, 15.18. c 2 Sm 7, 12–14; Pss 89, 3–4; 132, 11; Mi 5, 1; Mt 2, 5–6. d 12, 42. e 3, 1; 19, 39. f Dt 1, 16–17. g Lk 21, 37–38. h Lv 20, 10; Dt 22, 22–29.

him. Jesus bent down and began to write on the ground with his finger. [7 i]*But when they continued asking him, he straightened up and said to them, "Let the one among you who is without sin be the first to throw a stone at her." [8]Again he bent down and wrote on the ground. [9]And in response, they went away one by one, beginning with the elders. So he was left alone with the woman before him. [10 j]Then Jesus straightened up and said to her, "Woman, where are they? Has no one condemned you?" [11 k]She replied, "No one, sir." Then Jesus said, "Neither do I condemn you. Go, [and] from now on do not sin any more."]

The Light of the World [12 l]*Jesus spoke to them again, saying, "I am the light of the world. Whoever follows me will not walk in darkness, but will have the light of life." [13]So the Pharisees said to him, "You testify on your own behalf, so your testimony cannot be verified." [14 m]*Jesus answered and said to them, "Even if I do testify on my own behalf, my testimony can be verified, because I know where I came from and where I am going. But you do not know where I come from or where I am going. [15 n]*You judge by appearances, but I do not judge anyone. [16 o]And even if I should judge, my judgment is valid, because I am not alone, but it is I and the Father who sent me. [17 p]*Even in your law it is written that the testimony of two men can be verified. [18 q]I testify on my behalf and so does the Father who sent me." [19 r]So they said to him, "Where is your father?" Jesus answered, "You know neither me nor my Father. If you knew me, you would know my Father also." [20 s]He spoke these words while teaching in the treasury in the temple area. But no one arrested him, because his hour had not yet come.

Jesus, the Father's Ambassador [21 t]*He said to them again, "I am going away and you will look for me, but you will die in your sin. Where I am going you cannot come." [22]*So the Jews said, "He is not going to kill himself, is he, because he said, 'Where I am going you cannot come'?" [23 u]He said to them, "You belong to what is below, I belong to what is above. You belong to this world, but I do not belong to this world. [24 v]*That is why I told you that you will die in your sins. For if you do not believe that I AM, you will die in your sins." [25 w]*So they said to him, "Who are you?" Jesus said to them, "What I told you from the beginning. [26 x]I have much to say about you in condemnation. But the one who sent me is true, and what I heard from him I tell the world." [27]They did not realize that he was speaking to them of the Father. [28 y]So Jesus said [to them], "When you lift up the Son of Man, then you will realize that I AM, and that I do nothing on my own, but I say only what the Father taught me. [29]The one who sent me is with me. He has not left me alone, because I always do what is pleasing to him." [30]Because he spoke this way, many came to believe in him.

Jesus and Abraham [31]*Jesus then said to those Jews who believed in him, "If you remain

8, 7: The first stones were to be thrown by the witnesses (Dt 17, 7).

8, 12–20: Jesus the light of the world. Jesus replaces the four torches of the illumination of the temple as the light of joy.

8, 14: My testimony can be verified: this seems to contradict 5, 31, but the emphasis here is on Jesus' origin from the Father and his divine destiny. **Where I am going:** indicates Jesus' passion and glorification.

8, 15: By appearances: literally, "according to the flesh." **I do not judge anyone:** superficial contradiction of 5, 22.27.30; here the emphasis is that the judgment is not by material standards.

8, 17: Your law: a reflection of later controversy between church and synagogue.

8, 21–30: He whose ambassador I am is with me. Jesus' origin is from God; he can reveal God.

8, 21: You will die in your sin: i.e., of disbelief; cf v 24. **Where I am going you cannot come:** except through faith in Jesus' passion-resurrection.

8, 22: The Jews suspect that he is referring to his death. Johannine irony is apparent here; Jesus' death will not be self-inflicted but destined by God.

8, 24.28: I AM: an expression that late Jewish tradition understood as Yahweh's own self-designation (Is 43, 10); see the note on 4, 26. Jesus is here placed on a par with Yahweh.

8, 25: What I told you from the beginning: this verse seems textually corrupt, with several other possible translations: "(I am) what I say to you"; "Why do I speak to you at all?" The earliest attested reading (Bodmer Papyrus P^{66}) has (in a second hand), "I told you at the beginning what I am also telling you (now)." The answer here (cf Prv 8, 22) seems to hinge on a misunderstanding of v 24 "**that I AM**" as "**what I am.**"

8, 31–59: Jesus' origin ("before Abraham") and destiny are developed; the truth will free them from sin (34) and death (51).

8, 31: Those Jews who believed in him: a rough editorial suture, since in v 37 they are described as trying to kill Jesus.

i Dt 17, 7. j Ez 33, 11. k 5, 14. l 1, 4–5.9; 12, 46; Ex 13, 22; Is 42, 6; Zec 14, 8. m 5, 31. n 12, 47; 1 Sm 16, 7. o 5, 30. p Dt 17, 6; 19, 15; Nm 35, 30. q 5, 23.37. r 7, 28; 14, 7; 15, 21. s 7, 30. t 7, 34; 13, 33. u 3, 31; 17, 14; 18, 36. v Ex 3, 14; Dt 32, 39; Is 43, 10. w 10, 24. x 12, 44–50. y 3, 14; 12, 32.34.

in my word, you will truly be my disciples, 32 [z]and you will know the truth, and the truth will set you free." 33 [a]*They answered him, "We are descendants of Abraham and have never been enslaved to anyone. How can you say, 'You will become free'?" 34 [b]Jesus answered them, "Amen, amen, I say to you, everyone who commits sin is a slave of sin. 35 [c]*A slave does not remain in a household forever, but a son always remains. 36 So if a son frees you, then you will truly be free. 37 I know that you are descendants of Abraham. But you are trying to kill me, because my word has no room among you. 38 *I tell you what I have seen in the Father's presence; then do what you have heard from the Father."

39 [d]*They answered and said to him, "Our father is Abraham." Jesus said to them, "If you were Abraham's children, you would be doing the works of Abraham. 40 But now you are trying to kill me, a man who has told you the truth that I heard from God; Abraham did not do this. 41 [e]You are doing the works of your father!" [So] they said to him, "We are not illegitimate. We have one Father, God." 42 [f]Jesus said to them, "If God were your Father, you would love me, for I came from God and am here; I did not come on my own, but he sent me. 43 Why do you not understand what I am saying? Because you cannot bear to hear my word. 44 [g]You belong to your father the devil and you willingly carry out your father's desires. He was a murderer from the beginning and does not stand in truth, because there is no truth in him. When he tells a lie, he speaks in character, because he is a liar and the father of lies. 45 But because I speak the truth, you do not believe me. 46 [h]Can any of you charge me with sin? If I am telling the truth, why do you not believe me? 47 [i]Whoever belongs to God hears the words of God; for this reason you do not listen, because you do not belong to God."

48 *The Jews answered and said to him, "Are we not right in saying that you are a Samaritan and are possessed?" 49 Jesus answered, "I am not possessed; I honor my Father, but you dishonor me. 50 [j]I do not seek my own glory; there is one who seeks it and he is the one who judges. 51 [k]Amen, amen, I say to you, whoever keeps my word will never see death." 52 [So] the Jews said to him, "Now we are sure that you are possessed. Abraham died, as did the prophets, yet you say, 'Whoever keeps my word will never taste death.' 53 [l]*Are you greater than our father Abraham, who died? Or the prophets, who died? Who do you make yourself out to be?" 54 Jesus answered, "If I glorify myself, my glory is worth nothing; but it is my Father who glorifies me, of whom you say, 'He is our God.' 55 [m]You do not know him, but I know him. And if I should say that I do not know him, I would be like you a liar. But I do know him and I keep his word. 56 [n]*Abraham your father rejoiced to see my day; he saw it and was glad. 57 *So the Jews said to him, "You are not yet fifty years old and you have seen Abraham?" 58 [o]*Jesus said to them, "Amen, amen, I say to you, before Abraham came to be, I AM." 59 [p]So they picked up stones to throw at him; but Jesus hid and went out of the temple area.

8, 33: Have never been enslaved to anyone: since, historically, the Jews were enslaved almost continuously, this verse is probably Johannine irony, about slavery to sin.

8, 35: A slave . . . a son: an allusion to Ishmael and Isaac (Gn 16 and 21), or to the release of a slave after six years (Ex 21, 2; Dt 15, 12).

8, 38: The Father: i.e., God. It is also possible, however, to understand the second part of the verse as a sarcastic reference to descent of the Jews from the devil (44), "You do what you have heard from [your] father."

8, 39: The works of Abraham: Abraham believed; cf Rom 4, 11–17; Jas 2, 21–23.

8, 48: Samaritan: therefore interested in magical powers; cf Acts 7, 14–24.

8, 53: Are you greater than our father Abraham?: cf 4, 12.

8, 56: He saw it: this seems a reference to the birth of Isaac (Gn 17, 7; 21, 6), the beginning of the fulfillment of promises about Abraham's seed.

8, 57: The evidence of the third-century Bodmer Papyrus P^{75} and the first hand of Codex Sinaiticus indicates that the text originally read: "How can Abraham have seen you?"

8, 58: Came to be, I AM: the Greek word used for "came to be" is the one used of all creation in the prologue, while the word used for "am" is the one reserved for the Logos.

z Is 42, 7; Gal 4, 31. a Mt 3, 9. b Rom 6, 16–17. c Gn 21, 10; Gal 4, 30; Heb 3, 5–6. d Gn 26, 5; Rom 4, 11–17; Jas 2, 21–23. e Mal 2, 10. f 1 Jn 5, 1. g Gn 3, 4; Wis 1, 13; 2, 24; Acts 13, 10; 1 Jn 3, 8–15. h Heb 4, 15; 1 Pt 2, 22; 1 Jn 3, 5. i 10, 26; 1 Jn 4, 6. j 7, 18. k 5, 24–29; 6, 40.47; 11, 25–26. l 4, 12. m 7, 28–29. n Gn 17, 17; Mt 13, 17; Lk 17, 22. o 1, 30; 17, 5. p 10, 31.39; 11, 8; Lk 4, 29–30.

CHAPTER 9

The Man Born Blind [1][q]*As he passed by he
saw a man blind from birth. [2][r]*His disciples
asked him, "Rabbi, who sinned, this man or his
parents, that he was born blind?" [3][s]Jesus an-
swered, "Neither he nor his parents sinned; it is
so that the works of God might be made visible
through him. [4][t]We have to do the works of the
one who sent me while it is day. Night is coming
when no one can work. [5][u]While I am in the
world, I am the light of the world." [6][v]When he
had said this, he spat on the ground and made
clay with the saliva, and smeared the clay on his
eyes, [7][w]*and said to him, "Go wash in the Pool
of Siloam" (which means Sent). So he went and
washed, and came back able to see.

[8]His neighbors and those who had seen him
earlier as a beggar said, "Isn't this the one who
used to sit and beg?" [9]Some said, "It is," but
others said, "No, he just looks like him." He said,
"I am." [10]So they said to him, "[So] how were
your eyes opened?" [11]He replied, "The man
called Jesus made clay and anointed my eyes and
told me, 'Go to Siloam and wash.' So I went
there and washed and was able to see." [12]And
they said to him, "Where is he?" He said, "I
don't know."

[13]They brought the one who was once blind
to the Pharisees. [14][x]*Now Jesus had made clay
and opened his eyes on a sabbath. [15]So then the
Pharisees also asked him how he was able to see.
He said to them, "He put clay on my eyes, and I
washed, and now I can see." [16][y]So some of the
Pharisees said, "This man is not from God,
because he does not keep the sabbath." [But]
others said, "How can a sinful man do such
signs?" And there was a division among them.
[17][z]So they said to the blind man again, "What
do you have to say about him, since he opened
your eyes?" He said, "He is a prophet."

[18]Now the Jews did not believe that he had
been blind and gained his sight until they
summoned the parents of the one who had
gained his sight. [19]They asked them, "Is this
your son, who you say was born blind? How
does he now see?" [20]His parents answered and
said, "We know that this is our son and that he
was born blind. [21]We do not know how he sees
now, nor do we know who opened his eyes. Ask
him, he is of age; he can speak for himself."
[22][a]*His parents said this because they were
afraid of the Jews, for the Jews had already
agreed that if anyone acknowledged him as the
Messiah, he would be expelled from the syna-
gogue. [23][b]For this reason his parents said, "He is
of age; question him."

[24][c]*So a second time they called the man
who had been blind and said to him, "Give God
the praise! We know that this man is a sinner."
[25]He replied, "If he is a sinner, I do not know.
One thing I do know is that I was blind and now
I see." [26]So they said to him, "What did he do to
you? How did he open your eyes?" [27]He an-
swered them, "I told you already and you did
not listen. Why do you want to hear it again? Do
you want to become his disciples, too?" [28]They
ridiculed him and said, "You are that man's
disciple; we are disciples of Moses! [29][d]We know
that God spoke to Moses, but we do not know
where this one is from." [30]The man answered
and said to them, "This is what is so amazing,
that you do not know where he is from, yet he
opened my eyes. [31][e]We know that God does not
listen to sinners, but if one is devout and does his

9, 1—10, 21: Sabbath healing of the man born blind. This fifth sign is introduced to illustrate the saying, "I am the light of the world" (8, 12; 9, 5). The narrative of conflict about Jesus contrasts Jesus (light) with the Jews (blindness, 39–41). The theme of water is reintroduced in the reference to the pool of Siloam. Ironically, Jesus is being judged by the Jews, yet the Jews are judged by the Light of the world; cf 3, 19–21.

9, 2: See the note on 5, 14, and Ex 20, 5, that parents' sins were visited upon their children. Jesus denies such a cause and emphasizes the purpose: the infirmity was providential.

9, 7: Go wash: perhaps a test of faith; cf 2 Kgs 5, 10–14. The water tunnel Siloam (= Sent) is used as a symbol of Jesus, sent by his Father.

9, 14: In using spittle, kneading clay, and healing, Jesus had broken the sabbath rules laid down by Jewish tradition.

9, 22: This comment of the evangelist (in terms used again in 12, 42 and 16, 2) envisages a situation after Jesus' ministry. Rejection/excommunication from the synagogue of Jews who confessed Jesus as Messiah seems to have begun ca. A.D. 85, when the curse against the **mînîm** or heretics was introduced into the "Eighteen Benedictions."

9, 24: Give God the praise!: an Old Testament formula of adjuration to tell the truth; cf Jos 7, 19; 1 Sm 6, 5 LXX. Cf 5, 41.

q Is 42, 7. r Ex 20, 5; Ez 18, 20; Lk 13, 2. s 5, 14; 11, 4. t 11, 9–10; 12, 35–36. u 8, 12. v 5, 11; Mk 7, 33; 8, 23. w 2 Kgs 5, 10–14. x 5, 9. y 3, 2; Mt 12, 10–11; Lk 13, 10–11; 14, 1–4. z 4, 19. a 7, 13; 12, 42; 16, 2; 19, 38. b 12, 42. c Jos 7, 19; 1 Sm 6, 5 LXX. d Ex 33, 11. e 10, 21; Pss 34, 16; 66, 18; Prv 15, 29; Is 1, 15.

will, he listens to him. 32 *It is unheard of that anyone ever opened the eyes of a person born blind. 33 [f]If this man were not from God, he would not be able to do anything." 34 They answered and said to him, "You were born totally in sin, and are you trying to teach us?" Then they threw him out.

35 When Jesus heard that they had thrown him out, he found him and said, "Do you believe in the Son of Man?" 36 He answered and said, "Who is he, sir, that I may believe in him?" 37 [g]Jesus said to him, "You have seen him and the one speaking with you is he." 38 He said, "I do believe, Lord," and he worshiped him. 39 [h]*Then Jesus said, "I came into this world for judgment, so that those who do not see might see, and those who do see might become blind."

40 [i]Some of the Pharisees who were with him heard this and said to him, "Surely we are not also blind, are we?" 41 [j]Jesus said to them, "If you were blind, you would have no sin; but now you are saying, 'We see,' so your sin remains.

CHAPTER 10

The Good Shepherd 1 [k]*"Amen, amen, I say to you, whoever does not enter a sheepfold through the gate but climbs over elsewhere is a thief and a robber. 2 But whoever enters through the gate is the shepherd of the sheep. 3 The gatekeeper opens it for him, and the sheep hear his voice, as he calls his own sheep by name and leads them out. 4 [l]*When he has driven out all his own, he walks ahead of them, and the sheep follow him, because they recognize his voice. 5 But they will not follow a stranger; they will run away from him, because they do not recognize the voice of strangers." 6 *Although Jesus used this figure of speech, they did not realize what he was trying to tell them.

7 *So Jesus said again, "Amen, amen, I say to you, I am the gate for the sheep. 8 *All who came [before me] are thieves and robbers, but the sheep did not listen to them. 9 I am the gate. Whoever enters through me will be saved, and will come in and go out and find pasture. 10 A thief comes only to steal and slaughter and destroy; I came so that they might have life and have it more abundantly. 11 [m]I am the good shepherd. A good shepherd lays down his life for the sheep. 12 [n]A hired man, who is not a shepherd and whose sheep are not his own, sees a wolf coming and leaves the sheep and runs away, and the wolf catches and scatters them. 13 This is because he works for pay and has no concern for the sheep. 14 I am the good shepherd, and I know mine and mine know me, 15 [o]just as the Father knows me and I know the Father; and I will lay down my life for the sheep. 16 [p]*I have other sheep that do not belong to this fold. These also I must lead, and they will hear my voice, and there will be one flock, one shepherd. 17 [q]This is why the Father loves me, because I lay down my life in order to take it up again. 18 [r]*No one takes it from me, but I lay it down on my own. I have power to lay it down, and power to take it up again. This command I have received from my Father."

9, 32: A person born blind: the only Old Testament cure from blindness is found in Tobit (cf Tb 7, 7; 11, 7–13; 14, 1–2), but Tobit was not born blind.

9, 39–41: These verses spell out the symbolic meaning of the cure; the Pharisees are not the innocent blind, willing to accept the testimony of others.

10, 1–21: The good shepherd discourse continues the theme of attack on the Pharisees that ends ch 9. The figure is allegorical: the hired hands are the Pharisees who excommunicated the cured blind man. It serves as a commentary on ch 9. For the shepherd motif, used of Yahweh in the Old Testament, cf Ex 34; Gn 48, 15; 49, 24; Mi 7, 14; Pss 23, 1–4; 80, 1.

10, 1: Sheepfold: a low stone wall open to the sky.

10, 4: Recognize his voice: the Pharisees do not recognize Jesus, but the people of God, symbolized by the blind man, do.

10, 6: Figure of speech: John uses a different word for illustrative speech than the "parable" of the synoptics, but the idea is similar.

10, 7–10: In vv 7–8, the figure is of a gate for the shepherd to come to the sheep; in vv 9–10, the figure is of a gate for the sheep to **come in and go out.**

10, 8: [Before me]: these words are omitted in many good early manuscripts and versions.

10, 16: Other sheep: the Gentiles, possibly a reference to "God's dispersed children" of 11, 52 destined to be gathered into one, or "apostolic Christians" at odds with the community of the beloved disciple.

10, 18: Power to take it up again: contrast the role of the Father as the efficient cause of the resurrection in Acts 2, 24; 4, 10; etc.; Rom 1, 4; 4, 24. Yet even here is added: **This command I have received from my Father.**

f 3, 2. g 4, 26; Dn 7, 13. h Mt 13, 33–35. i Mt 15, 14; 23, 26; Rom 2, 19. j 15, 22. k Gn 48, 15; 49, 24; Pss 23, 1–4; 80, 2; Jer 23, 1–4; Ez 34, 1–31; Mi 7, 14. l Mi 2, 12–13. m Ps 23, 1–4; Is 40, 11; 49, 9–10; Heb 13, 20; Rv 7, 17. n Zec 11, 17. o 15, 13; 1 Jn 3, 16. p 11, 52; Is 56, 8; Jer 23, 3; Ez 34, 23; 37, 24; Mi 2, 12. q Heb 10, 10. r 19,11.

19 [s]Again there was a division among the Jews
because of these words. 20 [t]Many of them said,
"He is possessed and out of his mind; why listen
to him?" 21 [u]Others said, "These are not the
words of one possessed; surely a demon cannot
open the eyes of the blind, can he?"

Feast of the Dedication 22 [v]*The feast of the
Dedication was then taking place in Jerusalem. It
was winter. 23 *And Jesus walked about in the
temple area on the Portico of Solomon. 24 [w]*So
the Jews gathered around him and said to him,
"How long are you going to keep us in suspense?
If you are the Messiah, tell us plainly." 25 [x]*Jesus
answered them, "I told you and you do not
believe. The works I do in my Father's name
testify to me. 26 [y]But you do not believe, because
you are not among my sheep. 27 My sheep hear
my voice; I know them, and they follow me.
28 [z]I give them eternal life, and they shall never
perish. No one can take them out of my hand.
29 [a]*My Father, who has given them to me, is
greater than all, and no one can take them out of
the Father's hand. 30 [b]*The Father and I are
one."

31 [c]The Jews again picked up rocks to stone
him. 32 Jesus answered them, "I have shown you
many good works from my Father. For which of
these are you trying to stone me?" 33 [d]The Jews
answered him, "We are not stoning you for a
good work but for blasphemy. You, a man, are
making yourself God." 34 [e]*Jesus answered
them, "Is it not written in your law, 'I said, "You
are gods" '? 35 If it calls them gods to whom the
word of God came, and scripture cannot be set
aside, 36 [f]*can you say that the one whom the
Father has consecrated and sent into the world
blasphemes because I said, 'I am the Son of
God'? 37 If I do not perform my Father's works,
do not believe me; 38 [g]but if I perform them,
even if you do not believe me, believe the works,
so that you may realize [and understand] that the
Father is in me and I am in the Father." 39 [Then]
they tried again to arrest him; but he escaped
from their power.

40 [h]He went back across the Jordan to the
place where John first baptized, and there he
remained. 41 *Many came to him and said, "John
performed no sign, but everything John said
about this man was true." 42 [i]And many there
began to believe in him.

CHAPTER 11

The Raising of Lazarus 1 [j]*Now a man was ill,
Lazarus from Bethany, the village of Mary and
her sister Martha. 2 Mary was the one who had
anointed the Lord with perfumed oil and dried
his feet with her hair; it was her brother Lazarus
who was ill. 3 So the sisters sent word to him,

10, 22: **Feast of the Dedication:** an eight-day festival of lights (Hebrew, Hanukkah) held in December, three months after the feast of Tabernacles (7, 2), to celebrate the Maccabees' rededication of the altar and reconsecration of the temple in 164 B.C., after their desecration by Antiochus IV Epiphanes (Dn 8, 13; 9, 27; cf 1 Mc 4, 36–59; 2 Mc 1, 18—2, 19; 10, 1–8).

10, 23: **Portico of Solomon:** on the east side of the temple area, offering protection against the cold winds from the desert.

10, 24: **Keep us in suspense:** literally, "How long will you take away our life?" Cf 11, 48–50. **If you are the Messiah, tell us plainly:** cf Lk 22, 67. This is the climax of Jesus' encounters with the Jewish authorities. There has never yet been an open confession before them.

10, 25: **I told you:** probably at 8, 25, which was an evasive answer.

10, 29: The textual evidence for the first clause is very divided; it may also be translated: "As for the Father, what he has given me is greater than all," or "My Father is greater than all, in what he has given me."

10, 30: This is justification for v 29; it asserts unity of power and reveals that the words and deeds of Jesus are the words and deeds of God.

10, 34: This is a reference to the judges of Israel who, since they exercised the divine prerogative to judge (Dt 1, 17), were called "gods"; cf Ex 21, 6, besides Ps 82, 6, from which the quotation comes.

10, 36: **Consecrated:** this may be a reference to the rededicated altar at the Hanukkah feast; see the note on 10, 22.

10, 41: **Performed no sign:** this is to stress the inferior role of John the Baptist. The Transjordan topography recalls the great witness of John the Baptist to Jesus, as opposed to the hostility of the authorities in Jerusalem.

11, 1–44: The raising of Lazarus, the longest continuous narrative in John outside of the Passion account, is the climax of the signs. It leads directly to the decision of the Sanhedrin to kill Jesus. The theme of life predominates. Lazarus is a token of the real life that Jesus dead and raised will give to all who believe in him. Johannine irony is found in the fact that Jesus' gift of life leads to his own death. The story is not found in the synoptics, but cf Mk 5, 21 and parallels; Lk 7, 11–17. There are also parallels between this story and Luke's parable of the rich man and poor Lazarus (Lk 16, 19–31). In both a man named Lazarus dies; in Luke, there is a request that he return to convince his contemporaries of the need for faith and repentance, while in John, Lazarus does return and some believe but others do not.

s 7, 43; 9, 16. t 7, 20; 8, 48. u 3, 2. v 1 Mc 4, 54.59. w Lk 22, 67. x 8, 25 / 5, 36; 10, 38. y 8, 45.47. z Dt 32, 39. a Wis 3, 1; Is 43, 13. b 1, 1; 12, 45; 14, 9; 17, 21. c 8, 59. d 5, 18; 19, 7; Lv 24, 16. e Ps 82, 6. f 5, 18. g 14, 10–11.20. h 1, 28. i 2, 23; 7, 31; 8, 30. j 12, 1–8; Lk 10, 38–42; 16, 19–31.

saying, "Master, the one you love is ill."
4 k*When Jesus heard this he said, "This illness is
not to end in death, but is for the glory of God,
that the Son of God may be glorified through it."
5Now Jesus loved Martha and her sister and
Lazarus. 6So when he heard that he was ill, he
remained for two days in the place where he
was. 7Then after this he said to his disciples, "Let
us go back to Judea." 8 lThe disciples said to him,
"Rabbi, the Jews were just trying to stone you,
and you want to go back there?" 9 m nJesus
answered, "Are there not twelve hours in a day?
If one walks during the day, he does not
stumble, because he sees the light of this world.
10*But if one walks at night, he stumbles,
because the light is not in him." 11He said this,
and then told them, "Our friend Lazarus is
asleep, but I am going to awaken him." 12So the
disciples said to him, "Master, if he is asleep, he
will be saved." 13 oBut Jesus was talking about
his death, while they thought that he meant
ordinary sleep. 14So then Jesus said to them
clearly, "Lazarus has died. 15And I am glad for
you that I was not there, that you may believe.
Let us go to him." 16 p*So Thomas, called
Didymus, said to his fellow disciples, "Let us also
go to die with him."

17When Jesus arrived, he found that Lazarus
had already been in the tomb for four days.
18*Now Bethany was near Jerusalem, only about
two miles away. 19 qAnd many of the Jews had
come to Martha and Mary to comfort them
about their brother. 20When Martha heard that
Jesus was coming, she went to meet him; but
Mary sat at home. 21 rMartha said to Jesus,
"Lord, if you had been here, my brother would
not have died. 22[But] even now I know that
whatever you ask of God, God will give you."
23Jesus said to her, "Your brother will rise."
24 sMartha said to him, "I know he will rise, in
the resurrection on the last day." 25 tJesus told
her, "I am the resurrection and the life; whoever
believes in me, even if he dies, will live, 26and
everyone who lives and believes in me will
never die. Do you believe this?" 27 u*She said to
him, "Yes, Lord. I have come to believe that you
are the Messiah, the Son of God, the one who is
coming into the world."

28When she had said this, she went and called
her sister Mary secretly, saying, "The teacher is
here and is asking for you." 29As soon as she
heard this, she rose quickly and went to him.
30For Jesus had not yet come into the village, but
was still where Martha had met him. 31So when
the Jews who were with her in the house
comforting her saw Mary get up quickly and go
out, they followed her, presuming that she was
going to the tomb to weep there. 32When Mary
came to where Jesus was and saw him, she fell at
his feet and said to him, "Lord, if you had been
here, my brother would not have died."
33*When Jesus saw her weeping and the Jews
who had come with her weeping, he became
perturbed and deeply troubled, 34and said,
"Where have you laid him?" They said to him,
"Sir, come and see." 35 vAnd Jesus wept. 36So the
Jews said, "See how he loved him." 37But some
of them said, "Could not the one who opened
the eyes of the blind man have done something
so that this man would not have died?"

38So Jesus, perturbed again, came to the
tomb. It was a cave, and a stone lay across it.
39Jesus said, "Take away the stone." Martha, the
dead man's sister, said to him, "Lord, by now
there will be a stench; he has been dead for four
days." 40Jesus said to her, "Did I not tell you that

11, 4: Not to end in death: this is misunderstood by the disciples as referring to physical death, but it is meant as spiritual death.

11, 10: The light is not in him: the ancients apparently did not grasp clearly the entry of light **through** the eye; they seem to have thought of it as being **in** the eye; cf Lk 11, 34; Mt 6, 23.

11, 16: Called Didymus: Didymus is the Greek word for twin. Thomas is derived from the Aramaic word for twin; in an ancient Syriac version and in the Gospel of Thomas (80, 11–12) his given name, Judas, is supplied.

11, 18: About two miles: literally, "about fifteen stades"; a stade was 607 feet.

11, 27: The titles here are a summary of titles given to Jesus earlier in the gospel.

11, 33: Became perturbed: a startling phrase in Greek, literally, "He snorted in spirit," perhaps in anger at the presence of evil (death).

k 9, 3.24. 18, 59; 10, 31. m 8, 12; 9, 4. n 12, 35; 1 Jn 2, 10. o Mt 9, 24. p 14, 5.22. q 12, 9.17–18. r 11, 32. s 5, 29; 6, 39–40.44.54; 12, 48; Is 2, 2; Mi 4, 1; Acts 23, 8;24, 15. t 5, 24; 8, 51; 14, 6; Dn 12, 2. u 1, 9; 6, 69. v Lk 19, 41.

if you believe you will see the glory of God?"
41 *So they took away the stone. And Jesus raised
his eyes and said, "Father, I thank you for
hearing me. 42 [w]I know that you always hear me;
but because of the crowd here I have said this,
that they may believe that you sent me." 43 *And
when he had said this, he cried out in a loud
voice, "Lazarus, come out!" 44 The dead man
came out, tied hand and foot with burial bands,
and his face was wrapped in a cloth. So Jesus
said to them, "Untie him and let him go."

Session of the Sanhedrin 45 [x]Now many of
the Jews who had come to Mary and seen what
he had done began to believe in him. 46 But some
of them went to the Pharisees and told them
what Jesus had done. 47 [y]So the chief priests and
the Pharisees convened the Sanhedrin and said,
"What are we going to do? This man is perform-
ing many signs. 48 *If we leave him alone, all will
believe in him, and the Romans will come and
take away both our land and our nation."
49 [z]*But one of them, Caiaphas, who was high
priest that year, said to them, "You know noth-
ing, 50 nor do you consider that it is better for you
that one man should die instead of the people, so
that the whole nation may not perish." 51 He did
not say this on his own, but since he was high
priest for that year, he prophesied that Jesus was
going to die for the nation, 52 *and not only for
the nation, but also to gather into one the
dispersed children of God. 53 [a]So from that day
on they planned to kill him.

54 *So Jesus no longer walked about in public
among the Jews, but he left for the region near
the desert, to a town called Ephraim, and there
he remained with his disciples.

The Last Passover 55 [b]*Now the Passover of
the Jews was near, and many went up from the
country to Jerusalem before Passover to purify
themselves. 56 They looked for Jesus and said to
one another as they were in the temple area,
"What do you think? That he will not come to
the feast?" 57 For the chief priests and the Phari-
sees had given orders that if anyone knew where
he was, he should inform them, so that they
might arrest him.

CHAPTER 12

The Anointing at Bethany 1 [c d]*Six days be-
fore Passover Jesus came to Bethany, where
Lazarus was, whom Jesus had raised from the
dead. 2 [e]They gave a dinner for him there, and
Martha served, while Lazarus was one of those
reclining at table with him. 3 [f]*Mary took a liter
of costly perfumed oil made from genuine aro-
matic nard and anointed the feet of Jesus and
dried them with her hair; the house was filled
with the fragrance of the oil. 4 Then Judas the
Iscariot, one [of] his disciples, and the one who
would betray him, said, 5 *"Why was this oil not
sold for three hundred days' wages and given to
the poor?" 6 [g]He said this not because he cared
about the poor but because he was a thief and
held the money bag and used to steal the
contributions. 7 *So Jesus said, "Leave her alone.
Let her keep this for the day of my burial. 8 [h]You
always have the poor with you, but you do not
always have me."

11, 41: Father: in Aramaic, *'abbā.'* See the note on Mk 14, 36.

11, 43: Cried out in a loud voice: a dramatization of 5, 28: "the hour is coming when all who are in the tombs will hear his voice."

11, 48: The Romans will come: Johannine irony; this is precisely what happened after Jesus' death.

11, 49: That year: emphasizes the conjunction of the office and the year. Actually, Caiaphas was high priest A.D. 18–36. The Jews attributed a gift of prophecy, sometimes unconscious, to the high priest.

11, 52: Dispersed children of God: perhaps the "other sheep" of 10, 16.

11, 54: Ephraim is usually located about twelve miles northeast of Jerusalem, where the mountains descend into the Jordan valley.

11, 55: Purify: prescriptions for purity were based on Ex 19, 10–11.15; Nm 9, 6–14; 2 Chr 30, 1–3.15–18.

12, 1–8: This is probably the same scene of anointing found in Mk 14, 3–9 (see the note there) and Mt 26, 6–13. The anointing by a penitent woman in Lk 7, 36–38 is different. Details from these various episodes have become interchanged.

12, 3: The feet of Jesus: so Mk 14, 3; but in Mt 26, 6, Mary anoints Jesus' head as a sign of regal, messianic anointing.

12, 5: Days' wages: literally, "denarii." A denarius is a day's wage in Mt 20, 2; see the note on 6, 7.

12, 7: Jesus' response reflects the rabbinical discussion of what was the greatest act of mercy, almsgiving or burying the dead. Those who favored proper burial of the dead thought it an essential condition for sharing in the resurrection.

w 12, 30. x Lk 16, 31. y 12, 19; Mt 26, 3–5; Lk 22, 2; Acts 4, 16. z 18, 13–14. a 5, 18; 7, 1; Mt 12, 14. b 2, 13; 5, 1; 6, 4; 18, 28; Ex 19, 10–11.15; Nm 9, 6–14; 19, 12; Dt 16, 6; 2 Chr 30, 1–3.15–18. c Mt 26, 6–13; Mk 14, 3–9. d 11, 1. e Lk 10, 38–42. f 11, 2. g 13, 29. h Dt 15, 11.

[9 i][The] large crowd of the Jews found out that
he was there and came, not only because of
Jesus, but also to see Lazarus, whom he had
raised from the dead. [10]And the chief priests
plotted to kill Lazarus too, [11 j]because many of
the Jews were turning away and believing in
Jesus because of him.

The Entry into Jerusalem [12 k]*On the next
day, when the great crowd that had come to the
feast heard that Jesus was coming to Jerusalem,
[13 l]*they took palm branches and went out to
meet him, and cried out:

"Hosanna!
Blessed is he who comes in the name of the
Lord,
[even] the king of Israel."

[14]Jesus found an ass and sat upon it, as is
written:

[15 m]*"Fear no more, O daughter Zion;
see, your king comes, seated upon an ass's
colt."

[16 n]*His disciples did not understand this at first,
but when Jesus had been glorified they remem-
bered that these things were written about him
and that they had done this for him. [17]*So the
crowd that was with him when he called Laza-
rus from the tomb and raised him from death
continued to testify. [18]This was [also] why the
crowd went to meet him, because they heard
that he had done this sign. [19 o]*So the Pharisees
said to one another, "You see that you are
gaining nothing. Look, the whole world has
gone after him."

The Coming of Jesus' Hour [20 p]*Now there
were some Greeks among those who had come
up to worship at the feast. [21 q]*They came to
Philip, who was from Bethsaida in Galilee, and
asked him, "Sir, we would like to see Jesus."
[22 r]Philip went and told Andrew; then Andrew
and Philip went and told Jesus. [23 s]*Jesus an-
swered them, "The hour has come for the Son of
Man to be glorified. [24 t]*Amen, amen, I say to
you, unless a grain of wheat falls to the ground
and dies, it remains just a grain of wheat; but if it
dies, it produces much fruit. [25 u]*Whoever loves
his life loses it, and whoever hates his life in this
world will preserve it for eternal life.
[26 v]Whoever serves me must follow me, and
where I am, there also will my servant be. The
Father will honor whoever serves me.

[27 w]*"I am troubled now. Yet what should I
say? 'Father, save me from this hour'? But it was
for this purpose that I came to this hour.
[28 x]Father, glorify your name." Then a voice

12, 12–19: In Jn, the entry into Jerusalem follows the anointing whereas in the synoptics it precedes. In John, the crowd, not the disciples, are responsible for the triumphal procession.

12, 13: Palm branches: used to welcome great conquerors; cf 1 Mc 13, 51; 2 Mc 10, 7. They may be related to the lûlāb, the twig bundles used at the feast of Tabernacles. **Hosanna:** see Ps 118, 25–26. The Hebrew word means: "(O Lord), grant salvation." **He who comes in the name of the Lord:** referred in Ps 118, 26 to a pilgrim entering the temple gates, but here a title for Jesus (see the notes on Mt 11, 3 and Jn 6, 14; 11, 27). **The king of Israel:** perhaps from Zep 3, 14–15, in connection with the next quotation from Zec 9, 9.

12, 15: Daughter Zion: Jerusalem. **Ass's colt:** symbol of peace, as opposed to the war-horse.

12, 16: They had done this: the antecedent of **they** is ambiguous.

12, 17–18: There seem to be two different crowds in these verses. There are some good witnesses to the text that have another reading for v 17: "Then the crowd that was with him began to testify that he had called Lazarus out of the tomb and raised him from the dead."

12, 19: The whole world: the sense is that everyone is following Jesus, but John has an ironic play on **world;** he alludes to the universality of salvation (3, 17; 4, 42).

12, 20–36: This announcement of glorification by death is an illustration of "the whole world" (19) going after him.

12, 20: Greeks: not used here in a nationalistic sense. These are probably Gentile proselytes to Judaism; cf 7, 35.

12, 21–22: Philip . . . Andrew: the approach is made through disciples who have distinctly Greek names, suggesting that access to Jesus was mediated to the Greek world through his disciples. Philip and Andrew were from Bethsaida (1, 44); Galileans were mostly bilingual. **See:** here seems to mean "have an interview with."

12, 23: Jesus' response suggests that only after the crucifixion could the gospel encompass both Jew and Gentile.

12, 24: This verse implies that through his death Jesus will be accessible to all. **It remains just a grain of wheat:** this saying is found in the synoptic triple and double traditions (Mk 8, 35 // Mt 16, 25 // Lk 9, 24; Mt 10, 39 // Lk 17, 33). John adds the phrases (25) **in this world** and **for eternal life.**

12, 25: His life: the Greek word **psychē** refers to a person's natural life. It does not mean "soul," for Hebrew anthropology did not postulate body/soul dualism in the way that is familiar to us.

12, 27: I am troubled: perhaps an allusion to the Gethsemane agony scene of the synoptics.

i 11, 19. j 11, 45. k Mt 21, 1–16; Mk 11, 1–10; Lk 19, 28–40. l 1, 49; Lv 23, 40; 1 Mc 13, 51; 2 Mc 10, 7; Rv 7, 9. m Is 40, 9; Zec 9, 9. n 2, 22. o 11, 47–48. p Acts 10, 2. q 1, 44. r 1, 40. s 2, 4. t Is 53, 10–12; 1 Cor 15, 36. u Mt 10, 39; 16, 25; Mk 8, 35; Lk 9, 24; 17, 33. v 14, 3; 17, 24; Mt 16, 24; Mk 8, 34; Lk 9, 23. w 6, 38; 18, 11; Mt 26, 38–39; Mk 14, 34–36; Lk 22, 42; Heb 5, 7–8. x 2, 11; 17, 5; Dn 4, 31.34.

came from heaven, "I have glorified it and will
glorify it again." 29 [y]The crowd there heard it and
said it was thunder; but others said, "An angel
has spoken to him." 30 [z]Jesus answered and said,
"This voice did not come for my sake but for
yours. 31 [a]*Now is the time of judgment on this
world; now the ruler of this world will be driven
out. 32 [b]And when I am lifted up from the earth,
I will draw everyone to myself." 33 He said this
indicating the kind of death he would die.
34 [c]*So the crowd answered him, "We have
heard from the law that the Messiah remains
forever. Then how can you say that the Son of
Man must be lifted up? Who is this Son of
Man?" 35 [d]Jesus said to them, "The light will be
among you only a little while. Walk while you
have the light, so that darkness may not over-
come you. Whoever walks in the dark does not
know where he is going. 36 [e]While you have the
light, believe in the light, so that you may
become children of the light."

Unbelief and Belief among the Jews After
he had said this, Jesus left and hid from them.
37 [f]*Although he had performed so many signs
in their presence they did not believe in him,
38 [g]*in order that the word which Isaiah the
prophet spoke might be fulfilled:

"Lord, who has believed our preaching,
to whom has the might of the Lord been
revealed?"

39 For this reason they could not believe,
because again Isaiah said:

40 [h]"He blinded their eyes
and hardened their heart,
so that they might not see with their eyes
and understand with their heart and be
converted,
and I would heal them."

41 [i]*Isaiah said this because he saw his glory and
spoke about him. 42 [j]Nevertheless, many, even
among the authorities, believed in him, but
because of the Pharisees they did not acknowl-
edge it openly in order not to be expelled from
the synagogue. 43 [k]For they preferred human
praise to the glory of God.

Recapitulation 44 [l]Jesus cried out and said,
"Whoever believes in me believes not only in me
but also in the one who sent me, 45 [m]and
whoever sees me sees the one who sent me. 46 [n]I
came into the world as light, so that everyone
who believes in me might not remain in dark-
ness. 47 [o]And if anyone hears my words and does
not observe them, I do not condemn him, for I
did not come to condemn the world but to save
the world. 48 [p]Whoever rejects me and does not
accept my words has something to judge him:
the word that I spoke, it will condemn him on
the last day, 49 [q]because I did not speak on my
own, but the Father who sent me commanded
me what to say and speak. 50 And I know that his
commandment is eternal life. So what I say, I say
as the Father told me."

III: The Book of Glory*

CHAPTER 13

The Washing of the Disciples' Feet

1 [r]*Before the feast of Passover, Jesus knew that

12, 31: **Ruler of this world:** Satan.

12, 34: There is no passage in the Old Testament that states precisely that **the Messiah remains forever.** Perhaps the closest is Ps 89, 37.

12, 37–50: These verses, on unbelief of the Jews, provide an epilogue to the Book of Signs.

12, 38–41: John gives a historical explanation of the disbelief of the Jewish people, not a psychological one. The Old Testament had to be fulfilled; the disbelief that met Isaiah's message was a foreshadowing of the disbelief that Jesus encountered. In v 42 and also in 3, 20, we see that there is no negation of freedom.

12, 41: **His glory:** Isaiah saw the glory of Yahweh enthroned in the heavenly temple, but in John the antecedent of **his** is Jesus.

13, 1—19, 42: The Book of Glory. There is a major break here; the word "sign" is used again only in 20, 30. In this phase of Jesus' return to the Father, the discourses (chs 13–17) precede the traditional narrative of the passion (chs 18–20) to interpret them for the Christian reader. This is the only extended example of esoteric teaching of disciples in John.

13, 1–20: Washing of the disciples' feet. This episode occurs in John at the place of the narration of the institution of the Eucharist in the synoptics. It may be a dramatization of Lk 22, 27: "I am your servant." It is presented as a "model" ("pattern") of the crucifixion. It symbolizes cleansing from sin by sacrificial death.

13, 1: **Before the feast of Passover:** this would be Thursday

y Ex 9, 28; 2 Sm 22, 14; Jb 37, 4; Ps 29, 3; Lk 22, 43; Acts 23, 9. z 11, 42. a 16, 11; Lk 10, 18; Rv 12, 9. b 3, 14; 8, 28; Is 52, 13. c Pss 89, 5; 110, 4; Is 9, 7; Dn 7, 13–14; Rv 20, 1–6. d 9, 4; 11, 10; Jb 5, 14. e Eph 5, 8. f Dt 29, 2–4; Mk 4, 11–12; Rom 9–11. g Is 53, 1; Rom 10, 16. h Is 6, 9–10; Mt 13, 13–15; Mk 4, 12. i 5, 39; Is 6, 1.4. j 9, 22. k 5, 44. l 13, 20; 14, 1. m 14, 7–9. n 1, 9; 8, 12. o 3, 17. p Lk 10, 16; Heb 4, 12. q 14, 10.31; Dt 18, 18–19. r 2, 4; 7, 30; 8, 20; Mt 26, 17.45; Mk 14, 12.41; Lk 22, 7.

his hour had come to pass from this world to the Father. He loved his own in the world and he loved them to the end. 2 [s]*The devil had already induced Judas, son of Simon the Iscariot, to hand him over. So, during supper, 3 [t]fully aware that the Father had put everything into his power and that he had come from God and was returning to God, 4 he rose from supper and took off his outer garments. He took a towel and tied it around his waist. 5 [u]*Then he poured water into a basin and began to wash the disciples' feet and dry them with the towel around his waist. 6 He came to Simon Peter, who said to him, "Master, are you going to wash my feet?" 7 Jesus answered and said to him, "What I am doing, you do not understand now, but you will understand later." 8 [v]Peter said to him, "You will never wash my feet." Jesus answered him, "Unless I wash you, you will have no inheritance with me." 9 Simon Peter said to him, "Master, then not only my feet, but my hands and head as well." 10 [w]*Jesus said to him, "Whoever has bathed has no need except to have his feet washed, for he is clean all over; so you are clean, but not all." 11 [x]For he knew who would betray him; for this reason, he said, "Not all of you are clean."

12 So when he had washed their feet [and] put his garments back on and reclined at table again, he said to them, "Do you realize what I have done for you? 13 [y]You call me 'teacher' and 'master,' and rightly so, for indeed I am. 14 If I, therefore, the master and teacher, have washed your feet, you ought to wash one another's feet. 15 [z]I have given you a model to follow, so that as I have done for you, you should also do. 16 [a]*Amen, amen, I say to you, no slave is greater than his master nor any messenger greater than the one who sent him. 17 If you understand this, blessed are you if you do it. 18 [b]I am not speaking of all of you. I know those whom I have chosen. But so that the scripture might be fulfilled, 'The one who ate my food has raised his heel against me.' 19 From now on I am telling you before it happens, so that when it happens you may believe that I AM. 20 [c]Amen, amen, I say to you, whoever receives the one I send receives me, and whoever receives me receives the one who sent me."

Announcement of Judas's Betrayal

21 [d]When he had said this, Jesus was deeply troubled and testified, "Amen, amen, I say to you, one of you will betray me." 22 The disciples looked at one another, at a loss as to whom he meant. 23 [e]*One of his disciples, the one whom Jesus loved, was reclining at Jesus' side. 24 So Simon Peter nodded to him to find out whom he meant. 25 [f]He leaned back against Jesus' chest and said to him, "Master, who is it?" 26 *Jesus answered, "It is the one to whom I hand the morsel after I have dipped it." So he dipped the morsel and [took it and] handed it to Judas, son of Simon the Iscariot. 27 [g]After he took the morsel, Satan entered him. So Jesus said to him, "What you are going to do, do quickly." 28 [Now] none of those reclining at table realized why he said this to him. 29 [h]Some thought that since Judas kept the money bag, Jesus had told him, "Buy what we need for the feast," or to give something to the poor. 30 So he took the morsel and left at once. And it was night.

---

evening, before the day of preparation; in the synoptics, the Last Supper is a Passover meal taking place, in John's chronology, on Friday evening. **To the end:** or, "completely."

13, 2: Induced: literally, "The devil put into the heart that Judas should hand him over."

13, 5: The act of washing another's feet was one that could not be required of the lowliest Jewish slave. It is an allusion to the humiliating death of the crucifixion.

13, 10: Bathed: many have suggested that this passage is a symbolic reference to baptism. The Greek root involved is used in baptismal contexts in 1 Cor 6, 11; Eph 5, 26; Ti 3, 5; Heb 10, 22.

13, 16: Messenger: the Greek has **apostolos,** the only occurrence of the term in John. It is not used in the technical sense here.

13, 23: The one whom Jesus loved: also mentioned in 19, 26; 20, 2; 21, 7. A disciple, called "another disciple" or "the other disciple," is mentioned in 18, 15 and 20, 2; in the latter reference he is identified with the disciple whom Jesus loved. There is also an unnamed disciple in 1, 35–40; see the note on 1, 37.

13, 26: Morsel: probably the bitter herb dipped in salt water.

s 6, 71; 17, 12; Mt 26, 20–21; Mk 14, 17–18; Lk 22, 3. t 3, 35. u 1 Sm 25, 41. v 2 Sm 20, 1. w 15, 3. x 6, 70. y Mt 23, 8.10. z Lk 22, 27; 1 Pt 2, 21. a 15, 20; Mt 10, 24; Lk 6, 40. b Ps 41, 10. c Mt 10, 40; Mk 9, 37; Lk 9, 48. d Mt 26, 21–25; Mk 14, 18–21; Lk 22, 21–23. e 19, 26; 20, 2; 21, 7.20; Mt 10, 37. f 21, 20. g 13, 2; Lk 22, 3. h 12, 5–6.

The New Commandment 31 *When he had left, Jesus said, "Now is the Son of Man glorified, and God is glorified in him. 32 i [If God is glorified in him,] God will also glorify him in himself, and he will glorify him at once. 33 j My children, I will be with you only a little while longer. You will look for me, and as I told the Jews, 'Where I go you cannot come,' so now I say it to you. 34 k *I give you a new commandment: love one another. As I have loved you, so you also should love one another. 35 This is how all will know that you are my disciples, if you have love for one another."

Peter's Denial Predicted 36 l Simon Peter said to him, "Master, where are you going?" Jesus answered [him], "Where I am going, you cannot follow me now, though you will follow later." 37 Peter said to him, "Master, why can't I follow you now? I will lay down my life for you." 38 m Jesus answered, "Will you lay down your life for me? Amen, amen, I say to you, the cock will not crow before you deny me three times.

CHAPTER 14

Last Supper Discourses 1 *"Do not let your hearts be troubled. You have faith in God; have faith also in me. 2 In my Father's house there are many dwelling places. If there were not, would I have told you that I am going to prepare a place for you? 3 n *And if I go and prepare a place for you, I will come back again and take you to myself, so that where I am you also may be. 4 *Where [I] am going you know the way." 5 Thomas said to him, "Master, we do not know where you are going; how can we know the way?" 6 o *Jesus said to him, "I am the way and the truth and the life. No one comes to the Father except through me. 7 p *If you know me, then you will also know my Father. From now on you do know him and have seen him." 8 q *Philip said to him, "Master, show us the Father, and that will be enough for us." 9 r Jesus said to him, "Have I been with you for so long a time and you still do not know me, Philip? Whoever has seen me has seen the Father. How can you say, 'Show us the Father'? 10 s Do you not believe that I am in the Father and the Father is in me? The words that I speak to you I do not speak on my own. The Father who dwells in me is doing his works. 11 t Believe me that I am in the Father and the Father is in me, or else, believe because of the works themselves. 12 u Amen, amen, I say to you, whoever believes in me will do the works that I do, and will do greater ones than these, because I am going to the Father. 13 v And whatever you ask in my name, I will do, so that the Father may be glorified in the Son. 14 If you ask anything of me in my name, I will do it.

The Advocate 15 w "If you love me, you will keep my commandments. 16 x *And I will ask

13, 31—17, 26: Two farewell discourses and a prayer. These seem to be Johannine compositions, including sayings of Jesus at the Last Supper and on other occasions, modeled on similar farewell discourses in Greek literature and the Old Testament (of Moses, Joshua, David).

13, 31–38: Introduction: departure and return. Terms of coming and going predominate. These verses form an introduction to the last discourse of Jesus, which extends through chs 14 to 17. In it John has collected Jesus' words to **his own** (13, 1). There are indications that several speeches have been fused together, e.g., in 14, 31 and 17, 1.

13, 34: I give you a new commandment: this puts Jesus on a par with Yahweh. The commandment itself is not new; cf Lv 19, 18 and the note there.

14, 1–31: Jesus' departure and return. This section is a dialogue marked off by a literary inclusion in vv 1 and 27: "Do not let your hearts be troubled."

14, 1: You have faith: could also be imperative: "Have faith."

14, 3: Come back again: a rare Johannine reference to the parousia; cf 1 Jn 2, 28.

14, 4: The way: here, of Jesus himself; also a designation of Christianity in Acts 9, 2; 19, 9.23; 22, 4; 24, 14.22.

14, 6: The truth: in John, the divinely revealed reality of the Father manifested in the person and works of Jesus. The possession of truth confers knowledge and liberation from sin (8, 32).

14, 7: An alternative reading, "If you knew me, then you would have known my Father also," would be a rebuke, as in 8, 19.

14, 8: Show us the Father: Philip is pictured asking for a theophany like Ex 24, 9–10; 33, 18.

14, 16: Another Advocate: Jesus is the first advocate (paraclete); see 1 Jn 2, 1, where Jesus is an advocate in the sense of intercessor in heaven. The Greek term derives from legal terminology for an advocate or defense attorney, and can mean spokesman, mediator, intercessor, comforter, consoler, although no one of these terms encompasses the meaning in John. The Paraclete in John is a teacher, a witness to Jesus, and a prosecutor of the world, who represents the continued presence on earth of the Jesus who has returned to the Father.

i 17, 1–5. j 7, 33; 8, 21. k 15, 12–13.17; Lv 19, 18; 1 Thes 4, 9; 1 Jn 2, 7–10; 3, 23; 2 Jn 5. l Mk 14, 27; Lk 22, 23. m 18, 27; Mt 26, 33–35; Mk 14, 29–31; Lk 22, 33–34. n 12, 26; 17, 24; 1 Jn 2, 28. o 8, 31–47. p 8, 19; 12, 45. q Ex 24, 9–10; 33, 18. r 1, 18; 10, 30; 12, 45; 2 Cor 4, 4; Col 1, 15; Heb 1, 3. s 1, 1; 10, 37–38; 12, 49. t 10, 38. u 1, 50; 5, 20. v 15, 7.16; 16, 23–24; Mt 7, 7–11. w 15, 10; Dt 6, 4–9; Ps 119; Wis 6, 18; 1 Jn 5, 3; 2 Jn 6. x 15, 26; Lk 24, 49; 1 Jn 2, 1.

the Father, and he will give you another Advo-
cate to be with you always, [17][y]*the Spirit of
truth, which the world cannot accept, because
it neither sees nor knows it. But you know it,
because it remains with you, and will be in
you. [18]*I will not leave you orphans; I will
come to you. [19][z]In a little while the world will
no longer see me, but you will see me, because
I live and you will live. [20][a]On that day you will
realize that I am in my Father and you are in
me and I in you. [21][b]Whoever has my command-
ments and observes them is the one who loves
me. And whoever loves me will be loved by my
Father, and I will love him and reveal myself to
him." [22][c]*Judas, not the Iscariot, said to him,
"Master, [then] what happened that you will
reveal yourself to us and not to the world?"
[23][d]Jesus answered and said to him, "Whoever
loves me will keep my word, and my Father
will love him, and we will come to him and
make our dwelling with him. [24]Whoever does
not love me does not keep my words; yet the
word you hear is not mine but that of the
Father who sent me.

[25]"I have told you this while I am with you.
[26][e]The Advocate, the holy Spirit that the Father
will send in my name—he will teach you
everything and remind you of all that [I] told you.
[27][f]*Peace I leave with you; my peace I give to
you. Not as the world gives do I give it to you.
Do not let your hearts be troubled or afraid.
[28][g]*You heard me tell you, 'I am going away and
I will come back to you.' If you loved me, you
would rejoice that I am going to the Father; for
the Father is greater than I. [29][h]And now I have
told you this before it happens, so that when it
happens you may believe. [30]*I will no longer
speak much with you, for the ruler of the world
is coming. He has no power over me, [31][i]but the
world must know that I love the Father and that
I do just as the Father has commanded me. Get
up, let us go.

CHAPTER 15

The Vine and the Branches [1][j]*"I am the true
vine, and my Father is the vine grower. [2]*He
takes away every branch in me that does not
bear fruit, and everyone that does he prunes so
that it bears more fruit. [3][k]You are already
pruned because of the word that I spoke to you.
[4]Remain in me, as I remain in you. Just as a
branch cannot bear fruit on its own unless it
remains on the vine, so neither can you unless
you remain in me. [5]I am the vine, you are the
branches. Whoever remains in me and I in him
will bear much fruit, because without me you
can do nothing. [6][l]*Anyone who does not re-
main in me will be thrown out like a branch and
wither; people will gather them and throw them
into a fire and they will be burned. [7][m]If you
remain in me and my words remain in you, ask
for whatever you want and it will be done for
you. [8][n]By this is my Father glorified, that you

14, 17: The Spirit of truth: this term is also used at Qumran, where it is a moral force put into a person by God, as opposed to the spirit of perversity. It is more personal in John; it will teach the realities of the new order (26), and testify to the truth (6). While it has been customary to use masculine personal pronouns in English for the Advocate, the Greek word for "spirit" is neuter, and the Greek text and manuscript variants fluctuate between masculine and neuter pronouns.

14, 18: I will come to you: indwelling, not parousia.

14, 22: Judas, not the Iscariot: probably not the brother of Jesus in Mk 6, 3 // Mt 13, 55 or the apostle named Jude in Lk 6, 16, but Thomas (see the note on 11, 16), although other readings have "Judas the Cananean."

14, 27: Peace: the traditional Hebrew salutation šālôm; but Jesus' "Shalom" is a gift of salvation, connoting the bounty of messianic blessing.

14, 28: The Father is greater than I: because he sent, gave, etc., and Jesus is "a man who has told you the truth that I heard from God" (8, 40).

14, 30: The ruler of the world: Satan; cf 12, 31; 16, 11.

15, 1—16, 4: Discourse on the union of Jesus with his disciples. His words become a monologue and go beyond the immediate crisis of the departure of Jesus.

15, 1–17: Like 10, 1–5, this passage resembles a parable. Israel is spoken of as a vineyard at Is 5, 1–7; Mt 21, 33–46 and as a vine at Ps 80, 9–17; Jer 2, 21; Ez 15, 2; 17, 5–10; 19, 10; Hos 10, 1. The identification of the vine as the Son of Man in Ps 80, 16, and Wisdom's description of herself as a vine in Sir 24, 17, are further background for portrayal of Jesus by this figure. There may be secondary eucharistic symbolism here; cf Mk 14, 25, "the fruit of the vine."

15, 2: Takes away . . . prunes: in Greek there is a play on two related verbs.

15, 6: Branches were cut off and dried on the wall of the vineyard for later use as fuel.

y 16, 13; Mt 28, 20; 2 Jn 1–2. z 16, 16. a 10, 38; 17, 21; Is 2, 17; 4, 2–3. b 16, 27; 1 Jn 2, 5; 3, 24. c 7, 4; Acts 10, 40–41. d Rv 3, 20. e 15, 26; 16, 7.13–14; Ps 51, 13; Is 63, 10. f 16, 33; Eph 2, 14–18. g 8, 40. h 13, 19; 16, 4. i 6, 38. j Ps 80, 9–17; Is 5, 1–7; Jer 2, 21; Ez 15, 2; 17, 5–10; 19, 10. k 13, 10. l Ez 15, 6–7; 19, 10–14. m 14, 13; Mt 7, 7; Mk 11, 24; 1 Jn 5, 14. n Mt 5, 16.

bear much fruit and become my disciples. 9 [o]As the Father loves me, so I also love you. Remain in my love. 10 [p]If you keep my commandments, you will remain in my love, just as I have kept my Father's commandments and remain in his love.

11 [q]"I have told you this so that my joy might be in you and your joy might be complete. 12 [r]This is my commandment: love one another as I love you. 13 [s]*No one has greater love than this, to lay down one's life for one's friends. 14You are my friends if you do what I command you. 15 [t]*I no longer call you slaves, because a slave does not know what his master is doing. I have called you friends, because I have told you everything I have heard from my Father. 16 [u]It was not you who chose me, but I who chose you and appointed you to go and bear fruit that will remain, so that whatever you ask the Father in my name he may give you. 17 [v]This I command you: love one another.

The World's Hatred 18 [w]*"If the world hates you, realize that it hated me first. 19 [x]If you belonged to the world, the world would love its own; but because you do not belong to the world, and I have chosen you out of the world, the world hates you. 20 [y]*Remember the word I spoke to you, 'No slave is greater than his master.' If they persecuted me, they will also persecute you. If they kept my word, they will also keep yours. 21 [z]*And they will do all these things to you on account of my name, because they do not know the one who sent me. 22 [a]*If I had not come and spoken to them, they would have no sin; but as it is they have no excuse for their sin. 23 [b]Whoever hates me also hates my Father. 24 [c]If I had not done works among them that no one else ever did, they would not have sin; but as it is, they have seen and hated both me and my Father. 25 [d]*But in order that the word written in their law might be fulfilled, 'They hated me without cause.'

26 [e]*"When the Advocate comes whom I will send you from the Father, the Spirit of truth that proceeds from the Father, he will testify to me. 27 [f]And you also testify, because you have been with me from the beginning.

CHAPTER 16

1"I have told you this so that you may not fall away. 2 [g]*They will expel you from the synagogues; in fact, the hour is coming when everyone who kills you will think he is offering worship to God. 3 [h]They will do this because they have not known either the Father or me. 4 [i]*I have told you this so that when their hour comes you may remember that I told you.

Jesus' Departure; Coming of the Advocate "I did not tell you this from the beginning, because I was with you. 5 [j]*But now I am going

15, 13: For one's friends: or: "those whom one loves." In 9–13a, the words for love are related to the Greek **agapaō.** In 13b-15, the words for love are related to the Greek **phileō.** For John, the two roots seem synonymous and mean "to love"; cf also 21, 15–17. The word **philos** is used here.

15, 15: Slaves . . . friends: in the Old Testament, Moses (Dt 34, 5), Joshua (Jos 24, 29), and David (Ps 89, 21) were called "servants" or "slaves of Yahweh"; only Abraham (Is 41, 8; 2 Chr 20, 7; cf Jas 2, 23) was called a "friend of God."

15, 18—16, 4: The hostile reaction of the world. There are synoptic parallels, predicting persecution, especially at Mt 10, 17–25; 24, 9–10.

15, 20: The word I spoke to you: a reference to 13, 16.

15, 21: On account of my name: the idea of persecution for Jesus' name is frequent in the New Testament (Mt 10, 22; 24, 9; Acts 9, 14). For John, association with Jesus' name implies union with Jesus.

15, 22.24: Jesus' words (**spoken**) and deeds (**works**) are the great motives of credibility. **They have seen and hated:** probably means that they have seen his works and still have hated; but the Greek can be read: "have seen both me and my Father and still have hated both me and my Father." **Works . . . that no one else ever did:** so Yahweh in Dt 4, 32–33.

15, 25: In their law: law is here used as a larger concept than the Pentateuch, for the reference is to Ps 35, 19 or 69, 5. See the notes on 10, 34; 12, 34. **Their** law reflects the argument of the church with the synagogue.

15, 26: Whom I will send: in 14, 16.26, the Paraclete is to be sent by the Father, at the request of Jesus. Here the Spirit comes from both Jesus and the Father in mission; there is no reference here to the eternal procession of the Spirit.

16, 2: Hour: of persecution, not Jesus' "hour" (see the note on 2, 4).

16, 4b–33: A duplicate of 14, 1–31 on departure and return.

16, 5: Not one of you asks me: the difficulty of reconciling this with Simon Peter's question in 13, 36 and Thomas' words in 14, 5 strengthens the supposition that the last discourse has been made up of several collections of Johannine material.

o 17, 23. p 8, 29; 14, 15. q 16, 22; 17, 13. r 13, 34. s Rom 5, 6–8; 1 Jn 3, 16. t Dt 34, 5; Jos 24, 29; 2 Chr 20, 7; Ps 89, 21; Is 41, 8; Rom 8, 15; Gal 4, 7; Jas 2, 23. u 14, 13; Dt 7, 6. v 13, 34; 1 Jn 3, 23; 4, 21. w 7, 7; 14, 17; Mt 10, 22; 24, 9; Mk 13, 13; Lk 6, 22; 1 Jn 3, 13. x 17, 14–16; 1 Jn 4, 5. y 13, 16; Mt 10, 24. z 8, 19; 16, 3. a 8, 21.24; 9, 41. b 5, 23; Lk 10, 16; 1 Jn 2, 23. c 3, 2; 9, 32; Dt 4, 32–33. d Ps 35, 19; 69, 4. e 14, 16.26; Mt 10, 19–20. f Lk 1, 2; Acts 1, 8. g 9, 22; 12, 42; Mt 10, 17; Lk 21, 12; Acts 26, 11. h 15, 21. i 13, 19; 14, 29. j 7, 33; 13, 36; 14, 5.

to the one who sent me, and not one of you asks
me, 'Where are you going?' 6 But because I told
you this, grief has filled your hearts. 7 [k]But I tell
you the truth, it is better for you that I go. For if I
do not go, the Advocate will not come to you.
But if I go, I will send him to you. 8 *And when
he comes he will convict the world in regard to
sin and righteousness and condemnation: 9 [l]sin,
because they do not believe in me; 10 righteous-
ness, because I am going to the Father and you
will no longer see me; 11 [m]condemnation, be-
cause the ruler of this world has been con-
demned.

12 "I have much more to tell you, but you
cannot bear it now. 13 [n]*But when he comes, the
Spirit of truth, he will guide you to all truth. He
will not speak on his own, but he will speak
what he hears, and will declare to you the things
that are coming. 14 He will glorify me, because
he will take from what is mine and declare it to
you. 15 Everything that the Father has is mine;
for this reason I told you that he will take from
what is mine and declare it to you.

16 [o]"A little while and you will no longer see
me, and again a little while later and you will see
me." 17 So some of his disciples said to one
another, "What does this mean that he is saying
to us, 'A little while and you will not see me, and
again a little while and you will see me,' and
'Because I am going to the Father'?" 18 So they
said, "What is this 'little while' [of which he
speaks]? We do not know what he means."
19 Jesus knew that they wanted to ask him, so he
said to them, "Are you discussing with one
another what I said, 'A little while and you will
not see me, and again a little while and you will
see me'? 20 [p]Amen, amen, I say to you, you will
weep and mourn, while the world rejoices; you
will grieve, but your grief will become joy.
21 [q]When a woman is in labor, she is in anguish
because her hour has arrived; but when she has
given birth to a child, she no longer remembers
the pain because of her joy that a child has been
born into the world. 22 [r]So you also are now in
anguish. But I will see you again, and your hearts
will rejoice, and no one will take your joy away
from you. 23 [s]On that day you will not question
me about anything. Amen, amen, I say to you,
whatever you ask the Father in my name he will
give you. 24 Until now you have not asked
anything in my name; ask and you will receive,
so that your joy may be complete.

25 [t]*"I have told you this in figures of speech.
The hour is coming when I will no longer speak
to you in figures but I will tell you clearly about
the Father. 26 [u]On that day you will ask in my
name, and I do not tell you that I will ask the
Father for you. 27 For the Father himself loves
you, because you have loved me and have come
to believe that I came from God. 28 [v]I came from
the Father and have come into the world. Now I
am leaving the world and going back to the
Father." 29 His disciples said, "Now you are
talking plainly, and not in any figure of speech.
30 *Now we realize that you know everything
and that you do not need to have anyone
question you. Because of this we believe that
you came from God." 31 Jesus answered them,
"Do you believe now? 32 [w]*Behold, the hour is
coming and has arrived when each of you will be
scattered to his own home and you will leave me
alone. But I am not alone, because the Father is
with me. 33 [x]I have told you this so that you
might have peace in me. In the world you will

16, 8–11: These verses illustrate the forensic character of the Paraclete's role: in the forum of the disciples' conscience he prosecutes the world. He leads believers to see (a) that the basic sin was and is refusal to believe in Jesus; (b) that, although Jesus was found guilty and apparently died in disgrace, in reality righteousness has triumphed, for Jesus has returned to his Father; (c) finally, that it is **the ruler of this world,** Satan, who has been condemned through Jesus' death (12, 32).

16, 13: Declare to you the things that are coming: not a reference to new predictions about the future, but interpretation of what has already occurred or been said.

16, 25: See the note on 10, 6. Here, possibly a reference to 15, 1–16 or 16, 21.

16, 30: The reference is seemingly to the fact that Jesus could anticipate their question in v 19. The disciples naively think they have the full understanding that is the climax of "the hour" of Jesus' death, resurrection, and ascension (25), but the only part of the hour that is at hand for them is their share in the passion (32).

16, 32: You will be scattered: cf Mk 14, 27 and Mt 26, 31, where both cite Zec 13, 7 about the sheep being dispersed.

k 7, 39; 14, 16–17.26; 15, 26. l 8, 21–24; 15, 22. m 12, 31. n 14, 17.26; 15, 26; Pss 25, 5; 143, 10; 1 Jn 2, 27; Rv 7, 17. o 7, 33; 14, 19. p Ps 126, 6. q Is 26, 17–18; Jer 31, 13; Mic 4, 9. r 14, 19; 15, 11; 20, 20. s 14, 13. t Mt 13, 34–35. u 14, 13. v 1, 1. w 8, 29; Zec 13, 7; Mt 26, 31; Mk 14, 27. x 14, 27.

have trouble, but take courage, I have con-
quered the world."

CHAPTER 17

The Prayer of Jesus 1 [y]*When Jesus had said
this, he raised his eyes to heaven and said,
"Father, the hour has come. Give glory to your
son, so that your son may glorify you, 2 [z]*just as
you gave him authority over all people, so that
he may give eternal life to all you gave him.
3 [a]*Now this is eternal life, that they should
know you, the only true God, and the one
whom you sent, Jesus Christ. 4 I glorified you on
earth by accomplishing the work that you gave
me to do. 5 [b]Now glorify me, Father, with you,
with the glory that I had with you before the
world began.

6*"I revealed your name to those whom you
gave me out of the world. They belonged to you,
and you gave them to me, and they have kept
your word. 7 Now they know that everything you
gave me is from you, 8 because the words you
gave to me I have given to them, and they
accepted them and truly understood that I came
from you, and they have believed that you sent
me. 9 [c]I pray for them. I do not pray for the
world but for the ones you have given me,
because they are yours, 10 [d]and everything of
mine is yours and everything of yours is mine,
and I have been glorified in them. 11 And now I
will no longer be in the world, but they are in
the world, while I am coming to you. Holy
Father, keep them in your name that you have
given me, so that they may be one just as we are.
12 [e]When I was with them I protected them in
your name that you gave me, and I guarded
them, and none of them was lost except the son
of destruction, in order that the scripture might
be fulfilled. 13 [f]But now I am coming to you. I
speak this in the world so that they may share
my joy completely. 14 [g]I gave them your word,
and the world hated them, because they do not
belong to the world any more than I belong to
the world. 15 [h]*I do not ask that you take them
out of the world but that you keep them from
the evil one. 16 They do not belong to the world
any more than I belong to the world.
17 [i]Consecrate them in the truth. Your word is
truth. 18 [j]As you sent me into the world, so I sent
them into the world. 19 And I consecrate myself
for them, so that they also may be consecrated in
truth.

20 "I pray not only for them, but also for those
who will believe in me through their word,
21 [k]so that they may all be one, as you, Father,
are in me and I in you, that they also may be in
us, that the world may believe that you sent me.
22 And I have given them the glory you gave me,
so that they may be one, as we are one, 23 I in
them and you in me, that they may be brought
to perfection as one, that the world may know
that you sent me, and that you loved them even
as you loved me. 24 [l]*Father, they are your gift to
me. I wish that where I am they also may be
with me, that they may see my glory that you
gave me, because you loved me before the
foundation of the world. 25 [m]Righteous Father,
the world also does not know you, but I know
you, and they know that you sent me. 26*I made
known to them your name and I will make it

17, 1–26: Climax of the last discourse(s). Since the sixteenth century, this chapter has been called the "high priestly prayer" of Jesus. He speaks as intercessor, with words addressed directly to the Father and not to the disciples, who supposedly only overhear. Yet the prayer is one of petition, for immediate (6–19) and future (20–21) disciples. Many phrases reminiscent of the Lord's Prayer occur. Although still in the world (13), Jesus looks on his earthly ministry as a thing of the past (4.12). Whereas Jesus has up to this time stated that the disciples could follow him (13, 33.36), now he wishes them to be with him in union with the Father (12–14).

17, 1: The action of looking up to heaven and the address **Father** are typical of Jesus at prayer; cf 11, 41 and Lk 11, 2.

17, 2: Another possible interpretation is to treat the first line of the verse as parenthetical and the second as an appositive to the clause that ends v 1: **so that your son may glorify you (just as . . . all people), so that he may give eternal life. . . .**

17, 3: This verse was clearly added in the editing of the gospel as a reflection on the preceding verse; Jesus nowhere else refers to himself as Jesus Christ.

17, 6: I revealed your name: perhaps the name **I AM**; cf 8, 24. 28.58; 13, 19.

17, 15: Note the resemblance to the petition of the Lord's Prayer, "deliver us from the evil one." Both probably refer to the devil rather than to abstract evil.

17, 24: Where I am: Jesus prays for the believers ultimately to join him in heaven. Then they will not see his glory as in a mirror but clearly (2 Cor 3, 18; 1 Jn 3, 2).

17, 26: I will make it known: through the Advocate.

y 13, 31. z 3, 35; Mt 28, 18. a 1, 17; Wis 14, 7; 15, 3; 1 Jn 5, 20. b 1, 1.2; 12, 28; Phil 2, 6.9–11. c 17, 20. d 16, 15; 2 Thes 1, 10.12. e 13, 18; 18, 9; Ps 41, 10; Mt 26, 24; Acts 1, 16. f 15, 11. g 15, 19. h Mt 6, 13; 2 Thes 3, 3; 1 Jn 5, 18. i 1 Pt 1, 22 j 20, 21–22. k 10, 30; 14, 10–11.20. l 14, 3; 1 Thes 4, 17. m 1, 10.

known, that the love with which you loved me may be in them and I in them."

CHAPTER 18

Jesus Arrested 1 n*When he had said this, Jesus went out with his disciples across the Kidron valley to where there was a garden, into which he and his disciples entered. 2 Judas his betrayer also knew the place, because Jesus had often met there with his disciples. 3 o*So Judas got a band of soldiers and guards from the chief priests and the Pharisees and went there with lanterns, torches, and weapons. 4 Jesus, knowing everything that was going to happen to him, went out and said to them, "Whom are you looking for?" 5 *They answered him, "Jesus the Nazorean." He said to them, "I AM." Judas his betrayer was also with them. 6 When he said to them, "I AM," they turned away and fell to the ground. 7 So he again asked them, "Whom are you looking for?" They said, "Jesus the Nazorean." 8 Jesus answered, "I told you that I AM. So if you are looking for me, let these men go." 9 p*This was to fulfill what he had said, "I have not lost any of those you gave me." 10 *Then Simon Peter, who had a sword, drew it, struck the high priest's slave, and cut off his right ear. The slave's name was Malchus. 11 q*Jesus said to Peter, "Put your sword into its scabbard. Shall I not drink the cup that the Father gave me?"

12 r So the band of soldiers, the tribune, and the Jewish guards seized Jesus, bound him, 13 s*and brought him to Annas first. He was the father-in-law of Caiaphas, who was high priest that year. 14 t It was Caiaphas who had counseled the Jews that it was better that one man should die rather than the people.

Peter's First Denial 15 u*Simon Peter and another disciple followed Jesus. Now the other disciple was known to the high priest, and he entered the courtyard of the high priest with Jesus. 16 But Peter stood at the gate outside. So the other disciple, the acquaintance of the high priest, went out and spoke to the gatekeeper and brought Peter in. 17 Then the maid who was the gatekeeper said to Peter, "You are not one of this man's disciples, are you?" He said, "I am not." 18 Now the slaves and the guards were standing around a charcoal fire that they had made, because it was cold, and were warming themselves. Peter was also standing there keeping warm.

The Inquiry before Annas 19 v The high priest questioned Jesus about his disciples and about his doctrine. 20 w*Jesus answered him, "I have spoken publicly to the world. I have always taught in a synagogue or in the temple area where all the Jews gather, and in secret I have said nothing. 21 Why ask me? Ask those who heard me what I said to them. They know what I said." 22 x When he had said this, one of the temple guards standing there struck Jesus and

18, 1–14: John does not mention the agony in the garden and the kiss of Judas, nor does he identify the place as Gethsemane or the Mount of Olives.

18, 1: Jesus went out: see 14, 31, where it seems he is leaving the supper room. **Kidron valley:** literally, "the winter-flowing Kidron"; this wadi has water only during the winter rains.

18, 3: Band of soldiers: seems to refer to Roman troops, either the full cohort of 600 men (1/10 of a legion), or more likely the maniple of 200 under their tribune (12). In this case, John is hinting at Roman collusion in the action against Jesus before he was brought to Pilate. The lanterns and torches may be symbolic of the hour of darkness.

18, 5: Nazorean: the form found in Mt 26, 71 (see the note on Mt 2, 23) is here used, not **Nazarene** of Mark. **I AM:** or "I am he," but probably intended by the evangelist as an expression of divinity (cf their appropriate response in 6); see the note on 8, 24. John sets the confusion of the arresting party against the background of Jesus' divine majesty.

18, 9: The citation may refer to 6, 39; 10, 28; or 17, 12.

18, 10: Only John gives the names of the two antagonists; both John and Luke mention the right ear.

18, 11: The theme of the cup is found in the synoptic account of the agony (Mk 14, 36 and parallels).

18, 13: Annas: only John mentions an inquiry before Annas; cf 16.19–24; see the note on Lk 3, 2. It is unlikely that this nighttime interrogation before Annas is the same as the trial before Caiaphas placed by Matthew and Mark at night and by Luke in the morning.

18, 15–16: Another disciple . . . the other disciple: see the note on 13, 23.

18, 20: I have always taught . . . in the temple area: cf Mk 14, 49 for a similar statement.

n 2 Sm 15, 23; Mt 26, 30.36; Mk 14, 26.32; Lk 22, 39. o Mt 26, 47–51; Mk 14, 43–44; Lk 22, 47. p 6, 39; 10, 28; 17, 12. q Mt 20, 22; 26, 39; Mk 10, 38; Lk 22, 42. r Mt 26, 57–58; Mk 14, 53–54; Lk 22, 54–55. s Lk 3, 2. t 11, 49–50. u Mt 26, 58.69–70; Mk 14, 54.66–68; Lk 22, 54–57. v Mt 26, 59–66; Mk 14, 55–64; Lk 22, 66–71. w 6, 59; 7, 14.26; Is 48, 16; Mt 26, 55; Mk 4, 23; Lk 19, 47; 22, 53. x Acts 23, 2.

said, "Is this the way you answer the high priest?" [23]Jesus answered him, "If I have spoken wrongly, testify to the wrong; but if I have spoken rightly, why do you strike me?" [24] [y]*Then Annas sent him bound to Caiaphas the high priest.

Peter Denies Jesus Again [25] [z]Now Simon Peter was standing there keeping warm. And they said to him, "You are not one of his disciples, are you?" He denied it and said, "I am not." [26]One of the slaves of the high priest, a relative of the one whose ear Peter had cut off, said, "Didn't I see you in the garden with him?" [27]*Again Peter denied it. And immediately the cock crowed.

The Trial before Pilate [28] [a]*Then they brought Jesus from Caiaphas to the praetorium. It was morning. And they themselves did not enter the praetorium, in order not to be defiled so that they could eat the Passover. [29]So Pilate came out to them and said, "What charge do you bring [against] this man?" [30]They answered and said to him, "If he were not a criminal, we would not have handed him over to you." [31]*At this, Pilate said to them, "Take him yourselves, and judge him according to your law." The Jews answered him, "We do not have the right to execute anyone," [32] [b]*in order that the word of Jesus might be fulfilled that he said indicating the kind of death he would die. [33]So Pilate went back into the praetorium and summoned Jesus and said to him, "Are you the King of the Jews?" [34]Jesus answered, "Do you say this on your own or have others told you about me?" [35] [c]Pilate answered, "I am not a Jew, am I? Your own nation and the chief priests handed you over to me. What have you done?" [36] [d]Jesus answered, "My kingdom does not belong to this world. If my kingdom did belong to this world, my attendants [would] be fighting to keep me from being handed over to the Jews. But as it is, my kingdom is not here." [37] [e]*So Pilate said to him, "Then you are a king?" Jesus answered, "You say I am a king. For this I was born and for this I came into the world, to testify to the truth. Everyone who belongs to the truth listens to my voice." [38] [f]Pilate said to him, "What is truth?"

When he had said this, he again went out to the Jews and said to them, "I find no guilt in him. [39]*But you have a custom that I release one prisoner to you at Passover. Do you want me to release to you the King of the Jews?" [40]*They cried out again, "Not this one but Barabbas!" Now Barabbas was a revolutionary.

CHAPTER 19

[1] [g]*Then Pilate took Jesus and had him scourged. [2]And the soldiers wove a crown out of thorns and placed it on his head, and clothed him in a purple cloak, [3]and they came to him and said, "Hail, King of the Jews!" And they struck him repeatedly. [4] [h]Once more Pilate went out and said to them, "Look, I am bringing him out to you, so that you may know that I find no guilt in him." [5] [i]So Jesus came out, wearing the crown of thorns and the purple cloak. And he said to them, "Behold, the man!" [6] [j]When the chief priests and the guards saw him they cried out, "Crucify him, crucify him!" Pilate said to

18, 24: Caiaphas: see Mt 26, 3.57; Lk 3, 2; and the notes there. John may leave room here for the trial before Caiaphas described in the synoptic gospels.

18, 27: Cockcrow was the third Roman division of the night, lasting from midnight to 3 a.m.

18, 28: Praetorium: see the note on Mt 27, 27. **Morning:** literally, "the early hour," or fourth Roman division of the night, 3 to 6 a.m. **The Passover:** the synoptic gospels give the impression that the Thursday night supper was the Passover meal (Mk 14, 12); for John that meal is still to be eaten Friday night.

18, 31: We do not have the right to execute anyone: only John gives this reason for their bringing Jesus to Pilate. Jewish sources are not clear on the competence of the Sanhedrin at this period to sentence and to execute for political crimes.

18, 32: The Jewish punishment for blasphemy was stoning (Lv 24, 16). In coming to the Romans to ensure that Jesus would be crucified, the Jewish authorities fulfilled his prophecy that he would be **exalted** (3, 14; 12, 32–33). There is some historical evidence, however, for Jews crucifying Jews.

18, 37: You say I am a king: see Mt 26, 64 for a similar response to the high priest. It is at best a reluctant affirmative.

18, 39: See the note on Mt 27, 15.

18, 40: Barabbas: see the note on Mt 27, 16–17. **Revolutionary:** a guerrilla warrior fighting for nationalistic aims, though the term can also denote a robber. See the note on Mt 27, 38.

19, 1: Luke places the mockery of Jesus at the midpoint in the trial when Jesus was sent to Herod. Mark and Matthew place the scourging and mockery at the end of the trial after the sentence of death. Scourging was an integral part of the crucifixion penalty.

y Mt 26, 57. z Mt 26, 71–75; Mk 14, 69–72; Lk 22, 58–62. a Mt 27, 1–2.11–25; Mk 15, 1–5; Lk 23, 1–5. b 3, 14; 8, 28; 12, 32–33. c 1, 11. d 1, 10; 8, 23. e 8, 47; 1 Tm 6, 13. f Mt 27, 15–26; Mk 15, 6–15; Lk 23, 18–25; Acts 3, 14. g Mt 27, 27–31; Mk 15, 16–20; Lk 23, 13–25. h 18, 38. i Is 52, 14. j 18, 31; 19, 15.

them, "Take him yourselves and crucify him. I
find no guilt in him." [7 k]*The Jews answered,
"We have a law, and according to that law he
ought to die, because he made himself the Son of
God." [8]Now when Pilate heard this statement,
he became even more afraid, [9 l]and went back
into the praetorium and said to Jesus, "Where
are you from?" Jesus did not answer him. [10]So
Pilate said to him, "Do you not speak to me? Do
you not know that I have power to release you
and I have power to crucify you?" [11 m]Jesus
answered [him], "You would have no power
over me if it had not been given to you from
above. For this reason the one who handed me
over to you has the greater sin." [12 n]*Con-
sequently, Pilate tried to release him; but the
Jews cried out, "If you release him, you are not a
Friend of Caesar. Everyone who makes himself a
king opposes Caesar."
[13]*When Pilate heard these words he brought
Jesus out and seated him on the judge's bench in
the place called Stone Pavement, in Hebrew,
Gabbatha. [14]*It was preparation day for Pass-
over, and it was about noon. And he said to the
Jews, "Behold, your king!" [15]They cried out,
"Take him away, take him away! Crucify him!"
Pilate said to them, "Shall I crucify your king?"
The chief priests answered, "We have no king
but Caesar." [16]*Then he handed him over to
them to be crucified.

The Crucifixion of Jesus So they took Jesus,
[17 o]*and carrying the cross himself he went out
to what is called the Place of the Skull, in
Hebrew, Golgotha. [18]There they crucified him,
and with him two others, one on either side,
with Jesus in the middle. [19]*Pilate also had an
inscription written and put on the cross. It read,
"Jesus the Nazorean, the King of the Jews."
[20]Now many of the Jews read this inscription,
because the place where Jesus was crucified was
near the city; and it was written in Hebrew,
Latin, and Greek. [21 p]So the chief priests of the
Jews said to Pilate, "Do not write 'The King of
the Jews,' but that he said, 'I am the King of the
Jews.' " [22]Pilate answered, "What I have writ-
ten, I have written."
[23 q r]*When the soldiers had crucified Jesus,
they took his clothes and divided them into four
shares, a share for each soldier. They also took
his tunic, but the tunic was seamless, woven in
one piece from the top down. [24]So they said to
one another, "Let's not tear it, but cast lots for it
to see whose it will be," in order that the passage
of scripture might be fulfilled [that says]:

"They divided my garments among them,
and for my vesture they cast lots."

This is what the soldiers did. [25 s]*Standing by
the cross of Jesus were his mother and his
mother's sister, Mary the wife of Clopas, and

19, 7: Made himself the Son of God: this question was not raised in John's account of the Jewish interrogations of Jesus as it was in the synoptic account. Nevertheless, see 5, 18; 8, 53; 10, 36.

19, 12: Friend of Caesar: a Roman honorific title bestowed upon high-ranking officials for merit.

19, 13: Seated him: others translate "(Pilate) sat down." In John's thought, Jesus is the real judge of the world, and John may here be portraying him seated on the judgment bench. **Stone Pavement:** in Greek **lithostrotos;** under the fortress Antonia, one of the conjectured locations of the praetorium, a massive stone pavement has been excavated. **Gabbatha** (Aramaic rather than Hebrew) probably means "ridge, elevation."

19, 14: Noon: Mk 15, 25 has Jesus crucified "at the third hour," which means either 9 a.m. or the period from 9 to 12. Noon, the time when, according to John, Jesus was sentenced to death, was the hour at which the priests began to slaughter Passover lambs in the temple; see Jn 1, 29.

19, 16: He handed him over to them to be crucified: in context this would seem to mean "handed him over to the chief priests." Lk 23, 25 has a similar ambiguity. There is a polemic tendency in the gospels to place the guilt of the crucifixion on the Jewish authorities and to exonerate the Romans from blame. But John later mentions the Roman soldiers (23), and it was to these soldiers that Pilate handed Jesus over.

19, 17: Carrying the cross himself: a different picture from that of the synoptics, especially Lk 23, 26, where Simon of Cyrene is made to carry the cross, walking behind Jesus. In John's theology, Jesus remained in complete control and master of his destiny (cf 10, 18). **Place of the Skull:** the Latin word for skull is **Calvaria;** hence "Calvary." **Golgotha** is actually an Aramaic rather than a Hebrew word.

19, 19: The inscription differs with slightly different words in each of the four gospels. John's form is fullest and gives the equivalent of the Latin **INRI = Iesus Nazarenus Rex Iudaeorum.** Only John mentions its polyglot character (20) and Pilate's role in keeping the title unchanged (21–22).

19, 23–25a: While all four gospels describe the soldiers casting lots to divide Jesus' garments (see the note on Mt 27, 35), only John quotes the underlying passage from Ps 22, 19, and only John sees each line of the poetic parallelism literally carried out in two separate actions (23a; 23b-24).

19, 25: It is not clear whether four women are meant, or three (i.e., **Mary the wife of Cl[e]opas** [cf Lk 24, 18] is in apposition

k 10, 33–36; Lv 24, 16. 17, 28. **m** 3, 27; 10, 18; Rom 13, 1. **n** Acts 17, 7. **o** Mt 27, 32–37; Mk 15, 21–26; Lk 23, 26–35. **p** 18, 33; Lk 19, 14. **q** Mt 27, 38–44; Mk 15, 27–32; Lk 23, 36–43. **r** Ps 22, 19; Mt 27, 35; Mk 15, 24; Lk 23, 34. **s** Mt 27, 55; Mk 15, 40–41; Lk 8, 2; 23, 49.

Mary of Magdala. [26] [t]*When Jesus saw his mother and the disciple there whom he loved, he said to his mother, "Woman, behold, your son." [27]Then he said to the disciple, "Behold, your mother." And from that hour the disciple took her into his home.

[28] [u v]*After this, aware that everything was now finished, in order that the scripture might be fulfilled, Jesus said, "I thirst." [29]*There was a vessel filled with common wine. So they put a sponge soaked in wine on a sprig of hyssop and put it up to his mouth. [30] [w]*When Jesus had taken the wine, he said, "It is finished." And bowing his head, he handed over the spirit.

The Blood and Water [31] [x]Now since it was preparation day, in order that the bodies might not remain on the cross on the sabbath, for the sabbath day of that week was a solemn one, the Jews asked Pilate that their legs be broken and they be taken down. [32]So the soldiers came and broke the legs of the first and then of the other one who was crucified with Jesus. [33]But when they came to Jesus and saw that he was already dead, they did not break his legs, [34] [y]*but one soldier thrust his lance into his side, and immediately blood and water flowed out. [35] [z]*An eyewitness has testified, and his testimony is true; he knows that he is speaking the truth, so that you also may [come to] believe. [36] [a]For this happened so that the scripture passage might be fulfilled:

"Not a bone of it will be broken."

[37] [b]And again another passage says:

"They will look upon him whom they have pierced."

The Burial of Jesus [38] [c]*After this, Joseph of Arimathea, secretly a disciple of Jesus for fear of the Jews, asked Pilate if he could remove the body of Jesus. And Pilate permitted it. So he came and took his body. [39] [d]Nicodemus, the one who had first come to him at night, also came bringing a mixture of myrrh and aloes weighing about one hundred pounds. [40]They took the body of Jesus and bound it with burial cloths along with the spices, according to the Jewish burial custom. [41]Now in the place where he had been crucified there was a garden, and in the garden a new tomb, in which no one had yet been buried. [42]So they laid Jesus there because of the Jewish preparation day; for the tomb was close by.

CHAPTER 20

The Empty Tomb [1] [e f]*On the first day of the week, Mary of Magdala came to the tomb early

---

with **his mother's sister**) or two (his mother and his mother's sister, i.e., Mary of Cl[e]opas and Mary of Magdala). Only John mentions the mother of Jesus here. The synoptics have a group of women looking on from a distance at the cross (Mk 15, 40).

19, 26–27: This scene has been interpreted literally, of Jesus' concern for his mother; and symbolically, e.g., in the light of the Cana story in ch 2 (the presence of the mother of Jesus, the address **woman,** and the mention of the **hour**) and of the upper room in ch 13 (the presence of the beloved disciple; the **hour**). Now that the hour has come (28), Mary (a symbol of the church?) is given a role as the mother of Christians (personified by the beloved disciple); or, as a representative of those seeking salvation, she is supported by the disciple who interprets Jesus' revelation; or Jewish and Gentile Christianity (or Israel and the Christian community) are reconciled.

19, 28: The scripture . . . fulfilled: either in the scene of vv 25–27, or in the **I thirst** of v 28. If the latter, Pss 22, 16 and 69, 22 deserve consideration.

19, 29: Wine: John does not mention the drugged wine, a narcotic that Jesus refused as the crucifixion began (Mk 15, 23), but only this final gesture of kindness at the end (Mk 15, 36). **Hyssop,** a small plant, is scarcely suitable for carrying a sponge (Mark mentions a reed) and may be a symbolic reference to the hyssop used to daub the blood of the paschal lamb on the doorpost of the Hebrews (Ex 12, 22).

19, 30: Handed over the spirit: there is a double nuance of dying (giving up the last breath or spirit) and that of passing on the holy Spirit; see 7, 39, which connects the giving of the Spirit with Jesus' glorious return to the Father, and 20, 22, where the author portrays the conferral of the Spirit.

19, 34–35: John probably emphasizes these verses to show the reality of Jesus' death, against the docetic heretics. In the blood and water there may also be a symbolic reference to the Eucharist and baptism.

19, 35: He knows: it is not certain from the Greek that this **he** is the **eyewitness** of the first part of the sentence. **May [come to] believe:** see the note on 20, 31.

19, 38–42: In the first three gospels there is no anointing on Friday. In Mt and Lk, the women come to the tomb on Sunday morning precisely to anoint Jesus.

20, 1–31: The risen Jesus reveals his glory and confers the Spirit. This story fulfills the basic need for testimony to the

t 13, 23. u Mt 27, 45–56; Mk 15, 33–41; Lk 23, 44–49. v Pss 22, 16; 69, 22. w 4, 34; 10, 18; 17, 4; Lk 23, 46. x Ex 12, 16; Dt 21, 23. y Nm 20, 11; 1 Jn 5, 6. z 7, 37–39; 21, 24. a Ex 12, 46; Nm 9, 12; Ps 34, 21. b Nm 21, 9; Zec 12, 10; Rv 1, 7. c Mt 27, 57–60; Mk 15, 42–46; Lk 34, 50–54. d 3, 1–2; 7, 50; Ps 45, 9. e Mt 28, 1–10; Mk 16, 1–11; Lk 24, 1–12. f 19,25.

in the morning, while it was still dark, and saw the stone removed from the tomb. [2]*So she ran and went to Simon Peter and to the other disciple whom Jesus loved, and told them, "They have taken the Lord from the tomb, and we don't know where they put him." [3]*So Peter and the other disciple went out and came to the tomb. [4]They both ran, but the other disciple ran faster than Peter and arrived at the tomb first; [5]he bent down and saw the burial cloths there, but did not go in. [6 g]*When Simon Peter arrived after him, he went into the tomb and saw the burial cloths there, [7 h]and the cloth that had covered his head, not with the burial cloths but rolled up in a separate place. [8]Then the other disciple also went in, the one who had arrived at the tomb first, and he saw and believed. [9 i]*For they did not yet understand the scripture that he had to rise from the dead. [10]Then the disciples returned home.

The Appearance to Mary of Magdala [11 j]*But Mary stayed outside the tomb weeping. And as she wept, she bent over into the tomb [12]and saw two angels in white sitting there, one at the head and one at the feet where the body of Jesus had been. [13]And they said to her, "Woman, why are you weeping?" She said to them, "They have taken my Lord, and I don't know where they laid him." [14 k]When she had said this, she turned around and saw Jesus there, but did not know it was Jesus. [15 l]Jesus said to her, "Woman, why are you weeping? Whom are you looking for?" She thought it was the gardener and said to him, "Sir, if you carried him away, tell me where you laid him, and I will take him." [16]*Jesus said to her, "Mary!" She turned and said to him in Hebrew, "Rabbouni," which means Teacher. [17 m]*Jesus said to her, "Stop holding on to me, for I have not yet ascended to the Father. But go to my brothers and tell them, 'I am going to my Father and your Father, to my God and your God.' " [18]Mary of Magdala went and announced to the disciples, "I have seen the Lord," and what he told her.

Appearance to the Disciples [19 n]*On the evening of that first day of the week, when the doors were locked, where the disciples were, for fear of the Jews, Jesus came and stood in their midst and said to them, "Peace be with you." [20 o]*When he had said this, he showed them his hands and his side. The disciples rejoiced when they saw the Lord. [21 p]*[Jesus] said to them

---

resurrection. What we have here is not a record but a series of single stories.

20, 1–10: The story of the empty tomb is found in both the Matthean and the Lucan traditions; John's version seems to be a fusion of the two.

20, 1: Still dark: according to Mark the sun had risen, Matthew describes it as "dawning," and Luke refers to early dawn. Mary sees the stone removed, not the empty tomb.

20, 2: Mary runs away, not directed by an angel/young man as in the synoptic accounts. The plural "we" in the second part of her statement might reflect a tradition of more women going to the tomb.

20, 3–10: The basic narrative is told of Peter alone in Lk 24, 12, a verse missing in important manuscripts and which may be borrowed from tradition similar to John. Cf also Lk 24, 24.

20, 6–8: Some special feature about the state of the burial cloths caused the beloved disciple to believe. Perhaps the details emphasized that the grave had not been robbed.

20, 9: Probably a general reference to the scriptures is intended, as in Lk 24, 26 and 1 Cor 15, 4. Some individual Old Testament passages suggested are Ps 16, 10; Hos 6, 2; Jon 2, 1.2.11.

20, 11–18: This appearance to Mary is found only in Jn, but cf Mt 28, 8–10 and Mk 16, 9–11.

20, 16: Rabbouni: Hebrew or Aramaic for "my master."

20, 17: Stop holding on to me: see Mt 28, 9, where the women take hold of his feet. **I have not yet ascended:** for John and many of the New Testament writers, the ascension in the theological sense of going to the Father to be glorified took place with the resurrection as one action. This scene in John dramatizes such an understanding, for by Easter night Jesus is glorified and can give the Spirit. Therefore his ascension takes place immediately after he has talked to Mary. In such a view, the ascension after forty days described in Acts 1, 1–11 would be simply a termination of earthly appearances or, perhaps better, an introduction to the conferral of the Spirit upon the early church, modeled on Elisha's being able to have a (double) share in the spirit of Elijah if he saw him being taken up (same verb as ascending) into heaven (2 Kgs 2, 9–12). **To my Father and your Father, to my God and your God:** this echoes Ru 1, 16: "Your people shall be my people, and your God my God." The Father of Jesus will now become the Father of the disciples because, once ascended, Jesus can give them the Spirit that comes from the Father and they can be reborn as God's children (3, 5). That is why he calls them **my brothers.**

20, 19–29: The appearances to the disciples, without or with Thomas (cf 11, 16; 14, 5), have rough parallels in the other gospels only for vv 19–23; cf Lk 24, 36–39; Mk 16, 14–18.

20, 19: The disciples: by implication from v 24, this means ten of the Twelve, presumably in Jerusalem. **Peace be with you:** although this could be an ordinary greeting, John intends here to echo 14, 27. The theme of rejoicing in v 20 echoes 16, 22.

20, 20: Hands and . . . side: Lk 24, 39–40 mentions "hands and feet," based on Ps 22, 17.

20, 21: By means of this sending, the Eleven were made apostles, that is, "those sent" (cf 17, 18), though John does not use the noun in reference to them (see the note on 13, 16). A solemn

g Lk 24, 12. h 11, 44; 19, 40. i Acts 2, 26–27; 1 Cor 15, 4. j Mk 16, 9–11. k 21, 4; Mk 16, 12; Lk 24, 16; 1 Cor 15, 43–44. l Mt 28, 9–10. m Acts 1, 9. n Mt 28, 16–20; Mk 16, 14–18; Lk 24, 36–44. o 14, 27. p 17, 18; Mt 28, 19; Mk 16, 15; Lk 24, 47–48.

again, "Peace be with you. As the Father has
sent me, so I send you." 22 [q]*And when he had
said this, he breathed on them and said to them,
"Receive the holy Spirit. 23 [r]*Whose sins you
forgive are forgiven them, and whose sins you
retain are retained."
Thomas 24Thomas, called Didymus, one of the
Twelve, was not with them when Jesus came.
25 [s]So the other disciples said to him, "We have
seen the Lord." But he said to them, "Unless I
see the mark of the nails in his hands and put my
finger into the nailmarks and put my hand into
his side, I will not believe." 26 [t]Now a week later
his disciples were again inside and Thomas was
with them. Jesus came, although the doors were
locked, and stood in their midst and said, "Peace
be with you." 27Then he said to Thomas, "Put
your finger here and see my hands, and bring
your hand and put it into my side, and do not be
unbelieving, but believe." 28 [u]*Thomas an-
swered and said to him, "My Lord and my God!"
29 [v]*Jesus said to him, "Have you come to
believe because you have seen me? Blessed are
those who have not seen and have believed."
Conclusion 30 [w]*Now Jesus did many other
signs in the presence of [his] disciples that are not
written in this book. 31 [x]But these are written
that you may [come to] believe that Jesus is the
Messiah, the Son of God, and that through this
belief you may have life in his name.

IV: Epilogue

The Resurrection Appearance in Galilee

CHAPTER 21

The Appearance to the Seven Disciples
1 [y]*After this, Jesus revealed himself again to his
disciples at the Sea of Tiberias. He revealed
himself in this way. 2*Together were Simon
Peter, Thomas called Didymus, Nathanael from
Cana in Galilee, Zebedee's sons, and two others
of his disciples. 3 [z]*Simon Peter said to them, "I
am going fishing." They said to him, "We also
will come with you." So they went out and got
into the boat, but that night they caught noth-
ing. 4 [a]When it was already dawn, Jesus was
standing on the shore; but the disciples did not
realize that it was Jesus. 5 [b]Jesus said to them,
"Children, have you caught anything to eat?"
They answered him, "No." 6So he said to them,
"Cast the net over the right side of the boat and
you will find something." So they cast it, and
were not able to pull it in because of the number
of fish. 7So the disciple whom Jesus loved said to
Peter, "It is the Lord." When Simon Peter heard
that it was the Lord, he tucked in his garment,
for he was lightly clad, and jumped into the sea.
8The other disciples came in the boat, for they
were not far from shore, only about a hundred
yards, dragging the net with the fish. 9 [c]*When

---

mission or "sending" is also the subject of the post-resurrection appearances to the Eleven in Mt 28, 19; Lk 24, 47; Mk 16, 15.

20, 22: This action recalls Gn 2, 7, where God breathed on the first man and gave him life; just as Adam's life came from God, so now the disciples' new spiritual life comes from Jesus. Cf also the revivification of the dry bones in Ez 37. This is the author's version of Pentecost. Cf also the note on 19, 30.

20, 23: The Council of Trent defined that this power to forgive sins is exercised in the sacrament of penance. See Mt 16, 19 and 18, 18.

20, 28: My Lord and my God: this forms a literary inclusion with the first verse of the gospel: "and the Word was God."

20, 29: This verse is a beatitude on future generations; faith, not sight, matters.

20, 30–31: These verses are clearly a conclusion to the gospel and express its purpose. While many manuscripts read **come to believe,** possibly implying a missionary purpose for John's gospel, a small number of quite early ones read "continue to believe," suggesting that the audience consists of Christians whose faith is to be deepened by the book; cf 19, 35.

21, 1–23: There are many non-Johannine peculiarities in this chapter, some suggesting Lucan Greek style; yet this passage is closer to John than 7, 53—8, 11. There are many Johannine features as well. Its closest parallels in the synoptic gospels are found in Lk 5, 1–11 and Mt 14, 28–31. Perhaps the tradition was ultimately derived from John but preserved by some disciple other than the writer of the rest of the gospel. The appearances narrated seem to be independent of those in ch 20. Even if a later addition, the chapter was added before publication of the gospel, for it appears in all manuscripts.

21, 2: Zebedee's sons: the only reference to James and John in this gospel (but see the note on 1, 37). Perhaps the phrase was originally a gloss to identify, among the five, the **two others of his disciples.** The anonymity of the latter phrase is more Johannine (1, 35). The total of seven may suggest the community of the disciples in its fullness.

21, 3–6: This may be a variant of Luke's account of the catch of fish; see the note on Lk 5, 1–11.

21, 9.12–13: It is strange that Jesus already has fish since none have yet been brought ashore. This meal may have had eucharistic

q Gn 2, 7; Ez 37, 9; 1 Cor 15, 45. r Mt 16, 19; 18, 18. s 1 Jn 1, 1. t 21, 14. u 1, 1. v 4, 48; Lk 1, 45; 1 Pt 1, 8. w 21, 25. x 3, 14.15; 1 Jn 5, 13. y Mt 26, 32; 28, 7. z Mt 4, 18; Lk 5, 4–10. a 20, 14; Mt 28, 17; Lk 24, 16. b Lk 24, 41. c Lk 24, 41–43.

they climbed out on shore, they saw a charcoal
fire with fish on it and bread. [10]Jesus said to
them, "Bring some of the fish you just caught."
[11][d]*So Simon Peter went over and dragged the
net ashore full of one hundred fifty-three large
fish. Even though there were so many, the net
was not torn. [12]*Jesus said to them, "Come,
have breakfast." And none of the disciples dared
to ask him, "Who are you?" because they
realized it was the Lord. [13][e]Jesus came over and
took the bread and gave it to them, and in like
manner the fish. [14][f]*This was now the third
time Jesus was revealed to his disciples after
being raised from the dead.
Jesus and Peter [15]*When they had finished
breakfast, Jesus said to Simon Peter, "Simon, son
of John, do you love me more than these?" He
said to him, "Yes, Lord, you know that I love
you." He said to him, "Feed my lambs." [16]He
then said to him a second time, "Simon, son of
John, do you love me?" He said to him, "Yes,
Lord, you know that I love you." He said to him,
"Tend my sheep." [17][g]He said to him the third
time, "Simon, son of John, do you love me?"
Peter was distressed that he had said to him a
third time, "Do you love me?" and he said to
him, "Lord, you know everything; you know
that I love you." [Jesus] said to him, "Feed my
sheep. [18][h]*Amen, amen, I say to you, when you
were younger, you used to dress yourself and go
where you wanted; but when you grow old, you
will stretch out your hands, and someone else
will dress you and lead you where you do not
want to go." [19][i]He said this signifying by what
kind of death he would glorify God. And when
he had said this, he said to him, "Follow me."
The Beloved Disciple [20][j]Peter turned and
saw the disciple following whom Jesus loved, the
one who had also reclined upon his chest during
the supper and had said, "Master, who is the one
who will betray you?" [21]When Peter saw him,
he said to Jesus, "Lord, what about him?"
[22][k]*Jesus said to him, "What if I want him to
remain until I come? What concern is it of
yours? You follow me." [23]*So the word spread
among the brothers that that disciple would not
die. But Jesus had not told him that he would
not die, just "What if I want him to remain until
I come? [What concern is it of yours?]"
Conclusion [24][l]*It is this disciple who testifies
to these things and has written them, and we
know that his testimony is true. [25][m]There are
also many other things that Jesus did, but if these
were to be described individually, I do not think
the whole world would contain the books that
would be written.

---

significance for early Christians since v 13 recalls Jn 6, 11, which uses the vocabulary of Jesus' action at the Last Supper; but see also the note on Mt 14, 19.

21, 11: The exact number 153 is probably meant to have a symbolic meaning in relation to the apostles' universal mission; Jerome claims that Greek zoologists catalogued 153 species of fish. Or 153 is the sum of the numbers from 1 to 17. Others invoke Ez 47, 10.

21, 12: None . . . dared to ask him: is Jesus' appearance strange to them? Cf Lk 24, 16; Mk 16, 12; Jn 20, 14. The disciples do, however, recognize Jesus **before** the breaking of the bread (opposed to Lk 24, 35).

21, 14: This verse connects chs 20 and 21; cf 20, 19.26.

21, 15–23: This section constitutes Peter's rehabilitation and emphasizes his role in the church.

21, 15–17: In these three verses there is a remarkable variety of synonyms: two different Greek verbs for **love** (see the note on 15, 13); two verbs for **feed/tend;** two nouns for **sheep;** two verbs for **know.** But apparently there is no difference of meaning. The threefold confession of Peter is meant to counteract his earlier threefold denial (18, 17.25.27). The First Vatican Council cited these verses in defining that Jesus after his resurrection gave Peter the jurisdiction of supreme shepherd and ruler over the whole flock.

21, 15: More than these: probably "more than these disciples do" rather than "more than you love them" or "more than you love these things [fishing, etc.]."

21, 18: Originally probably a proverb about old age, now used as a figurative reference to the crucifixion of Peter.

21, 22: Until I come: a reference to the parousia.

21, 23: This whole scene takes on more significance if the disciple is already dead. The death of the apostolic generation caused problems in the church because of a belief that Jesus was to have returned first. Loss of faith sometimes resulted; cf 2 Pt 3, 4.

21, 24: Who . . . has written them: this does not necessarily mean he wrote them with his own hand. The same expression is used in 19, 22 of Pilate, who certainly would not have written the inscription himself. **We know:** i.e., the Christian community; cf 1, 14.16.

d 2 Chr 2, 16. e Lk 24, 42. f 20, 19.26. g 13, 37–38; 18, 15–18.25–27; Mt 26, 69–75; Mk 14, 66–72; Lk 22, 55–62. h Acts 21, 11.14; 2 Pt 1, 14. i 13, 36. j 13, 25. k Mt 16, 28. l 19, 35. m 20, 30.

THE ACTS OF THE APOSTLES

The Acts of the Apostles, the second volume of Luke's two-volume work, continues Luke's presentation of biblical history, describing how the salvation promised to Israel in the Old Testament and accomplished by Jesus has now under the guidance of the holy Spirit been extended to the Gentiles. This was accomplished through the divinely chosen representatives (10, 41) whom Jesus prepared during his historical ministry (1, 21-22) and commissioned after his resurrection as witnesses to all that he taught (1, 8; 10, 37-43; Lk 24, 48). Luke's preoccupation with the Christian community as the Spirit-guided bearer of the word of salvation rules out of his book detailed histories of the activity of most of the preachers. Only the main lines of the roles of Peter and Paul serve Luke's interest.

Peter was the leading member of the Twelve (1, 13.15), a miracle worker like Jesus in the gospel (3, 1-10; 5, 1-11.15; 9, 32-35.36-42), the object of divine care (5, 17-21; 12, 6-11), and the spokesman for the Christian community (2, 14-36; 3, 12-26; 4, 8-12; 5, 29-32; 10, 34-43; 15, 7-11), who, according to Luke, was largely responsible for the growth of the community in the early days (2, 4; 4, 4). Paul eventually joined the community at Antioch (11, 25-26), which subsequently commissioned him and Barnabas to undertake the spread of the gospel to Asia Minor. This missionary venture generally failed to win the Jews of the diaspora to the gospel but enjoyed success among the Gentiles (13, 14—14, 27).

Paul's refusal to impose the Mosaic law upon his Gentile converts provoked very strong objection among the Jewish Christians of Jerusalem (15, 1), but both Peter and James supported his position (15, 6-21). Paul's second and third missionary journeys (16, 36—21, 16) resulted in the same pattern of failure among the Jews generally but of some success among the Gentiles. Paul, like Peter, is presented as a miracle worker (14, 8-18; 19, 12; 20, 7-12; 28, 7-10) and the object of divine care (16, 25-31).

In Acts, Luke has provided a broad survey of the church's development from the resurrection of Jesus to Paul's first Roman imprisonment, the point at which the book ends. In telling this story, Luke describes the emergence of Christianity from its origins in Judaism to its position as a religion of worldwide status and appeal. Originally a Jewish Christian community in Jerusalem, the church was placed in circumstances impelling it to include within its membership people of other cultures: the Samaritans (8, 4-25), at first an occasional Gentile (8, 26-30; 10, 1-48), and finally the Gentiles on principle (11, 20-21). Fear on the part of the Jewish people that Christianity, particularly as preached to the Gentiles, threatened their own cultural heritage caused them to be suspicious of Paul's gospel (13, 42-45; 15, 1-5; 28, 17-24). The inability of Christian missionaries to allay this apprehension inevitably created a situation in which the gospel was preached more and more to the Gentiles. Toward the end of Paul's career, the Christian communities, with the exception of those in Palestine itself (9, 31), were mainly of Gentile membership. In tracing the emergence of Christianity from Judaism, Luke is insistent upon the prominence of Israel in the divine plan of salvation (see the note on 1, 26; see also 2, 5-6; 3, 13-15; 10, 36; 13, 16-41; 24, 14-15) and that the extension of salvation to the Gentiles has been a part of the divine plan from the beginning (see 15, 13-18; 26, 22-23).

In the development of the church from a Jewish Christian origin in Jerusalem, with its roots in Jewish religious tradition, to a series of Christian communities among the Gentiles of the Roman empire, Luke perceives the action of God in history laying open the heart of all humanity to the divine message of salvation. His approach to the history of the church is motivated by his theological interests. His history of the apostolic church is the story of a Spirit-guided community and a Spirit-guided spread of the Word of God (1, 8). The travels of Peter and Paul are in reality the travels of the Word of God as it spreads from Jerusalem, the city of destiny for Jesus, to Rome, the capital of the civilized world of Luke's day. Nonetheless, the historical data he utilizes are of value for the understanding of the church's early life and development and as general background to the Pauline epistles. In the interpretation of Acts, care must be exercised to determine Luke's theological aims and interests and to evaluate his historical data without either exaggerating their literal accuracy or underestimating their factual worth.

Finally, an apologetic concern is evident throughout Acts. By stressing the continuity between Judaism and Christianity (13, 16-41; 23, 6-9; 24, 10-21; 26, 2-23), Luke argues that Christianity is deserving of the same toleration accorded Judaism by Rome. Part of Paul's defense before Roman authorities is to show that Christianity is not a disturber of the peace of the Roman Empire (24, 5.12-13; 25, 7-8). Moreover, when he stands before Roman authorities, he is declared innocent of any crime against the empire (18, 13-15; 23, 29; 25, 25-27; 26, 31–32). Luke tells his story with the hope that Christianity will be treated as fairly.

Concerning the date of Acts, see the Introduction to the Gospel according to Luke.

The principal divisions of the Acts of the Apostles are the following:

I. The Preparation for the Christian Mission (1, 1—2, 13)
II. The Mission in Jerusalem (2, 14—8, 3)
III. The Mission in Judea and Samaria (8, 4—9, 43)
IV. The Inauguration of the Gentile Mission (10, 1—15, 35)
V. The Mission of Paul to the Ends of the Earth (15, 36—28, 31)

I: The Preparation for the Christian Mission

CHAPTER 1

The Promise of the Spirit [1][a]*In the first
book, Theophilus, I dealt with all that Jesus did
and taught [2][b]until the day he was taken up, after
giving instructions through the holy Spirit to the
apostles whom he had chosen. [3][c]*He presented
himself alive to them by many proofs after he
had suffered, appearing to them during forty
days and speaking about the kingdom of God.
[4][d]*While meeting with them, he enjoined them
not to depart from Jerusalem, but to wait for
"the promise of the Father about which you
have heard me speak; [5][e]for John baptized with
water, but in a few days you will be baptized
with the holy Spirit."

The Ascension of Jesus [6]*When they had gath-
ered together they asked him, "Lord, are you at

1, 1–26: This introductory material (1–2) connects Acts with the Gospel of Luke, shows that the apostles were instructed by the risen Jesus (3–5), points out that the parousia or second coming in glory of Jesus will occur as certainly as his ascension occurred (6–11), and lists the members of the Twelve, stressing their role as a body of divinely mandated witnesses to his life, teaching, and resurrection (12–26).

1, 3: **Appearing to them during forty days:** Luke considered especially sacred the interval in which the appearances and instructions of the risen Jesus occurred and expressed it therefore in terms of the sacred number forty (cf Dt 8, 2). In his gospel, however, Luke connects the ascension of Jesus with the resurrection by describing the ascension on Easter Sunday evening (Lk 24, 50–53). What should probably be understood as one event (resurrection, glorification, ascension, sending of the Spirit—the paschal mystery) has been historicized by Luke when he writes of a visible ascension of Jesus after forty days and the descent of the Spirit at Pentecost. For Luke, the ascension marks the end of the appearances of Jesus except for the extraordinary appearance to Paul. With regard to Luke's understanding of salvation history, the ascension also marks the end of the time of Jesus (Lk 24, 50–53) and signals the beginning of the time of the church.

1, 4: **The promise of the Father:** the holy Spirit, as is clear from the next verse. This gift of the Spirit was first promised in Jesus' final instructions to his chosen witnesses in Luke's gospel (Lk 24, 49) and formed part of the continuing instructions of the risen Jesus on the kingdom of God, of which Luke speaks in v 3.

1, 6: The question of the disciples implies that in believing Jesus to be the Christ (see the note on Lk 2, 11) they had expected him to be a political leader who would restore self-rule to Israel during his historical ministry. When this had not taken place, they ask if it is to take place at this time, the period of the church.

a Lk 1, 1–4. b Mt 28, 19–20; Lk 24, 44–49; Jn 20, 22; 1 Tm 3, 16. c 10, 41; 13, 31. d Jn 14, 16.17.26. e 11, 16; Mt 3, 11; Mk 1, 8; Lk 3, 16; Jn 1, 26; Eph 1, 13.

this time going to restore the kingdom to Israel?" [7][f]*He answered them, "It is not for you to know the times or seasons that the Father has established by his own authority. [8][g]*But you will receive power when the holy Spirit comes upon you, and you will be my witnesses in Jerusalem, throughout Judea and Samaria, and to the ends of the earth." [9][h]When he had said this, as they were looking on, he was lifted up, and a cloud took him from their sight. [10][i]While they were looking intently at the sky as he was going, suddenly two men dressed in white garments stood beside them. [11][j]They said, "Men of Galilee, why are you standing there looking at the sky? This Jesus who has been taken up from you into heaven will return in the same way as you have seen him going into heaven." [12][k]Then they returned to Jerusalem from the mount called Olivet, which is near Jerusalem, a sabbath day's journey away.

The First Community in Jerusalem [13]When they entered the city they went to the upper room where they were staying, Peter and John and James and Andrew, Philip and Thomas, Bartholomew and Matthew, James son of Alphaeus, Simon the Zealot, and Judas son of James. [14][l]All these devoted themselves with one accord to prayer, together with some women, and Mary the mother of Jesus, and his brothers.

The Choice of Judas's Successor [15]During those days Peter stood up in the midst of the brothers (there was a group of about one hundred and twenty persons in the one place). He said, [16][m]"My brothers, the scripture had to be fulfilled which the holy Spirit spoke beforehand through the mouth of David, concerning Judas, who was the guide for those who arrested Jesus. [17]He was numbered among us and was allotted a share in this ministry. [18][n]*He bought a parcel of land with the wages of his iniquity, and falling headlong, he burst open in the middle, and all his insides spilled out. [19]This became known to everyone who lived in Jerusalem, so that the parcel of land was called in their language 'Akeldama,' that is, Field of Blood. [20][o]For it is written in the Book of Psalms:

> 'Let his encampment become desolate,
> and may no one dwell in it.'

And:

> 'May another take his office.'

[21]Therefore, it is necessary that one of the men who accompanied us the whole time the Lord Jesus came and went among us, [22][p]beginning from the baptism of John until the day on which he was taken up from us, become with us a witness to his resurrection." [23]So they proposed two, Joseph called Barsabbas, who was also known as Justus, and Matthias. [24]Then they prayed, "You, Lord, who know the hearts of all, show which one of these two you have chosen [25]to take the place in this apostolic ministry from which Judas turned away to go to his own place." [26][q]*Then they gave lots to them, and the lot fell upon Matthias, and he was counted with the eleven apostles.

CHAPTER 2

The Coming of the Spirit [1][r]*When the time for Pentecost was fulfilled, they were all in one

1, 7: This verse echoes the tradition that the precise time of the parousia is not revealed to human beings; cf Mk 13, 32; 1 Thes 5, 1–3.

1, 8: Just as Jerusalem was the city of destiny in the Gospel of Luke (the place where salvation was accomplished), so here at the beginning of Acts, Jerusalem occupies a central position. It is the starting point for the mission of the Christian disciples to "the ends of the earth," the place where the apostles were situated and the doctrinal focal point in the early days of the community (15, 2.6). **The ends of the earth:** for Luke, this means Rome.

1, 18: Luke records a popular tradition about the death of Judas that differs from the one in Mt 27, 5, according to which Judas hanged himself. Here, although the text is not certain, Judas is depicted as purchasing a piece of property with the betrayal money and being killed on it in a fall.

1, 26: The need to replace Judas was probably dictated by the symbolism of the number twelve, recalling the twelve tribes of Israel. This symbolism also indicates that for Luke (see Lk 22, 30) the Christian church is a reconstituted Israel.

2, 1–41: Luke's pentecostal narrative consists of an introduction (1–13), a speech ascribed to Peter declaring the resurrection of Jesus and its messianic significance (14–36), and a favorable response from the audience (37–41). It is likely that the narrative telescopes events that took place over a period of time and on a less dramatic scale. The Twelve were not originally in a position to proclaim publicly the messianic office of Jesus without incurring immediate reprisal from those religious authorities in Jerusalem

f Mt 24, 36; 1 Thes 5, 1–2. g 2, 1–13; 10, 39; Is 43, 10; Mt 28, 19; Lk 24, 47–48. h 2 Kgs 2, 11; Mk 16, 19; Lk 24, 51. i Jn 20, 17. j Lk 24, 51; Eph 4, 8–10; 1 Pt 3, 22; Rv 1, 7. k Lk 6, 14–16. l Lk 23, 49. m Ps 41, 10; Lk 22, 47. n Mt 27, 3–10. o Pss 69, 26; 109, 8; Jn 17, 12. p 1, 8–9; 10, 39. q Prv 16, 33. r Lv 23, 15–21; Dt 16, 9–11.

place together. 2 s*And suddenly there came
from the sky a noise like a strong driving wind,
and it filled the entire house in which they
were. 3 t*Then there appeared to them tongues
as of fire, which parted and came to rest on
each one of them. 4 u*And they were all filled
with the holy Spirit and began to speak in
different tongues, as the Spirit enabled them to
proclaim.

5 Now there were devout Jews from every
nation under heaven staying in Jerusalem. 6 At
this sound, they gathered in a large crowd, but
they were confused because each one heard
them speaking in his own language. 7 vThey
were astounded, and in amazement they asked,
"Are not all these people who are speaking
Galileans? 8 Then how does each of us hear them
in his own native language? 9 We are Parthians,
Medes, and Elamites, inhabitants of Mesopota-
mia, Judea and Cappadocia, Pontus and Asia,
10 Phrygia and Pamphylia, Egypt and the districts
of Libya near Cyrene, as well as travelers from
Rome, 11 wboth Jews and converts to Judaism,
Cretans and Arabs, yet we hear them speaking in
our own tongues of the mighty acts of God."
12 They were all astounded and bewildered, and
said to one another, "What does this mean?"
13 xBut others said, scoffing, "They have had too
much new wine."

II: The Mission in Jerusalem

Peter's Speech at Pentecost 14*Then Peter
stood up with the Eleven, raised his voice, and
proclaimed to them, "You who are Jews, indeed
all of you staying in Jerusalem. Let this be known
to you, and listen to my words. 15 These people
are not drunk, as you suppose, for it is only nine
o'clock in the morning. 16 No, this is what was
spoken through the prophet Joel:

17 y'It will come to pass in the last days,'
God says,
'that I will pour out a portion of my spirit
upon all flesh.
Your sons and your daughters shall prophesy,
your young men shall see visions,
your old men shall dream dreams.
18 Indeed, upon my servants and my handmaids
I will pour out a portion of my spirit in those
days,
and they shall prophesy.
19 And I will work wonders in the heavens above
and signs on the earth below:
blood, fire, and a cloud of smoke.
20 The sun shall be turned to darkness,
and the moon to blood,
before the coming of the great and
splendid day of the Lord,
21 zand it shall be that everyone shall be saved
who calls on the name of the Lord.'

22 aYou who are Israelites, hear these words.
Jesus the Nazorean was a man commended to
you by God with mighty deeds, wonders, and
signs, which God worked through him in your
midst, as you yourselves know. 23 bThis man,
delivered up by the set plan and foreknowledge
of God, you killed, using lawless men to crucify
him. 24 cBut God raised him up, releasing him
from the throes of death, because it was impossi-
ble for him to be held by it. 25 dFor David says of
him:

'I saw the Lord ever before me,
with him at my right hand I shall not be
disturbed.

---

who had brought about Jesus' death precisely to stem the rising tide in his favor.

2, 2: There came from the sky a noise like a strong driving wind: wind and spirit are associated in Jn 3, 8. The sound of a great rush of wind would herald a new action of God in the history of salvation.

2, 3: Tongues as of fire: see Ex 19, 18 where fire symbolizes the presence of God to initiate the covenant on Sinai. Here the holy Spirit acts upon the apostles, preparing them to proclaim the new covenant with its unique gift of the Spirit (38).

2, 4: To speak in different tongues: ecstatic prayer in praise of God, interpreted in vv 6 and 11 as speaking in foreign languages, symbolizing the worldwide mission of the church.

2, 14–36: The first of six discourses in Acts (along with 3, 12–26; 4, 8–12; 5, 29–32; 10, 34–43; 13, 16–41) dealing with the resurrection of Jesus and its messianic import. Five of these are attributed to Peter, the final one to Paul. Modern scholars term these discourses in Acts the "kerygma," the Greek word for proclamation (cf 1 Cor 15, 11).

s Jn 3, 8. t Lk 3, 16. u 1, 5; 4, 31; 8, 15.17; 10, 44; 11, 15–16; 15, 8; 19, 6; Ps 104, 30; Jn 20, 33. v 1, 11. w 10, 46. x 1 Cor 14, 23. y Is 2, 2; 44, 3; Jl 3, 1–5. z Rom 10, 13. a 10, 38; Lk 24, 19. b 1 Thes 2, 15. c 13, 34. d Ps 16, 8–11.

26 Therefore my heart has been glad and my
tongue has exulted;
my flesh, too, will dwell in hope,
27 [e]because you will not abandon my soul to the
nether world,
nor will you suffer your holy one to see
corruption.
28 You have made known to me the paths of life;
you will fill me with joy in your presence.'

29 My brothers, one can confidently say to you
about the patriarch David that he died and was
buried, and his tomb is in our midst to this day.
30 [f]But since he was a prophet and knew that
God had sworn an oath to him that he would set
one of his descendants upon his throne, 31 [g]he
foresaw and spoke of the resurrection of the
Messiah, that neither was he abandoned to the
netherworld nor did his flesh see corruption.
32 God raised this Jesus; of this we are all
witnesses. 33 [h]*Exalted at the right hand of God,
he received the promise of the holy Spirit from
the Father and poured it forth, as you [both] see
and hear. 34 [i]For David did not go up into
heaven, but he himself said:

'The Lord said to my Lord,
"Sit at my right hand
35 until I make your enemies your footstool." '

36 [j]Therefore let the whole house of Israel know
for certain that God has made him both Lord and
Messiah, this Jesus whom you crucified."
37 [k]Now when they heard this, they were cut
to the heart, and they asked Peter and the other
apostles, "What are we to do, my brothers?"
38 [l]*Peter [said] to them, "Repent and be bap-
tized, every one of you, in the name of Jesus
Christ for the forgiveness of your sins; and you
will receive the gift of the holy Spirit. 39 [m]For the
promise is made to you and to your children and
to all those far off, whomever the Lord our God
will call." 40 [n]He testified with many other argu-
ments, and was exhorting them, "Save yourselves
from this corrupt generation." 41 [o]Those who ac-
cepted his message were baptized, and about
three thousand persons were added that day.
Communal Life 42 [p q]*They devoted them-
selves to the teaching of the apostles and to the
communal life, to the breaking of the bread and to
the prayers. 43 [r]Awe came upon everyone, and
many wonders and signs were done through the
apostles. 44 [s]All who believed were together and
had all things in common; 45 they would sell their
property and possessions and divide them among
all according to each one's need. 46 Every day they
devoted themselves to meeting together in the
temple area and to breaking bread in their homes.
They ate their meals with exultation and sincerity
of heart, 47 praising God and enjoying favor with
all the people. And every day the Lord added to
their number those who were being saved.

CHAPTER 3

Cure of a Crippled Beggar 1 *Now Peter and
John were going up to the temple area for the

2, 33: At the right hand of God: or "by the right hand of God."

2, 38: Repent and be baptized: repentance is a positive concept, a change of mind and heart toward God reflected in the actual goodness of one's life. It is in accord with the apostolic teaching derived from Jesus (42) and ultimately recorded in the four gospels. Luke presents baptism in Acts as the expected response to the apostolic preaching about Jesus and associates it with the conferring of the Spirit (1, 5; 10, 44–48; 11, 16).

2, 42–47: The first of three summary passages (along with 4, 32–37 and 5, 12–16) that outline, somewhat idyllically, the chief characteristics of the Jerusalem community: adherence to the teachings of the Twelve and the centering of its religious life in the eucharistic liturgy (42); a system of distribution of goods that led wealthier Christians to sell their possessions when the needs of the community's poor required it (44 and the note on 4, 32–37); and continued attendance at the temple, since in this initial stage there was little or no thought of any dividing line between Christianity and Judaism (46).

3, 1—4, 31: This section presents a series of related events: the dramatic cure of a lame beggar (3, 1–10) produces a large audience for the kerygmatic discourse of Peter (3, 11–26). The Sadducees, taking exception to the doctrine of resurrection, have Peter, John, and apparently the beggar as well, arrested (4, 1–4) and brought to trial before the Sanhedrin. The issue concerns the authority by which Peter and John publicly teach religious doctrine in the temple (4, 5–7). Peter replies with a brief summary of the kerygma, implying that his authority is prophetic (4, 8–12). The court warns the apostles to abandon their practice of invoking prophetic authority in the name of Jesus (4, 13–18). When Peter and John reply that the prophetic role cannot be abandoned to satisfy human objections, the court nevertheless releases them, afraid to do otherwise since the beggar, lame from birth and over forty years old, is a well-known figure in Jerusalem and the facts of his cure are common property (4, 19–22). The narrative concludes with a prayer of the Christian community imploring divine aid against threats of persecution (4, 23–31).

3, 1: For the three o'clock hour of prayer: literally,

e 13, 35. f 2 Sm 7, 12; Ps 132, 11. g 13, 35; Ps 16, 10. h 1, 4–5. i Ps 110, 1. j 9, 22; Rom 10, 9; Phil 2, 11. k Lk 3, 10. l 3, 19; 16, 31; Lk 3, 3. m Is 57, 19; Jl 3, 5; Eph 2, 17. n Dt 32, 5; Ps 78, 8; Lk 9, 41; Phil 2, 15. o 2, 47; 4, 4; 5, 14; 6, 7; 11, 21.24; 21, 20. p 4, 32–35. q 1, 14; 6, 4. r 5, 12–16. s 4, 32.34–35.

three o'clock hour of prayer. 2 [t]And a man crippled from birth was carried and placed at the gate of the temple called "the Beautiful Gate" every day to beg for alms from the people who entered the temple. 3 When he saw Peter and John about to go into the temple, he asked for alms. 4 But Peter looked intently at him, as did John, and said, "Look at us." 5 He paid attention to them, expecting to receive something from them. 6 [u]*Peter said, "I have neither silver nor gold, but what I do have I give you: in the name of Jesus Christ the Nazorean, [rise and] walk." 7 Then Peter took him by the right hand and raised him up, and immediately his feet and ankles grew strong. 8 [v]He leaped up, stood, and walked around, and went into the temple with them, walking and jumping and praising God. 9 When all the people saw him walking and praising God, 10 they recognized him as the one who used to sit begging at the Beautiful Gate of the temple, and they were filled with amazement and astonishment at what had happened to him.

Peter's Speech 11 [w]As he clung to Peter and John, all the people hurried in amazement toward them in the portico called "Solomon's Portico." 12 [x]When Peter saw this, he addressed the people, "You Israelites, why are you amazed at this, and why do you look so intently at us as if we had made him walk by our own power or piety? 13 [y]*The God of Abraham, [the God] of Isaac, and [the God] of Jacob, the God of our ancestors, has glorified his servant Jesus whom you handed over and denied in Pilate's presence, when he had decided to release him. 14 [z]*You denied the Holy and Righteous One and asked that a murderer be released to you. 15 [a]*The author of life you put to death, but God raised him from the dead; of this we are witnesses. 16 And by faith in his name, this man, whom you see and know, his name has made strong, and the faith that comes through it has given him this perfect health, in the presence of all of you. 17 [b]*Now I know, brothers, that you acted out of ignorance, just as your leaders did; 18 [c]*but God has thus brought to fulfillment what he had announced beforehand through the mouth of all the prophets, that his Messiah would suffer. 19 [d]Repent, therefore, and be converted, that your sins may be wiped away, 20 *and that the Lord may grant you times of refreshment and send you the Messiah already appointed for you, Jesus, 21 *whom heaven must receive until the times of universal restoration of which God

---

"at the ninth hour of prayer." With the day beginning at 6 a.m., the ninth hour would be 3 p.m.

3, 6–10: The miracle has a dramatic cast; it symbolizes the saving power of Christ and leads the beggar to enter the temple, where he hears Peter's proclamation of salvation through Jesus.

3, 13: Has glorified: through the resurrection and ascension of Jesus, God reversed the judgment against him on the occasion of his trial. **Servant:** the Greek word can also be rendered as "son" or even "child" here and also in 3, 26; 4, 25 (applied to David); 4, 27; and 4, 30. Scholars are of the opinion, however, that the original concept reflected in the words identified Jesus with the suffering Servant of the Lord of Is 52, 13—53, 12.

3, 14: The Holy and Righteous One: so designating Jesus emphasizes his special relationship to the Father (see Lk 1, 35; 4, 34) and emphasizes his sinlessness and religious dignity that are placed in sharp contrast with the guilt of those who rejected him in favor of Barabbas.

3, 15: The author of life: other possible translations of the Greek title are "leader of life" or "pioneer of life." The title clearly points to Jesus as the source and originator of salvation.

3, 17: Ignorance: a Lucan motif, explaining away the actions not only of the people but also of their leaders in crucifying Jesus. On this basis the presbyters in Acts could continue to appeal to the Jews in Jerusalem to believe in Jesus, even while affirming their involvement in his death because they were unaware of his messianic dignity. See also 13, 27 and Lk 23, 34.

3, 18: Through the mouth of all the prophets: Christian prophetic insight into the Old Testament saw the crucifixion and death of Jesus as the main import of messianic prophecy. The Jews themselves did not anticipate a suffering Messiah; they usually understood the Servant Song in Is 52, 13—53, 12 to signify their own suffering as a people. In his typical fashion (cf Lk 18, 31; 24, 25.27.44), Luke does not specify the particular Old Testament prophecies that were fulfilled by Jesus. See also the note on Lk 24, 26.

3, 20: The Lord . . . and send you the Messiah already appointed for you, Jesus: an allusion to the parousia or second coming of Christ, judged to be imminent in the apostolic age. This reference to its nearness is the only explicit one in Acts. Some scholars believe that this verse preserves a very early christology, in which the title "Messiah" (Greek "Christ") is applied to him as of his parousia, his second coming (contrast 2, 36). This view of a future messiahship of Jesus is not found elsewhere in the New Testament.

3, 21: The times of universal restoration: like "the times of refreshment" (20), an apocalyptic designation of the messianic age, fitting in with the christology of v 20 that associates the messiahship of Jesus with his future coming.

t 14, 8–10. u 4, 10. v Is 35, 6; Lk 7, 22. w 5, 12; Jn 10, 23. x 14, 15. y Ex 3, 6.15; Is 52, 13; Lk 23, 14–25. z Mt 27, 20–21; Mk 15, 11; Lk 23, 18; Jn 18, 40. a 4, 10; 5, 31 / 1, 8; 2, 32. b 13, 27; Lk 23, 34; 1 Cor 2, 8; 1 Tm 1, 13. c Lk 18, 31. d 2, 38.

spoke through the mouth of his holy prophets
from of old. [22][e]*For Moses said:

'A prophet like me will the Lord, your God,
raise up for you
from among your own kinsmen;
to him you shall listen in all that he may say to
you.
[23][f]Everyone who does not listen to that prophet
will be cut off from the people.'

[24]Moreover, all the prophets who spoke, from
Samuel and those afterwards, also announced
these days. [25][g]You are the children of the
prophets and of the covenant that God made
with your ancestors when he said to Abraham,
'In your offspring all the families of the earth
shall be blessed.' [26][h]For you first, God raised up
his servant and sent him to bless you by turning
each of you from your evil ways."

CHAPTER 4

[1]*While they were still speaking to the people,
the priests, the captain of the temple guard, and
the Sadducees confronted them, [2][i]disturbed that
they were teaching the people and proclaiming
in Jesus the resurrection of the dead. [3]They laid
hands on them and put them in custody until the
next day, since it was already evening. [4]But
many of those who heard the word came to
believe and [the] number of men grew to [about]
five thousand.

Before the Sanhedrin [5]On the next day, their
leaders, elders, and scribes were assembled in
Jerusalem, [6]with Annas the high priest, Caia-
phas, John, Alexander, and all who were of the
high-priestly class. [7]They brought them into
their presence and questioned them, "By what
power or by what name have you done this?"
[8][j]Then Peter, filled with the holy Spirit, an-
swered them, "Leaders of the people and elders:
[9]If we are being examined today about a good
deed done to a cripple, namely, by what means
he was saved, [10]then all of you and all the people
of Israel should know that it was in the name of
Jesus Christ the Nazorean whom you crucified,
whom God raised from the dead; in his name
this man stands before you healed. [11][k]*He is
'the stone rejected by you, the builders, which
has become the cornerstone.' [12][l]*There is no
salvation through anyone else, nor is there any
other name under heaven given to the human
race by which we are to be saved."

[13]Observing the boldness of Peter and John
and perceiving them to be uneducated, ordinary
men, they were amazed, and they recognized
them as the companions of Jesus. [14]Then when
they saw the man who had been cured standing
there with them, they could say nothing in reply.
[15]So they ordered them to leave the Sanhedrin,
and conferred with one another, saying,
[16]"What are we to do with these men? Everyone
living in Jerusalem knows that a remarkable sign
was done through them, and we cannot deny it.
[17][m]But so that it may not be spread any further
among the people, let us give them a stern
warning never again to speak to anyone in this
name."

[18]So they called them back and ordered them
not to speak or teach at all in the name of Jesus.
[19][n]Peter and John, however, said to them in
reply, "Whether it is right in the sight of God for
us to obey you rather than God, you be the
judges. [20]It is impossible for us not to speak
about what we have seen and heard." [21]After
threatening them further, they released them,

3, 22: A loose citation of Dt 18, 15, which teaches that the Israelites are to learn the will of Yahweh from no one but their prophets. At the time of Jesus, some Jews expected a unique prophet to come in fulfillment of this text. Early Christianity applied this tradition and text to Jesus and used them especially in defense of the divergence of Christian teaching from traditional Judaism.

4, 1: The priests, the captain of the temple guard, and the Sadducees: the priests performed the temple liturgy; the temple guard was composed of Levites, whose captain ranked next after the high priest. The Sadducees, a party within Judaism at this time, rejected those doctrines, including bodily resurrection, which they believed alien to the ancient Mosaic religion. The Sadducees were drawn from priestly families and from the lay aristocracy.

4, 11: Early Christianity applied this citation from Ps 118, 22 to Jesus; cf Mk 12, 10; 1 Pt 2, 7.

4, 12: In the Roman world of Luke's day, salvation was often attributed to the emperor who was hailed as "savior" and "god." Luke, in the words of Peter, denies that deliverance comes through anyone other than Jesus.

e 7, 37; Dt 18, 15.18. f Lv 23, 29; Dt 18, 19. g Gn 12, 3; 18, 18; 22, 18; Sir 44, 19–21; Gal 3, 8–9. h 13, 46; Rom 1, 16. i 23, 6–8; 24, 21. j Mt 10, 20. k Ps 118, 22; Is 28, 16; Mt 21, 42; Mk 12, 10; Lk 20, 17; Rom 9, 33; 1 Pt 2, 7. l Mt 1, 21; 1 Cor 3, 11. m 5, 28. n 5, 29–32.

finding no way to punish them, on account of the people who were all praising God for what had happened. [22]For the man on whom this sign of healing had been done was over forty years old.

Prayer of the Community [23]After their release they went back to their own people and reported what the chief priests and elders had told them. [24]And when they heard it, they raised their voices to God with one accord and said, "Sovereign Lord, maker of heaven and earth and the sea and all that is in them, [25] [o]you said by the holy Spirit through the mouth of our father David, your servant:

'Why did the Gentiles rage
and the peoples entertain folly?
[26]The kings of the earth took their stand
and the princes gathered together
against the Lord and against his
anointed.'

[27] [p]*Indeed they gathered in this city against your holy servant Jesus whom you anointed, Herod and Pontius Pilate, together with the Gentiles and the peoples of Israel, [28]to do what your hand and [your] will had long ago planned to take place. [29]And now, Lord, take note of their threats, and enable your servants to speak your word with all boldness, [30]as you stretch forth [your] hand to heal, and signs and wonders are done through the name of your holy servant Jesus." [31] [q]*As they prayed, the place where they were gathered shook, and they were all filled with the holy Spirit and continued to speak the word of God with boldness.

Life in the Christian Community [32]*The community of believers was of one heart and mind, and no one claimed that any of his possessions was his own, but they had everything in common. [33]With great power the apostles bore witness to the resurrection of the Lord Jesus, and great favor was accorded them all. [34] [r]There was no needy person among them, for those who owned property or houses would sell them, bring the proceeds of the sale, [35]and put them at the feet of the apostles, and they were distributed to each according to need.

[36] [s]Thus Joseph, also named by the apostles Barnabas (which is translated "son of encouragement"), a Levite, a Cypriot by birth, [37]sold a piece of property that he owned, then brought the money and put it at the feet of the apostles.

CHAPTER 5

Ananias and Sapphira [1]*A man named Ananias, however, with his wife Sapphira, sold a piece of property. [2]He retained for himself, with his wife's knowledge, some of the purchase price, took the remainder, and put it at the feet of the apostles. [3] [t]But Peter said, "Ananias, why has Satan filled your heart so that you lied to the holy Spirit and retained part of the price of the land? [4]While it remained unsold, did it not remain yours? And when it was sold, was it not still under your control? Why did you contrive this deed? You have lied not to human beings, but to God." [5]When Ananias heard these words, he fell down and breathed his last, and great fear came upon all who heard of it. [6]The young men came and wrapped him up, then carried him out and buried him.

[7]After an interval of about three hours, his wife came in, unaware of what had happened. [8]Peter said to her, "Tell me, did you sell the land

4, 27: Herod: Herod Antipas, ruler of Galilee and Perea from 4 B.C. to A.D. 39, who executed John the Baptist and before whom Jesus was arraigned; cf Lk 23, 6–12.

4, 31: The place . . . shook: the earthquake is used as a sign of the divine presence in Ex 19, 18; Is 6, 4. Here the shaking of the building symbolizes God's favorable response to the prayer. Luke may have had as an additional reason for using the symbol in this sense the fact that it was familiar in the Hellenistic world. Ovid and Virgil also employ it.

4, 32–37: This is the second summary characterizing the Jerusalem community (see the note on 2, 42–47). It emphasizes the system of the distribution of goods and introduces Barnabas, who appears later in Acts as the friend and companion of Paul, and who, as noted here (37), endeared himself to the community by a donation of money through the sale of property. This sharing of material possessions continues a practice that Luke describes during the historical ministry of Jesus (Lk 8, 3) and is in accord with the sayings of Jesus in Luke's gospel (Lk 12, 33; 16, 9.11.13).

5, 1–11: The sin of Ananias and Sapphira did not consist in the withholding of part of the money but in their deception of the community. Their deaths are ascribed to a lie to the holy Spirit (3.9), i.e., they accepted the honor accorded them by the community for their generosity, but in reality they were not deserving of it.

o Ps 2, 1–2. p Lk 23, 12–13. q 2, 4. r 2, 44–45. s 9, 27; 11, 22.30; 12, 25; 13, 15; 1 Cor 9, 6; Gal 2, 1.9.13; Col 4, 10. t Lk 22, 3; Jn 13, 2.

for this amount?" She answered, "Yes, for that amount." 9Then Peter said to her, "Why did you agree to test the Spirit of the Lord? Listen, the footsteps of those who have buried your husband are at the door, and they will carry you out." 10At once, she fell down at his feet and breathed her last. When the young men entered they found her dead, so they carried her out and buried her beside her husband. 11 [u]And great fear came upon the whole church and upon all who heard of these things.

Signs and Wonders of the Apostles 12 [v]*Many signs and wonders were done among the people at the hands of the apostles. They were all together in Solomon's portico. 13None of the others dared to join them, but the people esteemed them. 14Yet more than ever, believers in the Lord, great numbers of men and women, were added to them. 15 [w]Thus they even carried the sick out into the streets and laid them on cots and mats so that when Peter came by, at least his shadow might fall on one or another of them. 16A large number of people from the towns in the vicinity of Jerusalem also gathered, bringing the sick and those disturbed by unclean spirits, and they were all cured.

Trial before the Sanhedrin 17 [x]*Then the high priest rose up and all his companions, that is, the party of the Sadducees, and, filled with jealousy, 18laid hands upon the apostles and put them in the public jail. 19 [y]But during the night, the angel of the Lord opened the doors of the prison, led them out, and said, 20"Go and take your place in the temple area, and tell the people everything about this life." 21When they heard this, they went to the temple early in the morning and taught. When the high priest and his companions arrived, they convened the Sanhedrin, the full senate of the Israelites, and sent to the jail to have them brought in. 22But the court officers who went did not find them in the prison, so they came back and reported, 23"We found the jail securely locked and the guards stationed outside the doors, but when we opened them, we found no one inside." 24When they heard this report, the captain of the temple guard and the chief priests were at a loss about them, as to what this would come to. 25Then someone came in and reported to them, "The men whom you put in prison are in the temple area and are teaching the people." 26 [z]Then the captain and the court officers went and brought them in, but without force, because they were afraid of being stoned by the people.

27When they had brought them in and made them stand before the Sanhedrin, the high priest questioned them, 28 [a]"We gave you strict orders [did we not?] to stop teaching in that name. Yet you have filled Jerusalem with your teaching and want to bring this man's blood upon us." 29 [b]But Peter and the apostles said in reply, "We must obey God rather than men. 30 [c]*The God of our ancestors raised Jesus, though you had him killed by hanging him on a tree. 31 [d]*God exalted him at his right hand as leader and savior to grant Israel repentance and forgiveness of sins. 32 [e]We are witnesses of these things, as is the holy Spirit that God has given to those who obey him."

33When they heard this, they became infuriated and wanted to put them to death. 34 [f]*But a Pharisee in the Sanhedrin named Gamaliel, a

5, 12–16: This, the third summary portraying the Jerusalem community, underscores the Twelve as its bulwark, especially because of their charismatic power to heal the sick; cf 2, 42–47; 4, 32–37.

5, 17–42: A second action against the community is taken by the Sanhedrin in the arrest and trial of the Twelve; cf 4, 1–3. The motive is the jealousy of the religious authorities over the popularity of the apostles (17) who are now charged with the defiance of the Sanhedrin's previous order to them to abandon their prophetic role (28; cf 4, 18). In this crisis the apostles are favored by a miraculous release from prison (18–24). (For similar incidents involving Peter and Paul, see 12, 6–11; 16, 25–29.) The real significance of such an event, however, would be manifest only to people of faith, not to unbelievers; since the Sanhedrin already judged the Twelve to be inauthentic prophets, it could disregard reports of their miracles. When the Twelve immediately resumed public teaching, the Sanhedrin determined to invoke upon them the penalty of death (33) prescribed in Dt 13, 6–10. Gamaliel's advice against this course finally prevailed, but it did not save the Twelve from the punishment of scourging (40) in a last endeavor to shake their conviction of their prophetic mission.

5, 30: **Hanging him on a tree:** that is, crucifying him (cf also Gal 3, 13).

5, 31: **At his right hand:** see the note on 2, 33.

5, 34: **Gamaliel:** in 22, 3, Paul identifies himself as a disciple of this Rabbi Gamaliel I who flourished in Jerusalem between A.D. 25 and 50.

u 2, 43; 5, 5; 19, 17. v 2, 43; 6, 8; 14, 3; 15, 12. w 19, 11–12; Mk 6, 56. x 4, 1–3.6. y 12, 7–10; 16, 25–26. z Lk 20, 19. a Mt 27, 25. b 4, 19. c 2, 23–24. d 2, 38. e Lk 24, 48; Jn 15, 26. f 22,3.

teacher of the law, respected by all the people,
stood up, ordered the men to be put outside for
a short time, 35 and said to them, "Fellow Israel-
ites, be careful what you are about to do to
these men. 36 *Some time ago, Theudas ap-
peared, claiming to be someone important, and
about four hundred men joined him, but he
was killed, and all those who were loyal to him
were disbanded and came to nothing. 37 After
him came Judas the Galilean at the time of the
census. He also drew people after him, but he
too perished and all who were loyal to him
were scattered. 38 So now I tell you, have noth-
ing to do with these men, and let them go. For
if this endeavor or this activity is of human
origin, it will destroy itself. 39 But if it comes
from God, you will not be able to destroy them;
you may even find yourselves fighting against
God." They were persuaded by him. 40 [g]After
recalling the apostles, they had them flogged,
ordered them to stop speaking in the name of
Jesus, and dismissed them. 41 [h]So they left the
presence of the Sanhedrin, rejoicing that they
had been found worthy to suffer dishonor for
the sake of the name. 42 [i]And all day long, both
at the temple and in their homes, they did not
stop teaching and proclaiming the Messiah,
Jesus.

CHAPTER 6

The Need for Assistants 1 [j]*At that time, as
the number of disciples continued to grow, the
Hellenists complained against the Hebrews be-
cause their widows were being neglected in the
daily distribution. 2 *So the Twelve called to-
gether the community of the disciples and said,
"It is not right for us to neglect the word of God
to serve at table. 3 Brothers, select from among
you seven reputable men, filled with the Spirit
and wisdom, whom we shall appoint to this
task, 4 whereas we shall devote ourselves to
prayer and to the ministry of the word." 5 The
proposal was acceptable to the whole commu-
nity, so they chose Stephen, a man filled with
faith and the holy Spirit, also Philip, Prochorus,
Nicanor, Timon, Parmenas, and Nicholas of
Antioch, a convert to Judaism. 6 [k]*They pre-
sented these men to the apostles who prayed
and laid hands on them. 7 [l]The word of God
continued to spread, and the number of the
disciples in Jerusalem increased greatly; even a
large group of priests were becoming obedient to
the faith.

Accusation against Stephen 8 *Now Stephen,
filled with grace and power, was working great
wonders and signs among the people. 9 Certain
members of the so-called Synagogue of Freed-

5, 36–37: Gamaliel offers examples of unsuccessful contemporary movements to argue that if God is not the origin of this movement preached by the apostles it will perish by itself. The movement initiated by Theudas actually occurred when C. Cuspius Fadus was governor, A.D. 44–46. Luke's placing of Judas the Galilean after Theudas and at the time of the census (see the note on Lk 2, 1–2) is an indication of the vagueness of his knowledge of these events.

6, 1–7: The Hellenists . . . the Hebrews: the Hellenists were not necessarily Jews from the diaspora, but were more probably Palestinian Jews who spoke only Greek. The Hebrews were Palestinian Jews who spoke Hebrew or Aramaic and who may also have spoken Greek. Both groups belong to the Jerusalem Jewish Christian community. The conflict between them leads to a restructuring of the community that will better serve the community's needs. The real purpose of the whole episode, however, is to introduce Stephen as a prominent figure in the community whose long speech and martyrdom will be recounted in ch 7.

6, 2–4: The essential function of the Twelve is the "service of the word," including development of the kerygma by formulation of the teachings of Jesus.

6, 2: To serve at table: some commentators think that it is not the serving of food that is described here but rather the keeping of the accounts that recorded the distribution of food to the needy members of the community. In any case, after Stephen and the others are chosen, they are never presented carrying out the task for which they were appointed (2–3). Rather, two of their number, Stephen and Philip, are presented as preachers of the Christian message. They, the Hellenist counterpart of the Twelve, are active in the ministry of the word.

6, 6: They . . . laid hands on them: the customary Jewish way of designating persons for a task and invoking upon them the divine blessing and power to perform it.

6, 8—8, 1: The summary (6, 7) on the progress of the Jerusalem community, illustrated by the conversion of the priests, is followed by a lengthy narrative regarding Stephen. Stephen's defense is not a response to the charges made against him but takes the form of a discourse that reviews the fortunes of God's word to Israel and leads to a prophetic declaration: a plea for the hearing of that word as announced by Christ and now possessed by the Christian community.

The charges that Stephen depreciated the importance of the temple and the Mosaic law and elevated Jesus to a stature above Moses (6, 13–14) were in fact true. Before the Sanhedrin, no defense against them was possible. With Stephen, who thus perceived the fuller implications of the teachings of Jesus, the differences between Judaism and Christianity began to appear. Luke's account of Stephen's martyrdom and its aftermath shows how the major impetus behind the Christian movement passed from Jerusalem, where the temple and law prevailed, to Antioch in Syria, where these influences were less pressing.

g Mt 10, 17; Acts 4, 17–18. h Mt 5, 10–11; 1 Pt 4, 13. i 2, 46; 5, 20–21.25; 8, 35; 17, 3; 18, 5.28; 19, 4–5. j 2, 45; 4, 34–35. k 1, 24; 13, 3; 14, 23. l 9, 31; 12, 24; 16, 5; 19, 20; 28, 30–31.

men, Cyrenians, and Alexandrians, and people from Cilicia and Asia, came forward and debated with Stephen, 10 [m]but they could not withstand the wisdom and the spirit with which he spoke. 11 [n]Then they instigated some men to say, "We have heard him speaking blasphemous words against Moses and God." 12 They stirred up the people, the elders, and the scribes, accosted him, seized him, and brought him before the Sanhedrin. 13 [*]They presented false witnesses who testified, "This man never stops saying things against [this] holy place and the law. 14 [o]For we have heard him claim that this Jesus the Nazorean will destroy this place and change the customs that Moses handed down to us." 15 All those who sat in the Sanhedrin looked intently at him and saw that his face was like the face of an angel.

CHAPTER 7

Stephen's Discourses 1 Then the high priest asked, "Is this so?" 2 [p][*]And he replied, "My brothers and fathers, listen. The God of glory appeared to our father Abraham while he was in Mesopotamia, before he had settled in Haran, 3 [q]and said to him, 'Go forth from your land and [from] your kinsfolk to the land that I will show you.' 4 [r]So he went forth from the land of the Chaldeans and settled in Haran. And from there, after his father died, he made him migrate to this land where you now dwell. 5 [s]Yet he gave him no inheritance in it, not even a foot's length, but he did promise to give it to him and his descendants as a possession, even though he was childless. 6 [t]And God spoke thus, 'His descendants shall be aliens in a land not their own, where they shall be enslaved and oppressed for four hundred years; 7 [u]but I will bring judgment on the nation they serve,' God said, 'and after that they will come out and worship me in this place.' 8 [v]Then he gave him the covenant of circumcision, and so he became the father of Isaac, and circumcised him on the eighth day, as Isaac did Jacob, and Jacob the twelve patriarchs.

9 [w]"And the patriarchs, jealous of Joseph, sold him into slavery in Egypt; but God was with him 10 [x]and rescued him from all his afflictions. He granted him favor and wisdom before Pharaoh, the king of Egypt, who put him in charge of Egypt and [of] his entire household. 11 [y]Then a famine and great affliction struck all Egypt and Canaan, and our ancestors could find no food; 12 [z]but when Jacob heard that there was grain in Egypt, he sent our ancestors there a first time. 13 [a]The second time, Joseph made himself known to his brothers, and Joseph's family became known to Pharaoh. 14 [b]Then Joseph sent for his father Jacob, inviting him and his whole clan, seventy-five persons; 15 [c]and Jacob went down to Egypt. And he and our ancestors died 16 [d]and were brought back to Shechem and placed in the tomb that Abraham had purchased for a sum of money from the sons of Hamor at Shechem.

17 [e]"When the time drew near for the fulfillment of the promise that God pledged to Abraham, the people had increased and become very numerous in Egypt, 18 [f]until another king who knew nothing of Joseph came to power [in Egypt]. 19 He dealt shrewdly with our people and oppressed [our] ancestors by forcing them to expose their infants, that they might not survive. 20 [g]At this time Moses was born, and he was

6, 13: False witnesses: here, and in his account of Stephen's execution (7, 54–60), Luke parallels the martyrdom of Stephen with the death of Jesus.

7, 2–53: Stephen's speech represents Luke's description of Christianity's break from its Jewish matrix. Two motifs become prominent in the speech: (1) Israel's reaction to God's chosen leaders in the past reveals that the people have consistently rejected them; and (2) Israel has misunderstood God's choice of the Jerusalem temple as the place where he is to be worshiped.

7, 2: God . . . appeared to our father Abraham . . . in Mesopotamia: the first of a number of minor discrepancies between the data of the Old Testament and the data of Stephen's discourse. According to Gn 12, 1, God first spoke to Abraham in Haran. The main discrepancies are these: in v 16 it is said that Jacob was buried in Shechem, whereas Gn 50, 13 says he was buried at Hebron; in the same verse it is said that the tomb was purchased by Abraham, but in Gn 33, 19 and Jos 24, 32 the purchase is attributed to Jacob himself.

m Lk 21, 15. n Mt 26, 59–61; Mk 14, 55–58; Acts 21, 21. o Mt 26, 59–61; 27, 40; Jn 2, 19. p Gn 11, 31; 12, 1; Ps 29, 3. q Gn 12, 1. r Gn 12, 5; 15, 7. s Gn 12, 7; 13, 15; 15, 2; 16, 1; Dt 2, 5. t Gn 15, 13–14. u Ex 3, 12. v Gn 17, 10–14; 21, 2–4. w Gn 37, 11.28; 39, 2.3.21.23. x Gn 41, 37–43; Ps 105, 21; Wis 10, 13–14. y Gn 41, 54–57; 42, 5. z Gn 42, 1–2. a Gn 45, 3–4.16. b Gn 45, 9–11.18–19; 46, 27; Ex 1, 5 LXX; Dt 10, 22. c Gn 46, 5–6; 49, 33. d Gn 23, 3–20; 33, 19; 49, 29–30; 50, 13; Jos 24, 32. e Ex 1, 7. f Ex 1, 8. g Ex 2, 2; Heb 11, 23.

extremely beautiful. For three months he was nursed in his father's house; [21] [h]but when he was exposed, Pharaoh's daughter adopted him and brought him up as her own son. [22]Moses was educated [in] all the wisdom of the Egyptians and was powerful in his words and deeds.

[23] [i]"When he was forty years old, he decided to visit his kinsfolk, the Israelites. [24]When he saw one of them treated unjustly, he defended and avenged the oppressed man by striking down the Egyptian. [25]He assumed [his] kinsfolk would understand that God was offering them deliverance through him, but they did not understand. [26] [j]The next day he appeared to them as they were fighting and tried to reconcile them peacefully, saying, 'Men, you are brothers. Why are you harming one another?' [27]Then the one who was harming his neighbor pushed him aside, saying, 'Who appointed you ruler and judge over us? [28]Are you thinking of killing me as you killed the Egyptian yesterday?' [29] [k]Moses fled when he heard this and settled as an alien in the land of Midian, where he became the father of two sons.

[30] [l]"Forty years later, an angel appeared to him in the desert near Mount Sinai in the flame of a burning bush. [31]When Moses saw it, he was amazed at the sight, and as he drew near to look at it, the voice of the Lord came, [32]'I am the God of your fathers, the God of Abraham, of Isaac, and of Jacob.' Then Moses, trembling, did not dare to look at it. [33]But the Lord said to him, 'Remove the sandals from your feet, for the place where you stand is holy ground. [34]I have witnessed the affliction of my people in Egypt and have heard their groaning, and I have come down to rescue them. Come now, I will send you to Egypt.' [35] [m]This Moses, whom they had rejected with the words, 'Who appointed you ruler and judge?' God sent as [both] ruler and deliverer, through the angel who appeared to him in the bush. [36] [n]This man led them out, performing wonders and signs in the land of Egypt, at the Red Sea, and in the desert for forty years. [37] [o]It was this Moses who said to the Israelites, 'God will raise up for you, from among your own kinsfolk, a prophet like me.' [38] [p]It was he who, in the assembly in the desert, was with the angel who spoke to him on Mount Sinai and with our ancestors, and he received living utterances to hand on to us.

[39] [q]"Our ancestors were unwilling to obey him; instead, they pushed him aside and in their hearts turned back to Egypt, [40] [r]saying to Aaron, 'Make us gods who will be our leaders. As for that Moses who led us out of the land of Egypt, we do not know what has happened to him.' [41] [s]So they made a calf in those days, offered sacrifice to the idol, and reveled in the works of their hands. [42] [t] [u]Then God turned and handed them over to worship the host of heaven, as it is written in the book of the prophets:

'Did you bring me sacrifices and offerings
  for forty years in the desert, O house of
    Israel?
[43] No, you took up the tent of Moloch
  and the star of [your] god Rephan,
    the images that you made to worship.
  So I shall take you into exile beyond Babylon.'

[44] [v]Our ancestors had the tent of testimony in the desert just as the One who spoke to Moses directed him to make it according to the pattern he had seen. [45] [w]Our ancestors who inherited it brought it with Joshua when they dispossessed the nations that God drove out from before our ancestors, up to the time of David, [46] [x]who found favor in the sight of God and asked that he might find a dwelling place for the house of Jacob. [47] [y]But Solomon built a house for him. [48] [z]Yet the Most High does not dwell in houses made by human hands. As the prophet says:

[49] [a]'The heavens are my throne,
  the earth is my footstool.
What kind of house can you build for me?
    says the Lord,
  or what is to be my resting place?
[50] Did not my hand make all these things?'

h Ex 2, 3–10. i Ex 2, 11–12. j Ex 2, 13–14. k Ex 2, 15.21–22; 18, 3–4. l Ex 3, 2–3. m Ex 2, 14. n Ex 7, 3.10; 14, 21; Nm 14, 33. o Dt 18, 15; Acts 3, 22. p Ex 19, 3; 20, 1–17; Dt 5, 4–22; 6, 4–25. q Nm 14, 3. r Ex 32, 1.23. s Ex 32, 4–6. t Am 5, 25–27. u Jer 7, 18; 8, 2; 19, 13. v Ex 25, 9.40. w Jos 3, 14–17; 18, 1; 2 Sm 7, 5–7. x 2 Sm 7, 1–2; 1 Kgs 8, 17; Ps 132, 1–5. y 1 Kgs 6, 1; 1 Chr 17, 12. z 17, 24. a Is 66, 1–2.

Conclusion 51 “You stiff-necked people, uncir-
cumcised in heart and ears, you always oppose
the holy Spirit; you are just like your ancestors.
52 [b]Which of the prophets did your ancestors not
persecute? They put to death those who foretold
the coming of the righteous one, whose betray-
ers and murderers you have now become.
53 [c]You received the law as transmitted by an-
gels, but you did not observe it.”
Stephen's Martyrdom 54 When they heard
this, they were infuriated, and they ground their
teeth at him. 55 [d]*But he, filled with the holy
Spirit, looked up intently to heaven and saw the
glory of God and Jesus standing at the right hand
of God, 56 and he said, “Behold, I see the
heavens opened and the Son of Man standing at
the right hand of God.” 57 *But they cried out in
a loud voice, covered their ears, and rushed
upon him together. 58 [e]They threw him out of
the city, and began to stone him. The witnesses
laid down their cloaks at the feet of a young man
named Saul. 59 [f]*As they were stoning Stephen,
he called out, “Lord Jesus, receive my spirit.”
60 [g]Then he fell to his knees and cried out in a
loud voice, “Lord, do not hold this sin against
them”; and when he said this, he fell asleep.

CHAPTER 8

1 [h]*Now Saul was consenting to his execution.
Persecution of the Church On that day, there
broke out a severe persecution of the church in
Jerusalem, and all were scattered throughout the
countryside of Judea and Samaria, except the
apostles. 2 Devout men buried Stephen and made
a loud lament over him. 3 [i]*Saul, meanwhile,
was trying to destroy the church; entering house
after house and dragging out men and women,
he handed them over for imprisonment.

III: The Mission in Judea and Samaria

Philip in Samaria 4 [j]Now those who had been
scattered went about preaching the word.
5 [k]Thus Philip went down to [the] city of Samaria
and proclaimed the Messiah to them. 6 With one
accord, the crowds paid attention to what was
said by Philip when they heard it and saw the
signs he was doing. 7 [l]For unclean spirits, crying
out in a loud voice, came out of many possessed
people, and many paralyzed and crippled people
were cured. 8 There was great joy in that city.
Simon the Magician 9 *A man named Simon
used to practice magic in the city and astounded
the people of Samaria, claiming to be someone
great. 10 All of them, from the least to the
greatest, paid attention to him, saying, “This
man is the ‘Power of God’ that is called
‘Great.’ ” 11 They paid attention to him because
he had astounded them by his magic for a long
time, 12 [m]but once they began to believe Philip as
he preached the good news about the kingdom
of God and the name of Jesus Christ, men and
women alike were baptized. 13 Even Simon him-

7, 55: He . . . saw . . . Jesus standing at the right hand of God: Stephen affirms to the Sanhedrin that the prophecy Jesus made before them has been fulfilled (Mk 14, 62).

7, 57: Covered their ears: Stephen's declaration, like that of Jesus, is a scandal to the court, which regards it as blasphemy.

7, 59: Compare Lk 23, [34].46.

8, 1–40: Some idea of the severity of the persecution that now breaks out against the Jerusalem community can be gathered from 22, 4 and 26, 9–11. Luke, however, concentrates on the fortunes of the word of God among people, indicating how the dispersal of the Jewish community resulted in the conversion of the Samaritans (4–17.25). His narrative is further expanded to include the account of Philip's acceptance of an Ethiopian (26–39).

8, 1: All were scattered . . . except the apostles: this observation leads some modern scholars to conclude that the persecution was limited to the Hellenist Christians and that the Hebrew Christians were not molested, perhaps because their attitude toward the law and temple was still more in line with that of their fellow Jews (see the charge leveled against the Hellenist Stephen in 6, 13–14). Whatever the facts, it appears that the Twelve took no public stand regarding Stephen's position, choosing, instead, to await the development of events.

8, 3: Saul . . . was trying to destroy the church: like Stephen, Saul was able to perceive that the Christian movement contained the seeds of doctrinal divergence from Judaism. A pupil of Gamaliel, according to 22, 3, and totally dedicated to the law as the way of salvation (Gal 1, 13–14), Saul accepted the task of crushing the Christian movement, at least insofar as it detracted from the importance of the temple and the law. His vehement opposition to Christianity reveals how difficult it was for a Jew of his time to accept a messianism that differed so greatly from the general expectation.

8, 9–13.18–24: Sorcerers were well known in the ancient world. Probably the incident involving Simon and his altercation with Peter is introduced to show that the miraculous charisms possessed by members of the Christian community (6–7) were not to be confused with the magic of sorcerers.

b 2 Chr 36, 16; Mt 23, 31.34. c Gal 3, 19; Heb 2, 2. d Mt 26, 64; Mk 14, 62; Lk 22, 69; Acts 2, 34. e 22, 20. f Ps 31, 6; Lk 23, 46. g Mt 27, 46.50; Mk 15, 34; Lk 23, 46. h 22, 20. i 9, 1.13; 22, 4; 26, 9–11; 1 Cor 5, 9; Gal 1, 13. j 11, 19. k 6, 5; 21, 8–9. l Mk 16, 17. m 1, 3; 19, 8; 28, 23.31.

self believed and, after being baptized, became devoted to Philip; and when he saw the signs and mighty deeds that were occurring, he was astounded.

14 Now when the apostles in Jerusalem heard that Samaria had accepted the word of God, they sent them Peter and John, 15 who went down and prayed for them, that they might receive the holy Spirit, 16 *for it had not yet fallen upon any of them; they had only been baptized in the name of the Lord Jesus. 17 [n]Then they laid hands on them and they received the holy Spirit.

18 *When Simon saw that the Spirit was conferred by the laying on of the apostles' hands, he offered them money 19 and said, "Give me this power too, so that anyone upon whom I lay my hands may receive the holy Spirit." 20 But Peter said to him, "May your money perish with you, because you thought that you could buy the gift of God with money. 21 You have no share or lot in this matter, for your heart is not upright before God. 22 Repent of this wickedness of yours and pray to the Lord that, if possible, your intention may be forgiven. 23 For I see that you are filled with bitter gall and are in the bonds of iniquity." 24 Simon said in reply, "Pray for me to the Lord, that nothing of what you have said may come upon me." 25 So when they had testified and proclaimed the word of the Lord, they returned to Jerusalem and preached the good news to many Samaritan villages.

Philip and the Ethiopian 26 *Then the angel of the Lord spoke to Philip, "Get up and head south on the road that goes down from Jerusalem to Gaza, the desert route." 27 [o]*So he got up and set out. Now there was an Ethiopian eunuch, a court official of the Candace, that is, the queen of the Ethiopians, in charge of her entire treasury, who had come to Jerusalem to worship, 28 and was returning home. Seated in his chariot, he was reading the prophet Isaiah. 29 The Spirit said to Philip, "Go and join up with that chariot." 30 *Philip ran up and heard him reading Isaiah the prophet and said, "Do you understand what you are reading?" 31 [p]He replied, "How can I, unless someone instructs me?" So he invited Philip to get in and sit with him. 32 [q]This was the scripture passage he was reading:

"Like a sheep he was led to the slaughter,
and as a lamb before its shearer is silent,
so he opened not his mouth.
33 In [his] humiliation justice was denied him.
Who will tell of his posterity?
For his life is taken from the earth."

34 Then the eunuch said to Philip in reply, "I beg you, about whom is the prophet saying this? About himself, or about someone else?" 35 Then Philip opened his mouth and, beginning with this scripture passage, he proclaimed Jesus to him. 36 [r]As they traveled along the road they came to some water, and the eunuch said, "Look, there is water. What is to prevent my being baptized?" [37]* 38 Then he ordered the chariot to stop, and Philip and the eunuch both went down into the water, and he baptized him. 39 [s]When they came out of the water, the Spirit of the Lord snatched Philip away, and the

8, 16: Here and in 10, 44–48 and 19, 1–6, Luke distinguishes between baptism in the name of the Lord Jesus and the reception of the Spirit. In each case, the Spirit is conferred through members of the Twelve (Peter and John) or their representative (Paul). This may be Luke's way of describing the role of the church in the bestowal of the Spirit. Elsewhere in Acts, baptism and the Spirit are more closely related (1, 5; 11, 16).

8, 18–20: Simon attempts to buy the gift of God (20) with money. Peter's cursing of Simon's attempt so to use his money expresses a typically Lucan attitude toward material wealth (cf Lk 6, 24; 12, 16–21; 16, 13).

8, 26–40: In the account of the conversion of the Ethiopian eunuch, Luke adduces additional evidence to show that the spread of Christianity outside the confines of Judaism itself was in accord with the plan of God. He does not make clear whether the Ethiopian was originally a convert to Judaism or, as is more probable, a "God-fearer" (10, 1), i.e., one who accepted Jewish monotheism and ethic and attended the synagogue but did not consider himself bound by other regulations such as circumcision and observance of the dietary laws. The story of his conversion to Christianity is given a strong supernatural cast by the introduction of an angel (26), instruction from the holy Spirit (29), and the strange removal of Philip from the scene (39).

8, 27: The Candace: Candace is not a proper name here but the title of a Nubian queen.

8, 30–34: Philip is brought alongside the carriage at the very moment when the Ethiopian is pondering the meaning of Is 53, 7–8, a passage that Christianity, from its earliest origins, has applied to Jesus; cf the note on 3, 13.

8, 37: The oldest and best manuscripts of Acts omit this verse, which is a Western text reading: "And Philip said, 'If you believe with all your heart, you may.' And he said in reply, 'I believe that Jesus Christ is the Son of God.' "

n 2, 4; 4, 31; 10, 44–47; 15, 8–9; 19, 2.6. o Is 56, 3–5. p Jn 16, 13. q Is 53, 7–8 LXX. r 10, 47. s 1 Kgs 18, 12.

eunuch saw him no more, but continued on his way rejoicing. [40 t]Philip came to Azotus, and went about proclaiming the good news to all the towns until he reached Caesarea.

CHAPTER 9

Saul's Conversion [1 u v]*Now Saul, still breathing murderous threats against the disciples of the Lord, went to the high priest [2]*and asked him for letters to the synagogues in Damascus, that, if he should find any men or women who belonged to the Way, he might bring them back to Jerusalem in chains. [3 w]On his journey, as he was nearing Damascus, a light from the sky suddenly flashed around him. [4 x]He fell to the ground and heard a voice saying to him, "Saul, Saul, why are you persecuting me?" [5 y]He said, "Who are you, sir?" The reply came, "I am Jesus, whom you are persecuting. [6 z]Now get up and go into the city and you will be told what you must do." [7 a]The men who were traveling with him stood speechless, for they heard the voice but could see no one. [8 b]*Saul got up from the ground, but when he opened his eyes he could see nothing; so they led him by the hand and brought him to Damascus. [9]For three days he was unable to see, and he neither ate nor drank.

Saul's Baptism [10 c]There was a disciple in Damascus named Ananias, and the Lord said to him in a vision, "Ananias." He answered, "Here I am, Lord." [11 d]The Lord said to him, "Get up and go to the street called Straight and ask at the house of Judas for a man from Tarsus named Saul. He is there praying, [12]and [in a vision] he has seen a man named Ananias come in and lay [his] hands on him, that he may regain his sight." [13 e]*But Ananias replied, "Lord, I have heard from many sources about this man, what evil things he has done to your holy ones in Jerusalem. [14 f]And here he has authority from the chief priests to imprison all who call upon your name." [15 g]But the Lord said to him, "Go, for this man is a chosen instrument of mine to carry my name before Gentiles, kings, and Israelites, [16]and I will show him what he will have to suffer for my name." [17]So Ananias went and entered the house; laying his hands on him, he said, "Saul, my brother, the Lord has sent me, Jesus who appeared to you on the way by which you came, that you may regain your sight and be filled with the holy Spirit." [18]Immediately things like scales fell from his eyes and he regained his sight. He got up and was baptized, [19]*and when he had eaten, he recovered his strength.

Saul Preaches in Damascus He stayed some days with the disciples in Damascus, [20]*and he began at once to proclaim Jesus in the synagogues, that he is the Son of God. [21]All who heard him were astounded and said, "Is not this the man who in Jerusalem ravaged those who call upon this name, and came here expressly to take them back in chains to the chief priests?" [22]But Saul grew all the stronger and confounded [the] Jews who lived in Damascus, proving that this is the Messiah.

Saul Visits Jerusalem [23]After a long time had passed, the Jews conspired to kill him, [24 h]but

9, 1–19: This is the first of three accounts of Paul's conversion (with 22, 3–16 and 26, 2–18) with some differences of detail owing to Luke's use of different sources. Paul's experience was not visionary but was precipitated by the appearance of Jesus, as he insists in 1 Cor 15, 8. The words of Jesus, "Saul, Saul, why are you persecuting me?" related by Luke with no variation in all three accounts, exerted a profound and lasting influence on the thought of Paul. Under the influence of this experience he gradually developed his understanding of justification by faith (see the letters to the Galatians and Romans) and of the identification of the Christian community with Jesus Christ (see 1 Cor 12, 27). That Luke would narrate this conversion three times is testimony to the importance he attaches to it. This first account occurs when the word is first spread to the Gentiles. At this point, the conversion of the hero of the Gentile mission is recounted. The emphasis in the account is on Paul as a divinely chosen instrument (15).

9, 2: The Way: a name used by the early Christian community for itself (18, 26; 19, 9.23; 22, 4; 24, 14.22). The Essene community at Qumran used the same designation to describe its mode of life.

9, 8: He could see nothing: a temporary blindness (18) symbolizing the religious blindness of Saul as persecutor (cf 26, 18).

9, 13: Your holy ones: literally, "your saints."

9, 19–30: This is a brief resume of Paul's initial experience as an apostolic preacher. At first he found himself in the position of being regarded as an apostate by the Jews and suspect by the Christian community of Jerusalem. His acceptance by the latter was finally brought about through his friendship with Barnabas (27).

9, 20: Son of God: the title "Son of God" occurs in Acts only here, but cf the citation of Ps 2, 7 in Paul's speech at Antioch in Pisidia (13, 33).

t 21, 8. u 8, 3; 9, 13; 22, 4; 1 Cor 15, 9; Gal 1, 13–14. v 9, 14; 26, 10. w 1 Cor 9, 1; 15, 8; Gal 1, 16. x 22, 6; 26, 14. y 22, 8; 26, 15; Mt 25, 40. z 22, 10; 26, 16. a 22, 9; 26, 13–14. b 22, 11. c 22, 12–16. d 21, 39. e 8, 3; 9, 1. f 9, 1–2; 26, 10; 1 Cor 1, 2; 2 Tm 2, 22. g 22, 15; 26, 1; 27, 24. h 2 Cor 11, 32–33.

their plot became known to Saul. Now they were keeping watch on the gates day and night so as to kill him, 25 but his disciples took him one night and let him down through an opening in the wall, lowering him in a basket.

26 [i]*When he arrived in Jerusalem he tried to join the disciples, but they were all afraid of him, not believing that he was a disciple. 27 Then Barnabas took charge of him and brought him to the apostles, and he reported to them how on the way he had seen the Lord and that he had spoken to him, and how in Damascus he had spoken out boldly in the name of Jesus. 28 He moved about freely with them in Jerusalem, and spoke out boldly in the name of the Lord. 29*He also spoke and debated with the Hellenists, but they tried to kill him. 30 [j]And when the brothers learned of this, they took him down to Caesarea and sent him on his way to Tarsus.

The Church at Peace 31*The church throughout all Judea, Galilee, and Samaria was at peace. It was being built up and walked in the fear of the Lord, and with the consolation of the holy Spirit it grew in numbers.

Peter Heals Aeneas at Lydda 32 As Peter was passing through every region, he went down to the holy ones living in Lydda. 33 There he found a man named Aeneas, who had been confined to bed for eight years, for he was paralyzed. 34 Peter said to him, "Aeneas, Jesus Christ heals you. Get up and make your bed." He got up at once. 35 And all the inhabitants of Lydda and Sharon saw him, and they turned to the Lord.

Peter Restores Tabitha to Life 36*Now in Joppa there was a disciple named Tabitha (which translated means Dorcas). She was completely occupied with good deeds and almsgiving. 37 Now during those days she fell sick and died, so after washing her, they laid [her] out in a room upstairs. 38 Since Lydda was near Joppa, the disciples, hearing that Peter was there, sent two men to him with the request, "Please come to us without delay." 39 So Peter got up and went with them. When he arrived, they took him to the room upstairs where all the widows came to him weeping and showing him the tunics and cloaks that Dorcas had made while she was with them. 40 [k]Peter sent them all out and knelt down and prayed. Then he turned to her body and said, "Tabitha, rise up." She opened her eyes, saw Peter, and sat up. 41 He gave her his hand and raised her up, and when he had called the holy ones and the widows, he presented her alive. 42 This became known all over Joppa, and many came to believe in the Lord. 43 [l]*And he stayed a long time in Joppa with Simon, a tanner.

IV: The Inauguration of the Gentile Mission

CHAPTER 10

The Vision of Cornelius 1 [m]*Now in Caesarea there was a man named Cornelius, a centurion of the Cohort called the Italica, 2*devout and God-fearing along with his whole household, who used to give alms generously to the Jewish

9, 26: This visit of Paul to Jerusalem is mentioned by Paul in Gal 1, 18.

9, 29: Hellenists: see the note on 6, 1–7.

9, 31–43: In the context of the period of peace enjoyed by the community through the cessation of Paul's activities against it, Luke introduces two traditions concerning the miraculous power exercised by Peter as he was making a tour of places where the Christian message had already been preached. The towns of Lydda, Sharon, and Joppa were populated by both Jews and Gentiles and their Christian communities may well have been mixed.

9, 36: Tabitha (Dorcas), respectively the Aramaic and Greek words for "gazelle," exemplifies the right attitude toward material possessions expressed by Jesus in the Lucan Gospel (Lk 6, 30; 11, 41; 12, 33; 18, 22; 19, 8).

9, 43: The fact that Peter lodged with a tanner would have been significant to both the Gentile and Jewish Christians, for Judaism considered the tanning occupation unclean.

10, 1–48: The narrative centers on the conversion of Cornelius, a Gentile and a "God-fearer" (see the note on 8, 26–40). Luke considers the event of great importance, as is evident from his long treatment of it. The incident is again related in 11, 1–18 where Peter is forced to justify his actions before the Jerusalem community and alluded to in 15, 7–11 where at the Jerusalem "Council" Peter supports Paul's missionary activity among the Gentiles. The narrative divides itself into a series of distinct episodes, concluding with Peter's presentation of the Christian kerygma (34–43) and a pentecostal experience undergone by Cornelius' household preceding their reception of baptism (44–48).

10, 1: The Cohort called the Italica: this battalion was an auxiliary unit of archers formed originally in Italy but transferred to Syria shortly before A.D. 69.

10, 2: Used to give alms generously: like Tabitha (9, 36), Cornelius exemplifies the proper attitude toward wealth (see the note on 9, 36).

i Gal 1, 18. j 11, 25. k Mk 5, 40–41. l 10, 6. m 10,30–33.

people and pray to God constantly. [3]*One afternoon about three o'clock, he saw plainly in a vision an angel of God come in to him and say to him, "Cornelius." [4]He looked intently at him and, seized with fear, said, "What is it, sir?" He said to him, "Your prayers and almsgiving have ascended as a memorial offering before God. [5]Now send some men to Joppa and summon one Simon who is called Peter. [6 n]He is staying with another Simon, a tanner, who has a house by the sea." [7]*When the angel who spoke to him had left, he called two of his servants and a devout soldier from his staff, [8]explained everything to them, and sent them to Joppa.

The Vision of Peter [9]*The next day, while they were on their way and nearing the city, Peter went up to the roof terrace to pray at about noontime. [10]He was hungry and wished to eat, and while they were making preparations he fell into a trance. [11 o]He saw heaven opened and something resembling a large sheet coming down, lowered to the ground by its four corners. [12]In it were all the earth's four-legged animals and reptiles and the birds of the sky. [13]A voice said to him, "Get up, Peter. Slaughter and eat." [14 p]But Peter said, "Certainly not, sir. For never have I eaten anything profane and unclean." [15 q]The voice spoke to him again, a second time, "What God has made clean, you are not to call profane." [16]This happened three times, and then the object was taken up into the sky.

[17]*While Peter was in doubt about the meaning of the vision he had seen, the men sent by Cornelius asked for Simon's house and arrived at the entrance. [18]They called out inquiring whether Simon, who is called Peter, was staying there. [19 r]As Peter was pondering the vision, the Spirit said [to him], "There are three men here looking for you. [20]So get up, go downstairs, and accompany them without hesitation, because I have sent them." [21]Then Peter went down to the men and said, "I am the one you are looking for. What is the reason for your being here?" [22 s]They answered, "Cornelius, a centurion, an upright and God-fearing man, respected by the whole Jewish nation, was directed by a holy angel to summon you to his house and to hear what you have to say." [23]So he invited them in and showed them hospitality.

The next day he got up and went with them, and some of the brothers from Joppa went with him. [24]*On the following day he entered Caesarea. Cornelius was expecting them and had called together his relatives and close friends. [25 t]When Peter entered, Cornelius met him and, falling at his feet, paid him homage. [26]Peter, however, raised him up, saying, "Get up. I myself am also a human being." [27]While he conversed with him, he went in and found many people gathered together [28 u]*and said to them, "You know that it is unlawful for a Jewish man to associate with, or visit, a Gentile, but God has shown me that I should not call any person profane or unclean. [29]And that is why I came without objection when sent for. May I ask, then, why you summoned me?"

[30]*Cornelius replied, "Four days ago at this hour, three o'clock in the afternoon, I was at prayer in my house when suddenly a man in dazzling robes stood before me and said, [31]'Cornelius, your prayer has been heard and your almsgiving remembered before God. [32]Send therefore to Joppa and summon Simon, who is called Peter. He is a guest in the house of Simon,

10, 3: About three o'clock: literally, "about the ninth hour." See the note on 3, 1.

10, 7: A devout soldier: by using this adjective, Luke probably intends to classify him as a "God-fearer" (see the note on 8, 26–40).

10, 9–16: The vision is intended to prepare Peter to share the food of Cornelius' household without qualms of conscience (48). The necessity of such instructions to Peter reveals that at first not even the apostles fully grasped the implications of Jesus' teaching on the law. In Acts, the initial insight belongs to Stephen.

10, 9: At about noontime: literally, "about the sixth hour."

10, 17–23: The arrival of the Gentile emissaries with their account of the angelic apparition illuminates Peter's vision: he is to be prepared to admit Gentiles, who were considered unclean like the animals of his vision, into the Christian community.

10, 24–27: So impressed is Cornelius with the apparition that he invites close personal friends to join him in his meeting with Peter. But his understanding of the person he is about to meet is not devoid of superstition, suggested by his falling down before him. For a similar experience of Paul and Barnabas, see 14, 11–18.

10, 28: Peter now fully understands the meaning of his vision; see the note on 10, 17–23.

10, 30: Four days ago: literally, "from the fourth day up to this hour."

n 9, 43. o 11, 5–12. p Lv 11, 1–47; Ez 4, 14. q Mk 7, 15–19; Gal 2, 12. r 13, 2. s Lk 7, 4–5. t 14, 13–15; Rv 19, 10. u Gal 2, 11–16.

a tanner, by the sea.’ 33 So I sent for you immediately, and you were kind enough to come. Now therefore we are all here in the presence of God to listen to all that you have been commanded by the Lord.”

Peter’s Speech 34 v*Then Peter proceeded to speak and said, “In truth, I see that God shows no partiality. 35 Rather, in every nation whoever fears him and acts uprightly is acceptable to him. 36 w*You know the word [that] he sent to the Israelites as he proclaimed peace through Jesus Christ, who is Lord of all, 37 xwhat has happened all over Judea, beginning in Galilee after the baptism that John preached, 38 y*how God anointed Jesus of Nazareth with the holy Spirit and power. He went about doing good and healing all those oppressed by the devil, for God was with him. 39 *We are witnesses of all that he did both in the country of the Jews and [in] Jerusalem. They put him to death by hanging him on a tree. 40 This man God raised [on] the third day and granted that he be visible, 41 znot to all the people, but to us, the witnesses chosen by God in advance, who ate and drank with him after he rose from the dead. 42 a*He commissioned us to preach to the people and testify that he is the one appointed by God as judge of the living and the dead. 43 To him all the prophets bear witness, that everyone who believes in him will receive forgiveness of sins through his name.”

The Baptism of Cornelius 44 b*While Peter was still speaking these things, the holy Spirit fell upon all who were listening to the word. 45 The circumcised believers who had accompanied Peter were astounded that the gift of the holy Spirit should have been poured out on the Gentiles also, 46 for they could hear them speaking in tongues and glorifying God. Then Peter responded, 47 c“Can anyone withhold the water for baptizing these people, who have received the holy Spirit even as we have?” 48 He ordered them to be baptized in the name of Jesus Christ. 49 Then they invited him to stay for a few days.

CHAPTER 11

The Baptism of the Gentiles Explained 1 *Now the apostles and the brothers who were in Judea heard that the Gentiles too had accepted the word of God. 2 So when Peter went up to Jerusalem the circumcised believers confronted him, 3 *saying, “You entered the house of uncircumcised people and ate with them.” 4 Peter began and explained it to them step by step, saying, 5 d“I was at prayer in the city of Joppa when in a trance I had a vision, something

10, 34–43: Peter’s speech to the household of Cornelius typifies early Christian preaching to Gentiles.

10, 34–35: The revelation of God’s choice of Israel to be the people of God did not mean he withheld the divine favor from other people.

10, 36–43: These words are more directed to Luke’s Christian readers than to the household of Cornelius, as indicated by the opening words, “You know.” They trace the continuity between the preaching and teaching of Jesus of Nazareth and the proclamation of Jesus by the early community. The emphasis on this divinely ordained continuity (41) is meant to assure Luke’s readers of the fidelity of Christian tradition to the words and deeds of Jesus.

10, 36: To the Israelites: Luke, in the words of Peter, speaks of the prominent position occupied by Israel in the history of salvation.

10, 38: Jesus of Nazareth: God’s revelation of his plan for the destiny of humanity through Israel culminated in Jesus of Nazareth. Consequently, the ministry of Jesus is an integral part of God’s revelation. This viewpoint explains why the early Christian communities were interested in conserving the historical substance of the ministry of Jesus, a tradition leading to the production of the four gospels.

10, 39: We are witnesses: the apostolic testimony was not restricted to the resurrection of Jesus but also included his historical ministry. This witness, however, was theological in character; the Twelve, divinely mandated as prophets, were empowered to interpret his sayings and deeds in the light of his redemptive death and resurrection. The meaning of these words and deeds was to be made clear to the developing Christian community as the bearer of the word of salvation (cf 1, 21–26). **Hanging him on a tree:** see the note on 5, 30.

10, 42: As judge of the living and the dead: the apostolic preaching to the Jews appealed to their messianic hope, while the preaching to Gentiles stressed the coming divine judgment; cf 1 Thes 1, 10.

10, 44: Just as the Jewish Christians received the gift of the Spirit, so too do the Gentiles.

11, 1–18: The Jewish Christians of Jerusalem were scandalized to learn of Peter’s sojourn in the house of the Gentile Cornelius. Nonetheless, they had to accept the divine directions given to both Peter and Cornelius. They concluded that the setting aside of the legal barriers between Jew and Gentile was an exceptional ordinance of God to indicate that the apostolic kerygma was also to be directed to the Gentiles. Only in ch 15 at the “Council” in Jerusalem does the evangelization of the Gentiles become the official position of the church leadership in Jerusalem.

11, 3: You entered . . . : alternatively, this could be punctuated as a question.

v Dt 17, 2; 2 Chr 19, 7; Jb 34, 19; Wis 6, 7; Rom 2, 11; Gal 2,6; Eph 6, 9; 1 Pt 1, 17. w Is 52, 7; Na 2, 1. x Mt 4, 12; Mk 1, 14; Lk 4, 14. y Is 61, 1; Lk 4, 18. z Lk 24, 41–43. a 1, 8; 3, 15; 17, 31; Lk 24, 48; Rom 14, 9; 2 Tm 4, 1. b 11, 15; 15, 8. c 8, 36. d 10, 11–20.

resembling a large sheet coming down, lowered from the sky by its four corners, and it came to me. 6 Looking intently into it, I observed and saw the four-legged animals of the earth, the wild beasts, the reptiles, and the birds of the sky. 7 I also heard a voice say to me, 'Get up, Peter. Slaughter and eat.' 8 But I said, 'Certainly not, sir, because nothing profane or unclean has ever entered my mouth.' 9 But a second time a voice from heaven answered, 'What God has made clean, you are not to call profane.' 10 This happened three times, and then everything was drawn up again into the sky. 11 Just then three men appeared at the house where we were, who had been sent to me from Caesarea. 12 *The Spirit told me to accompany them without discriminating. These six brothers also went with me, and we entered the man's house. 13 [e]He related to us how he had seen [the] angel standing in his house, saying, 'Send someone to Joppa and summon Simon, who is called Peter, 14 who will speak words to you by which you and all your household will be saved.' 15 [f]As I began to speak, the holy Spirit fell upon them as it had upon us at the beginning, 16 [g]and I remembered the word of the Lord, how he had said, 'John baptized with water but you will be baptized with the holy Spirit.' 17 [h]If then God gave them the same gift he gave to us when we came to believe in the Lord Jesus Christ, who was I to be able to hinder God?" 18 When they heard this, they stopped objecting and glorified God, saying, "God has then granted life-giving repentance to the Gentiles too."

The Church at Antioch 19 [i]*Now those who had been scattered by the persecution that arose because of Stephen went as far as Phoenicia, Cyprus, and Antioch, preaching the word to no one but Jews. 20 There were some Cypriots and Cyrenians among them, however, who came to Antioch and began to speak to the Greeks as well, proclaiming the Lord Jesus. 21 The hand of the Lord was with them and a great number who believed turned to the Lord. 22 The news about them reached the ears of the church in Jerusalem, and they sent Barnabas [to go] to Antioch. 23 When he arrived and saw the grace of God, he rejoiced and encouraged them all to remain faithful to the Lord in firmness of heart, 24 for he was a good man, filled with the holy Spirit and faith. And a large number of people was added to the Lord. 25 Then he went to Tarsus to look for Saul, 26 *and when he had found him he brought him to Antioch. For a whole year they met with the church and taught a large number of people, and it was in Antioch that the disciples were first called Christians.

The Prediction of Agabus 27 *At that time some prophets came down from Jerusalem to Antioch, 28 [j]and one of them named Agabus stood up and predicted by the Spirit that there would be a severe famine all over the world, and it happened under Claudius. 29 [k]So the disciples determined that, according to ability, each should send relief to the brothers who lived in Judea. 30 *This they did, sending it to the presbyters in care of Barnabas and Saul.

CHAPTER 12

Herod's Persecution of the Christians

1 *About that time King Herod laid hands upon

11, 12: **These six brothers:** companions from the Christian community of Joppa (see 10, 23).

11, 19–26: The Jewish Christian antipathy to the mixed community was reflected by the early missionaries generally. The few among them who entertained a different view succeeded in introducing Gentiles into the community at Antioch (in Syria). When the disconcerted Jerusalem community sent Barnabas to investigate, he was so favorably impressed by what he observed that he persuaded his friend Saul to participate in the Antioch mission.

11, 26: **Christians:** "Christians" is first applied to the members of the community at Antioch because the Gentile members of the community enable it to stand out clearly from Judaism.

11, 27–30: It is not clear whether the prophets from Jerusalem came to Antioch to request help in view of the coming famine or whether they received this insight during their visit there. The former supposition seems more likely. Suetonius and Tacitus speak of famines during the reign of Claudius (A.D. 41–54), while the Jewish historian Josephus mentions a famine in Judea in A.D. 46–48. Luke is interested, rather, in showing the charity of the Antiochene community toward the Jewish Christians of Jerusalem despite their differences on mixed communities.

11, 30: **Presbyters:** this is the same Greek word that elsewhere is translated "elders," primarily in reference to the Jewish community.

12, 1–19: Herod Agrippa ruled Judea A.D. 41–44. While Luke does not assign a motive for his execution of James and his intended execution of Peter, the broad background lies in Herod's support of Pharisaic Judaism. The Jewish Christians had lost the

e 10, 3–5.22.30–32. f 10, 44. g 1, 5; 19, 4; Lk 3, 16. h 15, 8–9. i 8, 1–4. j 21, 10. k 12,25.

some members of the church to harm them. [2]*He had James, the brother of John, killed by the sword, [3]*and when he saw that this was pleasing to the Jews he proceeded to arrest Peter also. (It was [the] feast of Unleavened Bread.) [4]He had him taken into custody and put in prison under the guard of four squads of four soldiers each. He intended to bring him before the people after Passover. [5] [l]Peter thus was being kept in prison, but prayer by the church was fervently being made to God on his behalf.

[6]On the very night before Herod was to bring him to trial, Peter, secured by double chains, was sleeping between two soldiers, while outside the door guards kept watch on the prison. [7]Suddenly the angel of the Lord stood by him and a light shone in the cell. He tapped Peter on the side and awakened him, saying, "Get up quickly." The chains fell from his wrists. [8]The angel said to him, "Put on your belt and your sandals." He did so. Then he said to him, "Put on your cloak and follow me." [9]So he followed him out, not realizing that what was happening through the angel was real; he thought he was seeing a vision. [10]They passed the first guard, then the second, and came to the iron gate leading out to the city, which opened for them by itself. They emerged and made their way down an alley, and suddenly the angel left him. [11]Then Peter recovered his senses and said, "Now I know for certain that [the] Lord sent his angel and rescued me from the hand of Herod and from all that the Jewish people had been expecting." [12] [m]When he realized this, he went to the house of Mary, the mother of John who is called Mark, where there were many people gathered in prayer. [13]When he knocked on the gateway door, a maid named Rhoda came to answer it. [14]She was so overjoyed when she recognized Peter's voice that, instead of opening the gate, she ran in and announced that Peter was standing at the gate. [15]They told her, "You are out of your mind," but she insisted that it was so. But they kept saying, "It is his angel." [16]But Peter continued to knock, and when they opened it, they saw him and were astounded. [17]*He motioned to them with his hand to be quiet and explained [to them] how the Lord had led him out of the prison, and said, "Report this to James and the brothers." Then he left and went to another place. [18] [n]At daybreak there was no small commotion among the soldiers over what had become of Peter. [19]Herod, after instituting a search but not finding him, ordered the guards tried and executed. Then he left Judea to spend some time in Caesarea.

Herod's Death [20]*He had long been very angry with the people of Tyre and Sidon, who now came to him in a body. After winning over Blastus, the king's chamberlain, they sued for peace because their country was supplied with food from the king's territory. [21]On an appointed day, Herod, attired in royal robes, [and] seated on the rostrum, addressed them publicly. [22]The assembled crowd cried out, "This is the voice of a god, not of a man." [23]At once the angel of the Lord struck him down because he did not ascribe the honor to God, and he was eaten by worms and breathed his last. [24] [o]But the word of God continued to spread and grow.

Mission of Barnabas and Saul [25] [p]*After Barnabas and Saul completed their relief mission, they returned to Jerusalem, taking with them John, who is called Mark.

---

popularity they had had in Jerusalem (2, 47), perhaps because of suspicions against them traceable to the teaching of Stephen.

12, 2: James, the brother of John: this James, the son of Zebedee, was beheaded by Herod Agrippa ca. A.D. 44.

12, 3.4: Feast of Unleavened Bread . . . Passover: see the note on Lk 22, 1.

12, 17: To James: this James is not the son of Zebedee mentioned in v 2, but is James, the "brother of the Lord" (Gal 1, 19), who in chs 15 and 21 is presented as leader of the Jerusalem Christian community. **He left and went to another place:** the conjecture that Peter left for Rome at this time has nothing to recommend it. His chief responsibility was still the leadership of the Jewish Christian community in Palestine (see Gal 2, 7). The concept of the great missionary effort of the church was yet to come (see 13, 1–3).

12, 20–23: Josephus gives a similar account of Herod's death that occurred in A.D. 44. Early Christian tradition considered the manner of it to be a divine punishment upon his evil life. See 2 Kgs 19, 35 for the figure of the angel of the Lord in such a context.

12, 25: They returned to Jerusalem: many manuscripts read "from Jerusalem," since 11, 30 implies that Paul and Barnabas are already in Jerusalem. This present verse could refer to a return visit or subsequent relief mission.

l Jas 5, 16. m 12, 25; 15, 37. n 5, 22–24. o 6, 7. p 11,29–30.

CHAPTER 13

1*Now there were in the church at Antioch prophets and teachers: Barnabas, Symeon who was called Niger, Lucius of Cyrene, Manaen who was a close friend of Herod the tetrarch, and Saul. 2While they were worshiping the Lord and fasting, the holy Spirit said, "Set apart for me Barnabas and Saul for the work to which I have called them." 3Then, completing their fasting and prayer, they laid hands on them and sent them off.

First Mission Begins in Cyprus 4*So they, sent forth by the holy Spirit, went down to Seleucia and from there sailed to Cyprus. 5*When they arrived in Salamis, they proclaimed the word of God in the Jewish synagogues. They had John also as their assistant. 6*When they had traveled through the whole island as far as Paphos, they met a magician named Bar-Jesus who was a Jewish false prophet. 7He was with the proconsul Sergius Paulus, a man of intelligence, who had summoned Barnabas and Saul and wanted to hear the word of God. 8But Elymas the magician (for that is what his name means) opposed them in an attempt to turn the proconsul away from the faith. 9*But Saul, also known as Paul, filled with the holy Spirit, looked intently at him 10and said, "You son of the devil, you enemy of all that is right, full of every sort of deceit and fraud. Will you not stop twisting the straight paths of [the] Lord? 11Even now the hand of the Lord is upon you. You will be blind, and unable to see the sun for a time." Immediately a dark mist fell upon him, and he went about seeking people to lead him by the hand. 12When the proconsul saw what had happened, he came to believe, for he was astonished by the teaching about the Lord.

Paul's Arrival at Antioch in Pisidia 13 [q]From Paphos, Paul and his companions set sail and arrived at Perga in Pamphylia. But John left them and returned to Jerusalem. 14They continued on from Perga and reached Antioch in Pisidia. On the sabbath they entered [into] the synagogue and took their seats. 15After the reading of the law and the prophets, the synagogue officials sent word to them, "My brothers, if one of you has a word of exhortation for the people, please speak."

Paul's Address in the Synagogue 16*So Paul got up, motioned with his hand, and said, "Fellow Israelites and you others who are God-fearing, listen. 17 [r]The God of this people Israel chose our ancestors and exalted the people during their sojourn in the land of Egypt. With uplifted arm he led them out of it 18 [s]*and for about forty years he put up with them in the desert. 19 [t]When he had destroyed seven nations in the land of Canaan, he gave them their land as an inheritance 20 [u]*at the end of about four hundred and fifty years. After these things he provided judges up to Samuel [the] prophet.

13, 1–3: The impulse for the first missionary effort in Asia Minor is ascribed to the prophets of the Antiochene community, under the inspiration of the holy Spirit. Just as the Jerusalem community had earlier been the center of missionary activity, so too Antioch becomes the center from which the missionaries Barnabas and Saul are sent out.

13, 4—14, 27: The key event in Luke's account of the first missionary journey is the experience of Paul and Barnabas at Pisidian Antioch (13, 14–52). The Christian kerygma proclaimed by Paul in the synagogue was favorably received. Some Jews and "God-fearers" (see the note on 8, 26–40) became interested and invited the missionaries to speak again on the following sabbath (13, 42). By that time, however, the appearance of a large number of Gentiles from the city had so disconcerted the Jews that they became hostile toward the apostles (13, 44–50). This hostility of theirs appears in all three accounts of Paul's missionary journeys in Acts, the Jews of Iconium (14, 1–2) and Beroea (17, 11) being notable exceptions.

13, 5: John: that is, John Mark (see 12, 12.25).

13, 6: A magician named Bar-Jesus who was a Jewish false prophet: that is, he posed as a prophet. Again Luke takes the opportunity to dissociate Christianity from the magical acts of the time (7–11); see also 8, 18–24.

13, 9: Saul, also known as Paul: there is no reason to believe that his name was changed from Saul to Paul upon his conversion. The use of a double name, one Semitic (Saul), the other Greco-Roman (Paul), is well attested (cf 1, 23, Joseph Justus; 12, 12.25, John Mark).

13, 16–41: This is the first of several speeches of Paul to Jews proclaiming that the Christian church is the logical development of Pharisaic Judaism (see also 24, 10–21; 26, 2–23).

13, 16: Who are God-fearing: see the note on 8, 26–40.

13, 18: Put up with: some manuscripts read "sustained."

13, 20: At the end of about four hundred and fifty years: the manuscript tradition makes it uncertain whether the mention of four hundred and fifty years refers to the sojourn in Egypt before the Exodus, the wilderness period and the time of the conquest (see Ex 12, 40–41), as the translation here suggests, or to the time between the conquest and the time of Samuel, the period of the judges, if the text is read, "After these things, for about four hundred and fifty years, he provided judges."

q 15, 38. r Ex 6, 1.6; 12, 51. s Ex 16, 1.35; Nm 14, 34. t Dt 7, 1; Jos 14, 1–2. u Jgs 2, 16; 1 Sm 3, 20.

21 [v]Then they asked for a king. God gave them
Saul, son of Kish, a man from the tribe of
Benjamin, for forty years. 22 [w]Then he removed
him and raised up David as their king; of him he
testified, 'I have found David, son of Jesse, a man
after my own heart; he will carry out my every
wish.' 23 [x]From this man's descendants God,
according to his promise, has brought to Israel a
savior, Jesus. 24 [y]John heralded his coming by
proclaiming a baptism of repentance to all the
people of Israel; 25 [z]and as John was completing
his course, he would say, 'What do you suppose
that I am? I am not he. Behold, one is coming
after me; I am not worthy to unfasten the
sandals of his feet.'

26 "My brothers, children of the family of
Abraham, and those others among you who are
God-fearing, to us this word of salvation has
been sent. 27 The inhabitants of Jerusalem and
their leaders failed to recognize him, and by
condemning him they fulfilled the oracles of the
prophets that are read sabbath after sabbath.
28 [a]For even though they found no grounds for a
death sentence, they asked Pilate to have him
put to death, 29 [b]and when they had accom-
plished all that was written about him, they took
him down from the tree and placed him in a
tomb. 30 [c]But God raised him from the dead,
31 [d]*and for many days he appeared to those
who had come up with him from Galilee to
Jerusalem. These are [now] his witnesses before
the people. 32 We ourselves are proclaiming this
good news to you that what God promised our
ancestors 33 [e]he has brought to fulfillment for us,
[their] children, by raising up Jesus, as it is
written in the second psalm, 'You are my son;
this day I have begotten you.' 34 [f]And that he
raised him from the dead never to return to
corruption he declared in this way, 'I shall give
you the benefits assured to David.' 35 [g]That is
why he also says in another psalm, 'You will not
suffer your holy one to see corruption.' 36 [h]Now
David, after he had served the will of God in his
lifetime, fell asleep, was gathered to his ances-
tors, and did see corruption. 37 But the one
whom God raised up did not see corruption.
38 *You must know, my brothers, that through
him forgiveness of sins is being proclaimed to
you, [and] in regard to everything from which
you could not be justified under the law of
Moses, 39 [i]in him every believer is justified. 40 Be
careful, then, that what was said in the prophets
not come about:

41 [j]'Look on, you scoffers,
be amazed and disappear.
For I am doing a work in your days,
a work that you will never believe even if
someone tells you.' "

42 As they were leaving, they invited them to
speak on these subjects the following sabbath.
43 After the congregation had dispersed, many
Jews and worshipers who were converts to
Judaism followed Paul and Barnabas, who spoke
to them and urged them to remain faithful to the
grace of God.

Address to the Gentiles 44 On the following
sabbath almost the whole city gathered to hear
the word of the Lord. 45 When the Jews saw the
crowds, they were filled with jealousy and with
violent abuse contradicted what Paul said.
46 [k]*Both Paul and Barnabas spoke out boldly

13, 31: The theme of the Galilean witnesses is a major one in the Gospel of Luke and in Acts and is used to signify the continuity between the teachings of Jesus and the teachings of the church and to guarantee the fidelity of the church's teachings to the words of Jesus.

13, 38–39: Justified: the verb is the same as that used in Paul's letters to speak of the experience of justification and, as in Paul, is here connected with the term "to have faith" ("every believer"). But this seems the only passage about Paul in Acts where justification is mentioned. In Lucan fashion it is paralleled with "forgiveness of sins" (a theme at 2, 38; 3, 19; 5, 31; 10, 43) based on Jesus' resurrection (37) rather than his cross, and is put negatively (38). Therefore, some would translate, "in regard to everything from which you could not be acquitted . . . every believer is acquitted."

13, 46: The refusal to believe frustrates God's plan for his chosen people; however, no adverse judgment is made here concerning their ultimate destiny. Again, Luke, in the words of Paul, speaks of the priority of Israel in the plan for salvation (see 10, 36).

v 1 Sm 8, 5.19; 9, 16; 10, 1.20–21.24; 11, 15. w 1 Sm 13, 14; 16, 12–13; Ps 89, 20–21. x Is 11, 1. y Mt 3, 1–2; Mk 1, 4–5; Lk 3, 2–3. z Mt 3, 11; Mk 1, 7; Lk 3, 16; Jn 1, 20.27. a Mt 27, 20.22–23; Mk 15, 13–14; Lk 23, 4.14–15.21–23; Jn 19, 4–6.15. b Mt 27, 59–60; Mk 15, 46; Lk 23, 53; Jn 19, 38.41–42. c 2, 24.32; 3, 15; 4, 10; 17, 31. d 1, 3.8; 10, 39.41; Mt 28, 8–10.16–20; Mk 16, 9.12–20; Lk 24, 13–53; Jn 20, 11–29; 21, 1–23. e Ps 2, 7. f Is 55, 3. g Ps 16, 10. h 2, 29; 1 Kgs 2, 10. i Rom 3, 20. j Hb 1, 5. k 3, 26; Rom 1, 16.

and said, "It was necessary that the word of God be spoken to you first, but since you reject it and condemn yourselves as unworthy of eternal life, we now turn to the Gentiles. [47] [l]For so the Lord has commanded us, 'I have made you a light to the Gentiles, that you may be an instrument of salvation to the ends of the earth.' "

[48]The Gentiles were delighted when they heard this and glorified the word of the Lord. All who were destined for eternal life came to believe, [49]and the word of the Lord continued to spread through the whole region. [50]The Jews, however, incited the women of prominence who were worshipers and the leading men of the city, stirred up a persecution against Paul and Barnabas, and expelled them from their territory. [51] [m]*So they shook the dust from their feet in protest against them and went to Iconium. [52]The disciples were filled with joy and the holy Spirit.

CHAPTER 14

Paul and Barnabas at Iconium [1]In Iconium they entered the Jewish synagogue together and spoke in such a way that a great number of both Jews and Greeks came to believe, [2]although the disbelieving Jews stirred up and poisoned the minds of the Gentiles against the brothers. [3] [n]So they stayed for a considerable period, speaking out boldly for the Lord, who confirmed the word about his grace by granting signs and wonders to occur through their hands. [4]The people of the city were divided: some were with the Jews; others, with the apostles. [5] [o]When there was an attempt by both the Gentiles and the Jews, together with their leaders, to attack and stone them, [6]they realized it and fled to the Lycaonian cities of Lystra and Derbe and to the surrounding countryside, [7]where they continued to proclaim the good news.

Paul and Barnabas at Lystra [8]*At Lystra there was a crippled man, lame from birth, who had never walked. [9]He listened to Paul speaking, who looked intently at him, saw that he had the faith to be healed, [10]and called out in a loud voice, "Stand up straight on your feet." He jumped up and began to walk about. [11] [p]When the crowds saw what Paul had done, they cried out in Lycaonian, "The gods have come down to us in human form." [12]*They called Barnabas "Zeus" and Paul "Hermes," because he was the chief speaker. [13]And the priest of Zeus, whose temple was at the entrance to the city, brought oxen and garlands to the gates, for he together with the people intended to offer sacrifice.

[14]*The apostles Barnabas and Paul tore their garments when they heard this and rushed out into the crowd, shouting, [15] [q]*"Men, why are you doing this? We are of the same nature as you, human beings. We proclaim to you good news that you should turn from these idols to the living God, 'who made heaven and earth and sea and all that is in them.' [16] [r]In past generations he allowed all Gentiles to go their own ways; [17] [s]yet, in bestowing his goodness, he did not leave himself without witness, for he gave you rains from heaven and fruitful seasons, and filled you with nourishment and gladness for your hearts." [18]Even with these words, they scarcely restrained the crowds from offering sacrifice to them.

[19] [t]However, some Jews from Antioch and Iconium arrived and won over the crowds. They stoned Paul and dragged him out of the city, supposing that he was dead. [20]But when the disciples gathered around him, he got up and entered the city. On the following day he left with Barnabas for Derbe.

13, 51: See the note on Lk 9, 5.

14, 8–18: In an effort to convince his hearers that the divine power works through his word, Paul cures the cripple. However, the pagan tradition of the occasional appearance of gods among human beings leads the people astray in interpreting the miracle. The incident reveals the cultural difficulties with which the church had to cope. Note the similarity of the miracle worked here by Paul to the one performed by Peter in 3, 2–10.

14, 12: Zeus . . . Hermes: in Greek religion, Zeus was the chief of the Olympian gods, the "father of gods and men"; Hermes was a son of Zeus and was usually identified as the herald and messenger of the gods.

14, 14: Tore their garments: a gesture of protest.

14, 15–17: This is the first speech of Paul to Gentiles recorded by Luke in Acts (cf 17, 22–31). Rather than showing how Christianity is the logical outgrowth of Judaism, as he does in speeches before Jews, Luke says that God excuses past Gentile ignorance and then presents a natural theology arguing for the recognition of God's existence and presence through his activity in natural phenomena.

l Is 49, 6. m Mt 10, 14; Mk 6, 11; Lk 9, 5; 10, 11. n Mk 16, 17–20. o 2 Tm 3, 11. p 28, 6. q 3, 12; 10, 26; Ex 20, 11; Ps 146, 6. r 17, 30. s Wis 13, 1. t 2 Cor 11, 25; 2 Tm 3, 11.

End of the First Mission 21After they had proclaimed the good news to that city and made a considerable number of disciples, they returned to Lystra and to Iconium and to Antioch. 22 [u]They strengthened the spirits of the disciples and exhorted them to persevere in the faith, saying, "It is necessary for us to undergo many hardships to enter the kingdom of God." 23*They appointed presbyters for them in each church and, with prayer and fasting, commended them to the Lord in whom they had put their faith. 24Then they traveled through Pisidia and reached Pamphylia. 25After proclaiming the word at Perga they went down to Attalia. 26 [v]From there they sailed to Antioch, where they had been commended to the grace of God for the work they had now accomplished. 27And when they arrived, they called the church together and reported what God had done with them and how he had opened the door of faith to the Gentiles. 28Then they spent no little time with the disciples.

CHAPTER 15

Council of Jerusalem 1 [wx]*Some who had come down from Judea were instructing the brothers, "Unless you are circumcised according to the Mosaic practice, you cannot be saved." 2Because there arose no little dissension and debate by Paul and Barnabas with them, it was decided that Paul, Barnabas, and some of the others should go up to Jerusalem to the apostles and presbyters about this question. 3They were sent on their journey by the church, and passed through Phoenicia and Samaria telling of the conversion of the Gentiles, and brought great joy to all the brothers. 4When they arrived in Jerusalem, they were welcomed by the church, as well as by the apostles and the presbyters, and they reported what God had done with them. 5But some from the party of the Pharisees who had become believers stood up and said, "It is necessary to circumcise them and direct them to observe the Mosaic law."

6*The apostles and the presbyters met together to see about this matter. 7 [y]*After much debate had taken place, Peter got up and said to them, "My brothers, you are well aware that from early days God made his choice among you that through my mouth the Gentiles would hear the word of the gospel and believe. 8 [z]And God, who knows the heart, bore witness by granting them the holy Spirit just as he did us. 9 [a]He made no distinction between us and them, for by faith he purified their hearts. 10 [b]Why, then, are you now putting God to the test by placing on the shoulders of the disciples a yoke that neither our ancestors nor we have been able to bear? 11 [c]*On the contrary, we believe that we are saved through the grace of the Lord Jesus, in the same way as they." 12The whole assembly fell silent, and they listened while Paul and Barnabas described the signs and wonders God had worked among the Gentiles through them.

James on Dietary Law 13*After they had fallen silent, James responded, "My brothers,

14, 23: They appointed presbyters: the communities are given their own religious leaders by the traveling missionaries. The structure in these churches is patterned on the model of the Jerusalem community (11, 30; 15, 2.5.22; 21, 18).

15, 1–35: The Jerusalem "Council" marks the official rejection of the rigid view that Gentile converts were obliged to observe the Mosaic law completely. From here to the end of Acts, Paul and the Gentile mission become the focus of Luke's writing.

15, 1–5: When some of the converted Pharisees of Jerusalem discover the results of the first missionary journey of Paul, they urge that the Gentiles be taught to follow the Mosaic law. Recognizing the authority of the Jerusalem church, Paul and Barnabas go there to settle the question of whether Gentiles can embrace a form of Christianity that does not include this obligation.

15, 6–12: The gathering is possibly the same as that recalled by Paul in Gal 2, 1–10. Note that in v 2 it is only the apostles and presbyters, a small group, with whom Paul and Barnabas are to meet. Here Luke gives the meeting a public character because he wishes to emphasize its doctrinal significance (see 22).

15, 7–11: Paul's refusal to impose the Mosaic law on the Gentile Christians is supported by Peter on the ground that within his own experience God bestowed the holy Spirit upon Cornelius and his household without preconditions concerning the adoption of the Mosaic law (see 10, 44–47).

15, 11: In support of Paul, Peter formulates the fundamental meaning of the gospel: that all are invited to be saved through faith in the power of Christ.

15, 13–35: Some scholars think that this apostolic decree suggested by James, the immediate leader of the Jerusalem community, derives from another historical occasion than the meeting in question. This seems to be the case if the meeting is the same as the one related in Gal 2, 1–10. According to that account, nothing was imposed upon Gentile Christians in respect to Mosaic law; whereas the decree instructs Gentile Christians of mixed communities to abstain from meats sacrificed to idols and from blood-meats, and to avoid marriage within forbidden degrees of consanguinity and affinity (Lv 18), all of which practices were especially abhorrent to Jews. Luke seems to have telescoped two originally independent incidents here: the first a Jerusalem "Coun-

u 1 Thes 3, 3. v 13, 1–3. w Gal 2, 1–9. x Lv 12, 3; Gal 5, 2. y 10, 27–43. z 10, 44–48. a 10, 34–35. b Mt 23, 4; Gal 5, 1. c Gal 2, 16; 3, 11; Eph 2, 5–8.

listen to me. 14 *Symeon has described how God first concerned himself with acquiring from among the Gentiles a people for his name. 15 The words of the prophets agree with this, as is written:

16 [d]'After this I shall return
and rebuild the fallen hut of David;
from its ruins I shall rebuild it
and raise it up again,
17 so that the rest of humanity may seek out the Lord,
even all the Gentiles on whom my name is invoked.
Thus says the Lord who accomplishes these things,
18 known from of old.'

19 [e]It is my judgment, therefore, that we ought to stop troubling the Gentiles who turn to God, 20 [f]but tell them by letter to avoid pollution from idols, unlawful marriage, the meat of strangled animals, and blood. 21 For Moses, for generations now, has had those who proclaim him in every town, as he has been read in the synagogues every sabbath."

Letter of the Apostles 22 Then the apostles and presbyters, in agreement with the whole church, decided to choose representatives and to send them to Antioch with Paul and Barnabas. The ones chosen were Judas, who was called Barsabbas, and Silas, leaders among the brothers. 23 This is the letter delivered by them: "The apostles and the presbyters, your brothers, to the brothers in Antioch, Syria, and Cilicia of Gentile origin: greetings. 24 Since we have heard that some of our number [who went out] without any mandate from us have upset you with their teachings and disturbed your peace of mind, 25 we have with one accord decided to choose representatives and to send them to you along with our beloved Barnabas and Paul, 26 who have dedicated their lives to the name of our Lord Jesus Christ. 27 So we are sending Judas and Silas who will also convey this same message by word of mouth: 28 [g]'It is the decision of the holy Spirit and of us not to place on you any burden beyond these necessities, 29 [h]namely, to abstain from meat sacrificed to idols, from blood, from meats of strangled animals, and from unlawful marriage. If you keep free of these, you will be doing what is right. Farewell.' "

Delegates at Antioch 30 And so they were sent on their journey. Upon their arrival in Antioch they called the assembly together and delivered the letter. 31 When the people read it, they were delighted with the exhortation. 32 Judas and Silas, who were themselves prophets, exhorted and strengthened the brothers with many words. 33 After they had spent some time there, they were sent off with greetings of peace from the brothers to those who had commissioned them. [34]* 35 But Paul and Barnabas remained in Antioch, teaching and proclaiming with many others the word of the Lord.

V: The Mission of Paul to the Ends of the Earth

Paul and Barnabas Separate 36 *After some time, Paul said to Barnabas, "Come, let us make a return visit to see how the brothers are getting

---

cil" that dealt with the question of circumcision, and the second a Jerusalem decree dealing mainly with Gentile observance of dietary laws (see 21, 25 where Paul seems to be learning of the decree for the first time).

15, 14: Symeon: elsewhere in Acts he is called either Peter or Simon. The presence of the name Symeon here suggests that, in the source Luke is using for this part of the Jerusalem "Council" incident, the name may have originally referred to someone other than Peter (see 13, 1 where the Antiochene Symeon Niger is mentioned). As the text now stands, however, it is undoubtedly a reference to Simon Peter (7).

15, 34: Some manuscripts add, in various wordings, "But Silas decided to remain there."

15, 36—18, 22: This continuous narrative recounts Paul's second missionary journey. On the internal evidence of the Lucan account, it lasted about three years. Paul first visited the communities he had established on his first journey (16, 1–5), then pushed on into Macedonia, where he established communities at Philippi, Thessalonica, and Beroea (16, 7—17, 5). To escape the hostility of the Jews of Thessalonica, he left for Greece and while resident in Athens attempted, without success, to establish an effective Christian community there. From Athens he proceeded to Corinth and, after a stay of a year and a half, returned to Antioch by way of Ephesus and Jerusalem (17, 16—18, 22). Luke does not concern himself with the structure or statistics of the communities but aims to show the general progress of the gospel in the Gentile world as well as its continued failure to take root in the Jewish community.

d Am 9, 11–12. e 15, 28–29; 21, 25. f Gn 9, 4; Lv 3, 17; 17, 10–14. g 15, 19–20. h Gn 9, 4; Lv 3, 17; 17, 10–14.

on in all the cities where we proclaimed the
word of the Lord." [37]Barnabas wanted to take
with them also John, who was called Mark,
[38][i]but Paul insisted that they should not take
with them someone who had deserted them at
Pamphylia and who had not continued with
them in their work. [39]So sharp was their dis-
agreement that they separated. Barnabas took
Mark and sailed to Cyprus. [40]But Paul chose
Silas and departed after being commended by
the brothers to the grace of the Lord. [41]He
traveled through Syria and Cilicia bringing
strength to the churches.

CHAPTER 16

Paul in Lycaonia: Timothy [1][j]He reached
[also] Derbe and Lystra where there was a
disciple named Timothy, the son of a Jewish
woman who was a believer, but his father was a
Greek. [2][k]The brothers in Lystra and Iconium
spoke highly of him, [3]*and Paul wanted him to
come along with him. On account of the Jews of
that region, Paul had him circumcised, for they
all knew that his father was a Greek. [4]As they
traveled from city to city, they handed on to the
people for observance the decisions reached by
the apostles and presbyters in Jerusalem. [5]Day
after day the churches grew stronger in faith and
increased in number.

Through Asia Minor [6]They traveled through
the Phrygian and Galatian territory because they
had been prevented by the holy Spirit from
preaching the message in the province of Asia.
[7]*When they came to Mysia, they tried to go on
into Bithynia, but the Spirit of Jesus did not allow
them, [8]so they crossed through Mysia and came
down to Troas. [9]During [the] night Paul had a
vision. A Macedonian stood before him and
implored him with these words, "Come over to
Macedonia and help us." [10]*When he had seen
the vision, we sought passage to Macedonia at
once, concluding that God had called us to
proclaim the good news to them.

Into Europe [11]*We set sail from Troas, making
a straight run for Samothrace, and on the next
day to Neapolis, [12]and from there to Philippi, a
leading city in that district of Macedonia and a
Roman colony. We spent some time in that city.
[13]On the sabbath we went outside the city gate
along the river where we thought there would
be a place of prayer. We sat and spoke with the
women who had gathered there. [14]*One of
them, a woman named Lydia, a dealer in purple
cloth, from the city of Thyatira, a worshiper of
God, listened, and the Lord opened her heart to
pay attention to what Paul was saying. [15]After
she and her household had been baptized, she
offered us an invitation, "If you consider me a
believer in the Lord, come and stay at my
home," and she prevailed on us.

Imprisonment at Philippi [16]*As we were go-
ing to the place of prayer, we met a slave girl
with an oracular spirit, who used to bring a large
profit to her owners through her fortune-telling.
[17]She began to follow Paul and us, shouting,
"These people are slaves of the Most High God,
who proclaim to you a way of salvation." [18]She
did this for many days. Paul became annoyed,
turned, and said to the spirit, "I command you in
the name of Jesus Christ to come out of her."
Then it came out at that moment.

[19]When her owners saw that their hope of
profit was gone, they seized Paul and Silas and
dragged them to the public square before the

16, 3: Paul had him circumcised: he did this in order that Timothy might be able to associate with the Jews and so perform a ministry among them. Paul did not object to the Jewish Christians' adherence to the law. But he insisted that the law could not be imposed on the Gentiles. Paul himself lived in accordance with the law, or as exempt from the law, according to particular circumstances (see 1 Cor 9, 19–23).

16, 7: The Spirit of Jesus: this is an unusual formulation in Luke's writings. The parallelism with v 6 indicates its meaning, the holy Spirit.

16, 10–17: This is the first of the so-called "we-sections" in Acts, where Luke writes as one of Paul's companions. The other passages are 20, 5–15; 21, 1–18; 27, 1—28, 16. Scholars debate whether Luke may not have used the first person plural simply as a literary device to lend color to the narrative. The realism of the narrative, however, lends weight to the argument that the "we" includes Luke or another companion of Paul whose data Luke used as a source.

16, 11–40: The church at Philippi became a flourishing community to which Paul addressed one of his letters (see Introduction to the Letter to the Philippians).

16, 14: A worshiper of God: a "God-fearer." See the note on 8, 26–40.

16, 16: With an oracular spirit: literally, "with a Python spirit." The Python was the serpent or dragon that guarded the Delphic oracle. It later came to designate a "spirit that pronounced oracles" and also a ventriloquist who, it was thought, had such a spirit in the belly.

i 13, 13. j 1 Tm 1, 2; 2 Tm 1, 5. k Phil 2, 20.

local authorities. [20]*They brought them before the magistrates and said, "These people are Jews and are disturbing our city [21]and are advocating customs that are not lawful for us Romans to adopt or practice." [22] [l]The crowd joined in the attack on them, and the magistrates had them stripped and ordered them to be beaten with rods. [23]After inflicting many blows on them, they threw them into prison and instructed the jailer to guard them securely. [24]When he received these instructions, he put them in the innermost cell and secured their feet to a stake.

Deliverance from Prison [25]About midnight, while Paul and Silas were praying and singing hymns to God as the prisoners listened, [26]there was suddenly such a severe earthquake that the foundations of the jail shook; all the doors flew open, and the chains of all were pulled loose. [27]When the jailer woke up and saw the prison doors wide open, he drew [his] sword and was about to kill himself, thinking that the prisoners had escaped. [28]But Paul shouted out in a loud voice, "Do no harm to yourself; we are all here." [29]He asked for a light and rushed in and, trembling with fear, he fell down before Paul and Silas. [30]Then he brought them out and said, "Sirs, what must I do to be saved?" [31]And they said, "Believe in the Lord Jesus and you and your household will be saved." [32]So they spoke the word of the Lord to him and to everyone in his house. [33]He took them in at that hour of the night and bathed their wounds; then he and all his family were baptized at once. [34]He brought them up into his house and provided a meal and with his household rejoiced at having come to faith in God.

[35]*But when it was day, the magistrates sent the lictors with the order, "Release those men." [36]The jailer reported the[se] words to Paul, "The magistrates have sent orders that you be released. Now, then, come out and go in peace." [37] [m]*But Paul said to them, "They have beaten us publicly, even though we are Roman citizens and have not been tried, and have thrown us into prison. And now, are they going to release us secretly? By no means. Let them come themselves and lead us out." [38] [n]The lictors reported these words to the magistrates, and they became alarmed when they heard that they were Roman citizens. [39]So they came and placated them, and led them out and asked that they leave the city. [40]When they had come out of the prison, they went to Lydia's house where they saw and encouraged the brothers, and then they left.

CHAPTER 17

Paul in Thessalonica [1] [o]When they took the road through Amphipolis and Apollonia, they reached Thessalonica, where there was a synagogue of the Jews. [2]Following his usual custom, Paul joined them, and for three sabbaths he entered into discussions with them from the scriptures, [3] [p]expounding and demonstrating that the Messiah had to suffer and rise from the dead, and that "This is the Messiah, Jesus, whom I proclaim to you." [4]Some of them were convinced and joined Paul and Silas; so, too, a great number of Greeks who were worshipers, and not a few of the prominent women. [5] [q]But the Jews became jealous and recruited some worthless men loitering in the public square, formed a mob, and set the city in turmoil. They marched on the house of Jason, intending to bring them before the people's assembly. [6]*When they could not find them, they dragged Jason and some of the brothers before the city magistrates, shouting, "These people who have been creating a disturbance all over the world have now come here, [7] [r]*and Jason has wel-

16, 20: Magistrates: in Greek, **stratēgoi,** the popular designation of the **duoviri,** the highest officials of the Roman colony of Philippi.

16, 35: The lictors: the equivalent of police officers, among whose duties were the apprehension and punishment of criminals.

16, 37: Paul's Roman citizenship granted him special privileges in regard to criminal process. Roman law forbade under severe penalty the beating of Roman citizens (see also 22, 25).

17, 6–7: The accusations against Paul and his companions echo the charges brought against Jesus in Lk 23, 2.

17, 7: There is another king, Jesus: a distortion into a political sense of the apostolic proclamation of Jesus and the kingdom of God (see 8, 12).

l 2 Cor 11, 25; Phil 1, 30; 1 Thes 2, 2. m 22, 25. n 22, 29. o 1 Thes 2, 1–2. p 3, 18; Lk 24, 25–26.46. q Rom 16, 21. r Lk 23, 2; Jn 19, 12–15.

comed them. They all act in opposition to the decrees of Caesar and claim instead that there is another king, Jesus." [8]They stirred up the crowd and the city magistrates who, upon hearing these charges, [9]took a surety payment from Jason and the others before releasing them.

Paul in Beroea [10]The brothers immediately sent Paul and Silas to Beroea during the night. Upon arrival they went to the synagogue of the Jews. [11] [s]These Jews were more fair-minded than those in Thessalonica, for they received the word with all willingness and examined the scriptures daily to determine whether these things were so. [12]Many of them became believers, as did not a few of the influential Greek women and men. [13]But when the Jews of Thessalonica learned that the word of God had now been proclaimed by Paul in Beroea also, they came there too to cause a commotion and stir up the crowds. [14] [t]So the brothers at once sent Paul on his way to the seacoast, while Silas and Timothy remained behind. [15]After Paul's escorts had taken him to Athens, they came away with instructions for Silas and Timothy to join him as soon as possible.

Paul in Athens [16]*While Paul was waiting for them in Athens, he grew exasperated at the sight of the city full of idols. [17]So he debated in the synagogue with the Jews and with the worshipers, and daily in the public square with whoever happened to be there. [18]*Even some of the Epicurean and Stoic philosophers engaged him in discussion. Some asked, "What is this scavenger trying to say?" Others said, "He sounds like a promoter of foreign deities," because he was preaching about 'Jesus' and 'Resurrection.' [19] [u]*They took him and led him to the Areopagus and said, "May we learn what this new teaching is that you speak of? [20]For you bring some strange notions to our ears; we should like to know what these things mean." [21]Now all the Athenians as well as the foreigners residing there used their time for nothing else but telling or hearing something new.

Paul's Speech at the Areopagus [22]*Then Paul stood up at the Areopagus and said:

"You Athenians, I see that in every respect you are very religious. [23]*For as I walked around looking carefully at your shrines, I even discovered an altar inscribed, 'To an Unknown God.' What therefore you unknowingly worship, I proclaim to you. [24] [v]The God who made the world and all that is in it, the Lord of heaven and earth, does not dwell in sanctuaries made by human hands, [25]nor is he served by human hands because he needs anything. Rather it is he who gives to everyone life and breath and everything. [26]*He made from one the whole

17, 16–21: Paul's presence in Athens sets the stage for the great discourse before a Gentile audience in vv 22–31. Although Athens was a politically insignificant city at this period, it still lived on the glories of its past and represented the center of Greek culture. The setting describes the conflict between Christian preaching and Hellenistic philosophy.

17, 18: Epicurean and Stoic philosophers: for the followers of Epicurus (342–271 B.C.), the goal of life was happiness attained through sober reasoning and the searching out of motives for all choice and avoidance. The Stoics were followers of Zeno, a younger contemporary of Alexander the Great. Zeno and his followers believed in a type of pantheism that held that the spark of divinity was present in all reality and that, in order to be free, each person must live "according to nature." **This scavenger:** literally, "seed-picker," as of a bird that picks up grain. The word is later used of scrap collectors and of people who take other people's ideas and propagate them as if they were their own. **Promoter of foreign deities:** according to Xenophon, Socrates was accused of promoting new deities. The accusation against Paul echoes the charge against Socrates. **'Jesus' and 'Resurrection':** the Athenians are presented as misunderstanding Paul from the outset; they think he is preaching about Jesus and a goddess named **Anastasis,** i.e., Resurrection.

17, 19: To the Areopagus: the "Areopagus" refers either to the Hill of Ares west of the Acropolis or to the Council of Athens, which at one time met on the hill but which at this time assembled in the Royal Colonnade (**Stoa Basileios**).

17, 22–31: In Paul's appearance at the Areopagus he preaches his climactic speech to Gentiles in the cultural center of the ancient world. The speech is more theological than christological. Paul's discourse appeals to the Greek world's belief in divinity as responsible for the origin and existence of the universe. It contests the common belief in a multiplicity of gods supposedly exerting their powers through their images. It acknowledges that the attempt to find God is a constant human endeavor. It declares, further, that God is the judge of the human race, that the time of the judgment has been determined, and that it will be executed through a man whom God raised from the dead. The speech reflects sympathy with pagan religiosity, handles the subject of idol worship gently, and appeals for a new examination of divinity, not from the standpoint of creation but from the standpoint of judgment.

17, 23: 'To an Unknown God': ancient authors such as Pausanias, Philostratus, and Tertullian speak of Athenian altars with no specific dedication as altars of "unknown gods" or "nameless altars."

17, 26: From one: many manuscripts read "from one blood." **Fixed . . . seasons:** or "fixed limits to the epochs."

s Jn 5, 39. t 1 Thes 3, 1–2. u 1 Cor 1, 22. v 7, 48–50; Gn 1, 1; 1 Kgs 8, 27; Is 42, 5.

human race to dwell on the entire surface of the earth, and he fixed the ordered seasons and the boundaries of their regions, 27 [w]so that people might seek God, even perhaps grope for him and find him, though indeed he is not far from any one of us. 28 *For 'In him we live and move and have our being,' as even some of your poets have said, 'For we too are his offspring.' 29 [x]Since therefore we are the offspring of God, we ought not to think that the divinity is like an image fashioned from gold, silver, or stone by human art and imagination. 30 God has overlooked the times of ignorance, but now he demands that all people everywhere repent 31 [y]because he has established a day on which he will 'judge the world with justice' through a man he has appointed, and he has provided confirmation for all by raising him from the dead."

32 When they heard about resurrection of the dead, some began to scoff, but others said, "We should like to hear you on this some other time." 33 And so Paul left them. 34 But some did join him, and became believers. Among them were Dionysius, a member of the Court of the Areopagus, a woman named Damaris, and others with them.

CHAPTER 18

Paul in Corinth 1 After this he left Athens and went to Corinth.. 2 [z]*There he met a Jew named Aquila, a native of Pontus, who had recently come from Italy with his wife Priscilla because Claudius had ordered all the Jews to leave Rome. He went to visit them 3 and, because he practiced the same trade, stayed with them and worked, for they were tentmakers by trade. 4 Every sabbath, he entered into discussions in the synagogue, attempting to convince both Jews and Greeks.

5 When Silas and Timothy came down from Macedonia, Paul began to occupy himself totally with preaching the word, testifying to the Jews that the Messiah was Jesus. 6 [a]*When they opposed him and reviled him, he shook out his garments and said to them, "Your blood be on your heads! I am clear of responsibility. From now on I will go to the Gentiles." 7 [b]*So he left there and went to a house belonging to a man named Titus Justus, a worshiper of God; his house was next to a synagogue. 8 [c]*Crispus, the synagogue official, came to believe in the Lord along with his entire household, and many of the Corinthians who heard believed and were baptized. 9 [d]One night in a vision the Lord said to Paul, "Do not be afraid. Go on speaking, and do not be silent, 10 for I am with you. No one will attack and harm you, for I have many people in this city." 11 He settled there for a year and a half and taught the word of God among them.

Accusations before Gallio 12 *But when Gallio was proconsul of Achaia, the Jews rose up together against Paul and brought him to the tribunal, 13 *saying, "This man is inducing people to worship God contrary to the law." 14 When Paul was about to reply, Gallio spoke to the Jews, "If it were a matter of some crime or malicious fraud, I should with reason hear the complaint of you Jews; 15 but since it is a question of arguments over doctrine and titles and your own law, see to it yourselves. I do not wish to be a judge of such matters." 16 And he drove them away from the tribunal. 17 They all seized Sosthenes, the synagogue official, and

17, 28: 'In him we live and move and have our being': some scholars understand this saying to be based on an earlier saying of Epimenides of Knossos (6th century B.C.). **'For we too are his offspring'**: here Paul is quoting Aratus of Soli, a third-century B.C. poet from Cilicia.

18, 2: Aquila . . . Priscilla: both may already have been Christians at the time of their arrival in Corinth (see 26). According to 1 Cor 16, 19, their home became a meeting place for Christians. **Claudius**: the Emperor Claudius expelled the Jews from Rome ca. A.D. 40. The Roman historian Suetonius gives as reason for the expulsion disturbances among the Jews "at the instigation of Chrestos," probably meaning disputes about the messiahship of Jesus.

18, 6: Shook out his garments: a gesture indicating Paul's repudiation of his mission to the Jews there; cf 28, 17–31.

18, 7: A worshiper of God: see the note on 8, 26–40.

18, 8: Crispus: in 1 Cor 1, 14, Paul mentions that Crispus was one of the few he himself baptized at Corinth.

18, 12: When Gallio was proconsul of Achaia: Gallio's proconsulship in Achaia is dated to A.D. 51–52 from an inscription discovered at Delphi. This has become an important date in establishing a chronology of the life and missionary work of Paul.

18, 13: Contrary to the law: Gallio (15) understands this to be a problem of Jewish, not Roman, law.

w Jer 23, 23; Wis 13, 6; Rom 1, 19. x 19, 26; Is 40, 18–20; 44, 10–17; Rom 1, 22–23. y 10, 42. z Rom 16, 3. a 13, 51; Mt 10, 14; 27, 24–25; Mk 6, 11; Lk 9, 5; 10, 10–11. b 13, 46–47; 28, 28. c 1 Cor 1, 14. d Jer 1, 8.

beat him in full view of the tribunal. But none of this was of concern to Gallio.

Return to Syrian Antioch [18][e]*Paul remained for quite some time, and after saying farewell to the brothers he sailed for Syria, together with Priscilla and Aquila. At Cenchreae he had his hair cut because he had taken a vow. [19]When they reached Ephesus, he left them there, while he entered the synagogue and held discussions with the Jews. [20]Although they asked him to stay for a longer time, he did not consent, [21]but as he said farewell he promised, "I shall come back to you again, God willing." Then he set sail from Ephesus. [22]*Upon landing at Caesarea, he went up and greeted the church and then went down to Antioch. [23]*After staying there some time, he left and traveled in orderly sequence through the Galatian country and Phrygia, bringing strength to all the disciples.

Apollos [24][f]*A Jew named Apollos, a native of Alexandria, an eloquent speaker, arrived in Ephesus. He was an authority on the scriptures. [25]He had been instructed in the Way of the Lord and, with ardent spirit, spoke and taught accurately about Jesus, although he knew only the baptism of John. [26]*He began to speak boldly in the synagogue; but when Priscilla and Aquila heard him, they took him aside and explained to him the Way [of God] more accurately. [27]And when he wanted to cross to Achaia, the brothers encouraged him and wrote to the disciples there to welcome him. After his arrival he gave great assistance to those who had come to believe through grace. [28]He vigorously refuted the Jews in public, establishing from the scriptures that the Messiah is Jesus.

CHAPTER 19

Paul in Ephesus [1]*While Apollos was in Corinth, Paul traveled through the interior of the country and came [down] to Ephesus where he found some disciples. [2]He said to them, "Did you receive the holy Spirit when you became believers?" They answered him, "We have never even heard that there is a holy Spirit." [3]He said, "How were you baptized?" They replied, "With the baptism of John." [4][g]Paul then said, "John baptized with a baptism of repentance, telling the people to believe in the one who was to come after him, that is, in Jesus." [5]When they heard this, they were baptized in the name of the Lord Jesus. [6][h]And when Paul laid [his] hands on them, the holy Spirit came upon them, and they spoke in tongues and prophesied. [7]Altogether there were about twelve men.

[8]He entered the synagogue, and for three months debated boldly with persuasive arguments about the kingdom of God. [9]But when some in their obstinacy and disbelief disparaged the Way before the assembly, he withdrew and took his disciples with him and began to hold daily discussions in the lecture hall of Tyrannus. [10]This continued for two years with the result that all the inhabitants of the province of Asia heard the word of the Lord, Jews and Greeks alike. [11]So extraordinary were the mighty deeds God accomplished at the hands of Paul [12][i]that when face cloths or aprons that touched his skin were applied to the sick, their diseases left them and the evil spirits came out of them.

The Jewish Exorcists [13]Then some itinerant Jewish exorcists tried to invoke the name of the Lord Jesus over those with evil spirits, saying, "I adjure you by the Jesus whom Paul preaches."

18, 18: He had his hair cut because he had taken a vow: a reference to a Nazirite vow (see Nm 6, 1–21, especially, 6, 18) taken by Paul (see also 21, 23–27).

18, 22: He went up and greeted the church: "going up" suggests a visit to the church in Jerusalem.

18, 23—21, 16: Luke's account of Paul's third missionary journey devotes itself mainly to his work at Ephesus (19, 1—20, 1). There is a certain restiveness on Paul's part and a growing conviction that the Spirit bids him return to Jerusalem and prepare to go to Rome (19, 21).

18, 24–25: Apollos appears as a preacher who knows the teaching of Jesus in the context of John's baptism of repentance. Aquila and Priscilla instruct him more fully. He is referred to in 1 Cor 1, 12; 3, 5–6.22.

18, 26: The Way [of God]: for the Way, see the note on 9, 2. Other manuscripts here read "the Way of the Lord," "the word of the Lord," or simply "the Way."

19, 1–6: Upon his arrival in Ephesus, Paul discovers other people at the same religious stage as Apollos, though they seem to have considered themselves followers of Christ, not of the Baptist. On the relation between baptism and the reception of the Spirit, see the note on 8, 16.

e 21, 24; Nm 6, 18. f 1 Cor 1, 12. g 1, 5; 11, 16; 13, 24–25; Mt 3, 11; Mk 1, 8; Lk 3, 16. h 8, 15–17; 10, 44.46. i 5, 15–16; Lk 8, 44–47.

14 When the seven sons of Sceva, a Jewish high priest, tried to do this, 15 the evil spirit said to them in reply, "Jesus I recognize, Paul I know, but who are you?" 16 The person with the evil spirit then sprang at them and subdued them all. He so overpowered them that they fled naked and wounded from that house. 17 When this became known to all the Jews and Greeks who lived in Ephesus, fear fell upon them all, and the name of the Lord Jesus was held in great esteem. 18 Many of those who had become believers came forward and openly acknowledged their former practices. 19 Moreover, a large number of those who had practiced magic collected their books and burned them in public. They calculated their value and found it to be fifty thousand silver pieces. 20 Thus did the word of the Lord continue to spread with influence and power.

Paul's Plans 21 [j]When this was concluded, Paul made up his mind to travel through Macedonia and Achaia, and then to go on to Jerusalem, saying, "After I have been there, I must visit Rome also." 22 Then he sent to Macedonia two of his assistants, Timothy and Erastus, while he himself stayed for a while in the province of Asia.

The Riot of the Silversmiths 23 About that time a serious disturbance broke out concerning the Way. 24 *There was a silversmith named Demetrius who made miniature silver shrines of Artemis and provided no little work for the craftsmen. 25 He called a meeting of these and other workers in related crafts and said, "Men, you know well that our prosperity derives from this work. 26 [k]As you can now see and hear, not only in Ephesus but throughout most of the province of Asia this Paul has persuaded and misled a great number of people by saying that gods made by hands are not gods at all. 27 The danger grows, not only that our business will be discredited, but also that the temple of the great goddess Artemis will be of no account, and that she whom the whole province of Asia and all the world worship will be stripped of her magnificence."

28 When they heard this, they were filled with fury and began to shout, "Great is Artemis of the Ephesians!" 29 [l]The city was filled with confusion, and the people rushed with one accord into the theater, seizing Gaius and Aristarchus, the Macedonians, Paul's traveling companions. 30 Paul wanted to go before the crowd, but the disciples would not let him, 31 *and even some of the Asiarchs who were friends of his sent word to him advising him not to venture into the theater. 32 Meanwhile, some were shouting one thing, others something else; the assembly was in chaos, and most of the people had no idea why they had come together. 33 Some of the crowd prompted Alexander, as the Jews pushed him forward, and Alexander signaled with his hand that he wished to explain something to the gathering. 34 But when they recognized that he was a Jew, they all shouted in unison, for about two hours, "Great is Artemis of the Ephesians!" 35 *Finally the town clerk restrained the crowd and said, "You Ephesians, what person is there who does not know that the city of the Ephesians is the guardian of the temple of the great Artemis and of her image that fell from the sky? 36 Since these things are undeniable, you must calm yourselves and not do anything rash. 37 The men you brought here are not temple robbers, nor have they insulted our goddess. 38 If Demetrius and his fellow craftsmen have a complaint against anyone, courts are in session, and there are proconsuls. Let them bring charges against one another. 39 If you have anything further to investigate, let the matter be settled in the lawful

19, 24: Miniature silver shrines of Artemis: the temple of Artemis at Ephesus was one of the seven wonders of the ancient world. Artemis, originally the Olympian virgin hunter, moon goddess, and goddess of wild nature, was worshiped at Ephesus as an Asian mother goddess and goddess of fertility. She was one of the most widely worshiped female deities in the Hellenistic world (see 18, 27).

19, 31: Asiarchs: the precise status and role of the Asiarchs is disputed. They appear to have been people of wealth and influence who promoted the Roman imperial cult and who may also have been political representatives in a league of cities in the Roman province of Asia.

19, 35: Guardian of the temple: this title was accorded by Rome to cities that provided a temple for the imperial cult. Inscriptional evidence indicates that Ephesus was acknowledged as the temple keeper of Artemis and of the imperial cult. **That fell from the sky:** many scholars think that this refers to a meteorite that was worshiped as an image of the goddess.

j 23, 11; Rom 1, 13; 15, 22–32. k 17, 29. l Col 4, 10.

assembly, 40*for, as it is, we are in danger of being charged with rioting because of today's conduct. There is no cause for it. We shall [not] be able to give a reason for this demonstration." With these words he dismissed the assembly.

CHAPTER 20

Journey to Macedonia and Greece 1 [m]When the disturbance was over, Paul had the disciples summoned and, after encouraging them, he bade them farewell and set out on his journey to Macedonia. 2As he traveled throughout those regions, he provided many words of encouragement for them. Then he arrived in Greece, 3where he stayed for three months. But when a plot was made against him by the Jews as he was about to set sail for Syria, he decided to return by way of Macedonia.

Return to Troas 4 [n]Sopater, the son of Pyrrhus, from Beroea, accompanied him, as did Aristarchus and Secundus from Thessalonica, Gaius from Derbe, Timothy, and Tychicus and Trophimus from Asia 5 [o]*who went on ahead and waited for us at Troas. 6*We sailed from Philippi after the feast of Unleavened Bread, and rejoined them five days later in Troas, where we spent a week.

Eutychus Restored to Life 7*On the first day of the week when we gathered to break bread, Paul spoke to them because he was going to leave on the next day, and he kept on speaking until midnight. 8There were many lamps in the upstairs room where we were gathered, 9and a young man named Eutychus who was sitting on the window sill was sinking into a deep sleep as Paul talked on and on. Once overcome by sleep, he fell down from the third story and when he was picked up, he was dead. 10 [p]*Paul went down, threw himself upon him, and said as he embraced him, "Don't be alarmed; there is life in him." 11Then he returned upstairs, broke the bread, and ate; after a long conversation that lasted until daybreak, he departed. 12And they took the boy away alive and were immeasurably comforted.

Journey to Miletus 13We went ahead to the ship and set sail for Assos where we were to take Paul on board, as he had arranged, since he was going overland. 14When he met us in Assos, we took him aboard and went on to Mitylene. 15We sailed away from there on the next day and reached a point off Chios, and a day later we reached Samos, and on the following day we arrived at Miletus. 16*Paul had decided to sail past Ephesus in order not to lose time in the province of Asia, for he was hurrying to be in Jerusalem, if at all possible, for the day of Pentecost.

Paul's Farewell Speech at Miletus 17From Miletus he had the presbyters of the church at Ephesus summoned. 18When they came to him, he addressed them, "You know how I lived among you the whole time from the day I first came to the province of Asia. 19I served the Lord with all humility and with the tears and trials that came to me because of the plots of the Jews, 20and I did not at all shrink from telling you what was for your benefit, or from teaching you in public or in your homes. 21I earnestly bore witness for both Jews and Greeks to repentance before God and to faith in our Lord Jesus. 22But now, compelled by the Spirit, I am going to Jerusalem. What will happen to me there I do not know, 23 [q]except that in one city after another the holy Spirit has been warning me that

19, 40: Some manuscripts omit the negative in **[not] be able,** making the meaning, "There is no cause for which we shall be able to give a reason for this demonstration."

20, 5: The second "we-section" of Acts begins here. See the note on 16, 10–17.

20, 6: Feast of Unleavened Bread: see the note on Lk 22, 1.

20, 7: The first day of the week: the day after the sabbath and the first day of the Jewish week, apparently chosen originally by the Jerusalem community for the celebration of the liturgy of the Eucharist in order to relate it to the resurrection of Christ.

20, 10: The action of Paul in throwing himself upon the dead boy recalls that of Elijah in 1 Kgs 17, 21 where the son of the widow of Zarephath is revived and that of Elisha in 2 Kgs 4, 34 where the Shunamite woman's son is restored to life.

20, 16–35: Apparently aware of difficulties at Ephesus and neighboring areas, Paul calls the presbyters together at Miletus, about thirty miles from Ephesus. He reminds them of his dedication to the gospel (18–21), speaks of what he is about to suffer for the gospel (22–27), and admonishes them to guard the community against false prophets, sure to arise upon his departure (28–31). He concludes by citing a saying of Jesus (35) not recorded in the gospel tradition. Luke presents this farewell to the Ephesian presbyters as Paul's last will and testament.

m 1 Cor 16, 1. n Rom 16, 21. o 21, 29; 2 Tm 4, 20. p 1 Kgs 17, 17–24; 2 Kgs 4, 30–37; Mt 9, 24; Mk 5, 39; Lk 8, 52. q 9, 16.

imprisonment and hardships await me. [24] [r]Yet I consider life of no importance to me, if only I may finish my course and the ministry that I received from the Lord Jesus, to bear witness to the gospel of God's grace.

[25]"But now I know that none of you to whom I preached the kingdom during my travels will ever see my face again. [26]And so I solemnly declare to you this day that I am not responsible for the blood of any of you, [27]for I did not shrink from proclaiming to you the entire plan of God. [28] [s]*Keep watch over yourselves and over the whole flock of which the holy Spirit has appointed you overseers, in which you tend the church of God that he acquired with his own blood. [29] [t]I know that after my departure savage wolves will come among you, and they will not spare the flock. [30] [u]And from your own group, men will come forward perverting the truth to draw the disciples away after them. [31] [v]So be vigilant and remember that for three years, night and day, I unceasingly admonished each of you with tears. [32]And now I commend you to God and to that gracious word of his that can build you up and give you the inheritance among all who are consecrated. [33]I have never wanted anyone's silver or gold or clothing. [34] [w]You know well that these very hands have served my needs and my companions. [35] [x]In every way I have shown you that by hard work of that sort we must help the weak, and keep in mind the words of the Lord Jesus who himself said, 'It is more blessed to give than to receive.' "

[36]When he had finished speaking he knelt down and prayed with them all. [37]They were all weeping loudly as they threw their arms around Paul and kissed him, [38]for they were deeply distressed that he had said that they would never see his face again. Then they escorted him to the ship.

CHAPTER 21

Arrival at Tyre [1]*When we had taken leave of them we set sail, made a straight run for Cos, and on the next day for Rhodes, and from there to Patara. [2]Finding a ship crossing to Phoenicia, we went on board and put out to sea. [3]We caught sight of Cyprus but passed by it on our left and sailed on toward Syria and put in at Tyre where the ship was to unload cargo. [4]There we sought out the disciples and stayed for a week. They kept telling Paul through the Spirit not to embark for Jerusalem. [5]At the end of our stay we left and resumed our journey. All of them, women and children included, escorted us out of the city, and after kneeling on the beach to pray, [6]we bade farewell to one another. Then we boarded the ship, and they returned home.

Arrival at Ptolemais and Caesarea [7]We continued the voyage and came from Tyre to Ptolemais, where we greeted the brothers and stayed a day with them. [8] [y]*On the next day we resumed the trip and came to Caesarea, where we went to the house of Philip the evangelist, who was one of the Seven, and stayed with him. [9]He had four virgin daughters gifted with prophecy. [10]*We had been there several days when a prophet named Agabus came down from Judea. [11] [z]*He came up to us, took Paul's belt, bound his own feet and hands with it, and said, "Thus says the holy Spirit: This is the way the Jews will bind the owner of this belt in Jerusalem, and they will hand him over to the Gentiles." [12]When we heard this, we and the local residents begged him not to go up to Jerusalem. [13] [a]Then Paul replied, "What are you doing, weeping and breaking my heart? I am prepared not only to be bound but even to die in Jerusalem for the name of the Lord

20, 28: **Overseers:** see the note on Phil 1, 1. **The church of God:** because the clause "that he acquired with his own blood" following "the church of God" suggests that "his own blood" refers to God's blood, some early copyists changed "the church of God" to "the church of the Lord." Some prefer the translation "acquired with the blood of his own," i.e., Christ.

21, 1–18: The third "we-section" of Acts (see the note on 16, 10–17).

21, 8: **One of the Seven:** see the note on 6, 2–4.

21, 10: **Agabus:** mentioned in 11, 28 as the prophet who predicted the famine that occurred when Claudius was emperor.

21, 11: The symbolic act of Agabus recalls those of Old Testament prophets. Compare Is 20, 2; Ez 4, 1; Jer 13, 1.

r 2 Tm 4, 7. s Jn 21, 15–17; 1 Pt 5, 2. t Jn 10, 12. u Mt 7, 15; 2 Pt 2, 1–3; 1 Jn 2, 18–19. v 1 Thes 2, 11. w 1 Cor 4, 12; 1 Thes 2, 9; 2 Thes 3, 8. x Sir 4, 31. y 6, 5; 8, 5–6. z 11, 28; 20, 23. a 19, 15–16.

Jesus." 14 [b]*Since he would not be dissuaded we let the matter rest, saying, "The Lord's will be done."

Paul and James in Jerusalem 15 After these days we made preparations for our journey, then went up to Jerusalem. 16 Some of the disciples from Caesarea came along to lead us to the house of Mnason, a Cypriot, a disciple of long standing, with whom we were to stay. 17 *When we reached Jerusalem the brothers welcomed us warmly. 18 The next day, Paul accompanied us on a visit to James, and all the presbyters were present. 19 He greeted them, then proceeded to tell them in detail what God had accomplished among the Gentiles through his ministry. 20 They praised God when they heard it but said to him, "Brother, you see how many thousands of believers there are from among the Jews, and they are all zealous observers of the law. 21 They have been informed that you are teaching all the Jews who live among the Gentiles to abandon Moses and that you are telling them not to circumcise their children or to observe their customary practices. 22 What is to be done? They will surely hear that you have arrived. 23 [c]*So do what we tell you. We have four men who have taken a vow. 24 *Take these men and purify yourself with them, and pay their expenses that they may have their heads shaved. In this way everyone will know that there is nothing to the reports they have been given about you but that you yourself live in observance of the law. 25 [d]*As for the Gentiles who have come to believe, we sent them our decision that they abstain from meat sacrificed to idols, from blood, from the meat of strangled animals, and from unlawful marriage." 26 [e]So Paul took the men, and on the next day after purifying himself together with them entered the temple to give notice of the day when the purification would be completed and the offering made for each of them.

Paul's Arrest 27 When the seven days were nearly completed, the Jews from the province of Asia noticed him in the temple, stirred up the whole crowd, and laid hands on him, 28 [f]*shouting, "Fellow Israelites, help us. This is the man who is teaching everyone everywhere against the people and the law and this place, and what is more, he has even brought Greeks into the temple and defiled this sacred place." 29 For they had previously seen Trophimus the Ephesian in the city with him and supposed that Paul had brought him into the temple. 30 The whole city was in turmoil with people rushing together. They seized Paul and dragged him out of the temple, and immediately the gates were closed. 31 *While they were trying to kill him, a report reached the cohort commander that all Jerusalem was rioting. 32 He immediately took soldiers and centurions and charged down on them. When they saw the commander and the soldiers they stopped beating Paul. 33 The cohort commander came forward, arrested him, and ordered him to be secured with two chains; he tried to find out who he might be and what he had done. 34 Some in the mob shouted one thing,

21, 14: The Christian disciples' attitude reflects that of Jesus (see Lk 22, 42).

21, 17–26: The leaders of the Jewish Christians of Jerusalem inform Paul that the Jews there believe he has encouraged the Jews of the diaspora to abandon the Mosaic law. According to Acts, Paul had no objection to the retention of the law by the Jewish Christians of Jerusalem and left the Jews of the diaspora who accepted Christianity free to follow the same practice.

21, 23–26: The leaders of the community suggest that Paul, on behalf of four members of the Jerusalem community, make the customary payment for the sacrifices offered at the termination of the Nazirite vow (see Nm 6, 1–24) in order to impress favorably the Jewish Christians in Jerusalem with his high regard for the Mosaic law. Since Paul himself had once made this vow (18, 18), his respect for the law would be on public record.

21, 24: Pay their expenses: according to Nm 6, 14–15 the Nazirite had to present a yearling lamb for a holocaust, a yearling ewe lamb for a sin offering, and a ram for a peace offering, along with food and drink offerings, upon completion of the period of the vow.

21, 25: Paul is informed about the apostolic decree, seemingly for the first time (see the note on 15, 13–35). The allusion to the decree was probably introduced here by Luke to remind his readers that the Gentile Christians themselves were asked to respect certain Jewish practices deriving from the law.

21, 28: The charges against Paul by the diaspora Jews are identical to the charges brought against Stephen by diaspora Jews in 6, 13. **Brought Greeks into the temple:** non-Jews were forbidden, under penalty of death, to go beyond the Court of the Gentiles. Inscriptions in Greek and Latin on a stone ballustrade marked off the prohibited area.

21, 31: Cohort commander: literally, "the leader of a thousand in a cohort." At this period the Roman cohort commander usually led six hundred soldiers, a tenth of a legion; but the number in a cohort varied.

b Mt 6, 10; 26, 39; Mk 14, 36; Lk 22, 42. c 18, 18; Nm 6, 1–21. d 15, 19–20.28–29. e 1 Cor 9, 20. f Rom 15, 31.

others something else; so, since he was unable
to ascertain the truth because of the uproar, he
ordered Paul to be brought into the compound.
35 When he reached the steps, he was carried by
the soldiers because of the violence of the mob,
36 g*for a crowd of people followed and shouted,
"Away with him!"

37 Just as Paul was about to be taken into the
compound, he said to the cohort commander,
"May I say something to you?" He replied, "Do
you speak Greek? 38 h*So then you are not the
Egyptian who started a revolt some time ago and
led the four thousand assassins into the desert?"
39 Paul answered, "I am a Jew, of Tarsus in
Cilicia, a citizen of no mean city; I request you
to permit me to speak to the people." 40 *When
he had given his permission, Paul stood on the
steps and motioned with his hand to the people;
and when all was quiet he addressed them in
Hebrew.

CHAPTER 22

Paul's Defense before the Jerusalem Jews

1 *"My brothers and fathers, listen to what I am
about to say to you in my defense." 2 When they
heard him addressing them in Hebrew they
became all the more quiet. And he continued,
3 i"I am a Jew, born in Tarsus in Cilicia, but
brought up in this city. At the feet of Gamaliel I
was educated strictly in our ancestral law and
was zealous for God, just as all of you are today.
4 jI persecuted this Way to death, binding both
men and women and delivering them to prison.
5 Even the high priest and the whole council of
elders can testify on my behalf. For from them I
even received letters to the brothers and set out
for Damascus to bring back to Jerusalem in
chains for punishment those there as well.

6 k"On that journey as I drew near to Damas-
cus, about noon a great light from the sky
suddenly shone around me. 7 lI fell to the ground
and heard a voice saying to me, 'Saul, Saul, why
are you persecuting me?' 8 mI replied, 'Who are
you, sir?' And he said to me, 'I am Jesus the
Nazorean whom you are persecuting.' 9 nMy
companions saw the light but did not hear the
voice of the one who spoke to me. 10 oI asked,
'What shall I do, sir?' The Lord answered me,
'Get up and go into Damascus, and there you
will be told about everything appointed for you
to do.' 11 pSince I could see nothing because of
the brightness of that light, I was led by hand by
my companions and entered Damascus.

12 q"A certain Ananias, a devout observer of
the law, and highly spoken of by all the Jews
who lived there, 13 came to me and stood there
and said, 'Saul, my brother, regain your sight.'
And at that very moment I regained my sight
and saw him. 14 Then he said, 'The God of our
ancestors designated you to know his will, to see
the Righteous One, and to hear the sound of his
voice; 15 *for you will be his witness before all to
what you have seen and heard. 16 Now, why
delay? Get up and have yourself baptized and
your sins washed away, calling upon his name.'

17 "After I had returned to Jerusalem and
while I was praying in the temple, I fell into a
trance 18 and saw the Lord saying to me, 'Hurry,
leave Jerusalem at once, because they will not
accept your testimony about me.' 19 rBut I re-
plied, 'Lord, they themselves know that from
synagogue to synagogue I used to imprison and

21, 36: Away with him: at the trial of Jesus before Pilate in Lk 23, 18, the people similarly shout, "Away with this man."

21, 38: The Egyptian: according to the Jewish historian Josephus, an Egyptian gathered a large crowd on the Mount of Olives to witness the destruction of the walls of Jerusalem that would fall at the Egyptian "prophet's" word. The commotion was put down by the Roman authorities and the Egyptian escaped, but only after thousands had been killed. **Four thousand assassins:** literally, **sicarii.** According to Josephus, these were political nationalists who removed their opponents by assassination with a short dagger, called in Latin a **sica.**

21, 40: In Hebrew: meaning, perhaps, in Aramaic, which at this time was the Semitic tongue in common use.

22, 1–21: Paul's first defense speech is presented to the Jerusalem crowds. Luke here presents Paul as a devout Jew (3) and zealous persecutor of the Christian community (4–5), and then recounts the conversion of Paul for the second time in Acts (see the note on 9, 1–19).

22, 15: His witness: like the Galilean followers during the historical ministry of Jesus, Paul too, through his experience of the risen Christ, is to be a witness to the resurrection (compare 1, 8; 10, 39–41; Lk 24, 48).

g 22, 22; Lk 23, 18; Jn 19, 15. h 5, 36–37. i 5, 34; 26, 4–5; 2 Cor 11, 22; Gal 1, 13–14; Phil 3, 5–6. j 8, 3; 9, 1–2; 22, 19; 26, 9–11; Phil 3, 6. k 9, 3; 26, 13; 1 Cor 15, 8. l 9, 4; 26, 14. m 9, 5; 26, 15; Mt 25, 40. n 9, 7; 26, 13–14. o 9, 6; 26, 16. p 9, 8. q 9, 10–19. r 8, 3; 9, 1–2; 22, 4–5; 26, 9–11.

beat those who believed in you. 20 [s]And when the blood of your witness Stephen was being shed, I myself stood by giving my approval and keeping guard over the cloaks of his murderers.' 21 [t]*Then he said to me, 'Go, I shall send you far away to the Gentiles.' "

Paul Imprisoned 22 [u]*They listened to him until he said this, but then they raised their voices and shouted, "Take such a one as this away from the earth. It is not right that he should live." 23 And as they were yelling and throwing off their cloaks and flinging dust into the air, 24 the cohort commander ordered him to be brought into the compound and gave instruction that he be interrogated under the lash to determine the reason why they were making such an outcry against him. 25 [v]*But when they had stretched him out for the whips, Paul said to the centurion on duty, "Is it lawful for you to scourge a man who is a Roman citizen and has not been tried?" 26 When the centurion heard this, he went to the cohort commander and reported it, saying, "What are you going to do? This man is a Roman citizen." 27 Then the commander came and said to him, "Tell me, are you a Roman citizen?" "Yes," he answered. 28 The commander replied, "I acquired this citizenship for a large sum of money." Paul said, "But I was born one." 29 At once those who were going to interrogate him backed away from him, and the commander became alarmed when he realized that he was a Roman citizen and that he had had him bound.

Paul before the Sanhedrin 30 The next day, wishing to determine the truth about why he was being accused by the Jews, he freed him and ordered the chief priests and the whole Sanhedrin to convene. Then he brought Paul down and made him stand before them.

CHAPTER 23

1 [w]Paul looked intently at the Sanhedrin and said, "My brothers, I have conducted myself with a perfectly clear conscience before God to this day." 2 *The high priest Ananias ordered his attendants to strike his mouth. 3 [x]*Then Paul said to him, "God will strike you, you whitewashed wall. Do you indeed sit in judgment upon me according to the law and yet in violation of the law order me to be struck?" 4 The attendants said, "Would you revile God's high priest?" 5 [y]*Paul answered, "Brothers, I did not realize he was the high priest. For it is written, 'You shall not curse a ruler of your people.' "

6 [z]Paul was aware that some were Sadducees and some Pharisees, so he called out before the Sanhedrin, "My brothers, I am a Pharisee, the son of Pharisees; [I] am on trial for hope in the resurrection of the dead." 7 When he said this, a dispute broke out between the Pharisees and Sadducees, and the group became divided. 8 [a]For the Sadducees say that there is no resurrection or angels or spirits, while the Pharisees acknowledge all three. 9 A great uproar occurred, and some scribes belonging to the Pharisee party stood up and sharply argued, "We find nothing wrong with this man. Suppose a spirit or an angel has spoken to him?" 10 The dispute was so serious that the commander, afraid that Paul would be torn to pieces by them, ordered his troops to go down and rescue him from their midst and take him into the compound. 11 [b]*The following night the Lord stood by him and said, "Take courage. For just as you have borne

22, 21: Paul endeavors to explain that his position on the law has not been identical with that of his audience because it has been his prophetic mission to preach to the Gentiles to whom the law was not addressed and who had no faith in it as a way of salvation.

22, 22: Paul's suggestion that his prophetic mission to the Gentiles did not involve his imposing the law on them provokes the same opposition as occurred in Pisidian Antioch (13, 45).

22, 25: Is it lawful for you to scourge a man who is a Roman citizen and has not been tried?: see the note on 16, 37.

23, 2: The high priest Ananias: Ananias, son of Nedebaeus, was high priest from A.D. 47 to 59.

23, 3: God will strike you: Josephus reports that Ananias was later assassinated in A.D. 66 at the beginning of the First Revolt.

23, 5: Luke portrays Paul as a model of one who is obedient to the Mosaic law. Paul, because of his reverence for the law (Ex 22, 27), withdraws his accusation of hypocrisy, "whitewashed wall" (cf Mt 23, 27), when he is told Ananias is the high priest.

23, 11: The occurrence of the vision of Christ consoling Paul and assuring him that he will be his witness in Rome prepares the reader for the final section of Acts: the journey of Paul and the word he preaches to Rome under the protection of the Romans.

s 7, 58; 8, 1. t 9, 15; Gal 2, 7–9. u 21, 36; Lk 23, 18; Jn 19, 15. v 16, 37. w 24, 16. x Ez 13, 10–15; Mt 23, 27. y Ex 22, 27. z 24, 15.21; 26, 5; Phil 3, 5. a Mt 22, 23; Lk 20, 27. b 19, 21.

witness to my cause in Jerusalem, so you must
also bear witness in Rome."
Transfer to Caesarea 12 When day came, the
Jews made a plot and bound themselves by oath
not to eat or drink until they had killed Paul.
13 There were more than forty who formed this
conspiracy. 14 They went to the chief priests and
elders and said, "We have bound ourselves by a
solemn oath to taste nothing until we have killed
Paul. 15 You, together with the Sanhedrin, must
now make an official request to the commander
to have him bring him down to you, as though
you meant to investigate his case more thor-
oughly. We on our part are prepared to kill him
before he arrives." 16 The son of Paul's sister,
however, heard about the ambush; so he went
and entered the compound and reported it to
Paul. 17 *Paul then called one of the centurions
and requested, "Take this young man to the
commander; he has something to report to
him." 18 So he took him and brought him to the
commander and explained, "The prisoner Paul
called me and asked that I bring this young man
to you; he has something to say to you." 19 The
commander took him by the hand, drew him
aside, and asked him privately, "What is it you
have to report to me?" 20 He replied, "The Jews
have conspired to ask you to bring Paul down to
the Sanhedrin tomorrow, as though they meant
to inquire about him more thoroughly, 21 but do
not believe them. More than forty of them are
lying in wait for him; they have bound them-
selves by oath not to eat or drink until they have
killed him. They are now ready and only wait for
your consent." 22 As the commander dismissed
the young man he directed him, "Tell no one
that you gave me this information."
23 *Then he summoned two of the centurions
and said, "Get two hundred soldiers ready to go
to Caesarea by nine o'clock tonight, along with
seventy horsemen and two hundred auxiliaries.
24 Provide mounts for Paul to ride and give him
safe conduct to Felix the governor." 25 Then he
wrote a letter with this content: 26 *"Claudius
Lysias to his excellency the governor Felix,
greetings. 27 [c]This man, seized by the Jews and
about to be murdered by them, I rescued after
intervening with my troops when I learned that
he was a Roman citizen. 28 I wanted to learn the
reason for their accusations against him so I
brought him down to their Sanhedrin. 29 [d]I
discovered that he was accused in matters of
controversial questions of their law and not of
any charge deserving death or imprisonment.
30 Since it was brought to my attention that there
will be a plot against the man, I am sending him
to you at once, and have also notified his
accusers to state [their case] against him before
you."
31 So the soldiers, according to their orders,
took Paul and escorted him by night to Antipa-
tris. 32 The next day they returned to the com-
pound, leaving the horsemen to complete the
journey with him. 33 When they arrived in Caesa-
rea they delivered the letter to the governor and
presented Paul to him. 34 When he had read it
and asked to what province he belonged, and
learned that he was from Cilicia, 35 he said, "I
shall hear your case when your accusers arrive."
Then he ordered that he be held in custody in
Herod's praetorium.

CHAPTER 24

Trial before Felix 1 Five days later the high
priest Ananias came down with some elders and
an advocate, a certain Tertullus, and they pre-
sented formal charges against Paul to the gover-
nor. 2 When he was called, Tertullus began to
accuse him, saying, "Since we have attained
much peace through you, and reforms have been

23, 17: Centurions: a centurion was a military officer in charge of one hundred soldiers.

23, 23: By nine o'clock tonight: literally, "by the third hour of the night." The night hours began at 6 p.m. **Two hundred auxiliaries:** the meaning of the Greek is not certain. It seems to refer to spearmen from the local police force and not from the cohort of soldiers, which would have numbered only 500–1000 men.

23, 26–30: The letter emphasizes the fact that Paul is a Roman citizen and asserts the lack of evidence that he is guilty of a crime against the empire. The tone of the letter implies that the commander became initially involved in Paul's case because of his Roman citizenship, but this is not an exact description of what really happened (see 21, 31–33; 22, 25–29).

23, 26: M. Antonius Felix was procurator of Judea from A.D. 52 to 60. His procuratorship was marked by cruelty toward and oppression of his Jewish subjects.

c 21, 30–34; 22, 27. d 18, 14–15; 25, 18–19.

accomplished in this nation through your provident care, [3]we acknowledge this in every way and everywhere, most excellent Felix, with all gratitude. [4]But in order not to detain you further, I ask you to give us a brief hearing with your customary graciousness. [5] [e]*We found this man to be a pest; he creates dissension among Jews all over the world and is a ringleader of the sect of the Nazoreans. [6] [f]He even tried to desecrate our temple, but we arrested him. [7]* [8]If you examine him you will be able to learn from him for yourself about everything of which we are accusing him." [9]The Jews also joined in the attack and asserted that these things were so.

[10]*Then the governor motioned to him to speak and Paul replied, "I know that you have been a judge over this nation for many years and so I am pleased to make my defense before you. [11]As you can verify, not more than twelve days have passed since I went up to Jerusalem to worship. [12]Neither in the temple, nor in the synagogues, nor anywhere in the city did they find me arguing with anyone or instigating a riot among the people. [13]Nor can they prove to you the accusations they are now making against me. [14] [g]But this I do admit to you, that according to the Way, which they call a sect, I worship the God of our ancestors and I believe everything that is in accordance with the law and written in the prophets. [15] [h]I have the same hope in God as they themselves have that there will be a resurrection of the righteous and the unrighteous. [16] [i]Because of this, I always strive to keep my conscience clear before God and man. [17] [j]After many years, I came to bring alms for my nation and offerings. [18] [k]While I was so engaged, they found me, after my purification, in the temple without a crowd or disturbance. [19]But some Jews from the province of Asia, who should be here before you to make whatever accusation they might have against me— [20]or let these men themselves state what crime they discovered when I stood before the Sanhedrin, [21] [l]unless it was my one outcry as I stood among them, that 'I am on trial before you today for the resurrection of the dead.' "

[22]Then Felix, who was accurately informed about the Way, postponed the trial, saying, "When Lysias the commander comes down, I shall decide your case." [23]He gave orders to the centurion that he should be kept in custody but have some liberty, and that he should not prevent any of his friends from caring for his needs.

Captivity in Caesarea [24]*Several days later Felix came with his wife Drusilla, who was Jewish. He had Paul summoned and listened to him speak about faith in Christ Jesus. [25]But as he spoke about righteousness and self-restraint and the coming judgment, Felix became frightened and said, "You may go for now; when I find an opportunity I shall summon you again." [26]At the same time he hoped that a bribe would be offered him by Paul, and so he sent for him very often and conversed with him.

[27]*Two years passed and Felix was succeeded by Porcius Festus. Wishing to ingratiate himself with the Jews, Felix left Paul in prison.

CHAPTER 25

Appeal to Caesar [1]Three days after his arrival in the province, Festus went up from Caesarea to Jerusalem [2]*where the chief priests and Jewish leaders presented him their formal charges against Paul. They asked him [3]as a favor to have him sent to Jerusalem, for they were plotting to kill him along the way. [4]Festus replied that Paul was being held in custody in Caesarea

24, 5: Nazoreans: that is, followers of Jesus of Nazareth.

24, 7: The Western text has added here a verse (really 6b-8a) that is not found in the best Greek manuscripts. It reads, "and would have judged him according to our own law, but the cohort commander Lysias came and violently took him out of our hands and ordered his accusers to come before you."

24, 10–21: Whereas the advocate Tertullus referred to Paul's activities on his missionary journeys, the apostle narrowed the charges down to the riot connected with the incident in the temple (see 21, 27–30; 24, 17–20). In his defense, Paul stresses the continuity between Christianity and Judaism.

24, 24–25: The way of Christian discipleship greatly disquiets Felix, who has entered into an adulterous marriage with Drusilla, daughter of Herod Agrippa I. This marriage provides the background for the topics Paul speaks about and about which Felix does not want to hear.

24, 27: Very little is known of Porcius Festus who was a procurator of Judea from A.D. 60 to 62.

25, 2: Even after two years the animosity toward Paul in Jerusalem had not subsided (see 24, 27).

e 24, 14; Lk 23, 2. f 21, 28. g 24, 5. h Dn 12, 2; Jn 5, 28–29. i 23, 1. j Rom 15, 25–26; Gal 2, 10. k 21, 26–30. l 23, 6; 24, 15.

and that he himself would be returning there shortly. [5]He said, "Let your authorities come down with me, and if this man has done something improper, let them accuse him."

[6]After spending no more than eight or ten days with them, he went down to Caesarea, and on the following day took his seat on the tribunal and ordered that Paul be brought in. [7]When he appeared, the Jews who had come down from Jerusalem surrounded him and brought many serious charges against him, which they were unable to prove. [8]In defending himself Paul said, "I have committed no crime either against the Jewish law or against the temple or against Caesar." [9]*Then Festus, wishing to ingratiate himself with the Jews, said to Paul in reply, "Are you willing to go up to Jerusalem and there stand trial before me on these charges?" [10]Paul answered, "I am standing before the tribunal of Caesar; this is where I should be tried. I have committed no crime against the Jews, as you very well know. [11]If I have committed a crime or done anything deserving death, I do not seek to escape the death penalty; but if there is no substance to the charges they are bringing against me, then no one has the right to hand me over to them. I appeal to Caesar." [12]Then Festus, after conferring with his council, replied, "You have appealed to Caesar. To Caesar you will go."

Paul before King Agrippa [13]*When a few days had passed, King Agrippa and Bernice arrived in Caesarea on a visit to Festus. [14] [m]Since they spent several days there, Festus referred Paul's case to the king, saying, "There is a man here left in custody by Felix. [15]When I was in Jerusalem the chief priests and the elders of the Jews brought charges against him and demanded his condemnation. [16]I answered them that it was not Roman practice to hand over an accused person before he has faced his accusers and had the opportunity to defend himself against their charge. [17]So when [they] came together here, I made no delay; the next day I took my seat on the tribunal and ordered the man to be brought in. [18] [n]His accusers stood around him, but did not charge him with any of the crimes I suspected. [19]Instead they had some issues with him about their own religion and about a certain Jesus who had died but who Paul claimed was alive. [20]Since I was at a loss how to investigate this controversy, I asked if he were willing to go to Jerusalem and there stand trial on these charges. [21]And when Paul appealed that he be held in custody for the Emperor's decision, I ordered him held until I could send him to Caesar." [22]Agrippa said to Festus, "I too should like to hear this man." He replied, "Tomorrow you will hear him."

[23]The next day Agrippa and Bernice came with great ceremony and entered the audience hall in the company of cohort commanders and the prominent men of the city and, by command of Festus, Paul was brought in. [24]And Festus said, "King Agrippa and all you here present with us, look at this man about whom the whole Jewish populace petitioned me here and in Jerusalem, clamoring that he should live no longer. [25]I found, however, that he had done nothing deserving death, and so when he appealed to the Emperor, I decided to send him. [26]But I have nothing definite to write about him to our sovereign; therefore I have brought him before all of you, and particularly before you, King Agrippa, so that I may have something to write as a result of this investigation. [27]For it seems senseless to me to send up a prisoner without indicating the charges against him."

CHAPTER 26

King Agrippa Hears Paul [1]Then Agrippa said to Paul, "You may now speak on your own behalf." So Paul stretched out his hand and began his defense. [2]*"I count myself fortunate,

25, 9–12: Paul refuses to acknowledge that the Sanhedrin in Jerusalem has any jurisdiction over him now (11). Paul uses his right as a Roman citizen to appeal his case to the jurisdiction of the Emperor (Nero, ca. A.D. 60) (12). This move broke the deadlock between Roman protective custody of Paul and the plan of his enemies to kill him (3).

25, 13: King Agrippa and Bernice: brother and sister, children of Herod Agrippa I whose activities against the Jerusalem community are mentioned in 12, 1–19. Agrippa II was a petty ruler over small areas in northern Palestine and some villages in Perea. His influence on the Jewish population of Palestine was insignificant.

26, 2–23: Paul's final defense speech in Acts is now made before a king (see 9, 15). In the speech Paul presents himself as a zealous Pharisee and Christianity as the logical development of

m 24, 27. n 18, 14–15; 23, 29.

King Agrippa, that I am to defend myself before
you today against all the charges made against
me by the Jews, 3 especially since you are an
expert in all the Jewish customs and controver-
sies. And therefore I beg you to listen patiently.
4 *My manner of living from my youth, a life
spent from the beginning among my people and
in Jerusalem, all [the] Jews know. 5 [o]They have
known about me from the start, if they are
willing to testify, that I have lived my life as a
Pharisee, the strictest party of our religion. 6 [p]But
now I am standing trial because of my hope in
the promise made by God to our ancestors. 7 Our
twelve tribes hope to attain to that promise as
they fervently worship God day and night; and
on account of this hope I am accused by Jews, O
king. 8 Why is it thought unbelievable among
you that God raises the dead? 9 [q]I myself once
thought that I had to do many things against the
name of Jesus the Nazorean, 10 [r]and I did so in
Jerusalem. I imprisoned many of the holy ones
with the authorization I received from the chief
priests, and when they were to be put to death I
cast my vote against them. 11 Many times, in
synagogue after synagogue, I punished them in
an attempt to force them to blaspheme; I was so
enraged against them that I pursued them even
to foreign cities.
12 "On one such occasion I was traveling to
Damascus with the authorization and commis-
sion of the chief priests. 13 [s] [t]At midday, along the
way, O king, I saw a light from the sky, brighter
than the sun, shining around me and my travel-
ing companions. 14 [u]*We all fell to the ground
and I heard a voice saying to me in Hebrew,
'Saul, Saul, why are you persecuting me? It is
hard for you to kick against the goad.' 15 [v]And I
said, 'Who are you, sir?' And the Lord replied, 'I
am Jesus whom you are persecuting. 16 [w]*Get up
now, and stand on your feet. I have appeared to
you for this purpose, to appoint you as a servant
and witness of what you have seen [of me] and
what you will be shown. 17 [x]I shall deliver you
from this people and from the Gentiles to whom
I send you, 18 [y]*to open their eyes that they may
turn from darkness to light and from the power
of Satan to God, so that they may obtain
forgiveness of sins and an inheritance among
those who have been consecrated by faith in
me.'
19 "And so, King Agrippa, I was not disobedi-
ent to the heavenly vision. 20 On the contrary,
first to those in Damascus and in Jerusalem and
throughout the whole country of Judea, and
then to the Gentiles, I preached the need to
repent and turn to God, and to do works giving
evidence of repentance. 21 [z]That is why the Jews
seized me [when I was] in the temple and tried
to kill me. 22 [a]*But I have enjoyed God's help to
this very day, and so I stand here testifying to
small and great alike, saying nothing different
from what the prophets and Moses foretold,
23 [b]*that the Messiah must suffer and that, as the
first to rise from the dead, he would proclaim
light both to our people and to the Gentiles."
Reactions to Paul's Speech 24 While Paul was
so speaking in his defense, Festus said in a loud
voice, "You are mad, Paul; much learning is
driving you mad." 25 But Paul replied, "I am not
mad, most excellent Festus; I am speaking
words of truth and reason. 26 *The king knows
about these matters and to him I speak boldly,

Pharisaic Judaism. The story of his conversion is recounted for the third time in Acts in this speech (see the note on 9, 1–19).

26, 4: Among my people: that is, among the Jews.

26, 14: In Hebrew: see the note on 21, 40. **It is hard for you to kick against the goad:** this proverb is commonly found in Greek literature and in this context signifies the senselessness and ineffectiveness of any opposition to the divine influence in his life.

26, 16: The words of Jesus directed to Paul here reflect the dialogues between Christ and Ananias (9, 15) and between Ananias and Paul (22, 14–15) in the two previous accounts of Paul's conversion.

26, 18: To open their eyes: though no mention is made of Paul's blindness in this account (cf 9, 8–9.12.18; 22, 11–13), the task he is commissioned to perform is the removal of other people's spiritual blindness.

26, 22: Saying nothing different from what the prophets and Moses foretold: see the note on Lk 18, 31.

26, 23: That the Messiah must suffer: see the note on Lk 24, 26.

26, 26: Not done in a corner: for Luke, this Greek proverb expresses his belief that he is presenting a story about Jesus and the church that is already well known. As such, the entire history of Christianity is public knowledge and incontestable. Luke pres-

o Phil 3, 5–6; Gal 1, 13–14; 2 Cor 11, 22. p 23, 6; 24, 15.21; 28, 20. q 8, 3; 9, 1–2; 22, 19; Phil 3, 6. r 9, 14. s 9, 7. t 9, 3; 22, 6. u 9, 4; 22, 7. v 9, 5; 22, 8; Mt 25, 40. w 9, 6; 22, 10; Ez 2, 1. x Jer 1, 7. y Is 42, 7.16; 61, 1 LXX; Col 1, 13. z 21, 31. a 3, 18; Lk 24, 26–27.44–47. b Is 42, 6; 49, 6; Lk 2, 32; 1 Cor 15, 20–23.

for I cannot believe that [any] of this has escaped
his notice; this was not done in a corner.
27*King Agrippa, do you believe the prophets? I
know you believe." 28Then Agrippa said to Paul,
"You will soon persuade me to play the Chris-
tian." 29Paul replied, "I would pray to God that
sooner or later not only you but all who listen to
me today might become as I am except for these
chains."
30Then the king rose, and with him the
governor and Bernice and the others who sat
with them. 31*And after they had withdrawn
they said to one another, "This man is doing
nothing [at all] that deserves death or imprison-
ment." 32[c]And Agrippa said to Festus, "This
man could have been set free if he had not
appealed to Caesar."

CHAPTER 27

Departure for Rome 1*When it was decided
that we should sail to Italy, they handed Paul
and some other prisoners over to a centurion
named Julius of the Cohort Augusta. 2[d]We went
on board a ship from Adramyttium bound for
ports in the province of Asia and set sail.
Aristarchus, a Macedonian from Thessalonica,
was with us. 3On the following day we put in at
Sidon where Julius was kind enough to allow
Paul to visit his friends who took care of him.
4From there we put out to sea and sailed around
the sheltered side of Cyprus because of the
headwinds, 5and crossing the open sea off the
coast of Cilicia and Pamphylia we came to Myra
in Lycia.
Storm and Shipwreck 6There the centurion
found an Alexandrian ship that was sailing to
Italy and put us on board. 7For many days we
made little headway, arriving at Cnidus only
with difficulty, and because the wind would not
permit us to continue our course we sailed for
the sheltered side of Crete off Salmone. 8We
sailed past it with difficulty and reached a place
called Fair Havens, near which was the city of
Lasea.
9[e]*Much time had now passed and sailing
had become hazardous because the time of the
fast had already gone by, so Paul warned them,
10"Men, I can see that this voyage will result in
severe damage and heavy loss not only to the
cargo and the ship, but also to our lives." 11The
centurion, however, paid more attention to the
pilot and to the owner of the ship than to what
Paul said. 12Since the harbor was unfavorably
situated for spending the winter, the majority
planned to put out to sea from there in the hope
of reaching Phoenix, a port in Crete facing west-
northwest, there to spend the winter.
13A south wind blew gently, and thinking they
had attained their objective, they weighed an-
chor and sailed along close to the coast of Crete.
14Before long an offshore wind of hurricane
force called a "Northeaster" struck. 15Since the
ship was caught up in it and could not head into
the wind we gave way and let ourselves be
driven. 16We passed along the sheltered side of
an island named Cauda and managed only with
difficulty to get the dinghy under control. 17They
hoisted it aboard, then used cables to undergird
the ship. Because of their fear that they would
run aground on the shoal of Syrtis, they lowered
the drift anchor and were carried along in this
way. 18We were being pounded by the storm so
violently that the next day they jettisoned some
cargo, 19and on the third day with their own

ents his story in this way to provide "certainty" to his readers about the instructions they have received (Lk 1, 4).

26, 27–28: If the Christian missionaries proclaim nothing different from what the Old Testament prophets had proclaimed (22–23), then the logical outcome for the believing Jew, according to Luke, is to become a Christian.

26, 31–32: In recording the episode of Paul's appearance before Agrippa, Luke wishes to show that, when Paul's case was judged impartially, no grounds for legal action against him were found (see 23, 29; 25, 25).

27, 1—28, 16: Here Luke has written a stirring account of adventure on the high seas, incidental to his main purpose of showing how well Paul got along with his captors and how his prophetic influence saved the lives of all on board. The recital also establishes the existence of Christian communities in Puteoli and Rome. This account of the voyage and shipwreck also constitutes the final "we-section" in Acts (see the note on 16, 10–17).

27, 1: Cohort Augusta: the presence of a Cohort Augusta in Syria during the first century A.D. is attested in inscriptions. Whatever the historical background to this information given by Luke may be, the name Augusta serves to increase the prominence and prestige of the prisoner Paul whose custodians bear so important a Roman name.

27, 9: The time of the fast: the fast kept on the occasion of the Day of Atonement (Lv 16, 29–31), which occurred in late September or early October.

c 25, 11–12. d 19, 29; 20, 4. e Lv 16, 29–31.

hands they threw even the ship's tackle overboard. 20Neither the sun nor the stars were visible for many days, and no small storm raged. Finally, all hope of our surviving was taken away.

21When many would no longer eat, Paul stood among them and said, "Men, you should have taken my advice and not have set sail from Crete and you would have avoided this disastrous loss. 22I urge you now to keep up your courage; not one of you will be lost, only the ship. 23For last night an angel of the God to whom [I] belong and whom I serve stood by me 24f and said, 'Do not be afraid, Paul. You are destined to stand before Caesar; and behold, for your sake, God has granted safety to all who are sailing with you.' 25Therefore, keep up your courage, men; I trust in God that it will turn out as I have been told. 26We are destined to run aground on some island."

27On the fourteenth night, as we were still being driven about on the Adriatic Sea, toward midnight the sailors began to suspect that they were nearing land. 28They took soundings and found twenty fathoms; a little farther on, they again took soundings and found fifteen fathoms. 29Fearing that we would run aground on a rocky coast, they dropped four anchors from the stern and prayed for day to come. 30The sailors then tried to abandon ship; they lowered the dinghy to the sea on the pretext of going to lay out anchors from the bow. 31But Paul said to the centurion and the soldiers, "Unless these men stay with the ship, you cannot be saved." 32So the soldiers cut the ropes of the dinghy and set it adrift.

33Until the day began to dawn, Paul kept urging all to take some food. He said, "Today is the fourteenth day that you have been waiting, going hungry and eating nothing. 34I urge you, therefore, to take some food; it will help you survive. Not a hair of the head of anyone of you will be lost." 35 g*When he said this, he took bread, gave thanks to God in front of them all, broke it, and began to eat. 36They were all encouraged, and took some food themselves. 37In all, there were two hundred seventy-six of us on the ship. 38After they had eaten enough, they lightened the ship by throwing the wheat into the sea.

39When day came they did not recognize the land, but made out a bay with a beach. They planned to run the ship ashore on it, if they could. 40So they cast off the anchors and abandoned them to the sea, and at the same time they unfastened the lines of the rudders, and hoisting the foresail into the wind, they made for the beach. 41But they struck a sandbar and ran the ship aground. The bow was wedged in and could not be moved, but the stern began to break up under the pounding [of the waves]. 42The soldiers planned to kill the prisoners so that none might swim away and escape, 43but the centurion wanted to save Paul and so kept them from carrying out their plan. He ordered those who could swim to jump overboard first and get to the shore, 44and then the rest, some on planks, others on debris from the ship. In this way, all reached shore safely.

CHAPTER 28

Winter in Malta 1Once we had reached safety we learned that the island was called Malta. 2The natives showed us extraordinary hospitality; they lit a fire and welcomed all of us because it had begun to rain and was cold. 3Paul had gathered a bundle of brushwood and was putting it on the fire when a viper, escaping from the heat, fastened on his hand. 4*When the natives saw the snake hanging from his hand, they said to one another, "This man must certainly be a murderer; though he escaped the sea, Justice has not let him remain alive." 5But he shook the snake off into the fire and suffered no harm. 6 hThey were expecting him to swell up or suddenly to fall down dead but, after waiting a long time and seeing nothing unusual happen to him, they changed their minds and began to say that he was a god. 7In the vicinity of that place

27, 35: He took bread . . . : the words recall the traditional language of the celebration of the Eucharist (see Lk 22, 19).

28, 4: Justice: in Greek mythology, the pursuing goddess of vengeance and justice.

f 23, 11. g Mt 15, 36; Mk 6, 41; 8, 6; Lk 22, 19; 1 Cor 11, 23–24. h 14, 11.

were lands belonging to a man named Publius, the chief of the island. He welcomed us and received us cordially as his guests for three days. [8]It so happened that the father of Publius was sick with a fever and dysentery. Paul visited him and, after praying, laid his hands on him and healed him. [9]After this had taken place, the rest of the sick on the island came to Paul and were cured. [10]They paid us great honor and when we eventually set sail they brought us the provisions we needed.

Arrival in Rome [11]*Three months later we set sail on a ship that had wintered at the island. It was an Alexandrian ship with the Dioscuri as its figurehead. [12]We put in at Syracuse and stayed there three days, [13]and from there we sailed round the coast and arrived at Rhegium. After a day, a south wind came up and in two days we reached Puteoli. [14]There we found some brothers and were urged to stay with them for seven days. And thus we came to Rome. [15]The brothers from there heard about us and came as far as the Forum of Appius and Three Taverns to meet us. On seeing them, Paul gave thanks to God and took courage. [16]*When he entered Rome, Paul was allowed to live by himself, with the soldier who was guarding him.

Testimony to Jews in Rome [17][i]*Three days later he called together the leaders of the Jews. When they had gathered he said to them, "My brothers, although I had done nothing against our people or our ancestral customs, I was handed over to the Romans as a prisoner from Jerusalem. [18][j]After trying my case the Romans wanted to release me, because they found nothing against me deserving the death penalty. [19][k]But when the Jews objected, I was obliged to appeal to Caesar, even though I had no accusation to make against my own nation. [20][l]*This is the reason, then, I have requested to see you and to speak with you, for it is on account of the hope of Israel that I wear these chains." [21]They answered him, "We have received no letters from Judea about you, nor has any of the brothers arrived with a damaging report or rumor about you. [22][m]But we should like to hear you present your views, for we know that this sect is denounced everywhere."

[23]So they arranged a day with him and came to his lodgings in great numbers. From early morning until evening, he expounded his position to them, bearing witness to the kingdom of God and trying to convince them about Jesus from the law of Moses and the prophets. [24]Some were convinced by what he had said, while others did not believe. [25]*Without reaching any agreement among themselves they began to leave; then Paul made one final statement. "Well did the holy Spirit speak to your ancestors through the prophet Isaiah, saying:

[26][n]'Go to this people and say:
You shall indeed hear but not understand.
You shall indeed look but never see.
[27]Gross is the heart of this people;
they will not hear with their ears;
they have closed their eyes,
so they may not see with their eyes
and hear with their ears
and understand with their heart and be
converted,
and I heal them.'

[28][o]Let it be known to you that this salvation of

28, 11: **Dioscuri:** that is, the Twin Brothers, Castor and Pollux, the sons of Zeus and the patrons of the sailors.

28, 16: With Paul's arrival in Rome, the programmatic spread of the word of the Lord to "the ends of the earth" (1, 8) is accomplished. In Rome, Paul is placed under house arrest, and under this mild form of custody he is allowed to proclaim the word in the capital of the civilized world of his day.

28, 17–22: Paul's first act in Rome is to learn from the leaders of the Jewish community whether the Jews of Jerusalem plan to pursue their case against him before the Roman jurisdiction. He is informed that no such plan is afoot, but that the Jews of Rome have heard the Christian teaching denounced. Paul's offer to explain it to them is readily accepted.

28, 20: **The hope of Israel:** in the words of Paul (23, 6), Luke has identified this hope as hope in the resurrection of the dead.

28, 25–28: Paul's final words in Acts reflect a major concern of Luke's writings: how the salvation promised in the Old Testament, accomplished by Jesus, and offered first to Israel (13, 26), has now been offered to and accepted by the Gentiles. Quoting Is 6, 9–10, Paul presents the scriptural support for his indictment of his fellow Jews who refuse to accept the message he proclaims. Their rejection leads to its proclamation among the Gentiles.

i 24, 12–13; 25, 8. j 23, 29; 25, 25; 26, 31–32. k 25, 11. l 23, 6; 24, 15.21; 26, 6–8. m 24, 5.14. n Is 6, 9–10; Mt 13, 14–15; Mk 4, 12; Lk 8, 10; Jn 12, 40; Rom 11, 8. o 13, 46; 18, 6; Ps 67, 2; Is 40, 5 LXX; Lk 3, 6.

God has been sent to the Gentiles; they will listen." [29]*

30 *He remained for two full years in his lodgings. He received all who came to him,
31 and with complete assurance and without hindrance he proclaimed the kingdom of God and taught about the Lord Jesus Christ.

28, 29: The Western text has added here a verse that is not found in the best Greek manuscripts: "And when he had said this, the Jews left, seriously arguing among themselves."

28, 30–31: Although the ending of Acts may seem to be abrupt, Luke has now completed his story with the establishment of Paul and the proclamation of Christianity in Rome. Paul's confident and unhindered proclamation of the gospel in Rome forms the climax to the story whose outline was provided in 1, 8: "You will be my witnesses in Jerusalem . . . and to the ends of the earth."

NEW TESTAMENT LETTERS

In the New Testament canon, between the Acts of the Apostles and Revelation, there are twenty-one documents that take the form of letters or epistles. Most of these are actual letters, but some are more like treatises in the guise of letters. In a few cases even some of the more obvious elements of the letter form are absent; see the Introductions to Hebrews and to 1 John.

The virtually standard form found in these documents, though with some variation, is dependent upon the conventions of letter writing common in the ancient world, but these were modified to suit the purposes of Christian writers. The New Testament letters usually begin with a greeting including an identification of the sender or senders and of the recipients. Next comes a prayer, usually in the form of a thanksgiving. The body of the letter provides an exposition of Christian teaching, usually provoked by concrete circumstances, and generally also draws conclusions regarding ethical behavior. There often follows a discussion of practical matters, such as the writer's travel plans, and the letter concludes with further advice and a formula of farewell.

Fourteen of the twenty-one letters have been traditionally attributed to Paul. One of these, the Letter to the Hebrews, does not itself claim to be the work of Paul; when it was accepted into the canon after much discussion, it was attached at the very end of the Pauline corpus. The other thirteen identify Paul as their author, but most scholars believe that some of them were actually written by his disciples; see the Introductions to Ephesians, Colossians, 2 Thessalonians, and 1 Timothy.

Four of the letters in the Pauline corpus (Ephesians, Philippians, Colossians, and Philemon) are called the "Captivity Epistles" because in each of them the author speaks of being in prison at the time of writing. Three others (1–2 Timothy and Titus) are known as the "Pastoral Epistles" because, addressed to individuals rather than communities, they give advice to disciples about caring for the flock. The letters of the Pauline corpus are arranged in roughly descending order of length from Romans to Philemon, with Hebrews added at the end.

The other seven letters of the New Testament that follow the Pauline corpus are collectively referred to as the "Catholic Epistles." This term, which means "universal," refers to the fact that most of them are directed not to a single Christian community, as are most of the Pauline letters, but to a wider audience; see the Introduction to the catholic letters. Three of them (1–2–3 John) are closely related to the fourth gospel and thus belong to the Johannine corpus. The catholic letters, like those of the Pauline corpus, are also arranged in roughly descending order of length, but the three Johannine letters are kept together and Jude is placed at the end.

The genuine letters of Paul are earlier in date than any of our written gospels. The dates of the other New Testament letters are more difficult to determine, but for the most part they belong to the second and third Christian generations rather than to the first.

THE LETTER TO THE ROMANS

Of all the letters of Paul, that to the Christians at Rome has long held pride of place. It is the longest and most systematic unfolding of the apostle's thought, expounding the gospel of God's righteousness that saves all who believe (1, 16-17); it reflects a universal outlook, with special implications for Israel's relation to the church (chs 9—11). Yet, like all Paul's letters, Romans too arose out of a specific situation, when the apostle wrote from Greece, likely Corinth, between A.D. 56 and 58 (cf Acts 20, 2-3).

Paul at that time was about to leave for Jerusalem with a collection of funds for the impoverished Jewish Christian believers there, taken up from his predominantly Gentile congregations (15, 25-27). He planned then to travel on to Rome and to enlist support there for a mission to Spain (15, 24.28). Such a journey had long been on his mind (1, 9-13; 15, 23). Now, with much missionary preaching successfully accomplished in the East (15, 19), he sought new opportunities in the West (15, 20-21), in order to complete the divine plan of evangelization in the Roman world. Yet he recognized that the visit to Jerusalem would be hazardous (15, 30-32), and we know from Acts that Paul was arrested there and came to Rome only in chains, as a prisoner (Acts 21—28, especially 21, 30-33 and 28, 14.30-31).

The existence of a Christian community in Rome antedates Paul's letter there. When it arose, likely within the sizable Jewish population at Rome, and how, we do not know. The Roman historian Suetonius mentions an edict of the Emperor Claudius about A.D. 49 ordering the expulsion of Jews from Rome in connection with a certain "Chrestus," probably involving a dispute in the Jewish community over Jesus as the Messiah ("Christus"). According to Acts 18, 2, Aquila and Priscilla (or Prisca, as in Rom 16, 3) were among those driven out; from them, in Corinth, Paul may have learned about conditions in the church at Rome.

Opinions vary as to whether Jewish or Gentile Christians predominated in the house churches (cf 16, 5) in the capital city of the empire at the time Paul wrote. Perhaps already by then Gentile Christians were in the majority. Paul speaks in Romans of both Jews and Gentiles (3, 9.29; see the note on 1, 14). The letter also refers to those "weak in faith" (14, 1) and those "who are strong" (15, 1); this terminology may reflect not so much differences between believers of Jewish and of Gentile background, respectively, as an ascetic tendency in some converts (14, 2) combined with Jewish laws about clean and unclean foods (14, 14.20). The issues were similar to problems that Paul had faced in Corinth (1 Cor 8). If Romans 16 is part of the letter to Rome (see the note on 16, 1-23), then Paul had considerable information about conditions in Rome through all these people there whom he knew, and our letter does not just reflect a generalized picture of an earlier situation in Corinth.

In any case, Paul writes to introduce himself and his message to the Christians at Rome, seeking to enlist their support for the proposed mission to Spain. He therefore employs formulations likely familiar to the Christians at Rome; see the note on the confessional material at 1, 3-4 and compare 3, 25-26 and 4, 25. He cites the Old Testament frequently (1, 17; 3, 10-18; ch 4; 9, 7.12-13.15.17.25- 29.33; 10, 5-13.15-21; 15, 9-12). The gospel Paul presents is meant to be a familiar one to those in Rome, even though they heard it first from other preachers.

As the outline below shows, this gospel of Paul (see 16, 25) finds its center in salvation and justification through faith in Christ (1, 16-17). While God's wrath is revealed against all sin and wickedness of Gentile and Jew alike (1, 18—3, 20), God's power to save by divine righteous or justifying action in Christ is also revealed (1, 16-17; 3, 21—5, 21). The consequences and implications for those who believe are set forth (6, 1—8, 39), as are results for those in Israel (chs 9—11) who, to Paul's great sorrow (9, 1-5), disbelieve. The apostle's hope is that, just as rejection of the gospel by some in Israel has led to a ministry of salvation for non-Jews, so one day, in God's mercy, "all Israel" will be saved (11, 11-15.25-29.30-32). The fuller ethical response of believers is also drawn out, both with reference to life in Christ's body (ch 12) and with regard to the world (13, 1-7), on the basis of the eschatological situation (13, 11–14) and conditions in the community (14, 1—15, 13).

Others have viewed Romans more in the light of Paul's earlier, quite polemical Letter to the Galatians and so see the theme as the relationship between Judaism and Christianity, a topic judged to be much in the minds of the Roman Christians. Each of these religious faiths claimed to be the way of salvation based upon a covenant between God and a people chosen and made the beneficiary of divine gifts. But Christianity regarded itself as the prophetic development and fulfillment of the faith of the Old Testament, declaring that the preparatory Mosaic covenant must now give way to the new and more perfect covenant in Jesus Christ. Paul himself had been the implacable advocate of freedom of Gentiles from the laws of the Mosaic covenant and, especially in Galatia, had refused to allow attempts to impose them on Gentile converts to the gospel. He had witnessed the personal hostilities that developed between the adherents of the two faiths and had written his strongly worded letter to the Galatians against those Jewish Christians who were seeking to persuade Gentile Christians to adopt the religious practices of Judaism. For him, the purity of the religious understanding of Jesus as the source of salvation would be seriously impaired if Gentile Christians were obligated to amalgamate the two religious faiths.

Still others find the theme of Israel and the church as expressed in Romans 9—11 to be the heart of Romans. Then the implication of Paul's exposition of justification by faith rather than by means of law is that the divine plan of salvation works itself out on a broad theological plane to include the whole of humanity, despite the differences in the content of the given religious system to which a human culture is heir. Romans presents a plan of salvation stretching from Adam through Abraham and Moses to Christ (chs 4 and 5) and on to the future revelation at Christ's parousia (8, 18-25). Its outlook is universal.

Paul's Letter to the Romans is a powerful exposition of the doctrine of the supremacy of Christ and of faith in Christ as the source of salvation. It is an implicit plea to the Christians at Rome, and to all Christians, to hold fast to that faith. They are to resist any pressure put on them to accept a doctrine of salvation through works of the law (see the note on 10, 4). At the same time they are not to exaggerate Christian freedom as an abdication of responsibility for others (12, 1-2) or as a repudiation of God's law and will (see the notes on 3, 9-26; 3, 31; 7, 7-12.13-25).

The principal divisions of the Letter to the Romans are the following:

I. Address (1, 1-15)
II. Humanity Lost without the Gospel (1, 16—3, 20)
III. Justification through Faith in Christ (3, 21—5, 21)
IV. Justification and the Christian Life (6, 1—8, 39)
V. Jews and Gentiles in God's Plan (9, 1—11, 36)
VI. The Duties of Christians (12, 1—15, 13)
VII. Conclusion (15, 14—16, 27)

I: Address

CHAPTER 1

Greeting 1 [a]*Paul, a slave of Christ Jesus, called
to be an apostle and set apart for the gospel of
God, 2 [b]which he promised previously through
his prophets in the holy scriptures, 3 [c]*the gospel
about his Son, descended from David according
to the flesh, 4 [d]but established as Son of God in
power according to the spirit of holiness through
resurrection from the dead, Jesus Christ our
Lord. 5 [e]*Through him we have received the
grace of apostleship, to bring about the obedi-
ence of faith, for the sake of his name, among all
the Gentiles, 6 [f]among whom are you also, who
are called to belong to Jesus Christ; 7 [g]*to all the
beloved of God in Rome, called to be holy. Grace
to you and peace from God our Father and the
Lord Jesus Christ.

Thanksgiving 8 [h]*First, I give thanks to my
God through Jesus Christ for all of you, because
your faith is heralded throughout the world.
9 [i]God is my witness, whom I serve with my
spirit in proclaiming the gospel of his Son, that I
remember you constantly, 10 [j]*always asking in
my prayers that somehow by God's will I may at
last find my way clear to come to you. 11 [k]For I
long to see you, that I may share with you some
spiritual gift so that you may be strengthened,
12 that is, that you and I may be mutually
encouraged by one another's faith, yours and
mine. 13 [l]*I do not want you to be unaware,
brothers, that I often planned to come to you,
though I was prevented until now, that I might
harvest some fruit among you, too, as among the
rest of the Gentiles. 14 *To Greeks and non-
Greeks alike, to the wise and the ignorant, I am

1, 1–7: In Paul's letters the greeting or **praescriptio** follows a standard form, though with variations. It is based upon the common Greco-Roman epistolary practice, but with the addition of Semitic and specifically Christian elements. The three basic components are: name of sender; name of addressee; greeting. In identifying himself, Paul often adds phrases to describe his apostolic mission; this element is more developed in Rom than in any other letter. Elsewhere he associates co-workers with himself in the greeting: Sosthenes (1 Cor), Timothy (2 Cor; Phil; Phlm), Silvanus (1–2 Thes). The standard secular greeting was the infinitive **chairein,** "greetings." Paul uses instead the similar-sounding **charis,** "grace," together with the Semitic greeting **šālôm** (Greek **eirēnē**), "peace." These gifts, foreshadowed in God's dealings with Israel (see Nm 6, 24–26), have been poured out abundantly in Christ, and Paul wishes them to his readers. In Rom the Pauline **praescriptio** is expanded and expressed in a formal tone; it emphasizes Paul's office as apostle to the Gentiles. Verses 3–4 stress the gospel or kerygma, v 2 the fulfillment of God's promise, and vv 1 and 5 Paul's office. On his call, see Gal 1, 15–16; 1 Cor 9, 1; 15, 8–10; Acts 9, 1–22; 22, 3–16; 26, 4–18.

1, 1: Slave of Christ Jesus: Paul applies the term slave to himself in order to express his undivided allegiance to the Lord of the church, the Master of all, including slaves and masters. "No one can serve (i.e., be a slave to) two masters," said Jesus (Mt 6, 24). It is this aspect of the slave-master relationship rather than its degrading implications that Paul emphasizes when he discusses Christian commitment.

1, 3–4: Paul here cites an early confession that proclaims Jesus' sonship as messianic descendant of David (cf Mt 22, 42; 2 Tm 2, 8; Rv 22, 16) and as Son of God by the resurrection. As "life-giving spirit" (1 Cor 15, 45), Jesus Christ is able to communicate the Spirit to those who believe in him.

1, 5: Paul recalls his apostolic office, implying that the Romans know something of his history. **The obedience of faith:** as Paul will show at length in chs 6–8 and 12–15, faith in God's justifying action in Jesus Christ relates one to God's gift of the new life that is made possible through the death and resurrection of Jesus Christ and the activity of the holy Spirit (see especially 8, 1–11).

1, 7: Called to be holy: Paul often refers to Christians as "the holy ones" or "the saints." The Israelite community was called a "holy assembly" because they had been separated for the worship and service of the Lord (see Lv 11, 44; 23, 1–44). The Christian community regarded its members as sanctified by baptism (6, 22; 15, 16; 1 Cor 6, 11; Eph 5, 26–27). Christians are called to holiness (1 Cor 1, 2; 1 Thes 4, 7), that is, they are called to make their lives conform to the gift they have already received.

1, 8: In Greco-Roman letters, the greeting was customarily followed by a prayer. The Pauline letters usually include this element (except Gal and Ti), expressed in Christian thanksgiving formulas and usually stating the principal theme of the letter. In 2 Cor the thanksgiving becomes a blessing, and in Eph it is preceded by a lengthy blessing. Sometimes the thanksgiving is blended into the body of the letter, especially in 1 Thes. In Rom it is stated briefly.

1, 10–12: Paul lays the groundwork for his more detailed statement in 15, 22–24 about his projected visit to Rome.

1, 13: Brothers is idiomatic for all Paul's "kin in Christ," all those who believe in the gospel; it includes women as well as men (cf 4, 3).

1, 14: Greeks and non-Greeks: literally, "Greeks and barbarians." As a result of Alexander's conquests, Greek became the standard international language of the Mediterranean world. **Greeks** in Paul's statement therefore means people who know Greek or who have been influenced by Greek culture. **Non-Greeks** were people whose cultures remained substantially unaffected by Greek influences. Greeks called such people "barbarians" (cf Acts 28, 2), meaning people whose speech was foreign. Roman citizens would scarcely classify themselves as such, and Nero, who was reigning when Paul wrote this letter, prided himself on his admiration for Greek culture. **Under obligation:** Paul will expand on the theme of obligation in 13, 8; 15, 1.27.

a Gal 1, 10; Phil 1, 1; Jas 1, 1 / Acts 9, 15; 13, 2; 1 Cor 1, 1; Gal 1, 15; Ti 1, 1. b 16, 25–26; Ti 1, 2. c 9, 5; 2 Sm 7, 12; Mt 1, 1; Mk 12, 35; Jn 7, 42; Acts 13, 22–23;2 Tm 2, 8; Rv 22, 16. d 10, 9; Acts 13, 33; Phil 3, 10. e 15, 15; Gal 2, 7.9 / 15, 18; Acts 9, 15; 26, 16–18; Gal 1, 16; 2, 7.9. f 1 Cor 1, 9. g Nm 6, 25–26; 1 Cor 1, 2–3; 2 Cor 1, 1–2. h 16, 19; 1 Thes 1, 8. i 2 Cor 1, 23; Eph 1, 16; Phil 1, 8; 1 Thes 1, 2; 2, 5.10;2 Tm 1, 3. j 15, 23.32; Acts 18, 21; 1 Cor 4, 19; 1 Thes 2, 17. k 1 Thes 2, 17; 3, 10. l 15, 22; Jn 15, 16; Acts 19, 21.

under obligation; [15] [m]that is why I am eager to preach the gospel also to you in Rome.

II: Humanity Lost Without the Gospel

God's Power for Salvation [16] [n]*For I am not ashamed of the gospel. It is the power of God for the salvation of everyone who believes: for Jew first, and then Greek. [17] [o]*For in it is revealed the righteousness of God from faith to faith; as it is written, "The one who is righteous by faith will live."

Punishment of Idolators [18] [p]*The wrath of God is indeed being revealed from heaven against every impiety and wickedness of those who suppress the truth by their wickedness. [19] [q]For what can be known about God is evident to them, because God made it evident to them. [20] [r]Ever since the creation of the world, his invisible attributes of eternal power and divinity have been able to be understood and perceived in what he has made. As a result, they have no excuse; [21] [s]for although they knew God they did not accord him glory as God or give him thanks. Instead, they became vain in their reasoning, and their senseless minds were darkened. [22] [t]While claiming to be wise, they became fools [23] [u]and exchanged the glory of the immortal God for the likeness of an image of mortal man or of birds or of four-legged animals or of snakes.

[24] [v]*Therefore, God handed them over to impurity through the lusts of their hearts for the mutual degradation of their bodies. [25] [w]They exchanged the truth of God for a lie and revered and worshiped the creature rather than the creator, who is blessed forever. Amen. [26]Therefore, God handed them over to degrading passions. Their females exchanged natural relations for unnatural, [27] [x]and the males likewise gave up natural relations with females and burned with lust for one another. Males did shameful things with males and thus received in their own persons the due penalty for their perversity. [28]And since they did not see fit to acknowledge God, God handed them over to their undiscerning mind to do what is improper. [29] [y]They are filled with every form of wickedness, evil, greed, and malice; full of envy, murder, rivalry, treachery, and spite. They are gossips [30]and scandalmongers and they hate God. They are inso-

1, 16–17: The principal theme of the letter is salvation through faith. **I am not ashamed of the gospel:** Paul is not ashamed to proclaim the gospel, despite the criticism that Jews and Gentiles leveled against the proclamation of the crucified savior; cf 1 Cor 1, 23–24. Paul affirms, however, that it is precisely through the crucifixion and resurrection of Jesus that God's saving will and power become manifest. **Jew first** (cf 2, 9–10) means that Jews especially, in view of the example of Abraham (ch 4), ought to be the leaders in the response of faith.

1, 17: In it is revealed the righteousness of God from faith to faith: the gospel centers in Jesus Christ, in whom God's saving presence and righteousness in history have been made known. Faith is affirmation of the basic purpose and meaning of the Old Testament as proclamation of divine promise (2; 4, 13) and exposure of the inability of humanity to effect its salvation even through covenant law. Faith is the gift of the holy Spirit and denotes acceptance of salvation as God's righteousness, that is, God's gift of a renewed relationship in forgiveness and power for a new life. Faith is response to God's total claim on people and their destiny. **The one who is righteous by faith will live:** see the note on Hb 2, 4.

1, 18—3, 20: Paul aims to show that all humanity is in a desperate plight and requires God's special intervention if it is to be saved.

1, 18–32: In this passage Paul uses themes and rhetoric common in Jewish-Hellenistic mission proclamation (cf Wis 13, 1—14, 31) to indict especially the non-Jewish world. The close association of idolatry and immorality is basic, but the generalization needs in all fairness to be balanced against the fact that non-Jewish Christian society on many levels displayed moral attitudes and performance whose quality would challenge much of contemporary Christian culture. Romans themselves expressed abhorrence over devotion accorded to animals in Egypt. Paul's main point is that the wrath of God does not await the end of the world but goes into action at each present moment in humanity's history when misdirected piety serves as a facade for self-interest.

1, 18: The wrath of God: God's reaction to human sinfulness, an Old Testament phrase that expresses the irreconcilable opposition between God and evil (see Is 9, 11.16.18.20; 10, 4; 30, 27). It is not contrary to God's universal love for his creatures, but condemns Israel's turning aside from the covenant obligations. Hosea depicts Yahweh as suffering intensely at the thought of having to punish Israel (Hos 11, 8–9). God's wrath was to be poured forth especially on the "Day of Yahweh" and thus took on an eschatological connotation (see Zep 1, 15).

1, 24: In order to expose the depth of humanity's rebellion against the Creator, **God handed them over to impurity through the lusts of their hearts.** Instead of curbing people's evil interests, God abandoned them to self-indulgence, thereby removing the facade of apparent conformity to the divine will. Subsequently Paul will show that the Mosaic law produces the same effect; cf 5, 20; 7, 13–24. The divine judgment expressed here is related to the theme of hardness of heart described in 9, 17–18.

m Acts 28, 30–31. n Ps 119, 46; 1 Cor 1, 18.24 / 2, 9; Acts 3, 26; 13, 46. o 3, 21–22; Hb 2, 4; Gal 3, 11; Heb 10, 38. p 2, 5.8–9; Is 66, 15; Eph 5, 6; Col 3, 6. q Wis 13–19; Acts 14, 15–17; 17, 23–29. r Jb 12, 7–9; Pss 8, 4; 19, 2; Sir 17, 7–9; Is 40, 26; Acts 14, 17;17, 25–28. s Eph 4, 17–18. t Wis 13, 1–9; Is 5, 21; Jer 10, 14; Acts 17, 29–30;1 Cor 1, 19–21. u Dt 4, 15–19; Ps 106, 20; Wis 11, 15; 12, 24; 13, 10–19; Jer 2, 11. v Wis 12, 25; 14, 22–31; Acts 7, 41–42; Eph 4, 19. w 9, 5; Jer 13, 25–27. x Lv 18, 22; 20, 13; Wis 14, 26; 1 Cor 6, 9; 1 Tm 1, 10. y 13, 13; Mt 15, 19; Mk 7, 21–22; Gal 5, 19–21; 2 Tm 3, 2–4.

lent, haughty, boastful, ingenious in their wickedness, and rebellious toward their parents. 31 They are senseless, faithless, heartless, ruthless. 32 [z]Although they know the just decree of God that all who practice such things deserve death, they not only do them but give approval to those who practice them.

CHAPTER 2

God's Just Judgment 1 [a]*Therefore, you are without excuse, every one of you who passes judgment. For by the standard by which you judge another you condemn yourself, since you, the judge, do the very same things. 2 We know that the judgment of God on those who do such things is true. 3 [b]Do you suppose, then, you who judge those who engage in such things and yet do them yourself, that you will escape the judgment of God? 4 [c]Or do you hold his priceless kindness, forbearance, and patience in low esteem, unaware that the kindness of God would lead you to repentance? 5 [d]By your stubbornness and impenitent heart, you are storing up wrath for yourself for the day of wrath and revelation of the just judgment of God, 6 [e]*who will repay everyone according to his works: 7 eternal life to those who seek glory, honor, and immortality through perseverance in good works, 8 [f]but wrath and fury to those who selfishly disobey the truth and obey wickedness. 9 Yes, affliction and distress will come upon every human being who does evil, Jew first and then Greek. 10 [g]But there will be glory, honor, and peace for everyone who does good, Jew first and then Greek. 11 [h]*There is no partiality with God.

Judgment by the Interior Law 12 [i]*All who sin outside the law will also perish without reference to it, and all who sin under the law will be judged in accordance with it. 13 [j]For it is not those who hear the law who are just in the sight of God; rather, those who observe the law will be justified. 14 [k]For when the Gentiles who do not have the law by nature observe the prescriptions of the law, they are a law for themselves even though they do not have the law. 15 *They show that the demands of the law are written in their hearts, while their conscience also bears witness and their conflicting thoughts accuse or even defend them 16 [l]on the day when, according to my gospel, God will judge people's hidden works through Christ Jesus.

Judgment by the Mosaic Law 17 [m]*Now if you call yourself a Jew and rely on the law and boast of God 18 [n]and know his will and are able to discern what is important since you are instructed from the law, 19 [o]and if you are confident that you are a guide for the blind and a light for those in darkness, 20 [p]that you are a trainer of the foolish and teacher of the simple, because in the law you have the formulation of knowledge and truth— 21 [q]then you who teach another, are you failing to teach yourself? You who preach against stealing, do you steal? 22 You

2, 1—3, 20: After his general indictment of the Gentile, Paul shows that in spite of special revelation Jews enjoy no advantage in moral status before God (3, 1–8). With the entire human race now declared guilty before God (3, 9–20), Paul will then be able to display the solution for the total problem: salvation through God's redemptive work that is revealed in Christ Jesus for all who believe (3, 21–31).

2, 1–11: As a first step in his demonstration that Jews enjoy no real moral supremacy over Gentiles, Paul explains that the final judgment will be a review of performance, not of privilege. From this perspective Gentiles stand on an equal footing with Jews, and Jews cannot condemn the sins of Gentiles without condemning themselves.

2, 6: Will repay everyone according to his works: Paul reproduces the Septuagint text of Ps 62, 12 and Prv 24, 12.

2, 11: No partiality with God: this sentence is not at variance with the statements in vv 9–10. Since Jews are the first to go under indictment, it is only fair that they be given first consideration in the distribution of blessings. Basic, of course, is the understanding that God accepts no bribes (Dt 10, 17).

2, 12–16: Jews cannot reasonably demand from Gentiles the standard of conduct inculcated in the Old Testament since God did not address its revelation to them. Rather, God made it possible for Gentiles to know instinctively the difference between right and wrong. But, as Paul explained in 1, 18–32, humanity misread the evidence of God's existence, power, and divinity, and "while claiming to be wise, they became fools" (1, 22).

2, 15: Paul expands on the thought of Jer 31, 33; Wis 17, 11.

2, 17–29: Mere possession of laws is no evidence of virtue. By eliminating circumcision as an elitist moral sign, Paul clears away the last obstacle to his presentation of justification through faith without claims based on the receipt of circumcision and its attendant legal obligations.

z Acts 8, 1; 2 Thes 2, 12. a Mt 7, 1–2. b Wis 16, 15–16. c 3, 25–26; 9, 22; Wis 11, 23; 15, 1; 2 Pt 3, 9.15. d Ex 33, 3; Acts 7, 51; Rv 6, 17; 11, 18. e Ps 62, 12; Prv 24, 12; Sir 16, 14; Mt 16, 27; Jn 5, 29;2 Cor 5, 10. f 2 Thes 1, 8. g 1, 16; 3, 9. h Dt 10, 17; 2 Chr 19, 7; Sir 35, 12–13; Acts 10, 34; Gal 2, 6; Eph 6, 9; Col 3, 25; 1 Pt 1, 17. i 3, 19. j Mt 7, 21; Lk 6, 46–49; 8, 21; Jas 1, 22–25; 1 Jn 3, 7. k Acts 10, 35. l Acts 10, 42; 17, 31. m Is 48, 1–2; Mi 3, 11; Phil 3, 4–6. n Phil 1, 10. o Mt 15, 14; Lk 6, 39. p 2 Tm 3, 15. q Ps 50, 16–21; Mt 23, 3–4.

who forbid adultery, do you commit adultery?
You who detest idols, do you rob temples? 23You
who boast of the law, do you dishonor God by
breaking the law? 24 r*For, as it is written,
"Because of you the name of God is reviled
among the Gentiles."

25 s tCircumcision, to be sure, has value if you
observe the law; but if you break the law, your
circumcision has become uncircumcision.
26 uAgain, if an uncircumcised man keeps the
precepts of the law, will he not be considered
circumcised? 27Indeed, those who are physically
uncircumcised but carry out the law will pass
judgment on you, with your written law and
circumcision, who break the law. 28 vOne is not a
Jew outwardly. True circumcision is not out-
ward, in the flesh. 29 wRather, one is a Jew
inwardly, and circumcision is of the heart, in the
spirit, not the letter; his praise is not from
human beings but from God.

CHAPTER 3

Answers to Objections 1*What advantage is
there then in being a Jew? Or what is the value
of circumcision? 2 xMuch, in every respect. [For]
in the first place, they were entrusted with the
utterances of God. 3 yWhat if some were unfaith-
ful? Will their infidelity nullify the fidelity of
God? 4 z*Of course not! God must be true,
though every human being is a liar, as it is
written:

"That you may be justified in your words,
and conquer when you are judged."

5 aBut if our wickedness provides proof of God's
righteousness, what can we say? Is God unjust,
humanly speaking, to inflict his wrath? 6Of
course not! For how else is God to judge the
world? 7But if God's truth redounds to his glory
through my falsehood, why am I still being
condemned as a sinner? 8 bAnd why not say—as
we are accused and as some claim we say—that
we should do evil that good may come of it?
Their penalty is what they deserve.

Universal Bondage to Sin 9 c*Well, then, are
we better off? Not entirely, for we have already
brought the charge against Jews and Greeks alike
that they are all under the domination of sin,
10 das it is written:

"There is no one just, not one,
11 there is no one who understands,
there is no one who seeks God.
12 All have gone astray; all alike are worthless;
there is not one who does good,
[there is not] even one.
13 eTheir throats are open graves;
they deceive with their tongues;
the venom of asps is on their lips;
14 ftheir mouths are full of bitter cursing.
15 gTheir feet are quick to shed blood;
16 ruin and misery are in their ways,
17 and the way of peace they know not.
18 hThere is no fear of God before their eyes."

19 i*Now we know that what the law says is
addressed to those under the law, so that every
mouth may be silenced and the whole world
stand accountable to God, 20 j*since no human

2, 24: According to Is 52, 5 the suffering of Israel prompts her enemies to revile God. Paul uses the passage in support of his point that the present immorality of Israelites is the cause of such defamation.

3, 1–4: In keeping with the popular style of diatribe, Paul responds to the objection that his teaching on the sinfulness of all humanity detracts from the religious prerogatives of Israel. He stresses that Jews have remained the vehicle of God's revelation despite their sins, though this depends on the fidelity of God.

3, 4: Though every human being is a liar: these words reproduce the Greek text of Ps 116, 11. The rest of the verse is from Ps 51, 6.

3, 9–20: Well, then, are we better off?: this phrase can also be translated "Are we at a disadvantage?" but the latter version does not substantially change the overall meaning of the passage. Having explained that Israel's privileged status is guaranteed by God's fidelity, Paul now demonstrates the infidelity of the Jews by a catena of citations from scripture, possibly derived from an existing collection of **testimonia.** These texts show that all human beings share the common burden of sin. They are linked together by mention of organs of the body: throat, tongue, lips, mouth, feet, eyes.

3, 19: The law: Paul here uses the term in its broadest sense to mean all of the scriptures; none of the preceding texts is from the Torah or Pentateuch.

3, 20: No human being will be justified in his sight: these

r Is 52, 5; Ez 36, 20; 2 Pt 2, 2. s Jer 4, 4; 9, 24–25. t 1 Cor 7, 19; Gal 5, 3. u Gal 5, 6. v Jn 7, 24; 8, 15.39. w Dt 30, 6; Jer 4, 4; 9, 25; Col 2, 11 / 1 Cor 4, 5; 2 Cor 10, 18. x 9, 4; Dt 4, 7–8; Pss 103, 7; 147, 19–20. y 9, 6; 11, 1.29; Ps 89, 30–37; 2 Tm 2, 13. z Ps 116, 11 / Ps 51, 6. a 9, 14; Jb 34, 12–17. b 6, 1. c 1, 18—2, 25; 3, 23; Sir 8, 5. d Pss 14, 1–3; 53, 2–4; Eccl 7, 20. e Pss 5, 10; 140, 4. f Ps 10, 7. g Prv 1, 16; Is 59, 7–8. h Ps 36, 2. i 7, 7. j Ps 143, 2; Gal 2, 16 / 7, 7.

being will be justified in his sight by observing
the law; for through the law comes conscious-
ness of sin.

III: Justification Through Faith in Christ

Justification apart from the Law 21 k*But
now the righteousness of God has been mani-
fested apart from the law, though testified to by
the law and the prophets, 22 l the righteousness
of God through faith in Jesus Christ for all who
believe. For there is no distinction; 23 m all have
sinned and are deprived of the glory of God.
24 n They are justified freely by his grace through
the redemption in Christ Jesus, 25 o*whom God
set forth as an expiation, through faith, by his
blood, to prove his righteousness because of the
forgiveness of sins previously committed,
26 through the forbearance of God—to prove his
righteousness in the present time, that he might
be righteous and justify the one who has faith in
Jesus.
27 p*What occasion is there then for boasting?
It is ruled out. On what principle, that of works?
No, rather on the principle of faith. 28 q For we
consider that a person is justified by faith apart
from works of the law. 29 r Does God belong to
Jews alone? Does he not belong to Gentiles, too?
Yes, also to Gentiles, 30 s for God is one and will
justify the circumcised on the basis of faith and
the uncircumcised through faith. 31 t*Are we
then annulling the law by this faith? Of course
not! On the contrary, we are supporting the law.

CHAPTER 4

Abraham Justified by Faith 1 u*What then
can we say that Abraham found, our ancestor
according to the flesh? 2*Indeed, if Abraham
was justified on the basis of his works, he has
reason to boast; but this was not so in the sight
of God. 3 v*For what does the scripture say?
"Abraham believed God, and it was credited to
him as righteousness." 4 w A worker's wage is
credited not as a gift, but as something due. 5 But
when one does not work, yet believes in the one
who justifies the ungodly, his faith is credited as

words are freely cited from Ps 143, 2. In place of the psalmist's "no living person," Paul substitutes "no human being" (literally "no flesh," a Hebraism), and he adds "by observing the law."

3, 21–31: These verses provide a clear statement of Paul's "gospel," i.e., the principle of justification by faith in Christ. God has found a means of rescuing humanity from its desperate plight: Paul's general term for this divine initiative is **the righteousness of God** (21). Divine mercy declares the guilty innocent and makes them so. God does this not as a result of the law but apart from it (21), and not because of any merit in human beings but through forgiveness of their sins (24), in virtue of the redemption wrought in Christ Jesus for all who believe (22.24–25). God has manifested his righteousness in the coming of Jesus Christ, whose saving activity inaugurates a new era in human history.

3, 21: But now: Paul adopts a common phrase used by Greek authors to describe movement from disaster to prosperity. The expressions indicate that vv 21–26 are the consolatory answer to vv 9–20.

3, 25: Expiation: this rendering is preferable to "propitiation," which suggests hostility on the part of God toward sinners. As Paul will be at pains to point out (5, 8–10), it is humanity that is hostile to God.

3, 27–31: People cannot boast of their own holiness, since it is God's free gift (27), both to the Jew who practices circumcision out of faith and to the Gentile who accepts faith without the Old Testament religious culture symbolized by circumcision (29–30).

3, 27: Principle of faith: literally, "law of faith." Paul is fond of wordplay involving the term "law"; cf 7, 21.23; 8, 2. Since "law" in Greek may also connote "custom" or "principle," his readers and hearers would have sensed no contradiction in the use of the term after the negative statement concerning law in v 20.

3, 31: We are supporting the law: giving priority to God's intentions. God is the ultimate source of law, and the essence of law is fairness. On the basis of the Mosaic covenant, God's justice is in question if those who sinned against the law are permitted to go free (see 23–26). In order to rescue all humanity rather than condemn it, God thinks of an alternative: the law or "principle" of faith (27). What can be more fair than to admit everyone into the divine presence on the basis of forgiveness grasped by faith? Indeed, this principle of faith antedates the Mosaic law, as Paul will demonstrate in ch 4, and does not therefore mark a change in divine policy.

4, 1–25: This is an expanded treatment of the significance of Abraham's faith, which Paul discusses in Gal 3, 6–18; see the notes there.

4, 2–5: Verse 2 corresponds to v 4, and v 3 to v 5. The Greek term here rendered **credited** means "made an entry." The context determines whether it is credit or debit. Verse 8 speaks of "recording sin" as a debit. Paul's repeated use of accountants' terminology in this and other passages can be traced both to the Old Testament texts he quotes and to his business activity as a tentmaker. The commercial term in Gn 15, 6, "credited it to him," reminds Paul in vv 7–8 of Ps 32, 2, in which the same term is used and applied to forgiveness of sins. Thus Paul is able to argue that Abraham's faith involved receipt of forgiveness of sins and that all believers benefit as he did through faith.

4, 3: Jas 2, 24 appears to conflict with Paul's statement. However, James combats the error of extremists who used the doctrine of justification through faith as a screen for moral self-determination. Paul discusses the subject of holiness in greater detail than does James and beginning with ch 6 shows how justification through faith introduces one to the gift of a new life in Christ through the power of the holy Spirit.

k Is 51, 6–8; Acts 10, 43. l 1, 17; Gal 2, 16; Phil 3, 9. m 3, 9; 5, 12. n Eph 2, 8; Ti 3, 7 / 5, 1–2; Eph 1, 7. o Lv 16, 12–15; Acts 17, 31; 1 Jn 4, 10. p 8, 2; 1 Cor 1, 29–31. q 5, 1; Gal 2, 16. r 10, 12. s Dt 6, 4; Gal 3, 20; Jas 2, 19 / 4, 11–12. t 8, 4; Mt 5, 17. u Gal 3, 6–9. v Gn 15, 6; Gal 3, 6; Jas 2, 14.20–24. w 11, 6.

righteousness. 6 So also David declares the blessedness of the person to whom God credits righteousness apart from works:

7 [x]“Blessed are they whose iniquities are
forgiven
and whose sins are covered.
8 Blessed is the man whose sin the Lord does
not record.”

9 [y]*Does this blessedness apply only to the circumcised, or to the uncircumcised as well? Now we assert that “faith was credited to Abraham as righteousness.” 10 Under what circumstances was it credited? Was he circumcised or not? He was not circumcised, but uncircumcised. 11 [z]And he received the sign of circumcision as a seal on the righteousness received through faith while he was uncircumcised. Thus he was to be the father of all the uncircumcised who believe, so that to them [also] righteousness might be credited, 12 as well as the father of the circumcised who not only are circumcised but also follow the path of faith that our father Abraham walked while still uncircumcised.

Inheritance through Faith 13 [a]It was not through the law that the promise was made to Abraham and his descendants that he would inherit the world, but through the righteousness that comes from faith. 14 [b]For if those who adhere to the law are the heirs, faith is null and the promise is void. 15 [c]*For the law produces wrath; but where there is no law, neither is there violation. 16 [d]For this reason, it depends on faith, so that it may be a gift, and the promise may be guaranteed to all his descendants, not to those who only adhere to the law but to those who follow the faith of Abraham, who is the father of all of us, 17 [e]as it is written, “I have made you father of many nations.” He is our father in the sight of God, in whom he believed, who gives life to the dead and calls into being what does not exist. 18 [f]He believed, hoping against hope, that he would become “the father of many nations,” according to what was said, “Thus shall your descendants be.” 19 [g]He did not weaken in faith when he considered his own body as [already] dead (for he was almost a hundred years old) and the dead womb of Sarah. 20 *He did not doubt God’s promise in unbelief; rather, he was empowered by faith and gave glory to God 21 [h]and was fully convinced that what he had promised he was also able to do. 22 [i]That is why “it was credited to him as righteousness.” 23 But it was not for him alone that it was written that “it was credited to him”; 24 [j]it was also for us, to whom it will be credited, who believe in the one who raised Jesus our Lord from the dead, 25 [k]who was handed over for our transgressions and was raised for our justification.

CHAPTER 5

Faith, Hope, and Love 1 [l]*Therefore, since we have been justified by faith, we have peace with God through our Lord Jesus Christ, 2 [m]through whom we have gained access [by

4, 9: Blessedness: evidence of divine favor.

4, 15: Law has the negative function of bringing the deep-seated rebellion against God to the surface in specific sins; see the note on 1, 18–32.

4, 20: He did not doubt God’s promise in unbelief: any doubts Abraham might have had were resolved in commitment to God’s promise. Heb 11, 8–12 emphasizes the faith of Abraham and Sarah.

5, 1–11: Popular piety frequently construed reverses and troubles as punishment for sin; cf Jn 9, 2. Paul therefore assures believers that God’s justifying action in Jesus Christ is a declaration of peace. The crucifixion of Jesus Christ displays God’s initiative in certifying humanity for unimpeded access into the divine presence. Reconciliation is God’s gift of pardon to the entire human race. Through faith one benefits personally from this pardon or, in Paul’s term, is justified. The ultimate aim of God is to liberate believers from the pre-Christian self as described in chs 1–3. Since this liberation will first find completion in the believer’s resurrection, salvation is described as future in 5, 10. Because this fullness of salvation belongs to the future it is called the Christian **hope.** Paul’s Greek term for **hope** does not, however, suggest a note of uncertainty, to the effect: “I wonder whether God really means it.” Rather, God’s promise in the gospel fills believers with expectation and anticipation for the climactic gift of unalloyed commitment in the holy Spirit to the performance of the will of God. The persecutions that attend Christian commitment are to teach believers patience and to strengthen this hope, which will not disappoint them because the holy Spirit dwells in their hearts and imbues them with God’s love (5).

5, 1: We have peace: a number of manuscripts, versions, and church Fathers read “Let us have peace”; cf 14, 19.

x Ps 32, 1–2. y 4, 3. z Gn 17, 10–11; Gal 3, 6–8. a Gn 12, 7; 18, 18; 22, 17–18; Sir 44, 21; Gal 3, 16–18.29. b Gal 3, 18. c 3, 20; 5, 13; 7, 8; Gal 3, 19. d Sir 44, 19; Gal 3, 7–9. e Gn 17, 5; Heb 11, 19 / Is 48, 13. f Gn 15, 5. g Gn 17, 17; Heb 11, 11. h Gn 18, 14; Lk 1, 37. i Gn 15, 6. j 10, 9; 1 Pt 1, 21. k Is 53, 4–5.12; 1 Cor 15, 17; 1 Pt 1, 3 / 8, 11. 13, 24–28; Gal 2, 16. m Eph 2, 18; 3, 12.

faith] to this grace in which we stand, and we boast in hope of the glory of God. [3]Not only that, but we even boast of our afflictions, knowing that affliction produces endurance, [4][n]and endurance, proven character, and proven character, hope, [5][o]and hope does not disappoint, because the love of God has been poured out into our hearts through the holy Spirit that has been given to us. [6]For Christ, while we were still helpless, yet died at the appointed time for the ungodly. [7]*Indeed, only with difficulty does one die for a just person, though perhaps for a good person one might even find courage to die. [8][p]But God proves his love for us in that while we were still sinners Christ died for us. [9][q]How much more then, since we are now justified by his blood, will we be saved through him from the wrath. [10][r]Indeed, if, while we were enemies, we were reconciled to God through the death of his Son, how much more, once reconciled, will we be saved by his life. [11]Not only that, but we also boast of God through our Lord Jesus Christ, through whom we have now received reconciliation.

Humanity's Sin through Adam [12][s]*Therefore, just as through one person sin entered the world, and through sin, death, and thus death came to all, inasmuch as all sinned— [13][t]for up to the time of the law, sin was in the world, though sin is not accounted when there is no law. [14][u]But death reigned from Adam to Moses, even over those who did not sin after the pattern of the trespass of Adam, who is the type of the one who was to come.

Grace and Life through Christ [15]But the gift is not like the transgression. For if by that one person's transgression the many died, how much more did the grace of God and the gracious gift of the one person Jesus Christ overflow for the many. [16]And the gift is not like the result of the one person's sinning. For after one sin there was the judgment that brought condemnation; but the gift, after many transgressions, brought acquittal. [17]For if, by the transgression of one person, death came to reign through that one, how much more will those who receive the abundance of grace and of the gift of justification come to reign in life through the one person Jesus Christ. [18][v]In conclusion, just as through one transgression condemnation came upon all, so through one righteous act acquittal and life came to all. [19][w]For just as through the disobedience of one person the many were made sinners, so through the obedience of one the many will be made righteous. [20][x]*The law entered in so that transgression might increase but, where sin increased, grace overflowed all the more, [21][y]so that, as sin reigned in death, grace also might reign through justification for eternal life through Jesus Christ our Lord.

IV: Justification and the Christian Life

CHAPTER 6

Freedom from Sin; Life in God [1][z]*What then shall we say? Shall we persist in sin that grace may abound? Of course not! [2][a]How can

5, 7: In the world of Paul's time the **good person** is especially one who is magnanimous to others.

5, 12–21: Paul reflects on the sin of Adam (Gn 3, 1–13) in the light of the redemptive mystery of Christ. Sin, as used in the singular by Paul, refers to the dreadful power that has gripped humanity, which is now in revolt against the Creator and engaged in the exaltation of its own desires and interests. But no one has a right to say, "Adam made me do it," for all are culpable (12): Gentiles under the demands of the law written in their hearts (2, 14–15), and Jews under the Mosaic covenant. Through the Old Testament law, the sinfulness of humanity that was operative from the beginning (13) found further stimulation, with the result that sins were generated in even greater abundance. According to vv 15–21, God's act in Christ is in total contrast to the disastrous effects of the virus of sin that invaded humanity through Adam's crime.

5, 12: Inasmuch as all sinned: others translate "because all sinned," and understand v 13 as a parenthetical remark. Unlike Wis 2, 24, Paul does not ascribe the entry of death to the devil.

5, 20: The law entered in: sin had made its entrance (12); now the law comes in alongside sin. See the notes on 1, 18–32; 5, 12–21. **Where sin increased, grace overflowed all the more:** Paul declares that grace outmatches the productivity of sin.

6, 1–11: To defend the gospel against the charge that it promotes moral laxity (cf 3, 5–8), Paul expresses himself in the typical style of spirited diatribe. God's display of generosity or grace is not evoked by sin but, as stated in 5, 8, is the expression of God's love, and this love pledges eternal life to all believers (5, 21). Paul views the present conduct of the believers from the perspective of God's completed salvation when the body is resurrected and directed totally by the holy Spirit. Through baptism believers share the

n 2 Cor 12, 9–10; Jas 1, 2–4; 1 Pt 1, 5–7; 4, 12–14. o 8, 14–16; Pss 22, 5–6; 25, 20. p Jn 3, 16; 1 Jn 4, 10.19. q 1, 18; 1 Thes 1, 10. r 8, 7–8; 2 Cor 5, 18; Col 1, 21–22. s Gn 2, 17; 3, 1–19; Wis 2, 24 / 3, 19.23. t 4, 15. u 1 Cor 15, 21. v 1 Cor 15, 21–22. w Is 53, 11; Phil 2, 8–9. x 4, 15; 7, 7–8; Gal 3, 19. y 6, 23. z 3, 5–8. a 1 Pt 4, 1.

we who died to sin yet live in it? [3][b]Or are you unaware that we who were baptized into Christ Jesus were baptized into his death? [4][c]We were indeed buried with him through baptism into death, so that, just as Christ was raised from the dead by the glory of the Father, we too might live in newness of life.

[5][d]For if we have grown into union with him through a death like his, we shall also be united with him in the resurrection. [6][e]We know that our old self was crucified with him, so that our sinful body might be done away with, that we might no longer be in slavery to sin. [7]For a dead person has been absolved from sin. [8][f]If, then, we have died with Christ, we believe that we shall also live with him. [9][g]We know that Christ, raised from the dead, dies no more; death no longer has power over him. [10][h]As to his death, he died to sin once and for all; as to his life, he lives for God. [11][i]Consequently, you too must think of yourselves as [being] dead to sin and living for God in Christ Jesus.

[12][j]*Therefore, sin must not reign over your mortal bodies so that you obey their desires. [13][k]And do not present the parts of your bodies to sin as weapons for wickedness, but present yourselves to God as raised from the dead to life and the parts of your bodies to God as weapons for righteousness. [14][l]For sin is not to have any power over you, since you are not under the law but under grace.

[15][m]What then? Shall we sin because we are not under the law but under grace? Of course not! [16][n][o]Do you not know that if you present yourselves to someone as obedient slaves, you are slaves of the one you obey, either of sin, which leads to death, or of obedience, which leads to righteousness? [17]*But thanks be to God that, although you were once slaves of sin, you have become obedient from the heart to the pattern of teaching to which you were entrusted. [18]Freed from sin, you have become slaves of righteousness. [19]I am speaking in human terms because of the weakness of your nature. For just as you presented the parts of your bodies as slaves to impurity and to lawlessness for lawlessness, so now present them as slaves to righteousness for sanctification. [20][p]*For when you were slaves of sin, you were free from righteousness. [21][q]But what profit did you get then from the things of which you are now ashamed? For the end of those things is death. [22][r]*But now that you have been freed from sin and have become slaves of God, the benefit that you have leads to sanctification, and its end is eternal life. [23][s]For the wages of sin is death, but the gift of God is eternal life in Christ Jesus our Lord.

CHAPTER 7

Freedom from the Law [1]*Are you unaware, brothers (for I am speaking to people who know the law), that the law has jurisdiction over one as long as one lives? [2][t]Thus a married woman is bound by law to her living husband; but if her

death of Christ and thereby escape from the grip of sin. Through the resurrection of Christ the power to live anew becomes reality for them, but the fullness of participation in Christ's resurrection still lies in the future. But life that is lived in dedication to God now is part and parcel of that future. Hence anyone who sincerely claims to be interested in that future will scarcely be able to say, "Let us sin so that grace may prosper" (cf 1).

6, 12–19: Christians have been released from the grip of sin, but sin endeavors to reclaim its victims. The antidote is constant remembrance that divine grace has claimed them and identifies them as people who are alive only for God's interests.

6, 17: In contrast to humanity, which was handed over to self-indulgence (1, 24–32), believers are **entrusted** ("handed over") to God's **pattern of teaching,** that is, the new life God aims to develop in Christians through the productivity of the holy Spirit. Throughout this passage Paul uses the slave-master model in order to emphasize the fact that one cannot give allegiance to both God and sin.

6, 20: You were free from righteousness: expressed ironically, for such freedom is really tyranny. The commercial metaphors in vv 21–23 add up only one way: sin is a bad bargain.

6, 22: Sanctification: or holiness.

7, 1–6: Paul reflects on the fact that Christians have a different understanding of the law because of their faith in Christ. Law binds the living, not the dead, as exemplified in marriage, which binds in life but is dissolved through death. Similarly, Christians who through baptism have died with Christ to sin (cf 6, 2–4) are freed from the law that occasioned transgressions, which in turn were productive of death. Now that Christians are joined to Christ, the power of Christ's resurrection makes it possible for them to bear the fruit of newness of life for God.

b Gal 3, 27. c Col 2, 12; 1 Pt 3, 21–22. d Phil 3, 10–11; 2 Tm 2, 11. e Gal 5, 24; 6, 14; Eph 4, 22–23. f 1 Thes 4, 17. g Acts 13, 34; 1 Cor 15, 26; 2 Tm 1, 10; Rv 1, 18. h Heb 9, 26–28; 1 Pt 3, 18. i 2 Cor 5, 15; 1 Pt 2, 24. j Gn 4, 7. k 12, 1; Eph 2, 5; 5, 14 / Col 3, 5. l Gal 5, 18; 1 Jn 3, 6. m 5, 17.21. n Jn 8, 31–34; 2 Pt 2, 19. o Jn 8, 32–36. p Jn 8, 34. q 8, 6.13; Prv 12, 28; Ez 16, 61.63. r 1 Pt 1, 9. s Gn 2, 17; Gal 6, 7–9; Jas 1, 15. t 1 Cor 7, 39.

husband dies, she is released from the law in
respect to her husband. [3]Consequently, while her
husband is alive she will be called an adulteress if
she consorts with another man. But if her hus-
band dies she is free from that law, and she is not
an adulteress if she consorts with another man.

[4]In the same way, my brothers, you also were
put to death to the law through the body of
Christ, so that you might belong to another, to
the one who was raised from the dead in order
that we might bear fruit for God. [5] [u]For when we
were in the flesh, our sinful passions, awakened
by the law, worked in our members to bear fruit
for death. [6] [v]But now we are released from the
law, dead to what held us captive, so that we
may serve in the newness of the spirit and not
under the obsolete letter.

Acquaintance with Sin through the Law
[7] [w]*What then can we say? That the law is sin?
Of course not! Yet I did not know sin except
through the law, and I did not know what it is to
covet except that the law said, "You shall not
covet." [8] [x]But sin, finding an opportunity in the
commandment, produced in me every kind of
covetousness. Apart from the law sin is dead. [9]I
once lived outside the law, but when the com-
mandment came, sin became alive; [10] [y]then I
died, and the commandment that was for life
turned out to be death for me. [11] [z]For sin, seizing
an opportunity in the commandment, deceived
me and through it put me to death. [12] [a]So then
the law is holy, and the commandment is holy
and righteous and good.

Sin and Death [13] [b]*Did the good, then, be-
come death for me? Of course not! Sin, in order
that it might be shown to be sin, worked death
in me through the good, so that sin might
become sinful beyond measure through the
commandment. [14] [c]We know that the law is
spiritual; but I am carnal, sold into slavery to sin.
[15]What I do, I do not understand. For I do not do
what I want, but I do what I hate. [16]Now if I do
what I do not want, I concur that the law is
good. [17]So now it is no longer I who do it, but
sin that dwells in me. [18] [d]For I know that good
does not dwell in me, that is, in my flesh. The
willing is ready at hand, but doing the good is
not. [19]For I do not do the good I want, but I do
the evil I do not want. [20]Now if [I] do what I do
not want, it is no longer I who do it, but sin that
dwells in me. [21]So, then, I discover the principle
that when I want to do right, evil is at hand.
[22]For I take delight in the law of God, in my
inner self, [23] [e]*but I see in my members another
principle at war with the law of my mind, taking
me captive to the law of sin that dwells in my
members. [24]Miserable one that I am! Who will
deliver me from this mortal body? [25] [f]Thanks be
to God through Jesus Christ our Lord. Therefore,
I myself, with my mind, serve the law of God
but, with my flesh, the law of sin.

CHAPTER 8

The Flesh and the Spirit [1] *Hence, now there
is no condemnation for those who are in Christ

7, 7–25: In this passage Paul uses the first person singular in the style of diatribe for the sake of argument. He aims to depict the disastrous consequences when a Christian reintroduces the law as a means to attain the objective of holiness pronounced in 6, 22.

7, 7–12: The apostle defends himself against the charge of identifying the law with sin. Sin does not exist in law but in human beings, whose sinful inclinations are not overcome by the proclamation of law.

7, 13–25: Far from improving the sinner, law encourages sin to expose itself in transgressions or violations of specific commandments (see 1, 24; 5, 20). Thus persons who do not experience the justifying grace of God, and Christians who revert to dependence on law as the criterion for their relationship with God, will recognize a rift between their reasoned desire for the goodness of the law and their actual performance that is contrary to the law. Unable to free themselves from the slavery of sin and the power of death, they can only be rescued from defeat in the conflict by the power of God's grace working through Jesus Christ.

7, 23: As in 3, 27, Paul plays on the term **law,** which in Greek can connote custom, system, or **principle.**

8, 1–13: After his warning in ch 7 against the wrong route to fulfillment of the objective of holiness expressed in 6, 22, Paul points his addressees to the correct way. Through the redemptive work of Christ, Christians have been liberated from the terrible forces of sin and death. Holiness was impossible so long as the **flesh** (or our "old self"), that is, self-interested hostility toward God (7), frustrated the divine objectives expressed in the law. What is worse, sin used the law to break forth into all manner of lawlessness (8). All this is now changed. At the cross God broke the power of sin and pronounced sentence on it (3). Christians still retain the flesh, but it is alien to their new being, which is life in the spirit, namely the new self, governed by the holy Spirit.

u 6, 21; 8, 6.13. v 8, 2; 2 Cor 3, 6. w 3, 20; Ex 20, 17; Dt 5, 21. x 5, 13.20; 1 Cor 15, 56 / 4, 15. y Lv 18, 5. z Gn 3, 13; Heb 3, 13. a 1 Tm 1, 8. b 4, 15; 5, 20. c 8, 7–8; Ps 51, 7. d Gn 6, 5; 8, 21; Phil 2, 13. e Gal 5, 17; 1 Pt 2, 11. f 1 Cor 15, 57.

Jesus. 2 *g*For the law of the spirit of life in Christ Jesus has freed you from the law of sin and death. 3 *h*For what the law, weakened by the flesh, was powerless to do, this God has done: by sending his own Son in the likeness of sinful flesh and for the sake of sin, he condemned sin in the flesh, 4 *i*so that the righteous decree of the law might be fulfilled in us, who live not according to the flesh but according to the spirit. 5For those who live according to the flesh are concerned with the things of the flesh, but those who live according to the spirit with the things of the spirit. 6 *j*The concern of the flesh is death, but the concern of the spirit is life and peace. 7 *k*For the concern of the flesh is hostility toward God; it does not submit to the law of God, nor can it; 8 *l*and those who are in the flesh cannot please God. 9 *m*But you are not in the flesh; on the contrary, you are in the spirit, if only the Spirit of God dwells in you. Whoever does not have the Spirit of Christ does not belong to him. 10 *n*But if Christ is in you, although the body is dead because of sin, the spirit is alive because of righteousness. 11If the Spirit of the one who raised Jesus from the dead dwells in you, the one who raised Christ from the dead will give life to your mortal bodies also, through his Spirit that dwells in you. 12Consequently, brothers, we are not debtors to the flesh, to live according to the flesh. 13 *o*For if you live according to the flesh, you will die, but if by the spirit you put to death the deeds of the body, you will live.

Children of God through Adoption 14 *p**For those who are led by the Spirit of God are children of God. 15 *q**For you did not receive a spirit of slavery to fall back into fear, but you received a spirit of adoption, through which we cry, "*Abba,* Father!" 16 *r*The Spirit itself bears witness with our spirit that we are children of God, 17 *s*and if children, then heirs, heirs of God and joint heirs with Christ, if only we suffer with him so that we may also be glorified with him.

Destiny of Glory 18 *t**I consider that the sufferings of this present time are as nothing compared with the glory to be revealed for us. 19For creation awaits with eager expectation the revelation of the children of God; 20 *u*for creation was made subject to futility, not of its own accord but because of the one who subjected it, in hope 21 *v*that creation itself would be set free from slavery to corruption and share in the glorious freedom of the children of God. 22 *w*We know that all creation is groaning in labor pains even until now; 23 *x*and not only that, but we ourselves, who have the firstfruits of the Spirit, we also groan within ourselves as we wait for adoption, the redemption of our bodies. 24 *y*For in hope we were saved. Now hope that sees for itself is not hope. For who hopes for what one sees? 25But if we hope for what we do not see, we wait with endurance.

26In the same way, the Spirit too comes to the aid of our weakness; for we do not know how to pray as we ought, but the Spirit itself intercedes with inexpressible groanings. 27 *z*And the one who searches hearts knows what is the intention of the Spirit, because it intercedes for the holy ones according to God's will.

Under the direction of the holy Spirit Christians are able to fulfill the divine will that formerly found expression in the law (4). The same Spirit who enlivens Christians for holiness will also resurrect their bodies at the last day (11). Christian life is therefore the experience of a constant challenge to put to death the evil deeds of the body through life of the spirit (13).

8, 14–17: Christians, by reason of the Spirit's presence within them, enjoy not only new life but also a new relationship to God, that of adopted children and heirs through Christ, whose sufferings and glory they share.

8, 15: Abba: see the note on Mk 14, 36.

8, 18–27: The glory that believers are destined to share with Christ far exceeds the sufferings of the present life. Paul considers the destiny of the created world to be linked with the future that belongs to the believers. As it shares in the penalty of corruption brought about by sin, so also will it share in the benefits of redemption and future glory that comprise the ultimate liberation of God's people (19–22). After patient endurance in steadfast expectation, the full harvest of the Spirit's presence will be realized. On earth believers enjoy the firstfruits, i.e., the Spirit, as a guarantee of the total liberation of their bodies from the influence of the rebellious old self (23).

g 7, 23–24; 2 Cor 3, 17. h Acts 13, 38; 15, 10 / Jn 3, 16–17; 2 Cor 5, 21; Gal 3, 13; 4, 4; Phil 2, 7; Col 1, 22; Heb 2, 17; 4, 15; 1 Jn 4, 9. i Gal 5, 16–25. j 6, 21; 7, 5; 8, 13; Gal 6, 8. k 5, 10; Jas 4, 4. l 1 Jn 2, 16. m 1 Cor 3, 16. n Gal 2, 20; 1 Pt 4, 6. o Gal 5, 24; 6, 8; Eph 4, 22–24. p Gal 5, 18. q Mk 14, 36; Gal 4, 5–6; 2 Tm 1, 7. r Jn 1, 12; Gal 3, 26–29. s Gal 4, 7; 1 Pt 4, 13; 5, 1. t 2 Cor 4, 17. u Gn 3, 17–19. v 2 Pt 3, 12–13; Rv 21, 1. w 2 Cor 5, 2–5. x 2 Cor 1, 22; Gal 5, 5. y 2 Cor 5, 7; Heb 11, 1. z Ps 139, 1; 1 Cor 4, 5.

God's Indomitable Love in Christ 28 a*We
know that all things work for good for those who
love God, who are called according to his
purpose. 29 b*For those he foreknew he also
predestined to be conformed to the image of his
Son, so that he might be the firstborn among
many brothers. 30 cAnd those he predestined he
also called; and those he called he also justified;
and those he justified he also glorified.
31 d*What then shall we say to this? If God is
for us, who can be against us? 32 eHe who did
not spare his own Son but handed him over for
us all, how will he not also give us everything
else along with him? 33 fWho will bring a charge
against God's chosen ones? It is God who
acquits us. 34 gWho will condemn? It is Christ
[Jesus] who died, rather, was raised, who also is
at the right hand of God, who indeed intercedes
for us. 35What will separate us from the love of
Christ? Will anguish, or distress, or persecution,
or famine, or nakedness, or peril, or the sword?
36 hAs it is written:

"For your sake we are being slain all the day;
we are looked upon as sheep to be
slaughtered."

37 iNo, in all these things we conquer overwhelm-
ingly through him who loved us. 38 j*For I am
convinced that neither death, nor life, nor an-
gels, nor principalities, nor present things, nor
future things, nor powers, 39*nor height, nor
depth, nor any other creature will be able to
separate us from the love of God in Christ Jesus
our Lord.

V: Jews and Gentiles in God's Plan

CHAPTER 9

Paul's Love for Israel 1 k*I speak the truth in
Christ, I do not lie; my conscience joins with the
holy Spirit in bearing me witness 2that I have
great sorrow and constant anguish in my heart.
3 lFor I could wish that I myself were accursed
and separated from Christ for the sake of my
brothers, my kin according to the flesh. 4 mThey
are Israelites; theirs the adoption, the glory, the
covenants, the giving of the law, the worship,
and the promises; 5 n*theirs the patriarchs, and
from them, according to the flesh, is the Mes-
siah. God who is over all be blessed forever.
Amen.

8, 28–30: These verses outline the Christian vocation as it was designed by God: **to be conformed to the image of his Son,** who is to **be the firstborn among many brothers** (29). God's redemptive action on behalf of the believers has been in process before the beginning of the world. Those whom God chooses are **those he foreknew** (29) or elected. Those who are **called** (30) are **predestined** or predetermined. These expressions do not mean that God is arbitrary. Rather, Paul uses them to emphasize the thought and care that God has taken for the Christian's salvation.

8, 28: We know that all things work for good for those who love God: a few ancient authorities have God as the subject of the verb, and some translators render: "We know that God makes everything work for good for those who love God . . . ."

8, 29: Image: while man and woman were originally created in God's image (Gn 1, 26–27), it is through baptism into Christ, the image of God (2 Cor 4, 4; Col 1, 15), that we are renewed according to the image of the Creator (Col 3, 10).

8, 31–39: The all-conquering power of God's love has overcome every obstacle to Christians' salvation and every threat to separate them from God. That power manifested itself fully when God's own Son was delivered up to death for their salvation. Through him Christians can overcome all their afflictions and trials.

8, 38: Present things and **future things** may refer to astrological data. Paul appears to be saying that the gospel liberates believers from dependence on astrologers.

8, 39: Height, depth may refer to positions in the zodiac, positions of heavenly bodies relative to the horizon. In astrological documents the term for "height" means "exaltation" or the position of greatest influence exerted by a planet. Since hostile spirits were associated with the planets and stars, Paul includes **powers** (38) in his list of malevolent forces.

9, 1—11, 36: Israel's unbelief and its rejection of Jesus as savior astonished and puzzled Christians. It constituted a serious problem for them in view of God's specific preparation of Israel for the advent of the Messiah. Paul addresses himself here to the essential question of how the divine plan could be frustrated by Israel's unbelief. At the same time, he discourages both complacency and anxiety on the part of Gentiles. To those who might boast of their superior advantage over Jews, he warns that their enjoyment of the blessings assigned to Israel can be terminated. To those who might anxiously ask, "How can we be sure that Israel's fate will not be ours?" he replies that only unbelief can deprive one of salvation.

9, 1–5: The apostle speaks in strong terms of the depth of his grief over the unbelief of his own people. He would willingly undergo a curse himself for the sake of their coming to the knowledge of Christ (3; cf Lv 27, 28–29). His love for them derives from God's continuing choice of them and from the spiritual benefits that God bestows on them and through them on all of humanity (4–5).

9, 5: Some editors punctuate this verse differently and prefer the translation, "Of whom is Christ according to the flesh, who is God over all." However, Paul's point is that **God who is over all** aimed to use Israel, which had been entrusted with every privilege, in outreach to the entire world through the Messiah.

a Eph 1, 4–14; 3, 11. b Eph 1, 5; 1 Pt 1, 2. c Is 45, 25; 2 Thes 2, 13–14. d Ps 118, 6; Heb 13, 6. e Jn 3, 16. f Is 50, 8. g Ps 110, 1; Heb 7, 25; 1 Jn 2, 1. h Ps 44, 23; 1 Cor 4, 9; 15, 30; 2 Cor 4, 11; 2 Tm 3, 12. i 1 Jn 5, 4. j 1 Cor 3, 22; Eph 1, 21; 1 Pt 3, 22. k 2 Cor 11, 31; 1 Tm 2, 7. l Ex 32, 32. m 3, 2; Ex 4, 22; Dt 7, 6; 14, 1–2. n Mt 1, 1–16; Lk 3, 23–38 / 1, 25; Ps 41, 14.

God's Free Choice 6 [o]But it is not that the
word of God has failed. For not all who are of
Israel are Israel, 7 [p]nor are they all children of
Abraham because they are his descendants; but
"It is through Isaac that descendants shall bear
your name." 8 [q]This means that it is not the
children of the flesh who are the children of
God, but the children of the promise are counted
as descendants. 9 [r]For this is the wording of the
promise, "About this time I shall return and
Sarah will have a son." 10 [s]*And not only that,
but also when Rebecca had conceived children
by one husband, our father Isaac— 11 before they
had yet been born or had done anything, good or
bad, in order that God's elective plan might
continue, 12 [t]not by works but by his call—she
was told, "The older shall serve the younger."
13 [u]*As it is written:

> "I loved Jacob
> but hated Esau."

14 [v]*What then are we to say? Is there injustice
on the part of God? Of course not! 15 [w]For he
says to Moses:

> "I will show mercy to whom I will,
> I will take pity on whom I will."

16 [x]So it depends not upon a person's will or
exertion, but upon God, who shows mercy.
17 [y]For the scripture says to Pharaoh, "This is
why I have raised you up, to show my power
through you that my name may be proclaimed
throughout the earth." 18 [z]*Consequently, he
has mercy upon whom he wills, and he hardens
whom he wills.

19 [a]*You will say to me then, "Why [then]
does he still find fault? For who can oppose his
will?" 20 [b]But who indeed are you, a human
being, to talk back to God? Will what is made
say to its maker, "Why have you created me so?"
21 Or does not the potter have a right over the
clay, to make out of the same lump one vessel for
a noble purpose and another for an ignoble one?
22 [c]What if God, wishing to show his wrath and
make known his power, has endured with much
patience the vessels of wrath made for destruc-
tion? 23 This was to make known the riches of his
glory to the vessels of mercy, which he has
prepared previously for glory, 24 namely, us
whom he has called, not only from the Jews but
also from the Gentiles.

Witness of the Prophets 25 [d]*As indeed he
says in Hosea:

> "Those who were not my people I will call 'my
> people,'
> and her who was not beloved I will call
> 'beloved.'

> 26 [e]And in the very place where it was said to
> them, 'You are not my people,'
> there they shall be called children of the
> living God."

9, 10: Children by one husband, our father Isaac: Abraham had two children, Ishmael and Isaac, by two wives, Hagar and Sarah, respectively. In that instance Isaac, although born later than Ishmael, became the bearer of the messianic promise. In the case of twins born to Rebecca, God's elective procedure is seen even more dramatically, and again the younger, contrary to Semitic custom, is given the preference.

9, 13: The literal rendering, **"Jacob I loved, but Esau I hated,"** suggests an attitude of divine hostility that is not implied in Paul's statement. In Semitic usage "hate" means to love less; cf Lk 14, 26 with Mt 10, 37. Israel's unbelief reflects the mystery of the divine election that is always operative within it. Mere natural descent from Abraham does not ensure the full possession of the divine gifts; it is God's sovereign prerogative to bestow this fullness upon, or to withhold it from, whomsoever he wishes; cf Mt 3, 9; Jn 8, 39. The choice of Jacob over Esau is a case in point.

9, 14–18: The principle of divine election does not invite Christians to theoretical inquiry concerning the nonelected, nor does this principle mean that God is unfair in his dealings with humanity. The instruction concerning divine election is a part of the gospel and reveals that the gift of faith is the enactment of God's mercy (16). God raised up Moses to display that mercy, and Pharaoh to display divine severity in punishing those who obstinately oppose their Creator.

9, 18: The basic biblical principle is: those who will not see or hear **shall** not see or hear. On the other hand, the same God who thus makes stubborn or hardens the heart can reconstruct it through the work of the holy Spirit.

9, 19–29: The apostle responds to the objection that if God rules over faith through the principle of divine election, God cannot then accuse unbelievers of sin (19). For Paul, this objection is in the last analysis a manifestation of human insolence, and his "answer" is less an explanation of God's ways than the rejection of an argument that places humanity on a level with God. At the same time, Paul shows that God is far less arbitrary than appearances suggest, for God endures **with much patience** (22) a person like the Pharaoh of the Exodus.

9, 25: Beloved: in Semitic discourse means "preferred" or "favorite" (cf 13). See Hos 2, 1, which is transposed after Hos 3, 5 in the NAB.

o Nm 23, 19 / Mt 3, 9. p Gn 21, 12; Gal 3, 29. q Gal 4, 23.28. r Gn 18, 10.14. s Gn 25, 21. t 11, 5–6 / Gn 25, 23–24. u Mal 1, 3. v Dt 32, 4. w Ex 33, 19. x Eph 2, 8; Ti 3, 5. y Ex 9, 16. z 11, 30–32; Ex 4, 21; 7, 3. a 3, 7; Wis 12, 12. b Wis 15, 7; Is 29, 16; 45, 9; Jer 18, 6. c 2, 4; Wis 12, 20–21; Jer 50, 25. d Hos 2, 25. e Hos 2, 1.

27 f And Isaiah cries out concerning Israel,
"Though the number of the Israelites were like
the sand of the sea, only a remnant will be
saved; 28 for decisively and quickly will the Lord
execute sentence upon the earth." 29 g And as
Isaiah predicted:

"Unless the Lord of hosts had left us
descendants,
we would have become like Sodom
and have been made like Gomorrah."

Righteousness Based on Faith 30 h *What
then shall we say? That Gentiles, who did not
pursue righteousness, have achieved it, that is,
righteousness that comes from faith; 31 i but that
Israel, who pursued the law of righteousness, did
not attain to that law? 32 j *Why not? Because
they did it not by faith, but as if it could be done
by works. They stumbled over the stone that
causes stumbling, 33 k as it is written:

"Behold, I am laying a stone in Zion
that will make people stumble
and a rock that will make them fall,
and whoever believes in him shall not be put
to shame."

CHAPTER 10

1 l *Brothers, my heart's desire and prayer to God
on their behalf is for salvation. 2 m I testify with
regard to them that they have zeal for God, but it
is not discerning. 3 n For, in their unawareness of
the righteousness that comes from God and their
attempt to establish their own [righteousness],
they did not submit to the righteousness of God.
4 o *For Christ is the end of the law for the
justification of everyone who has faith.
5 p *Moses writes about the righteousness that
comes from [the] law, "The one who does these
things will live by them." 6 q But the righteous-
ness that comes from faith says, "Do not say in
your heart, 'Who will go up into heaven?' (that
is, to bring Christ down) 7 r *or 'Who will go
down into the abyss?' (that is, to bring Christ up
from the dead)." 8 s But what does it say?

"The word is near you,
in your mouth and in your heart"

(that is, the word of faith that we preach), 9 t *for,
if you confess with your mouth that Jesus is Lord
and believe in your heart that God raised him
from the dead, you will be saved. 10 For one
believes with the heart and so is justified, and
one confesses with the mouth and so is saved.
11 u For the scripture says, "No one who believes
in him will be put to shame." 12 v For there is no
distinction between Jew and Greek; the same
Lord is Lord of all, enriching all who call upon
him. 13 w For "everyone who calls on the name of
the Lord will be saved."
14 x *But how can they call on him in whom

9, 30–33: In the conversion of the Gentiles and, by contrast, of relatively few Jews, the Old Testament prophecies are seen to be fulfilled; cf 25–29. Israel feared that the doctrine of justification through faith would jeopardize the validity of the Mosaic law, and so they never reached their goal of righteousness that they had sought to attain through meticulous observance of the law (31). Since Gentiles, including especially Greeks and Romans, had a great regard for righteousness, Paul's statement concerning Gentiles in v 30 is to be understood from a Jewish perspective: quite evidently they had not been interested in "God's" righteousness, for it had not been revealed to them; but now in response to the proclamation of the gospel they respond in faith.

9, 32: Paul discusses Israel as a whole from the perspective of contemporary Jewish rejection of Jesus as Messiah. The Old Testament and much of Jewish noncanonical literature in fact reflect a fervent faith in divine mercy.

10, 1–13: Despite Israel's lack of faith in God's act in Christ, Paul does not abandon hope for her salvation (1). However, Israel must recognize that the Messiah's arrival in the person of Jesus Christ means the termination of the Mosaic law as the criterion for understanding oneself in a valid relationship to God. Faith in God's saving action in Jesus Christ takes precedence over any such legal claim (6).

10, 4: The Mosaic legislation has been superseded by God's action in Jesus Christ. Others understand **end** here in the sense that Christ is the goal of the law, i.e., the true meaning of the Mosaic law, which cannot be correctly understood apart from him. Still others believe that both meanings are intended.

10, 5–6: The subject of the verb **says** (6) is **righteousness** personified. Both of the statements in vv 5 and 6 derive from Moses, but Paul wishes to contrast the language of law and the language of faith.

10, 7: Here Paul blends Dt 30, 13 and Ps 107, 26.

10, 9–11: To confess Jesus as Lord was frequently quite hazardous in the first century (cf Mt 10, 18; 1 Thes 2, 2; 1 Pt 2, 18–21; 3, 14). For a Jew it could mean disruption of normal familial and other social relationships, including great economic sacrifice. In the face of penalties imposed by the secular world, Christians are assured that **no one who believes** in Jesus **will be put to shame** (11).

10, 14–21: The gospel has been sufficiently proclaimed to

f Is 10, 22–23; Hos 2, 1 / 11, 5 / Is 28, 22. g Is 1, 9; Mt 10, 15. h 10, 4.20. i 10, 3. j Is 8, 14. k Is 28, 16; 1 Pt 2, 6–8. l 9, 1.3. m Acts 22, 3. n 9, 31–32; Phil 3, 9. o Acts 13, 38–39; 2 Cor 3, 14; Heb 8, 13. p Lv 18, 5; Gal 3, 12. q Dt 9, 4; 30, 12. r Dt 30, 13; 1 Pt 3, 19. s Dt 30, 14. t 1 Cor 12, 3. u 9, 33; Is 28, 16. v 1, 16; 3, 22.29; Acts 10, 34; 15, 9.11; Gal 3, 28; Eph 2, 14. w Jl 3, 5; Acts 2, 21. x Acts 8, 31.

they have not believed? And how can they
believe in him of whom they have not heard?
And how can they hear without someone to
preach? 15 [y]*And how can people preach unless
they are sent? As it is written, "How beautiful
are the feet of those who bring [the] good news!"
16 [z]But not everyone has heeded the good news;
for Isaiah says, "Lord, who has believed what
was heard from us?" 17 [a]Thus faith comes from
what is heard, and what is heard comes through
the word of Christ. 18 [b]But I ask, did they not
hear? Certainly they did; for

"Their voice has gone forth to all the earth,
and their words to the ends of the world."

19 [c]But I ask, did not Israel understand? First
Moses says:

"I will make you jealous of those who are not a nation;
with a senseless nation I will make you angry."

20 [d]Then Isaiah speaks boldly and says:

"I was found [by] those who were not seeking me;
I revealed myself to those who were not asking for me."

21 But regarding Israel he says, "All day long I
stretched out my hands to a disobedient and
contentious people."

CHAPTER 11

The Remnant of Israel 1 [ef]*I ask, then, has
God rejected his people? Of course not! For I too
am an Israelite, a descendant of Abraham, of the
tribe of Benjamin. 2 God has not rejected his
people whom he foreknew. Do you not know
what the scripture says about Elijah, how he
pleads with God against Israel? 3 [g]"Lord, they
have killed your prophets, they have torn down
your altars, and I alone am left, and they are
seeking my life." 4 [h]But what is God's response
to him? "I have left for myself seven thousand
men who have not knelt to Baal." 5 [i]So also at
the present time there is a remnant, chosen by
grace. 6 [j]But if by grace, it is no longer because of
works; otherwise grace would no longer be
grace. 7 [k]What then? What Israel was seeking it
did not attain, but the elect attained it; the rest
were hardened, 8 [l]as it is written:

"God gave them a spirit of deep sleep,
eyes that should not see
and ears that should not hear,
down to this very day."

9 [m]And David says:

"Let their table become a snare and a trap,
a stumbling block and a retribution for them;
10 let their eyes grow dim so that they may not see,
and keep their backs bent forever."

The Gentiles' Salvation 11 [n]*Hence I ask, did
they stumble so as to fall? Of course not! But
through their transgression salvation has come
to the Gentiles, so as to make them jealous.
12 Now if their transgression is enrichment for
the world, and if their diminished number is
enrichment for the Gentiles, how much more
their full number.

13 [o]Now I am speaking to you Gentiles. Inas-
much then as I am the apostle to the Gentiles, I

Israel, and Israel has adequately understood God's plan for the messianic age, which would see the gospel brought to the uttermost parts of the earth. As often in the past, Israel has not accepted the prophetic message; cf Acts 7, 51–53.

10, 15: **How beautiful are the feet of those who bring [the] good news:** in Semitic fashion, the parts of the body that bring the messenger with welcome news are praised; cf Lk 11, 27.

11, 1–10: Although Israel has been unfaithful to the prophetic message of the gospel (10, 14–21), God remains faithful to Israel. Proof of the divine fidelity lies in the existence of Jewish Christians like Paul himself. The unbelieving Jews, says Paul, have been blinded by the Christian teaching concerning the Messiah.

11, 11–15: The unbelief of the Jews has paved the way for the preaching of the gospel to the Gentiles and for their easier acceptance of it outside the context of Jewish culture. Through his mission to the Gentiles Paul also hopes to fill his fellow Jews with jealousy. Hence he hastens to fill the entire Mediterranean world with the gospel. Once all the Gentile nations have heard the gospel, Israel as a whole is expected to embrace it. This will be tantamount to resurrection of the dead, that is, the reappearance of Jesus Christ with all the believers at the end of time.

y Is 52, 7; Na 2, 1; Eph 6, 15. z Is 53, 1; Jn 12, 38. a Jn 17, 20. b Ps 19, 5; Mt 24, 14. c 11, 11.14; Dt 32, 21. d 9, 30; Is 65, 1–2. e 2 Cor 11, 22; Phil 3, 5. f 1 Sm 12, 22; Ps 94, 14. g 1 Kgs 19, 10.14. h 1 Kgs 19, 18. i 9, 27. j 4, 4; Gal 3, 18. k 9, 31. l Dt 29, 3; Is 29, 10; Mt 13, 13–15; Acts 28, 26–27. m Pss 69, 23–24; 35, 8. n Acts 13, 46; 18, 6; 28, 28 / 10, 19; Dt 32, 21. o 1,5.

glory in my ministry 14in order to make my race
jealous and thus save some of them. 15For if their
rejection is the reconciliation of the world, what
will their acceptance be but life from the dead?
16 p*If the firstfruits are holy, so is the whole
batch of dough; and if the root is holy, so are the
branches.
17 qBut if some of the branches were broken
off, and you, a wild olive shoot, were grafted in
their place and have come to share in the rich
root of the olive tree, 18 rdo not boast against the
branches. If you do boast, consider that you do
not support the root; the root supports you.
19Indeed you will say, "Branches were broken
off so that I might be grafted in." 20 sThat is so.
They were broken off because of unbelief, but
you are there because of faith. So do not become
haughty, but stand in awe. 21 tFor if God did not
spare the natural branches, [perhaps] he will not
spare you either. 22 uSee, then, the kindness and
severity of God: severity toward those who fell,
but God's kindness to you, provided you remain
in his kindness; otherwise you too will be cut
off. 23 vAnd they also, if they do not remain in
unbelief, will be grafted in, for God is able to
graft them in again. 24For if you were cut from
what is by nature a wild olive tree, and grafted,
contrary to nature, into a cultivated one, how
much more will they who belong to it by nature
be grafted back into their own olive tree.

God's Irrevocable Call 25 w*I do not want you
to be unaware of this mystery, brothers, so that
you will not become wise [in] your own estima-
tion: a hardening has come upon Israel in part,
until the full number of the Gentiles comes in,
26 x yand thus all Israel will be saved, as it is
written:

"The deliverer will come out of Zion,
he will turn away godlessness from Jacob;
27 zand this is my covenant with them
when I take away their sins."

28 aIn respect to the gospel, they are enemies on
your account; but in respect to election, they are
beloved because of the patriarchs. 29 bFor the
gifts and the call of God are irrevocable.

Triumph of God's Mercy 30*Just as you once
disobeyed God but have now received mercy
because of their disobedience, 31so they have
now disobeyed in order that, by virtue of the
mercy shown to you, they too may [now] receive
mercy. 32 cFor God delivered all to disobedience,
that he might have mercy upon all.
33 d*Oh, the depth of the riches and wisdom
and knowledge of God! How inscrutable are his
judgments and how unsearchable his ways!

34 e*"For who has known the mind of the Lord
or who has been his counselor?"
35 f*"Or who has given him anything
that he may be repaid?"

36 gFor from him and through him and for him
are all things. To him be glory forever. Amen.

11, 16–24: Israel remains holy in the eyes of God and stands as a witness to the faith described in the Old Testament because of **the firstfruits** (or the first piece baked) (16), that is, the converted remnant, and **the root** that **is holy,** that is, the patriarchs (16). The Jews' failure to believe in Christ is a warning to Gentile Christians to be on guard against any semblance of anti-Jewish arrogance, that is, failure to recognize their total dependence on divine grace.

11, 25–29: In God's design, Israel's unbelief is being used to grant the light of faith to the Gentiles. Meanwhile, Israel remains dear to God (cf 9, 13), still the object of special providence, the mystery of which will one day be revealed.

11, 30–32: Israel, together with the Gentiles who have been handed over to all manner of vices (ch 1), has been **delivered . . . to disobedience.** The conclusion of v 32 repeats the thought of 5, 20, "Where sin increased, grace overflowed all the more."

11, 33–36: This final reflection celebrates the wisdom of God's plan of salvation. As Paul has indicated throughout these chapters, both Jew and Gentile, despite the religious recalcitrance of each, have received the gift of faith. The methods used by God in making this outreach to the world stagger human comprehension but are at the same time a dazzling invitation to abiding faith.

11, 34: The citation is from the Greek text of Is 40, 13. Paul does not explicitly mention Isaiah in this verse, nor Job in v 35.

11, 35: Paul quotes from an old Greek version of Jb 41, 3a, which differs from the Hebrew text (Jb 41, 11a).

p Nm 15, 17–21; Ez 44, 30; Neh 10, 36–38. q Eph 2, 11–19. r 1 Cor 1, 31. s 12, 16. t 1 Cor 10, 12. u Jn 15, 2.4; Heb 3, 14. v 2 Cor 3, 16. w Prv 3, 7 / 12, 16; Mk 13, 10; Lk 21, 24; Jn 10, 16. x Mt 23, 39. y Ps 14, 7; Is 59, 20–21. z Is 27, 9; Jer 31, 33–34. a 15, 8; 1 Thes 2, 15–16. b 9, 6; Nm 23, 19; Is 54, 10. c Gal 3, 22; 1 Tm 2, 4. d Jb 11, 7–8; Ps 139, 6.17–18; Wis 17, 1; Is 55, 8–9. e Jb 15, 8; Wis 9, 13; Is 40, 13; Jer 23, 18; 1 Cor 2, 11–16. f Jb 41, 3; Is 40, 14. g 1 Cor 8, 6; Col 1, 16–17.

VI: The Duties of Christians

CHAPTER 12

Sacrifice of Body and Mind [1][h]*I urge you
therefore, brothers, by the mercies of God, to
offer your bodies as a living sacrifice, holy and
pleasing to God, your spiritual worship. [2][i]Do not
conform yourself to this age but be transformed
by the renewal of your mind, that you may
discern what is the will of God, what is good and
pleasing and perfect.

Many Parts in One Body [3][j]For by the grace
given to me I tell everyone among you not to
think of himself more highly than one ought to
think, but to think soberly, each according to the
measure of faith that God has apportioned. [4][k]For
as in one body we have many parts, and all the
parts do not have the same function, [5]*so we,
though many, are one body in Christ and indi-
vidually parts of one another. [6][l]*Since we have
gifts that differ according to the grace given to
us, let us exercise them: if prophecy, in propor-
tion to the faith; [7]if ministry, in ministering; if
one is a teacher, in teaching; [8]*if one exhorts, in
exhortation; if one contributes, in generosity; if
one is over others, with diligence; if one does
acts of mercy, with cheerfulness.

Mutual Love [9][m]Let love be sincere; hate what
is evil, hold on to what is good; [10][n]love one an-
other with mutual affection; anticipate one an-
other in showing honor. [11][o]Do not grow slack in
zeal, be fervent in spirit, serve the Lord.
[12][p]Rejoice in hope, endure in affliction, perse-
vere in prayer. [13][q]Contribute to the needs of the
holy ones, exercise hospitality. [14][r s]*Bless those
who persecute [you], bless and do not curse
them. [15][t]Rejoice with those who rejoice, weep
with those who weep. [16][u]Have the same regard
for one another; do not be haughty but associate
with the lowly; do not be wise in your own esti-
mation. [17][v]Do not repay anyone evil for evil; be
concerned for what is noble in the sight of all.
[18][w]If possible, on your part, live at peace with all.
[19][x]Beloved, do not look for revenge but leave
room for the wrath; for it is written, "Vengeance
is mine, I will repay, says the Lord." [20][y]Rather, "if
your enemy is hungry, feed him; if he is thirsty,
give him something to drink; for by so doing you
will heap burning coals upon his head." [21]Do not
be conquered by evil but conquer evil with good.

CHAPTER 13

Obedience to Authority [1][z]*Let every person
be subordinate to the higher authorities, for

12, 1—13, 14: Since Christ marks the termination of the Mosaic law as the primary source of guidance for God's people (10, 4), the apostle explains how Christians can function, in the light of the gift of justification through faith, in their relation to one another and the state.

12, 1–8: The Mosaic code included elaborate directions on sacrifices and other cultic observances. The gospel, however, invites believers to present their **bodies as a living sacrifice** (1). Instead of being limited by specific legal maxims, Christians are liberated for the exercise of good judgment as they are confronted with the many and varied decisions required in the course of daily life. To assist them, God distributes a variety of gifts to the fellowship of believers, including those of prophecy, teaching, and exhortation (6–8). Prophets assist the community to understand the will of God as it applies to the present situation (6). Teachers help people to understand themselves and their responsibilities in relation to others (7). One who **exhorts** offers encouragement to the community to exercise their faith in the performance of all that is pleasing to God (8). Indeed, this very section, beginning with v 1, is a specimen of Paul's own style of exhortation.

12, 5: One body in Christ: on the church as the body of Christ, see 1 Cor 12, 12–27.

12, 6: Everyone has some gift that can be used for the benefit of the community. When the instruction on justification through faith is correctly grasped, the possesser of a gift will understand that it is not an instrument of self-aggrandizement. Possession of a gift is not an index to quality of faith. Rather, the gift is a challenge to faithful use.

12, 8: Over others: usually taken to mean "rule over" but possibly "serve as a patron." Wealthier members in Greco-Roman communities were frequently asked to assist in public service projects. In view of the references to contributing **in generosity** and to **acts of mercy,** Paul may have in mind people like Phoebe (16, 1–2), who is called a **benefactor** (or "patron") because of the services she rendered to many Christians, including Paul.

12, 14–21: Since God has justified the believers, it is not necessary for them to take justice into their own hands by taking vengeance. God will ultimately deal justly with all, including those who inflict injury on the believers. This question of personal rights as a matter of justice prepares the way for more detailed consideration of the state as adjudicator.

13, 1–7: Paul must come to grips with the problem raised by a message that declares people free from the law. How are they to relate to Roman authority? The problem was exacerbated by the fact that imperial protocol was interwoven with devotion to various deities. Paul builds on the traditional instruction exhibited in Wis 6, 1–3, according to which kings and magistrates rule by

h 2 Cor 1, 3 / 6, 13; 1 Pt 2, 5. i Eph 4, 17.22–23; 1 Pt 1, 14 / Eph 5, 10.17; Phil 1, 10. j 15, 15 / Phil 2, 3 / 1 Cor 12, 11; Eph 4, 7. k 1 Cor 12, 12.27; Eph 4, 25. l 1 Cor 12, 4–11.28–31; Eph 4, 7–12; 1 Pt 4, 10–11 / 2 Cor 9, 7. m 2 Cor 6, 6; 1 Tm 1, 5; 1 Pt 1, 22 / Am 5, 15. n Jn 13, 34; 1 Thes 4, 9; 1 Pt 2, 17; 2 Pt 1, 7 / Phil 2, 3. o Acts 18, 25. p 5, 2–3; Col 4, 2; 1 Thes 5, 17. q Heb 13, 2; 1 Pt 4, 9. r Mt 5, 38–48; 1 Cor 4, 12; 1 Pt 3, 9. s Lk 6, 27–28. t Ps 35, 13; Sir 7, 34; 1 Cor 12, 26. u 15, 5; Phil 2, 2–3 / 11, 20; Prv 3, 7; Is 5, 21. v Prv 3, 4; 1 Thes 5, 15; 1 Pt 3, 9. w Heb 12, 14. x Lv 19, 18; Dt 32, 35.41; Mt 5, 39; 1 Cor 6, 6–7; Heb 10, 30. y Prv 25, 21–22; Mt 5, 44. z Prv 8, 15–16; Wis 6, 3; Jn 19, 11; 1 Pt 2, 13–17; Ti 3, 1.

there is no authority except from God, and those that exist have been established by God. 2 Therefore, whoever resists authority opposes what God has appointed, and those who oppose it will bring judgment upon themselves. 3 [a]For rulers are not a cause of fear to good conduct, but to evil. Do you wish to have no fear of authority? Then do what is good and you will receive approval from it, 4 [b]for it is a servant of God for your good. But if you do evil, be afraid, for it does not bear the sword without purpose; it is the servant of God to inflict wrath on the evildoer. 5 [c]Therefore, it is necessary to be subject not only because of the wrath but also because of conscience. 6 This is why you also pay taxes, for the authorities are ministers of God, devoting themselves to this very thing. 7 [d]Pay to all their dues, taxes to whom taxes are due, toll to whom toll is due, respect to whom respect is due, honor to whom honor is due.

Love Fulfills the Law 8 [e]*Owe nothing to anyone, except to love one another; for the one who loves another has fulfilled the law. 9 [f]The commandments, "You shall not commit adultery; you shall not kill; you shall not steal; you shall not covet," and whatever other commandment there may be, are summed up in this saying, [namely] "You shall love your neighbor as yourself." 10 [g]Love does no evil to the neighbor; hence, love is the fulfillment of the law.

Awareness of the End of Time 11 [h]*And do this because you know the time; it is the hour now for you to awake from sleep. For our salvation is nearer now than when we first believed; 12 [i]the night is advanced, the day is at hand. Let us then throw off the works of darkness [and] put on the armor of light; 13 [j]*let us conduct ourselves properly as in the day, not in orgies and drunkenness, not in promiscuity and licentiousness, not in rivalry and jealousy. 14 [k]But put on the Lord Jesus Christ, and make no provision for the desires of the flesh.

CHAPTER 14

To Live and Die for Christ 1 [l] [m]*Welcome anyone who is weak in faith, but not for disputes over opinions. 2 [n]One person believes that one may eat anything, while the weak person eats only vegetables. 3 [o]The one who eats must not despise the one who abstains, and the one who abstains must not pass judgment on the one who eats; for God has welcomed him. 4 [p]Who are you to pass judgment on someone else's servant? Before his own master he stands or falls. And he will be upheld, for the Lord is able to make him stand. 5 [q]*[For] one person considers one day more important than another, while another person considers all days alike. Let everyone be fully persuaded in his own mind. 6 Whoever observes the day, observes it for the Lord. Also

consent of God. From this perspective, then, believers who render obedience to the governing authorities are obeying the one who is highest in command. At the same time, it is recognized that Caesar has the responsibility to make just ordinances and to commend uprightness; cf Wis 6, 4–21. That Caesar is not entitled to obedience when such obedience would nullify God's prior claim to the believers' moral decision becomes clear in the light of the following verses.

13, 8–10: When love directs the Christian's moral decisions, the interest of law in basic concerns, such as familial relationships, sanctity of life, and security of property, is safeguarded (9). Indeed, says Paul, the same applies to any **other commandment** (9), whether one in the Mosaic code or one drawn up by local magistrates under imperial authority. Love anticipates the purpose of public legislation, namely, to secure the best interests of the citizenry. Since Caesar's obligation is to punish the wrongdoer (4), the Christian who acts in love is free from all legitimate indictment.

13, 11–14: These verses provide the motivation for the love that is encouraged in vv 8–10.

13, 13: Let us conduct ourselves properly as in the day: the behavior described in 1, 29–30 is now to be reversed. Secular moralists were fond of making references to people who could not wait for nightfall to do their carousing. Paul says that Christians claim to be people of the new day that will dawn with the return of Christ. Instead of planning for nighttime behavior they should be concentrating on conduct that is consonant with avowed interest in the Lord's return.

14, 1—15, 6: Since Christ spells termination of the law, which included observance of specific days and festivals as well as dietary instruction, the jettisoning of long-practiced customs was traumatic for many Christians brought up under the Mosaic code. Although Paul acknowledges that in principle no food is a source of moral contamination (14), he recommends that the consciences of Christians who are scrupulous in this regard be respected by other Christians (21). On the other hand, those who have scruples are not to sit in judgment on those who know that the gospel has liberated them from such ordinances (10). See 1 Cor 8 and 10.

14, 5: Since the problem to be overcome was humanity's perverted mind or judgment (1, 28), Paul indicates that the **mind** of the Christian is now able to function with appropriate discrimination (cf 12, 2).

a 1 Pt 2, 13–14; 3, 13. b 12, 19. c 1 Pt 2, 19. d Mt 22, 21; Mk 12, 17; Lk 20, 25. e Jn 13, 34; Gal 5, 14. f Ex 20, 13–17 / Lv 19, 18; Dt 5, 17–21; Mt 5, 43–44; 19, 18–19;22, 39; Mk 12, 31; Lk 10, 27; Gal 5, 14; Jas 2, 8. g Mt 22, 40; 1 Cor 13, 4–7. h Eph 5, 8–16; 1 Thes 5, 5–7. i Jn 8, 12; 1 Thes 5, 4–8; 1 Jn 2, 8 / 2 Cor 6, 7; 10, 4; Eph 5, 11; 6, 13–17. j Lk 21, 34; Eph 5, 18. k Gal 3, 27; 5, 16; Eph 4, 24; 6, 11. l 1 Cor 8, 1–13. m 15, 1.7; 1 Cor 9, 22. n Gn 1, 29; 9, 3; 1 Cor 8, 1–13; 10, 14–33. o Col 2, 16. p 2, 1; Mt 7, 11; Jas 4, 11–12. q Gal 4, 10.

whoever eats, eats for the Lord, since he gives thanks to God; while whoever abstains, abstains for the Lord and gives thanks to God. [7]None of us lives for oneself, and no one dies for oneself. [8][r]*For if we live, we live for the Lord, and if we die, we die for the Lord; so then, whether we live or die, we are the Lord's. [9][s]For this is why Christ died and came to life, that he might be Lord of both the dead and the living. [10][t]Why then do you judge your brother? Or you, why do you look down on your brother? For we shall all stand before the judgment seat of God; [11][u]for it is written:

"As I live, says the Lord, every knee shall bend
 before me,
 and every tongue shall give praise to God."

[12][v]So [then] each of us shall give an account of himself [to God].

Consideration for the Weak Conscience [13][w]Then let us no longer judge one another, but rather resolve never to put a stumbling block or hindrance in the way of a brother. [14][x]I know and am convinced in the Lord Jesus that nothing is unclean in itself; still, it is unclean for someone who thinks it unclean. [15][y]If your brother is being hurt by what you eat, your conduct is no longer in accord with love. Do not because of your food destroy him for whom Christ died. [16][z]So do not let your good be reviled. [17][a]For the kingdom of God is not a matter of food and drink, but of righteousness, peace, and joy in the holy Spirit; [18]whoever serves Christ in this way is pleasing to God and approved by others. [19][b]*Let us then pursue what leads to peace and to building up one another. [20][c]For the sake of food, do not destroy the work of God. Everything is indeed clean, but it is wrong for anyone to become a stumbling block by eating; [21]it is good not to eat meat or drink wine or do anything that causes your brother to stumble. [22]Keep the faith [that] you have to yourself in the presence of God; blessed is the one who does not condemn himself for what he approves. [23][d]*But whoever has doubts is condemned if he eats, because this is not from faith; for whatever is not from faith is sin.

CHAPTER 15

Patience and Self-Denial [1][e]We who are strong ought to put up with the failings of the weak and not to please ourselves; [2][f]let each of us please our neighbor for the good, for building up. [3][g]*For Christ did not please himself; but, as it is written, "The insults of those who insult you fall upon me." [4][h]For whatever was written previously was written for our instruction, that by endurance and by the encouragement of the scriptures we might have hope. [5][i]*May the God of endurance and encouragement grant you to think in harmony with one another, in keeping with Christ Jesus, [6]that with one accord you may with one voice glorify the God and Father of our Lord Jesus Christ.

God's Fidelity and Mercy [7][j]*Welcome one another, then, as Christ welcomed you, for the glory of God. [8][k]For I say that Christ became a

14, 8: The Lord: Jesus, our Master. The same Greek word, **kyrios,** was applied to both rulers and holders of slaves. Throughout the Letter to the Romans Paul emphasizes God's total claim on the believer; see the note on 1, 1.

14, 19: Some manuscripts, versions, and church Fathers read, "We then pursue . . ."; cf 5, 1.

14, 23: Whatever is not from faith is sin: Paul does not mean that all the actions of unbelievers are sinful. He addresses himself to the question of intracommunity living. **Sin** in the singular is the dreadful power described in 5, 12–14.

15, 3: Liberation from the law of Moses does not make the scriptures of the old covenant irrelevant. Much consolation and motivation for Christian living can be derived from the Old Testament, as in the citation from Ps 69, 10. Because this psalm is quoted several times in the New Testament, it has been called indirectly messianic.

15, 5: Think in harmony: a Greco-Roman ideal. Not rigid uniformity of thought and expression but thoughtful consideration of other people's views finds expression here.

15, 7–13: True oneness of mind is found in pondering the ultimate mission of the church: to bring it about that God's name be glorified throughout the world and that Jesus Christ be universally recognized as God's gift to all humanity. Paul here prepares his addressees for the climactic appeal he is about to make.

r Lk 20, 38; 2 Cor 5, 15; Gal 2, 20; 1 Thes 5, 10. s Acts 10, 42. t Acts 17, 31; 2 Cor 5, 10. u Is 49, 18 / Is 45, 23; Phil 2, 10–11. v Gal 6, 5. w 1 Cor 8, 9.13. x Mk 7, 5.20; Acts 10, 15; 1 Cor 10, 25–27; 1 Tm 4, 4. y 1 Cor 8, 11–13. z 2, 24; Ti 2, 5. a 1 Cor 8, 8. b 12, 18 / 15, 2. c 1 Cor 8, 11–13; 10, 28–29; Ti 1, 15. d Ti 1, 15; Jas 4, 17. e 14, 1–2. f 14, 1.19; 1 Cor 9, 19; 10, 24.33. g Ps 69, 10. h 4, 23–24; 1 Mc 12, 9; 1 Cor 10, 11; 2 Tm 3, 16. i 12, 16; Phil 2, 2; 4, 2. j 14, 1. k Mt 15, 24 / Mi 7, 20; Acts 3, 25.

minister of the circumcised to show God's truthfulness, to confirm the promises to the patriarchs, [9 l]but so that the Gentiles might glorify God for his mercy. As it is written:

"Therefore, I will praise you among the
Gentiles
and sing praises to your name."

[10 m*]And again it says:

"Rejoice, O Gentiles, with his people."

[11 n]And again:

"Praise the Lord, all you Gentiles,
and let all the peoples praise him."

[12 o]And again Isaiah says:

"The root of Jesse shall come,
raised up to rule the Gentiles;
in him shall the Gentiles hope."

[13 p]May the God of hope fill you with all joy and peace in believing, so that you may abound in hope by the power of the holy Spirit.

VII: Conclusion

Apostle to the Gentiles [14*]I myself am convinced about you, my brothers, that you yourselves are full of goodness, filled with all knowledge, and able to admonish one another. [15 q]But I have written to you rather boldly in some respects to remind you, because of the grace given me by God [16 r]to be a minister of Christ Jesus to the Gentiles in performing the priestly service of the gospel of God, so that the offering up of the Gentiles may be acceptable, sanctified by the holy Spirit. [17]In Christ Jesus, then, I have reason to boast in what pertains to God. [18 s]For I will not dare to speak of anything except what Christ has accomplished through me to lead the Gentiles to obedience by word and deed, [19*]by the power of signs and wonders, by the power of the Spirit [of God], so that from Jerusalem all the way around to Illyricum I have finished preaching the gospel of Christ. [20 t*]Thus I aspire to proclaim the gospel not where Christ has already been named, so that I do not build on another's foundation, [21 u*]but as it is written:

"Those who have never been told of him shall
see,
and those who have never heard of him
shall understand."

Paul's Plans; Need for Prayers [22]That is why I have so often been prevented from coming to you. [23 v]But now, since I no longer have any opportunity in these regions and since I have desired to come to you for many years, [24 w]I hope to see you in passing as I go to Spain and to be sent on my way there by you, after I have enjoyed being with you for a time. [25 x*]Now, however, I am going to Jerusalem to minister to the holy ones. [26 y*]For Macedonia and Achaia have decided to make some contribution for the poor among the holy ones in Jerusalem; [27 z]they decided to do it, and in fact they are indebted to them, for if the Gentiles have come to share in their spiritual blessings, they ought also to serve

15, 10: Paul's citation of Dt 32, 43 follows the Greek version.

15, 14–33: Paul sees himself as apostle and benefactor in the priestly service of the gospel and so sketches plans for a mission in Spain, supported by those in Rome.

15, 14: **Full of goodness:** the opposite of what humanity was filled with according to 1, 29–30.

15, 19: **Illyricum:** Roman province northwest of Greece on the eastern shore of the Adriatic.

15, 20: **I aspire:** Paul uses terminology customarily applied to philanthropists. Unlike some philanthropists of his time, Paul does not engage in cheap competition for public acclaim. This explanation of his missionary policy is to assure the Christians in Rome that he is also not planning to remain in that city and build on other people's foundations (cf 2 Cor 10, 12–18). However, he does solicit their help in sending him on his way to Spain, which was considered the limit of the western world. Thus Paul's addressees realize that evangelization may be understood in the broader sense of mission or, as in Rom 1, 15, of instruction within the Christian community that derives from the gospel.

15, 21: The citation from Is 52, 15 concerns the Servant of the Lord. According to Isaiah, the Servant is first of all Israel, which was to bring the knowledge of Yahweh to the nations. In chs 9–11 Paul showed how Israel failed in this mission. Therefore, he himself undertakes almost singlehandedly Israel's responsibility as the Servant and moves as quickly as possible with the gospel through the Roman empire.

15, 25–27: Paul may have viewed the contribution he was gathering from Gentile Christians for the poor in Jerusalem (cf 2 Cor 8 and 9) as a fulfillment of the vision of Is 60, 5–6. In confidence that the messianic fulfillment was taking place, Paul stresses in chs 14–16 the importance of harmonious relationships between Jews and Gentiles.

15, 26: **Achaia:** the Roman province of southern Greece.

l 11, 30 / 2 Sm 22, 50; Ps 18, 50. m Dt 32, 43. n Ps 117, 1. o Is 11, 10; Rv 5, 5; 22, 16. p 5, 1–2. q 1, 5; 12, 3. r 11, 13; Phil 2, 17. s Acts 15, 12; 2 Cor 12, 12. t 2 Cor 10, 13–18. u Is 52, 15. v 1, 10–13; Acts 19, 21–22. w 1 Cor 16, 6. x Acts 19, 21; 20, 22. y 1 Cor 16, 1; 2 Cor 8, 1–4; 9, 2.12. z 9, 4 / 1 Cor 9, 11.

them in material blessings. [28]So when I have completed this and safely handed over this contribution to them, I shall set out by way of you to Spain; [29]and I know that in coming to you I shall come in the fullness of Christ's blessing.

[30] [a]I urge you, [brothers,] by our Lord Jesus Christ and by the love of the Spirit, to join me in the struggle by your prayers to God on my behalf, [31]that I may be delivered from the disobedient in Judea, and that my ministry for Jerusalem may be acceptable to the holy ones, [32]so that I may come to you with joy by the will of God and be refreshed together with you. [33] [b]The God of peace be with all of you. Amen.

CHAPTER 16

Phoebe Commended [1] [c]*I commend to you Phoebe our sister, who is [also] a minister of the church at Cenchreae, [2]that you may receive her in the Lord in a manner worthy of the holy ones, and help her in whatever she may need from you, for she has been a benefactor to many and to me as well.

Paul's Greetings [3] [d]*Greet Prisca and Aquila, my co-workers in Christ Jesus, [4]who risked their necks for my life, to whom not only I am grateful but also all the churches of the Gentiles; [5] [e]*greet also the church at their house. Greet my beloved Epaenetus, who was the firstfruits in Asia for Christ. [6]Greet Mary, who has worked hard for you. [7]*Greet Andronicus and Junia, my relatives and my fellow prisoners; they are prominent among the apostles and they were in Christ before me. [8]Greet Ampliatus, my beloved in the Lord. [9]Greet Urbanus, our co-worker in Christ, and my beloved Stachys. [10]Greet Apelles, who is approved in Christ. Greet those who belong to the family of Aristobulus. [11]Greet my relative Herodion. Greet those in the Lord who belong to the family of Narcissus. [12]Greet those workers in the Lord, Tryphaena and Tryphosa. Greet the beloved Persis, who has worked hard in the Lord. [13] [f]*Greet Rufus, chosen in the Lord, and his mother and mine. [14]Greet Asyncritus, Phlegon, Hermes, Patrobas, Hermas, and the brothers who are with them. [15]Greet Philologus, Julia, Nereus and his sister, and Olympas, and all the holy ones who are with them. [16] [g]Greet one another with a holy kiss. All the churches of Christ greet you.

Against Factions [17] [h]*I urge you, brothers, to watch out for those who create dissensions and obstacles, in opposition to the teaching that you learned; avoid them. [18] [i]For such people do not serve our Lord Christ but their own appetites, and by fair and flattering speech they deceive the hearts of the innocent. [19] [j]For while your obedience is known to all, so that I rejoice over you, I want you to be wise as to what is good, and simple as to what is evil; [20] [k]*then the God of peace will quickly crush Satan under your feet. The grace of our Lord Jesus be with you.

Greetings from Corinth [21] [l]Timothy, my co-worker, greets you; so do Lucius and Jason and Sosipater, my relatives. [22]I, Tertius, the writer of

16, 1–23: Some authorities regard these verses as a later addition to the letter, but in general the evidence favors the view that they were included in the original. Paul endeavors through the long list of greetings (3–16; 21–23) to establish strong personal contact with congregations that he has not personally encountered before. The combination of Jewish and Gentile names dramatically attests the unity in the gospel that transcends previous barriers of nationality, religious ceremony, or racial status.

16, 1: Minister: in Greek, **diakonos;** see the note on Phil 1, 1.

16, 3: Prisca and Aquila: presumably the couple mentioned at Acts 18, 2; 1 Cor 16, 19; 2 Tm 4, 19.

16, 5: The church at their house: i.e., that meets there. Such local assemblies (cf 1 Cor 16, 19; Col 4, 15; Phlm 2) might consist of only one or two dozen Christians each. It is understandable, therefore, that such smaller groups might experience difficulty in relating to one another on certain issues. **Firstfruits:** cf 8, 23; 11, 16; 1 Cor 16, 15.

16, 7: The name Junia is a woman's name. One ancient Greek manuscript and a number of ancient versions read the name "Julia." Most editors have interpreted it as a man's name, Junias.

16, 13: This Rufus cannot be identified to any degree of certainty with the Rufus of Mk 15, 21.

16, 17–18: Paul displays genuine concern for the congregations in Rome by warning them against self-seeking teachers. It would be a great loss, he intimates, if their obedience, which is known to all (cf 1, 8), would be diluted.

16, 20: This verse contains the only mention of Satan in Romans.

a 2 Cor 1, 11; Phil 1, 27; Col 4, 3; 2 Thes 3, 1. b 16, 20; 2 Cor 13, 11; Phil 4, 9; 1 Thes 5, 23; 2 Thes 3, 16; Heb 13, 20. c Acts 18, 18. d Acts 18, 2.18–26; 1 Cor 16, 19; 2 Tm 4, 19. e 1 Cor 16, 19; Col 4, 15; Phlm 2 / 1 Cor 16, 15. f Mk 15, 21. g 1 Cor 16, 20; 2 Cor 13, 12; 1 Thes 5, 26; 1 Pt 5, 14. h Mt 7, 15; Ti 3, 10. i Phil 3, 18–19 / Col 2, 4; 2 Pt 2, 3. j 1, 8; Mt 10, 16; 1 Cor 14, 20. k 15, 33; Gn 3, 15; Lk 10, 19 / 1 Cor 16, 23; 1 Thes 5, 28;2 Thes 3, 18. l Acts 16, 1–2; 19, 22; 20, 4; 1 Cor 4, 17; 16, 10; Phil 2, 19–22; Heb 13, 23.

this letter, greet you in the Lord. 23 m*Gaius, who is host to me and to the whole church, greets you. Erastus, the city treasurer, and our brother Quartus greet you. [24]*

Doxology [25 n*Now to him who can strengthen you, according to my gospel and the proclamation of Jesus Christ, according to the revelation of the mystery kept secret for long ages 26 obut now manifested through the prophetic writings and, according to the command of the eternal God, made known to all nations to bring about the obedience of faith, 27 pto the only wise God, through Jesus Christ be glory forever and ever. Amen.]

16, 23: This Erastus is not necessarily to be identified with the Erastus of Acts 19, 22 or of 2 Tm 4, 20.

16, 24: Some manuscripts add, similarly to v 20, "The grace of our Lord Jesus Christ be with you all. Amen."

16, 25–27: This doxology is assigned variously to the end of chs 14, 15, and 16 in the manuscript tradition. Some manuscripts omit it entirely. Whether written by Paul or not, it forms an admirable conclusion to the letter at this point.

16, 25: Paul's gospel reveals **the mystery kept secret for long ages:** justification and salvation through faith, with all the implications for Jews and Gentiles that Paul has developed in the letter.

m Acts 19, 29; 1 Cor 1, 14 / 2 Tm 4, 20. n 1 Cor 2, 7; Eph 1, 9; 3, 3–9; Col 1, 26. o 2 Tm 1, 10 / 1, 5; Eph 3, 4–5.9; 1 Pt 1, 20. p 11, 36; Gal 1, 5; Eph 3, 20–21; Phil 4, 20; 1 Tm 1, 17; 2 Tm 4, 18; Heb 13, 21; 1 Pt 4, 11; 2 Pt 3, 18; Jude 25, Rev 1, 6.

THE FIRST LETTER TO THE CORINTHIANS

Paul's first letter to the church of Corinth provides us with a fuller insight into the life of an early Christian community of the first generation than any other book of the New Testament. Through it we can glimpse both the strengths and the weaknesses of this small group in a great city of the ancient world, men and women who had accepted the good news of Christ and were now trying to realize in their lives the implications of their baptism. Paul, who had founded the community and continued to look after it as a father, responds both to questions addressed to him and to situations of which he had been informed. In doing so, he reveals much about himself, his teaching, and the way in which he conducted his work of apostleship. Some things are puzzling because we have the correspondence only in one direction. For the person studying this letter, it seems to raise as many questions as it answers, but without it our knowledge of church life in the middle of the first century would be much poorer.

Paul established a Christian community in Corinth about the year 51, on his second missionary journey. The city, a commercial crossroads, was a melting pot full of devotees of various pagan cults and marked by a measure of moral depravity not unusual in a great seaport. The Acts of the Apostles suggests that moderate success attended Paul's efforts among the Jews in Corinth at first, but that they soon turned against him (Acts 18, 1-8). More fruitful was his year and a half spent among the Gentiles (Acts 18, 11), which won to the faith many of the city's poor and underprivileged (1, 26). After his departure the eloquent Apollos, an Alexandrian Jewish Christian, rendered great service to the community, expounding "from the scriptures that the Messiah is Jesus" (Acts 18, 24-28).

While Paul was in Ephesus on his third journey (16, 8; Acts 19, 1-20), he received disquieting news about Corinth. The community there was displaying open factionalism, as certain members were identifying themselves exclusively with individual Christian leaders and interpreting Christian teaching as a superior wisdom for the initiated few (1, 10—4, 21). The community lacked the decisiveness to take appropriate action against one of its members who was living publicly in an incestuous union (5, 1-13). Other members engaged in legal conflicts in pagan courts of law (6, 1-11); still others may have participated in religious prostitution (6, 12-20) or temple sacrifices (10, 14-22).

The community's ills were reflected in its liturgy. In the celebration of the Eucharist certain members discriminated against others, drank too freely at the agape, or fellowship meal, and denied Christian social courtesies to the poor among the membership (11, 17-22). Charisms such as ecstatic prayer, attributed freely to the impulse of the holy Spirit, were more highly prized than works of charity (13, 1-2.8), and were used at times in a disorderly way (14, 1-40). Women appeared at the assembly without the customary head-covering (11, 3-16), and perhaps were quarreling over their right to address the assembly (14, 34-35).

Still other problems with which Paul had to deal concerned matters of conscience discussed among the faithful members of the community: the eating of meat that had been sacrificed to idols (8, 1-13), the use of sex in marriage (7, 1-7), and the attitude to be taken by the unmarried toward marriage in view of the possible proximity of Christ's second coming (7, 25-40). There was also a doctrinal matter that called for Paul's attention, for some members of the community, despite their belief in the resurrection of Christ, were denying the possibility of general bodily resurrection.

To treat this wide spectrum of questions, Paul wrote this letter from Ephesus about the year A.D. 56. The majority of the Corinthian Christians may well have been quite faithful. Paul writes on their behalf to guard against the threats posed to the community by the views and conduct of various minorities. He writes with confidence in the authority of his apostolic mission, and he presumes that the Corinthians, despite their deficiencies, will recognize and accept it. On the other hand, he does not hesitate to exercise his authority as his judgment dictates in each situation, even going so far as to promise a direct confrontation with recalcitrants, should the abuses he scores remain uncorrected (4, 18-21).

The letter illustrates well the mind and character of Paul. Although he is impelled to insist on his office as founder of the community, he recognizes that he is only one servant of God among many and generously acknowledges the labors of Apollos (3, 5-8). He provides us in this letter with many valuable examples of his method of theological reflection and exposition. He always treats the questions at issue on the level of the purity of Christian teaching and conduct. Certain passages of the letter are of the greatest importance for the understanding of early Christian teaching on the Eucharist (10, 14-22; 11, 17-34) and on the resurrection of the body (15, 1-58).

Paul's authorship of 1 Corinthians, apart from a few verses that some regard as later interpolations, has never been seriously questioned. Some scholars have proposed, however, that the letter as we have it contains portions of more than one original Pauline letter. We know that Paul wrote at least two other letters to Corinth (see 5, 9; 2 Cor 2, 3-4) in addition to the two that we now have; this theory holds that the additional letters are actually contained within the two canonical ones. Most commentators, however, find 1 Corinthians quite understandable as a single coherent work.

The principal divisions of the First Letter to the Corinthians are the following:

I. Address (1, 1-9)
II. Disorders in the Corinthian Community (1, 10—6, 20)
  A. Divisions in the Church (1, 10—4, 21)
  B. Moral Disorders (5, 1—6, 20)

III. Answers to the Corinthians' Questions (7, 1—11, 1)
A. Marriage and Virginity (7, 1-40)
B. Offerings to Idols (8, 1—11, 1)
IV. Problems in Liturgical Assemblies (11, 2—14, 40)
A. Women's Headdresses (11, 3-16)
B. The Lord's Supper (11, 17-34)
C. Spiritual Gifts (12, 1—14, 40)
V. The Resurrection (15, 1-58)
A. The Resurrection of Christ (15, 1-11)
B. The Resurrection of the Dead (15, 12-34)
C. The Manner of the Resurrection (15, 35-58)
VI. Conclusion (16, 1-24)

I: Address

CHAPTER 1

Greeting [1a*]Paul, called to be an apostle of
Christ Jesus by the will of God, and Sosthenes
our brother, [2b]to the church of God that is in
Corinth, to you who have been sanctified in
Christ Jesus, called to be holy, with all those
everywhere who call upon the name of our Lord
Jesus Christ, their Lord and ours. [3]Grace to you
and peace from God our Father and the Lord
Jesus Christ.
Thanksgiving [4]I give thanks to my God always
on your account for the grace of God bestowed
on you in Christ Jesus, [5]that in him you were
enriched in every way, with all discourse and all
knowledge, [6*]as the testimony to Christ was
confirmed among you, [7c]so that you are not
lacking in any spiritual gift as you wait for the
revelation of our Lord Jesus Christ. [8d]He will
keep you firm to the end, irreproachable on the
day of our Lord Jesus [Christ]. [9e]God is faithful,
and by him you were called to fellowship with
his Son, Jesus Christ our Lord.

II: Disorders in the Corinthian Community

A. Divisions in the Church

Groups and Slogans [10f*]I urge you, brothers,
in the name of our Lord Jesus Christ, that all of
you agree in what you say, and that there be no
divisions among you, but that you be united in
the same mind and in the same purpose. [11]For it
has been reported to me about you, my brothers,
by Chloe's people, that there are rivalries among
you. [12g*]I mean that each of you is saying, "I
belong to Paul," or "I belong to Apollos," or "I
belong to Kephas," or "I belong to Christ." [13*]Is
Christ divided? Was Paul crucified for you? Or
were you baptized in the name of Paul? [14h]I give

1, 1–9: Paul follows the conventional form for the opening of a Hellenistic letter (cf Rom 1, 1–7), but expands the opening with details carefully chosen to remind the readers of their situation and to suggest some of the issues the letter will discuss.

1, 1: **Called . . . by the will of God:** Paul's mission and the church's existence are grounded in God's initiative. God's call, grace, and fidelity are central ideas in this introduction, emphasized by repetition and wordplays in the Greek.

1, 6: **The testimony:** this defines the purpose of Paul's mission (see also 15, 15 and the note on 2, 1). The forms of his testimony include oral preaching and instruction, his letters, and the life he leads as an apostle.

1, 10—4, 21: The first problem Paul addresses is that of divisions within the community. Although we are unable to reconstruct the situation in Corinth completely, Paul clearly traces the divisions back to a false self-image on the part of the Corinthians, coupled with a false understanding of the apostles who preached to them (cf 4, 6.9; 9, 1–5) and of the Christian message itself. In these chapters he attempts to deal with those underlying factors and to bring the Corinthians back to a more correct perspective.

1, 12: **I belong to:** the activities of Paul and Apollos in Corinth are described in Acts 18. **Kephas** (i.e., "the Rock," a name by which Paul designates Peter also in 3, 22; 9, 5; 15, 5 and in Gal 1, 18; 2, 9.11.14) may well have passed through Corinth; he could have baptized some members of the community either there or elsewhere. The reference to **Christ** may be intended ironically here.

1, 13–17: The reference to baptism and the contrast with preaching the gospel in v 17a suggest that some Corinthians were paying special allegiance to the individuals who initiated them into the community.

a Rom 1, 1. b Acts 18, 1–11. c Ti 2, 13. d Phil 1, 6. e 1 Jn 1, 3. f Phil 2, 2. g 3, 4.22; 16, 12; Acts 18, 24–28. h Acts 18, 8 / Rom 16, 23.

thanks [to God] that I baptized none of you except Crispus and Gaius, 15 so that no one can say you were baptized in my name. 16 *i*(I baptized the household of Stephanas also; beyond that I do not know whether I baptized anyone else.) 17 *j**For Christ did not send me to baptize but to preach the gospel, and not with the wisdom of human eloquence, so that the cross of Christ might not be emptied of its meaning.

Paradox of the Cross 18 *k*The message of the cross is foolishness to those who are perishing, but to us who are being saved it is the power of God. 19 *l*For it is written:

"I will destroy the wisdom of the wise,
and the learning of the learned I will set aside."

20 *m*Where is the wise one? Where is the scribe? Where is the debater of this age? Has not God made the wisdom of the world foolish? 21 *For since in the wisdom of God the world did not come to know God through wisdom, it was the will of God through the foolishness of the proclamation to save those who have faith. 22 *n*For Jews demand signs and Greeks look for wisdom, 23 *o*but we proclaim Christ crucified, a stumbling block to Jews and foolishness to Gentiles, 24 but to those who are called, Jews and Greeks alike, Christ the power of God and the wisdom of God. 25 For the foolishness of God is wiser than human wisdom, and the weakness of God is stronger than human strength.

The Corinthians and Paul 26 *Consider your own calling, brothers. Not many of you were wise by human standards, not many were powerful, not many were of noble birth. 27 *p*Rather, God chose the foolish of the world to shame the wise, and God chose the weak of the world to shame the strong, 28 and God chose the lowly and despised of the world, those who count for nothing, to reduce to nothing those who are something, 29 *q**so that no human being might boast before God. 30 *r*It is due to him that you are in Christ Jesus, who became for us wisdom from God, as well as righteousness, sanctification, and redemption, 31 *s*so that, as it is written, "Whoever boasts, should boast in the Lord."

CHAPTER 2

1 *t**When I came to you, brothers, proclaiming the mystery of God, I did not come with sublimity of words or of wisdom. 2 *u*For I resolved to know nothing while I was with you except Jesus Christ, and him crucified. 3 *I came

1, 17b-18: The basic theme of chs 1–4 is announced. Adherence to individual leaders has something to do with differences in rhetorical ability and also with certain presuppositions regarding wisdom, eloquence, and effectiveness (power), which Paul judges to be in conflict with the gospel and the cross.

1, 17b: Not with the wisdom of human eloquence: both of the nouns employed here involve several levels of meaning, on which Paul deliberately plays as his thought unfolds. **Wisdom (sophia)** may be philosophical and speculative, but in biblical usage the term primarily denotes practical knowledge such as is demonstrated in the choice and effective application of means to achieve an end. The same term can designate the arts of building (cf 3, 10) or of persuasive speaking (cf 2, 4) or effectiveness in achieving salvation. **Eloquence (logos)**: this translation emphasizes one possible meaning of the term **logos** (cf the references to rhetorical style and persuasiveness in 2, 1.4). But the term itself may denote an internal reasoning process, plan, or intention, as well as an external word, speech, or message. So by his expression **ouk en sophia logou** in the context of gospel preaching, Paul may intend to exclude both human ways of reasoning or thinking about things and human rhetorical technique. **Human:** this adjective does not stand in the Greek text but is supplied from the context. Paul will begin immediately to distinguish between **sophia** and **logos** from their divine counterparts and play them off against each other.

1, 21-25: True wisdom and power are to be found paradoxically where one would least expect them, in the place of their apparent negation. To human eyes the crucified Christ symbolizes impotence and absurdity.

1, 26—2, 5: The pattern of God's wisdom and power is exemplified in their own experience, if they interpret it rightly (1, 26–31), and can also be read in their experience of Paul as he first appeared among them preaching the gospel (2, 1–5).

1, 29-31: "Boasting (about oneself)" is a Pauline expression for the radical sin, the claim to autonomy on the part of a creature, the illusion that we live and are saved by our own resources. "Boasting in the Lord" (31), on the other hand, is the acknowledgment that we live only from God and for God.

2, 1: The mystery of God: God's secret, known only to himself, is his plan for the salvation of his people; it is clear from 1, 18–25; 2, 2.8–10 that this secret involves Jesus and the cross. In place of **mystery**, other good manuscripts read "testimony" (cf 1, 6).

2, 3: The **weakness** of the crucified Jesus is reflected in Paul's own bearing (cf 2 Cor 10—13). **Fear and much trembling:** reverential fear based on a sense of God's transcendence permeates Paul's existence and preaching. Compare his advice to the Philippians to work out their salvation with "fear and trembling" (Phil 2, 12), because God is at work in them just as his exalting power was paradoxically at work in the emptying, humiliation, and obedience of Jesus to death on the cross (Phil 2, 6–11).

i 16, 15–17. j 2, 1.4. k 2, 14 / Rom 1, 16. l Is 29, 14. m Is 19, 12. n Mt 12, 38; 16, 1 / Acts 17, 18–21. o 2, 2; Gal 3, 1 / Gal 5, 11. p Jas 2, 5. q Eph 2, 9. r Rom 4, 17 / 6, 11; Rom 3, 24–26; 2 Cor 5, 21 / Eph 1, 7; Col 1, 14; 1 Thes 5, 23. s Jer 9, 23; 2 Cor 10, 17. t 1, 17. u 1, 23; Gal 6, 14.

to you in weakness and fear and much trembling, [4][v]*and my message and my proclamation were not with persuasive [words of] wisdom, but with a demonstration of spirit and power, [5][w]so that your faith might rest not on human wisdom but on the power of God.

The True Wisdom [6]*Yet we do speak a wisdom to those who are mature, but not a wisdom of this age, nor of the rulers of this age who are passing away. [7]*Rather we speak God's wisdom, mysterious, hidden, which God predetermined before the ages for our glory, [8]*and which none of the rulers of this age knew for, if they had known it, they would not have crucified the Lord of glory. [9][x]But as it is written:

"What eye has not seen, and ear has not
heard,
and what has not entered the human heart,
what God has prepared for those who love
him,"

[10][y]this God has revealed to us through the Spirit.

For the Spirit scrutinizes everything, even the depths of God. [11]Among human beings, who knows what pertains to a person except the spirit of the person that is within? Similarly, no one knows what pertains to God except the Spirit of God. [12]We have not received the spirit of the world but the Spirit that is from God, so that we may understand the things freely given us by God. [13]*And we speak about them not with words taught by human wisdom, but with words taught by the Spirit, describing spiritual realities in spiritual terms.

[14]*Now the natural person does not accept what pertains to the Spirit of God, for to him it is foolishness, and he cannot understand it, because it is judged spiritually. [15]*The spiritual person, however, can judge everything but is not subject to judgment by anyone.

[16][z]For "who has known the mind of the Lord, so as to counsel him?" But we have the mind of Christ.

CHAPTER 3

[1]*Brothers, I could not talk to you as spiritual people, but as fleshly people, as infants in Christ. [2][a]I fed you milk, not solid food, because you were unable to take it. Indeed, you are still not able, even now, [3][b]*for you are still of the flesh. While there is jealousy and rivalry among you,

2, 4: Among many manuscript readings here the best is either "not with the persuasion of wisdom" or "not with persuasive words of wisdom," which differ only by a nuance. Whichever reading is accepted, the inefficacy of human wisdom for salvation is contrasted with the power of the cross.

2, 6—3, 4: Paul now asserts paradoxically what he has previously been denying. To the Greeks who "are looking for wisdom" (1, 22), he does indeed bring a wisdom, but of a higher order and an entirely different quality, the only wisdom really worthy of the name. The Corinthians would be able to grasp Paul's preaching as wisdom and enter into a wisdom-conversation with him if they were more open to the Spirit and receptive to the new insight and language that the Spirit teaches.

2, 7–10a: God's wisdom: his plan for our salvation. This was his own eternal secret that no one else could fathom, but in this new age of salvation he has graciously revealed it to us. For the pattern of God's secret, hidden to others and now revealed to the Church, cf also Rom 11, 25–36; 16, 25–27; Eph 1, 3–10; 3, 3–11; Col 1, 25–28.

2, 8: The rulers of this age: this suggests not only the political leaders of the Jews and Romans under whom Jesus was crucified (cf Acts 4, 25–28) but also the cosmic powers behind them (cf Eph 1, 20–23; 3, 10). **They would not have crucified the Lord of glory:** they became the unwitting executors of God's plan, which will paradoxically bring about their own conquest and submission (15, 24–28).

2, 13: In spiritual terms: the Spirit teaches spiritual people a new mode of perception (12) and an appropriate language by which they can share their self-understanding, their knowledge about what God has done in them. The final phrase in v 13 can also be translated "describing spiritual realities to spiritual people," in which case it prepares for vv 14–16.

2, 14: The natural person: see the note on 3, 1.

2, 15: The spiritual person . . . is not subject to judgment: since spiritual persons have been given knowledge of what pertains to God (11–12), they share in God's own capacity to judge. One to whom the mind of the Lord (and of Christ) is revealed (16) can be said to share in some sense in God's exemption from counseling and criticism.

3, 1–4: The Corinthians desire a sort of wisdom dialogue or colloquy with Paul; they are looking for solid, adult food, and he appears to disappoint their expectations. Paul counters: if such a dialogue has not yet taken place, the reason is that they are still at an immature stage of development (cf 2, 6).

3, 1: Spiritual people . . . fleshly people: Paul employs two clusters of concepts and terms to distinguish what later theology will call the "natural" and the "supernatural." (1) The natural person (2, 14) is one whose existence, perceptions, and behavior are determined by purely natural principles, the **psychē** (2, 14) and the **sarx** (flesh, a biblical term that connotes creatureliness, 1.3). Such persons are only infants (1); they remain on a purely human level (**anthrōpoi,** 4). (2) On the other hand, they are called to be animated by a higher principle, the **pneuma,** God's spirit. They are to become spiritual (**pneumatikoi,** 1) and mature (2, 6) in their perceptions and behavior (cf Gal 5, 16–26). The culmination of existence in the Spirit is described in 15, 44–49.

3, 3–4: Jealousy, rivalry, and divisions in the community are symptoms of their arrested development; they reveal the immaturity both of their self-understanding (4) and of the judgments about their apostles (21).

v 4, 20; Rom 15, 19; 1 Thes 1, 5. w 2 Cor 4, 7. x Is 64, 3. y Mt 11, 25; 13, 11; 16, 17. z Wis 9, 13; Is 40, 13; Rom 11, 34. a Heb 5, 12–14. b Jas 3, 13–16.

are you not of the flesh and behaving in an
ordinary human way? 4 [c]Whenever someone
says, "I belong to Paul," and another, "I belong
to Apollos," are you not merely human?

The Role of God's Ministers 5 *What is Apol-
los, after all, and what is Paul? Ministers through
whom you became believers, just as the Lord
assigned each one. 6 [d]I planted, Apollos watered,
but God caused the growth. 7 Therefore, neither
the one who plants nor the one who waters is
anything, but only God, who causes the growth.
8 The one who plants and the one who waters
are equal, and each will receive wages in propor-
tion to his labor. 9 [e]For we are God's co-workers;
you are God's field, God's building.

10 *According to the grace of God given to me,
like a wise master builder I laid a foundation,
and another is building upon it. But each one
must be careful how he builds upon it, 11 for no
one can lay a foundation other than the one that
is there, namely, Jesus Christ. 12 If anyone builds
on this foundation with gold, silver, precious
stones, wood, hay, or straw, 13 [f]*the work of
each will come to light, for the Day will disclose
it. It will be revealed with fire, and the fire [itself]
will test the quality of each one's work. 14 If the
work stands that someone built upon the founda-
tion, that person will receive a wage. 15 *But if
someone's work is burned up, that one will
suffer loss; the person will be saved, but only as
through fire. 16 [g]Do you not know that you are
the temple of God, and that the Spirit of God
dwells in you? 17 *If anyone destroys God's
temple, God will destroy that person; for the
temple of God, which you are, is holy.

18 [h]Let no one deceive himself. If anyone
among you considers himself wise in this age, let
him become a fool so as to become wise. 19 [i]For
the wisdom of this world is foolishness in the
eyes of God, for it is written:

"He catches the wise in their own ruses,"

20 [j]and again:

"The Lord knows the thoughts of the wise,
that they are vain."

21 [k]*So let no one boast about human beings, for
everything belongs to you, 22 Paul or Apollos or
Kephas, or the world or life or death, or the
present or the future: all belong to you, 23 and
you to Christ, and Christ to God.

CHAPTER 4

1 [l]Thus should one regard us: as servants of
Christ and stewards of the mysteries of God.
2 Now it is of course required of stewards that
they be found trustworthy. 3 It does not concern
me in the least that I be judged by you or any
human tribunal; I do not even pass judgment on
myself; 4 [m]I am not conscious of anything against
me, but I do not thereby stand acquitted; the
one who judges me is the Lord. 5 Therefore, do

3, 5—4, 5: The Corinthians tend to evaluate their leaders by the criteria of human wisdom and to exaggerate their importance. Paul views the role of the apostles in the light of his theology of spiritual gifts (cf chs 12–14, where the charism of the apostle heads the lists). The essential aspects of all spiritual gifts (12, 4–6 presents them as gifts of grace, as services, and as modes of activity) are exemplified by the apostolate, which is a gift of grace (3, 10) through which God works (3, 9) and a form of service (3, 5) for the common good (elsewhere expressed by the verb "build up," suggested here by the image of the building, 3, 9). The apostles serve the church, but their accountability is to God and to Christ (4, 1–5).

3, 5: Ministers: for other expressions of Paul's understanding of himself as minister or steward to the church, cf 4, 1; 9, 17.19–27; 2 Cor 3, 6–9; 4, 1; 5, 18; 6, 3–4; and 11, 23 (the climax of Paul's defense).

3, 10–11: There are diverse functions in the service of the community, but each individual's task is serious, and each will stand accountable for the quality of his contribution.

3, 13: The Day: the great day of Yahweh, the day of judgment, which can be a time of either gloom or joy. **Fire** both destroys and purifies.

3, 15: Will be saved: although Paul can envision very harsh divine punishment (cf 17), he appears optimistic about the success of divine corrective means both here and elsewhere (cf 5, 5; 11, 32 [discipline]). The text of v 15 has sometimes been used to support the notion of purgatory, though it does not envisage this.

3, 17: Holy: i.e., "belonging to God." The cultic sanctity of the community is a fundamental theological reality to which Paul frequently alludes (cf 1, 2.30; 6, 11; 7, 14).

3, 21–23: These verses pick up the line of thought of 1, 10–13. If the Corinthians were genuinely wise (18–20), their perceptions would be reversed, and they would see everything in the world and all those with whom they exist in the church in their true relations with one another. Paul assigns all the persons involved in the theological universe a position on a scale: God, Christ, church members, church leaders. Read from top to bottom, the scale expresses ownership; read from bottom to top, the obligation to serve. This picture should be complemented by similar statements such as those in 8, 6 and 15, 20–28.

c 1, 12. d Acts 18, 1–11.24–28. e Eph 2, 20–22; 1 Pt 2, 5. f Mt 3, 11–12; 2 Thes 1, 7–10. g 6, 19; 2 Cor 6, 16; Eph 2, 20–22. h 8, 2; Is 5, 21; Gal 6, 3. i 1, 20 / Jb 5, 13. j Ps 94, 11. k 4, 6 / Rom 8, 32. l Ti 1, 7; 1 Pt 4, 10. m 2 Cor 1, 12 / Rom 2, 16; 2 Cor 5, 10.

not make any judgment before the appointed
time, until the Lord comes, for he will bring to
light what is hidden in darkness and will mani-
fest the motives of our hearts, and then everyone
will receive praise from God.
Paul's Life as Pattern 6 *I have applied these
things to myself and Apollos for your benefit,
brothers, so that you may learn from us not to
go beyond what is written, so that none of you
will be inflated with pride in favor of one
person over against another. 7 Who confers dis-
tinction upon you? What do you possess that
you have not received? But if you have received
it, why are you boasting as if you did not
receive it? 8 *You are already satisfied; you have
already grown rich; you have become kings
without us! Indeed, I wish that you had be-
come kings, so that we also might become
kings with you.
9 n *For as I see it, God has exhibited us
apostles as the last of all, like people sentenced
to death, since we have become a spectacle to
the world, to angels and human beings alike.
10 o We are fools on Christ's account, but you are
wise in Christ; we are weak, but you are strong;
you are held in honor, but we in disrepute. 11 p To
this very hour we go hungry and thirsty, we are
poorly clad and roughly treated, we wander
about homeless 12 q and we toil, working with
our own hands. When ridiculed, we bless; when
persecuted, we endure; 13 when slandered, we
respond gently. We have become like the world's
rubbish, the scum of all, to this very moment.
14 *I am writing you this not to shame you,
but to admonish you as my beloved children.
15 r Even if you should have countless guides to
Christ, yet you do not have many fathers, for I
became your father in Christ Jesus through the
gospel. 16 s Therefore, I urge you, be imitators of
me. 17 t For this reason I am sending you Timo-
thy, who is my beloved and faithful son in the
Lord; he will remind you of my ways in Christ
[Jesus], just as I teach them everywhere in every
church.
18 *Some have become inflated with pride, as
if I were not coming to you. 19 But I will come to
you soon, if the Lord is willing, and I shall
ascertain not the talk of these inflated people but
their power. 20 u For the kingdom of God is not a
matter of talk but of power. 21 v Which do you
prefer? Shall I come to you with a rod, or with
love and a gentle spirit?

4, 6–21: This is an emotionally charged peroration to the discussion about divisions. It contains several exhortations and statements of Paul's purpose in writing (cf 6.14–17.21) that counterbalance the initial exhortation at 1, 10.

4, 6: That you may learn from us not to go beyond what is written: the words "to go" are not in the Greek, but have here been added as the minimum necessary to elicit sense from this difficult passage. It probably means that the Corinthians should avoid the false wisdom of vain speculation, contenting themselves with Paul's proclamation of the cross, which is the fulfillment of God's promises in the Old Testament (what is written). **Inflated with pride:** literally, "puffed up," i.e., arrogant, filled with a sense of self-importance. The term is particularly Pauline, found in the New Testament only in 1 Cor 4, 6.18–19; 5, 2; 8, 1; 13, 4; Col 2, 18 (cf the related noun at 2 Cor 12, 20). It sometimes occurs in conjunction with the theme of "boasting," as in vv 6–7 here.

4, 8: Satisfied . . . rich . . . kings: these three statements could also be punctuated as questions continuing the series begun in v 7. In any case these expressions reflect a tendency at Corinth toward an overrealized eschatology, a form of self-deception that draws Paul's irony. The underlying attitude has implications for the Corinthians' thinking about other issues, notably morality and the resurrection, that Paul will address later in the letter.

4, 9–13: A rhetorically effective catalogue of the circumstances of apostolic existence, in the course of which Paul ironically contrasts his own sufferings with the Corinthians' illusion that they have passed beyond the folly of the passion and have already reached the condition of glory. His language echoes that of the beatitudes and woes, which assert a future reversal of present conditions. Their present sufferings ("to this very hour," 11) place the apostles in the class of those to whom the beatitudes promise future relief (Mt 5, 3–11; Lk 6, 20–23); whereas the Corinthians' image of themselves as "already" filled, rich, ruling (8), as wise, strong, and honored (10) places them paradoxically in the position of those whom the woes threaten with future undoing (Lk 6, 24–26). They have lost sight of the fact that the reversal is predicted for the future.

4, 14–17: My beloved children: the close of the argument is dominated by the tender metaphor of the father who not only gives his children life but also educates them. Once he has begotten them through his preaching, Paul continues to present the gospel to them existentially, by his life as well as by his word, and they are to learn, as children do, by imitating their parents (16). The reference to the **rod** in v 21 belongs to the same image-complex. So does the image of the **ways** in v 17: the ways that Paul teaches everywhere, "his ways in Christ Jesus," mean a behavior pattern quite different from the human ways along which the Corinthians are walking (3, 3).

4, 18–21: Verse 20 picks up the contrast between a certain kind of talk (**logos**) and true power (**dynamis**) from 1, 17–18 and 2, 4–5. The kingdom, which many of them imagine to be fully present in their lives (8), will be rather unexpectedly disclosed in the strength of Paul's encounter with them, if they make a powerful intervention on his part necessary. Compare the similar ending to an argument in 2 Cor 13, 1–4.10.

n 15, 31; Rom 8, 36; 2 Cor 4, 8–12; 11, 23 / Heb 10, 33. o 1, 18; 3, 18; 2 Cor 11, 19 / 2, 3; 2 Cor 13, 9. p Rom 8, 35; 2 Cor 11, 23–27. q Acts 9, 6–14; 18, 3; 20, 34; 1 Thes 2, 9 / 1 Pt 3, 9. r Gal 4, 19; Phlm 10. s 11, 1; Phil 3, 17; 4, 9; 1 Thes 1, 6; 2 Thes 3, 7.9. t 16, 10; Acts 19, 22. u 2, 4; 1 Thes 1, 5. v 2 Cor 1, 23; 10, 2.

B. Moral Disorders

CHAPTER 5

A Case of Incest [1] [w]*It is widely reported that there is immorality among you, and immorality of a kind not found even among pagans—a man living with his father's wife. [2]*And you are inflated with pride. Should you not rather have been sorrowful? The one who did this deed should be expelled from your midst. [3] [x]I, for my part, although absent in body but present in spirit, have already, as if present, pronounced judgment on the one who has committed this deed, [4]in the name of [our] Lord Jesus: when you have gathered together and I am with you in spirit with the power of the Lord Jesus, [5] [y]*you are to deliver this man to Satan for the destruction of his flesh, so that his spirit may be saved on the day of the Lord.

[6] [z]*Your boasting is not appropriate. Do you not know that a little yeast leavens all the dough? [7] [a]*Clear out the old yeast, so that you may become a fresh batch of dough, inasmuch as you are unleavened. For our paschal lamb, Christ, has been sacrificed. [8] [b]Therefore, let us celebrate the feast, not with the old yeast, the yeast of malice and wickedness, but with the unleavened bread of sincerity and truth.

[9]*I wrote you in my letter not to associate with immoral people, [10] [c]not at all referring to the immoral of this world or the greedy and robbers or idolaters; for you would then have to leave the world. [11] [d]But I now write to you not to associate with anyone named a brother, if he is immoral, greedy, an idolater, a slanderer, a drunkard, or a robber, not even to eat with such a person. [12]For why should I be judging outsiders? Is it not your business to judge those within? [13] [e]God will judge those outside. "Purge the evil person from your midst."

CHAPTER 6

Lawsuits before Unbelievers [1]*How can any one of you with a case against another dare to bring it to the unjust for judgment instead of to the holy ones? [2] [f]*Do you not know that the holy ones will judge the world? If the world is to be judged by you, are you unqualified for the lowest law courts? [3]Do you not know that we will judge angels? Then why not everyday matters? [4]If, therefore, you have courts for everyday matters, do you seat as judges people of no standing in the church? [5]I say this to shame you. Can it be that there is not one among you wise enough to be able to settle a case between brothers? [6]But rather brother goes to court against brother, and that before unbelievers?

[7] [g]Now indeed [then] it is, in any case, a failure

5, 1—6, 20: Paul now takes up a number of other matters that require regulation. These have come to his attention by hearsay (5, 1), probably in reports brought by "Chloe's people" (1, 11).

5, 1–13: Paul first deals with the incestuous union of a man with his stepmother (1–8) and then attempts to clarify general admonitions he has given about associating with fellow Christians guilty of immorality (9–13). Each of these three brief paragraphs expresses the same idea: the need of separation between the holy and the unholy.

5, 2: Inflated with pride: this remark and the reference to **boasting** in v 6 suggest that they are proud of themselves despite the infection in their midst, tolerating and possibly even approving the situation. The attitude expressed in 6, 2.13 may be influencing their thinking in this case.

5, 5: Deliver this man to Satan: once the sinner is expelled from the church, the sphere of Jesus' lordship and victory over sin, he will be in the region outside over which Satan is still master. **For the destruction of his flesh:** the purpose of the penalty is medicinal: through affliction, sin's grip over him may be destroyed and the path to repentance and reunion laid open. With Paul's instructions for an excommunication ceremony here, contrast his recommendations for the reconciliation of a sinner in 2 Cor 2, 5–11.

5, 6: A little yeast: yeast, which induces fermentation, is a natural symbol for a source of corruption that becomes all-pervasive. The expression is proverbial.

5, 7–8: In the Jewish calendar, Passover was followed immediately by the festival of Unleavened Bread. In preparation for this feast all traces of old bread were removed from the house, and during the festival only unleavened bread was eaten. The sequence of these two feasts provides Paul with an image of Christian existence: Christ's death (the true Passover celebration) is followed by the life of the Christian community, marked by newness, purity, and integrity (a perpetual feast of unleavened bread). Paul may have been writing around Passover time (cf 16, 5); this is a little Easter homily, the earliest in Christian literature.

5, 9–13: Paul here corrects a misunderstanding of his earlier directives against associating with immoral fellow Christians. He concedes the impossibility of avoiding contact with sinners in society at large but urges the Corinthians to maintain the inner purity of their own community.

6, 1–11: Christians at Corinth are suing one another before pagan judges in Roman courts. A barrage of rhetorical questions (1–9) betrays Paul's indignation over this practice, which he sees as an infringement upon the holiness of the Christian community.

6, 2–3: The principle to which Paul appeals is an eschatological prerogative promised to Christians: they are to share with Christ the judgment of the world (cf Dn 7, 22.27). Hence they ought to be able to settle minor disputes within the community.

w Lv 18, 7–8; 20, 11; Dt 27, 20. x Col 2, 5. y 1 Tm 1, 20. z Gal 5, 9. a Ex 12, 1–13; Dt 16, 1–2; 1 Pt 1, 19. b Ex 12, 15–20; 13, 7; Dt 16, 3. c 10, 27; Jn 17, 15. d Mt 18, 17; 2 Thes 3, 6.14; 2 Jn 10. e Dt 13, 6; 17, 7; 22, 24. f Wis 3, 8; Mt 19, 28; Rv 20, 4. g Mt 5, 38–42; Rom 12, 17–21; 1 Thes 5, 15.

on your part that you have lawsuits against one another. Why not rather put up with injustice? Why not rather let yourselves be cheated? [8]Instead, you inflict injustice and cheat, and this to brothers. [9] [h]*Do you not know that the unjust will not inherit the kingdom of God? Do not be deceived; neither fornicators nor idolaters nor adulterers nor boy prostitutes nor sodomites [10]nor thieves nor the greedy nor drunkards nor slanderers nor robbers will inherit the kingdom of God. [11] [i]That is what some of you used to be; but now you have had yourselves washed, you were sanctified, you were justified in the name of the Lord Jesus Christ and in the Spirit of our God.

Sexual Immorality [12] [j]*"Everything is lawful for me," but not everything is beneficial. "Everything is lawful for me," but I will not let myself be dominated by anything. [13]"Food for the stomach and the stomach for food," but God will do away with both the one and the other. The body, however, is not for immorality, but for the Lord, and the Lord is for the body; [14] [k]God raised the Lord and will also raise us by his power. [15] [l]*Do you not know that your bodies are members of Christ? Shall I then take Christ's members and make them the members of a prostitute? Of course not! [16] [m][Or] do you not know that anyone who joins himself to a prostitute becomes one body with her? For "the two," it says, "will become one flesh." [17] [n]But whoever is joined to the Lord becomes one spirit with him. [18]*Avoid immorality. Every other sin a person commits is outside the body, but the immoral person sins against his own body. [19] [o]*Do you not know that your body is a temple of the holy Spirit within you, whom you have from God, and that you are not your own? [20] [p]For you have been purchased at a price. Therefore glorify God in your body.

III: Answers to the Corinthians' Questions

A. Marriage and Virginity

CHAPTER 7

Advice to the Married [1]*Now in regard to the matters about which you wrote: "It is a good

6, 9–10: A catalogue of typical vices that exclude from the kingdom of God and that should be excluded from God's church. Such lists (cf 5, 10) reflect the common moral sensibility of the New Testament period.

6, 9: The Greek word translated as **boy prostitutes** may refer to catamites, i.e., boys or young men who were kept for purposes of prostitution, a practice not uncommon in the Greco-Roman world. In Greek mythology this was the function of Ganymede, the "cupbearer of the gods," whose Latin name was Catamitus. The term translated **sodomites** would then refer to adult males who indulged in homosexual practices with such boys. See similar condemnations of such practices in Rom 1, 26–27; 1 Tm 1, 10.

6, 12–20: Paul now turns to the opinion of some Corinthians that sexuality is a morally indifferent area (12–13). This leads him to explain the mutual relation between the Lord Jesus and our bodies (13b) in a densely packed paragraph that contains elements of a profound theology of sexuality (15–20).

6, 12–13: Everything is lawful for me: the Corinthians may have derived this slogan from Paul's preaching about Christian freedom, but they mean something different by it: they consider sexual satisfaction a matter as indifferent as food, and they attribute no lasting significance to bodily functions (13a). Paul begins to deal with the slogan by two qualifications, which suggest principles for judging sexual activity. **Not everything is beneficial:** cf 10, 23, and the whole argument of chs 8–10 on the finality of freedom and moral activity. **Not let myself be dominated:** certain apparently free actions may involve in fact a secret servitude in conflict with the lordship of Jesus.

6, 15b-16: A prostitute: the reference may be specifically to religious prostitution, an accepted part of pagan culture at Corinth and elsewhere; but the prostitute also serves as a symbol for any sexual relationship that conflicts with Christ's claim over us individually. **The two . . . will become one flesh:** the text of Gn 2, 24 is applied positively to human marriage in Mt and Mk, and in Eph 5, 29–32: love of husband and wife reflect the love of Christ for his church. The application of the text to union with a prostitute is jarring, for such a union is a parody, an antitype of marriage, which does conflict with Christ's claim over us. This explains the horror expressed in 15b.

6, 18: Against his own body: expresses the intimacy and depth of sexual disorder, which violates the very orientation of our bodies.

6, 19–20: Paul's vision becomes trinitarian. **A temple:** sacred by reason of God's gift, his indwelling Spirit. **Not your own:** but "for the Lord," who acquires ownership by the act of redemption. **Glorify God in your body:** the argument concludes with a positive imperative to supplement the negative "avoid immorality" of v 18. Far from being a terrain that is morally indifferent, the area of sexuality is one in which our relationship with God (and his Christ and his Spirit) is very intimately expressed: he is either highly glorified or deeply offended.

7, 1–40: Paul now begins to answer questions addressed to him by the Corinthians (7, 1—11, 1). The first of these concerns marriage. This chapter contains advice both to the married (1–16) and to the unmarried (25–38) or widowed (39–40); these two parts are separated by vv 17–24, which enunciate a principle applicable to both.

7, 1–16: It seems that some Christians in Corinth were advocating asceticism in sexual matters. The pattern **it is a good thing . . . , but** occurs twice (1–2.8–9; cf 26), suggesting that in

h 15, 50; Gal 5, 19–21; Eph 5, 5. i Ti 3, 3–7. j 10, 23. k Rom 8, 11; 2 Cor 4, 14. l 12, 27; Rom 6, 12–13; 12, 5; Eph 5, 30. m Gn 2, 24; Mt 19, 5; Mk 10, 8; Eph 5, 31. n Rom 8, 9–10; 2 Cor 3, 17. o 3, 16–17; Rom 5, 5. p 3, 23; 7, 23; Acts 20, 28 / Rom 12, 1; Phil 1, 20.

thing for a man not to touch a woman," [2]but because of cases of immorality every man should have his own wife, and every woman her own husband. [3]The husband should fulfill his duty toward his wife, and likewise the wife toward her husband. [4]A wife does not have authority over her own body, but rather her husband, and similarly a husband does not have authority over his own body, but rather his wife. [5]Do not deprive each other, except perhaps by mutual consent for a time, to be free for prayer, but then return to one another, so that Satan may not tempt you through your lack of self-control. [6]*This I say by way of concession, however, not as a command. [7 q]*Indeed, I wish everyone to be as I am, but each has a particular gift from God, one of one kind and one of another.

[8 r]*Now to the unmarried and to widows I say: it is a good thing for them to remain as they are, as I do, [9]but if they cannot exercise self-control they should marry, for it is better to marry than to be on fire. [10 s]*To the married, however, I give this instruction (not I, but the Lord): a wife should not separate from her husband [11]—and if she does separate she must either remain single or become reconciled to her husband—and a husband should not divorce his wife.

[12]*To the rest I say (not the Lord): if any brother has a wife who is an unbeliever, and she is willing to go on living with him, he should not divorce her; [13]and if any woman has a husband who is an unbeliever, and he is willing to go on living with her, she should not divorce her husband. [14 t]For the unbelieving husband is made holy through his wife, and the unbelieving wife is made holy through the brother. Otherwise your children would be unclean, whereas in fact they are holy.

[15]*If the unbeliever separates, however, let him separate. The brother or sister is not bound in such cases; God has called you to peace. [16]For how do you know, wife, whether you will save your husband; or how do you know, husband, whether you will save your wife?

The Life That the Lord Has Assigned

[17]*Only, everyone should live as the Lord has assigned, just as God called each one. I give this order in all the churches. [18 u]Was someone called after he had been circumcised? He should not try to undo his circumcision. Was an uncircumcised person called? He should not be circumcised. [19 v]Circumcision means nothing, and uncircumcision means nothing; what matters is keeping God's commandments. [20]Everyone should remain in the state in which he was called.

[21]Were you a slave when you were called? Do not be concerned but, even if you can gain your freedom, make the most of it. [22 w]For the slave called in the Lord is a freed person in the Lord, just as the free person who has been called is a

---

this matter as in others the Corinthians have seized upon a genuine value but are exaggerating or distorting it in some way. Once again Paul calls them to a more correct perspective and a better sense of their own limitations. The phrase **it is a good thing** (1) may have been the slogan of the ascetic party at Corinth.

7, 1–7: References to Paul's own behavior (7–8) suggest that his celibate way of life and his preaching to the unmarried (cf 25–35) have given some the impression that asceticism within marriage, i.e., suspension of normal sexual relations, would be a laudable ideal. Paul points to their experience of widespread immorality to caution them against overestimating their own strength (2); as individuals they may not have the particular gift that makes such asceticism feasible (7) and hence are to abide by the principle to be explained in vv 17–24.

7, 6: By way of concession: this refers most likely to the concession mentioned in v 5a: temporary interruption of relations for a legitimate purpose.

7, 7: A particular gift from God: use of the term **charisma** suggests that marriage and celibacy may be viewed in the light of Paul's theology of spiritual gifts (chs 12–14).

7, 8: Paul was obviously unmarried when he wrote this verse. Some interpreters believe that he had previously been married and widowed; there is no clear evidence either for or against this view, which was expressed already at the end of the second century by Clement of Alexandria.

7, 10–11: (Not I, but the Lord): Paul reminds the married of Jesus' principle of nonseparation (Mk 10, 9). This is one of his rare specific references to the teaching of Jesus.

7, 12–14: To the rest: marriages in which only one partner is a baptized Christian. Jesus' prohibition against divorce is not addressed to them, but Paul extends the principle of nonseparation to such unions, provided they are marked by peacefulness and shared sanctification.

7, 15–16: If the unbeliever separates: the basis of the "Pauline privilege" in Catholic marriage legislation.

7, 17–24: On the ground that distinct human conditions are less significant than the whole new existence opened up by God's call, Paul urges them to be less concerned with changing their states of life than with answering God's call where it finds them. The principle applies both to the married state (1–16) and to the unmarried (25–38).

q Mt 19, 11–12. r 1 Tm 5, 11–16 / 9, 5; s Mt 5, 32; 19, 9. t Rom 11, 16. u 1 Mc 1, 15 / Acts 15, 1–2. v Rom 2, 25.29; Gal 5, 6; 6, 15. w Eph 6, 5–9; Col 3, 11; Phlm 16.

slave of Christ. 23 [x]You have been purchased at a
price. Do not become slaves to human beings.
24 Brothers, everyone should continue before
God in the state in which he was called.

Advice to Virgins and Widows 25 *Now in
regard to virgins I have no commandment from
the Lord, but I give my opinion as one who by
the Lord's mercy is trustworthy. 26 [y]So this is
what I think best because of the present distress:
that it is a good thing for a person to remain as
he is. 27 Are you bound to a wife? Do not seek a
separation. Are you free of a wife? Then do not
look for a wife. 28 If you marry, however, you do
not sin, nor does an unmarried woman sin if she
marries; but such people will experience afflic-
tion in their earthly life, and I would like to spare
you that.

29 [z]*I tell you, brothers, the time is running
out. From now on, let those having wives act as
not having them, 30 those weeping as not weep-
ing, those rejoicing as not rejoicing, those buying
as not owning, 31 those using the world as not
using it fully. For the world in its present form is
passing away.

32 I should like you to be free of anxieties. An
unmarried man is anxious about the things of
the Lord, how he may please the Lord. 33 [a]But a
married man is anxious about the things of the
world, how he may please his wife, 34 [b]and he is
divided. An unmarried woman or a virgin is
anxious about the things of the Lord, so that she
may be holy in both body and spirit. A married
woman, on the other hand, is anxious about the
things of the world, how she may please her
husband. 35 [c]I am telling you this for your own
benefit, not to impose a restraint upon you, but
for the sake of propriety and adherence to the
Lord without distraction.

36 *If anyone thinks he is behaving improperly
toward his virgin, and if a critical moment has
come and so it has to be, let him do as he
wishes. He is committing no sin; let them get
married. 37 The one who stands firm in his
resolve, however, who is not under compulsion
but has power over his own will, and has made
up his mind to keep his virgin, will be doing
well. 38 So then, the one who marries his virgin
does well; the one who does not marry her will
do better.

39 [d]*A wife is bound to her husband as long as
he lives. But if her husband dies, she is free to be
married to whomever she wishes, provided that
it be in the Lord. 40 [e]She is more blessed, though,
in my opinion, if she remains as she is, and I
think that I too have the Spirit of God.

B. Offerings to Idols

CHAPTER 8

Knowledge Insufficient 1 [f]*Now in regard to
meat sacrificed to idols: we realize that "all of us

7, 25–28: Paul is careful to explain that the principle of v 17 does not bind under sin but that present earthly conditions make it advantageous for the unmarried to remain as they are (28). These remarks must be complemented by the statement about "particular gifts" from v 7.

7, 29–31: The world . . . is passing away: Paul advises Christians to go about the ordinary activities of life in a manner different from those who are totally immersed in them and unaware of their transitoriness.

7, 36–38: The passage is difficult to interpret, because it is unclear whether Paul is thinking of a father and his unmarried daughter (or slave), or of a couple engaged in a betrothal or spiritual marriage. The general principles already enunciated apply: there is no question of sin, even if they should marry, but staying as they are is "better" (for the reasons mentioned in 28–35). Once again the **charisma** of v 7, which applies also to the unmarried (8–9), is to be presupposed.

7, 36: A critical moment has come: either because the woman will soon be beyond marriageable age, or because their passions are becoming uncontrollable (cf 9).

7, 39–40: Application of the principles to the case of widows. If they do choose to remarry, they ought to prefer Christian husbands.

8, 1—11, 1: The Corinthians' second question concerns meat that has been sacrificed to idols; in this area they were exhibiting a disordered sense of liberation that Paul here tries to rectify. These chapters contain a sustained and unified argument that illustrates Paul's method of theological reflection on a moral dilemma. Although the problem with which he is dealing is dated, the guidelines for moral decisions that he offers are of lasting validity.

Essentially Paul urges them to take a communitarian rather than an individualistic view of their Christian freedom. Many decisions that they consider pertinent only to their private relationship with God have, in fact, social consequences. Nor can moral decisions be determined by merely theoretical considerations; they must be based on concrete circumstances, specifically on the value and needs of other individuals and on mutual responsibility within the community. Paul here introduces the theme of "building up" (**oikodomē**), i.e., of contributing by individual action to the welfare and growth of the community. This theme will be further developed in ch 14; see the note on 14, 3b-5. Several years later Paul would again deal with the problem of meat sacrificed to idols in Rom 14, 1—15, 6.

8, 1a: Meat sacrificed to idols: much of the food consumed in the city could have passed through pagan religious ceremonies before finding its way into markets and homes. **"All of us have**

x 6, 20. y 8. z Rom 13, 11. a Lk 14, 20. b 1 Tm 5, 5. c Lk 10, 39–42. d Rom 7, 2. e 25. f Rom 15, 14 / 13, 1–13; Rom 14, 15.19.

have knowledge"; knowledge inflates with pride, but love builds up. 2 If anyone supposes he knows something, he does not yet know as he ought to know. 3 [g]But if one loves God, one is known by him.

4 [h]So about the eating of meat sacrificed to idols: we know that "there is no idol in the world," and that "there is no God but one." 5 Indeed, even though there are so-called gods in heaven and on earth (there are, to be sure, many "gods" and many "lords"), 6 [i]*yet for us there is

one God, the Father,
from whom all things are and for whom we exist,
and one Lord, Jesus Christ,
through whom all things are and through whom we exist.

Practical Rules 7 [j]But not all have this knowledge. There are some who have been so used to idolatry up until now that, when they eat meat sacrificed to idols, their conscience, which is weak, is defiled.

8 [k]*Now food will not bring us closer to God. We are no worse off if we do not eat, nor are we better off if we do. 9 [l]But make sure that this liberty of yours in no way becomes a stumbling block to the weak. 10 If someone sees you, with your knowledge, reclining at table in the temple of an idol, may not his conscience too, weak as it is, be "built up" to eat the meat sacrificed to idols? 11 [m]Thus through your knowledge, the weak person is brought to destruction, the brother for whom Christ died. 12 When you sin in this way against your brothers and wound their consciences, weak as they are, you are sinning against Christ. 13 [n]*Therefore, if food causes my brother to sin, I will never eat meat again, so that I may not cause my brother to sin.

CHAPTER 9

Paul's Rights as an Apostle 1 [o]*Am I not free? Am I not an apostle? Have I not seen Jesus our Lord? Are you not my work in the Lord? 2 Although I may not be an apostle for others, certainly I am for you, for you are the seal of my apostleship in the Lord.

3 *My defense against those who would pass judgment on me is this. 4 *Do we not have the right to eat and drink? 5 Do we not have the right to take along a Christian wife, as do the rest of the apostles, and the brothers of the Lord, and Kephas? 6 [p]Or is it only myself and Barnabas who do not have the right not to work? 7 [q]Who ever serves as a soldier at his own expense? Who plants a vineyard without eating its produce? Or who shepherds a flock without using some of the

---

knowledge": a slogan, similar to 6, 12, which reveals the self-image of the Corinthians. Verse 4 will specify the content of this knowledge.

8, 6: This verse rephrases the monotheistic confession of v 4 in such a way as to contrast it with polytheism (5) and to express our relationship with the one God in concrete, i.e., in personal and Christian terms. **And for whom we exist:** since the Greek contains no verb here and the action intended must be inferred from the preposition **eis,** another translation is equally possible: "toward whom we return." **Through whom all things:** the earliest reference in the New Testament to Jesus' role in creation.

8, 8–9: Although the food in itself is morally neutral, extrinsic circumstances may make the eating of it harmful. **A stumbling block:** the image is that of tripping or causing someone to fall (cf 13; 9, 12; 10, 12.32; 2 Cor 6, 3; Rom 14, 13.20–21). This is a basic moral imperative for Paul, a counterpart to the positive imperative to "build one another up"; compare the expression "giving offense" as opposed to "pleasing" in 10, 32–33.

8, 13: His own course is clear: he will avoid any action that might harm another Christian. This statement prepares for the paradigmatic development in ch 9.

9, 1–27: This chapter is an emotionally charged expansion of Paul's appeal to his own example in 8, 13; its purpose is to reinforce the exhortation of 8, 9. The two opening questions introduce the themes of Paul's freedom and his apostleship (1), themes that the chapter will develop in reverse order, vv 1–18 treating the question of his apostleship and the rights that flow from it, and vv 19–27 exploring dialectically the nature of Paul's freedom. The language is highly rhetorical, abounding in questions, wordplays, paradoxes, images, and appeals to authority and experience. The argument is unified by repetitions; its articulations are highlighted by inclusions and transitional verses.

9, 3: **My defense against those who would pass judgment on me:** the reference to a defense (**apologia**) is surprising, and suggests that Paul is incorporating some material here that he has previously used in another context. The defense will touch on two points: the fact of Paul's rights as an apostle (4–12a and 13–14) and his nonuse of those rights (12b and 15–18).

9, 4–12a: Apparently some believe that Paul is not equal to the other apostles and therefore does not enjoy equal privileges. His defense on this point (here and in 13–14) reinforces the assertion of his apostolic character in v 2. It consists of a series of analogies from natural equity (7) and religious custom (13) designed to establish his equal right to support from the churches (4–6.11–12a); these analogies are confirmed by the authority of the law (8–10) and of Jesus himself (14).

g Rom 8, 29; Gal 4, 9; h 10, 19; Dt 6, 4. i Mal 2, 10 / Rom 11, 36; Eph 4, 5–6 / 1, 2–3 / Jn 1, 3; Col 1, 16. j 10, 28; Rom 14, 23 / Rom 14, 1; 15, 1. k Rom 14, 17. l Rom 14, 13.20–21. m Rom 14, 15.20. n Mt 18, 6; Rom 14, 20–21. o 19 / 2 Cor 12, 12 / 15, 8–9; Acts 9, 17; 26, 16. p Acts 4, 36–37; 13, 1–2; Gal 2, 1.9.13; Col 4, 10. q 2 Tm 2, 3–4.

milk from the flock? [8]Am I saying this on human authority, or does not the law also speak of these things? [9] [r]It is written in the law of Moses, "You shall not muzzle an ox while it is treading out the grain." Is God concerned about oxen, [10] [s]or is he not really speaking for our sake? It was written for our sake, because the plowman should plow in hope, and the thresher in hope of receiving a share. [11] [t]If we have sown spiritual seed for you, is it a great thing that we reap a material harvest from you? [12] [u]*If others share this rightful claim on you, do not we still more?

Reason for Not Using His Rights Yet we have not used this right. On the contrary, we endure everything so as not to place an obstacle to the gospel of Christ. [13] [v]*Do you not know that those who perform the temple services eat [what] belongs to the temple, and those who minister at the altar share in the sacrificial offerings? [14] [w]In the same way, the Lord ordered that those who preach the gospel should live by the gospel.

[15] [x]*I have not used any of these rights, however, nor do I write this that it be done so in my case. I would rather die. Certainly no one is going to nullify my boast. [16] [y]If I preach the gospel, this is no reason for me to boast, for an obligation has been imposed on me, and woe to me if I do not preach it! [17] [z]If I do so willingly, I have a recompense, but if unwillingly, then I have been entrusted with a stewardship. [18] [a]What then is my recompense? That, when I preach, I offer the gospel free of charge so as not to make full use of my right in the gospel.

All Things to All [19] [b]*Although I am free in regard to all, I have made myself a slave to all so as to win over as many as possible. [20]To the Jews I became like a Jew to win over Jews; to those under the law I became like one under the law—though I myself am not under the law—to win over those under the law. [21]To those outside the law I became like one outside the law—though I am not outside God's law but within the law of Christ—to win over those outside the law. [22] [c]To the weak I became weak, to win over the weak. I have become all things to all, to save at least some. [23]All this I do for the sake of the gospel, so that I too may have a share in it.

[24] [d]*Do you not know that the runners in the stadium all run in the race, but only one wins the prize? Run so as to win. [25] [e]Every athlete exercises discipline in every way. They do it to win a perishable crown, but we an imperishable one. [26]Thus I do not run aimlessly; I do not fight as if I were shadowboxing. [27]*No, I drive my body and train it, for fear that, after having preached to others, I myself should be disqualified.

CHAPTER 10

Warning against Overconfidence [1] [f]*I do not want you to be unaware, brothers, that our ances-

9, 12b: It appears, too, that suspicion or misunderstanding has been created by Paul's practice of not living from his preaching. The first reason he asserts in defense of this practice is an entirely apostolic one; it anticipates the developments to follow in vv 19–22. He will give a second reason in vv 15–18.

9, 13–14: The position of these verses produces an interlocking of the two points of Paul's defense. These arguments by analogy (13) and from authority (14) belong with those of vv 7–10 and ground the first point. But Paul defers them until he has had a chance to mention "the gospel of Christ" (12b), after which it is more appropriate to mention Jesus' injunction to his preachers and to argue by analogy from the sacred temple service to his own liturgical service, the preaching of the gospel (cf Rom 1, 9; 15, 16).

9, 15–18: Paul now assigns a more personal motive to his nonuse of his right to support. His preaching is not a service spontaneously undertaken on his part but a stewardship imposed by a sort of divine compulsion. Yet to merit any reward he must bring some spontaneous quality to his service, and this he does by freely renouncing his right to support. The material here is quite similar to that contained in Paul's "defense" at 2 Cor 11, 5–12; 12, 11–18.

9, 19–23: In a rhetorically balanced series of statements Paul expands and generalizes the picture of his behavior and explores the paradox of apostolic freedom. It is not essentially freedom from restraint but freedom for service—a possibility of constructive activity.

9, 24–27: A series of miniparables from sports, appealing to readers familiar with Greek gymnasia and the nearby Isthmian games.

9, 27: For fear that . . . I myself should be disqualified: a final paradoxical turn to the argument: what appears at first a free, spontaneous renunciation of rights (12–18) seems subsequently to be required for fulfillment of Paul's stewardship (to preach effectively he must reach his hearers wherever they are, 19–22), and finally is seen to be necessary for his own salvation (23–27). Mention of the possibility of disqualification provides a transition to ch 10.

10, 1–5: Paul embarks unexpectedly upon a panoramic survey of the events of the Exodus period. The privileges of Israel in the

r Dt 25, 4; 1 Tm 5, 18. s 2 Tm 2, 6. t Rom 15, 27. u 2 Cor 11, 7–12; 12, 13–18; 2 Thes 3, 6–12. v Nm 18, 8.31; Dt 18, 1–5. w Mt 10, 10; Lk 10, 7–8. x 2 Cor 11, 9–10. y Acts 26, 14–18. z 4, 1; Gal 2, 7. a 2 Cor 11, 7–12. b Mt 20, 26–27. c 10, 33; Rom 15, 1; 2 Cor 11, 29. d Heb 12, 1. e 2 Tm 2, 5 / 2 Tm 4, 7–8; Jas 1, 12; 1 Pt 5, 4. f Ex 13, 21–22; 14, 19–20 / Ex 14, 21–22.26–30.

tors were all under the cloud and all passe
through the sea, [2][g]and all of them were baptized
into Moses in the cloud and in the sea. [3]All ate the
same spiritual food, [4][h]*and all drank the same
spiritual drink, for they drank from a spiritual rock
that followed them, and the rock was the Christ.
[5][i]Yet God was not pleased with most of them, for
they were struck down in the desert.
[6][j]*These things happened as examples for us,
so that we might not desire evil things, as they
did. [7][k]And do not become idolaters, as some of
them did, as it is written, "The people sat down
to eat and drink, and rose up to revel." [8][l]Let us
not indulge in immorality as some of them did,
and twenty-three thousand fell within a single
day. [9][m]*Let us not test Christ as some of them
did, and suffered death by serpents. [10][n]Do not
grumble as some of them did, and suffered death
by the destroyer. [11]*These things happened to
them as an example, and they have been written
down as a warning to us, upon whom the end of
the ages has come. [12]*Therefore, whoever
thinks he is standing secure should take care not
to fall. [13][o]No trial has come to you but what is
human. God is faithful and will not let you be
tried beyond your strength; but with the trial he
will also provide a way out, so that you may be
able to bear it.

Warning against Idolatry [14][p]*Therefore, my
beloved, avoid idolatry. [15]I am speaking as to
sensible people; judge for yourselves what I am
saying. [16][q]The cup of blessing that we bless, is it
not a participation in the blood of Christ? The
bread that we break, is it not a participation in
the body of Christ? [17][r]Because the loaf of bread
is one, we, though many, are one body, for we all
partake of the one loaf.
[18][s]Look at Israel according to the flesh; are
not those who eat the sacrifices participants in
the altar? [19]So what am I saying? That meat
sacrificed to idols is anything? Or that an idol is
anything? [20][t]*No, I mean that what they sacri-
fice, [they sacrifice] to demons, not to God, and I
do not want you to become participants with
demons. [21][u]You cannot drink the cup of the
Lord and also the cup of demons. You cannot
partake of the table of the Lord and of the table
of demons. [22][v]Or are we provoking the Lord to
jealous anger? Are we stronger than he?

Seek the Good of Others [23][w]*"Everything is
lawful," but not everything is beneficial. "Every-
thing is lawful," but not everything builds up.

---

wilderness are described in terms that apply strictly only to the realities of the new covenant ("baptism," "spiritual food and drink"); interpreted in this way they point forward to the Christian experience (1–4). But those privileges did not guarantee God's permanent pleasure (5).

10, 4: A spiritual rock that followed them: the Torah speaks only about a rock from which water issued, but rabbinic legend amplified this into a spring that followed the Israelites throughout their migration. Paul uses this legend as a literary type: he makes the rock itself accompany the Israelites, and he gives it a spiritual sense. **The rock was the Christ:** in the Old Testament, Yahweh is the Rock of his people (cf Dt 32, Moses' song to Yahweh the Rock). Paul now applies this image to the Christ, the source of the living water, the true Rock that accompanied Israel, guiding their experiences in the desert.

10, 6–13: This section explicitates the typological value of these Old Testament events: the desert experiences of the Israelites are examples, meant as warnings, to deter us from similar sins (idolatry, immorality, etc.) and from a similar fate.

10, 9: Christ: to avoid Paul's concept of Christ present in the wilderness events, some manuscripts read "the Lord."

10, 11: Upon whom the end of the ages has come: it is our period in time toward which past ages have been moving and in which they arrive at their goal.

10, 12–13: Take care not to fall: the point of the whole comparison with Israel is to caution against overconfidence, a sense of complete security (12). This warning is immediately balanced by a reassurance, based, however, on God (13).

10, 14–22: The warning against idolatry from v 7 is now repeated (14) and explained in terms of the effect of sacrifices: all sacrifices, Christian (16–17), Jewish (18), or pagan (20), establish communion. But communion with Christ is exclusive, incompatible with any other such communion (21). Compare the line of reasoning at 6, 15.

10, 20: To demons: although Jews denied divinity to pagan gods, they often believed that there was some nondivine reality behind the idols, such as the dead, or angels, or demons. The explanation Paul offers in v 20 is drawn from Dt 32, 7: the power behind the idols, with which the pagans commune, consists of demonic powers hostile to God.

10, 23—11, 1: By way of peroration Paul returns to the opening situation (ch 8) and draws conclusions based on the intervening considerations (chs 9–10).

10, 23–24: He repeats in the context of this new problem the slogans of liberty from 6, 12, with similar qualifications. Liberty is not merely an individual perfection, nor an end in itself, but is to be used for the common good. The language of v 24 recalls the description of Jesus' self-emptying in Phil 2.

g Rom 6, 3; Gal 3, 27 / Ex 16, 4–35. h Ex 17, 1–7; Nm 20, 7–11; Dt 8, 15. i Nm 14, 28–38; Jude 5. j Nm 11, 4.34. k Ex 32, 6. l Nm 25, 1–9. m Nm 21, 5–9. n Nm 14, 2–37; 16, 1–35. o Mt 6, 13; Jas 1, 13–14 / 1, 9. p 1 Jn 5, 21. q Mt 26, 26–29; Acts 2, 42. r Rom 12, 5; Eph 4, 4. s Lv 7, 6. t Dt 32, 17. u 2 Cor 6, 14–18. v Dt 32, 21 / Eccl 6, 10. w 6,12.

[24 x]No one should seek his own advantage, but
that of his neighbor. [25]*Eat anything sold in the
market, without raising questions on grounds of
conscience, [26 y]for "the earth and its fullness are
the Lord's." [27]If an unbeliever invites you and
you want to go, eat whatever is placed before
you, without raising questions on grounds of
conscience. [28]But if someone says to you, "This
was offered in sacrifice," do not eat it on
account of the one who called attention to it
and on account of conscience; [29]I mean not
your own conscience, but the other's. For why
should my freedom be determined by someone
else's conscience? [30 z]If I partake thankfully,
why am I reviled for that over which I give
thanks?

[31]So whether you eat or drink, or whatever
you do, do everything for the glory of God.
[32]*Avoid giving offense, whether to Jews or
Greeks or the church of God, [33 a]just as I try to
please everyone in every way, not seeking my
own benefit but that of the many, that they may
be saved.

CHAPTER 11

[1 b]Be imitators of me, as I am of Christ.

IV: Problems in Liturgical Assemblies

[2 c]*I praise you because you remember me in
everything and hold fast to the traditions, just as
I handed them on to you.

A. Women's Headdresses

Man and Woman [3 d]*But I want you to know
that Christ is the head of every man, and a
husband the head of his wife, and God the head
of Christ. [4]*Any man who prays or prophesies
with his head covered brings shame upon his
head. [5]But any woman who prays or prophesies
with her head unveiled brings shame upon her
head, for it is one and the same thing as if she
had had her head shaved. [6]For if a woman does
not have her head veiled, she may as well have
her hair cut off. But if it is shameful for a woman
to have her hair cut off or her head shaved, then
she should wear a veil.

[7 e]*A man, on the other hand, should not

10, 25–30: A summary of specific situations in which the eating of meat sacrificed to idols could present problems of conscience. Three cases are considered. In the first (the marketplace, 25–26) and the second (at table, 27), there is no need to be concerned with whether food has passed through a pagan sacrifice or not, for the principle of 8, 4–6 still stands, and the whole creation belongs to the one God. But in the third case (28), the situation changes if someone present explicitly raises the question of the sacrificial origin of the food; eating in such circumstances may be subject to various interpretations, some of which could be harmful to individuals. Paul is at pains to insist that the enlightened Christian conscience need not change its judgment about the neutrality, even the goodness, of the food in itself (29–30); yet the total situation is altered to the extent that others are potentially endangered, and this calls for a different response, for the sake of others.

10, 32—11, 1: In summary, the general rule of mutually responsible use of their Christian freedom is enjoined first negatively (32), then positively, as exemplified in Paul (33), and finally grounded in Christ, the pattern for Paul's behavior and theirs (11, 1; cf Rom 15, 1–3).

11, 2—14, 40: This section of the letter is devoted to regulation of conduct at the liturgy. The problems Paul handles have to do with the dress of women in the assembly (11, 3–16), improprieties in the celebration of community meals (11, 17–34), and the use of charisms or spiritual gifts (12, 1—14, 40). The statement in 11, 2 introduces all of these discussions, but applies more appropriately to the second (cf the mention of praise in 11, 17 and of tradition in 11, 23).

11, 3–16: Women have been participating in worship at Corinth without the head-covering normal in Greek society of the period. Paul's stated goal is to bring them back into conformity with contemporary practice and propriety. In his desire to convince, he reaches for arguments from a variety of sources, though he has space to develop them only sketchily and is perhaps aware that they differ greatly in persuasiveness.

11, 3: A husband the head of his wife: the specific problem suggests to Paul the model of the head as a device for clarifying relations within a hierarchical structure. The model is similar to that developed later in greater detail and nuance in Eph 5, 21–33. It is a hybrid model, for it grafts onto a strictly theological scale of existence (cf 3, 21–23) the hierarchy of sociosexual relations prevalent in the ancient world: men, dominant, reflect the active function of Christ in relation to his church; women, submissive, reflect the passive role of the church with respect to its savior. This gives us the functional scale: God, Christ, man, woman.

11, 4–6: From man's direct relation to Christ, Paul infers that his head should not be covered. But woman, related not directly to Christ on the scale but to her husband, requires a covering as a sign of that relationship. **Shameful . . . to have her hair cut off:** certain less honored classes in society, such as lesbians and prostitutes, are thought to have worn their hair close-cropped.

11, 7–9: The hierarchy of v 3 is now expressed in other metaphors: the image (**eikōn**) and the reflected glory (**doxa**). Paul is alluding basically to the text of Gn 1, 27, in which mankind as a whole, the male-female couple, is created in God's image and given the command to multiply and together dominate the lower creation. But Gn 1, 24 is interpreted here in the light of the second creation narrative in Gn 2, in which each of the sexes is created separately (first the man and then the woman **from** man and **for** him, to be his helpmate, Gn 2, 20–23), and under the influence of the story of the fall, as a result of which the husband rules over the woman (Gn 3, 16). This interpretation splits the single image of God into two, at different degrees of closeness.

x Rom 15, 2; Phil 2, 4.21. y Pss 24, 1; 50, 12. z Rom 14, 6; 1 Tm 4, 3–4. a 9, 22; Rom 15, 2. b 4, 16; Phil 3, 17. c 15, 3; 2 Thes 2, 15. d Eph 5, 23. e Gn 1, 26–27; 5, 1.

cover his head, because he is the image and glory
of God, but woman is the glory of man. [8][f]For
man did not come from woman, but woman
from man; [9][g]nor was man created for woman,
but woman for man; [10]*for this reason a woman
should have a sign of authority on her head, be-
cause of the angels. [11][h]*Woman is not indepen-
dent of man or man of woman in the Lord. [12][i]For
just as woman came from man, so man is born of
woman; but all things are from God.

[13]*Judge for yourselves: is it proper for a
woman to pray to God with her head unveiled?
[14]Does not nature itself teach you that if a man
wears his hair long it is a disgrace to him,
[15]whereas if a woman has long hair it is her
glory, because long hair has been given [her] for a
covering? [16]But if anyone is inclined to be
argumentative, we do not have such a custom,
nor do the churches of God.

B. The Lord's Supper

An Abuse at Corinth [17]*In giving this instruc-
tion, I do not praise the fact that your meetings are
doing more harm than good. [18][j]First of all, I hear
that when you meet as a church there are divi-
sions among you, and to a degree I believe it;
[19]*there have to be factions among you in order
that [also] those who are approved among you
may become known. [20]When you meet in one
place, then, it is not to eat the Lord's supper, [21]for
in eating, each one goes ahead with his own supper,
and one goes hungry while another gets drunk.
[22][k]Do you not have houses in which you can eat
and drink? Or do you show contempt for the
church of God and make those who have nothing
feel ashamed? What can I say to you? Shall I praise
you? In this matter I do not praise you.

Tradition of the Institution [23][l]*For I received
from the Lord what I also handed on to you, that
the Lord Jesus, on the night he was handed over,
took bread, [24]and, after he had given thanks,
broke it and said, "This is my body that is for
you. Do this in remembrance of me." [25][m]In the
same way also the cup, after supper, saying,
"This cup is the new covenant in my blood. Do
this, as often as you drink it, in remembrance of
me." [26]For as often as you eat this bread and
drink the cup, you proclaim the death of the
Lord until he comes.

[27]*Therefore, whoever eats the bread or
drinks the cup of the Lord unworthily will have
to answer for the body and blood of the Lord.
[28]*A person should examine himself, and so eat
the bread and drink the cup. [29]*For anyone who

11, 10: A sign of authority: "authority" (**exousia**) may possibly be due to mistranslation of an Aramaic word for "veil"; in any case, the connection with v 9 indicates that the covering is a sign of woman's subordination. **Because of the angels:** a surprising additional reason, which the context does not clarify. Presumably the reference is to cosmic powers who might inflict harm on women or whose function is to watch over women or the cult.

11, 11–12: These parenthetical remarks relativize the argument from Gn 2—3. **In the Lord:** in the Christian economy the relation between the sexes is characterized by a mutual dependence, which is not further specified. And even in the natural order conditions have changed: the mode of origin described in Gn 2 has been reversed (12a). But the ultimately significant fact is the origin that all things have in common (12b).

11, 13–16: The argument for conformity to common church practice is summed up and pressed home. Verses 14–15 contain a final appeal to the sense of propriety that contemporary Greek society would consider "natural" (cf 5–6).

11, 17–34: Paul turns to another abuse connected with the liturgy, and a more serious one, for it involves neglect of basic Christian tradition concerning the meaning of the Lord's Supper. Paul recalls that tradition for them and reminds them of its implications.

11, 19: That . . . those who are approved among you may become known: Paul situates their divisions within the context of the eschatological separation of the authentic from the inauthentic and the final revelation of the difference. The notion of authenticity-testing recurs in the injunction to self-examination in view of present and future judgment (28–32).

11, 23–25: This is the earliest written account of the institution of the Lord's Supper in the New Testament. The narrative emphasizes Jesus' action of self-giving (expressed in the words over the bread and the cup) and his double command to repeat his own action.

11, 27: It follows that the only proper way to celebrate the Eucharist is one that corresponds to Jesus' intention, which fits with the meaning of his command to reproduce his action in the proper spirit. If the Corinthians eat and drink unworthily, i.e., without having grasped and internalized the meaning of his death for them, they **will have to answer for the body and blood,** i.e., will be guilty of a sin against the Lord himself (cf 8, 12).

11, 28: Examine himself: the Greek word is similar to that for "approved" in v 19, which means "having been tested and found true." The self-testing required for proper eating involves **discerning the body** (29), which, from the context, must mean understanding the sense of Jesus' death (26), perceiving the imperative to unity that follows from the fact that Jesus gives himself to all and requires us to repeat his sacrifice in the same spirit (18–25).

11, 29–32: Judgment: there is a series of wordplays in these verses that would be awkward to translate literally into English; it includes all the references to judgment (**krima,** 29.34; **krinō,** 31.32), discernment (**diakrinō,** 29.31), and condemnation (**katakrinō,** 32). The judgment is concretely described as the illness, infirmity, and death that have visited the community. These are signs that the power of Jesus' death is not yet com-

f Gn 2, 21–23. g Gn 2, 18. h Gal 3, 27–28. i 8, 6; Rom 11, 36. j 1, 10–12; Gal 5, 20. k Jas 2, 1–7. 12; 15, 3 / 10, 16–17; Mt 26, 26–29; Mk 14, 22–25; Lk 22, 14–20. m Ex 24, 8; 2 Cor 3, 6; Heb 8, 6–13.

eats and drinks without discerning the body, eats and drinks judgment on himself. [30]That is why many among you are ill and infirm, and a considerable number are dying. [31]If we discerned ourselves, we would not be under judgment; [32 n]but since we are judged by [the] Lord, we are being disciplined so that we may not be condemned along with the world.

[33]Therefore, my brothers, when you come together to eat, wait for one another. [34]If anyone is hungry, he should eat at home, so that your meetings may not result in judgment. The other matters I shall set in order when I come.

C. Spiritual Gifts

CHAPTER 12

Unity and Variety [1]*Now in regard to spiritual gifts, brothers, I do not want you to be unaware. [2 o]*You know how, when you were pagans, you were constantly attracted and led away to mute idols. [3 p]Therefore, I tell you that nobody speaking by the spirit of God says, "Jesus be accursed." And no one can say, "Jesus is Lord," except by the holy Spirit.

[4 q]*There are different kinds of spiritual gifts but the same Spirit; [5]there are different forms of service but the same Lord; [6]there are different workings but the same God who produces all of them in everyone. [7]To each individual the manifestation of the Spirit is given for some benefit. [8 r]To one is given through the Spirit the expression of wisdom; to another the expression of knowledge according to the same Spirit; [9]to another faith by the same Spirit; to another gifts of healing by the one Spirit; [10 s]to another mighty deeds; to another prophecy; to another discernment of spirits; to another varieties of tongues; to another interpretation of tongues. [11 t]But one and the same Spirit produces all of these, distributing them individually to each person as he wishes.

One Body, Many Parts [12 u]*As a body is one though it has many parts, and all the parts of the body, though many, are one body, so also Christ. [13 v]For in one Spirit we were all baptized into one body, whether Jews or Greeks, slaves or free persons, and we were all given to drink of one Spirit.

[14]Now the body is not a single part, but many. [15]If a foot should say, "Because I am not a hand I do not belong to the body," it does not for this reason belong any less to the body. [16]Or if an ear should say, "Because I am not an eye I do not belong to the body," it does not for this reason belong any less to the body. [17]If the whole body were an eye, where would the hearing be? If the whole body were hearing, where would the sense of smell be? [18]But as it is, God placed the parts, each one of them, in the body as he intended. [19]If they were all one part, where would the body be? [20]But as it is, there are many parts, yet one body. [21]The eye cannot say to the hand, "I do not need you," nor again the head to the feet, "I do not need you." [22]Indeed, the parts of the body that seem to be weaker are all the more necessary, [23]and those parts of the body that we consider less honorable we surround with greater honor, and our less presentable

---

pletely recognized and experienced. Yet even the judgment incurred is an expression of God's concern; it is a medicinal measure meant to rescue us from condemnation with God's enemies.

12, 1—14, 40: Ecstatic and charismatic activity were common in early Christian experience, as they were in other ancient religions. But the Corinthians seem to have developed a disproportionate esteem for certain phenomena, especially tongues, to the detriment of order in the liturgy. Paul's response to this development provides us with the fullest exposition we have of his theology of the charisms.

12, 2–3: There is an experience of the Spirit and an understanding of ecstatic phenomena that are specifically Christian and that differ, despite apparent similarities, from those of the pagans. It is necessary to discern which spirit is leading one; ecstatic phenomena must be judged by their effect (2). Verse 3 illustrates this by an example: power to confess Jesus as Lord can come only from the Spirit, and it is inconceivable that the Spirit would move anyone to curse the Lord.

12, 4–6: There are some features common to all charisms, despite their diversity: all are **gifts** (**charismata**), grace from outside ourselves; all are **forms of service** (**diakoniai**), an expression of their purpose and effect; and all are **workings** (**energēmata**), in which God is at work. Paul associates each of these aspects with what later theology will call one of the persons of the Trinity, an early example of "appropriation."

12, 12–26: The image of **a body** is introduced to explain Christ's relationship with believers (12). Verse 13 applies this model to the church: by baptism all, despite diversity of ethnic or social origins, are integrated into one organism. Verses 14–26 then develop the need for diversity of function among the parts of a body without threat to its unity.

n Dt 8, 5; Heb 12, 5–11. o Eph 2, 11–18. p Rom 10, 9; 1 Jn 4, 2–3. q Rom 12, 6; Eph 4, 7.11. r 2, 6–13. s 14, 5.26.39; Acts 2, 4. t 7, 7; Eph 4, 7. u 10, 17; Rom 12, 4–5; Eph 2, 16; Col 3, 15. v Gal 3, 28; Eph 2, 13–18; Col 3, 11 / Jn 7, 37–39.

parts are treated with greater propriety, [24]whereas our more presentable parts do not need this. But God has so constructed the body as to give greater honor to a part that is without it, [25]so that there may be no division in the body, but that the parts may have the same concern for one another. [26]If [one] part suffers, all the parts suffer with it; if one part is honored, all the parts share its joy.

Application to Christ [27] [w]*Now you are Christ's body, and individually parts of it. [28] [x]*Some people God has designated in the church to be, first, apostles; second, prophets; third, teachers; then, mighty deeds; then gifts of healing, assistance, administration, and varieties of tongues. [29]Are all apostles? Are all prophets? Are all teachers? Do all work mighty deeds? [30]Do all have gifts of healing? Do all speak in tongues? Do all interpret? [31]Strive eagerly for the greatest spiritual gifts.

The Way of Love But I shall show you a still more excellent way.

CHAPTER 13

[1] [y]*If I speak in human and angelic tongues but do not have love, I am a resounding gong or a clashing cymbal. [2] [z]And if I have the gift of prophecy and comprehend all mysteries and all knowledge; if I have all faith so as to move mountains, but do not have love, I am nothing. [3] [a]If I give away everything I own, and if I hand my body over so that I may boast but do not have love, I gain nothing.

[4] [b]*Love is patient, love is kind. It is not jealous, [love] is not pompous, it is not inflated, [5] [c]it is not rude, it does not seek its own interests, it is not quick-tempered, it does not brood over injury, [6]it does not rejoice over wrongdoing but rejoices with the truth. [7] [d]It bears all things, believes all things, hopes all things, endures all things.

[8]*Love never fails. If there are prophecies, they will be brought to nothing; if tongues, they will cease; if knowledge, it will be brought to nothing. [9]For we know partially and we prophesy partially, [10]but when the perfect comes, the partial will pass away. [11]When I was a child, I used to talk as a child, think as a child, reason as a child; when I became a man, I put aside childish things. [12] [e]At present we see indistinctly, as in a mirror, but then face to face. At present I know partially; then I shall know fully, as I am fully known. [13] [f]*So faith, hope, love remain, these three; but the greatest of these is love.

CHAPTER 14

Prophecy Greater than Tongues [1] [g]*Pursue love, but strive eagerly for the spiritual gifts,

12, 27–30: Paul now applies the image again to the church as a whole and its members (27). The lists in vv 28–30 spell out the parallelism by specifying the diversity of functions found in the church (cf Rom 12, 6–8; Eph 4, 11).

12, 28: **First, apostles:** apostleship was not mentioned in vv 8–10, nor is it at issue in these chapters, but Paul gives it pride of place in his listing. It is not just one gift among others but a prior and fuller gift that includes the others. They are all demonstrated in Paul's apostolate, but he may have developed his theology of charisms by reflecting first of all on his own grace of apostleship (cf 3, 5—4, 14; 9, 1–27; 2 Cor 2, 14—6, 13; 10, 1—13, 30, esp. 11, 23 and 12, 12).

13, 1–13: This chapter involves a shift of perspective and a new point. All or part of the material may once have been an independent piece in the style of Hellenistic eulogies of virtues, but it is now integrated, by editing, into the context of chs 12–14 (cf the reference to tongues and prophecy) and into the letter as a whole (cf the references to knowledge and to behavior). The function of ch 13 within the discussion of spiritual gifts is to relativize all the charisms by contrasting them with the more basic, pervasive, and enduring value that gives them their purpose and their effectiveness. The rhetoric of this chapter is striking.

13, 1–3: An inventory of gifts, arranged in careful gradation: neither tongues (on the lowest rung), nor prophecy, knowledge, or faith, nor even self-sacrifice has value unless informed by love.

13, 4–7: This paragraph is developed by personification and enumeration, defining love by what it does or does not do. The Greek contains fifteen verbs; it is natural to translate many of them by adjectives in English.

13, 8–13: The final paragraph announces its topic, **Love never fails** (8), then develops the permanence of love in contrast to the charisms (9–12), and finally asserts love's superiority even over the other "theological virtues" (13).

13, 13: In speaking of love, Paul is led by spontaneous association to mention faith and hope as well. They are already a well-known triad (cf 1 Thes 1, 3), three interrelated (cf 7) features of Christian life, more fundamental than any particular charism. **The greatest . . . is love:** love is operative even within the other members of the triad (7), so that it has a certain primacy among them. Or, if the perspective is temporal, love will remain (cf "never fails," 8) even when faith has yielded to sight and hope to possession.

14, 1–5: Verse 1b returns to the thought of 12, 31a and reveals Paul's primary concern. The series of contrasts in vv 2–5 discloses the problem at Corinth: a disproportionate interest in tongues, with a corresponding failure to appreciate the worth of prophecy. Paul attempts to clarify the relative values of those gifts by indicat-

w Rom 12, 5–8; Eph 1, 23; 4, 12; 5, 30; Col 1, 18.24. x Eph 2, 20; 3, 5; 4, 11. y 8, 1; 16, 14; Rom 12, 9–10; 13, 8–10. z 4, 1; 14, 2 / 1, 5; 8, 1–3; 12, 8 / Mt 17, 20; 21, 21; Col 2, 3. a Mt 6, 2. b Eph 4, 2 / 4, 6.18; 5, 2; 8, 1. c 10, 24.33; Phil 2, 4.21; 1 Thes 5, 15. d Prv 10, 12; 1 Pt 4, 8. e 2 Cor 5, 7; Heb 11, 1 / 2 Tm 2, 19; 1 Jn 3, 2. f Col 1, 4; 1 Thes 1, 3; 5, 8. g 5.12.39.

above all that you may prophesy. 2*For one who speaks in a tongue does not speak to human beings but to God, for no one listens; he utters mysteries in spirit. 3 h*On the other hand, one who prophesies does speak to human beings, for their building up, encouragement, and solace. 4Whoever speaks in a tongue builds himself up, but whoever prophesies builds up the church. 5Now I should like all of you to speak in tongues, but even more to prophesy. One who prophesies is greater than one who speaks in tongues, unless he interprets, so that the church may be built up.

6*Now, brothers, if I should come to you speaking in tongues, what good will I do you if I do not speak to you by way of revelation, or knowledge, or prophecy, or instruction? 7Likewise, if inanimate things that produce sound, such as flute or harp, do not give out the tones distinctly, how will what is being played on flute or harp be recognized? 8And if the bugle gives an indistinct sound, who will get ready for battle? 9Similarly, if you, because of speaking in tongues, do not utter intelligible speech, how will anyone know what is being said? For you will be talking to the air. 10It happens that there are many different languages in the world, and none is meaningless; 11but if I do not know the meaning of a language, I shall be a foreigner to one who speaks it, and one who speaks it a foreigner to me. 12So with yourselves: since you strive eagerly for spirits, seek to have an abundance of them for building up the church.

Need for Interpretation 13*Therefore, one who speaks in a tongue should pray to be able to interpret. 14*[For] if I pray in a tongue, my spirit is at prayer but my mind is unproductive. 15 iSo what is to be done? I will pray with the spirit, but I will also pray with the mind. I will sing praise with the spirit, but I will also sing praise with the mind. 16Otherwise, if you pronounce a blessing [with] the spirit, how shall one who holds the place of the uninstructed say the "Amen" to your thanksgiving, since he does not know what you are saying? 17For you may be giving thanks very well, but the other is not built up. 18I give thanks to God that I speak in tongues more than any of you, 19but in the church I would rather speak five words with my mind, so as to instruct others also, than ten thousand words in a tongue.

Functions of These Gifts 20 j*Brothers, stop being childish in your thinking. In respect to evil be like infants, but in your thinking be mature. 21 kIt is written in the law:

"By people speaking strange tongues
and by the lips of foreigners

---

ing the kind of communication achieved in each and the kind of effect each produces.

14, 2–3a: They involve two kinds of communication: tongues, private speech toward God in inarticulate terms that need interpretation to be intelligible to others (see 27–28); prophecy, communication with others in the community.

14, 3b-5: They produce two kinds of effect. One who speaks in tongues **builds himself up;** it is a matter of individual experience and personal perfection, which inevitably recalls Paul's previous remarks about being inflated, seeking one's own good, pleasing oneself. But a prophet **builds up the church:** the theme of "building up" or "edifying" others, the main theme of the letter, comes to clearest expression in this chapter (3.4.5.12.17). It has been anticipated at 8, 1 and 10, 23, and by the related concept of "the beneficial" in 6, 12; 10, 23; 12, 7; etc.

14, 6–12: Sound, in order to be useful, must be intelligible. This principle is illustrated by a series of analogies from music (7–8) and from ordinary human speech (10–11); it is applied to the case at hand in v 9 and v 12.

14, 13–19: The charism of interpretation lifts tongues to the level of intelligibility, enabling them to produce the same effect as prophecy (cf 5.26–28).

14, 14–15: My spirit: Paul emphasizes the exclusively ecstatic, nonrational quality of tongues. The tongues at Pentecost are also described as an ecstatic experience (Acts 2, 4.12–13), though Luke superimposes further interpretations of his own. **My mind:** the ecstatic element, dominant in earliest Old Testament prophecy as depicted in 1 Sam 10, 5–13; 19, 20–24, seems entirely absent from Paul's notion of prophecy and completely relegated to tongues. He emphasizes the role of reason when he specifies instruction as a function of prophecy (6.19.31). But he does not exclude intuition and emotion; cf references to encouragement and consolation (3.31) and the scene describing the ideal exercise of prophecy (24–25).

14, 20–22: The Corinthians pride themselves on tongues as a sign of God's favor, a means of direct communication with him (2.28). To challenge them to a more mature appraisal, Paul draws from scripture a less flattering explanation of what speaking in tongues may signify. Isaiah threatened the people that if they failed to listen to their prophets, the Lord would speak to them (in punishment) through the lips of Assyrian conquerors (Is 28, 11–12). Paul compresses Isaiah's text and makes God address his people directly. Equating tongues with foreign languages (cf 10–11), Paul concludes from Isaiah that **tongues are a sign not for those who believe,** i.e., not a mark of God's pleasure for those who listen to him but a mark of his displeasure with those in the community who are faithless, who have not heeded the message that he has sent through the prophets.

h 4–5.12.17.26; 3, 9; 8, 1.10; 10, 23. i Eph 5, 19; Col 3, 16. j Mt 10, 16; Rom 16, 19; Eph 4, 14. k Is 28, 11–12; Dt 28, 49.

I will speak to this people,
and even so they will not listen to me,

says the Lord." 22 Thus, tongues are a sign not for those who believe but for unbelievers, whereas prophecy is not for unbelievers but for those who believe.

23 [l]*So if the whole church meets in one place and everyone speaks in tongues, and then uninstructed people or unbelievers should come in, will they not say that you are out of your minds? 24 But if everyone is prophesying, and an unbeliever or uninstructed person should come in, he will be convinced by everyone and judged by everyone, 25 [m]and the secrets of his heart will be disclosed, and so he will fall down and worship God, declaring, "God is really in your midst."

Rules of Order 26 [n]*So what is to be done, brothers? When you assemble, one has a psalm, another an instruction, a revelation, a tongue, or an interpretation. Everything should be done for building up. 27 If anyone speaks in a tongue, let it be two or at most three, and each in turn, and one should interpret. 28 But if there is no interpreter, the person should keep silent in the church and speak to himself and to God.

29 Two or three prophets should speak, and the others discern. 30 But if a revelation is given to another person sitting there, the first one should be silent. 31 For you can all prophesy one by one, so that all may learn and all be encouraged. 32 Indeed, the spirits of prophets are under the prophets' control, 33 *since he is not the God of disorder but of peace.

As in all the churches of the holy ones, 34 [o]women should keep silent in the churches, for they are not allowed to speak, but should be subordinate, as even the law says. 35 But if they want to learn anything, they should ask their husbands at home. For it is improper for a woman to speak in the church. 36 Did the word of God go forth from you? Or has it come to you alone?

37 If anyone thinks that he is a prophet or a spiritual person, he should recognize that what I am writing to you is a commandment of the Lord. 38 If anyone does not acknowledge this, he is not acknowledged. 39 So, [my] brothers, strive eagerly to prophesy, and do not forbid speaking in tongues, 40 but everything must be done properly and in order.

V: The Resurrection

A. The Resurrection of Christ

CHAPTER 15

The Gospel Teaching 1 *Now I am reminding you, brothers, of the gospel I preached to you, which you indeed received and in which you

14, 23–25: Paul projects the possible missionary effect of two hypothetical liturgical experiences, one consisting wholly of tongues, the other entirely of prophecy. **Uninstructed (idiōtai):** the term may simply mean people who do not speak or understand tongues, as in v 16, where it seems to designate Christians. But coupled with the term "unbelievers" it may be another way of designating those who have not been initiated into the community of faith; some believe it denotes a special class of non-Christians who are close to the community, such as catechumens. **Unbelievers (apistoi):** he has shifted from the inner-community perspective of v 22; the term here designates non-Christians (cf 6, 6; 7, 15; 10, 27).

14, 26–33a: Paul concludes with specific directives regarding exercise of the gifts in their assemblies. Verse 26 enunciates the basic criterion in the use of any gift: it must contribute to "building up."

14, 33b-36: Verse 33b may belong with what precedes, so that the new paragraph would begin only with v 34. Verses 34–35 change the subject. These two verses have the theme of submission in common with ch 11, despite differences in vocabulary, and a concern with what is or is not becoming; but it is difficult to harmonize the injunction to silence here with ch 11, which appears to take it for granted that women do pray and prophesy aloud in the assembly (cf 11, 5.13). Hence the verses are often considered an interpolation, reflecting the discipline of later churches; such an interpolation would have to have antedated our manuscripts, all of which contain them, though some transpose them to the very end of the chapter.

15, 1–58: Some consider this chapter an earlier Pauline composition inserted into the present letter. The problem that Paul treats is clear to a degree: some of the Corinthians are denying the resurrection of the dead (12), apparently because of their inability to imagine how any kind of bodily existence could be possible after death (35). It is plausibly supposed that their attitude stems from Greek anthropology, which looks with contempt upon matter and would be content with the survival of the soul, and perhaps also from an overrealized eschatology of gnostic coloration, such as that reflected in 2 Tm 2, 18, which considers the resurrection a purely spiritual experience already achieved in baptism and in the forgiveness of sins. Paul, on the other hand, will affirm both the essential corporeity of the resurrection and its futurity.

His response moves through three steps: a recall of the basic kerygma about Jesus' resurrection (1–11), an assertion of the logical inconsistencies involved in denial of the resurrection (12–34), and an attempt to perceive theologically what the properties of the resurrected body must be (35–58).

15, 1–11: Paul recalls the tradition (3–7), which he can presuppose as common ground and which provides a starting point for

l Acts 2, 6.13. m 4, 5 / Is 45, 14; Zec 8, 23. n Eph 4, 12. o 1 Tm 2, 11–15; 1 Pt 3, 1.

also stand. 2 Through it you are also being saved,
if you hold fast to the word I preached to you,
unless you believed in vain. 3 [p]*For I handed on
to you as of first importance what I also re-
ceived: that Christ died for our sins in accor-
dance with the scriptures; 4 [q]that he was buried;
that he was raised on the third day in accordance
with the scriptures; 5 [r]that he appeared to
Kephas, then to the Twelve. 6 After that, he
appeared to more than five hundred brothers at
once, most of whom are still living, though some
have fallen asleep. 7 After that he appeared to
James, then to all the apostles. 8 [s]Last of all, as to
one born abnormally, he appeared to me. 9 [t]*For
I am the least of the apostles, not fit to be called
an apostle, because I persecuted the church of
God. 10 But by the grace of God I am what I am,
and his grace to me has not been ineffective.
Indeed, I have toiled harder than all of them; not
I, however, but the grace of God [that is] with
me. 11 Therefore, whether it be I or they, so we
preach and so you believed.

B. The Resurrection of the Dead

Results of Denial 12 *But if Christ is preached
as raised from the dead, how can some among
you say there is no resurrection of the dead?
13 [u]If there is no resurrection of the dead, then
neither has Christ been raised. 14 And if Christ
has not been raised, then empty [too] is our
preaching; empty, too, your faith. 15 [v]Then we
are also false witnesses to God, because we
testified against God that he raised Christ, whom
he did not raise if in fact the dead are not raised.
16 For if the dead are not raised, neither has
Christ been raised, 17 *and if Christ has not been
raised, your faith is vain; you are still in your
sins. 18 Then those who have fallen asleep in
Christ have perished. 19 If for this life only we
have hoped in Christ, we are the most pitiable
people of all.

Christ the Firstfruits 20 [w]*But now Christ has
been raised from the dead, the firstfruits of those
who have fallen asleep. 21 *For since death came
through a human being, the resurrection of the
dead came also through a human being. 22 [x]For
just as in Adam all die, so too in Christ shall all
be brought to life, 23 [y]but each one in proper
order: Christ the firstfruits; then, at his coming,
those who belong to Christ; 24 [z]*then comes the
end, when he hands over the kingdom to his
God and Father, when he has destroyed every

---

his argument. This is the fundamental content of all Christian preaching and belief (1–2.11).

15, 3–7: The language by which Paul expresses the essence of the "gospel" (1) is not his own but is drawn from older credal formulas. This credo highlights Jesus' death for our sins (confirmed by his burial) and Jesus' resurrection (confirmed by his appearances) and presents both of them as fulfillment of prophecy. **In accordance with the scriptures:** conformity of Jesus' passion with the scriptures is asserted in Mt 16, 1; Lk 24, 25–27.32.44–46. Application of some Old Testament texts (Pss 2, 7; 16, 8–11) to his resurrection is illustrated by Acts 2, 27–31; 13, 29–39; and Is 52, 13—53, 12 and Hos 6, 2 may also have been envisaged.

15, 9–11: A persecutor may have appeared disqualified (**ouk . . . hikanos**) from apostleship, but in fact God's grace has qualified him. Cf the remarks in 2 Cor about his qualifications (2, 16; 3, 5) and his greater labors (11, 23). These verses are parenthetical, but a nerve has been touched (the references to his abnormal birth and his activity as a persecutor may echo taunts from Paul's opponents), and he is instinctively moved to self-defense.

15, 12–19: Denial of the resurrection (12) involves logical inconsistencies. The basic one, stated twice (13.16), is that if there is no such thing as (bodily) resurrection, then it has not taken place even in Christ's case.

15, 17–18: The consequences for the Corinthians are grave: both forgiveness of sins and salvation are an illusion, despite their strong convictions about both. Unless Christ is risen, their faith does not save.

15, 20–28: After a triumphant assertion of the reality of Christ's resurrection (20a), Paul explains its positive implications and consequences. As a soteriological event of both human (20–23) and cosmic (24–28) dimensions, Jesus' resurrection logically and necessarily involves ours as well.

15, 20: The firstfruits: the portion of the harvest offered in thanksgiving to God implies the consecration of the entire harvest to come. Christ's resurrection is not an end in itself; its finality lies in the whole harvest, ourselves.

15, 21–22: Our human existence, both natural and supernatural, is corporate, involves solidarity. **In Adam . . . in Christ:** the Hebrew word **'adām** in Genesis is both a common noun for mankind and a proper noun for the first man. Paul here presents Adam as at least a literary type of Christ; the parallelism and contrast between them will be developed further in vv 45–49 and in Rom 5, 12–21.

15, 24–28: Paul's perspective expands to cosmic dimensions, as he describes the climax of history, **the end.** His viewpoint is still christological, as in vv 20–23. Verses 24 and 28 describe Christ's final relations to his enemies and his Father in language that is both royal and military; vv 25–28 insert a proof from scripture (Pss 110, 1; 8, 7) into this description. But the viewpoint is also theological, for God is the ultimate agent and end, and likewise soteriological, for we are the beneficiaries of all the action.

p 11, 23 / 1 Pt 2, 24; 3, 18 / Is 53, 4–12. q Acts 2, 23–24 / Ps 16, 8–11; Hos 6, 1–2; Jon 2, 1. r Mk 16, 14; Mt 28, 16–17; Lk 24, 36; Jn 20, 19. s 9, 1; Acts 9, 3–6; Gal 1, 16. t Acts 8, 3; 9, 1–2; Gal 1, 23; Eph 3, 8; 1 Tm 1, 15. u 1 Thes 4, 14. v Acts 5, 32. w Rom 8, 11; Col 1, 18; 1 Thes 4, 14. x Gn 3, 17–19; Rom 5, 12–19. y 1 Thes 4, 15–17. z Eph 1, 22.

sovereignty and every authority and power.
25 [a]For he must reign until he has put all his
enemies under his feet. 26 [b]*The last enemy to
be destroyed is death, 27 [c]*for "he subjected
everything under his feet." But when it says that
everything has been subjected, it is clear that it
excludes the one who subjected everything to
him. 28 [d]When everything is subjected to him,
then the Son himself will [also] be subjected to
the one who subjected everything to him, so that
God may be all in all.
Practical Arguments 29 *Otherwise, what will
people accomplish by having themselves bap-
tized for the dead? If the dead are not raised at
all, then why are they having themselves bap-
tized for them?
30 [e]*Moreover, why are we endangering our-
selves all the time? 31 [f]Every day I face death; I
swear it by the pride in you [brothers] that I have
in Christ Jesus our Lord. 32 [g]If at Ephesus I fought
with beasts, so to speak, what benefit was it to
me? If the dead are not raised:

"Let us eat and drink,
for tomorrow we die."

33 Do not be led astray:

"Bad company corrupts good morals."

34 [h]Become sober as you ought and stop sinning.
For some have no knowledge of God; I say this
to your shame.

C. The Manner of the Resurrection

35 *But someone may say, "How are the dead
raised? With what kind of body will they come
back?"
The Resurrection Body 36 [i]*You fool! What
you sow is not brought to life unless it dies.
37 And what you sow is not the body that is to be
but a bare kernel of wheat, perhaps, or of some
other kind; 38 [j]but God gives it a body as he
chooses, and to each of the seeds its own body.
39 *Not all flesh is the same, but there is one kind
for human beings, another kind of flesh for
animals, another kind of flesh for birds, and
another for fish. 40 There are both heavenly
bodies and earthly bodies, but the brightness of
the heavenly is one kind and that of the earthly
another. 41 The brightness of the sun is one kind,
the brightness of the moon another, and the
brightness of the stars another. For star differs
from star in brightness.
42 *So also is the resurrection of the dead. It is
sown corruptible; it is raised incorruptible. 43 [k]It
is sown dishonorable; it is raised glorious. It is
sown weak; it is raised powerful. 44 It is sown a

15, 26: The last enemy . . . is death: a parenthesis that specifies the final fulfillment of the two Old Testament texts just referred to, Ps 110, 1 and Ps 8, 7. Death is not just one cosmic power among many, but the ultimate effect of sin in the universe (cf 56; Rom 5, 12). Christ defeats death where it prevails, in our bodies. The destruction of the last enemy is concretely the "coming to life" (22) of "those who belong to Christ" (23).

15, 27b-28: The one who subjected everything to him: the Father is the ultimate agent in the drama, and the final end of the process, to whom the Son and everything else is ordered (24.28). **That God may be all in all:** his reign is a dynamic exercise of creative power, an outpouring of life and energy through the universe, with no further resistance. This is the supremely positive meaning of "subjection": that God may fully be God.

15, 29–34: Paul concludes his treatment of logical inconsistencies with a listing of miscellaneous Christian practices that would be meaningless if the resurrection were not a fact.

15, 29: Baptized for the dead: this practice is not further explained here, nor is it necessarily mentioned with approval, but Paul cites it as something in their experience that attests in one more way to belief in the resurrection.

15, 30–34: A life of sacrifice, such as Paul describes in 4, 9–13 and 2 Cor, would be pointless without the prospect of resurrection; a life of pleasure, such as that expressed in the Epicurean slogan of v 32, would be far more consistent. **I fought with beasts:** since Paul does not elsewhere mention a combat with beasts at Ephesus, he may be speaking figuratively about struggles with adversaries.

15, 35–58: Paul imagines two objections that the Corinthians could raise: one concerning the manner of the resurrection (**how?**), the other pertaining to the qualities of the risen body (**what kind?**). These questions probably lie behind their denial of the resurrection (12), and seem to reflect the presumption that no kind of body other than the one we now possess would be possible. Paul deals with these objections in inverse order, in vv 36–49 and vv 50–58. His argument is fundamentally theological and its appeal is to the understanding.

15, 35–49: Paul approaches the question of the nature of the risen body (**what kind of body?**) by means of two analogies: the seed (36–44) and the first man, Adam (45–49).

15, 36–38: The analogy of the seed: there is a change of attributes from seed to plant; the old life-form must be lost for the new to emerge. By speaking about the seed as a **body** that dies and comes to life, Paul keeps the point of the analogy before the reader's mind.

15, 39–41: The expression "its own body" (38) leads to a development on the marvelous diversity evident in bodily life.

15, 42–44: The principles of qualitative difference before and after death (36–38) and of diversity on different levels of creation (39–41) are now applied to the human body. Before: a body

a Ps 110, 1. b Rom 6, 9; 2 Tm 1, 10; Rv 20, 14; 21, 4. c Ps 8, 7; Eph 1, 22; Phil 3, 21. d Eph 4, 6; Col 3, 11. e 2 Cor 4, 8–12; 11, 23–27. f Ps 44, 23; Rom 8, 36. g 4, 9; 2 Cor 4, 10–11 / Wis 2, 5–7; Is 22, 13. h Mt 22, 29; Mk 12, 24. i Jn 12, 24. j Gn 1, 11. k Phil 3, 20–21; Col 3, 4.

natural body; it is raised a spiritual body. If there
is a natural body, there is also a spiritual one.
[45] [l]*So, too, it is written, "The first man,
Adam, became a living being," the last Adam a
life-giving spirit. [46]But the spiritual was not first;
rather the natural and then the spiritual. [47]The
first man was from the earth, earthly; the second
man, from heaven. [48]As was the earthly one, so
also are the earthly, and as is the heavenly one,
so also are the heavenly. [49] [m]*Just as we have
borne the image of the earthly one, we shall also
bear the image of the heavenly one.
The Resurrection Event [50] [n]*This I declare,
brothers: flesh and blood cannot inherit the
kingdom of God, nor does corruption inherit
incorruption. [51] [o]*Behold, I tell you a mystery.
We shall not all fall asleep, but we will all be
changed, [52] [p]in an instant, in the blink of an eye,
at the last trumpet. For the trumpet will sound,
the dead will be raised incorruptible, and we
shall be changed. [53] [q]For that which is corrupt-
ible must clothe itself with incorruptibility, and
that which is mortal must clothe itself with
immortality. [54] [r]*And when this which is corrupt-
ible clothes itself with incorruptibility and this
which is mortal clothes itself with immortality,
then the word that is written shall come about:

"Death is swallowed up in victory.
[55] [s]Where, O death, is your victory?
Where, O death, is your sting?"

[56] [t]*The sting of death is sin, and the power of
sin is the law. [57] [u]But thanks be to God who
gives us the victory through our Lord Jesus
Christ.
[58]Therefore, my beloved brothers, be firm,
steadfast, always fully devoted to the work of the
Lord, knowing that in the Lord your labor is not
in vain.

VI: Conclusion

CHAPTER 16

The Collection [1] [v]*Now in regard to the collec-
tion for the holy ones, you also should do as I
ordered the churches of Galatia. [2]On the first
day of the week each of you should set aside and
save whatever he can afford, so that collections
will not be going on when I come. [3]And when I
arrive, I shall send those whom you have ap-

---

animated by a lower, natural life-principle (**psychē**) and endowed with the properties of natural existence (corruptibility, lack of glory, weakness). After: a body animated by a higher life-principle (**pneuma**; cf 45) and endowed with other qualities (incorruptibility, glory, power, spirituality), which are properties of God himself.

15, 45: The analogy of **the first man, Adam,** is introduced by a citation from Gn 2, 7. Paul alters the text slightly, adding the adjective **first**, and translating the Hebrew **'adām** twice, so as to give it its value both as a common noun (**man**) and as a proper name (**Adam**). Verse 45b then specifies similarities and differences between the two Adams. **The last Adam,** Christ (cf 21–22) has become **a . . . spirit (pneuma)**, a life-principle transcendent with respect to the natural soul (**psychē**) of the first Adam (on the terminology here, cf the note on 3, 1). Further, he is not just alive, but **life-giving,** a source of life for others.

15, 49: We shall also bear the image: although it has less manuscript support, this reading better fits the context's emphasis on futurity and the transforming action of God; on future transformation as conformity to the image of the Son, cf Rom 8, 29; Phil 3, 21. The majority reading, "let us bear the image," suggests that the image of the heavenly man is already present and exhorts us to conform to it.

15, 50–57: These verses, an answer to the first question of v 35, explain theologically how the change of properties from one image to another will take place: God has the power to transform, and he will exercise it.

15, 50–53: Flesh and blood . . . corruption: living persons and the corpses of the dead, respectively. In both cases, the gulf between creatures and God is too wide to be bridged unless God himself transforms us.

15, 51–52: A mystery: the last moment in God's plan is disclosed; cf the notes on 2, 1.7–10a. The final trumpet and the awakening of the dead are stock details of the apocalyptic scenario. **We shall not all fall asleep:** Paul expected that some of his contemporaries might still be alive at Christ's return; after the death of Paul and his whole generation, copyists altered this statement in various ways. **We will all be changed:** the statement extends to all Christians, for Paul is not directly speaking about anyone else. Whether they have died before the end or happen still to be alive, all must be transformed.

15, 54–55: Death is swallowed up in victory: scripture itself predicts death's overthrow. **O death:** in his prophetic vision Paul may be making Hosea's words his own, or imagining this cry of triumph on the lips of the risen church.

15, 56: The sting of death is sin: an explanation of Hosea's metaphor. Death, scorpion-like, is equipped with a sting, sin, by which it injects its poison. Christ defeats sin, the cause of death (Gn 3, 19; Rom 5, 12).

16, 1–4: This paragraph contains our earliest evidence for a project that became a major undertaking of Paul's ministry. The collection for the church at Jerusalem was a symbol in his mind for the unity of Jewish and Gentile Christianity. Cf Gal 2, 10; Rom 15, 25–29; 2 Cor 8—9 and the notes to this last passage.

16, 1: In regard to the collection: it has already begun in Galatia and Macedonia (cf 2 Cor 8), and presumably he has already instructed the Corinthians about its purpose.

l Gn 2, 7 / Jn 5, 21–29; 2 Cor 3, 6.17. m Gn 5, 3 / Rom 8, 29; Phil 3, 21. n Jn 3, 3–6. o 1 Thes 4, 14–17. p Jl 2, 1; Zec 9, 14; Mt 24, 31; Rv 11, 15–18. q 2 Cor 5, 2–4. r Is 25, 8; 2 Cor 5, 4; 2 Tm 1, 10; Heb 2, 14–15. s Hos 13, 14. t Rom 4, 15; 7, 7.13. u Jn 16, 33; 1 Jn 5, 4. v Acts 24, 17; Rom 15, 25–32; 2 Cor 8–9; Gal 2, 10.

proved with letters of recommendation to take your gracious gift to Jerusalem. 4*If it seems fitting that I should go also, they will go with me.

Paul's Travel Plans 5 w*I shall come to you after I pass through Macedonia (for I am going to pass through Macedonia), 6and perhaps I shall stay or even spend the winter with you, so that you may send me on my way wherever I may go. 7 xFor I do not wish to see you now just in passing, but I hope to spend some time with you, if the Lord permits. 8 y*I shall stay in Ephesus until Pentecost, 9 zbecause a door has opened for me wide and productive for work, but there are many opponents.

10 aIf Timothy comes, see that he is without fear in your company, for he is doing the work of the Lord just as I am. 11Therefore, no one should disdain him. Rather, send him on his way in peace that he may come to me, for I am expecting him with the brothers. 12 bNow in regard to our brother Apollos, I urged him strongly to go to you with the brothers, but it was not at all his will that he go now. He will go when he has an opportunity.

Exhortation and Greetings 13Be on your guard, stand firm in the faith, be courageous, be strong. 14Your every act should be done with love.

15 cI urge you, brothers—you know that the household of Stephanas is the firstfruits of Achaia and that they have devoted themselves to the service of the holy ones— 16be subordinate to such people and to everyone who works and toils with them. 17I rejoice in the arrival of Stephanas, Fortunatus, and Achaicus, because they made up for your absence, 18 dfor they refreshed my spirit as well as yours. So give recognition to such people.

19 e*The churches of Asia send you greetings. Aquila and Prisca together with the church at their house send you many greetings in the Lord. 20 fAll the brothers greet you. Greet one another with a holy kiss.

21 gI, Paul, write you this greeting in my own hand. 22 h*If anyone does not love the Lord, let him be accursed. *Marana tha.* 23 iThe grace of the Lord Jesus be with you. 24My love to all of you in Christ Jesus.

16, 4: That I should go also: presumably Paul delivered the collection on his final visit to Jerusalem; cf Rom 15, 25–32; Acts 24, 14.

16, 5–12: The travel plans outlined here may not have materialized precisely as Paul intended; cf 2 Cor 1, 8—2, 13; 7, 4–16.

16, 8: In Ephesus until Pentecost: this tells us the place from which he wrote the letter and suggests he may have composed it about Easter time (cf 5, 7–8).

16, 19–24: These paragraphs conform to the normal epistolary conclusion, but their language is overlaid with liturgical coloration as well. The **greetings** of the Asian churches are probably to be read, along with the letter, in the liturgy at Corinth, and the union of the church is to be expressed by **a holy kiss** (19–20). Paul adds to this his own greeting (21) and blessings (23–24).

16, 22: Accursed: literally, "anathema." This expression (cf 12, 3) is a formula for exclusion from the community; it may imply here a call to self-examination before celebration of the Eucharist, in preparation for the Lord's coming and judgment (cf 11, 17–34). **Marana tha:** an Aramaic expression, probably used in the early Christian liturgy. As understood here ("O Lord, come!"), it is a prayer for the early return of Christ. If the Aramaic words are divided differently (**Maran atha,** "Our Lord has come"), it becomes a credal declaration. The former interpretation is supported by what appears to be a Greek equivalent of this acclamation in Rv 22, 20: "Amen. Come, Lord Jesus!"

w Acts 19, 21; Rom 15, 26; 2 Cor 1, 15–16. x Acts 18, 21. y 15, 32; Acts 18, 19; 19, 1–10. z Acts 14, 27; 2 Cor 2, 12. a 4, 17; Acts 16, 1; 19, 22; Phil 2, 19–23. b 1, 12; 3, 4–6.22; Acts 18, 24–28. c 1, 16. d 1 Thes 5, 12–13. e Acts 18, 2.18.26; Rom 16, 3–5. f Rom 16, 16; 2 Cor 13, 12; 1 Thes 5, 26; 1 Pt 5, 14. g Gal 6, 11; Col 4, 18; 2 Thes 3, 17. h 12, 3; Rom 9, 3; Gal 1, 8–9; Rv 22, 20. i Rom 16, 20.

THE SECOND LETTER TO THE CORINTHIANS

The Second Letter to the Corinthians is the most personal of all of Paul's extant writings, and it reveals much about his character. In it he deals with one or more crises that have arisen in the Corinthian church. The confrontation with these problems caused him to reflect deeply on his relationship with the community and to speak about it frankly. One moment he is venting his feelings of frustration and uncertainty, the next he is pouring out his relief and affection. The importance of the issues at stake between them calls forth from him an enormous effort of personal persuasion, as well as doctrinal considerations that are of great value for us. Paul's ability to produce profound theological foundations for what may at first sight appear to be rather commonplace circumstances is perhaps nowhere better exemplified than in Second Corinthians. The emotional tone of the letter, its lack of order, and our ignorance of some of its background do not make it easy to follow, but it amply repays the effort required of the reader.

Second Corinthians is rich and varied in content. The interpretation of Exodus in chapter 3, for instance, offers a striking example of early apologetic use of the Old Testament. Paul's discussion of the collection in chs 8–9 contains a theology of sharing of possessions, of community of goods among Christian churches, which is both balanced and sensitive. Furthermore, the closing chapters provide an illustration of early Christian invective and polemic, because the conflict with intruders forces Paul to assert his authority. But in those same chapters Paul articulates the vision and sense of values that animate his own apostolate, revealing his faith that Jesus' passion and resurrection are the pattern for all Christian life and expressing a spirituality of ministry unsurpassed in the New Testament.

The letter is remarkable for its rhetoric. Paul falls naturally into the style and argumentation of contemporary philosophic preachers, employing with ease the stock devices of the "diatribe." By a barrage of questions, by challenges both serious and ironic, by paradox heaped upon paradox, even by insults hurled at his opponents, he strives to awaken in his hearers a true sense of values and an appropriate response. All his argument centers on the destiny of Jesus, in which a paradoxical reversal of values is revealed. But Paul appeals to his own personal experience as well. In passages of great rhetorical power (4, 7-15; 6, 3-10; 11, 21-29; 12, 5-10; 13, 3-4) he enumerates the circumstances of his ministry and the tribulations he has had to endure for Jesus and the gospel, in the hope of illustrating the pattern of Jesus' existence in his own and of drawing the Corinthians into a reappraisal of the values they cherish. Similar passages in the same style in his other letters (cf especially Rom 8, 31-39; 1 Cor 1, 26-31; 4, 6-21; 9, 1-27; 13, 1-13; Phil 4, 10-19) confirm Paul's familiarity with contemporary rhetoric and demonstrate how effectively it served to express his vision of Christian life and ministry.

Second Corinthians was occasioned by events and problems that developed after Paul's first letter reached Corinth. We have no information about these circumstances except what is contained in the letter itself, which of course supposes that they are known to the readers. Consequently the reconstruction of the letter's background is an uncertain enterprise about which there is not complete agreement.

The letter deals principally with these three topics: (1) a crisis between Paul and the Corinthians, occasioned at least partially by changes in his travel plans (1, 12—2, 13), and the successful resolution of that crisis (7, 5-16); (2) further directives and encouragement in regard to the collection for the church in Jerusalem (8, 1—9, 15); (3) the definition and defense of Paul's ministry as an apostle. Paul's reflections on this matter are occasioned by visitors from other churches who passed through Corinth, missionaries who differed from Paul in a variety of ways, both in theory and in practice. Those differences led to comparisons. Either the visitors themselves or some of the local church members appear to have sown confusion among the Corinthians with regard to Paul's authority or his style, or both. Paul deals at length with aspects of this situation in 2, 14—7, 4 and again in 10, 1—13, 10, though the manner of treatment and the thrust of the argument differ in each of these sections.

Scholars have noticed a lack of continuity in this document. For example, the long section of 2, 14—7, 4 seems abruptly spliced into the narrative of a crisis and its resolution. Identical or similar topics, moreover, seem to be treated several times during the letter (compare 2, 14—7, 4 with 10, 1—13, 10, and 8, 1-24 with 9, 1-15). Many judge, therefore, that this letter as it stands incorporates several briefer letters sent to Corinth over a certain span of time. If this is so, then Paul himself or, more likely, some other editor clearly took care to gather those letters together and impose some literary unity upon the collection, thus producing the document that has come down to us as the Second Letter to the Corinthians. Others continue to regard it as a single letter, attributing its inconsistencies to changes of perspective in Paul that may have been occasioned by the arrival of fresh news from Corinth during its composition. The letter, or at least some sections of it, appears to have been composed in Macedonia (2, 12-13; 7, 5-6; 8, 1-4; 9, 2-4). It is generally dated about the autumn of A.D. 57; if it is a compilation, of course, the various parts may have been separated by intervals of at least some months.

The principal divisions of the Second Letter to the Corinthians are the following:

- I. Address (1, 1-11)
- II. The Crisis between Paul and the Corinthians (1, 12—7, 16)
  - A. Past Relationships (1, 12—2, 13)
  - B. Paul's Ministry (2, 14—7, 4)
  - C. Resolution of the Crisis (7, 5–16)
- III. The Collection for Jerusalem (8, 1—9, 15)
- IV. Paul's Defense of His Ministry (10, 1—13, 10)
- V. Conclusion (13, 11-13)

I: Address

CHAPTER 1

Greeting 1 [a]*Paul, an apostle of Christ Jesus by
the will of God, and Timothy our brother, to the
church of God that is in Corinth, with all the holy
ones throughout Achaia: 2 grace to you and peace
from God our Father and the Lord Jesus Christ.
Thanksgiving 3 [b]*Blessed be the God and Fa-
ther of our Lord Jesus Christ, the Father of
compassion and God of all encouragement,
4 [c]who encourages us in our every affliction, so
that we may be able to encourage those who are
in any affliction with the encouragement with
which we ourselves are encouraged by God.
5 *For as Christ's sufferings overflow to us, so
through Christ does our encouragement also
overflow. 6 If we are afflicted, it is for your
encouragement and salvation; if we are encour-

1, 1–11: The opening follows the usual Pauline form, except that the thanksgiving takes the form of a doxology or glorification of God (3). This introduces a meditation on the experience of suffering and encouragement shared by Paul and the Corinthians (4–7), drawn, at least in part, from Paul's reflections on a recent affliction (8–10). The section ends with a modified and delayed allusion to thanksgiving (11).

1, 3: **God of all encouragement:** Paul expands a standard Jewish blessing so as to state the theme of the paragraph. The theme of "encouragement" or "consolation" (**paraklēsis**) occurs ten times in this opening, against a background formed by multiple references to "affliction" and "suffering."

1, 5: **Through Christ:** the Father of compassion is the Father of our Lord Jesus (3); Paul's sufferings and encouragement (or "consolation") are experienced in union with Christ. Cf Lk 2, 25: the "consolation of Israel" is Jesus himself.

a Eph 1, 1; Col 1, 1 / 1, 19; Acts 16 / Rom 1, 7; 1 Cor 1, 2. b 1 Cor 15, 24; Eph 1, 3; 1 Pt 1, 3 / Rom 15, 5. c 7,6–7.13; 1 Thes 3, 6–8; 2 Thes 2, 16.

aged, it is for your encouragement, which en-
ables you to endure the same sufferings that we
suffer. [7]*Our hope for you is firm, for we know
that as you share in the sufferings, you also share
in the encouragement.
[8] [d]*We do not want you to be unaware,
brothers, of the affliction that came to us in the
province of Asia; we were utterly weighed down
beyond our strength, so that we despaired even
of life. [9] [e]*Indeed, we had accepted within
ourselves the sentence of death, that we might
trust not in ourselves but in God who raises the
dead. [10] [f]He rescued us from such great danger
of death, and he will continue to rescue us; in
him we have put our hope [that] he will also
rescue us again, [11] [g]as you help us with prayer,
so that thanks may be given by many on our
behalf for the gift granted us through the prayers
of many.

II: The Crisis between Paul and the Corinthians

A. Past Relationships

Paul's Sincerity and Constancy [12]*For our
boast is this, the testimony of our conscience
that we have conducted ourselves in the world,
and especially toward you, with the simplicity
and sincerity of God, [and] not by human
wisdom but by the grace of God. [13]For we
write you nothing but what you can read and
understand, and I hope that you will under-
stand completely, [14] [h]as you have come to un-
derstand us partially, that we are your boast as
you also are ours, on the day of [our] Lord
Jesus.
[15]*With this confidence I formerly intended
to come to you so that you might receive a
double favor, [16] [i]namely, to go by way of you to
Macedonia, and then to come to you again on
my return from Macedonia, and have you send
me on my way to Judea. [17] [j]*So when I intended
this, did I act lightly? Or do I make my plans
according to human considerations, so that with
me it is "yes, yes" and "no, no"? [18]*As God is
faithful, our word to you is not "yes" and "no."
[19] [k]For the Son of God, Jesus Christ, who was
proclaimed to you by us, Silvanus and Timothy
and me, was not "yes" and "no," but "yes" has
been in him. [20] [l]For however many are the
promises of God, their Yes is in him; therefore,
the Amen from us also goes through him to God

1, 7: You also share in the encouragement: the eschatological reversal of affliction and encouragement that Christians expect (cf Mt 5, 4; Lk 6, 24) permits some present experience of reversal in the Corinthians' case, as in Paul's.

1, 8: Asia: a Roman province in western Asia Minor, the capital of which was Ephesus.

1, 9–10: The sentence of death: it is unclear whether Paul is alluding to a physical illness or to an external threat to life. The result of the situation was to produce an attitude of faith in God alone. **God who raises the dead:** rescue is the constant pattern of God's activity; his final act of encouragement is the resurrection.

1, 12—2, 13: The autobiographical remarks about the crisis in Asia Minor lead into consideration of a crisis that has arisen between Paul and the Corinthians. Paul will return to this question, after a long digression, in 7, 5–16. Both of these sections deal with travel plans Paul had made, changes in the plans, alternative measures adopted, a breach that opened between him and the community, and finally a reconciliation between them.

1, 12–14: Since Paul's own conduct will be under discussion here, he prefaces the section with a statement about his habitual behavior and attitude toward the community. He protests his openness, single-mindedness, and conformity to God's grace; he hopes that his relationship with them will be marked by mutual understanding and pride, which will constantly increase until it reaches its climax at the judgment. Two references to boasting frame this paragraph (12.14), the first appearances of a theme that will be important in the letter, especially in chs 10–13; the term is used in a positive sense here (cf the note on 1 Cor 1, 29–31).

1, 15: I formerly intended to come: this plan reads like a revision of the one mentioned in 1 Cor 16, 5. Not until 1, 23—2, 1 will Paul tell us something his original readers already knew, that he has canceled one or the other of these projected visits.

1, 17: Did I act lightly?: the subsequent change of plans casts suspicion on the original intention, creating the impression that Paul is vacillating and inconsistent or that **human considerations** keep dictating shifts in his goals and projects (cf the counterclaim of 12). **"Yes, yes" and "no, no":** stating something and denying it in the same or the next breath; being of two minds at once, or from one moment to the next.

1, 18–22: As God is faithful: unable to deny the change in plans, Paul nonetheless asserts the firmness of the original plan and claims a profound constancy in his life and work. He grounds his defense in God himself, who is firm and reliable; this quality can also be predicated in various ways of those who are associated with him. Christ, Paul, and the Corinthians all participate in analogous ways in the constancy of God. A number of the terms here, which appear related only conceptually in Greek or English, would be variations of the same root, **'mn**, in a Semitic language, and thus naturally associated in a Semitic mind, such as Paul's. These include the words **yes** (17–20), **faithful** (18), **Amen** (20), **gives us security** (21), **faith, stand firm** (24).

d Acts 20, 18–19; 1 Cor 15, 32. e 4, 7–11; Rom 4, 17. f 2 Tm 4, 18. g 4, 15; 9, 12. h Phil 2, 16; 1 Thes 2, 19–20. i 1 Cor 16, 5–9; Acts 19, 21. j Mt 5, 37; Jas 5, 12. k Acts 16, 1–3; 1 Thes 1, 1; 2 Thes 1, 1. l 1 Cor 14, 16; Rv 3, 14.

for glory. [21] [m]*But the one who gives us security with you in Christ and who anointed us is God; [22] [n]he has also put his seal upon us and given the Spirit in our hearts as a first installment.

Paul's Change of Plan [23] [o]*But I call upon God as witness, on my life, that it is to spare you that I have not yet gone to Corinth. [24]Not that we lord it over your faith; rather, we work together for your joy, for you stand firm in the faith.

CHAPTER 2

[1]For I decided not to come to you again in painful circumstances. [2]For if I inflict pain upon you, then who is there to cheer me except the one pained by me? [3]*And I wrote as I did so that when I came I might not be pained by those in whom I should have rejoiced, confident about all of you that my joy is that of all of you. [4]For out of much affliction and anguish of heart I wrote to you with many tears, not that you might be pained but that you might know the abundant love I have for you.

The Offender [5]*If anyone has caused pain, he has caused it not to me, but in some measure (not to exaggerate) to all of you. [6]This punishment by the majority is enough for such a person, [7] [p]so that on the contrary you should forgive and encourage him instead, or else the person may be overwhelmed by excessive pain. [8]Therefore, I urge you to reaffirm your love for him. [9] [q]For this is why I wrote, to know your proven character, whether you were obedient in everything. [10]Whomever you forgive anything, so do I. For indeed what I have forgiven, if I have forgiven anything, has been for you in the presence of Christ, [11] [r]so that we might not be taken advantage of by Satan, for we are not unaware of his purposes.

Paul's Anxiety [12] [s]*When I went to Troas for the gospel of Christ, although a door was opened for me in the Lord, [13] [t]*I had no relief in my spirit because I did not find my brother Titus. So I took leave of them and went on to Macedonia.

B. Paul's Ministry

Ministers of a New Covenant [14]*But thanks be to God, who always leads us in triumph in

1, 21–22: The commercial terms **gives us security, seal, first installment** are here used analogously to refer to the process of initiation into the Christian life, perhaps specifically to baptism. The passage is clearly trinitarian. The Spirit is the **first installment** or "down payment" of the full messianic benefits that God guarantees to Christians. Cf Eph 1, 13–14.

1, 23–24: I have not yet gone to Corinth: some suppose that Paul received word of some affair in Corinth, which he decided to regulate by letter even before the first of his projected visits (cf 16). Others conjecture that he did pay the first visit, was offended there (cf 2, 5), returned to Ephesus, and sent a letter (2, 3–9) in place of the second visit. The expressions **to spare you** (23) and **work together for your joy** (24) introduce the major themes of the next two paragraphs, which are remarkable for insistent repetition of key words and ideas. These form two clusters of terms in the English translation: (1) cheer, rejoice, encourage, joy; (2) pain, affliction, anguish. These clusters reappear when Paul resumes treatment of this subject in 7, 5–16.

2, 3–4: I wrote as I did: we learn for the first time about the sending of a letter in place of the proposed visit. Paul mentions the letter in passing, but emphasizes his motivation in sending it: to avoid being saddened by them (cf 1), and to help them realize the depth of his love. Another motive will be added in 7, 12: to bring to light their own concern for him. **With many tears:** it has been suggested that we may have all or part of this "tearful letter" somewhere in the Corinthian correspondence, either in 1 Cor 5 (the case of the incestuous man), or in 1 Cor as a whole, or in 2 Cor 10—13. None of these hypotheses is entirely convincing. See the note on 13, 1.

2, 5–11: The nature of the **pain** (5) is unclear, though some believe an individual at Corinth rejected Paul's authority, thereby scandalizing many in the community. In any case, action has been taken, and Paul judges the measures adequate to right the situation (6). The follow-up directives he now gives are entirely positive: forgive, encourage, love. **Overwhelmed** (7): a vivid metaphor (literally "swallowed") that Paul employs positively at 5, 4 and in 1 Cor 15, 54 (7). It is often used to describe satanic activity (cf 1 Pt 5, 8); note the reference to Satan here in v 11.

2, 12–13: I had no relief: Paul does not explain the reason for his anxiety until he resumes the thread of his narrative at 7, 5: he was waiting to hear how the Corinthians would respond to his letter. Since 7, 5–16 describes their response in entirely positive terms, we never learn in detail why he found it necessary to defend and justify his change of plans, as in 1, 15–24. Was this portion of the letter written before the arrival of Titus with his good news (7, 6–7)?

2, 13: Macedonia: a Roman province in northern Greece.

2, 14—7, 4: This section constitutes a digression within the narrative of the crisis and its resolution (1, 12—2, 13 and 7, 5–16). The main component (2, 14—6, 10) treats the nature of Paul's ministry and his qualifications for it; this material bears some similarity to the defense of his ministry in chs 10–13, but it may well come from a period close to the crisis. This is followed by a supplementary block of material quite different in character and tone (6, 14—7, 1). These materials may have been brought together into their present position during final editing of the letter; appeals to the Corinthians link them to one another (6, 11–13) and lead back to the interrupted narrative (7, 2–4).

2, 14—6, 10: The question of Paul's adequacy (16; cf 3, 5) and his credentials (3, 1–2) has been raised. Paul responds by an extended treatment of the nature of his ministry. It is a ministry of glory (3, 7—4, 6), of life (4, 7—5, 10), of reconciliation (5, 11—6, 10).

2, 14–16a: The initial statement plunges us abruptly into an-

m 1 Jn 2, 20.27. n Eph 1, 13–14; 4, 30 / 5, 5; Rom 5, 5; 8, 16.23. o 13, 2. p Col 3, 13. q 7, 15. r Eph 4, 27. s Acts 16, 8. t 7, 6; 1 Tm 1, 3.

Christ and manifests through us the odor of the knowledge of him in every place. 15 [u]For we are the aroma of Christ for God among those who are being saved and among those who are perishing, 16 *to the latter an odor of death that leads to death, to the former an odor of life that leads to life. Who is qualified for this? 17 [v]For we are not like the many who trade on the word of God; but as out of sincerity, indeed as from God and in the presence of God, we speak in Christ.

CHAPTER 3

1 [w]*Are we beginning to commend ourselves again? Or do we need, as some do, letters of recommendation to you or from you? 2 *You are our letter, written on our hearts, known and read by all, 3 [x]*shown to be a letter of Christ administered by us, written not in ink but by the Spirit of the living God, not on tablets of stone but on tablets that are hearts of flesh.

4 *Such confidence we have through Christ toward God. 5 [y]Not that of ourselves we are qualified to take credit for anything as coming from us; rather, our qualification comes from God, 6 [z]*who has indeed qualified us as ministers of a new covenant, not of letter but of spirit; for the letter brings death, but the Spirit gives life.

Contrast with the Old Covenant 7 [a]*Now if the ministry of death, carved in letters on stone, was so glorious that the Israelites could not look intently at the face of Moses because of its glory

---

other train of thought. Paul describes his personal existence and his function as a preacher in two powerful images (14) that constitute a prelude to the development to follow.

2, 14a: Leads us in triumph in Christ: this metaphor of a festive parade in honor of a conquering military hero can suggest either a positive sharing in Christ's triumph or an experience of defeat, being led in captivity and submission (cf 4, 8–11; 1 Cor 4, 9). Paul is probably aware of the ambiguity, as he is in the case of the next metaphor.

2, 14b-16a: The odor of the knowledge of him: incense was commonly used in triumphal processions. The metaphor suggests the gradual diffusion of the knowledge of God through the apostolic preaching. **The aroma of Christ:** the image shifts from the fragrance Paul diffuses to the aroma that he is. Paul is probably thinking of the "sweet odor" of the sacrifices in the Old Testament (e.g., Gn 8, 21; Ex 29, 18) and perhaps of the metaphor of wisdom as a sweet odor (Sir 24, 15). **Death . . . life:** the aroma of Christ that comes to them through Paul is perceived differently by various classes of people. To some his preaching and his life (cf 1 Cor 1, 17—2, 6) are perceived as **death,** and the effect is death for them; others perceive him, despite appearances, as **life,** and the effect is life for them. This fragrance thus produces a separation and a judgment (cf the function of the "light" in John's gospel).

2, 16b-17: Qualified: Paul may be echoing either the self-satisfied claims of other preachers or their charges about Paul's deficiencies. No one is really qualified, but the apostle contrasts himself with those who dilute or falsify the preaching for personal advantage and insists on his totally good conscience: his ministry is from God, and he has exercised it with fidelity and integrity (cf 3, 5–6).

3, 1: Paul seems to allude to certain preachers who pride themselves on their written credentials. Presumably they reproach him for not possessing similar credentials and compel him to spell out his own qualifications (4, 2; 5, 12; 6, 4). The Corinthians themselves should have performed this function for Paul (5, 12; cf 12, 11). Since he is forced to find something that can recommend him, he points to them: their very existence constitutes his **letter of recommendation** (1–2). Others who engage in self-commendation will also be mentioned in 10, 12–18.

3, 2–3: Mention of "letters of recommendation" generates a series of metaphors in which Paul plays on the word "letter": (1) the community is Paul's letter of recommendation (2a); (2) they are a letter engraved on his affections for all to see and read (2b); (3) they are a letter from Christ that Paul merely delivers (3a); (4) they are a letter written by the Spirit on the tablets of human hearts (3b). One image dissolves into another.

3, 3b: This verse contrasts Paul's letter with those **written . . . in ink** (like the credentials of other preachers) and those **written . . . on tablets of stone** (like the law of Moses). These contrasts suggest that the other preachers may have claimed special relationship with Moses. If they were Judaizers zealous for the Mosaic law, that would explain the detailed contrast between the old and the new covenants (6; 4, 7—6, 10). If they were charismatics who claimed Moses as their model, that would explain the extended treatment of Moses himself and his glory (3, 7—4, 6). **Hearts of flesh:** cf Ezekiel's contrast between the heart of flesh that the Spirit gives and the heart of stone that it replaces (Ez 36, 26); the context is covenant renewal and purification that makes observance of the law possible.

3, 4–6: These verses resume 2, 1—3, 3. Paul's confidence (4) is grounded in his sense of God-given mission (2, 17), the specifics of which are described in vv 1–3. Verses 5–6 return to the question of his qualifications (2, 16), attributing them entirely to God. Verse 6 further spells out the situation described in v 3b and "names" it: Paul is living within **a new covenant,** characterized by the Spirit, which **gives life.** The usage of a **new covenant** is derived from Jer 31, 31–33, a passage that also speaks of writing on the heart; cf 2.

3, 6b: This verse serves as a topic sentence for 3, 7—6, 10. For the contrast between **letter** and **spirit,** cf Rom 2, 29; 7, 5–6.

3, 7—4, 6: Paul now develops the contrast enunciated in 3, 6b in terms of the relative glory of the two covenants, insisting on the greater glory of the new. His polemic seems directed against individuals who appeal to the glorious Moses and fail to perceive any comparable glory either in Paul's life as an apostle or in the gospel he preaches. He asserts in response that Christians have a glory of their own that far surpasses that of Moses.

3, 7: The ministry of death: from his very first words, Paul describes the Mosaic covenant and ministry from the viewpoint of their limitations. They lead to **death** rather than life (6–7; cf 4, 7—5, 10), to **condemnation** rather than reconciliation (9; cf 5, 11—6, 10). **Was so glorious:** the basic text to which Paul alludes is Ex 34, 29–35, to which his opponents have undoubtedly laid claim. **Going to fade:** Paul concedes the glory of Moses' covenant and ministry, but grants them only temporary significance.

u 4, 3; 1 Cor 1, 18. v 4, 2; 1 Cor 5, 8. w Acts 18, 27; Rom 16, 1; 1 Cor 16, 3. x Ex 24, 12; 31, 18; 32, 15–19 / Jer 31, 33; Ez 11, 19; 36, 26–27. y Jn 3, 27. z Eph 3, 7 / Jer 31, 31–34. a Ex 34, 29–35.

that was going to fade, 8*how much more will
the ministry of the Spirit be glorious? 9For if the
ministry of condemnation was glorious, the
ministry of righteousness will abound much
more in glory. 10Indeed, what was endowed
with glory has come to have no glory in this
respect because of the glory that surpasses it.
11For if what was going to fade was glorious,
how much more will what endures be glorious.

12*Therefore, since we have such hope, we
act very boldly 13*and not like Moses, who put a
veil over his face so that the Israelites could not
look intently at the cessation of what was fading.
14*Rather, their thoughts were rendered dull, for
to this present day the same veil remains unlifted
when they read the old covenant, because
through Christ it is taken away. 15 [b]To this day, in
fact, whenever Moses is read, a veil lies over
their hearts, 16 [c]but whenever a person turns to
the Lord the veil is removed. 17*Now the Lord is
the Spirit, and where the Spirit of the Lord is,
there is freedom. 18 [d]*All of us, gazing with
unveiled face on the glory of the Lord, are being
transformed into the same image from glory to
glory, as from the Lord who is the Spirit.

CHAPTER 4

Integrity in the Ministry 1*Therefore, since
we have this ministry through the mercy shown
us, we are not discouraged. 2 [e]Rather, we have
renounced shameful, hidden things; not acting
deceitfully or falsifying the word of God, but by
the open declaration of the truth we commend
ourselves to everyone's conscience in the sight
of God. 3 [f]*And even though our gospel is
veiled, it is veiled for those who are perishing,
4 [g]in whose case the god of this age has blinded
the minds of the unbelievers, so that they may
not see the light of the gospel of the glory of
Christ, who is the image of God. 5*For we do
not preach ourselves but Jesus Christ as Lord,
and ourselves as your slaves for the sake of Jesus.
6 [h]*For God who said, "Let light shine out of

3, 8–11: How much more: the argument "from the less to the greater" is repeated three times (8.9.11). Verse 10 expresses another point of view: the difference in glory is so great that only the new covenant and ministry can properly be called "glorious" at all.

3, 12: Such hope: the glory is not yet an object of experience, but that does not lessen Paul's confidence. **Boldly:** the term **parrēsia** expresses outspoken declaration of Christian conviction (cf 4, 1–2). Paul has nothing to hide and no reason for timidity.

3, 13–14a: Not like Moses: in Exodus Moses veiled his face to protect the Israelites from God's reflected glory. Without impugning Moses' sincerity, Paul attributes another effect to the veil. Since it lies between God's glory and the Israelites, it explains how they could fail to notice the glory disappearing. **Their thoughts were rendered dull:** the problem lay with their understanding. This will be expressed in vv 14b-16 by a shift in the place of the veil: it is no longer over Moses' face but over their perception.

3, 14b-16: The parallelism in these verses makes it necessary to interpret corresponding parts in relation to one another. **To this present day:** this signals the shift of Paul's attention to his contemporaries; his argument is typological, as in 1 Cor 10. The Israelites of Moses' time typify the Jews of Paul's time, and perhaps also Christians of Jewish origin or mentality who may not recognize the temporary character of Moses' glory. **When they read the old covenant:** the lasting dullness prevents proper appraisal of Moses' person and covenant. When his writings are read in the synagogue, a veil still impedes their understanding. **Through Christ:** i.e., in the new covenant. **Whenever a person turns to the Lord:** Moses in Exodus appeared before God without the veil and gazed on his face unprotected. Paul applies that passage to converts to Christianity: when they turn to the Lord fully and authentically, the impediment to their understanding is removed.

3, 17: The Lord is the Spirit: the "Lord" to whom the Christian turns (16) is the Spirit of whom Paul has been speaking, the life-giving Spirit of the living God (6.8), the inaugurator of the new covenant and ministry, who is also the Spirit of Christ. **The Spirit of the Lord:** the Lord here is the living God (3), but there may also be an allusion to Christ as Lord (14.16). **Freedom:** i.e., from the ministry of death (7) and the covenant that condemned (9).

3, 18: Another application of the veil image. **All of us . . . with unveiled face:** Christians (Israelites from whom the veil has been removed) are like Moses, standing in God's presence, beholding and reflecting his glory. **Gazing:** the verb may also be translated "contemplating as in a mirror"; 4, 6 would suggest that the mirror is Christ himself. **Are being transformed:** elsewhere Paul speaks of transformation, conformity to Jesus, God's image, as a reality of the end time, and even v 12 speaks of the glory as an object of hope. But the life-giving Spirit, the distinctive gift of the new covenant, is already present in the community (cf 1, 22, the "first installment"), and the process of transformation has already begun. **Into the same image:** into the image of God, which is Christ (4, 4).

4, 1–2: A ministry of this sort generates confidence and forthrightness; cf 1, 12–14; 2, 17.

4, 3–4: Though our gospel is veiled: the final application of the image. Paul has been reproached either for obscurity in his preaching or for his manner of presenting the gospel. But he confidently asserts that there is no veil over his gospel. If some fail to perceive its light, that is because of unbelief. The veil lies over their eyes (3, 14), a blindness induced by Satan, and a sign that they are headed for destruction (cf 2, 15).

4, 5: We do not preach ourselves: the light seen in his gospel is the glory of Christ (4). Far from preaching himself, the preacher should be a transparent medium through whom Jesus is perceived (cf 10–11). **Your slaves:** Paul draws attention away from individuals as such and toward their role in relation to God, Christ, and the community; cf 1 Cor 3, 5; 4, 1.

4, 6: Autobiographical allusion to the episode at Damascus

b Rom 11, 7–10. c Ex 34, 34. d Rom 8, 29–30; 12, 2; Gal 4, 19; Phil 3, 10.20–21 / 4, 4–6;1 Cor 15, 49; Col 1, 15; 3, 9–11; 1 Jn 3, 2. e 2, 17; 1 Thes 2, 4–7. f 2, 15–16; 2 Thes 2, 10. g Jn 12, 31–36 / 1 Tm 1, 11. h Gn 1, 3; Is 9, 1; Acts 26, 13–23; Gal 1, 15–16 / Jn 8, 12; Heb 1, 3.

darkness," has shone in our hearts to bring to
light the knowledge of the glory of God on the
face of [Jesus] Christ.
The Paradox of the Ministry 7*But we hold
this treasure in earthen vessels, that the surpass-
ing power may be of God and not from us.
8 i*We are afflicted in every way, but not con-
strained; perplexed, but not driven to despair;
9persecuted, but not abandoned; struck down,
but not destroyed; 10 j*always carrying about in
the body the dying of Jesus, so that the life of
Jesus may also be manifested in our body. 11 kFor
we who live are constantly being given up to
death for the sake of Jesus, so that the life of
Jesus may be manifested in our mortal flesh.
12*So death is at work in us, but life in you.
13 l*Since, then, we have the same spirit of faith,
according to what is written, "I believed, there-
fore I spoke," we too believe and therefore
speak, 14 mknowing that the one who raised the
Lord Jesus will raise us also with Jesus and place
us with you in his presence. 15 nEverything
indeed is for you, so that the grace bestowed in
abundance on more and more people may cause
the thanksgiving to overflow for the glory of
God.
16 o*Therefore, we are not discouraged;
rather, although our outer self is wasting away,
our inner self is being renewed day by day.
17 pFor this momentary light affliction is produc-
ing for us an eternal weight of glory beyond all
comparison, 18 qas we look not to what is seen
but to what is unseen; for what is seen is
transitory, but what is unseen is eternal.

CHAPTER 5

Our Future Destiny 1 r*For we know that if
our earthly dwelling, a tent, should be de-
stroyed, we have a building from God, a dwell-
ing not made with hands, eternal in heaven.
2 s*For in this tent we groan, longing to be

clarifies the origin and nature of Paul's service; cf Acts 9, 1–19; 22, 3–16; 26, 2–18. **"Let light shine out of darkness":** Paul seems to be thinking of Gn 1, 3 and presenting his apostolic ministry as a new creation. There may also be an allusion to Is 9, 1, suggesting his prophetic calling as servant of the Lord and light to the nations; cf Is 42, 6.16; 49, 6; 60, 1–2, and the use of light imagery in Acts 26, 13–23. **To bring to light the knowledge:** Paul's role in the process of revelation, expressed at the beginning under the image of the odor and aroma (2, 14–15), is restated now, at the end of this first moment of the development, in the imagery of light and glory (3–6).

4, 7—5, 10: Paul now confronts the difficulty that his present existence does not appear glorious at all; it is marked instead by suffering and death. He deals with this by developing the topic already announced in 3, 3.6, asserting his faith in the presence and ultimate triumph of life, in his own and every Christian existence, despite the experience of death.

4, 7: This treasure: the glory that he preaches and into which they are being transformed. **In earthen vessels:** the instruments God uses are human and fragile; some imagine small terracotta lamps in which light is carried.

4, 8–9: A catalogue of his apostolic trials and afflictions. Yet in these the negative never completely prevails; there is always some experience of rescue, of salvation.

4, 10–11: Both the negative and the positive sides of the experience are grounded christologically. The logic is similar to that of 1, 3–11. His sufferings are connected with Christ's, and his deliverance is a sign that he is to share in Jesus' resurrection.

4, 12–15: His experience does not terminate in himself, but in others (12.15; cf 1, 4–5). Ultimately, everything is ordered even beyond the community, toward God (15; cf 1, 11).

4, 13–14: Like the Psalmist, Paul clearly proclaims his faith, affirming life within himself despite death (10–11) and the life-giving effect of his experience upon the church (12.14–15). **And place us with you in his presence:** Paul imagines God presenting him and them to Jesus at the parousia and the judgment; cf 11, 2; Rom 14, 10.

4, 16–18: In a series of contrasts Paul explains the extent of his faith in life. Life is not only already present and revealing itself (8–11.16) but will outlast his experience of affliction and dying: it is eternal (17–18).

4, 16: Not discouraged: i.e., despite the experience of death. Paul is still speaking of himself personally, but he assumes his faith and attitude will be shared by all Christians. **Our outer self:** the individual subject of ordinary perception and observation, in contrast to the interior and hidden self, which undergoes renewal. **Is being renewed day by day:** this suggests a process that has already begun; cf 3, 18. The renewal already taking place even in Paul's dying is a share in the life of Jesus, but this is recognized only by faith (13.18; 5, 7).

5, 1: Our earthly dwelling: the same contrast is restated in the imagery of a dwelling. The language recalls Jesus' saying about the destruction of the temple and the construction of another building **not made with hands** (Mk 14, 58), a prediction later applied to Jesus' own body (Jn 2, 20).

5, 2–5: Verses 2–3 and 4 are largely parallel in structure. **We groan, longing:** see the note on 5, 5. **Clothed with our heavenly habitation:** Paul mixes his metaphors, adding the image of the garment to that of the building. **Further clothed:** the verb means strictly "to put one garment on over another." Paul may desire to put the resurrection body on over his mortal body, without dying; vv 2 and 4 permit this meaning but do not impose it. Or perhaps he imagines the resurrection body as a garment put on over the Christ-garment first received in baptism (Gal 3, 27) and preserved by moral behavior (Rom 13, 12–14; Col 3, 12; cf Mt 22, 11–13). Some support for this interpretation may be found in the context; cf the references to baptism (5), to judgment according to works (10), and to present renewal (4, 16), an idea elsewhere combined with the image of "putting on" a new nature (Eph 4, 22–24; Col 3, 1–5.9–10).

i 6, 4–10; 1 Cor 4, 9–13. j Col 1, 24. k Rom 8, 36; 1 Cor 15, 31. l Ps 116, 10. m Rom 4, 24–25; 8, 11; 1 Cor 6, 14; 1 Thes 4, 14. n 1, 11. o 4, 1.1. p Mt 5, 11–12; Rom 8, 18. q Rom 8, 24–25; Heb 11, 1. r Is 38, 12 / Col 3, 1–4 / Mk 14, 58; Col 2, 11; Heb 9, 11.24. s Rom 8, 23 / 1 Cor 15, 51–54.

further clothed with our heavenly habitation [3]*if
indeed, when we have taken it off, we shall not
be found naked. [4][t]*For while we are in this tent
we groan and are weighed down, because we do
not wish to be unclothed but to be further
clothed, so that what is mortal may be swal-
lowed up by life. [5][u]*Now the one who has
prepared us for this very thing is God, who has
given us the Spirit as a first installment.

[6]*So we are always courageous, although we
know that while we are at home in the body we
are away from the Lord, [7]for we walk by faith,
not by sight. [8][v]Yet we are courageous, and we
would rather leave the body and go home to the
Lord. [9]Therefore, we aspire to please him,
whether we are at home or away. [10][w]*For we
must all appear before the judgment seat of
Christ, so that each one may receive recom-
pense, according to what he did in the body,
whether good or evil.

The Ministry of Reconciliation [11][x]*There-
fore, since we know the fear of the Lord, we try
to persuade others; but we are clearly apparent
to God, and I hope we are also apparent to your
consciousness. [12][y]We are not commending our-
selves to you again but giving you an opportunity
to boast of us, so that you may have something
to say to those who boast of external appearance
rather than of the heart. [13]*For if we are out of
our minds, it is for God; if we are rational, it is
for you. [14][z]*For the love of Christ impels us,
once we have come to the conviction that one
died for all; therefore, all have died. [15][a]He
indeed died for all, so that those who live might
no longer live for themselves but for him who for
their sake died and was raised.

[16]*Consequently, from now on we regard no
one according to the flesh; even if we once
knew Christ according to the flesh, yet now we
know him so no longer. [17][b]So whoever is in
Christ is a new creation: the old things have
passed away; behold, new things have come.
[18]*And all this is from God, who has reconciled
us to himself through Christ and given us the

5, 3: When we have taken it off: the majority of witnesses read "when we have put it on," i.e., when we have been clothed (in the resurrection body), then we shall not be without a body (naked). This seems mere tautology, though some understand it to mean: whether we are "found" (by God at the judgment) clothed or naked depends upon whether we have preserved or lost our original investiture in Christ (cf the previous note). In this case to "put it on" does not refer to the resurrection body, but to keeping intact the Christ-garment of baptism. The translation follows the western reading (Codex Bezae, Tertullian), the sense of which is clear: to "take it off" is to shed our mortal body in death, after which we shall be clothed in the resurrection body and hence not "naked" (cf 1 Cor 15, 51–53).

5, 4: We do not wish to be unclothed: a clear allusion to physical death (4, 16; 5, 1). Unlike the Greeks, who found dissolution of the body desirable (cf Socrates), Paul has a Jewish horror of it. He seems to be thinking of the "intermediate period," an interval between death and resurrection. **Swallowed up by life:** cf 1 Cor 15, 54.

5, 5: God has created us for resurrected bodily life and already prepares us for it by the gift of the Spirit in baptism. **The Spirit as a first installment:** the striking parallel to 5, 1–5 in Rom 8, 17–30 describes Christians who have received the "firstfruits" (cf "first installment" here) of the Spirit as "groaning" (cf 2.4 here) for the resurrection, the complete redemption of their bodies. In place of clothing and building, Rom 8 uses other images for the resurrection: adoption and conformity to the image of the Son.

5, 6–9: Tension between present and future is expressed by another spatial image, the metaphor of the country and its citizens. At present we are like citizens in exile or far away from home. The Lord is the distant homeland, believed in but unseen (7).

5, 10: We must all appear: the verb is ambiguous: we are scheduled to "appear" for judgment, at which we will be "revealed" as we are (cf 11; 2, 14; 4, 10–11).

5, 11–15: This paragraph is transitional. Paul sums up much that has gone before. Still playing on the term "appearance," he reasserts his transparency before God and the Corinthians, in contrast to the self-commendation, boasting, and preoccupation with externals that characterize some others (cf 1, 12–14; 2, 14; 3, 1; 3, 7—4, 6). Verse 14 recalls 3, 7—4, 6, and sums up 4, 7—5, 10.

5, 13: Out of our minds: this verse confirms that a concern for ecstasy and charismatic experience may lie behind the discussion about "glory" in 3, 7—4, 6. Paul also enjoys such experiences but, unlike others, does not make a public display of them or consider them ends in themselves. **Rational:** the Greek virtue **sōphrosynē,** to which Paul alludes, implies reasonableness, moderation, good judgment, self-control.

5, 14–15: These verses echo 4, 14 and resume the treatment of "life despite death" from 4, 7—5, 10.

5, 16–17: Consequently: the death of Christ described in vv 14–15 produces a whole new order (17) and a new mode of perception (16). **According to the flesh:** the natural mode of perception, characterized as "fleshly," is replaced by a mode of perception proper to the Spirit. Elsewhere Paul contrasts what Christ looks like according to the old criteria (weakness, powerlessness, folly, death) and according to the new (wisdom, power, life); cf vv 15.21; 1 Cor 1, 17—3, 3. Similarly, he describes the paradoxical nature of Christian existence, e.g., in 4, 10–11.14. **A new creation:** rabbis used this expression to describe the effect of the entrance of a proselyte or convert into Judaism or of the remission of sins on the Day of Atonement. The new order created **in Christ** is the new covenant (3, 6).

5, 18–21: Paul attempts to explain the meaning of God's action by a variety of different categories; his attention keeps moving rapidly back and forth from God's act to his own ministry as well. **Who has reconciled us to himself:** i.e., he has brought all into oneness. **Not counting their trespasses:** the reconciliation is described as an act of justification (cf "righteousness," 21); this

t Is 25, 8; 1 Cor 15, 54. u 1, 22. v Phil 1, 21–23. w Mt 16, 27; 25, 31–46; Rom 2, 16; 14, 10–11. x 1, 12–14. y 3, 1 / 1, 14; Phil 1, 26. z Rom 6, 1–6. a Rom 4, 25; 6, 4–11; 14, 9; Col 3, 3–4. b Gal 6, 15; Eph 2, 15 / Is 43, 18–21; Rv 21, 5.

ministry of reconciliation, [19] [c]namely, God was reconciling the world to himself in Christ, not counting their trespasses against them and entrusting to us the message of reconciliation. [20] [d]So we are ambassadors for Christ, as if God were appealing through us. We implore you on behalf of Christ, be reconciled to God. [21] [e]*For our sake he made him to be sin who did not know sin, so that we might become the righteousness of God in him.

CHAPTER 6

The Experience of the Ministry [1] [f]*Working together, then, we appeal to you not to receive the grace of God in vain. [2] [g]*For he says:

"In an acceptable time I heard you,
 and on the day of salvation I helped you."

Behold, now is a very acceptable time; behold, now is the day of salvation. [3] [h]*We cause no one to stumble in anything, in order that no fault may be found with our ministry; [4] [i]*on the contrary, in everything we commend ourselves as ministers of God, through much endurance, in afflictions, hardships, constraints, [5] [j]beatings, imprisonments, riots, labors, vigils, fasts; [6] [k]*by purity, knowledge, patience, kindness, in a holy spirit, in unfeigned love, [7] [l]in truthful speech, in the power of God; with weapons of righteousness at the right and at the left; [8] *through glory and dishonor, insult and praise. We are treated as deceivers and yet are truthful; [9] [m]as unrecognized and yet acknowledged; as dying and behold we live; as chastised and yet not put to death; [10] [n]as sorrowful yet always rejoicing; as poor yet enriching many; as having nothing and yet possessing all things.

[11] *We have spoken frankly to you, Corinthians; our heart is open wide. [12] [o]You are not constrained by us; you are constrained by your own affections. [13] [p]As recompense in kind (I speak as to my children), be open yourselves.

Call to Holiness [14] *Do not be yoked with those who are different, with unbelievers. For

contrasts with the covenant that condemned (3, 8). **The ministry of reconciliation:** Paul's role in the wider picture is described: entrusted with the message of reconciliation (19), he is Christ's ambassador, through whom God appeals (20a). In v 20b Paul acts in the capacity just described.

5, 21: This is a statement of God's purpose, expressed paradoxically in terms of sharing and exchange of attributes. As Christ became our righteousness (1 Cor 1, 30), we become God's righteousness (cf vv 14–15).

6, 1–10: This paragraph is a single long sentence in the Greek, interrupted by the parenthesis of v 2. The one main verb is "we appeal." In this paragraph Paul both exercises his ministry of reconciliation (cf 5, 20) and describes how his ministry is exercised: the "message of reconciliation" (5, 19) is lived existentially in his apostolic experience.

6, 1: Not to receive . . . in vain: i.e., conform to the gift of justification and new creation. The context indicates how this can be done concretely: become God's righteousness (5, 21), not live for oneself (5, 15), be reconciled with Paul (6, 11–13; 7, 2–3).

6, 2: In an acceptable time: Paul cites the Septuagint text of Is 49, 8; the Hebrew reads "in a time of favor"; it is parallel to "on the day of salvation." **Now:** God is bestowing favor and salvation at this very moment, as Paul is addressing his letter to them.

6, 3: Cause no one to stumble: the language echoes that of 1 Cor 8—10, as does the expression "no longer live for themselves" in 5, 15. **That no fault may be found:** i.e., at the eschatological judgment (cf 1 Cor 4, 2–5).

6, 4a: This is the central assertion, the topic statement for the catalogue that follows. **We commend ourselves:** Paul's self-commendation is ironical (with an eye on the charges mentioned in 3, 1–3) and paradoxical (pointing mostly to experiences that would not normally be considered points of pride but are perceived as such by faith). Cf also the self-commendation in 11, 23–29. **As ministers of God:** the same Greek word, **diakonos,** means "minister" and "servant"; cf 11, 23, the central assertion in a similar context, and 1 Cor 3, 5.

6, 4b-5: Through much endurance: this phrase functions as a subtitle; it is followed by an enumeration of nine specific types of trials endured.

6, 6–7a: A list of virtuous qualities in two groups of four, the second fuller than the first.

6, 8b-10: A series of seven rhetorically effective antitheses, contrasting negative external impressions with positive inner reality. Paul perceives his existence as a reflection of Jesus' own and affirms an inner reversal that escapes outward observation. The final two members illustrate two distinct kinds of paradox or apparent contradiction that are characteristic of apostolic experience.

6, 11–13: Paul's tone becomes quieter, but his appeal for acceptance and affection is emotionally charged. References to the heart and their mutual relations bring the development begun in 2, 14—3, 3 to an effective conclusion.

6, 14—7, 1: Language and thought shift noticeably here. Suddenly we are in a different atmosphere, dealing with a quite different problem. Both the vocabulary and the thought, with their contrast between good and evil, are more characteristic of Qumran documents or the Book of Revelation than they are of Paul. Hence, critics suspect that this section was inserted by another hand.

6, 14–16a: The opening injunction to separate from unbelievers is reinforced by five rhetorical questions to make the point that Christianity is not compatible with paganism. Their opposition is emphasized also by the accumulation of five distinct designations for each group. These verses are a powerful statement of God's holiness and the exclusiveness of his claims.

c Rom 5, 10–11; Col 1, 20. d Eph 6, 20; Phlm 9. e Is 53, 6–9; Gal 3, 13 / Rom 3, 24–26; 1 Cor 1, 30; 1 Pt 2, 24;1 Jn 3, 5–8. f 1 Cor 3, 9; 1 Thes 3, 2. g Is 49, 8. h 1 Cor 9, 12; 10, 32 / 8, 20–21. i 4, 8–11; 11, 23–27; 1 Cor 4, 9–13. j Acts 16, 23. k Gal 5, 22–23. l 10, 4; Rom 13, 12; Eph 6, 11–17. m 4, 10–11; Rom 8, 36. n Rom 8, 32; 1 Cor 3, 21. o 7, 3. p Gal 4, 19.

what partnership do righteousness and lawless-
ness have? Or what fellowship does light have
with darkness? 15 What accord has Christ with
Beliar? Or what has a believer in common with
an unbeliever? 16 q*What agreement has the
temple of God with idols? For we are the temple
of the living God; as God said:

"I will live with them and move among them,
and I will be their God
and they shall be my people.
17 rTherefore, come forth from them
and be separate," says the Lord,
"and touch nothing unclean;
then I will receive you
18 sand I will be a father to you,
and you shall be sons and daughters to me,
says the Lord Almighty."

CHAPTER 7

1 Since we have these promises, beloved, let us
cleanse ourselves from every defilement of flesh
and spirit, making holiness perfect in the fear of
God.

2*Make room for us; we have not wronged
anyone, or ruined anyone, or taken advantage of
anyone. 3 tI do not say this in condemnation, for
I have already said that you are in our hearts,
that we may die together and live together. 4I
have great confidence in you, I have great pride
in you; I am filled with encouragement, I am
overflowing with joy all the more because of all
our affliction.

C. Resolution of the Crisis

Paul's Joy in Macedonia 5 u*For even when
we came into Macedonia, our flesh had no rest,
but we were afflicted in every way—external
conflicts, internal fears. 6 vBut God, who encour-
ages the downcast, encouraged us by the arrival
of Titus, 7and not only by his arrival but also by
the encouragement with which he was encour-
aged in regard to you, as he told us of your
yearning, your lament, your zeal for me, so that I
rejoiced even more. 8 w*For even if I saddened
you by my letter, I do not regret it; and if I did
regret it ([for] I see that that letter saddened you,
if only for a while), 9I rejoice now, not because
you were saddened, but because you were
saddened into repentance; for you were sad-
dened in a godly way, so that you did not suffer
loss in anything because of us. 10For godly
sorrow produces a salutary repentance without
regret, but worldly sorrow produces death. 11For
behold what earnestness this godly sorrow has
produced for you, as well as readiness for a
defense, and indignation, and fear, and yearning,
and zeal, and punishment. In every way you
have shown yourselves to be innocent in the
matter. 12 xSo then even though I wrote to you, it
was not on account of the one who did the
wrong, or on account of the one who suffered

6, 16c-18: This is a chain of scriptural citations carefully woven together. God's covenant relation to his people and his presence among them (16) is seen as conditioned on cultic separation from the profane and cultically impure (17); that relation is translated into the personal language of the parent-child relationship, an extension to the community of the language of 2 Sm 7, 14 (18). Some remarkable parallels to this chain are found in the final chapters of Revelation. God's presence among his people (21, 22) is expressed there, too, by applying 2 Sm 7, 14 to the community (21, 7). There is a call to separation (18, 4) and exclusion of the unclean from the community and its liturgy (21, 27). The title "Lord Almighty" (**Pantokratōr**) occurs in the New Testament only here in 18 and nine times in Rv.

7, 2-4: These verses continue the thought of 6, 11–13, before the interruption of 6, 14—7, 1. Verse 4 serves as a transition to the next section: the four themes it introduces (confidence; pride or "boasting"; encouragement; joy in affliction) are developed in vv 5–16. All have appeared previously in the letter.

7, 5-16: This section functions as a peroration or formal summing up of the whole first part of the letter, chs 1–7. It deals with the restoration of right relations between Paul and the Corinthians, and it is marked by fullness and intensity of emotion.

7, 5-7: Paul picks up the thread of the narrative interrupted at 2, 13 (5) and describes the resolution of the tense situation there depicted (6–7). Finally Titus arrives and his coming puts an end to Paul's restlessness (2, 13; 7, 5), casts out his fears, and reverses his mood. The theme of encouragement and affliction is reintroduced (cf 1, 3–11); here, too, encouragement is traced back to God and is described as contagious (6). The language of joy and sorrow also reappears in v 7 (cf 1, 23—2, 1 and the note on 1, 23–24).

7, 5: Macedonia: see the note on 2, 13.

7, 8-12: Paul looks back on the episode from the viewpoint of its ending. The goal of their common activity, promotion of their joy (1, 24), has been achieved, despite and because of the sorrow they felt. That sorrow was God-given. Its salutary effects are enumerated fully and impressively in vv 10–11; not the least important of these is that it has revealed to them the attachment they have to Paul.

q 1 Cor 10, 20–21 / 1 Cor 3, 16–17; 6, 19 / Ex 25, 8; 29, 45; Lv 26, 12; Jer 31, 1; 32, 38; Ez 37, 27. r Is 52, 11; Ez 20, 34.41; Rv 18, 4; 21, 27. s 2 Sm 7, 14; Ps 2, 7; Is 43, 6; Jer 31, 9; Rv 21, 7 / Rv 4, 8;11, 17; 15, 3; 21, 22. t 6,11–13. u 2, 13. v 7, 13–14; 1 Thes 3, 6–8. w 2, 2–4; Heb 12, 11. x 2, 3.9; 7, 8.

the wrong, but in order that your concern for us
might be made plain to you in the sight of God.
13 *For this reason we are encouraged.

And besides our encouragement, we rejoice
even more because of the joy of Titus, since his
spirit has been refreshed by all of you. 14 For if I
have boasted to him about you, I was not put to
shame. No, just as everything we said to you was
true, so our boasting before Titus proved to be
the truth. 15 [y]And his heart goes out to you all
the more, as he remembers the obedience of all
of you, when you received him with fear and
trembling. 16 I rejoice, because I have confidence
in you in every respect.

III: The Collection for Jerusalem

CHAPTER 8

Generosity in Giving 1 [z]*We want you to
know, brothers, of the grace of God that has
been given to the churches of Macedonia, 2 *for
in a severe test of affliction, the abundance of
their joy and their profound poverty overflowed
in a wealth of generosity on their part. 3 *For
according to their means, I can testify, and
beyond their means, spontaneously, 4 [a]they
begged us insistently for the favor of taking part
in the service to the holy ones, 5 *and this, not as
we expected, but they gave themselves first to
the Lord and to us through the will of God,
6 [b]*so that we urged Titus that, as he had already
begun, he should also complete for you this
gracious act also. 7 [c]*Now as you excel in every
respect, in faith, discourse, knowledge, all ear-
nestness, and in the love we have for you, may
you excel in this gracious act also.

8 I say this not by way of command, but to test
the genuineness of your love by your concern for
others. 9 [d]*For you know the gracious act of our

7, 13–16: Paul summarizes the effect of the experience on Titus: encouragement, joy, love, relief. Finally, he describes its effects on himself: encouragement, joy, confidence, pride or "boasting" (i.e., the satisfaction resulting from a boast that proves well-founded; cf 4; 1, 12.14).

8, 1—9, 15: Paul turns to a new topic, the collection for the church in Jerusalem. There is an early precedent for this project in the agreement mentioned in Gal 2, 6–10. According to Acts, the church at Antioch had sent Saul and Barnabas to Jerusalem with relief (Acts 11, 27–30). Subsequently Paul organized a project of relief for Jerusalem among his own churches. Our earliest evidence for it comes in 1 Cor 16, 1–4, after it had already begun (see the notes there); by the time Paul wrote Rom 15, 25–28 the collection was completed and ready for delivery. Chapters 8 and 9 contain what appear to be two letters on the subject. In them Paul gives us his fullest exposition of the meaning he sees in the enterprise, presenting it as an act of Christian charity and as an expression of the unity of the church, both present and eschatological. These chapters are especially rich in the recurrence of key words, on which Paul plays; it is usually impossible to do justice to these wordplays in the translation.

8, 1–24: This is a letter of recommendation for Titus and two unnamed companions, written from Macedonia probably at least a year later than 1 Cor 16. The recommendation proper is prefaced by remarks about the ideals of sharing and equality within the Christian community (1–15). Phil 4, 10–20 shows that Paul has reflected on his personal experience of need and relief in his relations with the community at Philippi; he now develops his reflections on the larger scale of relations between his Gentile churches and the mother church in Jerusalem.

8, 1–5: The example of the Macedonians, a model of what ought to be happening at Corinth, provides Paul with the occasion for expounding his theology of "giving."

8, 1: The grace of God: the fundamental theme is expressed by the Greek noun **charis,** which will be variously translated throughout these chapters as "grace" (8, 1; 9, 8.14), "favor" (8, 4), "gracious act" (8, 6.7.9) or "gracious work" (8, 19), to be compared to "gracious gift" (1 Cor 16, 3). The related term, **eucharistia,** "thanksgiving," also occurs at 9, 11.12. The wordplay is not superficial; various mutations of the same root signal inner connection between aspects of a single reality, and Paul consciously exploits the similarities in vocabulary to highlight that connection.

8, 2: Three more terms are now introduced. **Test (dokimē):** the same root is translated as "to test" (8) and "evidence" (9, 13); it means to be tried and found genuine. **Abundance:** variations on the same root lie behind "overflow" (8, 2; 9, 12), "excel" (8, 7), "surplus" (8, 14), "superfluous" (9, 1), "make abundant" and "have an abundance" (9, 8). These expressions of fullness contrast with references to need (8, 14; 9, 12). **Generosity:** the word **haplotēs** has nuances of both simplicity and sincerity; here and in 9, 11.13 it designates the singleness of purpose that manifests itself in generous giving.

8, 3–4: Paul emphasizes the spontaneity of the Macedonians and the nature of their action. **They begged us insistently:** the same root is translated as "urge," "appeal," "encourage" (8, 6.17; 9, 5). **Taking part:** the same word is translated "contribution" in 9, 13 and a related term as "partner" in 8, 23. **Service (diakonia):** this word occurs also in 9, 1.13 as "service"; in 9, 12 it is translated "administration," and in 8, 19.20 the corresponding verb is rendered "administer."

8, 5: They gave themselves . . . to the Lord and to us: on its deepest level their attitude is one of self-giving.

8, 6: Titus: 1 Cor 16 seemed to leave the organization up to the Corinthians, but apparently Paul has sent Titus to initiate the collection as well; 8, 16–17 will describe Titus' attitude as one of shared concern and cooperation.

8, 7: The charitable service Paul is promoting is seen briefly and in passing within the perspective of Paul's theology of the charisms. **Earnestness (spoudē):** this or related terms occur also in v 22 ("earnest") and 8, 8.16.17 ("concern").

8, 9: The dialectic of Jesus' experience, expressed earlier in terms of life and death (5, 15), sin and righteousness (5, 21), is now rephrased in terms of poverty and wealth. Many scholars think this is a reference to Jesus' preexistence with God (his "wealth") and to his incarnation and death (his "poverty"), and they point to the similarity between this verse and Phil 2, 6–8. Others interpret the wealth and poverty as succeeding phases of

y 2, 9. z 11, 9; Rom 15, 26. a Acts 24, 17; Rom 15, 31. b 2, 13; 7, 6–7.13–14; 8, 16.23; 12, 18. c 1 Cor 1, 5. d 6, 10; Phil 2, 6–8.

Lord Jesus Christ, that for your sake he became poor although he was rich, so that by his poverty you might become rich. [10][e]And I am giving counsel in this matter, for it is appropriate for you who began not only to act but to act willingly last year: [11]*complete it now, so that your eager willingness may be matched by your completion of it out of what you have. [12]*For if the eagerness is there, it is acceptable according to what one has, not according to what one does not have; [13]not that others should have relief while you are burdened, but that as a matter of equality [14]your surplus at the present time should supply their needs, so that their surplus may also supply your needs, that there may be equality. [15][f]As it is written:

"Whoever had much did not have more,
and whoever had little did not have less."

Titus and His Collaborators [16]*But thanks be to God who put the same concern for you into the heart of Titus, [17]for he not only welcomed our appeal but, since he is very concerned, he has gone to you of his own accord. [18][g]*With him we have sent the brother who is praised in all the churches for his preaching of the gospel. [19][h]And not only that, but he has also been appointed our traveling companion by the churches in this gracious work administered by us for the glory of the Lord [himself] and for the expression of our eagerness. [20]*This we desire to avoid, that anyone blame us about this lavish gift administered by us, [21][i]for we are concerned for what is honorable not only in the sight of the Lord but also in the sight of others. [22]And with them we have sent our brother whom we often tested in many ways and found earnest, but who is now much more earnest because of his great confidence in you. [23]As for Titus, he is my partner and co-worker for you; as for our brothers, they are apostles of the churches, the glory of Christ. [24]*So give proof before the churches of your love and of our boasting about you to them.

CHAPTER 9

God's Indescribable Gift [1]*Now about the service to the holy ones, it is superfluous for me to write to you, [2][j]*for I know your eagerness, about which I boast of you to the Macedonians, that Achaia has been ready since last year; and your zeal has stirred up most of them. [3]*Nonetheless, I sent the brothers so that our boast about you might not prove empty in this case, so that you might be ready, as I said, [4]for fear that if any Macedonians come with me and find you not ready we might be put to shame (to say nothing of you) in this conviction. [5]So I thought it necessary to encourage the brothers to go on ahead to you and arrange in advance for your promised gift, so that in this way it might be ready as a bountiful gift and not as an exaction.

Jesus' earthly existence, e.g., his sense of intimacy with God and then the desolation and the feeling of abandonment by God in his death (cf Mk 15, 34).

8, 11: Eager: the word **prothymia** also occurs in 8, 12.19; 9, 2.

8, 12–15: Paul introduces the principle of **equality** into the discussion. The goal is not impoverishment but sharing of resources; balance is achieved at least over the course of time. In v 15 Paul grounds his argument unexpectedly in the experience of Israel gathering manna in the desert: equality was achieved, independently of personal exertion, by God, who gave with an even hand according to need. Paul touches briefly here on the theme of "living from God."

8, 16–24: In recommending Titus and his companions, Paul stresses their personal and apostolic qualities, their good dispositions toward the Corinthians, and their authority as messengers of the churches and representatives of Christ.

8, 18: The brother: we do not know the identity of this co-worker of Paul, nor of the third companion mentioned below in v 22.

8, 20–22: That anyone blame us: 12, 16–18 suggests that misunderstandings may indeed have arisen concerning Paul's management of the collection through the messengers mentioned here, but those same verses seem to imply that the Corinthians by and large would recognize the honesty of Paul's conduct in this area as in others (cf 6, 3).

8, 24: As Paul began by holding up the Macedonians as examples to be imitated, he closes by exhorting the Corinthians to show their love (by accepting the envoys and by cooperating as the Macedonians do), thus justifying the pride Paul demonstrates because of them before other churches.

9, 1–15: Quite possibly this was originally an independent letter, though it deals with the same subject and continues many of the same themes. In that case, it may have been written a few weeks later than ch 8, while the delegation there mentioned was still on its way.

9, 2: Achaia: see the note on Rom 15, 26.

9, 3: I sent the brothers: the Greek aorist tense here could be epistolary, referring to the present; in that case Paul would be sending them now, and ch 9 would merely conclude the letter of recommendation begun in ch 8. But the aorist may also refer to a sending that is past as Paul writes; then ch 9, with its apparently fresh beginning, is a follow-up message entrusted to another carrier.

e 9, 2; 1 Cor 16, 1–4. f Ex 16, 18. g 12, 18. h 1 Cor 16, 3–4. i Rom 12, 17. j 8, 10; Rom 15, 26.

[6] [k]Consider this: whoever sows sparingly will
also reap sparingly, and whoever sows bounti-
fully will also reap bountifully. [7] [l]Each must do as
already determined, without sadness or compul-
sion, for God loves a cheerful giver. [8] *Moreover,
God is able to make every grace abundant for
you, so that in all things, always having all you
need, you may have an abundance for every
good work. [9] [m]As it is written:

> "He scatters abroad, he gives to the poor;
> his righteousness endures forever."

[10] [n]The one who supplies seed to the sower and
bread for food will supply and multiply your seed
and increase the harvest of your righteousness.

[11] *You are being enriched in every way for all
generosity, which through us produces thanksgiv-
ing to God, [12] for the administration of this public
service is not only supplying the needs of the
holy ones but is also overflowing in many acts of
thanksgiving to God. [13] [o]Through the evidence
of this service, you are glorifying God for your
obedient confession of the gospel of Christ and
the generosity of your contribution to them and
to all others, [14] while in prayer on your behalf
they long for you, because of the surpassing
grace of God upon you. [15] [p]Thanks be to God for
his indescribable gift!

IV: Paul's Defense of His Ministry

CHAPTER 10

Accusation of Weakness [1] *Now I myself,
Paul, urge you through the gentleness and
clemency of Christ, I who am humble when face
to face with you, but brave toward you when
absent, [2] [q]*I beg you that, when present, I may
not have to be brave with that confidence with
which I intend to act boldly against some who
consider us as acting according to the flesh.
[3] *For, although we are in the flesh, we do not
battle according to the flesh, [4] [r]for the weapons
of our battle are not of flesh but are enormously
powerful, capable of destroying fortresses. We
destroy arguments [5] and every pretension raising
itself against the knowledge of God, and take
every thought captive in obedience to Christ,

9, 8–10: The behavior to which he exhorts them is grounded in God's own pattern of behavior. God is capable of overwhelming generosity, as scripture itself attests (9), so that they need not fear being short. He will provide in abundance, both supplying their natural needs and increasing their righteousness. Paul challenges them to godlike generosity and reminds them of the fundamental motive for encouragement: God himself cannot be outdone.

9, 11–15: Paul's vision broadens to take in all the interested parties in one dynamic picture. His language becomes liturgically colored and conveys a sense of fullness. With a final play on the words **charis** and **eucharistia** (see the note on 8, 1), he describes a circle that closes on itself: the movement of grace overflowing from God to them and handed on from them through Paul to others is completed by the prayer of praise and thanksgiving raised on their behalf to God.

10, 1—13, 10: These final chapters have their own unity of structure and theme and could well have formed the body of a separate letter. They constitute an **apologia** on Paul's part, i.e., a legal defense of his behavior and his ministry; the writing is emotionally charged and highly rhetorical. In the central section (11, 16—12, 10), the **apologia** takes the form of a boast. This section is prepared for by a prologue (11, 1–15) and followed by an epilogue (12, 11–18), which are similar in content and structure. These sections, in turn, are framed by an introduction (10, 1–18) and a conclusion (12, 19—13, 10), both of which assert Paul's apostolic authority and confidence and define the purpose of the letter. The structure that results from this disposition of the material is chiastic, i.e., the first element corresponds to the last, the second to the second last, etc., following the pattern **abcb'a'**.

10, 1–18: Paul asserts his apostolic authority and expresses the confidence this generates in him. He writes in response to certain opinions that have arisen in the community and certain charges raised against him and in preparation for a forthcoming visit in which he intends to set things in order. This section gives us an initial glimpse of the situation in Corinth that Paul must address; much of its thematic material will be taken up again in the finale (12, 19—13, 10).

10, 1–2: A strong opening plunges us straight into the conflict. Contrasts dominate here: presence versus absence, gentleness-clemency-humility versus boldness-confidence-bravery. **Through the gentleness and clemency of Christ:** the figure of the gentle Christ, presented in a significant position before any specifics of the situation are suggested, forms a striking contrast to the picture of the bold and militant Paul (2–6); this tension is finally resolved in 13, 3–4. **Absent . . . present:** this same contrast, with a restatement of the purpose of the letter, recurs in 13, 10, which forms an inclusion with 10, 1–2.

10, 2b-4a: Flesh: the Greek word **sarx** can express both the physical life of the body without any pejorative overtones (as in "we are in the flesh," 3) and our natural life insofar as it is marked by limitation and weakness (as in the other expressions) in contrast to the higher life and power conferred by the Spirit; cf the note on 1 Cor 3, 1. The wordplay is intended to express the paradoxical situation of a life already taken over by the Spirit but not yet seen as such except by faith. Lack of empirical evidence of the Spirit permits misunderstanding and misjudgment, but Paul resolutely denies that his behavior and effectiveness are as limited as some suppose.

10, 3b-6: Paul is involved in combat. The strong military language and imagery are both an assertion of his confidence in the divine power at his disposal and a declaration of war against those who underestimate his resources. The threat is echoed in 13, 2–3.

k Prv 11, 24–25. **l** Prv 22, 8 LXX. **m** Ps 112, 9. **n** Is 55, 10. **o** 8, 4; Rom 15, 31. **p** Rom 5, 15–16. **q** 13, 2.10; 1 Cor 4, 21. **r** 6, 7; 13, 2–3; 1 Cor 1, 25; Eph 6, 10–14.

6 [s]and we are ready to punish every disobedi-
ence, once your obedience is complete.
7 [t]*Look at what confronts you. Whoever is
confident of belonging to Christ should consider
that as he belongs to Christ, so do we. 8 [u]And
even if I should boast a little too much of our
authority, which the Lord gave for building you
up and not for tearing you down, I shall not be
put to shame. 9 *May I not seem as one frighten-
ing you through letters. 10 [v]For someone will say,
"His letters are severe and forceful, but his
bodily presence is weak, and his speech con-
temptible." 11 [w]Such a person must understand
that what we are in word through letters when
absent, that we also are in action when present.
12 [x]*Not that we dare to class or compare
ourselves with some of those who recommend
themselves. But when they measure themselves
by one another and compare themselves with
one another, they are without understanding.
13 *But we will not boast beyond measure but
will keep to the limits God has apportioned us,
namely, to reach even to you. 14 For we are not
overreaching ourselves, as though we did not
reach you; we indeed first came to you with the
gospel of Christ. 15 We are not boasting beyond
measure, in other people's labors; yet our hope
is that, as your faith increases, our influence
among you may be greatly enlarged, within our
proper limits, 16 [y]so that we may preach the
gospel even beyond you, not boasting of work
already done in another's sphere. 17 [z]*"Whoever
boasts, should boast in the Lord." 18 [a]*For it is
not the one who recommends himself who is
approved, but the one whom the Lord recom-
mends.

CHAPTER 11

Preaching without Charge 1 [b]*If only you
would put up with a little foolishness from me!
Please put up with me. 2 [c]*For I am jealous of
you with the jealousy of God, since I betrothed
you to one husband to present you as a chaste
virgin to Christ. 3 [d]*But I am afraid that, as the
serpent deceived Eve by his cunning, your
thoughts may be corrupted from a sincere [and
pure] commitment to Christ. 4 [e]*For if someone

10, 7–8: Belonging to Christ . . . so do we: these phrases already announce the pattern of Paul's boast in 11, 21b-29, especially 11, 22–23. **For building you up and not for tearing you down:** Paul draws on the language by which Jeremiah described the purpose of the prophetic power the Lord gave to him (Jer 1, 9–10; 12, 16–17; 24, 6). Though Paul's power may have destructive effects on others (2–6), its intended effect on the community is entirely constructive (cf 13, 10). **I shall not be put to shame:** his assertions will not be refuted; they will be revealed as true at the judgment.

10, 9–10: Paul cites the complaints of some who find him lacking in personal forcefulness and holds out the threat of a personal **parousia** (both "return" and "presence") that will be forceful, indeed will be a demonstration of Christ's own power (cf 13, 2–4).

10, 12–18: Paul now qualifies his claim to boldness, indicating its limits. He distinguishes his own behavior from that of others, revealing those "others" as they appear to him: as self-recommending, immoderately boastful, encroaching on territory not assigned to them, and claiming credit not due to them.

10, 13: Will keep to the limits: the notion of proper limits is expressed here by two terms with overlapping meanings, **metron** and **kanōn**, which are played off against several expressions denoting overreaching or expansion beyond a legitimate sphere.

10, 17: Boast in the Lord: there is a legitimate boasting, in contrast to the immoderate boasting to which vv 13 and 15 allude. God's work through Paul in the community is the object of his boast (13–16; 1, 12–14) and constitutes his recommendation (3, 1–3). Cf the notes on 1, 12–14 and 1 Cor 1, 29–31.

10, 18: Approved: to be approved is to come successfully through the process of testing for authenticity (cf 13, 3–7 and the note on 8, 2). **Whom the Lord recommends:** self-commendation is a premature and unwarranted anticipation of the final judgment, which the Lord alone will pass (cf 1 Cor 4, 3–5). Paul alludes to this judgment throughout chs 10–13, frequently in final or transitional positions; cf 11, 15; 12, 19a; 13, 3–7.

11, 1–15: Although these verses continue to reveal information about Paul's opponents and the differences he perceives between them and himself, 11, 1 signals a turn in Paul's thought. This section constitutes a prologue to the boasting that he will undertake in 11, 16—12, 10, and it bears remarkable similarities to the section that follows the central boast, 12, 11–18.

11, 1: Put up with a little foolishness from me: this verse indicates more clearly than the general statement of intent in 10, 13 the nature of the project Paul is about to undertake. He alludes ironically to the Corinthians' toleration for others. **Foolishness:** Paul qualifies his project as folly from beginning to end; see the note on 11, 16—12, 10.

11, 2: Paul gives us a sudden glimpse of the theological values that are at stake. **The jealousy of God:** the perspective is that of the covenant, described in imagery of love and marriage, as in the prophets; cf 1 Cor 10, 22. **I betrothed you:** Paul, like a father (cf 12, 14), betroths the community to Christ as his bride (cf Eph 5, 21–33) and will present her to him at his second coming. Cf Mt 25, 1–13 and the nuptial imagery in Rv 21.

11, 3: As the serpent deceived Eve: before Christ can return for the community Paul fears a repetition of the primal drama of seduction. Corruption of minds is satanic activity (see 2, 11; 4, 4). Satanic imagery recurs in 11, 13–15.20; 12, 7b.16–17; see the notes on these passages.

11, 4: Preaches another Jesus: the danger is specified, and Paul's opponents are identified with the cunning serpent. The battle for minds has to do with the understanding of Jesus, the Spirit, the gospel; the Corinthians have flirted with another under-

s 2, 9. t 1 Cor 1, 12. u 13, 10. v 1 Cor 2, 3. w 13, 1–2. x 3, 1–2; 4, 2; 5, 12; 6, 4; 10, 18; 12, 11. y Rom 15, 20–21. z Jer 9, 22–23; 1 Cor 1, 31. a 13, 3–9. b 11, 21; 12, 11. c Hos 2, 21–22; Eph 5, 26–27. d Gn 3, 1–6. e Gal 1, 6–9.

comes and preaches another Jesus than the one we preached, or if you receive a different spirit from the one you received or a different gospel from the one you accepted, you put up with it well enough. 5f*For I think that I am not in any way inferior to these "superapostles." 6g*Even if I am untrained in speaking, I am not so in knowledge; in every way we have made this plain to you in all things.

7h*Did I make a mistake when I humbled myself so that you might be exalted, because I preached the gospel of God to you without charge? 8I plundered other churches by accepting from them in order to minister to you. 9iAnd when I was with you and in need, I did not burden anyone, for the brothers who came from Macedonia supplied my needs. So I refrained and will refrain from burdening you in any way. 10jBy the truth of Christ in me, this boast of mine shall not be silenced in the regions of Achaia. 11k*And why? Because I do not love you? God knows I do!

12And what I do I will continue to do, in order to end this pretext of those who seek a pretext for being regarded as we are in the mission of which they boast. 13*For such people are false apostles, deceitful workers, who masquerade as apostles of Christ. 14And no wonder, for even Satan masquerades as an angel of light. 15So it is not strange that his ministers also masquerade as ministers of righteousness. Their end will correspond to their deeds.

Paul's Boast: His Labors 16*I repeat, no one should consider me foolish; but if you do, accept me as a fool, so that I too may boast a little. 17What I am saying I am not saying according to the Lord but as in foolishness, in this boastful state. 18Since many boast according to the flesh, I too will boast. 19For you gladly put up with fools, since you are wise yourselves. 20*For you put up with it if someone enslaves you, or

---

standing than the one that Paul handed on to them as traditional and normative.

11, 5: These "superapostles": this term, employed again in 12, 11b, designates the opponents of whom Paul has spoken in ch 10 and again in 11, 4. They appear to be intruders at Corinth. Their preaching is marked at least by a different emphasis and style, and they do not hesitate to accept support from the community. Perhaps these itinerants appeal to the authority of church leaders in Jerusalem and even carry letters of recommendation from them. But it is not those distant leaders whom Paul is attacking here. The intruders are "superapostles" not in the sense of the "pillars" at Jerusalem (Gal 2), but in their own estimation. They consider themselves superior to Paul as apostles and ministers of Christ, and they are obviously enjoying some success among the Corinthians. Paul rejects their claim to be apostles in any superlative sense (**hyperlian**), judging them bluntly as "false apostles," ministers of Satan masquerading as apostles of Christ (13–15). On the contrary, he himself will claim to be a superminister of Christ (**hyper egō**, 23).

11, 6: Apparently found deficient in both rhetorical ability (cf 10, 10) and knowledge (cf 10, 5), Paul concedes the former charge but not the latter. **In every way:** in all their contacts with him revelation has been taking place. Paul, through whom God reveals the knowledge of himself (2, 14), and in whom the death and life of Jesus are revealed (4, 10–11; cf 6, 4), also demonstrates his own role as the bearer of true knowledge. Cf 1 Cor 1, 18—2, 16.

11, 7–10: Abruptly Paul passes to another reason for complaints: his practice of preaching without remuneration (cf 1 Cor 9, 3–18). He deftly defends his practice by situating it from the start within the pattern of Christ's own self-humiliation (cf 10, 1) and reduces objections to absurdity by rhetorical questions (cf 12, 13).

11, 11–12: Paul rejects lack of affection as his motive (possibly imputed to him by his opponents) and states his real motive, a desire to emphasize the disparity between himself and the others (cf 19–21). The topic of his gratuitous service will be taken up once more in 12, 13–18. 1 Cor 9, 15–18 gives a different but complementary explanation of his motivation.

11, 13–15: Paul picks up again the imagery of v 3 and applies it to the opponents: they are false apostles of Christ, really serving another master. **Deceitful . . . masquerade:** deception and simulation, like cunning (3), are marks of the satanic. **Angel of light:** recalls the contrast between light and darkness, Christ and Beliar at 6, 14–15. **Ministers of righteousness:** recalls the earlier contrast between the ministry of condemnation and that of righteousness (3, 9). **Their end:** the section closes with another allusion to the judgment, when all participants in the final conflict will be revealed or unmasked and dealt with as they deserve.

11, 16—12, 10: Paul now accepts the challenge of his opponents and indulges in boasting similar to theirs, but with differences that he has already signaled in 10, 12–18 and that become clearer as he proceeds. He defines the nature of his project and unmistakably labels it as folly at the beginning and the end (11, 16–23; 12, 11). Yet his boast does not spring from ignorance (11, 21; 12, 6) nor is it concerned merely with human distinctions (11, 18). Paul boasts "in moderation" (10, 13.15) and "in the Lord" (10, 17).

11, 16–29: The first part of Paul's boast focuses on labors and afflictions, in which authentic service of Christ consists.

11, 16–21: These verses recapitulate remarks already made about the foolishness of boasting and the excessive toleration of the Corinthians. They form a prelude to the boast proper.

11, 20: Paul describes the activities of the "others" in terms that fill out the picture drawn in vv 3–4.13–15. Much of the vocabulary suggests fleshly or even satanic activity. **Enslaves:** cf Gal 2, 4. **Devours:** cf 1 Pt 5, 8. **Gets the better:** the verb **lambanō** means "to take," but is used in a variety of senses; here it may imply financial advantage, as in the English colloquialism "to take someone." It is similarly used at 12, 16 and is there connected with cunning and deceit. **Puts on airs:** the same verb is rendered "raise oneself" (10, 5) and "be too elated" (12, 7).

f 12, 11. g 1 Cor 1, 5.17; 2, 1–5. h 12, 13–18; Acts 18, 3; 1 Cor 9, 6–18. i Phil 4, 15.18. j 1 Cor 9, 15. k 12, 15.

devours you, or gets the better of you, or puts on airs, or slaps you in the face. 21 *To my shame I say that we were too weak!

But what anyone dares to boast of (I am speaking in foolishness) I also dare. 22 [l]*Are they Hebrews? So am I. Are they Israelites? So am I. Are they descendants of Abraham? So am I. 23 [m]*Are they ministers of Christ? (I am talking like an insane person.) I am still more, with far greater labors, far more imprisonments, far worse beatings, and numerous brushes with death. 24 [n]Five times at the hands of the Jews I received forty lashes minus one. 25 [o]Three times I was beaten with rods, once I was stoned, three times I was shipwrecked, I passed a night and a day on the deep; 26 on frequent journeys, in dangers from rivers, dangers from robbers, dangers from my own race, dangers from Gentiles, dangers in the city, dangers in the wilderness, dangers at sea, dangers among false brothers; 27 [p]in toil and hardship, through many sleepless nights, through hunger and thirst, through frequent fastings, through cold and exposure. 28 And apart from these things, there is the daily pressure upon me of my anxiety for all the churches. 29 [q]Who is weak, and I am not weak? Who is led to sin, and I am not indignant?

Paul's Boast: His Weakness 30 *If I must boast, I will boast of the things that show my weakness. 31 *The God and Father of the Lord Jesus knows, he who is blessed forever, that I do not lie. 32 At Damascus, the governor under King Aretas guarded the city of Damascus, in order to seize me, 33 [r]but I was lowered in a basket through a window in the wall and escaped his hands.

CHAPTER 12

1 *I must boast; not that it is profitable, but I will go on to visions and revelations of the Lord. 2 I know someone in Christ who, fourteen years ago (whether in the body or out of the body I do not know, God knows), was caught up to the third heaven. 3 And I know that this person (whether in the body or out of the body I do not know, God knows) 4 [s]was caught up into Paradise and heard ineffable things, which no one may utter. 5 *About this person I will boast, but about myself I will not boast, except about my weaknesses. 6 Although if I should wish to boast, I would not be foolish, for I would be telling the truth. But I refrain, so that no one may think more of me than what he sees in me or hears from me 7 [t]*because of the abundance of the

11, 21: Paul ironically concedes the charge of personal weakness from 10, 1–18 but will refute the other charge there mentioned, that of lack of boldness, accepting the challenge to demonstrate it by his boast.

11, 22: The opponents apparently pride themselves on their "Jewishness." Paul, too, can claim to be a Jew by race, religion, and promise. **Descendants of Abraham:** elsewhere Paul distinguishes authentic from inauthentic heirs of Abraham and the promise (Rom 4, 13–18; 9, 7–13; 11, 1; Gal 3, 9.27–29; cf Jn 8, 33–47). Here he grants his opponents this title in order to concentrate on the principal claim that follows.

11, 23a: Ministers of Christ . . . I am still more: the central point of the boast (cf the note on 11, 5). **Like an insane person:** the climax of his folly.

11, 23b-29: Service of the humiliated and crucified Christ is demonstrated by trials endured for him. This rhetorically impressive catalogue enumerates many of the labors and perils Paul encountered on his missionary journeys.

11, 30—12, 10: The second part of Paul's boast, marked by a change of style and a shift in focus. After recalling the project in which he is engaged, he states a new topic: his weaknesses as matter for boasting. Everything in this section, even the discussion of privileges and distinctions, will be integrated into this perspective.

11, 31–32: The episode at Damascus is symbolic. It aptly illustrates Paul's weakness but ends in deliverance (cf 4, 7–11).

12, 1–4: In the body or out of the body: he seemed no longer confined to bodily conditions, but he does not claim to understand the mechanics of the experience. **Caught up:** i.e., in ecstasy. **The third heaven . . . Paradise:** ancient cosmologies depicted a multitiered universe. Jewish intertestamental literature contains much speculation about the number of heavens. Seven is the number usually mentioned, but the Testament of Levi (Lev 2, 7–10; 3, 1–4) speaks of three; God himself dwelt in the third of these. Without giving us any clear picture of the cosmos, Paul indicates a mental journey to a nonearthly space, set apart by God, in which secrets were revealed to him. **Ineffable things:** i.e., privileged knowledge, which it was not possible or permitted to divulge.

12, 5–7: This person: the indirect way of referring to himself has the effect of emphasizing the distance between that experience and his everyday life, just as the indirect **someone in Christ** (2) and all the passive verbs emphasize his passivity and receptivity in the experience. The revelations were not a personal achievement, nor were they meant to draw attention to any quality of his own.

12, 7b: That I might not become too elated: God assures that there is a negative component to his experience, so that he cannot lose proper perspective; cf 1, 9; 4, 7–11. **A thorn in the flesh:** variously interpreted as a sickness or physical disability, a temptation, or a handicap connected with his apostolic activity. But since Hebrew "thorn in the flesh," like English "thorn in my side," refers to persons (cf Nm 33, 55; Ez 28, 24), Paul may be referring to some especially persistent and obnoxious opponent. The language of vv 7–8 permits this interpretation. If this is correct, the

l Acts 22, 3 / Rom 11, 1; Phil 3, 5–6. m 6, 5; Acts 16, 22–24; 1 Cor 15, 31–32. n Dt 25, 2–3. o Acts 14, 19; 27, 43–44. p 1 Cor 4, 11. q 1 Cor 9, 22. r Acts 9, 23–25. s Lk 23, 43; Rv 2, 7. t Nm 33, 55; Jos 23, 13; Ez 28, 24.

revelations. Therefore, that I might not become
too elated, a thorn in the flesh was given to me,
an angel of Satan, to beat me, to keep me from
being too elated. [8][u]*Three times I begged the
Lord about this, that it might leave me, [9][v]*but
he said to me, "My grace is sufficient for you, for
power is made perfect in weakness." I will
rather boast most gladly of my weaknesses, in
order that the power of Christ may dwell with
me. [10][w]*Therefore, I am content with weak-
nesses, insults, hardships, persecutions, and con-
straints, for the sake of Christ; for when I am
weak, then I am strong.
Selfless Concern for the Church [11][x]*I have
been foolish. You compelled me, for I ought to
have been commended by you. For I am in no
way inferior to these "superapostles," even
though I am nothing. [12][y]*The signs of an apostle
were performed among you with all endurance,
signs and wonders, and mighty deeds. [13][z]*In
what way were you less privileged than the rest
of the churches, except that on my part I did not
burden you? Forgive me this wrong!
[14]Now I am ready to come to you this third
time. And I will not be a burden, for I want not
what is yours, but you. Children ought not to
save for their parents, but parents for their
children. [15]I will most gladly spend and be
utterly spent for your sakes. If I love you more,
am I to be loved less? [16][a]But granted that I
myself did not burden you, yet I was crafty and
got the better of you by deceit. [17]Did I take
advantage of you through any of those I sent to
you? [18][b]I urged Titus to go and sent the brother
with him. Did Titus take advantage of you? Did
we not walk in the same spirit? And in the same
steps?
Final Warnings and Appeals [19]*Have you
been thinking all along that we are defending
ourselves before you? In the sight of God we are
speaking in Christ, and all for building you up,
beloved. [20][c]*For I fear that when I come I may

---

frequent appearance of singular pronouns in depicting the opposition may not be merely a stylistic variation; the singular may be provoked and accompanied by the image of one individual in whom criticism of Paul's preaching, way of life, and apostolic consciousness is concentrated, and who embodies all the qualities Paul attributes to the group. **An angel of Satan:** a personal messenger from Satan; cf the satanic language already applied to the opponents in 11, 3.13–15.20.

12, 8: Three times: his prayer was insistent, like that of Jesus in Gethsemane, a sign of how intolerable he felt the thorn to be.

12, 9: But he said to me: Paul's petition is denied; release and healing are withheld for a higher purpose. The Greek perfect tense indicates that Jesus' earlier response still holds at the time of writing. **My grace is sufficient for you:** this is not a statement about the sufficiency of grace in general. Jesus speaks directly to Paul's situation. **Is made perfect:** i.e., is given most fully and manifests itself fully.

12, 9b-10a: Paul draws the conclusion from the autobiographical anecdote and integrates it into the subject of this part of the boast. **Weaknesses:** the apostolic hardships he must endure, including active personal hostility, as specified in a final catalogue (10a). **That the power of Christ may dwell with me:** Paul pinpoints the ground for the paradoxical strategy he has adopted in his self-defense.

12, 10b: When I am weak, then I am strong: Paul recognizes a twofold pattern in the resolution of the weakness-power (and death-life) dialectic, each of which looks to Jesus as the model and is experienced in him. The first is personal, involving a reversal in oneself (Jesus, 13, 4a; Paul, 1, 9–10; 4, 10–11; 6, 9). The second is apostolic, involving an effect on others (Jesus, 5, 14–15; Paul, 1, 6; 4, 12; 13, 9). The specific kind of "effectiveness in ministry" that Paul promises to demonstrate on his arrival (13, 4b; cf 10, 1–11) involves elements of both; this, too, will be modeled on Jesus' experience and a participation in that experience (9; 13, 3b).

12, 11–18: This brief section forms an epilogue or concluding observation to Paul's boast, corresponding to the prologue in 11, 1–15. A four-step sequence of ideas is common to these two sections: Paul qualifies his boast as folly (11, 1; 12, 11a), asserts his noninferiority to the "superapostles" (11, 5; 12, 11b), exemplifies this by allusion to charismatic endowments (11, 6; 12, 12), and finally denies that he has been a financial burden to the community (11, 7–12; 12, 13–18).

12, 12: Despite weakness and affliction (suggested by the mention of **endurance**), his ministry has been accompanied by demonstrations of power (cf 1 Cor 2, 3–4). **Signs of an apostle:** visible proof of belonging to Christ and of mediating Christ's power, which the opponents require as touchstones of apostleship (11; cf 13, 3).

12, 13–18: Paul insists on his intention to continue refusing support from the community (cf 11, 8–12). In defending his practice and his motivation, he once more protests his love (cf 11, 11) and rejects the suggestion of secret self-enrichment. He has recourse here again to language applied to his opponents earlier: "cunning" (11, 3), "deceit" (11, 13), "got the better of you" (see the note on 11, 20), "take advantage" (2, 11).

12, 19—13, 10: This concludes the development begun in ch 10. In the chiastic arrangement of the material (see the note on 10, 1—13, 10), this final part corresponds to the opening; there are important similarities of content between the two sections as well.

12, 19: This verse looks back at the previous chapters and calls them by their proper name, a defense, an **apologia** (cf 1 Cor 9, 3). Yet Paul insists on an important distinction: he has indeed been speaking for their benefit, but the ultimate judgment to which he submits is God's (cf 1 Cor 4, 3–5). This verse also leads into the final section, announcing two of its themes: judgment and building up.

12, 20: I fear that . . . : earlier Paul expressed fear that the Corinthians were being victimized, exploited, seduced from right thinking by his opponents (11, 3–4.19–21). Here he alludes unexpectedly to moral disorders among the Corinthians themselves. The catalogue suggests the effects of factions that have grown up around rival apostles.

u Mt 26, 39–44. v 4, 7. w 6, 4–5; Rom 5, 3 / Phil 4, 13. x 11, 5. y Rom 15, 19; 1 Thes 1, 5. z 11, 9–12. a 11, 3.13. b 2, 13; 8, 16.23. c 1 Cor 1, 11; 3, 3.

find you not such as I wish, and that you may
find me not as you wish; that there may be
rivalry, jealousy, fury, selfishness, slander, gossip,
conceit, and disorder. 21*I fear that when I come
again my God may humiliate me before you, and
I may have to mourn over many of those who
sinned earlier and have not repented of the
impurity, immorality, and licentiousness they
practiced.

CHAPTER 13

1 [d]*This third time I am coming to you. "On the
testimony of two or three witnesses a fact shall
be established." 2*I warned those who sinned
earlier and all the others, and I warn them now
while absent, as I did when present on my
second visit, that if I come again I will not be
lenient, 3*since you are looking for proof of
Christ speaking in me. He is not weak toward
you but powerful in you. 4For indeed he was
crucified out of weakness, but he lives by the
power of God. So also we are weak in him, but
toward you we shall live with him by the power
of God.

5*Examine yourselves to see whether you are
living in faith. Test yourselves. Do you not
realize that Jesus Christ is in you?—unless, of
course, you fail the test. 6I hope you will
discover that we have not failed. 7But we pray to
God that you may not do evil, not that we may
appear to have passed the test but that you may
do what is right, even though we may seem to
have failed. 8For we cannot do anything against
the truth, but only for the truth. 9For we rejoice
when we are weak but you are strong. What we
pray for is your improvement.

10 [e]*I am writing this while I am away, so that
when I come I may not have to be severe in
virtue of the authority that the Lord has given
me to build up and not to tear down.

V: Conclusion

11*Finally, brothers, rejoice. Mend your ways,
encourage one another, agree with one another,
live in peace, and the God of love and peace will
be with you. 12 [f]Greet one another with a holy
kiss. All the holy ones greet you.

13 [g]The grace of the Lord Jesus Christ and the
love of God and the fellowship of the holy Spirit
be with all of you.

12, 21: Again: one can also translate, "I fear that when I come my God may again humiliate me." Paul's allusion to the humiliation and mourning that may await him recall the mood he described in 2, 1–4, but there is no reference here to any individual such as there is in 2, 5–11. The crisis of ch 2 has happily been resolved by integration of the offender and repentance (7, 4–16), whereas 12, 21 is preoccupied with still unrepentant sinners. The sexual sins recall 1 Cor 5–7.

13, 1: This third time I am coming: designation of the forthcoming visit as the "third" (cf 12, 14) may indicate that, in addition to his founding sojourn in Corinth, Paul had already made the first of two visits mentioned as planned in 1, 15, and the next visit will be the long-postponed second of these. If so, the materials in 1, 12—2, 13 plus 7, 4–16 and chs 10–13 may date from the same period of time, presumably of some duration, between Paul's second and third visit, though it is not clear that they are addressing the same crisis. The chronology is too unsure and the relations between sections of 2 Cor too unclear to yield any certainty. The hypothesis that chs 10–13 are themselves the "tearful letter" mentioned at 2, 3–4 creates more problems than it solves.

13, 2: I warned those who sinned earlier: mention of unrepentant sinners (12, 21 and here) and of an oral admonition given them on an earlier visit complicates the picture at the very end of Paul's development. It provides, in fact, a second explanation for the show of power that has been threatened from the beginning (10, 1–6), but a different reason for it, quite unsuspected until now. It is not clear whether Paul is merely alluding to a dimension of the situation that he has not previously had occasion to mention, or whether some other community crisis, not directly connected with that behind chs 10–13, has influenced the final editing. **I will not be lenient:** contrast Paul's hesitation and reluctance to inflict pain in 1, 23 and 2, 1–4. The next visit will bring the showdown.

13, 3–4: Paul now gives another motive for severity when he comes, the charge of weakness leveled against him as an apostle. The motive echoes more closely the opening section (10, 1–18) and the intervening development (especially 11, 30—12, 10). **Proof of Christ speaking in me:** the threat of 10, 1–2 is reworded to recall Paul's conformity with the pattern of Christ, his insertion into the interplay of death and life, weakness and power (cf the note on 12, 10b).

13, 5–9: Paul turns the challenge mentioned in v 3 on them: they are to put themselves to the test to demonstrate whether Christ is in them. These verses involve a complicated series of plays on the theme of **dokimē** (testing, proof, passing and failing a test). Behind this stands the familiar distinction between present human judgment and final divine judgment. This is the final appearance of the theme (cf 10, 18; 11, 15; 12, 19).

13, 10: Authority . . . to build up and not to tear down: Paul restates the purpose of his letter in language that echoes 10, 2.8, emphasizing the positive purpose of his authority in their regard. This verse forms an inclusion with the topic sentence of the section (12, 19), as well as with the opening of this entire portion of the letter (10, 1–2).

13, 11–13: These verses may have originally concluded chs 10–13, but they have nothing specifically to do with the material of that section. It is also possible to consider them a conclusion to the whole of 2 Cor in its present edited form. The exhortations are general, including a final appeal for peace in the community. The letter ends calmly, after its many storms, with the prospect of ecclesial unity and divine blessing. The final verse is one of the clearest trinitarian passages in the New Testament.

d Dt 19, 15; Mt 18, 16; Jn 8, 17; Heb 10, 28. e 10, 8. f Rom 16, 16; 1 Cor 16, 20 / Phil 4, 22; 1 Thes 5, 26; 1 Pt 5, 14. g Rom 16, 20; 1 Cor 16, 23.

THE LETTER TO THE GALATIANS

The Galatians to whom the letter is addressed were Paul's converts, most likely among the descendants of Celts who had invaded western and central Asia Minor in the third century B.C. and had settled in the territory around Ancyra (modern Ankara, Turkey). Paul had passed through this area on his second missionary journey (Acts 16, 6) and again on his third (Acts 18, 23). It is less likely that the recipients of this letter were Paul's churches in the southern regions of Pisidia, Lycaonia, and Pamphylia where he had preached earlier in the Hellenized cities of Perge, Iconium, Pisidian Antioch, Lystra, and Derbe (Acts 13, 13—14, 27); this area was part of the Roman province of Galatia, and some scholars think that South Galatia was the destination of this letter.

If it is addressed to the Galatians in the north, the letter was probably written around A.D. 54 or 55, most likely from Ephesus after Paul's arrival there for a stay of several years on his third missionary journey (Acts 19; 20, 31). On the South Galatian theory, the date would be earlier, perhaps A.D. 48–50. Involved is the question of how one relates the events of 2, 1-10 to the "Council of Jerusalem" described in Acts 15 (see the notes on each passage).

In any case, the new Christians whom Paul is addressing were converts from paganism (4, 8-9) who were now being enticed by other missionaries to add the observances of the Jewish law, including the rite of circumcision, to the cross of Christ as a means of salvation. For, since Paul's visit, some other interpretation of Christianity had been brought to these neophytes, probably by converts from Judaism (the name "Judaizers" is sometimes applied to them); it has specifically been suggested that they were Jewish Christians who had come from the austere Essene sect.

These interlopers insisted on the necessity of following certain precepts of the Mosaic law along with faith in Christ. They were undermining Paul's authority also, asserting that he had not been trained by Jesus himself, that his gospel did not agree with that of the original and true apostles in Jerusalem, that he had kept from his converts in Galatia the necessity of accepting circumcision and other key obligations of the Jewish law, in order more easily to win them to Christ, and that his gospel was thus not the full and authentic one held by "those of repute" in Jerusalem (2, 2). Some scholars also see in chapters 5 and 6 another set of opponents against whom Paul writes, people who in their emphasis on the Spirit set aside all norms for conduct and became libertines in practice.

When Paul learned of the situation, he wrote this defense of his apostolic authority and of the correct understanding of the faith. He set forth the unique importance of Christ and his redemptive sacrifice on the cross, the freedom that Christians enjoy from the old burdens of the law, the total sufficiency of Christ and of faith in Christ as the way to God and to eternal life, and the beauty of the new life of the Spirit. Galatians is thus a summary of basic Pauline theology. Its themes were more fully and less polemically developed in the Letter to the Romans.

Autobiographically, the letter gives us Paul's own accounts of how he came to faith (1, 15-24), the agreement in "the truth of the gospel" (2, 5.14) that he shared with the Jewish Christian leaders in Jerusalem, James, Kephas, and John (2, 1-10), and the rebuke he had to deliver to Kephas in Antioch for inconsistency, contrary to the gospel, on the issue of table fellowship in the racially mixed church of Jewish and Gentile Christians in Antioch (2, 11-14; cf 15-21). At the conclusion of the letter (6, 11-18), Paul wrote in his own hand (cf 2 Thes 3, 17-18) a vivid summary of the message to the Galatians.

In his vigorous emphasis on the absolute preeminence of Christ and his cross as God's way to salvation and holiness, Paul stresses Christian freedom and the ineffectiveness of the Mosaic law for gaining divine favor and blessings (3, 19-29). The pious Jew saw in the law a way established by God to win divine approval by a life of meticulous observance of ritual, social, and moral regulations. But Paul's profound insight into the higher designs of God in Christ led him to understand and welcome the priority of promise and faith (shown in the experience of Abraham, 3, 6-18) and the supernatural gifts of the Spirit (3, 2-5; 5, 16—6, 10). His enthusiasm for this new vision of the life of grace in Christ and of the uniquely salvific role of Christ's redemptive death on the cross shines through this whole letter.

The principal divisions of the Letter to the Galatians are the following:

I. Address (1, 1-5)
II. Loyalty to the Gospel (1, 6-10)
III. Paul's Defense of His Gospel and His Authority (1, 11—2, 21)
IV. Faith and Liberty (3, 1—4, 31)
V. Exhortation to Christian Living (5, 1—6, 10)
VI. Conclusion (6, 11-18)

I: Address

CHAPTER 1

Greeting [1 a b]*Paul, an apostle not from human
beings nor through a human being but through
Jesus Christ and God the Father who raised him
from the dead, [2]*and all the brothers who are
with me, to the churches of Galatia: [3]grace to
you and peace from God our Father and the Lord
Jesus Christ, [4 c]*who gave himself for our sins
that he might rescue us from the present evil age
in accord with the will of our God and Father,
[5 d]to whom be glory forever and ever. Amen.

II: Loyalty to the Gospel

[6 e]*I am amazed that you are so quickly
forsaking the one who called you by [the] grace
[of Christ] for a different gospel [7](not that there is
another). But there are some who are disturbing
you and wish to pervert the gospel of Christ.
[8 f]*But even if we or an angel from heaven
should preach [to you] a gospel other than the
one that we preached to you, let that one be
accursed! [9]As we have said before, and now I
say again, if anyone preaches to you a gospel
other than the one that you received, let that
one be accursed!

[10 g]*Am I now currying favor with human
beings or God? Or am I seeking to please people?
If I were still trying to please people, I would not
be a slave of Christ.

1, 1–5: See the note on Rom 1, 1–7, concerning the greeting.

1, 1: **Apostle:** because of attacks on his authority in Galatia, Paul defends his apostleship. He is not an apostle commissioned by a congregation (Phil 2, 25; 2 Cor 8, 23) or even by prophets (1 Tm 1, 18 and 4, 14) but **through Jesus Christ and God the Father.**

1, 2: **All the brothers:** fellow believers in Christ, male and female; cf 3, 27–28. Paul usually mentions the co-sender(s) at the start of a letter, but the use of **all** is unique, adding weight to the letter. **Galatia:** central Turkey more likely than the Roman province of Galatia; see Introduction.

1, 4: The greeting in v 3 is expanded by a christological formula that stresses deliverance through the Lord Jesus from a world dominated by Satan; cf 2 Cor 4, 4; Eph 2, 2; 6, 12.

1, 6–10: In place of the usual thanksgiving (see the note on Rom 1, 8), Paul, with little to be thankful for in the Galatian situation, expresses amazement at the way his converts are deserting the gospel of Christ for a perverted message. He reasserts the one gospel he has preached (7–9) and begins to defend himself (10).

1, 6: **The one who called you:** God or Christ, though in actuality Paul was the divine instrument to call the Galatians.

1, 8: **Accursed:** in Greek, **anathema;** cf Rom 9, 3; 1 Cor 12, 3; 16, 22.

1, 10: This charge by Paul's opponents, that he sought to conciliate people with flattery and to curry favor with God, might refer to his mission practices (cf 1 Cor 9, 19–23) but the word **still** suggests it refers to his pre-Christian days (cf 14; Phil 3, 6). The self-description **slave of Christ** is one Paul often uses in a greeting (Rom 1, 1).

a Rom 1, 1–7; 1 Cor 1, 1–3. b 1, 11–12. c 2, 20; Eph 5, 2; 1 Tm 2, 6 / 1 Jn 5, 19 / Rom 12, 2; Eph 5, 16; Heb 10, 10. d Rom 16, 27; 2 Tm 4, 18. e 5, 8.10; Acts 15, 1.24; 2 Cor 11, 4. f 1 Cor 16, 22 / 5, 3.21; 2 Cor 13, 2. g 2 Cor 5, 11 / 1 Thes 2, 4.

III: Paul's Defense of His Gospel and His Authority

His Call by Christ 11 [h]*Now I want you to
know, brothers, that the gospel preached by me
is not of human origin. 12 *For I did not receive it
from a human being, nor was I taught it, but it
came through a revelation of Jesus Christ.
13 [i]*For you heard of my former way of life in
Judaism, how I persecuted the church of God
beyond measure and tried to destroy it, 14 [j]and
progressed in Judaism beyond many of my
contemporaries among my race, since I was
even more a zealot for my ancestral traditions.
15 [k]But when [God], who from my mother's
womb had set me apart and called me through
his grace, was pleased 16 [l]*to reveal his Son to
me, so that I might proclaim him to the Gentiles,
I did not immediately consult flesh and blood,
17 *nor did I go up to Jerusalem to those who
were apostles before me; rather, I went into
Arabia and then returned to Damascus.
18 [m]*Then after three years I went up to
Jerusalem to confer with Kephas and remained
with him for fifteen days. 19 [n]*But I did not see
any other of the apostles, only James the brother
of the Lord. 20 [o](As to what I am writing to you,
behold, before God, I am not lying.) 21 [p]Then I
went into the regions of Syria and Cilicia. 22 And
I was unknown personally to the churches of
Judea that are in Christ; 23 [q]they only kept
hearing that "the one who once was persecuting
us is now preaching the faith he once tried to
destroy." 24 So they glorified God because of me.

CHAPTER 2

The Council of Jerusalem 1 [r]*Then after four-
teen years I again went up to Jerusalem with
Barnabas, taking Titus along also. 2 [s]*I went up

1, 11—2, 21: Paul's presentation on behalf of his message and of his apostleship reflects rhetorical forms of his day: he first narrates the facts about certain past events (1, 12—2, 14) and then states his contention regarding justification by faith as the gospel message (2, 15–21). Further arguments follow from both experience and scripture in chs 3 and 4, before he draws out the ethical consequences (5, 1—6, 10). The specific facts that he takes up here to show that his gospel is not a human invention (1, 11) but **came through a revelation of Jesus Christ** (1, 12) deal with his own calling as a Christian missionary (1, 13–17), his initial relations with the apostles in Jerusalem (1, 18–24), a later journey to Jerusalem (2, 1–10), and an incident in Antioch involving Kephas and persons from James (2, 11–14). The content of Paul's revealed gospel is then set forth in the heart of the letter (2, 15–21).

1, 12: Although Paul received his gospel **through a revelation** from Christ, this did not exclude his use of early Christian confessional formulations. See the note on 1, 4.

1, 13–17: Along with Phil 3, 4–11, which also moves from autobiography to its climax in a discussion on justification by faith (cf Gal 2, 15–21), this passage is Paul's chief account of the change from his **former way of life** (13) to service as a Christian missionary (16); cf Acts 9, 1–22; 22, 4–16; 26, 9–18. Paul himself does not use the term "conversion" but stresses revelation (12.16). In v 15 his language echoes the Old Testament prophetic call of Jeremiah. Unlike the account in Acts (cf 22, 4–16), the calling of Paul here includes the mission to proclaim Christ **to the Gentiles** (16).

1, 16: Flesh and blood: human authorities (cf Mt 16, 17; 1 Cor 15, 50). Paul's apostleship comes from God (1).

1, 17: Arabia: probably the region of the Nabataean Arabs, east and south of Damascus.

1, 18–24: Paul's first journey to Jerusalem as a Christian, according to Galatians (cf Acts 9, 23–31 and the note on Acts 12, 25). He is quite explicit about contacts there, testifying under oath (20). On returning to **Syria** (perhaps specifically Damascus, cf v 17) **and Cilicia** (including his home town Tarsus, cf Acts 9, 30; 22, 3), Paul most likely engaged in missionary work. He underscores the fact that Christians in Judea knew of him only by reputation.

1, 18: After three years: two years and more, since Paul's call. To **confer with** Kephas may mean simply "pay a visit" or more specifically "get information from" him about Jesus, over a two-week period. **Kephas:** Aramaic name of Simon (Peter); cf Mt 16, 16–18 and the notes there.

1, 19: James the brother of the Lord: not one of the Twelve, but a brother of Jesus (see the note on Mk 6, 3). He played an important role in the Jerusalem church (see the note on Gal 2, 9), the leadership of which he took over from Peter (Acts 12, 17). Paul may have regarded James as an apostle.

2, 1–10: Paul's second journey to Jerusalem, according to Galatians, involved a private meeting with **those of repute** (2). At issue was a Gentile, Titus, and the question of circumcision, which **false brothers** (4) evidently demanded for him. Paul insists that the gospel he preaches (2; cf 1, 9.11) remained intact with no addition by those of repute (6); that **Titus** was not **compelled** to accept circumcision (3); and that he and the reputed **pillars** in Jerusalem agreed on how each would advance the missionary task (7–10). Usually, 1–10 is equated with the "Council of Jerusalem," as it is called, described in Acts 15. See the notes on Acts 15, 6–12 and 15, 13–35, the latter concerning the "decree" that Paul does not mention.

2, 1: After fourteen years: thirteen or more years, probably reckoned from the return to Syria and Cilicia (1, 21), though possibly from Paul's calling as a Christian (1, 15). **Barnabas:** cf 9.13; 1 Cor 9, 6. A Jewish Christian missionary, with whom Paul worked (Acts 4, 36–37; 11, 22.25.30; 12, 25; 13, 1–3; 15, 2). **Titus:** a missionary companion of Paul (2 Cor 2, 13; 7, 6.13–15; 8, 6.16.23; 12, 18), non-Jewish (Gal 2, 3), never mentioned in Acts.

2, 2: A revelation: cf 1, 1.12. Paul emphasizes it was God's will, not Jerusalem authority, that led to the journey. Acts 15, 2 states that the church in Antioch appointed Paul and Barnabas for the task. **Those of repute:** leaders of the Jerusalem church; the term, while positive, may be slightly ironic (cf 6.9). **Run, in vain:** while Paul presents a positive picture in what follows, his missionary work in Galatia would have been to no purpose if his oppo-

h 1 Cor 15, 1 / 1, 1; Eph 3, 3. i Acts 8, 1–3; 9, 1–2; 1 Cor 15, 9. j Acts 26, 4–5. k Is 49, 1; Jer 1, 4. l 1, 11–12; Rom 1, 5; 1 Cor 15, 10; Acts 9, 3–9 / 2, 2.7 /Mt 16, 17. m Acts 9, 26–30 / Jn 1, 42. n 2, 9; Mt 13, 55; Acts 12, 17. o Rom 9, 1; 2 Cor 11, 31. p Acts 9, 30. q 1, 13. r Acts 15, 2. s 1, 11–12.16 / 1, 16 / Phil 2, 16.

in accord with a revelation, and I presented to
them the gospel that I preach to the Gentiles—
but privately to those of repute—so that I might
not be running, or have run, in vain.
3 t*Moreover, not even Titus, who was with me,
although he was a Greek, was compelled to be
circumcised, 4 u*but because of the false broth-
ers secretly brought in, who slipped in to spy on
our freedom that we have in Christ Jesus, that
they might enslave us— 5 v*to them we did not
submit even for a moment, so that the truth of
the gospel might remain intact for you. 6 wBut
from those who were reputed to be important
(what they once were makes no difference to
me; God shows no partiality)—those of repute
made me add nothing. 7 x*On the contrary,
when they saw that I had been entrusted with
the gospel to the uncircumcised, just as Peter to
the circumcised, 8for the one who worked in
Peter for an apostolate to the circumcised
worked also in me for the Gentiles, 9 y*and
when they recognized the grace bestowed upon
me, James and Kephas and John, who were
reputed to be pillars, gave me and Barnabas their
right hands in partnership, that we should go to
the Gentiles and they to the circumcised.
10 z*Only, we were to be mindful of the poor,
which is the very thing I was eager to do.

Peter's Inconsistency at Antioch
11 a*And
when Kephas came to Antioch, I opposed him to
his face because he clearly was wrong. 12 b*For,
until some people came from James, he used to
eat with the Gentiles; but when they came, he
began to draw back and separated himself,
because he was afraid of the circumcised.
13 c*And the rest of the Jews [also] acted hypo-
critically along with him, with the result that
even Barnabas was carried away by their hypoc-
risy. 14 d*But when I saw that they were not on
the right road in line with the truth of the gospel,
I said to Kephas in front of all, "If you, though a
Jew, are living like a Gentile and not like a Jew,
how can you compel the Gentiles to live like
Jews?"

Faith and Works
15 *We, who are Jews by
nature and not sinners from among the Gentiles,

---

nents were correct that circumcision is needed for complete faith in Christ.

2, 3: Not even a Gentile Christian like Titus was compelled to receive the rite of circumcision. The Greek text could be interpreted that he voluntarily accepted circumcision, but this is unlikely in the overall argument.

2, 4: False brothers: Jewish Christians who took the position that Gentile Christians must first become Jews through circumcision and observance of the Mosaic law in order to become Christians; cf Acts 15, 1.

2, 5: The truth of the gospel: the true gospel, in contrast to the false one of the opponents (1, 6–9); the gospel of grace, used as a norm (14).

2, 7–9: Some think that actual "minutes" of the meeting are here quoted. Paul's apostleship to the Gentiles (1, 16) is recognized alongside that of Peter to the Jews. Moreover, the right to proclaim the gospel without requiring circumcision and the Jewish law is sealed by a handshake. That Paul and colleagues **should go to the Gentiles** did not exclude his preaching to the Jews as well (Rom 1, 13–16) or Kephas to Gentile areas.

2, 9: James and Kephas and John: see the notes on 1, 18 and 19; on Peter and John as leaders in the Jerusalem church, cf Acts 3, 1 and 8, 14. The order here, with James first, may reflect his prominence in Jerusalem after Peter (Kephas) departed (Acts 12, 17).

2, 10: The poor: Jerusalem Christians or a group within the church there (cf Rom 15, 26). The collection for them was extremely important in Paul's thought and labor (cf Rom 15, 25–28; 1 Cor 16, 1–4; 2 Cor 8 and 9).

2, 11–14: The decision reached in Jerusalem (3–7) recognized the freedom of Gentile Christians from the Jewish law. But the problem of table fellowship between Jewish Christians, who possibly still kept kosher food regulations, and Gentile believers was not yet settled. When Kephas first came to the racially mixed community of Jewish and Gentile Christians in Antioch (12), he ate with non-Jews. Pressure from persons arriving later from Jerusalem caused him and Barnabas to draw back. Paul therefore publicly rebuked Peter's inconsistency toward the gospel (14). Some think that what Paul said on that occasion extends through v 16 or v 21.

2, 11: Clearly was wrong: literally, "stood condemned," by himself and also by Paul. His action in breaking table fellowship was especially grievous if the eating involved the meal at the Lord's supper (cf 1 Cor 11, 17–25).

2, 12: Some people came from James: strict Jewish Christians (cf Acts 15, 1.5; 21, 20–21), either sent by James (1, 19; 2, 9) or claiming to be from the leader of the Jerusalem church. **The circumcised:** presumably Jewish Christians, not Jews.

2, 13: The Jews: Jewish Christians, like Barnabas. **Hypocrisy:** literally, "pretense," "play-acting"; moral insincerity.

2, 14: Compel the Gentiles to live like Jews: that is, conform to Jewish practices, such as circumcision (3–5) or regulations about food (12).

2, 15–21: Following on the series of incidents cited above, Paul's argument, whether spoken to Kephas at Antioch or only now articulated, is pertinent to the Galatian situation, where believers were having themselves circumcised (6, 12–13) and obeying other aspects of Jewish law (4, 9–10; 5, 1–4). He insists that salvation is by faith in Christ, not by works of the law. His teaching on the gospel concerns justification by faith (16) in relation to sin (17), law (19), life in Christ (19–20), and grace (21).

t 2 Cor 2, 13; 7, 6–7; 8, 16–17; 12, 18; Ti 1, 4 / 2, 14; 6, 12. u 5, 1; Acts 15, 1.24. v 2, 14; 4, 16. w Dt 10, 17; Rom 2, 11. x 1, 15–16; Acts 9, 15; 15, 12; 22, 21; Rom 1, 5. y Rom 15, 15 / 1, 18–19; Jn 1, 42; Acts 12, 17 / 2, 1. z Acts 11, 29–30; Rom 15, 25–28; 1 Cor 16, 1–4; 2 Cor 8, 9. a 1, 18 / Acts 11, 19–30; 15, 1–2. b Acts 10, 15.28; 11, 3. c 2, 1.9. d 2, 5 / 1, 18; 2, 9 / 2, 3.

16 [e]*[yet] who know that a person is not justified
by works of the law but through faith in Jesus
Christ, even we have believed in Christ Jesus
that we may be justified by faith in Christ and
not by works of the law, because by works of the
law no one will be justified. 17*But if, in seeking
to be justified in Christ, we ourselves are found
to be sinners, is Christ then a minister of sin? Of
course not! 18*But if I am building up again
those things that I tore down, then I show
myself to be a transgressor. 19 [f]*For through the
law I died to the law, that I might live for God. I
have been crucified with Christ; 20 [g]yet I live, no
longer I, but Christ lives in me; insofar as I now
live in the flesh, I live by faith in the Son of God
who has loved me and given himself up for me.
21 [h]I do not nullify the grace of God; for if
justification comes through the law, then Christ
died for nothing.

IV: Faith and Liberty

CHAPTER 3

Justification by Faith 1 [i]*O stupid Galatians!
Who has bewitched you, before whose eyes
Jesus Christ was publicly portrayed as crucified?
2 [j]*I want to learn only this from you: did you
receive the Spirit from works of the law, or from
faith in what you heard? 3 [k]*Are you so stupid?
After beginning with the Spirit, are you now
ending with the flesh? 4*Did you experience so
many things in vain?—if indeed it was in vain.
5 [l]Does, then, the one who supplies the Spirit to
you and works mighty deeds among you do so
from works of the law or from faith in what you
heard? 6 [m]*Thus Abraham "believed God, and it
was credited to him as righteousness."
7 [n]*Realize then that it is those who have faith
who are children of Abraham. 8 [o]Scripture,
which saw in advance that God would justify the
Gentiles by faith, foretold the good news to
Abraham, saying, "Through you shall all the
nations be blessed." 9 [p]Consequently, those who
have faith are blessed along with Abraham who
had faith. 10 [q]*For all who depend on works of
the law are under a curse; for it is written,
"Cursed be everyone who does not persevere in
doing all the things written in the book of the
law." 11 [r]And that no one is justified before God
by the law is clear, for "the one who is righteous

2, 16: No one will be justified: Ps 143, 2 is reflected.

2, 17: A minister of sin: literally, "a servant of sin" (cf Rom 15, 8), an agent of sin, one who promotes it. This is possibly a claim by opponents that justification on the basis of faith in Christ makes Christ an abettor of sin when Christians **are found to be sinners.** Paul denies the conclusion (cf Rom 6, 1–4).

2, 18: To return to observance of the law as the means to salvation would entangle one not only in inevitable transgressions of it but also in the admission that it was wrong to have abandoned the law in the first place.

2, 19: Through the law I died to the law: this is variously explained: the law revealed sin (Rom 7, 7–9) and led to death and then to belief in Christ; or, the law itself brought the insight that law cannot justify (16; Ps 143, 2); or, the "law of Christ" (6, 2) led to abandoning the Mosaic law; or, the law put Christ to death (cf 3, 13) and so provided a way to our salvation, through baptism into Christ, through which we die (**crucified with Christ;** see Rom 6, 6). Cf also 3, 19–25 on the role of the law in reference to salvation.

3, 1–14: Paul's contention that justification comes not through the law or the works of the law but by faith in Christ and in his death (2, 16.21) is supported by appeals to Christian experience (1–5) and to scripture (6–14). The gift of God's Spirit to the Galatians came from the gospel received in faith, not from doing what the law enjoins. The story of Abraham shows that faith in God brings **righteousness** (6; Gn 15, 6). The promise to Abraham (8; Gn 12, 3) extends to the Gentiles (14).

3, 1: Stupid: not just senseless, for they were in danger of deserting their salvation.

3, 2: Faith in what you heard: Paul's message received with faith. The Greek can also mean "the proclamation of the faith" or "a hearing that comes from faith."

3, 3: On the contrast of **Spirit** and **flesh,** cf Rom 8, 1–11. Having received the Spirit, they need not be circumcised now.

3, 4: Experience so many things: probably the **mighty deeds** of v 5 but possibly the experience of sufferings.

3, 6: Abraham . . . righteousness: see Gn 15, 6; Rom 4, 3. The Galatians like Abraham heard with faith and experienced justification. This first argument forms the basis for the further scriptural evidence that follows.

3, 7–9: Faith is what matters, for **Abraham** and the **children of Abraham,** in contrast to the claims of the opponents that circumcision and observance of the law are needed to bring the promised blessing of Gn 12, 3; cf Gn 18, 18; Sir 44, 21; Acts 3, 25.

3, 10–14: Those **who depend** not on promise and faith but **on works of the law are under a curse** because they do **not persevere in doing all the things written in the book of the law** (10; Dt 27, 26) in order to gain life (12; Lv 18, 5; cf Rom 10, 5). But scripture teaches that **no one is justified before God by the law** (11; Hb 2, 4, adapted from the Greek version of Habakkuk; cf Rom 1, 17; Heb 10, 38). Salvation, then, depends on faith in Christ who died on the cross (13), taking upon himself a curse found in Dt 21, 23 (about executed criminals hanged in public view), to free us from **the curse of the law** (13). That the Gentile Galatians have received the promised Spirit (14) by faith and in no other way returns the argument to the experience cited in vv 1–5.

e 3, 2.11; Ps 143, 1–2; Rom 3, 20.28; 4, 5; 11, 6; Eph 2, 8–9; Phil 3, 9. f 6, 14; Rom 6, 6.8.10; 7, 6. g 1, 4; Rom 8, 10–11; Col 3, 3–4. h 5, 2. i 5, 7; 1 Cor 1, 23. j 2, 16 / 3, 14; Rom 10, 17. k 5, 16–18. l 2, 16. m Gn 15, 6; Rom 4, 3; Jas 2, 23. n 3, 29; Rom 4, 11–12 / Sir 44, 19–21. o Gn 12, 3; 18, 17–19; Acts 3, 25. p Rom 4, 16. q Dt 27, 26; Jas 2, 10. r 2, 16; Hb 2, 4; Rom 1, 17.

by faith will live." [12] [s]But the law does not depend on faith; rather, "the one who does these things will live by them." [13] [t]Christ ransomed us from the curse of the law by becoming a curse for us, for it is written, "Cursed be everyone who hangs on a tree," [14] [u]that the blessing of Abraham might be extended to the Gentiles through Christ Jesus, so that we might receive the promise of the Spirit through faith.

The Law Did Not Nullify the Promise

[15] [v]*Brothers, in human terms I say that no one can annul or amend even a human will once ratified. [16] [w]*Now the promises were made to Abraham and to his descendant. It does not say, "And to descendants," as referring to many, but as referring to one, "And to your descendant," who is Christ. [17] [x]*This is what I mean: the law, which came four hundred and thirty years afterward, does not annul a covenant previously ratified by God, so as to cancel the promise. [18] [y]*For if the inheritance comes from the law, it is no longer from a promise; but God bestowed it on Abraham through a promise.

[19] [z]*Why, then, the law? It was added for transgressions, until the descendant came to whom the promise had been made; it was promulgated by angels at the hand of a mediator. [20] [a]Now there is no mediator when only one party is involved, and God is one. [21] [b]Is the law then opposed to the promises [of God]? Of course not! For if a law had been given that could bring life, then righteousness would in reality come from the law. [22] [c]But scripture confined all things under the power of sin, that through faith in Jesus Christ the promise might be given to those who believe.

What Faith Has Brought Us [23] [d]*Before faith came, we were held in custody under law, confined for the faith that was to be revealed. [24] [e]*Consequently, the law was our disciplinarian for Christ, that we might be justified by faith. [25] [f]But now that faith has come, we are no longer under a disciplinarian. [26] [g]*For through faith you are all children of God in Christ Jesus. [27] [h]*For all of you who were baptized into Christ have clothed yourselves with Christ. [28] [i]There is neither Jew nor Greek, there is neither slave nor free person, there is not male and female; for

3, 15–18: A third argument to support Paul's position that salvation is not through the law but by promise (1–14) comes from legal practice and scriptural history. A legal agreement or **human will, duly ratified,** is unalterable (15). God's **covenant** with **Abraham** and its repeated promises (Gn 12, 2–3.7; 13, 15; 17, 7–8; 22, 16–18; 24, 7) is not superseded by **the law,** which came much later, in the time of Moses. **The inheritance** (of the Spirit and the blessings) is by promise, not by law (18). Paul's argument hinges on the fact that the same Greek word, **diathēkē,** can be rendered as **will** or testament (15) and as **covenant** (17).

3, 16: Descendant: literally, "and to his seed." The Hebrew, as in Gn 12, 7; 15, 18; 22, 17–18, is a collective singular, traditionally rendered as a plural, **descendants,** but taken by Paul in its literal number to refer to **Christ** as descendant of Abraham.

3, 17: Four hundred and thirty years afterward: follows Ex 12, 40 in the Greek (Septuagint) version, in contrast to Gn 15, 13 and Acts 7, 6, for chronology.

3, 18: This refutes the opponents' contention that the promises of God are fulfilled only as a reward for human observance of the law.

3, 19–22: A digression: if the Mosaic law, then, does not save or **bring life,** why was it given? Elsewhere, Paul says the law served to show what sin is (Rom 3, 20; 7, 7–8). Here the further implication is that the law in effect served to produce transgressions. Moreover, it was received at second hand **by angels,** through a **mediator,** not directly from God (19). The law does not, however, oppose God's purposes, for it carries out its function (22), so that **righteousness** comes by **faith** and **promise,** not by human works of the law.

3, 19: The descendant: Christ (16). **By angels:** Dt 33, 2–4 stressed their presence as enhancing the importance of the law; Paul uses their role to diminish its significance (cf Acts 7, 38.53). **A mediator:** Moses. But in a covenant of promise, where all depends on the one God, no mediator is needed (20).

3, 23–29: Paul adds a further argument in support of righteousness or justification by faith and through God's promise rather than by works of the law (2, 16; 3, 22): as **children of God, baptized into Christ,** the Galatians are all **Abraham's descendant** and **heirs of the promise** to Abraham (8.14.16–18.29). The teaching in 23–25, that since **faith** (Christianity) **has come, we are no longer under** the law, could be taken with the previous paragraph on the role of the Mosaic law, but it also fits here as a contrast between the situation **before faith** (23) and the results after faith has come (25–29).

3, 24–25: Disciplinarian: the Greek **paidagōgos** referred to a slave who escorted a child to school but did not teach or tutor; hence, a guardian or monitor. Applying this to the law fits the role of the law described in vv 19–25.

3, 26: Children of God: literally "sons," in contrast to the young child under the disciplinarian in vv 24–25. The term includes males and females (28).

3, 27: Clothed yourselves with Christ: literally, "have put on Christ"; cf Rom 13, 14; Eph 4, 24; Col 3, 10. Baptismal imagery, traceable to the Old Testament (Jb 29, 14; Is 59, 17) but also found in pagan mystery cults.

s Lv 18, 5; Rom 10, 5. t Dt 21, 23; Rom 8, 3; 2 Cor 5, 21. u 3, 2–3.5; Is 44, 3; Jl 3, 1–2; Acts 2, 33. v Rom 3, 5 / Heb 9, 16–17. w Gn 12, 7; 13, 15; 17, 8; 22, 17; 24, 7; Mt 1, 1. x Ex 12, 40. y Rom 4, 16; 11, 6. z Rom 4, 15; 5, 20; 7, 7.13 / Acts 7, 38.53. a Dt 6, 4. b Rom 7, 7.10; 8, 2–4. c Rom 3, 9–20.23; 11, 32. d 4, 3–5; 5, 18. e 2, 16. f Rom 10, 4. g 4, 5–7; Jn 1, 12; Rom 8, 14–17. h Rom 6, 3; 13, 14; Eph 4, 24. i Rom 10, 12; 1 Cor 12, 13; Col 3, 11.

you are all one in Christ Jesus. [29 j]And if you belong to Christ, then you are Abraham's descendant, heirs according to the promise.

CHAPTER 4

God's Free Children in Christ [1 *]I mean that as long as the heir is not of age, he is no different from a slave, although he is the owner of everything, [2]but he is under the supervision of guardians and administrators until the date set by his father. [3 k*]In the same way we also, when we were not of age, were enslaved to the elemental powers of the world. [4 l]But when the fullness of time had come, God sent his Son, born of a woman, born under the law, [5 m]to ransom those under the law, so that we might receive adoption. [6 n*]As proof that you are children, God sent the spirit of his Son into our hearts, crying out, "Abba, Father!" [7 o]So you are no longer a slave but a child, and if a child then also an heir, through God.

Do Not Throw This Freedom Away [8 p*]At a time when you did not know God, you became slaves to things that by nature are not gods; [9 q]but now that you have come to know God, or rather to be known by God, how can you turn back again to the weak and destitute elemental powers? Do you want to be slaves to them all over again? [10 r*]You are observing days, months, seasons, and years. [11 *]I am afraid on your account that perhaps I have labored for you in vain.

Appeal to Former Loyalty [12 s*]I implore you, brothers, be as I am, because I have also become as you are. You did me no wrong; [13 *]you know that it was because of a physical illness that I originally preached the gospel to you, [14]and you did not show disdain or contempt because of the trial caused you by my physical condition, but rather you received me as an angel of God, as Christ Jesus. [15 *]Where now is that blessedness of yours? Indeed, I can testify to you that, if it had been possible, you would have torn out your eyes and given them to me. [16]So now have I become your enemy by telling you the truth? [17 t*]They show interest in you, but not in a good way; they want to isolate you, so that you may show interest in them. [18]Now it is good to be shown interest for good reason at all times, and not only when I am with you. [19 u]My children, for whom I am again in labor until Christ be formed in you! [20]I would like to be with you now and to change my tone, for I am perplexed because of you.

An Allegory on Christian Freedom [21 *]Tell me, you who want to be under the law, do you

4, 1–7: What Paul has argued in 3, 26–29 is now elaborated in terms of the Christian as **the heir** (1.7; cf 3, 18.29) freed from control by others. Again, as in 3, 2–5, the proof that Christians are children of God is the gift of the Spirit of Christ relating them intimately to God.

4, 1.3: Not of age: an infant or minor.

4, 3: The elemental powers of the world: while the term can refer to the "elements" like earth, air, fire, and water or to elementary forms of religion, the sense here is more likely that of celestial beings that were thought in pagan circles to control the world; cf 8; Col 2, 8.20.

4, 6: Children: see the note on 3, 26; here in contrast to the infant or young person **not of age** (1.3). **Abba:** cf Mk 14, 36 and the note; Rom 8, 15.

4, 8–11: On the basis of the arguments advanced from 3, 1 through 4, 7, Paul now launches his appeal to the Galatians with the question, **how can you turn back** to the slavery of the law (9)? The question is posed with reference to bondage to the **elemental powers** (see the note on 4, 3) because the Galatians had originally been converted to Christianity from paganism, not Judaism (8). The use of the direct question is like 3, 3–5.

4, 8: Things that by nature are not gods: or "gods that by nature do not exist."

4, 10: This is likely a reference to ritual observances from the Old Testament, promoted by opponents: sabbaths or Yom Kippur, new moon, Passover or Pentecost, sabbatical years.

4, 11: Cf 2, 2. If the Galatians become **slaves . . . all over again** to the law (9), Paul will have worked in vain among them.

4, 12–20: A strongly personal section. Paul appeals to past ties between the Galatians and himself. He speaks sharply of the opponents (17–18) and pastorally to the Galatians (19–20).

4, 12: Because I have also become as you are: a terse phrase in Greek, meaning "Be as I, Paul, am," i.e., living by faith, independent of the law, for, in spite of my background in Judaism (1, 13), I have become as you Galatians are now, a brother in Christ.

4, 13: Physical illness: because its nature is not described, some assume an eye disease (15); others, epilepsy; some relate it to 2 Cor 12, 7–9. **Originally:** this may also be translated "formerly" or "on the first (of two) visit(s)"; cf Acts 16, 6; 18, 23.

4, 15: That blessedness of yours: possibly a reference to the Galatians' initial happy reception of Paul (14) and of his gospel (1, 6; 3, 1–4) and their felicitation at such blessedness, but the phrase could also refer ironically to earlier praise by Paul of the Galatians, no longer possible when they turn from the gospel to the claims of the opponents (17–18; 1, 7). If the word is a more literal reference to a beatitude, Gal 3, 26–28 may be in view.

4, 17: Isolate you: that is, from the blessings of the gospel and/or from Paul.

4, 21–31: Paul supports his appeal for the gospel (9; 1, 6–9; 2,

j 3, 7.14.16.18; Rom 4, 16–17; 9, 7 / 4, 1.7; Rom 4, 13–14; 8, 17; Heb 6, 12; Jas 2, 5. k 3, 23 / 4, 9; Col 2, 20. l Mk 1, 15. m 3, 13.26. n 3, 26; Rom 8, 15. o 3, 29; Rom 8, 16–17. p 1 Cor 12, 2. q 4, 3; Col 2, 20. r Col 2, 16–20. s 1 Cor 11, 1. t 1, 7; 6, 12; Acts 20, 30. u 1 Cor 4, 14–15; 2 Cor 6, 13; 1 Thes 2, 7–8.

not listen to the law? 22 vFor it is written that
Abraham had two sons, one by the slave woman
and the other by the freeborn woman. 23 wThe
son of the slave woman was born naturally, the
son of the freeborn through a promise. 24 xNow
this is an allegory. These women represent two
covenants. One was from Mount Sinai, bearing
children for slavery; this is Hagar. 25 *Hagar
represents Sinai, a mountain in Arabia; it corre-
sponds to the present Jerusalem, for she is in
slavery along with her children. 26 yBut the
Jerusalem above is freeborn, and she is our
mother. 27 z*For it is written:

"Rejoice, you barren one who bore no
children;
break forth and shout, you who were not in
labor;
for more numerous are the children of the
deserted one
than of her who has a husband."

28 aNow you, brothers, like Isaac, are children of
the promise. 29 But just as then the child of the
flesh persecuted the child of the spirit, it is the
same now. 30 bBut what does the scripture say?

"Drive out the slave woman and her son!
For the son of the slave woman shall not
share the inheritance with the son"

of the freeborn. 31 cTherefore, brothers, we are
children not of the slave woman but of the
freeborn woman.

V: Exhortation to Christian Living

CHAPTER 5

The Importance of Faith 1 d*For freedom
Christ set us free; so stand firm and do not
submit again to the yoke of slavery.
2 eIt is I, Paul, who am telling you that if you
have yourselves circumcised, Christ will be of no
benefit to you. 3 f*Once again I declare to every
man who has himself circumcised that he is
bound to observe the entire law. 4 You are
separated from Christ, you who are trying to be
justified by law; you have fallen from grace.
5 gFor through the Spirit, by faith, we await the
hope of righteousness. 6 h*For in Christ Jesus,
neither circumcision nor uncircumcision counts
for anything, but only faith working through
love.

Be Not Misled 7 *You were running well; who
hindered you from following [the] truth? 8 i*That
enticement does not come from the one who
called you. 9 jA little yeast leavens the whole
batch of dough. 10 kI am confident of you in the
Lord that you will not take a different view, and
that the one who is troubling you will bear the
condemnation, whoever he may be. 11 l*As for

16; 3, 2) by a further argument from scripture (cf 3, 6–18). It involves the relationship of **Abraham** (3, 6–16) to his wife, Sarah, the **freeborn woman,** and to Hagar, **the slave woman,** and the contrast between the sons born to each, **Isaac,** child of promise, and Ishmael, son of Hagar (Gn 16 and 21). Only through Isaac is the promise of God preserved. This **allegory** (24), with its equation of the Sinai covenant and Mosaic law with slavery and of the promise of God with freedom, Paul uses only in light of previous arguments. His quotation of Gn 21, 10 at v 30 suggests on a scriptural basis that the Galatians should expel those who are troubling them (1, 7).

4, 25: Hagar represents Sinai . . . : some manuscripts have what seems a geographical note, "For Sinai is a mountain in Arabia."

4, 27: Is 54, 1 in the Septuagint translation is applied to Sarah as the **barren one** (in Gn 15) who ultimately becomes the mother not only of Isaac but now of numerous children, i.e., of all those who believe, the **children of the promise** (28).

5, 1–6: Paul begins the exhortations, continuing through 6, 10, with an appeal to the Galatians to side with freedom instead of slavery (1). He reiterates his message of justification or righteousness by faith instead of law and circumcision (2–5); cf 2, 16; 3, 3. Faith, not circumcision, is what counts (6).

5, 1: Freedom: Paul stresses as the conclusion from the allegory in 4, 21–31 this result of Christ's work for us. It is a principle previously mentioned (2, 4), the responsible use of which v 13 will emphasize.

5, 3: Cf 3, 10–12. Just as those who seek to live by the law must carry out all its contents, so those who have faith and live by promise must stand firm in their freedom (1.13).

5, 6: Cf Rom 2, 25–26; 1 Cor 7, 19; Gal 6, 15. The Greek for **faith working through love** or "faith expressing itself through love" can also be rendered as "faith energized by (God's) love."

5, 7–12: Paul addresses the Galatians directly: with questions (7.11), a proverb (9), a statement (8), and biting sarcasm (12), seeking to persuade the Galatians to break with those trying to add law and circumcision to Christ as a basis for salvation.

5, 7: Running well: as in an athletic contest; cf 2, 2; 1 Cor 9, 24–26; Phil 2, 16; 3, 14.

5, 8: The one who called you: see the note on 1, 6.

5, 11: Preaching circumcision: this could refer to Paul's pre-Christian period (possibly as a missionary for Judaism); more

v Gn 16, 15; 21, 2–3. w Gn 17, 16; Rom 4, 19–20; 9, 7–9. x 3, 17 / Ex 19, 20 / Gn 16, 1. y Heb 12, 22; Rv 21, 2. z Is 54, 1. a Rom 9, 8. b Gn 21, 10. c 3, 29; Jn 8, 35. d 2, 4; 4, 5.9; Jn 8, 32.36. e 2, 21; Acts 15, 1–29. f 3, 10; Rom 2, 25; Jas 2, 10. g Rom 8, 23.25. h 3, 28; 6, 15; 1 Cor 7, 19. i 1, 6. j 1 Cor 5, 6. k 1, 7. 16, 12.14; 1 Cor 1, 23.

me, brothers, if I am still preaching circumcision,
why am I still being persecuted? In that case, the
stumbling block of the cross has been abolished.
12 *Would that those who are upsetting you
might also castrate themselves!

Freedom for Service 13 m *For you were called
for freedom, brothers. But do not use this
freedom as an opportunity for the flesh; rather,
serve one another through love. 14 n *For the
whole law is fulfilled in one statement, namely,
"You shall love your neighbor as yourself." 15 But
if you go on biting and devouring one another,
beware that you are not consumed by one
another.

16 o *I say, then: live by the Spirit and you will
certainly not gratify the desire of the flesh.
17 p For the flesh has desires against the Spirit,
and the Spirit against the flesh; these are op-
posed to each other, so that you may not do
what you want. 18 q But if you are guided by the
Spirit, you are not under the law. 19 r *Now the
works of the flesh are obvious: immorality,
impurity, licentiousness, 20 s idolatry, sorcery, ha-
treds, rivalry, jealousy, outbursts of fury, acts of
selfishness, dissensions, factions, 21 *occasions of
envy, drinking bouts, orgies, and the like. I warn
you, as I warned you before, that those who do
such things will not inherit the kingdom of God.
22 t In contrast, the fruit of the Spirit is love, joy,
peace, patience, kindness, generosity, faithful-
ness, 23 u gentleness, self-control. Against such
there is no law. 24 v Now those who belong to
Christ [Jesus] have crucified their flesh with its
passions and desires. 25 w If we live in the Spirit,
let us also follow the Spirit. 26 x Let us not be
conceited, provoking one another, envious of
one another.

CHAPTER 6

Life in the Community of Christ

1 y *Brothers, even if a person is caught in some
transgression, you who are spiritual should cor-
rect that one in a gentle spirit, looking to
yourself, so that you also may not be tempted.
2 z *Bear one another's burdens, and so you will
fulfill the law of Christ. 3 a For if anyone thinks he
is something when he is nothing, he is deluding
himself. 4 *Each one must examine his own
work, and then he will have reason to boast with
regard to himself alone, and not with regard to
someone else; 5 b for each will bear his own load.
6 c *One who is being instructed in the word
should share all good things with his instructor.
7 Make no mistake: God is not mocked, for a
person will reap only what he sows, 8 d because
the one who sows for his flesh will reap corrup-
tion from the flesh, but the one who sows for the
spirit will reap eternal life from the spirit. 9 e Let

---

probably it arose as a charge from opponents, based perhaps on the story in Acts 16, 1–3 that Paul had circumcised Timothy "on account of the Jews." Unlike the Gentile Titus in Gal 2, 3, Timothy was the son of a Jewish mother. **The stumbling block of the cross:** cf 1 Cor 1, 23.

5, 12: A sarcastic half-wish that their knife would go beyond mere circumcision; cf Phil 3, 2 and the note there.

5, 13–26: In light of another reminder of the freedom of the gospel (13; cf 1), Paul elaborates on what believers are called to do and be: they fulfill the law by love of neighbor (14–15), walking in the Spirit (16–26), as is illustrated by concrete **fruit of the Spirit** in their lives.

5, 13: Serve . . . through love: cf v 6.

5, 14: Lv 19, 18, emphasized by Jesus (Mt 22, 39; Lk 10, 27); cf Rom 13, 8–10.

5, 16–25: Spirit . . . flesh: cf 3, 3 and the note on Rom 8, 1–13.

5, 19–23: Such lists of vices and virtues (cf Rom 1, 29–31; 1 Cor 6, 9–10) were common in the ancient world. Paul contrasts **works of the flesh** (19) with **fruit** (not "works") **of the Spirit** (22). Not law, but the Spirit, leads to such traits.

5, 21: Occasions of envy: after the Greek word **phthonoi,** "envies," some manuscripts add a similar sounding one, **phonoi,** "murders."

6, 1–10: The ethical exhortations begun at 5, 1 continue with a variety of admonitions to the community (**brothers:** see the note on 1, 2). Nearly every sentence contains a separate item of practical advice; the faith and freedom of the gospel underlie each maxim. Tensions and temptation within communal life have previously been addressed in 5, 15.26, and v 1 continues with a case in which **a person is caught in some transgression** such as those in 5, 19–21; cf 2, 17.

6, 2: The law of Christ: cf Rom 8, 2; 1 Cor 9, 21; Gal 5, 14. The principle of love for others is meant. To **bear one another's burdens** is to "serve one another through love" (5, 13).

6, 4–5: Self-examination is the cure for self-deception. Compare what you are with what you were before, and give the glory to God; cf Rom 6, 19–22. **Load:** used elsewhere of a soldier's pack. Correcting one's own conduct avoids burdening others with it.

6, 6: Implies oral instruction in the faith by catechists; these are to be remunerated for their service; cf Rom 15, 27.

m 5, 1 / Rom 6, 18; 1 Cor 8, 9; 1 Pt 2, 16. n Lv 19, 18; Mt 22, 39; Rom 13, 8–10. o 5, 24–25; Rom 8, 5. p Rom 7, 15.23; 8, 6. q Rom 6, 14; 8, 14. r Rom 1, 29–31; 1 Cor 6, 9–10; Col 3, 5–6.8. s Rv 22, 15. t Eph 5, 9 / 1 Cor 13, 4–7; 2 Cor 6, 6; 1 Tm 4, 12; 2 Pt 1, 6. u 1 Tm 1, 9. v 2, 19; Rom 6, 6; 8, 13. w 5, 16. x Phil 2, 3. y Mt 18, 15; Jas 5, 19 / 1 Cor 10, 12–13. z Col 3, 13 / 1 Cor 9, 21. a 1 Cor 3, 18; 8, 2; 2 Cor 12, 11. b Rom 14, 12. c 1 Cor 9, 14. d Prv 11, 18; Rom 8, 6.13. e 2 Thes 3, 13; Heb 12, 1–3.

us not grow tired of doing good, for in due time
we shall reap our harvest, if we do not give up.
[10f]*So then, while we have the opportunity, let
us do good to all, but especially to those who
belong to the family of the faith.

VI: Conclusion

Final Appeal [11g]*See with what large letters I
am writing to you in my own hand! [12h]*It is
those who want to make a good appearance in
the flesh who are trying to compel you to have
yourselves circumcised, only that they may not
be persecuted for the cross of Christ. [13]*Not
even those having themselves circumcised ob-
serve the law themselves; they only want you to
be circumcised so that they may boast of your
flesh. [14i]*But may I never boast except in the
cross of our Lord Jesus Christ, through which
the world has been crucified to me, and I to the
world. [15j]*For neither does circumcision mean
anything, nor does uncircumcision, but only a
new creation. [16k]*Peace and mercy be to all
who follow this rule and to the Israel of God.

[17l]*From now on, let no one make troubles
for me; for I bear the marks of Jesus on my body.

[18m]The grace of our Lord Jesus Christ be with
your spirit, brothers. Amen.

6, 10: **The family of the faith:** the Christian household or church. Doing good has a universal object (**to all**), but the local community makes specific the reality of those to be served.

6, 11–18: A postscript in Paul's own hand, as was his practice (see 1 Cor 16, 21; 2 Thes 3, 17). Paul summarizes his appeal against his opponents (12–13), then returns to his message of glorying in the cross, not in circumcision, as the means of salvation (14–15; cf 5, 11). A benediction follows at v 16. In the polemical spirit that the attack on his apostleship called forth (1, 11—2, 21), Paul reasserts his missionary credentials (17) before giving a final benediction (18).

6, 11: **Large letters:** in contrast to the finer hand of the scribe who wrote the letter up to this point. The larger Greek letters make Paul's message even more emphatic. Some find a hint of poor eyesight on Paul's part. See the note on 4, 13.

6, 12–15: The Jewish Christian opponents wished **not to be persecuted,** possibly by Jews. But since Judaism seems to have had a privileged status as a religion in the Roman empire, circumcised Christians might, if taken as Jews, thereby avoid persecution from the Romans. In any case, Paul instead stresses conformity with **the cross of our Lord Jesus Christ;** cf 2, 19–21; 5, 11.

6, 13: **Those having themselves circumcised:** other manuscripts read, "those who have had themselves circumcised."

6, 14: **Through which:** or "through whom."

6, 15: **New creation:** or "new creature"; cf 2 Cor 5, 17.

6, 16: **This rule:** the principle in vv 14 and 15. **The Israel of God:** while the church may be meant (the phrase can be translated "to all who follow this rule, even the Israel of God"; cf 10; 1 Cor 10, 18), the reference may also be to God's ancient people, Israel; cf Pss 125, 5; 128, 6.

6, 17: **The marks of Jesus:** slaves were often branded by marks (**stigmata**) burned into their flesh to show to whom they belonged; so also were devotees of pagan gods. Paul implies that instead of outdated circumcision, his body bears the scars of his apostolic labors (2 Cor 11, 22–31), such as floggings (Acts 16, 22; 2 Cor 11, 25) and stonings (Acts 14, 19), that mark him as belonging to the Christ who suffered (cf Rom 6, 3; 2 Cor 4, 10; Col 1, 24) and will protect his own.

f 1 Thes 5, 15. g 1 Cor 16, 21. h 5, 2.11. i 2, 20; 1 Cor 2, 2. j 5, 6; 1 Cor 7, 19 / 2 Cor 5, 17. k Pss 125, 5; 128, 6. l 2 Cor 4, 10. m Phil 4, 23; 2 Tm 4, 22; Phlm 25.

THE LETTER TO THE EPHESIANS

Ephesians is the great Pauline letter about the church. It deals, however, not so much with a congregation in the city of Ephesus in Asia Minor as with the worldwide church, the head of which is Christ (4, 15), the purpose of which is to be the instrument for making God's plan of salvation known throughout the universe (3, 9-10). Yet this ecclesiology is anchored in God's saving love, shown in Jesus Christ (2, 4-10), and the whole of redemption is rooted in the plan and accomplishment of the triune God (1, 3-14). The language is often that of doxology (1, 3-14) and prayer (cf 1, 15-23; 3, 14-19), indeed of liturgy and hymns (3, 20-21; 5, 14).

The majestic chapters of Ephesians emphasize the unity in the church of Christ that has come about for both Jews and Gentiles within God's household (1, 15—2, 22, especially 2, 11-22) and indeed the "seven unities" of church, Spirit, hope; one Lord, faith, and baptism; and the one God (4, 4-6). Yet the concern is not with the church for its own sake but rather as the means for mission in the world (3, 1—4, 24). The gifts Christ gives its members are to lead to growth and renewal (4, 7-24). Ethical admonition is not lacking either; all aspects of human life and relationships are illumined by the light of Christ (4, 25—6, 20).

The letter is seemingly addressed by Paul to Christians in Ephesus (1, 1), a place where the apostle labored for well over two years (Acts 19, 10). Yet there is a curiously impersonal tone to the writing for a community with which Paul was so intimately acquainted (cf 3, 2 and 4, 21). There are no personal greetings (cf 6, 23). More significantly, important early manuscripts omit the words "in Ephesus" (see the note on 1, 1). Many therefore regard the letter as an encyclical or "circular letter" sent to a number of churches in Asia Minor, the addressees to be designated in each place by its bearer, Tychicus (6, 21-22). Others think that Ephesians is the letter referred to in Colossians 4, 16 as "to the Laodiceans."

Paul, who is designated as the sole author at 1, 1, is described in almost unparalleled terms with regard to the significant role he has in God's plan for bringing the Gentiles to faith in Christ (3, 1-12). Yet at the time of writing he is clearly in prison (3, 1; 4, 1; 6, 20), suffering afflictions (3, 13). Traditionally this "Captivity Epistle" has, along with Colossians, Philippians, and Philemon, been dated to an imprisonment in Rome, likely in A.D. 61–63. Others appeal to an earlier imprisonment, perhaps in Caesarea (Acts 23, 27—27, 2). Since the early ninteenth century, however, much of critical scholarship has considered the letter's style and use of words (especially when compared with Colossians), its concept of the church, and other points of doctrine put forward by the writer as grounds for serious doubt about authorship by Paul. The letter may then be the work of a secretary writing at the apostle's direction or of a later disciple who sought to develop Paul's ideas for a new situation around A.D. 80–100.

The principal divisions of the Letter to the Ephesians are the following:

I. Address (1, 1-14)
II. Unity of the Church in Christ (1, 15—2, 22)
III. World Mission of the Church (3, 1—4, 24)
IV. Daily Conduct, an Expression of Unity (4, 25—6, 20)
V. Conclusion (6, 21-24)

I: Address

CHAPTER 1

Greeting [1] [a]*Paul, an apostle of Christ Jesus by
the will of God, to the holy ones who are [in
Ephesus] faithful in Christ Jesus: [2] [b]grace to you
and peace from God our Father and the Lord
Jesus Christ.

The Father's Plan of Salvation [3] [c]*Blessed be
the God and Father of our Lord Jesus Christ,
who has blessed us in Christ with every spiritual
blessing in the heavens, [4] [d]as he chose us in him,
before the foundation of the world, to be holy
and without blemish before him. In love [5] [e]he
destined us for adoption to himself through Jesus

1, 1–2: For the epistolary form used at the beginning of letters, see the note on Rom 1, 1–7. Twenty-two of the thirty Greek words in vv 1–2 also occur in Col 1, 1–2.

1, 1: [In Ephesus]: the phrase is lacking in important early witnesses such as P^{46} (3rd cent.), and Sinaiticus and Vaticanus (4th cent.), appearing in the latter two as a fifth-century addition. Basil and Origen mention its absence from manuscripts. See Introduction. Without the phrase, the Greek can be rendered, as in Col 1, 2, "to the holy ones and faithful brothers in Christ."

1, 3–14: While a Pauline letter usually continues after the greeting with a prayer of thanksgiving, as in 15–23 below, Ephesians first inserts a blessing of God for the blessings Christians have experienced, as in 2 Cor 1, 3–4 and 1 Pt 1, 3–12. The blessing here, akin to a Jewish **berakah,** is rich in images almost certainly drawn from hymns and liturgy. Many ideas here are also found in Col 1, 3–23. Certain phrases are frequently repeated, such as **in Christ** (3.10.12) or **in him** (4.7.9.11.13) or **in the Beloved** (6) and **(for) the praise of (his) glory** (6.12.14). Some terms like **chose** (4) and **destined** (5) reflect Old Testament theology (Dt 7, 7; 9, 4–6; 23, 5) or Pauline themes (**redemption,** 7.14; **grace,** 6.7) or specific emphases in Col (**forgiveness,** Col 1, 14).

A triadic structure is discernible in vv 3–14: **God the Father**

a Rom 1, 7; 1 Cor 1, 1–2; Col 1, 1. b Col 1, 2. c 2, 6; 2 Cor 1, 3. d 5, 27; Jn 15, 16; 17, 24; Rom 8, 29; 2 Thes 2, 13. e Jn 1, 12; 1 Jn 3, 1.

Christ, in accord with the favor of his will, [6] [f]for the praise of the glory of his grace that he granted us in the beloved.

Fulfillment through Christ [7] [g]In him we have redemption by his blood, the forgiveness of transgressions, in accord with the riches of his grace [8] [h]that he lavished upon us. In all wisdom and insight, [9] [i]*he has made known to us the mystery of his will in accord with his favor that he set forth in him [10] [j]as a plan for the fullness of times, to sum up all things in Christ, in heaven and on earth.

Inheritance through the Spirit [11] [k]In him we were also chosen, destined in accord with the purpose of the One who accomplishes all things according to the intention of his will, [12] *so that we might exist for the praise of his glory, we who first hoped in Christ. [13] [l]*In him you also, who have heard the word of truth, the gospel of your salvation, and have believed in him, were sealed with the promised holy Spirit, [14] [m]*which is the first installment of our inheritance toward redemption as God's possession, to the praise of his glory.

II: Unity of the Church in Christ

The Church as Christ's Body [15] [n]*Therefore, I, too, hearing of your faith in the Lord Jesus and of your love for all the holy ones, [16] [o]do not cease giving thanks for you, remembering you in my prayers, [17] [p]that the God of our Lord Jesus Christ, the Father of glory, may give you a spirit of wisdom and revelation resulting in knowledge of him. [18] [q]May the eyes of [your] hearts be enlightened, that you may know what is the hope that belongs to his call, what are the riches of glory in his inheritance among the holy ones, [19] [r]and what is the surpassing greatness of his power for us who believe, in accord with the exercise of his great might, [20] [s]which he worked in Christ, raising him from the dead and seating him at his right hand in the heavens, [21] [t]far above every principality, authority, power, and dominion, and every name that is named not only in this age but also in the one to come. [22] [u]And he put all things beneath his feet and gave him as head over all things to the church, [23] [v]*which is his body, the fullness of the one who fills all things in every way.

(3–6.8.11), **Christ** (3.5.7–10.12), and the **Spirit** (13–14). The spiritual blessings Christians have received through Christ (3) are gratefully enumerated: the call to holiness (4; cf Col 1, 22); the gift of divine **adoption** establishing a unique spiritual relationship with God the Father through Christ (5; cf Gal 4, 5); liberation from sin through Christ's sacrificial death (7); revelation of God's plan of salvation in Christ (9; cf 3, 3–4; Rom 16, 25); the gift of election and faith in Christ bestowed upon Jewish Christians (see the note on 12, **we who first hoped in Christ**); and finally, the same gift granted to Gentiles (13, **you also**). In the Christ-centered faith and existence of the Christian communities the apostle sees the predetermined **plan** of God to bring all creation under the final rule of Christ (4–5.9–10) being **made known** (9) and carried through, to God's **glory** (6.12.14). ened in them through the message of the gospel (13.17–19). Those blessings are seen in the context of God's **might** in establishing the sovereignty of Christ over all other creatures (19–21) and in appointing him **head** of the church (22–23). For the allusion to angelic spirits in v 21, see Rom 8, 38 and Col 1, 16. Here, as in 1 Cor 15, 24–25 and Col 2, 15, every such **principality** and **power** is made subject to Christ.

1, 3: **In the heavens:** literally, "in the heavenlies" or "in the heavenly places," a term in Eph for the divine realm.

1, 9: **Mystery:** as in Rom 16, 25; Col 1, 26.27 and elsewhere, a secret of God now revealed in the **plan** to save and **sum up all things in Christ** (10); cf 3, 3–6.

1, 12: **We who first hoped:** probably Jewish Christians (contrast 13, **you**, the Gentiles); possibly the people of Israel, "we who already enjoyed the hope of Christ," or perhaps present hope in contrast to future redemption (cf 14).

1, 13: **Sealed:** by God, in baptism; cf 4, 30; 2 Cor 1, 22.

1, 14: **First installment:** down payment by God on full salvation, as at 2 Cor 1, 22.

1, 15–23: See the note on Rom 1, 8 for the thanksgiving form in a letter. Much of the content parallels thoughts in Col 1, 3–20. The prayer moves from God and Christ (17.20–21) to the Ephesians (17–19) and the church (22–23). Paul asks that the blessing imparted by God the Father (3) to the Ephesians will be strength-

1, 15: **Your faith . . . your love:** some manuscripts omit the latter phrase, but cf Col 1, 4.

1, 23: **His body:** the church (22); cf the note on Col 1, 18. Only in Eph and Col is Christ the **head** of the **body**, in contrast to the view in 1 Cor 12 and Rom 12, 4–8 where Christ is equated with the entire body or community. **Fullness:** see the note on Col 1, 19. Some take **the one who fills** as God, others as Christ (cf 4, 10). If in Christ "dwells the fullness of the deity bodily" (Col 2, 9), then, as God "fills" Christ, Christ in turn fills the church and the believer (3, 19; 5, 18). But the difficult phrases here may also allow the church to be viewed as the "complement" of Christ who is "being filled" as God's plan for the universe is carried out through the church (cf 3, 9–10).

f Mt 3, 17; Col 1, 13. g 2, 7–13; Rom 3, 24; Col 1, 14.20. h Col 1, 9. i 3, 3.9; Rom 16, 25. j Gal 4, 4; Col 1, 16.20. k Is 46, 10; Rom 8, 28; Col 1, 12; Rv 4, 11. l 4, 30; Acts 2, 33; Col 1, 5–6. m 2 Cor 1, 22; 5, 5. n Col 1, 3–4; Phlm 4–5. o Col 1, 3.9. p 3, 14.16; Col 1, 9–10; 1 Jn 5, 20. q 4, 4; Col 1, 12.27. r 2 Cor 13, 4; Col 1, 11; 2, 12. s Ps 110, 1; Heb 1, 3. t Phil 2, 9; Col 1, 16; 1 Pt 3, 22. u 4, 15; Ps 8, 7; Mt 28, 18; Col 1, 18. v 4, 10.12; Rom 12, 5; 1 Cor 12, 27; Col 1, 19.

CHAPTER 2

Generosity of God's Plan [1 w]*You were dead
in your transgressions and sins [2 x]*in which you
once lived following the age of this world,
following the ruler of the power of the air, the
spirit that is now at work in the disobedient.
[3 y]All of us once lived among them in the desires
of our flesh, following the wishes of the flesh and
the impulses, and we were by nature children of
wrath, like the rest. [4]But God, who is rich in
mercy, because of the great love he had for us,
[5 z]*even when we were dead in our transgres-
sions, brought us to life with Christ (by grace
you have been saved), [6 a]raised us up with him,
and seated us with him in the heavens in Christ
Jesus, [7 b]that in the ages to come he might show
the immeasurable riches of his grace in his
kindness to us in Christ Jesus. [8 c]For by grace you
have been saved through faith, and this is not
from you; it is the gift of God; [9 d]it is not from
works, so no one may boast. [10 e]For we are his
handiwork, created in Christ Jesus for the good
works that God has prepared in advance, that
we should live in them.
One in Christ [11]*Therefore, remember that at
one time you, Gentiles in the flesh, called the
uncircumcision by those called the circumcision,
which is done in the flesh by human hands,
[12 f]*were at that time without Christ, alienated
from the community of Israel and strangers to
the covenants of promise, without hope and
without God in the world. [13 g]But now in Christ
Jesus you who once were far off have become
near by the blood of Christ.

[14 h]*For he is our peace, he who made both
one and broke down the dividing wall of enmity,
through his flesh, [15 i]*abolishing the law with its
commandments and legal claims, that he might
create in himself one new person in place of the
two, thus establishing peace, [16 j]and might recon-
cile both with God, in one body, through the
cross, putting that enmity to death by it. [17 k]He
came and preached peace to you who were far
off and peace to those who were near, [18 l]for

2, 1–22: The gospel of **salvation** (1, 13) that God **worked in Christ** (1, 20) is reiterated in terms of what God's **great love** (4), expressed in Christ, means for us. The passage sometimes addresses **you,** Gentiles (1–2.8.11–13.19.22), but other times speaks of **all of us** who believe (3–7.10.14.18). In urging people to **remember** their grim past when they were **dead** in sins (1–3.11–12) and what they are **now in Christ** (4–10.13), the author sees both Jew and Gentile reconciled with God, now **one new person,** a new humanity, **one body, the household of God, a temple** and **dwelling place** of God's Spirit (15–16.19–22). The presentation falls into two parts, the second stressing more the meaning for the church.

2, 1–10: The recipients of Paul's letter have experienced, in their redemption from **transgressions and sins,** the effect of Christ's supremacy over the power of the devil (1–2; cf 6, 11–12), who rules not from the netherworld but from the **air** between God in heaven and human beings on earth. Both Jew and Gentile have experienced, through Christ, God's free gift of salvation that already marks them for a future heavenly destiny (3–7). The language **dead, raised us up,** and **seated us . . . in the heavens** closely parallels Jesus' own passion and Easter experience. The terms in vv 8–9 describe salvation in the way Paul elsewhere speaks of justification: **by grace, through faith, the gift of God, not from works;** cf Gal 2, 16–21; Rom 3, 24–28. Christians are a newly created people in Christ, fashioned by God for a life of goodness (10).

2, 1–7: These verses comprise one long sentence in Greek, the main verb coming in v 5, God **brought us to life,** the object you/us **dead in . . . transgressions** being repeated in 1 and 5; cf Col 2, 13.

2, 2: Age of this world: or "aeon," a term found in gnostic thought, possibly synonymous with **the rulers of this world,** but also reflecting the Jewish idea of "two ages," this present evil age and "the age to come"; cf 1 Cor 3, 19; 5, 10; 7, 31; Gal 1, 4; Ti 2, 12. **The disobedient:** literally, "the sons of disobedience," a Semitism as at Is 30, 9.

2, 5: Our relation through baptism **with Christ,** the risen Lord, is depicted in terms of realized eschatology, as already exaltation, though v 7 brings in the future aspect too.

2, 11–22: The Gentiles lacked Israel's messianic expectation, lacked the various **covenants** God made with **Israel,** lacked **hope** of salvation and knowledge of the true **God** (11–12); but through Christ all these religious barriers between Jew and Gentile have been transcended (13–14) by the abolition of the Mosaic covenant-law (15) for the sake of uniting Jew and Gentile into a single religious community (15–16), imbued with the same holy **Spirit** and worshiping the same **Father** (18). The Gentiles are now included in God's **household** (19) as it arises upon the **foundation** of **apostles** assisted by those endowed with the prophetic gift (3, 5), the preachers of Christ (20; cf 1 Cor 12, 28). With Christ as the **capstone** (20; cf Is 28, 16; Mt 21, 42), they are being built into the holy **temple** of God's people where the divine presence dwells (21–22).

2, 12: The community of Israel: or "commonwealth"; cf 4, 18. **The covenants:** cf Rom 9, 4: with Abraham, with Moses, with David.

2, 14–16: The elaborate imagery here combines pictures of Christ as **our peace** (Is 9, 5), his crucifixion, the ending of the Mosaic law (cf Col 2, 14), reconciliation (2 Cor 5, 18–21), and the destruction of **the dividing wall** such as kept people from God in the temple or a barrier in the heavens.

2, 15: One new person: a corporate body, the Christian community, made up of Jews and Gentiles, replacing ancient divisions; cf Rom 1, 16.

w Col 1, 21; 2, 13. x 6, 12; Jn 12, 31; Col 1, 13. y Col 3, 6–7. z Rom 5, 8; 6, 13; Col 2, 13. a Rom 8, 10–11; Phil 3, 20; Col 2, 12. b 1, 7. c Rom 3, 24; Gal 2, 16. d 1 Cor 1, 29. e 4, 24; Ti 2, 14. f Rom 9, 4; Col 1, 21.27. g 2, 17; Is 57, 19; Col 1, 20. h Gal 3, 28. i 2 Cor 5, 17; Col 2, 14. j Col 1, 20.22. k Is 57, 19; Zec 9, 10. 13, 12.

through him we both have access in one Spirit to the Father.
[19] [m]So then you are no longer strangers and sojourners, but you are fellow citizens with the holy ones and members of the household of God, [20] [n]*built upon the foundation of the apostles and prophets, with Christ Jesus himself as the capstone. [21] [o]Through him the whole structure is held together and grows into a temple sacred in the Lord; [22] [p]in him you also are being built together into a dwelling place of God in the Spirit.

III: World Mission of the Church

CHAPTER 3

Commission to Preach God's Plan [1] [q]*Because of this, I, Paul, a prisoner of Christ [Jesus] for you Gentiles— [2] [r]*if, as I suppose, you have heard of the stewardship of God's grace that was given to me for your benefit, [3] [s]*[namely, that] the mystery was made known to me by revelation, as I have written briefly earlier. [4]When you read this you can understand my insight into the mystery of Christ, [5] [t]which was not made known to human beings in other generations as it has now been revealed to his holy apostles and prophets by the Spirit, [6] [u]that the Gentiles are coheirs, members of the same body, and copartners in the promise in Christ Jesus through the gospel.

[7] [v]Of this I became a minister by the gift of God's grace that was granted me in accord with the exercise of his power. [8] [w]To me, the very least of all the holy ones, this grace was given, to preach to the Gentiles the inscrutable riches of Christ, [9] [x]*and to bring to light [for all] what is the plan of the mystery hidden from ages past in God who created all things, [10] [y]*so that the manifold wisdom of God might now be made known through the church to the principalities and authorities in the heavens. [11]This was according to the eternal purpose that he accomplished in Christ Jesus our Lord, [12] [z]in whom we have boldness of speech and confidence of access through faith in him. [13] [a]So I ask you not to lose heart over my afflictions for you; this is your glory.

Prayer for the Readers [14]*For this reason I kneel before the Father, [15]from whom every family in heaven and on earth is named, [16] [b]that he may grant you in accord with the riches of his glory to be strengthened with power through his Spirit in the inner self, [17] [c]and that Christ may dwell in your hearts through faith; that you, rooted and grounded in love, [18] [d]may have strength to comprehend with all the holy ones what is the breadth and length and height and

2, 20: Capstone: the Greek can also mean cornerstone or keystone.

3, 1–13: Paul reflects on his mission to the Gentiles. He alludes to his call and appointment to the apostolic office (2–3) and how his **insight** through revelation, as well as that of the other apostles and charismatic prophets in the church (4–5), has deepened understanding of God's plan of salvation in Christ. Paul is the special herald (7) of a new **promise** to the **Gentiles** (6): that the divine plan includes them in the spiritual benefits promised to Israel. Not only is this unique apostolic role his; Paul also has been given the task of explaining to all the divine **plan** of salvation (8–9), once **hidden.** Through **the church,** God's plan to save through Christ is becoming manifest to angelic beings (10; cf 1, 21), in accord with God's **purpose** (11). The fulfillment of the plan in Christ gives the whole church more **confidence** through **faith** in God (12). The readers of this letter are also thereby encouraged to greater confidence despite Paul's imprisonment (13).

3, 1: A prisoner of Christ: see Introduction. Paul abruptly departs from his train of thought at the end of v 1, leaving an incomplete sentence.

3, 2: Stewardship: the Greek is the same term employed at 1, 10 for the **plan** that God administers (Col 1, 25) and in which Paul plays a key role.

3, 3–4: The mystery: God's resolve to deliver Gentiles along with Israel through Christ; cf the notes on 1, 10; 3, 9.

3, 9: [For all]: while some think this phrase was added so as to yield the sense "to enlighten all about the plan . . . ," it is more likely that some manuscripts and Fathers omitted it accidentally or to avoid the idea that **all** conflicted with Paul's assignment to preach to **the Gentiles** (8) specifically.

3, 10: Principalities and authorities: see the note on 1, 15–23 regarding v 21.

3, 14–21: The apostle prays that those he is addressing may, like the rest of the church, deepen their understanding of God's plan of salvation in Christ. It is a plan that affects the whole universe (15) with **the breadth and length and height and depth** of God's love in Christ (18) or possibly the universe in all its dimensions. The apostle prays that they may perceive the redemptive love of Christ for them and be completely immersed in the fullness of God (19). The prayer concludes with a doxology to God (20–21).

3, 14–15: Every family: in the Greek there is wordplay on the word for **the Father (patria, patēr)**. The phrase could also mean "God's whole family" (cf 2, 21).

m Heb 12, 22–23. n Is 28, 16; Rv 21, 14. o 1 Cor 3, 16; Col 2, 19. p 1 Pt 2, 5. q Phil 1, 7.13; Col 1, 24–29; 4, 18; Phlm 1, 9; 2 Tm 2, 9. r Col 1, 25. s 1, 9–10; Col 1, 26. t Col 1, 26. u 2, 13.18–19. v Rom 15, 15; Col 1, 25.29. w 1 Cor 15, 8–10; Gal 1, 16; 2, 7–9. x Rom 16, 25; Col 1, 26–27. y 1 Pt 1, 12. z Rom 5, 1–2; Heb 4, 16. a Col 1, 22.24; 2 Tm 2, 10. b 6, 10; Rom 7, 22; 2 Cor 4, 16; Col 1, 11. c Jn 14, 23; Col 1, 23; 2, 7. d Col 2, 2.

depth, [19][e]and to know the love of Christ that surpasses knowledge, so that you may be filled with all the fullness of God.

[20][f]Now to him who is able to accomplish far more than all we ask or imagine, by the power at work within us, [21]to him be glory in the church and in Christ Jesus to all generations, forever and ever. Amen.

CHAPTER 4

Unity in the Body [1][g]*I, then, a prisoner for the Lord, urge you to live in a manner worthy of the call you have received, [2][h]with all humility and gentleness, with patience, bearing with one another through love, [3][i]striving to preserve the unity of the spirit through the bond of peace: [4][j]*one body and one Spirit, as you were also called to the one hope of your call; [5][k]one Lord, one faith, one baptism; [6][l]one God and Father of all, who is over all and through all and in all.

Diversity of Gifts [7][m]But grace was given to each of us according to the measure of Christ's gift. [8][n]*Therefore, it says:

> "He ascended on high and took prisoners
> captive;
> he gave gifts to men."

[9]What does "he ascended" mean except that he also descended into the lower [regions] of the earth? [10]The one who descended is also the one who ascended far above all the heavens, that he might fill all things.

[11][o]*And he gave some as apostles, others as prophets, others as evangelists, others as pastors and teachers, [12]*to equip the holy ones for the work of ministry, for building up the body of Christ, [13][p]*until we all attain to the unity of faith and knowledge of the Son of God, to mature manhood, to the extent of the full stature of Christ, [14][q]so that we may no longer be infants, tossed by waves and swept along by every wind of teaching arising from human trickery, from their cunning in the interests of deceitful scheming. [15][r]*Rather, living the truth in love, we should grow in every way into him who is the head, Christ, [16][s]from whom the whole body, joined and held together by every supporting ligament, with the proper functioning of each part, brings about the body's growth and builds itself up in love.

Renewal in Christ [17][t]*So I declare and testify in the Lord that you must no longer live as the Gentiles do, in the futility of their minds; [18][u]darkened in understanding, alienated from the life of God because of their ignorance, because of their hardness of heart, [19][v]they have become callous and have handed themselves over to licentiousness for the practice of every

4, 1–16: A general plea for unity in the church. Christians have been fashioned through the **Spirit** into a single harmonious religious community (**one body,** 4.12; cf 16), belonging to a single **Lord** (in contrast to the many gods of the pagan world), and by one way of salvation through **faith,** brought out especially by the significance of **baptism** (1–6; cf Rom 6, 1–11). But Christian unity is more than adherence to a common belief. It is manifested in the exalted Christ's gifts to individuals to serve so as to make the community more Christlike (11–16). This teaching on Christ as the source of the gifts is introduced in v 8 by a citation of Ps 68, 18, which depicts Yahweh triumphantly leading Israel to salvation in Jerusalem. It is here understood of Christ, ascending **above all the heavens,** the **head** of the church; through his redemptive death, resurrection, and ascension he has become the source of the church's spiritual gifts. The "descent" of Christ (9–10) refers more probably to the incarnation (cf Phil 2, 6–8) than to Christ's presence after his death in the world of the dead (cf 1 Pt 3, 19).

4, 4–6: The "seven unities" (church, **Spirit, hope; Lord, faith** in Christ [1, 13], **baptism; one God**) reflect the triune structure of later creeds in reverse.

4, 8–10: While the emphasis is on an ascension and gift-giving by Christ, there is also a reference in taking **prisoners captive** to the aeons and powers mentioned at 1, 21; 2, 2; 3, 10; and 6, 12.

4, 11: Concerning this list of ministers, cf 1 Cor 12, 28 and Rom 12, 6–8. **Evangelists:** missionary preachers (cf Acts 21, 8 and 2 Tm 4, 5), not those who wrote gospels. **Pastors and teachers:** a single group in the Greek, shepherding congregations.

4, 12: The ministerial leaders in v 11 are to equip the whole people of God for their **work of ministry.**

4, 13: Mature manhood: literally, "a perfect man" (cf Col 1, 28), possibly the "one new person" of 2, 15, though there **anthrōpos** suggests humanity, while here **anēr** is the term for male. This personage becomes visible in the church's growing to its fullness in the unity of those who believe in Christ.

4, 15–16: The head, Christ: cf Col 1, 18 and contrast 1 Cor 12, 12–27 and Rom 12, 4–5 where Christ is identified with the whole body, including the head. The imagery may derive from ancient views in medicine, the **head** coordinating and caring for the body, each **ligament** (perhaps the ministers of v 11) supporting the whole. But as at 2, 19–22, where the temple is depicted as a growing organism, there may also be the idea here of growing toward the capstone, Christ.

4, 17–24: Paul begins to indicate how the new life in Christ contrasts with the Gentiles' old way of existence. Literally, **the old self** (22) and **the new self** (24) are "the old man" and "the new man" (**anthrōpos,** person), as at 2, 15; cf the note on 4, 13.

e Col 2, 3.9. f Rom 16, 25–27; Col 1, 29. g 3, 1; Col 1, 10. h Col 3, 12–13. i Col 3, 14–15. j Rom 12, 5; 1 Cor 10, 17; 12, 12–13. k 1 Cor 8, 6. l 1 Cor 12, 6. m Rom 12, 3.6; 1 Cor 12, 28. n Ps 68, 19; Col 2, 15. o 1 Cor 12, 28. p Col 1, 28. q 1 Cor 14, 20; Col 2, 4.8; Heb 13, 9; Jas 1, 6. r 1 Cor 11, 3; Col 1, 18; 2, 19. s Col 2, 19. t Rom 1, 21. u Col 1, 21; 1 Pt 1, 14. v Col 3, 5.

kind of impurity to excess. [20]That is not how you learned Christ, [21]assuming that you have heard of him and were taught in him, as truth is in Jesus, [22][w]that you should put away the old self of your former way of life, corrupted through deceitful desires, [23][x]and be renewed in the spirit of your minds, [24][y]*and put on the new self, created in God's way in righteousness and holiness of truth.

IV: Daily Conduct, an Expression of Unity

Rules for the New Life [25][z]*Therefore, putting away falsehood, speak the truth, each one to his neighbor, for we are members one of another. [26][a]*Be angry but do not sin; do not let the sun set on your anger, [27][b]and do not leave room for the devil. [28][c]*The thief must no longer steal, but rather labor, doing honest work with his [own] hands, so that he may have something to share with one in need. [29][d]No foul language should come out of your mouths, but only such as is good for needed edification, that it may impart grace to those who hear. [30]*And do not grieve the holy Spirit of God, with which you were sealed for the day of redemption. [31][e]All bitterness, fury, anger, shouting, and reviling must be removed from you, along with all malice. [32][f][And] be kind to one another, compassionate, forgiving one another as God has forgiven you in Christ.

CHAPTER 5

[1][g]*So be imitators of God, as beloved children, [2][h]and live in love, as Christ loved us and handed himself over for us as a sacrificial offering to God for a fragrant aroma. [3][i]Immorality or any impurity or greed must not even be mentioned among you, as is fitting among holy ones, [4][j]no obscenity or silly or suggestive talk, which is out of place, but instead, thanksgiving. [5][k]Be sure of this, that no immoral or impure or greedy person, that is, an idolater, has any inheritance in the kingdom of Christ and of God.

Duty to Live in the Light [6][l]*Let no one deceive you with empty arguments, for because of these things the wrath of God is coming upon the disobedient. [7]So do not be associated with them. [8][m]For you were once darkness, but now you are light in the Lord. Live as children of light, [9][n]for light produces every kind of goodness and righteousness and truth. [10][o]Try to learn what is pleasing to the Lord. [11][p]Take no part in the fruitless works of darkness; rather expose them, [12]for it is shameful even to mention the things done by them in secret; [13][q]but everything exposed by the light becomes visible, [14][r]*for everything that becomes visible is light. Therefore, it says:

"Awake, O sleeper,
  and arise from the dead,
and Christ will give you light."

[15][s]*Watch carefully then how you live, not as foolish persons but as wise, [16]making the most of the opportunity, because the days are evil. [17]Therefore, do not continue in ignorance, but try to understand what is the will of the Lord. [18][t]And do not get drunk on wine, in which lies debauchery, but be filled with the Spirit, [19][u]addressing one another [in] psalms and hymns and spiritual songs, singing and playing to the Lord in your hearts, [20][v]giving thanks always and for everything in the name of our Lord Jesus Christ to God the Father.

4, 24: Put on: in baptism. See the note on Gal 3, 27.

4, 25—6, 20: For similar exhortations to a morally good life in response to God's gift of faith, see the notes on Rom 12, 1—13, 14 and Gal 5, 13–26.

4, 26: If angry, seek reconciliation that day, not giving the devil (6, 11) opportunity to lead into sin.

4, 28: Honest work: literally, "the good." **His [own] hands:** some manuscripts have the full phrase as in 1 Cor 4, 12.

4, 30: See the note on 1, 13.

5, 1: Imitators of God: in forgiving (4, 32) and in loving (as exhibited in how **Christ loved us**).

5, 6: See the note on 2, 2.

5, 14: An early Christian hymn, possibly from a baptismal liturgy. For the content compare 2, 5–6; 3, 9 and Is 60, 1.

5, 15–16.19–20: The wording is similar to Col 4, 5 and 3, 16–17.

w Rom 8, 13; Gal 6, 8; Col 3, 9. x Rom 12, 2. y Gn 1, 26–27; Col 3, 10. z Zec 8, 16. a Ps 4, 5 LXX; Mt 5, 22. b 2 Cor 2, 11. c 1 Thes 4, 11. d 5, 4; Col 3, 16; 4, 6. e Col 3, 8. f Mt 6, 14; Col 3, 12–13. g Mt 5, 45.48. h Ex 29, 18; Ps 40, 7; Gal 2, 20; 1 Jn 3, 16. i Gal 5, 19; Col 3, 5. j 4, 29; Col 3, 8. k 1 Cor 6, 9–10; Gal 5, 21; Col 3, 5. l Rom 1, 18; Col 2, 4.8. m 2, 11–13; Jn 12, 36; Col 1, 12–13. n Gal 5, 22. o Rom 12, 2. p Rom 13, 12. q Jn 3, 20–21. r Is 26, 19; 60, 1. s Col 4, 5. t Prv 23, 31 LXX; Lk 21, 34. u Ps 33, 2–3; Col 3, 16. v Col 3, 17.

Wives and Husbands 21 [w]*Be subordinate to one another out of reverence for Christ. 22 [x]Wives should be subordinate to their husbands as to the Lord. 23 [y]For the husband is head of his wife just as Christ is head of the church, he himself the savior of the body. 24 As the church is subordinate to Christ, so wives should be subordinate to their husbands in everything. 25 [z]Husbands, love your wives, even as Christ loved the church and handed himself over for her 26 [a]to sanctify her, cleansing her by the bath of water with the word, 27 [b]that he might present to himself the church in splendor, without spot or wrinkle or any such thing, that she might be holy and without blemish. 28 So [also] husbands should love their wives as their own bodies. He who loves his wife loves himself. 29 For no one hates his own flesh but rather nourishes and cherishes it, even as Christ does the church, 30 [c]because we are members of his body.

31 [d]"For this reason a man shall leave [his] father
and [his] mother
and be joined to his wife,
and the two shall become one flesh."

32 [e]This is a great mystery, but I speak in reference to Christ and the church. 33 In any case, each one of you should love his wife as himself, and the wife should respect her husband.

CHAPTER 6

Children and Parents 1 [f]Children, obey your parents [in the Lord], for this is right. 2 [g]"Honor your father and mother." This is the first commandment with a promise, 3 "that it may go well with you and that you may have a long life on earth." 4 [h]Fathers, do not provoke your children to anger, but bring them up with the training and instruction of the Lord.

Slaves and Masters 5 [i]Slaves, be obedient to your human masters with fear and trembling, in sincerity of heart, as to Christ, 6 [j]not only when being watched, as currying favor, but as slaves of Christ, doing the will of God from the heart, 7 willingly serving the Lord and not human beings, 8 knowing that each will be requited from the Lord for whatever good he does, whether he is slave or free. 9 [k]Masters, act in the same way toward them, and stop bullying, knowing that both they and you have a Master in heaven and that with him there is no partiality.

Battle against Evil 10 *Finally, draw your strength from the Lord and from his mighty power. 11 [l]Put on the armor of God so that you may be able to stand firm against the tactics of the devil. 12 [m]For our struggle is not with flesh and blood but with the principalities, with the powers, with the world rulers of this present darkness, with the evil spirits in the heavens. 13 [n]Therefore, put on the armor of God, that you may be able to resist on the evil day and, having done everything, to hold your ground. 14 [o]So stand fast with your loins girded in truth, clothed

5, 21—6, 9: Cf the notes on Col 3, 18—4, 1 and 1 Pt 2, 18—3, 7 for a similar listing of household duties where the inferior is admonished first (**wives,** 5, 22; **children,** 6, 1; **slaves,** 6, 5), then the superior (**husbands,** 5, 25; **fathers,** 6, 4; **masters,** 6, 9). Paul varies this pattern by an emphasis on mutuality (see 5, 20); use of Old Testament material about **father and mother** in 6, 2; the judgment to come for slave-owners (**you have a Master in heaven,** 6, 9); and above all the initial principle of subordination **to one another** under **Christ,** thus effectively undermining exclusive claims to domination by one party. Into the section on **wives** and **husbands** an elaborate teaching on **Christ** and **the church** has been woven (5, 22–33).

5, 21–33: The apostle exhorts married Christians to a strong mutual love. Holding with Gn 2, 24 that marriage is a divine institution (31), Paul sees Christian marriage as taking on a new meaning symbolic of the intimate relationship of love between Christ and the church. The wife should serve her husband in the same spirit as that of the church's service to Christ (22.24), and the husband should care for his wife with the devotion of Christ to the church (25–30). Paul gives to the Genesis passage its highest meaning in the light of the union of Christ and the church, of which Christlike loyalty and devotion in Christian marriage are a clear reflection (31–33).

6, 10–20: A general exhortation to courage and prayer. Drawing upon the imagery and ideas of Is 11, 5; 59, 16–17; and Wis 5, 17–23, Paul describes the Christian in terms of the dress and equipment of Roman soldiers. He observes, however, that the Christian's readiness for combat is not directed against human beings but against the spiritual powers of evil (10–17; cf 1, 21; 2, 2; 3, 10). Unique importance is placed upon prayer (18–20).

w 1 Pt 5, 5. x Col 3, 18—4, 1; 1 Pt 3, 1–7. y 1 Cor 11, 3; Col 1, 18. z Col 3, 19; 1 Tm 2, 6. a Rom 6, 4; Ti 3, 5–7. b 2 Cor 11, 2; Col 1, 22. c Rom 12, 5; 1 Cor 6, 15. d Gn 2, 24; Mt 19, 5; Mk 10, 7–8. e Rv 19, 7. f Prv 6, 20; Sir 3, 1–6; Col 3, 20. g Ex 20, 12; Dt 5, 16. h Col 3, 21–22. i Col 3, 22–25; 1 Tm 6, 1–2; Ti 2, 9–10. j 1 Pt 2, 18. k Col 4, 1. l Rom 13, 12; 2 Cor 6, 7; 10, 4; Jas 4, 7. m 1, 21; 2, 2; Col 1, 13. n Rom 13, 12. o Wis 5, 17–20; Is 11, 5; Lk 12, 35; 1 Thes 5, 8.

with righteousness as a breastplate, 15 [p]and your feet shod in readiness for the gospel of peace. 16 [q]In all circumstances, hold faith as a shield, to quench all [the] flaming arrows of the evil one. 17 [r]And take the helmet of salvation and the sword of the Spirit, which is the word of God.

Constant Prayer 18 [s]With all prayer and supplication, pray at every opportunity in the Spirit. To that end, be watchful with all perseverance and supplication for all the holy ones 19 [t]and also for me, that speech may be given me to open my mouth, to make known with boldness the mystery of the gospel 20 [u]for which I am an ambassador in chains, so that I may have the courage to speak as I must.

6, 21–24: **Tychicus:** the bearer of the letter; see the note on Col 4, 7. Verses 21–22 parallel Col 4, 7–8, often word for word. If Ephesians is addressed to several Christian communities (see Introduction), it is understandable that no greetings to individual members of these communities should have been included in it.

V: Conclusion

A Final Message 21 [v]*So that you also may have news of me and of what I am doing, Tychicus, my beloved brother and trustworthy minister in the Lord, will tell you everything. 22 [w]I am sending him to you for this very purpose, so that you may know about us and that he may encourage your hearts.

23 Peace be to the brothers, and love with faith, from God the Father and the Lord Jesus Christ. 24 [x]Grace be with all who love our Lord Jesus Christ in immortality.

p Is 52, 7. q 1 Pt 5, 9. r Is 59, 17; 1 Thes 5, 8. s Mt 26, 41; Col 4, 2–3. t Acts 4, 29; Col 4, 3; 2 Thes 3, 1. u 2 Cor 5, 20; Col 4, 4. v Acts 20, 4; Col 4, 7; 2 Tm 4, 12. w Col 4, 8. x 1 Pt 1, 8.

THE LETTER TO THE PHILIPPIANS

Philippi, in northeastern Greece, was a city of some importance in the Roman province of Macedonia. Lying on the great road from the Adriatic coast to Byzantium, the Via Egnatia, and in the midst of rich agricultural plains near the gold deposits of Mt. Pangaeus, it was in Paul's day a Roman town (Acts 16, 21), with a Greek-Macedonian population and a small group of Jews (see Acts 16, 13). Originally founded in the sixth century B.C. as Krenides by the Thracians, the town was taken over after 360 B.C. by Philip II of Macedon, the father of Alexander the Great, and was renamed for himself, "Philip's City." The area became Roman in the second century B.C. On the plains near Philippi in October 42 B.C., Antony and Octavian decisively defeated the forces of Brutus and Cassius, the slayers of Julius Caesar. Octavian (Augustus) later made Philippi a Roman colony and settled many veterans of the Roman armies there.

Paul, according to Acts (16, 9-40), established at Philippi the first Christian community in Europe. He came to Philippi, via its harbor town of Neapolis (modern Kavalla), on his second missionary journey, probably in A.D. 49 or 50, accompanied by Silas and Timothy (Acts 15, 40; 16, 3; cf Phil 1, 1) and Luke, if he is to be included in the "we" references of Acts 16, 10-17. The Acts account tells of the conversion of a business woman, Lydia; the exorcism of a slave girl; and, after an earthquake, while Paul and Silas were imprisoned in Philippi, the faith and baptism of a jailer and his family. None of these persons, however, is directly mentioned in Philippians (cf the notes on 4, 2 and 4, 3). Acts 16 concludes its account by describing how Paul (and Silas), asked by the magistrates to leave Philippi, went on to Thessalonica (Acts 17, 1-10), where several times his loyal Philippians continued to support him with financial aid (Phil 4,

16). Later, Paul may have passed through Philippi on his way from Ephesus to Greece (Acts 20, 1-2), and he definitely stopped there on his fateful trip to Jerusalem (Acts 20, 6).

Paul's letter to the Christians at Philippi was written while he was in a prison somewhere (1, 7.13.14.17), indeed in danger of death (1, 20-23). Although under guard for preaching Christ, Paul rejoices at the continuing progress of the gospel (1, 12-26) and expresses gratitude for the Philippians' renewed concern and help in an expression of thanks most clearly found at 4, 10-20. Much of the letter is devoted to instruction about unity and humility within the Christian community at Philippi (1, 27—2, 18) and exhortations to growth, joy, and peace in their life together (4, 1-9). The letter seems to be drawing to a close at the end of what we number as ch 2, as Paul reports the plans of his helper Timothy and of Epaphroditus (whom the Philippians had sent to aid Paul) to come to Philippi (2, 19—3, 1), and even Paul's own expectation that he will go free and come to Philippi (1, 25-26; 2, 24). Yet quite abruptly at 3, 2, Paul erupts into warnings against false teachers who threaten to impose on the Philippians the burdens of the Mosaic law, including circumcision. The section that follows, 3, 2-21, is a vigorous attack on these Judaizers (cf Gal 2, 11—3, 29) or Jewish Christian teachers (cf 2 Cor 11, 12-23), giving us insights into Paul's own life story (3, 4-6) and into the doctrine of justification, the Christian life, and ultimate hope (3, 7-21).

The location of Paul's imprisonment when he wrote to the Philippians, and thus the date of the letter, are uncertain. The traditional view has been that it stems from Paul's confinement in Rome, between A.D. 59 and 63 (cf Acts 28, 14-31). One modern view suggests the period when he was imprisoned at Caesarea, on the coast of Palestine, A.D. 57 or 58 (Acts 23, 23—26, 32); another suggests Corinth (cf 2 Cor 11, 9). Much recent scholarship favors Ephesus, around A.D. 55, a situation referred to in 2 Cor 1, 8 concerning "the affliction that came to us" in Asia Minor (cf also 1 Cor 15, 32). The reference at 1, 13 to the "praetorium" (cf also 4, 22) can be understood to mean the imperial guard or government house at Ephesus (or Caesarea), or the praetorian camp in Rome. Involved in a decision are the several journeys back and forth between Philippi and wherever Paul is imprisoned, mentioned in the letter (2, 25-28; 4, 14); this factor causes many to prefer Ephesus because of its proximity to Philippi. The Ephesian hypothesis dates the composition of Philippians to the mid-50s when most of Paul's major letters were written.

There is also a likelihood, according to some scholars, that the letter as we have it is a composite from parts of three letters by Paul to the Philippians. Seemingly 4, 10-20 is a brief note of appreciation for help sent through Epaphroditus. The long section from 1, 3 to 3, 1 is then another letter, with news of Paul's imprisonment and reports on Timothy and Epaphroditus (who has fallen ill while with Paul), along with exhortations to the Philippians about Christian conduct; and 3, 2-21 a third communication warning about threats to Philippian Christianity. The other verses in ch 4 and 1, 1-2, are variously assigned by critics to these three underlying letters, which an editor presumably put together to produce a picture of Paul writing earnestly from prison (chs 1–2), facing opponents of the faith (ch 3), and with serene joy advising and thanking his Philippians (ch 4). If all four chapters were originally a unity, then one must assume that a break occurred between the writing of 3, 1 and 3, 2, possibly involving the receipt of bad news from Philippi, and that Paul had some reasons for delaying his words of thanks for the aid brought by Epaphroditus till the end of his letter.

This beautiful letter is rich in insights into Paul's theology and his apostolic love and concern for the gospel and his converts. In Philippians, Paul reveals his human sensitivity and tenderness, his enthusiasm for Christ as the key to life and death (1, 21), and his deep feeling for those in Christ who dwell in Philippi. With them he shares his hopes and convictions, his anxieties and fears, revealing the total confidence in Christ that constitutes faith (3, 8-10). The letter incorporates a hymn about the salvation that God has brought about through Christ (2, 6-11), applied by Paul to the relations of Christians with one another (2, 1-5). Philippians has been termed "the letter of joy" (4, 4.10). It is the rejoicing of faith, based on true understanding of Christ's unique role in the salvation of all who profess his lordship (2, 11; 3, 8-12.14.20-21).

The principal divisions of the Letter to the Philippians are the following:

I. Address (1, 1-11)
II. Progress of the Gospel (1, 12-26)
III. Instructions for the Community (1, 27—2, 18)
IV. Travel Plans of Paul and His Assistants (2, 19—3, 1)
V. Polemic: Righteousness and the Goal in Christ (3, 2-21)
VI. Instructions for the Community (4, 1-9)
VII. Gratitude for the Philippians' Generosity (4, 10-20)
VIII. Farewell (4, 21-23)

I: Address

CHAPTER 1

Greeting 1 [a]*Paul and Timothy, slaves of Christ Jesus, to all the holy ones in Christ Jesus who are in Philippi, with the overseers and ministers: 2 [b]*grace to you and peace from God our Father and the Lord Jesus Christ.

Thanksgiving 3 [c]*I give thanks to my God at every remembrance of you, 4 praying always with joy in my every prayer for all of you, 5 because of your partnership for the gospel from the first day until now. 6 [d]*I am confident of this, that the one who began a good work in you will continue to complete it until the day of Christ Jesus. 7 It is right that I should think this way about all of you, because I hold you in my heart, you who are all partners with me in grace, both in my imprisonment and in the defense and confirmation of the gospel. 8 [e]For God is my witness, how I long for all of you with the affection of Christ Jesus. 9 [f]And this is my prayer: that your love may increase ever more and more in knowledge and every kind of perception,

1, 1–2: See the note on Rom 1, 1–7, concerning the greeting.

1, 1: **Slaves:** Paul usually refers to himself at the start of a letter as an apostle. Here he substitutes a term suggesting the unconditional obligation of himself and Timothy to the service of Christ, probably because, in view of the good relationship with the Philippians, he wishes to stress his status as a co-servant rather than emphasize his apostolic authority. Reference to Timothy is a courtesy: Paul alone writes the letter, as the singular verb throughout shows (3–26), and the reference (2, 19–24) to Timothy in the third person. **Overseers:** the Greek term **episkopos** literally means "one who oversees" or "one who supervises," but since the second century it has come to designate the "bishop," the official who heads a local church. In New Testament times this office had not yet developed into the form that it later assumed, though it seems to be well on the way to such development in the Pastorals; see 1 Tm 3, 2 and Ti 1, 7, where it is translated **bishop.** At Philippi, however (and at Ephesus, according to Acts 20, 28), there was more than one **episkopos,** and the precise function of these officials is uncertain. In order to distinguish this office from the later stages into which it developed, the term is here translated as **overseers. Ministers:** the Greek term **diakonoi** is used frequently in the New Testament to designate "servants," "attendants," or "ministers." Paul refers to himself and to other apostles as "ministers of God" (2 Cor 6, 4) or "ministers of Christ" (2 Cor 11, 23). In the Pastorals (1 Tm 3, 8.12) the **diakonos** has become an established official in the local church; hence the term is there translated as **deacon.** The **diakonoi** at Philippi seem to represent an earlier stage of development of the office; we are uncertain about their precise functions. Hence the term is here translated as **ministers.** See Rom 16, 1, where Phoebe is described as a **diakonos (minister)** of the church of Cenchreae.

1, 2: The gifts come **from** Christ the Lord, not simply through him from the Father; compare the christology in 2, 6–11.

1, 3–11: As in Rom 1, 8–15 and all the Pauline letters except Galatians, a thanksgiving follows, including a direct prayer for the Philippians (9–11); see the note on Rom 1, 8. On their **partnership for the gospel** (5), cf 29–30; 4, 10–20. Their devotion to the faith and to Paul made them his pride and joy (4, 1). The characteristics thus manifested are evidence of the community's continuing preparation for the Lord's parousia (6.10). Paul's especially warm relationship with the Philippians is suggested here (7.8) as elsewhere in the letter. The eschatology serves to underscore a concern for ethical growth (9–11), which appears throughout the letter.

1, 6: **The day of Christ Jesus:** the parousia or triumphant return of Christ, when those loyal to him will be with him and share in his eternal glory; cf 10; 2, 16; 3, 20–21; 1 Thes 4, 17; 5, 10; 2 Thes 1, 10; 1 Cor 1, 8.

a Rom 1, 1; 2 Cor 1, 1; 1 Thes 1, 1; Phlm 1 / 1 Tm 3, 1–13. b Rom 1, 7; Gal 1, 3; Phlm 3. c Rom 1, 8; 1 Cor 1, 4; 1 Thes 1, 2. d 2, 13 / 1, 10; 2, 16; 1 Cor 1, 8. e Rom 1, 9; 2 Cor 1, 23; 1 Thes 2, 5. f Eph 3, 14–19; Col 1, 9–10; Phlm 6.

[10][g]to discern what is of value, so that you may be pure and blameless for the day of Christ, [11][h]filled with the fruit of righteousness that comes through Jesus Christ for the glory and praise of God.

II: Progress of the Gospel

[12][i]*I want you to know, brothers, that my situation has turned out rather to advance the gospel, [13][j]*so that my imprisonment has become well known in Christ throughout the whole praetorium and to all the rest, [14]*and so that the majority of the brothers, having taken encouragement in the Lord from my imprisonment, dare more than ever to proclaim the word fearlessly.

[15]Of course, some preach Christ from envy and rivalry, others from good will. [16]The latter act out of love, aware that I am here for the defense of the gospel; [17]the former proclaim Christ out of selfish ambition, not from pure motives, thinking that they will cause me trouble in my imprisonment. [18][k]*What difference does it make, as long as in every way, whether in pretense or in truth, Christ is being proclaimed? And in that I rejoice.

Indeed I shall continue to rejoice, [19][l]*for I know that this will result in deliverance for me through your prayers and support from the Spirit of Jesus Christ. [20][m]My eager expectation and hope is that I shall not be put to shame in any way, but that with all boldness, now as always, Christ will be magnified in my body, whether by life or by death. [21][n]For to me life is Christ, and death is gain. [22][o]If I go on living in the flesh, that means fruitful labor for me. And I do not know which I shall choose. [23][p]I am caught between the two. I long to depart this life and be with Christ, [for] that is far better. [24]Yet that I remain [in] the flesh is more necessary for your benefit. [25]And this I know with confidence, that I shall remain and continue in the service of all of you for your progress and joy in the faith, [26]so that your boasting in Christ Jesus may abound on account of me when I come to you again.

III: Instructions for the Community

Steadfastness in Faith [27][q]*Only, conduct yourselves in a way worthy of the gospel of Christ, so that, whether I come and see you or am absent, I may hear news of you, that you are standing firm in one spirit, with one mind struggling together for the faith of the gospel, [28]not intimidated in any way by your opponents. This is proof to them of destruction, but of your salvation. And this is God's doing. [29][r]For to you has been granted, for the sake of Christ, not only to believe in him but also to suffer for him. [30][s]*Yours is the same struggle as you saw in me and now hear about me.

1, 12–26: The body of the letter begins with an account of Paul's present **situation,** i.e., his **imprisonment** (12–13; see Introduction), and then goes on with advice for the Philippians (1, 27—2, 18). The **advance of the gospel** (12) and the **progress** of the Philippians **in the faith** (25) frame what is said.

1, 13: **Praetorium:** either the praetorian guard in the city where Paul was imprisoned or the governor's official residence in a Roman province (cf Mk 15, 16; Acts 23, 35). See Introduction on possible sites.

1, 14–18: Although Paul is imprisoned, Christians there nonetheless go on preaching Christ. But they do so with varied motives, **some** with personal hostility toward Paul, others out of personal ambition.

1, 18: **Rejoice:** a major theme in the letter; see Introduction.

1, 19–25: Paul earnestly debates his prospects of martyrdom or continued missionary labor. While he may **long to depart this life** and thus **be with Christ** (23), his overall and final expectation is that he will be delivered from this imprisonment and **continue in the service** of the Philippians and of others (19.25; 2, 24). In either case, Christ is central (20.21); if to live means Christ for Paul, death means to be united with Christ in a deeper sense.

1, 19: **Result in deliverance for me:** an echo of Jb 13, 16, hoping that God will turn suffering to ultimate good and deliverance from evil.

1, 27–30: Ethical admonition begins at this early point in the letter, emphasizing steadfastness and congregational unity in the face of possible suffering. The **opponents** (28) are those in Philippi, probably pagans, who oppose the gospel cause. **This is proof . . .** (28) may refer to the whole outlook and conduct of the Philippians, turning out for their salvation but to the judgment of the opponents (cf 2 Cor 2, 15–16), or possibly the sentence refers to the opinion of the opponents, who hold that the obstinacy of the Christians points to the destruction of such people as defy Roman authority (though in reality, Paul holds, such faithfulness leads to salvation).

1, 30: A reference to Paul's earlier imprisonment in Philippi (Acts 16, 19–24; 1 Thes 2, 2) and to his present confinement.

g Rom 2, 18; 12, 2 / 1, 6. h Jn 15, 8. i Eph 3, 1; 6, 20; 2 Tm 2, 9; Phlm 9. j 4, 22. k 4, 10. l Jb 13, 16 / 2 Cor 1, 11. m 1 Cor 6, 20; 1 Pt 4, 16. n Gal 2, 20. o Rom 1, 13. p 2 Cor 5, 8. q Eph 4, 1; Col 1, 10; 1 Thes 2, 12 / 4, 3. r Mt 5, 10; 10, 38; Mk 8, 34; Acts 5, 41. s 1, 13; Acts 16, 22–24.

CHAPTER 2

Plea for Unity and Humility [1]*If there is any
encouragement in Christ, any solace in love, any
participation in the Spirit, any compassion and
mercy, [2 t]complete my joy by being of the same
mind, with the same love, united in heart,
thinking one thing. [3 u]Do nothing out of selfish-
ness or out of vainglory; rather, humbly regard
others as more important than yourselves,
[4 v]each looking out not for his own interests, but
[also] everyone for those of others.
[5]*Have among yourselves the same attitude
that is also yours in Christ Jesus,

6 [w]*Who, though he was in the form of God,
did not regard equality with God something
to be grasped.
7 [x]*Rather, he emptied himself,
taking the form of a slave,
coming in human likeness;
and found human in appearance,
8 [y]*he humbled himself,
becoming obedient to death,
even death on a cross.
9 [z]*Because of this, God greatly exalted him
and bestowed on him the name
that is above every name,
10 [a]*that at the name of Jesus
every knee should bend,
of those in heaven and on earth and under
the earth,
11 [b]*and every tongue confess that
Jesus Christ is Lord,
to the glory of God the Father.

Obedience and Service in the World [12 c]*So
then, my beloved, obedient as you have always
been, not only when I am present but all the
more now when I am absent, work out your
salvation with fear and trembling. [13 d]For God is
the one who, for his good purpose, works in you
both to desire and to work. [14 e]Do everything
without grumbling or questioning, [15 f]*that you
may be blameless and innocent, children of God
without blemish in the midst of a crooked and
perverse generation, among whom you shine
like lights in the world, [16 g]as you hold on to the
word of life, so that my boast for the day of
Christ may be that I did not run in vain or labor

2, 1–11: The admonition to likemindedness and unity (2–5) is based on the believers' threefold experience with Christ, God's love, and the Spirit. The appeal to humility (3) and to obedience (12) is rooted in christology, specifically in a statement about Christ Jesus (6–11) and his humbling of self and obedience to the point of death (8).

2, 5: Have . . . the same attitude that is also yours in Christ Jesus: or, "that also Christ Jesus had." While it is often held that Christ here functions as a model for moral imitation, it is not the historical Jesus but the entire Christ event that vv 6–11 depict. Therefore, the appeal is to have in relations among yourselves that same relationship you have in Jesus Christ, i.e., serving one another as you serve Christ (4).

2, 6–11: Perhaps an early Christian hymn quoted here by Paul. The short rhythmic lines fall into two parts, vv 6–8 where the subject of every verb is Christ, and vv 9–11 where the subject is God. The general pattern is thus of Christ's humiliation and then exaltation. More precise analyses propose a division into six three-line stanzas (6; 7abc; 7d-8; 9; 10; 11) or into three stanzas (6–7ab; 7cd-8; 9–11). Phrases such as **even death on a cross** (8c) are considered by some to be additions (by Paul) to the hymn, as are vv 10c and 11c.

2, 6: Either a reference to Christ's preexistence and those aspects of divinity that he was willing to give up in order to serve in human form, or to what the man Jesus refused to grasp at to attain divinity. Many see an allusion to the Genesis story: unlike Adam, Jesus, **though . . . in the form of God** (Gn 1, 26–27), did not reach out for **equality with God,** in contrast with the first Adam in Gn 3, 5–6.

2, 7: Taking the form of a slave, coming in human likeness: or ". . . taking the form of a slave. // Coming in human likeness, and found human in appearance." While it is common to take vv 6 and 7 as dealing with Christ's preexistence and v 8 with his incarnate life, so that lines 7b and c are parallel, it is also possible to interpret so as to exclude any reference to preexistence (see the note on 2, 6) and to take vv 6–8 as presenting two parallel stanzas about Jesus' human state (6–7b; 7cd-8); in the latter alternative, **coming in human likeness** begins the second stanza and parallels 6a to some extent.

2, 8: There may be reflected here language about the servant of the Lord, Is 52, 13—53, 12, especially 53, 12.

2, 9: The name: "Lord" (11), revealing the true nature of the one who is named.

2, 10–11: Every knee should bend . . . every tongue confess: into this language of Is 45, 23 there has been inserted a reference to the three levels in the universe, according to ancient thought, **heaven, earth, under the earth.**

2, 11: Jesus Christ is Lord: a common early Christian acclamation; cf 1 Cor 12, 3; Rom 10, 9. But doxology to God the Father is not overlooked here (11c) in the final version of the hymn.

2, 12–18: Paul goes on to draw out further ethical implications for daily life (14–18) from the salvation God works in Christ.

2, 12: Fear and trembling: a common Old Testament expression indicating awe and seriousness in the service of God (cf Ex 15, 16; Jdt 2, 28; Ps 2, 11; Is 19, 16).

2, 15–16: Generation . . . as you hold on to . . . : or ". . . generation. Among them shine like lights in the world because you hold the word of life . . . ."

t Rom 15, 5; 1 Cor 1, 10. u Rom 12, 3.10; Gal 5, 26. v 1 Cor 10, 24.33; 13, 5. w Jn 1, 1–2; 17, 5; Col 2, 9; Heb 1, 3. x Is 53, 3.11; Jn 1, 14; Rom 8, 3; 2 Cor 8, 9; Gal 4, 4; Heb 2, 14.17. y Mt 26, 39; Jn 10, 17; Heb 5, 8; 12, 2. z Acts 2, 33; Mt 23, 12; Eph 1, 20–21; Heb 1, 3–4. a Is 45, 23; Jn 5, 23; Rom 14, 11; Rv 5, 13. b Acts 2, 36; Rom 10, 9; 1 Cor 12, 3. c Ps 2, 11; 1 Cor 2, 3; 2 Cor 7, 15. d 1, 6; 1 Cor 12, 6; 15, 10; 2 Cor 3, 5. e 1 Cor 10, 10; 1 Pt 4, 9. f 1 Thes 3, 13 / Dt 32, 5; Mt 10, 16; Acts 2, 40 / Dn 12, 3; Mt 5, 14.16; Eph 5, 8. g 1 Thes 2, 19 / Is 49, 4; 65, 23; Gal 2, 2.

in vain. [17][h]*But, even if I am poured out as a libation upon the sacrificial service of your faith, I rejoice and share my joy with all of you. [18][i]In the same way you also should rejoice and share your joy with me.

IV: Travel Plans of Paul and His Assistants

Timothy and Paul [19][j]*I hope, in the Lord Jesus, to send Timothy to you soon, so that I too may be heartened by hearing news of you. [20]For I have no one comparable to him for genuine interest in whatever concerns you. [21][k]For they all seek their own interests, not those of Jesus Christ. [22]But you know his worth, how as a child with a father he served along with me in the cause of the gospel. [23]He it is, then, whom I hope to send as soon as I see how things go with me, [24]*but I am confident in the Lord that I myself will also come soon.

Epaphroditus [25][l]*With regard to Epaphroditus, my brother and co-worker and fellow soldier, your messenger and minister in my need, I consider it necessary to send him to you. [26]For he has been longing for all of you and was distressed because you heard that he was ill. [27]He was indeed ill, close to death; but God had mercy on him, not just on him but also on me, so that I might not have sorrow upon sorrow. [28]I send him therefore with the greater eagerness, so that, on seeing him, you may rejoice again, and I may have less anxiety. [29][m]Welcome him then in the Lord with all joy and hold such people in esteem, [30]because for the sake of the work of Christ he came close to death, risking his life to make up for those services to me that you could not perform.

CHAPTER 3

Concluding Admonitions [1][n]*Finally, my brothers, rejoice in the Lord. Writing the same things to you is no burden for me but is a safeguard for you.

V: Polemic: Righteousness and the Goal in Christ

Against Legalistic Teachers [2][o]*Beware of the dogs! Beware of the evil-workers! Beware of the mutilation! [3][p]*For we are the circumcision, we who worship through the Spirit of God, who boast in Christ Jesus and do not put our confidence in flesh, [4][q]although I myself have grounds for confidence even in the flesh.

Paul's Autobiography If anyone else thinks he can be confident in flesh, all the more can I.

2, 17: Libation: in ancient religious ritual, the pouring out on the ground of a liquid offering as a sacrifice. Paul means that he may be facing death.

2, 19—3, 1: The plans of Paul and his assistants for future travel are regularly a part of a Pauline letter near its conclusion; cf Rom 15, 22–29; 1 Cor 16, 5–12.

2, 19: Timothy: already known to the Philippians (Acts 16, 1–15; cf 1 Cor 4, 17; 16, 10).

2, 24: I myself will also come soon: cf 1, 19–25 for the significance of this statement.

2, 25: Epaphroditus: sent by the Philippians as their **messenger** (literally, "apostle") to aid Paul in his imprisonment, he had fallen seriously ill; Paul commends him as he sends him back to Philippi.

3, 1: Finally . . . rejoice: the adverb often signals the close of a letter; cf 4, 8; 2 Cor 13, 11. While the verb could also be translated "good-bye" or "farewell," although it is never so used in Greek epistolography, the theme of joy has been frequent in the letter (1, 18; 2, 2.18); note also 4, 4 and the addition of "always" there as evidence for the meaning "rejoice." To write **the same things** may refer to what Paul has previously taught in Philippi or to what he has just written or to what follows.

3, 2–21: An abrupt change in content and tone, either because Paul at this point responds to disturbing news he has just heard about a threat to the faith of the Philippians in the form of false teachers, or because part of another Pauline letter was inserted here; see Introduction. The chapter describes these teachers in strong terms as **dogs.** The persons meant are evidently different from the rival preachers of 1, 14–18 and the opponents of 1, 28. Since vv 2–4 emphasize Jewish terms like **circumcision** (2–3.5), some relate them to the "Judaizers" of the Letter to the Galatians. Other phrases make them appear more like the false teachers of 2 Cor 11, 12–15, the **evil-workers.** The latter part of the chapter depicts the **many** who are **enemies** of Christ's cross in terms that may sound more Gentile or even "gnostic" than Jewish (18–19). Accordingly, some see two groups of false teachers in ch 3, others one group characterized by a claim of having attained "perfect maturity" (12–15).

3, 2–11: Paul sets forth the Christian claim, especially using personal, autobiographical terms that are appropriate to the situation. He presents his own experience in coming to know Christ Jesus in terms of **righteousness** or justification (cf Rom 1, 16–17; 3, 21—5, 11; Gal 2, 5–11), contrasting **the righteousness from God** through faith and that of one's own **based on the law** as two exclusive ways of pleasing God.

3, 2: Beware of the mutilation: literally, "incision," an ironic wordplay on "circumcision"; cf Gal 5, 12. There may be an association with the self-inflicted mutilations of the prophets of Baal (1 Kgs 18, 28) and of devotees of Cybele who slashed themselves in religious frenzy.

3, 3: We are the circumcision: the true people of God, seed and offspring of Abraham (Gal 3, 7.29; 6, 15). **Spirit of God:** some manuscripts read "worship God by the Spirit."

h Rom 15, 16; 2 Tm 4, 6. i 3, 1; 4, 4. j Acts 16, 1–3; 17, 14–15; 1 Cor 4, 17; 16, 10. k 1 Cor 13, 5; 2 Tm 4, 10. l 4, 10–11.15–16.18. m 1 Cor 16, 18. n 2, 18; 4, 4. o Ps 22, 17.21; Rv 22, 15 / 2 Cor 11, 13 / Gal 5, 6.12. p Rom 2, 28–29; Col 2, 11. q 2 Cor 11, 18.21–23.

[5] r*Circumcised on the eighth day, of the race of Israel, of the tribe of Benjamin, a Hebrew of Hebrew parentage, in observance of the law a Pharisee, [6] sin zeal I persecuted the church, in righteousness based on the law I was blameless.
Righteousness from God [7] t*[But] whatever gains I had, these I have come to consider a loss because of Christ. [8]More than that, I even consider everything as a loss because of the supreme good of knowing Christ Jesus my Lord. For his sake I have accepted the loss of all things and I consider them so much rubbish, that I may gain Christ [9] uand be found in him, not having any righteousness of my own based on the law but that which comes through faith in Christ, the righteousness from God, depending on faith [10] vto know him and the power of his resurrection and [the] sharing of his sufferings by being conformed to his death, [11] wif somehow I may attain the resurrection from the dead.
Forward in Christ [12] x*It is not that I have already taken hold of it or have already attained perfect maturity, but I continue my pursuit in hope that I may possess it, since I have indeed been taken possession of by Christ [Jesus]. [13]Brothers, I for my part do not consider myself to have taken possession. Just one thing: forgetting what lies behind but straining forward to what lies ahead, [14] yI continue my pursuit toward the goal, the prize of God's upward calling, in Christ Jesus. [15]Let us, then, who are "perfectly mature" adopt this attitude. And if you have a different attitude, this too God will reveal to you. [16]*Only, with regard to what we have attained, continue on the same course.
Wrong Conduct and Our Goal [17] z*Join with others in being imitators of me, brothers, and observe those who thus conduct themselves according to the model you have in us. [18] aFor many, as I have often told you and now tell you even in tears, conduct themselves as enemies of the cross of Christ. [19] bTheir end is destruction. Their God is their stomach; their glory is in their "shame." Their minds are occupied with earthly things. [20] c*But our citizenship is in heaven, and from it we also await a savior, the Lord Jesus Christ. [21] dHe will change our lowly body to conform with his glorified body by the power that enables him also to bring all things into subjection to himself.

VI: Instructions for the Community

CHAPTER 4

Live in Concord [1] e*Therefore, my brothers, whom I love and long for, my joy and crown, in this way stand firm in the Lord, beloved.

[2]*I urge Euodia and I urge Syntyche to come to a mutual understanding in the Lord. [3] f*Yes, and I ask you also, my true yokemate, to help them, for they have struggled at my side in

3, 5: Circumcised on the eighth day: as the law required (Gn 17, 12; Lv 12, 3).

3, 7: Loss: his knowledge of Christ led Paul to reassess the ways of truly pleasing and serving God. His reevaluation indicates the profound and lasting effect of his experience of the meaning of Christ on the way to Damascus some twenty years before (Gal 1, 15–16; Acts 9, 1–22).

3, 12–16: To be **taken possession of by Christ** does not mean that one has already arrived at perfect spiritual maturity. Paul and the Philippians instead press on, trusting in God.

3, 12: Attained perfect maturity: possibly an echo of the concept in the mystery religions of being an initiate, admitted to divine secrets.

3, 16: Some manuscripts add, probably to explain Paul's cryptic phrase, "thinking alike."

3, 17–21: Paul and those who live a life centered in Christ, envisaging both his suffering and resurrection, provide a model that is the opposite of opponents who reject Christ's cross (cf 1 Cor 1, 23).

3, 17: Being imitators of me: not arrogance, but humble simplicity, since all his converts know that Paul is wholly dedicated to imitating Christ (1 Cor 11, 1; cf also Phil 4, 9; 1 Thes 1, 6; 2 Thes 3, 7.9; 1 Cor 4, 6).

3, 20: Citizenship: Christians constitute a colony of heaven, as Philippi was a **colonia** of Rome (Acts 16, 12). The hope Paul expresses involves the final coming of Christ, not a status already attained, such as the opponents claim.

4, 1–9: This series of ethical admonitions rests especially on the view of Christ and his coming (cf 5) in 3, 20–21. Paul's instructions touch on unity within the congregation, joy, prayer, and the Christian outlook on life.

4, 2: Euodia . . . Syntyche: two otherwise unknown women in the Philippian congregation; on the advice to them, cf 2, 2–4.

4, 3: Yokemate: or "comrade," although the Greek **syzygos** could also be a proper name. **Clement:** otherwise unknown, although later writers sought to identify him with Clement, bishop of Rome (Eusebius, **Ecclesiastical History** 3.15.1).

r Lk 1, 59; 2, 21 / Acts 22, 3; 23, 6; 26, 5. s Acts 8, 3; 22, 4; 26, 9–11. t Mt 13, 44.46; Lk 14, 33. u Rom 3, 21–22. v Rom 6, 3–5; 8, 17; Gal 6, 17. w Jn 11, 23–26; Acts 4, 2; Rv 20, 5–6. x 1 Tm 6, 12.19. y 1 Cor 9, 24–25; 2 Tm 4, 7. z 1 Cor 4, 16; 11, 1; 1 Thes 1, 7; 1 Pt 5, 3. a 1 Cor 1, 17.23; Gal 6, 12. b Rom 8, 5–6; 16, 18. c Eph 2, 6.19; Col 3, 1–3; Heb 12, 22. d Rom 8, 23.29; 1 Cor 15, 42–57; 2 Cor 3, 18; 5, 1–5 /1 Cor 15, 27–28. e 1 Thes 2, 19–20. f Ex 32, 32–33; Ps 69, 29; Dn 12, 1; Lk 10, 20; Rv 3, 5; 13, 8;17, 8; 20, 12.15; 21, 27.

promoting the gospel, along with Clement and my other co-workers, whose names are in the book of life.

Joy and Peace 4 g *Rejoice in the Lord always. I shall say it again: rejoice! 5 h *Your kindness should be known to all. The Lord is near. 6 i Have no anxiety at all, but in everything, by prayer and petition, with thanksgiving, make your requests known to God. 7 j Then the peace of God that surpasses all understanding will guard your hearts and minds in Christ Jesus.

8 k *Finally, brothers, whatever is true, whatever is honorable, whatever is just, whatever is pure, whatever is lovely, whatever is gracious, if there is any excellence and if there is anything worthy of praise, think about these things. 9 l *Keep on doing what you have learned and received and heard and seen in me. Then the God of peace will be with you.

VII: Gratitude for the Philippians' Generosity

10 m *I rejoice greatly in the Lord that now at last you revived your concern for me. You were, of course, concerned about me but lacked an opportunity. 11 n Not that I say this because of need, for I have learned, in whatever situation I find myself, to be self-sufficient. 12 I know indeed how to live in humble circumstances; I know also how to live with abundance. In every circumstance and in all things I have learned the secret of being well fed and of going hungry, of living in abundance and of being in need. 13 o I have the strength for everything through him who empowers me. 14 Still, it was kind of you to share in my distress.

15 *You Philippians indeed know that at the beginning of the gospel, when I left Macedonia, not a single church shared with me in an account of giving and receiving, except you alone. 16 For even when I was at Thessalonica you sent me something for my needs, not only once but more than once. 17 It is not that I am eager for the gift; rather, I am eager for the profit that accrues to your account. 18 p *I have received full payment and I abound. I am very well supplied because of what I received from you through Epaphroditus, "a fragrant aroma," an acceptable sacrifice, pleasing to God. 19 q My God will fully supply whatever you need, in accord with his glorious riches in Christ Jesus. 20 r To our God and Father, glory forever and ever. Amen.

VIII: Farewell

21 *Give my greetings to every holy one in Christ Jesus. The brothers who are with me send you their greetings; 22 s *all the holy ones send you their greetings, especially those of Caesar's household. 23 The grace of the Lord Jesus Christ be with your spirit.

4, 4: Rejoice: see the note on 3, 1.

4, 5: Kindness: considerateness, forbearance, fairness. **The Lord is near:** most likely a reference to Christ's parousia (1, 6.10; 3, 20–21; 1 Cor 16, 22), although some sense an echo of Ps 119, 151 and the perpetual presence of the Lord.

4, 8: The language employs terms from Roman Stoic thought.

4, 9: Cf the note on 3, 17.

4, 10–20: Paul, more directly than anywhere else in the letter (cf 1, 3–5), here thanks the Philippians for their gift of money sent through Epaphroditus (2, 25). Paul's own policy was **to be self-sufficient** as a missionary, supporting himself by his own labor (1 Thes 2, 5–9; 1 Cor 9, 15–18; cf Acts 18, 2–3). In spite of this reliance on self and on God to provide (11–13), Paul accepted gifts from the Philippians **not only once but more than once** (16) when he was in Thessalonica (Acts 17, 1–9), as he does now, in prison (**my distress,** 14). While commercial terms appear in the passage, like **an account of giving and receiving** (15) and **received full payment** (18), Paul is most concerned about the spiritual growth of the Philippians (10.17.19); he emphasizes that God will care for their needs, through Christ.

4, 15: The beginning of the gospel: it was at Philippi that Paul first preached Christ in Europe, going on from there to Thessalonica and Beroea (Acts 16, 9—17, 14).

4, 18: Aroma . . . sacrifice: Old Testament cultic language (cf Gn 8, 21; Ex 29, 18.25.41; Lv 1, 9.13; Ez 20, 41) applied to the Philippians' gift; cf Eph 5, 2; 2 Cor 2, 14–16.

4, 21–23: On the usual greetings at the conclusion of a letter, see the note on 1 Cor 16, 19–24. Inclusion of greetings from **all the holy ones** in the place from which Paul writes would involve even the Christians of 1, 14–18 who had their differences with Paul.

4, 22: Those of Caesar's household: minor officials or even slaves and freedmen, found in Ephesus or Rome, among other places.

g 2, 18; 3, 1. h Ti 3, 2 / Ps 145, 18; Heb 10, 37; Jas 5, 8–9. i Mt 6, 25–34; 1 Pt 5, 7 / Col 4, 2. j Jn 14, 27; Col 3, 15. k Rom 12, 17. l 1 Thes 4, 1 / Rom 15, 33; 16, 20; 1 Cor 14, 33; 1 Thes 5, 23. m 1, 18; 2, 25; 1 Cor 9, 11; 2 Cor 11, 9. n 1 Cor 4, 11; 2 Cor 6, 10; 11, 27 / 2 Cor 12, 9–10. o Col 1, 29; 2 Tm 4, 17. p Gn 8, 21; Ex 29, 18; Eph 5, 2; Heb 13, 16. q 1 Thes 3, 11.13. r Rom 16, 27; Eph 5, 20. s 1, 13.

THE LETTER TO THE COLOSSIANS

This letter is addressed to a congregation at Colossae in the Lycus Valley in Asia Minor, east of Ephesus. At the time of writing, Paul had not visited there, the letter says (1, 4; 2, 1). The community had apparently been established by Epaphras of Colossae (1, 7; 4, 12; Phlm 23). Problems, however, had arisen, brought on by teachers who emphasized Christ's relation to the universe (cosmos). Their teachings stressed angels (2, 18; "principalities and powers," 2, 15), which were connected with astral powers and cultic practices (see the note on 2, 16) and rules about food and drink and ascetical disciplines (2, 16.18). These teachings, Paul insists, detract from the person and work of Christ for salvation as set forth magnificently in a hymnic passage at 1, 15-20 and reiterated throughout the letter. Such teachings are but "shadows"; Christ is "reality" (2, 17).

For help in dealing with these problems that the new teachers posed at Colossae, Epaphras sought out Paul, who was then imprisoned (4, 10.18) at a place that the letter does not mention. Paul, without entering into debate over the existence of angelic spirits or their function, simply affirms that Christ possesses the sum total of redemptive power (1, 19) and that the spiritual renewal of the human person occurs through contact in baptism with the person of Christ, who died and rose again (2, 9-14). It is unnecessary for the Christian to be concerned about placating spirits (2, 15) or avoiding imagined defilement through ascetical practices in regard to food and drink (2, 20-23). True Christian asceticism consists in the conquering of personal sins (3, 5-10) and the practice of love of neighbor in accordance with the standard set by Christ (3, 12-16).

Paul commends the community as a whole (1, 3-8); this seems to indicate that, though the Colossians have been under pressure to adopt the false doctrines, they have not yet succumbed. The apostle expresses his prayerful concern for them (1, 9-14). His preaching has cost him persecution, suffering, and imprisonment, but he regards these as reflective of the sufferings of Christ, a required discipline for the sake of the gospel (see the note on 1, 24; cf 1, 29; 2, 1). His instructions to the Christian family and to slaves and masters require a new spirit of reflection and action. Love, obedience, and service are to be rendered "in the Lord" (3, 18—4, 1).

Colossians follows the outline of a typical Pauline letter. It is distinguished by the poetic lines in 1, 15-20 concerning who Christ is and what Christ means in creation and redemption. This hymn may be compared with similar passages in Philippians 2, 6-11; 1 Timothy 3, 16; and John 1, 1-18. It was apparently familiar liturgical material to the author, the audience, and the false teachers. In 1, 21—2, 7, however, Paul interprets the relation between the body of Christ, which he insists is the church (1, 18), and the world or cosmos to be one not simply of Christ's preexistence and rule but one of missionary advance into the world by the spreading of the word (1, 25.28). In this labor of the missionary body of Christ, Paul as a minister plays a prime part in bringing Christ and the gospel as hope to the Gentiles (1, 23.25.27). To "every creature under heaven" the word is to be proclaimed, so that everyone receives Christ, is established in faith, and walks in Christ (1, 28; 2, 6.7).

Paul wrote the Letter to the Colossians while in prison, but his several imprisonments leave the specific place and date of composition uncertain. On this point the same problem exists as with Ephesians and Philippians (see the Introductions to these letters). Traditionally the house arrest at Rome, in which Paul enjoyed a certain restricted freedom in preaching (see Acts 28, 16-28), or a second Roman imprisonment has been claimed as the setting. Others suggest a still earlier imprisonment at Caesarea (see Acts 23, 12—27, 1) or in Ephesus (see Acts 19). Still others regard the letter as the work of some pupil or follower of Paul, writing in his name. In any case, the contents are often closely paralleled by thoughts in Ephesians.

The principal divisions of the Letter to the Colossians are the following:

I. Address (1, 1-14)
II. The Preeminence of Christ (1, 15—2, 3)
III. Warnings against False Teachers (2, 4-23)
IV. The Ideal Christian Life in the World (3, 1—4, 6)
V. Conclusion (4, 7-18)

I: Address

CHAPTER 1

Greeting 1 [a]*Paul, an apostle of Christ Jesus by the will of God, and Timothy our brother, 2 to the holy ones and faithful brothers in Christ in Colossae: grace to you and peace from God our Father.

Thanksgiving 3 [b]*We always give thanks to God, the Father of our Lord Jesus Christ, when we pray for you, 4 for we have heard of your faith in Christ Jesus and the love that you have for all the holy ones 5 [c]because of the hope reserved for you in heaven. Of this you have already heard through the word of truth, the gospel, 6 that has come to you. Just as in the whole world it is bearing fruit and growing, so also among you, from the day you heard it and came to know the grace of God in truth, 7 [d]*as you learned it from Epaphras our beloved fellow slave, who is a trustworthy minister of Christ on your behalf 8 and who also told us of your love in the Spirit.

Prayer for Continued Progress 9 [e]*Therefore, from the day we heard this, we do not cease praying for you and asking that you may be filled with the knowledge of his will through all spiritual wisdom and understanding 10 to live in a manner worthy of the Lord, so as to be fully pleasing, in every good work bearing fruit and growing in the knowledge of God, 11 strengthened with every power, in accord with his glorious might, for all endurance and patience, with joy 12 [f]*giving thanks to the Father, who has made you fit to share in the inheritance of the holy ones in light. 13 He delivered us from the power of darkness and transferred us to the kingdom of his beloved Son, 14 [g]in whom we have redemption, the forgiveness of sins.

1, 1–2: For the epistolary form used by Paul at the beginning of his letters, see the note on Rom 1, 1–7. On **holy ones** or "God's people," see the note on Rom 1, 7. Awareness of their calling helps this group to be **faithful brothers** and sisters **in Christ,** i.e., dedicated to the tasks implied in their calling.

1, 3–8: On thanksgiving at the start of a letter, see the note on Rom 1, 8. The apostle, recalling his own prayers for them and the good report about them he has received (3–4), congratulates the Colossians upon their acceptance of Christ and their faithful efforts to live the gospel (3, 6–8). To encourage them he mentions the success of the gospel elsewhere (6) and assures them that his knowledge of their community is accurate, since he has been in personal contact with Epaphras (7–8), who likely had evangelized Colossae and other cities in the Lycus Valley of Asia Minor (cf 4, 12.13; Phlm 23). On **faith, love,** and **hope** (4.5.8), see the note on 1 Cor 13, 13; cf 1 Thes 1, 3; 5, 8.

1, 7: Epaphras: now with Paul but a Colossian, founder of the church there.

1, 9–14: Moved by Epaphras' account, the apostle has prayed and continues to pray fervently for the Colossians that, in their response to the gospel, they **may be filled with the knowledge of** God's **will** (9; cf 3, 10). Paul expects a mutual interaction between their life according to the gospel and this knowledge (10), yielding results (**fruit,** 10; cf 6) **in every good work:** growth, strength, **endurance, patience, with joy** (11), and the further giving of thanks (12).

1, 12–14: A summary about **redemption by the Father** precedes the statement in vv 15–20 about the **beloved Son** who is God's love in person (13). Christians share **the inheritance . . . in light** with **the holy ones,** here probably the angels (12). The imagery reflects the Exodus (**delivered . . . transferred**) and Jesus' theme of **the kingdom. Redemption** is explained as **forgiveness of sins** (cf Acts 2, 38; Rom 3, 24–25; Eph 1, 7).

a Eph 1, 1. b Eph 1, 15–16; Phlm 4–5. c Eph 1, 13.18; 1 Pt 1, 4. d Phlm 23. e Eph 1, 15–17; 5, 17; Phil 1, 9. f 3, 17; Jn 8, 12; Acts 26, 18; 1 Tm 6, 16; 1 Pt 2, 9. g Eph 1, 7.

II: The Preeminence of Christ

His Person and Work

15 h*He is the image of the invisible God,
the firstborn of all creation.
16 i*For in him were created all things in heaven
and on earth,
the visible and the invisible,
whether thrones or dominions or
principalities or powers;
all things were created through him and for
him.
17 He is before all things,
and in him all things hold together.
18 j*He is the head of the body, the church.
He is the beginning, the firstborn from the
dead,
that in all things he himself might be
preeminent.
19 *For in him all the fullness was pleased to
dwell,
20 k*and through him to reconcile all things
for him,
making peace by the blood of his cross
[through him], whether those on earth or
those in heaven.

21 l*And you who once were alienated and
hostile in mind because of evil deeds 22he has
now reconciled in his fleshly body through his
death, to present you holy, without blemish, and
irreproachable before him, 23provided that you
persevere in the faith, firmly grounded, stable,
and not shifting from the hope of the gospel that
you heard, which has been preached to every
creature under heaven, of which I, Paul, am a
minister.

Christ in Us 24*Now I rejoice in my sufferings
for your sake, and in my flesh I am filling up
what is lacking in the afflictions of Christ on
behalf of his body, which is the church, 25of
which I am a minister in accordance with God's
stewardship given to me to bring to completion

1, 15–20: As the poetic arrangement indicates, these lines are probably an early Christian hymn, known to the Colossians and taken up into the letter from liturgical use (cf Phil 2, 6–11; 1 Tm 3, 16). They present Christ as the mediator of creation (15–18a) and of redemption (18b-20). There is a parallelism between **firstborn of all creation** (15) and **firstborn from the dead** (18). While many of the phrases were at home in Greek philosophical use and even in gnosticism, the basic ideas also reflect Old Testament themes about Wisdom found in Prv 8, 22–31; Wis 7, 22—8, 1; and Sir 1, 4. See also the notes on what is possibly a hymn in Jn 1, 1–18.

1, 15: Image: cf Gn 1, 27. Whereas the man and the woman were originally created in the image and likeness of God (see also Gn 1, 26), Christ as image (2 Cor 4, 4) of **the invisible God** (Jn 1, 18) now shares this new nature in baptism with those redeemed (cf 3, 10–11).

1, 16–17: Christ (though not mentioned by name) is preeminent and supreme as God's agent in the creation of **all things** (cf Jn 1, 3), as prior to **all things** (17; cf Heb 1, 3).

1, 18: Church: such a reference seemingly belongs under "redemption" in the following lines, not under the "creation" section of the hymn. Stoic thought sometimes referred to the world as "the body of Zeus." Pauline usage is to speak of the church as the body of Christ (1 Cor 12, 12–27; Rom 12, 4–5). Some think that the author of Colossians has inserted the reference to the church here so as to define "head of the body" in Paul's customary way. See v 24. **Preeminent:** when Christ was raised by God as **firstborn from the dead** (cf Acts 26, 23; Rv 1, 5), he was placed over the community, the church, that he had brought into being, but he is also indicated as crown of the whole new creation, over **all things**. His further role is to **reconcile all things** (20) for God or possibly "to himself."

1, 19: Fullness: in gnostic usage this term referred to a spiritual world of beings above, between God and the world; many later interpreters take it to refer to **the fullness of the deity** (2, 9); the reference could also be to the fullness of grace (cf Jn 1, 16).

1, 20: The blood of his cross: the most specific reference in the hymn to redemption through Christ's death, a central theme in Paul; cf 2, 14–15; 1 Cor 1, 17.18.23. **[Through him]:** the phrase, lacking in some manuscripts, seems superfluous but parallels the reference to reconciliation through Christ earlier in the verse.

1, 21–23: Paul, in applying this hymn to the Colossians, reminds them that they have experienced the reconciling effect of Christ's death. He sees the effects of the cross in the redemption of human beings, not of cosmic powers such as those referred to in vv 16 and 20 (**all things**). Paul also urges adherence to Christ in faith and begins to point to his own role as minister (23), sufferer (24), and proclaimer (27–28) of this gospel.

1, 24—2, 3: As the community at Colossae was not personally known to Paul (see Introduction), he here invests his teaching with greater authority by presenting a brief sketch of his apostolic ministry and sufferings as they reflect those of Christ on behalf of the church (24). The preaching of God's word (25) carries out the divine plan (**the mystery,** 26) to make Christ known to the Gentiles (27). It teaches the God-given wisdom about Christ (28), whose power works mightily in the apostle (29). Even in those communities that do not know him personally (2, 1), he can increase the perception of God in Christ, unite the faithful more firmly in love, and so bring encouragement to them (2). He hopes that his apostolic authority will make the Colossians perceive more readily the defects in the teaching of others who have sought to delude them, the next concern in the letter.

1, 24: What is lacking: although variously interpreted, this phrase does not imply that Christ's atoning death on the cross was defective. It may refer to the apocalyptic concept of a quota of "messianic woes" to be endured before the end comes; cf Mk 13, 8.19–20.24 and the note on Mt 23, 29–32. Others suggest that Paul's mystical unity with Christ allowed him to call his own **sufferings the afflictions of Christ.**

h Ps 89, 28; Jn 1, 3.18; 2 Cor 4, 4. i 1 Cor 8, 6; Eph 1, 10.21. j 1 Cor 11, 3; 12, 12.27; 15, 20; Eph 1, 22–23; Rv 1, 5. k 2 Cor 5, 18–19; Eph 1, 10. l Eph 2, 14–16.

for you the word of God, [26][m]the mystery hidden
from ages and from generations past. But now it
has been manifested to his holy ones, [27][n]to
whom God chose to make known the riches of
the glory of this mystery among the Gentiles; it
is Christ in you, the hope for glory. [28][o]It is he
whom we proclaim, admonishing everyone and
teaching everyone with all wisdom, that we may
present everyone perfect in Christ. [29][p]For this I
labor and struggle, in accord with the exercise of
his power working within me.

CHAPTER 2

[1]*For I want you to know how great a struggle I
am having for you and for those in Laodicea and
all who have not seen me face to face, [2][q]that
their hearts may be encouraged as they are
brought together in love, to have all the richness
of fully assured understanding, for the knowl-
edge of the mystery of God, Christ, [3][r]in whom
are hidden all the treasures of wisdom and
knowledge.

III: Warnings against False Teachers

A General Admonition [4][s]*I say this so that
no one may deceive you by specious arguments.
[5][t]For even if I am absent in the flesh, yet I am
with you in spirit, rejoicing as I observe your
good order and the firmness of your faith in
Christ. [6]So, as you received Christ Jesus the
Lord, walk in him, [7][u]rooted in him and built
upon him and established in the faith as you
were taught, abounding in thanksgiving. [8][v]*See
to it that no one captivate you with an empty,
seductive philosophy according to human tradi-
tion, according to the elemental powers of the
world and not according to Christ.

Sovereign Role of Christ [9][w]*For in him
dwells the whole fullness of the deity bodily,
[10]and you share in this fullness in him, who is
the head of every principality and power. [11][x]*In
him you were also circumcised with a circumci-
sion not administered by hand, by stripping off
the carnal body, with the circumcision of Christ.
[12][y]You were buried with him in baptism, in
which you were also raised with him through
faith in the power of God, who raised him from
the dead. [13][z]And even when you were dead [in]
transgressions and the uncircumcision of your
flesh, he brought you to life along with him,
having forgiven us all our transgressions;
[14][a]*obliterating the bond against us, with its
legal claims, which was opposed to us, he also
removed it from our midst, nailing it to the
cross; [15][b]*despoiling the principalities and the
powers, he made a public spectacle of them,
leading them away in triumph by it.

2, 1: Laodicea: chief city in Phrygia, northwest of Colossae; cf 4, 13.16; Rv 3, 14–22.

2, 4–23: In face of the threat posed by false teachers (4), the Colossians are admonished to adhere to the gospel as it was first preached to them (6), steeping themselves in it with grateful hearts (7). They must reject religious teachings originating in any source except the gospel (8) because in Christ alone will they have access to God, **the deity** (9). So fully has Christ enlightened them that they need no other source of religious knowledge or virtue (10). They do not require **circumcision** (11), for **in baptism** their whole being has been affected by Christ (12) through forgiveness of sin and resurrection to a new life (13; cf 3, 1 and Rom 6, 1–11).

On the cross Christ canceled the record of the debt that stood against us with all its claims (14), i.e., he eliminated the law (cf Eph 2, 15) that human beings could not observe—and that could not save them. He forgave sins against the law (14) and exposed as false and misleading (15) all other powers (cf 1, 16) that purport to offer salvation. Therefore, the Colossians are not to accept judgments from such teachers on **food and drink** or to keep certain religious festivals or engage in certain cultic practices (16), for the Colossians would thereby risk severing themselves from Christ (19). If, when they accepted the gospel, they believed in Christ as their savior, they must be convinced that their salvation cannot be achieved by appeasing ruling spirits through dietary practices or through a wisdom gained simply by means of harsh asceticism (20–23).

2, 8: Elemental powers of the world: see the note on Gal 4, 3.

2, 9: Fullness of the deity: the divine nature, not just attributes; see the note on 1, 19.

2, 11: A description of baptism (12) in symbolic terms of the Old Testament rite for entry into the community. The false teachers may have demanded physical circumcision of the Colossians.

2, 14: The elaborate metaphor here about how God canceled the legal claims against us through Christ's cross depicts not Christ being nailed to the cross by men but **the bond . . . with its legal claims** being nailed to the cross by God.

2, 15: The picture derives from the **public spectacle** and **triumph** of a Roman emperor's victory parade, where captives marched in subjection. **The principalities and the powers** are here conquered, not reconciled (cf 1, 16.20). An alternate rendering for **by it** (the cross) is "by him" (Christ).

m Rom 16, 25–26; 1 Cor 2, 7; Eph 3, 3.9. n 3, 4; Rom 8, 10. o Eph 4, 13. p 2, 1; 4, 12; Phil 4, 13. q 1, 26–27; Eph 3, 18–19. r Prv 2, 4–5; Is 45, 3; Rom 11, 33; 1 Cor 1, 30. s Eph 4, 14. t 1 Cor 5, 3; Phil 1, 27. u Eph 2, 20–22; 3, 17. v Gal 4, 3; Eph 5, 6. w 1, 19; Eph 3, 19. x 1, 22; Jer 4, 4; Rom 2, 25–29; Phil 3, 3. y Rom 6, 3–4. z Eph 2, 1.5. a Eph 2, 14–15. b 1, 16.20; 2 Cor 2, 14; Eph 1, 21.

Practices Contrary to Faith [16][c]*Let no one, then, pass judgment on you in matters of food and drink or with regard to a festival or new moon or sabbath. [17][d]These are shadows of things to come; the reality belongs to Christ. [18][e]*Let no one disqualify you, delighting in self-abasement and worship of angels, taking his stand on visions, inflated without reason by his fleshly mind, [19][f]and not holding closely to the head, from whom the whole body, supported and held together by its ligaments and bonds, achieves the growth that comes from God.

[20]If you died with Christ to the elemental powers of the world, why do you submit to regulations as if you were still living in the world? [21]"Do not handle! Do not taste! Do not touch!" [22][g]These are all things destined to perish with use; they accord with human precepts and teachings. [23]While they have a semblance of wisdom in rigor of devotion and self-abasement [and] severity to the body, they are of no value against gratification of the flesh.

IV: The Ideal Christian Life in the World

CHAPTER 3

Mystical Death and Resurrection [1][h]*If then you were raised with Christ, seek what is above, where Christ is seated at the right hand of God. [2]Think of what is above, not of what is on earth. [3][i]For you have died, and your life is hidden with Christ in God. [4]When Christ your life appears, then you too will appear with him in glory.

Renunciation of Vice [5][j]*Put to death, then, the parts of you that are earthly: immorality, impurity, passion, evil desire, and the greed that is idolatry. [6][k]*Because of these the wrath of God is coming [upon the disobedient]. [7]By these you too once conducted yourselves, when you lived in that way. [8][l]*But now you must put them all away: anger, fury, malice, slander, and obscene language out of your mouths. [9][m]Stop lying to one another, since you have taken off the old self with its practices [10][n]*and have put on the new self, which is being renewed, for knowledge, in the image of its creator. [11][o]*Here there is not Greek and Jew, circumcision and uncircumcision, barbarian, Scythian, slave, free; but Christ is all and in all.

[12][p]Put on then, as God's chosen ones, holy and beloved, heartfelt compassion, kindness, humility, gentleness, and patience, [13][q]bearing with one another and forgiving one another, if one has a grievance against another; as the Lord has forgiven you, so must you also do. [14][r]And over all these put on love, that is, the bond of perfection. [15][s]And let the peace of Christ control your hearts, the peace into which you were also called in one body. And be thankful. [16][t]Let the word of Christ dwell in you richly, as in all wisdom you teach and admonish one another, singing psalms, hymns, and spiritual songs with gratitude in your hearts to God. [17][u]And whatever you do, in word or in deed, do everything in the name of the Lord Jesus, giving thanks to God the Father through him.

2, 16: Festival or new moon or sabbath: yearly, monthly, and weekly observances determined by religious powers associated with a calendar set by the heavenly bodies, sun, moon, and stars (cf 8).

2, 18: Ascetic practices encouraged by the false teachers included subjection of self humbly to their rules, worship of angels, and cultivation of visions, though exact details are unclear.

3, 1–4: By retaining the message of the gospel that the risen, living Christ is the source of their salvation, the Colossians will be free from false religious evaluations of the things of the world (1–2). They have died to these; but one day **when Christ . . . appears,** they will live with Christ in the presence of God (3–4).

3, 5–17: In lieu of false asceticism and superstitious festivals, the apostle reminds the Colossians of the moral life that is to characterize their response to God through Christ. He urges their participation in the liturgical hymns and prayers that center upon God's plan of salvation in Christ (16).

3, 5.8: The two lists of five vices each are similar to enumerations at Rom 1, 29–31 and Gal 5, 19–21.

3, 6: The wrath of God: see the note on Rom 1, 18. Many manuscripts add, as at Eph 5, 6, "upon the disobedient."

3, 8–10: Put . . . away; have taken off; have put on: the terms may reflect baptismal practice, taking off garments and putting on new ones after being united with Christ, here translated into ethical terms.

3, 10: Image: see the note on 1, 15.

3, 11: Scythian: a barbarous people from north of the Black Sea.

c Rom 14, 3–4; 1 Tm 4, 3. d Heb 8, 5; 10, 1. e 2, 23; Mt 24, 4. f Eph 2, 21–22; 4, 16. g Is 29, 13. h 2, 12; Ps 110, 1; Phil 3, 20; Eph 2, 6. i Rom 6, 2–5. j Mt 15, 19; Rom 1, 29–30; Gal 5, 19–21; Eph 5, 3.5. k Rom 1, 18. l Eph 4, 22.25.31. m Rom 6, 4.6; Eph 4, 22–25; Heb 12, 1; 1 Pt 2, 1; 4, 2. n Gn 1, 26–27. o 1 Cor 12, 13; Gal 3, 27–28. p Eph 4, 1–2.32; 1 Thes 5, 15. q Mt 6, 14; 18, 21–35; Eph 4, 32. r Rom 13, 8–10. s Rom 12, 5; 1 Cor 12, 12; Eph 2, 16; 4, 3–4; Phil 4, 7. t Eph 5, 19–20. u 1 Cor 10, 31.

The Christian Family 18 [v]*Wives, be subordinate to your husbands, as is proper in the Lord. 19 Husbands, love your wives, and avoid any bitterness toward them. 20 [w]Children, obey your parents in everything, for this is pleasing to the Lord. 21 [x]Fathers, do not provoke your children, so they may not become discouraged.

Slaves and Masters 22 [y]*Slaves, obey your human masters in everything, not only when being watched, as currying favor, but in simplicity of heart, fearing the Lord. 23 Whatever you do, do from the heart, as for the Lord and not for others, 24 knowing that you will receive from the Lord the due payment of the inheritance; be slaves of the Lord Christ. 25 [z]For the wrongdoer will receive recompense for the wrong he committed, and there is no partiality.

CHAPTER 4

1 Masters, treat your slaves justly and fairly, realizing that you too have a Master in heaven.

Prayer and Apostolic Spirit 2 [a]Persevere in prayer, being watchful in it with thanksgiving; 3 [b]at the same time, pray for us, too, that God may open a door to us for the word, to speak of the mystery of Christ, for which I am in prison, 4 that I may make it clear, as I must speak. 5 [c]Conduct yourselves wisely toward outsiders, making the most of the opportunity. 6 Let your speech always be gracious, seasoned with salt, so that you know how you should respond to each one.

V: Conclusion

Tychicus and Onesimus 7 [d]*Tychicus, my beloved brother, trustworthy minister, and fellow slave in the Lord, will tell you all the news of me. 8 I am sending him to you for this very purpose, so that you may know about us and that he may encourage your hearts, 9 [e]together with Onesimus, a trustworthy and beloved brother, who is one of you. They will tell you about everything here.

From Paul's Co-Workers 10 [f]*Aristarchus, my fellow prisoner, sends you greetings, as does Mark the cousin of Barnabas (concerning whom you have received instructions; if he comes to you, receive him), 11 *and Jesus, who is called Justus, who are of the circumcision; these alone are my co-workers for the kingdom of God, and they have been a comfort to me. 12 [g]*Epaphras sends you greetings; he is one of you, a slave of Christ [Jesus], always striving for you in his prayers so that you may be perfect and fully assured in all the will of God. 13 *For I can testify that he works very hard for you and for those in Laodicea and those in Hierapolis. 14 [h]*Luke the beloved physician sends greetings, as does Demas.

A Message for the Laodiceans 15 *Give greetings to the brothers in Laodicea and to Nympha and to the church in her house. 16 *And when this letter is read before you, have it read also in the church of the Laodiceans, and you your-

3, 18—4, 6: After general recommendations that connect family life and the social condition of slavery with the service of Christ (3, 18—4, 1), Paul requests prayers for himself, especially in view of his imprisonment (2–3), and recommends friendly relations and meaningful discussions of Christian teaching with **outsiders,** i.e., non-Christians (5–6). See the note on Eph 5, 21—6, 9.

3, 22–25: Slaves: within this table of duties in family and societal relations, involving wives and husbands, children and parents (18–21), such as also appears in Eph 5, 22—6, 9, slaves here receive special attention because of the case of Onesimus the slave returning to his master (4, 9; Phlm 10–12).

4, 7–18: Paul concludes with greetings and information concerning various Christians known to the Colossians.

4, 7: Tychicus: Acts 20, 4 mentions his role in the collection for Jerusalem; Eph 6, 21 repeats what is said here; see also 2 Tm 4, 12; Ti 3, 12.

4, 10: Aristarchus: a Thessalonian who was with Paul at Ephesus and Caesarea and on the voyage to Rome (Acts 19, 29; 20, 4; 27, 2). **Mark:** also referred to at Phlm 24 and 2 Tm 4, 11 and, as "John Mark," in Acts (12, 12.25; 13, 13; 15, 37–40). See also 1 Pt 5, 13 and the note there. Traditionally the author of the second gospel.

4, 11: Jesus: a then common Jewish name, the Greek form of Joshua.

4, 12: Epaphras: see the notes on 1, 3–8 and 1, 7.

4, 13: Laodicea: see the note on 2, 1. **Hierapolis:** a city northeast of Laodicea and northwest of Colossae.

4, 14: Luke: only here described as a medical doctor; cf Phlm 24 and 2 Tm 4, 11. Traditionally the author of the third gospel. **Demas:** cf Phlm 24; he later deserted Paul (2 Tm 4, 10).

4, 15: Nympha and . . . her house: some manuscripts read a masculine for the house-church leader, "Nymphas and . . . his house."

4, 16: The one from Laodicea: either a letter by Paul that has been lost or the Letter to the Ephesians (cf the note on Eph 1, 1, **in Ephesus**).

v Eph 5, 22; Ti 2, 5; 1 Pt 3, 1. w Eph 6, 1. x Eph 6, 4. y Eph 6, 5; 1 Tm 6, 1; Ti 2, 9–10; 1 Pt 2, 18. z Rom 2, 11. a Lk 18, 1; Rom 12, 12; Eph 6, 18–20; 1 Thes 5, 17. b Rom 15, 30; 1 Cor 16, 9; Eph 6, 19; 2 Thes 3, 1. c Eph 5, 15–16. d Acts 20, 4; Eph 6, 21–22; Phil 1, 12. e Phlm 10–11. f Acts 19, 29; 20, 4; 27, 2 / Acts 12, 12.25; 13, 13; 15, 37.40;2 Tm 4, 11; Phlm 24; 1 Pt 5, 13. g 1, 7; Rom 15, 30. h Phlm 24; 2 Tm 4, 10–11.

selves read the one from Laodicea. [17] [i]*And tell Archippus, "See that you fulfill the ministry that you received in the Lord."

4, 17: **Fulfill the ministry:** usually taken to mean that **Archippus**, the son of Philemon and Apphia (Phlm 1–2), is "pastor" at Colossae. An alternate interpretation is that Archippus, not Philemon, is the owner of the slave Onesimus and that Paul is asking Archippus to complete the service he has received in the Lord by sending Onesimus back to minister to Paul in his captivity (cf Phlm 20).

[18] [j]*The greeting is in my own hand, Paul's. Remember my chains. Grace be with you.

4, 18: **My own hand:** a postscript in Paul's own hand was his custom; cf Gal 6, 11–18 and 2 Thes 3, 17–18.

i Phlm 2. j 1 Cor 16, 21; Gal 6, 11; Eph 3, 1; 2 Thes 3, 17.

THE FIRST LETTER TO THE THESSALONIANS

When Paul parted from Barnabas (Acts 15, 36-41) at the beginning of what is called his second missionary journey, he chose Silvanus (Silas) as his traveling companion. Soon afterwards he took Timothy along with him (Acts 16, 1-3). Paul was now clearly at the head of his own missionary band. About A.D. 50, he arrived in Greece for the first time. In making converts in Philippi and, soon afterwards, in Thessalonica, he was beset by persecution from Jews and Gentiles alike. Moving on to Beroea, he was again harassed by enemies from Thessalonica and hurriedly left for Athens (Acts 16, 11—17, 15). Silvanus and Timothy remained behind for a while. Paul soon sent Timothy back to Thessalonica to strengthen that community in its trials (3, 1-5). Timothy and Silvanus finally returned to Paul when he reached Corinth (Acts 18, 1-18), probably in the early summer of A.D. 51. Timothy's return with a report on conditions at Thessalonica served as the occasion for Paul's first letter (3, 6-8).

The letter begins with a brief address (1, 1) and concludes with a greeting (5, 26-28). The body of the letter consists of two major parts. The first (1, 2—3, 13) is a set of three sections of thanksgiving connected by two *apologiae* (defenses) dealing, respectively, with the missionaries' previous conduct and their current concerns. Paul's thankful optimism regarding the Thessalonians' spiritual welfare is tempered by his insistence on their recognition of the selfless love shown by the missionaries. In an age of itinerant peddlers of new religions, Paul found it necessary to emphasize not only the content of his gospel but also his manner of presenting it, for both attested to God's grace as freely bestowed and powerfully effected.

The second part of the letter (4, 1—5, 25) is specifically hortatory or parenetic. The superabundant love for which Paul has just prayed (3, 12-13) is to be shown practically by living out the norms of conduct that he has communicated to them. Specific "imperatives" of Christian life, principles for acting morally, stem from the "indicative" of one's relationship to God through Christ by the sending of the holy Spirit. Thus, moral conduct is the practical, personal expression of one's Christian faith, love, and hope.

The principal divisions of the First Letter to the Thessalonians are the following:

I. Address (1, 1-10)
II. Previous Relations with the Thessalonians (2, 1—3, 13)
III. Specific Exhortations (4, 1—5, 25)
IV. Final Greeting (5, 26-28)

I: Address

CHAPTER 1

Greeting 1 [a]*Paul, Silvanus, and Timothy to the church of the Thessalonians in God the Father and the Lord Jesus Christ: grace to you and peace.

Thanksgiving for Their Faith 2 [b]We give thanks to God always for all of you, remembering you in our prayers, unceasingly 3 *calling to mind your work of faith and labor of love and endurance in hope of our Lord Jesus Christ, before our God and Father, 4 [c]knowing, brothers loved by God, how you were chosen. 5 [d]For our gospel did not come to you in word alone, but also in power and in the holy Spirit and [with] much conviction. You know what sort of people we were [among] you for your sake. 6 *And you became imitators of us and of the Lord, receiving the word in great affliction, with joy from the holy Spirit, 7 [e]so that you became a model for all the believers in Macedonia and in Achaia. 8 [f]For from you the word of the Lord has sounded forth not only in Macedonia and [in] Achaia, but in every place your faith in God has gone forth, so that we have no need to say anything. 9 [g]For they themselves openly declare about us what sort of reception we had among you, and how you turned to God from idols to serve the living and true God 10 [h]and to await his Son from heaven, whom he raised from [the] dead, Jesus, who delivers us from the coming wrath.

II: Previous Relations with the Thessalonians

CHAPTER 2

Paul's Ministry Among Them 1 For you yourselves know, brothers, that our reception among you was not without effect. 2 [i]Rather, after we had suffered and been insolently treated, as you know, in Philippi, we drew courage through our God to speak to you the gospel of God with much struggle. 3 Our exhortation was not from delusion or impure motives, nor did it work through deception. 4 [j]*But as we were judged worthy by God to be entrusted with the gospel, that is how we speak, not as trying to please human beings, but rather God, who judges our hearts. 5 Nor, indeed, did we ever appear with flattering speech, as you know, or with a pretext for greed—God is witness— 6 [k]nor did we seek praise from human beings, either from you or from others, 7 *although we were able to impose our weight as apostles of Christ. Rather, we were gentle among you, as a nursing mother cares for her children. 8 With such affection for you, we were determined to share with you not only the gospel of God, but our very selves as well, so dearly beloved had you become to us. 9 [l]You recall, brothers, our toil and drudgery. Working night and day in order not to burden any of you, we proclaimed to you the gospel of God. 10 You are witnesses, and so is God, how devoutly and justly and blamelessly we behaved toward you believers. 11 [m]As you know, we treated each one of you as a father treats his children, 12 [n]exhorting and encouraging you and insisting that you conduct yourselves as worthy of the God who calls you into his kingdom and glory.

Further Thanksgiving 13 And for this reason we too give thanks to God unceasingly, that, in receiving the word of God from hearing us, you received not a human word but, as it truly is, the word of God, which is now at work in you who believe. 14 *For you, brothers, have become

1, 1: On the address, see the note on Rom 1, 1–7.

1, 3: Faith . . . love . . . hope: this, along with 5, 8, is the earliest mention in Christian literature of the three "theological virtues" (see 1 Cor 13, 13). The order here stresses eschatological hope, in line with the letter's emphasis on the Lord's second, triumphal coming, or parousia (10; 2, 12.19; 3, 13; 4, 13—5, 11; 5, 23).

1, 6: Imitators: the Pauline theme of "imitation" (see 2, 14; 1 Cor 4, 16; 11, 1; 2 Thes 3, 9) is rooted in Paul's view of solidarity in Christ through sharing in Jesus' cross and in the Spirit of the risen Lord.

2, 4: Judged worthy: Paul regards "worthiness" not as grounded in one's own talent or moral self-righteousness but in God's discernment of genuinely selfless attitudes and actions (see 2 Cor 10, 17–18).

2, 7: Gentle: many excellent manuscripts read "infants" (nēpioi), but "gentle" (ēpioi) better suits the context here.

2, 14: Luke's picture of the persecutions at Philippi (by Gen-

a Acts 15, 40; 16, 1–3.19; 17, 14–15; 2 Thes 1, 1–2. b 2 Thes 1, 3. c 2 Thes 2, 13. d Acts 13, 52; 17, 1–9. e 2 Thes 1, 4; 1 Cor 4, 16; 11, 1 / 2, 14; Phil 3, 17. f Rom 1, 8. g Acts 14, 15; Gal 4, 8 / 4, 5. h Rom 2, 1–16; 5, 9; 13, 4 / 5, 9. i Acts 16, 19—17, 10. j Gal 1, 10. k Jn 5, 41.44; 1 Cor 10, 31; 2 Cor 4, 17. l Acts 20, 34; 1 Cor 4, 12; 9, 3–18; 2 Thes 3, 7–9. m Acts 20, 31. n 1 Pt 5, 10 / 4, 7; 2 Thes 2, 14.

imitators of the churches of God that are in Judea in Christ Jesus. For you suffer the same things from your compatriots as they did from the Jews, [15][o]*who killed both the Lord Jesus and the prophets and persecuted us; they do not please God, and are opposed to everyone, [16][p]trying to prevent us from speaking to the Gentiles that they may be saved, thus constantly filling up the measure of their sins. But the wrath of God has finally begun to come upon them.

Paul's Recent Travel Plans [17][q]Brothers, when we were bereft of you for a short time, in person, not in heart, we were all the more eager in our great desire to see you in person. [18][r]We decided to go to you—I, Paul, not only once but more than once—yet Satan thwarted us. [19][s]For what is our hope or joy or crown to boast of in the presence of our Lord Jesus at his coming if not you yourselves? [20]For you are our glory and joy.

CHAPTER 3

[1][t]That is why, when we could bear it no longer, we decided to remain alone in Athens [2][u]and sent Timothy, our brother and co-worker for God in the gospel of Christ, to strengthen and encourage you in your faith, [3]*so that no one be disturbed in these afflictions. For you yourselves know that we are destined for this. [4][v]For even when we were among you, we used to warn you in advance that we would undergo affliction, just as has happened, as you know. [5]For this reason, when I too could bear it no longer, I sent to learn about your faith, for fear that somehow the tempter had put you to the test and our toil might come to nothing.

[6]But just now Timothy has returned to us from you, bringing us the good news of your faith and love, and that you always think kindly of us and long to see us as we long to see you. [7]Because of this, we have been reassured about you, brothers, in our every distress and affliction, through your faith. [8]For we now live, if you stand firm in the Lord.

Concluding Thanksgiving and Prayer [9]*What thanksgiving, then, can we render to God for you, for all the joy we feel on your account before our God? [10]Night and day we pray beyond measure to see you in person and to remedy the deficiencies of your faith. [11]Now may God himself, our Father, and our Lord Jesus direct our way to you, [12][w]and may the Lord make you increase and abound in love for one another and for all, just as we have for you, [13][x]so as to strengthen your hearts, to be blameless in holiness before our God and Father at the coming of our Lord Jesus with all his holy ones. [Amen.]

III: Specific Exhortations

CHAPTER 4

General Exhortations [1]Finally, brothers, we earnestly ask and exhort you in the Lord Jesus that, as you received from us how you should conduct yourselves to please God—and as you are conducting yourselves—you do so even

---

tiles) and in Thessalonica and Beroea (by Jews) seems to be considerably schematized (Acts 16, 11–40; 17, 1–15). Paul pictures the Thessalonian community as composed of converts from paganism (1, 9) and speaks here of persecution by their (pagan) compatriots rather than by Jews.

2, 15–16: Paul is speaking of historical opposition on the part of Palestinian Jews in particular and does so only some twenty years after Jesus' crucifixion. Even so, he quickly proceeds to depict the persecutors typologically, in apocalyptic terms. His remarks give no grounds for anti-Semitism to those willing to understand him, especially in view of Paul's pride in his own ethnic and religious background (Rom 9, 1–5; 10, 1; 11, 1–3; Phil 3, 4–6). Sinful conduct (16) is itself an anticipation of the ultimate wrath or judgment of God (Rom 1, 18—2, 5), whether or not it is perceived as such.

3, 3: We are destined: the Greek phraseology and the context suggest Paul's concern to alert his readers to difficulties he knew they would necessarily face and to enable them to see their present experience in the light of what he warned them would happen in the future. This line of thought is followed in 2 Thes 2, 1–15.

3, 9–10: The tension between Paul's optimism concerning the Thessalonians' faith and his worries about their perseverance remains unresolved. Perhaps this is accounted for not only by the continuing harassment but also by the shortness of his own stay in Thessalonica (even if that were over twice as long as the conventional three weeks that Luke assigns to it, Acts 17, 2).

o Acts 2, 23; 7, 52. p Gn 15, 16; 2 Mc 6, 14 / Rom 1, 18; 2, 5–6. q 3, 10; Rom 1, 10–11. r Rom 15, 22. s 2 Cor 1, 14; Phil 2, 16; 4, 1. t Acts 17, 14. u Acts 16, 1-2; 1 Cor 3, 5–9. v Acts 14, 22; 2 Thes 2, 5–7; 2 Tm 3, 12. w 4, 9–10; 2 Thes 1, 3. x 5, 23; 1 Cor 1, 8.

more. 2 *For you know what instructions we gave you through the Lord Jesus.

Holiness in Sexual Conduct 3 *This is the will of God, your holiness: that you refrain from immorality, 4 that each of you know how to acquire a wife for himself in holiness and honor, 5 [y]not in lustful passion as do the Gentiles who do not know God; 6 not to take advantage of or exploit a brother in this matter, for the Lord is an avenger in all these things, as we told you before and solemnly affirmed. 7 For God did not call us to impurity but to holiness. 8 [z]Therefore, whoever disregards this, disregards not a human being but God, who [also] gives his holy Spirit to you.

Mutual Charity 9 [a]On the subject of mutual charity you have no need for anyone to write you, for you yourselves have been taught by God to love one another. 10 [b]Indeed, you do this for all the brothers throughout Macedonia. Nevertheless we urge you, brothers, to progress even more, 11 and to aspire to live a tranquil life, to mind your own affairs, and to work with your [own] hands, as we instructed you, 12 that you may conduct yourselves properly toward outsiders and not depend on anyone.

Hope for the Christian Dead 13 We do not want you to be unaware, brothers, about those who have fallen asleep, so that you may not grieve like the rest, who have no hope. 14 [c]For if we believe that Jesus died and rose, so too will God, through Jesus, bring with him those who have fallen asleep. 15 [d]*Indeed, we tell you this, on the word of the Lord, that we who are alive, who are left until the coming of the Lord, will surely not precede those who have fallen asleep. 16 [e]For the Lord himself, with a word of command, with the voice of an archangel and with the trumpet of God, will come down from heaven, and the dead in Christ will rise first. 17 *Then we who are alive, who are left, will be caught up together with them in the clouds to meet the Lord in the air. Thus we shall always be with the Lord. 18 Therefore, console one another with these words.

CHAPTER 5

Vigilance 1 [f]Concerning times and seasons, brothers, you have no need for anything to be written to you. 2 [g]For you yourselves know very well that the day of the Lord will come like a thief at night. 3 When people are saying, "Peace and security," then sudden disaster comes upon them, like labor pains upon a pregnant woman, and they will not escape.

4 [h]But you, brothers, are not in darkness, for that day to overtake you like a thief. 5 *For all of you are children of the light and children of the day. We are not of the night or of darkness. 6 [i]Therefore, let us not sleep as the rest do, but let us stay alert and sober. 7 Those who sleep go to sleep at night, and those who are drunk get drunk at night. 8 [j]But since we are of the day, let us be sober, putting on the breastplate of faith and love and the helmet that is hope for salvation. 9 For God did not destine us for wrath, but

4, 2: Instructions: these include specific guidelines on the basis of the Lord's authority, not necessarily sayings Jesus actually uttered. More profoundly, as v 8 implies, the instructions are practical principles that Paul worked out in accordance with his understanding of the role of the Spirit.

4, 3–8: Many think that this passage deals with a variety of moral regulations (fornication, adultery, sharp business practices). It can be more specifically interpreted as bringing general norms to bear on a specific problem, namely, marriage within degrees of consanguinity (as between uncle and niece) forbidden in Jewish law but allowed according to a Greek heiress law, which would insure retention of an inheritance within the family and perhaps thereby occasion divorce. In that case, "immorality" (3) should be rendered as "unlawful marriage" and "this matter" (6) as "a lawsuit." The phrase in v 4, "acquire a wife for himself," has often been interpreted to mean "control one's body."

4, 15: Coming of the Lord: Paul here assumes that the second coming, or parousia, will occur within his own lifetime but insists that the time or season is unknown (5, 1–2). Nevertheless, the most important aspect of the parousia for him was the fulfillment of union with Christ. His pastoral exhortation focuses first on hope for the departed faithful, then (5, 1–3) on the need of preparedness for those who have to achieve their goal.

4, 17: Will be caught up together: literally, snatched up, carried off; cf 2 Cor 12, 2; Rv 12, 5. From the Latin verb here used, **rapiemur,** has come the idea of "the rapture," when believers will be transported away from the woes of the world; this construction combines this verse with Mt 24, 40–41 (see the note there) // Lk 17, 34–35 and passages from Rv in a scheme of millennial dispensationalism.

5, 5: Children of the light: that is, belonging to the daylight of God's personal revelation and expected to achieve it (an analogous development of imagery that appears in Jn 12, 36).

y Ps 79, 6; Jer 10, 25; 2 Thes 1, 8; 1 Pt 3, 7. z Lk 10, 16. a Jn 6, 45; 13, 34; 1 Jn 2, 20–21.27; 4, 7. b 2 Thes 3, 6–12. c 1 Cor 15, 3–4.12.20. d 1 Cor 15, 51; Rv 14, 13; 20, 4–6. e Mt 24, 31; 1 Cor 15, 23.52. f Mt 24, 36–45. g 2 Pt 3, 10. h Eph 5, 8–9. i Mt 24, 42; Rom 13, 12–13; 1 Pt 5, 8. j Is 59, 17; Rom 13, 11–14; Eph 6, 11.14–17.

to gain salvation through our Lord Jesus Christ,
10*who died for us, so that whether we are
awake or asleep we may live together with him.
11 [k]Therefore, encourage one another and build
one another up, as indeed you do.
Church Order 12We ask you, brothers, to
respect those who are laboring among you and
who are over you in the Lord and who admonish
you, 13and to show esteem for them with special
love on account of their work. Be at peace
among yourselves.
14We urge you, brothers, admonish the idle,
cheer the fainthearted, support the weak, be
patient with all. 15 [l]See that no one returns evil
for evil; rather, always seek what is good [both]
for each other and for all. 16Rejoice always.
17Pray without ceasing. 18 [m]In all circumstances
give thanks, for this is the will of God for you in
Christ Jesus. 19*Do not quench the Spirit. 20Do
not despise prophetic utterances. 21Test every-
thing; retain what is good. 22Refrain from every
kind of evil.
Concluding Prayer 23 [n]*May the God of peace
himself make you perfectly holy and may you
entirely, spirit, soul, and body, be preserved
blameless for the coming of our Lord Jesus
Christ. 24The one who calls you is faithful, and
he will also accomplish it. 25Brothers, pray for us
[too].

IV: Final Greeting

26*Greet all the brothers with a holy kiss. 27I
adjure you by the Lord that this letter be read to
the brothers. 28The grace of our Lord Jesus
Christ be with you.

5, 10: Characteristically, Paul plays on words suggesting ultimate and anticipated death and life. Union with the crucified and risen Lord at his parousia is anticipated in some measure in contrasted states of our temporal life. The essential element he urges is our indestructible personal union in Christ's own life (see Rom 5, 1–10).

5, 19–21: Paul's buoyant encouragement of charismatic freedom sometimes occasioned excesses that he or others had to remedy (see 1 Cor 14; 2 Thes 2, 1–15; 2 Pt 3, 1–16).

5, 23: Another possible translation is, "May the God of peace himself make you perfectly holy and sanctify your spirit fully, and may both soul and body be preserved blameless for the coming of our Lord Jesus Christ." In either case, Paul is not offering an anthropological or philosophical analysis of human nature. Rather, he looks to the wholeness of what may be called the supernatural and natural aspects of a person's service of God.

5, 26: **Kiss:** the holy embrace (see Rom 16, 16; 1 Cor 16, 20; 2 Cor 13, 12; 1 Pt 5, 14) was a greeting of respect and affection, perhaps given during a liturgy at which Paul's letter would have been read.

k Rom 15, 2; 1 Cor 8, 1; 14, 12.26; Eph 4, 29. l Prv 20, 22; Mt 5, 38–42; Rom 12, 17. m Eph 5, 20. n 2 Thes 3, 16.

THE SECOND LETTER TO THE THESSALONIANS

This letter is addressed to the same church as the letter that precedes it in the canon and contains many expressions parallel to those in the First Letter to the Thessalonians, indeed verbatim with them. Yet other aspects of the contents of the Second Letter to the Thessalonians suggest a more impersonal tone and changed circumstances in the situation at Thessalonica.

The letter begins with an address (1, 1-2) that expands only slightly on that of 1 Thes 1, 1. It ends with a greeting insisting on its Pauline authority in the face of false claims made in Paul's name (see the note on 2, 2). The body of the letter falls into three short parts, of which the second is notoriously difficult (ch 2).

The opening thanksgiving and prayer (1, 3-12) speak of the Thessalonians' increasing faith and love in the face of outside persecution. God's eventual judgment against persecutors and his salvation for the faithful are already evidenced by the very fact of persecution. The second part (2, 1-17), the heart of the letter, deals with a problem threatening the faith of the community. A message involving a prophetic oracle and apparently a forged letter, possibly presented at a liturgical gathering (cf 2, 2 and 1 Cor 14, 26-33), to the effect that the day of the Lord and all that it means have already come, has upset the life of the Thessalonian church.

The writer counters their preoccupation with the date of the parousia (or coming again of the Lord Jesus from heaven, 2, 1) by recalling Paul's teaching concerning what must happen first and by going on to describe what will happen at the Lord's coming (2, 8); he indicates the twofold process by which the "activity of Satan" and God's actions (2, 9-11) are working out, namely, a growing division between believers and those who succumb to false prophecy and "the lie." He concludes by insisting on Pauline traditions and by praying for divine strength (2, 13-17). The closing part of the letter (3, 1-16) deals in particular with the apostle's directives and model style of life and with correction of disorderly elements within the community.

Traditional opinion holds that this letter was written shortly after 1 Thessalonians. Occasionally it has been argued that 2 Thessalonians was written first or that the two letters are addressed to different segments within the church at Thessalonica (2 Thessalonians being directed to the Jewish Christians there) or even that 2 Thessalonians was originally written to some other nearby place where Paul carried out mission work, such as Philippi or Beroea. Increasingly in recent times, however, the opinion has been advanced that 2 Thessalonians is a pseudepigraph, that is, a letter written authoritatively in Paul's name, to maintain apostolic traditions in a later period, perhaps during the last two decades of the first century.

In any case, the presumed audience of Second Thessalonians and certain features of its style and content require that it be read and studied in a Pauline context, particularly that provided by 1 Thessalonians. At the same time, and especially if the letter is regarded as not by Paul himself, its apocalyptic presentation of preconditions for the parousia (2, 1-12) may profit from and require recourse to a wider biblical basis for interpretation, namely Old Testament books such as Daniel and Isaiah and especially, in the New Testament, the synoptic apocalyptic discourse (Mk 13; Mt 24–25; Lk 21, 5-36) and the Book of Revelation.

The principal divisions of the Second Letter to the Thessalonians are the following:

I. Address (1, 1-12)
II. Warning against Deception Concerning the Parousia (2, 1-17)
III. Concluding Exhortations (3, 1-16)
IV. Final Greetings (3, 17-18)

I: Address

CHAPTER 1

Greeting 1 [a]*Paul, Silvanus, and Timothy to the church of the Thessalonians in God our Father and the Lord Jesus Christ: 2grace to you and peace from God [our] Father and the Lord Jesus Christ.

Thanksgiving 3 [b]*We ought to thank God always for you, brothers, as is fitting, because your
faith flourishes ever more, and the love of every one of you for one another grows ever greater.
4Accordingly, we ourselves boast of you in the churches of God regarding your endurance and faith in all your persecutions and the afflictions you endure.

5 [c]This is evidence of the just judgment of God, so that you may be considered worthy of the kingdom of God for which you are suffering.
6For it is surely just on God's part to repay with

1, 1–2: On the address, see the note on Rom 1, 1–7 and cf 1 Thes 1, 1.

1, 3–12: On the thanksgiving, see the note on Rom 1, 8 and cf 1 Thes 1, 2–10. Paul's gratitude to God for the faith and love of the Thessalonians (3) and his Christian pride in their faithful endurance (4–5) contrast with the condemnation announced for those who afflict them, a judgment to be carried out at the parousia (6–10), which is described in vivid language drawn from Old Testament apocalyptic. A prayer for the fulfillment of God's purpose in the Thessalonians (11–12) completes the section, as is customary in a Pauline letter (cf 1 Thes 1, 2–3).

a 1 Thes 1, 1. b 1 Cor 1, 4; 1 Thes 1, 2; 3, 12. c Phil 1, 28; 1 Thes 2, 12.

afflictions those who are afflicting you, 7and to
grant rest along with us to you who are undergo-
ing afflictions, at the revelation of the Lord Jesus
from heaven with his mighty angels, 8 [d]in blazing
fire, inflicting punishment on those who do not
acknowledge God and on those who do not obey
the gospel of our Lord Jesus. 9 [e]These will pay
the penalty of eternal ruin, separated from the
presence of the Lord and from the glory of his
power, 10 [f]*when he comes to be glorified
among his holy ones and to be marveled at on
that day among all who have believed, for our
testimony to you was believed.

Prayer 11 [g]To this end, we always pray for you,
that our God may make you worthy of his calling
and powerfully bring to fulfillment every good
purpose and every effort of faith, 12 [h]*that the
name of our Lord Jesus may be glorified in you,
and you in him, in accord with the grace of our
God and Lord Jesus Christ.

II: Warning against Deception Concerning the Parousia

CHAPTER 2

Christ and the Lawless One 1 [i]*We ask you,
brothers, with regard to the coming of our Lord
Jesus Christ and our assembling with him,
2 [j]*not to be shaken out of your minds suddenly,
or to be alarmed either by a "spirit," or by an
oral statement, or by a letter allegedly from us to
the effect that the day of the Lord is at hand.
3*Let no one deceive you in any way. For unless
the apostasy comes first and the lawless one is
revealed, the one doomed to perdition, 4 [k]*who
opposes and exalts himself above every so-called
god and object of worship, so as to seat himself
in the temple of God, claiming that he is a god—
5do you not recall that while I was still with you
I told you these things? 6*And now you know
what is restraining, that he may be revealed in

1, 10: Among his holy ones: in the Old Testament, this term can refer to an angelic throng (cf also Jude 14), but here, in parallel with **among all who have believed,** it can refer to the triumphant people of God.

1, 12: The grace of our God and Lord Jesus Christ: the Greek can also be translated, "the grace of our God and of the Lord Jesus Christ."

2, 1–17: The Thessalonians have been **shaken** by a message purporting to come from Paul himself that **the day of the Lord** is already present. He warns against this deception in eschatology by citing a scenario of events that must first occur (3–12) before the end will come. The overall point Paul makes is the need to reject such lies as Satan sends; he also reaffirms the Thessalonians in their calling (13–14). They are to uphold what Paul himself has taught (15). There is a concluding prayer for their strengthening (16–17). As in 1, 8–10, the Old Testament provides a good deal of coloring; cf especially Is 14, 13–14; 66, 15.18–21; Ez 28, 2–9; Dn 11, 36–37. The contents of 2, 3b-8 may come from a previously existing apocalypse. The details have been variously interpreted.

An alternative to the possibilities noted below understands that an oracular utterance, supposedly coming from a prophetic spirit (2–3a), has so disrupted the community's thinking that its effects may be compared to those of the mania connected with the worship of the Greek god Dionysus. On this view, the writer seems to allude in vv 6–8 to Dionysiac "seizure," although, of course, ironically, somewhat as Paul alludes to witchcraft ("an evil eye") in Gal 3, 1 in speaking of the threat to faith posed by those disturbing the Galatians (Gal 1, 6–7; 5, 10b). On this view of 2 Thes 2, the Greek participles **katechon** (rendered above as **what is restraining**) and **katechōn (the one who restrains)** are to be translated "the seizing power" in v 6 and "the seizer" in v 7. They then allude to a pseudocharismatic force or spirit of Dionysiac character that has suddenly taken hold of the Thessalonian community (see 2). The addressees **know** (6) this force or spirit because of the problem it is causing. This pseudocharismatic force or spirit is a kind of anticipation and advance proof of the ultimate, climactic figure (**the lawless one** or the rebel, 3), of which the community has been warned (see the note on 1 Thes 3, 3). It is, however, only the beginning of the end that the latter's manifestation entails; the end is not yet. For in the course of the **mystery of lawlessness** (7), false prophetism, after it ceases in the Thessalonian community, will be manifested in the world at large (8–12), where it will also be eliminated in turn by the Lord Jesus.

2, 2: "Spirit": a Spirit-inspired utterance or ecstatic revelation. **An oral statement:** literally, a "word" or pronouncement, not necessarily of ecstatic origin. **A letter allegedly sent by us:** possibly a forged letter, so that Paul calls attention in 3, 17 to his practice of concluding a genuine letter with a summary note or greeting in his own hand, as at Gal 6, 11–18 and elsewhere.

2, 3b-5: This incomplete sentence (anacoluthon, 4) recalls what the Thessalonians had already been taught, an apocalyptic scenario depicting, in terms borrowed especially from Dn 11, 36–37 and related verses, human self-assertiveness against God in **the temple of God** itself. **The lawless one** represents the climax of such activity in this account.

2, 4: Seat himself in the temple of God: a reflection of the language in Dn 7, 23–25; 8, 9–12; 9, 27; 11, 36–37; and 12, 11 about the attempt of Antiochus IV Epiphanes to set up a statue of Zeus in the Jerusalem temple and possibly of the Roman emperor Caligula to do a similar thing (Mk 13, 14). Here the imagery suggests an attempt to install someone in the place of God, **claiming that he is a god** (cf Ez 28, 2). Usually, it is the Jerusalem temple that is assumed to be meant; on the alternative view sketched above (see the note on 2, 1–17), **the temple** refers to the Christian community.

2, 6–7: What is restraining . . . the one who restrains: neuter and masculine, respectively, of a force and person holding back the lawless one. The Thessalonians know what is meant (6), but the terms, seemingly found only in this passage and in writings dependent on it, have been variously interpreted. Traditionally, v 6 has been applied to the Roman empire and v 7 to the Roman emperor (in Paul's day, Nero) as bulwarks holding back chaos (cf Rom 13, 1–7). A second interpretation suggests that cosmic or angelic powers are binding Satan (9) and so restraining him; some relate this to an anti-Christ figure (1 Jn 2, 18) or to Michael the archangel (Rv 12, 7–9; 20, 1–3). A more recent view suggests

d Ps 79, 5–6; Is 66, 15; Jer 10, 25. e Is 2, 10.19.21. f Ps 89, 8; Dn 7, 18–22.27; 1 Thes 3, 13. g 1 Thes 1, 2–3. h Is 66, 5. i 1 Thes 4, 13–17. j Mt 24, 6; 1 Cor 14, 26.32–33; 1 Thes 5, 1-2. k Dn 11, 36–37; Ez 28, 2.

his time. 7 [l]*For the mystery of lawlessness is
already at work. But the one who restrains is to
do so only for the present, until he is removed
from the scene. 8 [m]And then the lawless one will
be revealed, whom the Lord [Jesus] will kill with
the breath of his mouth and render powerless by
the manifestation of his coming, 9 [n]the one
whose coming springs from the power of Satan
in every mighty deed and in signs and wonders
that lie, 10 and in every wicked deceit for those
who are perishing because they have not ac-
cepted the love of truth so that they may be
saved. 11 Therefore, God is sending them a
deceiving power so that they may believe the lie,
12 that all who have not believed the truth but
have approved wrongdoing may be condemned.

13 [o]*But we ought to give thanks to God for
you always, brothers loved by the Lord, because
God chose you as the firstfruits for salvation
through sanctification by the Spirit and belief in
truth. 14 [p]To this end he has [also] called you
through our gospel to possess the glory of our
Lord Jesus Christ. 15 *Therefore, brothers, stand
firm and hold fast to the traditions that you were
taught, either by an oral statement or by a letter
of ours.

16 May our Lord Jesus Christ himself and God
our Father, who has loved us and given us
everlasting encouragement and good hope
through his grace, 17 encourage your hearts and
strengthen them in every good deed and word.

III: Concluding Exhortations

CHAPTER 3

Request for Prayers 1 [q]*Finally, brothers, pray
for us, so that the word of the Lord may speed
forward and be glorified, as it did among you,
2 and that we may be delivered from perverse
and wicked people, for not all have faith. 3 [r]But
the Lord is faithful; he will strengthen you and
guard you from the evil one. 4 [s]We are confident
of you in the Lord that what we instruct you,
you [both] are doing and will continue to do.
5 May the Lord direct your hearts to the love of
God and to the endurance of Christ.

Neglect of Work 6 *We instruct you, brothers,
in the name of [our] Lord Jesus Christ, to shun
any brother who conducts himself in a disorderly
way and not according to the tradition they
received from us. 7 For you know how one must
imitate us. For we did not act in a disorderly way
among you, 8 [t]nor did we eat food received free
from anyone. On the contrary, in toil and drudg-
ery, night and day we worked, so as not to
burden any of you. 9 [u]Not that we do not have
the right. Rather, we wanted to present our-
selves as a model for you, so that you might

---

that it is the preaching of the Christian gospel that restrains the end, for in God's plan the end cannot come until the gospel is preached to all nations (Mk 13, 10); in that case, Paul as missionary preacher par excellence is "the one who restrains," whose removal (death) will bring the end (7). On the alternative view (see the note on 2, 1–17), the phrases should be referred to that which and to him who seizes (a prophet) in ecstasy so as to have him speak pseudo-oracles.

2, 7–12: The lawless one and **the one who restrains** are involved in an activity or process, **the mystery of lawlessness,** behind which **Satan** stands (9). The action of **the Lord [Jesus]** in overcoming the lawless one is described in Old Testament language (**with the breath of his mouth;** cf Is 11, 4; Jb 4, 9; Rv 19, 15). His **coming** is literally the Lord's "parousia." The biblical concept of the "holy war," eschatologically conceived, may underlie the imagery.

2, 13: As the firstfruits: there is also strong manuscript evidence for the reading, "God chose you from the beginning," thus providing a focus on God's activity from beginning to end; **firstfruits** is a Pauline term, however; cf Rom 8, 23; 11, 16; 16, 5, among other references.

2, 15: Reference to **an oral statement** and **a letter** (2) and the content here, including a formula of conclusion (cf 1 Cor 16, 13; Gal 5, 1), suggest that vv 1–15 or even 1–17 are to be taken as a literary unit, notwithstanding the incidental thanksgiving formula in v 13.

3, 1–18: The final chapter urges the Thessalonians to pray for Paul and his colleagues (1–2) and reiterates confidence in the Thessalonians (3–5), while admonishing them about a specific problem in their community that has grown out of the intense eschatological speculation, namely, not to work but to become instead disorderly busybodies (6–15). A benediction (16) and postscript in Paul's own hand round out the letter. On vv 17–18, cf the note on 2, 2.

3, 6: Some members of the community, probably because they regarded the parousia as imminent or the new age of the Lord to be already here (2, 2), had apparently ceased to work for a living. The disciplinary problem they posed could be rooted in distorted thinking about Paul's own teaching (cf 1 Thes 2, 16; 3, 3–4; 5, 4–5) or, more likely, in a forged letter (2, 2) and the type of teaching dealt with in 2, 1–15. The apostle's own moral teaching, reflected in his selfless labors for others, was rooted in a deep doctrinal concern for the gospel message (cf 1 Thes 2, 3–10).

l Mt 13, 36–43; Acts 20, 29; Gal 5, 10; 2 Pt 2, 1; Rv 22, 11. m Is 11, 4; Rv 19, 15. n Mt 24, 24; Rv 13, 13. o 1 Thes 2, 13; 5, 9. p Rom 5, 1–10; 8, 29–30; 1 Thes 4, 7; 5, 9. q Eph 6, 19; Col 4, 3. r 1 Thes 5, 24 / 1 Cor 16, 13 / Mt 6, 13. s 2 Cor 7, 16; 1 Thes 4, 1–2. t 1 Thes 2, 9. u Mt 10, 10; Phil 3, 17.

imitate us. 10 [v]In fact, when we were with you,
we instructed you that if anyone was unwilling
to work, neither should that one eat. 11 [w]We
hear that some are conducting themselves
among you in a disorderly way, by not keeping
busy but minding the business of others. 12 Such
people we instruct and urge in the Lord Jesus
Christ to work quietly and to eat their own food.
13 But you, brothers, do not be remiss in doing
good. 14 If anyone does not obey our word as
expressed in this letter, take note of this person
not to associate with him, that he may be put to
shame. 15 [x]Do not regard him as an enemy but
admonish him as a brother. 16 [y]May the Lord of
peace himself give you peace at all times and in
every way. The Lord be with all of you.

IV: Final Greetings

17 [z]This greeting is in my own hand, Paul's.
This is the sign in every letter; this is how I
write. 18 The grace of our Lord Jesus Christ be
with all of you.

v 1 Thes 4, 11. w 1 Thes 5, 14. x 2 Cor 2, 7; Gal 6, 1. y Jn 14, 27; Rom 15, 33. z 1 Cor 16, 21; Gal 6, 11.

THE FIRST LETTER TO TIMOTHY

The three letters, First and Second Timothy and Titus, form a distinct group within the Pauline corpus. In the collection of letters by the Apostle to the Gentiles, they differ from the others in form and contents. All three suggest they were written late in Paul's career. The opponents are not "Judaizers" as in Galatians but false teachers stressing "knowledge" (*gnōsis;* see the note on 1 Tm 6, 20-21). Attention is given especially to correct doctrine and church organization. Jesus' second coming recedes into the background compared to references in Paul's earlier letters (though not Colossians and Ephesians). The three letters are addressed not to congregations but to those who shepherd congregations (Latin, *pastores*). These letters were first named "Pastoral Epistles" in the eighteenth century because they all are concerned with the work of a pastor in caring for the community or communities under his charge.

The first of the Pastorals, 1 Timothy, is presented as having been written from Macedonia. Timothy, whom Paul converted, was of mixed Jewish and Gentile parentage (Acts 16, 1-3). He was the apostle's companion on both the second and the third missionary journeys (Acts 16, 3; 19, 22) and was often sent by him on special missions (Acts 19, 22; 1 Cor 4, 17; 1 Thes 3, 2). In 1 Timothy (1, 3), he is described as the administrator of the entire Ephesian community.

The letter instructs Timothy on his duty to restrain false and useless teaching (1, 3-11; 4, 1-5; 6, 3-16) and proposes principles pertaining to his relationship with the older members of the community (5, 1-2) and with the presbyters (5, 17-22). It gives rules for aid to widows (5, 3-8) and their selection for charitable ministrations (5, 9-16) and also deals with liturgical celebrations (2, 1-15), selections for the offices of bishop and deacon (3, 1-13), relation of slaves with their masters (6, 1-2), and obligations of the wealthier members of the community (6, 17-19). This letter also reminds Timothy of the prophetic character of his office (1, 12-20) and encourages him in his exercise of it (4, 6-16). The central passage of the letter (3, 14-16) expresses the principal motive that should guide the conduct of Timothy—preservation of the purity of the church's doctrine against false teaching. On this same note the letter concludes (6, 20-21).

From the late second century to the nineteenth, Pauline authorship of the three Pastoral Epistles went unchallenged. Since then, the attribution of these letters to Paul has been questioned. Most scholars are convinced that Paul could not have been responsible for the vocabulary and style, the concept of church organization, or the theological expressions found in these letters. A second group believes, on the basis of statistical evidence, that the vocabulary and style are Pauline, even if at first sight the contrary seems to be the case. They state that the concept of church organization in the letters is not as advanced as the questioners of Pauline authorship hold since the notion of hierarchical order in a religious community existed in Israel before the time of Christ, as evidenced in the Dead Sea Scrolls. Finally, this group sees affinities between the theological thought of the Pastorals and that of the unquestionably genuine letters of Paul. Other scholars, while conceding a degree of validity to the positions mentioned above, suggest that the apostle made use of a secretary who was responsible for the composition of the letters. A fourth group of scholars believes that these letters are the work of a compiler, that they are based on traditions about Paul in his later years, and that they include, in varying amounts, actual fragments of genuine Pauline correspondence.

If Paul is considered the more immediate author, the Pastorals are to be dated between the end of his first Roman imprisonment (Acts 28, 16) and his execution under Nero (A.D. 63–67); if they are regarded as only more remotely Pauline, their date may be as late as the early second century. In spite of these problems of authorship and dating, the Pastorals are illustrative of early Christian life and remain an important element of canonical scripture.

The principal divisions of the First Letter to Timothy are the following:

I. Address (1, 1-2)
II. Sound Teaching (1, 3-20)
III. Problems of Discipline (2, 1—4, 16)
IV. Duties toward Others (5, 1—6, 2a)
V. False Teaching and True Wealth (6, 2b-19)
VI. Final Recommendation and Warning (6, 20-21)

I: Address

CHAPTER 1

Greeting 1 [a]*Paul, an apostle of Christ Jesus by
command of God our savior and of Christ Jesus
our hope, 2 [b]to Timothy, my true child in faith:
grace, mercy, and peace from God the Father
and Christ Jesus our Lord.

II: Sound Teaching

Warning against False Doctrine 3 [c]*I repeat
the request I made of you when I was on my
way to Macedonia, that you stay in Ephesus to
instruct certain people not to teach false doc-
trines 4 [d]*or to concern themselves with myths
and endless genealogies, which promote specula-
tions rather than the plan of God that is to be
received by faith. 5 [e]The aim of this instruction is
love from a pure heart, a good conscience, and a
sincere faith. 6 [f]Some people have deviated from
these and turned to meaningless talk, 7 wanting
to be teachers of the law, but without under-
standing either what they are saying or what
they assert with such assurance.
8 [g]*We know that the law is good, provided

1, 1–2: For the Pauline use of the conventional epistolary form, see the note on Rom 1, 1–7.

1, 3–7: Here Timothy's initial task **in Ephesus** (cf Acts 20, 17–35) is outlined: to suppress the idle religious speculations, probably about Old Testament figures (3–4, but see the note on 6, 20–21), which do not contribute to the development of love within the community (5) but rather encourage similar useless conjectures (6–7).

1, 4: **The plan of God that is to be received by faith:** the Greek may also possibly mean "God's trustworthy plan" or "the training in faith that God requires."

1, 8–11: Those responsible for the speculations that are to be suppressed by Timothy do not present the Old Testament from the Christian viewpoint. The Christian values the Old Testament not

a 2, 3; Lk 1, 47; Ti 1, 3; 2, 10 / Col 1, 27. b 2 Tm 1, 2; Ti 1, 4. c Acts 20, 1. d 4, 7; Ti 1, 14; 3, 9; 2 Pt 1, 16. e Rom 13, 10. f 6, 4.20; Ti 1, 10. g Rom 7, 12.16.

that one uses it as law, [9]with the understanding that law is meant not for a righteous person but for the lawless and unruly, the godless and sinful, the unholy and profane, those who kill their fathers or mothers, murderers, [10 h]*the unchaste, sodomites, kidnapers, liars, perjurers, and whatever else is opposed to sound teaching, [11 i]according to the glorious gospel of the blessed God, with which I have been entrusted.

Gratitude for God's Mercy [12 j]*I am grateful to him who has strengthened me, Christ Jesus our Lord, because he considered me trustworthy in appointing me to the ministry. [13 k]I was once a blasphemer and a persecutor and an arrogant man, but I have been mercifully treated because I acted out of ignorance in my unbelief. [14 l]Indeed, the grace of our Lord has been abundant, along with the faith and love that are in Christ Jesus. [15 m]*This saying is trustworthy and deserves full acceptance: Christ Jesus came into the world to save sinners. Of these I am the foremost. [16]But for that reason I was mercifully treated, so that in me, as the foremost, Christ Jesus might display all his patience as an example for those who would come to believe in him for everlasting life. [17 n]*To the king of ages, incorruptible, invisible, the only God, honor and glory forever and ever. Amen.

Responsibility of Timothy [18 o]*I entrust this charge to you, Timothy, my child, in accordance with the prophetic words once spoken about you. Through them may you fight a good fight [19 p]by having faith and a good conscience. Some, by rejecting conscience, have made a shipwreck of their faith, [20 q]*among them Hymenaeus and Alexander, whom I have handed over to Satan to be taught not to blaspheme.

III: Problems of Discipline

CHAPTER 2

Prayer and Conduct [1 r]*First of all, then, I ask that supplications, prayers, petitions, and thanksgivings be offered for everyone, [2]for kings and for all in authority, that we may lead a quiet and tranquil life in all devotion and dignity. [3 s]This is good and pleasing to God our savior, [4 t]who wills everyone to be saved and to come to knowledge of the truth.

---

as a system of law but as the first stage in God's revelation of his saving plan, which is brought to fulfillment in the good news of salvation through faith in Jesus Christ.

1, 10: **Sodomites:** see 1 Cor 6, 9 and the note there.

1, 12–17: Present gratitude for the Christian apostleship leads Paul to recall an earlier time when he had been a fierce persecutor of the Christian communities (cf Acts 26, 9–11) until his conversion by intervention of divine mercy through the appearance of Jesus. This and his subsequent apostolic experience testify to the saving purpose of Jesus' incarnation. The fact of his former ignorance of the truth has not kept the apostle from regarding himself as having been the worst of sinners (15). Yet he was chosen to be an apostle, that God might manifest his firm will to save sinful humanity through Jesus Christ (16). The recounting of so great a mystery leads to a spontaneous outpouring of adoration (17).

1, 15: **This saying is trustworthy:** this phrase regularly introduces in the Pastorals a basic truth of early Christian faith; cf 3, 1; 4, 9; 2 Tm 2, 11; Ti 3, 8.

1, 17: **King of ages:** through Semitic influence, the Greek expression could mean "everlasting king"; it could also mean "king of the universe."

1, 18–20: Timothy is to be mindful of his calling, which is here compared to the way Barnabas and Saul were designated by Christ as prophets for missionary service; cf Acts 13, 1–3. Such is probably the sense of the allusion to the prophetic words (18). His task is not to yield, whether in doctrine or in conduct, to erroneous opinions, taking warning from what has already happened at Ephesus in the case of Hymenaeus and Alexander (19–20).

1, 18: **The prophetic words once spoken about you:** the Greek may also be translated, "the prophecies that led (me) to you." It probably refers to testimonies given by charismatic figures in the Christian communities. **Fight a good fight:** this translation preserves the play on words in Greek. The Greek terms imply a lengthy engagement in battle and might well be translated "wage a good campaign."

1, 20: **Hymenaeus:** mentioned in 2 Tm 2, 17 as saying that the resurrection has already taken place (in baptism). **Alexander:** probably the Alexander mentioned in 2 Tm 4, 14 as the coppersmith who "did me a great deal of harm." **Whom I have handed over to Satan:** the same terms are used in the condemnation of the incestuous man in 1 Cor 5, 5.

2, 1–7: This marked insistence that the liturgical prayer of the community concern itself with the needs of all, whether Christian or not, and especially of those in authority, may imply that a disposition existed at Ephesus to refuse prayer for pagans. In actuality, such prayer aids the community to achieve peaceful relationships with non-Christians (2) and contributes to salvation, since it derives its value from the presence within the community of Christ, who is the one and only savior of all (3–6). The vital apostolic mission to the Gentiles (7) reflects Christ's purpose of universal salvation.

Verse 5 contains what may well have been a very primitive creed. Some interpreters have called it a Christian version of the Jewish **shema:** "Hear, O Israel, the LORD is our God, the LORD alone . . ." (Dt 6, 4–5). The assertion in v 7, "I am speaking the truth, I am not lying," reminds one of similar affirmations in Rom 9, 1; 2 Cor 11, 31; and Gal 1, 20.

h 4, 6; 6, 3; 2 Tm 4, 3; Ti 1, 9; 2, 1. i Ti 1, 3. j Phil 4, 13 / Acts 9, 15; Gal 1, 15–16. k Acts 8, 3; 9, 1–2; 1 Cor 15, 9; Gal 1, 13. l Rom 5, 20; 2 Tm 1, 13. m Lk 15, 2; 19, 10. n Rom 16, 27. o 4, 14 / 6, 12; 2 Tm 4, 7; Jude 3. p 3, 9. q 2 Tm 2, 17; 4, 14 / 1 Cor 5, 5. r Eph 6, 18; Phil 4, 6. s 1, 1; 4, 10. t 2 Tm 3, 7; 2 Pt 3, 9.

5 [u]For there is one God.
There is also one mediator between God and
the human race,
Christ Jesus, himself human,
6 [v]*who gave himself as ransom for all.

This was the testimony at the proper time. 7 [w]For this I was appointed preacher and apostle (I am speaking the truth, I am not lying), teacher of the Gentiles in faith and truth.

8 *It is my wish, then, that in every place the men should pray, lifting up holy hands, without anger or argument. 9 [x]Similarly, [too,] women should adorn themselves with proper conduct, with modesty and self-control, not with braided hairstyles and gold ornaments, or pearls, or expensive clothes, 10 [y]but rather, as befits women who profess reverence for God, with good deeds. 11 [z]A woman must receive instruction silently and under complete control. 12 *I do not permit a woman to teach or to have authority over a man. She must be quiet. 13 [a]For Adam was formed first, then Eve. 14 [b]Further, Adam was not deceived, but the woman was deceived and transgressed. 15 [c]But she will be saved through motherhood, provided women persevere in faith and love and holiness, with self-control.

CHAPTER 3

Qualifications of Various Ministers 1 [d]*This saying is trustworthy: whoever aspires to the office of bishop desires a noble task. 2 Therefore, a bishop must be irreproachable, married only once, temperate, self-controlled, decent, hospitable, able to teach, 3 [e]not a drunkard, not aggressive, but gentle, not contentious, not a lover of money. 4 He must manage his own household well, keeping his children under control with perfect dignity; 5 for if a man does not know how to manage his own household, how can he take care of the church of God? 6 *He should not be a recent convert, so that he may not become conceited and thus incur the devil's punishment. 7 [f]He must also have a good reputation among outsiders, so that he may not fall into disgrace, the devil's trap.

8 *Similarly, deacons must be dignified, not deceitful, not addicted to drink, not greedy for sordid gain, 9 holding fast to the mystery of the faith with a clear conscience. 10 Moreover, they should be tested first; then, if there is nothing against them, let them serve as deacons. 11 [g]*Women, similarly, should be dignified, not slanderers, but temperate and faithful in everything. 12 Deacons may be married only once and

2, 6: The testimony: to make sense of this overly concise phrase, many manuscripts supply "to which" (or "to whom"); two others add "was given." The translation has supplied "this was."

2, 8–15: The prayer of the community should be unmarred by internal dissension (8); cf Mt 5, 21–26; 6, 14; Mk 11, 25. At the liturgical assembly the dress of women should be appropriate to the occasion (9); their chief adornment is to be reputation for good works (10). Women are not to take part in the charismatic activity of the assembly (11–12; cf 1 Cor 14, 34) or exercise authority; their conduct there should reflect the role of man's helpmate (13; cf Gn 2, 18) and not the later relationship of Eve to Adam (14; cf Gn 3, 6–7). As long as women perform their role as wives and mothers in faith and love, their salvation is assured (15).

2, 12: A man: this could also mean "her husband."

3, 1–7: The passage begins by commending those who aspire to the office of bishop (**episkopos;** see the note on Phil 1, 1) within the community, but this first sentence (1) may also imply a warning about the great responsibilities involved. The writer proceeds to list the qualifications required: personal stability and graciousness; talent for teaching (2); moderation in habits and temperament (3); managerial ability (4); and experience in Christian living (5–6). Moreover, the candidate's previous life should provide no grounds for the charge that he did not previously practice what he now preaches. No list of qualifications for presbyters appears in 1 Tm. The presbyter-bishops here and in Ti (see the note on Ti 1, 5–9) lack certain functions reserved here for Paul and Timothy.

3, 1: This saying is trustworthy: the saying introduced is so unlike others after this phrase that some later Western manuscripts read, "This saying is popular." It is understood by some interpreters as concluding the preceding section (2, 8–15). **Bishop:** literally, "overseer"; see the note on Phil 1, 1.

3, 6: The devil's punishment: this phrase could mean the punishment once incurred by the devil (objective genitive) or a punishment brought about by the devil (subjective genitive).

3, 8–13: Deacons, besides possessing the virtue of moderation (8), are to be outstanding for their faith (9) and well respected within the community (10). Women in the same role, although some interpreters take them to mean wives of deacons, must be dignified, temperate, dedicated, and not given to malicious talebearing (11). Deacons must have shown stability in marriage and have a good record with their families (12), for such experience prepares them well for the exercise of their ministry on behalf of the community (13). See further the note on Phil 1, 1.

3, 11: Women: this seems to refer to women deacons but may possibly mean wives of deacons. The former is preferred because the word is used absolutely; if deacons' wives were meant, a possessive "their" would be expected. Moreover, they are also introduced by the word "similarly," as in v 8; this parallel suggests that they too exercised ecclesiastical functions.

u 1 Cor 8, 6; Heb 8, 6; 9, 15; 12, 24 / Rom 5, 15. v Mk 10, 45; Gal 1, 4; 2, 20; Eph 5, 25; Ti 2, 14. w Acts 9, 15; 1 Cor 9, 1; Gal 2, 7–8. x 1 Pt 3, 3–5. y 5, 10; 1 Pt 3, 1. z 1 Cor 14, 34–35. a Gn 1, 27; 2, 7.22; 1 Cor 11, 8–9. b Gn 3, 6.13; 2 Cor 11, 3. c 5, 14. d Ti 1, 6–9. e Heb 13, 5. f 2 Cor 8, 21; 2 Tm 2, 26. g Ti 2, 3.

must manage their children and their households well. [13]Thus those who serve well as deacons gain good standing and much confidence in their faith in Christ Jesus.

The Mystery of Our Religion [14]*I am writing you about these matters, although I hope to visit you soon. [15 h]But if I should be delayed, you should know how to behave in the household of God, which is the church of the living God, the pillar and foundation of truth. [16 i]*Undeniably great is the mystery of devotion,

Who was manifested in the flesh,
vindicated in the spirit,
seen by angels,
proclaimed to the Gentiles,
believed in throughout the world,
taken up in glory.

CHAPTER 4

False Asceticism [1 j]*Now the Spirit explicitly says that in the last times some will turn away from the faith by paying attention to deceitful spirits and demonic instructions [2]through the hypocrisy of liars with branded consciences. [3 k]They forbid marriage and require abstinence from foods that God created to be received with thanksgiving by those who believe and know the truth. [4 l]For everything created by God is good, and nothing is to be rejected when received with thanksgiving, [5]*for it is made holy by the invocation of God in prayer.

Counsel to Timothy [6]*If you will give these instructions to the brothers, you will be a good minister of Christ Jesus, nourished on the words of the faith and of the sound teaching you have followed. [7 m]Avoid profane and silly myths. Train yourself for devotion, [8 n]for, while physical training is of limited value, devotion is valuable in every respect, since it holds a promise of life both for the present and for the future. [9 o]This saying is trustworthy and deserves full acceptance. [10 p]*For this we toil and struggle, because we have set our hope on the living God, who is the savior of all, especially of those who believe.

[11]*Command and teach these things. [12 q]*Let no one have contempt for your youth, but set an example for those who believe, in speech, conduct, love, faith, and purity. [13]*Until I arrive, attend to the reading, exhortation, and teaching. [14 r]*Do not neglect the gift you have, which was

3, 14–16: In case there is some delay in the visit to Timothy at Ephesus planned for the near future, the present letter is being sent on ahead to arm and enlighten him in his task of preserving sound Christian conduct in the Ephesian church. The care he must exercise over this community is required by the profound nature of Christianity. It centers in Christ, appearing in human flesh, vindicated by the holy Spirit; the mystery of his person was revealed to the angels, announced to the Gentiles, and accepted by them in faith. He himself was taken up (through his resurrection and ascension) to the divine glory (16). This passage apparently includes part of a liturgical hymn used among the Christian communities in and around Ephesus. It consists of three couplets in typical Hebrew balance: flesh-spirit (contrast), seen-proclaimed (complementary), world-glory (contrast).

3, 16: Who: the reference is to Christ, who is himself "the mystery of our devotion." Some predominantly Western manuscripts read "which," harmonizing the gender of the pronoun with that of the Greek word for mystery; many later (eighth/ninth century on), predominantly Byzantine manuscripts read "God," possibly for theological reasons.

4, 1–5: Doctrinal deviations from the true Christian message within the church have been prophesied, though the origin of the prophecy is not specified (1–2); cf Acts 20, 29–30. The letter warns against a false asceticism that prohibits marriage and regards certain foods as forbidden, though they are part of God's good creation (3).

4, 5: The invocation of God in prayer: literally, "the word of God and petition." The use of "word of God" without an article in Greek suggests that it refers to the name of God being invoked in blessing rather than to the "word of God" proclaimed to the community.

4, 6–10: Timothy is urged to be faithful, both in his teaching and in his own life, as he looks only to God for salvation.

4, 10: Struggle: other manuscripts and patristic witnesses read "suffer reproach."

4, 11–16: Timothy is urged to preach and teach with confidence, relying on the gifts and the mission that God has bestowed on him.

4, 12: Youth: some commentators find this reference a sign of pseudepigraphy. Timothy had joined Paul as a missionary already in A.D. 49, some fifteen years before the earliest supposed date of composition.

4, 13: Reading: the Greek word refers to private or public reading. Here, it probably designates the public reading of scripture in the Christian assembly.

4, 14: Prophetic word: this may mean the utterance of a Christian prophet designating the candidate or a prayer of blessing accompanying the rite. **Imposition of hands:** this gesture was used in the Old Testament to signify the transmission of authority from Moses to Joshua (Nm 27, 18–23; Dt 34, 9). The early Christian community used it as a symbol of installation into an office: the Seven (Acts 6, 6) and Paul and Barnabas (Acts 13, 3). **Of the presbyterate:** this would mean that each member of the college of presbyters imposed hands and appears to contradict 2 Tm 1, 6, in which Paul says that he imposed hands on Timothy. This latter text, however, does not exclude participation by others in the rite. Some prefer to translate "for the presbyterate," and thus understand it to designate the office into which Timothy was installed rather than the agents who installed him.

h Eph 2, 19–22. i Jn 1, 14; Rom 1, 3–4. j 2 Tm 3, 1; 4, 3; 2 Pt 3, 3; Jude 18. k Gn 9, 3; Rom 14, 6; 1 Cor 10, 30–31. l Gn 1, 31; Acts 10, 15. m 1, 4; 2 Tm 2, 16; Ti 1, 14. n 6, 6. o 1, 15; 2 Tm 2, 11; Ti 3, 8. p 2, 4; Ti 2, 11. q 1 Cor 16, 11; Ti 2, 15 / Phil 3, 17. r 5, 22; Acts 6, 6; 8, 17; 2 Tm 1, 6.

conferred on you through the prophetic word with the imposition of hands of the presbyterate. 15 Be diligent in these matters, be absorbed in them, so that your progress may be evident to everyone. 16 Attend to yourself and to your teaching; persevere in both tasks, for by doing so you will save both yourself and those who listen to you.

IV: Duties toward Others

CHAPTER 5

1 [s]*Do not rebuke an older man, but appeal to him as a father. Treat younger men as brothers, 2 older women as mothers, and younger women as sisters with complete purity.

Rules for Widows 3 Honor widows who are truly widows. 4 But if a widow has children or grandchildren, let these first learn to perform their religious duty to their own family and to make recompense to their parents, for this is pleasing to God. 5 [t]The real widow, who is all alone, has set her hope on God and continues in supplications and prayers night and day. 6 But the one who is self-indulgent is dead while she lives. 7 Command this, so that they may be irreproachable. 8 And whoever does not provide for relatives and especially family members has denied the faith and is worse than an unbeliever.

9 Let a widow be enrolled if she is not less than sixty years old, married only once, 10 [u]with a reputation for good works, namely, that she has raised children, practiced hospitality, washed the feet of the holy ones, helped those in distress, involved herself in every good work. 11 But exclude younger widows, for when their sensuality estranges them from Christ, they want to marry 12 and will incur condemnation for breaking their first pledge. 13 [v]And furthermore, they learn to be idlers, going about from house to house, and not only idlers but gossips and busybodies as well, talking about things that ought not to be mentioned. 14 [w]So I would like younger widows to marry, have children, and manage a home, so as to give the adversary no pretext for maligning us. 15 For some have already turned away to follow Satan. 16 *If any woman believer has widowed relatives, she must assist them; the church is not to be burdened, so that it will be able to help those who are truly widows.

Rules for Presbyters 17 [x]*Presbyters who preside well deserve double honor, especially those who toil in preaching and teaching. 18 [y]For the scripture says, "You shall not muzzle an ox when it is threshing," and, "A worker deserves his pay." 19 [z]Do not accept an accusation against a presbyter unless it is supported by two or three witnesses. 20 [a]Reprimand publicly those who do sin, so that the rest also will be afraid. 21 I charge you before God and Christ Jesus and the elect angels to keep these rules without prejudice, doing nothing out of favoritism. 22 [b]Do not lay hands too readily on anyone, and do not share in

5, 1–16: After a few words of general advice based on common sense (1–2), the letter takes up, in its several aspects, the subject of widows. The first responsibility for their care belongs to the family circle, not to the Christian community as such (3–4.16). The widow left without the aid of relatives may benefit the community by her prayer, and the community should consider her material sustenance its responsibility (5–8). Widows who wish to work directly for the Christian community should not be accepted unless they are well beyond the probability of marriage, i.e., sixty years of age, married only once, and with a reputation for good works (9–10). Younger widows are apt to be troublesome and should be encouraged to remarry (11–15).

5, 16: Woman believer: some early Latin manuscripts and Fathers have a masculine here, while most later manuscripts and patristic quotations conflate the two readings, perhaps to avoid unfair restriction to women.

5, 17–25: The function of presbyters is not exactly the same as that of the **episkopos,** "bishop" (3, 1); in fact, the relation of the two at the time of this letter is obscure (but cf the note on Ti 1, 5–9). The Pastorals seem to reflect a transitional stage that developed in many regions of the church into the monarchical episcopate of the second and third centuries. The presbyters possess the responsibility of preaching and teaching, for which functions they are supported by the community (17–18). The realization that their position subjects them to adverse criticism is implied in the direction to Timothy (19–20) to make sure of the truth of any accusation against them before public reproof is given. He must be as objective as possible in weighing charges against presbyters (21), learning from his experience to take care in selecting them (22). Some scholars take v 22 as a reference not to ordination of presbyters but to reconciliation of public sinners. The letter now sounds an informal note of personal concern in its advice to Timothy not to be so ascetic that he even avoids wine (23). Judgment concerning the fitness of candidates to serve as presbyters is easy with persons of open conduct, more difficult and prolonged with those of greater reserve (24–25).

s Lv 19, 32; Ti 2, 2. t Jer 49, 11; Lk 2, 37; 18, 7. u Jn 13, 14; Heb 13, 2. v 2 Thes 3, 11. w 1 Cor 7, 9. x 1 Cor 16, 18; Phil 2, 29. y Dt 25, 4; 1 Cor 9, 8 / Mt 10, 10; Lk 10, 7. z Dt 17, 6; 19, 15; Mt 18, 16; 2 Cor 13, 1. a Gal 2, 14; Eph 5, 11; 2 Tm 4, 2; Ti 1, 9.13. b 4, 14; 2 Tm 1, 6.

another's sins. Keep yourself pure. 23 Stop drinking only water, but have a little wine for the sake of your stomach and your frequent illnesses.

24 Some people's sins are public, preceding them to judgment; but other people are followed by their sins. 25 Similarly, good works are also public; and even those that are not cannot remain hidden.

CHAPTER 6

Rules for Slaves 1 [c]*Those who are under the yoke of slavery must regard their masters as worthy of full respect, so that the name of God and our teaching may not suffer abuse. 2 [d]*Those whose masters are believers must not take advantage of them because they are brothers but must give better service because those who will profit from their work are believers and are beloved.

V: False Teaching and True Wealth

Teach and urge these things. 3 [e]Whoever teaches something different and does not agree with the sound words of our Lord Jesus Christ and the religious teaching 4 is conceited, understanding nothing, and has a morbid disposition for arguments and verbal disputes. From these come envy, rivalry, insults, evil suspicions, 5 [f]and mutual friction among people with corrupted minds, who are deprived of the truth, supposing religion to be a means of gain. 6 [g]*Indeed, religion with contentment is a great gain. 7 [h]For we brought nothing into the world, just as we shall not be able to take anything out of it. 8 [i]If we have food and clothing, we shall be content with that. 9 [j]Those who want to be rich are falling into temptation and into a trap and into many foolish and harmful desires, which plunge them into ruin and destruction. 10 For the love of money is the root of all evils, and some people in their desire for it have strayed from the faith and have pierced themselves with many pains.

Exhortations to Timothy 11 [k]*But you, man of God, avoid all this. Instead, pursue righteousness, devotion, faith, love, patience, and gentleness. 12 [l]Compete well for the faith. Lay hold of eternal life, to which you were called when you made the noble confession in the presence of many witnesses. 13 [m]I charge [you] before God, who gives life to all things, and before Christ Jesus, who gave testimony under Pontius Pilate for the noble confession, 14 to keep the commandment without stain or reproach until the appearance of our Lord Jesus Christ 15 [n]that the blessed and only ruler will make manifest at the proper time, the King of kings and Lord of lords, 16 [o]who alone has immortality, who dwells in unapproachable light, and whom no human being has seen or can see. To him be honor and eternal power. Amen.

Right Use of Wealth 17 [p]*Tell the rich in the present age not to be proud and not to rely on so uncertain a thing as wealth but rather on God, who richly provides us with all things for our enjoyment. 18 Tell them to do good, to be rich in good works, to be generous, ready to share, 19 [q]thus accumulating as treasure a good foundation for the future, so as to win the life that is true life.

6, 1–2: Compare the tables for household duties, such as that of Col 3, 18—4, 1. Domestic relationships derive new meaning from the Christian faith.

6, 1: **Our teaching:** this refers to the teaching of the Christian community.

6, 2b-10: Timothy is exhorted to maintain steadfastly the position outlined in this letter, not allowing himself to be pressured into any other course. He must realize that false teachers can be discerned by their pride, envy, quarrelsomeness, and greed for material gain. Verse 6 is rather obscure and is interpreted, and therefore translated, variously. The suggestion seems to be that the important gain that religion brings is spiritual, but that there is material gain, too, up to the point of what is needed for physical sustenance (cf 17–19).

6, 6: **Contentment:** the word **autarkeia** is a technical Greek philosophical term for the virtue of independence from material goods (Aristotle, Cynics, Stoics).

6, 11–16: Timothy's position demands total dedication to God and faultless witness to Christ (11–14) operating from an awareness, through faith, of the coming revelation in Jesus of the invisible God (15–16).

6, 11: **Man of God:** a title applied to Moses and the prophets (Dt 33, 1; 1 Sm 2, 27; 1 Kgs 12, 22; 13, 1; etc.).

6, 17–19: Timothy is directed to instruct the rich, advising them to make good use of their wealth by aiding the poor.

c Eph 6, 5; Ti 2, 9–10. d Phlm 16. e Gal 1, 6–9; 2 Tm 1, 13; Ti 1, 1. f 2 Tm 3, 8; 4, 4; Ti 1, 14. g 4, 8; Phil 4, 11–12; Heb 13, 5. h Jb 1, 21; Eccl 5, 14. i Prv 30, 8. j Prv 23, 4; 28, 22. k 2 Tm 2, 22. l 1 Cor 9, 26; 2 Tm 4, 7. m Jn 18, 36–37; 19, 11. n 2 Mc 13, 4; Rv 17, 14. o Ex 33, 20; Ps 104, 2. p Ps 62, 11; Lk 12, 20. q Mt 6, 20.

VI: Final Recommendation and Warning

20 r*O Timothy, guard what has been entrusted to you. Avoid profane babbling and the absurdities of so-called knowledge. 21 sBy professing it, some people have deviated from the faith.

Grace be with all of you.

6, 20–21: A final solemn warning against the heretical teachers, with what seems to be a specific reference to gnosticism, the great rival and enemy of the church for two centuries and more (the Greek word for "knowledge" is **gnōsis**). If gnosticism is being referred to here, it is probable that the warnings against "speculations" and "myths and genealogies" (cf especially 1, 4; Ti 3, 9) involve allusions to that same kind of heresy. Characteristic of the various gnostic systems of speculation was an elaborate mythology of innumerable superhuman intermediaries, on a descending scale ("genealogies"), between God and the world. Thus would be explained the emphasis upon Christ's being the **one** mediator (as in 2, 5). Although fully developed gnosticism belonged to the second and later centuries, there are signs that incipient forms of it belonged to Paul's own period.

r 2 Tm 1, 14 / 4, 7. s 1, 6; 2 Tm 2, 18.

THE SECOND LETTER TO TIMOTHY

The authorship and date of this letter, as one of the Pastoral Epistles, are discussed in the Introduction to the First Letter to Timothy.

The tone here is more personal than in First Timothy, for this letter addresses Timothy in vivid terms (1, 6-14; 2, 1-13) and depicts Paul's courage and hope in the face of discouragements late in the course of his apostolic ministry (1, 15-18; 3, 10-17; 4, 9-18). Indeed, the letter takes on the character of a final exhortation and testament from Paul to the younger Timothy (4, 1-8). Paul is portrayed as a prisoner (1, 8.16; 2, 9) in Rome (1, 17), and there is a hint that Timothy may be in Ephesus (2, 17). The letter reveals that, with rare exceptions, Christians have not rallied to Paul's support (1, 15-18) and takes a pessimistic view of the outcome of his case (4, 6). It describes Paul as fully aware of what impends, looking to God, not to human beings, for his deliverance (4, 3-8.18). It recalls his mission days with Timothy (1, 3-5; cf Acts 16, 1-4). It points to his preaching of the gospel as the reason for his imprisonment and offers Timothy, as a motive for steadfastness, his own example of firmness in faith despite adverse circumstances (1, 6-14). The letter suggests that Timothy should prepare others to replace himself as Paul has prepared Timothy to replace him (2, 1-2). Paul urges him not to desist out of fear from preserving and spreading the Christian message (2, 3-7). It presents the resurrection of Jesus and his messianic role as the heart of the gospel for which Paul has been ready to lay down his life (2, 8-9) and thus not only to express his own conviction fully but to support the conviction of others (2, 10-13).

This letter, like the preceding one, urges Timothy to protect the community from the inevitable impact of false teaching (2, 14—3, 9), without fear of the personal attacks that may result (3, 10-13). It recommends that he rely on the power of the scriptures, on proclamation of the word, and on sound doctrine (3, 14—4, 2), without being troubled by those who do not accept him (4, 3-5). The letter poignantly observes in passing that Paul has need of his reading materials and his cloak (4, 13) and, what will be best of all, a visit from Timothy.

On the theory of authorship by Paul himself, Second Timothy appears to be the last of the three Pastoral Epistles. The many scholars who argue that the Pastorals are products of the Pauline school often incline toward Second Timothy as the earliest of the three and the one most likely to have actual fragments of material from Paul himself.

The principal divisions of the Second Letter to Timothy are the following:

I. Address (1, 1-5)
II. Exhortations to Timothy (1, 6—2, 13)
III. Instructions Concerning False Teaching (2, 14—4, 8)
IV. Personal Requests and Final Greetings (4, 9-22)

I: Address

CHAPTER 1

Greeting [1][a]*Paul, an apostle of Christ Jesus by the will of God for the promise of life in Christ Jesus, [2]to Timothy, my dear child: grace, mercy, and peace from God the Father and Christ Jesus our Lord.

Thanksgiving [3][b]*I am grateful to God, whom I worship with a clear conscience as my ancestors did, as I remember you constantly in my prayers, night and day. [4]*I yearn to see you again, recalling your tears, so that I may be filled with joy, [5][c]as I recall your sincere faith that first lived in your grandmother Lois and in your mother Eunice and that I am confident lives also in you.

II: Exhortations to Timothy

The Gifts Timothy Has Received [6][d]*For this reason, I remind you to stir into flame the gift of God that you have through the imposition of my hands. [7][e]For God did not give us a spirit of cowardice but rather of power and love and self-control. [8][f]*So do not be ashamed of your testimony to our Lord, nor of me, a prisoner for his sake; but bear your share of hardship for the gospel with the strength that comes from God.

[9][g]*He saved us and called us to a holy life, not according to our works but according to his own design and the grace bestowed on us in Christ Jesus before time began, [10][h]but now made manifest through the appearance of our savior Christ Jesus, who destroyed death and brought life and immortality to light through the gospel, [11][i]*for which I was appointed preacher and apostle and teacher. [12][j]*On this account I am suffering these things; but I am not ashamed, for I know him in whom I have believed and am confident that he is able to guard what has been entrusted to me until that day. [13][k]Take as your norm the sound words that you heard from me, in the faith and love that are in Christ Jesus. [14][l]Guard this rich trust with the help of the holy Spirit that dwells within us.

Paul's Suffering [15][m]*You know that everyone in Asia deserted me, including Phygelus and Hermogenes. [16][n]*May the Lord grant mercy to

1, 1–2: For the formula of address and greeting, see the note on Rom 1, 1–7.

1, 1: **The promise of life in Christ Jesus:** that God grants through union with Christ in faith and love; cf Col 3, 4; 1 Tm 4, 8.

1, 3: **As my ancestors did:** this emphasizes the continuity of Judaism and Christianity; for a similar view, see Rom 9, 3–5; Phil 3, 4–6.

1, 4–5: Purportedly written from prison in Rome (8.17; 4, 6–8) shortly before the writer's death, the letter recalls the earlier sorrowful parting from Timothy, commending him for his faith and expressing the longing to see him again.

1, 6: **The gift of God:** the grace resulting from the conferral of an ecclesiastical office. **The imposition of my hands:** see the note on 1 Tm 4, 14.

1, 8: **Do not be ashamed of your testimony to our Lord:** i.e., of preaching and suffering for the sake of the gospel.

1, 9–10: Redemption from sin and the call to holiness of life are not won by personal deeds but are freely and graciously bestowed according to God's eternal plan; cf Eph 1, 4.

1, 11: **Teacher:** the overwhelming majority of manuscripts and Fathers read "teacher of the nations," undoubtedly a harmonization with 1 Tm 2, 7.

1, 12: **He is able to guard . . . until that day:** the intervening words can also be translated "what I have entrusted to him" (i.e., the fruit of his ministry) as well as "what has been entrusted to me" (i.e., the faith). The same difficult term occurs in v 14, where it is modified by the adjective "rich" and used without a possessive.

1, 15: Keen disappointment is expressed, here and later (4, 16), that the Christians of the province of Asia, especially Phygelus and Hermogenes, should have abandoned the writer and done nothing to defend his case in court.

1, 16–18: **The family of Onesiphorus because he . . . of my chains:** Onesiphorus seems to have died before this letter was written. His family is mentioned twice (here and in 4, 19), though it was Onesiphorus himself who was helpful to Paul in prison and rendered much service to the community of Ephesus. Because the apostle complains of abandonment by all in Asia during his second imprisonment and trial, the assistance of Onesiphorus seems to have been given to Paul during his first Roman imprisonment (A.D. 61–63).

a 1 Tm 4, 8. b 1 Tm 3, 9 / Phil 3, 5. c 1 Tm 1, 5 / Acts 16, 1. d 1 Tm 4, 14; 5, 22 / Acts 6, 6; 8, 17. e Rom 5, 5; 8, 15; 1 Cor 2, 4. f 2, 3.15; Rom 1, 16. g Eph 2, 8–9; Ti 3, 5 / Eph 1, 4; Ti 1, 2. h Rom 16, 26; 1 Pt 1, 20 / 1 Tm 6, 14 / Phil 3, 20; Ti 1, 4; 2, 13; 2 Pt 1, 11 / 1 Cor 15, 54–55; Heb 2, 14 / 1 Cor 15, 53–54. i 1 Tm 2, 7. j 1 Pt 4, 16 / 1 Tm 1, 10–11. k 1 Tm 1, 14. l 1 Tm 6, 20 / Rom 8, 11. m 4, 16. n 4, 19.

the family of Onesiphorus because he often gave me new heart and was not ashamed of my chains. 17 But when he came to Rome, he promptly searched for me and found me. 18 o*May the Lord grant him to find mercy from the Lord on that day. And you know very well the services he rendered in Ephesus.

CHAPTER 2

Timothy's Conduct 1 *So you, my child, be strong in the grace that is in Christ Jesus. 2 And what you heard from me through many witnesses entrust to faithful people who will have the ability to teach others as well. 3 p Bear your share of hardship along with me like a good soldier of Christ Jesus. 4 q To satisfy the one who recruited him, a soldier does not become entangled in the business affairs of life. 5 r Similarly, an athlete cannot receive the winner's crown except by competing according to the rules. 6 s The hardworking farmer ought to have the first share of the crop. 7 t Reflect on what I am saying, for the Lord will give you understanding in everything.

8 u*Remember Jesus Christ, raised from the dead, a descendant of David: such is my gospel, 9 v for which I am suffering, even to the point of chains, like a criminal. But the word of God is not chained. 10 w Therefore, I bear with everything for the sake of those who are chosen, so that they too may obtain the salvation that is in Christ Jesus, together with eternal glory. 11 x This saying is trustworthy:

If we have died with him
  we shall also live with him;
12 y if we persevere
  we shall also reign with him.
But if we deny him
  he will deny us.
13 z If we are unfaithful
  he remains faithful,
  for he cannot deny himself.

III: Instructions Concerning False Teaching

Warning against Useless Disputes
14 a*Remind people of these things and charge them before God to stop disputing about words. This serves no useful purpose since it harms those who listen. 15 b Be eager to present yourself as acceptable to God, a workman who causes no disgrace, imparting the word of truth without deviation. 16 c Avoid profane, idle talk, for such people will become more and more godless, 17 d and their teaching will spread like gangrene. Among them are Hymenaeus and Philetus, 18 e who have deviated from the truth by saying that [the] resurrection has already taken place and are upsetting the faith of some. 19 f Nevertheless, God's solid foundation stands, bearing this inscription, "The Lord knows those who are his"; and, "Let everyone who calls upon the name of the Lord avoid evil."

20 In a large household there are vessels not only of gold and silver but also of wood and clay, some for lofty and others for humble use. 21 g If

1, 18: Lord . . . Lord: the first "Lord" here seems to refer to Christ, the second "Lord" to the Father.

2, 1–7: This passage manifests a characteristic deep concern for safeguarding the faith and faithfully transmitting it through trustworthy people (1–2; cf 1, 14; 1 Tm 6, 20; Ti 1, 9). Comparisons to the soldier's detachment, the athlete's sportsmanship, and the farmer's arduous work as the price of recompense (4–6) emphasize the need of singleness of purpose in preaching the word, even at the cost of hardship, for the sake of Christ (3).

2, 8–13: The section begins with a sloganlike summary of Paul's gospel about Christ (8) and concludes with what may be part of an early Christian hymn (11b-12a; most exegetes include the rest of v 12 and all of v 13 as part of the quotation). The poetic lines suggest that through baptism Christians die spiritually with Christ and hope to live with him and reign with him forever, but the Christian life includes endurance, witness, and even suffering, as the final judgment will show and as Paul's own case makes clear; while he is imprisoned for preaching the gospel (9), his sufferings are helpful to the elect for obtaining the salvation and glory available in Christ (10), who will be true to those who are faithful and will disown those who deny him (12–13).

2, 14–19: For those who dispute about mere words (cf 23–24) and indulge in irreligious talk to the detriment of their listeners (16–19), see the notes on 1 Tm 1, 3–7; 6, 20–21. Hymenaeus and Philetus (17), while accepting the Christian's mystical death and resurrection in Christ through baptism, claimed that baptized Christians are already risen with Christ in this life and thus that there is no future bodily resurrection or eternal glory to come. The first quotation in v 19 is from Nm 16, 5; the other quotation is from some unidentified Jewish or Christian writing.

2, 14: Before God: many ancient manuscripts read "before the Lord."

o Jude 21. p 1, 8; 4, 5; Phlm 2. q 1 Cor 9, 6. r 1 Cor 9, 25. s 1 Cor 9, 7–10. t Prv 2, 6. u Rom 1, 3; 1 Cor 15, 4.20 / Rom 2, 16; Gal 1, 11; 2, 2. v Phil 1, 12–14. w Col 1, 24; 1 Tm 1, 15. x Rom 6, 8. y Mt 10, 22.33; Lk 12, 9. z Nm 23, 19; Rom 3, 3–4; 1 Cor 10, 13; Ti 1, 2. a 1 Tm 6, 4. b 1, 8; 2 Cor 6, 7; Eph 1, 13; Col 1, 5. c 1 Tm 4, 7. d 1 Tm 1, 20. e 2 Thes 2, 2. f Is 28, 16; 1 Cor 3, 10–15 / Nm 16, 5; Jn 10, 14. g 3, 17.

anyone cleanses himself of these things, he will be a vessel for lofty use, dedicated, beneficial to the master of the house, ready for every good work. [22] [h]*So turn from youthful desires and pursue righteousness, faith, love, and peace, along with those who call on the Lord with purity of heart. [23] [i]Avoid foolish and ignorant debates, for you know that they breed quarrels. [24] [j]A slave of the Lord should not quarrel, but should be gentle with everyone, able to teach, tolerant, [25] [k]correcting opponents with kindness. It may be that God will grant them repentance that leads to knowledge of the truth, [26] [l]*and that they may return to their senses out of the devil's snare, where they are entrapped by him, for his will.

CHAPTER 3

The Dangers of the Last Days [1] [m]*But understand this: there will be terrifying times in the last days. [2] [n]People will be self-centered and lovers of money, proud, haughty, abusive, disobedient to their parents, ungrateful, irreligious, [3]callous, implacable, slanderous, licentious, brutal, hating what is good, [4]traitors, reckless, conceited, lovers of pleasure rather than lovers of God, [5] [o]as they make a pretense of religion but deny its power. Reject them. [6] [p]For some of these slip into homes and make captives of women weighed down by sins, led by various desires, [7] [q]always trying to learn but never able to reach a knowledge of the truth. [8] [r]Just as Jannes and Jambres opposed Moses, so they also oppose the truth—people of depraved mind, unqualified in the faith. [9]But they will not make further progress, for their foolishness will be plain to all, as it was with those two.

Paul's Example and Teaching [10]*You have followed my teaching, way of life, purpose, faith, patience, love, endurance, [11] [s]persecutions, and sufferings, such as happened to me in Antioch, Iconium, and Lystra, persecutions that I endured. Yet from all these things the Lord delivered me. [12] [t]In fact, all who want to live religiously in Christ Jesus will be persecuted. [13]But wicked people and charlatans will go from bad to worse, deceivers and deceived. [14] [u]But you, remain faithful to what you have learned and believed, because you know from whom you learned it, [15] [v]and that from infancy you have known [the] sacred scriptures, which are capable of giving you wisdom for salvation through faith in Christ Jesus. [16] [w]*All scripture is inspired by God and is useful for teaching, for refutation, for correction, and for training in righteousness, [17] [x]so that one who belongs to God may be competent, equipped for every good work.

CHAPTER 4

Solemn Charge [1] [y]*I charge you in the presence of God and of Christ Jesus, who will judge the living and the dead, and by his appearing and

2, 22: Those who call on the Lord: those who believe in Christ and worship him as Lord, i.e., Christians (Acts 9, 14–16.20–21; Rom 10, 12–13; cf 19, literally, "Everyone who names the name of the Lord").

2, 26: Some interpreters would render this passage, "Thus they may come to their senses and, forced to do his (i.e., God's) will, may escape the devil's trap." This interpretation of the Greek is possible, but the one accepted in the text seems more likely.

3, 1–9: The moral depravity and false teaching that will be rampant in the last days are already at work (1–5). The frivolous and superficial, too, devoid of the true spirit of religion, will be easy victims of those who pervert them by falsifying the truth (6–8), just as Jannes and Jambres, Pharaoh's magicians of Egypt (Ex 7, 11–12.22), discredited the truth in Moses' time. Exodus does not name the magicians, but the two names are widely found in much later Jewish, Christian, and even pagan writings. Their origins are legendary.

3, 10–17: Paul's example for Timothy includes persecution, a frequent emphasis in the Pastorals. Timothy is to be steadfast to what he has been taught and to scripture. The scriptures are the source of wisdom, i.e., of belief in and loving fulfillment of God's word revealed in Christ, through whom salvation is given.

3, 16: All scripture is inspired by God: this could possibly also be translated, "All scripture inspired by God is useful for . . . ." In this classic reference to inspiration, God is its principal author, with the writer as the human collaborator. Thus the scriptures are the word of God in human language. See also 2 Pt 1, 20–21.

3, 16–17: Useful for teaching . . . every good work: because as God's word the scriptures share his divine authority. It is exercised through those who are ministers of the word.

4, 1–5: The gravity of the obligation incumbent on Timothy to preach the word can be gauged from the solemn adjuration: in the presence of God, and of Christ coming as universal judge, and by his appearance and his kingly power (1). Patience, courage, constancy, and endurance are required despite the opposition, hostility, indifference, and defection of many to whom the truth has been preached (2–5).

h Gal 5, 22; 1 Tm 6, 11 / Rom 10, 13; 1 Cor 1, 2. i 1 Tm 1, 4; 4, 7; 6, 4; Ti 3, 9. j 1 Tm 3, 2–3. k 3, 7; 1 Tm 2, 4. l 1 Tm 3, 7. m 1 Tm 4, 1; 2 Pt 3, 3; Jude 18. n Rom 1, 29–31. o Rom 2, 20–22; Ti 1, 16. p Ti 1, 11. q 2, 25. r Ex 7, 11.22; 1 Tm 6, 5. s Acts 13, 50; 14, 5.19 / Ps 34, 20. t Jn 15, 20; Acts 14, 22. u 2, 2. v Jn 5, 39. w Rom 15, 4; 2 Pt 1, 19–21. x 2, 21. y 1 Tm 5, 21; 6, 14 / Acts 10, 42; Rom 14, 9–10; 1 Pt 4, 5.

his kingly power: 2 [z]proclaim the word; be
persistent whether it is convenient or inconve-
nient; convince, reprimand, encourage through
all patience and teaching. 3 [a]*For the time will
come when people will not tolerate sound
doctrine but, following their own desires and
insatiable curiosity, will accumulate teachers
4 [b]and will stop listening to the truth and will be
diverted to myths. 5 But you, be self-possessed in
all circumstances; put up with hardship; per-
form the work of an evangelist; fulfill your
ministry.
Reward for Fidelity 6 [c]*For I am already being
poured out like a libation, and the time of my
departure is at hand. 7 [d]*I have competed well; I
have finished the race; I have kept the faith.
8 [e]*From now on the crown of righteousness
awaits me, which the Lord, the just judge, will
award to me on that day, and not only to me, but
to all who have longed for his appearance.

IV: Personal Requests and Final Greetings

Paul's Loneliness 9 *Try to join me soon,
10 [f]*for Demas, enamored of the present world,
deserted me and went to Thessalonica, Crescens
to Galatia, and Titus to Dalmatia. 11 [g]Luke is the
only one with me. Get Mark and bring him with
you, for he is helpful to me in the ministry. 12 [h]I
have sent Tychicus to Ephesus. 13 [i]When you
come, bring the cloak I left with Carpus in Troas,
the papyrus rolls, and especially the parchments.
14 [j]*Alexander the coppersmith did me a great
deal of harm; the Lord will repay him according
to his deeds. 15 You too be on guard against him,
for he has strongly resisted our preaching.
16 [k]At my first defense no one appeared on my
behalf, but everyone deserted me. May it not be
held against them! 17 [l]But the Lord stood by me
and gave me strength, so that through me the
proclamation might be completed and all the
Gentiles might hear it. And I was rescued from
the lion's mouth. 18 [m]The Lord will rescue me
from every evil threat and will bring me safe to
his heavenly kingdom. To him be glory forever
and ever. Amen.
Final Greeting 19 [n]*Greet Prisca and Aquila
and the family of Onesiphorus. 20 [o]*Erastus re-
mained in Corinth, while I left Trophimus sick at
Miletus. 21 *Try to get here before winter. Eubu-
lus, Pudens, Linus, Claudia, and all the brothers
send greetings.
22 [p]The Lord be with your spirit. Grace be
with all of you.

4, 3: Insatiable curiosity: literally, "with itching ears."

4, 6: The apostle recognizes his death through martyrdom to be imminent. He regards it as an act of worship in which his blood will be poured out in sacrifice; cf Ex 29, 38–40; Phil 2, 17.

4, 7: At the close of his life Paul could testify to the accomplishment of what Christ himself foretold concerning him at the time of his conversion, "I will show him what he will have to suffer for my name" (Acts 9, 16).

4, 8: When the world is judged at the parousia, all who have eagerly looked for the Lord's appearing and have sought to live according to his teachings will be rewarded. The crown is a reference to the laurel wreath placed on the heads of victorious athletes and conquerors in war; cf 2, 5; 1 Cor 9, 25.

4, 9–13: Demas either abandoned the work of the ministry for worldly affairs or, perhaps, gave up the faith itself (10). Luke (11) may have accompanied Paul on parts of his second and third missionary journeys (Acts 16, 10–12; 20, 5–7). Notice the presence of the first personal pronoun "we" in these Acts passages, suggesting to some that Luke (or at least some traveling companion of Paul's) was the author of Acts. Mark, once rejected by Paul (Acts 13, 13; 15, 39), is now to render him a great service (11); cf Col 4, 10; Phlm 24. For Tychicus, see Eph 6, 21; cf also Acts 20, 4; Col 4, 7.

4, 10: Galatia: some manuscripts read "Gaul" or "Gallia."

4, 14–18: Alexander: an opponent of Paul's preaching (14–15), perhaps the one who is mentioned in 1 Tm 1, 20. Despite Paul's abandonment by his friends in the province of Asia (cf 1, 15–16), the divine assistance brought this first trial to a successful issue, even to the point of making the gospel message known to those who participated in or witnessed the trial (16–17).

4, 19: Prisca and Aquila: they assisted Paul in his ministry in Corinth (Acts 18, 2–3) and Ephesus (Acts 18, 19.26; 1 Cor 16, 19). They risked death to save his life, and all the Gentile communities are indebted to them (Rom 16, 3–5).

4, 20: Erastus: he was the treasurer of the city of Corinth (Rom 16, 24); cf also Acts 19, 22. **Trophimus:** from the province of Asia, he accompanied Paul from Greece to Troas (Acts 20, 4–5).

4, 21: Linus: Western tradition sometimes identified this Linus with the supposed successor of Peter as bishop of Rome, and Claudia as the mother of Linus (**Apostolic Constitutions,** fourth century).

z Acts 20, 20.31; 1 Tm 5, 20. a 1 Tm 4, 1. b 1 Tm 1, 4; 4, 7; Ti 1, 14. c Phil 2, 17. d 1 Tm 1, 18; 6, 12; Jude 3 / Acts 20, 24; 1 Cor 9, 24; Heb 12, 1. e 2, 5; Wis 5, 16; 1 Cor 9, 25; Phil 3, 14; Jas 1, 12; 1 Pt 5, 4; Rv 2, 10. f Col 4, 14; Phlm 24 / 2 Cor 2, 13; 7, 6–7; 8, 23; Gal 2, 3; Ti 1, 4. g Col 4, 14; Phlm 24 / Col 4, 10; Phlm 24. h Acts 20, 4; Eph 6, 21; Col 4, 7. i Acts 16, 8; 20, 6. j 1 Tm 1, 20 / 2 Sm 3, 39; Pss 28, 4; 62, 12; Prv 24, 12; Rom 2, 6. k 1, 15. l Acts 23, 11; 27, 23; Phil 4, 13 / 1 Mc 2, 60; Ps 22, 22; Dn 6, 23. m 2 Cor 1, 10 / Rom 16, 27. n Acts 18, 2; Rom 16, 3; 1 Cor 16, 19 / 1, 16. o Acts 19, 22; Rom 16, 24 / Acts 20, 4; 21, 29. p Gal 6, 18; Phil 4, 23; Col 4, 18; 1 Tm 6, 21; Ti 3, 15.

THE LETTER TO TITUS

The third of the Pastoral Epistles in the New Testament is addressed to a different co-worker of Paul than are First and Second Timothy. The situation is different, too, for Titus is addressed as the person in charge of developing the church on the large Mediterranean island of Crete (1, 5), a place Paul had never, according to the New Testament, visited. The tone is closer to that of First Timothy as three topics of church life and structure are discussed: presbyter-bishops (see the note on 1, 5-9), groups with which one must work in the church (2, 1-10), and admonitions for conduct based on the grace and love of God that appeared in Jesus Christ (2, 11—3, 10). The warmer personal tone of Second Timothy is replaced by emphasis on church office and on living in the society of the day, in which deceivers and heretics abound (1, 10-16; 3, 9-10).

The Pauline assistant who is addressed, Titus, was a Gentile Christian, but we are nowhere informed of his place of birth or residence. He went from Antioch with Paul and Barnabas to Jerusalem (Gal 2, 1; cf Acts 15, 2). According to 2 Corinthians (2, 13; 7, 6.13-14), he was with Paul on his third missionary journey; his name, however, does not appear in Acts. Besides being the bearer of Paul's severe letter to the Corinthians (2 Cor 7, 6-8), he had the responsibility of taking up the collection in Corinth for the Christian community of Jerusalem (2 Cor 8, 6.16-19.23). In the present letter (1, 5), he is mentioned as the administrator of the Christian community in Crete, charged with the task of organizing it through the appointment of presbyters and bishops (1, 5-9; here the two terms refer to the same personages).

The letter instructs Titus about the character of the assistants he is to choose in view of the pastoral difficulties peculiar to Crete (1, 5-16). It suggests the special individual and social virtues that the various age groups and classes in the Christian community should be encouraged to acquire (2, 1-10). The motivation for transformation of their lives comes from christology, especially the redemptive sacrifice of Christ and his future coming, as applied through baptism and justification (2, 11-14; 3, 4-8). The community is to serve as a leaven for Christianizing the social world about it (3, 1-3). Good works are to be the evidence of their faith in God (3, 8); those who engage in religious controversy are, after suitable warning, to be ignored (3, 9-11).

The authorship and date of the Letter to Titus are discussed in the Introduction to 1 Timothy. Those who assume authorship by Paul himself usually place Titus after 1 Timothy and before 2 Timothy. Others see it as closely related to 1 Timothy, in a growing emphasis on church structure and opposition to heresy, later than the letters of Paul himself and 2 Timothy. It has also been suggested that, if the three Pastorals once circulated as a literary unit, Titus was meant to be read ahead of 1 and 2 Timothy.

The principal divisions of the Letter to Titus are the following:

I. Address (1, 1-4)
II. Pastoral Charge (1, 5-16)
III. Teaching the Christian Life (2, 1—3, 15)

I: Address

CHAPTER 1

Greeting 1 [a] *Paul, a slave of God and apostle of Jesus Christ for the sake of the faith of God's chosen ones and the recognition of religious truth, 2 [b] in the hope of eternal life that God, who does not lie, promised before time began, 3 [c] who indeed at the proper time revealed his word in the proclamation with which I was entrusted by the command of God our savior, 4 [d] to Titus, my true child in our common faith: grace and peace from God the Father and Christ Jesus our savior.

II: Pastoral Charge

Titus in Crete 5 *For this reason I left you in Crete so that you might set right what remains to be done and appoint presbyters in every town, as I directed you, 6 [e] on condition that a man be blameless, married only once, with believing children who are not accused of licentiousness or rebellious. 7 For a bishop as God's steward must be blameless, not arrogant, not irritable, not a drunkard, not aggressive, not greedy for sordid gain, 8 but hospitable, a lover of goodness, temperate, just, holy, and self-controlled, 9 [f] holding fast to the true message as taught so that he will be able both to exhort with sound doctrine and to refute opponents. 10 *For there are also many rebels, idle talkers and deceivers, especially the Jewish Christians. 11 It is imperative to silence them, as they are upsetting whole families by teaching for sordid gain what they should not. 12 *One of them, a prophet of their own, once said, "Cretans have always been liars, vicious beasts, and lazy gluttons." 13 [g] That testimony is true. Therefore, admonish them sharply, so that they may be sound in the faith, 14 [h] instead of paying attention to Jewish myths and regulations of people who have repudiated the truth. 15 [i] To the clean all things are clean, but to those who are defiled and unbelieving nothing is clean; in fact, both their minds and their consciences are tainted. 16 They claim to know God, but by their deeds they deny him. They are vile and disobedient and unqualified for any good deed.

III: Teaching the Christian Life

CHAPTER 2

Christian Behavior 1 [j] *As for yourself, you must say what is consistent with sound doctrine, namely, 2 that older men should be temperate, dignified, self-controlled, sound in faith, love, and endurance. 3 Similarly, older women should be reverent in their behavior, not slanderers, not addicted to drink, teaching what is good, 4 so that they may train younger women to love their husbands and children, 5 [k] to be self-controlled, chaste, good homemakers, under the control of their husbands, so that the word of God may not be discredited.

6 Urge the younger men, similarly, to control themselves, 7 showing yourself as a model of good deeds in every respect, with integrity in your teaching, dignity, 8 and sound speech that cannot be criticized, so that the opponent will be put to shame without anything bad to say about us.

1, 1–4: On the epistolary form, see the note on Rom 1, 1–7. The apostolate is the divinely appointed mission to lead others to the true faith and through it to eternal salvation (1–3).

1, 5–9: This instruction on the selection and appointment of presbyters, substantially identical with that in 1 Tm 3, 1–7 on a bishop (see the note there), was aimed at strengthening the authority of Titus by apostolic mandate; cf 2, 15. In vv 5.7 and Acts 20, 17.28, the terms **episkopos** and **presbyteros** ("bishop" and "presbyter") refer to the same persons. Deacons are not mentioned in Titus. See also the note on Phil 1, 1.

1, 10–16: This adverse criticism of the defects within the community is directed especially against certain Jewish Christians, who busy themselves with useless speculations over persons mentioned in the Old Testament, insist on the observance of Jewish ritual purity regulations, and thus upset whole families by teaching things they have no right to teach; cf 3, 9; 1 Tm 1, 3–10.

1, 10: Jewish Christians: literally, "those of the circumcision."

1, 12: Cretans . . . gluttons: quoted from Epimenides, a Cretan poet of the sixth century B.C.

2, 1–10: One of Titus' main tasks in Crete is to become acquainted with the character of the Cretans and thereby learn to cope with its deficiencies (see 1, 12). The counsel is not only for Titus himself but for various classes of people with whom he must deal: older men and women (2–4), younger women and men (4–7), and slaves (9–10); cf Eph 6, 1–9; Col 3, 18—4, 1.

a 1 Tm 2, 4; 4, 3; 2 Tm 2, 25; 3, 7; Heb 10, 26. b 3, 7; 2 Tm 1, 1; 1 Jn 2, 25. c 2, 10; 3, 4; Ps 24, 5; 1 Tm 1, 1; 2, 3; 4, 10; Jude 25. d 2, 13; 3, 6; Phil 3, 20; 2 Tm 1, 10; 2 Pt 1, 1.11; 2, 20; 3, 2.18. e 1 Tm 3, 2–7; 2 Tm 2, 24–26. f 1, 13; 2, 1–2.8; 1 Tm 1, 10; 6, 3; 2 Tm 1, 13; 4, 3. g 1, 9. h 3, 9; 1 Tm 1, 4; 4, 7; 2 Tm 4, 4; 2 Pt 1, 16. i Mk 7, 18–23; Acts 10, 15; Rom 14, 14–23. j 1, 9.13; 2, 8; 1 Tm 1, 10; 6, 3; 2 Tm 1, 13; 4, 3. k 1 Cor 11, 3; 14, 34; Eph 5, 22–24; Col 3, 18; 1 Tm 2, 11–15;1 Pt 3, 1–6.

9 [l]Slaves are to be under the control of their
masters in all respects, giving them satisfaction,
not talking back to them 10 [m]or stealing from
them, but exhibiting complete good faith, so as to
adorn the doctrine of God our savior in every way.
Transformation of Life 11 [n]*For the grace of
God has appeared, saving all 12 and training us to
reject godless ways and worldly desires and to
live temperately, justly, and devoutly in this age,
13 [o]*as we await the blessed hope, the appear-
ance of the glory of the great God and of our
savior Jesus Christ, 14 [p]who gave himself for us
to deliver us from all lawlessness and to cleanse
for himself a people as his own, eager to do what
is good.

15 [q]Say these things. Exhort and correct with
all authority. Let no one look down on you.

CHAPTER 3

1 [r]*Remind them to be under the control of
magistrates and authorities, to be obedient, to be
open to every good enterprise. 2 They are to
slander no one, to be peaceable, considerate,
exercising all graciousness toward everyone.
3 [s]For we ourselves were once foolish, disobedi-
ent, deluded, slaves to various desires and plea-
sures, living in malice and envy, hateful our-
selves and hating one another.

4 [t]But when the kindness and generous love
of God our savior appeared,
5 [u]not because of any righteous deeds we had
done
but because of his mercy,
he saved us through the bath of rebirth
and renewal by the holy Spirit,
6 [v]whom he richly poured out on us
through Jesus Christ our savior,
7 [w]so that we might be justified by his grace
and become heirs in hope of eternal life.

8 [x]*This saying is trustworthy.
Advice to Titus I want you to insist on these
points, that those who have believed in God be
careful to devote themselves to good works;
these are excellent and beneficial to others.
9 [y]*Avoid foolish arguments, genealogies, rival-
ries, and quarrels about the law, for they are
useless and futile. 10 [z]After a first and second
warning, break off contact with a heretic, 11 real-
izing that such a person is perverted and sinful
and stands self-condemned.
Directives, Greetings, and Blessing
12 [a]*When I send Artemas to you, or Tychicus,
try to join me at Nicopolis, where I have decided
to spend the winter. 13 [b]Send Zenas the lawyer
and Apollos on their journey soon, and see to it
that they have everything they need. 14 [c]But let
our people, too, learn to devote themselves to
good works to supply urgent needs, so that they
may not be unproductive.

15 [d]All who are with me send you greetings.
Greet those who love us in the faith.

Grace be with all of you.

2, 11–15: Underlying the admonitions for moral improvement in 1–10 as the moving force is the constant appeal to God's revelation of salvation in Christ, with its demand for transformation of life.

2, 13: The blessed hope, the appearance: literally, "the blessed hope and appearance," but the use of a single article in Greek strongly suggests an epexegetical, i.e., explanatory sense. **Of the great God and of our savior Jesus Christ:** another possible translation is "of our great God and savior Jesus Christ."

3, 1–8: The list of Christian duties continues from 2, 9–10, undergirded again as in 2, 11–13 by appeal to what God in Christ has done (4–7; cf 2, 11–14). The spiritual renewal of the Cretans, signified in God's merciful gift of baptism (4–7), should be reflected in their improved attitude toward civil authority and in their Christian relationship with all (1–3).

3, 1: Magistrates and authorities: some interpreters understand these terms as referring to the principalities and powers of the heavenly hierarchy. **To be open to every good enterprise:** this implies being good citizens. It could also be translated "ready to do every sort of good work" (as Christians); cf 14.

3, 8–11: In matters of good conduct and religious doctrine, Titus is to stand firm.

3, 9: See the note on 1 Tm 6, 20–21.

3, 12–15: Artemas or **Tychicus** (2 Tm 4, 12) is to replace Titus, who will join Paul in his winter sojourn at Nicopolis in Epirus, on the western coast of Greece.

l 1 Cor 7, 21–22; Eph 6, 5–8; Col 3, 22–25; 1 Tm 6, 1–2;1 Pt 2, 18. m 1, 3; 3, 4; Ps 24, 5; 1 Tm 1, 1; 2, 3; 4, 10; Jude 25. n 1 Tm 2, 4; 4, 10. o 1 Cor 1, 7; Phil 3, 20; 1 Thes 1, 10 / 2 Tm 1, 10 / 1, 4; 3, 6;2 Pt 1, 1.11; 2, 20; 3, 2.18. p Gal 1, 4; 2, 20; Eph 5, 2.25; 1 Tm 2, 6; 1 Pt 1, 18–19 /Ps 130, 8. q 1 Tm 4, 12. r Rom 13, 1–7; 1 Tm 2, 1–2; 1 Pt 2, 13–14. s 1 Cor 6, 9–11; Eph 2, 1–3; 5, 8; Col 3, 5–7; 1 Pt 4, 3. t 1, 3; 2, 10; Ps 24, 5; 1 Tm 1, 1; 2, 3; 4, 10; Jude 25. u Dt 9, 5; Eph 2, 4–5.8–9; 2 Tm 1, 9. v 1, 4; 2, 13; Phil 3, 20; 2 Tm 1, 10; 2 Pt 1, 1.11; 2, 20; 3, 2.18. w 1, 2; 2 Tm 1, 1; 1 Jn 2, 25. x 1 Tm 1, 15; 3, 1; 4, 9; 2 Tm 2, 11. y 1 Tm 1, 4; 4, 7; 2 Tm 2, 23. z Mt 18, 15–18; Rom 16, 17; 1 Cor 5, 11; 2 Thes 3, 6.14–15. a Acts 20, 4; Eph 6, 21; Col 4, 7; 2 Tm 4, 12. b Acts 18, 24–26; 1 Cor 1, 12; 3, 4–6.22; 4, 6; 16, 12. c 2, 14; 3, 8; Heb 10, 24; 1 Pt 3, 13. d Heb 13, 25.

THE LETTER TO PHILEMON

This short letter addressed to three specific individuals was written by Paul during an imprisonment, perhaps in Rome between A.D. 61 and 63 (see the Introduction to Colossians for other possible sites). It concerns Onesimus, a slave from Colossae (Col 4, 9), who had run away from his master, perhaps guilty of theft in the process (18). Onesimus was converted to Christ by Paul (10). Paul sends him back to his master (12) with this letter asking that he be welcomed willingly by his old master (8-10.14.17) not just as a slave but as a brother in Christ (16). Paul uses very strong arguments (especially 19) in his touching appeal on behalf of Onesimus. It is unlikely that Paul is subtly hinting that he would like to retain Onesimus as his own slave, lent to Paul by his master. Rather, he suggests he would like to have Onesimus work with him for the gospel (13.20-21). There is, however, little evidence connecting this Onesimus with a bishop of Ephesus of the same name mentioned by Ignatius of Antioch (ca. A.D. 110).

Paul's letter deals with an accepted institution of antiquity, human slavery. But Paul breathes into this letter the spirit of Christ and of equality within the Christian community. He does not attack slavery directly, for this is something the Christian communities of the first century were in no position to do, and the expectation that Christ would soon come again militated against social reforms. Yet Paul, by presenting Onesimus as "brother, beloved . . . to me, but even more so to you" (16), voiced an idea revolutionary in that day and destined to break down worldly barriers of division "in the Lord."

Address and Greeting [1] [a]*Paul, a prisoner for Christ Jesus, and Timothy our brother, to Philemon, our beloved and our co-worker, [2] [b]*to Apphia our sister, to Archippus our fellow soldier, and to the church at your house. [3] [c]*Grace to you and peace from God our Father and the Lord Jesus Christ.

Thanksgiving [4] [d]*I give thanks to my God always, remembering you in my prayers, [5]*as I hear of the love and the faith you have in the Lord Jesus and for all the holy ones, [6] [e]*so that your partnership in the faith may become effective in recognizing every good there is in us that leads to Christ.

Plea for Onesimus [7] [f]*For I have experienced much joy and encouragement from your love, because the hearts of the holy ones have been refreshed by you, brother. [8]*Therefore, although I have the full right in Christ to order you to do what is proper, [9] [g]*I rather urge you out of love, being as I am, Paul, an old man, and now also a prisoner for Christ Jesus. [10] [h]I urge you on behalf of my child Onesimus, whose father I have become in my imprisonment, [11]*who was once

1: **Prisoner:** as often elsewhere (cf Rom, 1 Cor, Gal especially), the second word in Greek enunciates the theme and sets the tone of the letter. Here it is the prisoner appealing rather than the apostle commanding.

2: **Apphia our sister:** sister is here used (like brother) to indicate a fellow Christian. **The church at your house: your** here is singular. It more likely refers to Philemon than to the last one named, Archippus; Philemon is then the owner of the slave Onesimus (10). An alternate view is that the actual master of the slave is Archippus and that the one to whom the letter is addressed, Philemon, is the most prominent Christian there; see the note on Col 4, 17.

3: **Grace . . . and peace:** for this greeting, which may be a combination of Greek and Aramaic epistolary formulae, see the note on Rom 1, 1–7.

4: **In my prayers:** literally, "at the time of my prayers."

5: **Holy ones:** a common term for members of the Christian community (so also 7).

6: **In us:** some good ancient manuscripts have **in you** (plural). **That leads to Christ: leads** to translates the Greek preposition **eis,** indicating direction or purpose.

7: **Encouragement:** the Greek word **paraklēsis** is cognate with the verb translated "urge" in vv 9.10, and serves as an introduction to Paul's plea. **Hearts:** literally, "bowels," expressing in Semitic fashion the seat of the emotions, one's "inmost self." The same Greek word is used in v 12 and again in v 20, where it forms a literary inclusion marking off the body of the letter.

8: **Full right:** often translated "boldness," the Greek word **parrēsia** connotes the full franchise of speech, as the right of a citizen to speak before the body politic, claimed by the Athenians as their privilege (Euripides).

9: **Old man:** some editors conjecture that Paul here used a similar Greek word meaning "ambassador" (cf Eph 6, 20). This conjecture heightens the contrast with "prisoner" but is totally without manuscript support.

11: **Useless . . . useful:** here Paul plays on the name Onesi-

a 9; Eph 3, 1; 4, 1; Phil 1, 7.13. b Col 4, 17. c Rom 1, 7; Gal 1, 3; Phil 1, 2. d Rom 1, 8–9; Eph 1, 15–16. e Phil 1, 9; Col 1, 9. f 2 Cor 7, 4. g 1; Eph 3, 1; 4, 1; Phil 1, 7.13. h 1 Cor 4, 14–15; Gal 4, 19; Col 4, 9.

useless to you but is now useful to [both] you and
me. 12I am sending him, that is, my own heart,
back to you. 13 [i]*I should have liked to retain
him for myself, so that he might serve me on
your behalf in my imprisonment for the gospel,
14 [j]but I did not want to do anything without
your consent, so that the good you do might not
be forced but voluntary. 15*Perhaps this is why
he was away from you for a while, that you
might have him back forever, 16 [k]*no longer as a
slave but more than a slave, a brother, beloved
especially to me, but even more so to you, as a
man and in the Lord. 17So if you regard me as a
partner, welcome him as you would me. 18*And
if he has done you any injustice or owes you
anything, charge it to me. 19 [l]I, Paul, write this in
my own hand: I will pay. May I not tell you that
you owe me your very self. 20Yes, brother, may I
profit from you in the Lord. Refresh my heart in
Christ.
21With trust in your compliance I write to
you, knowing that you will do even more than I
say. 22 [m]At the same time prepare a guest room
for me, for I hope to be granted to you through
your prayers.

Final Greetings 23 [n]*Epaphras, my fellow pris-
oner in Christ Jesus, greets you, 24 [o]as well as
Mark, Aristarchus, Demas, and Luke, my co-
workers. 25The grace of the Lord Jesus Christ be
with your spirit.

mus, which means "useful" or "beneficial." The verb translated "profit" in v 20 is cognate.

13: **Serve:** the Greek **diakoneō** could connote a ministry.

15: **Was away from:** literally, "was separated from," but the same verb means simply "left" in Acts 18, 1. It is a euphemism for his running away.

16: **As a man:** literally, "in the flesh." With this and the following phrase, Paul describes the natural and spiritual orders.

18–19: **Charge it to me . . . I will pay:** technical legal and commercial terms in account keeping and acknowledgment of indebtedness.

23–24: **Epaphras:** a Colossian who founded the church there (Col 1, 7) and perhaps also in Laodicea and Hierapolis (Col 2, 1; 4, 12–13). **Aristarchus:** a native of Thessalonica and fellow worker of Paul (Acts 19, 29; 20, 4; 27, 2). For Mark, Demas, and Luke, see 2 Tm 4, 9–13 and the note there.

i Phil 2, 30. j 2 Cor 9, 7; 1 Pt 5, 2. k 1 Tm 6, 2. l Gal 6, 11; 2 Thes 3, 17. m Heb 13, 19. n Col 1, 7; 4, 12–13. o Acts 12, 12.15; 13, 13; 15, 37–39; 19, 29; 20, 4; 27, 2; Col 4, 10.14; 2 Tm 4, 10–13.

THE LETTER TO THE HEBREWS

As early as the second century, this treatise, which is of great rhetorical power and force in its admonition to faithful pilgrimage under Christ's leadership, bore the title "To the Hebrews." It was assumed to be directed to Jewish Christians. Usually Hebrews was attached in Greek manuscripts to the collection of letters by Paul. Although no author is mentioned (for there is no address), a reference to Timothy (13, 23) suggested connections to the circle of Paul and his assistants. Yet the exact audience, the author, and even whether Hebrews is a letter have long been disputed.

The author saw the addressees in danger of apostasy from their Christian faith. This danger was due not to any persecution from outsiders but to a weariness with the demands of Christian life and a growing indifference to their calling (2, 1; 4, 14; 6, 1-12; 10, 23-32). The author's main theme, the priesthood and sacrifice of Jesus (chs 3–10), is not developed for its own sake but as a means of restoring their lost fervor and strengthening them in their faith. Another important theme of the letter is that of the pilgrimage of the people of God to the heavenly Jerusalem (11, 10; 12, 1-3.18-29; 13, 14). This theme is intimately connected with that of Jesus' ministry in the heavenly sanctuary (9, 11—10, 22).

The author calls this work a "message of encouragement" (13, 22), a designation that is given to a synagogue sermon in Acts 13, 15. Hebrews is probably therefore a written homily, to which the author gave an epistolary ending (13, 22-25).

The author begins with a reminder of the preexistence, incarnation, and exaltation of Jesus (1, 3) that proclaimed him the climax of God's word to humanity (1, 1-3). He dwells upon the dignity of the person of Christ, superior to the angels (1, 4—2, 2). Christ is God's final word of salvation communicated (in association with accredited witnesses to his teaching: cf 2, 3-4) not merely by word but through his suffering in the humanity common to him and to all others (2, 5-16). This enactment of salvation went beyond the pattern known to Moses, faithful prophet of God's word though he was, for Jesus as high priest expiated sin and was faithful to God with the faithfulness of God's own Son (2, 17—3, 6).

Just as the infidelity of the people thwarted Moses' efforts to save them, so the infidelity of any Christian may thwart God's plan in Christ (3, 6—4, 13). Christians are to reflect that it is their humanity that Jesus took upon himself, with all its defects save sinfulness, and that he bore the burden of it until death out of obedience to God. God declared this work of his Son to be the cause of salvation for all (4, 14—5, 10). Although Christians recognize this fundamental teaching, they may grow weary of it and of its implications, and therefore require other reflections to stimulate their faith (5, 11—6, 20).

Therefore, the author presents to the readers for their reflection the everlasting priesthood of Christ (7, 1-28), a priesthood that fulfills the promise of the Old Testament (8, 1-13). It also provides the meaning God ultimately intended in the sacrifices of the Old Testament (9, 1-28): these pointed to the unique sacrifice of Christ, which alone obtains forgiveness of sins (10, 1-18). The trial of faith experienced by the readers should resolve itself through their consideration of Christ's ministry in the heavenly sanctuary and his perpetual intercession there on their behalf (7, 25; 8, 1-13). They should also be strengthened by the assurance of his foreordained parousia, and by the fruits of faith that they have already enjoyed (10, 19-39).

It is in the nature of faith to recognize the reality of what is not yet seen and is the object of hope, and the saints of the Old Testament give striking example of that faith (11, 1-40). The perseverance to which the author exhorts the readers is shown forth in the early life of Jesus. Despite the afflictions of his ministry and the supreme trial of his suffering and death, he remained confident of the triumph that God would bring him (12, 1-3). The difficulties of human life have meaning when they are accepted as God's discipline (12, 4-13), and if Christians persevere in fidelity to the word in which they have believed, they are assured of possessing forever the unshakable kingdom of God (12, 14-29).

The letter concludes with specific moral commandments (13, 1-17), in the course of which the author recalls again his central theme of the sacrifice of Jesus and the courage needed to associate oneself with it in faith (13, 9-16).

As early as the end of the second century, the church of Alexandria in Egypt accepted Hebrews as a letter of Paul, and that became the view commonly held in the East. Pauline authorship was contested in the West into the fourth century, but then accepted. In the sixteenth century, doubts about that position were again raised, and the modern consensus is that the letter was not written by Paul. There is, however, no widespread agreement on any of the other suggested authors, e.g., Barnabas, Apollos, or Prisc(ill)a and Aquila. The document itself has no statement about its author.

Among the reasons why Pauline authorship has been abandoned are the great difference of vocabulary and style between Hebrews and Paul's letters, the alternation of doctrinal teaching with moral exhortation, the different manner of citing the Old Testament, and the resemblance between the thought of Hebrews and that of Alexandrian Judaism. The Greek of the letter is in many ways the best in the New Testament.

Since the letter of Clement of Rome to the Corinthians, written about A.D. 96, most probably cites Hebrews, the upper limit for the date of composition is reasonably certain. While the letter's references in the present tense to the Old Testament sacrificial worship do not necessarily show that temple worship was still going on, many older commentators and a growing number of recent ones favor the view that it was and that the author wrote before the destruction of the temple of Jerusalem in A.D. 70. In that case, the argument of the letter is more easily explained as directed toward Jewish Christians rather than those of Gentile origin, and the persecutions they have suffered in the past (cf 10, 32-34) may have been connected with the disturbances that preceded the expulsion of the Jews from Rome in A.D. 49 under the emperor Claudius. These were probably caused by disputes between Jews who accepted Jesus as the Messiah and those who did not.

The principal divisions of the Letter to the Hebrews are the following:

I. Introduction (1, 1-4)
II. The Son Higher than the Angels (1, 5—2, 18)
III. Jesus, Faithful and Compassionate High Priest (3, 1—5, 10)
IV. Jesus' Eternal Priesthood and Eternal Sacrifice (5, 11—10, 39)
V. Examples, Discipline, Disobedience (11, 1—12, 29)
VI. Final Exhortation, Blessing, Greetings (13, 1-25)

I: Introduction

CHAPTER 1

1 *In times past, God spoke in partial and
various ways to our ancestors through the proph-
ets; 2 [a]in these last days, he spoke to us through
a son, whom he made heir of all things and
through whom he created the universe,

3 [b]who is the refulgence of his glory,
the very imprint of his being,
and who sustains all things by his mighty word.
When he had accomplished purification from sins,
he took his seat at the right hand of the Majesty on high,
4 [c]as far superior to the angels
as the name he has inherited is more excellent than theirs.

1, 1–4: The letter opens with an introduction consisting of a reflection on the climax of God's revelation to the human race in his Son. The divine communication was initiated and maintained during Old Testament times in fragmentary and varied ways through **the prophets** (1), including Abraham, Moses, and all through whom God spoke. But now **in these last days** (2), the final age, God's revelation of his saving purpose is achieved **through a son,** i.e., one who is Son, whose role is redeemer and mediator of creation. He was made **heir of all things** through his death and exaltation to glory, yet he existed before he appeared as man; through him God **created the universe.** Verses 3–4, which may be based upon a liturgical hymn, assimilate the Son to the personified Wisdom of the Old Testament as **refulgence of** God's **glory** and **imprint of his being** (3; cf Wis 7, 26). These same terms are used of the Logos in Philo. The author now turns from the cosmological role of the preexistent Son to the redemptive work of Jesus: he brought about purification from sins and has been exalted to the right hand of God (see Ps 110, 1). The once-humiliated and crucified Jesus has been declared God's Son, and this name shows his superiority to the angels. The reason for the author's insistence on that superiority is, among other things, that in some Jewish traditions angels were mediators of the old covenant (see Acts 7, 53; Gal 3, 19). Finally, Jesus' superiority to the angels emphasizes the superiority of the new covenant to the old because of the heavenly priesthood of Jesus.

a Is 2, 2; Jer 23, 20; Ez 38, 16; Dn 10, 14 / Jn 3, 17; Rom 8, 3; Gal 4, 4 / Prv 8, 30; Wis 7, 22; Jn 1, 3; 1 Cor 8, 6; Col 1, 16. b Wis 7, 26; 2 Cor 4, 4; Col 1, 15 / 8, 1; 10, 12; 12, 2; Mk 16, 19; Acts 2, 33; 7, 55–56; Rom 8, 34; Eph 1, 20; Col 3, 1; 1 Pt 3, 22. c Eph 1, 21; Phil 2, 9–11.

II: The Son Higher Than the Angels

Messianic Enthronement 5 [d]*For to which of the angels did God ever say:

"You are my son; this day I have begotten
you"?

Or again:

"I will be a father to him, and he shall be a son
to me"?

6 [e]*And again, when he leads the first-born into the world, he says:

"Let all the angels of God worship him."

7 [f]Of the angels he says:

"He makes his angels winds
and his ministers a fiery flame";

8 [g]*but of the Son:

"Your throne, O God, stands forever and ever;
and a righteous scepter is the scepter of
your kingdom.
9 You loved justice and hated wickedness;
therefore God, your God, anointed you
with the oil of gladness above your
companions";

10 [h]and:

"At the beginning, O Lord, you established the
earth,
and the heavens are the works of your
hands.
11 They will perish, but you remain;
and they will all grow old like a garment.
12 You will roll them up like a cloak,
and like a garment they will be changed.
But you are the same, and your years will have
no end."

13 [i]But to which of the angels has he ever said:

"Sit at my right hand
until I make your enemies your footstool"?

14 [j]Are they not all ministering spirits sent to serve, for the sake of those who are to inherit salvation?

CHAPTER 2

Exhortation to Faithfulness 1 *Therefore, we
must attend all the more to what we have heard,
so that we may not be carried away. 2 [k]For if the
word announced through angels proved firm,
and every transgression and disobedience re-
ceived its just recompense, 3 [l]how shall we
escape if we ignore so great a salvation? An-
nounced originally through the Lord, it was
confirmed for us by those who had heard.
4 [m]God added his testimony by signs, wonders,
various acts of power, and distribution of the
gifts of the holy Spirit according to his will.
Exaltation through Abasement 5 *For it was
not to angels that he subjected the world to

1, 5–14: Jesus' superiority to the angels is now demonstrated by a series of seven Old Testament texts. Some scholars see in the stages of Jesus' exaltation an order corresponding to that of enthronement ceremonies in the ancient Near East, especially in Egypt, namely, elevation to divine status (5–6); presentation to the angels and proclamation of everlasting lordship (7–12); enthronement and conferral of royal power (13). The citations from the Psalms in vv 5 and 13 were traditionally used of Jesus' messianic sonship (cf Acts 13, 33) through his resurrection and exaltation (cf Acts 2, 33–35); those in vv 8 and 10–12 are concerned with his divine kingship and his creative function. The central quotation in v 7 serves to contrast the angels with the Son. The author quotes it according to the Septuagint translation, which is quite different in meaning from that of the Hebrew ("You make the winds your messengers, and flaming fire your ministers"). The angels are only **sent to serve . . . those who are to inherit salvation** (14).

1, 6: And again, when he leads: the Greek could also be translated "And when he again leads" in reference to the parousia.

1, 8–12: O God: the application of the name "God" to the Son derives from the preexistence mentioned in vv 2–3; the psalmist had already used it of the Hebrew king in the court style of the original. See the note on Ps 45, 7. It is also important for the author's christology that in vv 10–12 an Old Testament passage addressed to God is redirected to Jesus.

2, 1–4: The author now makes a transition into exhortation, using an a fortiori argument (as at 7, 21–22; 9, 13–14; 10, 28–29; 12, 25). The **word announced through angels** (2), the Mosaic law, is contrasted with the more powerful word that Christians have received (3–4). Christ's supremacy strengthens Christians against being **carried away** from their faith.

2, 5–18: The humanity and the suffering of Jesus do not constitute a valid reason for relinquishing the Christian faith. Ps 8 (6–7) is also applied to Jesus in 1 Cor 15, 27; Eph 1, 22; and probably 1 Pt 3, 22. This christological interpretation, therefore, probably reflects a common early Christian tradition, which may have originated in the expression **the son of man** (6). The psalm contrasts God's greatness with man's relative insignificance but also stresses the superiority of man to the rest of creation, of which he is lord. Heb applies this christologically: Jesus lived a truly human existence, **lower than the angels,** in the days of his

d Ps 2, 7 / 2 Sm 7, 14. e Dt 32, 43 LXX; Ps 97, 7. f Ps 104, 4 LXX. g Ps 45, 7–8. h Ps 102, 26–28. i Ps 110, 1. j Ps 91, 11; Dn 7, 10. k Acts 7, 38.53; Gal 3, 19. l 10, 29; 12, 25. m Mk 16, 20; Acts 14, 3; 19, 11.

come, of which we are speaking. 6 [n]Instead,
someone has testified somewhere:

"What is man that you are mindful of him,
or the son of man that you care for him?
7 You made him for a little while lower than the
angels;
you crowned him with glory and honor,
8 [o]subjecting all things under his feet."

In "subjecting" all things [to him], he left nothing not "subject to him." Yet at present we do not
see "all things subject to him," 9 [p]but we do see
Jesus "crowned with glory and honor" because he suffered death, he who "for a little while" was made "lower than the angels," that by the grace of God he might taste death for everyone.
10 [q]For it was fitting that he, for whom and through whom all things exist, in bringing many children to glory, should make the leader to their
salvation perfect through suffering. 11 He who
consecrates and those who are being consecrated all have one origin. Therefore, he is not
ashamed to call them "brothers," 12 [r]saying:

"I will proclaim your name to my brothers,
in the midst of the assembly I will praise
you";

13 [s]and again:

"I will put my trust in him";

and again:

"Behold, I and the children God has given
me."

14 [t]Now since the children share in blood and flesh, he likewise shared in them, that through death he might destroy the one who has the
power of death, that is, the devil, 15 and free
those who through fear of death had been
subject to slavery all their life. 16 Surely he did
not help angels but rather the descendants of
Abraham; 17 [u]therefore, he had to become like
his brothers in every way, that he might be a merciful and faithful high priest before God to
expiate the sins of the people. 18 Because he
himself was tested through what he suffered, he is able to help those who are being tested.

III: Jesus, Faithful and Compassionate High Priest

CHAPTER 3

Jesus, Superior to Moses 1 *Therefore, holy
"brothers," sharing in a heavenly calling, reflect

---

earthly life, particularly in his suffering and death; now, **crowned with glory and honor,** he is raised above all creation. The author considers all things as already **subject to him** because of his exaltation (8–9), though **we do not see** this yet. The reference to Jesus as **leader** (10) sounds the first note of an important leitmotif in Heb: the journey of the people of God to the sabbath rest (4, 9), the heavenly sanctuary, following Jesus, their "forerunner" (6, 20). It was fitting that God should make him **perfect through suffering,** consecrated by obedient suffering. Because he is perfected as high priest, Jesus is then able to consecrate his people (11); access to God is made possible by each of these two consecrations. If Jesus is able to help human beings, it is because he has become one of us; we are his "brothers." The author then cites three Old Testament texts as proofs of this unity between ourselves and the Son. Psalm 22, 23 is interpreted so as to make Jesus the singer of this lament, which ends with joyful praise of the Lord in the assembly of "brothers." The other two texts are from Is 8, 17.18. The first of these seems intended to display in Jesus an example of the trust in God that his followers should emulate. The second curiously calls these followers "children"; probably this is to be understood to mean children of Adam, but the point is our solidarity with Jesus. By sharing human nature, including the ban of death, Jesus broke the power of the devil over death (14); the author shares the view of Hellenistic Judaism that death was not intended by God and that it had been introduced into the world by the devil. The **fear of death** (15) is a religious fear based on the false conception that death marks the end of a person's relations with God (cf Ps 115, 17–18; Is 38, 18). Jesus deliberately allied himself with **the descendants of Abraham** (16) in order to be **a merciful and faithful high priest.** This is the first appearance of the central theme of Heb, Jesus the great high priest expiating **the sins of the people** (17), as one who experienced the same tests as they (18).

3, 1–6: The author now takes up the two qualities of Jesus mentioned in 2, 17, but in inverse order: faithfulness (3, 1—4, 13) and mercy (4, 14—5, 10). Christians are called **holy "brothers"** because of their common relation to him (2, 11), the **apostle,** a designation for Jesus used only here in the New Testament (cf Jn 13, 16; 17, 3), meaning one sent as God's final word to us (1, 2). He is compared with Moses probably because he is seen as mediator of the new covenant (9, 15) just as Moses was of the old (9, 19–22, including his sacrifice). But when the author of Heb speaks of Jesus' sacrifice, he does not consider Moses as the Old Testament antitype, but rather the high priest on the Day of Atonement (9, 6–15). Moses' faithfulness **"in [all] his house"** refers back to Nm 12, 7, on which this section is a midrashic commentary. In vv 3–6, the author does not indicate that he thinks of either Moses or Christ as the founder of the household. **His house** (2.5.6) means God's house, not that of Moses or

n Ps 8, 5–7. o Mt 28, 18; 1 Cor 15, 25–28; Eph 1, 20–23; Phil 3, 21; 1 Pt 3, 22. p Phil 2, 6–11. q 12, 2; Is 53, 4 / Rom 11, 36; 1 Cor 8, 6. r Ps 22, 23. s Is 8, 17.18. t Is 25, 8; Hos 13, 14; Jn 12, 31; Rom 6, 9; 1 Cor 15, 54–55;2 Tm 1, 10; Rv 12, 10. u 4, 15; 5, 1–3.

on Jesus, the apostle and high priest of our confession, [2] [v]who was faithful to the one who appointed him, just as Moses was "faithful in [all] his house." [3] [w]But he is worthy of more "glory" than Moses, as the founder of a house has more "honor" than the house itself. [4]Every house is founded by someone, but the founder of all is God. [5]Moses was "faithful in all his house" as a "servant" to testify to what would be spoken, [6] [x]*but Christ was faithful as a son placed over his house. We are his house, if [only] we hold fast to our confidence and pride in our hope.

Israel's Infidelity a Warning [7] [y]*Therefore, as the holy Spirit says:

"Oh, that today you would hear his voice,
8 'Harden not your hearts as at the rebellion
in the day of testing in the desert,
9 [z]where your ancestors tested and tried me
and saw my works [10]for forty years.
Because of this I was provoked with that
generation
and I said, "They have always been of
erring heart,
and they do not know my ways."
11 As I swore in my wrath,
"They shall not enter into my rest." ' "

[12]Take care, brothers, that none of you may have an evil and unfaithful heart, so as to forsake the living God. [13]Encourage yourselves daily while it is still "today," so that none of you may grow hardened by the deceit of sin. [14] [a]We have become partners of Christ if only we hold the beginning of the reality firm until the end, [15] [b]for it is said:

"Oh, that today you would hear his voice:
'Harden not your hearts as at the rebellion.' "

[16] [c]Who were those who rebelled when they heard? Was it not all those who came out of Egypt under Moses? [17] [d]With whom was he "provoked for forty years"? Was it not those who had sinned, whose corpses fell in the desert? [18] [e]And to whom did he "swear that they should not enter into his rest," if not to those who were disobedient? [19]And we see that they could not enter for lack of faith.

CHAPTER 4

The Sabbath Rest [1]Therefore, let us be on our guard while the promise of entering into his rest remains, that none of you seem to have failed. [2]For in fact we have received the good news just as they did. But the word that they heard did not profit them, for they were not united in faith with those who listened. [3] [f]For we who believed enter into [that] rest, just as he has said:

"As I swore in my wrath,
'They shall not enter into my rest,' "

and yet his works were accomplished at the foundation of the world. [4] [g]For he has spoken

---

Christ; in the case of Christ, compare v 6 with 10, 21. The **house** of v 6 is the Christian community; the author suggests its continuity with Israel by speaking not of two houses but of only one. Verse 6 brings out the reason why Jesus is superior to Moses: the latter was the faithful **servant** laboring **in** the house founded by God, but Jesus is God's **son,** placed **over** the house.

3, 6: The majority of manuscripts add "firm to the end," but these words are not found in the three earliest and best witnesses and are probably an interpolation derived from v 14.

3, 7—4, 13: The author appeals for steadfastness of faith in Jesus, basing his warning on the experience of Israel during the Exodus. In the Old Testament the Exodus had been invoked as a symbol of the return of Israel from the Babylonian exile (Is 42, 9; 43, 16–21; 51, 9–11). In the New Testament the redemption was similarly understood as a new exodus, both in the experience of Jesus himself (Lk 9, 31) and in that of his followers (1 Cor 10, 1–4). The author cites Ps 95, 7–11, a salutary example of hardness of heart, as a warning against the danger of growing weary and giving up the journey. To call God **living** (12) means that he reveals himself in his works (cf Jos 3, 10; Jer 10, 10). The **rest** (11) into which Israel was to enter was only a foreshadowing of that rest to which Christians are called. They are to remember the example of Israel's revolt in the desert that cost a whole generation the loss of the promised land (15–19; cf Nm 14, 20–29). In 4, 1–11, the symbol of **rest** is seen in deeper dimension: because the promise to the ancient Hebrews foreshadowed that given to Christians, it is **good news;** and because the promised land was the place of rest that God provided for his people, it was a share in his own rest, which he enjoyed after he had finished his creative work (3–4; cf Gn 2, 2). The author attempts to read this meaning of God's rest into Ps 95, 7–11 (6–9). The Greek form of the name of Joshua, who led Israel into the promised land, is Jesus (8). The author plays upon the name but stresses the superiority of Jesus, who leads his followers into heavenly rest. Verses 12 and 13 are meant as a continuation of the warning, for the word of God brings judgment as well as salvation. Some would capitalize **the word of God** and see it as a personal title of Jesus, comparable to that of Jn 1, 1–18.

v Nm 12, 7. w 2 Cor 3, 7–8. x 10, 21; Eph 2, 19; 1 Tm 3, 15; 1 Pt 4, 17. y Ps 95, 7–11. z Ex 17, 7; Nm 20, 2–5. a Rom 8, 17. b Ps 95, 7–8. c Nm 14, 1–38; Dt 1, 19–40. d Nm 14, 29. e Nm 14, 22–23; Dt 1, 35. f 3, 11; Ps 95, 11. g Gn 2, 2.

somewhere about the seventh day in this man-
ner, "And God rested on the seventh day from
all his works"; 5 [h]and again, in the previously
mentioned place, "They shall not enter into my
rest." 6 Therefore, since it remains that some will
enter into it, and those who formerly received
the good news did not enter because of disobedi-
ence, 7 [i]he once more set a day, "today," when
long afterwards he spoke through David, as
already quoted:

"Oh, that today you would hear his voice:
'Harden not your hearts.' "

8 [j]Now if Joshua had given them rest, he would
not have spoken afterwards of another day.
9 Therefore, a sabbath rest still remains for the
people of God. 10 And whoever enters into God's
rest, rests from his own works as God did from
his. 11 Therefore, let us strive to enter into that
rest, so that no one may fall after the same
example of disobedience.
12 [k]Indeed, the word of God is living and
effective, sharper than any two-edged sword,
penetrating even between soul and spirit, joints
and marrow, and able to discern reflections and
thoughts of the heart. 13 [l]No creature is con-
cealed from him, but everything is naked and
exposed to the eyes of him to whom we must
render an account.

Jesus, Compassionate High Priest

14 [m]*Therefore, since we have a great high priest
who has passed through the heavens, Jesus, the
Son of God, let us hold fast to our confession.
15 [n]For we do not have a high priest who is
unable to sympathize with our weaknesses, but
one who has similarly been tested in every way,
yet without sin. 16 [o]So let us confidently ap-
proach the throne of grace to receive mercy and
to find grace for timely help.

CHAPTER 5

1 *Every high priest is taken from among men
and made their representative before God, to of-
fer gifts and sacrifices for sins. 2 *He is able to deal
patiently with the ignorant and erring, for he him-
self is beset by weakness 3 [p]and so, for this reason,
must make sin offerings for himself as well as for
the people. 4 [q]No one takes this honor upon him-
self but only when called by God, just as Aaron
was. 5 [r]In the same way, it was not Christ who
glorified himself in becoming high priest, but
rather the one who said to him:

"You are my son;
this day I have begotten you";

6 [s]*just as he says in another place:

"You are a priest forever
according to the order of Melchizedek."

4, 14–16: These verses, which return to the theme first sounded in 2, 16—3, 1, serve as an introduction to the section that follows. The author here alone calls Jesus **a great high priest** (14), a designation used by Philo for the Logos; perhaps he does so in order to emphasize Jesus' superiority over the Jewish high priest. He has **been tested in every way, yet without sin** (15); this indicates an acquaintance with the tradition of Jesus' temptations, not only at the beginning (as in Mk 1, 13) but throughout his public life (cf Lk 22, 28). Although the reign of the exalted Jesus is a theme that occurs elsewhere in Heb, and Jesus' throne is mentioned in 1, 8, **the throne of grace** (16) refers to the throne of God. The similarity of v 16 to 10, 19–22 indicates that the author is thinking of our confident access to God, made possible by the priestly work of Jesus.

5, 1–10: The true humanity of Jesus (see the note on 2, 5–18) makes him a more rather than a less effective high priest to the Christian community. In Old Testament tradition, the high priest was identified with the people, guilty of personal sin just as they were (1–3). Even so, the office was of divine appointment (4), as was also the case with the sinless Christ (5). For v 6, see the note on Ps 110, 4. Although Jesus was Son of God, he was destined as a human being to learn obedience by accepting the suffering he had to endure (8). Because of his perfection through this experience of human suffering, he is the cause of salvation for all (9), a **high priest according to the order of Melchizedek** (10; cf 6 and 7, 3).

5, 1: To offer gifts and sacrifices for sins: the author is thinking principally of the Day of Atonement rite, as is clear from 9, 7. This ritual was celebrated to atone for "all the sins of the Israelites" (Lv 16, 34).

5, 2: Deal patiently: the Greek word **metriopathein** occurs only here in the Bible; this term was used by the Stoics to designate the golden mean between excess and defect of passion. Here it means rather the ability to sympathize.

5, 6–8: The author of Heb is the only New Testament writer to cite v 4 of Ps 110, here and in 7, 17.21, to show that Jesus has been called by God to his role as priest. Verses 7–8 deal with his ability to sympathize with sinners, because of his own experience of the trials and weakness of human nature, especially fear of death. In his present exalted state, weakness is foreign to him, but he understands what we suffer because of his previous earthly experience.

h Ps 95, 11. i 3, 7–8.15; Ps 95, 7–8. j Dt 31, 7; Jos 22, 4. k Wis 18, 15–16; Is 49, 2; Eph 6, 17; Rv 1, 16; 2, 12. l Jb 34, 21–22; Pss 90, 8; 139, 2–4. m 9, 11.24. n 2, 17–18; 5, 2. o 8, 1; 10, 19.22.35; 12, 2; Eph 3, 12. p Lv 9, 7; 16, 15–17.30.34. q Ex 28, 1. r Ps 2, 7. s Ps 110, 4.

[7] [t]*In the days when he was in the flesh, he offered prayers and supplications with loud cries and tears to the one who was able to save him from death, and he was heard because of his reverence. [8] [u]*Son though he was, he learned obedience from what he suffered; [9] [v]and when he was made perfect, he became the source of eternal salvation for all who obey him, [10] [w]declared by God high priest according to the order of Melchizedek.

IV: Jesus' Eternal Priesthood and Eternal Sacrifice

Exhortation to Spiritual Renewal [11] *About this we have much to say, and it is difficult to explain, for you have become sluggish in hearing. [12] [x]Although you should be teachers by this time, you need to have someone teach you again the basic elements of the utterances of God. You need milk, [and] not solid food. [13]Everyone who lives on milk lacks experience of the word of righteousness, for he is a child. [14]But solid food is for the mature, for those whose faculties are trained by practice to discern good and evil.

CHAPTER 6

[1] [y]Therefore, let us leave behind the basic teaching about Christ and advance to maturity, without laying the foundation all over again: repentance from dead works and faith in God, [2] [z]*instruction about baptisms and laying on of hands, resurrection of the dead and eternal judgment. [3]And we shall do this, if only God permits. [4] [a]*For it is impossible in the case of those who have once been enlightened and tasted the heavenly gift and shared in the holy Spirit [5] *and tasted the good word of God and the powers of the age to come, [6] [b]*and then have fallen away, to bring them to repentance again, since they are recrucifying the Son of God for themselves and holding him up to contempt. [7] [c]Ground that has absorbed the rain falling upon it repeatedly and brings forth crops useful to those for whom it is cultivated receives a blessing from God. [8] [d]But if it produces thorns and thistles, it is rejected; it will soon be cursed and finally burned.

[9]But we are sure in your regard, beloved, of better things related to salvation, even though we speak in this way. [10]For God is not unjust so as to overlook your work and the love you have demonstrated for his name by having served and continuing to serve the holy ones. [11] [e]We earnestly desire each of you to demonstrate the same eagerness for the fulfillment of

5, 7: He offered prayers . . . to the one who was able to save him from death: at Gethsemane (cf Mk 14, 35), though some see a broader reference (see the note on Jn 12, 27).

5, 8: Son though he was: two different though not incompatible views of Jesus' sonship coexist in Heb, one associating it with his exaltation, the other with his preexistence. The former view is the older one (cf Rom 1, 4).

5, 11—6, 20: The central section of Heb (5, 11—10, 39) opens with a reprimand and an appeal. Those to whom the author directs his teaching about Jesus' priesthood, which is **difficult to explain,** have become **sluggish in hearing** and forgetful of even **the basic elements** (5, 12). But rather than treating of basic teachings, the author apparently believes that the challenge of more advanced ones may shake them out of their inertia (**therefore,** 6, 1). The six examples of **basic teaching** in 6, 1–3 are probably derived from a traditional catechetical list. No effort is made to address apostates, for their very hostility to the Christian message cuts them off completely from Christ (6, 4–8). This harsh statement seems to rule out repentance after apostasy, but perhaps the author deliberately uses hyperbole in order to stress the seriousness of abandoning Christ. With 6, 9 a milder tone is introduced, and the criticism of the community (6, 1–3.9) is now balanced by an expression of confidence that its members are living truly Christian lives, and that God will justly reward their efforts (10). The author is concerned especially about their persevering (11–12), citing in this regard the achievement of Abraham, who relied on God's promise and on God's oath (13–18; cf Gn 22, 16), and proposes to them as a firm anchor of Christian hope the high priesthood of Christ, who is now living with God (19–20).

6, 2: Instruction about baptisms: not simply about Christian baptism but about the difference between it and similar Jewish rites, such as proselyte baptism, John's baptism, and the washings of the Qumran sectaries. **Laying on of hands:** in Acts 8, 17; 19, 6 this rite effects the infusion of the holy Spirit; in Acts 6, 6; 13, 3; 1 Tm 4, 14; 5, 22; 2 Tm 1, 6 it is a means of conferring some ministry or mission in the early Christian community.

6, 4: Enlightened and tasted the heavenly gift: this may refer to baptism and the Eucharist, respectively, but more probably means the neophytes' enlightenment by faith and their experience of salvation.

6, 5: Tasted the good word of God and the powers of the age to come: the proclamation of the **word of God** was accompanied by signs of the Spirit's power (1 Thes 1, 5; 1 Cor 2, 4).

6, 6: They are recrucifying the Son of God for themselves: a colorful description of the malice of apostasy, which is portrayed as again crucifying and deriding the Son of God.

t Mt 26, 38–44; Mk 14, 34–40; Lk 22, 41–46; Jn 12, 27. u Rom 5, 19; Phil 2, 8. v 7, 24–25.28. w 6, 20; Ps 110, 4. x 1 Cor 3, 1–3. y 9, 14. z 9, 10; Mk 7, 4 / Acts 6, 6; 8, 17; 13, 3; 19, 6; 1 Tm 4, 14; 5, 22; 2 Tm 1, 6. a 10, 26.32; Ps 34, 6; 2 Cor 4, 6. b 2 Pt 2, 21. c Gn 1, 11–12; Dt 11, 11. d Gn 3, 17–18; Mt 7, 16; 13, 7; Mk 4, 7; Lk 8, 7. e 3,14.

hope until the end, [12f]*so that you may not
become sluggish, but imitators of those who,
through faith and patience, are inheriting the
promises.
God's Promise Immutable [13g]*When God
made the promise to Abraham, since he had no
one greater by whom to swear, "he swore by
himself," [14h]and said, "I will indeed bless you
and multiply" you. [15i]*And so, after patient
waiting, he obtained the promise. [16]Human
beings swear by someone greater than them-
selves; for them an oath serves as a guarantee
and puts an end to all argument. [17j]So when
God wanted to give the heirs of his promise an
even clearer demonstration of the immutability
of his purpose, he intervened with an oath,
[18k]*so that by two immutable things, in which
it was impossible for God to lie, we who have
taken refuge might be strongly encouraged to
hold fast to the hope that lies before us.
[19l]*This we have as an anchor of the soul, sure
and firm, which reaches into the interior be-
hind the veil, [20m]where Jesus has entered on
our behalf as forerunner, becoming high priest
forever according to the order of Melchizedek.

CHAPTER 7

Melchizedek, a Type of Christ [1n]*This "Mel-
chizedek, king of Salem and priest of God Most
High," "met Abraham as he returned from his
defeat of the kings" and "blessed him." [2]*And
Abraham apportioned to him "a tenth of every-
thing." His name first means righteous king, and
he was also "king of Salem," that is, king of
peace. [3o]*Without father, mother, or ancestry,
without beginning of days or end of life, thus
made to resemble the Son of God, he remains a
priest forever.
[4p]*See how great he is to whom the patriarch
"Abraham [indeed] gave a tenth" of his spoils.
[5q]The descendants of Levi who receive the
office of priesthood have a commandment ac-
cording to the law to exact tithes from the
people, that is, from their brothers, although
they also have come from the loins of Abraham.
[6]But he who was not of their ancestry received
tithes from Abraham and blessed him who had
received the promises. [7]*Unquestionably, a
lesser person is blessed by a greater. [8]In the one
case, mortal men receive tithes; in the other, a
man of whom it is testified that he lives on.
[9]*One might even say that Levi himself, who

6, 12: Imitators of those . . . inheriting the promises: the author urges the addressees to imitate the faith of the holy people of the Old Testament, who now possess the promised goods of which they lived in hope. This theme will be treated fully in ch 11.

6, 13: He swore by himself: God's promise to Abraham, which he confirmed by an oath ("I swear by myself," Gen 22, 16) was the basis for the hope of all Abraham's descendants.

6, 15: He obtained the promise: this probably refers not to Abraham's temporary possession of the land but to the eschatological blessings that Abraham and the other patriarchs have now come to possess.

6, 18: Two immutable things: the promise and the oath, both made by God.

6, 19: Anchor . . . into the interior behind the veil: a mixed metaphor. The Holy of Holies, beyond the veil that separates it from the Holy Place (Ex 26, 31–33), is seen as the earthly counterpart of the heavenly abode of God. This theme will be developed in ch 9.

7, 1–3: Recalling the meeting between Melchizedek and Abraham described in Gn 14, 17–20, the author enhances the significance of this priest by providing the popular etymological meaning of his name and that of the city over which he ruled (2). Since Genesis gives no information on the parentage or the death of Melchizedek, he is seen here as a type of Christ, representing a priesthood that is unique and eternal (3).

7, 1: The author here assumes that Melchizedek was a priest of the God of Israel (cf Gn 14, 22 and the note there).

7, 2: In Gn 14, the Hebrew text does not state explicitly who gave tithes to whom. The author of Heb supplies Abraham as the subject, according to a contemporary interpretation of the passage. This supports the argument of the midrash and makes it possible to see in Melchizedek a type of Jesus. The messianic blessings of righteousness and peace are foreshadowed in the names "Melchizedek" and "Salem."

7, 3: Without father, mother, or ancestry, without beginning of days or end of life: this is perhaps a quotation from a hymn about Melchizedek. The rabbis maintained that anything not mentioned in the Torah does not exist. Consequently, since the Old Testament nowhere mentions Melchizedek's ancestry, birth, or death, the conclusion can be drawn that he **remains . . . forever.**

7, 4–10: The tithe that Abraham gave to Melchizedek (4), a practice later followed by the levitical priesthood (5), was a gift (6) acknowledging a certain superiority in Melchizedek, the foreign priest (7). This is further indicated by the fact that the institution of the levitical priesthood was sustained by hereditary succession in the tribe of Levi, whereas the absence of any mention of Melchizedek's death in Gn implies that his personal priesthood is permanent (8). The levitical priesthood itself, through Abraham, its ancestor, paid tithes to Melchizedek, thus acknowledging the superiority of his priesthood over its own (9–10).

7, 7: A lesser person is blessed by a greater: though this sounds like a principle, there are some examples in the Old Testament that do not support it (cf 2 Sm 14, 22; Jb 31, 20). The author may intend it as a statement of a liturgical rule.

7, 9: Levi: for the author this name designates not only the son

f 5, 11; Gal 3, 14; Eph 1, 13–14. g Gn 22, 16. h Gn 22, 17. i 12; Rom 4, 20. j 12. k Nm 23, 19; 1 Sm 15, 29; Jn 8, 17; 2 Tm 2, 13. l 10, 20; Ex 26, 31–33; Lv 16, 2. m 5, 10; Ps 110, 4. n Gn 14, 17–20. o 4, 14; 6, 6; 10, 29. p Gn 14, 20. q Nm 18, 21 / Gn 35, 11.

receives tithes, was tithed through Abraham,
10 for he was still in his father's loins when
Melchizedek met him.

11 r*If, then, perfection came through the
levitical priesthood, on the basis of which the
people received the law, what need would there
still have been for another priest to arise accord-
ing to the order of Melchizedek, and not reck-
oned according to the order of Aaron? 12 When
there is a change of priesthood, there is necessar-
ily a change of law as well. 13 *Now he of whom
these things are said belonged to a different
tribe, of which no member ever officiated at the
altar. 14 s*It is clear that our Lord arose from
Judah, and in regard to that tribe Moses said
nothing about priests. 15 *It is even more obvious
if another priest is raised up after the likeness of
Melchizedek, 16 *who has become so, not by a
law expressed in a commandment concerning
physical descent but by the power of a life that
cannot be destroyed. 17 tFor it is testified:

"You are a priest forever
according to the order of Melchizedek."

18 uOn the one hand, a former commandment is
annulled because of its weakness and useless-
ness, 19 *for the law brought nothing to perfec-
tion; on the other hand, a better hope is
introduced, through which we draw near to
God. 20 *And to the degree that this happened
not without the taking of an oath—for others
became priests without an oath, 21 vbut he with
an oath, through the one who said to him:

"The Lord has sworn, and he will not repent:
'You are a priest forever' "—

22 w*to that same degree has Jesus [also] become
the guarantee of an [even] better covenant.
23 Those priests were many because they were
prevented by death from remaining in office,
24 xbut he, because he remains forever, has a
priesthood that does not pass away.
25 y*Therefore, he is always able to save those
who approach God through him, since he lives
forever to make intercession for them.

26 z*It was fitting that we should have such a
high priest: holy, innocent, undefiled, separated

---

of Jacob mentioned in Genesis but the priestly tribe that was thought to be descended from him.

7, 11–14: The levitical priesthood was not typified by the priesthood of Melchizedek, for Ps 110, 4 speaks of a priesthood of a new order, the order of Melchizedek, to arise in messianic times (11). Since the levitical priesthood served the Mosaic law, a new priesthood (12) would not come into being without a change in the law itself. Thus Jesus was not associated with the Old Testament priesthood, for he was a descendant of the tribe of Judah, which had never exercised the priesthood (13–14).

7, 13: He of whom these things are said: Jesus, the priest "according to the order of Melchizedek." According to the author's interpretation, Ps 110 spoke prophetically of Jesus.

7, 14: Judah: the author accepts the early Christian tradition that Jesus was descended from the family of David (cf Mt 1, 1–2.16.20; Lk 1, 27; 2, 4; Rom 1, 3). The Qumran community expected two Messiahs, one descended from Aaron and one from David; Heb shows no awareness of this view or at least does not accept it. Our author's view is not attested in contemporaneous Judaism.

7, 15–19: Jesus does not exercise a priesthood through family lineage but through his immortal existence (15–16), fulfilling Ps 110, 4 (17; cf 3). Thus he abolishes forever both the levitical priesthood and the law it serves, because neither could effectively sanctify people (18) by leading them into direct communication with God (19).

7, 16: A life that cannot be destroyed: the life to which Jesus has attained by virtue of his resurrection; it is his exaltation rather than his divine nature that makes him priest. The Old Testament speaks of the Aaronic priesthood as eternal (see Ex 40, 15); our author does not explicitly consider this possible objection to his argument but implicitly refutes it in vv 23–24.

7, 19: A better hope: this hope depends upon the sacrifice of the Son of God; through it we "approach the throne of grace" (4, 16); cf 6, 19.20.

7, 20–25: As was the case with the promise to Abraham (6, 13), though not with the levitical priesthood, the eternal priesthood of the order of Melchizedek was confirmed by God's oath (20–21); cf Ps 110, 4. Thus Jesus becomes the guarantee of a permanent covenant (22) that does not require a succession of priests as did the levitical priesthood (23) because his high priesthood is eternal and unchangeable (24). Consequently, Jesus is able to save all who draw near to God through him since he is their ever-living intercessor (25).

7, 20: An oath: God's oath in Ps 110, 4.

7, 22: An [even] better covenant: better than the Mosaic covenant because it will be eternal, like the priesthood of Jesus upon which it is based. Verse 12 argued that a change of priesthood involves a change of law; since "law" and "covenant" are used correlatively, a new covenant is likewise instituted.

7, 25: To make intercession: the intercession of the exalted Jesus, not the sequel to his completed sacrifice but its eternal presence in heaven; cf Rom 8, 34.

7, 26–28: Jesus is precisely the high priest whom the human race requires, holy and sinless, installed far above humanity (26); one having no need to offer sacrifice daily for sins but making a single offering of himself (27) once for all. The law could only appoint high priests with human limitations, but the fulfillment of God's oath regarding the priesthood of Melchizedek (Ps 110, 4) makes the Son of God the perfect priest forever (28).

7, 26: This verse with its list of attributes is reminiscent of v 3 and is perhaps a hymnic counterpart to it, contrasting the exalted Jesus with Melchizedek.

r 5, 6; Ps 110, 4. s Gn 49, 10; Is 11, 1; Mt 1, 1–2.16.20; 2, 6; Lk 1, 27; 2, 4; Rom 1, 3; Rv 5, 5. t 5, 6; Ps 110, 4. u 10, 1. v Ps 110, 4. w 8, 6–10; 9, 15–20; 10, 29; 12, 24; 13, 20. x 5, 6; 13, 8. y Rom 8, 34; 1 Jn 2, 1; Rv 1, 18. z 4, 14.15.

from sinners, higher than the heavens. [27] [a] *He has no need, as did the high priests, to offer sacrifice day after day, first for his own sins and then for those of the people; he did that once for all when he offered himself. [28] [b] For the law appoints men subject to weakness to be high priests, but the word of the oath, which was taken after the law, appoints a son, who has been made perfect forever.

CHAPTER 8

Heavenly Priesthood of Jesus [1] [c] *The main point of what has been said is this: we have such a high priest, who has taken his seat at the right hand of the throne of the Majesty in heaven, [2] [d] *a minister of the sanctuary and of the true tabernacle that the Lord, not man, set up. [3] [e] Now every high priest is appointed to offer gifts and sacrifices; thus the necessity for this one also to have something to offer. [4] [f] If then he were on earth, he would not be a priest, since there are those who offer gifts according to the law. [5] [g] They worship in a copy and shadow of the heavenly sanctuary, as Moses was warned when he was about to erect the tabernacle. For he says, "See that you make everything according to the pattern shown you on the mountain." [6] [h] Now he has obtained so much more excellent a ministry as he is mediator of a better covenant, enacted on better promises.

Old and New Covenants [7] *For if that first covenant had been faultless, no place would have been sought for a second one. [8] [i] *But he finds fault with them and says:

"Behold, the days are coming, says the Lord,
when I will conclude a new covenant with the house of Israel and the house of Judah.
[9] It will not be like the covenant I made with their fathers
the day I took them by the hand to lead them forth from the land of Egypt;
for they did not stand by my covenant
and I ignored them, says the Lord.
[10] [j] But this is the covenant I will establish with the house of Israel
after those days, says the Lord:
I will put my laws in their minds
and I will write them upon their hearts.
I will be their God,
and they shall be my people.
[11] And they shall not teach, each one his fellow citizen
and kinsman, saying, 'Know the Lord,'
for all shall know me,
from least to greatest.
[12] For I will forgive their evildoing
and remember their sins no more."

7, 27: Such daily sacrifice is nowhere mentioned in the Mosaic law; only on the Day of Atonement is it prescribed that the high priest must **offer sacrifice . . . for his own sins and then for those of the people** (Lv 16, 11–19). **Once for all:** this translates the Greek words **ephapax/hapax** that occur eleven times in Heb.

8, 1–6: The Christian community has in Jesus the kind of high priest described in 7, 26–28. In virtue of his ascension Jesus has taken his place at God's right hand in accordance with Ps 110, 1 (1), where he presides over the heavenly sanctuary established by God himself (2). Like every high priest, he has his offering to make (3; cf 9, 12.14), but it differs from that of the levitical priesthood in which he had no share (4) and which was in any case but a shadowy reflection of the true offering in the heavenly sanctuary (5). But Jesus' ministry in the heavenly sanctuary is that of mediator of a superior covenant that accomplishes what it signifies (6).

8, 2: The sanctuary: the Greek term could also mean "holy things" but bears the meaning "sanctuary" elsewhere in Heb (9, 8.12.24.25; 10, 19; 13, 11). **The true tabernacle:** the heavenly tabernacle **that the Lord . . . set up** is contrasted with the earthly tabernacle that Moses set up in the desert. **True** means "real" in contradistinction to a mere "copy and shadow" (5); compare the Johannine usage (e.g., Jn 1, 9; 6, 32; 15, 1). The idea that the earthly sanctuary is a reflection of a heavenly model may be based upon Ex 25, 9, but probably also derives from the Platonic concept of a real world of which our observable world is merely a shadow.

8, 7–13: Since the first covenant was deficient in accomplishing what it signified, it had to be replaced (7), as Jeremiah (31, 31–34) had prophesied (8–12). Even in the time of Jeremiah, the first covenant was antiquated (13). In 7, 22–24, the superiority of the new covenant was seen in the permanence of its priesthood; here the superiority is based on better promises, made explicit in the citation of Jer 31 (LXX: 38), 31–34, namely, in the immediacy of the people's knowledge of God (11) and in the forgiveness of sin (12).

8, 8–12: In citing Jer the author follows the Septuagint; some apparent departures from it may be the result of a different Septuagintal text rather than changes deliberately introduced.

a 5, 3; 9, 12.25–28; 10, 11–14; Ex 29, 38–39; Lv 16, 6.11.15–17; Nm 28, 3–4; Is 53, 10; Rom 6, 10. b 5, 1.2.9. c 1, 3; 4, 14; 7, 26–28. d 9, 11; Ex 33, 7; Nm 24, 6 LXX. e 5, 1. f 7, 13. g 9, 23; Ex 25, 40; Acts 7, 44; Col 2, 17. h 7, 22; 9, 15. i Jer 31, 31–34. j 10, 16–17.

13 k*When he speaks of a "new" covenant, he
declares the first one obsolete. And what has
become obsolete and has grown old is close to
disappearing.

CHAPTER 9

The Worship of the First Covenant 1 *Now
[even] the first covenant had regulations for
worship and an earthly sanctuary. 2 l*For a
tabernacle was constructed, the outer one, in
which were the lampstand, the table, and the
bread of offering; this is called the Holy Place.
3 m*Behind the second veil was the tabernacle
called the Holy of Holies, 4 n*in which were the
gold altar of incense and the ark of the covenant
entirely covered with gold. In it were the gold jar
containing the manna, the staff of Aaron that
had sprouted, and the tablets of the covenant.
5 o*Above it were the cherubim of glory over-
shadowing the place of expiation. Now is not the
time to speak of these in detail.

6 p*With these arrangements for worship, the
priests, in performing their service, go into the
outer tabernacle repeatedly, 7 q*but the high
priest alone goes into the inner one once a year,
not without blood that he offers for himself and
for the sins of the people. 8 In this way the holy
Spirit shows that the way into the sanctuary had
not yet been revealed while the outer tabernacle
still had its place. 9 *This is a symbol of the
present time, in which gifts and sacrifices are
offered that cannot perfect the worshiper in
conscience 10 r but only in matters of food and
drink and various ritual washings: regulations
concerning the flesh, imposed until the time of
the new order.

Sacrifice of Jesus 11 s*But when Christ came
as high priest of the good things that have come
to be, passing through the greater and more
perfect tabernacle not made by hands, that is,
not belonging to this creation, 12 t he entered
once for all into the sanctuary, not with the
blood of goats and calves but with his own
blood, thus obtaining eternal redemption.
13 u*For if the blood of goats and bulls and the
sprinkling of a heifer's ashes can sanctify those
who are defiled so that their flesh is cleansed,
14 v*how much more will the blood of Christ,

8, 13: Close to disappearing: from the prophet's perspective, not that of the author of Heb.

9, 1–10: The regulations for worship under the old covenant permitted all the priests to enter the Holy Place (2, 6), but only the high priest to enter the Holy of Holies and then only once a year (3–5.7). The description of the sanctuary and its furnishings is taken essentially from Ex 25–26. This exclusion of the people from the Holy of Holies signified that they were not allowed to stand in God's presence (8) because their offerings and sacrifices, which were merely symbols of their need of spiritual renewal (10), could not obtain forgiveness of sins (9).

9, 2: The outer one: the author speaks of **the outer tabernacle** (6) and **the inner one** (7) rather than of one Mosaic tabernacle divided into two parts or sections.

9, 3: The second veil: what is meant is the veil that divided the Holy Place from the Holy of Holies. It is here called **the second,** because there was another veil at the entrance to the Holy Place, or "outer tabernacle" (Ex 26, 36).

9, 4: The gold altar of incense: Ex 30, 6 locates this altar in the Holy Place, i.e., the first tabernacle, rather than in the Holy of Holies. Neither is there any Old Testament support for the assertion that the jar of manna and the staff of Aaron were in the ark of the covenant. For the tablets of the covenant, see Ex 25, 16.

9, 5: The place of expiation: the gold "mercy seat" (Greek **hilastērion,** as in Rom 3, 25), where the blood of the sacrificial animals was sprinkled on the Day of Atonement (Lv 16, 14–15). This rite achieved "expiation" or atonement for the sins of the preceding year.

9, 6: In performing their service: the priestly services that had to be performed regularly in the Holy Place or **outer tabernacle** included burning incense on the incense altar twice each day (Ex 30, 7), replacing the loaves on the table of the bread of offering once each week (Lv 24, 8), and constantly caring for the lamps on the lampstand (Ex 27, 21).

9, 7: Not without blood: blood was essential to Old Testament sacrifice because it was believed that life was located in the blood. Hence blood was especially sacred, and its outpouring functioned as a meaningful symbol of cleansing from sin and reconciliation with God. Unlike Heb, the Old Testament never says that the blood is "offered." The author is perhaps retrojecting into his description of Mosaic ritual a concept that belongs to the New Testament antitype, as Paul does when he speaks of the Israelites' passage through the sea as a "baptism" (1 Cor 10, 2).

9, 9: The present time: this expression is equivalent to the "present age," used in contradistinction to the "age to come."

9, 11–14: Christ, the high priest of the spiritual blessings foreshadowed in the Old Testament sanctuary, has actually entered the true sanctuary of heaven that is not of human making (11). His place there is permanent, and his offering is his own blood that won eternal redemption (12). If the sacrifice of animals could bestow legal purification (13), how much more effective is the blood of the sinless, divine Christ who spontaneously offered himself to purge the human race of sin and render it fit for the service of God (14).

9, 11: The good things that have come to be: the majority of later manuscripts here read "the good things to come"; cf 10, 1.

9, 13: A heifer's ashes: ashes from a red heifer that had been burned were mixed with water and used for the cleansing of those who had become ritually defiled by touching a corpse; see Nm 19, 9.14–21.

9, 14: Through the eternal spirit: this expression does not

k Rom 10, 4. l Ex 25, 23–30. m Ex 26, 31–34. n Ex 16, 32–34; 25, 10.16.21; 30, 1–10; Lv 16, 12–13; Nm 17, 2–7.16–26. o Ex 25, 16–22; 26, 34; Lv 16, 14–15. p Ex 27, 21; 30, 7; Lv 24, 8. q Ex 30, 10; Lv 16, 1–14. r 13, 9; Lv 11; 14, 8; Nm 19, 11–21; Col 2, 16. s 4, 14; 10, 1.20. t 7, 27; Mt 26, 28. u 10, 4; Lv 16, 6–16; Nm, 19, 9.14–21. v 10, 10; Rom 5, 9; 1 Tm 3, 9; Ti 2, 14; 1 Pt 1, 18–19; 1 Jn 1, 7; Rv 1, 5.

who through the eternal spirit offered himself unblemished to God, cleanse our consciences from dead works to worship the living God.

15 [w]*For this reason he is mediator of a new covenant: since a death has taken place for deliverance from transgressions under the first covenant, those who are called may receive the promised eternal inheritance.
16 *Now where there is a will, the death of the testator must be established.
17 For a will takes effect only at death; it has no force while the testator is alive.
18 Thus not even the first covenant was inaugurated without blood.
19 [x]*When every commandment had been proclaimed by Moses to all the people according to the law, he took the blood of calves [and goats], together with water and crimson wool and hyssop, and sprinkled both the book itself and all the people,
20 [y]saying, "This is 'the blood of the covenant which God has enjoined upon you.' "
21 [z]*In the same way, he sprinkled also the tabernacle and all the vessels of worship with blood.
22 [a]*According to the law almost everything is purified by blood, and without the shedding of blood there is no forgiveness.

23 [b]*Therefore, it was necessary for the copies of the heavenly things to be purified by these rites, but the heavenly things themselves by better sacrifices than these.
24 [c]For Christ did not enter into a sanctuary made by hands, a copy of the true one, but heaven itself, that he might now appear before God on our behalf.
25 Not that he might offer himself repeatedly, as the high priest enters each year into the sanctuary with blood that is not his own;
26 [d]*if that were so, he would have had to suffer repeatedly from the foundation of the world. But now once for all he has appeared at the end of the ages to take away sin by his sacrifice.
27 [e]Just as it is appointed that human beings die once, and after this the judgment,
28 [f]*so also Christ, offered once to take away the sins of many, will appear a second time, not to take away sin but to bring salvation to those who eagerly await him.

---

refer either to the holy Spirit or to the divine nature of Jesus but to the life of the risen Christ, "a life that cannot be destroyed" (7, 16).

9, 15–22: Jesus' role as **mediator of the new covenant** is based upon his sacrificial **death** (cf 8, 6). His death has effected **deliverance from transgressions**, i.e., deliverance from sins committed under the old covenant, which the Mosaic sacrifices were incapable of effacing. Until this happened, the **eternal inheritance** promised by God could not be obtained (15). This effect of his work follows the human pattern by which a last will and testament becomes effective only with the death of the testator (16–17). The Mosaic covenant was also associated with death, for Moses made use of blood to seal the pact between God and the people (18–21). In Old Testament tradition, guilt could normally not be remitted without the use of blood (22; cf Lv 17, 11).

9, 16–17: A will . . . death of the testator: the same Greek word **diathēkē,** meaning "covenant" in vv 15 and 18, is used here with the meaning **will.** The new covenant, unlike the old, is at the same time a will that requires **the death of the testator.** Jesus as eternal Son is the one who established the new covenant together with his Father, author of both covenants; at the same time he is the testator whose death puts his **will** into effect.

9, 19–20: A number of details here are different from the description of this covenant rite in Ex 24, 5–8. Exodus mentions only calves ("young bulls," NAB), not goats (but this addition in Heb is of doubtful authenticity), says nothing of the use of **water and crimson wool and hyssop** (these features probably came from a different rite; cf Lv 14, 3–7; Nm 19, 6–18), and describes Moses as splashing blood on the altar, whereas Heb says he sprinkled it on the book (but both book and altar are meant to symbolize the agreement of God). The words of Moses are also slightly different from those in Exodus and are closer to the words of Jesus at the Last Supper in Mk 14, 24 // Mt 26, 28.

9, 21: According to Ex, the tabernacle did not yet exist at the time of the covenant rite. Moreover, nothing is said of sprinkling it with blood at its subsequent dedication (Ex 40, 9–11).

9, 22: Without the shedding of blood there is no forgiveness: in fact, ancient Israel did envisage other means of obtaining forgiveness; the Old Testament mentions contrition of heart (Ps 51, 19), fasting (Jl 2, 12), and almsgiving (Sir 3, 29). The author is limiting his horizon to the sacrificial cult, which did always involve the shedding of blood for its expiatory and unitive value.

9, 23–28: Since the blood of animals became a cleansing symbol among Old Testament prefigurements, it was necessary that the realities foreshadowed be brought into being by a shedding of blood that was infinitely more effective by reason of its worth (23). Christ did not simply prefigure the heavenly realities (24) by performing an annual sacrifice with a blood not his own (25); he offered the single sacrifice of himself as the final annulment of sin (26). Just as death is the unrepeatable act that ends a person's life, so Christ's offering of himself for all is the unrepeatable sacrifice that has once for all achieved redemption (27–28).

9, 26: At the end of the ages: the use of expressions such as this shows that the author of Heb, despite his interest in the Platonic concept of an eternal world above superior to temporal reality here below, nevertheless still clings to the Jewish Christian eschatology with its sequence of "the present age" and "the age to come."

9, 28: To take away the sins of many: the reference is to Is 53, 12. Since the Greek verb **anapherō** can mean both "to take away" and "to bear," the author no doubt intended to play upon both senses: Jesus took away sin by bearing it himself. See the similar wordplay in Jn 1, 29. **Many** is used in the Semitic meaning of "all" in the inclusive sense, as in Mk 14, 24. **To those who eagerly await him:** Jesus will appear **a second time** at the parousia, as the high priest reappeared on the Day of Atonement, emerging from the Holy of Holies, which he had entered **to take away sin.** This dramatic scene is described in Sir 50, 5–11.

w 1 Tm 2, 5. x 12–13. y Ex 24, 3–8; Mt 26, 28; Mk 14, 24. z Ex 40, 9; Lv 8, 15.19. a Lv 17, 11. b Jb 15, 15. c 7, 25; Rom 8, 34; 1 Jn 2, 1–2. d 7, 27; Jn 1, 29; Gal 4, 4. e Gn 3, 19. f 10, 10; Is 53, 12.

CHAPTER 10

One Sacrifice instead of Many [1][g]*Since the
law has only a shadow of the good things to
come, and not the very image of them, it can
never make perfect those who come to worship
by the same sacrifices that they offer continually
each year. [2]Otherwise, would not the sacrifices
have ceased to be offered, since the worshipers,
once cleansed, would no longer have had any
consciousness of sins? [3][h]But in those sacrifices
there is only a yearly remembrance of sins, [4][i]for
it is impossible that the blood of bulls and goats
take away sins. [5][j]*For this reason, when he
came into the world, he said:

"Sacrifice and offering you did not desire,
but a body you prepared for me;
[6]holocausts and sin offerings you took no
delight in.
[7]Then I said, 'As is written of me in the scroll,
Behold, I come to do your will, O God.' "

[8][k]*First he says, "Sacrifices and offerings, holo-
causts and sin offerings, you neither desired nor
delighted in." These are offered according to the
law. [9][l]Then he says, "Behold, I come to do your
will." He takes away the first to establish the
second. [10][m]By this "will," we have been conse-
crated through the offering of the body of Jesus
Christ once for all.

[11][n]*Every priest stands daily at his ministry,
offering frequently those same sacrifices that can
never take away sins. [12][o]But this one offered
one sacrifice for sins, and took his seat forever at
the right hand of God; [13]*now he waits until his
enemies are made his footstool. [14][p]For by one
offering he has made perfect forever those who
are being consecrated. [15]*The holy Spirit also
testifies to us, for after saying:

[16][q]"This is the covenant I will establish with
them after those days, says the Lord:
'I will put my laws in their hearts,
and I will write them upon their minds,' "

[17][r]*he also says:

"Their sins and their evildoing
I will remember no more."

[18]Where there is forgiveness of these, there is no
longer offering for sin.

Recalling the Past [19][s]*Therefore, brothers,
since through the blood of Jesus we have confi-

10, 1–10: Christian faith now realizes that the Old Testament sacrifices did not effect the spiritual benefits to come but only prefigured them (1). For if the sacrifices had actually effected the forgiveness of sin, there would have been no reason for their constant repetition (2). They were rather a continual reminder of the people's sins (3). It is not reasonable to suppose that human sins could be removed by the blood of animal sacrifices (4). Christ, therefore, is here shown to understand his mission in terms of Ps 40, 6–8, cited according to the Septuagint (5–7). Jesus acknowledged that the Old Testament sacrifices did not remit the sins of the people and so, perceiving the will of God, offered his own body for this purpose (8–10).

10, 1: A shadow of the good things to come: the term **shadow** was used in 8, 5 to signify the earthly counterpart of the Platonic heavenly reality. But here it means a prefiguration of what is to come in Christ, as it is used in the Pauline literature; cf Col 2, 17.

10, 5–7: A passage from Ps 40, 7–9a is placed in the mouth of the Son at his incarnation. As usual, the author follows the Septuagint text. There is a notable difference in v 5 (= Ps 40, 7b), where the Masoretic text reads "ears you have dug for me" ("ears open to obedience you gave me," NAB), but most Septuagint manuscripts have "a body you prepared for me," a reading obviously more suited to the interpretation of Heb.

10, 8: Sacrifices and offerings, holocausts and sin offerings: these four terms taken from the preceding passage of Ps 40 (with the first two changed to plural forms) are probably intended as equivalents to the four principal types of Old Testament sacrifices: peace offerings (Lv 3, here called **sacrifices**); cereal offerings (Lv 2, here called **offerings**); **holocausts** (Lv 1); and **sin offerings** (Lv 4—5). This last category includes the guilt offerings of Lv 5, 14–26.

10, 11–18: Whereas the levitical priesthood offered daily sacrifices that were ineffectual in remitting sin (11), Jesus offered a single sacrifice that won him a permanent place at God's right hand. There he has only to await the final outcome of his work (12–13; cf Ps 110, 1). Thus he has brought into being in his own person the new covenant prophesied by Jeremiah (31, 33–34) that has rendered meaningless all other offerings for sin (14–18).

10, 13: Until his enemies are made his footstool: Ps 110, 1 is again used; the reference here is to the period of time between the enthronement of Jesus and his second coming. The identity of the **enemies** is not specified; cf 1 Cor 15, 25–27.

10, 15–17: The testimony of the scriptures is now invoked to support what has just preceded. The passage cited is a portion of the new covenant prophecy of Jer 31, 31–34, which the author previously used in 8, 8–12.

10, 17: He also says: these words are not in the Greek text, which has only **kai**, "also," but the expression **after saying** in v 15 seems to require such a phrase to divide the Jeremiah text into two sayings. Others understand "the Lord says" of v 16 (here rendered **says the Lord**) as outside the quotation and consider v 16b as part of the second saying. Two ancient versions and a number of minuscules introduce the words "then he said" or a similar expression at the beginning of v 17.

10, 19–39: Practical consequences from these reflections on

g 8, 5; Col 2, 17. h Lv 16, 21; Nm 5, 15 LXX. i Is 1, 11; Mi 6, 6–8. j Ps 40, 7–9. k 5–6; Ps 40, 7. 17; Ps 40, 8; Mt 26, 39; Mk 14, 36; Lk 22, 42; Jn 6, 38. m 9, 12.14. n 7, 27; Dt 10, 8; 18, 7. o Ps 110, 1. p 9, 28. q 8, 10; Jer 31, 33. r 8, 12; Jer 31, 34. s 3, 6; 4, 16; 6, 19–20; Eph 1, 7; 3, 12.

dence of entrance into the sanctuary 20 t*by the new and living way he opened for us through the veil, that is, his flesh, 21 u*and since we have "a great priest over the house of God," 22 v*let us approach with a sincere heart and in absolute trust, with our hearts sprinkled clean from an evil conscience and our bodies washed in pure water. 23 wLet us hold unwaveringly to our confession that gives us hope, for he who made the promise is trustworthy. 24 We must consider how to rouse one another to love and good works. 25 x*We should not stay away from our assembly, as is the custom of some, but encourage one another, and this all the more as you see the day drawing near.

26 y*If we sin deliberately after receiving knowledge of the truth, there no longer remains sacrifice for sins 27 zbut a fearful prospect of judgment and a flaming fire that is going to consume the adversaries. 28 a*Anyone who rejects the law of Moses is put to death without pity on the testimony of two or three witnesses. 29 bDo you not think that a much worse punishment is due the one who has contempt for the Son of God, considers unclean the covenant-blood by which he was consecrated, and insults the spirit of grace? 30 cWe know the one who said:

"Vengeance is mine; I will repay,"

and again:

"The Lord will judge his people."

31 dIt is a fearful thing to fall into the hands of the living God.

32 e*Remember the days past when, after you had been enlightened, you endured a great contest of suffering. 33 fAt times you were publicly exposed to abuse and affliction; at other times you associated yourselves with those so treated. 34 gYou even joined in the sufferings of those in prison and joyfully accepted the confiscation of your property, knowing that you had a better and lasting possession. 35 hTherefore, do not throw away your confidence; it will have great recompense. 36 iYou need endurance to do the will of God and receive what he has promised.

37 j*"For, after just a brief moment,
he who is to come shall come;
he shall not delay.

---

the priesthood and the sacrifice of Christ should make it clear that Christians may now have direct and confident access to God through the person of Jesus (19–20), who rules God's house as high priest (21). They should approach God with sincerity and faith, in the knowledge that through baptism their sins have been remitted (22), reminding themselves of the hope they expressed in Christ at that event (23). They are to encourage one another to Christian love and activity (24), not refusing, no matter what the reason, to participate in the community's assembly, especially in view of the parousia (25; cf 1 Thes 4, 13–18). If refusal to participate in the assembly indicates rejection of Christ, no sacrifice exists to obtain forgiveness for so great a sin (26); only the dreadful judgment of God remains (27). For if violation of the Mosaic law could be punished by death, how much worse will be the punishment of those who have turned their backs on Christ by despising his sacrifice and disregarding the gifts of the holy Spirit (28–29). Judgment belongs to the Lord, and he enacts it by his living presence (30–31). There was a time when the spirit of their community caused them to welcome and share their sufferings (32–34). To revitalize that spirit is to share in the courage of the Old Testament prophets (cf Is 26, 20; Hb 2, 3–4), the kind of courage that must distinguish the faith of the Christian (35–39).

10, 20: Through the veil, that is, his flesh: the term **flesh** is used pejoratively. As the temple veil kept people from entering the Holy of Holies (it was rent at Christ's death, Mk 15, 38), so the flesh of Jesus constituted an obstacle to approaching God.

10, 21: The house of God: this refers back to 3, 6, "we are his house."

10, 22: With our hearts sprinkled clean from an evil conscience: as in 9, 13 (see the note there), the sprinkling motif refers to the Mosaic rite of cleansing from ritual impurity. This could produce only an external purification, whereas sprinkling with the blood of Christ (9, 14) cleanses the **conscience. Washed in pure water:** baptism is elsewhere referred to as a washing; cf 1 Cor 6, 11; Eph 5, 26.

10, 25: Our assembly: the liturgical **assembly** of the Christian community, probably for the celebration of the Eucharist. **The day:** this designation for the parousia also occurs in the Pauline letters, e.g., Rom 2, 16; 1 Cor 3, 13; 1 Thes 5, 2.

10, 26: If we sin deliberately: verse 29 indicates that the author is here thinking of apostasy; cf 3, 12; 6, 4–8.

10, 28: Rejects the law of Moses: evidently not any sin against the law, but idolatry. Dt 17, 2–7 prescribed capital punishment for idolaters who were convicted on the testimony of two or three witnesses.

10, 32: After you had been enlightened: "enlightenment" is an ancient metaphor for baptism (cf Eph 5, 14; Jn 9, 11), but see 6, 4 and the note there.

10, 37–38: In support of his argument, the author uses Hb 2, 3–4 in a wording almost identical with the text of the Codex Alexandrinus of the Septuagint but with the first and second lines of v 4 inverted. He introduces it with a few words from Is 26, 20: **after just a brief moment.** Note the Pauline usage of Hb 2, 4 in Rom 1, 17; Gal 3, 11.

t Jn 14, 6 / 6, 19–20; 9, 8.11–12; Mt 27, 51; Mk 15, 38; Lk 23, 45. u 3, 6. v 9, 13–14; Ez 36, 25; 1 Cor 6, 11; Ti 3, 5; 1 Pt 3, 21. w 3, 1.6; 4, 14; 1 Cor 10, 13. x Rom 13, 12; 1 Cor 3, 13. y 3, 12; 6, 4–8. z 31; 9, 27; Is 26, 11 LXX; Zep 1, 18. a Dt 17, 6. b 6, 6. c Dt 32, 35.36; Rom 12, 19. d 27; Mt 10, 28; Lk 12, 4–5. e 6, 4. f 1 Cor 4, 9. g 13, 3; Mt 6, 19–20; Lk 12, 33–34. h 4, 16. i Lk 21, 19. j Is 26, 20; Hb 2, 3.

38 [k]But my just one shall live by faith,
and if he draws back I take no pleasure in
him."

39 We are not among those who draw back and perish, but among those who have faith and will possess life.

V: Examples, Discipline, Disobedience

CHAPTER 11

Faith of the Ancients 1 [l]*Faith is the realization of what is hoped for and evidence of things not seen. 2 Because of it the ancients were well attested. 3 [m]*By faith we understand that the universe was ordered by the word of God, so that what is visible came into being through the invisible. 4 [n]*By faith Abel offered to God a sacrifice greater than Cain's. Through this he was attested to be righteous, God bearing witness to his gifts, and through this, though dead, he still speaks. 5 [o]By faith Enoch was taken up so that he should not see death, and "he was found no more because God had taken him." Before he was taken up, he was attested to have pleased God. 6 [p]*But without faith it is impossible to please him, for anyone who approaches God must believe that he exists and that he rewards those who seek him. 7 [q]By faith Noah, warned about what was not yet seen, with reverence built an ark for the salvation of his household. Through this he condemned the world and inherited the righteousness that comes through faith.

8 [r]By faith Abraham obeyed when he was called to go out to a place that he was to receive as an inheritance; he went out, not knowing where he was to go. 9 [s]By faith he sojourned in the promised land as in a foreign country, dwelling in tents with Isaac and Jacob, heirs of the same promise; 10 [t]for he was looking forward to the city with foundations, whose architect and maker is God. 11 [u]By faith he received power to generate, even though he was past the normal age—and Sarah herself was sterile—for he thought that the one who had made the promise was trustworthy. 12 [v]So it was that there came forth from one man, himself as good as dead, descendants as numerous as the stars in the sky and as countless as the sands on the seashore.

13 [w]All these died in faith. They did not receive what had been promised but saw it and greeted it from afar and acknowledged them-

11, 1–40: This chapter draws upon the people and events of the Old Testament to paint an inspiring portrait of religious faith, firm and unyielding in the face of any obstacles that confront it. These pages rank among the most eloquent and lofty to be found in the Bible. They expand the theme announced in 6, 12, to which the author now returns (10, 39). The material of this chapter is developed chronologically. Verses 3–7 draw upon the first nine chapters of Gn; vv 8–22, upon the period of the patriarchs; vv 23–31, upon the time of Moses; vv 32–38, upon the history of the judges, the prophets, and the Maccabean martyrs. The author gives the most extensive description of faith provided in the New Testament, though his interest does not lie in a technical, theological definition. In view of the needs of his audience he describes what authentic faith does, not what it is in itself. Through faith God guarantees the blessings to be hoped for from him, providing evidence in the gift of faith that what he promises will eventually come to pass (1). Because they accepted in faith God's guarantee of the future, the biblical personages discussed in vv 3–38 were themselves commended by God (2). Christians have even greater reason to remain firm in faith since they, unlike the Old Testament men and women of faith, have perceived the beginning of God's fulfillment of his messianic promises (39–40).

11, 1: Faith is the realization . . . evidence: the author is not attempting a precise definition. There is dispute about the meaning of the Greek words **hypostasis** and **elenchos,** here translated **realization** and **evidence,** respectively. **Hypostasis** usually means "substance," "being" (as translated in 1, 3), or "reality" (as translated in 3, 14); here it connotes something more subjective, and so **realization** has been chosen rather than "assurance" (RSV). **Elenchos,** usually "proof," is used here in an objective sense and so translated **evidence** rather than the transferred sense of "(inner) conviction" (RSV).

11, 3: By faith . . . God: this verse does not speak of the faith of the Old Testament men and women but is in the first person plural. Hence it seems out of place in the sequence of thought.

11, 4: The "Praise of the Ancestors" in Sir 44, 1—50, 21 gives a similar list of heroes. The Cain and Abel narrative in Gn 4, 1–16 does not mention Abel's faith. It says, however, that God "looked with favor on Abel and his offering" (Gn 4, 4); in view of v 6 the author probably understood God's favor to have been activated by Abel's faith. **Though dead, he still speaks:** possibly because his blood "cries out to me from the soil" (Gn 4, 10), but more probably a way of saying that the repeated story of Abel provides ongoing witness to faith.

11, 6: One must believe not only that God **exists** but that he is concerned about human conduct; the Old Testament defines folly as the denial of this truth; cf Ps 52, 2.

k Hb 2, 4; Rom 1, 17; Gal 3, 11. l 1, 3; 3, 14; Rom 8, 24; 2 Cor 4, 18. m Gn 1, 3; Ps 33, 6; Wis 9, 1; Jn 1, 3. n 12, 24; Gn 4, 4.10. o Gn 5, 24; Sir 44, 16. p Wis 4, 10. q Gn 6, 8–22; Sir 44, 17–18; Mt 24, 37–39; Lk 17, 26–27;1 Pt 3, 20; 2, Pt 2, 5. r Gn 12, 1–4; 15, 7–21; Sir 44, 19–22; Acts 7, 2–8; Rom 4, 16–22. s Gn 12, 8; 13, 12; 23, 4; 26, 3; 35, 27. t 12, 22; 13, 14; Rv 21, 10–22. u Gn 17, 19; 21, 2; Rom 4, 19–21 / 1 Cor 10, 13. v Gn 15, 5; 22, 17; 32, 13; Ex 32, 13; Dt 10, 22; Dn 3, 36 LXX. w Gn 23, 4; Ps 39, 13.

selves to be strangers and aliens on earth, [14]for those who speak thus show that they are seeking a homeland. [15]If they had been thinking of the land from which they had come, they would have had opportunity to return. [16][x]But now they desire a better homeland, a heavenly one. Therefore, God is not ashamed to be called their God, for he has prepared a city for them.

[17][y]By faith Abraham, when put to the test, offered up Isaac, and he who had received the promises was ready to offer his only son, [18][z]of whom it was said, "Through Isaac descendants shall bear your name." [19][a]*He reasoned that God was able to raise even from the dead, and he received Isaac back as a symbol. [20][b]*By faith regarding things still to come Isaac blessed Jacob and Esau. [21][c]By faith Jacob, when dying, blessed each of the sons of Joseph and "bowed in worship, leaning on the top of his staff." [22][d]By faith Joseph, near the end of his life, spoke of the Exodus of the Israelites and gave instructions about his bones.

[23][e]By faith Moses was hidden by his parents for three months after his birth, because they saw that he was a beautiful child, and they were not afraid of the king's edict. [24][f]*By faith Moses, when he had grown up, refused to be known as the son of Pharaoh's daughter; [25]he chose to be ill-treated along with the people of God rather than enjoy the fleeting pleasure of sin. [26]He considered the reproach of the Anointed greater wealth than the treasures of Egypt, for he was looking to the recompense. [27][g]By faith he left Egypt, not fearing the king's fury, for he persevered as if seeing the one who is invisible. [28][h]By faith he kept the Passover and sprinkled the blood, that the Destroyer of the firstborn might not touch them. [29][i]By faith they crossed the Red Sea as if it were dry land, but when the Egyptians attempted it they were drowned. [30][j]By faith the walls of Jericho fell after being encircled for seven days. [31][k]By faith Rahab the harlot did not perish with the disobedient, for she had received the spies in peace.

[32][l]What more shall I say? I have not time to tell of Gideon, Barak, Samson, Jephthah, of David and Samuel and the prophets, [33][m]who by faith conquered kingdoms, did what was righteous, obtained the promises; they closed the mouths of lions, [34][n]put out raging fires, escaped the devouring sword; out of weakness they were made powerful, became strong in battle, and turned back foreign invaders. [35][o]Women received back their dead through resurrection. Some were tortured and would not accept deliverance, in order to obtain a better resurrection. [36][p]Others endured mockery, scourging, even chains and imprisonment. [37][q]They were stoned, sawed in two, put to death at sword's point; they went about in skins of sheep or goats, needy, afflicted, tormented. [38][r]The world was not worthy of them. They wandered about in deserts and on mountains, in caves and in crevices in the earth.

[39]Yet all these, though approved because of their faith, did not receive what had been promised. [40]*God had foreseen something better for us, so that without us they should not be made perfect.

11, 19: As a symbol: Isaac's "return from death" is seen as a **symbol** of Christ's resurrection. Others understand the words **en parabolē** to mean "in figure," i.e., the word **dead** is used figuratively of Isaac, since he did not really die. But in the one other place that **parabolē** occurs in Heb, it means symbol (9, 9).

11, 20–22: Each of these three patriarchs, Isaac, Jacob, and Joseph, had faith in the future fulfillment of God's promise and renewed this faith when near death.

11, 24–27: The reason given for Moses' departure from Egypt differs from the account in Ex 2, 11–15. The author also gives a christological interpretation of his decision to share the trials of his people.

11, 40: So that without us they should not be made perfect: the heroes of the Old Testament obtained their recompense only after the saving work of Christ had been accomplished. Thus they already enjoy what Christians who are still struggling do not yet possess in its fullness.

x 13, 14; Ex 3, 6. y Gn 22, 1–10; Sir 44, 20; 1 Mc 2, 52; Jas 2, 21. z Gn 21, 12 LXX; Rom 9, 7. a Rom 4, 16–22. b Gn 27, 27–40. c Gn 27, 38–40; 47, 31 LXX; 48, 15–16. d Gn 50, 24–25. e Ex 2, 2; Acts 7, 20. f Ex 2, 10–15; Acts 7, 23–29. g Ex 2, 15; Acts 7, 29. h Ex 12, 21–23; Wis 18, 25; 1 Cor 10, 10. i Ex 14, 22–28. j Jos 6, 12–21. k Jos 2, 1–21; 6, 22–25; Jas 2, 25. l Jgs 4, 6—22; 6, 11—8, 32; 11, 1–12, 7. m Dn 6, 23. n Dn 3, 22–25.49–50. o 1 Kgs 17, 17–24; 2 Kgs 4, 18–37; 2 Mc 6, 18—7, 42. p 2 Chr 36, 16; Jer 20, 2; 37, 15. q 2 Chr 24, 21. r 1 Mc 2, 28–30.

CHAPTER 12

God our Father 1 *Therefore, since we are
surrounded by so great a cloud of witnesses, let
us rid ourselves of every burden and sin that
clings to us and persevere in running the race
that lies before us 2 [s]while keeping our eyes fixed
on Jesus, the leader and perfecter of faith. For
the sake of the joy that lay before him he
endured the cross, despising its shame, and has
taken his seat at the right of the throne of God.
3 Consider how he endured such opposition from
sinners, in order that you may not grow weary
and lose heart. 4 In your struggle against sin you
have not yet resisted to the point of shedding
blood. 5 [t]You have also forgotten the exhortation
addressed to you as sons:

"My son, do not disdain the discipline of the
Lord
or lose heart when reproved by him;
6 for whom the Lord loves, he disciplines;
he scourges every son he acknowledges."

7 [u]Endure your trials as "discipline"; God treats
you as sons. For what "son" is there whom his
father does not discipline? 8 If you are without
discipline, in which all have shared, you are not
sons but bastards. 9 [v]Besides this, we have had
our earthly fathers to discipline us, and we
respected them. Should we not [then] submit all
the more to the Father of spirits and live? 10 They
disciplined us for a short time as seemed right to
them, but he does so for our benefit, in order
that we may share his holiness. 11 [w]At the time,
all discipline seems a cause not for joy but for
pain, yet later it brings the peaceful fruit of
righteousness to those who are trained by it.

12 [x]So strengthen your drooping hands and
your weak knees. 13 [y]Make straight paths for
your feet, that what is lame may not be dislo-
cated but healed.

Penalties of Disobedience 14 [z]Strive for peace
with everyone, and for that holiness without
which no one will see the Lord. 15 [a]*See to it
that no one be deprived of the grace of God, that
no bitter root spring up and cause trouble,
through which many may become defiled,
16 [b]that no one be an immoral or profane person
like Esau, who sold his birthright for a single
meal. 17 [c]For you know that later, when he
wanted to inherit his father's blessing, he was
rejected because he found no opportunity to
change his mind, even though he sought the
blessing with tears.

18 [d]*You have not approached that which
could be touched and a blazing fire and gloomy
darkness and storm 19 [e]and a trumpet blast and a
voice speaking words such that those who heard
begged that no message be further addressed to
them, 20 [f]for they could not bear to hear the
command: "If even an animal touches the moun-
tain, it shall be stoned." 21 [g]Indeed, so fearful
was the spectacle that Moses said, "I am terrified
and trembling." 22 [h]No, you have approached
Mount Zion and the city of the living God, the

12, 1–13: Christian life is to be inspired not only by the Old Testament men and women of faith (1) but above all by Jesus. As the architect of Christian faith, he had himself to endure the cross before receiving the glory of his triumph (2). Reflection on his sufferings should give his followers courage to continue the struggle, if necessary even to the shedding of blood (3–4). Christians should regard their own sufferings as the affectionate correction of the Lord, who loves them as a father loves his children.

12, 1: That clings to us: the meaning is uncertain, since the Greek word **euperistatos,** translated **cling,** occurs only here. The papyrus P^{46} and one minuscule read **euperispastos,** "easily distracting," which also makes good sense.

12, 15–17: Esau serves as an example in two ways: his **profane** attitude illustrates the danger of apostasy, and his inability to secure a blessing afterward illustrates the impossibility of repenting after falling away (see 6, 4–6).

12, 18–29: As a final appeal for adherence to Christian teaching, the two covenants, of Moses and of Christ, are compared. The Mosaic covenant, the author argues, is shown to have originated in fear of God and threats of divine punishment (18–21). The covenant in Christ gives us direct access to God (22), makes us members of the Christian community, God's children, a sanctified people (23), who have Jesus as mediator to speak for us (24). Not to heed the voice of the risen Christ is a graver sin than the rejection of the word of Moses (25–26). Though Christians fall away, God's kingdom in Christ will remain and his justice will punish those guilty of deserting it (28–29).

12, 18–24: This remarkably beautiful passage contrasts two great assemblies of people: that of the Israelites gathered at Mount Sinai for the sealing of the old covenant and the promulgation of the Mosaic law, and that of the followers of Jesus gathered at **Mount Zion, the heavenly Jerusalem,** the assembly of the **new covenant.** This latter scene, marked by the presence of **countless angels** and of **Jesus** with his redeeming **blood,** is reminiscent of the celestial liturgies of the Book of Revelation.

s 2, 10; Ps 110, 1; Phil 2, 6–8. t Prv 3, 11–12 / Dt 8, 5; 1 Cor 11, 32. u Prv 13, 24; Sir 30, 1. v Nm 16, 22; 27, 16 LXX. w 2 Cor 4, 17; Phil 1, 11; Jas 3, 18. x Is 35, 3; Sir 25, 23; Jb 4, 3–4. y Prv 4, 26 LXX. z Rom 12, 18; 14, 19. a Dt 29, 18 (17 LXX). b Gn 25, 33. c Gn 27, 34–38. d Ex 19, 12–14; Dt 4, 11; 5, 22–23. e Ex 19, 16.19; 20, 18–19. f Ex 19, 12–13. g Dt 9, 19. h Gal 4, 26; Rv 21, 2.

heavenly Jerusalem, and countless angels in festal gathering, [23] [i]*and the assembly of the firstborn enrolled in heaven, and God the judge of all, and the spirits of the just made perfect, [24] [j]*and Jesus, the mediator of a new covenant, and the sprinkled blood that speaks more eloquently than that of Abel.

[25] [k]See that you do not reject the one who speaks. For if they did not escape when they refused the one who warned them on earth, how much more in our case if we turn away from the one who warns from heaven. [26] [l]His voice shook the earth at that time, but now he has promised, "I will once more shake not only earth but heaven." [27] [m]That phrase, "once more," points to [the] removal of shaken, created things, so that what is unshaken may remain. [28] [n]Therefore, we who are receiving the unshakable kingdom should have gratitude, with which we should offer worship pleasing to God in reverence and awe. [29] [o]For our God is a consuming fire.

VI: Final Exhortation, Blessing, Greetings

CHAPTER 13

[1] *Let mutual love continue. [2] [p]Do not neglect hospitality, for through it some have unknowingly entertained angels. [3] [q]Be mindful of prisoners as if sharing their imprisonment, and of the ill-treated as of yourselves, for you also are in the body. [4] [r]Let marriage be honored among all and the marriage bed be kept undefiled, for God will judge the immoral and adulterers. [5] [s]Let your life be free from love of money but be content with what you have, for he has said, "I will never forsake you or abandon you." [6] [t]Thus we may say with confidence:

"The Lord is my helper,
[and] I will not be afraid.
What can anyone do to me?"

[7] Remember your leaders who spoke the word of God to you. Consider the outcome of their way of life and imitate their faith. [8] [u]Jesus Christ is the same yesterday, today, and forever.

[9] [v]*Do not be carried away by all kinds of strange teaching. It is good to have our hearts strengthened by grace and not by foods, which do not benefit those who live by them. [10] *We have an altar from which those who serve the tabernacle have no right to eat. [11] [w]The bodies of the animals whose blood the high priest brings into the sanctuary as a sin offering are burned outside the camp. [12] [x]Therefore, Jesus also suffered outside the gate, to consecrate the people by his own blood. [13] Let us then go to him outside the camp, bearing the reproach that he bore. [14] [y]For here we have no lasting city, but we seek the one that is to come. [15] [z]Through him [then] let us continually offer God a sacrifice of praise, that is, the fruit of lips that confess his name. [16] [a]Do not neglect to do good and to share what you have; God is pleased by sacrifices of that kind.

12, 23: The assembly of the firstborn enrolled in heaven: this expression may refer to the angels of v 22, or to the heroes of the Old Testament (see ch 11), or to the entire assembly of the new covenant.

12, 24: Speaks more eloquently: the blood of Abel, the first human blood to be shed, is contrasted with that of Jesus. Abel's blood cried out from the earth for vengeance, but the blood of Jesus has opened the way for everyone, providing cleansing and access to God (10, 19).

13, 1–16: After recommendations on social and moral matters (1–6), the letter turns to doctrinal issues. The fact that the original leaders are dead should not cause the recipients of this letter to lose their faith (7), for Christ still lives and he remains always the same (8). They must not rely for their personal sanctification on regulations concerning foods (9), nor should they entertain the notion that Judaism and Christianity can be intermingled (10; cf the notes on Gal 2, 11–14 and 2, 15–21). As Jesus died separated from his own people, so must the Christian community remain apart from the religious doctrines of Judaism (11–14). Christ must be the heart and center of the community (15–16).

13, 9: Strange teaching: this doctrine about **foods** probably refers to the Jewish food laws; in view of v 10, however, the author may be thinking of the Mosaic sacrificial banquets.

13, 10: We have an altar: this does not refer to the Eucharist, which is never clearly mentioned in Heb, but to the sacrifice of Christ.

i Lk 10, 20; Rv 5, 11. j 7, 22; 8, 6; 9, 15 / 11, 4; Gn 4, 10. k Ex 20, 19. l Ex 19, 18; Jgs 5, 4–5; Ps 68, 9; Hg 2, 6. m Is 66, 22; Mt 24, 35; Mk 13, 31; Lk 21, 33. n Dn 7, 14.18 / Rom 1, 9. o Dt 4, 24; Is 33, 14. p Gn 18, 3; 19, 2–3; Jgs 6, 11–22; Tb 5, 4. q Mt 25, 36. r 1 Cor 5, 13; Eph 5, 5. s Dt 31, 6.8; Jos 1, 5. t Pss 27, 1–3; 118, 6. u 1, 12; 7, 24; Rv 1, 17. v Rom 14, 17; 1 Cor 8, 8; Eph 4, 14; Col 2, 16. w Ex 29, 14; Lv 16, 27. x Mt 21, 39; Mk 12, 8; Lk 20, 15; Jn 19, 17. y 11, 10.14. z Hos 14, 3. a Phil 4, 18.

17 *Obey your leaders and defer to them, for
they keep watch over you and will have to give
an account, that they may fulfill their task with
joy and not with sorrow, for that would be of no
advantage to you.
18 Pray for us, for we are confident that we
have a clear conscience, wishing to act rightly in
every respect. 19 I especially ask for your prayers
that I may be restored to you very soon.
20 [b] *May the God of peace, who brought up
from the dead the great shepherd of the sheep by
the blood of the eternal covenant, Jesus our
Lord, 21 furnish you with all that is good, that you
may do his will. May he carry out in you what is
pleasing to him through Jesus Christ, to whom
be glory forever [and ever]. Amen.
22 Brothers, I ask you to bear with this mes-
sage of encouragement, for I have written to you
rather briefly. 23 [c] I must let you know that our
brother Timothy has been set free. If he comes
soon, I shall see you together with him. 24 Greet-
ings to all your leaders and to all the holy ones.
Those from Italy send you greetings. 25 [d] Grace be
with all of you.

13, 17–25: Recommending obedience to the leaders of the community, the author asks for prayers (17–19). The letter concludes with a blessing (20–21), a final request for the acceptance of its message (22), information regarding Timothy (23), and general greetings (24–25).

13, 20–21: These verses constitute one of the most beautiful blessings in the New Testament. The resurrection of Jesus is presupposed throughout Heb, since it is included in the author's frequently expressed idea of his exaltation, but this is the only place where it is explicitly mentioned.

b Is 63, 11; Zec 9, 11; Jn 10, 11; Acts 2, 24; Rom 15, 33.
c Acts 16, 1. d Ti 3, 15.

THE CATHOLIC LETTERS

In addition to the thirteen letters attributed to Paul and the Letter to the Hebrews, the New Testament contains seven other letters. Three of these are attributed to John, two to Peter, and one each to James and Jude, all personages of the apostolic age. The term "catholic letter" first appears, with reference only to 1 John, in the writings of Apollonius of Ephesus, a second-century apologist, known only from a citation in Eusebius's *Ecclesiastical History.* Eusebius himself (A.D. 260–340) used the term to refer to all seven letters.

The reason for the term "catholic," which means "universal," was the perception that these letters, unlike those of Paul, which were directed to a particular local church, were apparently addressed more generally to the universal church. This designation is not entirely accurate, however. On the one hand, Hebrews has no specifically identified addressees, and originally this was probably true of Ephesians as well. On the other hand, 3 John is addressed to a named individual, 2 John to a specific, though unnamed, community, and 1 Peter to a number of churches that are specified as being located in Asia Minor.

While all seven of these writings begin with an epistolary formula, several of them do not appear to be real letters in the modern sense of the term. In the ancient world it was not unusual to cast an exhortation in the form of a letter for literary effect, a phenomenon comparable to the "open letter" that is sometimes used today.

With the exception of 1 Peter and 1 John, the ancient church showed reluctance to include the catholic letters in the New Testament canon. The reason for this was widespread doubt whether they had actually been written by the apostolic figures to whom they are attributed. The early Christians saw the New Testament as the depository of apostolic faith; therefore, they wished to include only the testimony of apostles. Today we distinguish more clearly between the authorship of a work and its canonicity: even though written by other, later witnesses than those whose names they bear, these writings nevertheless testify to the apostolic faith and constitute canonical scripture. By the late fourth or early fifth centuries, most objections had been overcome in both the Greek and Latin churches (though not in the Syriac), and all seven of the catholic letters have since been acknowledged as canonical.

THE LETTER OF JAMES

The person to whom this letter is ascribed can scarcely be one of the two members of the Twelve who bore the name James (see Mt 10, 2-3; Mk 3, 17-18; Lk 6, 14-15), for he is not identified as an apostle but only as "slave of God and of the Lord Jesus Christ" (1, 1). This designation most probably refers to the third New Testament personage named James, a relative of Jesus who is usually called "brother of the Lord" (see Mt 13, 55; Mk 6, 3). He was the leader of the Jewish Christian community in Jerusalem whom Paul acknowledged as one of the "pillars" (Gal 2, 9). In Acts he appears as the authorized spokesman for the Jewish Christian position in the early Church (Acts 12, 17; 15, 13-21). According to the Jewish historian Josephus (Antiquities 20, 9, 1 §§200–203), he was stoned to death by the Jews under the high priest Ananus II in A.D. 62.

The letter is addressed to "the twelve tribes in the dispersion." In Old Testament terminology the term "twelve tribes" designates the people of Israel; the "dispersion" or "diaspora" refers to the non-Palestinian Jews who had settled throughout the Greco-Roman world (see Jn 7, 35). Since in Christian thought the church is the new Israel, the address probably designates the Jewish Christian churches located in Palestine, Syria, and elsewhere. Or perhaps the letter is meant more generally for all Christian communities, and the "dispersion" has the symbolic meaning of exile from our true home, as it has in the address of 1 Peter (1, 1). The letter is so markedly Jewish in character that some scholars have regarded it as a Jewish document subsequently "baptized" by a few Christian insertions, but such an origin is scarcely tenable in view of the numerous contacts discernible between the Letter of James and other New Testament literature.

From the viewpoint of its literary form, James is a letter only in the most conventional sense; it has none of the characteristic features of a real letter except the address. It belongs rather to the genre of *parenesis* or exhortation and is concerned almost exclusively with ethical conduct. It therefore falls within the tradition of Jewish wisdom literature, such as can be found in the Old Testament (Proverbs, Sirach) and in the extracanonical Jewish literature (*Testaments of the Twelve Patriarchs,* the *Books of Enoch,* the *Manual of Discipline* found at Qumran). More specifically, it consists of sequences of didactic proverbs, comparable to Tob 4, 5-19, to many passages in Sirach, and to sequences of sayings in the synoptic gospels. Numerous passages in James treat of subjects that also appear in the synoptic sayings of Jesus, especially in Matthew's Sermon on the Mount, but the correspondences are too general to establish any literary dependence. James represents a type of early Christianity that emphasized sound teaching and responsible moral behavior. Ethical norms are derived not primarily from christology, as in Paul, but from a concept of salvation that involves conversion, baptism, forgiveness of sin, and expectation of judgment (1, 17; 4, 12).

Paradoxically, this very Jewish work is written in an excellent Greek style, which ranks among the best in the New Testament and appears to be the work of a trained Hellenistic writer. Those who continue to regard James of Jerusalem as its author are therefore obliged to suppose that a secretary must have put the letter into its present literary form. This assumption is not implausible in the light of ancient practice. Some regard the letter as one of the earliest writings in the New Testament and feel that its content accurately reflects what we would expect of the leader of Jewish Christianity. Moreover, they argue that the type of Jewish Christianity reflected in the letter cannot be situated historically after the fall of Jerusalem in A.D. 70.

Others, however, believe it more likely that James is a pseudonymous work of a later period. In addition to its Greek style, they observe further that (a) the prestige that the writer is assumed to enjoy points to the later legendary reputation of James; (b) the discussion of the importance of good works seems to presuppose a debate subsequent to that in Paul's own day; (c) the author does not rely upon prescriptions of the Mosaic law, as we would expect from the historical James; (d) the letter contains no allusions to James's own history and to his relationship with Jesus or to the early Christian community of Jerusalem. For these reasons, many recent interpreters assign James to the period A.D. 90–100.

The principal divisions of the Letter of James are the following:

I. Address (1, 1)
II. The Value of Trials and Temptation (1, 2-18)
III. Exhortations and Warnings (1, 19—5, 12)
IV. The Power of Prayer (5, 13-20)

I: Address

CHAPTER 1

[1][a]*James, a slave of God and of the Lord Jesus Christ, to the twelve tribes in the dispersion, greetings.

II: The Value of Trials and Temptation

Perseverance in Trial [2][b]*Consider it all joy, my brothers, when you encounter various trials, [3]*for you know that the testing of your faith produces perseverance. [4]And let perseverance be perfect, so that you may be perfect and complete, lacking in nothing. [5][c]*But if any of you lacks wisdom, he should ask God who gives to all generously and ungrudgingly, and he will be given it. [6][d]But he should ask in faith, not doubting, for the one who doubts is like a wave of the sea that is driven and tossed about by the wind. [7]For that person must not suppose that he will receive anything from the Lord, [8]since he is a man of two minds, unstable in all his ways.

[9][e]*The brother in lowly circumstances should take pride in his high standing, [10][f]and the rich one in his lowliness, for he will pass away "like the flower of the field." [11]For the sun comes up with its scorching heat and dries up the grass, its flower droops, and the beauty of its appearance vanishes. So will the rich person fade away in the midst of his pursuits.

Temptation [12][g]*Blessed is the man who perseveres in temptation, for when he has been proved he will receive the crown of life that he promised to those who love him. [13][h]*No one experiencing temptation should say, "I am being tempted by God"; for God is not subject to temptation to evil, and he himself tempts no one. [14]Rather, each person is tempted when he is lured and enticed by his own desire. [15]Then desire conceives and brings forth sin, and when sin reaches maturity it gives birth to death.

[16]*Do not be deceived, my beloved brothers: [17]*all good giving and every perfect gift is from above, coming down from the Father of lights, with whom there is no alteration or shadow caused by change. [18][i]*He willed to give us birth by the word of truth that we may be a kind of firstfruits of his creatures.

III: Exhortations and Warnings

Doers of the Word [19][j]*Know this, my dear brothers: everyone should be quick to hear, slow to speak, slow to wrath, [20][k]for the wrath of a

1, 1: **James, a slave of God and of the Lord Jesus Christ:** a declaration of the writer's authority for instructing the Christian communities; cf Rom 1, 1. Regarding the identity of the author, see Introduction. **Dispersion:** see Introduction.

1, 2: **Consider it all joy . . . various trials:** a frequent teaching of the New Testament derived from the words and sufferings of Jesus (Mt 5, 10–12; Jn 10, 11; Acts 5, 41).

1, 3–8: The sequence of testing, perseverance, and being perfect and complete indicates the manner of attaining spiritual maturity and full preparedness for the coming of Christ (5, 7–12; cf 1 Pt 1, 6–7; Rom 5, 3–5). These steps require wisdom (5).

1, 5: **Wisdom:** a gift that God readily grants to all who ask in faith and that sustains the Christian in times of trial. It is a kind of knowledge or understanding not accessible to the unbeliever or those who doubt, which gives the recipient an understanding of the real importance of events. In this way a Christian can deal with adversity with great calm and hope (cf 1 Cor 2, 6–12).

1, 9–11: Throughout his letter (see 2, 5; 4, 10.13–16; 5, 1–6), the author reaffirms the teaching of Jesus that worldly prosperity is not necessarily a sign of God's favor but can even be a hindrance to proper humility before God (cf Lk 6, 20–25; 12, 16–21; 16, 19–31).

1, 12: **Temptation:** the Greek word used here is the same one used for "trials" in v 2. **The crown of life:** in ancient Palestine, crowns or wreaths of flowers were worn at festive occasions as signs of joy and honor. In the Hellenistic world, wreaths were given as a reward to great statesmen, soldiers, athletes. **Life:** here means eternal life. **He promised:** some manuscripts read "God" or "the Lord," while the best witnesses do not specify the subject of "promised."

1, 13–15: It is contrary to what we know of God for God to be the author of human temptation (13). In the commission of a sinful act, one is first beguiled by passion (14), then consent is given, which in turn causes the sinful act. When sin permeates the entire person, it incurs the ultimate penalty of death (15).

1, 16–18: The author here stresses that God is the source of all good and of good alone, and the evil of temptation does not come from him.

1, 17: **All good giving and every perfect gift** may be a proverb written in hexameter. **Father of lights:** God is here called the Father of the heavenly luminaries, i.e., the stars, sun, and moon that he created (Gn 1, 14–18). Unlike orbs moving from nadir to zenith, he never changes or diminishes in brightness.

1, 18: Acceptance of the gospel message, **the word of truth,** constitutes new birth (Jn 3, 5–6) and makes the recipient the **firstfruits** (i.e., the cultic offering of the earliest grains, symbolizing the beginning of an abundant harvest) of a new creation; cf 1 Cor 15, 20; Rom 8, 23.

1, 19–25: **To be quick to hear** the gospel is to accept it readily and to act in conformity with it, removing from one's soul whatever is opposed to it, so that it may take root and effect salvation (19–21). To listen to the gospel message but not practice it is failure to improve oneself (22–24). Only conformity of life to the perfect law of true freedom brings happiness (25).

a Jn 7, 35; 1 Pt 1, 1. b Rom 5, 3–5; 1 Pt 1, 6; 4, 13–16. c Prv 2, 2–6; Wis 9, 4.9–12. d Mt 7, 7; Mk 11, 24. e 2, 5. f Is 40, 6–7. g 1 Cor 9, 25; 2 Tm 4, 8; 1 Pt 5, 4; Rv 2, 10. h Sir 15, 11–20; 1 Cor 10, 13. i Jn 1, 12–13; 1 Pt 1, 23. j Prv 14, 17; Sir 5, 11. k Eph 4, 26.

man does not accomplish the righteousness of God. [21] [l]Therefore, put away all filth and evil excess and humbly welcome the word that has been planted in you and is able to save your souls.

[22] [m]Be doers of the word and not hearers only, deluding yourselves. [23]For if anyone is a hearer of the word and not a doer, he is like a man who looks at his own face in a mirror. [24]He sees himself, then goes off and promptly forgets what he looked like. [25] [n]*But the one who peers into the perfect law of freedom and perseveres, and is not a hearer who forgets but a doer who acts, such a one shall be blessed in what he does.

[26] [o]*If anyone thinks he is religious and does not bridle his tongue but deceives his heart, his religion is vain. [27] [p]*Religion that is pure and undefiled before God and the Father is this: to care for orphans and widows in their affliction and to keep oneself unstained by the world.

CHAPTER 2

Sin of Partiality [1]*My brothers, show no partiality as you adhere to the faith in our glorious Lord Jesus Christ. [2]For if a man with gold rings on his fingers and in fine clothes comes into your assembly, and a poor person in shabby clothes also comes in, [3]and you pay attention to the one wearing the fine clothes and say, "Sit here, please," while you say to the poor one, "Stand there," or "Sit at my feet," [4]*have you not made distinctions among yourselves and become judges with evil designs?

[5] [q]*Listen, my beloved brothers. Did not God choose those who are poor in the world to be rich in faith and heirs of the kingdom that he promised to those who love him? [6]But you dishonored the poor person. Are not the rich oppressing you? And do they themselves not haul you off to court? [7] [r]Is it not they who blaspheme the noble name that was invoked over you? [8] [s]*However, if you fulfill the royal law according to the scripture, "You shall love your neighbor as yourself," you are doing well. [9] [t]But if you show partiality, you commit sin, and are convicted by the law as transgressors. [10] [u]For whoever keeps the whole law, but falls short in one particular, has become guilty in respect to all of it. [11] [v]For he who said, "You shall not commit adultery," also said, "You shall not kill." Even if you do not commit adultery but kill, you have become a transgressor of the law. [12] [w]*So speak and so act as people who will be judged by the law of freedom. [13] [x]For the judgment is merciless to one who has not shown mercy; mercy triumphs over judgment.

Faith and Works [14] [y]*What good is it, my brothers, if someone says he has faith but does not have works? Can that faith save him? [15]If a

1, 25: Peers into the perfect law: the image of a person doing this is paralleled to that of hearing God's word. The **perfect law** applies the Old Testament description of the Mosaic law to the gospel of Jesus Christ that brings freedom.

1, 26–27: A practical application of v 22 is now made.

1, 26: For control of the tongue, see the note on 3, 1–12.

1, 27: In the Old Testament, orphans and widows are classical examples of the defenseless and oppressed.

2, 1–13: In the Christian community there must be no discrimination or favoritism based on status or wealth (2–4; cf Mt 5, 3; 11, 5; 23, 6; 1 Cor 1, 27–29). Divine favor rather consists in God's election and promises (5). The rich who oppress the poor blaspheme the name of Christ (6–7). By violating one law of love of neighbor, they offend against the whole law (8–11). On the other hand, conscious awareness of the final judgment helps the faithful to fulfill the whole law (12).

2, 4: When Christians show favoritism to the rich they are guilty of the worst kind of prejudice and discrimination. The author says that such Christians set themselves up as judges who judge not by divine law but by the basest, self-serving motives.

2, 5: The poor, "God's poor" of the Old Testament, were seen by Jesus as particularly open to God for belief in and reliance on him alone (Lk 6, 20). God's law cannot tolerate their oppression in any way (9).

2, 8: Royal: literally, "kingly"; because the Mosaic law came from God, the universal king. There may be an allusion to Jesus' uses of this commandment in his preaching of the kingdom of God (Mt 22, 39; Mk 12, 31; Lk 10, 27).

2, 12–13: The law upon which the last judgment will be based is the law of freedom. As Jesus taught, mercy (which participates in God's own loving mercy) includes forgiveness of those who wrong us (see Mt 6, 12.14–15).

2, 14–26: The theme of these verses is the relationship of faith and works (deeds). It has been argued that the teaching here contradicts that of Paul (see especially Rom 4, 5–6). The problem can only be understood if the different viewpoints of the two authors are seen. Paul argues against those who claim to participate in God's salvation because of their good deeds as well as because they have committed themselves to trust in God through Jesus Christ (Paul's concept of faith). Paul certainly understands, however, the implications of true faith for a life of love and generosity (see Gal 5, 6.13–15). The author of James is well aware that proper conduct can only come about with an authentic commitment to God in faith (18.26). Many think he was seeking to correct a misunderstanding of Paul's view.

l Col 3, 8. m Mt 7, 26; Rom 2, 13. n 2, 12; Ps 19, 8; Rom 8, 2. o 3, 2; Ps 34, 14. p Ex 22, 21. q 1 Cor 1, 26–28; Rv 2, 9. r 1 Pt 4, 4. s Lv 19, 18; Mt 22, 39; Rom 13, 9. t Dt 1, 17. u Gal 3, 10. v Ex 20, 13–14; Dt 5, 17–18. w 1, 25; Rom 8, 2. x Mt 5, 7; 6, 14–15; 18, 32–33. y Mt 25, 31–46; Gal 5, 6.

brother or sister has nothing to wear and has no food for the day, [16] [z]and one of you says to them, "Go in peace, keep warm, and eat well," but you do not give them the necessities of the body, what good is it? [17]So also faith of itself, if it does not have works, is dead.

[18]Indeed someone might say, "You have faith and I have works." Demonstrate your faith to me without works, and I will demonstrate my faith to you from my works. [19]You believe that God is one. You do well. Even the demons believe that and tremble. [20]Do you want proof, you ignoramus, that faith without works is useless? [21] [a]Was not Abraham our father justified by works when he offered his son Isaac upon the altar? [22]You see that faith was active along with his works, and faith was completed by the works. [23] [b]Thus the scripture was fulfilled that says, "Abraham believed God, and it was credited to him as righteousness," and he was called "the friend of God." [24]See how a person is justified by works and not by faith alone. [25] [c]And in the same way, was not Rahab the harlot also justified by works when she welcomed the messengers and sent them out by a different route? [26]For just as a body without a spirit is dead, so also faith without works is dead.

CHAPTER 3

Power of the Tongue [1]*Not many of you should become teachers, my brothers, for you realize that we will be judged more strictly, [2] [d]for we all fall short in many respects. If anyone does not fall short in speech, he is a perfect man, able to bridle his whole body also. [3]If we put bits into the mouths of horses to make them obey us, we also guide their whole bodies. [4]It is the same with ships: even though they are so large and driven by fierce winds, they are steered by a very small rudder wherever the pilot's inclination wishes. [5]In the same way the tongue is a small member and yet has great pretensions.

Consider how small a fire can set a huge forest ablaze. [6]The tongue is also a fire. It exists among our members as a world of malice, defiling the whole body and setting the entire course of our lives on fire, itself set on fire by Gehenna. [7]For every kind of beast and bird, of reptile and sea creature, can be tamed and has been tamed by the human species, [8] [e]but no human being can tame the tongue. It is a restless evil, full of deadly poison. [9]With it we bless the Lord and Father, and with it we curse human beings who are made in the likeness of God. [10]From the same mouth come blessing and cursing. This need not be so, my brothers. [11]Does a spring gush forth from the same opening both pure and brackish water? [12] [f]Can a fig tree, my brothers, produce olives, or a grapevine figs? Neither can salt water yield fresh.

True Wisdom [13] [g]*Who among you is wise and understanding? Let him show his works by a good life in the humility that comes from wisdom. [14]But if you have bitter jealousy and selfish ambition in your hearts, do not boast and be false to the truth. [15]Wisdom of this kind does not come down from above but is earthly, unspiritual, demonic. [16]For where jealousy and selfish ambition exist, there is disorder and every foul practice. [17] [h]But the wisdom from above is first of all pure, then peaceable, gentle, compliant, full of mercy and good fruits, without inconstancy or insincerity. [18] [i]And the fruit of righteousness is sown in peace for those who cultivate peace.

CHAPTER 4

Causes of Division [1] [j]*Where do the wars and where do the conflicts among you come from? Is

3, 1–12: The use and abuse of the important role of teaching in the church (1) are here related to the good and bad use of the tongue (9–12), the instrument through which teaching was chiefly conveyed (see Sir 5, 11—6, 1; 28, 12–26).

3, 13–18: This discussion of true wisdom is related to the previous reflection on the role of the teacher as one who is in control of his speech. The qualities of the wise man endowed from above are detailed (17–18; cf Gal 5, 22–23), in contrast to the qualities of earthbound wisdom (14–16; cf 2 Cor 12, 20).

4, 1–12: The concern here is with the origin of conflicts in the Christian community. These are occasioned by love of the world, which means enmity with God (4). Further, the conflicts are bound up with failure to pray properly (cf Mt 7, 7–11; Jn 14, 13; 15, 7; 16, 23), that is, not asking God at all or using God's kindness only for one's pleasure (2–3). In contrast, the proper dispositions are submission to God, repentance, humility, and resistance to evil (7–10).

4, 1: Passions: the Greek word here (literally, "pleasures") does

z 1 Jn 3, 17. a Gn 22, 9–12; Heb 11, 17. b Gn 15, 6; Rom 4, 3; Gal 3, 6 / 2 Chr 20, 7; Is 41, 8. c Jos 2, 1–21. d 1, 26; Prv 13, 3; Sir 28, 12–26. e Ps 140, 4. f Mt 7, 16–17. g Eph 4, 1–2. h 1, 17; Wis 7, 22–23. i Mt 5, 9. j Rom 7, 23; 1 Pt 2, 11.

it not from your passions that make war within your members? 2 You covet but do not possess. You kill and envy but you cannot obtain; you fight and wage war. You do not possess because you do not ask. 3 You ask but do not receive, because you ask wrongly, to spend it on your passions. 4 [k]*Adulterers! Do you not know that to be a lover of the world means enmity with God? Therefore, whoever wants to be a lover of the world makes himself an enemy of God. 5 *Or do you suppose that the scripture speaks without meaning when it says, "The spirit that he has made to dwell in us tends toward jealousy"? 6 [l]*But he bestows a greater grace; therefore, it says:

"God resists the proud,
but gives grace to the humble."

7 [m]So submit yourselves to God. Resist the devil, and he will flee from you. 8 [n]Draw near to God, and he will draw near to you. Cleanse your hands, you sinners, and purify your hearts, you of two minds. 9 Begin to lament, to mourn, to weep. Let your laughter be turned into mourning and your joy into dejection. 10 [o]Humble yourselves before the Lord and he will exalt you.

11 *Do not speak evil of one another, brothers. Whoever speaks evil of a brother or judges his brother speaks evil of the law and judges the law. If you judge the law, you are not a doer of the law but a judge. 12 [p]There is one lawgiver and judge who is able to save or to destroy. Who then are you to judge your neighbor?

Warning against Presumption 13 *Come now, you who say, "Today or tomorrow we shall go into such and such a town, spend a year there doing business, and make a profit"— 14 [q]*you have no idea what your life will be like tomorrow. You are a puff of smoke that appears briefly and then disappears. 15 *Instead you should say, "If the Lord wills it, we shall live to do this or that." 16 But now you are boasting in your arrogance. All such boasting is evil. 17 [r]*So for one who knows the right thing to do and does not do it, it is a sin.

CHAPTER 5

Warning to the Rich 1 [s]*Come now, you rich, weep and wail over your impending miseries. 2 [t]Your wealth has rotted away, your clothes have become moth-eaten, 3 [u]your gold and silver have corroded, and that corrosion will be a testimony against you; it will devour your flesh like a fire. You have stored up treasure for the last days. 4 [v]Behold, the wages you withheld from the workers who harvested your fields are crying aloud, and the cries of the harvesters have

not indicate that pleasure is evil. Rather, as the text points out (2–3), it is the manner in which one deals with needs and desires that determines good or bad. The motivation for any action can be wrong, especially if one does not pray properly but seeks only selfish enjoyment (3).

4, 4: Adulterers: a common biblical image for the covenant between God and his people is the marriage bond. In this image, breaking the covenant with God is likened to the unfaithfulness of adultery.

4, 5: The meaning of this saying is difficult because the author of Jas cites, probably from memory, a passage that is not in any extant manuscript of the Bible. Other translations of the text with a completely different meaning are possible: "The Spirit that he (God) made to dwell in us yearns (for us) jealously," or, "He (God) yearns jealously for the spirit that he has made to dwell in us." If this last translation is correct, the author perhaps had in mind an apocryphal religious text that echoes the idea that God is zealous for his creatures; cf Ex 20, 5; Dt 4, 24; Zec 8, 2.

4, 6: The point of this whole argument is that God wants the happiness of all, but that selfishness and pride can make that impossible. We must work with him in humility (10).

4, 11: Slander of a fellow Christian does not break just one commandment but makes mockery of the authority of law in general and therefore of God.

4, 13–17: The uncertainty of life (14), its complete dependence on God, and the necessity of submitting to God's will (15) all help one know and do what is right (17). To disregard this is to live in pride and arrogance (16); failure to do what is right is a sin (17).

4, 14: Some important Greek manuscripts here have, "You who have no idea what tomorrow will bring. Why, what is your life?"

4, 15: If the Lord wills it: often in piety referred to as the **"conditio Jacobaea,"** the condition James says we should employ to qualify all our plans.

4, 17: It is a sin: those who live arrogantly, forgetting the contingency of life and our dependence on God (13–16), are guilty of sin.

5, 1–6: Continuing with the theme of the transitory character of life on earth, the author points out the impending ruin of the godless. He denounces the unjust rich, whose victims cry to heaven for judgment on their exploiters (4–6). The decay and corrosion of the costly garments and metals, which symbolize wealth, prove them worthless and portend the destruction of their possessors (2–3).

k Mt 6, 24; Lk 16, 13; Rom 8, 7; 1 Jn 2, 15–16. l Jb 22, 29; Prv 3, 34; Mt 23, 12; 1 Pt 5, 5. m 1 Pt 5, 8–9. n Zec 1, 3; Mal 3, 7. o Jb 5, 11; Mt 23, 12; Lk 14, 11; 18, 14; 1 Pt 5, 6. p Mt 7, 1; Rom 2, 1; 14, 4. q Prv 27, 1 / Ps 39, 6–7. r Lk 12, 47. s Lk 6, 24. t Mt 6, 19. u Ps 21, 10; Prv 11, 4; Jdt 16, 17. v Lv 19, 13; Dt 24, 14–15; Mal 3, 5.

reached the ears of the Lord of hosts. [5] [w]You have lived on earth in luxury and pleasure; you have fattened your hearts for the day of slaughter. [6] [x]*You have condemned; you have murdered the righteous one; he offers you no resistance.

Patience and Oaths [7] *Be patient, therefore, brothers, until the coming of the Lord. See how the farmer waits for the precious fruit of the earth, being patient with it until it receives the early and the late rains. [8] [y]You too must be patient. Make your hearts firm, because the coming of the Lord is at hand. [9] Do not complain, brothers, about one another, that you may not be judged. Behold, the Judge is standing before the gates. [10] Take as an example of hardship and patience, brothers, the prophets who spoke in the name of the Lord. [11] [z]Indeed we call blessed those who have persevered. You have heard of the perseverance of Job, and you have seen the purpose of the Lord, because "the Lord is compassionate and merciful."

[12] [a]*But above all, my brothers, do not swear, either by heaven or by earth or with any other oath, but let your "Yes" mean "Yes" and your "No" mean "No," that you may not incur condemnation.

IV: The Power of Prayer

Anointing of the Sick [13] Is anyone among you suffering? He should pray. Is anyone in good spirits? He should sing praise. [14] [b]*Is anyone among you sick? He should summon the presbyters of the church, and they should pray over him and anoint [him] with oil in the name of the Lord, [15] *and the prayer of faith will save the sick person, and the Lord will raise him up. If he has committed any sins, he will be forgiven.

Confession and Intercession [16] Therefore, confess your sins to one another and pray for one another, that you may be healed. The fervent prayer of a righteous person is very powerful. [17] [c]Elijah was a human being like us; yet he prayed earnestly that it might not rain, and for three years and six months it did not rain upon the land. [18] [d]Then he prayed again, and the sky gave rain and the earth produced its fruit.

Conversion of Sinners [19] [e]My brothers, if anyone among you should stray from the truth and someone bring him back, [20] [f]*he should know that whoever brings back a sinner from the error of his way will save his soul from death and will cover a multitude of sins.

5, 6: The author does not have in mind any specific crime in his readers' communities but rather echoes the Old Testament theme of the harsh oppression of the righteous poor (see Prv 1, 11; Wis 2, 10.12.20).

5, 7–11: Those oppressed by the unjust rich are reminded of the need for patience, both in bearing the sufferings of human life (9) and in their expectation of the coming of the Lord. It is then that they will receive their reward (7–8.10–11; cf Heb 10, 25; 1 Jn 2, 18).

5, 7: The early and the late rains: an expression related to the agricultural season in ancient Palestine (see Dt 11, 14; Jer 5, 24; Jl 2, 23).

5, 12: This is the threat of condemnation for the abuse of swearing oaths (cf Mt 5, 33–37). **By heaven or by earth:** these words were substitutes for the original form of an oath, to circumvent its binding force and to avoid pronouncing the holy name of God (see Ex 22, 10).

5, 14: In case of sickness a Christian should ask for the presbyters of the church, i.e., those who have authority in the church (cf Acts 15, 2.22–23; 1 Tm 5, 17; Ti 1, 5). They are to pray over the person and anoint with oil; oil was used for medicinal purposes in the ancient world (see Is 1, 6; Lk 10, 34). In Mk 6, 13, the Twelve anoint the sick with oil on their missionary journey. **In the name of the Lord:** by the power of Jesus Christ.

5, 15: The results of the prayer and anointing are physical health and forgiveness of sins. The Roman Catholic Church (Council of Trent, Session 14) declared that this anointing of the sick is a sacrament "instituted by Christ and promulgated by blessed James the apostle."

5, 20: When a Christian is instrumental in the conversion of a sinner, the result is forgiveness of sins and a reinstatement of the sinner to the life of grace.

w Jer 12, 3; Lk 16, 19–25. x Wis 2, 10–20. y Lk 21, 19; Heb 10, 36 / Heb 10, 25; 1 Pt 4, 7. z Ex 34, 6; Ps 103, 8. a Mt 5, 34–37. b Mk 6, 13. c 1 Kgs 17, 1; Lk 4, 25. d 1 Kgs 18, 45. e Mt 18, 15; Gal 6, 1. f Prv 10, 12; 1 Pt 4, 8.

THE FIRST LETTER OF PETER

This letter begins with an address by Peter to Christian communities located in five provinces of Asia Minor (1, 1), including areas evangelized by Paul (Acts 16, 6-7; 18, 23). Christians there are encouraged to remain faithful to their standards of belief and conduct in spite of threats of persecution. Numerous allusions in the letter suggest that the churches addressed were largely of Gentile composition (1, 14.18; 2, 9-10; 4, 3-4), though considerable use is made of the Old Testament (1, 24; 2, 6-7.9-10.22; 3, 10-12).

The contents following the address both inspire and admonish these "chosen sojourners" (1, 1) who, in seeking to live as God's people, feel an alienation from their previous religious roots and the society around them. Appeal is made to Christ's resurrection and the future hope it provides (1, 3-5) and to the experience of baptism as new birth (1, 3.23-25; 3, 21). The suffering and death of Christ serve as both source of salvation and example (1, 19; 2, 21-25; 3, 18). What Christians are in Christ, as a people who have received mercy and are to proclaim and live according to God's call (2, 9-10), is repeatedly spelled out for all sorts of situations in society (2, 11-17), work (even as slaves, 2, 18-20), the home (3, 1-7), and general conduct (3, 8-12; 4, 1-11). But over all hangs the possibility of suffering as a Christian (3, 13-17). In 4, 12-19 persecution is described as already occurring, so that some have supposed the letter was addressed both to places where such a "trial by fire" was already present and to places where it might break out.

The letter constantly mingles moral exhortation (*paraklēsis*) with its catechetical summaries of mercies in Christ. Encouragement to fidelity in spite of suffering is based upon a vision of the meaning of Christian existence. The emphasis on baptism and allusions to various features of the baptismal liturgy suggest that the author has incorporated into his exposition numerous homiletic, credal, hymnic, and sacramental elements of the baptismal rite that had become traditional at an early date.

From Irenaeus in the late second century until modern times, Christian tradition regarded Peter the apostle as author of this document. Since he was martyred at Rome during the persecution of Nero between A.D. 64 and 67, it was supposed that the letter was written from Rome shortly before his death. This is supported by its reference to "Babylon" (5, 13), a code name for Rome in the early church.

Some modern scholars, however, on the basis of a number of features that they consider incompatible with Petrine authenticity, regard the letter as the work of a later Christian writer. Such features include the cultivated Greek in which it is written, difficult to attribute to a Galilean fisherman, together with its use of the Greek Septuagint translation when citing the Old Testament; the similarity in both thought and expression to the Pauline literature; and the allusions to widespread persecution of Christians, which did not occur until at least the reign of Domitian (A.D. 81–96). In this view the letter would date from the end of the first century or even the beginning of the second, when there is evidence for persecution of Christians in Asia Minor (the letter of Pliny the Younger to Trajan, A.D. 111–12).

Other scholars believe, however, that these objections can be met by appeal to use of a secretary, Silvanus, mentioned in 5, 12. Such secretaries often gave literary expression to the author's thoughts in their own style and language. The persecutions may refer to local harassment rather than to systematic repression by the state. Hence there is nothing in the document incompatible with Petrine authorship in the 60s.

Still other scholars take a middle position. The many literary contacts with the Pauline literature, James, and 1 John suggest a common fund of traditional formulations rather than direct dependence upon Paul. Such liturgical and catechetical traditions must have been very ancient and in some cases of Palestinian origin.

Yet it is unlikely that Peter addressed a letter to the Gentile churches of Asia Minor while Paul was still alive. This suggests a period after the death of the two apostles, perhaps A.D. 70–90. The author would be a disciple of Peter in Rome, representing a Petrine group that served as a bridge between the Palestinian origins of Christianity and its flowering in the Gentile world. The problem addressed would not be official persecution but the difficulty of living the Christian life in a hostile, secular environment that espoused different values and subjected the Christian minority to ridicule and oppression.

The principal divisions of the First Letter of Peter are the following:

I. Address (1, 1-2)
II. The Gift and Call of God in Baptism (1, 3—2, 10)
III. The Christian in a Hostile World (2, 11—4, 11)
IV. Advice to the Persecuted (4, 12—5, 11)
V. Conclusion (5, 12-14)

I: Address

CHAPTER 1

Greeting 1 [a]*Peter, an apostle of Jesus Christ,
to the chosen sojourners of the dispersion in
Pontus, Galatia, Cappadocia, Asia, and Bithynia,
2 [b]in the foreknowledge of God the Father,
through sanctification by the Spirit, for obedi-
ence and sprinkling with the blood of Jesus
Christ: may grace and peace be yours in abun-
dance.

II: The Gift and Call of God in Baptism

Blessing 3 [c]*Blessed be the God and Father of
our Lord Jesus Christ, who in his great mercy
gave us a new birth to a living hope through the
resurrection of Jesus Christ from the dead, 4 [d]to
an inheritance that is imperishable, undefiled,
and unfading, kept in heaven for you 5who by
the power of God are safeguarded through faith,
to a salvation that is ready to be revealed in the
final time. 6 [e]*In this you rejoice, although now
for a little while you may have to suffer through
various trials, 7 [f]so that the genuineness of your
faith, more precious than gold that is perishable
even though tested by fire, may prove to be for
praise, glory, and honor at the revelation of Jesus
Christ. 8 [g]Although you have not seen him you
love him; even though you do not see him now
yet believe in him, you rejoice with an indescrib-
able and glorious joy, 9as you attain the goal of
[your] faith, the salvation of your souls.
10*Concerning this salvation, prophets who
prophesied about the grace that was to be yours

1, 1–2: The introductory formula names **Peter** as the writer (but see Introduction). In his comments to the presbyters (5, 1), the author calls himself a "fellow presbyter." He addresses himself to the Gentile converts of Asia Minor. Their privileged status as a **chosen** and sanctified people makes them worthy of God's **grace** and **peace.** In contrast is their actual existence as aliens and **sojourners,** scattered among pagans, far from their true country.

1, 1: **Dispersion:** literally, diaspora; see Jas 1, 1 and Introduction to that letter. **Pontus . . . Bithynia:** five provinces in Asia Minor, listed in clockwise order from the north, perhaps in the sequence in which a messenger might deliver the letter.

1, 3–5: A prayer of praise and thanksgiving to God who bestows the gift of new life and hope in baptism (**new birth,** 3) **through the resurrection of Jesus Christ from the dead.** The new birth is a sign of an **imperishable inheritance** (4), of **salvation** that is still in the future (**to be revealed in the final time,** 5).

1, 6–9: As the glory of Christ's resurrection was preceded by his sufferings and death, the new life of faith that it bestows is to be subjected to many **trials** (6) while achieving its goal: the glory of the fullness of **salvation** (9) at the coming of Christ (7).

1, 10–12: The **Spirit of Christ** (11) is here shown to have been present in the prophets, moving them to search, investigate, and prophesy about the **grace of salvation** that was to come (10), and in the apostles impelling them to preach the fulfillment of salvation in the message of Christ's sufferings and glory (12).

a Jas 1, 1. b Rom 8, 29. c Ti 3, 5. d Mt 6, 19–20. e Jas 1, 2–3. f 1 Cor 3, 13. g 2 Cor 5, 6–7.

searched and investigated it, [11] [h]investigating the
time and circumstances that the Spirit of Christ
within them indicated when it testified in ad-
vance to the sufferings destined for Christ and
the glories to follow them. [12]It was revealed to
them that they were serving not themselves but
you with regard to the things that have now
been announced to you by those who preached
the good news to you [through] the holy Spirit
sent from heaven, things into which angels
longed to look.

Obedience [13]*Therefore, gird up the loins of
your mind, live soberly, and set your hopes
completely on the grace to be brought to you at
the revelation of Jesus Christ. [14]*Like obedient
children, do not act in compliance with the
desires of your former ignorance [15] [i]but, as he
who called you is holy, be holy yourselves in
every aspect of your conduct, [16] [j]for it is written,
"Be holy because I [am] holy."

Reverence [17] [k]Now if you invoke as Father him
who judges impartially according to each one's
works, conduct yourselves with reverence dur-
ing the time of your sojourning, [18] [l]realizing that
you were ransomed from your futile conduct,
handed on by your ancestors, not with perish-
able things like silver or gold [19] [m]*but with the
precious blood of Christ as of a spotless unblem-
ished lamb. [20]He was known before the founda-
tion of the world but revealed in the final time
for you, [21]who through him believe in God who
raised him from the dead and gave him glory, so
that your faith and hope are in God.

Mutual Love [22] [n]*Since you have purified your-
selves by obedience to the truth for sincere
mutual love, love one another intensely from a
[pure] heart. [23] [o]*You have been born anew, not
from perishable but from imperishable seed,
through the living and abiding word of God,
[24] [p]for:

"All flesh is like grass,
and all its glory like the flower of the field;
the grass withers,
and the flower wilts;
[25]but the word of the Lord remains forever."

This is the word that has been proclaimed to
you.

CHAPTER 2

God's House and People [1] [q]*Rid yourselves
of all malice and all deceit, insincerity, envy, and
all slander; [2]like newborn infants, long for pure
spiritual milk so that through it you may grow
into salvation, [3] [r]*for you have tasted that the
Lord is good. [4] [s]*Come to him, a living stone,
rejected by human beings but chosen and pre-
cious in the sight of God, [5] [t]*and, like living
stones, let yourselves be built into a spiritual
house to be a holy priesthood to offer spiritual
sacrifices acceptable to God through Jesus
Christ. [6] [u]For it says in scripture:

"Behold, I am laying a stone in Zion,
a cornerstone, chosen and precious,
and whoever believes in it shall not be put to
shame."

1, 13–25: These verses are concerned with the call of God's people to holiness and to mutual love by reason of their redemption through the blood of Christ (18–21).

1, 13: Gird up the loins of your mind: a figure reminiscent of the rite of Passover when the Israelites were in flight from their oppressors (Ex 12, 11), and also suggesting the vigilance of the Christian people in expectation of the parousia of Christ (Lk 12, 35).

1, 14–16: The **ignorance** here referred to (14) was their former lack of knowledge of God, leading inevitably to godless conduct. Holiness (15–16), on the contrary, is the result of their call to the knowledge and love of God.

1, 19: Christians have received the redemption prophesied by Isaiah (52, 3), through the blood (Jewish symbol of life) of the spotless lamb (Is 53, 7.10; Jn 1, 29; Rom 3, 24–25; cf 1 Cor 6, 20).

1, 22–25: The new birth of Christians (23) derives from Christ, the **imperishable seed** or sowing that produces a new and lasting existence in those who accept the gospel (24–25), with the consequent duty of loving **one another** (22).

1, 23: The living and abiding word of God: or, "the word of the living and abiding God."

2, 1–3: Growth toward salvation is seen here as two steps: first, stripping away all that is contrary to the new life in Christ; second, the nourishment **(pure spiritual milk)** that the newly baptized have received.

2, 3: Tasted that the Lord is good: cf Ps 34, 9.

2, 4–8: Christ is the cornerstone (cf Is 28, 16) that is the foundation of the spiritual edifice of the Christian community (5). To unbelievers, Christ is an obstacle and a stumbling block on which they are destined to fall (8); cf Rom 11, 11.

2, 5: Let yourselves be built: the form of the Greek word could also be indicative passive, "you are being built" (cf 9).

h Is 52, 13—53, 12; Dn 9, 24. i Mt 5, 48; 1 Jn 3, 3. j Lv 11, 44; 19, 2. k 2, 11. l Is 52, 3; 1 Cor 6, 20. m Ex 12, 5; Jn 1, 29; Heb 9, 14. n Rom 12, 10. o 1 Jn 3, 9. p Is 40, 6–8. q Jas 1, 21. r Ps 34, 9. s Ps 118, 22; Mt 21, 42; Acts 4, 11. t Eph 2, 21–22. u Is 28, 16.

7 [v]Therefore, its value is for you who have faith,
but for those without faith:

"The stone which the builders rejected
has become the cornerstone,"

8 [w]and

"A stone that will make people stumble,
and a rock that will make them fall."

They stumble by disobeying the word, as is their
destiny.
9 [x]*But you are "a chosen race, a royal priest-
hood, a holy nation, a people of his own, so that
you may announce the praises" of him who
called you out of darkness into his wonderful
light.

10 [y]Once you were "no people"
but now you are God's people;
you "had not received mercy"
but now you have received mercy.

III: The Christian in a Hostile World

Christian Examples 11 [z]*Beloved, I urge you
as aliens and sojourners to keep away from
worldly desires that wage war against the soul.
12 Maintain good conduct among the Gentiles, so
that if they speak of you as evildoers, they may
observe your good works and glorify God on the
day of visitation.
Christian Citizens 13 [a]*Be subject to every
human institution for the Lord's sake, whether it
be to the king as supreme 14 or to governors as
sent by him for the punishment of evildoers and
the approval of those who do good. 15 For it is the
will of God that by doing good you may silence
the ignorance of foolish people. 16 [b]Be free, yet
without using freedom as a pretext for evil, but
as slaves of God. 17 [c]Give honor to all, love the
community, fear God, honor the king.
Christian Slaves 18 [d]*Slaves, be subject to your
masters with all reverence, not only to those
who are good and equitable but also to those
who are perverse. 19 For whenever anyone bears
the pain of unjust suffering because of conscious-
ness of God, that is a grace. 20 But what credit is
there if you are patient when beaten for doing
wrong? But if you are patient when you suffer
for doing what is good, this is a grace before
God. 21 [e]*For to this you have been called,
because Christ also suffered for you, leaving you
an example that you should follow in his foot-
steps.

22 [f]*"He committed no sin,
and no deceit was found in his mouth."

2, 9–10: The prerogatives of ancient Israel mentioned here are now more fully and fittingly applied to the Christian people: "a chosen race" (cf Is 43, 20–21) indicates their divine election (Eph 1, 4–6); "a royal priesthood" (cf Ex 19, 6) to serve and worship God in Christ, thus continuing the priestly functions of his life, passion, and resurrection; "a holy nation" (Ex 19, 6) reserved for God, a people he claims for his own (cf Mal 3, 17) in virtue of their baptism into his death and resurrection. This transcends all natural and national divisions and unites the people into one community to glorify the one who led them from the darkness of paganism to the light of faith in Christ. From being "no people" deprived of all mercy, they have become the very people of God, the chosen recipients of his mercy (cf Hos 1, 9; 2, 25).

2, 11—3, 12: After explaining the doctrinal basis for the Christian community, the author makes practical applications in terms of the virtues that should prevail in all the social relationships of the members of the community: good example to Gentile neighbors (2, 11–12); respect for human authority (2, 13–17); obedience, patience, and endurance of hardship in domestic relations (2, 18–25); Christian behavior of husbands and wives (3, 1–7); mutual charity (3, 8–12).

2, 11: Aliens and sojourners: no longer signifying absence from one's native land (Gn 23, 4), this image denotes rather their estrangement from the world during their earthly pilgrimage (see also 1, 1.17).

2, 13–17: True Christian freedom is the result of being servants of God (16; see the note on 2, 18–23). It includes reverence for God, esteem for every individual, and committed love for fellow Christians (17). Although persecution may threaten, subjection to human government is urged (13.17) and concern for the impact of Christians' conduct on those who are not Christians (12.15).

2, 18–21: Most of the labor in the commercial cities of first-century Asia Minor was performed by a working class of slaves. The sense of freedom contained in the gospel undoubtedly caused great tension among Christian slaves: witness the special advice given concerning them here and in 1 Cor 7, 21–24; Eph 6, 5–8; Col 3, 22–25; Phlm. The point made here does not have so much to do with the institution of slavery, which the author does not challenge, but with the nonviolent reaction (20) of slaves to unjust treatment. Their patient suffering is compared to that of Jesus (21), which won righteousness for all humanity.

2, 21: Suffered: some ancient manuscripts and versions read "died" (cf 3, 18).

2, 22–25: After the quotation of Is 53, 9b, the passage describes Jesus' passion with phrases concerning the Suffering Servant from Is 53, 4–12, perhaps as employed in an early Christian confession of faith; cf 1, 18–21 and 3, 18–22.

v Ps 118, 22; Mt 21, 42; Lk 20, 17; Acts 4, 11. w Is 8, 14; Rom 9, 33. x Ex 19, 6; Is 61, 6; Rv 1, 6; 20, 6. y Hos 1, 9; 2, 25 / Hos 1, 6. z Gal 5, 24. a Rom 13, 1–7. b Gal 5, 13. c Prv 24, 21; Mt 22, 21. d Eph 6, 5. e Mt 16, 24. f Is 53, 9.

[23] [g]When he was insulted, he returned no insult;
when he suffered, he did not threaten; instead,
he handed himself over to the one who judges
justly. [24] [h]He himself bore our sins in his body
upon the cross, so that, free from sin, we might
live for righteousness. By his wounds you have
been healed. [25] [i]*For you had gone astray like
sheep, but you have now returned to the shep-
herd and guardian of your souls.

CHAPTER 3

Christian Spouses [1]*Likewise, you wives
should be subordinate to your husbands so that,
even if some disobey the word, they may be won
over without a word by their wives' conduct
[2] [j]when they observe your reverent and chaste
behavior. [3] [k]Your adornment should not be an
external one: braiding the hair, wearing gold
jewelry, or dressing in fine clothes, [4]but rather
the hidden character of the heart, expressed in
the imperishable beauty of a gentle and calm
disposition, which is precious in the sight of
God. [5]For this is also how the holy women who
hoped in God once used to adorn themselves
and were subordinate to their husbands; [6]thus
Sarah obeyed Abraham, calling him "lord." You
are her children when you do what is good and
fear no intimidation.
[7] [l]*Likewise, you husbands should live with
your wives in understanding, showing honor to
the weaker female sex, since we are joint heirs
of the gift of life, so that your prayers may not be
hindered.

Christian Conduct [8]*Finally, all of you, be of
one mind, sympathetic, loving toward one an-
other, compassionate, humble. [9] [m]Do not return
evil for evil, or insult for insult; but, on the
contrary, a blessing, because to this you were
called, that you might inherit a blessing. [10] [n]For:

"Whoever would love life
and see good days
must keep the tongue from evil
and the lips from speaking deceit,
[11] must turn from evil and do good,
seek peace and follow after it.
[12] For the eyes of the Lord are on the righteous
and his ears turned to their prayer,
but the face of the Lord is against evildoers."

Christian Suffering [13]*Now who is going to
harm you if you are enthusiastic for what is
good? [14]But even if you should suffer because of
righteousness, blessed are you. Do not be afraid
or terrified with fear of them, [15] [o]but sanctify
Christ as Lord in your hearts. Always be ready to
give an explanation to anyone who asks you for
a reason for your hope, [16]but do it with gentle-
ness and reverence, keeping your conscience
clear, so that, when you are maligned, those
who defame your good conduct in Christ may
themselves be put to shame. [17]For it is better to
suffer for doing good, if that be the will of God,
than for doing evil.

2, 25: The shepherd and guardian of your souls: the familiar shepherd and flock figures express the care, vigilance, and love of God for his people in the Old Testament (Ps 23; Is 40, 11; Jer 23, 4–5; Ez 34, 11–16) and of Jesus for all humanity in the New Testament (Mt 18, 10–14; Lk 15, 4–7; Jn 10, 1–16; Heb 13, 20).

3, 1–6: The typical marital virtues of women of the ancient world, obedience, reverence, and chastity (1–2), are outlined here by the author, who gives them an entirely new motivation: Christian wives are to be virtuous so that they may be instrumental in the conversion of their husbands. In imitation of **holy women** in the past (5) they are to cultivate the interior life (4) instead of excessive concern with their appearance (3).

3, 7: Husbands who do not respect their wives will have as little success in prayer as those who, according to Paul, have no love: their prayers will be "a resounding gong or a clashing cymbal" (1 Cor 13, 1). Consideration for others is shown as a prerequisite for effective prayer also in Mt 5, 23–24; 1 Cor 11, 20–22; Jas 4, 3. After all, whatever the social position of women in the world and in the family, they are equal recipients of the gift of God's salvation. Paul is very clear on this point, too (see 1 Cor 11, 11–12; Gal 3, 28).

3, 8–12: For the proper ordering of Christian life in its various aspects as described in 2, 11—3, 9, there is promised the blessing expressed in Ps 34, 13–17. In the Old Testament this refers to longevity and prosperity; here, it also refers to eternal life.

3, 13–22: This exposition, centering on v 17, runs as follows: by his suffering and death Christ the righteous one saved the unrighteous (18); by his resurrection he received new life in the spirit, which he communicates to believers through the baptismal bath that cleanses their consciences from sin. As Noah's family was saved **through water,** so Christians are saved through the waters of baptism (19–22). Hence they need not share the fear of sinners; they should rather rejoice in suffering because of their hope in Christ. Thus their innocence disappoints their accusers (13–16; cf Mt 10, 28; Rom 8, 35–39).

g Mt 5, 39. h Is 53, 4.12 / Is 53, 5. i Is 53, 6. j 1 Cor 7, 12–16; Eph 5, 22–24; Col 3, 18; 1 Tm 2, 9–15. k 1 Tm 2, 9–10. l Eph 5, 25–33; Col 3, 19. m Mt 5, 44; Lk 6, 28; Rom 12, 14. n Ps 34, 13–17. o Is 8, 12.

[18][p]*For Christ also suffered for sins once, the righteous for the sake of the unrighteous, that he might lead you to God. Put to death in the flesh, he was brought to life in the spirit. [19]*In it he also went to preach to the spirits in prison, [20][q]who had once been disobedient while God patiently waited in the days of Noah during the building of the ark, in which a few persons, eight in all, were saved through water. [21][r]*This prefigured baptism, which saves you now. It is not a removal of dirt from the body but an appeal to God for a clear conscience, through the resurrection of Jesus Christ, [22][s]who has gone into heaven and is at the right hand of God, with angels, authorities, and powers subject to him.

CHAPTER 4

Christian Restraint [1]*Therefore, since Christ suffered in the flesh, arm yourselves also with the same attitude (for whoever suffers in the flesh has broken with sin), [2]so as not to spend what remains of one's life in the flesh on human desires, but on the will of God. [3][t]For the time that has passed is sufficient for doing what the Gentiles like to do: living in debauchery, evil desires, drunkenness, orgies, carousing, and wanton idolatry. [4]They are surprised that you do not plunge into the same swamp of profligacy, and they vilify you; [5][u]but they will give an account to him who stands ready to judge the living and the dead. [6]*For this is why the gospel was preached even to the dead that, though condemned in the flesh in human estimation, they might live in the spirit in the estimation of God.

Christian Charity [7]*The end of all things is at hand. Therefore, be serious and sober for prayers. [8][v]*Above all, let your love for one another be intense, because love covers a multitude of sins. [9][w]Be hospitable to one another without complaining. [10][x]As each one has received a gift, use it to serve one another as good stewards of God's varied grace. [11][y]*Whoever preaches, let it be with the words of God; whoever serves, let it be with the strength that God supplies, so that in all things God may be glorified through Jesus Christ, to whom belong glory and dominion forever and ever. Amen.

IV: Advice to the Persecuted

Trial of Persecution [12][z]*Beloved, do not be surprised that a trial by fire is occurring among you, as if something strange were happening to you. [13][a]But rejoice to the extent that you share in the sufferings of Christ, so that when his glory is revealed you may also rejoice exultantly. [14][b]If you are insulted for the name of Christ, blessed are you, for the Spirit of glory and of God rests upon you. [15]But let no one among you be made to suffer as a murderer, a thief, an evildoer, or as

3, 18: Suffered: very many ancient manuscripts and versions read "died." **Put to death in the flesh:** affirms that Jesus truly died as a human being. **Brought to life in the spirit:** that is, in the new and transformed existence freed from the limitations and weaknesses of natural human life (cf 1 Cor 15, 45).

3, 19: The spirits in prison: it is not clear just who these spirits are. They may be the spirits of the sinners who died in the flood, or angelic powers, hostile to God, who have been overcome by Christ (cf 22; Gn 6, 4; Enoch 6–36, especially 21, 6; 2 Enoch 7, 1–5).

3, 21: Appeal to God: this could also be translated "pledge," that is, a promise on the part of Christians to live with a good conscience before God, or a pledge from God of forgiveness and therefore a good conscience for us.

4, 1–6: Willingness to suffer with Christ equips the Christian with the power to conquer sin (1). Christ is here portrayed as the judge to whom those guilty of pagan vices must render an account (5; cf Jn 5, 22–27; Acts 10, 42; 2 Tm 4, 1).

4, 6: The dead: these may be the sinners of the flood generation who are possibly referred to in 3, 19. But many scholars think that there is no connection between these two verses, and that **the dead** here are Christians who have died since hearing the preaching of the gospel.

4, 7–11: The inner life of the eschatological community is outlined as **the end** (the parousia of Christ) and the judgment draws near in terms of seriousness, sobriety, prayer, and love expressed through hospitality and the use of one's gifts for the glory of God and of Christ.

4, 8: Love covers a multitude of sins: a maxim based on Prv 10, 12; see also Ps 32, 1; Jas 5, 20.

4, 11: Some scholars feel that this doxology concludes the part of the homily addressed specifically to the newly baptized, begun in 1, 3; others that it concludes a baptismal liturgy. Such doxologies do occur within a New Testament letter, e.g., Rom 9, 5. Some propose that v 11 was an alternate ending, with 4, 12—5, 14 being read in places where persecution was more pressing. But such doxologies usually do not occur at the end of letters (the only examples are 2 Pt 3, 18, Jude 25, and Rom 16, 27, the last probably a liturgical insertion).

4, 12–19: The suffering to which the author has already frequently referred is presented in more severe terms. This has led some scholars to see these verses as referring to an actual persecution. Others see the heightening of the language as only a rhetorical device used at the end of the letter to emphasize the suffering motif.

p 1 Cor 15, 45. q Gn 7, 7.17; 2 Pt 2, 5. r Eph 5, 26; Heb 10, 22. s Eph 1, 20–21. t Eph 2, 2–3; 4, 17–19; Col 3, 7; Ti 3, 3. u Acts 10, 42; 2 Tm 4, 1. v Prv 10, 12; Jas 5, 20. w Heb 13, 2. x Rom 12, 6–8; 1 Cor 12, 4–11. y 1 Cor 10, 31. z 1, 6–7; 3, 14.17. a Rom 5, 3–5; 8, 17; 2 Tm 2, 12. b Acts 5, 41 / Is 11, 2.

an intriguer. 16But whoever is made to suffer as a
Christian should not be ashamed but glorify God
because of the name. 17[c]For it is time for the
judgment to begin with the household of God; if
it begins with us, how will it end for those who
fail to obey the gospel of God?

18[d]"And if the righteous one is barely saved,
where will the godless and the sinner
appear?"

19As a result, those who suffer in accord with
God's will hand their souls over to a faithful
creator as they do good.

CHAPTER 5

Advice to Presbyters 1*So I exhort the pres-
byters among you, as a fellow presbyter and
witness to the sufferings of Christ and one who
has a share in the glory to be revealed. 2[e]Tend
the flock of God in your midst, [overseeing] not
by constraint but willingly, as God would have
it, not for shameful profit but eagerly. 3Do not
lord it over those assigned to you, but be
examples to the flock. 4[f]*And when the chief
Shepherd is revealed, you will receive the unfad-
ing crown of glory.
Advice to the Community 5[g]*Likewise, you
younger members, be subject to the presbyters.
And all of you, clothe yourselves with humility
in your dealings with one another, for:

"God opposes the proud
but bestows favor on the humble."

6[h]So humble yourselves under the mighty hand
of God, that he may exalt you in due time.
7[i]Cast all your worries upon him because he
cares for you.
8[j]Be sober and vigilant. Your opponent the
devil is prowling around like a roaring lion
looking for [someone] to devour. 9Resist him,
steadfast in faith, knowing that your fellow
believers throughout the world undergo the
same sufferings. 10[k]The God of all grace who
called you to his eternal glory through Christ
[Jesus] will himself restore, confirm, strengthen,
and establish you after you have suffered a little.
11To him be dominion forever. Amen.

V: Conclusion

12*I write you this briefly through Silvanus,
whom I consider a faithful brother, exhorting
you and testifying that this is the true grace of
God. Remain firm in it. 13*The chosen one at
Babylon sends you greeting, as does Mark, my
son. 14[l]Greet one another with a loving kiss.
Peace to all of you who are in Christ.

5, 1–4: In imitation of Christ, the chief shepherd, those entrusted with a pastoral office are to tend the flock by their care and example.

5, 1: Presbyters: the officially appointed leaders and teachers of the Christian community (cf 1 Tm 5, 17–18; Ti 1, 5–8; Jas 5, 14).

5, 4: See the note on 2, 25.

5, 5–11: The community is to be subject to the presbyters and to show humility toward one another and trust in God's love and care (5–7). With sobriety, alertness, and steadfast faith they must resist the evil one; their sufferings are shared with Christians everywhere (8–9). They will be strengthened and called to eternal glory (10–11).

5, 5: Younger members: this may be a designation for office-holders of lesser rank.

5, 12: Silvanus: the companion of Paul (see 2 Cor 1, 19; 1 Thes 1, 1; 2 Thes 1, 1). Jews and Jewish Christians, like Paul, often had a Hebrew name (Saoul, Silas) and a Greek or Latin name (Paul, Silvanus). On Silvanus's possible role as amanuensis, see Introduction.

5, 13: The chosen one: feminine, referring to the Christian community **(ekklēsia)** at **Babylon,** the code name for Rome in Rv 14, 8; 17, 5; 18, 2. **Mark, my son:** traditionally a prominent disciple of Peter and co-worker at the church in Rome, perhaps the John Mark referred to in Acts 12, 12.25; 13, 5.13; and in 15, 37–39, a companion of Barnabas. Perhaps this is the same Mark mentioned as Barnabas's cousin in Col 4, 10, a co-worker with Paul in Phlm 24 (see also 2 Tm 4, 11).

c Lk 23, 31; 2 Thes 1, 8. d Prv 11, 31 LXX. e Acts 20, 28; Ti 1, 7. f Wis 5, 15–16; 1 Cor 9, 25; 2 Tm 4, 8; Jas 1, 12. g Prv 3, 34. h Jb 22, 29; Jas 4, 10. i Ps 55, 23; Mt 6, 25–33; Lk 12, 22–31; Phil 4, 6. j 1 Thes 5, 6. k Rom 8, 18; 2 Cor 4, 17. l Rom 16, 16; 1 Cor 16, 20; 2 Cor 13, 12.

THE SECOND LETTER OF PETER

This letter can be appreciated both for its positive teachings and for its earnest warnings. It seeks to strengthen readers in faith (1, 1), hope for the future (3, 1-10), knowledge (1, 2.6.8), love (1, 7), and other virtues (1, 5-6). This aim is carried out especially by warning against false teachers, the condemnation of whom occupies the long central section of the letter (2, 1-22). A particular crisis is the claim by "scoffers" that there will be no second coming of Jesus, a doctrine that the author vigorously affirms (3, 1-10). The concept of God's "promises" is particularly precious in the theology of 2 Peter (1, 4; 3, 4.9.13). Closing comments at 3, 17-18 well sum up the twin concerns: that you not "be led into" error and "fall" but instead "grow in grace" and "knowledge" of Jesus Christ.

Second Peter is clearly structured in its presentation of these points. It reminds its readers of the divine authenticity of Christ's teaching (1, 3-4), continues with reflections on Christian conduct (1, 5-15), then returns to the exalted dignity of Jesus by incorporating into the text the apostolic witness to his transfiguration (1, 16-18). It takes up the question of the interpretation of scripture by pointing out that it is possible to misunderstand the sacred writings (1, 19-21) and that divine punishment will overtake false teachers (2, 1-22). It proclaims that the parousia is the teaching of the Lord and of the apostles and is therefore an eventual certainty (3, 1-13). At the same time, it warns that the meaning of Paul's writings on this question should not be distorted (3, 14-18).

In both content and style this letter is very different from 1 Peter, which immediately precedes it in the canon. The opening verse attributes it to "Symeon Peter, a slave and apostle of Jesus Christ." Moreover, the author in 3, 1 calls his work a "second letter," referring probably to 1 Peter as his first, and in 1, 18 counts himself among those present at the transfiguration of Jesus.

Nevertheless, acceptance of 2 Peter into the New Testament canon met with great resistance in the early church. The oldest certain reference to it comes from Origen in the early third century. While he himself accepted both Petrine letters as canonical, he testifies that others rejected 2 Peter. As late as the fifth century some local churches still excluded it from the canon, but eventually it was universally adopted. The principal reason for the long delay was the persistent doubt that the letter stemmed from the apostle Peter.

Among modern scholars there is wide agreement that 2 Peter is a pseudonymous work, i.e., one written by a later author who attributed it to Peter according to a literary convention popular at the time. It gives the impression of being more remote in time from the apostolic period than 1 Peter; indeed, many think it is the latest work in the New Testament and assign it to the first or even the second quarter of the second century.

The principal reasons for this view are the following. The author refers to the apostles and "our ancestors" as belonging to a previous generation, now dead (3, 2-4). A collection of Paul's letters exists and appears to be well known, but disputes have arisen about the interpretation of them (3, 14-16). The passage about false teachers (2, 1-18) contains a number of literary contacts with Jude 4-16, and it is generally agreed that 2 Peter depends upon Jude, not vice versa. Finally, the principal problem exercising the author is the false teaching of "scoffers" who have concluded from the delay of the parousia that the Lord is not going to return. This could scarcely have been an issue during the lifetime of Simon Peter.

The Christians to whom the letter is addressed are not identified, though it may be the intent of 3, 1 to identify them with the churches of Asia Minor to which 1 Peter was sent. Except for the epistolary greeting in 1, 1-2, 2 Peter does not have the features of a genuine letter at all, but is rather a general exhortation cast in the form of a letter. The author must have been a Jewish Christian of the dispersion for, while his Jewish heritage is evident in various features of his thought and style, he writes in the rather stilted literary Greek of the Hellenistic period. He appeals to tradition against the twin threat of doctrinal error and moral laxity, which appear to reflect an early stage of what later developed into full-blown gnosticism. Thus he forms a link between the apostolic period and the church of subsequent ages.

The principal divisions of the Second Letter of Peter are the following:

I. Address (1, 1-2)
II. Exhortation to Christian Virtue (1, 3-21)
III. Condemnation of the False Teachers (2, 1-22)
IV. The Delay of the Second Coming (3, 1-16)
V. Final Exhortation and Doxology (3, 17-18)

I: Address

CHAPTER 1

Greeting [1] *Symeon Peter, a slave and apostle of Jesus Christ, to those who have received a faith of equal value to ours through the righteousness of our God and savior Jesus Christ: [2] *may grace and peace be yours in abundance through knowledge of God and of Jesus our Lord.

II: Exhortation to Christian Virtue

The Power of God's Promise [3] [a] *His divine power has bestowed on us everything that makes for life and devotion, through the knowledge of him who called us by his own glory and power. [4] [b] Through these, he has bestowed on us the precious and very great promises, so that through them you may come to share in the divine nature, after escaping from the corruption that is in the world because of evil desire. [5] [c] *For this very reason, make every effort to supplement your faith with virtue, virtue with knowledge, [6] knowledge with self-control, self-control with endurance, endurance with devotion, [7] devotion with mutual affection, mutual affection with love. [8] If these are yours and increase in abundance, they will keep you from being idle or unfruitful in the knowledge of our Lord Jesus Christ. [9] [d] Anyone who lacks them is blind and shortsighted, forgetful of the cleansing of his past sins. [10] *Therefore, brothers, be all the more eager to make your call and election firm, for, in doing so, you will never stumble. [11] For, in this way, entry into the eternal kingdom of our Lord and savior Jesus Christ will be richly provided for you.

Apostolic Witness [12] *Therefore, I will always remind you of these things, even though you

1, 1: Symeon Peter: on the authorship of 2 Peter, see Introduction; on the spelling here of the Hebrew name **Šimʿôn,** cf Acts 15, 14. The greeting is especially similar to those in 1 Peter and Jude. The words translated **our God and savior Jesus Christ** could also be rendered "our God and the savior Jesus Christ"; cf 11; 2, 20; 3, 2.18.

1, 2: Knowledge: a key term in the letter (3.8; 2, 20; 3, 18), perhaps used as a Christian emphasis against gnostic claims.

1, 3–4: Christian life in its fullness is a gift of divine power effecting a knowledge of Christ and the bestowal of divine promises (3, 4.9). **To share in the divine nature,** escaping from a corrupt world, is a thought found elsewhere in the Bible but expressed only here in such Hellenistic terms, since it is said to be accomplished through **knowledge** (3); cf 2; 2, 20; but see also Jn 15, 4; 17, 22–23; Rom 8, 14–17; Heb 3, 14; 1 Jn 1, 3; 3, 2.

1, 3: By his own glory and power: the most ancient papyrus and the best codex read "through glory and power."

1, 5–9: Note the climactic gradation of qualities (5–7), beginning with faith and leading to the fullness of Christian life, which is love; cf Rom 5, 3–4; Gal 5, 6.22 for a similar series of "virtues," though the program and sense here are different than in Paul. The fruit of these is knowledge of Christ (8) referred to in v 3; their absence is spiritual blindness (9).

1, 10–11: Perseverance in the Christian vocation is the best preventative against losing it and the safest provision for attaining its goal, the kingdom. **Kingdom of . . . Christ,** instead of "God," is unusual; cf Col 1, 13 and Mt 13, 41, as well as the **righteousness of . . . Christ** (1).

1, 12–19: The purpose in writing is to call to mind the apostle's witness to the truth, even as he faces the end of his life (12–15), his eyewitness testimony to Christ (16–18), and the true pro-

a 2 Cor 4, 6; 1 Pt 2, 9. b 2 Cor 7, 1; 1 Jn 2, 15. c Gal 5, 22–23. d 1 Jn 2, 9.11.

already know them and are established in the
truth you have. [13]*I think it right, as long as I
am in this "tent," to stir you up by a reminder,
[14][e]since I know that I will soon have to put it
aside, as indeed our Lord Jesus Christ has
shown me. [15]I shall also make every effort to
enable you always to remember these things
after my departure.

[16][f]*We did not follow cleverly devised myths
when we made known to you the power and
coming of our Lord Jesus Christ, but we had
been eyewitnesses of his majesty. [17][g]*For he
received honor and glory from God the Father
when that unique declaration came to him from
the majestic glory, "This is my Son, my beloved,
with whom I am well pleased." [18]*We ourselves
heard this voice come from heaven while we
were with him on the holy mountain.
[19][h]Moreover, we possess the prophetic message
that is altogether reliable. You will do well to be
attentive to it, as to a lamp shining in a dark
place, until day dawns and the morning star rises
in your hearts. [20]*Know this first of all, that
there is no prophecy of scripture that is a matter
of personal interpretation, [21]for no prophecy
ever came through human will; but rather
human beings moved by the holy Spirit spoke
under the influence of God.

III: Condemnation of the False Teachers

CHAPTER 2

False Teachers [1][i]*There were also false proph-
ets among the people, just as there will be false
teachers among you, who will introduce destruc-
tive heresies and even deny the Master who
ransomed them, bringing swift destruction on
themselves. [2][j]Many will follow their licentious
ways, and because of them the way of truth will
be reviled. [3][k]In their greed they will exploit you
with fabrications, but from of old their condem-
nation has not been idle and their destruction
does not sleep.

Lessons from the Past [4][l]*For if God did not
spare the angels when they sinned, but con-
demned them to the chains of Tartarus and
handed them over to be kept for judgment;
[5][m]*and if he did not spare the ancient world,
even though he preserved Noah, a herald of
righteousness, together with seven others, when

---

phetic message (19) through the Spirit in scripture (20–21), in contrast to what false teachers are setting forth (ch 2).

1, 13: Tent: a biblical image for transitory human life (Is 38, 12), here combined with a verb that suggests not folding or packing up a tent but its being discarded in death (cf 2 Cor 5, 1–4).

1, 16: Coming: in Greek **parousia,** used at 3, 4.12 of the second coming of Christ. The word was used in the extrabiblical writings for the visitation of someone in authority; in Greek cult and Hellenistic Judaism it was used for the manifestation of the divine presence. What the apostles **made known** has been interpreted to refer to Jesus' transfiguration (17) or to his entire first coming or to his future coming in power (ch 3).

1, 17: The author assures the readers of the reliability of the apostolic message (including Jesus' power, glory, and coming; cf the note on 1, 16) by appeal to the transfiguration of Jesus in glory (cf Mt 17, 1–8 and parallels) and by appeal to the prophetic message (19; perhaps Nm 24, 17). Here, as elsewhere, the New Testament insists on continued reminders as necessary to preserve the historical facts about Jesus and the truths of the faith; cf 3, 1–2; 1 Cor 11, 2; 15, 1–3. **My Son, my beloved:** or, "my beloved Son."

1, 18: We: at Jesus' transfiguration, referring to Peter, James, and John (Mt 17, 1).

1, 20–21: Often cited, along with 2 Tm 3, 16, on the "inspiration" of scripture or against private interpretation, these verses in context are directed against the false teachers of ch 2 and clever tales (16). The prophetic word in scripture comes admittedly through **human beings** (21), but **moved by the holy Spirit,** not from their own interpretation, and is a matter of what the author and Spirit intended, not the **personal interpretation** of false teachers. Instead of **under the influence of God,** some manuscripts read "holy ones of God."

2, 1–3: The pattern of **false prophets** among the Old Testament people of God will recur through **false teachers** in the church. Such destructive opinions of heretical sects bring loss of faith in Christ, contempt for the way of salvation (cf 21), and immorality.

2, 4–6: The false teachers will be punished just as surely and as severely as were the fallen **angels** (4; cf Jude 6; Gn 6, 1–4), the sinners of Noah's day (5; Gn 7, 21–23), and the inhabitants of the cities of the Plain (6; Jude 7; Gn 19, 25). Whereas there are three examples in Jude 5–7 (Exodus and wilderness; rebellious angels; Sodom and Gomorrah), 2 Peter omitted the first of these, has inserted a new illustration about Noah (5) between Jude's second and third examples, and listed the resulting three examples in their Old Testament order (Gn 6; 7; 19).

2, 4: Chains of Tartarus: cf Jude 6; other manuscripts in 2 Peter read "pits of Tartarus." **Tartarus:** a term borrowed from Greek mythology to indicate the infernal regions.

2, 5–10a: Although God did not spare the sinful, he kept and saved the righteous, such as **Noah** (5) and **Lot** (7), and he **knows how to rescue the devout** (9), who are contrasted with the false teachers of the author's day. On Noah, cf Gn 5, 32—9, 29, especially 7, 1. On Lot, cf Gn 13 and 19.

e Is 38, 12; Jn 21, 18–19. f Lk 9, 28–36; Jn 1, 14. g Ps 2, 7; Mt 17, 4–6. h Lk 1, 78–79; Rv 2, 28. i Mt 24, 11.24; 1 Tm 4, 1; Jude 4. j Is 52, 5. k Rom 16, 18. l Jude 6. m Gn 8, 15–19; Heb 11, 7.

he brought a flood upon the godless world;
6 [n]and if he condemned the cities of Sodom and Gommorah [to destruction], reducing them to ashes, making them an example for the godless [people] of what is coming;
7 and if he rescued Lot, a righteous man oppressed by the licentious conduct of unprincipled people
8 (for day after day that righteous man living among them was tormented in his righteous soul at the lawless deeds that he saw and heard),
9 [o]then the Lord knows how to rescue the devout from trial and to keep the unrighteous under punishment for the day of judgment,
10 [p]*and especially those who follow the flesh with its depraved desire and show contempt for lordship.

False Teachers Denounced Bold and arrogant, they are not afraid to revile glorious beings,
11 [q]*whereas angels, despite their superior strength and power, do not bring a reviling judgment against them from the Lord.
12 [r]But these people, like irrational animals born by nature for capture and destruction, revile things that they do not understand, and in their destruction they will also be destroyed,
13 [s]*suffering wrong as payment for wrongdoing. Thinking daytime revelry a delight, they are stains and defilements as they revel in their deceits while carousing with you.
14 Their eyes are full of adultery and insatiable for sin. They seduce unstable people, and their hearts are trained in greed. Accursed children!
15 [t]*Abandoning the straight road, they have gone astray, following the road of Balaam, the son of Bosor, who loved payment for wrongdoing,
16 [u]but he received a rebuke for his own crime: a mute beast spoke with a human voice and restrained the prophet's madness.
17 [v]These people are waterless springs and mists driven by a gale; for them the gloom of darkness has been reserved.
18 [w]*For, talking empty bombast, they seduce with licentious desires of the flesh those who have barely escaped from people who live in error.
19 [x]They promise them freedom, though they themselves are slaves of corruption, for a person is a slave of whatever overcomes him.
20 [y]For if they, having escaped the defilements of the world through the knowledge of [our] Lord and savior Jesus Christ, again become entangled and overcome by them, their last condition is worse than their first.
21 [z]*For it would have been better for them not to have known the way of righteousness than after knowing it to turn back from the holy commandment handed down to them.
22 [a]*What is expressed in the true proverb has happened to them, "The dog returns to its own vomit," and "A bathed sow returns to wallowing in the mire."

IV: The Delay of the Second Coming

CHAPTER 3

Denial of the Parousia
1 *This is now, beloved, the second letter I am writing to you;

2, 10b-22: Some take 10b and 11 with the preceding paragraph. Others begin the new paragraph with 10a, supplying from v 9 **The Lord knows how . . . to keep . . . under punishment,** with reference to God and probably specifically Christ (1). The conduct of the false teachers is described and condemned in language similar to that of Jude 8–16. This arrogance knows no bounds; animal-like, they are due to be caught and destroyed. They seduce even those who have knowledge of Christ (20).

2, 10b: Glorious beings: literally, "glories"; cf Jude 8. While some think that illustrious personages are meant or even political officials behind whom (fallen) angels stand, it is more likely that the reference is to glorious angelic beings (cf Jude 9).

2, 11: From the Lord: some manuscripts read "before the Lord"; cf Jude 9.

2, 13: Suffering wrong: some manuscripts read "receiving a reward." **In their deceits:** some manuscripts read "in their love feasts" (Jude 12).

2, 15: Balaam, the son of Bosor: in Nm 22, 5, Balaam is said to be the son of Beor, and it is this name that turns up in a few ancient Greek manuscripts by way of "correction" of the text. Balaam is not portrayed in such a bad light in Nm 22. His evil reputation and his **madness** (16), and possibly his surname Bosor, may have come from a Jewish tradition about him in the first/second century, of which we no longer have any knowledge.

2, 18: Barely escaped: some manuscripts read "really escaped."

2, 21: Commandment handed down: cf 3, 2 and Jude 3.

2, 22: The second proverb is of unknown origin, while the first appears in Prv 26, 11.

3, 1–4: The false teachers not only flout Christian morality (cf Jude 8–19); they also deny the second coming of Christ and the judgment (4; cf 7). They seek to justify their licentiousness by arguing that the promised return of Christ has not been realized and the world is the same, no better than it was before (3–4). The author wishes to strengthen the faithful against such errors by reminding them in this **second letter** of the instruction in 1 Pt and of the teaching of the **prophets** and of Christ, conveyed through the **apostles** (1–2; cf Jude 17); cf 1 Pt 1, 10–12.16–21, especially 16–21; Eph 2, 20.

n Gn 19, 24–25; Jude 7. o 1 Cor 10, 13; Rv 3, 10. p Jude 8. q Jude 9. r Ps 49, 13–15; Jude 10. s Jude 12. t Nm 31, 16; Jude 11. u Nm 22, 28–33. v Jude 12–13. w Jude 16. x Jn 8, 34; Rom 6, 16–17. y Mt 12, 45. z Ez 3, 20. a Prv 26, 11.

through them by way of reminder I am trying to
stir up your sincere disposition, [2][b]to recall the
words previously spoken by the holy prophets
and the commandment of the Lord and savior
through your apostles. [3][c]*Know this first of all,
that in the last days scoffers will come [to] scoff,
living according to their own desires [4][d]*and
saying, "Where is the promise of his coming?
From the time when our ancestors fell asleep,
everything has remained as it was from the
beginning of creation." [5][e]*They deliberately
ignore the fact that the heavens existed of old
and earth was formed out of water and through
water by the word of God; [6][f]*through these the
world that then existed was destroyed, deluged
with water. [7][g]The present heavens and earth
have been reserved by the same word for fire,
kept for the day of judgment and of destruction
of the godless.

[8][h]*But do not ignore this one fact, beloved,
that with the Lord one day is like a thousand
years and a thousand years like one day. [9][i]The
Lord does not delay his promise, as some regard
"delay," but he is patient with you, not wishing
that any should perish but that all should come
to repentance. [10][j]*But the day of the Lord will
come like a thief, and then the heavens will pass
away with a mighty roar and the elements will
be dissolved by fire, and the earth and every-
thing done on it will be found out.

Exhortation to Preparedness [11][k]*Since
everything is to be dissolved in this way, what
sort of persons ought [you] to be, conducting
yourselves in holiness and devotion, [12][l]*waiting
for and hastening the coming of the day of God,
because of which the heavens will be dissolved
in flames and the elements melted by fire.
[13][m]*But according to his promise we await new
heavens and a new earth in which righteousness
dwells.

[14]Therefore, beloved, since you await these
things, be eager to be found without spot or
blemish before him, at peace. [15][n]And consider
the patience of our Lord as salvation, as our
beloved brother Paul, according to the wisdom
given to him, also wrote to you, [16]*speaking of
these things as he does in all his letters. In them
there are some things hard to understand that
the ignorant and unstable distort to their own
destruction, just as they do the other scriptures.

3, 3: **Scoffers:** cf Jude 18, where, however, only the passions of the scoffers are mentioned, not a denial on their part of Jesus' parousia.

3, 4–7: The false teachers tried to justify their immorality by pointing out that the promised **coming (parousia)** of the Lord has not yet occurred, even though early Christians expected it in their day. They thus insinuate that God is not guiding the world's history anymore, since nothing has changed and the first generation of Christians, **our ancestors** (4), has all died by this time. The author replies that, just as God destroyed the earth by water in the flood (5–6, cf 2, 5), so he will destroy it along with the false teachers on judgment day (7). **The word of God,** which called the world into being (Gn 1; Ps 33, 6) and **destroyed** it by the waters of a flood, will destroy it again by fire on **the day of judgment** (5–7).

3, 5: **Formed out of water and through water:** Gn 1, 2.6–8 is reflected as well as Greek views that water was the basic element from which all is derived.

3, 6: **Destroyed, deluged with water:** cf 2, 5; Gn 7, 11—8, 2.

3, 8–10: The scoffers' objection (4) is refuted also by showing that **delay** of the Lord's second coming is not a failure to fulfill his word but rather a sign of his patience: God is giving time for repentance before the final judgment (cf Wis 11, 23–26; Ez 18, 23; 33, 11).

3, 8: Cf Ps 90, 4.

3, 10: **Like a thief:** Mt 24, 43; 1 Thes 5, 2; Rv 3, 3. **Will be found out:** cf 1 Cor 3, 13–15. Some few versions read, as the sense may demand, "will not be found out"; many manuscripts read "will be burned up"; there are further variants in other manuscripts, versions, and Fathers. Total destruction is assumed (11).

3, 11–16: The second coming of Christ and the judgment of the world are the doctrinal bases for the moral exhortation to readiness through vigilance and a virtuous life; cf Mt 24, 42.50–51; Lk 12, 40; 1 Thes 5, 1–11; Jude 20–21.

3, 12: **Flames . . . fire:** although this is the only New Testament passage about a final conflagration, the idea was common in apocalyptic and Greco-Roman thought. **Hastening:** eschatology is here used to motivate ethics (11), as elsewhere in the New Testament. Jewish sources and Acts 3, 19–20 assume that proper ethical conduct can help bring the promised day of the Lord; cf 9. Some render the phrase, however, "desiring it earnestly."

3, 13: **New heavens and a new earth:** cf Is 65, 17; 66, 22. The divine promises will be fulfilled after the day of judgment will have passed. The universe will be transformed by the reign of God's **righteousness** or justice; cf Is 65, 17–18; Acts 3, 21; Rom 8, 18–25; Rv 21, 1.

3, 16: **These things:** the teachings of this letter find parallels in Paul, e.g., God's will to save (Rom 2, 4; 9, 22–23; 1 Cor 1, 7–8), the coming of Christ (1 Thes 4, 16–17; 1 Cor 15, 23–52), and preparedness for the judgment (Col 1, 22–23; Eph 1, 4–14; 4, 30; 5, 5–14). **Other scriptures:** used to guide the faith and life of the Christian community. The letters of Paul are thus here placed on the same level as books of the Old Testament. Possibly other New Testament writings could also be included.

b Jude 17. c 1 Tm 4, 1; 2 Tm 3, 1; Jude 18. d Is 5, 19. e Gn 1, 2.6.8; Ps 24, 2. f Gn 7, 21. g Is 51, 6; Mt 3, 12. h Ps 90, 4. i Ez 18, 23; 1 Tm 2, 4. j Is 66, 15–16; Mt 24, 29. k Acts 3, 19–21. l Is 34, 4; Heb 10, 27. m Is 65, 17; 66, 22; Rom 8, 21; Rv 21, 1.27. n Rom 8, 19; Jude 24.

V: Final Exhortation and Doxology

17 o*Therefore, beloved, since you are forewarned, be on your guard not to be led into the error of the unprincipled and to fall from your own stability. 18 pBut grow in grace and in the knowledge of our Lord and savior Jesus Christ. To him be glory now and to the day of eternity. [Amen.]

3, 17–18: To avoid the dangers of **error** and loss of **stability,** Christians are **forewarned** to be **on guard** and to **grow in grace and knowledge** (1, 2) of Christ. The doxology (18) recalls 1 Pt 4, 11. Some manuscripts add **Amen.**

o Mk 13, 5; Heb 2, 1. p Rom 16, 27.

THE FIRST LETTER OF JOHN

Early Christian tradition identified this work as a letter of John the apostle. Because of its resemblance to the fourth gospel in style, vocabulary, and ideas, it is generally agreed that both works are the product of the same school of Johannine Christianity. The terminology and the presence or absence of certain theological ideas in 1 John suggest that it was written after the gospel; it may have been composed as a short treatise on ideas that were developed more fully in the fourth gospel. To others, the evidence suggests that 1 John was written after the fourth gospel as part of a debate on the proper interpretation of that gospel. Whatever its relation to the gospel, 1 John may be dated toward the end of the first century. Unlike 2 and 3 John, it lacks in form the salutation and epistolary conclusion of a letter. These features, its prologue, and its emphasis on doctrinal teaching make it more akin to a theological treatise than to most other New Testament letters.

The purpose of the letter is to combat certain false ideas, especially about Jesus, and to deepen the spiritual and social awareness of the Christian community (3, 17). Some former members (2, 19) of the community refused to acknowledge Jesus as the Christ (2, 22) and denied that he was a true man (4, 2). The specific heresy described in this letter cannot be identified exactly, but it is a form of docetism or gnosticism; the former doctrine denied the humanity of Christ to insure that his divinity was untainted, and the latter viewed the appearance of Christ as a mere stepping-stone to higher knowledge of God. These theological errors are rejected by an appeal to the reality and continuity of the apostolic witness to Jesus. The author affirms that authentic Christian love, ethics, and faith take place only within the historical revelation and sacrifice of Jesus Christ. The fullness of Christian life as fellowship with the Father must be based on true belief and result in charitable living; knowledge of God and love for one another are inseparable, and error in one area inevitably affects the other. Although the author recognizes that Christian doctrine presents intangible mysteries of faith about Christ, he insists that the concrete Christian life brings to light the deeper realities of the gospel.

The structure and language of the letter are straightforward yet repetitious. The author sets forth the striking contrasts between light and darkness, Christians and the world, and truth and error to illustrate the threats and responsibilities of Christian life. The result is not one of theological argument but one of intense religious conviction expressed in simple truths. The letter is of particular value for its declaration of the humanity and divinity of Christ as an apostolic teaching and for its development of the intrinsic connection between Christian moral conduct and Christian doctrine.

The principal divisions of the First Letter of John are the following:

I. Prologue (1, 1-4)
II. God as Light (1, 5—3, 10)
III. Love for One Another (3, 11—5, 12)
IV. Epilogue (5, 13-21)

I: Prologue

CHAPTER 1

The Word of Life

1 [a] *What was from the beginning,
what we have heard,
what we have seen with our eyes,
what we looked upon
and touched with our hands
concerns the Word of life—
2 [b] for the life was made visible;
we have seen it and testify to it
and proclaim to you the eternal life
that was with the Father and was made
visible to us—
3 [c] what we have seen and heard
we proclaim now to you,
so that you too may have fellowship with
us;
for our fellowship is with the Father
and with his Son, Jesus Christ.
4 [d] We are writing this so that our joy may be
complete.

II: God As Light

God is Light [5]*Now this is the message that
we have heard from him and proclaim to you:
God is light, and in him there is no darkness at
all. [6] [e]If we say, "We have fellowship with him,"
while we continue to walk in darkness, we lie
and do not act in truth. [7] [f]But if we walk in the
light as he is in the light, then we have fellow-
ship with one another, and the blood of his Son
Jesus cleanses us from all sin. [8] [g]*If we say, "We
are without sin," we deceive ourselves, and the
truth is not in us. [9] [h]If we acknowledge our sins,
he is faithful and just and will forgive our sins
and cleanse us from every wrongdoing. [10] [i]If we
say, "We have not sinned," we make him a liar,
and his word is not in us.

CHAPTER 2

Christ and His Commandments [1] [j]*My chil-
dren, I am writing this to you so that you may
not commit sin. But if anyone does sin, we have
an Advocate with the Father, Jesus Christ the
righteous one. [2] [k]He is expiation for our sins, and
not for our sins only but for those of the whole
world. [3] [l]*The way we may be sure that we
know him is to keep his commandments.
[4] [m]Whoever says, "I know him," but does not
keep his commandments is a liar, and the truth is
not in him. [5] [n]But whoever keeps his word, the
love of God is truly perfected in him. This is the

1, 1–4: There is a striking parallel to the prologue of the gospel of John (Jn 1, 1–18), but the emphasis here is not on the preexistent Word but rather on the apostles' witness to the incarnation of **life** by their experience of the historical Jesus. He is **the Word of life** (1; cf Jn 1, 4), **the eternal life that was with the Father and was made visible** (2; cf Jn 1, 14), and was **heard, seen, looked upon,** and **touched** by the apostles. The purpose of their teaching is to share that **life,** called **fellowship . . . with the Father and with his Son, Jesus Christ,** with those who receive their witness (3; Jn 1, 14.16).

1, 5–7: Light is to be understood here as truth and goodness; **darkness** here is error and depravity (cf Jn 3, 19–21; 17, 17; Eph 5, 8). To **walk** in light or darkness is to live according to truth or error, not merely intellectual but moral as well. Fellowship with God and with one another consists in a life according to the truth as found in God and in Christ.

1, 8–10: Denial of the condition of sin is self-deception and even contradictory of divine revelation; there is also the continual possibility of sin's recurrence. Forgiveness and deliverance from sin through Christ are assured through acknowledgment of them and repentance.

2, 1: Children: like the term "beloved," this is an expression of pastoral love (cf Jn 13, 33; 21, 5; 1 Cor 4, 14). **Advocate:** for the use of the term, see Jn 14, 16. Forgiveness of sin is assured through Christ's intercession and expiation or "offering"; the death of Christ effected the removal of sin.

2, 3–6: The way we may be sure: to those who claim, "I have known Christ and therefore I know him," our author insists on not mere intellectual knowledge but obedience to God's commandments in a life conformed to the example of Christ; this confirms our knowledge of him and is **the love of God . . . perfected.** Disparity between moral life and the commandments proves improper belief.

a 2, 13; Jn 1, 1.14; 20, 20.25.27. b Jn 15, 27; 17, 5. c Jn 17, 21; Acts 4, 20. d Jn 15, 11; 2 Jn 12. e Jn 12, 35. f Mt 26, 28; Rom 3, 24–25; Heb 9, 14; 1 Pt 1, 19; Rv 1, 5. g 2 Chr 6, 36; Prv 20, 9. h Prv 28, 13; Jas 5, 16. i 5, 10. j Jn 14, 16; Heb 7, 25. k 4, 10. l Jn 14, 15; 15, 10. m 4, 20. n Jn 14, 23.

way we may know that we are in union with him: [6]whoever claims to abide in him ought to live [just] as he lived.

The New Commandment [7 o]*Beloved, I am writing no new commandment to you but an old commandment that you had from the beginning. The old commandment is the word that you have heard. [8 p]*And yet I do write a new commandment to you, which holds true in him and among you, for the darkness is passing away, and the true light is already shining. [9 q]Whoever says he is in the light, yet hates his brother, is still in the darkness. [10 r]Whoever loves his brother remains in the light, and there is nothing in him to cause a fall. [11]Whoever hates his brother is in darkness; he walks in darkness and does not know where he is going because the darkness has blinded his eyes.

Members of the Community [12 s]*I am writing to you, children, because your sins have been forgiven for his name's sake.

[13 t]I am writing to you, fathers, because you know him who is from the beginning.

I am writing to you, young men, because you have conquered the evil one.

[14]I write to you, children, because you know the Father.

I write to you, fathers, because you know him who is from the beginning.

I write to you, young men, because you are strong and the word of God remains in you, and you have conquered the evil one.

[15 u]*Do not love the world or the things of the world. If anyone loves the world, the love of the Father is not in him. [16]*For all that is in the world, sensual lust, enticement for the eyes, and a pretentious life, is not from the Father but is from the world. [17 v]Yet the world and its enticement are passing away. But whoever does the will of God remains forever.

Antichrists [18 w]*Children, it is the last hour; and just as you heard that the antichrist was coming, so now many antichrists have appeared. Thus we know this is the last hour. [19]*They went out from us, but they were not really of our number; if they had been, they would have remained with us. Their desertion shows that none of them was of our number. [20 x]*But you have the anointing that comes from the holy one, and you all have knowledge. [21 y]I write to you not because you do not know the truth but because you do, and because every lie is alien to the truth. [22 z]*Who is the liar? Whoever denies that Jesus is the Christ. Whoever denies the Father and the Son, this is the antichrist. [23 a]No one who denies the Son has the Father, but whoever confesses the Son has the Father as well.

Life from God's Anointing [24 b]*Let what you heard from the beginning remain in you. If what

2, 7–11: The author expresses the continuity and freshness of mutual charity in Christian experience. Through Christ the commandment of love has become the **light** defeating the **darkness** of evil in a new age. All hatred as darkness is incompatible with the light and Christian life. Note also the characteristic Johannine polemic in which a positive assertion is emphasized by the negative statement of its opposite.

2, 8: Which holds true in him and among you: literally, "a thing that holds true in him and in you."

2, 12–17: The Christian community that has experienced the grace of God through forgiveness of sin and knowledge of Christ is armed against the evil one.

2, 12: For his name's sake: because of Christ our sins are forgiven.

2, 15: The world: all that is hostile toward God and alienated from him. Love of the **world** and love of God are thus mutually exclusive; cf Jas 4, 4.

2, 16: Sensual lust: literally, "the lust of the flesh," inordinate desire for physical gratification. **Enticement for the eyes:** literally, "the lust of the eyes," avarice or covetousness; the eyes are regarded as the windows of the soul. **Pretentious life:** literally, "pride of life," arrogance or ostentation in one's earthly style of life that reflects a willful independence from God and others.

2, 18: It is the last hour: literally, "a last hour," the period between the death and resurrection of Christ and his second coming. **The antichrist:** opponent or adversary of Christ; the term appears only in 1–2 John, but "pseudochrists" (translated "false messiahs") in Mt 24, 24 and Mk 13, 22, and Paul's "lawless one" in 2 Thes 2, 3, are similar figures. **Many antichrists:** Mt, Mk, and Rv seem to indicate a collectivity of persons, here related to the false teachers.

2, 19: Not really of our number: the apostate teachers only proved their lack of faith by leaving the community.

2, 20: The anointing that comes from the holy one: this anointing is in the Old Testament sense of receiving the Spirit of God. The **Holy One** probably refers to Christ. True knowledge is the gift of the Spirit (cf Is 11, 2), and the function of the Spirit is to lead Christians to the truth (Jn 14, 17.26; 16, 13).

2, 22–23: Certain gnostics denied that the earthly Jesus was the Christ; to deny knowledge of the Son is to deny the Father, since only through the Son has God been fully revealed (Jn 1, 18; 14, 8–9).

2, 24: Continuity with the apostolic witness as proclaimed in the prologue is the safeguard of right belief.

o 3, 11; Dt 6, 5; Mt 22, 37–40. p Jn 13, 34 / Jn 1, 5; Rom 13, 12. q Jn 8, 12. r Eccl 2, 14; Jn 11, 10. s 1 Cor 6, 11. t 1, 1; Jn 1, 1. u Rom 8, 7–8; Jas 4, 4; 2 Pt 1, 4. v Is 40, 8; Mt 7, 21; 1 Cor 7, 31; 1 Pt 4, 2. w 1 Tim 4, 1. x Jn 14, 26. y 3, 19; 2 Pt 1, 12. z 2 Thes 2, 4. a Jn 14, 7–9. b Jn 14, 23.

you heard from the beginning remains in you, then you will remain in the Son and in the Father. 25 [c]And this is the promise that he made us: eternal life. 26 I write you these things about those who would deceive you. 27 As for you, the anointing that you received from him remains in you, so that you do not need anyone to teach you. But his anointing teaches you about everything and is true and not false; just as it taught you, remain in him.

Children of God 28 *And now, children, remain in him, so that when he appears we may have confidence and not be put to shame by him at his coming. 29 If you consider that he is righteous, you also know that everyone who acts in righteousness is begotten by him.

CHAPTER 3

1 [d]*See what love the Father has bestowed on us that we may be called the children of God. Yet so we are. The reason the world does not know us is that it did not know him. 2 [e]*Beloved, we are God's children now; what we shall be has not yet been revealed. We do know that when it is revealed we shall be like him, for we shall see him as he is. 3 [f]Everyone who has this hope based on him makes himself pure, as he is pure.

Avoiding Sin 4 *Everyone who commits sin commits lawlessness, for sin is lawlessness. 5 [g]You know that he was revealed to take away sins, and in him there is no sin. 6 No one who remains in him sins; no one who sins has seen him or known him. 7 Children, let no one deceive you. The person who acts in righteousness is righteous, just as he is righteous. 8 [h]Whoever sins belongs to the devil, because the devil has sinned from the beginning. Indeed, the Son of God was revealed to destroy the works of the devil. 9 *No one who is begotten by God commits sin, because God's seed remains in him; he cannot sin because he is begotten by God. 10 In this way, the children of God and the children of the devil are made plain; no one who fails to act in righteousness belongs to God, nor anyone who does not love his brother.

III: Love for One Another

11 [i]*For this is the message you have heard from the beginning: we should love one another, 12 [j]unlike Cain who belonged to the evil one and slaughtered his brother. Why did he slaughter him? Because his own works were evil, and those of his brother righteous. 13 [k]Do not be amazed, [then,] brothers, if the world hates you. 14 [l]We know that we have passed from death to life because we love our brothers. Whoever does not love remains in death. 15 [m]Everyone who hates his brother is a murderer, and you know that no murderer has eternal life remaining in him. 16 [n]The way we came to know love was that he laid down his life for us; so we ought to lay down our lives for our brothers. 17 [o]If someone who has worldly means sees a brother in need and refuses him compassion, how can the love of God remain in him? 18 [p]Children, let us love not in word or speech but in deed and truth.

2, 28–29: Our confidence at his judgment is based on the daily assurance of salvation. Our actions reflect our true relation to him.

3, 1–3: The greatest sign of God's love is the gift of his Son (Jn 3, 16) that has made Christians true children of God. This relationship is a present reality and also part of the life to come; true knowledge of God will ultimately be gained, and Christians prepare themselves now by virtuous lives in imitation of the Son.

3, 2: When it is revealed: or "when he is revealed" (the subject of the verb could be Christ).

3, 4: Lawlessness: a reference to the activity of the antichrist, so it is expressed as hostility toward God and a rejection of Christ. The author goes on to contrast the states of sin and righteousness. Christians do not escape sin but realize that when they sin they cease to have fellowship with God. Virtue and sin distinguish the children of God from the children of the devil.

3, 9: A habitual sinner is a child of the devil, while a child of God, who by definition is in fellowship with God, cannot sin. **Seed:** Christ or the Spirit who shares the nature of God with the Christian.

3, 11–18: Love, even to the point of self-sacrifice, is the point of the commandment. The story of Cain and Abel (12–15; Gn 4, 1–16) presents the rivalry of two brothers, in a contrast of evil and righteousness, where envy led to murder. For Christians, proof of deliverance is love toward others, after the example of Christ. This includes concrete acts of charity, out of our material abundance.

c Jn 5, 24; 10, 28; 17, 2. d Jn 1, 12; Eph 1, 5 / Jn 15, 21; 17, 25. e Phil 3, 21. f 2, 6. g Is 53, 9; Jn 1, 29; 8, 46; 1 Pt 2, 22. h Jn 8, 44; 12, 31–32. i 2, 7; Jn 13, 34; 15, 12.17. j Gn 4, 8; Jude 11. k Mt 24, 9; Jn 15, 18; 17, 14. l Lv 19, 17; Jn 5, 24. m Jn 8, 44. n Mt 20, 28; Jn 10, 11; 15, 13. o Dt 15, 7.11; Jas 2, 15–16. p Jas 1, 22.

Confidence before God [19]*[Now] this is how
we shall know that we belong to the truth and
reassure our hearts before him [20]in whatever our
hearts condemn, for God is greater than our
hearts and knows everything. [21]Beloved, if [our]
hearts do not condemn us, we have confidence
in God [22] [q]and receive from him whatever we
ask, because we keep his commandments and
do what pleases him. [23] [r]And his commandment
is this: we should believe in the name of his Son,
Jesus Christ, and love one another just as he
commanded us. [24] [s]Those who keep his com-
mandments remain in him, and he in them, and
the way we know that he remains in us is from
the Spirit that he gave us.

CHAPTER 4

Testing the Spirits [1] [t]*Beloved, do not trust
every spirit but test the spirits to see whether
they belong to God, because many false prophets
have gone out into the world. [2] [u]This is how you
can know the Spirit of God: every spirit that
acknowledges Jesus Christ come in the flesh
belongs to God, [3] [v]*and every spirit that does not
acknowledge Jesus does not belong to God. This
is the spirit of the antichrist that, as you heard, is
to come, but in fact is already in the world. [4]You
belong to God, children, and you have con-
quered them, for the one who is in you is greater
than the one who is in the world. [5] [w]They belong
to the world; accordingly, their teaching belongs
to the world, and the world listens to them.
[6] [x]We belong to God, and anyone who knows
God listens to us, while anyone who does not
belong to God refuses to hear us. This is how we
know the spirit of truth and the spirit of deceit.
God's Love and Christian Life [7]*Beloved, let
us love one another, because love is of God;
everyone who loves is begotten by God and
knows God. [8]Whoever is without love does not
know God, for God is love. [9] [y]In this way the
love of God was revealed to us: God sent his
only Son into the world so that we might have
life through him. [10] [z]In this is love: not that we
have loved God, but that he loved us and sent
his Son as expiation for our sins. [11]Beloved, if
God so loved us, we also must love one another.
[12] [a]No one has ever seen God. Yet, if we love one
another, God remains in us, and his love is
brought to perfection in us.

[13]*This is how we know that we remain in
him and he in us, that he has given us of his
Spirit. [14]Moreover, we have seen and testify that
the Father sent his Son as savior of the world.
[15]Whoever acknowledges that Jesus is the Son of
God, God remains in him and he in God. [16]We
have come to know and to believe in the love
God has for us.

God is love, and whoever remains in love
remains in God and God in him. [17] [b]In this is
love brought to perfection among us, that we
have confidence on the day of judgment because
as he is, so are we in this world. [18]There is no
fear in love, but perfect love drives out fear
because fear has to do with punishment, and so
one who fears is not yet perfect in love. [19]We

3, 19–24: Living a life of faith in Jesus and of Christian love assures us of abiding in God no matter what our feelings may at times tell us. Our obedience gives us confidence in prayer and trust in God's judgment. This obedience includes our belief in Christ and love for one another.

3, 19b-20: This difficult passage may also be translated "we shall be at peace before him in whatever our hearts condemn, for . . ." or "and before God we shall convince our hearts, if our hearts condemn us, that God is greater than our hearts."

4, 1–6: Deception is possible in spiritual phenomena and may be tested by its relation to Christian doctrine (cf 1 Cor 12, 3): those who fail to acknowledge Jesus Christ in the flesh are false prophets and belong to the antichrist. Even though these false prophets are well received in the world, the Christian who belongs to God has a greater power in the truth.

4, 3: Does not acknowledge Jesus: some ancient manuscripts add "Christ" and/or "to have come in the flesh" (cf 2), and others read "every spirit that annuls (or severs) Jesus."

4, 7–12: Love as we share in it testifies to the nature of God and to his presence in our lives. One who loves shows that one is a child of God and knows God, for God's very being is love; one without love is without God. The revelation of the nature of God's love is found in the free gift of his Son to us, so that we may share life with God and be delivered from our sins. The love we have for one another must be of the same sort: authentic, merciful; this unique Christian love is our proof that we know God and can "see" the invisible God.

4, 13–21: The testimony of the Spirit and that of faith join the testimony of love to confirm our knowledge of God. Our love is grounded in the confession of Jesus as the Son of God and the example of God's love for us. Christian life is founded on the knowledge of God as love and on his continuing presence that relieves us from fear of judgment (16–18). What Christ is gives us confidence, even as we live and love in this world. Yet Christian love is not abstract but lived in the concrete manner of love for one another.

q 5, 15; Mt 7, 7–11; 21, 22; Jn 14, 13–14. r Jn 13, 34; 15, 17. s 4, 13; Jn 14, 21–23. t 2, 18; Mt 24, 24. u 1 Cor 12, 3; 1 Thes 5, 21. v 1, 22. w Jn 15, 19. x Jn 8, 47; 10, 16. y Jn 3, 16. z Rom 5, 8. a Jn 1, 18; 1 Tm 6, 16. b 2, 28.

love because he first loved us. [20] [c]*If anyone says, "I love God," but hates his brother, he is a liar; for whoever does not love a brother whom he has seen cannot love God whom he has not seen. [21] [d]This is the commandment we have from him: whoever loves God must also love his brother.

CHAPTER 5

Faith is Victory over the World [1] [e]*Everyone who believes that Jesus is the Christ is begotten by God, and everyone who loves the father loves [also] the one begotten by him. [2]In this way we know that we love the children of God when we love God and obey his commandments. [3] [f]For the love of God is this, that we keep his commandments. And his commandments are not burdensome, [4] [g]for whoever is begotten by God conquers the world. And the victory that conquers the world is our faith. [5] [h]Who [indeed] is the victor over the world but the one who believes that Jesus is the Son of God?

[6] [i]*This is the one who came through water and blood, Jesus Christ, not by water alone, but by water and blood. The Spirit is the one that testifies, and the Spirit is truth. [7]So there are three that testify, [8] [j]the Spirit, the water, and the blood, and the three are of one accord. [9] [k]If we accept human testimony, the testimony of God is surely greater. Now the testimony of God is this, that he has testified on behalf of his Son. [10] [l]Whoever believes in the Son of God has this testimony within himself. Whoever does not believe God has made him a liar by not believing the testimony God has given about his Son. [11] [m]And this is the testimony: God gave us eternal life, and this life is in his Son. [12]Whoever possesses the Son has life; whoever does not possess the Son of God does not have life.

IV: Epilogue

Prayer for Sinners [13] [n]*I write these things to you so that you may know that you have eternal life, you who believe in the name of the Son of God. [14] [o]And we have this confidence in him, that if we ask anything according to his will, he hears us. [15]And if we know that he hears us in regard to whatever we ask, we know that what we have asked him for is ours. [16] [p]If anyone sees his brother sinning, if the sin is not deadly, he should pray to God and he will give him life. This is only for those whose sin is not deadly. There is such a thing as deadly sin, about which I do not say that you should pray. [17]All wrongdoing is sin, but there is sin that is not deadly.

[18]We know that no one begotten by God sins; but the one begotten by God he protects, and the evil one cannot touch him. [19]We know that we belong to God, and the whole world is under the power of the evil one. [20] [q]We also know that the Son of God has come and has given us discernment to know the one who is true. And we are in the one who is true, in his Son Jesus Christ. He is the true God and eternal life. [21]Children, be on your guard against idols.

4, 20: **Cannot love God:** some ancient manuscripts read "how can he love . . . ?"

5, 1–5: Children of God are identified not only by their love for others (4, 7–9) and for God (5, 1–2) but by their belief in the divine sonship of Jesus Christ. Faith, the acceptance of Jesus in his true character and the obedience in love to God's commands (3), is the source of the Christian's power in the world and conquers the world of evil (4–5), even as Christ overcame the world (Jn 16, 33).

5, 6–12: **Water and blood** (6) refers to Christ's baptism (Mt 3, 16–17) and to the shedding of his blood on the cross (Jn 19, 34). **The Spirit** was present at the baptism (Mt 3, 16; Mk 1, 10; Lk 3, 22; Jn 1, 32.34). **The testimony** to Christ as the Son of God is confirmed by divine witness (7–9), greater by far than the two legally required human witnesses (Dt 17, 6). To deny this is to deny God's truth; cf Jn 8, 17–18. The gist of the divine witness or **testimony** is that **eternal life** (11–12) is given in Christ and nowhere else. To **possess the Son** is not acceptance of a doctrine but of a person who lives now and provides life.

5, 13–21: As children of God we have confidence in prayer because of our intimate relationship with him (14–15). In love, we pray (16–17) for those who are in **sin,** but not in **deadly sin** (literally, "sin unto death"), probably referring to apostasy or activities brought on under the antichrist; cf Mk 3, 29; Heb 6, 4–6; 10, 26–31. Even in the latter case, however, prayer, while not enjoined, is not forbidden. The letter concludes with a summary of the themes of the letter (18–20). There is a sharp antithesis between the children of God and those belonging to the world and to the evil one. The Son reveals the God of truth; Christians dwell in the true God, **in his Son,** and have eternal life. The final verse (21) voices a perennial warning about **idols,** any type of rival to God.

c 2, 4. d Jn 13, 34; 14, 15.21; 15, 17. e Jn 8, 42; 1 Pt 1, 23. f Jn 14, 15. g Jn 16, 33. h 1 Cor 15, 57. i Jn 15, 26; 19, 34. j Jn 5, 32.36; 15, 26. k Jn 5, 32.37. 13, 33. m 1, 2; Jn 1, 4; 5, 21.26; 17, 3. n Jn 1, 12; 20, 31. o 3, 21–22; Mt 7, 7; Jn 14, 13–14. p Mt 12, 31. q Jer 24, 7; Jn 17, 3; Eph 1, 17.

THE SECOND LETTER OF JOHN

Written in response to similar problems, the Second and Third Letters of John are of the same length, perhaps determined by the practical consideration of the writing space on one piece of papyrus. In each letter the writer calls himself "the Presbyter," and their common authorship is further evidenced by internal similarities in style and wording, especially in the introductions and conclusions. The literary considerations that link 2 and 3 John also link them with the First Letter and the Gospel of John. The concern with "truth," christology, mutual love, the new commandment, antichrist, and the integrity of witness to the earthly Jesus mark these works as products of the Johannine school. The identity of the Presbyter is problematic. The use of the title implies more than age, and refers to his position of leadership in the early church. The absence of a proper name indicates that he was well known and acknowledged in authority by the communities to which he writes. Although traditionally attributed to John the apostle, these letters were probably written by a disciple or scribe of an apostle. The traditional place and date of composition, Ephesus at the end of the first century, are plausible for both letters.

The Second Letter is addressed to "the chosen Lady" and "to her children." This literary image of a particular Christian community reflects the specific destination and purpose of the letter. Unlike 1 John, this brief letter is not a theological treatise but a reply to problems within the church. The Johannine themes of love and truth are used to support practical advice on Christian living. The Presbyter encourages community members to show their Christianity by adhering to the great commandment of mutual love and to the historical truth about Jesus. The false teaching present among them is a spiritualizing christology that may tempt some members to discount teachings about the incarnation and death of Jesus the Christ; cf 1 Jn 4, 2. For their protection the Presbyter forbids hospitality toward unknown or "progressive" Christians to prevent their infiltration of the community. The Second Letter preserves the Johannine concerns of doctrinal purity and active love in the form of pastoral advice to a threatened community.

1 [a]*The Presbyter to the chosen Lady and to
her children whom I love in truth—and not only
I but also all who know the truth— 2 because of
the truth that dwells in us and will be with us
forever. 3 *Grace, mercy, and peace will be with
us from God the Father and from Jesus Christ
the Father's Son in truth and love.

4 [b]*I rejoiced greatly to find some of your
children walking in the truth just as we were
commanded by the Father. 5 [c]But now, Lady, I
ask you, not as though I were writing a new
commandment but the one we have had from
the beginning: let us love one another. 6 [d]*For
this is love, that we walk according to his
commandments; this is the commandment, as
you heard from the beginning, in which you
should walk.

7 [e]*Many deceivers have gone out into the
world, those who do not acknowledge Jesus

1: **The chosen Lady:** literally "elected"; this could also be translated "Kyria (a woman's name) chosen (by God)" or "the lady Electa" or "Electa Kyria." The adjective "chosen" is applied to all Christians at the beginning of other New Testament letters (1 Pt 1, 1; Ti 1, 1). The description is of a specific community with "children" who are its members. **The truth:** the affirmation of Jesus in the flesh and in contrast to false teaching (7).

3: **Grace, mercy, and peace:** like 1 and 2 Tm this letter adds **mercy** to the terms used frequently in a salutation to describe Christian blessing; it appears only here in the Johannine writings. The author also puts the blessing in relation to **truth** and **love**, the watchwords of the Johannine teaching. **The Father's Son:** the title that affirms the close relationship of Christ to God; similar variations of this title occur elsewhere (Jn 1, 14; 3, 35), but the precise wording is not found elsewhere in the New Testament.

4: **Some of your children:** this refers to those whom the Presbyter has recently encountered, but it may also indicate the presence of false doctrine in the community: the Presbyter encourages those who have remained faithful. **Walking in the truth:** an expression used in the Johannine writings to describe a way of living in which the Christian faith is visibly expressed; cf 1 Jn 1, 6–7; 2, 6.11; 3 Jn 3.

6: **His commandments:** cf 1 Jn 3, 23; 2, 7–8; 4, 21; obedience to the commandment of faith and love includes all others.

7: **The antichrist:** see 1 Jn 2, 18–19.22; 4, 3.

a Jn 8, 32; 3 Jn 1. b 3 Jn 3. c Jn 13, 34; 15, 12; 1 Jn 4, 7. d Jn 13, 34; 14, 15; 1 Jn 5, 3. e 1 Jn 2, 22; 4, 2.

Christ as coming in the flesh; such is the
deceitful one and the antichrist. 8*Look to
yourselves that you do not lose what we worked
for but may receive a full recompense.
9f*Anyone who is so "progressive" as not to
remain in the teaching of the Christ does not
have God; whoever remains in the teaching has
the Father and the Son. 10g*If anyone comes to
you and does not bring this doctrine, do not
receive him in your house or even greet him;
11for whoever greets him shares in his evil
works.

12h*Although I have much to write to you, I
do not intend to use paper and ink. Instead, I
hope to visit you and to speak face to face so that
our joy may be complete. 13*The children of
your chosen sister send you greetings.

8: You (plural): it is not certain whether this means the Christians addressed or includes the Presbyter, since some of the ancient Greek manuscripts and Greek Fathers have "we."

9: Anyone who is so "progressive": literally, "Anyone who goes ahead." Some gnostic groups held the doctrine of the Christ come in the flesh to be a first step in belief, which the more advanced and spiritual believer surpassed and abandoned in his knowledge of the spiritual Christ. The author affirms that fellowship with God may be gained only by holding to the complete doctrine of Jesus Christ (1 Jn 2, 22–23; 4, 2; 5, 5–6).

10–11: At this time false teachers were considered so dangerous and divisive as to be shunned completely. From this description they seem to be wandering preachers. We see here a natural suspicion of early Christians concerning such itinerants and can envisage the problems faced by missionaries such as those mentioned in 3 Jn 10.

12: Our joy: a number of other Greek manuscripts read "your joy."

13: Chosen sister: the community of which the Presbyter is now a part greets you (singular), the community of the Lady addressed.

f Jn 8, 31; 1 Jn 2, 23; 4, 15. g Rom 16, 17; 2 Thes 3, 6. h Jn 15, 11; 1 Jn 1, 4; 3 Jn 13.

THE THIRD LETTER OF JOHN

The Third Letter of John preserves a brief glimpse into the problems of missionary activity and local autonomy in the early church. In contrast to the other two letters of John, this work was addressed to a specific individual, Gaius. This letter is less theological in content and purpose. The author's goal was to secure hospitality and material support for his missionaries, and the Presbyter is writing to another member of the church who has welcomed missionaries in the past. The Presbyter commends Gaius for his hospitality and encourages his future help. He indicates he may come to challenge the policy of Diotrephes that is based on evil gossip.

The problems of the Presbyter in this short letter provide us with valuable evidence of the flexible and personal nature of authority in the early church. The Presbyter writes to Gaius, whom perhaps he had converted or instructed, on the basis of their personal links. The brothers have also confirmed him as a loyal Christian in action and belief. Gaius accepted the missionaries from the Presbyter and presumably will accept Demetrius on the Presbyter's recommendation. In contrast, Diotrephes refuses to receive either letters or friends of the Presbyter. Although he is portrayed as ambitious and hostile, he perhaps exemplifies the cautious and sectarian nature of early Christianity; for its own protection the local community mistrusted missionaries as false teachers. Most interestingly, Diotrephes seems comfortable in ignoring the requests of the Presbyter. The Presbyter seems to acknowledge that only a personal confrontation with Diotrephes will remedy the situation (10). The division, however, may also rest on doctrinal disagreement in which Gaius and the other "friends" accept the teaching of the Presbyter, and Diotrephes does not; the missionaries are not received for suspicion of theological error. Diotrephes has thus been viewed by some as an overly ambitious local upstart trying to thwart the advance of orthodox Christianity, by others as an orthodox church official suspicious of the teachings of the Presbyter and those in the Johannine school who think as he does, or by still others as a local leader anxious to keep the debates in the Johannine community out of his own congregation.

This brief letter and the situation that it mirrors show us how little we know about some details of early development in the church: schools of opinion existed around which questions of faith and life were discussed, and personal ties as well as doctrine and authority played a role in what happened amid divisions and unity.

1 [a]*The Presbyter to the beloved Gaius whom
I love in truth.
2 Beloved, I hope you are prospering in every
respect and are in good health, just as your soul
is prospering. 3 [b]*I rejoiced greatly when some of
the brothers came and testified to how truly you
walk in the truth. 4 [c]Nothing gives me greater joy
than to hear that my children are walking in the
truth.
5 [d]*Beloved, you are faithful in all you do for
the brothers, especially for strangers; 6 [e]*they
have testified to your love before the church.
Please help them in a way worthy of God to
continue their journey. 7*For they have set out
for the sake of the Name and are accepting
nothing from the pagans. 8 Therefore, we ought
to support such persons, so that we may be co-
workers in the truth.
9*I wrote to the church, but Diotrephes, who
loves to dominate, does not acknowledge us.
10*Therefore, if I come, I will draw attention to
what he is doing, spreading evil nonsense about
us. And not content with that, he will not
receive the brothers, hindering those who wish
to do so and expelling them from the church.
11 [f]*Beloved, do not imitate evil but imitate
good. Whoever does what is good is of God;
whoever does what is evil has never seen God.
12 [g]*Demetrius receives a good report from all,
even from the truth itself. We give our testimo-
nial as well, and you know our testimony is true.
13 [h]I have much to write to you, but I do not
wish to write with pen and ink. 14 Instead, I hope
to see you soon, when we can talk face to face.
15 [i]*Peace be with you. The friends greet you;
greet the friends there each by name.

1: **Beloved Gaius:** a frequent form of address for fellow Christians in New Testament epistolary literature.

3: **The brothers:** in this letter, the term may refer to Christians who have been missionaries and received hospitality from Gaius (5–6). **Walk in the truth:** the common Johannine term to describe Christian living; this description presents Gaius as following the teachings of the Presbyter in contrast to Diotrephes.

5: **You are faithful in all you do:** Gaius's aid to the missionaries is a manifestation of his true Christian faith.

6: **Help them . . . to continue their journey:** the Presbyter asks Gaius not only to continue to welcome the missionaries to his community but also to equip them for further travels.

7: **The Name:** of Jesus Christ (cf Acts 5, 41; 1 Jn 2, 12; 3, 23; 5, 13). **Accepting nothing:** not expecting support from the pagans to whom they preach the gospel, so that they will not be considered as beggars; they required support from other Christians; cf Paul's complaints to the Corinthians (1 Cor 9, 3–12).

9: **Who loves to dominate:** the Presbyter does not deny Diotrephes's place as leader but indicates that his ambition may have caused him to disregard his letter and his influence.

10: **If I come:** the Presbyter may visit the community to challenge the actions of Diotrephes toward himself and the missionaries. **Will not receive the brothers:** Diotrephes may have been critical of the teachings of the Presbyter and sought to maintain doctrinal purity; cf 1 Jn 2, 19 and 2 Jn 10–11.

11: **Do not imitate evil:** Gaius should not be influenced by the behavior of Diotrephes.

12: **Demetrius:** because of the fear of false teachers, Demetrius, perhaps the bearer of the letter, is provided with a recommendation from the Presbyter; cf 2 Cor 3, 1; Rom 16, 1. **Even from the truth itself:** this refers probably to the manner of Demetrius's life that testifies to his true belief; cf Gaius above (v 3).

15: **Friends:** although a Johannine term for Christians (Jn 15, 15), the word here may refer to those in the community loyal to the Presbyter and to Gaius.

a 2 Jn 1. b 5; Gal 6, 10; 2 Jn 4. c 1 Thes 2, 11–12; 1 Tm 1, 2; 2 Tm 1, 2; 1 Jn 2, 1; 2 Jn 4. d Rom 12, 13; Gal 6, 10; Heb 13, 2. e Acts 15, 3; Col 1, 10; 1 Thes 2, 12. f 1 Jn 2, 29; 3, 6.10. g Jn 19, 35; 21, 24; 1 Tm 3, 7. h 2 Jn 12. i Jn 20, 19.21.26; Eph 6, 23; 1 Pt 5, 14.

THE LETTER OF JUDE

This letter is by its address attributed to "Jude, a slave of Jesus Christ and brother of James" (1). Since he is not identified as an apostle, this designation can hardly be meant to refer to the Jude or Judas who is listed as one of the Twelve (Lk 6, 16; Acts 1, 13; cf Jn 14, 22). The person intended is almost certainly the other Jude, named in the gospels among the relatives of Jesus (Mt 13, 55; Mk 6, 3), and the James who is listed there as his brother is the one to whom the Letter of James is attributed (see the Introduction to James). Nothing else is known of this Jude, and the apparent need to identify him by reference to his better-known brother indicates that he was a rather obscure personage in the early church.

The letter is addressed in the most general terms to "those who are called, beloved in God the Father and kept safe for Jesus Christ" (1), hence apparently to all Christians. But since its purpose is to warn the addressees against false teachers, the author must have had in mind one or more specific Christian communities located in the unidentified region where the errors in question constituted a danger. While the letter contains some Semitic features, there is nothing to identify the addressees specifically as Jewish Christians; indeed, the errors envisaged seem to reflect an early form of gnosticism, opposed to law, that points rather to the cultural context of the Gentile world. Like James and 2 Peter, the Letter of Jude manifests none of the typical features of the letter form except the address.

There is so much similarity between Jude and 2 Peter, especially Jude 4-16 and 2 Peter 2, 1-18, that there must be a literary relationship between them. Since there is no evidence for the view that both authors borrowed from the same source, it is usually supposed that one of them borrowed from the other. Most scholars believe that Jude is the earlier of the two, principally because he quotes two apocryphal Jewish works, the Assumption of Moses (9) and the Book of Enoch (14-15) as part of his structured argument, whereas 2 Peter omits both references. Since there was controversy in the early church about the propriety of citing noncanonical literature that included legendary material, it is more probable that a later writer would omit such references than that he would add them.

Many interpreters today consider Jude a pseudonymous work dating from the end of the first century or even later. In support of this view they adduce the following arguments: (a) the apostles are referred to as belonging to an age that has receded into the past (17-18); (b) faith is understood as a body of doctrine handed down by a process of tradition (3); (c) the author's competent Greek style shows that he must have had a Hellenistic cultural formation; (d) the gnostic character of the errors envisaged fits better into the early second century than into a period several decades earlier. While impressive, these arguments are not entirely compelling and do not completely rule out the possibility of composition around the year A.D. 80, when the historical Jude may still have been alive.

This little letter is an urgent note by an author who intended to write more fully about salvation to an unknown group of readers, but who was forced by dangers from false teachers worming their way into the community (3-4) to dash off a warning against them (5-16) and to deliver some pressing Christian admonitions (17-23). The letter is justly famous for its majestic closing doxology (24-25).

Address and Greeting [1][a]*Jude, a slave of
Jesus Christ and brother of James, to those who
are called, beloved in God the Father and kept
safe for Jesus Christ: [2][b]may mercy, peace, and
love be yours in abundance.
Occasion for Writing [3][c]*Beloved, although I
was making every effort to write to you about
our common salvation, I now feel a need to
write to encourage you to contend for the faith
that was once for all handed down to the holy
ones. [4][d]For there have been some intruders,
who long ago were designated for this condem-
nation, godless persons, who pervert the grace of
our God into licentiousness and who deny our
only Master and Lord, Jesus Christ.
The False Teachers [5][e]*I wish to remind you,
although you know all things, that [the] Lord
who once saved a people from the land of Egypt
later destroyed those who did not believe.
[6][f]*The angels too, who did not keep to their
own domain but deserted their proper dwelling,
he has kept in eternal chains, in gloom, for the
judgment of the great day. [7][g]*Likewise, Sodom,
Gomorrah, and the surrounding towns, which,
in the same manner as they, indulged in sexual
promiscuity and practiced unnatural vice, serve
as an example by undergoing a punishment of
eternal fire.
[8]*Similarly, these dreamers nevertheless also
defile the flesh, scorn lordship, and revile glori-
ous beings. [9][h]*Yet the archangel Michael, when
he argued with the devil in a dispute over the
body of Moses, did not venture to pronounce a
reviling judgment upon him but said, "May the
Lord rebuke you!" [10][i]But these people revile
what they do not understand and are destroyed
by what they know by nature like irrational
animals. [11][j]*Woe to them! They followed the
way of Cain, abandoned themselves to Balaam's
error for the sake of gain, and perished in the
rebellion of Korah. [12][k]*These are blemishes on
your love feasts, as they carouse fearlessly and
look after themselves. They are waterless clouds
blown about by winds, fruitless trees in late
autumn, twice dead and uprooted. [13]They are
like wild waves of the sea, foaming up their
shameless deeds, wandering stars for whom the
gloom of darkness has been reserved forever.
[14][l]*Enoch, of the seventh generation from
Adam, prophesied also about them when he

1: Jude . . . brother of James: for the identity of the author of this letter, see Introduction. **To those who are called:** the vocation to the Christian faith is God's free gift to those whom he loves and whom he safely protects in Christ until the Lord's second coming.

3–4: Our common salvation: the teachings of the Christian faith derived from the apostolic preaching and to be kept by the Christian community.

5: For this first example of divine punishment on those who had been saved but did not then keep faith, see Nm 14, 28–29 and the note there. Some manuscripts have the word "once" (**hapax** as at 3) after "you know"; some commentators have suggested that it means "knowing one thing" or "you know all things once for all." Instead of "[the] Lord" manuscripts vary, having "Jesus," "God," or no subject stated.

6: This second example draws on Gn 6, 1–4 as elaborated in the apocryphal Book of Enoch (cf 14): heavenly beings came to earth and had sexual intercourse with women. God punished them by casting them out of heaven into darkness and bondage.

7: Practiced unnatural vice: literally, "went after alien flesh." This example derives from Gn 19, 1–25, especially 4–11, when the townsmen of Sodom violated both hospitality and morality by demanding that Lot's two visitors (really messengers of Yahweh) be handed over to them so that they could abuse them sexually. **Unnatural vice:** this refers to the desire for intimacies by human beings with angels (the reverse of the example in 6). Sodom (whence "sodomy") and Gomorrah became proverbial as object lessons for God's punishment on sin (Is 1, 9; Jer 50, 40; Am 4, 11; Mt 10, 15; 2 Pt 2, 6).

8: Dreamers: the writer returns to the false teachers of v 4, applying charges from the three examples in vv 5, 6, 7. This may apply to claims they make for revelations they have received by night (to the author, hallucinations). **Defile the flesh:** this may mean bodily pollutions from the erotic dreams of sexual license (7). **Lordship . . . glorious beings:** these may reflect the Lord (5; Jesus, 4) whom they spurn and the angels (6; cf the note on 2 Pt 2, 10, here, as there, literally, "glories").

9: The archangel Michael . . . judgment: a reference to an incident in the apocryphal Assumption of Moses. Dt 34, 6 had said of Moses, literally in Greek, "they buried him" or "he (God?) buried him" (taken to mean "he was buried"). The later account tells how Michael, who was sent to bury him, was challenged by the devil's interest in the body. Our author draws out the point that if an archangel refrained from reviling even the devil, how wrong it is for mere human beings to revile glorious beings (angels).

11: Cain . . . Balaam . . . Korah: examples of rebellious men and of the punishment their conduct incurred; cf Gn 4, 8–16; Nm 16, 1–35; 31, 16. See the note on 2 Pt 2, 15.

12: Blemishes on your love feasts: or "hidden rocks" or "submerged reefs" (cf 13). The opponents engaged in scandalous conduct in connection with community gatherings called **love feasts** (agape meals), which were associated with eucharistic celebrations at certain stages of early Christian practice; cf 1 Cor 11, 18–34 and the note on 2 Pt 2, 13.

14–15: Cited from the apocryphal Book of Enoch 1, 9.

a Mt 13, 55; Mk 6, 3; Acts 12, 17; Rom 1, 7. b Gal 6, 16; 1 Tm 1, 2; 2 Pt 1, 2. c 17.20; 1 Tm 6, 12. d Gal 2, 4; 2 Tm 3, 6; 2 Pt 2, 1. e Nm 14, 35; 1 Cor 10, 5; Heb 3, 16.17. f 2 Pt 2, 4.9. g Dt 29, 22–24; Mt 25, 41; 2 Thes 1, 8–9; 2 Pt 2, 6; 3, 7. h Dn 10, 21; 12, 1. i 2 Pt 2, 12. j Gn 4, 8–16; 1 Jn 3, 12 / Nm 31, 15–16; 2 Pt 2, 15; Rv 2, 14 / Nm 16, 19–35. k 2 Pt 2, 13.17. l Mt 16, 27; Heb 12, 22–23.

said, "Behold, the Lord has come with his countless holy ones [15]to execute judgment on all and to convict everyone for all the godless deeds that they committed and for all the harsh words godless sinners have uttered against him." [16] [m]These people are complainers, disgruntled ones who live by their desires; their mouths utter bombast as they fawn over people to gain advantage.

Exhortations [17] [n]But you, beloved, remember the words spoken beforehand by the apostles of our Lord Jesus Christ, [18] [o]*for they told you, "In [the] last time there will be scoffers who will live according to their own godless desires." [19] [p]These are the ones who cause divisions; they live on the natural plane, devoid of the Spirit. [20] [q]But you, beloved, build yourselves up in your most holy faith; pray in the holy Spirit. [21] [r]Keep yourselves in the love of God and wait for the mercy of our Lord Jesus Christ that leads to eternal life. [22]*On those who waver, have mercy; [23]*save others by snatching them out of the fire; on others have mercy with fear, abhorring even the outer garment stained by the flesh.

Doxology [24] [s]*To the one who is able to keep you from stumbling and to present you unblemished and exultant, in the presence of his glory, [25] [t]to the only God, our savior, through Jesus Christ our Lord be glory, majesty, power, and authority from ages past, now, and for ages to come. Amen.

18: This is the substance of much early Christian preaching rather than a direct quotation of any of the various New Testament passages on this theme (see Mk 13, 22; Acts 20, 30; 1 Tm 4, 1–3; 2 Pt 3, 3).

22: Have mercy: some manuscripts read "convince," "confute," or "reprove." Others have "even though you waver" or "doubt" instead of **who waver.**

23: With fear: some manuscripts connect the phrase "with fear" with the imperative "save" or with the participle "snatching." Other manuscripts omit the phrase "on others have mercy," so that only two groups are envisioned. Rescue of those led astray and caution in the endeavor are both enjoined. **Outer garment stained by the flesh:** the imagery may come from Zec 3, 3–5, just as that of **snatching . . . out of the fire** comes from Zec 3, 2; the very garments of the godless are to be abhorred because of their contagion.

24–25: With this liturgical statement about the power of God to keep the faithful from stumbling, and praise to him through Jesus Christ, the letter reaches its conclusion by returning to the themes with which it began (1–2).

m 18; 1 Cor 10, 10; 2 Pt 2, 10.18. n Heb 2, 3; 2 Pt 3, 2. o 1 Tm 4, 1; 2 Tm 3, 1–5; 2 Pt 3, 3. p 1 Cor 2, 14; Jas 3, 15. q 2; Eph 6, 18; Col 2, 7. r Ti 2, 13. s 2 Cor 4, 14; 1 Pt 4, 13. t Rom 11, 36; 1 Tm 1, 17.

THE REVELATION TO JOHN

The Apocalypse, or Revelation to John, the last book of the Bible, is one of the most difficult to understand because it abounds in unfamiliar and extravagant symbolism, which at best appears unusual to the modern reader. Symbolic language, however, is one of the chief characteristics of apocalyptic literature, of which this book is an outstanding example. Such literature enjoyed wide popularity in both Jewish and Christian circles from ca. 200 B.C. to A.D. 200.

This book contains an account of visions in symbolic and allegorical language borrowed extensively from the Old Testament, especially Ezekiel, Zechariah, and Daniel. Whether or not these visions were real experiences of the author or simply literary conventions employed by him is an open question.

This much, however, is certain: symbolic descriptions are not to be taken as literal descriptions, nor is the symbolism meant to be pictured realistically. One would find it difficult and repulsive to visualize a lamb with seven horns and seven eyes; yet Jesus Christ is described in precisely such words (5, 6). The author used these images to suggest Christ's universal (seven) power (horns) and knowledge (eyes). A significant feature of apocalyptic writing is the use of symbolic colors, metals, garments (1, 13-16; 3, 18; 4, 4; 6, 1-8; 17, 4; 19, 8), and numbers (*four* signifies the world, *six* imperfection, *seven* totality of perfection, *twelve* Israel's tribes or the apostles, *one thousand* immensity). Finally the vindictive language in the book (6, 9-10; 18, 1—19, 4) is also to be understood symbolically and not literally. The cries for vengeance on the lips of Christian martyrs that sound so harsh are in fact literary devices the author employed to evoke in the reader and hearer a feeling of horror for apostasy and rebellion that will be severely punished by God.

The lurid descriptions of the punishment of Jezebel (2, 22) and of the destruction of the great harlot, Babylon (16, 9—19, 2), are likewise literary devices. The metaphor of Babylon as harlot would be wrongly construed if interpreted literally. On the other hand, the stylized figure of the woman clothed with the sun (12, 1-6), depicting the New Israel, may seem to be a negative stereotype. It is necessary to look beyond the literal meaning to see that these images mean to convey a sense of God's wrath at sin in the former case and trust in God's providential care over the church in the latter.

The Book of Revelation cannot be adequately understood except against the historical background that occasioned its writing. Like Daniel and other apocalypses, it was composed as resistance literature to meet a crisis. The book itself suggests that the crisis was ruthless persecution of the early church by the Roman authorities; the harlot Babylon symbolizes pagan Rome, the city on seven hills (17, 9). The book is, then, an exhortation and admonition to Christians of the first century to stand firm in the faith and to avoid compromise with paganism, despite the threat of adversity and martyrdom; they are to await patiently the fulfillment of God's mighty promises. The triumph of God in the world of men and women remains a mystery, to be accepted in faith and longed for in hope. It is a triumph that unfolded in the history of Jesus of Nazareth and continues to unfold in the history of the individual Christian who follows the way of the cross, even, if necessary, to a martyr's death.

Though the perspective is eschatological—ultimate salvation and victory are said to take place at the end of the present age when Christ will come in glory at the parousia—the book presents the decisive struggle of Christ and his followers against Satan and his cohorts as already over. Christ's overwhelming defeat of the kingdom of Satan ushered in the everlasting reign of God (11, 15; 12, 10). Even the forces of evil unwittingly carry out the divine plan (17, 17), for God is the sovereign Lord of history.

The Book of Revelation had its origin in a time of crisis, but it remains valid and meaningful for Christians of all time. In the face of apparently insuperable evil, either from within or from without, all Christians are called to trust in Jesus' promise, "Behold, I am with you always, until the end of the age" (Mt 28, 20). Those who remain steadfast in their faith and confidence in the risen Lord need have no fear. Suffering, persecution, even death by martyrdom, though remaining impenetrable mysteries of evil, do not comprise an absurd dead end. No matter what adversity or sacrifice Christians may endure, they will in the end triumph over Satan and his forces because of their fidelity to Christ the victor. This is the enduring message of the book; it is a message of hope and consolation and challenge for all who dare to believe.

The author of the book calls himself John (1, 1.4.9; 22, 8), who because of his Christian faith has been exiled to the rocky island of Patmos, a Roman penal colony. Although he never claims to be John the apostle, whose name is attached to the fourth gospel, he was so identified by several of the early church Fathers, including Justin, Irenaeus, Clement of Alexandria, Tertullian, Cyprian, and Hippolytus. This identification, however, was denied by other Fathers, including Denis of Alexandria, Eusebius of Caesarea, Cyril of Jerusalem, Gregory Nazianzen, and John Chrysostom. Indeed, vocabulary, grammar, and style make it doubtful that the book could have been put into its present form by the same person(s) responsible for the fourth gospel. Nevertheless, there are definite linguistic and theological affinities between the two books. The tone of the letters to the seven churches (1, 4—3, 22) is indicative of the great authority the author enjoyed over the Christian communities in Asia. It is possible, therefore, that he was a disciple of John the apostle, who is traditionally associated with that part of the world. The date of the book in its present form is probably near the end of the reign of Domitian (A.D. 81–96), a fierce persecutor of the Christians.

The principal divisions of the Book of Revelation are the following:

I. Prologue (1, 1-3)
II. Letters to the Churches of Asia (1, 4—3, 22)
III. God and the Lamb in Heaven (4, 1—5, 14)
IV. The Seven Seals, Trumpets, and Plagues, with Interludes (6, 1—16, 21)
V. The Punishment of Babylon and the Destruction of Pagan Nations (17, 1—20, 15)
VI. The New Creation (21, 1—22, 5)
VII. Epilogue (22, 6-21)

I: Prologue

CHAPTER 1

1 [a]*The revelation of Jesus Christ, which God
gave to him, to show his servants what must
happen soon. He made it known by sending his
angel to his servant John, 2 who gives witness to
the word of God and to the testimony of Jesus
Christ by reporting what he saw. 3 [b]*Blessed is
the one who reads aloud and blessed are those
who listen to this prophetic message and heed
what is written in it, for the appointed time is
near.

II: Letters to the Churches of Asia

Greeting 4 [c]*John, to the seven churches in
Asia: grace to you and peace from him who is
and who was and who is to come, and from the
seven spirits before his throne, 5 [d]*and from
Jesus Christ, the faithful witness, the firstborn of
the dead and ruler of the kings of the earth. To
him who loves us and has freed us from our sins
by his blood, 6 [e]who has made us into a kingdom, priests for his God and Father, to him be
glory and power forever [and ever]. Amen.

7 [f]Behold, he is coming amid the clouds,
and every eye will see him,
even those who pierced him.
All the peoples of the earth will lament him.
Yes. Amen.

8 [g]*"I am the Alpha and the Omega," says the
Lord God, "the one who is and who was and
who is to come, the almighty."

1, 1-3: This prologue describes the source, contents, and audience of the book and forms an inclusion with the epilogue (22, 6-21), with its similar themes and expressions.

1, 3: **Blessed is the one:** this is the first of seven beatitudes in this book; the others are in 14, 13; 16, 15; 19, 9; 20, 6; 22, 7.14. **This prophetic message:** literally, "the words of the prophecy"; so 22, 7.10.18.19 by inclusion. **The appointed time:** when Jesus will return in glory; cf 1, 7; 3, 11; 22, 7.10.12.20.

1, 4-8: Although Revelation begins and ends (22, 21) with Christian epistolary formulae, there is nothing between chs 4 and 22 resembling a letter. The author here employs the standard word order for greetings in Greek letter writing: "N. to N., greetings . . ."; see the note on Rom 1, 1.

1, 4: **Seven churches in Asia:** Asia refers to the Roman province of that name in western Asia Minor (modern Turkey); these representative churches are mentioned by name in v 11, and each is the recipient of a message (2, 1—3, 22). **Seven** is the biblical number suggesting fullness and completeness; thus the seer is writing for the whole church.

1, 5: **Freed us:** the majority of Greek manuscripts and several early versions read "washed us"; but "freed us" is supported by the best manuscripts and fits well with Old Testament imagery, e.g., Is 40, 2.

1, 8: **The Alpha and the Omega:** the first and last letters of the Greek alphabet. In 22, 13 the same words occur together with the expressions "the First and the Last, the Beginning and the End"; cf 17; 2, 8; 21, 6; Is 41, 4; 44, 6.

a 22, 6-8.20; Dn 2, 28 / 19, 10. b 22, 7 / Lk 11, 28. c 8; 4, 8; 11, 17; 16, 5; Ex 3, 14. d 3, 14; 1 Cor 15, 20; Col 1, 18 / Heb 9, 14; 1 Pt 1, 19;1 Jn 1, 7. e Ex 19, 6; 1 Pt 2, 9. f Dn 7, 13 / Zec 12, 10; Mt 24, 30; Jn 19, 37. g 17; 21, 6; 22, 13; Is 41, 4; 44, 6; 48, 12.

The First Vision 9*I, John, your brother, who
share with you the distress, the kingdom, and
the endurance we have in Jesus, found myself on
the island called Patmos because I proclaimed
God's word and gave testimony to Jesus. 10*I
was caught up in spirit on the Lord's day and
heard behind me a voice as loud as a trumpet,
11*which said, "Write on a scroll what you see
and send it to the seven churches: to Ephesus,
Smyrna, Pergamum, Thyatira, Sardis, Philadel-
phia, and Laodicea." 12*Then I turned to see
whose voice it was that spoke to me, and when I
turned, I saw seven gold lampstands 13 [h]*and in
the midst of the lampstands one like a son of
man, wearing an ankle-length robe, with a gold
sash around his chest. 14*The hair of his head
was as white as white wool or as snow, and his
eyes were like a fiery flame. 15*His feet were like
polished brass refined in a furnace, and his voice
was like the sound of rushing water. 16 [i]*In his
right hand he held seven stars. A sharp two-
edged sword came out of his mouth, and his face
shone like the sun at its brightest.

17 [j]*When I caught sight of him, I fell down at
his feet as though dead. He touched me with
his right hand and said, "Do not be afraid. I am
the first and the last, 18*the one who lives.
Once I was dead, but now I am alive forever
and ever. I hold the keys to death and the
netherworld. 19*Write down, therefore, what
you have seen, and what is happening, and
what will happen afterwards. 20*This is the
secret meaning of the seven stars you saw in
my right hand, and of the seven gold
lampstands: the seven stars are the angels of
the seven churches, and the seven lampstands
are the seven churches.

CHAPTER 2

To Ephesus 1*"To the angel of the church in
Ephesus, write this:

" 'The one who holds the seven stars in his
right hand and walks in the midst of the seven

1, 9–20: In this first vision, the seer is commanded to write what he sees to the seven churches (9–11). He sees Christ in glory, whom he depicts in stock apocalyptic imagery (12–16), and hears him describe himself in terms meant to encourage Christians by emphasizing his victory over death (17–20).

1, 9: Island called Patmos: one of the Sporades islands in the Aegean Sea, some fifty miles south of Ephesus, used by the Romans as a penal colony. **Because I proclaimed God's word:** literally, "on account of God's word."

1, 10: The Lord's day: Sunday. **As loud as a trumpet:** the imagery is derived from the theophany at Sinai (Ex 19, 16.19; cf Heb 12, 19 and the trumpet in other eschatological settings in Is 27, 13; Jl 2, 1; Mt 24, 31; 1 Cor 15, 52; 1 Thes 4, 16).

1, 11: Scroll: a papyrus roll.

1, 12–16: A symbolic description of Christ in glory. The metaphorical language is not to be understood literally; cf Introduction.

1, 13: Son of man: see the note on Mk 8, 31. **Ankle-length robe:** Christ is priest; cf Ex 28, 4; 29, 5; Wis 18, 24; Zec 3, 4. **Gold sash:** Christ is king; cf Ex 28, 4; 1 Mc 10, 89; 11, 58; Dn 10, 5.

1, 14: Hair . . . as white as white wool or as snow: Christ is eternal, clothed with the dignity that belonged to the "Ancient of Days"; cf 18; Dn 7, 9. **His eyes were like a fiery flame:** Christ is portrayed as all-knowing; cf 2, 23; Ps 7, 10; Jer 17, 10; and similar expressions in 2, 18; 19, 12; cf Dn 10, 6.

1, 15: His feet . . . furnace: Christ is depicted as unchangeable; cf Ez 1, 27; Dn 10, 6. The Greek word translated "refined" is unconnected grammatically with any other word in the sentence. **His voice . . . water:** Christ speaks with divine authority; cf Ez 1, 24.

1, 16: Seven stars: in the pagan world, Mithras and the Caesars were represented with seven stars in their right hand, symbolizing their universal dominion. **A sharp two-edged sword:** this refers to the word of God (cf Eph 6, 17; Heb 4, 12) that will destroy unrepentant sinners; cf 2, 16; 19, 15; Wis 18, 15; Is 11, 4; 49, 2. **His face . . . brightest:** this symbolizes the divine majesty of Christ; cf 10, 1; 21, 23; Jgs 5, 31; Is 60, 19; Mt 17, 2.

1, 17: It was an Old Testament belief that for sinful human beings to see God was to die; cf Ex 19, 21; 33, 20; Jgs 6, 22–23; Is 6, 5.

1, 18: Netherworld: Greek Hades, Hebrew Sheol, the abode of the dead; cf 20, 13–14; Nm 16, 33.

1, 19: What you have seen, and what is happening, and what will happen afterwards: the three parts of the Book of Revelation, the vision (10–20), the situation in the seven churches (chs 2–3), and the events of chs 6–22.

1, 20: Secret meaning: literally, "mystery." **Angels:** these are the presiding spirits of the seven churches. Angels were thought to be in charge of the physical world (cf 7, 1; 14, 18; 16, 5) and of nations (Dn 10, 13; 12, 1), communities (the seven churches), and individuals (Mt 18, 10; Acts 12, 15). Some have seen in the "angel" of each of the seven churches its pastor or a personification of the spirit of the congregation.

2, 1—3, 22: Each of the seven letters follows the same pattern: address; description of the exalted Christ; blame and/or praise for the church addressed; threat and/or admonition; final exhortation and promise to all Christians.

2, 1–7: The letter to Ephesus praises the members of the church there for their works and virtues, including discerning false teachers (2–3), but admonishes them to repent and return to their former devotion (4–5). It concludes with a reference to the Nicolaitans (see the note on 6) and a promise that the victor will have access to eternal life (7).

2, 1: Ephesus: this great ancient city had a population of ca. 250,000; it was the capital of the Roman province of Asia and the commercial, cultural, and religious center of Asia. The other six churches were located in the same province, situated roughly in a circle; they were selected for geographical reasons rather than for the size of their Christian communities. **Walks in the midst of the seven gold lampstands:** this signifies that Christ is always present in the church; see the note on 1, 4.

h Dn 7, 13; 10, 5. i Heb 4, 12. j Dn 8, 18 / 1, 8.

gold lampstands says this: 2*"I know your
works, your labor, and your endurance, and that
you cannot tolerate the wicked; you have tested
those who call themselves apostles but are not,
and discovered that they are impostors. 3More-
over, you have endurance and have suffered for
my name, and you have not grown weary. 4Yet I
hold this against you: you have lost the love you
had at first. 5Realize how far you have fallen.
Repent, and do the works you did at first.
Otherwise, I will come to you and remove your
lampstand from its place, unless you repent.
6*But you have this in your favor: you hate the
works of the Nicolaitans, which I also hate.

7 k*" ' "Whoever has ears ought to hear what
the Spirit says to the churches. To the victor I
will give the right to eat from the tree of life that
is in the garden of God." '

To Smyrna 8*"To the angel of the church in
Smyrna, write this:

" 'The first and the last, who once died but
came to life, says this: 9 l*"I know your tribula-
tion and poverty, but you are rich. I know the
slander of those who claim to be Jews and are
not, but rather are members of the assembly of
Satan. 10Do not be afraid of anything that you
are going to suffer. Indeed, the devil will throw
some of you into prison, that you may be tested,
and you will face an ordeal for ten days. Remain
faithful until death, and I will give you the
crown of life.

11 m*" ' "Whoever has ears ought to hear
what the Spirit says to the churches. The victor
shall not be harmed by the second death." '

To Pergamum 12*"To the angel of the church
in Pergamum, write this:

" 'The one with the sharp two-edged sword
says this: 13*"I know that you live where Satan's
throne is, and yet you hold fast to my name and
have not denied your faith in me, not even in the
days of Antipas, my faithful witness, who was
martyred among you, where Satan lives. 14 n*Yet
I have a few things against you. You have some
people there who hold to the teaching of Ba-
laam, who instructed Balak to put a stumbling
block before the Israelites: to eat food sacrificed
to idols and to play the harlot. 15Likewise, you
also have some people who hold to the teaching
of [the] Nicolaitans. 16Therefore, repent. Other-
wise, I will come to you quickly and wage war
against them with the sword of my mouth.

17 o*" ' "Whoever has ears ought to hear what
the Spirit says to the churches. To the victor I
shall give some of the hidden manna; I shall also

2, 2: Who call themselves . . . impostors: this refers to unauthorized and perverse missionaries; cf Acts 20, 29–30.

2, 6: Nicolaitans: these are perhaps the impostors of v 2; see the note on vv 14–15. There is little evidence for connecting this group with Nicolaus, the proselyte from Antioch, mentioned in Acts 6, 5.

2, 7: Victor: referring to any Christian individual who holds fast to the faith and does God's will in the face of persecution. **The tree of life that is in the garden of God:** this is a reference to the tree in the primeval paradise (Gn 2, 9); cf 22, 2.14.19. The decree excluding humanity from the tree of life has been revoked by Christ.

2, 8–11: The letter to Smyrna encourages the Christians in this important commercial center by telling them that although they are impoverished, they are nevertheless rich, and calls those Jews who are slandering them members of the assembly of Satan (9). There is no admonition; rather, the Christians are told that they will suffer much, even death, but the time of tribulation will be short compared to their eternal reward (10), and they will thus escape final damnation (11).

2, 8: Smyrna: modern Izmir, ca. thirty miles north of Ephesus, and the chief city of Lydia, with a temple to the goddess Roma. It was renowned for its loyalty to Rome, and it also had a large Jewish community very hostile toward Christians.

2, 9–10: The church in Smyrna was materially poor but spiritually rich. Accusations made by Jewish brethren there occasioned the persecution of Christians; cf Acts 14, 2.19; 17, 5.13.

2, 11: The second death: this refers to the eternal death, when sinners will receive their final punishment; cf 20, 6.14–15; 21, 8.

2, 12–17: The letter to Pergamum praises the members of the church for persevering in their faith in Christ even in the midst of a pagan setting and in face of persecution and martyrdom (13). But it admonishes them about members who advocate an unprincipled morality (14; cf 2 Pt 2, 15; Jude 11) and others who follow the teaching of the Nicolaitans (15; see the note there). It urges them to repent (16) and promises them the hidden manna and Christ's amulet (17).

2, 12: Pergamum: modern Bergama, ca. forty-five miles northeast of Smyrna, a center for various kinds of pagan worship. It also had an outstanding library (the word **parchment** is derived from its name).

2, 13: Satan's throne: the reference is to emperor worship and other pagan practices that flourished in Pergamum, perhaps specifically to the white marble altar erected and dedicated to Zeus by Eumenes II (197–160 B.C.).

2, 14–15: Like Balaam, the biblical prototype of the religious compromiser (cf Nm 25, 1–3; 31, 16; 2 Pt 2, 15; Jude 11), the Nicolaitans in Pergamum and Ephesus (6) accommodated their Christian faith to paganism. They abused the principle of liberty enunciated by Paul (1 Cor 9, 19–23).

2, 17: The hidden manna: this is the food of life; cf Ps 78, 24–25. **White amulet:** literally, "white stone," on which was written a magical name, whose power could be tapped by one who knew the secret name. It is used here as a symbol of victory and joy; cf 3, 4–5. **New name:** this is a reference to the Christian's rebirth in Christ; cf 3, 12; 19, 12; Is 62, 2; 65, 15.

k 11.17.29; 3, 6.13.22; 13, 9; Mt 11, 15. l Jas 2, 5. m 20, 6.14; 21, 8. n Nm 22–24; 25, 1–3; 31, 16; 2 Pt 2, 15; Jude 11. o Is 62, 2; 65, 15.

give a white amulet upon which is inscribed a
new name, which no one knows except the one
who receives it." '

To Thyatira 18*"To the angel of the church in
Thyatira, write this:

" 'The Son of God, whose eyes are like a fiery
flame and whose feet are like polished brass, says
this: 19"I know your works, your love, faith,
service, and endurance, and that your last works
are greater than the first. 20*Yet I hold this
against you, that you tolerate the woman Jeze-
bel, who calls herself a prophetess, who teaches
and misleads my servants to play the harlot and
to eat food sacrificed to idols. 21I have given her
time to repent, but she refuses to repent of her
harlotry. 22So I will cast her on a sickbed and
plunge those who commit adultery with her into
intense suffering unless they repent of her
works. 23 p*I will also put her children to death.
Thus shall all the churches come to know that I
am the searcher of hearts and minds and that I
will give each of you what your works deserve.
24*But I say to the rest of you in Thyatira, who
do not uphold this teaching and know nothing of
the so-called deep secrets of Satan: on you I will
place no further burden, 25except that you must
hold fast to what you have until I come.

26 q*" ' "To the victor, who keeps to my ways
until the end,
I will give authority over the nations.
27 He will rule them with an iron rod.
Like clay vessels will they be smashed,

28just as I received authority from my Father.
And to him I will give the morning star.

29" ' "Whoever has ears ought to hear what
the Spirit says to the churches." '

CHAPTER 3

To Sardis 1*"To the angel of the church in
Sardis, write this:

" 'The one who has the seven spirits of God
and the seven stars says this: "I know your
works, that you have the reputation of being
alive, but you are dead. 2Be watchful and
strengthen what is left, which is going to die, for
I have not found your works complete in the
sight of my God. 3 rRemember then how you
accepted and heard; keep it, and repent. If you
are not watchful, I will come like a thief, and
you will never know at what hour I will come
upon you. 4 sHowever, you have a few people in
Sardis who have not soiled their garments; they
will walk with me dressed in white, because
they are worthy.

5 t*" ' "The victor will thus be dressed in
white, and I will never erase his name from the
book of life but will acknowledge his name in
the presence of my Father and of his angels.

6" ' "Whoever has ears ought to hear what
the Spirit says to the churches." '

2, 18–29: The letter to Thyatira praises the progress in virtue of this small Christian community (19) but admonishes them for tolerating a false prophet who leads them astray (20). Her fate is sealed, but there is hope of repentance for her followers (21–22). Otherwise, they too shall die (23). They are warned against Satanic power or knowledge (24–25). Those who remain faithful will share in the messianic reign, having authority over nations (26–27), and will in fact possess Christ himself (28).

2, 18: Thyatira: modern Akhisar, ca. forty miles southeast of Pergamum, a frontier town famous for its workers' guilds (cf Acts 16, 14), membership in which may have involved festal meals in pagan temples.

2, 20: The scheming and treacherous Jezebel of old (cf 1 Kgs 19, 1–2; 21, 1–14; 2 Kgs 9, 22.30–34) introduced pagan customs into the religion of Israel; this new Jezebel was doing the same to Christianity.

2, 23: Children: spiritual descendants.

2, 24: The so-called deep secrets of Satan: literally, "the deep things of Satan," a scathing reference to the perverse teaching of the Nicolaitans (15).

2, 26–28: The Christian who perseveres in faith will share in Christ's messianic authority (cf Ps 2, 8–9) and resurrection victory over death, symbolized by the morning star; cf 22, 16.

2, 26: Who keeps to my ways: literally, "who keeps my works."

3, 1–6: The letter to Sardis does not praise the community but admonishes its members to watchfulness, mutual support, and repentance (2–3). The few who have remained pure and faithful will share Christ's victory and will be inscribed in the book of life (4–5).

3, 1: Sardis: this city, located ca. thirty miles southeast of Thyatira, was once the capital of Lydia, known for its wealth at the time of Croesus (6th century B.C.). Its citadel, reputed to be unassailable, was captured by surprise, first by Cyrus and later by Antiochus. The church is therefore warned to be on guard.

3, 5: In white: white is a sign of victory and joy as well as resurrection; see the note on 2, 17. **The book of life:** the roll in which the names of the redeemed are kept; cf 13, 8; 17, 8; 20, 12.15; 21, 27; Phil 4, 3; Dn 12, 1. They will be acknowledged by Christ in heaven; cf Mt 10, 32.

p 1 Sm 16, 7; Jer 11, 20; 17, 10. q 12, 5; Ps 2, 8–9. r Mt 24, 42–44; Mk 13, 33; 1 Thes 5, 2; 2 Pt 3, 10. s 7, 13–14. t Ps 69, 29; Dn 12, 1 / Mt 10, 32.

To Philadelphia [7][u]*"To the angel of the
church in Philadelphia, write this:

" 'The holy one, the true,
who holds the key of David,
who opens and no one shall close,
who closes and no one shall open,

says this:
[8]*" ' "I know your works (behold, I have left
an open door before you, which no one can
close). You have limited strength, and yet you
have kept my word and have not denied my
name. [9][v]Behold, I will make those of the assem-
bly of Satan who claim to be Jews and are not,
but are lying, behold I will make them come and
fall prostrate at your feet, and they will realize
that I love you. [10]*Because you have kept my
message of endurance, I will keep you safe in the
time of trial that is going to come to the whole
world to test the inhabitants of the earth. [11][w]I
am coming quickly. Hold fast to what you have,
so that no one may take your crown.
[12][x]*" ' "The victor I will make into a pillar in
the temple of my God, and he will never leave it
again. On him I will inscribe the name of my
God and the name of the city of my God, the
new Jerusalem, which comes down out of
heaven from my God, as well as my new name.
[13]" ' "Whoever has ears ought to hear what
the Spirit says to the churches." '
To Laodicea [14][y]*"To the angel of the church
in Laodicea, write this:
" 'The Amen, the faithful and true witness,
the source of God's creation, says this: [15]*"I
know your works; I know that you are neither
cold nor hot. I wish you were either cold or hot.
[16]*So, because you are lukewarm, neither hot
nor cold, I will spit you out of my mouth.
[17][z]*For you say, 'I am rich and affluent and have
no need of anything,' and yet do not realize that
you are wretched, pitiable, poor, blind, and
naked. [18]*I advise you to buy from me gold
refined by fire so that you may be rich, and
white garments to put on so that your shameful
nakedness may not be exposed, and buy oint-
ment to smear on your eyes so that you may see.
[19][a]Those whom I love, I reprove and chastise.
Be earnest, therefore, and repent.
[20]*" ' "Behold, I stand at the door and knock.
If anyone hears my voice and opens the door,
[then] I will enter his house and dine with him,
and he with me. [21][b]I will give the victor the

3, 7–13: The letter to Philadelphia praises the Christians there for remaining faithful even with their limited strength (8). Members of the assembly of Satan are again singled out (9; see 2, 9 above). There is no admonition; rather, the letter promises that they will be kept safe at the great trial (10–11) and that the victors will become pillars of the heavenly temple, upon which three names will be inscribed: God, Jerusalem, and Christ (12).

3, 7: Philadelphia: modern Alasehir, ca. thirty miles southeast of Sardis, founded by Attalus II Philadelphus of Pergamum to be an "open door" (8) for Greek culture; it was destroyed by an earthquake in A.D. 17. Rebuilt by money from the Emperor Tiberius, the city was renamed Neo-Caesarea; this may explain the allusions to "name" in v 12. **Key of David:** to the heavenly city of David (cf Is 22, 22), "the new Jerusalem" (12), over which Christ has supreme authority.

3, 8: An open door: opportunities for sharing and proclaiming the faith; cf Acts 14, 27; 1 Cor 16, 9; 2 Cor 2, 12.

3, 10: My message of endurance: this does not refer to a saying of Jesus about patience but to the example of Christ's patient endurance. **The inhabitants of the earth:** literally, "those who live on the earth." This expression, which also occurs in 6, 10; 8, 13; 11, 10; 13, 8.12.14; 17, 2.8, always refers to the pagan world.

3, 12: Pillar: this may be an allusion to the rebuilding of the city; see the note on v 7. **New Jerusalem:** it is described in 21, 10—22, 5.

3, 14–22: The letter to Laodicea reprimands the community for being lukewarm (15–16), but no particular faults are singled out. Their material prosperity is contrasted with their spiritual poverty, the violet tunics that were the source of their wealth with the white robe of baptism, and their famous eye ointment with true spiritual perception (17–18). But Christ's chastisement is inspired by love and a desire to be allowed to share the messianic banquet with his followers in the heavenly kingdom (19–21).

3, 14: Laodicea: ca. forty miles southeast of Philadelphia and ca. eighty miles east of Ephesus, a wealthy industrial and commercial center, with a renowned medical school. It exported fine woolen garments and was famous for its eye salves. It was so wealthy that it was proudly rebuilt without outside aid after the devastating earthquake of A.D. 60/61. **The Amen:** this is a divine title (cf Hebrew text of Is 65, 16) applied to Christ; cf 2 Cor 1, 20. **Source of God's creation:** literally, "the beginning of God's creation," a concept found also in Jn 1, 3; Col 1, 16–17, Heb 1, 2; cf Prv 8, 22–31; Wis 9, 1–2.

3, 15–16: Halfhearted commitment to the faith is nauseating to Christ; cf Rom 12, 11.

3, 16: Spit: literally, "vomit." The image is that of a beverage that should be either hot or cold. Perhaps there is an allusion to the hot springs of Hierapolis across the Lycus river from Laodicea, which would have been lukewarm by the time they reached Laodicea.

3, 17: Economic prosperity occasioned spiritual bankruptcy.

3, 18: Gold . . . fire: God's grace. **White garments:** symbol of an upright life; the city was noted for its violet/purple cloth. **Ointment . . . eyes:** to remove spiritual blindness; one of the city's exports was eye ointment (see the note on 3, 14).

3, 20: Christ invites all to the messianic banquet in heaven; cf Is 25, 6; Lk 14, 15; 22, 30.

u Is 22, 22; Mt 16, 19. v 2, 9 / Is 45, 14; 60, 14. w 2, 25; 22, 7.20. x 21, 2–3; Ez 48, 35 / 19, 13. y 1, 5. z Prv 13, 7; Lk 12, 21. a Prv 3, 11–12; 1 Cor 11, 32; Heb 12, 5–11. b Lk 22, 28–30; Mt 19, 28.

right to sit with me on my throne, as I myself
first won the victory and sit with my Father on
his throne.

22" ' "Whoever has ears ought to hear what
the Spirit says to the churches." ' "

III: God and the Lamb in Heaven

CHAPTER 4

Vision of Heavenly Worship 1*After this I
had a vision of an open door to heaven, and I
heard the trumpetlike voice that had spoken to
me before, saying, "Come up here and I will
show you what must happen afterwards." 2[c]*At
once I was caught up in spirit. A throne was
there in heaven, and on the throne sat 3one
whose appearance sparkled like jasper and car-
nelian. Around the throne was a halo as brilliant
as an emerald. 4[d]*Surrounding the throne I saw
twenty-four other thrones on which twenty-four
elders sat, dressed in white garments and with
gold crowns on their heads. 5*From the throne
came flashes of lightning, rumblings, and peals of
thunder. Seven flaming torches burned in front
of the throne, which are the seven spirits of God.
6[e]*In front of the throne was something that
resembled a sea of glass like crystal.

In the center and around the throne, there
were four living creatures covered with eyes in
front and in back. 7*The first creature resembled
a lion, the second was like a calf, the third had a
face like that of a human being, and the fourth
looked like an eagle in flight. 8[f]*The four living
creatures, each of them with six wings, were
covered with eyes inside and out. Day and night
they do not stop exclaiming:

"Holy, holy, holy is the Lord God almighty,
who was, and who is, and who is to come."

9Whenever the living creatures give glory and
honor and thanks to the one who sits on the
throne, who lives forever and ever, 10the twenty-
four elders fall down before the one who sits on
the throne and worship him, who lives forever
and ever. They throw down their crowns before
the throne, exclaiming:

11[g]"Worthy are you, Lord our God,
to receive glory and honor and power,
for you created all things;
because of your will they came to be and
were created."

CHAPTER 5

The Scroll and the Lamb 1[h]*I saw a scroll in
the right hand of the one who sat on the throne.
It had writing on both sides and was sealed with
seven seals. 2Then I saw a mighty angel who
proclaimed in a loud voice, "Who is worthy to
open the scroll and break its seals?" 3But no one
in heaven or on earth or under the earth was
able to open the scroll or to examine it. 4I shed
many tears because no one was found worthy to

4, 1–11: The seer now describes a vision of the heavenly court in worship of God enthroned. He reverently avoids naming or describing God but pictures twenty-four elders in priestly and regal attire (4) and God's throne and its surroundings made of precious gems and other symbols that traditionally express the majesty of God (5–6). Universal creation is represented by the four living creatures (6–7). Along with the twenty-four elders, they praise God unceasingly in humble adoration (8–11).

4, 1: The ancients viewed heaven as a solid vault, entered by way of actual doors.

4, 2–8: Much of the imagery here is taken from Ez 1 and 10.

4, 4: **Twenty-four elders:** these represent the twelve tribes of Israel and the twelve apostles; cf 21, 12–14.

4, 5: **Flashes of lightning, rumblings, and peals of thunder:** as in other descriptions of God's appearance or activity; cf 8, 5; 11, 19; 16, 18; Ex 19, 16; Ez 1, 4.13. **The seven spirits of God:** the seven "angels of the presence" as in 8, 2 and Tb 12, 15.

4, 6: **A sea of glass like crystal:** an image adapted from Ez 1, 22–26. **Four living creatures:** these are symbols taken from Ez 1, 5–21; they are identified as cherubim in Ez 10, 20. **Covered with eyes:** these suggest God's knowledge and concern.

4, 7: **Lion . . . calf . . . human being . . . eagle:** these symbolize, respectively, what is noblest, strongest, wisest, and swiftest in creation. **Calf:** traditionally translated "ox," the Greek word refers to a heifer or young bull. Since the second century, these four creatures have been used as symbols of the evangelists Mark, Luke, Matthew, and John, respectively.

4, 8: **Six wings:** like the seraphim of Is 6, 2.

5, 1–14: The seer now describes a papyrus roll in God's right hand (1) with seven seals indicating the importance of the message. A mighty angel asks who is worthy to open the scroll, i.e., who can accomplish God's salvific plan (2). There is despair at first when no one in creation can do it (3–4). But the seer is comforted by an elder who tells him that Christ, called the lion of the tribe of Judah, has won the right to open it (5). Christ then appears as a Lamb, coming to receive the scroll from God (6–7), for which he is acclaimed as at a coronation (8–10). This is followed by a doxology of the angels (11–12) and then finally by the heavenly church united with all of creation (13–14).

5, 1: **A scroll:** a papyrus roll possibly containing a list of afflictions for sinners (cf Ez 2, 9–10) or God's plan for the world. **Sealed with seven seals:** it is totally hidden from all but God. Only the Lamb (7–9) has the right to carry out the divine plan.

c Is 6, 1 / Ez 1, 26–28. d Is 24, 23. e Ex 24, 10. f Is 6, 2–3 / 1, 4.8; 11, 17; 16, 5. g Rom 4, 17; 16, 27. h Is 29, 11.

open the scroll or to examine it. 5 [i]*One of the
elders said to me, "Do not weep. The lion of the
tribe of Judah, the root of David, has triumphed,
enabling him to open the scroll with its seven
seals."

6 [j]*Then I saw standing in the midst of the
throne and the four living creatures and the
elders a Lamb that seemed to have been slain.
He had seven horns and seven eyes; these are
the [seven] spirits of God sent out into the whole
world. 7 He came and received the scroll from
the right hand of the one who sat on the throne.
8 When he took it, the four living creatures and
the twenty-four elders fell down before the
Lamb. Each of the elders held a harp and gold
bowls filled with incense, which are the prayers
of the holy ones. 9 They sang a new hymn:

"Worthy are you to receive the scroll
and to break open its seals,
for you were slain and with your blood you
purchased for God
those from every tribe and tongue, people
and nation.
10 [k]You made them a kingdom and priests for our
God,
and they will reign on earth."

11 [l]*I looked again and heard the voices of many
angels who surrounded the throne and the living
creatures and the elders. They were countless in
number, 12 and they cried out in a loud voice:

"Worthy is the Lamb that was slain
to receive power and riches, wisdom and
strength,
honor and glory and blessing."

13 Then I heard every creature in heaven and on
earth and under the earth and in the sea,
everything in the universe, cry out:

"To the one who sits on the throne and to the
Lamb
be blessing and honor, glory and might,
forever and ever."

14 The four living creatures answered, "Amen,"
and the elders fell down and worshiped.

IV: The Seven Seals, Trumpets, and Plagues, with Interludes

CHAPTER 6

The First Six Seals 1 *Then I watched while
the Lamb broke open the first of the seven seals,
and I heard one of the four living creatures cry
out in a voice like thunder, "Come forward."
2 [m]*I looked, and there was a white horse, and
its rider had a bow. He was given a crown, and
he rode forth victorious to further his victories.
3 When he broke open the second seal, I heard
the second living creature cry out, "Come for-
ward." 4 [n]*Another horse came out, a red one.
Its rider was given power to take peace away

5, 5: The lion of the tribe of Judah, the root of David: these are the messianic titles applied to Christ to symbolize his victory; cf 22, 16; Gn 49, 9; Is 11, 1.10; Mt 1, 1.

5, 6: Christ is the Paschal Lamb without blemish, whose blood saved the new Israel from sin and death; cf Ex 12; Is 53, 7; Jn 1, 29.36; Acts 8, 32; 1 Pt 1, 18–19. This is the main title for Christ in Rv, used twenty-eight times. **Seven horns and seven eyes:** Christ has the fullness (see the note on 1, 4) of power (horns) and knowledge (eyes); cf Zec 4, 10. **[Seven] spirits:** as in 1, 4; 3, 1; and 4, 5.

5, 11: Countless: literally, "100,000,000 plus 1,000,000," used by the author to express infinity.

6, 1—16, 21: A series of seven disasters now begins as each seal is broken (6, 1—8, 1), followed by a similar series as seven trumpets sound (8, 2—11, 19) and as seven angels pour bowls on the earth causing plagues (15, 1—16, 21). These gloomy sequences are interrupted by longer or shorter scenes suggesting the triumph of God and his witnesses (e.g., chs 7, 10, 11, 12, 13, 14).

6, 1–17: This chapter provides a symbolic description of the contents of the sealed scroll. The breaking of the first four seals reveals four riders. The first rider (of a white horse) is a conquering power (1–2), the second (red horse) a symbol of bloody war (3–4), the third (black horse) a symbol of famine (5–6), the fourth (pale green horse) a symbol of Death himself, accompanied by Hades (the netherworld) as his page (7–8). Verse 8b summarizes the role of all four riders. The breaking of the fifth seal reveals Christian martyrs in an attitude of sacrifice as blood poured out at the foot of an altar begging God for vindication, which will come only when their quota is filled; but they are given a white robe symbolic of victory (9–11). The breaking of the sixth seal reveals typical apocalyptic signs in the sky and the sheer terror of all people at the imminent divine judgment (12–17).

6, 1–8: The imagery is adapted from Zec 1, 8–10; 6, 1–8.

6, 2: White horse . . . bow: this may perhaps allude specifically to the Parthians on the eastern border of the Roman empire. Expert in the use of the bow, they constantly harassed the Romans and won a major victory in A.D. 62; see the note on 9, 13–21. But the Old Testament imagery typifies the history of oppression of God's people at all times.

6, 4: Huge sword: this is a symbol of war and violence; cf Ez 21, 14–17.

i Is 11, 1.10; Rom 15, 12. j Jn 1, 29. k 1, 6; Ex 19, 6; Is 61, 6. l Dn 7, 10; Jude 14–15. m Zec 1, 8–10; 6, 1–3. n Ez 21, 14–16.

from the earth, so that people would slaughter
one another. And he was given a huge sword.
5 *When he broke open the third seal, I heard
the third living creature cry out, "Come for-
ward." I looked, and there was a black horse,
and its rider held a scale in his hand. 6 [o]*I heard
what seemed to be a voice in the midst of the
four living creatures. It said, "A ration of wheat
costs a day's pay, and three rations of barley cost
a day's pay. But do not damage the olive oil or
the wine."
7 When he broke open the fourth seal, I heard
the voice of the fourth living creature cry out,
"Come forward." 8 [p]*I looked, and there was a
pale green horse. Its rider was named Death, and
Hades accompanied him. They were given au-
thority over a quarter of the earth, to kill with
sword, famine, and plague, and by means of the
beasts of the earth.
9 *When he broke open the fifth seal, I saw
underneath the altar the souls of those who had
been slaughtered because of the witness they
bore to the word of God. 10 *They cried out in a
loud voice, "How long will it be, holy and true
master, before you sit in judgment and avenge
our blood on the inhabitants of the earth?"
11 Each of them was given a white robe, and they
were told to be patient a little while longer until
the number was filled of their fellow servants
and brothers who were going to be killed as they
had been.
12 [q]*Then I watched while he broke open the
sixth seal, and there was a great earthquake; the
sun turned as black as dark sackcloth and the
whole moon became like blood. 13 *The stars in
the sky fell to the earth like unripe figs shaken
loose from the tree in a strong wind. 14 [r]*Then
the sky was divided like a torn scroll curling up,
and every mountain and island was moved from
its place. 15 *The kings of the earth, the nobles,
the military officers, the rich, the powerful, and
every slave and free person hid themselves in
caves and among mountain crags. 16 [s]They cried
out to the mountains and the rocks, "Fall on us
and hide us from the face of the one who sits on
the throne and from the wrath of the Lamb,
17 *because the great day of their wrath has
come and who can withstand it?"

CHAPTER 7

The 144,000 Sealed 1 [t]*After this I saw four
angels standing at the four corners of the earth,
holding back the four winds of the earth so that
no wind could blow on land or sea or against any
tree. 2 *Then I saw another angel come up from

6, 5: Black horse: this is a symbol of famine, the usual accompaniment of war in antiquity; cf Lv 26, 26; Ez 4, 16–17. The **scale** is a symbol of shortage of food with a corresponding rise in price.

6, 6: A day's pay: literally, "a denarius," a Roman silver coin that constitutes a day's wage in Mt 20, 2. Because of the famine, food was rationed and sold at an exorbitant price. A liter of flour was considered a day's ration in the Greek historians Herodotus and Diogenes Laertius. **Barley:** food of the poor (Jn 6, 9.13; cf 2 Kgs 7, 1.16.18); it was also used to feed animals; cf 1 Kgs 5, 8. **Do not damage:** the olive and the vine are to be used more sparingly in time of famine.

6, 8: Pale green: symbol of death and decay; cf Ez 14, 21.

6, 9: The altar: this altar corresponds to the altar of holocausts in the temple in Jerusalem; see also 11, 1. **Because of the witness . . . word of God:** literally, "because of the word of God and the witness they had borne."

6, 10: Holy and true master: Old Testament usage as well as the context indicates that this is addressed to God rather than to Christ.

6, 12–14: Symbolic rather than literal description of the cosmic upheavals attending the day of the Lord when the martyrs' prayer for vindication (10) would be answered; cf Am 8, 8–9; Is 34, 4; 50, 3; Jl 2, 10; 3, 3–4; Mt 24, 4–36; Mk 13, 5–37; Lk 21, 8–36.

6, 12: Dark sackcloth: for mourning, sackcloth was made from the skin of a black goat.

6, 13: Unripe figs: literally, "summer (or winter) fruit."

6, 14: Was divided: literally, "was split," like a broken papyrus roll torn in two, each half then curling up to form a roll on either side.

6, 15: Nobles: literally, "courtiers," "grandees." **Military officers:** literally, "commanders of 1,000 men," used in Josephus and other Greek authors as the equivalent of the Roman **tribunus militum.** The listing of various ranks of society represents the universality of terror at the impending doom.

6, 17: Their: this reading is attested in the best manuscripts, but the vast majority read "his" in reference to the wrath of the Lamb in the preceding verse.

7, 1–17: An interlude of two visions precedes the breaking of the seventh seal, just as two more will separate the sixth and seventh trumpets (ch 10). In the first vision (1–8), the elect receive the seal of the living God as protection against the coming cataclysm; cf 14, 1; Ez 9, 4–6; 2 Cor 1, 22; Eph 1, 13; 4, 30. The second vision (9–17) portrays the faithful Christians before God's throne to encourage those on earth to persevere to the end, even to death.

7, 1: The four corners of the earth: the earth is seen as a table or rectangular surface.

7, 2: East: literally, "rising of the sun." The east was considered the source of light and the place of paradise (Gn 2, 8). **Seal:** whatever was marked by the impression of one's signet ring belonged to that person and was under his protection.

o Lv 26, 26; Ez 4, 16–17. p Ez 14, 21. q Jl 3, 4; Mt 24, 29. r Is 34, 4 / 16, 20. s Is 2, 19; Hos 10, 8; Lk 23, 30. t Jer 49, 36; Zec 6, 5.

the East, holding the seal of the living God. He
cried out in a loud voice to the four angels who
were given power to damage the land and the
sea, 3 [u]*“Do not damage the land or the sea or the
trees until we put the seal on the foreheads of
the servants of our God.” 4 [v]*I heard the number
of those who had been marked with the seal,
one hundred and forty-four thousand marked
from every tribe of the Israelites: 5 *twelve
thousand were marked from the tribe of Judah,
twelve thousand from the tribe of Reuben,
twelve thousand from the tribe of Gad, 6 twelve
thousand from the tribe of Asher, twelve thou-
sand from the tribe of Naphtali, twelve thousand
from the tribe of Manasseh, 7 twelve thousand
from the tribe of Simeon, twelve thousand from
the tribe of Levi, twelve thousand from the tribe
of Issachar, 8 twelve thousand from the tribe of
Zebulun, twelve thousand from the tribe of
Joseph, and twelve thousand were marked from
the tribe of Benjamin.

Triumph of the Elect 9 *After this I had a
vision of a great multitude, which no one could
count, from every nation, race, people, and
tongue. They stood before the throne and before
the Lamb, wearing white robes and holding
palm branches in their hands. 10 *They cried out
in a loud voice:

“Salvation comes from our God, who is seated
on the throne,
and from the Lamb.”

11 All the angels stood around the throne and
around the elders and the four living creatures.
They prostrated themselves before the throne,
worshiped God, 12 and exclaimed:

“Amen. Blessing and glory, wisdom and
thanksgiving,
honor, power, and might
be to our God forever and ever. Amen.”

13 Then one of the elders spoke up and said to
me, “Who are these wearing white robes, and
where did they come from?” 14 [w]*I said to him,
“My lord, you are the one who knows.” He said
to me, “These are the ones who have survived
the time of great distress; they have washed
their robes and made them white in the blood of
the Lamb.

15 “For this reason they stand before God’s
throne
and worship him day and night in his
temple.
The one who sits on the throne will shelter
them.
16 [x]They will not hunger or thirst anymore,
nor will the sun or any heat strike them.
17 [y]*For the Lamb who is in the center of the
throne will shepherd them
and lead them to springs of life-giving water,
and God will wipe away every tear from
their eyes.”

CHAPTER 8

The Seven Trumpets 1 [z]*When he broke open
the seventh seal, there was silence in heaven for
about half an hour. 2 [a]And I saw that the seven

7, 4–9: One hundred and forty-four thousand: the square of twelve (the number of Israel’s tribes) multiplied by a thousand, symbolic of the new Israel (cf 14, 1–5; Gal 6, 16; Jas 1, 1) that embraces people **from every nation, race, people, and tongue** (9).

7, 5–8: Judah is placed first because of Christ; cf “the Lion of the tribe of Judah” (5, 5). Dan is omitted because of a later tradition that the antichrist would arise from it.

7, 9: White robes . . . palm branches: symbols of joy and victory; see the note on 3, 5.

7, 10: Salvation comes from: literally, “(let) salvation (be ascribed) to.” A similar hymn of praise is found at the fall of the dragon (12, 10) and of Babylon (19, 1).

7, 14: Time of great distress: fierce persecution by the Romans; cf Introduction.

7, 17: Life-giving water: literally, “the water of life,” God’s grace, which flows from Christ; cf 21, 6; 22, 1.17; Jn 4, 10.14.

8, 1–13: The breaking of the seventh seal produces at first silence and then seven symbolic disasters, each announced by a trumpet blast, of which the first four form a unit as did the first four seals. A minor liturgy (3–5) is enclosed by a vision of seven angels (2.6). Then follow the first four trumpet blasts, each heralding catastrophes modeled on the plagues of Egypt affecting the traditional prophetic third (cf Ez 5, 12) of the earth, sea, fresh water, and stars (7–12). Finally, there is a vision of an eagle warning of the last three trumpet blasts (13).

8, 1: Silence in heaven: as in Zep 1, 7, a prelude to the eschatological woes that are to follow; cf Introduction.

u Ex 12, 7–14; Ez 9, 4; 2 Cor 1, 22; Eph 1, 13; 4, 30. v 14, 1. w Mt 24, 21. x Is 49, 10. y 21, 4; Is 25, 8. z Hb 2, 20; Zep 1, 7; Zec 2, 17. a 4, 5; Tb 12, 15.

angels who stood before God were given seven trumpets.

The Gold Censer 3 [b]*Another angel came and stood at the altar, holding a gold censer. He was given a great quantity of incense to offer, along with the prayers of all the holy ones, on the gold altar that was before the throne. 4 The smoke of the incense along with the prayers of the holy ones went up before God from the hand of the angel. 5 [c]Then the angel took the censer, filled it with burning coals from the altar, and hurled it down to the earth. There were peals of thunder, rumblings, flashes of lightning, and an earthquake.

The First Four Trumpets 6 [d]The seven angels who were holding the seven trumpets prepared to blow them.

7 *When the first one blew his trumpet, there came hail and fire mixed with blood, which was hurled down to the earth. A third of the land was burned up, along with a third of the trees and all green grass.

8 [e]*When the second angel blew his trumpet, something like a large burning mountain was hurled into the sea. A third of the sea turned to blood, 9 *a third of the creatures living in the sea died, and a third of the ships were wrecked.

10 [f]When the third angel blew his trumpet, a large star burning like a torch fell from the sky. It fell on a third of the rivers and on the springs of water. 11 [g]*The star was called "Wormwood," and a third of all the water turned to wormwood. Many people died from this water, because it was made bitter.

12 [h]When the fourth angel blew his trumpet, a third of the sun, a third of the moon, and a third of the stars were struck, so that a third of them became dark. The day lost its light for a third of the time, as did the night.

13 *Then I looked again and heard an eagle flying high overhead cry out in a loud voice, "Woe! Woe! Woe to the inhabitants of the earth from the rest of the trumpet blasts that the three angels are about to blow!"

CHAPTER 9

The Fifth Trumpet 1 [i]*Then the fifth angel blew his trumpet, and I saw a star that had fallen from the sky to the earth. It was given the key for the passage to the abyss. 2 [j]It opened the passage to the abyss, and smoke came up out of the passage like smoke from a huge furnace. The sun and the air were darkened by the smoke from the passage. 3 [k]*Locusts came out of the smoke onto the land, and they were given the same power as scorpions of the earth. 4 They were told not to harm the grass of the earth or any plant or any tree, but only those people who did not have the seal of God on their foreheads. 5 *They were not allowed to kill them but only to torment them for five months; the torment they inflicted was like that of a scorpion when it stings a person. 6 [l]During that time these people will seek death but will not find it, and they will long to die but death will escape them.

7 [m]*The appearance of the locusts was like that of horses ready for battle. On their heads

8, 3: Altar: there seems to be only one altar in the heavenly temple, corresponding to the altar of holocausts in 6, 9, and here to the altar of incense in Jerusalem; cf also 9, 13; 11, 1; 14, 18; 16, 7.

8, 7: This woe resembles the seventh plague of Egypt (Ex 9, 23–24); cf Jl 3, 3.

8, 8–11: The background of these two woes is the first plague of Egypt (Ex 7, 20–21).

8, 9: Creatures living in the sea: literally, "creatures in the sea that had souls."

8, 11: Wormwood: an extremely bitter and malignant plant symbolizing the punishment God inflicts on the ungodly; cf Jer 9, 12–14; 23, 15.

8, 13: Woe! Woe! Woe: each of the three woes pronounced by the angel represents a separate disaster; cf 9, 12; 11, 14. The final woe, released by the seventh trumpet blast, includes the plagues of ch 16.

9, 1–12: The fifth trumpet heralds a woe containing elements from the eighth and ninth plagues of Egypt (Ex 10, 12–15.21–23) but specifically reminiscent of the invasion of locusts in Jl 1, 4—2, 10.

9, 1: A star: late Judaism represented fallen powers as stars (Is 14, 12–15; Lk 10, 18; Jude 13), but a comparison with 1, 20 and 20, 1 suggests that here it means an angel. **The passage to the abyss:** referring to Sheol, the netherworld, where Satan and the fallen angels are kept for a thousand years, to be cast afterwards into the pool of fire; cf 20, 7–10. The abyss was conceived of as a vast subterranean cavern full of fire. Its only link with the earth was a kind of passage or mine shaft, which was kept locked.

9, 3: Scorpions: their poisonous sting was proverbial; Ez 2, 6; Lk 11, 12.

9, 5: For five months: more or less corresponding to the life-span of locusts.

9, 7–10: Eight characteristics are listed to show the eschatological and diabolical nature of these locusts.

b Ps 141, 2; Tb 12, 12. c Ez 10, 2; Ps 11, 6 / 4, 5; 11, 19; 16, 18. d 16, 1–21. e Ex 7, 20. f Is 14, 12. g Jer 9, 14. h Ex 10, 21–23. i 20, 1. j Gn 19, 28. k Ex 10, 12–15; Wis 16, 9. l Jb 3, 21. m Jl 2, 4.

they wore what looked like crowns of gold; their faces were like human faces, 8 [n]and they had hair like women's hair. Their teeth were like lions' teeth, 9and they had chests like iron breastplates. The sound of their wings was like the sound of many horse-drawn chariots racing into battle. 10They had tails like scorpions, with stingers; with their tails they had power to harm people for five months. 11*They had as their king the angel of the abyss, whose name in Hebrew is Abaddon and in Greek Apollyon.

12The first woe has passed, but there are two more to come.

The Sixth Trumpet 13 [o]*Then the sixth angel blew his trumpet, and I heard a voice coming from the [four] horns of the gold altar before God, 14*telling the sixth angel who held the trumpet, "Release the four angels who are bound at the banks of the great river Euphrates." 15So the four angels were released, who were prepared for this hour, day, month, and year to kill a third of the human race. 16The number of cavalry troops was two hundred million; I heard their number. 17 [p]*Now in my vision this is how I saw the horses and their riders. They wore red, blue, and yellow breastplates, and the horses' heads were like heads of lions, and out of their mouths came fire, smoke, and sulfur. 18By these three plagues of fire, smoke, and sulfur that came out of their mouths a third of the human race was killed. 19For the power of the horses is in their mouths and in their tails; for their tails are like snakes, with heads that inflict harm.

20 [q]*The rest of the human race, who were not killed by these plagues, did not repent of the works of their hands, to give up the worship of demons and idols made from gold, silver, bronze, stone, and wood, which cannot see or hear or walk. 21Nor did they repent of their murders, their magic potions, their unchastity, or their robberies.

CHAPTER 10

The Angel with the Small Scroll 1*Then I saw another mighty angel come down from heaven wrapped in a cloud, with a halo around his head; his face was like the sun and his feet were like pillars of fire. 2*In his hand he held a small scroll that had been opened. He placed his right foot on the sea and his left foot on the land, 3 [r]and then he cried out in a loud voice as a lion roars. When he cried out, the seven thunders raised their voices, too. 4When the seven thunders had spoken, I was about to write it down; but I heard a voice from heaven say, "Seal up what the seven thunders have spoken, but do not write it down." 5Then the angel I saw standing on the sea and on the land raised his right hand to heaven 6 [s]*and swore by the one who lives forever and ever, who created heaven and earth and sea and all that is in them, "There shall be no more delay. 7 [t]*At the time when you hear the seventh angel blow his trumpet, the mysterious plan of God shall be fulfilled, as he promised to his servants the prophets."

8Then the voice that I had heard from heaven

9, 11: Abaddon: Hebrew (more precisely, Aramaic) for destruction or ruin. **Apollyon:** Greek for the "Destroyer."

9, 13–21: The sixth trumpet heralds a woe representing another diabolical attack symbolized by an invasion by the Parthians living east of the Euphrates; see the note on 6, 2. At the appointed time (15), the frightful horses act as God's agents of judgment. The imaginative details are not to be taken literally; see Introduction and the note on 6, 12–14.

9, 13: [Four]: many Greek manuscripts and versions omit the word. The horns were situated at the four corners of the altar (Ex 27, 2; 30, 2–3); see the note on 8, 3.

9, 14–15: The four angels: they are symbolic of the destructive activity that will be extended throughout the universe.

9, 17: Blue: literally, "hyacinth-colored." **Yellow:** literally, "sulfurous."

9, 20: The works of their hands: i.e., the gods their hands had made.

10, 1—11, 14: An interlude in two scenes (10, 1–11 and 11, 1–14) precedes the sounding of the seventh trumpet; cf 7, 1–17. The first vision describes an angel astride sea and land like a colossus, with a small scroll open, the contents of which indicate that the end is imminent (ch 10). The second vision is of the measuring of the temple and of two witnesses, whose martyrdom means that the kingdom of God is about to be inaugurated.

10, 1–4: The seven thunders: God's voice announcing judgment and doom; cf Ps 29, 3–9, where thunder, as the voice of Yahweh, is praised seven times.

10, 2: He placed . . . on the land: this symbolizes the universality of the angel's message, as does the figure of the small scroll open to be read.

10, 6: Heaven and earth and sea: the three parts of the universe. **No more delay:** cf Dn 12, 7; Hb 2, 3.

10, 7: The mysterious plan of God: literally, "the mystery of God," the end of the present age when the forces of evil will be put down (17, 1—19, 4.11–21; 20, 7–10; cf 2 Thes 2, 6–12; Rom 16, 25–26), and the establishment of the reign of God when all creation will be made new (21, 1—22, 5).

n Jl 1, 6. o Ex 30, 1–3. p Jb 41, 10–13. q Ps 135, 15–17; Is 17, 8; Dn 5, 4. r Ps 29, 3–9; Jer 25, 30; Am 3, 8. s Dt 32, 40; Dn 12, 7 / Ez 12, 28. t Am 3, 7.

spoke to me again and said, "Go, take the scroll that lies open in the hand of the angel who is standing on the sea and on the land." 9 *So I went up to the angel and told him to give me the small scroll. He said to me, "Take and swallow it. It will turn your stomach sour, but in your mouth it will taste as sweet as honey." 10 [u]I took the small scroll from the angel's hand and swallowed it. In my mouth it was like sweet honey, but when I had eaten it, my stomach turned sour. 11 *Then someone said to me, "You must prophesy again about many peoples, nations, tongues, and kings."

CHAPTER 11

The Two Witnesses 1 [v]*Then I was given a measuring rod like a staff and I was told, "Come and measure the temple of God and the altar, and count those who are worshiping in it. 2 *But exclude the outer court of the temple; do not measure it, for it has been handed over to the Gentiles, who will trample the holy city for forty-two months. 3 *I will commission my two witnesses to prophesy for those twelve hundred and sixty days, wearing sackcloth." 4 [w]*These are the two olive trees and the two lampstands that stand before the Lord of the earth. 5 *If anyone wants to harm them, fire comes out of their mouths and devours their enemies. In this way, anyone wanting to harm them is sure to be slain. 6 [x]They have the power to close up the sky so that no rain can fall during the time of their prophesying. They also have power to turn water into blood and to afflict the earth with any plague as often as they wish.

7 [y]*When they have finished their testimony, the beast that comes up from the abyss will wage war against them and conquer them and kill them. 8 *Their corpses will lie in the main street of the great city, which has the symbolic names "Sodom" and "Egypt," where indeed their Lord was crucified. 9 *Those from every people, tribe, tongue, and nation will gaze on their corpses for three and a half days, and they will not allow their corpses to be buried. 10 The inhabitants of the earth will gloat over them and be glad and exchange gifts because these two prophets tormented the inhabitants of the earth. 11 [z]But after the three and a half days, a breath of life from God entered them. When they stood on their feet, great fear fell on those who saw them. 12 [a]Then they heard a loud voice from heaven say to them, "Come up here." So they went up to heaven in a cloud as their enemies looked on. 13 *At that moment there was a great earthquake, and a tenth of the city fell in ruins. Seven thousand people were killed during the earthquake; the rest were terrified and gave glory to the God of heaven.

10, 9–10: The small scroll was sweet because it predicted the final victory of God's people; it was sour because it also announced their sufferings. Cf Ez 3, 1–3.

10, 11: This further prophecy is contained in chs 12–22.

11, 1: The temple and altar symbolize the new Israel; see the note on 7, 4–9. The worshipers represent Christians. The measuring of the temple (cf Ez 40, 3—42, 20; 47, 1–12; Zec 2, 5–6) suggests that God will preserve the faithful remnant (cf Is 4, 2–3) who remain true to Christ (14, 1–5).

11, 2: The outer court: the Court of the Gentiles. **Trample . . . forty-two months:** the duration of the vicious persecution of the Jews by Antiochus IV Epiphanes (Dn 7, 25; 12, 7); this persecution of three and a half years (half of seven, counted as 1260 days in 3; 12, 6) became the prototype of periods of trial for God's people; cf Lk 4, 25; Jas 5, 17. The reference here is to the persecution by the Romans; cf Introduction.

11, 3: The two witnesses, wearing sackcloth symbolizing lamentation and repentance, cannot readily be identified. Do they represent Moses and Elijah, or the Law and the Prophets, or Peter and Paul? Most probably they refer to the universal church, especially the Christian martyrs, fulfilling the office of witness (two because of Dt 19, 15; cf Mk 6, 7; Jn 8, 17).

11, 4: The two olive trees and the two lampstands: the martyrs who stand in the presence of the Lord; the imagery is taken from Zec 4, 1–3.11–14, where the olive trees refer to Zerubbabel and Joshua.

11, 5–6: These details are derived from stories of Moses, who turned **water into blood** (Ex 7, 17–20), and of Elijah, who called down fire from heaven (1 Kgs 18, 36–40; 2 Kgs 1, 10) and closed up the sky for three years (1 Kgs 17, 1; cf 18, 1).

11, 7: The beast . . . from the abyss: the Roman emperor Nero, who symbolizes the forces of evil, or the antichrist (13, 1.8; 17, 8); cf Dn 7, 2–8.11–12.19–22 and Introduction.

11, 8: The great city: this expression is used constantly in Rv for Babylon, i.e., Rome; cf 14, 8; 16, 19; 17, 18; 18, 2.10.21. **"Sodom" and "Egypt":** symbols of immorality (cf Is 1, 10) and oppression of God's people (cf Ex 1, 11–14). **Where indeed their Lord was crucified:** not the geographical but the symbolic Jerusalem that rejects God and his witnesses, i.e., Rome, called Babylon in chs 16–18; see the note on 17, 9 and Introduction.

11, 9–12: Over the martyrdom (7) of the two witnesses, now called prophets, the ungodly rejoice **for three and a half days,** a symbolic period of time; see the note on v 2. Afterwards they go in triumph to heaven, as did Elijah (2 Kgs 2, 11).

11, 13: Seven thousand people: a symbolic sum to represent all social classes (seven) and large numbers (thousands); cf Introduction.

u Ez 3, 1–3. v Ez 40, 3–5 / Zec 2, 5–9. w Zec 4, 3.14. x Ex 7, 17. y Dn 7, 21. z Ez 37, 5.10. a 2 Kgs 2, 11.

14 The second woe has passed, but the third is
coming soon.
The Seventh Trumpet 15 *Then the seventh
angel blew his trumpet. There were loud voices
in heaven, saying, "The kingdom of the world
now belongs to our Lord and to his Anointed,
and he will reign forever and ever." 16 The
twenty-four elders who sat on their thrones
before God prostrated themselves and wor-
shiped God 17 and said:

"We give thanks to you, Lord God almighty,
who are and who were.
For you have assumed your great power
and have established your reign.
18 [b]The nations raged,
but your wrath has come,
and the time for the dead to be judged,
and to recompense your servants, the
prophets,
and the holy ones and those who fear your
name,
the small and the great alike,
and to destroy those who destroy the earth."

19 Then God's temple in heaven was opened, and
the ark of his covenant could be seen in the
temple. There were flashes of lightning, rum-
blings, and peals of thunder, an earthquake, and
a violent hailstorm.

CHAPTER 12

The Woman and the Dragon 1 [c]*A great sign
appeared in the sky, a woman clothed with the
sun, with the moon under her feet, and on her
head a crown of twelve stars. 2 *She was with
child and wailed aloud in pain as she labored to
give birth. 3 [d]*Then another sign appeared in the
sky; it was a huge red dragon, with seven heads
and ten horns, and on its heads were seven
diadems. 4 [e]Its tail swept away a third of the stars
in the sky and hurled them down to the earth.
Then the dragon stood before the woman about
to give birth, to devour her child when she gave
birth. 5 [f]*She gave birth to a son, a male child,
destined to rule all the nations with an iron rod.
Her child was caught up to God and his throne.
6 *The woman herself fled into the desert where
she had a place prepared by God, that there she
might be taken care of for twelve hundred and
sixty days.

7 *Then war broke out in heaven; Michael
and his angels battled against the dragon. The
dragon and its angels fought back, 8 but they did
not prevail and there was no longer any place for
them in heaven. 9 [g]*The huge dragon, the an-
cient serpent, who is called the Devil and Satan,
who deceived the whole world, was thrown
down to earth, and its angels were thrown down
with it.

11, 15–19: The seventh trumpet proclaims the coming of God's reign after the victory over diabolical powers; see the note on 10, 7.

12, 1—14, 20: This central section of Rv portrays the power of evil, represented by a dragon, in opposition to God and his people. First, the dragon pursues the woman about to give birth, but her son is saved and "caught up to God and his throne" (12, 5). Then Michael and his angels cast the dragon and his angels out of heaven (12, 7–9). After this, the dragon tries to attack the boy indirectly by attacking members of his church (12, 13–18). A beast, symbolizing the Roman empire, then becomes the dragon's agent, mortally wounded but restored to life and worshiped by all the world (13, 1–10). A second beast arises from the land, symbolizing the antichrist, which leads people astray by its prodigies to idolize the first beast (13, 11–18). This is followed by a vision of the Lamb and his faithful ones, and the proclamation of imminent judgment upon the world in terms of the wine of God's wrath (14, 1–20).

12, 1–6: The woman adorned with the sun, the moon, and the stars (images taken from Gn 37, 9–10) symbolizes God's people in the Old and the New Testament. The Israel of old gave birth to the Messiah (5) and then became the new Israel, the church, which suffers persecution by the dragon (6.13–17); cf Is 50, 1; 66, 7; Jer 50, 12. This corresponds to a widespread myth throughout the ancient world that a goddess pregnant with a savior was pursued by a horrible monster; by miraculous intervention, she bore a son who then killed the monster.

12, 2: Because of Eve's sin, the woman gives birth in distress and pain (Gn 3, 16; cf Is 66, 7–14).

12, 3: **Huge red dragon:** the Devil or Satan (cf 9; 20, 2), symbol of the forces of evil, a mythical monster known also as Leviathan (Ps 74, 13–14) or Rahab (Jb 26, 12–13; Ps 89, 11). **Seven diadems:** these are symbolic of the fullness of the dragon's sovereignty over the kingdoms of this world; cf Christ with many diadems (19, 12).

12, 5: **Rule . . . iron rod:** fulfilled in 19, 15; cf Ps 2, 9. **Was caught up to God:** reference to Christ's ascension.

12, 6: God protects the persecuted church in the desert, the traditional Old Testament place of refuge for the afflicted, according to the typology of the Exodus; see the note on 11, 2.

12, 7–12: Michael, mentioned only here in Rv, wins a victory over the dragon. A hymn of praise follows.

12, 7: **Michael:** the archangel, guardian and champion of Israel; cf Dn 10, 13.21; 12, 1; Jude 9. In Hebrew, the name Michael means "Who can compare with God?"; cf 13, 4.

12, 9: **The ancient serpent:** who seduced Eve (Gn 3, 1–6), mother of the human race; cf 20, 2; Eph 6, 11–12. **Was thrown down:** allusion to the expulsion of Satan from heaven; cf Lk 10, 18.

b Ps 2, 1.5 / Am 3, 7. c Gn 37, 9. d Dn 7, 7. e Dn 8, 10. f Is 66, 7 / Ps 2, 9. g Gn 3, 1–4 / Lk 10, 18.

10 *Then I heard a loud voice in heaven say:
"Now have salvation and power come,
and the kingdom of our God
and the authority of his Anointed.
For the accuser of our brothers is cast out,
who accuses them before our God day and night.
11 They conquered him by the blood of the Lamb
and by the word of their testimony;
love for life did not deter them from death.
12 Therefore, rejoice, you heavens,
and you who dwell in them.
But woe to you, earth and sea,
for the Devil has come down to you in great fury,
for he knows he has but a short time."
13 [h]When the dragon saw that it had been
thrown down to the earth, it pursued the
woman who had given birth to the male child.
14 [i]*But the woman was given the two wings of
the great eagle, so that she could fly to her place
in the desert, where, far from the serpent, she
was taken care of for a year, two years, and a
half-year. 15 *The serpent, however, spewed a
torrent of water out of his mouth after the
woman to sweep her away with the current.
16 But the earth helped the woman and opened
its mouth and swallowed the flood that the
dragon spewed out of its mouth. 17 [j]*Then the
dragon became angry with the woman and went
off to wage war against the rest of her offspring,
those who keep God's commandments and bear
witness to Jesus. 18 *It took its position on the
sand of the sea.

CHAPTER 13

The First Beast 1 [k]*Then I saw a beast come
out of the sea with ten horns and seven heads;
on its horns were ten diadems, and on its heads
blasphemous name[s]. 2 [l]*The beast I saw was
like a leopard, but it had feet like a bear's, and its
mouth was like the mouth of a lion. To it the
dragon gave its own power and throne, along
with great authority. 3 *I saw that one of its
heads seemed to have been mortally wounded,
but this mortal wound was healed. Fascinated,
the whole world followed after the beast.
4 *They worshiped the dragon because it gave its
authority to the beast; they also worshiped the
beast and said, "Who can compare with the
beast or who can fight against it?"
5 [m]*The beast was given a mouth uttering
proud boasts and blasphemies, and it was given
authority to act for forty-two months. 6 It opened
its mouth to utter blasphemies against God,
blaspheming his name and his dwelling and
those who dwell in heaven. 7 [n]It was also
allowed to wage war against the holy ones and
conquer them, and it was granted authority over
every tribe, people, tongue, and nation. 8 [o]All the
inhabitants of the earth will worship it, all whose
names were not written from the foundation of
the world in the book of life, which belongs to
the Lamb who was slain.

12, 10: The accuser: the meaning of the Hebrew word "Satan," found in v 9; Jb 1—2; Zec 3, 1; 1 Chr 21, 1; he continues to accuse Christ's disciples.

12, 14: Great eagle: symbol of the power and swiftness of divine help; cf Ex 19, 4; Dt 32, 11; Is 40, 31.

12, 15: The serpent is depicted as the sea monster; cf 13, 1; Is 27, 1; Ez 32, 2; Ps 74, 13–14.

12, 17: Although the church is protected by God's special providence (16), the individual Christian is to expect persecution and suffering.

12, 18: It took its position: many later manuscripts and versions read "I took my position," thus connecting the sentence to the following paragraph.

13, 1–10: This wild beast, combining features of the four beasts in Dn 7, 2–28, symbolizes the Roman empire; the seven heads represent the emperors; see the notes on 17, 10 and 17, 12–14. The blasphemous names are the divine titles assumed by the emperors.

13, 2: Satan (12, 9), the prince of this world (Jn 12, 31), commissioned the beast to persecute the church (5–7).

13, 3: This may be a reference to the popular legend that Nero would come back to life and rule again after his death (which occurred in A.D. 68 from a self-inflicted stab wound in the throat); cf v 14; 17, 8. Domitian (A.D. 81–96) embodied all the cruelty and impiety of Nero. Cf Introduction.

13, 4: Worshiped the beast: allusion to emperor worship, which Domitian insisted upon and ruthlessly enforced. **Who can compare with the beast:** perhaps a deliberate parody of the name Michael; see the note on 12, 7.

13, 5–6: Domitian, like Antiochus IV Epiphanes (Dn 7, 8.11.25), demanded that he be called by divine titles such as "our lord and god" and "Jupiter." See the note on 11, 2.

13, 5: Forty-two months: this is the same duration as the profanation of the holy city (11, 2), the prophetic mission of the two witnesses (11, 3), and the retreat of the woman into the desert (12, 6.14).

h Gn 3, 15. i Ex 19, 4; Dn 7, 25; 12, 7. j Gn 3, 15. k 2 Thes 2, 3–12. l Dn 7, 3–6. m Dn 7, 8.11.25; 8, 14; 9, 27; 11, 36; 12, 7. n Dn 7, 21. o 3, 5; 17, 8; 20, 12.

9 [p]Whoever has ears ought to hear these words.
10 [q]Anyone destined for captivity goes into
captivity.
Anyone destined to be slain by the sword shall
be slain by the sword.
Such is the faithful endurance of the holy ones.
The Second Beast 11 *Then I saw another
beast come up out of the earth; it had two horns
like a lamb's but spoke like a dragon. 12 It
wielded all the authority of the first beast in its
sight and made the earth and its inhabitants
worship the first beast, whose mortal wound
had been healed. 13 [r]It performed great signs,
even making fire come down from heaven to
earth in the sight of everyone. 14 It deceived the
inhabitants of the earth with the signs it was
allowed to perform in the sight of the first beast,
telling them to make an image for the beast who
had been wounded by the sword and revived.
15 [s]It was then permitted to breathe life into the
beast's image, so that the beast's image could
speak and [could] have anyone who did not
worship it put to death. 16 [t]It forced all the
people, small and great, rich and poor, free and
slave, to be given a stamped image on their right
hands or their foreheads, 17 so that no one could
buy or sell except one who had the stamped
image of the beast's name or the number that
stood for its name.
18 [u]*Wisdom is needed here; one who under-
stands can calculate the number of the beast, for
it is a number that stands for a person. His
number is six hundred and sixty-six.

CHAPTER 14

The Lamb's Companions 1 [v]*Then I looked
and there was the Lamb standing on Mount Zion,
and with him a hundred and forty-four thousand
who had his name and his Father's name written
on their foreheads. 2 I heard a sound from heaven
like the sound of rushing water or a loud peal of
thunder. The sound I heard was like that of harp-
ists playing their harps. 3 [w]They were singing
[what seemed to be] a new hymn before the
throne, before the four living creatures and the
elders. No one could learn this hymn except the
hundred and forty-four thousand who had been
ransomed from the earth. 4 [x]*These are they who
were not defiled with women; they are virgins
and these are the ones who follow the Lamb
wherever he goes. They have been ransomed as
the firstfruits of the human race for God and the
Lamb. 5 [y]*On their lips no deceit has been found;
they are unblemished.
The Three Angels 6 *Then I saw another an-
gel flying high overhead, with everlasting good

13, 11–18: The second beast is described in terms of the false prophets (cf 16, 13; 19, 20; 20, 10) who accompany the false messiahs (the first beast); cf Mt 24, 24; Mk 13, 22; 2 Thes 2, 9; cf also Dt 13, 2–4. Christians had either to worship the emperor and his image or to suffer martyrdom.

13, 18: Each of the letters of the alphabet in Hebrew as well as in Greek has a numerical value. Many possible combinations of letters will add up to 666, and many candidates have been nominated for this infamous number. The most likely is the emperor Caesar Nero (see the note on 13, 3), the Greek form of whose name in Hebrew letters gives the required sum. (The Latin form of this name equals 616, which is the reading of a few manuscripts.) Nero personifies the emperors who viciously persecuted the church. It has also been observed that "6" represents imperfection, falling short of the perfect number "7," and is represented here in a triple or superlative form.

14, 1–5: Now follows a tender and consoling vision of the Lamb and his companions.

14, 1: Mount Zion: in Jerusalem, the traditional place where the true remnant, the Israel of faith, is to be gathered in the messianic reign; cf 2 Kgs 19, 30–31; Jl 3, 5; Ob 17; Mi 4, 6–8; Zep 3, 12–20. **A hundred and forty-four thousand:** see the note on 7, 4–9. **His Father's name . . . foreheads:** in contrast to the pagans who were marked with the name or number of the beast (13, 16–17).

14, 4: Virgins: metaphorically, because they never indulged in any idolatrous practices, which are considered in the Old Testament to be adultery and fornication (2, 14–15.20–22; 17, 1–6; cf Ez 16, 1–58; 23, 1–49). The parallel passages (7, 3; 22, 4) indicate that the 144,000 whose foreheads are sealed represent all Christian people.

14, 5: No deceit: because they did not deny Christ or do homage to the beast. Lying is characteristic of the opponents of Christ (Jn 8, 44), but the Suffering Servant spoke no falsehood (Is 53, 9; 1 Pt 2, 22). **Unblemished:** a cultic term taken from the vocabulary of sacrificial ritual.

14, 6–13: Three angels proclaim imminent judgment on the pagan world, calling all peoples to worship God the creator. Babylon (Rome) will fall, and its supporters will be tormented forever.

14, 6: Everlasting good news: that God's eternal reign is about to begin; see the note on 10, 7.

p Mt 13, 9. q Jer 15, 2. r Dt 13, 2–4; Mt 24, 24; 2 Thes 2, 9–10. s Dn 3, 5–7.15. t 14, 9; 16, 2; 19, 20; 20, 4. u 17, 9. v Jl 3, 5; Ob 17; Acts 2, 21. w Pss 33, 3; 96, 1; 98, 1; Is 42, 10. x Jer 2, 2; Jas 1, 18. y Zep 3, 13.

news to announce to those who dwell on earth,
to every nation, tribe, tongue, and people. [7][z]He
said in a loud voice, "Fear God and give him
glory, for his time has come to sit in judgment.
Worship him who made heaven and earth and
sea and springs of water."

[8][a]*A second angel followed, saying:
"Fallen, fallen is Babylon the great,
that made all the nations drink
the wine of her licentious passion."

[9]A third angel followed them and said in a loud
voice, "Anyone who worships the beast or its
image, or accepts its mark on forehead or hand,
[10]*will also drink the wine of God's fury, poured
full strength into the cup of his wrath, and will
be tormented in burning sulfur before the holy
angels and before the Lamb. [11][b]The smoke of
the fire that torments them will rise forever and
ever, and there will be no relief day or night for
those who worship the beast or its image or
accept the mark of its name." [12][c]*Here is what
sustains the holy ones who keep God's commandments and their faith in Jesus.

[13][d]*I heard a voice from heaven say, "Write
this: Blessed are the dead who die in the Lord
from now on." "Yes," said the Spirit, "let them
find rest from their labors, for their works
accompany them."

The Harvest of the Earth [14][e]*Then I looked
and there was a white cloud, and sitting on the
cloud one who looked like a son of man, with a
gold crown on his head and a sharp sickle in his
hand. [15][f]Another angel came out of the temple,
crying out in a loud voice to the one sitting on
the cloud, "Use your sickle and reap the harvest,
for the time to reap has come, because the
earth's harvest is fully ripe." [16]So the one who
was sitting on the cloud swung his sickle over
the earth, and the earth was harvested.

[17]Then another angel came out of the temple
in heaven who also had a sharp sickle. [18]*Then
another angel [came] from the altar, [who] was in
charge of the fire, and cried out in a loud voice
to the one who had the sharp sickle, "Use your
sharp sickle and cut the clusters from the earth's
vines, for its grapes are ripe." [19][g]So the angel
swung his sickle over the earth and cut the
earth's vintage. He threw it into the great wine
press of God's fury. [20]*The wine press was
trodden outside the city and blood poured out of
the wine press to the height of a horse's bridle
for two hundred miles.

CHAPTER 15

The Seven Last Plagues [1]*Then I saw in
heaven another sign, great and awe-inspiring:
seven angels with the seven last plagues, for
through them God's fury is accomplished.

[2][h]*Then I saw something like a sea of glass
mingled with fire. On the sea of glass were standing those who had won the victory over the
beast and its image and the number that signified
its name. They were holding God's harps,

14, 8: This verse anticipates the lengthy dirge over Babylon (Rome) in 18, 1—19, 4. The oracle of Is 21, 9 to Babylon is applied here.

14, 10–11: **The wine of God's fury**: image taken from Is 51, 17; Jer 25, 15–16; 49, 12; 51, 7; Ez 23, 31–34. Eternal punishment in the fiery pool of burning sulfur (or "fire and brimstone"; cf Gn 19, 24) is also reserved for the Devil, the beast, and the false prophet (19, 20; 20, 10; 21, 8).

14, 12: In addition to **faith in Jesus,** the seer insists upon the necessity and value of works, as in 2, 23; 20, 12–13; 22, 12; cf Mt 16, 27; Rom 2, 6.

14, 13: See the note on 1, 3. According to Jewish thought, people's actions followed them as witnesses before the court of God.

14, 14–20: The reaping of the harvest symbolizes the gathering of the elect in the final judgment, while the reaping and treading of the grapes symbolizes the doom of the ungodly (cf Jl 4, 12–13; Is 63, 1–6) that will come in 19, 11–21.

14, 18: **Altar:** there was only one altar in the heavenly temple; see the notes above on 6, 9; 8, 3; 11, 1.

14, 20: **Two hundred miles:** literally sixteen hundred stades. The **stadion,** a Greek unit of measurement, was about 607 feet in length, approximately the length of a furlong.

15, 1—16, 21: The seven bowls, the third and last group of seven after the seven seals and the seven trumpets, foreshadow the final cataclysm. Again, the series is introduced by a heavenly prelude, in which the victors over the beast sing the canticle of Moses (15, 2–4).

15, 1–4: A vision of the victorious martyrs precedes the vision of woe in 15, 5—16, 21; cf 7, 9–12.

15, 2: **Mingled with fire:** fire symbolizes the sanctity involved in facing God, reflected in the trials that have prepared the victorious Christians or in God's wrath.

z 2, 10; Mt 10, 28. a 18, 2–3; Is 21, 9; Jer 51, 8 / Is 51, 17; Jer 25, 15–17. b 19, 3. c 12, 17. d Mt 11, 28–29; 2 Thes 1, 7; Heb 4, 10. e 1, 7; Dn 7, 13. f Jl 4, 13; Mt 13, 36–43. g 19, 15; Is 63, 1–6. h 7, 9.14; 13, 15–18.

3 [i]*and they sang the song of Moses, the servant
of God, and the song of the Lamb:

"Great and wonderful are your works,
 Lord God almighty.
Just and true are your ways,
 O king of the nations.
4 [j]Who will not fear you, Lord,
 or glorify your name?
For you alone are holy.
 All the nations will come
 and worship before you,
 for your righteous acts have been revealed."

5*After this I had another vision. The temple
that is the heavenly tent of testimony opened,
6 [k]and the seven angels with the seven plagues
came out of the temple. They were dressed in
clean white linen, with a gold sash around their
chests. 7One of the four living creatures gave the
seven angels seven gold bowls filled with the
fury of God, who lives forever and ever. 8 [l]Then
the temple became so filled with the smoke from
God's glory and might that no one could enter it
until the seven plagues of the seven angels had
been accomplished.

CHAPTER 16

The Seven Bowls 1*I heard a loud voice
speaking from the temple to the seven angels,
"Go and pour out the seven bowls of God's fury
upon the earth."
2*The first angel went and poured out his
bowl on the earth. Festering and ugly sores
broke out on those who had the mark of the
beast or worshiped its image.
3*The second angel poured out his bowl on
the sea. The sea turned to blood like that from a
corpse; every creature living in the sea died.
4 [m]The third angel poured out his bowl on the
rivers and springs of water. These also turned to
blood. 5 [n]Then I heard the angel in charge of the
waters say:

"You are just, O Holy One,
 who are and who were,
 in passing this sentence.
6 [o]For they have shed the blood of the holy ones
 and the prophets,
 and you [have] given them blood to drink;
 it is what they deserve."

7 [p]Then I heard the altar cry out,

"Yes, Lord God almighty,
 your judgments are true and just."

8The fourth angel poured out his bowl on the
sun. It was given the power to burn people with
fire. 9 [q]People were burned by the scorching heat
and blasphemed the name of God who had
power over these plagues, but they did not
repent or give him glory.
10 [r]*The fifth angel poured out his bowl on
the throne of the beast. Its kingdom was plunged
into darkness, and people bit their tongues in
pain 11 [s]and blasphemed the God of heaven
because of their pains and sores. But they did not
repent of their works.
12*The sixth angel emptied his bowl on the
great river Euphrates. Its water was dried up to
prepare the way for the kings of the East. 13 [t]*I
saw three unclean spirits like frogs come from
the mouth of the dragon, from the mouth of the
beast, and from the mouth of the false prophet.
14 [u]These were demonic spirits who performed

15, 3: The song of Moses: the song that Moses and the Israelites sang after their escape from the oppression of Egypt (Ex 15, 1–18). The martyrs have escaped from the oppression of the Devil. **Nations:** many other Greek manuscripts and versions read "ages."

15, 5–8: Seven angels receive the bowls of God's wrath.

15, 5: Tent of testimony: the name of the meeting tent in the Greek text of Ex 40. Cf 2 Mc 2, 4–7.

16, 1–21: These seven bowls, like the seven seals (6, 1–17; 8, 1) and the seven trumpets (8, 2—9, 21; 11, 15–19), bring on a succession of disasters modeled in part on the plagues of Egypt (Ex 7—12). See the note on 6, 12–14.

16, 2: Like the sixth Egyptian plague (Ex 9, 8–11).

16, 3–4: Like the first Egyptian plague (Ex 7, 20–21). The same woe followed the blowing of the second trumpet (8, 8–9).

16, 10: The throne of the beast: symbol of the forces of evil. **Darkness:** like the ninth Egyptian plague (Ex 10, 21–23); cf 9, 2.

16, 12: The kings of the East: Parthians; see the notes on 6, 2 and 17, 12–13. **East:** literally, "rising of the sun," as in 7, 2.

16, 13: Frogs: possibly an allusion to the second Egyptian plague (Ex 7, 26—8, 11). **The false prophet:** identified with the two-horned second beast (13, 11–18 and the note there).

i Pss 92, 6; 98, 1 / Dt 32, 4; Ps 145, 17. j Ps 86, 9–10; Jer 10, 7. k 19, 8. l 1 Kgs 8, 10; Is 6, 4. m Ex 7, 14–24. n 1, 4. o Ez 35, 6; Mt 23, 34–35. p Dn 3, 27; Tb 3, 2. q Am 4, 6. r Ex 10, 21–23. s Ex 9, 8–11 / Jer 5, 3. t Ex 8, 2–3. u 1 Cor 1, 8.

signs. They went out to the kings of the whole world to assemble them for the battle on the great day of God the almighty. [15 v]*("Behold, I am coming like a thief." Blessed is the one who watches and keeps his clothes ready, so that he may not go naked and people see him exposed.) [16]*They then assembled the kings in the place that is named Armageddon in Hebrew.

[17 w]The seventh angel poured out his bowl into the air. A loud voice came out of the temple from the throne, saying, "It is done." [18 x]Then there were lightning flashes, rumblings, and peals of thunder, and a great earthquake. It was such a violent earthquake that there has never been one like it since the human race began on earth. [19]*The great city was split into three parts, and the gentile cities fell. But God remembered great Babylon, giving it the cup filled with the wine of his fury and wrath. [20]*Every island fled, and mountains disappeared. [21 y]Large hailstones like huge weights came down from the sky on people, and they blasphemed God for the plague of hail because this plague was so severe.

V: The Punishment of Babylon and the Destruction of Pagan Nations

CHAPTER 17

Babylon the Great [1 z]*Then one of the seven angels who were holding the seven bowls came and said to me, "Come here. I will show you the judgment on the great harlot who lives near the many waters. [2 a]*The kings of the earth have had intercourse with her, and the inhabitants of the earth became drunk on the wine of her harlotry." [3 b]*Then he carried me away in spirit to a deserted place where I saw a woman seated on a scarlet beast that was covered with blasphemous names, with seven heads and ten horns. [4 c]*The woman was wearing purple and scarlet and adorned with gold, precious stones, and pearls. She held in her hand a gold cup that was filled with the abominable and sordid deeds of her harlotry. [5]On her forehead was written a name, which is a mystery, "Babylon the great, the mother of harlots and of the abominations of the earth." [6]*I saw that the woman was drunk on the blood of the holy ones and on the blood of the witnesses to Jesus.

Meaning of the Beast and Harlot When I saw her I was greatly amazed. [7]The angel said to me, "Why are you amazed? I will explain to you the mystery of the woman and of the beast that carries her, the beast with the seven heads and the ten horns. [8 d]*The beast that you saw existed once but now exists no longer. It will come up from the abyss and is headed for destruction. The inhabitants of the earth whose names have not been written in the book of life from the foundation of the world shall be amazed when they see the beast, because it existed once but exists no longer, and yet it will come again. [9 e]*Here is a clue for one who has wisdom. The seven heads represent seven hills upon which the woman sits. They also represent seven kings: [10]*five have already fallen, one still lives, and

16, 15: Like a thief: as in 3, 3 (cf Mt 24, 42–44; 1 Thes 5, 2). **Blessed:** see the note on 1, 3.

16, 16: Armageddon: in Hebrew, this means "Mountain of Megiddo." Since Megiddo was the scene of many decisive battles in antiquity (Jgs 5, 19–20; 2 Kgs 9, 27; 2 Chr 35, 20–24), the town became the symbol of the final disastrous rout of the forces of evil.

16, 19: The great city: Rome and the empire.

16, 20–21: See the note on 6, 12–14. **Hailstones:** as in the seventh Egyptian plague (Ex 9, 23–24); cf 8, 7. **Like huge weights:** literally, "weighing a talent," about one hundred pounds.

17, 1—19, 10: The punishment of Babylon is now described as a past event and, metaphorically, under the image of the great harlot who leads people astray into idolatry.

17, 1–6: Babylon, the symbolic name (5) of Rome, is graphically described as "the great harlot."

17, 2: Intercourse . . . harlotry: see the note on 14, 4. The pagan kings subject to Rome adopted the cult of the emperor.

17, 3: Scarlet beast: see the note on 13, 1–10. **Blasphemous names:** divine titles assumed by the Roman emperors; see the note on 13, 5–6.

17, 4: Reference to the great wealth and idolatrous cults of Rome.

17, 6b-18: An interpretation of the vision is here given.

17, 8: Allusion to the belief that the dead Nero would return to power (11); see the note on 13, 3.

17, 9: Here is a clue: literally, "Here a mind that has wisdom." **Seven hills:** of Rome.

17, 10: There is little agreement as to the identity of the Roman emperors alluded to here. The number seven (9) suggests that all the emperors are meant; see the note on 1, 4.

v Mt 24, 42–44 / 3, 17. w Is 66, 6. x Mk 13, 19. y Ex 9, 22–26. z Jer 50, 38; 51, 13. a Jer 51, 7. b 13, 1. c 18, 16. d 13, 3–4 / 3, 5; 13, 8; 20, 12. e 13, 18.

the last has not yet come, and when he comes he must remain only a short while. 11 *The beast that existed once but exists no longer is an eighth king, but really belongs to the seven and is headed for destruction. 12 f *The ten horns that you saw represent ten kings who have not yet been crowned; they will receive royal authority along with the beast for one hour. 13 They are of one mind and will give their power and authority to the beast. 14 g They will fight with the Lamb, but the Lamb will conquer them, for he is Lord of lords and king of kings, and those with him are called, chosen, and faithful."

15 Then he said to me, "The waters that you saw where the harlot lives represent large numbers of peoples, nations, and tongues. 16 h *The ten horns that you saw and the beast will hate the harlot; they will leave her desolate and naked; they will eat her flesh and consume her with fire. 17 For God has put it into their minds to carry out his purpose and to make them come to an agreement to give their kingdom to the beast until the words of God are accomplished. 18 The woman whom you saw represents the great city that has sovereignty over the kings of the earth."

CHAPTER 18

The Fall of Babylon 1 i *After this I saw another angel coming down from heaven, having great authority, and the earth became illumined by his splendor. 2 j *He cried out in a mighty voice:

"Fallen, fallen is Babylon the great.
She has become a haunt for demons.
She is a cage for every unclean spirit,
a cage for every unclean bird,
[a cage for every unclean] and disgusting
[beast].
3 k *For all the nations have drunk
the wine of her licentious passion.
The kings of the earth had intercourse with
her,
and the merchants of the earth grew rich
from her drive for luxury."

4 l *Then I heard another voice from heaven say:

"Depart from her, my people,
so as not to take part in her sins
and receive a share in her plagues,
5 m for her sins are piled up to the sky,
and God remembers her crimes.
6 n Pay her back as she has paid others.
Pay her back double for her deeds.
Into her cup pour double what she poured.
7 o To the measure of her boasting and
wantonness
repay her in torment and grief;
for she said to herself,
'I sit enthroned as queen;
I am no widow,
and I will never know grief.'
8 Therefore, her plagues will come in one day,
pestilence, grief, and famine;
she will be consumed by fire.
For mighty is the Lord God who judges her."

9 The kings of the earth who had intercourse with her in their wantonness will weep and mourn over her when they see the smoke of her pyre. 10 They will keep their distance for fear of the torment inflicted on her, and they will say:

"Alas, alas, great city,

17, 11: The beast: Nero; see the note on v 8.

17, 12–13: Ten kings who have not yet been crowned: perhaps Parthian satraps who are to accompany the revived Nero (the beast) in his march on Rome to regain power; see the note on 13, 3. In 19, 11–21, the Lamb and his companions will conquer them.

17, 16–18: The ten horns: the ten pagan kings (12) who unwittingly fulfill God's will against harlot Rome, the great city; cf Ez 16, 37.

18, 1—19, 4: A stirring dirge over the fall of Babylon-Rome. The perspective is prophetic, as if the fall of Rome had already taken place. The imagery here, as elsewhere in this book, is not to be taken literally. The vindictiveness of some of the language, borrowed from the scathing Old Testament prophecies against Babylon, Tyre, and Nineveh (Is 23; 24; 27; Jer 50—51; Ez 26—27), is meant to portray symbolically the inexorable demands of God's holiness and justice; cf Introduction. The section concludes with a joyous canticle on the future glory of heaven.

18, 2: Many Greek manuscripts and versions omit **a cage for every unclean . . . beast.**

18, 3–24: Rome is condemned for her immorality, symbol of idolatry (see the note on 14, 4), and for persecuting the church; cf 19, 2.

18, 4: Depart from her: not evacuation of the city but separation from sinners, as always in apocalyptic literature.

f Dn 7, 24. g 19, 11–21; 2 Mc 13, 4; 1 Tm 6, 15 / Rom 1, 6; 1 Pt 2, 9; Jude 1. h Ez 16, 37–41; 23, 25–29. i Ez 43, 2. j 14, 8; Is 21, 9; Jer 50, 2–3; 51, 8. k 17, 2; Jer 51, 7. l Is 48, 20; Jer 50, 8. m Jer 51, 9. n Jer 50, 15 / Jer 16, 18. o Is 47, 8–9.

Babylon, mighty city.
In one hour your judgment has come."

11 *The merchants of the earth will weep and mourn for her, because there will be no more markets for their cargo: 12 their cargo of gold, silver, precious stones, and pearls; fine linen, purple silk, and scarlet cloth; fragrant wood of every kind, all articles of ivory and all articles of the most expensive wood, bronze, iron, and marble; 13 *cinnamon, spice, incense, myrrh, and frankincense; wine, olive oil, fine flour, and wheat; cattle and sheep, horses and chariots, and slaves, that is, human beings.

14 [p]"The fruit you craved
has left you.
All your luxury and splendor are gone,
never again will one find them."

15 The merchants who deal in these goods, who grew rich from her, will keep their distance for fear of the torment inflicted on her. Weeping and mourning, 16 [q]they cry out:

"Alas, alas, great city,
wearing fine linen, purple and scarlet,
adorned [in] gold, precious stones, and pearls.
17 In one hour this great wealth has been ruined."

Every captain of a ship, every traveler at sea, sailors, and seafaring merchants stood at a distance 18 and cried out when they saw the smoke of her pyre, "What city could compare with the great city?" 19 [r]They threw dust on their heads and cried out, weeping and mourning:

"Alas, alas, great city,
in which all who had ships at sea
grew rich from her wealth.
In one hour she has been ruined.
20 [s]Rejoice over her, heaven,
you holy ones, apostles, and prophets.
For God has judged your case against her."

21 [t]A mighty angel picked up a stone like a huge millstone and threw it into the sea and said:

"With such force will Babylon the great city be thrown down,
and will never be found again.
22 [u]No melodies of harpists and musicians,
flutists and trumpeters,
will ever be heard in you again.
No craftsmen in any trade
will ever be found in you again.
No sound of the millstone
will ever be heard in you again.
23 [v]No light from a lamp
will ever be seen in you again.
No voices of bride and groom
will ever be heard in you again.
Because your merchants were the great ones of the world,
all nations were led astray by your magic potion.
24 [w]In her was found the blood of prophets and holy ones
and all who have been slain on the earth."

CHAPTER 19

1 *After this I heard what sounded like the loud voice of a great multitude in heaven, saying:

"Alleluia!
Salvation, glory, and might belong to our God,
2 [x]for true and just are his judgments.
He has condemned the great harlot
who corrupted the earth with her harlotry.
He has avenged on her the blood of his servants."

3 [y]They said a second time:

"Alleluia! Smoke will rise from her forever and ever."

18, 11: Ironically, the merchants weep not so much for Babylon-Rome, but for their lost markets; cf Ez 27, 36.

18, 13: Spice: an unidentified spice plant called in Greek **amōmon.**

19, 1.3.4.6: Alleluia: found only here in the New Testament, this frequent exclamation of praise in the Hebrew psalms was important in Jewish liturgy.

p Hos 10, 5 / Am 6, 7. q 17, 4. r Ez 27, 27–32. s 19, 1–2; Dt 32, 43. t Jer 51, 63–64; Ez 26, 21. u Is 24, 8; Ez 26, 13. v Jer 7, 34; 16, 9; 25, 10. w 16, 6. x Dn 3, 27 / Jer 51, 48–49. y 14, 11; Is 34, 10.

4 The twenty-four elders and the four living
creatures fell down and worshiped God who sat
on the throne, saying, "Amen. Alleluia."

The Victory Song 5 [z]*A voice coming from the
throne said:

"Praise our God, all you his servants,
[and] you who revere him, small and great."

6 Then I heard something like the sound of a
great multitude or the sound of rushing water or
mighty peals of thunder, as they said:

"Alleluia!
The Lord has established his reign,
[our] God, the almighty.
7 [a]*Let us rejoice and be glad
and give him glory.
For the wedding day of the Lamb has come,
his bride has made herself ready.
8 [b]*She was allowed to wear
a bright, clean linen garment."

(The linen represents the righteous deeds of the
holy ones.)
9 [c]*Then the angel said to me, "Write this:
Blessed are those who have been called to the
wedding feast of the Lamb." And he said to me,
"These words are true; they come from God."
10 [d]*I fell at his feet to worship him. But he said
to me, "Don't! I am a fellow servant of yours and
of your brothers who bear witness to Jesus.
Worship God. Witness to Jesus is the spirit of
prophecy."

The King of Kings 11 [e]*Then I saw the heav-
ens opened, and there was a white horse; its
rider was [called] "Faithful and True." He judges
and wages war in righteousness. 12 [f]*His eyes
were [like] a fiery flame, and on his head were
many diadems. He had a name inscribed that no
one knows except himself. 13 [g]*He wore a cloak
that had been dipped in blood, and his name was
called the Word of God. 14 [h]The armies of
heaven followed him, mounted on white horses
and wearing clean white linen. 15 [i]*Out of his
mouth came a sharp sword to strike the nations.
He will rule them with an iron rod, and he
himself will tread out in the wine press the wine
of the fury and wrath of God the almighty. 16 [j]He
has a name written on his cloak and on his thigh,
"King of kings and Lord of lords."

17 *Then I saw an angel standing on the sun.
He cried out [in] a loud voice to all the birds
flying high overhead, "Come here. Gather for
God's great feast, 18 [k]to eat the flesh of kings, the
flesh of military officers, and the flesh of war-
riors, the flesh of horses and of their riders, and
the flesh of all, free and slave, small and great."
19 Then I saw the beast and the kings of the earth
and their armies gathered to fight against the one
riding the horse and against his army. 20 [l]*The
beast was caught and with it the false prophet
who had performed in its sight the signs by
which he led astray those who had accepted the
mark of the beast and those who had worshiped
its image. The two were thrown alive into the
fiery pool burning with sulfur. 21 The rest were

19, 5–10: A victory song follows, sung by the entire church, celebrating the marriage of the Lamb, the union of the Messiah with the community of the elect.

19, 7: The wedding day of the Lamb: symbol of God's reign about to begin (21, 1—22, 5); see the note on 10, 7. **His bride:** the church; cf 2 Cor 11, 2; Eph 5, 22–27. Marriage is one of the biblical metaphors used to describe the covenant relationship between God and his people; cf Hos 2, 16–22; Is 54, 5–6; 62, 5; Ez 16, 6–14. Hence, idolatry and apostasy are viewed as adultery and harlotry (Hos 2, 4–15; Ez 16, 15–63); see the note on 14, 4.

19, 8: See the note on 14, 12.

19, 9: Blessed: see the note on 1, 3.

19, 10: The spirit of prophecy: as the prophets were inspired to proclaim God's word, so the Christian is called to give witness to the Word of God (13) made flesh; cf 1, 2; 6, 9; 12, 17.

19, 11–16: Symbolic description of the exalted Christ (cf 1, 13–16) who together with the armies of heaven overcomes the beast and its followers; cf 17, 14.

19, 12: A name: in Semitic thought, the name conveyed the reality of the person; cf Mt 11, 27; Lk 10, 22.

19, 13: Had been dipped in: other Greek manuscripts and versions read "had been sprinkled with"; cf v 15. **The Word of God:** Christ is the revelation of the Father; cf Jn 1, 1.14; 1 Jn 2, 14.

19, 15: The treading of the wine press is a prophetic symbol used to describe the destruction of God's enemies; cf Is 63, 1–6; Jl 4, 13.

19, 17–21: The certainty of Christ's victory is proclaimed by an angel, followed by a reference to the mustering of enemy forces and a fearsome description of their annihilation. The gruesome imagery is borrowed from Ez 39, 4.17–20.

19, 20: Beast . . . false prophet: see the notes on ch 13. **The fiery pool . . . sulfur:** symbol of God's punishment (14, 10; 20, 10.14–15), different from the abyss; see the note on 9, 1.

z 11, 18; Ps 115, 13. a Mt 22, 9; Eph 5, 27. b 15, 6; Is 61, 10; Mt 22, 11–12. c Mt 8, 11; Lk 14, 15. d 22, 8–9. e Is 11, 4. f 1, 14–16; 2, 18 / Lk 10, 22. g Is 63, 1 / Jn 1, 1. h 15, 6; 19, 8. i 14, 20; Is 63, 3. j 17, 14; 2 Mc 13, 4. k Ez 39, 17–20. l 14, 10.

killed by the sword that came out of the mouth
of the one riding the horse, and all the birds
gorged themselves on their flesh.

CHAPTER 20

The Thousand-year Reign 1 m*Then I saw an
angel come down from heaven, holding in his
hand the key to the abyss and a heavy chain.
2 n*He seized the dragon, the ancient serpent,
which is the Devil or Satan, and tied it up for a
thousand years 3and threw it into the abyss,
which he locked over it and sealed, so that it
could no longer lead the nations astray until the
thousand years are completed. After this, it is to
be released for a short time.
4 o*Then I saw thrones; those who sat on
them were entrusted with judgment. I also saw
the souls of those who had been beheaded for
their witness to Jesus and for the word of God,
and who had not worshiped the beast or its
image nor had accepted its mark on their fore-
heads or hands. They came to life and they
reigned with Christ for a thousand years. 5The
rest of the dead did not come to life until the
thousand years were over. This is the first
resurrection. 6*Blessed and holy is the one who
shares in the first resurrection. The second death
has no power over these; they will be priests of
God and of Christ, and they will reign with him
for [the] thousand years.
7*When the thousand years are completed,
Satan will be released from his prison. 8 p*He
will go out to deceive the nations at the four
corners of the earth, Gog and Magog, to gather
them for battle; their number is like the sand of
the sea. 9 q*They invaded the breadth of the
earth and surrounded the camp of the holy ones
and the beloved city. But fire came down from
heaven and consumed them. 10The Devil who
had led them astray was thrown into the pool of
fire and sulfur, where the beast and the false
prophet were. There they will be tormented day
and night forever and ever.
The Large White Throne 11 r*Next I saw a
large white throne and the one who was sitting
on it. The earth and the sky fled from his
presence and there was no place for them. 12 s*I
saw the dead, the great and the lowly, standing
before the throne, and scrolls were opened.
Then another scroll was opened, the book of life.
The dead were judged according to their deeds,
by what was written in the scrolls. 13*The sea
gave up its dead; then Death and Hades gave up
their dead. All the dead were judged according
to their deeds. 14 t*Then Death and Hades were
thrown into the pool of fire. (This pool of fire is
the second death.) 15Anyone whose name was
not found written in the book of life was thrown
into the pool of fire.

VI: The New Creation

CHAPTER 21

The New Heaven and the New Earth
1 u*Then I saw a new heaven and a new earth.
The former heaven and the former earth had
passed away, and the sea was no more. 2 v*I also
saw the holy city, a new Jerusalem, coming

20, 1–6: Like the other numerical values in this book, the thousand years are not to be taken literally; they symbolize the long period of time between the chaining up of Satan (a symbol for Christ's resurrection-victory over death and the forces of evil) and the end of the world. During this time God's people share in the glorious reign of God that is present to them by virtue of their baptismal victory over death and sin; cf Rom 6, 1–8; Jn 5, 24–25; 16, 33; 1 Jn 3, 14; Eph 2, 1.

20, 1: Abyss: see the note on 9, 1.

20, 2: Dragon . . . serpent . . . Satan: see the notes on 12, 3.9.10.15.

20, 4: Beast . . . mark: see ch 13 and its notes.

20, 6: Blessed: see the note on 1, 3. **Second death:** see the note on 2, 11. **Priests:** as in 1, 6; 5, 10; cf 1 Pt 2, 9.

20, 7–10: A description of the symbolic battle to take place when Satan is released at the end of time, when the thousand years are over; see the note on vv 1–6.

20, 8: Gog and Magog: symbols of all pagan nations; the names are taken from Ez 38, 1—39, 20.

20, 9: The breadth of the earth: Palestine. **The beloved city:** Jerusalem; see the note on 14, 1.

20, 11–15: A description of the final judgment. After the intermediate reign of Christ, all the dead are raised and judged, thus inaugurating the new age.

20, 12: The book of life: see the note on 3, 5. **Judged . . . scrolls:** see the note on 14, 12.

20, 13: Hades: the netherworld; see the note on 1, 18.

20, 14: Second death: see the note on 2, 11.

21, 1—22, 5: A description of God's eternal kingdom in heaven under the symbols of a new heaven and a new earth; cf Is 65, 17–25; 66, 22; Mt 19, 28.

21, 1: Sea . . . no more: because as home of the dragon it was doomed to disappear; cf Jb 7, 12.

21, 2: New Jerusalem . . . bride: symbol of the church (Gal 4, 26); see the note on 19, 7.

m 9, 1. n Gn 3, 1. o Mt 19, 28. p Ez 38, 2.9.16. q Ez 38, 22. r 2 Pt 3, 7.10.12. s Rom 2, 6. t 1 Cor 15, 26.54–55. u Is 65, 17; 66, 22; Rom 8, 19–23; 2 Pt 3, 13. v 19, 7–9.

down out of heaven from God, prepared as a
bride adorned for her husband. 3 [w]*I heard a
loud voice from the throne saying, "Behold,
God's dwelling is with the human race. He will
dwell with them and they will be his people and
God himself will always be with them [as their
God]. 4 [x]He will wipe every tear from their eyes,
and there shall be no more death or mourning,
wailing or pain, [for] the old order has passed
away."

5 [y]*The one who sat on the throne said,
"Behold, I make all things new." Then he said,
"Write these words down, for they are trustwor-
thy and true." 6 [z]*He said to me, "They are
accomplished. I [am] the Alpha and the Omega,
the beginning and the end. To the thirsty I will
give a gift from the spring of life-giving water.
7 [a]*The victor will inherit these gifts, and I shall
be his God, and he will be my son. 8 [b]*But as for
cowards, the unfaithful, the depraved, murder-
ers, the unchaste, sorcerers, idol-worshipers, and
deceivers of every sort, their lot is in the burning
pool of fire and sulfur, which is the second
death."

The New Jerusalem 9 *One of the seven an-
gels who held the seven bowls filled with the
seven last plagues came and said to me, "Come
here. I will show you the bride, the wife of the
Lamb." 10 [c]He took me in spirit to a great, high
mountain and showed me the holy city Jerusa-
lem coming down out of heaven from God. 11 [d]It
gleamed with the splendor of God. Its radiance
was like that of a precious stone, like jasper,
clear as crystal. 12 It had a massive, high wall,
with twelve gates where twelve angels were
stationed and on which names were inscribed,
[the names] of the twelve tribes of the Israelites.
13 [e]There were three gates facing east, three
north, three south, and three west. 14 [f]*The wall
of the city had twelve courses of stones as its
foundation, on which were inscribed the twelve
names of the twelve apostles of the Lamb.

15 *The one who spoke to me held a gold
measuring rod to measure the city, its gates, and
its wall. 16 *The city was square, its length the
same as [also] its width. He measured the city
with the rod and found it fifteen hundred miles
in length and width and height. 17 *He also
measured its wall: one hundred and forty-four
cubits according to the standard unit of measure-
ment the angel used. 18 *The wall was con-
structed of jasper, while the city was pure gold,
clear as glass. 19 [g]The foundations of the city wall
were decorated with every precious stone; the
first course of stones was jasper, the second
sapphire, the third chalcedony, the fourth emer-
ald, 20 the fifth sardonyx, the sixth carnelian, the
seventh chrysolite, the eighth beryl, the ninth
topaz, the tenth chrysoprase, the eleventh hya-
cinth, and the twelfth amethyst. 21 The twelve
gates were twelve pearls, each of the gates made
from a single pearl; and the street of the city was
of pure gold, transparent as glass.

21, 3: People: other ancient manuscripts read a plural, "peoples."

21, 3–4: Language taken from Ez 37, 27; Is 25, 8; 35, 10; cf 7, 17.

21, 5: The one . . . on the throne: God himself; cf 4, 1–11.

21, 6: They are accomplished: God's reign has already begun; see the note on 20, 1–6. **Alpha . . . Omega:** see the note on 1, 8. **Life-giving water:** see the note on 7, 17.

21, 7: The victor: over the forces of evil; see the conclusions of the seven letters (2, 7.11.17.26; 3, 5.12.21). **He will be my son:** the victorious Christian enjoys divine affiliation by adoption (Gal 4, 4–7; Rom 8, 14–17); see the note on 2, 26–28.

21, 8: Cowards: their conviction is so weak that they deny Christ in time of trial and become traitors. **Second death:** see the note on 2, 11.

21, 9—22, 5: Symbolic descriptions of the new Jerusalem, the church. Most of the images are borrowed from Ez 40—48.

21, 9: The bride, the wife of the Lamb: the church (2), the new Jerusalem (10); cf 2 Cor 11, 2.

21, 14: Courses of stones . . . apostles: literally, "twelve foundations"; cf Eph 2, 19–20.

21, 15–17: The city is shaped like a gigantic cube, a symbol of perfection (cf 1 Kgs 6, 19–20). The measurements of the city and its wall are multiples of the symbolic number twelve; see the note on 7, 4–9.

21, 16: Fifteen hundred miles: literally, twelve thousand stades, about 12,000 furlongs (see the note on 14, 20); the number is symbolic: twelve (the apostles as leaders of the new Israel) multiplied by 1,000 (the immensity of Christians); cf Introduction. **In length and width and height:** literally, "its length and width and height are the same."

21, 17: One hundred and forty-four cubits: the cubit was about eighteen inches in length. **Standard unit of measurement the angel used:** literally, "by a human measure, i.e., an angel's."

21, 18–21: The gold and precious gems symbolize the beauty and excellence of the church; cf Ex 28, 15–21; Tb 13, 16–17; Is 54, 11–12.

w Ez 37, 27. x 7, 17; Is 25, 8; 35, 10. y Is 43, 19; 2 Cor 5, 17. z 22, 17; Ps 36, 8–9; Is 55, 1. a 2 Sm 7, 14. b 22, 15; Rom 1, 29–32. c Ez 40, 2. d Heb 11, 10. e Ez 48, 31–35. f Eph 2, 20. g Is 54, 11–12.

22 [h]*I saw no temple in the city, for its temple is the Lord God almighty and the Lamb. 23 [i]*The city had no need of sun or moon to shine on it, for the glory of God gave it light, and its lamp was the Lamb. 24 [j]*The nations will walk by its light, and to it the kings of the earth will bring their treasure. 25 During the day its gates will never be shut, and there will be no night there. 26 The treasure and wealth of the nations will be brought there, 27 [k]but nothing unclean will enter it, nor any[one] who does abominable things or tells lies. Only those will enter whose names are written in the Lamb's book of life.

CHAPTER 22

1 [l]*Then the angel showed me the river of life-giving water, sparkling like crystal, flowing from the throne of God and of the Lamb 2 *down the middle of its street. On either side of the river grew the tree of life that produces fruit twelve times a year, once each month; the leaves of the trees serve as medicine for the nations. 3 Nothing accursed will be found there anymore. The throne of God and of the Lamb will be in it, and his servants will worship him. 4 *They will look upon his face, and his name will be on their foreheads. 5 [m]Night will be no more, nor will they need light from lamp or sun, for the Lord God shall give them light, and they shall reign forever and ever.

VII: Epilogue

6 [n]*And he said to me, "These words are trustworthy and true, and the Lord, the God of prophetic spirits, sent his angel to show his servants what must happen soon." 7 [o]*"Behold, I am coming soon." Blessed is the one who keeps the prophetic message of this book.

8 It is I, John, who heard and saw these things, and when I heard and saw them I fell down to worship at the feet of the angel who showed them to me. 9 [p]But he said to me, "Don't! I am a fellow servant of yours and of your brothers the prophets and of those who keep the message of this book. Worship God."

10 *Then he said to me, "Do not seal up the prophetic words of this book, for the appointed time is near. 11 Let the wicked still act wickedly, and the filthy still be filthy. The righteous must still do right, and the holy still be holy."

12 [q]"Behold, I am coming soon. I bring with me the recompense I will give to each according to his deeds. 13 [r]*I am the Alpha and the Omega, the first and the last, the beginning and the end."

14 [s]*Blessed are they who wash their robes so as to have the right to the tree of life and enter the city through its gates. 15 [t]Outside are the dogs, the sorcerers, the unchaste, the murderers, the idol-worshipers, and all who love and practice deceit.

16 [u]*"I, Jesus, sent my angel to give you this testimony for the churches. I am the root and offspring of David, the bright morning star."

17 [v]*The Spirit and the bride say, "Come." Let the hearer say, "Come." Let the one who thirsts come forward, and the one who wants it receive the gift of life-giving water.

18 I warn everyone who hears the prophetic words in this book: if anyone adds to them, God will add to him the plagues described in this book, 19 [w]and if anyone takes away from the

21, 22: Christ is present throughout the church; hence, no temple is needed as an earthly dwelling for God; cf Mt 18, 20; 28, 20; Jn 4, 21.

21, 23: Lamp . . . Lamb: cf Jn 8, 12.

21, 24–27: All men and women of good will are welcome in the church; cf Is 60, 1.3.5.11. **The . . . book of life:** see the note on 3, 5.

22, 1.17: Life-giving water: see the note on 7, 17.

22, 2: The tree of life: cf v 14; see the note on 2, 7. **Fruit . . . medicine:** cf Ez 47, 12.

22, 4: Look upon his face: cf Mt 5, 8; 1 Cor 13, 12; 1 Jn 3, 2.

22, 6–21: The book ends with an epilogue consisting of a series of warnings and exhortations and forming an inclusion with the prologue by resuming its themes and expressions; see the note on 1, 1–3.

22, 7.12.20: I am coming soon: Christ is the speaker; see the note on 1, 3.

22, 7.14: Blessed: see the note on 1, 3.

22, 10: The appointed time: see the note on 1, 3.

22, 13: Christ applies to himself words used by God in 1, 8.

22, 14: The city: heavenly Jerusalem; see the note on 21, 2.

22, 16: The root . . . of David: see the note on 5, 5. **Morning star:** see the note on 2, 26–28.

22, 17: Bride: the church; see the note on 21, 2.

h Jn 2, 19–20. i Is 60, 1–2.19–20. j Is 60, 11. k Is 35, 8; 52, 1; Zec 13, 2 / Rv 3, 5; 20, 12. l Ez 47, 1–12. m Is 60, 20. n 1, 1. o 12.20 / 1, 3. p 19, 10. q 7.20 / Ps 62, 12; 2 Tm 4, 14. r 1, 8; 21, 6; Is 41, 4; 44, 6. s 7, 14–15; 22, 2. t 21, 8; Rom 1, 29–32. u 1, 1.11–12; 22, 6 / 2, 28. v 21, 6; Is 55, 1. w Dt 4, 2.

words in this prophetic book, God will take
away his share in the tree of life and in the holy
city described in this book.
20 x*The one who gives this testimony says,
"Yes, I am coming soon." Amen! Come, Lord
Jesus!
21 The grace of the Lord Jesus be with all.

22, 20: Come, Lord Jesus: a liturgical refrain, similar to the Aramaic expression **Marana tha**—"Our Lord, come!"—in 1 Cor 16, 22; cf the note there. It was a prayer for the coming of Christ in glory at the parousia; see the note on 1, 3.

x 7.12 / Acts 3, 20–21; 1 Cor 15, 23; 16, 22.

GLOSSARY

LIST OF SUNDAY READINGS

READINGS FOR THE MAJOR FEASTS OF THE YEAR

COLLABORATORS ON THE OLD TESTAMENT,
THE REVISED PSALMS, THE REVISED NEW TESTAMENT

ACKNOWLEDGMENTS

Glossary

Acrostic a poetic form in which the first letter of each new line or series of lines within a larger group follows the order of letters in the Hebrew alphabet. The supreme example in the Bible is Psalm 119 and, outside the psalter, the Book of Lamentations.

Allegory an extended comparison in which persons or objects stand for abstract ideas, moral qualities, or spiritual realities. Some people read the Song of Songs, which uses the language of a passionate love affair, as an allegory of God's love for the people of God, or of Christ's love for the church. Allegorical: characterized by allegory; symbolic.

Alleluia a Greek and Latin form of a Hebrew verb, meaning "praise the Lord." *See* hallelujah.

Anawim the Hebrew word for "the poor," "the afflicted," "the meek or humble."

Aphorism a short memorable saying. Many of the Proverbs are aphorisms, and so are many of Jesus' statements. Aphorisms are easy to remember.

Apocalypse the Greek word for "revelation." It is also used as the name for a type of literature that contains mysterious revelations, usually veiled in symbolic language and interpreted by an angel. The subject matter of an apocalypse deals with the heavenly world and with the future, especially the final judgment. Biblical examples are found in Daniel 7–12 and in the Book of Revelation.

Apocrypha a Greek word meaning "hidden," describing pious literature related to the Scriptures but not included in the canon. Protestants regard several books of the Catholic Old Testament as apocryphal because they are not found in the Hebrew Bible (Sirach, Wisdom, Baruch, 1 and 2 Maccabees, Tobit, Judith). *See* canon; deuterocanonical.

Apologia Greek, "explanation." A defense of one's actions or beliefs, usually given in a formal speech or written document.

Apostasy the act of abandoning a set of beliefs, or the position of having abandoned them.

Base Community a translation of a Spanish term, *comunidad de base:* "basic or foundational society," for certain popular church groups in Central and South America that are empowering cultural, educational, and political organizations among the oppressed—particularly peasants.

Basilica a church built according to an ancient Roman plan, with a rectangular nave and a semicircular apse at one end; also, a Catholic church with certain ceremonial or liturgical privileges.

Booths, Feast of the final harvest festival of grapes and olives, falling within our month of October. It was called "Booths" because the harvesters lived in the field in makeshift tents or booths. *See* Tabernacles; *Sukkoth.*

Canaan the land infiltrated by the Israelites after the Exodus. It was more extensive than biblical Israel. Canaanite: an inhabitant of that land.

Canon a Greek word meaning "measuring rod," and later the rule by which something was judged. Christian tradition uses the word for the official list of the individual books that make up the Scriptures. The canon of the Catholic Church is more extensive than that of the Protestant churches, but less extensive than that of the Orthodox churches. *See* apocrypha; pseudepigraphy. Canonical: conforming to the canon.

Canonical Criticism a way of reading the text of the Bible that tries to understand its final form, rather than working only with the parts that make it up or trying to reconstruct earlier versions of it. *See* form criticism; historical-critical method; literary criticism; redaction criticism.

Casemate two parallel walls that are joined by short cross walls. They form small rooms that are used for storage or are filled with earth to strengthen fortifications.

Ceramic Typology a way of dating different levels of an archaeological site by classifying the pieces of pottery found in them according to the approximate eras in which they were made.

Chaos complete lack of order. In the mythology of the ancient Near East, chaos was sometimes personified as divine beings who had to be conquered by other gods in order to establish an orderly and habitable universe.

Charisma a gift of spiritual grace, particularly a gift of one of the manifestations of the Holy Spirit in the New Testament church, such as speaking in tongues. Charismatic: gifted with charisma.

Christ the Greek word for the Hebrew *masiah* (*see* messiah). Both words mean anointed, that is, blessed by having oil poured over the head. By applying this title to Jesus, the early Christians expressed their belief that he was the messiah of Israel.

Christology the theological doctrines covering the nature of Jesus as the Christ. High christology emphasizes the divinity of Jesus; low christology stresses his humanity.

Chronicler scholarly name for the author, or group of authors, of the books of 1 and 2 Chronicles, Ezra, and Nehemiah.

Circumcision the ritual removal of the foreskin of the penis in male infants. It symbolized, for Jews, the membership of the infant in the people of God (Genesis 17,9–14). It came to have spiritual significance, an image of repentance (Jeremiah 4,4). In Paul's writings (see in particular Galatians 5,2–6), it means the reliance upon one's own good deeds, rather than on God's mercy, for salvation.

Cisjordan Latin for "this side of Jordan," that is, the western bank of the river Jordan ("this side" as viewed from Jerusalem). *See* Transjordan.

Codex a manuscript made up of separate leaves of writing that are bound into a unit along one edge. Our modern books are a development of the codex form. *See* scroll.

Cosmos Greek for "order, regularity." The cosmos is the created world of order, stability, and relative permanence, as opposed to the impermanence and disorder of chaos.

Council of Trent the twenty-ninth ecumenical council of the Catholic Church, held 1545–1563, after the Protestant Reformation had begun. Among other things, it defined the books that are part of the Catholic canon of Scripture.

Covenant an agreement between two parties. There are several important covenants in the Old Testament. After the Flood, God made a covenant with Noah not to destroy the earth again. The covenants with Abraham and David have the character of unconditional promises by God. The most central covenant is that made with Moses on Mt. Sinai, and described in the Books of Exodus and Deuteronomy. That covenant has specific requirements (the commandments) and resembles the international treaties of the ancient Near East.

Cult the rituals and religious practices at a temple or other place of worship. For instance, the cult of the Jerusalem Temple means the religious practices observed there, with no judgment about their value implied in the term.

Dead Sea Scrolls a group of manuscripts that were found in 1947 in caves near the Dead Sea, at a place called *wadi Qumran* (Qumran gulch). The scrolls appear to have been the library of an Essene settlement, which flourished at the site from the late second century B.C. until it was destroyed by the Romans in 68 A.D. The importance of the scrolls for biblical studies in twofold. They include Hebrew manuscripts of biblical books that are several centuries older than those previously known, and they shed new light on Jewish beliefs and practices around the time of Jesus. *See* Essenes.

Decalogue Greek, "ten words." The traditional name for the list of commandments given in Exodus 20,1–17 and Deuteronomy 5,6–21.

Demon a spiritual or nonphysical being, generally hostile to human beings, but in most Old Testament passages still under God's control (*see* Job 1 and 2). A common Hebrew name was *satan,* meaning "adversary." By the time of the New Testament demons were generally regarded as hostile to God as well, and therefore evil, or the cause of bad influences—disease, mental distress—on human beings. Demonic: marked by spiritual evil, like a demon.

Deuterocanonical Greek, "second canon." The name for those books in the Catholic Old Testament that are not in the Hebrew canon, but were added in the Greek translation, the Septuagint, and taken over into the Latin versions. The deuterocanonical books (and additions) are: Sirach, Wisdom, Baruch, 1 and 2 Maccabees, Tobit, Judith, and additions to Esther and Daniel. *See* canon, Septuagint.

Deuteronomic History the books of Joshua, Judges, 1 and 2 Samuel, and 1 and 2 Kings, giving a history of Israel from the conquest of the land to the exile. The Book of Deuteronomy serves as a sort of preface to this work.

Deuteronomic Reform the religious reform and revival that took place under King Josiah beginning in 621 B.C. Scholars generally assume that the book from which the religious instructions were read to the people was the newly rediscovered Book of Deuteronomy (see 2 Kings 22,8–23,25). During this reform the Temple worship was purged of many pagan influences that had crept in under the political overlordship of the Assyrian Empire.

Deuteronomist the scholarly name for the author or authors of the books of Joshua, Judges, 1 and 2 Samuel, and 1 and 2 Kings, which form a continuous history of Israel from the conquest of the land to the exile in Babylon. *See* Deuteronomic History.

Discernment the ability to distinguish between what is valuable and what is not, especially in the spiritual or moral realms.

Disciple a follower. The disciples of Jesus were those who followed, or tried to follow, his teachings.

Doctrine a systematic set of beliefs or teachings.

Ecclesiology the theology of the meaning of the church or the study of the church's forms, structures, importance, etc.

Ecumenism from the Greek *oikoumene,* "the whole inhabited world." Any attempts to deal with the relations between different Christian groups, or to think about ways in which divisions might be overcome. Since the Second Vatican Council (1963–65) ecumenical activity has become a major goal of the Catholic Church. Ecumenical: aimed at fostering ecumenism, or characterized by ecumenical aims; having the character of ecumenism.

Elohist the scholarly name for the author of one of the source documents for the Pentateuch. The Elohist's writing is marked by the use of Hebrew *'elohim* (God) rather than the proper name *yahweh* (LORD) in the period before Moses. *See* Yahwist.

Ephraim the most important tribe of the Northern Kingdom. *See* Northern Kingdom.

Epicurean a follower of the Greek philosopher Epicurus, who taught (among other things) that more permanent pleasures should be preferred to passing ones, and that one should remain unaffected as far as possible by the changes and passions of everyday life.

Epigraph an inscription, usually carved or etched in stone. Epigraphs, which can be recovered from archaeological sites, provide information about the language and customs of the time when they were written.

Epistle a letter, generally intended for public reading and written according to a set literary style. Epistolary: having the form of a letter.

Eschatology teaching about "the end." In the Hebrew prophets, the end in question is that of Israel or Judah as independent nations. In later apocalyptic writings it came to mean the end of the world.

Essenes a Jewish sect around the time of Jesus. They are described by the first-century Jewish authors Philo and Josephus, and by the Roman Pliny. The Dead Sea Scrolls are believed to be the documents of an Essene community. *See* Dead Sea Scrolls.

Ethnology the study of races or ethnic groups.

Etiology an account or story that gives the cause of something. Many stories in the Bible may have originated in this way; for instance, the story of Lot's wife (Genesis 19,26) may have been told to explain the existence of a pillar of salt.

Exegesis the explanation of a text.

Exile removal from one's own country. In the context of the Old Testament, "the Exile" refers to the period between 586 and 539 B.C. when the upper classes of Judah were exiles in Babylon. A previous exile, from the Northern Kingdom of Israel, had been enforced in 722–721 B.C. Exilic: taking place during the Exile, or dealing with it.

Festival a religious celebration.

Form Criticism an approach to a text that focuses on the smaller literary forms contained in a larger work (for instance, parables or miracle stories in the Gospels) and tries to discover the historical settings in which they might have originated, before they were incorporated in the larger work.

Former Prophets the name in the Hebrew Scriptures for the first part of the larger section called the Prophets. The Former Prophets consist of Joshua, Judges, 1 and 2 Samuel, and 1 and 2 Kings. *See* Latter Prophets; Prophets; Writings.

Fundamentalist in its narrow meaning, a fundamentalist is a conservative Protestant who believes in the five fundamentals: the sole authority of Scripture; the Virgin Birth of Jesus Christ; the doctrine of the substitutionary atonement of the death of Christ; the physical, bodily resurrection of Christ; and the literal Second Coming of Christ to judge the world. In its larger meaning, fundamentalist has come to mean any rigidly conservative adherent to a belief system, who regards all those outside the belief system as without hope of salvation, and who treats the sacred text of the tradition as an infallible guide to belief and action.

Gemara *see* Talmud.

Genre a literary form or type. Biblical genres include oracles, laments, hymns, parables, letters, gospels, and apocalypses.

Gentile a non-Jew.

Gnosticism from the Greek word *gnosis,* "knowledge." A kind of religion that claims secret knowledge about the real nature of the universe. Gnosticism flourished in the second to fourth centuries A.D., but tendencies to it can also be found in New Testament times. Gnostic philosophies differ greatly in their actual beliefs, but all claim to have and impart secret knowledge to those who join their group. Some New Testament writings, such as the letters of Paul and John, may be combatting forms of gnosticism in some of their passages. Gnosticism was denounced as heretical by the early theologians of the church. A major library of gnostic documents was discovered at Nag Hammadi in Egypt in 1946. Gnostic: an adherent of gnosticism, or a person or writing with characteristics of gnosticism.

Haggadah Jewish tales, anecdotes, and other materials in the Talmud that are distinguished from the legal traditions that also became part of the Talmud. *See* Talmud.

Halakah Jewish laws and regulations, other than those found in the Bible, that make up the legal part of the Talmud. *See* Talmud.

Hallelujah a Hebrew word meaning "praise the Lord." The Greek and Latin spelling of it, alleluia, is more familiar in the liturgy.

Hasmonean the name given to the dynasty descended from the Maccabee brothers. It ruled Israel from 135 to 36 B.C.; the last Hasmonean was overthrown by Herod the Great.

Hellenic conforming to, or characterized by, the ideals of Greek culture. The Greek conquest of the countries of the eastern Mediterranean by Alexander the Great, during the years 333–323 B.C., was followed by the adoption of the Greek language and educational practices in the areas under Greek political influence. Hellenistic: having this Greek cultural character or idealizing it. Hellenization: the process of adopting Greek culture and practices.

Herem the practice of sacrificing all the spoils of war to God.

Heresy from the Greek word *hairesis,* "choice." Heresy is a belief or teaching that is chosen in opposition to officially approved doctrine. Heretical: having the character of heresy; unorthodox.

Herodian followers and members of the court of the dynasty of Herod the Great and his sons (about 40 B.C. to A.D. 40).

Historical-Critical Method any method of reading a text that tries to understand it in its historical context, that is, its original setting and what it meant to its original hearers or readers. For example, a historical-critical reading of Isaiah 7,14 ("the virgin shall be with child") asks what this prophecy meant to the people of Jerusalem in the eighth century B.C., not what it later came to mean for the Christian faith. The method uses the tools of historical research to understand the conditions of the past, and critical tools to understand the traditions and development that lie behind the surface of the text. Historical criticism is an umbrella term that includes such methods as form criticism and redaction criticism.

Holocaust a sacrifice entirely consumed by fire, a whole burnt offering. This sacrifice was one of adoration of God.

Holocaust, The the European persecution of the Jews, 1938–1945, that culminated in the death-camp slaughter of up to six million European Jews.

Holocausts, Altar of in the Temple, the altar on which the whole burnt offerings were made.

Humanist one who upholds the value and dignity of the human person and human culture. Some humanists believe in God; others do not, but believe that human endeavors and accomplishments are the highest ones we know of. Some scholars have thought that humanism marks some of the passages in Ecclesiastes and other wisdom materials.

Hymn a religious poem set to music and sung as part of worship.

Hypostasization (or Hypostatization) speaking of an abstract quality as if it were a living being, for instance, Wisdom in Proverbs 8 or Sirach 24.

Hyksos Egyptian dynasty (1850–1500 B.C.) that may have been of Semitic origin, and therefore have provided the historical basis for the stories of the Israelite patriarchs in Egypt (Genesis 37–50).

Inerrancy the doctrine that the biblical materials are without error. In its strict form, as held, for instance, by Protestant fundamentalists, inerrancy includes the assertion that in the original manuscripts of the biblical books there are no errors of fact, whether theological, historical, or scientific. A more restrained version of the doctrine would claim that the Bible is an inerrant guide in matters of faith, but that it may contain historical errors or assertions that cannot be reconciled with present-day science. Vatican II expressed it this way: "Therefore, since everything asserted by the inspired authors or sacred writers must be held to be asserted by the Holy Spirit, it follows that the books of Scripture must be acknowledged as teaching firmly, faithfully, and without error that truth which God wanted put into the sacred writings for the sake of our salvation" (Document on Revelation, *Dei Verbum,* n. 11). The final phrase, "for the sake of our salvation"—that is, not for the sake of giving us historical or scientific information—establishes the limits of inerrancy.

Inspiration the belief that words uttered by a human being are really the words of a divinity. In the ancient world, prophets and oracles were thought to be inspired. In Christian tradition, the notion of inspiration was eventually applied to the whole Bible. Inspiration in a more expanded sense speaks of an inspired tradition, in which numerous authors, anonymous contributors, editors, and others all worked together more or less consciously to create the biblical materials; in this view, God used all these people and their human traditions to express the Bible's teachings. The Second Vatican Council affirms the inspiration of Scripture, but warns that God speaks "through men in human fashion" so that careful attention must be given "to what the sacred writers really intended" (*Dogmatic Constitution on Divine Revelation,* III.12).

Israel the name for both the kingdom of twelve tribal groups, of which David and Solomon were kings, and for the northern section of this kingdom, which split off after the death of Solomon and began a separate political existence under Jeroboam I (1 Kings 12). *See* Northern Kingdom, Southern Kingdom.

Jahvist the author of one of the source documents of the Pentateuch (German spelling). *See* Yahwist.

Josephus a Roman Jewish historian of the first century A.D., whose works of Jewish history were written partly to make the Jewish religion and people more acceptable to the Roman government. His two major works are the *Jewish Wars* and the *Jewish Antiquities,* which provide valuable information about the background of the later Old Testament writings and the New Testament.

Judah the major tribal group of the Southern Kingdom. *See* Southern Kingdom.

Kosher according to specific regulations; fit or proper. Food that is *kosher* does not fall into any of the forbidden food groups and has been prepared according to the cleanliness regulations.

Lament a Hebrew verse form that is used for poetic elegies, psalms of suffering or anguish, and other treatments of painful parts of the human condition. The Book of Lamentations and many psalms are in the form of laments. See *qinah.*

Latter Prophets the name given in Jewish tradition to the second part of the section of the Hebrew Scriptures called the Prophets. The Latter Prophets are Isaiah, Jeremiah, Ezekiel, and the Book of Twelve (Hosea, Joel, Amos, Obadiah, Jonah, Micah, Nahum, Habakkuk, Zephaniah, Haggai, Zechariah, Malachi). *See* Prophets.

Law the usual English translation of the Hebrew word *Torah,* which means "guidance" or "teaching." The Torah in the narrower sense of the Pentateuch (Genesis, Exodus, Leviticus, Numbers, and Deuteronomy) is the first of the three divisions of the Hebrew Scriptures (followed by the Prophets and the Writings). It is often called the "Law of Moses" although it contains much else besides legal material. Despite Paul's attacks on attempts to win salvation through the Law, the dominant biblical attitude to law sees it as a gift of God and source of joy. It is the opportunity to show faithfulness to God in one's daily activities. *See* Pentateuch; Prophets; Torah; Writings.

Levite a member of the tribe charged with responsibility for Israel's worship. The Levites owned no land of their own, but rather lived on the offerings of the Temple sacrifices.

Levirate Marriage from Latin *levir,* "husband's brother." A practice in the earlier stages of Judaism in which a man had to take his dead brother's wife as his own if his brother had died before fathering any children who could carry on his name. The children that would result from the union of the widow and her brother-in-law would be treated as if they were the dead man's offspring, inheriting his property and carrying on his name. It is generally agreed that the practice died out well before the time of Jesus (along with the practice of polygamy), but it forms the basis of the question that the Sadducees present to Jesus (Matthew 22,23–33; Mark 12,18–27; Luke 20,27–40): in the next life, which of seven brothers will be the husband of a woman whom they all successively married under the levirate law.

Libation from the Latin for "pour." Pouring out a liquid (such as wine or oil) onto the ground as a sacrifice to a deity.

Literal Meaning the plain sense of a text, whether historical, instructional, or otherwise. The literal meaning was traditionally treated in opposition to the allegorical meaning. *See* allegory.

Literary Criticism in older usage literary criticism meant what is now called "source criticism," that is, the search for the underlying documents in a biblical text. The isolation of the Yahwistic, Elohistic, and other basic documents in the first four books of the Bible is an example of this. More recently, a form of literary criticism has arisen which accepts the text in its final form and does not try to reconstruct earlier stages of it. This more recent type of criticism is concerned with the meaning of the text for the modern reader rather than with its historical context. *See* canonical criticism; historical-critical method; source criticism.

Liturgy originally a term for a public good work, paid for by a wealthy citizen but intended to benefit everyone. Liturgy now means the official public worship of the church. "The Liturgy" is increasingly used, following Orthodox writers, to mean the celebration of the Eucharist.

Love Feasts early Christian celebrations, perhaps held together with the Eucharist or as part of it, that included a full meal for the whole church community. Paul criticizes some of the church members in Corinth for the fact that in their assemblies they do not share food and drink, but rather the wealthy bring their own and consume it, while the poor have nothing extra to eat (1 Corinthians 11,17–22). Perhaps because of such abuses, the institution of the love feast seems to have disappeared at a relatively early date.

Matriarch Greek "mother-ruler," a female leader, elder, or ruler. *See* patriarch.

***Megillah,* (plural *Megilloth*)** Hebrew, "scroll," a long strip of parchment or papyrus on which the text of a book was written. The festal *megilloth* are the books of Ruth, Song of Songs, Ecclesiastes, Esther, and Lamentations, each of which is read in the synagogue at a specific special feast.

Messiah Hebrew for "anointed." It could be applied to various officials, including priests, but came to refer especially to the king who was descended from David. (As part of the ritual when a king was enthroned, his head was anointed with oil.) In the period after the Exile, when there was no longer a king in Judah, the "messiah" came to mean an ideal figure who would restore the kingdom of Israel in the future. *See also* Christ (the Greek translation of Messiah).

Metaphor a direct comparison, one that does not use the words "like" or "as," between two things. Jesus used a metaphor when he said, "I am the gate for the sheep" (John 10,7). *See* simile.

Midrash Hebrew, "explanation." A method of interpretation, developed among Jewish teachers before the time of Christ, in which a biblical passage is quoted up to the point of contemporary application. At that point the passage is discontinued and the explanation or application is given. A New Testament example is found in Matthew 2,16–23. Matthew alludes to Jeremiah 31,15–17, but quotes only Jeremiah 31,15 (the tears of Rachel). Whereas Jeremiah goes on to announce the reward of those tears and the return of the Israelites from Exile, Matthew writes of the return of Jesus, Mary, and Joseph from Egypt.

Millennium a thousand years. In Revelation 20,1–5, the thousand-year reign of Christ is predicted, and this reign has been called "the Millennium" because it is supposed to bring in an era of peace and well-being. A millennarian is one who takes this passage as predicting a literal, physical reign of Christ on Earth (as opposed to treating it as a metaphor for heaven, for example) and who tries to identify the events that will occur in order to bring the Millennium about.

Mishnah *see* Talmud.

Motif a characteristic image or theme in a work.

Mystery a spiritual reality that can never be fully understood. A mystery is not opaque to reason, but rather has a character that human reason cannot fully comprehend. The love of God for us is a mystery, not because we cannot understand what love is, but because we cannot comprehend the fullness of God's love, no matter how hard we try.

Myth a story that expresses a spiritual truth or basic conviction of a culture through narrative. In particular, myths give explanations of origins, often through the struggles of divine beings or superhuman creatures. Because the Bible firmly believes in only one God, in biblical myths the presence of multiple deities has faded out, but the titantic struggle between good and evil is still maintained, as in the story of Paradise in Genesis 2–3, or the Tower of Babel story in Genesis 11,1–9. (For an alternate form of the Paradise myth, see Ezekiel 28,11–19.) Such stories, for example, express the impossibility of human efforts to attain the level of God.

Nazirite one who takes a religious vow of strict observance to dedicate himself or herself to the Lord, as explained in Numbers 6,1–21. The vow involves keeping purity laws very strictly, abstaining from alcoholic drink, and refraining from cutting one's hair. Samson, whose story is told in Judges 13–16, was a Nazirite, though his observance was marked by a number of relapses. Paul took the Nazirite vow (Acts 18,18; 21,23–24).

Northern Kingdom the political assembly of tribal groups that split off from the kingdom of Israel after Solomon's death (1 Kings 12). This newly-formed kingdom was itself called Israel, and in some of the prophets (for instance, Hosea 8,11), Ephraim, after its most important tribe.

Oracle a message from God to a priest or prophet, and by the prophet to others, often in response to an inquiry. The content and style vary, from a call to prophesy to a message of salvation or a statement of threat and condemnation. Prophetic books are often made up of a series of oracles, usually in poetical form, which were collected and written down later, not necessarily in the order in which the prophet originally spoke them.

Ostraca pieces of pottery with writing scratched on them. Ostraca are recovered from archaeological digs and provide evidence about the language at the time they were written; their existence reflects the fact that paper was a relatively rare and valuable substance, and was not used for casual writing, such as messages intended to be read once and thrown away, lists, and the like. Instead, people scratched a few words on a piece of broken pottery—useless for anything else—and thousands of these casual messages have been discovered.

Palaeography the study of ancient forms of writing. Palaeography can be used to date manuscripts, since writing styles changed over the years and different manuscripts of the same book can be arranged in the likely order in which they were written. Palaeography can also classify the writing in inscriptions (epigraphs) and scratched on broken pieces of pottery (ostraca).

Paraenesis moral exhortation, urging the reader or hearer to better behavior or a better mode of living, usually accompanied with or in the form of proverbial wisdom. The Letter of James contains much of this sort of moral exhortation.

Parousia Greek, "presence," by extension "appearance." The second coming of Christ.

Passover the Jewish feast commemorating the Exodus from Egypt.

Patriarch Greek, "father-ruler," a male leader, elder, or ruler. *See* matriarch.

Patristic (from the Greek word for "father"). Having to do with, or in the period of, the early theologians of the Christian church, usually referred to as "the fathers." The patristic period begins with the close of the New Testament writings, sometime after 100 A.D., and continues for several centuries. During this time creeds and many classic Christian doctrines, such as the Incarnation, were worked out and put in final form.

Pentateuch a Greek word meaning "five scrolls" that is used to designate the first five books of the Bible (Genesis, Exodus, Leviticus, Numbers, Deuteronomy). Modern scholars now hold that the first four of these books are a later compilation (perhaps assembled during or after the Exile) of earlier independent sources, which are distinguished by various literary characteristics. The oldest of these, the "J" source (from the German name for it, Jahvist), uses the Hebrew word *Yahweh* as the name of God from the beginning, and may be connected to the court of King David. Another source, "E," uses *'elohim* instead of Yahweh before the time of Moses, and reflects traditions (about sites of worship, for instance) that probably derive from the northern tribes of the kingdom of Israel rather than from the southern sources of the kingdom of Judah that are contained in "J." A third source, "P," is a compilation of laws and Temple practices that the priests developed. The fourth source, "D," is found almost exclusively in the book of Deuteronomy. *See* Law; source criticism; Torah.

Personification a literary device that takes an abstract quality or spiritual reality and speaks of it in human terms. The Book of Proverbs, 3,16 says of Wisdom, "Long life is in her right hand,/in her left are riches and honor." Speaking of wisdom as if it were a human being is personification.

Pharisaism a reform movement in Judaism that probably began in the century before the birth of Jesus and, after the destruction of Jerusalem in 70 A.D., became an increasingly important influence in the religious life of Judaism. Essentially a lay movement, Pharisaism sought to invigorate Jewish life by emphasizing fidelity to Jewish law. Its base was the local synagogue with its study of the Jewish Scriptures and traditions and its strong sense of piety. Although Jesus may have shared many of the goals of Pharisaism, the Gospels report him in conflict with it over interpretation of the religious law. *See* Pharisee.

Pharisee Hebrew, "separatist." One of a group of observant Jews, beginning before the time of Jesus and continuing with important leadership roles afterwards. They helped to develop an elaborate system of oral laws to apply the written law of Moses to Jewish life after the destruction of the Temple and the Roman conquest of their homeland. They were influential in the evolution of the synagogue and staunchly defended new doctrinal developments, such as belief in angels, bodily resurrection, and life after death. Some of the negative image of Pharisees in the Gospels may reflect later clashes between these Jewish leaders and the early church. *See* Pharisaism; Torah.

Platonism a philosophical system, derived in part from Plato but going beyond what he taught, that (among other things) saw a distinct separation between the worlds of the spirit and of material things, and that regarded the material world as inferior. There has certainly been Platonic influence on Christianity, though how much is difficult to say; but the Christian doctrine of the goodness of creation has helped to moderate the harshness of the Platonic judgment about the evil of material existence in and of itself.

Pogrom the organized killing of a group, especially of Jews.

Polemic a denunciation or condemnation of an opponent.

Potsherd a broken piece (sherd or shard) of pottery. By studying decoration, shape, materials, etc., archaeologists can tell the level of pottery-making in a given era by examining the broken pieces from archaeological sites. *See* ceramic typology; ostraca; stratigraphy.

Pre-Exilic before the Exile of the Jewish people, that is, either before 721 B.C., when the Northern Kingdom (Israel) went into exile, or before 587–86 B.C., when the Southern Kingdom (Judah) was exiled by the Babylonians.

Priestly Source the source that scholars assume was put together by the remains of the Israelite priesthood in Exile, containing the rules and regulations for worship in the Temple and other geneaological and legal information. This source, usually abbreviated "P," is one of the documents assumed to make up the Pentateuch *(see).*

Primeval History the term for the first ten chapters and part of the eleventh chapter of Genesis, dealing with events before the time of Abraham, who was regarded as the direct ancestor of the Israelites. "Primeval" designates the long stretch of time before literary documents enable us to reconstruct historical data.

Prophet Greek, "one who speaks out." A prophet, called by God to speak the truth no matter what the cost, was one of the main participants in classical Israelite religion. The prophet was charged with the role of delivering God's message to the rulers, whether religious or political, and, as a result, many prophets were unpopular with the kings and priests. Prophets did not specialize in predicting the future, but rather in analyzing the present and announcing the consequences of current behavior. Most prophets spoke in a very memorable poetic form, delivering their statements orally in the streets or sanctuaries; only later were these written down, and still later put in some sort of order.

Prophets the second of the three divisions of the classical Hebrew Scriptures (the other two divisions are the Law and the Writings). The Prophets, in turn, are divided into the Former Prophets—Joshua, Judges, 1 and 2 Samuel, and 1 and 2 Kings—and the Latter Prophets—Isaiah, Jeremiah, Ezekiel, and the Twelve Minor Prophets. *See* canon; Former Prophets; Latter Prophets; Law; Writings.

Proverb a statement of traditional wisdom, supported by long experience and expressed in memorable form. Generally the second line repeats or develops, sometimes by contrast, the thought of the first line. This feature is called parallelism, and is common in Hebrew poetry. Proverbs are quoted in many books of the Bible, but the major collection is in Proverbs. There are also proverbs in Wisdom and, in a longer "essay" form, in Sirach. *See* wisdom.

Psalm from the Greek, a song accompanied by musical instruments. In the Bible these songs cover a wide variety of style and content; psalms appear in many places, but the principal collection of them is found in the Book of Psalms. The Hebrew name for this book is *Tehillim,* meaning "praises," even though the majority of the psalms are not hymns of praise but spread over many other categories such as laments, prayers of thanksgiving and confidence, wisdom, and psalms of royalty.

Pseudepigraphy Greek, "false attributions," meaning a false claim to authorship. The term is used for those ancient writings, Jewish and Christian, which went under the name of an important or fascinating biblical person, like Solomon or Enoch, or the apostles Thomas or James. Such works purported to be of equal status with works whose authority was already accepted. Some found their way into the Bible, at least in the Catholic and Orthodox canon: for instance, the Wisdom of Solomon. *See* apocrypha; canon; deuterocanonical.

Pseudonymous under a false name. A pseudonymous writing is one that is published under the name of a well-known figure (usually long dead) in order to establish its authority or to continue the traditions of a revered but now dead leader. In the ancient world this was an accepted literary device. *See* pseudepigraphy.

Q the abbreviation of the German word *quelle,* "source." It designates one of the original sources of Matthew and Luke, containing sayings of Jesus that they added to material they took from Mark's Gospel. *See* Synoptic Gospels.

Qinah a Hebrew poetical form (the lament) usually characterized by a two-line structure in which the first line has three stresses and the second line has two stresses. Normally in Hebrew poetry, each line of a strophe has the same number of stresses.

Qoheleth the Hebrew name, meaning "one who leads the assembly," of Ecclesiastes.

Rabbi a teacher of the Jewish laws and traditions. Some of the followers of Jesus called him "rabbi"; in the time after Jesus, and after the Romans had destroyed the Temple in 70 A.D., the rabbis reconstituted the Jewish religion as one of study and meditation on the Scripture.

Reader-Response Criticism a method for analyzing a literary text that focuses on the relationship between the text and its reader, paying attention to the literary clues in the text that guide the reader in drawing meaning from it.

Redaction Criticism the analysis of how a text was put together by an editor (or redactor) from already existing sources. The editor sometimes adds bridging sentences, uses characteristic language, adds or subtracts material, or uses the sources in a particular way, that reveal the concerns of the author and the audience at a point later in time than the original sources. Chapter 5 of Vatican II's document on Revelation speaks of the Gospels as the product of redactors: "The sacred authors wrote the four Gospels, selecting some things from the many which had been handed on by word of mouth or in writing, reducing some of them to a synthesis, explicating some things in view of the situation of their churches, and preserving the form of proclamation, but always in such fashion that they told us the honest truth about Jesus" (*Dei Verbum,* n. 19).

Revelation Latin, "taking away the veil" (a translation of Greek, *apokalypsis*). The Book of Revelation in the Bible is an example of the apocalyptic genre (*see* apocalypse), which explains current happenings by means of a heavenly interpreter so that the reader understands the real importance of what is going on. The idea of revelation in theology is that what is revealed either could not have been discovered by unaided human reason or would take the reason too long to discover.

Rhetorical Criticism analysis of a text that shows how it uses literary devices to achieve its aims and effects.

Rosh Hashanah Hebrew, "head of the year." The Jewish New Year.

Sacrifice the practice of giving something of value to God, in order to show one's devotion or commitment. In Israelite religion, sacrifice, usually of an animal or bird (though grain was also offered), was carried out by the ritual destruction of part or all of it by fire on an altar. This symbolized the bonding of oneself with God or the reunion with God after a sinful or unclean person received forgiveness and purification. Christianity took over this idea of sacrifice and applied it to the death of Jesus Christ, teaching that Christ's sacrifice was in atonement for human sin. In modern-day Christianity, sacrifice usually entails doing without things of value (money, material possessions, or time) by giving them away, to the church to promote its work of worship and service, to any organization engaged in the service of others, or directly to those in need.

Sadducee a member of the priestly family descended from Zadok, one of the two high priestly families under King David (2 Samuel 8,17). They were granted supreme control over the Temple by King Solomon (1 Kings 2,35) and were further secured in their position by Ezekiel (Ezekiel 44,10–31). The Sadducees formed one of the ruling parties of Judaism from the time of the Hasmonean Dynasty (around 146 B.C.) to the destruction of the Temple in 70 A.D. They believed in the religious authority only of the Torah, or first five books of the Bible, and opposed the new interpretations advanced by the Pharisees, especially belief in the resurrection, life after death, and the existence of angels (*see* Acts 23,6–11). The Sadducees, despite their religious conservatism, were strongly influenced by the secular aspects of Greek culture and may have been willing to sacrifice strict Jewish ideals to maintain their power and wealth. *See* Pharisees.

Saga a popular account of the prehistory or early heroic period of a people. Sagas are usually tales about the ancestors of a particular group, or the founders of a country. Many of the stories in the early chapters of Genesis are sagas.

Samaritan a member of a group resident in Israel at the time of the New Testament, and descended from the survivors in the land at the time of the Exile, who had intermarried with non-Israelites brought into the land by the Assyrians (2 Kings 17,24). After the restoration of the nation of Israel under Ezra and Nehemiah, they had not been reassimilated into the Hebrew nation. The Jews of Jesus' time looked down on Samaritans as not being true adherents of the Jewish religion, though the Samaritans themselves thought otherwise. Jesus, characteristically, treated the Samaritans with respect (John 4,4–42), and told one of his best-known parables using a Samaritan to illustrate true neighborliness, against two presumably religious characters who do not stop to help someone in need (Luke 10,30–37).

Scroll a long strip of parchment or papyrus on which a manuscript was written. A scroll was difficult to handle and refer to, since in order to be read it had to be unrolled and it could be thirty or more feet long. It was replaced, some time after the first century A.D., by the bound book, or codex *(see)*, but synagogues even today have scrolls of the Hebrew Scriptures for religious use.

Second Temple the reconstruction of Solomon's Temple, after the return from Exile, under the encouragement of the prophets Haggai and Zechariah and the direction of Ezra and Nehemiah. The Second Temple period began at the end of the sixth century B.C. and lasted through the extensive reconstruction of the Temple under Herod the Great's initiative until the fiery destruction by the Romans in 70 A.D.

Septuagint from the Latin for "seventy," therefore abbreviated LXX, the Latin numeral for seventy. It is the name of the main ancient Greek translation of the Hebrew Bible (with additions originally in Greek), undertaken by the Jewish community in Greek-speaking Egypt beginning about 250 B.C. This version included a larger number of books than was eventually accepted by the Jews for their collection of the Scriptures. It became very popular among Christians and was in fact their premier edition of the Bible. The name "seventy" derives from a legend that Ptolemy II (285–247 B.C.) commissioned seventy (or seventy-two) learned elders to prepare this translation, a task they accomplished in seventy-two days. Because the Septuagint is not a literal translation, but rather introduces modifications and explanatory remarks, it witnesses to Jewish interpretation of the Bible in the one or two centuries before Christ.

Simile a comparison between two things, using "like" or "as." Malachi speaks of the Lord as "like the refiner's fire" (3,2) and the Psalms say the soul longs for God "as the hind longs for the running waters" (42,1). *See* metaphor.

Soteriology from the Greek word for "savior." The study of the theology of salvation, or the explanation of different understandings of salvation.

Source Criticism the isolation and study of the different sources that go to make up a text. The most famous hypotheses of source criticism include the theory that the Books of Genesis through Numbers are made up of three sources ("J," or Yahwist, "E," or Elohist, "P," or Priestly) that were combined by later editors or redactors. Another source hypothesis is that Matthew and Luke used the

Gospel of Mark and another source (called "Q") when they wrote their Gospels. *See* redaction criticism.

Southern Kingdom the remaining part of the undivided kingdom of Israel, after the northern tribes withdrew from Israel at Solomon's death (1 Kings 12). It is also called Judah. *See* Northern Kingdom.

Stoa a covered walkway or portico.

Stratigraphy the analysis of the sequence of layers, or strata, of a tell, or mound, at an archaeological site formed by successive periods of human occupation.

Strophe (Greek, "turning"). Two or more lines of poetry that are treated as a unit; a stanza.

Structural Analysis a critical method that studies a text by looking for recurring patterns of meaning or imagery common to all languages and cultures. It wrestles with the text itself and is not concerned with the meaning intended by the original author nor with the historical context of the first composition.

Sukkoth Hebrew, "booths" or "tents," temporary structures built in the fields for the laborers to live in while the crops were being harvested. The Feast of *Sukkoth* is the major harvest festival. *See* Booths; Tabernacles.

Synoptic Gospels Matthew, Mark, and Luke. They are called "synoptic" because they can be "viewed together" or compared in parallel fashion. Similarities in the order of events, material, and even language, suggest that the Synoptics have a literary interrelationship. Scholars have theorized that Matthew and Luke are based on Mark and on another source, a list of Jesus' sayings, that is called "Q" (from the German word *Quelle,* "source"). This common basis would account for their similar character.

Tabernacles, Feast of the Hebrew harvest festival. *See* Booths; *Sukkoth.*

Talmud from the Hebrew, "learning" or "instruction." A collection of laws, regulations, and other material that, after the Hebrew Scriptures, is the authoritative religious document of Judaism. It consists primarily of the Mishnah, a collection of legal and procedural interpretations and practices from the Pharisees and other respected teachers. These materials themselves were further explained and expanded in the Gemara, which is a commentary on the Mishnah. All these materials were handed down orally until they were given a written form in what is called the Palestinian or Jerusalem Talmud (fourth century A.D.). A century later, the scholars of Judaism living outside the land of Israel put together the longer and more authoritative version called the Babylonian Talmud (which contains over two and a half million words, more than twice as many words as are in the entire Bible, and about four times as many words as are in the Hebrew Scriptures). See *Haggadah, Halakah.*

Temple a place of worship. The Temple in Hebrew religion was a permanent structure in Jerusalem, built by Solomon as a substitute for the tent of worship that the Israelites had used in the wilderness and continued to use through David's reign. This Temple was destroyed by the Babylonians in 587–86 B.C. A Second Temple was constructed under Ezra and Nehemiah in the fifth century, after the return from Exile. *See* Second Temple.

Testament a documentary witness or testifier to something; in the Bible, specifically, the two Testaments are witnesses, respectively, to the relations between God and Israel, and to the work of God in Jesus Christ and in the beginnings of the Christian church.

Text any unit of writing that is the subject of critical reading. It can be as small as one word (in the case of determining misprints, copying errors, etc.) or as large as an entire section or book. In biblical studies the term strictly applies only to editions of the Bible in the original language; very early renditions into another language are called versions; modern language versions are called translations. *See* Septuagint; Vulgate.

Textual Criticism the examination of the written text (usually in a number of different manuscripts) in order to determine what its accurate form is. Textual criticism compares one manuscript with another, to choose the variant form that is preferable in cases where the manuscripts disagree about a particular word. In translations, textual variations are sometimes explained in footnotes. *The New American Bible* says that it is "Translated from the Original Languages with Critical Use of All the Ancient Sources" (*see* the title page).

Theodicy the theological effort to "justify God," that is, to explain the existence of evil while maintaining the goodness and power of God. The Book of Job is a long argument in theodicy.

Theophany a Greek word meaning "appearance of God," that is, the manifestation of the divine to human perception in some way.

Toledoth Hebrew, "generations, descendants, offspring"; a list of descendants; a genealogical account. There is a list of generations in Genesis 5,1–32 or in the first nine chapters of 1 Chronicles. Biblical genealogies generally, like the ones for Jesus in Matthew 1,1–7 and Luke 3,23–38, communicate a religious message within the list of names.

Torah a Hebrew word meaning "guide" or "teaching." The Torah consists of the first five books of the Bible (Genesis, Exodus, Leviticus, Numbers, Deuteronomy) and is the most important part of the Hebrew Scriptures for the Jewish religion. *See* Law; Pentateuch.

Tradition the means by which beliefs, customs, stories, laws, religious practices, and other cultural phenomena are handed down from one generation to the next. The Bible is in part a record of traditions, first among the Hebrew people and then among the Christians. The Bible itself was first represented in tradition: in traditional stories and beliefs, in religious practices, and so on; only later was it written down and handed on in that form. The study of tradition—of how things are handed on, and how they change or stay the same during the process—is of great importance for understanding the Bible and the beliefs that are based upon it. *See* redaction criticism.

Transcendence the quality of going beyond ordinary experience. In theology, transcendence teaches that God is not contained in creation, or identical with it, but surpasses it in an absolute sense.

Transjordan Latin for "the other side of the (river) Jordan" as seen from Jerusalem. *See* Cisjordan.

Transmission History the account of how a text came down to us from its originator. The transmission can begin in spoken form: a story told to others, a proverbial saying. It may then result in a written document, which is copied and combined with other documents or oral traditions, until it is in the form in which we have it. Scholars studying the text of the books of the Bible have assumed that, because of such things as two different accounts of the same event, or different names for God, the text as we have it is the result of a complicated process. Their efforts to understand this process are transmission history.

Trent, Council of *see* Council of Trent.

Typology from the Greek word *typos,* the raised design on a seal for imprinting in wax, then a pattern or model; a theological way of understanding persons, events, or explanations, especially in the New Testament, by referring back to Old Testament "types." A type can be an event, like the Exodus from Egypt (1 Corinthians 10,1–6); a real person, like Solomon (Luke 11,31); or a story or parable like that of Jonah (Luke 11,29–30).

Typology, Ceramic *see* ceramic typology.

Vatican II the council of the Church held in the Vatican from 1962–65. The Second Vatican Council made many far-reaching decisions about the life of the Church, such as putting the liturgy into the language of the people. The Council also promoted the study and reading of the Scriptures and encouraged new Catholic translations and commentaries to help the understanding of nonexperts.

Vulgate the Latin translation of the Bible by St. Jerome, made in the fifth century A.D. Jerome went back to the original languages, Greek and Hebrew, in making his translation; it is called the Vulgate (from the Latin meaning "of the common people") because Latin was the language that most people spoke at that time.

Wisdom the tradition of human learning, handed down from teacher to pupil and from parent to child. Wisdom relied on seeing recurring patterns in human behavior and in moral consequences of action, and in presenting these in a memorable form, usually a proverb. Wisdom Literature: the collection of wisdom writings in the Bible, consisting of the books of Proverbs, Ecclesiastes, Wisdom, and Sirach, and including parts of Job and Psalms as well.

Writings the third part of the Hebrew Scriptures, after the Law (Torah) and Prophets. The Writings consisted of Psalms, Proverbs, Job, The Song of Songs, Ruth, Lamentations, Ecclesiastes, Esther, Daniel, Ezra, Nehemiah, and 1 and 2 Chronicles.

Yahweh the Hebrew name for God. It is usually explained as based on the Hebrew verb for "to be or become," but it is not easy to translate. "The one who is" or "who causes to be" are possibilities. *The New American Bible,* following a tradition of English-language translations, uses the word LORD (or occasionally GOD) to indicate when the word Yahweh appears in the text. Yahweh is given as God's name to Moses in Exodus 3,14.

Yahwist the name for the author of one of the source documents of the Pentateuch. The Yahwist, from the beginning of his work (Genesis 2,4), habitually uses the name Yahweh for God (as opposed to the author of another of the documents, the Elohist, who uses the Hebrew word *'elohim,* or God). It is generally agreed among scholars that the Yahwist's account is the oldest of the documents. *See* Elohist; Pentateuch; Priestly.

Yom Kippur Hebrew, "Day of Atonement." The Jewish holy day of fasting and repentance.

Zealot a Jew who was committed to the violent overthrow of the Roman rulers of Israel. Zealots were not a unified party or group but formed a number of sometimes conflicting factions, united only by their aversion to Roman oppression. They practiced assassination and other terror tactics, as well as engaging in political agitation. Although Zealots may have been active during Jesus' lifetime, there is little evidence of their emergence as a significant movement and force in Judaism until the time of the Jewish revolt that began about thirty years after the death of Jesus. The Zealots captured by the Romans were usually crucified as a deterrent to their followers. The Zealot-inspired revolt in 66–70 A.D. was crushed by the Romans and the Temple in Jerusalem was pulled down.

Zion original meaning uncertain. It is sometimes spelled according to its Greek form, Sion. The name refers to the fortification within ancient Jerusalem conquered by David or to the entire city (2 Samuel 5,6–10). Still later Zion designated the area immediately north of this original city where Solomon built the Temple (Psalms 2,6; 48,2), and in some prophetical writings it stood for the heavenly Jerusalem (Isaiah 60,14; see Hebrews 12,22). From the fourth century A.D. the name has been attached to the southwest part of Jerusalem, where the tomb of David was relocated and the upper room of the Last Supper is pointed out. At the present time it is outside the medieval walls of Jerusalem.

The New 3-Year Cycle of Readings for Sunday Mass

[See p. 448 for Readings of Feasts that displace the Sunday Readings.]

Year A: 1993 1996 1999 2002 2005 2008 2011 2014

Guide: **1** *refers to Reading I* **2** *refers to Reading II* **3** *refers to Gospel*

ADVENT SEASON

1st Sunday of Advent
1 Is 2,1–5
2 Rom 13,11–14
3 Mt 24,37–44

2nd Sunday of Advent
1 Is 11,1–10
2 Rom 15,4–9
3 Mt 3,1–12

3rd Sunday of Advent
1 Is 35,1–6a.10
2 Jas 5,7–10
3 Mt 11,2–11

4th Sunday of Advent
1 Is 7,10–14
2 Rom 1,1–7
3 Mt 1,18–24

CHRISTMAS SEASON

Christmas Vigil
1 Is 62,1–5
2 Acts 13,16–17.22–25
3 Mt 1,1–25

Christmas (At Midnight)
1 Is 9,1–6
2 Ti 2,11–14
3 Lk 2,1–14

Christmas (At Dawn)
1 Is 62,11–12
2 Ti 3,4–7
3 Lk 2,15–20

Christmas (During the Day)
1 Is 52,7–10
2 Heb 1,1–6
3 Jn 1,1–18

Sunday After Christmas (Holy Family)
1 Sir 3,3–7.14–17a
2 Col 3,12–21
3 Mt 2,13–15.19–23

January 1 (Solemnity of Mary, Mother of God)
1 Nm 6,22–27
2 Gal 4,4–7
3 Lk 2,16–21

2nd Sunday After Christmas
1 Sir 24,1–4.12–16
2 Eph 1,3–6.15–18
3 Jn 1,1–18

Epiphany
1 Is 60,1–6
2 Eph 3,2–3a.5–6
3 Mt 2,1–12

Sunday After Epiphany (Baptism of the Lord)
1 Is 42,1–4.6–7
2 Acts 10,34–38
3 Mt 3,13–17

LENTEN SEASON

Ash Wednesday
1 Jl 2,12–18
2 2 Cor 5,20 – 6,2
3 Mt 6,1–6.16–18

1st Sunday of Lent
1 Gn 2,7–9; 3,1–7
2 Rom 5,12–19
3 Mt 4,1–11

2nd Sunday of Lent
1 Gn 12,1–4a
2 2 Tm 1,8b–10
3 Mt 17,1–9

3rd Sunday of Lent
1 Ex 17,3–7
2 Rom 5,1–2.5–8
3 Jn 4,5–42

4th Sunday of Lent
1 1 Sm 16,1b.6–7.10–13a
2 Eph 5,8–14
3 Jn 9,1–41

5th Sunday of Lent
1 Ez 37,12–14
2 Rom 8,8–11
3 Jn 11,1–45

Passion Sunday (Palm Sunday)
Procession: Mt 21,1–11
1 Is 50,4–7
2 Phil 2,6–11
3 Mt 26,14 – 27,66

EASTER TRIDUUM AND EASTER SEASON

Mass of Lord's Supper
1 Ex 12,1–8.11–14
2 1 Cor 11,23–26
3 Jn 13,1–15

Good Friday
1 Is 52,13 – 53,12
2 Heb 4,14–16; 5,7–9
3 Jn 18,1 – 19,42

Easter Vigil
1 Gn 1,1 – 2,2
Gn 22,1–18
Ex 14,15 – 15,1
Is 54,5–14
Is 55,1–11
Bar 3,9–15; 3,32 – 4,4
Ez 36,16–17a.18–28
2 Rom 6,3–11
3 Mt 28,1–10

Easter Sunday
1 Acts 10,34a.37–43
2 Col 3,1–4
or 1 Cor 5,6b–8
3 Jn 20,1–9 or Mt 28,1–10
Evening:
3 Lk 24,13–35

2nd Sunday of Easter
1 Acts 2,42–47
2 1 Pt 1,3–9
3 Jn 20,19–31

3rd Sunday of Easter
1 Acts 2,14.22–33
2 1 Pt 1,17–21
3 Lk 24,13–35

4th Sunday of Easter
1 Acts 2,14a.36–41
2 1 Pt 2,20b–25
3 Jn 10,1–10

5th Sunday of Easter
1 Acts 6,1–7
2 1 Pt 2,4–9
3 Jn 14,1–12

6th Sunday of Easter
1 Acts 8,5–8.14–17
2 1 Pt 3,15–18
3 Jn 14,15–21

Ascension of Our Lord
1 Acts 1,1–11
2 Eph 1,17–23
3 Mt 28,16–20

7th Sunday of Easter
1 Acts 1,12–14
2 1 Pt 4,13–16
3 Jn 17,1–11a

Pentecost Vigil
1 Gn 11,1–9
or Ex 19,3–8a.16–20b
or Ez 37,1–14
or Jl 3,1–5
2 Rom 8,22–27
3 Jn 7,37–39

Mass of the Day
1 Acts 2,1–11
2 1 Cor 12,3b–7.12–13
3 Jn 20,19–23

SOLEMNITIES OF THE LORD DURING ORDINARY TIME

Trinity Sunday (Sunday after Pentecost)
1 Ex 34,4b–6.8–9
2 2 Cor 13,11–13
3 Jn 3,16–18

Corpus Christi
1 Dt 8,2–3.14b–16a
2 1 Cor 10,16–17
3 Jn 6,51–58

Sacred Heart of Jesus
1 Dt 7,6–11
2 1 Jn 4,7–16
3 Mt 11,25–30

ORDINARY TIME

1st Sunday
(See Baptism of the Lord, above)

2nd Sunday
1 Is 49,3.5–6
2 1 Cor 1,1–3
3 Jn 1,29–34

3rd Sunday
1 Is 8,23b – 9,3
2 1 Cor 1,10–13.17
3 Mt 4,12–23

4th Sunday
1 Zep 2,3; 3,12–13
2 1 Cor 1,26–31
3 Mt 5,1–12a

5th Sunday
1 Is 58,7–10
2 1 Cor 2,1–5
3 Mt 5,13–16

6th Sunday
1 Sir 15,16–21
2 1 Cor 2,6–10
3 Mt 5,17–37

7th Sunday
1 Lv 19,1–2.17–18
2 1 Cor 3,16–23
3 Mt 5,38–48

8th Sunday
1 Is 49,14–15
2 1 Cor 4,1–5
3 Mt 6,24–34

9th Sunday
1 Dt 11,18.26–28.32
2 Rom 3,21–25a.28
3 Mt 7,21–27

10th Sunday
1 Hos 6,3–6
2 Rom 4,18–25
3 Mt 9,9–13

11th Sunday
1 Ex 19,2–6a
2 Rom 5,6–11
3 Mt 9,36 – 10,8

12th Sunday
1 Jer 20,10–13
2 Rom 5,12–15
3 Mt 10,26–33

13th Sunday
1 2 Kgs 4,8–11.14–16a
2 Rom 6,3–4.8–11
3 Mt 10,37–42

14th Sunday
1 Zec 9,9–10
2 Rom 8,9.11–13
3 Mt 11,25–30

15th Sunday
1 Is 55,10–11
2 Rom 8,18–23
3 Mt 13,1–23

16th Sunday
1 Wis 12,13.16–19
2 Rom 8,26–27
3 Mt 13,24–43

17th Sunday
1 1 Kgs 3,5.7–12
2 Rom 8,28–30
3 Mt 13,44–52

18th Sunday
1 Is 55,1–3
2 Rom 8,35.37–39
3 Mt 14,13–21

19th Sunday
1 1 Kgs 19,9a.11–13a
2 Rom 9,1–5
3 Mt 14,22–33

20th Sunday
1 Is 56,1.6–7
2 Rom 11,13–15.29–32
3 Mt 15,21–28

21st Sunday
1 Is 22,19–23
2 Rom 11,33–36
3 Mt 16,13–20

22nd Sunday
1 Jer 20,7–9
2 Rom 12,1–2
3 Mt 16,21–27

23rd Sunday
1 Ez 33,7–9
2 Rom 13,8–10
3 Mt 18,15–20

24th Sunday
1 Sir 27,30—28,7
2 Rom 14,7–9
3 Mt 18,21–35

25th Sunday
1 Is 55,6–9
2 Phil 1,20c–24.27a
3 Mt 20,1–16a

26th Sunday
1 Ez 18,25–28
2 Phil 2,1–11
3 Mt 21,28–32

27th Sunday
1 Is 5,1–7
2 Phil 4,6–9
3 Mt 21,33–43

28th Sunday
1 Is 25,6–10a
2 Phil 4,12–14.19–20
3 Mt 22,1–14

29th Sunday
1 Is 45,1.4–6
2 1 Thes 1,1–5b
3 Mt 22,15–21

30th Sunday
1 Ex 22,20–26
2 1 Thes 1,5c–10
3 Mt 22,34–40

31st Sunday
1 Mal 1,14b—2,2b.8–10
2 1 Thes 2,7b–9.13
3 Mt 23,1–12

32nd Sunday
1 Wis 6,12–16
2 1 Thes 4,13–18
3 Mt 25,1–13

33rd Sunday
1 Prv 31,10–13.
19–20.30–31
2 1 Thes 5,1–6
3 Mt 25,14–30

34th Sunday (Christ the King)
1 Ez 34,11–12.15–17
2 1 Cor 15,20–26.28
3 Mt 25,31–46

Year B: 1994 1997 2000 2003 2006 2009 2012 2015

Guide: **1** *refers to Reading I* **2** *refers to Reading II* **3** *refers to Gospel*

ADVENT SEASON

1st Sunday of Advent
1 Is 63,16b–17.19b;
64,2b–7
2 1 Cor 1,3–9
3 Mk 13,33–37

2nd Sunday of Advent
1 Is 40,1–5.9–11
2 2 Pt 3,8–14
3 Mk 1,1–8

3rd Sunday of Advent
1 Is 61,1–2a.10–11
2 1 Thes 5,16–24
3 Jn 1,6–8.19–28

4th Sunday of Advent
1 2 Sm 7,1–5.8b–12.14a.16
2 Rom 16,25–27
3 Lk 1,26–38

CHRISTMAS SEASON

Christmas Vigil
1 Is 62,1–5
2 Acts 13,16–17.22–25
3 Mt 1,1–25

Christmas (At Midnight)
1 Is 9,1–6
2 Ti 2,11–14
3 Lk 2,1–14

Christmas (At Dawn)
1 Is 62,11–12
2 Ti 3,4–7
3 Lk 2,15–20

Christmas (During the Day)
1 Is 52,7–10
2 Heb 1,1–6
3 Jn 1,1–18

Sunday After Christmas (Holy Family)
1 Gen 15,1–6; 21,1–3
2 Heb 11,8.11–12.17–19
3 Lk 2,22–40
or 2,22.39–40

January 1 (Solemnity of Mary, Mother of God)
1 Nm 6,22–27
2 Gal 4,4–7
3 Lk 2,16–21

2nd Sunday After Christmas
1 Sir 24,1–2.8–12
2 Eph 1,3–6.15–18
3 Jn 1,1–18

Epiphany
1 Is 60,1–6
2 Eph 3,2–3a.5–6
3 Mt 2,1–12

Sunday After Epiphany (Baptism of the Lord)
1 Is 55,1–11
2 1 Jn 5,1–9
3 Mk 1,7–11

LENTEN SEASON

Ash Wednesday
1 Jl 2,12–18
2 2 Cor 5,20 – 6,2
3 Mt 6,1–6.16–18

1st Sunday of Lent
1 Gn 9,8–15
2 1 Pt 3,18–22
3 Mk 1,12–15

2nd Sunday of Lent
1 Gn 22,1–2.9a.10–13.15–18
2 Rom 8,31b–34
3 Mk 9,2–10

3rd Sunday of Lent
1 Ex 20,1–17
2 1 Cor 1,22–25
3 Jn 2,13–25

4th Sunday of Lent
1 2 Chr 36,14–16.19–23
2 Eph 2,4–10
3 Jn 3,14–21

5th Sunday of Lent
1 Jer 31,31–34
2 Heb 5,7–9
3 Jn 12,20–33

Passion Sunday (Palm Sunday)
Procession: Mk 11,1–10 or Jn 12,12–16
1 Is 50,4–7
2 Phil 2,6–11
3 Mk 14,1 – 15,47

EASTER TRIDUUM AND EASTER SEASON

Mass of Lord's Supper
1 Ex 12,1–8.11–14
2 1 Cor 11,23–26
3 Jn 13,1–15

Good Friday
1 Is 52,13 – 53,12
2 Heb 4,14–16.5,7–9
3 Jn 18,1 – 19,42

Easter Vigil
1 Gn 1,1 – 2,2
Gn 22,1–18
Ex 14,15 – 15,1
Is 54,5–14
Is 55,1–11
Bar 3,9–15; 3,32 – 4,4
Ez 36,16–28
2 Rom 6,3–11
3 Mk 16,1–7

Easter Sunday
1 Acts 10,34a.37–43
2 Col 3,1–4
or 1 Cor 5,6b–8
3 Jn 20,1–9
or Mk 16,1–8
Evening:
3 Lk 24,13–35

2nd Sunday of Easter
1 Acts 4,32–35
2 1 Jn 5,1–6
3 Jn 20,19–31

3rd Sunday of Easter
1 Acts 3,13–15.17–19
2 1 Jn 2,1–5a
3 Lk 24,35–48

4th Sunday of Easter
1 Acts 4,8–12
2 1 Jn 3,1–2
3 Jn 10,11–18

5th Sunday of Easter
1 Acts 9,26–31
2 1 Jn 3,18–24
3 Jn 15,1–8

6th Sunday of Easter
1 Acts 10,25–26.34–35.44–48
2 1 Jn 4,7–10
3 Jn 15,9–17

Ascension of Our Lord
1 Acts 1,1–11
2 Eph 1,17–23 or 4,1–13
3 Mk 16,15–20

7th Sunday of Easter
1 Acts 1,15–17.20a.20c–26
2 1 Jn 4,11–16
3 Jn 17,11b–19

Pentecost Vigil
1 Gn 11,1–9 or Ex 19,3–8a.16–20b or Ez 37,1–14 or Jl 3,1–5
2 Rom 8,22–27
3 Jn 7,37–39

Mass of the Day
1 Acts 2,1–11
2 1 Cor 12,3b–7.12–13
3 Jn 20,19–23
Pentecost-Optional
2 Gal 5,16–25
3 Jn 15,26–27; 16,12–15

SOLEMNITIES OF THE LORD DURING ORDINARY TIME

Trinity Sunday (Sunday after Pentecost)
1 Dt 4,32–34.39–40
2 Rom 8,14–17
3 Mt 28,16–20

Corpus Christi
1 Ex 24,3–8
2 Heb 9,11–15
3 Mk 14,12–16.22–26

Sacred Heart of Jesus
1 Hos 11,1.3–4.8c–9
2 Eph 3,8–12.14–19
3 Jn 19,31–37

ORDINARY TIME

1st Sunday
(See Baptism of the Lord, above)

2nd Sunday
1 1 Sm 3,3b–10.19
2 1 Cor 6,13c–15a.17–20
3 Jn 1,35–42

3rd Sunday
1 Jon 3,1–5.10
2 1 Cor 7,29–31
3 Mk 1,14–20

4th Sunday
1 Dt 18,15–20
2 1 Cor 7,32–35
3 Mk 1,21–28

5th Sunday
1 Jb 7,1–4.6–7
2 1 Cor 9,16–19.22–23
3 Mk 1,29–39

6th Sunday
1 Lv 13,1–2.45–46
2 1 Cor 10,31 – 11,1
3 Mk 1,40–45

7th Sunday
1 Is 43,18–19.21–22. 24b–25
2 2 Cor 1,18–22
3 Mk 2,1–12

8th Sunday
1 Hos 2,16b.17b.21–22
2 2 Cor 3,1b–6
3 Mk 2,18–22

9th Sunday
1 Dt 5,12–15
2 2 Cor 4,6–11
3 Mk 2,23 – 3,6

10th Sunday
1 Gn 3,9–15
2 2 Cor 4,13 – 5,1
3 Mk 3,20–35

11th Sunday
1 Ez 17,22–24
2 2 Cor 5,6–10
3 Mk 4,26–34

12th Sunday
1 Jb 38,1.8–11
2 2 Cor 5,14–17
3 Mk 4,35–41

13th Sunday
1 Wis 1,13–15; 2,23–24
2 2 Cor 8,7.9.13–15
3 Mk 5,21–43

14th Sunday
1 Ez 2,2–5
2 2 Cor 12,7–10
3 Mk 6,1–6

15th Sunday
1 Am 7,12–15
2 Eph 1,3–14
3 Mk 6,7–13

16th Sunday
1 Jer 23,1–6
2 Eph 2,13–18
3 Mk 6,30–34

17th Sunday
1 2 Kgs 4,42–44
2 Eph 4,1–6
3 Jn 6,1–15

18th Sunday
1 Ex 16,2–4.12–15
2 Eph 4,17.20–24
3 Jn 6,24–35

19th Sunday
1 1 Kgs 19,4–8
2 Eph 4,30 – 5,2
3 Jn 6,41–51

20th Sunday
1 Prv 9,1–6
2 Eph 5,15–20
3 Jn 6,51–58

21st Sunday
1 Jos 24,1–2a.15–17.18b
2 Eph 5,21–32
3 Jn 6,60–69

22nd Sunday
1 Dt 4,1–2.6–8
2 Jas 1,17–18.21b–22.27
3 Mk 7,1–8.14–15.21–23

23rd Sunday
1 Is 35,4–7a
2 Jas 2,1–5
3 Mk 7,31–37

24th Sunday
1 Is 50,5–9a
2 Jas 2,14–18
3 Mk 8,27–35

25th Sunday
1 Wis 2,12.17–20
2 Jas 3,16 – 4,3
3 Mk 9,30–37

26th Sunday
1 Nm 11,25–29
2 Jas 5,1–6
3 Mk 9,38–43.45.47–48

27th Sunday
1 Gn 2,18–24
2 Heb 2,9–11
3 Mk 10,2–16

28th Sunday
1 Wis 7,7–11
2 Heb 4,12–13
3 Mk 10,17–30

29th Sunday
1 Is 53,10–11
2 Heb 4,14–16
3 Mk 10,35–45

30th Sunday
1 Jer 31,7–9
2 Heb 5,1–6
3 Mk 10,46–52

31st Sunday
1 Dt 6,2–6
2 Heb 7,23–28
3 Mk 12,28b–34

32nd Sunday
1 1 Kgs 17,10–16
2 Heb 9,24–28
3 Mk 12,38–44

33rd Sunday
1 Dn 12,1–3
2 Heb 10,11–14.18
3 Mk 13,24–32

34th Sunday (Christ the King)
1 Dn 7,13–14
2 Rv 1,5–8
3 Jn 18,33b–37

Year C: 1992 1995 1998 2001 2004 2007 2010 2013 2016

Guide: **1** *refers to Reading I* **2** *refers to Reading II* **3** *refers to Gospel*

ADVENT SEASON

1st Sunday of Advent
1 Jer 33,14–16
2 1 Thes 3,12 – 4,2
3 Lk 21,25–28.34–36

2nd Sunday of Advent
1 Bar 5,1–9
2 Phil 1,4–6.8–11
3 Lk 3,1–6

3rd Sunday of Advent
1 Zep 3,14–18a
2 Phil 4,4–7
3 Lk 3,10–18

4th Sunday of Advent
1 Mi 5,1–4a
2 Heb 10,5–10
3 Lk 1,39–45

CHRISTMAS SEASON

Christmas Vigil
1 Is 62,1–6
2 Acts 13,16–17.22–25
3 Mt 1,1–25

Christmas (At Midnight)
1 Is 9,1–6
2 Ti 2,11–14
3 Lk 2,1–14

Christmas (At Dawn)
1 Is 62,11–12
2 Ti 3,4–7
3 Lk 2,15–20

Christmas (During the Day)
1 Is 57,7–10
2 Heb 1,1–6
3 Jn 1,1–18

Sunday After Christmas (Holy Family)
1 1 Sm 1,20–22.24–28
2 1 Jn 3,1–2.21–24
3 Lk 2,41–52

January 1 (Solemnity of Mary, Mother of God)
1 Nm 6,22–27
2 Gal 4,4–7
3 Lk 2,16–21

2nd Sunday After Christmas
1 Sir 24,1–2.8–12
2 Eph 1,3–6.15–18
3 Jn 1,1–18

Epiphany
1 Is 60,1–6
2 Eph 3,2–3a.5–6
3 Mt 2,1–12

Sunday After Epiphany (Baptism of the Lord)
1 Is 40,1–5.9–11
2 Ti 2,11–14; 3,4–7
3 Lk 3,15–16.21–22

LENTEN SEASON

Ash Wednesday
1 Jl 2,12–18
2 2 Cor 5,20 – 6,2
3 Mt 6,1–6.16–18

1st Sunday of Lent
1 Dt 26,4–10
2 Rom 10,8–13
3 Lk 4,1–13

2nd Sunday of Lent
1 Gn 15,5–12.17–18
2 Phil 3,17 – 4,1
3 Lk 9,28b–36

3rd Sunday of Lent
1 Ex 3,1–8a.13–15
2 1 Cor 10,1–6.10–12
3 Lk 13,1–9

4th Sunday of Lent
1 Jos 5,9a.10–12
2 2 Cor 5,17–21
3 Lk 15,1–3.11–32

5th Sunday of Lent
1 Is 43,16–21
2 Phil 3,8–14
3 Jn 8,1–11

Passion Sunday (Palm Sunday)
Procession: Lk 19,28–40
1 Is 50,4–7
2 Phil 2,6–11
3 Lk 22,14 – 23,56

EASTER TRIDUUM AND EASTER SEASON

Mass of Lord's Supper
1 Ex 12,1–8.11–14
2 1 Cor 11,23–26
3 Jn 13,1–15

Good Friday
1 Is 52,13 – 53,12
2 Heb 4,14–16; 5,7–9
3 Jn 18,1 – 19,42

Easter Vigil
1 Gn 1,1 – 2,2
Gn 22,1–18
Ex 14,15 – 15,1
Is 54,5–14
Is 55,1–11
Bar 3,9–15; 3,32 – 4,4
Ez 36,16–28
2 Rom 6,3–11
3 Lk 24,1–12

Easter Sunday
1 Acts 10,34a.37–43
2 Col 3,1–4 or 1 Cor 5,6b–8
3 Jn 20,1–9 or Lk 24,1–12
Evening:
3 Lk 24,13–35

2nd Sunday of Easter
1 1 Acts 5,12–16
2 Rv 1,9–11a.12–13.17–19
3 Jn 20,19–31

3rd Sunday of Easter
1 Acts 5,27b–32.40b–41
2 Rv 5,11–14
3 Jn 21,1–19 or 1–14

4th Sunday of Easter
1 Acts 13,14.43–52
2 Rv 7,9.14b–17
3 Jn 10,27–30

5th Sunday of Easter
1 Acts 14,21b–27
2 Rv 21,1–5a
3 Jn 13,31–33a.34–35

6th Sunday of Easter
1 Acts 15,1–2.22–29
2 Rv 21,10–14.22–23
3 Jn 14,23–29

Ascension of the Lord
1 Acts 1,1–11
2 Eph 1,17–23 or Heb 9,24–28; 10,19–23
3 Lk 24,46–53

7th Sunday of Easter
1 Acts 7,55–60
2 Rv 22,12–14.16–17.20
3 Jn 17,20–26

Pentecost Vigil
1 Gn 11,1–9 or Ex 19,3–8a.16–20b or Ez 37,1–14 or Jl 3,1–5
2 Rom 8,22–27
3 Jn 7,37–39

Mass of the Day
1 Acts 2,1–11
2 1 Cor 12,3b–7.12–13 or Rom 8,8–27
3 Jn 20,19–23 or Jn 14,15–16.23b–26

SOLEMNITIES OF THE LORD DURING ORDINARY TIME

Trinity Sunday (Sunday After Pentecost)
1 Prv 8,22–31
2 Rom 5,1–5
3 Jn 16,12–15

Corpus Christi
1 Gn 14,18–20
2 1 Cor 11,23–26
3 Lk 9,11b–17

Sacred Heart of Jesus
1 Ez 34,11–16
2 Rom 5,5b–11
3 Lk 15,3–7

ORDINARY TIME

1st Sunday
(See Baptism of the Lord, above)

2nd Sunday
1 Is 62,1–5
2 1 Cor 12,4–11
3 Jn 2,1–12

3rd Sunday
1 Neh 8,2–4a.5–6.8–10
2 1 Cor 12,12–30
3 Lk 1,1–4; 4,14–21

4th Sunday
1 Jer 1,4–5.17–19
2 1 Cor 12,31 – 13,13
3 Lk 4,21–30

5th Sunday
1 Is 6,1–2a.3–8
2 1 Cor 15,1–11
3 Lk 5,1–11

6th Sunday
1 Jer 17,5–8
2 1 Cor 15,12.16–20
3 Lk 6,17.20–26

7th Sunday
1 1 Sm 26,2.7–9.12–13.22–23
2 1 Cor 15,45–49
3 Lk 6,27–38

8th Sunday
1 Sir 27,5–8
2 1 Cor 15,54–58
3 Lk 6,39–45

9th Sunday
1 1 Kgs 8,41–43
2 Gal 1,1–2.6–10
3 Lk 7,1–10

10th Sunday
1 1 Kgs 17,17–24
2 Gal 1,11–19
3 Lk 7,11–17

11th Sunday
1 2 Sm 12,7–10.13
2 Gal 2,16.19–21
3 Lk 7,36 – 8,3

12th Sunday
1 Zec 12,10–11
2 Gal 3,26–29
3 Lk 9,18–24

13th Sunday
1 1 Kgs 19,16b.19–21
2 Gal 5,1.13–18
3 Lk 9,51–62

14th Sunday
1 Is 66,10–14c
2 Gal 6,14–18
3 Lk 10,1–12.17–20

15th Sunday
1 Dt 30,10–14
2 Col 1,15–20
3 Lk 10,25–37

16th Sunday
1 Gn 18,1–10a
2 Col 1,24–28
3 Lk 10,38–42

17th Sunday
1 Gn 18,20–32
2 Col 2,12–14
3 Lk 11,1–13

18th Sunday
1 Eccl 1,2; 2,21–23
2 Col 3,1–5.9–11
3 Lk 12,13–31

19th Sunday
1 Wis 18,6–9
2 Heb 11,1–2.8–19
3 Lk 12,32–48

20th Sunday
1 Jer 38,4–6.8–10
2 Heb 12,1–4
3 Lk 12,49–53

21st Sunday
1 Is 66,18–21
2 Heb 12,5–7.11–13
3 Lk 13,22–30

22nd Sunday
1 Sir 3,19–21.30–31

2 Heb 12,18–19.22–24a
3 Lk 14,1.7–14

23rd Sunday
1 Wis 9,13–19
2 Phlm 9b–10.12–17
3 Lk 14,25–33

24th Sunday
1 Ex 32,7–11.13–14
2 1 Tm 1,12–17
3 Lk 15,1–32

25th Sunday
1 Am 8,4–7
2 1 Tm 2,1–8
3 Lk 16,1–13

26th Sunday
1 Am 6,1a.4–7
2 1 Tm 6,11–16
3 Lk 16,19–31

27th Sunday
1 Hb 1,2–3; 2,2–4
2 2 Tm 1,6–8.13–14
3 Lk 17,5–10

28th Sunday
1 2 Kgs 5,14–17
2 2 Tm 2,8–13
3 Lk 17,11–19

29th Sunday
1 Ex 17,8–13
2 2 Tm 3,14 – 4,2
3 Lk 18,1–8

30th Sunday
1 Sir 35,15b–17. 20–22a
2 2 Tm 4,6–8.16–18
3 Lk 18,9–14

31st Sunday
1 Wis 11,23 – 12,2
2 2 Thes 1,11 – 2,2
3 Lk 19,1–10

32nd Sunday
1 2 Mc 7,1–2.9–14
2 2 Thes 2,16 – 3,5
3 Lk 20,27–38

33rd Sunday
1 Mal 3, 19–20a
2 2 Thes 3,7–12
3 Lk 21,5–19

34th Sunday (Christ the King)
1 2 Sm 5,1–3
2 Col 1, 12–20
3 Lk 23, 35–43

Readings for the Major Feasts of the Year

Feb. 2: Presentation of the Lord
1 Mal 3,1–4
2 Heb 2,14–18
3 Lk 2,22–40

Mar. 19: Joseph, Husband of Mary
1 2 Sm 7,4–5a.12–14a.16
2 Rom 4,13.16–18.22
3 Mt 1,16.18–21.24a or Lk 2,41–51a

Mar. 25: Annunciation
1 Is 7,10–14
2 Heb 10,4–10
3 Lk 1,26–28

June 24: John the Baptist Vigil
1 Jer 1,4–10
2 1 Pt 1,8–12
3 Lk 1,5–17

Mass of the Day
1 Is 49,1–6
2 Acts 13,22–26
3 Lk 1,57–66.80

June 29: Peter and Paul Vigil
1 Acts 3,1–10
2 Gal 1,11–20
3 Jn 21,15–19

Mass of the Day
1 Acts 12,1–11
2 2 Tm 4,6–8.17–18
3 Mt 16,13–19

Aug. 6: Transfiguration
1 Dn 7,9–10.13–14
2 2 Pt 1,16–19
3 (A) Mt 7,1–9 (B) Mk 9,2–10 (C) Lk 9,28b–36

Aug. 15: Assumption Vigil
1 1 Chr 15,3–4.15; 16,1–2
2 1 Cor 15,54–57
3 Lk 11,27–28

Mass of the Day
1 Rv 11,19a; 12,1–6a.10ab
2 1 Cor 15,20–26
3 Lk 1,39–56

Sept. 14: Triumph of the Cross
1 Nm 21,4–9
2 Phil 2,6–11
3 Jn 3,13–17

Nov. 1: All Saints
1 Rv 7,2–4.9–14
2 1 Jn 3,1–3
3 Mt 5,1–12a

Nov. 2: All Souls First Mass
1 Jb 19,1.23–27
2 1 Cor 15,51–57
3 Jn 6,37–40

Second Mass
1 Wis 3,1–9
2 Phil 3,20–21
3 Jn 11,17–27

Third Mass
1 2 Mc 12,43–46
2 Rv 14,13
3 Jn 14,1–6

(Other Readings may be chosen)

Nov. 9: Dedication of St. John Lateran
1 2 Chr 5,6–10; 5,13 – 6,2
2 1 Cor 3,9–13.16–17
3 Lk 19,1–10

(Other Readings may be chosen)

Dec. 8: Immaculate Conception
1 Gn 3,9–15.20
2 Eph 1,3–6.11–12
3 Lk 1,26–38

Collaborators on the Old Testament of the New American Bible

BISHOPS' COMMITTEE OF THE CONFRATERNITY OF CHRISTIAN DOCTRINE

Most Rev. Charles P. Greco, D.D., *Chairman*
Most Rev. Joseph T. McGucken, S.T.D.
Most Rev. Vincent S. Waters, D.D.
Most Rev. Romeo Blanchette, D.D.
Most Rev. Christopher J. Weldon, .D.D.

EDITORS IN CHIEF

Rev. Louis F. Hartman, C.SS.R., S.S.L., LING. OR. L., *Chairman*
Rev. Msgr. Patrick W. Skehan, S.T.D., LL.D., *Vice-Chairman*
Rev. Stephen J. Hartdegen, O.F.M., S.S.L., *Secretary*

ASSOCIATE EDITORS AND TRANSLATORS

Rev. Edward P. Arbez, S.S., S.T.D.
Rev. Msgr. Edward J. Byrne, PH.D., S.T.D.
Rev. Edward A. Cerny, S.S., S.T.D.
Rev. James E. Coleran, S.J., S.T.L., S.S.L.
Rev. John J. Collins, S.J., M.A., S.S.L.
Sr. M. Emmanuel Collins, O.S.F., PH.D.
Prof. Frank M. Cross, Jr., PH.D.
Rev. Patrick Cummins, O.S.B., S.T.D.
Rev. Antonine A. DeGuglielmo, O.F.M., S.T.D., S.S.L., S.S.LECT. GEN.
Rev. Alexander A. DiLella, O.F.M., S.T.L., S.S.L., PH.D.
Most Rev. John J. Dougherty, S.T.L., S.S.D.
William A. Dowd, S.J., S.T.D., S.S.L.
Prof. David Noel Freedman, PH.D.
Rev. Michael J. Gruenthaner, S.J., S.T.D., S.S.D.
Rev. Msgr. Maurice A. Hofer, S.S.L.
Rev. Justin Krellner, O.S.B., S.T.D.
Rev. Joseph L. Lilly, C.M., S.T.D., S.S.L.
Rev. Roderick F. MacKenzie, S.J., M.A., S.S.D.
Rev. Edward A. Mangan, C.SS.R., S.S.L.
Rev. Daniel W. Martin, C.M., S.T.L., S.S.L.
Rev. William H. McClellan, S.J.
Rev. James McGlinchey, C.M., S.T.D.
Rev. Frederick Moriarty, S.J., S.S.L., S.T.D.
Rev. Richard T. Murphy, O.P., S.T.D., S.S.D.
Rev. Roland E. Murphy, O. CARM., M.A., S.T.D., S.S.L.
Rev. Msgr. William R. Newton, M.S., S.S.D.
Rev. Eberhard Olinger, O.S.B.
Rev. Charles H. Pickar, O.S.A., S.T.L., S.S.L.
Rev. Christopher Rehwinkel, O.F.M., S.T.D., S.S. LECT. GEN.
Rev. Msgr. John R. Rowan, S.T.D., S.S.L
Prof. J. A. Sanders, PH.D.
Rev. Edward F. Siegman, C.PP.S., S.T.D., S.S.L.
Rev. Msgr. Matthew P. Stapleton, S.T.D., S.S.L.
Rev. Msgr. John E. Steinmueller, S.T.D., S.S.L.
Rev. John Ujlaki, O.S.B., LITT.D.
Rev. Bruce Vawter, C.M., S.T.L., S.S.D.
Rev. John B. Weisengoff, S.T.D., S.S.L.

Collaborators on the Revised Psalms of the New American Bible

BISHOPS' AD HOC COMMITTEE

Most Rev. Enrique San Pedro, S.J.
Most Rev. Richard Sklba, D.D.
Most Rev. Donald W. Troutman, S.T.D., S.S.L.
Most Rev. Emil A. Wcela
Most Rev. John F. Whealon, S.S.L., *Chairman*

BOARD OF EDITORS

Rev. Richard Clifford, S.J.
Brother Aloysius Fitzgerald, F.S.C.
Rev. Joseph Jensen, O.S.B.
Rev. Roland Murphy, O. CARM.
Sr. Irene Nowell, O.S.B
Dr. Judith Sanderson

REVISERS

Prof. Gary Anderson
Rev. Michael L. Barré
Rev. Christopher T. Begg
Dr. Joseph Blenkinsopp
Rev. Anthony R. Ceresko, O.S.F.S.
Rev. Richard J. Clifford, S.J.
Rev. Aelred Cody, O.S.B.
Prof. Michael D. Coogan
Rev. Alexander A. Di Lella, O.F.M.
Dr. Robert A. Di Vito
Bro. Aloysius Fitzgerald, F.S.C.
Rev. Michael D. Guinan, O.F.M.
Rev. William L. Holladay
Rev. William Irwin, C.S.B.
Rev. Joseph Jensen, O.S.B.
Rev. John S. Kselman
Dr. Conrad E. L'Heureux
Rev. Leo Laberge, O.M.I.
Dr. Paul G. Mosca
Rev. Dr. Roland E. Murphy, O. CARM.
Dr. Michael Patrick O'Connor
Rev. Brian J. Peckham, S.J.
Prof. Jimmy J. Roberts
Sr. Eileen M. Schuller, O.S.U.
Dr. Byron E. Shafer
Prof. Mark S. Smith
Prof. Matitiahu Tsevat
Dr. Eugene C. Ulrich
Prof. James C. VanderKam
Rev. Jerome T. Walsh

ENGLISH CONSULTANTS

Dr. Catherine Dunn
Bro. Daniel Burke, F.S.C.

BUSINESS MANAGER

Charles A. Buggé

Collaborators on the Revised New Testament of the New American Bible

BISHOPS' AD HOC COMMITTEE

Most Rev. Theodore E. McCarrick, D.D.
Most Rev. Richard J. Sklba, D.D.
Most Rev. J. Francis Stafford, D.D.
Most Rev. John F. Whealon, D.D., *Chairman*

BOARD OF EDITORS

Rev. Msgr. Myles M. Bourke
Rev. Francis T. Gignac, S.J., *Chairman*
Rev. Stephen J. Hartdegen, O.F.M., *Secretary*
Rev. Claude J. Peifer, O.S.B.
Rev. John H. Reumann

REVISERS

Rev. Msgr. Myles M. Bourke
Rev. Frederick W. Danker
Rev. Alexander A. Di Lella, O.F.M.
Rev. Charles H. Giblin, S.J.
Rev. Francis T. Gignac, S.J.
Rev. Stephen J. Hartdegen, O.F.M.
Dr. Maurya P. Horgan
Rev. John R. Keating, S.J.
Rev. John Knox
Dr. Paul J. Kobelski
Dr. J. Rebecca Lyman
Bro. Elliott C. Maloney, O.S.B.
Dr. Janet A. Timbie

CONSULTANTS

Rev. Joseph Jensen, O.S.B.
Rev. Aidan Kavanagh, O.S.B.
Dr. Marianne Sawicki

BUSINESS MANAGER

Charles A. Buggé

WORD PROCESSOR

Suzanna Jordan

Acknowledgments

The editor and contributors wish to thank all those whose efforts have made the publication of this volume possible. The staff at Oxford University Press included Donald Kraus, who was involved with the initial planning of the book and oversaw every step of the writing, editing, and production; Clifton Harris, who handled the many details involved in assembling the final manuscript; Katrina Gettman, who prepared the manuscript for typesetting and kept track of endless details; and Leslie Phillips, who designed the book and directed the typesetting.

June and Doug Gunden, Mildred and Frederick Tripp, and the other members of the proofreading team helped us to avoid numerous errors.

Particular thanks are due also to Father Donald Senior and Professors Mary Ann Getty and John J. Collins, who provided their scholarly expertise. Father Carroll Stuhlmueller, who was also involved with the early stages of the project, died before it was completed. The worlds of biblical scholarship and teaching, having gained so much from his lifetime of contributions, mourn his loss and are grateful for his time among us.